Bowker's Guide To CHARACTERS IN FICTION 2004

This edition of
BOWKER'S GUIDE TO CHARACTERS IN FICTION 2004
was prepared by R.R. Bowker's Database Publishing Group in collaboration with the Information Technology Department.

Michael Cairns, President
Gary Aiello, Senior Vice President, Operations
Belinda Tseo, Senior Vice President, Finance
Angela D'Agostino, Vice President, Product Development and Marketing
Boe Horton, Vice President, Worldwide Sales
Roy Crego, Senior Managing Director, Editorial
Andrew Grabois, Senior Director, Publisher Relations and Content Development
Doreen Gravesande, Senior Director, ISBN/SAN/PAD and Data Acquisition
Constance Harbison, Senior Director, BIP Editorial, Quality Assurance, and Subject Guide
Galen Strazza, Creative Director

International Standard Book Number/Standard Address Number Agency/Publishers Authority Database
Don Riseborough, Senior Managing Editor
Paula Kurdi, Diana Luongo, and James Motley, Senior Editors
Beverly Palacio, Associate Editor
Venus Ayers, David Brassler, Leon Gravesande, Adriana Santiago, and Heidi Weber, Assistant Editors

Data Acquisition
Joseph Kalina, Director
Stephanie Halpern, Managing Editor
Patricia McCraney, Public Relations Specialist - Canada
Gladys Osofisan, Data Analyst

Editorial
Andrew LaCroix, Manager, Editorial Production
Kathleen Cunningham, Lisa Heft, and Eleanor Schubauer, Managing Editors
Adrene Allen, Senior Editor
Misty Harmon, Ila Joseph-Corley, Tom Lucas, and Dorothy Perry-Gilchrist, Associate Editors
Stacey Volanto, Lynda Williams, and Steve Zaffuto, Assistant Editors

Subject Guide
Michael Olenick, Database Analyst
Angela Barrett, Senior Associate Editor
Dafina Moore, Assistant Editor

Data Collection & Processing Group
Valerie Harris, Director of Operations, Tampa
Mervaine Ricks, Editorial Manager
Diane Johnson, Office Manager
John Litzenberger, Network Technician
Cheryl Patrick and Rhonda McKendrick, Editorial Specialists
Janet Foltz and Kathy Griner, Editorial Coordinators
Lori Burnett, Rita Phillips and Sally Snelling, Editorial Assistants
Joyce Bashista and Tasi Peterika, Assistant Editors

Production
Gordon MacPherson, Director, Electronic and Print Production
Myriam Nunez, Project Manager, Content Integrity
Megan Roxberry, Managing Editor
Kennard McGill, Senior Editor
Jocelyn Kwiatkowski, Associate Editor

Manufacturing
Delia Tedoff, Director

Editorial Systems, Information Technology Group
Mark Heinzelman, Director
Frank Morris, Project Manager
Youliang Zhou, Programmer

Computer Operations Group
John Nesselt, UNIX Administrator
Daniel O'Malley, Manager, Network Administration and Operations

Bowker's Guide To CHARACTERS IN FICTION

2004 VOLUME 2 CHILDREN'S FICTION

Published by
R.R. Bowker LLC
630 Central Avenue, New Providence
New Jersey 07974

Michael Cairns, President

Telephone: 908-286-1090; Toll-free: 800-521-8110
Fax: 908-219-0098
E-mail address: customerservice@bowker.com
URL: http://www.bowker.com

Readers may send any corrections and/or updates to the information in this work to R.R. Bowker through the corrections option on the Bowker Web site at http://www.bowker.com or may send e-mail directly to the address: Corrections@bowker.com. Publishers may update or add to their listings by accessing the BowkerLink Publisher Access System at http://www.bowkerlink.com. Books In Print is also available via subscription on the web at www.booksinprint.com.

International Standard Book Number
Set: 0-8352-4608-6
Volume 1: 0-8352-4609-4
Volume 2: 0-8352-4610-8

Printed in the United States of America

ISBN 0-8352-4608-6

9 780835 246088

CONTENTS

Volume 1—Adult Fiction

Volume 2 —Children's Fiction

HOW TO USE BOWKER'S GUIDE TO CHARACTERS IN FICTION 2004

This is the introductory edition of **Bowker's Guide to Characters In Fiction**, with Volume 1 devoted to adult fiction and Volume 2 to children's fiction. As the title implies, a large portion of this book is dedicated to fiction featuring a specific character; however, other topics covered in a fictional manner are also addressed (such as ethnic groups and settings). Like most of Bowker's bibliographic directories, it was produced from the Books In Print database. Unlike most of our directories, it brings together books published in three different formats (print, audio, electronic) and includes out-of-print, out-of-stock, and on-demand titles alongside active titles. Virtually none of the items listed in either volume appear in Bowker's **Subject Guide to Books In Print**, making this the perfect companion to our more established publication. Besides the main index, each volume features a List of Subject Headings, a Publisher Index, and a Wholesaler & Distributor Index.

CLASSIFICATION

Bowker's Guide to Characters In Fiction follows the headings assigned by the Library of Congress for cases where LC has established a fiction-related heading. It should be noted that while children's fiction has long been classified by topic, it has been only ten years since LC began classifying children's fiction by fictitious character or imaginary setting, and adult fiction at all. For already established headings, "—FICTION" was merely added as a subdivision (e.g., POLICEWOMEN—FICTION). However, for characters and settings, thousands of new headings had to be created, from BAMBI (FICTITIOUS CHARACTER) to BENNET, ELIZABETH (FICTITIOUS CHARACTER) to BOND, JAMES (FICTITIOUS CHARACTER), before "—FICTION" could be appended. Bowker has always patterned our classification after LC, so we also started to create fiction-related headings in the manner of LC and began applying these to incoming data as well as to titles already in our database (like LC, we had already been classifying children's fiction by topic). As you can imagine, retroactive classification was a massive undertaking. To focus our efforts, we commissioned research to determine under which broad topics readers were most likely to request fiction. The results of this research enabled us to target our efforts, and have also determined the seven topical sections of each main index: Characters, Ethnic Groups, Historical Events, Miscellaneous, Occupations, Relationships, and Settings (each of which is discussed in detail below under ARRANGEMENT AND USAGE OF SUBJECTS). We used classification by the Library of Congress when possible to help determine the headings assigned. However, for areas in which LC is not strong (for example, original paperbacks), other sources were used as well. Several appropriate subjects were assigned, so a book may appear multiple times per section, as well as in several sections.

Bowker's Guide to Characters In Fiction Volume 1 (Adult Fiction) contains approximately 142,550 entries appearing 154,000 times under 4,180 populated headings. Volume 2 (Children's Fiction) contains some 64,000 entries appearing 68,000 times under 1,090 subject headings. This first edition includes roughly 88,300 in-print books, 8,700 audiobooks, and 3,270 e-books. We also include 3,065 on-demand titles in addition to titles recently declared out-of stock or out-of-print. No entries appear in both volumes.

For the headings in the Ethnic Groups, Historical Events, Miscellaneous, Occupations, and Relationships sections we based the style of the heading on that of LC. For the Characters and Settings sections, we based any real characters and settings on LC, as well as any fictitious characters or imaginary settings for which LC had authority records. However, we have gone well beyond LC classification in this regard. LC generally only establishes a heading for fictitious characters and imaginary settings if they appear in three or more works - we decided not to set such a limit and have added headings whenever we thought that they would be useful. When this was done, we still adhered to general LC policy for these types of headings (for example, characters are listed under their surnames, when appropriate). LC bibliographic and subject authority information can be found at http://catalog.loc.gov.

In general, **Bowker's Guide to Characters In Fiction** includes any work of adult or children's fiction that has been assigned a Bowker subject ending with "—FICTION" that fits into one of the topical sections (and note that the "—FICTION" subdivision has been retained for each heading). There is no distinction made between novels, single-author short story collections, and multiple author anthologies (although it is less common for anthologies to focus on a specific character, occupation, setting, etc., so the majority of works included are by a single author). That being said, there are several types of related works that it might help to specifically state are excluded:

- Literary criticism dealing with a fictitious character or imaginary setting is not included, but can be found in **Subject Guide to Books In Print** under unsubdivided subjects; (e.g., COMPSON, CADDY (FICTITIOUS CHARACTER); YOKNAPATAWPHA COUNTY (IMAGINARY PLACE).
- Drama and poetry are excluded, even if they feature a character, setting, etc. that has been included.
- Works discussing other aspects of a character are excluded (e.g, no works on Mickey Mouse collectibles or James Bond movies).

Much effort has been put into identifying children's versions of classics and classifying them appropriately. In some cases, this has led to a character appearing in both volumes (e.g., HEATHCLIFF (FICTITIOUS CHARACTER)—FICTION). We tried to limit the definition of "children's version" to mean cases where works generally considered as being for adults were abridged or adapted specifically for younger readers. However, in cases where we were not able to determine this, we went with the publisher's information

- if they told us that their edition of *Wuthering Heights* was a children's edition, then we listed it in the Children's volume, even if it was textually the same as the standard edition.

GENERAL EDITORIAL POLICIES

Current information was solicited from all publishers in the Books In Print database. These publishers include participants in Bowker's Electronic Data Interchange (EDI) program as well as publishers who regularly submit Advance Book Information (ABI) forms and their current book catalogs. Less active publishers are asked to review their active titles on checklists or online at www.bowker-link.com and every effort was made to get up-to-date, complete information on all titles included in **Bowker's Guide to Characters In Fiction**. All prices and availability are subject to change without notice.

ARRANGEMENT AND USAGE OF SUBJECTS

The first principle of **Bowker's Guide to Characters In Fiction** was to classify a book using the most specific heading(s) under which someone was likely to look. So if you are interested in a book taking place in a particular city, first look under that city (or even under an area within a city). If nothing is found, then try the next broadest area (such as a state or province) and then continue in this manner through broader terms (such as country, region, or continent). It is possible that a book will be found under both a city and state, or a country and a continent, but it is advised to try the narrowest term first. It should be noted that publishers do not always distinguish between England and Great Britain when conveying information to us, so users are advised to try both place names. Each volume is divided into sections as noted below. Any rules or explanations given apply to both volumes unless stated. Examples may appear in one or both volumes, but a heading will only appear in one section of each volume.

■ Characters

This section includes headings for real people (e.g., ROOSEVELT, ELEANOR, 1884-1962—FICTION), as well as fictitious and legendary characters (e.g., BROWN, CHARLIE (FICTITIOUS CHARACTER)—FICTION; MERLIN (LEGENDARY CHARACTER)—FICTION). If a character has a surname, he or she will generally be listed under that name. If someone is known primarily (or only) by a title or rank, then that will be included in the heading, but the person will still be listed under his or her surname (e.g., AHAB, CAPTAIN (FICTITIOUS CHARACTER) —FICTION); COLUMBO, LIEUTENANT (FICTITIOUS CHARACTER —FICTION). Superheroes are generally listed under their assumed identity (e.g., CAPTAIN UNDERPANTS (FICTITIOUS CHARACTER)—FICTION; SPIDER-MAN (FICTITIOUS CHARACTER)—FICTION). Characters with the same name are differentiated by including the author's surname in the heading (e.g., ARTHUR (FICTITIOUS CHARACTER : BROWN)—FICTION; ARTHUR (FICTITIOUS CHARACTER : HOBAN)—FICTION). Besides individual characters, there are headings for combinations of characters, which can take the forms of relatives, families, or other types of groupings (e.g., ARMITAGE SISTERS (FICTITIOUS CHARACTERS)—FICTION; ADDAMS FAMILY (FICTITIOUS CHARACTERS)—FICTION; X-MEN (FICTITIOUS CHARACTERS)—FICTION). Sometimes two characters who always appear together have heen combined into one heading (e.g., WALLACE AND GROMIT (FICTITIOUS CHARACTERS)—FICTION).

■ Ethnic Groups

This section includes headings for ethnic groups (e.g., CHINESE AMERICANS—FICTION), headings that are usually associated with ethnic groups (e.g., KIBBUTZIM—FICTION; KWANZAA—FICTION), and headings related to a specific religion, whether or not that religion is primarily associated with an ethnic group (e.g., MENNONITES—FICTION).

■ Historical Events

The history-related headings in the Adult volume (Volume 1) almost all pertain to a particular war or conflict (e.g., UNITED STATES—HISTORY—WAR OF 1812—FICTION; VIETNAMESE CONFLICT, 1961-1975—FICTION), with an occasional non-military heading (e.g., FRONTIER AND PIONEER LIFE—FICTION). The history-related headings in the Children's volume (Volume 2) include most of what's in the Adult volume plus headings that relate to an event, place, time period, or other aspect of history (e.g., BOSTON TEA PARTY, 1773—FICTION; BRONZE AGE—FICTION; EGYPT—HISTORY—FICTION; MOGUL EMPIRE—FICTION; PONY EXPRESS—FICTION). Note that the Historical Events and Settings sections are both worth checking if you are looking for a book that takes place in a real setting in the past.

■ Miscellaneous

For the Adult volume this section represents the handful of headings ending with "—FICTION" that did not fit into any other section. There were about 1,000 children's fiction headings that did not fit into the other sections (remembering that children's fiction classification has been going on much longer than adult fiction classification), so for the Children's volume we decided to offer a selection of headings related to fantasy or the supernatural (e.g., DRAGONS—FICTION; GHOSTS—FICTION; GIANTS—FICTION; MERMAIDS—FICTION; WIZARDS—FICTION). The **Subject Guide to Children's Books In Print** contains all children's fiction (and, of course, nonfiction).

■ Occupations

While most headings in this section relate to what one would generally call an occupation (e.g., COLLEGE TEACHERS—FICTION; JOURNALISTS—FICTION), some headings in the Children's volume might be more accurately described as "things people do" (e.g., APPRENTICES—FICTION; EXPLORERS—FICTION).

■ Relationships

This section includes headings dealing with family and interpersonal relationships (e.g., DATING (SOCIAL CUSTOMS)—FICTION; FATHERS AND SONS—FICTION; GRANDPARENTS—FICTION; MARRIAGE—FICTION; TWINS—FICTION; WIDOWS—FICTION). It has been extended somewhat to include GAY MEN—FICTION and LESBIANS—FICTION as well. Note that relationships involving recognizable characters may be covered by a heading in the Characters section.

■ Settings

Included here are headings for real places (e.g., BEVERLY HILLS (CALIF.)—FICTION; CALIFORNIA—FICTION; WEST (U.S.)—FICTION), as well as imaginary and legendary places (e.g., CAMELOT (LEGENDARY PLACE)—FICTION; TREASURE ISLAND (IMAGINARY PLACE)—FICTION). If an imaginary setting has been identified as existing within a real place, that will be noted (e.g., CABOT COVE (ME : IMAGINARY PLACE)—FICTION). Settings can range from specific schools, streets, hotels, etc. (e.g., FORTY-THREE LIGHT STREET (IMAGINARY PLACE)—FICTION; ROSWELL HIGH (NM : IMAGINARY PLACE)—FICTION) to planets (e.g., DUNE (IMAGINARY PLACE)—FICTION). Note that the Settings and Historical Events sections are both worth checking if you are looking for a book that takes place in a real setting in the past.

Within each section, the presentation of subject headings is alphabetical; however, in accordance with the Library of Congress, the following rules are followed:

- Headings beginning with "Da" and "De" are treated as if there were no space.
- Headings beginning with "Mc" and "Mac" are treated as if they all began with "Mac".
- "Saint" and "St." are treated as alphabetical equals.
- Apostrophes are ignored.
- Hyphens are treated as spaces.
- Real people and fictitious characters are interfiled alphabetically (as are real settings and imaginary ones).

Below are some examples of sequencing. Note that headings may appear between the examples given, and that the examples are all from the Characters section in the Adult volume (although the rules apply to all sections in both volumes).

AUSTEN, CAT (FICTITIOUS CHARACTER)—FICTION

AUSTEN, JANE, 1775-1817—FICTION

AUSTEN, KATE (FICTITIOUS CHARACTER)—FICTION

DASH (FICTITIOUS CHARACTER)—FICTION

DA SILVA, JANE (FICTITIOUS CHARACTER)—FICTION

DATA (FICTITIOUS CHARACTER)—FICTION

MABRY, BUBBA (FICTITIOUS CHARACTER)—FICTION

MCALISTER, HALEY (FICTITIOUS CHARACTER)—FICTION

MACK, RUDYARD (FICTITIOUS CHARACTER)—FICTION

MCVAY, LIZZIE (FICTITIOUS CHARACTER)—FICTION

MADDOCK, JOREY (FICTITIOUS CHARACTER)—FICTION

O'BRIEN, MILES (FICTITIOUS CHARACTER)—FICTION

ODO (FICTITIOUS CHARACTER)—FICTION

O'NEILL, PEGGY (FICTITIOUS CHARACTER)—FICTION

SAINT (FICTITIOUS CHARACTER)—FICTION

SAINT, AUGUST (FICTITIOUS CHARACTER)—FICTION

SAINT-GERMAIN (FICTITIOUS CHARACTER)—FICTION

ST. IVES, PHILIP (FICTITIOUS CHARACTER)—FICTION

SAINT JAMES, QUIN (FICTITIOUS CHARACTER)—FICTION

There are also "see" references provided to lead users from the heading they are looking at to the heading under which books are actually listed, although these are not as extensive as in **Subject Guide to Books In Print**. Subjects with a "see" reference do not have books listed under them. References have generally been added when a person or place is known by more than one name, or when it is not clear if a person is listed under his or her full name or surname. For example:

ADEPT, THE (FICTITIOUS CHARACTER)—FICTION
see Sinclair, Adam (Fictitious Character)—Fiction

BEDELIA, AMELIA (FICTITIOUS CHARACTER)—FICTION
see Amelia-Bedelia (Fictitious Character)—Fiction

CASTLE AMBER (IMAGINARY PLACE)—FICTION
see Amber (Imaginary Place)—Fiction

HANSEN, ANNIKA (FICTITIOUS CHARACTER)—FICTION
see Seven of Nine (Fictitious Character)—Fiction

HIGHLANDER (FICTITIOUS CHARACTER)—FICTION
see MacLeod, Duncan (Fictitious Character)—Fiction

OBI-WAN KENOBI (FICTITIOUS CHARACTER)—FICTION
see Kenobi, Obi-Wan (Fictitious Character)—Fiction

SHIRLEY, ANNE (FICTITIOUS CHARACTER)—FICTION
see Anne of Green Gables (Fictitious Character)—Fiction

Note that "see" references will only appear in the volumes and sections in which they are appropriate.

LIST OF SUBJECT HEADINGS

While in most cases it will be obvious what section a heading will be in (and where it will appear in that section), there are cases where it may not be immediately apparent. To help in the search, we have provided an index at the beginning of each volume that is arranged first by section and then within each section by the sequence in which the headings appear. Furthermore, page references are provided to lead you directly to the heading. Below is an example from the Characters index in Volume 1:

BATMAN (FICTITIOUS CHARACTER) p.49
BATTLE, SUPERINTENDENT (FICTITIOUS CHARACTER) p.50
BAUER, TORY (FICTITIOUS CHARACTER) p.50
BAUER, VICKY (FICTITIOUS CHARACTER) p.50
BAUM, STEVEN (FICTITIOUS CHARACTER) p.51

Note that in this list, the subdivision "—FICTION" has been suppressed from the end of the heading.

ALPHABETICAL ARRANGEMENT OF ENTRIES WITHIN SUBJECT

After arrangement by section and by subject, entries are arranged alphabetically by author (or other contributor, if no author is given). If no contributor is present, the entry is filed by title within the contributor arrangement. Contributors' names in **Bowker's Guide**

to Characters In Fiction have been alphabetized using the following rules:

- Proper names beginning with "Mc" and "Mac" are filed in strict alphabetical order. For example, entries for names such as Mac Adam, MacAvory, and MacCarthy are located prior to entries for names such as McAdam, McCoy, and McDermott.
- Compound names are listed under their first component. For example, Van Holland is listed under Van.
- When contributor names are represented with initials, they are alphabetized before contributor first names. For example, Smith, H. C. appears before Smith, Harold A.
- If more than two contributors performing the same function are responsible for a given title, then only the name of the first is given, followed by "et al".

INFORMATION INCLUDED IN ENTRIES

Entries include the following bibliographic information (when available): author, co-author, editor, co-editor, translator, co-translator, original language, title, subtitle, title volume number, number of volumes, edition, publication year, series information, original title, current language if other than English, whether or not illustrated, number of pages, whether a book is an original paperback, audience, grade range, binding/format if other than cloth over boards, price, status if other than active or on-demand, ISBN, order number, imprint, and publisher name.

PUBLISHER NAME INDEX

Indexes to publisher names are found in both volumes (containing more than 2,690 publishers used in the bibliographic entries of Volume 1 and over 2,560 publishers used in the bibliographic entries of Volume 2). Entries in these indexes contain (when available): publisher name, ISBN prefix(es), business affiliation, ordering address(es), SAN (Standard Address Number), telephone number(s), fax and toll-free number(s), editorial address(es) and associated contact numbers, imprints, e-mail and Web site address(es), and the distributors who handle this publisher. Publishers with like or similar names include a "Do not confuse with..." notation within the entry. A dagger (†) preceding a publisher's name and the note "CIP" at the end of an entry indicate that the publisher participates in the Cataloging in Publication Program of the Library of Congress. Full information for distributors, as well as 1,000 book wholesalers, is found in the Wholesaler & Distributor Name Index (in both volumes). Note that publishers who also serve as distributors may be listed both here and in the Publisher Name Index. Foreign publishers with U.S. distributors are listed, followed by their three-character ISO (International Standards Organization) country code ("GBR," "CAN," etc.), ISBN prefix(es), if available, and a cross-reference to their U.S. distributor, as shown below:

Addison-Wesley Longman, Ltd. (GBR) (0-582) Dist. by **Trans-Atl Phila**.

In addition, cross-references are provided from imprints to their publisher and from former company name to new name.

WHOLESALER & DISTRIBUTOR NAME INDEX

The Wholesaler & Distributor Name Index is arranged alphabetically by company name and contains (when available): company name, ISBN prefix(es), business affiliation, full address and ordering information, SAN(s), telephone number(s), fax and toll-free number(s), e-mail and Web site address(es). Wholesalers and distributors with like or similar names include a "Do not confuse with..." notation within the entry.

ISBN AGENCY

164,700 of the entries included in **Bowker's Guide to Characters In Fiction** have been assigned an International Standard Book Number (ISBN) by the publisher. All ISBNs listed in this volume have been validated by using the check digit control, ensuring accuracy.

Note: The ISBN prefix 0-615 is for decentralized use by the U.S. ISBN Agency and has been assigned to numerous publishers. This prefix is not unique to one exclusive publisher.

ISBNs allow order transmission and bibliographic information updating using the Book Industry Standards and Communications (BISAC) standard format for data transmission. Publishers not currently participating in the ISBN system may request the assignment of an ISBN Publisher Prefix from the ISBN Agency by calling 877-310-7333, fax 908-219-0188, or through the ISBN/SAN Web site at www.isbn.org.

SAN AGENCY

A feature of the publishers, distributors, and wholesalers entries is the Standard Address Number (SAN). The SAN is a unique identification number assigned to each address of an organization in or served by the publishing industry. It facilitates communications and repetitive transactions with other members of the industry. The SAN functions in its application to activities such as purchasing, billing, shipping, receiving, paying, crediting, and refunding, and can be used for any other communication or transaction between participating organizations. To obtain an application or further information on the SAN system, please contact Diana Luongo, SAN Manager, by calling 908-219-0283, fax 908-219-0188, or visit the ISBN/SAN Web site at www.isbn.org.

ADDITIONAL RESOURCES

A wealth of current bibliographic data (more than 4.6 million records, including videos) can also be searched by customers on Bowker's Web site: www.booksinprint.com. The Books In Print database is also available on CD-ROM. For further information about subscribing to these services, contact Bowker at 1-888-269-5372. Out-of-print titles are also available on our Web site at www.booksoutofprint.com.

LIST OF ABBREVIATIONS

abr.	abridged
adapt.	adapted
addr.	address
affil.	affiliate
aft.	afterword
Amer.	American
anno.	annotated by
annot.	annotation(s)
ans.	answer(s)
app.	appendix
Apple II	Apple II disk
approx.	approximately
Apt.	apartment
assn.	association
assoc(s).	associate
Ave.	Avenue
audio	analog audio cassette
auth.	author
bd.	bound
bdg.	binding
bds.	boards
bibl(s).	bibliography(ies)
bk(s).	book(s)
bklet(s).	booklet(s)
Bldg.	building
Blvd.	boulevard
boxed	boxed set, slipcase, or caseboard
Bro.	Brother
C	college audience level
c/o	care of
Cir.	Circle
co.	company
comm.	commission, committee
comment.	commentaries
comp.	compiled
cond.	condensed
contrib.	contributed
corp.	corporation
Ct.	Court
Ctr(s)	Center(s)
Cty.	county
dept.	department
des.	designed
diag(s).	diagram(s)
digital-audio	digital audio cassette
dir.	director
disk	software disk or diskette
dist.	distributed
Div.	Division
doz.	dozen
Dr.	Drive
E	East
ea.	each
ed.	edited, edition, editor
edit.	editorial
eds.	editions, editors
educ.	education
elem.	elementary
ency.	encyclopedia
ENG	English
enl.	enlarged
epil.	epilogue
exp.	expurgated
expr.	experiments
fac.	facsimile
fasc.	fascicule
fict.	fiction
fig(s).	figure(s)
flmstrp.	filmstrip
flr.	floor
footn.	footnotes
for.	foreign
Ft.	Fort
frwd.	foreword
gen.	general
G.P.O.	General Post Office
gr.	grade(s)
hdbk.	handbook
hse.	house
Hwy.	Highway
Illus.	illustrated, illustration(s), illustrator(s)
in prep.	in preparation
Inc.	Incorporated
incl.	includes, including
info.	information
inst.	institute
intro.	introduction
ISBN	International Standard Book Number
ISO	International Standards Organization
i.t.a.	initial teaching alphabet
J	juvenile audience level
Jr.	Junior
jt. auth.	joint author
jt. ed.	joint editor
k	kindergarten audience level
lab	laboratory
lang(s).	languages(s)
LC	Library of Congress
lea.	leather
lib.	library
lib. bdg.	library binding
lit.	literature, literary
Ln.	Lane
lp	record, album, long playing
LTD	Limited
ltd. ed.	limited edition
mac hd	144M, Mac
mac ld	800K, Mac
mass mkt.	mass market paperbound
math.	mathematics
mic. film	microfilm
mic. form	microform
mod.	modern
mor.	morocco
MS(S)	manuscript(s)
N	North
NE	Northeast
natl.	national
net	net price (see publisher for specific pricing policies)
NW	Northwest
no(s).	number(s)
o.p.	out of print
orig.	original text, not a reprint (paperback)
o.s.i.	out of stock indefinitely
p.	pages
pap.	paper
per.	perfect binding
photos	photographer, photographs
Pk.	Park

LIST OF ABBREVIATIONS

Pkwy.	Parkway
Pl.	Place
P.O.	post office
pop. ed.	popular edition
pr.	press
prep.	preparation
probs.	problems
prog. bk.	programmed books
ps	preschool audience level
pseud.	pseudonym
pt(s).	part(s)
pub.	published, publisher, publishing
pubn.	publication
R.D.	rural delivery
Rd.	Road
ref(s).	reference(s)
reprod(s).	reproduction(s)
ret.	retold by
rev.	revised
R.F.D.	rural free delivery
Rm.	Room
rpm	revolutions per minute (phono records)
R.R.	Rural Route
Rte.	Route
S	South
SAN	Standard Address Number
S&L	Signed and Limited
SE	Southeast
sec.	section
sel.	selected
ser.	series
Soc.	Society
sols.	solutions
s.p.	school price
Sq.	Square
Sr. (after given name)	Senior
Sr. (before given name)	Sister
St.	Saint, Street
Sta.	Station
subs.	subsidiary
subscr.	subscription
suppl.	supplement
SW	Southwest
tech.	technical
Terr.	Terrace
text ed.	text edition
Tpke	Turnpike
tr.	translated, translation, translator
trans.	transparencies
Univ.	University
vdisk	videodisk
VHS	video, VHS format
vol(s).	volume(s)
W	West
wkbk.	workbook
YA	young adult audience level
yrbk.	yearbook
3.5 hd	1.44M, 3.5″ disk, DOS
3.5 ld	720, 3.5″ Disk, DOS
5.25hd	1.2M, 5.25″ Disk, DOS
5.25 ld	360 K, 5.25″ Disk, DOS

PUBLISHER COUNTRY CODES

Foreign publishers are listed in **Bowker's Guide to Characters In Fiction** with the three-letter International Standards Organization (ISO) code for their country of domicile. This is the complete list of ISO codes, though not all countries may be represented in **Bowker's Guide to Characters In Fiction**. The codes are mnemonic in most cases. The country names listed here may have been shortened to a more common usage form.

ABW	Aruba
AFG	Afghanistan
AGO	Angola
AIA	Anguilla
ALB	Albania
AND	Andorra
ANT	Netherland Antilles
ARE	United Arab Emirates
ARG	Argentina
ARM	Armenia
ASM	American Samoa
ATA	Antarctica
ATF	French Southern Territories
ATG	Antigua and Barbuda
AUS	Australia
AUT	Austria
AZE	Azerbaijan
BDI	Burundi
BEL	Belgium
BEN	Benin
BFA	Burkina Faso
BGD	Bangladesh
BGR	Bulgaria
BHR	Bahrain
BHS	Bahamas
BIH	Bosnia and Herzegovina
BLR	Belarus
BLZ	Belize
BMU	Bermuda
BOL	Bolivia
BRA	Brazil
BRB	Barbados
BUL	Bulgaria
BRD	West Germany
BRN	Brunei Darussalam
BTN	Bhutan
BVT	Bouvet Island
BWA	Botswana
CAF	Central African Republic
CAN	Canada
CCK	Cocos (Keeling) Islands
CHE	Switzerland
CHL	Chile
CHN	China
CIV	Cote D'Ivoire
CMR	Cameroon
COD	Congo, Democratic Republic of
COG	Congo
COK	Cook Islands
COL	Colombia
COM	Comoros
CPV	Cape Verde
CRI	Costa Rica
CSK	Czechoslovakia
CUB	Cuba
CXR	Christmas Island
CYN	Cayman Islands
CYP	Cyprus
CZE	Czech Republic
DDR	East Germany
DEU	Germany
DJI	Djibouti
DMA	Dominica
DNK	Denmark
DOM	Dominican Republic
DZA	Algeria
ECU	Ecuador
EGY	Egypt
ERI	Eritrea
ESH	Western Sahara
ESP	Spain
EST	Estonia
ETH	Ethiopia
FIN	Finland
FJI	Fiji
FLK	Falkland Islands
FRA	France
FRO	Faeroe Islands
FSM	Fed. States of Micronesia
GAB	Gabon
GBR	United Kingdom
GEO	Georgia
GHA	Ghana
GIB	Gibralter
GIN	Guinea
GLP	Guadaloupe
GMB	Gambia
GNB	Guinea-Bissau
GNQ	Equatorial Guinea
GRC	Greece
GRD	Grenada
GRL	Greenland
GTM	Guatemala
GUF	French Guiana
GUM	Guam
GUY	Guyana
HKG	Hong Kong
HMD	Heard Island and McDonald Islands
HND	Honduras
HRV	Croatia
HTI	Haiti
HUN	Hungary
IDN	Indonesia
IND	India
IOT	British Indian Ocean Territory
IRL	Ireland
IRN	Iran
IRQ	Iraq
ISL	Iceland
ISR	Israel
ITA	Italy
JAM	Jamaica
JOR	Jordan
JPN	Japan
KAZ	Kazakstan
KEN	Kenya
KGZ	Kyrgyzstan
KHM	Cambodia
KIR	Kiribati
KNA	Saint Kitts and Nevis
KOR	Korea, Republic of
KWT	Kuwait
LAO	Laos
LBN	Lebanon
LBR	Liberia
LBY	Libya
LCA	St. Lucia
LIE	Liechtenstein
LKA	Sri Lanka
LSO	Lesotho
LTU	Lithuania
LUX	Luxembourg
LVA	Latvia
MAC	Macau
MAR	Morocco
MCO	Monaco
MDA	Moldova
MDG	Madagascar
MDV	Maldive Islands

PUBLISHER COUNTRY CODES

MEX	Mexico
MHL	Marshall Islands
MKD	Macedonia
MLI	Mali
MLT	Malta
MMR	Myanmar
MNG	Mongolia
MNP	Northern Mariana Islands
MOZ	Mozambique
MRT	Mauritania
MSR	Montserrat
MTQ	Martinique
MUS	Mauritius
MWI	Malawi
MYS	Malaysia
MYT	Mayotte
NAM	Namibia
NCL	New Caledonia
NER	Niger
NFK	Norfolk Island
NGA	Nigeria
NIC	Nicauragua
NIU	Niue
NLD	Netherlands
NOR	Norway
NPL	Nepal
NRU	Nauru
NZL	New Zealand
OMN	Oman
PAK	Pakistan
PAN	Panama
PCN	Pitcairn Islands
PER	Peru
PHL	Philippines
PLW	Palau
PNG	Papua New Guinea
POL	Poland
PRI	Puerto Rico
PRK	Korea, Democratic People's Rep. of
PRT	Portugal
PRY	Paraguay
PSE	Occupied Palestinian Territory
PYF	French Polynesia
QAT	Qatar
REU	Reunion
ROM	Romania
RUS	Russia
RWA	Rwanda
SAU	Saudi Arabia
ADN	Sudan
SEN	Senegal
SGP	Singapore
SGS	South Georgia and Sandwich Islands
SHN	Saint Helena
SJM	Svalbard and Jan Mayen
SLB	Solomen Islands
SLE	Sierra Leone
SLV	El Salvador
SMR	San Marino
SOM	Somalia
SPM	Saint Pierre and Miquelon
STP	Sao Tome e Principe
SUN	U.S.S.R.
SUR	Suriname
SVK	Slovakia
SVN	Slovenia
SWE	Sweden
SWZ	Swaziland
SYC	Seychelles
SYR	Syrian Arab Republic
TCA	Turks and Caicos Islands
TCG	Togo
THA	Thailand
TJK	Tajikistan
TKL	Tokelau
TKM	Turkmenistan
TNP	East Timor
TON	Tonga
TTO	Trinidad and Tobago
TUN	Tunisia
TUR	Turkey
TUV	Tuvalu
TWN	Taiwan
TZA	Tanzania
UGA	Uganda
UKR	Ukraine
URY	Uruguay
USA	United States
UZB	Uzbekistan
VAT	Vatican City
VCT	St. Vincents and Grenadines
VEN	Venezuela
VGB	Virgin Islands, British
VIR	Virgin Islands, U.S.
VNM	Vietnam
VUT	Vanuatu
WLF	Wallis and Futuna
WSM	Somoa
YEM	Yemen
YUG	Yugoslavia
ZAF	South Africa
ZAR	Zaire
ZMB	Zambia
ZWE	Zimbabwe

LANGUAGE CODES

ACE	Acholi
AFR	Afrikaans
AFA	Afro-Asiatic
AKK	Akkadian
ALB	Albanian
ALE	Aleut
ALG	Algonquin
AMH	Amharic
ANG	Anglo-Saxon
APA	Apache
ARA	Arabic
ARC	Aramaic
ARP	Arapaho
ARM	Armenian
ASM	Assamese
AVA	Avar
AVE	Avesta
AYM	Aymara
AZE	Azerbaijani
BAT	Baltic
BAL	Baluchi
BAM	Bambara
BAK	Bashkir
BAQ	Basque
BEJ	Beja
BEL	Belorussian
BEM	Bemba
BEN	Bengali
BER	Berber Group
BIH	Bihari
BLA	Blackfoot
BRE	Breton
BUL	Bulgarian
BUR	Burmese
CAD	Caddo
CAM	Cambodian
CAR	Carib
CAT	Catalan
CAU	Caucasian
CEL	Celtic Group
CAI	Central American Indian
CHE	Chechen
CHR	Cherokee
CHY	Cheyenne
CHB	Chibcha
CHI	Chinese
CHN	Chinook
CHO	Choctaw
CHU	Church Slavic
CHV	Chuvash
COP	Coptic
COR	Cornish
CRE	Cree
CRP	Creole and Pidgin
CRO	Croatian
CUS	Cushitic
CZE	Czech
DAK	Dakota
DAN	Danish
DEL	Delaware
DIN	Dinka
DOI	Dogri
DRA	Dravidian
DUA	Duala
DUT	Dutch
EFI	Efik
EGY	Egyptian
ELX	Elamite
ENG	English
ENM	English, Middle
ESK	Eskimo
ESP	Esperanto
EST	Estonian
ETH	Ethiopic
EWE	Ewe
FAN	Fang
FAR	Faroese
FIJ	Finnish
FIU	Finno-Ugrian
FLE	Flemish
FON	Fon
FRE	French
FEM	French, Middle
FRO	French, Old
FRI	Frisian
GAA	Ga
GAE	Gaelic
GAL	Galla
GAG	Gallegan
GEO	Georgian
GER	German
GEH	Germanic
GON	Gondi
GOT	Gothic
GRE	Greek
GEC	Greek, Classical
GUA	Guarani
HAU	Hausa
HAW	Hawaiian
HEB	Hebrew
HER	Hereo
HIL	Hiligaynon
HIN	Hindi
HUN	Hungarian
HUP	Hupa
IBA	Iban
ICE	Icelandic
IBO	Icelandic
IBO	Igbo
ILO	Ilocano
INC	Indic
INE	Indo-European
IND	Indonesian
INT	Interlingua
IKU	Inuktitut
IRA	Iranian
IRI	Irish
IRO	Iroquois
ITA	Italian
JPN	Japanese
JAV	Javanese
KAC	Kachin
KAM	Kamba
KAN	Kannada
KAU	Kanuri
KAA	Karakalpak
KAR	Karen
KAS	Kashmiri
KAZ	Kazakh
KHA	Khasi
KIK	Kikuyu
KIN	Kinyarwanda
KIR	Kirghiz
KON	Kongo
KOK	Konkani
KOR	Korean
KPE	Kpelle
KRO	Kru
KUR	Kurdish
KRU	Kurukh
KUA	Kwanyama
LAD	Ladino
LAH	Lahnda
LAM	Lamba
LAO	Laotian
LAP	Lapp
LAT	Latin

LANGUAGE CODES

LAV	Latvian
LIN	Lingala
LIT	Lithuanian
LOL	Lolo
LUB	Luba
LUG	Luganda
LUI	Luiseno
MAC	Macedonian
MAI	Maithili
MLA	Malagasy
MAY	Malay
MAL	Malayalam
MAP	Malayo-Polynesian
MAN	Mandingo
MNO	Manobo
Mao	Maori
Mar	Marathi
MAS	Masai
MYN	Mayan
MEN	Mende
MIC	Micmac
MIS	Miscellaneous
MOL	Moldavian
MON	Mongol
MOS	Mossi
MUL	Multiple languages
MUS	Muskogee
NAV	Navaho
NDE	Ndebele, Northern
NBL	Ndebele, Southern
NEP	Nepali
NEW	Newari
NIC	Niger-Congo
NAI	North American Indian
NOR	Norwegian
NUB	Nubian
NYM	Nyamwezi
NYA	Nyanja
NYO	Nyoro Group
OJI	Ojibwa
ORI	Oriya
OSA	Osage
OES	Ossetic
OTO	Otomi
PAH	Pahari
PAL	Pahlavi
PLI	Pali
PAN	Panjabi
PAA	Papuan-Australian
PER	Persian, Modern
PEO	Persian, Old
POL	Polish
POR	Portuguese
PRO	Provencal
PUS	Pushto
QUE	Quechua
RAJ	Rajasthani
ROA	Romance
RUM	Romanian
ROH	Romansh
ROM	Romanian
RUN	Rundi
RUS	Russian
SAM	Samaritan
SAO	Sampan
SAD	Sandawe
SAG	Sango
SAN	Sanskrit
SRD	Sardinian
SCO	Scots
SEL	Selkup
SEM	Semitic
SER	Serbian
SBC	Serbo-Croatian
SRR	Serer
SHN	Shan
SHO	Shona
SID	Sidamo
SND	Sindhi
SNH	Singhalese
SIT	Sino-Tibetan
SIO	Siouan languages
SLA	Slavik
SLO	Slovak
SLV	Slovenian
SOG	Sogdian
SOM	Somali
SON	Songhai
NSO	Sotho, Northern
SOT	Sotho, Southern
SAI	South American Indian
SPA	Spanish
SSA	Sub-Saharan African
SUK	Sukuma
SUX	Sumerian
SUN	Sudanese
SUS	Susu
SWA	Swahili
SWE	Swedish
SYR	Syriac
TAG	Tagalong
TAJ	Tajik
TAM	Tamil
TAR	Tatar
TEl	Telugu
TEM	Temne
TER	Tereno
THA	Thai
TIB	Tibetan
TIG	Tigre
TIR	Tigrinya
TOG	Tonga, Nyasa
TON	Tonga, Tonga Islands
TSI	Tsimshian
TSO	Tsonga
TSW	Tswana
TUR	Turkish
TUK	Turkmen
TUT	Turko-Tataric
TWI	Twi
UGA	Ugaritic
UKR	Ukrainian
UMB	Umbundu
UND	Undetermined
URD	Urdu
UZB	Uzbek
VIE	Vietnamese
VOT	Votic
WAL	Walamo
WAS	Washo
WEL	Welsh
WEN	Wendic
WOL	Wolof
XHO	Xhosa
YAO	Yao
YID	Yiddish
YOR	Yoruba
ZAP	Zapotec
ZEN	Zenaga
ZUL	Zulu
ZUN	Zuni

List of Subject Headings
Children's Fiction

CHARACTERS

ETHNIC GROUPS

HISTORICAL EVENTS

MISCELLANEOUS

OCCUPATIONS

RELATIONSHIPS

SETTINGS

Bowker's Guide to Characters In Fiction® 2004

Volume 2

Children's Fiction

CHARACTERS

A

ADAMS, JILLY (FICTITIOUS CHARACTER)—FICTION

Press, Skip. A Rave of Snakes. 1994. (You-Solve-It Mysteries Ser.: No. 1). 78p. (YA). mass mkt. 3.50 o.p. (*0-8217-4546-8*, Zebra Bks.) Kensington Publishing Corp.

—A Shift of Coyotes. 1994. (You-Solve-It Mysteries Ser.: No. 6). (YA). mass mkt. 3.50 o.s.i (*0-8217-4706-1*, Zebra Bks.) Kensington Publishing Corp.

—A Web of Ya Yas. 1994. (You-Solve-It Mysteries Ser.: No. 4). 224p. (YA). mass mkt. 3.50 o.s.i (*0-8217-4643-X*) Kensington Publishing Corp.

ADAMS, JOHN, 1735-1826—FICTION

Adkins, Jan E. John Adams. 2002. (Childhood of Famous Americans Ser.). (Illus.). 256p. (J). (gr. 3-7). pap. 4.99 (*0-689-85135-9*, Aladdin) Simon & Schuster Children's Publishing.

Bourne, Miriam A. Nabby Adams' Diary. 1975. (Illus.). 128p. (J). (gr. 5-11). 5.95 o.p. (*0-698-20312-7*) Putnam Publishing Group, The.

Hering, Marianne. The Secret of the Missing Teacup. (White House Adventures Ser.: Vol. 2). 64p. (J). (gr. 2-5). pap. 4.99 (*0-7814-3064-X*) Cook Communications Ministries.

Krensky, Stephen. Dangerous Crossing: The Revolutionary Voyage of John & John Quincy Adams. Harlin, Greg, tr. & illus. by. 2005. 32p. (J). 16.99 (*0-525-46966-4*, Dutton Children's Bks.) Penguin Putnam Bks. for Young Readers.

ADDAMS FAMILY (FICTITIOUS CHARACTERS)—FICTION

The Addams Family. 1991. 128p. (J). pap. 2.95 o.p. (*0-590-45541-9*) Scholastic, Inc.

Calmenson, Stephanie. The Addams Family Digest. 1991. 96p. (J). mass mkt. 2.95 o.p. (*0-590-45540-0*) Scholastic, Inc.

Hodgman, Ann. Addams Family Values. Ashby, Ruth, ed. 1993. 96p. (Orig.). (J). pap. 3.99 (*0-671-88001-2*, Aladdin) Simon & Schuster Children's Publishing.

Horowitz, Jordan. The Addams Family. 1991. 32p. (J). (gr. k-2). mass mkt. 2.50 o.p. (*0-590-45539-7*) Scholastic, Inc.

Kash, Conrad, adapted by. The Addams Family in "Sir Pugsley" 1993. (Sound Story Bks.). (Illus.). 24p. (J). (ps-4). 9.95 o.p. (*0-307-74031-5*, 64031, Golden Bks.) Random Hse. Children's Bks.

AHAB, CAPTAIN (FICTITIOUS CHARACTER)—FICTION

Capdevila, Roser. Moby Dick. 2002. (Cuentos Fantasticos de las Tres Mellizas Coleccion: Vol. 1). (SPA.). (J). (gr. k-2). pap. 5.95 (*1-930332-38-6*, LC6629) Lectorum Pubns., Inc.

Dalmatian Press Staff, adapted by. Moby Dick. 2002. (Spot the Classics Ser.). (Illus.). 192p. (J). (gr. k-5). 4.99 (*1-57759-547-5*) Dalmatian Pr.

—Moby Dick. (J). 9.95 (*1-56156-308-0*) Kidsbooks, Inc.

Hagerty, Carol, ed. Moby Dick. 1998. (Classics Ser.: Set II). 77p. (YA). (gr. 5-12). pap. text 7.95 (*1-56254-258-3*, SP2583) Saddleback Publishing, Inc.

Melville, Herman. Moby Dick. 2002. (Great Illustrated Classics). (Illus.). 240p. (J). (gr. 3-8). lib. bdg. 21.35 (*1-57765-695-4*, ABDO & Daughters) ABDO Publishing Co.

—Moby Dick. 1997. (Classics Illustrated Study Guides). (Illus.). 64p. (YA). (gr. 7 up). mass mkt., stu. ed. 4.99 o.p. (*1-57840-013-9*) Acclaim Bks.

—Moby Dick. 1991. (YA). (gr. 5-12). pap. 9.95 (*0-8224-9350-0*) Globe Fearon Educational Publishing.

—Moby Dick. 2002. (Illus.). 48p. (J). tchr. ed. 16.00 (*0-618-26571-6*) Houghton Mifflin Co.

—Moby Dick. Carlson, Donna, ed. 1992. (Illustrated Classics Ser.). (Illus.). 128p. (J). pap. 2.95 o.p. (*1-56156-093-6*) Kidsbooks, Inc.

—Moby Dick. Teresa Agnes, ed. Heller, Rudolf, tr. 1979. (SPA., Illus.). 64p. (J). stu. ed. 1.50 (*0-88301-574-9*); pap. text 3.95 (*0-88301-454-8*) Pendulum Pr., Inc.

—Moby Dick. Shapiro, Irwin, ed. 1973. (Now Age Illustrated Ser.). (Illus.). 64p. (J). (gr. 5-10). 7.50 o.p. (*0-88301-212-X*); pap. 2.95 (*0-88301-099-2*) Pendulum Pr., Inc.

—Moby Dick. Vogel, Malvina, ed. 1990. (Great Illustrated Classics Ser.: Vol. 16). (Illus.). 240p. (J). (gr. 3-6). 9.95 (*0-86611-967-1*) Playmore, Inc., Pubs.

—Moby Dick. 1987. (Regents Illustrated Classics Ser.). (Illus.). 62p. (J). (gr. 7 up). pap. text 5.25 net. o.p. (*0-13-586272-8*, 20381) Prentice Hall, ESL Dept.

—Moby Dick. (American Collection Short Classics). (J). (gr. 4-7). 1993. pap. 4.95 o.p. (*0-8114-6834-8*); 1983. (Illus.). 48p. pap. 9.27 o.p. (*0-8172-2016-X*); 1982. (Illus.). 48p. lib. bdg. 22.83 o.p. (*0-8172-1679-0*) Raintree Pubs.

—Moby Dick. 2000. (Coleccion "Clasicos Juveniles" Ser.). (SPA.). 224p. pap. 12.95 (*0-595-13218-9*) iUniverse, Inc.

—Moby Dick. 2001. (J). (Illus.). 32p. (gr. 4-7). 15.95 (*1-56163-293-7*); pap. 7.95 (*1-56163-294-5*); (Illus.). viii, 119p. pap. 7.95 (*1-56163-291-0*) NBM Publishing Co.

—Moby Dick. 1990. (Illus.). (J). 3.75 o.s.i (*0-425-12023-6*, Classics Illustrated) Berkley Publishing Group.

—Moby Dick. 2nd ed. 2000. (Historias de Siempre Ser.). (SPA., Illus.). 194p. (YA). (gr. 5-8). 9.95 (*84-204-5732-9*) Alfaguara, Ediciones, S.A.- Grupo Santillana ESP. *Dist:* Santillana USA Publishing Co., Inc.

—Moby Dick. 2nd ed. 1998. (Illustrated Classic Book Ser.). (Illus.). 61p. (J). (gr. 3 up). reprint ed. pap. text 4.95 (*1-56767-235-3*) Educational Insights, Inc.

—Moby Dick. adapted ed. (YA). (gr. 5-12). pap. text 9.95 (*0-8359-0225-0*) Globe Fearon Educational Publishing.

—Moby Dick. rev. ed. 1987. (American Classics: Bk. 2). (J). (gr. 9 up). pap. text 5.75 o.p. (*0-13-024416-3*, 18121) Prentice Hall, ESL Dept.

—Moby Dick, RS. 1997. (Illus.). 32p. (J). (gr. k-3). 16.00 o.p. (*0-374-34997-5*, Farrar, Straus & Giroux (BYR)) Farrar, Straus & Giroux.

—Moby Dick: Level 5. (Illus.). 72p. (YA). (gr. 4 up). pap. 7.95 (*1-55576-326-X*, EDN508B) AV Concepts Corp.

—Moby Dick: Or, the White Whale. 1997. (Oxford Illustrated Classics Ser.). (Illus.). 104p. (J). (gr. 4 up). 25.00 o.p. (*0-19-274156-X*) Oxford Univ. Pr., Inc.

—Moby Dick: The White Whale. 1998. (Oxford Illustrated Classics Ser.). (Illus.). 104p. reprint ed. pap. 12.95 (*0-19-278153-7*) Oxford Univ. Pr., Inc.

—Moby Dick, Grades 5-12. adapted ed. pap. text, tchr. ed. 4.95 (*0-8359-0123-8*) Globe Fearon Educational Publishing.

—Moby Dick Readalong. 1994. (Illustrated Classics Collection). 64p. pap. 14.95 incl. audio (*0-7854-0709-X*, 40351); (J). pap. 13.50 o.p. incl. audio (*1-56103-434-7*) American Guidance Service, Inc.

—Moby Dick Readalong, 2 cass., Set. 1986. (Read-Along Ser.). (YA). pap., stu. ed. 34.95 incl. audio (*0-88432-967-4*, S23908) Norton Pubs., Inc., Jeffrey /Audio-Forum.

Melville, Herman & Schwartz, Lew Sayre. Moby Dick. 2002. (Illus.). 48p. (J). pap. 6.95 (*0-618-26572-4*) Houghton Mifflin Co.

Melville, Herman, et al. Moby Dick. (Classics Illustrated Ser.). (Illus.). 52p. (YA). pap. 4.95 (*1-57209-003-0*) Classics International Entertainment, Inc.

Raintree Steck-Vaughn Staff. Moby Dick. 1988. (Short Classics Learning Files Ser.). (J). (gr. 4 up). 22.00 o.p. (*0-8172-2186-7*) Raintree Pubs.

Scott, James, adapted by. Moby Dick: Reproducible Teaching Unit. 2001. 110p. (YA). (gr. 7-12). tchr. ed., ring bd. 29.50 (*1-58049-283-5*, TU169) Prestwick Hse., Inc.

Selden, Bernice, adapted by. Moby Dick. 1988. (Troll Illustrated Classics). (Illus.). (J). 10.15 o.p. (*0-606-03619-9*) Turtleback Bks.

ALADDIN (FICTITIOUS CHARACTER)—FICTION

Aladdin. 1994. 32p. pap. 2.95 (*0-7935-3161-6*) Leonard, Hal Corp.

Aladdin. (Little Library). (J). (ps up). 1995. 126p. 5.98 o.p. (*1-57082-010-4*); 1994. (Illus.). 96p. 7.98 o.p. (*1-57082-015-5*) Mouse Works.

Aladdin. 2004. (J). bds. (*1-4127-0324-7*, 7217801) Publications International, Ltd.

Aladdin. 1995. (Disney Ser.). (Illus.). 24p. (J). (ps-2). bds. o.p. (*0-307-00124-5*, Golden Bks.) Random Hse. Children's Bks.

Aladdin. unabr. ed. 1993. (Read-Along Ser.). (J). (ps-3). 7.99 incl. audio (*1-55723-362-4*) Walt Disney Records.

Aladdin: Here Comes a Parade. unabr. ed. (My First Read Along Ser.). (Illus.). (J). 7.99 incl. audio (*1-55723-748-4*) Walt Disney Records.

Aladdin: Magic Carpet Ride. 1995. (Illus.). 24p. (J). (ps-2). bds. o.p. (*0-307-30144-3*, Golden Bks.) Random Hse. Children's Bks.

Aladdin: The Genie Gets Wet. 1994. (Bath Bk.). 4p. (J). 5.98 o.p. (*1-57082-011-2*) Mouse Works.

Aladdin & His Magic Lamp. 1992. (Paint with Water Fairy Tales Ser.). 32p. (J). (gr. k-2). pap. 1.95 o.s.i (*1-56144-138-4*, Honey Bear Bks.) Modern Publishing.

Aladdin & the Magic Lamp. (Fun-to-Read Fairy Tales Ser.). (Illus.). (J). (gr. k-3). 1992. 24p. pap. 2.50 (*1-56144-169-4*, Honey Bear Bks.); 1988. 12p. bds. 4.95 o.s.i (*0-87449-497-4*) Modern Publishing.

Aladdin Coloring & Activity Books. 1992. (Illus.). (J). (gr. k-3). Bk. 1. pap. 0.99 o.s.i (*1-56144-155-4*); Bk. 2. pap. 0.99 o.s.i (*1-56144-156-2*); Bk. 3. pap. 0.99 o.s.i (*1-56144-157-0*); Bk. 4. pap. 0.99 o.s.i (*1-56144-158-9*) Modern Publishing. (Honey Bear Bks.).

Alistir, K. A. Disney's Aladdin Level 3: Genie School. 1997. (Disney's First Readers Ser.). (Illus.). 40p. (J). (gr. 2-4). pap. 3.50 o.p. (*0-7868-4073-0*) Disney Pr.

Applegate, K. A. Tales from Agrabah: Seven Original Stories of Aladdin & Jasmine. 1995. (Illus.). 96p. (J). (gr. 1-4). 14.95 (*0-7868-3023-9*); 14.89 (*0-7868-5038-8*) Disney Pr.

Barry, Jean & Disney Staff. Aladdin. 1994. (Little Nugget Bks.). (Illus.). 28p. (J). (ps-3). o.p. (*0-307-12547-5*, Golden Bks.) Random Hse. Children's Bks.

Bazaldua, Barbara. Fine-Feathered Friend: Disney's Aladdin. 1995. (Illus.). 24p. (J). (ps-3). pap. text 2.25 o.p. (*0-307-12883-0*, Golden Bks.) Random Hse. Children's Bks.

—Mixed-Up Magic: Disney's Aladdin. 1995. (Illus.). 24p. (J). (ps-3). pap. text 2.25 o.p. (*0-307-12882-2*, Golden Bks.) Random Hse. Children's Bks.

—Monkey Business: Disney's Aladdin. 1993. (Illus.). 24p. (J). (ps-3). pap. o.p. (*0-307-12788-5*, Golden Bks.) Random Hse. Children's Bks.

Braybrooks, Ann. Aladdin. 1993. (J). o.p. (*0-307-62692-X*, Golden Bks.) Random Hse. Children's Bks.

—The Cave of Wonders: Disney's Aladdin. 1993. (Illus.). (J). (ps-3). o.p. (*0-307-11565-8*); pap. o.p. (*0-307-15974-4*) Random Hse. Children's Bks. (Golden Bks.).

Braybrooks, Ann & Disney Staff. Aladdin. 1992. (Golden Look-Look Bks.). (Illus.). 24p. (J). (ps-3). pap. o.p. (*0-307-12692-7*, 12692, Golden Bks.) Random Hse. Children's Bks.

Burton, Richard F., tr. from ARA. Aladdin & His Wonderful Lamp. 1982. (Illus.). 48p. (J). (gr. 1-4). 10.95 o.s.i (*0-440-00302-4*); lib. bdg. 10.89 o.s.i (*0-440-00304-0*) Dell Publishing. (Delacorte Pr.).

Carrick, Carol. Aladdin & the Wonderful Lamp. 1989. (Illus.). (J). (ps-3). 12.95 o.p. (*0-590-41679-0*) Scholastic, Inc.

Carrick, Donald. Aladdin & the Wonderful Lamp. 1992. (J). mass mkt. 4.95 o.p. (*0-590-41680-4*) Scholastic, Inc.

Chen, Ju-Hong, illus. The Tale of Aladdin & the Wonderful Lamp. 1992. 32p. (J). (ps-3). tchr. ed. 14.95 (*0-8234-0938-4*) Holiday Hse., Inc.

Daniels, Patricia. Aladdin & the Magic Lamp. 1980. (Fairy Tales Ser.). (Illus.). 24p. (J). (gr. k-5). lib. bdg. 9.95 o.s.i (*0-8393-0257-6*) Raintree Pubs.

Daniels, Patricia, retold by. Aladdin & the Magic Lamp. 1981. (Fairy Tale Clippers Ser.). (Illus.). 24p. (J). (gr. k-5). lib. bdg. 29.28 o.s.i (*0-8393-1832-4*) Raintree Pubs.

Dawood, N. J. Aladdin: And Other Tales from the Arabian Nights. 1990. 176p. (J). (gr. 4 up). pap. 3.50 o.p. (*0-14-035105-1*, Puffin Bks.) Penguin Putnam Bks. for Young Readers.

—Aladdin & Other Tales from the Arabian Nights. 1997. (Puffin Classics Ser.). (Illus.). 208p. (YA). (gr. 5-9). pap. 3.99 (*0-14-036782-9*) Penguin Putnam Bks. for Young Readers.

—Aladdin & Other Tales from the Arabian Nights. 1996. (Puffin Classics). (J). 10.04 (*0-606-02968-0*) Turtleback Bks.

Dawood, N. J., tr. Aladdin & the Enchanted Lamp. abr. ed. 1996. (Classic Ser.). (J). audio 10.95 o.s.i (*0-14-086230-7*, Penguin AudioBooks) Viking Penguin.

Deighton, Jo, adapted by. Scheherezade Presents. (Scheherezade Presents Ser.: No. 1). (Illus.). (J). 44p. pap. (*1-85964-091-5*); 43p. pap. (*1-85964-100-8*); 44p. pap. (*1-85964-092-3*); 44p. pap. (*1-85964-093-1*); 43p. pap. (*1-85964-094-X*); 42p. pap. (*1-85964-095-8*); 44p. pap. (*1-85964-096-6*); 57p. pap. (*1-85964-097-4*); 43p. pap. (*1-85964-098-2*); 42p. pap. (*1-85964-099-0*) Garnet Publishing, Ltd. (Ithaca Pr.).

Disney Book Club Staff. Aladdin & the Wonderful Lamp. 1999. (J). lib. bdg. (*0-394-93937-9*, Random Hse. Bks. for Young Readers) Random Hse. Children's Bks.

Disney Staff. Aladdin. (FRE.). 96p. (J). (gr. k-5). pap. 9.95 (*0-7859-8852-1*) French & European Pubns., Inc.

—Aladdin. (J). 1993. (SPA.). 7.98 o.p. (*0-453-03164-1*); 1992. (Illus.). 96p. 7.98 o.p. (*0-453-03058-0*) Mouse Works.

—Aladdin: Little Library. 1993. (Illus.). (J). (ps). 5.98 o.p. (*0-453-03170-6*) Mouse Works.

—Aladdin: The Genie Gets Wet Bath Book. 1993. (Illus.). (J). (ps). text 5.98 o.p. (*0-453-03169-2*) Mouse Works.

—Aladdin: Travels with Genie. 1993. (J). (ps-3). 1.09 o.p. (*0-453-03138-2*) Mouse Works.

—Aladdin: Wishful Thinking. 1997. (Disney's "Storytime Treasures" Library: Vol. 3). (Illus.). 44p. (J). (gr. 1-6). 3.49 o.p. (*1-885222-99-8*) Advance Pubs. LLC.

—Aladdin Bath Book. 1992. (Penguin-Disney Ser.). (J). (ps-3). 5.98 o.p. (*0-453-03060-2*) Mouse Works.

—Aladdin Little Library. 1992. (Penguin-Disney Ser.). (J). (ps-3). 5.98 o.p. (*0-453-03059-9*) Mouse Works.

—The Secret of Aladdin's Lamp. 1993. (J). (ps-3). pap. 5.98 o.s.i (*0-453-03098-X*) Mouse Works.

—Squeak Abu! Aladdin. 1994. (Illus.). 9p. (J). (ps). 6.98 o.p. (*0-453-03243-5*) NAL.

Disney's Aladdin. 1995. (Play Lights Bks.). (Illus.). (J). 5p. bds. o.p. (*0-307-75303-4*); 14p. bds. o.p. (*0-307-74102-8*) Random Hse. Children's Bks. (Golden Bks.).

Disney's Aladdin: A Postcard Book. 1993. (Disney Postcard Bk.). (Illus.). 64p. (Orig.). (J). pap. 8.95 o.s.i (*1-56138-257-4*) Running Pr. Bk. Pubs.

Disney's How to Draw Aladdin. 1993. (Hardback Disney's Classic Character Ser.). (Illus.). 48p. 9.95 o.p. (*1-56010-112-1*, DC04); 40p. (YA). (gr. 3 up). pap. 8.95 (*1-56010-163-6*, DC04) Foster, Walter Publishing, Inc.

Elder, Vanessa. Jasmine's Story. 1997. (Disney Chapters Ser.). 64p. (J). (gr. 2-4). pap. 3.50 o.p. (*0-7868-4153-2*) Disney Pr.

Falken, Linda C., ed. Aladdin & the Wonderful Lamp & Other Tales of Adventure. 1987. (Golden Junior Classics Ser.). (Illus.). 48p. (J). (ps-3). o.p. (*0-307-12808-3*, Golden Bks.) Random Hse. Children's Bks.

Fontes, Justine. Aladdin: The Genie's Wish. 1997. (Golden Book Ser.). (Illus.). (J). pap. text o.p. (*0-307-13043-6*, Golden Bks.) Random Hse. Children's Bks.

Glennon, William. Aladdin. rev. ed. 1990. 63p. pap. 5.60 (*0-87129-072-3*, A46) Dramatic Publishing Co.

Goldberg, Moses. Aladdin: A Participation Play. 1977. (J). 6.00 (*0-87602-101-1*) Anchorage Pr.

Golden Books Staff. Aladdin. 1998. 2.22 o.s.i (*0-307-34047-3*); 1994. o.p. (*0-307-03022-9*); 1994. 48p. pap. 2.22 o.s.i (*0-307-03892-0*) Random Hse. Children's Bks. (Golden Bks.).

—Aladdin Giant Color Activity Book. 9999. (J). o.p. (*0-307-03336-8*, Golden Bks.) Random Hse. Children's Bks.

—Aladdin Giant Paint with Water. 9999. 3.99 o.p. (*0-307-02790-2*, Golden Bks.) Random Hse. Children's Bks.

—Thief among Us. 1997. (Golden Book Ser.). 70p. (J). (ps-4). pap. text o.p. (*0-307-03445-3*, Golden Bks.) Random Hse. Children's Bks.

Guile, Gill. Aladdin. 1996. (Once Upon a Time Ser.). (Illus.). 24p. (J). (ps-1). 3.98 (*1-85854-415-7*) Brimax Bks., Ltd.

Haas, Kenny. Disney's Aladdin. 1995. (Look & Find Ser.). (Illus.). 24p. (J). (ps-6). lib. bdg. 14.95 (*1-56674-143-2*, HTS Bks.) Forest Hse. Publishing Co., Inc.

Hal Leonard Corporation Staff. Aladdin: Illustrated Songbook. 1994. (Illus.). 48p. pap. 14.95 (*0-7935-3412-7*) Leonard, Hal Corp.

Harris, Sarah, adapted by. Aladdin. 1995. (Comes to Life Bks.). (DUT & ENG.). 16p. (J). (ps-2). (*1-57234-034-7*) YES! Entertainment Corp.

Hautzig, Deborah. Aladdin & the Magic Lamp. 1993. (Step into Reading Ser.). (Illus.). 48p. (J). (ps-3). pap. 3.99 o.s.i (*0-679-83241-6*, Random Hse. Bks. for Young Readers) Random Hse. Children's Bks.

Hildebrandt, Greg, illus. Aladdin & the Magic Lamp. 1992. (Read-to-Me Ser.). 48p. (J). (ps-2). 5.95 o.p. (*0-88101-266-1*) Unicorn Publishing Hse., Inc., The.

Horowitz, Jordan. Aladdin & the Magic Lamp. 1993. 32p. (J). (ps-3). mass mkt. 2.50 o.p. (*0-590-46417-5*) Scholastic, Inc.

Humphrey, L. Spencer. Aladdin. 1995. 32p. (J). (ps-3). pap. text 2.95 (*0-8125-2319-9*, Tor Bks.) Doherty, Tom Assocs., LLC.

Johnson-Davies, Denys, tr. from ARA. Aladdin & the Lamp. 1995. (Tales from Egypt & the Arab World Ser.). (Illus.). 48p. (Orig.). (J). (gr. 3-8). pap. 6.95 (*977-5325-38-2*) Hoopoe Bks. EGY. *Dist:* AMIDEAST.

Junger, Ernst. Aladdin's Problem. Neugroschel, Joachim, tr. from GER. 1992. (Eridanos Library). 136p. 19.00 (*0-941419-58-4*, Eridanos Library) Marsilio Pubs.

Kerven, Rosalind. Aladdin. 2000. (Classic Readers Ser.). (Illus.). 32p. (J). (gr. 2-3). pap. 12.95 (*0-7894-5700-8*, D K Ink) Dorling Kindersley Publishing, Inc.

—Aladdin: And Other Tales from the Arabian Nights. 1998. (Eyewitness Classics Ser.). (Illus.). 64p. (J). (gr. 3-6). pap. 14.95 o.p. (*0-7894-2789-3*) Dorling Kindersley Publishing, Inc.

Kerven, Rosalind & Mistry, Nilesh. Aladdin. 2000. (Classic Readers Ser.). (Illus.). 32p. (J). (gr. 2-3). pap. 3.95 (*0-7894-5389-4*, D K Ink) Dorling Kindersley Publishing, Inc.

Kliros. Aladdin Sticker Storybook. 1997. (J). pap. 1.00 (*0-486-29907-4*) Dover Pubns., Inc.

Kreider, Karen. The Genie's Tale: Disney's Aladdin. 1993. (Golden Super Shape Book Ser.). (Illus.). 24p. (J). (ps). pap. o.p. (*0-307-10019-7*, 10019, Golden Bks.) Random Hse. Children's Bks.

Kreider, Karen & Disney Staff. Aladdin. 1992. (Big Golden Bks.). (Illus.). 24p. (J). (ps-3). o.p. (*0-307-12348-0*, 12348, Golden Bks.) Random Hse. Children's Bks.

Kuntsler, James Howard. Aladdin & the Magic Lamp. 1995. (J). (ps-3). 19.95 o.p. incl. audio (*0-689-80063-0*, Simon & Schuster Children's Publishing) Simon & Schuster Children's Publishing.

Ladybird Books Staff. Aladdin & Ali Baba. 1997. (Classic Ser.). 56p. (J). 2.99 o.s.i (*0-7214-5615-4*, Ladybird Bks.) Penguin Group (USA) Inc.

Landes, William-Alan. Aladdin n' His Magic Lamp. rev. ed. 1985. (Wondrawhopper Ser.). 51p. (J). (gr. 3-12). pap. 6.00 (*0-88734-102-0*) Players Pr., Inc.

—Aladdin n' His Magic Lamp: Music & Lyrics. rev. ed. 1985. (Wondrawhopper Ser.). (J). (gr. 3-12). pap. text 15.00 (*0-88734-002-4*) Players Pr., Inc.

Lang, Andrew. Aladdin. 1983. (Illus.). 32p. (J). (gr. 4-7). pap. 5.99 o.s.i (*0-14-050389-7*, Puffin Bks.) Penguin Putnam Bks. for Young Readers.

—Aladdin & the Wonderful Lamp. 1981. (Illus.). 32p. (J). (gr. 1 up). 12.50 o.p. (*0-670-11146-5*) Viking Penguin.

Leibold, Jay. The Search for Aladdin's Lamp. 1991. (Choose Your Own Adventure Ser.: No. 117). 128p. (J). (gr. 4-8). pap. 3.50 o.s.i (*0-553-29185-8*) Bantam Bks.

—The Search for Aladdin's Lamp. l.t. ed. 1995. (Choose Your Own Adventure Ser.: No. 117). (Illus.). 128p. (J). (gr. 4-8). lib. bdg. 21.27 o.p. (*0-8368-1311-1*) Stevens, Gareth Inc.

Lubin, Leonard. Aladdin & His Wonderful Lamp. Burton, Richard T., tr. from ARA. 1982. (Illus.). 48p. (J). (ps-3). 12.95 o.s.i (*0-385-28033-5*, Delacorte Pr.) Dell Publishing.

Mayer, Marianna. Aladdin & the Enchanted Lamp. 1985. (Illus.). 96p. (J). (gr. 4-6). 15.95 o.s.i (*0-02-765360-9*, Simon & Schuster Children's Publishing) Simon & Schuster Children's Publishing.

McGee, Marni. Forest Child. 1999. (Illus.). 40p. (J). (ps-3). pap. 5.99 (*0-689-82578-1*, 076714005990, Aladdin) Simon & Schuster Children's Publishing.

Michelinie, David, et al. The Aladdin Effect. 1985. 64p. 5.95 o.p. (*0-87135-081-5*) Marvel Enterprises.

Miller, A. G., ed. Pop-Up Aladdin & the Wonderful Lamp. 1970. (Pop-Up Classics Ser.: No. 7). (Illus.). (J). 3.95 o.p. (*0-394-81105-4*, Random Hse. Bks. for Young Readers) Random Hse. Children's Bks.

Morris, Neil & Morris, Ting. Aladdin. 1991. (Evans Illustrated Stories Ser.). (Illus.). 48p. (J). (gr. 2-5). 13.95 o.p. (*0-237-50933-4*) Evans Brothers, Ltd. GBR. *Dist:* Trafalgar Square.

Mouse Works Staff. Aladdin. (J). 1997. (SPA., Illus.). (*1-57082-809-1*); 1997. (Illus.). 7.98 (*1-57082-794-X*); 1995. 7.98 o.s.i (*1-57082-030-9*) Mouse Works.

—Aladdin - Peter Pan, 2. 75th anniv. ed. 1998. (Illus.). (ps-3). 9.99 (*0-7364-0086-9*) Mouse Works.

Norris, James. Aladdin & the Wonderful Lamp. 1940. (J). 6.00 (*0-87602-102-X*) Anchorage Pr.

Plumb, A. R. Birds of a Feather. 1994. (Further Adventures of Aladdin Ser.: No. 2). (Illus.). 64p. (J). (gr. k-3). pap. 3.50 o.p. (*0-7868-4017-X*) Disney Pr.

—Iago's Promise. 1995. (Further Adventures of Aladdin Ser.: Bk. 4). (Illus.). 64p. (J). (gr. 1-4). pap. 3.50 o.p. (*0-7868-4024-2*) Disney Pr.

—A Thief in the Night. 1994. (Further Adventures of Aladdin Ser.: No. 1). (Illus.). 64p. (J). (gr. k-3). pap. 3.50 o.p. (*0-7868-4016-1*) Disney Pr.

Resnick, Mike & Greenberg, Martin H., eds. Aladdin: Master of the Lamp. 1992. 352p. (Orig.). mass mkt. 4.99 o.p. (*0-88677-545-0*) DAW Bks., Inc.

Roberts, Fulton. Jasmine's Magic Charm: Disney's Aladdin. 1994. (Golden Book Ser.). (Illus.). 32p. (J). (ps-3). o.p. (*0-307-16154-4*, Golden Bks.) Random Hse. Children's Bks.

Roffey, Maureen, illus. Aladdin. 1997. (Duplo Fold-Out Playbks.). 10p. (J). (ps up). 12.95 (*0-316-85342-9*) Little Brown & Co.

Rovinson, W. Heath. Aladdin & Other Tales from the Arabian Nights. 1993. (Everyman's Library Children's Classics Ser.). (gr. 2 up). 12.95 (*0-679-42533-0*) Knopf, Alfred A. Inc.

Schreiber, Anne. Disney's Aladdin: Abu Monkeys Around, Vol. 1. 1997. (Disney's First Readers Ser.). (Illus.). 32p. (J). (gr. 1-3). pap. 2.95 o.p. (*0-7868-4071-4*) Disney Pr.

Shane, Harold G. Aladdin & the Wonderful Lamp. Clark, William, ed. 1980. (Hero Legends Bks.). (Illus.). 16p. (J). (gr. 4-8). pap. 29.95 o.p. (*0-89290-080-6*, BC15-3) S V E & Churchill Media.

Singer, A. L. Aladdin: Illustrated Classic (Mini Edition) 1996. (Illus.). 96p. (J). 5.95 o.p. (*0-7868-3073-5*) Disney Pr.

Singer, A. L., adapted by. Disney's Aladdin. 1992. (Junior Novelization Ser.). (Illus.). 64p. (J). (gr. 1-4). pap. 3.50 o.p. (*1-56282-241-1*) Disney Pr.

Smith, Philip, ed. Aladdin & Other Favorite Arabian Nights Stories. 1993. (Children's Thrift Classics Ser.). (Illus.). 96p. (J). (gr. 3 up). reprint ed. pap. 1.00 (*0-486-27571-X*) Dover Pubns., Inc.

—Listen & Read Aladdin & Other Favorite Arabian Nights Stories. 1998. 5.95 (*0-486-40108-1*) Dover Pubns., Inc.

Stempleski. Aladdin & the Magic Lamp. Date not set. pap. text 72.95 (*0-582-03043-9*) Addison-Wesley Longman, Ltd. GBR. *Dist:* Trans-Atlantic Pubns., Inc.

Stewart, Pat L. Aladdin Stickers. 1994. (Dover Little Activity Bks.). (J). (ps-3). pap. 1.00 (*0-486-28158-2*) Dover Pubns., Inc.

Stewart, Pat Ronson. Aladdin & the Magic Lamp: Full-Color Picture Book. 1995. (Illus.). 16p. (Orig.). (J). pap. text 1.00 (*0-486-28524-3*) Dover Pubns., Inc.

The Story of Aladdin. 1997. (Scheherezade Children's Stories Ser.). (Illus.). 16p. (J). (*1-873938-84-5*, Ithaca Pr.) Garnet Publishing, Ltd.

Suben, Eric. Aladdin & the Magic Lamp. 1995. (Storytime Bks.). (Illus.). 24p. (J). (ps-2). pap. 1.29 o.p. (*1-56293-542-9*, McClanahan Bk.) Learning Horizons, Inc.

Suire, Diane Dow, tr. from SPA. Aladdin's Lamp: A Classic Tale. 1988. (Classic Tales Ser.).Tr. of Aladino y la Lampara Maravillosa. (Illus.). 32p. (J). (ps-3). lib. bdg. 19.93 o.p. (*0-89565-481-4*) Child's World, Inc.

Thompkins, Kenny & Gallego, James, illus. Disney's Aladdin. 1992. (Illustrated Classics Ser.). 96p. (J). 14.95 o.p. (*1-56282-240-3*); lib. bdg. 14.89 o.s.i (*1-56282-275-6*) Disney Pr.

Tyrrell, Melissa. Aladdin. 2002. (Fairytale Foil Bks.). (Illus.). 10p. (J). bds. 4.99 (*0-8431-4868-3*, Price Stern Sloan) Penguin Putnam Bks. for Young Readers.

Vaccaro Associates Staff, illus. Aladdin: The Magic Carpet Ride. 1993. (Tiny Changing Pictures Bk.). 10p. (J). (ps-k). 4.95 o.p. (*1-56282-396-5*) Disney Pr.

Vaccaro Associates Staff & Durrell, Dennis, illus. Aladdin: Peek Abu. 1993. (Surprise Lift-the-Flap Bk.). 18p. (J). (ps-1). 9.95 o.p. (*1-56282-389-2*) Disney Pr.

Varley, Chris. Aladdin & the King of Thieves. 1996. (My Favorite Sound Story Bks.). (Illus.). 32p. (J). o.p. (*0-307-71136-6*, 61136-30, Golden Bks.) Random Hse. Children's Bks.

Wakeman, Diana, illus. Aladdin: Pop-Up Book. 1993. 12p. (J). (ps-3). 11.95 o.p. (*1-56282-242-X*) Disney Pr.

Walt Disney Productions Staff. Aladdin. 1993. (Disney Miniature Editions Ser.). (Illus.). 144p. (J). (ps-3). 5.95 o.p. (*1-56138-251-5*) Running Pr. Bk. Pubs.

—Alladin Music Fun. 1992. 49p. (J). (ps-3). 9.95 (*0-7935-1828-8*) Leonard, Hal Corp.

Walt Disney's Feature Animation Department Staff. Disney's Aladdin Postcard Book. 1995. (Illus.). 64p. (J). pap. 8.95 (*0-7868-8059-7*) Hyperion Pr.

—Walt Disney's Aladdin: An Animated Flip Book. 1992. (Illus.). 96p. (J). pap. 3.95 o.s.i (*1-56282-889-4*) Hyperion Pr.

ALCOTT, LOUISA MAY, 1832-1888—FICTION

Atkins, Jeannine. Becoming Little Women: Louisa May at Fruitlands. 2001. (Illus.). 176p. (J). (gr. 4-7). 16.99 (*0-399-23619-8*, G. P. Putnam's Sons) Penguin Group (USA) Inc.

Klass, Sheila S. Little Women Next Door. 2000. (Illus.). 188p. (J). (gr. 3-7). tchr. ed. 15.95 (*0-8234-1472-8*) Holiday Hse., Inc.

Wallner, Alexandra. An Alcott Family Christmas. 1996. (Illus.). 32p. (J). (gr. k-3). tchr. ed. 15.95 (*0-8234-1265-2*) Holiday Hse., Inc.

ALEXANDER, THE GREAT, 356-323 B.C.—FICTION

Love, Ann. Taking Control: Historical Adventure. rev. ed. 1996. reprint ed. pap. 5.00 (*0-88092-998-7*) Royal Fireworks Publishing Co.

ALFRED, KING OF ENGLAND, 849-899—FICTION

Ross, Stewart. Find King Alfred! Alfred the Great & the Danes. 1998. (Coming Alive Ser.). (Illus.). 62p. (J). (gr. 4-6). 17.95 (*0-237-51786-8*) Evans Brothers, Ltd. GBR. *Dist:* Trafalgar Square.

Tingle, Rebecca. The Edge on the Sword. 2003. (Sailing Mystery Ser.). 288p. (J). pap. 6.99 (*0-14-250058-5*, Puffin Bks.) Penguin Putnam Bks. for Young Readers.

ALICE (FICTITIOUS CHARACTER: CARROLL)—FICTION

Alice in Wonderland. 2003. (J). 12.99 (*0-7868-3476-5*) Disney Pr.

Alice in Wonderland. 2003. (Illus.). 288p. (J). 9.98 (*1-4054-1674-2*) Parragon, Inc.

Alice in Wonderland. 2004. (J). bds. (*1-4127-0325-5*, 7217802) Publications International, Ltd.

Alice in Wonderland. unabr. ed. Incl. Alice in Wonderland: A Mad Tea-Party. audio Alice in Wonderland: Advice from a Caterpillar. audio Alice in Wonderland: Alice's Evidence. audio Alice in Wonderland: Down the Rabbit Hole. audio Alice in Wonderland: Pig & Pepper. audio Alice in Wonderland: The Cheshire-Cat. audio Alice in Wonderland: The Mock Turtle's Story. audio Alice in Wonderland: The Pool of Tears. audio Alice in Wonderland: The Queen's Croquet-Ground. audio Alice in Wonderland: Who Stole the Tarts. audio (J). 1984. Set audio 9.95 (*0-89845-899-4*, CPN 1097, Caedmon) HarperTrade.

Alice in Wonderland: A Mad Tea-Party. (J). audio HarperTrade.

Alice in Wonderland: Advice from a Caterpillar. (J). audio HarperTrade.

Alice in Wonderland: Alice's Evidence. (J). audio HarperTrade.

Alice in Wonderland: Down the Rabbit Hole. (J). audio HarperTrade.

Alice in Wonderland: Pig & Pepper. (J). audio HarperTrade.

Alice in Wonderland: The Cheshire-Cat. (J). audio HarperTrade.

Alice in Wonderland: The Mock Turtle's Story. (J). audio HarperTrade.

Alice in Wonderland: The Pool of Tears. (J). audio HarperTrade.

Alice in Wonderland: The Queen's Croquet-Ground. (J). audio HarperTrade.

Alice in Wonderland: Who Stole the Tarts. (J). audio HarperTrade.

Bassett, Jennifer, ed. Through the Looking Glass: And What Alice Found There. 1995. (Illus.). 64p. pap. text 5.95 o.p. (*0-19-422749-9*) Oxford Univ. Pr., Inc.

Brown, Michele. New Tales From Alice's Wonderland: Collection One. 2000. pap. 13.95 (*0-233-99610-9*) Andre Deutsch GBR. *Dist:* Trafalgar Square, Trans-Atlantic Pubns., Inc.

Brownlow, Paul. Alice in Wonderland. 1993. 140p. 7.99 o.p. (*1-877719-66-8*) Brownlow Publishing Co., Inc.

Bryer, Denise, reader. Alice in Wonderland. (J). (ps-2). audio 2.98 (*1-55886-031-2*); audio 3.98 o.p. (*1-55886-039-8*) Smarty Pants.

Carroll, Lewis, pseud. Alice im Wunderland. 1999. Tr. of Alice in Wonderland. (GER., Illus.). (ps up). 12.95 (*3-499-20733-8*) Rowohlt Taschenbuch Verlag GmbH DEU. *Dist:* Distribooks, Inc.

—Alice in Wonderland. 1999. (J). pap. 4.99 o.p. (*1-57840-191-7*) Acclaim Bks.

—Alice in Wonderland. Date not set. (J). lib. bdg. 16.95 (*0-8488-1262-X*) Amereon, Ltd.

—Alice in Wonderland. unabr. ed. (J). audio 23.80 Audio Bk. Co.

—Alice in Wonderland, unabr. ed. 1997. audio 17.95 (*0-7861-1214-X*, 1997) Blackstone Audio Bks., Inc.

—Alice in Wonderland. (J). 2001. per. 12.50 (*1-891355-26-0*); 2000. per. 15.50 (*1-58396-193-3*) Blue Unicorn Editions.

—Alice in Wonderland. Date not set. (Illus.). 248p. (YA). 14.95 (*1-884807-19-4*) Blushing Rose Publishing.

—Alice in Wonderland. unabr. ed. (J). audio 16.95 (*1-55686-118-4*, 118) Books in Motion.

—Alice in Wonderland. unabr. ed. (J). audio 20.00 o.p. Books on Tape, Inc.

—Alice in Wonderland. 1994. (Children's Classics Ser.). (J). 112p. 9.98 (*0-86112-457-X*); 64p. 5.98 (*0-86112-942-3*) Brimax Bks., Ltd.

—Alice in Wonderland. 1981. (J). reprint ed. 299p. lib. bdg. 12.95 o.s.i (*0-89967-019-9*, Harmony Raine & Co.); 215p. lib. bdg. 15.95 o.s.i (*0-89966-345-1*) Buccaneer Bks., Inc.

—Alice in Wonderland. audio 18.95 California Artists Radio Theater Productions.

—Alice in Wonderland. 2003. (Illus.). 208p. (J). pap. 12.99 (*0-7636-2049-1*) Candlewick Pr.

—Alice in Wonderland. (J). (gr. 2-4). audio 19.95 Cover to Cover Cassettes, Ltd.

—Alice in Wonderland. 1988. (Illus.). 144p. (J). 3.95 o.s.i (*0-517-50858-3*); 7.95 o.s.i (*0-517-50857-5*) Crown Publishing Group. (Clarkson Potter).

—Alice in Wonderland. Carruth, Jane, ed. 2000. (Illus.). 93p. (J). (gr. 4-6). reprint ed. 25.00 (*0-7881-9229-9*) DIANE Publishing Co.

—Alice in Wonderland. 1992. 12p. (J). pap. 14.00 (*0-440-80312-8*) Dell Publishing.

—Alice in Wonderland. (Juvenile Classics). (Illus.). (J). 2001. 160p. 2.00 (*0-486-41658-5*); 1998. 80p. pap. 1.00 (*0-486-40345-9*) Dover Pubns., Inc.

—Alice in Wonderland. 1965. 124p. (J). (gr. 1 up). pap. 5.60 (*0-87129-241-6*, A13) Dramatic Publishing Co.

—Alice in Wonderland. abr. ed. (J). 1986. (gr. 5-7). audio 29.95 o.p. (*0-88646-801-9*, 7063); 1983. audio 4.99 (*0-88646-647-4*); 1982. audio 15.95 o.p. (*0-88646-046-8*, TC-LFP 7063) Durkin Hayes Publishing Ltd.

—Alice in Wonderland. 1992. (Children's Classics Ser.). (Illus.). (J). (*0-89434-121-9*, Ferguson Publishing Co.) Facts on File Inc.

—Alice in Wonderland. Steadman, Ralph, tr. & illus. by. 2003. 128p. (J). 29.95 (*1-55297-754-4*) Firefly Bks., Ltd.

—Alice in Wonderland, Set. unabr. ed. (J). audio 14.95 Halvorson Assocs.

—Alice in Wonderland. Date not set. (Illus.). 176p. (J). 14.95 (*0-06-095770-0*) HarperCollins Children's Bk. Group.

—Alice in Wonderland. Date not set. 192p. (YA). (gr. 3 up). mass mkt. 8.99 (*0-06-440929-5*) HarperCollins Pubs.

—Alice in Wonderland. abr. ed. (J). audio 29.95 o.p. (*0-89845-390-9*, SBC 127, HarperAudio) HarperTrade.

—Alice in Wonderland. 1989. (J). (gr. 4 up). audio 21.00 Jimcin Recordings.

—Alice in Wonderland. 1981. (English As a Second Language Bk.). (J). pap. text 5.95 o.p. (*0-582-53414-3*, 74058) Longman Publishing Group.

—Alice in Wonderland. (J). 1999. (gr. 4-7). 20.00 (*0-7871-1978-4*); 1993. audio 4.95 o.p. (*1-55800-676-1*, 390104) NewStar Media, Inc.

—Alice in Wonderland. 1999. (Illus.). 104p. (J). (gr. 4-7). 19.95 (*0-7358-1166-0*) North-South Bks., Inc.

—Alice in Wonderland. Gray, Donald J., ed. 1971. (Critical Editions Ser.). (Illus.). (J). 10.00 o.p. (*0-393-04343-6*); pap. o.p. (*0-393-09977-6*) Norton, W. W. & Co., Inc.

—Alice in Wonderland. Grey, Donald J., ed. 2nd ed. 1992. (Critical Editions Ser.). (Illus.). 408p. (C). pap. text 14.20 (*0-393-95804-3*) Norton, W. W. & Co., Inc.

—Alice in Wonderland. 2003. audio 17.99 (*1-58926-167-4*, C05M-0060) Oasis Audio.

—Alice in Wonderland. (Classic Ser.). (Illus.). 1996. 56p. 2.99 o.s.i (*0-7214-5676-6*); 1994. 52p. (J). text 3.50 (*0-7214-1654-3*, Ladybird Bks.) Penguin Group (USA) Inc.

—Alice in Wonderland. 1986. (Illus.). 120p. (YA). (gr. 5 up). 10.95 o.p. (*0-448-18983-6*, Grosset & Dunlap) Penguin Putnam Bks. for Young Readers.

—Alice in Wonderland. 1984. (Classics Ser.). (Illus.). 162p. (J). (gr. 2 up). reprint ed. 7.00 o.p. (*0-88088-902-0*, 889020) Peter Pauper Pr. Inc.

—Alice in Wonderland. 1987. (Radiobook Ser.). (J). audio 4.98 (*0-929541-09-X*) Radiola Co.

—Alice in Wonderland. 1944. (Windermere Classics Ser.). (Illus.). 240p. (gr. 3 up). pap. 1.50 o.p. (*0-528-87166-8*) Rand McNally.

—Alice in Wonderland. (Little Golden Bks.). (J). pap. 4.99 o.p. (*0-307-02149-1*, 98104, Golden Bks.) Random Hse. Children's Bks.

—Alice in Wonderland. 1990. 7.99 o.p. (*0-517-05738-7*); 1988. (Illus.). (J). 12.99 o.s.i (*0-517-65961-1*); 1930. (J). 7.99 o.s.i (*0-517-05191-5*) Random Hse. Value Publishing.

—Alice in Wonderland. 1968. (Pop-up Books Ser. No. 3). (Illus.). (J). 3.95 o.p. (*0-394-80898-3*) Random Hse., Inc.

—Alice in Wonderland. (Illus.). (J). 2002. 160p. (gr. 2). mass mkt. 3.99 (*0-439-29149-6*); 1988. 160p. (gr. 4-7). mass mkt. 4.50 (*0-590-42035-6*, Scholastic Paperbacks); 1972. reprint ed. pap. 1.95 o.p. (*0-590-08503-4*) Scholastic, Inc.

—Alice in Wonderland. (J). (gr. k-6). 1997. (Illus.). 60p. 7.98 o.p. (*0-7651-9188-1*); 1990. 7.98 o.p. (*0-8317-1351-8*) Smithmark Pubs., Inc.

—Alice in Wonderland. abr. ed. (Children's Classics Ser.). (J). 1998. audio 13.95 o.p. (*1-55935-161-6*); 1972. pap. 5.95 o.p. incl. audio (*0-88142-320-3*, 320) Soundelux Audio Publishing.

—Alice in Wonderland. 1929. 110p. (J). pap. 2.95 o.p. (*0-460-87107-2*, Everyman's Classic Library in Paperback) Tuttle Publishing.

—Alice in Wonderland. abr. unabr. ed. 1997. (Children's Classics Ser.). (J). audio 10.95 o.s.i (*0-14-086219-6*, Penguin AudioBooks) Viking Penguin.

—Alice in Wonderland. (Children's Classics). 272p. (J). 2001. pap. 3.95 (*1-85326-118-1*); 1998. pap. 3.95 (*1-85326-002-9*, 0029WW) Wordsworth Editions, Ltd. GBR. *Dist:* Advanced Global Distribution Services, Casemate Pubs. & Bk. Distributors, LLC, Combined Publishing.

—Alice in Wonderland: A Classic Tale. Riehecky, Janet, tr. from SPA. 1988. (Classic Tales Ser.).Tr. of Alicia en el Pais de las Maravillas. (Illus.). 32p. (J). (ps-3). lib. bdg. 19.93 o.p. (*0-89565-467-9*) Child's World, Inc.

—Alice in Wonderland: Fairy Tales. Tallarico, Tony, ed. 1987. (Tuffy Story Bks.). 32p. (J). (ps-3). 2.95 o.s.i (*0-89828-328-0*, 83280, Tuffy Bks.) Putnam Publishing Group, The.

—Alice in Wonderland: Giant Illustrated Edition. 1976. (Illus.). (J). pap. 4.95 o.p. (*0-312-01855-X*, Saint Martin's Griffin) St. Martin's Pr.

—Alice in Wonderland: Through the Looking Glass. 1984. (Classics Ser.). (Illus.). 346p. (J). (gr. 2 up). reprint ed. 25.00 o.p. (*0-88088-903-9*, 889039) Peter Pauper Pr. Inc.

—Alice in Wonderland: Through the Looking Glass. 1995. (Illus.). 307p. (J). 12.98 o.p. (*0-8317-6694-8*) Smithmark Pubs., Inc.

—Alice in Wonderland: Through the Looking Glass. unabr. ed. 1993. (J). audio 13.95 o.p. (*1-55935-112-8*) Soundelux Audio Publishing.

—Alice in Wonderland & Other Favorites. 1983. (Illus.). 288p. (J). (gr. 5 up). mass mkt. 2.95 o.s.i (*0-671-46688-7*, Pocket) Simon & Schuster.

—Alice in Wonderland & Through the Looking Glass. unabr. ed. 1993. (J). audio 20.00 Books on Tape, Inc.

—Alice in Wonderland & Through the Looking Glass. l.t. ed. 710p. pap. 56.62 (*0-7583-0142-1*); 167p. pap. 18.46 (*0-7583-0136-7*); 469p. pap. 40.34 (*0-7583-0140-5*); 209p. pap. 20.82 (*0-7583-0137-5*); 286p. pap. 26.18 (*0-7583-0138-3*); 367p. pap. 32.62 (*0-7583-0139-1*); 823p. pap. 65.75 (*0-7583-0143-X*); 577p. pap. 48.32 (*0-7583-0141-3*); 286p. lib. bdg. 32.18 (*0-7583-0130-8*); 167p. lib. bdg. 24.46 (*0-7583-0128-6*); 367p. lib. bdg. 38.62 (*0-7583-0131-6*); 469p. lib. bdg. 46.34 (*0-7583-0132-4*); 710p. lib. bdg. 62.62 (*0-7583-0134-0*); 209p. lib. bdg. 26.82 (*0-7583-0129-4*); 577p. lib. bdg. 54.46 (*0-7583-0133-2*); 823p. lib. bdg. 84.45 (*0-7583-0135-9*) Huge Print Pr.

—Alice in Wonderland & Through the Looking Glass. 1988. (Illus.). 296p. (YA). pap. 7.95 o.p. (*0-8092-4488-8*) McGraw-Hill/Contemporary.

—Alice in Wonderland & Through the Looking Glass. l.t. ed. 1996. 270p. reprint ed. lib. bdg. 25.00 (*0-939495-07-4*) North Bks.

—Alice in Wonderland & Through the Looking Glass. (Illustrated Junior Library). (Illus.). (J). (gr. 4 up). 1981. 304p. 7.95 o.s.i (*0-448-11004-0*); 1946. 5.95 o.p. (*0-448-05804-9*); 1946. 320p. 16.99 (*0-448-06004-3*) Penguin Putnam Bks. for Young Readers. (Grosset & Dunlap).

—Alice in Wonderland & Through the Looking Glass. abr. unabr. ed. 1997. (BBC Radio Presents Ser.). audio 16.99 o.s.i (*0-553-47812-5*, Listening Library) Random Hse. Audio Publishing Group.

—Alice in Wonderland & Through the Looking Glass. unabr. ed. 2002. (J). audio compact disk 29.95 (*1-58472-202-9*, 022); audio compact disk 18.95 (*1-58472-379-3*) Sound Room Pubs., Inc. (In Audio).

—Alice in Wonderland Book & Charm. 2000. (Charming Classics Ser.). (Illus.). 176p. (J). (gr. 3-7). pap. 6.99 (*0-694-01454-0*, Harper Festival) HarperCollins Children's Bk. Group.

—Alice in Wonderland Coloring Book. 81st ed. 1972. (Illus.). 64p. (J). (gr. k-3). pap. 3.50 (*0-486-22853-3*) Dover Pubns., Inc.

—Alice in Wonderland Jigsaw Book. 2003. (Illus.). (J). 19.95 (*0-333-76291-6*) Macmillan U.K. GBR. *Dist:* Trafalgar Square.

—Alice in Wonderland Pop-Up Book. 1980. (Illus.). 12p. (J). (gr. k-4). pap. 6.95 o.s.i (*0-385-28038-6*, Delacorte Pr.) Dell Publishing.

—Alice in Wonderland Pop-Up Book. 1991. 12p. (J). (ps-3). pap. 14.00 o.s.i (*0-440-40540-8*, Yearling) Random Hse. Children's Bks.

—Alice's Abenteuer im Wunderland. Zimmermann, Antonie, tr. from GER. 1974. (Illus.). 178p. (J). reprint ed. 6.95 (*0-486-20668-8*) Dover Pubns., Inc.

—Alice's Adventures in Wonderland. 2000. 252p. (J). E-Book 9.95 (*0-594-04068-X*) 1873 Pr.

—Alice's Adventures in Wonderland. 2003. (Illus.). 152p. (J). tchr. ed. 25.00 (*1-885183-47-X*, 85047) Artisan.

—Alice's Adventures in Wonderland, Set. unabr. ed. 1995. (J). audio 18.95 (*1-85549-763-8*, CTC 020) BBC Audiobooks America.

—Alice's Adventures in Wonderland. 1984. (Bantam Classics Ser.). (Illus.). 256p. (YA). (gr. 6-12). mass mkt. 1.95 o.s.i (*0-553-21173-0*) Bantam Bks.

—Alice's Adventures in Wonderland. 1994. (Children's Library). (Illus.). (J). 10.95 o.p. (*0-681-00644-7*) Borders Pr.

—Alice's Adventures in Wonderland. (Illus.). (J). pap. 3.95 o.s.i (*0-8283-1423-3*, 19) Branden Bks.

—Alice's Adventures in Wonderland. ltd. ed. 1999. (Illus.). (J). 75.00 (*0-7636-1057-7*) Candlewick Pr.

—Alice's Adventures in Wonderland. 1998. (Illus.). 192p. (J). (gr. 3-5). pap. 3.99 (*0-87406-864-9*, Silver Elm Classic) Darby Creek Publishing.

—Alice's Adventures in Wonderland. 1977. (Illus.). (J). 7.95 o.s.i (*0-440-00069-6*); lib. bdg. 7.45 o.s.i (*0-440-00075-0*) Dell Publishing. (Delacorte Pr.).

—Alice's Adventures in Wonderland. 1992. 110p. (J). mass mkt. 2.99 (*0-8125-0418-6*, Tor Classics); 1988. mass mkt. 1.95 (*0-938819-65-8*, Aerie) Doherty, Tom Assocs., LLC.

—Alice's Adventures in Wonderland. E-Book 2.49 (*1-58627-094-X*) Electric Umbrella Publishing.

—Alice's Adventures in Wonderland, Vol. 1. 1999. (Selected Classic Fairy Tales Ser.). (Illus.). 20p. (J). (gr. k-7). lib. bdg. 13.95 (*1-56674-220-X*) Forest Hse. Publishing Co., Inc.

—Alice's Adventures in Wonderland. l.t. ed. 1980. (Reader's Request Ser.). (J). 11.95 o.p. (*0-8161-3070-1*, Macmillan Reference USA) Gale Group.

—Alice's Adventures in Wonderland. Goodacre, Selwyn H., ed. 1991. (J). 160p. pap. 16.95 (*0-15-604426-9*, Harvest Bks.); (Illus.). 145p. (gr. 2 up). 34.95 o.s.i (*0-15-104230-6*) Harcourt Trade Pubs.

—Alice's Adventures in Wonderland. (Illus.). (J). 2001. 192p. (gr. 3 up). 21.95 (*0-06-029150-8*); 2001. 192p. (gr. 3 up). lib. bdg. 21.89 (*0-06-029498-1*); 1992. 240p. (gr. 2 up). 16.99 (*0-688-11087-8*) HarperCollins Children's Bk. Group.

—Alice's Adventures in Wonderland, ERS. 1985. (Illus.). (J). (gr. 4-6). 128p. 19.95 o.p. (*0-8050-0212-X*); 120p. 14.95 o.p. (*0-03-002037-9*) Holt, Henry & Co. (Holt, Henry & Co. Bks. For Young Readers).

—Alice's Adventures in Wonderland. l.t. ed. 1997. (Large Print Heritage Ser.). 140p. (YA). (gr. 7-12). lib. bdg. 24.95 (*1-58118-010-1*, 21962) LRS.

—Alice's Adventures in Wonderland. 2002. (Illus.). 208p. (J). 19.95 (*1-58717-152-X*) North-South Bks., Inc.

—Alice's Adventures in Wonderland. (Oxford Progressive English Readers Ser.). (Illus.). 1982. (YA). (gr. 7-12). pap. 4.95 o.p. (*0-19-580713-8*); 2nd ed. 1993. 62p. pap. text 5.95 (*0-19-585274-5*) Oxford Univ. Pr., Inc.

—Alice's Adventures in Wonderland, Level 2. Hedge, Tricia, ed. 2000. (Bookworms Ser.). (Illus.). 64p. pap. text 5.95 (*0-19-422964-5*) Oxford Univ. Pr., Inc.

—Alice's Adventures in Wonderland. (Illus.). 1998. 128p. (J). (gr. 4-7). 19.99 o.p. (*0-525-46094-2*, Dutton Children's Bks.); 1994. 160p. (YA). (gr. 4-7). pap. 4.99 (*0-14-036675-X*, Puffin Bks.); 1989. 224p. (J). (gr. 3 up). 17.95 o.p. (*0-399-22241-3*, Philomel); 1985. 160p. (YA). (gr. 7 up). pap. 3.50 o.p. (*0-14-035038-1*, Puffin Bks.); 1950. 352p. (J). pap. 3.99 o.s.i (*0-14-030169-0*, Puffin Bks.) Penguin Putnam Bks. for Young Readers.

—Alice's Adventures in Wonderland. 1999. 174p. E-Book 5.99 incl. cd-rom (*1-891595-04-0*) Quiet Vision Publishing.

—Alice's Adventures in Wonderland. (Illus.). (J). 1991. 4.99 o.p. (*0-517-07842-2*); 1984. 160p. (gr. 3 up). 3.99 o.p. (*0-517-55591-3*); 1995. 200p. 15.99 o.s.i (*0-517-12420-3*) Random Hse. Value Publishing.

—Alice's Adventures in Wonderland. 2001. (Illus.). 248p. (J). 15.99 o.s.i (*0-517-21865-8*) Random Hse., Inc.

—Alice's Adventures in Wonderland. 1993. (Miniature Editions Ser.). (Illus.). 192p. (J). text 4.95 o.p. (*1-56138-246-9*) Running Pr. Bk. Pubs.

—Alice's Adventures in Wonderland. 1962. 315p. (J). (gr. 4-6). pap. 2.95 o.s.i (*0-02-042350-0*, Scribner Paper Fiction) Simon & Schuster.

—Alice's Adventures in Wonderland. (Illus.). (J). 2003. 6p. 24.95 (*0-689-84743-2*, Little Simon); 2000. 176p. (gr. 3-7). pap. 3.99 (*0-689-83375-X*, Aladdin); 1994. 96p. (gr. 2 up). text 16.95 o.p. (*0-689-31864-2*, Atheneum); 1986. (ps up). pap. 14.95 o.p. (*0-671-63565-4*, Simon & Schuster Children's Publishing); 2003. 6p. 250.00 (*0-689-85968-6*, Little Simon) Simon & Schuster Children's Publishing.

—Alice's Adventures in Wonderland. 2003. (Illus.). (J). (*1-894965-00-0*) Simply Read Bks.

—Alice's Adventures in Wonderland. unabr. ed. 1994. (Carroll Ser.). (J). 16.95 incl. audio (*1-883049-40-7*, 390330, Commuters Library) Sound Room Pubs., Inc.

—Alice's Adventures in Wonderland. 1969. (Illus.). 224p. (J). reprint ed. 13.95 o.p. (*0-312-01820-7*) St. Martin's Pr.

—Alice's Adventures in Wonderland. 2003. (Illus.). (J). 165p. (*0-7862-6108-0*); 175p. 28.95 (*0-7862-5653-2*) Thorndike Pr.

—Alice's Adventures in Wonderland. 1992. (Illus.). (J). 9.04 (*0-606-18634-4*) Turtleback Bks.

—Alice's Adventures in Wonderland. 1982. (Illus.). 148p. (J). (gr. 8 up). 32.50 o.p. (*0-520-04815-6*); 225.00 o.p. (*0-520-04820-2*) Univ. of California Pr.

—Alice's Adventures in Wonderland. Rackham, Arthur, ed. 1975. (Illus.). 161p. (J). 6.95 o.p. (*0-670-11277-1*) Viking Penguin.

—Alice's Adventures in Wonderland Promo. 2003. pap. 3.99 o.p. (*0-14-250093-3*, Puffin Bks.) Penguin Putnam Bks. for Young Readers.

—Alice's Adventures under Ground. 2000. (Cottage Classics). (Illus.). 88p. (YA). (gr. 3-12). 29.95 (*1-892847-00-0*) Word Play Pubns.

—Alicia en el Pais de las Maravillas. 2000. (Coleccion "Clasicos Juveniles" Ser.). (SPA.). 156p. pap. 10.95 (*0-595-13544-7*) iUniverse, Inc.

—Las Aventuras de Alicia. 2002. (Classics for Young Readers Ser.). (SPA.). (YA). 14.95 (*84-392-0920-7*, EV30607) Lectorum Pubns., Inc.

—Las Aventuras de Alicia. (Coleccion Clasicos de la Juventud). (SPA., Illus.). 240p. (J). 12.95 (*84-7189-060-7*, ORT308) Ortells, Alfredo Editorial S.L. ESP. *Dist:* Continental Bk. Co., Inc.

—The Best of Lewis Carroll. 2001. 440p. (J). (gr. 4-7). pap. 7.99 (*0-7858-1326-8*) Book Sales, Inc.

—Through the Looking Glass. Date not set. 176p. (J). 19.95 (*0-8488-2629-9*) Amereon, Ltd.

—Through the Looking Glass, Set. unabr. ed. 1984. (J). audio 20.95 (*1-55685-069-7*) Audio Bk. Contractors, Inc.

—Through the Looking Glass. unabr. ed. 1997. audio 23.95 (*0-7861-1224-7*, 2160); 1986. (J). audio 23.95 (*0-7861-0576-3*, 2066) Blackstone Audio Bks., Inc.

—Through the Looking Glass. 1984. pap. 2.00 o.s.i (*0-8283-1459-4*, 20) Branden Bks.

—Through the Looking Glass. 1981. (J). reprint ed. lib. bdg. 15.95 o.s.i (*0-89966-419-9*) Buccaneer Bks., Inc.

—Through the Looking Glass. abr. ed. (J). audio 15.95 o.p. (*0-88646-096-4*, TC-LFP 7116); 1986. (J). (gr. 5-7). audio 29.95 o.p. (*0-88646-807-8*, R 7116); audio 9.99 (*1-55204-004-6*, 9004) Durkin Hayes Publishing Ltd.

—Through the Looking Glass. 1993. (Books of Wonder). (Illus.). 240p. (J). (gr. 2 up). 16.95 (*0-688-12049-0*) HarperCollins Children's Bk. Group.

—Through the Looking Glass. audio HarperTrade.

—Through the Looking Glass. 1989. (J). audio 21.00 Jimcin Recordings.

—Through the Looking Glass. l.t. ed. 1997. (Large Print Heritage Ser.). 161p. (YA). (gr. 7-12). lib. bdg. 26.95 (*1-58118-007-1*, 21495) LRS.

—Through the Looking Glass. (Illus.). 176p. 1996. (YA). (gr. 5-9). pap. 4.99 (*0-14-036709-8*); 1985. (J). (gr. 7 up). pap. 2.99 o.p. (*0-14-035039-X*) Penguin Putnam Bks. for Young Readers. (Puffin Bks.).

—Through the Looking Glass, unabr. ed. 1980. (J). (gr. 6). audio 19.00 (*1-55690-514-9*, 80061E7) Recorded Bks., LLC.

—Through the Looking Glass. abr. ed. 1993. (Illus.). 128p. (J). (gr. 2 up). reprint ed. lib. bdg. 16.95 o.s.i (*0-689-31863-4*, Atheneum) Simon & Schuster Children's Publishing.

—Through the Looking Glass. abr. ed. 1972. (Mind's Eye Ser.). (J). pap. 5.95 o.p. incl. audio (*0-88142-332-7*, 332); pap. 5.95 o.p. incl. audio (*0-88142-332-7*, 332) Soundelux Audio Publishing.

—Through the Looking Glass. 1977. (Illus.). (J). pap. 4.95 o.p. (*0-312-80377-X*, Saint Martin's Griffin); 224p. reprint ed. 14.95 (*0-312-80374-5*) St. Martin's Pr.

—Through the Looking Glass. abr. unabr. ed. 1997. (Children's Classics Ser.). 2p. (J). pap. 10.95 o.s.i incl. audio (*0-14-086421-0*, Penguin AudioBooks) Viking Penguin.

—Through the Looking Glass: And What Alice Found There. 1999. (Thrift Editions Ser.). 128p. (J). pap. 2.00 (*0-486-40878-7*) Dover Pubns., Inc.

—Through the Looking Glass: And What Alice Found There, audio 24.95 o.p. (*0-89845-547-2*, SBC 129, Caedmon) HarperTrade.

—Through the Looking Glass: And What Alice Found There. (Illus.). 224p. o.p. (*0-333-73837-3*) Macmillan Children's Bks.

—Through the Looking Glass: And What Alice Found There. abr. ed. 1998. (J). audio 13.98 (*962-634-642-6*, NA214214); audio compact disk 15.98 (*962-634-142-4*, NA214212) Naxos of America, Inc. (Naxos AudioBooks).

—Through the Looking Glass: And What Alice Found There. abr. ed. 1995. (Dove Kids' Ser.). (J). (gr. 4-7). 6.95 o.p. (*0-7871-0337-3*) NewStar Media, Inc.

—Through the Looking Glass: And What Alice Found There. 1984. (Classics Ser.). (Illus.). 184p. (J). (gr. 2 up). reprint ed. 6.95 o.p. (*0-88088-991-8*, 889918) Peter Pauper Pr. Inc.

—Through the Looking Glass: And What Alice Found There. (Children's Classics Ser.). (J). 1990. 12.99 o.s.i (*0-517-03346-1*); 1989. (Illus.). 127p. 7.99 o.p. (*0-517-00233-7*) Random Hse. Value Publishing.

—Through the Looking Glass: And What Alice Found There, Set. unabr. ed. 1994. (J). 16.95 incl. audio (*1-883049-41-5*, Commuters Library) Sound Room Pubs., Inc.

—Through the Looking Glass: And What Alice Found There. Goodacres, Selwyn H. & Kincaid, James R., eds. Incl. Deluxe Edition. 198p. 1983. 225.00 o.p. (*0-520-05026-6*); (Illus.). 198p. 1983. 35.00 o.p. (*0-520-05039-8*) Univ. of California Pr.

—A Traves del Espejo. 2002. (Clover Ser.). (SPA., Illus.). 204p. (YA). 11.50 (*84-392-8028-9*, EV5540) Lectorum Pubns., Inc.

Carroll, Lewis, pseud & Baker, Kyle. Through the Looking Glass. (Classics Illustrated Ser.). (Illus.). 52p. (YA). pap. 4.95 (*1-57209-002-2*) Classics International Entertainment, Inc.

Carroll, Lewis, pseud & Golden Books Staff. Alice in Wonderland. 1986. (Golden Classics Ser.). (Illus.). 128p. (J). (ps-3). pap. 8.95 o.s.i (*0-307-17111-6*, Golden Bks.) Random Hse. Children's Bks.

Carroll, Lewis, pseud & Kipling, Rudyard. Alice in Wonderland. 2003. (J). cd-rom (*0-9724995-2-0*) Alcazar Audioworks.

Carroll, Lewis, pseud & Mitchell, Kathy. Alice in Wonderland & Through the Looking Glass. 1986. (Golden Classics Ser.). (Illus.). 254p. (J). (*0-307-67111-9*) Whitman Publishing LLC.

Carroll, Lewis, pseud & Tenniel, John. Alice's Adventures in Wonderland. 1977. (Illus.). (YA). (gr. 5 up). 14.95 (*0-312-01821-5*) St. Martin's Pr.

Clark, Faye. Through the Looking Glasses II. 1993. 72p. pap. 8.95 (*0-9639110-0-7*) Lavender Lady Pr.

Cronk, Lee. Through the Looking Glass. Bryant, Vaughn M., ed. 2nd ed. 1999. 256p. pap. 29.38 (*0-07-228605-9*, McGraw-Hill Humanities, Social Sciences & World Languages) McGraw-Hill Higher Education.

Cuddy, Robbin, illus. Alice in Wonderland down the Rabbit Hole: A Lift-the-Flap Rebus Book. 1994. 16p. (J). (ps-3). 12.95 o.s.i (*0-7868-3000-X*) Disney Pr.

Disney Staff. Alice in Wonderland: It's about Time! 1997. (Disney's "Storytime Treasures" Library: Vol. 17). (Illus.). 44p. (J). (gr. 1-6). 3.49 o.p. (*1-57973-013-2*) Advance Pubs. LLC.

Disney, Walter Elias. Alice in Wonderland. 1988. (Disney Animated Ser.). (J). 5.99 o.p. (*0-517-67008-9*) Random Hse. Value Publishing.

Ettleson, Abraham. Through the Looking Glass Decoded. 1967. 3.75 o.p. (*0-8022-0460-0*) Philosophical Library, Inc.

Fior, Jane & Carroll, Lewis. Alice in Wonderland. 2001. (Young Classics Ser.). (Illus.). 48p. (J). (gr. 1-3). pap. 9.95 o.p. (*0-7894-5902-7*) Dorling Kindersley Publishing, Inc.

Fischer, Kathleen M. Alice in Wonderland. Friedland, J. & Kessler, Rikki, eds. 1996. (Novel-Ties Ser.). (Illus.). 30p. (J). (gr. 6). pap., stu. ed. 15.95 (*1-56982-651-X*, S0218) Learning Links, Inc.

Golden Books Staff. Alice in Wonderland. 1997. (J). pap. text o.p. (*0-307-08659-3*, Golden Bks.) Random Hse. Children's Bks.

—Alice in Wonderland: Follow the White Rabbit. 1998. 48p. (J). (gr. k-3). pap. text o.p. (*0-307-09327-1*, Golden Bks.) Random Hse. Children's Bks.

Guile, Gill. Alice in Wonderland. 1997. (Classics for Children 8 & Younger Ser.). (Illus.). 48p. (J). (ps-3). 6.98 (*1-85854-602-8*) Brimax Bks., Ltd.

Hildebrandt, Greg, illus. Alice in Wonderland. 1991. (Gateway Classic Ser.). 48p. (J). (gr. 2-5). 6.95 o.p. (*0-88101-109-6*) Unicorn Publishing Hse., Inc., The.

Howe, D. H., ed. Through the Looking Glass. 2nd ed. 1993. (Illus.). 78p. pap. text 5.95 (*0-19-585268-0*) Oxford Univ. Pr., Inc.

Jackson, Elizabeth. Alice in Wonderland. 1987. 1.00 o.p. (*0-435-23465-X*) Heinemann.

Landes, William-Alan. Alice n' Wonderland. 1984. (Wondrawhopper Ser.). 32p. (Orig.). (J). (gr. 3 up). pap. 6.00 (*0-88734-112-8*) Players Pr., Inc.

Metropolitan Museum of Art. Alice in Wonderland: A Book of Ornaments. 1997. 9.95 o.p. (*0-8109-1985-0*) Abrams, Harry N. , Inc.

Miller, Madge. Alice in Wonderland. 1953. (J). 6.00 (*0-87602-104-6*) Anchorage Pr.

Mitchell, Melisa, ed. Through the Looking Glass. 1997. 19.95 (*1-57553-401-0*) National Library of Poetry.

Mouse Works Staff. Alice in Wonderland. (Classic Storybook Ser.). (J). 2002. 7.99 (*1-57082-976-4*); 1997. (Illus.). 7.98 (*1-57082-795-8*) Mouse Works.

Noble, Marty. Alice in Wonderland Stained Glass Coloring Book. 1998. (Illus.). 8p. (J). pap. 1.00 (*0-486-40305-X*) Dover Pubns., Inc.

—Alice in Wonderland Sticker Activity Book. 1998. (J). pap. 1.00 (*0-486-40314-9*) Dover Pubns., Inc.

Nursey-Bray, Rosemary. Through the Looking Glass & What Alice Found There: Playscript. 1988. (J). (ps up). 6.50 (*0-87602-276-X*) Anchorage Pr.

Richardson, Miranda, et al. Alice in Wonderland. abr. ed. 1999. audio 18.00 (*0-7871-1948-2*) NewStar Media, Inc.

Rodriguez, Edel. Alice in Wonderland. abr. l.t. ed. 1995. (Illus.). 32p. (Orig.). (J). (gr. k up). pap. 14.95 (*1-886201-01-3*) Nana Banana Classics.

Seibold, J. Otto. Alice in Wonderland. 2001. (Illus.). (J). 5.00 (*0-7636-1757-1*) Candlewick Pr.

—Alice in Wonderland. (Illus.). (J). (gr. k-2). 1994. (Paint with Water Fairy Tales Ser.: No. II). 32p. pap. (*1-56144-486-3*, Honey Bear Bks.); 1993. (Fun-to-Read Fairy Tales Ser.). 24p. pap. 2.50 (*1-56144-294-1*, Honey Bear Bks.); 1990. (Giant Pop-Up Bks.). 8p. pap. 6.95 o.p. (*0-87449-881-3*) Modern Publishing.

—Alice in Wonderland. 1994. (Classics Ser.). (Illus.). 96p. (J). (ps-4). 7.98 o.p. (*1-57082-031-7*) Mouse Works.

—Alice in Wonderland. 9999. (Children's Classics Ser.: No. 740-23). (Illus.). (J). (gr. 3-5). pap. 3.50 o.p. (*0-7214-0967-9*, Ladybird Bks.) Penguin Group (USA) Inc.

—Alice in Wonderland. (J). (gr. k-3). o.p. (*0-8431-4173-5*, Price Stern Sloan) Penguin Putnam Bks. for Young Readers.

—Alice in Wonderland. abr. l.t. ed. 1996. (Great Illustrated Classics Ser.: Vol. 50). (Illus.). 240p. (J). (gr. 3-7). 9.95 (*0-86611-873-X*) Playmore, Inc., Pubs.

—Alice in Wonderland. 1993. (Look & Find Ser.). (Illus.). 24p. (J). 7.98 (*0-7853-0065-1*) Publications International, Ltd.

—Alice in Wonderland. 1978. (Disney Classics Ser.). (Illus.). (J). (gr. 3-8). pap. 0.95 o.s.i (*0-448-16105-2*) Putnam Publishing Group, The.

—Alice in Wonderland. 1997. (Little Golden Bks.). (J). (ps-3). o.p. (*0-307-09322-0*, Golden Bks.) Random Hse. Children's Bks.

—Alice in Wonderland. 2003. (Illus.). 6p. (J). (gr. k-3). bds. 19.95 (*0-439-41184-X*, Orchard Bks.) Scholastic, Inc.

Senna, Carl. CliffsNotes TM Alice in Wonderland. 1999. E-Book 4.95 (*0-8220-7003-0*, Cliff Notes) Wiley, John & Sons, Inc.

Sibley, Brian, intro. Alice in Wonderland. 1988. (Illus.). 64p. 14.95 o.p. (*0-8109-1872-2*) Abrams, Harry N. , Inc.

Slater. Alice in Wonderland. 1994. (Illus.). (J). (ps-3). o.p. (*0-307-62341-6*, Golden Bks.) Random Hse. Children's Bks.

Slater, Teddy. Alice in Wonderland: Illustrated Classic. 1995. (Illus.). 96p. (J). 14.95 (*0-7868-3034-4*); lib. bdg. 15.49 (*0-7868-5017-5*) Disney Pr.

—Alice in Wonderland: Junior Novelization. 1995. (Illus.). 64p. (J). (gr. 2-6). pap. 3.50 o.p. (*0-7868-4027-7*) Disney Pr.

—Alice in Wonderland Junior Novel. 1995. (J). pap. 42.00 (*0-7868-5741-2*) Disney Pr.

Through the Looking Glass. Incl. Through the Looking Glass: Humpty Dumpty. audio o.p. Through the Looking Glass: Looking Glass House. audio o.p. Through the Looking Glass: Queen Alice. audio o.p. Through the Looking Glass: Shaking. audio o.p. Through the Looking Glass: The Garden of Live Flowers. audio o.p. Through the Looking Glass: The White Knight. audio o.p. Through the Looking Glass: The White Queen. audio o.p. Through the Looking Glass: Tweedledum & Tweedledee. audio o.p. Through the Looking Glass: Waking. audio o.p. (J). Set audio 9.95 o.p. (*0-694-50655-9*, CDL5 1098, Caedmon) HarperTrade.

Through the Looking Glass. (J). audio Audio Bk. Co.

Through the Looking Glass. (Read-along Ser.). 34.95 incl. audio. (YA). pap., stu. ed. 34.95 incl. audio (*0-88432-971-2*, S23946) Norton Pubs., Inc., Jeffrey /Audio-Forum.

Through the Looking Glass: Humpty Dumpty. (J). audio o.p. HarperTrade.

Through the Looking Glass: Looking Glass House. (J). audio o.p. HarperTrade.

Through the Looking Glass: Queen Alice. (J). audio o.p. HarperTrade.

Through the Looking Glass: Shaking. (J). audio o.p. HarperTrade.

Through the Looking Glass: The Garden of Live Flowers. (J). audio o.p. HarperTrade.

Through the Looking Glass: The White Knight. (J). audio o.p. HarperTrade.

Through the Looking Glass: The White Queen. (J). audio o.p. HarperTrade.

Through the Looking Glass: Tweedledum & Tweedledee. (J). audio o.p. HarperTrade.

Tierney, Tom. Alice in Wonderland Paper Doll. 1992. (Illus.). (J). (gr. k-3). pap. 1.00 (*0-486-27368-7*) Dover Pubns., Inc.

Titlebaum, Ellen. Alice in Wonderland Read Aloud: Storybook. 2000. 64p. (J). 6.99 (*0-7364-1051-1*) Hyperion Bks. for Children.

Van Gool Studio Staff, illus. Alice in Wonderland. 1994. (Classic Ser.). 64p. (J). 4.98 o.p. (*0-8317-1651-7*) Smithmark Pubs., Inc.

Verrier, Anthony. Through the Looking Glass. 1983. 18.50 o.p. (*0-393-01648-X*) Norton, W. W. & Co., Inc.

Wakeling, Edward. Alice in Wonderland Puzzle & Game Book. 1995. (Illus.). 86p. (J). pap. 7.95 (*1-57281-006-8*, CBK905, Cove Pr.) U.S. Games Systems, Inc.

—Alice in Wonderland's Deck/Book Set. 1996. (Illus.). 86p. (YA). (gr. 5-9). 19.95 (*0-88079-704-5*, ALW100) U.S. Games Systems, Inc.

Walt Disney Productions Staff. Alice in Wonderland. 1991. (J). 7.98 o.p. (*0-453-03079-3*) Mouse Works.

Walt Disney Productions Staff, prod. Alice in Wonderland. 1998. (J). audio 19.95 (*0-7634-0388-1*) Walt Disney Records.

ALLEN, ETHAN, 1738-1789—FICTION

Gauthier, Gail. The Hero of Ticonderoga. 2001. 231p. (J). (gr. 5 up). 16.99 (*0-399-23559-0*) Penguin Group (USA) Inc.

—The Hero of Ticonderoga. 2002. 240p. (YA). (gr. 5-9). pap. 6.99 (*0-698-11968-1*, PaperStar) Penguin Putnam Bks. for Young Readers.

AMELIA-BEDELIA (FICTITIOUS CHARACTER)—FICTION

Parish, Herman. Amelia Bedelia 4 Mayor. (I Can Read Bks.). (Illus.). (J). 2001. 64p. (gr. k-2). pap. 3.99 (*0-06-444309-4*, Harper Trophy); 1999. 48p. (gr. 1 up). 15.99 (*0-688-16721-7*, Greenwillow Bks.); 1999. 48p. (gr. 1 up). lib. bdg. 15.89 (*0-688-16722-5*, Greenwillow Bks.); No. 2. 2003. 8.99 incl. audio (*0-06-009345-5*) HarperCollins Children's Bk. Group.

—Bravo Amelia Bedelia, Vol. 2. 2002. (I Can Read Bks.). (Illus.). 48p. (J). pap. 3.99 (*0-06-444318-3*, Harper Trophy) HarperCollins Children's Bk. Group.

—Calling Doctor Amelia Bedelia. 2002. (Illus.). 64p. (J). (gr. 1-2). 15.99 (*0-06-001421-0*); lib. bdg. 17.89 (*0-06-001422-9*) HarperCollins Children's Bk. Group. (Greenwillow Bks.).

—Good Driving, Amelia Bedelia. 2002. (I Can Read Bks.). (Illus.). 48p. (J). (gr. 1-3). pap. 3.99 (*0-06-008092-2*, Harper Trophy) HarperCollins Children's Bk. Group.

Parish, Herman S., 3rd. Amelia Bedelia 4 Mayor. 1999. (I Can Read Bks.). (Illus.). (J). 10.10 (*0-606-21026-1*) Turtleback Bks.

Parish, Peggy. Amelia Bedelia. 1999. (I Can Read Bks.). (J). (gr. 1-3). 11.50 (*0-88103-916-0*); (SPA.). (*0-613-09959-1*) Econo-Clad Bks.

—Amelia Bedelia. 1999. (I Can Read Bks.). (Illus.). 64p. (J). (ps-3). 15.99 (*0-694-01296-3*, Harper Festival) HarperCollins Children's Bk. Group.

—Amelia Bedelia. Canetti, Yanitzia, tr. 1996. (I Can Read Bks.). (SPA., Illus.). 64p. (J). (gr. 1-3). 15.95 o.s.i (*0-06-026247-8*); pap. 4.95 o.p. (*0-06-444200-4*) HarperCollins Children's Bk. Group.

—Amelia Bedelia. (I Can Read Bks.). (Illus.). (J). 1992. 64p. (gr. k-3). 15.99 (*0-06-020186-X*); 1992. 64p. (gr. k-3). pap. 3.99 (*0-06-444155-5*, Harper Trophy); 1992. 64p. (gr. k-3). lib. bdg. 16.89 (*0-06-020187-8*); 1983. 32p. (gr. 1-3). pap. 3.50 o.p. (*0-06-443036-7*, Harper Trophy); 1963. 80p. (gr. 1-3). 13.00 o.p. (*0-06-024640-5*); 1963. 80p. (gr. 1-3). lib. bdg. 12.89 o.p. (*0-06-024641-3*) HarperCollins Children's Bk. Group.

—Amelia Bedelia. 1993. (I Can Read Bks.). (Illus.). 64p. (J). (gr. k-3). 8.99 incl. audio (*1-55994-782-9*, HarperAudio) HarperTrade.

—Amelia Bedelia. 2000. (Coleccion Ya Se Leer). (SPA., Illus.). (J). (gr. 1-3). 15.95 (*1-880507-76-5*, LC0355); pap. 6.95 (*1-880507-75-7*, LC0360) Lectorum Pubns., Inc.

—Amelia Bedelia. 1999. (J). (gr. 1-3). 9.95 (*1-56137-023-1*) Novel Units, Inc.

—Amelia Bedelia. (J). 2001. (SPA., Illus.). 12.10 (*0-606-21546-8*); 1996. (gr. 1-3). 10.15 o.p. (*0-606-10377-5*); 1963. (gr. 1-3). 10.10 (*0-606-01041-6*) Turtleback Bks.

—Amelia Bedelia & Her Wacky World Boxed Set: Amelia Bedelia & the Baby; Amelia Bedelia Goes Camping; Amelia Bedelia Helps Out; Good Work, Amelia Bedelia, 4 vols., Set. 1986. (Amelia Bedelia Ser.). (Illus.). (J). (gr. k-2). 15.96 o.p. (*0-380-75238-7*, Avon Bks.) Morrow/Avon.

—Amelia Bedelia & the Baby. 1999. (Amelia Bedelia Ser.). (J). (gr. k-2). 11.50 (*0-88103-914-4*) Econo-Clad Bks.

—Amelia Bedelia & the Baby. (I Can Read Book 2 Ser.). (Illus.). 64p. (J). 2004. pap. 3.99 (*0-06-051105-2*, Harper Trophy); 1981. 16.00 (*0-688-00316-8*, Greenwillow Bks.); 1981. lib. bdg. 16.89 (*0-688-00321-4*, Greenwillow Bks.) HarperCollins Children's Bk. Group.

—Amelia Bedelia & the Baby. (Amelia Bedelia Ser.). (Illus.). 64p. (J). (gr. k-2). 1996. pap. 3.99 (*0-380-72795-1*); 1982. pap. 3.99 (*0-380-57067-X*) Morrow/Avon. (Avon Bks.).

—Amelia Bedelia & the Baby. unabr. ed. 2001. (Amelia Bedelia Ser.). (J). (gr. k-2). audio 10.00 (*0-7887-0369-2*, 94561E7) Recorded Bks., LLC.

—Amelia Bedelia & the Baby. 1986. (Amelia Bedelia Ser.). (J). (gr. k-2). 31.99 incl. audio (*0-394-69327-2*) SRA/McGraw-Hill.

—Amelia Bedelia & the Baby. 1996. (Amelia Bedelia Ser.). (J). (gr. k-2). 10.10 (*0-606-00368-1*) Turtleback Bks.

—Amelia Bedelia & the Surprise Shower. (I Can Read Bks.). (Illus.). 64p. (J). 9999. (gr. 1-3). 5.98 o.p. incl. audio (*0-694-00161-9*, JC-144, Harper Trophy); 9999. (gr. 1-3). 5.98 o.p. incl. audio (*0-694-00161-9*, JC-144, Harper Trophy); 1979. (ps-3). pap. 3.99 (*0-06-444019-2*, Harper Trophy); 1966. (gr. k-3). 15.95 (*0-06-024642-1*); 1966. (gr. k-3). lib. bdg. 15.89 (*0-06-024643-X*) HarperCollins Children's Bk. Group.

—Amelia Bedelia & the Surprise Shower. unabr. ed. 1990. (I Can Read Bks.). (Illus.). 64p. (J). (gr. k-3). pap. 8.99 incl. audio (*1-55994-216-9*, Caedmon) HarperTrade.

—Amelia Bedelia & the Surprise Shower. 1994. (I Can Read Bks.). (J). (gr. 1-3). 10.10 (*0-606-02009-8*) Turtleback Bks.

—Amelia Bedelia Goes Camping. (I Can Read Bks.). (Illus.). (J). (gr. k-3). 2003. 64p. pap. 3.99 (*0-06-051106-0*, Harper Trophy); 1997. 64p. pap. 3.99 (*0-380-72917-2*, Harper Trophy); 1985. 56p. 15.95 (*0-688-04057-8*, Greenwillow Bks.); 1985. 56p. lib. bdg. 16.89 (*0-688-04058-6*, Greenwillow Bks.) HarperCollins Children's Bk. Group.

—Amelia Bedelia Goes Camping. 1986. (Amelia Bedelia Ser.). (Illus.). 48p. (J). (gr. k-2). pap. 3.99 (*0-380-70067-0*, Avon Bks.) Morrow/Avon.

—Amelia Bedelia Goes Camping. 1985. (Amelia Bedelia Ser.). (J). (gr. k-2). 10.10 (*0-606-01980-4*) Turtleback Bks.

—Amelia Bedelia Helps Out. 1979. (Amelia Bedelia Ser.). (Illus.). 64p. (J). (gr. k-3). 15.99 (*0-688-80231-1*); lib. bdg. 16.89 (*0-688-84231-3*) HarperCollins Children's Bk. Group. (Greenwillow Bks.).

—Amelia Bedelia Helps Out. (Amelia Bedelia Ser.). (Illus.). 64p. (J). (gr. k-2). 1997. pap. 3.99 (*0-380-72796-X*); 1981. pap. 3.99 (*0-380-53405-3*) Morrow/Avon. (Avon Bks.).

—Amelia Bedelia Helps Out. 1997. (Amelia Bedelia Ser.). (J). (gr. k-2). 10.14 (*0-606-02010-1*) Turtleback Bks.

—Amelia Bedelia Treasury. 1995. (Amelia Bedelia Ser.). (Illus.). 192p. (J). (gr. k-2). 4.50 o.s.i (*0-06-026787-9*) HarperCollins Pubs.

—Amelia Bedelia's Birthday Package, 5 bks., Set. 1988. (Amelia Bedelia Ser.). (Illus.). (J). (gr. k-2). pap. 17.50 (*0-06-444123-7*, Harper Trophy) HarperCollins Children's Bk. Group.

—Amelia Bedelia's Family Album. (I Can Read Bks.). (Illus.). 48p. (J). (gr. k-3). 2003. pap. 3.99 (*0-06-051116-8*, Harper Trophy); 1997. pap. 3.95 (*0-380-72860-5*, Harper Trophy); 1988. 15.99 (*0-688-07676-9*, Greenwillow Bks.); 1988. lib. bdg. 16.89 (*0-688-07677-7*, Greenwillow Bks.) HarperCollins Children's Bk. Group.

—Amelia Bedelia's Family Album. (Amelia Bedelia Ser.). (J). (gr. k-2). 1991. (Illus.). pap. 3.99 (*0-380-71698-4*); 1989. 48p. mass mkt. 3.99 o.p. (*0-380-70760-8*) Morrow/Avon. (Avon Bks.).

—Amelia Bedelia's Family Album. 1988. (Amelia Bedelia Ser.). (J). (gr. k-2). 10.14 (*0-606-04154-0*) Turtleback Bks.

—Come Back, Amelia Bedelia. (I Can Read Bks.). (Illus.). (J). (gr. 1-3). 1986. 64p. 5.98 o.p. incl. audio (*0-694-00112-0*, JC-067, Harper Trophy); 1978. 80p. pap. 3.50 o.p. (*0-06-444016-8*, Harper Trophy); 1971. 64p. 14.95 o.p. (*0-06-024667-7*); 1971. 64p. lib. bdg. 14.89 o.p. (*0-06-024668-5*) HarperCollins Children's Bk. Group.

—Come Back, Amelia Bedelia. unabr. ed. 1990. (I Can Read Bks.). (Illus.). 64p. (J). (ps-3). pap. 8.99 incl. audio (*1-55994-225-8*, Caedmon) HarperTrade.

—Good Work, Amelia Bedelia. 1999. (Amelia Bedelia Ser.). (J). (gr. k-2). 11.55 (*0-88103-915-2*) Econo-Clad Bks.

—Good Work, Amelia Bedelia. (Illus.). (J). (gr. k-3). 1976. (Greenwillow Read-Alone Bks.: Vol. 1). 56p. 15.95 (*0-688-80022-X*, Greenwillow Bks.); 1976. (Greenwillow Read-Alone Bks.: Vol. 1). 56p. lib. bdg. 16.89 (*0-688-84022-1*, Greenwillow Bks.); Bk. 2. 2003. (I Can Read Book Ser.). 64p. pap. 3.99 (*0-06-051115-X*) HarperCollins Children's Bk. Group.

—Good Work, Amelia Bedelia. (Amelia Bedelia Ser.). (Illus.). (J). (gr. k-2). 1996. 64p. pap. 3.99 (*0-380-72831-1*); 1980. 164p. pap. 3.99 (*0-380-49171-0*) Morrow/Avon. (Avon Bks.).

—Good Work, Amelia Bedelia. 1996. (Amelia Bedelia Ser.). (J). (gr. k-2). 10.14 (*0-606-02124-8*) Turtleback Bks.

—I Can Read Amelia Bedelia. 40th anniv. ed. 2003. (Illus.). pap. 11.97 (*0-06-054238-1*) HarperCollins Children's Bk. Group.

—Merry Christmas, Amelia Bedelia. (Amelia Bedelia Ser.). (Illus.). 64p. (J). (gr. k-3). 1996. 3.95 (*0-380-72797-8*, Harper Trophy); 1986. 15.00 o.p. (*0-688-06101-X*, Greenwillow Bks.); 1986. lib. bdg. 15.89 (*0-688-06102-8*, Greenwillow Bks.) HarperCollins Children's Bk. Group.

—Merry Christmas, Amelia Bedelia. 1987. (Amelia Bedelia Ser.). (Illus.). 64p. (J). (gr. k-2). reprint ed. pap. 3.99 (*0-380-70325-4*, Avon Bks.) Morrow/Avon.

—Merry Christmas, Amelia Bedelia. 1996. (Amelia Bedelia Ser.). (J). (gr. k-2). 10.10 (*0-606-03615-6*) Turtleback Bks.

—Play Ball, Amelia Bedelia. (I Can Read Bks.). (Illus.). (J). 9999. 64p. (gr. 1-3). 5.98 o.p. incl. audio (*0-694-00037-X*, Harper Trophy); 9999. 64p. (gr. 1-3). 5.98 o.p. incl. audio (*0-694-00037-X*, Harper Trophy); 1978. 64p. (gr. 1-3). pap. 3.50 o.p. (*0-06-444005-2*, Harper Trophy); 1972. 192p. (gr. k-3). 14.95 (*0-06-024655-3*); 1972. 64p. (gr. 1-3). 14.89 (*0-06-024656-1*) HarperCollins Children's Bk. Group.

—Play Ball, Amelia Bedelia. unabr. ed. 1990. (I Can Read Bks.). (Illus.). 64p. (J). (ps-3). pap. 8.99 incl. audio (*1-55994-241-X*, HarperAudio) HarperTrade.

—Play Ball, Amelia Bedelia. 1986. (I Can Read Bks.). (Illus.). 64p. (J). (gr. 1-3). pap. 2.50 (*0-590-06203-4*) Scholastic, Inc.

—Play Ball, Amelia Bedelia. 1978. (I Can Read Bks.). (J). (gr. 1-3). 10.10 (*0-606-01549-3*) Turtleback Bks.

—Teach Us, Amelia Bedelia. 1999. (Amelia Bedelia Ser.). (J). (gr. k-2). 11.55 (*0-88103-912-8*) Econo-Clad Bks.

—Teach Us, Amelia Bedelia. 1977. (Illus.). 56p. (J). (gr. k-3). (Amelia Bedelia Ser.). 15.99 (*0-688-80069-6*); (Greenwillow Read-Alone Bks.: Vol. 1). lib. bdg. 16.89 (*0-688-84069-8*) HarperCollins Children's Bk. Group. (Greenwillow Bks.).

—Teach Us, Amelia Bedelia. (Hello Reader! Ser.). (Illus.). (J). 1995. 56p. (gr. 2-3). mass mkt. 3.99 (*0-590-53773-3*, Cartwheel Bks.); 1987. 64p. (gr. k-2). mass mkt. 2.95 o.p. (*0-590-43345-8*); 1980. (gr. k-2). pap. 1.95 o.p. (*0-590-05797-9*); 1980. (gr. k-2). pap. 2.50 o.p. (*0-590-33362-3*); 1987. 64p. (gr. k-2). reprint ed. pap. 2.50 o.p. (*0-590-40940-9*) Scholastic, Inc.

—Thank You, Amelia Bedelia. 1999. (I Can Read Bks.). (J). (gr. 1-3). 11.55 (*0-88103-910-1*) Econo-Clad Bks.

—Thank You, Amelia Bedelia. (I Can Read Bks.). (Illus.). (J). 1993. 64p. (gr. k-3). 15.99 (*0-06-022979-9*); 1993. 64p. (gr. k-3). lib. bdg. 16.89 (*0-06-022980-2*); 1993. 64p. (ps-3). pap. 3.99 (*0-06-444171-7*, Harper Trophy); 1983. 80p. (gr. 1-3). pap. 3.50 o.p. (*0-06-443037-5*, Harper Trophy); 1964. (gr. 1-3). 13.00 o.p. (*0-06-024665-0*); 1964. (gr. 1-3). lib. bdg. 12.89 o.p. (*0-06-024652-9*) HarperCollins Children's Bk. Group.

—Thank You, Amelia Bedelia. unabr. ed. 1995. (I Can Read Bks.). (Illus.). 64p. (J). (gr. k-3). pap. 8.99 incl. audio (*0-694-70002-9*, HarperAudio) HarperTrade.

—Thank You, Amelia Bedelia. 9999. (I Can Read Bks.). (J). (gr. 1-3). pap. 1.95 o.s.i (*0-590-38075-3*) Scholastic, Inc.

—Thank You, Amelia Bedelia. 1993. (I Can Read Bks.). (J). (gr. 1-3). 10.10 (*0-606-06053-7*) Turtleback Bks.

Parish, Peggy & Brookes, Diane. A Novel Study for Grade One & Two Based on Amelia Bedelia & the Surprise Shower Novel Study, 25 vols. 1998. pap., tchr. ed. (*0-9683234-4-8*) Raven Rock Publishing.

ANATOLE (FICTITIOUS CHARACTER)—FICTION

Titus, Eve. Anatole. 1990. 32p. (J). pap. 4.95 o.s.i (*0-553-34870-1*) Bantam Bks.

—Anatole & the Cat. 1990. 32p. (J). (ps-3). pap. 4.95 o.s.i (*0-553-34871-X*) Bantam Bks.

—Anatole & the Cat. 1957. (Illus.). (J). (gr. k-3). lib. bdg. 7.95 o.p. (*0-07-064910-3*) McGraw-Hill Cos., The.

—Anatole & the Cat. 1993. (J). mass mkt. o.s.i (*0-553-54123-4*, Dell Books for Young Readers) Random Hse. Children's Bks.

—Anatole & the Piano. 1990. 32p. (J). (ps-3). pap. 4.95 o.s.i (*0-553-34888-4*) Bantam Bks.

—Anatole & the Piano. 1966. (J). (gr. k-3). lib. bdg. o.p. (*0-07-064892-1*) McGraw-Hill Cos., The.

—Anatole & the Thirty Thieves. 1990. 32p. (J). (ps-3). pap. 4.95 o.s.i (*0-553-34889-2*) Bantam Bks.

—Anatole & the Thirty Thieves. 1969. (Adventures of Anatole Ser.). (Illus.). (J). (gr. k-3). lib. bdg. o.p. (*0-07-064888-3*) McGraw-Hill Cos., The.

—Anatole & the Toy Shop. 1991. (Illus.). 32p. (J). (ps-8). pap. 4.99 o.s.i (*0-553-35239-3*) Bantam Bks.

—Anatole & the Toy Shop. 1991. (J). mass mkt. o.p. (*0-553-53066-6*, Dell Books for Young Readers) Random Hse. Children's Bks.

—Anatole in Italy. 1973. (Adventures of Anatole Ser.). (Illus.). 40p. (J). (gr. k-3). lib. bdg. o.p. (*0-07-064899-9*) McGraw-Hill Cos., The.

—Anatole over Paris. 1991. (Illus.). 32p. (J). (ps-8). pap. 4.99 o.s.i (*0-553-35240-7*) Bantam Bks.

—Anatole over Paris. 1991. (J). mass mkt. o.p. (*0-553-53067-4*, Dell Books for Young Readers) Random Hse. Children's Bks.

Titus, Eve & Galdone, Paul. Anatole & the Pied Piper. 1979. (J). text 9.95 o.p. (*0-07-064897-2*) McGraw-Hill Cos., The.

ANDERSON, EINSTEIN (FICTITIOUS CHARACTER)—FICTION

Simon, Seymour. Einstein Anderson Goes to Bat. (Einstein Anderson, Science Sleuth Ser.). (Illus.). (J). (gr. 3-6). 1987. pap. 3.99 o.p. (*0-14-032303-1*, Puffin Bks.); 1982. 80p. 9.95 o.p. (*0-670-29068-8*, Viking Children's Bks.) Penguin Putnam Bks. for Young Readers.

—Einstein Anderson Lights up the Sky. (Einstein Anderson, Science Sleuth Ser.). (Illus.). (J). (gr. 3-6). 1982. 80p. 9.95 o.p. (*0-670-29066-1*, Viking Children's Bks.); 1987. reprint ed. pap. 3.95 o.p. (*0-14-032307-4*) Penguin Putnam Bks. for Young Readers.

—Einstein Anderson Makes up for Lost Time. (Einstein Anderson, Science Sleuth Ser.). (Illus.). 80p. (J). (gr. 3-6). 1986. pap. 3.95 o.p. (*0-14-032100-4*); 1981. 9.95 o.p. (*0-670-29067-X*, Viking Children's Bks.) Penguin Putnam Bks. for Young Readers.

—Einstein Anderson, Science Sleuth. (Einstein Anderson, Science Sleuth Ser.). (Illus.). 80p. (J). (gr. 3-6). 1986. pap. 3.99 o.p. (*0-14-032098-9*); 1980. 9.95 o.p. (*0-670-29069-6*, Viking Children's Bks.) Penguin Putnam Bks. for Young Readers.

—Einstein Anderson, Science Sleuth. 1981. (Einstein Anderson, Science Sleuth Ser.). (Illus.). 80p. (J). (gr. 3-6). reprint ed. pap. 2.50 o.s.i (*0-671-43168-4*, Simon & Schuster Children's Publishing) Simon & Schuster Children's Publishing.

—Einstein Anderson Sees Through the Invisible Man. (Einstein Anderson, Science Sleuth Ser.). (Illus.). (J). (gr. 3-6). 1987. pap. 3.95 o.p. (*0-14-032306-6*, Puffin Bks.); 1983. 80p. 9.95 o.p. (*0-670-29065-3*, Viking Children's Bks.) Penguin Putnam Bks. for Young Readers.

—Einstein Anderson Shocks His Friends. (Einstein Anderson, Science Sleuth Ser.). (Illus.). 80p. (J). (gr. 3-6). 1986. pap. 3.95 o.p. (*0-14-032099-7*); 1980. 9.95 o.p. (*0-670-29070-X*, Viking Children's Bks.) Penguin Putnam Bks. for Young Readers.

—Einstein Anderson Shocks His Friends. 1981. (Einstein Anderson, Science Sleuth Ser.). (Illus.). 80p. (J). (gr. 3-6). reprint ed. pap. 2.50 o.s.i (*0-671-43169-2*, Simon & Schuster Children's Publishing) Simon & Schuster Children's Publishing.

—Einstein Anderson Tells a Comet's Tale. (Einstein Anderson, Science Sleuth Ser.). (Illus.). (J). (gr. 3-6). 1987. pap. 3.95 o.p. (*0-14-032302-3*, Puffin Bks.); 1981. 80p. 9.95 o.p. (*0-670-29071-8*, Viking Children's Bks.) Penguin Putnam Bks. for Young Readers.

—The Gigantic Ants & Other Cases. 1997. (Einstein Anderson, Science Detective Ser.). (Illus.). 80p. (J). (gr. 3 up). reprint ed. 14.00 o.s.i (*0-688-14439-X*) HarperCollins Children's Bk. Group.

—The Gigantic Ants & Other Cases. 1998. (Einstein Anderson, Science Detective Ser.). (Illus.). (J). (gr. 3-6). pap. 3.99 (*0-380-72657-2*) Morrow/Avon.

—The Halloween Horror & Other Cases. (Einstein Anderson, Science Detective Ser.). (Illus.). (J). (gr. 3-6). 1997. 96p. reprint ed. 14.00 (*0-688-14437-3*, Morrow, William & Co.); Bk. 2. 1998. pap. 3.99 (*0-380-72656-4*, Avon Bks.) Morrow/Avon.

—The Halloween Horror & Other Cases. 1998. (Einstein Anderson, Science Detective Ser.). (J). (gr. 3-6). lib. bdg. 10.14 (*0-606-15519-8*) Turtleback Bks.

—The Howling Dog & Other Cases. 1997. (Einstein Anderson, Science Detective Ser.). (Illus.). 96p. (J). (gr. 3 up). reprint ed. 14.95 (*0-688-14435-7*) HarperCollins Children's Bk. Group.

—The Howling Dog & Other Cases. 1998. (Einstein Anderson, Science Detective Ser.). (Illus.). (J). (gr. 3-6). pap. 3.99 (*0-380-72655-6*) Morrow/Avon.

—The Howling Dog & Other Cases. 2000. (Einstein Anderson, Science Detective Ser.). (J). (gr. 3-6). pap. 32.00 incl. audio (*0-7887-4457-7*, 41148) Recorded Bks., LLC.

—The Invisible Man & Other Cases. (Einstein Anderson, Science Detective Ser.: Vol. 7). 96p. (J). (gr. 3-7). 1999. pap. 3.99 (*0-380-72661-0*, Harper Trophy); 1998. (Illus.). 14.95 (*0-688-14447-0*) HarperCollins Children's Bk. Group.

—The Invisible Man & Other Cases. 1999. (Einstein Anderson, Science Detective Ser.). (J). (gr. 3-6). 10.14 (*0-606-16358-1*) Turtleback Bks.

—The Mysterious Lights & Other Cases. rev. ed. 1998. (Einstein Anderson, Science Detective Ser.). (Illus.). 96p. (J). (gr. 3 up). 14.95 (*0-688-14445-4*) HarperCollins Children's Bk. Group.

—The Mysterious Lights & Other Cases. 1999. (Einstein Anderson, Science Detective Ser.). (Illus.). 96p. (J). (gr. 3-6). pap. 3.99 (*0-380-72660-2*, Avon Bks.) Morrow/Avon.

—The Mysterious Lights & Other Cases. 1999. (Einstein Anderson, Science Detective Ser.). (J). (gr. 3-6). 10.14 (*0-606-16354-9*) Turtleback Bks.

—The On-Line Spaceman & Other Cases. 1997. (Einstein Anderson, Science Detective Ser.). (Illus.). 224p. (J). (gr. 3-6). 14.95 (*0-688-14433-0*) HarperCollins Children's Bk. Group.

—The On-Line Spaceman & Other Cases. 1998. (Einstein Anderson, Science Detective Ser.). (Illus.). 96p. (J). (gr. 3-6). reprint ed. pap. 3.99 (*0-380-72662-9*, Avon Bks.) Morrow/Avon.

—The On-Line Spaceman & Other Cases. 1998. (Einstein Anderson, Science Detective Ser.). (J). (gr. 3-6). 10.14 (*0-606-13352-6*) Turtleback Bks.

—The Time Machine & Other Cases. 1997. (Einstein Anderson, Science Detective Ser.). (Illus.). 256p. (J). (gr. 7 up). reprint ed. 14.95 (*0-688-14441-1*) HarperCollins Children's Bk. Group.

—The Time Machine & Other Cases. 1999. (Einstein Anderson, Science Detective Ser.). (Illus.). (J). (gr. 3-6). pap. 3.99 (*0-380-72658-0*, Avon Bks.) Morrow/Avon.

—The Time Machine & Other Cases. 1999. (Einstein Anderson, Science Detective Ser.). (J). (gr. 3-6). 10.14 (*0-606-16005-1*) Turtleback Bks.

—The Wings of Darkness & Other Cases, Bk. 5. 1999. (Einstein Anderson, Science Detective Ser.). (Illus.). 80p. (J). (gr. 3-6). pap. 3.99 (*0-380-72659-9*, Harper Trophy) HarperCollins Children's Bk. Group.

—The Wings of Darkness & Other Cases. 1998. (Einstein Anderson, Science Detective Ser.). (Illus.). 80p. (J). (gr. 3-6). 14.00 o.p. (*0-688-14443-8*, Morrow, William & Co.) Morrow/Avon.

—The Wings of Darkness & Other Cases. 1999. (Einstein Anderson, Science Detective Ser.). (J). (gr. 3-6). 10.14 (*0-606-16341-7*) Turtleback Bks.

ANGEL (FICTITIOUS CHARACTER: HOLDER)—FICTION

Durgian, Doranna. Impressions. 2003. (Angel Ser.). (Illus.). 304p. (YA). mass mkt. 5.99 (*0-7434-2758-0*, Simon Pulse) Simon & Schuster Children's Publishing.

Holder, Nancy. The Angel Chronicles. (Buffy the Vampire Slayer Ser.). 2001. 224p. (J). E-Book 5.99 (*0-7434-3115-4*); 1999. (Illus.). 192p. (YA). (gr. 7 up). mass mkt. 4.99 (*0-671-02631-3*); Vol. 1. 1998. (Illus.). 224p. (YA). (gr. 7 up). mass mkt. 5.99 (*0-671-02133-8*) Simon & Schuster Children's Publishing. (Simon Pulse).

—City of Angel. 1999. (Angel Ser.: No. 1). 192p. (YA). (gr. 7 up). pap. 4.99 (*0-671-04144-4*, Simon Pulse) Simon & Schuster Children's Publishing.

—Not Forgotten. 2000. (Angel Ser.: No. 2). 256p. (YA). (gr. 7 up). mass mkt. 5.99 (*0-671-04145-2*, Simon Pulse) Simon & Schuster Children's Publishing.

Holder, Nancy & Mariotte, Jeff. The Unseen Book 1: The Burning. 2001. (Buffy the Vampire Slayer & Angel Crossover Ser.: No. 1). reprint ed. E-Book 6.99 (*0-7434-3289-4*, Simon Pulse) Simon & Schuster Children's Publishing.

—The Unseen Book 2: Door to Alternity. 2001. (Buffy the Vampire Slayer & Angel Crossover Ser.: No. 2). reprint ed. E-Book 6.99 (*0-7434-3290-8*, Simon Pulse) Simon & Schuster Children's Publishing.

—The Unseen Book 3: The Long Way Home. 2001. (Buffy the Vampire Slayer & Angel Crossover Ser.: No. 3). reprint ed. E-Book 6.99 (*0-7434-3291-6*, Simon Pulse) Simon & Schuster Children's Publishing.

ANGELINA BALLERINA (FICTITIOUS CHARACTER)—FICTION

Holabird, Katharine. Angelina & Alice. 1988. (Angelina Ballerina Ser.). (Illus.). 24p. (J). (ps-3). 16.00 o.p. (*0-517-56074-7*, Clarkson Potter) Crown Publishing Group.

—Angelina & Alice. (Angelina Ballerina Ser.). (Illus.). 24p. (J). (ps-3). 2002. 12.95 (*1-58485-651-3*); 2001. 9.95 (*1-58485-130-9*) Pleasant Co. Pubns.

—Angelina & Alice: Includes Alice Doll. 2001. (Angelina Ballerina Ser.). (Illus.). (J). (ps-3). 27.95 (*1-58485-332-8*) Pleasant Co. Pubns.

—Angelina & Henry. 2002. (Angelina Ballerina Ser.). (Illus.). 24p. (J). (ps-2). 12.95 (*1-58485-523-1*, American Girl) Pleasant Co. Pubns.

—Angelina & Henry: Includes Henry Doll. 2002. (Illus.). 24p. (J). 24.95 (*1-58485-576-2*, American Girl) Pleasant Co. Pubns.

—Angelina & the Princess. 1988. (Angelina Ballerina Ser.). (Illus.). 24p. (J). (ps-3). 16.00 o.p. (*0-517-55273-6*, Clarkson Potter) Crown Publishing Group.

—Angelina & the Princess. (Angelina Ballerina Ser.). (Illus.). 24p. (J). (ps-3). 2002. 12.95 (*1-58485-653-X*); 2000. 9.95 (*1-58485-148-1*) Pleasant Co. Pubns.

—Angelina at the Fair. 1988. (Angelina Ballerina Ser.). (Illus.). 24p. (J). (ps-3). 16.00 o.p. (*0-517-55744-4*, Clarkson Potter) Crown Publishing Group.

—Angelina at the Fair. (Angelina Ballerina Ser.). (Illus.). 24p. (J). (ps-3). 2002. 12.95 (*1-58485-654-8*); 2000. 9.95 (*1-58485-144-9*) Pleasant Co. Pubns.

—Angelina Ballerina. (Angelina Ballerina Ser.). (Illus.). (J). (ps-3). 1990. 24p. 5.99 o.p. (*0-517-57668-6*); 1988. 16.00 o.p. (*0-517-55083-0*) Crown Publishing Group. (Clarkson Potter).

—Angelina Ballerina. (Angelina Ballerina Ser.). (Illus.). 24p. (J). (ps-3). 2002. 12.95 (*1-58485-655-6*); 2000. 9.95 (*1-58485-135-X*) Pleasant Co. Pubns.

—Angelina Ballerina: Includes Doll. 2000. (Angelina Ballerina Ser.). (Illus.). 24p. (J). (ps-3). 27.95 (*1-58485-194-5*) Pleasant Co. Pubns.

—Angelina Ballerina & Other Stories. unabr. ed. 1986. (Angelina Ballerina Ser.). (J). (ps-3). audio 11.95 o.p. (*0-89845-632-0*, CPN 1790, Caedmon) HarperTrade.

—Angelina Ballerina & Other Stories. 1993. (Angelina Ballerina Ser.). (J). (ps-3). audio 9.98 Music for Little People, Inc.

—Angelina Ballerina's ABC. 2002. (Illus.). 20p. (J). bds. 5.95 (*1-58485-613-0*, American Girl) Pleasant Co. Pubns.

—Angelina Ballerina's Colors. 2002. (Illus.). 20p. (J). bds. 5.95 (*1-58485-615-7*, American Girl) Pleasant Co. Pubns.

—Angelina Ballerina's Invitation to the Ballet. 2003. (Angelina Ballerina Ser.). (Illus.). 32p. (J). 17.95 (*1-58485-757-9*, American Girl) Pleasant Co. Pubns.

—Angelina Ballerina's Shapes. 2002. (Angelina Ballerina Ser.). (Illus.). 20p. (J). bds. 5.95 (*1-58485-616-5*, American Girl) Pleasant Co. Pubns.

—Angelina Ballerina's 123. 2002. (Angelina Ballerina Ser.). (Illus.). 20p. (J). bds. 5.95 (*1-58485-614-9*, American Girl) Pleasant Co. Pubns.

—Angelina Ice Skates. 1994. (Angelina Ballerina Ser.). (Illus.). 32p. (J). (ps-3). 4.99 o.p. (*0-517-59982-1*, Clarkson Potter) Crown Publishing Group.

—Angelina Ice Skates. (Angelina Ballerina Ser.). (Illus.). 24p. (J). (ps-3). 2002. 12.95 (*1-58485-660-2*); 2nd ed. 2001. 9.95 (*1-58485-146-5*) Pleasant Co. Pubns.

—Angelina Loves: A Story of Love & Friendship. 2002. (Illus.). 24p. (J). pap. 6.95 (*1-58485-566-5*, American Girl) Pleasant Co. Pubns.

—Angelina on Stage. 1988. (Angelina Ballerina Ser.). (Illus.). 24p. (J). (ps-3). 16.00 o.p. (*0-517-56073-9*, Clarkson Potter) Crown Publishing Group.

—Angelina on Stage. (Angelina Ballerina Ser.). (Illus.). 24p. (J). (ps-3). 2002. 12.95 (*1-58485-656-4*); 2nd ed. 2001. 9.95 (*1-58485-150-3*) Pleasant Co. Pubns.

—Angelina's Baby Sister. 1991. (Angelina Ballerina Ser.). (J). (ps-3). 16.00 o.p. (*0-517-58600-2*, Clarkson Potter) Crown Publishing Group.

—Angelina's Baby Sister. (Angelina Ballerina Ser.). (Illus.). 24p. (J). (ps-3). 2002. 12.95 (*1-58485-657-2*); 2000. 9.95 (*1-58485-132-5*) Pleasant Co. Pubns.

—Angelina's Baby Sister: Includes Polly Doll. 2002. (Angelina Ballerina Ser.). (Illus.). (J). (ps-3). 24.95 (*1-58485-590-8*) Pleasant Co. Pubns.

—Angelina's Ballet Class. 2001. (Angelina Ballerina Ser.). (Illus.). 24p. (J). (ps up). pap. 7.95 (*1-58485-363-8*) Pleasant Co. Pubns.

—Angelina's Birthday. (Angelina Ballerina Ser.). (Illus.). 24p. (J). (ps-3). 2002. 12.95 (*1-58485-652-1*); 2nd ed. 2001. 9.95 (*1-58485-137-6*) Pleasant Co. Pubns.

—Angelina's Birthday Surprise. 1989. (Angelina Ballerina Ser.). (Illus.). 32p. (J). (ps-3). 16.00 o.p. (*0-517-57325-3*, Clarkson Potter) Crown Publishing Group.

—Angelina's Christmas. 1986. (Angelina Ballerina Ser.). (Illus.). 32p. (J). (ps-3). 16.00 o.p. (*0-517-55823-8*, Clarkson Potter) Crown Publishing Group.

—Angelina's Christmas. (Angelina Ballerina Ser.). (Illus.). 24p. (J). (ps-3). 2002. 12.95 (*1-58485-658-0*); 2000. 9.95 (*1-58485-140-6*) Pleasant Co. Pubns.

—Angelina's Christmas. 1988. (Angelina Ballerina Ser.). (J). (ps-3). 5.99 o.p. (*0-517-57188-9*) Random Hse. Value Publishing.

—Angelina's Halloween. (Angelina Ballerina Ser.). (Illus.). 24p. (J). (ps-3). 2002. 12.95 (*1-58485-659-9*); 2000. 9.95 (*1-58485-152-X*) Pleasant Co. Pubns.

—Angelina's Ice Skates. 1993. (Angelina Ballerina Ser.). (Illus.). 32p. (J). (ps-3). 16.00 o.p. (*0-517-59619-9*, Clarkson Potter) Crown Publishing Group.

—Dance with Angelina: A Sticker Storybook. Pleasant Company Staff, ed. 2000. (Angelina Ballerina Ser.). (Illus.). 20p. (J). (ps-3). pap. 6.95 (*1-58485-223-2*) Pleasant Co. Pubns.

—My Memory Book. 2003. (Angelina Ballerina Ser.). (Illus.). 32p. (J). 14.95 (*1-58485-715-3*) Pleasant Co. Pubns.

Holabird, Katharine & Lever, Sally-Ann. Angelina & the Rag Doll. 2002. (Angelina Ballerina Ser.). (Illus.). 24p. (J). pap. 3.50 (*1-58485-617-3*, American Girl) Pleasant Co. Pubns.

Lever, Sally-Ann. Angelina & the Butterfly. 2002. (Angelina Ballerina Ser.). (Illus.). 24p. (J). pap. 3.50 (*1-58485-618-1*, American Girl) Pleasant Co. Pubns.

Pleasant Company Staff. Angelina's Tea Party: An Activity Book. 2000. (Angelina Ballerina Ser.). (Illus.). 24p. (J). (ps-3). pap. 5.95 (*1-58485-222-4*) Pleasant Co. Pubns.

ANIMORPHS (FICTITIOUS CHARACTERS)—FICTION

Applegate, K. A. L' Alerte. 2nd ed. 1999. (Animorphs Ser.: No. 16). Tr. of Animorphs. (FRE.). (J). (gr. 3-7). pap. text 12.95 (*2-07-052191-5*) Distribooks, Inc.

—The Alien. 1997. (Animorphs Ser.: No. 8). 159p. (J). (gr. 3-7). mass mkt. 4.99 (*0-590-99728-9*) Scholastic, Inc.

—The Alien. 1997. (Animorphs Ser.: No. 8). (J). (gr. 3-7). 11.04 (*0-606-11050-X*) Turtleback Bks.

—The Andalite Chronicles. 1997. (Animorphs Ser.). 326p. (J). (gr. 3-7). mass mkt. 5.99 (*0-590-10971-5*, Scholastic Paperbacks) Scholastic, Inc.

—The Andalite Chronicles. 1997. (Animorphs Ser.). (J). (gr. 3-7). 12.04 (*0-606-12617-1*) Turtleback Bks.

—The Andalite's Gift. 1997. (Animorphs Ser.: No. 1). (J). (gr. 3-7). mass mkt. 4.99 (*0-590-21304-0*) Scholastic, Inc.

—The Andalite's Gift. 1997. (Animorphs: No. 1). (J). (gr. 3-7). 11.04 (*0-606-11052-6*) Turtleback Bks.

—The Android. 1997. (Animorphs Ser.: No. 10). (Illus.). 170p. (J). (gr. 3-7). mass mkt. 4.99 (*0-590-99730-0*) Scholastic, Inc.

—The Android. 1997. (Animorphs Ser.: No. 10). (J). (gr. 3-7). 11.04 (*0-606-11047-X*) Turtleback Bks.

—Animorphs, 12 bks. l.t. ed. Incl. Arrival. 148p. 2001. lib. bdg. 22.60 (*0-8368-2771-6*); Conspiracy. 138p. 2000. lib. bdg. 22.60 (*0-8368-2754-6*); Familiar. 143p. 2001. lib. bdg. 22.60 (*0-8368-2774-0*); Hidden. 121p. 2001. lib. bdg. 22.60 (*0-8368-2772-4*); Illusion. 156p. 2000. lib. bdg. 22.60 (*0-8368-2755-4*); Journey. 139p. 2001. lib. bdg. 22.60 (*0-8368-2775-9*); Mutation. 142p. 2000. lib. bdg. 22.60 (*0-8368-2756-2*); Other. 130p. 2001. lib. bdg. 22.60 (*0-8368-2773-2*); Prophecy. 141p. 2000. lib. bdg. 22.60 (*0-8368-2757-0*); Proposal. 147p. 2000. lib. bdg. 22.60 (*0-8368-2758-9*); Separation. 158p. 2000. lib. bdg. 22.60 (*0-8368-2759-7*); Weakness. (Illus.). 129p. 2001. lib. bdg. 22.60 (*0-8368-2770-8*); (J). (gr. 4 up). 2001. Set lib. bdg. 271.20 (*0-8368-2862-3*) Stevens, Gareth Inc.

—Animorphs Boxed Set No. 1: Books 1-4. 2001. (Animorphs Ser.). (J). (gr. 3-7). pap. 19.96 (*0-590-38187-3*) Scholastic, Inc.

—Animorphs Boxed Set No. 2: Books 5-8. 2001. (Animorphs Ser.). (J). (gr. 3-7). 19.96 (*0-590-90725-5*) Scholastic, Inc.

—Animorphs Boxed Set No. 4: Books 13-16. 2001. (Animorphs Ser.). (J). (gr. 3-7). pap. 19.96 (*0-590-28434-7*, Scholastic Paperbacks) Scholastic, Inc.

—Animorphs Boxed Set No. 6: Books 21-24. 2001. (Animorphs Ser.). (J). (gr. 3-7). pap. 19.96 (*0-590-28497-5*, Scholastic Paperbacks) Scholastic, Inc.

—Animorphs Boxed Set No. 7: Books 25-28. 2001. (Animorphs Ser.). (J). pap. 19.96 (*0-439-07341-3*) Scholastic, Inc.

—Animorphs Boxed Set No. 8: Books 29-32. 2001. (Animorphs Ser.: 29-32). (J). 19.96 (*0-439-10684-2*) Scholastic, Inc.

—Animorphs Series Boxed Set. 1998. (Animorphs Ser.). (J). (gr. 3-7). pap. 143.64 (*0-590-51066-5*) Scholastic, Inc.

—Animorphs Series Boxed Set: The Secret; The Android; The Forgotten; The Reaction, 4 vols., No. 3. 1997. (Animorphs Ser.: Nos. 9-12). (J). (gr. 3-7). 19.96 (*0-590-35020-X*) Scholastic, Inc.

—Animorphs Series Boxed Set: The Threat; The Solution; The Pretender; The Suspicion, 4 vols., No. 6. 2001. (Animorphs Ser.: Nos. 21-24). (J). (gr. 3-7). pap. 19.96 (*0-590-28543-2*) Scholastic, Inc.

—Animorphs Series Boxed Set: The Weakness; The Arrival; The Hidden; The Other. 2000. (Animorphs Ser.: Nos. 37-40). (Illus.). (J). (gr. 3-7). pap. 19.96 (*0-439-10688-5*, Scholastic Paperbacks) Scholastic, Inc.

—The Arrival. 2000. (Animorphs Ser.: No. 38). (Illus.). 160p. (J). (gr. 3-7). mass mkt. 4.99 (*0-439-10677-X*, Scholastic Paperbacks) Scholastic, Inc.

—The Arrival. 2000. (Animorphs Ser.: No. 38). (Illus.). (J). (gr. 3-7). 11.04 (*0-606-18509-7*) Turtleback Bks.

—The Attack, No. 26. 1999. (Animorphs Ser.: No. 26). 145p. (J). (gr. 3-7). mass mkt. 4.99 (*0-590-76259-1*) Scholastic, Inc.

—The Attack. 1999. (Animorphs Ser.: No. 26). (J). (gr. 3-7). 11.04 (*0-606-15834-0*) Turtleback Bks.

—Back to Before, No. 4. 2000. (Animorphs Ser.: No. 4). (Illus.). 240p. (J). (gr. 3-7). mass mkt. 5.99 (*0-439-17307-8*) Scholastic, Inc.

—Back to Before. 2000. (Animorphs: No. 4). (Illus.). (J). (gr. 3-7). 12.04 (*0-606-18513-5*) Turtleback Bks.

—The Capture. 1997. (Animorphs Ser.: No. 6). 154p. (J). (gr. 3-7). mass mkt. 4.99 (*0-590-62982-4*) Scholastic, Inc.

—The Capture. 1997. (Animorphs Ser.: No. 6). (J). (gr. 3-7). 11.04 (*0-606-10742-8*) Turtleback Bks.

—The Change. 1997. (Animorphs Ser.: No. 13). 162p. (J). (gr. 3-7). mass mkt. 4.99 (*0-590-49418-X*, Scholastic Paperbacks) Scholastic, Inc.

—The Change. 1997. (Animorphs Ser.: No. 13). (J). (gr. 3-7). 11.04 (*0-606-12619-8*) Turtleback Bks.

—The Conspiracy. 31st ed. 1999. (Animorphs Ser.: No. 31). 139p. (J). (gr. 3-7). mass mkt. 4.99 (*0-439-07031-7*) Scholastic, Inc.

—The Conspiracy. l.t. ed. 2000. (Animorphs Ser.: No. 31). 138p. (J). (gr. 4 up). lib. bdg. 22.60 (*0-8368-2754-6*) Stevens, Gareth Inc.

—The Conspiracy. 1999. (Animorphs Ser.: No. 31). (Illus.). (J). (gr. 3-7). 11.04 (*0-606-16928-8*) Turtleback Bks.

—The Decision. 1998. (Animorphs Ser.: No. 18). 168p. (J). (gr. 3-7). mass mkt. 4.99 (*0-590-49441-4*, Scholastic Paperbacks) Scholastic, Inc.

—The Decision. 1998. (Animorphs Ser.: No. 18). (J). (gr. 3-7). 11.04 (*0-606-13138-8*) Turtleback Bks.

—The Departure. 1998. (Animorphs Ser.: No. 19). 159p. (J). (gr. 3-7). mass mkt. 4.99 (*0-590-49451-1*, Scholastic Paperbacks) Scholastic, Inc.

—The Departure. 1998. (Animorphs Ser.: No. 19). (J). (gr. 3-7). 11.04 (*0-606-13139-6*) Turtleback Bks.

—The Discovery. 1998. (Animorphs Ser.: No. 20). 153p. (J). (gr. 3-7). mass mkt. 4.99 (*0-590-49637-9*, Scholastic Paperbacks) Scholastic, Inc.

—The Discovery. 1998. (Animorphs Ser.: No. 20). (J). (gr. 3-7). 11.04 (*0-606-13140-X*) Turtleback Bks.

—Elfangor's Secret. 1999. (Animorphs Ser.: No. 3). 208p. (J). (gr. 3-7). mass mkt. 5.99 (*0-590-03639-4*) Scholastic, Inc.

—Elfangor's Secret. 1999. (Animorphs Ser.: No. 3). (J). (gr. 3-7). 12.04 (*0-606-16619-X*) Turtleback Bks.

—The Ellimist Chronicles. 2000. (Animorphs Ser.). 288p. (J). (gr. 3-7). mass mkt. 5.99 (*0-439-21798-9*) Scholastic, Inc.

—The Ellimist Chronicles. 2000. (Animorphs Ser.). (J). (gr. 3-7). 12.04 (*0-606-19533-5*) Turtleback Bks.

—The Encounter. 1996. (Animorphs Ser.: No. 3). 157p. (J). (gr. 3-7). mass mkt. 4.99 (*0-590-62979-4*) Scholastic, Inc.

—The Encounter. 1996. (Animorphs Ser.: No. 3). (J). (gr. 3-7). 11.04 (*0-606-09004-5*) Turtleback Bks.

—El Encuentro. 1999. (Animorphs Ser.: Vol. 3). (SPA., Illus.). (J). (gr. 4-7). pap. 4.99 (*0-439-08627-2*, SO1649) Scholastic, Inc.

—El Encuentro. 1999. (Animorphs Ser.: No. 3). (J). (gr. 3-7). 11.04 (*0-606-17286-6*) Turtleback Bks.

—The Escape. 1998. (Animorphs Ser.: No. 15). 170p. (J). (gr. 3-7). mass mkt. 4.99 (*0-590-49424-4*) Scholastic, Inc.

—The Escape. 1998. (Animorphs Ser.: No. 15). (J). (gr. 3-7). 11.04 (*0-606-12876-X*) Turtleback Bks.

—The Experiment. 1999. (Animorphs Ser.: No. 28). 139p. (J). (gr. 3-7). mass mkt. 4.99 (*0-590-76261-3*) Scholastic, Inc.

—The Experiment. 1999. (Animorphs Ser.: No. 28). (J). (gr. 3-7). 11.04 (*0-606-16608-4*) Turtleback Bks.

—The Exposed. 1999. (Animorphs Ser.: No. 27). 154p. (J). (gr. 3-7). mass mkt. 4.99 (*0-590-76260-5*) Scholastic, Inc.

—The Exposed. 1999. (Animorphs Ser.: No. 27). (J). (gr. 3-7). 11.04 (*0-606-16589-4*) Turtleback Bks.

—The Extreme. 1999. (Animorphs Ser.: No. 25). (J). (gr. 3-7). pap. text 179.64 (*0-439-04365-4*);No. 25. 146p. mass mkt. 4.99 (*0-590-76258-3*) Scholastic, Inc.

—The Extreme. 1999. (Animorphs Ser.: No. 25). (J). (gr. 3-7). 11.04 (*0-606-15437-X*) Turtleback Bks.

—The Familiar. 2000. (Animorphs Ser.: No. 41). (Illus.). (J). (gr. 3-7). 11.04 (*0-606-18512-7*) Turtleback Bks.

—The First Journey. 1999. (Animorphs Ser.: No. 1). 115p. (J). (gr. 3-7). mass mkt. 4.99 (*0-439-06164-4*) Scholastic, Inc.

—The First Journey. 1999. (Animorphs: No. 1). (J). (gr. 3-7). 11.04 (*0-606-16606-8*) Turtleback Bks.

—The Forgotten. 1997. (Animorphs Ser.: No. 11). 162p. (J). (gr. 3-7). mass mkt. 4.99 (*0-590-99732-7*) Scholastic, Inc.

—The Forgotten. 1997. (Animorphs Ser.: No. 11). (J). (gr. 3-7). 11.04 (*0-606-11048-8*) Turtleback Bks.

—The Hidden. 2000. (Animorphs Ser.: No. 39). 160p. (J). (gr. 3-7). mass mkt. 4.99 (*0-439-10678-8*) Scholastic, Inc.

—The Hork-Bajir Chronicles. (Animorphs Ser.). (J). (gr. 3-7). 1999. 206p. mass mkt. 5.99 (*0-590-03646-7*); 1998. 206p. pap. 13.95 (*0-439-04291-7*); 1998. 12.95 (*0-590-38198-9*) Scholastic, Inc.

—The Hork-Bajir Chronicles. 1999. (Animorphs Ser.). (J). (gr. 3-7). 12.04 (*0-606-17284-X*) Turtleback Bks.

—The Illusion. 1999. (Animorphs Ser.: No. 33). 156p. (J). (gr. 3-7). mass mkt. 4.99 (*0-439-07033-3*) Scholastic, Inc.

—The Illusion. l.t. ed. 2000. (Animorphs Ser.: No. 33). 156p. (J). (gr. 4 up). lib. bdg. 22.60 (*0-8368-2755-4*) Stevens, Gareth Inc.

—The Illusion. 1999. (Animorphs Ser.: No. 33). (J). (gr. 3-7). 11.04 (*0-606-17287-4*) Turtleback Bks.

—In the Time of Dinosaurs. 1999. (Animorphs: No. 2). (J). (gr. 3-7). 12.40 (*0-613-07252-9*) Econo-Clad Bks.

—In the Time of Dinosaurs. 1998. (Animorphs Ser.: No. 2). 229p. (J). (gr. 3-7). mass mkt. 4.99 (*0-590-95615-9*, Scholastic Paperbacks) Scholastic, Inc.

—In the Time of Dinosaurs. 1998. (Animorphs: No. 2). (J). (gr. 3-7). 11.04 (*0-606-13142-6*) Turtleback Bks.

—The Invasion. 1996. (Animorphs Ser.: No. 1). (Illus.). 144p. (J). (gr. 3-7). mass mkt. 4.99 (*0-590-62977-8*) Scholastic, Inc.

—The Invasion. 1996. (Animorphs Ser.: No. 1). (J). (gr. 3-7). 11.04 (*0-606-09002-9*) Turtleback Bks.

—L' Invasion. 1999. (Animorphs Ser.: No. 1). Tr. of Invasion. (FRE & SPA.). 128p. (J). (gr. 3-7). pap. text 4.99 (*0-439-05602-0*) Scholastic, Inc.

—The Journey. 42nd ed. 2000. (Animorphs Ser.: No. 42). (Illus.). 144p. (J). (gr. 3-7). mass mkt. 4.99 (*0-439-11516-7*) Scholastic, Inc.

—The Journey. 2000. (Animorphs Ser.: No. 42). (Illus.). (J). (gr. 3-7). 11.04 (*0-606-18860-6*) Turtleback Bks.

—El Mensaje. 1999. (Animorphs Ser.: No. 4). (SPA.). (J). (gr. 3-7). pap. text 4.99 (*0-439-08783-X*, SO5398) Scholastic, Inc.

—El Mensaje. 1999. No. 4. 11.04 (*0-606-17290-4*) Turtleback Bks.

—The Message. 1996. (Animorphs Ser.: No. 4). 151p. (J). (gr. 3-7). mass mkt. 4.99 (*0-590-62980-8*) Scholastic, Inc.

—The Message. 2000. (Animorphs Ser.: No. 4). (Illus.). (J). (gr. 3-7). 11.04 (*0-606-18510-0*) Turtleback Bks.

—Le Message. 1996. (Animorphs Ser.: No. 4). Tr. of Message. (FRE.). (J). (gr. 3-7). 11.04 (*0-606-10126-8*) Turtleback Bks.

—The Mutation. 36th ed. 1999. (Animorphs Ser.: No. 36). (Illus.). 142p. (J). (gr. 3-7). mass mkt. 4.99 (*0-439-10675-3*) Scholastic, Inc.

—The Mutation. l.t. ed. 2000. (Animorphs Ser.: No. 36). 142p. (J). (gr. 4 up). lib. bdg. 22.60 (*0-8368-2756-2*) Stevens, Gareth Inc.

—The Mutation. 1999. (Animorphs Ser.: No. 36). (Illus.). (J). (gr. 3-7). 11.04 (*0-606-18507-0*) Turtleback Bks.

—The Next Passage. 2000. (Animorphs Ser.: No. 2). (Illus.). 128p. (J). (gr. 3-7). mass mkt. 4.99 (*0-439-14263-6*) Scholastic, Inc.

—The Next Passage. 2000. (Animorphs: No. 2). (Illus.). (J). (gr. 3-7). 11.04 (*0-606-18506-2*) Turtleback Bks.

—The Other. 2000. (Animorphs Ser.: No. 40). (Illus.). 160p. (J). (gr. 3-7). mass mkt. 4.99 (*0-439-10679-6*) Scholastic, Inc.

—The Other. 2000. (Animorphs Ser.: No. 40). (Illus.). (J). (gr. 3-7). 11.04 (*0-606-18511-9*) Turtleback Bks.

—The Predator. 1996. (Animorphs Ser.: No. 5). 152p. (J). (gr. 3-7). mass mkt. 4.99 (*0-590-62981-6*) Scholastic, Inc.

—The Predator. 1996. (Animorphs Ser.: No. 5). (J). (gr. 3-7). 11.04 (*0-606-10127-6*) Turtleback Bks.

—The Pretender. 1998. (Animorphs Ser.: No. 23). 154p. (J). (gr. 3-7). mass mkt. 4.99 (*0-590-76256-7*) Scholastic, Inc.

—The Pretender. 1998. (Animorphs Ser.: No. 23). (J). (gr. 3-7). 11.04 (*0-606-15435-3*) Turtleback Bks.

—The Prophecy. 1999. (Animorphs Ser.: No. 34). 141p. (J). (gr. 3-7). mass mkt. 4.99 (*0-439-07034-1*) Scholastic, Inc.

—The Prophecy. l.t. ed. 2000. (Animorphs Ser.: No. 34). 141p. (J). (gr. 4 up). lib. bdg. 22.60 (*0-8368-2757-0*) Stevens, Gareth Inc.

—The Prophecy. 1999. (Animorphs Ser.: No. 34). (J). (gr. 3-7). 11.04 (*0-606-17283-1*) Turtleback Bks.

—The Proposal. 1999. (Animorphs Ser.: No. 35). 147p. (J). (gr. 3-7). mass mkt. 4.99 (*0-439-07035-X*) Scholastic, Inc.

—The Proposal. l.t. ed. 2000. (Animorphs Ser.: No. 35). 147p. (J). (gr. 4 up). lib. bdg. 22.60 (*0-8368-2758-9*) Stevens, Gareth Inc.

—The Proposal. 1999. (Animorphs Ser.: No. 35). (J). (gr. 3-7). 11.04 (*0-606-17289-0*) Turtleback Bks.

—The Reaction. 1997. (Animorphs Ser.: No. 12). 152p. (J). (gr. 3-7). mass mkt. 4.99 (*0-590-99734-3*) Scholastic, Inc.

—The Reaction. 1997. (Animorphs Ser.: No. 12). (J). (gr. 3-7). 11.04 (*0-606-12618-X*) Turtleback Bks.

—The Resistance. 2000. (Animorphs Ser.: No. 47). 160p. (J). (gr. 3-7). mass mkt. 4.99 (*0-439-11521-3*) Scholastic, Inc.

—The Resistance. 2000. (Animorphs Ser.: No. 47). (J). (gr. 3-7). 11.04 (*0-606-19530-0*) Turtleback Bks.

—The Reunion. 1999. (Animorphs Ser.: No. 30). 156p. (J). (gr. 3-7). mass mkt. 4.99 (*0-590-76263-X*) Scholastic, Inc.

—The Reunion. 1999. (Animorphs: No. 30). 11.04 (*0-606-16657-2*) Turtleback Bks.

—The Revelation. 2000. (Animorphs Ser.: No. 45). (Illus.). 160p. (J). (gr. 3-7). mass mkt. 4.99 (*0-439-11519-1*) Scholastic, Inc.

—The Revelation. 2000. (Animorphs Ser.: No. 45). (Illus.). (J). (gr. 3-7). 11.04 (*0-606-18863-0*) Turtleback Bks.

—The Secret. 1997. (Animorphs Ser.: No. 9). 158p. (J). (gr. 3-7). mass mkt. 4.99 (*0-590-99729-7*) Scholastic, Inc.

—The Secret. 1997. (Animorphs Ser.: No. 9). (J). (gr. 3-7). 11.04 (*0-606-11051-8*) Turtleback Bks.

—The Separation. 1999. (Animorphs Ser.: No. 32). 158p. (J). (gr. 3-7). mass mkt. 4.99 (*0-439-07032-5*) Scholastic, Inc.

—The Separation. l.t. ed. 2000. (Animorphs Ser.: No. 32). 158p. (J). (gr. 4 up). lib. bdg. 22.60 (*0-8368-2759-7*) Stevens, Gareth Inc.

—The Separation. 1999. (Animorphs Ser.: No. 32). (J). (gr. 3-7). 11.04 (*0-606-17060-X*) Turtleback Bks.

—The Sickness. 1999. (Animorphs Ser.: No. 29). 152p. (J). (gr. 3-7). mass mkt. 4.99 (*0-590-76262-1*) Scholastic, Inc.

—The Sickness. 1999. (Animorphs Ser.: No. 29). 11.04 (*0-606-16618-1*) Turtleback Bks.

—The Solution. 1998. (Animorphs Ser.: No. 22). 152p. (J). (gr. 3-7). mass mkt. 4.99 (*0-590-76255-9*) Scholastic, Inc.

—The Solution. 1998. (Animorphs Ser.: No. 22). (J). (gr. 3-7). 11.04 (*0-606-15434-5*) Turtleback Bks.

—The Stranger. 1997. (Animorphs Ser.: No. 7). 163p. (J). (gr. 3-7). mass mkt. 4.99 (*0-590-99726-2*) Scholastic, Inc.

—The Stranger. 1997. (Animorphs Ser.: No. 7). (J). (gr. 3-7). 11.04 (*0-606-11049-6*) Turtleback Bks.

—The Suspicion. 1998. (Animorphs Ser.: No. 24). (J). (gr. 3-7). pap. text 179.64 (*0-590-63052-0*);No. 24. 155p. mass mkt. 4.99 (*0-590-76257-5*) Scholastic, Inc.

—The Suspicion. 1998. (Animorphs Ser.: No. 24). (J). (gr. 3-7). 11.04 (*0-606-15436-1*) Turtleback Bks.

—The Test. 2000. (Animorphs Ser.: No. 43). (Illus.). 144p. (J). (gr. 3-7). mass mkt. 4.99 (*0-439-11517-5*) Scholastic, Inc.

—The Test. 2000. (Animorphs Ser.: No. 43). (Illus.). (J). (gr. 3-7). 11.04 (*0-606-18861-4*) Turtleback Bks.

—The Threat. 1998. (Animorphs Ser.: No. 21). 158p. (J). (gr. 3-7). mass mkt. 4.99 (*0-590-76254-0*, Scholastic Paperbacks) Scholastic, Inc.

—The Threat. 1998. (Animorphs Ser.: No. 21). (J). (gr. 3-7). 11.04 (*0-606-13141-8*) Turtleback Bks.

—The Underground. 1998. (Animorphs Ser.: No. 17). 167p. (J). (gr. 3-7). mass mkt. 4.99 (*0-590-49436-8*, Scholastic Paperbacks) Scholastic, Inc.

—The Underground. 1998. (Animorphs Ser.: No. 17). (J). (gr. 3-7). 11.04 (*0-606-13137-X*) Turtleback Bks.

—The Unexpected. 2000. (Animorphs Ser.: No. 44). (Illus.). 160p. (J). (gr. 3-7). mass mkt. 4.99 (*0-439-11518-3*) Scholastic, Inc.

—The Unexpected. 2000. (Animorphs Ser.: No. 44). (Illus.). (J). (gr. 3-7). 11.04 (*0-606-18862-2*) Turtleback Bks.

—The Unknown. 1998. (Animorphs Ser.: No. 14). 166p. (J). (gr. 3-7). mass mkt. 4.99 (*0-590-49423-6*, Scholastic Paperbacks) Scholastic, Inc.

—The Unknown. 1998. (Animorphs Ser.: No. 14). (J). (gr. 3-7). 11.04 (*0-606-12875-1*) Turtleback Bks.

—El Visitante. 1999. (Animorphs Ser.: No. 2). (SPA., Illus.). 192p. (J). (gr. 3-7). pap. 4.99 (*0-439-07163-1*, SO5396) Scholastic, Inc.

—El Visitante. 1999. (Animorphs Ser.: No. 2). (J). (gr. 3-7). 11.04 (*0-606-16929-6*) Turtleback Bks.

—The Visitor. 1996. (Animorphs Ser.: No. 2). (Illus.). 144p. (J). (gr. 3-7). mass mkt. 4.99 (*0-590-62978-6*) Scholastic, Inc.

—The Visitor. 1996. (Animorphs Ser.: No. 2). (J). (gr. 3-7). 11.04 (*0-606-09003-7*) Turtleback Bks.

—The Warning. 1998. (Animorphs Ser.: No. 16). 151p. (J). (gr. 3-7). mass mkt. 4.99 (*0-590-49430-9*, Scholastic Paperbacks) Scholastic, Inc.

—The Warning. 1998. (Animorphs Ser.: No. 16). (J). (gr. 3-7). 11.04 (*0-606-13136-1*) Turtleback Bks.

—The Weakness. 37th ed. 2000. (Animorphs Ser.: No. 37). 160p. (J). (gr. 3-7). mass mkt. 4.99 (*0-439-10676-1*, Scholastic Paperbacks) Scholastic, Inc.

—The Weakness. 2000. (Animorphs Ser.: No. 37). (Illus.). (J). (gr. 3-7). 11.04 (*0-606-18508-9*) Turtleback Bks.

Reisfeld, Randi. Meet the Stars of Animorphs. 1999. (Animorphs Ser.). (J). (gr. 3-7). pap. text 59.88 (*0-439-07272-7*); 144p. mass mkt. 4.99 (*0-439-06165-2*) Scholastic, Inc.

ANNE OF GREEN GABLES (FICTITIOUS CHARACTER)—FICTION

Alcott, Louisa May & Montgomery, L. M. Anne of Green Gables & Little Women. l.t. ed. 1999. E-Book 24.95 incl. cd-rom (*1-929077-40-8*, Books OnScreen) PageFree Publishing, Inc.

Burke, Betty. Anne of Green Gables. Cain, Janet, ed. 1994. (Literature Units Ser.). (Illus.). 48p. pap. 7.99 (*1-55734-438-8*, TCM0438) Teacher Created Materials, Inc.

Center for Learning Network Staff. Anne of Green Gables: Curriculum Unit, Grades 6-12. 1995. (Novel Ser.). 89p. tchr. ed., spiral bd. 18.95 (*1-56077-333-2*) Ctr. for Learning, The.

Collins, Carolyn Strom & Eriksson, Christina Wyss. The Anne of Green Gables Treasury. annuals 1997. (Illus.). 208p. (J). (gr. 4-7). pap. 12.95 o.p. (*0-14-017231-9*) Penguin Group (USA) Inc.

—The Anne of Green Gables Treasury. 1991. (Illus.). 160p. (J). 24.95 o.s.i (*0-670-82591-3*, Viking) Viking Penguin.

—The Anne of Green Gables Treasury of Days. 1994. (Illus.). 128p. 15.95 o.p. (*0-670-85508-1*, Viking) Viking Penguin.

Dussling, Jennifer. Anne of Green Gables. 2001. (All Aboard Reading Ser.). (Illus.). 48p. (J). (gr. 4-7). 13.89 o.s.i (*0-448-42460-6*); pap. 3.99 (*0-448-42459-2*) Penguin Putnam Bks. for Young Readers. (Philomel).

Green, Donna. Anne of Green Gables Journal. 1997. (Illus.). 112p. (J). (gr. 4-7). 10.98 (*0-7651-9438-4*) Smithmark Pubs., Inc.

—Anne of Green Gables Journal. 1997. (Illus.). 112p. (gr. 4-7). (YA). 12.95 (*1-883746-15-9*); (J). 14.95 (*1-883746-14-0*) Vermilion.

Helldorfer, Mary-Claire. Anne of Green Gables. 2003. (Illus.). 32p. (J). pap. 6.99 (*0-440-41614-0*, Dragonfly Bks.) Random Hse. Children's Bks.

Levine, Gloria. Anne of Green Gables, Level 6. 1989. (Novel-Ties Ser.). pap., tchr. ed. 15.95 (*0-88122-056-6*, S0521) Learning Links, Inc.

Macdonald, Kate. Anne of Green Gables Cookbook. 1987. (Illus.). 48p. (J). 14.95 o.p. (*0-19-540496-3*) Oxford Univ. Pr., Inc.

McHugh, Fiona, adapted by. The Anne of Green Gables Storybook. 2003. (Illus.). 80p. (J). (gr. 2-7). 19.95 (*0-920668-43-7*); pap. 9.95 (*0-920668-42-9*) Firefly Bks., Ltd.

Montgomery, L. M. Anne au Domaine des Peupliers. 1989. (Avonlea Ser.: No. 9). Tr. of Anne of Windy Poplars. (FRE.). 89p. (YA). (gr. 5-8). pap. 10.95 o.p. (*0-921556-08-X*) Ragweed Pr. CAN. *Dist:* LPC/InBook.

—Anne d'Avonlea. 1998. (Avonlea Ser.: No. 2). Tr. of Anne of Avonlea. (FRE.). 194p. (YA). (gr. 5-8). pap. 10.95 (*0-920304-88-5*) Ragweed Pr. CAN. *Dist:* Univ. of Toronto Pr.

—Anne of Avonlea. 1984. (Avonlea Ser.: No. 2). (YA). (gr. 5-8). mass mkt. 2.95 o.p. (*0-8049-0219-4*, CL219) Airmont Publishing Co., Inc.

—Anne of Avonlea. 1976. (Avonlea Ser.: No. 2). 376p. (YA). (gr. 5-8). 22.95 (*0-89190-155-8*) Amereon, Ltd.

—Anne of Avonlea. unabr. ed. 1987. (Avonlea Ser.: No. 2). (YA). (gr. 5-8). audio 41.95 (*1-55685-089-1*) Audio Bk. Contractors, Inc.

—Anne of Avonlea. (Avonlea Ser.: No. 2). (gr. 5-8). 1992. 288p. (YA). pap. 3.25 o.s.i (*0-553-15114-2*); 1984. 288p. (J). mass mkt. 2.95 o.s.i (*0-553-24740-9*); 1984. 288p. (YA). mass mkt. 3.95 (*0-7704-2206-3*); No. 2. 1984. 304p. (YA). mass mkt. 4.50 (*0-553-21314-8*) Bantam Bks.

—Anne of Avonlea. unabr. ed. (Avonlea Ser.: No. 2). (YA). (gr. 5-8). 1998. audio (*0-7861-1428-2*, 896061); 1992. audio 49.95 (*0-7861-0314-0*, 2289) Blackstone Audio Bks., Inc.

—Anne of Avonlea. (Avonlea Ser.: No. 2). (YA). (gr. 5-8). 2001. per. 12.50 (*1-891355-33-3*); 2000. per. 15.50 (*1-58396-201-8*) Blue Unicorn Editions.

—Anne of Avonlea. unabr. ed. 1992. (Avonlea Ser.: Bk. 2). (YA). (gr. 5-8). audio 49.95 (*1-55686-448-5*, 448) Books in Motion.

—Anne of Avonlea. 1992. (Avonlea Ser.: No. 2). (Illus.). xiv, 204p. (YA). (gr. 5-8). 12.99 o.s.i (*0-517-08127-X*) Crown Publishing Group.

—Anne of Avonlea. 1995. (Avonlea Ser.: No. 2). 291p. (YA). (gr. 5-8). mass mkt. 2.99 (*0-8125-5196-6*, Tor Classics) Doherty, Tom Assocs., LLC.

—Anne of Avonlea. unabr. ed. 2002. (Juvenile Classics). 272p. (J). pap. 3.00 (*0-486-42239-9*) Dover Pubns., Inc.

—Anne of Avonlea. 1997. (Avonlea Ser.: No. 2). (YA). (gr. 5-8). pap. 5.60 (*0-87129-791-4*, A72) Dramatic Publishing Co.

—Anne of Avonlea. (Avonlea Ser.: No. 2). (YA). (gr. 5-8). E-Book 2.49 (*0-7574-3111-9*) Electric Umbrella Publishing.

—Anne of Avonlea, RS. 1950. (Avonlea Ser.: No. 2). (YA). (gr. 5-8). o.p. (*0-374-30354-1*, Farrar, Straus & Giroux (BYR)) Farrar, Straus & Giroux.

—Anne of Avonlea. 2002. (Charming Classics Ser.). 256p. (J). (ps-1). pap. 6.99 (*0-694-01584-9*, Harper Festival) HarperCollins Children's Bk. Group.

—Anne of Avonlea. unabr. ed. 1999. (Avonlea Ser.: No. 2). (YA). (gr. 5-8). audio 49.95 Highsmith Inc.

—Anne of Avonlea. 2001. 248p. (gr. 8-12). 24.99 (*1-58827-590-6*); per. 20.99 (*1-58827-591-4*) IndyPublish.com.

—Anne of Avonlea. (Avonlea Ser.: No. 2). (YA). (gr. 5-8). E-Book 1.95 (*1-57799-878-2*) Logos Research Systems, Inc.

—Anne of Avonlea. 1987. (Avonlea Ser.: No. 2). 288p. (YA). (gr. 5-8). mass mkt. 3.95 o.s.i (*0-451-52113-7*, Signet Classics) NAL.

—Anne of Avonlea. abr. ed. 1999. (Avonlea Ser.: No. 2). (YA). (gr. 5-8). audio 13.98 (*962-634-669-8*, NA216914); audio compact disk 15.98 (*962-634-169-6*, NA216912) Naxos of America, Inc. (Naxos AudioBooks).

—Anne of Avonlea. 1998. (Avonlea Ser.: No. 2). 270p. (YA). (gr. 5-8). reprint ed. lib. bdg. 25.00 (*1-58287-013-6*) North Bks.

—Anne of Avonlea. (Avonlea Ser.: No. 2). (YA). (gr. 5-8). 1997. (Illus.). 336p. pap. 4.99 (*0-14-036798-5*); 1992. 240p. pap. 2.99 o.p. (*0-14-032565-4*, Puffin Bks.); 1990. (Illus.). 320p. 15.99 (*0-448-40063-4*, Grosset & Dunlap) Penguin Putnam Bks. for Young Readers.

—Anne of Avonlea. 1999. (Avonlea Ser.: No. 2). (YA). (gr. 5-8). E-Book 8.99 o.p. incl. cd-rom (*1-57646-053-3*) Quiet Vision Publishing.

—Anne of Avonlea. abr. unabr. ed. 1989. (Avonlea Ser.: No. 2). (J). (gr. 4-7). audio 18.00 (*0-553-45200-2*, Listening Library) Random Hse. Audio Publishing Group.

—Anne of Avonlea. (Avonlea Ser.: No. 2). (YA). (gr. 5-8). 1994. pap. o.s.i (*0-553-85021-0*); 1993. pap. o.s.i (*0-553-56709-8*) Random Hse. Children's Bks. (Dell Books for Young Readers).

—Anne of Avonlea, unabr. ed. 2001. (Avonlea Ser.: No. 2). (YA). (gr. 5-8). audio 62.00 (*0-7887-0535-0*, 94730E7) Recorded Bks., LLC.

—Anne of Avonlea. 1994. (Avonlea Ser.: No. 2). 256p. (YA). (gr. 5-8). text 5.98 o.p. (*1-56138-368-6*, Courage Bks.) Running Pr. Bk. Pubs.

—Anne of Avonlea. 1991. (Avonlea Ser.: No. 2). 336p. (YA). (gr. 5-8). mass mkt. 4.50 (*0-590-44556-1*, Scholastic Paperbacks) Scholastic, Inc.

—Anne of Avonlea. 1976. (Avonlea Ser.: No. 2). (YA). (gr. 5-8). 10.04 (*0-606-00791-1*) Turtleback Bks.

—Anne of Avonlea. 2002. (Children's Classics). 288p. (J). pap. 3.95 (*1-85326-162-9*) Wordsworth Editions, Ltd. GBR. *Dist:* Advanced Global Distribution Services.

—Anne of Green Gables. 1984. (Avonlea Ser.: No. 1). (YA). (gr. 5-8). mass mkt. 1.95 o.p. (*0-8049-0218-6*, CL218) Airmont Publishing Co., Inc.

—Anne of Green Gables. 1976. (Avonlea Ser.: No. 1). 244p. (YA). (gr. 5-8). 23.95 (*0-8488-0584-4*) Amereon, Ltd.

—Anne of Green Gables, 3 vols. (Avonlea Ser.: No. 1). (YA). (gr. 5-8). 1997. mass mkt. 13.50 (*0-553-33307-0*); 1987. mass mkt. 8.85 o.s.i (*0-553-30838-6*); 1986. mass mkt. o.s.i (*0-553-16646-8*); 1983. 320p. pap. 3.95 (*0-7704-2205-5*); 1982. 336p. mass mkt. 4.50 (*0-553-21313-X*, Bantam Classics); 1982. 320p. mass mkt. 2.95 o.s.i (*0-553-24295-4*) Bantam Bks.

—Anne of Green Gables. 1998. (J). E-Book 5.00 (*0-7607-1341-3*) Barnes & Noble, Inc.

—Anne of Green Gables. 2001. (J). per. 12.50 (*1-891355-34-1*) Blue Unicorn Editions.

—Anne of Green Gables. (Avonlea Ser.: No. 1). (Illus.). (YA). (gr. 5-8). 1995. 352p. o.p. (*0-681-00770-2*); 1988. 240p. 11.95 o.p. (*0-681-40501-5*) Borders Pr.

—Anne of Green Gables. 2000. (Avonlea Ser.: No. 1). 280p. (YA). (gr. 5-8). pap. text 15.00 (*0-7881-9155-1*) DIANE Publishing Co.

—Anne of Green Gables. 1995. (Avonlea Ser.: No. 1). 307p. (YA). (gr. 5-8). pap. text 2.99 (*0-8125-5152-4*, Tor Classics); 1994. mass mkt. 2.50 (*1-55902-906-4*, Aerie) Doherty, Tom Assocs., LLC.

—Anne of Green Gables. (Avonlea Ser.: No. 1). (YA). (gr. 5-8). 2000. 320p. pap. 3.00 (*0-486-41025-0*); 1995. (Illus.). iv, 91p. pap. text 1.00 (*0-486-28366-6*) Dover Pubns., Inc.

—Anne of Green Gables. 1989. (Avonlea Ser.: No. 1). (YA). (gr. 5-8). pap. 5.60 (*0-87129-242-4*, A41) Dramatic Publishing Co.

—Anne of Green Gables. (J). E-Book 2.49 (*0-7574-3112-7*) Electric Umbrella Publishing.

—Anne of Green Gables. 1999. (Focus on the Family Great Stories Ser.). (Illus.). 368p. (J). (gr. 4-7). 15.99 o.p. (*1-56179-625-5*) Focus on the Family Publishing.

—Anne of Green Gables. 1999. (Avonlea Ser.: No. 1). (YA). (gr. 5-8). 23.95 (*0-8057-8090-4*, Macmillan Reference USA) Gale Group.

—Anne of Green Gables. 1989. (Avonlea Ser.: No. 1). (Illus.). 320p. (YA). (gr. 5-8). 19.95 o.s.i (*0-87923-783-X*) Godine, David R. Pub.

—Anne of Green Gables. (Avonlea Ser.: No. 1). (YA). (gr. 5-8). 2000. (*0-06-028227-4*); 1999. (Illus.). 80p. 2.99 o.s.i (*0-694-01284-X*, Harper Festival) HarperCollins Children's Bk. Group.

—Anne of Green Gables. (Avonlea Ser.: No. 1). (YA). (gr. 5-8). pap. 3.50 (*0-340-71500-6*) Hodder & Stoughton, Ltd. GBR. *Dist:* Lubrecht & Cramer, Ltd., Trafalgar Square.

—Anne of Green Gables. Greenwood, Barbara, ed. 2001. (Avonlea Ser.: No. 1). 94p. (YA). (gr. 5-8). pap. 9.95 (*1-55013-431-0*) Key Porter Bks. CAN. *Dist:* Firefly Bks., Ltd.

—Anne of Green Gables. 1995. (Avonlea Ser.: No. 1). (Illus.). 416p. (gr. 5-8). 14.95 (*0-679-44475-0*, Everyman's Library) Knopf Publishing Group.

—Anne of Green Gables. 1994. (Avonlea Ser.: No. 1). (Illus.). 256p. (YA). (gr. 5-8). 25.00 (*0-88363-994-7*) Levin, Hugh Lauter Assocs.

—Anne of Green Gables. (Avonlea Ser.: No. 1). (YA). (gr. 5-8). E-Book 1.95 (*1-57799-946-0*) Logos Research Systems, Inc.

—Anne of Green Gables. MQ Publications Staff, ed. 1998. (Little Brown Notebooks Ser.). (Illus.). 256p. 9.99 (*1-84072-063-8*) M Q Pubns. GBR. *Dist:* Watson-Guptill Pubns., Inc.

—Anne of Green Gables. 1992. (Avonlea Ser.: No. 1). 338p. (YA). (gr. 5-8). mass mkt. 4.95 (*0-7710-9883-9*) McClelland & Stewart/Tundra Bks.

—Anne of Green Gables. (Avonlea Ser.: No. 1). (YA). (gr. 5-8). E-Book 1.95 (*1-58515-198-X*) MesaView, Inc.

—Anne of Green Gables. 1987. (Avonlea Ser.: No. 1). 320p. (YA). (gr. 5-8). mass mkt. 4.95 o.p. (*0-451-52112-9*, Signet Classics) NAL.

—Anne of Green Gables. 1998. 354p. (J). pap. (*1-55109-249-2*) Nimbus Publishing, Ltd.

—Anne of Green Gables. Bassett, Jennifer, ed. 1995. (Avonlea Ser.: No. 1). (Illus.). 48p. (YA). (gr. 5-8). pap. text 5.95 o.p. (*0-19-422725-1*) Oxford Univ. Pr., Inc.

—Anne of Green Gables. (Avonlea Ser.: No. 1). (YA). (gr. 5-8). 1996. (Illus.). 384p. 4.99 (*0-14-036741-1*, Puffin Bks.); 1994. 256p. pap. 2.99 o.p. (*0-14-035148-5*, Puffin Bks.); 1993. (Illus.). 16p. o.p. (*0-525-45173-0*); 1992. 256p. pap. 2.99 o.p. (*0-14-032462-3*, Puffin Bks.); 1983. (Illus.). 384p. 17.99 (*0-448-06030-2*, Grosset & Dunlap) Penguin Putnam Bks. for Young Readers.

—Anne of Green Gables. Hanft, Joshua, ed. 1995. (Great Illustrated Classics Ser.: Vol. 42). (Illus.). 240p. (J). (gr. 3-6). 9.95 (*0-86611-993-0*) Playmore, Inc., Pubs.

—Anne of Green Gables. (YA). (gr. 5-8). 2000. (Anne of Green Gables Ser.: Vol. No. 1). 220p. pap. 12.99 (*1-57646-300-1*); 2000. (Anne of Green Gables Ser.: Vol. No.1). 220p. lib. bdg. 32.99 (*1-57646-301-X*); 1999. (Avonlea Ser.: No. 1). E-Book 8.99 o.p. incl. cd-rom (*1-57646-052-5*) Quiet Vision Publishing.

—Anne of Green Gables. 2004. 112p. (J). (gr. 3-5). lib. bdg. 11.99 (*0-679-99428-9*, Random Hse. Bks. for Young Readers); 1999. (Avonlea Ser.: No. 1). (Illus.). 112p. (gr. 5-8). pap. text 3.99 (*0-440-41356-7*, Dell Books for Young Readers); 1998. (Avonlea Ser.: No. 1). 352p. (gr. 5-8). mass mkt. 2.99 o.s.i (*0-440-22787-9*, Yearling); 1994. (Avonlea Ser.: No. 1). (YA). (gr. 5-8). mass mkt. o.s.i (*0-553-85018-0*, Dell Books for Young Readers); 1994. (Step into Classics Ser.). (Illus.). 112p. (J). (gr. 3-5). pap. 3.99 (*0-679-85467-3*, Random Hse. Bks. for Young Readers); 1993. (Avonlea Ser.: No. 1). (YA). (gr. 5-8). pap. o.s.i (*0-553-56712-8*, Dell Books for Young Readers) Random Hse. Children's Bks.

—Anne of Green Gables. (Children's Classics Ser.: No. 1). 1998. (Illus.). 256p. (J). (gr. 4-7). 5.99 (*0-517-18968-2*); 1995. (YA). (gr. 5-8). 1.10 o.s.i (*0-517-14154-X*); 1988. (Illus.). xvi, 240p. (YA). (gr. 5-8). 12.99 o.s.i (*0-517-65958-1*) Random Hse. Value Publishing.

—Anne of Green Gables. 1993. (Avonlea Ser.: No.1). 287p. (YA). (gr. 5-8). text 5.98 o.p. (*1-56138-324-4*, Courage Bks.) Running Pr. Bk. Pubs.

—Anne of Green Gables. (YA). 2002. (Scholastic Classic Ser.). 400p. mass mkt. 4.99 (*0-439-29577-7*); 1989. (Avonlea Ser.: No. 1). 384p. (gr. 5-8). mass mkt. 4.50 (*0-590-42243-X*, Scholastic Paperbacks) Scholastic, Inc.

—Anne of Green Gables, 3 vol. set. 1997. (YA). (*0-7704-2218-7*) Seal Bks. CAN. *Dist:* Random Hse. of Canada, Ltd.

—Anne of Green Gables. 2001. (Aladdin Classics Ser.). (Illus.). 480p. (J). pap. 3.99 (*0-689-84622-3*, Aladdin) Simon & Schuster Children's Publishing.

—Anne of Green Gables. 1994. (Avonlea Ser.: No. 1). (Illus.). 256p. (YA). (gr. 5-8). 9.99 o.p. (*1-897954-26-3*) Sterling Publishing Co., Inc.

—Anne of Green Gables. 2000. (Avonlea Ser.: No. 1). (Illus.). 328p. (J). (gr. 5-8). 24.95 (*0-88776-515-7*) Tundra Bks. of Northern New York.

—Anne of Green Gables. Morgan, Sally, ed. 1994. (Avonlea Ser.: No. 1). (YA). (gr. 5-8). 9.09 o.p. (*0-606-09006-1*) Turtleback Bks.

—Anne of Green Gables. 1987. (Avonlea Ser.: No. 1). (YA). (gr. 5-8). 10.55 (*0-606-00282-0*) Turtleback Bks.

—Anne of Green Gables. 2001. (Illus.). 40p. (J). (gr. k-3). 15.95 o.p. (*0-385-32715-3*, Doubleday Bks. for Young Readers) Random Hse. Children's Bks.

—Anne of Green Gables, unabr. ed. 1986. (Avonlea Ser.: No. 1). (YA). (gr. 5-8). audio 53.95 (*1-55685-045-X*) Audio Bk. Contractors, Inc.

—Anne of Green Gables. abr. ed. 1986. (Avonlea Ser.: No. 1). (YA). (gr. 5-8). pap. 12.95 incl. audio (*1-882071-07-7*, 009) B&B Audio, Inc.

—Anne of Green Gables, Vol. 1. 1984. (Avonlea Ser.: Vol. 1). 320p. (gr. 5-8). pap. text 4.50 (*0-553-15327-7*) Bantam Bks.

—Anne of Green Gables. unabr. ed. (Avonlea Ser.: No. 1). (YA). (gr. 5-8). 1998. audio 56.95 (*0-7861-1315-4*, 2240); 1991. audio 62.95 (*0-7861-0247-0*, 1216) Blackstone Audio Bks., Inc.

—Anne of Green Gables. l.t. ed. 2001. (Avonlea Ser.: No. 1). (YA). (gr. 5-8). per. 15.50 (*1-58396-202-6*) Blue Unicorn Editions.

—Anne of Green Gables. unabr. ed. 1992. (Avonlea Ser.: Bk. 1). (J). audio 49.95 (*1-55686-447-7*, 447) Books in Motion.

—Anne of Green Gables. unabr. collector's ed. 1998. (Avonlea Ser.: No. 1). (YA). (gr. 5-8). audio 56.00 (*0-7366-4150-5*, 896035) Books on Tape, Inc.

—Anne of Green Gables. 1977. (Avonlea Ser.: No. 1). 429p. (YA). (gr. 5-8). reprint ed. lib. bdg. 27.95 (*0-89966-262-5*) Buccaneer Bks., Inc.

—Anne of Green Gables. abr. ed. 1997. (Avonlea Ser.: No. 1). (YA). (gr. 5-8). audio 4.99 (*0-88646-954-6*, 7954) Durkin Hayes Publishing Ltd.

—Anne of Green Gables, RS. 1950. (Avonlea Ser.: No. 1). (YA). (gr. 5-8). pap. o.p. (*0-374-40403-8*, Sunburst) Farrar, Straus & Giroux.

—Anne of Green Gables. unabr. ed. 1999. (Avonlea Ser.: No. 1). (YA). (gr. 5-8). audio 56.95 Highsmith Inc.

—Anne of Green Gables, ERS. 1994. (Avonlea Ser.: No. 1). (FRE., Illus.). xx, 486p. (YA). (gr. 5-8). 15.95 o.p. (*0-8050-3126-X*, Holt, Henry & Co. Bks. For Young Readers) Holt, Henry & Co.

—Anne of Green Gables. l.t. ed. (Avonlea Ser.: No. 1). (YA). (gr. 5-8). 614p. pap. 44.14 (*0-7583-0235-5*); 786p. pap. 62.17 (*0-7583-0236-3*); 966p. pap. 72.70 (*0-7583-0237-1*); 1189p. pap. 83.30 (*0-7583-0238-X*); 350p. pap. 28.82 (*0-7583-0233-9*); 280p. pap. 24.84 (*0-7583-0232-0*); 480p. pap. 35.78 (*0-7583-0234-7*); 1379p. pap. 93.47 (*0-7583-0239-8*); 786p. lib. bdg. 74.17 (*0-7583-0228-2*); 1189p. lib. bdg. 95.30 (*0-7583-0230-4*); 350p. lib. bdg. 34.82 (*0-7583-0225-8*); 480p. lib. bdg. 41.78 (*0-7583-0226-6*); 280p. lib. bdg. 30.84 (*0-7583-0224-X*); 614p. lib. bdg. 50.14 (*0-7583-0227-4*); 1379p. lib. bdg. 105.47 (*0-7583-0231-2*); 966p. lib. bdg. 84.70 (*0-7583-0229-0*) Huge Print Pr.

—Anne of Green Gables. l.t. ed. 1991. (Avonlea Ser.: No. 1). 376p. (YA). (gr. 5-8). 17.95 o.p. (*1-85089-895-2*) ISIS Large Print Bks. GBR. *Dist:* Transaction Pubs.

—Anne of Green Gables. Stemach, Jerry, ed. l.t. ed. 2002. text 150.00 (*1-58702-021-1*) Johnston, Don Inc.

—Anne of Green Gables, Vol. 6. Stemach, Jerry et al, eds. 2000. (Start-to-Finish Books). (J). (gr. 2-3). audio 35.00 (*1-58702-501-9*); audio (*1-893376-99-0*, F22K2) Johnston, Don Inc.

—Anne of Green Gables. l.t. ed. 1998. (Avonlea Ser.: No. 1). 472p. (YA). (gr. 5-8). lib. bdg. 35.95 (*1-58118-035-7*, 22019) LRS.

—Anne of Green Gables. unabr. ed. 2001. (Audio Theatre Ser.). (YA). (gr. 5 up). audio 16.95 (*1-56994-533-0*, Monterey SoundWorks) Monterey Media, Inc.

—Anne of Green Gables. abr. ed. 1997. (Junior Classics Ser.: No. 1). (YA). (gr. 4-7). audio 13.98 (*962-634-623-X*, NA212314); (gr. 5-8). audio compact disk 15.98 (*962-634-123-8*, NA212312) Naxos of America, Inc. (Naxos AudioBooks).

—Anne of Green Gables. abr. ed. 1997. (Avonlea Ser.: No. 1). (YA). (gr. 5-8). audio 7.00 (*0-7871-1221-6*); audio 20.00 (*0-7871-1222-4*) NewStar Media, Inc. (Dove Audio).

—Anne of Green Gables. 1998. (Avonlea Ser.). 352p. (YA). (gr. 5-8). reprint ed. (*1-55109-013-9*) Nimbus Publishing, Ltd.

—Anne of Green Gables. l.t. ed. (Avonlea Ser.: No. 1). (YA). (gr. 5-8). reprint ed. 1993. 494p. lib. bdg. 26.00 (0-939495-25-2); 1998. 310p. lib. bdg. 25.00 (1-58287-014-4) North Bks.

—Anne of Green Gables, Level 2. Hedge, Tricia, ed. 2000. (Bookworms Ser.). (Illus.). 64p. (J). pap. text 5.95 (0-19-422965-3) Oxford Univ. Pr., Inc.

—Anne of Green Gables. l.t. ed. 2000. (Anne of Green Gables Ser.: Vol. 1). 414p. (YA). (gr. 5-8). pap. 24.99 (1-57646-302-8); lib. bdg. 37.99 (1-57646-303-6) Quiet Vision Publishing.

—Anne of Green Gables. abr. ed. 1991. (Avonlea Ser.: No. 1). (YA). (gr. 5-8). 27.99 o.s.i incl. audio (0-7704-2492-9, RH Audio); 1987. (Avonlea Ser.: No. 1). (YA). (gr. 4-7). audio 18.00 (0-553-45091-3, 390221, Listening Library); 2001. audio 32.00 (0-8072-0646-6, Listening Library); 2000. (Avonlea Ser.: No. 1). 38p. (YA). (gr. 5-8). audio 9.99 o.s.i (0-8072-8278-2, Listening Library); Set. 1991. (Avonlea Ser.: No. 1). (J). (gr. 5-8). 24.99 o.s.i incl. audio (0-553-47020-5, RH Audio) Random Hse. Audio Publishing Group.

—Anne of Green Gables, Set. 1992. (Avonlea Ser.: No. 1). (YA). (gr. 5-8). 16.24 o.p. (0-553-62867-4, Dell Books for Young Readers) Random Hse. Children's Bks.

—Anne of Green Gables, unabr. ed. 1989. (Avonlea Ser.: No. 1). (YA). (gr. 5-8). audio 60.00 (1-55690-022-8, 89150E7) Recorded Bks., LLC.

—Anne of Green Gables, 8 vols., Set. 1997. (YA). (0-7704-2407-4) Seal Bks. CAN. Dist: Random Hse. of Canada, Ltd.

—Anne of Green Gables. unabr. ed. 2003. (J). audio compact disk 45.00 (1-4001-0071-2); audio compact disk 20.00 (1-4001-5071-X) Tantor Media, Inc.

—Anne of Green Gables. abr. ed. 1997. (Avonlea Ser.: No. 1). (YA). (gr. 5-8). mass mkt. 16.95 o.p. incl. audio (1-85998-749-4); audio 14.95 (1-85998-080-5) Trafalgar Square.

—Anne of Green Gables. abr. ed. 1997. (Avonlea Ser.: No. 1). (YA). (gr. 5-8). 2p. audio 10.95 o.s.i (0-14-086331-1, Penguin AudioBooks); (Illus.). 112p. 22.95 o.p. (0-670-87031-5) Viking Penguin.

—Anne of Green Gables: A Musical in Two Acts. 1997. (Illus.). 98p. (YA). (gr. 7 up). pap. 5.95 (0-87129-760-4, A08) Dramatic Publishing Co.

—Anne of Green Gables: Address & Birthday Book, 2 vols., Set. 2001. (Illus.). 238p. (J). 12.95 (1-55263-180-X) Key Porter Bks. CAN. Dist: Firefly Bks., Ltd.

—Anne of Green Gables: Anne of Avonlea. 1996. (Avonlea Ser.: No. 1). (YA). (gr. 5-8). 12.98 o.p. (0-7651-9979-3) Smithmark Pubs., Inc.

—Anne of Green Gables: Anne of Avonlea; Anne of the Island; Anne of Green Gables. 1997. (Avonlea Ser.: No. 1). (YA). (gr. 5-8). mass mkt. 13.50 (0-553-33306-2) Bantam Bks.

—Anne of Green Gables: Press Out Model House. 1994. 28p. (J). (gr. 4-7). pap. 12.95 (0-7704-2590-9) Bantam Bks.

—Anne of Green Gables: Seal Edition. abr. ed. 1987. (Avonlea Ser.: No. 1). (YA). (gr. 5-8). audio 18.99 o.s.i (0-7704-3998-5, RH Audio) Random Hse. Audio Publishing Group.

—Anne of Green Gables Birthday Book. 1990. (Illus.). 128p. (J). 8.95 o.s.i (0-7704-2362-0) Bantam Bks.

—Anne of Green Gables Book & Charm. 1999. (Charming Classic Bks.). 400p. (J). (ps up). pap. 6.99 (0-694-01251-3, Harper Festival) HarperCollins Children's Bk. Group.

—The Anne of Green Gables Collection. 1999. (Workhorse Library Ser.). E-Book 19.99 incl. cd-rom (1-891595-36-9) Quiet Vision Publishing.

—Anne of Green Gables Coloring Book. 1995. pap. text 2.95 (0-486-28589-8) Dover Pubns., Inc.

—Anne of Green Gables Cookbook. 22.95 (0-8488-2657-4) Amereon, Ltd.

—Anne of Green Gables Diary. 22.95 (0-8488-2654-X) Amereon, Ltd.

—Anne of Green Gables Holiday Diary. 2000. (Illus.). 96p. (YA). pap. (0-7704-2853-3) Doubleday Publishing.

—Anne of Ingleside. (Avonlea Ser.: No. 10). (YA). (gr. 5-8). 23.95 (0-8488-0890-8); 1976. 286p. 23.95 (0-8488-1101-1) Amereon, Ltd.

—Anne of Ingleside. 1984. (Avonlea Ser.: No. 10). (YA). (gr. 5-8). mass mkt. 3.50 o.s.i (0-7704-2144-X); 288p. mass mkt. 2.95 o.s.i (0-553-24648-8); 6th ed. 304p. mass mkt. 3.95 (0-7704-2207-1);No. 6. 304p. mass mkt. 4.50 (0-553-21315-6, Bantam Classics) Bantam Bks.

—Anne of Ingleside. (Avonlea Ser.: No. 10). (Illus.). 341p. (YA). (gr. 5-8). 6.98 (0-7710-6180-3) McClelland & Stewart/Tundra Bks.

—Anne of Ingleside. 1999. (Avonlea Ser.: No. 10). 320p. (YA). (gr. 5-8). mass mkt. 3.95 (0-451-52643-0, Signet Classics) NAL.

—Anne of Ingleside, Vol. 6. 1999. 384p. (J). pap. 3.99 (0-14-036801-9, Puffin Bks.) Penguin Putnam Bks. for Young Readers.

—Anne of Ingleside. 1970. (Avonlea Ser.: No. 10). (YA). (gr. 5-8). 6.95 o.p. (0-448-02546-9) Putnam Publishing Group, The.

—Anne of Ingleside. 1967. (Avonlea Ser.: No. 10). (YA). (gr. 5-8). 10.55 (0-606-00375-4) Turtleback Bks.

—Anne of the Island. 1976. (Avonlea Ser.: No. 4). 252p. (YA). (gr. 5-8). 22.95 (0-8488-0585-2) Amereon, Ltd.

—Anne of the Island, unabr. ed. 1999. (Avonlea Ser.: No. 4). (YA). (gr. 5-8). audio 35.95 (1-55685-580-X) Audio Bk. Contractors, Inc.

—Anne of the Island. (Avonlea Ser.: No. 4). (YA). 1992. 256p. (gr. 3-7). pap. 4.50 o.s.i (0-553-48066-9); 1983. 256p. (gr. 5-8). mass mkt. 2.95 o.s.i (0-553-24158-3); 1983. 272p. (gr. 5-8). mass mkt. 4.50 (0-553-21317-2, Bantam Classics); 1983. 274p. (gr. 5-8). mass mkt. 3.95 (0-7704-2204-7) Bantam Bks.

—Anne of the Island, unabr. ed. 1999. (Avonlea Ser.: No. 4). (YA). (gr. 5-8). audio 44.95 (0-7861-1905-5, P2698) Blackstone Audio Bks., Inc.

—Anne of the Island. (Avonlea Ser.: No. 4). (YA). (gr. 5-8). 2001. per. 12.50 (1-891355-36-8); 2000. per. 15.50 (1-58396-204-2) Blue Unicorn Editions.

—Anne of the Island. unabr. ed. 1993. (Avonlea Ser.: Bk. 4). (YA). (gr. 5-8). audio 39.95 (1-55686-461-2, 461) Books in Motion.

—Anne of the Island. 2000. (Avonlea Ser.: No. 4). (YA). (gr. 5-8). E-Book 2.49 (1-58744-132-2) Electric Umbrella Publishing.

—Anne of the Island, RS. 1950. (Avonlea Ser.: No. 4). (YA). (gr. 5-8). pap. o.p. (0-374-40404-6, Sunburst) Farrar, Straus & Giroux.

—Anne of the Island, unabr. ed. 1999. (Avonlea Ser.: No. 4). (YA). (gr. 5-8). audio 49.95 Highsmith Inc.

—Anne of the Island. l.t. ed. (Avonlea Ser.: No. 4). (YA). (gr. 5-8). 278p. pap. 27.17 (0-7583-0249-5); 488p. pap. 41.99 (0-7583-0251-7); 768p. pap. 61.80 (0-7583-0253-3); 1095p. pap. 90.63 (0-7583-0255-X); 944p. pap. 74.29 (0-7583-0254-1); 381p. pap. 34.45 (0-7583-0250-9); 624p. pap. 51.65 (0-7583-0252-5); 222p. lib. bdg. 28.58 (0-7583-0240-1); 488p. lib. bdg. 48.59 (0-7583-0243-6); 278p. lib. bdg. 33.74 (0-7583-0241-X); 768p. lib. bdg. 82.51 (0-7583-0245-2) Huge Print Pr.

—Anne of the Island. l.t. ed. 1998. (Avonlea Ser.: No. 4). 376p. (YA). (gr. 5-8). lib. bdg. 34.95 (1-58118-036-5, 22020) LRS.

—Anne of the Island. (Avonlea Ser.: No. 4). (YA). (gr. 5-8). E-Book 1.95 (1-57799-879-0) Logos Research Systems, Inc.

—Anne of the Island. l.t. ed. 1991. (Avonlea Ser.: No. 4). 256p. (YA). (gr. 5-8). mass mkt. 2.95 o.p. (0-451-52534-5, Signet Classics) NAL.

—Anne of the Island. (Avonlea Ser.: No. 4). (YA). (gr. 5-8). 1998. 304p. pap. 4.99 (0-14-036777-2); 1992. 304p. pap. 2.99 o.p. (0-14-032567-0, Puffin Bks.); 1992. (Illus.). 282p. 14.95 o.s.i (0-448-40311-0, Grosset & Dunlap); 1956. 3.95 o.p. (0-448-02513-2, Planet Dexter) Penguin Putnam Bks. for Young Readers.

—Anne of the Island. 1970. (Avonlea Ser.: No. 4). (YA). (gr. 5-8). 6.95 o.p. (0-448-02547-7) Putnam Publishing Group, The.

—Anne of the Island. (YA). (gr. 5-8). 1999. (Avonlea Ser.: No. 4). E-Book 8.99 o.p. incl. cd-rom (1-57646-054-1); 2000. (Anne of Green Gables Ser.: Vol. 3). 336p. pap. 24.99 (1-57646-310-9); 2000. (Anne of Green Gables Ser.: Vol. No. 3). 336p. lib. bdg. 33.99 (1-57646-311-7) Quiet Vision Publishing.

—Anne of the Island. abr. ed. 1990. (Avonlea Ser.: No. 4). (J). (gr. 4-7). audio 18.00 (0-553-45201-0, Listening Library) Random Hse. Audio Publishing Group.

—Anne of the Island. 1994. (Avonlea Ser.: No. 4). (YA). (gr. 5-8). pap. o.s.i (0-553-85024-5, Dell Books for Young Readers) Random Hse. Children's Bks.

—Anne of the Island, unabr. ed. 1996. (Avonlea Ser.: No. 4). (YA). (gr. 5-8). audio 53.00 (0-7887-0598-9, 94776E7) Recorded Bks., LLC.

—Anne of the Island. 1994. (Avonlea Ser.: No. 4). 239p. (YA). (gr. 5-8). text 5.98 o.p. (1-56138-369-4, Courage Bks.) Running Pr. Bk. Pubs.

—Anne of the Island. 1993. (Avonlea Ser.: No. 4). 320p. (YA). (gr. 5-8). mass mkt. 3.25 (0-590-46163-X, Scholastic Paperbacks) Scholastic, Inc.

—Anne of the Island. 1976. (Avonlea Ser.: No. 4). (YA). (gr. 5-8). 10.04 (0-606-00792-X) Turtleback Bks.

—Anne of the Islands & Tales of Avonlea. 1991. (Avonlea Ser.: No. 4). (Illus.). xv, 573p. (YA). (gr. 5-8). 11.99 o.s.i (0-517-03705-X) Random Hse. Value Publishing.

—Anne of Windy Poplars. 1976. (Avonlea Ser.: No. 9). 268p. (YA). (gr. 5-8). 22.95 (0-8488-0586-0) Amereon, Ltd.

—Anne of Windy Poplars. (Avonlea Ser.: No. 9). (YA). (gr. 5-8). 1992. 288p. pap. 3.99 o.s.i (0-553-48065-0); 1983. 272p. mass mkt. 2.95 o.s.i (0-553-24397-7); 1983. 288p. mass mkt. 4.50 (0-553-21316-4, Bantam Classics); 4th ed. 1983. 288p. mass mkt. 3.95 (0-7704-2167-9) Bantam Bks.

—Anne of Windy Poplars. (Avonlea Ser.: No. 9). 274p. (YA). (gr. 5-8). pap. 4.98 o.p. (0-7710-6164-1) McClelland & Stewart/Tundra Bks.

—Anne of Windy Poplars, Vol. 4. 1999. 336p. (J). pap. 3.99 (0-14-036800-0, Puffin Bks.) Penguin Putnam Bks. for Young Readers.

—Anne of Windy Poplars. 1970. (Avonlea Ser.: No. 9). (YA). (gr. 5-8). 6.95 o.p. (0-448-02548-5) Putnam Publishing Group, The.

—Anne of Windy Poplars. 1987. (Avonlea Ser.: No. 9). (YA). (gr. 5-8). 10.04 (0-606-02371-2) Turtleback Bks.

—Anne's House of Dreams. 1976. (Avonlea Ser.: No. 5). 192p. (YA). (gr. 5-8). 20.95 (0-8488-0587-9) Amereon, Ltd.

—Anne's House of Dreams, unabr. ed. 1999. (Avonlea Ser.: No. 5). (YA). (gr. 5-8). audio 35.95 (1-55685-586-9) Audio Bk. Contractors, Inc.

—Anne's House of Dreams. 1983. (Avonlea Ser.: No. 5). (YA). (gr. 5-8). 256p. mass mkt. 4.50 (0-553-21318-0, Bantam Classics); 5th ed. 256p. mass mkt. 3.95 (0-7704-2210-1);No. 5. 240p. mass mkt. 2.95 o.s.i (0-553-24195-8) Bantam Bks.

—Anne's House of Dreams, unabr. ed. 1997. (Avonlea Ser.: No. 5). (YA). (gr. 5-8). audio 44.95 (0-7861-1230-1, 1976) Blackstone Audio Bks., Inc.

—Anne's House of Dreams. 2001. (Avonlea Ser.: No. 5). (YA). (gr. 5-8). per. 12.50 (1-891355-35-X); per. 15.50 (1-58396-203-4) Blue Unicorn Editions.

—Anne's House of Dreams. (Avonlea Ser.: No. 5). (YA). (gr. 5-8). E-Book 2.49 (0-7574-3113-5) Electric Umbrella Publishing.

—Anne's House of Dreams, unabr. ed. 1999. (Avonlea Ser.: No. 5). (YA). (gr. 5-8). audio 44.95 Highsmith Inc.

—Anne's House of Dreams. l.t. ed. 1999. (Avonlea Ser.: No. 5). 364p. (YA). (gr. 5-8). lib. bdg. 34.95 (1-58118-048-9, 22517) LRS.

—Anne's House of Dreams. (Avonlea Ser.: No. 5). (YA). (gr. 5-8). E-Book 1.95 (1-57799-880-4) Logos Research Systems, Inc.

—Anne's House of Dreams. 1989. (J). pap. o.p. (0-7710-6161-7) McClelland & Stewart/Tundra Bks.

—Anne's House of Dreams. 1989. (Avonlea Ser.: No. 5). (YA). (gr. 5-8). mass mkt. 2.95 o.p. (0-451-52319-9, Signet Classics) NAL.

—Anne's House of Dreams. 1992. (Avonlea Ser.: No. 5). 304p. (YA). (gr. 5-8). pap. 2.99 o.p. (0-14-032569-7, Puffin Bks.); 1970. (Avonlea Ser.: No. 5). (YA). (gr. 5-8). 6.95 o.p. (0-448-02549-3, Grosset & Dunlap); Vol. 5. 1999. 320p. (J). pap. 3.99 (0-14-036799-3, Puffin Bks.) Penguin Putnam Bks. for Young Readers.

—Anne's House of Dreams. (YA). (gr. 5-8). 2000. (Anne of Green Gables Ser.: Vol. No. 5). 182p. pap. 14.99 (1-57646-312-5); 2000. (Anne of Green Gables Ser.: Vol. No. 5). 182p. lib. bdg. 30.99 (1-57646-313-3); 1999. (Avonlea Ser.: No. 5). E-Book 8.99 o.p. incl. cd-rom (1-57646-055-X); 2000. (Anne of Green Gables Ser.: Vol. 5). 336p. pap. 24.99 (1-57646-314-1); 2000. (Anne of Green Gables Ser.: Vol. No. 5). 336p. lib. bdg. 33.99 (1-57646-315-X) Quiet Vision Publishing.

—Anne's House of Dreams. 1994. (Avonlea Ser.: No. 5). (YA). (gr. 5-8). o.s.i (0-553-85030-X, Dell Books for Young Readers) Random Hse. Children's Bks.

—Anne's House of Dreams. 1996. (Avonlea Ser.: No. 5). viii, 193p. (YA). (gr. 5-8). 8.99 o.s.i (0-517-14820-X) Random Hse. Value Publishing.

—Anne's House of Dreams. 1994. (Avonlea Ser.: No. 5). 238p. (YA). (gr. 5-8). text 5.98 o.p. (1-56138-430-5, Courage Bks.) Running Pr. Bk. Pubs.

—Anne's House of Dreams. 1972. (Avonlea Ser.: No. 5). (YA). (gr. 5-8). 10.55 (0-606-00376-2) Turtleback Bks.

—Avonlea Boxed Set: Anne of the Island; Anne's House of Dreams. (Avonlea Ser.: No. 4-5). 464p. (YA). (gr. 5-8). reprint ed. 2000. 9.00 o.p. (0-7624-0561-9); 1997. text 8.98 o.p. (0-7624-0113-3, Courage Bks.) Running Pr. Bk. Pubs.

—The Complete Anne of Green Gables: Anne of Green Gables; Anne of the Island; Anne of Avonlea; Anne of Windy Poplars; Anne's House of Dreams; Anne of Ingleside; Rainbow Valley; Rilla of Ingleside, 8 vols. gif. ed. 1997. (J). (gr. 4-7). mass mkt. 36.00 (0-553-60941-6) Bantam Bks.

—Rainbow Valley. 1976. (Avonlea Ser.: No. 6). 234p. (YA). (gr. 5-8). 21.95 (0-8488-0591-7) Amereon, Ltd.

—Rainbow Valley. (Avonlea Ser.: No. 6). (gr. 5-8). 1987. 256p. (J). mass mkt. 4.99 (0-7704-2268-3); 1985. 240p. (YA). mass mkt. 2.95 o.s.i (0-553-25213-5) Bantam Bks.

—Rainbow Valley, unabr. ed. 1995. (Avonlea Ser.: No. 6). (YA). (gr. 5-8). audio 44.95 (0-7861-0913-0, 1704) Blackstone Audio Bks., Inc.

—Rainbow Valley. unabr. ed. 1999. (Avonlea Ser.: No. 6). (YA). (gr. 5-8). audio 44.95 Highsmith Inc.

—Rainbow Valley. 1985. (Avonlea Ser.: No. 6). 256p. (YA). (gr. 5-8). mass mkt. 4.50 (0-553-26921-6, Dell Books for Young Readers) Random Hse. Children's Bks.

—Rainbow Valley. 1985. (Avonlea Ser.: No. 6). (YA). (gr. 5-8). 10.04 (0-606-02613-4) Turtleback Bks.

—Rilla of Ingleside. 1976. (Avonlea Ser.: No. 8). 286p. (YA). (gr. 5-8). 23.95 (0-8488-0592-5) Amereon, Ltd.

—Rilla of Ingleside. (Avonlea Ser.: No. 8). (YA). (gr. 5-8). 1987. 288p. mass mkt. 3.99 (0-7704-2185-7); 1985. 304p. mass mkt. 4.50 (0-553-26922-4) Bantam Bks.

—Rilla of Ingleside. unabr. ed. 1998. (Avonlea Ser.: No. 8). (YA). (gr. 5-8). audio 56.95 (0-7861-1275-1, 2172) Blackstone Audio Bks., Inc.

—Rilla of Ingleside. 1985. (Avonlea Ser.: No. 8). 288p. (YA). (gr. 5-8). mass mkt. 2.95 o.s.i (0-553-25241-0, Starfire) Random Hse. Children's Bks.

—Rilla of Ingleside. 1997. (Avonlea Ser.: No. 8). (Illus.). (YA). (gr. 5-8). 7.99 (0-517-18083-9) Random Hse. Value Publishing.

—Rilla of Ingleside. 1985. (Avonlea Ser.: No. 8). (YA). (gr. 5-8). 10.04 (0-606-00747-4) Turtleback Bks.

Montgomery, L. M. & Outlet Book Company Staff. Rainbow Valley. 1995. (Avonlea Ser.: No. 6). (Illus.). xi, 256p. (YA). (gr. 5-8). 7.99 o.s.i (0-517-10192-0) Random Hse. Value Publishing.

Montgomery, L. M. & Sandberg, R. N. Anne of Green Gables: Playscript. 1995. (Avonlea Ser.: No. 1). (YA). (gr. 5-8). pap. 6.50 (0-87602-335-9) Anchorage Pr.

Montgomery, L. M. & Tanaka, Shelley. Anne of Green Gables. 1998. (Avonlea Ser.: No. 1). 112p. (gr. 5-8). text 12.95 o.s.i (0-385-32333-6, Dell Books for Young Readers) Random Hse. Children's Bks.

Morton, Elizabeth. Anne: Six Titles Based on Anne of Green Gables. 2001. (Illus.). 64p. (J). (ps-3). 6.99 (0-694-01587-3, Harper Festival) HarperCollins Children's Bk. Group.

—Anne: The Animated Series Storybook. 2001. (Illus.). (J). (ps-4). 119.75 (0-694-01542-3) HarperCollins Children's Bk. Group.

Peterson. Anne of Green Gables. 1999. (Avonlea Ser.: No. 1). 32p. (YA). (gr. 5-8). pap. 4.95 (0-06-443535-0) HarperCollins Children's Bk. Group.

Row, Richard. Anne of Green Gables: Pop-up Dollhouse. 1994. (Illus.). (J). (ps-3). 18.00 o.s.i (0-679-86391-5, Random Hse. Bks. for Young Readers) Random Hse. Children's Bks.

Stiles, John D. The Insolent Boy. 2001. 192p. pap. (1-895837-04-9) Insomniac Pr.

Tanaka, Shelley. Anne of Green Gables. 1998. (Avonlea Ser.: No. 1). 112p. (gr. 5-8). mass mkt. 5.99 (0-7704-2744-8) Bantam Bks.

APPLESEED, JOHNNY, 1774-1845—FICTION

Crompton, Anne E. Johnny's Trail. 1986. 112p. 6.95 (0-87785-131-X) Swedenborg Foundation, Inc.

Durrant, Lynda. The Sun, the Rain, & the Apple Seed: A Novel of Johnny Appleseed's Life. 2003. 208p. (J). (gr. 5-9). tchr. ed. 15.00 (0-618-23487-X, Clarion Bks.) Houghton Mifflin Co. Trade & Reference Div.

Glass, Andrew. Folks Call Me Appleseed John. 1995. (Illus.). 48p. (J). (gr. 1-5). 15.95 o.p. (0-385-32045-0) Doubleday Publishing.

—Folks Call Me Appleseed John. 1998. (Picture Yearling Book Ser.). (Illus.). 48p. (gr. 1-4). pap. text 6.99 o.s.i (0-440-41466-0, Dell Books for Young Readers) Random Hse. Children's Bks.

—Folks Call Me Appleseed John. unabr. ed. 1998. (J). Class Set. 102.70 incl. audio (0-7887-2552-1, 46722); Homework. 27.24 incl. audio (0-7887-2247-6, 40731) Recorded Bks., LLC.

—Folks Call Me Appleseed John. 1998. 13.14 (0-606-13393-3) Turtleback Bks.

ARABUS FAMILY (FICTITIOUS CHARACTER)—FICTION

Collier, James Lincoln. Jump Ship to Freedom. 1996. (J). pap. 5.99 (0-440-91158-3, Dell Books for Young Readers) Random Hse. Children's Bks.

—Jump Ship to Freedom. 1987. (Arabus Family Saga Ser.). (J). 11.55 (0-606-02265-1) Turtleback Bks.

Collier, James Lincoln & Collier, Christopher. Jump Ship to Freedom. 1981. 192p. (J). (gr. 4-6). pap. 13.95 o.s.i (0-385-28484-5, Delacorte Pr.) Dell Publishing.

—Jump Ship to Freedom. 1987. (Arabus Family Saga Ser.: Vol. 2). 208p. (gr. 4-7). pap. text 5.50 (0-440-44323-7, Yearling) Random Hse. Children's Bks.

—Who Is Carrie? 1984. 192p. (J). (gr. 4-6). 14.95 o.s.i (0-385-29295-3, Delacorte Pr.) Dell Publishing.

—Who Is Carrie? 1987. (Arabus Family Saga Ser.: Vol. 3). 176p. (gr. 5-7). pap. text 4.99 o.s.i (0-440-49536-9, Yearling) Random Hse. Children's Bks.

—Who Is Carrie? 1987. (Arabus Family Saga Ser.). (J). 11.04 (0-606-03505-2) Turtleback Bks.

Characters

ARCHER, JENNY (FICTITIOUS CHARACTER)—FICTION

Conford, Ellen. Can Do, Jenny Archer. 1991. (Springboard Bks.). (Illus.). (J). (gr. 2-4). 11.95 o.p. (*0-316-15356-7*) Little Brown & Co.

—Can Do, Jenny Archer. 1993. 64p. (J). (ps-3). pap. 4.95 (*0-316-15372-9*, Tingley, Megan Bks.) Little Brown Children's Bks.

—Can Do, Jenny Archer. 1991. (Springboard Bks.). (J). 10.65 (*0-606-05778-1*) Turtleback Bks.

—A Case for Jenny Archer. 1988. (Springboard Bks.). (Illus.). (J). (gr. 2-4). 12.95 o.p. (*0-316-15266-8*) Little Brown & Co.

—A Case for Jenny Archer. 1990. (Illus.). 64p. (J). (ps-3). pap. 4.95 (*0-316-15352-4*, Tingley, Megan Bks.) Little Brown Children's Bks.

—A Case for Jenny Archer. 1988. (Springboard Bks.). (J). 10.65 (*0-606-04628-3*) Turtleback Bks.

—Get the Picture, Jenny Archer? 2000. (Illus.). 64p. (J). (gr. 3-7). pap. 4.95 (*0-316-15393-1*) Little Brown Children's Bks.

—Get the Picture, Jenny Archer? 2000. 11.10 (*0-606-19838-5*) Turtleback Bks.

—Jenny Archer, Author. 1989. (Springboard Bks.). (Illus.). 64p. (J). (gr. 2-4). 13.95 o.p. (*0-316-15255-2*) Little Brown & Co.

—Jenny Archer, Author. 2002. (Illus.). 64p. (J). pap. 4.95 (*0-316-15353-2*) Little Brown Children's Bks.

—Jenny Archer to the Rescue. 1990. (J). (ps-3). 10.95 o.p. (*0-316-15351-6*) Little Brown & Co.

—Jenny Archer to the Rescue. 1992. 64p. (J). (gr. k-3). pap. 4.95 (*0-316-15369-9*) Little Brown Children's Bks.

—Jenny Archer to the Rescue. 1990. (Springboard Bks.). (J). 11.10 (*0-606-02230-9*) Turtleback Bks.

—A Job for Jenny Archer. 1988. (Illus.). 76p. (J). (gr. 3-5). 9.95 o.p. (*0-316-15262-5*) Little Brown & Co.

—A Job for Jenny Archer. 1990. (Springboard Bks.). 80p. (J). (gr. 4-7). pap. 4.95 (*0-316-15349-4*, Tingley, Megan Bks.) Little Brown Children's Bks.

—A Job for Jenny Archer. 1988. (Springboard Bks.). (J). 10.65 (*0-606-04452-3*) Turtleback Bks.

—Nibble, Nibble, Jenny Archer. 1993. (Springboard Bks.). (Illus.). 61p. (J). (ps-3). 14.95 o.p. (*0-316-15371-0*) Little Brown & Co.

—Nibble, Nibble, Jenny Archer. 1999. (Illus.). 64p. (J). (gr. 2-4). pap. 4.95 (*0-316-15206-4*, Tingley, Megan Bks.) Little Brown Children's Bks.

—Nibble, Nibble, Jenny Archer. 1999. 10.65 (*0-606-17505-9*) Turtleback Bks.

—What's Cooking, Jenny Archer? 1989. (Illus.). (J). (gr. 2-4). 12.95 o.p. (*0-316-15254-4*) Little Brown & Co.

—What's Cooking, Jenny Archer? 1991. 80p. (J). (gr. 2-4). pap. 4.95 (*0-316-15357-5*) Little Brown Children's Bks.

—What's Cooking, Jenny Archer? 1989. 11.10 (*0-606-00820-9*) Turtleback Bks.

ARCHIMEDES—FICTION

Lexau, Joan M. Archimedes Takes a Bath. 1969. (Illus.). (J). (gr. 2-5). lib. bdg. 6.89 o.p. (*0-690-09900-2*) HarperCollins Children's Bk. Group.

ARNOLD, BENEDICT, 1741-1801—FICTION

Fritz, Jean. Traitor: The Case of Benedict Arnold. 1997. (J). 12.04 (*0-606-12001-7*) Turtleback Bks.

Rinaldi, Ann. Finishing Becca: A Story about Peggy Shippen & Benedict Arnold. (Great Episodes Ser.). 384p. (YA). 2004. pap. (*0-15-205079-5*); 1994. (gr. 7 up). 12.00 (*0-15-200880-2*); 1994. (gr. 7 up). pap. 6.00 o.s.i (*0-15-200879-9*) Harcourt Children's Bks. (Gulliver Bks.).

—Finishing Becca: A Story about Peggy Shippen & Benedict Arnold. 1994. 12.05 (*0-606-14207-X*) Turtleback Bks.

Wolf, William J. Benedict Arnold, a Novel. 1990. (Illus.). 413p. (YA). (gr. 10-12). 30.00 o.p. (*0-913993-13-1*) Paideia Pubs.

ARTHUR (FICTITIOUS CHARACTER: BROWN)—FICTION

Arthur. 2001. (Illus.). (J). 7.95 (*0-7853-4852-2*) Publications International, Ltd.

Brown, Marc. Arthur Accused! 1998. (Arthur Chapter Book Ser.: No. 5). (J). (gr. 3-6). pap. 3.95 (*0-316-12150-9*); (Illus.). 64p. pap. 3.95 (*0-316-11556-8*) Little Brown Children's Bks.

—Arthur Accused! (Arthur Chapter Book Ser.: No. 5). (J). (gr. 3-6). 58p. pap. 3.95 (*0-8072-1299-7*); 1998. 58p. pap. 17.00 incl. audio (*0-8072-0385-8*, FTR191SP);Vol. 5. 2001. audio compact disk 18.00 (*0-8072-6200-5*) Random Hse. Audio Publishing Group. (Listening Library).

—Arthur Accused! 1998. (Arthur Chapter Book Ser.: No. 5). (J). (gr. 3-6). 10.10 (*0-606-15914-2*) Turtleback Bks.

—Arthur & the Babysitter. 2004. (J). 15.95 (*0-316-12128-2*) Little Brown & Co.

—Arthur & the Bad-Luck Brain. 2003. 64p. (J). (gr. 2-4). pap. 4.25 (*0-316-12377-3*) Little Brown & Co.

—Arthur & the Bad-Luck Brain. 2003. (Arthur Chapter Book Ser.). (J). (gr. 3-6). 14.95 (*0-316-12650-0*) Little Brown Children's Bks.

—Arthur & the Best Coach Ever. 2001. (Arthur Good Sports Chapter Book Ser.: No. 4). (Illus.). 64p. (J). (gr. 3-6). 13.95 (*0-316-11965-2*); pap. 3.95 (*0-316-12117-7*) Little Brown Children's Bks.

—Arthur & the Best Coach Ever. 2001. (Arthur Chapter Book Ser.). (Illus.). (J). 10.00 (*0-606-21910-2*) Turtleback Bks.

—Arthur & the Big Blow-up. 2000. (Arthur Chapter Book Ser.: No. 20). (Illus.). (J). (gr. 3-6). 10.10 (*0-606-18251-9*) Turtleback Bks.

—Arthur & the Big Blow-Up. (Arthur Chapter Book Ser.: No. 20). (J). (gr. 3-6). 2000. (Illus.). 64p. 12.95 (*0-316-12129-0*); 2000. (Illus.). 64p. pap. 3.95 (*0-316-12203-3*); 1999. pap. 3.95 (*0-316-12326-9*) Little Brown Children's Bks.

—Arthur & the Comet Crisis. 2002. (Arthur Chapter Book Ser.: No. 27). (Illus.). 64p. (J). (gr. 2-4). 14.95 (*0-316-12462-1*); pap. 4.25 (*0-316-12199-1*) Little Brown Children's Bks.

—Arthur & the Cootie-Catcher. 1999. (Arthur Chapter Book Ser.: No. 15). (J). (gr. 3-6). (Illus.). 64p. pap. 4.25 (*0-316-12266-1*); pap. 3.95 (*0-316-12085-5*) Little Brown Children's Bks.

—Arthur & the Crunch Cereal Contest. 1998. (Arthur Chapter Book Ser.: No. 4). (J). (gr. 3-6). pap. 3.95 (*0-316-10546-5*); (Illus.). 64p. 13.95 (*0-316-11552-5*); (Illus.). 64p. pap. 3.95 (*0-316-11553-3*) Little Brown Children's Bks.

—Arthur & the Crunch Cereal Contest. (Arthur Chapter Book Ser.: No. 4). (J). (gr. 3-6). 61p. pap. 3.95 (*0-8072-1298-9*); 1998. 58p. pap. 17.00 incl. audio (*0-8072-0382-3*, FTR190SP);4. 1999. audio 18.00 (*0-8072-8146-8*, YA107CXR) Random Hse. Audio Publishing Group. (Listening Library).

—Arthur & the Crunch Cereal Contest. 1998. (Arthur Chapter Book Ser.: No. 4). (J). (gr. 3-6). 10.10 (*0-606-13150-7*) Turtleback Bks.

—Arthur & the Double Dare. 2002. (Arthur Chapter Book Ser.: No. 25). (Illus.). 64p. (J). (gr. 2-4). pap. 4.25 (*0-316-12087-1*); (gr. 3-6). 13.95 (*0-316-12264-5*) Little Brown Children's Bks.

—Arthur & the Goalie Ghost. 2001. (Arthur Chapter Book Ser.). (Illus.). (J). 10.10 (*0-606-22027-5*) Turtleback Bks.

—Arthur & the Lost Diary. 1999. (Arthur Chapter Book Ser.: No. 9). (Illus.). (J). (gr. 3-6). pap. 11.05 (*0-613-11277-6*) Econo-Clad Bks.

—Arthur & the Lost Diary. 1998. (Arthur Chapter Book Ser.: No. 9). (J). (gr. 3-6). pap. 3.95 (*0-316-61004-6*); (Illus.). 64p. pap. 3.95 (*0-316-11537-1*) Little Brown Children's Bks.

—Arthur & the Lost Diary. (Arthur Chapter Book Ser.: No. 9). 55p. (J). (gr. 3-6). pap. 3.95 (*0-8072-1305-5*); 1999. pap. 17.00 incl. audio (*0-8072-0404-8*, EFTR200SP) Random Hse. Audio Publishing Group. (Listening Library).

—Arthur & the Lost Diary. 1998. (Arthur Chapter Book Ser.: No. 9). (J). (gr. 3-6). 10.10 (*0-606-15441-8*) Turtleback Bks.

—Arthur & the Nerves of Steal. 2004. (J). (gr. 3-6). 13.95 (*0-316-12895-3*); pap. 4.25 (*0-316-12618-7*) Little Brown Children's Bks.

—Arthur & the New Kid. 2004. (Step into Reading Sticker Book Ser.). (J). (*0-375-91381-5*); pap. (*0-375-81381-0*) Random Hse., Inc.

—Arthur & the No-Brainer. 2002. (Arthur Chapter Book Ser.: No. 26). (Illus.). 64p. (J). (gr. 2-4). 14.95 (*0-316-12332-3*); pap. 4.25 (*0-316-12132-0*) Little Brown Children's Bks.

—Arthur & the Pen-Pal Playoff. 2001. (Arthur Good Sports Chapter Book Ser.: No. 6). (Illus.). (J). (gr. 3-6). 64p. 14.95 (*0-316-12054-5*); 55p. pap. 4.25 (*0-316-12170-3*) Little Brown Children's Bks.

—Arthur & the Perfect Brother. 2000. (Arthur Chapter Book Ser.: No. 21). (Illus.). 64p. (J). (gr. 3-6). 13.95 (*0-316-12163-0*); pap. 3.95 (*0-316-12226-2*) Little Brown Children's Bks.

—Arthur & the Perfect Brother. 2000. (Arthur Chapter Book Ser.: No. 21). (Illus.). (J). (gr. 3-6). 10.10 (*0-606-18252-7*) Turtleback Bks.

—Arthur & the Poetry Contest. 1999. (Arthur Chapter Book Ser.: No. 18). (J). (gr. 3-6). pap. 3.95 (*0-316-12153-3*); (Illus.). 64p. 13.95 (*0-316-12062-6*); (Illus.). 64p. pap. 3.95 (*0-316-12295-5*) Little Brown Children's Bks.

—Arthur & the Poetry Contest. 1999. (Arthur Chapter Book Ser.: No. 18). (J). (gr. 3-6). 10.10 (*0-606-17238-6*) Turtleback Bks.

—Arthur & the Popularity Test. 1999. (Arthur Chapter Book Ser.: No. 12). (Illus.). (J). (gr. 3-6). pap. 11.05 (*0-613-11278-4*) Econo-Clad Bks.

—Arthur & the Popularity Test. (Arthur Chapter Book Ser.: No. 12). (J). (gr. 3-6). 1999. pap. 3.95 (*0-316-11999-7*); 1998. (Illus.). 64p. 12.95 (*0-316-11544-4*); 1998. (Illus.). 64p. pap. 3.95 (*0-316-11545-2*) Little Brown Children's Bks.

—Arthur & the Popularity Test. (Arthur Chapter Book Ser.: No. 12). 58p. (J). (gr. 3-6). pap. 3.95 (*0-8072-1308-X*); 1999. pap. 17.00 incl. audio (*0-8072-0413-7*, FTR204SP) Random Hse. Audio Publishing Group. (Listening Library).

—Arthur & the Popularity Test. 1998. (Arthur Chapter Book Ser.: No. 12). (J). (gr. 3-6). 10.10 (*0-606-16974-1*) Turtleback Bks.

—Arthur & the Race to Read. 2001. (Arthur Chapter Book Ser.). (Illus.). (J). 10.10 (*0-606-21041-5*) Turtleback Bks.

—Arthur & the Recess Rookie. 2001. (Arthur Good Sports Chapter Book Ser.: No. 3). (Illus.). 64p. (J). (gr. 3-6). 13.95 (*0-316-11916-4*); pap. 3.95 (*0-316-12105-3*) Little Brown Children's Bks.

—Arthur & the Recess Rookie. 2001. (Arthur Chapter Book Ser.). (Illus.). (J). 10.00 (*0-606-21909-9*) Turtleback Bks.

—Arthur & the Scare-Your-Pants-Off Club. (Arthur Chapter Book Ser.: No. 2). (J). (gr. 3-6). 1998. pap. 3.95 (*0-316-10496-5*); 1998. (Illus.). 64p. 12.95 (*0-316-11548-7*); 1998. (Illus.). 64p. pap. 4.25 (*0-316-11549-5*); Bks. 1-3. 2000. (Illus.). 196p. 9.95 (*0-316-12096-0*) Little Brown Children's Bks.

—Arthur & the Scare-Your-Pants-Off Club. (Arthur Chapter Book Ser.: No. 2). (J). (gr. 3-6). 58p. pap. 3.95 (*0-8072-1296-2*); 1998. 58p. pap. 17.00 incl. audio (*0-8072-0376-9*, FTR188SP);2. 2000. audio 18.00 (*0-8072-8040-2*, YA970CXR) Random Hse. Audio Publishing Group. (Listening Library).

—Arthur & the Scare-Your-Pants-Off Club. 1998. (Arthur Chapter Book Ser.: No. 2). (J). (gr. 3-6). 10.10 (*0-606-13151-5*) Turtleback Bks.

—Arthur & the School Pet. 2003. (Step into Reading Sticker Books). (Illus.). 24p. (J). 3.99 (*0-375-81001-3*, Golden Bks.) Random Hse. Children's Bks.

—Arthur & the Seventh-Inning Stretcher. 2001. (Arthur Good Sports Chapter Book Ser.: No. 2). (Illus.). 64p. (J). (gr. 3-6). 13.95 (*0-316-11861-3*); pap. 4.25 (*0-316-12094-4*) Little Brown Children's Bks.

—Arthur & the True Francine. (Arthur Adventure Ser.). (Illus.). 32p. (J). (gr. k-3). 1998. pap. 9.95 incl. audio (*0-316-11946-6*); 1998. pap. 9.95 incl. audio (*0-316-11946-6*); 1996. pap. 5.95 (*0-316-10949-5*) Little Brown Children's Bks.

—Arthur & the True Francine. (Arthur Adventure Ser.). (J). (gr. k-3). 7.98 incl. audio. 7.98 incl. audio NewSound, LLC.

—Arthur & the True Francine. 1996. (Arthur Adventure Ser.). (J). (gr. k-3). 12.10 (*0-606-09012-6*) Turtleback Bks.

—Arthur & the World Record, Bks. 33. 2004. (J). 13.95 (*0-316-12949-6*) Little Brown & Co.

—Arthur Babysits. 2002. (Arthur Picture Bks.). (Illus.). (J). 13.15 (*0-7587-1971-X*) Book Wholesalers, Inc.

—Arthur Babysits. 1999. (Arthur Adventure Ser.). (Illus.). (J). (gr. k-3). pap. 13.35 (*0-7857-5838-0*) Econo-Clad Bks.

—Arthur Babysits. 1997. (Arthur Adventure Ser.). (Illus.). 32p. (J). (gr. k-3). 5.95 (*0-316-11134-1*) Little Brown Children's Bks.

—Arthur Babysits. 1994. (Arthur Adventure Ser.). (J). (gr. k-3). 12.10 (*0-606-06185-1*) Turtleback Bks.

—Arthur Breaks the Bank. 2005. (J). (*0-375-81002-1*); lib. bdg. (*0-375-91002-6*) Random Hse., Inc.

—Arthur Chapter Books #4-6, 3 bks. in 1. 2002. (Illus.). 196p. (J). (gr. 2-4). 9.95 (*0-316-07595-7*) Little Brown Children's Bks.

—Arthur, Clean Your Room! (Step into Reading Sticker Bks.). (ps-3). 2003. 24p. lib. bdg. 11.99 (*0-679-98467-4*); 1999. (J). 0.75 o.s.i (*0-375-80872-8*); 1999. 24p. (J). pap. 3.99 o.s.i (*0-375-80873-6*) Random Hse. Children's Bks. (Random Hse. Bks. for Young Readers).

—Arthur Counts! 1998. (Arthur Ser.). (Illus.). 22p. (J). (ps). bds. 3.99 (*0-679-88462-9*, Random Hse. Bks. for Young Readers) Random Hse. Children's Bks.

—Arthur Decks the Hall. 1998. (Arthur Ser.). (Illus.). 12p. (J). (ps). bds. 7.99 (*0-679-88472-6*, Random Hse. Bks. for Young Readers) Random Hse. Children's Bks.

—Arthur Goes to Camp. 2002. (Arthur Picture Bks.). (Illus.). (J). 13.15 (*0-7587-1972-8*) Book Wholesalers, Inc.

—Arthur Goes to Camp. 1982. (Arthur Adventure Ser.). (J). (gr. k-3). 12.10 (*0-606-03970-8*) Turtleback Bks.

—Arthur Goes to School. 1998. (Arthur Ser.). (J). (ps-k). 313.40 o.s.i (*0-676-76375-8*, Random Hse. Bks. for Young Readers) Random Hse. Children's Bks.

—Arthur Goes to School. 1995. (Arthur Ser.). (Illus.). 12p. (J). (ps-k). bds. 11.99 (*0-679-86734-1*) Random Hse., Inc.

—Arthur in a Pickle. 1999. (Step into Reading Sticker Bks.). (Illus.). 24p. (J). (ps-3). pap. 3.99 (*0-679-88469-6*, Random Hse. Bks. for Young Readers) Random Hse. Children's Bks.

—Arthur, Its Only Rock 'n' Roll. 2002. (Illus.). 32p. (J). 15.95 (*0-316-11854-0*) Little Brown Children's Bks.

—Arthur Loses His Marbles, Bk. 31. 2004. (J). 13.95 (*0-316-12711-6*); pap. 4.25 (*0-316-12557-1*) Little Brown & Co.

—Arthur Lost & Found. ed. 2000. (YA). (gr. 2). spiral bd. (*0-616-11102-9*) Canadian National Institute for the Blind/Institut National Canadien pour les Aveugles.

—Arthur Lost & Found. 1998. (Arthur Adventure Ser.). (Illus.). 32p. (J). (gr. k-3). 15.95 (*0-316-10912-6*) Little Brown Children's Bks.

—Arthur Lost & Found. 2000. (Arthur Adventure Ser.). (J). (gr. k-3). 12.10 (*0-606-19835-0*) Turtleback Bks.

—Arthur Makes the Team. 1998. (Arthur Chapter Book Ser.: No. 3). (J). (gr. 3-6). pap. 3.95 (*0-316-10536-8*); (Illus.). 64p. 12.95 (*0-316-11550-9*); (Illus.). 64p. pap. 3.95 (*0-316-11551-7*) Little Brown Children's Bks.

—Arthur Makes the Team. (Arthur Chapter Book Ser.: No. 3). (J). (gr. 3-6). audio 12.78 NewSound, LLC.

—Arthur Makes the Team. (Arthur Chapter Book Ser.: No. 3). (J). (gr. 3-6). 61p. pap. 3.95 (*0-8072-1297-0*); 1998. 61p. pap. 17.00 incl. audio (*0-8072-0379-3*, FTR189SP);3. 2000. audio 18.00 (*0-8072-8090-9*, YA988CXR) Random Hse. Audio Publishing Group. (Listening Library).

—Arthur Makes the Team. 1998. (Arthur Chapter Book Ser.: No. 3). (J). (gr. 3-6). 10.10 (*0-606-13152-3*) Turtleback Bks.

—Arthur Meets the President. (Arthur Adventure Ser.). (J). (gr. k-3). pap. o.p. (*0-316-10291-1*); 1998. pap. 5.95 o.p. (*0-316-10554-6*); 1997. (Illus.). pap. 5.95 (*0-316-11578-9*); 1992. (Illus.). 32p. pap. 5.95 (*0-316-11291-7*) Little Brown Children's Bks.

—Arthur Meets the President. 1992. (Golden Book Ser.). (J). (gr. k-3). pap. 2.99 o.s.i (*0-307-05882-4*, Golden Bks.) Random Hse. Children's Bks.

—Arthur Meets the President. 1991. (Arthur Adventure Ser.). (J). (gr. k-3). 12.10 (*0-606-02222-8*) Turtleback Bks.

—Arthur on the Farm. 1998. (Arthur Ser.). (Illus.). 22p. (J). (ps). bds. 3.99 (*0-679-88461-0*, Random Hse. Bks. for Young Readers) Random Hse. Children's Bks.

—Arthur Plays the Blues. 2003. 64p. (J). pap. 4.25 (*0-316-12314-5*) Little Brown & Co.

—Arthur Plays the Blues. 2003. (Arthur Chapter Book Ser.). (J). (gr. 3-6). 14.95 (*0-316-12586-5*) Little Brown Children's Bks.

—Arthur Rocks with Binky. 2002. (Arthur Chapter Bks.). (Illus.). (J). 11.70 (*0-7587-0439-9*) Book Wholesalers, Inc.

—Arthur Rocks with Binky. 1999. (Arthur Chapter Book Ser.: No. 11). (Illus.). (J). (gr. 3-6). pap. 11.05 (*0-613-11281-4*) Econo-Clad Bks.

—Arthur Rocks with Binky. 1998. (Arthur Chapter Book Ser.: No. 11). (Illus.). 64p. (J). (gr. 3-6). 12.95 (*0-316-11542-8*); pap. 4.25 (*0-316-11543-6*) Little Brown Children's Bks.

—Arthur Rocks with Binky. (Arthur Chapter Book Ser.: No. 11). 61p. (J). (gr. 3-6). pap. 3.95 (*0-8072-1307-1*); 1999. 17.00 incl. audio (*0-8072-0410-2*, FTR203SP) Random Hse. Audio Publishing Group. (Listening Library).

—Arthur Rocks with Binky. 1998. (Arthur Chapter Book Ser.: No. 11). (J). (gr. 3-6). 10.10 (*0-606-15913-4*) Turtleback Bks.

—Arthur Rocks with Binky Special Scholastic Edition. 1999. (Arthur Chapter Book Ser.: No. 11). (J). (gr. 3-6). pap. 3.95 (*0-316-10422-1*) Little Brown Children's Bks.

—Arthur Tricks the Tooth Fairy. 1998. (Step into Reading Sticker Bks.). (Illus.). 24p. (J). (ps-3). pap. 3.99 (*0-679-88464-5*); lib. bdg. 11.99 (*0-679-98464-X*) Random Hse. Children's Bks. (Random Hse. Bks. for Young Readers).

—Arthur Writes a Story. 2002. (Illus.). (J). 13.15 (*0-7587-1974-4*) Book Wholesalers, Inc.

—Arthur Writes a Story. ed. 2000. (J). (gr. 1). spiral bd. (*0-616-01604-2*); (gr. 2). spiral bd. (*0-616-01605-0*) Canadian National Institute for the Blind/Institut National Canadien pour les Aveugles.

—Arthur Writes a Story. 2003. (Illus.). 14.95 (*1-59319-021-2*) LeapFrog Enterprises, Inc.

—Arthur Writes a Story. (Arthur Adventure Ser.). (J). (gr. k-3). 1999. (Illus.). 32p. 9.95 incl. audio (*0-316-11976-8*); 1998. (Illus.). 32p. pap. 5.95 (*0-316-11164-3*); 1998. pap. 5.95 o.s.i (*0-316-11973-3*); 1996. (Illus.). 32p. 15.95 (*0-316-10916-9*) Little Brown Children's Bks.

—Arthur Writes a Story. 1998. (Arthur Adventure Ser.). (J). (gr. k-3). 12.10 (*0-606-13153-1*) Turtleback Bks.

—Arthur's Animal Adventure. 2002. (Arthur Ser.). (Illus.). 12p. (J). (ps-2). bds. 7.99 (*0-375-80699-7*) Random Hse., Inc.

—Arthur's April Fool. (Arthur Adventure Ser.). (J). (gr. k-3). 1998. pap. 5.95 o.p. (*0-316-10555-4*); 1997. (Illus.). pap. 5.95 (*0-316-11581-9*); 1995. (Illus.). 32p. 9.95 incl. audio (*0-316-11181-3*); 1995. (Illus.). 32p. 9.95 incl. audio (*0-316-11181-3*) Little Brown Children's Bks.

—Arthur's April Fool. 1986. (Arthur Adventure Ser.). (J). (gr. k-3). audio 42.66 (*0-676-30730-2*) SRA/McGraw-Hill.

—Arthur's April Fool. 1983. (Arthur Adventure Ser.). (J). (gr. k-3). 12.10 (*0-606-03987-2*) Turtleback Bks.

—Arthur's Baby. (Arthur Adventure Ser.). (gr. k-3). 1998. (Illus.). 30p. (J). 5.95 (*0-316-11858-3*); 1997. 9.95 incl. audio; 1990. (Illus.). 32p. (J). pap. 5.95 (*0-316-11007-8*) Little Brown Children's Bks.

—Arthur's Baby. 1987. (Arthur Adventure Ser.). (J). (gr. k-3). 12.10 (*0-606-03035-2*) Turtleback Bks.

—Arthur's Back-to-School Surprise. 2002. (Illus.). 24p. (J). pap. 3.99 (*0-375-81000-5*); lib. bdg. 11.99 (*0-375-91000-X*) Random Hse., Inc.

—Arthur's Birthday. 1997. (Arthur Adventure Ser.). (J). (gr. k-3). cd-rom 23.75 (*1-57135-301-1*) Broderbund Software, Inc.

—Arthur's Birthday. 1998. (Arthur Adventure Ser.). (Illus.). (J). (gr. k-3). 32p. pap. 17.95 (*0-316-11588-6*); 30p. bds. 5.95 (*0-316-11857-5*) Little Brown Children's Bks.

—Arthur's Birthday. 1989. (Arthur Adventure Ser.). (J). (gr. k-3). 12.10 (*0-606-06186-X*) Turtleback Bks.

—Arthur's Birthday Activity Book: With Reusable Vinyl Stickers. 2001. (Arthur Activity Book Ser.). (Illus.). 18p. (J). (ps-3). 7.95 (*0-316-11851-6*) Little Brown & Co.

—Arthur's Birthday; Arthur's Pet Business; Arthur's Baby; Arthur Meets the President, 3 bks. 1996. (Arthur Adventure Ser.). (Illus.). 32p. (J). (gr. k-3). 14.95 (*0-316-10953-3*) Little Brown Children's Bks.

—Arthur's Birthday Surprise. 2004. (Illus.). 24p. (J). (ps-3). mass mkt. 3.99 (*0-316-73379-2*) Little Brown Children's Bks.

—Arthur's Boo-Boo Book: With Peel-Off Stickers for First Aid Fun! 1998. (Arthur Ser.). (Illus.). 12p. (ps). bds. 7.99 (*0-679-88465-3*, Random Hse. Bks. for Young Readers) Random Hse. Children's Bks.

—Arthur's Chicken Pox. 2002. (Arthur Picture Bks.). (Illus.). (J). 13.15 (*0-7587-1978-7*) Book Wholesalers, Inc.

—Arthur's Chicken Pox. (Arthur Adventure Ser.). (J). (gr. k-3). 1999. (Illus.). 30p. 5.95 (*0-316-11953-9*); 1998. 32p. pap. 9.95 incl. audio (*0-316-11947-4*); 1998. 32p. pap. 9.95 incl. audio (*0-316-11947-4*) Little Brown Children's Bks.

—Arthur's Chicken Pox. 1994. (Arthur Adventure Ser.). (J). (gr. k-3). 12.10 (*0-606-08691-9*) Turtleback Bks.

—Arthur's Christmas. 2002. (Arthur Picture Bks.). (Illus.). (J). 13.15 (*0-7587-1979-5*) Book Wholesalers, Inc.

—Arthur's Christmas. ed. 1995. (J). (gr. 1). spiral bd. (*0-616-01599-2*); (gr. 2). spiral bd. (*0-616-01600-X*) Canadian National Institute for the Blind/Institut National Canadien pour les Aveugles.

—Arthur's Christmas. (Arthur Adventure Ser.). (J). (gr. k-3). 1999. 32p. pap. 9.95 incl. audio (*0-316-11964-4*); 1999. 32p. pap. 9.95 incl. audio (*0-316-11964-4*); 1996. pap. 5.95 o.p. (*0-316-11536-3*) Little Brown Children's Bks.

—Arthur's Christmas. 1984. (Arthur Adventure Ser.). (J). (gr. k-3). 12.10 (*0-606-03988-0*) Turtleback Bks.

—Arthur's Computer Disaster. (Arthur Adventure Ser.). (J). (gr. k-3). 1999. pap. 5.95 (*0-316-12373-0*); 1999. (Illus.). 32p. pap. 5.95 (*0-316-10534-1*); 1997. (Illus.). 32p. 15.95 (*0-316-11016-7*) Little Brown Children's Bks.

—Arthur's Computer Disaster. 1997. (Arthur Adventure Ser.). (J). (gr. k-3). 12.10 (*0-606-17382-X*) Turtleback Bks.

—Arthur's Eyes. 1986. (Arthur Adventure Ser.). (Illus.). 32p. (J). (gr. k-3). pap. 5.95 (*0-316-11069-8*) Little Brown Children's Bks.

—Arthur's Eyes. 1981. (Arthur Adventure Ser.). (Illus.). 32p. (J). (gr. k-3). pap. 2.25 o.p. (*0-380-53389-8*, 70000-X, Avon Bks.) Morrow/Avon.

—Arthur's Eyes. 1979. (Arthur Adventure Ser.). (J). (gr. k-3). 12.10 (*0-606-03716-0*) Turtleback Bks.

—Arthur's Family Feud. 2003. (J). 15.95 (*0-316-12093-6*) Little Brown & Co.

—Arthur's Family Treasury. 2000. (Illus.). 112p. (J). (ps-3). 18.95 (*0-316-12147-9*) Little Brown & Co.

—Arthur's Family Vacation. 2002. (Arthur Picture Bks.). (Illus.). (J). 13.15 (*0-7587-1981-7*) Book Wholesalers, Inc.

—Arthur's Family Vacation. ed. 2000. (J). (gr. 1). spiral bd. (*0-616-01601-8*); (gr. 2). spiral bd. (*0-616-01602-6*) Canadian National Institute for the Blind/Institut National Canadien pour les Aveugles.

—Arthur's Family Vacation. (Arthur Adventure Ser.). (J). (gr. k-3). 1998. (Illus.). pap. 5.95 (*0-316-11528-2*); 1997. pap. 1.00 o.s.i (*0-316-10569-4*); 1996. (Illus.). 32p. pap. 9.95 incl. audio (*0-316-11043-4*); 1996. (Illus.). 32p. pap. 9.95 incl. audio (*0-316-11043-4*); 1995. (Illus.). 32p. pap. 5.95 (*0-316-10958-4*) Little Brown Children's Bks.

—Arthur's Family Vacation. 1993. (Arthur Adventure Ser.). (J). (gr. k-3). 12.10 (*0-606-07209-8*) Turtleback Bks.

—Arthur's First Kiss. 2001. (Step into Reading Sticker Bks.). (Illus.). 24p. (J). (ps-3). pap. 3.99 (*0-375-80602-4*); lib. bdg. 11.99 (*0-375-90602-9*) Random Hse. Children's Bks. (Random Hse. Bks. for Young Readers).

—Arthur's First Sleepover. 2002. (Arthur Picture Bks.). (Illus.). (J). 13.15 (*0-7587-1982-5*) Book Wholesalers, Inc.

—Arthur's First Sleepover. (Arthur Adventure Ser.). (J). (gr. k-3). 1999. (Illus.). 30p. bds. 5.95 (*0-316-10560-0*); 1998. pap. 5.95 (*0-316-11974-1*); 1998. 32p. pap. 9.95 incl. audio (*0-316-11948-2*); 1998. 32p. pap. 9.95 incl. audio (*0-316-11948-2*); 1996. (Illus.). 32p. pap. 5.95 (*0-316-11049-3*); 1994. 32p. 15.95 (*0-316-11445-6*) Little Brown Children's Bks.

—Arthur's First Sleepover. 1994. (Arthur Adventure Ser.). (J). (gr. k-3). 12.10 (*0-606-10128-4*) Turtleback Bks.

—Arthur's Halloween. 2002. (Arthur Picture Bks.). (Illus.). (J). 13.15 (*0-7587-1983-3*) Book Wholesalers, Inc.

—Arthur's Halloween. (Arthur Adventure Ser.). (J). (gr. k-3). 1996. pap. 5.95 o.p. (*0-316-11516-9*); 1996. (Illus.). 32p. pap. 9.95 incl. audio (*0-316-11105-8*); 1996. (Illus.). 32p. pap. 9.95 incl. audio (*0-316-11105-8*); 1989. pap. (*0-316-11004-3*) Little Brown Children's Bks.

—Arthur's Halloween. 1982. (Arthur Adventure Ser.). (J). (gr. k-3). 12.10 (*0-606-03989-9*) Turtleback Bks.

—Arthur's Heart Mix-Up. 2004. (Illus.). 24p. (J). pap. 3.99 (*0-316-73381-4*) Little Brown & Co.

—Arthur's Hiccups. 2001. (Step into Reading Sticker Bks.). (Illus.). (J). (gr. k-3). 24p. lib. bdg. 11.99 (*0-375-90698-3*); 24p. pap. 3.99 (*0-375-80698-9*); lib. bdg. (*0-375-90699-1*) Random Hse. Children's Bks. (Random Hse. Bks. for Young Readers).

—Arthur's Jelly Beans. 2004. (Illus.). 24p. (J). pap. 3.99 (*0-316-73382-2*) Little Brown & Co.

—Arthur's Lost & Found. 2000. (Arthur Adventure Ser.). (Illus.). 32p. (J). (ps-3). pap. 5.95 (*0-316-10824-3*) Little Brown Children's Bks.

—Arthur's Lost Puppy. 2003. (Step into Reading Sticker Bks.). (Illus.). 24p. (J). (ps-3). 3.99 (*0-679-88466-1*, Golden Bks.) Random Hse. Children's Bks.

—Arthur's Messy Room. 1999. (Step into Reading Ser.). (Illus.). 24p. (J). (ps-3). pap. 3.99 (*0-679-88467-X*) Random Hse., Inc.

—Arthur's Mystery Envelope. 1998. (Arthur Chapter Book Ser.: No. 1). (J). (gr. 3-6). pap. 3.95 (*0-316-10464-7*); (Illus.). 64p. 13.95 (*0-316-11546-0*); (Illus.). 64p. pap. 3.95 (*0-316-11547-9*) Little Brown Children's Bks.

—Arthur's Mystery Envelope. (Arthur Chapter Book Ser.: No. 1). (J). (gr. 3-6). 13.58 o.p. incl. audio. 13.58 o.p. incl. audio. 12.78 incl. audio NewSound, LLC.

—Arthur's Mystery Envelope. (Arthur Chapter Book Ser.: No. 1). (J). (gr. 3-6). 58p. pap. 3.95 (*0-8072-1295-4*); 2000. audio 18.00 (*0-8072-8015-1*, TYA966-1CX); 2000. audio 18.00 (*0-8072-8015-1*, TYA966-1CX); 1998. 58p. pap. 17.00 incl. audio (*0-8072-0372-6*, FTR187SP) Random Hse. Audio Publishing Group. (Listening Library).

—Arthur's Mystery Envelope. 1998. (Arthur Chapter Book Ser.: No. 1). (J). (gr. 3-6). 10.10 (*0-606-13154-X*) Turtleback Bks.

—Arthur's Neighborhood. 1996. (Arthur Ser.). (Illus.). 12p. (J). (ps-k). bds. 11.99 (*0-679-86737-6*) Random Hse., Inc.

—Arthur's New Baby Book: A Lift-The-Flap Guide to Being a Great Big-Brother or Sister. 1999. (Arthur Ser.). (Illus.). 12p. (J). (ps-k). bds. 11.99 (*0-679-88463-7*, Random Hse. Bks. for Young Readers) Random Hse. Children's Bks.

—Arthur's New Puppy. 2002. (Arthur Picture Bks.). (Illus.). (J). 13.15 (*0-7587-1984-1*) Book Wholesalers, Inc.

—Arthur's New Puppy. (Arthur Adventure Ser.). (Illus.). 32p. (J). (gr. k-3). 1998. pap. 9.95 incl. audio (*0-316-11949-0*); 1998. pap. 9.95 incl. audio (*0-316-11949-0*); 1997. bds. 5.95 (*0-316-11133-3*); 1995. pap. 5.95 (*0-316-10921-5*) Little Brown Children's Bks.

—Arthur's New Puppy. (Arthur Adventure Ser.). (J). (gr. k-3). 7.98 incl. audio. 7.98 incl. audio NewSound, LLC.

—Arthur's New Puppy. 1993. (Arthur Adventure Ser.). (J). (gr. k-3). 12.10 (*0-606-07210-1*) Turtleback Bks.

—Arthur's Nose. 1981. (Arthur Adventure Ser.). (Illus.). 32p. (J). (gr. k-3). pap. 2.25 o.p. (*0-380-53397-9*, 68940-5, Avon Bks.) Morrow/Avon.

—Arthur's Nose. 1976. (Arthur Adventure Ser.). (J). (gr. k-3). 12.10 (*0-606-03971-6*) Turtleback Bks.

—Arthur's off to School. 2004. (Illus.). 24p. (J). (ps-3). mass mkt. 3.99 (*0-316-73378-4*) Little Brown Children's Bks.

—Arthur's Perfect Christmas. 2000. (Arthur Adventure Ser.). (Illus.). 40p. (J). (gr. k-3). 15.95 (*0-316-11968-7*) Little Brown Children's Bks.

—Arthur's Pet Business. (Arthur Adventure Ser.). (J). (gr. k-3). 1997. pap. 1.00 o.s.i (*0-316-10570-8*); 1993. (Illus.). 32p. pap. 5.95 (*0-316-11316-6*); 1990. 32p. 15.95 (*0-316-11262-3*) Little Brown Children's Bks.

—Arthur's Pet Business. 1990. (Arthur Adventure Ser.). (J). (gr. k-3). 12.10 (*0-606-05126-0*) Turtleback Bks.

—Arthur's Reading Race. 1996. (Step into Reading Sticker Bks.). (Illus.). (J). (ps-3). o.p. (*0-679-88042-9*) Random Hse., Inc.

—Arthur's Really Helpful Bedtime Stories. 1998. (Arthur Ser.). (Illus.). 48p. (J). (ps-3). 14.99 (*0-679-88468-8*); lib. bdg. 15.99 (*0-679-98468-2*) Random Hse. Children's Bks. (Random Hse. Bks. for Young Readers).

—Arthur's Science Fair Trouble. 2003. (Illus.). 24p. (J). (gr. 1-3). pap. 3.99 (*0-375-81003-X*); lib. bdg. 11.99 (*0-375-91003-4*) Random Hse., Inc.

—Arthur's Spookiest Halloween. 2003. (Illus.). 10p. (J). (ps-1). bds. 7.99 (*0-375-81004-8*) Random Hse. Children's Bks.

—Arthur's Teacher Moves In. 2000. (Arthur Adventure Ser.). (J). (gr. k-3). (Illus.). 32p. 15.95 (*0-316-11979-2*); 15.95 (*0-316-11856-7*) Little Brown Children's Bks.

—Arthur's Teacher Trouble. (Arthur Adventure Ser.). (J). (gr. k-3). 1995. lib. bdg. 99.95 (*1-57135-019-5*); 1994. pap. 23.75 net. incl. cd-rom (*1-57135-017-9*) Broderbund Software, Inc.

—Arthur's Teacher Trouble. ed. 1999. (J). (gr. 1). spiral bd. (*0-616-01603-4*); (gr. 2). spiral bd. (*0-616-00406-0*) Canadian National Institute for the Blind/Institut National Canadien pour les Aveugles.

—Arthur's Teacher Trouble. 1986. (Arthur Adventure Ser.). (J). (gr. k-3). 12.10 (*0-606-04161-3*) Turtleback Bks.

—Arthur's Teacher Trouble Class Set. 1995. (Arthur Adventure Ser.). (J). (gr. k-3). pap. 79.95 (*1-57135-018-7*) Broderbund Software, Inc.

—Arthur's Thanksgiving. (Arthur Adventure Ser.). (J). (gr. k-3). 1996. pap. 5.95 o.p. (*0-316-11513-4*); 1989. pap. (*0-316-11005-1*) Little Brown Children's Bks.

—Arthur's Thanksgiving. 1984. (Arthur Adventure Ser.). (J). (gr. k-3). 12.10 (*0-606-03990-2*) Turtleback Bks.

—Arthur's Tooth. 2002. (Arthur Picture Bks.). (Illus.). (J). 13.15 (*0-7587-1989-2*) Book Wholesalers, Inc.

—Arthur's Tooth. 1985. (Arthur Adventure Ser.). (J). (gr. k-3). 13.95 o.p. (*0-87113-006-8*) Grove/Atlantic, Inc.

—Arthur's Tooth. 1985. (Arthur Adventure Ser.). (J). (gr. k-3). 12.10 (*0-606-11058-5*) Turtleback Bks.

—Arthur's Truck Adventure. Schulman, Janet, ed. 2000. (Arthur Ser.). (Illus.). 12p. (J). (ps-3). bds. 7.99 (*0-679-88470-X*, Random Hse. Bks. for Young Readers) Random Hse. Children's Bks.

—Arthur's TV Trouble. 2002. (Arthur Picture Bks.). (Illus.). (J). 13.15 (*0-7587-1990-6*) Book Wholesalers, Inc.

—Arthur's TV Trouble. (Arthur Adventure Ser.). (J). (gr. k-3). 1999. (Illus.). 32p. 9.95 incl. audio (*0-316-11594-0*); 1997. (Illus.). 32p. reprint ed. pap. 5.95 (*0-316-11047-7*); 1997. pap. 5.95 (*0-316-11959-8*) Little Brown Children's Bks.

—Arthur's TV Trouble. 1997. (Arthur Adventure Ser.). (J). (gr. k-3). 12.10 (*0-606-12620-1*) Turtleback Bks.

—Arthur's Underwear. ed. 2003. (gr. 1). spiral bd. (*0-616-14563-2*); (gr. 2). spiral bd. (*0-616-14564-0*) Canadian National Institute for the Blind/Institut National Canadien pour les Aveugles.

—Arthur's Underwear. (Arthur Adventure Ser.). (Illus.). 32p. (J). (gr. k-3). 2001. pap. 5.95 (*0-316-10619-4*); 1999. 15.95 (*0-316-11012-4*) Little Brown Children's Bks.

—Arthur's Valentine. 2002. (Arthur Picture Bks.). (Illus.). (J). 13.15 (*0-7587-1991-4*) Book Wholesalers, Inc.

—Arthur's Valentine. (Arthur Adventure Ser.). (J). (gr. k-3). 2000. 32p. pap. 9.95 incl. audio (*0-316-11866-4*); 1997. (Illus.). pap. 5.95 (*0-316-11590-8*) Little Brown Children's Bks.

—Arthur's Valentine. 1982. (Arthur Adventure Ser.). (Illus.). 32p. (J). (gr. k-3). pap. 1.95 o.p. (*0-380-57075-0*, 57075-0, Avon Bks.) Morrow/Avon.

—Arthur's Valentine. 1986. (Arthur Adventure Ser.). (J). (gr. k-3). 42.52 incl. audio (*0-394-69884-3*) SRA/McGraw-Hill.

—Arthur's Valentine. 1980. (Arthur Adventure Ser.). (J). (gr. k-3). 12.10 (*0-606-03717-9*) Turtleback Bks.

—Arthur's Valentine Countdown. 1999. (Arthur Ser.). (Illus.). 12p. (J). (ps-3). bds. 7.99 (*0-679-88475-0*, Random Hse. Bks. for Young Readers) Random Hse. Children's Bks.

—Arthur's $10 Allowance. 1996. (Illus.). (J). 10.00 (*0-316-11512-6*) Little Brown & Co.

—Arturo Tiene Varicela. Sarfatti, Esther, tr. from ENG. 2001. (SPA., Illus.). (J). (gr. k-2). pap. 6.95 (*1-930332-00-9*, LC30182) Lectorum Pubns., Inc.

—Arturo y el Destrastre de la Computadora. 2001. Tr. of Arthur's Computer Disaster. (SPA., Illus.). (J). 13.10 (*0-606-21044-X*) Turtleback Bks.

—Arturo y el Negocio de Mascotas. Sarfatti, Esther, tr. (SPA.). (J). (gr. k-2). pap. 6.95 (*1-880507-94-3*, LC8511) Lectorum Pubns., Inc.

—Arturo y el Negocio de Mascotas. 2001. (Arthur's Adventures in Spanish Ser.). (SPA., Illus.). (J). 13.10 (*0-606-21045-8*) Turtleback Bks.

—Arturo y los Terribles Gemelos. Sarfatti, Esther, tr. from ENG. 2000. (Arthur Adventure Ser.). (SPA., Illus.). (J). (gr. k-3). pap. 6.95 (*1-880507-65-X*, LC2344) Lectorum Pubns., Inc.

—Arturo y los Terribles Gemelos. 2000. (Arthur Adventure Ser.). (J). (gr. k-3). 13.10 (*0-606-17569-5*) Turtleback Bks.

—Arturo y Sus Problemas con el Profesor. 1994. (Arthur Adventure Ser.). (SPA.). (J). (gr. k-3). 15.95 o.p. (*0-316-11379-4*) Little Brown Children's Bks.

—Arturo y Sus Problemas con el Profesor. 1986. (Arthur Adventure Ser.). (SPA.). (J). (gr. k-3). 12.10 (*0-606-06188-6*) Turtleback Bks.

—Binky Rules. 2000. (Arthur Chapter Book Ser.: No. 24). (Illus.). 64p. (J). (gr. 3-6). pap. 3.95 (*0-316-12333-1*) Little Brown & Co.

—Binky Rules. 2000. (Arthur Chapter Book Ser.: No. 24). (Illus.). 64p. (J). (gr. 3-6). 13.95 (*0-316-12193-2*) Little Brown Children's Bks.

—Binky Rules. 2000. (Arthur Chapter Book Ser.: No. 24). (J). (gr. 3-6). 10.10 (*0-606-19447-9*) Turtleback Bks.

—Buster Makes the Grade. 1999. (Arthur Chapter Book Ser.: No. 16). (J). (gr. 3-6). pap. 3.95 (*0-316-12262-9*); (Illus.). 64p. pap. 3.95 (*0-316-12277-7*) Little Brown Children's Bks.

—Buster Makes the Grade. 1999. (Arthur Chapter Book Ser.: No. 16). (J). (gr. 3-6). 10.10 (*0-606-17235-1*) Turtleback Bks.

—Buster's Dino Dilemma. 1998. (Arthur Chapter Book Ser.: No. 7). (Illus.). 64p. (J). (gr. 3-6). pap. 3.95 (*0-316-11560-6*); 13.95 (*0-316-11559-2*) Little Brown Children's Bks.

—Buster's Dino Dilemma. (Arthur Chapter Book Ser.: No. 7). 58p. (J). (gr. 3-6). pap. 3.95 (*0-8072-1303-9*); 1999. pap. 17.00 incl. audio (*0-8072-0397-1*, FTR198SP) Random Hse. Audio Publishing Group. (Listening Library).

—Buster's Dino Dilemma. 1998. (Arthur Chapter Book Ser.: No. 7). (J). (gr. 3-6). 10.10 (*0-606-15906-1*) Turtleback Bks.

—Buster's New Friend, Vol. 23. 2000. (Arthur Chapter Book Ser.: No. 23). (Illus.). 64p. (J). (gr. 3-6). pap. 4.25 (*0-316-12307-2*) Little Brown & Co.

—Buster's New Friend. 2000. (Arthur Chapter Book Ser.: No. 23). (Illus.). 64p. (J). (gr. 3-6). 13.95 (*0-316-12212-2*) Little Brown Children's Bks.

—Buster's New Friend. 2000. (Arthur Chapter Book Ser.: No. 23). (J). (gr. 3-6). 10.10 (*0-606-19446-0*) Turtleback Bks.

—D. W., Go to Your Room! 1999. (D. W. Ser.). (Illus.). 32p. (J). (gr. k-2). 13.95 (*0-316-10905-3*) Little Brown Children's Bks.

—D. W. Thinks Big. 1999. (D. W. Ser.). (Illus.). 32p. (J). (gr. k-2). pap. 17.95 (*0-316-11966-0*) Little Brown Children's Bks.

—D. W.'s Lost Blankie. 2002. (D.W. Ser.). (Illus.). (J). 13.15 (*0-7587-2330-X*) Book Wholesalers, Inc.

—D. W.'s Lost Blankie. 2000. (D. W. Ser.). (Illus.). 24p. (J). (gr. k-2). pap. 5.95 (*0-316-11595-9*) Little Brown Children's Bks.

—D. W.'s Lost Blankie. 1998. (D. W. Ser.). (J). (gr. k-2). 12.10 (*0-606-17848-1*) Turtleback Bks.

—La Fiesta de Arturo. 1999. (Arthur Adventure Ser.). (SPA., Illus.). (J). (gr. k-3). pap. 6.95 (*1-880507-64-1*, LC2343) Lectorum Pubns., Inc.

—La Fiesta de Arturo. 1996. (Arthur Adventure Ser.). (J). (gr. k-3). 13.10 (*0-606-17582-2*) Turtleback Bks.

—Francine, Believe It or Not. 1999. (Arthur Chapter Book Ser.: No. 14). (Illus.). 64p. (J). (gr. 3-6). 13.95 (*0-316-12011-1*); pap. 3.95 (*0-316-12258-0*) Little Brown Children's Bks.

—Francine, Believe It or Not Special Scholastic Edition. 1999. (Arthur Chapter Book Ser.: No. 14). (J). (gr. 3-6). pap. 3.95 (*0-316-10463-9*) Little Brown Children's Bks.

—King Arthur. 2002. (Arthur Chapter Bks.). (Illus.). (J). 11.45 (*0-7587-0631-6*) Book Wholesalers, Inc.

—King Arthur. 1999. (Arthur Chapter Book Ser.: No. 13). (J). (gr. 3-6). pap. 3.95 (*0-316-10667-4*); (Illus.). 64p. pap. 3.95 (*0-316-12241-6*) Little Brown Children's Bks.

—King Arthur. unabr. ed. 2001. (Arthur Chapter Bks.: Vol. 13). 58p. (J). (gr. 1-3). pap. 17.00 incl. audio (*0-8072-0344-0*, Listening Library) Random Hse. Audio Publishing Group.

—King Arthur. 1999. (Arthur Chapter Book Ser.: No. 13). (J). (gr. 3-6). 10.10 (*0-606-16804-4*) Turtleback Bks.

—Kiss Hello, Kiss Good-Bye. 1997. (Arthur Ser.). 12p. (J). (ps-k). bds. 4.99 o.s.i (*0-679-86739-2*, Random Hse. Bks. for Young Readers) Random Hse. Children's Bks.

—Locked in the Library. 1999. (Arthur Chapter Book Ser.: No. 6). (Illus.). (J). (gr. 3-6). pap. 11.05 (*0-613-07017-8*) Econo-Clad Bks.

—Locked in the Library. 1998. (Arthur Chapter Book Ser.: No. 6). (Illus.). 64p. (J). (gr. 3-6). 12.95 (*0-316-11557-6*); pap. 4.25 (*0-316-11558-4*) Little Brown Children's Bks.

—Locked in the Library. (Arthur Chapter Book Ser.: No. 6). 58p. (J). (gr. 3-6). pap. 3.95 (*0-8072-1300-4*); 1998. pap. 17.00 incl. audio (*0-8072-0388-2*, FTR192SP) Random Hse. Audio Publishing Group. (Listening Library).

—Locked in the Library. 1998. (Arthur Chapter Book Ser.: No. 6). (J). (gr. 3-6). 10.10 (*0-606-15915-0*) Turtleback Bks.

—Muffy's Secret Admirer. 1999. (Arthur Chapter Book Ser.: No. 17). (J). (gr. 3-6). pap. 3.95 (*0-316-12047-2*); (Illus.). 64p. 13.95 (*0-316-12017-0*); (Illus.). 64p. pap. 3.95 (*0-316-12230-0*) Little Brown Children's Bks.

—Muffy's Secret Admirer. 1999. (Arthur Chapter Book Ser.: No. 17). (J). (gr. 3-6). 10.10 (*0-606-17237-8*) Turtleback Bks.

—The Mystery of the Stolen Bike. 1998. (Arthur Chapter Book Ser.: No. 8). (Illus.). 64p. (J). (gr. 3-6). 12.95 (*0-316-11570-3*); pap. 3.95 (*0-316-11571-1*) Little Brown Children's Bks.

—The Mystery of the Stolen Bike. (Arthur Chapter Book Ser.: No. 8). 59p. (J). (gr. 3-6). pap. 3.95 (*0-8072-1304-7*); 1999. pap. 17.00 incl. audio (*0-8072-0401-3*, EFTR199SP) Random Hse. Audio Publishing Group. (Listening Library).

—The Mystery of the Stolen Bike. 1998. (Arthur Chapter Book Ser.: No. 8). (J). (gr. 3-6). 10.10 (*0-606-15916-9*) Turtleback Bks.

—Say the Magic Word. 1997. (Arthur Ser.). 12p. (J). (ps-k). bds. 4.99 o.s.i (*0-679-86736-8*, Random Hse. Bks. for Young Readers) Random Hse. Children's Bks.

—Untitled Marc Brown: Arthur Chapter Book, Vol. 33. 2004. (J). pap. 4.25 (*0-316-12681-0*) Little Brown & Co.

—La Visita del Señor Rataquemada. Sarfatti, Esther, tr. from ENG. 2003. (SPA.). (J). (gr. k-2). pap. 6.95 (*1-930332-41-6*) Lectorum Pubns., Inc.

—Who's in Love with Arthur? (Arthur Chapter Book Ser.: No. 10). (J). (gr. 3-6). 1999. pap. 3.95 (*0-316-10671-2*); 1998. (Illus.). 64p. 12.95 (*0-316-11539-8*); 1998. (Illus.). 64p. pap. 4.25 (*0-316-11540-1*) Little Brown Children's Bks.

—Who's in Love with Arthur? (Arthur Chapter Book Ser.: No. 10). (J). (gr. 3-6). 57p. pap. 3.95 (*0-8072-1306-3*); 1999. 15.98 incl. audio Random Hse. Audio Publishing Group.

Brown, Marc, illus. Arthur & the Big Blow-Up. 2002. (Arthur Chapter Bks.). (J). 11.45 (*0-7587-0000-8*) Book Wholesalers, Inc.

—Arthur & the Comet Crisis. 2002. (Arthur Chapter Bks.). (J). 11.70 (*1-4046-1061-8*) Book Wholesalers, Inc.

—Arthur & the Double Dare. 2002. (Arthur Chapter Bks.). (J). 11.70 (*0-7587-9423-1*) Book Wholesalers, Inc.

—Arthur & the Goalie Ghost. 2002. (Arthur Chapter Bks.). (J). 11.45 (*0-7587-6862-1*) Book Wholesalers, Inc.

—Arthur & the Pen-Pal Playoff. 2002. (Arthur Chapter Bks.). (J). 11.70 (*0-7587-6863-X*) Book Wholesalers, Inc.

Brown, Marc, reader. Arthur Goes to Camp. 1994. (Arthur Adventure Ser.). (J). (gr. k-3). 9.95 incl. audio (*0-316-11388-3*) Little Brown Children's Bks.

—Arthur's Eyes. 1993. (Arthur Adventure Ser.). (Illus.). (J). (gr. k-3). pap. 9.95 incl. audio (*0-316-11338-7*) Little Brown Children's Bks.

—Arthur's Pet Business. 1995. (Arthur Adventure Ser.). (Illus.). 32p. (J). (gr. k-3). 9.95 incl. audio (*0-316-11182-1*) Little Brown Children's Bks.

—Arthur's Teacher Trouble. 1994. (Arthur Adventure Ser.). (Illus.). (J). (gr. k-3). pap. 9.95 incl. audio (*0-316-11389-1*) Little Brown Children's Bks.

—Arthur's Tooth. 1993. (Arthur Adventure Ser.). (Illus.). (J). (gr. k-3). pap. 9.95 incl. audio (*0-316-11339-5*) Little Brown Children's Bks.

Brown, Marc & LeapFrog Staff, compiled by. Arthur & the Lost Diary. 2002. (Illus.). (J). (gr. k-3). 14.95 (*1-58605-916-5*, LeapFrog Schl. Hse.) LeapFrog Enterprises, Inc.

—Arthur Makes the Team. 2002. (J). (gr. k-3). 14.95 (*1-58605-914-9*, LeapFrog Schl. Hse.) LeapFrog Enterprises, Inc.

Brown, Marc & Nelson, Judith A. ABC Reach for the Stars! 1998. (Arthur Ser.). (Illus.). 24p. (J). (ps-3). pap. 3.99 o.s.i (*0-679-89284-2*, Random Hse. Bks. for Young Readers) Random Hse. Children's Bks.

—1, 2, 3 Monsters on Parade! 1998. (Arthur Ser.). 24p. (J). (ps-3). pap. 3.99 o.s.i (*0-679-89283-4*, Random Hse. Bks. for Young Readers) Random Hse. Children's Bks.

Brown, Marc & Sarfatti, Esther. Arturo y la Navidad. 2003. (J). pap. 6.95 (*1-930332-48-3*) Lectorum Pubns., Inc.

Brown, Marc, et al. Arthur Accused! 1998. (Arthur Chapter Book Ser.: No. 5). (Illus.). 64p. (J). (gr. 3-6). 12.95 (*0-316-11554-1*) Little Brown Children's Bks.

—Arthur & the Cootie-Catcher. 1999. (Arthur Chapter Book Ser.: No. 15). (Illus.). 64p. (J). (gr. 3-6). 13.95 (*0-316-11993-8*) Little Brown Children's Bks.

—Arthur & the Lost Diary. 1998. (Arthur Chapter Book Ser.: No. 9). (Illus.). 64p. (J). (gr. 3-6). 12.95 (*0-316-11573-8*) Little Brown Children's Bks.

—Arthur & the True Francine. 1996. (Arthur Adventure Ser.). (Illus.). 32p. (J). (gr. k-3). reprint ed. 15.95 (*0-316-11136-8*) Little Brown Children's Bks.

—Arthur Babysits. (Arthur Adventure Ser.). (J). (gr. k-3). 1996. 32p. pap. 9.95 incl. audio (*0-316-11103-1*); 1996. 32p. pap. 9.95 incl. audio (*0-316-11103-1*); 1994. (Illus.). 32p. pap. 5.95 (*0-316-11442-1*); 1993. (Illus.). pap. 9.95 incl. audio (*0-316-11336-0*); 1993. (Illus.). pap. 9.95 incl. audio (*0-316-11336-0*); 1992. (Illus.). 32p. 15.95 (*0-316-11293-3*) Little Brown Children's Bks.

—Arthur Goes to Camp. (Arthur Adventure Ser.). (Illus.). 32p. (J). (gr. k-3). 1984. pap. 5.95 (*0-316-11058-2*); 1982. 15.95 (*0-316-11218-6*) Little Brown Children's Bks.

—Arthur Meets the President. (Arthur Adventure Ser.). 32p. (J). (gr. k-3). 1996. pap. 9.95 incl. audio (*0-316-11044-2*); 1991. 15.95 (*0-316-11265-8*) Little Brown Children's Bks.

—Arthur's April Fool. 1983. (Arthur Adventure Ser.). (Illus.). 32p. (J). (gr. k-3). 16.95 (*0-316-11196-1*) Little Brown Children's Bks.

—Arthur's Baby. 1987. (Arthur Adventure Ser.). 32p. (J). (gr. k-3). 15.95 (*0-316-11123-6*) Little Brown Children's Bks.

—Arthur's Birthday. (Arthur Adventure Ser.). (Illus.). (J). (gr. k-3). 1993. pap. 9.95 incl. audio (*0-316-11337-9*); 1993. pap. 9.95 incl. audio (*0-316-11337-9*); 1991. 32p. pap. 5.95 (*0-316-11074-4*); 1989. 32p. 15.95 (*0-316-11073-6*) Little Brown Children's Bks.

—Arthur's Chicken Pox. (Arthur Adventure Ser.). 32p. (J). (gr. k-3). 1996. (Illus.). pap. 5.95 (*0-316-11050-7*); 1994. 15.95 (*0-316-11384-0*) Little Brown Children's Bks.

—Arthur's Christmas. (Arthur Adventure Ser.). (Illus.). (J). (gr. k-3). 1985. 30p. pap. 5.95 (*0-316-10993-2*); 1984. 32p. 15.95 (*0-316-11180-5*) Little Brown Children's Bks.

—Arthur's Eyes. 1979. (Arthur Adventure Ser.). (Illus.). 32p. (J). (gr. k-3). 15.95 (*0-316-11063-9*) Little Brown Children's Bks.

—Arthur's Family Vacation. 1993. (Arthur Adventure Ser.). 32p. (J). (gr. k-3). 15.95 (*0-316-11312-3*) Little Brown Children's Bks.

—Arthur's Halloween. (Arthur Adventure Ser.). (Illus.). 32p. (J). (gr. k-3). 1983. pap. 5.95 (*0-316-11059-0*); 1982. 15.95 (*0-316-11116-3*) Little Brown Children's Bks.

—Arthur's New Puppy. 1993. (Arthur Adventure Ser.). 32p. (J). (gr. k-3). 15.95 (*0-316-11355-7*) Little Brown Children's Bks.

—Arthur's Nose. (Arthur Adventure Ser.). (Illus.). 32p. (J). (gr. k-3). 1986. pap. 5.95 (*0-316-11070-1*); 1976. 15.95 (*0-316-11193-7*) Little Brown Children's Bks.

—Arthur's Teacher Trouble. (Arthur Adventure Ser.). (Illus.). (J). (gr. k-3). 1989. 30p. pap. 5.95 (*0-316-11186-4*); 1987. 32p. 16.95 (*0-316-11244-5*) Little Brown Children's Bks.

—Arthur's Thanksgiving. (Arthur Adventure Ser.). (Illus.). (J). (gr. k-3). 1984. 30p. pap. 5.95 (*0-316-11232-1*); 1983. 32p. 15.95 (*0-316-11060-4*) Little Brown Children's Bks.

—Arthur's Tooth. (Arthur Adventure Ser.). (Illus.). 32p. (J). (gr. k-3). 1986. pap. 5.95 (*0-316-11246-1*); 1985. 15.95 (*0-316-11245-3*) Little Brown Children's Bks.

—Arthur's TV Trouble. 1995. (Arthur Adventure Ser.). (Illus.). 32p. (J). (gr. k-3). 16.95 (*0-316-10919-3*) Little Brown Children's Bks.

—Arthur's Valentine. (Arthur Adventure Ser.). 32p. (J). (gr. k-3). 1988. (Illus.). pap. 5.95 (*0-316-11187-2*); 1980. 15.95 (*0-316-11062-0*) Little Brown Children's Bks.

—Buster Makes the Grade. 1999. (Arthur Chapter Book Ser.: No. 16). (Illus.). 64p. (J). (gr. 3-6). 13.95 (*0-316-11960-1*) Little Brown Children's Bks.

—King Arthur. 1999. (Arthur Chapter Book Ser.: No. 13). (Illus.). 64p. (J). (gr. 3-6). 13.95 (*0-316-12178-9*) Little Brown Children's Bks.

Coren, Alan. Arthur & the Great Detective. 1980. (Illus.). 80p. (J). (gr. 3-7). 7.95 o.p. (*0-316-15736-8*) Little Brown & Co.

—Buffalo Arthur. 1978. (Illus.). (J). (gr. 4-6). 7.95 o.p. (*0-316-15738-4*) Little Brown & Co.

—Klondike Arthur. 1979. (Illus.). (J). (gr. 4-6). 7.95 o.p. (*0-316-15733-3*) Little Brown & Co.

—The Lone Arthur. 1978. (Illus.). (J). (gr. 4-6). 10.45 o.p. (*0-316-15739-2*) Little Brown & Co.

—Railroad Arthur. 1978. (Illus.). (J). (gr. 4-6). 7.95 o.p. (*0-316-15737-6*) Little Brown & Co.

Syverson-Stork, Jill, tr. Arturo y Sus Problemas con el Profesor. 1994. (Arthur Adventure Ser.). (SPA.). 32p. (J). (gr. k-3). pap. 5.95 (*0-316-11380-8*) Little Brown Children's Bks.

ARTHUR (FICTITIOUS CHARACTER: HOBAN)—FICTION

Hoban, Lillian. Arthur's Back to School Day. (I Can Read Bks.). (Illus.). 48p. (J). (gr. k-3). 1996. lib. bdg. 16.89 (*0-06-024956-0*); 1996. 15.95 o.p. (*0-06-024955-2*); 64th ed. 1998. pap. 3.95 (*0-06-444245-4*, Harper Trophy) HarperCollins Children's Bk. Group.

—Arthur's Back to School Day. 1998. (I Can Read Bks.). 10.10 (*0-606-16759-5*) Turtleback Bks.

—Arthur's Birthday Party. 1999. (I Can Read Bks.). (Illus.). 64p. (J). (gr. k-4). lib. bdg. 14.89 (*0-06-027799-8*); 14.95 (*0-06-027798-X*) HarperCollins Children's Bk. Group.

—Arthur's Camp-Out. (I Can Read Bks.). (Illus.). 64p. (J). 1994. (gr. k-3). pap. 3.99 (*0-06-444175-X*, Harper Trophy); 1993. (gr. k-3). lib. bdg. 16.89 (*0-06-020526-1*); 1993. (gr. 1-3). 14.00 o.p. (*0-06-020525-3*) HarperCollins Children's Bk. Group.

—Arthur's Camp-Out. 1994. (I Can Read Bks.). (J). (gr. 1-3). 10.10 (*0-606-06187-8*) Turtleback Bks.

—Arthur's Christmas Cookies. (I Can Read Bks.). (J). (gr. k-3). 1984. (Illus.). 64p. pap. 3.99 (*0-06-444055-9*, Harper Trophy); 1972. (Illus.). 64p. 14.00 (*0-06-022367-7*); 1972. (Illus.). 64p. lib. bdg. 15.89 (*0-06-022368-5*); Level 2. 1986. 5.98 incl. audio (*0-694-00162-7*, JC-145); Level 2. 1986. (Illus.). 64p. 5.98 o.p. (*0-694-00160-0*, Harper Trophy) HarperCollins Children's Bk. Group.

—Arthur's Christmas Cookies. unabr. ed. 1990. (I Can Read Bks.). (Illus.). 64p. (J). (gr. k-3). pap. 8.99 incl. audio (*1-55994-217-7*, HarperAudio) HarperTrade.

—Arthur's Christmas Cookies. 1984. (I Can Read Bks.). (J). (gr. k-3). 10.10 (*0-606-01986-3*) Turtleback Bks.

—Arthur's Funny Money. 2002. (Arthur the Chimpanzee Ser.). (Illus.). (J). 12.34 (*0-7587-5985-1*) Book Wholesalers, Inc.

—Arthur's Funny Money. (I Can Read Bks.). (Illus.). 64p. (J). 1984. (gr. k-3). pap. 3.99 (*0-06-444048-6*, Harper Trophy); 1981. (gr. k-3). lib. bdg. 15.89 (*0-06-022344-8*); 1981. (gr. 1-3). 11.95 (*0-06-022343-X*); 1990. (gr. k-3). pap. 8.99 incl. audio (*1-55994-218-5*); level 2. 1987. (gr. 1-3). 5.98 o.p. incl. audio (*0-694-00173-2*, JC-166, Harper Trophy) HarperCollins Children's Bk. Group.

—Arthur's Funny Money. 1984. (I Can Read Bks.). (J). (gr. 1-3). 10.10 (*0-606-03367-X*) Turtleback Bks.

—Arthur's Great Big Valentine. (I Can Read Bks.). (Illus.). 64p. (J). 1991. (gr. k-3). pap. 3.95 (*0-06-444149-0*, Harper Trophy); 1989. (gr. k-3). lib. bdg. 15.89 (*0-06-022407-X*); 1989. (gr. 1-3). 14.00 (*0-06-022406-1*) HarperCollins Children's Bk. Group.

—Arthur's Great Big Valentine. 1991. (I Can Read Bks.). (J). (gr. 1-3). 10.10 (*0-606-04609-7*) Turtleback Bks.

—Arthur's Halloween Costume. 2002. (Arthur the Chimpanzee Ser.). (Illus.). (J). 12.30 (*0-7587-5553-8*) Book Wholesalers, Inc.

—Arthur's Halloween Costume. (I Can Read Bks.). (Illus.). 64p. (J). (gr. k-3). 1986. pap. 3.95 (*0-06-444101-6*, Harper Trophy); 1984. 13.00 (*0-06-022387-1*); 1984. lib. bdg. 15.89 (*0-06-022391-X*) HarperCollins Children's Bk. Group.

—Arthur's Halloween Costume. 1986. (I Can Read Bks.). (J). (gr. 1-3). 10.10 (*0-606-03180-4*) Turtleback Bks.

—Arthur's Honey Bear. 2002. (Arthur the Chimpanzee Ser.). (Illus.). (J). 11.91 (*0-7587-5986-X*) Book Wholesalers, Inc.

—Arthur's Honey Bear. (I Can Read Bks.). (Illus.). 64p. (J). 1999. (ps-3). 12.95 o.p. (*0-694-01307-2*); 1982. (gr. k-3). pap. 3.99 (*0-06-444033-8*, Harper Trophy); 1974. (gr. k-3). 15.95 (*0-06-022369-3*); 1974. (gr. k-3). lib. bdg. 15.89 (*0-06-022370-7*); Level 2. 1986. (gr. 1-3). 5.98 o.p. incl. audio (*0-694-00116-3*, JC-066, Harper Trophy) HarperCollins Children's Bk. Group.

—Arthur's Honey Bear. unabr. ed. 1990. (I Can Read Bks.). (Illus.). 64p. (J). (gr. k-3). pap. 8.99 incl. audio (*1-55994-219-3*, Caedmon) HarperTrade.

—Arthur's Honey Bear. 1982. (I Can Read Bks.). (J). (gr. 1-3). pap. 1.95 (*0-590-10263-X*) Scholastic, Inc.

—Arthur's Loose Tooth. 2002. (Arthur the Chimpanzee Ser.). (Illus.). (J). 11.37 (*0-7587-5987-8*) Book Wholesalers, Inc.

—Arthur's Loose Tooth. (I Can Read Book 2 Ser.). (Illus.). 64p. (J). 2003. (ps-3). 8.99 incl. audio (*0-694-01578-4*); 2003. (ps-3). 8.99 incl. audio (*0-694-01578-4*); 1987. (gr. k-3). pap. 3.99 (*0-06-444093-1*, Harper Trophy); 1985. (gr. k-3). lib. bdg. 15.89 (*0-06-022354-5*); 1985. (gr. 1-3). 11.95 (*0-06-022353-7*) HarperCollins Children's Bk. Group.

—Arthur's Loose Tooth. 1992. (J). 16.25 o.p. (*0-8446-6555-X*) Smith, Peter Pub., Inc.

—Arthur's Loose Tooth. 1985. (I Can Read Bks.: Level 2). (J). (gr. 1-3). 10.10 (*0-606-03545-1*) Turtleback Bks.

—Arthur's Pen Pal. 2002. (Arthur the Chimpanzee Ser.). (Illus.). (J). 12.34 (*0-7587-5989-4*) Book Wholesalers, Inc.

—Arthur's Pen Pal. 1982. (gr. 1-3). pap. 11.05 (*0-8085-3054-2*) Econo-Clad Bks.

—Arthur's Pen Pal. (I Can Read Bks.). (Illus.). 64p. (J). (gr. k-3). 1982. pap. 3.99 (*0-06-444032-X*, Harper Trophy); 1976. lib. bdg. 15.89 (*0-06-022372-3*) HarperCollins Children's Bk. Group.

—Arthur's Pen Pal. 1990. (I Can Read Bks.). (Illus.). (J). 32p. (gr. 1-3). pap. 6.95 incl. audio (*0-00-004236-6*, Caedmon); 64p. (gr. k-3). pap. 8.99 incl. audio (*1-55994-238-X*, HarperAudio) HarperTrade.

—Arthur's Pen Pal. 1976. (I Can Read Bks.). (J). (gr. 1-3). 10.10 (*0-606-00380-0*) Turtleback Bks.

—Arthur's Prize Reader. 2002. (Arthur the Chimpanzee Ser.). (Illus.). (J). 12.30 (*0-7587-5554-6*) Book Wholesalers, Inc.

—Arthur's Prize Reader. (I Can Read Bks.). (Illus.). 64p. (J). 1985. (gr. 1-3). 5.98 o.p. incl. audio (*0-694-00016-7*, Harper Trophy); 1985. (gr. 1-3). 5.98 o.p. incl. audio (*0-694-00016-7*, Harper Trophy); 1984. (gr. k-3). pap. 3.95 (*0-06-444049-4*, Harper Trophy); 1978. (gr. k-3). lib. bdg. 15.89 (*0-06-022380-4*); 1978. (gr. 1-3). 13.00 o.p. (*0-06-022379-0*) HarperCollins Children's Bk. Group.

—Arthur's Prize Reader. unabr. ed. 1990. (I Can Read Bks.). (Illus.). 64p. (J). (gr. k-3). pap. 8.95 incl. audio (*1-55994-220-7*, HarperAudio) HarperTrade.

—Arthur's Prize Reader. 1978. (I Can Read Bks.). (J). (gr. 1-3). 10.10 (*0-606-03365-3*) Turtleback Bks.

Hoban, Lillian, et al. Arthur's Camp-Out. 1996. (I Can Read Bks.). (Illus.). 64p. (J). (gr. k-3). 8.95 incl. audio (*0-694-70040-1*) HarperCollins Pubs.

ARTHUR, KING—FICTION

Barkan, Joanne. A Pup in King Arthur's Court. 1998. (Adventures of Wishbone Ser.: No. 15). (Illus.). 164p. (J). (gr. 2-5). pap. 3.99 o.p. (*1-57064-325-3*) Lyrick Publishing.

—A Pup in King Arthur's Court. l.t. ed. 1999. (Adventures of Wishbone Ser.: No. 15). (Illus.). 164p. (J). (gr. 2-5). lib. bdg. 22.60 (*0-8368-2593-4*) Stevens, Gareth Inc.

Brown, Marc. King Arthur. 2002. (Arthur Chapter Bks.). (Illus.). (J). 11.45 (*0-7587-0631-6*) Book Wholesalers, Inc.

—King Arthur. 1999. (Arthur Chapter Book Ser.: No. 13). (J). (gr. 3-6). pap. 3.95 (*0-316-10667-4*) Little Brown Children's Bks.

—King Arthur. unabr. ed. 2001. (Arthur Chapter Bks.: Vol. 13). 58p. (J). (gr. 1-3). pap. 17.00 incl. audio (*0-8072-0344-0*, Listening Library) Random Hse. Audio Publishing Group.

—King Arthur. 1999. (Arthur Chapter Book Ser.: No. 13). (J). (gr. 3-6). 10.10 (*0-606-16804-4*) Turtleback Bks.

Brown, Marc, et al. King Arthur. 1999. (Arthur Chapter Book Ser.: No. 13). (Illus.). 64p. (J). (gr. 3-6). 13.95 (*0-316-12178-9*) Little Brown Children's Bks.

Browne, N. M. Warriors of Camlann. 2003. (Illus.). 275p. (YA). 16.95 (*1-58234-817-0*, Bloomsbury Children) Bloomsbury Publishing.

Bulla, Clyde Robert. The Sword in the Tree. 1956. (Illus.). (J). (gr. 2-5). 12.95 (*0-690-79908-X*) HarperCollins Children's Bk. Group.

Los Caballeros del Rey Arturo. (SPA., Illus.). (YA). 14.95 (*84-7281-107-7*, AF1107) Auriga, Ediciones S.A. ESP. *Dist:* Continental Bk. Co., Inc.

Crossley-Holland, Kevin. At the Crossing-Places. 2002. (Arthur Trilogy: Bk. 2). (J). 394p. pap. 5.99 (*0-439-26599-1*); 352p. (gr. 9 up). 17.95 (*0-439-26598-3*) Scholastic, Inc. (Levine, Arthur A. Bks.).

—At the Crossing Places. unabr. ed. 2002. (J). (gr. 4-7). audio 30.00 (*0-8072-0540-0*, Listening Library) Random Hse. Audio Publishing Group.

—The Seeing Stone. unabr. ed. 2001. (YA). audio 30.00 (*0-8072-0538-9*, Listening Library) Random Hse. Audio Publishing Group.

—The Seeing Stone. 2002. (Arthur Trilogy: Vol. 1). 352p. (YA). (gr. 5 up). pap. 6.99 (*0-439-43524-2*); 2002. (Arthur Trilogy: Bk. 1). (Illus.). 352p. (J). (gr. 4-7). pap. 6.99 (*0-439-26327-1*); 2001. (Illus.). 368p. (J). (gr. 5-8). trans. 17.95 (*0-439-26326-3*) Scholastic, Inc. (Levine, Arthur A. Bks.).

Characters

Dixon, Andy. Los Caballeros del Rey Arturo. 2001. (SPA., Illus.). 32p. (YA). (gr. 3 up). pap. 8.95 (*0-7460-3896-8*); lib. bdg. 16.95 (*1-58086-318-3*) EDC Publishing. (Usborne).

—King Arthur's Knight Quest. 1999. (Usborne Fantasy Adventure Ser.). (Illus.). 32p. (YA). (gr. 3 up). pap. 8.95 (*0-7460-3394-X*) EDC Publishing.

Gelders-Sterne, Emma. King Arthur & the Knights of the Round Table. 2002. (Illus.). 160p. (J). (gr. 1). lib. bdg. 21.99 (*0-307-90432-6*, Golden Bks.) Random Hse. Children's Bks.

Green, Roger Lancelyn. King Arthur & His Knights of the Round Table. 1993. (Everyman's Library Children's Classics Ser.). 368p. (gr. 2 up). 14.95 (*0-679-42311-7*) Knopf, Alfred A. Inc.

—King Arthur & His Knights of the Round Table. (Puffin Classics Ser.). (J). 1995. (Illus.). 352p. (gr. 4-7). pap. 4.99 (*0-14-036670-9*, Puffin Bks.); 1990. 288p. (gr. 5 up). pap. 3.99 o.p. (*0-14-035100-0*, Puffin Bks.); 1974. 288p. (gr. 5-7). pap. 2.95 o.p. (*0-14-030073-2*, Viking Children's Bks.) Penguin Putnam Bks. for Young Readers.

—King Arthur & His Knights of the Round Table. abr. ed. 1997. (Children's Classics Ser.). 2p. (J). pap. 10.95 o.s.i incl. audio (*0-14-086369-9*, Penguin AudioBooks) Viking Penguin.

Hill, Pamela Smith. The Last Grail Keeper. 2001. 288p. (J). (gr. 6-8). tchr. ed. 17.95 (*0-8234-1574-0*) Holiday Hse., Inc.

Hoffman, Mary. Women of Camelot: Queens & Enchantresses at the Court of King Arthur. 2000. (Illus.). 72p. (J). 19.95 (*0-7892-0646-3*) Abbeville Pr., Inc.

Lister, Robin. The Story of King Arthur. 1996. (Kingfisher Classics Ser.). (Illus.). 96p. (J). (gr. 4 up). pap. 15.95 (*0-7534-5101-8*, Kingfisher) Houghton Mifflin Co. Trade & Reference Div.

McCafferty, Catherine. Quest for Camelot. 1998. (J). (*0-7853-2383-X*) Publications International, Ltd.

Morpurgo, Michael. Arthur, High King of Britain. 1995. (Illus.). 144p. (YA). (gr. 4-7). 22.00 (*0-15-200080-1*) Harcourt Children's Bks.

Morris, Gerald. Parsifal's Page. 240p. (J). (gr. 5-9). 2004. pap. 5.95 (*0-618-43237-X*); 2001. (Illus.). tchr. ed. 15.00 (*0-618-05509-6*) Houghton Mifflin Co.

Springer, Nancy. I Am Mordred: A Tale from Camelot. 2002. (Firebird Ser.). 192p. (YA). (gr. 7 up). pap. 5.99 (*0-698-11841-3*, Firebird) Penguin Putnam Bks. for Young Readers.

—I Am Mordred: A Tale from Camelot. unabr. ed. 2000. (YA). pap. 68.99 incl. audio (*0-7887-3006-1*, 40888X4) Recorded Bks., LLC.

—I Am Morgan Le Fay: A Tale from Camelot. 2001. ix, 227p. (J). (gr. 7 up). 17.99 (*0-399-23451-9*, Philomel) Penguin Putnam Bks. for Young Readers.

—I Am Morgan le Fay: A Tale from Camelot. 2002. (Firebird Ser.). 240p. (J). pap. 5.99 (*0-698-11974-6*, Firebird) Penguin Putnam Bks. for Young Readers.

Sutcliff, Rosemary. The Light Beyond the Forest: The Quest for the Holy Grail. 1994. 144p. (J). (gr. 7 up). pap. 4.99 (*0-14-037150-8*, Puffin Bks.) Penguin Putnam Bks. for Young Readers.

—The Light Beyond the Forest: The Quest for the Holy Grail. 1994. 11.04 (*0-606-07024-9*) Turtleback Bks.

Thomson, Sarah L. The Dragon's Son. 2001. (Illus.). 181p. (J). (gr. 7 up). pap. 17.95 (*0-531-30333-0*, Orchard Bks.) Scholastic, Inc.

Twain, Mark. A Connecticut Yankee in King Arthur's Court. 1997. (Classics Illustrated Study Guides). (Illus.). 64p. (YA). (gr. 7 up). mass mkt., stu. ed. 4.99 o.p. (*1-57840-016-3*) Acclaim Bks.

—A Connecticut Yankee in King Arthur's Court. 1964. (Airmont Classics Ser.). (J). (gr. 5 up). mass mkt. 3.25 (*0-8049-0029-9*, CL-29) Airmont Publishing Co., Inc.

—A Connecticut Yankee in King Arthur's Court. 1999. (YA). reprint ed. pap. text 28.00 (*1-4047-1121-X*) Classic Textbooks.

—A Connecticut Yankee in King Arthur's Court. 1991. 333p. (gr. 4-7). mass mkt. 3.99 (*0-8125-0436-4*, Tor Classics) Doherty, Tom Assocs., LLC.

—A Connecticut Yankee in King Arthur's Court. 1988. (Books of Wonder). (Illus.). 384p. (J). (ps-3). 24.99 (*0-688-06346-2*) HarperCollins Children's Bk. Group.

—A Connecticut Yankee in King Arthur's Court. deluxe ltd. ed. 1988. (Books of Wonder). (Illus.). 384p. (YA). (gr. 5 up). 100.00 o.p. (*0-688-08258-0*, Morrow, William & Co.) Morrow/Avon.

—A Connecticut Yankee in King Arthur's Court. 1963. (Signet Classics). 336p. (YA). mass mkt. 4.95 (*0-451-52475-6*, Signet Classics) NAL.

—A Connecticut Yankee in King Arthur's Court. Fago, John N., ed. abr. ed. 1977. (Now Age Illustrated III Ser.). (Illus.). (gr. 4-12). (J). pap. text 2.95 (*0-88301-263-4*); (YA). text 7.50 o.p. (*0-88301-275-8*) Pendulum Pr., Inc.

Wein, Elizabeth. Winter Prince. 2003. (Firebird Ser.). (Illus.). 224p. (YA). pap. 6.99 (*0-14-250014-3*, Puffin Bks.) Penguin Putnam Bks. for Young Readers.

Wein, Elizabeth E. Coalition of Lions. 2003. 224p. (J). 16.99 (*0-670-03618-8*) Viking Penguin.

White, T. H. The Sword in the Stone. 1978. 288p. (YA). (gr. 5-12). mass mkt. 5.99 (*0-440-98445-9*, Laurel) Dell Publishing.

—The Sword in the Stone. (Illus.). 1993. 256p. (J). (gr. 2 up). 22.99 (*0-399-22502-1*, Philomel); 1972. 11.95 o.s.i (*0-399-10783-5*, G. P. Putnam's Sons) Penguin Putnam Bks. for Young Readers.

—The Sword in the Stone. 1963. 11.55 (*0-606-05065-5*) Turtleback Bks.

Williams, Marcia, illus. & retold by. King Arthur & the Knights of the Round Table. 1997. 32p. (J). (gr. 2-6). reprint ed. bds. 7.99 o.p. (*0-7636-0152-7*) Candlewick Pr.

Yolen, Jane. The Dragon's Boy: A Tale of Young King Arthur. 2001. (Illus.). (J). 11.00 (*0-606-21161-6*) Turtleback Bks.

—Sword of the Rightful King: A Novel of King Arthur. 2003. (Illus.). 368p. (J). 17.00 (*0-15-202527-8*) Harcourt Children's Bks.

ASTERIX (FICTITIOUS CHARACTER)—FICTION

Distribooks Inc. Staff. Asterix Bind-Ups: Asterix & Friends. 1998. (Asterix Ser.). (Illus.). (J). 29.95 (*0-340-72755-1*) Hodder & Stoughton, Ltd. GBR. *Dist:* Distribooks, Inc., Lubrecht & Cramer, Ltd., Trafalgar Square.

Goscinny, René. Absolutely Asterix. 1998. (Illus.). (J). text 29.95 (*0-340-72756-X*) Hodder & Stoughton, Ltd. GBR. *Dist:* Lubrecht & Cramer, Ltd., Trafalgar Square.

—Asterix: La Galere D'Obelix. 1996. (FRE.). 48p. (J). 24.95 (*0-7859-9352-5*) French & European Pubns., Inc.

—Asterix & Caesar's Gift. 1995. (Asterix Ser.). (Illus.). 44p. (J). (gr. 4-7). reprint ed. pap. 10.95 (*0-917201-68-X*) Dargaud Publishing Co. FRA. *Dist:* Distribooks, Inc.

—Asterix & Caesar's Gift, No. 19. (Illus.). 48p. (J). pap. text 9.95 (*0-340-23301-X*) International Language Centre.

—Asterix & Cleopatra. 1995. (Asterix Ser.). (Illus.). 44p. (J). (gr. 4-7). pap. 10.95 (*0-917201-75-2*) Dargaud Publishing Co. FRA. *Dist:* Distribooks, Inc.

—Asterix & Cleopatra, No. 4. 1976. (Asterix Ser.). (Illus.). (J). pap. text 9.95 (*0-340-17220-7*) International Language Centre.

—Asterix & Obelix All at Sea. 1996. 64p. (J). 24.95 (*0-7859-9452-1*) French & European Pubns., Inc.

—Asterix & the Banquet. 1995. (Asterix Ser.). (Illus.). 44p. (J). (gr. 4-7). reprint ed. pap. 10.95 (*0-917201-71-X*) Dargaud Publishing Co. FRA. *Dist:* Distribooks, Inc.

—Asterix & the Big Fight. 1995. (Asterix Ser.). (Illus.). 44p. (J). (gr. 4-7). reprint ed. pap. 10.95 (*0-917201-58-2*) Dargaud Publishing Co. FRA. *Dist:* Distribooks, Inc.

—Asterix & the Big Fight. 1976. (Asterix Ser.: No. 9). (Illus.). (J). pap. text 9.95 (*0-340-19167-8*) International Language Centre.

—Asterix & the Black Gold. 1984. (J). (gr. 4-7). pap. 10.95 (*0-340-32367-1*) Hodder & Stoughton, Ltd. GBR. *Dist:* Distribooks, Inc.

—Asterix & the Cauldron. 1995. (Asterix Ser.). (Illus.). 44p. (J). (gr. 4-7). reprint ed. pap. 10.95 (*0-917201-66-3*) Dargaud Publishing Co. FRA. *Dist:* Distribooks, Inc.

—Asterix & the Cauldron, No. 17. 1976. (Asterix Ser.). (Illus.). 48p. (J). pap. text 9.95 (*0-340-22711-7*) International Language Centre.

—Asterix & the Chieftain's Shield. 1995. (Asterix Ser.). (Illus.). 44p. (J). (gr. 4-7). reprint ed. pap. 10.95 (*0-917201-67-1*) Dargaud Publishing Co. FRA. *Dist:* Distribooks, Inc.

—Asterix & the Golden Sickle. 1995. (Asterix Ser.). (Illus.). 44p. (J). (gr. 4-7). reprint ed. pap. 10.95 (*0-917201-64-7*) Dargaud Publishing Co. FRA. *Dist:* Distribooks, Inc.

—Asterix & the Great Crossing. 1995. (Asterix Ser.). (Illus.). 44p. (J). (gr. 4-7). pap. 10.95 (*0-917201-65-5*) Dargaud Publishing Co. FRA. *Dist:* Distribooks, Inc.

—Asterix & the Great Divide. 1982. (Adventures of Asterix Ser.: No. 26). (J). pap. text 10.95 (*0-340-27627-4*) Hodder & Stoughton, Ltd. GBR. *Dist:* Distribooks, Inc.

—Asterix & the Laurel Wreath. 1995. (Asterix Ser.). (Illus.). 44p. (J). (gr. 4-7). reprint ed. pap. 10.95 (*0-917201-62-0*) Dargaud Publishing Co. FRA. *Dist:* Distribooks, Inc.

—Asterix & the Normans. 1995. (Asterix Ser.). (Illus.). 44p. (J). (gr. 4-7). reprint ed. pap. 10.95 (*0-917201-69-8*) Dargaud Publishing Co. FRA. *Dist:* Distribooks, Inc.

—Asterix & the Normans. (Illus.). (J). pap. 9.95 (*0-02-497290-8*) International Language Centre.

—Asterix & the Roman Agent. 1995. (Asterix Adventure Ser.). (Illus.). 44p. (J). reprint ed. pap. 10.95 (*0-917201-59-0*) Dargaud Publishing Co. FRA. *Dist:* Distribooks, Inc.

—Asterix & the Roman Agent, No. 10. 1976. (Asterix Ser.: No. 10). (Illus.). (J). pap. text 9.95 (*0-340-19168-6*) International Language Centre.

—Asterix & the Soothsayer. 1995. (Asterix Ser.). (Illus.). 44p. (J). (gr. 4-7). reprint ed. pap. 10.95 (*0-917201-63-9*) Dargaud Publishing Co. FRA. *Dist:* Distribooks, Inc.

—Asterix & the Soothsayer, No. 14. 1976. (Asterix Ser.). (Illus.). 48p. (J). pap. text 9.95 (*0-340-20697-7*) International Language Centre.

—Asterix at the Olympic Games. 1995. (Asterix Ser.). (Illus.). 44p. (J). (gr. 4-7). pap. 10.95 (*0-917201-61-2*) Dargaud Publishing Co. FRA. *Dist:* Distribooks, Inc.

—Asterix at the Olympic Games, No. 12. 1976. (Asterix Ser.: No. 12). (Illus.). (J). pap. text 9.95 (*0-340-19169-4*) International Language Centre.

—Asterix aux Jeux Olympiques. 1990. (FRE.). (J). (gr. 7-9). 24.95 (*0-8288-5109-3*, FC884) French & European Pubns., Inc.

—Asterix Chez les Bretons. 1990. (FRE.). (J). (gr. 7-9). 24.95 (*0-8288-5108-5*, FC880) French & European Pubns., Inc.

—Asterix Chez les Helvetes. 1990. (FRE., Illus.). (J). (gr. 7-9). 24.95 (*0-8288-5110-7*, FC889) French & European Pubns., Inc.

—Asterix Conquers America. 1997. (Asterix Ser.: Vol. 34). (J). pap. text 10.95 (*0-340-65347-7*) Hodder & Stoughton, Ltd. GBR. *Dist:* Distribooks, Inc., Lubrecht & Cramer, Ltd., Trafalgar Square.

—Asterix et Cleopatre. 1990. (FRE.). (J). (gr. 7-9). 24.95 (*0-8288-5112-3*, FC878) French & European Pubns., Inc.

—Asterix et la Serpe d'or. 1990. (FRE., Illus.). (J). (gr. 3-8). 24.95 (*0-8288-4939-0*) French & European Pubns., Inc.

—Asterix et la Surprise de Cesar. 1993. (FRE.). 64p. (J). lib. bdg. 24.95 (*0-7859-3651-3*, 2865030044) French & European Pubns., Inc.

—Asterix et le Chaudron. 1990. (FRE., Illus.). (J). (gr. 7-9). 24.95 (*0-8288-5113-1*, FC885) French & European Pubns., Inc.

—Asterix et les Goths. 1990. (FRE.). (J). (gr. 7-9). 24.95 (*0-8288-5114-X*, FC875) French & European Pubns., Inc.

—Asterix et les Normands. 1990. (FRE.). (J). (gr. 7-9). 24.95 (*0-8288-5115-8*, FC881) French & European Pubns., Inc.

—Asterix Gladiateur. 1990. (FRE.). (J). (gr. 7-9). 24.95 (*0-8288-5116-6*, FC876) French & European Pubns., Inc.

—Asterix in Belgium. 1995. (Asterix Ser.). (Illus.). 44p. (J). (gr. 4-7). reprint ed. pap. 10.95 (*0-917201-73-6*) Dargaud Publishing Co. FRA. *Dist:* Distribooks, Inc.

—Asterix in Belgium, No. 25. (Illus.). (J). pap. text 9.95 (*0-340-27753-X*) International Language Centre.

—Asterix in Britain. 1995. (Asterix Ser.). (Illus.). 44p. (J). (gr. 4-7). pap. 10.95 (*0-917201-74-4*) Dargaud Publishing Co. FRA. *Dist:* Distribooks, Inc.

—Asterix in Britain, No. 3. 1976. (Asterix Ser.). (Illus.). (J). pap. text 9.95 (*0-340-17221-5*) International Language Centre.

—Asterix in Corsica. 1995. (Asterix Ser.). (Illus.). 44p. (J). (gr. 4-7). reprint ed. pap. 10.95 (*0-917201-72-8*) Dargaud Publishing Co. FRA. *Dist:* Distribooks, Inc.

—Asterix in Corsica, No. 24. (Illus.). 48p. (J). pap. text 9.95 (*0-340-27754-8*) International Language Centre.

—Asterix in Spain. 1995. (Asterix Ser.). (Illus.). 44p. (J). (gr. 4-7). reprint ed. pap. 10.95 (*0-917201-51-5*) Dargaud Publishing Co. FRA. *Dist:* Distribooks, Inc.

—Asterix in Spain, No. 2. 1976. (Asterix Ser.). (Illus.). (J). pap. text 9.95 (*0-340-18326-8*) International Language Centre.

—Asterix in Switzerland. 1995. (Asterix Ser.). (Illus.). 44p. (J). (gr. 4-7). reprint ed. pap. 10.95 (*0-917201-57-4*) Dargaud Publishing Co. FRA. *Dist:* Distribooks, Inc.

—Asterix in Switzerland. 1976. (Asterix Ser.: No. 8). (Illus.). (J). pap. text 9.95 (*0-340-19270-4*) International Language Centre.

—Asterix la Zizanie. 1990. (FRE., Illus.). (J). (gr. 7-9). 24.95 (*0-8288-5117-4*, FC888) French & European Pubns., Inc.

—Asterix le Gaulois. 1990. (FRE.). (J). (gr. 7-9). 24.95 (*0-8288-5118-2*, FC873) French & European Pubns., Inc.

—Asterix Legionnaire. 1990. (FRE.). (J). (gr. 7-9). 24.95 (*0-8288-5119-0*, FC882) French & European Pubns., Inc.

—Asterix the Gaul. (Illus.). (J). pap. text 9.95 (*0-340-17210-X*) International Language Centre.

—Asterix the Gladiator. 1995. (Asteric Comic Book Ser.). (Illus.). 44p. (J). (gr. 4-7). reprint ed. pap. 10.95 (*0-917201-55-8*) Dargaud Publishing Co. FRA. *Dist:* Distribooks, Inc.

—Asterix the Gladiator. 1976. (Asterix Ser.: No. 6). (Illus.). (J). pap. text 9.95 (*0-340-18320-9*) International Language Centre.

—Asterix the Legionary. 1995. (Asterix Ser.). (Illus.). 44p. (J). (gr. 4-7). pap. 10.95 (*0-917201-56-6*) Dargaud Publishing Co. FRA. *Dist:* Distribooks, Inc.

—Asterix the Legionary. 1976. (Asterix Ser.: No. 7). (Illus.). (J). pap. text 9.95 (*0-340-18321-7*) International Language Centre.

—Asterix vs. Caesar. 1997. (Adventures of Asterix Ser.: No. 29). (J). pap. text 10.95 (*0-340-39723-3*) Hodder & Stoughton, Ltd. GBR. *Dist:* Distribooks, Inc.

—The Banquet, No. 23. (Illus.). (J). pap. text 9.95 (*0-340-26429-2*) International Language Centre.

—The Chieftain's Shield, No. 18. 1977. (Asterix Ser.). (Illus.). 48p. (J). pap. text 9.95 (*0-340-22710-9*) International Language Centre.

—The Golden Sickle, No. 15. 1976. (Asterix Ser.). (Illus.). 48p. (J). pap. text 9.95 (*0-340-21209-8*) International Language Centre.

—The Great Crossing, No. 16. 1976. (Asterix Ser.). (Illus.). 48p. (J). pap. text 9.95 (*0-340-21589-5*) International Language Centre.

—The Laurel Wreath, No. 13. 1976. (Asterix Ser.). (Illus.). 48p. (J). pap. text 9.95 (*0-340-20699-3*) International Language Centre.

—The Mansion of the Gods. 1976. (Asterix Ser.: No. 11). (Illus.). (J). pap. text 9.95 (*0-340-19269-0*) International Language Centre.

—The Mansions of the Gods. 1995. (Asterix Ser.). (Illus.). 44p. (J). (gr. 4-7). reprint ed. pap. 10.95 (*0-917201-60-4*) Dargaud Publishing Co. FRA. *Dist:* Distribooks, Inc.

—Obelix & Company. 1995. (Asterix Ser.). (Illus.). 44p. (J). (gr. 4-7). reprint ed. pap. 10.95 (*0-917201-70-1*) Dargaud Publishing Co. FRA. *Dist:* Distribooks, Inc.

—Obelix & Company, No. 22. (Illus.). 48p. (J). pap. text 9.95 (*0-340-25307-X*) International Language Centre.

—The Twelve Tasks of Asterix, No. 21. (Illus.). 56p. (J). pap. text 9.95 (*0-340-27647-9*) International Language Centre.

Goscinny, René & Uderzo, Albert. Asterix Aetepekioe en Oayammie. 1992. (GRE.). (J). 24.95 (*0-7859-1040-9*, 9602202661) French & European Pubns., Inc.

—Asterix & Maestria. 1992. (GER.). (J). 24.95 (*0-7859-1025-5*, 3770400291) French & European Pubns., Inc.

—Asterix & Son. 1992. (J). 19.95 (*0-7859-1047-6*, 0-340-330082) French & European Pubns., Inc.

—Asterix & Son. 1983. (Asterix Ser.: No. 28). (J). pap. text 10.95 (*0-340-35331-7*) Hodder & Stoughton, Ltd. GBR. *Dist:* Distribooks, Inc.

—Asterix & the Banquet. 1992. (J). 19.95 (*0-7859-1042-5*, 0-340-231742) French & European Pubns., Inc.

—Asterix & the Black Gold. 1992. (J). 19.95 (*0-7859-1046-8*, 0-340-27476X) French & European Pubns., Inc.

—Asterix & the Great Divide. 1992. (J). 19.95 (*0-7859-1045-X*, 0-340-259884) French & European Pubns., Inc.

—Asterix & the Magic Carpet. 1992. (J). 19.95 (*0-7859-1048-4*, 0-340-409576) French & European Pubns., Inc.

—Asterix Apud Brittannos. 1992. (LAT.). (J). 24.95 (*0-7859-1029-8*, 3770400593) French & European Pubns., Inc.

—Asterix Atque Olla Cypria. 1992. (LAT.). (J). 24.95 (*0-7859-1033-6*, 3770400666) French & European Pubns., Inc.

—Asterix aux Jeux Olympiques. 1992. (FRE.). (J). 19.95 (*0-7859-0986-9*, 2205003208) French & European Pubns., Inc.

—Asterix Certamen Principum. 1992. (LAT.). (J). 24.95 (*0-7859-1027-1*, 3770400577) French & European Pubns., Inc.

—Asterix Chez les Bretons. 1992. (FRE.). (J). 19.95 (*0-7859-1075-1*, 220500185X) French & European Pubns., Inc.

—Asterix Chez les Helvetes. 1992. (FRE.). (J). 19.95 (*0-7859-0989-3*, 2205005162) French & European Pubns., Inc.

—Asterix Chez Rahazade. 1992. (FRE.). (J). 19.95 (*0-7859-1016-6*, 2864970201) French & European Pubns., Inc.

—Asterix Clipeus Arvernus. 1992. (LAT.). (J). 24.95 (*0-7859-1077-8*, 377040064X) French & European Pubns., Inc.

—Asterix en Corse. 1992. (FRE.). (J). 19.95 (*0-7859-0991-5*, 2205006940) French & European Pubns., Inc.

—Asterix en Hispania. 1992. (SPA.). (J). 24.95 (*0-7859-1039-5*, 8475100287) French & European Pubns., Inc.

—Asterix en Hispanie. 1992. (FRE.). (J). 24.95 (*0-7859-0988-5*, 2205003941) French & European Pubns., Inc.

—Asterix et Cleopatra. 1992. (LAT.). (J). 24.95 (*0-7859-1026-3*, 3770400569) French & European Pubns., Inc.

—Asterix et Cleopatre. 1992. (FRE.). (J). 19.95 (*0-7859-0981-8*, 2205001574) French & European Pubns., Inc.

—Asterix et la Surprise de Cesar. 1992. (FRE.). (J). 24.95 (*0-7859-0993-1*, 2205030044) French & European Pubns., Inc.

—Asterix et le Chaudron. 1992. (FRE.). (J). 19.95 (*0-7859-0987-7*, 2205003364) French & European Pubns., Inc.

—Asterix et les Normands. 1992. (FRE.). (J). 19.95 (*0-7859-0983-4*, 2205001906) French & European Pubns., Inc.

—Asterix et Normanni. 1992. (LAT.). (J). 24.95 (*0-7859-1031-X*, 3770400615) French & European Pubns., Inc.

—Asterix Gladiateur. 1992. (FRE.). (J). 19.95 (*0-7859-0980-X*, 2205001345) French & European Pubns., Inc.

—Asterix in Belgium. 1992. (J). 19.95 (*0-7859-1044-1*, 0-340-257350) French & European Pubns., Inc.

—Asterix in Corsica. 1992. (J). 19.95 (*0-7859-1043-3*, 240741) French & European Pubns., Inc.

—Asterix in Hispania. 1992. (LAT.). (J). 24.95 (*0-7859-1034-4*, 3770400674) French & European Pubns., Inc.

—Asterix la Rosa y la Espada. 1992. (SPA.). (J). 24.95 (*0-7859-1038-7*, 8474199123) French & European Pubns., Inc.

—Asterix la Rose et le Glaive. 1992. (FRE.). (J). 24.95 (*0-7859-1017-4*, 2864970538) French & European Pubns., Inc.

—Asterix le Gaulois. 1992. (FRE.). (J). 19.95 (*0-7859-0979-6*, 2205000969) French & European Pubns., Inc.

—Asterix Legionnaire. 1992. (FRE.). (J). 19.95 (*0-7859-0984-2*, 2205002309) French & European Pubns., Inc.

—Asterix Olympius. 1992. (LAT.). (J). 24.95 (*0-7859-0959-1*, 0-377-040658) French & European Pubns., Inc.

—Asterix Orientalis. 1992. (LAT.). (J). 24.95 (*0-7859-1035-2*, 3770400682) French & European Pubns., Inc.

—Filius Asterix. 1992. (LAT.). (J). 24.95 (*0-7859-1032-8*, 3770400623) French & European Pubns., Inc.

—Der Sohn des Asterix. 1992. (GER.). (J). 24.95 (*0-7859-1024-7*, 3770400275) French & European Pubns., Inc.

—Uderzo de Flamberge a Asterix. 1993. (FRE.). 64p. (J). 24.95 (*0-7859-3653-X*, 2865030077) French & European Pubns., Inc.

Goscinny, René & Uderzo, M. Asterix: Comment Obelix est Tombe dans la Marmite du Druide Quand Il Etait Petit. 1990. (FRE.). (J). 24.95 (*0-8288-8597-4*) French & European Pubns., Inc.

—Asterix: How Obelix Fell into the Magic Cauldron When He Was a Little Boy. 1990. (J). 24.95 (*0-8288-8594-X*) French & European Pubns., Inc.

—Asterix als Gladiator. 1992. (GER., Illus.). (J). (gr. 7-10). 24.95 (*0-8288-4923-4*) French & European Pubns., Inc.

—Asterix als Legionar. 1992. (GER., Illus.). (J). (gr. 7-10). 24.95 (*0-8288-4924-2*) French & European Pubns., Inc.

—Asterix & Caesar's Gift. 1990. (Illus.). (J). (gr. 7-10). 24.95 (*0-8288-4915-3*) French & European Pubns., Inc.

—Asterix & Cleopatra. 1990. (Illus.). (J). (gr. 7-10). 24.95 (*0-8288-4916-1*) French & European Pubns., Inc.

—Asterix & Operation Getafix. 1990. (J). 24.95 (*0-8288-8570-2*) French & European Pubns., Inc.

—Asterix & Son. 1990. (J). 24.95 (*0-8288-8568-0*) French & European Pubns., Inc.

—Asterix & the Banquet. 1990. (J). 24.95 (*0-8288-8590-7*) French & European Pubns., Inc.

—Asterix & the Big Fight. 1990. (Illus.). (J). (gr. 7-10). 24.95 (*0-8288-4917-X*) French & European Pubns., Inc.

—Asterix & the Black Gold. 1990. (J). 24.95 (*0-8288-8592-3*) French & European Pubns., Inc.

—Asterix & the Chieftain's Shield. 1990. (Illus.). (J). (gr. 7-10). 24.95 (*0-8288-4918-8*) French & European Pubns., Inc.

—Asterix & the Goths. 1990. (Illus.). (J). (gr. 7-10). 24.95 (*0-8288-4919-6*) French & European Pubns., Inc.

—Asterix & the Great Divide. 1990. (J). 24.95 (*0-8288-8567-2*) French & European Pubns., Inc.

—Asterix & the Laurel Wreath. 1990. (Illus.). (J). (gr. 7-10). 24.95 (*0-8288-4920-X*) French & European Pubns., Inc.

—Asterix & the Magic Carpet. 1990. (J). 24.95 (*0-8288-8569-9*) French & European Pubns., Inc.

—Asterix & the Normans. 1990. (Illus.). (J). (gr. 7-10). 24.95 (*0-8288-4921-8*) French & European Pubns., Inc.

—Asterix & the Roman Agent. 1990. (Illus.). (J). (gr. 7-10). 24.95 (*0-8288-4922-6*) French & European Pubns., Inc.

—Asterix apud Gothos. 1990. (LAT., Illus.). (J). (gr. 7-10). lib. bdg. 24.95 (*0-8288-4925-0*) French & European Pubns., Inc.

—Asterix at the Olympic Games. 1990. (Illus.). (J). (gr. 7-10). 24.95 (*0-8288-4926-9*) French & European Pubns., Inc.

—Asterix auf Korsika. 1990. (GER., Illus.). (J). (gr. 7-10). lib. bdg. 24.95 (*0-8288-4927-7*) French & European Pubns., Inc.

—Asterix bei den Briten. 1990. (GER., Illus.). (J). (gr. 7-10). lib. bdg. 24.95 (*0-8288-4928-5*) French & European Pubns., Inc.

—Asterix bei den Olympischen Spielen. 1990. (GER., Illus.). (J). (gr. 7-10). lib. bdg. 24.95 (*0-8288-4929-3*) French & European Pubns., Inc.

—Asterix bei den Schweizern. 1990. (GER., Illus.). (J). (gr. 7-10). lib. bdg. 24.95 (*0-8288-4930-7*) French & European Pubns., Inc.

—Asterix chez les Belges. 1990. (FRE., Illus.). (J). (gr. 7-10). 24.95 (*0-8288-4931-5*) French & European Pubns., Inc.

—Asterix Chez Rahazade. 1990. (FRE.). (J). 24.95 (*0-8288-8572-9*) French & European Pubns., Inc.

—Asterix der Gallier. 1990. (GER., Illus.). (J). (gr. 7-10). lib. bdg. 24.95 (*0-8288-4932-3*) French & European Pubns., Inc.

—Asterix el Galo. (SPA., Illus.). (J). (gr. 7-10). 24.95 (*0-8288-4933-1*) French & European Pubns., Inc.

—Asterix en Bretana. 1990. (SPA., Illus.). (J). (gr. 7-10). lib. bdg. 24.95 (*0-8288-4934-X*) French & European Pubns., Inc.

—Asterix en Corcega. 1990. (SPA., Illus.). (J). (gr. 7-10). lib. bdg. 24.95 (*0-8288-4935-8*) French & European Pubns., Inc.

—Asterix en Corse. 1990. (FRE., Illus.). (J). (gr. 7-10). 24.95 (*0-8288-4936-6*) French & European Pubns., Inc.

—Asterix en Helvecia. 1990. (SPA., Illus.). (J). (gr. 7-10). lib. bdg. 24.95 (*0-8288-4937-4*) French & European Pubns., Inc.

—Asterix en los Juegos Olimpicos. 1990. (SPA., Illus.). (J). (gr. 7-10). lib. bdg. 24.95 (*0-8288-4938-2*) French & European Pubns., Inc.

—Asterix et la Rose et le Glaive. 1990. (FRE.). (J). 24.95 (*0-8288-8573-7*) French & European Pubns., Inc.

—Asterix Gallus. 1990. (LAT., Illus.). (J). (gr. 7-10). lib. bdg. 24.95 (*0-8288-4941-2*) French & European Pubns., Inc.

—Asterix Gladiador. 1990. (SPA., Illus.). (J). (gr. 7-10). lib. bdg. 24.95 (*0-8288-4942-0*) French & European Pubns., Inc.

—Asterix Gladiator. 1990. (LAT., Illus.). (J). 24.95 (*0-8288-4943-9*) French & European Pubns., Inc.

—Asterix in Belgium. 1990. (J). 24.95 (*0-8288-8591-5*) French & European Pubns., Inc.

—Asterix in Britain. 1990. (Illus.). (J). 24.95 (*0-8288-4944-7*) French & European Pubns., Inc.

—Asterix in Corsica. 1990. (J). 24.95 (*0-8288-8566-4*) French & European Pubns., Inc.

—Asterix in Spain. 1990. (Illus.). (J). 24.95 (*0-8288-4945-5*) French & European Pubns., Inc.

—Asterix in Spanien. 1990. (GER., Illus.). (J). lib. bdg. 24.95 (*0-8288-4946-3*) French & European Pubns., Inc.

—Asterix in Switzerland. 1990. (Illus.). (J). lib. bdg. 24.95 (*0-8288-4947-1*) French & European Pubns., Inc.

—Asterix iter Gallicum. 1990. (LAT., Illus.). (J). lib. bdg. 24.95 (*0-8288-4948-X*) French & European Pubns., Inc.

—Asterix Legionario. 1990. (SPA., Illus.). (J). lib. bdg. 24.95 (*0-8288-4949-8*) French & European Pubns., Inc.

—Asterix, Obelix & Company. 1990. (J). 24.95 (*0-8288-8565-6*) French & European Pubns., Inc.

—Asterix the Gaul. 1990. (Illus.). (J). 24.95 (*0-8288-4950-1*) French & European Pubns., Inc.

—Asterix the Gladiator. 1990. (Illus.). (J). 24.95 (*0-8288-4951-X*) French & European Pubns., Inc.

—Asterix the Legionary. 1990. (Illus.). (J). 24.95 (*0-8288-4952-8*) French & European Pubns., Inc.

—Asterix und die Goten. 1990. (GER., Illus.). (J). lib. bdg. 24.95 (*0-8288-4953-6*) French & European Pubns., Inc.

—Asterix und Kleopatra. 1990. (GER., Illus.). (J). lib. bdg. 24.95 (*0-8288-4954-4*) French & European Pubns., Inc.

—Asterix Versus Caesar. 1990. (J). 24.95 (*0-8288-8593-1*) French & European Pubns., Inc.

—Asterix y Cleopatra. 1990. (SPA., Illus.). (J). lib. bdg. 24.95 (*0-8288-4955-2*) French & European Pubns., Inc.

—Asterix y el Caldero. 1990. (SPA., Illus.). (J). lib. bdg. 24.95 (*0-8288-4956-0*) French & European Pubns., Inc.

—Asterix y los Godos. 1990. (SPA., Illus.). (J). lib. bdg. 24.95 (*0-8288-4957-9*) French & European Pubns., Inc.

—Asterix y los Normandos. 1990. (SPA., Illus.). (J). lib. bdg. 24.95 (*0-8288-4958-7*) French & European Pubns., Inc.

—Streit um Asterix. (GER., Illus.). (J). 24.95 (*0-8288-4906-4*) French & European Pubns., Inc.

Goscinny, René, et al. Asterix & the Goths. 1995. (Asterix Ser.). (Illus.). 44p. (J). (gr. 4-7). reprint ed. pap. 10.95 (*0-917201-54-X*) Dargaud Publishing Co. FRA. *Dist:* Distribooks, Inc.

—Asterix the Gaul. 1995. (Asterix Ser.). (Illus.). 44p. (J). (gr. 4-7). reprint ed. pap. 10.95 (*0-917201-50-7*) Dargaud Publishing Co. FRA. *Dist:* Distribooks, Inc.

Uderzo, Albert. Asterix & Obelix All at Sea. 2002. (Asterix Ser.). (Illus.). 48p. (YA). pap. 9.95 (*0-7528-4778-3*) Orion Publishing Group, Ltd. GBR. *Dist:* Trafalgar Square.

—Asterix & the Actress. Bell, Anthea & Hockridge, Derek, trs. from FRE. 2001. (Illus.). 48p. (J). (gr. 5). 12.95 (*0-7528-4657-4*) Sterling Publishing Co., Inc.

—Asterix & the Secret Weapon. 2002. (Asterix Ser.). (Illus.). 48p. (YA). pap. 9.95 (*0-7528-4777-5*) Orion Publishing Group, Ltd. GBR. *Dist:* Trafalgar Square.

Uderzo, Albert & Goscinny, René. Asterix & the Actress. 2002. (Asterix Ser.). (Illus.). 48p. pap. 9.95 (*0-7528-4658-2*) Orion Publishing Group, Ltd. GBR. *Dist:* Trafalgar Square.

—The Complete Guide to Asterix. Bell, Anthea & Hockridge, Derek, trs. from FRE. 1997. (Adventures of Asterix Ser.). (Illus.). 105p. (J). reprint ed. 29.95 o.p. (*0-340-65346-9*) Distribooks, Inc.

AUDUBON, JOHN JAMES, 1785-1851—FICTION

Brenner, Barbara. On the Frontier with Mr. Audubon. 1977. (Illus.). (J). (gr. 3-6). 12.95 o.p. (*0-698-20385-2*, Coward-McCann) Putnam Publishing Group, The.

AUNT EATER (FICTITIOUS CHARACTER)—FICTION

Cushman, Doug. Aunt Eater Loves a Mystery. 2002. (Aunt Eater Mysteries Ser.). (Illus.). (J). 12.30 (*0-7587-5990-8*) Book Wholesalers, Inc.

—Aunt Eater Loves a Mystery. 2001. (First Readers Ser.). (J). lib. bdg. (*1-59054-001-8*) Fitzgerald Bks.

—Aunt Eater Loves a Mystery. (I Can Read Bks.). (Illus.). 64p. (J). 1989. (gr. k-3). pap. 3.99 (*0-06-444126-1*, Harper Trophy); 1987. (gr. k-3). lib. bdg. 15.89 (*0-06-021327-2*); 1987. (gr. 1-3). 13.00 (*0-06-021326-4*) HarperCollins Children's Bk. Group.

—Aunt Eater Loves a Mystery. unabr. ed. 1991. (I Can Read Bks.). (Illus.). 64p. (J). (gr. k-3). pap. 8.95 incl. audio (*1-55994-435-8*, HarperAudio) HarperTrade.

—Aunt Eater Loves a Mystery. 1987. (I Can Read Bks.). (J). (gr. 1-3). 10.10 (*0-606-04162-1*) Turtleback Bks.

—Aunt Eater's Mystery Christmas. 2002. (Aunt Eater Mysteries Ser.). (Illus.). (J). 12.30 (*0-7587-5991-6*) Book Wholesalers, Inc.

—Aunt Eater's Mystery Christmas. (I Can Read Bks.). (Illus.). 64p. (J). 1996. (ps-3). pap. 3.99 (*0-06-444221-7*, Harper Trophy); 1995. (gr. 1-3). lib. bdg. 14.89 (*0-06-023580-2*); 1995. (gr. 1-3). 14.95 o.p. (*0-06-023579-9*) HarperCollins Children's Bk. Group.

—Aunt Eater's Mystery Christmas. 1996. (I Can Read Bks.). (J). (gr. 1-3). 10.10 (*0-606-10130-6*) Turtleback Bks.

—Aunt Eater's Mystery Halloween. 2002. (Aunt Eater Mysteries Ser.). (Illus.). (J). 11.91 (*0-7587-5992-4*) Book Wholesalers, Inc.

—Aunt Eater's Mystery Halloween. (I Can Read Bks.). (Illus.). (J). (gr. k-3). 1999. 64p. pap. 3.99 (*0-06-444266-7*, Harper Trophy); 1998. 40p. lib. bdg. 14.89 (*0-06-027804-8*) HarperCollins Children's Bk. Group.

—Aunt Eater's Mystery Halloween. 1998. (I Can Read Bks.). (Illus.). 64p. (J). (gr. k-3). 14.95 (*0-06-027803-X*, Perennial) HarperTrade.

—Aunt Eater's Mystery Halloween. 1999. (I Can Read Bks.). 10.10 (*0-606-17301-3*) Turtleback Bks.

—Aunt Eater's Mystery Vacation. 2002. (Aunt Eater Mysteries Ser.). (Illus.). (J). 12.30 (*0-7587-5993-2*) Book Wholesalers, Inc.

—Aunt Eater's Mystery Vacation. (I Can Read Bks.). (Illus.). 64p. (J). 1993. (gr. k-3). pap. 3.99 (*0-06-444169-5*, Harper Trophy); 1992. (gr. 1-3). 14.95 o.p. (*0-06-020513-X*); 1992. (ps-3). lib. bdg. 15.89 (*0-06-020514-8*) HarperCollins Children's Bk. Group.

—Aunt Eater's Mystery Vacation. 1993. (I Can Read Bks.). (J). (gr. 1-3). 10.10 (*0-606-05732-3*) Turtleback Bks.

AUSTIN FAMILY (FICTITIOUS CHARACTERS)—FICTION

L'Engle, Madeleine. The Anti-Muffins. 1981. (Education of the Public & the Public School Ser.). (Illus.). 48p. (J). (gr. 3-6). 7.95 o.p. (*0-8298-0415-3*) Pilgrim Pr., The/United Church Pr.

—A Full House: An Austin Family Christmas. 2000. (Illus.). 48p. (J). (gr. 4-7). 12.99 o.s.i (*0-87788-020-4*, Shaw) WaterBrook Pr.

—Meet the Austins. 2002. (Illus.). (J). 13.94 (*0-7587-8955-6*) Book Wholesalers, Inc.

—Meet the Austins. 1981. 192p. (YA). (gr. 4-7). mass mkt. 5.50 (*0-440-95777-X*, Laurel) Dell Publishing.

—Meet the Austins, RS. 1997. (Austin Family Ser.). (Illus.). 224p. (J). (gr. 5-9). 17.00 (*0-374-34929-0*, Farrar, Straus & Giroux (BYR)) Farrar, Straus & Giroux.

—Meet the Austins. 1960. (J). 10.55 (*0-606-02172-8*) Turtleback Bks.

—The Moon by Night. 1981. (Austin Family Ser.: Vol. 2). 256p. (YA). (gr. 5-9). mass mkt. 4.99 (*0-440-95776-1*, Laurel) Dell Publishing.

—The Moon by Night, RS. 1963. 224p. (J). (gr. 5-9). 16.00 o.s.i (*0-374-35049-3*, Farrar, Straus & Giroux (BYR)) Farrar, Straus & Giroux.

—The Moon by Night. 1963. (Austin Family Ser.). (J). 11.04 (*0-606-02181-7*) Turtleback Bks.

—A Ring of Endless Light, RS. 1980. 336p. (J). (gr. 4-7). 20.00 (*0-374-36299-8*, Farrar, Straus & Giroux (BYR)) Farrar, Straus & Giroux.

—A Ring of Endless Light. 1995. (J). mass mkt. 5.99 (*0-440-91081-1*, Dell Books for Young Readers); 1981. (Austin Family Ser.: Vol. 3). 336p. (YA). (gr. 4-7). mass mkt. 5.99 (*0-440-97232-9*, Laurel Leaf) Random Hse. Children's Bks.

—A Ring of Endless Light. 1980. (Austin Family Ser.). (J). 12.04 (*0-606-02243-0*) Turtleback Bks.

—The Twenty-Four Days Before Christmas: An Austin Family Story. 1987. (Young Yearling Ser.). 80p. (ps-3). pap. text 3.99 o.s.i (*0-440-40105-4*, Yearling) Random Hse. Children's Bks.

—The Twenty-Four Days Before Christmas: An Austin Family Story. 1984. (Dell Young Yearling Ser.). (J). 10.14 (*0-606-04059-5*) Turtleback Bks.

—The Young Unicorns, RS. 1968. 256p. (J). (gr. 5-9). 16.00 o.s.i (*0-374-38778-8*, Farrar, Straus & Giroux (BYR)) Farrar, Straus & Giroux.

—The Young Unicorns. 1989. 288p. (YA). (gr. 4-7). mass mkt. 5.50 (*0-440-99919-7*, Laurel Leaf) Random Hse. Children's Bks.

—The Young Unicorns. 1968. (J). 11.04 (*0-606-01893-X*) Turtleback Bks.

B

BABAR (FICTITIOUS CHARACTER)—FICTION

Babar Comes to America. (J). audio o.p. HarperTrade.

de Brunhoff, Jean. A. B. C. de Babar. 1978. (FRE.). 46p. (J). 15.95 o.p. (*0-8288-4858-0*, M11808); (Illus.). 24.95 (*0-7859-8776-2*) French & European Pubns., Inc.

—Babar: Lemon Surprise. 1997. (Babar Ser.). (Illus.). (J). (ps-3). (*0-7853-2358-9*) Publications International, Ltd.

—Babar & Father Christmas. Haas, Merle S., tr. unabr. ed. 1984. (Babar Ser.).Tr. of Babar et le Pere Noel. (J). (ps-3). audio 9.95 (*1-55994-067-0*, CPN 1488, Caedmon) HarperTrade.

—Babar & Father Christmas. Haas, Merle, tr. from FRE. 2001. Tr. of Babar et le Pere Noel. 48p. (J). (gr. 3). 15.95 (*0-375-81444-2*); (Illus.). (ps-2). lib. bdg. 17.99 (*0-375-91444-7*) Random Hse. Children's Bks. (Random Hse. Bks. for Young Readers).

—Babar & Father Christmas. 1949. (Babar Ser.).Tr. of Babar et le Pere Noel. (Illus.). (J). (ps-3). 10.00 o.s.i (*0-394-80578-X*, Random Hse. Bks. for Young Readers) Random Hse. Children's Bks.

—Babar & His Children. (Babar Ser.).Tr. of Babar en Famille. (J). (ps-3). audio. audio o.p. HarperTrade.

—Babar & His Children. 1989. (Babar Ser.).Tr. of Babar en Famille. (Illus.). 48p. (J). (ps-3). 16.95 o.s.i (*0-679-80165-0*, Random Hse. Bks. for Young Readers) Random Hse. Children's Bks.

—Babar & His Children. Haas, Merle, tr. from FRE. (Babar Ser.).Tr. of Babar en Famille. (Illus.). 48p. (J). (ps-3). 1969. lib. bdg. 17.99 (*0-394-90577-6*); 1954. 15.95 (*0-394-80577-1*) Random Hse. Children's Bks. (Random Hse. Bks. for Young Readers).

—Babar & Zephir. Haas, Merle, tr. (Babar Ser.). (Illus.). 48p. (J). (ps-3). 1969. lib. bdg. 17.99 o.p. (*0-394-90579-2*); 1942. 15.95 (*0-394-80579-8*) Random Hse. Children's Bks. (Random Hse. Bks. for Young Readers).

—Babar Comes to America. Craig, Jean M., tr. unabr. ed. 1984. (Babar Ser.). (J). (ps-3). audio 9.95 (*0-89845-931-1*, CPN 1551, Caedmon) HarperTrade.

Characters

—Babar en Famille. 1975. (Babar Ser.).Tr. of Babar & His Children. (FRE., Illus.). 26p. (J). (ps-3). 15.95 (*0-7859-0672-X*, FC589) French & European Pubns., Inc.

—Babar et le Crocodile. 1975. (Babar Ser.). (FRE., Illus.). 16p. (J). (ps-3). 4.95 (*0-7859-0673-8*, FC242) French & European Pubns., Inc.

—Babar et le Pere Noel. 1975. (Babar Ser.).Tr. of Babar & Father Christmas. (FRE., Illus.). 29p. (J). (ps-3). 15.95 (*0-7859-0674-6*, FC582) French & European Pubns., Inc.

—Babar et le Pere Noel. 1991. (Babar Ser.).Tr. of Babar & Father Christmas. (FRE.). (J). (ps-3). 14.95 incl. audio Olivia & Hill Pr., The.

—Babar Retrouve Ses Amis. 1994. (Babar Ser.). (FRE., Illus.). (J). (ps-3). pap. 17.95 (*0-7859-8790-8*) French & European Pubns., Inc.

—Babar the King. ed. 1984. Tr. of Roi Babar. (J). (gr. 2). spiral bd. (*0-616-01629-8*) Canadian National Institute for the Blind/Institut National Canadien pour les Aveugles.

—Babar the King. (Babar Ser.).Tr. of Roi Babar. (J). (ps-3). audio o.p. HarperTrade.

—Babar the King. Haas, Merle S., tr. unabr. ed. 1994. (Babar Ser.).Tr. of Roi Babar. (Illus.). (J). (ps-3). audio 9.95 (*0-89845-930-3*, CPN 1487, Caedmon) HarperTrade.

—Babar the King. (Babar Ser.).Tr. of Roi Babar. (Illus.). (J). (ps-3). 1986. 48p. 14.95 o.s.i (*0-394-88245-8*); 1967. 56p. lib. bdg. 17.99 (*0-394-90580-6*); 1937. 56p. 15.95 (*0-394-80580-1*) Random Hse. Children's Bks. (Random Hse. Bks. for Young Readers).

—Babar y Papa Noel. (Babar Ser.).Tr. of Babar & Father Christmas. (SPA., Illus.). 56p. (J). (ps-3). 12.95 o.p. (*84-204-3702-6*) Santillana USA Publishing Co., Inc.

—Bonjour, Babar! The Six Unabridged Classics by the Creator of Barbar. Schulman, Janet, ed. Haas, Merle, tr. unabr. ed. 2000. (Babar Ser.). (Illus.). 280p. (J). (ps-3). 29.95 (*0-375-81060-9*, Random Hse. Bks. for Young Readers) Random Hse. Children's Bks.

—Le Couronnement de Babar. 1975. (Babar Ser.). (FRE., Illus.). 16p. (J). (ps-3). 4.95 (*0-7859-0930-3*, FC251) French & European Pubns., Inc.

—Histoire de Babar, le Petit Elephant. 2001. (Babar Ser.).Tr. of Story of Babar, the Little Elephant. (J). (ps-3). 13.95 (*2-01-002519-9*) Istra FRA. *Dist:* Distribooks, Inc.

—El Rey Babar. (Babar Ser.).Tr. of Babr the King. (SPA., Illus.). 56p. (J). (ps-3). 11.50 o.p. (*84-204-3038-2*) Santillana USA Publishing Co., Inc.

—The Story of Babar. braille ed. 1992. (J). (gr. 2). spiral bd. (*0-616-01628-X*) Canadian National Institute for the Blind/Institut National Canadien pour les Aveugles.

—The Story of Babar. (Babar Ser.). (Illus.). (J). (ps-3). 1967. 56p. lib. bdg. 17.99 o.p. (*0-394-90575-X*, Random Hse. Bks. for Young Readers); 1937. 56p. 15.95 (*0-394-80575-5*, Random Hse. Bks. for Young Readers); 1984. 48p. 19.00 o.s.i (*0-394-86823-4*, Random Hse. Bks. for Young Readers); 1991. 48p. 4.95 o.s.i (*0-679-81049-8*, Random Hse. Bks. for Young Readers); 1989. 48p. reprint ed. pap. 5.99 o.s.i (*0-394-82940-9*, Knopf Bks. for Young Readers) Random Hse. Children's Bks.

—The Story of Babar. 9999. (Babar Ser.). (Illus.). (J). (ps-3). pap. 2.25 o.p. (*0-590-10235-4*) Scholastic, Inc.

—The Travels of Babar. (Babar Ser.). (Illus.). 56p. (J). (ps-3). 1967. lib. bdg. 17.99 (*0-394-90576-8*); 1937. 15.95 (*0-394-80576-3*) Random Hse. Children's Bks. (Random Hse. Bks. for Young Readers).

—Les Vacances de Zephyr. 1983. 40p. (J). 24.95 (*0-7859-8797-5*) French & European Pubns., Inc.

—Les Vacances de Zephyr. 2000. (Babar Ser.). (FRE.). (J). 13.95 (*2-01-003571-2*) Istra FRA. *Dist:* Distribooks, Inc.

—Vive le Roi Babar. 1976. (Babar Ser.). (FRE., Illus.). 20p. (J). (ps-3). 4.95 (*0-7859-0675-4*, FC253) French & European Pubns., Inc.

—Le Voyage de Babar. 1975. (Babar Ser.). (FRE., Illus.). 27p. (J). (ps-3). 15.95 (*0-7859-0676-2*, FC581) French & European Pubns., Inc.

—Le Voyage de Babar. 1999. (Babar Ser.). (FRE., Illus.). (J). (ps-3). 13.95 (*2-01-002518-0*) Istra FRA. *Dist:* Distribooks, Inc.

de Brunhoff, Jean & de Brunhoff, Laurent. Babar: Royal Parade. 1997. (Babar Ser.). (Illus.). (J). (ps-3). (*0-7853-2357-0*) Publications International, Ltd.

—Babar: Snapshots from Celesteville. 1997. (Babar Ser.). (Illus.). (J). (ps-3). (*0-7853-2365-1*) Publications International, Ltd.

—Babar a la Ferme. 1990. (Babar Ser.). (FRE., Illus.). 48p. (J). (ps-3). 17.95 (*0-7859-8778-9*) French & European Pubns., Inc.

—Babar a la Fete. 1990. (Babar Ser.). (FRE., Illus.). 48p. (J). (ps-3). 17.95 (*0-7859-8779-7*) French & European Pubns., Inc.

—Babar a la Maison. 1990. (Babar Ser.). (Illus.). 48p. (J). (ps-3). 17.95 (*0-7859-8780-0*) French & European Pubns., Inc.

—Babar a la Ville. 1990. (Babar Ser.). (FRE., Illus.). 48p. (J). (ps-3). 17.95 (*0-7859-8781-9*) French & European Pubns., Inc.

—Babar & Father Christmas. (Babar Ser.).Tr. of Babar et le Pere Noel. (J). (ps-3). audio o.p. HarperTrade.

—Babar & His Friends In Celesteville. 1991. (Babar Ser.). (Illus.). 48p. (J). (ps-3). 6.99 o.s.i (*0-517-05213-X*) Random Hse. Value Publishing.

—Babar & His Friends In the Forest. 1991. (Babar Ser.). (Illus.). 48p. (J). (ps-3). 6.99 o.s.i (*0-517-05212-1*) Random Hse. Value Publishing.

—Babar Concierto para Piano. 2001. Tr. of Babar in the Piano Concert. (SPA., Illus.). (*84-7546-546-3*) Beascoa, Ediciones S.A.

—Babar en el Fantasma de la Opera. 2001. Tr. of Babar in the Phantom of the Opera. (SPA., Illus.). (*84-7546-545-5*) Beascoa, Ediciones S.A.

—Babar en Famille. 1999. (Babar Ser.).Tr. of Babar & His Children. (FRE., Illus.). (J). (ps-3). 13.95 (*2-01-002516-4*) Distribooks, Inc.

—Babar en Foret. 1990. (Babar Ser.). (FRE., Illus.). 48p. (J). (ps-3). 17.95 (*0-7859-8782-7*) French & European Pubns., Inc.

—Babar en la Carrera a la Luna. 2001. Tr. of Babar & the Race to the Moon. (SPA., Illus.). (*84-7546-547-1*) Beascoa, Ediciones S.A.

—Babar en Pequenos Amigos. 2001. Tr. of Babar in Little Friends. (SPA., Illus.). (*84-7546-556-0*) Beascoa, Ediciones S.A.

—Babar en Vacances. 1990. (Babar Ser.). (FRE., Illus.). 48p. (J). (ps-3). 17.95 (*0-7859-8783-5*) French & European Pubns., Inc.

—Babar Fait Ses Courses. 1991. (Babar Ser.). (FRE., Illus.). 48p. (J). (ps-3). 17.95 (*0-7859-8788-6*) French & European Pubns., Inc.

—Babar y Sus Amigos Van de Compras. 2001. Tr. of Babar & Friends Go Shopping. (SPA.). (*84-7546-679-6*) Beascoa, Ediciones S.A.

—Babar y Sus Amigos Van de Viaje. 2001. Tr. of Babar & Friends Go on a Trip. (*84-7546-677-X*) Beascoa, Ediciones S.A.

—Babar's Anniversary Album. 1981. (Babar Ser.). (Illus.). 144p. (J). (ps-3). 18.00 o.s.i (*0-394-84813-6*); 16.99 o.s.i (*0-394-94813-0*) Random Hse. Children's Bks. (Random Hse. Bks. for Young Readers).

—Le Grand Album de Babar. 1982. (Babar Ser.). (FRE., Illus.). 142p. (J). (ps-3). 39.95 (*0-7859-8793-2*) French & European Pubns., Inc.

de Brunhoff, Jean & Lokvig, Tor. Le Livre Anime de Voyage de Babar. 1991. (Babar Ser.). (FRE., Illus.). (J). (ps-3). pap. 39.95 (*0-7859-8795-9*) French & European Pubns., Inc.

de Brunhoff, Jean, et al. Babar & His Friends at Home. 1991. (Babar Ser.). (Illus.). 48p. (J). (ps-3). 6.99 o.s.i (*0-517-05210-5*) Random Hse. Value Publishing.

—Babar & His Friends at the Farm. 1991. (Babar Ser.). (Illus.). 48p. (J). (ps-3). 6.99 o.s.i (*0-517-05211-3*) Random Hse. Value Publishing.

de Brunhoff, Laurent. L' Anniversaire de Babar. 1975. (Babar Ser.). (FRE., Illus.). 28p. (J). (ps-3). 17.95 (*0-7859-0677-0*, M11806) French & European Pubns., Inc.

—L' Anniversaire de Babar. (Babar Ser.). (FRE., Illus.). (J). (ps-3). 13.95 (*2-01-002551-2*) Istra FRA. *Dist:* Distribooks, Inc.

—Babar: Le Livre des Chiffres. 1986. (Babar Ser.). (FRE., Illus.). (J). (ps-3). 24.95 (*0-7859-8789-4*) French & European Pubns., Inc.

—Babar: Le Livre des Couleurs. 1985. (Babar Ser.). (FRE., Illus.). (J). (ps-3). 24.95 (*0-7859-8777-0*) French & European Pubns., Inc.

—Babar a Celesteville. 1974. (Babar Ser.). (FRE., Illus.). 16p. (J). (ps-3). 4.95 (*0-7859-0678-9*, F12062) French & European Pubns., Inc.

—Babar a New York. 1975. (Babar Ser.). (FRE., Illus.). (J). (ps-3). bds. 15.95 (*0-7859-5281-0*, 2010025520) French & European Pubns., Inc.

—Babar a New York. 1999. (Babar Ser.). (FRE., Illus.). (J). (ps-3). 13.95 (*2-01-002552-0*) Istra FRA. *Dist:* Distribooks, Inc.

—Babar & His Friends On Vacation. 1991. (Babar Ser.). (Illus.). 48p. (J). (ps-3). 6.99 o.s.i (*0-517-05214-8*) Random Hse. Value Publishing.

—Babar & the Ghost. (Babar Ser.). (Illus.). (J). (ps-3). 1986. 48p. 7.99 o.s.i (*0-394-97908-7*); 1986. 48p. pap. 3.99 o.s.i (*0-394-87908-2*); 1981. 32p. 4.95 o.s.i (*0-394-84660-5*); 1981. 32p. 11.99 o.s.i (*0-394-94660-X*) Random Hse. Children's Bks. (Random Hse. Bks. for Young Readers).

—Babar & the Ghost. 1986. (Babar Ser.). (J). (ps-3). 8.70 o.p. (*0-606-00847-0*) Turtleback Bks.

—Babar & the Professor. 1966. (Babar Ser.). (Illus.). (J). (ps-3). 6.99 o.s.i (*0-394-90590-3*); 4.95 o.s.i (*0-394-80590-9*) Random Hse. Children's Bks. (Random Hse. Bks. for Young Readers).

—Babar & the Succotash Bird. 2000. (Babar Ser.). (Illus.). 38p. (J). (ps-3). 16.95 (*0-8109-5700-0*) Abrams, Harry N. , Inc.

—Babar & the Wully-Wully. 1975. (Babar Ser.). (Illus.). 36p. (J). (ps-3). 4.95 o.s.i (*0-394-83077-6*); lib. bdg. 5.99 o.s.i (*0-394-93077-0*) Random Hse. Children's Bks. (Random Hse. Bks. for Young Readers).

—Babar Artiste Peintre. 1991. (Babar Ser.). (FRE., Illus.). (J). (ps-3). 15.95 (*0-7859-5285-3*, 209201417X) French & European Pubns., Inc.

—Babar at School. 1991. (Babar Ser.). (Illus.). 8p. (J). (ps-3). 3.99 o.s.i (*0-517-05219-9*) Random Hse. Value Publishing.

—Babar aux Sports d'Hiver. 1976. (Babar Ser.). (FRE., Illus.). 20p. (J). (ps-3). 4.95 (*0-7859-0679-7*, FC250) French & European Pubns., Inc.

—Babar Aviateur. 1974. (Babar Ser.). (FRE., Illus.). 16p. (J). (ps-3). 4.95 (*0-7859-0680-0*, M5989) French & European Pubns., Inc.

—The Babar Baby Book. 1990. (Babar Ser.). (Illus.). 80p. (J). (ps-3). 15.95 o.p. (*1-55670-080-6*) Stewart, Tabori & Chang.

—Babar Comes to America. 1965. (Babar Ser.). (Illus.). (J). (ps-3). 7.99 o.s.i (*0-394-90588-1*); 7.95 o.s.i (*0-394-80588-7*) Random Hse. Children's Bks. (Random Hse. Bks. for Young Readers).

—Babar Dans l'Ile aux Oiseaux. (Babar Ser.). (FRE.). (J). (ps-3). 19.95 o.p. incl. audio Olivia & Hill Pr., The.

—Babar dans l'Ile aux Oiseaux. (Babar Ser.).Tr. of Babar in the Jungle. (FRE., Illus.). 29p. (J). (ps-3). 15.95 (*0-7859-0681-9*, F2002) French & European Pubns., Inc.

—Babar dans l'Ile aux Oiseaux. 1999. (Babar Ser.).Tr. of Babar in the Jungle. (FRE., Illus.). (J). (ps-3). 13.95 (*2-01-002547-4*) Istra FRA. *Dist:* Distribooks, Inc.

—Babar Eats Lunch. 1991. (Babar Ser.). (Illus.). 8p. (J). (ps-3). 3.99 o.s.i (*0-517-05236-9*) Random Hse. Value Publishing.

—Babar en Amerique. 1999. (Babar Ser.).Tr. of Babar in America. (FRE., Illus.). (J). (ps-3). 13.95 (*2-01-002553-9*) Istra FRA. *Dist:* Distribooks, Inc.

—Babar et la Vieille Dame. (Babar Ser.). (FRE., Illus.). (J). (ps-3). pap. 15.95 (*0-7859-0614-2*, FC254) French & European Pubns., Inc.

—Babar et le Fantome. 1981. (Babar Ser.). (FRE., Illus.). 32p. (J). (ps-3). pap. 17.95 (*0-7859-8784-3*) French & European Pubns., Inc.

—Babar et le Pere Noel. 1999. (Babar Ser.).Tr. of Babar & Father Christmas. (FRE., Illus.). (J). (ps-3). 13.95 (*2-01-002549-0*) Istra FRA. *Dist:* Distribooks, Inc.

—Babar et le Professeur Grifton. 1999. (Babar Ser.).Tr. of Babar & Professor Grifton. (FRE., Illus.). (J). (ps-3). 13.95 (*2-01-002550-4*) Istra FRA. *Dist:* Distribooks, Inc.

—Babar et le Wouly-Wouly. (Babar Ser.).Tr. of Babar & the Wully-Wully. (FRE., Illus.). 26p. (J). (ps-3). 15.95 (*0-7859-0682-7*, M11805) French & European Pubns., Inc.

—Babar et le Wouly-Wouly. 1999. (Babar Ser.).Tr. of Babar & the Wully-Wully. (FRE., Illus.). (J). (ps-3). 13.95 (*2-01-004209-3*) Istra FRA. *Dist:* Distribooks, Inc.

—Babar et les Quatre Voleurs. 1979. (Babar Ser.). (FRE., Illus.). 28p. (J). (ps-3). pap. 17.95 (*0-7859-8785-1*) French & European Pubns., Inc.

—Babar et Moi: Le Livre de mes Secrets. 1987. (Babar Ser.). (FRE., Illus.). (J). (ps-3). 24.95 (*0-7859-8786-X*) French & European Pubns., Inc.

—Babar et Sa Petite Fille Isabelle. 1988. (Babar Ser.). (FRE., Illus.). (J). (ps-3). 24.95 (*0-7859-8787-8*) French & European Pubns., Inc.

—Babar et Ses Amis a la Ferme. (Babar Ser.). (FRE., Illus.). 48p. (J). (ps-3). 19.95 (*0-7859-8805-X*) French & European Pubns., Inc.

—Babar et Ses Amis a la Fete. (Babar Ser.). (FRE., Illus.). 48p. (J). (ps-3). 19.95 (*0-7859-8806-8*) French & European Pubns., Inc.

—Babar et Ses Amis a la Maison. (Babar Ser.). (FRE., Illus.). 48p. (J). (ps-3). 19.95 (*0-7859-8804-1*) French & European Pubns., Inc.

—Babar et Ses Amis a la Ville. (Babar Ser.). (FRE., Illus.). 48p. (J). (ps-3). 19.95 (*0-7859-8809-2*) French & European Pubns., Inc.

—Babar et Ses Amis a L'Ecole. (Babar Ser.). (FRE., Illus.). 48p. (J). (ps-3). 19.95 (*0-7859-8802-5*) French & European Pubns., Inc.

—Babar et Ses Amis au Spectacle. (Babar Ser.). (FRE., Illus.). 48p. (J). (ps-3). 19.95 (*0-7859-8803-3*) French & European Pubns., Inc.

—Babar et Ses Amis en Foret. (Babar Ser.). (FRE., Illus.). 48p. (J). (ps-3). 19.95 (*0-7859-8811-4*) French & European Pubns., Inc.

—Babar et Ses Amis en Vacances. (Babar Ser.). (FRE., Illus.). 48p. (J). (ps-3). 19.95 (*0-7859-8808-4*) French & European Pubns., Inc.

—Babar et Ses Amis Font les Courses. (Babar Ser.). (FRE., Illus.). 48p. (J). (ps-3). 19.95 (*0-7859-8810-6*) French & European Pubns., Inc.

—Babar et Ses Amis Visitent le Royaume. (Babar Ser.). (FRE., Illus.). 48p. (J). (ps-3). 19.95 (*0-7859-8807-6*) French & European Pubns., Inc.

—Babar Learns to Cook. 1979. (Babar Ser.). (Illus.). 32p. (J). (ps-3). pap. 3.25 o.s.i (*0-394-84108-5*, Random Hse. Bks. for Young Readers) Random Hse. Children's Bks.

—Babar Learns to Cook. 1989. (Babar Ser.). (Illus.). (J). (ps-3). 8.45 o.p. (*0-606-12173-0*) Turtleback Bks.

—Babar les 500 Premiers Mots. (Babar Ser.). (FRE., Illus.). 48p. (J). (ps-3). 19.95 (*0-7859-8812-2*) French & European Pubns., Inc.

—Babar Loses His Crown. 1967. (Babar Ser.). (Illus.). 72p. (J). (ps-3). 7.99 o.s.i (*0-394-90045-6*); 3.95 o.s.i (*0-394-80045-1*) Beginner Bks.

—Babar Loses His Crown. 1975. (Babar Ser.). (Illus.). (J). (ps-3). 28.37 incl. audio (*0-394-03636-0*) SRA/McGraw-Hill.

—Babar Packs His Trunk. 1978. (Babar Ser.). (Illus.). (J). (ps-3). 2.95 o.s.i (*0-394-83960-9*, Random Hse. Bks. for Young Readers) Random Hse. Children's Bks.

—Babar Raconte Flore Reporter. (Babar Ser.). (FRE., Illus.). 48p. (J). (ps-3). 19.95 (*0-7859-8813-0*) French & European Pubns., Inc.

—Babar Raconte Halte a la Pollution. (Babar Ser.). (FRE., Illus.). 48p. (J). (ps-3). 19.95 (*0-7859-8816-5*) French & European Pubns., Inc.

—Babar Raconte la Course a la Lune. (Babar Ser.). (FRE., Illus.). 48p. (J). (ps-3). 19.95 (*0-7859-8820-3*) French & European Pubns., Inc.

—Babar Raconte l'Affaire de la Couronne. (Babar Ser.). (FRE., Illus.). 48p. (J). (ps-3). 19.95 (*0-7859-8818-1*) French & European Pubns., Inc.

—Babar Raconte l'Arrivee du Bebe Elephant. (Babar Ser.). (FRE., Illus.). 48p. (J). (ps-3). 19.95 (*0-7859-8815-7*) French & European Pubns., Inc.

—Babar Raconte le Fantome. (Babar Ser.). (FRE., Illus.). 48p. (J). (ps-3). 19.95 (*0-7859-8819-X*) French & European Pubns., Inc.

—Babar Raconte le Meilleur Ami des Elephants. (Babar Ser.). (FRE., Illus.). 48p. (J). (ps-3). 19.95 (*0-7859-8823-8*) French & European Pubns., Inc.

—Babar Raconte le Pianiste. (Babar Ser.). (FRE., Illus.). 48p. (J). (ps-3). 19.95 (*0-7859-8822-X*) French & European Pubns., Inc.

—Babar Raconte le Plus Beau Cadeau du Monde. (Babar Ser.). (FRE., Illus.). 48p. (J). (ps-3). 19.95 (*0-7859-8821-1*) French & European Pubns., Inc.

—Babar Raconte Que la Fete Continue. (Babar Ser.). (FRE., Illus.). 48p. (J). (ps-3). 19.95 (*0-7859-8824-6*) French & European Pubns., Inc.

—Babar Raconte un Diner Chez Rataxes. (Babar Ser.). (FRE., Illus.). 48p. (J). (ps-3). 19.95 (*0-7859-8817-3*) French & European Pubns., Inc.

—Babar Raconte Zephir Fait le Singe. (Babar Ser.). (FRE., Illus.). 48p. (J). (ps-3). 19.95 (*0-7859-8814-9*) French & European Pubns., Inc.

—Babar Saves the Day. 1976. (Babar Ser.). (Illus.). 32p. (J). (ps-3). pap. 3.25 o.s.i (*0-394-83341-4*, Random Hse. Bks. for Young Readers) Random Hse. Children's Bks.

—Babar Says Goodnight. 1991. (Babar Ser.). (Illus.). 8p. (J). (ps-3). 3.99 o.s.i (*0-517-05235-0*) Random Hse. Value Publishing.

—Babar sur la Planete Molle. 1980. (Babar Ser.). (FRE., Illus.). (J). (ps-3). pap. 17.95 (*0-7859-8791-6*) French & European Pubns., Inc.

—Babar sur la Planete Molle. 2000. (Babar Ser.). (FRE., Illus.). (J). (ps-3). 13.95 (*2-01-006867-X*) Istra FRA. *Dist:* Distribooks, Inc.

—Babar the Magician. 1980. (Babar Ser.). (Illus.). 24p. (J). (ps-3). 2.50 o.p. (*0-394-84360-6*) Random Hse., Inc.

—Babar Visits Another Planet. 2003. (Illus.). 38p. (J). 16.95 (*0-8109-4244-5*) Abrams, Harry N. , Inc.

—Babar Visits Another Planet. 1972. (Babar Ser.). (Illus.). (J). (ps-3). 13.99 o.s.i (*0-394-92429-0*); 4.95 o.s.i (*0-394-82429-6*) Random Hse. Children's Bks. (Random Hse. Bks. for Young Readers).

—Babar, 7 Families. 1990. (Babar Ser.). (Illus.). (J). (ps-3). 6.00 o.p. (*1-56021-034-6*) W.J. Fantasy, Inc.

—Babar's Bath Book. 1992. (Babar Ser.). (Illus.). 10p. (J). (ps-3). bds. 4.99 o.s.i (*0-679-83434-6*, Random Hse. Bks. for Young Readers) Random Hse. Children's Bks.

—Babar's Birthday Surprise. (Babar Ser.). (J). (ps-3). audio. (Illus.). audio o.p. HarperTrade.

—Babar's Book of Color. 1984. (Babar Ser.). (Illus.). 36p. (J). (ps-3). 13.00 o.s.i (*0-394-86896-X*); 10.99 o.s.i (*0-394-96896-4*) Random Hse. Children's Bks. (Random Hse. Bks. for Young Readers).

—Babar's Bookmobile. 1974. (Babar Ser.). (Illus.). 24p. (J). (ps-3). 9.95 o.s.i (*0-394-82660-4*, Random Hse. Bks. for Young Readers) Random Hse. Children's Bks.

—Babar's Castle. Haas, Merle, tr. 1962. (Babar Ser.). (Illus.). (J). (ps-3). 4.95 o.s.i (*0-394-80586-0*, Random Hse. Bks. for Young Readers) Random Hse. Children's Bks.

—Babar's Counting Book. 2003. (Illus.). 38p. (J). 16.95 (*0-8109-4243-7*) Abrams, Harry N. , Inc.

—Babar's Counting Book. 1986. (Babar Ser.). (Illus.). 36p. (J). (ps-3). 10.99 o.s.i (*0-394-97517-0*); 10.00 o.s.i (*0-394-87517-6*) Random Hse. Children's Bks. (Random Hse. Bks. for Young Readers).

—Babar's Cousin. Haas, Merle, tr. (Babar Ser.). (Illus.). (J). (ps-3). 1967. lib. bdg. 5.99 o.s.i (*0-394-90581-4*); 1952. 4.95 o.s.i (*0-394-80581-X*) Random Hse. Children's Bks. (Random Hse. Bks. for Young Readers).

—Babar's Fair. Haas, Merle, tr. (Babar Ser.). (Illus.). (J). (ps-3). 1969. lib. bdg. 7.99 o.s.i (*0-394-90584-9*); 1961. 4.95 o.s.i (*0-394-80584-4*) Random Hse. Children's Bks. (Random Hse. Bks. for Young Readers).

—Babar's Family Album: Five Favorite Stories. 1991. (Babar Ser.). (Illus.). 112p. (J). (ps-3). 17.00 o.s.i (*0-679-81167-2*, Random Hse. Bks. for Young Readers) Random Hse. Children's Bks.

—Babar's French Lessons. 1963. (Babar Ser.). (Illus.). (J). (ps-3). lib. bdg. 5.99 o.s.i (*0-394-90587-3*); 11.00 o.s.i (*0-394-80587-9*) Random Hse. Children's Bks. (Random Hse. Bks. for Young Readers).

—Babar's Games. 1968. (Babar Ser.). (Illus.). (J). (ps-3). 3.95 o.p. (*0-394-81527-0*) Random Hse., Inc.

—Babar's Little Circus Star. 1988. (Babar Ser.). (Illus.). 32p. (J). (ps-3). 7.99 o.s.i (*0-394-98959-7*); pap. 3.99 o.s.i (*0-394-88959-2*) Random Hse. Children's Bks. (Random Hse. Bks. for Young Readers).

—Babar's Little Circus Star. 1988. (Babar Ser.). (J). (ps-3). 9.19 o.p. (*0-606-03720-9*) Turtleback Bks.

—Babar's Little Girl. 1987. (Babar Ser.). (Illus.). 36p. (J). (ps-3). 11.00 o.s.i (*0-394-88689-5*); 9.99 o.s.i (*0-394-98689-X*) Random Hse. Children's Bks. (Random Hse. Bks. for Young Readers).

—Babar's Moon Trip. 1969. (Babar Ser.). (Illus.). (J). (ps-3). 3.95 o.p. (*0-394-80583-6*) Random Hse., Inc.

—Babar's Museum of Art. 2003. (Illus.). 48p. (J). (gr. k-3). 16.95 (*0-8109-4597-5*) Abrams, Harry N. , Inc.

—Babar's Paint Box Book. 1989. (Babar Ser.). (Illus.). (J). (ps-3). pap. 0.71 o.s.i (*0-394-82281-1*, Random Hse. Bks. for Young Readers) Random Hse. Children's Bks.

—Babar's Picnic. 1991. (Babar Ser.). (Illus.). 24p. (Orig.). (J). (ps-3). 2.25 o.s.i (*0-679-81245-8*, Random Hse. Bks. for Young Readers) Random Hse. Children's Bks.

—Babar's Spanish Lessons. (Babar Ser.). (Illus.). (J). (ps-3). 1966. lib. bdg. 4.99 o.s.i (*0-394-90589-X*); 1965. 5.95 o.s.i (*0-394-80589-5*) Random Hse. Children's Bks. (Random Hse. Bks. for Young Readers).

—Babar's Trunk, 4 bks., Set. 1969. (Babar Ser.). (Illus.). (J). (ps-3). 9.95 o.s.i (*0-394-80585-2*, Random Hse. Bks. for Young Readers) Random Hse. Children's Bks.

—Le Chateau de Babar. 1999. (Babar Ser.).Tr. of Babar's House. (FRE., Illus.). (J). (ps-3). 13.95 (*2-01-002515-6*) Distribooks, Inc.

—Le Chateau de Babar. 1991. (Babar Ser.).Tr. of Babar's House. (FRE.). (J). (ps-3). 14.95 incl. audio Olivia & Hill Pr., The.

—Fifty Years of Babar: Watercolors by Jean & Laurent de Brunhoff. John, Angela G., ed. 1983. (Babar Ser.). (Illus.). (J). (ps-3). pap. 5.50 o.p. (*0-88397-047-3*) Art Services International.

—Hello, Babar! 1991. (Babar Ser.). (Illus.). 12p. (J). (ps-3). 4.99 o.s.i (*0-679-81073-0*, Random Hse. Bks. for Young Readers) Random Hse. Children's Bks.

—Isabelle's New Friend: A Babar Book. 1990. (Babar Ser.). (Illus.). 32p. (J). (ps-3). pap. 2.25 o.s.i (*0-394-82880-1*, Random Hse. Bks. for Young Readers) Random Hse. Children's Bks.

—Une Journee de Babar. 1985. (Babar Ser.). (FRE., Illus.). 8p. (J). (ps-3). 14.95 (*0-7859-8794-0*) French & European Pubns., Inc.

—Meet Babar & His Family. (Babar Ser.). (Illus.). 32p. (J). (ps-3). 1985. pap. 5.95 o.s.i incl. audio (*0-394-87653-9*); 1973. pap. 3.25 o.s.i (*0-394-82682-5*) Random Hse. Children's Bks. (Random Hse. Bks. for Young Readers).

—La Petite Boite Babar: Le Feu, l'Eau, l'Air, la Terre. 1980. (Babar Ser.). (FRE., Illus.). 192p. (J). (ps-3). 39.95 (*0-7859-8796-7*) French & European Pubns., Inc.

—Le Roi Babar. 1999. (Babar Ser.).Tr. of Babar the King. (FRE., Illus.). (J). (ps up). 13.95 (*2-01-002517-2*) Distribooks, Inc.

Dorfman, Ariel. The Empire's Old Clothes: What the Lone Ranger Babar, & Other Innocent Heroes do to Our Minds. Hansen, Clark, tr. 1983. 225p. pap. 12.95 o.s.i (*0-394-71486-5*, Pantheon) Knopf Publishing Group.

—The Empire's Old Clothes: What the Lone Ranger Babar & Other Innocent Heroes do to Our Minds. Hansen, Clark, tr. 1983. 225p. 14.95 o.p. (*0-394-52723-2*, Pantheon) Knopf Publishing Group.

Favorite Songs of Babar. 1994. (Babar Ser.). (Illus.). (J). (ps-3). 21.95 o.p. (*0-316-54562-7*) Little Brown & Co.

Grenard, Fernand. Babar, First of the Moguls. White, Homer & Glaenzer, Richard, trs. 1977. (Select Bibliographies Reprint Ser.). reprint ed. 19.95 (*0-8369-5424-6*) Ayer Co. Pubs., Inc.

Haas, Merle, tr. Babar's Castle. 1994. (Babar Ser.). (Illus.). (J). (ps-3). lib. bdg. 5.99 (*0-394-90586-5*, Random Hse. Bks. for Young Readers) Random Hse. Children's Bks.

Herman, Gail. Babar the Boy King. 1989. (Babar Ser.). (Illus.). 32p. (Orig.). (J). (ps-3). 1.50 o.s.i (*0-394-84533-1*, Random Hse. Bks. for Young Readers) Random Hse. Children's Bks.

Outlet Book Company Staff. Babar & His Friends at the Amusement Park. 1991. (Babar Ser.). (Illus.). 48p. (J). (ps-3). 6.99 o.s.i (*0-517-05209-1*) Random Hse. Value Publishing.

—Babar Story Book: An Elephant's Best Friend. 1990. (Babar Ser.). (Illus.). 48p. (J). (ps-3). 6.99 o.s.i (*0-517-05207-5*) Random Hse. Value Publishing.

—Babar Story Book: The Best Present in the World. 1990. (Babar Ser.). (Illus.). 48p. (J). (ps-3). 6.99 o.s.i (*0-517-05197-4*) Random Hse. Value Publishing.

—Babar Story Book: The Phantom. 1990. (Babar Ser.). (Illus.). 48p. (J). (ps-3). 6.99 o.s.i (*0-517-05196-6*) Random Hse. Value Publishing.

—Babar Story Book: The Race to the Moon. 1990. (Babar Ser.). (Illus.). 48p. (J). (ps-3). 6.99 o.s.i (*0-517-05208-3*) Random Hse. Value Publishing.

—Babar Story Book: The Show Must Go On. 1990. (Babar Ser.). (Illus.). 48p. (J). (ps-3). 6.99 o.s.i (*0-517-05206-7*) Random Hse. Value Publishing.

—Babar Story Book: To Duet or Not to Duet. 1990. (Babar Ser.). (Illus.). 48p. (J). (ps-3). 6.99 o.s.i (*0-517-05195-8*) Random Hse. Value Publishing.

Wallant, Leslie. Babar Sees the World. 1996. (Babar Ser.). (Illus.). 32p. (J). (ps-3). pap. 14.95 (*1-886201-07-2*) Nana Banana Classics.

Weiss, Ellen. Babar: A Gift for Mother. 2004. (Illus.). (J). 9.95 (*0-8109-4837-0*) Abrams, Harry N. , Inc.

Weiss, Ellen & de Brunhoff, Laurent. Babar Goes to School. 2003. (Illus.). 32p. (J). 9.95 (*0-8109-4582-7*) Abrams, Harry N. , Inc.

BABBITT, SPENCER (FICTITIOUS CHARACTER)—FICTION

Abbott, Tony. The Fake Teacher. 1999. (Don't Touch That Remote Ser.: No. 2). 160p. (J). (gr. 3-6). pap. 3.99 (*0-671-02782-4*, Aladdin) Simon & Schuster Children's Publishing.

—Sitcom School. 1999. (Don't Touch That Remote Ser.: No. 1). 160p. (J). (gr. 4-7). pap. 3.99 (*0-671-02781-6*, Aladdin) Simon & Schuster Children's Publishing.

—Stinky Business. 2000. (Don't Touch That Remote Ser.: No. 3). 160p. (J). (gr. 3-6). pap. 3.99 (*0-671-02783-2*, Aladdin) Simon & Schuster Children's Publishing.

BAGGINS, BILBO (FICTITIOUS CHARACTER)—FICTION

The Hobbit. 1999. (YA). 9.95 (*1-56137-253-6*) Novel Units, Inc.

Tolkien, J. R. R. The Hobbit. 2002. 16.60 (*0-7587-7961-5*) Book Wholesalers, Inc.

—The Hobbit. (YA). 2002. 320p. (gr. 5). pap. 10.00 (*0-618-26030-7*); 1997. (Illus.). 289p. (gr. 7). 35.00 (*0-395-87346-0*); 1984. (Illus.). 304p. (gr. 7 up). 29.95 (*0-395-36290-3*); 1973. (Illus.). 320p. (gr. 7). 35.00 (*0-395-17711-1*); 1938. (Illus.). 320p. (gr. 7). 16.00 (*0-395-07122-4*) Houghton Mifflin Co.

—The Hobbit. 1989. (Illus.). 304p. (YA). (gr. 7-5). pap. 17.95 (*0-395-52021-5*) Houghton Mifflin Co. Trade & Reference Div.

—The Hobbit. unabr. ed. 2000. (YA). audio 25.95 (*0-8072-8883-7*, Listening Library) Random Hse. Audio Publishing Group.

—The Hobbit. (J). 1984. pap. 29.95 o.p. incl. audio (*0-88142-269-X*, 269); 1984. pap. 29.95 o.p. incl. audio (*0-88142-269-X*, 269); 1994. audio compact disk 29.95 (*1-55935-119-5*) Soundelux Audio Publishing.

—The Hobbit: A 3-D Pop-Up Adventure. 1999. (Illus.). 12p. (J). (gr. 2 up). 9.98 o.s.i (*0-694-01436-2*) HarperCollins Children's Bk. Group.

BAGGINS, FRODO (FICTITIOUS CHARACTER)—FICTION

The Lord of the Rings. (Lord of the Rings Ser.). (J). audio o.p. HarperTrade.

Tolkien, J. R. R. The Lord of the Rings. abr. ed. (Lord of the Rings Ser.). 2001. audio compact disk 59.95 (*1-55935-120-9*); 1979. 12p. pap. 59.95 o.p. incl. audio (*0-88142-270-3*, 102629); 1979. 12p. pap. 59.95 o.p. incl. audio (*0-88142-270-3*, 102629) Soundelux Audio Publishing.

BAGGS, BILLY (FICTITIOUS CHARACTER)—FICTION

Weaver, Will. Farm Team. 288p. 1999. (J). (gr. 6 up). pap. 5.99 (*0-06-447118-7*, Harper Trophy); 1995. (YA). (gr. 7 up). 14.95 o.p. (*0-06-023588-8*); 1995. (Illus.). (YA). (gr. 6 up). lib. bdg. 15.89 (*0-06-023589-6*) HarperCollins Children's Bk. Group.

—Farm Team. 1999. 11.00 (*0-606-15860-X*) Turtleback Bks.

—Hard Ball. (gr. 6 up). 1999. 256p. (J). pap. 5.99 (*0-06-447208-6*, Harper Trophy); 1998. 240p. (YA). 15.95 (*0-06-027121-3*); 1998. 240p. (YA). lib. bdg. 15.89 (*0-06-027122-1*) HarperCollins Children's Bk. Group.

—Hard Ball. 1999. 11.00 (*0-606-16706-4*) Turtleback Bks.

—Hard Ball: A Billy Baggs Novel. l.t. ed. 2000. (Illus.). 270p. (YA). (gr. 8-12). 20.95 (*0-7862-2752-4*) Thorndike Pr.

—Striking Out. (J). 1995. (Illus.). 304p. (gr. 6 up). pap. 6.99 (*0-06-447113-6*, Harper Trophy); 1993. 288p. (gr. 5 up). 15.00 o.p. (*0-06-023346-X*); 1993. 288p. (gr. 5 up). lib. bdg. 14.89 o.p. (*0-06-023347-8*) HarperCollins Children's Bk. Group.

—Striking Out. 1995. (J). 11.00 (*0-606-08211-5*) Turtleback Bks.

BAILEY CITY MONSTERS (FICTITIOUS CHARACTERS)—FICTION

Dadey, Debbie & Jones, Marcia Thornton. Frankenstein Doesn't Start Food Fights. 2003. (Adventures of the Bailey School Kids Ser.: No. 47). 80p. (J). mass mkt. 3.99 (*0-439-55999-5*, Scholastic Paperbacks) Scholastic, Inc.

Jones, Marcia Thornton & Dadey, Debbie. Double Trouble Monsters. 1999. (Bailey City Monsters Ser.: No. 5). (Illus.). 80p. (J). (gr. 2-4). mass mkt. 3.99 (*0-439-05870-8*) Scholastic, Inc.

—Double Trouble Monsters. 1999. (Bailey City Monsters Ser.: No. 5). (J). (gr. 2-4). 10.14 (*0-606-16604-1*) Turtleback Bks.

—Happy Boo Day. 2000. (Bailey City Monsters Ser.: No. 9). (Illus.). 80p. (J). (gr. 2-4). mass mkt. 3.99 (*0-439-15009-4*, Scholastic Paperbacks) Scholastic, Inc.

—The Hauntlys' Hairy Surprise. 1999. (Bailey City Monsters Super Special Ser.: No. 1). (Illus.). 112p. (J). (gr. 2-4). mass mkt. 3.99 (*0-590-04302-1*) Scholastic, Inc.

—The Hauntlys' Hairy Surprise. 1999. (Bailey City Monsters Super Special Ser.: No. 1). (J). (gr. 2-4). 10.14 (*0-606-19911-X*) Turtleback Bks.

—Howling at the Hauntlys' 1998. (Bailey City Monsters Ser.: No.2). (Illus.). (J). (gr. 2-4). mass mkt. 3.99 (*0-590-10845-X*) Scholastic, Inc.

—Howling at the Hauntlys' 1998. (Bailey City Monsters Ser.: No. 2). (Illus.). (J). (gr. 2-4). 10.14 (*0-606-15448-5*) Turtleback Bks.

—Kilmer's Pet Monster. 1999. (Bailey City Monsters Ser.: No. 4). (Illus.). 72p. (J). (gr. 2-4). mass mkt. 3.99 (*0-590-10847-6*) Scholastic, Inc.

—Kilmer's Pet Monster. 1998. (Bailey City Monsters Ser.: No. 4). (J). (gr. 2-4). 10.14 (*0-606-15899-5*) Turtleback Bks.

—The Monsters Next Door. 1998. (Bailey City Monsters Ser.: No. 1). (Illus.). 71p. (J). (gr. 2-4). mass mkt. 3.99 (*0-590-10787-9*) Scholastic, Inc.

—The Monsters Next Door. 1997. (Bailey City Monsters Ser.: No. 1). (J). (gr. 2-4). 10.14 (*0-606-15447-7*) Turtleback Bks.

—Snow Monster Mystery. 1999. (Bailey City Monsters Ser.: No. 8). (Illus.). (J). (gr. 2-4). 10.14 (*0-606-18514-3*) Turtleback Bks.

—The Snow Monster Mystery. 1999. (Bailey City Monsters Ser.: No. 8). (Illus.). 80p. (J). (gr. 2-4). mass mkt. 3.99 (*0-439-05873-2*) Scholastic, Inc.

—Spooky Spells. 1999. (Bailey City Monsters Ser.: No. 6). (Illus.). 80p. (J). (gr. 2-4). mass mkt. 3.99 (*0-439-05871-6*) Scholastic, Inc.

—Spooky Spells. 1999. (Bailey City Monsters Ser.: No. 6). (J). (gr. 2-4). 10.14 (*0-606-16656-4*) Turtleback Bks.

—Vampire Baby. 1999. (Bailey City Monsters Ser.: No. 7). (Illus.). 80p. (J). (gr. 2-4). mass mkt. 3.99 (*0-439-05872-4*) Scholastic, Inc.

—Vampire Baby. 1999. (Bailey City Monsters Ser.: No. 7). (J). (gr. 2-4). 10.14 (*0-606-17059-6*) Turtleback Bks.

—Vampire Trouble. 1998. (Bailey City Monsters Ser.: No. 3). (Illus.). 80p. (J). (gr. 2-4). mass mkt. 3.99 (*0-590-10846-8*) Scholastic, Inc.

—Vampire Trouble. 1998. (Bailey City Monsters Ser.: No. 3). (J). (gr. 2-4). 10.14 (*0-606-15449-3*) Turtleback Bks.

BAILEY SCHOOL KIDS (FICTITIOUS CHARACTERS)—FICTION

Dadey, Debbie. Angels Don't Know Karate. 1996. (Adventures of the Bailey School Kids Ser.: No. 23). (J). (gr. 2-4). 10.14 (*0-606-10124-1*) Turtleback Bks.

—Mrs. Jeepers in Outer Space. 1999. (Adventures of the Bailey School Kids Super Special Ser.: No. 4). (J). (gr. 2-4). 10.04 (*0-606-19912-8*) Turtleback Bks.

—Witches Don't Do Back Flips. 1994. (Adventures of the Bailey School Kids Ser.: No. 10). (J). (gr. 2-4). 10.14 (*0-606-06888-0*) Turtleback Bks.

—Wizards Don't Need Computers. 1996. (Adventures of the Bailey School Kids Ser.: No. 20). (Illus.). 63p. (J). (gr. 2-4). mass mkt. 3.99 (*0-590-50962-4*) Scholastic, Inc.

—Wizards Don't Need Computers. 1996. (Adventures of the Bailey School Kids Ser.: No. 20). (J). (gr. 2-4). 10.14 (*0-606-10079-2*) Turtleback Bks.

Dadey, Debbie & Jones, Marcia Thornton. Aliens Don't Carve Jack-O-Lanterns. 2002. (Bailey School Kids Holiday Special Ser.). 112p. (J). mass mkt. 3.99 (*0-439-40831-8*, Scholastic Paperbacks) Scholastic, Inc.

—Aliens Don't Wear Braces. 1993. (Adventures of the Bailey School Kids Ser.: No. 7). (J). (gr. 2-4). 10.14 (*0-606-05112-0*) Turtleback Bks.

—Angels Don't Know Karate. 1996. (Adventures of the Bailey School Kids Ser.: No. 23). (Illus.). 67p. (J). (gr. 2-4). mass mkt. 3.99 (*0-590-84902-6*) Scholastic, Inc.

—Bigfoot Doesn't Square Dance. 1997. (Adventures of the Bailey School Kids Ser.: No. 25). 80p. (J). (gr. 2-4). mass mkt. 3.99 (*0-590-84905-0*, Scholastic Paperbacks) Scholastic, Inc.

—Bigfoot Doesn't Square Dance. 1997. (Adventures of the Bailey School Kids Ser.: No. 25). (J). (gr. 2-4). 10.14 (*0-606-11128-X*) Turtleback Bks.

—Bogeymen Don't Play Football. 1997. (Adventures of the Bailey School Kids Ser.: No. 27). (Illus.). 80p. (J). (gr. 2-4). mass mkt. 3.99 (*0-590-25701-3*) Scholastic, Inc.

—Bogeymen Don't Play Football. 1997. (Adventures of the Bailey School Kids Ser.: No. 27). (Illus.). (J). (gr. 2-4). 10.14 (*0-606-11145-X*) Turtleback Bks.

—Cupid Doesn't Flip Hamburgers. 1995. (Adventures of the Bailey School Kids Ser.: No. 12). (Illus.). 96p. (J). (gr. 2-4). mass mkt. 3.99 (*0-590-48114-2*) Scholastic, Inc.

—Cupid Doesn't Flip Hamburgers. 1995. (Adventures of the Bailey School Kids Ser.: No. 12). (J). (gr. 2-4). 10.14 (*0-606-07405-8*) Turtleback Bks.

—Cyclops Doesn't Roller Skate. 1996. (Adventures of the Bailey School Kids Ser.: No. 22). (J). (gr. 2-4). mass mkt. 3.99 o.s.i (*0-590-84886-0*) Scholastic, Inc.

—Cyclops Doesn't Roller Skate. 1996. (Adventures of the Bailey School Kids Ser.: No. 22). (J). (gr. 2-4). 10.14 (*0-606-09176-9*) Turtleback Bks.

—Dracula Doesn't Drink Lemonade. 1995. (Adventures of the Bailey School Kids Ser.: No. 16). (Illus.). 80p. (J). (gr. 2-4). mass mkt. 3.99 o.s.i (*0-590-22638-X*) Scholastic, Inc.

—Dracula Doesn't Drink Lemonade. 1995. (Adventures of the Bailey School Kids Ser.: No. 16). (J). (gr. 2-4). 10.14 (*0-606-07444-9*) Turtleback Bks.

—Dracula Doesn't Rock & Roll. 2000. (Adventures of the Bailey School Kids Ser.: No. 39). (Illus.). 80p. (J). (gr. 2-4). mass mkt. 3.99 (*0-439-04399-9*, Scholastic Paperbacks) Scholastic, Inc.

—Dracula Doesn't Rock & Roll. 2000. (Adventures of the Bailey School Kids Ser.: No. 39). (Illus.). (J). (gr. 2-4). 10.14 (*0-606-18537-2*) Turtleback Bks.

—Dragons Don't Cook Pizza. 1997. (Adventures of the Bailey School Kids Ser.: No. 24). 80p. (J). (gr. 2-4). mass mkt. 3.99 (*0-590-84904-2*) Scholastic, Inc.

—Dragons Don't Cook Pizza. 1997. (Adventures of the Bailey School Kids Ser.: No. 24). (J). (gr. 2-4). 10.14 (*0-606-10790-8*) Turtleback Bks.

—Elves Don't Wear Hard Hats. 1995. (Adventures of the Bailey School Kids Ser.: No. 17). (J). (gr. 2-4). mass mkt. 3.99 (*0-590-22637-1*) Scholastic, Inc.

—Elves Don't Wear Hard Hats. 1995. (Adventures of the Bailey School Kids Ser.: No. 17). (J). (gr. 2-4). 10.14 (*0-606-08514-9*) Turtleback Bks.

—Frankenstein Doesn't Plant Petunias. (Adventures of the Bailey School Kids Ser.: No. 6). (J). (gr. 2-4). 9999. (FRE., Illus.). pap. 5.99 o.p. (*0-590-24497-3*); 1993. 80p. mass mkt. 3.99 o.s.i (*0-590-47071-X*) Scholastic, Inc.

—Frankenstein Doesn't Plant Petunias. 1993. (Adventures of the Bailey School Kids Ser.: No. 6). (J). (gr. 2-4). 8.70 (*0-606-05298-4*) Turtleback Bks.

—Frankenstein Doesn't Slam Hockey Pucks. 1999. (Adventures of the Bailey School Kids Ser.: No. 34). (Illus.). 76p. (J). (gr. 2-4). mass mkt. 3.99 (*0-590-18984-0*) Scholastic, Inc.

—Frankenstein Doesn't Slam Hockey Pucks. 1998. (Adventures of the Bailey School Kids Ser.: No. 34). (J). (gr. 2-4). 10.14 (*0-606-15898-7*) Turtleback Bks.

—Gargoyles Don't Drive School Buses. 1996. (Adventures of the Bailey School Kids Ser.: No. 19). (Illus.). 80p. (J). (gr. 2-4). mass mkt. 3.99 (*0-590-50961-6*) Scholastic, Inc.

—Gargoyles Don't Drive School Buses. 1996. (Adventures of the Bailey School Kids Ser.: No. 19). (J). (gr. 2-4). 10.14 (*0-606-08750-8*) Turtleback Bks.

—Genies Don't Ride Bicycles. (Adventures of the Bailey School Kids Ser.: No. 8). (J). (gr. 2-4). (FRE., Illus.). pap. 5.99 (*0-590-24377-2*); 1994. 80p. mass mkt. 3.99 (*0-590-47297-6*) Scholastic, Inc.

—Genies Don't Ride Bicycles. 1993. (Adventures of the Bailey School Kids Ser.: No. 8). (J). (gr. 2-4). 10.14 (*0-606-06403-6*) Turtleback Bks.

—Ghosts Don't Eat Potato Chips. (Adventures of the Bailey School Kids Ser.: No. 5). (J). (gr. 2-4). (FRE.). pap. 5.99 (*0-590-74836-X*); 1992. (Illus.). 96p. mass mkt. 3.99 (*0-590-45854-X*) Scholastic, Inc.

—Ghosts Don't Eat Potato Chips. 1992. (Adventures of the Bailey School Kids Ser.: No. 5). (J). (gr. 2-4). 10.14 (*0-606-01843-3*) Turtleback Bks.

—Ghouls Don't Scoop Ice Cream. 1998. (Adventures of the Bailey School Kids Ser.: No. 31). (J). (gr. 2-4). 10.14 (*0-606-13426-3*) Turtleback Bks.

—Giants Don't Go Snowboarding. 1998. (Adventures of the Bailey School Kids Ser.: No. 33). (Illus.). 76p. (J). (gr. 2-4). mass mkt. 3.99 (*0-590-18983-2*) Scholastic, Inc.

—Giants Don't Go Snowboarding. 1998. (Adventures of the Bailey School Kids Ser.: No. 33). (J). (gr. 2-4). 10.14 (*0-606-15547-3*) Turtleback Bks.

—Goblins Don't Play Video Games. 1999. (Adventures of the Bailey School Kids Ser.: No. 37). (Illus.). 82p. (J). (gr. 2-4). mass mkt. 3.99 (*0-439-04397-2*) Scholastic, Inc.

—Goblins Don't Play Video Games. 1999. (Adventures of the Bailey School Kids Ser.: No. 37). (J). (gr. 2-4). 10.14 (*0-606-17276-9*) Turtleback Bks.

—Gremlins Don't Chew Bubble Gum. 1995. (Adventures of the Bailey School Kids Ser.: No. 13). 96p. (J). (gr. 2-4). mass mkt. 3.99 (*0-590-48115-0*) Scholastic, Inc.

—Gremlins Don't Chew Bubble Gum. 1995. (Adventures of the Bailey School Kids Ser.: No. 13). (J). (gr. 2-4). 10.04 (*0-606-07602-6*) Turtleback Bks.

—Hercules Doesn't Pull Teeth. 1998. (Adventures of the Bailey School Kids Ser.: No. 30). (Illus.). 70p. (J). (gr. 2-4). mass mkt. 3.99 (*0-590-25809-5*, Scholastic Paperbacks) Scholastic, Inc.

—Hercules Doesn't Pull Teeth. 1998. (Adventures of the Bailey School Kids Ser.: No. 30). (J). (gr. 2-4). 10.14 (*0-606-13475-1*) Turtleback Bks.

—Knights Don't Teach Piano. 1998. (Adventures of the Bailey School Kids Ser.: No. 29). (Illus.). 66p. (J). (gr. 2-4). mass mkt. 3.99 (*0-590-25804-4*, Scholastic Paperbacks) Scholastic, Inc.

—Knights Don't Teach Piano. 1998. (Adventures of the Bailey School Kids Ser.: No. 29). (J). (gr. 2-4). 10.14 (*0-606-12975-8*) Turtleback Bks.

—Leprechauns Don't Play Basketball. 1992. (Adventures of the Bailey School Kids Ser.: No. 4). (J). (gr. 2-4). 10.14 (*0-606-14110-3*) Turtleback Bks.

—Leprechauns Don't Play Fetch. 2003. (Bailey School Kids Holiday Special Ser.). (Illus.). 96p. (J). (gr. 2-4). mass mkt. 3.99 (*0-439-40833-4*, Scholastic Paperbacks) Scholastic, Inc.

—Martians Don't Take Temperatures. 1996. (Adventures of the Bailey School Kids Ser.: No. 18). 67p. (J). (gr. 2-4). mass mkt. 3.99 (*0-590-50960-8*) Scholastic, Inc.

—Martians Don't Take Temperatures. 1995. (Adventures of the Bailey School Kids Ser.: No. 18). (J). (gr. 2-4). 10.14 (*0-606-08565-3*) Turtleback Bks.

—Mermaids Don't Run Track. 1997. (Adventures of the Bailey School Kids Ser.: No. 26). (Illus.). 72p. (J). (gr. 2-4). mass mkt. 3.99 (*0-590-84906-9*, Scholastic Paperbacks) Scholastic, Inc.

—Mermaids Don't Run Track. 1997. (Adventures of the Bailey School Kids Ser.: No. 26). (J). (gr. 2-4). 10.14 (*0-606-11620-6*) Turtleback Bks.

—Monsters Don't Scuba Dive. (Adventures of the Bailey School Kids Ser.: No. 14). (Illus.). (J). (gr. 2-4). (FRE.). 80p. pap. 5.99 (*0-590-24550-3*); 1995. 96p. mass mkt. 3.99 (*0-590-22635-5*) Scholastic, Inc.

—Monsters Don't Scuba Dive. 1995. (Adventures of the Bailey School Kids Ser.: No. 14). (J). (gr. 2-4). 10.14 (*0-606-07884-3*) Turtleback Bks.

—Mrs. Jeepers' Batty Vacation. 1997. (Adventures of the Bailey School Kids Super Special Ser.: No. 2). (Illus.). (J). (gr. 2-4). 4.99 (*0-590-21243-5*) Scholastic, Inc.

—Mrs. Jeepers in Outer Space. 1999. (Adventures of the Bailey School Kids Super Special Ser.: No. 4). (Illus.). 124p. (J). (gr. 2-4). mass mkt. 3.99 (*0-439-04396-4*) Scholastic, Inc.

—Mrs. Jeepers Is Missing. 1996. (Adventures of the Bailey School Kids Super Special Ser.: No. 1). (Illus.). (J). (gr. 2-4). 4.99 (*0-590-88134-5*) Scholastic, Inc.

—Mrs. Jeepers' Monster Class Trip. 2001. (Adventures of the Bailey School Kids Super Special Ser.: No. 5). (J). (gr. 2-4). 10.04 (*0-606-19930-6*) Turtleback Bks.

—Mrs. Jeepers on Vampire Island. 2002. (Bailey School Kids Ser.: No. 6). (Illus.). 128p. (J). mass mkt. 3.99 (*0-439-30641-8*, Scholastic Paperbacks) Scholastic, Inc.

—Mrs. Jeepers' Secret Cave. 1998. (Adventures of the Bailey School Kids Super Special Ser.: No. 3). (Illus.). 128p. (J). (gr. 2-4). pap. 4.99 (*0-590-11712-2*, Scholastic Paperbacks) Scholastic, Inc.

—Mrs. Jeepers' Secret Cave. 1998. (Adventures of the Bailey School Kids Super Special Ser.: No. 3). (J). (gr. 2-4). 10.09 o.p. (*0-606-13626-6*) Turtleback Bks.

—Mummies Don't Coach Softball. 1996. (Adventures of the Bailey School Kids Ser.: No. 21). (J). (gr. 2-4). mass mkt. 3.99 (*0-590-22639-8*) Scholastic, Inc.

—Mummies Don't Coach Softball. 1996. (Adventures of the Bailey School Kids Ser.: No. 21). (J). (gr. 2-4). 10.14 (*0-606-09644-2*) Turtleback Bks.

—Ninjas Don't Bake Pumpkin Pies. 1999. (Adventures of the Bailey School Kids Ser.: No. 38). (Illus.). 70p. (J). (gr. 2-4). mass mkt. 3.99 (*0-439-04398-0*) Scholastic, Inc.

—Ninjas Don't Bake Pumpkin Pies. 1999. (Adventures of the Bailey School Kids Ser.: No. 38). (J). (gr. 2-4). 10.14 (*0-606-18588-7*) Turtleback Bks.

—Phantoms Don't Drive Sports Cars. 1998. (Adventures of the Bailey School Kids Ser.: No. 32). (Illus.). 76p. (J). (gr. 2-4). mass mkt. 3.99 (*0-590-18982-4*, Scholastic Paperbacks) Scholastic, Inc.

—Phantoms Don't Drive Sports Cars. 1998. (Adventures of the Bailey School Kids Ser.: No. 32). (J). (gr. 2-4). 10.14 (*0-606-13702-5*) Turtleback Bks.

—Pirates Don't Wear Pink Sunglasses. 1994. (Adventures of the Bailey School Kids Ser.: No. 9). (Illus.). 80p. (J). (gr. 2-4). mass mkt. 3.99 (*0-590-47298-4*) Scholastic, Inc.

—Pirates Don't Wear Pink Sunglasses. 1994. (Adventures of the Bailey School Kids Ser.: No. 9). (J). (gr. 2-4). 10.14 (*0-606-06671-3*) Turtleback Bks.

—Santa Claus Doesn't Mop Floors. 1991. (Adventures of the Bailey School Kids Ser.: No. 3). 80p. (J). (gr. 2-4). mass mkt. 3.99 (*0-590-44477-8*) Scholastic, Inc.

—Santa Claus Doesn't Mop Floors. 1991. (Adventures of the Bailey School Kids Ser.: No. 3). (J). (gr. 2-4). 10.14 (*0-606-01936-7*) Turtleback Bks.

—Sea Monsters Don't Ride Motorcycles. 2000. (Adventures of the Bailey School Kids Ser.: No. 40). (Illus.). 80p. (J). (gr. 2-4). mass mkt. 3.99 (*0-439-04401-4*, Scholastic Paperbacks) Scholastic, Inc.

—Sea Monsters Don't Ride Motorcycles. 2000. (Adventures of the Bailey School Kids Ser.: No. 40). (J). (gr. 2-4). 10.14 (*0-606-18601-8*) Turtleback Bks.

—Sea Serpents Don't Juggle Water Balloons. 2002. (Bailey School Kids Ser.: Bk. 46). 80p. (J). mass mkt. 3.99 (*0-439-36805-7*, Scholastic Paperbacks) Scholastic, Inc.

—Skeletons Don't Play Tubas. 1994. (Adventures of the Bailey School Kids Ser.: No. 11). 96p. (J). (gr. 2-4). mass mkt. 3.99 (*0-590-48113-4*) Scholastic, Inc.

—Sorciers/Ne Croient/Ordinateur. (Adventures of the Bailey School Kids Ser.). (FRE., Illus.). 88p. (J). mass mkt. 5.99 (*0-590-16024-9*) Scholastic, Inc.

—Trolls Don't Ride Roller Coasters. 1999. (Adventures of the Bailey School Kids Ser.: No. 35). (Illus.). 68p. (J). (gr. 2-4). mass mkt. 3.99 (*0-590-18985-9*, Scholastic Paperbacks) Scholastic, Inc.

—Trolls Don't Ride Roller Coasters. 1999. (Adventures of the Bailey School Kids Ser.: No. 35). (J). (gr. 2-4). 10.14 (*0-606-16587-8*) Turtleback Bks.

—Unicorns Don't Give Sleigh Rides. 1997. (Adventures of the Bailey School Kids Ser.: No. 28). (Illus.). (J). (gr. 2-4). mass mkt. 3.99 (*0-590-25783-8*) Scholastic, Inc.

—Unicorns Don't Give Sleigh Rides. 1997. (Adventures of the Bailey School Kids Ser.: No. 28). (J). (gr. 2-4). 10.14 (*0-606-12837-9*) Turtleback Bks.

—Vampires Don't Wear Polka Dots. (Adventures of the Bailey School Kids Ser.: No. 1). Tr. of Vampires Ne Portent Pas de Robe a Pois. (J). (gr. 2-4). 9999. (FRE.). pap. 5.99 o.p. (*0-590-73545-4*); 1990. (Illus.). 78p. mass mkt. 3.99 (*0-590-43411-X*) Scholastic, Inc.

—Vampires Don't Wear Polka Dots. 1990. (Adventures of the Bailey School Kids Ser.: No. 1). Tr. of Vampires Ne Portent Pas de Robe a Pois. (J). (gr. 2-4). 10.14 (*0-606-04839-1*) Turtleback Bks.

—Werewolves Don't Go to Summer Camp. 9999. (Adventures of the Bailey School Kids Ser.: No. 2). (FRE.). (J). (gr. 2-4). pap. 5.99 o.p. (*0-590-73940-9*) Scholastic, Inc.

—Werewolves Don't Go to Summer Camp. 1991. (Adventures of the Bailey School Kids Ser.: No. 2). (J). (gr. 2-4). 10.14 (*0-606-14111-1*) Turtleback Bks.

—Wizards Don't Wear Graduation Gowns. 2002. (Bailey School Kids Ser.: Vol. 45). (Illus.). 80p. (J). (gr. 4-6). mass mkt. 3.99 (*0-439-36803-0*) Scholastic, Inc.

—Wolfmen Don't Hula Dance. 1999. (Adventures of the Bailey School Kids Ser.: No. 36). (Illus.). 71p. (J). (gr. 2-4). mass mkt. 3.99 (*0-590-18986-7*) Scholastic, Inc.

—Wolfmen Don't Hula Dance. 1999. (Adventures of the Bailey School Kids Ser.: No. 36). (J). (gr. 2-4). 10.14 (*0-606-16938-5*) Turtleback Bks.

—Zombies Don't Play Soccer. 1995. (Adventures of the Bailey School Kids Ser.: No. 15). (Illus.). 70p. (J). (gr. 2-4). mass mkt. 3.99 (*0-590-22636-3*, Scholastic Paperbacks) Scholastic, Inc.

—Zombies Don't Play Soccer. 1995. (Adventures of the Bailey School Kids Ser.: No. 15). (J). (gr. 2-4). 10.14 (*0-606-08417-7*) Turtleback Bks.

Dadey, Debbie, et al. Aliens Don't Wear Braces. 1993. (Adventures of the Bailey School Kids Ser.: No. 7). (Illus.). 74p. (J). (gr. 2-4). mass mkt. 3.99 (*0-590-47070-1*) Scholastic, Inc.

—Ghouls Don't Scoop Ice Cream. 1998. (Adventures of the Bailey School Kids Ser.: No. 31). (Illus.). 66p. (J). (gr. 2-4). mass mkt. 3.99 (*0-590-25819-2*, Scholastic Paperbacks) Scholastic, Inc.

—Leprechauns Don't Play Basketball. 1992. (Adventures of the Bailey School Kids Ser.: No. 4). (Illus.). 71p. (J). (gr. 2-4). mass mkt. 3.99 (*0-590-44822-6*) Scholastic, Inc.

—Skeletons Don't Play Tubas. 1994. (Adventures of the Bailey School Kids Ser.: No. 11). (J). (gr. 2-4). 10.14 (*0-606-07086-9*) Turtleback Bks.

—Werewolves Don't Go to Summer Camp. 1991. (Adventures of the Bailey School Kids Ser.: No. 2). (Illus.). 93p. (J). (gr. 2-4). mass mkt. 3.99 (*0-590-44061-6*) Scholastic, Inc.

—Witches Don't Do Back Flips. 1994. (Adventures of the Bailey School Kids Ser.: No. 10). 96p. (J). (gr. 2-4). mass mkt. 3.99 (*0-590-48112-6*) Scholastic, Inc.

BAMBI (FICTITIOUS CHARACTER)—FICTION

Alvin S. White Studio Staff, illus. Bambi Looks for His Forest Friends. 1992. (Surprise Lift-the-Flap Bk.). 18p. (J). (ps-k). 9.95 o.p. (*1-56282-074-5*) Disney Pr.

Balducci, Rita. Walt Disney's Bambi: Thumper's Book of Opposites. 1993. (Golden Board Bks.). (Illus.). 12p. (J). (ps). bds. o.p. (*0-307-06124-8*, 6124, Golden Bks.) Random Hse. Children's Bks.

Bambi: A Little Spring Shower. unabr. ed. Date not set. (My First Read Along Ser.). (Illus.). 18p. (J). 7.99 incl. audio (*1-55723-749-2*) Walt Disney Records.

Bambi: Paint with Water. (J). 0.99 o.p. (*0-307-08720-4*, 08720, Golden Bks.) Random Hse. Children's Bks.

Bambi: Walt Disney. 1986. (Big Golden Bks.). (Illus.). 24p. (J). (ps). o.p. (*0-307-10380-3*, Golden Bks.) Random Hse. Children's Bks.

Bambi & the Big Clean Up. 1984. (Disney Puppet Bks.). (Illus.). 4.95 o.p. (*0-531-05156-0*, Watts, Franklin) Scholastic Library Publishing.

Bambi en Espanol. 1994. (Spanish Classics Ser.). (Illus.). 96p. (J). 7.98 o.p. (*1-57082-055-4*) Mouse Works.

Birney, Betty. Bambi's Snowy Day. 1992. (Golden Fuzzy Wuzzy Bks.). (Illus.). 32p. (J). (ps). o.p. (*0-307-15704-0*, 15704, Golden Bks.) Random Hse. Children's Bks.

Carr, Jan. Bambi. 1988. (J). pap. 2.50 o.p. (*0-590-41664-2*) Scholastic, Inc.

Covey, Stephen R. Bambi. 1997. (J). pap. o.p. (*0-307-30227-X*, Golden Bks.) Random Hse. Children's Bks.

DeVita, James. Bambi, a Life in the Woods. 1995. (J). (gr. 4 up). pap. 7.00 (*0-87602-347-2*) Anchorage Pr.

Disney Staff. Bambi. 1980. (Illus.). (J). (ps). 1.95 o.p. (*0-525-69512-5*, Dutton) Dutton/Plume.

—Bambi. (FRE.). 96p. (J). (gr. k-5). pap. 9.95 (*0-7859-8850-5*) French & European Pubns., Inc.

—Bambi. 1991. (J). 7.98 o.p. (*0-453-03080-7*) Mouse Works.

—Bambi. 1988. (Disney Animated Ser.). 5.99 o.p. (*0-517-66193-4*) Random Hse. Value Publishing.

—Bambi. (Penguin-Disney Ser.). (ps-3). 1992. (J). 6.98 o.p. (*0-453-03019-X*); 1987. 6.98 o.p. (*0-8317-0681-3*) Viking Penguin.

—Bambi: A Noisy Neighbor. 1997. (Disney's "Storytime Treasures" Library: Vol. 12). (Illus.). 44p. (J). (gr. 1-6). 3.49 o.p. (*1-57973-008-6*) Advance Pubs. LLC.

—Bambi & the Four Seasons. 1988. (J). bds. 5.98 o.p. (*0-8317-0684-8*) Smithmark Pubs., Inc.

—Bambi Gets Lost. 1982. 2.50 o.p. (*0-531-05159-5*, Watts, Franklin) Scholastic Library Publishing.

—Bambi Saves the Day. 1976. (J). (ps-3). 3.50 o.p. (*0-525-61554-7*, Dutton) Dutton/Plume.

—Bambi's Big Day. 1976. (J). (ps-1). 1.50 o.p. (*0-525-61549-0*, Dutton) Dutton/Plume.

—Bambi's Hide & Seek. (Step into Reading Ser.). (Illus.). 32p. (J). 2003. 3.99 (*0-7364-1347-2*); 2002. lib. bdg. 11.99 (*0-7364-8009-9*) Random Hse. Children's Bks. (RH/Disney).

—It's Naptime. 2001. (Illus.). 12p. (J). bds. 5.99 (*0-7364-1199-2*, RH/Disney) Random Hse. Children's Bks.

Disney's How to Draw Bambi. 1992. (Hardback Disney's Classic Character Ser.). (Illus.). 48p. 9.95 o.p. (*1-56010-109-1*, DC01); 40p. (YA). (gr. 3 up). pap. 8.95 (*1-56010-160-1*, DC01) Foster, Walter Publishing, Inc.

Fanning, Jim. Disney's Sing-Along Song Book. 2nd ed. 1997. (Illus.). 144p. (ps-3). pap. 11.95 (*0-7868-8282-4*) Hyperion Pr.

Fun Time with Bambi. 1997. (Disney Toddler Coloring Books I). (Illus.). (J). (ps). pap. (*0-7666-0027-0*, Honey Bear Bks.) Modern Publishing.

Golden Books Staff. Bambi: Good Friends. 1997. (Illus.). (J). pap. text 1.99 o.p. (*0-307-15110-7*, Golden Bks.) Random Hse. Children's Bks.

—Bambi & His Forest Adventures: A Book about Friendship. 1987. (Disney Ser.). (Illus.). 32p. (J). (ps-2). pap. 3.95 o.s.i (*0-307-11675-1*, Golden Bks.) Random Hse. Children's Bks.

Isaacson, Michael. Bambi: Good Morning. 1996. (My First Sound Story Bks.). (Illus.). 14p. (J). o.p. (*0-307-74058-7*, 64058-30, Golden Bks.) Random Hse. Children's Bks.

Johnston, Ollie & Thomas, Frank. Walt Disney's Bambi: The Story & the Film. 1990. (Illus.). 200p. 29.95 o.p. (*1-55670-160-8*) Stewart, Tabori & Chang.

Little Golden Books Staff. Bambi. 1997. (Illus.). (J). (ps-2). bds. 2.99 (*0-307-01061-9*, 98071, Golden Bks.) Random Hse. Children's Bks.

—Walt Disney's Bambi & the Butterfly. 1983. (First Little Golden Bks.). (Illus.). 24p. (J). (ps). bds. 3.99 o.p. (*0-307-10152-5*, Golden Bks.) Random Hse. Children's Bks.

Marvin, Fred, illus. Bambi: The New Prince. 1994. (Tiny Changing Pictures Bk.). 10p. (J). (ps-k). 4.95 o.p. (*1-56282-601-8*) Disney Pr.

Miller, A. G. Walt Disney's Bambi Gets Lost. 1973. (Disney's Wonderful World of Reading Ser.: No. 2). (J). (ps-3). 6.95 o.s.i (*0-394-82520-9*); lib. bdg. 4.99 o.s.i (*0-394-92520-3*) Random Hse. Children's Bks. (Random Hse. Bks. for Young Readers).

Miller, Mona. Disney's Bambi. 1997. (Super Shape Bks.). (Illus.). 24p. (J). (ps-3). 6.99 o.p. (*0-307-10055-3*, 10055, Golden Bks.) Random Hse. Children's Bks.

Mones, Isidre, illus. Walt Disney's Bambi. 1992. (Little Nugget Bks.). 28p. (J). (ps). bds. o.p. (*0-307-12535-1*, 12535, Golden Bks.) Random Hse. Children's Bks.

Mouse Works Staff. Bambi, Vol. 1. 1996. 96p. (J). 7.98 o.p. (*1-57082-403-7*) Little Brown & Co.

—Bambi. 1996. (Spanish Classics Ser.). (Illus.). (J). 7.98 (*1-57082-402-9*) Mouse Works.

—Bambi: A Read-Aloud Storybook. Baker, Liza, ed. 1999. (Disney's Read-Aloud Storybooks Ser.). (Illus.). 64p. (J). (ps-2). 8.99 (*0-7364-0121-0*) Mouse Works.

—Bambi's Favorite Things - Mother's Favorite Things. 1996. (J). bds. 6.98 o.p. (*1-57082-327-8*) Mouse Works.

—It's Hard to Share: Little Lessons for Bambi. 1998. (Disneys Ser.). (Illus.). 16p. (J). (ps). 3.99 o.p. (*1-57082-953-5*) Mouse Works.

—The Jungle Book/Bambi, 2 vols. 75th anniv. ed. 1998. (*0-7364-0090-7*) Mouse Works.

Muldron, Diane. Walt Disney's Bambi Bambi Count to Five. 1991. (Golden Board Bks.). (Illus.). 12p. (J). (ps). bds. o.p. (*0-307-06114-0*, Golden Bks.) Random Hse. Children's Bks.

Pacheco, David & Clay, Jesse, illus. Bambi. 1993. (Illustrated Classic Ser.). 96p. (J). lib. bdg. 15.49 o.s.i (*1-56282-443-0*) Disney Pr.

—Walt Disney's Bambi. 1993. (Sketchbook Ser.). 96p. (J). 14.95 o.p. (*1-56282-442-2*) Disney Pr.

Packard, Mary. Disney's Bambi: Opossum Problems. 1997. (Little Super Shape Bks.). (Illus.). 24p. (J). (ps). pap. text 2.79 o.p. (*0-307-10581-4*, 10581, Golden Bks.) Random Hse. Children's Bks.

Patrick, Denise L. Disney's Bambi. 1997. (Shaped Little Nugget Bks.). (Illus.). 18p. (J). (ps). o.p. (*0-307-12746-X*, Golden Bks.) Random Hse. Children's Bks.

—Disney's Peek-a-Boo Bambi. 1992. (Golden Sturdy Bks.). (Illus.). 14p. (J). (ps-3). o.p. (*0-307-12392-8*, 12392, Golden Bks.) Random Hse. Children's Bks.

Phillips, Joan. Bambi's Game: Walt Disney. 1991. (Golden Book Ser.). (Illus.). (J). (ps-1). o.p. (*0-307-11599-2*, Golden Bks.) Random Hse. Children's Bks.

—Walt Disney Bambi's Game. 1992. (Golden Book Ser.: Level 1). (Illus.). 32p. (J). (ps-1). pap. o.p. (*0-307-15968-X*, 15968, Golden Bks.) Random Hse. Children's Bks.

Random House Disney Staff. Bambi. (FRE.). (J). (gr. 3-8). 13.95 (*0-7859-0613-4*, S26622) French & European Pubns., Inc.

—Bambi. (J). 1996. 5.98 o.p. (*1-57082-435-5*); 1994. (Illus.). 96p. 7.98 o.p. (*1-57082-033-3*) Mouse Works.

—Bambi. (Illus.). (J). 2002. 12p. bds. 6.99 (*0-7364-1250-6*, RH/Disney); 1991. 24p. o.p. (*0-307-74017-X*, Golden Bks.) Random Hse. Children's Bks.

—Bambi. unabr. ed. (Read-Along Ser.). (J). 7.99 incl. audio (*1-55723-008-0*) Walt Disney Records.

Ryder, Joanne. Walt Disney's Bambi's Forest: A Year in the Life of the Forest. 1994. (Illus.). 32p. (J). (gr. k-3). 11.95 o.p. (*1-56282-643-3*); lib. bdg. 12.49 o.p. (*1-56282-698-0*) Disney Pr.

Ryder, Joanne, adapted by. Walt Disney's Bambi. 1993. (Sketchbook Ser.). (Illus.). 64p. (J). (gr. 2-6). pap. 3.50 o.p. (*1-56282-444-9*) Disney Pr.

—Walt Disney's Bambi: Illustrated Classics. 1993. (Sketchbook Ser.). (Illus.). 97p. (J). 14.95 o.p. (*1-56282-000-1*) Disney Pr.

—Walt Disney's Bambi: The Sketchbook Series. 1993. (Sketchbook Ser.). (Illus.). (J). 64p. pap. 2.95 o.p. (*1-56282-237-3*); 97p. lib. bdg. 14.89 o.p. (*1-56282-001-X*) Disney Pr.

Salten, Felix. Bambi: A Life in the Woods. 1981. (J). reprint ed. 112p. lib. bdg. 16.95 (*0-89967-032-6*, Harmony Raine & Co.); 134p. (gr. 2 up). lib. bdg. 17.95 (*0-89966-358-3*) Buccaneer Bks., Inc.

—Bambi: A Life in the Woods. unabr. ed. (J). (gr. 4-6). audio 5.99 (*1-55994-916-3*) HarperChildren's Audio.

—Bambi: A Life in the Woods. unabr. ed. 1988. (J). (ps-3). audio 9.95 o.p. (*0-89845-815-3*, CPN 1419, Caedmon) HarperTrade.

—Bambi: A Life in the Woods. 1969. (Thrushwood Bks.). (Illus.). (J). (gr. k-3). 3.95 o.p. (*0-448-02518-3*) Putnam Publishing Group, The.

—Bambi: A Life in the Woods. Schulman, Janet, ed. 1999. (Illus.). 47p. (J). (ps-3). 18.00 (*0-689-81954-4*, Atheneum/Anne Schwartz Bks.) Simon & Schuster Children's Publishing.

—Bambi: A Life in the Woods. (Illus.). (J). 1992. 160p. (gr. 1 up). pap. 18.00 o.s.i (*0-671-73937-9*, Simon & Schuster Children's Publishing); 1988. mass mkt. 3.50 (*0-671-67469-2*, Simon Pulse); 1988. 192p. (gr. 4-7). pap. 4.99 (*0-671-66607-X*, Aladdin); 1982. (gr. k up). pap. 7.00 (*0-671-46138-9*, Simon Pulse) Simon & Schuster Children's Publishing.

—Bambi - Life in the Woods. (J). 20.95 (*0-8488-1467-3*) Amereon, Ltd.

—Bambi's Children. 1992. (Illus.). 316p. (YA). reprint ed. lib. bdg. 21.95 o.p. (*0-89966-894-1*) Buccaneer Bks., Inc.

—Walt Disney's Bambi Comic Album. 1988. (Gladstone Comic Album Ser.: No. 9). (Illus.). 48p. (Orig.). (J). (ps up). pap. 5.95 o.p. (*0-944599-09-5*) Gladstone Publishing.

Stevens, Stacey. Bambi. 1997. (Illus.). 32p. (J). (ps-k). pap. 4.95 o.p. (*0-7868-4149-4*) Disney Pr.

Story Time with Bambi. 1997. (Disney Toddler Coloring Books II). (Illus.). (J). (ps). pap. (*0-7666-0031-9*, Honey Bear Bks.) Modern Publishing.

Suromex Staff. Bambi. 1997. (Illus.). 12p. (J). (ps-3). pap. (*968-855-235-6*) Suromex, Ediciones, S.A.

Thomas, Frank & Johnston, Ollie. Walt Disney's Bambi: The Sketchbook Series. 1997. (Sketchbook Ser.). (Illus.). 88p. (J). 29.95 (*0-7868-6302-1*) Hyperion Pr.

Walt Disney Bambi. 9999. (J). pap. o.p. (*0-307-07100-6*, Golden Bks.) Random Hse. Children's Bks.

Walt Disney Productions Staff. Bambi in the Woods: Things to Touch, See, & Sniff. 1984. (Illus.). 14p. (J). (ps). 5.95 o.p. (*0-394-86771-8*, Random Hse. Bks. for Young Readers) Random Hse. Children's Bks.

Walt Disney Productions Staff, illus. Bambi's Forest Friends. 1982. (Golden Book Ser.). 8p. (J). (ps). o.p. (*0-307-11501-1*, Golden Bks.) Random Hse. Children's Bks.

Walt Disney Studios Staff. Walt Disney's Bambi. Johnston, Ollie & Thomas, Frank, eds. ltd. ed. 1997. (Sketchbook Ser.). (Illus.). 104p. 100.00 (*1-55709-342-3*) Applewood Bks.

Walt Disney's Bambi. 2002. (J). pap. (*0-9720651-0-5*) Story Reader, Inc.

Walt Disney's Bambi's Fragrant Forest. 1988. (Golden Scratch & Sniff Bks.). (Illus.). 32p. (J). (ps-2). o.p. (*0-307-13530-6*, Golden Bks.) Random Hse. Children's Bks.

Walt Disney's Favorites: Twelve Favorite Little Golden Books - Classics Ser. 1992. (Illus.). 288p. (J). (ps). o.p. (*0-307-15491-2*, 15491, Golden Bks.) Random Hse. Children's Bks.

Walt Disney's Play with Bambi. 1991. (Touch & Feel Bks.). (Illus.). (J). (ps). o.p. (*0-307-12002-3*, Golden Bks.) Random Hse. Children's Bks.

BARBIE (FICTITIOUS CHARACTER)—FICTION

Aber, Linda Williams. Barbie of Swan Lake. 2003. (Barbie Ser.). 48p. (J). mass mkt. 3.99 (*0-439-54523-4*, Scholastic Paperbacks) Scholastic, Inc.

—The Clue in the Castle Wall. 2004. (Barbie Mystery Ser.). 48p. (J). pap. 3.99 (*0-439-55709-7*, Scholastic Paperbacks) Scholastic, Inc.

—The Haunted Mansion Mystery. 2002. (Barbie Mystery Files Ser.: No. 1). 64p. (J). (gr. 1-4). mass mkt. 3.99 (*0-439-37204-6*) Scholastic, Inc.

—The Mystery of the Jeweled Mask. 2002. (Barbie Mystery Files Ser.: No. 2). (Illus.). 80p. (J). (gr. 1-3). mass mkt. 3.99 (*0-439-37205-4*) Scholastic, Inc.

—The Mystery of the Lost Valentine. 2004. (Barbie Mystery Ser.). 48p. (J). mass mkt. 3.99 (*0-439-55708-9*, Scholastic Paperbacks) Scholastic, Inc.

—The Mystery of the Missing Stallion. 2003. (Barbie Mystery Files Ser.: No. 4). 80p. (J). mass mkt. 3.99 (*0-439-37207-0*) Scholastic, Inc.

—Mystery Unplugged. 2003. (Barbie Mystery Files Ser.: No. 3). 80p. (J). (gr. 1-4). mass mkt. 3.99 (*0-439-37206-2*) Scholastic, Inc.

Barbie Birthday. 2004. (Touch & Feel Ser.). 12p. (J). bds. 6.99 (*0-7566-0334-X*) Dorling Kindersley Publishing, Inc.

Barbie Farm Animals. 2004. (Touch & Feel Ser.). 12p. (J). bds. 6.99 (*0-7566-0335-8*) Dorling Kindersley Publishing, Inc.

Gikow, Louise. No Teasing Allowed. 2003. (Barbie Rules Ser.). (Illus.). 24p. (J). 3.25 (*0-307-10357-9*, Golden Bks.) Random Hse. Children's Bks.

Gillian, Lisa. Barbie My Glamour Night. 2002. (Illus.). 10p. (J). (ps-k). bds. 8.99 (*0-7944-0005-1*) Reader's Digest Children's Publishing, Inc.

Golden Books Staff. Barbie: Lost & Found. 2002. 32p. (J). lib. bdg. 11.99 (*0-307-46219-6*, Golden Bks.) Random Hse. Children's Bks.

—Barbie of Swan Lake. 2003. (Illus.). 32p. (J). 11.99 (*0-375-82639-4*, Golden Bks.) Random Hse. Children's Bks.

—Barbie of Swan Lake: A Storybook. movie tie-in ed. 2003. (Illus.). 24p. (J). 3.99 (*0-375-82640-8*, Golden Bks.) Random Hse. Children's Bks.

—The Best of Barbie. 2003. (Illus.). (J). 17.99 (*0-375-82676-9*, Golden Bks.) Random Hse. Children's Bks.

—Gala Evening Fashions. 2003. (Illus.). 12p. (J). pap. 3.99 (*0-375-82539-8*, Golden Bks.) Random Hse. Children's Bks.

—Rising Stars. 2004. (Illus.). (J). pap. 2.99 (*0-375-82649-1*, Golden Bks.) Random Hse. Children's Bks.

—Spring into Fashion. 2004. (Illus.). (J). pap. 3.99 (*0-375-82648-3*, Golden Bks.) Random Hse. Children's Bks.

Goldowsky, Jill. Barbie Wheel of Fashion. 2002. (Illus.). 10p. (J). bds. 8.99 (*0-7944-0009-4*) Reader's Digest Children's Publishing, Inc.

Goldowsky, Jill L. Barbie of Swan Lake: A Panorama Sticker Storybook. 2003. (Illus.). 16p. (J). pap. 7.99 (*0-7944-0280-1*) Reader's Digest Children's Publishing, Inc.

Inches, Alison. Starring Barbie: A Dream Come True. 2003. (Illus.). 32p. (J). 7.99 (*0-307-10589-X*, Golden Bks.) Random Hse. Children's Bks.

Man-Kong, Mary. Fashion Show Fun. 2004. (Illus.). (J). pap. 3.99 (*0-375-82746-3*, Golden Bks.) Random Hse. Children's Bks.

Miller, Sara. A Wedding to Remember. 2003. (Illus.). 32p. (J). (gr. 1-3). 5.99 (*0-307-10424-9*, Golden Bks.) Random Hse. Children's Bks.

Muldrow, Diane. My Barbie Fun Box. 2003. (Illus.). (J). 48p. bds. 9.99 (*0-7364-2228-5*); bds. 9.99 (*0-307-10441-9*) Random Hse. Children's Bks. (Golden Bks.).

O'Neill, Cynthia, ed. Barbie Career Girl. 2004. (SPA.). 48p. (J). pap. 6.99 (*0-7566-0448-6*) Dorling Kindersley Publishing, Inc.

Pagliano, Carol. Barbie: A Day at the Fair. 2003. (Step into Reading Ser.). (Illus.). 32p. (J). lib. bdg. 11.99 (*0-375-92368-3*); pap. 3.99 (*0-375-82368-9*) Random Hse., Inc.

Parker, Jessie & Kilgras, Heidi. Barbie: A Dress-Up Day. 2003. (J). pap. 3.99 (*0-375-82501-0*); lib. bdg. 11.99 (*0-375-92501-5*) Random Hse. Children's Bks. (Random Hse. Bks. for Young Readers).

Random House Staff. The Swan Princess. 2003. (Illus.). 64p. (J). 3.99 (*0-375-82535-5*, Golden Bks.) Random Hse. Children's Bks.

Rogers, Beth. Barbie As Rapunzel: A Magical Princess Story. 2002. (Illus.). 10p. (J). (ps-4). bds. 9.99 (*0-7944-0030-2*, Reader's Digest Children's Bks.) Reader's Digest Children's Publishing, Inc.

Weinberger, Kimberly. Barbie as Rapunzel. 2002. (Junior Chapter Bk.). 48p. (J). (ps-3). mass mkt. 3.99 (*0-439-44295-8*) Scholastic, Inc.

BARNABY (FICTITIOUS CHARACTER: HOLDER)—FICTION

Rouillard, Wendy W. Barnaby-Seasons in the Park. Rouillard, Wendy W., ed. 2000. (Barnaby Ser.: Vol. 5). (Illus.). 32p. (J). 15.95 (*0-9642836-9-7*) Barnaby & Co.

—Barnaby's Aspen Coloring Book. 1996. 16p. (J). (ps-4). pap. 2.50 (*0-9642836-5-4*) Barnaby & Co.

—Barnaby's Cape Cod Coloring Book. 1996. 16p. (J). (ps-4). pap. 2.50 (*0-9642836-4-6*) Barnaby & Co.

—Barnaby's Faraway Land. 1993. (Illus.). 28p. (J). (ps-4). pap. 8.95 (*0-9642836-0-3*) Barnaby & Co.

—Barnaby's Kite Ride. l.t. ed. 1998. (Illus.). 32p. (J). (gr. 1-3). 15.95 (*0-9642836-6-2*) Barnaby & Co.

—Barnaby's Legend: The Nantucket Love Story of Wonoma & Autopscot. 1996. (Illus.). (J). (ps-4). pap. 8.95 (*0-9642836-3-8*) Barnaby & Co.

—Barnaby's Martha's Vineyard Coloring Book. 1995. 24p. (J). (ps-4). pap. 5.95 (*0-9642836-2-X*) Barnaby & Co.

—Barnaby's Nantucket Coloring Book. 1994. (Illus.). 32p. (J). (ps-4). pap. 5.95 (*0-9642836-1-1*) Barnaby & Co.

BARNAVELT, LEWIS (FICTITIOUS CHARACTER)—FICTION

Bellairs, John. The Doom of the Haunted Opera. 1998. (John Bellairs Ser.). (Illus.). 160p. (gr. 3-7). pap. 5.99 o.s.i (*0-14-037657-7*) Penguin Putnam Bks. for Young Readers.

—The Doom of the Haunted Opera. 1998. (J). 10.55 (*0-606-13343-7*) Turtleback Bks.

—The Figure in the Shadows. (Lewis Barnavelt Ser.). (Illus.). (J). (gr. 4-7). 1993. 160p. pap. 5.99 (*0-14-036337-8*, Puffin Bks.); 1975. 168p. 6.95 o.p. (*0-8037-4916-3*, Dial Bks. for Young Readers); 1975. 168p. 13.89 o.p. (*0-8037-4917-1*, Dial Bks. for Young Readers) Penguin Putnam Bks. for Young Readers.

—The Figure in the Shadows. 1999. (J). (gr. 3 up). 20.75 (*0-8446-7009-X*) Smith, Peter Pub., Inc.

—The Figure in the Shadows. 1993. (J). 11.04 (*0-606-05286-0*) Turtleback Bks.

—The House with a Clock in Its Walls. (Lewis Barnavelt Ser.). (Illus.). 192p. (J). 1993. (gr. 3-7). pap. 5.99 (*0-14-036336-X*, Puffin Bks.); 1984. (gr. 4-7). 13.95 o.p. (*0-8037-3821-8*, Dial Bks. for Young Readers); 1984. (gr. 4-7). 13.89 o.p. (*0-8037-3823-4*, Dial Bks. for Young Readers) Penguin Putnam Bks. for Young Readers.

—The House with a Clock in Its Walls. 179p. (J). (gr. 4-6). pap. 4.50 (*0-8072-1423-X*, Listening Library) Random Hse. Audio Publishing Group.

—The House with a Clock in Its Walls. 1974. 192p. (J). (gr. 3 up). pap. 3.50 o.s.i (*0-440-43742-3*, Yearling) Random Hse. Children's Bks.

—The House with a Clock in Its Walls, unabr. ed. 1992. (J). (gr. 5). audio 27.00 (*1-55690-587-4*, 92124E7) Recorded Bks., LLC.

—The House with a Clock in Its Walls. 1994. (J). 20.50 (*0-8446-6758-7*) Smith, Peter Pub., Inc.

—The House with a Clock in Its Walls. 1993. (J). 11.04 (*0-606-05353-0*) Turtleback Bks.

—The Vengeance of the Witch-Finder. (Illus.). 1995. 160p. (J). (gr. 4-7). pap. 5.99 (*0-14-037511-2*, Puffin Bks.); 1993. 176p. (YA). (gr. 5 up). 14.89 o.p. (*0-8037-1451-3*, Dial Bks. for Young Readers); 1993. 160p. (YA). (gr. 5 up). 14.99 o.s.i (*0-8037-1450-5*, Dial Bks. for Young Readers) Penguin Putnam Bks. for Young Readers.

—The Vengeance of the Witch-Finder. 1995. (J). 11.04 (*0-606-08343-X*) Turtleback Bks.

Bellairs, John & Strickland, Brad. The Doom of the Haunted Opera. 1995. 160p. (J). 14.89 o.s.i (*0-8037-1465-3*); (Illus.). 14.99 o.s.i (*0-8037-1464-5*) Penguin Putnam Bks. for Young Readers. (Dial Bks. for Young Readers).

—The Specter from the Magician's Museum. 1998. 149 p. (J). 20.01 (*0-8037-2204-4*, Dial Bks. for Young Readers) Penguin Putnam Bks. for Young Readers.

Strickland, Brad & Bellairs, John. The Specter from the Magician's Museum. 1998. (Lewis Barnavelt Ser.). 160p. (J). (gr. 3-7). 15.99 o.s.i (*0-8037-2202-8*, Dial Bks. for Young Readers) Penguin Putnam Bks. for Young Readers.

BARNEY (FICTITIOUS CHARACTER)—FICTION

Amaral, Gayla. Barney Happy, Mad, Silly, Sad. 2001. (Barney Ser.). 20p. (J). (ps-k). bds. 3.99 (*1-57064-722-4*) Scholastic, Inc.

—Barney on the Go! A Treasury of "Go To" Books. 2000. (Barney's Go to Ser.). (Illus.). 164p. (J). (ps). pap. 10.95 o.p. (*1-57064-732-1*, 97983) Lyrick Publishing.

—Barney's Animal Activity Fun: Matches, Mazes, & More! 2003. (Barney Ser.). (Illus.). 80p. (J). (ps-k). mass mkt. 2.99 (*1-58668-303-9*) Lyrick Publishing.

—Barney's C is for Christmas. 2001. (Barney Ser.). (Illus.). 16p. (J). (ps-k). bds. 6.99 (*1-57064-726-7*) Scholastic, Inc.

—Barney's Color Train Readalong. 2000. (Illus.). 24p. (J). (ps-2). 6.95 (*1-57064-713-5*, 97964) Scholastic, Inc.

—Barney's First Picture Words. 2000. (Barney Ser.). (Illus.). 84p. (J). (ps-k). wbk. ed. 1.99 (*1-57064-730-5*) Scholastic, Inc.

—Barney's Sing-Along Stories: B-I-N-G-O. 2002. (Barney Ser.). 24p. (J). (ps-1). mass mkt. 3.50 o.p. (*1-58668-290-3*) Lyrick Publishing.

—Barney's Star Light, Star Bright. 2000. (Barney Ser.). (Illus.). 20p. (J). (ps-k). pap. 6.95 o.p. (*1-57064-708-9*) Lyrick Publishing.

—Hooray for Mommies! Babies & Barney. 2002. (Barney Ser.). (Illus.). 22p. (J). (ps-k). bds. 5.99 o.p. (*1-58668-220-2*) Lyrick Publishing.

Amaral, Gayla, ed. Barney, Let's Discover. 2001. (Barney Ser.). (Illus.). 32p. (J). (ps-3). pap. 0.99 (*1-58668-134-6*) Scholastic, Inc.

—Barney Let's Pretend. 2001. (Barney Ser.). (Illus.). 32p. (J). (ps-3). pap., wbk. ed. 0.99 o.p. (*1-58668-133-8*) Lyrick Publishing.

—Barney's Favorite Easter Stories, 2 vols., Set. 2001. (Barney Ser.). (Illus.). 48p. (J). (ps-k). bds. 4.99 (*1-58668-072-2*) Scholastic, Inc.

—Barney's I Love Animals. 2003. (Barney Ser.). (Illus.). 112p. (J). 2.99 o.p. (*1-58668-131-1*) Lyrick Publishing.

—Barney's I Love Nursery Rhymes! 2001. (Barney Ser.). (Illus.). 64p. (J). (ps-3). 1.99 (*1-58668-132-X*) Scholastic, Inc.

—Barney's Paint & Play. 2001. (Barney Ser.). (Illus.). 32p. (J). (ps-1). act. bk. ed. 2.99 (*1-58668-142-7*) Scholastic, Inc.

Baby Bop Pretends. 2002. (Barney Ser.). 32p. (J). (ps-k). bds. 5.95 o.p. (*1-58668-156-7*) Lyrick Publishing.

Barney: My First Telephone Book. 2000. (Illus.). (J). (*0-7853-4538-8*) Publications International, Ltd.

Barney & Baby Bop Go to School. 2002. (Barney's Go to Ser.). 32p. (J). (ps-k). bds. 5.95 o.p. (*1-58668-240-7*) Lyrick Publishing.

Barney & Baby Bop Go to the Doctor. 2002. (Barney's Go to Ser.). 32p. (J). (ps-k). bds. 5.95 o.p. (*1-58668-245-8*) Lyrick Publishing.

Barney & Baby Bop Go to the Grocery Store. 2001. (Barney's Go to Ser.). 32p. (J). (ps-k). bds. 5.95 o.p. (*1-58668-147-8*) Lyrick Publishing.

Barney & Baby Bop Go to the Library. 2002. (Barney's Go to Ser.). 32p. (J). (ps-k). bds. 5.95 o.p. (*1-58668-238-5*) Lyrick Publishing.

Barney & Baby Bop Go to the Restaurant. 2002. (Barney's Go to Ser.). 32p. (J). (ps-k). bds. 5.95 o.p. (*1-58668-236-9*) Lyrick Publishing.

Barney & BJ Go to the Fire Station. 2002. (Barney's Go to Ser.). 32p. (J). (ps-k). bds. 5.95 o.p. (*1-58668-228-8*) Lyrick Publishing.

Barney & BJ Go to the Police Station. 2002. (Barney's Go to Ser.). 32p. (J). (ps-k). bds. 5.95 (*1-58668-231-8*) Lyrick Studios.

Barney & BJ Go to the Zoo. 2001. (Barney's Go to Ser.). 32p. (J). (ps-k). bds. 5.95 o.p. (*1-58668-148-6*) Lyrick Publishing.

Barney Design Staff, illus. Barney's Water Fun. 1997. (Barney Ser.). 10p. (J). (ps-k). pap. 4.99 o.p. (*1-57064-199-4*) Scholastic, Inc.

Barney Goes to School Collection. 1996. (Barney's Go to Ser.). (J). (ps-k). 23.00 o.p. incl. VHS (*1-57064-112-9*) Lyrick Publishing.

Barney Goes to the Dentist. 2002. (Barney's Go to Ser.). 32p. (J). (ps-k). bds. 5.95 (*1-58668-248-2*) Scholastic, Inc.

Barney Goes to the Fair. 2002. (Barney's Go to Ser.). 32p. (J). (ps-k). bds. 5.95 o.p. (*1-58668-154-0*) Lyrick Publishing.

Barney Goes to the Farm. 2002. (Barney's Go to Ser.). 32p. (J). (ps-k). bds. 5.95 o.p. (*1-58668-157-5*) Lyrick Publishing.

Barney Goes to the Pet Shop. 2002. (Barney's Go to Ser.). 32p. (J). (ps-k). bds. 5.95 o.p. (*1-58668-151-6*) Lyrick Publishing.

Barney Goes to Town. 2003. pap. text 3.99 o.p. (*1-58668-308-X*) Lyrick Publishing.

Barney Let's Go to the Zoo. 2001. (Barney Ser.). (Illus.). 60p. (J). (ps-k). 1.99 (*1-57064-940-5*) Scholastic, Inc.

Barney Meets the New Baby. 2002. (Barney Ser.). 32p. (J). (ps-k). bds. 5.95 (*1-58668-246-6*) Scholastic, Inc.

Barney Plays Piano. 2002. (Illus.). (J). 16.95 (*0-7853-5234-1*) Publications International, Ltd.

Barney Publishing Staff. Opposites. 1997. (Barney's Beginnings Ser.). 32p. (J). (ps-k). pap. text, wbk. ed. 2.95 (*1-57064-123-4*) Scholastic, Inc.

Barney Publishing Staff & Bernthal, Mark S. Barney's Book of Colors. 1999. (Barney Ser.). (Illus.). 22p. (J). (ps-3). bds. 5.99 (*1-57064-454-3*) Scholastic, Inc.

—Barney's Outer Space Adventure. 1999. (Barney Ser.). (Illus.). 24p. (J). (ps-k). pap. 3.25 o.p. (*1-57064-456-X*) Scholastic, Inc.

Barney Publishing Staff & Kearns, Kimberly. Barney & Me on Safari. 1999. (Barney Ser.). (Illus.). 16p. (J). (ps-k). 5.95 o.p. (*1-57064-448-9*) Scholastic, Inc.

Barney Puppet & Farm Animals Book. (J). 9.95 o.p. (*1-57064-056-4*) Scholastic, Inc.

Barney Says. 2002. (Barney Ser.). 32p. (J). (ps-1). bds. 5.95 o.p. (*1-58668-239-3*); bds. 5.95 o.p. (*1-58668-229-6*) Lyrick Publishing.

Barney Song Sampler. 1998. (Barney Ser.). (J). (ps-k). audio 3.99 o.p. (*1-57132-225-6*, 9421) Lyrick Studios.

Barney Staff. Barney's Great Adventure. (Barney Ser.). (J). (ps-k). audio 7.98. audio NewSound, LLC.

Barney's a Great Day for Learning. 1999. (Barney Ser.). (J). (ps-k). audio compact disk 14.98 o.p. (*1-57132-310-4*, 9442) Lyrick Studios.

Barney's ABC Animals! 1999. (Barney Ser.). (Illus.). 32p. (J). (ps-k). 6.95 (*1-57064-624-4*) Scholastic, Inc.

Barney's Alphabet Fun. 2002. (Barney Ser.). 32p. (J). (ps-k). bds. 5.95 o.p. (*1-58668-241-5*) Lyrick Publishing.

Barney's Big Balloon. 2002. (Barney Ser.). 32p. (J). (ps-k). bds. 5.95 o.p. (*1-58668-237-7*) Lyrick Publishing.

Barney's Big Surprise. 1997. (Barney Ser.). (J). (ps-k). audio 9.98 o.p. (*1-57132-149-7*, 9565) Lyrick Studios.

Barney's Book of Hugs. 2002. (Barney Ser.). 32p. (J). (ps-k). bds. 5.95 o.p. (*1-58668-232-6*) Lyrick Publishing.

Barney's Christmas. 2003. (Barney Ser.). (J). pap. text 3.99 o.p. (*1-58668-312-8*) Lyrick Publishing.

Barney's Great Adventure Soundtrack. 1998. (Barney Ser.). (J). (ps-k). audio 9.98 o.p. (*1-57132-201-9*, 9420); audio 9.98 o.p. (*1-57132-197-7*, 9416); audio 9.98 o.p. (*1-57132-198-5*, 9417); audio compact disk 14.98 o.p. (*1-57132-200-0*, 9419); audio compact disk 14.98 o.p. (*1-57132-199-3*, 9418) Lyrick Studios.

Barney's Great Day for Learning. 1999. (Barney Ser.). (J). (ps-k). audio 9.98 o.p. (*1-57132-307-4*, 9439); audio compact disk 9.98 (*1-57132-309-0*, 9441); audio compact disk 9.98 o.p. (*1-57132-308-2*, 9440); audio compact disk 14.98 o.p. (*1-57132-311-2*, 9443) Lyrick Studios.

Barney's Halloween. 2003. (Barney Ser.). (J). pap. text 3.99 o.p. (*1-58668-311-X*) Lyrick Publishing.

Barney's Love & Lullabies. 1999. (Barney Ser.). (J). (ps-k). audio 6.98 o.p. (*1-57132-458-5*, 9490); audio 6.98 o.p. (*1-57132-459-3*, 9491); audio compact disk 10.98 o.p. (*1-57132-461-5*, 9493); audio compact disk 10.98 o.p. (*1-57132-460-7*, 9492) Lyrick Studios.

Barney's Song Sampler. 1998. (Barney Ser.). (J). (ps-k). audio 3.99 o.p. (*1-57132-335-X*, 9453) Lyrick Studios.

Barney's Tenth Anniversary: I Love to Sing with Barney. 1999. (Barney Ser.). (J). (ps-k). audio 9.98 o.p. (*1-57132-355-4*, 9460); audio compact disk 9.98 o.p. (*1-57132-357-0*, 9462); audio compact disk 14.98 o.p. (*1-57132-358-9*, 9463); audio compact disk 14.98 o.p. (*1-57132-359-7*, 9464) Lyrick Studios.

Barney's Tenth Anniversary: I Love to Sing with Barney. 1999. (Barney Ser.). (J). (ps-k). pap. 9.98 o.p. (*1-57132-356-2*, 9461) Scholastic, Inc.

Berk, Sheryl. Barney's Little Lessons: Be My Friend! 2002. (Barney Ser.). 8p. (J). (ps-1). bds. 5.99 (*1-58668-293-8*) Lyrick Publishing.

—Barney's Little Lessons: The New Babysitter. 2003. (Barney Ser.). 224p. (J). (ps-1). bds. 5.99 (*1-58668-302-0*) Lyrick Publishing.

—Going to My Big Bed! Barney's Little Lessons. 2002. (Barney Ser.). (Illus.). (J). bds. 5.99 o.p. (*1-58668-039-0*) Lyrick Publishing.

—Mine, Mine, Mine! Barney's Little Lessons. 2002. (Barney Ser.). (Illus.). 16p. (J). bds. 5.99 o.p. (*1-57064-727-5*) Lyrick Publishing.

Bernthal, Mark S. Baby Bop Goes to School. Dowdy, Linda Cress, ed. 1994. (Barney Ser.). (Illus.). 24p. (J). (ps-k). 4.95 o.p. (*1-57064-020-3*) Scholastic, Inc.

—Baby Bop's ABC Book. Hartley, Linda, ed. 1993. (Barney Ser.). (Illus.). 26p. (J). (ps-k). mass mkt. 3.50 (*1-57064-008-4*) Scholastic, Inc.

—La Banda de Barney y Babybop: La Alegria de Comparti. 1997. (SPA., Illus.). 32p. (J). pap. 2.95 o.p. (*1-57064-169-2*) Scholastic, Inc.

—Barney: Catch That Hat. 1999. (Barney Ser.). (Illus.). 24p. (J). (ps-k). 2.29 o.s.i (*0-307-98807-4*, 98807, Golden Bks.) Random Hse. Children's Bks.

—Barney: Sharing is Caring. 1999. (Barney Ser.). (J). (ps-k). 2.29 o.s.i (*0-307-98790-6*, Golden Bks.) Random Hse. Children's Bks.

—Barney & Baby Bop Go to School. Larsen, Margie, ed. 1996. (Barney's Go to Ser.). (Illus.). 24p. (J). (ps-k). mass mkt. 3.25 (*1-57064-075-0*) Scholastic, Inc.

—Barney & Baby Bop Go to the Library. 1999. (Barney's Go to Ser.). (Illus.). 21p. (J). (ps-k). mass mkt. 3.50 (*1-57064-447-0*) Scholastic, Inc.

—Barney & Baby Bop's Band: A Story about Sharing. 1995. (Barney Ser.). (Illus.). 32p. (J). (ps-k). pap. 6.95 (*1-57064-024-6*, 99616) Scholastic, Inc.

—Barney & BJ Go to the Fire Station. Larsen, Margie, ed. 1996. (Barney's Go to Ser.). (Illus.). 24p. (J). (ps-k). mass mkt. 3.25 o.s.i (*1-57064-072-6*) Scholastic, Inc.

—Barney & BJ Go to the Police Station. 1998. (Barney's Go to Ser.). (Illus.). 24p. (J). (ps-k). mass mkt. 3.50 (*1-57064-238-9*) Scholastic, Inc.

—Barney & BJ Go to the Zoo. 1999. (Barney's Go to Ser.). (Illus.). 24p. (J). (ps-k). mass mkt. 3.50 (*1-57064-446-2*) Scholastic, Inc.

—Barney Goes to the Fair. Davis, Guy, ed. 2000. (Barney's Go to Ser.). (Illus.). 24p. (J). (ps). mass mkt. 3.50 o.p. (*1-57064-721-6*) Lyrick Publishing.

—Barney Goes to the Farm. 1998. (Barney's Go to Ser.). (Illus.). 24p. (J). (ps-k). mass mkt. 3.50 (*1-57064-261-3*) Scholastic, Inc.

—Barney Va a la Granja. 2002. (Barney's Go to Ser.). (SPA., Illus.). 24p. (J). (ps-k). pap. 3.50 (*1-57064-418-7*) Lyrick Publishing.

—Barney y BJ Van a la Estacion de Bomberos. 1997. (Barney's Go to Ser.).Tr. of Barney & BJ Go to the Fire Station. (SPA., Illus.). 24p. (J). (ps-k). pap. 2.95 o.p. (*1-57064-167-6*) Scholastic, Inc.

—Barney's ABC Animals! 1999. (Barney Ser.). (Illus.). 32p. (J). (ps-k). mass mkt. 3.50 (*1-57064-453-5*) Scholastic, Inc.

—Barney's Adventure Hunt. 1998. (Barney Ser.). (Illus.). 18p. (J). (ps-k). bds. 5.95 (*1-57064-263-X*) Scholastic, Inc.

—Barney's Big Balloon. 1995. (Barney Ser.). (Illus.). 24p. (J). (ps-k). mass mkt. 3.50 o.p. (*1-57064-044-0*) Scholastic, Inc.

—Barney's Book of Shapes. 1998. (Barney Ser.). (Illus.). 22p. (J). (ps). bds. 5.95 o.p. (*1-57064-242-7*) Lyrick Publishing.

—Barney's Book of Shapes. 2001. (Illus.). E-Book (*1-59019-632-5*) ipicturebooks, LLC.

—Barney's Christmas Surprise. 1997. (Barney Ser.). (Illus.). 24p. (J). (ps-k). reprint ed. pap. 6.95 (*1-57064-131-5*); mass mkt. 3.50 (*1-57064-047-5*) Scholastic, Inc.

—Barney's Great Adventure. 1998. (Barney Ser.). (Illus.). 24p. (J). (ps-k). 6.95 o.p. (*1-57064-249-4*); 3.25 o.p. (*1-57064-262-1*) Scholastic, Inc.

—Barney's Number Friends. Larsen, Margie, ed. 1996. (Barney Ser.). (Illus.). 24p. (J). (ps-k). bds. 5.95 (*1-57064-079-3*) Scholastic, Inc.

—Barney's Trick or Treat. 1997. (Barney Ser.). (Illus.). 24p. (J). (ps-k). mass mkt. 3.50 (*1-57064-178-1*) Scholastic, Inc.

—Barney's 12 Days of Christmas. 2000. (Barney Ser.). (Illus.). 26p. (J). (ps). bds. 9.95 o.p. (*1-57064-835-2*) Lyrick Publishing.

—Barney's 12 Days of Christmas. 1998. (Barney Ser.). 26p. (J). (ps-k). bds. 13.95 (*1-57064-241-9*) Scholastic, Inc.

—La Gran Aventura de Barney. 1998. (Barney Ser.). (SPA.). (J). (ps-k). pap. 3.25 o.p. (*1-57064-419-5*) Lyrick Publishing.

—El Gran Globo de Barney: Una Aventura de Escondidillas. 1997. (SPA., Illus.). 24p. (J). pap. 2.95 o.p. (*1-57064-168-4*) Scholastic, Inc.

Bernthal, Mark S. & Wormser, Deborah. Barney's Storybook Treasury. 1999. (Barney Ser.). (Illus.). 176p. (J). (ps-k). pap. 10.99 (*1-57064-579-5*) Scholastic, Inc.

BJ & Scooter. 2002. (Barney Ser.). (J). pap. text o.p. (*1-58668-282-2*) Lyrick Publishing.

Come on over to Barney's House. 2001. (Barney Ser.). 32p. (J). (ps-k). bds. 5.95 o.p. (*1-58668-144-3*) Lyrick Publishing.

Coomer, Donna. Barney's Animal Homes. 1998. (Barney Ser.). (Illus.). 18p. (J). (ps-k). bds. 5.99 (*1-57064-258-3*) Scholastic, Inc.

Cooner, Donna D. Barney & Baby Bop Go to the Grocery Store. 1997. (Barney's Go to Ser.). (Illus.). 20p. (J). (ps-k). mass mkt. 3.25 o.p. (*1-57064-117-X*) Scholastic, Inc.

—Barney & BJ, I See an Insect. 1997. (Barney Ser.). (Illus.). 26p. (J). (ps-k). 8.95 o.p. (*1-57064-132-3*) Scholastic, Inc.

—Barney & BJ's Treehouse. Larsen, Margie, ed. 1996. (Barney Ser.). (Illus.). 22p. (J). (ps-k). 5.95 o.p. (*1-57064-080-7*) Scholastic, Inc.

—Barney Makes Music. Davis, Guy, ed. 1999. (Barney Ser.). (Illus.). 24p. (J). (ps-k). 4.95 (*1-57064-461-6*) Scholastic, Inc.

—Barney's Toolbox. 1998. (Barney Ser.). (Illus.). 14p. (J). (ps-k). 5.95 (*1-57064-244-3*) Scholastic, Inc.

—Bedtime for Baby Bop. Larsen, Margie, ed. 1996. (Barney Ser.). (Illus.). 20p. (J). (ps-k). bds. 4.95 (*1-57064-078-5*) Scholastic, Inc.

Davis, Guy. Barney, Is It Time Yet? 2001. (Barney Ser.). (Illus.). 16p. (J). (ps). bds. 6.95 o.p. (*1-57064-725-9*) Lyrick Publishing.

—Barney, Is It Time Yet? 2001. (Illus.). E-Book (*1-58824-586-1*) ipicturebooks, LLC.

—Barney Says "Night-Night" 1998. (Barney Ser.). (Illus.). 12p. (J). (ps-k). 6.95 (*1-57064-455-1*) Scholastic, Inc.

—Barney's ABC, 123 & More. 1999. (Barney Ser.). (Illus.). 14p. (J). (ps-k). bds. 9.99 (*1-57064-243-5*) Scholastic, Inc.

—Barney's Alphabet Fun. 1998. (Barney Ser.). (Illus.). 32p. (J). (ps-k). mass mkt. 3.50 (*1-57064-257-5*) Scholastic, Inc.

—Barney's Baby Farm Animals. 1998. (Barney Ser.). (Illus.). 22p. (J). (ps-k). 4.95 o.p. (*1-57064-260-5*) Scholastic, Inc.

—Barney's Easter Parade. 1998. (Barney Ser.). (Illus.). 21p. (J). (ps-k). pap. 3.25 o.p. (*1-57064-256-7*) Scholastic, Inc.

—Barney's Favorite Farm Animals. 2001. (Barney Ser.). (Illus.). 20p. (J). (ps-k). bds. 3.95 (*1-58668-129-X*) Scholastic, Inc.

—Barney's Happy Halloween! 2000. (Barney Ser.). (Illus.). 16p. (J). (ps). 5.99 o.p. (*1-57064-989-8*, 97999) Lyrick Publishing.

—Barney's Musical Castle. 2001. (Barney Ser.). (Illus.). 24p. (J). (ps-k). mass mkt. 3.50 (*1-57064-710-0*) Scholastic, Inc.

—Barney's Neighborhood. 1999. (Barney Ser.). (Illus.). 18p. (J). (ps-k). 6.95 (*1-57064-463-2*) Scholastic, Inc.

—Barney's Peekaboo Halloween! 1999. (Barney Ser.). (Illus.). 20p. (J). (ps-k). bds. 5.95 o.p. (*1-57064-464-0*) Lyrick Publishing.

—Barney's Rainbow. 2000. (Barney Ser.). (Illus.). 16p. (J). (ps). bds. 7.95 o.p. (*1-57064-715-1*) Lyrick Publishing.

—Barney's Shake, Rattle & Roll. 2001. (Barney Ser.). (Illus.). 22p. (J). (ps-k). bds. 5.95 o.p. (*1-58668-130-3*) Scholastic, Inc.

—Barney's Sleepytime Gift Set with Plush. 1999. (Barney Ser.). (Illus.). (ps-k). pap. 12.99 o.p. (*1-57064-656-2*) Scholastic, Inc.

—Barney's Treasure Hunt. 1997. (Barney Ser.). (Illus.). 18p. (J). (ps-k). bds. 5.95 o.p. (*1-57064-135-8*) Scholastic, Inc.

—Freddi Fish & the Pirate's Treasure. 2001. (Humongous Ser.). 12p. (J). bds. 9.99 incl. cd-rom (*1-58668-066-8*) Lyrick Studios.

—Love & Lullabies. 2000. (Barney Ser.). (Illus.). 48p. (J). (ps-k). pap. 7.95 o.p. (*1-57064-904-9*, 97988) Scholastic, Inc.

—Playtime at Barney's House! 2001. (Barney Ser.). (Illus.). 12p. (J). (ps). bds. 9.95 o.p. (*1-58668-051-X*) Lyrick Publishing.

—Twinken Plays Peek-a-Boo. 1998. (Barney's Great Adventure Ser.). (Illus.). 20p. (J). (ps-k). 6.95 o.p. (*1-57064-266-4*) Scholastic, Inc.

Davis, Guy, ed. Barney's We Wish You a Merry Christmas. 1999. (Barney Ser.). (Illus.). 14p. (J). (ps-k). pap. 5.95 (*1-57064-750-X*) Scholastic, Inc.

Davis, Guy & Valentine, June. Baby Bop's Blankey. 1999. (Barney Ser.). (Illus.). 14p. (J). (ps-k). 5.95 (*1-57064-613-9*) Scholastic, Inc.

Dowdy, Linda Cress. Barney Goes to the Zoo. Hartley, Linda, ed. 1993. (Lift & Peek Ser.). (Illus.). 18p. (J). (ps). bds. 5.99 (*1-57064-011-4*) Scholastic, Inc.

—Barney Meets the New Baby. 1997. (Barney Ser.). (Illus.). 24p. (J). (ps-k). mass mkt. 5.95 (*1-57064-116-1*) Scholastic, Inc.

—Barney's Puppet Show. Davis, Guy, ed. 1999. (Barney Ser.). (Illus.). 14p. (J). (ps). bds. 6.95 o.p. (*1-57064-597-3*) Lyrick Publishing.

—Make Believe with Barney. 1996. (Barney Ser.). (Illus.). 14p. (J). (ps-k). 7.95 o.p. (*1-57064-094-7*) Scholastic, Inc.

Dudko, Mary Ann. Barney's Alphabet Soup. Larsen, Margie, ed. 1997. (Barney Ser.). (Illus.). 18p. (J). (ps-k). bds. 4.95 (*1-57064-118-8*) Scholastic, Inc.

—Barney's Clothes. 1997. (Barney Ser.). (Illus.). 20p. (J). (ps-k). 3.95 o.p. (*1-57064-119-6*) Scholastic, Inc.

—Los Sombreros de Barney. 1997. (SPA., Illus.). 24p. (J). pap. 2.95 o.p. (*1-57064-162-5*) Scholastic, Inc.

Dudko, Mary Ann & Larsen, Margie. Baby Bop Imagina. 1996. (Barney Ser.).Tr. of Baby Bop Pretends. (SPA., Illus.). 24p. (J). (ps-k). pap. 3.25 o.p. (*1-57064-163-3*) Scholastic, Inc.

—Baby Bop Pretends. Dowdy, Linda Cress, ed. 1994. (Barney Ser.). (Illus.). 24p. (J). (ps-k). mass mkt. 3.25 (*1-57064-022-X*) Scholastic, Inc.

—Baby Bop's Counting Book. Hartley, Linda, ed. 1993. (Barney Ser.). (Illus.). 20p. (J). (ps-k). reprint ed. bds. 3.95 (*1-57064-006-8*) Scholastic, Inc.

—Baby Bop's Foods. Dowdy, Linda Cress, ed. 1994. (Barney Ser.). (Illus.). 24p. (J). (ps-k). 3.95 o.p. (*1-57064-014-9*) Scholastic, Inc.

—Barney & Baby Bop at the Beach. 1995. (Barney Ser.). (Illus.). 14p. (J). (ps-k). 7.95 o.p. (*1-57064-036-X*) Scholastic, Inc.

—Barney's Book of Foods. 2000. (Barney Ser.). (Illus.). 24p. (J). (ps-k). 5.95 o.p. (*1-57064-711-9*, 97962) Scholastic, Inc.

—Barney's Book of Opposites. 1994. (Barney Ser.). (Illus.). 18p. (J). (ps). bds. 4.95 o.p. (*1-57064-016-5*) Lyrick Publishing.

—Barney's Color Surprise. Hartley, Linda, ed. 1993. (Barney Ser.). (Illus.). 18p. (J). (ps-k). bds. 3.95 (*1-57064-007-6*) Scholastic, Inc.

—Barney's Hats. Hartley, Linda, ed. 1993. (Barney Ser.). (Illus.). 24p. (J). (ps-k). 2.25 o.p. (*1-57064-005-X*) Scholastic, Inc.

—Barney's in, Out & All Around. 1999. (Barney Ser.). (Illus.). 24p. (J). (ps-k). bds. 4.99 (*1-57064-445-4*) Scholastic, Inc.

—Barney's Weather Book. 1995. (Barney Ser.). (Illus.). 22p. (J). (ps-k). bds. 3.95 (*1-57064-037-8*) Scholastic, Inc.

—Barney's 5 Senses. Davis, Guy, ed. 2000. (Barney Ser.). (Illus.). 22p. (J). (ps-k). bds. 4.99 o.s.i (*1-57064-706-2*) Scholastic, Inc.

—BJ's Fun Week. 1994. (Barney Ser.). (Illus.). 20p. (J). (ps-k). 3.95 o.p. (*1-57064-015-7*) Scholastic, Inc.

—A Day with Barney. Dowdy, Linda Cress, ed. 1994. (Barney Ser.). (Illus.). 26p. (J). (ps-k). 3.95 o.p. (*1-57064-013-0*) Scholastic, Inc.

Fabulous Funtime Tales. (Barney Ser.). (J). (ps-k). 6.38 incl. audio NewSound, LLC.

Flack, Roberta, et al. Barney's Great Adventure. (Barney Ser.). (J). (ps-k). audio 7.98. audio 5.58. audio compact disk 11.98 NewSound, LLC.

Funtime Stories: 3 Little Pigs. 1998. (J). (ps-3). pap. 7.95 o.p. (*1-57132-220-5*, 9572) Scholastic, Inc.

Golden Books Staff. At the Zoo. 1999. (Barney Ser.). 70p. (J). pap. 2.29 o.s.i (*0-307-08437-X*, Golden Bks.) Random Hse. Children's Bks.

—Barney: Color Surprise. 1999. (Barney Ser.). (Illus.). 32p. (J). (ps-k). pap. 3.99 o.s.i (*0-307-15283-9*, Golden Bks.) Random Hse. Children's Bks.

—A Barney Christmas. 1999. (Barney Ser.). (Illus.). 16p. (J). (ps-k). pap. 2.69 o.s.i (*0-307-08503-1*, Golden Bks.) Random Hse. Children's Bks.

—Barney's Great Adventure. 1998. (Barney Ser.). 12p. (J). (ps-k). o.p. (*0-307-75756-0*, Golden Bks.) Random Hse. Children's Bks.

—I Love Nursery Rhymes. 1999. (Barney Ser.). 70p. (J). pap. 2.29 o.s.i (*0-307-08533-3*, Golden Bks.) Random Hse. Children's Bks.

—I Love Puppies, Kitties & Other Furry Fuzzies. 1999. (Barney Ser.). (Illus.). 70p. (J). pap. 2.29 o.s.i (*0-307-08285-7*, Golden Bks.) Random Hse. Children's Bks.

—Let's Discover. 1999. (Barney Ser.). (Illus.). 40p. (J). pap. 1.19 o.s.i (*0-307-09331-X*, Golden Bks.) Random Hse. Children's Bks.

Goodnight Barney. 2001. (Illus.). (J). 7.95 (*0-7853-4752-6*) Publications International, Ltd.

Griswold, Mike, illus. BJ's Little Boy Blue. 1997. (Barney Ser.). 20p. (J). (ps-k). 6.95 o.p. (*1-57064-269-9*) Scholastic, Inc.

Halfmann, Janet. Barney's Christmas Fun: A Dino-Mite Color & Activity Book. Davis, Guy, ed. 1999. (Barney Ser.). (Illus.). 80p. (J). (ps-k). 1.99 (*1-57064-466-7*) Scholastic, Inc.

—Barney's Egg-Citing Easter: A Dino-Mite Color & Activity Book. Davis, Guy, ed. 1999. (Barney Ser.). (Illus.). 80p. (J). (ps-k). 1.99 o.p. (*1-57064-451-9*) Lyrick Publishing.

—Barney's Four Seasons. Davis, Guy, ed. 1999. (Illus.). 80p. (J). (ps-3). 1.99 (*1-57064-465-9*) Scholastic, Inc.

—Barney's Fun with Rhymes. Davis, Guy, ed. 2003. (Barney Ser.). (Illus.). 112p. (J). (ps-k). 2.99 o.p. (*1-57064-458-6*) Lyrick Publishing.

—Barney's Springtime Fun. Davis, Guy, ed. 1999. (Barney Ser.). (Illus.). 80p. (J). (ps-k). mass mkt. 1.99 (*1-57064-452-7*) Scholastic, Inc.

Halfmann, Janet, et al. Barney's Favorite Songs. Davis, Guy, ed. 2003. (Barney Ser.). (Illus.). 112p. (J). (ps-k). 2.99 o.p. (*1-57064-457-8*) Lyrick Publishing.

Hippity Hop It's Baby Bop. 2002. (Barney Ser.). 32p. (J). bds. 5.95 o.p. (*1-58668-153-2*) Lyrick Publishing.

Holiday Hugs Gift Set: Barney Book & Plush Gift Set. 1997. (Illus.). (J). text 12.99 (*1-57064-138-2*) Scholastic, Inc.

Johnson, Jay B., illus. This Little Piggy. 1997. (Barney Ser.). 22p. (J). (ps up). bds. 6.95 o.p. (*1-57064-225-7*) Lyrick Publishing.

Kearns, Kimberly. Barney & Me at the Circus. 1997. (Barney Ser.). (Illus.). 18p. (J). (ps-k). 5.95 o.p. (*1-57064-125-0*) Scholastic, Inc.

—Barney's Twinkle, Twinkle, Little Star. 1998. (Barney Ser.). (Illus.). 14p. (J). (ps). 5.95 o.p. (*1-57064-406-3*) Lyrick Publishing.

Kearns, Kimberly & Amaral, Gayla. BJ's Rub a Dub Dub. Davis, Guy, ed. 1999. (Barney Ser.). (Illus.). 14p. (J). (ps-k). 5.95 (*1-57064-612-0*) Scholastic, Inc.

Kearns, Kimberly & O'Brien, Marie. Baby Bop's Toys. Hartley, Linda, ed. 1993. (Barney Ser.). (Illus.). 24p. (J). (ps-k). 3.95 o.p. (*1-57064-003-3*) Scholastic, Inc.

—Barney's Farm Animals. Hartley, Linda, ed. 1993. (Barney Ser.). (Illus.). 24p. (J). (ps-k). 3.95 o.p. (*1-57064-002-5*) Scholastic, Inc.

Larsen, Margie. Barney Plays Nose to Toes. Dudko, Mary Ann, ed. 1996. (Barney Ser.). (Illus.). 22p. (J). (ps-k). bds. 4.95 (*1-57064-077-7*) Scholastic, Inc.

—Barney Works with One Hammer. 1997. (Illus.). 14p. (J). 8.95 o.p. (*1-57064-039-4*) Scholastic, Inc.

—Barney y Baby Bop Van al Doctor. 1997. (Barney's Go to Ser.). (SPA., Illus.). 24p. (J). (ps-k). pap. 2.95 o.p. (*1-57064-166-8*) Scholastic, Inc.

—Barney's Halloween Box of Treats. 1998. (Barney Ser.). (Illus.). (J). (ps-k). 9.99 o.p. (*1-57064-515-9*) Lyrick Publishing.

—Barney's Halloween Party. 1996. (Barney Ser.). (Illus.). 24p. (J). (ps-k). mass mkt. 3.50 (*1-57064-046-7*) Scholastic, Inc.

Larsen, Margie, ed. Barney's Friends. 1996. (Barney Ser.). (Illus.). 16p. (J). (ps-k). 4.95 o.p. (*1-57064-114-5*) Scholastic, Inc.

Larsen, Margie & Dudko, Mary Ann. Barney Says "Play Safely" 1996. (Barney Ser.). (Illus.). 24p. (J). (ps-k). mass mkt. 3.50 (*1-57064-073-4*) Scholastic, Inc.

—Barney's "Let's Learn" Boxed Set, Set. 1998. (Barney Ser.). (Illus.). (J). (ps-k). pap. 9.99 (*1-57064-517-5*) Scholastic, Inc.

—Colors: Barney's Balloons. rev. ed. 1997. (Barney's Beginnings Ser.). (Illus.). 32p. (J). (ps-k). pap. 2.95 o.p. (*1-57064-223-0*) Lyrick Publishing.

—Numbers: Barney's Number Circus. 1997. (Barney's Beginnings Ser.). (Illus.). 32p. (J). (ps-k). pap., wbk. ed. 2.95 o.p. (*1-57064-175-7*) Lyrick Publishing.

—Same & Different: Barney Pretends. 1997. (Barney's Beginnings Ser.). 32p. (J). (ps-k). pap., wbk. ed. 2.95 o.p. (*1-57064-176-5*) Scholastic, Inc.

—Shapes: Barney's Shape Picnic. 1997. (Barney's Beginnings Ser.). (Illus.). 32p. (J). (ps-k). pap., wbk. ed. 2.95 o.p. (*1-57064-224-9*) Lyrick Publishing.

Larsen, Margie, et al. Barney Goes to the Doctor. 1997. (Barney's Go to Ser.). (Illus.). 24p. (J). (ps). mass mkt. 3.50 (*1-57064-074-2*) Lyrick Publishing.

—Colors: Barney's Balloons. 1996. (Barney's Beginnings Ser.). (Illus.). 16p. (J). (ps-k). pap. 2.95 o.p. (*1-57064-090-4*) Lyrick Publishing.

—Numbers: Barney's Number Circus. 1996. (Barney's Beginnings Ser.). (Illus.). 16p. (J). (ps-k). pap., wbk. ed. 2.95 o.p. (*1-57064-092-0*) Lyrick Publishing.

—Same & Different: Barney Pretends. 1996. (Barney's Beginnings Ser.). (Illus.). 16p. (J). (ps-k). pap., wbk. ed. 2.95 o.p. (*1-57064-093-9*) Lyrick Publishing.

—Shapes: Barney's Shape Picnic. 1996. (Barney's Beginnings Ser.). (Illus.). 16p. (J). (ps-k). pap., wbk. ed. 2.95 o.p. (*1-57064-091-2*) Scholastic, Inc.

Leach, Sheryl. What Would Barney Say? Larsen, Margie, ed. collector's ed. 1996. (Barney Ser.). (Illus.). 22p. (J). (ps-k). mass mkt. 3.50 (*1-57064-121-8*) Scholastic, Inc.

Leach, Sheryl & Leach, Patrick. Barney's Book of Hugs. Larsen, Margie, ed. 1996. (Barney Ser.). (Illus.). 24p. (J). (ps-k). mass mkt. 3.25 (*1-57064-120-X*) Scholastic, Inc.

Levy, Paul. Turtle Who Lost His Shell. Larsen, Margie, ed. 1996. (Barney Ser.). (Illus.). 24p. (J). (ps-k). pap. 6.95 o.p. (*1-57064-096-3*) Scholastic, Inc.

Lyons, Group. Barney's Christmas Surprise. 1996. (Barney Ser.). (J). (ps-k). pap. text 70.80 o.p. (*1-57064-147-1*) Lyrick Publishing.

Lyons Group Staff & Vedral, Joyce L. Barney & Baby Bop: Seasons & Weather. 1999. (Barney Ser.). (Illus.). 32p. (J). (ps-k). pap. 1.19 o.s.i (*0-307-03521-2*, Golden Bks.) Random Hse. Children's Bks.

Lyrick Publishing Staff, contrib. by. Barney in Outer Space Sing Along. 1999. (Barney Ser.). (Illus.). 16p. (J). (ps-k). pap. 7.95 o.p. (*1-57132-388-0*, 9470) Scholastic, Inc.

Lyrick Studios Staff. Barney's Count to 10. 1999. (Barney Ser.). (Illus.). 24p. (J). (ps-k). 7.95 (*1-57064-623-6*) Scholastic, Inc.

—Barney's Great Adventure: A Super-Dee-Duper Color & Activity Book. 1998. (Barney Ser.). 112p. (J). (ps-k). pap. 3.25 o.p. (*1-57064-314-8*) Scholastic, Inc.

—Barney's Great Adventure: The Chase Is On! 1998. (Barney Ser.). 24p. (J). (ps-k). pap. 3.25 o.p. (*1-57064-247-8*) Scholastic, Inc.

—Barney's Great Adventure Activity Pad. 1998. (Barney Ser.). 48p. (J). (ps-k). pap. 1.95 o.p. (*1-57064-333-4*) Scholastic, Inc.

—Barney's Great Adventure Singalong. 1998. (Barney Ser.). (J). (ps-k). pap. 7.95 o.p. incl. audio (*1-57132-313-9*, 9445) Lyrick Studios.

—Barney's Great Adventure Sticker Book. 1997. (Barney Ser.). (J). (ps-k). pap. 1.95 o.p. (*1-57064-316-4*) Scholastic, Inc.

—Storytime Three: Three Billy Goats Gruff. 1998. (Story Time with Barney Ser.). (Illus.). (J). pap. 7.95 o.p. (*1-57132-150-0*, 9570) Scholastic, Inc.

Lyrick Studios Staff, ed. Barney's I Love You. 2000. (Barney Ser.). (Illus.). 10p. (J). (ps-k). pap. 6.95 o.p. (*1-57064-707-0*) Scholastic, Inc.

—Barney's Puppet Show. 2000. (Barney Ser.). (Illus.). (J). (ps-k). pap. 9.99 o.p. (*1-57064-952-9*) Scholastic, Inc.

Lyrick Studios Staff & Halfmann, Janet. Barney's Run, Jump, Skip & Sing! 2000. (Barney Ser.). (Illus.). 84p. (J). (ps-k). 1.99 (*1-57064-729-1*, 97980) Scholastic, Inc.

McAdam, Christine. Barney's Shapes. 1999. (Barney Ser.). (Illus.). 22p. (J). (ps-k). 5.95 (*1-57064-651-1*) Scholastic, Inc.

Mcadams, Christine. Barney's Colors. 1998. (Barney's Beginnings Ser.). (Illus.). 12p. (J). (ps-k). 5.95 o.p. (*1-57064-310-5*) Lyrick Publishing.

McKee, Darren. Barney Visits the Zoo. 2003. (Barney Ser.). (Illus.). 64p. (J). (ps). 2.99 (*1-58668-313-6*) Lyrick Publishing.

Mody, Monica. Barney's Book of Airplanes. 1998. (Barney's Transportation Ser.). (Illus.). 24p. (J). (ps-k). pap. 3.25 o.p. (*1-57064-236-2*) Scholastic, Inc.

—Barney's Book of Boats. 1997. (Barney's Transportation Ser.). (Illus.). 24p. (J). (ps-k). pap. 3.25 o.p. (*1-57064-129-3*) Scholastic, Inc.

—Barney's Book of Trains. 1998. (Barney's Transportation Ser.). (Illus.). 24p. (J). (ps-k). pap. 3.25 o.p. (*1-57064-237-0*) Scholastic, Inc.

—Barney's Book of Trucks. 1997. (Barney's Transportation Ser.). (Illus.). 24p. (J). (ps-k). pap. 3.25 o.p. (*1-57064-128-5*) Scholastic, Inc.

—Barney's Easter Party! 2000. (Barney Ser.). (Illus.). 22p. (J). (ps-k). bds. 5.99 (*1-57064-714-3*) Scholastic, Inc.

—Barney's Mother Goose Hunt. 1999. (Barney Ser.). (Illus.). 16p. (J). (ps-k). bds. 5.99 (*1-57064-444-6*) Scholastic, Inc.

—Zoomba in Toyland. Larsen, Margie, ed. 1996. (Barney Ser.). (Illus.). 24p. (J). (ps-k). pap. 6.95 o.p. (*1-57064-095-5*, 99645) Scholastic, Inc.

—Zoomba in Toyland. Larsen, Margie, ed. 1995. (Barney Ser.). (Illus.). 24p. (J). (ps-k). 5.95 o.p. (*1-57064-045-9*) Scholastic, Inc.

Neusner, Dena. At the Park: A Touch-and-Feel Book. 2003. (Barney Ser.). (Illus.). 5p. (J). bds. 9.99 (*1-58668-314-4*, Barney Bks.) Lyrick Publishing.

Neusner, Dena Wallenstein. Barney Is So Big! 2003. (Barney Ser.). (Illus.). 176p. (J). bds. 6.99 (*1-58668-301-2*) Lyrick Publishing.

Nickel, Scott. Barney's Halloween Fun. 2000. (Barney Ser.). (Illus.). 84p. (J). (ps-k). 1.99 (*1-57064-780-1*, 97986) Scholastic, Inc.

—Barney's World of Trucks. 2001. (Barney Ser.). (Illus.). 40p. (J). (ps-k). pap. 6.99 (*1-58668-135-4*) Scholastic, Inc.

Parent, Nancy. Barney's Book of Clothes. 2004. (Illus.). 8p. (J). pap. text 5.99 (*1-58668-309-8*) Lyrick Publishing.

—Barney's Zoo Friends. 2001. (Barney Ser.). (Illus.). 12p. (J). (ps-1). bds. 9.99 (*1-58668-233-4*) Scholastic, Inc.

—Where's Barney? 2002. (Barney Ser.). (Illus.). (J). bds. 5.99 o.p. (*1-58668-141-9*) Lyrick Publishing.

Payne, Sandra J. Barney, I Did It Myself! 2000. (Barney Ser.). (Illus.). 20p. (J). (ps). bds. 5.95 o.p. (*1-57064-719-4*) Lyrick Publishing.

—Barney's Neighborhood Friends. 2000. (Barney Ser.). (Illus.). 84p. (J). (ps-k). 1.99 (*1-57064-779-8*, 97985) Scholastic, Inc.

—Barney's Time for Counting. Davis, Guy, ed. 1999. (Barney Ser.). (Illus.). 24p. (J). (ps-k). mass mkt. 2.99 o.s.i (*1-57064-449-7*) Scholastic, Inc.

Payne, Sandra J., et al. Barney's Alphabet Fun with Mother Goose. Davis, Guy, ed. 1999. (Barney Ser.). (Illus.). 64p. (J). (ps-k). mass mkt. 1.99 (*1-57064-450-0*) Scholastic, Inc.

Rillo, Cary, illus. Barney's Play & Learn Book Set, 4 vols. 1999. 18p. (J). (ps-k). 9.99 (*1-57064-754-2*, 97428) Scholastic, Inc.

Ruppe, Juan V., illus. Barney's Happy Valentine's Day. 1997. (Barney Ser.). 24p. (J). (ps-k). mass mkt. 3.50 (*1-57064-294-X*, 97752) Scholastic, Inc.

Ryan, Lisa. Barney's Many Hats! What Can Barney Be? 2002. (Barney Ser.). 5p. (J). (ps-1). bds. 6.99 (*1-58668-291-1*) Lyrick Publishing.

—The Wheels on Barney's Bus. 2002. (Barney Ser.). 6p. (J). (ps-1). pap. 9.99 (*1-58668-292-X*) Lyrick Publishing.

Sander, Sonia. Getting Ready for 123 Fun. 2003. (Barney Ser.). 64p. (J). mass mkt. 2.99 (*1-58668-310-1*) Scholastic, Inc.

Scholastic, Inc. Staff. Barney Goes to the Zoo; Barney's Book of Hugs; Barney Says Please & Thank You; Barney & Baby Bop Go to School; Barney's Alphabet Fun; Barney Goes to the Pet Shop, 6 vols., Set. 2002. (Illus.). 144p. (J). pap. 14.00 (*0-439-44306-7*) Scholastic, Inc.

—Barney y Bebe Bop Van a la Escuela. 2002. (Barney Ser.). (Illus.). 24p. (J). (ps). pap. 2.95 (*1-57064-353-9*) Lyrick Publishing.

—Barneys Sing-along Stories: Clean-Up. 2004. (Barney Ser.). (Illus.). 24p. (J). pap. 3.50 (*1-58668-307-1*) Lyrick Publishing.

—Barney's Sing-along Stories: If You're Happy & You Know It! 2004. (Barney Ser.). (Illus.). 24p. (J). mass mkt. 3.50 (*0-439-45862-5*) Scholastic, Inc.

—Merry Christmas! 2003. (Barney Ser.). 64p. (J). mass mkt. 2.99 (*0-439-52451-2*, Scholastic Paperbacks) Scholastic, Inc.

—Play Time! 2004. (Barney Ser.). 144p. (J). mass mkt. 3.99 (*0-439-60700-0*) Scholastic, Inc.

Scholastic, Inc. Staff, contrib. by. Barney's Color Train. 2000. (Barney Ser.). (Illus.). 32p. (J). mass mkt. 128.00 (*1-58668-250-4*) Scholastic, Inc.

—Barney's Count to 10. 1999. (Barney Ser.). (Illus.). 32p. (J). mass mkt. 3.50 (*1-58668-249-0*) Scholastic, Inc.

Scholastic, Inc. Staff, et al. Barney's Colorful World. 2003. (Barney Ser.). 32p. (J). mass mkt. 3.99 (*0-439-56881-1*) Scholastic, Inc.

Shrode, Mary. Just Imagine with Barney. White, Stephen, ed. 1992. (Barney Ser.). (Illus.). 32p. (J). (ps-1). 7.95 o.p. (*1-57064-000-9*) Scholastic, Inc.

Sleepytime Slumber Stories. (Barney Ser.). (J). 6.38 incl. audio NewSound, LLC.

Sleepytime Storytime Two: Ugly Duckling. 1998. (J). (ps-3). pap. 7.95 o.p. (*1-57132-221-3*, 9577) Scholastic, Inc.

Storytime Four: The Lion & the Mouse. 1997. (J). pap. 7.95 o.p. (*1-57132-155-1*, 9575) Scholastic, Inc.

Storytime with Barney: 3 Billy Goats Gruff. 1997. (Barney Ser.). (J). (ps-k). audio 7.95 Lyrick Studios.

Tait, Katie. Babies & Barney: Hooray for Puppies & Kittens! 2003. (Barney Ser.). (Illus.). 192p. (J). (ps-1). bds. 5.99 (*1-58668-300-4*) Lyrick Publishing.

—Barney's Forest Friends. 2003. (Barney Ser.). (Illus.). 23p. (J). mass mkt. 3.99 (*1-58668-296-2*) Lyrick Publishing.

A Tent Too Full. 2002. (Barney Ser.). 32p. (J). (ps-k). bds. 5.95 o.p. (*1-58668-150-8*) Lyrick Publishing.

Three Billy Goats Gruff & Other Tee-riffic Tales. (Barney Ser.). (J). 6.38 incl. audio NewSound, LLC.

Valentine, June, illus. Barney's Christmas Songs. 1998. (Barney Ser.). (J). (ps-k). (*0-7853-2727-4*) Publications International, Ltd.

Valentine-Ruppe, June, illus. Baby Bop's Hey Diddle Diddle! 1997. (Barney Ser.). 20p. (J). (ps-k). 6.95 o.p. (*1-57064-268-0*) Scholastic, Inc.

—Barney's Friends. 1996. (Barney Ser.). 18p. (J). (ps-k). pap. 4.95 o.p. (*1-57064-066-1*) Scholastic, Inc.

—Barney's Sing-along Stories: I Love You. 2003. (Barney Ser.). 24p. (J). (ps-1). mass mkt. 3.50 (*1-58668-299-7*) Lyrick Publishing.

Valvassori, Maureen M. Barney & Baby Bop Go to the Restaurant. 1998. (Barney's Go to Ser.). (Illus.). 24p. (J). (ps). mass mkt. 3.25 o.p. (*1-57064-239-7*) Lyrick Publishing.

—Barney & Baby Bop's Garden. 1997. (Barney Ser.). (Illus.). 26p. (J). (ps-k). 8.95 o.p. (*1-57064-133-1*) Scholastic, Inc.

—Barney Goes to the Dentist. 1998. (Barney's Go to Ser.). (Illus.). 24p. (J). (ps-k). mass mkt. 5.95 o.p. (*1-57064-240-0*) Scholastic, Inc.

—Barney Goes to the Pet Shop. Davis, Guy, ed. 2000. (Barney's Go to Ser.). (Illus.). 24p. (J). (ps-k). mass mkt. 3.50 (*1-57064-720-8*) Scholastic, Inc.

—Barney, What Will I Be When I Grow Up? 2000. (Barney Ser.). (Illus.). 16p. (J). (ps). pap. 5.95 o.p. (*1-57064-712-7*, 97963) Lyrick Publishing.

—My Day with Barney. 2001. (Barney Ser.). (Illus.). 12p. (J). bds. 5.99 (*1-58668-139-7*) Scholastic, Inc.

What Would Barney Say? 2002. (Barney Ser.). 32p. (J). (ps-k). bds. 5.95 o.p. (*1-58668-227-X*) Lyrick Publishing.

White, Stephen. Baby Bop Discovers Shapes. 1997. (Barney Ser.). (Illus.). (J). (ps-k). (*0-7853-2143-8*) Publications International, Ltd.

—Baby Bop Discovers Shapes. Hartley, Linda, ed. 1993. (Barney Ser.). (Illus.). 14p. (J). (ps-k). 4.95 o.p. (*1-57064-010-6*) Scholastic, Inc.

—Barney. 1997. (Barney Ser.). (Illus.). (J). (ps-k). (*0-7853-2144-6*) Publications International, Ltd.

—Barney & Baby Bop: A Tent Too Full. Dowdy, Linda Cress, ed. 1993. (Barney Ser.). (Illus.). 24p. (J). (ps-k). pap. 3.25 o.p. (*1-57064-009-2*) Scholastic, Inc.

—Barney & Baby Bop Follow That Cat! 1996. (Barney Ser.). (Illus.). 14p. (J). (ps-k). 5.95 o.p. (*1-57064-081-5*) Scholastic, Inc.

—Barney & Baby Bop Follow That Cat! Dowdy, Linda Cress, ed. 1994. (Barney Ser.). (Illus.). 14p. (J). (ps-k). pap. 4.95 o.p. (*1-57064-017-3*) Scholastic, Inc.

—Barney Dice Por Favor y Gracias. 2002. (Barney Ser.). (SPA., Illus.). 24p. (J). (ps-k). pap. 3.50 (*1-57064-164-1*) Scholastic, Inc.

—Barney Says "I Love You" 1997. (Barney Ser.). (Illus.). 26p. (J). (ps-k). 12.95 o.p. (*1-57064-122-6*) Scholastic, Inc.

—Barney Says "Please & Thank You" Dowdy, Linda Cress, ed. 1994. (Barney Ser.). (Illus.). 24p. (J). (ps-k). mass mkt. 3.50 (*1-57064-023-8*) Scholastic, Inc.

—Barney's Christmas Wishes. 1997. (Barney Ser.). (Illus.). 24p. (J). (ps-k). mass mkt. 3.50 (*1-57064-179-X*) Scholastic, Inc.

—Barney's Easter Egg Hunt. 1996. (Barney Ser.). (Illus.). 24p. (J). (ps-k). mass mkt. 3.50 (*1-57064-134-X*) Scholastic, Inc.

—Barney's Happy Holiday Set. 1998. (Barney Ser.). (Illus.). (J). (ps-k). 12.99 o.p. (*1-57064-552-3*) Lyrick Publishing.

—Barney's Imagination Island: Bedtime with Barney. Dowdy, Linda Cress, ed. 1994. (Barney Ser.). (Illus.). 32p. (J). (ps-k). 7.95 o.p. (*1-57064-028-9*) Scholastic, Inc.

—Barney's Night Before Christmas. Davis, Guy, ed. 1999. (Barney Ser.). (Illus.). 24p. (J). (ps-k). mass mkt. 3.50 (*1-57064-462-4*) Scholastic, Inc.

—Barney's Thanksgiving. 1998. (Barney Ser.). (Illus.). 24p. (J). (ps-k). mass mkt. 3.50 (*1-57064-459-4*) Scholastic, Inc.

—Barney's Wonderful Winter Day. (Barney Ser.). (Illus.). 32p. (J). (ps-k). 1995. pap. 6.95 o.p. (*1-57064-049-1*); 1994. 4.95 o.p. (*1-57064-027-0*); 1997. reprint ed. mass mkt. 3.50 (*1-57064-202-8*) Scholastic, Inc.

—Just Like You. 1995. (Barney Ser.). (Illus.). 32p. (J). (ps-k). 6.95 o.p. (*1-57064-021-1*) Scholastic, Inc.

—A Tent Too Full. Larsen, Margie, ed. 1996. (Barney Ser.). (Illus.). 24p. (J). (ps-k). pap. 6.95 o.p. (*1-57064-070-X*) Scholastic, Inc.

—What Can It Be? Dowdy, Linda Cress, ed. 1994. (Barney Ser.). (Illus.). 32p. (J). (ps-k). 4.95 o.p. (*1-57064-019-X*) Lyrick Publishing.

—What Can It Be? Larsen, Margie, ed. 1996. (Barney Ser.). (Illus.). 32p. (J). (ps-k). pap. 6.95 o.p. (*1-57064-071-8*) Scholastic, Inc.

BARTH, SEBASTIAN (FICTITIOUS CHARACTER)—FICTION

Howe, James. Dew Drop Dead: A Sebastian Barth Mystery. 1991. 128p. (YA). (gr. 5 up). pap. 4.50 o.p. (*0-380-71301-2*, Avon Bks.) Morrow/Avon.

—Dew Drop Dead: A Sebastian Barth Mystery. 160p. (J). (gr. 3-7). 2000. pap. 4.50 (*0-689-80760-0*, Aladdin); 1990. 16.00 (*0-689-31425-6*, Atheneum) Simon & Schuster Children's Publishing.

—Dew Drop Dead: A Sebastian Barth Mystery. 2000. 10.55 (*0-606-17314-5*); 1990. 9.60 o.p. (*0-606-04906-1*) Turtleback Bks.

—Eat Your Poison, Dear: A Sebastian Barth Mystery. (J). 1991. 144p. (gr. 4-7). pap. 3.99 (*0-380-71332-2*); 1987. pap. 2.95 (*0-380-70359-9*) Morrow/Avon. (Avon Bks.).

—Eat Your Poison, Dear: A Sebastian Barth Mystery. (Sebastian Barth Mysteries Ser.). 144p. (J). (gr. 4-7). 1995. pap. 4.99 (*0-689-80339-7*, Aladdin); 1986. 16.00 (*0-689-31206-7*, Atheneum) Simon & Schuster Children's Publishing.

—Eat Your Poison, Dear: A Sebastian Barth Mystery. 1995. 11.04 (*0-606-07463-5*) Turtleback Bks.

—Stage Fright: A Sebastian Barth Mystery. 1991. 144p. (J). pap. 3.99 o.p. (*0-380-71331-4*); 1987. (YA). pap. 2.95 (*0-380-70173-1*) Morrow/Avon. (Avon Bks.).

—Stage Fright: A Sebastian Barth Mystery. (Sebastian Barth Mysteries Ser.). 160p. (J). 1995. (gr. 4-7). pap. 4.99 (*0-689-80338-9*, Aladdin); 1986. (gr. 3-7). 12.95 o.s.i (*0-689-31160-5*, Atheneum); 2nd ed. 1990. (gr. 3-7). 15.00 (*0-689-31701-8*, Atheneum) Simon & Schuster Children's Publishing.

—Stage Fright: A Sebastian Barth Mystery. 1995. 11.04 (*0-606-08193-3*) Turtleback Bks.

—What Eric Knew: A Sebastian Barth Mystery. 1991. 128p. (J). pap. 3.99 (*0-380-71330-6*); 1986. 144p. pap. 3.50 (*0-380-70171-5*) Morrow/Avon. (Avon Bks.).

—What Eric Knew: A Sebastian Barth Mystery. (J). 1995. (Sebastian Barth Mysteries Ser.: Vol. 1). 156p. (gr. 4-7). pap. 4.99 (*0-689-80340-0*, Aladdin); 1985. (gr. 3-7). 12.95 o.s.i (*0-689-31159-1*, 467190, Atheneum); 2nd ed. 1990. 126p. (gr. 4-7). 15.00 (*0-689-31702-6*, Atheneum) Simon & Schuster Children's Publishing.

—What Eric Knew: A Sebastian Barth Mystery. 1995. 11.04 (*0-606-08359-6*) Turtleback Bks.

BARTON, CLARA, 1821-1912—FICTION

Osborne, Mary Pope. Civil War on Sunday. 2000. (Magic Tree House Ser.: No. 21). (Illus.). 96p. (J). (gr. k-3). lib. bdg. 11.99 (*0-679-99067-4*); pap. 3.99 (*0-679-89067-X*) Random Hse. Children's Bks. (Random Hse. Bks. for Young Readers).

—Civil War on Sunday. 2000. (Magic Tree House Ser.: No. 21). (Illus.). (J). (gr. k-3). 10.04 (*0-606-18852-5*) Turtleback Bks.

Woodworth, Deborah. Compassion: The Story of Clara Barton. 1997. (Value Biographies Ser.). (Illus.). 32p. (J). (gr. 2-6). lib. bdg. 22.79 (*1-56766-227-7*) Child's World, Inc.

BASIL OF BAKER STREET (FICTITIOUS CHARACTER)—FICTION

Titus, Eve. Basil & the Lost Colony. (Illus.). (J). (gr. 3-6). 1989. pap. 2.50 (*0-671-64120-4*, Aladdin); 1981. pap. (*0-671-41602-2*, Simon Pulse) Simon & Schuster Children's Publishing.

—Basil & the Lost Colony. 1992. (J). 15.75 o.p. (*0-8446-6548-7*) Smith, Peter Pub., Inc.

—Basil & the Pygmy Cats. 1982. (Illus.). (J). (gr. 3-6). pap. (*0-671-45531-1*, Simon Pulse) Simon & Schuster Children's Publishing.

—Basil & the Pygmy Cats. 1992. (J). 16.00 o.p. (*0-8446-6549-5*) Smith, Peter Pub., Inc.

—Basil & the Pygmy Cats: A Basil of Baker Street Mystery. 1989. (Illus.). (J). (gr. 3-6). pap. 2.75 (*0-671-64119-0*, Aladdin) Simon & Schuster Children's Publishing.

—Basil in Mexico. 1976. (Illus.). (J). (gr. 4-6). text 7.95 o.p. *(0-07-064898-0)*; lib. bdg. 7.95 o.p. *(0-07-064900-6)* McGraw-Hill Cos., The.

—Basil in Mexico. (Illus.). (J). (gr. 3-6). 1990. 96p. pap. 2.75 *(0-671-64117-4*, Aladdin); 1986. pap. *(0-671-62436-9*, Simon Pulse) Simon & Schuster Children's Publishing.

—Basil in the Wild West. 1981. (Illus.). (J). (gr. 4-6). text 9.95 o.p. *(0-07-064934-0)* McGraw-Hill Cos., The.

—Basil in the Wild West. 1990. (Illus.). 86p. (J). (gr. 4-7). per. 2.75 *(0-671-64118-2*, Aladdin) Simon & Schuster Children's Publishing.

—Basil of Baker Street. (J). (gr. 3-6). 1989. mass mkt. 3.99 *(0-671-70287-4)*; 1988. (Illus.). pap. 2.50 *(0-671-63517-4)* Simon & Schuster Children's Publishing. (Aladdin).

—Basil of Baker Street. 1958. (J). 9.09 o.p. *(0-606-04104-4)* Turtleback Bks.

Titus, Eve & Galdone, Paul. Basil of Baker Street. 1958. (J). (gr. 3-6). lib. bdg. 8.95 o.p. *(0-07-064907-3)* McGraw-Hill Cos., The.

BATMAN (FICTITIOUS CHARACTER)—FICTION

Bader, Hilary J. Batman Beyond. 2000. (Illus.). 140p. pap. 9.95 *(1-56389-604-4)* DC Comics.

Batman Sticker Book. 2001. 16p. (J). pap. 6.99 *(0-7894-7866-8)* Dorling Kindersley Publishing, Inc.

Byrne, John. Generations: An Imaginary Tale. Crain, Dale, ed. 2000. (Illus.). 191p. pap. 14.95 *(1-56389-605-2)* DC Comics.

Campbell, Tom. Batman & Robin. Sahler, John, ed. 1997. (Magic Touch Talking Bks.). (Illus.). (J). (ps-2). 19.99 *(1-888208-34-1)* Hasbro, Inc.

Colon, Suzan. Batman: Terror of Two-Face. 1999. (Illus.). 24p. (J). (ps-3). pap. 3.99 o.s.i *(0-307-13070-3*, Golden Bks.) Random Hse. Children's Bks.

DC Comics Staff. Batman: The Animated Series Pop-up Playbook. 1994. (Illus.). (J). (ps-3). 24.95 o.p. *(0-316-17788-1)* Little Brown & Co.

—Batman 3. 1995. (J). pap. *(0-316-15441-5)* Little Brown & Co.

—Superman. novel ed. 2001. 32p. (J). pap. *(0-316-17799-7)* Little Brown Children's Bks.

Fisch, Sholly. Batman Beyond: No Place Like Home. Milliron, Kerry, ed. 2000. (Pictureback Ser.). (Illus.). 24p. (J). (ps-3). pap. 3.25 *(0-375-80652-0*, Random Hse. Bks. for Young Readers) Random Hse. Children's Bks.

Goetz, Ann & Golden Books Staff. Heroes & Villains. 1997. (Golden Look-Look Bks.). (Illus.). 24p. (J). (ps-3). pap. 3.29 o.s.i *(0-307-12967-5*, 12967, Golden Bks.) Random Hse. Children's Bks.

Golden Books Staff. Batman & Mr. Freeze: Subzero (On Thin Ice!) Coloring Book. 1997. (Golden Book Ser.). (Illus.). 70p. (J). pap. 2.29 o.s.i *(0-307-08435-3*, Golden Bks.) Random Hse. Children's Bks.

—Batman & Robin. 1999. 48p. pap. 1.69 o.s.i *(0-307-09291-7*, Golden Bks.) Random Hse. Children's Bks.

—Batman & Robin: Gotham Nights Coloring Book. 1997. (Illus.). 32p. (J). pap. 1.79 o.s.i *(0-307-15119-0*, Golden Bks.) Random Hse. Children's Bks.

—Batman Redemption: Paint with Water. 1997. 32p. (J). pap. 1.79 o.s.i *(0-307-08724-7*, Golden Bks.) Random Hse. Children's Bks.

Golden Western Staff. Batman TV. (Illus.). (J). (ps-3). 9999. pap. o.p. *(0-307-08238-5)*; 9999. pap. o.p. *(0-307-08324-1)*; 1999. 56p. pap. 1.69 o.s.i *(0-307-03997-8)* Random Hse. Children's Bks. (Golden Bks.).

Grayson, Devin, et al. Batman: The Copycat Crime. 2003. (Reader Ser.). 48p. (J). mass mkt. 3.99 *(0-439-47097-8*, Cartwheel Bks.) Scholastic, Inc.

Knowledge Adventures Staff. Batman & Robin Cartoon Maker. 1995. cd-rom 15.00 o.s.i *(1-56997-219-2)* Random Hse., Inc.

Lovitt, Chip. Batman & the Ninja. 1995. (Illus.). 24p. (J). (ps-3). pap. 3.29 o.s.i *(0-307-12837-7*, Golden Bks.) Random Hse. Children's Bks.

McCann, Jesse Leon, et al. Batman: Time Thaw. 2003. (Reader Ser.). 48p. (J). mass mkt. 3.99 *(0-439-47096-X)* Scholastic, Inc.

Peterson, Scott. Batman Beyond: New Hero in Town. Milliron, Kerry, ed. 2000. (Pictureback Ser.). (Illus.). 24p. (J). (ps-3). pap. 3.25 *(0-375-80653-9*, Random Hse. Bks. for Young Readers) Random Hse. Children's Bks.

Puckett, Kelley. Batman's Dark Secret. 2000. (Hello Reader! Ser.). (Illus.). (J). 10.14 *(0-606-18517-8)* Turtleback Bks.

Random House U. K. Ltd. Staff. Batman Beyond: Gene Splicers. 2002. 24p. (J). pap. 3.25 *(0-375-80655-5*, Random Hse. Bks. for Young Readers) Random Hse. Children's Bks.

Raven, James. Subzero: Batman & Mr. Freeze. 1997. (Illus.). 128p. (J). (gr. 4-6). pap. 3.50 *(0-316-17696-6)* Little Brown Children's Bks.

Simonson, Louise. Batman: Mystery of the Batwoman. 2003. (Illus.). 176p. (gr. 3-7). pap. text 4.99 *(0-553-48777-9*, Bantam Bks. for Young Readers) Random Hse. Children's Bks.

Slavkovic, Sibin. Just Imagine Stan Lee Creating Batman. 2001. (Illus.). 48p. pap. *(1-56389-822-5)* DC Comics.

Sonneborn, Scott & Lewis, Liz. Batman Beyond Files. 2000. (Illus.). 48p. (J). pap. 12.95 o.p. *(0-8230-0462-7*, Watson-Guptill Bks.) Watson-Guptill Pubns., Inc.

Starlog Presents: A Salute to Batman & Other Heroes. 1997. (Starlog Movie Ser.). (YA). pap. 5.99 *(0-934551-17-0)* Profile Entertainment, Inc.

Teitelbaum, Michael. Batman Beyond: The Return of the Joker. 2000. 144p. (J). (gr. 4-7). mass mkt. 4.99 *(0-439-20769-X)* Scholastic, Inc.

—The Penguin's Plot. 1992. (Batman Returns Ser.). (Illus.). 24p. (J). (ps-3). pap. 3.29 o.s.i *(0-307-12687-0*, 12687, Golden Bks.) Random Hse. Children's Bks.

Templeton, Ty, illus. How to Draw Batman. 1997. (DC Comics Ser.). 40p. (J). (gr. 3 up). pap. 8.95 *(1-56010-326-4*, CB01) Foster, Walter Publishing, Inc.

Timm, Bruce, prod. Batman Beyond: Original Television Soundtrack. 2002. (J). audio 9.98 Rhino Entertainment.

Vincenzo, Darren & Golden Books Staff. Batman Book of Masks. 1999. (Golden Book Ser.). (Illus.). (J). (ps-1). pap. 3.49 o.s.i *(0-307-12990-X*, Golden Bks.) Random Hse. Children's Bks.

Wenk, Richard. The Doomsday Prophecy. 1989. (Which Way Bks.: No. 4). (Illus.). (J). (gr. 4-7). pap. 3.99 *(0-671-68312-8*, Simon Pulse) Simon & Schuster Children's Publishing.

BEDELIA, AMELIA (FICTITIOUS CHARACTER)—FICTION

see Amelia-Bedelia (Fictitious Character)—Fiction

BELDEN, TRIXIE (FICTITIOUS CHARACTER)—FICTION

Campbell, Julie. The Mystery in Arizona. 2004. (Trixie Belden Ser.: No. 6). 272p. (gr. 3-7). lib. bdg. 9.99 *(0-375-92741-7*, Random Hse. Bks. for Young Readers) Random Hse. Children's Bks.

—The Red Trailer Mystery. (Trixie Belden Ser.: No. 2). 2003. (Illus.). 272p. (gr. 3-7). text 6.99 *(0-375-82411-1*, Random Hse. Bks. for Young Readers); 1977. (J). (gr. 4 up). pap. o.p. *(0-307-21525-3*, Golden Bks.) Random Hse. Children's Bks.

—The Secret of the Mansion. 2003. (Trixie Belden Ser.: No. 1). (Illus.). 272p. (gr. 3-7). text 6.99 *(0-375-82412-X*, Random Hse. Bks. for Young Readers) Random Hse. Children's Bks.

Kenny, Kathryn. The Mysterious Code. 2004. (Trixie Belden Ser.: No. 7). 272p. (gr. 3-7). lib. bdg. 9.99 *(0-375-92978-9*, Random Hse. Bks. for Young Readers) Random Hse. Children's Bks.

—The Red Trailer Mystery. 1977. (Trixie Belden Ser.: No. 2). (J). (gr. 4 up). lib. bdg. o.p. *(0-307-61525-1*, Golden Bks.) Random Hse. Children's Bks.

—Trixie Belden #8: The Black Jacket Mystery. 2004. 272p. (gr. 3-7). lib. bdg. 9.99 *(0-375-92979-7*, Random Hse. Bks. for Young Readers) Random Hse. Children's Bks.

BENNET, ELIZABETH (FICTITIOUS CHARACTER)—FICTION

Austen, Jane. Pride & Prejudice. 1999. (YA). 11.95 *(1-56137-767-8)* Novel Units, Inc.

—Pride & Prejudice, Level 6. Hedge, Tricia, ed. 2000. (Bookworms Ser.). (Illus.). 121p. (YA). pap. text 5.95 *(0-19-423093-7)* Oxford Univ. Pr., Inc.

—Pride & Prejudice. 1979. (Now Age Illustrated V Ser.). (Illus.). 64p. (gr. 4-12). (J). stu. ed. 1.25 o.p. *(0-88301-419-X)*; (J). text 5.00 o.p. *(0-88301-407-6)*; pap. text 1.95 o.p. *(0-88301-395-9)* Pendulum Pr., Inc.

—Pride & Prejudice. (Illustrated Junior Library). (Illus.). 384p. 1984. (J). (gr. 4 up). 10.95 o.s.i *(0-448-06032-9*, Grosset & Dunlap); 1995. (YA). (gr. 7 up). pap. 4.99 *(0-14-037337-3*, Puffin Bks.) Penguin Putnam Bks. for Young Readers.

—Pride & Prejudice. abr. Lt. ed. 1996. (Great Illustrated Classics Ser.: Vol. 52). (Illus.). 240p. (J). (gr. 3-7). 9.95 *(0-86611-871-3)* Playmore, Inc., Pubs.

—Pride & Prejudice. (J). 1998. 47p. pap. 6.95 *(0-8114-6836-4)*; 1996. (Illus.). 48p. (gr. 4 up). lib. bdg. 22.83 o.p. *(0-8172-1673-1)*; 1988. (gr. 4 up). 22.00 *(0-8172-2188-3)*; 1983. (Illus.). 48p. (gr. 4 up). pap. 9.27 o.p. *(0-8172-2018-6)* Raintree Pubs.

—Pride & Prejudice. 1996. (J). pap. 2.25 *(0-590-08576-X)* Scholastic, Inc.

—Pride & Prejudice. 1994. (Enriched Classics Ser.). (YA). (gr. 9-12). 3.95 o.p. *(0-671-00601-0*, Pocket) Simon & Schuster.

—Pride & Prejudice. 1994. 9.04 *(0-606-18651-4)* Turtleback Bks.

—Pride & Prejudice: Penguin Readers Level 5. 1998. 80p. pap. 7.00 *(0-14-081507-4)* Viking Penguin.

Austen, Jane & Kerrigan, Michael. Pride & Prejudice. 1999. (Literature Made Easy Ser.). (Illus.). 96p. (YA). pap. 4.95 *(0-7641-0834-4)* Barron's Educational Series, Inc.

Raintree Steck-Vaughn Staff. Pride & Prejudice, 5 vols., Set. 1991. (Short Classics Ser.). (Illus.). (J). pap. 32.69 *(0-8114-6972-7)* Raintree Pubs.

BERENSTAIN BEARS (FICTITIOUS CHARACTERS)—FICTION

The Bears' Picnic & Other Stories. unabr. ed. Incl. Bear Scouts. Berenstain, Stan & Berenstain, Jan. audio Bears in the Night. Berenstain, Stan & Berenstain, Jan. audio Bears' New Baby. audio Bears' Vacation. Berenstain, Stan & Berenstain, Jan. audio Big Honey Hunt. Berenstain, Stan & Berenstain, Jan. audio (J). (ps-3). (Berenstain Bears Beginner Bks.). 1984. Set audio 9.95 *(0-89845-884-6*, CP 1549, Caedmon) HarperTrade.

Berenstain Bears & the Missing Dinosaur Bone. 2001. (Dr. Seuss & Friends Ser.). lib. bdg. *(1-59054-279-7)* Fitzgerald Bks.

Berenstain Enterprises Staff. The Berenstain Bears: Chunky Book. 2000. (J). 4.99 o.s.i *(0-679-89325-3)*; 4.99 o.s.i *(0-679-89324-5)* Discovery Bks.

Berenstain, Jan, et al. The Berenstain Bears Save Christmas. 2003. (Berenstain Bears Ser.). (Illus.). 48p. (J). 12.99 *(0-06-052670-X)*; lib. bdg. 13.89 *(0-06-052671-8)* HarperCollins Pubs.

Berenstain, Stan. The Bear Scouts. 1997. (Los Osos Scouts Ser.). (SPA.). (J). mass mkt. 3.50 *(0-590-94478-9*, Scholastic Paperbacks) Scholastic, Inc.

—Berenstain Activity Book. 1997. (J). (gr. 2-5). pap. *(0-590-06706-0)* Scholastic, Inc.

—The Berenstain Bears Accept No Substitutes. 1993. (Berenstain Bears Big Chapter Bks.). (Illus.). 112p. (J). (gr. 2-6). pap. 3.99 o.s.i *(0-679-84035-4*, Random Hse. Bks. for Young Readers) Random Hse. Children's Bks.

—The Berenstain Bears & the Bad Dream. ed. 2000. (J). (gr. 1). spiral bd. *(0-616-01555-0)*; (gr. 2). spiral bd. *(0-616-01556-9)* Canadian National Institute for the Blind/Institut National Canadien pour les Aveugles.

—The Berenstain Bears & the Galloping Ghost. 1994. (Berenstain Bears Big Chapter Bks.). (J). (gr. 2-6). 9.55 *(0-606-14003-4)* Turtleback Bks.

—The Berenstain Bears & the Giddy Grandma. 1994. (Berenstain Bears Big Chapter Bks.). (J). (gr. 2-6). 10.04 *(0-606-14004-2)* Turtleback Bks.

—The Berenstain Bears & the In-Crowd. 1992. (Berenstain Bears First Time Bks.). (Illus.). (J). (gr. k-2). 3.99 o.p. *(0-517-08949-1)* Random Hse. Value Publishing.

—The Berenstain Bears & the Papa's Day Roast. 2003. (Illus.). 32p. (J). lib. bdg. 8.99 *(0-375-91129-4)*; pap. 3.25 *(0-375-81129-X)* Random Hse. Children's Bks.

—Berenstain Bears & The Phantom of the Gymnasium. 2000. (Illus.). (J). pap. 3.99 *(0-679-88949-3*, Random Hse. Bks. for Young Readers) Random Hse. Children's Bks.

—The Berenstain Bears & the Sitter. 1985. (Berenstain Bears First Time Bks.). (J). (gr. k-2). o.s.i *(0-394-87795-0*, Random Hse. Bks. for Young Readers) Random Hse. Children's Bks.

—The Berenstain Bears & the Week at Grandma's. 1990. pap. 2.25 o.s.i *(0-679-81275-X)* Random Hse., Inc.

—The Berenstain Bears & Too Much Junk Food. 1999. (Berenstain Bears First Time Bks.). (Illus.). (J). (gr. k-2). pap. 10.25 *(0-8085-3551-X)* Econo-Clad Bks.

—The Berenstain Bears & Too Much TV. 1990. (Berenstain Bears First Time Bks.). (J). (gr. k-2). pap. 2.25 o.s.i *(0-679-81268-7)* Random Hse., Inc.

—The Berenstain Bears & Too Much Vacation. 1992. (Berenstain Bears First Time Bks.). (Illus.). (J). (gr. k-2). 3.99 o.p. *(0-517-08937-8)* Random Hse. Value Publishing.

—The Berenstain Bears Around the Clock Coloring Book. 1987. (Berenstain Bears Ser.). (J). (ps-3). pap. 0.49 o.p. *(0-394-88263-6*, Random Hse. Bks. for Young Readers) Random Hse. Children's Bks.

—The Berenstain Bears Bear Scout Coloring Book. 1987. (Berenstain Bear Scouts Ser.). (J). (gr. 3-6). pap. 0.49 o.p. *(0-394-88260-1*, Random Hse. Bks. for Young Readers) Random Hse. Children's Bks.

—The Berenstain Bears Count on Numbers Coloring Book. 1987. (Berenstain Bears Ser.). (J). (ps-3). pap. 0.49 o.p. *(0-394-88264-4*, Random Hse. Bks. for Young Readers) Random Hse. Children's Bks.

—The Berenstain Bears Go In & Out. 2000. (Early Step into Reading Ser.). (Illus.). (J). 10.14 *(0-606-18488-0)* Turtleback Bks.

—The Berenstain Bears Learn about Strangers. 1985. (Berenstain Bears First Time Bks.). (Illus.). 32p. (gr. k-2). lib. bdg. 8.99 *(0-394-97334-8*, Random Hse. Bks. for Young Readers) Random Hse. Children's Bks.

—The Berenstain Bears Meet Santa Bear. 1984. (Berenstain Bears First Time Bks.). (Illus.). 30p. (J). (gr. k-2). 5.99 o.s.i *(0-394-96880-8*, Random Hse. Bks. for Young Readers) Random Hse. Children's Bks.

—The Berenstain Bears' Nature Guide. 1984. (Berenstain Bears Bear Facts Library). (Illus.). 72p. (J). (gr. 1-4). pap. 7.95 o.s.i *(0-394-86602-9*, Random Hse. Bks. for Young Readers) Random Hse. Children's Bks.

—Berenstain Bears On the Farm Coloring Book. 1987. (Berenstain Bears Ser.). (J). (ps-3). pap. 0.49 o.p. *(0-394-88262-8*, Random Hse. Bks. for Young Readers) Random Hse. Children's Bks.

—Berenstain Bears Safety First Coloring Book. 1987. (Berenstain Bears Ser.). (J). (ps-3). pap. 0.49 o.p. *(0-394-88259-8*, Random Hse. Bks. for Young Readers) Random Hse. Children's Bks.

—The Berenstain Bears Think of Those in Need. 1999. (Berenstain Bears Ser.). (Illus.). (J). 9.40 *(0-606-20465-2)* Turtleback Bks.

—Los Osos Berenstain Sombrero Viejo Sombrero Nuevo. 2003. (SPA., Illus.). 24p. (J). bds. 4.99 *(0-375-82360-3*, RH Para Ninos) Random Hse. Children's Bks.

—Los Pajaros, las Abejitas y los Osos Berenstain. 2001. (SPA., Illus.). 32p. (J). (-1). pap. 3.25 *(0-375-81504-X)* Random Hse. Children's Bks.

—El Robot Chiflado. 1997. Tr. of Run Amuck Robot. 9.55 *(0-606-11576-5)* Turtleback Bks.

Berenstain, Stan & Berenstain, Jan. The Bear Detectives: The Case of the Missing Pumpkin. 1975. (Berenstain Bears Beginner Bks.). (Illus.). 48p. (J). (ps-3). lib. bdg. 12.99 *(0-394-93127-0)*; 8.99 *(0-394-83127-6)* Beginner Bks.

—The Bear Detectives: The Case of the Missing Pumpkin. 1988. (I Can Read It All by Myself Ser.). (Illus.). 42p. (J). (ps-3). pap. 5.95 o.s.i *(0-394-80499-6*, Random Hse. Bks. for Young Readers) Random Hse. Children's Bks.

—The Bear Scouts. 1967. (Berenstain Bears Beginner Bks.). (Illus.). 72p. (J). (ps-3). lib. bdg. 12.99 *(0-394-90046-4)*; 8.99 *(0-394-80046-X)* Beginner Bks.

—The Bears' Christmas. 1970. (Illus.). 72p. (J). (ps-3). 8.99 *(0-394-80090-7)*; lib. bdg. 12.99 *(0-394-90090-1)* Beginner Bks.

—Bears in the Night. 2002. (Berenstain Bears Bright & Early Bks.). (Illus.). (J). 16.70 *(0-7587-0922-6)* Book Wholesalers, Inc.

—Bears in the Night. 1971. (Berenstain Bears Bright & Early Bks.). (Illus.). (J). (ps-3). 36p. 8.99 *(0-394-82286-2)*; 35p. lib. bdg. 12.99 *(0-394-92286-7)* Random Hse. Children's Bks. (Random Hse. Bks. for Young Readers).

—Bears on Wheels. 1969. (Berenstain Bears Bright & Early Bks.). (Illus.). 36p. (J). (ps-3). 8.99 *(0-394-80967-X*, Random Hse. Bks. for Young Readers) Random Hse. Children's Bks.

—The Bears' Picnic. 1966. (Berenstain Bears Beginner Bks.). (Illus.). 72p. (J). (ps-3). lib. bdg. 12.99 *(0-394-90041-3)*; 8.99 *(0-394-80041-9)* Beginner Bks.

—The Bears' Picnic. 2002. (Berenstain Bears Beginner Bks.). (Illus.). (J). 15.74 *(0-7587-0924-2)* Book Wholesalers, Inc.

—The Bears' Picnic. 1999. (Berenstain Bears Beginner Bks.). (J). (ps-3). audio 49.32 *(0-394-12834-6)* McKay, David Co., Inc.

—The Bears' Picnic & Other Stories. 1994. (Berenstain Bears Beginner Bks.). (J). (ps-3). audio 5.99 *(1-55994-903-1)* HarperChildren's Audio.

—The Bears' Vacation. 1968. (Berenstain Bears Beginner Bks.). (Illus.). 72p. (J). (ps-3). 8.99 *(0-394-80052-4)* Beginner Bks.

—El Bebe de los Osos Berenstain. De Cuenca, Pilar & Alvarez, Inés, trs. 1982. (Pictureback Ser.). (ENG & SPA., Illus.). 32p. (ps-3). pap. 3.25 o.s.i *(0-394-85144-7*, Random Hse. Bks. for Young Readers) Random Hse. Children's Bks.

—El Bebe de los Osos Berenstain. 1992. (Berenstain Bears Ser.). (SPA., Illus.). (J). 9.40 *(0-606-20565-9)* Turtleback Bks.

—Berenstain Bear Scouts. 1995. (J). pap. 71.76 *(0-590-59726-4)* Scholastic, Inc.

—The Berenstain Bear Scouts & the Coughing Catfish. 1998. (Berenstain Bear Scouts Ser.). (Illus.). 32p. (J). (gr. 3-8). mass mkt. 3.50 *(0-590-60384-1)* Scholastic, Inc.

—The Berenstain Bear Scouts & the Coughing Catfish. 1996. (Berenstain Bear Scouts Ser.). (J). (gr. 3-6). 10.04 *(0-606-09065-7)* Turtleback Bks.

—Berenstain Bear Scouts & the Evil Eye. 1998. (Berenstain Bear Scouts Ser.). (J). (gr. 3-6). mass mkt. 3.99 *(0-590-94488-6*, Scholastic Paperbacks) Scholastic, Inc.

—The Berenstain Bear Scouts & the Humongous Pumpkin. (Berenstain Bear Scouts Ser.). (J). (gr. 3-6). 1996. 32p. mass mkt. 3.99 *(0-590-60386-8)*; 1995. (Illus.). 64p. mass mkt. 3.99 *(0-590-60380-9)* Scholastic, Inc.

—The Berenstain Bear Scouts & the Humongous Pumpkin. 1995. (Berenstain Bear Scouts Ser.). (J). (gr. 3-6). 10.04 (*0-606-07276-4*) Turtleback Bks.

—The Berenstain Bear Scouts & the Ice Monster. 1997. (Berenstain Bear Scouts Ser.). (Illus.). 32p. (J). (gr. 3-6). mass mkt. 3.99 (*0-590-94479-7*, Scholastic Paperbacks) Scholastic, Inc.

—Berenstain Bear Scouts & the Magic Crystal Caper. 1997. (Berenstain Bear Scouts Ser.). 32p. (J). (gr. 3-6). mass mkt. 3.99 (*0-590-94475-4*, Scholastic Paperbacks) Scholastic, Inc.

—Berenstain Bear Scouts & the Magic Crystal Caper. 1997. (Berenstain Bear Scouts Ser.). (J). (gr. 3-6). 10.04 (*0-606-11107-7*) Turtleback Bks.

—The Berenstain Bear Scouts & the Missing Merit Badges. 1998. (Berenstain Bear Scouts Ser.). (Illus.). 32p. (J). (gr. 3-6). mass mkt. 3.50 (*0-590-56390-4*) Scholastic, Inc.

—The Berenstain Bear Scouts & the Missing Merit Badges. 1998. (Berenstain Bear Scouts Ser.). (J). (gr. 3-6). 9.65 (*0-606-13191-4*) Turtleback Bks.

—Berenstain Bear Scouts & the Really Big Disaster. 1998. (Berenstain Bear Scouts Ser.). (Illus.). 32p. (J). (gr. 3-6). mass mkt. 3.99 (*0-590-94481-9*, Scholastic Paperbacks) Scholastic, Inc.

—Berenstain Bear Scouts & the Ripoff Queen. 1998. (Berenstain Bear Scouts Ser.). (Illus.). 112p. (J). (gr. 3-6). mass mkt. 3.99 (*0-590-94493-2*) Scholastic, Inc.

—Berenstain Bear Scouts & the Ripoff Queen. 1998. (Berenstain Bear Scouts Ser.). (J). (gr. 3-6). 10.04 (*0-606-15457-4*) Turtleback Bks.

—Berenstain Bear Scouts & the Run-Amuck Robot. 1997. (Berenstain Bear Scouts Ser.). (Illus.). 32p. (J). (gr. 3-6). mass mkt. 3.99 (*0-590-94477-0*, Scholastic Paperbacks) Scholastic, Inc.

—Berenstain Bear Scouts & the Run-Amuck Robot. 1997. (Berenstain Bear Scouts Ser.). (J). (gr. 3-6). 9.55 (*0-606-11108-5*) Turtleback Bks.

—The Berenstain Bear Scouts & the Sci-Fi Pizza. 1996. (Berenstain Bear Scouts Ser.). (J). (gr. 3-6). mass mkt. 3.99 (*0-590-60385-X*) Scholastic, Inc.

—The Berenstain Bear Scouts & the Sci-Fi Pizza. 1997. (Berenstain Bear Scouts Ser.). (J). (gr. 3-6). 10.04 (*0-606-11109-3*) Turtleback Bks.

—The Berenstain Bear Scouts & the Search for Naughty Ned. 1998. (Berenstain Bear Scouts Ser.). (Illus.). 32p. (J). (gr. 3-6). mass mkt. 3.50 (*0-590-56509-5*) Scholastic, Inc.

—The Berenstain Bear Scouts & the Search for Naughty Ned. 1998. (Berenstain Bear Scouts Ser.). (J). (gr. 3-6). 9.65 (*0-606-13193-0*) Turtleback Bks.

—The Berenstain Bear Scouts & the Sinister Smoke Ring. 1997. (Berenstain Bear Scouts Ser.). 32p. (J). (gr. 3-6). mass mkt. 3.99 (*0-590-94473-8*) Scholastic, Inc.

—The Berenstain Bear Scouts & the Stinky Milk Mystery. 1999. (Berenstain Bear Scouts Ser.). (Illus.). 32p. (J). (gr. 3-6). mass mkt. 3.50 (*0-590-56524-9*, Cartwheel Bks.) Scholastic, Inc.

—Berenstain Bear Scouts & the Terrible Talking Termite. 1996. (Berenstain Bear Scouts Ser.). (Illus.). (J). (gr. 3-6). mass mkt. 3.99 (*0-590-60383-3*) Scholastic, Inc.

—Berenstain Bear Scouts & the Terrible Talking Termite. 1996. (Berenstain Bear Scouts Ser.). (J). (gr. 3-6). 10.04 (*0-606-09066-5*) Turtleback Bks.

—The Berenstain Bear Scouts & the White-Water Mystery. 1999. (Berenstain Bear Scouts Ser.). 32p. (J). (gr. 3-6). mass mkt. 3.50 (*0-590-56522-2*) Scholastic, Inc.

—The Berenstain Bear Scouts & the White-Water Mystery. 1999. (Berenstain Bear Scouts Ser.). (J). (gr. 3-6). 9.65 (*0-606-16598-3*) Turtleback Bks.

—Berenstain Bear Scouts Ghost Versus Ghost. 1996. (Berenstain Bear Scouts Ser.). (J). (gr. 3-6). 10.04 (*0-606-11111-5*) Turtleback Bks.

—The Berenstain Bear Scouts in the Giant Bat Cave. 1995. (Berenstain Bear Scouts Ser.). 64p. (J). (gr. 4-7). mass mkt. 3.99 (*0-590-60379-5*) Scholastic, Inc.

—The Berenstain Bear Scouts in the Giant Bat Cave. 1995. (Berenstain Bear Scouts Ser.). (J). (gr. 3-6). 10.04 (*0-606-07277-2*) Turtleback Bks.

—Berenstain Bear Scouts Meet Bigpaw. 1996. (Berenstain Bear Scouts Ser.). 32p. (J). (gr. 3-6). mass mkt. 3.99 (*0-590-60381-7*) Scholastic, Inc.

—Berenstain Bear Scouts Save That Backscratcher. 1996. (Berenstain Bear Scouts Ser.). (Illus.). (J). (gr. 3-6). mass mkt. 3.99 (*0-590-60382-5*) Scholastic, Inc.

—Berenstain Bear Scouts Save That Backscratcher. 1996. (Berenstain Bear Scouts Ser.). (J). (gr. 3-6). 10.04 (*0-606-09067-3*) Turtleback Bks.

—The Berenstain Bear Scouts Scream Their Heads Off. 1998. (Berenstain Bear Scouts Ser.). (Illus.). 32p. (J). (gr. 3-6). mass mkt. 3.99 (*0-590-94484-3*, Scholastic Paperbacks) Scholastic, Inc.

—The Berenstain Bear Scouts Scream Their Heads Off. 1998. (Berenstain Bear Scouts Ser.). (J). (gr. 3-6). 10.04 (*0-606-13194-9*) Turtleback Bks.

—The Berenstain Bears, 7 vols., Date not set. (Early Childhood First Bks.). (Illus.). (J). (ps-2). lib. bdg. 97.65 (*1-56674-942-5*) Forest Hse. Publishing Co., Inc.

—Berenstain Bears: A Visit to the Big City. 1996. (Magic Touch Talking Bks.). (Illus.). 22p. (J). (ps-2). 19.99 (*1-888208-08-2*) Hasbro, Inc.

—Berenstain Bears: A Visit to the Big Museum. 1996. (Magic Touch Talking Bks.). (Illus.). 22p. (J). (ps-2). 19.99 (*1-888208-09-0*) Hasbro, Inc.

—The Berenstain Bears: Back to School. l.t. ed. 1998. (Early Childhood First Bks.). (Illus.). 24p. (J). (ps-2). lib. bdg. 13.95 (*1-56674-213-7*) Forest Hse. Publishing Co., Inc.

—The Berenstain Bears: Hold Hands at the Big Mall. l.t. ed. 1998. (Early Childhood First Bks.). (Illus.). 24p. (J). (ps-2). lib. bdg. 13.95 (*1-56674-216-1*) Forest Hse. Publishing Co., Inc.

—The Berenstain Bears: How to Get Along at School with Your Fellow Bear. 1984. (Berenstain Bears Ser.). 32p. (J). (ps-3). 8.98 o.p. (*0-87660-014-3*) I. J. E. Bk. Publishing, Inc./Kid Stuff.

—The Berenstain Bears: No Girls Allowed. 1986. (Berenstain Bears First Time Bks.). (Illus.). 32p. (J). (gr. k-2). pap. 3.25 (*0-394-87331-9*, Random Hse. Bks. for Young Readers) Random Hse. Children's Bks.

—The Berenstain Bears: No Girls Allowed. 1986. (Berenstain Bears First Time Bks.). (J). (gr. k-2). 9.40 (*0-606-01993-6*) Turtleback Bks.

—Berenstain Bears: When I Grow Up. 1996. (Magic Touch Talking Bks.). (Illus.). 22p. (J). (ps-2). 19.99 (*1-888208-10-4*) Hasbro, Inc.

—The Berenstain Bears' Almanac. 1984. (Berenstain Bears Bear Facts Library). (Illus.). 72p. (J). (gr. 1-4). pap. 6.99 o.s.i (*0-394-86601-0*, Random Hse. Bks. for Young Readers) Random Hse. Children's Bks.

—The Berenstain Bears & Baby Makes Five. 2000. (Berenstain Bears First Time Bks.). (Illus.). 32p. (J). (gr. k-1). pap. 3.25 (*0-679-88960-4*); lib. bdg. 8.99 (*0-679-98960-9*) Random Hse. Children's Bks. (Random Hse. Bks. for Young Readers).

—The Berenstain Bears & Baby Makes Five. 2000. (Berenstain Bears First Time Bks.). (Illus.). (J). (gr. k-2). 9.40 (*0-606-18485-6*) Turtleback Bks.

—The Berenstain Bears & Baby Makes Five. 2002. (J). E-Book (*1-59019-223-0*); 2002. (J). E-Book (*1-59019-222-2*); 2000. E-Book (*1-59019-224-9*) ipicturebooks, LLC.

—The Berenstain Bears & Mama's New Job. 1999. (Berenstain Bears First Time Bks.). (Illus.). (J). (gr. k-2). pap. 10.25 (*0-88103-144-5*) Econo-Clad Bks.

—The Berenstain Bears & Mama's New Job. 1984. (Berenstain Bears First Time Bks.). (Illus.). 32p. (gr. k-2). (J). 5.99 o.s.i (*0-394-96881-6*); pap. 3.25 (*0-394-86881-1*) Random Hse. Children's Bks. (Random Hse. Bks. for Young Readers).

—The Berenstain Bears & No Guns Allowed. 2000. (Berenstain Bears Big Chapter Bks.). (Illus.). 112p. (gr. 3-5). lib. bdg. 11.99 (*0-679-98953-6*); pap. text 3.99 (*0-679-88953-1*) Random Hse. Children's Bks. (Random Hse. Bks. for Young Readers).

—The Berenstain Bears & No Guns Allowed. 2000. (Berenstain Bears Big Chapter Bks.). (Illus.). (J). 10.04 (*0-606-18486-4*) Turtleback Bks.

—The Berenstain Bears & Queenie's Crazy Crush. 1997. (Berenstain Bears Big Chapter Bks.). (J). (gr. 2-6). 11.99 o.s.i (*0-679-98745-2*); (Illus.). 112p. pap. 3.99 o.s.i (*0-679-88745-8*) Random Hse. Children's Bks. (Random Hse. Bks. for Young Readers).

—The Berenstain Bears & Queenie's Crazy Crush. 1997. (Berenstain Bears Big Chapter Bks.). (J). (gr. 2-6). 9.09 (*0-606-12628-7*) Turtleback Bks.

—The Berenstain Bears & the Bad Dream. 2002. (Berenstain Bears 1st Time Ser.). (Illus.). (J). 11.19 (*0-7587-0957-9*) Book Wholesalers, Inc.

—The Berenstain Bears & the Bad Dream. (Berenstain Bears First Time Bks.). (J). (gr. k-2). audio o.s.i (*0-679-82760-9*) McKay, David Co., Inc.

—The Berenstain Bears & the Bad Dream. (Berenstain Bears First Time Bks.). (Illus.). 32p. (gr. k-2). 1992. (J). 6.95 o.s.i incl. audio (*0-679-82761-7*); 1988. (J). 6.99 o.s.i (*0-394-97341-0*); 1988. pap. 3.25 (*0-394-87341-6*) Random Hse. Children's Bks. (Random Hse. Bks. for Young Readers).

—The Berenstain Bears & the Bad Dream. 1988. (Berenstain Bears First Time Bks.). 32p. (J). (gr. k-2). 9.40 (*0-606-03730-6*) Turtleback Bks.

—The Berenstain Bears & the Bad Habit. 1987. (Berenstain Bears First Time Bks.). (Illus.). 32p. (gr. k-2). (J). 6.99 o.s.i (*0-394-97340-2*); pap. 3.25 (*0-394-87340-8*) Random Hse. Children's Bks. (Random Hse. Bks. for Young Readers).

—The Berenstain Bears & the Bad Habit. 1986. (Berenstain Bears First Time Bks.). (J). (gr. k-2). 9.40 (*0-606-00616-8*) Turtleback Bks.

—The Berenstain Bears & the Bermuda Triangle. 1997. (Berenstain Bears Big Chapter Bks.). (J). (gr. 2-6). 11.99 o.s.i (*0-679-97649-3*); (Illus.). 112p. pap. 3.99 o.s.i (*0-679-87649-9*) Random Hse., Inc.

—The Berenstain Bears & the Bermuda Triangle. 1997. (Berenstain Bears Big Chapter Bks.). (J). (gr. 2-6). 8.60 (*0-606-11112-3*) Turtleback Bks.

—The Berenstain Bears & the Big Blooper. Klimo, Kate, ed. 2000. (First Time Bks.). (Illus.). 32p. (J). (gr. k-3). pap. 3.25 (*0-679-88962-0*); lib. bdg. 8.99 (*0-679-98962-5*) Random Hse. Children's Bks. (Random Hse. Bks. for Young Readers).

—The Berenstain Bears & the Big Blooper. 2000. (Berenstain Bears First Time Bks.). (J). (gr. k-2). 9.40 (*0-606-19887-3*) Turtleback Bks.

—The Berenstain Bears & the Big Blooper. 2002. (J). E-Book (*1-59019-225-7*); 2000. E-Book (*1-59019-226-5*); 2000. E-Book (*1-59019-227-3*) ipicturebooks, LLC.

—The Berenstain Bears & the Big Date. 1998. (Berenstain Bears Big Chapter Bks.). (J). (gr. 2-6). 11.99 o.s.i (*0-679-98941-2*); (Illus.). 112p. pap. 3.99 o.s.i (*0-679-88941-8*) Knopf Publishing Group. (Vintage).

—The Berenstain Bears & the Big Date. 1998. (Berenstain Bears Big Chapter Bks.). (J). (gr. 2-6). 10.04 (*0-606-13951-6*) Turtleback Bks.

—The Berenstain Bears & the Big Election. 1984. (Berenstain Bears Mini-Storybooks). (Illus.). 32p. (J). (ps-3). pap. 1.50 o.s.i (*0-394-86542-1*, Random Hse. Bks. for Young Readers) Random Hse. Children's Bks.

—The Berenstain Bears & the Big Question. 1999. (Berenstain Bears First Time Bks.). (Illus.). (J). (gr. k-2). 24p. lib. bdg. 8.99 (*0-679-98961-7*); 32p. pap. 3.25 (*0-679-88961-2*) Random Hse. Children's Bks. (Random Hse. Bks. for Young Readers).

—The Berenstain Bears & the Big Road Race. 1987. (Berenstain Bears First Time Readers Ser.). (Illus.). 32p. (ps-3). (J). 5.99 o.s.i (*0-394-99134-6*); pap. 3.25 (*0-394-89134-1*) Random Hse. Children's Bks. (Random Hse. Bks. for Young Readers).

—The Berenstain Bears & the Big Road Race. 1987. (Berenstain Bears First Time Readers Ser.). 32p. (J). (ps-3). 9.40 (*0-606-00617-6*) Turtleback Bks.

—The Berenstain Bears & the Birds & the Bees. (Berenstain Bears First Time Bks.). (Illus.). 32p. (J). (gr. k-2). 2000. lib. bdg. 8.99 (*0-679-98959-5*); 1999. pap. 3.25 (*0-679-88958-2*) Random Hse., Inc.

—The Berenstain Bears & the Blame Game. 2002. (Berenstain Bears 1st Time Ser.). (Illus.). (J). 11.19 (*0-7587-0965-X*) Book Wholesalers, Inc.

—The Berenstain Bears & the Blame Game. ed. 2003. (gr. 1). spiral bd. (*0-616-14559-4*); (gr. 2). spiral bd. (*0-616-14560-8*) Canadian National Institute for the Blind/Institut National Canadien pour les Aveugles.

—The Berenstain Bears & the Blame Game. 1997. (Berenstain Bears First Time Bks.). (J). (gr. k-2). 8.99 o.s.i (*0-679-98743-6*); (Illus.). 32p. pap. 3.25 (*0-679-88743-1*) Random Hse. Children's Bks. (Random Hse. Bks. for Young Readers).

—The Berenstain Bears & the Blame Game. 1997. (Berenstain Bears First Time Bks.). (J). (gr. k-2). 9.40 (*0-606-12629-5*) Turtleback Bks.

—The Berenstain Bears & the Bully. 1993. (Berenstain Bears First Time Bks.). (Illus.). 32p. (J). (ps-3). pap. 3.25 (*0-679-84805-3*, Random Hse. Bks. for Young Readers) Random Hse. Children's Bks.

—The Berenstain Bears & the Bully. 1993. (Berenstain Bears First Time Bks.). (J). (gr. k-2). 9.40 (*0-606-05754-4*) Turtleback Bks.

—The Berenstain Bears & the Dinosaurs. (Berenstain Bears Mini-Storybooks). (J). (ps-3). 1995. pap. o.s.i (*0-679-87978-1*); 1984. (Illus.). 32p. pap. 1.50 o.s.i (*0-394-86883-8*) Random Hse. Children's Bks. (Random Hse. Bks. for Young Readers).

—The Berenstain Bears & the Double Dare. 2002. (Berenstain Bears 1st Time Ser.). (Illus.). (J). 11.19 (*0-7587-0956-0*) Book Wholesalers, Inc.

—The Berenstain Bears & the Double Dare. 1988. (Berenstain Bears First Time Bks.). (Illus.). 32p. (gr. k-2). (J). 5.99 o.s.i (*0-394-99748-4*); pap. 3.25 (*0-394-89748-X*) Random Hse. Children's Bks. (Random Hse. Bks. for Young Readers).

—The Berenstain Bears & the Double Dare. 1988. (Berenstain Bears First Time Bks.). (Illus.). 32p. (J). (gr. k-2). 9.40 (*0-606-03729-2*) Turtleback Bks.

—The Berenstain Bears & the Dress Code. 1994. (Berenstain Bears Big Chapter Bks.). (Illus.). (gr. 2-5). 103p. (J). 11.99 o.s.i (*0-679-96665-X*); 112p. pap. 3.99 (*0-679-86665-5*) Random Hse. Children's Bks. (Random Hse. Bks. for Young Readers).

—The Berenstain Bears & the Dress Code. 1994. (Berenstain Bears Big Chapter Bks.). (J). (gr. 2-5). 10.04 (*0-606-14002-6*) Turtleback Bks.

—The Berenstain Bears & the Drug Free Zone. 2002. (Berenstain Bears Big Chapters Ser.). (Illus.). (J). 11.91 (*0-7587-0941-2*) Book Wholesalers, Inc.

—The Berenstain Bears & the Drug Free Zone. 1993. (Berenstain Bears Big Chapter Bks.). (Illus.). 100p. (J). (ps-3). 11.99 (*0-679-93612-2*); 112p. (gr. 4-7). pap. 3.99 o.s.i (*0-679-83612-8*) Random Hse. Children's Bks. (Random Hse. Bks. for Young Readers).

—The Berenstain Bears & the Escape of the Bogg Brothers. Klimo, Kate, ed. 2003. (Step into Reading Step 3 Bks.). (Illus.). 48p. (J). (gr. 2-4). pap. 3.99 (*0-679-89228-1*); lib. bdg. 11.99 (*0-679-99228-6*) Random Hse. Children's Bks. (Random Hse. Bks. for Young Readers).

—The Berenstain Bears & the Excuse Note. 2002. (Berenstain Bears 1st Time Ser.). (Illus.). (J). 11.19 (*0-7587-6916-4*) Book Wholesalers, Inc.

—The Berenstain Bears & the Excuse Note. 2001. (First Time Bks.). (Illus.). 32p. (J). (gr. k-3). pap. 3.25 (*0-375-81125-7*); lib. bdg. 8.99 (*0-375-91125-1*) Random Hse. Children's Bks. (Random Hse. Bks. for Young Readers).

—The Berenstain Bears & the G-Rex Bones. (Berenstain Bears Big Chapter Bks.). (J). (gr. 2-6). 2001. lib. bdg. 11.99 (*0-679-98949-8*); 1999. (Illus.). 112p. pap. 3.99 o.s.i (*0-679-88945-0*) Random Hse. Children's Bks. (Random Hse. Bks. for Young Readers).

—The Berenstain Bears & the G-Rex Bones. 1999. (Berenstain Bears Big Chapter Bks.). (J). (gr. 2-6). 11.99 o.s.i (*0-679-98945-5*) Random Hse., Inc.

—The Berenstain Bears & the Galloping Ghost. 1994. (Berenstain Bears Big Chapter Bks.). (Illus.). 104p. (J). (gr. 2-6). 11.99 o.s.i (*0-679-95815-0*); pap. 3.50 o.s.i (*0-679-85815-6*) Random Hse. Children's Bks. (Random Hse. Bks. for Young Readers).

—The Berenstain Bears & the Ghost of the Auto Graveyard. 1997. (Berenstain Bears Big Chapter Bks.). (J). (gr. 2-6). 11.99 o.s.i (*0-679-97651-5*); (Illus.). 102p. pap. 3.99 o.s.i (*0-679-87651-0*) Random Hse. Children's Bks. (Random Hse. Bks. for Young Readers).

—The Berenstain Bears & the Ghost of the Auto Graveyard. 1997. (Berenstain Bears Big Chapter Bks.). (J). (gr. 2-6). 10.04 (*0-606-11113-1*) Turtleback Bks.

—The Berenstain Bears & the Ghost of the Forest. 1988. (Berenstain Bears First Time Readers Ser.). (Illus.). (J). (ps-3). 30p. 5.99 o.s.i (*0-394-90565-2*); 32p. pap. 3.25 (*0-394-80565-8*) Random Hse. Children's Bks. (Random Hse. Bks. for Young Readers).

—The Berenstain Bears & the Ghost of the Forest. 1988. (Berenstain Bears First Time Readers Ser.). 30p. (J). (ps-3). 9.40 (*0-606-03984-8*) Turtleback Bks.

—The Berenstain Bears & the Giddy Grandma. 1994. (Berenstain Bears Big Chapter Bks.). (Illus.). 112p. (J). (gr. 2-6). lib. bdg. 11.99 o.s.i (*0-679-95814-2*); pap. 3.99 o.s.i (*0-679-85814-8*) Random Hse. Children's Bks. (Random Hse. Bks. for Young Readers).

—The Berenstain Bears & the Goofy, Goony Guy. 2001. (Berenstain Bears First Time Chapter Bks.). (Illus.). 96p. (J). (gr. 1-3). pap. 3.99 (*0-375-81270-9*); lib. bdg. 11.99 o.s.i (*0-375-91270-3*) Random Hse. Children's Bks. (Random Hse. Bks. for Young Readers).

—The Berenstain Bears & the Great Ant Attack. 2000. (Berenstain Bears Big Chapter Bks.). (Illus.). 112p. (gr. 3-7). lib. bdg. 11.99 o.s.i (*0-679-98950-1*, Random Hse. Bks. for Young Readers) Random Hse. Children's Bks.

—The Berenstain Bears & the Great Ant Attack. 2000. (Berenstain Bears Big Chapter Bks.). (Illus.). 112p. (gr. 3-7). pap. text 3.99 o.s.i (*0-679-88950-7*) Random Hse., Inc.

—The Berenstain Bears & the Great Ant Attack. 2000. (Berenstain Bears Big Chapter Bks.). (Illus.). (J). (gr. 2-6). 10.04 (*0-606-18487-2*) Turtleback Bks.

—The Berenstain Bears & the Green-Eyed Monster. 2002. (Berenstain Bears 1st Time Ser.). (Illus.). (J). 11.19 (*0-7587-0946-3*) Book Wholesalers, Inc.

—The Berenstain Bears & the Green-Eyed Monster. 1995. (Berenstain Bears First Time Bks.). (Illus.). (gr. k-2). (J). 8.99 o.s.i (*0-679-96434-7*); 32p. pap. 3.25 (*0-679-86434-2*) Random Hse. Children's Bks. (Random Hse. Bks. for Young Readers).

—The Berenstain Bears & the Green-Eyed Monster. 1995. (Berenstain Bears First Time Bks.). (J). (gr. k-2). 9.40 (*0-606-07278-0*) Turtleback Bks.

—The Berenstain Bears & the Haunted Hayride. 1997. (Berenstain Bears Big Chapter Bks.). (J). (gr. 2-6). 11.99 o.s.i (*0-679-97650-7*, Vintage) Knopf Publishing Group.

—The Berenstain Bears & the Haunted Hayride. 1997. (Berenstain Bears Big Chapter Bks.). (Illus.). 112p. (J). (gr. 2-6). pap. 3.99 o.s.i (*0-679-87650-2*, Random Hse. Bks. for Young Readers) Random Hse. Children's Bks.

—The Berenstain Bears & the Haunted Hayride. 1997. (Berenstain Bears Big Chapter Bks.). (J). (gr. 2-6). 10.04 (*0-606-12630-9*) Turtleback Bks.

Characters

—The Berenstain Bears & the Haunted Lighthouse. 2001. (Berenstain Bears First Time Chapter Bks.). (Illus.). 96p. (J). (gr. 1-3). pap. 3.99 (*0-375-81269-5*); lib. bdg. 11.99 (*0-375-91269-X*) Random Hse. Children's Bks. (Random Hse. Bks. for Young Readers).

—The Berenstain Bears & the Homework Hassle. 2002. (Berenstain Bears 1st Time Ser.). (Illus.). (J). 11.19 (*0-7587-0966-8*) Book Wholesalers, Inc.

—The Berenstain Bears & the Homework Hassle. 1997. (Berenstain Bears First Time Bks.). 32p. (J). (gr. k-2). lib. bdg. 8.99 (*0-679-98744-4*); (Illus.). pap. 3.25 (*0-679-88744-X*) Random Hse. Children's Bks. (Random Hse. Bks. for Young Readers).

—The Berenstain Bears & the Homework Hassle. 1997. (Berenstain Bears First Time Bks.). (J). (gr. k-2). 9.40 (*0-606-12631-7*) Turtleback Bks.

—The Berenstain Bears & the In-Crowd. 2002. (Berenstain Bears 1st Time Ser.). (Illus.). (J). 11.19 (*0-7587-0940-4*) Book Wholesalers, Inc.

—The Berenstain Bears & the In-Crowd. 1989. (Berenstain Bears First Time Bks.). (Illus.). 32p. (gr. k-2). pap. 3.25 (*0-394-83013-X*, Random Hse. Bks. for Young Readers) Random Hse. Children's Bks.

—The Berenstain Bears & the In-Crowd. 1989. (Berenstain Bears First Time Bks.). 32p. (J). (gr. k-2). 9.40 (*0-606-04168-0*) Turtleback Bks.

—The Berenstain Bears & the Love Match. 1998. (Berenstain Bears Big Chapter Bks.). (J). (gr. 2-6). 11.99 o.s.i (*0-679-98942-0*, Random Hse. Bks. for Young Readers) Random Hse. Children's Bks.

—The Berenstain Bears & the Love Match. 1998. (Berenstain Bears Big Chapter Bks.). (Illus.). 112p. (J). (gr. 2-6). pap. 3.99 o.s.i (*0-679-88942-6*) Random Hse., Inc.

—The Berenstain Bears & the Love Match. 1998. (Berenstain Bears Big Chapter Bks.). (J). (gr. 2-6). 10.04 (*0-606-13952-4*) Turtleback Bks.

—The Berenstain Bears & the Messy Room. (Berenstain Bears First Time Bks.). (Illus.). 32p. (J). (gr. k-2). 1987. pap. 3.50 o.s.i (*0-394-88892-8*); 1985. Random Hse. Children's Bks.

—The Berenstain Bears & the Messy Room. Lerner, Sharon, ed. 1983. (Berenstain Bears First Time Bks.). (Illus.). 32p. (gr. k-2). lib. bdg. 6.99 (*0-394-95639-7*); pap. 3.25 (*0-394-85639-2*) Random Hse. Children's Bks. (Random Hse. Bks. for Young Readers).

—The Berenstain Bears & the Messy Room. 1986. (Berenstain Bears First Time Bks.). (J). (gr. k-2). 7.95 o.s.i incl. audio (*0-394-88009-9*); 7.95 o.s.i incl. audio (*0-394-88009-9*) Random Hse., Inc.

—The Berenstain Bears & the Messy Room. 1983. (Berenstain Bears First Time Bks.). 32p. (J). (gr. k-2). 9.40 (*0-606-01640-6*) Turtleback Bks.

—The Berenstain Bears & the Missing Dinosaur Bone. 1980. (Berenstain Bears Beginner Bks.). (Illus.). 48p. (J). (ps-3). 8.99 (*0-394-84447-5*); lib. bdg. 12.99 (*0-394-94447-X*) Beginner Bks.

—The Berenstain Bears & the Missing Dinosaur Bone. 2002. (Illus.). (J). 16.70 (*0-7587-0962-5*) Book Wholesalers, Inc.

—The Berenstain Bears & the Missing Honey. 1987. (Berenstain Bears First Time Readers Ser.). (Illus.). 32p. (ps-3). (J). 5.99 o.s.i (*0-394-99133-8*); pap. 3.25 (*0-394-89133-3*) Random Hse. Children's Bks. (Random Hse. Bks. for Young Readers).

—The Berenstain Bears & the Missing Honey. 1987. (Berenstain Bears First Time Readers Ser.). 32p. (J). (ps-3). 9.40 (*0-606-00611-7*) Turtleback Bks.

—The Berenstain Bears & the Missing Watermelon Money. 2001. (Step into Reading Ser.). (Illus.). 48p. (J). (gr. 1-3). lib. bdg. 11.99 (*0-679-99230-8*, Random Hse. Bks. for Young Readers) Random Hse. Children's Bks.

—Berenstain Bears & the Missing Watermelon Money. 2001. (Step into Reading Ser.). (Illus.). (J). 10.14 (*0-606-21056-3*) Turtleback Bks.

—The Berenstain Bears & the Missing Watermelon Money. l.t. ed. 2001. (Step into Reading Ser.). (Illus.). 48p. (J). (gr. 1-3). pap. 3.99 (*0-679-89230-3*, Random Hse. Bks. for Young Readers) Random Hse. Children's Bks.

—The Berenstain Bears & the Neighborly Skunk. 1984. (Berenstain Bears Mini-Storybooks). (Illus.). 32p. (J). (ps-3). pap. 1.25 o.s.i (*0-394-86882-X*, Random Hse. Bks. for Young Readers) Random Hse. Children's Bks.

—The Berenstain Bears & the Nerdy Nephew. 1993. (Berenstain Bears Big Chapter Bks.). (Illus.). 98p. (J). (gr. 2-6). pap. 3.99 o.s.i (*0-679-83610-1*, Random Hse. Bks. for Young Readers) Random Hse. Children's Bks.

—The Berenstain Bears & the New Girl in Town. 1993. (Berenstain Bears Big Chapter Bks.). (Illus.). 112p. (gr. 4-6). pap. 3.99 (*0-679-83613-6*, Random Hse. Bks. for Young Readers) Random Hse. Children's Bks.

—The Berenstain Bears & the Perfect Crime (Almost) 1998. (Berenstain Bears Big Chapter Bks.). 112p. (J). (gr. 2-6). 11.99 o.s.i (*0-679-98943-9*, Random Hse. Bks. for Young Readers) Random Hse. Children's Bks.

—The Berenstain Bears & the Perfect Crime (Almost) 1998. (Berenstain Bears Big Chapter Bks.). (Illus.). 112p. (J). (gr. 2-6). pap. 3.99 o.s.i (*0-679-88943-4*) Random Hse., Inc.

—The Berenstain Bears & the Prize Pumpkin. 2002. (Berenstain Bears 1st Time Ser.). (Illus.). (J). 11.19 (*0-7587-0959-5*) Book Wholesalers, Inc.

—The Berenstain Bears & the Prize Pumpkin. 1990. (Berenstain Bears First Time Bks.). (Illus.). 32p. (gr. k-2). (J). 8.99 (*0-679-90847-1*); pap. 3.25 (*0-679-80847-7*) Random Hse. Children's Bks. (Random Hse. Bks. for Young Readers).

—The Berenstain Bears & the Real Easter Eggs. 2002. (Berenstain Bears 1st Time Ser.). (Illus.). (J). 11.19 (*0-7587-8978-5*) Book Wholesalers, Inc.

—The Berenstain Bears & the Real Easter Eggs. 2002. (Illus.). 32p. (J). (gr. k-3). pap. 3.25 (*0-375-81133-8*); lib. bdg. 8.99 (*0-375-91133-2*) Random Hse. Children's Bks. (Random Hse. Bks. for Young Readers).

—The Berenstain Bears & the Red-Handed Thief. 1993. (Berenstain Bears Big Chapter Bks.). (Illus.). (gr. 2-6). 102p. (J). 11.99 o.s.i (*0-679-94033-2*); 112p. pap. 3.99 (*0-679-84033-8*) Random Hse. Children's Bks. (Random Hse. Bks. for Young Readers).

—Berenstain Bears & the Scavenger Hunt. 1997. (J). pap. 5.99 (*0-679-87325-2*, Random Hse. Bks. for Young Readers) Random Hse. Children's Bks.

—The Berenstain Bears & the School Scandal Sheet. 1994. (Berenstain Bears Big Chapter Bks.). (Illus.). (gr. 2-6). 103p. (J). 11.99 o.s.i (*0-679-95812-6*); 112p. pap. 3.99 (*0-679-85812-1*) Random Hse. Children's Bks. (Random Hse. Bks. for Young Readers).

—The Berenstain Bears & the Showdown at Chainsaw Gap. 1995. (Berenstain Bears Big Chapter Bks.). (Illus.). 112p. (J). (gr. 2-6). pap. 3.99 o.s.i (*0-679-87571-9*) Random Hse., Inc.

—The Berenstain Bears & the Showdown at Chainsaw Gap. 1995. (Berenstain Bears Big Chapter Bks.). (J). (gr. 2-6). 8.60 o.p. (*0-606-08489-4*) Turtleback Bks.

—The Berenstain Bears & the Sitter. (Berenstain Bears First Time Bks.). 32p. (gr. k-2). 1987. (J). pap. 2.95 o.s.i (*0-394-88890-1*); 1985. (Illus.). (J).; 1981. (Illus.). (J). 6.99 o.s.i (*0-394-94837-8*); 1981. (Illus.). pap. 3.25 (*0-394-84837-3*) Random Hse. Children's Bks. (Random Hse. Bks. for Young Readers).

—The Berenstain Bears & the Sitter. 1989. (Berenstain Bears First Time Bks.). (J). (gr. k-2). audio 21.26 (*0-676-31506-2*) SRA/McGraw-Hill.

—The Berenstain Bears & the Sitter. 1981. (Berenstain Bears First Time Bks.). (J). (gr. k-2). 9.40 (*0-606-00389-4*) Turtleback Bks.

—The Berenstain Bears & the Slumber Party. 1990. (Berenstain Bears First Time Bks.). (Illus.). 32p. (gr. k-2). (J). 6.99 o.s.i (*0-679-90419-0*); pap. 3.25 (*0-679-80419-6*) Random Hse. Children's Bks. (Random Hse. Bks. for Young Readers).

—The Berenstain Bears & the Spooky Old Tree. 1978. (Berenstain Bears Bright & Early Bks.). (Illus.). 48p. (J). (ps-3). lib. bdg. 12.99 (*0-394-93910-7*); 8.99 (*0-394-83910-2*) Random Hse. Children's Bks. (Random Hse. Bks. for Young Readers).

—The Berenstain Bears & the Spooky Old Tree. 1978. (Berenstain Bears Bright & Early Bks.). (J). (ps-3). audio 18.66 (*0-07-507095-2*) SRA/McGraw-Hill.

—Berenstain Bears & the Spooky Old Tree. 2001. (Dr. Seuss & Friends Ser.). lib. bdg. (*1-59054-280-0*) Fitzgerald Bks.

—The Berenstain Bears & the Tic-Tac-Toe Mystery. 2001. (Step into Reading Ser.). (Illus.). 48p. (J). (gr. 1-3). pap. 3.99 (*0-679-89229-X*); lib. bdg. 11.99 (*0-679-99229-4*) Random Hse. Children's Bks. (Random Hse. Bks. for Young Readers).

—Berenstain Bears & the Tic-Tac-Toe Mystery. 2001. (Step into Reading Ser.). (Illus.). (J). 10.14 (*0-606-20569-1*) Turtleback Bks.

—The Berenstain Bears & the Trouble with Bedtime. (J). 2005. (*0-375-91128-6*); 2003. (*0-375-81128-1*) Random Hse., Inc.

—The Berenstain Bears & the Trouble with Friends. 1987. (Berenstain Bears First Time Bks.). (Illus.). 32p. (gr. k-2). (J). 6.99 o.s.i (*0-394-97339-9*); pap. 3.25 (*0-394-87339-4*) Random Hse. Children's Bks. (Random Hse. Bks. for Young Readers).

—The Berenstain Bears & the Trouble with Grownups. 2002. (Berenstain Bears 1st Time Ser.). (Illus.). (J). 11.19 (*0-7587-0958-7*) Book Wholesalers, Inc.

—The Berenstain Bears & the Trouble with Grownups. 1992. (Berenstain Bears First Time Bks.). (Illus.). 32p. (J). (gr. k-2). pap. 3.25 (*0-679-83000-6*, Random Hse. Bks. for Young Readers) Random Hse. Children's Bks.

—The Berenstain Bears & the Trouble with Grownups. 1992. (Berenstain Bears First Time Bks.). (J). (gr. k-2). 9.40 (*0-606-01494-2*) Turtleback Bks.

—The Berenstain Bears & the Truth. (Berenstain Bears First Time Bks.). (Illus.). 32p. (gr. k-2). 1988. (J). 6.95 o.s.i incl. audio (*0-394-89771-4*); 1988. (J). pap. 3.50 o.s.i (*0-394-89794-3*); 1983. (J). 5.99 o.s.i (*0-394-95640-0*); 1983. pap. 3.25 (*0-394-85640-6*) Random Hse. Children's Bks. (Random Hse. Bks. for Young Readers).

—The Berenstain Bears & the Truth. 1983. (Berenstain Bears First Time Bks.). 32p. (J). (gr. k-2). 9.40 (*0-606-02779-3*) Turtleback Bks.

—The Berenstain Bears & the Wax Museum. 1999. (Berenstain Bears Big Chapter Bks.). (Illus.). 101p. (J). (gr. 3-5). lib. bdg. 11.99 o.s.i (*0-679-98947-1*); pap. 3.99 o.s.i (*0-679-88947-7*) Random Hse. Children's Bks. (Random Hse. Bks. for Young Readers).

—The Berenstain Bears & the Wax Museum. 1999. (Berenstain Bears Big Chapter Bks.). (J). (gr. 2-6). 10.04 (*0-606-16943-1*) Turtleback Bks.

—The Berenstain Bears & the Week at Grandma's. 2002. (Berenstain Bears 1st Time Ser.). (Illus.). (J). 11.19 (*0-7587-6632-7*) Book Wholesalers, Inc.

—The Berenstain Bears & the Week at Grandma's. 1986. (Berenstain Bears First Time Bks.). (Illus.). 32p. (gr. k-2). (J). 6.99 o.s.i (*0-394-97335-6*); pap. 3.25 (*0-394-87335-1*) Random Hse. Children's Bks. (Random Hse. Bks. for Young Readers).

—The Berenstain Bears & the Week at Grandma's. 1986. (Berenstain Bears First Time Bks.). 32p. (J). (gr. k-2). 9.40 (*0-606-00629-X*) Turtleback Bks.

—The Berenstain Bears & the Wheelchair Commando. 1993. (Berenstain Bears Big Chapter Bks.). (Illus.). 112p. (gr. 2-6). pap. 3.99 (*0-679-84034-6*, Random Hse. Bks. for Young Readers) Random Hse. Children's Bks.

—The Berenstain Bears & the Wild, Wild Honey. (Berenstain Bears Mini-Storybooks). (J). (ps-3). 1995. pap. o.s.i (*0-679-87973-0*); 1983. (Illus.). 32p. pap. 1.50 o.s.i (*0-394-85924-3*) Random Hse. Children's Bks. (Random Hse. Bks. for Young Readers).

—The Berenstain Bears & the Wrong Crowd. 2001. (Berenstain Bears First Time Chapter Bks.). (Illus.). 96p. (J). (gr. 1-3). pap. 3.99 (*0-375-81268-7*); lib. bdg. 11.99 o.s.i (*0-375-91268-1*) Random Hse. Children's Bks. (Random Hse. Bks. for Young Readers).

—The Berenstain Bears & Too Much Birthday. 1986. (Berenstain Bears First Time Bks.). (Illus.). 32p. (gr. k-2). (J). 5.99 o.s.i (*0-394-97332-1*); pap. 3.25 (*0-394-87332-7*) Random Hse. Children's Bks. (Random Hse. Bks. for Young Readers).

—The Berenstain Bears & Too Much Birthday. 1986. (Berenstain Bears First Time Bks.). 32p. (J). (gr. k-2). 9.40 (*0-606-01992-8*) Turtleback Bks.

—The Berenstain Bears & Too Much Junk Food. Lerner, Sharon, ed. 1985. (Berenstain Bears First Time Bks.). (Illus.). 32p. (gr. k-2). pap. 3.25 (*0-394-87217-7*); lib. bdg. 6.99 (*0-394-97217-1*) Random Hse. Children's Bks. (Random Hse. Bks. for Young Readers).

—The Berenstain Bears & Too Much Junk Food. 1985. (Berenstain Bears First Time Bks.). 30p. (J). (gr. k-2). 9.40 (*0-606-03420-X*) Turtleback Bks.

—The Berenstain Bears & Too Much Pressure. 1992. (Berenstain Bears First Time Bks.). (Illus.). 32p. (J). (gr. k-2). pap. 3.25 (*0-679-83671-3*, Random Hse. Bks. for Young Readers) Random Hse. Children's Bks.

—The Berenstain Bears & Too Much Pressure. 1992. (Berenstain Bears First Time Bks.). (J). (gr. k-2). 9.40 (*0-606-02314-3*) Turtleback Bks.

—The Berenstain Bears & Too Much Teasing. 1995. (Berenstain Bears First Time Bks.). (Illus.). 32p. (gr. k-2). lib. bdg. 8.99 (*0-679-97706-6*); (J). pap. 3.25 (*0-679-87706-1*) Random Hse., Inc.

—The Berenstain Bears & Too Much Teasing. 1995. (Berenstain Bears First Time Bks.). (J). (gr. k-2). 9.40 (*0-606-08490-8*) Turtleback Bks.

—The Berenstain Bears & Too Much TV. 2002. (Berenstain Bears 1st Time Ser.). (Illus.). (J). 11.19 (*0-7587-0943-9*) Book Wholesalers, Inc.

—The Berenstain Bears & Too Much TV. (Berenstain Bears First Time Bks.). (Illus.). (gr. k-2). 1989. (J). 7.95 o.s.i incl. audio (*0-394-82894-1*); 1989. (J). 7.95 o.s.i incl. audio (*0-394-82894-1*); 1985. 32p. (J).; 1984. 32p. (J). 6.99 o.s.i (*0-394-96570-1*); 1984. 32p. pap. 3.25 (*0-394-86570-7*) Random Hse. Children's Bks. (Random Hse. Bks. for Young Readers).

—The Berenstain Bears & Too Much TV. 1984. (Berenstain Bears First Time Bks.). 32p. (J). (gr. k-2). 9.40 (*0-606-03165-0*) Turtleback Bks.

—The Berenstain Bears & Too Much Vacation. 2002. (Berenstain Bears 1st Time Ser.). (Illus.). (J). 11.19 (*0-7587-0954-4*) Book Wholesalers, Inc.

—The Berenstain Bears & Too Much Vacation. 1990. (J). 6.95 o.s.i (*0-679-80311-4*); 1989. (Illus.). 32p. pap. 3.25 (*0-394-83014-8*) Random Hse. Children's Bks. (Random Hse. Bks. for Young Readers).

—The Berenstain Bears & Too Much Vacation. 1989. (Berenstain Bears First Time Bks.). 32p. (J). (gr. k-2). 9.40 (*0-606-04169-9*) Turtleback Bks.

—The Berenstain Bears Are a Family. (Berenstain Bears Toddler Bks.). (J). (ps). 1996. 23p. bds. 3.99 o.s.i (*0-679-88185-9*); 1991. (Illus.). 24p. pap. 2.95 o.s.i (*0-679-80746-2*) Random Hse. Children's Bks. (Random Hse. Bks. for Young Readers).

—The Berenstain Bears at Camp Crush. 1994. (Berenstain Bears Big Chapter Bks.). (J). (gr. 2-6). 28.00 o.s.i (*0-679-85961-6*); (Illus.). 112p. 11.99 o.s.i (*0-679-96028-7*); (Illus.). 112p. pap. 3.99 o.s.i (*0-679-86028-2*) Random Hse. Children's Bks. (Random Hse. Bks. for Young Readers).

—The Berenstain Bears at Camp Crush. 1994. (Berenstain Bears Big Chapter Bks.). (J). (gr. 2-6). 10.04 (*0-606-14005-0*) Turtleback Bks.

—The Berenstain Bears at the Mansion. 1996. (Berenstain Bears Big Chapter Bks.). (J). (gr. 4-7). 11.99 o.s.i (*0-679-98156-X*, Random Hse. Bks. for Young Readers) Random Hse. Children's Bks.

—The Berenstain Bears at the Spooky Fun House. 1991. (Deluxe Golden Sound Story Bks.). (Illus.). 23p. (J). (ps-2). o.p. (*0-307-74013-7*, Golden Bks.) Random Hse. Children's Bks.

—The Berenstain Bears at the Super-Duper Market. 1991. (Berenstain Bears Toddler Bks.). 24p. (J). (ps). pap. 2.95 o.s.i (*0-679-80748-9*, Random Hse. Bks. for Young Readers) Random Hse. Children's Bks.

—The Berenstain Bears at the Teen Rock Cafe. 1996. (Berenstain Bears Big Chapter Bks.). (Illus.). (J). (gr. 2-6). 11.99 o.s.i (*0-679-97570-5*); 112p. pap. 3.99 o.s.i (*0-679-87570-0*) Random Hse., Inc.

—The Berenstain Bears at the Teen Rock Cafe. 1996. (Berenstain Bears Big Chapter Bks.). (J). (gr. 2-6). 10.04 (*0-606-10753-3*) Turtleback Bks.

—Berenstain Bears' Bad Habit. 1987. (J). pap. text 1.95 (*0-394-89341-7*) Random Hse., Inc.

—The Berenstain Bears' Bath Book. (Berenstain Bears Ser.). (Illus.). 10p. (J). (ps-3). 1986. 3.95 o.s.i (*0-394-88015-3*); 1985. bds. 3.95 o.s.i (*0-394-87116-2*) Random Hse. Children's Bks. (Random Hse. Bks. for Young Readers).

—The Berenstain Bears Bedtime Story. l.t. ed. 1998. (Berenstain Bears Ser.). (Illus.). 24p. (J). (ps-3). lib. bdg. 13.95 (*1-56674-214-5*) Forest Hse. Publishing Co., Inc.

—The Berenstain Bears Big Bear, Small Bear. 1998. (Early Step into Reading Ser.). 32p. (J). (ps-k). lib. bdg. 11.99 (*0-679-98717-7*, Random Hse. Bks. for Young Readers) Random Hse. Children's Bks.

—The Berenstain Bears Big Bear, Small Bear. 1998. (Early Step into Reading Ser.). (Illus.). 32p. (J). (ps-k). pap. 3.99 (*0-679-88717-2*) Random Hse., Inc.

—The Berenstain Bears' Big Book of Science & Nature. 1991. (Berenstain Bears Ser.). (Illus.). 192p. (J). (ps-3). pap. 12.99 o.s.i (*0-679-81238-5*, Random Hse. Bks. for Young Readers) Random Hse. Children's Bks.

—The Berenstain Bears' Big Rummage Sale. 1992. (Berenstain Bears Ser.). 24p. (J). (ps-3). o.p. (*0-307-74020-X*, 64020, Golden Bks.) Random Hse. Children's Bks.

—The Berenstain Bears Blaze a Trail. 1987. (Berenstain Bears First Time Readers Ser.). (Illus.). 32p. (ps-3). (J). 6.99 o.s.i (*0-394-99132-X*); pap. 3.25 (*0-394-89132-5*) Random Hse. Children's Bks. (Random Hse. Bks. for Young Readers).

—The Berenstain Bears Blaze a Trail. 1987. (Berenstain Bears First Time Readers Ser.). 32p. (J). (ps-3). 9.40 (*0-606-00619-2*) Turtleback Bks.

—The Berenstain Bears Bunny Hop, 2. 2000. (Coloring Bks.). (Illus.). 64p. (J). (ps-3). pap. 1.99 o.s.i (*0-679-89474-8*, Random Hse. Bks. for Young Readers) Random Hse. Children's Bks.

—The Berenstain Bears by the Sea. 2002. (Illus.). (J). 11.91 (*0-7587-0969-2*) Book Wholesalers, Inc.

—The Berenstain Bears by the Sea. 1998. (Early Step into Reading Ser.). (Illus.). 32p. (ps-k). lib. bdg. 11.99 (*0-679-98719-3*, Random Hse. Bks. for Young Readers) Random Hse. Children's Bks.

—The Berenstain Bears by the Sea. 1998. (Early Step into Reading Ser.). (Illus.). 32p. (J). (ps-k). pap. 3.99 (*0-679-88719-9*) Random Hse., Inc.

—The Berenstain Bears Catch the Bus. 2002. (Berenstain Bears Step into Reading Ser.). (Illus.). (J). 11.91 (*0-7587-0977-3*) Book Wholesalers, Inc.

—The Berenstain Bears Catch the Bus. 1999. (Step into Reading Step 1 Bks.). (Illus.). 32p. (J). (gr. k-3). lib. bdg. 11.99 (*0-679-99227-8*); pap. 3.99 (*0-679-89227-3*) Random Hse. Children's Bks.

—The Berenstain Bears' Christmas Tree. l.t. ed. (Berenstain Bears Ser.). (Illus.). (J). (ps-3). 1991. 64p. 8.95 o.s.i (*0-679-81974-6*); 1980. 72p. 9.99 o.s.i (*0-394-94566-2*); 1980. 32p. pap. 14.00 o.s.i (*0-394-84566-8*) Random Hse. Children's Bks. (Random Hse. Bks. for Young Readers).

—Berenstain Bears Collect It. 1997. (Illus.). lib. bdg. o.s.i (*0-679-97841-0*); (J). pap. o.s.i (*0-679-87841-6*) Random Hse., Inc.

—The Berenstain Bears' Comic Valentine. l.t. ed. 1998. (Berenstain Bears Ser.). (Illus.). 48p. (J). (ps-3). pap. 10.95 (*0-590-94729-X*) Scholastic, Inc.

—The Berenstain Bears Cook-It! Breakfast for Mama! 1996. (Berenstain Bears First Time Do-It! Bks.). (Illus.). (J). (ps-3). 8.99 o.s.i (*0-679-97316-8*); 24p. pap. 3.25 o.s.i (*0-679-87316-3*) Random Hse., Inc.

—The Berenstain Bears Cook-It! Breakfast for Mama! 1996. (Berenstain Bears First Time Do-It! Bks.). (J). (ps-3). 9.40 (*0-606-09068-1*) Turtleback Bks.

—The Berenstain Bears Count Their Blessings. 1995. (Berenstain Bears First Time Bks.). (Illus.). 32p. (gr. k-2). (J). lib. bdg. 8.99 (*0-679-97707-4*); pap. 3.25 (*0-679-87707-X*) Random Hse., Inc.

—The Berenstain Bears Count Their Blessings. 1995. (Berenstain Bears First Time Bks.). (J). (gr. k-2). 9.40 (*0-606-08491-6*) Turtleback Bks.

—The Berenstain Bears Count Their Blessings. 2002. (J). E-Book (*1-59019-228-1*); 1995. E-Book (*1-59019-229-X*); 1995. E-Book (*1-59019-230-3*) ipicturebooks, LLC.

—The Berenstain Bears' Counting Book. 1976. (Berenstain Bears Ser.). (Illus.). 14p. (J). (ps-3). pap. 3.50 o.s.i (*0-394-83246-9*) Random Hse., Inc.

—Berenstain Bears Create It. 1997. (Illus.). (J). pap. o.s.i (*0-679-87839-4*); lib. bdg. o.s.i (*0-679-97839-9*) Random Hse., Inc.

—The Berenstain Bears' Dollars & Sense. Klimo, Kate, ed. 2001. (Berenstain Bears First Time Bks.). (Illus.). 32p. (J). (gr. k-3). lib. bdg. 8.99 (*0-375-91124-3*, Random Hse. Bks. for Young Readers) Random Hse. Children's Bks.

—The Berenstain Bears Don't Pollute (Anymore) 1999. (Berenstain Bears First Time Bks.). (Illus.). (J). (gr. k-2). pap. 10.25 (*0-8335-6545-1*) Econo-Clad Bks.

—The Berenstain Bears Don't Pollute (Anymore) (Berenstain Bears First Time Bks.). (Illus.). (gr. k-2). 1993. 32p. (J). 6.95 o.s.i incl. audio (*0-679-83889-9*); 1991. 32p. (J). 8.99 o.s.i (*0-679-92351-9*); 1991. (J). o.p. (*0-679-83230-0*); 1991. 32p. pap. 3.25 (*0-679-82351-4*) Random Hse. Children's Bks. (Random Hse. Bks. for Young Readers).

—The Berenstain Bears Don't Pollute (Anymore) 1996. (Berenstain Bears First Time Bks.). (J). (gr. k-2). pap. o.p. (*0-679-88176-X*) Random Hse., Inc.

—The Berenstain Bears Draw-It! Drawing Lessons from Stan & Jan. 1996. (Berenstain Bears First Time Do-It! Bks.). (Illus.). (J). (ps-3). 8.99 o.s.i (*0-679-97314-1*); 23p. pap. 3.25 o.s.i (*0-679-87314-7*) Random Hse., Inc.

—The Berenstain Bears Draw-It! Drawing Lessons from Stan & Jan. 1996. (Berenstain Bears First Time Do-It! Bks.). (J). (ps-3). 9.40 (*0-606-10754-1*) Turtleback Bks.

—The Berenstain Bears' Easter Surprise. l.t. ed. 1998. (Berenstain Bears Ser.). (Illus.). 48p. (J). (ps-3). pap. 10.95 (*0-590-94730-3*) Scholastic, Inc.

—The Berenstain Bears Family Tree House. 1993. (Berenstain Bears Ser.). 2p. (J). (ps-3). (*1-883366-06-2*) YES! Entertainment Corp.

—The Berenstain Bears Fly-It! Up, Up, & Away. 1996. (Berenstain Bears First Time Do-It! Bks.). (Illus.). (J). (ps-3). 8.99 o.s.i (*0-679-97317-6*); 23p. pap. 3.25 o.s.i (*0-679-87317-1*) Random Hse., Inc.

—The Berenstain Bears Fly-It! Up, Up, & Away. 1996. (Berenstain Bears First Time Do-It! Bks.). (J). (ps-3). 9.40 (*0-606-10755-X*) Turtleback Bks.

—The Berenstain Bears Forget Their Manners. (Berenstain Bears First Time Bks.). (Illus.). (J). (gr. k-2). 1988. 32p. pap. 3.50 o.s.i (*0-394-89798-6*); 1986. pap. 7.95 o.s.i incl. audio (*0-394-88343-8*); 1985. 32p. 5.99 o.s.i (*0-394-97333-X*); 1985. 32p. pap. 3.25 (*0-394-87333-5*) Random Hse. Children's Bks. (Random Hse. Bks. for Young Readers).

—The Berenstain Bears Forget Their Manners. 1985. (Berenstain Bears First Time Bks.). 32p. (J). (gr. k-2). 9.40 (*0-606-00260-X*) Turtleback Bks.

—The Berenstain Bears Four Seasons. (Berenstain Bears Toddler Bks.). (J). (ps). 1996. 23p. bds. 3.99 o.s.i (*0-679-88182-4*); 1991. (Illus.). 24p. pap. 2.95 o.s.i (*0-679-80749-7*) Random Hse. Children's Bks. (Random Hse. Bks. for Young Readers).

—The Berenstain Bears Get in a Fight. 1995. (Berenstain Bears First Time Bks.). (J). (gr. k-2). lib. bdg. 113.00 (*1-57135-127-2*); 23.75 net. (*1-57135-122-1*);Set. pap. 45.00 (*1-57135-126-4*) Broderbund Software, Inc.

—The Berenstain Bears Get in a Fight. (Berenstain Bears First Time Bks.). (Illus.). 32p. (gr. k-2). 1988. (J). pap. 5.95 o.s.i incl. audio (*0-394-89778-1*); 1987. (J). pap. 3.50 o.s.i (*0-394-88893-6*); 1982. (J). 5.99 o.s.i (*0-394-95132-8*); 1982. pap. 3.25 (*0-394-85132-3*) Random Hse. Children's Bks. (Random Hse. Bks. for Young Readers).

—The Berenstain Bears Get in a Fight. 1982. (Berenstain Bears First Time Bks.). (J). (gr. k-2). 9.40 (*0-606-00390-8*) Turtleback Bks.

—The Berenstain Bears Get Stage Fright. 1986. (Berenstain Bears First Time Bks.). (Illus.). 32p. (gr. k-2). (J). 5.99 o.s.i (*0-394-97337-2*); pap. 3.25 (*0-394-87337-8*) Random Hse. Children's Bks. (Random Hse. Bks. for Young Readers).

—The Berenstain Bears Get Stage Fright. 1986. (Berenstain Bears First Time Bks.). 32p. (J). (gr. k-2). 9.40 (*0-606-00620-6*) Turtleback Bks.

—The Berenstain Bears Get the Don't Haftas. 1998. (Library of American Biography). (J). (ps-3). 7.99 o.s.i (*0-679-99236-7*);No. 2. (Illus.). 24p. 1.99 o.s.i (*0-679-89236-2*) Random Hse. Children's Bks. (Random Hse. Bks. for Young Readers).

—The Berenstain Bears Get the Gimmies. (Berenstain Bears First Time Bks.). (Illus.). 32p. (gr. k-2). 1988. (J). 8.99 o.s.i (*0-394-90566-0*); 1988. (J). pap. 3.25 (*0-394-80566-6*); 1990. reprint ed. 7.95 o.s.i incl. audio (*0-679-80313-0*) Random Hse. Children's Bks. (Random Hse. Bks. for Young Readers).

—The Berenstain Bears Get the Gimmies. 1988. (Berenstain Bears First Time Bks.). 32p. (J). (gr. k-2). 9.40 (*0-606-03731-4*) Turtleback Bks.

—The Berenstain Bears Get the Grouchies. l.t. ed. 1998. (Berenstain Bears Family Time Bks.). (Illus.). 24p. (J). (ps-3). lib. bdg. 13.95 (*1-56674-253-6*) Forest Hse. Publishing Co., Inc.

—The Berenstain Bears Get the Noisies. 1999. (Jellybean Bks.). (Illus.). 24p. (J). (ps-3). 1.99 o.s.i (*0-679-89266-4*, Random Hse. Bks. for Young Readers) Random Hse. Children's Bks.

—The Berenstain Bears Get the Noisies. 1999. (Jellybean Bks.). (Illus.). 20p. (J). (ps-3). 7.99 o.s.i (*0-679-99266-9*) Random Hse., Inc.

—The Berenstain Bears Get the Scaredies. 1999. (Jellybean Bks.). (Illus.). 24p. (J). (ps-3). lib. bdg. 7.99 (*0-679-99323-1*);Bk. 4. 1.99 o.s.i (*0-679-89323-7*) Random Hse. Children's Bks. (Random Hse. Bks. for Young Readers).

—The Berenstain Bears Get the Screamies. 1998. (Library of American Biography). (J). (ps-3). 7.99 o.s.i (*0-679-99235-9*); (Illus.). 24p. 1.99 o.s.i (*0-679-89235-4*) Random Hse. Children's Bks. (Random Hse. Bks. for Young Readers).

—The Berenstain Bears Get the Twitchies. 2000. (Jellybean Bks.). (Illus.). 24p. (J). (ps). 2.99 o.s.i (*0-375-80127-8*, Random Hse. Bks. for Young Readers) Random Hse. Children's Bks.

—The Berenstain Bears Get Their Kicks. 1998. (Berenstain Bears First Time Bks.). 32p. (gr. k-2). (J). lib. bdg. 8.99 (*0-679-98955-2*); (Illus.). pap. 3.25 (*0-679-88955-8*) Random Hse. Children's Bks. (Random Hse. Bks. for Young Readers).

—The Berenstain Bears Get Their Kicks. 1998. (Berenstain Bears First Time Bks.). (J). (gr. k-2). 9.40 (*0-606-13955-9*) Turtleback Bks.

—The Berenstain Bears Go Fly a Kite. (Berenstain Bears Mini-Storybooks). (J). (ps-3). 1995. pap. o.s.i (*0-679-87974-9*); 1983. (Illus.). 32p. pap. 1.50 o.s.i (*0-394-85921-9*) Random Hse. Children's Bks. (Random Hse. Bks. for Young Readers).

—The Berenstain Bears Go Hollywood. 1999. (Berenstain Bears Big Chapter Bks.). (Illus.). 112p. (gr. 3-5). (J). lib. bdg. 11.99 o.s.i (*0-679-98948-X*); pap. text 3.99 o.s.i (*0-679-88948-5*) Random Hse., Inc.

—The Berenstain Bears Go Hollywood. 1999. (Berenstain Bears Big Chapter Bks.). (J). (gr. 2-6). 10.04 (*0-606-17264-5*) Turtleback Bks.

—The Berenstain Bears Go In & Out. 2000. (Early Step into Reading Ser.). (Illus.). 31p. (J). (ps-3). pap. 3.99 (*0-679-89225-7*); 5th ed. lib. bdg. 11.99 (*0-679-99225-1*) Random Hse. Children's Bks. (Random Hse. Bks. for Young Readers).

—The Berenstain Bears Go Out for the Team. (Berenstain Bears First Time Bks.). (Illus.). 32p. (gr. k-2). 1991. (J). 8.95 o.s.i incl. audio (*0-679-81495-7*); 1987. (J). 5.99 o.s.i (*0-394-97338-0*); 1987. pap. 3.25 (*0-394-87338-6*) Random Hse. Children's Bks. (Random Hse. Bks. for Young Readers).

—The Berenstain Bears Go Platinum. 1998. (Berenstain Bears Big Chapter Bks.). (Illus.). (J). (gr. 2-6). 112p. 11.99 o.s.i (*0-679-98944-7*); 106p. pap. 3.99 o.s.i (*0-679-88944-2*) Random Hse. Children's Bks. (Random Hse. Bks. for Young Readers).

—The Berenstain Bears Go Platinum. 1998. (Berenstain Bears Big Chapter Bks.). (J). (gr. 2-6). 10.04 (*0-606-15459-0*) Turtleback Bks.

—The Berenstain Bears Go to Camp. (Berenstain Bears First Time Bks.). (Illus.). (gr. k-2). 1989. (J). 5.95 o.s.i (*0-394-82896-8*); 1982. 32p. (J). 5.99 o.s.i (*0-394-95131-X*); 1982. 32p. pap. 3.25 (*0-394-85131-5*) Random Hse. Children's Bks. (Random Hse. Bks. for Young Readers).

—The Berenstain Bears Go to Camp. 1982. (Berenstain Bears First Time Bks.). (J). (gr. k-2). 9.40 (*0-606-00392-4*) Turtleback Bks.

—The Berenstain Bears Go to School. (Berenstain Bears First Time Bks.). (Illus.). 32p. (gr. k-2). 1987. (J). pap. 2.95 o.s.i (*0-394-88888-X*); 1978. lib. bdg. 6.99 (*0-394-93736-8*); 1978. pap. 3.25 (*0-394-83736-3*) Random Hse. Children's Bks. (Random Hse. Bks. for Young Readers).

—The Berenstain Bears Go to School. 1987. (Berenstain Bears First Time Bks.). (Illus.). (J). (gr. k-2). 9.40 (*0-606-01481-0*) Turtleback Bks.

—The Berenstain Bears Go to the Doctor. (Berenstain Bears First Time Bks.). (Illus.). 32p. (gr. k-2). 1987. (J). pap. 2.95 o.s.i (*0-394-88889-8*); 1981. lib. bdg. 8.99 (*0-394-94835-1*); 1981. pap. 3.25 (*0-394-84835-7*) Random Hse. Children's Bks. (Random Hse. Bks. for Young Readers).

—The Berenstain Bears Go to the Doctor. 1985. (Berenstain Bears First Time Bks.). (J). (gr. k-2). pap. 7.95 o.s.i incl. audio (*0-394-87663-6*); pap. 7.95 o.s.i incl. audio (*0-394-87663-6*) Random Hse., Inc.

—The Berenstain Bears Go to the Doctor. 1981. (Berenstain Bears First Time Bks.). (J). (gr. k-2). 9.40 (*0-606-00393-2*) Turtleback Bks.

—The Berenstain Bears Go up & Down. 1999. (Early Step into Reading Ser.). (Illus.). 32p. (J). (ps-k). lib. bdg. 11.99 (*0-679-98720-7*, Random Hse. Bks. for Young Readers) Random Hse. Children's Bks.

—The Berenstain Bears Go up & Down. 1999. (Early Step into Reading Ser.). (Illus.). 32p. (J). (ps-k). pap. 3.99 (*0-679-88720-2*) Random Hse., Inc.

—The Berenstain Bears Go up & Down. 1999. (Early Step into Reading Ser.). (J). (ps-k). lib. bdg. 10.14 (*0-606-15895-2*) Turtleback Bks.

—The Berenstain Bears Gotta Dance. 1993. (Berenstain Bears Big Chapter Bks.). (Illus.). 101p. (J). (gr. 2-6). pap. 3.50 o.s.i (*0-679-84032-X*, Random Hse. Bks. for Young Readers) Random Hse. Children's Bks.

—The Berenstain Bears Grow-It! Mother Nature Has Such a Green Thumb! 1996. (Berenstain Bears First Time Do-It! Bks.). (Illus.). 24p. (J). (ps-3). pap. 3.25 o.s.i (*0-679-87315-5*, Random Hse. Bks. for Young Readers) Random Hse. Children's Bks.

—The Berenstain Bears Grow-It! Mother Nature Has Such a Green Thumb! 1996. (Berenstain Bears First Time Do-It! Bks.). (Illus.). (J). (ps-3). 8.99 o.s.i (*0-679-97315-X*) Random Hse., Inc.

—The Berenstain Bears Grow-It! Mother Nature Has Such a Green Thumb! 1996. (Berenstain Bears First Time Do-It! Bks.). (J). (ps-3). 9.40 (*0-606-09069-X*) Turtleback Bks.

—The Berenstain Bears Help Around the House. l.t. ed. 1998. (Berenstain Bears Family Time Bks.). (Illus.). 24p. (J). (ps-3). lib. bdg. 13.95 (*1-56674-215-3*) Forest Hse. Publishing Co., Inc.

—The Berenstain Bears' Home Sweet Tree. 1997. (Berenstain Bears Ser.). (Illus.). 12p. (J). (ps-3). bds. 11.99 o.s.i (*0-679-87328-7*, Random Hse. Bks. for Young Readers) Random Hse. Children's Bks.

—The Berenstain Bears' Home Sweet Tree. 1995. (Berenstain Bears Ser.). 16p. (J). (ps-3). (*1-57234-061-4*) YES! Entertainment Corp.

—The Berenstain Bears in Big Bear City. 1996. (Berenstain Bears Ser.). (Illus.). (J). (ps-3). pap. 4.99 o.s.i (*0-679-87324-4*, Random Hse. Bks. for Young Readers) Random Hse. Children's Bks.

—The Berenstain Bears in Maniac Mansion. 1996. (Berenstain Bears Big Chapter Bks.). (J). (gr. 2-6). pap. 3.50 o.s.i (*0-679-88156-5*, Random Hse. Bks. for Young Readers) Random Hse. Children's Bks.

—The Berenstain Bears in Maniac Mansion. 1996. (Berenstain Bears Big Chapter Bks.). (J). (gr. 2-6). 9.55 (*0-606-10756-8*) Turtleback Bks.

—The Berenstain Bears in the Dark. (Berenstain Bears First Time Bks.). (J). (gr. k-2). 1997. 32p. cd-rom 49.95 (*1-57135-204-X*); 1996. 23.75 (*1-57135-200-7*) Broderbund Software, Inc.

—The Berenstain Bears in the Dark. (Berenstain Bears First Time Bks.). 32p. (gr. k-2). 1985. (Illus.). (J).; 1982. (J). 5.99 o.s.i (*0-394-95443-2*); 1982. pap. 3.25 (*0-394-85443-8*) Random Hse. Children's Bks. (Random Hse. Bks. for Young Readers).

—The Berenstain Bears in the Dark. 1982. (Berenstain Bears First Time Bks.). 32p. (J). (gr. k-2). 9.40 (*0-606-00394-0*) Turtleback Bks.

—The Berenstain Bears in the Freaky Funhouse. 1995. (Berenstain Bears Big Chapter Bks.). (Illus.). 112p. (J). (gr. 2-6). pap. 3.99 o.s.i (*0-679-87244-2*) Random Hse., Inc.

—The Berenstain Bears in the Freaky Funhouse. 1995. (Berenstain Bears Big Chapter Bks.). (J). (gr. 2-6). 10.04 (*0-606-07279-9*) Turtleback Bks.

—The Berenstain Bears in the House of Mirrors. 2002. (Berenstain Bears Step into Reading Ser.). (Illus.). (J). 11.91 (*0-7587-0974-9*) Book Wholesalers, Inc.

—The Berenstain Bears in the House of Mirrors. 1999. (Early Step into Reading Ser.). (J). (ps-k). lib. bdg. 11.99 (*0-679-99226-X*); (Illus.). 32p. pap. 3.99 (*0-679-89226-5*) Random Hse., Inc.

—The Berenstain Bears in the House of Mirrors. 1999. (Early Step into Reading Ser.). (J). (ps-k). 10.14 (*0-606-16837-0*) Turtleback Bks.

—The Berenstain Bears Learn about Strangers. (Berenstain Bears First Time Bks.). (Illus.). 32p. (J). (gr. k-2). 1986. pap. 7.95 o.s.i incl. audio (*0-394-88346-2*); 1986. pap. 7.95 o.s.i incl. audio (*0-394-88346-2*); 1985. pap. 3.25 (*0-394-87334-3*) Random Hse. Children's Bks. (Random Hse. Bks. for Young Readers).

—The Berenstain Bears Learn about Strangers. 1989. (Berenstain Bears First Time Bks.). (J). (gr. k-2). audio 26.66 (*0-676-31929-7*) SRA/McGraw-Hill.

—The Berenstain Bears Learn about Strangers. 1985. (Berenstain Bears First Time Bks.). 32p. (J). (gr. k-2). 9.40 (*0-606-00259-6*) Turtleback Bks.

—The Berenstain Bears Lend a Helping Hand. 1998. (Berenstain Bears First Time Bks.). (Illus.). 32p. (J). (gr. k-2). lib. bdg. 8.99 o.s.i (*0-679-98956-0*, Random Hse. Bks. for Young Readers) Random Hse. Children's Bks.

—The Berenstain Bears Lend a Helping Hand. 1998. (Berenstain Bears First Time Bks.). (Illus.). 32p. (J). (gr. k-2). pap. 3.25 (*0-679-88956-6*) Random Hse., Inc.

—The Berenstain Bears Lend a Helping Hand. 1998. (Berenstain Bears First Time Bks.). (J). (gr. k-2). 9.40 (*0-606-15460-4*) Turtleback Bks.

—The Berenstain Bears Lost in Cyberspace. 1999. (Berenstain Bears Big Chapter Bks.). 112p. (J). (gr. 2-6). lib. bdg. 11.99 o.s.i (*0-679-98946-3*); (Illus.). (gr. 3-5). pap. 3.99 o.s.i (*0-679-88946-9*) Random Hse., Inc.

—The Berenstain Bears' Mad, Mad, Mad Toy Craze. 1999. (Berenstain Bears First Time Bks.). (Illus.). 24p. (J). (gr. k-2). lib. bdg. 8.99 o.s.i (*0-679-98958-7*) Random Hse., Inc.

—The Berenstain Bears' Mad, Mad, Mad Toy Craze. 1999. (Berenstain Bears First Time Bks.). (J). (gr. k-2). 9.40 (*0-606-15979-7*) Turtleback Bks.

—The Berenstain Bears' Make & Do Book. 1984. (Berenstain Bears Ser.). (Illus.). 64p. (J). (ps-3). pap. 3.95 o.s.i (*0-394-86895-1*, Random Hse. Bks. for Young Readers) Random Hse. Children's Bks.

—Berenstain Bears Make It. 1997. (Illus.). (J). pap. o.s.i (*0-679-87842-4*) Random Hse., Inc.

—The Berenstain Bears' Media Madness. 1995. (Berenstain Bears Big Chapter Bks.). (Illus.). (J). (gr. 2-6). 100p. 11.99 o.s.i (*0-679-96664-1*); 112p. pap. 3.99 o.s.i (*0-679-86664-7*) Random Hse., Inc.

—The Berenstain Bears' Media Madness. 1995. (Berenstain Bears Big Chapter Bks.). (J). (gr. 2-6). 8.60 (*0-606-07280-2*) Turtleback Bks.

—Berenstain Bears Meet Questron: Left Right Stop Go & Other Things You Need to Know. 9999. (J). 4.95 o.p. (*0-8431-3175-6*, Price Stern Sloan) Penguin Putnam Bks. for Young Readers.

—The Berenstain Bears Meet Santa Bear. (Berenstain Bears First Time Bks.). (Illus.). 32p. (gr. k-2). 1989. (J). pap. 5.95 o.s.i incl. audio (*0-394-85228-1*); 1988. (J). pap. 2.95 o.s.i (*0-394-89797-8*); 1984. pap. 3.25 (*0-394-86880-3*) Random Hse. Children's Bks. (Random Hse. Bks. for Young Readers).

—The Berenstain Bears Meet Santa Bear. 1984. (Berenstain Bears First Time Bks.). (J). (gr. k-2). 9.40 (*0-606-12632-5*) Turtleback Bks.

—The Berenstain Bears' Moving Day. 1981. (Berenstain Bears First Time Bks.). (Illus.). 32p. (gr. k-2). lib. bdg. 6.99 o.s.i (*0-394-94838-6*); (J). pap. 3.25 (*0-394-84838-1*) Random Hse. Children's Bks. (Random Hse. Bks. for Young Readers).

—The Berenstain Bears' Moving Day. 1981. (Berenstain Bears First Time Bks.). (J). (gr. k-2). 9.40 (*0-606-00395-9*) Turtleback Bks.

—The Berenstain Bears' New Baby. (Berenstain Bears First Time Bks.). (gr. k-2). 1988. (Illus.). 32p. (J). pap. 2.95 o.s.i (*0-394-89796-X*); 1985. (Illus.). 32p. (J). pap. 6.95 o.s.i incl. audio (*0-394-87661-X*); 1978. (J). pap.; 1974. (Illus.). 32p. pap. 3.25 (*0-394-82908-5*) Random Hse. Children's Bks. (Random Hse. Bks. for Young Readers).

—The Berenstain Bears' New Baby. 1974. (Berenstain Bears First Time Bks.). (Illus.). (J). (gr. k-2). 9.40 (*0-606-01483-7*) Turtleback Bks.

—Berenstain Bears New Baby. 2001. (Early Readers Ser.: Vol. 3). (J). lib. bdg. (*1-59054-386-6*) Fitzgerald Bks.

—The Berenstain Bears' New Neighbors. 1994. (Berenstain Bears First Time Bks.). (Illus.). 32p. (gr. k-2). pap. 3.25 (*0-679-86435-0*, Random Hse. Bks. for Young Readers) Random Hse. Children's Bks.

—The Berenstain Bears' New Neighbors. 1994. (Berenstain Bears First Time Bks.). (J). (gr. k-2). 9.40 (*0-606-06227-0*) Turtleback Bks.

—The Berenstain Bears New Neighbors. 1994. (Berenstain Bears First Time Bks.). (Illus.). 32p. (gr. k-2). lib. bdg. 8.99 (*0-679-96435-5*, Random Hse. Bks. for Young Readers) Random Hse. Children's Bks.

—The Berenstain Bears No Girls Allowed! 1986. (Berenstain Bears First Time Bks.). (Illus.). 32p. (gr. k-2). lib. bdg. 8.99 (*0-394-97331-3*, Random Hse. Bks. for Young Readers) Random Hse. Children's Bks.

—The Berenstain Bears' Nursery Tales. 1973. (Berenstain Bears First Time Bks.). (Illus.). 32p. (J). (ps-3). pap. 3.25 o.s.i (*0-394-82665-5*, Random Hse. Bks. for Young Readers) Random Hse. Children's Bks.

—The Berenstain Bears' Nursery Tales. 1973. (Berenstain Bears First Time Bks.). (J). (gr. k-2). 9.40 (*0-606-01484-5*) Turtleback Bks.

—The Berenstain Bears Olympics. 1983. (Texas Instruments Magic Wand Speaking Library). (Illus.). 50p. (J). text 7.30 o.p. *(0-89512-070-4)* Texas Instruments, Inc.

—The Berenstain Bears on the Job. 1987. (Berenstain Bears First Time Readers Ser.). (Illus.). 32p. (ps-3). (J). 6.99 o.s.i *(0-394-99131-1)*; pap. 3.25 o.s.i *(0-394-89131-7)* Random Hse. Children's Bks. (Random Hse. Bks. for Young Readers).

—The Berenstain Bears on the Job. 1983. (Berenstain Bears First Time Readers Ser.). (Illus.). 49p. (J). (ps-3). text 7.30 o.p. *(0-89512-069-0)* Texas Instruments, Inc.

—The Berenstain Bears on the Job. 1987. (Berenstain Bears First Time Readers Ser.). 32p. (J). (ps-3). 9.40 *(0-606-00625-7)* Turtleback Bks.

—The Berenstain Bears on the Moon. 1985. (Berenstain Bears Bright & Early Bks.). (Illus.). (ps-3). 38p. (J). 11.99 o.s.i *(0-394-97180-9)*; 48p. 7.99 o.s.i *(0-394-87180-4)* Random Hse. Children's Bks. (Random Hse. Bks. for Young Readers).

—The Berenstain Bears on the Road. l.t. ed. 1998. (Berenstain Bears Family Time Bks.). (Illus.). 24p. (J). (ps-3). lib. bdg. 13.95 *(1-56674-217-X)* Forest Hse. Publishing Co., Inc.

—The Berenstain Bears on Wheels. 1992. (Little Wheel Bks.). (Illus.). 14p. (J). (ps up). pap. 4.99 o.s.i *(0-679-83245-9*, Random Hse. Bks. for Young Readers) Random Hse. Children's Bks.

—The Berenstain Bears Phenom in the Family. Klimo, Kate, ed. 2000. (Berenstain Bears Big Chapter Bks.). (Illus.). 112p. (J). (gr. 3-5). pap. 3.99 o.s.i *(0-679-88952-3)*; lib. bdg. 11.99 o.s.i *(0-679-98952-8)* Random Hse. Children's Bks. (Random Hse. Bks. for Young Readers).

—The Berenstain Bears Phenom in the Family. 2000. (Berenstain Bears Big Chapter Bks.). (J). (gr. 2-6). 10.04 *(0-606-19888-1)* Turtleback Bks.

—The Berenstain Bears Play Ball. l.t. ed. 1998. (Berenstain Bears Ser.). (Illus.). 48p. (J). (ps-3). pap. 10.95 *(0-590-94732-X)* Scholastic, Inc.

—The Berenstain Bears Ready, Get Set, Go! 1988. (Berenstain Bears First Time Readers Ser.). (Illus.). 32p. (ps-3). (J). 5.99 o.s.i *(0-394-90564-4)*; pap. 3.25 *(0-394-80564-X)* Random Hse. Children's Bks. (Random Hse. Bks. for Young Readers).

—The Berenstain Bears Ready, Get Set, Go! 1988. (Berenstain Bears First Time Readers Ser.). (J). (ps-3). 9.40 *(0-606-03985-6)* Turtleback Bks.

—Berenstain Bears Ready Get Set Go. 2001. (First Readers Ser.: Vol. 1). (J). lib. bdg. *(1-59054-387-4)* Fitzgerald Bks.

—Berenstain Bears Recycle It. 1997. (Illus.). (J). pap. o.s.i *(0-679-87840-8)*; lib. bdg. o.s.i *(0-679-97840-2)* Random Hse., Inc.

—The Berenstain Bears Ride the Thunderbolt. 1998. (Early Step into Reading Ser.). (Illus.). 32p. (ps-k). lib. bdg. 11.99 *(0-679-98718-5*, Random Hse. Bks. for Young Readers) Random Hse. Children's Bks.

—The Berenstain Bears Ride the Thunderbolt. 1998. (Early Step into Reading Ser.). (Illus.). 32p. (ps-k). pap. 3.99 *(0-679-88718-0)* Random Hse., Inc.

—The Berenstain Bears Ride the Thunderbolt. 1998. (Early Step into Reading Ser.). (J). (ps-k). 10.14 *(0-606-13956-7)* Turtleback Bks.

—The Berenstain Bears' Sampler: The Best of Bear Country. 1995. (Berenstain Bears First Time Bks.). (Illus.). 160p. (J). (gr. k-2). pap. 14.99 o.s.i *(0-679-87790-8*, Random Hse. Bks. for Young Readers) Random Hse. Children's Bks.

—The Berenstain Bears Say Goodnight. 1996. (Berenstain Bears Toddler Bks.). 23p. (J). (ps). bds. 3.99 o.s.i *(0-679-88183-2)* McKay, David Co., Inc.

—The Berenstain Bears Say Goodnight. 1991. (Berenstain Bears Toddler Bks.). (Illus.). 24p. (J). (ps). pap. 2.95 o.s.i *(0-679-80747-0*, Random Hse. Bks. for Young Readers) Random Hse. Children's Bks.

—The Berenstain Bears Say Please & Thank You. l.t. ed. 1998. (Berenstain Bears Family Time Bks.). (Illus.). 24p. (J). (ps-3). lib. bdg. 13.95 *(1-56674-218-8)* Forest Hse. Publishing Co., Inc.

—The Berenstain Bears' Science Fair. (Berenstain Bears Bear Facts Library). (Illus.). (J). (gr. 1-4). 1984. 72p. pap. 7.99 o.s.i *(0-394-86603-7)*; 1977. 11.99 o.s.i *(0-394-93294-3)*; 1977. pap. 5.95 o.s.i *(0-394-83294-9)* Random Hse. Children's Bks. (Random Hse. Bks. for Young Readers).

—The Berenstain Bears' Science Fair. 1977. (Berenstain Bears Bear Facts Library). (J). (gr. 1-4). 14.14 *(0-606-03166-9)* Turtleback Bks.

—The Berenstain Bears Shoot the Rapids. (Berenstain Bears Mini-Storybooks). (Illus.). (J). (ps-3). 1995. pap. o.s.i *(0-679-87977-3)*; 1984. 32p. pap. 1.50 o.s.i *(0-394-86543-X)* Random Hse. Children's Bks. (Random Hse. Bks. for Young Readers).

—The Berenstain Bears' Soccer Star. (Berenstain Bears Mini-Storybooks). (J). (ps-3). 1995. pap. o.s.i *(0-679-87976-5)*; 1983. (Illus.). 32p. pap. 1.50 o.s.i *(0-394-85922-7)* Random Hse. Children's Bks. (Random Hse. Bks. for Young Readers).

—The Berenstain Bears' Spring Fling. 2000. (Coloring Bks.). (Illus.). 64p. (J). (ps-3). pap. 1.99 o.s.i *(0-679-89473-X*, Random Hse. Bks. for Young Readers) Random Hse. Children's Bks.

—The Berenstain Bears' Take-Along Library. Incl. Berenstain Bears & the Messy Room. Berenstain Bears & the Sitter. Berenstain Bears & Too Much TV. Berenstain Bears in the Dark. Berenstain Bears Visit the Dentist. 32p. (J). (gr. k-2). (Berenstain Bears Ser.). (Illus.). 1985. 16.25 o.s.i *(0-394-87615-6*, Random Hse. Bks. for Young Readers) Random Hse. Children's Bks.

—The Berenstain Bears' Thanksgiving. l.t. ed. 1997. (Berenstain Bears Ser.). (Illus.). 48p. (J). (ps-3). pap. 10.95 *(0-590-94731-1)* Scholastic, Inc.

—The Berenstain Bears' That Stump Must Go! 2000. (I Can Read It All by Myself: Beginner Books). (Illus.). 48p. (J). (gr. k-3). lib. bdg. 11.99 o.s.i *(0-679-98963-3*, Random Hse. Bks. for Young Readers) Random Hse. Children's Bks.

—The Berenstain Bears, the Birds & the Bees. 2000. (Berenstain Bears First Time Bks.). (Illus.). 32p. (J). (gr. k-3). pap. 3.25 *(0-679-88959-0*, Random Hse. Bks. for Young Readers) Random Hse. Children's Bks.

—The Berenstain Bears, the Birds & the Bees. 1999. (Berenstain Bears First Time Bks.). (J). (gr. k-2). *(0-679-88971-X)* Random Hse., Inc.

—The Berenstain Bears the Whole Year Through: With Earthsaver Tips & Things to Do for Each & Every Month of the Year. 1997. (Berenstain Bears Ser.). (J). (ps-3). *(0-590-94462-2)* Scholastic, Inc.

—The Berenstain Bears Think of Those in Need. 1999. (Berenstain Bears First Time Bks.). (Illus.). 32p. (J). (gr. k-2). lib. bdg. 8.99 *(0-679-98957-9)*; pap. 3.25 *(0-679-88957-4)* Random Hse., Inc.

—The Berenstain Bears to the Rescue. (Berenstain Bears Mini-Storybooks). (J). (ps-3). 1995. pap. o.s.i *(0-679-87975-7)*; 1983. (Illus.). 32p. pap. 1.50 o.s.i *(0-394-85923-5)* Random Hse. Children's Bks. (Random Hse. Bks. for Young Readers).

—The Berenstain Bears' Toy Time. 1985. (Berenstain Bears Ser.). (Illus.). 12p. (J). (ps-3). pap. 4.99 o.s.i *(0-394-87449-8*, Random Hse. Bks. for Young Readers) Random Hse. Children's Bks.

—The Berenstain Bears Trick or Treat. (Berenstain Bears First Time Bks.). (Illus.). 32p. (gr. k-2). 1991. (J). 6.00 o.s.i incl. audio *(0-679-81497-3)*; 1991. (J). 6.00 o.s.i incl. audio *(0-679-81497-3)*; 1989. (J). 5.99 o.s.i *(0-679-90091-8)*; 1989. pap. 3.25 *(0-679-80091-3)* Random Hse. Children's Bks. (Random Hse. Bks. for Young Readers).

—The Berenstain Bears' Trouble at School. 1987. (Berenstain Bears First Time Bks.). 32p. (J). (gr. k-2). 5.99 o.s.i *(0-394-97336-4)*; (Illus.). pap. 3.25 *(0-394-87336-X)* Random Hse. Children's Bks. (Random Hse. Bks. for Young Readers).

—The Berenstain Bears' Trouble at School. 1986. (Berenstain Bears First Time Bks.). 32p. (J). (gr. k-2). 9.40 *(0-606-00626-5)* Turtleback Bks.

—The Berenstain Bears' Trouble with Money. 1983. (Berenstain Bears First Time Bks.). (Illus.). 32p. (J). (gr. k-2). pap. 3.25 *(0-394-85917-0*, Random Hse. Bks. for Young Readers) Random Hse. Children's Bks.

—The Berenstain Bears' Trouble with Money. 1983. (Berenstain Bears First Time Bks.). 32p. (J). (gr. k-2). 9.40 *(0-606-02777-7)* Turtleback Bks.

—The Berenstain Bears Trouble with Money. 1983. (Berenstain Bears First Time Bks.). (Illus.). 32p. (J). (gr. k-2). 5.99 o.s.i *(0-394-95917-5*, Random Hse. Bks. for Young Readers) Random Hse. Children's Bks.

—The Berenstain Bears' Trouble with Pets. 1990. (Berenstain Bears First Time Bks.). (Illus.). 32p. (gr. k-2). pap. 3.25 *(0-679-80848-5*, Random Hse. Bks. for Young Readers) Random Hse. Children's Bks.

—The Berenstain Bears' Trouble with Pets. 1990. (Berenstain Bears First Time Bks.). (J). (gr. k-2). 9.40 *(0-606-04615-1)* Turtleback Bks.

—The Berenstain Bears Visit the Dentist. (Berenstain Bears First Time Bks.). (Illus.). 32p. (gr. k-2). 1987. (J). pap. 2.95 o.s.i *(0-394-88894-4)*; 1985. (J).; 1981. lib. bdg. 8.99 *(0-394-94836-X)*; 1981. pap. 3.25 *(0-394-84836-5)* Random Hse. Children's Bks. (Random Hse. Bks. for Young Readers).

—The Berenstain Bears Visit the Dentist. 1981. (Berenstain Bears First Time Bks.). (J). (gr. k-2). 9.40 *(0-606-00396-7)* Turtleback Bks.

—The Berenstain Bears Yike! Yike! Where's My Trike? 1996. (Berenstain Bears Ser.). (Illus.). 14p. (J). (ps-3). bds. 4.99 o.s.i *(0-679-87577-8*, Random Hse. Bks. for Young Readers) Random Hse. Children's Bks.

—Berenstain Make It. 1997. (Illus.). (J). lib. bdg. o.s.i *(0-679-97842-9)* Random Hse., Inc.

—The Big Honey Hunt. 1962. (Berenstain Bears Beginner Bks.). (Illus.). 72p. (J). (ps-3). 8.99 *(0-394-80028-1*, Random Hse. Bks. for Young Readers) Random Hse. Children's Bks.

—The Bike Lesson. 1964. (Berenstain Bears Beginner Bks.). (Illus.). 72p. (J). (ps-3). 8.99 *(0-394-80036-2)*; lib. bdg. 12.99 *(0-394-90036-7)* Random Hse. Children's Bks. (Random Hse. Bks. for Young Readers).

—The Birds, Bees & the Berenstain Bears. 2000. 9.40 *(0-606-17523-7)* Turtleback Bks.

—Eager Beavers: The Berenstain Bears. (Comes to Life Bks.). 16p. (J). (ps-2). 1994. *(1-883366-73-9)*; 1993. *(1-883366-02-X)* YES! Entertainment Corp.

—En de Bezige Bevers: The Berenstain Bears. DigiPro Staff, tr. from ENG. 1994. (Comes to Life Bks.).Tr. of Eager Beavers. (DUT.). 16p. (J). (ps-2). *(1-883366-89-5)* YES! Entertainment Corp.

—En de Geheimzinnige Getallen: The Berenstain Bears. DigiPro Staff, tr. from ENG. 1994. (Comes to Life Bks.).Tr. of Mysterious Numbers. (DUT.). 16p. (J). (ps-2). *(1-883366-90-9)* YES! Entertainment Corp.

—Et les Castors Consciencieux: The Berenstain Bears. DigiPro Staff, tr. from ENG. 1994. (Comes to Life Bks.).Tr. of Eager Beavers. (FRE.). 16p. (J). (ps-2). *(1-883366-64-X)* YES! Entertainment Corp.

—Et les Nombres Mysterieux: The Berenstain Bears. DigiPro Staff, tr. from ENG. 1994. (Comes to Life Bks.).Tr. of Mysterious Numbers. (FRE.). 16p. (J). (ps-2). *(1-883366-65-8)* YES! Entertainment Corp.

—The Goofy, Goony Guy. 2001. (Berenstain Bears First Time Bks.). (Illus.). (J). 10.14 *(0-606-21057-1)* Turtleback Bks.

—The Haunted Lighthouse. 2001. (Berenstain Bears First Time Bks.). (Illus.). (J). 10.14 *(0-606-21058-X)* Turtleback Bks.

—He Bear, She Bear. 2002. (Berenstain Bears Bright & Early Bks.). (Illus.). (J). 16.70 *(0-7587-1253-7)* Book Wholesalers, Inc.

—He Bear, She Bear. (Berenstain Bears Bright & Early Bks.). (Illus.). (J). (ps-3). 1999. 24p. bds. 4.99 *(0-679-89426-8)*; 1974. 48p. 11.99 o.s.i *(0-394-92997-7)* Random Hse. Children's Bks. (Random Hse. Bks. for Young Readers).

—Inside, Outside, Upside Down. 1968. (Berenstain Bears Bright & Early Bks.). (Illus.). 36p. (ps-3). 8.99 *(0-394-81142-9)*; lib. bdg. 11.99 *(0-394-91142-3)* Random Hse. Children's Bks. (Random Hse. Bks. for Young Readers).

—Inside, Outside, Upside Down. (Berenstain Bears Bright & Early Bks.). (ps-3). 2000. (J). 7.99 *(0-375-80253-3)*; 1997. 12p. bds. 4.99 *(0-679-88632-X)* Random Hse., Inc.

—Life with Pa Pa: The Berenstain Bears. 1993. (Comes to Life Bks.). 16p. (J). (ps-2). *(1-883366-01-1)* YES! Entertainment Corp.

—Me First! Me First! Coping on the Playground. 2000. (Berenstain Bears Baby Bears Ser.). (Illus.). 7p. (J). (ps). bds. 4.99 o.s.i *(0-679-89332-6*, Random Hse. Bks. for Young Readers) Random Hse. Children's Bks.

—My New Bed: From Crib to Bed. 2nd ed. 1999. (Berenstain Bears Baby Bears Ser.). (Illus.). 7p. (J). (ps). bds. 4.99 o.s.i *(0-679-89333-4*, Random Hse. Bks. for Young Readers) Random Hse. Children's Bks.

—My Potty & I: A Friend In Need. 4th ed. 1999. (Berenstain Bears Baby Bears Ser.). (Illus.). 7p. (J). (ps). bds. 4.99 o.s.i *(0-679-89335-0*, Random Hse. Bks. for Young Readers) Random Hse. Children's Bks.

—My Trusty Car Seat: Buckling Up For Safety. 3rd ed. 1999. (Berenstain Bears Baby Bears Ser.). (Illus.). 7p. (J). (ps). bds. 4.99 o.s.i *(0-679-89334-2*, Random Hse. Bks. for Young Readers) Random Hse. Children's Bks.

—Mysterious Numbers: The Berenstain Bears. (Comes to Life Bks.). 16p. (J). (ps-2). 1994. *(1-883366-74-7)*; 1993. *(1-883366-00-3)* YES! Entertainment Corp.

—Not So Buried Treasure: The Berenstain Bears. 1995. (Comes to Life Bks.). 16p. (J). (ps-2). *(1-57234-057-6)* YES! Entertainment Corp.

—Old Hat, New Hat. 1997. (Berenstain Bears Bright & Early Bks.). 24p. (ps-3). bds. 4.99 *(0-679-88630-3*, Random Hse. Bks. for Young Readers) Random Hse. Children's Bks.

—Los Osos Berenstain & la Ninera. Guibert, Rita, tr. from ENG. 1993. (Berenstain Bears First Time Bks.).Tr. of Berenstain Bears & the Sitter. (SPA., Illus.). 32p. (J). (gr. k-2). pap. 3.25 *(0-679-84746-4*, Random Hse. Bks. for Young Readers) Random Hse. Children's Bks.

—Los Osos Berenstain Dia de Mudanza. 1992. (Berenstain Bears Ser.).Tr. of Berenstain Bears' Moving Day. (Illus.). (J). 9.40 *(0-606-20837-2)* Turtleback Bks.

—Los Osos Berenstain en la Oscuridad. 1992. (Berenstain Bears Ser.).Tr. of Berenstain Bears in the Dark. (Illus.). (J). 9.40 *(0-606-20838-0)* Turtleback Bks.

—Los Osos Berenstain, No Se Permiten Ninas. 1992. (Berenstain Bears Ser.).Tr. of Berenstain Bears No Girls Allowed. (Illus.). (J). 9.40 *(0-606-20839-9)* Turtleback Bks.

—Los Osos Berenstain y Demasiada Fiesta. ed. 2003. Tr. of Berenstain Bears & Too Much Birthday. (gr. 1). spiral bd. *(0-616-14610-8)* Canadian National Institute for the Blind/Institut National Canadien pour les Aveugles.

—Los Osos Berenstain y Demasiada Fiesta. Guibert, Rita, tr. from ENG. 1993. (Berenstain Bears First Time Bks.).Tr. of Berenstain Bears & Too Much Birthday. (SPA., Illus.). 32p. (J). (gr. k-2). pap. 3.25 *(0-679-84745-6*, Random Hse. Bks. for Young Readers) Random Hse. Children's Bks.

—Los Osos Berenstain y Demasiada Fiesta. 1992. (Berenstain Bears Ser.).Tr. of Berenstain Bears & Too Much Birthday. (Illus.). (J). 9.40 *(0-606-20840-2)* Turtleback Bks.

—Los Osos Berenstain y el Cuarto Desordenado. 1992. (Berenstain Bears Ser.).Tr. of Berenstain Bears & the Messy Bedroom. (Illus.). (J). 9.40 *(0-606-20841-0)* Turtleback Bks.

—Los Osos Berenstain y las Paleas Entre Amigos. Guibert, Rita, tr. from ENG. 1993. (Berenstain Bears First Time Bks.). (SPA., Illus.). 32p. (J). (gr. k-2). pap. 3.25 *(0-679-84006-0*, Random Hse. Bks. for Young Readers) Random Hse. Children's Bks.

—Los Osos Scouts Berenstain & el Bagre Que Tose. 1996. (Berenstain Bear Scouts Ser.).Tr. of Berenstain Bear Scouts & the Coughing Catfish. (SPA.). (J). (gr. 3-6). pap. text 3.50 *(0-590-87729-1)* Scholastic, Inc.

—Los Osos Scouts Berenstain & el Bagre Que Tose. 1996. (Berenstain Bear Scouts Ser.).Tr. of Berenstain Bear Scouts & the Coughing Catfish. (SPA.). (J). (gr. 3-6). 8.09 o.p. *(0-606-09719-8)* Turtleback Bks.

—Los Osos Scouts Berenstain & el Complot de la Gran Calabaza. 1995. (Berenstain Bear Scouts Ser.).Tr. of Berenstain Bear Scouts & the Humongous Pumpkin. (SPA., Illus.). 64p. (J). (gr. 3-6). pap. 2.99 *(0-590-59750-7)* Scholastic, Inc.

—Los Osos Scouts Berenstain & el Complot de la Gran Calabaza. 1995. (Berenstain Bear Scouts Ser.).Tr. of Berenstain Bear Scouts & the Humongous Pumpkin. (SPA.). (J). (gr. 3-6). 8.09 o.p. *(0-606-07805-3)* Turtleback Bks.

—Los Osos Scouts Berenstain & el Desastre Colosal. 1998. (Berenstain Bear Scouts Ser.).Tr. of Berenstain Bear Scouts & the Really Big Disaster. (SPA.). (J). (gr. 3-6). pap. text 3.50 *(0-590-94482-7*, Scholastic Paperbacks) Scholastic, Inc.

—Los Osos Scouts Berenstain & el Desastre Colosal. 1998. (Berenstain Bear Scouts Ser.).Tr. of Berenstain Bear Scouts & the Really Big Disaster. (SPA.). (J). (gr. 3-6). 8.60 o.p. *(0-606-13581-2)* Turtleback Bks.

—Los Osos Scouts Berenstain & el Monstruo de Hielo. 1997. (Berenstain Bear Scouts Ser.).Tr. of Berenstain Bear Scouts & the Ice Monster. (SPA.). (J). (gr. 3-6). pap. text 3.50 *(0-590-94480-0)* Scholastic, Inc.

—Los Osos Scouts Berenstain & el Monstruo de Hielo. 1997. (Berenstain Bear Scouts Ser.).Tr. of Berenstain Bear Scouts & the Ice Monster. (SPA.). (J). (gr. 3-6). 9.55 *(0-606-12760-7)* Turtleback Bks.

—Los Osos Scouts Berenstain & la Bola de Cristal Magica. 1997. (Berenstain Bear Scouts Ser.).Tr. of Berenstain Bear Scouts & the Magic Crystal Ball. (SPA.). (J). (gr. 3-6). pap. text 3.50 *(0-590-94476-2)* Scholastic, Inc.

—Los Osos Scouts Berenstain & la Bola de Cristal Magica. 1997. (Berenstain Bear Scouts Ser.).Tr. of Berenstain Bear Scouts & the Magic Crystal Ball. (SPA.). (J). (gr. 3-6). 9.55 *(0-606-11577-3)* Turtleback Bks.

—Los Osos Scouts Berenstain & la Guerra de los Fantasmas. 1996. (Berenstain Bear Scouts Ser.).Tr. of Berenstain Bear Scouts & the War of the Ghosts. (SPA.). (J). (gr. 3-6). pap. text 2.99 *(0-590-93381-7)* Scholastic, Inc.

—Los Osos Scouts Berenstain & la Pizza Voladora. 1996. (Berenstain Bear Scouts Ser.).Tr. of Berenstain Bear Scouts & the Sci-Fi Pizza. (SPA., Illus.). (J). (gr. 3-6). pap. text 2.99 o.p. *(0-590-93380-9)* Scholastic, Inc.

—Los Osos Scouts Berenstain & la Pizza Voladora. 1996. (Berenstain Bear Scouts Ser.).Tr. of Berenstain Bear Scouts & the Sci-Fi Pizza. (SPA.). (J). (gr. 3-6). 8.09 o.p. *(0-606-10481-X)* Turtleback Bks.

—Los Osos Scouts Berenstain & la Terrible Termita Habladora. 1996. (Berenstain Bear Scouts Ser.).Tr. of Berenstain Bear Scouts & the Terrible Talking Termite. (SPA.). (J). (gr. 3-6). mass mkt. 2.99 *(0-590-73850-X)* Scholastic, Inc.

—Los Osos Scouts Berenstain & la Terrible Termita Habladora. 1996. (Berenstain Bear Scouts Ser.).Tr. of Berenstain Bear Scouts & the Terrible Talking Termite. (SPA.). (J). (gr. 3-6). 8.09 o.p. *(0-606-09576-4)* Turtleback Bks.

—Los Osos Scouts Berenstain & los Siniestros Anillos de Humo. 1997. (Berenstain Bear Scouts Ser.).Tr. of Berenstain Bear Scouts & the Sinister Smoke Rings. (SPA.). (J). (gr. 3-6). pap. 3.50 *(0-590-94474-6)* Scholastic, Inc.

—Los Osos Scouts Berenstain & los Siniestros Anillos de Humo. 1997. (Berenstain Bear Scouts Ser.).Tr. of Berenstain Bear Scouts & the Sinister Smoke Rings. (J). (gr. 3-6). 8.70 o.p. (*0-606-11578-1*) Turtleback Bks.

—Los Osos Scouts Berenstain en la Cueva del Murcielago Gigante. 1995. (Berenstain Bear Scouts Ser.).Tr. of Berenstain Bear Scouts & the Giant Bat Cave. (SPA.). 64p. (J). (gr. 3-6). pap. 2.99 (*0-590-59749-3*) Scholastic, Inc.

—Los Osos Scouts Berenstain Gritan de Terror. 1998. (Berenstain Bear Scouts Ser.).Tr. of Berenstain Bear Scouts Scream Their Heads Off. (SPA.). (J). (gr. 3-6). 8.60 o.p. (*0-606-13580-4*) Turtleback Bks.

—Los Osos Scouts Berenstain Salvan a Rascaespaldas. 1996. (Berenstain Bear Scouts Ser.).Tr. of Berenstain Bear Scouts Save that Backscratcher. (SPA., Illus.). (J). (gr. 3-6). mass mkt. 2.99 (*0-590-69766-8*) Scholastic, Inc.

—Los Osos Scouts Berenstain Salvan a Rascaespaldas. 1996. (Berenstain Bear Scouts Ser.).Tr. of Berenstain Bear Scouts Save that Backscratcher. (SPA.). (J). (gr. 3-6). 9.55 (*0-606-09575-6*) Turtleback Bks.

—Los Osos Scouts Berenstain Se Encuentran Con Patagrande. 1996. (Berenstain Bear Scouts Ser.).Tr. of Berenstain Bear Scouts Meet Bigpaw. (SPA.). (J). (gr. 3-6). pap. 2.99 (*0-590-67664-4*) Scholastic, Inc.

—Los Osos Scouts Berenstain Se Encuentran Con Patagrande. 1995. (Berenstain Bear Scouts Ser.).Tr. of Berenstain Bear Scouts Meet Bigpaw. (SPA.). (J). (gr. 3-6). 8.09 o.p. (*0-606-08563-7*) Turtleback Bks.

—Pacifier Days: A Fond Farewell, 1999. (Berenstain Bears Baby Bears Ser.). (Illus.). 14p. (J). (ps). bds. 4.99 o.s.i (*0-679-89336-9*) Random Hse., Inc.

—The Runamuck Dog Show. 2001. (Berenstain Bears First Time Bks.). (Illus.). (J). 10.14 (*0-606-21059-8*) Turtleback Bks.

—Sister Bear's Jewelry Box. 1996. (J). o.s.i (*0-679-87327-9*, Random Hse. Bks. for Young Readers) Random Hse. Children's Bks.

—That Stump Must Go! 2000. (Berenstain Bears Bright & Early Bks.). (Illus.). 48p. (J). (ps-3). 7.99 o.s.i (*0-679-88963-9*, Random Hse. Bks. for Young Readers) Random Hse. Children's Bks.

—The Wrong Crowd. 2001. (Berenstain Bears First Time Bks.). (Illus.). (J). 10.14 (*0-606-21060-1*) Turtleback Bks.

—Y los Castores Trabajadores: The Berenstain Bears. DigiPro Staff, tr. from ENG. 1994. (Comes to Life Bks.).Tr. of Eager Beavers. (SPA.). 16p. (J). (ps-2). (*1-57234-007-X*) YES! Entertainment Corp.

Berenstain, Stan, et al. The Berenstain Bears & the Messy Room. 1998. (Berenstain Bears First Time Bks.). (Illus.). 32p. (J). (gr. k-2). pap. 3.99 o.s.i (*0-679-88774-1*, Random Hse. Bks. for Young Readers) Random Hse. Children's Bks.

—The Berenstain Bears & Too Much Junk Food. 1986. (Berenstain Bears First Time Bks.). (J). (gr. k-2). 7.95 o.s.i incl. audio (*0-394-88008-0*) Random Hse., Inc.

—The Berenstain Bears at the Super-Duper Market. 1996. (Berenstain Bears Toddler Bks.). 21p. (J). (ps). pap. 3.99 o.s.i (*0-679-88184-0*, Random Hse. Bks. for Young Readers) Random Hse. Children's Bks.

—The Berenstain Bears' Big Book of Science & Nature. 1997. (Berenstain Bears Ser.). 192p. (ps-3). pap. 12.99 o.s.i (*0-679-88652-4*, Random Hse. Bks. for Young Readers) Random Hse. Children's Bks.

—The Berenstain Bears Get the Gimmies. 1998. (Berenstain Bears First Time Bks.). (Illus.). 32p. (J). (gr. k-2). pap., wbk. ed. 3.99 o.s.i (*0-679-88772-5*, Random Hse. Bks. for Young Readers) Random Hse. Children's Bks.

—The Berenstain Bears in the Dark First Time Workbook. 1998. (Berenstain Bears First Time Bks.). (Illus.). 32p. (J). (gr. k-2). pap., wbk. ed. 3.99 o.s.i (*0-679-88773-3*, Random Hse. Bks. for Young Readers) Random Hse. Children's Bks.

—The Berenstain Bears in the Movies. 1994. (Berenstain Bears Ser.). 12p. (J). (ps-3). (*1-883366-59-3*) YES! Entertainment Corp.

—The Berenstain Bears Save Christmas. 2003. (Illus.). (J). 129.90 (*0-06-056995-6*) HarperCollins Children's Bk. Group.

—The Berenstain Bears' Trouble with Money. 1998. (Berenstain Bears First Time Bks.). (Illus.). 32p. (J). (gr. k-2). pap., wbk. ed. 3.99 o.s.i (*0-679-88775-X*, Random Hse. Bks. for Young Readers) Random Hse. Children's Bks.

—Comes to Life StoryPlayer & the Berenstain Bears & les Nombres Mysterieux. DigiPro Staff, tr. from ENG. 1994. (Comes to Life Bks.). (FRE.). 16p. (J). (ps-2). (*1-57234-002-9*) YES! Entertainment Corp.

—He Bear, She Bear. 1974. (Berenstain Bears Bright & Early Bks.). (Illus.). 48p. (ps-3). 8.99 (*0-394-82997-2*, Random Hse. Bks. for Young Readers) Random Hse. Children's Bks.

Koontz, Dean & Berenstain, Stan. The Berenstain Bears & the Spooky Old Tree. 1978. (Berenstain Bears Bright & Early Bks.). (J). (ps-3). 18.66 incl. audio (*0-394-00940-1*) Random Hse., Inc.

Where's Waldo, Inc. Staff, et al. Comes to Life Books: Berenstain Bears - Life with Papa; The Boy Who Became a Frog; Where's Waldo; Waldo in Dinoland, 4 bks., Set. 16p ea. 1993. (J). (ps-2). (*1-883366-39-9*) YES! Entertainment Corp.

YES! Entertainment Corporation Staff, et al. Comes to Life Story Player & Berenstain Bears: Mysterious Numbers & Berenstain Bears Eager Beavers Books. 1993. (Comes to Life Bks.). 16p. (J). (ps-2). (*1-883366-29-1*) YES! Entertainment Corp.

—Comes to Life Story Player & Berenstain Bears: Mysterious Numbers Book Set. 1993. (Comes to Life Bks.). 16p. (J). (ps-2). (*1-883366-07-0*) YES! Entertainment Corp.

—Comes to Life StoryPlayer & Berenstain Bears: Eager Beavers Book Set. 1994. (Comes to Life Bks.). 16p. (J). (ps-2). (*1-883366-50-X*) YES! Entertainment Corp.

—Comes to Life StoryPlayer & y los Numeros Misteriosos: The Berenstain Bears. 1994. (Comes to Life Bks.). (SPA.). 16p. (J). (ps-2). (*1-57234-006-1*) YES! Entertainment Corp.

BILLINGTON, JOHN, D. 1630—FICTION

Bulla, Clyde Robert. John Billington, Friend of Squanto. 1956. (Illus.). (J). (gr. 2-5). 11.49 o.p. (*0-690-46253-0*) HarperCollins Children's Bk. Group.

Hays, Wilma P. Naughty Little Pilgrim. 1969. (Illus.). (J). (gr. 1-3). 4.95 o.p. (*0-679-24057-8*, 240967) McKay, David Co., Inc.

BINDER, AMOS (FICTITIOUS CHARACTER)—FICTION

Paulsen, Gary. Amos & the Alien. 1994. (Culpepper Adventures Ser.). 80p. (J). (gr. 3-5). pap. 3.50 (*0-440-40990-X*) Dell Publishing.

—Amos & the Chameleon Caper. 1996. (Culpepper Adventures Ser.). 80p. (J). (gr. 3-5). pap. 3.99 o.s.i (*0-440-41047-9*) Dell Publishing.

—Amos & the Chameleon Caper. 1996. (Culpepper Adventures Ser.). (J). (gr. 3-5). 9.19 o.p. (*0-606-11039-9*) Turtleback Bks.

—Amos & the Vampire. 1996. (Culpepper Adventures Ser.). 80p. (J). (gr. 3-5). pap. 3.99 o.s.i (*0-440-41043-6*, Yearling) Random Hse. Children's Bks.

—Amos & the Vampire. 1996. (Culpepper Adventures Ser.). (J). (gr. 3-5). 9.19 o.p. (*0-606-08996-9*) Turtleback Bks.

—Amos Binder, Secret Agent. 1996. (Culpepper Adventures Ser.). 80p. (gr. 3-5). pap. text 3.99 o.s.i (*0-440-41050-9*) Dell Publishing.

—Amos Binder, Secret Agent. 1997. (Culpepper Adventures Ser.). (J). (gr. 3-5). 9.19 o.p. (*0-606-11040-2*) Turtleback Bks.

—Amos Gets Famous. 1992. (Culpepper Adventures Ser.). 80p. (J). (gr. 3-5). pap. 3.99 o.s.i (*0-440-40749-4*) Dell Publishing.

—Amos Gets Married. 1995. (Culpepper Adventures Ser.). 112p. (J). (gr. 3-5). pap. 3.50 o.s.i (*0-440-40933-0*) Dell Publishing.

—Amos Gets Married. 1995. (Culpepper Adventures Ser.). (J). (gr. 3-5). 8.60 o.p. (*0-606-07187-3*) Turtleback Bks.

—Amos Goes Bananas. 1996. (Culpepper Adventures Ser.). 80p. (J). (gr. 3-5). pap. 3.99 o.s.i (*0-440-41008-8*) Dell Publishing.

—Amos Goes Bananas. 1995. (Culpepper Adventures Ser.). (J). (gr. 3-5). 9.19 o.p. (*0-606-08997-7*) Turtleback Bks.

—Amos's Killer Concert Caper. 1994. (Culpepper Adventures Ser.). 96p. (J). (gr. 3-5). pap. 3.50 o.s.i (*0-440-40989-6*) Dell Publishing.

—Amos's Killer Concert Caper. 1995. (Culpepper Adventures Ser.). (J). (gr. 3-5). 8.60 o.p. (*0-606-07188-1*) Turtleback Bks.

—Amos's Last Stand. 1993. (Culpepper Adventures Ser.). 80p. (J). (gr. 3-5). pap. 3.25 o.s.i (*0-440-40775-3*) Dell Publishing.

—Dunc & the Haunted Castle. 1993. (Culpepper Adventures Ser.). (J). (gr. 3-5). 9.19 o.p. (*0-606-05817-6*) Turtleback Bks.

BISCUIT (FICTITIOUS CHARACTER: CAPUCILLI)—FICTION

Capucilli, Alyssa Satin. Bathtime for Biscuit. (My First I Can Read Bks.). (Illus.). 32p. (J). (ps up). 1999. pap. 3.99 (*0-06-444264-0*, Harper Trophy); 1998. 12.95 (*0-06-027937-0*); 1998. lib. bdg. 14.89 (*0-06-027938-9*) HarperCollins Children's Bk. Group.

—Biscuit. (My First I Can Read Bks.). (Illus.). (J). (ps-k). 1999. 8.99 incl. audio (*0-694-70101-7*, Harper Festival); 1996. 32p. 14.99 (*0-06-026197-8*); 1996. 32p. lib. bdg. 15.89 (*0-06-026198-6*); 1997. 32p. reprint ed. pap. 3.99 (*0-06-444212-8*, Harper Trophy) HarperCollins Children's Bk. Group.

—Biscuit. 1997. (My First I Can Read Bks.). (Illus.). (J). (ps-k). 10.10 (*0-606-11135-2*) Turtleback Bks.

—Biscuit & Daisy. 2002. (Biscuit Ser.). (Illus.). 16p. (J). (ps-1). bds. 4.95 (*0-694-01520-2*, Harper Festival) HarperCollins Children's Bk. Group.

—Biscuit & Puddles. 2002. (Biscuit Ser.). (Illus.). 16p. (J). (ps-1). bds. 4.95 (*0-694-01523-7*, Harper Festival) HarperCollins Children's Bk. Group.

—Biscuit Finds a Friend. (My First I Can Read Bks.). (Illus.). 32p. (J). (ps up). 1998. pap. 3.99 (*0-06-444243-8*, Harper Trophy); 1997. 15.99 (*0-06-027412-3*); 1997. lib. bdg. 14.89 (*0-06-027413-1*); 2001. pap. 8.99 incl. audio (*0-06-029324-1*) HarperCollins Children's Bk. Group.

—Biscuit Finds a Friend. 1998. (My First I Can Read Bks.). (Illus.). (J). (ps-k). 10.10 (*0-606-13203-1*) Turtleback Bks.

—Biscuit Goes to School. (Biscuit Ser.). (Illus.). (J). (ps-k). 2003. 8.99 incl. audio (*0-06-009426-5*); 2002. 32p. 14.99 (*0-06-028682-2*); 2002. 32p. lib. bdg. 16.89 (*0-06-028683-0*) HarperCollins Children's Bk. Group.

—Biscuit Goes to School. 2003. (Biscuit Ser.). (Illus.). 24p. (J). (ps up). pap. 3.99 (*0-06-443616-0*) HarperCollins Pubs.

—Biscuit Mini Book & Puppy. 1999. (Biscuit Ser.). (Illus.). (J). (ps-1). 14.95 (*0-694-01444-3*) HarperCollins Children's Bk. Group.

—Biscuit Treasury. 2000. (Biscuit Ser.). (Illus.). (J). (ps-1). (*0-06-029128-1*) HarperCollins Children's Bk. Group.

—Biscuit Wants to Play. (My First I Can Read Bks.). (Illus.). 32p. (J). (ps-k). 2002. pap. 3.99 (*0-06-444315-9*, Harper Trophy); 2001. 14.99 (*0-06-028069-7*); 2001. lib. bdg. 14.89 (*0-06-028070-0*) HarperCollins Children's Bk. Group.

—Biscuit's Christmas. 2000. (Biscuit Ser.). (Illus.). 16p. (J). (ps-1). 6.95 (*0-694-01516-4*, Harper Festival) HarperCollins Children's Bk. Group.

—Biscuit's Day at the Beach. 2001. (Biscuit Ser.). (Illus.). 16p. (J). (ps-1). 3.95 (*0-694-01521-0*, Harper Festival) HarperCollins Children's Bk. Group.

—Biscuit's New Trick. 2000. (My First I Can Read Bks.). (Illus.). 32p. (J). (ps-k). 12.95 (*0-06-028067-0*); lib. bdg. 15.89 (*0-06-028068-9*) HarperCollins Children's Bk. Group.

—Biscuit's Picnic. 1998. (Biscuit Ser.). (Illus.). 24p. (J). (ps-1). 12.95 (*0-06-028072-7*) HarperCollins Children's Bk. Group.

—Biscuit's Vacation. 2002. (Biscuit Ser.). (Illus.). 24p. (J). (ps-1). lib. bdg. 12.89 (*0-06-028681-4*) HarperCollins Children's Bk. Group.

BISHOP, ELVIN (FICTITIOUS CHARACTER)—FICTION

Lynch, Chris. Extreme Elvin. 240p. (gr. 7 up). 2001. (J). pap. 5.95 (*0-06-447142-X*, Harper Trophy); 1999. (J). lib. bdg. 15.89 (*0-06-028210-X*); 1999. (YA). 15.95 (*0-06-028040-9*) HarperCollins Children's Bk. Group.

—Slot Machine. 256p. 1996. (Illus.). (J). (gr. 7 up). pap. 5.99 (*0-06-447140-3*, Harper Trophy); 1995. (YA). (gr. 12 up). lib. bdg. 14.89 o.s.i (*0-06-023585-3*); 1995. (YA). (gr. 7 up). 14.95 o.p. (*0-06-023584-5*) HarperCollins Children's Bk. Group.

—Slot Machine. 1996. (J). 12.00 (*0-606-09867-4*) Turtleback Bks.

BLACK HAWK, SAUK CHIEF, 1767-1838—FICTION

Le Sueur, Meridel. Sparrow Hawk. 1966. (Illus.). (J). (gr. 5 up). lib. bdg. 5.19 o.s.i (*0-394-91658-1*, Knopf Bks. for Young Readers) Random Hse. Children's Bks.

BLACK STALLION (FICTITIOUS CHARACTER)—FICTION

The Black Stallion & Satan. (Black Stallion Ser.). (J). (gr. 4-6). Random Hse. Children's Bks.

Farley, Steven. The Black Stallion's Shadow. 2000. (Black Stallion Ser.). (Illus.). 192p. (gr. 5-8). pap. text 5.99 (*0-679-89046-7*, Random Hse. Bks. for Young Readers) Random Hse. Children's Bks.

—The Black Stallion's Shadow. 1996. (Black Stallion Ser.). 182p. (J). (gr. 4-6). 16.00 o.s.i (*0-679-85004-X*) Random Hse., Inc.

—The Black Stallion's Steeplechaser. 1997. (Black Stallion Ser.). (J). (gr. 4-6). 17.00 o.s.i (*0-679-88200-6*); 19.99 o.s.i (*0-679-98200-0*) Random Hse., Inc.

—Hard Lessons. 1999. (Young Black Stallion Ser.: No. 6). (Illus.). 144p. (gr. 5-8). pap. text 3.99 o.s.i (*0-375-80092-1*); (J). (gr. 4-6). lib. bdg. 11.99 (*0-375-90092-6*) Random Hse. Children's Bks. (Random Hse. Bks. for Young Readers).

—Hard Lessons. 1999. (Young Black Stallion Ser.: No. 6). (J). (gr. 4-6). 10.04 (*0-606-16965-2*) Turtleback Bks.

—The Homecoming. 1999. (Young Black Stallion Ser.: No. 3). (Illus.). (J). 128p. (gr. 3-5). lib. bdg. 11.99 o.s.i (*0-679-99358-4*); 3rd ed. 110p. (gr. 5-8). pap. 3.99 o.s.i (*0-679-89358-X*) Random Hse. Children's Bks. (Random Hse. Bks. for Young Readers).

—The Homecoming. 1999. (Young Black Stallion Ser.: No. 3). (J). (gr. 4-6). 10.04 (*0-606-16962-8*) Turtleback Bks.

—A Horse Called Raven. 1998. (Young Black Stallion Ser.: No. 2). 144p. (J). (gr. 4-6). 11.99 o.s.i (*0-679-99142-5*); 2nd ed. pap. 3.99 o.s.i (*0-679-89142-0*) Random Hse. Children's Bks. (Random Hse. Bks. for Young Readers).

—A Horse Called Raven. 1998. (Young Black Stallion Ser.: No. 2). (J). (gr. 4-6). 10.04 (*0-606-16961-X*) Turtleback Bks.

—The Promise. 1998. (Young Black Stallion Ser.: No. 1). 132p. (J). (gr. 4-6). 11.99 o.s.i (*0-679-99141-7*, Random Hse. Bks. for Young Readers) Random Hse. Children's Bks.

—The Promise. 1998. (Young Black Stallion Ser.: No. 1). 132p. (J). (gr. 4-6). pap. 3.99 o.s.i (*0-679-89141-2*) Random Hse., Inc.

—The Promise, Vol. 1. 1998. (Young Black Stallion Ser.: No.1). (J). (gr. 4-6). 10.04 (*0-606-16960-1*) Turtleback Bks.

—South Wind Spring. 2000. (Young Black Stallion Ser.: No. 7). (Illus.). 144p. (J). (gr. 4-6). pap. 3.99 (*0-375-80139-1*); lib. bdg. 11.99 o.p. (*0-375-90139-6*) Random Hse. Children's Bks. (Random Hse. Bks. for Young Readers).

Farley, Walter. The Black Stallion. (Black Stallion Ser.). 1991. 224p. (YA). (gr. 5-8). pap. 5.99 (*0-679-81343-8*); 1982. (Illus.). 192p. (J). (gr. 4-6). 8.95 o.s.i (*0-394-85114-5*); 1977. (Illus.). (J). (gr. 4-6). pap. 3.95 o.s.i (*0-394-83609-X*); 1963. (Illus.). (J). (gr. k-3). 1.95 o.s.i (*0-394-80635-2*); 1963. (Illus.). (J). (gr. k-3). lib. bdg. 3.99 o.s.i (*0-394-90635-7*); 1944. (Illus.). (J). (gr. 4-6). pap. 3.95 o.s.i (*0-394-80601-8*); 1944. (Illus.). 192p. (gr. 4-6). lib. bdg. 11.99 (*0-394-90601-2*); 1991. (Illus.). 232p. (J). (gr. 5-8). reprint ed. 17.00 (*0-679-81349-7*) Random Hse. Children's Bks. (Random Hse. Bks. for Young Readers).

—The Black Stallion. 2000. (Black Stallion Ser.). (Illus.). 192p. (J). (gr. 5-8). mass mkt. 2.99 o.s.i (*0-375-80671-7*) Random Hse., Inc.

—The Black Stallion. 9999. (Black Stallion Ser.). (J). (gr. 4-6). pap. 2.25 o.s.i (*0-590-31564-1*) Scholastic, Inc.

—The Black Stallion. 1941. (Black Stallion Ser.). (J). (gr. 4-6). 12.04 (*0-606-02376-3*) Turtleback Bks.

—The Black Stallion: Beginner Book. 1986. (Black Stallion Ser.). (Illus.). 48p. (J). (ps-3). 7.99 o.p. (*0-394-86876-5*, Random Hse. Bks. for Young Readers) Random Hse. Children's Bks.

—The Black Stallion: Comic Book Album. 1983. (Black Stallion Comic Bks.). (Illus.). 48p. (J). (gr. 3-7). pap. 2.95 o.p. (*0-394-86025-X*, Random Hse. Bks. for Young Readers) Random Hse. Children's Bks.

—The Black Stallion An Easy-to-Read Adaptation. 1986. (Black Stallion Ser.). (Illus.). 48p. (J). (gr. 4-6). 11.99 o.p. (*0-394-96876-X*, Random Hse. Bks. for Young Readers) Random Hse. Children's Bks.

—The Black Stallion & Flame. (Black Stallion Ser.). (Illus.). (J). (gr. 4-6). 1980. pap. 3.95 o.s.i (*0-394-84372-X*); 1960. 11.99 o.p. (*0-394-90615-2*); 1960. pap. 3.95 o.s.i (*0-394-80615-8*) Random Hse. Children's Bks. (Random Hse. Bks. for Young Readers).

—The Black Stallion & Flame. 1960. (Black Stallion Ser.). (J). (gr. 4-6). 11.04 (*0-606-00439-4*) Turtleback Bks.

—The Black Stallion & Satan. (Black Stallion Ser.). (Illus.). (J). (gr. 4-6). 1978. pap. 2.95 o.s.i (*0-394-83914-5*); 1949. 8.99 o.s.i (*0-394-90605-5*); 1949. pap. 3.95 o.s.i (*0-394-80605-0*) Random Hse. Children's Bks. (Knopf Bks. for Young Readers).

—The Black Stallion & the Girl. (Black Stallion Ser.). (J). (gr. 4-6). 1977. pap. 3.95 o.s.i (*0-394-83614-6*); 1971. 3.95 o.s.i (*0-394-82145-9*); 1971. 10.99 o.s.i (*0-394-92145-3*) Random Hse. Children's Bks. (Knopf Bks. for Young Readers).

—The Black Stallion Challenged. 1964. (Black Stallion Ser.). (Illus.). (J). (gr. 4-6). 10.99 o.s.i (*0-394-90617-9*); pap. 3.95 o.s.i (*0-394-80617-4*) Random Hse. Children's Bks. (Random Hse. Bks. for Young Readers).

—The Black Stallion Challenged. 2003. (Black Stallion Ser.). (Illus.). 240p. (YA). (gr. 5-8). pap. 5.99 (*0-394-84371-1*) Random Hse., Inc.

—The Black Stallion Legend. 1985. (Black Stallion Ser.). (Illus.). 192p. (J). (gr. 4-6). pap. 3.95 o.s.i (*0-394-87500-1*, Random Hse. Bks. for Young Readers) Random Hse. Children's Bks.

—The Black Stallion Mystery. (Black Stallion Ser.). (J). (gr. 4-6). 1965. (J). (gr. 4-6). 10.99 o.s.i (*0-394-90613-6*); 1957. (J). (gr. 4-6). 3.95 o.s.i (*0-394-80613-1*); 2004. 240p. (YA). (gr. 5-8). reprint ed. pap. 5.99 (*0-679-82700-5*) Random Hse. Children's Bks. (Random Hse. Bks. for Young Readers).

—The Black Stallion Mystery. 1957. (Black Stallion Ser.). (J). (gr. 4-6). 10.09 (*0-606-02046-2*) Turtleback Bks.

—The Black Stallion Returns. (Black Stallion Ser.). 1991. 240p. (YA). (gr. 5-8). pap. 5.99 *(0-679-81344-6*, Random Hse. Bks. for Young Readers); 1977. (Illus.). 208p. (J). (gr. 4-6). pap. 2.95 o.s.i *(0-394-83610-3*, Knopf Bks. for Young Readers) Random Hse. Children's Bks.

—The Black Stallion Returns. 1945. (Black Stallion Ser.). (J). (gr. 4-6). pap. 3.95 o.s.i *(0-394-80602-6)* Random Hse., Inc.

—The Black Stallion Returns. 9999. (Black Stallion Ser.). (J). (gr. 4-6). pap. 2.50 o.s.i *(0-590-32872-7)* Scholastic, Inc.

—The Black Stallion Returns. 1973. (Black Stallion Ser.). (J). (gr. 4-6). 11.04 *(0-606-02047-0)* Turtleback Bks.

—The Black Stallion Returns: A Comic Book Album. 1984. (Black Stallion Comic Bks.). (Illus.). (J). (gr. 4-6). pap. 3.95 o.p. *(0-394-86341-0*, Random Hse. Bks. for Young Readers) Random Hse. Children's Bks.

—The Black Stallion Revolts. (Black Stallion Ser.). (J). 2002. 288p. (gr. 5-8). pap. 5.99 *(0-394-83613-8)*; 1953. (gr. 4-6). 6.99 o.s.i *(0-394-90609-8)*; 1953. (gr. 4-6). pap. 3.95 o.s.i *(0-394-80609-3)* Random Hse. Children's Bks. (Random Hse. Bks. for Young Readers).

—The Black Stallion's Blood Bay Colt. 1994. (Black Stallion Ser.). 288p. (J). (gr. 5-8). pap. 4.99 o.s.i *(0-679-81347-0*, Random Hse. Bks. for Young Readers) Random Hse. Children's Bks.

—The Black Stallion's Blood Bay Colt. 1994. (Black Stallion Ser.). (J). (gr. 4-6). 10.09 *(0-606-06939-9)* Turtleback Bks.

—The Black Stallion's Courage. (Black Stallion Ser.). (Illus.). 2004. 224p. (YA). (gr. 5-8). pap. 5.99 *(0-394-83918-8)*; 1963. (J). (gr. 4-6). 6.99 o.s.i *(0-394-90612-8)*; 1956. (J). (gr. 4-6). pap. 3.95 o.s.i *(0-394-80612-3)* Random Hse. Children's Bks. (Knopf Bks. for Young Readers).

—The Black Stallion's Filly. (Black Stallion Ser.). (Illus.). (J). 2002. 288p. (gr. 5-8). pap. 5.99 *(0-394-83916-1)*; 1952. (gr. 4-6). lib. bdg. 8.99 o.s.i *(0-394-90608-X)* Random Hse. Children's Bks. (Random Hse. Bks. for Young Readers).

—The Black Stallion's Ghost. (Black Stallion Ser.). (Illus.). 1995. 208p. (YA). (gr. 5-8). pap. 5.99 *(0-679-86950-6)*; 1978. (J). (gr. 4-6). pap. 3.95 o.s.i *(0-394-83919-6)*; 1969. 208p. (gr. 4-6). lib. bdg. 11.99 *(0-394-90618-7)* Random Hse. Children's Bks. (Random Hse. Bks. for Young Readers).

—The Black Stallion's Ghost. 1995. (Black Stallion Ser.). (J). (gr. 4-6). 11.04 *(0-606-07292-6)* Turtleback Bks.

—The Black Stallion's Sulky Colt. (Black Stallion Ser.). (Illus.). (J). (gr. 4-6). 1978. 3.95 o.s.i *(0-394-80610-7)*; 1978. pap. 3.95 o.s.i *(0-394-83917-X)*; 1954. 10.99 o.s.i *(0-394-90610-1)* Random Hse. Children's Bks. (Random Hse. Bks. for Young Readers).

—The Horse-Tamer. (Black Stallion Ser.). 160p. (J). (gr. 4-6). 1980. pap. 3.95 o.s.i *(0-394-84374-6)*; 1963. 6.99 o.s.i *(0-394-90614-4)*; 1958. 3.95 o.s.i *(0-394-80614-X)* Random Hse. Children's Bks. (Random Hse. Bks. for Young Readers).

—The Island Stallion. 1948. (Black Stallion Ser.). (Illus.). (J). (gr. 4-6). 3.95 o.s.i *(0-394-80604-2)*; 11.99 o.s.i *(0-394-90604-7)* Random Hse. Children's Bks. (Random Hse. Bks. for Young Readers).

—The Island Stallion. 2003. (Black Stallion Ser.). (Illus.). 240p. (YA). (gr. 5-8). pap. 5.99 *(0-394-84376-2)* Random Hse., Inc.

—The Island Stallion. 1948. (Black Stallion Ser.). (J). (gr. 4-6). 10.09 o.p. *(0-606-01731-3)* Turtleback Bks.

—The Island Stallion Races. (Black Stallion Ser.). (Illus.). (J). (gr. 4-6). 1964. 6.99 o.s.i *(0-394-90611-X)*; 1955. pap. 3.95 o.s.i *(0-394-80611-5)* Random Hse. Children's Bks. (Random Hse. Bks. for Young Readers).

—The Island Stallion Races. 2003. (Black Stallion Ser.). (Illus.). 256p. (YA). (gr. 5-8). pap. 5.99 *(0-394-84375-4)* Random Hse., Inc.

—The Island Stallion's Fury. 1951. (Black Stallion Ser.). (Illus.). (J). (gr. 4-6). 3.95 o.s.i *(0-394-80607-7)*; 6.99 o.s.i *(0-394-90607-1)* Random Hse. Children's Bks. (Random Hse. Bks. for Young Readers).

—The Island Stallion's Fury. 2003. (Black Stallion Ser.). (Illus.). 224p. (YA). (gr. 5-8). pap. 5.99 *(0-394-84373-8)* Random Hse., Inc.

—Son of the Black Stallion. (Black Stallion Ser.). (Illus.). (J). (gr. 4-6). 1977. pap. 3.95 o.s.i *(0-394-83612-X)*; 1963. 10.99 o.s.i *(0-394-90603-9)*; 1947. pap. 3.95 o.s.i *(0-394-80603-4)* Random Hse. Children's Bks. (Knopf Bks. for Young Readers).

—Son of the Black Stallion. 9999. (Black Stallion Ser.). (J). (gr. 4-6). pap. 2.25 o.s.i *(0-590-30387-2)* Scholastic, Inc.

—Son of the Black Stallion. 1991. (Black Stallion Ser.). (J). (gr. 4-6). 10.09 o.p. *(0-606-02266-X)* Turtleback Bks.

Farley, Walter & Farley, Steven. The Young Black Stallion. 2003. 160p. (YA). (gr. 5-8). pap. 5.99 *(0-375-82935-0)*; 1989. 192p. (J). (gr. 4-6). 10.95 o.s.i *(0-394-84562-5)* Random Hse. Children's Bks. (Random Hse. Bks. for Young Readers).

—The Young Black Stallion. 1993. (Black Stallion Ser.). (J). (gr. 4-6). 2.99 o.p. *(0-517-11121-7)* Random Hse. Value Publishing.

—The Young Black Stallion. 1991. (Black Stallion Ser.). (J). (gr. 4-6). 11.04 *(0-606-05051-5)* Turtleback Bks.

BLAKE, JENNA (FICTITIOUS CHARACTER)—FICTION

Golden, Christopher. Body Bags. 1999. (Body of Evidence Ser.: Vol. 1). 272p. (YA). (gr. 7-12). mass mkt. 4.99 *(0-671-03492-8*, Simon Pulse) Simon & Schuster Children's Publishing.

—Head Games. 2000. (Body of Evidence Ser.: No. 5). (Illus.). 256p. (YA). (gr. 7-12). mass mkt. 4.99 *(0-671-77582-0*, Simon Pulse) Simon & Schuster Children's Publishing.

—Meets the Eye. 2000. (Body of Evidence Ser.: No. 4). 256p. (YA). (gr. 7 up). mass mkt. 4.99 *(0-671-03495-2*, Simon Pulse) Simon & Schuster Children's Publishing.

—Skin Deep. 2000. (Body of Evidence Ser.: Vol. 6). (Illus.). 288p. (YA). mass mkt. 5.99 o.s.i *(0-671-77583-9*, Simon Pulse) Simon & Schuster Children's Publishing.

—Soul Survivor. 1999. (Body of Evidence Ser.: Vol. 3). 256p. (YA). (gr. 7-12). pap. 4.99 *(0-671-03494-4*, Simon Pulse) Simon & Schuster Children's Publishing.

—Thief of Hearts. 1999. (Body of Evidence Ser.: Vol. 2). (Illus.). 272p. (YA). (gr. 8-12). pap. 4.99 *(0-671-03493-6*, Simon Pulse) Simon & Schuster Children's Publishing.

BLUE (FICTITIOUS CHARACTER)—FICTION

Albee, Sarah. Blue's Checkup. 2003. (Blue's Clues Ser.). (Illus.). 24p. (J). pap. 3.50 *(0-689-85449-8*, Simon Spotlight/Nickelodeon) Simon & Schuster Children's Publishing.

—Blue's Lunchbox. 2000. (Blue's Clues Ser.). (Illus.). 16p. (J). (ps-k). pap. 3.99 *(0-689-83099-8*, Simon Spotlight/Nickelodeon) Simon & Schuster Children's Publishing.

—Blue's Travel Game. 2000. (Blue's Clues Ser.). (Illus.). 16p. (J). (ps-k). pap. 3.99 *(0-689-83098-X*, Simon Spotlight/Nickelodeon) Simon & Schuster Children's Publishing.

Bergen, Lara Rice. Blue's World of Words. 2002. (Blue's Clues Ser.). (Illus.). 32p. (J). (ps-k). 12.95 *(0-689-84741-6*, Simon Spotlight/Nickelodeon) Simon & Schuster Children's Publishing.

Blue's Clues. 2001. (Illus.). 48p. pap. 4.99 *(0-307-10852-X*, Golden Bks.) Random Hse. Children's Bks.

Blue's Clues Box Set. 1999. (Blue's Clues Ser.). (J). (ps-k). 19.96 *(0-689-83312-1*, Simon Spotlight) Simon & Schuster Children's Publishing.

Blue's Clues Nature Game. 2001. (Illus.). 32p. pap. 4.99 *(0-307-16431-4*, Golden Bks.) Random Hse. Children's Bks.

Blue's Treasury of Stories. 2003. (Illus.). (J). 15.25 *(0-689-85883-3*, Simon Spotlight/Nickelodeon) Simon & Schuster Children's Publishing.

Boczkowski, Tricia. Blue's Favorite Things. 2003. (Blue's Clues Ser.). (Illus.). 12p. (J). bds. 7.99 *(0-689-84840-4*, Simon Spotlight/Nickelodeon) Simon & Schuster Children's Publishing.

Fry, Sonali. Blue's Colors. 2003. (Baby Blue's Clues Ser.). (Illus.). 14p. (J). bds. 7.99 *(0-689-85502-8*, Simon Spotlight/Nickelodeon) Simon & Schuster Children's Publishing.

Golden Books Staff. Adventures with Blue. 2001. pap. 5.99 o.s.i *(0-307-34132-1)* Random Hse., Inc.

—Blue's Friendship Day/What's Blue Building? 2003. 64p. (J). pap. 2.99 *(0-307-10122-3*, Golden Bks.) Random Hse. Children's Bks.

—Outside with Blue: Blue's Big Day. 2001. 128p. (J). (ps-k). pap. 3.99 *(0-307-25260-4*, Golden Bks.) Random Hse. Children's Bks.

—A Scavenger Hunt with Blue. 2001. 32p. (J). (ps-k). pap. 4.99 *(0-307-16443-8*, Golden Bks.) Random Hse. Children's Bks.

—Spending Time with Blue. 2001. 32p. (J). (ps-k). pap. 4.99 *(0-307-27623-6*, Golden Bks.) Random Hse. Children's Bks.

Inches, Alison. Blue's First Holiday. 2003. (Blue's Clues Ser.). (Illus.). 24p. (J). 9.99 *(0-689-86167-2*, Simon Spotlight/Nickelodeon) Simon & Schuster Children's Publishing.

Johnson, Traci Paige. Crayon World. 1999. (Blue's Clues Ser.). 14p. (J). (ps-k). 4.99 *(0-689-83333-4*, Simon Spotlight/Nickelodeon) Simon & Schuster Children's Publishing.

Johnson, Traci Paige & Kim, Soo Kyung, illus. Crayon World. 1999. (Blue's Clues Ser.). 6p. (J). (ps-k). 4.99 *(0-689-82448-3*, Simon Spotlight/ Nickelodeon) Simon & Schuster Children's Publishing.

Landy, Sarah. Blue's Snack Party A Lift-the-Flap Story. 2000. (Blue's Clues Ser.). (Illus.). 16p. (J). (ps-k). 5.99 *(0-689-83432-2*, Simon Spotlight/ Nickelodeon) Simon & Schuster Children's Publishing.

Lissy, Jessica. A Blue's Clues Chanukah. 2003. (Blue's Clues Ser.). (Illus.). 24p. (J). (ps-2). pap. 3.99 *(0-689-85840-X*, Simon Spotlight/Nickelodeon) Simon & Schuster Children's Publishing.

Lukas, Catherine. Blue's 12 Days of Christmas. 2002. (Blue's Clues Ser.). (Illus.). 32p. (J). 9.99 *(0-689-84971-0*, Simon Spotlight/Nickelodeon) Simon & Schuster Children's Publishing.

Miglis, Jenny. Blue's. 2003. (Blue's Clues Ser.). (Illus.). 14p. (J). bds. 4.99 *(0-689-85231-2*, Simon Spotlight/Nickelodeon) Simon & Schuster Children's Publishing.

—Faces. 2002. (Blue's Clues Ser.). (Illus.). 12p. (J). bds. 5.99 *(0-689-84842-0*, Simon Spotlight/ Nickelodeon) Simon & Schuster Children's Publishing.

—Feelings. 2002. (Blue's Clues Ser.). (Illus.). 12p. (J). bds. 5.99 *(0-689-84843-9*, Simon Spotlight/ Nickelodeon) Simon & Schuster Children's Publishing.

Peltzman, Adam. Blue's Big Pajama Party. 1999. (Blue's Clues Ser.). (Illus.). 24p. (J). (ps-k). 9.99 *(0-689-82896-9*, Simon Spotlight/Nickelodeon) Simon & Schuster Children's Publishing.

Perello, Jennifer Twomey, et al. Blue's Guess Who! 1999. (Blue's Clues Ser.). (Illus.). 16p. (J). (ps-k). pap. 3.99 *(0-689-82951-5*, Simon Spotlight/ Nickelodeon) Simon & Schuster Children's Publishing.

Reber, Deborah. Blue's ABC Detective Game. 2002. (Blue's Clues Ser.). (Illus.). 16p. (J). 9.99 *(0-689-84346-1*, Simon Spotlight/Nickelodeon) Simon & Schuster Children's Publishing.

—Blue's Egg Hunt. 2001. (Blue's Clues Ser.). (Illus.). 24p. (J). (ps-k). pap. 3.50 *(0-689-83873-5*, Simon Spotlight/Nickelodeon) Simon & Schuster Children's Publishing.

—Blue's Valentine's Day. 2000. (Blue's Clues Ser.). (Illus.). 16p. (J). (ps-k). pap. 3.99 *(0-689-83062-9*, Simon Spotlight/Nickelodeon) Simon & Schuster Children's Publishing.

—Guess Who Loves Blue! 2002. (Blue's Clues Ser.). (Illus.). 14p. (J). bds. 4.99 *(0-689-84870-6*, Simon Spotlight/Nickelodeon) Simon & Schuster Children's Publishing.

—Magenta & Me. 2000. (Blues Clue's Ready to Read Ser.: No. 2). (Illus.). 24p. (J). (ps-1). pap. 3.99 *(0-689-83123-4*, Simon Spotlight/Nickelodeon) Simon & Schuster Children's Publishing.

—Magenta Gets Glasses! 2002. (Blue's Clues Ser.). (Illus.). 24p. (J). pap. 3.50 *(0-689-84745-9*, Simon Spotlight/Nickelodeon) Simon & Schuster Children's Publishing.

—Weather Games with Blue. 1999. (Blue's Clues Ser.). (Illus.). 10p. (J). (ps-k). bds. 4.99 *(0-689-82949-3*, Simon Spotlight/Nickelodeon) Simon & Schuster Children's Publishing.

Santomero, Angela C. Blue Skidoos to the Farm A Storybook with 63 Stickers. 1998. (Blue's Clues Ser.). (Illus.). 24p. (J). (ps-k). pap. 3.99 *(0-689-81698-7*, Simon Spotlight/Nickelodeon) Simon & Schuster Children's Publishing.

—Blue Skidoos to the Planets! Includes 27 Stickers. 1999. (Blue's Clues Ser.). (Illus.). 20p. (J). (ps-k). pap. 5.99 *(0-689-82446-7*, Simon Spotlight/ Nickelodeon) Simon & Schuster Children's Publishing.

—Blue's Big Birthday. (Blue's Clues Ser.). (Illus.). 24p. (J). (ps-1). 2002. pap. 3.50 *(0-689-85103-0)*; 1998. 9.99 *(0-689-82151-4)* Simon & Schuster Children's Publishing. (Simon Spotlight/ Nickelodeon).

—Blue's Big Treasure Hunt. 1999. (Blue's Clues Ser.). (J). (ps-k). 5.99 o.s.i *(0-689-83111-0)*; (Illus.). 24p. 5.99 *(0-689-82540-4)* Simon & Schuster Children's Publishing. (Simon Spotlight/Nickelodeon).

—A Blue's Clues Holiday. 1999. (Blue's Clues Ser.). (Illus.). 24p. (J). (ps-k). 9.99 *(0-689-82947-7*, Simon Spotlight/Nickelodeon) Simon & Schuster Children's Publishing.

—Blue's Felt Friends. 1998. (Blue's Clues Ser.). (Illus.). 20p. (J). (ps-k). bds. 4.99 *(0-689-81910-2*, Simon Spotlight/Nickelodeon) Simon & Schuster Children's Publishing.

—Blue's Treasure Hunt Notebook. 1999. (Blue's Clues Ser.). (J). (ps-k). 14p. 4.99 *(0-689-83332-6)*; (Illus.). 6p. bds. 4.99 *(0-689-82541-2)* Simon & Schuster Children's Publishing. (Simon Spotlight/ Nickelodeon).

—Good Night, Blue. 1999. (Blue's Clues Ser.). (Illus.). 10p. (J). (ps-k). bds. 4.99 *(0-689-82950-7*, Simon Spotlight/Nickelodeon) Simon & Schuster Children's Publishing.

—Hide-&-Seek with Blue. 1999. (Blue's Clues Ser.). (J). (ps-k). mass mkt. 3.99 o.s.i *(0-689-83353-9)*; (Illus.). 16p. pap. 3.99 *(0-689-82445-9)* Simon & Schuster Children's Publishing. (Simon Spotlight/ Nickelodeon).

—Lights On! Lights Off! 1999. (Blue's Clues Ser.). (Illus.). 140p. (J). (ps-k). pap. 9.00 *(0-7416-1009-4)* Havoc Publishing.

—The Shape Detectives. 1998. (Blue's Clues Ser.). (Illus.). 14p. (J). (ps-k). bds. 5.99 *(0-689-81747-9*, Simon Spotlight/Nickelodeon) Simon & Schuster Children's Publishing.

—Welcome to Blue's Clues. 1999. (Blue's Clues Ser.). (Illus.). 12p. (J). (ps-k). bds. 10.95 *(0-689-82952-3*, Simon Spotlight/Nickelodeon) Simon & Schuster Children's Publishing.

—We're Thankful. 1999. (Blue's Clues Ser.). (Illus.). 16p. (J). (ps-k). pap. 3.99 *(0-689-82900-0*, Simon Spotlight/Nickelodeon) Simon & Schuster Children's Publishing.

—What Is Blue Feeling? 1999. (Blue's Clues Ser.). (J). (ps-k). 14p. 4.99 o.s.i *(0-689-83330-X)*; (Illus.). 12p. bds. 7.99 *(0-689-82675-3)* Simon & Schuster Children's Publishing. (Simon Spotlight/ Nickelodeon).

—What to Do, Blue? 1999. (Blue's Clues Ser.: Vol. 2). (Illus.). 24p. (J). (ps-k). pap. 3.50 *(0-689-82444-0*, 076714003507, Simon Spotlight/Nickelodeon) Simon & Schuster Children's Publishing.

Santomero, Angela C. & Alexander, Liza. Blue & the Color Detectives A Storybook with 53 Stickers. 1998. (Blue's Clues Ser.). (Illus.). 24p. (J). (ps-k). 3.99 *(0-689-81697-9*, Simon Spotlight/ Nickelodeon) Simon & Schuster Children's Publishing.

Santomero, Angela C. & Craig, Karen. Blue Is My Name. 2000. (Blues Clue's Ready to Read Ser.: No. 1). (Illus.). 24p. (J). (ps-1). pap. 3.99 *(0-689-83122-6*, Simon Spotlight/Nickelodeon) Simon & Schuster Children's Publishing.

Santomero, Angela C., et al. Lights On! Lights Off! 1998. (Blue's Clues Ser.). (Illus.). 20p. (J). (ps-k). bds. 4.99 *(0-689-81909-9*, Simon Spotlight/ Nickelodeon) Simon & Schuster Children's Publishing.

—What to Do, Blue? 1999. (Blue's Clues Ser.). (Illus.). 24p. (J). (gr. k-3). pap. 3.50 *(0-689-83214-1*, Simon Spotlight/Nickelodeon) Simon & Schuster Children's Publishing.

Silverhardt, Lauryn. Blue's Friends. 2001. (Blue's Clues Ser.). (Illus.). 14p. (J). bds. 4.99 *(0-689-84544-8*, Simon Spotlight/Nickelodeon) Simon & Schuster Children's Publishing.

—Counting with Blue. 2001. (Blue's Clues Ser.). (Illus.). 14p. (J). bds. 4.99 *(0-689-84543-X*, Simon Spotlight/Nickelodeon) Simon & Schuster Children's Publishing.

—Get Dressed. 2003. (Blue's Clues Ser.). (Illus.). 12p. (J). bds. 5.99 *(0-689-85488-9*, Simon Spotlight/ Nickelodeon) Simon & Schuster Children's Publishing.

—I Can Get Dressed! 2003. (Baby Blue's Clues Ser.). (Illus.). 8p. (J). 17.95 *(0-689-85977-5*, Simon Spotlight/Nickelodeon) Simon & Schuster Children's Publishing.

Smith, Michael T. Blue's Halloween Hide-&-Seek. 2000. (Blue's Clues Ser.). (Illus.). 16p. (J). (ps-k). 5.99 *(0-689-83433-0*, Simon Spotlight/ Nickelodeon) Simon & Schuster Children's Publishing.

—Periwinkle Moves In. 2000. (Blue's Clues Ser.). 14p. (J). (ps-k). bds. 4.99 *(0-689-83584-1*, Simon Spotlight/Nickelodeon) Simon & Schuster Children's Publishing.

Style Guide Staff, illus. Blue's Bedtime. 2001. (Blue's Clues Ser.). 8p. (J). 12.95 *(0-689-84041-1*, Simon Spotlight/Nickelodeon) Simon & Schuster Children's Publishing.

Wilder, Alice. Blue's Lost Backpack. 1999. (Blue's Clues Ser.). (J). (ps-k). mass mkt. 3.99 o.s.i *(0-689-83352-0*, Simon Spotlight/Nickelodeon) Simon & Schuster Children's Publishing.

—It's Present Day! 1999. (Blue's Clues Ser.). (Illus.). 16p. (J). (ps-k). 5.99 *(0-689-82898-5*, Simon Spotlight/Nickelodeon) Simon & Schuster Children's Publishing.

—Who Am I? 2000. (Blue's Clues Ser.). (Illus.). 14p. (J). (ps-k). bds. 9.99 *(0-689-83338-5*, Simon Spotlight/Nickelodeon) Simon & Schuster Children's Publishing.

Wilder, Alice & Smith, Michael T. Blue's Lost Backpack. 1999. (Blue's Clues Ser.). (Illus.). 16p. (J). (ps-k). pap. 3.99 *(0-689-82442-4*, Simon Spotlight/Nickelodeon) Simon & Schuster Children's Publishing.

Wilder, Alice, et al. Blue's Costume Party. 1999. (Blue's Clues Ser.). (Illus.). 16p. (J). (ps-k). pap. 3.99 *(0-689-82899-3*, Simon Spotlight/ Nickelodeon) Simon & Schuster Children's Publishing.

Willson, Sarah. Blue's Big Beach Party. 2004. (Illus.). 8p. (J). mass mkt. *(0-689-85162-6*, Simon Spotlight/Nickelodeon) Simon & Schuster Children's Publishing.

Yablonsky, Buster. Blue's #1 Picnic. 1998. (Blue's Clues Ser.). (Illus.). 14p. (J). (ps-k). 5.99 *(0-689-81746-0*, Simon Spotlight/Nickelodeon) Simon & Schuster Children's Publishing.

BOB THE BUILDER (FICTITIOUS CHARACTER)—FICTION

Auerbach, Annie. Bob's Busy World. 2001. (Bob the Builder Ser.). (Illus.). 12p. (J). bds. 10.95 (*0-689-84418-2*, Simon Spotlight) Simon & Schuster Children's Publishing.

—Bob's Egg Hunt: A Lift-the-Flap Story. 2002. (Bob the Builder Ser.). (Illus.). 24p. (J). pap. 5.99 (*0-689-84590-1*, Simon Spotlight) Simon & Schuster Children's Publishing.

—Bob's Snowy Day: A Lift-the-Flap Story. 2002. (Bob the Builder Ser.). (Illus.). 24p. pap. 5.99 (*0-689-84589-8*, Simon Spotlight) Simon & Schuster Children's Publishing.

—A Day at the Barn. 2001. (Bob the Builder Ser.). (Illus.). 12p. (J). pap. 5.99 (*0-689-84380-1*, Simon Spotlight) Simon & Schuster Children's Publishing.

—Lego's a Day at the Barn. 2001. (Bob the Builder Ser.). (Illus.). 12p. (J). bds. 7.99 (*0-689-84929-X*, Simon Spotlight) Simon & Schuster Children's Publishing.

Beinstein, Phoebe, adapted by. Good Job, Bob! 2004. (Bob the Builder Ser.). (Illus.). 12p. (J). pap. 5.99 (*0-689-86270-9*, Simon Spotlight) Simon & Schuster Children's Publishing.

Boczkowski, Tricia. Bob's Busy Year. 2003. (Bob the Builder Ser.). (Illus.). 22p. (J). bds. 4.99 (*0-689-85893-0*, Simon Spotlight) Simon & Schuster Children's Publishing.

Chicko, Joe & Chicko, Terri, illus. Dizzy & Muck Work It Out. 2002. (Bob the Builder Ser.: Bk. 4). 24p. (J). (ps-2). pap. 3.50 (*0-689-84756-4*, Simon Spotlight) Simon & Schuster Children's Publishing.

Collins, Terry. Bob's Bedtime. 2003. (Bob the Builder Ser.). (Illus.). 22p. bds. 4.99 (*0-689-85292-4*, Simon Spotlight) Simon & Schuster Children's Publishing.

Driscoll, Laura. Where's Pilchard? 2003. (Bob the Builder Ser.). (Illus.). 16p. (J). pap. 5.99 (*0-689-85303-3*, Simon Spotlight) Simon & Schuster Children's Publishing.

Farrell, Melissa. Roley & the Rock Star. 2003. (Bob the Builder Ser.: No. 7). (Illus.). 24p. pap. 3.50 (*0-689-85461-7*, Simon Spotlight) Simon & Schuster Children's Publishing.

Golden Books Staff. Be Careful, Bob! 2002. (Illus.). 48p. (J). (ps-1). pap. 4.99 (*0-307-27634-1*, Golden Bks.) Random Hse. Children's Bks.

—Bob's Handy Hammer. 2003. (Fix It with Bob Ser.). (Illus.). 14p. 9.99 (*0-375-82645-9*) Random Hse. Children's Bks.

—Bob's Toolbox. 2002. (Illus.). 12p. (J). (ps-k). bds. 7.99 (*0-307-20064-7*, Golden Bks.) Random Hse. Children's Bks.

—Dizzy's Days. 2002. (Bob the Builder Ser.). (Illus.). 48p. (J). (ps-1). pap. 3.99 (*0-307-27900-6*, Golden Bks.) Random Hse. Children's Bks.

—Paint It. 2002. (Bob the Builder Ser.). (Illus.). 32p. (J). (ps-1). pap. 4.99 (*0-307-29961-9*, Golden Bks.) Random Hse. Children's Bks.

—Team Work. 2002. (Bob the Builder Ser.). (Illus.). 48p. (J). (ps-1). pap. 4.99 (*0-307-10851-1*, Golden Bks.) Random Hse. Children's Bks.

Hot Animation Staff, Animation, illus. The Knights of Fix-a-Lot. 2004. (Bob the Builder Ser.). 24p. (J). pap. 3.50 (*0-689-86288-1*, Simon Spotlight) Simon & Schuster Children's Publishing.

Inches, Alison. Bob's White Christmas. 2001. (Bob the Builder Ser.). (Illus.). 24p. (J). bds. 9.99 (*0-689-84436-0*, Simon Spotlight) Simon & Schuster Children's Publishing.

—Dizzy's Bird Watch. 2001. (Bob the Builder Ready-to-Read Ser.: Vol. 1). (Illus.). 24p. (J). pap. 3.99 (*0-689-84390-9*, Simon Spotlight) Simon & Schuster Children's Publishing.

—Run-Away Roley. 2002. (Bob the Builder Ready-to-Read Ser.: Bk. 3). (Illus.). 32p. (J). (ps-1). pap. 3.99 (*0-689-84753-X*, Simon Spotlight) Simon & Schuster Children's Publishing.

—A Surprise for Wendy. 2002. (Bob the Builder Ready-to-Read Ser.: Vol. 4). (Illus.). 24p. (J). pap. 3.99 (*0-689-84754-8*, Simon Spotlight) Simon & Schuster Children's Publishing.

—Wendy Helps Out. 2001. (Bob the Builder Ready-to-Read Ser.: Vol. 2). (Illus.). 32p. (J). pap. 3.99 (*0-689-84391-7*, Simon Spotlight) Simon & Schuster Children's Publishing.

McCune, Krisha. Meet Lofty. 2003. (Bob the Builder Ser.). (Illus.). 12p. (J). bds. 5.99 (*0-689-85777-2*, Simon Spotlight) Simon & Schuster Children's Publishing.

—Meet Scoop. 2003. (Bob the Builder Ser.). (Illus.). 12p. (J). bds. 5.99 (*0-689-85776-4*, Simon Spotlight) Simon & Schuster Children's Publishing.

Miglis, Jenny. Building With Bob. 2003. (Bob the Builder Ser.). (Illus.). 12p. (J). bds. 10.95 (*0-689-85367-X*, Simon Spotlight) Simon & Schuster Children's Publishing.

Ostrow, Kim. Bob Builder Ine Party. 2003. (Bob the Builder Ser.). 12p. pap. 5.99 (*0-689-84941-9*, Simon Spotlight) Simon & Schuster Children's Publishing.

—Bob's Valentine Surprise. 2002. (Bob the Builder Ser.). (Illus.). 14p. (J). bds. 5.99 (*0-689-84633-9*, Simon Spotlight) Simon & Schuster Children's Publishing.

—Rock-and-Roll Bob. 2003. (Bob the Builder Ser.). (Illus.). 24p. (J). pap. 3.99 (*0-689-85832-9*, Simon Spotlight) Simon & Schuster Children's Publishing.

Redmond, Diane. Bob's Birthday. 2001. (Bob the Builder Ser.). (Illus.). 24p. (J). pap. 3.50 (*0-689-84545-6*, Simon Spotlight) Simon & Schuster Children's Publishing.

Running Press Staff. Opposites, 4 vols., Set 2. 2001. (Mini Board Bks.). (Illus.). 10p. (J). bds. 12.95 (*0-7548-0826-2*, Lorenz Bks.) Anness Publishing, Inc.

—Opposites. 2001. (Early Learning Ser.). (J). (gr. k-12). vinyl bd. 4.95 (*1-58845-055-4*) McGraw-Hill Children's Publishing.

—Opposites. 1998. (Fit-a-Shape Ser.). (Illus.). 10p. (J). (ps-k). pap. text 6.95 o.p. (*0-7624-0935-5*) Running Pr. Bk. Pubs.

—Opposites. 1998. (Fleurus Peek-a-Boo Ser.). (J). 4.98 o.p. (*0-7651-9140-7*) Smithmark Pubs., Inc.

—Opposites. 2003. (Bounce-Along Bks.). (Illus.). 12p. (J). bds. 4.95 (*0-8069-8091-5*) Sterling Publishing Co., Inc.

—Opposites. 2001. (Sticker Math Ser.). 24p. (J). pap. 4.95 (*0-7945-0042-0*) Usborne Publishing, Inc.

Silverhardt, Lauryn. Bob Builder Bobs Building Yard. 2003. (Bob the Builder Ser.). (Illus.). 20p. bds. 6.99 (*0-689-85312-2*, Simon Spotlight) Simon & Schuster Children's Publishing.

—Bob Builder Busy Screwdriver. 2003. (Bob the Builder Ser.). (Illus.). 12p. (J). bds. 5.99 (*0-689-84949-4*, Simon Spotlight) Simon & Schuster Children's Publishing.

—A Christmas to Remember. 2003. (Bob the Builder Ser.). (Illus.). 32p. (J). bds. 9.99 (*0-689-84972-9*, Simon Spotlight) Simon & Schuster Children's Publishing.

Thorpe, Kiki. Bob Builder Busy Wrench. 2003. (Bob the Builder Ser.). (Illus.). 12p. (J). bds. 5.99 (*0-689-84948-6*, Simon Spotlight) Simon & Schuster Children's Publishing.

—Bob's Toolbox Mix Up. 2002. (Bob the Builder Ser.). (Illus.). 14p. (J). bds. 5.99 (*0-689-84634-7*, Simon Spotlight) Simon & Schuster Children's Publishing.

—Muck's Sleepover. 2002. (Bob the Builder Ser.: Bk. 3). (Illus.). 24p. (J). (ps-2). pap. 3.50 (*0-689-84755-6*, Simon Spotlight) Simon & Schuster Children's Publishing.

Willson, Sarah. Bob Builder & Scoop's Big Race. 2003. (Bob the Builder Ser.). (Illus.). 16p. (J). pap. 5.99 (*0-689-85302-5*, Simon Spotlight) Simon & Schuster Children's Publishing.

BOBBSEY TWINS (FICTITIOUS CHARACTERS)—FICTION

Hope, Laura Lee. The Bobbsey Twins. (Bobbsey Twins Ser.). (J). (gr. 3-5). 1990. 11.80 (*0-671-96364-3*, Aladdin); 1979. (Illus.). 10.00 (*0-671-95521-7*, Simon & Schuster Children's Publishing) Simon & Schuster Children's Publishing.

—The Bobbsey Twins' Adventure in the Country. 1989. (Bobbsey Twins Ser.). (Illus.). 180p. (J). (gr. 3-5). 5.95 o.s.i (*0-448-09072-4*, Grosset & Dunlap) Penguin Putnam Bks. for Young Readers.

—The Bobbsey Twins' Adventure in Washington. (Bobbsey Twins Ser.). (J). (gr. 3-5). 1991. 4.50 o.s.i (*0-448-40111-8*, Platt & Munk); 1963. 4.50 o.p. (*0-448-08012-5*, Grosset & Dunlap); 1963. 5.90 o.p. (*0-448-40118-5*, Grosset & Dunlap) Penguin Putnam Bks. for Young Readers.

—The Bobbsey Twins' Adventures with Baby May. 1967. (Bobbsey Twins Ser.). (Illus.). (J). (gr. 3-5). 4.50 o.s.i (*0-448-08017-6*, Grosset & Dunlap) Penguin Putnam Bks. for Young Readers.

—The Bobbsey Twins & Double Trouble. 1983. (Bobbsey Twins Ser.: No. 7). (Illus.). 128p. (J). (gr. 3-5). pap. (*0-671-43584-1*); pap. 3.50 (*0-671-43585-X*) Simon & Schuster Children's Publishing. (Aladdin).

—The Bobbsey Twins & Dr. Funnybone's Secret. 1972. (Bobbsey Twins Ser.). 196p. (J). (gr. 3-5). 4.50 o.s.i (*0-448-08065-6*, Grosset & Dunlap) Penguin Putnam Bks. for Young Readers.

—The Bobbsey Twins & the Big Adventure at Home. 1990. (Bobbsey Twins Ser.). (Illus.). 120p. (J). (gr. 3-5). 4.50 o.p. (*0-448-09134-8*, Grosset & Dunlap) Penguin Putnam Bks. for Young Readers.

—The Bobbsey Twins & the Big River Mystery. 1962. (Bobbsey Twins Ser.). (J). (gr. 3-5). 4.50 o.s.i (*0-448-08056-7*, Grosset & Dunlap) Penguin Putnam Bks. for Young Readers.

—The Bobbsey Twins & the Blue Poodle Mystery. 1980. (Bobbsey Twins Ser.: No. 1). (Illus.). 128p. (J). (gr. 3-5). pap. (*0-671-95546-2*); pap. 3.50 (*0-671-95554-3*) Simon & Schuster Children's Publishing. (Aladdin).

—The Bobbsey Twins & the Camp Fire Mystery. 1982. (Bobbsey Twins Ser.: No. 6). (Illus.). 128p. (J). (gr. 3-5). (*0-671-43374-1*); pap. 3.50 (*0-671-43373-3*) Simon & Schuster Children's Publishing. (Aladdin).

—The Bobbsey Twins & the Cedar Camp Mystery. 1967. (Bobbsey Twins Ser.). (J). (gr. 3-5). 4.50 o.p. (*0-448-08014-1*, Grosset & Dunlap) Penguin Putnam Bks. for Young Readers.

—The Bobbsey Twins & the Circus Surprise. 1932. (Bobbsey Twins Ser.). (J). (gr. 3-5). 4.50 o.s.i (*0-448-08025-7*, Grosset & Dunlap) Penguin Putnam Bks. for Young Readers.

—The Bobbsey Twins & the Coral Turtle Mystery. 1978. (Bobbsey Twins Ser.). 196p. (J). (gr. 3-5). 4.50 o.s.i (*0-448-08072-9*, Grosset & Dunlap) Penguin Putnam Bks. for Young Readers.

—The Bobbsey Twins & the County Fair Mystery. 1922. (Bobbsey Twins Ser.). (J). (gr. 3-5). 4.50 o.s.i (*0-448-08015-X*, Grosset & Dunlap) Penguin Putnam Bks. for Young Readers.

—The Bobbsey Twins & the Doodlebug Mystery. 1969. (Bobbsey Twins Ser.). (Illus.). (J). (gr. 3-5). 4.50 o.s.i (*0-448-08062-1*, Grosset & Dunlap) Penguin Putnam Bks. for Young Readers.

—The Bobbsey Twins & the Dune Buggy Mystery. 1981. (Bobbsey Twins Ser.: No. 3). (Illus.). 112p. (J). (gr. 3-5). pap. (*0-671-42293-6*); pap. 3.50 (*0-671-42294-4*) Simon & Schuster Children's Publishing. (Aladdin).

—The Bobbsey Twins & the Flying Clown. (Bobbsey Twins Ser.). (J). (gr. 3-5). 1978. 3.29 o.p. (*0-448-18067-7*); 1974. 196p. 4.50 o.s.i (*0-448-08067-2*) Penguin Putnam Bks. for Young Readers. (Grosset & Dunlap).

—The Bobbsey Twins & the Four-Leaf Clover Mystery. rev. ed. 1968. (Bobbsey Twins Ser.). (Illus.). (J). (gr. 3-5). 4.50 o.s.i (*0-448-08019-2*, Grosset & Dunlap) Penguin Putnam Bks. for Young Readers.

—The Bobbsey Twins & the Freedom Bell Mystery. 1975. (Bobbsey Twins Ser.). 196p. (J). (gr. 3-5). 4.50 o.s.i (*0-448-08069-9*, Grosset & Dunlap) Penguin Putnam Bks. for Young Readers.

—The Bobbsey Twins & the Ghost in the Computer. 1984. (Bobbsey Twins Ser.: No. 10). (J). (gr. 3-5). pap. 3.50 (*0-671-43591-4*, Aladdin) Simon & Schuster Children's Publishing.

—The Bobbsey Twins & the Ghost in the Computer. Barish, Wendy, ed. 1984. (Bobbsey Twins Ser.: No. 10). (Illus.). 128p. (J). (gr. 3-5). pap. 3.50 o.p. (*0-671-43590-6*, Aladdin) Simon & Schuster Children's Publishing.

—The Bobbsey Twins & the Goldfish Mystery. 1962. (Bobbsey Twins Ser.). (Illus.). (J). (gr. 3-5). 4.50 o.s.i (*0-448-08055-9*, Grosset & Dunlap) Penguin Putnam Bks. for Young Readers.

—The Bobbsey Twins & the Greek Hat Mystery. 1964. (Bobbsey Twins Ser.). (J). (gr. 3-5). 4.50 o.s.i (*0-448-08057-5*, Grosset & Dunlap) Penguin Putnam Bks. for Young Readers.

—The Bobbsey Twins & the Haunted House Mystery. Arico, Diane, ed. 1985. (Bobbsey Twins Ser.: No. 12). (Illus.). 128p. (J). (gr. 3-5). pap. 3.50 (*0-671-54996-0*, Aladdin) Simon & Schuster Children's Publishing.

—The Bobbsey Twins & the Missing Pony Mystery. 1981. (Bobbsey Twins Ser.: No. 4). (Illus.). 112p. (J). (gr. 3-5). pap. 3.50 (*0-671-42296-0*, Aladdin); 7.95 (*0-671-42295-2*, Simon & Schuster Children's Publishing) Simon & Schuster Children's Publishing.

—The Bobbsey Twins & the Music Box Mystery. Barish, Wendy, ed. 1983. (Bobbsey Twins Ser.: No. 9). (Illus.). 128p. (J). (gr. 3-5). pap. 3.50 (*0-671-43589-2*); (*0-671-43588-4*) Simon & Schuster Children's Publishing. (Aladdin).

—The Bobbsey Twins & the Mystery at Cherry Corner. rev. ed. 1971. (Bobbsey Twins Ser.). (Illus.). (J). (gr. 3-5). 4.50 o.s.i (*0-448-08020-6*, Grosset & Dunlap) Penguin Putnam Bks. for Young Readers.

—The Bobbsey Twins & the Mystery at Meadowbrook. 1990. (Bobbsey Twins Ser.). (Illus.). 180p. (J). (gr. 3-5). 4.50 o.s.i (*0-448-09100-3*, Grosset & Dunlap) Penguin Putnam Bks. for Young Readers.

—The Bobbsey Twins & the Mystery at School. 1989. (Bobbsey Twins Ser.). (Illus.). 180p. (J). (gr. 3-5). 4.95 o.p. (*0-448-09074-0*, Grosset & Dunlap) Penguin Putnam Bks. for Young Readers.

—The Bobbsey Twins & the Mystery at Snow Lodge. (Bobbsey Twins Ser.). (J). (gr. 3-5). 1990. (Illus.). 180p. 4.95 o.s.i (*0-448-09098-8*); 1930. 4.50 o.s.i (*0-448-08005-2*) Penguin Putnam Bks. for Young Readers. (Grosset & Dunlap).

—The Bobbsey Twins & the Mystery of the Hindu Temple. Barish, Wendy, ed. 1985. (Bobbsey Twins Ser.: No. 13). (Illus.). 128p. (Orig.). (J). (gr. 3-5). pap. 3.50 (*0-671-55499-9*, Aladdin) Simon & Schuster Children's Publishing.

—The Bobbsey Twins & the Mystery of the King's Puppet. 1967. (Bobbsey Twins Ser.). (J). (gr. 3-5). 4.50 o.s.i (*0-448-08060-5*, Grosset & Dunlap) Penguin Putnam Bks. for Young Readers.

—The Bobbsey Twins & the Mystery of the Laughing Dinosaur. Barish, Wendy, ed. 1983. (Bobbsey Twins Ser.: No. 8). (Illus.). 128p. (J). (gr. 3-5). pap. (*0-671-43586-8*); pap. 3.50 (*0-671-43587-6*) Simon & Schuster Children's Publishing. (Aladdin).

—The Bobbsey Twins & the Play House Secret. rev. ed. 1968. (Bobbsey Twins Ser.). (Illus.). (J). (gr. 3-5). 4.50 o.s.i (*0-448-08018-4*, Grosset & Dunlap) Penguin Putnam Bks. for Young Readers.

—The Bobbsey Twins & the Rose Parade Mystery. 1981. (Bobbsey Twins Ser.: No. 5). (Illus.). 112p. (Orig.). (J). (gr. 3-5). pap. (*0-671-43372-5*); pap. 3.50 (*0-671-43371-7*) Simon & Schuster Children's Publishing. (Aladdin).

—The Bobbsey Twins & the Secret at the Seashore. 1989. (Bobbsey Twins Ser.). (Illus.). 180p. (J). (gr. 3-5). 4.95 o.p. (*0-448-09073-2*, Grosset & Dunlap) Penguin Putnam Bks. for Young Readers.

—The Bobbsey Twins & the Secret in the Pirate's Cave. 1980. (Bobbsey Twins Ser.: No. 2). (Illus.). 128p. (J). (gr. 3-5). pap. (*0-671-41118-7*); pap. 3.50 (*0-671-41113-6*) Simon & Schuster Children's Publishing. (Aladdin).

—The Bobbsey Twins & the Secret of Candy Castle. 1968. (Bobbsey Twins Ser.). (Illus.). (J). (gr. 3-5). 4.50 o.p. (*0-448-08061-3*, Grosset & Dunlap) Penguin Putnam Bks. for Young Readers.

—The Bobbsey Twins & the Smokey Mountain Mystery. 1976. (Bobbsey Twins Ser.). (Illus.). (J). (gr. 3-5). 4.50 o.s.i (*0-448-08070-2*, Grosset & Dunlap) Penguin Putnam Bks. for Young Readers.

—The Bobbsey Twins & the Tagalong Giraffe. 1973. (Bobbsey Twins Ser.). (J). (gr. 3-5). 4.50 o.s.i (*0-448-08066-4*, Grosset & Dunlap) Penguin Putnam Bks. for Young Readers.

—The Bobbsey Twins & the Talking Fox Mystery. 1970. (Bobbsey Twins Ser.). (Illus.). (J). (gr. 3-5). 4.50 o.s.i (*0-448-08063-X*, Grosset & Dunlap) Penguin Putnam Bks. for Young Readers.

—The Bobbsey Twins & the TV Mystery Show. 1978. (Bobbsey Twins Ser.). (Illus.). (J). (gr. 3-5). 4.50 o.s.i (*0-448-08071-0*, Grosset & Dunlap) Penguin Putnam Bks. for Young Readers.

—The Bobbsey Twins & Their Camel Adventure. 1978. (Bobbsey Twins Ser.). (J). (gr. 3-5). 3.29 o.p. (*0-448-18059-6*, Grosset & Dunlap) Penguin Putnam Bks. for Young Readers.

—The Bobbsey Twins at Big Bear Pond. 1954. (Bobbsey Twins Ser.). (J). (gr. 3-5). 4.50 o.p. (*0-448-08047-8*, Grosset & Dunlap) Penguin Putnam Bks. for Young Readers.

—The Bobbsey Twins at London Tower. 1959. (Bobbsey Twins Ser.). (Illus.). (J). (gr. 3-5). 4.50 o.s.i (*0-448-08052-4*, Grosset & Dunlap) Penguin Putnam Bks. for Young Readers.

—The Bobbsey Twins at Pilgrim Rock. 1957. (Bobbsey Twins Ser.). (J). (gr. 3-5). 4.50 o.s.i (*0-448-08050-8*, Grosset & Dunlap) Penguin Putnam Bks. for Young Readers.

—The Bobbsey Twins Camping Out. 1923. (Bobbsey Twins Ser.). (J). (gr. 3-5). 4.50 o.s.i (*0-448-08016-8*, Grosset & Dunlap) Penguin Putnam Bks. for Young Readers.

—The Bobbsey Twins' Forest Adventure. 1958. (Bobbsey Twins Ser.). (J). (gr. 3-5). 4.50 o.s.i (*0-448-08051-6*, Grosset & Dunlap) Penguin Putnam Bks. for Young Readers.

—The Bobbsey Twins in the Mystery Cave. 1960. (Bobbsey Twins Ser.). (Illus.). (J). (gr. 3-5). 4.50 o.s.i (*0-448-08053-2*, Grosset & Dunlap) Penguin Putnam Bks. for Young Readers.

—The Bobbsey Twins in Volcano Land. 1961. (Bobbsey Twins Ser.). (Illus.). (J). (gr. 3-5). 4.50 o.s.i (*0-448-08054-0*, Grosset & Dunlap) Penguin Putnam Bks. for Young Readers.

—The Bobbsey Twins of Lakeport. (Bobbsey Twins Ser.). (J). (gr. 3-5). 1989. (Illus.). 180p. 5.99 (*0-448-09071-6*); 1936. 4.50 o.s.i (*0-448-08001-X*) Penguin Putnam Bks. for Young Readers. (Grosset & Dunlap).

—The Bobbsey Twins on a Bicycle Trip. 1955. (Bobbsey Twins Ser.). (J). (gr. 3-5). 4.50 o.s.i (*0-448-08048-6*, Grosset & Dunlap) Penguin Putnam Bks. for Young Readers.

—The Bobbsey Twins on a Houseboat. (Bobbsey Twins Ser.). (J). (gr. 3-5). 1990. (Illus.). 180p. 4.95 o.s.i (*0-448-09099-6*); 1930. 4.50 o.s.i (*0-448-08006-0*) Penguin Putnam Bks. for Young Readers. (Grosset & Dunlap).

—The Bobbsey Twins on Blueberry Island. (Bobbsey Twins Ser.). (J). (gr. 3-5). 1991. (Illus.). 4.50 o.s.i (*0-448-40110-X*); 1930. 4.50 o.s.i (*0-448-08010-9*) Penguin Putnam Bks. for Young Readers. (Grosset & Dunlap).

Characters

Characters

—The Bobbsey Twins on the Deep Blue Sea. unabr. ed. 1993. (Bobbsey Twins Ser.). (J). (gr. 3-5). audio 24.95 (*1-55685-277-0*) Audio Bk. Contractors, Inc.

—The Bobbsey Twins on the Deep Blue Sea. 1991. (Bobbsey Twins Ser.). (Illus.). (J). (gr. 3-5). 4.50 o.s.i (*0-448-40113-4*, Grosset & Dunlap) Penguin Putnam Bks. for Young Readers.

—The Bobbsey Twins on the Sun-Moon Cruise. 1975. (Bobbsey Twins Ser.). (Illus.). 196p. (J). (gr. 3-5). 4.50 o.s.i (*0-448-08068-0*, Grosset & Dunlap) Penguin Putnam Bks. for Young Readers.

—The Bobbsey Twins' Own Little Ferryboat. 1956. (Bobbsey Twins Ser.). (J). (gr. 3-5). 4.50 o.s.i (*0-448-08049-4*, Grosset & Dunlap) Penguin Putnam Bks. for Young Readers.

—The Bobbsey Twins' Red, White, & Blue Mystery. 1971. (Bobbsey Twins Ser.). (Illus.). (J). (gr. 3-5). 4.50 o.s.i (*0-448-08064-8*, Grosset & Dunlap) Penguin Putnam Bks. for Young Readers.

—The Bobbsey Twins' Scarecrow Mystery. Barish, Wendy, ed. 1984. (Bobbsey Twins Ser.: No. 11). (Illus.). 128p. (J). (gr. 3-5). pap. 3.50 (*0-671-53238-3*, Aladdin) Simon & Schuster Children's Publishing.

—The Bobbsey Twins' Search for the Green Rooster. 1964. (Bobbsey Twins Ser.). (J). (gr. 3-5). 4.50 o.s.i (*0-448-08058-3*, Grosset & Dunlap) Penguin Putnam Bks. for Young Readers.

—The Bobbsey Twins' Search in the Great City. 1930. (Bobbsey Twins Ser.). (J). (gr. 3-6). 4.50 o.s.i (*0-448-08009-5*, Grosset & Dunlap) Penguin Putnam Bks. for Young Readers.

—The Bobbsey Twins Solve a Mystery. 1934. (Bobbsey Twins Ser.). (J). (gr. 3-5). 4.50 o.s.i (*0-448-08027-3*, Grosset & Dunlap) Penguin Putnam Bks. for Young Readers.

—The Bobbsey Twins' Visit to the Great West. (Bobbsey Twins Ser.). (J). (gr. 3-5). 1991. (Illus.). 4.50 o.s.i (*0-448-40112-6*); 1966. 4.50 o.s.i (*0-448-08013-3*) Penguin Putnam Bks. for Young Readers. (Grosset & Dunlap).

—The Bobbsey Twins' Wonderful Winter Secret. 1931. (Bobbsey Twins Ser.). (J). (gr. 3-5). 4.50 o.s.i (*0-448-08024-9*, Grosset & Dunlap) Penguin Putnam Bks. for Young Readers.

BOND, JAMES (FICTITIOUS CHARACTER)—FICTION

Mascott, R. D. Double O Three & One-Half: The Adventures of James Bond Junior. 1968. (Illus.). (J). (gr. 4-7). lib. bdg. 4.99 o.s.i (*0-394-91211-X*, Random Hse. Bks. for Young Readers) Random Hse. Children's Bks.

Vincent, John. The Eiffel Target. 1992. (James Bond Adventure Ser.: Bk. 2). (Illus.). 128p. (J). (gr. 3-7). mass mkt. 2.99 o.p. (*0-14-036012-3*, Puffin Bks.) Penguin Putnam Bks. for Young Readers.

—High Stakes. 1992. (James Bond Adventure Ser.: No. 6). (Illus.). 128p. (J). (gr. 3-7). mass mkt. 2.99 o.p. (*0-14-036048-4*, Puffin Bks.) Penguin Putnam Bks. for Young Readers.

—Live & Let's Dance. 1992. (James Bond Adventure Ser.: Bk. 3). (Illus.). 128p. (J). (gr. 3-7). mass mkt. 2.99 o.p. (*0-14-036013-1*, Puffin Bks.) Penguin Putnam Bks. for Young Readers.

—Sandblast! 1992. (James Bond Adventure Ser.: Bk. 4). (Illus.). 128p. (J). (gr. 3-7). mass mkt. 2.99 o.p. (*0-14-036014-X*, Puffin Bks.) Penguin Putnam Bks. for Young Readers.

—The Sword of Death. 1992. (James Bond Adventure Ser.: No. 5). (Illus.). 128p. (J). (gr. 3-7). mass mkt. 2.99 o.p. (*0-14-036049-2*, Puffin Bks.) Penguin Putnam Bks. for Young Readers.

—A View to a Thrill. 1992. (James Bond Adventure Ser.: Bk. 1). (Illus.). 128p. (J). (gr. 3-7). mass mkt. 2.99 o.s.i (*0-14-036011-5*, Puffin Bks.) Penguin Putnam Bks. for Young Readers.

BOONE, DANIEL, 1734-1820—FICTION

Glass, Andrew. Bewildered for Three Days: As to Why Daniel Boone Never Wore His Coonskin Cap. 2000. (Illus.). 32p. (J). (gr. 1-5). tchr. ed. 16.95 (*0-8234-1446-9*) Holiday Hse., Inc.

Gleiter, Jan & Thompson, Kathleen. Daniel Boone. 1984. (Story Clippers Ser.). (Illus.). (J). (gr. 2-5). pap. 23.95 o.p. incl. audio (*0-8172-2273-1*); pap. 9.27 o.p. (*0-8172-2263-4*); lib. bdg. 32.10 o.p. incl. audio (*0-8172-2242-1*); lib. bdg. 19.97 o.p. (*0-8172-2120-4*) Raintree Pubs.

Ingoglia, Gina. Daniel Boone, No. 2. 2nd ed. 2000. (J). lib. bdg. 13.49 (*0-7868-5021-3*) Disney Pr.

Korm. Daniel Boone, No. 1. 1999. (J). lib. bdg. 13.49 o.p. (*0-7868-5019-1*) Disney Pr.

Steele, William O. Daniel Boone's Echo. 1957. (Illus.). (J). (gr. k-3). 5.95 o.p. (*0-15-221980-3*) Harcourt Children's Bks.

Winston, Annie. Admiral Wright's Heroical Stroricals: Daniel Boone & the Battle of Boonesborough. 2002. 120p. per. 9.95 (*0-9717009-6-6*, Sonship Pr.) 21st Century Pr.

BORROWERS (FICTITIOUS CHARACTERS)—FICTION

Norton, Mary. The Adventures of the Borrowers. (Borrowers Ser.). (Illus.). (J). (gr. 3-7). 1986. pap. 20.75 o.p. (*0-15-210529-8*); 1975. 784p. reprint ed. pap. 11.95 o.p. (*0-15-613605-8*) Harcourt Children's Bks. (Voyager Bks./Libros Viajeros).

—The Borrowers. unabr. ed. 1993. (Borrowers Ser.). (J). (gr. 3-7). 24.95 incl. audio (*0-7451-8551-7*, CCA 3002, Chivers Children's Audio Bks.) BBC Audiobooks America.

—The Borrowers. l.t. unabr. ed. 1986. (Borrowers Ser.). (J). (gr. 3-7). lib. bdg. 12.95 o.p. (*0-7451-0331-6*, Macmillan Reference USA) Gale Group.

—The Borrowers. (Illus.). 2003. 192p. (YA). pap. 5.95 (*0-15-204737-9*, Odyssey Classics); 1991. 160p. (J). (gr. 3-7). 22.95 o.s.i (*0-15-209991-3*); 1989. 192p. (YA). (gr. 3-7). pap. 6.00 o.s.i (*0-15-209990-5*, Odyssey Classics); 1965. 192p. (J). (gr. 3-7). pap. 4.95 o.p. (*0-15-613600-7*, Voyager Bks./Libros Viajeros); 1953. 192p. (J). (gr. 3-7). 17.00 (*0-15-209987-5*); 50th anniv. ed. 2003. 176p. (J). 19.95 (*0-15-204928-2*) Harcourt Children's Bks.

—The Borrowers. 1993. (Borrowers Ser.). (Illus.). 180p. (J). (gr. 3-7). pap. 6.00 (*0-15-200086-0*) Harcourt Trade Pubs.

—The Borrowers. abr. ed. (Borrowers Ser.). (J). (gr. 3-7). audio 9.95 o.p. (*0-89845-807-2*, CPN 1459, HarperAudio) HarperTrade.

—The Borrowers. 1981. (Borrowers Ser.). (J). (gr. 3-7). 12.05 (*0-606-02413-1*) Turtleback Bks.

—The Borrowers Afield. unabr. ed. 1993. (Borrowers Ser.). (J). (gr. 3-7). 32.95 incl. audio (*0-7451-8552-5*, CCA 3143, Chivers Children's Audio Bks.) BBC Audiobooks America.

—The Borrowers Afield. l.t. ed. 1987. (Borrowers Ser.). (J). (gr. 3-7). lib. bdg. 15.95 o.p. (*0-7451-0549-1*, Macmillan Reference USA) Gale Group.

—The Borrowers Afield. (Illus.). 2003. 224p. (YA). pap. 5.95 (*0-15-204732-8*, Odyssey Classics); 1990. 224p. (YA). (gr. 3-7). pap. 6.00 o.s.i (*0-15-210535-2*, Odyssey Classics); 1955. 224p. (J). (gr. 3-7). 17.00 (*0-15-210166-7*); 1970. (J). (gr. 3-7). reprint ed. pap. 4.95 o.p. (*0-15-613601-5*, Voyager Bks./Libros Viajeros) Harcourt Children's Bks.

—The Borrowers Afield. 1983. (Borrowers Ser.). (J). (gr. 3-7). 12.05 (*0-606-02414-X*) Turtleback Bks.

—The Borrowers Afloat. unabr. ed. 1999. (Borrowers Ser.). (J). (gr. 3-7). audio 32.95 (*0-7540-5069-6*, CCA3507, Chivers Children's Audio Bks.) BBC Audiobooks America.

—The Borrowers Afloat. l.t. ed. 1988. (Borrowers Ser.). 216p. (J). (gr. 3-7). 13.95 o.p. (*0-8161-4441-9*, Macmillan Reference USA) Gale Group.

—The Borrowers Afloat. (Illus.). 192p. 2003. (YA). pap. 5.95 (*0-15-204733-6*, Odyssey Classics); 1990. (YA). (gr. 3-7). pap. 6.00 o.s.i (*0-15-210534-4*, Odyssey Classics); 1959. (J). (gr. 3-7). 17.00 (*0-15-210345-7*); 1973. (J). (gr. 3-7). reprint ed. pap. 4.95 o.p. (*0-15-613603-1*, Voyager Bks./Libros Viajeros) Harcourt Children's Bks.

—The Borrowers Afloat. 1987. (Borrowers Ser.). (J). (gr. 3-7). 12.05 (*0-606-02417-4*) Turtleback Bks.

—The Borrowers Aloft. unabr. ed. 1999. (Borrowers Ser.). (J). (gr. 3-7). audio 32.95 (*0-7540-5099-8*, CCA3537, Chivers Children's Audio Bks.) BBC Audiobooks America.

—The Borrowers Aloft. (Borrowers Ser.). (Illus.). (gr. 3-7). reprint ed. 1990. 224p. (YA). pap. 6.00 o.s.i (*0-15-210533-6*, Odyssey Classics); 1974. 192p. (J). pap. 4.95 o.p. (*0-15-613604-X*, Voyager Bks./Libros Viajeros) Harcourt Children's Bks.

—The Borrowers Aloft. 1961. (Borrowers Ser.). (J). (gr. 3-7). 12.05 (*0-606-02416-6*) Turtleback Bks.

—The Borrowers Aloft: Plus the Short Tale, Poor Stainless. (Illus.). 224p. (gr. 3-7). 2003. (YA). pap. 5.95 (*0-15-204734-4*, Odyssey Classics); 1961. (J). reprint ed. 17.00 (*0-15-210524-7*) Harcourt Children's Bks.

—The Borrowers Avenged. (Illus.). 2003. 304p. (YA). pap. 5.95 (*0-15-204731-X*, Odyssey Classics); 1990. 304p. (YA). (gr. 3-7). pap. 6.00 o.s.i (*0-15-210532-8*, Odyssey Classics); 1984. 300p. (J). (gr. 3-7). pap. 4.95 o.p. (*0-15-210531-X*, Voyager Bks./Libros Viajeros); 1982. 304p. (J). (gr. 3-7). 17.00 (*0-15-210530-1*) Harcourt Children's Bks.

—The Borrowers Avenged. 1988. (Borrowers Ser.). (J). (gr. 3-7). 18.05 o.p. (*0-8446-6358-1*) Smith, Peter Pub., Inc.

—The Borrowers Avenged. 1982. (Borrowers Ser.). (J). (gr. 3-7). 12.05 (*0-606-03322-X*) Turtleback Bks.

—Poor Stainless. 1985. (Borrowers Ser.). (Illus.). 32p. (J). (gr. 3-7). 7.95 o.p. (*0-15-263221-2*) Harcourt Children's Bks.

Smith, Sherwood. The Borrowers: Movie Tie-In. 1997. (Borrowers Ser.). (J). (gr. 3-7). pap. 4.99 o.s.i (*0-15-201779-8*) Harcourt Trade Pubs.

BOXCAR CHILDREN (FICTITIOUS CHARACTERS)—FICTION

Bailey, Linda. How Come the Best Clues Are Always in the Garbage? 1996. (Stevie Diamond Mystery Ser.: No. 1). (Illus.). 175p. (J). (gr. 4-7). lib. bdg. 13.95 o.p. (*0-8075-3409-9*) Whitman, Albert & Co.

Barkan, Joanne. Boxcar. 1992. (Come Aboard Bks.). (Illus.). 12p. (J). (ps). pap. 3.50 (*0-689-71573-0*, Little Simon) Simon & Schuster Children's Publishing.

Chandler Warner, Gertrude. The Mystery in the Computer Game. 2003. (Boxcar Children Mystery Ser.: No. 78). (J). audio compact disk 14.99 (*1-58926-126-7*, A65L-011D); audio 12.99 (*1-58926-120-8*, A65L-0110) Oasis Audio.

Christopher, Garrett. The Boxcar Children, Level 3. Friedland, J. & Kessler, Rikki, eds. 1993. (Novel-Ties Ser.). (J). (gr. 3). pap., stu. ed. 15.95 (*0-88122-879-6*, S0378) Learning Links, Inc.

Duffy, Daniel M., illus. Benny Goes into Business. 1999. (Adventures of Benny & Watch: Vol. No. 5). 32p. (J). (gr. 1-3). pap. 3.95 (*0-8075-0637-0*) Whitman, Albert & Co.

—Benny's New Friend. 1998. (Adventures of Benny & Watch: Vol. No. 3). 32p. (J). (gr. 1-3). pap. 3.95 (*0-8075-0649-4*) Whitman, Albert & Co.

—The Magic Show Mystery. 1998. (Adventures of Benny & Watch: Vol. No. 4). 32p. (J). (gr. 1-3). mass mkt. 3.95 (*0-8075-4939-8*) Whitman, Albert & Co.

—Meet the Boxcar Children. 1998. (Adventures of Benny & Watch: Vol. No. 1). 46p. (J). (gr. 1-3). pap. 3.95 (*0-8075-5034-5*) Whitman, Albert & Co.

—A Present for Grandfather. 1998. (Adventures of Benny & Watch: Vol. No. 2). 32p. (J). (gr. 1-3). pap. 3.95 (*0-8075-6625-X*) Whitman, Albert & Co.

—Watch Runs Away. 1999. (Adventures of Benny & Watch: Vol. No. 6). 32p. (J). (gr. 1-3). mass mkt. 3.95 (*0-8075-8681-1*) Whitman, Albert & Co.

Kennedy, Richard. The Boxcar at the Center of the Universe. 1982. (Illus.). 96p. (J). (gr. 6 up). lib. bdg. 11.89 o.p. (*0-06-023187-4*) HarperCollins Children's Bk. Group.

LinguiSystems Staff. Access to Literature: The Boxcar Children. 1993. stu. ed. 16.95 o.p. (*1-55999-360-X*) LinguiSystems, Inc.

Long, Donna Lee. A Guide for Using Boxcar Children: Surprise Island in the Classroom. 2000. (Literature Units Ser.). (Illus.). 48p. pap., tchr. ed. 7.99 (*1-57690-338-9*, TCM 2338) Teacher Created Materials, Inc.

Tang, Charles, illus. The Basketball Mystery. 1999. (Boxcar Children Ser.: No. 68). 128p. (J). (gr. 2-5). pap. 3.95 (*0-8075-0576-5*) Whitman, Albert & Co.

—The Black Pearl Mystery. 1998. (Boxcar Children Ser.: No. 64). 128p. (J). (gr. 2-7). pap. 3.95 (*0-8075-0784-9*) Whitman, Albert & Co.

—The Cereal Box Mystery. 1998. (Boxcar Children Ser.: No. 65). (J). (gr. 2-5). 10.00 (*0-606-13214-7*) Turtleback Bks.

—The Cereal Box Mystery. 1998. (Boxcar Children Ser.: No. 65). (J). (gr. 2-5). 111p. pap. 3.95 (*0-8075-1115-3*); 128p. lib. bdg. 13.95 (*0-8075-1114-5*) Whitman, Albert & Co.

—The Chocolate Sundae Mystery. 1995. (Boxcar Children Ser.: No. 46). 120p. (J). (gr. 2-5). pap. 3.95 (*0-8075-1145-5*); lib. bdg. 13.95 (*0-8075-1146-3*) Whitman, Albert & Co.

—The Ghost Ship Mystery. 1994. (Boxcar Children Ser.: No. 39). 122p. (J). (gr. 2-5). lib. bdg. 13.95 (*0-8075-2856-0*); mass mkt. 3.95 (*0-8075-2855-2*) Whitman, Albert & Co.

—The Mystery Bookstore. 1995. (Boxcar Children Ser.: No. 48). (J). (gr. 2-5). lib. bdg. 13.95 (*0-8075-5421-9*); mass mkt. 3.95 (*0-8075-5422-7*) Whitman, Albert & Co.

—The Mystery in New York. 1999. (Boxcar Children Special Ser.: No. 13). 121p. (J). (gr. 2-5). lib. bdg. 13.95 (*0-8075-5459-6*); mass mkt. 3.95 (*0-8075-5460-X*) Whitman, Albert & Co.

—The Mystery in the Cave. 1996. (Boxcar Children Ser.: No. 50). (J). (gr. 2-5). lib. bdg. 13.95 (*0-8075-5411-1*); mass mkt. 3.95 (*0-8075-5412-X*) Whitman, Albert & Co.

—The Mystery of the Empty Safe. 2000. (Boxcar Children Ser.: No. 75). (J). (gr. 2-5). 10.00 (*0-606-18768-5*) Turtleback Bks.

—The Mystery of the Empty Safe. 2000. (Boxcar Children Ser.: No. 75). 120p. (J). (gr. 2-5). mass mkt. 3.95 (*0-8075-5463-4*) Whitman, Albert & Co.

—The Mystery of the Hidden Painting. l.t. ed. 1995. (Boxcar Children Ser.: No. 24). (J). (gr. 2-5). 9.00 (*0-395-73243-3*) Houghton Mifflin Co.

—The Mystery of the Stolen Boxcar. 1995. (Boxcar Children Ser.: No. 49). (J). (gr. 2-5). lib. bdg. 13.95 (*0-8075-5423-5*); mass mkt. 3.95 (*0-8075-5424-3*) Whitman, Albert & Co.

—The Mystery of the Stolen Music. 1995. (Boxcar Children Ser.: No. 45). 118p. (J). (gr. 2-5). lib. bdg. 13.95 (*0-8075-5415-4*); mass mkt. 3.95 (*0-8075-5416-2*) Whitman, Albert & Co.

—The Mystery of the Stolen Sword. 1998. (Boxcar Children Ser.: No. 67). 121p. (J). (gr. 2-5). mass mkt. 3.95 (*0-8075-7623-9*) Whitman, Albert & Co.

—The Pilgrim Village Mystery. 1995. (Boxcar Children Special Ser.: No. 5). (J). (gr. 2-5). pap. 3.95 (*0-8075-6531-8*); lib. bdg. 13.95 (*0-8075-6530-X*) Whitman, Albert & Co.

—The Pizza Mystery. 1993. (Boxcar Children Ser.: No. 33). 128p. (J). (gr. 2-5). lib. bdg. 13.95 (*0-8075-6534-2*); mass mkt. 3.95 (*0-8075-6535-0*) Whitman, Albert & Co.

Warner, Gertrude Chandler. Benny Goes into Business. 1999. (Adventures of Benny & Watch: No.5). (J). (gr. 1-3). 10.10 (*0-606-16916-4*) Turtleback Bks.

—Benny Uncovers a Mystery. 1976. (Boxcar Children Ser.: No. 19). (J). (gr. 2-5). 10.00 (*0-606-04875-8*) Turtleback Bks.

—Benny Uncovers a Mystery. 1991. (Boxcar Children Ser.: No. 19). (J). (gr. 2-5). pap. 3.95 (*0-8075-0645-1*); 128p. lib. bdg. 13.95 (*0-8075-0644-3*) Whitman, Albert & Co.

—The Bicycle Mystery. 1970. (Boxcar Children Ser.: No. 15). (J). (gr. 2-5). 10.00 (*0-606-04878-2*) Turtleback Bks.

—The Bicycle Mystery. 1971. (Albert Whitman Pilot Bks.: No. 15). (Illus.). 128p. (J). (gr. 2-5). lib. bdg. 13.95 (*0-8075-0708-3*); mass mkt. 3.95 (*0-8075-0709-1*) Whitman, Albert & Co.

—Blue Bay Mystery. 1989. (Boxcar Children Ser.: No. 6). (J). (gr. 2-5). 10.00 (*0-606-00459-9*) Turtleback Bks.

—Blue Bay Mystery. 1961. (Boxcar Children Ser.: No. 6). (Illus.). (J). (gr. 2-5). pap. 3.95 (*0-8075-0794-6*); lib. bdg. 13.95 (*0-8075-0793-8*) Whitman, Albert & Co.

—The Boxcar Children. Date not set. (Boxcar Children Ser.: No. 1). (J). (gr. 2-5). lib. bdg. 18.95 (*0-8488-1712-5*) Amereon, Ltd.

—The Boxcar Children. unabr. ed. 1997. (Boxcar Children Mystery Ser.: No. 1). (J). (gr. 2-5). audio 23.00 BBC Audiobooks America.

—The Boxcar Children. (J). (gr. 2-5). (Boxcar Children Ser.: No. 1). 154p. pap. 3.95 (*0-8072-1447-7*);No. 1. 1991. pap. 28.00 incl. audio (*0-8072-7332-5*, YA 830SP);No. 1. 1991. audio 23.00 (*0-8072-7331-7*, YA 830CX) Random Hse. Audio Publishing Group. (Listening Library).

—The Boxcar Children. 1977. (Boxcar Children Ser.: No. 1). (J). (gr. 2-5). 10.00 (*0-606-04176-1*) Turtleback Bks.

—The Boxcar Children. 1942. (Boxcar Children Ser.: No. 1). (J). (gr. 2-5). reprint ed. lib. bdg. 13.95 (*0-8075-0851-9*); (Illus.). 154p. pap. 3.95 (*0-8075-0852-7*) Whitman, Albert & Co.

—The Boxcar Children Vol. 1-4: The Boxcar Children; Surprise Island; The Yellow House Mystery; Mystery Ranch. 1942. (Boxcar Children Ser.). (J). (gr. 2-5). reprint ed. pap. 15.80 (*0-8075-0854-3*) Whitman, Albert & Co.

—The Boxcar Children Vol. 5-8: Mike's Mystery; Blue Bay Mystery; The Woodshed Mystery; The Lighthouse Mystery. 1942. (Boxcar Children Ser.). (J). (gr. 2-5). reprint ed. pap. 15.80 (*0-8075-0857-8*) Whitman, Albert & Co.

—The Boxcar Children Mysteries. unabr. ed. 1996. (J). (gr. 2-5). Vol. 1. audio 34.00 (*0-7366-3508-4*, 4147); Vol. 2. (Boxcar Children Ser.: No.2). audio 30.00 (*0-7366-3509-2*, 4148) Books on Tape, Inc.

—The Bus Station Mystery. 1974. (Boxcar Children Ser.: No. 18). (J). (gr. 2-5). 10.00 (*0-606-04883-9*) Turtleback Bks.

—The Bus Station Mystery. 1974. (Boxcar Children Ser.: No. 18). (Illus.). 128p. (J). (gr. 2-5). pap. 3.95 (*0-8075-0976-0*); lib. bdg. 13.95 (*0-8075-0975-2*) Whitman, Albert & Co.

—The Caboose Mystery. 1999. (Boxcar Children Ser.: No. 11). 128p. (J). (gr. 2-5). pap. (*0-590-42681-8*) Scholastic, Inc.

—The Caboose Mystery. 1966. (Boxcar Children Ser.: No. 11). (J). (gr. 2-5). 10.00 (*0-606-03143-X*) Turtleback Bks.

—The Caboose Mystery. 1966. (Boxcar Children Ser.: No. 11). (Illus.). 128p. (J). (gr. 2-5). pap. 3.95 (*0-8075-1009-2*); lib. bdg. 13.95 (*0-8075-1008-4*) Whitman, Albert & Co.

—The Ghost Town Mystery. 1999. (Boxcar Children Ser.: No. 71). (J). (gr. 2-5). 10.00 (*0-606-18764-2*) Turtleback Bks.

—The Great Bicycle Race Mystery. 2000. (Boxcar Children Ser.: No. 76). (Illus.). (J). (gr. 2-5). 10.00 (*0-606-18907-6*) Turtleback Bks.

—The Gymnastics Mystery. 1999. (Boxcar Children Ser.: No. 73). (J). (gr. 2-5). 10.00 (*0-606-18766-9*) Turtleback Bks.

—The Hockey Mystery. 2001. (Boxcar Children Ser.: No. 80). 10.00 (*0-606-20318-4*) Turtleback Bks.

—The Hockey Mystery. 2001. (Boxcar Children Ser.: Vol. 80). (Illus.). 135p. (J). (gr. 2-5). lib. bdg. 13.95 (*0-8075-3342-4*);No. 80. mass mkt. 3.95 (*0-8075-3343-2*) Whitman, Albert & Co.

—The Homerun Mystery. 2000. (Boxcar Children Special Ser.: No. 14). (J). (gr. 2-5). 10.00 (*0-606-18772-3*) Turtleback Bks.

—The Honeybee Mystery. 2000. (Boxcar Children Special Ser.: No. 15). (J). (gr. 2-5). 10.00 *(0-606-20301-X)*; 10.00 *(0-606-20319-2)* Turtleback Bks.

—The Honeybee Mystery. 2000. (Boxcar Children Special Ser.: No. 15). (Illus.). 135p. (J). (gr. 2-5). pap. 3.95 *(0-8075-3374-2)*; lib. bdg. 13.95 *(0-8075-3373-4)* Whitman, Albert & Co.

—The Houseboat Mystery. 1967. (Boxcar Children Ser.: No. 12). (J). (gr. 2-5). 10.00 *(0-606-03737-3)* Turtleback Bks.

—The Houseboat Mystery. 1966. (Boxcar Children Ser.: No. 12). (Illus.). 128p. (J). (gr. 2-5). lib. bdg. 13.95 *(0-8075-3412-9)*; mass mkt. 3.95 *(0-8075-3413-7)* Whitman, Albert & Co.

—The Lighthouse Mystery. (Boxcar Children Ser.: No. 8). (J). (gr. 2-5). 147p. pap. 3.95 *(0-8072-1474-4)*; 1995. 147p. pap. 28.00 incl. audio *(0-8072-7541-7*, YA877SP); 1995. audio 23.00 *(0-8072-7540-9*, YA877CX) Random Hse. Audio Publishing Group. (Listening Library).

—The Lighthouse Mystery. 1963. (Boxcar Children Ser.: No. 8). (J). (gr. 2-5). 10.00 *(0-606-04467-1)* Turtleback Bks.

—The Lighthouse Mystery. (Boxcar Children Ser.: No. 8). (Illus.). 128p. (J). (gr. 2-5). 1990. mass mkt. 3.95 *(0-8075-4546-5)*; 1963. lib. bdg. 13.95 *(0-8075-4545-7)* Whitman, Albert & Co.

—The Magic Show Mystery. 1998. (Adventures of Benny & Watch: No.4). (J). (gr. 1-3). 10.10 *(0-606-16150-3)* Turtleback Bks.

—Mike's Mystery. (Boxcar Children Ser.: No. 5). (J). (gr. 2-5). 128p. pap. 3.95 *(0-8072-1462-0)*; 1994. 128p. pap. 28.00 incl. audio *(0-8072-7438-0*, YA859SP); 1994. audio 23.00 *(0-8072-7437-2*, YA859CX) Random Hse. Audio Publishing Group. (Listening Library).

—Mike's Mystery. 1988. (Boxcar Children Ser.: No. 5). (J). (gr. 2-5). 10.00 *(0-606-01921-9)* Turtleback Bks.

—Mike's Mystery. (Boxcar Children Ser.: No. 5). (Illus.). 128p. (J). (gr. 2-5). 1990. mass mkt. 3.95 *(0-8075-5141-4)*; 1960. lib. bdg. 14.95 *(0-8075-5140-6)* Whitman, Albert & Co.

—The Mountain Top Mystery. 1964. (Boxcar Children Ser.: No. 9). (J). (gr. 2-5). 10.00 *(0-606-04481-7)* Turtleback Bks.

—The Mountain Top Mystery. 1964. (Boxcar Children Ser.: No. 9). (Illus.). 128p. (J). (gr. 2-5). 19.95 *(0-8075-5292-5)*; pap. 5.95 *(0-8075-5293-3)* Whitman, Albert & Co.

—The Movie Star Mystery. 1999. (Boxcar Children Ser.: No. 69). (J). (gr. 2-5). 10.00 *(0-606-18762-6)* Turtleback Bks.

—The Mystery at Skeleton Point. 2002. (Boxcar Children Ser.: No. 91). (Illus.). 128p. (J). text 13.95 *(0-8075-5519-3)*; (gr. 4-7). mass mkt. 3.95 *(0-8075-5520-7)* Whitman, Albert & Co.

—The Mystery Behind the Wall. 1973. (Boxcar Children Ser.: No. 17). (J). (gr. 2-5). 10.00 *(0-606-04986-X)* Turtleback Bks.

—The Mystery Behind the Wall. 1973. (Boxcar Children Ser.: No. 17). (Illus.). 128p. (J). (gr. 2-5). lib. bdg. 13.95 *(0-8075-5364-6)*; mass mkt. 3.95 *(0-8075-5367-0)* Whitman, Albert & Co.

—The Mystery in New York. 1999. (Boxcar Children Special Ser.: No.13). (Illus.). (J). (gr. 2-5). 10.00 *(0-606-18771-5)* Turtleback Bks.

—The Mystery in the Computer Game. 2000. (Boxcar Children Ser.: No. 78). (J). (gr. 2-5). 10.00 *(0-606-20298-6)* Turtleback Bks.

—The Mystery in the Mall. 1999. (Boxcar Children Ser.: No. 72). (J). (gr. 2-5). 10.00 *(0-606-18765-0)* Turtleback Bks.

—The Mystery in the Sand. 1971. (Boxcar Children Ser.: No. 16). (J). (gr. 2-5). 10.00 *(0-606-04987-8)* Turtleback Bks.

—The Mystery in the Sand. 1971. (Boxcar Children Ser.: No. 16). (Illus.). 128p. (J). (gr. 2-5). lib. bdg. 13.95 *(0-8075-5373-5)*; mass mkt. 3.95 *(0-8075-5372-7)* Whitman, Albert & Co.

—The Mystery of Alligator Swamp. 2002. (Boxcar Children Special Ser.: No. 19). (Illus.). 144p. (J). text 13.95 *(0-8075-5516-9)*; (gr. 4-7). mass mkt. 3.95 *(0-8075-5517-7)* Whitman, Albert & Co.

—The Mystery of the Black Raven. 1999. (Boxcar Children Special Ser.: No. 12). (Illus.). (J). (gr. 2-5). 10.00 *(0-606-18770-7)* Turtleback Bks.

—The Mystery of the Crooked House. 2000. (Boxcar Children Ser.: No. 79). (J). (gr. 2-5). 10.00 *(0-606-20299-4)* Turtleback Bks.

—The Mystery of the Midnight Dog. 2001. (Boxcar Children Ser.). (Illus.). (J). 10.00 *(0-606-21080-6)* Turtleback Bks.

—The Mystery of the Mummy's Curse. 2002. (Boxcar Children Ser.: Vol. 88). 128p. (J). lib. bdg. 13.95 *(0-8075-5503-7)*;No. 88. pap. 3.95 *(0-8075-5504-5)* Whitman, Albert & Co.

—The Mystery of the Pirate's Map. 1999. (Boxcar Children Ser.: No. 70). (J). (gr. 2-5). 10.00 *(0-606-18763-4)* Turtleback Bks.

—The Mystery of the Queen's Jewels. 1998. (Boxcar Children Special Ser.: No. 11). (J). (gr. 2-5). 10.00 *(0-606-18769-3)* Turtleback Bks.

—The Mystery of the Screech Owl. 2001. (Boxcar Children Special Ser.). (Illus.). (J). 10.00 *(0-606-21085-7)* Turtleback Bks.

—The Mystery of the Star Ruby. 2002. (Boxcar Children Mystery Ser.: Vol. 89). (Illus.). 128p. (J). pap. 3.95 *(0-8075-5510-X)* Whitman, Albert & Co.

—The Mystery of the Star Ruby. 2002. (Boxcar Children Ser.: Vol. 89). (Illus.). 128p. (J). lib. bdg. 13.95 *(0-8075-5509-6)* Whitman, Albert & Co.

—The Mystery of the Stolen Sword. 1998. (Boxcar Children Ser.: No. 67). (J). (gr. 2-5). 10.00 *(0-606-17178-9)* Turtleback Bks.

—The Mystery of the Wild Ponies. 2000. (Boxcar Children Ser.: Vol. 77). (Illus.). (J). (gr. 2-5). 10.00 *(0-606-18908-4)* Turtleback Bks.

—Mystery Ranch. unabr. ed. 1997. (Boxcar Children Mystery Ser.: No. 4). (J). (gr. 2-5). audio 23.00 BBC Audiobooks America.

—Mystery Ranch. (Boxcar Children Ser.: No. 4). (J). (gr. 2-5). 128p. pap. 3.95 *(0-8072-1450-7)*; 2000. audio 18.00 o.s.i *(0-8072-7343-0*, YA833CX); 1993. pap. 28.00 incl. audio *(0-8072-7344-9*, YA 833 SP); 1993. pap. 28.00 incl. audio *(0-8072-7344-9*, YA 833 SP) Random Hse. Audio Publishing Group. (Listening Library).

—Mystery Ranch. 1986. (Boxcar Children Ser.: No. 4). (J). (gr. 2-5). 10.00 *(0-606-02084-5)* Turtleback Bks.

—Mystery Ranch. (Boxcar Children Ser.: No. 4). (Illus.). (J). (gr. 2-5). reprint ed. 1989. 127p. mass mkt. 3.95 *(0-8075-5391-3)*; 1958. 128p. lib. bdg. 13.95 *(0-8075-5390-5)* Whitman, Albert & Co.

—The Mystery Ranch. unabr. ed. 2000. (Boxcar Children Ser.: No. 4). (J). (gr. 4-7). audio 18.00 *(0-8072-7421-6*, YA 833 CXR, Listening Library) Random Hse. Audio Publishing Group.

—The Niagara Falls Mystery. 1997. (Boxcar Children Special Ser.: Vol. 8). (J). (gr. 2-5). pap. 3.95 *(0-8075-5603-3)* Whitman, Albert & Co.

—The Panther Mystery. 1998. (Boxcar Children Ser.: No.66). (J). (gr. 2-5). 10.00 *(0-606-16149-X)* Turtleback Bks.

—The Pizza Mystery. unabr. ed. 2003. audio compact disk 14.99 *(1-58926-293-X)* Oasis Audio.

—The Poison Frog Mystery. 2000. (Boxcar Children Ser.: No. 74). (J). (gr. 2-5). 10.00 *(0-606-18767-7)* Turtleback Bks.

—The Radio Mystery. unabr. ed. 2003. audio compact disk 14.99 *(1-58926-291-3)* Oasis Audio.

—The Schoolhouse Mystery. 1965. (Boxcar Children Ser.: No. 10). (J). (gr. 2-5). 10.00 *(0-606-04532-5)* Turtleback Bks.

—The Schoolhouse Mystery. 1965. (Boxcar Children Ser.: No. 10). (Illus.). 128p. (J). (gr. 2-5). reprint ed. lib. bdg. 13.95 *(0-8075-7262-4)*; mass mkt. 3.95 *(0-8075-7263-2)* Whitman, Albert & Co.

—The Secret under the Tree. 2001. (Boxcar Children Early Reader Ser.). (Illus.). (J). 10.10 *(0-606-21083-0)* Turtleback Bks.

—Snowbound Mystery. 1968. (Boxcar Children Ser.: No. 13). (J). (gr. 2-5). 10.00 *(0-606-05017-5)* Turtleback Bks.

—Snowbound Mystery. 1968. (Boxcar Children Ser.: No. 13). (Illus.). (J). (gr. 2-5). lib. bdg. 13.95 *(0-8075-7517-8)*; mass mkt. 3.95 *(0-8075-7516-X)* Whitman, Albert & Co.

—The Stuffed Bear Mystery. 2002. (Boxcar Children Ser.: No. 90). (Illus.). 128p. (J). text 13.95 *(0-8075-5512-6)*; (gr. 4-7). mass mkt. 3.95 *(0-8075-5513-4)* Whitman, Albert & Co.

—The Summer Camp Mystery. 2001. (Boxcar Children Ser.). (Illus.). (J). 10.00 *(0-606-21081-4)* Turtleback Bks.

—Surprise Island. unabr. ed. 1997. (Boxcar Children Mystery Ser.: No. 2). (J). (gr. 2-5). audio 23.00 BBC Audiobooks America.

—Surprise Island. unabr. ed. (Boxcar Children Ser.: No. 2). (J). (gr. 2-5). 2000. audio 18.00 *(0-8072-7391-0*, YA 831 CXR); 2000. audio 18.00 *(0-8072-7391-0*, YA 831 CXR); 1991. 178p. pap. 28.00 incl. audio *(0-8072-7336-8*, YA 831SP); 1991. 178p. pap. 28.00 incl. audio *(0-8072-7336-8*, YA 831SP); 1991. audio 23.00 *(0-8072-7335-X*, TA 831CX) Random Hse. Audio Publishing Group. (Listening Library).

—Surprise Island. 1977. (Boxcar Children Ser.: No. 2). (J). (gr. 2-5). 10.00 *(0-606-02701-7)* Turtleback Bks.

—Surprise Island. 1949. (Boxcar Children Ser.: No. 2). (Illus.). (J). (gr. 2-5). reprint ed. 178p. pap. 3.95 *(0-8075-7674-3)*; lib. bdg. 13.95 *(0-8075-7673-5)* Whitman, Albert & Co.

—The Tattletale Mystery. 2003. (Boxcar Children Ser.: No. 92). (Illus.). 128p. (J). text 13.95 *(0-8075-5525-8)*; mass mkt. 3.95 *(0-8075-5526-6)* Whitman, Albert & Co.

—The Tree House Mystery. 1969. (Boxcar Children Ser.: No. 14). (J). (gr. 2-5). 10.00 *(0-606-05036-1)* Turtleback Bks.

—The Tree House Mystery. 1969. (Pilot Bks.: No. 14). (Illus.). 128p. (J). (gr. 2-5). lib. bdg. 13.95 *(0-8075-8086-4)*; mass mkt. 5.95 *(0-8075-8087-2)* Whitman, Albert & Co.

—Watch Runs Away. 1999. (Adventures of Benny & Watch: No. 6). (J). (gr. 1-3). 10.10 *(0-606-16915-6)* Turtleback Bks.

—The Woodshed Mystery. 1990. (Boxcar Children Ser.: No. 7). (J). (gr. 2-5). 10.00 *(0-606-04592-9)* Turtleback Bks.

—The Woodshed Mystery. 1962. (Boxcar Children Ser.: No. 7). (Illus.). 128p. (J). (gr. 2-5). lib. bdg. 13.95 *(0-8075-9206-4)*; mass mkt. 3.95 *(0-8075-9207-2)* Whitman, Albert & Co.

—The Yellow House Mystery. (Boxcar Children Ser.: No. 3). (J). (gr. 2-5). 191p. pap. 3.95 *(0-8072-1449-3)*; 2000. audio 18.00 o.s.i *(0-8072-7339-2*, YA 832 CX); 2000. audio 18.00 *(0-8072-7395-3*, YA832CXR); 1992. pap. 28.00 incl. audio *(0-8072-7340-6*, YA 832 SP) Random Hse. Audio Publishing Group. (Listening Library).

—The Yellow House Mystery. 1993. (Boxcar Children Ser.: No. 3). (J). (gr. 2-5). audio 15.95 o.p. *(0-8161-7612-4)* Thorndike Pr.

—The Yellow House Mystery. 1981. (Boxcar Children Ser.: No. 3). (J). (gr. 2-5). 10.00 *(0-606-04428-0)* Turtleback Bks.

—The Yellow House Mystery. (Boxcar Children Ser.: No. 3). (J). (gr. 2-5). 1989. (Illus.). 191p. pap. 3.95 *(0-8075-9366-4)*; 1953. 128p. lib. bdg. 13.95 *(0-8075-9365-6)* Whitman, Albert & Co.

Warner, Gertrude Chandler, creator. The Amusement Park Mystery. 1992. (Boxcar Children Ser.: No. 25). (J). (gr. 2-5). 10.00 *(0-606-00272-3)* Turtleback Bks.

—The Amusement Park Mystery. 1992. (Boxcar Children Ser.: No. 25). (Illus.). 119p. (J). (gr. 2-5). pap. 3.95 *(0-8075-0319-3)*; lib. bdg. 13.95 *(0-8075-0320-7)* Whitman, Albert & Co.

—The Animal Shelter Mystery. 1991. (Boxcar Children Ser.: No. 22). (J). (gr. 2-5). 10.00 *(0-606-00285-5)* Turtleback Bks.

—The Animal Shelter Mystery. 1991. (Boxcar Children Ser.: No. 22). (Illus.). 121p. (J). (gr. 2-5). lib. bdg. 13.95 *(0-8075-0368-1)*; mass mkt. 3.95 *(0-8075-0367-3)* Whitman, Albert & Co.

—The Basketball Mystery. 1999. (Boxcar Children Ser.: No. 68). (J). (gr. 2-5). 10.00 *(0-606-17179-7)* Turtleback Bks.

—The Basketball Mystery. 1999. (Boxcar Children Ser.: No. 68). (Illus.). 128p. (J). (gr. 2-5). lib. bdg. 13.95 *(0-8075-0575-7)* Whitman, Albert & Co.

—Benny's New Friend. 1998. (Adventures of Benny & Watch: No. 3). (J). (gr. 1-3). 10.10 *(0-606-13217-1)* Turtleback Bks.

—The Black Pearl Mystery. 1998. (Boxcar Children Ser.: No. 64). (J). (gr. 2-5). 10.00 *(0-606-13213-9)* Turtleback Bks.

—The Black Pearl Mystery. 1998. (Boxcar Children Ser.: No. 64). (Illus.). 128p. (J). (gr. 2-5). lib. bdg. 19.95 *(0-8075-0783-0)* Whitman, Albert & Co.

—The Camp-Out Mystery. 1992. (Boxcar Children Ser.: No. 27). (J). (gr. 2-5). 10.00 *(0-606-02331-3)* Turtleback Bks.

—The Camp-Out Mystery. 1992. (Boxcar Children Ser.: No. 27). (Illus.). 192p. (J). (gr. 2-5). pap. 5.95 *(0-8075-1052-1)*; lib. bdg. 13.95 *(0-8075-1053-X)* Whitman, Albert & Co.

—The Canoe Trip Mystery. 1994. (Boxcar Children Ser.: No. 40). (J). (gr. 2-5). 10.00 *(0-606-06246-7)* Turtleback Bks.

—The Canoe Trip Mystery. 1994. (Boxcar Children Ser.: No. 40). 120p. (J). (gr. 2-5). pap. 5.95 *(0-8075-1059-9)*; lib. bdg. 13.95 *(0-8075-1058-0)* Whitman, Albert & Co.

—The Castle Mystery. 1993. (Boxcar Children Ser.: No. 36). (J). (gr. 2-5). 10.00 *(0-606-05765-X)* Turtleback Bks.

—The Castle Mystery. 1993. (Boxcar Children Ser.: No. 36). (J). (gr. 2-5). pap. 3.95 *(0-8075-1079-3)*; 121p. lib. bdg. 13.95 *(0-8075-1078-5)* Whitman, Albert & Co.

—The Chocolate Sundae Mystery. 1995. (Boxcar Children Ser.: No. 46). (J). (gr. 2-5). 10.00 *(0-606-07314-0)* Turtleback Bks.

—The Deserted Library Mystery. 1991. (Boxcar Children Ser.: No. 21). (J). (gr. 2-5). 10.00 *(0-606-00400-9)* Turtleback Bks.

—The Deserted Library Mystery. 1991. (Boxcar Children Ser.: No. 21). (Illus.). 121p. (J). (gr. 2-5). pap. 3.95 *(0-8075-1560-4)*; lib. bdg. 19.95 *(0-8075-1561-2)* Whitman, Albert & Co.

—The Dinosaur Mystery. 1995. (Boxcar Children Ser.: No. 44). (J). (gr. 2-5). 10.00 *(0-606-07149-0)* Turtleback Bks.

—The Dinosaur Mystery. 1995. (Boxcar Children Ser.: No. 44). (Illus.). 192p. (J). (gr. 2-5). pap. 3.95 *(0-8075-1604-X)*; lib. bdg. 13.95 *(0-8075-1603-1)* Whitman, Albert & Co.

—The Disappearing Friend Mystery. 1992. (Boxcar Children Ser.: No. 30). (J). (gr. 2-5). 10.00 *(0-606-02335-6)* Turtleback Bks.

—The Disappearing Friend Mystery. 1992. (Boxcar Children Ser.: No. 30). 192p. (J). (gr. 2-5). pap. 3.95 *(0-8075-1628-7)*; lib. bdg. 13.95 *(0-8075-1627-9)* Whitman, Albert & Co.

—The Firehouse Mystery. 1997. (Boxcar Children Ser.: No. 56). (J). (gr. 2-5). 10.00 *(0-606-10760-6)* Turtleback Bks.

—The Firehouse Mystery. 1997. (Boxcar Children Ser.: No. 56). (Illus.). 128p. (J). (gr. 2-5). pap. 3.95 *(0-8075-2448-4)*; lib. bdg. 13.95 *(0-8075-2447-6)* Whitman, Albert & Co.

—The Ghost Ship Mystery. 1994. (Boxcar Children Ser.: No. 39). (J). (gr. 2-5). 10.00 *(0-606-06245-9)* Turtleback Bks.

—The Ghost Town Mystery. 1999. (Boxcar Children Ser.: No. 71). (Illus.). 128p. (J). (gr. 2-5). lib. bdg. 13.95 *(0-8075-2858-7)*; mass mkt. 3.95 *(0-8075-2859-5)* Whitman, Albert & Co.

—The Great Bicycle Race Mystery. 2000. (Boxcar Children Ser.: No. 76). (Illus.). 115p. (J). (gr. 2-5). lib. bdg. 13.95 *(0-8075-3048-4)*; mass mkt. 13.95 *(0-8075-3049-2)* Whitman, Albert & Co.

—The Growling Bear Mystery. 1997. (Boxcar Children Ser.: No. 61). (J). (gr. 2-5). 10.00 *(0-606-12635-X)* Turtleback Bks.

—The Growling Bear Mystery. 1997. (Boxcar Children Ser.: No. 61). (Illus.). 128p. (J). (gr. 2-5). lib. bdg. 13.95 *(0-8075-3070-0)*; mass mkt. 3.95 *(0-8075-3071-9)* Whitman, Albert & Co.

—The Guide Dog Mystery. 1996. (Boxcar Children Ser.: No. 53). (J). (gr. 2-5). 10.00 *(0-606-09096-7)* Turtleback Bks.

—The Guide Dog Mystery. 1996. (Boxcar Children Ser.: No. 53). (Illus.). 128p. (J). (gr. 2-5). lib. bdg. 13.95 *(0-8075-3080-8)*; mass mkt. 3.95 *(0-8075-3081-6)* Whitman, Albert & Co.

—The Gymnastics Mystery. 1999. (Boxcar Children Ser.: No. 73). (Illus.). 128p. (J). (gr. 2-5). lib. bdg. 13.95 *(0-8075-3100-6)*; mass mkt. 3.95 *(0-8075-3101-4)* Whitman, Albert & Co.

—The Haunted Cabin Mystery. 1991. (Boxcar Children Ser.: No. 20). (J). (gr. 2-5). 10.00 *(0-606-00494-7)* Turtleback Bks.

—The Haunted Cabin Mystery. 1991. (Boxcar Children Ser.: No. 20). (Illus.). 121p. (J). (gr. 2-5). lib. bdg. 13.95 *(0-8075-3179-0)*; mass mkt. 3.95 *(0-8075-3178-2)* Whitman, Albert & Co.

—The Homerun Mystery. 2000. (Boxcar Children Special Ser.: No. 14). (Illus.). 120p. (J). (gr. 2-5). lib. bdg. 13.95 *(0-8075-3368-8)*;No. 14. mass mkt. 3.95 *(0-8075-3369-6)* Whitman, Albert & Co.

—The Hurricane Mystery. 1996. (Boxcar Children Ser.: No. 54). (J). (gr. 2-5). 10.00 *(0-606-10146-2)* Turtleback Bks.

—The Hurricane Mystery. 1996. (Boxcar Children Ser.: No. 54). (Illus.). 128p. (J). (gr. 2-5). lib. bdg. 13.95 *(0-8075-3436-6)*; mass mkt. 5.95 *(0-8075-3437-4)* Whitman, Albert & Co.

—Meet the Boxcar Children. 1998. (Adventures of Benny & Watch: No. 1). (J). (gr. 1-3). 10.10 *(0-606-13215-5)* Turtleback Bks.

—The Movie Star Mystery. 1999. (Boxcar Children Ser.: No. 69). (Illus.). 128p. (J). (gr. 2-5). lib. bdg. 13.95 *(0-8075-5303-4)*; mass mkt. 3.95 *(0-8075-5304-2)* Whitman, Albert & Co.

—The Mystery at Peacock Hall. 1998. (Boxcar Children Ser.: No. 63). (J). (gr. 2-5). 10.00 *(0-606-13212-0)* Turtleback Bks.

—The Mystery at Peacock Hall. 1998. (Boxcar Children Ser.: No. 63). (Illus.). 128p. (J). (gr. 2-5). lib. bdg. 13.95 *(0-8075-5444-8)*; mass mkt. 3.95 *(0-8075-5445-6)* Whitman, Albert & Co.

—The Mystery at Snowflake Inn. 1994. (Boxcar Children Special Ser.: No. 3). (J). (gr. 2-5). 10.00 *(0-606-13221-X)* Turtleback Bks.

—The Mystery at Snowflake Inn. 1994. (Boxcar Children Special Ser.: No. 3). (Illus.). 192p. (J). (gr. 2-5). lib. bdg. 13.95 *(0-8075-5345-X)*; mass mkt. 3.95 *(0-8075-5346-8)* Whitman, Albert & Co.

—The Mystery at the Alamo. 1997. (Boxcar Children Ser.: No. 58). (J). (gr. 2-5). 10.00 *(0-606-11161-1)* Turtleback Bks.

—The Mystery at the Alamo. 1997. (Boxcar Children Ser.: No. 58). (J). (gr. 2-5). lib. bdg. 13.95 *(0-8075-5436-7)*; mass mkt. 3.95 *(0-8075-5437-5)* Whitman, Albert & Co.

—The Mystery at the Ballpark. 1995. (Boxcar Children Special Ser.: No. 4). (J). (gr. 2-5). 10.00 *(0-606-13222-8)* Turtleback Bks.

—The Mystery at the Ballpark. 1995. (Boxcar Children Special Ser.: No. 4). 124p. (J). (gr. 2-5). lib. bdg. 13.95 *(0-8075-5340-9)*; mass mkt. 3.95 *(0-8075-5341-7)* Whitman, Albert & Co.

—The Mystery at the Dog Show. 1993. (Boxcar Children Ser.: No. 35). (J). (gr. 2-5). 10.00 *(0-606-08937-3)* Turtleback Bks.

—The Mystery at the Dog Show. 1993. (Boxcar Children Ser.: No. 35). (Illus.). 128p. (J). (gr. 2-5). lib. bdg. 13.95 *(0-8075-5395-6)*; mass mkt. 3.95 *(0-8075-5394-8)* Whitman, Albert & Co.

—The Mystery at the Fair. 1996. (Boxcar Children Special Ser.: No. 6). (J). (gr. 2-5). 10.00 *(0-606-08701-X)* Turtleback Bks.

—The Mystery at the Fair. 1996. (Boxcar Children Special Ser.: No. 6). (Illus.). 128p. (J). (gr. 2-5). lib. bdg. 13.95 *(0-8075-5336-0)*; mass mkt. 3.95 *(0-8075-5337-9)* Whitman, Albert & Co.

—The Mystery Bookstore. 1995. (Boxcar Children Ser.: No. 48). (J). (gr. 2-5). 10.00 (*0-606-08497-5*) Turtleback Bks.

—The Mystery Cruise. 1992. (Boxcar Children Ser.: No. 29). (J). (gr. 2-5). 10.00 (*0-606-02333-X*) Turtleback Bks.

—The Mystery Cruise. 1992. (Boxcar Children Ser.: No. 29). (Illus.). 192p. (J). (gr. 2-5). lib. bdg. 13.95 (*0-8075-5362-X*); mass mkt. 3.95 (*0-8075-5368-9*) Whitman, Albert & Co.

—The Mystery Girl. 1992. (Boxcar Children Ser.: No. 28). (J). (gr. 2-5). 10.00 (*0-606-02332-1*) Turtleback Bks.

—The Mystery Girl. 1992. (Boxcar Children Ser.: No. 28). (Illus.). 192p. (J). (gr. 2-5). lib. bdg. 13.95 (*0-8075-5370-0*); mass mkt. 3.95 (*0-8075-5371-9*) Whitman, Albert & Co.

—The Mystery Horse. 1993. (Boxcar Children Ser.: No. 34). (J). (gr. 2-5). 10.00 (*0-606-08936-5*) Turtleback Bks.

—The Mystery Horse. 1993. (Boxcar Children Ser.: No. 34). (Illus.). 128p. (J). (gr. 2-5). lib. bdg. 13.95 (*0-8075-5338-7*); mass mkt. 3.95 (*0-8075-5339-5*) Whitman, Albert & Co.

—The Mystery in San Francisco. 1997. (Boxcar Children Ser.: No. 57). (J). (gr. 2-5). 10.00 (*0-606-11160-3*) Turtleback Bks.

—The Mystery in San Francisco. 1997. (Boxcar Children Ser.: No. 57). (J). (gr. 2-5). lib. bdg. 13.95 (*0-8075-5433-2*); mass mkt. 3.95 (*0-8075-5434-0*) Whitman, Albert & Co.

—The Mystery in the Cave. 1995. (Boxcar Children Ser.: No. 50). (J). (gr. 2-5). 10.00 (*0-606-08499-1*) Turtleback Bks.

—The Mystery in the Computer Game. 2000. (Boxcar Children Ser.: No. 78). (Illus.). 115p. (J). (gr. 2-5). lib. bdg. 13.95 (*0-8075-5468-5*); mass mkt. 3.95 (*0-8075-5469-3*) Whitman, Albert & Co.

—The Mystery in the Mall. 1999. (Boxcar Children Ser.: No. 72). (Illus.). 128p. (J). (gr. 2-5). lib. bdg. 13.95 (*0-8075-5456-1*); mass mkt. 3.95 (*0-8075-5457-X*) Whitman, Albert & Co.

—The Mystery in the Old Attic. 1997. (Boxcar Children Special Ser.: No. 9). (J). (gr. 2-5). 10.00 (*0-606-12636-8*) Turtleback Bks.

—The Mystery in the Old Attic. 1997. (Boxcar Children Special Ser.: No. 9). (Illus.). 144p. (J). (gr. 2-5). lib. bdg. 13.95 (*0-8075-5438-3*); mass mkt. 3.95 (*0-8075-5439-1*) Whitman, Albert & Co.

—The Mystery in the Snow. 1992. (Boxcar Children Ser.: No. 32). (J). (gr. 2-5). 10.00 (*0-606-02337-2*) Turtleback Bks.

—The Mystery in the Snow. 1992. (Boxcar Children Ser.: No. 32). (Illus.). 192p. (J). (gr. 2-5). lib. bdg. 13.95 (*0-8075-5392-1*); mass mkt. 3.95 (*0-8075-5393-X*) Whitman, Albert & Co.

—The Mystery in Washington, D. C. 1994. (Boxcar Children Special Ser.: No. 2). (J). (gr. 2-5). 10.00 (*0-606-13220-1*) Turtleback Bks.

—The Mystery in Washington, D. C. 1994. (Boxcar Children Special Ser.: No. 2). 110p. (J). (gr. 2-5). lib. bdg. 13.95 (*0-8075-5409-X*); mass mkt. 3.95 (*0-8075-5410-3*) Whitman, Albert & Co.

—The Mystery of the Black Raven. 1999. (Boxcar Children Special Ser.: No. 12). (Illus.). 144p. (J). (gr. 2-5). lib. bdg. 13.95 (*0-8075-2988-5*); mass mkt. 3.95 (*0-8075-2989-3*) Whitman, Albert & Co.

—The Mystery of the Crooked House. 2000. (Boxcar Children Ser.: No. 79). (Illus.). 112p. (J). (gr. 2-5). lib. bdg. 13.95 (*0-8075-5471-5*); mass mkt. 3.95 (*0-8075-5472-3*) Whitman, Albert & Co.

—The Mystery of the Empty Safe. 2000. (Boxcar Children Ser.: No. 75). (Illus.). 120p. (J). (gr. 2-5). lib. bdg. 13.95 (*0-8075-5462-6*) Whitman, Albert & Co.

—The Mystery of the Hidden Beach. 1994. (Boxcar Children Ser.: No. 41). (J). (gr. 2-5). 10.00 (*0-606-06247-5*) Turtleback Bks.

—The Mystery of the Hidden Beach. 1994. (Boxcar Children Ser.: No. 41). 119p. (J). (gr. 2-5). lib. bdg. 13.95 (*0-8075-5403-0*); mass mkt. 3.95 (*0-8075-5404-9*) Whitman, Albert & Co.

—The Mystery of the Hidden Painting. 1992. (Boxcar Children Ser.: No. 24). (J). (gr. 2-5). 10.00 (*0-606-00631-1*) Turtleback Bks.

—The Mystery of the Hidden Painting. 1992. (Boxcar Children Ser.: No. 24). (Illus.). 117p. (J). (gr. 2-5). lib. bdg. 13.95 (*0-8075-5383-2*); mass mkt. 3.95 (*0-8075-5379-4*) Whitman, Albert & Co.

—The Mystery of the Hot Air Balloon. 1995. (Boxcar Children Ser.: No. 47). (J). (gr. 2-5). 9.55 (*0-606-07315-9*) Turtleback Bks.

—The Mystery of the Hot Air Balloon. 1995. (Boxcar Children Ser.: No. 47). 120p. (J). (gr. 2-5). lib. bdg. 13.95 (*0-8075-5419-7*); mass mkt. 3.95 (*0-8075-5420-0*) Whitman, Albert & Co.

—The Mystery of the Lake Monster. 1998. (Boxcar Children Ser.: No. 62). (J). (gr. 2-5). 10.00 (*0-606-13211-2*) Turtleback Bks.

—The Mystery of the Lake Monster. 1998. (Boxcar Children Ser.: No. 62). (Illus.). 128p. (J). (gr. 2-5). lib. bdg. 13.95 (*0-8075-5441-3*); mass mkt. 3.95 (*0-8075-5442-1*) Whitman, Albert & Co.

—The Mystery of the Lost Mine. 1996. (Boxcar Children Ser.: No. 52). (J). (gr. 2-5). 10.00 (*0-606-09095-9*) Turtleback Bks.

—The Mystery of the Lost Mine. 1996. (Boxcar Children Ser.: No. 52). (J). (gr. 2-5). lib. bdg. 13.95 (*0-8075-5427-8*); mass mkt. 3.95 (*0-8075-5428-6*) Whitman, Albert & Co.

—The Mystery of the Lost Village. 1993. (Boxcar Children Ser.: No. 37). (J). (gr. 2-5). 10.00 (*0-606-05766-8*) Turtleback Bks.

—The Mystery of the Lost Village. 1993. (Boxcar Children Ser.: No. 37). 121p. (J). (gr. 2-5). lib. bdg. 13.95 (*0-8075-5400-6*); mass mkt. 3.95 (*0-8075-5401-4*) Whitman, Albert & Co.

—The Mystery of the Missing Cat. 1994. (Boxcar Children Ser.: No. 42). (J). (gr. 2-5). 10.00 (*0-606-07147-4*) Turtleback Bks.

—The Mystery of the Missing Cat. 1994. (Boxcar Children Ser.: No. 42). (Illus.). 192p. (J). (gr. 2-5). lib. bdg. 13.95 (*0-8075-5405-7*); mass mkt. 3.95 (*0-8075-5406-5*) Whitman, Albert & Co.

—The Mystery of the Mixed-Up Zoo. 1992. (Boxcar Children Ser.: No. 26). (J). (gr. 2-5). 10.00 (*0-606-02330-5*) Turtleback Bks.

—The Mystery of the Mixed-Up Zoo. 1992. (Boxcar Children Ser.: No. 26). (Illus.). 192p. (J). (gr. 2-5). lib. bdg. 13.95 (*0-8075-5386-7*); mass mkt. 3.95 (*0-8075-5385-9*) Whitman, Albert & Co.

—The Mystery of the Pirate's Map. (Boxcar Children Ser.: No.70). (Illus.). (J). (gr. 2-5). 13.95 (*0-8075-5453-7*); 1999. 128p. mass mkt. 3.95 (*0-8075-5454-5*) Whitman, Albert & Co.

—The Mystery of the Purple Pool. 1994. (Boxcar Children Ser.: No. 38). (J). (gr. 2-5). 10.00 (*0-606-05767-6*) Turtleback Bks.

—The Mystery of the Purple Pool. (Boxcar Children Ser.: No. 38). 122p. (J). (gr. 2-5). 1994. mass mkt. 3.95 (*0-8075-5408-1*); 1993. lib. bdg. 13.95 (*0-8075-5407-3*) Whitman, Albert & Co.

—The Mystery of the Queen's Jewels. 1998. (Boxcar Children Special Ser.: No. 11). (Illus.). 144p. (J). (gr. 2-5). lib. bdg. 13.95 (*0-8075-5450-2*); mass mkt. 3.95 (*0-8075-5451-0*) Whitman, Albert & Co.

—The Mystery of the Secret Message. 1996. (Boxcar Children Ser.: No. 55). (J). (gr. 2-5). 10.00 (*0-606-10147-0*) Turtleback Bks.

—The Mystery of the Secret Message. 1996. (Boxcar Children Ser.: No. 55). (Illus.). 128p. (J). (gr. 2-5). pap. 3.95 (*0-8075-5430-8*); lib. bdg. 13.95 (*0-8075-5429-4*) Whitman, Albert & Co.

—The Mystery of the Singing Ghost. 1992. (Boxcar Children Ser.: No. 31). (J). (gr. 2-5). 10.00 (*0-606-02336-4*) Turtleback Bks.

—The Mystery of the Singing Ghost. 1992. (Boxcar Children Ser.: No. 31). (Illus.). 192p. (J). (gr. 2-5). lib. bdg. 13.95 (*0-8075-5397-2*); mass mkt. 3.95 (*0-8075-5398-0*) Whitman, Albert & Co.

—The Mystery of the Stolen Boxcar. 1995. (Boxcar Children Ser.: No. 49). (J). (gr. 2-5). 10.00 (*0-606-08498-3*) Turtleback Bks.

—The Mystery of the Stolen Music. 1995. (Boxcar Children Ser.: No. 45). (J). (gr. 2-5). 10.00 (*0-606-07313-2*) Turtleback Bks.

—The Mystery of the Stolen Sword. 1998. (Boxcar Children Ser.: No. 67). (Illus.). 128p. (J). (gr. 2-5). lib. bdg. 13.95 (*0-8075-7622-0*) Whitman, Albert & Co.

—The Mystery of the Wild Ponies. 2000. (Boxcar Children Ser.: No. 77). (Illus.). 135p. (J). (gr. 2-5). lib. bdg. 13.95 (*0-8075-5465-0*); mass mkt. 3.95 (*0-8075-5466-9*) Whitman, Albert & Co.

—The Mystery on Stage. 1994. (Boxcar Children Ser.: No. 43). (J). (gr. 2-5). 10.00 (*0-606-07148-2*) Turtleback Bks.

—The Mystery on Stage. 1994. (Boxcar Children Ser.: No. 43). (Illus.). 192p. (J). (gr. 2-5). lib. bdg. 13.95 (*0-8075-5417-0*); mass mkt. 3.95 (*0-8075-5418-9*) Whitman, Albert & Co.

—The Mystery on the Ice. 1993. (Boxcar Children Special Ser.: No. 1). (J). (gr. 2-5). 10.00 (*0-606-13218-X*) Turtleback Bks.

—The Mystery on the Ice. 1993. (Boxcar Children Special Ser.: No. 1). (J). (gr. 2-5). 118p. lib. bdg. 13.95 (*0-8075-5414-6*); mass mkt. 3.95 (*0-8075-5413-8*) Whitman, Albert & Co.

—The Mystery on the Train. 1996. (Boxcar Children Ser.: No. 51). (J). (gr. 2-5). 10.00 (*0-606-08699-4*) Turtleback Bks.

—The Mystery on the Train. 1996. (Boxcar Children Ser.: No. 51). (Illus.). 128p. (J). (gr. 2-5). lib. bdg. 13.95 (*0-8075-5425-1*); mass mkt. 3.95 (*0-8075-5426-X*) Whitman, Albert & Co.

—The Niagara Falls Mystery. 1997. (Boxcar Children Ser.: No. 8). (J). (gr. 2-5). 10.00 (*0-606-11163-8*) Turtleback Bks.

—The Niagara Falls Mystery. 1997. (Boxcar Children Special Ser.: No. 8). (J). (gr. 2-5). lib. bdg. 13.95 (*0-8075-5602-5*) Whitman, Albert & Co.

—The Old Motel Mystery. 1992. (Boxcar Children Ser.: No. 23). (J). (gr. 2-5). 10.00 (*0-606-00661-3*) Turtleback Bks.

—The Old Motel Mystery. 1991. (Boxcar Children Ser.: No. 23). (Illus.). 121p. (J). (gr. 2-5). lib. bdg. 19.95 (*0-8075-5967-9*); mass mkt. 5.95 (*0-8075-5966-0*) Whitman, Albert & Co.

—The Outer Space Mystery. 1997. (Boxcar Children Ser.: No. 59). (J). (gr. 2-5). 10.00 (*0-606-11162-X*) Turtleback Bks.

—The Outer Space Mystery. 1997. (Boxcar Children Ser.: No. 59). (J). (gr. 2-5). lib. bdg. 13.95 (*0-8075-6286-6*); mass mkt. 3.95 (*0-8075-6287-4*) Whitman, Albert & Co.

—The Panther Mystery. 1998. (Boxcar Children Ser.: No. 66). (Illus.). 128p. (J). (gr. 2-5). lib. bdg. 13.95 (*0-8075-6327-7*); mass mkt. 3.95 (*0-8075-6328-5*) Whitman, Albert & Co.

—The Pet Shop Mystery. 1996. (Boxcar Children Ser.: No. 7). (J). (gr. 2-5). 10.00 (*0-606-10761-4*) Turtleback Bks.

—The Pet Shop Mystery. 1996. (Boxcar Children Special Ser.: No. 7). (Illus.). 128p. (J). (gr. 2-5). lib. bdg. 13.95 (*0-8075-6527-X*); mass mkt. 3.95 (*0-8075-6528-8*) Whitman, Albert & Co.

—The Pilgrim Village Mystery. 1995. (Boxcar Children Special Ser.: No. 5). (J). (gr. 2-5). 10.00 (*0-606-08700-1*) Turtleback Bks.

—The Pizza Mystery. 1992. (Boxcar Children Ser.: No. 33). (J). (gr. 2-5). 10.00 (*0-606-08935-7*) Turtleback Bks.

—The Poison Frog Mystery. 2000. (Boxcar Children Ser.: No. 74). (Illus.). 128p. (J). (gr. 2-5). lib. bdg. 13.95 (*0-8075-6586-5*); mass mkt. 3.95 (*0-8075-6587-3*) Whitman, Albert & Co.

—A Present for Grandfather. 1998. (Adventures of Benny & Watch: No. 2). (J). (gr. 1-3). 10.10 (*0-606-13216-3*) Turtleback Bks.

—The Soccer Mystery. 1997. (Boxcar Children Ser.: No. 60). (J). (gr. 2-5). 10.00 (*0-606-12634-1*) Turtleback Bks.

—The Soccer Mystery. 1997. (Boxcar Children Ser.: No. 60). (Illus.). 128p. (J). (gr. 2-5). lib. bdg. 13.95 (*0-8075-7528-3*); mass mkt. 3.95 (*0-8075-7527-5*) Whitman, Albert & Co.

—The Windy City Mystery. 1998. (Boxcar Children Special Ser.: No. 10). (J). (gr. 2-5). 10.00 (*0-606-13219-8*) Turtleback Bks.

—The Windy City Mystery. 1998. (Boxcar Children Special Ser.: No. 10). (Illus.). 144p. (J). (gr. 2-5). lib. bdg. 13.95 (*0-8075-5447-2*); mass mkt. 3.95 (*0-8075-5448-0*) Whitman, Albert & Co.

BRENNEN, ASHLYN (FICTITIOUS CHARACTER)—FICTION

Haynes, Betsy. Deadly Deception. 224p. (YA). (gr. 6 up). 1995. mass mkt. 3.99 o.s.i (*0-440-21947-7*); 1994. 14.95 o.s.i (*0-385-32067-1*, Delacorte Pr.) Dell Publishing.

—Deadly Deception. 1995. (YA). (gr. 7-10). 9.09 o.p. (*0-606-07423-6*) Turtleback Bks.

BRONTE, CHARLOTTE, 1816-1855—FICTION

Bedard, Michael. Glasstown. 1997. (Illus.). 40p. (J). (gr. 1-4). 16.00 (*0-689-81185-3*, Atheneum) Simon & Schuster Children's Publishing.

BROWN, AMBER (FICTITIOUS CHARACTER)—FICTION

Danziger, Paula. Ambar en Cuarto y Sin Su Amigo, Level 3.7. 2001. (SPA., Illus.). 136p. (J). (gr. 3-5). pap. 10.95 (*84-204-4412-X*, SAN412X) Alfaguara, Ediciones, S.A.- Grupo Santillana ESP. *Dist:* Lectorum Pubns., Inc., Santillana USA Publishing Co., Inc.

—Amber Brown, Set 1. 2001. (Amber Brown Ser.). (Illus.). (J). (gr. 2-5). pap. 15.96 (*0-439-26011-6*) Scholastic, Inc.

—Amber Brown Boxed Set: Amber Brown Is Not a Crayon; You Can't Eat Your Chicken Pox, Amber Brown; Amber Brown Goes Fourth; Amber Brown Wants Extra Credit. 1997. (Amber Brown Ser.: Nos.1-4). (J). (gr. 3-6). pap. 15.96 (*0-590-30018-0*) Scholastic, Inc.

—The Amber Brown Collection: Amber Brown Is Not a Crayon; You Can't Eat Your Chicken Pox, Amber Brown; Amber Brown Goes Fourth. abr. unabr. ed. 2000. (Amber Brown Ser.: Nos. 1-3). (J). (gr. 3-6). audio 18.00 (*0-8072-7814-9*, YA 923 CXR, Listening Library) Random Hse. Audio Publishing Group.

—The Amber Brown Collection II. unabr. ed. 2000. (Amber Brown Ser.). (J). (gr. 3-6). audio 23.00 o.s.i (*0-8072-8019-4*, YA968CX); audio 18.00 (*0-8072-8037-2*, YA968CXR) Random Hse. Audio Publishing Group. (Listening Library).

—Amber Brown Goes Fourth. 1999. (Amber Brown Ser.: No. 3). (J). (gr. 3-6). 11.70 (*0-613-00276-8*) Econo-Clad Bks.

—Amber Brown Goes Fourth. 1995. (Amber Brown Ser.: No. 3). (Illus.). 112p. (J). (gr. 3-6). 15.99 (*0-399-22849-7*, G. P. Putnam's Sons) Penguin Group (USA) Inc.

—Amber Brown Goes Fourth. (Amber Brown Ser.: No. 3). 112p. (J). (gr. 3-6). pap. 3.99 (*0-8072-1291-1*); 1997. pap. 17.00 incl. audio (*0-8072-0360-2*, FTR 181 SP) Random Hse. Audio Publishing Group. (Listening Library).

—Amber Brown Goes Fourth. 1996. (Amber Brown Ser.: No. 3). (Illus.). 101p. (J). (gr. 3-6). mass mkt. 2.99 (*0-590-93425-2*, Scholastic Paperbacks) Scholastic, Inc.

—Amber Brown Goes Fourth. 1996. (Amber Brown Ser.: No. 3). (J). (gr. 3-6). 9.55 (*0-606-10120-9*) Turtleback Bks.

—Amber Brown Is Feeling Blue. 1998. (Amber Brown Ser.: No. 7). (Illus.). (J). (gr. 3-6). 13.95 o.s.i (*0-399-23219-2*) Penguin Group (USA) Inc.

—Amber Brown Is Feeling Blue. 1998. (Amber Brown Ser.: No. 7). (Illus.). 128p. (J). (gr. 3-6). 14.99 (*0-399-23179-X*, G. P. Putnam's Sons) Penguin Putnam Bks. for Young Readers.

—Amber Brown Is Feeling Blue. 1999. (Amber Brown Ser.: No. 7). (Illus.). 131p. (J). (gr. 3-6). mass mkt. 3.99 (*0-439-07168-2*) Scholastic, Inc.

—Amber Brown Is Feeling Blue. 1999. (Amber Brown Ser.: No.7). (J). (gr. 3-6). 10.04 (*0-606-17275-0*) Turtleback Bks.

—Amber Brown is Green with Envy. 2003. (Illus.). 160p. (J). 15.99 (*0-399-23181-1*, G. P. Putnam's Sons) Penguin Putnam Bks. for Young Readers.

—Amber Brown Is Not a Crayon. (Amber Brown Ser.: No. 1). (J). (gr. 3-6). 11.55 (*0-7857-7523-4*) Econo-Clad Bks.

—Amber Brown Is Not a Crayon. 1994. (Amber Brown Ser.: No. 1). (Illus.). 80p. (J). (gr. 3-6). 15.99 (*0-399-22509-9*, G. P. Putnam's Sons) Penguin Group (USA) Inc.

—Amber Brown Is Not a Crayon. (Amber Brown Ser.: No. 1). 80p. (J). (gr. 3-6). pap. 3.50 (*0-8072-1289-X*); 1997. pap. 17.00 incl. audio (*0-8072-0354-8*, FTR 179 SP) Random Hse. Audio Publishing Group. (Listening Library).

—Amber Brown Is Not a Crayon. 1995. (Amber Brown Ser.: No. 1). (Illus.). 80p. (J). (gr. 3-6). mass mkt. 3.99 (*0-590-45899-X*) Scholastic, Inc.

—Amber Brown Is Not a Crayon. 1995. (Amber Brown Ser.: No. 1). (J). (gr. 3-6). 10.14 (*0-606-07185-7*) Turtleback Bks.

—Amber Brown Sees Red. (Amber Brown Ser.: No. 6). (J). (gr. 3-6). 11.70 (*0-613-09442-5*) Econo-Clad Bks.

—Amber Brown Sees Red. 1997. (Amber Brown Ser.: No. 6). (Illus.). 112p. (J). (gr. 3-6). 15.99 (*0-399-22901-9*, G. P. Putnam's Sons) Penguin Group (USA) Inc.

—Amber Brown Sees Red. (Amber Brown Ser.: No. 6). 116p. (J). (gr. 3-6). pap. 3.99 (*0-8072-1294-6*); 1998. pap. 17.00 incl. audio (*0-8072-0369-6*, FTR186SP) Random Hse. Audio Publishing Group. (Listening Library).

—Amber Brown Sees Red. 1998. (Amber Brown Ser.: No. 6). (Illus.). 116p. (J). (gr. 3-6). mass mkt. 3.99 (*0-590-94728-1*) Scholastic, Inc.

—Amber Brown Sees Red. 1998. (Amber Brown Ser.: No. 6). (J). (gr. 3-6). 10.04 (*0-606-12874-3*) Turtleback Bks.

—Amber Brown Wants Extra Credit. (Amber Brown Ser.: No. 4). (J). (gr. 3-6). 11.55 (*0-613-02015-4*) Econo-Clad Bks.

—Amber Brown Wants Extra Credit. 1996. (Amber Brown Ser.: No. 4). (Illus.). 120p. (J). (gr. 3-6). 15.99 (*0-399-22900-0*, G. P. Putnam's Sons) Penguin Group (USA) Inc.

—Amber Brown Wants Extra Credit. (Amber Brown Ser.: No. 4). 120p. (J). (gr. 3-6). pap. 3.99 (*0-8072-1292-X*); 1997. pap. 17.00 incl. audio (*0-8072-0363-7*, FTR 182 SP) Random Hse. Audio Publishing Group. (Listening Library).

—Amber Brown Wants Extra Credit. 1997. (Amber Brown Ser.: No. 4). (Illus.). 120p. (J). (gr. 3-6). mass mkt. 3.99 (*0-590-94716-8*, Scholastic Paperbacks) Scholastic, Inc.

—Amber Brown Wants Extra Credit. 1997. (Amber Brown Ser.: No. 4). (J). (gr. 3-6). 10.04 (*0-606-11035-6*) Turtleback Bks.

—Forever Amber Brown. 1999. (Amber Brown Ser.: No. 5). (J). (gr. 3-6). 11.70 (*0-613-03623-9*) Econo-Clad Bks.

—Forever Amber Brown. (Amber Brown Ser.: No. 5). 101p. (J). (gr. 3-6). pap. 3.99 (*0-8072-1293-8*); 1998. pap. 17.00 incl. audio (*0-8072-0366-1*, FTR185SP) Random Hse. Audio Publishing Group. (Listening Library).

—Forever Amber Brown. 1998. (Amber Brown Ser.: No. 5). (Illus.). 96p. (J). (gr. 3-6). mass mkt. 3.99 (*0-590-94725-7*) Scholastic, Inc.

—I, Amber Brown. 1999. (Amber Brown Ser.: No. 8). (Illus.). 144p. (J). (gr. 3-6). 14.99 (*0-399-23180-3*, Ace/Putnam) Penguin Group (USA) Inc.

—I, Amber Brown. 2000. (Amber Brown Ser.: No. 8). (J). (gr. 3-6). (*0-399-23242-7*) Putnam Publishing Group, The.

—I, Amber Brown. 2000. (Amber Brown Ser.: No. 8). (Illus.). 144p. (J). (gr. 3-6). mass mkt. 3.99 (*0-439-07169-0*, Scholastic Paperbacks) Scholastic, Inc.

—I, Amber Brown. 2000. (Amber Brown Ser.: No. 8). (Illus.). (J). (gr. 3-6). 10.04 (*0-606-18877-0*) Turtleback Bks.

—It's a Fair Day, Amber Brown. 2002. (Illus.). 48p. (J). 12.99 (*0-399-23606-6*, G. P. Putnam's Sons) Penguin Putnam Bks. for Young Readers.

—It's Justin Time, Amber Brown. 2002. (J). pap., tchr.'s planning gde. ed. 29.95 incl. audio (*0-87499-908-1*); 25.95 incl. audio (*0-87499-907-3*); 25.95 incl. audio (*0-87499-907-3*); pap. 16.95 incl. audio (*0-87499-906-5*) Live Oak Media.

—It's Justin Time, Amber Brown. 2001. (Amber Brown Ser.: No. 10). (Illus.). 48p. (J). (gr. 3-6). 12.99 (*0-399-23470-5*, G. P. Putnam's Sons) Penguin Group (USA) Inc.

—It's Justin Time, Amber Brown. 2001. 10.14 (*0-606-22522-6*) Turtleback Bks.

—What a Trip, Amber Brown. 2002. (J). pap., tchr.'s planning gde. ed. 29.95 incl. audio (*0-87499-912-X*); pap., tchr.'s planning gde. ed. 29.95 incl. audio (*0-87499-912-X*); 25.95 incl. audio (*0-87499-911-1*); 25.95 incl. audio (*0-87499-911-1*) Live Oak Media.

—What a Trip, Amber Brown. 2001. (Amber Brown Ser.: No. 9). (Illus.). 48p. (J). (gr. 3-6). 12.99 (*0-399-23469-1*, G. P. Putnam's Sons) Penguin Group (USA) Inc.

—What a Trip, Amber Brown. 2001. (Illus.). 48p. (J). pap. 3.99 (*0-698-11908-8*, Puffin Bks.) Penguin Putnam Bks. for Young Readers.

—What a Trip, Amber Brown. 2001. 10.14 (*0-606-22523-4*) Turtleback Bks.

—You Can't Eat Your Chicken Pox, Amber Brown. (Amber Brown Ser.: No. 2). (J). (gr. 3-6). 11.70 (*0-7857-7522-6*) Econo-Clad Bks.

—You Can't Eat Your Chicken Pox, Amber Brown. 1995. (Amber Brown Ser.: No. 2). (Illus.). 80p. (J). (gr. 3-6). 14.99 (*0-399-22702-4*, G. P. Putnam's Sons) Penguin Group (USA) Inc.

—You Can't Eat Your Chicken Pox, Amber Brown. (Amber Brown Ser.: No. 2). 101p. (J). (gr. 3-6). pap. 3.50 (*0-8072-1290-3*); 1997. pap. 17.00 incl. audio (*0-8072-0357-2*, FTR 180 SP) Random Hse. Audio Publishing Group. (Listening Library).

—You Can't Eat Your Chicken Pox, Amber Brown. 1996. (Amber Brown Ser.: No. 2). (Illus.). 101p. (J). (gr. 3-6). mass mkt. 4.50 (*0-590-50207-7*, Scholastic Paperbacks) Scholastic, Inc.

—You Can't Eat Your Chicken Pox, Amber Brown. 1996. (Amber Brown Ser.: No. 2). (J). (gr. 3-6). 10.04 (*0-606-08911-X*) Turtleback Bks.

BROWN, CHARLIE (FICTITIOUS CHARACTER)—FICTION

LoBianco, Peter & LoBianco, Nick, illus. It's a Home Run, Charlie Brown! 2002. (Ready-to-Read Ser.). 32p. (J). (gr. 1-4). pap. 3.99 (*0-689-84939-7*); lib. bdg. 11.89 (*0-689-85263-0*) Simon & Schuster Children's Publishing. (Little Simon).

—It's Time for School, Charlie Brown. 2002. (Ready-to-Read Ser.). 32p. (J). (gr. 1-4). lib. bdg. 11.89 (*0-689-85147-2*, Little Simon) Simon & Schuster Children's Publishing.

Schulz, Charles M. A Boy Named Charlie Brown. 2001. (Illus.). 144p. (J). 9.98 (*1-58663-188-8*, MetroBooks) Friedman, Michael Publishing Group, Inc.

—A Charlie Brown Christmas. 1967. (J). (gr. 3 up). mass mkt. 2.50 o.p. (*0-451-12307-7*, AE2307, Signet Bks.) NAL.

—A Charlie Brown Christmas. 1988. (Illus.). (J). (ps-3). pap. 2.22 o.s.i (*0-307-13723-6*, Golden Bks.) Random Hse. Children's Bks.

—A Charlie Brown Christmas. (Peanuts Ser.). (Illus.). 32p. (J). 2002. 15.95 (*0-689-85357-2*); 2001. pap. 5.99 (*0-689-84608-8*) Simon & Schuster Children's Publishing. (Little Simon).

—A Charlie Brown Thanksgiving. 1975. mass mkt. 1.25 o.p. (*0-451-06885-8*, Y6885, Signet Bks.) NAL.

—A Charlie Brown Valentine. 2002. (Peanuts Ser.). (Illus.). 32p. (J). pap. 5.99 (*0-689-84821-8*, Little Simon) Simon & Schuster Children's Publishing.

—It's the Easter Beagle, Charlie Brown. 2002. (Peanuts Ser.). (Illus.). 32p. (J). (ps-3). pap. 5.99 (*0-689-84822-6*, Little Simon) Simon & Schuster Children's Publishing.

—It's the Great Pumpkin, Charlie Brown. 2001. (Peanuts Ser.). (Illus.). 32p. (J). (ps-3). pap. 5.99 (*0-689-84607-X*, Little Simon) Simon & Schuster Children's Publishing.

—It's Time for School, Charlie Brown. 2002. (Ready-to-Read Ser.). (Illus.). 32p. (J). (gr. 1-4). pap. 3.99 (*0-689-85146-4*, Little Simon) Simon & Schuster Children's Publishing.

—Kick the Football, Charlie Brown! 2001. (Ready-to-Read Ser.). (Illus.). 32p. (J). pap. 3.99 (*0-689-84594-4*, Little Simon) Simon & Schuster Children's Publishing.

—Snoopy's Doghouse. 2003. (Illus.). 16p. (J). 10.95 (*0-689-85854-X*, Little Simon) Simon & Schuster Children's Publishing.

—Why, Charlie Brown, Why? A Story about What Happens When a Friend is Very Ill. 2002. (Illus.). 64p. 15.95 (*0-345-45531-2*) Random Hse., Inc.

—Woodstock: Peanuts Backpack Book. 2003. (Illus.). 14p. (J). mass mkt. 6.99 (*0-689-85856-6*, Little Simon) Simon & Schuster Children's Publishing.

Schulz, Charles M. & Vrato, Elizabeth, contrib. by. A Charlie Brown Christmas. 2003. 128p. (J). text 4.95 (*0-7624-1601-7*) Running Pr. Bk. Pubs.

Schulz, Charles M., et al. A Charlie Brown Thanksgiving. 2002. (Peanuts Ser.). 32p. (J). pap. 5.99 (*0-689-85027-1*, Little Simon) Simon & Schuster Children's Publishing.

BROWN, ENCYCLOPEDIA (FICTITIOUS CHARACTER)—FICTION

Encyclopedia Brown. 1999. (J). 9.95 (*1-56137-282-X*) Novel Units, Inc.

Razzi, Jim. Encyclopedia Brown's First Book of Puzzles & Games. 1984. (Encyclopedia Brown Ser.). (J). (gr. 2-6). 1.25 o.p. (*0-553-15058-8*) Bantam Bks.

—Encyclopedia Brown's Fourth Book of Games & Puzzles. 1981. (Encyclopedia Brown Ser.). 64p. (J). (gr. 2-6). pap. 1.50 o.p. (*0-553-15110-X*) Bantam Bks.

—Encyclopedia Brown's Second Book of Puzzles & Games. 1984. (Encyclopedia Brown Ser.). (J). (gr. 2-6). 1.50 o.p. (*0-553-15099-5*) Bantam Bks.

—Encyclopedia Brown's Third Book of Games & Puzzles. 1981. (Encyclopedia Brown Ser.). 64p. (J). (gr. 2-6). pap. 1.50 o.p. (*0-553-15077-4*) Bantam Bks.

Searl, Duncan. Encyclopedia Brown: Boy Detective, Level 3. Friedland, J. & Kessler, Rikki, eds. 1995. (Encyclopedia Brown Ser.: No. 1). 29p. (J). (gr. 3). pap., stu. ed. 15.95 (*1-56982-275-1*, S0449) Learning Links, Inc.

Sobol, Donald J. The Best of Encyclopedia Brown, 4 vols. (Encyclopedia Brown Ser.). (J). (gr. 2-6). 9999. (Illus.). pap. 7.80 o.p. (*0-590-00662-2*, Scholastic Paperbacks); 1986. 9.00 o.p. (*0-590-63132-2*) Scholastic, Inc.

—Case of the Sleeping Dog. 1999. (Illus.). (J). 10.65 (*0-606-18628-X*) Turtleback Bks.

—Case of the Slippery Salamander. 1999. (Illus.). (J). 10.65 (*0-606-18629-8*) Turtleback Bks.

—Encyclopedia Brown & the Case of Pablo's Nose. (Encyclopedia Brown Ser.: No. 20). (Illus.). 80p. (gr. 2-6). 1997. pap. text 4.50 (*0-553-48513-X*, Skylark); 1996. text 14.95 o.s.i (*0-385-32184-8*, Dell Books for Young Readers) Random Hse. Children's Bks.

—Encyclopedia Brown & the Case of Pablo's Nose. 1997. (Encyclopedia Brown Ser.: No. 20). (J). (gr. 2-6). 10.65 (*0-606-11298-7*) Turtleback Bks.

—Encyclopedia Brown & the Case of the Dead Eagles. (Encyclopedia Brown Ser.: No. 12). (Illus.). 96p. (J). (gr. 2-6). reprint ed. 1979. 2.98 o.p. (*0-525-67801-8*); 1975. 13.99 o.s.i (*0-525-67220-6*) Penguin Putnam Bks. for Young Readers. (Dutton Children's Bks.).

—Encyclopedia Brown & the Case of the Dead Eagles. 1984. (Encyclopedia Brown Ser.: No. 12). (Illus.). 96p. (gr. 2-6). pap. text 4.50 (*0-553-48167-3*, Skylark) Random Hse. Children's Bks.

—Encyclopedia Brown & the Case of the Dead Eagles. (Encyclopedia Brown Ser.: No. 12). (J). (gr. 2-6). 1991. pap. 2.50 o.p. (*0-590-43343-1*); 1982. pap. 1.95 o.p. (*0-590-32565-5*); 1977. pap. 2.25 o.p. (*0-590-41466-6*, Scholastic Paperbacks) Scholastic, Inc.

—Encyclopedia Brown & the Case of the Dead Eagles. 1994. (Encyclopedia Brown Ser.: No. 12). (J). (gr. 2-6). 10.65 (*0-606-05823-0*) Turtleback Bks.

—Encyclopedia Brown & the Case of the Disgusting Sneakers. 1991. (Encyclopedia Brown Ser.: No. 18). 112p. (gr. 3-7). pap. text 4.50 (*0-553-15851-1*) Bantam Bks.

—Encyclopedia Brown & the Case of the Disgusting Sneakers. 1990. (Encyclopedia Brown Ser.: No. 18). (Illus.). 96p. (J). (ps-3). 15.95 (*0-688-09012-5*) HarperCollins Children's Bk. Group.

—Encyclopedia Brown & the Case of the Disgusting Sneakers. 1991. (Encyclopedia Brown Ser.: No. 18). (J). (gr. 2-6). 10.55 (*0-606-04666-6*) Turtleback Bks.

—Encyclopedia Brown & the Case of the Exploding Plumbing & Other Stories. 1984. (Encyclopedia Brown Ser.). (J). (gr. 2-6). pap. 1.95 o.p. (*0-590-32883-2*); (Illus.). 80p. reprint ed. pap. 2.25 o.p. (*0-590-40531-4*, Scholastic Paperbacks) Scholastic, Inc.

—Encyclopedia Brown & the Case of the Jumping Frogs. 2003. (Encyclopedia Brown Ser.). (Illus.). 80p. (gr. 3-7). text 14.95 (*0-385-72931-6*); lib. bdg. 16.99 (*0-385-90148-8*, Delacorte Bks. for Young Readers) Random Hse. Children's Bks.

—Encyclopedia Brown & the Case of the Midnight Visitor. 1982. (Encyclopedia Brown Ser.: No. 13). 128p. (gr. 2-6). pap. text 4.50 (*0-553-15738-8*) Bantam Bks.

—Encyclopedia Brown & the Case of the Midnight Visitor. 1979. (Encyclopedia Brown Ser.: No. 13). (Illus.). 96p. (J). (gr. 2-6). reprint ed. 2.98 o.p. (*0-525-67806-9*, Dutton Children's Bks.) Penguin Putnam Bks. for Young Readers.

—Encyclopedia Brown & the Case of the Midnight Visitor. 1977. (Encyclopedia Brown Ser.: No. 13). (J). (gr. 2-6). 10.55 (*0-606-02101-9*) Turtleback Bks.

—Encyclopedia Brown & the Case of the Mysterious Handprints. 1985. (Encyclopedia Brown Ser.: No. 16). (Illus.). 96p. (J). (gr. 4-7). 15.95 (*0-688-04626-6*) HarperCollins Children's Bk. Group.

—Encyclopedia Brown & the Case of the Mysterious Handprints. 1986. (Encyclopedia Brown Ser.). 96p. (gr. 2-6). (J). pap. 2.25 o.s.i (*0-553-15352-8*); pap. text 4.50 (*0-553-15739-6*) Random Hse. Children's Bks. (Skylark).

—Encyclopedia Brown & the Case of the Mysterious Handprints. 1986. (Encyclopedia Brown Ser.: No. 16). (J). (gr. 2-6). 10.65 (*0-606-00643-5*) Turtleback Bks.

—Encyclopedia Brown & the Case of the Secret Pitch. 1982. (Encyclopedia Brown Ser.: No. 2). 128p. (gr. 2-6). pap. text 4.50 (*0-553-15736-1*) Bantam Bks.

—Encyclopedia Brown & the Case of the Secret Pitch. (Encyclopedia Brown Ser.: No. 2). (Illus.). 96p. (J). (gr. 2-6). reprint ed. 1979. 2.98 o.p. (*0-525-67808-5*); 1965. 13.99 (*0-525-67202-8*) Penguin Putnam Bks. for Young Readers. (Dutton Children's Bks.).

—Encyclopedia Brown & the Case of the Secret Pitch. 1982. (Encyclopedia Brown Ser.: No. 2). (J). (gr. 2-6). pap. 2.50 o.s.i (*0-553-15587-3*, Skylark) Random Hse. Children's Bks.

—Encyclopedia Brown & the Case of the Secret Pitch. 1978. (Encyclopedia Brown Ser.: No. 2). (J). (gr. 2-6). 10.55 (*0-606-01142-0*) Turtleback Bks.

—Encyclopedia Brown & the Case of the Sleeping Dog. 1999. (Encyclopedia Brown Ser.: No. 21). 80p. (gr. 3-7). pap. text 4.50 (*0-553-48517-2*) Bantam Bks.

—Encyclopedia Brown & the Case of the Sleeping Dog, No. 21. 1998. (Encyclopedia Brown Ser.: No. 21). (Illus.). 80p. (gr. 2-6). text 14.95 o.s.i (*0-385-32576-2*, Delacorte Pr.) Dell Publishing.

—Encyclopedia Brown & the Case of the Slippery Salamander. (Encyclopedia Brown Ser.: No. 22). (Illus.). 96p. 2000. (gr. 3-7). pap. text 4.50 (*0-553-48521-0*, Skylark); 1999. (gr. 2-6). text 14.95 o.s.i (*0-385-32579-7*, Dell Books for Young Readers) Random Hse. Children's Bks.

—Encyclopedia Brown & the Case of the Treasure Hunt. 1988. (Encyclopedia Brown Ser.: No. 17). (Illus.). 96p. (J). (gr. 4-7). 15.99 (*0-688-06955-X*) HarperCollins Children's Bk. Group.

—Encyclopedia Brown & the Case of the Treasure Hunt. 1989. (Encyclopedia Brown Ser.: No. 17). (Illus.). 96p. (gr. 2-6). pap. text 4.50 (*0-553-15650-0*, Skylark) Random Hse. Children's Bks.

—Encyclopedia Brown & the Case of the Treasure Hunt. (J). 1995. (Illus.). 10.65 (*0-606-20485-7*); 1989. (Encyclopedia Brown Ser.: No. 17). (gr. 2-6). 10.65 (*0-606-04103-6*) Turtleback Bks.

—Encyclopedia Brown & the Case of the Two Spies. 1995. (Encyclopedia Brown Ser.: No. 19). 80p. (gr. 2-6). pap. text 4.50 (*0-553-48297-1*) Bantam Bks.

—Encyclopedia Brown & the Case of the Two Spies. 1994. (Encyclopedia Brown Ser.: No. 19). (J). (gr. 2-6). 9.19 o.p. (*0-606-07483-X*) Turtleback Bks.

—Encyclopedia Brown, Boy Detective. 1985. (Encyclopedia Brown Ser.: No. 1). (Illus.). 128p. (gr. 2-6). pap. text 4.50 (*0-553-15724-8*) Bantam Bks.

—Encyclopedia Brown, Boy Detective. 1995. (Encyclopedia Brown Ser.: No. 1). 128p. (J). (gr. 2-6). pap. 1.99 o.s.i (*0-553-56751-9*) Dell Publishing.

—Encyclopedia Brown, Boy Detective. (Encyclopedia Brown Ser.: No. 1). (Illus.). (J). (gr. 2-6). reprint ed. 1979. 96p. 2.98 o.p. (*0-525-67800-X*); 1964. 9p. 13.99 (*0-525-67200-1*) Penguin Putnam Bks. for Young Readers. (Dutton Children's Bks.).

—Encyclopedia Brown, Boy Detective. 1998. (Encyclopedia Brown Ser.: No. 1). 144p. (gr. 2-6). mass mkt. 2.99 o.s.i (*0-440-22799-2*, Yearling) Random Hse. Children's Bks.

—Encyclopedia Brown Carries On. (Encyclopedia Brown Ser.: No. 14). (J). (gr. 2-6). 1991. 80p. mass mkt. 2.95 o.p. (*0-590-44575-8*, Scholastic Paperbacks); 1982. pap. 1.95 o.p. (*0-590-32428-4*); 1981. 80p. pap. 2.25 o.p. (*0-590-40530-6*, Scholastic Paperbacks); 1980. (Illus.). 13.39 (*0-590-07562-4*, 833583) Scholastic, Inc.

—Encyclopedia Brown Carries On. 1984. (Encyclopedia Brown Ser.: No. 14). (Illus.). 80p. (J). (gr. 2-6). text 13.95 o.s.i (*0-02-786190-2*, Simon & Schuster Children's Publishing) Simon & Schuster Children's Publishing.

—Encyclopedia Brown Finds the Clues. 1982. (Encyclopedia Brown Ser.: No. 3). (gr. 2-6). (J). pap. 2.50 o.s.i (*0-553-15570-9*); (Illus.). 128p. pap. text 4.50 (*0-553-15725-6*) Bantam Bks.

—Encyclopedia Brown Finds the Clues. (Encyclopedia Brown Ser.: No. 3). (Illus.). 96p. (J). (gr. 2-6). 1979. 2.98 o.p. (*0-525-67802-6*); 1966. 13.99 o.s.i (*0-525-67204-4*) Penguin Putnam Bks. for Young Readers. (Dutton Children's Bks.).

—Encyclopedia Brown Finds the Clues. 1978. (Encyclopedia Brown Ser.: No. 3). (J). (gr. 2-6). 10.55 (*0-606-01143-9*) Turtleback Bks.

—Encyclopedia Brown Gets His Man. 1982. (Encyclopedia Brown Ser.: No. 4). 128p. (gr. 2-6). pap. text 4.50 (*0-553-15722-1*) Bantam Bks.

—Encyclopedia Brown Gets His Man. (Encyclopedia Brown Ser.: No. 4). (Illus.). 96p. (J). (gr. 2-6). reprint ed. 1979. 2.98 o.p. (*0-525-67803-4*); 1967. 15.99 (*0-525-67206-0*) Penguin Putnam Bks. for Young Readers. (Dutton Children's Bks.).

—Encyclopedia Brown Gets His Man, Vol. 4. 1982. (Encyclopedia Brown Ser.: No. 4). 128p. (J). (gr. 2-6). pap. 2.50 o.s.i (*0-553-15526-1*, Skylark) Random Hse. Children's Bks.

—Encyclopedia Brown Gets His Man. 1978. (Encyclopedia Brown Ser.: No. 4). (J). (gr. 2-6). 10.55 (*0-606-01503-5*) Turtleback Bks.

—Encyclopedia Brown Keeps the Peace. (Encyclopedia Brown Ser.: No. 6). (Illus.). 96p. (J). (gr. 2-6). 1979. 2.98 o.p. (*0-525-67804-2*); 1969. 13.99 o.s.i (*0-525-67208-7*) Penguin Putnam Bks. for Young Readers. (Dutton Children's Bks.).

—Encyclopedia Brown Keeps the Peace. 1982. (Encyclopedia Brown Ser.: No. 6). 128p. (gr. 2-6). pap. text 4.50 (*0-553-15735-3*, Skylark) Random Hse. Children's Bks.

—Encyclopedia Brown Keeps the Peace. 1978. (Encyclopedia Brown Ser.: No. 6). (J). (gr. 2-6). 10.55 (*0-606-01504-3*) Turtleback Bks.

—Encyclopedia Brown Lends a Hand. 1993. (Encyclopedia Brown Ser.: No. 11). 96p. (gr. 2-6). pap. text 4.50 (*0-553-48133-9*) Bantam Bks.

—Encyclopedia Brown Lends a Hand. (Encyclopedia Brown Ser.: No. 11). (Illus.). 96p. (J). (gr. 2-6). reprint ed. 1979. 2.98 o.p. (*0-525-67805-0*); 1974. 13.99 o.s.i (*0-525-67218-4*) Penguin Putnam Bks. for Young Readers. (Dutton Children's Bks.).

—Encyclopedia Brown Lends a Hand. 1993. (Encyclopedia Brown Ser.: No. 11). (J). (gr. 2-6). 10.65 (*0-606-05266-6*) Turtleback Bks.

—Encyclopedia Brown Saves the Day. 1982. (Encyclopedia Brown Ser.: No. 7). 128p. (gr. 2-6). pap. text 4.50 (*0-553-15734-5*) Bantam Bks.

—Encyclopedia Brown Saves the Day. (Encyclopedia Brown Ser.: No. 7). (Illus.). 96p. (J). (gr. 2-6). reprint ed. 1979. 2.98 o.p. (*0-525-67807-7*); 1970. 13.99 o.s.i (*0-525-67210-9*) Penguin Putnam Bks. for Young Readers. (Dutton Children's Bks.).

—Encyclopedia Brown Saves the Day. 1982. (Encyclopedia Brown Ser.: No. 7). (J). (gr. 2-6). pap. 2.50 o.s.i (*0-553-15539-3*, Skylark) Random Hse. Children's Bks.

—Encyclopedia Brown Saves the Day. 1971. (Encyclopedia Brown Ser.: No. 7). (J). (gr. 2-6). 10.55 (*0-606-03149-9*) Turtleback Bks.

—Encyclopedia Brown Sets the Pace. (Encyclopedia Brown Ser.: No. 15). (J). (gr. 2-6). 1991. 96p. pap. 4.50 (*0-590-44577-4*, Scholastic Paperbacks); 1989. pap. 2.50 o.p. (*0-590-43436-5*) Scholastic, Inc.

—Encyclopedia Brown Sets the Pace. 1984. (Encyclopedia Brown Ser.: No. 15). (Illus.). 96p. (J). (gr. 2-6). 13.95 o.p. (*0-02-786200-3*, Simon & Schuster Children's Publishing) Simon & Schuster Children's Publishing.

—Encyclopedia Brown Sets the Pace. 1982. (Encyclopedia Brown Ser.: No. 15). (J). (gr. 2-6). 10.65 (*0-606-03403-X*) Turtleback Bks.

—Encyclopedia Brown Shows the Way. (Encyclopedia Brown Ser.: No. 9). (Illus.). 96p. (J). (gr. 2-6). reprint ed. 1979. 2.98 o.p. (*0-525-67809-3*); 1972. 14.99 o.s.i (*0-525-67216-8*) Penguin Putnam Bks. for Young Readers. (Dutton Children's Bks.).

—Encyclopedia Brown Shows the Way. 1982. (Encyclopedia Brown Ser.: No. 9). 128p. (gr. 2-6). pap. text 4.50 (*0-553-15737-X*, Skylark) Random Hse. Children's Bks.

—Encyclopedia Brown Shows the Way. 1977. (Encyclopedia Brown Ser.: No. 9). (Illus.). (J). (gr. 2-6). pap. (*0-671-29863-1*, Simon Pulse) Simon & Schuster Children's Publishing.

—Encyclopedia Brown Shows the Way. 1981. (Encyclopedia Brown Ser.: No. 9). (J). (gr. 2-6). 10.55 (*0-606-02102-7*) Turtleback Bks.

—Encyclopedia Brown Solves Them All. 1992. (Encyclopedia Brown Ser.: No. 5). 96p. (gr. 2-6). pap. text 4.50 (*0-553-48080-4*) Bantam Bks.

—Encyclopedia Brown Solves Them All. (Encyclopedia Brown Ser.: No. 5). (Illus.). 96p. (J). (gr. 2-6). reprint ed. 1979. 2.98 o.p. (*0-525-67810-7*); 1968. 14.99 (*0-525-67212-5*) Penguin Putnam Bks. for Young Readers. (Dutton Children's Bks.).

—Encyclopedia Brown Solves Them All. (Encyclopedia Brown Ser.: No. 5). (J). (gr. 2-6). 1978. pap. 1.95 o.p. (*0-590-32884-0*); 1977. 96p. mass mkt. 2.25 o.p. (*0-590-40470-9*, Scholastic Paperbacks) Scholastic, Inc.

—Encyclopedia Brown Solves Them All. 1993. (Encyclopedia Brown Ser.: No. 5). (J). (gr. 2-6). 10.65 (*0-606-02632-0*) Turtleback Bks.

—Encyclopedia Brown Takes the Cake! A Cook & Case Book. (Encyclopedia Brown Ser.: No. 15.5). (J). (gr. 2-6). 1991. 128p. pap. 4.50 (*0-590-44576-6*); 1983. (Illus.). 13.39 (*0-590-07843-7*, 833794) Scholastic, Inc.

—Encyclopedia Brown Takes the Case. 1982. (Encyclopedia Brown Ser.: No. 10). (gr. 2-6). (J). pap. 2.50 o.s.i (*0-553-15528-8*); 128p. pap. text 4.50 (*0-553-15723-X*) Bantam Bks.

—Encyclopedia Brown Takes the Case. (Encyclopedia Brown Ser.: No. 10). (Illus.). 96p. (J). (gr. 2-6). reprint ed. 1979. 2.98 o.p. (*0-525-67811-5*); 1973. 14.99 (*0-525-66318-5*) Penguin Putnam Bks. for Young Readers. (Dutton Children's Bks.).

—Encyclopedia Brown Takes the Case. 1979. (Encyclopedia Brown Ser.: No. 10). (J). (gr. 2-6). pap. (*0-671-56016-6*, Simon Pulse) Simon & Schuster Children's Publishing.

—Encyclopedia Brown Takes the Case. 1981. (Encyclopedia Brown Ser.: No. 10). (J). (gr. 2-6). 10.55 (*0-606-03152-9*) Turtleback Bks.

—Encyclopedia Brown Tracks Them Down. 1982. (Encyclopedia Brown Ser.: No. 8). (gr. 2-6). 96p. (J). pap. 2.50 o.s.i (*0-553-15525-3*); 128p. pap. text 4.50 (*0-553-15721-3*) Bantam Bks.

—Encyclopedia Brown Tracks Them Down. 1979. (Encyclopedia Brown Ser.: No. 8). (Illus.). 96p. (J). (gr. 2-6). reprint ed. 2.98 o.p. (*0-525-67812-3*, Dutton Children's Bks.) Penguin Putnam Bks. for Young Readers.

—Encyclopedia Brown Tracks Them Down. 1977. (Encyclopedia Brown Ser.: No. 8). (J). (gr. 2-6). pap. (*0-671-29860-7*, Simon Pulse) Simon & Schuster Children's Publishing.

—Encyclopedia Brown Tracks Them Down. 1982. (Encyclopedia Brown Ser.: No. 8). (J). (gr. 2-6). 10.55 (*0-606-02103-5*) Turtleback Bks.

—Encyclopedia Brown Tracks Them down. 1971. (Encyclopedia Brown Ser.: No. 8). (Illus.). 96p. (J). (gr. 2-6). reprint ed. 14.99 (*0-525-67214-1*, Dutton Children's Bks.) Penguin Putnam Bks. for Young Readers.

—Encyclopedia Brown's Book of Strange but True Crimes. 1991. (Encyclopedia Brown Ser.). (J). (gr. 2-6). 10.55 (*0-606-01825-5*) Turtleback Bks.

—Encyclopedia Brown's Book of Strange but True Facts. 1991. (Encyclopedia Brown Ser.). (J). (gr. 2-6). pap. 12.95 o.p. (*0-590-44147-7*) Scholastic, Inc.

—Encyclopedia Brown's Book of Wacky Animals. 1985. (Encyclopedia Brown Ser.). (Illus.). 128p. (J). (gr. 2-6). 11.95 o.p. (*0-688-04152-3*, Morrow, William & Co.) Morrow/Avon.

—Encyclopedia Brown's Book of Wacky Animals. 1985. (Encyclopedia Brown Ser.). 128p. (J). (gr. 2-6). pap. 2.25 o.s.i (*0-553-15346-3*, Skylark) Random Hse. Children's Bks.

—Encyclopedia Brown's Book of Wacky Cars. 1987. (Encyclopedia Brown Ser.). (Illus.). 128p. (J). (gr. 2-6). 11.95 o.p. (*0-688-06222-9*, Morrow, William & Co.) Morrow/Avon.

—Encyclopedia Brown's Book of Wacky Cars. 1987. (Encyclopedia Brown Ser.). (Illus.). 128p. (J). (gr. 2-6). pap. 2.75 o.s.i (*0-553-15512-1*, Skylark) Random Hse. Children's Bks.

—Encyclopedia Brown's Book of Wacky Crimes. 1985. (Encyclopedia Brown Ser.). (Illus.). (J). (gr. 2-6). pap. 2.25 o.s.i (*0-553-15358-7*) Bantam Bks.

—Encyclopedia Brown's Book of Wacky Crimes. 1982. (Encyclopedia Brown Ser.). (Illus.). 12p. (J). (gr. 2-6). 12.95 o.p. (*0-525-66786-5*, Dutton Children's Bks.) Penguin Putnam Bks. for Young Readers.

—Encyclopedia Brown's Book of Wacky Spies. 1984. (Encyclopedia Brown Ser.). (Illus.). 128p. (J). (gr. 2-6). 15.00 o.p. (*0-688-02744-X*, Morrow, William & Co.) Morrow/Avon.

—Encyclopedia Brown's Book of Wacky Spies. 1984. (Encyclopedia Brown Ser.). (Illus.). 112p. (J). (gr. 2-6). pap. 2.25 o.s.i (*0-553-15369-2*, Skylark) Random Hse. Children's Bks.

—Encyclopedia Brown's Book of Wacky Sports. 1984. (Encyclopedia Brown Ser.). (Illus.). 128p. (J). (gr. 2-6). 16.00 (*0-688-03884-0*, Morrow, William & Co.) Morrow/Avon.

—Encyclopedia Brown's Book of Wacky Sports. 1984. (Encyclopedia Brown Ser.). (Illus.). 128p. (J). (gr. 2-6). pap. 2.50 o.s.i (*0-553-15497-4*, Skylark) Random Hse. Children's Bks.

—Encyclopedia Brown's Second Record Book of Weird & Wonderful Facts. 1981. (Encyclopedia Brown Ser.). (Illus.). 160p. (J). (gr. 2-6). 10.95 o.s.i (*0-385-28243-5*, Delacorte Pr.) Dell Publishing.

—Encyclopedia Brown's Third Record Book of Weird & Wonderful Facts. 1985. (Encyclopedia Brown Ser.). (Illus.). 144p. (J). (gr. 2-6). 11.95 o.p. (*0-688-05705-5*, Morrow, William & Co.) Morrow/Avon.

—Encyclopedia Brown's Third Record Book of Weird & Wonderful Facts. 1985. (Encyclopedia Brown Ser.). 144p. (J). (gr. 2-6). pap. 2.50 o.s.i (*0-553-15372-2*, Skylark) Random Hse. Children's Bks.

Sobol, Donald J. & Andrews, Glenn. Encyclopedia Brown Takes the Cake! A Cook & Case Book. 1984. (Encyclopedia Brown Ser.: No. 15.5). (J). (gr. 2-6). pap. 2.50 o.p. (*0-590-42901-9*); (Illus.). 128p. mass mkt. 2.25 o.p. (*0-590-40220-X*, Scholastic Paperbacks) Scholastic, Inc.

—Encyclopedia Brown Takes the Cake! A Cook & Case Book. 1984. (Encyclopedia Brown Ser.: No. 15.5). (Illus.). 128p. (J). (gr. 2-6). text 13.95 o.s.i (*0-02-786210-0*, Simon & Schuster Children's Publishing) Simon & Schuster Children's Publishing.

Sobol, Donald J. & Sobol, Rose. Encyclopedia Brown's Book of Strange but True Crimes. 1992. (Encyclopedia Brown Ser.). 128p. (J). (gr. 2-6). pap. 4.50 (*0-590-44148-5*, Scholastic Paperbacks) Scholastic, Inc.

Sobol, Donald J. & Velasquez, Eric. Eb & the Case of the Two Spies. 1994. (Encyclopedia Brown Ser.: No. 19). 80p. (J). (gr. 2-6). 13.95 o.s.i (*0-385-32036-1*, Delacorte Pr.) Dell Publishing.

BUDGIE, THE HELICOPTER (FICTITIOUS CHARACTER)—FICTION

Budgie Bedtime Book. 1999. (J). 15.00 (*0-689-81313-9*, Simon Spotlight) Simon & Schuster Children's Publishing.

Dutchess of York. Budgie the Little Helicopter. 1989. (Illus.). 40p. (J). (ps-1). mass mkt. 14.00 (*0-671-67683-0*, Simon & Schuster Children's Publishing) Simon & Schuster Children's Publishing.

Ferguson, Sarah. Budgie & the Blizzard. 1991. (Illus.). 40p. (J). (ps-1). pap. 14.00 o.p. (*0-671-73475-X*, Simon & Schuster Children's Publishing) Simon & Schuster Children's Publishing.

—Budgie Book, 1 cass. 1996. (J). 9.99 incl. audio (*0-689-80916-6*, Simon Spotlight) Simon & Schuster Children's Publishing.

—Budgie Goes to Sea. (Illus.). 40p. (J). (ps-1). 1996. pap. 5.99 (*0-689-80850-X*, Simon Spotlight); 1991. mass mkt. 13.00 (*0-671-73474-1*, Simon & Schuster Children's Publishing) Simon & Schuster Children's Publishing.

Krieger, Ellen & Ferguson, Sarah. Budgie & the Blizzard. 1996. (Illus.). 40p. (J). (ps-1). pap. 5.95 (*0-689-80817-8*, Simon Spotlight) Simon & Schuster Children's Publishing.

—Budgie the Little Helicopter. 1996. (Illus.). (J). pap. 5.95 (*0-689-80816-X*, Simon Spotlight) Simon & Schuster Children's Publishing.

BUFFY, THE VAMPIRE SLAYER (FICTITIOUS CHARACTER)—FICTION

Archway Press, Inc. Staff. The Essential Angel: A Poster Book. 1999. (Buffy the Vampire Slayer Ser.). (Illus.). 32p. (YA). (gr. 4-7). pap. 7.99 o.s.i (*0-671-03653-X*, Simon Pulse) Simon & Schuster Children's Publishing.

Boris, Cynthia. Pop Quiz. 1999. (Buffy the Vampire Slayer Ser.). (Illus.). 176p. (J). (gr. 7-12). mass mkt. 4.99 (*0-671-04258-0*, Simon Pulse) Simon & Schuster Children's Publishing.

Brereton, Dan & Ketcham, Rick. The Dust Waltz. 1998. (Buffy the Vampire Slayer Ser.). (Illus.). 80p. (YA). (gr. 7 up). pap. 9.95 (*1-56971-342-1*) Dark Horse Comics.

Buffy. 2002. (Buffy the Vampire Slayer Ser.: Vol. 19). (J). E-Book (*0-7434-2773-4*, Simon Pulse) Simon & Schuster Children's Publishing.

Buffy: Scriptbook Season 2. 2003. (Buffy the Vampire Slayer Ser.). (Illus.). 288p. (YA). pap. 14.99 (*0-689-85761-6*, Simon Pulse) Simon & Schuster Children's Publishing.

Buffy the Vampire Slayer. 1999. (Illus.). 144p. (YA). 10.95 o.p. (*0-7683-3639-2*) CEDCO Publishing.

Buffy the Vampire Slayer. 1998. pap. 12.99 o.p. (*1-56649-021-9*) Welcome Rain Pubs.

Buffy, the Vampire Slayer. 2002. (Buffy the Vampire Slayer Ser.: Vol. 18). (J). E-Book (*0-7434-2770-X*, Simon Pulse) Simon & Schuster Children's Publishing.

Buffy the Vampire Slayer: The Postcards. 1999. (Illus.). 44p. (J). pap. 8.00 (*0-671-03640-8*, Simon Pulse) Simon & Schuster Children's Publishing.

Buffy the Vampire Slayer Staff. The Script Book: Season Two. 2001. (Buffy the Vampire Slayer Ser.). 400p. (YA). pap. 14.00 (*0-7434-1014-9*, Simon Pulse) Simon & Schuster Children's Publishing.

Ciencin, Scott. Sweet Sixteen. 2002. (Buffy the Vampire Slayer Ser.: Bk. 24). (Illus.). 240p. (YA). pap. 5.99 (*0-7434-2732-7*, Simon Pulse) Simon & Schuster Children's Publishing.

Ciencin, Scott & Ciencin, Denise. Mortal Fear. 2003. (Buffy the Vampire Slayer Ser.). (Illus.). 496p. (YA). mass mkt. 6.99 (*0-7434-2771-8*, Simon Pulse) Simon & Schuster Children's Publishing.

Collins, Craig, et al. Visitors. 1999. (Buffy the Vampire Slayer Ser.: No. 9). 176p. (YA). (gr. 7 up). pap. 4.99 (*0-671-02628-3*, Simon Pulse) Simon & Schuster Children's Publishing.

Cover, Arthur Byron. Night of the Living Rerun. 1998. (Buffy the Vampire Slayer Ser.: No. 4). 192p. (YA). (gr. 7 up). mass mkt. 4.99 (*0-671-01715-2*, Simon Pulse) Simon & Schuster Children's Publishing.

Cusick, Richie Tankersley. Buffy the Vampire Slayer. 1993. (J). 14.95 o.p. (*1-55800-653-2*) NewStar Media, Inc.

—Buffy the Vampire Slayer. 1997. 192p. (J). (gr. 8-12). mass mkt. 5.99 (*0-671-01700-4*, Simon Pulse) Simon & Schuster Children's Publishing.

—Buffy the Vampire Slayer. MacDonald, Patricia, ed. 1992. 192p. (J). (gr. 7 up). mass mkt. 3.99 (*0-671-79220-2*, Simon Pulse) Simon & Schuster Children's Publishing.

—The Harvest. 1997. (Buffy the Vampire Slayer Ser.: No. 1). 160p. (YA). (gr. 7 up). pap. 5.99 (*0-671-01712-8*, Simon Pulse) Simon & Schuster Children's Publishing.

DeCandido, Keith R. A. The Xander Years, 1999. (Buffy the Vampire Slayer Ser.: No. 1). (Illus.). 240p. (YA). (gr. 7 up). mass mkt. 4.99 (*0-671-02629-1*, Simon Pulse) Simon & Schuster Children's Publishing.

Dokey, Cameron. Here Be Monsters. (Buffy the Vampire Slayer Ser.: No. 16). (YA). (gr. 7 up). 2000. 192p. mass mkt. 5.99 (*0-671-03921-0*); 2001. reprint ed. E-Book 5.99 (*0-7434-3125-1*) Simon & Schuster Children's Publishing. (Simon Pulse).

Fassbender, Tom, et al. Buffy the Vampire Slayer: Creatures of Habit. Allie, Scott, ed. Fassbender, Tom, tr. 2002. (Illus.). 96p. pap. 17.95 (*1-56971-563-7*) Dark Horse Comics.

Gallagher, Diana G. Obsidian Fate. 1999. (Buffy the Vampire Slayer Ser.: No. 7). 304p. (YA). mass mkt. 5.99 (*0-671-03929-6*, Simon Pulse) Simon & Schuster Children's Publishing.

—Prime Evil. 2000. (Buffy the Vampire Slayer Ser.: No. 10). 272p. (YA). pap. 5.99 (*0-671-03930-X*, Simon Pulse) Simon & Schuster Children's Publishing.

Gardner, Craig Shaw. Return to Chaos. 1998. (Buffy the Vampire Slayer Ser.: No. 2). 304p. (YA). pap. 5.99 (*0-671-02136-2*, Simon Pulse) Simon & Schuster Children's Publishing.

Garton, Ray. Resurrecting Ravana. 2000. (Buffy the Vampire Slayer Ser.: No. 9). 320p. (YA). pap. 5.99 (*0-671-02636-4*, Simon Pulse) Simon & Schuster Children's Publishing.

—Resurrecting Ravana. 1999. (Buffy the Vampire Slayer Ser.: No. 9). (Illus.). 12.04 (*0-606-18366-3*) Turtleback Bks.

Gilman, Laura Anne. Deep Water. 2000. (Buffy the Vampire Slayer Ser.: No. 14). (Illus.). (YA). (gr. 7 up). 11.04 (*0-606-18365-5*) Turtleback Bks.

Gilman, Laura Anne & Sherman, Josepha. Deep Water. 2000. (Buffy the Vampire Slayer Ser.: No. 14). 192p. (YA). (gr. 7 up). pap. 5.99 (*0-671-03919-9*, Simon Pulse) Simon & Schuster Children's Publishing.

Golden, Christopher. The Dark Times. 2001. (Buffy the Vampire Slayer Ser.: Vol. 2). 144p. (YA). pap. 2.99 (*0-7434-1186-2*, Simon Pulse) Simon & Schuster Children's Publishing.

—The King of the Dead. 2001. (Buffy the Vampire Slayer Ser.). E-Book 2.99 (*0-7434-3134-0*); 144p. (YA). pap. 2.99 (*0-7434-1187-0*) Simon & Schuster Children's Publishing. (Simon Pulse).

—Lost Slayer Pt. 1: The Prophecies. 2001. (Buffy the Vampire Slayer Ser.). reprint ed. E-Book 2.99 (*0-7434-3132-4*, Simon Pulse) Simon & Schuster Children's Publishing.

—The Lost Slayer Pt. 2: Dark Times. 2001. (Buffy the Vampire Slayer Ser.). reprint ed. E-Book 2.99 (*0-7434-3133-2*, Simon Pulse) Simon & Schuster Children's Publishing.

—The Lost Slayer Bind Up. 2003. (Buffy the Vampire Slayer Ser.). 592p. mass mkt. 6.99 (*0-7434-1226-5*, Simon Pulse) Simon & Schuster Children's Publishing.

—The Original Sins. 2001. (Buffy the Vampire Slayer Ser.). E-Book 2.99 (*0-7434-3135-9*); 192p. (YA). pap. 2.99 (*0-7434-1188-9*) Simon & Schuster Children's Publishing. (Simon Pulse).

—Oz: Into the Wild. 2002. (Buffy the Vampire Slayer Ser.). 288p. pap. 6.99 (*0-7434-0038-0*, Simon Pulse) Simon & Schuster Children's Publishing.

—Prophecies. 2001. (Buffy the Vampire Slayer Ser.: Vol. 1). 144p. (YA). mass mkt. 2.99 (*0-7434-1185-4*, Simon Pulse) Simon & Schuster Children's Publishing.

—Sins of the Father. 1999. (Buffy the Vampire Slayer Ser.: No. 8). 304p. (YA). mass mkt. 5.99 (*0-671-03928-8*, Simon Pulse) Simon & Schuster Children's Publishing.

—Spike & Dru: Pretty Maids All in a Row. 2000. (Buffy the Vampire Slayer Ser.). (Illus.). 320p. (YA). (gr. 8-12). 22.95 (*0-7434-0046-1*, Simon Pulse) Simon & Schuster Children's Publishing.

—The Watcher's Guide. 1999. (YA). mass mkt. 29.99 incl. audio compact disk (*0-671-04219-X*, Simon Pulse) Simon & Schuster Children's Publishing.

—The Wisdom of War. 2002. (Buffy the Vampire Slayer Ser.). 416p. (YA). pap. 6.99 (*0-7434-2760-2*, Simon Pulse) Simon & Schuster Children's Publishing.

Golden, Christopher & Holder, Nancy. Buffy the Vampire Slayer: Immortal. abr. ed. 1999. 18.00 (*0-671-04655-1*, Simon & Schuster Audioworks) Simon & Schuster Audio.

—Child of the Hunt. 1998. (Buffy the Vampire Slayer Ser.: No. 1). 336p. (YA). mass mkt. 5.99 (*0-671-02135-4*, Simon Pulse) Simon & Schuster Children's Publishing.

—The Gatekeeper Trilogy Book 3: Sons of Entropy, 3 vols. 1999. (Buffy the Vampire Slayer Ser.: No. 5). 336p. (YA). pap. 6.99 (*0-671-02750-6*, Simon Pulse) Simon & Schuster Children's Publishing.

—Ghost Roads, 3 vols. 1999. (Buffy the Vampire Slayer Ser.: No. 2). 384p. (YA). mass mkt. 6.99 (*0-671-02749-2*, Simon Pulse) Simon & Schuster Children's Publishing.

—Halloween Rain. 1997. (Buffy the Vampire Slayer Ser.: No. 2). 176p. (YA). (gr. 7 up). mass mkt. 5.99 (*0-671-01713-6*, Simon Pulse) Simon & Schuster Children's Publishing.

—Immortal. 2000. (Buffy the Vampire Slayer Ser.). 320p. (YA). reprint ed. pap. 5.99 (*0-671-04175-4*, Simon Pulse) Simon & Schuster Children's Publishing.

—The Official Sunnydale High School Yearbook. 1999. (Buffy the Vampire Slayer Ser.). (Illus.). 112p. (YA). (gr. 7 up). 16.95 (*0-671-03541-X*, Simon Pulse) Simon & Schuster Children's Publishing.

—The Watcher's Guide. rev. ed. 1998. (Buffy the Vampire Slayer Ser.). (Illus.). 304p. pap. 17.95 (*0-671-02433-7*, Simon Pulse) Simon & Schuster Children's Publishing.

Golden, Christopher, et al. The Blood of Carthage. 2001. (Buffy the Vampire Slayer Ser.). 128p. pap. 12.95 (*1-56971-534-3*) Dark Horse Comics.

—Blooded. 1998. (Buffy the Vampire Slayer Ser.: No. 5). 288p. (YA). (gr. 7 up). mass mkt. 4.99 (*0-671-02134-6*, Simon Pulse) Simon & Schuster Children's Publishing.

—How I Survived My Summer Vacation. 2000. (Buffy the Vampire Slayer Ser.: No. 17). 288p. (YA). (gr. 7 up). pap. 5.99 (*0-7434-0040-2*, Simon Pulse) Simon & Schuster Children's Publishing.

—The Origin. 1999. (Buffy the Vampire Slayer Ser.). 80p. (YA). (gr. 7 up). pap. 9.95 (*1-56971-429-0*) Dark Horse Comics.

—Out of the Madhouse, 1999. (Buffy the Vampire Slayer Ser.: No. 1). 384p. (YA). mass mkt. 5.99 (*0-671-02434-5*, Simon Pulse) Simon & Schuster Children's Publishing.

Holder, Nancy. The Angel Chronicles. (Buffy the Vampire Slayer Ser.). 2001. 224p. (J). E-Book 5.99 (*0-7434-3115-4*); 1999. (Illus.). 192p. (YA). (gr. 7 up). mass mkt. 4.99 (*0-671-02631-3*); Vol. 1. 1998. (Illus.). 224p. (YA). (gr. 7 up). mass mkt. 5.99 (*0-671-02133-8*) Simon & Schuster Children's Publishing. (Simon Pulse).

—Chosen: The One. novel ed. 2003. (Buffy the Vampire Slayer Ser.). 688p. (YA). mass mkt. 7.99 (*0-689-86625-9*, Simon Pulse) Simon & Schuster Children's Publishing.

—The Evil That Men Do. 2000. (Buffy the Vampire Slayer Ser.: No. 6). 352p. (YA). mass mkt. 6.99 (*0-671-02635-6*, Simon Pulse) Simon & Schuster Children's Publishing.

Holder, Nancy & Mariotte, Jeff. The Unseen Book 1: The Burning. 2001. (Buffy the Vampire Slayer & Angel Crossover Ser.: No. 1). reprint ed. E-Book 6.99 (*0-7434-3289-4*, Simon Pulse) Simon & Schuster Children's Publishing.

—The Unseen Book 2: Door to Alternity. 2001. (Buffy the Vampire Slayer & Angel Crossover Ser.: No. 2). reprint ed. E-Book 6.99 (*0-7434-3290-8*, Simon Pulse) Simon & Schuster Children's Publishing.

—The Unseen Book 3: The Long Way Home. 2001. (Buffy the Vampire Slayer & Angel Crossover Ser.: No. 3). reprint ed. E-Book 6.99 (*0-7434-3291-6*, Simon Pulse) Simon & Schuster Children's Publishing.

Holder, Nancy, et al. Tales of the Slayer. 2001. (Buffy the Vampire Slayer Ser.: Vol. 22). 288p. (YA). pap. 9.00 (*0-7434-0045-3*, Simon Pulse) Simon & Schuster Children's Publishing.

—The Watcher's Guide. 2000. (Buffy the Vampire Slayer Ser.: Vol. 2). (Illus.). 304p. (YA). pap. 17.95 (*0-671-04260-2*, Simon Pulse) Simon & Schuster Children's Publishing.

Koogler, Dori & McConnell, Ashley. These Our Actors. 2002. (Buffy the Vampire Slayer Ser.: Vol. 16). 320p. pap. 6.99 (*0-7434-0037-2*, Simon Pulse) Simon & Schuster Children's Publishing.

Mariotte, Jeff, contrib. by. The Xander Years, Vol. 2. 2000. (Buffy the Vampire Slayer Ser.: No. 15). (Illus.). 224p. (YA). (gr. 7 up). pap. 4.99 (*0-671-03920-2*, Simon Pulse) Simon & Schuster Children's Publishing.

Massie, Elizabeth. Power of Persuasion. (Buffy the Vampire Slayer Ser.: No. 12). 208p. 2001. (J). E-Book 4.99 (*0-7434-3121-9*); 1999. (YA). (gr. 7 up). pap. 5.99 (*0-671-02632-1*) Simon & Schuster Children's Publishing. (Simon Pulse).

Moesta, Rebecca. Little Things. 2002. (Buffy the Vampire Slayer Ser.: Bk. 26). 208p. (YA). pap. 5.99 (*0-7434-2736-X*, Simon Pulse) Simon & Schuster Children's Publishing.

Navarro, Yvonne. Paleo. 2000. (Buffy the Vampire Slayer Ser.: No. 11). 272p. (J). pap. 6.99 (*0-7434-0034-8*, Simon Pulse) Simon & Schuster Children's Publishing.

—Tempted Champions. 2002. (Buffy the Vampire Slayer Ser.: Vol. 13). (Illus.). 256p. (YA). pap. 6.99 (*0-7434-0036-4*, Simon Pulse) Simon & Schuster Children's Publishing.

—The Willow Files, Vol. 2. (Buffy the Vampire Slayer Ser.: No. 20). (YA). (gr. 7 up). E-Book 5.99 (*1-58945-554-1*) Adobe Systems, Inc.

—The Willow Files, Vol. 1. 1999. (Buffy the Vampire Slayer Ser.: No. 13). (Illus.). 208p. (YA). (gr. 7 up). pap. 4.99 (*0-671-03918-0*, Simon Pulse) Simon & Schuster Children's Publishing.

—The Willow Files, Vol. 1. 1999. (Buffy the Vampire Slayer Ser.: No. 13). (Illus.). (YA). (gr. 7 up). 11.04 (*0-606-18367-1*) Turtleback Bks.

Odom, Mel. Buffy the Vampire Slayer: Unnatural Selection. 1999. (J). 11.04 (*0-606-17065-0*) Turtleback Bks.

—Crossings. 2002. (Buffy the Vampire Slayer Ser.: Bk. 25). (Illus.). 256p. (YA). pap. 5.99 (*0-7434-2734-3*, Simon Pulse) Simon & Schuster Children's Publishing.

—Cursed. 2003. (Buffy the Vampire Slayer & Angel Crossover Ser.). (Illus.). 448p. (YA). mass mkt. 6.99 (*0-689-86437-X*, Simon Pulse) Simon & Schuster Children's Publishing.

—Unnatural Selection. 1999. (Buffy the Vampire Slayer Ser.: No. 10). 224p. (YA). (gr. 7 up). pap. 4.99 (*0-671-02630-5*, Simon Pulse) Simon & Schuster Children's Publishing.

Passarella, John. Ghoul Trouble. 2000. (Buffy the Vampire Slayer Ser.: No. 18). (Illus.). 256p. (YA). (gr. 7 up). pap. 5.99 (*0-7434-0042-9*, Simon Pulse) Simon & Schuster Children's Publishing.

Pelucir, Talis. The Buffy the Vampire Slayer New & Improved Internet Guide. 2000. 38p. pap. 10.00 o.p. (*1-883573-48-3*, Lightning Rod Limited) Windstorm Creative Ltd.

Petrie, Doug & Sook, Ryan. A Ring of Fire: Buffy the Vampire Slayer. 2000. (Buffy the Vampire Slayer Ser.). (Illus.). 80p. (YA). (gr. 7 up). pap. 9.95 (*1-56971-482-7*) Dark Horse Comics.

Pocket, G. Buffy the Vampire Slayer: Untitled G. Pocket. 2003. (Buffy the Vampire Slayer Ser.: Vol. 16). (Illus.). 304p. (YA). mass mkt. 6.99 (*0-7434-0039-9*, Simon Pulse) Simon & Schuster Children's Publishing.

Pocket, Gertrude. Buffy Fan Book. 2001. (Buffy the Vampire Slayer Ser.). E-Book 5.99 (*0-7434-3131-6*, Simon Pulse) Simon & Schuster Children's Publishing.

Scott, Stefanie. Meet the Stars of Buffy the Vampire Slayer. 1998. (Illus.). 128p. (J). (gr. 6-8). mass mkt. 4.99 (*0-590-51477-6*) Scholastic, Inc.

Script Books, Season Two, Vol. 1. 2001. (Buffy the Vampire Slayer Ser.). 352p. (YA). reprint ed. E-Book 14.00 (*0-7434-2784-X*, Simon Pulse) Simon & Schuster Children's Publishing.

Simon and Schuster Children's Staff. Buffy the Vampire Slayer Vol. 2: The Script Book, Season Three. 2003. (Buffy the Vampire Slayer Ser.). (Illus.). 336p. (YA). pap. 14.99 (*0-689-86346-2*, Simon Pulse) Simon & Schuster Children's Publishing.

Simon and Schuster Children's Staff, ed. Tales of the Slayer. 2003. (Buffy the Vampire Slayer Ser.). (Illus.). (YA). Vol. II. 368p. pap. 9.99 (*0-7434-2744-0*); Vol. 3. 336p. pap. 9.99 (*0-689-86436-1*) Simon & Schuster Children's Publishing. (Simon Pulse).

Stafford, Nikki. Bite Me! An Unofficial Guide to the World of Buffy the Vampire Slayer. 1998. (Illus.). 200p. (J). pap. 14.95 (*1-55022-361-5*) ECW Pr. CAN. *Dist:* LPC/InBook.

Tankersley, Richie. The Angel Chronicles, Vol. 2. 1998. (Buffy the Vampire Slayer Ser.: No. 7). (Illus.). 240p. (YA). (gr. 7 up). mass mkt. 5.99 (*0-671-02627-5*, Simon Pulse) Simon & Schuster Children's Publishing.

Tracy, Kathleen. The Girl's Got Bite: The Unofficial Guide to Buffy's World. 1998. (Illus.). 256p. pap. 14.95 o.p. (*1-58063-035-9*, Renaissance Bks.) St. Martin's Pr.

Vornholt, John. Coyote Moon. 1998. (Buffy the Vampire Slayer Ser.: No. 3). 176p. (YA). (gr. 7 up). pap. 4.99 (*0-671-01714-4*, Simon Pulse) Simon & Schuster Children's Publishing.

—Seven Crows. 2003. (Buffy the Vampire Slayer & Angel Crossover Ser.). (Illus.). 288p. (YA). mass mkt. 6.99 (*0-689-86014-5*, Simon Pulse) Simon & Schuster Children's Publishing.

Watson, Andi, et al. Bad Blood. 2000. (Buffy the Vampire Slayer Ser.). (Illus.). 88p. (YA). (gr. 7 up). pap. 9.95 (*1-56971-445-2*) Dark Horse Comics.

—Crash Test Demons. 2000. (Buffy the Vampire Slayer Ser.). (Illus.). 80p. (YA). (gr. 7 up). pap. 9.95 (*1-56971-461-4*) Dark Horse Comics.

—The Remaining Sunlight. 1999. (Buffy the Vampire Slayer Ser.). (Illus.). 88p. (YA). (gr. 7 up). pap. 9.95 (*1-56971-354-5*) Dark Horse Comics.

—Uninvited Guests. 1999. (Buffy the Vampire Slayer Ser.). (Illus.). 96p. (YA). (gr. 7 up). pap. 10.95 (*1-56971-436-3*) Dark Horse Comics.

Whedon, Joss, et al. Buffy the Vampire Slayer: Tales of the Slayer. 2002. (Illus.). 96p. (YA). pap. 14.95 (*1-56971-605-6*) Dark Horse Comics.

BUGS BUNNY (FICTITIOUS CHARACTER)—FICTION

Bugs Bunny & Friends. (Super Look & Find Ser.). (Illus.). 24p. (J). (ps-5). 1997. 14.98 (*0-7853-1131-9*, PI17); 1994. pap. text 7.98 (*0-7853-0700-1*) Publications International, Ltd.

Bugs Bunny & Friends. 1990. (J). o.p. (*0-307-15538-2*, Golden Bks.) Random Hse. Children's Bks.

Bugs Bunny & Friends Snap Pack. 1997. (Snap Pack Ser.). (Illus.). 40p. (J). (gr. 1 up). 12.95 o.p. (*1-56010-304-3*, LT01P) Foster, Walter Publishing, Inc.

Bugs Bunny in the Big Race. 1991. (Deluxe Golden Sound Story Bks.). (Illus.). 24p. (J). (ps-2). o.p. (*0-307-74002-1*, Golden Bks.) Random Hse. Children's Bks.

Carrotblanca. Date not set. (J). 7.98 incl. audio (*1-57042-320-2*) Warner Brothers Records.

Dougherty, Don. Bugs Bunny & Friends. 1996. (Look & Find Ser.). (Illus.). 24p. (J). (gr. k-6). lib. bdg. 14.95 (*1-56674-121-1*, HTS Bks.) Forest Hse. Publishing Co., Inc.

Glassman, Jackie. Looney Tunes Back in Action Reader. 2003. (Looney Tunes Ser.). (Illus.). 32p. (J). mass mkt. 3.99 (*0-439-52140-8*, Scholastic Paperbacks) Scholastic, Inc.

Golden Books Staff. Bugs Bunny. 1994. (Illus.). 56p. (J). (ps-3). pap. 1.69 o.s.i (*0-307-08572-4*, Golden Bks.) Random Hse. Children's Bks.

—Bugs Bunny. 1997. 48p. pap. 0.94 o.s.i (*0-307-93206-0*); 1995. 32p. pap. 1.79 o.s.i (*0-307-01788-5*); 1994. 32p. pap. 1.99 o.s.i (*0-307-01902-0*); 1991. 32p. pap. 3.49 o.s.i (*0-307-02893-3*); 1991. 48p. pap. 0.94 o.s.i (*0-307-02904-2*) Random Hse., Inc.

—Bugs Bunny & the Pink Flamingo. 1991. (Golden Book 'n' Tape Ser.). (Illus.). 24p. (J). (ps-3). pap. 5.99 o.s.i (*0-307-14167-5*, 14167, Golden Bks.) Random Hse. Children's Bks.

—Bugs Bunny Pirate. (J). o.p. (*0-307-00114-8*, Golden Bks.) Random Hse. Children's Bks.

—Bugs Bunny Stories. 1990. (Golden Treasury Ser.). (Illus.). (J). pap. 5.95 o.s.i (*0-307-15827-6*, Golden Bks.) Random Hse. Children's Bks.

—Bugs Bunny's Favorite Joke Book. 1995. (Golden Book Ser.). (Illus.). 96p. (J). (gr. 1-4). pap. 3.99 o.s.i (*0-307-13178-5*, Golden Bks.) Random Hse. Children's Bks.

—The Little Surprise. 1991. (Bugs Bunny Ser.). (Illus.). 24p. (J). (ps-3). pap. 5.99 o.s.i (*0-307-14177-2*, 14177, Golden Bks.) Random Hse. Children's Bks.

—Pirate Island. 1991. (Bugs Bunny Ser.). (Illus.). 24p. (J). (ps-3). pap. 5.99 o.s.i incl. audio (*0-307-14176-4*, 14176, Golden Bks.) Random Hse. Children's Bks.

Golden Staff. Bugs Bunny. 1997. 56p. pap. 1.69 o.s.i (*0-307-01140-2*, Golden Bks.) Random Hse. Children's Bks.

Golden Western Staff. Bugs Bunny. 9999. (Illus.). (J). (ps-3). pap. o.p. (*0-307-08215-6*, Golden Bks.) Random Hse. Children's Bks.

Happy Birthday, Bugs Bunny. 1990. (J). 5.98 o.p. (*1-55521-697-8*) Book Sales, Inc.

Herman, Gail. Space Jam Digest. 1996. (J). (gr. 2-5). mass mkt. 3.50 o.p. (*0-590-94555-6*) Scholastic, Inc.

Ingoglia, Gina. Bugs Bunny & His Sunburned Ears. 1990. (Golden Super Shape Book Ser.). (Illus.). 24p. (J). pap. 3.29 o.s.i (*0-307-10031-6*, Golden Bks.) Random Hse. Children's Bks.

—Bugs Bunny & the Pink Flamingos. 1987. (Golden Friendly Bks.). (Illus.). 32p. (J). (gr. 3-6). o.p. (*0-307-10912-7*, Golden Bks.) Random Hse. Children's Bks.

Lewis, Jean & Messerli, Joe. Bugs Bunny Rides Again. 1986. (Golden Tell-a-Tale Book Ser.). 26p. (J). (*0-307-07046-8*) Whitman Publishing LLC.

Markas, Jenny. Looney Tunes Back in Action Junior Novelization. 2003. (Looney Tunes Ser.). 80p. (J). mass mkt. 4.99 (*0-439-52136-X*, Scholastic Paperbacks) Scholastic, Inc.

Mason, Jane. Looney Tunes Back in Action Movie Storybook. 2003. (Looney Tunes Ser.). (Illus.). 48p. (J). mass mkt. 5.99 (*0-439-52137-8*, Scholastic Paperbacks) Scholastic, Inc.

McCann, Jesse Leon. Looney Tunes Back in Action. 2003. (Looney Tunes Ser.). 32p. (J). mass mkt. 3.50 (*0-439-52139-4*, Scholastic Paperbacks) Scholastic, Inc.

—Looney Tunes Back in Action Joke Book. 2003. (Looney Tunes Ser.). 64p. (J). mass mkt. 4.50 (*0-439-52138-6*, Scholastic Paperbacks) Scholastic, Inc.

Nolan, Billy. Bugs Bunny in the Big Race. 1989. (J). pap. o.p. (*0-88704-203-1*) Sight & Sound International, Inc.

Preller, James. Bugs Bunny in Space. 1996. mass mkt. 2.95 (*0-590-98480-2*) Scholastic, Inc.

Rhino Records Staff. Bugs Bunny Starring in Carrotblanca. 1998. (Illus.). 24p. (J). (ps-3). pap. 7.99 incl. audio (*1-56826-820-3*, KR8) Rhino Entertainment.

Ridgeway, Frank. Bugs Bunny in the Little Surprise. 1990. (Golden Little Look-Look Bks.). (Illus.). 24p. (J). (ps). pap. 1.79 o.s.i (*0-307-11668-9*, Golden Bks.) Random Hse. Children's Bks.

Scott, Vicki, illus. Wanted Bugs Bunny, Alias Wascally Wabbit. 1998. (*0-7853-2668-5*) Publications International, Ltd.

Sideline. Looney Tunes Musical Storybook: Bugs Bunny's Circus Job. 1989. (J). 12.99 (*0-88704-173-6*) Sight & Sound International, Inc.

Silver Dolphin Staff. Bugs Bunny & Friends, 2 vols. 1997. (Cartoon Works). (Illus.). 32p. 18.95 o.p. (*1-57145-308-3*, Silver Dolphin Bks.) Advantage Pubs. Group.

Sprague, Sydney, ed. Learn to Draw Bugs Bunny & Friends. 1997. (Looney Tunes Ser.). (Illus.). 40p. (J). (gr. 1 up). pap. 8.95 (*1-56010-200-4*, LT01) Foster, Walter Publishing, Inc.

BUMPPO, NATTY (FICTITIOUS CHARACTER)—FICTION

Cooper, James Fenimore. The Last of the Mohicans. 2002. (Great Illustrated Classics). (Illus.). 240p. (J). (gr. 3-8). lib. bdg. 21.35 (*1-57765-692-X*, ABDO & Daughters) ABDO Publishing Co.

—The Last of the Mohicans. 1964. (Airmont Classics Ser.). (J). (gr. 6 up). pap. 3.50 o.p. (*0-8049-0005-1*, CL-5) Airmont Publishing Co., Inc.

—The Last of the Mohicans. 1989. (Illus.). (J). (ps up). 26.95 (*0-89968-254-5*) Buccaneer Bks., Inc.

—The Last of the Mohicans. 1989. (gr. 4-6). audio 11.00 o.p. (*1-55994-075-1*, CPN 1239, Caedmon) HarperTrade.

—The Last of the Mohicans. Wright, Robin S., ed. & abr. by. 1976. (Illus.). (J). (gr. 7 up). 7.95 o.p. (*0-679-20372-9*) McKay, David Co., Inc.

—The Last of the Mohicans. 1962. 432p. (J). (gr. 7). mass mkt. 2.95 o.p. (*0-451-52329-6*); (Illus.). mass mkt. 4.95 o.s.i (*0-451-52503-5*) NAL. (Signet Classics).

—The Last of the Mohicans. Farr, Naunerle C., ed. abr. ed. 1977. (Now Age Illustrated III Ser.). (Illus.). (J). (gr. 4-12). text 7.50 o.p. (*0-88301-279-0*); pap. text 2.95 (*0-88301-267-7*) Pendulum Pr., Inc.

—The Last of the Mohicans. 9999. (Children's Classics Ser.: No. 740-14). (Illus.). (J). (gr. 3-5). text 3.50 o.p. (*0-7214-0789-7*, Ladybird Bks.) Penguin Group (USA) Inc.

—The Last of the Mohicans. Vogel, Malvina, ed. 1992. (Great Illustrated Classics Ser.: Vol. 24). (Illus.). 240p. (J). (gr. 3-6). 9.95 (*0-86611-975-2*) Playmore, Inc., Pubs.

—The Last of the Mohicans. 1987. (Regents Illustrated Classics Ser.). (J). (gr. 7-12). pap. text 3.75 o.p. (*0-13-523952-4*, 20569) Prentice Hall, ESL Dept.

—The Last of the Mohicans. 1993. (Step into Classics Ser.). (Illus.). 112p. (J). (gr. 3-5). pap. 3.99 (*0-679-84706-5*, Random Hse. Bks. for Young Readers) Random Hse. Children's Bks.

—The Last of the Mohicans. 1986. (Illus.). 376p. (J). 75.00 o.s.i (*0-684-18716-7*); (YA). (gr. 4-7). 28.00 (*0-684-18711-6*) Simon & Schuster Children's Publishing. (Atheneum).

—The Last of the Mohicans. (Saddleback Classics). (J). 2001. (Illus.). 13.10 (*0-606-21559-X*); 1993. 10.04 (*0-606-02705-X*) Turtleback Bks.

—The Last of the Mohicans. abr. ed. 2002. (Scribner Storybook Classic Ser.). (Illus.). 64p. (J). (gr. 3-6). 18.95 (*0-689-84068-3*, Atheneum) Simon & Schuster Children's Publishing.

—The Last of the Mohicans. adapted ed. 1997. (Living Classics Ser.). (Illus.). 32p. (J). (gr. 3-7). 14.95 o.p. (*0-7641-7048-1*) Barron's Educational Series, Inc.

—The Last of the Mohicans. 1826. 423p. (YA). reprint ed. pap. text 28.00 (*1-4047-2374-9*) Classic Textbooks.

—The Last of the Mohicans. 2nd ed. 1998. (Illustrated Classic Book Ser.). (Illus.). 61p. (J). (gr. 3 up). reprint ed. pap. text 4.95 (*1-56767-249-3*) Educational Insights, Inc.

—The Pioneers. 1964. (Airmont Classics Ser.). (J). (gr. 8 up). mass mkt. 1.95 o.p. (*0-8049-0049-3*, CL-49) Airmont Publishing Co., Inc.

—The Pioneers. 1823. 477p. (YA). reprint ed. pap. text 28.00 (*1-4047-2371-4*) Classic Textbooks.

—The Pioneers. 1964. 448p. (YA). mass mkt. 6.95 (*0-451-52521-3*); mass mkt. 4.50 o.p. (*0-451-52339-3*) NAL. (Signet Classics).

—Prairie. 1964. (Airmont Classics Ser.). (J). (gr. 8 up). mass mkt. 1.95 o.p. (*0-8049-0041-8*, CL-41) Airmont Publishing Co., Inc.

—Prairie. 1964. 416p. (YA). (gr. 10). mass mkt. 4.95 o.p. (*0-451-52516-7*, CE1780); mass mkt. 4.50 o.p. (*0-451-52235-4*) NAL. (Signet Classics).

BUNNICULA (FICTITIOUS CHARACTER)—FICTION

Howe, Deborah & Howe, James. Bunnicula: A Rabbit-Tale of Mystery. abr. ed. 1987. (Bunnicula Ser.). (J). (gr. 3-5). audio 11.95 (*0-89845-750-5*, CP 1700, Caedmon) HarperTrade.

—Bunnicula: A Rabbit-Tale of Mystery. 1980. (Bunnicula Ser.). (Illus.). 112p. (J). (gr. 3-5). pap. 3.99 (*0-380-51094-4*, Avon Bks.) Morrow/Avon.

—Bunnicula: A Rabbit-Tale of Mystery. 1994. (Bunnicula Ser.). (Illus.). (J). (gr. 3-5). 16.95 (*0-385-32153-8*, Cornerstone Bks.) Pages, Inc.

—Bunnicula: A Rabbit-Tale of Mystery. unabr. ed. 2000. (Bunnicula Ser.). (J). (gr. 3-5). audio 18.00 (*0-8072-8186-7*, LL0163, Listening Library) Random Hse. Audio Publishing Group.

—Bunnicula: A Rabbit-Tale of Mystery. (Kids' Picks Ser.). 112p. (J). (gr. 3-5). 2000. pap. 2.99 (*0-689-83863-8*, Aladdin); 1979. (Illus.). 16.95 (*0-689-30700-4*, Atheneum) Simon & Schuster Children's Publishing.

—Bunnicula: A Rabbit-Tale of Mystery. 1996. (Bunnicula Ser.). (J). (gr. 3-5). 10.04 (*0-606-10151-9*) Turtleback Bks.

—Bunnicula: The Vampire Bunny & His Friends, 4 vols., Set. (Bunnicula Ser.). (J). (gr. 3-5). 1989. pap. 14.00 (*0-380-70910-4*); 1986. 10.00 (*0-380-70281-9*) Morrow/Avon. (Avon Bks.).

Howe, James. Bunnicula Escapes. 1994. (Bunnicula Activity Book Ser.). (Illus.). 12p. (J). (gr. 2-6). 14.95 o.p. (*0-688-13212-X*, Morrow, William & Co.) Morrow/Avon.

—Bunnicula Fun Book. 1993. (Bunnicula Activity Book Ser.). (Illus.). 176p. (J). (gr. 2-6). pap. 9.95 o.p. (*0-688-11952-2*, Morrow, William & Co.) Morrow/Avon.

—Bunnicula Party Book. 1924. (Bunnicula Activity Book Ser.). (J). (gr. 3-5). pap. o.s.i (*0-688-11953-0*, Morrow, William & Co.) Morrow/Avon.

—Bunnicula Play Book. 1924. (Bunnicula Activity Book Ser.). (J). (gr. 3-5). o.s.i (*0-688-14191-9*, Morrow, William & Co.) Morrow/Avon.

—Bunnicula Strikes Again! (Bunnicula Ser.). 128p. (J). (gr. 3-5). 1999. (Illus.). 16.00 (*0-689-81463-1*, Atheneum); No. 6. 2001. pap. 4.99 (*0-689-81462-3*, Aladdin) Simon & Schuster Children's Publishing.

—Bunnicula's Frightfully Fabulous Factoids: A Book to Entertain Your Brain! 1999. (Bunnicula Activity Book Ser.). (Illus.). 48p. (J). (gr. 2-6). pap. 2.99 (*0-689-81666-9*, 076714002999, Little Simon) Simon & Schuster Children's Publishing.

—Bunnicula's Pleasantly Perplexing Puzzlers Book 2. 1998. (Bunnicula Activity Book Ser.). (Illus.). 48p. (J). (gr. 2-6). pap. 2.99 (*0-689-81664-2*, Little Simon) Simon & Schuster Children's Publishing.

—Bunnicula's Wickedly Wacky Word Games. 1998. (Bunnicula Activity Book Ser.). (Illus.). 48p. (J). (gr. 2-6). pap. 2.99 (*0-689-81663-4*, Little Simon) Simon & Schuster Children's Publishing.

—The Celery Stalks at Midnight. abr. ed. 1987. (Bunnicula Ser.). (J). (gr. 3-5). audio 11.95 (*0-89845-745-9*, CPN 1814, Caedmon) HarperTrade.

—The Celery Stalks at Midnight. 1984. (Bunnicula Ser.). (Illus.). 128p. (J). (gr. 3-5). pap. 4.95 (*0-380-69054-3*) Morrow/Avon.

—The Celery Stalks at Midnight. unabr. ed. 2000. (Bunnicula Ser.). (YA). (gr. 4-7). audio 18.00 (*0-8072-8235-9*, YA173CX, Listening Library) Random Hse. Audio Publishing Group.

—The Celery Stalks at Midnight. 1983. (Bunnicula Ser.). (Illus.). 128p. (J). (gr. 3-5). 16.95 (*0-689-30987-2*, Atheneum) Simon & Schuster Children's Publishing.

—The Celery Stalks at Midnight. 1984. (Bunnicula Ser.). (J). (gr. 3-5). 11.04 (*0-606-03352-1*) Turtleback Bks.

—The Celery Stalks at Midnight. 1995. (Bunnicula Ser.). (J). (gr. 3-5). audio 10.98 (*0-945267-39-8*, YM048-CN); audio compact disk 13.98 (*0-945267-40-1*, YM048-CD) Youngheart Music.

—Harold & Chester in Creepy-Crawly Birthday. (Bunnicula Ser.). (Illus.). 48p. (J). (gr. k-3). 1999. pap. 5.95 (*0-688-16700-4*, Morrow, William & Co.); 1992. pap. 5.99 (*0-380-75984-5*, Avon Bks.); 1991. 13.95 o.p. (*0-688-09687-5*, Morrow, William & Co.); 1991. lib. bdg. 13.88 (*0-688-09688-3*, Morrow, William & Co.) Morrow/Avon.

—Harold & Chester in Hot Fudge. 1999. (Bunnicula Ser.). (Illus.). 48p. (J). (gr. k-3). pap. 5.95 o.s.i (*0-688-17065-X*, Greenwillow Bks.) HarperCollins Children's Bk. Group.

—Harold & Chester in Hot Fudge. (Bunnicula Ser.). (Illus.). 48p. (J). (gr. k-3). 1991. pap. 5.99 *(0-380-70610-5,* Avon Bks.); 1990. 13.95 o.p. *(0-688-08237-8,* Morrow, William & Co.); 1990. lib. bdg. 13.88 o.p. *(0-688-09701-4,* Morrow, William & Co.) Morrow/Avon.

—Harold & Chester in Hot Fudge. 1999. (Bunnicula). (J). (gr. k-3). 12.10 *(0-606-17394-3)* Turtleback Bks.

—Harold & Chester in Rabbit-Cadabra. (Bunnicula Ser.). (Illus.). 48p. (J). (gr. k-3). 1999. pap. 5.95 *(0-688-16699-7,* Morrow, William & Co.); 1994. pap. 5.99 *(0-380-71336-5,* Avon Bks.); 1993. 15.00 *(0-688-10402-9,* Morrow, William & Co.); 1993. lib. bdg. 14.93 o.p. *(0-688-10403-7,* Morrow, William & Co.) Morrow/Avon.

—Harold & Chester in Sacred Silly: A Halloween Treat. 1990. (Bunnicula). (J). (gr. k-3). 11.19 o.p. *(0-606-04792-1)* Turtleback Bks.

—Harold & Chester in Scared Silly: A Halloween Treat. (Bunnicula Ser.). (Illus.). 48p. (J). (gr. k-3). 1998. pap. 4.95 *(0-688-16322-X,* Morrow, William & Co.); 1989. 16.00 o.p. *(0-688-07666-1,* Morrow, William & Co.); 1989. lib. bdg. 15.93 o.p. *(0-688-07667-X,* Morrow, William & Co.); 1990. reprint ed. pap. 5.99 *(0-380-70446-3,* Avon Bks.) Morrow/Avon.

—Harold & Chester in the Fright Before Christmas. 1999. (Bunnicula Ser.). (Illus.). 48p. (J). (ps-3). pap. 5.95 o.s.i *(0-688-16293-2,* Harper Trophy) HarperCollins Children's Bk. Group.

—Harold & Chester in the Fright Before Christmas. (Bunnicula Ser.). (Illus.). 48p. (J). (gr. k-3). 1989. pap. 5.95 *(0-380-70445-5,* Avon Bks.); 1988. 16.00 o.p. *(0-688-07664-5,* Morrow, William & Co.); 1988. 16.00 o.p. *(0-688-07664-5,* Morrow, William & Co.); 1988. lib. bdg. 15.93 o.p. *(0-688-07665-3,* Morrow, William & Co.) Morrow/Avon.

—Harold & Chester in the Fright Before Christmas. 1999. (Bunnicula). (J). (gr. k-3). 12.10 *(0-606-17244-0)* Turtleback Bks.

—Harold & Chester Stories. Date not set. (Bunnicula Ser.). (J). (gr. k-3). *(0-688-10298-0)*; lib. bdg. *(0-688-10299-9)* Morrow/Avon. (Morrow, William & Co.).

—Howliday Inn. unabr. ed. 1987. (Bunnicula Ser.). (J). (gr. 3-5). 11.95 o.p. incl. audio *(0-89845-751-3,* CPN 1748, Caedmon) HarperTrade.

—Howliday Inn. 1983. (Bunnicula Ser.). (Illus.). 208p. (J). (gr. 3-5). pap. 5.99 *(0-380-64543-2,* Avon Bks.) Morrow/Avon.

—Howliday Inn. unabr. ed. 2000. (Bunnicula Ser.). (J). (gr. 3-5). 195p. pap. 28.00 incl. audio *(0-8072-8382-7,* YA179SP); audio 23.00 *(0-8072-8381-9,* YA179CX) Random Hse. Audio Publishing Group. (Listening Library).

—Howliday Inn. (Bunnicula Ser.). (Illus.). 208p. (J). (gr. 3-5). 2001. pap. 4.99 *(0-689-84619-3,* Aladdin); 1982. 16.00 *(0-689-30846-9,* Atheneum) Simon & Schuster Children's Publishing.

—Howliday Inn. 1982. (Bunnicula Ser.). (J). (gr. 3-5). 11.04 *(0-606-00945-0)* Turtleback Bks.

—The Howliday Inn. unabr. ed. 2000. (Bunnicula Ser.). (YA). (gr. 3-5). audio 18.00 *(0-8072-8250-2,* LL0198, Listening Library) Random Hse. Audio Publishing Group.

—Nightly-Nightmare. 1987. (Bunnicula Ser.). (Illus.). 128p. (J). (gr. 3-5). 15.95 *(0-689-31207-5,* Atheneum) Simon & Schuster Children's Publishing.

—Nighty-Nightmare. abr. ed. 1988. (Bunnicula Ser.). (J). (gr. 3-5). audio 9.95 o.p. *(0-89845-790-4,* CPN 1833, Caedmon) HarperTrade.

—Nighty-Nightmare. 1988. (Bunnicula Ser.). (Illus.). (J). (gr. 3-5). reprint ed. pap. 3.99 *(0-380-70490-0,* Avon Bks.) Morrow/Avon.

—Nighty-Nightmare. unabr. ed. 2000. (Bunnicula Ser.). (J). 128p. (gr. 3-5). pap. 28.00 incl. audio *(0-8072-8397-5,* YA201SP); 128p. (gr. 3-5). pap. 28.00 incl. audio *(0-8072-8397-5,* YA201SP); (gr. 3-5). audio 23.00 *(0-8072-8396-7,* YA201CX); (gr. 4-7). audio 18.00 *(0-8072-8261-8,* LL0203) Random Hse. Audio Publishing Group. (Listening Library).

—Nighty-Nightmare. 1997. (Bunnicula Ser.). 128p. (J). (gr. 3-5). pap. 4.99 *(0-689-81724-X,* Aladdin) Simon & Schuster Children's Publishing.

—Nighty-Nightmare. 1997. (Bunnicula Ser.). (J). (gr. 3-5). 10.55 *(0-606-12453-5)* Turtleback Bks.

—Return to Howliday Inn. 1993. (Bunnicula Ser.). (Illus.). 128p. (J). (gr. 3-5). pap. 4.99 *(0-380-71972-X,* Avon Bks.) Morrow/Avon.

—Return to Howliday Inn. unabr. ed. 2000. (Bunnicula Ser.). (J). (gr. 3-5). audio 23.00 *(0-8072-8415-7,* YA192CX, Listening Library) Random Hse. Audio Publishing Group.

—Return to Howliday Inn. 1992. (Bunnicula Ser.). (Illus.). 168p. (J). (gr. 3-5). 16.95 *(0-689-31661-5,* Atheneum) Simon & Schuster Children's Publishing.

—Return to Howliday Inn. 1992. (Bunnicula Ser.). (J). (gr. 3-5). 11.00 *(0-606-02869-2)* Turtleback Bks.

Howe, James & Howe, Deborah. Bunnicula: A Rabbit Tale of Mystery. 1996. (Bunnicula Ser.). (Illus.). 112p. (J). (gr. 3-5). pap. 3.99 *(0-689-80659-0,* Aladdin) Simon & Schuster Children's Publishing.

Howe, James & Phillips, Louis. Bunnicula's Long-Lasting Laugh-Alouds: A Book of Jokes & Riddles to Tickle Your Bunny-Bone! 1999. (Bunnicula Activity Book Ser.). (Illus.). 46p. (J). (gr. 2-6). pap. 2.99 *(0-689-81665-0,* 076714002999, Little Simon) Simon & Schuster Children's Publishing.

BUTT-UGLY MARTIANS (FICTITIOUS CHARACTERS)—FICTION

Braunstein, Bill. Meet Gorgon. Szor, Henryk, tr. & illus. by. 2002. (Butt-Ugly Martians Chapter Bks.: No. 2). 80p. (J). (gr. k-7). mass mkt. 5.99 *(0-439-37024-8)* Scholastic, Inc.

Mason, Tom & Danko, Dan. Teenage Spaceland. 2002. (Butt-Ugly Martians Chapter Bks.: Bk. 4). 96p. (J). mass mkt. 4.50 *(0-439-40791-5)* Scholastic, Inc.

Scholastic, Inc. Staff. B. Bop's Brainwave. 2002. (Butt-Ugly Martians Adventure Storybook Ser.). 32p. (J). mass mkt. 4.99 *(0-439-40398-7)* Scholastic, Inc.

Scholastic, Inc. Staff, contrib. by. The Big Bang Theory. 2002. (Butt-Ugly Martians Chapter Bks.: No. 1). 80p. (J). (gr. k-7). mass mkt. 4.99 *(0-439-37023-X)* Scholastic, Inc.

—The Martians Have Landed. 2002. (Butt-Ugly Martians Adventure Storybook Ser.: No. 1). 32p. mass mkt. 5.99 *(0-439-37027-2)* Scholastic, Inc.

—That's No Puddle, That's Angela! 2002. (Butt-Ugly Martians Chapter Bks.: Vol. 3). (Illus.). 96p. (J). mass mkt. 5.99 *(0-439-39932-7)* Scholastic, Inc.

C

CABEZA DE VACA, ALVAR NUNEZ, 1490?-1557—FICTION

Baker, Betty. Walk the World's Rim. 1965. 80p. (J). (gr. 5 up). lib. bdg. 14.89 o.p. *(0-06-020381-1)* HarperCollins Children's Bk. Group.

CABOT, JOHN, D. 1498—FICTION

Garfield, Henry. The Lost Voyage of John Cabot. 2004. (YA). *(0-689-85173-1,* Atheneum/Richard Jackson Bks.) Simon & Schuster Children's Publishing.

CAILLOU (FICTITIOUS CHARACTER)—FICTION

Beaulieu, Jeannine & Sanschagrin, Joceline. Caillou: My House. 2002. (Illus.). 12p. (J). pap. 7.95 *(2-89450-266-4)* Editions Chouette, Inc. CAN. *Dist:* Client Distribution Services.

Harvey, Roger & CINAR Corporation Staff. Caillou Makes a Snowman. 2000. (Backpack Ser.). (Illus.). 24p. (J). (ps-k). pap. *(2-89450-180-3)* Editions Chouette, Inc. CAN. *Dist:* Client Distribution Services.

Johnson, Marion. Caillou: New Shoes. 2002. (Illus.). 24p. (J). (ps-k). 12.95 *(2-89450-327-X)* Editions Chouette, Inc. CAN. *Dist:* Client Distribution Services.

—Caillou Watches Rosie. 2002. (Illus.). 24p. (J). 12.95 *(2-89450-326-1)* Editions Chouette, Inc. CAN. *Dist:* Client Distribution Services.

L'Heureux, Christine. Caillou: Buenas Noches! 2004. (SPA.). (J). 3.95 *(1-58728-345-X)* Creative Publishing international, Inc.

Nadeau, Nicole & Lapierre, Claude. Caillou: The Shopping Trip. 2001. (Illus.). 24p. (YA). (ps up). pap. *(2-89450-234-6)* Editions Chouette, Inc.

Sanschagrin, Joceline & CINAR Corporation Staff. Caillou Plans a Surprise. 1999. (Backpack Ser.). (Illus.). 24p. (J). (ps-k). pap. *(2-89450-112-9)* Editions Chouette, Inc. CAN. *Dist:* Client Distribution Services.

CALRISSIAN, LANDO (FICTITIOUS CHARACTER)—FICTION

Disney Staff, ed. The Empire Strikes Back. (Read Along Star Wars Ser.). (J). 7.99 incl. audio *(0-7634-0194-3)* Walt Disney Records.

—The Empire Strikes Back: A Flip Book. 1997. 40p. (J). 2.98 o.s.i *(1-57082-578-5)* Mouse Works.

—Return of the Jedi. (Read Along Star Wars Ser.). (J). 7.99 incl. audio *(0-7634-0193-5)*; 14.99 incl. audio *(0-7634-0196-X)* Walt Disney Records.

Gardner, J. J. Return of the Jedi Storybook. 1997. (Illus.). (J). (gr. 5-7). mass mkt. 5.99 *(0-590-06659-5)* Scholastic, Inc.

Golden Books Staff. The Empire Strikes Back: With Tattoos. 1999. (Star Wars Ser.). (Illus.). 24p. pap. 3.99 o.s.i *(0-307-13068-1,* Golden Bks.) Random Hse. Children's Bks.

Golden, Christopher. The Empire Strikes Back. 1998. (Choose Your Own Star Wars Adventure Ser.). 128p. (gr. 4-8). pap. text 4.50 o.s.i *(0-553-48652-7,* Dell Books for Young Readers) Random Hse. Children's Bks.

Levy, Elizabeth, ed. Return of the Jedi Step-Up Movie Adventure. 1983. (Star Wars Ser.). (Illus.). 72p. (J). (gr. 1-3). 8.99 o.s.i *(0-394-96117-X,* Random Hse. Bks. for Young Readers) Random Hse. Children's Bks.

Lucas, George. The Empire Strikes Back Adventures. abr. ed. 1994. (J). (gr. k-3). audio 8.98 o.p. Time Warner AudioBooks.

—Return of the Jedi: A Flip Book. 1997. (Star Wars Ser.). 40p. (J). 2.98 o.s.i *(1-57082-579-3)* Mouse Works.

Scholastic, Inc. Staff, ed. The Empire Strikes Back. 9999. (J). pap. 2.50 o.s.i *(0-590-31791-1)* Scholastic, Inc.

—Return of the Jedi. 9999. (J). pap. 2.95 o.s.i *(0-590-32929-4)* Scholastic, Inc.

Vinge, Joan D., adapted by. Return of the Jedi: The Storybook Based on the Movie. 1983. (Storybook Based on the Movie Ser.). (Illus.). 64p. (J). (gr. 3-8). 7.99 o.p. *(0-394-95624-9,* Random Hse. Bks. for Young Readers) Random Hse. Children's Bks.

Whitman, John. Return of the Jedi. 1996. (Mighty Chronicles Ser.). (Illus.). 316p. (gr. 4-7). 9.95 o.s.i *(0-8118-1494-7)* Chronicle Bks. LLC.

Whitman, John, adapted by. The Empire Strikes Back. 1996. (Mighty Chronicles Ser.). (Illus.). 432p. (gr. 4-7). 9.95 o.s.i *(0-8118-1482-3)* Chronicle Bks. LLC.

CAMPBELL, ROSE (FICTITIOUS CHARACTER)—FICTION

Alcott, Louisa May. Eight Cousins. 1995. 288p. (J). 8.99 o.s.i *(0-517-14810-2)* Random Hse. Value Publishing.

—Rose in Bloom. 312p. (J). 1995. (gr. 5 up). pap. 9.99 *(0-316-03089-9)*; Vol. 1. 1996. 17.95 o.p. *(0-316-03782-6)* Little Brown & Co.

CAPTAIN UNDERPANTS (FICTITIOUS CHARACTER)—FICTION

Pilkey, Dav. The Adventures of Captain Underpants: An Epic Novel. 1997. (Captain Underpants Ser.: No. 1). (Illus.). 128p. (J). (gr. 2-5). pap. 16.95 *(0-590-84627-2)*; pap. 4.99 *(0-590-84628-0)* Scholastic, Inc.

—The Adventures of Captain Underpants: An Epic Novel. 1997. (Captain Underpants Ser.: No. 1). (J). (gr. 2-5). 10.04 *(0-606-15829-4)* Turtleback Bks.

—The All New Captain Underpants Extra Crunchy Book o' Fun 2. 2002. (Captain Underpants Ser.). 96p. (J). (gr. 1-5). pap. 3.99 *(0-439-37608-4)* Scholastic, Inc.

—Las Aventuras del Capitan Calzoncillos. 2000. (SPA., Illus.). 126p. (J). 10.95 *(84-348-7047-9)* SM Ediciones ESP. *Dist:* Distribooks, Inc.

—Las Aventuras del Capitan Calzoncillos. 2002. (SPA.). 128p. (J). (ps-4). pap. 4.99 *(0-439-22648-1,* SO3077, Scholastic en Espanola) Scholastic, Inc.

—El Capitan Calzoncillos y el Ataque de los Inodoros Parlantes. 2002. (SPA.). 144p. (J). (ps). pap. 4.99 *(0-439-31736-3,* SO31151, Scholastic en Espanola) Scholastic, Inc.

—El Capitan Calzoncillos y la Furia de la Supermujer Macroelastica. 2003. (Captain Underpants Ser.). (SPA., Illus.). 176p. (J). (gr. 2-5). mass mkt. 4.99 *(0-439-53820-3,* Scholastic en Espanola) Scholastic, Inc.

—Captain Underpants & the Attack of the Talking Toilets. 1999. (Captain Underpants Ser.: No. 2). (Illus.). (J). (gr. 2-5). 144p. pap. 16.95 *(0-590-63136-5)*; 139p. pap. 4.99 *(0-590-63427-5)* Scholastic, Inc. (Blue Sky Pr., The).

—Captain Underpants & the Attack of the Talking Toilets. 1999. (Captain Underpants Ser.: No. 2). (Illus.). (J). (gr. 2-5). 10.04 *(0-606-15830-8)* Turtleback Bks.

—Captain Underpants & the Big, Bad Battle of the Bionic Booger Boy Pt. 2: The Revenge of the Ridiculous Robo-Boogers. 2003. (Captain Underpants Ser.). 176p. (J). pap. 4.99 *(0-439-37612-2)*; (Illus.). pap. 16.95 *(0-439-37611-4)* Scholastic, Inc. (Blue Sky Pr., The).

—Captain Underpants & the Invasion of the Incredibly Naughty Cafeteria Ladies from Outer Space: And the Subsequent Assault of the Equally Evil Lunchroom Zombie Nerds. 1999. (Captain Underpants Ser.: No. 3). (Illus.). (J). (gr. 2-5). 112p. pap. 4.99 *(0-439-04996-2)*; 134p. pap. 16.95 *(0-439-04995-4)* Scholastic, Inc. (Blue Sky Pr., The).

—Captain Underpants & the Invasion of the Incredibly Naughty Cafeteria Ladies from Outer Space: And the Subsequent Assault of the Equally Evil Lunchroom Zombie Nerds. 1999. (Captain Underpants Ser.: No. 3). (J). (gr. 2-5). 10.04 *(0-606-17274-2)* Turtleback Bks.

—Captain Underpants & the Perilous Plot of Professor Poopypants. 2000. (Captain Underpants Ser.: No. 4). (Illus.). 160p. (J). (gr. 2-5). pap. 16.95 *(0-439-04997-0)*; pap. 3.99 *(0-439-04998-9)* Scholastic, Inc. (Blue Sky Pr., The).

—Captain Underpants & the Perilous Plot of Professor Poopypants. 2000. (Captain Underpants Ser.: No. 4). (Illus.). (J). (gr. 2-5). 10.04 *(0-606-18526-7)* Turtleback Bks.

—Captain Underpants & the Wrath of the Wicked Wedgie Woman. 2001. (Captain Underpants Ser.: No. 5). 176p. (J). (gr. 2-5). pap. 4.99 *(0-439-05000-6)*; (Illus.). pap. 16.95 *(0-439-04999-7)* Scholastic, Inc.

—Captain Underpants & the Wrath of the Wicked Wedgie Woman. 2001. (Adventures of Captain Underpants Ser.). (Illus.). (J). 11.04 *(0-606-21101-2)* Turtleback Bks.

—Captain Underpants Boxed Set with Whoopie Cushion: The Adventures of Captain Underpants; Captain Underpants & the Attack of the Talking Toilets; Captain Underpants & the Invasion of the Incredibly Naughty Cafeteria Ladies from Outer Space; Captain Underpants & the Perilous Plot of Professor Poopypants, 4 vols. 2000. (Captain Underpants Ser.: Nos. 1-4). (J). (gr. 2-5). 19.95 *(0-439-22700-3,* Blue Sky Pr., The) Scholastic, Inc.

—Captain Underpants Extra-Crunchy Book O' Fun 'N Games. 2001. (Captain Underpants Ser.). (Illus.). 80p. (J). (gr. 2-5). pap. 4.99 *(0-439-26761-7)* Scholastic, Inc.

—The New Captain Underpants Collection, Bks. 1-5. 2002. (Look-Inside Ser.). 128p. (J). (gr. 2-5). 24.95 *(0-439-41784-8,* Blue Sky Pr., The) Scholastic, Inc.

Pilkey, Dav, illus. Captain Underpants & the Big, Bad Battle of the Bionic Booger Boy Pt. 1: The Night of the Nasty Nostril Nuggets. 2003. (Captain Underpants Ser.: Bk. 6). 176p. (Orig.). (J). pap. 16.95 *(0-439-37609-2)*; pap. 4.99 *(0-439-37610-6)* Scholastic, Inc. (Blue Sky Pr., The).

CARE BEARS (FICTITIOUS CHARACTERS)—FICTION

Bright, J. E. What Makes You Happy? 2003. (Care Bears 8x8 Ser.). (Illus.). 24p. (J). (ps-1). mass mkt. 3.50 *(0-439-45543-X)* Scholastic, Inc.

del Sur, Duendes. ABC. 2003. (Care Bears Ser.). (Illus.). 8p. (J). bds. 5.99 o.s.i *(0-439-51804-0)* Scholastic, Inc.

Hudson, Eleanor. The Care Bears Help Out. 1983. (Care Bear Mini-Storybooks). (Illus.). 32p. (J). (gr. 1-6). 1.25 o.s.i *(0-394-85842-5,* Random Hse. Bks. for Young Readers) Random Hse. Children's Bks.

Johnson. Caring Is What Counts. 1985. (Care Bear Ser.). (J). pap. 11.95 o.p. *(0-516-09001-1,* Children's Pr.) Scholastic Library Publishing.

Johnson, Ward. Ben's New Buddy. 1985. (Care Bear Ser.). (J). pap. 11.95 o.p. *(0-516-09008-9,* Children's Pr.) Scholastic Library Publishing.

Kahn, Peggy. The Care Bears & the New Baby. 1983. (Care Bear Mini-Storybooks). (Illus.). 32p. (J). (gr. 1-6). 1.25 o.s.i *(0-394-85845-X,* Random Hse. Bks. for Young Readers) Random Hse. Children's Bks.

—The Care Bears' Book of ABC's. 1983. (Care Bear Mini-Storybooks). (Illus.). 40p. (J). (ps-2). 4.99 o.p. *(0-394-95808-X,* Random Hse. Bks. for Young Readers) Random Hse. Children's Bks.

—The Care Bears' Book of Feelings. 1984. (Care Bear Cuddle Bks.). (Illus.). 14p. (J). (ps). 1.95 o.s.i *(0-394-86447-6,* Random Hse. Bks. for Young Readers) Random Hse. Children's Bks.

—The Care Bears Help Santa. 1984. (Care Bear Bks.). (Illus.). 40p. (J). (ps-3). 4.99 o.p. *(0-394-96807-7,* Random Hse. Bks. for Young Readers) Random Hse. Children's Bks.

Katz, Bobbi. The Care Bears & the Big Cleanup. 1993. 2.49 o.p. *(0-517-10473-3)* Random Hse. Value Publishing.

Ladd, Frances Ann. Lucky Day. 2003. (Care Bears Ser.). (Illus.). 24p. (J). mass mkt. 3.50 *(0-439-45172-8)* Scholastic, Inc.

Lee, Quilan B. Care Bears: Una Entrega Especial. 2004. (Care Bears Ser.). 24p. (J). pap. 3.50 *(0-439-61713-8,* Scholastic en Espanola) Scholastic, Inc.

Lindenberger, Jan. Care Bears Collectibles: An Unauthorized Handbook & Price Guide. 1997. (Schiffer Book for Collectors Ser.). (Illus.). 192p. pap. 19.95 *(0-7643-0310-4)* Schiffer Publishing, Ltd.

Maison, Della. The Care Bears' Garden. 1983. (Care Bear Mini-Storybooks). (Illus.). 32p. (J). (gr. 1-6). 1.25 o.p. *(0-394-85827-1,* Random Hse. Bks. for Young Readers) Random Hse. Children's Bks.

Murad, Maria B. The Magic Words. 1985. (Care Bear Ser.). (J). pap. 11.95 o.p. *(0-516-09010-0,* Children's Pr.) Scholastic Library Publishing.

O'Connor, Jane. The Care Bears' Party Cookbook. 1985. (Step into Reading Step 2 Bks.). (Illus.). 48p. (J). (gr. 1-3). 6.99 o.p. *(0-394-97305-4)*; pap. 3.50 o.p. *(0-394-87305-X)* Random Hse. Children's Bks. (Random Hse. Bks. for Young Readers).

Parent, Nancy. The Care Bears Caring Contest. 2003. (Care Bears 8x8 Ser.). (Illus.). 24p. (J). (ps-1). mass mkt. 3.50 *(0-439-45158-2)* Scholastic, Inc.

—The Day Nobody Shared. 2003. (Care Bears Ser.). 24p. (J). pap. 3.50 *(0-439-45157-4,* Scholastic Paperbacks) Scholastic, Inc.

Reich, Ali. Meet the Care Bears. 1983. (Care Bear Mini-Storybooks). (Illus.). 32p. (J). (gr. 1-6). 1.25 o.s.i *(0-394-85844-1*, Random Hse. Bks. for Young Readers) Random Hse. Children's Bks.

Sander, Sonia. Care Bears Busy Busy Sunny Day. 2003. (Care Bears Ser.). (Illus.). 24p. (J). mass mkt. 3.50 *(0-439-53196-9)* Scholastic, Inc.

—The Caring Rainbow. 2003. (Care Bears Ser.). (Illus.). 8p. (J). (ps). bds. 5.99 o.s.i *(0-439-45178-7)* Scholastic, Inc.

—Find That Rainbow! Sticker Storybook. 2003. (Care Bears Ser.). 16p. (J). (ps-2). mass mkt. 5.99 o.s.i *(0-439-45176-0)* Scholastic, Inc.

—Who's Who? Sticker Storybook. 2003. (Care Bears Ser.). (Illus.). 16p. (J). mass mkt. 5.99 *(0-439-45544-8)* Scholastic, Inc.

Tait, Katie. Catch the Christmas Spirit! 2003. (Care Bears Ser.). (Illus.). 16p. (J). bds. 4.99 *(0-439-46023-9*, Scholastic Paperbacks) Scholastic, Inc.

Winthrop, Elizabeth. Being Brave Is Best. 1985. (Care Bear Ser.). (J). pap. 11.95 o.p. *(0-516-09007-0*, Children's Pr.) Scholastic Library Publishing.

CARSON, KIT, 1809-1868—FICTION

Osborne, Mary Pope. Adaline Falling Star. unabr. ed. 2001. (YA). (gr. 5-9). audio 18.00 *(0-8072-0430-7*, Listening Library) Random Hse. Audio Publishing Group.

—Adaline Falling Star. 2000. (Illus.). vi, 170p. (J). (gr. 7-12). pap. 16.95 *(0-439-05947-X*, Scholastic Reference) Scholastic, Inc.

CARVER, GEORGE WASHINGTON, 1864?-1943—FICTION

Jackson, Dave & Jackson, Neta. The Forty-Acre Swindle: George Washington Carver. 2000. (Trailblazer Bks.: Vol. 31). (Illus.). 144p. (J). (gr. 3-7). pap. 5.99 *(0-7642-2264-3)* Bethany Hse. Pubs.

Owens, Vivian. I Met a Great Man: John Meets Dr. Carver of Tuskegee. Owens, April, ed. unabr. ed. 1998. (Illus.). 64p. (J). (gr. 4-10). pap. 8.95 *(0-9623839-6-1)* Eschar Pubns.

CAT IN THE HAT (FICTITIOUS CHARACTER)—FICTION

McCann, Jesse Leon. The Cat in the Hat. 2003. (Illus.). 24p. (J). 0.33 *(0-375-82780-3*, Golden Bks.) Random Hse. Children's Bks.

Seuss, Dr. A Big Coloring Book: Wubbulous World of Dr. Seuss. 1998. 80p. (J). (ps-3). pap. 2.75 o.s.i *(0-679-89177-3*, Random Hse. Bks. for Young Readers) Random Hse. Children's Bks.

—The Cat in the Hat. 1999. (Illus.). (J). 12.99 *(0-679-89267-2)*; 1993. (J). 23.97 *(0-679-86348-6)*; 1987. (Illus.). 64p. (J). 9.95 incl. audio *(0-394-89218-6)*; 1987. (Illus.). 64p. (J). 9.95 incl. audio *(0-394-89218-6)*; 1967. (FRE.). 3.50 o.s.i *(0-394-80171-7)*; 1966. (Illus.). 72p. (J). lib. bdg. 11.99 *(0-394-90001-4)*; 1957. (Illus.). 72p. (J). 8.99 *(0-394-80001-X)* Random Hse. Children's Bks. (Random Hse. Bks. for Young Readers).

—The Cat in the Hat. 1991. o.s.i *(0-679-81985-1)*; 1997. (Illus.). (J). 19.00 o.s.i *(0-679-89111-0)* Random Hse., Inc.

—The Cat in the Hat. 1957. (J). 7.99 o.p. *(0-606-02568-5)* Turtleback Bks.

—The Cat in the Hat - el Gato Ensombrerado. 1993. (Bilingual Beginner Books & Cassettes Ser.). (ENG & SPA., Illus.). 72p. (J). (ps-3). 6.95 o.s.i incl. audio *(0-679-84329-9*, Random Hse. Bks. for Young Readers) Random Hse. Children's Bks.

—The Cat in the Hat Comes Back. 1986. audio 6.95 o.s.i *(0-394-88327-6)*; 1958. (Illus.). 72p. (J). 8.99 *(0-394-80002-8)*; 1958. (Illus.). 72p. (J). lib. bdg. 11.99 *(0-394-90002-2)* Random Hse. Children's Bks. (Random Hse. Bks. for Young Readers).

—The Cat in the Hat Comes Back. 1958. (J). 7.99 o.p. *(0-606-02569-3)* Turtleback Bks.

—The Cat in the Hat Cuddly Doll & Collectible Book. 1994. (Illus.). 70p. (J). (ps up). 15.00 o.s.i *(0-679-86011-8*, Random Hse. Bks. for Young Readers) Random Hse. Children's Bks.

—The Cat in the Hat in English & Spanish. Rivera, Carlos, tr. 1967. (Spanish Beginner Bks.: No. 1). (ENG & SPA., Illus.). 72p. (J). (gr. 1-2). 6.99 o.s.i *(0-394-91626-3)* Beginner Bks.

—The Cat in the Hat's Great Big Flap Book. 1999. (Illus.). 12p. (J). (ps-3). bds. 11.99 *(0-679-89360-1*, Random Hse. Bks. for Young Readers) Random Hse. Children's Bks.

—Green Eggs & Ham. (Nifty Lift-and-Look Bks.). (Illus.). (J). (ps). 2001. 12p. bds. 7.99 *(0-375-81088-9)*; 1987. 64p. pap. 9.95 incl. audio *(0-394-89220-8)*; 1987. 64p. pap. 9.95 incl. audio *(0-394-89220-8)*; 1960. 72p. 8.99 *(0-394-80016-8)*; 1960. 72p. lib. bdg. 11.99 *(0-394-90016-2)* Random Hse. Children's Bks. (Random Hse. Bks. for Young Readers).

—Green Eggs & Ham. deluxe l.t. ed. 1998. (Wubbulous World of Dr. Seuss Ser.). (Illus.). 72p. (ps-3). 19.00 *(0-679-89129-3)* Random Hse., Inc.

—Green Eggs & Ham. 1960. (J). audio 17.68 *(0-394-12953-9)* SRA/McGraw-Hill.

—Green Eggs & Ham, the Cat in the Hat. 1994. (J). 9.98 o.s.i *(0-679-85630-7)* Random Hse. Video.

Seuss, Dr. & Eastman, P. D. El Gato en el Sombrero. Rivera, Carlos, tr. 1967. (Spanish Beginner Bks.: No. 1). (SPA., Illus.). 72p. (J). (ps-3). 8.99 *(0-394-81626-9*, RH6269, Random Hse. Bks. for Young Readers) Random Hse. Children's Bks.

Seuss, Dr. & Lund, John. The Cat in the Hat's Fun Book. 1997. (Illus.). pap. 2.75 o.s.i *(0-679-88511-0*, Random Hse. Bks. for Young Readers) Random Hse. Children's Bks.

Williams, Susan. The Cat in the Hat. 1995. (Literature Unit Ser.). (Illus.). 48p. pap., tchr. ed. 7.99 *(1-55734-540-6*, TCA0540) Teacher Created Materials, Inc.

CAXTON, WILLIAM, CA. 1422-1491—FICTION

Grohskopf, Bernice. Blood & Roses. 1979. (Illus.). (J). (gr. 6-10). 8.95 o.p. *(0-689-30681-4*, Atheneum) Simon & Schuster Children's Publishing.

CHARLEMAGNE, 742-814—FICTION

Manson, Christopher. The Marvellous Blue Mouse, ERS. 1992. (Illus.). 32p. (J). (gr. k-3). 15.95 o.p. *(0-8050-1622-8*, Holt, Henry & Co. Bks. For Young Readers) Holt, Henry & Co.

Westwood, Jennifer. Stories of Charlemagne. 1976. (J). (gr. 6 up). 26.95 *(0-87599-213-7)* Phillips, S.G. Inc.

CHESTER CRICKET (FICTITIOUS CHARACTER)—FICTION

Jones, Chuck, illus. & adapted by. The Cricket in Times Square. 1984. (Chester Cricket Ser.). 48p. (J). (gr. 3-6). 5.95 o.p. *(0-8249-8074-3)* Ideals Pubns.

Selden, George. Chester Cricket's New Home, RS. 1983. (Chester Cricket Ser.). (Illus.). 144p. (J). (gr. 3-6). 15.00 o.s.i *(0-374-31240-0*, Farrar, Straus & Giroux (BYR)) Farrar, Straus & Giroux.

—Chester Cricket's New Home. 1984. (Chester Cricket Ser.). (Illus.). 160p. (gr. 3-6). pap. text 4.50 *(0-440-41246-3*, Yearling) Random Hse. Children's Bks.

—Chester Cricket's New Home. 1983. (Chester Cricket Ser.). (J). (gr. 3-6). 10.04 *(0-606-03355-6)* Turtleback Bks.

—Chester Cricket's Pigeon Ride, RS. 1981. (Chester Cricket Ser.). (Illus.). 64p. (J). (gr. 3-6). 15.00 o.s.i *(0-374-31239-7*, Farrar, Straus & Giroux (BYR)) Farrar, Straus & Giroux.

—Chester Cricket's Pigeon Ride. 1983. (Chester Cricket Ser.). (Illus.). 80p. (gr. 3-6). pap. text 3.50 o.s.i *(0-440-41389-3*, Yearling) Random Hse. Children's Bks.

—Chester Cricket's Pigeon Ride. 1983. (Chester Cricket Ser.). (J). (gr. 3-6). 9.65 *(0-606-01151-X)* Turtleback Bks.

—The Cricket in Times Square. 1999. (Chester Cricket Ser.). 176p. (gr. 3-6). mass mkt. 2.99 o.s.i *(0-440-22889-1)* Bantam Bks.

—The Cricket in Times Square. 2002. (Illus.). (J). 14.47 *(0-7587-0252-3)* Book Wholesalers, Inc.

—The Cricket in Times Square. 2000. (Chester Cricket Ser.). (J). (gr. 3-6). audio 18.00 *(0-7366-9062-X)* Books on Tape, Inc.

—The Cricket in Times Square. (Chester Cricket Ser.). 160p. (J). (gr. 3-6). 1996. mass mkt. 2.49 o.s.i *(0-440-22022-X)*; 1993. pap. 1.99 o.s.i *(0-440-21622-2)* Dell Publishing.

—The Cricket in Times Square, RS. 1960. (Chester Cricket Ser.). (Illus.). 144p. (J). (gr. 3-6). 16.00 *(0-374-31650-3*, Farrar, Straus & Giroux (BYR)) Farrar, Straus & Giroux.

—The Cricket in Times Square. 1999. (Chester Cricket Ser.). 32p. (J). (gr. 3-6). 9.95 *(1-56137-396-6)* Novel Units, Inc.

—The Cricket in Times Square. l.t. ed. 1990. (Chester Cricket Ser.). 192p. (J). (gr. 3-6). reprint ed. lib. bdg. 16.95 o.s.i *(1-55736-170-3*, Cornerstone Bks.) Pages, Inc.

—The Cricket in Times Square. (Chester Cricket Ser.). 151p. (J). (gr. 3-6). pap. 5.50 *(0-8072-8311-8)*; 2001. (J). (gr. 3-6). audio compact disk 28.00 *(0-8072-0503-6)*; 1995. (J). (gr. 3-6). audio 18.00 *(0-553-47406-5)*; 2004. (J). (gr. 5-6). audio compact disk 14.99 *(0-8072-0475-7)*; 2003. (YA). (gr. 4-7). audio 9.99 *(0-8072-8285-5)*; 2000. (J). (gr. 3-6). audio 23.00 *(0-8072-8309-6*, LL0178); 2000. 151p. (J). (gr. 3-6). pap. 23.00 incl. audio *(0-8072-8310-X*, YA158SP); 2000. 151p. (J). (gr. 3-6). pap. 23.00 incl. audio *(0-8072-8310-X*, YA158SP) Random Hse. Audio Publishing Group. (Listening Library).

—The Cricket in Times Square. 1997. (Chester Cricket Ser.). (J). (gr. 3-6). o.s.i *(0-440-70015-9*, Dell Books for Young Readers) Random Hse. Children's Bks.

—The Cricket in Times Square. unabr. ed. (Chester Cricket Ser.). (J). (gr. 3-6). 2000. audio compact disk 27.00 *(0-7887-3451-2*, C1057E7); 1995. audio 27.00 *(0-7887-0142-8*, 94367E7) Recorded Bks., LLC.

—The Cricket in Times Square. 1986. (Chester Cricket Ser.). (J). (gr. 3-6). audio 21.33 *(0-394-76814-0)* SRA/McGraw-Hill.

—The Cricket in Times Square. 1985. (Chester Cricket Ser.). (Illus.). (J). (gr. 3-6). pap. 11.93 o.p. *(0-516-09162-X*, Children's Pr.) Scholastic Library Publishing.

—The Cricket in Times Square. 1998. (Chester Cricket Ser.). (J). (gr. 3-6). pap. text 3.95 *(0-439-04463-4)* Scholastic, Inc.

—The Cricket in Times Square. 1960. (Chester Cricket Ser.). (J). (gr. 3-6). 11.55 *(0-606-02883-8)* Turtleback Bks.

—The Cricket in Times Square. unabr. ed. (Chester Cricket Ser.). (J). (gr. 3-6). pap. 23.00 incl. audio Weston Woods Studios, Inc.

—The Cricket in Times Square: All about Animals. 1970. (Chester Cricket Ser.). (Illus.). 160p. (gr. 3-6). pap. text 5.99 *(0-440-41563-2*, Yearling) Random Hse. Children's Bks.

—Harry Cat's Pet Puppy, RS. 1974. (Chester Cricket Ser.). (Illus.). 160p. (J). (gr. 3-6). 15.00 o.s.i *(0-374-32856-0*, Farrar, Straus & Giroux (BYR)) Farrar, Straus & Giroux.

—Harry Cat's Pet Puppy. 1975. (Chester Cricket Ser.). 176p. (gr. 3-6). pap. text 4.99 *(0-440-45647-9*, Yearling) Random Hse. Children's Bks.

—Harry Kitten & Tucker Mouse, RS. 1986. (Chester Cricket Ser.). (Illus.). 80p. (J). (gr. 3-6). 16.00 *(0-374-32860-9*, Farrar, Straus & Giroux (BYR)) Farrar, Straus & Giroux.

—Harry Kitten & Tucker Mouse. 1988. (Chester Cricket Ser.). 96p. (gr. 3-6). pap. text 3.99 o.s.i *(0-440-40124-0*, Yearling) Random Hse. Children's Bks.

—Harry Kitten & Tucker Mouse. 1989. (Chester Cricket Ser.). (J). (gr. 3-6). 9.09 o.p. *(0-606-12328-8)* Turtleback Bks.

—The Old Meadow, RS. (Chester Cricket Ser.). (Illus.). 208p. (J). (gr. 3-6). 2000. pap. 5.95 *(0-374-45605-4*, Sunburst); 1987. 15.00 o.s.i *(0-374-35616-5*, Farrar, Straus & Giroux (BYR)) Farrar, Straus & Giroux.

—The Old Meadow. 2000. (Chester Cricket Ser.). (J). (gr. 3-6). 12.00 *(0-606-20135-1)* Turtleback Bks.

—Tucker's Countryside, RS. 1969. (Chester Cricket Ser.). (Illus.). 176p. (J). (gr. 3-6). 16.00 o.s.i *(0-374-37854-1*, Farrar, Straus & Giroux (BYR)) Farrar, Straus & Giroux.

—Tucker's Countryside. 1979. (Chester Cricket Ser.). (Illus.). 167p. (J). (gr. 3-6). pap. 2.50 o.p. *(0-380-01584-6*, Avon Bks.) Morrow/Avon.

—Tucker's Countryside. 1989. (Chester Cricket Ser.). 176p. (gr. 3-6). reprint ed. pap. text 4.99 *(0-440-40248-4*, Yearling) Random Hse. Children's Bks.

—Tucker's Countryside. 1969. (Chester Cricket Ser.). (J). (gr. 3-6). 11.04 *(0-606-04414-0)* Turtleback Bks.

Selden, George & Williams, Garth. The Old Meadow. 1989. (Chester Cricket Ser.). 208p. (J). (gr. 3-6). pap. 3.25 o.s.i *(0-440-40238-7*, Yearling) Random Hse. Children's Bks.

CHET GECKO (FICTITIOUS CHARACTER)—FICTION

Hale, Bruce. The Big Nap. (Chet Gecko Mystery Ser.). (Illus.). (YA). (gr. 3-7). 2002. 132p. pap. 4.95 *(0-15-202479-4*, Harcourt Paperbacks); 2001. 128p. 14.00 *(0-15-202521-9)* Harcourt Children's Bks.

—The Chameleon Wore Chartreuse. 2000. (Chet Gecko Mystery Ser.). (Illus.). 112p. (YA). (gr. 2-5). 14.00 *(0-15-202281-3)* Harcourt Children's Bks.

—The Chameleon Wore Chartreuse: A Chet Gecko Mystery. 2001. (Illus.). (J). 11.00 *(0-606-21105-5)* Turtleback Bks.

—Chet Gecko - Private Eye. unabr. ed. 2001. (J). (gr. 2-5). audio 23.00 *(0-8072-8860-8)*; (gr. 4-7). audio 18.00 *(0-8072-6187-4)* Random Hse. Audio Publishing Group. (Listening Library).

—Farewell, My Lunchbag. (Chet Gecko Mystery Ser.). (Illus.). (YA). (gr. 3-7). 2002. 132p. pap. 4.95 *(0-15-202629-0*, Harcourt Paperbacks); 2001. 128p. 14.00 *(0-15-202275-9)* Harcourt Children's Bks.

—The Hamster of the Baskervilles. (Chet Gecko Mystery Ser.). (Illus.). (YA). 2003. 144p. pap. 4.95 *(0-15-202509-X*, Harcourt Paperbacks); 2002. 132p. (gr. 4-7). 14.00 *(0-15-202503-0)* Harcourt Children's Bks.

—The Malted Falcon. 2003. (Chet Gecko Mystery Ser.). (Illus.). 128p. (YA). 14.00 *(0-15-216706-4)* Harcourt Children's Bks.

—The Malted Falcon: A Chet Gecko Mystery. 2004. (Chet Gecko Mystery Ser.). (Illus.). 132p. (YA). pap. *(0-15-216712-9*, Harcourt Paperbacks) Harcourt Children's Bks.

—This Gum for Hire. (Chet Gecko Mystery Ser.). (Illus.). (YA). 2003. 144p. pap. 4.95 *(0-15-202497-2*, Harcourt Paperbacks); 2002. 136p. (gr. 3-7). 14.00 *(0-15-202491-3)* Harcourt Children's Bks.

CHRISTY (FICTITIOUS CHARACTER: MARSHALL)—FICTION

Marshall, Catherine. The Angry Intruder. 1995. (Christy Fiction Ser.: No. 3). 128p. (J). (gr. 4-8). pap. 4.99 o.s.i *(0-8499-3688-8)* Nelson, Tommy.

—The Bridge to Cutter Gap. 1995. (Christy Fiction Ser.: No. 1). 128p. (J). (gr. 4-8). mass mkt. 4.99 *(0-8499-3686-1)* Nelson, Tommy.

—Brotherly Love. 1997. (Christy Fiction Ser.: No. 12). 128p. (Orig.). (J). (gr. 4-8). mass mkt. 4.99 *(0-8499-3963-1)* Nelson, Tommy.

—Family Secrets. 1996. (Christy Fiction Ser.: No. 8). (Illus.). 128p. (Orig.). (J). (gr. 4-8). mass mkt. 4.99 *(0-8499-3959-3)* Nelson, Tommy.

—Goodbye, Sweet Prince. 1997. (Christy Fiction Ser.: No. 11). 128p. (Orig.). (J). (gr. 4-8). pap. 4.99 *(0-8499-3962-3)* Nelson, Tommy.

—Midnight Rescue. 1995. (Christy Fiction Ser.: No. 4). 128p. (J). (gr. 4-8). pap. 4.99 o.s.i *(0-8499-3689-6)* Nelson, Tommy.

—Mountain Madness. adapted ed. 1997. (Christy Fiction Ser.: No. 9). 128p. (Orig.). (J). (gr. 4-8). mass mkt. 4.99 *(0-8499-3960-7)* Nelson, Tommy.

—The Princess Club. 1996. (Christy Fiction Ser.: No. 7). 128p. (J). (gr. 4-8). pap. text 4.99 *(0-8499-3958-5)* Nelson, Tommy.

—The Proposal. 1995. (Christy Fiction Ser.: No. 5). 128p. (J). (gr. 4-8). mass mkt. 4.99 *(0-8499-3918-6)* Nelson, Tommy.

—Silent Superstitions. 1995. (Christy Fiction Ser.: No. 2). 128p. (J). (gr. 4-8). pap. 4.99 o.s.i *(0-8499-3687-X)* Nelson, Tommy.

—Stage Fright. 1997. (Christy Fiction Ser.: No. 10). (Illus.). 128p. (J). (gr. 4-8). mass mkt. 4.99 *(0-8499-3961-5)* Nelson, Tommy.

CLEOPATRA, QUEEN OF EGYPT, D. 30 B.C.—FICTION

Gregory, Kristiana. Cleopatra VII: Daughter of the Nile, Egypt, 57 B. C. 1999. (Royal Diaries Ser.). (Illus.). 221p. (J). (gr. 4-8). 10.95 *(0-590-81975-5*, Scholastic Pr.) Scholastic, Inc.

Lancaster, Peggy. Abby & the Golden Goddess. 1997. (Adventures of Abby Smith Through Time & Place Ser.: Vol. 3). 64p. (J). (gr. 3-5). pap. 6.95 *(0-87588-488-1)* Hobby Hse. Pr., Inc.

Shakespeare, William. Antony & Cleopatra. Gill, Roma, ed. 2002. (Oxford School Shakespeare Ser.). (Illus.). 224p. pap. text 7.95 *(0-19-832057-4)* Oxford Univ. Pr., Inc.

—Antony & Cleopatra. 2002. (Shakespeare Collection). (Illus.). 46p. (J). 9.95 o.p. *(0-19-521793-4)* Oxford Univ. Pr., Inc.

CLIFFORD, THE BIG RED DOG (FICTITIOUS CHARACTER)—FICTION

Barkly, Bob. A Puppy to Love. 2001. (Clifford, the Big Red Dog Ser.). (Illus.). (J). (gr. k-2). pap. *(0-439-22004-1)* Scholastic, Inc.

Bridwell, Norman. The Adventures of Clifford the Big Red Dog. 1994. (Comes to Life Bks.). 16p. (J). (ps-2). *(1-883366-42-9)* YES! Entertainment Corp.

—Bertrand dans la Tempete. 9999. (Clifford, the Big Red Dog Ser.).Tr. of Clifford & the Big Storm. (FRE., Illus.). (J). (gr. k-2). pap. 5.99 o.p. *(0-590-24553-8)* Scholastic, Inc.

—The Big Leaf Pile. 2002. (Big Red Readers Ser.). (Illus.). (J). 11.91 *(0-7587-6773-0)* Book Wholesalers, Inc.

—Las Buenas Acciones de Clifford. Palacios, Argentina, tr. 1996. (Clifford, the Big Red Dog Ser.). (SPA., Illus.). 32p. (J). (gr. k-2). pap. 3.50 *(0-590-40179-3*, SO2842, Scholastic en Espanola) Scholastic, Inc.

—Las Buenas Acciones de Clifford. 1980. (Clifford, the Big Red Dog Ser.). (SPA.). (J). (gr. k-2). 9.40 *(0-606-03108-1)* Turtleback Bks.

—Cleo Cooperates. 2002. (Clifford's Big Red Ideas Ser.). (Illus.). 7p. (J). bds. 4.99 *(0-439-39449-X)* Scholastic, Inc.

—Clifford: Clifford Gets a Job; Clifford's Riddles; Clifford's ABC, Clifford's Family; Clifford's Manners; Clifford Goes to Hollywood, 6 vols. 2002. (Illus.). (J). 14.00 *(0-439-44310-5)* Scholastic, Inc.

—Clifford al Rescate. 2000. (Clifford, the Big Red Dog Ser.). (SPA., Illus.). 32p. (J). (gr. k-2). pap. 3.50 *(0-439-12956-7*, SO2943, Scholastic en Espanola) Scholastic, Inc.

—Clifford al Rescate. 2000. (Clifford, the Big Red Dog Ser.). (SPA., Illus.). (J). (gr. k-2). 9.40 *(0-606-18534-8)* Turtleback Bks.

—Clifford & the Big Parade. 2002. (Clifford Bks.). (Illus.). (J). 11.45 *(0-7587-6372-7)* Book Wholesalers, Inc.

—Clifford & the Big Parade. 1998. (Clifford, the Big Red Dog Ser.). (Illus.). 32p. (J). (gr. k-2). mass mkt. 3.50 *(0-590-10811-5)* Scholastic, Inc.

—Clifford & the Big Parade. 1998. (Clifford, the Big Red Dog Ser.). (J). (gr. k-2). 9.65 *(0-606-13284-8)* Turtleback Bks.

—Clifford & the Big Storm. 1995. (Clifford, the Big Red Dog Ser.). (Illus.). 32p. (J). (gr. k-2). mass mkt. 3.25 (*0-590-25755-2*, Cartwheel Bks.) Scholastic, Inc.

—Clifford & the Big Storm. 1995. (Clifford, the Big Red Dog Ser.). (J). (gr. k-2). 9.40 (*0-606-07377-9*) Turtleback Bks.

—Clifford & the Grouchy Neighbors. 2002. (Clifford Bks.). (Illus.). (J). 11.45 (*0-7587-7030-8*) Book Wholesalers, Inc.

—Clifford & the Grouchy Neighbors. (Clifford, the Big Red Dog Ser.). (J). (gr. k-2). 1989. (Illus.). 32p. 7.95 (*0-590-63437-2*); 1988. audio 6.95 (*0-589-63437-2*); 1985. (Illus.). 32p. pap. 1.95 o.p. (*0-590-33461-1*); 1985. (Illus.). 32p. mass mkt. 3.25 (*0-590-44261-9*) Scholastic, Inc.

—Clifford & the Grouchy Neighbors. 1985. (Clifford, the Big Red Dog Ser.). (J). (gr. k-2). 9.40 (*0-606-03399-8*) Turtleback Bks.

—Clifford & the Halloween Parade. 2002. (Clifford, the Big Red Dog Ser.). (Illus.). 32p. (J). (gr. k-3). mass mkt. 3.99 (*0-439-09834-3*) Scholastic, Inc.

—Clifford & the Halloween Parade. 2000. (Clifford, the Big Red Dog Ser.). (Illus.). (J). (gr. k-2). 10.14 (*0-606-18867-3*) Turtleback Bks.

—Clifford at the Circus. 2002. (Clifford Bks.). (Illus.). (J). 11.45 (*0-7587-6707-2*) Book Wholesalers, Inc.

—Clifford at the Circus. (Clifford, the Big Red Dog Ser.). (J). (gr. k-2). (Illus.). 6.95 (*0-590-68639-9*); 1989. (Illus.). 32p. 7.95 (*0-590-63340-6*); 1985. (Illus.). 32p. pap. 1.95 o.p. (*0-590-33588-X*); 1985. (Illus.). 32p. mass mkt. 3.25 (*0-590-44293-7*); 1977. pap. 1.50 o.p. (*0-590-11835-8*) Scholastic, Inc.

—Clifford at the Circus. 1985. (Clifford, the Big Red Dog Ser.). (J). (gr. k-2). 9.65 (*0-606-03422-6*) Turtleback Bks.

—Clifford Barks! (Clifford, the Big Red Dog Ser.). (Illus.). 16p. (J). (ps-k). 2000. bds. 3.25 (*0-439-14999-1*); 1996. pap. 7.95 (*0-590-67093-X*) Scholastic, Inc. (Cartwheel Bks.).

—Clifford Celebrates the Year. 2002. (Clifford Ser.). (Illus.). 256p. (J). pap. 10.99 (*0-439-46770-5*) Scholastic, Inc.

—Clifford Counts Bubbles. 1992. (Clifford, the Big Red Dog Ser.). (Illus.). 16p. (J). (ps-k). bds. 3.25 (*0-590-45872-8*, 035, Cartwheel Bks.) Scholastic, Inc.

—Clifford Counts 1-2-3. 1998. (Clifford, the Big Red Dog Ser.). (Illus.). 14p. (J). (ps-k). bds. 5.99 (*0-590-37928-3*, Cartwheel Bks.) Scholastic, Inc.

—Clifford, el Cachorrito. 2003. (Clifford Ser.). (SPA., Illus.). 32p. (J). mass mkt. 3.50 (*0-439-54566-8*, Scholastic en Espanola) Scholastic, Inc.

—Clifford el Dolor de Barriga. 2003. (Big Red Reader Ser.). (SPA., Illus.). 32p. (J). (gr. k-2). pap. 3.99 (*0-439-55113-7*, Scholastic en Espanola) Scholastic, Inc.

—Clifford el Gran Perro Colorado. 1997. (Clifford, the Big Red Dog Ser.). (SPA.). (J). (ps-k). bds. 5.99 (*0-590-38178-4*, SO6873) Scholastic, Inc.

—Clifford el Gran Perro Colorado. Leos, Frances, tr. 1994. (Clifford, the Big Red Dog Ser.). (SPA., Illus.). 32p. (J). (gr. k-2). pap. 3.50 (*0-590-41380-5*, SO2840, Scholastic en Espanola) Scholastic, Inc.

—Clifford el Gran Perro Colorado. 1985. (Clifford, the Big Red Dog Ser.). (SPA.). (J). (gr. k-2). 9.40 (*0-606-03759-4*) Turtleback Bks.

—Clifford, el Pequeno Perro Colorado. 1998. (Clifford, the Big Red Dog Ser.). (SPA.). 32p. (J). (gr. k-2). pap. 3.50 (*0-590-04311-0*, SO8201, Scholastic en Espanola) Scholastic, Inc.

—Clifford, el Pequeno Perro Colorado. 1998. (Clifford, the Big Red Dog Ser.). (SPA.). (J). (gr. k-2). 9.40 (*0-606-15486-8*) Turtleback Bks.

—Clifford el Perro Bombero. 1994. (Clifford, the Big Red Dog Ser.).Tr. of Clifford the Firehouse Dog. (SPA.). (J). (gr. k-2). 9.40 (*0-606-06281-5*) Turtleback Bks.

—Clifford, el Perro Bombero. 1994. (Clifford, the Big Red Dog Ser.). (SPA., Illus.). 32p. (J). (gr. k-2). pap. 3.50 (*0-590-48808-2*, SO6031, Scholastic en Espanola) Scholastic, Inc.

—Clifford Follows His Nose. 1992. (Clifford, the Big Red Dog Ser.). 24p. (J). (ps-k). pap. 5.95 (*0-590-44345-3*) Scholastic, Inc.

—Clifford Gets a Job. 2002. (Clifford Bks.). (Illus.). (J). 11.45 (*0-7587-6390-5*) Book Wholesalers, Inc.

—Clifford Gets a Job. (Clifford, the Big Red Dog Ser.). (Illus.). (J). (gr. k-2). 1985. 32p. pap. 1.95 o.p. (*0-590-33555-3*); 1985. 32p. mass mkt. 3.25 (*0-590-44296-1*); 1972. pap. 3.95 o.p. (*0-590-04384-6*); 1972. pap. 1.50 o.p. (*0-590-01575-3*) Scholastic, Inc.

—Clifford Gets a Job. 1965. (Clifford, the Big Red Dog Ser.). (J). (gr. k-2). 9.65 (*0-606-01044-0*) Turtleback Bks.

—Clifford Goes Home. 1981. (Clifford, the Big Red Dog Ser.). (J). (gr. k-2). pap. 1.25 o.p. (*0-590-31607-9*) Scholastic, Inc.

—Clifford Goes to Dog School. 2002. (Clifford, the Big Red Dog Ser.). (Illus.). 32p. (J). (ps-3). mass mkt. 3.50 (*0-439-32788-1*) Scholastic, Inc.

—Clifford Goes to Hollywood. 2002. (Clifford Bks.). (Illus.). (J). 11.45 (*0-7587-7061-8*) Book Wholesalers, Inc.

—Clifford Goes to Hollywood. (Clifford, the Big Red Dog Ser.). (Illus.). (J). (gr. k-2). 1990. 32p. 7.95 (*0-590-63435-6*); 1986. pap. 1.95 o.p. (*0-590-40115-7*); 1986. 32p. mass mkt. 3.25 (*0-590-44289-9*) Scholastic, Inc.

—Clifford Goes to Hollywood. 1980. (Clifford, the Big Red Dog Ser.). (J). (gr. k-2). 9.65 (*0-606-03090-5*) Turtleback Bks.

—Clifford Grow Chart. 1990. (Clifford, the Big Red Dog Ser.). (J). (gr. k-2). pap. 2.95 (*0-590-63637-5*) Scholastic, Inc.

—Clifford Grows Up. 2002. (Clifford Bks.). (Illus.). (J). 11.45 (*0-7587-1071-2*) Book Wholesalers, Inc.

—Clifford Grows Up. 1999. (Clifford, the Big Red Dog Ser.). (Illus.). 32p. (J). (gr. k-2). mass mkt. 3.50 (*0-439-08233-1*) Scholastic, Inc.

—Clifford Grows Up. 1999. (Clifford, the Big Red Dog Ser.). (J). (gr. k-2). 9.65 (*0-606-16935-0*) Turtleback Bks.

—Clifford Keeps Cool. 2002. (Clifford Bks.). (Illus.). (J). 11.45 (*0-7587-5006-4*) Book Wholesalers, Inc.

—Clifford Keeps Cool. 1999. (Clifford, the Big Red Dog Ser.). (Illus.). 32p. (J). (gr. k-2). mass mkt. 3.50 (*0-439-04394-8*) Scholastic, Inc.

—Clifford Keeps Cool. 1999. (Clifford, the Big Red Dog Ser.). (J). (gr. k-2). 9.40 (*0-606-16626-2*) Turtleback Bks.

—Clifford Makes a Friend. 2002. (Clifford Bks.). (Illus.). (J). 11.91 (*0-7587-5017-X*) Book Wholesalers, Inc.

—Clifford Makes a Friend. 1998. (Clifford, the Big Red Dog Ser.). (Illus.). 32p. (J). (gr. k-2). mass mkt. 3.99 (*0-590-37930-5*) Scholastic, Inc.

—Clifford Makes a Friend. 1998. (Clifford, the Big Red Dog Ser.). (J). (gr. k-2). 10.14 (*0-606-15487-6*) Turtleback Bks.

—Clifford Plush Face Book. 1999. (Clifford, the Big Red Dog Ser.). (Illus.). 8p. (J). (ps-k). mass mkt. 7.95 (*0-439-06131-8*) Scholastic, Inc.

—Clifford Takes a Trip. 2002. (Clifford Bks.). (Illus.). (J). 11.45 (*0-7587-9335-9*) Book Wholesalers, Inc.

—Clifford Takes a Trip. (Clifford, the Big Red Dog Ser.). (J). (gr. k-2). 1991. 32p. 7.95 (*0-590-63823-8*, Cartwheel Bks.); 1985. (Illus.). 32p. pap. 1.95 o.p. (*0-590-33554-5*); 1985. (Illus.). 32p. mass mkt. 3.50 (*0-590-44260-0*); 1969. (Illus.). pap. 1.25 o.p. (*0-590-08029-6*) Scholastic, Inc.

—Clifford Takes a Trip. 1966. (Clifford, the Big Red Dog Ser.). (J). (gr. k-2). 9.40 (*0-606-01045-9*) Turtleback Bks.

—Clifford the Big Red Dog. (Clifford, the Big Red Dog Ser.). (J). (ps-k). 1997. (Illus.). 32p. bds. 5.99 (*0-590-34125-1*); 1997. 15.99 (*0-590-27359-0*); 1988. (Illus.). 32p. pap. 10.95 (*0-590-40743-0*); 1988. (Illus.). 32p. 7.95 (*0-590-63212-4*); 1985. (Illus.). 28p. mass mkt. 3.25 (*0-590-44297-X*); 1969. (Illus.). pap. 1.25 o.p. (*0-590-08028-8*); 1969. (Illus.). pap. 3.95 o.p. (*0-590-04385-4*); 40th anniv. deluxe ed. 2002. (Illus.). 32p. pap. 14.95 (*0-439-40396-0*, Cartwheel Bks.) Scholastic, Inc.

—Clifford the Big Red Dog. 1963. (Clifford, the Big Red Dog Ser.). (J). (gr. k-2). 9.40 (*0-606-01116-1*) Turtleback Bks.

—Clifford the Big Red Dog With Puppet. 1997. (Clifford, the Big Red Dog Ser.). (J). (gr. k-2). 23.99 (*0-590-27449-X*) Scholastic, Inc.

—Clifford the Firehouse Dog. (Clifford, the Big Red Dog Ser.). (Illus.). (J). (gr. k-2). (FRE.). pap. 5.99 (*0-590-24375-6*); 1994. 32p. mass mkt. 3.50 (*0-590-48419-2*, Cartwheel Bks.) Scholastic, Inc.

—Clifford the Firehouse Dog. 1994. (Clifford, the Big Red Dog Ser.). (J). (gr. k-2). 9.65 (*0-606-06282-3*) Turtleback Bks.

—Clifford the Small Red Puppy. (Clifford, the Big Red Dog Ser.). (J). (gr. k-2). 2000. 12.99 (*0-439-09260-4*); 1990. 32p. pap. 10.95 (*0-590-43496-9*); 1988. 32p. 7.95 (*0-590-63211-6*); 1988. 32p. 7.95 (*0-590-63211-6*); 1985. (Illus.). 32p. pap. 1.95 o.p. (*0-590-33583-9*); 1978. pap. 1.25 o.p. (*0-590-09349-5*); 1973. (Illus.). 32p. pap. 1.95 o.p. (*0-590-33726-2*); 1985. (Illus.). 32p. mass mkt. 3.50 (*0-590-44294-5*) Scholastic, Inc.

—Clifford the Small Red Puppy. 1972. (Clifford, the Big Red Dog Ser.). (J). (gr. k-2). 9.40 (*0-606-01046-7*) Turtleback Bks.

—Clifford the Weather Dog. 2002. (Clifford, the Big Red Dog Ser.). (Illus.). 5p. (J). bds. 6.99 (*0-439-39448-1*) Scholastic, Inc.

—Clifford to the Rescue. 2002. (Clifford Bks.). (Illus.). (J). 11.45 (*0-7587-5005-6*) Book Wholesalers, Inc.

—Clifford to the Rescue. 2000. (Clifford, the Big Red Dog Ser.). (Illus.). 32p. (J). (gr. k-2). mass mkt. 3.50 (*0-439-14038-2*, Cartwheel Bks.) Scholastic, Inc.

—Clifford to the Rescue. 2000. (Clifford, the Big Red Dog Ser.). (Illus.). (J). (gr. k-2). 9.40 (*0-606-18535-6*) Turtleback Bks.

—Clifford Treasury: Clifford the Small Red Puppy; Clifford the Big Red Dog; Clifford's Pals; Clifford & the Grouchy Neighbors, 4 vols., No. 1. 1991. (Clifford, the Big Red Dog Ser.). (J). (gr. k-2). pap. 9.00 (*0-590-63953-6*) Scholastic, Inc.

—Clifford Treasury: Clifford's Birthday Party; Clifford's Puppy Days; Clifford's Family; Clifford's Kitten, 4 vols., No. 2. 1991. (Clifford, the Big Red Dog Ser.). (J). (gr. k-2). pap. 9.00 (*0-590-63952-8*) Scholastic, Inc.

—Clifford Va a la Escuela. 1999. (Clifford, the Big Red Dog Ser.). (SPA., Illus.). 32p. (J). (gr. k-2). pap. 3.50 (*0-439-08729-5*, SO4319, Scholastic en Espanola) Scholastic, Inc.

—Clifford Va a la Escuela. 1999. (Clifford, the Big Red Dog Ser.). (SPA.). (J). (gr. k-2). 9.40 (*0-606-17052-9*) Turtleback Bks.

—Clifford Va de Viaje. Palacios, Argentina, tr. rev. ed. 1995. (Clifford, the Big Red Dog Ser.). (SPA., Illus.). 32p. (J). (ps-k). pap. 3.50 o.s.i (*0-590-40844-5*, SO2841, Scholastic en Espanola) Scholastic, Inc.

—Clifford Va de Viaje. 1987. (Clifford, the Big Red Dog Ser.). (SPA.). (J). (gr. k-2). 9.40 (*0-606-03188-X*) Turtleback Bks.

—Clifford Visita el Hospital. 2000. (Clifford, the Big Red Dog Ser.). (SPA., Illus.). 32p. (J). (ps-k). pap. 3.50 (*0-439-18897-0*, SO4989, Scholastic en Espanola) Scholastic, Inc.

—Clifford Visita el Hospital. 2000. (SPA., Illus.). (J). 9.40 (*0-606-18869-X*) Turtleback Bks.

—Clifford Visits the Hospital. 2002. (Clifford Bks.). (Illus.). (J). 11.45 (*0-7587-5004-8*) Book Wholesalers, Inc.

—Clifford Visits the Hospital. 2000. (Clifford, the Big Red Dog Ser.). (Illus.). 32p. (J). (ps-k). mass mkt. 3.50 (*0-439-14096-X*) Scholastic, Inc.

—Clifford Visits the Hospital. 2000. (Clifford, the Big Red Dog Ser.). (Illus.). (J). (gr. k-2). 9.40 (*0-606-18868-1*) Turtleback Bks.

—Clifford Wants a Cookie. 1988. (Clifford, the Big Red Dog Ser.). (Illus.). 16p. (J). (gr. k-2). pap. 3.95 (*0-590-63282-5*) Scholastic, Inc.

—Clifford, We Love You. (Clifford, the Big Red Dog Ser.). (J). (gr. k-2). 1994. 10.95 (*0-590-48612-8*); 1991. 32p. mass mkt. 3.50 (*0-590-43843-3*); 1991. 32p. 6.95 (*0-590-63604-9*); 1991. 32p. 6.95 (*0-590-63604-9*) Scholastic, Inc.

—Clifford, We Love You. 1991. (Clifford, the Big Red Dog Ser.). (J). (gr. k-2). 9.65 (*0-606-04638-0*) Turtleback Bks.

—Clifford y el Dia de Accion de Gracias. 2002. (Clifford, the Big Red Dog Ser.). (SPA., Illus.). 32p. (J). (gr. k-2). pap. 3.50 (*0-439-41832-1*, Scholastic en Espanola) Scholastic, Inc.

—Clifford y el Dia de Halloween. 2000. (Clifford, the Big Red Dog Ser.). (SPA., Illus.). 32p. (J). (gr. k-2). pap. 3.50 o.s.i (*0-439-17451-1*, SO1221, Scholastic en Espanola) Scholastic, Inc.

—Clifford y el Dia de Halloween. 2000. (Clifford, the Big Red Dog Ser.). (SPA., Illus.). (J). (gr. k-2). 9.65 (*0-606-18870-3*) Turtleback Bks.

—Clifford y el Dia de Pascua. 2003. (Clifford, the Big Red Dog Ser.). (SPA., Illus.). 32p. (J). (ps-k). pap. 3.50 (*0-590-11740-8*, SO7533, Scholastic en Espanola) Scholastic, Inc.

—Clifford y el Gran Desfile. 1998. (Clifford, the Big Red Dog Ser.). (SPA., Illus.). 32p. (J). (ps-k). pap. 3.50 (*0-590-50663-3*, SO7528, Scholastic en Espanola) Scholastic, Inc.

—Clifford y el Gran Desfile. 1998. (Clifford, the Big Red Dog Ser.). (SPA.). (J). (gr. k-2). 9.40 (*0-606-13285-6*) Turtleback Bks.

—Clifford y el Verano Caluroso. Mlawer, Teresa, tr. 1999. (Clifford, the Big Red Dog Ser.). (SPA., Illus.). 32p. (J). (gr. k-2). pap. 3.50 (*0-439-05014-6*, SO4995, Scholastic en Espanola) Scholastic, Inc.

—Clifford y la Hora del Bano. 2003. (Clifford Ser.).Tr. of Clifford's Bathtime. (SPA.). 16p. (J). pap. 3.95 (*0-439-54567-6*, Scholastic en Espanola) Scholastic, Inc.

—Clifford y la Limpieza de Primavera. 1997. (Clifford, the Big Red Dog Ser.). (SPA., Illus.). 32p. (J). (gr. k-2). pap. 3.50 o.s.i (*0-590-04158-4*, 691735Q, Scholastic en Espanola) Scholastic, Inc.

—Clifford y la Limpieza de Primavera. 1997. (Clifford, the Big Red Dog Ser.). (SPA.). (J). (gr. k-2). 9.40 (*0-606-11211-1*) Turtleback Bks.

—Clifford y la Tormenta. 1995. (Clifford, the Big Red Dog Ser.). (SPA., Illus.). 32p. (J). (ps-k). pap. 3.50 o.s.i (*0-590-25756-0*, SO0321, Scholastic en Espanola) Scholastic, Inc.

—Clifford y la Tormenta. 1995. (Clifford, the Big Red Dog Ser.). (SPA.). (J). (gr. k-2). 8.19 o.p. (*0-606-07378-7*) Turtleback Bks.

—Clifford y lod Opuestos. 2003. (Clifford Ser.).Tr. of Clifford's Opposites. (SPA., Illus.). 7p. (J). pap. 3.95 (*0-439-55110-2*, Scholastic en Espanola) Scholastic, Inc.

—Clifford y los Sondios de los Animales. 2003. (Clifford Ser.).Tr. of Clifford's Animal Sounds. (SPA.). 7p. (J). pap. 3.95 (*0-439-55109-9*, Scholastic en Espanola) Scholastic, Inc.

—Clifford's ABC. (Clifford, the Big Red Dog Ser.). (J). (gr. k-2). 1994. 10.95 (*0-590-48694-2*); 1986. 32p. mass mkt. 3.25 (*0-590-44286-4*); 1984. (Illus.). 32p. pap. 5.95 o.p. (*0-590-33154-X*); 1986. (Illus.). 32p. reprint ed. pap. 1.95 o.p. (*0-590-40453-9*) Scholastic, Inc.

—Clifford's ABC. 1983. (Clifford, the Big Red Dog Ser.). (J). (gr. k-2). 9.40 (*0-606-03087-5*) Turtleback Bks.

—Clifford's ABC Coloring Book. 1988. (Clifford, the Big Red Dog Ser.). (Illus.). 32p. (J). (gr. k-2). pap. 1.50 o.p. (*0-590-32953-7*) Scholastic, Inc.

—Clifford's Animal Sounds. 1991. (Clifford, the Big Red Dog Ser.). 16p. (J). (ps-k). bds. 3.25 (*0-590-44734-3*) Scholastic, Inc.

—Clifford's Bag of Fun. 1993. (Clifford, the Big Red Dog Ser.). 16p. (J). (gr. k-2). 5.95 (*0-590-69010-8*) Scholastic, Inc.

—Clifford's Bathtime. 1991. (Clifford, the Big Red Dog Ser.). 16p. (J). (ps-k). bds. 3.25 (*0-590-44735-1*) Scholastic, Inc.

—Clifford's Bedtime. (J). 2003. 7p. pap. 3.95 (*0-439-54568-4*, Scholastic en Espanola); 1991. 16p. bds. 3.25 (*0-590-44736-X*) Scholastic, Inc.

—Clifford's Best Friend: A Story about Emily Elizabeth. 2002. (Clifford Bks.). (Illus.). (J). 11.45 (*0-7587-5007-2*) Book Wholesalers, Inc.

—Clifford's Best Friend: A Story about Emily Elizabeth. 2001. (Clifford, the Big Red Dog Ser.). (Illus.). 32p. (J). (ps-k). mass mkt. 3.50 (*0-439-21997-3*) Scholastic, Inc.

—Clifford's Best Friend: A Story about Emily Elizabeth. 2000. (Clifford, the Big Red Dog Ser.). (J). (gr. k-2). 9.40 (*0-606-19551-3*) Turtleback Bks.

—Clifford's Big Book of Stories. 1994. (Clifford, the Big Red Dog Ser.). (Illus.). 64p. (J). (gr. k-2). pap. 9.95 (*0-590-47925-3*, Cartwheel Bks.) Scholastic, Inc.

—Clifford's Big Book of Things to Know: A Book of Fun Facts. 1999. (Clifford, the Big Red Dog Ser.). (Illus.). 40p. (J). (gr. k-2). pap. 10.95 (*0-590-00385-2*, Cartwheel Bks.) Scholastic, Inc.

—Clifford's Birthday Party. 2002. (Clifford Bks.). (Illus.). (J). 11.45 (*0-7587-6391-3*) Book Wholesalers, Inc.

—Clifford's Birthday Party. (Clifford, the Big Red Dog Ser.). (J). (gr. k-2). 1991. (Illus.). 32p. pap. 10.95 o.p. (*0-590-44232-5*); 1988. (Illus.). 32p. mass mkt. 3.50 (*0-590-44279-1*); 1988. (Illus.). 32p. 7.95 (*0-590-63237-X*); 1988. (Illus.). 32p. 7.95 (*0-590-63237-X*); 1993. bds. 19.95 o.p. (*0-590-73102-5*) Scholastic, Inc.

—Clifford's Birthday Party. 1988. (Clifford, the Big Red Dog Ser.). (J). (gr. k-2). 9.65 (*0-606-03561-3*) Turtleback Bks.

—Clifford's Busy Week. 2002. 32p. (J). mass mkt. 3.50 (*0-439-39452-X*) Scholastic, Inc.

—Clifford's Christmas. (Clifford, the Big Red Dog Ser.). (J). (gr. k-2). 1987. pap. 5.95 incl. audio; 1987. (Illus.). 32p. 5.95 (*0-590-63210-8*); 1984. (Illus.). pap. 1.95 o.p. (*0-590-40221-8*); 1984. (Illus.). 32p. mass mkt. 3.25 (*0-590-44288-0*); 1984. (Illus.). 32p. pap. 1.95 o.p. (*0-590-33277-5*) Scholastic, Inc.

—Clifford's Christmas. 1984. (Clifford, the Big Red Dog Ser.). (J). (gr. k-2). 9.40 (*0-606-03088-3*) Turtleback Bks.

—Clifford's Day with Dad. 2003. (Clifford Ser.). 32p. (J). mass mkt. 3.50 (*0-439-41073-8*) Scholastic, Inc.

—Clifford's Family. 2002. (Clifford Bks.). (Illus.). (J). 11.45 (*0-7587-6708-0*) Book Wholesalers, Inc.

—Clifford's Family. (Clifford, the Big Red Dog Ser.). (J). (gr. k-2). 1985. (Illus.). 32p. mass mkt. 3.25 (*0-590-44290-2*); 1984. pap. 1.50 o.p. (*0-590-33275-9*); 1984. (Illus.). 32p. pap. 1.95 o.p. (*0-590-33849-8*); 1993. 19.95 o.p. (*0-590-71584-4*) Scholastic, Inc.

—Clifford's Family. 1985. (Clifford, the Big Red Dog Ser.). (J). (gr. k-2). 9.65 (*0-606-03373-4*) Turtleback Bks.

—Clifford's Favorite Story Books. 2003. 14.00 (*0-439-55202-8*) Scholastic, Inc.

—Clifford's First Autumn. 1997. (Clifford, the Big Red Dog Ser.). (Illus.). 32p. (J). (gr. k-2). mass mkt. 3.50 (*0-590-34130-8*) Scholastic, Inc.

—Clifford's First Autumn. 1997. (Clifford, the Big Red Dog Ser.). (J). (gr. k-2). 9.40 (*0-606-11212-X*) Turtleback Bks.

—Clifford's First Christmas. (Clifford, the Big Red Dog Ser.). (Illus.). (J). (gr. k-2). (FRE.). pap. 5.99 (*0-590-24374-8*); 1994. 32p. mass mkt. 2.99 (*0-590-48420-6*, Cartwheel Bks.) Scholastic, Inc.

—Clifford's First Christmas. 1994. (Clifford, the Big Red Dog Ser.). (J). (gr. k-2). 9.40 (*0-606-06283-1*) Turtleback Bks.

—Clifford's First Easter. 1995. (Clifford, the Big Red Dog Ser.). (Illus.). 20p. (J). (gr. k-2). bds. 7.95 (*0-590-22241-4*, Cartwheel Bks.) Scholastic, Inc.

—Clifford's First Halloween. (Clifford, the Big Red Dog Ser.). (Illus.). 32p. (J). (gr. k-2). 1996. (FRE.). pap. 5.99 (*0-590-16034-6*); 1995. mass mkt. 3.25 (*0-590-50317-0*, Cartwheel Bks.) Scholastic, Inc.

—Clifford's First Halloween. 1995. (Clifford, the Big Red Dog Ser.). (J). (gr. k-2). 9.65 (*0-606-07379-5*) Turtleback Bks.

—Clifford's First School Day. 2002. (Clifford Bks.). (Illus.). (J). 11.45 (*0-7587-6587-8*) Book Wholesalers, Inc.

—Clifford's First School Day. 1999. (Clifford, the Big Red Dog Ser.). (Illus.). 32p. (J). (gr. k-2). mass mkt. 3.50 (*0-439-08284-6*, Cartwheel Bks.) Scholastic, Inc.

—Clifford's First School Day. 1999. (Cifford the Big Red Dog Ser.). (J). (gr. k-2). lib. bdg. 9.65 (*0-606-17051-0*) Turtleback Bks.

—Clifford's First Sleepover. 2004. (Clifford Ser.). 24p. (J). mass mkt. 3.50 (*0-439-47285-7*) Scholastic, Inc.

—Clifford's First Snow Day. 2002. (Clifford Bks.). (Illus.). (J). 11.45 (*0-7587-5008-0*) Book Wholesalers, Inc.

—Clifford's First Snow Day. 1998. (Clifford, the Big Red Dog Ser.). (Illus.). 32p. (J). (gr. k-2). mass mkt. 3.50 (*0-590-03480-4*, Cartwheel Bks.) Scholastic, Inc.

—Clifford's First Snow Day. 1998. (Clifford, the Big Red Dog Ser.). (J). (gr. k-2). 9.40 (*0-606-15488-4*) Turtleback Bks.

—Clifford's First Valentine's Day. 2002. (Clifford Bks.). (Illus.). (J). 11.45 (*0-7587-6533-9*) Book Wholesalers, Inc.

—Clifford's First Valentine's Day. 1997. (Clifford, the Big Red Dog Ser.). (Illus.). 32p. (J). (gr. k-2). mass mkt. 3.50 (*0-590-92162-2*, Cartwheel Bks.) Scholastic, Inc.

—Clifford's First Valentine's Day. 1997. (Clifford, the Big Red Dog Ser.). (J). (gr. k-2). 9.65 (*0-606-10774-6*) Turtleback Bks.

—Clifford's Furry Friends. (Clifford, the Big Red Dog Ser.). (Illus.). (J). (ps-k). 2001. 12p. bds. 6.99 (*0-439-24186-3*); 1996. 16p. mass mkt. 8.95 (*0-590-86402-5*, Cartwheel Bks.) Scholastic, Inc.

—Clifford's Good Deeds. (Clifford, the Big Red Dog Ser.). (J). (gr. k-2). 1991. 32p. 7.95 (*0-590-63824-6*); 1991. 32p. 7.95 (*0-590-63824-6*); 1987. pap. 3.95 o.p. (*0-590-20792-X*); 1985. (Illus.). pap. 1.95 o.p. (*0-590-33589-8*); 1985. (Illus.). 32p. mass mkt. 3.25 (*0-590-44292-9*); 1983. pap. 1.50 o.p. (*0-590-33749-1*) Scholastic, Inc.

—Clifford's Good Deeds. 1975. (Clifford, the Big Red Dog Ser.). (J). (gr. k-2). 9.40 (*0-606-01047-5*) Turtleback Bks.

—Clifford's Halloween. (Clifford, the Big Red Dog Ser.). (Illus.). (J). (gr. k-2). 1994. 6.95 (*0-590-66159-0*); 1989. 32p. 5.95 o.p. (*0-590-63436-4*); 1989. 32p. 5.95 o.p. (*0-590-63436-4*); 1986. pap. 1.95 o.p. (*0-590-40324-9*); 1986. 32p. mass mkt. 2.99 (*0-590-44287-2*) Scholastic, Inc.

—Clifford's Halloween. 1986. (Clifford, the Big Red Dog Ser.). (J). (gr. k-2). 9.14 (*0-606-03091-3*) Turtleback Bks.

—Clifford's Happy Christmas Lacing Book. 1995. (Clifford, the Big Red Dog Ser.). (Illus.). 24p. (J). (gr. k-2). 8.95 (*0-590-60494-5*, Cartwheel Bks.) Scholastic, Inc.

—Clifford's Happy Days: A Pop-up Book. 1990. (Clifford, the Big Red Dog Ser.). (Illus.). 12p. (J). (ps-k). pap. 12.95 (*0-590-42926-4*) Scholastic, Inc.

—Clifford's Happy Easter. 1994. (Clifford, the Big Red Dog Ser.). (Illus.). 32p. (J). (gr. k-2). mass mkt. 3.50 (*0-590-47782-X*, Cartwheel Bks.) Scholastic, Inc.

—Clifford's Happy Easter. 1994. (Clifford, the Big Red Dog Ser.). (J). (gr. k-2). 9.40 (*0-606-05790-0*) Turtleback Bks.

—Clifford's Happy Mother's Day. 2001. (Clifford, the Big Red Dog Ser.). (Illus.). 32p. (J). (gr. k-2). mass mkt. 3.50 (*0-439-22229-X*) Scholastic, Inc.

—Clifford's Happy New Year. 2004. (Clifford Ser.). 32p. (J). pap. 3.50 (*0-439-65087-9*, Cartwheel Bks.) Scholastic, Inc.

—Clifford's I Love You. 1994. (Clifford, the Big Red Dog Ser.). (Illus.). 10p. (J). (ps-k). pap. 4.95 o.p. (*0-590-47309-3*, Cartwheel Bks.) Scholastic, Inc.

—Clifford's Kitten. 1984. (Clifford, the Big Red Dog Ser.). (J). (gr. k-2). pap. 1.50 o.p. (*0-590-33276-7*); (Illus.). 32p. pap. 1.95 o.p. (*0-590-33967-2*); (Illus.). 32p. mass mkt. 3.50 (*0-590-44280-5*) Scholastic, Inc.

—Clifford's Kitten. 1984. (Clifford, the Big Red Dog Ser.). (J). (gr. k-2). 9.65 (*0-606-03372-6*) Turtleback Bks.

—Clifford's Manners. 1999. (Clifford, the Big Red Dog Ser.). (J). (gr. k-2). 10.40 (*0-8085-9621-7*) Econo-Clad Bks.

—Clifford's Manners. (Clifford, the Big Red Dog Ser.). (J). (gr. k-2). 1994. 10.95 (*0-590-48697-7*); 1987. (Illus.). 32p. pap. 1.95 o.p. (*0-590-40564-0*); 1987. (Illus.). 32p. mass mkt. 3.25 (*0-590-44285-6*); 1986. (Illus.). 32p. pap. 5.95 o.p. (*0-590-40111-4*) Scholastic, Inc.

—Clifford's Manners. 1987. (Clifford, the Big Red Dog Ser.). (J). (gr. k-2). 9.40 (*0-606-01309-1*) Turtleback Bks.

—Clifford's Noisy Day. 1992. (Clifford, the Big Red Dog Ser.). (Illus.). (J). (ps-k). bds. 3.25 (*0-590-45737-3*, 036, Cartwheel Bks.) Scholastic, Inc.

—Clifford's Opposites. 2000. (Clifford, the Big Red Dog Ser.). (Illus.). 16p. (J). (ps-k). bds. 3.25 (*0-439-15000-0*, Cartwheel Bks.) Scholastic, Inc.

—Clifford's Pals. (Clifford, the Big Red Dog Ser.). (Illus.). 32p. (J). (gr. k-2). 9999. (FRE.). pap. 5.99 o.p. (*0-590-16035-4*); 1985. pap. 1.95 o.p. (*0-590-33582-0*); 1985. mass mkt. 3.25 (*0-590-44295-3*) Scholastic, Inc.

—Clifford's Pals. 1985. (Clifford, the Big Red Dog Ser.). (J). (gr. k-2). 9.40 (*0-606-03423-4*) Turtleback Bks.

—Clifford's Peek-a-Boo. 1991. (Clifford, the Big Red Dog Ser.). 16p. (J). (ps-k). bds. 3.25 (*0-590-44737-8*) Scholastic, Inc.

—Clifford's Peek-&-Seek Animal Riddles. 1997. (Clifford, the Big Red Dog Ser.). (Illus.). 24p. (J). (ps-k). pap. 7.95 (*0-590-05704-9*) Scholastic, Inc.

—Clifford's Puppy Days. (Clifford, the Big Red Dog Ser.). (J). (ps-k). 1999. (Illus.). 32p. bds. 6.99 (*0-590-63608-1*, Cartwheel Bks.); 1994. (Illus.). 32p. pap. 10.95 (*0-590-43339-3*, Cartwheel Bks.); 1993. (Illus.). 32p. 19.95 o.p. (*0-590-66614-2*, Cartwheel Bks.); 1992. 19.95 o.p. (*0-590-72612-9*); 1989. pap. 1.95 (*0-590-42189-1*); 1989. (Illus.). 31p. mass mkt. 3.50 (*0-590-44262-7*) Scholastic, Inc.

—Clifford's Puppy Days. 1989. (Clifford, the Big Red Dog Ser.). (J). (gr. k-2). 9.65 (*0-606-04188-5*) Turtleback Bks.

—Clifford's Riddles. 2002. (Clifford Bks.). (Illus.). (J). 11.45 (*0-7587-6709-9*) Book Wholesalers, Inc.

—Clifford's Riddles. 1984. (Clifford, the Big Red Dog Ser.). (Illus.). 32p. (J). (gr. k-2). pap. 1.95 o.p. (*0-590-33361-5*); mass mkt. 3.25 (*0-590-44282-1*) Scholastic, Inc.

—Clifford's Riddles. 1974. (Clifford, the Big Red Dog Ser.). (J). (gr. k-2). 9.65 (*0-606-03089-1*) Turtleback Bks.

—Clifford's Scary Halloween. 2002. (Clifford, the Big Red Dog Ser.). (Illus.). 16p. (J). mass mkt. 4.99 (*0-439-39453-8*) Scholastic, Inc.

—Clifford's Schoolhouse. 2000. (Clifford, the Big Red Dog Ser.). (Illus.). (J). (gr. k-2). 87.60 (*0-439-21185-9*); 10p. bds. 10.95 (*0-439-16252-1*) Scholastic, Inc.

—Clifford's Sing Along Adventure. 1987. (Clifford, the Big Red Dog Ser.). (Illus.). 32p. (J). (gr. k-2). pap. 2.25 o.p. (*0-590-44283-X*) Scholastic, Inc.

—Clifford's Sports Day. 2002. (Clifford Bks.). (Illus.). (J). 11.45 (*0-7587-6710-2*) Book Wholesalers, Inc.

—Clifford's Sports Day. (Clifford, the Big Red Dog Ser.). (Illus.). 32p. (J). (gr. k-2). pap. 5.99 (*0-590-16002-8*); 1996. mass mkt. 3.25 (*0-590-62971-9*, Cartwheel Bks.) Scholastic, Inc.

—Clifford's Sports Day. 1996. (Clifford, the Big Red Dog Ser.). (J). (gr. k-2). 9.65 (*0-606-08715-X*) Turtleback Bks.

—Clifford's Spring Carnival. 2002. (Clifford, the Big Red Dog Ser.). (Illus.). 24p. (J). (gr. k-2). mass mkt. 5.99 (*0-439-34022-5*) Scholastic, Inc.

—Clifford's Spring Clean-Up. 2002. (Clifford Bks.). (Illus.). (J). 11.45 (*0-7587-6639-4*) Book Wholesalers, Inc.

—Clifford's Spring Clean-Up. 1997. (Clifford, the Big Red Dog Ser.). (Illus.). 32p. (J). (gr. k-2). mass mkt. 3.50 (*0-590-06012-0*, Cartwheel Bks.) Scholastic, Inc.

—Clifford's Spring Clean-Up. 1997. (Clifford, the Big Red Dog Ser.). (J). (gr. k-2). 9.40 (*0-606-11213-8*) Turtleback Bks.

—Clifford's Springtime. 1994. (Clifford, the Big Red Dog Ser.). (Illus.). 10p. (J). (gr. k-2). pap. 4.95 o.p. (*0-590-47293-3*, Cartwheel Bks.) Scholastic, Inc.

—Clifford's Sticker Book. 1995. (Clifford, the Big Red Dog Ser.). (Illus.). 24p. (J). (gr. k-2). mass mkt. 4.95 (*0-590-33657-6*) Scholastic, Inc.

—Clifford's Thanksgiving Visit. 2002. (Clifford Bks.). (Illus.). (J). 11.45 (*0-7587-6640-8*) Book Wholesalers, Inc.

—Clifford's Thanksgiving Visit. 1993. (Clifford, the Big Red Dog Ser.). (Illus.). 32p. (J). (gr. k-2). mass mkt. 3.25 (*0-590-46987-8*, Cartwheel Bks.) Scholastic, Inc.

—Clifford's Thanksgiving Visit. 1993. (Clifford, the Big Red Dog Ser.). (J). (gr. k-2). 8.19 o.p. (*0-606-05208-9*) Turtleback Bks.

—Clifford's Tricks. 2002. (Clifford Bks.). (Illus.). (J). 11.45 (*0-7587-7031-6*) Book Wholesalers, Inc.

—Clifford's Tricks. (Clifford, the Big Red Dog Ser.). (J). (gr. k-2). (FRE., Illus.). pap. 5.99 (*0-590-73954-9*); 9999. pap. 1.25 o.p. (*0-590-04439-7*); 1986. (Illus.). 32p. pap. 1.95 o.p. (*0-590-33612-6*); 1986. (Illus.). 32p. mass mkt. 2.99 (*0-590-44291-0*); 1971. (Illus.). pap. 1.50 o.p. (*0-590-33820-X*) Scholastic, Inc.

—Clifford's Tricks. 1969. (Clifford, the Big Red Dog Ser.). (J). (gr. k-2). 9.40 (*0-606-01048-3*) Turtleback Bks.

—Clifford's Valentine Bag of Fun. 1999. (Clifford, the Big Red Dog Ser.). (Illus.). 32p. (J). (gr. k-2). mass mkt. 6.95 (*0-590-00380-1*, Cartwheel Bks.) Scholastic, Inc.

—Clifford's Valentines. 2002. (Hello Reader! Ser.). (Illus.). 32p. (J). (ps-3). mass mkt. 3.99 (*0-439-18300-6*, Cartwheel Bks.) Scholastic, Inc.

—Clifford's Word Book. (Clifford, the Big Red Dog Ser.). (J). (ps-k). 1994. 10.95 (*0-590-48696-9*); 1990. (Illus.). 32p. mass mkt. 2.50 (*0-590-43095-5*) Scholastic, Inc.

—Clifford's Word Book. 1990. (Clifford, the Big Red Dog Ser.). (J). (ps-k). 9.65 (*0-606-04639-9*) Turtleback Bks.

—Clifford's Work Book.Tr. of Mots Preferes de Bertrand. (FRE., Illus.). (J). pap. 5.99 (*0-590-74326-0*) Scholastic, Inc.

—Cooking with Clifford. 1999. (Clifford, the Big Red Dog Ser.). 24p. (J). (gr. k-2). 9.95 (*0-590-68931-2*, Cartwheel Bks.) Scholastic, Inc.

—Count on Clifford. (Clifford, the Big Red Dog Ser.). (Illus.). 32p. (J). (ps-k). 1987. mass mkt. 3.50 (*0-590-44284-8*); 1985. 5.95 (*0-590-33614-2*) Scholastic, Inc.

—Count on Clifford. 1985. (Clifford, the Big Red Dog Ser.). (J). (ps-k). 9.65 (*0-606-03762-4*) Turtleback Bks.

—Cuenta con Clifford. 1999. (Clifford, the Big Red Dog Ser.). (SPA., Illus.). 32p. (J). (ps-k). pap. 3.50 (*0-590-87589-2*, SO6164, Scholastic en Espanola) Scholastic, Inc.

—Cuenta con Clifford. 1999. (Clifford, the Big Red Dog Ser.). (SPA.). (J). (gr. k-2). 9.40 (*0-606-16907-5*) Turtleback Bks.

—El Dia Deportivo de Clifford. 1996. (Clifford, the Big Red Dog Ser.). (SPA., Illus.). 32p. (J). (gr. k-2). pap. 3.50 (*0-590-69070-1*, SO2022, Scholastic en Espanola) Scholastic, Inc.

—El Dia Deportivo de Clifford. 1996. (Clifford, the Big Red Dog Ser.). (SPA.). (J). (gr. k-2). 9.14 (*0-606-08735-4*) Turtleback Bks.

—La Familia de Clifford. 1989. (Clifford, the Big Red Dog Ser.). (SPA.). (J). (gr. k-2). 32p. pap. 3.50 (*0-590-41992-7*, SO2844, Scholastic en Espanola); 19.95 (*0-590-73228-5*) Scholastic, Inc.

—La Familia de Clifford. 1999. (Clifford, the Big Red Dog Ser.). (SPA., Illus.). (J). (gr. k-2). 9.40 (*0-606-17004-9*) Turtleback Bks.

—Fun with Clifford Activity Book. 1989. (Clifford, the Big Red Dog Ser.). (J). (gr. k-2). 1.95 o.p. (*0-590-42032-1*) Scholastic, Inc.

—Glow-In-The-Dark Christmas. 2001. (Clifford, the Big Red Dog Ser.). (Illus.). 12p. (J). (ps-k). pap. 6.95 (*0-439-30567-5*, Cartwheel Bks.) Scholastic, Inc.

—Go, Clifford, Go! 2002. (Clifford, the Big Red Dog Ser.). (Illus.). 10p. (J). bds. 9.99 (*0-439-39447-3*) Scholastic, Inc.

—Hello, Clifford: A Puppet Book. 1991. (Clifford, the Big Red Dog Ser.). 12p. (J). (ps-k). 7.95 o.p. (*0-590-44673-8*) Scholastic, Inc.

—How to Care for Your Monster. (Illus.). (J). 1972. pap. 1.50 o.p. (*0-590-09177-8*); 1988. 64p. (gr. 4-6). reprint ed. pap. 2.50 o.p. (*0-590-40782-1*) Scholastic, Inc.

—Monster Holidays. 1975. (Illus.). (J). pap. 1.75 o.p. (*0-590-09930-2*) Scholastic, Inc.

—Monster Jokes & Riddles. 1972. (J). reprint ed. pap. 0.95 o.p. (*0-590-03451-0*) Scholastic, Inc.

—My Dog Clifford Plush Book. 2000. (Clifford, the Big Red Dog Ser.). (Illus.). 12p. (J). (ps-k). bds. 7.95 (*0-439-06046-X*, Cartwheel Bks.) Scholastic, Inc.

—La Navidad de Clifford. 2003. (Clifford Ser.).Tr. of Clifford's Christmas. (SPA., Illus.). 32p. (J). pap. 3.50 (*0-439-19891-7*, Scholastic en Espanola) Scholastic, Inc.

—Oops, Clifford! 2002. (Clifford Bks.). (Illus.). (J). 11.45 (*0-7587-5009-9*) Book Wholesalers, Inc.

—Oops, Clifford! 1999. (Clifford, the Big Red Dog Ser.). (Illus.). 32p. (J). (gr. k-2). mass mkt. 3.50 (*0-590-63117-9*, Cartwheel Bks.) Scholastic, Inc.

—Oops, Clifford! 1998. (Clifford, the Big Red Dog Ser.). (J). (gr. k-2). 9.65 (*0-606-17267-X*) Turtleback Bks.

—El Primer Halloween de Clifford. Mlawer, Teresa, tr. 1995. (Clifford, the Big Red Dog Ser.). (SPA., Illus.). 32p. (J). (gr. k-2). pap. 3.50 (*0-590-50928-4*, SO0530, Scholastic en Espanola) Scholastic, Inc.

—El Primer Halloween de Clifford. 1995. (Clifford, the Big Red Dog Ser.). (SPA.). (J). (gr. k-2). 9.40 (*0-606-07475-9*) Turtleback Bks.

—El Primer Otono de Clifford. 1997. (Clifford, the Big Red Dog Ser.). (SPA.). 32p. (J). (gr. k-2). pap. 3.50 o.s.i (*0-590-37332-3*, SO6874, Scholastic en Espanola) Scholastic, Inc.

—El Primer Otono de Clifford. 1997. (Clifford, the Big Red Dog Ser.). (SPA.). (J). (gr. k-2). 9.40 (*0-606-11295-2*) Turtleback Bks.

—El Primer San Valentin de Clifford. 1997. (Clifford, the Big Red Dog Ser.). (SPA., Illus.). 32p. (J). (ps-k). pap. 3.50 (*0-590-97469-6*, SO2149) Scholastic, Inc.

—El Primer San Valentin de Clifford. 1996. (Clifford, the Big Red Dog Ser.). (SPA.). (J). (gr. k-2). 8.19 o.p. (*0-606-10799-1*) Turtleback Bks.

—La Primera Navidad de Clifford. (Clifford, the Big Red Dog Ser.). (SPA., Illus.). 32p. (J). (ps-k). 1994. pap. 3.50 (*0-590-48852-X*, SO6033); 1998. reprint ed. pap. 3.50 (*0-590-63097-0*, SO8199) Scholastic, Inc. (Scholastic en Espanola).

—La Primera Navidad de Clifford. (Clifford, the Big Red Dog Ser.). (J). (gr. k-2). 1998. 9.40 (*0-606-15606-2*); 1994. (SPA.). 9.40 (*0-606-06516-4*) Turtleback Bks.

—T-Bone Tells the Truth. 2002. (Clifford's Big Red Ideas Ser.). (Illus.). 7p. (J). bds. 4.99 (*0-439-39450-3*) Scholastic, Inc.

—Take Me to School with You! 2002. (Clifford, the Big Red Dog Ser.). (Illus.). 16p. (J). mass mkt. 3.99 (*0-439-39454-6*) Scholastic, Inc.

—Teacher's Pet. 2001. (Clifford, the Big Red Dog Ser.). (Illus.). 24p. (J). (ps-1). mass mkt. 3.50 (*0-439-28336-1*, Cartwheel Bks.) Scholastic, Inc.

—A Tiny Family. 1999. (Hello Reader! Ser.). 32p. (J). (ps-1). mass mkt. 3.99 (*0-439-04019-1*) Scholastic, Inc.

—Los Trucos de Clifford. Palacios, Argentina, tr. 1994. (Clifford, the Big Red Dog Ser.). (SPA., Illus.). 32p. (J). (ps-k). pap. 3.50 (*0-590-40123-8*, SO2843, Scholastic en Espanola) Scholastic, Inc.

—Los Trucos de Clifford. 1981. (Clifford, the Big Red Dog Ser.). (SPA.). (J). (gr. k-2). 9.14 (*0-606-03109-X*) Turtleback Bks.

—What Time Is It, Clifford? Book & Clock Set. 1998. (Clifford, the Big Red Dog Ser.). (Illus.). 32p. (J). (ps-2). 9.95 (*0-590-76338-5*) Scholastic, Inc.

—Where Is Clifford? A Lift-a-Flap Book. 1989. (Clifford, the Big Red Dog Ser.). 10p. (J). (ps-k). pap. 11.95 (*0-590-42925-6*) Scholastic, Inc.

—Where Is the Big Red Doggie? 1998. (Clifford, the Big Red Dog Ser.). (Illus.). 14p. (J). (ps-k). bds. 5.99 (*0-590-04710-8*, Cartwheel Bks.) Scholastic, Inc.

—The Witch Goes to School. 1992. (Hello Reader! Ser.). (J). (ps-3). pap. 3.99 (*0-590-45831-0*) Scholastic, Inc.

—Witch Goes to School. 1992. (Hello Reader! Ser.). (J). 10.14 (*0-606-01981-2*) Turtleback Bks.

—The Witch Grows Up. 1987. (Illus.). 32p. (Orig.). (J). (gr. k-3). mass mkt. 2.99 o.p. (*0-590-40559-4*) Scholastic, Inc.

—The Witch Next Door. 1986. (Illus.). 32p. (J). (ps-3). mass mkt. 3.25 o.s.i (*0-590-40433-4*) Scholastic, Inc.

—The Witch Next Door. 1986. (J). 9.40 (*0-606-03148-0*) Turtleback Bks.

—Witch's Catalog. 1976. (J). (gr. 2-4). pap. 1.75 o.p. (*0-590-10332-6*) Scholastic, Inc.

—The Witch's Christmas. (Illus.). (J). (gr. k-3). 1986. 32p. pap. 2.50 (*0-590-40434-2*); 1972. pap. 1.50 (*0-590-09216-2*) Scholastic, Inc.

—Witch's Christmas. 1986. (J). 7.70 o.p. (*0-606-03150-2*) Turtleback Bks.

—The Witch's Vacation. (Illus.). (J). (gr. k-3). 1987. 32p. pap. 2.50 (*0-590-40558-6*); 1975. pap. 1.50 o.p. (*0-590-09839-X*); 1975. pap. 3.95 o.p. (*0-590-20697-4*) Scholastic, Inc.

Bridwell, Norman, illus. La Semana Atareada de Clifford. 2002. (Clifford, the Big Red Dog Ser.). (SPA.). 32p. (J). (ps-1). pap. 3.50 (*0-439-41833-X*, Scholastic en Espanola) Scholastic, Inc.

Bridwell, Norman & Lewison, Wendy Cheyette. Clifford's Loose Tooth. 2002. (Clifford Big Red Readers Ser.). (Illus.). 32p. (J). (ps-1). mass mkt. 3.99 (*0-439-33245-1*) Scholastic, Inc.

Bridwell, Norman & Page, Josephine. The Big Leaf Pile. 2001. (Clifford Big Red Readers Ser.). (Illus.). 32p. (J). (ps-1). mass mkt. 3.99 (*0-439-21357-6*, Cartwheel Bks.) Scholastic, Inc.

Clifford's Glow-in-the-Dark Halloween. 2001. (Clifford, the Big Red Dog Ser.). (Illus.). 12p. (J). (ps-k). pap. 6.95 (*0-439-30566-7*, Cartwheel Bks.) Scholastic, Inc.

Cuddy, Robin, illus. The Big Red Detective. 2003. (Clifford Big Red Chapter Book Ser.: No. 1). 64p. (J). mass mkt. 3.99 (*0-439-47315-2*) Scholastic, Inc.

Feldman, Thea. Clifford, Don't Wake the Puppies! 2003. (Clifford Ser.). 24p. (J). pap. 10.95 (*0-439-44941-3*) Scholastic, Inc.

—Clifford Love Me: Clifford Me Quiere. 2004. (Clifford Ser.). (ENG & SPA.). 24p. (J). pap. 3.50 (*0-439-62719-2*, Scholastic en Espanola) Scholastic, Inc.

—Clifford Loves Me! 2003. (Clifford, the Big Red Dog Ser.). (Illus.). 160p. (J). (ps-1). mass mkt. 3.50 (*0-439-45481-6*) Scholastic, Inc.

—Clifford's Big Day on the Farm. 2003. (Clifford, the Big Red Dog Ser.). (Illus.). 160p. (J). (ps-1). bds. 7.99 (*0-439-36628-3*) Scholastic, Inc.

Fry, Sonali. Clifford Digs a Dinosaur. 2003. (Clifford, the Big Red Dog Ser.). (Illus.). 176p. (J). mass mkt. 3.99 (*0-439-43429-7*) Scholastic, Inc.

—Clifford's Christmas Presents. 2002. (Clifford, the Big Red Dog Ser.). (Illus.). 7p. (J). bds. 8.99 (*0-439-39451-1*, Cartwheel Bks.) Scholastic, Inc.

—Thank You, Clifford. 2003. (Clifford, the Big Red Dog Ser.). (Illus.). 16p. (J). (ps-1). bds. 6.99 (*0-439-43427-0*) Scholastic, Inc.

Hamilton, Tisha. Clifford: Amazing Animals. 2004. (Clifford Ser.). 24p. (J). pap. 8.99 (*0-439-62748-6*) Scholastic, Inc.

Herman, Gail. Clifford Finds a Clue. 2004. (Clifford Ser.). 64p. (J). mass mkt. 3.99 (*0-439-53045-8*) Scholastic, Inc.

—Cookie Crazy! 2003. (Clifford Big Red Chapter Book Ser.: No. 2). (Illus.). 64p. (J). mass mkt. 3.99 (*0-439-47316-0*) Scholastic, Inc.

Jordan, Apple. Clifford Helps Out. 2004. (Clifford Ser.). 80p. (J). mass mkt. 2.99 (*0-439-55670-8*) Scholastic, Inc.

Kane, Barbara, ed. Clifford the Big Red Dog Window Art. 2003. 32p. (J). spiral bd. 14.95 (*1-59174-265-X*) Klutz.

Koeppel, Ruth. On the Road. movie tie-in ed. 2004. (Clifford Ser.). 24p. (J). mass mkt. 5.99 (*0-439-62815-6*) Scholastic, Inc.

Marguilies, Teddy. Clifford: El Conejo Fugitivo. 2002. (Clifford Big Red Readers Ser.). (SPA., Illus.). 32p. (J). pap. 3.99 (*0-439-25039-0*, SO0080) Scholastic, Inc.

—Clifford: El Dia de las Sorpresas. 2002. (Clifford Big Red Readers Ser.). (SPA., Illus.). 32p. (J). pap. 3.99 (*0-439-25038-2*, SO30537) Scholastic, Inc.

Margulies, Teddy Slater. Show & Tell Surprise. 2001. (J). 10.14 (*0-606-19913-6*) Turtleback Bks.

Margulies, Teddy Slater & Bridwell, Norman. The Runaway Rabbit. 2001. (Clifford, the Big Red Dog Ser.). (Illus.). 32p. (J). (gr. k-2). mass mkt. 3.99 (*0-439-21361-4*) Scholastic, Inc.

—The Show & Tell Surprise. 2001. (Clifford, the Big Red Dog Ser.). (Illus.). 32p. (J). (gr. k-2). mass mkt. 3.99 (*0-439-21359-2*) Scholastic, Inc.

Mills, Joanna E. A Special Friend. 2003. (Clifford's Big Red Ideas Ser.). (Illus.). 7p. (J). (ps-k). bds. 4.99 (*0-439-36636-4*) Scholastic, Inc.

Neusner, Dena. Clifford's Big Red Ideas: Clifford Plays Fair. 2004. (Clifford Ser.). 7p. (J). mass mkt. 4.99 (*0-439-45191-4*) Scholastic, Inc.

—The Star of the Show. 2004. (Clifford Ser.). 32p. (J). mass mkt. 3.99 (*0-439-62749-4*) Scholastic, Inc.

Neusner, Dena Wallenstein. Clifford's Touch & Feel Day. 2003. (Clifford Ser.). (Illus.). 5p. (J). bds. 9.99 (*0-439-44936-7*) Scholastic, Inc.

—Follow That School Bus! 2003. (Clifford Ser.). (Illus.). 5p. (J). bds. 7.99 (*0-439-44933-2*) Scholastic, Inc.

Page, Josephine. Tummy Trouble. 2001. (Clifford, the Big Red Dog Ser.). (Illus.). 32p. (J). (gr. k-2). mass mkt. 3.99 (*0-439-21358-4*) Scholastic, Inc.

—Tummy Trouble. 2001. (Clifford, the Big Red Dog Ser.). (J). (gr. k-2). 10.14 (*0-606-19916-0*) Turtleback Bks.

Parent, Nancy. Clifford's Big Red Easter. 2003. (Clifford, the Big Red Dog Ser.). (Illus.). 7p. (J). (ps up). bds. 4.99 (*0-439-43428-9*) Scholastic, Inc.

Scholastic, Inc. Staff. Clifford the Big Red Dog: The Big Leaf Pile. 2001. (Clifford, the Big Red Dog Ser.). (Illus.). (J). 10.14 (*0-606-21112-8*) Turtleback Bks.

—Clifford the Big Red Dog: The Dog Who Cried "Woof!" 2001. (Clifford, the Big Red Dog Ser.). (Illus.). (J). 10.14 (*0-606-21113-6*) Turtleback Bks.

—Clifford y el Monton de Hoyas. 2002. (Clifford Big Red Readers Ser.). (SPA., Illus.). 32p. (J). pap. 3.99 (*0-439-25040-4*, SO30514, Scholastic en Espanola) Scholastic, Inc.

—Clifford's Phonics Fun Box Set, Vol. 5. 2003. (Clifford Ser.). (Illus.). 16p. (J). (gr. k-3). pap. 12.99 (*0-439-40519-X*) Scholastic, Inc.

—El Diente Flojo de Clifford. 2002. (Clifford Big Red Readers Ser.). (SPA., Illus.). 32p. (J). pap. 3.99 (*0-439-35299-1*, Scholastic en Espanola) Scholastic, Inc.

—The Greatest Parade. 2004. (Clifford Ser.). 144p. (J). mass mkt. 3.99 (*0-439-60701-9*) Scholastic, Inc.

Scholastic, Inc. Staff, contrib. by. The Missing Beach Ball. 2002. (Clifford, the Big Red Dog Ser.). (Illus.). 24p. (J). (ps-3). mass mkt. 3.95 (*0-439-33799-2*, Cartwheel Bks.) Scholastic, Inc.

Scholastic, Inc. Staff, et al. Clifford the Small Red Puppy Learning & Growing Box Set. 2003. (Clifford Ser.). (J). 9.99 (*0-439-55405-5*) Scholastic, Inc.

—Clifford the Small Red Puppy Ring Rattle. 2003. (J). 6.99 (*0-439-56926-5*, Sidekicks) Scholastic, Inc.

—Clifford the Small Red Puppy Teething Rattle. 2003. (J). 6.99 (*0-439-56928-1*, Sidekicks) Scholastic, Inc.

—28 Clifford with Soundchip. 2003. (Clifford Ser.). (J). 49.99 (*0-439-48643-2*, Sidekicks) Scholastic, Inc.

Tait, Katie. Clifford Plays Peekaboo. 2004. (Clifford Ser.). (Illus.). 5p. (J). bds. 5.99 (*0-439-44938-3*) Scholastic, Inc.

Weinberger, Kimberly. Be-a-Good-Friend Sticker Book. 2001. (Clifford, the Big Red Dog Ser.). (Illus.). 24p. (J). (gr. k-2). 5.99 (*0-439-22945-6*) Scholastic, Inc.

—Clifford el dia de la Tormenta. 2003. (Big Red Reader Ser.). (SPA., Illus.). 32p. (J). (gr. k-3). pap. 3.99 (*0-439-55114-5*, Scholastic en Espanola) Scholastic, Inc.

—Share-&-Be-Fair Sticker Book. 2001. (Clifford, the Big Red Dog Ser.). (Illus.). 24p. (J). (gr. k-2). 5.99 (*0-439-22944-8*) Scholastic, Inc.

—The Stormy Day Rescue. 2001. 10.14 (*0-606-19914-4*) Turtleback Bks.

Weinberger, Kimberly & Bridwell, Norman. The Stormy Day Rescue. 2001. (Clifford, the Big Red Dog Ser.). (Illus.). 32p. (J). (gr. k-2). mass mkt. 3.99 (*0-439-21360-6*) Scholastic, Inc.

CLOUD, ALEX (FICTITIOUS CHARACTER)—FICTION

Press, Skip. A Rave of Snakes. 1994. (You-Solve-It Mysteries Ser.: No. 1). 78p. (YA). mass mkt. 3.50 o.p. (*0-8217-4546-8*, Zebra Bks.) Kensington Publishing Corp.

—A Shift of Coyotes. 1994. (You-Solve-It Mysteries Ser.: No. 6). (YA). mass mkt. 3.50 o.s.i (*0-8217-4706-1*, Zebra Bks.) Kensington Publishing Corp.

—A Web of Ya Yas. 1994. (You-Solve-It Mysteries Ser.: No. 4). 224p. (YA). mass mkt. 3.50 o.s.i (*0-8217-4643-X*) Kensington Publishing Corp.

COCHISE, APACHE CHIEF, D. 1874—FICTION

Sargent, Dave & Sargent, Pat. Charlie (Appaloosa) Be Brave #14. 2001. (Saddle Up Ser.). 36p. (J). pap. (*1-56763-608-X*); lib. bdg. 22.60 (*1-56763-607-1*) Ozark Publishing.

COLUMBUS, CHRISTOPHER, 1451-1506—FICTION

Carpenter, Eric. Young Christopher Columbus: Discoverer of New Worlds. 1992. (Troll First-Start Biography Ser.). (J). 9.65 (*0-606-02364-X*) Turtleback Bks.

Conrad, Pam. Pedro's Journal: A Voyage with Christopher Columbus, August 3, 1492-February 14, 1493. 1991. (J). 10.65 (*0-606-01924-3*) Turtleback Bks.

D'Aulaire, Ingri & D'Aulaire, Edgar P. Columbus. 1992. (Illus.). 64p. (J). (gr. 2-5). pap. 3.99 o.s.i (*0-440-40701-X*, Yearling) Random Hse. Children's Bks.

Dorris, Michael. Morning Girl. 80p. 1994. (YA). (gr. 4-7). pap. 4.95 (*1-56282-661-1*); 1992. (J). 12.95 o.p. (*1-56282-284-5*); 1992. (YA). (gr. 3 up). lib. bdg. 13.49 o.s.i (*1-56282-285-3*) Hyperion Bks. for Children.

—Morning Girl. 1999. 80p. (J). (gr. 4 up). pap. text 4.99 (*0-7868-1372-5*); mass mkt. 4.99 (*0-7868-1358-X*) Hyperion Pr.

—Morning Girl. 1994. (J). 11.14 (*0-606-06583-0*) Turtleback Bks.

Dyson, John. Westward with Columbus. 64p. (J). (gr. 4-7). 1993. (Illus.). pap. 6.95 (*0-590-43847-6*); 1991. 15.95 (*0-590-43846-8*) Scholastic, Inc.

Foreman, Michael. The Boy Who Sailed with Columbus. 1992. (Illus.). 80p. (J). (gr. 1-4). 16.95 o.p. (*1-55970-178-1*) Arcade Publishing, Inc.

Fritz, Jean. Where Do You Think You're Going, Christopher Columbus? 1980. (J). 12.14 (*0-606-04015-3*) Turtleback Bks.

Gardeski, Christina Mia. Columbus Day. 2001. (Rookie Read-About Holidays Ser.). (Illus.). 32p. (J). (gr. 1-2). lib. bdg. 19.00 (*0-516-22371-2*, Children's Pr.) Scholastic Library Publishing.

Hays, Wilma P. Noko, Captive of Columbus. 1967. (Illus.). (J). (gr. 3-7). 4.49 o.p. (*0-698-30259-1*) Putnam Publishing Group, The.

Holland, Margaret. Christopher Columbus. 1992. (People Who Shape Our World Ser.). (Illus.). 48p. (J). (gr. 3-5). pap. 2.99 (*0-87406-584-4*) Darby Creek Publishing.

Hughes, Alice D. Cajun Columbus. rev. ed. 1991. (Illus.). 40p. (J). (gr. k-4). 14.95 (*0-88289-875-2*) Pelican Publishing Co., Inc.

Lawson, Robert. I Discover Columbus. 1991. (Illus.). (J). (gr. 3-6). mass mkt. 4.95 o.p. (*0-316-51760-7*) Little Brown & Co.

Lewin, Waldtraut. Freedom Beyond the Sea. Crawford, Elizabeth D., tr. 2001. 272p. (YA). (gr. 9 up). 15.95 (*0-385-32705-6*, Delacorte Pr.) Dell Publishing.

—Freedom Beyond the Sea. 2003. 272p. (YA). (gr. 9-12). mass mkt. 5.50 (*0-440-22868-9*, Laurel Leaf) Random Hse. Children's Bks.

Litowinsky, Olga. The High Voyage: The Final Crossing of Christopher Columbus. 1992. (Illus.). 160p. (J). (gr. 5-9). pap. 3.50 o.s.i (*0-440-40703-6*, Yearling) Random Hse. Children's Bks.

Martin, Susan. I Sailed with Columbus: The Adventures of a Ship's Boy. 1991. (Illus.). 154p. (YA). (gr. 8-10). reprint ed. 18.00 (*0-7567-6043-7*) DIANE Publishing Co.

—I Sailed with Columbus: The Adventures of a Ship's Boy. 1991. (Illus.). 154p. (YA). (gr. 5 up). 17.95 o.p. (*0-87951-431-0*) Overlook Pr., The.

McAndrews, Anita. Blessed Be the Light of Day. 2001. 48p. (J). (gr. 2-5). 14.95 (*1-930093-02-0*) Brookfield Reader, Inc., The.

McGee, Marni. Diego Columbus: Adventures on the High Seas. 1992. (J). (gr. 4-7). pap. 6.99 o.p. (*0-8007-1671-X*); (Illus.). 128p. (gr. 3-7). pap. 6.99 o.p. (*0-8007-5433-6*) Revell, Fleming H. Co.

O'Connor, Genevieve A. The Admiral & the Deck Boy: One Boy's Journey with Christopher Columbus. 1991. (Illus.). 168p. (YA). (gr. 3 up). pap. 12.95 o.p. (*1-55870-218-0*, Betterway Bks.) F&W Pubns., Inc.

Roop, Peter & Roop, Connie, eds. I, Columbus: My Journal 1492-1493. 1991. (Illus.). 64p. (J). (gr. 5). reprint ed. mass mkt. 5.99 (*0-380-71545-7*, Avon Bks.) Morrow/Avon.

Schlein, Miriam. I Sailed with Columbus. (Trophy Bk.). (Illus.). 144p. (J). (gr. 3-6). 1992. pap. 3.95 o.p. (*0-06-440423-4*, Harper Trophy); 1991. 14.95 o.p. (*0-06-022513-0*); 1991. lib. bdg. 13.89 o.p. (*0-06-022514-9*) HarperCollins Children's Bk. Group.

Smith, Barry. The First Voyage of Christopher Columbus. 1992. (Illus.). 320p. (J). (ps-3). 12.95 o.p. (*0-670-84051-3*, Viking Children's Bks.) Penguin Putnam Bks. for Young Readers.

Smithmark Staff. Where's Columbus? 1992. (J). 4.98 o.p. (*0-8317-9284-1*) Smithmark Pubs., Inc.

Stewart, Charles, III. Columbus Sails to America. 1992. (Illus.). (J). (gr. k-4). 16.95 o.p. (*1-56282-132-6*) Disney Pr.

Templeton, Lee. Columbus' Cabin Boy. 1983. (Illus.). 192p. (J). (gr. 4-7). 8.95 o.p. (*0-89015-372-8*) Eakin Pr.

West with Columbus. 1991. (J). pap. o.p. (*0-590-28401-0*) Scholastic, Inc.

Whittier, Mary Ann. Tales from 1492. (YA). (gr. 7 up). lib. bdg. 19.99 (*0-89824-981-3*) Royal Fireworks Publishing Co.

Yolen, Jane. Encounter. (Illus.). (J). (gr. 4-7). 1996. 32p. pap. 6.00 (*0-15-201389-X*, Voyager Bks./Libros Viajeros); 1992. 40p. 16.00 (*0-15-225962-7*) Harcourt Children's Bks.

—Encounter. 1996. 12.15 (*0-606-10802-5*) Turtleback Bks.

—Encuentro. Ada, Alma Flor, tr. 1996. (SPA., Illus.). 32p. (J). (gr. 4-7). pap. 6.00 (*0-15-201342-3*, HB2056, Voyager Bks./Libros Viajeros) Harcourt Children's Bks.

COOK, DANIEL (FICTITIOUS CHARACTER)—FICTION

Kirby, Susan. Dead Man's Scam. 1994. (You-Solve-It Mysteries Ser.: No. 7). 224p. (YA). mass mkt. 3.50 (*0-8217-4734-7*, Zebra Bks.) Kensington Publishing Corp.

—The Field. 1995. 224p. mass mkt. 3.99 o.s.i (*0-8217-5118-2*) Kensington Publishing Corp.

—Prescription for Murder. 1994. (You-Solve-It Mysteries Ser.: No. 9). 224p. (YA). mass mkt. 3.50 (*0-8217-4791-6*) Kensington Publishing Corp.

COOK, JAMES, 1728-1779—FICTION

Hesse, Karen. Stowaway. unabr. ed. 2002. 328p. (J). (gr. 4-6). pap. 46.00 incl. audio (*0-8072-8760-1*, LYA 259 SP, Listening Library) Random Hse. Audio Publishing Group.

—Stowaway. (Illus.). (gr. 5-9). 2002. 320p. (YA). pap. 6.99 (*0-689-83989-8*, Aladdin); 2000. 328p. (J). 17.95 (*0-689-83987-1*, McElderry, Margaret K.) Simon & Schuster Children's Publishing.

—Stowaway. l.t. ed. 2002. (Young Adult Ser.). 375p. (YA). 24.95 (*0-7862-4789-4*) Thorndike Pr.

Van Rynbach, Iris. Captain Cook's Christmas Pudding. 1997. (Illus.). 32p. (J). (gr. k-4). 14.95 (*1-56397-644-7*) Boyds Mills Pr.

CORDUROY (FICTITIOUS CHARACTER)—FICTION

Freeman, Don. Corduroy. 1988. (Corduroy Ser.). (SPA., Illus.). 320p. (J). (gr. k-1). 11.95 o.s.i (*0-670-82265-5*, PG265, Viking Children's Bks.) Penguin Putnam Bks. for Young Readers.

Freeman, Don. Cp Corduroy Giant Board Ams. 2003. bds. 12.99 (*0-670-03690-0*, Viking) Viking Penguin.

Freeman, Don. Un Bolsillo para Corduroy. 1992. (Corduroy Ser.). (SPA., (gr. k-1). Illus.). (J). 22.95 incl. audio (*0-87499-294-X*); (Illus.). pap., tchr. ed. 33.95 incl. audio (*0-87499-295-8*); (J). audio 9.95. (Illus.). (J). pap. 15.95 incl. audio (*0-87499-293-1*, LK5313) Live Oak Media.

—Un Bolsillo para Corduroy. 1995. (Corduroy Ser.). (SPA., Illus.). 32p. (J). (gr. k-1). pap. 6.99 (*0-14-055283-9*, VK6507, Puffin Bks.) Penguin Putnam Bks. for Young Readers.

—Un Bolsillo para Corduroy. 1995. (Corduroy Ser.). (SPA.). (J). (gr. k-1). 13.14 (*0-606-08333-2*) Turtleback Bks.

—Un Bosillo Para Corduroy. 1992. (Corduroy Ser.).Tr. of Pocket for Corduroy. (ENG & SPA., Illus.). 32p. (J). (gr. k-1). 15.99 o.s.i (*0-670-84483-7*, Viking Children's Bks.) Penguin Putnam Bks. for Young Readers.

—Un Bosillo para Corduroy/a Pocket for Corduroy, 2 bks. unabr. ed. 1999. (Corduroy Ser.). (ENG & SPA., Illus.). (J). (gr. k-3). pap. 29.95 incl. audio (*0-87499-565-5*) Live Oak Media.

—Corduroy. 2002. (Corduroy Ser.). (Illus.). (J). 13.19 (*0-7587-2275-3*) Book Wholesalers, Inc.

—Corduroy. 2000. (Corduroy Ser.). (J). (gr. k-1). pap. 19.97 incl. audio (*0-7366-9201-0*); pap. 19.97 incl. audio (*0-7366-9201-0*) Books on Tape, Inc.

—Corduroy. ed. 1980. (J). (gr. 1). spiral bd. (*0-616-01642-5*); (gr. 2). spiral bd. (*0-616-01643-3*) Canadian National Institute for the Blind/Institut National Canadien pour les Aveugles.

—Corduroy. (Corduroy Ser.). (J). (gr. k-1). audio 32.95 o.p. 2001. (SPA.). audio 15.95 Kimbo Educational.

—Corduroy. (Corduroy Ser.). (gr. k-1). 1999. (SPA.). (J). pap. 29.95 incl. audio; 1983. (J). audio 32.95; 1982. (Illus.). pap., tchr. ed. 33.95 incl. audio (*0-941078-07-8*); 1990. (SPA., Illus.). (J). reprint ed. pap. 15.95 incl. audio (*0-87499-213-3*, LK3796); 1991. (SPA.). (J). audio 9.95; 1982. (Illus.). (J). 24.95 incl. audio (*0-941078-08-6*); 1982. (Illus.). (J). 24.95 incl. audio (*0-941078-08-6*); 1982. (Illus.). (J). pap. 15.95 incl. audio (*0-941078-06-X*); 1982. (Illus.). (J). pap. 15.95 incl. audio (*0-941078-06-X*) Live Oak Media.

—Corduroy. (Corduroy Ser.). (gr. k-1). 1993. (Illus.). 30p. (J). pap. 9.99 incl. audio (*0-14-095114-8*); 1990. (SPA., Illus.). 32p. (J). pap. 6.99 (*0-14-054252-3*, VK3790, Puffin Bks.); 1988. (Illus.). (J). 6.95 o.p. (*0-14-095063-X*, Puffin Bks.); 1976. (Illus.). 32p. (J). pap. 5.99 (*0-14-050173-8*, Puffin Bks.); 1970. pap. 0.95 o.p. (*0-670-05046-6*, Dutton Children's Bks.); 1968. (Illus.). 32p. (J). 15.99 (*0-670-24133-4*, Viking Children's Bks.); 1996. (Illus.). 32p. (J). pap. 19.99 o.p. (*0-14-055855-1*, Puffin Bks.) Penguin Putnam Bks. for Young Readers.

—Corduroy. 1992. (Golden Book Ser.). (J). (gr. k-1). pap. 2.99 o.s.i (*0-307-05887-5*, Golden Bks.) Random Hse. Children's Bks.

—Corduroy. 1989. (Corduroy Ser.). (J). (gr. k-1). 53.32 incl. audio (*0-676-31871-1*) SRA/McGraw-Hill.

—Corduroy. (Corduroy Ser.). (J). (gr. k-1). 1988. (SPA.). 12.14 (*0-606-03163-4*); 1976. (Illus.). 12.14 (*0-606-00490-4*) Turtleback Bks.

—Corduroy. (Corduroy Ser.). (gr. k-1). 1997. (J). pap. 14.98 (*0-670-78127-4*); 1968. 3.37 o.p. (*0-670-24134-2*, Viking) Viking Penguin.

—Corduroy. (Corduroy Ser.). (J). (gr. k-1). 24.95 incl. audio. pap. 32.75 incl. audio. (SPA.). pap. 15.95 incl. audio. audio 6.95 (*1-56008-445-6*); 2000. pap. 12.95 incl. audio Weston Woods Studios, Inc.

—Corduroy Edicion Espanola. Most, Bernard, tr. from ENG. 1993. (Corduroy Ser.). (SPA., Illus.). (J). (gr. k-1). reprint ed. 22.95 o.p. incl. audio (*0-87499-214-1*) Live Oak Media.

—Corduroy & Company: A Don Freeman Treasury. 2001. (Corduroy Ser.). (Illus.). 128p. (J). (gr. k-1). 25.00 (*0-670-03510-6*, Viking) Penguin Putnam Bks. for Young Readers.

—Corduroy at the Zoo. 2001. (Corduroy Ser.). (Illus.). 18p. (J). (gr. k-1). text 11.99 (*0-670-89288-2*, Viking Children's Bks.) Penguin Putnam Bks. for Young Readers.

—Corduroy; Corduroy, 2 vols., Set. unabr. ed. 1999. (Corduroy Ser.). (ENG & SPA., Illus.). (J). (gr. k-1). pap. 29.95 incl. audio (*0-87499-566-3*) Live Oak Media.

—Corduroy, Grades K-1. 1993. (Corduroy Ser.). (SPA., Illus.). (J). reprint ed. pap., tchr. ed. 33.95 incl. audio (*0-87499-215-X*) Live Oak Media.

—Corduroy's Best Halloween Ever. 2001. (Reading Railroad Bks.). (Illus.). 32p. (J). (gr. k-1). mass mkt. 3.49 (*0-448-42499-1*, Philomel) Penguin Putnam Bks. for Young Readers.

—Corduroy's Big Day. 2000. (Corduroy Ser.). (Illus.). 12p. (J). (gr. k-1). mass mkt. 6.99 o.p. (*0-8431-7566-4*, Price Stern Sloan) Penguin Putnam Bks. for Young Readers.

—Corduroy's Christmas. 1992. (Corduroy Ser.). (Illus.). 16p. (J). 12.99 (*0-670-84477-2*, Viking Children's Bks.) Penguin Putnam Bks. for Young Readers.

—Corduroy's Christmas Surprise. 2000. (Corduroy Ser.). (Illus.). 32p. (J). (gr. k-1). mass mkt. 3.49 (*0-448-42191-7*, Planet Dexter) Penguin Putnam Bks. for Young Readers.

—Corduroy's Day. 1985. (Corduroy Ser.). (Illus.). 144p. (J). (gr. k-1). bds. 3.99 (*0-670-80521-1*, Viking Children's Bks.) Penguin Putnam Bks. for Young Readers.

—Corduroy's Day & Corduroy's Party. (Corduroy Ser.). (J). (gr. k-1). audio 15.95 Kimbo Educational.

—Corduroy's Easter. 1999. (Corduroy Ser.). (Illus.). 8p. (J). (gr. k-1). 11.99 (*0-670-88101-5*) Penguin Putnam Bks. for Young Readers.

—Corduroy's Easter Party. 2000. (Corduroy Ser.). (Illus.). 32p. (J). (gr. k-1). mass mkt. 3.49 *(0-448-42154-2)* Penguin Putnam Bks. for Young Readers.
—Corduroy's Party. 1985. (Corduroy Ser.). (Illus.). 144p. (J). (gr. k-1). bds. 3.99 *(0-670-80520-3,* Viking Children's Bks.) Penguin Putnam Bks. for Young Readers.
—Corduroy's Playtime Activity Book. 1998. (Corduroy Ser.). (Illus.). 16p. (J). (gr. k-1). 7.99 *(0-670-88028-0)* Penguin Putnam Bks. for Young Readers.
—Corduroy's Toys. 1985. (Corduroy Ser.). (Illus.). 240p. (J). (gr. k-1). bds. 3.99 *(0-670-80522-X,* Viking Children's Bks.) Penguin Putnam Bks. for Young Readers.
—Corduroy's Trick or Treat. 2002. (Illus.). 12p. (J). bds. 5.99 *(0-670-03562-9,* Viking Children's Bks.) Penguin Putnam Bks. for Young Readers.
—Happy Easter, Corduroy. 2004. (Illus.). 16p. (J). bds. 5.99 *(0-670-03677-3,* Viking) Viking Penguin.
—A Pocket for Corduroy. 2002. (Corduroy Ser.). (Illus.). (J). 13.19 *(0-7587-3431-X)* Book Wholesalers, Inc.
—A Pocket for Corduroy. 2000. (Corduroy Ser.). (J). (gr. k-1). pap. 19.97 incl. audio *(0-7366-9202-9)*; pap. 19.97 incl. audio *(0-7366-9202-9)* Books on Tape, Inc.
—A Pocket for Corduroy. (Corduroy Ser.). (J). (gr. k-1). audio 32.95 o.p. Kimbo Educational.
—A Pocket for Corduroy. 1982. (Corduroy Ser.). (J). (gr. k-1). (Illus.). pap., stu. ed. 33.95 incl. audio *(0-941078-16-7)*; (Illus.). 24.95 incl. audio *(0-941078-17-5)*; (Illus.). 24.95 incl. audio *(0-941078-17-5)*; (Illus.). pap. 15.95 incl. audio *(0-941078-15-9)*; audio 9.95 Live Oak Media.
—A Pocket for Corduroy. (Corduroy Ser.). (Illus.). (J). (gr. k-1). 1997. 32p. pap. 18.99 o.s.i *(0-14-056230-3)*; 1993. pap. 9.99 incl. audio *(0-14-095124-5,* Puffin Bks.); 1989. 6.95 o.p. *(0-14-095036-2,* Puffin Bks.); 1980. 32p. pap. 5.99 *(0-14-050352-8,* Puffin Bks.); 1978. 32p. 14.99 *(0-670-56172-X,* Viking Children's Bks.) Penguin Putnam Bks. for Young Readers.
—A Pocket for Corduroy. 1986. (Corduroy Ser.). (J). (gr. k-1). 35.55 incl. audio *(0-676-31898-3)* SRA/McGraw-Hill.
—A Pocket for Corduroy. 9999. (Corduroy Ser.). (J). (gr. k-1). pap. 1.95 o.s.i *(0-590-31970-1)* Scholastic, Inc.
—A Pocket for Corduroy. 1980. (Corduroy Ser.). (Illus.). (J). (gr. k-1). 12.14 *(0-606-01785-2)* Turtleback Bks.
Freeman, Don & Inches, Alison. Corduroy Makes a Cake. 2003. (Illus.). 32p. pap. 3.99 *(0-14-250163-8,* Puffin Bks.) Penguin Putnam Bks. for Young Readers.
Hennessy, B. G. Corduroy's Birthday. 1997. (Corduroy Ser.). (Illus.). 16p. (J). (gr. k-1). 11.99 *(0-670-87065-X)* Penguin Putnam Bks. for Young Readers.
—Corduroy's Halloween: A Lift-the-Flap Book. 1995. (Corduroy Ser.). (Illus.). 16p. (J). (gr. k-1). 11.99 *(0-670-86193-6,* Viking Children's Bks.) Penguin Putnam Bks. for Young Readers.
Inches, Alison. Corduroy Makes a Cake. 2001. (Viking Easy-To-Read Ser.). (Illus.). 32p. (J). 13.99 *(0-670-88946-6,* Viking) Penguin Putnam Bks. for Young Readers.
—Corduroy's Garden. 2002. (Viking Easy To-Read Ser.). (Illus.). 32p. (J). (gr. k-3). 13.99 *(0-670-03547-5)* Penguin Putnam Bks. for Young Readers.
—Corduroy's Hike. (Illus.). 32p. 2003. pap. 3.99 *(0-14-250164-6,* Puffin Bks.); 2001. (J). 13.99 *(0-670-88945-8,* Viking) Penguin Putnam Bks. for Young Readers.
McCue, Lisa. Corduroy Goes to the Doctor. 1987. (Corduroy Ser.). (Illus.). 14p. (J). (gr. k-1). bds. 3.99 *(0-670-81495-4,* Viking Children's Bks.) Penguin Putnam Bks. for Young Readers.
—Corduroy on the Go. 1987. (Corduroy Ser.). (Illus.). 24p. (J). (gr. k-1). bds. 3.99 *(0-670-81497-0,* Viking Children's Bks.) Penguin Putnam Bks. for Young Readers.
—Corduroy's Busy Street. 1987. (Corduroy Ser.). (Illus.). 144p. (J). (gr. k-1). bds. 3.99 *(0-670-81496-2,* Viking Children's Bks.) Penguin Putnam Bks. for Young Readers.
—Corduroy's Busy Street & Corduroy Goes to the Doctor. (Corduroy Ser.). (J). (gr. k-1). audio 15.95 Kimbo Educational.
—Corduroy's Busy Street & Corduroy Goes to the Doctor. 1989. (Corduroy Ser.). (J). (gr. k-1). pap. 15.95 incl. audio. (Illus.). reprint ed. pap. 15.95 incl. audio *(0-87499-133-1)* Live Oak Media.
—Corduroy's Valentine Activity Book. Law, E., ed. 1999. (Corduroy Ser.). (Illus.). 16p. (J). (gr. k-1). 7.99 *(0-670-88862-1,* Viking Children's Bks.) Penguin Putnam Bks. for Young Readers.
McCue, Lisa, illus. Corduroy's Day & Corduroy's Party. 1987. (Corduroy Ser.). (J). (gr. k-1). bds. 15.95 incl. audio *(0-87499-041-6)* Live Oak Media.

CORTES, HERNANDO, 1485-1547—FICTION

Coleman, Eleanor S. Cross & the Sword of Cortes. 1981. (Illus.). (J). (gr. 5 up). 3.95 o.p. *(0-671-65018-1,* Simon & Schuster Children's Publishing) Simon & Schuster Children's Publishing.
Henty, G. A. By Right of Conquest: Or with Cortez in Mexico. (J). E-Book 3.95 *(0-594-02375-0)* 1873 Pr.

CREWE, SARA (FICTITIOUS CHARACTER)—FICTION

Brown, Janet Allison & Burnett, Frances Hodgson. A Little Princess. 2001. (Storytime Classics Ser.). (Illus.). 32p. (J). (ps-3). 15.99 o.p. *(0-670-89913-5,* Viking Children's Bks.) Penguin Putnam Bks. for Young Readers.
Burnett, Frances Hodgson. A Little Princess. (J). 16.95 *(0-8488-1253-0)* Amereon, Ltd.
—A Little Princess. unabr. ed. 1985. audio 29.95 *(1-55685-060-3)* Audio Bk. Contractors, Inc.
—A Little Princess. unabr. ed. 2000. (YA). (gr. 3 up). audio 24.95 *(0-945353-94-4,* H90394u, Audio Editions Bks. on Cassette) Audio Partners Publishing Corp.
—A Little Princess. 1987. (Classics Ser.). 208p. (J). mass mkt. 2.95 o.s.i *(0-553-21203-6,* Bantam Classics) Bantam Bks.
—A Little Princess. (J). audio 26.95 *(1-885546-01-7)* Big Ben Audio, Inc.
—A Little Princess. unabr. ed. 1993. audio 39.95 *(0-7861-0398-1,* 1350) Blackstone Audio Bks., Inc.
—A Little Princess. unabr. ed. 1991. (J). audio 39.95 *(1-55686-370-5,* 370) Books in Motion.
—A Little Princess. unabr. collector's ed. 1996. (J). audio 36.00 *(0-7366-3293-X,* 3948) Books on Tape, Inc.
—A Little Princess. 1981. 232p. (J). reprint ed. lib. bdg. 15.95 *(0-89966-327-3)* Buccaneer Bks., Inc.
—A Little Princess. 1995. 256p. (J). (gr. 5-8). pap. 3.50 *(0-87406-739-1)* Darby Creek Publishing.
—A Little Princess. abr. ed. 1996. (Children's Thrift Classics Ser.). (Illus.). 96p. (J). (gr. 1). pap. 1.00 *(0-486-29171-5)* Dover Pubns., Inc.
—A Little Princess. abr. ed. 1993. (J). audio 16.99 *(0-88646-359-9,* LFP 7359) Durkin Hayes Publishing Ltd.
—A Little Princess. (Illus.). (J). 2000. 32p. (ps-3). 16.95 *(0-06-027891-9)*; 1999. 336p. (gr. 4 up). 17.99 *(0-397-30693-8)*; 1963. 80p. (gr. 4-6). lib. bdg. 15.89 o.p. *(0-397-31339-X)*; 1987. 336p. (gr. 4 up). reprint ed. pap. 5.99 *(0-06-440187-1,* Harper Trophy) HarperCollins Children's Bk. Group.
—A Little Princess. l.t. ed. 1998. (Large Print Heritage Ser.). 324p. (YA). lib. bdg. 31.95 *(1-58118-021-7,* 21998) LRS.
—A Little Princess. 1995. (Signet Classics). 240p. (YA). mass mkt. 3.95 o.s.i *(0-451-52622-8,* Signet Classics) NAL.
—A Little Princess. abr. ed. 1997. (J). audio 6.95 *(0-7871-1213-5)*; (YA). audio 19.95 *(0-7871-1214-3)* NewStar Media, Inc. (Dove Audio).
—A Little Princess. (Illustrated Junior Library). (J). (gr. 4-7). 1995. (Illus.). 288p. 15.99 *(0-448-40949-6,* Grosset & Dunlap); 1989. (Illus.). 288p. 13.95 o.p. *(0-448-09299-9,* Grosset & Dunlap); 1984. 224p. pap. 3.50 o.p. *(0-14-035028-4,* Puffin Bks.) Penguin Putnam Bks. for Young Readers.
—A Little Princess. 1975. 240p. (J). (gr. 3-7). pap. 1.25 o.s.i *(0-440-44767-4,* Yearling) Random Hse. Children's Bks.
—A Little Princess. 1990. (Children's Classics Ser.). (J). 12.99 o.s.i *(0-517-01480-7)* Random Hse. Value Publishing.
—A Little Princess. 1994. (Step into Classics Ser.). 112p. (J). (gr. 3-8). pap. 3.99 *(0-679-85090-2)* Random Hse., Inc.
—A Little Princess, unabr. ed. 1997. (Illus.). (J). (gr. 5). audio 53.00 *(0-7887-0589-X,* 94766E7) Recorded Bks., LLC.
—A Little Princess. (J). 1996. 224p. 5.98 o.p. *(1-56138-742-8)*; 1997. 480p. reprint ed. text 8.98 o.p. *(0-7624-0115-X)* Running Pr. Bk. Pubs. (Courage Bks.).
—A Little Princess. (J). (Illus.). text 22.95 *(0-590-24079-X)*; 1995. 88p. (gr. 3-7). mass mkt. 3.50 o.p. *(0-590-48628-4)*; 1995. (Illus.). 256p. (gr. 4-7). mass mkt. 3.99 *(0-590-54307-5,* Scholastic Paperbacks) Scholastic, Inc.
—A Little Princess. deluxe ed. 1995. 48p. (J). (gr. 4-7). pap. 12.95 *(0-590-48627-6)* Scholastic, Inc.
—A Little Princess. abr. ed. 1997. (Children's Classics Ser.). (J). mass mkt. 14.95 o.p. *(1-85998-079-1)* Trafalgar Square.
—A Little Princess. Knoepflmacher, U. C., ed. & intro. by. 2002. (Classics Ser.). 272p. (J). 10.00 *(0-14-243701-8,* Penguin Classics) Viking Penguin.
—A Little Princess. (J). 1997. pap. 12.95 *(0-14-086079-7,* Puffin Bks.); 1996. audio 12.95 o.p. *(0-14-086283-8,* Penguin AudioBooks) Viking Penguin.
—A Little Princess. 1998. (Children's Classics). 192p. (J). (gr. 4-7). pap. 3.95 *(1-85326-136-X,* 136XWW) Wordsworth Editions, Ltd. GBR. *Dist:* Advanced Global Distribution Services.
—A Little Princess. Lindskoog, Kathryn, ed. & abr. by. 1993. (gr. 3 up). pap. 6.99 o.p. *(0-88070-527-2)* Zonderkidz.
—A Little Princess: Picture Book. 1995. (Illus.). 32p. (J). (gr. k-2). mass mkt. 2.95 *(0-590-55204-X)* Scholastic, Inc.
—A Little Princess & The Secret Garden. 2002. 480p. (J). (gr. 4-7). reprint ed. 9.00 o.p. *(0-7624-0564-3)* Running Pr. Bk. Pubs.
—A Little Princess Coloring Book. 1999. (Illus.). 48p. (J). pap. 2.95 *(0-486-40561-3)* Dover Pubns., Inc.
—A Little Princess Paper Dolls. 1999. (Illus.). 24p. (J). (ps-3). pap. 7.95 *(0-694-00970-9,* Harper Festival) HarperCollins Children's Bk. Group.
—Sara Crewe, or, What Happened at Miss Minchin's. (J). E-Book 2.49 *(1-58627-234-9)* Electric Umbrella Publishing.
Carabetta, Natalie, illus. A Little Princess. 1996. (All Aboard Reading Ser.: Level 3). 48p. (J). (gr. 2-3). 13.99 o.s.i *(0-448-41329-9,* Grosset & Dunlap) Penguin Putnam Bks. for Young Readers.

CROCKETT, DAVY, 1786-1836—FICTION

Cohen, Caron Lee. Sally Ann Thunder Ann Whirlwind Crockett. 1985. (Illus.). 40p. (J). (gr. 1-3). 14.00 o.p. *(0-688-04006-3)*; lib. bdg. 12.88 o.p. *(0-688-04007-1)* HarperCollins Children's Bk. Group. (Greenwillow Bks.).
Dewey, Ariane. The Narrow Escapes of Davy Crockett. 1990. (Illus.). (J). (gr. 1 up). 15.00 o.p. *(0-688-08914-3)*; lib. bdg. 14.93 o.p. *(0-688-08915-1)* HarperCollins Children's Bk. Group. (Greenwillow Bks.).
—Narrow Escapes Of Davy Crockett. 1993. 10.15 o.p. *(0-606-05503-7)* Turtleback Bks.
—The Narrow Escapes of Davy Crockett. 1993. (Illus.). 48p. (J). (gr. 1 up). reprint ed. pap. 4.95 o.p. *(0-688-12269-8,* Morrow, William & Co.) Morrow/Avon.
Dewey, Ariane, illus. Sally Ann Thunder Ann Whirlwind Crockett. 1993. 40p. (J). reprint ed. pap. 4.95 o.p. *(0-688-12331-7,* Morrow, William & Co.) Morrow/Avon.
Fontes, Justine. Davy Crockett & the Creek Indians. 1991. (Disney's American Frontier Ser.: Bk. 2). (Illus.). 80p. (J). (gr. 1-4). lib. bdg. 12.89 o.s.i *(1-56282-004-4)*; pap. 3.50 o.p. *(1-56282-005-2)* Disney Pr.
—Davy Crockett at the Alamo. 1991. (Disney's American Frontier Ser.: Bk. 4). (Illus.). 80p. (J). (gr. 1-4). lib. bdg. 12.89 o.s.i *(1-56282-008-7)*; pap. 3.50 *(1-56282-009-5)* Disney Pr.
Fontes, Ron & Fontes, Justine. Davy Crockett & the Highwaymen. 1992. (Disney's American Frontier Ser.: Bk. 6). (Illus.). 80p. (J). (gr. 1-4). pap. 3.50 o.s.i *(1-56282-260-8)*; lib. bdg. 12.89 o.s.i *(1-56282-261-6)* Disney Pr.
—Davy Crockett Meets Death Hug. 1993. (American Frontier Ser.: Bk. 12). (Illus.). 80p. (J). (gr. 1-4). lib. bdg. 12.89 o.s.i *(1-56282-496-1)*; pap. 3.50 o.p. *(1-56282-495-3)* Disney Pr.
Le Sueur, Meridel. Chanticleer of Wilderness Road: A Story of Davy Crockett. (Meridel Le Sueur Wilderness Bk.). (Illus.). (YA). (gr. 7-12). reprint ed. 2004. 160p. 13.95 *(0-930100-35-2)*; 2000. 153p. pap. 10.95 *(0-930100-87-5)* Holy Cow! Pr.
Schanzer, Rosalyn. American Journey. 2001. (Illus.). 32p. (J). lib. bdg. 16.89 *(0-688-16992-9,* Morrow, William & Co.) Morrow/Avon.
—Davy Crockett Saves the World. 2001. (Illus.). 32p. (J). 16.95 *(0-688-16991-0)* HarperCollins Pubs.
Singer, A. L. Davy Crockett & the King of the River. 1991. (Disney's American Frontier Ser.: Bk. 1). (Illus.). 80p. (J). (gr. 1-4). lib. bdg. 12.89 o.s.i *(1-56282-006-0)* Disney Pr.
—Davy Crockett & the Pirates at Cave-In Rock. 1991. (Disney's American Frontier Ser.: Bk. 3). (Illus.). 80p. (J). (gr. 1-4). lib. bdg. 12.89 o.s.i *(1-56282-002-8)*; pap. 3.50 *(1-56282-003-6)* Disney Pr.
Steele, William O. Davy Crockett's Earthquake. 1956. (Illus.). (J). (gr. k-3). 5.95 o.p. *(0-15-222696-6)* Harcourt Children's Bks.

CRUSOE, ROBINSON (FICTITIOUS CHARACTER)—FICTION

Defoe, Daniel. The Adventures of Robinson Crusoe. Vogel, Malvina, ed. 1990. (Great Illustrated Classics Ser.: Vol. 17). (Illus.). 240p. (J). (gr. 3-6). 9.95 *(0-86611-968-X)* Playmore, Inc., Pubs.
—The Farther Adventures of Robinson Crusoe, Being the Second & Last Part of His Life. (Illus.). reprint ed. 32.50 *(0-404-07912-1)* AMS Pr., Inc.
—The Life & Adventures of Robinson Crusoe. Marshall, Michael J., ed. abr. ed. 1997. (Core Classics Ser.: Vol. 2). (Illus.). 160p. (J). (gr. 4-6). pap. 5.95 *(1-890517-02-X)*; lib. bdg. 10.95 *(1-890517-03-8)* Core Knowledge Foundation.
—Robinson Crusoe. unabr. ed. 1963. (Classics Ser.). (YA). (gr. 6 up). mass mkt. 2.25 o.p. *(0-8049-0022-1,* CL-22) Airmont Publishing Co., Inc.
—Robinson Crusoe. 2nd ed. 2000. (Historias de Siempre Ser.). (SPA., Illus.). 92p. (YA). (gr. 5-8). pap. 12.95 *(84-204-5723-X)* Alfaguara, Ediciones, S.A.- Grupo Santillana ESP. *Dist:* Santillana USA Publishing Co., Inc.
—Robinson Crusoe. unabr. ed. 1990. (J). (gr. 4 up). audio 20.95 *(1-55685-164-2)* Audio Bk. Contractors, Inc.
—Robinson Crusoe. (Illustrated Christian Classics Ser.). (J). 1992. (gr. 3 up). 9.95 o.p. *(1-55748-277-2)*; 1990. (Illus.). 224p. (gr. 7 up). pap. text 1.39 o.p. *(1-55748-118-0)* Barbour Publishing, Inc.
—Robinson Crusoe. 1989. (Illus.). 192p. (J). (gr. 4 up). 1.50 o.p. *(0-8120-5967-0)* Barron's Educational Series, Inc.
—Robinson Crusoe. 1976. (Dent's Illustrated Children's Classics Ser.). (Illus.). (J). reprint ed. 6.95 o.p. *(0-460-05026-5)* Biblio Distribution.
—Robinson Crusoe. 2002. audio compact disk 72.00 *(0-7366-9121-9)*; 2002. (J). audio 64.00 *(0-7366-8953-2)*; 1977. (J). audio 64.00 *(0-7366-0007-8,* 1017) Books on Tape, Inc.
—Robinson Crusoe. abr. rev. ed. 1991. (Classics for Children Ser.). (Illus.). 64p. (J). (gr. 1-5). 8.95 o.p. *(0-89107-601-8)* Crossway Bks.
—Robinson Crusoe. 1989. 352p. (YA). (gr. 4-7). mass mkt. 2.99 *(0-8125-0482-8,* Tor Classics); Level 4. 1988. mass mkt. 2.25 *(0-938819-56-9,* Aerie) Doherty, Tom Assocs., LLC.
—Robinson Crusoe. 1998. (Eyewitness Classics Ser.). (Illus.). 64p. (J). (gr. 3-6). pap. 14.95 *(0-7894-3625-6,* D K Ink) Dorling Kindersley Publishing, Inc.
—Robinson Crusoe. abr. ed. 1998. (Children's Thrift Classics Ser.). (Illus.). 96p. (J). pap. 1.00 *(0-486-28816-1)* Dover Pubns., Inc.
—Robinson Crusoe. 2002. (Illus.). 46p. pap. 6.95 *(0-237-52283-7)* Evans Brothers, Ltd. GBR. *Dist:* Trafalgar Square.
—Robinson Crusoe. Exams Unlimited, Inc. Staff, ed. 2001. (Illus.). 104p. (J). reprint ed. cd-rom 5.20 *(1-59132-021-6)* Exams Unlimited, Inc.
—Robinson Crusoe. 1992. (Children's Classics Ser.). (Illus.). (J). *(0-89434-126-X,* Ferguson Publishing Co.) Facts on File Inc.
—Robinson Crusoe. 1967. (Illus.). (YA). (gr. 5-12). pap. 9.95 *(0-8224-9225-3)* Globe Fearon Educational Publishing.
—Robinson Crusoe. abr. ed. 2001. (Illus.). audio 14.95 *(0-00-105242-X)* HarperCollins Pubs. Ltd. GBR. *Dist:* Trafalgar Square.
—Robinson Crusoe. 1993. (Children's Classics Ser.). 294p. (J). (gr. 2 up). 13.95 *(0-679-42819-4,* Everyman's Library) Knopf Publishing Group.
—Robinson Crusoe. 1961. 320p. (J). (gr. 6). mass mkt. 5.95 o.s.i *(0-451-52236-2,* Signet Classics) NAL.
—Robinson Crusoe, Level 2. Hedge, Tricia, ed. 2001. (Bookworms Ser.). (Illus.). 64p. (J). pap. text 5.95 *(0-19-422984-X)* Oxford Univ. Pr., Inc.
—Robinson Crusoe. Lindskoog, Kathryn, ed. 2002. (Classics for Young Readers Ser.). (Illus.). 192p. (J). per. 6.99 *(0-87552-735-3)* P&R Publishing.
—Robinson Crusoe. Fago, John N., ed. 1978. (Now Age Illustrated IV Ser.). (Illus.). (J). (gr. 4-12). stu. ed. 1.25 *(0-88301-344-4)*; text 7.50 o.p. *(0-88301-332-0)*; pap. text 2.95 *(0-88301-320-7)* Pendulum Pr., Inc.
—Robinson Crusoe. 9999. (Read It Yourself Ser.: Level 5, No. 777-1). (Illus.). (J). (gr. 1). 3.50 o.p. *(0-7214-5123-3,* Ladybird Bks.) Penguin Group (USA) Inc.
—Robinson Crusoe. abr. ed. 1995. (Classics for Young Readers Ser.). (Illus.). 288p. (J). (gr. 4-7). pap. 4.99 *(0-14-036722-5,* Puffin Bks.) Penguin Putnam Bks. for Young Readers.
—Robinson Crusoe. 1987. (Regents Illustrated Classics Ser.). (Illus.). 62p. (YA). (gr. 7-12). pap. text 3.50 o.p. *(0-13-795410-7,* 20418) Prentice Hall, ESL Dept.
—Robinson Crusoe. (Illus.). (J). (gr. 4-6). 1964. 3.79 o.p. *(0-448-03260-0)*; 1963. 2.95 o.p. *(0-448-05467-1)*; 1952. 384p. 13.95 o.s.i *(0-448-06021-3)* Putnam Publishing Group, The.
—Robinson Crusoe. 2001. (Modern Library Classics). 320p. pap. 7.95 *(0-375-75732-5,* Modern Library) Random House Adult Trade Publishing Group.
—Robinson Crusoe. 1990. (Children's Classics Ser.). (J). 12.99 o.s.i *(0-517-01757-1)* Random Hse. Value Publishing.
—Robinson Crusoe. (Courage Unabridged Classics Ser.). (YA). 1998. 296p. pap. 6.00 o.p. *(0-7624-0551-1,* Courage Bks.); 1993. (Illus.). 384p. (gr. 7 up). reprint ed. text 16.95 o.p. *(1-56138-263-9)* Running Pr. Bk. Pubs.
—Robinson Crusoe. 1981. (Keith Jennison Large Type Bks.). (gr. 4-6). lib. bdg. 7.95 o.p. *(0-531-00273-X,* Watts, Franklin) Scholastic Library Publishing.
—Robinson Crusoe. (Junior Classics Ser.). 2001. (Illus.). 128p. (J). (gr. 8). mass mkt. 3.99 *(0-439-23621-5)*; 1990. 368p. (J). (gr. 7-9). pap. 4.50 *(0-590-43285-0)*; 1973. (YA). (gr. 7-12). pap. 1.50 o.p. *(0-590-01357-2)* Scholastic, Inc.

—Robinson Crusoe. Dolch, Edward W. et al, eds. 1988. 128p. (J). (gr. k-3). reprint ed. mass mkt. 2.99 (*0-590-41841-6*) Scholastic, Inc.

—Robinson Crusoe. (Illus.). (J). 2001. (Classics Ser.). 304p. (gr. 3-7). pap. 3.99 (*0-689-84408-5*, Aladdin); 1983. (Robinson Crusoe CL Ser.: Vol. 1). 368p. (gr. 4-7). 27.00 (*0-684-17946-6*, Atheneum) Simon & Schuster Children's Publishing.

—Robinson Crusoe. 1990. (Children's Treasury Ser.). (J). 7.98 o.p. (*0-8317-1356-9*) Smithmark Pubs., Inc.

—Robinson Crusoe. unabr. ed. 2002. (YA). audio compact disk 18.95 (*1-58472-397-1*, In Audio) Sound Room Pubs., Inc.

—Robinson Crusoe. abr. ed. 1995. (A+ Audio Ser.). audio 8.00 (*1-57042-164-1*, 4-521641) Time Warner AudioBooks.

—Robinson Crusoe. (SPA.). 9.95 (*84-241-5636-6*) Torres, Eliseo & Sons.

—Robinson Crusoe. (Saddleback Classics). 1999. (Illus.). (J). 13.10 (*0-606-21567-0*); 1990. 13.00 (*0-606-17593-8*) Turtleback Bks.

—Robinson Crusoe. Richetti, John, ed. & intro. by. 2001. (Classics Ser.). 288p. (J). 8.00 o.s.i (*0-14-043761-4*) Viking Penguin.

—Robinson Crusoe. Ross, Angus, ed. & intro. by. 1966. (Penguin Classics Ser.). 320p. (J). (gr. 9 up). pap. 7.95 o.s.i (*0-14-043007-5*, Penguin Classics) Viking Penguin.

—Robinson Crusoe. Lindskoog, Kathryn, ed. & abr. by. 1991. (Young Reader's Library). (J). (gr. 3-7). pap. 4.99 o.p. (*0-88070-438-1*) Zonderkidz.

—Robinson Crusoe. 1999. (Coleccion "Clasicos Juveniles" Ser.). (SPA., Illus.). 283p. (J). (gr. 4-7). pap. 13.95 (*1-58348-782-4*) iUniverse, Inc.

Defoe, Daniel & Chorpenning, Charlotte B. Robinson Crusoe. 1952. (J). (gr. 1-9). 6.00 (*0-87602-192-5*) Anchorage Pr.

Defoe, Daniel & Everyman's Library Staff. Robinson Crusoe. 1992. 294p. 15.00 (*0-679-40585-2*) Knopf, Alfred A. Inc.

Defoe, Daniel & Ladybird Books Staff. Robinson Crusoe. 1997. (Read It Yourself Ser.). 48p. (J). 3.50 o.s.i (*0-7214-5797-5*, Ladybird Bks.) Penguin Group (USA) Inc.

Defoe, Daniel & Van Gool Studio Staff. Robinson Crusoe. 1995. (Classic Ser.). (Illus.). 64p. (J). (ps-1). 4.98 o.p. (*0-8317-1665-7*) Smithmark Pubs., Inc.

Defoe, Daniel, et al. Robinson Crusoe. (Classics Illustrated Ser.). (Illus.). 52p. (YA). pap. 4.95 (*1-57209-021-9*) Classics International Entertainment, Inc.

Leavitt, Caroline. Robinhound Crusoe. 1997. (Adventures of Wishbone Ser.: No. 4). (Illus.). 144p. (J). (gr. 2-5). mass mkt. 3.99 o.p. (*1-57064-271-0*, Big Red Chair Bks.) Lyrick Publishing.

—Robinhound Crusoe. l.t. ed. 1999. (Adventures of Wishbone Ser.: No. 4). (Illus.). 144p. (J). (gr. 4 up). lib. bdg. 22.60 (*0-8368-2300-1*) Stevens, Gareth Inc.

Zorn, Steven & Defoe, Daniel. Robinson Crusoe: A Young Reader's Edition of the Classic Adventure by Daniel Defoe. 1998. (Illus.). 48p. (J). text 9.98 (*0-7624-1419-7*) Running Pr. Bk. Pubs.

CULPEPPER, DUNC (FICTITIOUS CHARACTER)—FICTION

Paulsen, Gary. Amos & the Alien. 1994. (Culpepper Adventures Ser.). 80p. (J). (gr. 3-5). pap. 3.50 (*0-440-40990-X*) Dell Publishing.

—Amos & the Chameleon Caper. 1996. (Culpepper Adventures Ser.). 80p. (J). (gr. 3-5). pap. 3.99 o.s.i (*0-440-41047-9*) Dell Publishing.

—Amos & the Chameleon Caper. 1996. (Culpepper Adventures Ser.). (J). (gr. 3-5). 9.19 o.p. (*0-606-11039-9*) Turtleback Bks.

—Amos & the Vampire. 1996. (Culpepper Adventures Ser.). 80p. (J). (gr. 3-5). pap. 3.99 o.s.i (*0-440-41043-6*, Yearling) Random Hse. Children's Bks.

—Amos & the Vampire. 1996. (Culpepper Adventures Ser.). (J). (gr. 3-5). 9.19 o.p. (*0-606-08996-9*) Turtleback Bks.

—Amos Binder, Secret Agent. 1996. (Culpepper Adventures Ser.). 80p. (gr. 3-5). pap. text 3.99 o.s.i (*0-440-41050-9*) Dell Publishing.

—Amos Binder, Secret Agent. 1997. (Culpepper Adventures Ser.). (J). (gr. 3-5). 9.19 o.p. (*0-606-11040-2*) Turtleback Bks.

—Amos Gets Famous. 1992. (Culpepper Adventures Ser.). 80p. (J). (gr. 3-5). pap. 3.99 o.s.i (*0-440-40749-4*) Dell Publishing.

—Amos Gets Married. 1995. (Culpepper Adventures Ser.). 112p. (J). (gr. 3-5). pap. 3.50 o.s.i (*0-440-40933-0*) Dell Publishing.

—Amos Gets Married. 1995. (Culpepper Adventures Ser.). (J). (gr. 3-5). 8.60 o.p. (*0-606-07187-3*) Turtleback Bks.

—Amos Goes Bananas. 1996. (Culpepper Adventures Ser.). 80p. (J). (gr. 3-5). pap. 3.99 o.s.i (*0-440-41008-8*) Dell Publishing.

—Amos Goes Bananas. 1995. (Culpepper Adventures Ser.). (J). (gr. 3-5). 9.19 o.p. (*0-606-08997-7*) Turtleback Bks.

—Amos's Killer Concert Caper. 1994. (Culpepper Adventures Ser.). 96p. (J). (gr. 3-5). pap. 3.50 o.s.i (*0-440-40989-6*) Dell Publishing.

—Amos's Killer Concert Caper. 1995. (Culpepper Adventures Ser.). (J). (gr. 3-5). 8.60 o.p. (*0-606-07188-1*) Turtleback Bks.

—Amos's Last Stand. 1993. (Culpepper Adventures Ser.). 80p. (J). (gr. 3-5). pap. 3.25 o.s.i (*0-440-40775-3*) Dell Publishing.

—The Case of the Dirty Bird. 1992. (Culpepper Adventures Ser.). 96p. (J). (gr. 3-5). pap. 3.50 o.s.i (*0-440-40598-X*, Yearling) Random Hse. Children's Bks.

—The Case of the Dirty Bird & Dunc's Doll. unabr. ed. (Culpepper Adventures Ser.). (J). (gr. 3-5). audio 16.95 (*1-55656-183-0*, DAB 075); 1993. audio 9.95 (*1-55656-182-2*) Dercum Audio.

—Coach Amos. 1994. (Culpepper Adventures Ser.). 80p. (J). (gr. 3-5). pap. 3.50 o.s.i (*0-440-40930-6*) Dell Publishing.

—Coach Amos. 1994. (Culpepper Adventures Ser.). (J). (gr. 3-5). 8.70 o.p. (*0-606-06284-X*) Turtleback Bks.

—Cowpokes & Desperadoes. 1993. (Culpepper Adventures Ser.). 80p. (J). (gr. 3-5). pap. 3.50 o.s.i (*0-440-40902-0*) Dell Publishing.

—Cowpokes & Desperadoes. 1994. (Culpepper Adventures Ser.). (J). (gr. 3-5). 9.65 (*0-606-05793-5*) Turtleback Bks.

—Culpepper's Cannon. 1992. (Culpepper Adventures Ser.). 96p. (J). (gr. 3-5). pap. 3.50 o.s.i (*0-440-40617-X*, Yearling) Random Hse. Children's Bks.

—Culpepper's Cannon. 1992. (Culpepper Adventures Ser.). (J). (gr. 3-5). 8.60 o.p. (*0-606-00890-X*) Turtleback Bks.

—Culpepper's Cannon & Dunc Gets Tweaked. unabr. ed. (Culpepper Adventures Ser.). (J). (gr. 3-5). audio 16.95 (*1-55656-185-7*, DAB 076); 1993. audio 9.95 (*1-55656-184-9*) Dercum Audio.

—Dunc & Amos & the Red Tatoos. 1993. (Culpepper Adventures Ser.). 80p. (J). (gr. 3-5). pap. 3.25 o.s.i (*0-440-40790-7*) Dell Publishing.

—Dunc & Amos Go to the Dogs. 1996. (Culpepper Adventures Ser.). 80p. (J). (gr. 3-5). pap. 3.99 o.s.i (*0-440-41040-1*, Yearling) Random Hse. Children's Bks.

—Dunc & Amos Go to the Dogs. 1996. (Culpepper Adventures Ser.). (J). (gr. 3-5). 9.19 o.p. (*0-606-09218-8*) Turtleback Bks.

—Dunc & Amos Hit the Big Top. 1993. (Culpepper Adventures Ser.). 96p. (J). (gr. 3-5). pap. 3.25 o.s.i (*0-440-40756-7*) Dell Publishing.

—Dunc & Amos Hit the Big Top & Dunc's Dump. unabr. ed. (Culpepper Adventures Ser.). (J). (gr. 3-5). audio 16.95 (*1-55656-191-1*, DAB 079); 1993. audio 9.95 (*1-55656-190-3*) Dercum Audio.

—Dunc & Amos Meet the Slasher. 1994. (Culpepper Adventures Ser.). 80p. (J). (gr. 3-5). pap. 3.50 o.s.i (*0-440-40939-X*) Dell Publishing.

—Dunc & Amos Meet the Slasher. 1994. (Culpepper Adventures Ser.). (J). (gr. 3-5). 8.70 o.p. (*0-606-06971-2*) Turtleback Bks.

—Dunc & Amos on Thin Ice. 1997. (Culpepper Adventures Ser.). 80p. (J). (gr. 3-5). pap. text 3.99 o.s.i (*0-440-41053-3*) Dell Publishing.

—Dunc & Amos on Thin Ice. 1997. (Culpepper Adventures Ser.). (J). (gr. 3-5). 34.00 o.p. (*0-606-12684-8*) Turtleback Bks.

—Dunc & the Flaming Ghost. 1992. (Culpepper Adventures Ser.). 96p. (J). (gr. 3-5). pap. 3.50 o.s.i (*0-440-40686-2*, Yearling) Random Hse. Children's Bks.

—Dunc & the Flaming Ghost & Amos Gets Famous. unabr. ed. (Culpepper Adventures Ser.). (J). (gr. 3-5). audio 16.95 (*1-55656-189-X*, DAB 078); 1993. audio 9.95 (*1-55656-188-1*, 396028) Dercum Audio.

—Dunc & the Greased Sticks of Doom. 1994. (Culpepper Adventures Ser.). 96p. (J). (gr. 3-5). pap. 3.50 o.s.i (*0-440-40940-3*) Dell Publishing.

—Dunc & the Haunted Castle. 1993. (Culpepper Adventures Ser.). 80p. (J). (gr. 3-5). pap. 3.99 o.s.i (*0-440-40893-8*) Dell Publishing.

—Dunc & the Haunted Castle. 1993. (Culpepper Adventures Ser.). (J). (gr. 3-5). 9.19 o.p. (*0-606-05817-6*) Turtleback Bks.

—Dunc & the Scam Artist & Dunc & Amos & the Red Tattoos. unabr. ed. (Culpepper Adventures Ser.). (J). (gr. 3-5). audio 16.95 (*1-55656-193-8*, DAB 080); 1993. audio 9.95 (*1-55656-192-X*) Dercum Audio.

—Dunc Breaks the Record. 1992. (Culpepper Adventures Ser.). 96p. (J). (gr. 3-5). pap. 3.99 o.s.i (*0-440-40678-1*, Yearling) Random Hse. Children's Bks.

—Dunc Gets Tweaked. 1992. (Culpepper Adventures Ser.). 96p. (J). (gr. 3-5). pap. 3.50 o.s.i (*0-440-40642-0*, Yearling) Random Hse. Children's Bks.

—Dunc's Doll. 1992. (Culpepper Adventures Ser.). 80p. (J). (gr. 3-5). pap. 3.50 o.s.i (*0-440-40601-3*, Yearling) Random Hse. Children's Bks.

—Dunc's Dump. 1993. (Culpepper Adventures Ser.). 80p. (J). (gr. 3-5). pap. 3.25 o.s.i (*0-440-40762-1*) Dell Publishing.

—Dunc's Halloween. 1993. (Culpepper Adventures Ser.). (J). (gr. 3-5). pap. o.p. (*0-440-90043-3*) Dell Publishing.

—Dunc's Halloween. 1992. (Culpepper Adventures Ser.). 96p. (J). (gr. 3-5). pap. 3.50 o.s.i (*0-440-40659-5*, Yearling) Random Hse. Children's Bks.

—Dunc's Halloween. 1992. (Culpepper Adventures Ser.). (J). (gr. 3-5). 8.60 o.p. (*0-606-05245-3*) Turtleback Bks.

—Dunc's Halloween & Dunc Breaks the Record. unabr. ed. (Culpepper Adventures Ser.). (J). (gr. 3-5). audio 12.95 o.p. (*1-55656-187-3*, DAB 077) BBC Audiobooks America.

—Dunc's Halloween & Dunc Breaks the Record. unabr. ed. 1993. (Culpepper Adventures Ser.). (J). (gr. 3-5). audio 9.95 (*1-55656-186-5*) Dercum Audio.

—Dunc's Undercover Christmas. 1993. (Culpepper Adventures Ser.). 96p. (J). (gr. 3-5). pap. 3.50 o.s.i (*0-440-40874-1*) Dell Publishing.

—Prince Amos. 1994. (Culpepper Adventures Ser.). 80p. (J). (gr. 3-5). pap. 3.50 o.s.i (*0-440-40928-4*) Dell Publishing.

—Prince Amos. 1994. (Culpepper Adventures Ser.). (J). (gr. 3-5). 8.70 o.p. (*0-606-05979-2*) Turtleback Bks.

—Super Amos. 1997. (Culpepper Adventures Ser.). 80p. (J). (gr. 3-5). pap. text 3.99 o.s.i (*0-440-41056-8*) Dell Publishing.

—Super Amos. 1997. (Culpepper Adventures Ser.). (J). (gr. 3-5). 9.19 o.p. (*0-606-12820-4*) Turtleback Bks.

—The Wild Culpepper Cruise. 1993. (Culpepper Adventures Ser.). 80p. (J). (gr. 3-5). pap. 3.50 o.s.i (*0-440-40883-0*) Dell Publishing.

CURIOUS GEORGE (FICTITIOUS CHARACTER)—FICTION

Becker, Fakkel. Curious George & the Hot Air Balloon. 1998. (Curious George Ser.). (J). (ps-2). 10.10 (*0-606-15496-5*) Turtleback Bks.

—Curious George & the Puppies. 1998. 10.10 (*0-606-15497-3*) Turtleback Bks.

—Curious George Feeds the Animals. 1998. (Curious George Ser.). (J). (ps-2). 10.10 (*0-606-16107-4*) Turtleback Bks.

—Curious George Goes to a Chocolate Factory. 1998. (Curious George Ser.). (J). (ps-2). 10.10 (*0-606-15498-1*) Turtleback Bks.

—Curious George Goes to a Movie. 1998. (Curious George Ser.). (J). (ps-2). 10.10 (*0-606-16108-2*) Turtleback Bks.

—Curious George Makes Pancakes. 1998. (Curious George Ser.). (J). (ps-2). 10.10 (*0-606-15499-X*) Turtleback Bks.

—Curious George's Dream. 1998. (Curious George Ser.). (J). (ps-2). 10.10 (*0-606-16109-0*) Turtleback Bks.

Carr, Jan. I Am Curious about Me. 1990. (Curious George Activity Bks.). (Illus.). 48p. (J). (gr. k-2). pap. 1.95 o.p. (*0-590-44032-2*) Scholastic, Inc.

—I Am Curious about the Four Seasons. 1988. (Curious George Activity Bks.). (Illus.). 48p. (J). (gr. k-2). pap. 1.95 o.p. (*0-590-41873-4*) Scholastic, Inc.

Epstein, Jolie. Curious George Goes to Town. 1986. (Curious George Ser.). (Illus.). 24p. (J). (gr. k-2). pap. 1.50 o.p. (*0-590-33990-7*) Scholastic, Inc.

—Curious George Joins the Show. 1985. (Curious George Ser.). (Illus.). 24p. (J). (ps-2). pap. 1.50 o.p. (*0-590-33810-2*) Scholastic, Inc.

Krulik, Nancy E. Curious George Makes a Splash. 1985. (Curious George Activity Bks.). (Illus.). 24p. (Orig.). (J). (gr. k-2). pap. 1.50 o.p. (*0-590-33828-5*) Scholastic, Inc.

—Curious George Saves the Day. 1986. (Curious George Activity Bks.). (Illus.). 24p. (Orig.). (J). (gr. k-2). pap. 1.50 o.p. (*0-590-40113-0*) Scholastic, Inc.

—I Am Curious about Numbers. 1987. (Curious George Activity Bks.). (Illus.). 48p. (Orig.). (J). (gr. k-2). pap. 1.95 o.p. (*0-590-41046-6*) Scholastic, Inc.

Leos, Frances. I Am Curious about Animals. 1988. (Curious George Activity Bks.). (Illus.). 48p. (J). (gr. k-2). pap. 1.95 o.p. (*0-590-41874-2*) Scholastic, Inc.

—I Am Curious about Reading. 1987. (Curious George Activity Bks.). (Illus.). 48p. (Orig.). (J). (gr. k-2). pap. 1.95 o.p. (*0-590-41045-8*) Scholastic, Inc.

Molleson, Diane. I Am Curious About Safety. 1989. (Curious George Activity Bks.). (J). (gr. k-2). pap. 1.95 o.p. (*0-590-42700-8*) Scholastic, Inc.

Rey, H. A. Curious George. 2002. (Curious George Picture Bks.). (Illus.). (J). 13.79 (*0-7587-2310-5*) Book Wholesalers, Inc.

—Curious George. 1995. (Curious George Ser.). (J). (ps-2). reprint ed. lib. bdg. 27.95 (*1-56849-658-3*) Buccaneer Bks., Inc.

—Curious George. ed. 1983. (J). (gr. 1). spiral bd. (*0-616-01768-5*); (gr. 2). spiral bd. (*0-616-01769-3*) Canadian National Institute for the Blind/Institut National Canadien pour les Aveugles.

—Curious George. unabr. ed. (Curious George Ser.). (J). (ps-2). audio 5.99 (*1-55994-915-5*) HarperChildren's Audio.

—Curious George. (Curious George Ser.). 56p. (J). (ps-3). 1994. (Illus.). pap. 24.00 (*0-395-69803-0*); 1993. pap. 9.95 incl. audio (*0-395-66490-X*, 494351); 1993. pap. 9.95 incl. audio (*0-395-66490-X*, 494351) Houghton Mifflin Co.

—Curious George. 2000. (Curious George Ser.). (J). (ps-2). pap. 9.95 incl. audio. pap. 9.95 incl. audio Houghton Mifflin Co. (Schl. Div.).

—Curious George. 1973. (Curious George Ser.). (Illus.). 56p. (J). (ps-3). reprint ed. pap. 5.95 (*0-395-15023-X*) Houghton Mifflin Co. Trade & Reference Div.

—Curious George. 2000. (J). pap., tchr. ed., wbk. ed (*1-56137-270-6*) Novel Units, Inc.

—Curious George. 1973. (Curious George Ser.). (J). (ps-2). 12.10 (*0-606-02923-0*) Turtleback Bks.

—Curious George. unabr. ed. Incl. Curious George Gets a Medal. audio Curious George Rides a Bike. audio Curious George Takes a Job. audio (J). (ps-2). (Curious George Ser.). 1984. Set audio 9.95 (*0-89845-109-4*, CPN 1420, Caedmon) HarperTrade.

—Curious George Comes Home, Vol. 2. 1997. (Curious George Ser.). (J). (ps-2). 10.30 (*0-395-85435-0*) Houghton Mifflin Co.

—Curious George Flies a Kite. 2002. (Curious George Picture Bks.). (Illus.). (J). 13.79 (*0-7587-2314-8*) Book Wholesalers, Inc.

—Curious George Flies a Kite. ed. 1999. (J). (gr. 1). spiral bd. (*0-616-01770-7*); (gr. 2). spiral bd. (*0-616-01771-5*) Canadian National Institute for the Blind/Institut National Canadien pour les Aveugles.

—Curious George Gets a Medal. 2002. (Curious George Picture Bks.). (Illus.). (J). 13.79 (*0-7587-2315-6*) Book Wholesalers, Inc.

—Curious George Gets a Medal. ed. 2000. (J). (gr. 1). spiral bd. (*0-616-01772-3*); (gr. 2). spiral bd. (*0-616-01773-1*) Canadian National Institute for the Blind/Institut National Canadien pour les Aveugles.

—Curious George Gets a Medal. (Curious George Ser.). (J). (ps-2). audio HarperTrade.

—Curious George Gets a Medal. 1974. (Curious George Ser.). (Illus.). 48p. (J). (ps-3). reprint ed. pap. 5.95 (*0-395-18559-9*) Houghton Mifflin Co. Trade & Reference Div.

—Curious George Gets a Medal. 1957. (Curious George Ser.). (J). (ps-2). 12.10 (*0-606-02909-5*) Turtleback Bks.

—Curious George Goes to a Chocolate Factory. 2002. (Illus.). 24p. (J). (ps-3). pap. 9.95 incl. audio (*0-618-21618-9*) Houghton Mifflin Co.

—Curious George in the Big City. 2001. (Curious George Ser.). (Illus.). 24p. (J). (ps-2). 7.95 (*0-618-15253-9*) Houghton Mifflin Co.

—Curious George Learns the Alphabet. 2002. (Curious George Picture Bks.). (Illus.). (J). 13.79 (*0-7587-2318-0*) Book Wholesalers, Inc.

—Curious George Learns the Alphabet. (Curious George Ser.). (Illus.). (J). (ps-3). 1973. 80p. pap. 5.95 (*0-395-13718-7*); 1998. 72p. pap. 9.95 incl. audio (*0-395-89113-2*, 482595, Clarion Bks.) Houghton Mifflin Co. Trade & Reference Div.

—Curious George Learns the Alphabet. 1963. (Curious George Ser.). (J). (ps-2). 12.10 (*0-606-00511-0*) Turtleback Bks.

—Curious George Paper Doll. 1982. (J). pap. 4.95 (*0-486-24386-9*) Dover Pubns., Inc.

—Curious George Rides a Bike. 2002. (Curious George Picture Bks.). (Illus.). 13.79 (*0-7587-2321-0*) Book Wholesalers, Inc.

—Curious George Rides a Bike. (Curious George Ser.). (J). (ps-2). audio HarperTrade.

—Curious George Rides a Bike. (Curious George Ser.). (Illus.). (J). (ps-3). 1997. 1p. pap. 9.95 incl. audio (*0-395-85760-0*); 1973. 48p. tchr. ed. 14.95 (*0-395-16964-X*) Houghton Mifflin Co.

—Curious George Rides a Bike. 1973. (Curious George Ser.). (Illus.). 48p. (J). (ps-3). reprint ed. pap. 5.95 (*0-395-17444-9*) Houghton Mifflin Co. Trade & Reference Div.

—Curious George Rides a Bike. 9999. (Curious George Ser.). (J). (ps-2). 48p. pap. 1.95 o.p. (*0-590-02045-5*); pap. 7.50 o.s.i (*0-590-20003-8*) Scholastic, Inc.

—Curious George Rides a Bike. 1973. (Curious George Ser.). (J). (ps-2). 12.10 (*0-606-02924-9*) Turtleback Bks.

—Curious George Rides a Bike. (Curious George Ser.). (J). (ps-2). 24.95 incl. audio. pap. 32.75 incl. audio. 1993. pap. 12.95 incl. audio (*1-56008-097-3*, PRA017); 1993. pap. text 12.95 incl. audio (*1-56008-116-3*, RAC017) Weston Woods Studios, Inc.

—Curious George Takes a Job. 2002. (Curious George Picture Bks.). (Illus.). (J). 13.79 (*0-7587-2322-9*) Book Wholesalers, Inc.

—Curious George Takes a Job. (Curious George Ser.). (J). (ps-2). audio HarperTrade.

—Curious George Takes a Job. (Curious George Ser.). 48p. (J). (ps-3). 1974. (Illus.). pap. 5.95 (*0-395-18649-8*); 1998. pap. 9.95 incl. audio (*0-395-89114-0*, 494388, Clarion Bks.) Houghton Mifflin Co. Trade & Reference Div.

—Curious George Takes a Job. 9999. (Curious George Ser.). (J). (ps-2). pap. 3.95 o.p. (*0-590-04426-5*); pap. 1.95 o.s.i (*0-590-02046-3*) Scholastic, Inc.

—Curious George Takes a Job. 1975. (Curious George Ser.). (J). (ps-2). 12.10 (*0-606-02925-7*) Turtleback Bks.

—Curious George Wins a Medal. 9999. (J). pap. 1.95 o.s.i (*0-590-02044-7*) Scholastic, Inc.

—Curious George's Box of Books, 4 vols. 2002. (Illus.). (J). (-ps). bds. 18.00 (*0-618-22611-7*) Houghton Mifflin Co.

—Jorge el Curioso. 1993. (Curious George Ser.). (SPA.). (J). (ps-2). pap. 10.44 (*0-395-64572-7*) Houghton Mifflin Co.

—Jorge el Curioso. 2001. (SPA., Illus.). (J). (gr. k-2). 7.96 net. (*1-56137-558-6*, NU6112) Novel Units, Inc.

—Jorge el Curioso. 1990. (Curious George Ser.). (SPA.). (J). (ps-2). 12.10 (*0-606-09494-6*) Turtleback Bks.

—Jorge el Curioso Monta en Bicicleta. Canetti, Yanitzia, tr. 2002. Tr. of Curious George Rides a Bike. (SPA., Illus.). 48p. (J). (ps-3). pap. 5.95 (*0-618-19677-3*); lib. bdg., tchr. ed. 14.95 (*0-618-21615-4*) Houghton Mifflin Co.

—Our George. 1974. (J). pap. 1.95 (*0-590-02043-9*) Scholastic, Inc.

Rey, H. A. & Rey, Margret. The Complete Adventures of Curious George. anniv. ed. 2001. (Curious George Ser.). (Illus.). 432p. (J). (ps-3). tchr. ed. 30.00 (*0-618-16441-3*) Houghton Mifflin Co.

—Curious George. (Curious George Ser.). (Illus.). (J). (ps-3). 1987. 12p. 15.95 (*0-395-45347-X*); 1973. 64p. lib. bdg., tchr. ed. 14.95 (*0-395-15993-8*); Set. 2001. bds. 18.00 (*0-618-15424-8*) Houghton Mifflin Co.

—Curious George & Friends: Favorite Stories by Margret & H. A. Rey. 2003. (Illus.). 272p. (J). (ps-3). tchr. ed. 25.00 (*0-618-22610-9*) Houghton Mifflin Co.

—Curious George & the Birthday Surprise. 2003. (Illus.). 24p. (J). (ps-3). 12.00 (*0-618-34688-0*); pap. 3.95 (*0-618-34687-2*) Houghton Mifflin Co.

—Curious George Gets a Medal. 1957. (Curious George Ser.). (Illus.). 48p. (J). (ps-3). tchr. ed. 15.00 (*0-395-16973-9*) Houghton Mifflin Co.

—Curious George Gets a Medal. unabr. ed. 1998. (Curious George Ser.). 48p. (J). (ps-ps). pap. 9.95 incl. audio (*0-395-89115-9*, 494862, Clarion Bks.) Houghton Mifflin Co. Trade & Reference Div.

—Curious George Goes to the Beach. 1999. (Curious George Ser.). (Illus.). 32p. (J). (ps-3). tchr. ed. 12.00 (*0-395-97834-3*); pap. 3.95 (*0-395-97838-6*); bds. 7.95 (*0-395-97846-7*) Houghton Mifflin Co.

—Curious George Learns the Alphabet. 1963. (Curious George Ser.). (Illus.). 80p. (J). (ps-2). tchr. ed. 14.95 (*0-395-16031-6*) Houghton Mifflin Co.

—Curious George Takes a Job. 1973. (Curious George Ser.). (Illus.). 48p. (J). (ps-ps). tchr. ed. 14.95 (*0-395-15086-8*) Houghton Mifflin Co.

—Curious George's Neighborhood. 2004. (Illus.). 10p. (J). (ps-3). bds. 11.99 (*0-618-41203-4*) Houghton Mifflin Co.

—Curious George's Pop-Up Storybook House. 1999. (Curious George Ser.). (Illus.). 43p. (J). (ps-3). 20.00 (*0-395-97908-0*) Houghton Mifflin Co.

—Jorge el Curioso. (Curious George Ser.). (SPA., Illus.). (J). (ps-3). 2001. 48p. pap. 9.95 incl. audio (*0-618-13159-0*, HM30407); 1989. 64p. lib. bdg. 14.95 (*0-395-17075-3*, HM0753); 1976. 64p. pap. 5.95 (*0-395-24909-0*, HM0825) Houghton Mifflin Co.

—The New Adventures of Curious George. 1999. (Curious George Ser.). (Illus.). 199p. (J). (ps-3). tchr. ed. 25.00 (*0-618-02251-1*) Houghton Mifflin Co.

—The Original Curious George: Collector's Edition. 1998. (Curious George Ser.). (Illus.). 64p. (J). (ps-3). lib. bdg., tchr. ed. 25.00 (*0-395-92272-0*) Houghton Mifflin Co.

Rey, H. A. & Rey, Margret, creators. Curious George & the Rocket. 2001. (Curious George Ser.). (Illus.). 22p. (J). (ps-ps). bds. 5.95 (*0-618-12069-6*) Houghton Mifflin Co.

—Curious George Rides. 2001. (Curious George Ser.). (Illus.). 22p. (J). (ps-ps). bds. 5.95 (*0-618-12075-0*) Houghton Mifflin Co.

—Curious George's 1 to 10 & Back Again. 2001. (Curious George Ser.). (Illus.). 26p. (J). (ps-ps). bds. 5.95 (*0-618-12074-2*) Houghton Mifflin Co.

—Jorge el Curioso y el Conejito. 2002. (SPA., Illus.). 26p. (J). (-ps). bds. 5.95 (*0-618-20316-8*) Houghton Mifflin Co.

—Opuestos con Jorge el Curioso. 2002. (SPA., Illus.). (J). (-ps). bds. 5.95 (*0-618-20317-6*) Houghton Mifflin Co.

Rey, H. A. & Shalleck, Alan J. Curious George Visits the Zoo. Rey, Margret, ed. 1985. (Curious George Ser.). (Illus.). 32p. (J). (ps-ps). pap. 3.95 (*0-395-39030-3*) Houghton Mifflin Co.

Rey, Margret. Curious George & the Dinosaur. 2002. (Curious George TV Bks.). (Illus.). (J). 11.87 (*0-7587-2311-3*) Book Wholesalers, Inc.

—Curious George & the Dinosaur. 1989. (Curious George Ser.). (Illus.). (J). 10.10 (*0-606-21722-3*) Turtleback Bks.

—Curious George & the Pizza. 2002. (Curious George TV Bks.). (Illus.). (J). 11.87 (*0-7587-2312-1*) Book Wholesalers, Inc.

—Curious George at the Fire Station. 2002. (Curious George TV Bks.). (Illus.). (J). 11.87 (*0-7587-2313-X*) Book Wholesalers, Inc.

—Curious George Goes to a Costume Party. 2001. (Curious George Ser.). (Illus.). 24p. (J). (ps-3). lib. bdg., tchr. ed. 12.00 (*0-618-06564-4*) Houghton Mifflin Co.

—Curious George Goes to School. 2002. (Curious George TV Bks.). (Illus.). (J). 11.87 (*0-7587-2316-4*) Book Wholesalers, Inc.

—Curious George Goes to the Aquarium. 2002. (Curious George TV Bks.). (Illus.). (J). 11.87 (*0-7587-2317-2*) Book Wholesalers, Inc.

—Curious George in the Big City. 2001. (Curious George Ser.). (Illus.). 24p. (J). (ps-3). pap. 3.95 (*0-618-15240-7*) Houghton Mifflin Co.

—Curious George in the Snow. 1998. (Curious George Ser.). (Illus.). (J). 10.10 (*0-606-21723-1*) Turtleback Bks.

—Curious George Plays Baseball. 1986. (Curious George Ser.). (Illus.). (J). 10.10 (*0-606-21892-0*) Turtleback Bks.

—Curious George Visits the Zoo. 2002. (Curious George TV Bks.). (Illus.). (J). 11.87 (*0-7587-2323-7*) Book Wholesalers, Inc.

Rey, Margret & Rey, H. A. The Complete Adventures of Curious George, 3 bks., Set. 1995. (Curious George Ser.). (Illus.). 424p. (J). (ps-ps). tchr. ed. 29.95 (*0-395-75410-0*) Houghton Mifflin Co.

—Curious George & the Bunny. 1998. (Curious George Ser.). (Illus.). 12p. (J). (ps-ps). bds. 5.95 (*0-395-89922-2*) Houghton Mifflin Co.

—Curious George & the Dinosaur. 1989. (Curious George Ser.). (Illus.). 32p. (J). (ps-2). 9.95 o.s.i (*0-395-51941-1*); pap. 3.95 (*0-395-51936-5*) Houghton Mifflin Co.

—Curious George & the Dinosaur. Shalleck, Alan J., ed. 1990. (Curious George Ser.). (Illus.). 1p. (J). (ps-3). pap. 9.95 incl. audio (*0-395-56484-0*, 494303, Clarion Bks.) Houghton Mifflin Co. Trade & Reference Div.

—Curious George & the Dump Truck. 1984. (Curious George Ser.). (Illus.). 32p. (J). (ps-2). 9.95 o.p. (*0-395-36635-6*); pap. 3.95 o.p. (*0-395-36629-1*) Houghton Mifflin Co.

—Curious George & the Dumptruck. 1999. (Curious George Ser.). (Illus.). (J). (ps-3). 24p. pap. 3.95 (*0-395-97836-X*); 32p. lib. bdg., tchr. ed. 12.00 (*0-395-97832-7*); 32p. bds. 7.95 (*0-395-97844-0*) Houghton Mifflin Co.

—Curious George & the Hot Air Balloon. 1998. (Curious George Ser.). (Illus.). (J). (ps-3). 24p. tchr. ed. 12.00 (*0-395-91918-5*); 24p. pap. 3.95 (*0-395-91909-6*); 64p. bds. 7.95 (*0-395-92338-7*) Houghton Mifflin Co.

—Curious George & the Pizza. Shalleck, Alan J., ed. (Curious George Ser.). (J). (ps-3). 1988. 1p. pap. 9.95 incl. audio (*0-395-48874-5*, 494294); 1985. 32p. tchr. ed. 12.00 (*0-395-39039-7*); 1985. 32p. pap. 3.95 (*0-395-39033-8*) Houghton Mifflin Co.

—Curious George & the Pizza. 1985. (Curious George Ser.). (J). (ps-2). 10.10 (*0-606-12232-X*) Turtleback Bks.

—Curious George & the Puppies. 1998. (Curious George Ser.). (J). (ps-3). 24p. tchr. ed. 12.00 (*0-395-91217-2*); (Illus.). 24p. pap. 3.95 (*0-395-91215-6*); (Illus.). 64p. bds. 7.95 (*0-395-92334-4*) Houghton Mifflin Co.

—Curious George at the Airport. (Curious George Ser.). (J). (ps-2). 1988. pap. 6.95 o.s.i (*0-395-48877-X*); 1987. (Illus.). 32p. 8.95 o.s.i (*0-395-45355-0*); 1987. (Illus.). 32p. pap. 2.95 o.p. (*0-395-45368-2*) Houghton Mifflin Co.

—Curious George at the Ballet. 1986. (Curious George Ser.). (Illus.). 32p. (J). (ps-2). 8.95 o.s.i (*0-395-42477-1*); pap. 3.95 o.s.i (*0-395-42474-7*) Houghton Mifflin Co.

—Curious George at the Beach. 1988. (Curious George Ser.). (Illus.). 32p. (J). (ps-2). 9.95 o.s.i (*0-395-48666-1*); pap. 2.95 o.s.i (*0-395-48660-2*) Houghton Mifflin Co.

—Curious George at the Fire Station. (Curious George Ser.). (Illus.). 32p. (J). (ps-ps). 1988. pap. 9.95 incl. audio (*0-395-48875-3*, 494295); 1985. tchr. ed. 12.00 (*0-395-39037-0*) Houghton Mifflin Co.

—Curious George at the Fire Station. Shalleck, Alan J., ed. 1985. (Curious George Ser.). (Illus.). 32p. (J). (ps-ps). pap. 3.95 (*0-395-39031-1*) Houghton Mifflin Co.

—Curious George at the Fire Station. 1985. (Curious George Ser.). (J). (ps-2). 10.10 (*0-606-19810-5*) Turtleback Bks.

—Curious George at the Laundromat. 1987. (Curious George Ser.). (Illus.). 32p. (Orig.). (J). (ps-2). 8.95 o.s.i (*0-395-45353-4*); pap. 2.95 o.s.i (*0-395-45367-4*) Houghton Mifflin Co.

—Curious George at the Parade. 1999. (Curious George Ser.). (Illus.). 32p. (J). (ps-3). pap. 3.95 (*0-395-97837-8*); lib. bdg., tchr. ed. 12.00 (*0-395-97833-5*); bds. 7.95 (*0-395-97845-9*) Houghton Mifflin Co.

—Curious George at the Railroad Station. 1988. (Curious George Ser.). (Illus.). 32p. (J). (ps-2). 9.95 o.s.i (*0-395-48667-X*); pap. 2.95 o.p. (*0-395-48657-2*) Houghton Mifflin Co.

—Curious George Bakes a Cake. 1990. (Curious George Ser.). (Illus.). 32p. (J). (ps-2). 9.95 o.s.i (*0-395-55725-9*); pap. 2.95 o.s.i (*0-395-55716-X*) Houghton Mifflin Co.

—Curious George Feeds the Animals. 1998. (Curious George Ser.). (Illus.). (J). (ps-3). 24p. pap. 3.95 (*0-395-91910-X*); 64p. bds. 7.95 (*0-395-92340-9*) Houghton Mifflin Co.

—Curious George Flies a Kite. (Curious George Ser.). (J). (ps-2). audio HarperTrade.

—Curious George Flies a Kite. (Curious George Ser.). (Illus.). 80p. (J). (ps-ps). 1997. pap. 9.95 incl. audio (*0-395-85759-7*); 1977. pap. 5.95 (*0-395-25937-1*); 1973. tchr. ed. 15.00 (*0-395-16965-8*) Houghton Mifflin Co.

—Curious George Flies a Kite. 1986. (Curious George Ser.). (J). (ps-2). 12.10 (*0-606-01093-9*) Turtleback Bks.

—Curious George Goes Camping. (Curious George Ser.). (Illus.). 32p. (J). (ps-3). 1999. pap. 3.95 (*0-395-97835-1*); 1999. lib. bdg., tchr. ed. 12.00 (*0-395-97831-9*); 1999. bds. 7.95 (*0-395-97843-2*); 1990. 9.95 o.s.i (*0-395-55726-7*); 1990. pap. 3.95 o.s.i (*0-395-55715-1*) Houghton Mifflin Co.

—Curious George Goes Fishing. 1987. (Curious George Ser.). (Illus.). 32p. (J). (ps-2). 8.95 o.s.i (*0-395-45351-8*); pap. 3.95 o.s.i (*0-395-45405-0*) Houghton Mifflin Co.

—Curious George Goes Hiking. 1985. (Curious George Ser.). 32p. (J). (ps-2). pap. 3.95 o.p. (*0-395-39032-X*); (Illus.). 8.95 o.p. (*0-395-39038-9*) Houghton Mifflin Co.

—Curious George Goes Sledding. 1984. (Curious George Ser.). (Illus.). 32p. (J). (ps-2). 9.95 o.p. (*0-395-36637-2*); pap. 3.95 o.p. (*0-395-36631-3*) Houghton Mifflin Co.

—Curious George Goes to a Chocolate Factory. 1998. (Curious George Ser.). (Illus.). (J). (ps-3). 64p. tchr. ed. 12.00 (*0-395-91216-4*); 24p. pap. 3.95 (*0-395-91214-8*); 24p. bds. 7.95 (*0-395-92331-X*) Houghton Mifflin Co.

—Curious George Goes to a Costume Party. 1986. (Curious George Ser.). (J). (ps-2). 8.95 o.s.i (*0-395-42478-X*); pap. 3.95 o.s.i (*0-395-42475-5*) Houghton Mifflin Co.

—Curious George Goes to a Restaurant. 1988. (Curious George Ser.). (Illus.). 32p. (J). (ps-2). 9.95 o.s.i (*0-395-48664-5*); pap. 2.95 o.p. (*0-395-48658-0*) Houghton Mifflin Co.

—Curious George Goes to a Toy Store. 1990. (Curious George Ser.). (Illus.). 32p. (J). (ps-2). 9.95 o.s.i (*0-395-55724-0*); pap. 2.95 o.s.i (*0-395-55714-3*) Houghton Mifflin Co.

—Curious George Goes to an Air Show. 1990. (Curious George Ser.). (Illus.). 32p. (J). (ps-2). 9.95 o.s.i (*0-395-55991-X*); pap. 2.95 o.s.i (*0-395-55989-8*) Houghton Mifflin Co.

—Curious George Goes to an Ice Cream Shop. 1989. (Curious George Ser.). (Illus.). 32p. (J). (ps-2). 9.95 o.s.i (*0-395-51943-8*) Houghton Mifflin Co.

—Curious George Goes to an Ice Cream Shop. 1989. (Curious George Ser.). (Illus.). (J). (ps-2). 10.10 (*0-606-19811-3*) Turtleback Bks.

—Curious George Goes to School. Shalleck, Alan J., ed. (Curious George Ser.). (Illus.). (J). (ps-3). 1990. 1p. pap. 9.95 incl. audio (*0-395-56483-2*, 494302); 1989. 32p. pap. 3.95 (*0-395-51939-X*); 1989. 32p. lib. bdg., tchr. ed. 12.00 (*0-395-51944-6*) Houghton Mifflin Co.

—Curious George Goes to School. 1989. (Curious George Ser.). (J). (ps-2). 10.10 (*0-606-19812-1*) Turtleback Bks.

—Curious George Goes to the Aquarium. Shalleck, Alan J., ed. 1984. (Curious George Ser.). (Illus.). 32p. (J). (ps-3). tchr. ed. 12.00 (*0-395-36634-8*); pap. 3.95 (*0-395-36628-3*) Houghton Mifflin Co.

—Curious George Goes to the Circus. 1984. (Curious George Ser.). (Illus.). 32p. (J). (ps-2). 9.95 o.p. (*0-395-36636-4*); pap. 3.95 o.p. (*0-395-36630-5*) Houghton Mifflin Co.

—Curious George Goes to the Hospital. (Curious George Ser.). (J). (ps-2). audio HarperTrade.

—Curious George Goes to the Hospital. (Curious George Ser.). (Illus.). (J). (ps-3). 1995. 1p. pap. 9.95 incl. audio (*0-395-72026-5*, 494395); 1995. 1p. pap. 9.95 incl. audio (*0-395-72026-5*, 494395); 1973. 48p. lib. bdg., tchr. ed. 14.95 (*0-395-18158-5*); 1966. 48p. pap. 5.95 (*0-395-07062-7*) Houghton Mifflin Co.

—Curious George Goes to the Hospital. 1988. (Curious George Ser.). (J). (ps-2). pap. 2.50 o.p. (*0-590-03426-X*) Scholastic, Inc.

—Curious George Goes to the Hospital. 1966. (Curious George Ser.). (J). (ps-2). 12.10 (*0-606-00836-5*) Turtleback Bks.

—Curious George Goes to the Movies. 1998. (Curious George Ser.). (Illus.). (J). (ps-3). 32p. pap. 3.95 (*0-395-91906-1*); 24p. lib. bdg., tchr. ed. 12.00 (*0-395-91901-0*); 24p. bds. 7.95 (*0-395-92335-2*) Houghton Mifflin Co.

—Curious George in the Snow. 1998. (Curious George Ser.). (Illus.). (J). (ps-3). 24p. tchr. ed. 12.00 (*0-395-91902-9*); 64p. bds. 7.95 (*0-395-92336-0*) Houghton Mifflin Co.

—Curious George Learns Phonics & Spelling. 1998. (Curious George Ser.). (J). (ps-2). 24.72 (*0-395-85431-8*) Houghton Mifflin Co.

—Curious George Learns the Alphabet. abr. ed. Incl. Curious George Flies a Kite. audio Curious George Goes to the Hospital. audio (J). (ps-2). (Curious George Ser.). 1984. Set audio 9.95 (*0-89845-812-9*, CPN 1421, Caedmon) HarperTrade.

—Curious George Makes Pancakes. 1998. (Curious George Ser.). (Illus.). (J). (ps-3). 24p. pap. 3.95 (*0-395-91908-8*); 24p. lib. bdg., tchr. ed. 12.00 (*0-395-91903-7*); 64p. bds. 7.95 (*0-395-92337-9*) Houghton Mifflin Co.

—Curious George Plays Baseball. Shalleck, Alan J., ed. 1986. (Curious George Ser.). (Illus.). 32p. (J). (ps-ps). tchr. ed. 12.00 (*0-395-39041-9*); pap. 3.95 (*0-395-39035-4*) Houghton Mifflin Co.

—Curious George Visits a Toy Store. 2002. (Illus.). 24p. (J). (ps-3). tchr. ed. 12.00 (*0-618-06398-6*) Houghton Mifflin Co.

—Curious George Visits an Amusement Park. 1988. (Curious George Ser.). (Illus.). 32p. (J). (ps-2). 9.95 o.s.i (*0-395-48665-3*); pap. 2.95 o.p. (*0-395-48659-9*) Houghton Mifflin Co.

—Curious George Visits the Police Station. 1987. (Curious George Ser.). (Illus.). 32p. (J). (ps-2). 8.95 o.s.i (*0-395-45349-6*); pap. 2.95 o.s.i (*0-395-45366-6*) Houghton Mifflin Co.

—Curious George Visits the Zoo. Shalleck, Alan J., ed. (Curious George Ser.). (J). (ps-3). 1988. 1p. pap. 9.95 incl. audio (*0-395-48876-1*, 494296); 1988. 1p. pap. 9.95 incl. audio (*0-395-48876-1*, 494296); 1985. 32p. tchr. ed. 12.00 (*0-395-39036-2*) Houghton Mifflin Co.

—Curious George Visits the Zoo. 1985. (Curious George Ser.). (J). (ps-2). 10.10 (*0-606-12233-8*) Turtleback Bks.

—Curious George Walks the Pets. 1986. (Curious George Ser.). (Illus.). 32p. (J). (ps-2). 8.95 o.p. (*0-395-39040-0*); pap. 2.95 o.p. (*0-395-39034-6*) Houghton Mifflin Co.

—Curious George's ABCs. 1998. (Curious George Ser.). (Illus.). 12p. (J). (ps-ps). bds. 5.95 (*0-395-89925-7*) Houghton Mifflin Co.

—Curious George's Are You Curious? 1998. (Curious George Ser.). (Illus.). 8p. (J). (ps-ps). bds. 5.95 (*0-395-89924-9*) Houghton Mifflin Co.

—Curious George's Dream. 1998. (Curious George Ser.). (Illus.). 24p. (J). (ps-3). tchr. ed. 12.00 (*0-395-91905-3*); pap. 3.95 (*0-395-91911-8*); bds. 7.95 (*0-395-92342-5*) Houghton Mifflin Co.

—Curious George's Opposites. 1998. (Curious George Ser.). (Illus.). 8p. (J). (ps-ps). bds. 5.95 (*0-395-89923-0*) Houghton Mifflin Co.

Rey, Margret & Rey, H. A., creators. Curious George Goes Fishing. 2001. (Curious George Ser.). (Illus.). 26p. (J). (ps-ps). bds. 5.95 (*0-618-12071-8*) Houghton Mifflin Co.

Rey, Margret & Shalleck, Alan J., eds. Curious George Goes to an Ice Cream Shop. 1989. (Curious George Ser.). (Illus.). 32p. (J). (ps-ps). pap. 3.95 (*0-395-51937-3*) Houghton Mifflin Co.

Rey, Margret, et al. Curious George & the Dinosaur. 1989. (Curious George Ser.). 32p. (J). (ps-ps). tchr. ed. 12.00 (*0-395-51942-X*) Houghton Mifflin Co.

—Curious George Goes to a Costume Party. 2001. (Curious George Ser.). (Illus.). 24p. (J). (ps-3). pap. 3.95 (*0-618-06569-5*) Houghton Mifflin Co.

Vipah Interactive Staff. Curious George & the Dump Truck. 1999. (Curious George Ser.). (J). (ps-2). 10.10 (*0-606-17365-X*) Turtleback Bks.

—Curious George at the Parade. 1999. (Curious George Ser.). (J). (ps-2). 10.10 (*0-606-17366-8*) Turtleback Bks.

—Curious George Goes Camping. 1999. (Curious George Ser.). (J). (ps-2). 10.10 (*0-606-17367-6*) Turtleback Bks.

—Curious George Goes to the Beach. 1999. (Curious George Ser.). (J). (ps-2). 10.10 (*0-606-17368-4*) Turtleback Bks.

Weston, Martha. Curious George Goes to a Costume Party. 2001. (Curious George Ser.). (Illus.). (J). 10.10 (*0-606-21931-5*) Turtleback Bks.

Weston, Martha, illus. Curious George in the Big City. 2001. (Curious George Ser.). 24p. (J). (ps-3). tchr. ed. 12.00 (*0-618-15252-0*) Houghton Mifflin Co.

—Curious George Takes a Train. 2002. 24p. (J). (ps-3). pap. 3.95 (*0-618-06567-9*); lib. bdg., tchr. ed. 12.00 (*0-618-06566-0*) Houghton Mifflin Co.

—Curious George Visits a Toy Store. 2002. 24p. (J). (ps-3). pap. 3.95 (*0-618-06570-9*) Houghton Mifflin Co.

—Curious George Visits the Library. 2003. 24p. (J). (ps-3). lib. bdg. 12.00 (*0-618-06565-2*) Houghton Mifflin Co.

Williams, Wendy. I Am Curious about Things That Go. 1990. (Curious George Activity Bks.). (J). (gr. k-2). pap. 1.95 o.p. (*0-590-42699-0*) Scholastic, Inc.

CUSTER, GEORGE ARMSTRONG, 1839-1876—FICTION

Burks, Brian. Soldier Boy. 1997. 160p. (YA). (gr. 7 up). 12.00 (*0-15-201218-4*); pap. 6.00 (*0-15-201219-2*, Harcourt Paperbacks) Harcourt Children's Bks.

Irwin, Hadley. Jim Dandy. 1994. 144p. (J). (gr. 5-9). 15.00 (*0-689-50594-9*, McElderry, Margaret K.) Simon & Schuster Children's Publishing.

Kremer, Kevin. Saved by Custer's Ghost. 1997. (Illus.). (J). (gr. 2-8). pap. 8.99 (*0-9632837-5-8*) Sweetgrass Communications, Inc.

D

DAFFY DUCK (FICTITIOUS CHARACTER)—FICTION

Daffy Duck Goes Animal Quackers. 1990. (J). 4.98 o.p. (*1-55521-686-2*) Book Sales, Inc.

Daffy's Rainy Day Zoo Tubbable. 1992. (Looney Tunes Adventures Ser.). (Illus.). 8p. (J). (ps). 4.95 o.p. (*0-681-41450-2*) Borders Pr.

Gilchrist, Brad. Daffy Duck Goes Animal Quackers! 1990. (Looney Tunes Library). (Illus.). 12p. (J). (gr. 1-3). 4.95 o.p. (*0-681-40553-8*) Borders Pr.

Glassman, Jackie. Looney Tunes Back in Action Reader. 2003. (Looney Tunes Ser.). (Illus.). 32p. (J). mass mkt. 3.99 (*0-439-52140-8*, Scholastic Paperbacks) Scholastic, Inc.

Jones, Chuck. Daffy Duck for President. 1997. (J). (*1-890371-00-9*) Warner Brothers Worldwide Publishing.

Markas, Jenny. Looney Tunes Back in Action Junior Novelization. 2003. (Looney Tunes Ser.). 80p. (J). mass mkt. 4.99 (*0-439-52136-X*, Scholastic Paperbacks) Scholastic, Inc.

Mason, Jane. Looney Tunes Back in Action Movie Storybook. 2003. (Looney Tunes Ser.). (Illus.). 48p. (J). mass mkt. 5.99 (*0-439-52137-8*, Scholastic Paperbacks) Scholastic, Inc.

McCann, Jesse Leon. Looney Tunes Back in Action. 2003. (Looney Tunes Ser.). 32p. (J). mass mkt. 3.50 (*0-439-52139-4*, Scholastic Paperbacks) Scholastic, Inc.

—Looney Tunes Back in Action Joke Book. 2003. (Looney Tunes Ser.). 64p. (J). mass mkt. 4.50 (*0-439-52138-6*, Scholastic Paperbacks) Scholastic, Inc.

Silver Dolphin Staff. Daffy Duck & Friends. 1997. (Cartoon Works). (Illus.). 32p. (gr. 3 up). 18.95 o.p. (*1-57145-309-1*, Silver Dolphin Bks.) Advantage Pubs. Group.

DANA GIRLS (FICTITIOUS CHARACTERS)—FICTION

Keene, Carolyn. The Curious Coronation. 1975. (Dana Girls Ser.: No. 14). (Illus.). 179p. (J). (gr. 3-5). 2.95 o.s.i (*0-448-09094-5*, Grosset & Dunlap) Penguin Putnam Bks. for Young Readers.

—The Ghost in the Gallery. 1975. (Dana Girls Ser.: No. 13). (Illus.). 180p. (J). (gr. 3-5). 2.95 o.p. (*0-448-09093-7*, Grosset & Dunlap) Penguin Putnam Bks. for Young Readers.

—The Haunted Lagoon. rev. ed. 1973. (Dana Girls Ser.: No. 8). (Illus.). 196p. (J). (gr. 3-5). 2.95 o.p. (*0-448-09088-0*, Grosset & Dunlap) Penguin Putnam Bks. for Young Readers.

—The Hundred Year Mystery. 1976. (Dana Girls Ser.: No. 15). (Illus.). 180p. (J). (gr. 3-5). 2.95 o.p. (*0-448-09095-3*, Grosset & Dunlap) Penguin Putnam Bks. for Young Readers.

—The Mountain-Peak Mystery. 1978. (Dana Girls Ser.: No. 16). (Illus.). 180p. (J). (gr. 3-5). 2.95 o.p. (*0-448-09096-1*, Grosset & Dunlap) Penguin Putnam Bks. for Young Readers.

—Mystery of the Bamboo Bird. 1973. (Dana Girls Ser.: No. 9). (Illus.). 192p. (J). (gr. 3-5). 2.95 o.p. (*0-448-09089-9*, Grosset & Dunlap) Penguin Putnam Bks. for Young Readers.

—Mystery of the Stone Tiger. 1972. (Dana Girls Ser.: No. 1). (Illus.). 175p. (J). (gr. 3-5). 2.95 o.p. (*0-448-09081-3*, Grosset & Dunlap) Penguin Putnam Bks. for Young Readers.

—Mystery of the Wax Queen. 1972. (Dana Girls Ser.: No. 4). (Illus.). 176p. (J). (gr. 3-5). 2.95 o.p. (*0-448-09084-8*, Grosset & Dunlap) Penguin Putnam Bks. for Young Readers.

—The Phantom Surfer. 1972. (Dana Girls Ser.: No. 6). (Illus.). 192p. (J). (gr. 3-5). 2.95 o.p. (*0-448-09086-4*, Grosset & Dunlap) Penguin Putnam Bks. for Young Readers.

—The Riddle of the Frozen Fountain. 1972. (Dana Girls Ser.: No. 2). (Illus.). 192p. (J). (gr. 3-5). 2.95 o.p. (*0-448-09082-1*, Grosset & Dunlap) Penguin Putnam Bks. for Young Readers.

—The Secret of the Lost Lake. 1974. (Dana Girls Ser.: No. 11). (J). (gr. 3-5). 2.95 o.p. (*0-448-09091-0*, Grosset & Dunlap) Penguin Putnam Bks. for Young Readers.

—The Secret of the Minstrel's Guitar. 1972. (Dana Girls Ser.: No. 5). (Illus.). 174p. (J). (gr. 3-5). 2.95 o.p. (*0-448-09085-6*, Grosset & Dunlap) Penguin Putnam Bks. for Young Readers.

—The Secret of the Silver Dolphin. 1972. (Dana Girls Ser.: No. 3). (Illus.). 192p. (J). (gr. 3-5). 2.95 o.p. (*0-448-09083-X*, Grosset & Dunlap) Penguin Putnam Bks. for Young Readers.

—The Secret of the Swiss Chalet. rev. ed. 1973. (Dana Girls Ser.: No. 7). (Illus.). 196p. (J). (gr. 3-5). 2.95 o.p. (*0-448-09087-2*, Grosset & Dunlap) Penguin Putnam Bks. for Young Readers.

—The Winking Ruby Mystery. 1974. (Dana Girls Ser.: No. 12). (Illus.). 192p. (J). (gr. 3-5). 2.95 o.p. (*0-448-09092-9*, Grosset & Dunlap) Penguin Putnam Bks. for Young Readers.

—The Witch's Omen. 1978. (Dana Girls Ser.: No. 17). (Illus.). 179p. (J). (gr. 3-5). 2.95 o.p. (*0-448-09097-X*, Grosset & Dunlap) Penguin Putnam Bks. for Young Readers.

DANGER JOE (FICTITIOUS CHARACTER)—FICTION

Schade, Susan & Buller, Jon. Bungee Baboon Rescue. 2002. (Danger Joe Show Ser.: No. 2). (Illus.). 112p. (J). mass mkt. 3.99 (*0-439-40976-4*, Scholastic Paperbacks) Scholastic, Inc.

—The Growling Grizzly. 2002. (Danger Joe Show Ser.: No. 1). (Illus.). 96p. (J). (gr. 1-3). mass mkt. 3.99 (*0-439-40140-2*, Scholastic Paperbacks) Scholastic, Inc.

—Hawk Talk. 2002. (Danger Joe Show Ser.: No. 3). (Illus.). 112p. (J). mass mkt. 3.99 (*0-439-40977-2*, Scholastic Paperbacks) Scholastic, Inc.

DARWIN, CHARLES, 1809-1882—FICTION

Johnson, Vargie. Charles Darwin, the Adventurer. 1992. (J). 10.00 o.p. (*0-533-10092-5*) Vantage Pr., Inc.

Weaver, Anne H. The Voyage of the Beetle: A Journey Around the World with Charles Darwin & the Search for the Solution to the Mystery of Mysteries, As Narrated by Rosie, an Articulate Beetle. Lawrence, George, tr. & illus. by. 2004. 80p. lib. bdg. 26.90 (*0-7613-2923-4*) Millbrook Pr., Inc.

DATA (FICTITIOUS CHARACTER)—FICTION

Barnes-Svarney, Patricia L. Loyalties. 1996. (Star Trek Ser.: No. 10). (Illus.). 128p. (J). (gr. 4-7). pap. 3.99 (*0-671-55280-5*, Aladdin) Simon & Schuster Children's Publishing.

—Loyalties. 1996. (Star Trek, The Next Generation: No. 10). (J). (gr. 3-6). 10.04 (*0-606-09893-3*) Turtleback Bks.

Friedman, Michael Jan. Mystery of the Missing Crew. Clancy, Lisa, ed. 1995. (Star Trek Ser.: No. 6). (Illus.). 128p. (J). (gr. 4-7). pap. 3.99 (*0-671-50108-9*, Aladdin) Simon & Schuster Children's Publishing.

—Mystery of the Missing Crew. 1995. (Star Trek, The Next Generation: No. 6). (J). (gr. 3-6). 10.04 (*0-606-11905-1*) Turtleback Bks.

—Secret of the Lizard People. Clancy, Lisa, ed. 1995. (Star Trek Ser.: No. 7). (Illus.). 128p. (J). (gr. 4-7). pap. 3.99 (*0-671-50109-7*, Aladdin) Simon & Schuster Children's Publishing.

—Secret of the Lizard People. 1995. (Star Trek, The Next Generation: No. 7). (J). (gr. 3-6). 10.04 (*0-606-11906-X*) Turtleback Bks.

Mason, Jane B. First Contact: The Movie Storybook. 1996. (Star Trek Ser.). (Illus.). 32p. (J). (ps-3). pap. 9.99 (*0-689-80899-2*, Simon Spotlight) Simon & Schuster Children's Publishing.

Vornholt, John. First Contact. 1996. (Star Trek Ser.: No. 8). (J). (ps-3). 10.04 (*0-606-11883-7*) Turtleback Bks.

Vornholt, John, et al. First Contact. 1996. (Star Trek Ser.: No. 8). (Illus.). 128p. (J). (gr. 8 up). per. 3.99 (*0-671-00128-0*, Aladdin) Simon & Schuster Children's Publishing.

Weiss, Bobbi J. G. & Weiss, David Cody. Deceptions. 1998. (Star Trek Ser.: No. 14). (Illus.). 128p. (J). (gr. 4-7). pap. 3.99 (*0-671-01723-3*, Aladdin) Simon & Schuster Children's Publishing.

—Deceptions. 1998. (Star Trek, The Next Generation: No. 14). (J). (gr. 3-6). 10.04 (*0-606-13812-9*) Turtleback Bks.

DAVE (FICTITIOUS CHARACTER: LAROCHELLE)—FICTION

LaRochelle, David. The Case of the Missing Lynx. 1995. (Mad Mysteries Ser.). (Illus.). 48p. (Orig.). (J). (gr. 2 up). 2.95 o.s.i (*0-8431-3797-5*, Price Stern Sloan) Penguin Putnam Bks. for Young Readers.

—Detective Dave: Space Case. 1998. (Mad Mysteries Ser.: Vol. 7). (Illus.). 48p. (J). (gr. 2-4). 3.50 o.s.i (*0-8431-7850-7*, Price Stern Sloan) Penguin Putnam Bks. for Young Readers.

—Detective Dave's Bummer Vacation. 1997. (Mad Mysteries Ser.: Vol. 5). (Illus.). 48p. (J). (gr. 2 up). 2.95 o.p. (*0-8431-7957-0*, Price Stern Sloan) Penguin Putnam Bks. for Young Readers.

—The Invisible Suit Case. 1995. (Mad Mysteries Ser.). (Illus.). 48p. (Orig.). (J). (gr. 2 up). 2.95 o.s.i (*0-8431-3798-3*, Price Stern Sloan) Penguin Putnam Bks. for Young Readers.

—Miss Taken's Identity. 1998. (Mad Mysteries Ser.: Vol. 8). (Illus.). 48p. (J). (gr. 2-4). 3.50 o.p. (*0-8431-7849-3*, Price Stern Sloan) Penguin Putnam Bks. for Young Readers.

—The Pirate's Yo-Ho Hoax. 1997. (Mad Mysteries Ser.: Vol. 6). (Illus.). 48p. (J). (gr. 2 up). 3.50 o.p. (*0-8431-7958-9*, Price Stern Sloan) Penguin Putnam Bks. for Young Readers.

—Trapped in Hill House. 1996. (Mad Mysteries Ser.). (Illus.). (J). (ps-3). 2.95 o.p. (*0-8431-3945-5*, Price Stern Sloan) Penguin Putnam Bks. for Young Readers.

DAVID, KING OF ISRAEL—FICTION

Bearman, Jane. David. 1975. (Illus.). (J). (gr. 3 up). 3.95 (*0-8246-0085-1*) Jonathan David Pubs., Inc.

Borchard, Therese J. Whitney Coaches David on Fighting Goliath: And Learns to Stand up for Herself. 2000. (Emerald Bible Collection). (Illus.). 80p. (J). (gr. 3-7). pap. 5.95 (*0-8091-6669-0*) Paulist Pr.

Bull, Geoffrey. I Wish I Lived When David Did. 1975. (Far-Away Bks.). (J). 1.95 o.p. (*0-87508-890-2*) Christian Literature Crusade, Inc.

Goldsboro, Bobby. Noah & the Ark/David & Goliath. 2002. (Adventures of Cheze & Kwackers Ser.: Bk. 1). (Illus.). 48p. (J). (gr. k-3). pap. 8.95 (*1-889658-27-8*) New Canaan Publishing Co., Inc.

Holly the Lamb Meets David. 1996. (J). 8.99 o.p. (*0-8054-7936-8*) Broadman & Holman Pubs.

Marsh, T. F. The Grouchy Giant: A Tale about Trusting God. (Tale Tellers Ser.). (Illus.). 32p. (J). (ps-2). 4.99 (*0-7814-3283-9*) Cook Communications Ministries.

Miyoshi, Sekiya, illus. Singing David. 1971. (J). (gr. k-3). lib. bdg. 4.90 o.p. (*0-531-01936-5*, Watts, Franklin) Scholastic Library Publishing.

Pakulak, Eric. At the Side of David: A Multiple-Ending Bible Adventure. 2000. (Illus.). 87p. (J). pap. 6.95 (*0-8198-0768-0*) Pauline Bks. & Media.

Petersham, Maud. The Story of David. 1900. (J). per. 5.99 (*0-689-81400-3*, Aladdin) Simon & Schuster Children's Publishing.

—The Story of Ruth & the Story of David. 1900. (J). per. 5.99 (*0-689-81399-6*, Aladdin) Simon & Schuster Children's Publishing.

DENNIS THE MENACE (FICTITIOUS CHARACTER)—FICTION

Dennis the Menace Takes the Cake. 1987. (Golden Story Book & Tape Ser.). (Illus.). 24p. (J). (ps-3). pap. o.p. (*0-307-13992-1*, Golden Bks.) Random Hse. Children's Bks.

Horowitz, Jordan. Dennis the Menace. 1993. (J). (gr. 4-7). mass mkt. 2.95 o.p. (*0-590-48219-X*); (ps-3). pap. 2.95 (*0-590-47399-9*); (Illus.). (gr. k-2). mass mkt. 2.95 (*0-590-47349-2*); (Illus.). 152p. (gr. 4-7). mass mkt. 3.25 o.p. (*0-590-47350-6*) Scholastic, Inc.

Ketcham, Hank. Dennis the Menace: Ain't Misbehavin' 1983. 125p. (Orig.). mass mkt. 2.95 o.s.i (*0-449-12679-X*, Fawcett) Ballantine Bks.

—Dennis the Menace: All American Kid. 1984. (Dennis the Menace Ser.). (Illus.). (J). mass mkt. 1.95 o.p. (*0-449-12700-1*, Fawcett) Ballantine Bks.

—Dennis the Menace: A.M. 1981. (Dennis the Menace Ser.). (Illus.). mass mkt. 1.75 o.s.i (*0-449-13733-3*, Fawcett) Ballantine Bks.

—Dennis the Menace: Busy Body. 1982. (Dennis the Menace Ser.). (Illus.). 128p. mass mkt. 3.95 o.s.i (*0-449-12529-7*, Fawcett) Ballantine Bks.

—Dennis the Menace: Dog's Best Friend. 1984. (Dennis the Menace Ser.: No. 43). 128p. (Orig.). mass mkt. 3.59 o.s.i (*0-449-12801-6*, Fawcett) Ballantine Bks.

—Dennis the Menace: Driving Mother up the Wall, No. 21. 1985. (Dennis the Menace Ser.). mass mkt. 3.59 o.s.i (*0-449-12944-6*, Fawcett) Ballantine Bks.

—Dennis the Menace: Everybody's Little Helper. 1984. (Dennis the Menace Ser.). (Illus.). 128p. (J). mass mkt. 1.95 o.s.i (*0-449-12732-X*, Fawcett) Ballantine Bks.

—Dennis the Menace: Five Years at the Same Location. 1987. (Illus.). 80p. pap. 4.95 o.p. (*0-399-51389-2*) Putnam Publishing Group, The.

—Dennis the Menace: Good Intenshuns. 1981. 128p. mass mkt. 1.50 o.p. (*0-449-14395-3*, Fawcett) Ballantine Bks.

—Dennis the Menace: Happy Half-Pint. 1982. (Dennis the Menace Ser.). (Illus.). mass mkt. 1.75 o.p. (*0-449-13649-3*, Fawcett) Ballantine Bks.

—Dennis the Menace: Here Comes Trouble. 1987. mass mkt. 3.59 o.s.i (*0-449-13389-3*, Ballantine Bks.); 1983. (Illus.). (J). mass mkt. 1.95 o.p. (*0-449-12585-8*, Fawcett) Ballantine Bks.

—Dennis the Menace: His First Forty Years. 1991. (Illus.). 224p. pap. 7.98 (*1-55859-157-5*) Abbeville Pr., Inc.

—Dennis the Menace: Household Hurricane. 1982. (Dennis the Menace Ser.). (Illus.). mass mkt. 1.75 o.s.i (*0-449-13679-5*, Fawcett) Ballantine Bks.

—Dennis the Menace: I Done It My Way. 1981. (Dennis the Menace Ser.). mass mkt. 1.95 o.s.i (*0-449-14095-4*, Fawcett) Ballantine Bks.

—Dennis the Menace: Just for Fun. 1981. (Dennis the Menace Ser.). (Illus.). mass mkt. 1.50 o.p. (*0-449-13777-5*, Fawcett) Ballantine Bks.

—Dennis the Menace: Little Man in a Big Hurry. 1984. (Dennis the Menace Ser.). (Illus.). 128p. (J). mass mkt. 1.95 o.s.i (*0-449-12778-8*, Fawcett) Ballantine Bks.

—Dennis the Menace: Little Pip-Squeak. 1980. (Dennis the Menace Ser.). (Illus.). 128p. mass mkt. 1.50 o.p. (*0-449-13851-8*, Fawcett) Ballantine Bks.

—Dennis the Menace: Make-Believe Angel. 1981. (Dennis the Menace Ser.). (Illus.). (J). mass mkt. 1.95 o.s.i (*0-449-13902-6*, Fawcett) Ballantine Bks.

—Dennis the Menace: Non-Stop Nuisance. 1981. (Dennis the Menace Ser.). (Illus.). mass mkt. 1.50 o.p. (*0-449-13737-6*, Fawcett) Ballantine Bks.

—Dennis the Menace: Non Stop Nuisance. 1984. mass mkt. 3.59 o.s.i (*0-449-12758-3*, Ballantine Bks.) Ballantine Bks.

—Dennis the Menace: Ol' Droopy Drawers. 1981. (Dennis the Menace Ser.). (Illus.). mass mkt. 1.50 o.p. (*0-449-14004-0*, Fawcett) Ballantine Bks.

—Dennis the Menace: Old Droopy Drawers. 1987. mass mkt. 3.59 o.s.i (*0-449-13432-6*, Ballantine Bks.) Ballantine Bks.

—Dennis the Menace: One More Time! 1981. 128p. mass mkt. 1.50 o.s.i (*0-449-14423-2*, Fawcett) Ballantine Bks.

—Dennis the Menace: Perpetual Motion. 1979. (Dennis the Menace Ser.). (Illus.). 128p. mass mkt. 1.25 o.s.i (*0-449-13647-7*, Fawcett) Ballantine Bks.

—Dennis the Menace: Prayers & Graces. 1993. (Illus.). (J). 64p. 11.95 o.p. (*0-664-21993-4*); 64p. pap. 9.95 (*0-664-25252-4*); pap. 72.00 (*0-664-25495-0*) Westminster John Knox Pr.

—Dennis the Menace: Short in the Saddle. 1981. mass mkt. 1.50 o.p. (*0-449-14287-6*, Fawcett) Ballantine Bks.

—Dennis the Menace: Short 'n Snappy. 1982. (Dennis the Menace Ser.). (Illus.). (J). mass mkt. 1.75 o.p. (*0-449-13872-0*, Fawcett) Ballantine Bks.

—Dennis the Menace: Stayin' Alive. 1981. (Dennis the Menace Ser.: No. 41). 128p. (Orig.). mass mkt. 1.50 o.s.i (*0-449-14363-5*, Fawcett) Ballantine Bks.

—Dennis the Menace: Sunrise Express. 1984. (Illus.). 128p. mass mkt. 2.95 o.s.i (*0-449-12787-7*, Fawcett) Ballantine Bks.

—Dennis the Menace: Surprise Package. 1981. (Dennis the Menace Ser.). (Illus.). (J). mass mkt. 1.95 o.p. (*0-449-13860-7*, Fawcett) Ballantine Bks.

—Dennis the Menace: Teacher's Threat. 1981. (Dennis the Menace Ser.). (Illus.). (J). mass mkt. 1.50 o.s.i (*0-449-13643-4*, Fawcett) Ballantine Bks.

—Dennis the Menace: The Kid Next Door. 1980. (Dennis the Menace Ser.). (Illus.). 128p. mass mkt. 1.50 o.p. (*0-449-13656-6*, Fawcett) Ballantine Bks.

—Dennis the Menace: The Short Swinger. 1981. (Dennis the Menace Ser.). (Illus.). (J). mass mkt. 1.50 o.s.i (*0-449-13641-8*, Fawcett) Ballantine Bks.

—Dennis the Menace: Voted Most Likely. 1982. (Dennis the Menace Ser.). (Illus.). (YA). (gr. 7 up). mass mkt. 1.75 o.s.i (*0-449-13747-3*, Fawcett) Ballantine Bks.

—Dennis the Menace: Where the Action Is. 1981. (Dennis the Menace Ser.). (Illus.). 128p. (J). mass mkt. 1.50 o.s.i (*0-449-13669-8*, Fawcett) Ballantine Bks.

—Dennis the Menace: Who Me? 1980. (Dennis the Menace Ser.). (Illus.). mass mkt. 1.50 o.p. (*0-449-13734-1*, Fawcett) Ballantine Bks.

—Dennis the Menace: Your Friendly Neighborhood Kid. 1979. (Dennis the Menace Ser.). (Illus.). (J). mass mkt. 1.25 o.s.i (*0-449-13778-3*, Fawcett) Ballantine Bks.

—Dennis the Menace: Your Mother's Calling! 1984. (Dennis the Menace Ser.). mass mkt. 2.95 o.s.i (*0-449-12725-7*, Fawcett) Ballantine Bks.

—The Mad Dog of Lobo Mountain. (D. J. Dillon Adventure Ser.: No. 5). 132p. (J). 1986. (gr. 3-7). pap. 4.99 o.p. (*0-89693-482-9*); 1996. pap. 5.99 (*1-56476-506-7*, 6-3506) Cook Communications Ministries.

—The Mystery of the Black Hole Mine. (D. J. Dillon Adventure Ser.). 132p. (J). 1996. pap. 5.99 (*1-56476-508-3*, 6-3508); 1987. (gr. 3-7). pap. 4.99 o.p. (*0-89693-320-2*) Cook Communications Ministries.

—The Secret of Mad River. 1996. (D. J. Dillon Adventure Ser.: No. 9). 132p. (J). (gr. 3-7). pap. 5.99 o.p. (*1-56476-510-5*, 6-3510) Cook Communications Ministries.

DIXON, JOHNNY (FICTITIOUS CHARACTER)—FICTION

Bellairs, John. The Chessmen of Doom. (John Bellairs Ser.). 2000. (Illus.). 160p. (gr. 3-7). pap. 5.99 (*0-14-130697-1*, Puffin Bks.); 1989. (J). 13.89 o.p. (*0-8037-0750-9*, Dial Bks. for Young Readers) Penguin Putnam Bks. for Young Readers.

—The Chessmen of Doom. 1992. (J). (gr. 4-8). 16.80 o.p. (*0-8446-6579-7*) Smith, Peter Pub., Inc.

—The Curse of the Blue Figurine. (Johnny Dixon Ser.). (Illus.). 1996. 208p. (J). (gr. 3-7). pap. 5.99 (*0-14-038005-1*); 1983. 224p. (YA). (gr. 5 up). 11.89 o.p. (*0-8037-1265-0*, Dial Bks. for Young Readers); 1983. 224p. (YA). (gr. 5 up). 11.95 o.p. (*0-8037-1119-0*, Dial Bks. for Young Readers) Penguin Putnam Bks. for Young Readers.

—The Curse of the Blue Figurine. 1984. pap. 2.75 o.s.i (*0-553-15429-X*, Yearling); 208p. (J). (gr. 4-6). pap. 3.50 o.s.i (*0-553-15540-7*, RL6IL4 + 15282-3, Skylark) Random Hse. Children's Bks.

—The Curse of the Blue Figurine. 1996. 11.04 (*0-606-10777-0*) Turtleback Bks.

—The Drum, the Doll & the Zombie. (Johnny Dixon Mystery Ser.). 176p. (J). 1997. (gr. 3-7). pap. 3.99 o.s.i (*0-14-037515-5*); 1994. (Illus.). 14.99 o.s.i (*0-8037-1462-9*, Dial Bks. for Young Readers); 1994. (Illus.). 14.89 o.p. (*0-8037-1463-7*, Dial Bks. for Young Readers) Penguin Putnam Bks. for Young Readers.

—The Drum, the Doll & the Zombie. 1997. (Johnny Dixon Mystery Ser.). (YA). 10.04 (*0-606-12683-X*) Turtleback Bks.

—The Eyes of the Killer Robot. (Johnny Dixon Mystery Ser.). 176p. 1998. (J). (gr. 3-7). pap. 5.99 (*0-14-130062-0*, Puffin Bks.); 1986. (YA). (gr. 5 up). 11.95 o.p. (*0-8037-0324-4*, Dial Bks. for Young Readers); 1986. (YA). (gr. 5 up). 11.89 o.p. (*0-8037-0325-2*, Dial Bks. for Young Readers) Penguin Putnam Bks. for Young Readers.

—The Eyes of the Killer Robot. 1987. (Illus.). 160p. (J). pap. 3.99 o.s.i (*0-553-15552-0*, Skylark) Random Hse. Children's Bks.

—The Eyes of the Killer Robot. 1998. (Johnny Dixon Mystery Ser.). 11.04 (*0-606-13371-2*) Turtleback Bks.

—The Mummy, the Will & the Crypt. 1985. 176p. pap. 3.99 o.s.i (*0-553-15701-9*); (J). (gr. 6). pap. 2.75 o.s.i (*0-553-15498-2*) Bantam Bks.

—The Mummy, the Will & the Crypt. (Johnny Dixon Ser.). (Illus.). 1996. 176p. (J). (gr. 3-7). pap. 5.99 (*0-14-038007-8*, Puffin Bks.); 1983. 192p. (YA). (gr. 5 up). 12.89 o.p. (*0-8037-0030-X*, Dial Bks. for Young Readers); 1983. 192p. (YA). (gr. 5 up). 12.95 o.p. (*0-8037-0029-6*, Dial Bks. for Young Readers) Penguin Putnam Bks. for Young Readers.

—The Mummy, the Will & the Crypt. 2001. (J). (gr. 4-8). 20.75 (*0-8446-7170-3*) Smith, Peter Pub., Inc.

—The Mummy, the Will & the Crypt. 1996. (J). 12.04 (*0-606-10883-1*) Turtleback Bks.

—The Revenge of the Wizard's Ghost. (Johnny Dixon Mystery Ser.). (Illus.). 160p. 1997. (J). (gr. 3-7). pap. 5.99 (*0-14-038043-4*); 1985. (YA). (gr. 5 up). 11.89 o.p. (*0-8037-0177-2*, Dial Bks. for Young Readers); 1985. (YA). (gr. 5 up). 13.95 o.p. (*0-8037-0170-5*, Dial Bks. for Young Readers) Penguin Putnam Bks. for Young Readers.

—The Revenge of the Wizard's Ghost. 1999. (J). (gr. 3 up). 20.25 (*0-8446-7010-3*) Smith, Peter Pub., Inc.

—The Revenge of the Wizard's Ghost. 1997. (Johnny Dixon Mystery Ser.). (J). 10.04 (*0-606-12798-4*) Turtleback Bks.

—The Secret of the Underground Room. (Johnny Dixon Ser.). (Illus.). (J). 1992. 144p. (gr. 3-7). pap. 4.99 o.p. (*0-14-034932-4*, Puffin Bks.); 1990. 12p. (ps-3). 13.89 o.p. (*0-8037-0864-5*, Dial Bks. for Young Readers); 1990. 160p. (ps-3). 14.00 o.s.i (*0-8037-0863-7*, Dial Bks. for Young Readers) Penguin Putnam Bks. for Young Readers.

—The Secret of the Underground Room. 1992. (J). 9.09 (*0-606-01744-5*) Turtleback Bks.

—The Spell of the Sorcerer's Skull. 1985. 176p. (J). pap. 3.99 o.s.i (*0-553-15726-4*) Bantam Bks.

—The Spell of the Sorcerer's Skull. (Johnny Dixon Mystery Ser.). 1997. (Illus.). 192p. (J). (gr. 3-7). pap. 5.99 (*0-14-038044-2*); 1985. (YA). (gr. 5 up). 11.89 o.p. (*0-8037-0122-5*, Dial Bks. for Young Readers); 1984. (YA). (gr. 5 up). 11.95 o.p. (*0-8037-0120-9*, Dial Bks. for Young Readers) Penguin Putnam Bks. for Young Readers.

—The Spell of the Sorcerer's Skull. 1985. 176p. (J). pap. 2.50 o.s.i (*0-553-15357-9*, Skylark) Random Hse. Children's Bks.

—The Spell of the Sorcerer's Skull. 2002. (YA). (gr. 3 up). 20.25 (*0-8446-7206-8*) Smith, Peter Pub., Inc.

—The Spell of the Sorcerer's Skull. 1997. (Johnny Dixon Mystery Ser.). 10.04 (*0-606-11867-5*) Turtleback Bks.

—The Trolley to Yesterday. 1990. 192p. (J). (gr. 4-7). pap. 4.50 o.s.i (*0-553-15795-7*) Bantam Bks.

—The Trolley to Yesterday. (Johnny Dixon Mystery Ser.). (Illus.). 192p. 1998. (J). (gr. 3-7). pap. 5.99 (*0-14-130092-2*, Puffin Bks.); 1989. (YA). (gr. 5 up). 13.89 o.p. (*0-8037-0582-4*, Dial Bks. for Young Readers); 1989. (YA). (gr. 5 up). 13.95 o.p. (*0-8037-0581-6*, Dial Bks. for Young Readers) Penguin Putnam Bks. for Young Readers.

—The Trolley to Yesterday. 1989. (J). 10.55 (*0-606-04566-X*) Turtleback Bks.

Strickland, Brad. The Bell, the Book & the Spellbinder. 2000. (John Bellairs Ser.). (Illus.). 160p. (gr. 3-7). pap. 5.99 (*0-14-130362-X*, Puffin Bks.) Penguin Putnam Bks. for Young Readers.

—The Hand of the Necromancer. (Johnny Dixon Mystery Ser.). 176p. 1998. (Illus.). (J). (gr. 3-7). pap. 4.99 o.p. (*0-14-038695-5*, Puffin Bks.); 1996. (YA). (gr. 5 up). 14.89 o.s.i (*0-8037-1830-6*, Dial Bks. for Young Readers); 1996. (YA). (gr. 5 up). 14.99 o.s.i (*0-8037-1829-2*, Dial Bks. for Young Readers) Penguin Putnam Bks. for Young Readers.

—The Wrath of the Grinning Ghost. Moore, Lisa, ed. 2001. (Johnny Dixon Ser.). 176p. (J). (gr. 3-7). pap. 5.99 (*0-14-131103-7*, Puffin Bks.) Penguin Putnam Bks. for Young Readers.

—The Wrath of the Grinning Ghost. Sherry, Toby, ed. 1999. (Johnny Dixon Mystery Ser.). (Illus.). 192p. (YA). (gr. 5-9). 16.99 o.s.i (*0-8037-2222-2*, Dial Bks. for Young Readers) Penguin Putnam Bks. for Young Readers.

Strickland, Brad & Bellairs, John. The Bell, the Book & the Spellbinder. (J). 1999. (Illus.). pap. 14.89 (*0-8037-1832-2*); 1997. 160p. (gr. 5-9). 14.99 o.s.i (*0-8037-1831-4*) Penguin Putnam Bks. for Young Readers. (Dial Bks. for Young Readers).

DOLITTLE, DOCTOR (FICTITIOUS CHARACTER)—FICTION

Berrien, Polly, adapted by. Doctor Dolittle & His Friends. 1967. (Illus.). (J). (gr. k-4). lib. bdg. 3.99 o.p. (*0-394-90739-6*, Random Hse. Bks. for Young Readers) Random Hse. Children's Bks.

Glasser, Robin Preiss, illus. Doctor Dolittle. 1998. (Doctor Dolittle Chapter Bks.). 128p. (gr. 1-4). pap. text 4.99 o.s.i (*0-440-41546-2*) Dell Publishing.

—Doctor Dolittle & His Animal Family: Based on the Original Text & Illustrations of Hugh Lofting. 1999. (Doctor Dolittle Chapter Bks.). 112p. (gr. 1-4). pap. text 3.99 o.s.i (*0-440-41544-6*) Bantam Bks.

—Doctor Dolittle & His Animal Family: Based on the Original Text & Illustrations of Hugh Lofting. 1999. (Doctor Dolittle Chapter Bks.). (J). (gr. 1-4). 10.04 (*0-606-16445-6*) Turtleback Bks.

—Doctor Dolittle & Tommy Stubbins. 1999. (Doctor Dolittle Chapter Bks.). 48p. (J). (gr. 1-4). pap. 3.99 o.s.i (*0-440-41553-5*, Dell Books for Young Readers) Random Hse. Children's Bks.

—Doctor Dolittle & Tommy Stubbins. 1999. (Doctor Dolittle Chapter Bks.). (J). (gr. 1-4). 10.14 (*0-606-16719-6*) Turtleback Bks.

—Doctor Dolittle Meets the Pushmi-Pullyu. 1999. (Doctor Dolittle Chapter Bks.). 41p. (J). (gr. 1-4). pap. 3.99 o.s.i (*0-440-41550-0*, Dell Books for Young Readers) Random Hse. Children's Bks.

—Doctor Dolittle Meets the Pushmi-Pullyu. 1999. (Doctor Dolittle Chapter Bks.). (J). (gr. 1-4). 10.14 (*0-606-16718-8*) Turtleback Bks.

—Doctor Dolittle's Journey. 1999. (Doctor Dolittle Chapter Bks.). 128p. (gr. 1-4). pap. text 3.99 o.s.i (*0-440-41547-0*, Dell Books for Young Readers) Random Hse. Children's Bks.

—Doctor Dolittle's Journey. 1999. (Doctor Dolittle Chapter Bks.). (J). (gr. 1-4). 10.04 (*0-606-16446-4*) Turtleback Bks.

Lawrence, Elliot. Doctor Dolittle's Animals. 1998. (Illus.). 32p. (ps-3). pap. text 4.99 o.s.i (*0-440-41556-X*) Dell Publishing.

Lofting, Hugh. Doctor Dolittle. unabr. ed. 2000. (Doctor Dolittle Ser.). (J). (gr. 4-6). audio compact disk 19.99 (*0-7861-9920-2*, z1698) Blackstone Audio Bks., Inc.

—Doctor Dolittle. unabr. ed. 1995. (Doctor Dolittle Ser.). (J). (gr. 4-6). audio 18.00 Books on Tape, Inc.

—Doctor Dolittle. 1976. (Doctor Dolittle Ser.). (J). (gr. 4-6). 5.60 (*0-87129-390-0*, D18) Dramatic Publishing Co.

—Doctor Dolittle: A Treasury. 1990. (Doctor Dolittle Ser.). (J). (gr. 4-6). reprint ed. lib. bdg. 37.95 (*0-89966-674-4*) Buccaneer Bks., Inc.

—Doctor Dolittle: A Treasury. 1986. (Doctor Dolittle Ser.). 336p. (J). (gr. 4-6). pap. 4.95 o.s.i (*0-440-41964-6*) Dell Publishing.

—Doctor Dolittle & the Green Canary. 1989. (Doctor Dolittle Ser.). (J). (gr. 4-6). pap. 14.95 o.s.i (*0-440-50141-5*); (Illus.). 288p. 14.95 o.s.i (*0-385-29748-3*, Delacorte Pr.) Dell Publishing.

—Doctor Dolittle & the Green Canary. 1950. (Doctor Dolittle Ser.). (Illus.). (J). (gr. 4-6). o.p. (*0-397-30166-9*) HarperCollins Children's Bk. Group.

—Doctor Dolittle & the Green Canary. (Doctor Dolittle Ser.). (J). (gr. 4-6). 1989. pap. o.s.i (*0-385-29854-4*, Dell Books for Young Readers); 1988. 288p. pap. 3.50 o.s.i (*0-440-40079-1*, Yearling) Random Hse. Children's Bks.

—Doctor Dolittle & the Secret Lake. 1948. (Doctor Dolittle Ser.). (Illus.). (J). (gr. 4-6). o.p. (*0-397-30135-9*) HarperCollins Children's Bk. Group.

—Doctor Dolittle in the Moon. 1988. (Doctor Dolittle Ser.). 224p. (J). (gr. 4-6). pap. 3.25 o.s.i (*0-440-40113-5*, Yearling) Random Hse. Children's Bks.

—Doctor Dolittle's Bag of Books. 1988. (J). (gr. 4-7). pap. o.s.i (*0-440-36000-5*) Dell Publishing.

—Doctor Dolittle's Birthday Book. 1968. (Doctor Dolittle Ser.). (Illus.). (J). (gr. 4-6). o.p. (*0-397-30996-1*) HarperCollins Children's Bk. Group.

—Doctor Dolittle's Caravan. 1988. (Doctor Dolittle Ser.). 256p. (J). (gr. 4-6). pap. 3.50 o.s.i (*0-440-40071-6*) Dell Publishing.

—Doctor Dolittle's Caravan. 1926. (Doctor Dolittle Ser.). (Illus.). (J). (gr. 4-6). 13.41 o.p. (*0-397-30011-5*) HarperCollins Children's Bk. Group.

—Doctor Dolittle's Circus. 1988. (Doctor Dolittle Ser.). 208p. (J). (gr. 4-6). pap. 3.50 o.s.i (*0-440-40058-9*) Dell Publishing.

—Doctor Dolittle's Circus. 1989. (Doctor Dolittle Ser.). (J). (gr. 4-6). 16.25 o.p. (*0-8446-6370-0*) Smith, Peter Pub., Inc.

—Doctor Dolittle's Garden. 1988. (Doctor Dolittle Ser.). 288p. (J). (gr. 4-6). pap. 3.50 o.s.i (*0-440-40103-8*, Yearling) Random Hse. Children's Bks.

—Doctor Dolittle's Post Office. 1988. (Doctor Dolittle Ser.). 288p. (J). (gr. 4-6). pap. 3.50 o.s.i (*0-440-40096-1*, Yearling) Random Hse. Children's Bks.

—Doctor Dolittle's Zoo. 1925. (Doctor Dolittle Ser.). (Illus.). (J). (gr. 4-6). o.p. (*0-397-30009-3*) HarperCollins Children's Bk. Group.

—Gub-Gub's Book, an Encyclopedia of Food. 1992. (Doctor Dolittle Ser.). (J). (gr. 4-6). pap. 15.00 (*0-671-78355-6*, Simon & Schuster Children's Publishing) Simon & Schuster Children's Publishing.

—The Story of Doctor Dolittle. unabr. ed. (Doctor Dolittle Ser.). (J). (gr. 4-6). 2000. audio compact disk 15.00 (*1-885608-37-3*); 1997. audio 14.95 (*1-885608-18-7*) Airplay.

—The Story of Doctor Dolittle. 1996. (Doctor Dolittle Ser.). (J). (gr. 4-6). audio 20.95 (*1-55685-451-X*) Audio Bk. Contractors, Inc.

—The Story of Doctor Dolittle. unabr. ed. 1996. (Doctor Dolittle Ser.). (J). (gr. 4-6). audio 17.95 (*0-7861-0946-7*, 1698) Blackstone Audio Bks., Inc.

—The Story of Doctor Dolittle. unabr. collector's ed. 1995. (Doctor Dolittle Ser.). (J). (gr. 4-6). audio 28.00 (*0-7366-3119-4*, 3795) Books on Tape, Inc.

—The Story of Doctor Dolittle. (Doctor Dolittle Ser.). (Illus.). 176p. (gr. 4-6). 1988. (J). 13.95 o.s.i (*0-385-29662-2*, Delacorte Pr.); 1968. pap. text 4.99 (*0-440-48307-7*) Dell Publishing.

—The Story of Doctor Dolittle. 1998. (Doctor Dolittle Ser.). 106p. (J). (gr. 4-6). pap. text 3.99 (*0-8125-8006-0*, Tor Classics) Doherty, Tom Assocs., LLC.

—The Story of Doctor Dolittle. unabr. ed. 1997. (Doctor Dolittle Ser.). (Illus.). 96p. (J). (gr. 4-6). reprint ed. pap. text 1.00 (*0-486-29350-5*) Dover Pubns., Inc.

—The Story of Doctor Dolittle. Exams Unlimited, Inc. Staff, ed. 2001. 116p. (J). reprint ed. cd-rom 5.95 (*1-885343-94-9*) Exams Unlimited, Inc.

—The Story of Doctor Dolittle. (Books of Wonder). (Illus.). (J). 1997. 176p. (ps-3). 24.99 (*0-688-14001-7*); 1920. (gr. 4-6). o.p. (*0-397-30000-X*) HarperCollins Children's Bk. Group.

—The Story of Doctor Dolittle. l.t. ed. (Doctor Dolittle Ser.). 257p. lib. bdg. 36.92 (*0-7583-2389-1*); 316p. (J). (gr. 4-6). pap. 29.84 (*0-7583-2398-0*); 257p. (J). (gr. 4-6). pap. 25.67 (*0-7583-2397-2*); 209p. (J). (gr. 4-6). pap. 22.27 (*0-7583-2396-4*); 366p. (J). (gr. 4-6). pap. 33.42 (*0-7583-2399-9*); 127p. (J). (gr. 4-6). pap. 16.51 (*0-7583-2394-8*); 93p. (J). (gr. 4-6). pap. 14.08 (*0-7583-2393-X*); 74p. (J). (gr. 4-6). pap. 12.74 (*0-7583-2392-1*); 163p. (J). (gr. 4-6). pap. 19.04 (*0-7583-2395-6*); 366p. (J). (gr. 4-6). lib. bdg. 44.67 (*0-7583-2391-3*); 127p. (J). (gr. 4-6). lib. bdg. 25.89 (*0-7583-2386-7*); 163p. (J). (gr. 4-6). lib. bdg. 30.29 (*0-7583-2387-5*); 209p. (J). (gr. 4-6). lib. bdg. 33.52 (*0-7583-2388-3*); 316p. (J). (gr. 4-6). lib. bdg. 41.09 (*0-7583-2390-5*); 74p. (J). (gr. 4-6). lib. bdg. 19.18 (*0-7583-2384-0*); 93p. (J). (gr. 4-6). lib. bdg. 21.58 (*0-7583-2385-9*) Huge Print Pr.

—The Story of Doctor Dolittle. abr. ed. 1998. (Doctor Dolittle Ser.). (J). (gr. 4-6). audio 18.00 o.s.i (*0-553-47769-2*, AD46R, Listening Library) Random Hse. Audio Publishing Group.

—The Story of Doctor Dolittle. adapted ed. 1997. (Doctor Dolittle Ser.). (Illus.). 128p. (gr. 4-6). pap. text 3.99 (*0-440-41233-1*, Yearling) Random Hse. Children's Bks.

—The Story of Doctor Dolittle. 1988. (Doctor Dolittle Ser.). (J). (gr. 4-6). 10.55 (*0-606-03929-5*) Turtleback Bks.

—Viages de Doctor Dolittle. 1999. (Espasa Juvenil Ser.: Vol. 94). Tr. of Voyages of Doctor Dolittle. (SPA., Illus.). 376p. (J). (gr. 4-7). 11.95 (*84-239-7060-4*) Espasa Calpe, S.A. ESP. *Dist:* Planeta Publishing Corp.

—The Voyages of Doctor Dolittle. 1999. (Doctor Dolittle Ser.). 352p. (gr. 4-6). mass mkt. 2.99 o.s.i (*0-440-22833-6*) Bantam Bks.

—The Voyages of Doctor Dolittle. unabr. ed. 2000. (Doctor Dolittle Ser.). (J). (gr. 4-6). audio 44.95 (*0-7861-1858-X*, 2657); audio compact disk 56.00 (*0-7861-9822-2*, z2657) Blackstone Audio Bks., Inc.

—The Voyages of Doctor Dolittle. (Doctor Dolittle Ser.). 336p. (J). (gr. 4-6). 1991. pap. 3.50 o.s.i (*0-440-70014-0*); 1988. (Illus.). 14.95 o.p. (*0-385-29663-0*, Delacorte Pr.) Dell Publishing.

—The Voyages of Doctor Dolittle. 2004. 224p. pap. 4.95 (*0-486-43491-5*) Dover Pubns., Inc.

—The Voyages of Doctor Dolittle. l.t. ed. (Doctor Dolittle Ser.). (J). (gr. 4-6). 440p. pap. 36.74 (*0-7583-2771-4*); 344p. pap. 29.61 (*0-7583-2770-6*); 563p. pap. 45.28 (*0-7583-2772-2*); 693p. pap. 54.26 (*0-7583-2773-0*); 852p. pap. 67.80 (*0-7583-2774-9*); 989p. pap. 77.45 (*0-7583-2775-7*); 251p. pap. 23.68 (*0-7583-2769-2*); 201p. pap. 20.38 (*0-7583-2768-4*); 201p. lib. bdg. 26.38 (*0-7583-2760-9*); 251p. lib. bdg. 29.68 (*0-7583-2761-7*); 344p. lib. bdg. 35.61 (*0-7583-2762-5*); 563p. lib. bdg. 51.28 (*0-7583-2764-1*); 693p. lib. bdg. 60.26 (*0-7583-2765-X*); 852p. lib. bdg. 83.30 (*0-7583-2766-8*); 989p. lib. bdg. 91.96 (*0-7583-2767-6*); 440p. lib. bdg. 42.74 (*0-7583-2763-3*) Huge Print Pr.

—The Voyages of Doctor Dolittle. 2001. (Doctor Dolittle Ser.). (Illus.). 368p. (J). (gr. 4-6). 24.99 (*0-688-14002-5*); 24.99 (*0-688-14002-5*) Morrow/Avon. (Morrow, William & Co.).

—The Voyages of Doctor Dolittle. 2000. (Doctor Dolittle Ser.). (Illus.). 272p. (J). (gr. 4-6). mass mkt. 4.95 (*0-451-52769-0*, Signet Bks.) NAL.

—The Voyages of Doctor Dolittle. 1998. (Doctor Dolittle Ser.). (Illus.). 288p. (J). (gr. 4-6). 15.99 (*0-448-41863-0*, Grosset & Dunlap) Penguin Putnam Bks. for Young Readers.

—The Voyages of Doctor Dolittle. abr. ed. 1999. (Doctor Dolittle Ser.). (J). (gr. 4-6). audio 18.00 o.s.i (*0-553-52602-2*, Listening Library) Random Hse. Audio Publishing Group.

—The Voyages of Doctor Dolittle. abr. ed. (Doctor Dolittle Ser.). (Illus.). (gr. 4-6). 1997. 240p. pap. text 4.50 (*0-440-41240-4*); 1988. 336p. pap. text 5.99 (*0-440-40002-3*) Random Hse. Children's Bks. (Yearling).

—The Voyages of Doctor Dolittle. 1994. (Doctor Dolittle Ser.). (J). (gr. 4-6). 11.55 (*0-606-03947-3*) Turtleback Bks.

Perkins, Al. Hugh Lofting's Travels of Doctor Dolittle. 1967. (Beginner Bks.). (Illus.). 64p. (J). (ps-2). 9.99 o.s.i (*0-394-90048-0*); 7.99 o.s.i (*0-394-80048-6*) Random Hse. Children's Bks. (Random Hse. Bks. for Young Readers).

Rivera, Carlos, tr. Hugh Lofting's Travels of Doctor Dolittle in English & Spanish. 1968. (Spanish Beginner Bks.). (Illus.). (J). (gr. k-3). lib. bdg. 5.99 o.p. (*0-394-91579-8*, Random Hse. Bks. for Young Readers) Random Hse. Children's Bks.

Vallier, Jean, tr. Hugh Lofting's Travels of Doctor Dolittle in English & French. 1968. (French Beginner Bks.). (Illus.). (J). (gr. k-3). lib. bdg. 5.99 o.p. (*0-394-90175-4*, Random Hse. Bks. for Young Readers) Random Hse. Children's Bks.

DON QUIXOTE (FICTITIOUS CHARACTER)—FICTION

Cervantes Saavedra, Miguel de. The Adventures of Don Quixote de la Mancha. Barret, Leighton, ed. 1962. (Illus.). (YA). (gr. 5 up). lib. bdg. 5.99 o.p. (*0-394-90892-9*, Knopf Bks. for Young Readers) Random Hse. Children's Bks.

—Don Quijote de la Mancha. 2002. (Classics for Young Readers Ser.). (SPA.). (YA). 14.95 (*84-392-0926-6*, EV30621) Lectorum Pubns., Inc.

—Don Quijote de la Mancha, Pt. 2. 1971. (SPA., Illus.). (YA). (gr. 11-12). pap. 3.95 o.p. (*0-88345-138-7*) Prentice Hall, ESL Dept.

—Don Quixote. Harrison, Michael, ed. 1999. (Oxford Illustrated Classics Ser.). (Illus.). 96p. (YA). pap. 12.95 o.p. (*0-19-274182-9*) Oxford Univ. Pr., Inc.

—Don Quixote. 1979. (Now Age Illustrated V Ser.). (Illus.). 64p. (J). (gr. 4-12). text 7.50 o.p. (*0-88301-399-1*); pap. text 2.95 (*0-88301-387-8*); stu. ed. 1.25 (*0-88301-411-4*) Pendulum Pr., Inc.

—Don Quixote. 1972. (Enriched Classics Ser.). (J). (gr. 9 up). pap. 0.95 o.s.i (*0-671-47873-7*, Washington Square Pr.) Simon & Schuster.

—Don Quixote. 1993. (Illus.). 32p. (J). (gr. 2 up). 13.95 o.p. (*1-56402-174-2*) Candlewick Pr.

—Don Quixote. 1995. (Oxford Illustrated Classics Ser.). (Illus.). 96p. (J). (gr. 4 up). 22.95 o.p. (*0-19-274165-9*) Oxford Univ. Pr., Inc.

—Don Quixote. Marshall, Michael J., ed. abr. ed. 1999. (Core Classics Ser.: Vol. 6). (Illus.). (J). (gr. 4-6). 264p. pap. 7.95 (*1-890517-10-0*); 256p. lib. bdg. 9.95 o.p. (*1-890517-11-9*) Core Knowledge Foundation.

—Don Quixote: Illustrated Classics. 1994. (Illustrated Classics Collection). 64p. (J). pap. 3.60 o.p. (*1-56103-621-8*) American Guidance Service, Inc.

—Don Quixote: Wishbone Classics. 1996. (Wishbone Classics Ser.: No. 1). (Illus.). 128p. (gr. 3-7). mass mkt. 4.25 (*0-06-106416-5*, HarperEntertainment) Morrow/Avon.

—Don Quixote: Wishbone Classics. 1996. (Wishbone Classics Ser.: No. 1). (J). (gr. 3-7). 10.30 (*0-606-10364-3*) Turtleback Bks.

—Don Quixote of Mancha. 1999. (Everyman's Library Children's Classics). (Illus.). 256p. (gr. 8-12). 14.95 (*0-375-40659-X*) Random Hse., Inc.

Fisher, Leonard Everett, illus. Don Quixote & the Windmills, RS. 2004. (J). 16.00 (*0-374-31825-5*, Farrar, Straus & Giroux (BYR)) Farrar, Straus & Giroux.

Marchesi, Stephen, illus. Don Quixote & Sancho Panza. 1992. 80p. (YA). (gr. 6 up). 16.95 (*0-684-19235-7*, Atheneum) Simon & Schuster Children's Publishing.

Williams, Marcia, illus. & retold by. Don Quixote. 1995. (J). (gr. 2 up). bds. 5.99 o.p. (*1-56402-070-3*) Candlewick Pr.

DONALD DUCK (FICTITIOUS CHARACTER)—FICTION

Barks, Carl, intro. Donald Duck. 1989. (Walt Disney's Best Comics Ser.). (Illus.). 195p. (J). 17.99 o.p. (*0-517-69714-9*) Random Hse. Value Publishing.

Disney Staff. Count on Donald, Vol. 2. 1997. (Illus.). 44p. (J). (gr. 1-6). 3.49 o.p. (*1-885222-77-7*) Advance Pubs. LLC.

—Donald Duck Directs, Vol. 14. 1997. (Illus.). 44p. (J). (gr. 1-6). 3.49 o.p. (*1-885222-89-0*) Advance Pubs. LLC.

—The Life of Donald Duck. deluxe ed. 1994. (Illus.). 72p. (J). 50.00 o.p. incl. audio compact disk (*1-55709-241-9*) Applewood Bks.

Disney Staff, illus. The Life of Donald Duck: Classic Edition. 1994. 72p. (J). 19.95 o.p. (*1-55709-242-7*) Applewood Bks.

Donald Duck & Sailboat. 9999. (J). (ps-2). o.p. (*0-307-02145-9*, Golden Bks.) Random Hse. Children's Bks.

Donald Duck Stories: Disney. 1990. (Illus.). (J). (ps). o.p. (*0-307-15829-2*, Golden Bks.) Random Hse. Children's Bks.

Mouse Works Staff. Donald Duck. 1998. (Friendly Tales Ser.). (Illus.). 10p. (J). (ps). 6.99 (*1-57082-927-6*) Mouse Works.

DORA THE EXPLORER (FICTITIOUS CHARACTER)—FICTION

Beinstein, Phoebe. Count with Dora! A Counting Book in Both English & Spanish. 2002. (Dora the Explorer Ser.). (Illus.). 14p. (J). bds. 4.99 (*0-689-84818-8*, Simon Spotlight/Nickelodeon) Simon & Schuster Children's Publishing.

—Dora. 2003. (Dora the Explorer Ser.). (Illus.). 12p. (J). bds. 7.99 (*0-689-85484-6*, Simon Spotlight/Nickelodeon) Simon & Schuster Children's Publishing.

—Dora Goes for a Ride. 2004. (Dora the Explorer Ser.). (Illus.). 22p. (J). bds. 4.99 (*0-689-86372-1*, Simon Spotlight/Nickelodeon) Simon & Schuster Children's Publishing.

Dora the Explorer. 2001. (Illus.). 64p. (J). pap. 4.99 (*0-307-23420-7*, Golden Bks.) Random Hse. Children's Bks.

Fruchter, Jason. Swiper, No Swiping. 2003. (Illus.). 14p. (J). 12.95 (*0-689-84773-4*, Simon Spotlight/Nickelodeon) Simon & Schuster Children's Publishing.

Golden Books Staff. It's Fiesta Time! 2004. (Dora the Explorer Ser.). (Illus.). 32p. (J). pap. 4.99 (*0-375-82650-5*, Golden Bks.) Random Hse. Children's Bks.

—Super Friends! 2004. (Dora the Explorer Ser.). (Illus.). 48p. (J). pap. 2.99 (*0-375-82651-3*, Golden Bks.) Random Hse. Children's Bks.

Hazen, Barbara Shook. The Circus Lion/Bouncy Ball. 2003. (Illus.). 64p. (J). (ps-2). pap. 2.99 (*0-307-10482-6*, Golden Bks.) Random Hse. Children's Bks.

Inches, Alison. Dora Loves Boots. 2004. (Dora the Explorer Ser.). (Illus.). 24p. (J). pap. 3.99 (*0-689-86373-X*, Simon Spotlight/Nickelodeon) Simon & Schuster Children's Publishing.

Little Simon Staff. Dora's Storytime Collection. 2003. (Dora the Explorer Ser.). (Illus.). 160p. (J). 10.95 (*0-689-86623-2*, Simon Spotlight/Nickelodeon) Simon & Schuster Children's Publishing.

Ricci, Christine. Dora in the Deep Sea. 2003. (Dora the Explorer Ser.). (Illus.). 24p. (J). pap. 3.99 (*0-689-85845-0*, Simon Spotlight/Nickelodeon) Simon & Schuster Children's Publishing.

—Dora the Explorer. Hall, Susan, tr. & illus. by. 2002. (J). 15.95 (*0-7853-6480-3*) Publications International, Ltd.

—Good Night, Dora! A Lift-the-Flap Story. 2002. (Dora the Explorer Ser.). (Illus.). 16p. (J). (ps-1). pap. 5.99 (*0-689-84774-2*, Simon Spotlight/Nickelodeon) Simon & Schuster Children's Publishing.

Silverhardt, Lauryn. A Day at the Beach. 2003. (Dora the Explorer Ser.). (Illus.). 22p. (J). bds. 4.99 (*0-689-85482-X*, Simon Spotlight/Nickelodeon) Simon & Schuster Children's Publishing.

—A Surprise Party. 2003. (Dora the Explorer Ser.). (Illus.). 22p. (J). bds. 4.99 (*0-689-85483-8*, Simon Spotlight/Nickelodeon) Simon & Schuster Children's Publishing.

Thorpe, Kiki. Where Is Boots? 2002. (Dora the Explorer Ser.). (Illus.). 16p. (J). (ps-1). pap. 5.99 (*0-689-84775-0*, Simon Spotlight/Nickelodeon) Simon & Schuster Children's Publishing.

Valdes, Leslie. Dora's Christmas Parade. 2003. (Dora the Explorer Ser.). (Illus.). 32p. (J). pap. 5.99 (*0-689-85843-4*, Simon Spotlight/Nickelodeon) Simon & Schuster Children's Publishing.

—Meet Diego! 2003. (Dora the Explorer Ser.). (Illus.). 24p. (J). pap. 3.50 (*0-689-85993-7*, Simon Spotlight/Nickelodeon) Simon & Schuster Children's Publishing.

Willson, Sarah. Dora's Easter Basket. 2003. (Dora the Explorer Ser.). (Illus.). 32p. (J). pap. 5.99 (*0-689-85240-1*, Simon Spotlight/Nickelodeon) Simon & Schuster Children's Publishing.

—Dora's Halloween Adventure. 2003. (Dora the Explorer Ser.). (Illus.). 14p. (J). bds. 5.99 (*0-689-85844-2*, Simon Spotlight/Nickelodeon) Simon & Schuster Children's Publishing.

—Dora's Thanksgiving. 2003. (Dora the Explorer Ser.). (Illus.). 24p. (J). pap. 3.99 (*0-689-85842-6*, Simon Spotlight/Nickelodeon) Simon & Schuster Children's Publishing.

DOUG (FICTITIOUS CHARACTER)—FICTION

Alan Novell Studios Staff, illus. Doug Gets His Wish: Look Look Book. 1999. (Golden Book Ser.). 32p. (J). (gr. k-3). pap. text 3.99 o.p. (*0-307-13140-8*, Golden Bks.) Random Hse. Children's Bks.

Campbell, Daniel. Bad to the Bone. (Funnie Mysteries Ser.: No. 6). 112p. (J). 2001. pap. o.p. (*0-7868-4473-6*); 2000. (Illus.). (gr. 3-7). pap. 4.99 (*0-7868-4412-4*) Disney Pr.

Campbell, Danny & Campbell, Kim. True Graffiti. 2000. (Doug: No. 2). (Illus.). 80p. (J). (gr. 3-7). pap. 4.99 (*0-7868-4383-7*) Disney Pr.

Campbell, Danny & Campbell, Kim S. Skeeter Loves Patti? 2000. (Doug Chronicles Ser.: No. 14). (Illus.). 64p. (J). (gr. 2-4). pap. 4.99 (*0-7868-4322-5*) Disney Pr.

Campbell, Kim. Invasion of the Judy Snatchers. 2000. (Doug: 1). (Illus.). 96p. (J). (gr. 3-7). pap. 4.99 (*0-7868-4382-9*) Disney Pr.

Carr, Jan. Doug's Secret Christmas. 1999. (Doug Ser.). (Illus.). 32p. (J). (gr. k-4). pap. 4.99 (*0-7868-4351-9*) Disney Pr.

Garvey, Dennis. Haunted House Hysteria. 2000. (Doug: No. 5). (Illus.). 109p. (J). (gr. 3-7). pap. 4.99 (*0-7868-4411-6*) Disney Pr.

Garvey, Dennis & Nichols, Tom. The Case of the Baffling Beast. 2000. (Doug: No. 3). (Illus.). 96p. (J). (gr. 3-7). pap. 4.99 (*0-7868-4384-5*) Disney Pr.

Garvey, Linda K. Doug & the End of the World. 1999. (Doug Chronicles Ser.: No. 12). (Illus.). 64p. (J). (gr. 2-4). pap. 4.99 o.p. (*0-7868-4300-4*) Disney Pr.

—Doug Cheats. 1999. (Doug Chronicles Ser.: No. 13). (Illus.). 64p. (J). (gr. 2-4). pap. 4.99 (*0-7868-4320-9*) Disney Pr.

—Doug's Twelve Days of Christmas. 1998. (Doug Ser.). (Illus.). 32p. (J). (ps-2). 8.95 o.p. (*0-7868-3197-9*) Disney Pr.

—A Picture for Patti. 1998. (Doug Chronicles Ser.: No. 3). (Illus.). 64p. (J). (gr. 2-4). pap. 3.99 (*0-7868-4236-9*) Disney Pr.

Goldman, Lisa. A Day with a Dirtbike. 1998. (Doug Chronicles Ser.: No. 4). (Illus.). 64p. (J). (gr. 2-4). pap. 3.99 (*0-7868-4233-4*) Disney Pr.

—A Day with Dirtbike. 1998. (Doug Chronicles Ser.). (J). (gr. 2-4). pap. 3.95 o.s.i (*0-7868-4321-7*) Disney Pr.

Gross, Bill. Poor Roger. 1998. (Doug Chronicles Ser.: No. 7). (Illus.). 64p. (J). (gr. 2-4). pap. 3.99 (*0-7868-4260-1*) Disney Pr.

Grundmann, Tim. The Funnie Haunted House. 1998. (Doug Chronicles Ser.: No. 6). 64p. (J). (gr. 2-4). pap. 3.95 o.s.i (*0-7868-4335-7*) Disney Pr.

—Lost in Space. 1998. (Doug Chronicles Ser.: No. 1). (Illus.). 64p. (J). (gr. 2-4). pap. 3.99 (*0-7868-4232-6*) Disney Pr.

—Winter Games. (Doug Chronicles Ser.: No. 8). 64p. (J). (gr. 2-4). 1999. (Illus.). pap. 3.95 (*0-7868-4264-4*); 1998. pap. 3.95 o.s.i (*0-7868-4336-5*) Disney Pr.

Jenkins, Jim. Doug's Doodle Desk. 1999. (Doug Ser.). (J). (gr. 4-7). 14.95 o.p. (*1-56010-470-8*) Foster, Walter Publishing, Inc.

Jinkins, Jim. Doug's Big Shoe Disaster. 1997. (Doug Ser.). (Illus.). 32p. (J). (gr. k-4). 8.95 o.p. (*0-7868-3142-1*) Disney Pr.

Jinkins, Jim & Aaron, Joe. Doug's Journal. 1997. (Doug Ser.). (Illus.). 96p. (J). (gr. k-4). 6.99 o.p. (*0-7868-4154-0*) Disney Pr.

Kassirer, Sue. Doug's Hoop Nightmare. 1997. (Disney Chapters Ser.). (J). (gr. 2-4). pap. 3.50 (*0-7868-4188-5*); (Illus.). 64p. pap. 3.99 (*0-7868-4151-6*) Disney Pr.

Kidd, Ronald. Money Madness. 1999. (Golden Book Ser.). (Illus.). 24p. (J). (gr. k-3). pap. 1.69 o.p. (*0-307-13257-9*, Golden Bks.) Random Hse. Children's Bks.

—Trading Places. 1999. (Golden Book Ser.). (Illus.). 24p. (J). (gr. k-3). pap. 1.69 o.p. (*0-307-13258-7*, Golden Bks.) Random Hse. Children's Bks.

Krulik, Nancy E. Doug Makes the Team. 1999. (Doug Ser.). (Illus.). 32p. (J). (gr. k-4). 8.99 o.p. (*0-7868-3193-6*) Disney Pr.

—Doug Puzzlers. 1998. (Doug Ser.). (Illus.). 64p. (J). (gr. 2-4). pap. 6.95 o.p. (*0-7868-4250-4*) Disney Pr.

—Doug Rules. 1999. (Doug Chronicles Ser.: No. 9). (Illus.). 56p. (J). (gr. 2-4). pap. 3.99 (*0-7868-4297-0*) Disney Pr.

—Doug's Big Comeback. 1997. (Disney Chapters Ser.). (J). (gr. 2-4). (Illus.). 64p. pap. 3.99 (*0-7868-4150-8*); pap. 3.50 (*0-7868-4218-0*); pap. 1.00 (*0-7868-4194-X*) Disney Pr.

—Doug's Vampire Caper. 1997. (Disney Chapters Ser.). (J). (gr. 2-4). pap. 3.50 o.s.i (*0-7868-4240-7*); (Illus.). 64p. pap. 3.99 (*0-7868-4157-5*) Disney Pr.

—Doug's 1st Movie. 1999. (Doug Ser.). (J). 48p. (gr. 2-4). pap. 3.99 o.s.i (*0-7868-1401-2*); (Illus.). 43p. (ps-3). pap. text 3.99 (*0-7868-4349-7*) Disney Pr.

—Untitled. 176p. (J). 2001. pap. 4.99 (*0-7868-1578-7*); No. 7. 2002. pap. 4.99 (*0-7868-1577-9*) Disney Pr.

Nodelman, Jeffrey. Itchy Situation. 1999. (Doug Chronicles Ser.: No. 11). (Illus.). 56p. (J). (gr. 2-4). pap. 3.99 (*0-7868-4299-7*) Disney Pr.

—Power Trip. 1998. (Doug Chronicles: No. 5). (Illus.). 64p. (J). (gr. 2-4). pap. 3.99 (*0-7868-4258-X*) Disney Pr.

Nodelman, Jeffrey. Disney's Doug Chronicles: Doug's Itchy Situation Club Book Club Edition, Vol. 11. 1999. 56p. (J). pap. 3.99 (*0-7868-4381-0*) Disney Pr.

Onish, Liane. Doug's Word Book. 1999. (Doug Ser.). (Illus.). 48p. (J). (gr. 2-4). 12.99 o.p. (*0-7364-0021-4*) Mouse Works.

Ostrow, Kim. Jurassic Doug. 2001. (Funnie Mysteries Ser.: No. 7). (Illus.). (J). 112p. pap. o.s.i (*0-7868-4490-6*); 96p. (gr. 3-7). pap. 4.99 (*0-7868-4458-2*) Disney Pr.

Peters, Matthew C., illus. Doug's Secret Christmas. 1997. (Doug Ser.). 32p. (J). (gr. k-4). 8.95 o.p. (*0-7868-3155-3*) Disney Pr.

Pollack, Pamela. The Curse of Beetenkaumun. 2000. (Doug: No. 4). (Illus.). 80p. (J). (gr. 3-7). pap. 4.99 (*0-7868-4410-8*) Disney Pr.

Rubin, Jim. Porkchop to the Rescue. 1998. (Doug Chronicles Ser.: No. 2). (Illus.). 64p. (J). (gr. 2-4). pap. 3.99 (*0-7868-4231-8*) Disney Pr.

Ryan, Pam Muñoz. Doug Counts Down. 1998. (Doug Ser.). (Illus.). 32p. (J). (gr. k-4). pap. 8.95 o.p. (*0-7868-3141-3*) Disney Pr.

—Doug's Treasure Hunt. 1999. (Doug Ser.). (Illus.). 10p. (J). (ps-4). 8.99 o.p. (*0-7364-0012-5*) Mouse Works.

—Funnie Family Vacation. 1999. (Doug Chronicles Ser.: No. 10). (Illus.). 55p. (J). (gr. 2-4). pap. 4.99 (*0-7868-4298-9*) Disney Pr.

Ultimate Buddies: Paint Box & Book. 1999. (Golden Book Ser.). 32p. (ps-3). pap. 0.99 o.p. (*0-307-09219-4*, Golden Bks.) Random Hse. Children's Bks.

Weiss, Ellen. The Bluffington Blob. 2001. (Funnie Mysteries Ser.: No. 8). (Illus.). 96p. (J). (gr. 3-7). reprint ed. pap. 4.99 (*0-7868-4462-0*) Disney Pr.

DOYLE, DARCY (FICTITIOUS CHARACTER)—FICTION

Maifair, Linda L. The Case of the Angry Actress. 1994. (Darcy J. Doyle, Daring Detective Ser.: Vol. 7). 64p. (J). (gr. 2-5). 3.99 (*0-310-43301-0*) Zondervan.

—The Case of the Bashed-Up Bicycle, Bk. 11. 1996. (Darcy J. Doyle, Daring Detective Ser.: 11). 64p. (J). (gr. 2-5). pap. 3.99 (*0-310-20736-3*) Zondervan.

—The Case of the Bashful Bully. 1994. (Darcy J. Doyle, Daring Detective Ser.: Vol. 6). 64p. (J). (gr. 2-5). pap. 3.99 (*0-310-43281-2*) Zondervan.

—The Case of the Choosey Cheater. 1993. (Darcy J. Doyle, Daring Detective Ser.: Vol. 2). 64p. (J). (gr. 2-5). mass mkt. 3.99 (*0-310-57901-5*) Zondervan.

—The Case of the Creepy Campout. 1994. (Darcy J. Doyle, Daring Detective Ser.: Vol. 5). 64p. (J). (gr. 2-5). pap. 3.99 (*0-310-43271-5*) Zondervan.

—The Case of the Giggling Ghost. 1993. (Darcy J. Doyle, Daring Detective Ser.: Vol. 3). 64p. (J). (gr. 2-5). mass mkt. 3.99 (*0-310-57911-2*) Zondervan.

—The Case of the Mixed-up Monsters. 1993. (Darcy J. Doyle, Daring Detective Ser.: Vol. 1). 64p. (J). mass mkt. 3.99 (*0-310-57921-X*) Zondervan.

—The Case of the Near-Sighted Neighbor, Bk. 12. 1996. (Darcy J. Doyle, Daring Detective Ser.: 12). 64p. (J). (gr. 2-5). pap. 3.99 (*0-310-20737-1*) Zondervan.

—The Case of the Pampered Poodle. 1993. (Darcy J. Doyle, Daring Detective Ser.: Vol. 4). 64p. (J). (gr. 2-5). mass mkt. 3.99 (*0-310-57891-4*) Zondervan.

—The Case of the Sweet-Toothed Shoplifter. 1996. (Darcy J. Doyle, Daring Detective Ser.: 10). 64p. (J). (gr. 2-5). pap. 3.99 (*0-310-20735-5*) Zondervan.

—The Case of the Troublesome Treasure. 1996. (Darcy J. Doyle, Daring Detective Ser.: 9). 64p. (J). (gr. 2-5). pap. 3.99 (*0-310-20734-7*) Zondervan.

—Darcy J. Doyle, Daring Detective, 4 vols., Set. 1995. pap. 15.96 o.p. (*0-310-20923-4*) Zondervan.

DRACULA, COUNT (FICTITIOUS CHARACTER)—FICTION

Abbott, Tony. Trapped in Transylvania: Dracula. 2002. (Cracked Classics Ser.). (Illus.). 144p. (J). (gr. 4-7). pap. 4.99 (*0-7868-1324-5*, Volo) Hyperion Bks. for Children.

Ambrus, Victor G. Count, Dracula! 1992. (Count Dracula Bks.). (Illus.). 24p. (J). (ps-1). 3.99 o.s.i (*0-517-58969-9*, Random Hse. Bks. for Young Readers) Random Hse. Children's Bks.

—Dracula. 1987. (Illus.). 32p. (J). (ps-6). 12.95 o.p. (*0-19-279746-8*); pap. 5.95 o.p. (*0-19-272121-6*) Oxford Univ. Pr., Inc.

—Dracula's Bedtime Storybook: Tales to Keep You Awake at Night. 1987. (Illus.). 32p. (J). (ps-6). 12.95 o.p. (*0-19-279762-X*); pap. 5.95 o.p. (*0-19-272077-5*) Oxford Univ. Pr., Inc.

—Son of Dracula. (Illus.). 32p. (J). (gr. 3-7). reprint ed. 1989. pap. 5.95 o.p. (*0-19-272191-7*); 1987. 12.95 o.p. (*0-19-279813-8*) Oxford Univ. Pr., Inc.

Arthur, Pat. Dracula's Castle. 1982. (Illus.). 12p. (J). (ps-4). pap. 2.95 o.p. (*0-89954-204-2*) Antioch Publishing Co.

Benjamin, Alan. Let's Count, Dracula: A Chubby Board Book. 1992. (Illus.). 16p. (J). (ps up). 3.95 (*0-671-77008-X*, Little Simon) Simon & Schuster Children's Publishing.

Bethlen, Julianna. Dracula Junior & the Fake Fangs: A 3-D Picture Book. 1996. (Illus.). 22p. (J). (gr. k up). 14.99 o.s.i (*0-8037-2008-4*, Dial Bks. for Young Readers) Penguin Putnam Bks. for Young Readers.

Brooks, Felicity. Dracula. 1996. (Library of Fear, Fantasy & Adventure). 96p. (YA). (gr. 5 up). (Illus.). pap. 9.95 (*0-7460-2365-0*); lib. bdg. 17.95 (*0-88110-811-1*) EDC Publishing. (Usborne).

Dadey, Debbie & Jones, Marcia Thornton. Dracula Doesn't Drink Lemonade. 1995. (Adventures of the Bailey School Kids Ser.: No. 16). (Illus.). 80p. (J). (gr. 2-4). mass mkt. 3.99 o.s.i (*0-590-22638-X*) Scholastic, Inc.

—Dracula Doesn't Drink Lemonade. 1995. (Adventures of the Bailey School Kids Ser.: No. 16). (J). (gr. 2-4). 10.14 (*0-606-07444-9*) Turtleback Bks.

—Dracula Doesn't Rock & Roll. 2000. (Adventures of the Bailey School Kids Ser.: No. 39). (Illus.). 80p. (J). (gr. 2-4). mass mkt. 3.99 (*0-439-04399-9*, Scholastic Paperbacks) Scholastic, Inc.

—Dracula Doesn't Rock & Roll. 2000. (Adventures of the Bailey School Kids Ser.: No. 39). (Illus.). (J). (gr. 2-4). 10.14 (*0-606-18537-2*) Turtleback Bks.

Dracula. 2002. (Illus.). 32p. (J). (*0-7868-0799-7*) Disney Pr.

Dracula. 1997. (Fx Packs Ser.). (Illus.). (J). (gr. 4-7). 6.95 o.p. (*0-7894-2284-0*) Dorling Kindersley Publishing, Inc.

Dracula. (J). 9.95 (*1-56156-373-0*) Kidsbooks, Inc.

Dracula. 1991. (Horror Classics Ser.: No. 841-1). (Illus.). (J). (gr. 4 up). pap. 3.50 o.p. (*0-7214-0812-5*, Ladybird Bks.) Penguin Group (USA) Inc.

Dracula. abr. l.t. ed. 1996. (Great Illustrated Classics Ser.: Vol. 51). (Illus.). 240p. (J). (gr. 3-7). 9.95 (*0-86611-872-1*) Playmore, Inc., Pubs.

Dracula's Den: Make Hundreds of Funny Faces with Re-Usable Stickers! 1999. (Funny Faces Ser.). (Illus.). 10p. (J). (ps-7). pap. 1.99 (*1-86091-124-2*) Trident Pr. International.

Farber, Erica & Sansevere, J. R. The Vampire Brides. 1996. (Mercer Mayer's Critters of the Night Ser.). (Illus.). 72p. (J). (ps-3). pap. 3.99 o.s.i (*0-679-87360-0*, Random Hse. Bks. for Young Readers) Random Hse. Children's Bks.

Faulkner, Keith. Dracula. 1993. (Illus.). 16p. (J). (ps-2). 10.95 o.p. (*0-694-00559-2*, Harper Festival) HarperCollins Children's Bk. Group.

Florescu, Radu R. Dracula, Prince of Many Faces, Vol. 1. 1989. (J). 19.95 o.s.i (*0-316-28655-9*) Little Brown & Co.

Garmon, Larry Mike. Dracula: Return of Evil. 2001. (Universal Monsters Ser.: No. 1). 160p. (J). (gr. 5 up). mass mkt. 4.50 (*0-439-20846-7*) Scholastic, Inc.

Greenburg, Dan. Don't Count on Dracula. 2000. (Zack Files Ser.: No. 21). (Illus.). 64p. (J). (gr. 2-5). mass mkt. 3.99 (*0-448-42175-5*, Planet Dexter) Penguin Putnam Bks. for Young Readers.

—Don't Count on Dracula. 2000. (Zack Files Ser.: No. 21). (J). (gr. 2-5). 10.14 (*0-606-20270-6*) Turtleback Bks.

Harvey, Jayne. Great-Uncle Dracula. 1992. (Stepping Stone Bks.). (Illus.). 80p. (J). (gr. 2-4). pap. 2.50 o.s.i (*0-679-82448-0*, Random Hse. Bks. for Young Readers) Random Hse. Children's Bks.

—Great-Uncle Dracula & the Dirty Rat. 1993. (Stepping Stone Book Ser.). (Illus.). 64p. (J). (gr. 2-4). pap. 2.50 o.s.i (*0-679-83457-5*, Random Hse. Bks. for Young Readers) Random Hse. Children's Bks.

Hatchigan, Jessica. Count Dracula, Me & Norma D. 1987. (J). (gr. 3-7). pap. 2.95 (*0-380-75414-2*, Avon Bks.) Morrow/Avon.

Hawthorn, P. & Blundell, Kim. Fangtastic Adventures of Dracula's Dentures. 1995. (Rhyming Stories Ser.). (Illus.). 24p. (gr. 2 up). (J). lib. bdg. 12.95 (*0-88110-721-2*); (YA). pap. 4.95 (*0-7460-1671-9*) EDC Publishing. (Usborne).

Hoffman, Mary. Dracula's Daughter. 1989. (Banana Bks.). (Illus.). 42p. (J). (gr. 2-4). 3.95 o.p. (*0-8120-6135-7*) Barron's Educational Series, Inc.

Kelly, Tim. Dracula: The Vampire Play. 1978. 56p. (J). (gr. 4 up). pap. 4.00 (*0-88680-043-9*) Clark, I. E. Pubns.

Kudalis, Eric. Dracula & Other Vampire Stories. 1994. (Classic Monster Stories Ser.). (Illus.). 48p. (J). (gr. 3-4). lib. bdg. 21.26 (*1-56065-212-8*, Capstone High-Interest Bks.) Capstone Pr., Inc.

—Dracula & Other Vampire Stories. 1994. (Classic Monster Stories Ser.). (Illus.). 48p. (J). (gr. 3-7). lib. bdg. 19.00 o.p. (*0-516-35212-1*, Children's Pr.) Scholastic Library Publishing.

Labatt, Mary. Spying on Dracula. 1999. (Sam - Dog Detective Ser.). (J). (gr. 2-5). 104p. pap. (*1-55074-632-4*); (Illus.). 210p. text 12.95 (*1-55074-634-0*) Kids Can Pr., Ltd.

—Spying on Dracula. 1999. (J). 11.00 (*0-606-19023-6*) Turtleback Bks.

Levy, Elizabeth. Dracula Is a Pain in the Neck. (Trophy Chapter Bks.). (Illus.). (J). (gr. 2-6). 1984. 96p. pap. 4.99 (*0-06-440146-4*, Harper Trophy); 1983. 80p. 12.95 o.p. (*0-06-023822-4*); 1983. 80p. lib. bdg. 14.89 o.p. (*0-06-023823-2*) HarperCollins Children's Bk. Group.

—Dracula Is a Pain in the Neck. 1990. (J). pap. 3.50 o.p. (*0-06-107014-9*) HarperCollins Pubs.

—Dracula Is a Pain in the Neck. 1984. (Trophy Chapter Bks.). 10.40 (*0-606-06335-8*) Turtleback Bks.

Lutzen, Hanna. Vlad the Undead. 192p. (YA). (gr. 8 up). 2001. pap. 5.95 (*0-88899-342-0*); 1998. 15.95 (*0-88899-341-2*) Groundwood Bks. CAN. *Dist:* Publishers Group West.

Martin, Ann M. Ma & Pa Dracula. 1989. (Illus.). 128p. (J). (gr. 3-7). 14.95 o.p. (*0-8234-0781-0*) Holiday Hse., Inc.

—Ma & Pa Dracula. 1991. 128p. (J). (gr. 4-6). mass mkt. 2.95 (*0-590-43828-X*) Scholastic, Inc.

McNaughton, Colin. Dracula's Tomb. 1998. (Illus.). 24p. (J). (gr. k-5). 15.99 o.p. (*0-7636-0495-X*) Candlewick Pr.

Pipe, Jim. Dracula. 1995. (In the Footsteps of Ser.: 6). (Illus.). 40p. (gr. 4-6). (J). 22.90 o.p. (*1-56294-646-3*); pap. 6.95 o.p. (*1-56294-186-0*) Millbrook Pr., Inc. (Copper Beech Bks.).

Platt, Kin. Dracula, Go Home. 1981. (Illus.). 96p. (J). (gr. 7 up). pap. 1.25 o.s.i (*0-440-92022-1*, Laurel) Dell Publishing.

Ratnett, Michael. Dracula Steps Out. 1998. (Illus.). 12p. (J). (ps-1). pap. 15.95 (*0-531-30100-1*, Orchard Bks.) Scholastic, Inc.

Saunders, Dudley. Dracula's Treasure. 1975. (J). 6.00 (*0-87602-123-2*) Anchorage Pr.

Schick, Joel & Schick, Alice. Bram Stoker's Dracula. 1980. (Illus.). 48p. (J). (gr. 4-6). pap. 6.95 o.s.i (*0-385-28141-2*, Delacorte Pr.) Dell Publishing.

Shelley, Mary Wollstonecraft. Frankenstein & Dracula Flip-Over Book. 2002. pap. 4.99 (*0-14-230171-X*) Penguin Putnam Bks. for Young Readers.

Sierra, Judy. The House That Drac Built. 1998. (Illus.). 32p. (J). (ps-2). pap. 6.00 (*0-15-201879-4*, Harcourt Paperbacks) Harcourt Children's Bks.

Smithmark Staff. Dracula - Frankenstein. 1995. (Illus.). 498p. (J). 12.98 o.p. (*0-8317-6696-4*) Smithmark Pubs., Inc.

Spinner, Stephanie. Dracula. 1982. (Step-Up Adventures Ser.). (J). 10.04 (*0-606-00426-2*) Turtleback Bks.

Stanley, George Edward. The Vampire Kittens of Count Dracula. 1997. (Scaredy Cats Ser.: No. 8). (Illus.). 80p. (J). (gr. 1-4). mass mkt. 3.99 (*0-689-81615-4*, Aladdin) Simon & Schuster Children's Publishing.

Stoker, Bram. Bram Stoker's Dracula. 1980. (Illus.). 48p. (J). (gr. 3 up). lib. bdg. 10.89 o.s.i (*0-440-01349-6*, Delacorte Pr.) Dell Publishing.

—Bram Stoker's Dracula. 1980. (Illus.). 48p. (J). (gr. 3 up). pap. 6.95 o.s.i (*0-440-01348-8*, Delacorte Pr.) Dell Publishing.

—Dracula. 1989. (J). pap. 2.50 o.s.i (*0-8125-0442-9*, Tor Classics); 1988. mass mkt. 2.25 (*0-938819-70-4*, Aerie) Doherty, Tom Assocs., LLC.

—Dracula. 1997. (Eyewitness Classics Ser.). (Illus.). 64p. (J). (gr. 3-6). pap. 14.95 o.p. (*0-7894-1489-9*) Dorling Kindersley Publishing, Inc.

—Dracula. 1997. (Children's Thrift Classics Ser.). (Illus.). 96p. (J). reprint ed. pap. text 1.00 (*0-486-29567-2*) Dover Pubns., Inc.

—Dracula. 1998. (Illustrated Classic Book Ser.). (Illus.). 61p. (J). (gr. 3 up). pap. text 4.95 (*1-56767-261-2*) Educational Insights, Inc.

—Dracula. 2000. (Books of Wonder). (Illus.). 430p. (J). (gr. 7-12). 21.95 (*0-688-13921-3*) Morrow/Avon.

—Dracula. Farr, Naunerle C., ed. 1973. (Now Age Illustrated Ser.). (Illus.). 64p. (J). (gr. 5-10). 7.50 o.p. (*0-88301-203-0*); stu. ed. 1.25 (*0-88301-175-1*); pap. 2.95 (*0-88301-100-X*) Pendulum Pr., Inc.

—Dracula. (Illustrated Junior Library). (J). 1994. (Illus.). 432p. 15.95 o.p. (*0-448-40559-8*, Grosset & Dunlap); 1986. 448p. (gr. 4-6). pap. 3.50 o.p. (*0-14-035048-9*, Puffin Bks.) Penguin Putnam Bks. for Young Readers.

—Dracula. Lafreniere, Kenneth, ed. 1982. (Stepping Stone Bks.: No. 1). (Illus.). 96p. (J). (gr. 3-7). pap. 3.99 (*0-394-84828-4*, Random Hse. Bks. for Young Readers) Random Hse. Children's Bks.

—Dracula. 2000. 528p. (gr. 4-7). mass mkt. 4.99 (*0-439-15411-1*); 1992. (J). mass mkt. 3.99 (*0-590-46029-3*, 067, Scholastic Paperbacks) Scholastic, Inc.

—Dracula. 1990. (Classic Pop-Up Ser.). (J). 3.98 o.p. (*0-8317-1483-2*) Smithmark Pubs., Inc.

—Dracula. (Saddleback Classics). (J). 1999. (Illus.). 13.10 (*0-606-21550-6*); 1971. 9.09 o.p. (*0-606-01821-2*) Turtleback Bks.

—Dracula. 1985. (J). (ps-3). 19.95 o.p. (*0-88101-020-0*) Unicorn Publishing Hse., Inc., The.

—Dracula - Frankenstein. 1989. (J). 5.98 o.p. (*0-86136-606-9*) Smithmark Pubs., Inc.

Stoker, Bram, et al. Dracula, Frankenstein, Dr. Jekyll & Mr. Hyde. 1978. 672p. (J). (gr. 7). mass mkt. 6.95 (*0-451-52363-6*, Signet Classics) NAL.

Stone, Tom B. Camp Dracula. 1995. (Graveyard School Ser.: No. 6). 128p. (J). (gr. 3-7). pap. 3.50 o.s.i (*0-553-48228-9*) Bantam Bks.

Stratemeyer Syndicate Staff. The Hardy Boys & Nancy Drew Meet Dracula. 1978. (Illus.). 109p. (J). (gr. 3-6). 3.95 o.p. (*0-448-16196-6*, Grosset & Dunlap) Penguin Putnam Bks. for Young Readers.

Waddell, Martin. Little Dracula at the Seashore. 1992. (Illus.). 32p. (J). (ps up). bds. 3.95 o.p. (*1-56402-026-6*) Candlewick Pr.

—Little Dracula Goes to School. 1992. (Illus.). 32p. (J). (ps up). bds. 3.95 o.p. (*1-56402-027-4*) Candlewick Pr.

—Little Dracula's Christmas. 1986. (Picture Puffin Ser.). (Illus.). 32p. (J). (gr. k up). pap. 3.95 o.p. (*0-14-050658-6*, Puffin Bks.) Penguin Putnam Bks. for Young Readers.

—Little Dracula's First Bite. 1986. (Stoney McTavish Ser.). (Illus.). 32p. (J). (gr. k up). pap. 3.95 o.p. (*0-14-050657-8*, Viking Children's Bks.) Penguin Putnam Bks. for Young Readers.

Wahl, Jan. Dracula's Cat & Frankenstein's Dog. 1990. (Illus.). (J). (ps-2). 13.95 o.p. (*0-671-70820-1*, Simon & Schuster Children's Publishing) Simon & Schuster Children's Publishing.

Wilson, Lionel. The Mystery of Dracula. 1984. (Unsolved Mysteries of the World Ser.). (J). 11.96 o.p. (*0-89547-065-9*) Silver, Burdett & Ginn, Inc.

DRAKE, FRANCIS, SIR, 1540?-1596—FICTION

Cadnum, Michael. Ship of Fire. 2003. 208p. (YA). 16.99 (*0-670-89907-0*, Viking) Viking Penguin.

DREW, NANCY (FICTITIOUS CHARACTER)—FICTION

Dixon, Franklin W. Sidetracked to Danger. Ashby, Ruth, ed. 1995. (Hardy Boys Mystery Stories Ser.: No. 130). 160p. (Orig.). (J). (gr. 3-6). pap. 3.99 (*0-671-87214-1*, Aladdin) Simon & Schuster Children's Publishing.

Keene, Carolyn. Against the Rules. (Nancy Drew Files Ser.: No. 119). (YA). (gr. 6 up). 1997. 160p. pap. 3.99 (*0-671-56877-9*); 1900. per. (*0-671-50377-4*) Simon & Schuster Children's Publishing. (Simon Pulse).

—Alien in the Classroom. 1998. (Nancy Drew Notebooks Ser.: No. 23). 80p. (J). (gr. k-3). pap. 3.99 (*0-671-00818-8*, Aladdin) Simon & Schuster Children's Publishing.

—Alien in the Classroom. 1998. (Nancy Drew Notebooks Ser.: No. 23). (J). (gr. k-3). 10.04 (*0-606-13653-3*) Turtleback Bks.

—Anything for Love. 1995. (Nancy Drew Files: No. 107). 160p. (YA). (gr. 6 up). mass mkt. 3.99 (*0-671-88198-1*, Simon Pulse) Simon & Schuster Children's Publishing.

—Anything for Love. 1995. (Nancy Drew Files: No. 107). (YA). (gr. 6 up). 9.09 o.p. (*0-606-07927-0*) Turtleback Bks.

—At All Costs. 1997. (Nancy Drew & Hardy Boys Super Mystery Ser.: No. 33). 224p. (YA). (gr. 6 up). pap. 3.99 (*0-671-00734-3*, Simon Pulse) Simon & Schuster Children's Publishing.

—At All Costs. 1997. (Nancy Drew & Hardy Boys Super Mystery Ser.: No. 33). (YA). (gr. 6 up). 10.04 (*0-606-12776-3*) Turtleback Bks.

—The Baby-Sitter Burglaries. 1996. (Nancy Drew Mystery Stories Ser.: No. 129). 160p. (J). (gr. 3-6). pap. 4.99 (*0-671-50507-6*, Aladdin) Simon & Schuster Children's Publishing.

—The Baby-Sitter Burglaries. 1996. (Nancy Drew Mystery Stories Ser.: No. 129). (J). (gr. 3-6). 9.09 o.p. (*0-606-09664-7*) Turtleback Bks.

—Bad Day for Ballet. 1995. (Nancy Drew Notebooks Ser.: No. 4). (Illus.). 80p. (J). (gr. k-3). pap. 3.99 (*0-671-87948-0*, Aladdin) Simon & Schuster Children's Publishing.

—Bad Day for Ballet. 1995. (Nancy Drew Notebooks Ser.: No. 4). (J). (gr. k-3). 10.14 (*0-606-07932-7*) Turtleback Bks.

—Bad Medicine. 1989. (Nancy Drew Files: No. 35). (Orig.). (YA). (gr. 6 up). pap. 2.95 (*0-671-64702-4*, Simon Pulse) Simon & Schuster Children's Publishing.

—The Best Detective. 1995. (Nancy Drew Notebooks Ser.: No. 8). 80p. (J). (gr. k-3). pap. 3.99 (*0-671-87952-9*, Aladdin) Simon & Schuster Children's Publishing.

—The Best Detective. 1995. (Nancy Drew Notebooks Ser.: No. 8). (J). (gr. k-3). 8.60 o.p. (*0-606-07936-X*) Turtleback Bks.

—Betrayed by Love. 1996. (Nancy Drew Files: No. 118). 160p. (YA). (gr. 6 up). mass mkt. 3.99 (*0-671-56876-0*, Simon Pulse) Simon & Schuster Children's Publishing.

—Betrayed by Love. 1996. (Nancy Drew Files: No. 118). (YA). (gr. 6 up). 10.04 (*0-606-11663-X*) Turtleback Bks.

—The Black Velvet Mystery. 1999. (Nancy Drew Notebooks Ser.: No. 32). 80p. (J). (gr. k-3). pap. 3.99 (*0-671-03474-X*, Aladdin) Simon & Schuster Children's Publishing.

—The Black Velvet Mystery. 1999. (Nancy Drew Notebooks Ser.: No. 32). (J). (gr. k-3). 10.14 (*0-606-19059-7*) Turtleback Bks.

—The Black Widow. 1989. (Nancy Drew Files: No. 28). (YA). (gr. 6 up). pap. 2.95 (*0-671-70357-9*, Simon Pulse) Simon & Schuster Children's Publishing.

—The Bluebeard Room. (Nancy Drew Mystery Stories Ser.: No. 77). (J). (gr. 3-6). 1988. pap. 3.50 (*0-671-66857-9*); 1985. 159p. pap. 3.50 (*0-671-49743-X*) Simon & Schuster Children's Publishing. (Aladdin).

—The Broken Anchor. (Nancy Drew Mystery Stories Ser.: No. 70). (J). (gr. 3-6). 1991. pap. 3.50 (*0-671-74228-0*, Aladdin); 1983. (Illus.). 189p. (*0-671-46462-0*, Simon & Schuster Children's Publishing); 1983. (Illus.). 189p. pap. 3.50 (*0-671-46461-2*, Aladdin) Simon & Schuster Children's Publishing.

—Broken Promises. 1996. (Nancy Drew on Campus Ser.: No. 9). 192p. (YA). (gr. 8 up). mass mkt. 3.99 (*0-671-52757-6*, Simon Pulse) Simon & Schuster Children's Publishing.

—The Bungalow Mystery. fac. ed. 2004. (Nancy Drew Mystery Stories Ser.: No. 3). iv, 204p. (J). (gr. 3-6). reprint ed. 17.95 (*1-55709-157-9*) Applewood Bks.

—The Bungalow Mystery, Vol. 3. 1930. (Nancy Drew Mystery Stories Ser.: No. 3). (Illus.). 180p. (J). (gr. 3-6). 5.99 (*0-448-09503-3*, Grosset & Dunlap) Penguin Putnam Bks. for Young Readers.

—The Bungalow Mystery. unabr. ed. 2002. (Nancy Drew Ser.: Vol. 3). (J). (gr. 4-7). audio 18.00 (*0-8072-0760-8*, Listening Library) Random Hse. Audio Publishing Group.

—Buried Secrets. l.t. ed. 1988. (Nancy Drew Files : No. 10). 153p. (YA). (gr. 6 up). reprint ed. 9.50 o.p. (*0-942545-41-9*); lib. bdg. 10.50 o.p. (*0-942545-36-2*) Grey Castle Pr.

—Buried Secrets. 1991. (Nancy Drew Files: No. 10). (YA). (gr. 6 up). pap. 3.50 (*0-671-73664-7*, Simon Pulse) Simon & Schuster Children's Publishing.

—Campus Exposures. 1996. (Nancy Drew on Campus Ser.: No. 13). 192p. (YA). (gr. 8 up). pap. 3.99 (*0-671-56802-7*, Simon Pulse) Simon & Schuster Children's Publishing.

—Captive Heart. 1995. (Nancy Drew Files: No. 108). (Illus.). 160p. (YA). (gr. 6 up). per. 3.99 (*0-671-88199-X*, Simon Pulse) Simon & Schuster Children's Publishing.

—Captive Heart. 1995. (Nancy Drew Files: No. 108). (YA). (gr. 6 up). 9.09 o.p. (*0-606-07928-9*) Turtleback Bks.

—Captive Witness. (Nancy Drew Mystery Stories Ser.: No. 64). (J). (gr. 3-6). 1990. 192p. pap. 3.50 (*0-671-70471-0*, Aladdin); 1987. pap. 3.50 (*0-671-62469-5*, Aladdin); 1981. (Illus.). 186p. pap. (*0-671-42360-6*, Simon & Schuster Children's Publishing); 1981. (Illus.). 186p. pap. 3.50 (*0-671-42361-4*, Aladdin) Simon & Schuster Children's Publishing.

—The Case of Capital Intrigue. 1998. (Nancy Drew Mystery Stories Ser.: No. 142). (J). (gr. 3-6). 10.04 (*0-606-13644-4*) Turtleback Bks.

—The Case of the Artful Crime. Winkler, Ellen, ed. 1992. (Nancy Drew Mystery Stories Ser.: No. 106). 160p. (J). (gr. 3-6). mass mkt. 3.99 (*0-671-73052-5*, Aladdin) Simon & Schuster Children's Publishing.

—The Case of the Artful Crime. 1992. (Nancy Drew Mystery Stories Ser.: No. 106). (J). (gr. 3-6). 9.09 o.p. (*0-606-02058-6*) Turtleback Bks.

—The Case of the Captured Queen. 1999. (Nancy Drew Mystery Stories Ser.: No. 147). 160p. (J). (gr. 3-6). pap. 4.99 (*0-671-02175-3*, Aladdin) Simon & Schuster Children's Publishing.

—The Case of the Creative Crime. 2002. (Nancy Drew Ser.: Vol. 166). (Illus.). 160p. (J). (gr. 3-6). pap. 4.99 (*0-7434-3748-9*, Aladdin) Simon & Schuster Children's Publishing.

—The Case of the Dangerous Solution. 1995. (Nancy Drew Mystery Stories Ser.: No. 127). 160p. (J). (gr. 3-6). pap. 3.99 (*0-671-50500-9*, Aladdin) Simon & Schuster Children's Publishing.

—The Case of the Dangerous Solution. 1995. (Nancy Drew Mystery Stories Ser.: No. 127). (J). (gr. 3-6). 10.04 (*0-606-08575-0*) Turtleback Bks.

—The Case of the Disappearing Deejay. (Nancy Drew Mystery Stories Ser.: No. 89). (J). (gr. 3-6). 1989. pap. 3.99 (*0-671-66314-3*); 1900. pap. 3.50 (*0-671-89512-5*) Simon & Schuster Children's Publishing. (Aladdin).

—The Case of the Disappearing Deejay. 1989. (Nancy Drew Mystery Stories Ser.: No. 89). (J). (gr. 3-6). 9.09 o.p. (*0-606-06599-7*) Turtleback Bks.

—The Case of the Disappearing Diamonds. 1987. (Nancy Drew Mystery Stories Ser.: No. 80). (J). (gr. 3-6). mass mkt. 3.99 (*0-671-64896-9*, Aladdin) Simon & Schuster Children's Publishing.

—The Case of the Floating Crime. 1994. (Nancy Drew Mystery Stories Ser.: No. 120). 160p. (J). (gr. 3-6). pap. 4.99 (*0-671-87203-6*, Aladdin) Simon & Schuster Children's Publishing.

—The Case of the Floating Crime. 1994. (Nancy Drew Mystery Stories Ser.: No. 120). (J). (gr. 3-6). 10.04 (*0-606-06598-9*) Turtleback Bks.

—The Case of the Lost Song. 2001. (Nancy Drew Mystery Stories Ser.: Vol. 162). (J). (gr. 3-6). (Illus.). 160p. pap. 4.99 (*0-7434-0688-5*); reprint ed. E-Book 4.99 (*0-7434-3701-2*) Simon & Schuster Children's Publishing. (Aladdin).

—The Case of the Photo Finish. Greenberg, Ann, ed. 1990. (Nancy Drew Mystery Stories Ser.: No. 96). 152p. (Orig.). (J). (gr. 3-6). pap. 3.99 (*0-671-69281-X*, Aladdin) Simon & Schuster Children's Publishing.

—The Case of the Rising Stars. Greenberg, Anne, ed. 1989. (Nancy Drew Mystery Stories Ser.: No. 87). 160p. (J). (gr. 3-6). pap. 3.99 (*0-671-66312-7*, Aladdin) Simon & Schuster Children's Publishing.

—The Case of the Safecracker's Secret. 1990. (Nancy Drew Mystery Stories Ser.: No. 93). 154p. (J). (gr. 3-6). pap. 3.99 (*0-671-66318-6*, Aladdin) Simon & Schuster Children's Publishing.

—The Case of the Twin Teddy Bears. 2001. (Nancy Drew Mystery Stories Ser.: Vol. 116). (J). (gr. 3-6). E-Book 3.99 (*0-7434-3708-X*, Aladdin) Simon & Schuster Children's Publishing.

—The Case of the Twin Teddy Bears. Winkler, Ellen, ed. rev. ed. 1993. (Nancy Drew Mystery Stories Ser.: Vol. 116). 160p. (J). (gr. 3-6). pap. 4.99 (*0-671-79302-0*, Aladdin) Simon & Schuster Children's Publishing.

—The Case of the Twin Teddy Bears. 1993. (Nancy Drew Mystery Stories Ser.: No. 116). (J). (gr. 3-6). 10.04 (*0-606-05938-5*) Turtleback Bks.

—The Case of the Vanishing Veil. 2001. (Nancy Drew Mystery Stories Ser.: Vol. 83). (J). (gr. 3-6). reprint ed. E-Book 4.99 (*0-7434-3424-2*, Aladdin) Simon & Schuster Children's Publishing.

—The Case of the Vanishing Veil. Greenberg, Anne, ed. rev. ed. 1988. (Nancy Drew Mystery Stories Ser.: No. 83). 160p. (J). (gr. 3-6). pap. 3.99 (*0-671-63413-5*, Aladdin) Simon & Schuster Children's Publishing.

—The Cheating Heart. Ashby, Ruth, ed. 1994. (Nancy Drew Files: No. 99). 160p. (YA). (gr. 6 up). mass mkt. 3.99 (*0-671-79491-4*, Simon Pulse) Simon & Schuster Children's Publishing.

—The Cheating Heart. 1994. (Nancy Drew Files: No. 99). (YA). (gr. 6 up). 10.04 (*0-606-06606-3*) Turtleback Bks.

—The Chocolate-Covered Contest. 1999. (Nancy Drew Mystery Stories Ser.: No. 151). 160p. (J). (gr. 3-6). pap. 3.99 (*0-671-03443-X*, Aladdin) Simon & Schuster Children's Publishing.

—The Chocolate-Covered Contest. 1999. (Nancy Drew Mystery Stories Ser.: No. 151). (J). (gr. 3-6). 10.04 (*0-606-19058-9*) Turtleback Bks.

—Choosing Sides. Greenberg, Anne, ed. 1993. (Nancy Drew Files: No. 84). 160p. (YA). (gr. 6 up). mass mkt. 3.99 (*0-671-73088-6*, Simon Pulse) Simon & Schuster Children's Publishing.

—Choosing Sides. 1993. (Nancy Drew Files: No. 84). (YA). (gr. 6 up). 10.04 (*0-606-05498-7*) Turtleback Bks.

—Circle of Evil. (Nancy Drew Files: No. 18). (Orig.). (YA). (gr. 6 up). 1988. 160p. pap. 2.95 (*0-671-68050-1*); 1987. pap. (*0-671-64142-5*) Simon & Schuster Children's Publishing. (Simon Pulse).

—The Clue in the Ancient Disguise. (Nancy Drew Mystery Stories Ser.: No. 69). (J). (gr. 3-6). 1987. pap. 3.50 (*0-671-64279-0*, Aladdin); 1983. (Illus.). 206p. (*0-671-45553-2*, Simon & Schuster Children's Publishing); 1982. (Illus.). 204p. pap. 3.50 (*0-671-45552-4*, Aladdin) Simon & Schuster Children's Publishing.

—The Clue in the Antique Trunk. 2001. (Nancy Drew Mystery Stories Ser.: Vol. 105). (J). reprint ed. E-Book 4.99 (*0-7434-3425-0*); (Illus.). 160p. (gr. 3-6). pap. 4.99 (*0-7434-2345-3*) Simon & Schuster Children's Publishing. (Aladdin).

—The Clue in the Antique Trunk. Greenberg, Ann, ed. rev. ed. 1992. (Nancy Drew Mystery Stories Ser.: No. 105). 160p. (J). (gr. 3-6). per. 3.99 (*0-671-73051-7*, Aladdin) Simon & Schuster Children's Publishing.

—The Clue in the Antique Trunk. 1992. (Nancy Drew Mystery Stories Ser.: No. 105). (J). (gr. 3-6). 9.09 o.p. (*0-606-00358-4*) Turtleback Bks.

—The Clue in the Camera. Greenberg, Ann, ed. 1988. (Nancy Drew Mystery Stories Ser.: No. 82). 148p. (J). (gr. 3-6). pap. 3.99 (*0-671-64962-0*, Aladdin) Simon & Schuster Children's Publishing.

—The Clue in the Crossword Cipher. (Nancy Drew Mystery Stories Ser.: No. 44). (J). (gr. 3-6). 1974. 3.29 o.p. (*0-448-19544-5*); Vol. 44. 1967. (Illus.). 180p. 5.99 (*0-448-09544-0*) Penguin Putnam Bks. for Young Readers. (Grosset & Dunlap).

—The Clue in the Crumbling Wall. 1945. (Nancy Drew Mystery Stories Ser.: No. 22). (Illus.). 180p. (J). (gr. 3-6). 5.99 (*0-448-09522-X*, Grosset & Dunlap) Penguin Putnam Bks. for Young Readers.

—The Clue in the Diary: Hardy Boys. fac. ed. 2004. (Nancy Drew Mystery Stories Ser.: No. 7). (Illus.). iv, 398p. (J). (gr. 3-6). reprint ed. 17.95 (*1-55709-161-7*) Applewood Bks.

—The Clue in the Diary: Hardy Boys. 1932. (Nancy Drew Mystery Stories Ser.: No. 7). (Illus.). 180p. (J). (gr. 3-6). 5.99 (*0-448-09507-6*, Grosset & Dunlap) Penguin Putnam Bks. for Young Readers.

—The Clue in the Glue. 1998. (Nancy Drew Notebooks Ser.: No. 22). (Illus.). 80p. (J). (gr. k-3). pap. 3.99 (*0-671-00816-1*, Aladdin) Simon & Schuster Children's Publishing.

—The Clue in the Glue. 1998. (Nancy Drew Notebooks Ser.: No. 22). (J). (gr. k-3). 10.04 (*0-606-12999-5*) Turtleback Bks.

—The Clue in the Jewel Box. 1943. (Nancy Drew Mystery Stories Ser.: No. 20). (Illus.). 180p. (J). (gr. 3-6). 5.99 (*0-448-09520-3*, Grosset & Dunlap) Penguin Putnam Bks. for Young Readers.

—The Clue in the Old Album. rev. ed. (Nancy Drew Mystery Stories Ser.: No. 24). (Illus.). 180p. (J). (gr. 3-6). 1974. 3.29 o.p. (*0-448-19524-0*); 1947. 5.99 (*0-448-09524-6*) Penguin Putnam Bks. for Young Readers. (Grosset & Dunlap).

—The Clue in the Old Stagecoach. 1959. (Nancy Drew Mystery Stories Ser.: No. 37). (Illus.). 180p. (J). (gr. 3-6). 5.99 (*0-448-09537-8*, Grosset & Dunlap) Penguin Putnam Bks. for Young Readers.

—The Clue of the Black Keys. rev. ed. 1951. (Nancy Drew Mystery Stories Ser.: No. 28). (Illus.). 180p. (J). (gr. 3-6). 5.99 (*0-448-09528-9*, Grosset & Dunlap) Penguin Putnam Bks. for Young Readers.

—The Clue of the Broken Locket. fac. ed. 2004. (Nancy Drew Mystery Stories Ser.: No. 11). (Illus.). 228p. (J). (gr. 3-6). reprint ed. 14.95 (*1-55709-165-X*) Applewood Bks.

—The Clue of the Broken Locket. 1943. (Nancy Drew Mystery Stories Ser.: No. 11). (Illus.). 180p. (J). (gr. 3-6). 5.99 (*0-448-09511-4*) Penguin Putnam Bks. for Young Readers.

—The Clue of the Dancing Puppet. 1962. (Nancy Drew Mystery Stories Ser.: No. 39). (Illus.). 180p. (J). (gr. 3-6). 5.99 (*0-448-09539-4*, Grosset & Dunlap) Penguin Putnam Bks. for Young Readers.

—The Clue of the Gold Doubloons. 1999. (Nancy Drew Mystery Stories Ser.: No. 149). 160p. (J). (gr. 3-6). pap. 3.99 (*0-671-02548-1*, Aladdin) Simon & Schuster Children's Publishing.

—The Clue of the Leaning Chimney. 1949. (Nancy Drew Mystery Stories Ser.: No. 26). (Illus.). 180p. (J). (gr. 3-6). 5.99 (*0-448-09526-2*, Grosset & Dunlap) Penguin Putnam Bks. for Young Readers.

—The Clue of the Tapping Heels. 1939. (Nancy Drew Mystery Stories Ser.: No. 16). (Illus.). 180p. (J). (gr. 3-6). 5.99 (*0-448-09516-5*, Grosset & Dunlap) Penguin Putnam Bks. for Young Readers.

—The Clue of the Velvet Mask. 1953. (Nancy Drew Mystery Stories Ser.: No. 30). (Illus.). 180p. (J). (gr. 3-6). 5.99 (*0-448-09530-0*, Grosset & Dunlap) Penguin Putnam Bks. for Young Readers.

—The Clue of the Whistling Bagpipes. 1964. (Nancy Drew Mystery Stories Ser.: No. 41). (Illus.). 180p. (J). (gr. 3-6). 5.99 (*0-448-09541-6*, Grosset & Dunlap) Penguin Putnam Bks. for Young Readers.

—The Clue on the Crystal Dove. 2001. (Nancy Drew Mystery Stories Ser.: Vol. 160). (J). (gr. 3-6). reprint ed. E-Book 4.99 (*0-7434-2765-3*, Aladdin) Simon & Schuster Children's Publishing.

—The Clue on the Silver Screen. Greenberg, Anne, ed. 1995. (Nancy Drew Mystery Stories Ser.: No. 123). 160p. (J). (gr. 3-6). pap. 3.99 (*0-671-87206-0*, Aladdin) Simon & Schuster Children's Publishing.

—Cold As Ice. 1990. (Nancy Drew Files: No. 54). (YA). (gr. 6 up). 9.80 (*0-606-04640-2*) Turtleback Bks.

—Cold as Ice. Greenberg, Ann, ed. 1990. (Nancy Drew Files: No. 54). 160p. (YA). (gr. 6 up). mass mkt. 3.75 (*0-671-70031-6*, Simon Pulse) Simon & Schuster Children's Publishing.

—Copper Canyon Conspiracy. Greenberg, Anne, ed. 1994. (Nancy Drew & Hardy Boys Super Mystery Ser.: No. 22). 224p. (YA). (gr. 6 up). pap. 3.99 (*0-671-88514-6*, Simon Pulse) Simon & Schuster Children's Publishing.

—Copper Canyon Conspiracy. 1994. (Nancy Drew & Hardy Boys Super Mystery Ser.: No. 22). (YA). (gr. 6 up). 10.04 (*0-606-07054-0*) Turtleback Bks.

—Counterfeit Christmas. Ashby, Ruth, ed. 1994. (Nancy Drew Files: No. 102). 160p. (YA). (gr. 6 up). per. 3.99 (*0-671-88193-0*, Simon Pulse) Simon & Schuster Children's Publishing.

—Counterfeit Christmas. 1994. (Nancy Drew Files: No. 102). (YA). (gr. 6 up). 9.09 o.p. (*0-606-07053-2*) Turtleback Bks.

—Courting Disaster. Greenberg, Anne, ed. 1993. (Nancy Drew & Hardy Boys Super Mystery Ser.: No. 15). 224p. (YA). (gr. 6 up). per. 3.99 (*0-671-78168-5*, Simon Pulse) Simon & Schuster Children's Publishing.

—Courting Disaster. 1993. (Nancy Drew & Hardy Boys Super Mystery Ser.: No. 15). (YA). (gr. 6 up). 9.09 o.p. (*0-606-05494-4*) Turtleback Bks.

—The Crazy Carnival Case. 2002. (Nancy Drew Notebooks Ser.: No. 48). (Illus.). 80p. (J). (gr. 1-4). pap. 3.99 (*0-7434-3747-0*, Aladdin) Simon & Schuster Children's Publishing.

—The Crazy Key Clue. 1996. (Nancy Drew Notebooks Ser.: No. 15). (Illus.). 80p. (J). (gr. k-3). pap. 3.99 (*0-671-56859-0*, Aladdin) Simon & Schuster Children's Publishing.

—The Crazy Key Clue. 1996. (Nancy Drew Notebooks Ser.: No. 15). (J). (gr. k-3). 8.60 o.p. (*0-606-10890-4*) Turtleback Bks.

—Crime at the Chat Cafe. 1997. (Nancy Drew Files: No. 124). 160p. (YA). (gr. 6 up). per. 3.99 (*0-671-00749-1*, Simon Pulse) Simon & Schuster Children's Publishing.

—A Crime for Christmas. 1988. (Nancy Drew & Hardy Boys Super Mystery Ser.). (Illus.). (YA). (gr. 6 up). mass mkt. 2.95 (*0-671-64918-3*, Simon Pulse) Simon & Schuster Children's Publishing.

—Crime in the Queen's Court. Winkler, Ellen, ed. 1993. (Nancy Drew Mystery Stories Ser.: No. 112). 160p. (J). (gr. 3-6). pap. 4.99 (*0-671-79298-9*, Aladdin) Simon & Schuster Children's Publishing.

—Crime in the Queen's Court. 1993. (Nancy Drew Mystery Stories Ser.: No. 112). (J). (gr. 3-6). 9.09 o.p. (*0-606-05490-1*) Turtleback Bks.

—The Crime Lab Case. 2002. (Nancy Drew Mystery Stories Ser.: Vol. 165). 160p. (J). E-Book 4.99 (*0-7434-3960-0*); (Illus.). pap. 4.99 (*0-7434-3744-6*) Simon & Schuster Children's Publishing. (Aladdin).

—The Crime Lab Case. l.t. ed. 2002. (J). 21.95 (*0-7862-4652-9*) Thorndike Pr.

—The Crooked Banister. 1971. (Nancy Drew Mystery Stories Ser.: No. 48). (Illus.). 180p. (J). (gr. 3-6). 5.99 (*0-448-09548-3*, Grosset & Dunlap) Penguin Putnam Bks. for Young Readers.

—Crosscurrents. Greenberg, Ann, ed. 1992. (Nancy Drew Files: No. 68). 160p. (Orig.). (YA). (gr. 6 up). pap. 3.75 (*0-671-73072-X*, Simon Pulse) Simon & Schuster Children's Publishing.

—The Curse of the Black Cat. 2001. (Nancy Drew Mystery Stories Ser.: Vol. 158). 160p. (J). (gr. 3-6). pap. 3.99 (*0-7434-0661-3*, Aladdin) Simon & Schuster Children's Publishing.

—Cutting Edge. Greenberg, Anne, ed. 1992. (Nancy Drew Files: No. 70). 160p. (Orig.). (YA). (gr. 6 up). pap. 3.99 (*0-671-73074-6*, Simon Pulse) Simon & Schuster Children's Publishing.

—Dance till You Die. Ashby, Ruth, ed. 1994. (Nancy Drew Files: No. 100). 160p. (YA). (gr. 6 up). mass mkt. 3.99 (*0-671-79492-2*, Simon Pulse) Simon & Schuster Children's Publishing.

—Dance till You Die. 1994. (Nancy Drew Files: No. 100). (YA). (gr. 6 up). 9.09 o.p. (*0-606-07051-6*) Turtleback Bks.

—Danger down Under. Greenberg, Anne, ed. 1995. (Nancy Drew & Hardy Boys Super Mystery Ser.: No. 20). 224p. (YA). (gr. 6 up). mass mkt. 3.99 (*0-671-88460-3*, Simon Pulse) Simon & Schuster Children's Publishing.

—Danger down Under. 1995. (Nancy Drew & Hardy Boys Super Mystery Ser.: No. 20). (YA). (gr. 6 up). 9.09 o.p. (*0-606-10265-5*) Turtleback Bks.

—Danger for Hire. Greenberg, Ann, ed. 1990. (Nancy Drew Files: No. 52). 160p. (Orig.). (YA). (gr. 6 up). pap. 2.95 (*0-671-70029-4*, Simon Pulse) Simon & Schuster Children's Publishing.

—Danger on Parade. Greenberg, Anne, ed. 1992. (Nancy Drew Files: No. 77). 160p. (YA). (gr. 6 up). mass mkt. 3.75 (*0-671-73081-9*, Simon Pulse) Simon & Schuster Children's Publishing.

—Danger on Parade. 1992. (Nancy Drew Files: No. 77). (YA). (gr. 6 up). 8.85 (*0-606-02793-9*) Turtleback Bks.

—Dangerous Loves. 1997. (Nancy Drew Files: No. 120). 160p. (YA). (gr. 6 up). per. 3.99 (*0-671-56878-7*, Simon Pulse) Simon & Schuster Children's Publishing.

—Dangerous Loves. 1997. (Nancy Drew Files: No. 120). (YA). (gr. 6 up). 9.09 o.p. (*0-606-11665-6*) Turtleback Bks.

—Dangerous Relations. Greenberg, Anne, ed. 1993. (Nancy Drew Files: No. 82). 160p. (YA). (gr. 6 up). mass mkt. 3.99 (*0-671-73086-X*, Simon Pulse) Simon & Schuster Children's Publishing.

—Dangerous Relations. 1993. (Nancy Drew Files: No. 82). (YA). (gr. 6 up). 9.09 (*0-606-05496-0*) Turtleback Bks.

—Dare at the Fair. 1998. (Nancy Drew Notebooks Ser.: No. 25). (Illus.). 80p. (J). (gr. k-3). pap. 3.99 (*0-671-00820-X*, Aladdin) Simon & Schuster Children's Publishing.

—Dare at the Fair. 1998. (Nancy Drew Notebooks Ser.: No. 25). (J). (gr. 2-4). 10.04 (*0-606-13655-X*) Turtleback Bks.

—The Dashing Dog Mystery. 2001. (Nancy Drew Notebooks Ser.: Vol. 45). (Illus.). 80p. (J). (gr. k-3). pap. 3.99 (*0-7434-0693-1*, Aladdin) Simon & Schuster Children's Publishing.

—A Date with Deception: A Summer Love Trilogy #1. 1990. (Nancy Drew Files: No. 48). 160p. (Orig.). (YA). (gr. 6 up). pap. 2.95 (*0-671-67500-1*, Simon Pulse) Simon & Schuster Children's Publishing.

—Dead on Arrival. 1995. (Nancy Drew & Hardy Boys Super Mystery Ser.: No. 23). (Illus.). 224p. (YA). (gr. 6 up). mass mkt. 3.99 (*0-671-88461-1*, Simon Pulse) Simon & Schuster Children's Publishing.

—Deadly Doubles. l.t. ed. 1988. (Nancy Drew Files : No. 7). 149p. (YA). (gr. 6 up). reprint ed. 9.50 o.p. (*0-942545-38-9*); lib. bdg. 10.50 o.p. (*0-942545-33-8*) Grey Castle Pr.

—Deadly Doubles. 1991. (Nancy Drew Files: No. 7). (YA). (gr. 6 up). pap. 3.50 (*0-671-73662-0*, Simon Pulse) Simon & Schuster Children's Publishing.

—Deadly Intent. l.t. ed. 1988. (Nancy Drew Files : No. 2). (YA). (gr. 6 up). 154p. 9.50 o.p. (*0-942545-23-0*); lib. bdg. 10.50 o.p. (*0-942545-28-1*) Grey Castle Pr.

—Deadly Intent. (Nancy Drew Files: No. 2). (YA). (gr. 6 up). 1991. 155p. mass mkt. 3.99 (*0-671-74611-1*); 1989. (Illus.). mass mkt. 2.95 (*0-671-68727-1*) Simon & Schuster Children's Publishing. (Simon Pulse).

—Deadly Intent. 1986. (Nancy Drew Files: No. 2). (YA). (gr. 6 up). 10.04 (*0-606-03066-2*) Turtleback Bks.

—Death by Design. (Nancy Drew Files: No. 30). (YA). (gr. 6 up). 1989. pap. 2.95 (*0-671-70358-7*); 1988. (Illus.). mass mkt. 2.75 (*0-671-64697-4*) Simon & Schuster Children's Publishing. (Simon Pulse).

—Deep Secrets: A Summer Love Trilogy #3. 1990. (Nancy Drew Files: No. 50). (YA). (gr. 6 up). mass mkt. 2.95 (*0-671-70027-8*, Simon Pulse) Simon & Schuster Children's Publishing.

—Deep Secrets: A Summer Love Trilogy #3. Greenberg, Ann, ed. 1991. (Nancy Drew Files: No. 50). 160p. (YA). (gr. 6 up). reprint ed. pap. 3.50 (*0-671-74525-5*, Simon Pulse) Simon & Schuster Children's Publishing.

—Designs in Crime. Greenberg, Anne, ed. 1993. (Nancy Drew Files: No. 89). 160p. (YA). (gr. 6 up). mass mkt. 3.99 (*0-671-79481-7*, Simon Pulse) Simon & Schuster Children's Publishing.

—Designs in Crime. 1993. (Nancy Drew Files: No. 89). (YA). (gr. 6 up). 10.04 (*0-606-05942-3*) Turtleback Bks.

—Desperate Measures. 1994. (Nancy Drew & Hardy Boys Super Mystery Ser.: No. 18). 224p. (YA). (gr. 6 up). mass mkt. 3.99 (*0-671-78174-X*, Simon Pulse) Simon & Schuster Children's Publishing.

—Desperate Measures. 1994. (Nancy Drew & Hardy Boys Super Mystery Ser.: No. 18). (YA). (gr. 6 up). 9.09 o.p. (*0-606-05947-4*) Turtleback Bks.

—Diamond Deceit. Greenberg, Anne, ed. 1993. (Nancy Drew Files: No. 83). 160p. (YA). (gr. 6 up). mass mkt. 3.99 (*0-671-73087-8*, Simon Pulse) Simon & Schuster Children's Publishing.

—Diamond Deceit. 1993. (Nancy Drew Files: No. 83). (YA). (gr. 6 up). 10.04 (*0-606-05497-9*) Turtleback Bks.

—Dinosaur Alert! 2001. (Nancy Drew Notebooks Ser.: Vol. 40). (J). (gr. k-3). reprint ed. E-Book 3.99 (*0-7434-2772-6*, Aladdin) Simon & Schuster Children's Publishing.

—Don't Look Back. 1995. (Nancy Drew on Campus Ser.: No. 3). 192p. (YA). (gr. 8 up). mass mkt. 3.99 (*0-671-52744-4*, Simon Pulse) Simon & Schuster Children's Publishing.

—Don't Look Twice. Greenberg, Ann, ed. 1991. (Nancy Drew Files: No. 55). 160p. (YA). (gr. 6 up). per. 3.75 (*0-671-70032-4*, Simon Pulse) Simon & Schuster Children's Publishing.

—Don't Look Twice. 1991. (Nancy Drew Files: No. 55). (YA). (gr. 6 up). 8.85 o.p. (*0-606-04655-0*) Turtleback Bks.

—The Door-to-Door Deception. 1997. (Nancy Drew Mystery Stories Ser.: No. 140). 160p. (J). (gr. 3-6). per. 3.99 (*0-671-00053-5*, Aladdin) Simon & Schuster Children's Publishing.

—The Door-to-Door Deception. 1997. (Nancy Drew Mystery Stories Ser.: No. 140). (J). (gr. 3-6). 10.04 (*0-606-13642-8*) Turtleback Bks.

—Double Crossing. (Nancy Drew & Hardy Boys Super Mystery Ser.: No. 1). (YA). (gr. 6 up). 1991. 224p. pap. 3.99 (*0-671-74616-2*); 1988. (Illus.). pap. (*0-671-64917-5*) Simon & Schuster Children's Publishing. (Simon Pulse).

—The Double Horror of Fenley Place. 2001. (Nancy Drew Mystery Stories Ser.: Vol. 79). (J). reprint ed. E-Book 4.99 (*0-7434-3423-4*); (Illus.). 160p. (gr. 3-6). pap. 4.99 (*0-7434-2343-7*) Simon & Schuster Children's Publishing. (Aladdin).

—The Double Horror of Fenley Place. Greenberg, Ann, ed. rev. ed. 1987. (Nancy Drew Mystery Stories Ser.: No. 79). 160p. (J). (gr. 3-6). per. 3.99 (*0-671-64387-8*, Aladdin) Simon & Schuster Children's Publishing.

—The Double Jinx Mystery. 1973. (Nancy Drew Mystery Stories Ser.: No. 50). (Illus.). 180p. (J). (gr. 3-6). 5.99 (*0-448-09550-5*, Grosset & Dunlap) Penguin Putnam Bks. for Young Readers.

—Dude Ranch Detective. 2000. (Nancy Drew Notebooks Ser.: No. 37). 80p. (J). (gr. k-3). pap. 3.99 (*0-671-04268-8*, Aladdin) Simon & Schuster Children's Publishing.

—The E-Mail Mystery. 1998. (Nancy Drew Mystery Stories Ser.: No. 144). 160p. (J). (gr. 3-6). pap. 4.99 (*0-671-00121-3*, Aladdin) Simon & Schuster Children's Publishing.

—The E-Mail Mystery. 1998. (Nancy Drew Mystery Stories Ser.: No. 144). (J). (gr. 3-6). 10.04 (*0-606-13646-0*) Turtleback Bks.

—Easy Marks. Greenberg, Anne, ed. 1991. (Nancy Drew Files: No. 62). 160p. (Orig.). (J). (gr. 6 up). pap. 3.50 (*0-671-73066-5*, Simon Pulse) Simon & Schuster Children's Publishing.

—The Elusive Heiress. (Nancy Drew Mystery Stories Ser.: No. 68). (J). (gr. 3-6). 1985. pap. 3.99 (*0-671-62478-4*, Aladdin); 1982. (Illus.). 206p. pap. (*0-671-44555-3*, Simon & Schuster Children's Publishing); 1982. (Illus.). 206p. pap. 3.50 (*0-671-44553-7*, Aladdin) Simon & Schuster Children's Publishing.

—The Emerald-Eyed Cat. (Nancy Drew Mystery Stories Ser.: No. 75). (J). (gr. 3-6). 1987. pap. 3.50 (*0-671-64282-0*, Aladdin); 1985. (Illus.). 173p. pap. (*0-671-49740-5*, Simon & Schuster Children's Publishing); 1984. (Illus.). 173p. pap. 3.50 (*0-671-49739-1*, Aladdin) Simon & Schuster Children's Publishing.

—Enemy Match. 1987. (Nancy Drew Mystery Stories Ser.: No. 73). 192p. (J). (gr. 3-6). pap. 3.50 (*0-671-64283-9*, Aladdin) Simon & Schuster Children's Publishing.

—Enemy Match. Barish, Wendy, ed. 1984. (Nancy Drew Mystery Stories Ser.: No. 73). (Illus.). 189p. (J). (gr. 3-6). pap. (*0-671-49736-7*, Simon & Schuster Children's Publishing); pap. 3.50 (*0-671-49735-9*, Aladdin) Simon & Schuster Children's Publishing.

—Evil in Amsterdam. Greenberg, Ann, ed. 1993. (Nancy Drew & Hardy Boys Super Mystery Ser.: No. 17). 224p. (YA). (gr. 6 up). mass mkt. 3.99 (*0-671-78173-1*, Simon Pulse) Simon & Schuster Children's Publishing.

—Evil in Amsterdam. Greenberg, Ann, ed. 1993. (Nancy Drew & Hardy Boys Super Mystery Ser.: No. 17). (YA). (gr. 6 up). 10.04 (*0-606-05948-2*) Turtleback Bks.

—Exhibition of Evil. 1997. (Nancy Drew & Hardy Boys Super Mystery Ser.: No. 32). 224p. (YA). (gr. 6 up). pap. 3.99 (*0-671-53750-4*, Simon Pulse) Simon & Schuster Children's Publishing.

—Exhibition of Evil. 1997. (Nancy Drew & Hardy Boys Super Mystery Ser.: No. 32). (YA). (gr. 6 up). 9.09 (*0-606-12777-1*) Turtleback Bks.

—False Friends. 1996. (Nancy Drew on Campus Ser.: No. 7). 192p. (YA). (gr. 8 up). pap. 3.99 (*0-671-52751-7*, Simon Pulse) Simon & Schuster Children's Publishing.

—False Impressions. (Nancy Drew Files: No. 43). (gr. 6 up). 1991. 160p. (J). per. 3.50 (*0-671-74392-9*); 1990. (Illus.). (YA). mass mkt. 2.95 (*0-671-67495-1*) Simon & Schuster Children's Publishing. (Simon Pulse).

—False Impressions. 1990. (Nancy Drew Files: No. 43). (YA). (gr. 6 up). 8.60 o.p. (*0-606-01007-6*) Turtleback Bks.

—False Moves. l.t. ed. 1988. (Nancy Drew Files : No. 9). 149p. (YA). (gr. 6 up). reprint ed. 9.50 o.p. (*0-942545-40-0*); lib. bdg. 10.50 o.p. (*0-942545-35-4*) Grey Castle Pr.

—False Moves. 1989. (Nancy Drew Files: No. 9). (YA). (gr. 6 up). pap. 3.75 (*0-671-70493-1*, Simon Pulse) Simon & Schuster Children's Publishing.

—False Pretenses. 1993. (Nancy Drew Files: No. 88). 160p. (YA). (gr. 6 up). pap. 3.99 (*0-671-79480-9*, Simon Pulse) Simon & Schuster Children's Publishing.

—Final Notes. Greenberg, Anne, ed. 1991. (Nancy Drew Files: No. 65). 160p. (Orig.). (YA). (gr. 6 up). pap. 3.75 (*0-671-73069-X*, Simon Pulse) Simon & Schuster Children's Publishing.

—The Fine Feathered Mystery. 1999. (Nancy Drew Notebooks Ser.: No. 31). (Illus.). 80p. (J). (gr. k-3). per. 3.99 (*0-671-02785-9*, Aladdin) Simon & Schuster Children's Publishing.

—Flower Power. 2001. (Nancy Drew Notebooks Ser.: No. 41). (Illus.). 80p. (J). (gr. k-3). pap. 3.99 (*0-7434-0664-8*); reprint ed. E-Book 3.99 (*0-7434-2435-2*) Simon & Schuster Children's Publishing. (Aladdin).

—The Flying Saucer Mystery. 1990. (Nancy Drew Mystery Stories Ser.: No. 58). (J). (gr. 3-6). pap. 3.99 (*0-671-72320-0*, Aladdin) Simon & Schuster Children's Publishing.

—Flying Too High. Greenberg, Anne, ed. 1995. (Nancy Drew Files: No. 106). 160p. (YA). (gr. 6 up). mass mkt. 3.99 (*0-671-88197-3*, Simon Pulse) Simon & Schuster Children's Publishing.

—Flying Too High. 1995. (Nancy Drew Files: No. 106). (YA). (gr. 6 up). 9.09 o.p. (*0-606-07926-2*) Turtleback Bks.

—For Love or Money. 1995. (Nancy Drew Files: No. 112). 160p. (YA). (gr. 6 up). pap. 3.99 (*0-671-88203-1*, Simon Pulse) Simon & Schuster Children's Publishing.

—For Love or Money. 1995. (Nancy Drew Files: No. 112). (YA). (gr. 6 up). 9.09 o.p. (*0-606-08578-5*) Turtleback Bks.

—The Fortune-Teller's Secret. Greenberg, Anne, ed. 1994. (Nancy Drew Mystery Stories Ser.: No. 121). 160p. (Orig.). (J). (gr. 3-6). pap. 3.99 (*0-671-87204-4*, Simon Pulse) Simon & Schuster Children's Publishing.

—The Fox Hunt Mystery. 1996. (Nancy Drew Mystery Stories Ser.: No. 132). 160p. (J). (gr. 3-6). pap. 3.99 (*0-671-50510-6*, Aladdin) Simon & Schuster Children's Publishing.

—The Fox Hunt Mystery. 1996. (Nancy Drew Mystery Stories Ser.: No. 132). (J). (gr. 3-6). 10.04 (*0-606-09667-1*) Turtleback Bks.

—The Funny Face Fight. 1996. (Nancy Drew Notebooks Ser.: No. 14). 80p. (J). (gr. k-3). pap. 3.99 (*0-671-53553-6*, Aladdin) Simon & Schuster Children's Publishing.

—The Funny Face Fight. 1996. (Nancy Drew Notebooks Ser.: No. 14). (J). (gr. k-3). 10.14 (*0-606-10889-0*) Turtleback Bks.

—Getting Closer. 1996. (Nancy Drew on Campus Ser.: No. 8). 192p. (YA). (gr. 8 up). pap. 3.99 (*0-671-52754-1*, Simon Pulse) Simon & Schuster Children's Publishing.

—The Ghost of Blackwood Hall. 1948. (Nancy Drew Mystery Stories Ser.: No. 25). (Illus.). 180p. (J). (gr. 3-6). 5.99 (*0-448-09525-4*, Grosset & Dunlap) Penguin Putnam Bks. for Young Readers.

—The Ghost of Craven Cove. Greenberg, Anne, ed. 1989. (Nancy Drew Mystery Stories Ser.: No. 92). 160p. (J). (gr. 3-6). pap. 3.99 (*0-671-66317-8*, Aladdin) Simon & Schuster Children's Publishing.

—The Ghost of the Lantern Lady. 1998. (Nancy Drew Mystery Stories Ser.: No. 146). 160p. (J). (gr. 3-6). pap. 4.99 (*0-671-02663-1*, Aladdin) Simon & Schuster Children's Publishing.

—The Girl Who Couldn't Remember. Greenberg, Ann, ed. 1989. (Nancy Drew Mystery Stories Ser.: No. 91). 160p. (Orig.). (J). (gr. 3-6). pap. 3.99 (*0-671-66316-X*, Aladdin) Simon & Schuster Children's Publishing.

—Going Home. 1996. (Nancy Drew on Campus Ser.: No. 16). 192p. (YA). (gr. 8 up). pap. 3.99 (*0-671-56805-1*, Simon Pulse) Simon & Schuster Children's Publishing.

—Going Too Far. 1990. (River Heights Ser.: No. 3). 160p. (YA). (gr. 6 up). pap. 2.95 (*0-671-67761-6*, Simon Pulse) Simon & Schuster Children's Publishing.

—The Gumdrop Ghost. 1999. (Nancy Drew Notebooks Ser.: No. 33). (Illus.). 80p. (J). (gr. k-3). pap. 3.99 (*0-671-03709-9*, Aladdin) Simon & Schuster Children's Publishing.

—The Gumdrop Ghost. 1999. (Nancy Drew Notebooks Ser.: No. 33). (J). (gr. k-3). 10.14 (*0-606-19060-0*) Turtleback Bks.

—Hannah's Secret. 1997. (Nancy Drew Notebooks Ser.: No. 20). (Illus.). 80p. (J). (gr. k-3). pap. 3.99 (*0-671-56864-7*, Aladdin) Simon & Schuster Children's Publishing.

—Hannah's Secret. 1997. (Nancy Drew Notebooks Ser.: No. 20). (J). (gr. k-3). 10.04 (*0-606-12778-X*) Turtleback Bks.

—Hard to Get. 1996. (Nancy Drew on Campus Ser.: No. 14). 192p. (YA). (gr. 8 up). pap. 3.99 (*0-671-56803-5*, Simon Pulse) Simon & Schuster Children's Publishing.

—The Haunted Bridge. 1938. (Nancy Drew Mystery Stories Ser.: No. 15). (Illus.). 180p. (J). (gr. 3-6). 5.99 (*0-448-09515-7*, Grosset & Dunlap) Penguin Putnam Bks. for Young Readers.

—The Haunted Carousel. 1988. (Nancy Drew Mystery Stories Ser.: No. 72). 192p. (Orig.). (J). (gr. 3-6). pap. 3.99 (*0-671-66227-9*, Aladdin) Simon & Schuster Children's Publishing.

—The Haunted Showboat. 1958. (Nancy Drew Mystery Stories Ser.: No. 35). (Illus.). 180p. (J). (gr. 3-6). 5.99 (*0-448-09535-1*, Grosset & Dunlap) Penguin Putnam Bks. for Young Readers.

—The Haunting of Horse Island. Greenberg, Ann, ed. 1990. (Nancy Drew Mystery Stories Ser.: No. 98). 160p. (Orig.). (J). (gr. 3-6). pap. 3.99 (*0-671-69284-4*, Aladdin) Simon & Schuster Children's Publishing.

—Heart of Danger. 1991. (Nancy Drew Files: No. 11). (YA). (gr. 6 up). per. 3.50 (*0-671-73665-5*, Simon Pulse) Simon & Schuster Children's Publishing.

—Heart of Danger. 1987. (Nancy Drew Files: No. 11). (YA). (gr. 6 up). 8.60 o.p. (*0-606-03009-3*) Turtleback Bks.

—Heart of Ice. Ashby, Ruth, ed. 1995. (Nancy Drew Files: No. 103). 160p. (YA). (gr. 6 up). mass mkt. 3.99 (*0-671-88194-9*, Simon Pulse) Simon & Schuster Children's Publishing.

—Heart of Ice. 1995. (Nancy Drew Files: No. 103). (YA). (gr. 6 up). 9.09 o.p. (*0-606-07923-8*) Turtleback Bks.

—The Hidden Inheritance. 1996. (Nancy Drew Mystery Stories Ser.: No. 131). 160p. (J). (gr. 3-6). pap. 3.99 (*0-671-50509-2*, Aladdin) Simon & Schuster Children's Publishing.

—Hidden Meanings. 1995. (Nancy Drew Files: No. 110). 160p. (YA). (gr. 6 up). mass mkt. 3.99 (*0-671-88201-5*, Simon Pulse) Simon & Schuster Children's Publishing.

—Hidden Meanings. 1995. (Nancy Drew Files: No. 110). (YA). (gr. 6 up). 9.09 o.p. (*0-606-07930-0*) Turtleback Bks.

—The Hidden Staircase. fac. ed. 2004. (Nancy Drew Mystery Stories Ser.: No. 2). (Illus.). iv, 408p. (J). (gr. 3-6). reprint ed. 17.95 (*1-55709-156-0*) Applewood Bks.

—The Hidden Staircase. (Nancy Drew Mystery Stories Ser.: No. 2). (J). (gr. 3-6). 1974. 3.29 o.p. (*0-448-19502-X*); 1930. (Illus.). 180p. 5.99 (*0-448-09502-5*) Penguin Putnam Bks. for Young Readers. (Grosset & Dunlap).

—The Hidden Staircase. unabr. ed. 2002. (Nancy Drew Ser.: No. 2). (J). (gr. 3 up). audio 18.00 (*0-8072-0757-8*, Listening Library) Random Hse. Audio Publishing Group.

—The Hidden Treasures. 1998. (Nancy Drew Notebooks Ser.: No. 24). (Illus.). 80p. (J). (gr. k-3). pap. 3.99 (*0-671-00819-6*, Aladdin) Simon & Schuster Children's Publishing.

—The Hidden Treasures. 1998. (Nancy Drew Notebooks Ser.: No. 24). (J). (gr. k-3). 10.04 (*0-606-13654-1*) Turtleback Bks.

—The Hidden Window Mystery. rev. ed. 1957. (Nancy Drew Mystery Stories Ser.: No. 34). (Illus.). 180p. (J). (gr. 3-6). 5.99 (*0-448-09534-3*, Grosset & Dunlap) Penguin Putnam Bks. for Young Readers.

—High Marks for Malice. 1991. (Nancy Drew Files: No. 32). (YA). (gr. 6 up). mass mkt. 3.50 (*0-671-74653-7*, Simon Pulse) Simon & Schuster Children's Publishing.

—High Risk. 2004. (Nancy Drew (All New) Girl Detective Ser.). 160p. (Orig.). (J). pap. 4.99 (*0-689-86569-4*, Aladdin) Simon & Schuster Children's Publishing.

—High Risk. Greenberg, Anne, ed. 1991. (Nancy Drew Files: No. 59). 160p. (Orig.). (YA). (gr. 6 up). mass mkt. 3.99 (*0-671-70036-7*, Simon Pulse) Simon & Schuster Children's Publishing.

—High Stakes. 1996. (Nancy Drew & Hardy Boys Super Mystery Ser.: No. 29). 224p. (YA). (gr. 6 up). per. 3.99 (*0-671-53747-4*, Simon Pulse) Simon & Schuster Children's Publishing.

—High Stakes. 1996. (Nancy Drew & Hardy Boys Super Mystery Ser.: No. 29). (YA). (gr. 6 up). 10.04 (*0-606-10888-2*) Turtleback Bks.

—High Survival. Greenberg, Ann, ed. 1991. (Nancy Drew & Hardy Boys Super Mystery Ser.: No. 10). 224p. (Orig.). (YA). (gr. 6 up). mass mkt. 3.99 (*0-671-67466-8*, Simon Pulse) Simon & Schuster Children's Publishing.

—Hit & Run Holiday. l.t. ed. 1989. (Nancy Drew Files : No. 5). 150p. (YA). (gr. 6 up). 9.50 o.p. (*0-942545-25-7*); lib. bdg. 10.50 o.p. (*0-942545-31-1*) Grey Castle Pr.

—Hit & Run Holiday. (Nancy Drew Files: No. 5). (YA). (gr. 6 up). 1991. pap. 3.99 (*0-671-73660-4*); 1989. pap. 2.95 (*0-671-70289-0*); 1986. pap. (*0-671-62560-8*) Simon & Schuster Children's Publishing. (Simon Pulse).

—Hit & Run Holiday. 1986. (Nancy Drew Files: No. 5). (YA). (gr. 6 up). 10.04 (*0-606-03047-6*) Turtleback Bks.

—Hits & Misses. Greenberg, Ann, ed. 1993. (Nancy Drew & Hardy Boys Super Mystery Ser.: No. 16). 224p. (YA). (gr. 6 up). mass mkt. 3.99 (*0-671-78169-3*, Simon Pulse) Simon & Schuster Children's Publishing.

—Hits & Misses. 1993. (Nancy Drew & Hardy Boys Super Mystery Ser.: No. 16). (YA). (gr. 6 up). 9.09 o.p. (*0-606-05495-2*) Turtleback Bks.

—Hollywood Horror. Greenberg, Anne, ed. 1994. (Nancy Drew & Hardy Boys Super Mystery Ser.: No. 21). 224p. (Orig.). (YA). (gr. 6 up). mass mkt. 3.99 (*0-671-78181-2*, Simon Pulse) Simon & Schuster Children's Publishing.

—Hot Pursuit. Greenberg, Anne, ed. 1991. (Nancy Drew Files: No. 58). 160p. (Orig.). (YA). (gr. 6 up). pap. 3.99 (*0-671-70035-9*, Simon Pulse) Simon & Schuster Children's Publishing.

—Hot Tracks. Greenberg, Anne, ed. 1992. (Nancy Drew Files: No. 71). 160p. (YA). (gr. 6 up). mass mkt. 3.75 (*0-671-73075-4*, Simon Pulse) Simon & Schuster Children's Publishing.

—Hot Tracks. 1992. (Nancy Drew Files: No. 71). (YA). (gr. 6 up). 9.80 (*0-606-02021-7*) Turtleback Bks.

—Hotline to Danger. Greenberg, Anne, ed. 1994. (Nancy Drew Files: No. 93). 160p. (Orig.). (YA). (gr. 6 up). mass mkt. 3.99 (*0-671-79485-X*, Simon Pulse) Simon & Schuster Children's Publishing.

—The Ice Cream Scoop. 1995. (Nancy Drew Notebooks Ser.: No. 6). (Illus.). 80p. (J). (gr. k-3). pap. 3.99 (*0-671-87950-2*, Aladdin) Simon & Schuster Children's Publishing.

—The Ice Cream Scoop. 1995. (Nancy Drew Notebooks Ser.: No. 6). (J). (gr. k-3). 10.14 (*0-606-07934-3*) Turtleback Bks.

—If Looks Could Kill. 1994. (Nancy Drew Files: No. 91). 160p. (YA). (gr. 6 up). mass mkt. 3.99 (*0-671-79483-3*, Simon Pulse) Simon & Schuster Children's Publishing.

—If Looks Could Kill. 1994. (Nancy Drew Files: No. 91). (YA). (gr. 6 up). 9.09 o.p. (*0-606-05944-X*) Turtleback Bks.

—Illusions of Evil. 1994. (Nancy Drew Files: No. 94). 160p. (YA). (gr. 6 up). pap. 3.99 (*0-671-79486-8*, Simon Pulse) Simon & Schuster Children's Publishing.

—Illusions of Evil. 1994. (Nancy Drew Files: No. 94). (YA). (gr. 6 up). 10.04 (*0-606-06601-2*) Turtleback Bks.

—In & Out of Love. 1997. (Nancy Drew on Campus Ser.: No. 22). 192p. (YA). (gr. 8 up). pap. 3.99 (*0-671-00214-7*, Simon Pulse) Simon & Schuster Children's Publishing.

—In Search of the Black Rose. 1997. (Nancy Drew Mystery Stories Ser.: No. 137). 160p. (J). (gr. 3-6). pap. 3.99 (*0-671-00051-9*, Aladdin) Simon & Schuster Children's Publishing.

—In Search of the Black Rose. 1997. (Nancy Drew Mystery Stories Ser.: No. 137). (J). (gr. 3-6). 10.04 (*0-606-11662-1*) Turtleback Bks.

—In the Name of Love. 1996. (Nancy Drew on Campus Ser.: No. 11). 192p. (YA). (gr. 8 up). pap. 3.99 (*0-671-52759-2*, Simon Pulse) Simon & Schuster Children's Publishing.

—In the Spotlight. 1997. (Nancy Drew on Campus Ser.: No. 24). 192p. (YA). (gr. 8 up). pap. 3.99 (*0-671-00216-3*, Simon Pulse) Simon & Schuster Children's Publishing.

—An Instinct for Trouble. Greenberg, Anne, ed. 1994. (Nancy Drew Files: No. 95). 160p. (YA). (gr. 6 up). mass mkt. 3.99 (*0-671-79487-6*, Simon Pulse) Simon & Schuster Children's Publishing.

—An Instinct for Trouble. 1994. (Nancy Drew Files: Vol. 95). (Illus.). (YA). (gr. 6 up). mass mkt. 3.99 (*0-671-89279-7*, Simon Pulse) Simon & Schuster Children's Publishing.

—An Instinct for Trouble. 1994. (Nancy Drew Files: No. 95). (YA). (gr. 6 up). 9.09 o.p. (*0-606-06602-0*) Turtleback Bks.

—Into Thin Air. Greenberg, Ann, ed. 1991. (Nancy Drew Files: No. 57). 160p. (YA). (gr. 6 up). mass mkt. 3.50 (*0-671-70034-0*, Simon Pulse) Simon & Schuster Children's Publishing.

—Into Thin Air. 1991. (Nancy Drew Files: No. 57). (YA). (gr. 6 up). 8.60 o.p. (*0-606-04704-2*) Turtleback Bks.

—The Invisible Intruder. 1969. (Nancy Drew Mystery Stories Ser.: No. 46). (Illus.). 180p. (J). (gr. 3-6). 5.99 (*0-448-09546-7*, Grosset & Dunlap) Penguin Putnam Bks. for Young Readers.

—Island of Secrets. 1994. (Nancy Drew Files: No. 98). 160p. (YA). (gr. 6 up). pap. 3.99 (*0-671-79490-6*, Simon Pulse) Simon & Schuster Children's Publishing.

—Islands of Intrigue. 1996. (Nancy Drew & Hardy Boys Super Mystery Ser.: No. 27). 224p. (YA). (gr. 6 up). per. 3.99 (*0-671-50294-8*, Simon Pulse) Simon & Schuster Children's Publishing.

—Islands of Intrigue. 1996. (Nancy Drew & Hardy Boys Super Mystery Ser.: No. 27). (YA). (gr. 6 up). 9.09 o.p. (*0-606-09672-8*) Turtleback Bks.

—It's No Joke. 1999. (Nancy Drew Notebooks Ser.: No. 30). 80p. (J). (gr. k-3). pap. 3.99 (*0-671-02493-0*, Aladdin) Simon & Schuster Children's Publishing.

—It's Your Move. 1996. (Nancy Drew on Campus Ser.: No. 6). 192p. (YA). (gr. 8 up). pap. 3.99 (*0-671-52748-7*, Simon Pulse) Simon & Schuster Children's Publishing.

—Jealous Feelings. 1997. (Nancy Drew on Campus Ser.: No. 20). 192p. (YA). (gr. 8 up). pap. 3.99 (*0-671-00212-0*, Simon Pulse) Simon & Schuster Children's Publishing.

—The Joker's Revenge. Greenberg, Ann, ed. 1988. (Nancy Drew Mystery Stories Ser.: No. 84). (J). (gr. 3-6). pap. 3.99 (*0-671-63414-3*); pap. 3.50 (*0-671-63426-7*) Simon & Schuster Children's Publishing. (Aladdin).

—Junior Class Trip: Super Sizzler. Greenberg, Ann, ed. 1991. (River Heights Ser.: No. 13). 224p. (Orig.). (YA). (gr. 6 up). pap. 2.95 (*0-671-73124-6*, Simon Pulse) Simon & Schuster Children's Publishing.

—Just the Two of Us. 1996. (Nancy Drew on Campus Ser.: No. 12). 192p. (YA). (gr. 8 up). pap. 3.99 (*0-671-52764-9*, Simon Pulse) Simon & Schuster Children's Publishing.

—The Kachina Doll Mystery. 1988. (Nancy Drew Mystery Stories Ser.: No. 62). (J). (gr. 3-6). pap. 3.99 (*0-671-67220-7*, Aladdin) Simon & Schuster Children's Publishing.

—Keeping Secrets. 1997. (Nancy Drew on Campus Ser.: No. 18). 192p. (YA). (gr. 8 up). pap. 3.99 (*0-671-56807-8*, Simon Pulse) Simon & Schuster Children's Publishing.

—The Key in the Satin Pocket. 2000. (Nancy Drew on Campus Ser.: No. 152). 160p. (J). (gr. 3-7). pap. 3.99 (*0-671-03871-0*, Aladdin) Simon & Schuster Children's Publishing.

—Kiss & Tell. Greenberg, Anne, ed. 1995. (Nancy Drew Files: No. 104). 160p. (YA). (gr. 6 up). pap. 3.99 (*0-671-88195-7*, Simon Pulse) Simon & Schuster Children's Publishing.

—Kiss & Tell. 1995. (Nancy Drew Files: No. 104). (YA). (gr. 6 up). 9.09 o.p. (*0-606-07924-6*) Turtleback Bks.

—Last Dance. (Nancy Drew Files: No. 37). (YA). (gr. 6 up). 1991. pap. 3.50 (*0-671-74657-X*); 1989. pap. 2.95 (*0-671-67489-7*) Simon & Schuster Children's Publishing. (Simon Pulse).

—The Legend of Miner's Creek. Greenberg, Anne, ed. 1992. (Nancy Drew Mystery Stories Ser.: No. 107). 160p. (Orig.). (YA). (gr. 3-6). pap. 3.99 (*0-671-73053-3*, Aladdin) Simon & Schuster Children's Publishing.

—The Legend of the Lost Gold. 1997. (Nancy Drew Mystery Stories Ser.: No. 138). 160p. (J). (gr. 3-6). pap. 3.99 (*0-671-00049-7*, Aladdin) Simon & Schuster Children's Publishing.

—The Legend of the Lost Gold. 1997. (Nancy Drew Mystery Stories Ser.: No. 138). (J). (gr. 3-6). 10.04 (*0-606-13640-1*) Turtleback Bks.

—The Lemonade Raid. 1997. (Nancy Drew Notebooks Ser.: No. 19). (Illus.). 80p. (J). (gr. k-3). pap. 3.99 (*0-671-56863-9*, Aladdin) Simon & Schuster Children's Publishing.

—The Lemonade Raid. 1997. (Nancy Drew Notebooks Ser.: No. 19). (J). (gr. k-3). 10.04 (*0-606-11672-9*) Turtleback Bks.

—Let's Talk Terror. 1993. (Nancy Drew Files: No. 86). 160p. (YA). (gr. 6 up). mass mkt. 3.99 (*0-671-79478-7*, Simon Pulse) Simon & Schuster Children's Publishing.

—Let's Talk Terror. 1993. (Nancy Drew Files: No. 86). (YA). (gr. 6 up). 10.04 (*0-606-05500-2*) Turtleback Bks.

—Lights! Camera! Clues! 1999. (Nancy Drew Notebooks Ser.: No. 29). (Illus.). 80p. (J). (gr. k-3). pap. 3.99 (*0-671-02463-9*, Aladdin) Simon & Schuster Children's Publishing.

—Lost in the Everglades. 2001. (Nancy Drew Mystery Stories Ser.: Vol. 161). (J). (gr. 3-6). (Illus.). 160p. pap. 4.99 (*0-7434-0687-7*); reprint ed. E-Book 4.99 (*0-7434-2766-1*) Simon & Schuster Children's Publishing. (Aladdin).

—The Lost Locket. 1994. (Nancy Drew Notebooks Ser.: No. 2). 80p. (J). (gr. k-3). pap. 3.99 (*0-671-87946-4*, Aladdin) Simon & Schuster Children's Publishing.

—The Lost Locket. 1994. (Nancy Drew Notebooks Ser.: No. 2). (J). (gr. k-3). 10.14 (*0-606-06608-X*) Turtleback Bks.

—Love & Betrayal. 1997. (Nancy Drew on Campus Ser.: No. 21). 192p. (YA). (gr. 8 up). pap. 3.99 (*0-671-00213-9*, Simon Pulse) Simon & Schuster Children's Publishing.

—Love Notes. 1995. (Nancy Drew Files: No. 109). 160p. (YA). (gr. 6 up). pap. 3.99 (*0-671-88200-7*, Simon Pulse) Simon & Schuster Children's Publishing.

—Love Notes. 1995. (Nancy Drew Files: No. 109). (YA). (gr. 6 up). 9.09 o.p. (*0-606-07929-7*) Turtleback Bks.

—Love On-Line. 1997. (Nancy Drew on Campus Ser.: No. 19). 192p. (YA). (gr. 8 up). pap. 3.99 (*0-671-00211-2*, Simon Pulse) Simon & Schuster Children's Publishing.

—Love Times Three. (River Heights Ser.: No. 1). (Orig.). (YA). (gr. 6 up). 1991. pap. 3.50 (*0-671-96703-7*); 1989. pap. 2.95 (*0-671-67759-4*) Simon & Schuster Children's Publishing. (Simon Pulse).

—Loving & Losing. 1996. (Nancy Drew on Campus Ser.: No. 15). 192p. (YA). (gr. 8 up). pap. 3.99 (*0-671-56804-3*, Simon Pulse) Simon & Schuster Children's Publishing.

—The Lucky Horseshoes. 1998. (Nancy Drew Notebooks Ser.: No. 26). (Illus.). 80p. (J). (gr. k-3). pap. 3.99 (*0-671-00822-6*, Aladdin) Simon & Schuster Children's Publishing.

—The Make Believe Mystery. 2000. (Nancy Drew Notebooks Ser.: Vol. 36). 80p. (J). (gr. k-3). per. 3.99 (*0-671-04267-X*, Aladdin) Simon & Schuster Children's Publishing.

—Make No Mistake. Greenberg, Ann, ed. 1991. (Nancy Drew Files: No. 56). 160p. (YA). (gr. 6 up). per. 3.50 (*0-671-70033-2*, Simon Pulse) Simon & Schuster Children's Publishing.

—Make No Mistake. 1991. (Nancy Drew Files: No. 56). (YA). (gr. 6 up). 8.60 (*0-606-04737-9*) Turtleback Bks.

—Making Waves. Greenberg, Ann, ed. 1993. (Nancy Drew Files: No. 81). 160p. (YA). (gr. 6 up). pap. 3.99 (*0-671-73085-1*, Simon Pulse) Simon & Schuster Children's Publishing.

—Making Waves. 1993. (Nancy Drew Files: No. 81). (YA). (gr. 6 up). 10.04 (*0-606-02803-X*) Turtleback Bks.

—The Mardi Gras Mystery. Greenberg, Ann, ed. 1988. (Nancy Drew Mystery Stories Ser.: No. 81). 160p. (J). (gr. 3-6). pap. 3.99 (*0-671-64961-2*, Aladdin) Simon & Schuster Children's Publishing.

—The Message in the Haunted Mansion. Greenberg, Anne, ed. 1994. (Nancy Drew Mystery Stories Ser.: No. 122). 160p. (J). (gr. 3-6). pap. 3.99 (*0-671-87205-2*, Simon Pulse) Simon & Schuster Children's Publishing.

—The Message in the Haunted Mansion. 2001. (Nancy Drew Mystery Stories Ser.: Vol. 122). reprint ed. E-Book 4.99 (*0-7434-3427-7*); (Illus.). 160p. (J). (gr. 3-6). pap. 4.99 (*0-7434-1937-5*) Simon & Schuster Children's Publishing. (Aladdin).

—The Message in the Hollow Oak. fac. ed. 2004. (Nancy Drew Mystery Stories Ser.: No. 12). (Illus.). 210p. (J). (gr. 3-6). 17.95 (*1-55709-258-3*) Applewood Bks.

—The Message in the Hollow Oak. (Nancy Drew Mystery Stories Ser.: No. 12). (Illus.). (J). (gr. 3-6). 1974. 196p. 3.29 o.p. (*0-448-19512-7*); Vol. 12. 1935. 180p. 5.99 (*0-448-09512-2*) Penguin Putnam Bks. for Young Readers. (Grosset & Dunlap).

—Mistletoe Mystery, Vol. 169. 2002. (Nancy Drew Ser.). 160p. (J). pap. 4.99 (*0-7434-3765-9*, Aladdin) Simon & Schuster Children's Publishing.

—Mixed Signals. Greenberg, Anne, ed. 1991. (Nancy Drew Files: No. 63). 160p. (Orig.). (YA). (gr. 6 up). pap. 3.50 (*0-671-73067-3*, Simon Pulse) Simon & Schuster Children's Publishing.

—A Model Crime. Greenberg, Ann, ed. 1990. (Nancy Drew Files: No. 51). 160p. (YA). (gr. 6 up). mass mkt. 3.75 (*0-671-70028-6*, Simon Pulse) Simon & Schuster Children's Publishing.

—A Model Crime. 1990. (Nancy Drew Files: No. 51). (YA). (gr. 6 up). 9.80 (*0-606-04479-5*) Turtleback Bks.

—The Moonstone Castle Mystery. 1962. (Nancy Drew Mystery Stories Ser.: No. 40). (Illus.). 180p. (J). (gr. 3-6). 5.99 (*0-448-09540-8*, Grosset & Dunlap) Penguin Putnam Bks. for Young Readers.

—Moving Target. Greenberg, Anne, ed. 1993. (Nancy Drew Files: No. 87). 160p. (J). (gr. 6 up). mass mkt. 3.99 (*0-671-79479-5*, Simon Pulse) Simon & Schuster Children's Publishing.

—Moving Target. 1993. (Nancy Drew Files: No. 87). (YA). (gr. 6 up). 9.09 o.p. (*0-606-05501-0*) Turtleback Bks.

—Murder on Ice. l.t. ed. 1988. (Nancy Drew Files : No. 3). 150p. (YA). (gr. 6 up). 9.50 o.p. (*0-942545-24-9*); lib. bdg. 10.50 o.p. (*0-942545-29-X*) Grey Castle Pr.

—Murder on Ice. (Nancy Drew Files: No. 3). (YA). (gr. 6 up). 1989. mass mkt. 3.75 (*0-671-68729-8*); 1986. pap. (*0-671-62566-7*) Simon & Schuster Children's Publishing. (Simon Pulse).

—Murder on Ice. 1986. (Nancy Drew Files: No. 3). (YA). (gr. 6 up). 9.80 (*0-606-03067-0*) Turtleback Bks.

—Murder on the Fourth of July. 1996. (Nancy Drew & Hardy Boys Super Mystery Ser.: No. 28). 224p. (YA). (gr. 6 up). mass mkt. 3.99 (*0-671-50295-6*, Simon Pulse) Simon & Schuster Children's Publishing.

—Murder on the Fourth of July. 1996. (Nancy Drew & Hardy Boys Super Mystery Ser.: No. 28). (YA). (gr. 6 up). 9.09 o.p. (*0-606-10266-3*) Turtleback Bks.

—My Deadly Valentine. Greenberg, Anne, ed. 1994. (Nancy Drew Files: No. 92). 160p. (YA). (gr. 6 up). per. 3.99 (*0-671-79484-1*, Simon Pulse) Simon & Schuster Children's Publishing.

—My Deadly Valentine. 1994. (Nancy Drew Files: No. 92). (YA). (gr. 6 up). 9.09 o.p. (*0-606-05945-8*) Turtleback Bks.

—The Mysterious Mannequin. 1970. (Nancy Drew Mystery Stories Ser.: No. 47). (Illus.). 180p. (J). (gr. 3-6). 5.99 (*0-448-09547-5*, Grosset & Dunlap) Penguin Putnam Bks. for Young Readers.

—The Mystery at Lilac Inn. fac. ed. 2004. (Nancy Drew Mystery Stories Ser.: No. 4). (Illus.). iv, 402p. (J). (gr. 3-6). reprint ed. 14.95 (*1-55709-158-7*) Applewood Bks.

—The Mystery at Lilac Inn, Vol. 4. 1930. (Nancy Drew Mystery Stories Ser.: No. 4). (Illus.). 180p. (J). (gr. 3-6). 5.99 (*0-448-09504-1*, Grosset & Dunlap) Penguin Putnam Bks. for Young Readers.

—The Mystery at Magnolia Mansion. Greenberg, Ann, ed. 1990. (Nancy Drew Mystery Stories Ser.: No. 97). 148p. (Orig.). (J). (gr. 3-6). pap. 3.99 (*0-671-69282-8*, Aladdin) Simon & Schuster Children's Publishing.

—Mystery at Moorsea Manor. 1999. (Nancy Drew Mystery Stories Ser.: No. 150). 160p. (J). (gr. 3-6). pap. 4.99 (*0-671-02787-5*, Aladdin) Simon & Schuster Children's Publishing.

—Mystery at Moorsea Manor. 1999. (Nancy Drew Mystery Stories Ser.: No. 150). (J). (gr. 3-6). 10.04 (*0-606-19038-4*) Turtleback Bks.

—The Mystery at the Crystal Palace. 1996. (Nancy Drew Mystery Stories Ser.: No. 133). 160p. (J). (gr. 3-6). per. 3.99 (*0-671-50515-7*, Aladdin) Simon & Schuster Children's Publishing.

—The Mystery at the Crystal Palace. 1996. (Nancy Drew Mystery Stories Ser.: No. 133). (J). (gr. 3-6). 9.09 o.p. (*0-606-10886-6*) Turtleback Bks.

—The Mystery at the Ski Jump. rev. ed. 1952. (Nancy Drew Mystery Stories Ser.: No. 29). (Illus.). 180p. (J). (gr. 3-6). 5.99 (*0-448-09529-7*, Grosset & Dunlap) Penguin Putnam Bks. for Young Readers.

—Mystery by Moonlight. 2002. (Nancy Drew Ser.: Vol. 167). 160p. (J). (gr. 3-7). pap. 4.99 (*0-7434-3762-4*, Aladdin) Simon & Schuster Children's Publishing.

—The Mystery of Crocodile Island. 1978. (Nancy Drew Mystery Stories Ser.: No. 55). (Illus.). 180p. (J). (gr. 3-6). 5.99 (*0-448-09555-6*); 7.25 o.p. (*0-448-19555-0*) Penguin Putnam Bks. for Young Readers. (Grosset & Dunlap).

—The Mystery of Misty Canyon. 1988. (Nancy Drew Mystery Stories Ser.: No. 86). (J). (gr. 3-6). mass mkt. 3.99 (*0-671-63417-8*, Aladdin) Simon & Schuster Children's Publishing.

—The Mystery of Mother Wolf. 2002. (Nancy Drew Mystery Stories Ser.: Vol. 164). 160p. (J). pap. 4.99 (*0-7434-3743-8*, Aladdin) Simon & Schuster Children's Publishing.

—The Mystery of the Brass Bound Trunk. (Nancy Drew Mystery Stories Ser.: No. 17). (Illus.). 180p. (J). 1974. (gr. 3-6). 3.29 o.p. (*0-448-19517-8*); 1940. (gr. 4-7). 5.99 (*0-448-09517-3*) Penguin Putnam Bks. for Young Readers. (Grosset & Dunlap).

—The Mystery of the Fire Dragon. 1961. (Nancy Drew Mystery Stories Ser.: No. 38). (Illus.). 180p. (J). (gr. 3-6). 5.99 (*0-448-09538-6*, Grosset & Dunlap) Penguin Putnam Bks. for Young Readers.

—The Mystery of the Glowing Eye. 1974. (Nancy Drew Mystery Stories Ser.: No. 51). (Illus.). 180p. (J). (gr. 3-6). 5.99 (*0-448-09551-3*, Grosset & Dunlap) Penguin Putnam Bks. for Young Readers.

—The Mystery of the Ivory Charm. 1936. (Nancy Drew Mystery Stories Ser.: No. 13). (Illus.). 180p. (J). (gr. 3-6). reprint ed. 5.95 (*0-448-09513-0*, Grosset & Dunlap) Penguin Putnam Bks. for Young Readers.

—The Mystery of the Jade Tiger. Greenberg, Anne, ed. 1991. (Nancy Drew Mystery Stories Ser.: No. 104). 160p. (J). (gr. 3-6). pap. 4.99 (*0-671-73050-9*, Aladdin) Simon & Schuster Children's Publishing.

—The Mystery of the Jade Tiger. 1991. (Nancy Drew Mystery Stories Ser.: No. 104). (J). (gr. 3-6). 10.04 (*0-606-00632-X*) Turtleback Bks.

—The Mystery of the Masked Rider. Winkler, Ellen, ed. 1992. (Nancy Drew Mystery Stories Ser.: No. 109). 160p. (Orig.). (J). (gr. 3-6). pap. 3.99 (*0-671-73055-X*, Aladdin) Simon & Schuster Children's Publishing.

—The Mystery of the Missing Mascot. Greenberg, Anne, ed. 1994. (Nancy Drew Mystery Stories Ser.: No. 119). 160p. (J). (gr. 3-6). pap. 3.99 (*0-671-87202-8*, Simon Pulse) Simon & Schuster Children's Publishing.

—The Mystery of the Missing Mascot. 1994. (Nancy Drew Mystery Stories Ser.: No. 119). (J). (gr. 3-6). 9.09 o.p. (*0-606-06597-0*) Turtleback Bks.

—The Mystery of the Missing Millionairess. Greenberg, Anne, ed. 1991. (Nancy Drew Mystery Stories Ser.: No. 101). 160p. (J). (gr. 3-6). pap. 3.99 (*0-671-69287-9*, Aladdin) Simon & Schuster Children's Publishing.

—The Mystery of the Moss-Covered Mansion. 2002. (Nancy Drew Mystery Stories Ser.). (Illus.). 228p. (YA). (gr. 7 up). 14.95 (*1-55709-264-8*) Applewood Bks.

—The Mystery of the Moss-Covered Mansion. 1941. (Nancy Drew Mystery Stories Ser.: No. 18). (Illus.). 180p. (J). (gr. 3-6). 5.99 (*0-448-09518-1*, Grosset & Dunlap) Penguin Putnam Bks. for Young Readers.

—The Mystery of the Mother Wolf. l.t. ed. 2002. 159p. (J). 21.95 (*0-7862-4654-5*) Thorndike Pr.

—The Mystery of the Ninety-Nine Steps. 1965. (Nancy Drew Mystery Stories Ser.: No. 43). (Illus.). 180p. (J). (gr. 3-6). 5.99 (*0-448-09543-2*, Grosset & Dunlap) Penguin Putnam Bks. for Young Readers.

—The Mystery of the Tolling Bell. (Nancy Drew Mystery Stories Ser.: No. 23). (Illus.). (J). (gr. 3-6). reprint ed. 1974. 192p. 3.29 o.p. (*0-448-19523-2*); 1946. 180p. 5.99 (*0-448-09523-8*) Penguin Putnam Bks. for Young Readers. (Grosset & Dunlap).

—Mystery on Maui. 1998. (Nancy Drew Mystery Stories Ser.: No. 143). (J). (gr. 3-6). 10.04 (*0-606-13645-2*) Turtleback Bks.

—Mystery on the Menu. Greenberg, Anne, ed. 1994. (Nancy Drew Mystery Stories Ser.: No. 117). 160p. (J). (gr. 3-6). per. 3.99 (*0-671-79303-9*, Aladdin) Simon & Schuster Children's Publishing.

—Nancy Drew Complete Set. 2003. mass mkt. 335.44 (*0-448-43439-3*, Grosset & Dunlap) Penguin Putnam Bks. for Young Readers.

—Nancy Drew Digest, 4 vols. (J). 1989. 14.00 (*0-671-92235-1*); 1987. 14.00 (*0-671-91515-0*) Simon & Schuster Children's Publishing. (Aladdin).

—Nancy Drew Files Boxed Set: Trouble in Tahiti; High Marks for Malice; Danger in Disguise; Vanishing Act; Over the Edge. 1991. (Nancy Drew Files: Nos. 31, 32, 33, 34, 36). (YA). (gr. 6 up). pap. 17.50 (*0-671-96785-1*, Simon Pulse) Simon & Schuster Children's Publishing.

—The Nancy Drew Files Collectors Edition: Danger for Hire; Make no Mistake; Poison Pen. 1998. (Nancy Drew Files: Nos. 52, 56, 60). 464p. (YA). (gr. 6 up). 4.99 (*0-671-01930-9*, Simon & Schuster Children's Publishing) Simon & Schuster Children's Publishing.

—The Nancy Drew Files Collector's Edition: The Wrong Chemistry; Out of Bounds; Flirting with Danger. 1998. (Nancy Drew Files: Nos. 42, 45, 47). 464p. (YA). (gr. 6 up). per. 4.99 (*0-671-01929-5*, Simon Pulse) Simon & Schuster Children's Publishing.

—The Nancy Drew Files Collector's Edition: The Wrong Track; Nobody's Business; Running Scared. 1998. (Nancy Drew Files: Nos. 64, 67, 69). 464p. (YA). (gr. 8-12). 4.99 (*0-671-01931-7*, Simon & Schuster Children's Publishing) Simon & Schuster Children's Publishing.

—Nancy Drew Files Gift Set: Secrets Can Kill; Heart of Danger; Never Say Die; Circle of Evil; Sisters in Crime. 1989. (Nancy Drew Files: Nos. 1, 11, 16, 18, 19). (YA). (gr. 6 up). pap. 14.75 (*0-671-92236-X*, Simon Pulse) Simon & Schuster Children's Publishing.

—Nancy Drew Ghost Stories. 2001. (Nancy Drew Ghost Stories Ser.: No. 1). (J). (gr. 3-7). E-Book 4.99 (*0-7434-3710-1*, Aladdin) Simon & Schuster Children's Publishing.

—Nancy Drew Ghost Stories. Greenberg, Ann, ed. 1989. (Nancy Drew Ghost Stories Ser.: No. 1). 160p. (J). (gr. 3-7). pap. 4.99 (*0-671-69132-5*, Aladdin) Simon & Schuster Children's Publishing.

—Nancy Drew Ghost Stories. Schneider, Meg F., ed. 1983. (Nancy Drew Mystery Stories Ser.). (Illus.). (J). (gr. 3-6). 151p. (*0-671-46466-3*, Simon & Schuster Children's Publishing); 160p. pap. 3.50 (*0-671-46468-X*, Aladdin) Simon & Schuster Children's Publishing.

—Nancy Drew Ghost Stories. 1900. (Nancy Drew Ghost Stories Ser.: No. 1). (J). (gr. 3-6). mass mkt. 3.50 (*0-671-67863-9*, Aladdin) Simon & Schuster Children's Publishing.

—Nancy Drew Ghost Stories. 1983. (Nancy Drew Mystery Stories Ser.). (J). (gr. 3-6). 9.09 o.p. (*0-606-02097-7*) Turtleback Bks.

—Nancy Drew Ghost Stories II. Arico, Diane, ed. 1985. (Nancy Drew Mystery Stories Ser.). (Illus.). 158p. (Orig.). (J). (gr. 3-6). pap. (*0-671-55075-6*, Simon & Schuster Children's Publishing); pap. 3.50 (*0-671-55070-5*, Aladdin) Simon & Schuster Children's Publishing.

—Nancy Drew Mystery Stories: The Secret of the Old Clock; The Hidden Staircase; The Bungalow Mystery. 1999. (Nancy Drew Mystery Stories Ser.: Nos. 1-3). (Illus.). 560p. (J). (gr. 4-7). 9.98 (*0-7651-1728-2*) Smithmark Pubs., Inc.

—Nancy Drew Mystery Stories Box Set: The Mystery at Lilac Inn; The Secret of Shadow Ranch; The Secret of Red Gate Farm, Vols. 1-6. 2000. (Nancy Drew Mystery Stories Ser.: Nos. 4-6). 560p. (J). (gr. 3-6). 9.98 (*0-7651-1766-5*) Smithmark Pubs., Inc.

—Nancy Drew Mystery Stories Box Set: The Nutcracker Ballet Mystery; Crime in the Queen's Court; The Baby-Sitter Burglaries. 1997. (Nancy Drew Mystery Stories Ser.: Nos. 110, 112, 129). (J). (gr. 3-6). pap. 15.96 (*0-671-87831-X*, Aladdin) Simon & Schuster Children's Publishing.

—Nancy's Mysterious Letter. fac. ed. 2004. (Nancy Drew Mystery Stories Ser.: No. 8). (Illus.). iv, 209p. (J). (gr. 3-6). reprint ed. 14.95 (*1-55709-162-5*) Applewood Bks.

—Nancy's Mysterious Letter. 1963. (Nancy Drew Mystery Stories Ser.: No. 8). (Illus.). 180p. (J). (gr. 3-6). 5.99 (*0-448-09508-4*, Grosset & Dunlap) Penguin Putnam Bks. for Young Readers.

—Natural Enemies. (Nancy Drew Files: No. 121). (YA). (gr. 6 up). 1997. 160p. mass mkt. 3.99 (*0-671-56879-5*); 1900. per. (*0-671-50396-0*) Simon & Schuster Children's Publishing. (Simon Pulse).

—Natural Enemies. 1997. (Nancy Drew Files: No. 121). (YA). (gr. 6 up). 10.04 (*0-606-11666-4*) Turtleback Bks.

—Never Say Die. (Nancy Drew Files: No. 16). (YA). (gr. 6 up). 1991. pap. 3.50 (*0-671-73666-3*); 1988. (Illus.). mass mkt. 2.95 (*0-671-68051-X*); 1987. pap. (*0-671-64140-9*) Simon & Schuster Children's Publishing. (Simon Pulse).

—New Beginnings. 1997. (Nancy Drew on Campus Ser.: No. 17). 192p. (YA). (gr. 8 up). pap. 3.99 (*0-671-56806-X*, Simon Pulse) Simon & Schuster Children's Publishing.

—New Lives, New Loves. 1995. (Nancy Drew on Campus Ser.: No. 1). 192p. (YA). (gr. 8 up). pap. 3.99 (*0-671-52737-1*, Simon Pulse) Simon & Schuster Children's Publishing.

—New Year's Evil. Greenberg, Anne, ed. 1991. (Nancy Drew & Hardy Boys Super Mystery Ser.: No. 11). 224p. (YA). (gr. 6 up). mass mkt. 3.99 (*0-671-67467-6*, Simon Pulse) Simon & Schuster Children's Publishing.

—New Year's Evil. 1991. (Nancy Drew & Hardy Boys Super Mystery Ser.: No. 11). (YA). (gr. 6 up). 9.09 (*0-606-00644-3*) Turtleback Bks.

—Nightmare in New Orleans. 1997. (Nancy Drew & Hardy Boys Super Mystery Ser.: No. 30). 224p. (YA). (gr. 6 up). pap. 3.99 (*0-671-53749-0*, Simon Pulse) Simon & Schuster Children's Publishing.

—Nightmare in New Orleans. 1997. (Nancy Drew & Hardy Boys Super Mystery Ser.: No. 30). (YA). (gr. 6 up). 9.09 o.p. (*0-606-11667-2*) Turtleback Bks.

—No Laughing Matter. Greenberg, Anne, ed. 1993. (Nancy Drew Files: No. 79). 160p. (YA). (gr. 6 up). mass mkt. 3.99 (*0-671-73083-5*, Simon Pulse) Simon & Schuster Children's Publishing.

—No Laughing Matter. 1993. (Nancy Drew Files: No. 79). (YA). (gr. 6 up). 9.09 (*0-606-02798-X*) Turtleback Bks.

—No Strings Attached. 2003. (Nancy Drew Ser.: Bk. 170). (Illus.). 144p. (J). pap. 4.99 (*0-689-85559-1*, Aladdin) Simon & Schuster Children's Publishing.

—Nobody's Business. Greenberg, Ann, ed. 1992. (Nancy Drew Files: No. 67). 160p. (Orig.). (YA). (gr. 6 up). pap. 3.50 (*0-671-73071-1*, Simon Pulse) Simon & Schuster Children's Publishing.

Characters

—Not Nice on Ice. 1996. (Nancy Drew Notebooks Ser.: No. 10). (Illus.). 80p. (J). (gr. k-3). pap. 3.99 (*0-671-52711-8*, Aladdin) Simon & Schuster Children's Publishing.
—Not Nice on Ice. 1996. (Nancy Drew Notebooks Ser.: No. 10). (J). (gr. k-3). 10.14 (*0-606-08579-3*) Turtleback Bks.
—The Nutcracker Ballet Mystery. 2001. (Nancy Drew Mystery Stories Ser.: Vol. 110). (J). E-Book 3.99 (*0-7434-3709-8*, Aladdin) Simon & Schuster Children's Publishing.
—The Nutcracker Ballet Mystery. Winkler, Ellen, ed. 1992. (Nancy Drew Mystery Stories Ser.: No. 110). 160p. (J). (gr. 3-6). reprint ed. pap. 4.99 (*0-671-73056-8*, Aladdin) Simon & Schuster Children's Publishing.
—The Nutcracker Ballet Mystery. 1992. (Nancy Drew Mystery Stories Ser.: No. 110). (J). (gr. 3-6). 9.09 o.p. (*0-606-02782-3*) Turtleback Bks.
—On Her Own. 1995. (Nancy Drew on Campus Ser.: No. 2). 192p. (YA). (gr. 8 up). pap. 3.99 (*0-671-52741-X*, Simon Pulse) Simon & Schuster Children's Publishing.
—On the Trail of Trouble. 1999. (Nancy Drew Mystery Stories Ser.: No. 148). 160p. (J). (gr. 3-6). pap. 3.99 (*0-671-02664-X*, Aladdin) Simon & Schuster Children's Publishing.
—Operation Titanic. 1998. (Nancy Drew & Hardy Boys Super Mystery Ser.: No. 35). 224p. (YA). (gr. 6 up). pap. 4.99 (*0-671-00737-8*, Simon Pulse) Simon & Schuster Children's Publishing.
—Operation Titanic. 1998. (Nancy Drew & Hardy Boys Super Mystery Ser.: No. 35). (YA). (gr. 6 up). 10.04 (*0-606-13650-9*) Turtleback Bks.
—Otherwise Engaged. 1997. (Nancy Drew on Campus Ser.: No. 23). 192p. (YA). (gr. 8 up). pap. 3.99 (*0-671-00215-5*, Simon Pulse) Simon & Schuster Children's Publishing.
—Out of Bounds. (Nancy Drew Files: No. 45). (YA). (gr. 6 up). 1991. 160p. pap. 3.50 (*0-671-73911-5*); 1990. (Illus.). mass mkt. 2.95 (*0-671-67497-8*) Simon & Schuster Children's Publishing. (Simon Pulse).
—Out of Bounds. 1990. (Nancy Drew Files: No. 45). (YA). (gr. 6 up). 8.60 o.p. (*0-606-04500-7*) Turtleback Bks.
—Out of Control. 1997. (Nancy Drew & Hardy Boys Super Mystery Ser.: No. 31). 224p. (YA). (gr. 6 up). pap. 3.99 (*0-671-53748-2*, Simon Pulse) Simon & Schuster Children's Publishing.
—Out of Control. 1997. (Nancy Drew & Hardy Boys Super Mystery Ser.: No. 31). (YA). (gr. 6 up). 10.04 (*0-606-11668-0*) Turtleback Bks.
—Over the Edge. (Nancy Drew Files: No. 36). (YA). (gr. 6 up). 1991. per. 3.50 (*0-671-74656-1*); 36. 1989. pap. 2.95 (*0-671-64703-2*) Simon & Schuster Children's Publishing. (Simon Pulse).
—Over the Edge. 1989. (Nancy Drew Files: No. 36). (YA). (gr. 6 up). 8.60 o.p. (*0-606-04294-6*) Turtleback Bks.
—Party Weekend. 1996. (Nancy Drew on Campus Ser.: No. 10). 192p. (YA). (gr. 8 up). mass mkt. 3.99 (*0-671-52758-4*, Simon Pulse) Simon & Schuster Children's Publishing.
—Passport to Danger. Greenberg, Anne, ed. 1994. (Nancy Drew & Hardy Boys Super Mystery Ser.: No. 19). 224p. (YA). (gr. 6 up). mass mkt. 3.99 (*0-671-78177-4*, Simon Pulse) Simon & Schuster Children's Publishing.
—Passport to Danger. 1994. (Nancy Drew & Hardy Boys Super Mystery Ser.: No. 19). (YA). (gr. 6 up). 10.04 (*0-606-06600-4*) Turtleback Bks.
—The Password to Larkspur Lane. fac. ed. 2004. (Nancy Drew Mystery Stories Ser.: No. 10). (Illus.). 210p. (J). (gr. 3-6). 17.95 (*1-55709-164-1*) Applewood Bks.
—The Password to Larkspur Lane. 1960. (Nancy Drew Mystery Stories Ser.: No. 10). (Illus.). 180p. (J). (gr. 3-6). 5.99 (*0-448-09510-6*, Grosset & Dunlap) Penguin Putnam Bks. for Young Readers.
—The Pen Pal Puzzle. 1996. (Nancy Drew Notebooks Ser.: No. 11). 80p. (J). (gr. k-3). pap. 3.99 (*0-671-53550-1*, Aladdin) Simon & Schuster Children's Publishing.
—The Pen Pal Puzzle. 1996. (Nancy Drew Notebooks Ser.: No. 11). (J). (gr. k-3). 8.60 o.p. (*0-606-09674-4*) Turtleback Bks.
—The Perfect Plot. Greenberg, Anne, ed. 1992. (Nancy Drew Files: No. 76). 160p. (Orig.). (J). (gr. 6 up). mass mkt. 3.99 (*0-671-73080-0*, Simon Pulse) Simon & Schuster Children's Publishing.
—The Phantom of Pine Hill. 1964. (Nancy Drew Mystery Stories Ser.: No. 42). (Illus.). 180p. (J). (gr. 3-6). 5.99 (*0-448-09542-4*, Grosset & Dunlap) Penguin Putnam Bks. for Young Readers.
—The Phantom of Venice. (Nancy Drew Mystery Stories Ser.: No. 78). Orig. Title: Ghost in the Gondola. (gr. 3-6). 1991. (YA). pap. 3.50 (*0-671-73422-9*); 1988. 160p. (J). pap. 3.50 (*0-671-66230-9*); 1985. 157p. (J). pap. 3.50 (*0-671-49745-6*) Simon & Schuster Children's Publishing. (Aladdin).
—The Picture of Guilt. Ashby, Ruth, ed. 1994. (Nancy Drew Files: No. 101). 160p. (YA). (gr. 6 up). pap. 3.99 (*0-671-88192-2*, Simon Pulse) Simon & Schuster Children's Publishing.
—The Picture of Guilt. 1994. (Nancy Drew Files: No. 101). (YA). (gr. 6 up). 9.09 o.p. (*0-606-07052-4*) Turtleback Bks.
—The Picture Perfect Mystery. 1990. (Nancy Drew Mystery Stories Ser.: No. 94). 160p. (J). (gr. 3-6). per. 3.99 (*0-671-66319-4*, Aladdin) Simon & Schuster Children's Publishing.
—The Picture Perfect Mystery. 1990. (Nancy Drew Mystery Stories Ser.: No. 94). (J). (gr. 3-6). 9.09 o.p. (*0-606-05941-5*) Turtleback Bks.
—Playing with Fire. 1989. (Nancy Drew Files: No. 26). (YA). (gr. 6 up). pap. 2.95 (*0-671-70356-0*, Simon Pulse) Simon & Schuster Children's Publishing.
—Portrait in Crime: A Summer Love Trilogy #2. Greenberg, Ann, ed. 1991. (Nancy Drew Files: No. 49). 160p. (Orig.). (J). (gr. 6 up). pap. 3.50 (*0-671-73996-4*, Simon Pulse) Simon & Schuster Children's Publishing.
—Portrait in Crime: A Summer Love Trilogy #2. 1990. (Nancy Drew Files: Vol. 49). (Illus.). (Orig.). (YA). (gr. 6 up). mass mkt. 2.95 (*0-671-70026-X*, Simon Pulse) Simon & Schuster Children's Publishing.
—Power of Suggestion. Greenberg, Anne, ed. 1993. (Nancy Drew Files: No. 80). 160p. (Orig.). (J). (gr. 6 up). pap. 3.75 (*0-671-73084-3*, Simon Pulse) Simon & Schuster Children's Publishing.
—Princess on Parade. 1997. (Nancy Drew Notebooks Ser.: No. 21). (Illus.). 80p. (J). (gr. k-3). pap. 3.99 (*0-671-00815-3*, Aladdin) Simon & Schuster Children's Publishing.
—Process of Elimination. 1998. (Nancy Drew & Hardy Boys Super Mystery Ser.: No. 36). 224p. (YA). (gr. 6 up). per. 3.99 (*0-671-00739-4*, Simon Pulse) Simon & Schuster Children's Publishing.
—Process of Elimination. 1998. (Nancy Drew & Hardy Boys Super Mystery Ser.: No. 36). (YA). (gr. 6 up). 9.09 o.p. (*0-606-13651-7*) Turtleback Bks.
—The Puppy Problem. 1996. (Nancy Drew Notebooks Ser.: No. 12). 80p. (J). (gr. k-3). pap. 3.99 (*0-671-53551-X*, Aladdin) Simon & Schuster Children's Publishing.
—The Puppy Problem. 1996. (Nancy Drew Notebooks Ser.: No. 12). (J). (gr. k-3). 8.60 o.p. (*0-606-09675-2*) Turtleback Bks.
—Pure Poison. 1988. (Nancy Drew Files: No. 29). (YA). (gr. 6 up). pap. 2.75 (*0-671-64696-6*, Simon Pulse) Simon & Schuster Children's Publishing.
—The Purple Fingerprint. 2001. (Nancy Drew Notebooks Ser.: Vol. 44). (J). (gr. k-3). E-Book 3.99 (*0-7434-3705-5*, Aladdin) Simon & Schuster Children's Publishing.
—The Puzzle at Pineview School. Greenberg, Ann, ed. 1989. (Nancy Drew Mystery Stories Ser.: No. 90). (Orig.). (J). (gr. 3-6). mass mkt. 3.99 (*0-671-66315-1*, Aladdin) Simon & Schuster Children's Publishing.
—The Quest of the Missing Map. 1942. (Nancy Drew Mystery Stories Ser.: No. 19). (Illus.). 180p. (J). (gr. 3-6). 5.99 (*0-448-09519-X*, Grosset & Dunlap) Penguin Putnam Bks. for Young Readers.
—A Question of Guilt. 1996. (Nancy Drew & Hardy Boys Super Mystery Ser.: No. 26). 224p. (YA). (gr. 6 up). per. 3.99 (*0-671-50293-X*, Simon Pulse) Simon & Schuster Children's Publishing.
—A Question of Guilt. 1996. (Nancy Drew & Hardy Boys Super Mystery Ser.: No. 26). (YA). (gr. 6 up). 9.09 o.p. (*0-606-09673-6*) Turtleback Bks.
—Race Against Time. (Nancy Drew Mystery Stories Ser.: No. 66). (J). (gr. 3-6). 1990. 208p. pap. 3.50 (*0-671-69485-5*, Aladdin); 1982. (Illus.). 206p. pap. (*0-671-42372-X*, Simon & Schuster Children's Publishing); 1982. (Illus.). 206p. pap. 3.50 (*0-671-42373-8*, Aladdin) Simon & Schuster Children's Publishing.
—Recipe for Murder. 1989. (Nancy Drew Files: No. 21). 160p. (Orig.). (YA). (gr. 6 up). pap. 2.95 (*0-671-68802-2*, Simon Pulse) Simon & Schuster Children's Publishing.
—Rehearsing for Romance. 1996. (Nancy Drew Files: No. 114). 160p. (YA). (gr. 6 up). mass mkt. 3.99 (*0-671-50355-3*, Simon Pulse) Simon & Schuster Children's Publishing.
—Rehearsing for Romance. 1996. (Nancy Drew Files: No. 114). (YA). (gr. 6 up). 9.09 o.p. (*0-606-09669-8*) Turtleback Bks.
—Rendezvous in Rome: Passport to Romance #2. Greenberg, Anne, ed. 1992. (Nancy Drew Files: No. 73). 160p. (Orig.). (YA). (gr. 6 up). pap. 3.75 (*0-671-73077-0*, Simon Pulse) Simon & Schuster Children's Publishing.
—Rich & Dangerous. 1989. (Nancy Drew Files: No. 25). (YA). (gr. 6 up). pap. 2.95 (*0-671-70139-8*, Simon Pulse) Simon & Schuster Children's Publishing.
—The Riddle in the Rare Book. 1995. (Nancy Drew Mystery Stories Ser.: No. 126). 160p. (J). (gr. 3-6). pap. 4.99 (*0-671-87209-5*, Aladdin) Simon & Schuster Children's Publishing.
—The Riddle in the Rare Book. 1995. (Nancy Drew Mystery Stories Ser.: No. 126). (J). (gr. 3-6). 9.09 o.p. (*0-606-07922-X*) Turtleback Bks.
—The Riddle of the Ruby Gazelle. 1997. (Nancy Drew Mystery Stories Ser.: No. 135). 160p. (J). (gr. 3-6). pap. 4.99 (*0-671-00048-9*, Aladdin) Simon & Schuster Children's Publishing.
—The Riddle of the Ruby Gazelle. 1997. (Nancy Drew Mystery Stories Ser.: No. 135). (J). (gr. 3-6). 10.04 (*0-606-11660-5*) Turtleback Bks.
—The Riding Club Crime, No. 172. 2003. (Nancy Drew Ser.). (Illus.). 160p. (J). pap. 4.99 (*0-689-86145-1*, Aladdin) Simon & Schuster Children's Publishing.
—The Ringmaster's Secret, Vol. 31. rev. ed. 1954. (Nancy Drew Mystery Stories Ser.: No. 31). (Illus.). 180p. (J). (gr. 3-6). reprint ed. 5.99 (*0-448-09531-9*, Grosset & Dunlap) Penguin Putnam Bks. for Young Readers.
—Royal Revenge. 1997. (Nancy Drew & Hardy Boys Super Mystery Ser.: No. 34). 224p. (YA). (gr. 6 up). pap. 3.99 (*0-671-00735-1*, Simon Pulse) Simon & Schuster Children's Publishing.
—Royal Revenge. 1997. (Nancy Drew & Hardy Boys Super Mystery Ser.: No. 34). (YA). (gr. 6 up). 10.04 (*0-606-13652-5*) Turtleback Bks.
—The Runaway Bride. Ashby, Rush, ed. 1994. (Nancy Drew Files: No. 96). 160p. (YA). (gr. 6 up). mass mkt. 3.99 (*0-671-79488-4*, Simon Pulse) Simon & Schuster Children's Publishing.
—The Runaway Bride. 1994. (Nancy Drew Files: No. 96). (YA). (gr. 6 up). 9.09 o.p. (*0-606-06603-9*) Turtleback Bks.
—Running into Trouble. 1996. (Nancy Drew Files: No. 115). 160p. (YA). (gr. 6 up). pap. 3.99 (*0-671-50358-8*, Simon Pulse) Simon & Schuster Children's Publishing.
—Running Scared. Greenberg, Anne, ed. 1992. (Nancy Drew Files: No. 69). 160p. (Orig.). (YA). (gr. 6 up). pap. 3.75 (*0-671-73073-8*, Simon Pulse) Simon & Schuster Children's Publishing.
—The Sand Castle Mystery. 2002. (Nancy Drew Notebooks Ser.: No. 48). (Illus.). 80p. (J). (gr. 1-4). pap. 3.99 (*0-7434-3767-5*, Aladdin) Simon & Schuster Children's Publishing.
—The Scarlet Slipper Mystery. rev. ed. (Nancy Drew Mystery Stories Ser.: No. 32). (Illus.). (J). (gr. 3-6). 1974. 196p. 3.29 o.p. (*0-448-19532-1*); 1955. 180p. 5.99 (*0-448-09532-7*) Penguin Putnam Bks. for Young Readers. (Grosset & Dunlap).
—The Scarytales Sleepover, Vol. 50. 2002. (Nancy Drew Notebooks Ser.). (Illus.). 80p. (J). pap. 3.99 (*0-7434-3768-3*, Aladdin) Simon & Schuster Children's Publishing.
—Scent of Danger. (Nancy Drew Files: No. 44). (YA). (gr. 6 up). 1991. mass mkt. 3.50 (*0-671-73749-X*); 1990. 160p. pap. 2.95 (*0-671-67496-X*) Simon & Schuster Children's Publishing. (Simon Pulse).
—Sea of Suspicion. Greenberg, Ann, ed. 1993. (Nancy Drew Files: No. 85). 160p. (YA). (gr. 6 up). per. 3.99 (*0-671-79477-9*, Simon Pulse) Simon & Schuster Children's Publishing.
—Sea of Suspicion. 1993. (Nancy Drew Files: No. 85). (YA). (gr. 6 up). 9.09 o.p. (*0-606-05499-5*) Turtleback Bks.
—The Search for Cindy Austin. 1989. (Nancy Drew Mystery Stories Ser.: No. 88). 150p. (Orig.). (J). (gr. 3-6). pap. 3.50 (*0-671-66313-5*, Aladdin) Simon & Schuster Children's Publishing.
—The Search for the Silver Persian. 1993. (Nancy Drew Mystery Stories Ser.: No. 114). 160p. (Orig.). (J). (gr. 3-6). pap. 3.99 (*0-671-79300-4*, Aladdin) Simon & Schuster Children's Publishing.
—The Secret at Seven Rocks. Greenberg, Ann, ed. 1991. (Nancy Drew Mystery Stories Ser.: No. 99). 160p. (J). (gr. 3-6). pap. 3.99 (*0-671-69285-2*, Aladdin) Simon & Schuster Children's Publishing.
—The Secret at Solaire. Winkler, Ellen, ed. 1993. (Nancy Drew Mystery Stories Ser.: No. 111). 160p. (J). (gr. 3-6). pap. 3.99 (*0-671-79297-0*, Aladdin) Simon & Schuster Children's Publishing.
—The Secret at Solaire. 1993. (Nancy Drew Mystery Stories Ser.: No. 111). (J). (gr. 3-6). 9.09 o.p. (*0-606-02789-0*) Turtleback Bks.
—The Secret in the Dark. Greenberg, Anne, ed. 1991. (Nancy Drew Mystery Stories Ser.: No. 102). 160p. (J). (gr. 3-6). pap. 3.99 (*0-671-69279-8*, Aladdin) Simon & Schuster Children's Publishing.
—The Secret in the Old Attic. (Nancy Drew Mystery Stories Ser.: No. 21). 180p. (J). (gr. 3-6). 1974. 3.29 o.p. (*0-448-19521-6*); 1955. (Illus.). 5.99 (*0-448-09521-1*) Penguin Putnam Bks. for Young Readers. (Grosset & Dunlap).
—A Secret in Time Nancy Drew's 100th Anniversary Edition. Greenberg, Anne, ed. anniv. ed. 1991. (Nancy Drew Mystery Stories Ser.: No. 100). 160p. (Orig.). (J). (gr. 3-6). mass mkt. 3.99 (*0-671-69286-0*, Aladdin) Simon & Schuster Children's Publishing.
—The Secret Lost at Sea. Winkler, Ellen, ed. 1993. (Nancy Drew Mystery Stories Ser.: No. 113). 160p. (Orig.). (J). (gr. 3-6). pap. 3.99 (*0-671-79299-7*, Aladdin) Simon & Schuster Children's Publishing.
—The Secret of Candlelight Inn. 1997. (Nancy Drew Mystery Stories Ser.: No. 139). 160p. (J). (gr. 3-6). pap. 3.99 (*0-671-00052-7*, Aladdin) Simon & Schuster Children's Publishing.
—The Secret of Candlelight Inn. 1997. (Nancy Drew Mystery Stories Ser.: No. 139). (J). (gr. 3-6). 10.04 (*0-606-13641-X*) Turtleback Bks.
—The Secret of Mirror Bay. (Nancy Drew Mystery Stories Ser.: No. 49). (Illus.). (J). (gr. 3-6). 1974. 196p. 3.29 o.p. (*0-448-19549-6*); 1972. 180p. 5.99 (*0-448-09549-1*) Penguin Putnam Bks. for Young Readers. (Grosset & Dunlap).
—The Secret of Red Gate Farm. fac. ed. 2004. (Nancy Drew Mystery Stories Ser.: No. 6). (Illus.). iv, 208p. (J). (gr. 3-6). reprint ed. 17.95 (*1-55709-160-9*) Applewood Bks.
—The Secret of Red Gate Farm. (J). 1974. (Nancy Drew Mystery Stories Ser.: No. 6). (gr. 3-6). 3.29 o.p. (*0-448-19506-2*); 1931. (Nancy Drew Mystery Stories Ser.: No. 6). (Illus.). 180p. (gr. 3-6). 5.99 (*0-448-09506-8*); Vols. 1-6. 1998. 19.98 (*0-448-41673-5*) Penguin Putnam Bks. for Young Readers. (Grosset & Dunlap).
—The Secret of Red Gate Farm. unabr. ed. 2003. (Nancy Drew Ser.: No. 6). (J). (gr. 3). audio 18.00 (*0-8072-1590-2*, Listening Library) Random Hse. Audio Publishing Group.
—The Secret of Shadow Ranch. fac. ed. 2004. (Nancy Drew Mystery Stories Ser.: No. 5). (Illus.). iv, 203p. (J). (gr. 3-6). reprint ed. 14.95 (*1-55709-159-5*) Applewood Bks.
—The Secret of Shadow Ranch. 1980. (Nancy Drew Mystery Stories Ser.: No. 5). (Illus.). 180p. (J). (gr. 3-6). 5.99 (*0-448-09505-X*, Grosset & Dunlap) Penguin Putnam Bks. for Young Readers.
—The Secret of Shadow Ranch. unabr. ed. 2003. (Nancy Drew Mystery Ser.: No. 6). (J). (gr. 3). audio 18.00 (*0-8072-1555-4*, Imagination Studio) Random Hse. Audio Publishing Group.
—The Secret of Shady Glen. Greenberg, Ann, ed. 1988. (Nancy Drew Mystery Stories Ser.: No. 85). 150p. (J). (gr. 3-6). pap. 3.99 (*0-671-63416-X*, Aladdin) Simon & Schuster Children's Publishing.
—The Secret of Shady Glen. 2001. (Nancy Drew Mystery Stories Ser.: Vol. 85). (J). reprint ed. E-Book 4.99 (*0-7434-3426-9*); 160p. (gr. 3-6). pap. 4.99 (*0-7434-1936-7*) Simon & Schuster Children's Publishing. (Aladdin).
—The Secret of the Forgotten Cave. 1996. (Nancy Drew Mystery Stories Ser.: No. 134). 160p. (J). (gr. 3-6). pap. 4.99 (*0-671-50516-5*, Aladdin) Simon & Schuster Children's Publishing.
—The Secret of the Forgotten Cave. 1996. (Nancy Drew Mystery Stories Ser.: No. 134). (J). (gr. 3-6). 10.04 (*0-606-11659-1*) Turtleback Bks.
—The Secret of the Forgotten City. 1975. (Nancy Drew Mystery Stories Ser.: No. 52). (Illus.). 180p. (J). (gr. 3-6). 5.99 (*0-448-09552-1*, Grosset & Dunlap) Penguin Putnam Bks. for Young Readers.
—The Secret of the Golden Pavilion. 1959. (Nancy Drew Mystery Stories Ser.: No. 36). (Illus.). 180p. (J). (gr. 3-6). 5.99 (*0-448-09536-X*, Grosset & Dunlap) Penguin Putnam Bks. for Young Readers.
—The Secret of the Old Clock. fac. ed. 2004. (Nancy Drew Mystery Stories Ser.: No. 1). (Illus.). iv, 408p. (J). (gr. 3-6). reprint ed. 17.95 (*1-55709-155-2*) Applewood Bks.
—The Secret of the Old Clock. 1930. (Nancy Drew Mystery Stories Ser.: No. 1). (Illus.). 180p. (J). (gr. 3-6). 5.99 (*0-448-09501-7*, Grosset & Dunlap) Penguin Putnam Bks. for Young Readers.
—The Secret of the Old Clock. unabr. ed. 2002. (Nancy Drew Mystery Ser.: No. 1). (J). (gr. 3 up). audio 18.00 (*0-8072-0754-3*, Listening Library) Random Hse. Audio Publishing Group.
—The Secret of the Old Clock: The Hidden Staircase. 1987. (Nancy Drew Mystery Stories Ser.: Nos. 1-2). (Illus.). 360p. (J). (gr. 3-6). 7.99 (*0-448-09570-X*, Grosset & Dunlap) Penguin Putnam Bks. for Young Readers.
—The Secret of the Old Clock; The Hidden Staircase; The Bungalow Mystery; The Mystery at Lilac Inn; The Secret of Shadow Ranch; The Secret of Red Gate Farm. 1996. (Nancy Drew Mystery Stories Ser.: Nos. 1-6). (J). (gr. 3-6). 19.98 o.s.i (*0-448-41674-3*, Grosset & Dunlap) Penguin Putnam Bks. for Young Readers.
—The Secret of the Scarlet Hand. Greenberg, Anne, ed. 1995. (Nancy Drew Mystery Stories Ser.: No. 124). 160p. (J). (gr. 3-6). pap. 3.99 (*0-671-87207-9*, Aladdin) Simon & Schuster Children's Publishing.
—The Secret of the Scarlet Hand. 1995. (Nancy Drew Mystery Stories Ser.: No. 124). (J). (gr. 3-6). 9.09 o.p. (*0-606-07920-3*) Turtleback Bks.

—The Secret of the Tibetan Treasure. Winkler, Ellen, ed. 1992. (Nancy Drew Mystery Stories Ser.: No. 108). 160p. (J). (gr. 3-6). pap. 3.99 (*0-671-73054-1*, Aladdin) Simon & Schuster Children's Publishing.

—The Secret of the Tibetan Treasure. 1992. (Nancy Drew Mystery Stories Ser.: No. 108). (J). (gr. 3-6). 9.09 o.p. (*0-606-02192-2*) Turtleback Bks.

—The Secret of the Wooden Lady. 1950. (Nancy Drew Mystery Stories Ser.: No. 27). (Illus.). 180p. (J). (gr. 3-6). 5.99 (*0-448-09527-0*, Grosset & Dunlap) Penguin Putnam Bks. for Young Readers.

—Secret Rules. 1996. (Nancy Drew on Campus Ser.: No. 5). 192p. (YA). (gr. 8 up). pap. 3.99 (*0-671-52746-0*, Simon Pulse) Simon & Schuster Children's Publishing.

—The Secret Santa. Greenberg, Anne, ed. 1994. (Nancy Drew Notebooks Ser.: No. 3). (Illus.). 80p. (J). (gr. k-3). pap. 3.99 (*0-671-87947-2*, Aladdin) Simon & Schuster Children's Publishing.

—The Secret Santa. 1994. (Nancy Drew Notebooks Ser.: No. 3). (J). (gr. k-3). 10.14 (*0-606-07056-7*) Turtleback Bks.

—Secrets Can Kill. l.t. ed. 1988. (Nancy Drew Files : No. 1). 152p. (YA). (gr. 6 up). 9.50 o.p. (*0-942545-22-2*); lib. bdg. 10.50 o.p. (*0-942545-27-3*) Grey Castle Pr.

—Secrets Can Kill. (Nancy Drew Files: No. 1). (YA). (gr. 6 up). 1991. pap. 3.99 (*0-671-74674-X*); 1989. pap. 2.95 (*0-671-68523-6*); 1986. pap. (*0-671-64193-X*) Simon & Schuster Children's Publishing. (Simon Pulse).

—Secrets of the Nile. 1995. (Nancy Drew & Hardy Boys Super Mystery Ser.: No. 25). 224p. (YA). (gr. 6 up). mass mkt. 3.99 (*0-671-50290-5*, Simon Pulse) Simon & Schuster Children's Publishing.

—Secrets of the Nile. 1995. (Nancy Drew & Hardy Boys Super Mystery Ser.: No. 25). (YA). (gr. 6 up). 9.09 o.p. (*0-606-08577-7*) Turtleback Bks.

—Shock Waves. 1989. (Nancy Drew & Hardy Boys Super Mystery Ser.: Vol. 3). (Illus.). (YA). (gr. 6 up). mass mkt. 2.95 (*0-671-64919-1*, Simon Pulse) Simon & Schuster Children's Publishing.

—The Sign of the Falcon. 1996. (Nancy Drew Mystery Stories Ser.: No. 130). 160p. (J). (gr. 3-6). pap. 3.99 (*0-671-50508-4*, Aladdin) Simon & Schuster Children's Publishing.

—The Sign of the Falcon. 1996. (Nancy Drew Mystery Stories Ser.: No. 130). (J). (gr. 3-6). 9.09 o.p. (*0-606-09665-5*) Turtleback Bks.

—The Sign of the Twisted Candles. fac. ed. 2004. (Nancy Drew Mystery Stories Ser.: No. 9). (Illus.). iv, 217p. (J). (gr. 3-6). reprint ed. 17.95 (*1-55709-163-3*) Applewood Bks.

—The Sign of the Twisted Candles. (Nancy Drew Mystery Stories Ser.: No. 9). (Illus.). (J). (gr. 3-6). 1959. 180p. 5.99 (*0-448-09509-2*); 1974. 3.29 o.p. (*0-448-19509-7*) Penguin Putnam Bks. for Young Readers. (Grosset & Dunlap).

—The Silent Suspect. 1990. (Nancy Drew Mystery Stories Ser.: No. 95). 160p. (Orig.). (J). (gr. 3-6). pap. 3.50 (*0-671-69280-1*, Aladdin) Simon & Schuster Children's Publishing.

—The Silver Cobweb. Greenberg, Ann, ed. 1990. (Nancy Drew Mystery Stories Ser.: No. 71). 208p. (J). (gr. 3-6). pap. 3.50 (*0-671-70992-5*, Aladdin) Simon & Schuster Children's Publishing.

—The Silver Cobweb. (Nancy Drew Mystery Stories Ser.: No. 71). (J). (gr. 3-6). 1987. pap. 3.50 (*0-671-62470-9*, Aladdin); 1983. (Illus.). 204p. (*0-671-46464-7*, Simon & Schuster Children's Publishing) Simon & Schuster Children's Publishing.

—The Silver Cobweb. Schneider, Meg F., ed. 1983. (Nancy Drew Mystery Stories Ser.: No. 71). (Illus.). 204p. (J). (gr. 3-6). pap. 3.50 (*0-671-46463-9*, Aladdin) Simon & Schuster Children's Publishing.

—The Sinister Omen. (Nancy Drew Mystery Stories Ser.: No. 67). (Illus.). (J). (gr. 3-6). 1991. 192p. pap. 3.50 (*0-671-73938-7*, Aladdin); 1982. 205p. pap. 3.50 (*0-671-44552-9*, Aladdin); 1982. 205p. pap. (*0-671-44554-5*, Simon & Schuster Children's Publishing); 67. 1986. 205p. pap. 3.50 (*0-671-62471-7*, Aladdin) Simon & Schuster Children's Publishing.

—Sinister Paradise. 1989. (Nancy Drew Files: No. 23). (YA). (gr. 6 up). pap. 2.95 (*0-671-68803-0*, Simon Pulse) Simon & Schuster Children's Publishing.

—Sisters in Crime. 1988. (Nancy Drew Files: No. 19). (Orig.). (YA). (gr. 6 up). 160p. pap. 3.75 (*0-671-67957-0*); pap. (*0-671-64225-1*) Simon & Schuster Children's Publishing. (Simon Pulse).

—The Ski Slope Mystery. 1997. (Nancy Drew Notebooks Ser.: No. 16). 80p. (J). (gr. k-3). pap. 3.99 (*0-671-56860-4*, Aladdin) Simon & Schuster Children's Publishing.

—The Ski Slope Mystery. 1997. (Nancy Drew Notebooks Ser.: No. 16). (J). (gr. k-3). 10.04 (*0-606-11669-9*) Turtleback Bks.

—Skipping a Beat. 1996. (Nancy Drew Files: No. 117). 160p. (YA). (gr. 6 up). per. 3.99 (*0-671-56875-2*, Simon Pulse) Simon & Schuster Children's Publishing.

—Skipping a Beat. 1996. (Nancy Drew Files: No. 117). (YA). (gr. 6 up). 9.09 o.p. (*0-606-10887-4*) Turtleback Bks.

—The Sky Phantom. 1975. (Nancy Drew Mystery Stories Ser.: No. 53). (Illus.). 180p. (J). (gr. 3-6). 5.99 (*0-448-09553-X*, Grosset & Dunlap) Penguin Putnam Bks. for Young Readers.

—The Slumber Party Secret. Greenberg, Anne, ed. 1994. (Nancy Drew Notebooks Ser.: No. 1). (Illus.). 80p. (J). (gr. k-3). pap. 3.99 (*0-671-87945-6*, Aladdin) Simon & Schuster Children's Publishing.

—The Slumber Party Secret. 1994. (Nancy Drew Notebooks Ser.: No. 1). (J). (gr. k-3). 9.09 o.p. (*0-606-06607-1*) Turtleback Bks.

—Smile & Say Murder. l.t. ed. 1988. (Nancy Drew Files : No. 4). 151p. (YA). (gr. 6 up). 9.50 o.p. (*0-942545-26-5*); lib. bdg. 10.50 o.p. (*0-942545-30-3*) Grey Castle Pr.

—Smile & Say Murder. (Nancy Drew Files: No. 4). (YA). (gr. 6 up). 1991. mass mkt. 3.75 (*0-671-73659-0*); 1988. (Illus.). mass mkt. 2.95 (*0-671-68053-6*); 1987. pap. (*0-671-64585-4*); 1986. pap. (*0-671-62557-8*) Simon & Schuster Children's Publishing. (Simon Pulse).

—Smile & Say Murder. 1986. (Nancy Drew Files: No. 4). (YA). (gr. 6 up). 8.85 o.p. (*0-606-03064-6*) Turtleback Bks.

—The Snow Queen's Surprise. (Nancy Drew Notebooks Ser.: No. 46). (J). (gr. k-3). E-Book 3.99 (*0-7434-3957-0*); 2002. (Illus.). 80p. pap. 3.99 (*0-7434-3666-0*) Simon & Schuster Children's Publishing. (Aladdin).

—Snowbound. 1998. (Nancy Drew on Campus Ser.: No. 25). 192p. (YA). (gr. 8 up). pap. 3.99 (*0-671-00779-3*, Simon Pulse) Simon & Schuster Children's Publishing.

—The Soccer Shoe Clue. Greenberg, Anne, ed. 1995. (Nancy Drew Notebooks Ser.: No. 5). (Illus.). 80p. (J). (gr. k-3). pap. 3.99 (*0-671-87949-9*, Aladdin) Simon & Schuster Children's Publishing.

—The Soccer Shoe Clue. 1995. (Nancy Drew Notebooks Ser.: No. 5). (J). (gr. k-3). 10.14 (*0-606-07933-5*) Turtleback Bks.

—Something to Hide. (Nancy Drew Files: No. 41). (YA). (gr. 6 up). 1991. 160p. pap. 3.50 (*0-671-74659-6*); 1989. (Illus.). mass mkt. 2.95 (*0-671-67493-5*) Simon & Schuster Children's Publishing. (Simon Pulse).

—The Spider Sapphire Mystery. 1967. (Nancy Drew Mystery Stories Ser.: No. 45). (Illus.). 180p. (J). (gr. 3-6). 5.99 (*0-448-09545-9*, Grosset & Dunlap) Penguin Putnam Bks. for Young Readers.

—Spies & Lies. Greenberg, Anne, ed. 1992. (Nancy Drew & Hardy Boys Super Mystery Ser.: No. 13). 224p. (YA). (gr. 6 up). pap. 3.99 (*0-671-73125-4*, Simon Pulse) Simon & Schuster Children's Publishing.

—Spies & Lies. 1992. (Nancy Drew & Hardy Boys Super Mystery Ser.: No. 13). (YA). (gr. 6 up). 9.09 o.p. (*0-606-02043-8*) Turtleback Bks.

—Squeeze Play. Ashby, Ruth, ed. 1994. (Nancy Drew Files: No. 97). 160p. (YA). (gr. 6 up). pap. 3.99 (*0-671-79489-2*, Simon Pulse) Simon & Schuster Children's Publishing.

—Squeeze Play. 1994. (Nancy Drew Files: No. 97). (YA). (gr. 6 up). 10.04 (*0-606-06604-7*) Turtleback Bks.

—Stage Fright. Greenberg, Anne, ed. 1993. (Nancy Drew Files: No. 90). 160p. (Orig.). (YA). (gr. 6 up). mass mkt. 3.99 (*0-671-79482-5*, Simon Pulse) Simon & Schuster Children's Publishing.

—Stay Tuned for Danger. (Nancy Drew Files: No. 17). (Orig.). (YA). (gr. 6 up). 1991. 160p. pap. 3.50 (*0-671-73667-1*); 1990. mass mkt. 2.95 (*0-671-72469-X*); 1987. (Illus.). mass mkt. (*0-671-64141-7*) Simon & Schuster Children's Publishing. (Simon Pulse).

—Stolen Affections. Ashby, Ruth, ed. 1995. (Nancy Drew Files: No. 105). 160p. (YA). (gr. 6 up). mass mkt. 3.99 (*0-671-88196-5*, Simon Pulse) Simon & Schuster Children's Publishing.

—Stolen Affections. 1995. (Nancy Drew Files: No. 105). (YA). (gr. 6 up). 9.09 o.p. (*0-606-07925-4*) Turtleback Bks.

—The Stolen Kiss. 1995. (Nancy Drew Files: No. 111). 160p. (YA). (gr. 6 up). mass mkt. 3.99 (*0-671-88202-3*, Simon Pulse) Simon & Schuster Children's Publishing.

—The Stolen Kiss. 1995. (Nancy Drew Files: No. 111). (YA). (gr. 6 up). 9.09 o.p. (*0-606-07931-9*) Turtleback Bks.

—The Stolen Unicorn. 1997. (Nancy Drew Notebooks Ser.: No. 18). (Illus.). 80p. (J). (gr. k-3). pap. 3.99 (*0-671-56862-0*, Aladdin) Simon & Schuster Children's Publishing.

—The Stolen Unicorn. 1997. (Nancy Drew Notebooks Ser.: No. 18). (J). (gr. k-3). 10.14 (*0-606-11671-0*) Turtleback Bks.

—Strange Memories. (Nancy Drew Files: No. 122). (YA). 1997. 160p. (gr. 7 up). per. 3.99 (*0-671-56880-9*); 1900. (gr. 6 up). per. (*0-671-50397-9*) Simon & Schuster Children's Publishing. (Simon Pulse).

—Strange Memories. 1997. (Nancy Drew Files: No. 122). (YA). (gr. 6 up). 10.04 (*0-606-13647-9*) Turtleback Bks.

—The Strange Message in the Parchment, Vol. 54. 1976. (Nancy Drew Mystery Stories Ser.: No. 54). (Illus.). 180p. (J). (gr. 3-6). 5.99 (*0-448-09554-8*, Grosset & Dunlap) Penguin Putnam Bks. for Young Readers.

—The Stranger in the Shadows. Greenberg, Anne, ed. 1991. (Nancy Drew Mystery Stories Ser.: No. 103). 160p. (Orig.). (J). (gr. 3-6). pap. 3.99 (*0-671-73049-5*, Aladdin) Simon & Schuster Children's Publishing.

—The Suspect in the Smoke. 1993. (Nancy Drew Mystery Stories Ser.: No. 115). 160p. (J). (gr. 3-6). pap. 3.99 (*0-671-79301-2*, Aladdin) Simon & Schuster Children's Publishing.

—The Suspect in the Smoke. 1993. (Nancy Drew Mystery Stories Ser.: No. 115). (J). (gr. 3-6). 9.09 o.p. (*0-606-05493-6*) Turtleback Bks.

—The Suspect Next Door. (Nancy Drew Files: No. 39). (Orig.). (YA). (gr. 6 up). 1991. pap. 3.50 (*0-671-74612-X*); 1989. (Illus.). mass mkt. 2.95 (*0-671-67491-9*) Simon & Schuster Children's Publishing. (Simon Pulse).

—The Swami's Ring. (Nancy Drew Mystery Stories Ser.: No. 61). (J). (gr. 3-6). 1986. pap. 3.50 (*0-671-62467-9*, Aladdin); 1981. (Illus.). 192p. (*0-671-42344-4*, Simon & Schuster Children's Publishing); 1981. (Illus.). 192p. pap. 3.50 (*0-671-42345-2*, Aladdin) Simon & Schuster Children's Publishing.

—Sweet Revenge. Greenberg, Ann, ed. 1991. (Nancy Drew Files: No. 61). 160p. (Orig.). (YA). (gr. 6 up). pap. 3.50 (*0-671-73065-7*, Simon Pulse) Simon & Schuster Children's Publishing.

—Swiss Secrets: Passport to Romance. Greenberg, Anne, ed. 1992. (Nancy Drew Files: No. 72). 160p. (YA). (gr. 6 up). mass mkt. 3.99 (*0-671-73076-2*, Simon Pulse) Simon & Schuster Children's Publishing.

—Swiss Secrets: Passport to Romance. 1992. (Nancy Drew Files: No. 72). (YA). (gr. 6 up). 9.09 o.p. (*0-606-02023-3*) Turtleback Bks.

—A Talent for Murder. Greenberg, Anne, ed. 1992. (Nancy Drew Files: No. 75). 160p. (Orig.). (YA). (gr. 6 up). mass mkt. 3.99 (*0-671-73079-7*, Simon Pulse) Simon & Schuster Children's Publishing.

—Tall, Dark & Deadly. Greenberg, Ann, ed. 1991. (Nancy Drew Files: No. 66). 160p. (YA). (gr. 6 up). pap. 3.99 (*0-671-73070-3*, Simon Pulse) Simon & Schuster Children's Publishing.

—Target for Terror. 1995. (Nancy Drew & Hardy Boys Super Mystery Ser.: No. 24). 224p. (YA). (gr. 6 up). mass mkt. 3.99 (*0-671-88462-X*, Simon Pulse) Simon & Schuster Children's Publishing.

—The Teen Model Mystery. 1995. (Nancy Drew Mystery Stories Ser.: No. 125). (Illus.). 160p. (J). (gr. 3-6). pap. 4.99 (*0-671-87208-7*, Aladdin) Simon & Schuster Children's Publishing.

—The Teen Model Mystery. 1995. (Nancy Drew Mystery Stories Ser.: No. 125). (J). (gr. 3-6). 9.09 o.p. (*0-606-07921-1*) Turtleback Bks.

—Tell Me the Truth. 1995. (Nancy Drew on Campus Ser.: No. 4). 192p. (YA). (gr. 8 up). pap. 3.99 (*0-671-52745-2*, Simon Pulse) Simon & Schuster Children's Publishing.

—The Thanksgiving Surprise. 1995. (Nancy Drew Notebooks Ser.: No. 9). (Illus.). 80p. (J). (gr. k-3). pap. 3.99 (*0-671-52707-X*, Aladdin) Simon & Schuster Children's Publishing.

—The Thanksgiving Surprise. 1995. (Nancy Drew Notebooks Ser.: No. 9). (J). (gr. k-3). 8.70 o.p. (*0-606-08580-7*) Turtleback Bks.

—Third-Grade Reporter. 2000. (Nancy Drew Notebooks Ser.: No. 35). (Illus.). 80p. (J). (gr. k-3). pap. 3.99 (*0-671-04266-1*, Aladdin) Simon & Schuster Children's Publishing.

—The Thirteenth Pearl. (Nancy Drew Mystery Stories Ser.: No. 56). (Illus.). (J). (gr. 3-6). 1979. 179p. 7.25 o.p. (*0-448-19556-9*); 1978. 180p. 5.99 (*0-448-09556-4*) Penguin Putnam Bks. for Young Readers. (Grosset & Dunlap).

—This Side of Evil. 1990. (Nancy Drew Files: No. 14). 160p. (Orig.). (YA). (gr. 6 up). pap. 2.95 (*0-671-72227-1*, Simon Pulse) Simon & Schuster Children's Publishing.

—Thrill on the Hill. 1998. (Nancy Drew Notebooks Ser.: No. 28). 80p. (J). (gr. k-3). pap. 3.99 (*0-671-02492-2*, Aladdin) Simon & Schuster Children's Publishing.

—Till Death Do Us Part. 1989. (Nancy Drew Files: No. 24). 160p. (YA). (gr. 6 up). pap. 2.95 (*0-671-68378-0*, Simon Pulse) Simon & Schuster Children's Publishing.

—Tour of Danger. Greenberg, Anne, ed. 1992. (Nancy Drew & Hardy Boys Super Mystery Ser.: No. 12). 224p. (YA). (gr. 6 up). pap. 3.99 (*0-671-67468-4*, Simon Pulse) Simon & Schuster Children's Publishing.

—Tour of Danger. 1992. (Nancy Drew & Hardy Boys Super Mystery Ser.: No. 12). (YA). (gr. 6 up). 9.09 o.p. (*0-606-02040-3*) Turtleback Bks.

—Trail of Lies. Greenberg, Ann, ed. 1990. (Nancy Drew Files: No. 53). 160p. (Orig.). (YA). (gr. 6 up). pap. 3.75 (*0-671-70030-8*, Simon Pulse) Simon & Schuster Children's Publishing.

—Trash or Treasure? 2000. (Nancy Drew Notebooks Ser.: No. 34). (Illus.). 80p. (J). (gr. k-3). pap. 3.99 (*0-671-03873-7*, Aladdin) Simon & Schuster Children's Publishing.

—The Treasure in the Royal Tower. 1995. (Nancy Drew Mystery Stories Ser.: No. 128). 160p. (J). (gr. 3-6). pap. 3.99 (*0-671-50502-5*, Aladdin) Simon & Schuster Children's Publishing.

—The Treasure in the Royal Tower. 1995. (Nancy Drew Mystery Stories Ser.: No. 128). (J). (gr. 3-6). 9.09 o.p. (*0-606-08576-9*) Turtleback Bks.

—Trial by Fire. (Nancy Drew Files: No. 15). (Orig.). (YA). (gr. 6 up). 1991. pap. 3.50 (*0-671-73750-3*); 1987. 160p. pap. (*0-671-64138-7*) Simon & Schuster Children's Publishing. (Simon Pulse).

—The Triple Hoax. (Nancy Drew Mystery Stories Ser.: No. 57). (J). (gr. 3-6). 1989. 192p. pap. 3.99 (*0-671-69153-8*); 1987. (Illus.). 192p. pap. 3.50 (*0-671-64278-2*); 1979. (Illus.). 184p. pap. 3.50 (*0-671-95512-8*) Simon & Schuster Children's Publishing. (Aladdin).

—Tropic of Fear. Greenberg, Anne, ed. 1992. (Nancy Drew & Hardy Boys Super Mystery Ser.: No. 14). 224p. (Orig.). (YA). (gr. 6 up). mass mkt. 3.99 (*0-671-73126-2*, Simon Pulse) Simon & Schuster Children's Publishing.

—Trouble at Camp Treehouse. 1995. (Nancy Drew Notebooks Ser.: No. 7). (Illus.). 80p. (J). (gr. k-3). pap. 3.99 (*0-671-87951-0*, Aladdin) Simon & Schuster Children's Publishing.

—Trouble at Camp Treehouse. 1995. (Nancy Drew Notebooks Ser.: No. 7). (J). (gr. k-3). 10.14 (*0-606-07935-1*) Turtleback Bks.

—Trouble at Lake Tahoe. 1994. (Nancy Drew Mystery Stories Ser.: No. 118). 160p. (YA). (gr. 3-6). pap. 3.99 (*0-671-79304-7*, Aladdin) Simon & Schuster Children's Publishing.

—Trouble at Lake Tahoe. 1994. (Nancy Drew Mystery Stories Ser.: No. 118). (J). (gr. 3-6). 9.09 o.p. (*0-606-06596-2*) Turtleback Bks.

—Trouble in Tahiti. (Nancy Drew Files: No. 31). (YA). (gr. 6 up). 1991. pap. 3.50 (*0-671-73912-3*); 1989. pap. 2.95 (*0-671-64698-2*) Simon & Schuster Children's Publishing. (Simon Pulse).

—Trouble Takes the Cake. 1998. (Nancy Drew Notebooks Ser.: No. 27). (Illus.). 80p. (J). (gr. k-3). per. 3.99 (*0-671-02141-9*, Aladdin) Simon & Schuster Children's Publishing.

—The Twin Dilemma. (Nancy Drew Mystery Stories Ser.: No. 63). (J). (gr. 3-6). 1988. mass mkt. 3.99 (*0-671-67301-7*, Aladdin); 1986. pap. 3.50 (*0-671-62473-3*, Aladdin); 1981. (Illus.). 190p. pap. (*0-671-42358-4*, Simon & Schuster Children's Publishing); 1981. (Illus.). 190p. pap. 3.50 (*0-671-42359-2*, Aladdin) Simon & Schuster Children's Publishing.

—Two Points to Murder. l.t. ed. 1988. (Nancy Drew Files : No. 8). 151p. (YA). (gr. 6 up). reprint ed. 9.50 o.p. (*0-942545-39-7*); lib. bdg. 10.50 o.p. (*0-942545-34-6*) Grey Castle Pr.

—Two Points to Murder. 1991. (Nancy Drew Files: No. 8). (YA). (gr. 6 up). pap. 3.50 (*0-671-73663-9*, Simon Pulse) Simon & Schuster Children's Publishing.

—Under His Spell. 1996. (Nancy Drew Files: No. 116). (Illus.). 160p. (YA). (gr. 6 up). mass mkt. 3.99 (*0-671-50372-3*, Simon Pulse) Simon & Schuster Children's Publishing.

—Under His Spell. 1996. (Nancy Drew Files: No. 116). (YA). (gr. 6 up). 9.09 o.p. (*0-606-09671-X*) Turtleback Bks.

—Update on Crime. 1996. 150p. (Orig.). 22.98 (*0-671-85154-3*, Star Trek) Simon & Schuster.

—Update on Crime. Greenberg, Anne, ed. 1992. (Nancy Drew Files: No. 78). 160p. (Orig.). (YA). (gr. 6 up). pap. 3.75 (*0-671-73082-7*, Simon Pulse) Simon & Schuster Children's Publishing.

—Vanishing Act. (Nancy Drew Files: No. 34). (YA). (gr. 6 up). 1991. pap. 3.50 (*0-671-74655-3*); 1989. pap. 2.95 (*0-671-64701-6*) Simon & Schuster Children's Publishing. (Simon Pulse).

—Very Deadly Yours. 1988. (Nancy Drew Files: No. 20). (YA). (gr. 6 up). 160p. pap. 2.95 (*0-671-68061-7*); pap. (*0-671-64226-X*) Simon & Schuster Children's Publishing. (Simon Pulse).

—The Walkie-Talkie Mystery. 2001. (Nancy Drew Notebooks Ser.: Vol. 43). (J). (gr. k-3). reprint ed. E-Book 3.99 (*0-7434-2769-6*, Aladdin) Simon & Schuster Children's Publishing.

—The Wedding Day Mystery. 1997. (Nancy Drew Mystery Stories Ser.: No. 136). 160p. (J). (gr. 3-6). pap. 4.99 (*0-671-00050-0*, Aladdin) Simon & Schuster Children's Publishing.

—The Wedding Day Mystery. 1997. (Nancy Drew Mystery Stories Ser.: No. 136). (J). (gr. 3-6). 10.04 (*0-606-11661-3*) Turtleback Bks.

—The Wedding Gift Goof. 1996. (Nancy Drew Notebooks Ser.: No. 13). (Illus.). 80p. (J). (gr. k-3). pap. 3.99 (*0-671-53552-8*, Aladdin) Simon & Schuster Children's Publishing.

—The Wedding Gift Goof. 1996. (Nancy Drew Notebooks Ser.: No. 13). (J). (gr. k-3). 10.04 (*0-606-10267-1*) Turtleback Bks.

—The Whispering Statue. 2004. (Nancy Drew Mystery Stories Ser.: No. 14). (Illus.). 217p. (J). (gr. 3-6). 17.95 (*1-55709-260-5*) Applewood Bks.

—The Whispering Statue. 1937. (Nancy Drew Mystery Stories Ser.: No. 14). (Illus.). 180p. (J). (gr. 3-6). 5.99 (*0-448-09514-9*, Grosset & Dunlap) Penguin Putnam Bks. for Young Readers.

—Whispers in the Fog. 2000. (Nancy Drew Mystery Stories Ser.: No. 153). 160p. (J). (gr. 3-6). pap. 3.99 (*0-671-04133-9*, Aladdin) Simon & Schuster Children's Publishing.

—White Water Terror. Lt. ed. 1988. (Nancy Drew Files : No. 6). 149p. (YA). (gr. 6 up). reprint ed. 9.50 o.p. (*0-942545-37-0*); lib. bdg. 10.50 o.p. (*0-942545-32-X*) Grey Castle Pr.

—White Water Terror. (Nancy Drew Files: No. 6). (YA). (gr. 6 up). 1991. pap. 3.50 (*0-671-73661-2*); 1990. mass mkt. 2.95 (*0-671-72650-1*); 1986. pap. (*0-671-63020-2*) Simon & Schuster Children's Publishing. (Simon Pulse).

—Whose Pet Is Best? 1997. (Nancy Drew Notebooks Ser.: No. 17). 80p. (J). (gr. k-3). pap. 3.99 (*0-671-56861-2*, Aladdin) Simon & Schuster Children's Publishing.

—Whose Pet Is Best? 1997. (Nancy Drew Notebooks Ser.: No. 17). (J). (gr. k-3). 10.14 (*0-606-11670-2*) Turtleback Bks.

—Wicked for the Weekend. (Nancy Drew Files: No. 123). (YA). (gr. 6 up). 1997. 160p. per. 3.99 (*0-671-00748-3*); 1900. per. (*0-671-50412-6*) Simon & Schuster Children's Publishing. (Simon Pulse).

—Wicked Ways. 1996. (Nancy Drew Files: No. 113). 160p. (YA). (gr. 6 up). mass mkt. 3.99 (*0-671-50353-7*, Simon Pulse) Simon & Schuster Children's Publishing.

—Wicked Ways. 1996. (Nancy Drew Files: No. 113). (YA). (gr. 6 up). 9.09 o.p. (*0-606-09668-X*) Turtleback Bks.

—The Wild Cat Crime. 1998. (Nancy Drew Mystery Stories Ser.: No. 141). 160p. (J). (gr. 3-6). pap. 4.99 (*0-671-00120-5*, Aladdin) Simon & Schuster Children's Publishing.

—Win, Place or Die. 1990. (Nancy Drew Files: No. 46). 160p. (YA). (gr. 6 up). per. 3.50 (*0-671-67498-6*, Simon Pulse) Simon & Schuster Children's Publishing.

—Win, Place or Die. 1990. (Nancy Drew Files: No. 46). (YA). (gr. 6 up). 8.60 o.p. (*0-606-04589-9*) Turtleback Bks.

—Wings of Fear. 1989. (Nancy Drew Files: No. 13). 160p. (Orig.). (YA). (gr. 6 up). pap. 2.95 (*0-671-70140-1*, Simon Pulse) Simon & Schuster Children's Publishing.

—The Witch Tree Symbol. rev. ed. (Nancy Drew Mystery Stories Ser.: No. 33). (Illus.). (J). (gr. 3-6). 1974. 179p. 3.29 o.p. (*0-448-19533-X*); Vol. 33. 1956. 180p. 5.99 (*0-448-09533-5*) Penguin Putnam Bks. for Young Readers. (Grosset & Dunlap).

—The Wrong Chemistry. 1989. (Nancy Drew Files: No. 42). (YA). (gr. 6 up). pap. 2.95 (*0-671-67494-3*, Simon Pulse) Simon & Schuster Children's Publishing.

—The Wrong Track. Greenberg, Anne, ed. 1991. (Nancy Drew Files: No. 64). 160p. (Orig.). (YA). (gr. 6 up). pap. 3.99 (*0-671-73068-1*, Simon Pulse) Simon & Schuster Children's Publishing.

Keene, Carolyn & Dixon, Franklin W. The Alaskan Mystery. Arico, Diane, ed. 1985. (Nancy Drew & Hardy Boys: No. 5). (Illus.). 120p. (Orig.). (J). (gr. 3-7). pap. 2.95 (*0-671-54550-7*, Aladdin) Simon & Schuster Children's Publishing.

—Best of Enemies. Greenberg, Ann, ed. 1991. (Nancy Drew & Hardy Boys Super Mystery Ser.: No. 9). 224p. (YA). (gr. 6 up). per. 3.99 (*0-671-67465-X*, Simon Pulse) Simon & Schuster Children's Publishing.

—Best of Enemies. 1991. (Nancy Drew & Hardy Boys Super Mystery Ser.: No. 9). (YA). (gr. 6 up). 9.09 o.p. (*0-606-04876-6*) Turtleback Bks.

—Buried in Time. Greenberg, Ann, ed. 1990. (Nancy Drew & Hardy Boys Super Mystery Ser.: No. 7). 224p. (YA). (gr. 6 up). reprint ed. mass mkt. 3.99 (*0-671-67463-3*, Simon Pulse) Simon & Schuster Children's Publishing.

—A Crime for Christmas. 1991. (Nancy Drew & Hardy Boys Super Mystery Ser.: No. 2). (YA). (gr. 7-12). pap. 3.99 (*0-671-74617-0*, Simon Pulse) Simon & Schuster Children's Publishing.

—A Crime for Christmas. 1988. (Nancy Drew & Hardy Boys Super Mystery Ser.: No. 2). (YA). (gr. 6 up). 10.04 (*0-606-04110-9*) Turtleback Bks.

—Danger on Ice. Schwartz, Betty Ann, ed. 1984. (Nancy Drew & Hardy Boys: No. 2). (Illus.). 117p. (Orig.). (J). (gr. 3-7). pap. 2.85 (*0-671-49920-3*, Aladdin) Simon & Schuster Children's Publishing.

—Dangerous Games. (Nancy Drew & Hardy Boys Super Mystery Ser.: No. 4). (Orig.). (YA). (gr. 6 up). 1991. mass mkt. 3.99 (*0-671-74108-X*); 1989. pap. 2.95 (*0-671-64920-5*) Simon & Schuster Children's Publishing. (Simon Pulse).

—Double Crossing. 1988. (Nancy Drew & Hardy Boys Super Mystery Ser.: No. 1). (YA). (gr. 6 up). 9.09 o.p. (*0-606-03772-1*) Turtleback Bks.

—The Feathered Serpent. Schwartz, Betty Ann, ed. 1984. (Nancy Drew & Hardy Boys: No. 3). (Illus.). 122p. (Orig.). (J). (gr. 3-7). pap. 3.50 (*0-671-49921-1*, Aladdin) Simon & Schuster Children's Publishing.

—Jungle of Evil. Arico, Diane, ed. 1985. (Nancy Drew & Hardy Boys: No. 7). (Illus.). 128p. (Orig.). (J). (gr. 3-7). pap. 2.95 (*0-671-55734-3*, Simon & Schuster Children's Publishing) Simon & Schuster Children's Publishing.

—The Last Resort. 1990. (Nancy Drew & Hardy Boys Super Mystery Ser.: No. 5). 224p. (YA). (gr. 6 up). mass mkt. 3.99 (*0-671-67461-7*, Simon Pulse) Simon & Schuster Children's Publishing.

—The Missing Money Mystery. Arico, Diane, ed. 1985. (Nancy Drew & Hardy Boys: No. 6). (Illus.). 117p. (J). (gr. 3-7). pap. 2.95 (*0-671-54551-5*, Aladdin) Simon & Schuster Children's Publishing.

—Mystery Train. Greenberg, Ann, ed. 1990. (Nancy Drew & Hardy Boys Super Mystery Ser.: No. 8). 224p. (YA). (gr. 6 up). pap. 3.99 (*0-671-67464-1*, Simon Pulse) Simon & Schuster Children's Publishing.

—Mystery Train. 1990. (Nancy Drew & Hardy Boys Super Mystery Ser.: No. 8). (YA). (gr. 6 up). 10.04 (*0-606-04758-1*) Turtleback Bks.

—Nancy Drew & the Hardy Boys Campfire Stories. 1984. (Illus.). 156p. (J). (gr. 2-7). pap. 3.50 (*0-671-50198-4*, Aladdin) Simon & Schuster Children's Publishing.

—Nancy Drew & the Hardy Boys Super Sleuths: Seven New Mysteries. 1982. (Illus.). 189p. (Orig.). (J). (gr. 3-7). pap. 8.95 o.p. (*0-671-44429-8*, Simon & Schuster Children's Publishing); pap. 3.50 (*0-671-43375-X*, Aladdin) Simon & Schuster Children's Publishing.

—Nancy Drew & the Hardy Boys Super Sleuths 2: Seven New Mysteries. 1984. (Illus.). 160p. (J). (gr. 3-7). pap. 3.50 (*0-671-50194-1*, Aladdin) Simon & Schuster Children's Publishing.

—The Paris Connection. (Nancy Drew & Hardy Boys Super Mystery Ser.: No. 6). (YA). (gr. 6 up). 1991. 224p. mass mkt. 3.99 (*0-671-74675-8*); 1990. mass mkt. 2.95 (*0-671-67462-5*) Simon & Schuster Children's Publishing. (Simon Pulse).

—Secret Cargo. Schwartz, Betty Ann, ed. 1984. (Nancy Drew & Hardy Boys: No. 4). (Illus.). 116p. (Orig.). (J). (gr. 3-7). pap. 3.50 (*0-671-49922-X*, Aladdin) Simon & Schuster Children's Publishing.

—The Secret of the Knight's Sword. Schwartz, Betty Ann, ed. 1984. (Nancy Drew & Hardy Boys: No. 1). (Illus.). 122p. (Orig.). (J). (gr. 3-7). pap. 3.50 (*0-671-49919-X*, Aladdin) Simon & Schuster Children's Publishing.

—Shock Waves. 1991. (Nancy Drew & Hardy Boys Super Mystery Ser.: No. 3). (YA). (gr. 6 up). pap. 3.99 (*0-671-74393-7*, Simon Pulse) Simon & Schuster Children's Publishing.

—Ticket to Intrigue. Arico, Diane, ed. 1985. (Nancy Drew & Hardy Boys: No. 8). (Illus.). 128p. (Orig.). (J). (gr. 3-7). pap. 2.95 (*0-671-55735-1*, Simon & Schuster Children's Publishing) Simon & Schuster Children's Publishing.

Keene, Carolyn & Greene, James. The Missing Horse Mystery. 1998. (Nancy Drew Mystery Stories Ser.: No. 145). 160p. (J). (gr. 3-6). pap. 4.99 (*0-671-00754-8*, Aladdin) Simon & Schuster Children's Publishing.

Keene, Carolyn & Jones, Jan Naimo. The Purple Fingerprint. 2001. (Nancy Drew Notebooks Ser.: Vol. 44). (Illus.). 80p. (J). (gr. k-3). pap. 3.99 (*0-7434-0692-3*, Aladdin) Simon & Schuster Children's Publishing.

Keene, Carolyn & Nugent, Elizabeth. The Case of Capital Intrigue. 1998. (Nancy Drew Mystery Stories Ser.: No. 142). 160p. (J). (gr. 3-6). pap. 3.99 (*0-671-00751-3*, Aladdin) Simon & Schuster Children's Publishing.

—Mystery on Maui. 1998. (Nancy Drew Mystery Stories Ser.: No. 143). 160p. (J). (gr. 3-6). pap. 4.99 (*0-671-00753-X*, Aladdin) Simon & Schuster Children's Publishing.

Keene, Carolyn & Schwarz, Joanie. The Carousel Mystery. 2003. (Nancy Drew Notebooks Ser.). (Illus.). 80p. (J). pap. 3.99 (*0-689-86342-X*, Aladdin) Simon & Schuster Children's Publishing.

Keene, Carolyn & Whelan, Patrick. Danger on the Great Lakes. 2003. (Nancy Drew Ser.). (Illus.). 160p. (J). pap. 4.99 (*0-689-86146-X*, 53545777, Aladdin) Simon & Schuster Children's Publishing.

—A Taste of Danger. 2003. (Nancy Drew Ser.). (Illus.). 176p. (J). pap. 4.99 (*0-689-86154-0*, Aladdin) Simon & Schuster Children's Publishing.

—Werewolf in a Winter Wonderland. 2003. (Nancy Drew Ser.). (Illus.). 160p. (J). pap. 4.99 (*0-689-86182-6*, Aladdin) Simon & Schuster Children's Publishing.

Schwarz, Joanie & Keene, Carolyn. The Stinky Cheese Surprise. 2003. (Nancy Drew Notebooks Ser.). (Illus.). 80p. (J). pap. 3.99 (*0-689-85694-6*, Aladdin) Simon & Schuster Children's Publishing.

—Turkey Trouble. 2003. (Nancy Drew Notebooks Ser.). (Illus.). 80p. (J). pap. 3.99 (*0-689-85696-2*, Aladdin) Simon & Schuster Children's Publishing.

Stratemeyer Syndicate Staff. The Hardy Boys & Nancy Drew Meet Dracula. 1978. (Illus.). 109p. (J). (gr. 3-6). 3.95 o.p. (*0-448-16196-6*, Grosset & Dunlap) Penguin Putnam Bks. for Young Readers.

E

EARHART, AMELIA, 1898-1937—FICTION

Ryan, Pam Muñoz. Amelia & Eleanor Go for a Ride. 1999. (Illus.). 40p. (J). (gr. k-4). pap. 16.95 (*0-590-96075-X*) Scholastic, Inc.

Sobol, Donald J. My Name Is Amelia. 1994. 112p. (J). (gr. 4-8). 14.00 o.p. (*0-689-31970-3*, Atheneum) Simon & Schuster Children's Publishing.

Wehr, Fred. Amelia. 1994. (J). 16.95 (*1-877853-33-X*) Nautical & Aviation Publishing Co. of America, Inc., The.

Wickham, Martha. Mysterious Journey: Amelia Earhart's Last Flight. 1997. (Smithsonian Odyssey Ser.). (Illus.). 32p. (J). (gr. 2-5). 14.95 (*1-56899-407-9*); (gr. 2-5). pap. 5.95 (*1-56899-408-7*); (gr. 4-7). 19.95 incl. audio (*1-56899-412-5*, BC6006); (gr. 4-7). 19.95 incl. audio (*1-56899-412-5*, BC6006);Incl. toy. (gr. 2-5). 29.95 (*1-56899-409-5*);Incl. toy. (gr. 2-5). 35.95 incl. audio (*1-56899-413-3*);Incl. toy. (gr. 2-5). pap. 17.95 (*1-56899-410-9*);Incl. toy. (gr. 2-5). pap. 25.95 incl. audio (*1-56899-411-7*);Incl. toy. (gr. 2-5). pap. 25.95 incl. audio (*1-56899-411-7*) Soundprints.

EDISON, THOMAS A. (THOMAS ALVA), 1847-1931—FICTION

Roop, Peter & Roop, Connie. Turn on the Light, Thomas Edison! 2003. (Illus.). 58p. (J). (*0-439-43927-2*) Scholastic, Inc.

Sargent, Dave & Sargent, Pat. Ginger (Lilac Roan) Be Likeable. 2003. (Saddle Up Ser.: Vol. 27). (Illus.). 42p. (J). lib. bdg. 22.60 (*1-56763-811-2*); mass mkt. 6.95 (*1-56763-812-0*) Ozark Publishing.

EDWARD VI, KING OF ENGLAND, 1537-1553—FICTION

Disney Staff. The Prince & the Pauper. 1990. (Penguin-Disney Ser.). (J). text 6.98 o.p. (*0-8317-2433-1*, Viking Children's Bks.) Penguin Putnam Bks. for Young Readers.

Disney, Walter Elias. The Prince & the Pauper. 1991. (Disney Little Libraries Ser.). (J). text 5.98 o.p. (*0-8317-2472-2*) Smithmark Pubs., Inc.

Fishkin, Shelley Fisher, ed. The Prince & the Pauper: A Tale for Young People of All Ages (1881) 1997. (Oxford Mark Twain Ser.). (Illus.). 496p. (J). text 22.00 o.p. (*0-19-511406-X*) Oxford Univ. Pr., Inc.

Krulik, Nancy E. The Prince & the Pauper. 1990. (J). mass mkt. 2.75 o.p. (*0-590-44364-X*) Scholastic, Inc.

Mayer, Marianna. The Prince & the Pauper. Arico, Diane, ed. deluxe ed. 1999. (Illus.). 48p. (J). 17.99 o.p. (*0-8037-2099-8*, Dial Bks. for Young Readers) Penguin Putnam Bks. for Young Readers.

Reynolds, Joyce. The Prince & the Pauper: Christmas Program. 1979. 32p. 2.25 o.p. (*0-88243-102-1*, 30-0102) Gospel Publishing Hse.

Twain, Mark. Historical Romances: The Prince & the Pauper; A Connecticut Yankee in King Arthur's Court; Personal Recollections of Joan of Arc. Harris, Susan K., ed. 1994. (Library of America: Vol. 71). 1050p. 35.00 (*0-940450-82-8*) Library of America, The.

—The Prince & the Pauper. (J). E-Book 3.95 (*0-594-05640-3*) 1873 Pr.

—The Prince & the Pauper. 2002. (Great Illustrated Classics). (Illus.). 240p. (J). (gr. 3-8). lib. bdg. 21.35 (*1-57765-698-9*, ABDO & Daughters) ABDO Publishing Co.

—The Prince & the Pauper. (Illus.). 72p. (YA). (gr. 4 up). pap. 7.95 (*1-55576-096-1*, EDN206B) AV Concepts Corp.

—The Prince & the Pauper. 1997. (Classics Illustrated Study Guides). (Illus.). 64p. (YA). (gr. 7 up). mass mkt., stu. ed. 4.99 o.p. (*1-57840-012-0*) Acclaim Bks.

—The Prince & the Pauper. 1977. (J). 1.50 o.s.i (*0-448-12942-6*) Ace Bks.

—The Prince & the Pauper. 1964. (Airmont Classics Ser.). (J). (gr. 5 up). mass mkt. 2.50 (*0-8049-0032-9*, CL-32) Airmont Publishing Co., Inc.

—The Prince & the Pauper. (J). 19.95 (*0-8488-0849-5*) Amereon, Ltd.

—The Prince & the Pauper. 1994. (Illustrated Classics Collection: No. 4). 64p. (J). pap. 4.95 (*0-7854-0751-0*, 40506) American Guidance Service, Inc.

—The Prince & the Pauper. 1996. (Andre Deutsch Classics). 240p. (J). (gr. 5-8). 11.95 (*0-233-99080-1*) Andre Deutsch GBR. *Dist:* Trafalgar Square, Trans-Atlantic Pubns., Inc.

—The Prince & the Pauper. 1983. (Bantam Classics Ser.). 240p. (gr. 4-11). mass mkt. 3.95 (*0-553-21256-7*) Bantam Bks.

—The Prince & the Pauper. 1982. (J). reprint ed. lib. bdg. 20.95 (*0-89966-380-X*) Buccaneer Bks., Inc.

—The Prince & the Pauper. 1999. (YA). reprint ed. pap. text 28.00 (*1-4047-1120-1*) Classic Textbooks.

—The Prince & the Pauper. 1985. 256p. (J). (gr. k-6). pap. 3.99 o.s.i (*0-440-47186-9*) Dell Publishing.

—The Prince & the Pauper. 1992. 234p. (YA). mass mkt. 2.99 (*0-8125-0477-1*, Tor Classics) Doherty, Tom Assocs., LLC.

—The Prince & the Pauper. 2000. (Dover Thrift Editions Ser.). 176p. (YA). pap. 2.00 (*0-486-41110-9*) Dover Pubns., Inc.

—The Prince & the Pauper. (J). E-Book 1.79 (*1-929120-66-4*) Electric Umbrella Publishing.

—The Prince & the Pauper. (YA). (gr. 5-12). pap. 9.95 (*0-8224-9344-6*) Globe Fearon Educational Publishing.

—The Prince & the Pauper. 1942. (Illus.). (J). reprint ed. lib. bdg. 11.89 o.p. (*0-06-014406-8*) Harper-Trade.

—The Prince & the Pauper. l.t. ed. (J). 375p. pap. 33.05 (*0-7583-1955-X*); 591p. pap. 49.06 (*0-7583-1957-6*); 293p. pap. 26.54 (*0-7583-1954-1*); 843p. pap. 67.14 (*0-7583-1959-2*); 727p. pap. 57.32 (*0-7583-1958-4*); 214p. pap. 21.12 (*0-7583-1953-3*); 480p. pap. 40.86 (*0-7583-1956-8*); 171p. pap. 18.68 (*0-7583-1952-5*); 293p. lib. bdg. 32.54 (*0-7583-1946-0*); 843p. lib. bdg. 85.24 (*0-7583-1951-7*); 171p. lib. bdg. 24.68 (*0-7583-1944-4*); 727p. lib. bdg. 63.32 (*0-7583-1950-9*); 591p. lib. bdg. 55.06 (*0-7583-1949-5*); 214p. lib. bdg. 27.12 (*0-7583-1945-2*); 375p. lib. bdg. 39.05 (*0-7583-1947-9*); 480p. lib. bdg. 46.86 (*0-7583-1948-7*) Huge Print Pr.

—The Prince & the Pauper. (J). 9.95 (*1-56156-311-0*) Kidsbooks, Inc.

—The Prince & the Pauper. l.t. ed. 2000. (Large Print Heritage Ser.). 364p. (J). lib. bdg. 33.95 (*1-58118-068-3*, 23662) LRS.

—The Prince & the Pauper. 1981. (English As a Second Language Bk.). (J). pap. text 5.95 o.p. (*0-582-53422-4*) Longman Publishing Group.

—The Prince & the Pauper. (J). 1982. 544p. mass mkt. 3.50 o.p. (*0-451-51628-1*, CE1628); 1964. 224p. (gr. 6). mass mkt. 3.95 o.s.i (*0-451-52193-5*) NAL. (Signet Classics).

—The Prince & the Pauper. abr. ed. 1996. (Children's Classics Ser.). (Illus.). (J). 6.95 o.p. (*0-7871-0639-9*); 19.95 o.p. (*0-7871-0638-0*, 694016) NewStar Media, Inc.

—The Prince & the Pauper. 1995. (Illus.). 78p. (J). pap. text 5.95 (*0-19-586304-6*) Oxford Univ. Pr., Inc.

—The Prince & the Pauper. Fago, John N., ed. 1978. (Now Age Illustrated IV Ser.). (Illus.). (J). (gr. 4-12). stu. ed. 1.25 (*0-88301-341-X*); text 7.50 o.p. (*0-88301-329-0*); pap. text 2.95 (*0-88301-317-7*) Pendulum Pr., Inc.

—The Prince & the Pauper. (Classics for Young Readers Ser.). 1983. 256p. (J). (gr. 3-7). pap. 3.50 o.p. (*0-14-035017-9*); 1996. (Illus.). 288p. (YA). (gr. 5-9). pap. 4.99 (*0-14-036749-7*) Penguin Putnam Bks. for Young Readers. (Puffin Bks.).

—The Prince & the Pauper. Vogel, Malvina, ed. 1992. (Great Illustrated Classics Ser.: Vol. 22). (Illus.). 240p. (J). (gr. 3-6). 9.95 (*0-86611-973-6*) Playmore, Inc., Pubs.

—The Prince & the Pauper. 1987. (Regents Illustrated Classics Ser.). (Illus.). 62p. (YA). (gr. 7-12). pap. text 3.75 o.p. (*0-13-703027-4*, 20494) Prentice Hall, ESL Dept.

—The Prince & the Pauper. 1965. (J). (gr. 4-6). 2.95 o.p. (*0-448-05477-9*) Putnam Publishing Group, The.

—The Prince & the Pauper. 2003. (Modern Library Classics). (Illus.). 240p. pap. 8.95 (*0-375-76112-8*, Modern Library) Random House Adult Trade Publishing Group.

—The Prince & the Pauper. (Illus.). 294p. 1994. (J). 12.99 o.s.i (*0-517-11815-7*); 1988. (YA). 0.99 o.s.i (*0-517-66845-9*) Random Hse. Value Publishing.

—The Prince & the Pauper. 1988. (Illus.). 238p. (J). 13.95 o.p. (*0-89577-295-7*) Reader's Digest Assn., Inc., The.

—The Prince & the Pauper. 1988. (Works of Mark Twain). (J). reprint ed. lib. bdg. 79.00 (*0-7812-1120-4*) Reprint Services Corp.

—The Prince & the Pauper. (J). 9999. pap. 2.25 o.s.i (*0-590-03126-0*); 1991. 3.50 o.p. (*0-590-44817-X*) Scholastic, Inc.

—The Prince & the Pauper. l.t. ed. 2000. (Perennial Bestsellers Ser.). 307p. (J). 26.95 (*0-7838-9061-3*) Thorndike Pr.

—The Prince & the Pauper. Fischer, Victor et al, eds. 1979. (Iowa-California Edition of the Works of Mark Twain: No. 6). (Illus.). 551p. (J). text 65.00 (*0-520-03622-0*) Univ. of California Pr.

—The Prince & the Pauper. 1997. 224p. (J). pap. 8.95 (*0-14-043669-3*, Penguin Classics) Viking Penguin.

—The Prince & the Pauper. 1998. (Children's Library). (J). pap. 3.95 (*1-85326-147-5*, 1475WW) Wordsworth Editions, Ltd. GBR. *Dist:* Combined Publishing.

—The Prince & the Pauper: A Tale for Young People of All Ages. 1964. (J). 10.00 (*0-606-01271-0*) Turtleback Bks.

—The Prince & the Pauper: With a Discussion of Respect. 2003. (Values in Action Illustrated Classics Ser.). (J). (*1-59203-052-1*) Learning Challenge, Inc.

Twain, Mark & Martens, Anne C. The Prince & the Pauper - Straight. 1970. (J). 3.60 (*0-87129-417-6*, P37) Dramatic Publishing Co.

Twain, Mark, et al. The Prince & the Pauper. abr. ed. 1997. (Children's Thrift Editions Ser.). (Illus.). 107p. (J). reprint ed. pap. text 1.00 (*0-486-29383-1*) Dover Pubns., Inc.

EEYORE (FICTITIOUS CHARACTER)—FICTION

The Book of Boo! 2002. (Illus.). 32p. (J). (ps-1). 5.99 (*0-7868-3364-5*) Disney Pr.

Disney Staff. Eeyore's Mail Surprise. 2001. (Illus.). 12p. (J). bds. 7.99 o.s.i (*0-7364-1201-8*, RH/Disney) Random Hse. Children's Bks.

Milne, A. A., pseud. Eeyore. 2000. (Pooh Giant Shaped Board Bks.). (Illus.). 10p. (YA). (ps up). bds. 7.99 (*0-525-46332-1*, Dutton Children's Bks.) Penguin Putnam Bks. for Young Readers.

—Eeyore Clip & Read. abr. ed. 1999. (Illus.). 24p. (ps-3). bds. 2.99 o.s.i (*0-525-46206-6*, Dutton Children's Bks.) Penguin Putnam Bks. for Young Readers.

—Eeyore Has a Birthday. (Easy-to-Read Ser.). (Illus.). 2001. 48p. (J). pap. 3.99 (*0-14-230042-X*, Puffin Bks.); 1999. 12p. bds. 5.99 o.s.i (*0-525-46118-3*); 1996. 24p. (J). bds. 3.99 o.s.i (*0-525-45528-0*, Dutton Children's Bks.) Penguin Putnam Bks. for Young Readers.

—Eeyore Has a Birthday. 2001. (Illus.). 48p. (J). 13.99 o.s.i (*0-525-46764-5*, Dutton Children's Bks.) Penguin Putnam Bks. for Young Readers.

—Eeyore Loses a Tail. (Winnie-the-Pooh Deluxe Picture Bks.). (Illus.). 32p. (J). (ps-3). 2000. 9.99 o.s.i (*0-525-46456-5*); 1993. 4.99 o.p. (*0-525-45137-4*); 1993. 13.99 o.p. (*0-525-45045-9*) Penguin Putnam Bks. for Young Readers. (Dutton Children's Bks.).

—Eeyore Loses a Tail. Ketchersid, Sarah, ed. abr. ed. 2001. (Illus.). 12p. (J). (ps-k). 6.99 o.s.i (*0-525-46703-3*, Dutton Children's Bks.) Penguin Putnam Bks. for Young Readers.

—Where Is Eeyore: Slide & Find Books. 2001. (Illus.). 4p. (J). (ps-k). 6.99 (*0-525-46540-5*, Dutton Children's Bks.) Penguin Putnam Bks. for Young Readers.

Random House Disney Staff. Eeyore's Not-So-Gloomy Day. 2003. (Illus.). 12p. (J). bds. 6.99 (*0-7364-2055-X*, RH/Disney) Random Hse. Children's Bks.

ELIZABETH I, QUEEN OF ENGLAND, 1533-1603—FICTION

King-Smith, Dick. Titus Rules! 2003. (Illus.). 96p. (J). (gr. 2-4). lib. bdg. 17.99 (*0-375-91461-7*); 15.95 (*0-375-81461-2*) Random Hse. Children's Bks. (Knopf Bks. for Young Readers).

Meyer, Carolyn. Beware, Princess Elizabeth. (Young Royals Ser.). 2002. (Illus.). 224p. (YA). pap. 5.95 (*0-15-204556-2*); 2001. (J). 17.00 (*0-15-202639-8*); 2001. (Illus.). 224p. (YA). (gr. 7 up). 17.00 (*0-15-202659-2*) Harcourt Children's Bks. (Gulliver Bks.).

Sheedy, Alexandra Elizabeth. She Was Nice to Mice. 1977. pap. 0.95 o.p. (*0-440-47844-8*) Dell Publishing.

Stainer, M. L. The Lyon's Throne. 1999. (Lyon Saga Ser.: Bk. 4). (Illus.). 153p. (YA). (gr. 5-9). pap. 6.95 (*1-893337-02-2*) Chicken Soup Pr., Inc.

ELMO (FICTITIOUS CHARACTER)—FICTION

Albee, Sarah. Elmo Goes to the Doctor. 2001. (Illus.). 32p. (J). (ps-k). 3.99 o.s.i (*0-375-81303-9*, Random Hse. Bks. for Young Readers) Random Hse. Children's Bks.

—Elmo Loves You. (Big Bird's Favorites Board Bks.). 24p. (J). (ps). 2002. (Illus.). bds. 4.99 (*0-375-81208-3*, Random Hse. Bks. for Young Readers); 1998. 3.99 o.s.i (*0-307-16188-9*, Golden Bks.) Random Hse. Children's Bks.

Elmo & the Monsters. 2001. (J). text (*1-931312-39-7*) SoftPlay, Inc.

Golden Books Staff. Elmo & the Baby Animals. 1999. (Golden's Sesame Street Ser.). 24p. (ps-3). pap. 6.98 incl. audio (*0-307-47703-7*, Golden Bks.) Random Hse. Children's Bks.

—Elmo Loves Easter. 1999. (Illus.). 32p. pap. 3.99 o.s.i (*0-307-09226-7*, Golden Bks.) Random Hse. Children's Bks.

Muntean, Michaela. Elmo & the Baby Animals. 1994. (Golden Book Ser.). (Illus.). 24p. (J). (ps-3). pap. o.p. incl. audio (*0-307-14352-X*, 14352, Golden Bks.) Random Hse. Children's Bks.

Samuels, Catherine. Elmo's New Puppy. 1999. (Golden's Sesame Street Ser.). 24p. 2.29 o.s.i (*0-307-98897-X*, Golden Bks.) Random Hse. Children's Bks.

—Elmo's New Puppy. 2000. (Jellybean Bks.). (Illus.). 24p. (J). (ps). 2.99 o.s.i (*0-375-80450-1*) Random Hse., Inc.

Stiles, Norman & Berger, Lou. Elmo Goes Around the Corner - on Sesame Street. 1994. (Please Read to Me Ser.). (Illus.). 32p. (Orig.). (J). (ps-3). pap. 3.25 o.s.i (*0-679-85455-X*, Random Hse. Bks. for Young Readers) Random Hse. Children's Bks.

ELOISE (FICTITIOUS CHARACTER)—FICTION

Thompson, Kay. Eloise. 1991. (Eloise Ser.). (Illus.). 66p. (J). reprint ed. 35.95 (*0-89966-833-X*) Buccaneer Bks., Inc.

—Eloise. 2002. (SPA., Illus.). 64p. (J). (gr. k-3). 17.00 (*84-264-3735-4*, LM30420) Editorial Lumen ESP. *Dist:* Lectorum Pubns., Inc.

—Eloise. 5th ed. 1998. (FRE.). (J). (ps-3). pap. 13.95 (*2-07-052125-7*) Gallimard, Editions FRA. *Dist:* Distribooks, Inc.

—Eloise. 2002. (SPA.). 68p. 18.95 (*1-4000-0173-0*) Random Hse., Inc.

—Eloise. 1982. (Eloise Ser). (FRE.). 116p. (J). (gr. 5-10). pap. 10.95 (*2-07-033223-3*) Schoenhof's Foreign Bks., Inc.

—Eloise. (Illus.). (ps). 2001. 64p. 22.00 incl. audio compact disk (*0-689-84311-9*); 2001. 64p. 22.00 incl. audio compact disk (*0-689-84311-9*); 1995. 64p. (J). 100.00 o.s.i (*0-689-80168-8*); 1969. 68p. (J). 18.00 (*0-671-22350-X*) Simon & Schuster Children's Publishing. (Simon & Schuster Children's Publishing).

—Eloise: The Absolutely Essential Edition. 1999. (Illus.). 80p. (J). (ps-3). 19.95 (*0-689-82703-2*); 150.00 o.s.i (*0-689-82883-7*) Simon & Schuster Children's Publishing. (Simon & Schuster Children's Publishing).

—Eloise: The Ultimate Edition. 2000. (Illus.). 304p. (J). (ps-3). 35.00 (*0-689-83990-1*, Simon & Schuster Children's Publishing) Simon & Schuster Children's Publishing.

—Eloise a Paris. 5th ed. 1999. Orig. Title: Eloise in Paris. (FRE., Illus.). (J). (ps-3). pap. 13.95 (*2-07-052625-9*) Gallimard, Editions FRA. *Dist:* Distribooks, Inc.

—Eloise at Christmastime. (J). 2003. 32p. 6.99 (*0-689-86982-7*, Simon Spotlight); 1999. (Illus.). 56p. 17.00 (*0-689-83039-4*, Simon & Schuster Children's Publishing); 1999. (Illus.). 100.00 o.s.i (*0-689-83286-9*, Simon & Schuster Children's Publishing) Simon & Schuster Children's Publishing.

—Eloise en Navidad. 2002. (SPA., Illus.). 56p. (J). (gr. k-3). 17.00 (*84-264-3748-6*, LM4922) Editorial Lumen ESP. *Dist:* Lectorum Pubns., Inc.

—Eloise en Navidad. 2002. (SPA.). 56p. 17.95 (*1-4000-0239-7*) Random Hse., Inc.

—Eloise in Moscow. 2000. 80p. (J). ltd. ed. 150.00 (*0-689-83328-8*); 40th ed. (Illus.). 17.00 (*0-689-83211-7*) Simon & Schuster Children's Publishing. (Simon & Schuster Children's Publishing).

—Eloise in Paris. 1991. (Eloise Ser.). (Illus.). 66p. (J). reprint ed. lib. bdg. 35.95 (*0-89966-834-8*) Buccaneer Bks., Inc.

—Eloise in Paris. 1999. (J). (ps-3). (Illus.). 72p. 17.00 (*0-689-82704-0*); 64p. 100.00 o.s.i (*0-689-82960-4*) Simon & Schuster Children's Publishing. (Simon & Schuster Children's Publishing).

—Eloise Takes a Bawth. ltd. ed. 2002. 300.00 (*0-689-84694-0*, Simon & Schuster Children's Publishing) Simon & Schuster Children's Publishing.

—Eloise's Guide to Life: Or How to Eat, Dress, Travel, Behave & Stay Six Forever. 2000. (Illus.). 48p. (J). (ps-3). 9.95 (*0-689-83310-5*, Simon & Schuster Children's Publishing) Simon & Schuster Children's Publishing.

Thompson, Kay & Crowley, Mart. Eloise Takes a Bawth. 2002. (Illus.). 62p. (J). (ps-3). 17.95 (*0-689-84288-0*, Simon & Schuster Children's Publishing) Simon & Schuster Children's Publishing.

EMILY (FICTITIOUS CHARACTER)—FICTION

Masurel, Claire. Emily & Her Daddy. 2003. (Lift-the-Flap Ser.). (Illus.). 16p. pap. 6.99 (*0-14-250080-1*, Puffin Bks.) Penguin Putnam Bks. for Young Readers.

Montgomery, L. M. Emily Climbs. 1976. 336p. (YA). 25.95 (*0-8488-0588-7*) Amereon, Ltd.

—Emily Climbs. 1984. 336p. (YA). mass mkt. 4.99 (*0-7704-2032-X*) Bantam Bks.

—Emily Climbs. 1996. 336p. (J). (gr. 7 up). mass mkt. 4.95 (*0-7710-9980-0*) McClelland & Stewart/Tundra Bks.

—Emily Climbs. 1983. 336p. (YA). (gr. 7 up). mass mkt. 4.99 (*0-553-26214-9*, Starfire) Random Hse. Children's Bks.

—Emily of New Moon. 1976. 360p. (J). 25.95 (*0-8488-0589-5*) Amereon, Ltd.

—Emily of New Moon. unabr. ed. Set. 1989. (YA). (gr. 8 up). 47.95 incl. audio; Set 1999. (J). (gr. 5-6). pap. 47.95 incl. audio (*1-55685-579-6*) Audio Bk. Contractors, Inc.

—Emily of New Moon. 1983. 352p. (YA). mass mkt. 4.99 (*0-7704-1798-1*); (gr. 4-7). mass mkt. 4.99 (*0-553-23370-X*) Bantam Bks.

—Emily of New Moon. unabr. ed. 1999. (YA). (gr. 4-7). audio 62.95 (*0-7861-1488-6*, 118471) Blackstone Audio Bks., Inc.

—Emily of New Moon, Set. unabr. ed. 1999. (J). audio 62.95 Highsmith Inc.

—Emily of New Moon. 1996. 368p. (J). (gr. 4-7). mass mkt. 4.95 (*0-7710-9979-7*) McClelland & Stewart/Tundra Bks.

—Emily of New Moon. 1999. 144p. (gr. 2-5). pap. text 3.99 (*0-440-41613-2*, Dell Books for Young Readers) Random Hse. Children's Bks.

—Emily of New Moon. l.t. ed. 1980. (Ulverscroft Large Print Ser.). 29.99 o.p. (*0-7089-0401-7*, Ulverscroft) Thorpe, F. A. Pubs. GBR. *Dist:* Ulverscroft Large Print Bks., Ltd., Ulverscroft Large Print Canada, Ltd.

—Emily's Quest. 1976. 236p. (J). 21.95 (*0-8488-0590-9*) Amereon, Ltd.

—Emily's Quest. 1984. 240p. (YA). mass mkt. 4.99 (*0-7704-2060-5*); 1983. (J). mass mkt. 2.95 o.s.i (*0-553-23323-8*); 1983. 240p. (YA). (gr. 4-7). mass mkt. 4.99 (*0-553-26493-1*) Bantam Bks.

—Emily's Quest. 1982. reprint ed. lib. bdg. 16.95 o.p. (*0-89966-418-0*) Buccaneer Bks., Inc.

—Emily's Quest. 1996. 248p. (J). (gr. 7 up). mass mkt. 4.95 (*0-7710-9981-9*) McClelland & Stewart/Tundra Bks.

ESTHER, QUEEN OF PERSIA—FICTION

Marsh, T. F. The Persian Plot: A Tale about Courage. (Tale Tellers Ser.). (Illus.). 32p. (J). (ps-3). 4.99 (*0-7814-3518-8*) Cook Communications Ministries.

Pakulak, Eric. At the Side of Esther: A Multiple-Ending Bible Adventure. 2000. (Illus.). 96p. (J). pap. 6.95 (*0-8198-0769-9*) Pauline Bks. & Media.

F

FELIX THE CAT (FICTITIOUS CHARACTER)—FICTION

The Comic Adventures of Felix the Cat. 1983. (Illus.). (J). pap. 3.95 (*0-915696-62-2*) Determined Productions, Inc.

FETT, BOBA (FICTITIOUS CHARACTER)—FICTION

Whitman, John. City of the Dead. 1997. (Star Wars: No. 2). (J). (gr. 4-7). 11.04 (*0-606-11889-6*) Turtleback Bks.

—The City of the Dead. ltd. ed. 1997. (Star Wars: No. 2). 160p. (J). (gr. 3-7). pap. 4.99 o.s.i (*0-553-48451-6*, Skylark) Random Hse. Children's Bks.

Windham, Ryder. Battle of the Bounty Hunters. unabr. ed. 1996. (Star Wars Ser.). (Illus.). 12p. (J). (ps up). 17.95 (*1-56971-129-1*) Dark Horse Comics.

FINN, HUCKLEBERRY (FICTITIOUS CHARACTER)—FICTION

Rosensfit, Gail R. Huckleberry Finn. 1988. (Living Literature Workbooks). (J). (gr. 7). pap. 1.50 o.p. (*0-671-09248-0*) Simon & Schuster.

Twain, Mark. The Adventures of Huckleberry Finn. 2002. (World Digital Library). (J). E-Book 3.95 (*0-594-08343-5*) 1873 Pr.

—The Adventures of Huckleberry Finn. 2002. (Great Illustrated Classics). (Illus.). 240p. (J). (gr. 3-8). lib. bdg. 21.35 (*1-57765-676-8*, ABDO & Daughters) ABDO Publishing Co.

—The Adventures of Huckleberry Finn. 2001. 7.95 (*0-8010-1220-1*) Baker Bks.

—The Adventures of Huckleberry Finn. 1981. (Bantam Classics Ser.). 320p. reprint ed. mass mkt. 4.95 (*0-553-21079-3*, Bantam Classics) Bantam Bks.

—The Adventures of Huckleberry Finn. 2002. (Spot the Classics Ser.). (Illus.). 192p. (J). (gr. k-5). 4.99 (*1-57759-553-X*) Dalmatian Pr.

—The Adventures of Huckleberry Finn. 1994. (Thrift Editions Ser.). 224p. (J). reprint ed. pap. 2.00 (*0-486-28061-6*) Dover Pubns., Inc.

—The Adventures of Huckleberry Finn. 2nd ed. 1998. (Illustrated Classic Book Ser.). (Illus.). 61p. (J). (gr. 3 up). reprint ed. pap. text 4.95 (*1-56767-255-8*) Educational Insights, Inc.

—The Adventures of Huckleberry Finn. (J). E-Book 2.49 (*1-929120-49-4*) Electric Umbrella Publishing.

—The Adventures of Huckleberry Finn. l.t. ed. 1371p. pap. 93.15 (*0-7583-0031-X*); 477p. pap. 35.64 (*0-7583-0026-3*); 610p. pap. 43.97 (*0-7583-0027-1*); 278p. pap. 24.74 (*0-7583-0024-7*); 348p. pap. 28.70 (*0-7583-0025-5*); 1182p. pap. 83.02 (*0-7583-0030-1*); 961p. pap. 72.45 (*0-7583-0029-8*); 781p. pap. 61.96 (*0-7583-0028-X*); 348p. lib. bdg. 34.70 (*0-7583-0017-4*); 1371p. lib. bdg. 105.15 (*0-7583-0023-9*); 961p. lib. bdg. 84.45 (*0-7583-0021-2*); 781p. lib. bdg. 73.96 (*0-7583-0020-4*); 610p. lib. bdg. 49.97 (*0-7583-0019-0*); 477p. lib. bdg. 41.64 (*0-7583-0018-2*); 1182p. lib. bdg. 95.02 (*0-7583-0022-0*); 2000. 278p. 30.74 (*0-7583-0016-6*) Huge Print Pr.

—The Adventures of Huckleberry Finn. l.t. ed. 1997. (Large Print Heritage Ser.). 491p. lib. bdg. 35.95 (*1-58118-015-2*, 21489) LRS.

—The Adventures of Huckleberry Finn. 1977. (American Classics). (J). (gr. 9-12). 6.12 o.p. (*0-88343-416-4*); audio 89.08 o.p. (*0-88343-426-1*) McDougal Littell Inc.

—The Adventures of Huckleberry Finn. 1959. 288p. (YA). (gr. 7). mass mkt. 1.75 o.p. (*0-451-51912-4*, Signet Classics) NAL.

—The Adventures of Huckleberry Finn, Level 2. Hedge, Tricia, ed. 2000. (Bookworms Ser.). (Illus.). 64p. (J). pap. text 5.95 (*0-19-422976-9*) Oxford Univ. Pr., Inc.

—The Adventures of Huckleberry Finn. 2003. (Illus.). 288p. (J). pap. 3.99 o.p. (*0-14-250098-4*, Puffin Bks.) Penguin Putnam Bks. for Young Readers.

—The Adventures of Huckleberry Finn. 1989. (Enriched Classics Ser.). 432p. (YA). (gr. 5-12). mass mkt. (*0-671-70136-3*, 46198, Washington Square Pr.) Simon & Schuster.

—The Adventures of Huckleberry Finn. abr. ed. 1972. (J). pap. 11.95 o.p. incl. audio (*0-88142-325-4*) Soundelux Audio Publishing.

—The Adventures of Huckleberry Finn. l.t. ed. 1996. (Perennial Bestsellers Ser.). 420p. (J). 24.95 (*0-7838-1609-X*) Thorndike Pr.

—The Adventures of Huckleberry Finn. 1999. 10.04 (*0-606-17508-3*); 1994. 11.04 (*0-606-12869-7*); 1982. (J). 11.00 (*0-606-13112-4*) Turtleback Bks.

—The Adventures of Huckleberry Finn. Fischer, Victor et al, eds. 2001. (Mark Twain Library). (Illus.). (J). 535p. 45.00 (*0-520-22806-5*); xxvii, 561p. pap. 14.95 (*0-520-22838-3*) Univ. of California Pr.

—The Adventures of Huckleberry Finn. 2002. (Classics Ser.). (Illus.). 368p. pap. 6.00 (*0-14-243717-4*, Penguin Classics) Viking Penguin.

—The Adventures of Huckleberry Finn. Seelye, John, ed. & intro. by. 1986. (Penguin Classics Ser.). 368p. (J). (gr. 4). pap. 5.95 o.s.i (*0-14-039046-4*) Viking Penguin.

—Las Aventuras de Huck Finn. 2002. (Classics for Young Readers Ser.). (SPA.). (YA). 14.95 (*84-392-0925-8*, EV30617) Gaviota Ediciones ESP. *Dist:* Lectorum Pubns., Inc.

—Las Aventuras de Tom Sawyer. 2000. (SPA., Illus.). 272p. (J). 7.95 (*84-406-8397-9*) B Ediciones S.A. ESP. *Dist:* Distribooks, Inc.

—Las Aventuras de Tom Sawyer. 2002. (SPA.). (YA). 7.95 (*956-13-1069-4*) Bello, Andres CHL. *Dist:* AIMS International Bks., Inc.

—Las Aventuras de Tom Sawyer. 2002. (Classics for Young Readers Ser.). (SPA.). (YA). 14.95 (*84-392-0908-8*, EV30591) Gaviota Ediciones ESP. *Dist:* Lectorum Pubns., Inc.

—Las Aventuras de Tom Sawyer. (Coleccion Estrella). (SPA., Illus.). 64p. (YA). 14.95 (*950-11-0012-X*, SGM012) Sigmar ARG. *Dist:* Continental Bk. Co., Inc.

—Huckleberry Finn. 1997. (Classics Illustrated Study Guides). (Illus.). 64p. (YA). (gr. 7 up). mass mkt., stu. ed. 4.99 o.p. (*1-57840-008-2*) Acclaim Bks.

—Huckleberry Finn. 1995. (Classroom Reading Plays Ser.). 32p. (YA). (gr. 6-12). pap. 2.40 o.p. (*1-56103-110-0*) American Guidance Service, Inc.

—Huckleberry Finn, unabr. ed. 1965. (J). audio 41.95 (*1-55685-353-X*) Audio Bk. Contractors, Inc.

—Huckleberry Finn. 1977. (Dent's Illustrated Children's Classics Ser.). (Illus.). 338p. (J). reprint ed. 10.00 o.p. (*0-460-05031-1*) Biblio Distribution.

—Huckleberry Finn. 1999. (YA). reprint ed. pap. text 28.00 (*1-4047-1118-X*) Classic Textbooks.

—Huckleberry Finn. 1988. (Study Texts Ser.). (YA). (gr. 7 up). pap. text 3.97 o.p. (*0-582-00264-8*, 73957) Longman Publishing Group.

—Huckleberry Finn. 1940. (J). audio 7.95 National Recording Co.

—Huckleberry Finn. Bassett, Jennifer, ed. 1995. (Illus.). 48p. (J). pap. text 5.95 o.p. (*0-19-422724-3*) Oxford Univ. Pr., Inc.

—Huckleberry Finn. Teresa Agnes, ed. Heller, Rudolf, tr. 1979. (SPA., Illus.). 64p. (YA). stu. ed. 1.50 (*0-88301-570-6*) Pendulum Pr., Inc.

—Huckleberry Finn. Farr, Naunerle C., ed. 1973. (Now Age Illustrated Ser.). (Illus.). 64p. (J). (gr. 5-10). 7.50 o.p. (*0-88301-207-3*); pap. 2.95 (*0-88301-098-4*) Pendulum Pr., Inc.

—Huckleberry Finn. (American Collection Short Classics). (J). (gr. 4-7). 1993. 32p. pap. 4.95 o.p. (*0-8114-6826-7*); 1988. 22.00 o.p. (*0-8172-2179-4*); 1983. (Illus.). 48p. pap. 9.27 o.p. (*0-8172-2009-7*); 1983. (Illus.). 48p. lib. bdg. 24.26 o.p. (*0-8172-1651-0*); Set. 1991. (Illus.). 48p. pap. 34.00 (*0-8114-6962-X*) Raintree Pubs.

—Huckleberry Finn. 1990. (Folio - Junior Ser.: No. 230). (FRE., Illus.). 380p. (J). (gr. 5-10). pap. 10.95 (*2-07-033230-6*) Schoenhof's Foreign Bks., Inc.

—Huckleberry Finn. unabr. ed. 2002. (YA). audio compact disk 39.95 (*1-58472-259-2*, 076); pap. incl. audio compact disk (*1-58472-261-4*); pap. incl. audio compact disk (*1-58472-261-4*) Sound Room Pubs., Inc. (In Audio).

FLATFOOT FOX (FICTITIOUS CHARACTER)—FICTION

Clifford, Eth. Flatfoot Fox. 9999. (J). pap. 12.95 o.p. (*0-395-56757-2*) Houghton Mifflin Co.

—Flatfoot Fox & the Case of the Bashful Beaver. 1995. (Illus.). 48p. (J). (gr. 4-6). lib. bdg., tchr. ed. 16.00 (*0-395-70560-6*) Houghton Mifflin Co.

—Flatfoot Fox & the Case of the Missing Eye. 1990. (Illus.). 48p. (J). (ps-3). lib. bdg., tchr. ed. 16.00 (*0-395-51945-4*) Houghton Mifflin Co.

—Flatfoot Fox & the Case of the Missing Eye. 1992. 48p. (J). (gr. 4-7). pap. 2.95 o.p. (*0-590-45812-4*) Scholastic, Inc.

—Flatfoot Fox & the Case of the Missing Schoolhouse. 1997. (Illus.). 48p. (J). (gr. 4-6). lib. bdg., tchr. ed. 15.00 (*0-395-81446-4*) Houghton Mifflin Co.

—Flatfoot Fox & the Case of the Missing Whoooo. 1993. (Illus.). 48p. (J). (gr. 2-5). tchr. ed. 13.95 o.p. (*0-395-65364-9*) Houghton Mifflin Co.

—Flatfoot Fox & the Case of the Missing Whoooo. 1994. 48p. (J). (gr. 4-7). pap. 2.95 o.p. (*0-590-48483-4*) Scholastic, Inc.

—Flatfoot Fox & the Case of the Nosy Otter. 1992. (Illus.). 48p. (J). (gr. 4-6). lib. bdg., tchr. ed. 16.00 (*0-395-60289-0*) Houghton Mifflin Co.

—Flatfoot Fox & the Case of the Nosy Otter. 1994. 48p. (J). (gr. 4-7). pap. 2.95 o.p. (*0-590-47336-0*) Scholastic, Inc.

FRANCIS, OF ASSISI, SAINT, 1182-1226—FICTION

Bernthal, Mark S. Gifts of Christmas. 1997. (Francesco's Friendly World Ser.). (Illus.). 24p. (J). (ps-3). pap. 2.95 o.p. (*1-57064-228-1*, 73100) Lyrick Publishing.

O'Dell, Scott. The Road to Damietta. 1987. 240p. (gr. 7 up). mass mkt. 6.50 (*0-449-70233-2*, Fawcett) Ballantine Bks.

—The Road to Damietta, 001. 1985. 256p. (J). (gr. 6 up). 14.95 o.p. (*0-395-38923-2*) Houghton Mifflin Co.

—The Road to Damietta. 1985. (J). 12.04 (*0-606-04403-5*) Turtleback Bks.

Rosen, Michael J. The Blessing of the Animals, RS. 2000. (Illus.). 96p. (J). (gr. 3-7). 15.00 (*0-374-30838-1*, Farrar, Straus & Giroux (BYR)) Farrar, Straus & Giroux.

Wintz, Jack. St. Francis in San Francisco. 2001. (Illus.). 32p. (J). (gr. k-3). 12.95 (*0-8091-6684-4*) Paulist Pr.

FRANKENSTEIN (FICTITIOUS CHARACTER)—FICTION

Campton, David, retold by. Frankenstein. 1988. (Fleshcreepers Ser.). 160p. (J). (gr. 6 up). pap. 2.95 o.p. (*0-8120-4076-7*) Barron's Educational Series, Inc.

Dadey, Debbie & Jones, Marcia Thornton. Frankenstein Doesn't Start Food Fights. 2003. (Adventures of the Bailey School Kids Ser.: No. 47). 80p. (J). mass mkt. 3.99 (*0-439-55999-5*, Scholastic Paperbacks) Scholastic, Inc.

Frankenstein. 2002. 32p. (J). (*0-7868-0798-9*) Disney Pr.

Frankenstein. 1988. mass mkt. 2.25 (*0-938819-54-2*, Aerie) Doherty, Tom Assocs., LLC.

Frankenstein. 1997. (Dk Classics Ser.). 64p. (J). pap. 14.95 (*0-7894-1750-2*) Dorling Kindersley Publishing, Inc.

Frankenstein. 1988. (Short Classics Learning Files Ser.). (J). (gr. 4 up). 22.00 o.p. (*0-8172-2178-6*) Raintree Pubs.

Garmon, Larry Mike. Frankenstein: Anatomy of Terror. 2001. (Universal Monsters Ser.: No. 3). 224p. (J). (gr. 5 up). mass mkt. 4.50 (*0-439-30344-3*) Scholastic, Inc.

Shelley, Mary Wollstonecraft. Frankenstein. 2002. (Great Illustrated Classics). (Illus.). 240p. (J). (gr. 3-8). lib. bdg. 21.35 (*1-57765-686-5*, ABDO & Daughters) ABDO Publishing Co.

—Frankenstein. 1984. (Modern Library Ser.). (J). E-Book 4.95 (*1-58945-004-3*) Adobe Systems, Inc.

—Frankenstein. 1995. (Classroom Reading Plays Ser.). 32p. (YA). (gr. 6-12). pap. 2.40 o.p. (*1-56103-106-2*) American Guidance Service, Inc.

—Frankenstein. Hutchinson, Emily, ed. 1995. (Classroom Reading Plays Ser.). 32p. (YA). (gr. 6-12). pap. 3.95 (*0-7854-1118-6*, 40206) American Guidance Service, Inc.

—Frankenstein. 1984. 240p. (YA). (gr. 9-12). mass mkt. 1.75 o.s.i (*0-553-21172-2*, Bantam Classics) Bantam Bks.

—Frankenstein. Stevens, David, ed. 1998. (Literature Ser.). (Illus.). 286p. pap. text 11.95 (*0-521-58702-6*) Cambridge Univ. Pr.

—Frankenstein. 1980. (Illus.). 48p. (J). (gr. 3 up). pap. 4.95 o.s.i (*0-440-02692-X*, Delacorte Pr.); 1980. (Illus.). 48p. (J). (gr. 3 up). lib. bdg. 10.89 o.s.i (*0-440-02693-8*, Delacorte Pr.); 1964. 221p. (YA). (gr. 7 up). pap. 1.95 o.s.i (*0-440-92717-X*, Laurel) Dell Publishing.

—Frankenstein. (YA). 1994. (Illus.). 236p. (gr. 7 up). mass mkt. 4.99 (*0-8125-5150-8*); 1989. (gr. 9-12). pap. 2.50 o.s.i (*0-8125-0457-7*) Doherty, Tom Assocs., LLC. (Tor Classics).

—Frankenstein. 2002. (Illus.). 46p. pap. 7.50 (*0-237-52280-2*) Evans Brothers, Ltd. GBR. *Dist:* Trafalgar Square.

—Frankenstein. 1986. (YA). (gr. 5-12). pap. 7.95 (*0-8224-9257-1*) Globe Fearon Educational Publishing.

—Frankenstein. (J). 9.95 (*1-56156-309-9*); 1992. (Illus.). 128p. pap. 2.95 o.p. (*1-56156-142-8*) Kidsbooks, Inc.

—Frankenstein. 1989. 256p. (YA). (gr. 7-12). 18.95 o.p. (*0-87226-190-5*, Bedrick, Peter Bks.) McGraw-Hill Children's Publishing.

—Frankenstein. 1965. (Illus.). 224p. (J). (ps up). mass mkt. 3.95 o.s.i (*0-451-52336-9*, Signet Classics) NAL.

—Frankenstein. Hunter, J. Paul, ed. 1995. (Critical Editions Ser.). (Illus.). 320p. (C). (gr. 7). pap. text (*0-393-96458-2*, Norton Paperbacks) Norton, W. W. & Co., Inc.

—Frankenstein. Binder, Otto, ed. 1973. (Now Age Illustrated Ser.). (Illus.). 64p. (J). (gr. 5-10). 7.50 o.p. (*0-88301-204-9*); stu. ed. 1.25 (*0-88301-177-8*); pap. 2.95 (*0-88301-097-6*) Pendulum Pr., Inc.

—Frankenstein. Sibley, Raymond, ed. 1991. (Horror Classics Ser.: No. 841-2). (Illus.). (J). (gr. 4 up). pap. 3.50 o.p. (*0-7214-0813-3*, Ladybird Bks.) Penguin Group (USA) Inc.

—Frankenstein. 1999. (J). (gr. 4-7). pap. 2.99 o.s.i (*0-14-130541-X*, Puffin Bks.); 1998. (Illus.). 256p. (J). (gr. 7-12). 25.99 o.s.i (*0-670-87800-6*); 1998. (Illus.). 256p. (J). (gr. 7-12). pap. 17.99 (*0-670-87801-4*, Viking); 1995. (Illus.). 288p. (J). 14.95 o.p. (*0-448-40966-6*, Platt & Munk); 1994. (Illus.). 288p. (YA). (gr. 5 up). pap. 4.99 (*0-14-036712-8*, Puffin Bks.) Penguin Putnam Bks. for Young Readers.

—Frankenstein. Hanft, Joshua, ed. 1993. (Great Illustrated Classics Ser.: Vol. 30). (Illus.). 240p. (J). (gr. 3-7). 9.95 (*0-86611-981-7*) Playmore, Inc., Pubs.

—Frankenstein. 1987. (Regents Illustrated Classics Ser.). (Illus.). 62p. (YA). (gr. 7-12). pap. text 5.25 net. o.p. (*0-13-330515-5*, 20507) Prentice Hall, ESL Dept.

—Frankenstein. 1983. (Short Classics Ser.). (Illus.). 48p. (J). (gr. 4 up). pap. 9.27 o.p. (*0-8172-2008-9*); lib. bdg. 24.26 o.p. (*0-8172-1674-X*) Raintree Pubs.

—Frankenstein. (Stepping Stone Bks.). (Illus.). 96p. (J). 2000. (gr. 3-5). pap. 3.99 (*0-394-84827-6*); 1982. (gr. 2-6). 4.99 o.s.i (*0-394-94827-0*) Random Hse. Children's Bks. (Random Hse. Bks. for Young Readers).

—Frankenstein. 2001. (Courage Unabridged Classics Ser.). 176p. (YA). pap. 6.00 o.p. (*0-7624-0545-7*, Courage Bks.) Running Pr. Bk. Pubs.

—Frankenstein. 1994. (Illus.). 272p. (J). (gr. 7 up). mass mkt. 3.50 (*0-590-48617-9*) Scholastic, Inc.

—Frankenstein. (Saddleback Classics). 1999. (Illus.). (J). 13.10 (*0-606-21551-4*); 1995. 11.04 (*0-606-12937-5*); 1983. (J). 10.00 (*0-606-21591-3*) Turtleback Bks.

—Frankenstein. 2001. (CliffsComplete Ser.). (Illus.). 233p. pap., stu. ed. 9.99 (*0-7645-8726-9*, Cliff Notes) Wiley, John & Sons, Inc.

—Frankenstein. Hegarty, Carol, ed. 1998. (Classics Ser.: Set I). (Illus.). 80p. (YA). (gr. 5-12). 6.95 (*1-56254-264-8*, SP2648) Saddleback Publishing, Inc.

—Frankenstein. unabr. ed. 1965. (Classics Ser.). (YA). (gr. 7 up). mass mkt. 3.95 (*0-8049-0019-1*, CL-19) Airmont Publishing Co., Inc.

—Frankenstein. unabr. collector's ed. 1980. (J). audio 48.00 (*0-7366-0314-X*, 1301) Books on Tape, Inc.

—Frankenstein. abr. ed. 1997. (Dover Children's Thrift Classics Ser.). (Illus.). (J). pap. 1.00 (*0-486-29930-9*) Dover Pubns., Inc.

—Frankenstein. abr. ed. 1984. audio 9.95 (*0-89845-882-X*, CP 1541, Caedmon) HarperTrade.

—Frankenstein, Vol. 5. Stemach, Jerry et al, eds. 2000. (Start-to-Finish Books). (J). (gr. 2-3). audio 35.00 (*1-58702-513-2*); audio (*1-58702-372-5*, F32K2) Johnston, Don Inc.

—Frankenstein. Howe, D. H., ed. 2nd ed. 1993. (Illus.). 126p. pap. text 5.95 (*0-19-585471-3*) Oxford Univ. Pr., Inc.

—Frankenstein, Level 3. Hedge, Tricia, ed. 2000. (Bookworms Ser.). (Illus.). 80p. (J). pap. text 5.95 (*0-19-423003-1*) Oxford Univ. Pr., Inc.

—Frankenstein: "The Modern Prometheus" Joseph, M. K., ed. & intro. by. 1998. (Oxford World's Classics Ser.). 264p. (YA). (gr. 7 up). pap. 6.95 (*0-19-283487-8*) Oxford Univ. Pr., Inc.

—Frankenstein & Dracula Flip-Over Book. 2002. pap. 4.99 (*0-14-230171-X*) Penguin Putnam Bks. for Young Readers.

Shelley, Mary Wollstonecraft, et al. Frankenstein. Munch, Philippe, tr. 2002. (SPA., Illus.). 284p. (J). 29.95 (*84-348-5617-4*) SM Ediciones ESP. *Dist:* AIMS International Bks., Inc.

Smithmark Staff. Dracula - Frankenstein. 1995. (Illus.). 498p. (J). 12.98 o.p. (*0-8317-6696-4*) Smithmark Pubs., Inc.

Stoker, Bram. Dracula - Frankenstein. 1989. (J). 5.98 o.p. (*0-86136-606-9*) Smithmark Pubs., Inc.

Stoker, Bram, et al. Dracula, Frankenstein, Dr. Jekyll & Mr. Hyde. 1978. 672p. (J). (gr. 7). mass mkt. 6.95 (*0-451-52363-6*, Signet Classics) NAL.

Weinberg, Larry. Frankenstein. 2000. (Golden Star Reader Ser.). (Illus.). (J). 10.14 (*0-606-18854-1*) Turtleback Bks.

FRANKLIN (FICTITIOUS CHARACTER: BOURGEOIS)—FICTION

Bourgeois, Paulette. Adventures with Franklin. 2000. (Franklin Color & Activity Bks.). (Illus.). 32p. (J). (ps-3). pap. (*0-7666-0492-6*) Modern Publishing.

—Benjamin et la Fee des Dents. ed. 1997. Tr. of Franklin & the Tooth Fairy. (FRE.). (J). (gr. 1). spiral bd. (*0-616-01825-8*) Canadian National Institute for the Blind/Institut National Canadien pour les Aveugles.

—Benjamin et Sa Petite Soeur. ed. 2003. Tr. of Franklin's Baby Sister. (gr. 1). spiral bd. (*0-616-14597-7*) Canadian National Institute for the Blind/ Institut National Canadien pour les Aveugles.

—Benjamin s'Est Perdu. braille ed. 1993. Tr. of Franklin Is Lost. (J). (gr. 1). spiral bd. (*0-616-01827-4*) Canadian National Institute for the Blind/Institut National Canadien pour les Aveugles.

—El Club Secreto de Franklin. 2001. (Franklin Ser.). (SPA., Illus.). (J). (ps-3). 10.95 (*1-930332-14-9*, LC6913) Lectorum Pubns., Inc.

—El Club Secreto de Franklin. Varela, Alejandra López, tr. from ENG. 1998. (Franklin Ser.). (SPA., Illus.). 32p. (J). (ps-3). pap. 5.95 (*1-880507-50-1*, LC8146) Lectorum Pubns., Inc.

—El Club Secreto de Franklin. 1998. (Franklin Ser.). (SPA.). (J). (ps-3). 11.10 (*0-606-16577-0*) Turtleback Bks.

—El Diente de Franklin. Vareta, Alejandra Lopez, tr. 2001. (Franklin Ser.). (SPA., Illus.). (J). (ps-3). pap. 5.95 (*1-880507-88-9*, LC1651); ring bd. 10.95 (*1-880507-89-7*, LC1736) Lectorum Pubns., Inc.

—El Diente de Franklin. 2001. (Franklin Ser.). (SPA., Illus.). (J). 12.10 (*0-606-21171-3*) Turtleback Bks.

—Finders Keepers for Franklin. 1997. (Franklin Ser.). (Illus.). 30p. (J). (ps-3). pap. (*1-55074-370-8*) Kids Can Pr., Ltd.

—Finders Keepers for Franklin. 1998. (Franklin Ser.). (Illus.). 260p. (J). (ps-3). 10.95 (*1-55074-368-6*) Kids Can Pr., Ltd. CAN. *Dist:* General Distribution Services, Inc.

—Finders Keepers for Franklin. 1998. (Franklin Ser.). (Illus.). 32p. (J). (ps-3). pap. 4.50 (*0-590-02633-X*) Scholastic, Inc.

—Finders Keepers for Franklin. 1998. (Franklin Ser.). (J). (ps-3). 10.65 (*0-606-12932-4*) Turtleback Bks.

—Franklin & Friends. 2000. (Franklin Color & Activity Bks.). (Illus.). 96p. (J). (ps-3). pap. (*0-7666-0495-0*) Modern Publishing.

—Franklin & Harriet. unabr. ed. 2001. (Franklin Ser.). (Illus.). 32p. (J). (ps-3). text 10.95 (*1-55074-874-2*) Kids Can Pr., Ltd.

—Franklin & Harriet. 2001. (Franklin Ser.). (Illus.). 32p. (J). (ps-3). pap. 4.50 (*0-439-20381-3*) Scholastic, Inc.

—Franklin & Me. 1997. (Franklin Ser.). (Illus.). 126p. (J). (ps-3). pap. (*1-55074-335-X*) Kids Can Pr., Ltd.

—Franklin & Me. unabr. ed. 1998. (Franklin Ser.). (Illus.). 32p. (J). (ps-3). text 9.95 (*1-55074-442-9*) Kids Can Pr., Ltd. CAN. *Dist:* General Distribution Services, Inc.

—Franklin & Me. 1995. (Franklin Ser.). (Illus.). 40p. (J). (ps-3). pap. 4.50 (*0-590-25488-X*) Scholastic, Inc.

—Franklin & the Hero. 2000. (Franklin TV-Tie In Ser.). (Illus.). 32p. (J). (ps-3). pap. 4.50 (*0-439-20380-5*) Scholastic, Inc.

—Franklin & the Hero. 2000. (Franklin TV Storybook Ser.). (J). (ps-3). 10.65 (*0-606-20057-6*) Turtleback Bks.

—Franklin & the Thunderstorm. 1998. (Franklin Ser.). 96p. (J). (ps-3). pap. (*1-55074-405-4*) Kids Can Pr., Ltd.

—Franklin & the Thunderstorm. 1998. (Franklin Ser.). (Illus.). 268p. (J). (ps-3). 10.95 (*1-55074-403-8*) Kids Can Pr., Ltd. CAN. *Dist:* General Distribution Services, Inc.

—Franklin & the Thunderstorm. 1998. (Franklin Ser.). (Illus.). 32p. (J). (ps-3). pap. 4.50 (*0-590-02635-6*, Cartwheel Bks.) Scholastic, Inc.

—Franklin & the Thunderstorm. 1998. (Franklin Ser.). (J). (ps-3). 10.65 (*0-606-13403-4*) Turtleback Bks.

—Franklin & the Tooth Fairy. ed. 1997. (J). (gr. 2). spiral bd. (*0-616-01568-2*) Canadian National Institute for the Blind/Institut National Canadien pour les Aveugles.

—Franklin & the Tooth Fairy. (Franklin Ser.). (Illus.). (J). (ps-3). 1999. 180p. pap. incl. audio (*1-55074-793-2*); 1995. 96p. pap. (*1-55074-280-9*) Kids Can Pr., Ltd.

—Franklin & the Tooth Fairy. 1997. (Franklin Ser.). (Illus.). 258p. (J). (ps-3). text 10.95 (*1-55074-270-1*) Kids Can Pr., Ltd. CAN. *Dist:* General Distribution Services, Inc.

—Franklin & the Tooth Fairy. 1996. (Franklin Ser.). (Illus.). 32p. (J). (ps-3). pap. 4.50 (*0-590-25469-3*) Scholastic, Inc.

—Franklin & the Tooth Fairy. 1996. (Franklin Ser.). (J). (ps-3). 10.65 (*0-606-08745-1*) Turtleback Bks.

—Franklin en el Museo. Varela, Alejandra López, tr. (SPA., Illus.). (J). (gr. k-2). ring bd. 10.95 (*1-930332-12-2*, LC30199) Lectorum Pubns., Inc.

—Franklin en el Museo. 1999. (Franklin Ser.). (SPA., Illus.). (J). (ps-3). pap. 5.95 (*1-880507-57-9*, LC2801) Lectorum Pubns., Inc.

—Franklin en el Museo. 1999. (Franklin Ser.). (SPA.). (J). (ps-3). 12.10 (*0-606-17007-3*) Turtleback Bks.

—Franklin en la Oscuridad. Varela, Alejandra López, tr. 2001. (SPA., Illus.). (J). ring bd. 10.95 (*1-880507-87-0*, LC3565) Lectorum Pubns., Inc.

—Franklin en la Oscuridad. 1998. (Franklin Ser.). (SPA.). (J). (ps-3). 11.10 (*0-606-15533-3*) Turtleback Bks.

—Franklin Es un Mandon. López Varela, Alejandra, tr. from ENG. 1998. (Franklin Ser.). (SPA., Illus.). 32p. (J). (ps-3). pap. 5.95 (*1-880507-42-0*, LC7795) Lectorum Pubns., Inc.

—Franklin Es un Mandon. (Franklin Ser.). (SPA.). (J). (ps-3). 1998. lib. bdg. 11.10 (*0-606-13404-2*); 1993. 10.65 (*0-606-06390-0*) Turtleback Bks.

—Franklin Fibs. ed. 1994. (J). (gr. 2). spiral bd. (*0-616-01569-0*) Canadian National Institute for the Blind/Institut National Canadien pour les Aveugles.

—Franklin Fibs. 1992. (Franklin Ser.). (Illus.). 96p. (J). (ps-3). pap. (*1-55074-077-6*) Kids Can Pr., Ltd.

—Franklin Fibs. 1991. (Franklin Ser.). (Illus.). 264p. (J). (ps-3). text 10.95 (*1-55074-038-5*) Kids Can Pr., Ltd. CAN. *Dist:* General Distribution Services, Inc.

—Franklin Fibs. 1992. (Franklin Ser.). (Illus.). 30p. (J). (ps-3). pap. 4.50 (*0-590-44647-9*) Scholastic, Inc.

—Franklin Fibs. 1991. (Franklin Ser.). (J). (ps-3). 10.65 (*0-606-01840-9*) Turtleback Bks.

—Franklin Forgets. 2000. (Franklin TV-Tie In Ser.). (Illus.). 32p. (J). (ps-3). pap. 4.50 (*0-439-08368-0*) Scholastic, Inc.

—Franklin Forgets. 2000. (Franklin TV Storybook Ser.). (J). (ps-3). 10.65 (*0-606-20058-4*) Turtleback Bks.

—Franklin Goes to Day Camp: A Story & Activity Book. (Franklin Ser.). (Illus.). 74p. (J). (ps-3). pap. (*1-55074-372-4*) Kids Can Pr., Ltd.

—Franklin Goes to Day Camp: A Story & Activity Book. 1998. (Franklin Ser.). (Illus.). (J). (ps-3). pap. text 4.50 (*0-590-06828-8*, Cartwheel Bks.) Scholastic, Inc.

—Franklin Goes to School. ed. 1997. (J). (gr. 1). spiral bd. (*0-616-01570-4*); (gr. 2). spiral bd. (*0-616-01571-2*) Canadian National Institute for the Blind/ Institut National Canadien pour les Aveugles.

—Franklin Goes to School. 1995. (Franklin Ser.). (Illus.). (J). (ps-3). 96p. pap. (*1-55074-276-0*); 32p. 10.95 (*1-55074-424-0*) Kids Can Pr., Ltd.

—Franklin Goes to School. 1995. (Franklin Ser.). (Illus.). 260p. (J). (ps-3). text 10.95 (*1-55074-268-X*) Kids Can Pr., Ltd. CAN. *Dist:* General Distribution Services, Inc.

—Franklin Goes to School. 1995. (Franklin Ser.). (Illus.). 32p. (J). (ps-3). pap. 4.50 (*0-590-25467-7*) Scholastic, Inc.

—Franklin Goes to School. 1995. (Franklin Ser.). (J). (ps-3). 10.65 (*0-606-07537-2*) Turtleback Bks.

—Franklin Goes to the Hospital. ed. 2001. (J). (gr. 1). spiral bd. (*0-616-03024-X*); (gr. 2). spiral bd. (*0-616-04547-6*) Canadian National Institute for the Blind/Institut National Canadien pour les Aveugles.

—Franklin Goes to the Hospital. 2000. (Franklin Ser.). (Illus.). 30p. (J). (ps-3). pap. (*1-55074-734-7*); text 10.95 (*1-55074-732-0*) Kids Can Pr., Ltd.

—Franklin Goes to the Hospital. 2000. (Franklin Ser.). (Illus.). 32p. (J). (ps-3). pap. 4.50 (*0-439-08370-2*) Scholastic, Inc.

—Franklin Goes to the Hospital. 2000. (Franklin Ser.). (Illus.). (J). (ps-3). 10.65 (*0-606-18547-X*) Turtleback Bks.

—Franklin Has a Sleepover. ed. 1997. (J). (gr. 1). spiral bd. (*0-616-01572-0*); (gr. 2). spiral bd. (*0-616-01573-9*) Canadian National Institute for the Blind/Institut National Canadien pour les Aveugles.

—Franklin Has a Sleepover. 1996. (Franklin Ser.). (Illus.). 96p. (J). (ps-3). pap. (*1-55074-302-3*) Kids Can Pr., Ltd.

—Franklin Has a Sleepover. 1997. (Franklin Ser.). (Illus.). 260p. (J). (ps-3). 10.95 (*1-55074-300-7*) Kids Can Pr., Ltd. CAN. *Dist:* General Distribution Services, Inc.

—Franklin Has a Sleepover. (Franklin Ser.). (Illus.). (J). (ps-3). 2000. 32p. pap. 6.95 incl. audio (*0-439-23283-X*); 2000. 32p. pap. 6.95 incl. audio (*0-439-23283-X*); 1996. 30p. pap. 4.50 (*0-590-61759-1*) Scholastic, Inc.

—Franklin Has a Sleepover. 1996. (Franklin Ser.). (J). (ps-3). 10.65 (*0-606-09295-1*) Turtleback Bks.

—Franklin Helps Out. 2000. (Franklin TV-Tie In Ser.). (Illus.). 32p. (J). (ps-3). pap. 4.50 (*0-439-20379-1*) Scholastic, Inc.

—Franklin Helps Out. 2000. (Franklin TV Storybook Ser.). (J). (ps-3). 10.65 (*0-606-20059-2*) Turtleback Bks.

—Franklin in the Dark. ed. 2000. (J). (gr. 1). spiral bd. (*0-616-01574-7*); (gr. 2). spiral bd. (*0-616-01575-5*) Canadian National Institute for the Blind/Institut National Canadien pour les Aveugles.

—Franklin in the Dark. 1992. (Franklin Ser.). (Illus.). 100p. (J). (ps-3). pap. (*0-921103-31-X*) Kids Can Pr., Ltd.

—Franklin in the Dark. 1986. (Franklin Ser.). (Illus.). 258p. (J). (ps-3). text 10.95 (*0-919964-93-1*) Kids Can Pr., Ltd. CAN. *Dist:* General Distribution Services, Inc.

—Franklin in the Dark. (Franklin Ser.). (J). (ps-3). 2000. (Illus.). 32p. pap. 6.95 incl. audio (*0-439-23282-1*); 2000. (Illus.). 32p. pap. 6.95 incl. audio (*0-439-23282-1*); 2000. (Illus.). 22p. 5.99 (*0-439-19425-3*); 1992. 19.95 (*0-590-72701-X*); 1987. (Illus.). 30p. reprint ed. pap. 4.50 (*0-590-44506-5*) Scholastic, Inc.

—Franklin in the Dark. 1987. (Franklin Ser.). (J). (ps-3). 10.65 (*0-606-03218-5*) Turtleback Bks.

—Franklin in the Dark: Mini-Book & Doll. 1996. (Franklin Ser.). (Illus.). 32p. (J). (ps-3). 10.95 o.p. (*0-590-96525-5*, 116931Q) Scholastic, Inc.

—Franklin Is Bossy. ed. 1994. (J). (gr. 2). spiral bd. (*0-616-01576-3*) Canadian National Institute for the Blind/Institut National Canadien pour les Aveugles.

—Franklin Is Bossy. 1995. (Franklin Ser.). (Illus.). 100p. (J). (ps-3). pap. (*1-55074-257-4*) Kids Can Pr., Ltd.

—Franklin Is Bossy. 1993. (Franklin Ser.). (Illus.). 260p. (J). (ps-3). text 10.95 (*1-55074-119-5*) Kids Can Pr., Ltd. CAN. *Dist:* General Distribution Services, Inc.

—Franklin Is Bossy. (Franklin Ser.). (Illus.). 30p. (J). (ps-3). 1998. 19.95 (*0-590-25764-1*); 1994. pap. 4.50 (*0-590-47757-9*) Scholastic, Inc.

—Franklin Is Lost. ed. 1993. (J). (gr. 2). spiral bd. (*0-616-01577-1*) Canadian National Institute for the Blind/Institut National Canadien pour les Aveugles.

—Franklin Is Lost. 1999. (Franklin Ser.). (Illus.). (J). (ps-3). pap. 11.70 (*0-7857-0678-X*) Econo-Clad Bks.

—Franklin Is Lost. 1992. (Franklin Ser.). (Illus.). 100p. (J). (ps-3). pap. (*1-55074-105-5*) Kids Can Pr., Ltd.

—Franklin Is Lost. 1992. (Franklin Ser.). (Illus.). 268p. (J). (ps-3). text 10.95 (*1-55074-053-9*) Kids Can Pr., Ltd. CAN. *Dist:* General Distribution Services, Inc.

—Franklin Is Lost. 1993. (Franklin Ser.). (Illus.). 32p. (J). (ps-3). pap. 4.50 (*0-590-46255-5*) Scholastic, Inc.

—Franklin Is Lost. 1992. (Franklin Ser.). (J). (ps-3). 10.65 (*0-606-05299-2*) Turtleback Bks.

—Franklin Is Messy. ed. 1997. (J). (gr. 1). spiral bd. (*0-616-01578-X*); (gr. 2). spiral bd. (*0-616-01579-8*) Canadian National Institute for the Blind/Institut National Canadien pour les Aveugles.

—Franklin Is Messy. 1994. (Franklin Ser.). (Illus.). 96p. (J). (ps-3). pap. (*1-55074-245-0*) Kids Can Pr., Ltd.

—Franklin Is Messy. 1994. (Franklin Ser.). (Illus.). (J). (ps-3). 256p. text 10.95 (*1-55074-243-4*); 32p. text 10.95 (*1-55074-426-7*) Kids Can Pr., Ltd. CAN. *Dist:* General Distribution Services, Inc.

—Franklin Is Messy. 1995. (Franklin Ser.). (Illus.). 30p. (J). (ps-3). pap. 4.50 (*0-590-48686-1*) Scholastic, Inc.

—Franklin Is Messy. 1994. (Franklin Ser.). (J). (ps-3). 10.65 (*0-606-07538-0*) Turtleback Bks.

—Franklin Juega al Futbol. Varela, Alejandra López, tr. (SPA., Illus.). (J). (gr. k-2). ring bd. 10.95 (*1-930332-17-3*, LC6563) Lectorum Pubns., Inc.

—Franklin Juega al Futbol. López Varela, Alejandra, tr. from ENG. 1998. (Franklin Ser.). (SPA., Illus.). 32p. (J). (ps-3). pap. 5.95 (*1-880507-44-7*, LC7851) Lectorum Pubns., Inc.

—Franklin Juega al Futbol. 1998. (Franklin Ser.). (SPA.). (J). (ps-3). 12.10 (*0-606-15534-1*) Turtleback Bks.

—Franklin Miente. 2000. (Franklin Ser.). (SPA., Illus.). (J). (ps-3). pap. 5.95 (*1-880507-69-2*, LC4551) Lectorum Pubns., Inc.

—Franklin Miente. 2000. (Franklin Ser.). (SPA., Illus.). (J). (ps-3). 12.10 (*0-606-18243-8*) Turtleback Bks.

—Franklin Plants a Tree. 2001. (Franklin TV-Tie In Ser.). (Illus.). 32p. (J). (ps-3). pap. 4.50 (*0-439-20382-1*) Scholastic, Inc.

—Franklin Plants a Tree. 2001. (Franklin Ser.). (Illus.). (J). 10.65 (*0-606-21196-9*) Turtleback Bks.

—Franklin Plays Hockey. 2002. (Franklin TV-Tie In Ser.: No. 14). (Illus.). 32p. (J). (ps-2). pap. 4.50 (*0-439-33880-8*) Scholastic, Inc.

—Franklin Plays the Game. ed. 1995. (J). (gr. 1). spiral bd. (*0-616-01580-1*); (gr. 2). spiral bd. (*0-616-01581-X*) Canadian National Institute for the Blind/Institut National Canadien pour les Aveugles.

—Franklin Plays the Game. 1995. (Franklin Ser.). (Illus.). 94p. (J). (ps-3). pap. (*1-55074-255-8*) Kids Can Pr., Ltd.

—Franklin Plays the Game. unabr. ed. 1997. (Franklin Ser.). (Illus.). 270p. (J). (ps-3). 10.95 (*1-55074-254-X*) Kids Can Pr., Ltd. CAN. *Dist:* General Distribution Services, Inc.

—Franklin Plays the Game. 1995. (Franklin Ser.). (Illus.). 32p. (J). (ps-3). pap. 4.50 (*0-590-22631-2*) Scholastic, Inc.

—Franklin Plays the Game. 1995. (Franklin Ser.). (J). (ps-3). 10.65 (*0-606-08519-X*) Turtleback Bks.

—Franklin Quiere una Mascota. Varela, Alejandra López, tr. from ENG. 1998. (Franklin Ser.). (SPA., Illus.). 32p. (J). (ps-3). pap. 5.95 (*1-880507-49-8*, LC8143) Lectorum Pubns., Inc.

—Franklin Quiere una Mascota. 1998. (Franklin Ser.). (SPA.). (J). (ps-3). 11.10 (*0-606-17015-4*) Turtleback Bks.

—Franklin Rides a Bike. ed. 1998. (J). (gr. 1). spiral bd. (*0-616-01582-8*); (gr. 2). spiral bd. (*0-616-01583-6*) Canadian National Institute for the Blind/Institut National Canadien pour les Aveugles.

—Franklin Rides a Bike. 1997. (Franklin Ser.). (Illus.). (J). (ps-3). 32p. 10.95 (*1-55074-414-3*); 96p. pap. (*1-55074-354-6*) Kids Can Pr., Ltd.

—Franklin Rides a Bike. 1997. (Franklin Ser.). (Illus.). 32p. (J). (ps-3). pap. 4.50 (*0-590-69333-6*) Scholastic, Inc.

—Franklin Rides a Bike. 1997. (Franklin Ser.). (J). (ps-3). 10.65 (*0-606-11351-7*) Turtleback Bks.

—Franklin Says I Love You. ed. 2003. (gr. 1). spiral bd. (*0-616-14561-6*); (gr. 2). spiral bd. (*0-616-14562-4*) Canadian National Institute for the Blind/Institut National Canadien pour les Aveugles.

—Franklin Says I Love You. 2002. (Franklin the Turtle Ser.). (Illus.). 32p. (J). (ps-3). 10.95 (*1-55337-035-X*) Kids Can Pr., Ltd.

—Franklin Says Sorry. 2000. (Franklin TV Storybook Ser.). (J). (ps-3). 10.65 (*0-606-20060-6*) Turtleback Bks.

—Franklin Se Pierde. 2000. (Franklin Ser.). (SPA., Illus.). (J). (ps-3). pap. 5.95 (*1-880507-70-6*, LC6163) Lectorum Pubns., Inc.

—Franklin Se Pierde. 2000. (Franklin Ser.). (SPA., Illus.). (J). (ps-3). 12.10 (*0-606-18244-6*) Turtleback Bks.

—Franklin Tiene un Mal Dia. Varela, Alejandra López, tr. (Franklin Ser.). (SPA.). (J). (ps-3). 2001. ring bd. 10.95 (*1-880507-86-2*, LC4083); 1999. (Illus.). pap. 5.95 (*1-880507-52-8*, LC8141) Lectorum Pubns., Inc.

—Franklin Tiene un Mal Dia. 1999. (Franklin Ser.). (SPA.). (J). (ps-3). 11.10 (*0-606-17011-1*) Turtleback Bks.

—Franklin Treasury. 2000. (Franklin Ser.). (Illus.). (J). (ps-3). 15.95 (*1-55337-018-X*) Kids Can Pr., Ltd.

—Franklin Va a la Escuela. López Varela, Alejandra, tr. (Franklin Ser.). (SPA., Illus.). (J). (ps-3). 2001. ring bd. 10.95 (*1-880507-85-4*, LC4919); 1998. 32p. pap. 5.95 (*1-880507-41-2*, LC7792) Lectorum Pubns., Inc.

—Franklin Va a la Escuela. 1998. (Franklin Ser.). (SPA.). (J). (ps-3). 12.10 (*0-606-13405-0*) Turtleback Bks.

—Franklin Va al Hospital. Varela, Alejandra López, tr. (SPA.). (J). (gr. k-2). pap. 5.95 (*1-930332-26-2*, LC1130); (Illus.). ring bd. 10.95 (*1-930332-27-0*, LC1301) Lectorum Pubns., Inc.

—Franklin Wants a Badge. 2003. (Franklin TV Storybook Ser.). (Illus.). 32p. (J). 10.95 (*1-55337-467-3*) Kids Can Pr., Ltd.

—Franklin Wants a Pet. ed. 1996. (J). (gr. 2). spiral bd. (*0-616-01584-4*) Canadian National Institute for the Blind/Institut National Canadien pour les Aveugles.

—Franklin Wants a Pet. (Franklin Ser.). (Illus.). (J). (ps-3). 2000. 180p. pap. incl. audio (*1-55074-795-9*); 1995. 96p. pap. (*1-55074-249-3*) Kids Can Pr., Ltd.

—Franklin Wants a Pet. 1994. (Franklin Ser.). (Illus.). 270p. (J). (ps-3). 10.95 (*1-55074-247-7*) Kids Can Pr., Ltd. CAN. *Dist:* General Distribution Services, Inc.

—Franklin Wants a Pet. 1995. (Franklin Ser.). (Illus.). 32p. (J). (ps-3). pap. 4.50 (*0-590-48915-1*) Scholastic, Inc.

—Franklin Wants a Pet. 1995. (Franklin Ser.). (J). (ps-3). 10.65 (*0-606-07539-9*) Turtleback Bks.

—Franklin y el Dia de Accion de Gracias. Varela, Alejandra López, tr. (SPA., Illus.). pap. 5.95 (*1-930332-06-8*, LC30183) Lectorum Pubns., Inc.

—Franklin y el Dia de Accion de Gracias. 2001. 12.10 (*0-606-22645-1*) Turtleback Bks.

—Franklin y el Regalo de Navidad. 1999. (Franklin Ser.). (SPA., Illus.). (J). (ps-3). pap. 5.95 (*1-880507-56-0*, LC2911) Lectorum Pubns., Inc.

—Franklin y el Regalo de Navidad. Varela, Alejandra López, tr. from ENG. 1999. (Franklin Ser.). (SPA., Illus.). (J). (ps-3). ring bd. 10.95 (*1-880507-67-6*, LC6006) Lectorum Pubns., Inc.

—Franklin y Harriet. 2001. (SPA., Illus.). (J). pap. 5.95 (*1-880507-96-X*, LC8512); ring bd. 10.95 (*1-880507-97-8*, LC0630) Lectorum Pubns., Inc.

—Franklin y Harriet. 2001. (Franklin Ser.). (SPA., Illus.). (J). 12.10 (*0-606-21197-7*) Turtleback Bks.

—Franklin's Baby Sister. ed. 2001. (J). (gr. 1). spiral bd. (*0-616-07218-X*) Canadian National Institute for the Blind/Institut National Canadien pour les Aveugles.

—Franklin's Baby Sister. (Franklin Ser.). (Illus.). (J). (ps-3). 96p. pap. (*1-55074-858-0*); 2000. 266p. text 10.95 (*1-55074-794-0*) Kids Can Pr., Ltd.

—Franklin's Baby Sister. 2000. (Franklin Ser.). (Illus.). 32p. (J). (ps-3). pap. text 4.50 (*0-439-20378-3*) Scholastic, Inc.

—Franklin's Baby Sister. 2000. (Franklin Ser.). (J). (ps-3). 10.65 (*0-606-19919-5*) Turtleback Bks.

—Franklin's Bad Day. 1996. (Franklin Ser.). 100p. (J). (ps-3). pap. (*1-55074-293-0*) Kids Can Pr., Ltd.

—Franklin's Bad Day. 1997. (Franklin Ser.). (Illus.). 260p. (J). (ps-3). 10.95 (*1-55074-291-4*) Kids Can Pr., Ltd. CAN. *Dist:* General Distribution Services, Inc.

—Franklin's Bad Day. 1997. (Franklin Ser.). (Illus.). 32p. (J). (ps-3). pap. 4.50 (*0-590-69332-8*) Scholastic, Inc.

—Franklin's Bad Day. 1997. (Franklin Ser.). (J). (ps-3). 10.65 (*0-606-10813-0*) Turtleback Bks.

—Franklin's Bicycle Helmet. 2000. (Franklin TV Storybook Ser.). (J). (ps-3). 10.65 (*0-606-20061-4*) Turtleback Bks.

—Franklin's Birthday Party. 2001. (Franklin TV Storybook Ser.). (Illus.). (J). 10.65 (*0-606-21198-5*) Turtleback Bks.

—Franklin's Blanket. ed. 1996. (J). (gr. 2). spiral bd. (*0-616-01585-2*) Canadian National Institute for the Blind/Institut National Canadien pour les Aveugles.

—Franklin's Blanket. (Franklin Ser.). (J). (ps-3). 2000. 180p. pap. incl. audio (*1-55074-686-3*); 1995. (Illus.). 96p. pap. (*1-55074-278-7*) Kids Can Pr., Ltd.

—Franklin's Blanket. 1997. (Franklin Ser.). (Illus.). 270p. (J). (ps-3). text 10.95 (*1-55074-154-3*) Kids Can Pr., Ltd. CAN. *Dist:* General Distribution Services, Inc.

—Franklin's Blanket. 1996. (Franklin Ser.). (Illus.). 32p. (J). (ps-3). pap. 4.50 (*0-590-25468-5*) Scholastic, Inc.

—Franklin's Blanket. 1995. (Franklin Ser.). (J). (ps-3). 10.65 (*0-606-08520-3*) Turtleback Bks.

—Franklin's Canoe Trip. 2002. (Franklin TV-Tie In Ser.: No. 11). 32p. (J). pap. 4.50 (*0-439-33877-8*) Scholastic, Inc.

—Franklin's Christmas: A Sticker Activity Book. 2003. (Franklin Ser.). (Illus.). 16p. (J). 6.95 (*1-55337-506-8*) Kids Can Pr., Ltd.

—Franklin's Christmas Gift. 1998. (Franklin Ser.). (Illus.). 96p. (J). (ps-3). pap. (*1-55074-468-2*) Kids Can Pr., Ltd.

—Franklin's Christmas Gift. 1998. (Franklin Ser.). (Illus.). 264p. (J). (ps-3). text 10.95 (*1-55074-466-6*) Kids Can Pr., Ltd. CAN. *Dist:* General Distribution Services, Inc.

—Franklin's Christmas Gift. 1998. (Franklin Ser.). (J). (ps-3). pap. 54.00 (*0-590-95169-6*); (Illus.). 32p. pap. 4.50 (*0-590-02611-9*) Scholastic, Inc. (Cartwheel Bks.).

—Franklin's Christmas Gift. 1998. (Franklin Ser.). (J). (ps-3). 10.65 (*0-606-15535-X*) Turtleback Bks.

—Franklin's Class Trip. 1999. (Franklin Ser.). (Illus.). (J). (ps-3). 30p. pap. (*1-55074-472-0*); 272p. text (*1-55074-470-4*) Kids Can Pr., Ltd.

—Franklin's Class Trip. 1999. (Franklin Ser.). (Illus.). 32p. (J). (ps-3). pap. 4.50 (*0-590-13002-1*) Scholastic, Inc.

—Franklin's Class Trip. 1999. (Franklin Ser.). (Illus.). (J). (ps-3). 10.65 (*0-606-18548-8*) Turtleback Bks.

—Franklin's Classic Treasury. (Franklin Ser.). (Illus.). (J). (ps-3). 1999. 608p. text (*1-55074-742-8*); 2000. 128p. text 15.95 (*1-55074-813-0*) Kids Can Pr., Ltd.

—Franklin's Friendship Treasury. 2000. (Franklin Ser.). (Illus.). 612p. (J). (ps-3). text 15.95 (*1-55074-872-6*) Kids Can Pr., Ltd.

—Franklin's Fun Book. 2000. (Franklin Color & Activity Bks.). (Illus.). 96p. (J). (ps-3). pap. (*0-7666-0494-2*) Modern Publishing.

—Franklin's Halloween. ed. 1997. (gr. 2). spiral bd. (*0-616-01587-9*); (Illus.). (J). (ps-2). spiral bd. (*0-616-01586-0*) Canadian National Institute for the Blind/Institut National Canadien pour les Aveugles.

—Franklin's Halloween. 1996. (Franklin Ser.). 100p. (J). (ps-3). pap. (*1-55074-285-X*) Kids Can Pr., Ltd.

—Franklin's Halloween. 1996. (Franklin Ser.). (Illus.). 260p. (J). (ps-3). 10.95 (*1-55074-283-3*) Kids Can Pr., Ltd. CAN. *Dist:* General Distribution Services, Inc.

—Franklin's Halloween. 1996. (Franklin Ser.). (Illus.). 32p. (J). (ps-3). pap. text 4.50 (*0-590-69330-1*) Scholastic, Inc.

—Franklin's Halloween. 1996. (Franklin Ser.). (J). (ps-3). 10.65 (*0-606-09296-X*) Turtleback Bks.

—Franklin's Holiday Treasury. 2002. (Franklin Ser.). (Illus.). 128p. (J). (ps-3). 15.95 (*1-55337-045-7*) Kids Can Pr., Ltd.

—Franklin's Neighborhood. ed. 2000. (gr. 1). spiral bd. (*0-616-01588-7*); (J). (gr. 2). spiral bd. (*0-616-01589-5*) Canadian National Institute for the Blind/Institut National Canadien pour les Aveugles.

—Franklin's Neighborhood. 1999. (Franklin Ser.). (J). (ps-3). 94p. pap. (*1-55074-704-5*); 270p. text (*1-55074-702-9*) Kids Can Pr., Ltd.

—Franklin's Neighborhood. 1999. (Franklin Ser.). (Illus.). 32p. (J). (ps-3). pap. text 4.50 (*0-439-08369-9*) Scholastic, Inc.

—Franklin's Neighborhood. 1999. (Franklin Ser.). (J). (ps-3). 10.65 (*0-606-17271-8*) Turtleback Bks.

—Franklin's New Friend. ed. 1999. (gr. 1). spiral bd. (*0-616-01590-9*); (J). (gr. 2). spiral bd. (*0-616-01591-7*) Canadian National Institute for the Blind/Institut National Canadien pour les Aveugles.

—Franklin's New Friend. (Franklin Ser.). 96p. (J). (ps-3). pap. (*1-55074-363-5*) Kids Can Pr., Ltd.

—Franklin's New Friend. 1997. (Franklin Ser.). (Illus.). 260p. (J). (ps-3). 10.95 (*1-55074-361-9*); 10.95 (*1-55074-352-X*) Kids Can Pr., Ltd. CAN. *Dist:* General Distribution Services, Inc.

—Franklin's New Friend. 1997. (Franklin Ser.). (Illus.). 32p. (J). (ps-3). pap. 4.50 (*0-590-02592-9*) Scholastic, Inc.

—Franklin's New Friend. 1997. (Franklin Ser.). (J). (ps-3). 10.65 (*0-606-11352-5*) Turtleback Bks.

—Franklin's Pet Problem. 2000. (Franklin Ser.). (Illus.). 22p. (J). (ps-3). 4.99 (*0-439-19424-5*) Scholastic, Inc.

—Franklin's School Play. ed. 1998. (J). (gr. 2). spiral bd. (*0-616-01592-5*) Canadian National Institute for the Blind/Institut National Canadien pour les Aveugles.

—Franklin's School Play. 1996. (Franklin Ser.). (Illus.). 96p. (J). (ps-3). pap. (*1-55074-289-2*) Kids Can Pr., Ltd.

—Franklin's School Play. 1997. (Franklin Ser.). (Illus.). 260p. (J). (ps-3). text 10.95 (*1-55074-287-6*) Kids Can Pr., Ltd. CAN. *Dist:* General Distribution Services, Inc.

—Franklin's School Play. 1996. (Franklin Ser.). (Illus.). (J). (ps-3). 30p. pap. 4.50 (*0-590-69331-X*); (FRE., 32p. pap. 6.99 (*0-590-16032-X*) Scholastic, Inc.

—Franklin's School Play. 1996. (Franklin Ser.). (J). (ps-3). 10.65 (*0-606-10188-8*) Turtleback Bks.

—Franklin's School Treasury. unabr. ed. 2001. (Franklin Ser.). (Illus.). 128p. (J). (ps-3). text 15.95 (*1-55074-877-7*) Kids Can Pr., Ltd.

—Franklin's Secret Club. ed. 2001. (J). (gr. 1). spiral bd. (*0-616-01593-3*); (gr. 2). spiral bd. (*0-616-01594-1*) Canadian National Institute for the Blind/Institut National Canadien pour les Aveugles.

—Franklin's Secret Club. 1999. (Franklin Ser.). (Illus.). (J). (ps-3). pap. 11.70 (*0-613-11556-2*) Econo-Clad Bks.

—Franklin's Secret Club. 1998. (Franklin Ser.). (Illus.). 96p. (J). (ps-3). pap. (*1-55074-476-3*) Kids Can Pr., Ltd.

—Franklin's Secret Club. 1998. (Franklin Ser.). (Illus.). 264p. (J). (ps-3). 10.95 (*1-55074-474-7*) Kids Can Pr., Ltd. CAN. *Dist:* General Distribution Services, Inc.

—Franklin's Secret Club. 1998. (Franklin Ser.). (Illus.). 32p. (J). (ps-3). pap. 4.50 (*0-590-13000-5*, Scholastic Paperbacks) Scholastic, Inc.

—Franklin's Secret Club. 1998. (Franklin Ser.). (J). (ps-3). 10.65 (*0-606-13406-9*) Turtleback Bks.

—Franklin's Special Blanket. 2000. (Franklin Ser.). (Illus.). 22p. (J). (ps-3). bds. 4.99 (*0-439-20299-X*) Scholastic, Inc.

—Franklin's Thanksgiving. 2001. (Franklin Ser.). (Illus.). (J). 10.65 (*0-606-22045-3*) Turtleback Bks.

—Franklin's Valentine Cards. 1998. (Franklin Ser.). (Illus.). 92p. (J). (ps-3). pap. (*1-55074-625-1*) Kids Can Pr., Ltd.

—Franklin's Valentine Cards. Burak, Hally, ed. 1999. (Franklin Ser.). (Illus.). 16p. (J). (ps up). pap. 2.99 (*0-439-05123-1*) Scholastic, Inc.

—Franklin's Valentines. 1998. (Franklin Ser.). (Illus.). 96p. (J). (ps-3). pap. (*1-55074-482-8*) Kids Can Pr., Ltd.

—Franklin's Valentines. 1998. (Franklin Ser.). (Illus.). 268p. (J). (ps-3). text 10.95 (*1-55074-480-1*) Kids Can Pr., Ltd. CAN. *Dist:* General Distribution Services, Inc.

—Franklin's Valentines. 1999. (Franklin Ser.). (J). (ps-3). pap. 54.00 (*0-439-04355-7*); (Illus.). 32p. pap. 4.50 (*0-590-13001-3*, Cartwheel Bks.) Scholastic, Inc.

—Franklin's Valentines. 1999. (Franklin Ser.). (J). (ps-3). 10.65 (*0-606-15536-8*) Turtleback Bks.

—Fun & Games with Franklin. 2000. (Franklin Color & Activity Bks.). (Illus.). 32p. (J). (ps-3). pap. (*0-7666-0493-4*) Modern Publishing.

—Fun with Franklin: A Learning to Read Book. (Franklin Ser.). (Illus.). (J). (ps-3). (*1-55074-646-4*); 1997. 86p. pap. (*1-55074-391-0*) Kids Can Pr., Ltd.

—Fun with Franklin: Activity Book. 1997. (Franklin Ser.). (Illus.). 86p. (J). (ps-3). pap. (*1-55074-392-9*) Kids Can Pr., Ltd.

—Fun with Franklin: Math Activity Book. 1998. (Franklin Ser.). (Illus.). 72p. (J). (ps-3). pap. (*1-55074-452-6*) Kids Can Pr., Ltd.

—Fun with Franklin: Puzzle Book. 1997. (Franklin Ser.). (Illus.). 86p. (J). (ps-3). pap. (*1-55074-394-5*) Kids Can Pr., Ltd.

—Fun with Franklin: Trace & Colour Book. 1997. (Franklin Ser.). (Illus.). 72p. (J). (ps-3). pap. (*1-55074-396-1*) Kids Can Pr., Ltd.

—El Hallazgo de Franklin. Varela, Alejandra López, tr. (SPA., Illus.). (J). (gr. k-2). ring bd. 10.95 (*1-930332-10-6*, LC1928); 1999. pap. 5.95 (*1-880507-51-X*, LC8142) Lectorum Pubns., Inc.

—La Hermanita de Franklin. 2000. (Franklin Ser.). (SPA., Illus.). (J). (ps-3). pap. 5.95 (*1-880507-83-8*, LC7611); ring bd. 10.95 (*1-880507-84-6*, LC3577) Lectorum Pubns., Inc.

—La Hermanita de Franklin. 2000. (Franklin Ser.). (SPA.). (J). (ps-3). 12.10 (*0-606-20188-2*) Turtleback Bks.

—Hurry up, Franklin. ed. 1997. (J). (gr. 2). spiral bd. (*0-616-01595-X*) Canadian National Institute for the Blind/Institut National Canadien pour les Aveugles.

—Hurry up, Franklin. 1992. (Franklin Ser.). (Illus.). 96p. (J). (ps-3). pap. (*1-55074-016-4*) Kids Can Pr., Ltd.

—Hurry up, Franklin. 1997. (Franklin Ser.). (Illus.). 270p. (J). (ps-3). text 10.95 (*0-921103-68-9*) Kids Can Pr., Ltd. CAN. *Dist:* General Distribution Services, Inc.

—Hurry up, Franklin. (Franklin Ser.). (J). (ps-3). 1991. (Illus.). 31p. pap. 3.95 (*0-590-42621-4*); 1990. pap. 11.95 o.p. (*0-590-42620-6*) Scholastic, Inc.

—Un Nouvel Ami pour Benjamin. ed. 1999. Tr. of Franklin's New Friend. (J). (gr. 1). spiral bd. (*0-616-01828-2*) Canadian National Institute for the Blind/Institut National Canadien pour les Aveugles.

—Time to Play with Franklin. 2000. (Franklin Color & Activity Bks.). (Illus.). 32p. (J). (ps-3). pap. (*0-7666-0491-8*) Modern Publishing.

—Welcome to Franklin's World. 2000. (Franklin Color & Activity Bks.). (Illus.). 32p. (J). (ps-3). pap. (*0-7666-0490-X*) Modern Publishing.

Bourgeois, Paulette & Clark, Brenda. Franklin & His Friend. 2002. (Franklin TV-Tie In Ser.: No. 12). (Illus.). 32p. (J). pap. 4.50 (*0-439-33878-6*) Scholastic, Inc.

—Franklin Fibs. 1999. (Franklin Ser.). (Illus.). 162p. (J). (ps-3). pap. incl. audio (*1-55074-668-5*) Kids Can Pr., Ltd.

—Franklin Forgets. 2000. (Franklin TV Storybook Ser.). (J). (ps-3). 96p. pap. (*1-55074-726-6*); (Illus.). 264p. text (*1-55074-722-3*) Kids Can Pr., Ltd.

—Franklin Has a Sleepover. 1999. (Franklin Ser.). (Illus.). 168p. (J). (ps-3). pap. incl. audio (*1-55074-664-2*) Kids Can Pr., Ltd.

—Franklin Is Lost. 1999. (Franklin Ser.). (Illus.). 162p. (J). (ps-3). pap. incl. audio (*1-55074-670-7*) Kids Can Pr., Ltd.

—Franklin Is Messy. 1999. (Franklin Ser.). 180p. (J). (ps-3). pap. incl. audio (*1-55074-678-2*) Kids Can Pr., Ltd.

—Franklin Makes a Deal. 2003. (Franklin TV-Tie In Ser.). 32p. (J). (gr. k-3). pap. 4.50 (*0-439-43126-3*) Scholastic, Inc.

—Franklin Says I Love You. 2002. (Franklin Ser.: Vol. 29). 32p. (J). pap. 4.50 (*0-439-33876-X*) Scholastic, Inc.

—Franklin Says Sorry. 1999. (Franklin TV Storybook Ser.). (J). (ps-3). 96p. pap. (*1-55074-714-2*); (Illus.). 262p. text (*1-55074-712-6*) Kids Can Pr., Ltd.

—Franklin Says Sorry. 2000. (Franklin TV-Tie In Ser.). (Illus.). 32p. (J). (ps-3). pap. 4.50 (*0-439-08366-4*) Scholastic, Inc.

—Franklin Wants a Badge. 2003. (Franklin TV-Tie In Ser.). (Illus.). 32p. (J). (gr. k-3). pap. 4.50 (*0-439-43122-0*, Scholastic Pr.) Scholastic, Inc.

—Franklin's Bicycle Helmet. 2000. (Franklin TV Storybook Ser.). (J). (ps-3). 96p. pap. (*1-55074-728-2*); (Illus.). 32p. (*1-55074-730-4*) Kids Can Pr., Ltd.

—Franklin's Bicycle Helmet. 2000. (Franklin TV-Tie In Ser.). (Illus.). 32p. (J). (ps-3). pap. 4.50 (*0-439-08367-2*) Scholastic, Inc.

—Franklin's Family Treasury. 2003. (Illus.). 128p. (J). (ps-3). 15.95 (*1-55337-479-7*) Kids Can Pr., Ltd.

—Franklin's Neighborhood. 1999. (Franklin Ser.). (Illus.). 194p. (J). (ps-3). pap. incl. audio (*1-55074-752-5*) Kids Can Pr., Ltd.

—Franklin's New Friend. 1999. (Franklin Ser.). (Illus.). 180p. (J). (ps-3). pap. incl. audio (*1-55074-797-5*) Kids Can Pr., Ltd.

—Franklin's Secret Club. 1999. (Franklin Ser.). (Illus.). 194p. (J). (ps-3). pap. incl. audio (*1-55074-672-3*) Kids Can Pr., Ltd.

Bourgeois, Paulette & Clark, Brenda, creators. Franklin's Birthday Party. 2001. (Franklin TV-Tie In Ser.). (Illus.). 32p. (J). (ps-3). pap. 4.50 (*0-439-20383-X*) Scholastic, Inc.

—Hurry up, Franklin. 2000. (Franklin Ser.). 180p. (J). (ps-3). pap. incl. audio (*1-55074-682-0*) Kids Can Pr., Ltd.

Bourgeois, Paulette & Jennings, Sharon. Franklin Plants a Tree. 2003. (Franklin TV Storybook Ser.). (Illus.). 32p. (J). 10.95 (*1-55074-878-5*) Kids Can Pr., Ltd.

—Franklin's Thanksgiving. 2001. (Franklin Ser.). (Illus.). 32p. (J). (ps-3). 10.95 (*1-55074-798-3*) Kids Can Pr., Ltd.

Bourgeois, Paulette & Moore, Eva. Franklin's First Day of School. 2000. (Franklin Ser.). (Illus.). 12p. (J). (ps-3). bds. 5.99 (*0-439-20298-1*) Scholastic, Inc.

Bourgeois, Paulette, et al. Franklin en la Oscuridad. López Varela, Alejandra, tr. from ENG. 1998. (Franklin Ser.). (SPA., Illus.). 32p. (J). (ps-3). pap. 5.95 (*1-880507-43-9*, LC7861) Lectorum Pubns., Inc.

—Franklin's Neighborhood. 1999. (Franklin Ser.). (Illus.). 32p. (J). (ps-3). text (*1-55074-729-0*) Kids Can Pr., Ltd.

Franklin's Surprise. 2003. (Kids Can Read Ser.). (Illus.). 32p. (J). 14.95 (*1-55337-465-7*); pap. 3.95 (*1-55337-466-5*) Kids Can Pr., Ltd.

Jenkins, Susan. Franklin & the Magic Show. 2003. (Kids Can Read with Help Ser.). (Illus.). 32p. (J). (gr. 1-2). 14.95 (*1-55074-990-0*); pap. 3.95 (*1-55074-992-7*) Kids Can Pr., Ltd.

—The Franklin Annual. 2002. (Illus.). 96p. (J). (ps-3). 14.95 (*1-55337-481-9*) Kids Can Pr., Ltd.

Jennings, Sharon. Franklin & Otter's Visit. 2003. (Franklin TV Storybooks Ser.). (Illus.). 32p. 10.95 (*1-55337-021-X*) Kids Can Pr., Ltd.

Jennings, Sharon & Bourgeois, Paulette. Franklin & the Big Kid. 2002. (Franklin TV-Tie In Ser.). (Illus.). 32p. (J). pap. 4.50 (*0-439-33879-4*) Scholastic, Inc.

Jennings, Sharon, et al. Franklin's Canoe Trip. 2003. (Franklin TV Storybooks Ser.). (Illus.). 32p. 10.95 (*1-55337-019-8*) Kids Can Pr., Ltd.

—Franklin's Music Lessons. 2003. (Kids Can Read with Help Ser.). (Illus.). 32p. (J). (gr. 1-2). 14.95 (*1-55337-171-2*); pap. 3.95 (*1-55337-172-0*) Kids Can Pr., Ltd.

Moore, Eva. Franklin & the Baby. 1999. (Franklin TV Storybook Ser.). (Illus.). 262p. (J). (ps-3). text (*1-55074-706-1*) Kids Can Pr., Ltd.

—Franklin & the Baby. 1999. (Franklin TV-Tie In Ser.). (Illus.). 32p. (J). (ps-3). pap. text 4.50 (*0-439-08365-6*) Scholastic, Inc.

—Franklin & the Baby. 1999. (Franklin TV Storybook Ser.). (J). (ps-3). 10.65 (*0-606-20056-8*) Turtleback Bks.

Moore, Eva & Nelvana Staff. Franklin & the Baby. 2000. (Franklin TV Storybook Ser.). (Illus.). 96p. (J). (ps-3). pap. (*1-55074-708-8*) Kids Can Pr., Ltd.

Scholastic, Inc. Staff. Franklin Forgives. 2004. (Franklin Ser.). 32p. (J). pap. 4.50 (*0-439-62054-6*) Scholastic, Inc.

—Franklin's Big Hockey Game: A Sticker Activity Book. 2002. (Franklin Ser.). (Illus.). 16p. (J). pap. 6.99 (*0-439-37573-8*) Scholastic, Inc.

Scholastic, Inc. Staff, et al. Franklin Dress-Up Doll. 2003. (Franklin Ser.). (J). 24.99 (*0-439-48588-6*, Sidekicks) Scholastic, Inc.

—Franklin Poseable. 2003. (Franklin Ser.). (J). 15.99 (*0-439-48591-6*, Sidekicks) Scholastic, Inc.

FRANKLIN, BENJAMIN, 1706-1790—FICTION

Bourne, Miriam A. What Is Papa up to Now? 1977. (Break-of-Day Bks.). (Illus.). 64p. (J). (gr. k-3). 6.99 o.p. (*0-698-30658-9*) Putnam Publishing Group, The.

Fleming, Candace. The Hatmaker's Sign. 1998. (Illus.). 40p. (J). (gr. k-4). pap. 16.95 (*0-531-30075-7*); lib. bdg. 17.99 (*0-531-33075-3*) Scholastic, Inc. (Orchard Bks.).

Gutman, Dan. Qwerty Stevens, Stuck in Time with Benjamin Franklin. 2002. (Illus.). 192p. (J). (gr. 5-8). 16.95 (*0-689-84553-7*, Simon & Schuster Children's Publishing) Simon & Schuster Children's Publishing.

Lawson, Robert. Ben & Me: An Astonishing Life of Benjamin Franklin by His Good Mouse Amos. (J). 1999. (*0-316-52533-2*); 1999. pap. (*0-316-52520-0*); 1988. (Illus.). 114p. (gr. 3-7). pap. 5.99 (*0-316-51730-5*); 1939. (Illus.). 114p. (gr. 3-7). 16.95 (*0-316-51732-1*) Little Brown & Co.

—Ben & Me: An Astonishing Life of Benjamin Franklin by His Good Mouse Amos. 1973. (J). (gr. 3-6). pap. 2.75 o.s.i (*0-440-42038-5*, Yearling) Random Hse. Children's Bks.

—Ben & Me: An Astonishing Life of Benjamin Franklin by His Good Mouse Amos. 1988. (J). 12.00 (*0-606-03968-6*) Turtleback Bks.

Murphy, Frank. Ben Franklin & the Magic Squares. 2001. (Step into Reading Ser.). (Illus.). 48p. (J). (gr. k-3). pap. 3.99 (*0-375-80621-0*); lib. bdg. 11.99 (*0-375-90621-5*) Random Hse. Children's Bks. (Random Hse. Bks. for Young Readers).

Sargent, Dave & Sargent, Pat. Sugar (cream) Curiosity Is Good #57. 2001. (Saddle Up Ser.). 36p. (J). pap. 6.95 (*1-56763-668-3*); lib. bdg. 22.60 (*1-56763-667-5*) Ozark Publishing.

The Spirited Philadelphia Adventure. 2000. (Illus.). 32p. (J). (gr. k-2). (*0-9626959-1-2*) Junior League of Philadelphia, Inc.

Stevens, Bryna. Ben Franklin's Glass Armonica. 1992. 48p. (J). (ps-3). pap. 3.25 o.s.i (*0-440-40584-X*) Dell Publishing.

Uglow, Loyd. Benjamin Franklin - You Know What to Say. 2000. (Another Great Achiever Ser.). (Illus.). 48p. (J). (gr. 3-6). lib. bdg. 16.95 (*1-57537-106-5*) Advance Publishing, Inc.

Zak & Ben. 1991. (Illus.). (J). (ps-2). pap. 5.10 (*0-8136-5661-3*); lib. bdg. 7.95 (*0-8136-5161-1*) Modern Curriculum Pr.

FREDDI FISH (FICTITIOUS CHARACTER)—FICTION

Davis, Guy. Freddi Fish. 2000. (Illus.). 112p. (J). (ps-2). pap. 2.99 o.p. (*1-57064-946-4*, 73113, Humongous Bks.) Lyrick Publishing.

Greenfield, N. S., illus. Freddi Fish the Missing Letters Mystery. 2000. 26p. (J). (ps-2). 7.99 o.p. (*1-57064-948-0*, 73115, Humongous Bks.) Lyrick Publishing.

Greenfield, N. S. & Alvord, R., illus. Freddi Fish the Big Froople Match. 2000. 24p. (J). (ps-2). pap. 3.99 o.p. (*1-57064-947-2*, 73114, Humongous Bks.) Lyrick Publishing.

Nickel, Scott. Freddi Fish a Whale of a Tale! 2001. (Humongous Ser.). (Illus.). 24p. (J). (ps-3). pap. text 4.99 (*1-58668-061-7*) Lyrick Studios.

FREDDY THE DETECTIVE (FICTITIOUS CHARACTER)—FICTION

Brooks, Walter R. Freddy & Mr. Camphor. 2000. (Illus.). 234p. (J). (gr. 3-7). 23.95 (*1-58567-027-8*) Overlook Pr., The.

—Freddy & Mr. Camphor. 2003. (Illus.). 256p. (J). pap. 7.99 (*0-14-230248-1*, Puffin Bks.) Penguin Putnam Bks. for Young Readers.

—Freddy & the Baseball Team from Mars. 1999. (Illus.). 256p. (YA). (gr. 3-7). 23.95 (*0-87951-942-8*) Overlook Pr., The.

—Freddy & the Baseball Team from Mars. 1963. (Illus.). (J). (gr. 3-7). 5.99 o.s.i (*0-394-90810-4*, Knopf Bks. for Young Readers) Random Hse. Children's Bks.

—Freddy & the Baseball Team from Mars. 2000. (J). pap. 67.95 incl. audio (*0-7887-4461-5*, 41150); pap. 67.95 incl. audio (*0-7887-4461-5*, 41150); wbk. ed. 284.80 incl. audio (*0-7887-4462-3*, 47147) Recorded Bks., LLC.

—Freddy & the Baseball Team From Mars. 1988. (Illus.). 256p. (J). (gr. 3-7). pap. 2.95 o.p. (*0-440-42724-X*) Dell Publishing.

—Freddy & the Baseball Team from Mars. unabr. ed. 2000. (J). (gr. 3-6). audio 37.00 (*0-7887-4077-6*, 96240E7) Recorded Bks., LLC.

—Freddy & the Bean Home News. 2000. (Freddy Ser.). (Illus.). 230p. (J). (gr. 3-7). 23.95 (*1-58567-081-2*) Overlook Pr., The.

—Freddy & the Dragon. 2000. (Illus.). 239p. (J). (gr. 3 up). 23.95 (*1-58567-026-X*) Overlook Pr., The.

—Freddy & the Flying Saucer Plans. 248p. (J). 22.95 o.s.i (*0-8488-2441-5*) Amereon, Ltd.

—Freddy & the Flying Saucer Plans. 1998. (Freddy Ser.). (Illus.). 256p. (J). (gr. 3-7). 23.95 (*0-87951-883-9*) Overlook Pr., The.

—Freddy & the Flying Saucer Plans. unabr. ed. 2000. (J). pap. 66.95 incl. audio (*0-7887-3639-6*, 41004X4); audio 283.80 (*0-7887-3668-X*, 46971) Recorded Bks., LLC.

—Freddy & the Ignormus. 288p. (J). 23.95 o.s.i (*0-8488-2440-7*) Amereon, Ltd.

—Freddy & the Ignormus. 1998. (Freddy Ser.). (Illus.). 288p. (J). (gr. 3-7). 23.95 (*0-87951-882-0*) Overlook Pr., The.

—Freddy & the Ignormus. 2001. (Illus.). 288p. (J). pap. 6.99 (*0-14-230043-8*, Puffin Bks.) Penguin Putnam Bks. for Young Readers.

—Freddy & the Ignormus. 1999. (J). pap. 66.95 incl. audio (*0-7887-2996-9*, 40878); (J). pap. 66.95 incl. audio (*0-7887-2996-9*, 40878); (YA). wbk. ed. 283.80 incl. audio (*0-7887-3026-6*, 46843); (YA). (gr. 3). audio 36.00 (*0-7887-2966-7*, 95740E7) Recorded Bks., LLC.

—Freddy & the Men from Mars. 1987. (Knopf Children's Paperbacks Ser.). (Illus.). 256p. (J). (gr. 3-7). 3.95 o.s.i (*0-394-88887-1*, Knopf Bks. for Young Readers) Random Hse. Children's Bks.

—Freddy & the Perilous Adventure. 1986. (Freddy the Pig Bks.). (Illus.). 256p. (J). (gr. 3-7). 9.99 o.s.i (*0-394-97601-0*, Knopf Bks. for Young Readers) Random Hse. Children's Bks.

—Freddy the Detective. 1997. (Freddy Ser.). (Illus.). 256p. (J). (gr. 3-7). 23.95 (*0-87951-809-X*) Overlook Pr., The.

—Freddy the Detective. (Knopf Children's Paperbacks Ser.). (Illus.). (J). (gr. 3-7). 1987. 272p. 4.95 o.s.i (*0-394-88885-5*); 1962. lib. bdg. 6.39 o.s.i (*0-394-90827-9*) Random Hse. Children's Bks. (Knopf Bks. for Young Readers).

—Freddy the Detective. unabr. ed. (J). 2000. (gr. 3). audio compact disk 45.00 (*0-7887-3453-9*, C1059E7); 1998. (gr. 3). audio 35.00 (*0-7887-1796-0*, 95268E7); Set 1998. (gr. 4). audio 64.70 (*0-7887-1958-0*, 40659) Recorded Bks., LLC.

—Freddy the Pilot. 1999. (Illus.). 288p. (YA). (gr. 3-7). 23.95 (*0-87951-941-X*) Overlook Pr., The.

—Freddy the Pilot. 2001. (Illus.). 256p. (J). pap. 6.99 (*0-14-230044-6*, Puffin Bks.) Penguin Putnam Bks. for Young Readers.

Brooks, Walter R., narrated by. Freddy & the Flying Saucer Plans. unabr. ed. 2000. (J). (gr. 3). audio 36.00 (*0-7887-3520-9*, 95842E7) Recorded Bks., LLC.

FREMONT, JOHN CHARLES, 1813-1890—FICTION

Nelson-Hernandez, Natalie. Mapmakers of the Western Trails: The Story of John Charles Fremont. 1997. (Illus.). 128p. (J). (gr. 3-8). pap. 9.95 o.p. (*0-9644386-2-3*) Santa Ines Pubns.

FROG AND TOAD (FICTITIOUS CHARACTERS)—FICTION

Addison, Donna & Lobel, Arnold. Frog & Toad All Year. 1982. (I Can Read It All by Myself: Beginner Books). (J). (gr. 1-3). 33.26 incl. audio (*0-394-69358-2*) Random Hse., Inc.

Clark, Lesile. Frog & Toad Together Study Guide, Classroom Ed. 1995. 34p. pap. text, stu. ed. 13.95 o.p. (*1-58609-035-6*, 115C) Progeny Pr.

—Frog & Toad Together Study Guide, Homeschool Ed. 1995. 34p. reprint ed. pap. text 5.49 o.p. (*1-58609-034-8*, 115H) Progeny Pr.

Frog & Toad Set. 1991. (J). pap. 14.00 o.p. (*0-06-449975-8*) HarperCollins Pubs.

Lobel, Arnold. The Adventures of Frog & Toad. 1998. (Illus.). (J). 12.95 (*0-06-028043-3*) HarperCollins Pubs.

—Frog & Toad. (Coloring Book Classics Ser.). (Illus.). (J). (ps-3). 1995. 32p. 3.50 o.p. (*0-694-00710-2*, Harper Festival); 1986. 12p. 9.95 o.s.i (*0-06-023986-7*) HarperCollins Children's Bk. Group.

—Frog & Toad All Year. 2002. (Frog & Toad Ser.). (Illus.). (J). 12.34 (*0-7587-1198-0*) Book Wholesalers, Inc.

—Frog & Toad All Year. (I Can Read Bks.). (Illus.). 64p. (J). 1985. (gr. 1-3). 5.98 o.p. incl. audio (*0-694-00026-4*); 1984. (gr. k-3). pap. 3.99 (*0-06-444059-1*); 1976. (gr. k-3). 15.99 (*0-06-023950-6*); 1976. (gr. k-3). lib. bdg. 16.89 (*0-06-023951-4*) HarperCollins Children's Bk. Group. (Harper Trophy).

—Frog & Toad All Year. unabr. ed. 1990. (I Can Read Bks.). (Illus.). 64p. (J). (ps-3). pap. 8.99 incl. audio (*1-55994-228-2*, HarperAudio) HarperTrade.

—Frog & Toad All Year. 1984. (I Can Read Bks.). (J). (gr. 1-3). 10.10 (*0-606-03379-3*) Turtleback Bks.

—Frog & Toad Are Friends. 2002. (Frog & Toad Ser.). (J). 12.34 (*0-7587-6105-8*) Book Wholesalers, Inc.

G

Characters

Mickey & Goofy: My Coloring Book. (Disney Ser.). (J). 9.95 o.p. (*0-307-08670-4*, 08670, Golden Bks.) Random Hse. Children's Bks.

GORDON, KATE (FICTITIOUS CHARACTER)—FICTION

Barron, T. A. The Ancient One. 2003. 320p. (J). mass mkt. 6.99 (*0-441-01032-6*) Ace Bks.

—The Ancient One. 1994. 352p. mass mkt. 5.99 o.s.i (*0-8125-3654-1*, Tor Bks.) Doherty, Tom Assocs., LLC.

—The Ancient One. 1992. (Illus.). 368p. (YA). (gr. 4-7). 19.99 (*0-399-21899-8*, Philomel) Penguin Putnam Bks. for Young Readers.

—The Ancient One. 1994. (J). 12.04 (*0-606-11042-9*) Turtleback Bks.

—Heartlight. 2003. 256p. mass mkt. 6.99 (*0-441-01036-9*) Ace Bks.

—Heartlight. 1995. 272p. mass mkt. 5.99 o.s.i (*0-8125-5170-2*, Tor Bks.) Doherty, Tom Assocs., LLC.

—Heartlight. 1990. 272p. (J). (gr. 4-7). 18.99 (*0-399-22180-8*, Philomel) Penguin Putnam Bks. for Young Readers.

—Heartlight. 1995. 11.04 (*0-606-11451-3*) Turtleback Bks.

—The Merlin Effect. 1996. (Lost Years of Merlin Ser.). 256p. (YA). mass mkt. 5.99 (*0-8125-5169-9*, Tor Bks.) Doherty, Tom Assocs., LLC.

—The Merlin Effect. 1994. 280p. (J). (gr. 5-9). 19.99 (*0-399-22689-3*, Philomel) Penguin Putnam Bks. for Young Readers.

—The Merlin Effect. 1996. 12.04 (*0-606-11618-4*) Turtleback Bks.

GRINCH (FICTITIOUS CHARACTER)—FICTION

Goode, Molly, et al. How the Grinch Got So Grinchy. 2000. (Step into Reading Step 2 Bks.). (Illus.). 48p. (ps-3). 11.99 (*0-375-91226-6*) Random Hse., Inc.

Grinch Plush with Book (English) 2000. (*1-58805-009-2*) DS-Max USA, Inc.

Random House Staff. How the Grinch Stole Christmas! Happy Who-Liday, Mr. Grinch. Terrill, Beth, ed. 2000. (Super Coloring Time Ser.). (Illus.). 80p. (J). (ps-3). pap. 2.99 (*0-375-80693-8*, Random Hse. Bks. for Young Readers) Random Hse. Children's Bks.

—How the Grinch Stole Christmas! Ornament Punch & Play Book. Jonaitis, Alice, ed. 2000. (Punch & Play Book Ser.). (Illus.). 8p. (J). (ps-3). pap. 3.99 o.s.i (*0-375-81011-0*, Random Hse. Bks. for Young Readers) Random Hse. Children's Bks.

—How the Grinch Stole Christmas! Who's Who in Who-Ville? Labrack, Joy, ed. 2000. (Super Coloring Time Ser.). (Illus.). 80p. (J). (ps-3). pap. 2.99 (*0-375-81013-7*, Random Hse. Bks. for Young Readers) Random Hse. Children's Bks.

—How the Grinch Stole Christmas! Grinch & Bear It: Life According to the Supreme Green Meany. Kleinberg, Naomi, ed. 2000. (Life Favors Ser.). (Illus.). 32p. (YA). 6.99 o.s.i (*0-375-81012-9*, Random Hse. Bks. for Young Readers) Random Hse. Children's Bks.

Seuss, Dr. The Grinch Meets His Max. 1998. (J). (ps-3). lib. bdg. 11.99 (*0-679-98836-X*, Random Hse. Bks. for Young Readers) Random Hse. Children's Bks.

—How the Grinch Stole Christmas! (J). 1999. 12.99 (*0-679-89270-2*); 1997. (Illus.). 64p. pap. 2.75 (*0-679-88793-8*); 1988. (Illus.). 64p. 10.00 o.s.i (*0-394-81339-1*); 1957. (Illus.). 64p. lib. bdg. 15.99 o.s.i (*0-394-90079-0*); 1957. (Illus.). 64p. 14.00 (*0-394-80079-6*) Random Hse. Children's Bks. (Random Hse. Bks. for Young Readers).

—How the Grinch Stole Christmas! Jonaitis, Alice, ed. deluxe ed. 2000. (Classic Seuss Ser.). (Illus.). 64p. (J). (ps-2). 25.00 o.s.i (*0-679-89153-6*, Random Hse. Bks. for Young Readers) Random Hse. Children's Bks.

—How the Grinch Stole Christmas! Kleinberg, Naomi, ed. movie tie-in ed. 2000. (Illus.). 128p. (J). (gr. 3-5). pap. 4.99 o.s.i (*0-375-81062-5*, Random Hse. Bks. for Young Readers) Random Hse. Children's Bks.

—How the Grinch Stole Christmas! audio 3.98 (*1-55886-143-2*, BB/PT 450) Smarty Pants.

—Quomodo Invidiosulus Nomine Grinchus Christi Natalem Abrogaverit: How the Grinch Stole Christmas. Tunberg, Jennifer Morrish & Tunberg, Terence O., trs. 1998. (LAT., Illus.). 64p. (ps-3). (J). 22.50 (*0-86516-419-3*); (YA). pap. 17.00 (*0-86516-420-7*) Bolchazy-Carducci Pubs.

Seuss, Dr. & Gikow, Louise. How the Grinch Stole Christmas! Movie Storybook. Jonaitis, Alice, ed. 2000. (Illus.). 48p. (J). (gr. 3-5). 6.99 (*0-375-81103-6*, Random Hse. Bks. for Young Readers) Random Hse. Children's Bks.

Target. How the Grinch Stole Christmas! 1990. 1.95 o.s.i (*0-679-81890-1*) Random Hse., Inc.

Worth, Bonnie. How the Grinch Got So Grinchy. Jonaitis, Alice, ed. 2001. (Step into Reading Step 2 Bks.). (Illus.). 48p. (J). (gr. k-3). pap. 3.99 o.s.i (*0-375-80662-8*); lib. bdg. 11.99 (*0-375-90662-2*) Random Hse. Children's Bks. (Random Hse. Bks. for Young Readers).

GROMIT (FICTITIOUS CHARACTER)—FICTION

see Wallace and Gromit (Fictitious Characters)—Fiction

GUMBY (FICTITIOUS CHARACTER)—FICTION

Harman, Holly. Gumby & Friends Fold & Mail Stationery. 2000. (Illus.). 40p. (J). 7.95 (*0-8118-2738-0*) Chronicle Bks. LLC.

—Gumby & Friends Notecards. 2000. (Illus.). 20p. 13.95 o.p. (*0-8118-2807-7*) Chronicle Bks. LLC.

—Gumby & Pokey Journal. 2000. (Illus.). 128p. 9.95 o.p. (*0-8118-2739-9*) Chronicle Bks. LLC.

—Gumby's Circus. 2000. (Illus.). 28p. (J). (ps-3). 12.95 o.p. (*0-8118-2733-X*) Chronicle Bks. LLC.

—Gumby's Circus. 2000. (Illus.). 22p. (J). (ps). reprint ed. 15.00 (*0-7567-5737-1*) DIANE Publishing Co.

—Gumby's Colors. 2000. (Illus.). 8p. (J). (ps-k). bds. 9.95 o.p. (*0-8118-2735-6*) Chronicle Bks. LLC.

Hyman, Jane. Gumby Book of Colors. 1986. (Illus.). 32p. (J). (ps-3). 5.95 o.s.i (*0-385-23454-6*); lib. bdg. 5.95 o.s.i (*0-385-23845-2*) Doubleday Publishing.

—Gumby Book of Forest Animals. 1987. (J). 5.95 (*0-385-23458-9*) Doubleday Publishing.

—Gumby Book of Music. 1987. (J). 5.95 (*0-385-23460-0*) Doubleday Publishing.

—Gumby Book of Numbers. 1986. (Illus.). 32p. (J). (ps-3). 5.95 o.s.i (*0-385-23455-4*); lib. bdg. 5.95 o.s.i (*0-385-23847-9*) Doubleday Publishing.

—Gumby Book of Shapes. 1986. (Illus.). 32p. (J). (ps-3). 5.95 o.s.i (*0-385-23453-8*); lib. bdg. 5.95 o.s.i (*0-385-23848-7*) Doubleday Publishing.

—Gumby Book of Toys. 1987. (ps-3). 5.95 (*0-385-23459-7*) Doubleday Publishing.

Oldfield, Pamela. The Gumby Gang on Holiday, Set. unabr. ed. (J). audio 18.95 (*0-7451-8559-2*, Chivers Children's Audio Bks.) BBC Audiobooks America.

—The Gumby Gang Strikes Again, Set. unabr. ed. 1993. (J). audio 18.95 (*0-7451-8560-6*, Chivers Children's Audio Bks.) BBC Audiobooks America.

—More about the Gumby Gang. unabr. ed. 1989. (J). audio 19.95 o.p. (*0-8161-9146-8*) Thorndike Pr.

—The Return of the Gumby Gang. unabr. ed. 1992. (J). (gr. 1 up). audio 18.95 (*0-7451-8561-4*, Chivers Children's Audio Bks.) BBC Audiobooks America.

H

HALE, NATHAN, 1755-1776—FICTION

Brown, Marion M. Young Nathan. 1949. (Illus.). (J). (gr. 5-9). 4.75 o.p. (*0-664-32050-3*) Westminster John Knox Pr.

HANNIBAL, 247-183 B.C.—FICTION

Hirsh, Marilyn. Hannibal & His Thirty-Seven Elephants. 1977. (Illus.). 32p. (J). (gr. 1-3). 5.95 o.p. (*0-8234-0300-9*) Holiday Hse., Inc.

HARDY BOYS (FICTITIOUS CHARACTERS)—FICTION

Cowan, Geoffrey. See No Evil. 1980. pap. 19.95 (*0-671-25411-1*, Touchstone) Simon & Schuster.

Dixon, Franklin W. The Abracadabra Case. 1998. (Hardy Boys Are: No. 7). (Illus.). 80p. (J). (gr. 2-4). pap. 3.99 (*0-671-00408-5*, Aladdin) Simon & Schuster Children's Publishing.

—The Abracadabra Case. 1998. (Hardy Boys Are: No. 7). (Illus.). (J). (gr. 2-4). 9.09 o.p. (*0-606-13402-6*) Turtleback Bks.

—Absolute Zero. 1997. (Hardy Boys Casefiles Ser.: No. 121). 160p. (YA). (gr. 6 up). pap. 3.99 (*0-671-56121-9*, Simon Pulse) Simon & Schuster Children's Publishing.

—Absolute Zero. 1997. (Hardy Boys Casefiles Ser.: No. 121). (YA). (gr. 6 up). 9.09 o.p. (*0-606-11435-1*) Turtleback Bks.

—Acting Up. 1996. (Hardy Boys Casefiles Ser.: No. 116). 160p. (YA). (gr. 6 up). pap. 3.99 (*0-671-50488-6*, Simon Pulse) Simon & Schuster Children's Publishing.

—Acting Up. 1996. (Hardy Boys Casefiles Ser.: No. 116). (YA). (gr. 6 up). 9.09 o.p. (*0-606-09388-5*) Turtleback Bks.

—Against All Odds. Greenberg, Anne, ed. 1995. (Hardy Boys Casefiles Ser.: No. 96). 160p. (YA). (gr. 6 up). pap. 3.99 (*0-671-88207-4*, Simon Pulse) Simon & Schuster Children's Publishing.

—Against All Odds. 1995. (Hardy Boys Casefiles Ser.: No. 96). (YA). (gr. 6 up). 10.04 (*0-606-07618-2*) Turtleback Bks.

—The Alaskan Adventure. 1996. (Hardy Boys Mystery Stories Ser.: No. 138). 160p. (J). (gr. 3-6). mass mkt. 3.99 (*0-671-50524-6*, Aladdin) Simon & Schuster Children's Publishing.

—The Alaskan Adventure. 1996. (Hardy Boys Mystery Stories Ser.: No. 138). (J). (gr. 3-6). 9.09 o.p. (*0-606-09378-8*) Turtleback Bks.

—The Alien Factor. Greenberg, Anne, ed. 1993. (Hardy Boys & Tom Swift Ultra Thrillers Ser.: No. 1). 224p. (Orig.). (J). (gr. 3-6). mass mkt. 3.99 (*0-671-79532-5*, Simon Pulse) Simon & Schuster Children's Publishing.

—All Eyes on First Prize. 1999. (Hardy Boys Are: No. 14). (J). (gr. 2-4). 10.14 (*0-606-19046-5*) Turtleback Bks.

—The Apeman's Secret. (Hardy Boys Mystery Stories Ser.: No. 62). (J). (gr. 3-6). 1989. pap. 3.50 (*0-671-69068-X*, Aladdin); 1986. pap. 3.50 (*0-671-62479-2*, Aladdin); 1980. (Illus.). 192p. pap. (*0-671-95530-6*, Simon & Schuster Children's Publishing); 1980. (Illus.). 192p. pap. 3.50 (*0-671-95482-2*, Aladdin) Simon & Schuster Children's Publishing.

—The Arctic Patrol Mystery. 1969. (Hardy Boys Mystery Stories Ser.: No. 48). (Illus.). 180p. (J). (gr. 3-6). 5.99 (*0-448-08948-3*, Grosset & Dunlap) Penguin Putnam Bks. for Young Readers.

—Attack of the Video Villians. Greenberg, Ann, ed. 1991. (Hardy Boys Mystery Stories Ser.: No. 106). 160p. (J). (gr. 3-6). pap. 3.99 (*0-671-69275-5*, Aladdin) Simon & Schuster Children's Publishing.

—Attack of the Video Villians. 1991. (Hardy Boys Mystery Stories Ser.: No. 106). (J). (gr. 3-6). 9.09 o.p. (*0-606-04610-0*) Turtleback Bks.

—Bad Chemistry. 1996. (Hardy Boys Casefiles Ser.: No. 110). 160p. (YA). (gr. 6 up). pap. 3.99 (*0-671-50433-9*, Simon Pulse) Simon & Schuster Children's Publishing.

—Bad Chemistry. 1996. (Hardy Boys Casefiles Ser.: No. 110). (J). (gr. 6 up). 9.09 o.p. (*0-606-09382-6*) Turtleback Bks.

—Bad Rap. Greenberg, Ann, ed. 1993. (Hardy Boys Casefiles Ser.: No. 73). 160p. (J). (gr. 6 up). pap. 3.99 (*0-671-73109-2*, Simon Pulse) Simon & Schuster Children's Publishing.

—Bad Rap. 1993. (Hardy Boys Casefiles Ser.: No. 73). (YA). (gr. 6 up). 9.09 o.p. (*0-606-02668-1*) Turtleback Bks.

—The Baseball Card Conspiracy. Winkler, Ellen, ed. 1992. (Hardy Boys Mystery Stories Ser.: No. 117). 160p. (Orig.). (J). (gr. 3-6). pap. 3.99 (*0-671-73064-9*, Aladdin) Simon & Schuster Children's Publishing.

—Beyond the Law. Greenberg, Anne, ed. 1991. (Hardy Boys Casefiles Ser.: No. 55). 160p. (Orig.). (J). (gr. 6 up). pap. 3.50 (*0-671-73091-6*, Simon Pulse) Simon & Schuster Children's Publishing.

—The Bike Race Ruckus. 2000. (Hardy Boys Are: No. 17). (Illus.). 80p. (J). (gr. 2-4). per. 3.99 (*0-671-04041-3*, Aladdin) Simon & Schuster Children's Publishing.

—The Billion Dollar Ransom. 1988. (Hardy Boys Mystery Stories Ser.: No. 73). 192p. (J). (gr. 3-6). pap. 3.50 (*0-671-66228-7*, Aladdin) Simon & Schuster Children's Publishing.

—The Billion Dollar Ransom. Barish, Wendy, ed. 1982. (Hardy Boys Mystery Stories Ser.: No. 73). (Illus.). 192p. (J). (gr. 3-6). pap. 3.50 (*0-671-42355-X*, Aladdin); pap. (*0-671-42352-5*, Simon & Schuster Children's Publishing) Simon & Schuster Children's Publishing.

—The Blackwing Puzzle. (Hardy Boys Mystery Stories Ser.: No. 82). (J). (gr. 3-6). 1990. 208p. pap. 3.50 (*0-671-70472-9*, Aladdin); 1984. pap. (*0-671-49726-X*, Simon & Schuster Children's Publishing); 1984. pap. 3.50 (*0-671-49725-1*, Aladdin) Simon & Schuster Children's Publishing.

—Blood Money. (Hardy Boys Casefiles Ser.: No. 32). (Orig.). 1991. 160p. (YA). (gr. 6 up). pap. 3.50 (*0-671-74665-0*); 1989. (Illus.). (J). mass mkt. 2.95 (*0-671-67480-3*) Simon & Schuster Children's Publishing. (Simon Pulse).

—Blood Relations. 1989. (Hardy Boys Casefiles Ser.: No. 15). (YA). (gr. 6 up). pap. 2.95 (*0-671-68779-4*, Simon Pulse) Simon & Schuster Children's Publishing.

—Blood Sport. 1996. (Hardy Boys Casefiles Ser.: No. 117). 160p. (YA). (gr. 6 up). per. 3.99 (*0-671-56117-0*, Simon Pulse) Simon & Schuster Children's Publishing.

—Blood Sport. 1996. (Hardy Boys Casefiles Ser.: No. 117). (J). (gr. 6 up). 10.04 (*0-606-10836-X*) Turtleback Bks.

—Blown Away. 1996. (Hardy Boys Casefiles Ser.: No. 108). 160p. (J). (gr. 6 up). pap. 3.99 (*0-671-50431-2*, Simon Pulse) Simon & Schuster Children's Publishing.

—Blown Away. 1996. (Hardy Boys Casefiles Ser.: No. 108). (YA). (gr. 6 up). 9.09 o.p. (*0-606-09380-X*) Turtleback Bks.

—The Bombay Boomerang. 1970. (Hardy Boys Mystery Stories Ser.: No. 49). (Illus.). 180p. (J). (gr. 3-6). 5.99 (*0-448-08949-1*, Grosset & Dunlap) Penguin Putnam Bks. for Young Readers.

—The Borderline Case. (Hardy Boys Casefiles Ser.: No. 25). 1990. (YA). (gr. 6 up). pap. 2.95 (*0-671-72452-5*); 1989. (Illus.). (J). mass mkt. 2.75 (*0-671-64688-5*) Simon & Schuster Children's Publishing. (Simon Pulse).

—The Borgia Dagger. (Orig.). 1991. (Hardy Boys Casefiles Ser.: No. 13). 160p. (YA). (gr. 6 up). pap. 3.50 (*0-671-73676-0*); 1988. (Hardy Boys Ser.: Vol. 13). (Illus.). (J). mass mkt. 2.95 (*0-671-67956-2*); 1988. (Hardy Boys Casefiles Ser.: No. 13). (YA). (gr. 6 up). pap. (*0-671-64463-7*) Simon & Schuster Children's Publishing. (Simon Pulse).

—Breakdown in Axeblade. 1989. (Hardy Boys Mystery Stories Ser.: No. 94). (Orig.). (J). (gr. 3-6). pap. 3.50 (*0-671-66311-9*, Aladdin) Simon & Schuster Children's Publishing.

—Brother Against Brother. (Hardy Boys Casefiles Ser.: No. 11). (Orig.). (YA). (gr. 6 up). 1991. pap. 3.50 (*0-671-74391-0*); 1989. 160p. mass mkt. 2.95 (*0-671-70712-4*) Simon & Schuster Children's Publishing. (Simon Pulse).

—Campaign of Crime. 1995. (Hardy Boys Casefiles Ser.: No. 103). 160p. (YA). (gr. 6 up). mass mkt. 3.99 (*0-671-88214-7*, Simon Pulse) Simon & Schuster Children's Publishing.

—Campaign of Crime. 1995. (Hardy Boys Casefiles Ser.: No. 103). (YA). (gr. 6 up). 9.09 o.p. (*0-606-07616-6*) Turtleback Bks.

—The Caribbean Cruise Caper. 1999. (Hardy Boys Mystery Stories Ser.: No. 154). 160p. (J). (gr. 3-6). pap. 4.99 (*0-671-02549-X*, Aladdin) Simon & Schuster Children's Publishing.

—The Caribbean Cruise Caper. 1999. (Hardy Boys Mystery Stories Ser.: No. 154). (J). (gr. 3-6). 10.04 (*0-606-17130-4*) Turtleback Bks.

—Carnival of Crime. 1993. (Hardy Boys Mystery Stories Ser.: No. 122). 160p. (Orig.). (J). (gr. 3-6). pap. 3.99 (*0-671-79312-8*, Aladdin) Simon & Schuster Children's Publishing.

—The Case of the Cosmic Kidnapping. Winkler, Ellen, ed. 1993. (Hardy Boys Mystery Stories Ser.: No. 120). 160p. (Orig.). (J). (gr. 3-6). pap. 3.99 (*0-671-79310-1*, Aladdin) Simon & Schuster Children's Publishing.

—The Case of the Counterfeit Criminals. Winkler, Ellen, ed. 1992. (Hardy Boys Mystery Stories Ser.: No. 114). 160p. (J). (gr. 3-6). pap. 3.99 (*0-671-73061-4*, Aladdin) Simon & Schuster Children's Publishing.

—The Case of the Counterfeit Criminals. 1992. (Hardy Boys Mystery Stories Ser.: No. 114). (J). (gr. 3-6). 10.04 (*0-606-02195-7*) Turtleback Bks.

—Cast of Criminals. 1989. (Hardy Boys Mystery Stories Ser.: No. 97). (Orig.). (J). (gr. 3-6). pap. 3.50 (*0-671-66307-0*, Aladdin) Simon & Schuster Children's Publishing.

—The Castle Conundrum. 2001. (Hardy Boys Mystery Stories Ser.: No. 168). (J). (gr. 3-6). (Illus.). 160p. pap. 4.99 (*0-7434-0683-4*); reprint ed. E-Book 4.99 (*0-7434-2768-8*) Simon & Schuster Children's Publishing. (Aladdin).

—Castle Fear. Greenberg, Ann, ed. 1991. (Hardy Boys Casefiles Ser.: No. 44). 160p. (YA). (gr. 6 up). per. 3.75 (*0-671-74615-4*, Simon Pulse) Simon & Schuster Children's Publishing.

—Castle Fear. 1990. (Hardy Boys Casefiles Ser.: Vol. 44). (Illus.). (J). mass mkt. 2.95 (*0-671-70041-3*, Simon Pulse) Simon & Schuster Children's Publishing.

—Castle Fear. 1990. (Hardy Boys Casefiles Ser.: No. 44). (YA). (gr. 6 up). 9.80 (*0-606-04630-5*) Turtleback Bks.

—Cave-In. 1990. (Hardy Boys Mystery Stories Ser.: No. 78). 192p. (J). (gr. 3-6). pap. 3.50 (*0-671-69486-3*, Aladdin) Simon & Schuster Children's Publishing.

—Cave Trap. 1996. (Hardy Boys Casefiles Ser.: No. 115). 160p. (YA). (gr. 6 up). pap. 3.99 (*0-671-50462-2*, Simon Pulse) Simon & Schuster Children's Publishing.

—Cave Trap. 1996. (Hardy Boys Casefiles Ser.: No. 115). (YA). (gr. 6 up). 9.09 o.p. (*0-606-09387-7*) Turtleback Bks.

—The Chase for the Mystery Twister. 1998. (Hardy Boys Mystery Stories Ser.: No. 149). 151p. (J). (gr. 3-6). pap. 3.99 (*0-671-00123-X*, Aladdin) Simon & Schuster Children's Publishing.

—The Chase for the Mystery Twister. 1998. (Hardy Boys Mystery Stories Ser.: No. 149). (J). (gr. 3-6). 9.09 o.p. (*0-606-13463-8*) Turtleback Bks.

—Choke Hold. Greenberg, Anne, ed. 1991. (Hardy Boys Casefiles Ser.: No. 51). 160p. (Orig.). (YA). (gr. 6 up). pap. 3.50 (*0-671-70048-0*, Simon Pulse) Simon & Schuster Children's Publishing.

—Clean Sweep. 1996. (Hardy Boys Casefiles Ser.: No. 114). 160p. (YA). (gr. 6 up). mass mkt. 3.99 (*0-671-50456-8*, Simon Pulse) Simon & Schuster Children's Publishing.

—Clean Sweep. 1996. (Hardy Boys Casefiles Ser.: No. 114). (YA). (gr. 6 up). 9.09 o.p. (*0-606-09386-9*) Turtleback Bks.

—Cliff Hanger. 1996. (Hardy Boys Casefiles Ser.: No. 112). 160p. (YA). (gr. 6 up). pap. 3.99 (*0-671-50453-3*, Simon Pulse) Simon & Schuster Children's Publishing.

—The Clue in the Embers. 1956. (Hardy Boys Mystery Stories Ser.: No. 35). (Illus.). 180p. (J). (gr. 3-6). 5.99 (*0-448-08935-1*, Grosset & Dunlap) Penguin Putnam Bks. for Young Readers.

—The Clue of the Broken Blade. 1942. (Hardy Boys Mystery Stories Ser.: No. 21). (Illus.). 180p. (J). (gr. 3-6). 5.99 (*0-448-08921-1*, Grosset & Dunlap) Penguin Putnam Bks. for Young Readers.

—The Clue of the Hissing Serpent. 1974. (Hardy Boys Mystery Stories Ser.: No. 53). (Illus.). 180p. (J). (gr. 3-6). 5.99 (*0-448-08953-X*, Grosset & Dunlap) Penguin Putnam Bks. for Young Readers.

—The Clue of the Screeching Owl. 1962. (Hardy Boys Mystery Stories Ser.: No. 41). (Illus.). 180p. (J). (gr. 3-6). 5.99 (*0-448-08941-6*, Grosset & Dunlap) Penguin Putnam Bks. for Young Readers.

—The Cold Cash Caper. 1996. (Hardy Boys Mystery Stories Ser.: No. 136). 160p. (J). (gr. 3-6). per. 3.99 (*0-671-50520-3*, Aladdin) Simon & Schuster Children's Publishing.

—The Cold Cash Caper. 1996. (Hardy Boys Mystery Stories Ser.: No. 136). (J). (gr. 3-6). 9.09 o.p. (*0-606-09376-1*) Turtleback Bks.

—Cold Sweat. Greenberg, Anne, ed. 1992. (Hardy Boys Casefiles Ser.: No. 63). 160p. (Orig.). (YA). (gr. 6 up). pap. 3.75 (*0-671-73099-1*, Simon Pulse) Simon & Schuster Children's Publishing.

—Collision Course. (Hardy Boys Casefiles Ser.: No. 33). 1991. 160p. (YA). (gr. 6 up). pap. 3.50 (*0-671-74666-9*); 1989. (Illus.). (J). mass mkt. 2.95 (*0-671-67481-1*) Simon & Schuster Children's Publishing. (Simon Pulse).

—Competitive Edge. 1996. (Hardy Boys Casefiles Ser.: No. 111). 160p. (YA). (gr. 6 up). mass mkt. 3.99 (*0-671-50446-0*, Simon Pulse) Simon & Schuster Children's Publishing.

—Competitive Edge. 1996. (Hardy Boys Casefiles Ser.: No. 111). (YA). (gr. 6 up). 9.09 o.p. (*0-606-09383-4*) Turtleback Bks.

—Countdown to Terror. (Hardy Boys Casefiles Ser.: No. 28). (Orig.). (YA). (gr. 6 up). 1991. pap. 3.50 (*0-671-74662-6*); 1989. pap. 2.95 (*0-671-64691-5*) Simon & Schuster Children's Publishing. (Simon Pulse).

—Crime in the Cards. 2001. (Hardy Boys Mystery Stories Ser.: No. 165). (J). (gr. 3-6). reprint ed. E-Book 3.99 (*0-7434-2350-X*, Aladdin) Simon & Schuster Children's Publishing.

—Crime in the Kennel. 1995. (Hardy Boys Mystery Stories Ser.: No. 133). 160p. (J). (gr. 3-6). per. 3.99 (*0-671-87217-6*, Aladdin) Simon & Schuster Children's Publishing.

—Crime in the Kennel. 1995. (Hardy Boys Mystery Stories Ser.: No. 133). (J). (gr. 3-6). 9.09 o.p. (*0-606-07612-3*) Turtleback Bks.

—The Crimson Flame. 1987. (Hardy Boys Mystery Stories Ser.: No. 77). (J). (gr. 3-6). pap. 3.99 (*0-671-64286-3*, Aladdin) Simon & Schuster Children's Publishing.

—The Crimson Flame. Barish, Wendy, ed. 1983. (Hardy Boys Mystery Stories Ser.: No. 77). 192p. (J). (gr. 3-6). pap. (*0-671-42366-5*, Simon & Schuster Children's Publishing); pap. 3.50 (*0-671-42367-3*, Aladdin) Simon & Schuster Children's Publishing.

—The Crisscross Crime. 1998. (Hardy Boys Mystery Stories Ser.: No. 150). 160p. (J). (gr. 3-6). per. 3.99 (*0-671-00743-2*, Simon Pulse) Simon & Schuster Children's Publishing.

—The Crisscross Crime, 1998. (Hardy Boys Mystery Stories Ser.: No. 150). (J). (gr. 3-6). 9.09 o.p. (*0-606-13464-6*) Turtleback Bks.

—The Crisscross Shadow. rev. ed. (Hardy Boys Mystery Stories Ser.: No. 33). (J). (gr. 3-6). 1975. 3.29 o.p. (*0-448-18932-1*); 1953. (Illus.). 180p. 5.95 (*0-448-08932-7*) Penguin Putnam Bks. for Young Readers. (Grosset & Dunlap).

—Cross Country Crime. 1995. (Hardy Boys Mystery Stories Ser.: No. 134). 160p. (J). (gr. 3-6). pap. 3.99 (*0-671-50517-3*, Aladdin) Simon & Schuster Children's Publishing.

—The Crowning Terror. l.t. ed. 1988. (Hardy Boys Casefiles Ser.: No. 6). 154p. (YA). (gr. 6 up). reprint ed. 9.50 o.p. (*0-942545-47-8*); lib. bdg. 10.50 o.p. (*0-942545-57-5*) Grey Castle Pr.

—The Crowning Terror. 1991. (Hardy Boys Casefiles Ser.: No. 6). 160p. (YA). (gr. 6 up). pap. 3.50 (*0-671-73670-1*); 1989. (Hardy Boys Ser.: Vol. 6). (Illus.). (J). mass mkt. 2.95 (*0-671-70713-2*); Vol. 6. 1987. mass mkt. (*0-671-62647-7*) Simon & Schuster Children's Publishing. (Simon Pulse).

—Crusade of the Flaming Sword. 1995. (Hardy Boys Mystery Stories Ser.: No. 131). (J). (gr. 3-6). 9.09 o.p. (*0-606-07610-7*) Turtleback Bks.

—Cult of Crime. l.t. ed. 1988. (Hardy Boys Casefiles Ser.: No. 3). 151p. (YA). (gr. 6 up). reprint ed. 9.50 o.p. (*0-942545-44-3*); lib. bdg. 10.50 o.p. (*0-942545-54-0*) Grey Castle Pr.

—Cult of Crime. (Hardy Boys Casefiles Ser.: No. 3). (YA). (gr. 6 up). 1989. mass mkt. 3.99 (*0-671-68726-3*); 1987. pap. (*0-671-62128-9*) Simon & Schuster Children's Publishing. (Simon Pulse).

—Cult of Crime. 1987. (Hardy Boys Casefiles Ser.: No. 3). (YA). (gr. 6 up). 9.09 o.p. (*0-606-02678-9*) Turtleback Bks.

—Danger in the Extreme. 1998. (Hardy Boys Mystery Stories Ser.: No. 152). 160p. (J). (gr. 3-6). pap. 4.99 (*0-671-02173-7*, Aladdin) Simon & Schuster Children's Publishing.

—Danger in the Fourth Dimension. Winkler, Ellen, ed. 1993. (Hardy Boys Mystery Stories Ser.: No. 118). 160p. (Orig.). (J). (gr. 3-6). pap. 3.99 (*0-671-79308-X*, Aladdin) Simon & Schuster Children's Publishing.

—Danger on the Air. 1989. (Hardy Boys Mystery Stories Ser.: No. 95). (Orig.). (J). (gr. 3-6). pap. 3.50 (*0-671-66305-4*, Aladdin) Simon & Schuster Children's Publishing.

—Danger on the Diamond. Greenberg, Anne, ed. 1988. (Hardy Boys Mystery Stories Ser.: No. 90). 160p. (J). (gr. 3-6). pap. 3.99 (*0-671-63425-9*, Aladdin) Simon & Schuster Children's Publishing.

—Danger on Vampire Trail. 1971. (Hardy Boys Mystery Stories Ser.: No. 50). (Illus.). 180p. (J). (gr. 3-6). 5.99 (*0-448-08950-5*, Grosset & Dunlap) Penguin Putnam Bks. for Young Readers.

—Danger Unlimited. Greenberg, Anne, ed. 1993. (Hardy Boys Casefiles Ser.: No. 79). 160p. (YA). (gr. 6 up). mass mkt. 3.99 (*0-671-79463-9*, Simon Pulse) Simon & Schuster Children's Publishing.

—Danger Unlimited. 1993. (Hardy Boys Casefiles Ser.: No. 79). (YA). (gr. 6 up). 10.04 (*0-606-05340-9*) Turtleback Bks.

—Danger Zone. (Hardy Boys Casefiles Ser.: No. 37). (YA). (gr. 6 up). 1991. pap. 3.75 (*0-671-73751-1*); 1990. 160p. pap. 2.95 (*0-671-67485-4*) Simon & Schuster Children's Publishing. (Simon Pulse).

—Daredevils. 2000. (Hardy Boys Mystery Stories Ser.: No. 159). 160p. (J). (gr. 3-6). pap. 4.99 (*0-671-03861-3*, Aladdin) Simon & Schuster Children's Publishing.

—Daredevils. 2003. (Hardy Boys Mystery Ser.). 139p. (J). 21.95 (*0-7862-5309-6*) Thorndike Pr.

—Darkness Falls. Ashby, Ruth, ed. abr. ed. 1994. (Hardy Boys Casefiles Ser.: No. 89). 160p. (YA). (gr. 6 up). pap. 3.99 (*0-671-79473-6*, Simon Pulse) Simon & Schuster Children's Publishing.

—Darkness Falls. 1994. (Hardy Boys Casefiles Ser.: No. 89). (J). (gr. 6 up). 10.04 (*0-606-06446-X*) Turtleback Bks.

—Day of the Dinosaur. Ashby, Ruth, ed. 1994. (Hardy Boys Mystery Stories Ser.: No. 128). 160p. (J). (gr. 3-6). mass mkt. 3.99 (*0-671-87212-5*, Simon Pulse) Simon & Schuster Children's Publishing.

—Day of the Dinosaur. 1994. (Hardy Boys Mystery Stories Ser.: No. 128). (J). (gr. 3-6). 9.09 o.p. (*0-606-06999-2*) Turtleback Bks.

—Dead in the Water. 1998. (Hardy Boys Casefiles Ser.: No. 127). 160p. (YA). (gr. 6 up). pap. 3.99 (*0-671-56242-8*, Simon Pulse) Simon & Schuster Children's Publishing.

—Dead in the Water. 1998. (Hardy Boys Casefiles Ser.: No. 127). (YA). (gr. 6 up). 9.09 o.p. (*0-606-13468-9*) Turtleback Bks.

—Dead Man in Deadwood. Greenberg, Anne, ed. 1994. (Hardy Boys Casefiles Ser.: No. 87). 160p. (YA). (gr. 6 up). pap. 3.99 (*0-671-79471-X*, Simon Pulse) Simon & Schuster Children's Publishing.

—Dead Man in Deadwood. 1994. (Hardy Boys Casefiles Ser.: Vol. 87). (Illus.). (J). mass mkt. 3.99 (*0-671-89281-9*, Simon Pulse) Simon & Schuster Children's Publishing.

—Dead Man in Deadwood. 1994. (Hardy Boys Casefiles Ser.: No. 87). (YA). (gr. 6 up). 9.09 o.p. (*0-606-06444-3*) Turtleback Bks.

—Dead of Night. 1993. (Hardy Boys Casefiles Ser.: No. 80). 160p. (YA). (gr. 6 up). mass mkt. 3.99 (*0-671-79464-7*, Simon Pulse) Simon & Schuster Children's Publishing.

—Dead of Night. 1993. (Hardy Boys Casefiles Ser.: No. 80). (YA). (gr. 6 up). 10.04 (*0-606-05341-7*) Turtleback Bks.

—Dead on Target. l.t. ed. 1988. (Hardy Boys Casefiles Ser.: No. 1). 153p. (YA). (gr. 6 up). reprint ed. 9.50 o.p. (*0-942545-42-7*); lib. bdg. 10.50 o.p. (*0-942545-52-4*) Grey Castle Pr.

—Dead on Target. (Hardy Boys Casefiles Ser.: No. 1). (YA). (gr. 6 up). 1991. mass mkt. 3.99 (*0-671-73992-1*); 1989. pap. 2.95 (*0-671-68524-4*) Simon & Schuster Children's Publishing. (Simon Pulse).

—Dead on Target. 1987. (Hardy Boys Casefiles Ser.: No. 1). (YA). (gr. 6 up). 10.04 (*0-606-02714-9*) Turtleback Bks.

—The Dead Season. (Hardy Boys Casefiles Ser.: No. 35). (YA). (gr. 6 up). 1991. 160p. pap. 3.50 (*0-671-74105-5*); 1990. mass mkt. 2.95 (*0-671-67483-8*) Simon & Schuster Children's Publishing. (Simon Pulse).

—The Dead Season. 1990. (Hardy Boys Casefiles Ser.: No. 35). (YA). (gr. 6 up). 8.60 o.p. (*0-606-00681-8*) Turtleback Bks.

—Deadfall. 1992. (Hardy Boys Casefiles Ser.: Vol. 60). (Illus.). 160p. (J). mass mkt. 3.75 (*0-671-73096-7*, Simon Pulse) Simon & Schuster Children's Publishing.

—Deadfall. 1992. (Hardy Boys Casefiles Ser.: No. 60). (YA). (gr. 6 up). 8.85 o.p. (*0-606-00388-6*) Turtleback Bks.

—The Deadliest Dare. (Hardy Boys Casefiles Ser.: No. 30). (Orig.). 1991. (YA). (gr. 6 up). pap. 3.50 (*0-671-74613-8*); 1989. (Illus.). (J). mass mkt. 2.95 (*0-671-67478-1*) Simon & Schuster Children's Publishing. (Simon Pulse).

—Deadly Chase. 1986. (Hardy Boys Mystery Stories Ser.: No. 68). Orig. Title: The Submarine Caper. (J). (gr. 3-6). pap. 3.50 (*0-671-62477-6*, Aladdin) Simon & Schuster Children's Publishing.

—Deadly Engagement. 1994. (Hardy Boys Casefiles Ser.: No. 90). 160p. (YA). (gr. 6 up). pap. 3.99 (*0-671-79474-4*, Simon Pulse) Simon & Schuster Children's Publishing.

—Deathgame. l.t. ed. 1988. (Hardy Boys Casefiles Ser.: No. 7). 151p. (YA). (gr. 6 up). reprint ed. 9.50 o.p. (*0-942545-48-6*); lib. bdg. 10.50 o.p. (*0-942545-58-3*) Grey Castle Pr.

—Deathgame. 1991. (Hardy Boys Casefiles Ser.: No. 7). 160p. (YA). (gr. 6 up). mass mkt. 3.99 (*0-671-73672-8*); 1989. (Hardy Boys Ser.: Vol. 7). (Illus.). (J). mass mkt. 2.95 (*0-671-69375-1*) Simon & Schuster Children's Publishing. (Simon Pulse).

—Deep Trouble. Greenberg, Anne, ed. 1991. (Hardy Boys Casefiles Ser.: No. 54). 160p. (YA). (gr. 6 up). pap. 3.99 (*0-671-73090-8*, Simon Pulse) Simon & Schuster Children's Publishing.

—Deep Trouble. 1991. (Hardy Boys Casefiles Ser.: No. 54). (YA). (gr. 6 up). 9.09 o.p. (*0-606-04905-3*) Turtleback Bks.

—The Demolition Mission. Greenberg, Ann, ed. 1992. (Hardy Boys Mystery Stories Ser.: No. 112). 160p. (Orig.). (J). (gr. 3-6). pap. 3.99 (*0-671-73058-4*, Aladdin) Simon & Schuster Children's Publishing.

—The Demon's Den. 1986. (Hardy Boys Mystery Stories Ser.: No. 81). (J). (gr. 3-6). pap. 3.50 (*0-671-62622-1*, Aladdin) Simon & Schuster Children's Publishing.

—The Demon's Den. Barish, Wendy, ed. (Hardy Boys Mystery Stories Ser.: No. 81). (Illus.). 208p. (J). (gr. 3-6). 1985. (*0-671-49724-3*, Simon & Schuster Children's Publishing); 1984. pap. 3.50 (*0-671-49723-5*, Aladdin) Simon & Schuster Children's Publishing.

—The Desert Thieves. 1996. (Hardy Boys Ser.: No. 141). 160p. (J). (gr. 3-6). pap. 4.99 o.s.i (*0-671-50527-0*, Aladdin) Simon & Schuster Children's Publishing.

—The Desert Thieves. 1996. (Hardy Boys Mystery Stories Ser.: No. 141). (J). (gr. 3-6). 10.04 (*0-606-11428-9*) Turtleback Bks.

—Dinosaur Disaster. 1998. (Hardy Boys Are: No. 5). (Illus.). 80p. (J). (gr. 2-4). pap. 3.99 (*0-671-00406-9*, Aladdin) Simon & Schuster Children's Publishing.

—Dinosaur Disaster, 5. 1998. (Hardy Boys Are: No. 5). (Illus.). (J). (gr. 2-4). 9.09 o.p. (*0-606-13400-X*) Turtleback Bks.

—Diplomatic Deceit. (Hardy Boys Casefiles Ser.: No. 38). (Orig.). (YA). (gr. 6 up). 1991. mass mkt. 3.50 (*0-671-74106-3*); 1990. 160p. pap. 2.95 (*0-671-67486-2*) Simon & Schuster Children's Publishing. (Simon Pulse).

—Dirty Deeds. Greenberg, Ann, ed. 1991. (Hardy Boys Casefiles Ser.: No. 49). 160p. (YA). (gr. 6 up). pap. 3.99 (*0-671-70046-4*, Simon Pulse) Simon & Schuster Children's Publishing.

—Dirty Deeds. 1991. (Hardy Boys Casefiles Ser.: No. 49). (YA). (gr. 6 up). 10.04 (*0-606-04654-2*) Turtleback Bks.

—The Disappearing Floor. 1940. (Hardy Boys Mystery Stories Ser.: No. 19). (Illus.). 180p. (J). (gr. 3-6). 5.99 (*0-448-08919-X*, Grosset & Dunlap) Penguin Putnam Bks. for Young Readers.

—Disaster for Hire. 1989. (Hardy Boys Casefiles Ser.: No. 23). (YA). (gr. 6 up). pap. 2.95 (*0-671-70491-5*); (Illus.). (J). mass mkt. 2.75 (*0-671-64686-9*) Simon & Schuster Children's Publishing. (Simon Pulse).

—The Doggone Detectives. 1998. (Hardy Boys Are: No. 8). (Illus.). 80p. (J). (gr. 2-4). pap. 3.99 (*0-671-00409-3*, Aladdin) Simon & Schuster Children's Publishing.

—Double Exposure. (Orig.). 1989. (Hardy Boys Casefiles Ser.: No. 22). (YA). (gr. 6 up). pap. 2.95 (*0-671-69376-X*); 1988. (Hardy Boys Ser.: Vol. 22). (Illus.). (J). mass mkt. 2.75 (*0-671-64685-0*) Simon & Schuster Children's Publishing. (Simon Pulse).

—Dungeon of Doom. 1989. (Hardy Boys Mystery Stories Ser.: No. 99). (J). (gr. 3-6). pap. 3.50 (*0-671-69449-9*, Aladdin) Simon & Schuster Children's Publishing.

—Edge of Destruction. l.t. ed. 1988. (Hardy Boys Casefiles Ser.: No. 5). 153p. (YA). (gr. 6 up). reprint ed. 9.50 o.p. (*0-942545-46-X*); lib. bdg. 10.50 o.p. (*0-942545-56-7*) Grey Castle Pr.

—Edge of Destruction. (Hardy Boys Casefiles Ser.: No. 5). (YA). (gr. 6 up). 1991. 160p. mass mkt. 3.99 (*0-671-73669-8*); 1989. mass mkt. 2.95 (*0-671-70360-9*) Simon & Schuster Children's Publishing. (Simon Pulse).

—The Emperor's Shield. 1997. (Hardy Boys Casefiles Ser.: No. 119). 160p. (YA). (gr. 6 up). mass mkt. 3.99 (*0-671-56119-7*, Simon Pulse) Simon & Schuster Children's Publishing.

—The Emperor's Shield. 1997. (Hardy Boys Casefiles Ser.: No. 119). (YA). (gr. 6 up). 10.04 (*0-606-11433-5*) Turtleback Bks.

—The End of the Trail. 2000. (Hardy Boys Mystery Stories Ser.: No. 162). 144p. (J). (gr. 3-6). pap. 3.99 (*0-671-04759-0*, Aladdin) Simon & Schuster Children's Publishing.

—Endangered Species. Greenberg, Anne, ed. 1992. (Hardy Boys Casefiles Ser.: No. 64). 160p. (Orig.). (YA). (gr. 6 up). pap. 3.99 (*0-671-73100-9*, Simon Pulse) Simon & Schuster Children's Publishing.

—Evil, Inc. l.t. ed. 1988. (Hardy Boys Casefiles Ser.: No. 2). 153p. (YA). (gr. 6 up). reprint ed. 9.50 o.p. (*0-942545-43-5*); lib. bdg. 10.50 o.p. (*0-942545-53-2*) Grey Castle Pr.

—Evil, Inc. (Hardy Boys Casefiles Ser.: No. 2). 1991. (YA). (gr. 6 up). pap. 3.99 (*0-671-73668-X*); 1989. (Illus.). (J). mass mkt. 2.95 (*0-671-70359-5*); 1988. (Illus.). (J). mass mkt. 2.75 (*0-671-67259-2*); 1987. (YA). (gr. 6 up). pap. (*0-671-62559-4*) Simon & Schuster Children's Publishing. (Simon Pulse).

—Evil, Inc. 1987. (Hardy Boys Casefiles Ser.: No. 2). (YA). (gr. 6 up). 10.04 (*0-606-02717-3*) Turtleback Bks.

—Eye on Crime. 1998. (Hardy Boys Mystery Stories Ser.: No. 153). 160p. (J). (gr. 3-6). pap. 3.99 (*0-671-02174-5*, Aladdin) Simon & Schuster Children's Publishing.

—False Alarm. Greenberg, Anne, ed. 1994. (Hardy Boys Casefiles Ser.: No. 84). 160p. (YA). (gr. 6 up). pap. 3.99 (*0-671-79468-X*, Simon Pulse) Simon & Schuster Children's Publishing.

—False Alarm. 1994. (Hardy Boys Casefiles Ser.: No. 84). (YA). (gr. 6 up). 10.04 (*0-606-05865-6*) Turtleback Bks.

—Fast Break. 1996. (Hardy Boys Casefiles Ser.: No. 107). 160p. (YA). (gr. 6 up). pap. 3.99 (*0-671-50430-4*, Simon Pulse) Simon & Schuster Children's Publishing.

—Fast Break. 1996. (Hardy Boys Casefiles Ser.: No. 107). (YA). (gr. 6 up). 10.04 (*0-606-08539-4*) Turtleback Bks.

—Fear on Wheels. Greenberg, Anne, ed. 1991. (Hardy Boys Mystery Stories Ser.: No. 108). 160p. (J). (gr. 3-6). per. 3.99 (*0-671-69277-1*, Aladdin) Simon & Schuster Children's Publishing.

—Fear on Wheels. 1991. (Hardy Boys Mystery Stories Ser.: No. 108). (J). (gr. 3-6). 9.09 o.p. (*0-606-04915-0*) Turtleback Bks.

—A Figure in Hiding. (Hardy Boys Mystery Stories Ser.: No. 16). (J). (gr. 3-6). 1975. 3.29 o.p. (*0-448-18916-X*); 1937. (Illus.). 180p. 5.99 (*0-448-08916-5*) Penguin Putnam Bks. for Young Readers. (Grosset & Dunlap).

—Final Cut. 1991. (Hardy Boys Casefiles Ser.: No. 34). (YA). (gr. 6 up). pap. 3.50 (*0-671-74667-7*, Simon Pulse) Simon & Schuster Children's Publishing.

—Final Gambit. Greenberg, Anne, ed. 1992. (Hardy Boys Casefiles Ser.: No. 62). 160p. (Orig.). (J). (gr. 6 up). pap. 3.75 (*0-671-73098-3*, Simon Pulse) Simon & Schuster Children's Publishing.

—Fire in the Sky. 1997. (Hardy Boys Casefiles Ser.: No. 126). 160p. (YA). (gr. 6 up). pap. 3.99 (*0-671-56125-1*, Simon Pulse) Simon & Schuster Children's Publishing.

—Fire in the Sky. 1997. (Hardy Boys Casefiles Ser.: No. 126). (YA). (gr. 6 up). 10.04 (*0-606-13467-0*) Turtleback Bks.

—The Firebird Rocket. 1978. (Hardy Boys Mystery Stories Ser.: No. 57). (Illus.). 180p. (J). (gr. 3-6). 5.99 (*0-448-08957-2*, Grosset & Dunlap) Penguin Putnam Bks. for Young Readers.

—First Day, Worst Day. 3rd ed. 1997. (Hardy Boys Are: No. 3). (Illus.). 80p. (J). (gr. 2-4). per. 3.99 (*0-671-00404-2*, Aladdin) Simon & Schuster Children's Publishing.

—First Day, Worst Day. 1997. (Hardy Boys Are: No. 3). (Illus.). (J). (gr. 2-4). 9.09 o.p. (*0-606-12935-9*) Turtleback Bks.

—The Fish-Faced Mask of Mystery. 2000. (Hardy Boys Are the Clue Brothers Ser.: No. 16). (Illus.). 80p. (J). (gr. 2-4). pap. 3.99 (*0-671-03872-9*, Aladdin) Simon & Schuster Children's Publishing.

—Flesh & Blood. (Hardy Boys Casefiles Ser.: No. 39). (Orig.). (YA). (gr. 6 up). 1991. mass mkt. 3.50 (*0-671-73913-1*); 1990. 160p. pap. 2.95 (*0-671-67487-0*) Simon & Schuster Children's Publishing. (Simon Pulse).

—The Flickering Torch Mystery. (Hardy Boys Mystery Stories Ser.: No. 22). (J). (gr. 3-6). 1975. 3.29 o.p. (*0-448-18922-4*); 1943. (Illus.). 180p. 5.99 (*0-448-08922-X*) Penguin Putnam Bks. for Young Readers. (Grosset & Dunlap).

—Flight into Danger. Greenberg, Ann, ed. 1991. (Hardy Boys Casefiles Ser.: No. 47). 160p. (Orig.). (J). (gr. 6 up). mass mkt. 3.99 (*0-671-70044-8*, Simon Pulse) Simon & Schuster Children's Publishing.

—Footprints under the Window. 2004. (Hardy Boys Mystery Stories Ser.: No. 12). (Illus.). 212p. (J). (gr. 3-6). 14.95 (*1-55709-270-2*) Applewood Bks.

—Footprints under the Window. (Hardy Boys Mystery Stories Ser.: No. 12). (J). (gr. 3-6). 1975. 3.29 o.p. (*0-448-18912-7*); 1933. (Illus.). 180p. 5.99 (*0-448-08912-2*) Penguin Putnam Bks. for Young Readers. (Grosset & Dunlap).

—Foul Play. Greenberg, Ann, ed. 1990. (Hardy Boys Casefiles Ser.: No. 46). 160p. (YA). (gr. 6 up). pap. 3.99 (*0-671-70043-X*, Simon Pulse) Simon & Schuster Children's Publishing.

—Foul Play. 1990. (Hardy Boys Casefiles Ser.: No. 46). (YA). (gr. 6 up). 9.09 o.p. (*0-606-04675-5*) Turtleback Bks.

—The Four-Headed Dragon. 1988. (Hardy Boys Mystery Stories Ser.: No. 69). 176p. (J). (gr. 3-6). pap. 3.50 (*0-671-65797-6*, Aladdin) Simon & Schuster Children's Publishing.

—Frame-Up. 1995. (Hardy Boys Casefiles Ser.: No. 99). 160p. (YA). (gr. 6 up). mass mkt. 3.99 (*0-671-88210-4*, Simon Pulse) Simon & Schuster Children's Publishing.

—Frame-Up. 1995. (Hardy Boys Casefiles Ser.: No. 99). (YA). (gr. 6 up). 10.04 (*0-606-07621-2*) Turtleback Bks.

—Fright Wave. (Hardy Boys Casefiles Ser.: No. 40). (Orig.). (YA). (gr. 6 up). 1991. 160p. pap. 3.50 (*0-671-73994-8*); 1990. mass mkt. 2.95 (*0-671-67488-9*) Simon & Schuster Children's Publishing. (Simon Pulse).

—A Game Called Chaos. 2000. (Hardy Boys Ser.: No. 160). 160p. (J). (gr. 3-6). pap. 3.99 (*0-671-03870-2*, Aladdin) Simon & Schuster Children's Publishing.

—Game Plan for Disaster. (Hardy Boys Mystery Stories Ser.: No. 76). (J). (gr. 3-6). 1990. mass mkt. 3.50 (*0-671-72321-9*); 1987. pap. 3.50 (*0-671-64288-X*) Simon & Schuster Children's Publishing. (Aladdin).

—Game Plan for Disaster. Schneider, Meg F., ed. 1982. (Hardy Boys Mystery Stories Ser.: No. 76). (Illus.). 208p. (J). (gr. 3-6). pap. (*0-671-42364-9*, Simon & Schuster Children's Publishing); pap. 3.50 (*0-671-42365-7*, Aladdin) Simon & Schuster Children's Publishing.

—The Genius Thieves. l.t. ed. 1988. (Hardy Boys Casefiles Ser.: No. 9). 153p. (YA). (gr. 6 up). reprint ed. 9.50 o.p. (*0-942545-50-8*); lib. bdg. 10.50 o.p. (*0-942545-60-5*) Grey Castle Pr.

—The Genius Thieves. 1991. (Hardy Boys Casefiles Ser.: No. 9). (J). (gr. 6 up). mass mkt. 3.50 (*0-671-73674-4*, Simon Pulse) Simon & Schuster Children's Publishing.

—The Ghost at Skeleton Rock. rev. ed. 1958. (Hardy Boys Mystery Stories Ser.: No. 37). (Illus.). 180p. (J). (gr. 3-6). 5.99 (*0-448-08937-8*, Grosset & Dunlap) Penguin Putnam Bks. for Young Readers.

—Ghost of a Chance. 2001. (Hardy Boys Mystery Stories Ser.: No. 169). (J). (gr. 3-6). 160p. pap. 4.99 (*0-7434-0684-2*); E-Book 4.99 (*0-7434-3703-9*) Simon & Schuster Children's Publishing. (Aladdin).

—Ghost Stories. 2001. (Hardy Boys Mystery Stories Ser.). (J). (gr. 3-6). E-Book 4.99 (*0-7434-3711-X*, Aladdin) Simon & Schuster Children's Publishing.

—Ghost Stories. Greenberg, Ann, ed. 1989. (Hardy Boys Mystery Stories Ser.). 144p. (J). (gr. 3-6). pap. 4.99 (*0-671-69133-3*, Aladdin) Simon & Schuster Children's Publishing.

—Ghost Stories. Schwartz, Betty Ann, ed. 1984. (Hardy Boys Mystery Stories Ser.). (Illus.). 160p. (J). (gr. 3-6). pap. 3.50 (*0-671-50808-3*, Aladdin) Simon & Schuster Children's Publishing.

—Ghost Stories. 1900. (Hardy Boys Mystery Stories Ser.). (J). (gr. 3-6). mass mkt. 3.50 (*0-671-67864-7*, Aladdin) Simon & Schuster Children's Publishing.

—The Giant Rat of Sumatra. 1997. (Hardy Boys Mystery Stories Ser.: No. 143). 160p. (J). (gr. 3-6). pap. 3.99 (*0-671-00055-1*, Aladdin) Simon & Schuster Children's Publishing.

—The Giant Rat of Sumatra. 1997. (Hardy Boys Mystery Stories Ser.: No. 143). (J). (gr. 3-6). 10.04 (*0-606-11430-0*) Turtleback Bks.

—Grave Danger. Greenberg, Anne, ed. 1992. (Hardy Boys Casefiles Ser.: No. 61). 160p. (YA). (gr. 6 up). pap. 3.99 (*0-671-73097-5*, Simon Pulse) Simon & Schuster Children's Publishing.

—Grave Danger. 1990. (Hardy Boys Casefiles Ser.: No. 61). (YA). (gr. 6 up). 9.09 (*0-606-02030-6*) Turtleback Bks.

—The Great Airport Mystery. 2004. (Hardy Boys Mystery Stories Ser.: No. 9). 228p. (J). (gr. 3-6). 14.95 (*1-55709-267-2*) Applewood Bks.

—The Great Airport Mystery. 1930. (Hardy Boys Mystery Stories Ser.: No. 9). (Illus.). 180p. (J). (gr. 3-6). 5.99 (*0-448-08909-2*, Grosset & Dunlap) Penguin Putnam Bks. for Young Readers.

—The Gross Ghost Mystery. 1997. (Hardy Boys Are: No. 1). (Illus.). 80p. (J). (gr. 2-4). mass mkt. 2.99 (*0-671-00402-6*, Aladdin) Simon & Schuster Children's Publishing.

—The Gross Ghost Mystery. 1997. (Hardy Boys Are: No. 1). (Illus.). (J). (gr. 2-4). 8.19 o.p. (*0-606-12705-4*) Turtleback Bks.

—The Hardy Boys, Vols. 1-6. 1998. (J). 19.98 (*0-448-41671-9*, Grosset & Dunlap) Penguin Putnam Bks. for Young Readers.

—The Hardy Boys Casefiles Boxed Set: Beyond the Law; Spiked; Open Season, 1998. (Hardy Boys Casefiles Ser.: Nos. 55, 58 & 59). 464p. (YA). (gr. 6 up). mass mkt. 4.99 (*0-671-02035-8*, Simon Pulse) Simon & Schuster Children's Publishing.

—The Hardy Boys Casefiles Boxed Set: Diplomatic Deceit; Flesh & Blood; Fright Wave. 1998. (Hardy Boys Casefiles Ser.: Nos. 38, 39 & 40). 464p. (YA). (gr. 6 up). pap. 4.99 (*0-671-02033-1*, Simon Pulse) Simon & Schuster Children's Publishing.

—The Hardy Boys Casefiles Boxed Set: Rock 'n' Revenge; Choke Hold; Uncivil War. 1998. (Hardy Boys Casefiles Ser.: Nos. 48, 51 & 52). (YA). (gr. 6 up). 464p. 4.99 (*0-671-02034-X*); 352p. pap. 4.99 (*0-671-02018-8*) Simon & Schuster Children's Publishing. (Simon Pulse).

—The Hardy Boys Casefiles Gift Set: Dead on Target; The Genius Thieves; Perfect Getaway; The Borgia Dagger; Blood Relations. 1989. (Hardy Boys Casefiles Ser.: Nos. 1, 9, 12, 13 & 15). (YA). (gr. 6 up). pap. 14.75 (*0-671-92250-5*, Simon Pulse) Simon & Schuster Children's Publishing.

—Hardy Boys Digest, 4 vols. gif. ed. (J). (gr. 3-7). 1989. 14.00 (*0-671-92234-3*); 1987. pap. 14.00 (*0-671-91514-2*) Simon & Schuster Children's Publishing. (Aladdin).

—The Hardy Boys Ghost Stories. 1989. (J). (gr. 3-7). 9.09 o.p. (*0-606-01308-3*) Turtleback Bks.

—The Hardy Boys Mystery Stories Boxed Set: Sky Blue Frame; Wipeout; The Crusade of the Flaming Sword; Crime in the Kennel. 1997. (Hardy Boys Mystery Stories Ser.: Nos. 89, 96, 131, & 133). (J). (gr. 3-6). 15.96 (*0-671-87830-1*, Aladdin) Simon & Schuster Children's Publishing.

—The Hardy Boys Mystery Stories Boxed Set: The Missing Chums; Hunting for Hidden Gold; The Shore Road Mystery. 2000. (Hardy Boys Mystery Stories Ser.: Nos. 4, 5 & 6). 560p. (J). (gr. 3-6). 9.98 (*0-7651-1767-3*) Smithmark Pubs., Inc.

—The Hardy Boys Mystery Stories Boxed Set: The Tower Treasure; The House on the Cliff; The Secret of the Old Mill, 1999. (Hardy Boys Mystery Stories Ser.: Nos. 1, 2 & 3). (Illus.). 560p. (J). (gr. 3-6). 9.98 (*0-7651-1727-4*) Smithmark Pubs., Inc.

—The Hardy Boys Starter Set: The Tower Treasure; The House on the Cliff; The Secret of the Old Mill; The Missing Chums; The Shore Road Mystery. 1996. (Hardy Boys Mystery Stories Ser.: Nos. 1-6). (J). (gr. 3-6). 19.98 o.p. (*0-448-41672-7*, Grosset & Dunlap) Penguin Putnam Bks. for Young Readers.

—The Hardy Boys Who-Dunnit Mystery Book. 1981. 64p. (J). (gr. 3-7). pap. 3.95 (*0-671-95721-X*, Aladdin) Simon & Schuster Children's Publishing.

—The Hardys on Holiday. 2002. (Hardy Boys Ser.). (Illus.). 464p. pap. 7.50 (*0-689-85620-2*, Aladdin) Simon & Schuster Children's Publishing.

—The Haunted Fort. 1964. (Hardy Boys Mystery Stories Ser.: No. 44). (Illus.). 180p. (J). (gr. 3-6). 5.99 (*0-448-08944-0*, Grosset & Dunlap) Penguin Putnam Bks. for Young Readers.

—Height of Danger. Greenberg, Anne, ed. 1991. (Hardy Boys Casefiles Ser.: No. 56). 160p. (J). (gr. 6 up). per. 3.99 (*0-671-73092-4*, Simon Pulse) Simon & Schuster Children's Publishing.

—Height of Danger. 1991. (Hardy Boys Casefiles Ser.: No. 56). (YA). (gr. 6 up). 9.09 o.p. (*0-606-04932-0*) Turtleback Bks.

—The Hidden Harbor Mystery. Date not set. (Hardy Boys Mystery Stories Ser.). (Illus.). 228p. (YA). (gr. 7 up). 14.95 (*1-55709-272-9*) Applewood Bks.

—The Hidden Harbor Mystery. 1935. (Hardy Boys Mystery Stories Ser.: No. 14). (Illus.). 180p. (J). (gr. 3-6). 5.99 (*0-448-08914-9*, Grosset & Dunlap) Penguin Putnam Bks. for Young Readers.

—Hide & Sneak, 2002. (Hardy Boys Ser.: Vol. 174). 144p. (J). pap. 4.99 (*0-7434-3758-6*, Aladdin) Simon & Schuster Children's Publishing.

—High-Speed Showdown. 1996. (Hardy Boys Mystery Stories Ser.: No. 137). 160p. (J). (gr. 3-6). pap. 3.99 (*0-671-50521-1*, Aladdin) Simon & Schuster Children's Publishing.

—High-Speed Showdown. 1996. (Hardy Boys Mystery Stories Ser.: No. 137). (J). (gr. 3-6). 9.09 (*0-606-09377-X*) Turtleback Bks.

—High-Wire Act. 1997. (Hardy Boys Casefiles Ser.: No. 123). 160p. (YA). (gr. 6 up). mass mkt. 3.99 (*0-671-56122-7*, Simon Pulse) Simon & Schuster Children's Publishing.

—High-Wire Act. 1997. (Hardy Boys Casefiles Ser.: No. 123). (YA). (gr. 6 up). 9.09 o.p. (*0-606-11437-8*) Turtleback Bks.

—Highway Robbery. Greenberg, Ann, ed. 1990. (Hardy Boys Casefiles Ser.: No. 41). 160p. (YA). (gr. 6 up). mass mkt. 3.75 (*0-671-70038-3*, Simon Pulse) Simon & Schuster Children's Publishing.

—Highway Robbery. 1990. (Hardy Boys Casefiles Ser.: No. 41). (YA). (gr. 6 up). 8.85 o.p. (*0-606-03538-9*) Turtleback Bks.

—The Hooded Hawk Mystery. rev. ed. (Hardy Boys Mystery Stories Ser.: No. 34). (Illus.). (J). (gr. 3-6). 1975. 3.29 o.p. (*0-448-18934-8*); 1955. 180p. 5.99 (*0-448-08934-3*) Penguin Putnam Bks. for Young Readers. (Grosset & Dunlap).

—Hostages of Hate. l.t. ed. 1988. (Hardy Boys Casefiles Ser.: No. 10). 153p. (YA). (gr. 6 up). reprint ed. 9.50 o.p. (*0-942545-51-6*); lib. bdg. 10.50 o.p. (*0-942545-61-3*) Grey Castle Pr.

—Hostages of Hate. 1989. (Hardy Boys Casefiles Ser.: No. 10). 160p. (YA). (gr. 6 up). pap. 2.95 (*0-671-69579-7*, Simon Pulse) Simon & Schuster Children's Publishing.

—Hot Wheels. Ashby, Ruth, ed. 1994. (Hardy Boys Casefiles Ser.: No. 91). 160p. (YA). (gr. 6 up). pap. 3.99 (*0-671-79475-2*, Simon Pulse) Simon & Schuster Children's Publishing.

—Hot Wheels. 1994. (Hardy Boys Casefiles Ser.: No. 91). (YA). (gr. 6 up). 10.04 (*0-606-06448-6*) Turtleback Bks.

—The House on the Cliff. 2004. (Hardy Boys Mystery Stories Ser.: No. 2). 212p. (J). (gr. 3-6). 14.95 (*1-55709-145-5*) Applewood Bks.

—The House on the Cliff. 1927. (Hardy Boys Mystery Stories Ser.: No. 2). (Illus.). 180p. (J). (gr. 3-6). 5.95 (*0-448-08902-5*, Grosset & Dunlap) Penguin Putnam Bks. for Young Readers.

—The House on the Cliff. abr. ed. 2002. (Hardy Boys: Vol. 2). (J). (gr. 4-6). 23.00 (*0-8072-0770-5*); (Hardy Boys Ser.: No. 2). (gr. 3 up). audio 18.00 (*0-8072-0769-1*) Random Hse. Audio Publishing Group. (Listening Library).

—The Hunt for the Four Brothers. 1999. (Hardy Boys Mystery Stories Ser.: No. 155). (J). (gr. 3-6). pap. 3.99 (*0-671-02550-3*, Aladdin) Simon & Schuster Children's Publishing.

—Hunting for Hidden Gold. 2004. (Hardy Boys Mystery Stories Ser.: No. 5). (Illus.). 210p. (J). (gr. 3-6). 14.95 (*1-55709-148-X*) Applewood Bks.

—Hunting for Hidden Gold. unabr. ed. 2003. (Hardy Boys Ser.: No. 5). (J). (gr. 3). audio 18.00 (*0-8072-1248-2*, Imagination Studio) Random Hse. Audio Publishing Group.

—The Hypersonic Secret. 1995. (Hardy Boys Mystery Stories Ser.: No. 135). 160p. (J). (gr. 3-6). pap. 3.99 (*0-671-50518-1*, Aladdin) Simon & Schuster Children's Publishing.

—The Hypersonic Secret. 1995. (Hardy Boys Mystery Stories Ser.: No. 135). (J). (gr. 3-6). 9.09 o.p. (*0-606-08535-1*) Turtleback Bks.

—The Ice Cold Case. 1998. (Hardy Boys Mystery Stories Ser.: No. 148). 147p. (J). (gr. 3-6). pap. 3.99 (*0-671-00122-1*, Aladdin) Simon & Schuster Children's Publishing.

—The Ice Cold Case. 1998. (Hardy Boys Mystery Stories Ser.: No. 148). (J). (gr. 3-6). 9.09 o.p. (*0-606-13462-X*) Turtleback Bks.

—Illegal Procedure. Ashby, Ruth, ed. 1995. (Hardy Boys Casefiles Ser.: No. 95). 160p. (YA). (gr. 6 up). mass mkt. 4.99 (*0-671-88206-6*, Simon Pulse) Simon & Schuster Children's Publishing.

—Illegal Procedure. 1995. (Hardy Boys Casefiles Ser.: No. 95). (YA). (gr. 6 up). 10.04 (*0-606-07617-4*) Turtleback Bks.

—In Plane Sight, No. 176. 2002. (Hardy Boys Ser.). (Illus.). 160p. pap. 4.99 (*0-7434-3760-8*, Aladdin) Simon & Schuster Children's Publishing.

—In Self-Defense. Greenberg, Ann, ed. 1990. (Hardy Boys Casefiles Ser.: No. 45). 160p. (YA). (gr. 6 up). pap. 3.75 (*0-671-70042-1*, Simon Pulse) Simon & Schuster Children's Publishing.

—In Self-Defense. 1990. (Hardy Boys Casefiles Ser.: No. 45). (YA). (gr. 6 up). 9.80 (*0-606-04702-6*) Turtleback Bks.

—Inferno of Fear. Ashby, Ruth, ed. 1994. (Hardy Boys Casefiles Ser.: No. 88). 160p. (Orig.). (YA). (gr. 6 up). pap. 3.99 (*0-671-79472-8*, Simon Pulse) Simon & Schuster Children's Publishing.

—The Infinity Clue. 1989. (Hardy Boys Mystery Stories Ser.: No. 70). 192p. (J). (gr. 3-6). pap. 3.50 (*0-671-69154-6*); 1981. (Hardy Boys Mystery Stories Ser.: No. 70). (Illus.). 192p. (J). (gr. 3-6). pap. 3.50 (*0-671-42343-6*); Vol. 70. 1986. mass mkt. 3.50 (*0-671-62475-X*) Simon & Schuster Children's Publishing. (Aladdin).

—Jump Shot Detectives. 1998. (Clues Brothers Ser.: No. 4). (Illus.). 80p. (J). (gr. 2-4). pap. 3.99 (*0-671-00405-0*, Aladdin) Simon & Schuster Children's Publishing.

—Jump Shot Detectives. 1998. (Hardy Boys Are: No. 4) (Illus.). (J). (gr. 2-4). 10.04 (*0-606-12936-7*) Turtleback Bks.

—The Jungle Pyramid. 1976. (Hardy Boys Mystery Stories Ser.: No. 56). (Illus.). (J). (gr. 3-6). 180p. 5.99 (*0-448-08956-4*); 7.25 o.p. (*0-448-18956-9*) Penguin Putnam Bks. for Young Readers. (Grosset & Dunlap).

—The Karate Clue. 1997. (Hardy Boys Are: No. 2). (Illus.). 80p. (J). (gr. 2-4). pap. 2.99 (*0-671-00403-4*, Aladdin) Simon & Schuster Children's Publishing.

—The Karate Clue. 1997. (Hardy Boys Are: No. 2). (J). (gr. 2-4). 8.19 o.p. (*0-606-12706-2*) Turtleback Bks.

—Kickoff to Danger. 2001. (Hardy Boys Mystery Stories Ser.: No. 170). (J). (gr. 3-6). 160p. pap. 4.99 (*0-7434-0685-0*); E-Book 4.99 (*0-7434-3704-7*) Simon & Schuster Children's Publishing. (Aladdin).

—A Killing in the Market. (Hardy Boys Casefiles Ser.: No. 18). (YA). (gr. 6 up). 1989. pap. 2.95 (*0-671-68472-8*); 1988. pap. (*0-671-64681-8*) Simon & Schuster Children's Publishing. (Simon Pulse).

—King for a Day. 1999. (Hardy Boys Are: No. 12). (Illus.). 80p. (J). (gr. 2-4). per. 3.99 (*0-671-02719-0*, Aladdin) Simon & Schuster Children's Publishing.

—The Last Laugh. 1990. (Hardy Boys Casefiles Ser.: No. 42). (YA). (gr. 6 up). mass mkt. 2.95 (*0-671-70039-1*, Simon Pulse) Simon & Schuster Children's Publishing.

—The Last Laugh. Greenberg, Ann, ed. 1991. (Hardy Boys Casefiles Ser.: No. 42). 160p. (YA). (gr. 6 up). reprint ed. pap. 3.50 (*0-671-74614-6*, Simon Pulse) Simon & Schuster Children's Publishing.

—The Last Leap. 1996. (Hardy Boys Casefiles Ser.: No. 118). 160p. (YA). (gr. 6 up). pap. 3.99 (*0-671-56118-9*, Simon Pulse) Simon & Schuster Children's Publishing.

—The Last Leap. 1996. (Hardy Boys Casefiles Ser.: No. 118). (YA). (gr. 6 up). 9.09 o.p. (*0-606-11432-7*) Turtleback Bks.

—Law of the Jungle. 1995. (Hardy Boys Casefiles Ser.: No. 105). 160p. (YA). (gr. 6 up). pap. 3.99 (*0-671-50428-2*, Simon Pulse) Simon & Schuster Children's Publishing.

—Law of the Jungle. 1995. (Hardy Boys Casefiles Ser.: No. 105). (YA). (gr. 6 up). 9.09 o.p. (*0-606-08537-8*) Turtleback Bks.

—The Lazarus Plot. l.t. ed. 1988. (Hardy Boys Casefiles Ser.: No. 4). 152p. (YA). (gr. 6 up). reprint ed. 9.50 o.p. (*0-942545-45-1*); lib. bdg. 10.50 o.p. (*0-942545-55-9*) Grey Castle Pr.

—The Lazarus Plot. (Hardy Boys Casefiles Ser.: No. 4). (YA). (gr. 6 up). 1991. mass mkt. 3.75 (*0-671-73995-6*); 1988. pap. 2.95 (*0-671-68048-X*); 1987. pap. (*0-671-62129-7*) Simon & Schuster Children's Publishing. (Simon Pulse).

—The Lazarus Plot. 1987. (Hardy Boys Casefiles Ser.: No. 4). (YA). (gr. 6 up). 9.80 (*0-606-02104-3*) Turtleback Bks.

—Lethal Cargo. Greenberg, Anne, ed. 1992. (Hardy Boys Casefiles Ser.: No. 67). 160p. (Orig.). (YA). (gr. 6 up). pap. 3.75 (*0-671-73103-3*, Simon Pulse) Simon & Schuster Children's Publishing.

—Line of Fire. (Illus.). (J). mass mkt. 2.95 (*0-671-70492-3*); 1989. (Hardy Boys Casefiles Ser.: No. 16). 160p. (YA). (gr. 6 up). pap. 2.95 (*0-671-68805-7*) Simon & Schuster Children's Publishing. (Simon Pulse).

—The London Deception. 1999. (Hardy Boys Mystery Stories Ser.: No. 158). 160p. (J). (gr. 3-6). pap. 3.99 (*0-671-03496-0*, Aladdin) Simon & Schuster Children's Publishing.

—The London Deception. 1999. (Hardy Boys Mystery Stories Ser.: No. 158). (J). (gr. 3-6). 10.04 (*0-606-19052-X*) Turtleback Bks.

—Lost in Gator Swamp. 1997. (Hardy Boys Mystery Stories Ser.: No. 142). 160p. (J). (gr. 3-6). per. 3.99 (*0-671-00054-3*, Aladdin) Simon & Schuster Children's Publishing.

—The Lure of the Italian Treasure. 1999. (Hardy Boys Mystery Stories Ser.: No. 157). 160p. (J). (gr. 3-6). pap. 3.99 (*0-671-03445-6*, Aladdin) Simon & Schuster Children's Publishing.

—The Mark of the Blue Tattoo. 1997. (Hardy Boys Mystery Stories Ser.: No. 146). 149p. (J). (gr. 3-6). per. 3.99 (*0-671-00058-6*, Aladdin) Simon & Schuster Children's Publishing.

—The Mark of the Blue Tattoo. 1997. (Hardy Boys Mystery Stories Ser.: No. 146). (J). (gr. 3-6). 9.09 o.p. (*0-606-13460-3*) Turtleback Bks.

—The Mark on the Door. rev. ed. (Hardy Boys Mystery Stories Ser.: No. 13). (J). (gr. 3-6). 1975. 3.29 o.p. (*0-448-18913-5*); 1934. (Illus.). 180p. 5.99 (*0-448-08913-0*) Penguin Putnam Bks. for Young Readers. (Grosset & Dunlap).

—The Masked Monkey. 1972. (Hardy Boys Mystery Stories Ser.: No. 51). (Illus.). 180p. (J). (gr. 3-6). 5.95 (*0-448-08951-3*, Grosset & Dunlap) Penguin Putnam Bks. for Young Readers.

—Maximum Challenge. 1995. (Hardy Boys Mystery Stories Ser.: No. 132). (Illus.). 160p. (J). (gr. 3-6). pap. 3.99 (*0-671-87216-8*, Aladdin) Simon & Schuster Children's Publishing.

—Maximum Challenge. 1995. (Hardy Boys Mystery Stories Ser.: No. 132). (J). (gr. 3-6). 9.09 o.p. (*0-606-07611-5*) Turtleback Bks.

—Mayhem in Motion. Greenberg, Anne, ed. 1992. (Hardy Boys Casefiles Ser.: No. 69). 160p. (YA). (gr. 6 up). pap. 3.75 (*0-671-73105-X*, Simon Pulse) Simon & Schuster Children's Publishing.

—Mayhem in Motion. 1992. (Hardy Boys Casefiles Ser.: No. 69). (YA). (gr. 6 up). 8.85 o.p. (*0-606-02665-7*) Turtleback Bks.

—The Melted Coins. (Hardy Boys Mystery Stories Ser.: No. 23). (Illus.). (J). (gr. 3-6). 1944. 180p. 5.99 (*0-448-08923-8*); 1975. 3.29 o.p. (*0-448-18923-2*) Penguin Putnam Bks. for Young Readers. (Grosset & Dunlap).

—The Million Dollar Nightmare. Greenberg, Ann, ed. 1990. (Hardy Boys Mystery Stories Ser.: No. 103). 160p. (Orig.). (J). (gr. 3-6). pap. 3.99 (*0-671-69272-0*, Aladdin) Simon & Schuster Children's Publishing.

—The Missing Chums. 2004. (Hardy Boys Mystery Stories Ser.: No. 4). (Illus.). 210p. (J). (gr. 3-6). reprint ed. 14.95 (*1-55709-147-1*) Applewood Bks.

—The Missing Chums. rev. ed. (Hardy Boys Mystery Stories Ser.: No. 4). (J). (gr. 3-6). 1975. 3.29 o.p. (*0-448-18904-6*); 1930. (Illus.). 180p. 5.95 (*0-448-08904-1*) Penguin Putnam Bks. for Young Readers. (Grosset & Dunlap).

—The Missing Chums. unabr. ed. 2002. (Hardy Boys Ser.: Vol. 4). (J). (gr. 4-7). audio 18.00 (*0-8072-0775-6*, Listening Library) Random Hse. Audio Publishing Group.

—Mission: Mayhem. Ashby, Ruth, ed. 1994. (Hardy Boys Casefiles Ser.: No. 93). 160p. (YA). (gr. 6 up). pap. 3.99 (*0-671-88204-X*, Simon Pulse) Simon & Schuster Children's Publishing.

—Mission: Mayhem. 1994. (Hardy Boys Casefiles Ser.: No. 93). (YA). (gr. 6 up). 10.04 (*0-606-07002-8*) Turtleback Bks.

—Moment of Truth. 1996. (Hardy Boys Casefiles Ser.: No. 109). 160p. (J). (gr. 6 up). mass mkt. 3.99 (*0-671-50432-0*, Simon Pulse) Simon & Schuster Children's Publishing.

—Moment of Truth. 1996. (Hardy Boys Casefiles Ser.: No. 109). (YA). (gr. 6 up). 9.09 o.p. (*0-606-09381-8*) Turtleback Bks.

—The Money Hunt. Greenberg, Ann, ed. 1990. (Hardy Boys Mystery Stories Ser.: No. 101). 160p. (J). (gr. 3-6). pap. 3.99 (*0-671-69451-0*, Aladdin) Simon & Schuster Children's Publishing.

—The Monster in the Lake. 1999. (Hardy Boys Are: No. 11). (Illus.). 80p. (J). (gr. 2-4). pap. 3.99 (*0-671-02662-3*, Aladdin) Simon & Schuster Children's Publishing.

—The Mummy Case. (Hardy Boys Mystery Stories Ser.: No. 63). 192p. (J). (gr. 3-6). 1987. mass mkt. 3.99 (*0-671-64289-8*, Aladdin); 1980. (Illus.). pap. (*0-671-41116-0*, Simon & Schuster Children's Publishing) Simon & Schuster Children's Publishing.

—Murder by Magic. Greenberg, Anne, ed. 1995. (Hardy Boys Casefiles Ser.: No. 98). 160p. (J). (gr. 6 up). pap. 3.99 (*0-671-88209-0*, Simon Pulse) Simon & Schuster Children's Publishing.

—Murder by Magic. 1995. (Hardy Boys Casefiles Ser.: No. 98). (YA). (gr. 6 up). 9.09 o.p. (*0-606-07620-4*) Turtleback Bks.

—The Mysterious Caravan. 1975. (Hardy Boys Mystery Stories Ser.: No. 54). (Illus.). 180p. (J). (gr. 3-6). 5.99 (*0-448-08954-8*, Grosset & Dunlap) Penguin Putnam Bks. for Young Readers.

—The Mystery at Devil's Paw. (Hardy Boys Mystery Stories Ser.: No. 38). (Illus.). (J). (gr. 3-6). reprint ed. 1975. 192p. 3.29 o.p. (*0-448-18938-0*); 1959. 180p. 5.99 (*0-448-08938-6*) Penguin Putnam Bks. for Young Readers. (Grosset & Dunlap).

—The Mystery in the Old Mine. 1993. (Hardy Boys Mystery Stories Ser.: No. 121). 160p. (Orig.). (J). (gr. 3-6). pap. 3.99 (*0-671-79311-X*, Aladdin) Simon & Schuster Children's Publishing.

—Mystery of Smugglers Cove. (Orig.). (J). 1991. (Hardy Boys Ser.: Vol. 64). (Illus.). pap. 3.50 (*0-671-73424-5*, Aladdin); 1988. (Hardy Boys Mystery Stories Ser.: No. 64). 176p. (gr. 3-6). pap. 3.50 (*0-671-66229-5*, Aladdin); 1980. (Hardy Boys Mystery Stories Ser.: No. 64). (Illus.). 192p. (gr. 3-6). pap. (*0-671-41117-9*, Simon & Schuster Children's Publishing); 1980. (Hardy Boys Mystery Stories Ser.: No. 64). (Illus.). 192p. (gr. 3-6). pap. (*0-671-41112-8*, Simon & Schuster Children's Publishing) Simon & Schuster Children's Publishing.

—The Mystery of the Aztec Warrior. (Hardy Boys Mystery Stories Ser.: No. 43). (J). (gr. 3-6). 1975. 3.29 o.p. (*0-448-18943-7*); 1964. (Illus.). 180p. 5.99 (*0-448-08943-2*) Penguin Putnam Bks. for Young Readers. (Grosset & Dunlap).

—The Mystery of the Chinese Junk. (Hardy Boys Mystery Stories Ser.: No. 39). (J). (gr. 3-6). 1975. 3.29 o.p. (*0-448-18939-9*); 1959. (Illus.). 180p. 5.99 (*0-448-08939-4*) Penguin Putnam Bks. for Young Readers. (Grosset & Dunlap).

—The Mystery of the Desert Giant. (Hardy Boys Mystery Stories Ser.: No. 40). (Illus.). (J). (gr. 3-6). 1975. 3.29 o.p. (*0-448-18940-2*); 1960. 180p. 5.99 (*0-448-08940-8*) Penguin Putnam Bks. for Young Readers. (Grosset & Dunlap).

—The Mystery of the Flying Express. (Hardy Boys Mystery Stories Ser.: No. 20). (Illus.). (J). (gr. 3-6). 1975. 3.29 o.p. (*0-448-18920-8*); 1941. 180p. 5.99 (*0-448-08920-3*) Penguin Putnam Bks. for Young Readers. (Grosset & Dunlap).

—The Mystery of the Samurai Sword. (Hardy Boys Mystery Stories Ser.: No. 60). (J). (gr. 3-6). 1988. 192p. pap. 3.99 (*0-671-67302-5*, Aladdin); 1979. (Illus.). pap. 3.50 (*0-671-95497-0*, Aladdin); 1979. (Illus.). pap. (*0-671-95506-3*, Simon & Schuster Children's Publishing) Simon & Schuster Children's Publishing.

—The Mystery of the Silver Star. 1987. (Hardy Boys Mystery Stories Ser.: No. 86). (J). (gr. 3-6). pap. 3.50 (*0-671-64374-6*, Aladdin) Simon & Schuster Children's Publishing.

—The Mystery of the Spiral Bridge. (Hardy Boys Mystery Stories Ser.: No. 45). (Illus.). (J). (gr. 3-6). 1975. 3.29 o.p. (*0-448-18945-3*); 1965. 180p. 5.99 (*0-448-08945-9*) Penguin Putnam Bks. for Young Readers. (Grosset & Dunlap).

—The Mystery of the Whale Tattoo. (Hardy Boys Mystery Stories Ser.: No. 47). (J). (gr. 3-6). 1975. 3.29 o.p. (*0-448-18947-X*); 1967. (Illus.). 180p. 5.99 (*0-448-08947-5*) Penguin Putnam Bks. for Young Readers. (Grosset & Dunlap).

—Mystery on Makatunk Island. 1994. (Hardy Boys Mystery Stories Ser.: No. 125). 160p. (J). (gr. 3-6). pap. 3.99 (*0-671-79315-2*, Aladdin) Simon & Schuster Children's Publishing.

—Mystery with a Dangerous Beat. 1994. (Hardy Boys Mystery Stories Ser.: No. 124). 160p. (J). (gr. 3-6). pap. 3.99 (*0-671-79314-4*, Aladdin) Simon & Schuster Children's Publishing.

—Mystery with a Dangerous Beat. 1994. (Hardy Boys Mystery Stories Ser.: No. 124). (J). (gr. 3-6). 9.09 o.p. (*0-606-05859-1*) Turtleback Bks.

—Night of the Werewolf. Greenberg, Ann, ed. 1990. (Hardy Boys Mystery Stories Ser.: No. 59). 192p. (J). (gr. 3-6). pap. 3.99 (*0-671-70993-3*, Aladdin) Simon & Schuster Children's Publishing.

—Night of the Werewolf. 1979. (Hardy Boys Mystery Stories Ser.: No. 59). (Illus.). (J). (gr. 3-6). pap. (*0-671-95520-9*); pap. (*0-671-95498-9*) Simon & Schuster Children's Publishing. (Simon & Schuster Children's Publishing).

—Nightmare in Angel City. (Hardy Boys Casefiles Ser.: No. 19). (Orig.). (YA). (gr. 6 up). 1989. pap. 2.95 (*0-671-69185-6*); 1988. pap. 2.75 (*0-671-64682-6*) Simon & Schuster Children's Publishing. (Simon Pulse).

—No Mercy. Greenberg, Anne, ed. 1992. (Hardy Boys Casefiles Ser.: No. 65). 176p. (Orig.). (YA). (gr. 6 up). pap. 3.99 (*0-671-73101-7*, Simon Pulse) Simon & Schuster Children's Publishing.

—No Way Out. Greenberg, Anne, ed. 1993. (Hardy Boys Casefiles Ser.: No. 75). 160p. (YA). (gr. 6 up). pap. 3.99 (*0-671-73111-4*, Simon Pulse) Simon & Schuster Children's Publishing.

—No Way Out. 1993. (Hardy Boys Casefiles Ser.: No. 75). (YA). (gr. 6 up). 10.04 (*0-606-05336-0*) Turtleback Bks.

—Nowhere to Run. 1989. (Hardy Boys Casefiles Ser.: No. 27). (Orig.). (YA). (gr. 6 up). pap. 2.95 (*0-671-64690-7*, Simon Pulse) Simon & Schuster Children's Publishing.

—The Number File. 1989. (Hardy Boys Casefiles Ser.: No. 17). (Orig.). (YA). (gr. 6 up). pap. 2.95 (*0-671-68806-5*, Simon Pulse) Simon & Schuster Children's Publishing.

—Open Season. Greenberg, Anne, ed. 1992. (Hardy Boys Casefiles Ser.: No. 59). 160p. (Orig.). (YA). (gr. 6 up). pap. 3.50 (*0-671-73095-9*, Simon Pulse) Simon & Schuster Children's Publishing.

—The Outlaw's Silver. (Hardy Boys Mystery Stories Ser.: No. 67). (J). (gr. 3-6). 1991. pap. 3.50 (*0-671-74229-9*, Aladdin); 1981. (Illus.). 192p. (*0-671-42336-3*, Simon & Schuster Children's Publishing); 1981. (Illus.). 192p. pap. 3.50 (*0-671-42337-1*, Aladdin); 1980. (Illus.). 192p. pap. 3.50 (*0-671-41111-X*, Aladdin) Simon & Schuster Children's Publishing.

—The Pacific Conspiracy. 1993. (Hardy Boys Casefiles Ser.: No. 78). 160p. (Orig.). (YA). (gr. 6 up). pap. 3.99 (*0-671-79462-0*, Simon Pulse) Simon & Schuster Children's Publishing.

—Panic on Gull Island. 1991. (Hardy Boys Mystery Stories Ser.: No. 107). 160p. (J). (gr. 3-6). mass mkt. 3.99 (*0-671-69276-3*, Aladdin) Simon & Schuster Children's Publishing.

—Panic on Gull Island. 1991. (Hardy Boys Mystery Stories Ser.: No. 107). (J). (gr. 3-6). 9.09 o.p. (*0-606-04998-3*) Turtleback Bks.

—Past & Present Danger. 2001. (Hardy Boys Mystery Stories Ser.: No. 166). 160p. (J). (gr. 3-6). E-Book 3.99 (*0-7434-2342-9*); (Illus.). pap. 3.99 (*0-7434-0660-5*) Simon & Schuster Children's Publishing. (Aladdin).

—Peak of Danger. 1995. (Hardy Boys Casefiles Ser.: No. 101). (Illus.). 160p. (J). (gr. 6 up). per. 3.99 (*0-671-88212-0*, Simon Pulse) Simon & Schuster Children's Publishing.

—Peak of Danger. 1995. (Hardy Boys Casefiles Ser.: No. 101). (YA). (gr. 6 up). 9.09 o.p. (*0-606-07614-X*) Turtleback Bks.

—The Pentagon Spy. Greenberg, Anne, ed. 1988. (Hardy Boys Mystery Stories Ser.: No. 61). 192p. (J). (gr. 3-6). pap. 3.99 (*0-671-67221-5*, Aladdin) Simon & Schuster Children's Publishing.

—The Pentagon Spy. 1980. (Hardy Boys Mystery Stories Ser.: No. 61). (Illus.). (J). (gr. 3-6). pap. 3.50 (*0-671-95570-5*, Aladdin); pap. (*0-671-95562-4*, Simon & Schuster Children's Publishing) Simon & Schuster Children's Publishing.

—Perfect Getaway. (Hardy Boys Casefiles Ser.: No. 12). (Orig.). (YA). (gr. 6 up). 1991. mass mkt. 3.50 (*0-671-73675-2*); 1988. 160p. pap. 2.95 (*0-671-68049-8*) Simon & Schuster Children's Publishing. (Simon Pulse).

—The Phantom Freighter. rev. ed. (Hardy Boys Mystery Stories Ser.: No. 26). (Illus.). (J). (gr. 3-6). 1975. 3.29 o.p. (*0-448-18926-7*); 1947. 180p. 5.99 (*0-448-08926-2*) Penguin Putnam Bks. for Young Readers. (Grosset & Dunlap).

—The Phoenix Equation. Greenberg, Anne, ed. 1992. (Hardy Boys Casefiles Ser.: No. 66). 176p. (Orig.). (YA). (gr. 6 up). pap. 3.99 (*0-671-73102-5*, Simon Pulse) Simon & Schuster Children's Publishing.

—Pirates Ahoy! 1999. (Hardy Boys Are: No. 13). (Illus.). 80p. (J). (gr. 2-4). pap. 3.99 (*0-671-02786-7*, Aladdin) Simon & Schuster Children's Publishing.

—Pirates Ahoy! 1999. (Hardy Boys Are: No. 13). (J). (gr. 2-4). 10.14 (*0-606-17731-0*) Turtleback Bks.

—Poisoned Paradise. Greenberg, Anne, ed. 1993. (Hardy Boys Casefiles Ser.: No. 82). 160p. (Orig.). (J). (gr. 6 up). pap. 3.99 (*0-671-79466-3*, Simon Pulse) Simon & Schuster Children's Publishing.

—Power Play. Greenberg, Anne, ed. 1991. (Hardy Boys Casefiles Ser.: No. 50). (Illus.). 160p. (YA). (gr. 6 up). pap. 3.99 (*0-671-70047-2*, Simon Pulse) Simon & Schuster Children's Publishing.

—Power Play. 1991. (Hardy Boys Casefiles Ser.: No. 50). (YA). (gr. 6 up). 10.04 (*0-606-05003-5*) Turtleback Bks.

—The Prime-Time Crime. Greenberg, Anne, ed. 1991. (Hardy Boys Mystery Stories Ser.: No. 109). 160p. (Orig.). (J). (gr. 3-6). pap. 3.99 (*0-671-69278-X*, Aladdin) Simon & Schuster Children's Publishing.

—Program for Destruction. Greenberg, Ann, ed. 1987. (Hardy Boys Mystery Stories Ser.: No. 87). (J). (gr. 3-6). pap. 3.99 (*0-671-64895-0*, Aladdin) Simon & Schuster Children's Publishing.

—The Pumped-up Pizza Problem. 1998. (Hardy Boys Are: No. 9). (Illus.). 80p. (J). (gr. 2-4). pap. 3.99 (*0-671-02142-7*, Aladdin) Simon & Schuster Children's Publishing.

—Pure Evil. Greenberg, Anne, ed. 1995. (Hardy Boys Casefiles Ser.: No. 97). 160p. (YA). (gr. 6 up). pap. 3.99 (*0-671-88208-2*, Simon Pulse) Simon & Schuster Children's Publishing.

—Pure Evil. 1995. (Hardy Boys Casefiles Ser.: No. 97). (YA). (gr. 6 up). 10.04 (*0-606-07619-0*) Turtleback Bks.

—Racing to Disaster. 1994. (Hardy Boys Mystery Stories Ser.: No. 126). 160p. (YA). (gr. 3-6). pap. 3.99 (*0-671-87210-9*, Aladdin) Simon & Schuster Children's Publishing.

—Racing to Disaster. 1994. (Hardy Boys Mystery Stories Ser.: No. 126). (J). (gr. 3-6). 9.09 o.p. (*0-606-06441-9*) Turtleback Bks.

—Radical Moves. Winkler, Ellen, ed. 1992. (Hardy Boys Mystery Stories Ser.: No. 113). 160p. (Orig.). (J). (gr. 3-6). pap. 3.99 (*0-671-73060-6*, Aladdin) Simon & Schuster Children's Publishing.

—Real Horror. Greenberg, Anne, ed. 1993. (Hardy Boys Casefiles Ser.: No. 71). 160p. (Orig.). (J). (gr. 6 up). pap. 3.99 (*0-671-73107-6*, Simon Pulse) Simon & Schuster Children's Publishing.

—Reel Thrills. 1994. (Hardy Boys Mystery Stories Ser.: No. 127). 160p. (YA). (gr. 3-6). pap. 3.99 (*0-671-87211-7*, Simon Pulse) Simon & Schuster Children's Publishing.

—Revenge of the Desert Phantom. (Hardy Boys Mystery Stories Ser.: No. 84). (J). (gr. 3-6). (*0-671-49730-8*, Simon & Schuster Children's Publishing); 1985. pap. 3.50 (*0-671-49729-4*, Aladdin) Simon & Schuster Children's Publishing.

—Rigged for Revenge. Greenberg, Anne, ed. 1992. (Hardy Boys Casefiles Ser.: No. 70). 160p. (Orig.). (YA). (gr. 6 up). pap. 3.75 (*0-671-73106-8*, Simon Pulse) Simon & Schuster Children's Publishing.

—River Rats. 1997. (Hardy Boys Casefiles Ser.: No. 122). 160p. (YA). (gr. 6 up). pap. 3.99 (*0-671-56123-5*, Simon Pulse) Simon & Schuster Children's Publishing.

—River Rats. 1997. (Hardy Boys Casefiles Ser.: No. 122). (YA). (gr. 6 up). 9.09 o.p. (*0-606-11436-X*) Turtleback Bks.

—Road Pirates. Greenberg, Anne, ed. 1993. (Hardy Boys Casefiles Ser.: No. 74). 160p. (Orig.). (YA). (gr. 6 up). pap. 3.99 (*0-671-73110-6*, Simon Pulse) Simon & Schuster Children's Publishing.

—The Roaring River Mystery. Schwartz, Betty Ann, ed. (Hardy Boys Mystery Stories Ser.: No. 80). (Orig.). (J). (gr. 3-6). 1991. pap. 3.50 (*0-671-73004-5*, Aladdin); 1984. pap. (*0-671-49722-7*, Simon & Schuster Children's Publishing) Simon & Schuster Children's Publishing.

—The Robot's Revenge. Winkler, Ellen, ed. 1993. (Hardy Boys Mystery Stories Ser.: No. 123). 160p. (J). (gr. 3-6). per. 3.99 (*0-671-79313-6*, Aladdin) Simon & Schuster Children's Publishing.

—The Robot's Revenge. 1993. (Hardy Boys Mystery Stories Ser.: No. 123). (J). (gr. 3-6). 10.04 (*0-606-05858-3*) Turtleback Bks.

—Rock 'n' Revenge. Greenberg, Ann, ed. 1991. (Hardy Boys Casefiles Ser.: No. 48). 160p. (YA). (gr. 6 up). pap. 3.50 (*0-671-70045-6*, Simon Pulse) Simon & Schuster Children's Publishing.

—Rock 'n' Revenge. 1991. (Hardy Boys Casefiles Ser.: No. 48). (YA). (gr. 6 up). 8.60 o.p. (*0-606-04782-4*) Turtleback Bks.

—Rock 'n' Roll Renegades. Winkler, Ellen, ed. 1992. (Hardy Boys Mystery Stories Ser.: No. 116). 160p. (J). (gr. 3-6). pap. 3.99 (*0-671-73063-0*, Aladdin) Simon & Schuster Children's Publishing.

—The Rocky Road to Revenge. 1998. (Hardy Boys Mystery Stories Ser.: No. 151). 147p. (J). (gr. 3-6). per. 3.99 (*0-671-02172-9*, Aladdin) Simon & Schuster Children's Publishing.

—The Rocky Road to Revenge, 1998. (Hardy Boys Mystery Stories Ser.: No. 151). (J). (gr. 3-6). 9.09 o.p. (*0-606-13465-4*) Turtleback Bks.

—Rough Riding. Greenberg, Anne, ed. 1992. (Hardy Boys Casefiles Ser.: No. 68). 160p. (Orig.). (J). (gr. 6 up). pap. 3.75 (*0-671-73104-1*, Simon Pulse) Simon & Schuster Children's Publishing.

—Running on Empty. (Hardy Boys Casefiles Ser.: No. 36). (YA). (gr. 6 up). 1991. 160p. pap. 3.50 (*0-671-74107-1*); 1990. mass mkt. 2.95 (*0-671-67484-6*) Simon & Schuster Children's Publishing. (Simon Pulse).

—Sabotage at Sea. Ashby, Ruth, ed. 1994. (Hardy Boys Casefiles Ser.: No. 92). 160p. (YA). (gr. 6 up). pap. 3.99 (*0-671-79476-0*, Simon Pulse) Simon & Schuster Children's Publishing.

—Sabotage at Sea. 1994. (Hardy Boys Casefiles Ser.: No. 92). (YA). (gr. 6 up). 10.04 (*0-606-07001-X*) Turtleback Bks.

—Sabotage at Sports City. Winkler, Ellen, ed. 1992. (Hardy Boys Mystery Stories Ser.: No. 115). 160p. (Orig.). (J). (gr. 3-6). pap. 3.99 (*0-671-73062-2*, Aladdin) Simon & Schuster Children's Publishing.

—Scene of the Crime. 1989. (Hardy Boys Casefiles Ser.: No. 24). (YA). (gr. 6 up). pap. 2.95 (*0-671-69377-8*); (Illus.). (J). mass mkt. 2.75 (*0-671-64687-7*) Simon & Schuster Children's Publishing. (Simon Pulse).

—Screamers. Greenberg, Anne, ed. 1993. (Hardy Boys Casefiles Ser.: No. 72). 160p. (Orig.). (J). (gr. 6 up). pap. 3.75 (*0-671-73108-4*, Simon Pulse) Simon & Schuster Children's Publishing.

—The Search for the Snow Leopard. 1996. (Hardy Boys Mystery Stories Ser.: No. 139). 160p. (J). (gr. 3-6). pap. 3.99 (*0-671-50525-4*, Aladdin) Simon & Schuster Children's Publishing.

—The Search for the Snow Leopard. 1996. (Hardy Boys Mystery Stories Ser.: No. 139). (J). (gr. 3-6). 10.04 (*0-606-09379-6*) Turtleback Bks.

—The Secret Agent on Flight 101. 1967. (Hardy Boys Mystery Stories Ser.: No. 46). (Illus.). 180p. (J). (gr. 3-6). 5.99 (*0-448-08946-7*, Grosset & Dunlap) Penguin Putnam Bks. for Young Readers.

—The Secret of Pirate's Hill. rev. ed. 1957. (Hardy Boys Mystery Stories Ser.: No. 36). (Illus.). 180p. (J). (gr. 3-6). 5.99 (*0-448-08936-X*, Grosset & Dunlap) Penguin Putnam Bks. for Young Readers.

—The Secret of Sigma Seven. 1991. (Hardy Boys Mystery Stories Ser.: No. 110). 160p. (J). (gr. 3-8). pap. 3.99 (*0-671-72717-6*, Aladdin) Simon & Schuster Children's Publishing.

—The Secret of Skeleton Reef. 1997. (Hardy Boys Mystery Stories Ser.: No. 144). 160p. (J). (gr. 3-6). per. 3.99 (*0-671-00056-X*, Aladdin) Simon & Schuster Children's Publishing.

—The Secret of Skeleton Reef. 1997. (Hardy Boys Mystery Stories Ser.: No. 144). (J). (gr. 3-6). 9.09 o.p. (*0-606-11431-9*) Turtleback Bks.

—The Secret of Skull Mountain. 1948. (Hardy Boys Mystery Stories Ser.: No. 27). (Illus.). 180p. (J). (gr. 3-6). 5.99 (*0-448-08927-0*, Grosset & Dunlap) Penguin Putnam Bks. for Young Readers.

—The Secret of the Caves. 2004. (Hardy Boys Mystery Stories Ser.: No. 7). (Illus.). 228p. (J). (gr. 3-6). reprint ed. 14.95 (*1-55709-150-1*) Applewood Bks.

—The Secret of the Caves. rev. ed. (Hardy Boys Mystery Stories Ser.: No. 7). (J). (gr. 3-6). 1975. 3.29 o.p. (*0-448-18907-0*); 1929. (Illus.). 180p. 5.99 (*0-448-08907-6*) Penguin Putnam Bks. for Young Readers. (Grosset & Dunlap).

Characters

—The Secret of the Island Treasure. 1990. (Hardy Boys Mystery Stories Ser.: No. 100). 160p. (J). (gr. 3-6). pap. 3.50 (*0-671-69450-2*, Aladdin) Simon & Schuster Children's Publishing.

—The Secret of the Lost Tunnel, Vol. 29. rev. ed. 1950. (Hardy Boys Mystery Stories Ser.: No. 29). (Illus.). 180p. (J). (gr. 3-6). 5.99 (*0-448-08929-7*, Grosset & Dunlap) Penguin Putnam Bks. for Young Readers.

—The Secret of the Old Mill. 1927. (Hardy Boys Mystery Stories Ser.: No. 3). (Illus.). 180p. (J). (gr. 3-6). 5.99 (*0-448-08903-3*, Grosset & Dunlap) Penguin Putnam Bks. for Young Readers.

—The Secret of the Old Mill. unabr. ed. 2002. (Hardy Boys: No. 3). (J). (gr. 4-7). audio 18.00 (*0-8072-0772-1*, Listening Library) Random Hse. Audio Publishing Group.

—The Secret of Wildcat Swamp. 1952. (Hardy Boys Mystery Stories Ser.: No. 31). (Illus.). 180p. (J). (gr. 3-6). 5.99 (*0-448-08931-9*, Grosset & Dunlap) Penguin Putnam Bks. for Young Readers.

—The Secret Panel. rev. ed. 1946. (Hardy Boys Mystery Stories Ser.: No. 25). (Illus.). 180p. (J). (gr. 3-6). 5.99 (*0-448-08925-4*, Grosset & Dunlap) Penguin Putnam Bks. for Young Readers.

—The Secret Warning. (Hardy Boys Mystery Stories Ser.: No. 17). (J). (gr. 3-6). 1975. 3.29 o.p. (*0-448-18917-8*); 1938. (Illus.). 180p. 5.99 (*0-448-08917-3*) Penguin Putnam Bks. for Young Readers. (Grosset & Dunlap).

—See No Evil. l.t. ed. 1988. (Hardy Boys Casefiles Ser.: No. 8). 152p. (YA). (gr. 6 up). reprint ed. 9.50 o.p. (*0-942545-49-4*); lib. bdg. 10.50 o.p. (*0-942545-59-1*) Grey Castle Pr.

—See No Evil. (Hardy Boys Casefiles Ser.: No. 8). (YA). (gr. 6 up). 1991. mass mkt. 3.50 (*0-671-73673-6*); 1990. mass mkt. 2.95 (*0-671-72959-4*) Simon & Schuster Children's Publishing. (Simon Pulse).

—See No Evil. 1987. (Hardy Boys Casefiles Ser.: No. 8). (YA). (gr. 6 up). 8.60 o.p. (*0-606-02109-4*) Turtleback Bks.

—The Serpent's Tooth Mystery. 1988. (Hardy Boys Mystery Stories Ser.: No. 93). (Orig.). (J). (gr. 3-6). pap. 3.99 (*0-671-66310-0*, Aladdin) Simon & Schuster Children's Publishing.

—The Shadow Killers. 1988. (Hardy Boys Mystery Stories Ser.: No. 92). (J). (gr. 3-6). pap. 3.99 (*0-671-66309-7*, Aladdin) Simon & Schuster Children's Publishing.

—The Shattered Helmet. (Hardy Boys Mystery Stories Ser.: No. 52). (Illus.). (J). (gr. 3-6). 1975. 196p. 3.29 o.p. (*0-448-18952-6*); 1973. 180p. 5.99 (*0-448-08952-1*) Penguin Putnam Bks. for Young Readers. (Grosset & Dunlap).

—Sheer Terror. 2001. (Hardy Boys Casefiles Ser.: No. 81). 160p. (YA). (gr. 6 up). mass mkt. 3.99 (*0-7434-0431-9*, Simon & Schuster Children's Publishing) Simon & Schuster Children's Publishing.

—Sheer Terror. Greenberg, Anne, ed. 1993. (Hardy Boys Casefiles Ser.: No. 81). 160p. (YA). (gr. 6 up). pap. 3.99 (*0-671-79465-5*, Simon Pulse) Simon & Schuster Children's Publishing.

—Shield of Fear. Greenberg, Ann, ed. 1988. (Hardy Boys Mystery Stories Ser.: No. 91). 160p. (J). (gr. 3-6). reprint ed. pap. 3.99 (*0-671-66308-9*, Aladdin) Simon & Schuster Children's Publishing.

—Shock Jock. 1995. (Hardy Boys Casefiles Ser.: No. 106). 160p. (YA). (gr. 6 up). pap. 3.99 (*0-671-50429-0*, Simon Pulse) Simon & Schuster Children's Publishing.

—Shock Jock. 1995. (Hardy Boys Casefiles Ser.: No. 106). (YA). (gr. 6 up). 9.09 o.p. (*0-606-08538-6*) Turtleback Bks.

—The Shore Road Mystery. fac. ed. 2004. (Hardy Boys Mystery Stories Ser.: No. 6). (Illus.). 210p. (J). (gr. 3-6). 14.95 (*1-55709-149-8*) Applewood Bks.

—The Shore Road Mystery. (Hardy Boys Mystery Stories Ser.: No. 6). (Illus.). (J). (gr. 3-6). 1975. 3.29 o.p. (*0-448-18906-2*); 1928. 180p. 5.99 (*0-448-08906-8*) Penguin Putnam Bks. for Young Readers. (Grosset & Dunlap).

—The Shore Road Mystery, No. 6. unabr. ed. 2003. (Hardy Boys Ser.). (J). (gr. 3). audio 18.00 (*0-8072-1587-2*, Listening Library) Random Hse. Audio Publishing Group.

—The Short-Wave Mystery. rev. ed. (Hardy Boys Mystery Stories Ser.: No. 24). (J). (gr. 3-6). 1975. 3.29 o.p. (*0-448-18924-0*); 1945. (Illus.). 180p. 5.99 (*0-448-08924-6*) Penguin Putnam Bks. for Young Readers. (Grosset & Dunlap).

—Sidetracked to Danger. Ashby, Ruth, ed. 1995. (Hardy Boys Mystery Stories Ser.: No. 130). 160p. (Orig.). (J). (gr. 3-6). pap. 3.99 (*0-671-87214-1*, Aladdin) Simon & Schuster Children's Publishing.

—Sidetracked to Danger. 1995. (Hardy Boys Mystery Stories Ser.: No. 130). (Orig.). (J). (gr. 3-6). 9.09 (*0-606-07609-3*) Turtleback Bks.

—The Sign of the Crooked Arrow. rev. ed. (Hardy Boys Mystery Stories Ser.: No. 28). (Illus.). (J). (gr. 3-6). 1975. 3.29 o.p. (*0-448-18928-3*); 1949. 180p. 5.99 (*0-448-08928-9*) Penguin Putnam Bks. for Young Readers. (Grosset & Dunlap).

—The Sinister Sign Post. (Hardy Boys Mystery Stories Ser.: No. 15). (J). (gr. 3-6). 1975. 3.29 o.p. (*0-448-18915-1*); 1936. (Illus.). 180p. 5.99 (*0-448-08915-7*) Penguin Putnam Bks. for Young Readers. (Grosset & Dunlap).

—Skin & Bones. 2000. (Hardy Boys Ser.: No. 164). 160p. (J). (gr. 3-6). pap. 3.99 (*0-671-04761-2*, Aladdin) Simon & Schuster Children's Publishing.

—The Sky Blue Frame. 1988. (Hardy Boys Mystery Stories Ser.: No. 89). 160p. (J). (gr. 3-6). mass mkt. 3.99 (*0-671-64974-4*, Aladdin) Simon & Schuster Children's Publishing.

—The Sky Blue Frame. 1988. (Hardy Boys Mystery Stories Ser.: No. 89). (J). (gr. 3-6). 9.09 o.p. (*0-606-03919-8*) Turtleback Bks.

—Sky High. 1996. (Hardy Boys Casefiles Ser.: No. 113). 160p. (YA). (gr. 6 up). pap. 3.99 (*0-671-50454-1*, Simon Pulse) Simon & Schuster Children's Publishing.

—Sky High. 1996. (Hardy Boys Casefiles Ser.: No. 113). (YA). (gr. 6 up). 9.09 o.p. (*0-606-09385-0*) Turtleback Bks.

—Sky Sabotage. 1986. (Hardy Boys Mystery Stories Ser.: No. 79). (Orig.). (J). (gr. 3-6). pap. 3.50 (*0-671-62625-6*, Aladdin) Simon & Schuster Children's Publishing.

—The Skyfire Puzzle. 1989. (Hardy Boys Mystery Stories Ser.: No. 85). (J). (gr. 3-6). pap. 3.50 (*0-671-67458-7*, Aladdin) Simon & Schuster Children's Publishing.

—The Skyfire Puzzle. Arico, Diane, ed. 1985. (Hardy Boys Mystery Stories Ser.: No. 85). 160p. (J). (gr. 3-6). pap. (*0-671-49732-4*, Simon & Schuster Children's Publishing); pap. 3.50 (*0-671-49731-6*, Aladdin) Simon & Schuster Children's Publishing.

—Slam Dunk Sabotage. 1996. (Hardy Boys Mystery Stories Ser.: No. 140). 160p. (J). (gr. 3-6). pap. 4.99 (*0-671-50526-2*, Aladdin) Simon & Schuster Children's Publishing.

—Slam Dunk Sabotage. 1996. (Hardy Boys Mystery Stories Ser.: No. 140). (J). (gr. 3-6). 10.04 (*0-606-10835-1*) Turtleback Bks.

—Slip, Slide & Slap Shot. 1999. (Hardy Boys Are: No. 15). (Illus.). 80p. (J). (gr. 2-4). pap. 3.99 (*0-671-03254-2*, Aladdin) Simon & Schuster Children's Publishing.

—Slip, Slide & Slap Shot. 1999. (Hardy Boys Are: No. 15). (J). (gr. 2-4). 10.14 (*0-606-19063-5*) Turtleback Bks.

—The Smoke Screen Mystery. Greenberg, Ann, ed. 1990. (Hardy Boys Mystery Stories Ser.: No. 105). 160p. (J). (gr. 3-6). per. 3.99 (*0-671-69274-7*, Aladdin) Simon & Schuster Children's Publishing.

—The Smoke Screen Mystery. 1990. (Hardy Boys Mystery Stories Ser.: No. 105). (J). (gr. 3-6). 9.09 o.p. (*0-606-04798-0*) Turtleback Bks.

—Spark of Suspicion. Greenberg, Ann, ed. 1989. (Hardy Boys Mystery Stories Ser.: No. 98). 160p. (Orig.). (YA). (gr. 3-6). pap. 3.99 (*0-671-66304-6*, Aladdin) Simon & Schuster Children's Publishing.

—Speed Times Five. 2002. (Hardy Boys Mystery Stories Ser.: No. 173). 160p. (J). (gr. 3-7). pap. 4.99 (*0-7434-3746-2*, Aladdin) Simon & Schuster Children's Publishing.

—Spiked! Greenberg, Anne, ed. 1991. (Hardy Boys Casefiles Ser.: No. 58). 160p. (Orig.). (YA). (gr. 6 up). pap. 3.50 (*0-671-73094-0*, Simon Pulse) Simon & Schuster Children's Publishing.

—The Spy That Never Lies. 2000. (Hardy Boys Mystery Stories Ser.: No. 163). 160p. (J). (gr. 3-6). mass mkt. 3.99 (*0-671-04760-4*, Aladdin) Simon & Schuster Children's Publishing.

—The Sting of the Scorpion. 1978. (Hardy Boys Mystery Stories Ser.: No. 58). (Illus.). (J). (gr. 3-6). 7.25 o.p. (*0-448-18958-5*); 180p. 5.99 (*0-448-08958-0*) Penguin Putnam Bks. for Young Readers. (Grosset & Dunlap).

—The Stone Idol. (Hardy Boys Mystery Stories Ser.: No. 65). 192p. (J). (gr. 3-6). 1990. pap. 3.50 (*0-671-69402-2*, Aladdin); 1981. (Illus.). pap. 2.65 (*0-671-42290-1*, Aladdin); 1981. (Illus.). pap. (*0-671-42289-8*, Simon & Schuster Children's Publishing) Simon & Schuster Children's Publishing.

—Strategic Moves. Greenberg, Ann, ed. 1990. (Hardy Boys Casefiles Ser.: No. 43). 160p. (Orig.). (YA). (gr. 6 up). pap. 2.95 (*0-671-70040-5*, Simon Pulse) Simon & Schuster Children's Publishing.

—Street Spies. 1989. (Hardy Boys Casefiles Ser.: No. 21). (YA). (gr. 6 up). pap. 2.95 (*0-671-69186-4*, Simon Pulse) Simon & Schuster Children's Publishing.

—Stress Point. 1997. (Hardy Boys Casefiles Ser.: No. 125). 160p. (YA). (gr. 6 up). pap. 3.99 (*0-671-56241-X*, Simon Pulse) Simon & Schuster Children's Publishing.

—Stress Point. 1997. (Hardy Boys Casefiles Ser.: No. 125). (YA). (gr. 6 up). 10.04 (*0-606-13466-2*) Turtleback Bks.

—The Submarine Caper. 1981. (Hardy Boys Mystery Stories Ser.: No. 68). (Illus.). 192p. (Orig.). (J). (gr. 3-7). pap. (*0-671-42338-X*, Simon & Schuster Children's Publishing); pap. 3.50 (*0-671-42339-8*, Aladdin) Simon & Schuster Children's Publishing.

—Survival of the Fittest. 1997. (Hardy Boys Casefiles Ser.: No. 120). 160p. (YA). (gr. 6 up). pap. 3.99 (*0-671-56120-0*, Simon Pulse) Simon & Schuster Children's Publishing.

—Survival of the Fittest. 1997. (Hardy Boys Casefiles Ser.: No. 120). (YA). (gr. 6 up). 9.09 o.p. (*0-606-11434-3*) Turtleback Bks.

—Survival Run. Greenberg, Ann, ed. 1993. (Hardy Boys Casefiles Ser.: No. 77). 160p. (J). (gr. 6 up). pap. 3.99 (*0-671-79461-2*, Simon Pulse) Simon & Schuster Children's Publishing.

—Survival Run. 1993. (Hardy Boys Casefiles Ser.: No. 77). (YA). (gr. 6 up). 9.09 o.p. (*0-606-05338-7*) Turtleback Bks.

—The Swamp Monster. 1989. (J). (Hardy Boys Mystery Stories Ser.: No. 83). (gr. 3-6). pap. 3.50 (*0-671-62681-7*); (Hardy Boys Ser.: Vol. 83). (Illus.). mass mkt. 3.50 (*0-671-49727-8*) Simon & Schuster Children's Publishing. (Aladdin).

—The Swamp Monster. Arico, Diane, ed. 1985. (Hardy Boys Mystery Stories Ser.: No. 83). 192p. (J). (gr. 3-6). pap. (*0-671-55054-3*, Simon & Schuster Children's Publishing); pap. 3.50 (*0-671-55048-9*, Aladdin) Simon & Schuster Children's Publishing.

—Tagged for Terror. Greenberg, Anne, ed. 1993. (Hardy Boys Casefiles Ser.: No. 76). 160p. (YA). (gr. 6 up). pap. 3.99 (*0-671-73112-2*, Simon Pulse) Simon & Schuster Children's Publishing.

—Tagged for Terror. 1993. (Hardy Boys Casefiles Ser.: No. 76). (YA). (gr. 6 up). 10.04 (*0-606-05337-9*) Turtleback Bks.

—A Taste for Terror. Ashby, Ruth, ed. 1994. (Hardy Boys Casefiles Ser.: No. 94). 160p. (YA). (gr. 6 up). pap. 3.99 (*0-671-88205-8*, Simon Pulse) Simon & Schuster Children's Publishing.

—A Taste for Terror. 1994. (Hardy Boys Casefiles Ser.: No. 94). (YA). (gr. 6 up). 9.09 (*0-606-07003-6*) Turtleback Bks.

—Terminal Shock. Greenberg, Ann, ed. 1990. (Hardy Boys Mystery Stories Ser.: No. 102). 160p. (J). (gr. 3-6). pap. 3.99 (*0-671-69288-7*, Aladdin) Simon & Schuster Children's Publishing.

—Terror at High Tide. 1997. (Hardy Boys Mystery Stories Ser.: No. 145). 160p. (J). (gr. 3-6). pap. 3.99 (*0-671-00057-8*, Aladdin) Simon & Schuster Children's Publishing.

—Terror at High Tide. 1997. (Hardy Boys Mystery Stories Ser.: No. 145). (J). (gr. 3-6). 9.09 o.p. (*0-606-13459-X*) Turtleback Bks.

—Terror on Track. 1991. (Hardy Boys Casefiles Ser.: No. 57). (YA). (gr. 6 up). 9.09 o.p. (*0-606-00799-7*) Turtleback Bks.

—The Test Case. 2002. (Hardy Boys Mystery Stories Ser.: No. 171). (J). (gr. 3-6). E-Book 4.99 (*0-7434-3961-9*); 160p. pap. 4.99 (*0-7434-3738-1*) Simon & Schuster Children's Publishing. (Aladdin).

—The Test Case. l.t. ed. 2002. 169p. (J). 21.95 (*0-7862-4657-X*) Thorndike Pr.

—Thick As Thieves. (Orig.). 1991. (Hardy Boys Casefiles Ser.: No. 29). (YA). (gr. 6 up). pap. 3.50 (*0-671-74663-4*); 1989. (Hardy Boys Ser.: Vol. 29). (Illus.). (J). mass mkt. (*0-671-67477-3*) Simon & Schuster Children's Publishing. (Simon Pulse).

—Three-Ring Terror. Greenberg, Anne, ed. 1991. (Hardy Boys Mystery Stories Ser.: No. 111). 160p. (Orig.). (J). (gr. 3-6). pap. 3.99 (*0-671-73057-6*, Aladdin) Simon & Schuster Children's Publishing.

—Tic-Tac Terror. (Hardy Boys Mystery Stories Ser.: No. 74). (J). (gr. 3-6). 1988. pap. 3.50 (*0-671-66858-7*, Aladdin); 1982. (Illus.). 192p. pap. (*0-671-42356-8*, Simon & Schuster Children's Publishing); 1982. (Illus.). 192p. pap. 3.50 (*0-671-42357-6*, Aladdin) Simon & Schuster Children's Publishing.

—Time Bomb. Greenberg, Anne, ed. 1992. (Hardy Boys & Tom Swift Ultra Thrillers Ser.: No. 2). 224p. (Orig.). (J). (gr. 3-6). pap. 3.75 (*0-671-75661-3*, Simon Pulse) Simon & Schuster Children's Publishing.

—Too Many Traitors. 1991. (Hardy Boys Casefiles Ser.: No. 14). 160p. (YA). (gr. 6 up). mass mkt. 3.50 (*0-671-73677-9*); 1989. (Hardy Boys Ser.: Vol. 14). (Illus.). (J). mass mkt. 2.95 (*0-671-68804-9*) Simon & Schuster Children's Publishing. (Simon Pulse).

—The Tower Treasure. 2004. (Hardy Boys Mystery Stories Ser.: No. 1). 214p. (J). (gr. 3-6). 17.95 (*1-55709-144-7*) Applewood Bks.

—The Tower Treasure. unabr. ed. 2002. (Hardy Boys Mystery Stories Ser.: No. 1). (J). (gr. 4 up). audio 24.95 (*1-55685-679-2*) Audio Bk. Contractors, Inc.

—The Tower Treasure. (Hardy Boys Mystery Stories Ser.: No. 1). (J). (gr. 3-6). 1975. 3.29 o.p. (*0-448-18901-1*); 1927. (Illus.). 180p. 5.99 (*0-448-08901-7*) Penguin Putnam Bks. for Young Readers. (Grosset & Dunlap).

—The Tower Treasure. abr. ed. 2002. (J). (Hardy Boys: Vol. 1). (Illus.). (gr. 4-6). 23.00 (*0-8072-0767-5*); (Hardy Boys Mystery Ser.: No. 1). (gr. 3 up). audio 18.00 (*0-8072-0766-7*) Random Hse. Audio Publishing Group. (Listening Library).

—The Tower Treasure & the House on the Cliff. 1987. (Hardy Boys Mystery Stories Ser.: Nos. 1 & 2). (Illus.). 360p. (J). (gr. 3-6). 7.99 (*0-448-08964-5*) Penguin Putnam Bks. for Young Readers.

—Toxic Revenge. 1994. (Hardy Boys Casefiles Ser.: No. 83). 160p. (YA). (gr. 6 up). pap. 3.99 (*0-671-79467-1*, Simon Pulse) Simon & Schuster Children's Publishing.

—Toxic Revenge. 1994. (Hardy Boys Casefiles Ser.: No. 83). (YA). (gr. 6 up). 9.09 o.p. (*0-606-05864-8*) Turtleback Bks.

—Track of the Zombie. (Hardy Boys Mystery Stories Ser.: No. 71). (J). (gr. 3-6). 1986. pap. 3.50 (*0-671-62623-X*, Aladdin); 1982. (Illus.). 192p. pap. (*0-671-42348-7*, Simon & Schuster Children's Publishing); 1982. (Illus.). 192p. pap. 3.50 (*0-671-42349-5*, Aladdin) Simon & Schuster Children's Publishing.

—Training for Trouble. 2000. (Hardy Boys Mystery Stories Ser.: No. 161). 160p. (J). (gr. 3-6). pap. 4.99 (*0-671-04758-2*, Aladdin) Simon & Schuster Children's Publishing.

—Trapped at Sea. 1987. (Hardy Boys Mystery Stories Ser.: No. 75). (J). (gr. 3-6). pap. 3.50 (*0-671-64290-1*, Aladdin) Simon & Schuster Children's Publishing.

—Trapped at Sea. Schneider, Meg F., ed. 1982. (Hardy Boys Mystery Stories Ser.: No. 75). (Illus.). 192p. (J). (gr. 3-6). pap. 3.50 (*0-671-42363-0*, Aladdin); pap. (*0-671-42362-2*, Simon & Schuster Children's Publishing) Simon & Schuster Children's Publishing.

—The Treasure at Dolphin Bay. Ashby, Ruth, ed. 1994. (Hardy Boys Mystery Stories Ser.: No. 129). 160p. (Orig.). (J). (gr. 3-6). pap. 3.99 (*0-671-87213-3*, Simon Pulse) Simon & Schuster Children's Publishing.

—Trial & Terror. 1997. (Hardy Boys Mystery Stories Ser.: No. 147). 160p. (J). (gr. 3-6). per. 3.99 (*0-671-00059-4*, Aladdin) Simon & Schuster Children's Publishing.

—Trial & Terror, 1997. (Hardy Boys Mystery Stories Ser.: No. 147). (J). (gr. 3-6). 10.04 (*0-606-13461-1*) Turtleback Bks.

—Tricks of the Trade. Greenberg, Ann, ed. 1990. (Hardy Boys Mystery Stories Ser.: No. 104). 160p. (J). (gr. 3-6). mass mkt. 3.99 (*0-671-69273-9*, Aladdin) Simon & Schuster Children's Publishing.

—Tricks of the Trade. 1990. (Hardy Boys Mystery Stories Ser.: No. 104). (J). (gr. 3-6). 9.09 o.p. (*0-606-04833-2*) Turtleback Bks.

—Tricky Business. Greenberg, Ann, ed. 1988. (Hardy Boys Mystery Stories Ser.: No. 88). 160p. (J). (gr. 3-6). per. 3.99 (*0-671-64973-6*, Aladdin) Simon & Schuster Children's Publishing.

—Tricky Business. 1988. (Hardy Boys Mystery Stories Ser.: No. 88). (J). (gr. 3-6). 9.09 o.p. (*0-606-03666-0*) Turtleback Bks.

—Trouble at Coyote Canyon. Winkler, Ellen, ed. 1993. (Hardy Boys Mystery Stories Ser.: No. 119). 160p. (Orig.). (J). (gr. 3-6). pap. 3.99 (*0-671-79309-8*, Aladdin) Simon & Schuster Children's Publishing.

—The Trouble in the Pipeline. (Hardy Boys Casefiles Ser.: No. 26). 1991. (YA). (gr. 6 up). pap. 3.50 (*0-671-74661-8*); 1989. (Illus.). (J). mass mkt. 2.95 (*0-671-64689-3*) Simon & Schuster Children's Publishing. (Simon Pulse).

—Trouble in Warp Space. 2002. (Hardy Boys Mystery Stories Ser.: No. 172). (J). (gr. 3-6). E-Book 4.99 (*0-7434-3962-7*, Aladdin) Simon & Schuster Children's Publishing.

—The Trouble in Warp Space. 2002. (Hardy Boys Mystery Stories Ser.: Vol. 172). 160p. (J). (gr. 3-6). pap. 4.99 (*0-7434-3754-3*, Aladdin) Simon & Schuster Children's Publishing.

—Trouble in Warp Space. l.t. ed. 2002. 181p. (J). 21.95 (*0-7862-4658-8*) Thorndike Pr.

—Trouble Times Two. 2001. (Hardy Boys Mystery Stories Ser.: No. 167). (J). (gr. 3-6). 160p. pap. 4.99 (*0-7434-0682-6*); reprint ed. E-Book 4.99 (*0-7434-2764-5*) Simon & Schuster Children's Publishing. (Aladdin).

—True Thriller. 1995. (Hardy Boys Casefiles Ser.: No. 100). (Illus.). 160p. (YA). (gr. 6 up). pap. 3.99 (*0-671-88211-2*, Simon Pulse) Simon & Schuster Children's Publishing.

—True Thriller. 1995. (Hardy Boys Casefiles Ser.: No. 100). (YA). (gr. 6 up). 9.09 o.p. (*0-606-07613-1*) Turtleback Bks.

—The Twisted Claw. rev. ed. 1939. (Hardy Boys Mystery Stories Ser.: No. 18). (Illus.). 180p. (J). (gr. 3-6). 5.99 (*0-448-08918-1*, Grosset & Dunlap) Penguin Putnam Bks. for Young Readers.

—Typhoon Island. l.t. ed. 2003. 200p. (J). 21.95 (*0-7862-5847-0*) Thorndike Pr.

—Uncivil War. Greenberg, Anne, ed. 1991. (Hardy Boys Casefiles Ser.: No. 52). 160p. (Orig.). (J). (gr. 6 up). pap. 3.50 (*0-671-70049-9*, Simon Pulse) Simon & Schuster Children's Publishing.

—The Vanishing Thieves. (Hardy Boys Mystery Stories Ser.: No. 66). (J). (gr. 3-6). 1987. mass mkt. 3.99 (*0-671-63890-4*, Aladdin); 1981. (Illus.). 176p. pap. (*0-671-42291-X*, Simon & Schuster Children's Publishing); 1981. (Illus.). 176p. pap. 3.50 (*0-671-42292-8*, Aladdin) Simon & Schuster Children's Publishing.

—The Viking Symbol Mystery. 1962. (Hardy Boys Mystery Stories Ser.: No. 42). (Illus.). 180p. (J). (gr. 3-6). 5.99 (*0-448-08942-4*, Grosset & Dunlap) Penguin Putnam Bks. for Young Readers.

—The Viking's Revenge. 1997. (Hardy Boys Casefiles Ser.: No. 124). 160p. (YA). (gr. 6 up). pap. 3.99 (*0-671-56124-3*, Simon Pulse) Simon & Schuster Children's Publishing.

—The Viking's Revenge. 1997. (Hardy Boys Casefiles Ser.: No. 124). (YA). (gr. 6 up). 9.09 o.p. (*0-606-11438-6*) Turtleback Bks.

—Virtual Villainy. 1994. (Hardy Boys Casefiles Ser.: No. 86). 160p. (YA). (gr. 6 up). pap. 3.99 (*0-671-79470-1*, Simon Pulse) Simon & Schuster Children's Publishing.

—Virtual Villainy. 1994. (Hardy Boys Casefiles Ser.: No. 86). (YA). (gr. 6 up). 9.09 o.p. (*0-606-06443-5*) Turtleback Bks.

—The Voodoo Plot. (Hardy Boys Mystery Stories Ser.: No. 72). (J). (gr. 3-6). 1987. pap. 3.99 (*0-671-64287-1*, Aladdin); 1982. (Illus.). 192p. pap. (*0-671-42350-9*, Simon & Schuster Children's Publishing); 1982. (Illus.). 192p. pap. 3.50 (*0-671-42351-7*, Aladdin) Simon & Schuster Children's Publishing.

—The Wailing Siren Mystery. rev. ed. (Hardy Boys Mystery Stories Ser.: No. 30). (Illus.). (J). (gr. 3-6). 1975. 3.29 o.p. (*0-448-18930-5*); 1951. 180p. 5.99 (*0-448-08930-0*) Penguin Putnam Bks. for Young Readers. (Grosset & Dunlap).

—The Walking Snowman. 1998. (Hardy Boys Are: No. 10). (Illus.). 80p. (J). (gr. 2-4). pap. 3.99 (*0-671-02560-0*, Aladdin) Simon & Schuster Children's Publishing.

—Web of Horror. Greenberg, Ann, ed. 1991. (Hardy Boys Casefiles Ser.: No. 53). 160p. (Orig.). (J). (gr. 6 up). pap. 3.99 (*0-671-73089-4*, Simon Pulse) Simon & Schuster Children's Publishing.

—What Happened at Midnight? 2004. (Hardy Boys Mystery Stories Ser.: No. 10). (Illus.). iv, 213p. (J). (gr. 3-6). 17.95 (*1-55709-268-0*) Applewood Bks.

—What Happened at Midnight?, Vol. 10. 1931. (Hardy Boys Mystery Stories Ser.: No. 10). (Illus.). 180p. (J). (gr. 3-6). 5.99 (*0-448-08910-6*, Grosset & Dunlap) Penguin Putnam Bks. for Young Readers.

—While the Clock Ticked. 2004. (Hardy Boys Mystery Stories Ser.: No. 11). (Illus.). 212p. (J). (gr. 3-6). 14.95 (*1-55709-269-9*) Applewood Bks.

—While the Clock Ticked. 1932. (Hardy Boys Mystery Stories Ser.: No. 11). (Illus.). 180p. (J). (gr. 3-6). 5.99 (*0-448-08911-4*, Grosset & Dunlap) Penguin Putnam Bks. for Young Readers.

—Who Took the Book? 1998. (Hardy Boys Are: No. 6). (Illus.). 80p. (J). (gr. 2-4). pap. 3.99 (*0-671-00407-7*, Aladdin) Simon & Schuster Children's Publishing.

—Who Took the Book? 1998. (Hardy Boys Are: No. 6). (Illus.). (J). (gr. 2-4). 9.09 o.p. (*0-606-13401-8*) Turtleback Bks.

—Wild Wheels. 1995. (Hardy Boys Casefiles Ser.: No. 104). 160p. (J). (gr. 6 up). pap. 3.99 (*0-671-88215-5*, Simon Pulse) Simon & Schuster Children's Publishing.

—Wild Wheels. 1995. (Hardy Boys Casefiles Ser.: No. 104). (YA). (gr. 6 up). 9.09 o.p. (*0-606-08536-X*) Turtleback Bks.

—A Will to Survive. 1999. (Hardy Boys Mystery Stories Ser.: No. 156). 160p. (J). (gr. 3-6). pap. 3.99 (*0-671-03464-2*, Aladdin) Simon & Schuster Children's Publishing.

—A Will to Survive. 1999. (Hardy Boys Mystery Stories Ser.: No. 156). (J). (gr. 3-6). 10.04 (*0-606-19051-1*) Turtleback Bks.

—Winner Take All. Ashby, Ruth, ed. 1994. (Hardy Boys Casefiles Ser.: No. 85). 160p. (YA). (gr. 6 up). pap. 3.99 (*0-671-79469-8*, Simon Pulse) Simon & Schuster Children's Publishing.

—Winner Take All. 1994. (Hardy Boys Casefiles Ser.: No. 85). (YA). (gr. 6 up). 10.04 (*0-606-05866-4*) Turtleback Bks.

—Wipeout. Ashby, Ruth, ed. 1989. (Hardy Boys Mystery Stories Ser.: No. 96). 160p. (J). (gr. 3-6). pap. 3.99 (*0-671-66306-2*, Aladdin) Simon & Schuster Children's Publishing.

—Wipeout. 1900. (Hardy Boys Mystery Stories Ser.: No. 96). (J). (gr. 3-6). pap. 3.50 (*0-671-89513-3*, Aladdin) Simon & Schuster Children's Publishing.

—Wipeout. 1989. (Hardy Boys Mystery Stories Ser.: No. 96). (J). (gr. 3-6). 9.09 o.p. (*0-606-04369-1*) Turtleback Bks.

—The Witchmaster's Key. 1975. (Hardy Boys Mystery Stories Ser.: No. 55). (Illus.). 180p. (J). (gr. 3-6). 5.99 (*0-448-08955-6*, Grosset & Dunlap) Penguin Putnam Bks. for Young Readers.

—Without a Trace. (Orig.). 1991. (Hardy Boys Casefiles Ser.: No. 31). (YA). (gr. 6 up). pap. 3.50 (*0-671-74664-2*); 1989. (Hardy Boys Ser.: Vol. 31). (Illus.). (J). mass mkt. 2.95 (*0-671-67479-X*) Simon & Schuster Children's Publishing. (Simon Pulse).

—Witness to Murder. 1989. (Hardy Boys Casefiles Ser.: No. 20). (Orig.). (YA). (gr. 6 up). pap. 2.95 (*0-671-69434-0*, Simon Pulse) Simon & Schuster Children's Publishing.

—Wrong Side of the Law. 1995. (Hardy Boys Casefiles Ser.: No. 102). 160p. (YA). (gr. 6 up). mass mkt. 3.99 (*0-671-88213-9*, Simon Pulse) Simon & Schuster Children's Publishing.

—Wrong Side of the Law. 1995. (Hardy Boys Casefiles Ser.: No. 102). (YA). (gr. 6 up). 9.09 o.p. (*0-606-07615-8*) Turtleback Bks.

—The Yellow Feather Mystery. (Hardy Boys Mystery Stories Ser.: No. 32). (J). (gr. 3-6). 1975. 3.29 o.p. (*0-448-18933-X*); 1954. (Illus.). 180p. 5.99 (*0-448-08933-5*) Penguin Putnam Bks. for Young Readers. (Grosset & Dunlap).

Dixon, Franklin W. & Barish, Wendy. Sky Sabotage. 1983. (Hardy Boys Mystery Stories Ser.: No. 79). (Illus.). 192p. (Orig.). (J). (gr. 3-6). pap. (*0-671-47556-8*, Simon & Schuster Children's Publishing); pap. 3.50 (*0-671-47557-6*, Aladdin) Simon & Schuster Children's Publishing.

Dixon, Franklin W. & Flynn, William F. The Hardy Boys Detective Handbook. rev. ed. 1972. (Hardy Boys Ser.). (Illus.). 180p. (J). (gr. 4-7). 5.99 (*0-448-01990-6*, Grosset & Dunlap) Penguin Putnam Bks. for Young Readers.

Dixon, Franklin W. & Greenberg, Anne. Crusade of the Flaming Sword. Greenberg, Anne, ed. 1995. (Hardy Boys Mystery Stories Ser.: No. 131). 160p. (J). (gr. 3-6). pap. 3.99 (*0-671-87215-X*, Aladdin) Simon & Schuster Children's Publishing.

—Terror on Track. 1991. (Hardy Boys Casefiles Ser.: No. 57). 160p. (YA). (gr. 6 up). pap. 3.99 (*0-671-73093-2*, Simon Pulse) Simon & Schuster Children's Publishing.

Dixon, Franklin W. & Link, Sheila. Hardy Boys Handbook: Seven Stories of Survival. 1980. (Illus.). 144p. (J). (gr. 3-7). (*0-671-95705-8*, Simon & Schuster Children's Publishing); pap. 3.95 (*0-671-95602-7*, Aladdin) Simon & Schuster Children's Publishing.

Dixon, Franklin W. & Spina, D. A. The Hardy Boys Detective Handbook. rev. ed. 1972. (Hardy Boys Ser.). (Illus.). 224p. (J). (gr. 4-7). 3.29 o.p. (*0-448-03227-9*, Grosset & Dunlap) Penguin Putnam Bks. for Young Readers.

Dixon, Franklin W. & Walker, Jeff. Double Jeopardy. 2003. (Hardy Boys Ser.). (Illus.). 160p. (J). pap. 4.99 (*0-689-85780-2*, Aladdin) Simon & Schuster Children's Publishing.

—The Mystery of the Black Rhino, No. 178. 2003. (Hardy Boys Ser.). (Illus.). 160p. (J). pap. 4.99 (*0-689-85598-2*, Aladdin) Simon & Schuster Children's Publishing.

—Passport to Danger. 2003. (Hardy Boys Ser.). (Illus.). 160p. (J). pap. 4.99 (*0-689-85779-9*, Aladdin) Simon & Schuster Children's Publishing.

—Typhoon Island. 2003. (Hardy Boys Ser.). (Illus.). 160p. (J). pap. 4.99 (*0-689-85884-1*, Aladdin) Simon & Schuster Children's Publishing.

Dixon, Franklin W., et al. Cave-In. (Hardy Boys Mystery Stories Ser.: No. 78). (Illus.). 192p. (J). (gr. 3-6). 1987. pap. 3.50 (*0-671-62621-3*, Aladdin); 1983. pap. (*0-671-42368-1*, Simon & Schuster Children's Publishing); 1983. pap. 3.50 (*0-671-42369-X*, Aladdin) Simon & Schuster Children's Publishing.

Franklin Nixon. Hardy Boys Complete Set. 2003. mass mkt. 347.42 (*0-448-43440-7*, Grosset & Dunlap) Penguin Putnam Bks. for Young Readers.

Keene, Carolyn. At All Costs. 1997. (Nancy Drew & Hardy Boys Super Mystery Ser.: No. 33). 224p. (YA). (gr. 6 up). pap. 3.99 (*0-671-00734-3*, Simon Pulse) Simon & Schuster Children's Publishing.

—At All Costs. 1997. (Nancy Drew & Hardy Boys Super Mystery Ser.: No. 33). (YA). (gr. 6 up). 10.04 (*0-606-12776-3*) Turtleback Bks.

—Copper Canyon Conspiracy. Greenberg, Anne, ed. 1994. (Nancy Drew & Hardy Boys Super Mystery Ser.: No. 22). 224p. (YA). (gr. 6 up). pap. 3.99 (*0-671-88514-6*, Simon Pulse) Simon & Schuster Children's Publishing.

—Copper Canyon Conspiracy. 1994. (Nancy Drew & Hardy Boys Super Mystery Ser.: No. 22). (YA). (gr. 6 up). 10.04 (*0-606-07054-0*) Turtleback Bks.

—Courting Disaster. Greenberg, Anne, ed. 1993. (Nancy Drew & Hardy Boys Super Mystery Ser.: No. 15). 224p. (YA). (gr. 6 up). per. 3.99 (*0-671-78168-5*, Simon Pulse) Simon & Schuster Children's Publishing.

—Courting Disaster. 1993. (Nancy Drew & Hardy Boys Super Mystery Ser.: No. 15). (YA). (gr. 6 up). 9.09 o.p. (*0-606-05494-4*) Turtleback Bks.

—A Crime for Christmas. 1988. (Nancy Drew & Hardy Boys Super Mystery Ser.). (Illus.). (YA). (gr. 6 up). mass mkt. 2.95 (*0-671-64918-3*, Simon Pulse) Simon & Schuster Children's Publishing.

—Danger down Under. Greenberg, Anne, ed. 1995. (Nancy Drew & Hardy Boys Super Mystery Ser.: No. 20). 224p. (YA). (gr. 6 up). mass mkt. 3.99 (*0-671-88460-3*, Simon Pulse) Simon & Schuster Children's Publishing.

—Danger down Under. 1995. (Nancy Drew & Hardy Boys Super Mystery Ser.: No. 20). (YA). (gr. 6 up). 9.09 o.p. (*0-606-10265-5*) Turtleback Bks.

—Dead on Arrival. 1995. (Nancy Drew & Hardy Boys Super Mystery Ser.: No. 23). (Illus.). 224p. (YA). (gr. 6 up). mass mkt. 3.99 (*0-671-88461-1*, Simon Pulse) Simon & Schuster Children's Publishing.

—Desperate Measures. 1994. (Nancy Drew & Hardy Boys Super Mystery Ser.: No. 18). 224p. (YA). (gr. 6 up). mass mkt. 3.99 (*0-671-78174-X*, Simon Pulse) Simon & Schuster Children's Publishing.

—Double Crossing. (Nancy Drew & Hardy Boys Super Mystery Ser.: No. 1). (YA). (gr. 6 up). 1991. 224p. pap. 3.99 (*0-671-74616-2*); 1988. (Illus.). pap. (*0-671-64917-5*) Simon & Schuster Children's Publishing. (Simon Pulse).

—Evil in Amsterdam. Greenberg, Ann, ed. 1993. (Nancy Drew & Hardy Boys Super Mystery Ser.: No. 17). 224p. (YA). (gr. 6 up). mass mkt. 3.99 (*0-671-78173-1*, Simon Pulse) Simon & Schuster Children's Publishing.

—Evil in Amsterdam. Greenberg, Ann, ed. 1993. (Nancy Drew & Hardy Boys Super Mystery Ser.: No. 17). (YA). (gr. 6 up). 10.04 (*0-606-05948-2*) Turtleback Bks.

—Exhibition of Evil. 1997. (Nancy Drew & Hardy Boys Super Mystery Ser.: No. 32). 224p. (YA). (gr. 6 up). pap. 3.99 (*0-671-53750-4*, Simon Pulse) Simon & Schuster Children's Publishing.

—Exhibition of Evil. 1997. (Nancy Drew & Hardy Boys Super Mystery Ser.: No. 32). (YA). (gr. 6 up). 9.09 (*0-606-12777-1*) Turtleback Bks.

—The Fine Feathered Mystery. 1999. (Nancy Drew Notebooks Ser.: No. 31). (Illus.). 80p. (J). (gr. k-3). per. 3.99 (*0-671-02785-9*, Aladdin) Simon & Schuster Children's Publishing.

—High Stakes. 1996. (Nancy Drew & Hardy Boys Super Mystery Ser.: No. 29). 224p. (YA). (gr. 6 up). per. 3.99 (*0-671-53747-4*, Simon Pulse) Simon & Schuster Children's Publishing.

—High Stakes. 1996. (Nancy Drew & Hardy Boys Super Mystery Ser.: No. 29). (YA). (gr. 6 up). 10.04 (*0-606-10888-2*) Turtleback Bks.

—High Survival. Greenberg, Ann, ed. 1991. (Nancy Drew & Hardy Boys Super Mystery Ser.: No. 10). 224p. (Orig.). (YA). (gr. 6 up). mass mkt. 3.99 (*0-671-67466-8*, Simon Pulse) Simon & Schuster Children's Publishing.

—Hits & Misses. Greenberg, Ann, ed. 1993. (Nancy Drew & Hardy Boys Super Mystery Ser.: No. 16). 224p. (YA). (gr. 6 up). mass mkt. 3.99 (*0-671-78169-3*, Simon Pulse) Simon & Schuster Children's Publishing.

—Hits & Misses. 1993. (Nancy Drew & Hardy Boys Super Mystery Ser.: No. 16). (YA). (gr. 6 up). 9.09 o.p. (*0-606-05495-2*) Turtleback Bks.

—Hollywood Horror. Greenberg, Anne, ed. 1994. (Nancy Drew & Hardy Boys Super Mystery Ser.: No. 21). 224p. (Orig.). (YA). (gr. 6 up). mass mkt. 3.99 (*0-671-78181-2*, Simon Pulse) Simon & Schuster Children's Publishing.

—Islands of Intrigue. 1996. (Nancy Drew & Hardy Boys Super Mystery Ser.: No. 27). 224p. (YA). (gr. 6 up). per. 3.99 (*0-671-50294-8*, Simon Pulse) Simon & Schuster Children's Publishing.

—Islands of Intrigue. 1996. (Nancy Drew & Hardy Boys Super Mystery Ser.: No. 27). (YA). (gr. 6 up). 9.09 o.p. (*0-606-09672-8*) Turtleback Bks.

—Murder on the Fourth of July. 1996. (Nancy Drew & Hardy Boys Super Mystery Ser.: No. 28). 224p. (YA). (gr. 6 up). mass mkt. 3.99 (*0-671-50295-6*, Simon Pulse) Simon & Schuster Children's Publishing.

—Murder on the Fourth of July. 1996. (Nancy Drew & Hardy Boys Super Mystery Ser.: No. 28). (YA). (gr. 6 up). 9.09 o.p. (*0-606-10266-3*) Turtleback Bks.

—New Year's Evil. Greenberg, Anne, ed. 1991. (Nancy Drew & Hardy Boys Super Mystery Ser.: No. 11). 224p. (YA). (gr. 6 up). mass mkt. 3.99 (*0-671-67467-6*, Simon Pulse) Simon & Schuster Children's Publishing.

—New Year's Evil. 1991. (Nancy Drew & Hardy Boys Super Mystery Ser.: No. 11). (YA). (gr. 6 up). 9.09 (*0-606-00644-3*) Turtleback Bks.

—Nightmare in New Orleans. 1997. (Nancy Drew & Hardy Boys Super Mystery Ser.: No. 30). 224p. (YA). (gr. 6 up). pap. 3.99 (*0-671-53749-0*, Simon Pulse) Simon & Schuster Children's Publishing.

—Nightmare in New Orleans. 1997. (Nancy Drew & Hardy Boys Super Mystery Ser.: No. 30). (YA). (gr. 6 up). 9.09 o.p. (*0-606-11667-2*) Turtleback Bks.

—On the Trail of Trouble. 1999. (Nancy Drew Mystery Stories Ser.: No. 148). 160p. (J). (gr. 3-6). pap. 3.99 (*0-671-02664-X*, Aladdin) Simon & Schuster Children's Publishing.

—Operation Titanic. 1998. (Nancy Drew & Hardy Boys Super Mystery Ser.: No. 35). 224p. (YA). (gr. 6 up). pap. 4.99 (*0-671-00737-8*, Simon Pulse) Simon & Schuster Children's Publishing.

—Operation Titanic. 1998. (Nancy Drew & Hardy Boys Super Mystery Ser.: No. 35). (YA). (gr. 6 up). 10.04 (*0-606-13650-9*) Turtleback Bks.

—Out of Control. 1997. (Nancy Drew & Hardy Boys Super Mystery Ser.: No. 31). 224p. (YA). (gr. 6 up). pap. 3.99 (*0-671-53748-2*, Simon Pulse) Simon & Schuster Children's Publishing.

—Out of Control. 1997. (Nancy Drew & Hardy Boys Super Mystery Ser.: No. 31). (YA). (gr. 6 up). 10.04 (*0-606-11668-0*) Turtleback Bks.

—Passport to Danger. Greenberg, Anne, ed. 1994. (Nancy Drew & Hardy Boys Super Mystery Ser.: No. 19). 224p. (YA). (gr. 6 up). mass mkt. 3.99 (*0-671-78177-4*, Simon Pulse) Simon & Schuster Children's Publishing.

—Passport to Danger. 1994. (Nancy Drew & Hardy Boys Super Mystery Ser.: No. 19). (YA). (gr. 6 up). 10.04 (*0-606-06600-4*) Turtleback Bks.

—Process of Elimination. 1998. (Nancy Drew & Hardy Boys Super Mystery Ser.: No. 36). 224p. (YA). (gr. 6 up). per. 3.99 (*0-671-00739-4*, Simon Pulse) Simon & Schuster Children's Publishing.

—Process of Elimination. 1998. (Nancy Drew & Hardy Boys Super Mystery Ser.: No. 36). (YA). (gr. 6 up). 9.09 o.p. (*0-606-13651-7*) Turtleback Bks.

—A Question of Guilt. 1996. (Nancy Drew & Hardy Boys Super Mystery Ser.: No. 26). 224p. (YA). (gr. 6 up). per. 3.99 (*0-671-50293-X*, Simon Pulse) Simon & Schuster Children's Publishing.

—A Question of Guilt. 1996. (Nancy Drew & Hardy Boys Super Mystery Ser.: No. 26). (YA). (gr. 6 up). 9.09 o.p. (*0-606-09673-6*) Turtleback Bks.

—Royal Revenge. 1997. (Nancy Drew & Hardy Boys Super Mystery Ser.: No. 34). 224p. (YA). (gr. 6 up). pap. 3.99 (*0-671-00735-1*, Simon Pulse) Simon & Schuster Children's Publishing.

—Royal Revenge. 1997. (Nancy Drew & Hardy Boys Super Mystery Ser.: No. 34). (YA). (gr. 6 up). 10.04 (*0-606-13652-5*) Turtleback Bks.

—Secrets of the Nile. 1995. (Nancy Drew & Hardy Boys Super Mystery Ser.: No. 25). 224p. (YA). (gr. 6 up). mass mkt. 3.99 (*0-671-50290-5*, Simon Pulse) Simon & Schuster Children's Publishing.

—Secrets of the Nile. 1995. (Nancy Drew & Hardy Boys Super Mystery Ser.: No. 25). (YA). (gr. 6 up). 9.09 o.p. (*0-606-08577-7*) Turtleback Bks.

—Shock Waves. 1989. (Nancy Drew & Hardy Boys Super Mystery Ser.: Vol. 3). (Illus.). (YA). (gr. 6 up). mass mkt. 2.95 (*0-671-64919-1*, Simon Pulse) Simon & Schuster Children's Publishing.

—Spies & Lies. Greenberg, Anne, ed. 1992. (Nancy Drew & Hardy Boys Super Mystery Ser.: No. 13). 224p. (YA). (gr. 6 up). pap. 3.99 (*0-671-73125-4*, Simon Pulse) Simon & Schuster Children's Publishing.

—Spies & Lies. 1992. (Nancy Drew & Hardy Boys Super Mystery Ser.: No. 13). (YA). (gr. 6 up). 9.09 o.p. (*0-606-02043-8*) Turtleback Bks.

—Target for Terror. 1995. (Nancy Drew & Hardy Boys Super Mystery Ser.: No. 24). 224p. (YA). (gr. 6 up). mass mkt. 3.99 (*0-671-88462-X*, Simon Pulse) Simon & Schuster Children's Publishing.

—Tour of Danger. Greenberg, Anne, ed. 1992. (Nancy Drew & Hardy Boys Super Mystery Ser.: No. 12). 224p. (YA). (gr. 6 up). pap. 3.99 (*0-671-67468-4*, Simon Pulse) Simon & Schuster Children's Publishing.

—Tour of Danger. 1992. (Nancy Drew & Hardy Boys Super Mystery Ser.: No. 12). (YA). (gr. 6 up). 9.09 o.p. (*0-606-02040-3*) Turtleback Bks.

—Tropic of Fear. Greenberg, Anne, ed. 1992. (Nancy Drew & Hardy Boys Super Mystery Ser.: No. 14). 224p. (Orig.). (YA). (gr. 6 up). mass mkt. 3.99 (*0-671-73126-2*, Simon Pulse) Simon & Schuster Children's Publishing.

Keene, Carolyn & Dixon, Franklin W. The Alaskan Mystery. Arico, Diane, ed. 1985. (Nancy Drew & Hardy Boys: No. 5). (Illus.). 120p. (Orig.). (J). (gr. 3-7). pap. 2.95 (*0-671-54550-7*, Aladdin) Simon & Schuster Children's Publishing.

—Best of Enemies. Greenberg, Ann, ed. 1991. (Nancy Drew & Hardy Boys Super Mystery Ser.: No. 9). 224p. (YA). (gr. 6 up). per. 3.99 (*0-671-67465-X*, Simon Pulse) Simon & Schuster Children's Publishing.

—Best of Enemies. 1991. (Nancy Drew & Hardy Boys Super Mystery Ser.: No. 9). (YA). (gr. 6 up). 9.09 o.p. (*0-606-04876-6*) Turtleback Bks.

—Buried in Time. Greenberg, Ann, ed. 1990. (Nancy Drew & Hardy Boys Super Mystery Ser.: No. 7). 224p. (YA). (gr. 6 up). reprint ed. mass mkt. 3.99 (*0-671-67463-3*, Simon Pulse) Simon & Schuster Children's Publishing.

—A Crime for Christmas. 1991. (Nancy Drew & Hardy Boys Super Mystery Ser.: No. 2). (YA). (gr. 7-12). pap. 3.99 (*0-671-74617-0*, Simon Pulse) Simon & Schuster Children's Publishing.

—A Crime for Christmas. 1988. (Nancy Drew & Hardy Boys Super Mystery Ser.: No. 2). (YA). (gr. 6 up). 10.04 (*0-606-04110-9*) Turtleback Bks.

—Danger on Ice. Schwartz, Betty Ann, ed. 1984. (Nancy Drew & Hardy Boys: No. 2). (Illus.). 117p. (Orig.). (J). (gr. 3-7). pap. 2.85 (*0-671-49920-3*, Aladdin) Simon & Schuster Children's Publishing.

—Dangerous Games. (Nancy Drew & Hardy Boys Super Mystery Ser.: No. 4). (Orig.). (YA). (gr. 6 up). 1991. mass mkt. 3.99 (*0-671-74108-X*); 1989. pap. 2.95 (*0-671-64920-5*) Simon & Schuster Children's Publishing. (Simon Pulse).

—Double Crossing. 1988. (Nancy Drew & Hardy Boys Super Mystery Ser.: No. 1). (YA). (gr. 6 up). 9.09 o.p. (*0-606-03772-1*) Turtleback Bks.

—The Feathered Serpent. Schwartz, Betty Ann, ed. 1984. (Nancy Drew & Hardy Boys: No. 3). (Illus.). 122p. (Orig.). (J). (gr. 3-7). pap. 3.50 (*0-671-49921-1*, Aladdin) Simon & Schuster Children's Publishing.

—Jungle of Evil. Arico, Diane, ed. 1985. (Nancy Drew & Hardy Boys: No. 7). (Illus.). 128p. (Orig.). (J). (gr. 3-7). pap. 2.95 (*0-671-55734-3*, Simon & Schuster Children's Publishing) Simon & Schuster Children's Publishing.

—The Last Resort. 1990. (Nancy Drew & Hardy Boys Super Mystery Ser.: No. 5). 224p. (YA). (gr. 6 up). mass mkt. 3.99 (*0-671-67461-7*, Simon Pulse) Simon & Schuster Children's Publishing.

—Mystery Train. Greenberg, Ann, ed. 1990. (Nancy Drew & Hardy Boys Super Mystery Ser.: No. 8). 224p. (YA). (gr. 6 up). pap. 3.99 (*0-671-67464-1*, Simon Pulse) Simon & Schuster Children's Publishing.

—Mystery Train. 1990. (Nancy Drew & Hardy Boys Super Mystery Ser.: No. 8). (YA). (gr. 6 up). 10.04 (*0-606-04758-1*) Turtleback Bks.

—Nancy Drew & the Hardy Boys Campfire Stories. 1984. (Illus.). 156p. (J). (gr. 2-7). pap. 3.50 (*0-671-50198-4*, Aladdin) Simon & Schuster Children's Publishing.

—Nancy Drew & the Hardy Boys Super Sleuths: Seven New Mysteries. 1982. (Illus.). 189p. (Orig.). (J). (gr. 3-7). pap. 8.95 o.p. (*0-671-44429-8*, Simon & Schuster Children's Publishing); pap. 3.50 (*0-671-43375-X*, Aladdin) Simon & Schuster Children's Publishing.

—Nancy Drew & the Hardy Boys Super Sleuths 2: Seven New Mysteries. 1984. (Illus.). 160p. (J). (gr. 3-7). pap. 3.50 (*0-671-50194-1*, Aladdin) Simon & Schuster Children's Publishing.

—The Paris Connection. (Nancy Drew & Hardy Boys Super Mystery Ser.: No. 6). (YA). (gr. 6 up). 1991. 224p. mass mkt. 3.99 (*0-671-74675-8*); 1990. mass mkt. 2.95 (*0-671-67462-5*) Simon & Schuster Children's Publishing. (Simon Pulse).

—Secret Cargo. Schwartz, Betty Ann, ed. 1984. (Nancy Drew & Hardy Boys: No. 4). (Illus.). 116p. (Orig.). (J). (gr. 3-7). pap. 3.50 (*0-671-49922-X*, Aladdin) Simon & Schuster Children's Publishing.

—The Secret of the Knight's Sword. Schwartz, Betty Ann, ed. 1984. (Nancy Drew & Hardy Boys: No. 1). (Illus.). 122p. (Orig.). (J). (gr. 3-7). pap. 3.50 (*0-671-49919-X*, Aladdin) Simon & Schuster Children's Publishing.

—Shock Waves. 1991. (Nancy Drew & Hardy Boys Super Mystery Ser.: No. 3). (YA). (gr. 6 up). pap. 3.99 (*0-671-74393-7*, Simon Pulse) Simon & Schuster Children's Publishing.

—Ticket to Intrigue. Arico, Diane, ed. 1985. (Nancy Drew & Hardy Boys: No. 8). (Illus.). 128p. (Orig.). (J). (gr. 3-7). pap. 2.95 (*0-671-55735-1*, Simon & Schuster Children's Publishing) Simon & Schuster Children's Publishing.

Stratemeyer Syndicate Staff. The Hardy Boys & Nancy Drew Meet Dracula. 1978. (Illus.). 109p. (J). (gr. 3-6). 3.95 o.p. (*0-448-16196-6*, Grosset & Dunlap) Penguin Putnam Bks. for Young Readers.

Tallarico, Tony. Hardy Boys Adventure Activity Book. (Activity Bks.). (Illus.). (J). (gr. 3-8). No. 1. 1976. 1.50 o.p. (*0-448-12872-1*); No. 3. 1978. 1.50 o.p. (*0-448-14770-X*) Putnam Publishing Group, The.

—Hardy Boys Adventure Activity Book: No. 2. 1977. (Elephant Books Ser.). (J). (gr. 3-8). 1.50 o.p. (*0-448-14423-9*) Putnam Publishing Group, The.

Turner, Mark. Hardy Boys. 1979. (TV & Movie Tie-Ins Ser.). (J). (gr. 4 up). lib. bdg. 18.50 o.p. (*0-87191-703-3*, Creative Education) Creative Co., The.

HAROLD (FICTITIOUS CHARACTER: JOHNSON)—FICTION

Johnson, Crockett. Harold & the Purple Crayon. 2001. (First Readers Ser.: Vol. 3). (J). lib. bdg. (*1-59054-063-8*) Fitzgerald Bks.

—Harold & the Purple Crayon. (Illus.). 64p. (J). (ps-3). 1981. pap. 5.99 (*0-06-443022-7*, Harper Trophy); 1955. 14.95 (*0-06-022935-7*); 1955. lib. bdg. 15.89 (*0-06-022936-5*) HarperCollins Children's Bk. Group.

—Harold & the Purple Crayon. 1983. (Purple Crayon Bks.). (J). 12.10 (*0-606-02126-4*) Turtleback Bks.

—Harold at the North Pole. 1998. (Harold & the Purple Crayon Ser.). (Illus.). 48p. (J). (ps-3). 14.95 (*0-06-028073-5*); lib. bdg. 14.89 (*0-06-028074-3*) HarperCollins Children's Bk. Group.

—Harold y el Lapiz Color Morado. Mlawer, Teresa, tr. 1995. (Coleccion Harper Arco Iris). (SPA., Illus.). 64p. (J). (gr. k-2). 15.95 (*0-06-025332-0*, HC6370); pap. 6.99 (*0-06-443402-8*, HC6371) HarperCollins Children's Bk. Group.

—Harold y el Lapiz Color Morado. 1995. 13.10 (*0-606-07622-0*) Turtleback Bks.

—Harold's ABC. 2002. (Illus.). (J). 14.43 (*0-7587-2696-1*) Book Wholesalers, Inc.

—Harold's ABC. 1981. (Purple Crayon Bks.). (Illus.). 64p. (J). (ps-3). pap. 5.99 (*0-06-443023-5*, Harper Trophy) HarperCollins Children's Bk. Group.

—Harold's ABC. 1963. (Illus.). (J). (gr. k-3). lib. bdg. 8.89 o.p. (*0-06-022956-X*) HarperCollins Pubs.

—Harold's ABC. 1963. (Purple Crayon Bks.). (J). 12.10 (*0-606-02127-2*) Turtleback Bks.

—Harold's Circus. 2002. (Illus.). (J). 14.47 (*0-7587-2697-X*) Book Wholesalers, Inc.

—Harold's Circus. (Purple Crayon Bks.). (J). (ps-3). 1981. (Illus.). 64p. pap. 5.99 (*0-06-443024-3*, Harper Trophy); 1959. lib. bdg. 13.89 o.p. (*0-06-022966-7*) HarperCollins Children's Bk. Group.

—Harold's Circus. 1959. (Purple Crayon Bks.). (J). 12.10 (*0-606-02128-0*) Turtleback Bks.

—Harold's Fairy Tale. (Further Adventures of the Purple Crayon Ser.). (Illus.). (J). (ps-3). 1994. 64p. pap. 5.99 (*0-06-443347-1*, Harper Trophy); 1986. 80p. lib. bdg. 13.89 o.p. (*0-06-022976-4*) HarperCollins Children's Bk. Group.

—Harold's Fairy Tale. 1984. (Further Adventures of the Purple Crayon Ser.). (J). 12.10 (*0-606-05867-2*) Turtleback Bks.

—Harold's Trip to the Sky. 2002. (Illus.). (J). 15.53 (*0-7587-2698-8*) Book Wholesalers, Inc.

—Harold's Trip to the Sky. (Trophy Picture Bk.). (Illus.). (J). (ps-3). 1981. 64p. pap. 6.99 (*0-06-443025-1*, Harper Trophy); 1957. lib. bdg. 14.89 o.p. (*0-06-022986-1*) HarperCollins Children's Bk. Group.

—A Picture for Harold's Room. 2002. (Illus.). (J). 12.30 (*0-7587-6236-4*) Book Wholesalers, Inc.

—A Picture for Harold's Room. 2001. (First Readers Ser.: Vol. 3). (J). lib. bdg. (*1-59054-082-4*) Fitzgerald Bks.

—A Picture for Harold's Room. (I Can Read Bks.). (Illus.). 64p. (J). (gr. k-3). 1985. pap. 3.99 (*0-06-444085-0*, Harper Trophy); 1960. lib. bdg. 16.89 (*0-06-023006-1*) HarperCollins Children's Bk. Group.

—A Picture for Harold's Room. 1960. (I Can Read Bks.). (Illus.). (J). (ps-1). 6.93 (*0-06-023005-3*, 495817) HarperCollins Pubs.

—A Picture for Harold's Room. 1985. (I Can Read Bks.). (J). (ps-1). 10.10 (*0-606-00383-5*) Turtleback Bks.

HARRIET THE SPY (FICTITIOUS CHARACTER)—FICTION

Ericson, Helen. Harriet Spies Again. 2002. 240p. (gr. 5 up). text 15.95 (*0-385-32786-2*, Delacorte Pr.) Dell Publishing.

Fitzhugh, Louise. Harriet the Spy. unabr. ed. 1999. (J). (gr. 1-8). audio 32.00 BBC Audiobooks America.

—Harriet the Spy. 1975. (J). pap. 2.95 o.s.i (*0-440-73447-9*) Dell Publishing.

—Harriet the Spy. (Illus.). 1996. 304p. (J). (gr. 4-7). pap. 5.95 o.p. (*0-06-440660-1*, Harper Trophy); 1996. 224p. (YA). (gr. 5 up). mass mkt. 4.50 o.s.i (*0-06-447165-9*, Harper Trophy); 1990. 304p. (J). (gr. 3-7). pap. 5.95 o.p. (*0-06-440331-9*, Harper Trophy); 1964. 304p. (J). (gr. 4-7). 15.95 o.p. (*0-06-021910-6*); 1964. 304p. (J). (gr. 4-7). lib. bdg. 15.89 o.p. (*0-06-021911-4*) HarperCollins Children's Bk. Group.

—Harriet the Spy. l.t. ed. 1987. (Illus.). 282p. (J). (gr. 2-6). reprint ed. lib. bdg. 16.95 o.s.i (*1-55736-012-X*, Cornerstone Bks.) Pages, Inc.

—Harriet the Spy. (J). (gr. 3-5). 298p. pap. 5.95 (*0-8072-1535-X*); 2000. audio 26.00 (*0-8072-8096-8*, 758471); 2000. audio 26.00 (*0-8072-8096-8*, 758471); 1999. 298p. pap. 37.00 incl. audio (*0-8072-8069-0*, YA993SP); 1999. 298p. pap. 37.00 incl. audio (*0-8072-8069-0*, YA993SP); 1999. audio 32.00 (*0-8072-8068-2*, YA993CX) Random Hse. Audio Publishing Group. (Listening Library).

—Harriet the Spy. (gr. 5-7). 2001. (Illus.). 320p. pap. 5.99 (*0-440-41679-5*, Yearling); 2000. (Illus.). 304p. text 15.95 (*0-385-32783-8*, Delacorte Bks. for Young Readers); 1978. 304p. (YA). mass mkt. 1.50 o.s.i (*0-440-93447-8*, Laurel Leaf) Random Hse. Children's Bks.

—Harriet the Spy. (J). 2001. (Illus.). 12.04 (*0-606-21226-4*); 1964. 10.05 o.p. (*0-606-03426-9*) Turtleback Bks.

—The Long Secret: Harriet the Spy Adventure. 2001. (Illus.). 288p. (gr. 5 up). text 15.95 (*0-385-32784-6*, Delacorte Bks. for Young Readers); 1978. (J). mass mkt. 1.50 o.s.i (*0-440-94977-7*, Dell Books for Young Readers) Random Hse. Children's Bks.

—The Long Secret: Harriet the Spy Adventure. 1965. (J). 10.05 o.p. (*0-606-04469-8*) Turtleback Bks.

HAYDN, FRANZ JOSEPH, 1732-1809—FICTION

Rachlin, Ann. Haydn: Famous Children. 1992. (J). mass mkt. 14.60 o.p. (*0-516-08793-2*, Children's Pr.) Scholastic Library Publishing.

HEATHCLIFF (FICTITIOUS CHARACTER)—FICTION

Bronte, Emily. Wuthering Heights. abr. ed. (Classics Illustrated Ser.). (Illus.). 52p. (YA). pap. 4.95 (*1-57209-011-1*) Classics International Entertainment, Inc.

—Wuthering Heights. abr. ed. 1995. (Classic Fiction Ser.). (YA). audio compact disk 19.98 (*962-634-063-0*, NA306312, Naxos AudioBooks) Naxos of America, Inc.

—Wuthering Heights. Farr, Naunerle C., ed. abr. ed. 1977. (Now Age Illustrated III Ser.). (Illus.). (YA). (gr. 4-12). text 7.50 o.p. (*0-88301-284-7*); pap. text 2.95 (*0-88301-272-3*) Pendulum Pr., Inc.

—Wuthering Heights. 1995. (Classics for Young Readers Ser.). (Illus.). 464p. (YA). (gr. 4-7). pap. 4.99 (*0-14-036694-6*, Puffin Bks.) Penguin Putnam Bks. for Young Readers.

—Wuthering Heights: Abridged for Children, Level 5. Hedge, Tricia, ed. 2000. (Bookworms Ser.). (Illus.). 112p. (YA). pap. text 5.95 (*0-19-423075-9*) Oxford Univ. Pr., Inc.

—Wuthering Heights: Abridged for Children. (gr. 4-7). 1998. (Illus.). 48p. (YA). pap. text 6.95 (*0-8114-6847-X*); 1988. (YA). 22.00 o.p. (*0-8172-2199-9*); 1982. (Illus.). 48p. (J). 22.83 o.p. (*0-8172-1682-0*); 1982. (Illus.). 48p. (YA). pap. 9.27 o.p. (*0-8172-2029-1*) Raintree Pubs.

Howe, D. H., ed. Wuthering Heights: Abridged for Children. 2nd ed. 1993. (Illus.). 126p. (J). pap. text 5.95 (*0-19-585474-8*) Oxford Univ. Pr., Inc.

Raintree Steck-Vaughn Staff. Wuthering Heights: Abridged for Children, 5 vols., Set. 1991. (Short Classics Ser.). (Illus.). (J). pap. 32.69 (*0-8114-6983-2*) Raintree Pubs.

Seymour, Peter S., adapted by. Wuthering Heights. 1971. (Hallmark Editions Ser.). 61p. (YA). (*0-87529-213-5*) Hallmark Card, Inc.

HENRY VI, KING OF ENGLAND, 1421-1471—FICTION

Williamson, Joanne S. To Dream upon a Crown. 1967. (Illus.). (J). (gr. 7 up). lib. bdg. 5.39 o.p. (*0-394-91980-0*, Knopf Bks. for Young Readers) Random Hse. Children's Bks.

HENRY VIII, KING OF ENGLAND, 1509-1574—FICTION

Davis, Susan. The Henry Game. 2003. 256p. (J). pap. (*0-552-54793-X*, Corgi) Bantam Bks.

Gould, Janet Hardy. Henry VIII & His Six Wives, Level 2. Hedge, Tricia, ed. 2000. (Bookworms Ser.). (Illus.). 64p. (J). pap. text 5.95 (*0-19-422975-0*) Oxford Univ. Pr., Inc.

Minard, Rosemary. Long Meg. 1982. (Illus.). 64p. (J). (gr. 8-11). 8.99 o.s.i (*0-394-94888-2*, Pantheon) Knopf Publishing Group.

Ross, Stewart. Beware of the King. 1996. (Illus.). 62p. (J). 17.95 (*0-237-51636-5*); pap. 8.95 (*0-237-51637-3*) Evans Brothers, Ltd. GBR. *Dist:* Trafalgar Square.

HENRY, PATRICK, 1736-1799—FICTION

Olasky, Susan. Annie Henry: Adventures in the American Revolution. 2003. (Illus.). 528p. (J). pap. 16.99 (*1-58134-521-6*) Crossway Bks.

—Annie Henry & the Birth of Liberty. 1995. (Adventures of the American Revolution Ser.: Vol. 2). 128p. (J). (gr. 3-7). pap. 5.99 (*0-89107-842-8*) Crossway Bks.

—Annie Henry & the Mysterious Stranger. 1996. (Adventures of the American Revolution Ser.: Vol. 3) 144p. (J). (gr. 3-7). pap. 5.99 (*0-89107-907-6*) Crossway Bks.

—Annie Henry & the Redcoats: Adventures of the American Revolution. 1996. (Adventures of the American Revolution Ser.: Vol. 4). 128p. (J). (gr. 3-7). pap. 5.99 (*0-89107-908-4*) Crossway Bks.

Rinaldi, Ann. Or Give Me Death: A Novel of Patrick Henry's Family. 2003. (Great Episodes Ser.). 240p. (J). 17.00 (*0-15-216687-4*) Harcourt Children's Bks.

HERCULES (ROMAN MYTHOLOGY)—FICTION

Acclaim Comics Staff. Hercules: The Making of a Hero. 1997. (Disney's Hercules Ser.). mass mkt. 5.95 (*1-57840-087-2*) Acclaim Bks.

Balzer, Elizabeth. Hercules. 1997. (Illus.). 96p. (J). lib. bdg. 15.49 (*0-7868-5050-7*) Disney Pr.

—Hercules Illustrated Classic. 1997. (Hercules Illustrated Classic Ser.: Vol. 1). (Illus.). 96p. (J). (gr. 4-7). 14.95 (*0-7868-3126-X*) Disney Pr.

Bazaldua, Barbara. A Budding Romance. 1997. (Hercules Ser.). 24p. (J). (ps-2). 9.98 o.p. (*1-57082-522-X*) Mouse Works.

—Hercules: A Race to the Rescue. 1997. (Disney Ser.). (Illus.). 24p. (J). (ps-k). o.p. (*0-307-98801-5*, 98801, Golden Bks.) Random Hse. Children's Bks.

Carr, Jan. Hercules: The Hero. 1997. (Illus.). 24p. (J). (ps-2). 13.95 (*0-7868-3130-8*) Disney Pr.

Caughill, Michael. Hercules: A Hero in the Making. 1997. (Smart Pages Bks.). (Illus.). 14p. (J). o.p. (*0-307-75751-X*, 65751, Golden Bks.) Random Hse. Children's Bks.

Charbonnet, Gabrielle. Hercules: I Made Herc a Hero by Phil. 1997. (Disney Chapters Ser.). (J). (gr. 2-4). 64p. pap. 3.50 o.p. (*0-7868-4116-8*); pap. 3.50 (*0-7868-4195-8*) Disney Pr.

Clark, Judith Holmes & Tilley, Scott, contrib. by. Disney's Hercules. 1997. (Little Library). 8p. (J). 5.98 o.p. (*1-57082-520-3*) Mouse Works.

DeCandido, Keith R. A. The Aries, Vol. 3. 1999. 144p. (J). (gr. 4-7). mass mkt. 3.99 (*0-671-03554-1*, Simon Pulse) Simon & Schuster Children's Publishing.

—Cheiron's Warriors. 1999. (Young Hercules Ser.: Vol. 2). 160p. (J). (gr. 4-7). mass mkt. 3.99 (*0-671-03552-5*, Aladdin) Simon & Schuster Children's Publishing.

Disney Staff. Best Gift of All. 1997. (Golden Book Ser.). 16p. (J). o.p. (*0-307-74060-9*, Golden Bks.) Random Hse. Children's Bks.

—Hercules: Lightning Strikes. 1997. (Disney's "Storytime Treasures" Library: Vol. 11). (Illus.). 44p. (J). (gr. 1-6). 3.49 o.p. (*1-57973-007-8*) Advance Pubs. LLC.

—Hercules: Zero to Hero. 1997. (Golden Book Ser.). (Illus.). 14p. (J). (ps-2). o.p. (*0-307-75700-5*, 65700, Golden Bks.) Random Hse. Children's Bks.

—Hercules 3-D Mask Book, Vol. 1. 1997. 14p. (J). (ps-2). pap. 10.95 o.p. (*0-7868-4129-X*) Disney Pr.

Disney Staff, illus. Hercules. 1997. (Read-Along Ser.). 24p. (J). 7.99 incl. audio (*0-7634-0202-8*) Walt Disney Records.

Disney, Walter Elias. Hercules: Feel the Pain, Pat the Panic. 1997. (Hercules Ser.). 12p. (J). (ps). 6.98 o.p. (*1-57082-521-1*) Mouse Works.

Dubowski, Cathy. Hercules. 1997. (J). pap. 3.95 (*0-7868-4196-6*) Disney Pr.

—Hercules Junior Novel. 1997. 96p. (J). (gr. 3-7). pap. 3.95 o.p. (*0-7868-4114-1*) Disney Pr.

Fontes, Justine. Disney's Hercules. 1997. (Little Golden Bks.). (Illus.). (J). o.p. (*0-307-98800-7*, 98800, Golden Bks.) Random Hse. Children's Bks.

—Hercules: A Hero Is Born. 1997. (Golden Super Shape Book Ser.). (Illus.). 24p. (J). (ps-k). pap. 2.99 o.p. (*0-307-10208-4*, 10208, Golden Bks.) Random Hse. Children's Bks.

Golden Books Staff. Hercules. 1999. (Song Book & Tape Ser.). (J). (ps-3). pap. 6.98 o.p. incl. audio (*0-307-47719-3*, Golden Bks.) Random Hse. Children's Bks.

—Hercules: Retelling of the Story. 1997. (Tell-a-Story Sticker Ser.). (Illus.). 18p. (J). (ps-3). pap. text o.p. (*0-307-05205-2*, Golden Bks.) Random Hse. Children's Bks.

—Hercules & the Monster. 1997. (Illus.). pap. text o.p. (*0-307-01913-6*, Golden Bks.) Random Hse. Children's Bks.

Gramatky, Hardie. Hercules. 1960. (Illus.). (J). (gr. k-3). 7.99 o.s.i (*0-399-60240-2*) Putnam Publishing Group, The.

HarperCollins Staff. Hercules Postcard Book. 1997. (Illus.). 64p. (J). pap. 9.95 (*0-7868-8236-0*) Hyperion Pr.

The Helpful Son. 1997. (Hercules Ser.). 10p. (J). (ps-1). 4.98 o.p. (*1-57082-523-8*) Mouse Works.

Hercules. 1997. (Spanish Classics Ser.). (SPA., Illus.). 96p. (J). (ps-4). 7.98 o.p. (*1-57082-519-X*) Mouse Works.

Hercules. (Play Packs Ser.). (J). 14.99 incl. audio (*0-7634-0261-3*); audio 13.99 (*0-7634-0232-X*); audio compact disk 22.99 (*0-7634-0234-6*); audio compact disk 22.99 (*0-7634-0235-4*); 1997. 11.99 incl. audio (*0-7634-0201-X*) Walt Disney Records.

Kennedy, Hunter. Hercules' Hugest Adventure! 1999. (Hercules Ser.). 128p. (Orig.). (gr. 4-7). mass mkt. 4.50 o.s.i (*0-425-16777-1*, JAM) Berkley Publishing Group.

Krulik, Nancy E. Hades: The Truth at Last. 1997. (Illus.). 32p. (J). (gr. k-4). 14.95 (*0-7868-3134-0*) Disney Pr.

Ladybird Books Staff. Hercules. 1997. (Ladybird Picture Classics Ser.). 56p. (J). (gr. 2-4). 2.99 o.s.i (*0-7214-5753-3*, Ladybird Bks.) Penguin Group (USA) Inc.

Layton, Bob. Hercules: Full Circle. 1988. 80p. 6.95 o.p. (*0-87135-397-0*) Marvel Enterprises.

—Hercules: Prince of Power. 1997. (Illus.). 192p. pap. text 19.99 o.p. (*0-7851-0555-7*); 1988. 96p. pap. 5.95 o.p. (*0-87135-365-2*) Marvel Enterprises.

Lundell, Margo. Friends & Foes. 1997. (Golden Book Ser.). pap. text o.p. (*0-307-11959-9*, Golden Bks.) Random Hse. Children's Bks.

Marsoli, Lisa A. Hercules. 1997. (Classic Storybook Ser.). (Illus.). 96p. (J). (ps-4). 7.98 o.s.i (*1-57082-518-1*) Mouse Works.

Marsoli, Lisa Ann, adapted by. Hercules. 2001. (Illus.). 128p. (J). (ps-k). text 6.00 o.p. (*0-7624-0231-8*) Running Pr. Bk. Pubs.

Menken, Alan. Hercules. 1997. (J). audio 13.99 (*0-7634-0233-8*) Walt Disney Records.

Moore, Robin. Hercules, Hero of the Night Sky. 1997. 10.14 (*0-606-11457-2*) Turtleback Bks.

Mouse Works Staff. Happy Birthday, Hercules! 1997. (Hercules Ser.). 18p. (J). (ps). 3.98 o.p. (*1-57082-540-8*) Mouse Works.

—Hercules Flip Book. 1996. (Illus.). 40p. (J). 2.98 o.p. (*1-57082-410-X*) Little Brown & Co.

Nelson, Ray, et al. Hercules' Spring Book. Siegel, Joseph & Habecker, Mary Beth, eds. 2000. (Illus.). 32p. (J). (gr. 1-3). pap. 12.00 (*1-883772-23-0*) Flying Rhinoceros, Inc.

Newman, Robert. The Twelve Labors of Hercules. 1972. (Hero Tales Ser.). (Illus.). 150p. (J). (gr. 3-5). 8.95 o.p. (*0-690-83920-0*) HarperCollins Children's Bk. Group.

Packard, Mary. Hercules: Friends Forever. 1997. (Golden Sturdy Bks.). (Illus.). 14p. (J). (ps). bds. o.p. (*0-307-12469-X*, 12469, Golden Bks.) Random Hse. Children's Bks.

Peterkin, Mike, illus. Hercules Pop-Up Book. 1997. 12p. (J). (gr. k-2). 13.95 (*0-7868-3128-6*) Disney Pr.

Snyder, Margaret. Hercules. 1997. (Golden Look-Look Bks.). (Illus.). 24p. (J). (ps-3). pap. o.p. (*0-307-11961-0*, 11961, Golden Bks.) Random Hse. Children's Bks.

Stamper, Judith Bauer & Keenan. Hercules & the Maze of the Minotaur. 1998. (Disney's First Readers Ser.: Vol. 3). 40p. (J). (gr. 2-4). pap. 3.50 o.p. (*0-7868-4171-0*) Disney Pr.

Stamper, Judith Bauer & Sol Studios Staff. Hercules & the Maze of the Minotaur. 1999. (Illus.). (*0-590-39387-1*) Scholastic, Inc.

Walt Disney Productions Staff, contrib. by. Disney's Hercules. 1997. (Illus.). 32p. (J). o.p. (*0-307-71145-5*, Golden Bks.) Random Hse. Children's Bks.

Weisbrot, Rob. Hercules: The Legendary Journeys. 1998. (Illus.). 288p. (YA). pap. 1.99 o.s.i (*0-385-32569-X*, Dell Books for Young Readers) Random Hse. Children's Bks.

Whitman, John. Hercules: The Legendary Journeys. 1998. (Hercules Ser.). (Illus.). 320p. (J). (gr. 3-7). 9.95 o.p. (*0-8118-2206-0*) Chronicle Bks. LLC.

—Xena: Warrior Princess. 1998. (Mighty Chronicles Ser.). (Illus.). 320p. (J). (gr. 3-7). 9.95 o.p. (*0-8118-2207-9*) Chronicle Bks. LLC.

HIDALGO Y COSTILLA, MIGUEL, 1753-1811—FICTION

Father Hidalgo: Mini-Play. 1978. (History of Mexico Ser.). (J). (gr. 5 up). 5.00 (*0-89550-326-3*) Stevens & Shea Pubs.

HILTON, TARA (FICTITIOUS CHARACTER)—FICTION

Kirby, Susan. Dead Man's Scam. 1994. (You-Solve-It Mysteries Ser.: No. 7). 224p. (YA). mass mkt. 3.50 (*0-8217-4734-7*, Zebra Bks.) Kensington Publishing Corp.

—Prescription for Murder. 1994. (You-Solve-It Mysteries Ser.: No. 9). 224p. (YA). mass mkt. 3.50 (*0-8217-4791-6*) Kensington Publishing Corp.

HOLMES, SHERLOCK (FICTITIOUS CHARACTER)—FICTION

Doyle, Arthur Conan. The Adventures of Sherlock Holmes. 1986. 304p. (YA). (gr. 4-7). mass mkt. 4.99 (*0-425-09838-9*) Berkley Publishing Group.

—The Adventures of Sherlock Holmes. 1994. 144p. (J). 12.98 o.p. (*0-86112-972-5*) Brimax Bks., Ltd.

—The Adventures of Sherlock Holmes. 1989. (Illus.). 259p. (YA). (gr. 7-12). mass mkt. 4.99 (*0-8125-0424-0*, Tor Classics) Doherty, Tom Assocs., LLC.

—The Adventures of Sherlock Holmes. 1992. (Books of Wonder: Vol. 1). (Illus.). 352p. (J). (gr. 2 up). 24.99 (*0-688-10782-6*) HarperCollins Children's Bk. Group.

—The Adventures of Sherlock Holmes. 1998. (Wordsworth Classics Ser.). (YA). (gr. 6-12). 5.27 (*0-89061-033-9*, R0339WW) Jamestown.

—The Adventures of Sherlock Holmes. 1981. (Illus.). (J). (gr. 4-7). Book 1. 140p. pap. 3.50 o.p. (*0-380-78089-5*); Book 2. 156p. pap. 2.95 (*0-380-78097-6*); Book 3. 112p. pap. 2.95 (*0-380-78105-0*); Book 4. 112p. pap. 3.50 (*0-380-78113-1*) Morrow/Avon. (Avon Bks.).

—The Adventures of Sherlock Holmes. abr. ed. 1998. 2p. audio 16.95 o.p. (*0-14-086600-0*, Penguin AudioBooks) Viking Penguin.

—Favorite Sherlock Holmes Detective Stories. unabr. ed. 2000. (Juvenile Classics). 208p. (J). pap. 2.00 (*0-486-41242-3*) Dover Pubns., Inc.

—The Hound of the Baskervilles. (Illus.). 72p. (YA). (gr. 4 up). pap. 7.95 (*0-931334-67-5*, EDN502B) AV Concepts Corp.

—The Hound of the Baskervilles. 1965. (Airmont Classics Ser.). (J). (gr. 8 up). mass mkt. 2.50 (*0-8049-0062-0*, CL-62) Airmont Publishing Co., Inc.

—The Hound of the Baskervilles. 1987. 176p. (J). (gr. 10 up). mass mkt. 4.99 (*0-425-10405-2*) Berkley Publishing Group.

—The Hound of the Baskervilles. 1994. 208p. (YA). (gr. 5 up). pap. 2.99 (*0-87406-698-0*) Darby Creek Publishing.

—The Hound of the Baskervilles. unabr. ed. 1994. (Thrift Editions Ser.). 128p. (J). pap. 1.50 (*0-486-28214-7*) Dover Pubns., Inc.

—The Hound of the Baskervilles. 1995. (Fiction Ser.). (YA). pap. text 7.88 (*0-582-09679-0*, 79819) Longman Publishing Group.

—The Hound of the Baskervilles. 1986. (YA). (gr. 7 up). 256p. mass mkt. 4.95 o.s.i (*0-451-52478-0*); mass mkt. 2.95 o.p. (*0-451-52385-7*) NAL. (Signet Classics).

—The Hound of the Baskervilles. 1982. (Oxford Progressive English Readers Ser.). (Illus.). (J). (gr. k-6). pap. 4.95 o.p. (*0-19-581211-5*) Oxford Univ. Pr., Inc.

—The Hound of the Baskervilles, Level 4. Hedge, Tricia, ed. 2000. (Bookworms Ser.). (Illus.). 105p. (J). pap. text 5.95 (*0-19-423035-X*) Oxford Univ. Pr., Inc.

—The Hound of the Baskervilles. Fago, John N., ed. abr. ed. 1977. (Now Age Illustrated III Ser.). (Illus.). (J). (gr. 4-12). text 7.50 o.p. (*0-88301-276-6*); pap. text 2.95 (*0-88301-264-2*) Pendulum Pr., Inc.

—The Hound of the Baskervilles. 1991. (Horror Classics Ser.: No. 841-5). (Illus.). (J). (gr. 4 up). pap. 3.50 o.p. (*0-7214-0719-6*, Ladybird Bks.) Penguin Group (USA) Inc.

—The Hound of the Baskervilles. (Whole Story Ser.). 2004. pap. 25.99 (*0-670-03653-6*, Viking Children's Bks.); 1995. (Illus.). 256p. (YA). (gr. 4-7). pap. 4.99 (*0-14-036699-7*, Puffin Bks.); 1986. 176p. (J). (gr. 4-6). pap. 3.50 o.p. (*0-14-035064-0*, Puffin Bks.) Penguin Putnam Bks. for Young Readers.

—The Hound of the Baskervilles. 1959. (Laurel-Leaf Bks.). 224p. (YA). (gr. 7-12). mass mkt. 4.50 (*0-440-93758-2*, Laurel Leaf) Random Hse. Children's Bks.

—The Hound of the Baskervilles. (Children's Classics Ser.). (Illus.). 272p. 1992. (J). (gr. 4 up). 12.99 o.p. (*0-517-07770-1*); 1988. (YA). 9.99 o.s.i (*0-517-67028-3*) Random Hse. Value Publishing.

—The Hound of the Baskervilles. 1972. (J). reprint ed. pap. 1.50 o.p. (*0-590-01355-6*) Scholastic, Inc.

—The Hound of the Baskervilles. 2001. (Saddleback Classics). (Illus.). (J). 13.10 (*0-606-21554-9*) Turtleback Bks.

—The Hound of the Baskervilles. 2004. (Whole Story Ser.). (J). bds. 17.99 (*0-670-03654-4*, Viking) Viking Penguin.

—The Lost World & Other Thrilling Tales. 2001. (Classics Ser.). (Illus.). 384p. (J). 9.00 (*0-14-043765-7*, Penguin Classics) Viking Penguin.

—The Memoirs of Sherlock Holmes. 1987. (YA). (gr. 10 up). mass mkt. 2.75 o.p. (*0-425-10402-8*) Berkley Publishing Group.

—The Return of Sherlock Holmes. l.t. ed. 1998. (Large Print Heritage Ser.). 278p. (YA). (gr. 7-12). lib. bdg. 29.95 (*1-58118-038-1*) LRS.

—El Sabueso de los Baskerville. 2nd ed. 2002. (Clover Ser.). (SPA., Illus.). 256p. (YA). (*84-392-8024-6*, EV5542) Gaviota Ediciones ESP. *Dist:* Lectorum Pubns., Inc.

—Sherlock Holmes Reader. (Courage Unabridged Classics Ser.). 224p. (YA). 1998. pap. 6.00 o.p. (*0-7624-0553-8*); 1994. text 5.98 o.p. (*1-56138-429-1*) Running Pr. Bk. Pubs. (Courage Bks.).

—A Study in Scarlet. 1986. (Illus.). 336p. (J). (gr. 7-12). 12.95 o.p. (*0-89577-254-X*) Reader's Digest Assn., Inc., The.

—A Study in Scarlet & The Sign of the Four. 1986. 256p. (YA). (gr. 10 up). mass mkt. 4.99 (*0-425-10240-8*) Berkley Publishing Group.

Doyle, Arthur Conan, ed. The Adventures of Sherlock Holmes. 2002. (Great Illustrated Classics). (Illus.). 240p. (J). (gr. 3-8). lib. bdg. 21.35 (*1-57765-678-4*, ABDO & Daughters) ABDO Publishing Co.

—The Adventures of Sherlock Holmes. 1988. mass mkt. 2.25 (*0-938819-62-3*, Aerie) Doherty, Tom Assocs., LLC.

Doyle, Arthur Conan & Vogel, Malvina, eds. The Adventures of Sherlock Holmes. 1993. (Great Illustrated Classics Ser.: Vol. 25). (Illus.). 240p. (J). (gr. 3-6). 9.95 (*0-86611-976-0*) Playmore, Inc., Pubs.

Greenwood, Marie, contrib. by. The Hound of the Baskervilles. 2000. (Dorling Kindersley Classics Ser.). (Illus.). 64p. (J). (gr. 2-5). pap. 14.95 o.p. (*0-7894-6108-0*) Dorling Kindersley Publishing, Inc.

Vanneman, Alan. Sherlock Holmes & the Giant Rat of Sumatra. 2003. 304p. pap. 14.00 (*0-7867-1125-6*); (Illus.). (J). 24.00 (*0-7867-0956-1*) Avalon Publishing Group. (Carroll & Graf Pubs.).

HOUSTON, SAM, 1793-1863—FICTION

Kutchinski, Marjorie. Liberty, Justice & F'Rall: The Dog Heroes of the Texas Republic. 1998. 152p. (J). (gr. k-5). 15.95 (*1-57168-217-1*) Eakin Pr.

Sargent, Dave & Sargent, Pat. Grady (Dappled Grey) Proud to Be an American. 2003. (Saddle Up Ser.: Vol. 30). 42p. (J). lib. bdg. 22.60 (*1-56763-813-9*); mass mkt. 6.95 (*1-56763-814-7*) Ozark Publishing.

HOWARD, BEVERLY (FICTITIOUS CHARACTER)—FICTION

Barnes-Svarney, Patricia L. Loyalties. 1996. (Star Trek Ser.: No. 10). (Illus.). 128p. (J). (gr. 4-7). pap. 3.99 (*0-671-55280-5*, Aladdin) Simon & Schuster Children's Publishing.

—Loyalties. 1996. (Star Trek, The Next Generation: No. 10). (J). (gr. 3-6). 10.04 (*0-606-09893-3*) Turtleback Bks.

HUDDLESTON, CHRISTY (FICTITIOUS CHARACTER)—FICTION

see Christy (Fictitious Character: Marshall)—Fiction

HUGGINS, HENRY (FICTITIOUS CHARACTER)—FICTION

Cleary, Beverly. Henry & Beezus. unabr. ed. 1999. (Henry Huggins Ser.). (J). (gr. 1-4). audio 17.95 Blackstone Audio Bks., Inc.

—Henry & Beezus. 2002. (Illus.). (J). 13.83 (*0-7587-0018-0*) Book Wholesalers, Inc.

—Henry & Beezus. 1923. (Henry Huggins Ser.). (J). (gr. 1-4). pap. 1.75 o.s.i (*0-440-73295-6*) Dell Publishing.

—Henry & Beezus, 4 vols. 50th anniv. ed. 1990. (Henry Huggins Ser.). (Illus.). 208p. (J). (gr. 1-4). pap. 5.99 (*0-380-70914-7*, Harper Trophy) HarperCollins Children's Bk. Group.

—Henry & Beezus. 1952. (Henry Huggins Ser.). (Illus.). 192p. (J). (gr. 1-4). 15.99 (*0-688-21383-9*); lib. bdg. 17.89 (*0-688-31383-3*) Morrow/Avon. (Morrow, William & Co.).

—Henry & Beezus. (Henry Huggins Ser.). (J). 192p. (gr. 1-4). pap. 4.99 (*0-8072-1484-1*); 2003. (gr. 2). audio 18.00 (*0-8072-1026-9*); 1997. 192p. (gr. 1-4). pap. 28.00 incl. audio (*0-8072-7607-3*, YA897SP); 1997. 192p. (gr. 1-4). pap. 28.00 incl. audio (*0-8072-7607-3*, YA897SP); 1997. 31p. (gr. 1-4). audio 23.00 (*0-8072-7606-5*, YA897CX) Random Hse. Audio Publishing Group. (Listening Library).

—Henry & Beezus. 1979. (Henry Huggins Ser.). (Illus.). 196p. (J). (gr. 1-4). pap. 3.25 o.s.i (*0-440-43295-2*, Yearling) Random Hse. Children's Bks.

—Henry & Beezus. 1981. (Henry Huggins Ser.). (J). (gr. 1-4). audio 16.00 (*0-394-66100-1*) SRA/McGraw-Hill.

—Henry & Beezus. 1952. (Henry Huggins Ser.). (J). (gr. 1-4). 11.04 (*0-606-03441-2*) Turtleback Bks.

—Henry & Ribsy. (Henry Huggins Ser.). (J). (gr. 1-4). 1988. pap. o.p. (*0-440-80052-8*); 1923. pap. 1.75 o.s.i (*0-440-73296-4*) Dell Publishing.

—Henry & Ribsy, 4 vols. (Henry Huggins Ser.). (Illus.). (J). (gr. 1-4). 1990. 208p. pap. 5.99 (*0-380-70917-1*, Harper Trophy); 1954. 192p. 15.99 (*0-688-21382-0*); 1954. 192p. lib. bdg. 16.89 (*0-688-31382-5*) HarperCollins Children's Bk. Group.

—Henry & Ribsy. 1973. (Henry Huggins Ser.). (Illus.). 192p. (J). (gr. 1-4). pap. 1.50 o.p. (*0-688-25382-2*, Morrow, William & Co.) Morrow/Avon.

—Henry & Ribsy. 1979. (Henry Huggins Ser.). 196p. (J). (gr. 1-4). pap. 3.25 o.s.i (*0-440-43296-0*, Yearling) Random Hse. Children's Bks.

—Henry & Ribsy. unabr. ed. (Henry Huggins Ser.). (J). (gr. 1-4). audio 19.00 (*0-7887-0534-2*, 94729E7) Recorded Bks., LLC.

—Henry & Ribsy. 1954. (Henry Huggins Ser.). (J). (gr. 1-4). 11.04 (*0-606-03446-3*) Turtleback Bks.

—Henry & the Clubhouse. 2002. (Illus.). (J). 13.83 (*0-7587-9142-9*) Book Wholesalers, Inc.

—Henry & the Clubhouse, 4 vols. (Henry Huggins Ser.). (Illus.). (J). (gr. 1-4). 1990. 208p. pap. 5.99 (*0-380-70915-5*, Harper Trophy); 1962. 192p. 15.99 (*0-688-21381-2*) HarperCollins Children's Bk. Group.

—Henry & the Clubhouse. 1962. (Henry Huggins Ser.). (Illus.). 192p. (J). (gr. 1-4). lib. bdg. 15.93 o.p. (*0-688-31381-7*, Morrow, William & Co.) Morrow/Avon.

—Henry & the Clubhouse. 1979. (Henry Huggins Ser.). (Illus.). 196p. (J). (gr. 1-4). pap. 1.75 o.p. (*0-440-43305-3*, Yearling) Random Hse. Children's Bks.

—Henry & the Clubhouse. unabr. ed. (Henry Huggins Ser.). (J). (gr. 1-4). audio 19.00 (*0-7887-0603-9*, 94782E7) Recorded Bks., LLC.

—Henry & the Clubhouse. 1962. (Henry Huggins Ser.). (J). (gr. 1-4). 11.04 (*0-606-03447-1*) Turtleback Bks.

—Henry & the Paper Route. 1923. (Henry Huggins Ser.). (J). (gr. 1-4). pap. 1.75 o.s.i (*0-440-73298-0*) Dell Publishing.

—Henry & the Paper Route. (Henry Huggins Ser.). (Illus.). (J). (gr. 1-4). 1957. 192p. 15.95 (*0-688-21380-4*); 1957. 192p. lib. bdg. 15.89 (*0-688-31380-9*); 1990. 208p. reprint ed. pap. 5.99 (*0-380-70921-X*, Harper Trophy) HarperCollins Children's Bk. Group.

—Henry & the Paper Route. (Henry Huggins Ser.). (J). (gr. 1-4). 1999. wbk. ed. 91.70 incl. audio; 2000. pap. 34.24 incl. audio (*0-7887-3797-X*, 41041X4); 2000. audio 21.00 (*0-7887-3821-6*, 96014E7) Recorded Bks., LLC.

—Henry & the Paper Route. 1990. (Henry Huggins Ser.). (J). (gr. 1-4). 11.04 (*0-606-04695-X*) Turtleback Bks.

—Henry Huggins. 2001. (J). audio 18.00 Blackstone Audio Bks., Inc.

—Henry Huggins. 1923. (Henry Huggins Ser.). (J). (gr. 1-4). pap. 1.75 o.s.i (*0-440-73551-3*) Dell Publishing.

—Henry Huggins. (Henry Huggins Ser.). 1950. (Illus.). 160p. (J). (gr. 1-4). 15.99 (*0-688-21385-5*); 1950. (Illus.). 160p. (J). (gr. 1-4). 15.99 (*0-688-21385-5*); 1950. (Illus.). 160p. (J). (gr. 5 up). lib. bdg. 16.89 (*0-688-31385-X*); 2001. (gr. 1-4). audio compact disk 20.00 (*0-694-52525-1*); 2001. (gr. 1-4). audio 18.00 (*0-694-52529-4*) HarperCollins Children's Bk. Group.

—Henry Huggins. 1996. (Henry Huggins Ser.). (SPA., Illus.). 160p. (J). (gr. 1-4). pap. 5.95 (*0-688-14887-5*, MR2292, Rayo) HarperTrade.

—Henry Huggins. 1996. (Henry Huggins Ser.). (J). (gr. 1-4). pap. 4.50 (*0-380-72800-1*, Avon Bks.) Morrow/Avon.

—Henry Huggins. Palacios, Argentina, tr. 1983. (Henry Huggins Ser.). (SPA., Illus.). (J). (gr. 1-4). 16.00 (*0-688-02014-3*, MR0792, Morrow, William & Co.) Morrow/Avon.

—Henry Huggins, 4 vols. 50th anniv. ed. 1990. (Henry Huggins Ser.). (Illus.). 160p. (J). (gr. 1-4). pap. 5.99 (*0-380-70912-0*, Morrow, William & Co.) Morrow/Avon.

—Henry Huggins. l.t. ed. 1989. (Henry Huggins Ser.). (J). (gr. 1-4). reprint ed. lib. bdg. 16.95 o.s.i (*1-55736-148-7*, Cornerstone Bks.) Pages, Inc.

—Henry Huggins. 1979. (Henry Huggins Ser.). 160p. (J). (gr. 1-4). pap. 1.75 o.s.i (*0-440-43551-X*, Yearling) Random Hse. Children's Bks.

—Henry Huggins. unabr. ed. (Henry Huggins Ser.). (J). (gr. 1-4). 2000. audio compact disk 27.00 (*0-7887-4218-3*, C1157E7); 1994. audio 19.00 (*0-7887-0020-0*, 94219E7) Recorded Bks., LLC.

—Henry Huggins. (Henry Huggins Ser.). (J). (gr. 1-4). 1996. 12.00 (*0-606-10426-7*); 1996. 9.60 o.p. (*0-606-09405-9*); 1978. 11.00 (*0-606-03501-X*) Turtleback Bks.

—Henry Huggins Series Boxed Set, 6 vols. 1990. (Henry Huggins Ser.). (J). (gr. 1-4). 19.50 (*0-440-36015-3*) Dell Publishing.

—Henry Huggins Series Boxed Set: Henry Huggins; Henry & Beezus; Henry & Ribsy; Henry & the Clubhouse, 4 vols., Set. 1990. (Henry Huggins Ser.). (Illus.). (J). (gr. 1-4). pap. 18.00 (*0-380-71206-7*, Avon Bks.) Morrow/Avon.

—Ribsy. 1923. (Henry Huggins Ser.). (J). (gr. 1-4). pap. 2.25 o.s.i (*0-440-77456-X*) Dell Publishing.

—Ribsy. (Henry Huggins Ser.). (Illus.). (J). (gr. 1-4). 1992. 208p. pap. 5.99 (*0-380-70955-4*, Harper Trophy); 1964. 192p. 15.99 (*0-688-21662-5*) HarperCollins Children's Bk. Group.

—Ribsy. (Henry Huggins Ser.). (J). (gr. 1-4). 1996. pap. 4.50 (*0-380-72803-6*, Avon Bks.); 1964. (Illus.). 192p. lib. bdg. 16.89 (*0-688-31662-X*, Morrow, William & Co.) Morrow/Avon.

—Ribsy. 1990. (Henry Huggins Ser.). (J). (gr. 1-4). pap. o.s.i (*0-440-80189-3*, Dell Books for Young Readers) Random Hse. Children's Bks.

—Ribsy. unabr. ed. (Henry Huggins Ser.). (J). (gr. 1-4). 2001. audio compact disk 39.00 (*0-7887-4963-3*, C1308E7); 1994. audio 27.00 (*0-7887-0021-9*, 94220E7) Recorded Bks., LLC.

—Ribsy. 1980. (Henry Huggins Ser.). (J). (gr. 1-4). pap. (*0-671-56090-5*, Simon Pulse) Simon & Schuster Children's Publishing.

—Ribsy. (Henry Huggins Ser.). (J). (gr. 1-4). 1996. 9.60 o.p. (*0-606-09788-0*); 1964. 11.00 (*0-606-00377-0*) Turtleback Bks.

J

JACKSON, ANDREW, 1767-1845—FICTION

Sargent, Dave & Sargent, Pat. Snow (white) Be Truthful #53. 2001. (Saddle Up Ser.). 36p. (J). pap. 6.95 (*1-56763-624-1*); lib. bdg. 22.60 (*1-56763-623-3*) Ozark Publishing.

Steele, William O. Andy Jackson's Water-Well. 1959. (Illus.). (J). (gr. 1-5). 4.50 o.p. (*0-15-203364-5*) Harcourt Children's Bks.

Characters

Stone, Irving. The President's Lady: A Novel about Rachel & Andrew Jackson. 1951. 360p. (J). 24.95 o.s.i (*0-385-04362-7*) Doubleday Publishing.

JACKSON, STONEWALL, 1824-1863—FICTION

Gibboney, Douglas Lee. Stonewall Jackson at Gettysburg. 2002. (Illus.). 132p. (YA). pap. 12.95 (*1-57249-317-8*, Burd Street Pr.) White Mane Publishing Co., Inc.

JANEWAY, KATHRYN MARGARET (FICTITIOUS CHARACTER)—FICTION

Barnes-Svarney, Patricia L. Quarantine. 1997. (Star Trek Voyager Ser.: No. 3). (Illus.). 128p. (J). (gr. 3-6). per. 3.99 (*0-671-00733-5*, Aladdin) Simon & Schuster Children's Publishing.

—Quarantine. 1997. (Star Trek Voyager: No. 3). (J). (gr. 3-6). 10.04 (*0-606-13803-X*) Turtleback Bks.

Cohen, Murray. The Chance Factor. 1997. (Star Trek Voyager Ser.: Vol. 2). (Illus.). 128p. (J). (gr. 2-4). per. 3.99 (*0-671-00732-7*, Aladdin) Simon & Schuster Children's Publishing.

Gallagher, Diana G. & Burke, Martin R. The Chance Factor. 1997. (Star Trek Voyager: No. 2). (J). (gr. 3-6). 10.04 (*0-606-13802-1*) Turtleback Bks.

Weiss, Bobbi J. G. & Weiss, David Cody. Lifeline. 1997. (Star Trek Voyager Ser.: No. 1). (Illus.). 128p. (J). (gr. 3-6). per. 3.99 (*0-671-00845-5*, Aladdin) Simon & Schuster Children's Publishing.

—Lifeline. 1997. (Star Trek Voyager: No. 1). (J). (gr. 3-6). 10.04 (*0-606-13801-3*) Turtleback Bks.

JANIE (FICTITIOUS CHARACTER: COONEY)—FICTION

Cooney, Caroline B. The Face on the Milk Carton. 192p. (YA). 1991. mass mkt. 3.50 o.s.i (*0-553-28958-6*); 1990. (gr. 7 up). 14.95 o.s.i (*0-553-05853-3*) Bantam Bks.

—The Face on the Milk Carton. 208p. 1996. (J). pap. 2.49 o.s.i (*0-440-22003-3*); 1991. (YA). (gr. 7-12). mass mkt. 5.99 (*0-440-22065-3*) Dell Publishing.

—The Face on the Milk Carton. abr. ed. 1993. (J). audio 17.99 o.s.i (*0-553-47188-0*, RH Audio) Random Hse. Audio Publishing Group.

—The Face on the Milk Carton. 1996. 192p. (YA). (gr. 7-12). 15.95 (*0-385-32328-X*, Dell Books for Young Readers); 1994. (J). mass mkt. 4.99 (*0-440-91009-9*, Laurel Leaf); 1991. (J). mass mkt. o.s.i (*0-553-54008-4*, Dell Books for Young Readers) Random Hse. Children's Bks.

—The Face on the Milk Carton. unabr. ed. 1998. (YA). (gr. 7). audio 35.00 (*0-7887-1916-5*, 95337E7); Set. (gr. 6). audio 49.24 (*0-7887-1944-0*, 40651); Set. (gr. 6). audio 115.70 (*0-7887-2463-0*, 46190) Recorded Bks., LLC.

—The Face on the Milk Carton. 1991. (J). 11.55 (*0-606-04871-5*) Turtleback Bks.

—The Voice on the Radio. 1996. (Illus.). 192p. (YA). (gr. 7-12). 15.95 (*0-385-32213-5*, Delacorte Pr.) Dell Publishing.

—The Voice on the Radio. 1998. 224p. (YA). (gr. 7-12). mass mkt. 5.50 (*0-440-21977-9*, Laurel Leaf) Random Hse. Children's Bks.

—The Voice on the Radio, unabr. ed. 1998. (YA). (gr. 7). audio 37.00 (*0-7887-2223-9*, 95522E7) Recorded Bks., LLC.

—The Voice on the Radio. 1998. (J). 11.55 (*0-606-13886-2*) Turtleback Bks.

—What Janie Found. 2000. 192p. (YA). (gr. 7-12). 15.95 (*0-385-32611-4*, Delacorte Pr.) Dell Publishing.

—What Janie Found. 2002. 192p. (YA). (gr. 7). mass mkt. 5.99 (*0-440-22772-0*, Laurel Leaf) Random Hse. Children's Bks.

—Whatever Happened to Janie? 1993. (J). o.s.i (*0-385-30937-6*, Dell Books for Young Readers) Random Hse. Children's Bks.

—Whatever Happened to Janie? unabr. ed. (YA). (gr. 7). 2000. audio compact disk 42.00 (*0-7887-3737-6*, C1108E7); 1998. audio 35.00 (*0-7887-2076-7*, 95429E7) Recorded Bks., LLC.

JANSEN, CAM (FICTITIOUS CHARACTER)—FICTION

Adler, David A. Cam Jansen & Mystery of Stolen Diamonds. 2004. (Cam Jansen Ser.). pap. 3.99 (*0-14-240010-6*, Puffin Bks.) Penguin Putnam Bks. for Young Readers.

—Cam Jansen & the Barking Treasure Mystery. 1999. (Cam Jansen Adventure Ser.: Vol. 19). (Illus.). 64p. (J). (gr. 2-5). 13.99 (*0-670-88516-9*) Penguin Putnam Bks. for Young Readers.

—Cam Jansen & the Birthday Mystery. 2000. (Cam Jansen Ser.: Vol. 20). (Illus.). 64p. (J). (gr. 2-5). 13.99 (*0-670-88877-X*, Viking Children's Bks.) Penguin Putnam Bks. for Young Readers.

—Cam Jansen & the Catnapping Mystery. (Cam Jansen Adventure Ser.: Vol. 18). (Illus.). 64p. (J). (gr. 2-5). 1998. text 13.99 (*0-670-88044-2*); Vol. 18. 2000. pap. 3.99 (*0-14-130897-4*, Puffin Bks.) Penguin Putnam Bks. for Young Readers.

—Cam Jansen & the Catnapping Mystery. 2000. 10.14 (*0-606-20353-2*); 10.14 (*0-606-20227-7*) Turtleback Bks.

—Cam Jansen & the Chocolate Fudge Mystery. 1995. (Cam Jansen Ser.: No. 14). (Illus.). 64p. (J). (gr. 2-5). pap. 3.99 o.s.i (*0-14-036421-8*, Puffin Bks.) Penguin Putnam Bks. for Young Readers.

—Cam Jansen & the Chocolate Fudge Mystery. 1995. (Cam Jansen Adventure Ser.). (J). 10.14 (*0-606-07334-5*) Turtleback Bks.

—Cam Jansen & the First Day of School Mystery. (Cam Jansen Ser.: No. 22). (Illus.). 2003. 64p. pap. 3.99 (*0-14-250114-X*, Puffin Bks.); Vol. 22. 2002. 80p. (J). 13.99 (*0-670-03575-0*, Viking Children's Bks.) Penguin Putnam Bks. for Young Readers.

—Cam Jansen & the Ghostly Mystery. (Cam Jansen Ser.: Vol. 16). (Illus.). 64p. (J). 1998. (gr. 2-5). pap. 3.99 (*0-14-038740-4*, Puffin Bks.); 1996. (gr. 1-4). 13.99 (*0-670-86872-8*, Viking Children's Bks.) Penguin Putnam Bks. for Young Readers.

—Cam Jansen & the Ghostly Mystery. 1998. 10.14 (*0-606-14174-X*) Turtleback Bks.

—Cam Jansen & the Mystery at the Haunted House. 1992. (Cam Jansen Adventure Ser.: No. 13). (Illus.). 64p. (J). (gr. 2-5). 13.99 (*0-670-83419-X*, Viking Children's Bks.) Penguin Putnam Bks. for Young Readers.

—Cam Jansen & the Mystery at the Haunted House. 1994. (Cam Jansen Adventure Ser.). 10.14 (*0-606-06264-5*) Turtleback Bks.

—Cam Jansen & the Mystery at the Monkey House. 2001. (Frequently Requested Ser.). lib. bdg. (*1-59054-252-5*) Fitzgerald Bks.

—Cam Jansen & the Mystery at the Monkey House. 1995. (Illus.). (J). (gr. 4). 9.00 (*0-395-73242-5*) Houghton Mifflin Co.

—Cam Jansen & the Mystery at the Monkey House. (Illus.). (gr. 2-5). 1999. (Cam Jansen Adventure Ser.: Vol. 10). 64p. pap. 3.99 (*0-14-130306-9*, Puffin Bks.); 1993. (Cam Jansen Ser.). 64p. (J). pap. 3.99 o.s.i (*0-14-036023-9*, Puffin Bks.); 1985. (Cam Jansen Ser.). 6p. (J). 13.99 (*0-670-80782-6*, Viking Children's Bks.) Penguin Putnam Bks. for Young Readers.

—Cam Jansen & the Mystery at the Monkey House. 1988. 64p. (J). (gr. k-6). pap. 3.25 o.s.i (*0-440-40047-3*, Yearling) Random Hse. Children's Bks.

—Cam Jansen & the Mystery at the Monkey House. 1993. (Young Puffin Ser.). (J). 10.14 (*0-606-05777-3*) Turtleback Bks.

—Cam Jansen & the Mystery of Flight 54. 1999. (Collections Ser.). (Illus.). (J). lib. bdg. 5.30 (*0-15-314312-6*) Harcourt School Pubs.

—Cam Jansen & the Mystery of Flight 54. (Cam Jansen Ser.: Vol. 12). (Illus.). 64p. (J). (gr. 2-5). 1999. pap. 3.99 (*0-14-130459-6*); 1992. pap. 3.99 o.s.i (*0-14-036104-9*, Puffin Bks.); 1989. 13.99 o.s.i (*0-670-81841-0*, Viking Children's Bks.) Penguin Putnam Bks. for Young Readers.

—Cam Jansen & the Mystery of Flight 54. 1992. (Cam Jansen Adventure Ser.). (J). 10.14 (*0-606-01682-1*) Turtleback Bks.

—Cam Jansen & the Mystery of the Babe Ruth Baseball. 1995. (Illus.). (J). (gr. 3). 8.60 (*0-395-73229-8*) Houghton Mifflin Co.

—Cam Jansen & the Mystery of the Babe Ruth Baseball. (J). 2004. pap. 3.99 (*0-14-240015-7*, Puffin Bks.); 1991. (Cam Jansen Ser.). (Illus.). 64p. (gr. 4-7). pap. 3.99 o.s.i (*0-14-034895-6*, Puffin Bks.); 1982. (Cam Jansen Ser.: No. 6). (Illus.). 64p. (gr. 2-5). 13.99 o.s.i (*0-670-20037-9*, Viking Children's Bks.); No. 6. 1998. (Cam Jansen Adventure Ser.: Vol. 6). (Illus.). 64p. (gr. 2-5). pap. 3.99 (*0-14-130090-6*, Puffin Bks.) Penguin Putnam Bks. for Young Readers.

—Cam Jansen & the Mystery of the Babe Ruth Baseball. (Cam Jansen Ser.). 57p. (J). (gr. 2-4). pap. 3.99 (*0-8072-1347-0*); 1985. pap. 17.00 incl. audio (*0-8072-0068-9*, FTR89SP) Random Hse. Audio Publishing Group. (Listening Library).

—Cam Jansen & the Mystery of the Babe Ruth Baseball. 1984. (Illus.). 64p. (J). (gr. 1-4). pap. 2.95 o.s.i (*0-440-41020-7*, Yearling) Random Hse. Children's Bks.

—Cam Jansen & the Mystery of the Babe Ruth Baseball. 1991. (Cam Jansen Adventure Ser.). 10.14 (*0-606-06146-0*) Turtleback Bks.

—Cam Jansen & the Mystery of the Carnival Prize. (Cam Jansen Ser.: No. 8). (Illus.). 2004. (J). pap. 3.99 (*0-14-240018-1*); 1999. 64p. (gr. 2-5). pap. 3.99 (*0-14-130307-7*); 1992. 64p. (J). (gr. 2-5). pap. 3.99 o.s.i (*0-14-036022-0*) Penguin Putnam Bks. for Young Readers. (Puffin Bks.).

—Cam Jansen & the Mystery of the Carnival Prize. 1992. (Cam Jansen Adventure Ser.). (J). 10.14 (*0-606-02446-8*) Turtleback Bks.

—Cam Jansen & the Mystery of the Chocolate Fudge Sale. 1993. (Cam Jansen Ser.: Vol. 14). (Illus.). 64p. (J). (gr. 2-5). 13.99 (*0-670-84968-5*, Viking Children's Bks.) Penguin Putnam Bks. for Young Readers.

—Cam Jansen & the Mystery of the Circus Clown. (Cam Jansen Ser.). 2004. pap. 3.99 (*0-14-240016-5*, Puffin Bks.); 1998. (Illus.). 64p. (J). (gr. 2-5). pap. 3.99 (*0-14-130091-4*, Puffin Bks.); 1991. (Illus.). 64p. (J). (gr. 4-7). pap. 3.99 o.s.i (*0-14-034897-2*, Puffin Bks.); 1983. (Illus.). 64p. (J). (gr. 2-4). 13.99 o.s.i (*0-670-20036-0*, Viking Children's Bks.) Penguin Putnam Bks. for Young Readers.

—Cam Jansen & the Mystery of the Circus Clown. 1985. (Illus.). 64p. (J). (gr. 1-4). pap. 2.75 o.s.i (*0-440-41021-5*, Yearling) Random Hse. Children's Bks.

—Cam Jansen & the Mystery of the Circus Clown. 1991. (Cam Jansen Adventure Ser.). 10.14 (*0-606-06262-9*) Turtleback Bks.

—Cam Jansen & the Mystery of the Dinosaur Bones. (Illus.). (J). 1997. (Cam Jansen Ser.: Vol. 3). 64p. (gr. 2-5). pap. 3.99 (*0-14-038715-3*, Puffin Bks.); 1991. (Cam Jansen Ser.: No. 3). 96p. (gr. 2-5). pap. 3.99 o.s.i (*0-14-034674-0*, Puffin Bks.); 1981. (Cam Jansen Adventure Ser.: Vol. 3). 64p. (gr. 4-7). 14.99 (*0-670-20040-9*, Viking Children's Bks.) Penguin Putnam Bks. for Young Readers.

—Cam Jansen & the Mystery of the Dinosaur Bones. unabr. ed. 1984. (Follow the Reader Ser.). 56p. (J). (gr. 2-4). pap., tchr.'s training gde. ed. 17.00 incl. audio (*0-8072-0056-5*, FTR 83SP); pap., tchr.'s training gde. ed. 17.00 incl. audio (*0-8072-0056-5*, FTR 83SP) Random Hse. Audio Publishing Group. (Listening Library).

—Cam Jansen & the Mystery of the Dinosaur Bones. 1982. (Illus.). 64p. (J). (gr. 1-4). pap. 2.75 o.s.i (*0-440-41199-8*, Yearling) Random Hse. Children's Bks.

—Cam Jansen & the Mystery of the Dinosaur Bones. unabr. ed. 1997. (J). (gr. 2). audio 10.00 (*0-7887-0673-X*, 94813E7) Recorded Bks., LLC.

—Cam Jansen & the Mystery of the Dinosaur Bones. 1997. (Puffin Chapters Ser.). (J). 10.14 (*0-606-04523-2*) Turtleback Bks.

—Cam Jansen & the Mystery of the Gold Coins. (Illus.). (J). 2004. (Cam Jansen Ser.). pap. 3.99 (*0-14-240014-9*, Puffin Bks.); 1991. (Cam Jansen Ser.). 64p. (gr. 4-7). pap. 3.99 o.s.i (*0-14-034896-4*, Puffin Bks.); 1982. (Cam Jansen Ser.: No. 5). 64p. (gr. 2-5). 13.99 o.s.i (*0-670-20038-7*, Viking Children's Bks.); Vol. 5. 1998. (Puffin Chapters Ser.: Vol. 5). 64p. (gr. 2-5). pap. 3.99 (*0-14-038954-7*, Puffin Bks.) Penguin Putnam Bks. for Young Readers.

—Cam Jansen & the Mystery of the Gold Coins. 1991. (Cam Jansen Adventure Ser.). 10.14 (*0-606-06263-7*) Turtleback Bks.

—Cam Jansen & the Mystery of the Haunted House, No. 13. 1994. (Cam Jansen Ser.). (Illus.). 64p. (J). (gr. 2-5). pap. 3.99 o.s.i (*0-14-034478-0*, Puffin Bks.) Penguin Putnam Bks. for Young Readers.

—Cam Jansen & the Mystery of the Monster Movie. (Illus.). 2004. (Cam Jansen Ser.). (J). pap. 3.99 (*0-14-240017-3*, Puffin Bks.); 1992. (Cam Jansen Ser.). 64p. (J). (gr. 2-5). pap. 3.99 o.s.i (*0-14-035021-2*, Puffin Bks.); 1984. (Cam Jansen Adventure Ser.: Vol. 8). 64p. (J). (gr. 4-7). 13.99 (*0-670-20935-2*, Viking Children's Bks.); Vol. 1 1999. (Cam Jansen Ser.: Vol. 8). 64p. (gr. 2-5). pap. 3.99 (*0-14-130460-X*, Puffin Bks.) Penguin Putnam Bks. for Young Readers.

—Cam Jansen & the Mystery of the Monster Movie. 1986. 64p. (J). (gr. k-3). pap. 2.99 o.s.i (*0-440-41922-3*, Yearling) Random Hse. Children's Bks.

—Cam Jansen & the Mystery of the Monster Movie. 1992. (Cam Jansen Adventure Ser.). (J). 10.14 (*0-606-02443-3*) Turtleback Bks.

—Cam Jansen & the Mystery of the Stolen Corn Popper. (Cam Jansen Ser.: No. 11). (Illus.). 64p. (gr. 2-5). 1992. (J). pap. 3.99 o.s.i (*0-14-036103-0*, Puffin Bks.); 1986. (J). 14.99 (*0-670-81118-1*, Viking Children's Bks.); Vol. 11. 1999. pap. 3.99 (*0-14-130461-8*, Puffin Bks.) Penguin Putnam Bks. for Young Readers.

—Cam Jansen & the Mystery of the Stolen Corn Popper. 1992. (Cam Jansen Adventure Ser.). (J). 10.14 (*0-606-01683-X*) Turtleback Bks.

—Cam Jansen & the Mystery of the Stolen Diamonds. (Illus.). (J). 1997. (Puffin Chapters Ser.). 64p. (gr. 2-5). pap. 3.99 (*0-14-038580-0*); 1991. (Cam Jansen Ser.: No. 1). 96p. (gr. 2-5). pap. 3.99 o.s.i (*0-14-034670-8*, Puffin Bks.); 1980. (Cam Jansen Adventure Ser.: Vol. 1). 64p. (gr. 4-7). 13.99 (*0-670-20039-5*, Viking Children's Bks.) Penguin Putnam Bks. for Young Readers.

—Cam Jansen & the Mystery of the Stolen Diamonds. 1982. (Illus.). 64p. (J). (gr. 1-4). pap. 2.75 o.s.i (*0-440-41111-4*, Yearling) Random Hse. Children's Bks.

—Cam Jansen & the Mystery of the Stolen Diamonds. 1997. (Cam Jansen Adventure Ser.). 10.14 (*0-606-11182-4*) Turtleback Bks.

—Cam Jansen & the Mystery of the Television Dog. (Illus.). (J). 2004. (Cam Jansen Ser.). pap. 3.99 (*0-14-240013-0*, Puffin Bks.); 1998. (Puffin Chapters Ser.). 64p. (gr. 2-5). pap. 3.99 (*0-14-038800-1*); 1991. (Cam Jansen Ser.: No. 4). 64p. (gr. 2-5). pap. 3.99 o.s.i (*0-14-034676-7*, Puffin Bks.); 1981. (Cam Jansen Ser.). 64p. (gr. 2-5). 11.99 o.s.i (*0-670-20042-5*, Viking Children's Bks.) Penguin Putnam Bks. for Young Readers.

—Cam Jansen & the Mystery of the Television Dog. 1982. (Illus.). 64p. (J). (gr. 1-4). pap. 2.75 o.s.i (*0-440-41196-3*, Yearling) Random Hse. Children's Bks.

—Cam Jansen & the Mystery of the Television Dog. 1991. (Cam Jansen Adventure Ser.). (J). 10.14 (*0-606-04625-9*) Turtleback Bks.

—Cam Jansen & the Mystery of the U.F.O. (Illus.). (J). 2004. pap. 3.99 (*0-14-240011-4*, Puffin Bks.); 1991. (Cam Jansen Ser.: No. 2). 96p. (gr. 2-5). pap. 3.99 o.s.i (*0-14-034672-4*, Puffin Bks.); 1980. (Cam Jansen Adventure Ser.: Vol. 2). 6p. (gr. 4-7). 13.99 (*0-670-20041-7*, Viking Children's Bks.); No. 2. 1997. (Cam Jansen Ser.: Vol. 2). 64p. (gr. 2-5). pap. 3.99 (*0-14-038579-7*, Puffin Bks.) Penguin Putnam Bks. for Young Readers.

—Cam Jansen & the Mystery of the U.F.O. 1982. (Illus.). 64p. (J). (gr. 1-4). pap. 2.75 o.p. (*0-440-41142-4*, Yearling) Random Hse. Children's Bks.

—Cam Jansen & the Mystery of the U.F.O. 1997. (Cam Jansen Adventure Ser.). 10.14 (*0-606-11183-2*) Turtleback Bks.

—Cam Jansen & the Scary Snake Mystery. (Cam Jansen Ser.: Vol. 17). (Illus.). 64p. (J). (gr. 2-5). 1999. pap. 3.99 (*0-14-130363-8*, Puffin Bks.); 1997. 13.99 (*0-670-87517-1*) Penguin Putnam Bks. for Young Readers.

—Cam Jansen & the Scary Snake Mystery. 1999. (Puffin Chapters Ser.). 10.14 (*0-606-17411-7*) Turtleback Bks.

—Cam Jansen & the School Play Mystery. (Illus.). 64p. 2001. (Cam Jansen Adventure Ser.: No. 21). (J). 13.99 (*0-670-89280-7*, Viking Children's Bks.); Vol. 21. 2003. (Cam Jansen Ser.). pap. 3.99 (*0-14-230244-9*, Puffin Bks.) Penguin Putnam Bks. for Young Readers.

—Cam Jansen & the Triceratops Pops Mystery. (Illus.). 64p. (J). (gr. 2-5). 1997. (Cam Jansen Ser.: Vol. 15). pap. 3.99 (*0-14-037512-0*, Puffin Bks.); 1995. (Cam Jansen Adventure Ser.: No. 15). 13.99 (*0-670-86027-1*, Viking Children's Bks.) Penguin Putnam Bks. for Young Readers.

—Cam Jansen & the Triceratops Pops Mystery. 1997. (Puffin Chapters Ser.). (J). 11.14 (*0-606-12641-4*) Turtleback Bks.

—The Cam Jansen Fun Book. (Cam Jansen Ser.). (Illus.). (J). (gr. 2-5). 2000. 32p. pap. 4.99 o.p. (*0-14-056756-9*); 1992. 320p. pap. 3.99 o.s.i (*0-14-034490-X*) Penguin Putnam Bks. for Young Readers. (Puffin Bks.).

—Cam Jansen 10 Mystery at Monkey House. 2004. (Cam Jansen Ser.). (Illus.). 64p. pap. 3.99 (*0-14-240019-X*, Puffin Bks.) Penguin Putnam Bks. for Young Readers.

—Young Cam Jansen & the Baseball Mystery. 1999. (Young Cam Jansen Ser.). (Illus.). 32p. (J). (gr. k-3). 13.99 (*0-670-88481-2*) Penguin Putnam Bks. for Young Readers.

—Young Cam Jansen & the Baseball Mystery, Vol. 5. Moore, Lisa, ed. 2001. (Young Cam Jansen Ser.: Vol. 5). (Illus.). 32p. (J). pap. 3.99 (*0-14-131106-1*, Puffin Bks.) Penguin Putnam Bks. for Young Readers.

—Young Cam Jansen & the Dinosaur Game. 1996. (Viking Easy-to-Read Ser.). (Illus.). 32p. (J). (gr. k-3). 13.99 (*0-670-86399-8*, Viking Children's Bks.) Penguin Putnam Bks. for Young Readers.

—Young Cam Jansen & the Dinosaur Game: Level 2. 1998. (Young Cam Jansen Ser.). (Illus.). 32p. (J). (gr. k-3). pap. 3.99 (*0-14-037779-4*) Penguin Putnam Bks. for Young Readers.

—Young Cam Jansen & the Dinosaur Game: Level 2. 1998. (Young Cam Jansen Ser.). (J). 10.14 (*0-606-13934-6*) Turtleback Bks.

—Young Cam Jansen & the Double Beach Mystery. (Illus.). 32p. 2002. (Viking Easy-To-Read Ser.: Vol. 8). (J). 13.99 (*0-670-03531-9*); Vol. 8. 2003. (Easy-to-Read Ser.). pap. 3.99 (*0-14-250079-8*, Puffin Bks.) Penguin Putnam Bks. for Young Readers.

—Young Cam Jansen & the Ice Skate Mystery. 1998. (Young Cam Jansen Ser.: Vol. 4). (Illus.). 48p. (J). (gr. k-3). 13.99 (*0-670-87791-3*) Penguin Putnam Bks. for Young Readers.

—Young Cam Jansen & the Library Mystery. (Viking Easy-to-Read Ser.). (Illus.). 32p. (J). (gr. k-3). 2001. 13.99 (*0-670-89281-5*, Viking Children's Bks.); Vol. 7. 2002. pap. 3.99 (*0-14-230202-3*) Penguin Putnam Bks. for Young Readers.

—Young Cam Jansen & the Lost Tooth. (Puffin Easy-to-Read Ser.). (Illus.). 32p. (gr. k-3). 1999. pap. 3.99 (*0-14-130273-9*, Puffin Bks.); 1997. (J). 13.99 (*0-670-87354-3*) Penguin Putnam Bks. for Young Readers.

—Young Cam Jansen & the Lost Tooth. 1997. 10.14 (*0-606-15993-2*) Turtleback Bks.

—Young Cam Jansen & the Missing Cookie. 1996. (Viking Easy-to-Read Series). (Illus.). 32p. (J). (ps-3). 13.99 o.s.i (*0-670-86772-1*, Viking Children's Bks.) Penguin Putnam Bks. for Young Readers.

—Young Cam Jansen & the Missing Cookie: Level 2. 1998. (Young Cam Jansen Ser.). (Illus.). 32p. (J). (gr. k-3). pap. 3.99 (*0-14-038050-7*, Puffin Bks.) Penguin Putnam Bks. for Young Readers.

—Young Cam Jansen & the Missing Cookie: Level 2. 1998. (Young Cam Jansen Ser.). (J). 10.14 (*0-606-13935-4*) Turtleback Bks.

—Young Cam Jansen & the New Girl Mystery. 2004. (Illus.). 13.99 (*0-670-05915-3*, Viking) Viking Penguin.

—Young Cam Jansen & the Pizza Shop Mystery. (Illus.). 32p. (J). 2001. (Young Cam Jansen Ser.: No. 6). pap. 3.99 (*0-14-230020-9*, Puffin Bks.); 2000. (Easy-to-Read Ser.). 13.99 (*0-670-88861-3*, Viking Children's Bks.) Penguin Putnam Bks. for Young Readers.

—Young Cam Jansen & the Zoo Note Mystery. 2003. (Illus.). 32p. (J). 13.99 (*0-670-03626-9*, Viking) Viking Penguin.

Adler, David A. & Natti, Susanna. Cam Jansen & the Mystery of the Carnival Prize. 1984. (Cam Jansen Ser.). (Illus.). 64p. (J). (gr. 2-5). 13.99 o.s.i (*0-670-20034-4*, Viking Children's Bks.) Penguin Putnam Bks. for Young Readers.

JEFFERSON, THOMAS, 1743-1826—FICTION

Armstrong, Jennifer. Thomas Jefferson: Letters from a Philadelphia Bookworm. 2001. (Dear Mr. President Ser.: Vol. 2). (Illus.). 117p. (J). (gr. 5-7). 8.95 (*1-890817-30-9*) Winslow Pr.

De Jong, David C. Seven Sayings of Mr. Jefferson. 1957. (Illus.). (J). (gr. 2-6). 2.95 o.p. (*0-87466-024-6*); lib. bdg. 2.87 o.p. (*0-87466-061-0*) Houghton Mifflin Co.

Fleming, Candace. A Big Cheese for the White House: The True Tale of a Tremendous Cheddar. 1999. (Illus.). 32p. (J). (gr. 1-5). pap. 16.95 o.p. (*0-7894-2573-4*) Dorling Kindersley Publishing, Inc.

—A Big Cheese for the White House: The True Tale of a Tremendous Cheddar, RS. 2004. (J). pap. 6.95 (*0-374-40627-8*, Sunburst) Farrar, Straus & Giroux.

—The Hatmaker's Sign. 1998. (Illus.). 40p. (J). (gr. k-4). pap. 16.95 (*0-531-30075-7*); lib. bdg. 17.99 (*0-531-33075-3*) Scholastic, Inc. (Orchard Bks.).

Hering, Marianne. Mockingbird Mystery. (White House Adventures Ser.: Vol. 1). 64p. (J). (gr. 2-5). pap. 4.99 (*0-7814-3065-8*) Cook Communications Ministries.

Rinaldi, Ann. Wolf by the Ears. (Point Ser.). 272p. (gr. 7-12). 1993. (YA). mass mkt. 4.99 (*0-590-43412-8*); 1991. (J). 13.95 (*0-590-43413-6*) Scholastic, Inc.

—Wolf by the Ears. 1991. (Point Ser.). (J). 11.04 (*0-606-02993-1*) Turtleback Bks.

Sargent, Dave & Sargent, Pat. Popcorn (Blue Corn) Work Hard #47. 2001. (Saddle Up Ser.). 36p. (J). pap. 6.95 (*1-56763-660-8*); lib. bdg. 22.60 (*1-56763-659-4*) Ozark Publishing.

Thomas Jefferson: Letters from a Philadelphia Bookworm. 2002. (Dear Mr. President Series). (J). (gr. 4-7). 25.95 incl. audio (*0-87499-989-8*) Live Oak Media.

Turner, Ann Warren. What Did I Know of Freedom? 2004. 32p. (J). (ps-3). 15.99 (*0-06-027579-0*); lib. bdg. 16.89 (*0-06-027580-4*) HarperCollins Children's Bk. Group.

JEKYLL, DOCTOR (FICTITIOUS CHARACTER)—FICTION

Dalmatian Press Staff, adapted by. Dr. Jekyll & Mr. Hyde. 2002. (Spot the Classics Ser.). (Illus.). 192p. (J). (gr. k-5). 4.99 (*1-57759-552-1*) Dalmatian Pr.

—Dr. Jekyll & Mr. Hyde. 1988. mass mkt. 4.95 (*0-938819-85-2*); mass mkt. 1.95 (*0-938819-12-7*) Doherty, Tom Assocs., LLC. (Aerie).

—Dr. Jekyll & Mr. Hyde. 2002. (YA). (gr. 9-12). stu. ed. (*1-58130-785-3*) Novel Units, Inc.

—Dr. Jekyll & Mr. Hyde. 1991. (Horror Classics Ser.: No. 841-4). (Illus.). (J). (gr. 4 up). pap. 3.50 o.p. (*0-7214-0884-2*, Ladybird Bks.) Penguin Group (USA) Inc.

Grant, John. Dr. Jekyll & Mr. Hyde. 1996. (Library of Fear, Fantasy & Adventure). (Illus.). 96p. (YA). (gr. 5 up). pap. 9.95 (*0-7460-2363-4*); lib. bdg. 17.95 (*0-88110-810-3*) EDC Publishing. (Usborne).

Halkin, John, ed. Dr. Jekyll & Mr. Hyde. 1988. (Flesh-creepers Ser.). 140p. (J). (gr. 6 up). pap. 2.95 o.p. (*0-8120-4072-4*) Barron's Educational Series, Inc.

Stevenson, Robert Louis. Dr. Jekyll & Mr. Hyde. (Illus.). 72p. (YA). (gr. 4 up). pap. 7.95 (*0-931334-50-0*, EDN402B) AV Concepts Corp.

—Dr. Jekyll & Mr. Hyde. 1981. (Tempo Classics Ser.). 176p. (J). 1.95 o.s.i (*0-448-17015-9*) Ace Bks.

—Dr. Jekyll & Mr. Hyde. 1964. (Airmont Classics Ser.). (YA). (gr. 8 up). mass mkt. 2.25 (*0-8049-0042-6*, CL-42) Airmont Publishing Co., Inc.

—Dr. Jekyll & Mr. Hyde. 1995. (Classroom Reading Plays Ser.). (YA). (gr. 6-12). 31p. pap. 2.40 o.p. (*1-56103-105-4*); 32p. pap. 3.95 (*0-7854-1117-8*, 40205) American Guidance Service, Inc.

—Dr. Jekyll & Mr. Hyde. 1996. (Andre Deutsch Classics). 107p. (J). (gr. 5-8). 11.95 (*0-233-99078-X*) Andre Deutsch GBR. *Dist:* Trafalgar Square, Trans-Atlantic Pubns., Inc.

—Dr. Jekyll & Mr. Hyde. abr. ed. (Classics Illustrated Bks.). (J). audio 5.95. audio Audio Bk. Co.

—Dr. Jekyll & Mr. Hyde. 1981. 128p. (YA). (gr. 7-12). pap. 1.95 o.s.i (*0-553-21087-4*, Bantam Classics) Bantam Bks.

—Dr. Jekyll & Mr. Hyde. (Classics Illustrated Ser.). (Illus.). 52p. (YA). pap. 4.95 (*1-57209-008-1*) Classics International Entertainment, Inc.

—Dr. Jekyll & Mr. Hyde. 1990. 82p. (J). mass mkt. 2.99 (*0-8125-0448-8*, Tor Classics) Doherty, Tom Assocs., LLC.

—Dr. Jekyll & Mr. Hyde. 2nd ed. 1998. (Illustrated Classic Book Ser.). (Illus.). 61p. (J). (gr. 3 up). reprint ed. pap. text 4.95 (*1-56767-237-X*) Educational Insights, Inc.

—Dr. Jekyll & Mr. Hyde. (YA). (gr. 5-12). pap. 7.95 (*0-8224-9255-5*) Globe Fearon Educational Publishing.

—Dr. Jekyll & Mr. Hyde. Harris, Raymond, ed. 1982. (Classics Ser.). (Illus.). 48p. (YA). (gr. 6-12). 17.96 incl. audio (*0-89061-255-2*, 452) Jamestown.

—Dr. Jekyll & Mr. Hyde, Level 4. Hedge, Tricia, ed. 2000. (Bookworms Ser.). (Illus.). 96p. (J). pap. text 5.95 (*0-19-423032-5*) Oxford Univ. Pr., Inc.

—Dr. Jekyll & Mr. Hyde. Platt, Kin, ed. 1973. (Now Age Illustrated Ser.). (Illus.). 64p. (J). (gr. 5-10). 7.50 o.p. (*0-88301-202-2*); stu. ed. 1.25 (*0-88301-176-X*); pap. 2.95 (*0-88301-096-8*) Pendulum Pr., Inc.

—Dr. Jekyll & Mr. Hyde. (YA). (gr. 5 up). 1997. (Illus.). 240p. pap. 3.99 o.s.i (*0-14-036764-0*); 1978. 6.95 o.p. (*0-448-41110-5*, Grosset & Dunlap) Penguin Putnam Bks. for Young Readers.

—Dr. Jekyll & Mr. Hyde. Vogel, Malvina, ed. 1990. (Great Illustrated Classics Ser.: Vol. 10). (Illus.). 240p. (J). (gr. 3-6). 9.95 (*0-86611-961-2*) Playmore, Inc., Pubs.

—Dr. Jekyll & Mr. Hyde. 1987. (Regents Illustrated Classics Ser.). (Illus.). (YA). (gr. 7-12). pap. text 5.25 net. o.p. (*0-13-216680-1*, 20432) Prentice Hall, ESL Dept.

—Dr. Jekyll & Mr. Hyde. Lafreniere, Kenneth, ed. 1984. (Stepping Stone Bks.: No. 9). (Illus.). 96p. (J). (gr. 3-7). reprint ed. pap. 3.99 (*0-394-86365-8*, Random Hse. Bks. for Young Readers) Random Hse. Children's Bks.

—Dr. Jekyll & Mr. Hyde. 208p. 2002. (YA). mass mkt. 3.99 (*0-439-29575-0*); 1991. (J). mass mkt. 3.25 o.p. (*0-590-45169-3*) Scholastic, Inc.

—Dr. Jekyll & Mr. Hyde. unabr. ed. 2002. (YA). audio compact disk 18.95 (*1-58472-243-6*, 014, In Audio) Sound Room Pubs., Inc.

—Dr. Jekyll & Mr. Hyde. 1990. (Illus.). (J). 9.04 (*0-606-18639-5*) Turtleback Bks.

—The Strange Case of Dr. Jekyll & Mr. Hyde. 2002. (Great Illustrated Classics). (Illus.). 240p. (J). (gr. 3-8). lib. bdg. 21.35 (*1-57765-800-0*, ABDO & Daughters) ABDO Publishing Co.

—The Strange Case of Dr. Jekyll & Mr. Hyde. 1997. (Eyewitness Classics Ser.). (Illus.). 64p. (J). (gr. 3-6). pap. 14.95 o.p. (*0-7894-2069-4*) Dorling Kindersley Publishing, Inc.

—The Strange Case of Dr. Jekyll & Mr. Hyde. (J). E-Book 2.49 (*1-58627-524-0*) Electric Umbrella Publishing.

—The Strange Case of Dr. Jekyll & Mr. Hyde. Harris, Raymond, ed. 1982. (Classics Ser.). (Illus.). 48p. (YA). (gr. 6-12). tchr. ed. 7.32 (*0-89061-254-4*, 453); pap. text 5.99 (*0-89061-253-6*, 451) Jamestown.

—The Strange Case of Dr. Jekyll & Mr. Hyde. (Young Collector's Illustrated Classics Ser.). (Illus.). 192p. (J). (gr. 3-7). 9.95 (*1-56156-460-5*) Kidsbooks, Inc.

—The Strange Case of Dr. Jekyll & Mr. Hyde. 1993. (Fiction Ser.). (YA). pap. text 6.50 (*0-582-08484-9*, 79829) Longman Publishing Group.

—The Strange Case of Dr. Jekyll & Mr. Hyde. 1996. (Wishbone Classics Ser.: No. 8). 128p. (J). (gr. 4-7). mass mkt. 3.99 (*0-06-106414-9*, HarperEntertainment) Morrow/Avon.

—The Strange Case of Dr. Jekyll & Mr. Hyde. abr. ed. 1996. (Classic Fiction Ser.). (YA). audio compact disk 15.98 o.p. (*962-634-090-8*, NA209012, Naxos AudioBooks) Naxos of America, Inc.

—The Strange Case of Dr. Jekyll & Mr. Hyde. 2000. (Dr. Jekyll & Mr. Hyde Ser.). (Illus.). (J). (gr. 7-12). 105p. 25.99 o.s.i (*0-670-88865-6*); 112p. pap. 17.99 (*0-670-88871-0*) Penguin Putnam Bks. for Young Readers. (Viking Children's Bks.).

—The Strange Case of Dr. Jekyll & Mr. Hyde. 1996. (Wishbone Classics Ser.: No. 8). (J). (gr. 3-7). 10.04 (*0-606-10371-6*) Turtleback Bks.

—The Strange Case of Dr. Jekyll & Mr. Hyde & the Suicide Club. 1986. (Classics for Young Readers Ser.). 176p. (J). (gr. 5 up). pap. 3.99 o.p. (*0-14-035047-0*, Puffin Bks.) Penguin Putnam Bks. for Young Readers.

—Treasure Island, The Master of Balantrae, Dr. Jekyll & Mr. Hyde, Kidnapped. 1985. (J). 15.45 (*0-671-52760-6*, Atheneum) Simon & Schuster Children's Publishing.

Stoker, Bram, et al. Dracula, Frankenstein, Dr. Jekyll & Mr. Hyde. 1978. 672p. (J). (gr. 7). mass mkt. 6.95 (*0-451-52363-6*, Signet Classics) NAL.

JESUS CHRIST—FICTION

Adams, Georgie. The First Christmas. 1997. (Illus.). 19p. (J). (ps-3). bds. 12.99 (*0-8054-0175-X*) Broadman & Holman Pubs.

Ahern, Denise. The Bread & the Wine: John 13:1-38; 1 Corinthians 11:23-24. 1979. (Arch Bks.). (Illus.). 24p. (J). (ps-3). pap. 1.99 (*0-570-06127-X*, 59-1245) Concordia Publishing Hse.

Alavedra, Joan. They Followed a Bright Star. 1994. (Illus.). 40p. (J). 16.99 (*0-399-22706-7*) Penguin Group (USA) Inc.

Alborghetti, Marci. The Miracle of the Myrrh. 2003. (J). 16.95 (*0-87946-249-3*, 708) ACTA Pubns.

—The Miracle of the Myrrh. 2000. (Illus.). 40p. (J). (ps-3). 16.95 (*1-890817-16-3*) Winslow Pr.

Animals Gift. 1994. (J). pap. 15.00 o.s.i (*0-671-72962-4*, Simon & Schuster Children's Publishing) Simon & Schuster Children's Publishing.

Aoki, Hisako. Santa's Favorite Story. 2nd ed. 1991. (Pixies Ser.). (Illus.). 28p. (J). (ps up). reprint ed. 4.95 (*0-88708-153-3*, Simon & Schuster Children's Publishing) Simon & Schuster Children's Publishing.

Aoki, Hisako & Gantschev, Ivan. Santa's Favorite Story. 1997. (Illus.). 28p. (J). (ps-3). pap. 5.99 (*0-689-81723-1*, Aladdin) Simon & Schuster Children's Publishing.

Barnes, Joyce B. Patches, the Blessed Beast of Burden. 1990. (Illus.). 36p. (J). 15.00 (*0-9628493-0-8*) Barnes, Joyce B.

Barrett, Ethel. God & a Boy Named Joe. 1975. (Regal Venture Stories Ser.). (Illus.). 144p. (J). (gr. 4-8). pap. 1.95 o.p. (*0-8307-0324-1*, 5700604, Regal Bks.) Gospel Light Pubns.

Berger, Barbara Helen. The Donkey's Dream. 1985. (Illus.). 32p. (J). (ps-3). 16.99 (*0-399-21233-7*, G. P. Putnam's Sons) Penguin Putnam Bks. for Young Readers.

Black, Auguste R. Miracles at the Inn. 1990. (Illus.). 24p. (Orig.). (J). (gr. 1-12). pap. 4.95 (*0-9628010-1-1*) Black, Auguste R.

Blaich, Ute. The Star. 2001. (Illus.). 32p. (J). (gr. k-3). lib. bdg. 16.50 (*0-7358-1510-0*, Michael Neugebauer Bks.) North-South Bks., Inc.

—The Star. Kazeroid, Sibylle, tr. from GER. 2001. (Illus.). 32p. (J). (gr. k-3). 15.95 (*0-7358-1509-7*, Michael Neugebauer Bks.) North-South Bks., Inc.

Boles, Paul D. Night of Vengeance. 1993. (J). o.p. (*0-88682-575-X*, Creative Education) Creative Co., The.

Bond, Katherine Grace. Sleepy-Time Dance. 2002. 12p. 5.99 (*0-310-70252-6*) Zondervan.

Bosca, Francesca. Caspar & the Star. 1991. (Illus.). 40p. (J). (gr. 1-8). 12.95 o.p. (*0-7459-2120-5*) Lion Publishing.

Bowman, Crystal. Room in the Stable: The Animals Share Christmas. (Illus.). 32p. (J). (ps-2). cd-rom 14.99 (*0-7814-3797-0*) Cook Communications Ministries.

Brantley, Steven & Brantley, Judi. The Legend of Snowflake, the Messenger Deer. l.t. ed. 2002. 40p. (J). 16.95 (*1-892570-04-1*) Spring Hse. Bks.

Brindle, Susan A., et al. The Little Caterpillar That Finds Jesus (La Oruguita que Encuentra a Jesus) A Parable of the Eucharist (Una Parabola Acerca de la Eucaristia) Emmanuelli Klosterman, Carmen A., tr. 1999. (Seven Sacraments Ser.). (ENG & SPA., Illus.). 72p. (gr. k-10). pap. 9.95 (*1-889733-08-3*, 01011) Precious Life Bks., Inc.

Briscoe, Jill. The Innkeeper's Daughter: A Delightful Discovery of a Wonderful Miracle. rev. ed. 1989. (Illus.). 48p. (J). (gr. 2 up). reprint ed. 7.99 o.p. (*0-929608-18-6*) Focus on the Family Publishing.

Brown, Margaret Wise. A Child Is Born. 2000. (Illus.). 32p. (J). 16.99 (*0-7868-0673-7*); lib. bdg. 17.49 (*0-7868-2564-2*) Hyperion Bks. for Children. (Jump at the Sun).

Brown, Margery W. Baby Jesus Like My Brother. 1995. (Illus.). 32p. (J). (ps-3). 15.95 (*0-940975-53-X*); pap. 7.95 (*0-940975-54-8*) Just Us Bks., Inc.

—Baby Jesus Like My Brother. 1995. (J). 13.20 o.p. (*0-606-09028-2*) Turtleback Bks.

—Baby Jesus Like My Brother. (Illus.). 2001. (J). E-Book (*1-59019-146-3*); 1995. E-Book (*1-59019-147-1*); 1995. E-Book 5.99 (*1-59019-148-X*) ipicturebooks, LLC.

Butterworth, Nick & Inkpen, Mick. The Fox's Story: Jesus Is Born. 1994. (Illus.). 24p. (J). pap. 5.99 (*0-551-02877-7*) Zondervan.

—The Mouse's Story: Jesus & the Storm. 1994. (Illus.). 24p. (J). pap. 5.99 (*0-551-02875-0*) Zondervan.

Byrd, Robert. Saint Francis & the Christmas Donkey. 2000. (Illus.). 40p. (J). (ps-3). 15.99 (*0-525-46480-8*, Dutton Children's Bks.) Penguin Putnam Bks. for Young Readers.

Cargas, Harry J. David's Decision: Betrayal or Trust? 1979. (J). pap. 2.25 o.p. (*0-570-07978-0*, 39-1118) Concordia Publishing Hse.

Carlson, Melody. Benjamin's Box: A Resurrection Story. 1997. (Illus.). 40p. (J). (gr. k-5). 10.99 o.p. (*1-57673-139-1*) Zonderkidz.

—Benjamin's Box: An Easter Story. 2000. (Illus.). 40p. (J). (gr. k-5). 10.99 (*0-310-70044-2*) Zondervan.

Carlyle, Linda Porter. Baby in the Laundry Basket. 1995. 32p. (J). 3.97 o.p. (*0-8163-1233-8*) Pacific Pr. Publishing Assn.

Christian, Mary Blount. Anna & the Strangers. 1981. (Illus.). 32p. (J). (gr. 1-3). pap. text 0.65 o.p. (*0-687-01529-4*) Abingdon Pr.

Clements, Andrew. Bright Christmas: An Angel Remembers. (Illus.). 32p. (J). (ps-3). 2000. pap. 5.95 (*0-618-05153-8*); 1996. lib. bdg., tchr. ed. 16.00 (*0-395-72096-6*) Houghton Mifflin Co. Trade & Reference Div. (Clarion Bks.).

Coe, Joyce. The Donkey Who Served the King. 1978. (Arch Bks.). (Illus.). (J). (gr. k-3). 1.29 o.s.i (*0-570-06120-2*, 59-1238) Concordia Publishing Hse.

Cook, Gladys M. Vashti & the Strange God. 1975. (Illus.). pap. 1.50 o.p. (*0-912692-57-X*) Cook, David C. Publishing Co.

Crawford, Sheryl Ann. The Baby Who Changed the World. (Illus.). 32p. (J). 12.99 o.p. (*0-7814-3431-9*) Cook Communications Ministries.

Currie, Robin. The Story of Easter. 1997. (Eyewitness Animals Ser.). (Illus.). 64p. (J). (ps-3). 12.99 (*0-7847-0593-3*, 03813, Bean Sprouts) Standard Publishing.

Curti, Anna, illus. Christmas Star. 1999. (Portable Holidays Ser.). 10p. (ps). (J). bds. 7.95 (*0-8109-5647-0*); bds. 7.95 (*0-8109-5638-1*) Abrams, Harry N. , Inc.

Damjan, Mischa. The Little Seahorse & the Christmas Pearl. Martens, Marianne, tr. from GER. 2001. (Illus.). 32p. (J). 15.95 (*0-7358-1505-4*); lib. bdg. 16.50 (*0-7358-1506-2*) North-South Bks., Inc.

Davidson, Alice Joyce. The "J" Is for Jesus: The Candy Cane Story. 1998. (Christmas Board Bks.). (Illus.). 14p. (J). (ps). 3.99 (*0-310-97553-0*) Zondervan.

Davis, Holly. My Birthday, Jesus' Birthday. 1998. (Illus.). 16p. (J). 5.99 (*0-310-97420-8*) Zondervan.

DeBoer, Jesslyn. Getting Ready for Christmas. 1998. (Christmas Board Bks.). (Illus.). 14p. (J). (ps). 3.99 (*0-310-97561-1*) Zonderkidz.

Di Silvestro, Frank. Boy Jesus & His Dog. 1998. (Illus.). 127p. (YA). (gr. 4-11). pap. 24.95 (*0-934591-03-2*) Songs & Stories Children Love.

Finley-Day, Linda. Donald the Dormouse Where's Our Baby Jesus? 1998. (Donald the Doormouse Ser.). (Illus.). 24p. (J). (ps-2). 14.99 o.p. (*0-8054-1247-6*) Broadman & Holman Pubs.

Fleetwood, Jenni. While Shepherds Watched. 1992. (Illus.). 32p. (J). (gr. k up). 14.00 o.p. (*0-688-11598-5*); lib. bdg. 13.93 o.p. (*0-688-11599-3*) HarperCollins Children's Bk. Group.

Flinn, Lisa & Younger, Barbara. The Christmas Garland. Corvino, Lucy, tr. & illus. by. 2003. 32p. (J). 14.95 (*0-8249-5460-2*, Ideals Pr.) Ideals Pubns.

—That's What a Friend Is! Corvino, Lucy, tr. & illus. by. 2003. 26p. (J). 6.95 (*0-8249-5468-8*, Ideals Pr.) Ideals Pubns.

Foreman, Michael. Cat in the Manger, ERS. 2001. (Illus.). 32p. (J). (ps-3). 16.95 (*0-8050-6677-2*, Holt, Henry & Co. Bks. For Young Readers) Holt, Henry & Co.

Frank, Penny. Jesus Gives the People Food. 1994. (Lion Story Bible Ser.). (J). (ps-3). pap. 1.99 o.p. (*0-7459-1781-X*) Lion Publishing.

—Jesus Gives the People Food. (Illus.). 24p. pap. 2.50 (*0-7459-4118-4*) Lion Publishing PLC GBR. *Dist:* Trafalgar Square.

—Jesus' Special Friends. 1994. (Illus.). 24p. (J). (ps-3). pap. 1.99 (*0-7459-1779-8*) Lion Publishing.

—Jesus' Special Friends. (Illus.). 24p. pap. 2.50 (*0-7459-4116-8*) Lion Publishing PLC GBR. *Dist:* Trafalgar Square.

Fryar, Jane L. Lost at the Mall. 1991. (Morris the Mouse Adventure Ser.). (Illus.). 32p. (J). (ps-1). 7.99 o.s.i (*0-570-04196-1*, 56-1655) Concordia Publishing Hse.

Geier, Marguerite E. Rama, the Holy Family Dog. 1991. (J). 11.95 o.p. (*0-533-09441-0*) Vantage Pr., Inc.

Ginolfi, Arthur. The Tiny Star. rev. ed. 1997. (Illus.). 32p. (J). (ps-3). 7.99 (*0-8499-1510-4*) Nelson, Tommy.

Greene, Carol. Jesus' Pig Picnic. 1994. (PassAlong Arch Bks.). (Illus.). 32p. (J). (ps-3). pap. 2.99 o.p. (*0-570-09049-0*, 59-1472) Concordia Publishing Hse.

Haley, Jan. The Gift. 1997. (Illus.). 48p. (J). (gr. 1-7). 17.95 (*1-885904-12-6*) Focus Publishing.

Hammer, Earl & Sipes, Don. Lassie: A Christmas Story. 1997. (Illus.). 48p. (J). pap. 14.99 o.p. (*0-8499-1427-2*) Nelson, Tommy.

Harder Tangvald, Christine. Hey, Mr. Angel! 1998. (Illus.). 32p. (J). (ps-k). 6.99 (*0-570-05058-8*) Concordia Publishing Hse.

—The Rinky Dinky Donkey. 1995. (Shaped Paperback Bks.). (Illus.). 24p. (J). (ps-k). pap. 3.99 (*0-7847-0168-7*, 03928, Bean Sprouts) Standard Publishing.

Hartman, Bob. Granny Mae's Christmas Play. 2004. (Illus.). 40p. (J). (gr. k-5). 16.99 (*0-8066-4063-4*, Augsburg Bks.) Augsburg Fortress, Pubs.

Hawse, Alberta. Encounter Christ Through the Dramatic Story of Vinegar Boy. 2002. 222p. (J). 9.99 (*0-8024-6588-9*) Moody Pr.

Head, Constance. The Man Who Carried the Cross for Jesus: Luke 23:26; Mark 15:21. 1979. (Arch Bks.). (Illus.). (J). (ps-3). pap. 1.99 (*0-570-06124-5*, 59-1242) Concordia Publishing Hse.

Heise, Robert F. 'Twas the Night Before Jesus. 1990. (Illus.). 28p. (J). (gr. 3-6). 12.95 (*0-9627049-0-3*) Dogwood Pr.

Helldorfer, Mary-Claire. Daniel's Gift. 1990. (Illus.). 32p. (J). (gr. k-3). reprint ed. pap. 4.95 (*0-689-71440-8*, Aladdin) Simon & Schuster Children's Publishing.

Hennessy, B. G. The First Night. 1993. (Illus.). 32p. (J). (ps-3). 13.99 o.s.i (*0-670-83026-7*, Viking Children's Bks.) Penguin Putnam Bks. for Young Readers.

Herold, Ann B. The Mysterious Passover Visitors. 1989. (Illus.). 112p. (Orig.). (J). (gr. 4-7). pap. 5.99 (*0-8361-3494-X*) Herald Pr.

Holcomb, Nan. Leah's Night of Wonder. Lt. ed. 1998. (Illus.). 32p. (J). (ps-3). lib. bdg. 16.95 (*0-944727-35-2*) Jason & Nordic Pubs.

Holly the Lamb Finds Baby Jesus. 1996. (Illus.). (J). 8.99 o.p. (*0-8054-7935-X*) Broadman & Holman Pubs.

Holmes, Marjorie. Three from Galilee: The Young Man from Nazareth. 1985. 224p. 13.95 o.p. (*0-06-015100-5*) HarperTrade.

—Three from Galilee: The Young Man from Nazareth. 1998. 330p. reprint ed. lib. bdg. 35.95 (*0-7351-0061-6*) Replica Bks.

Hooks, William H. The Legend of the Christmas Rose. 1999. (Illus.). 32p. (J). (gr. k-4). 14.95 (*0-06-027102-7*); lib. bdg. 14.89 (*0-06-027103-5*) HarperCollins Children's Bk. Group.

Hunt, Angela Elwell. Singing Shepherd. 1992. (Illus.). 32p. (J). (ps-6). 13.95 o.p. (*0-7459-2224-4*) Lion Publishing.

Janda, James A. The Lost Child: A Folk Tale. 1999. (Illus.). 32p. (J). (ps-2). pap. 6.95 (*0-8091-6646-1*) Paulist Pr.

Jeffs, Stephanie. Christopher Bear's First Christmas. 2004. (Christopher Bear Ser.). (Illus.). 30p. (J). 5.99 (*0-8066-4349-8*, Augsburg Bks.) Augsburg Fortress, Pubs.

—The Little Christmas Tree. 1991. (Illus.). 16p. (J). (ps-8). 12.95 o.p. (*0-7459-2118-3*) Lion Publishing.

Jesus Goes to a Wedding. 1983. (J). (ps-4). 0.50 o.p. (*0-570-08521-7*, 56-1436) Concordia Publishing Hse.

Jesus Goes to a Wedding. 2001. (Favorite Stories about Jesus Bks.). (Illus.). (J). bds. 0.99 (*0-8254-7229-6*) Kregel Pubns.

Johnson, Lissa Halls. The Worst Wish. 2000. (Kidwitness Tales Ser.). (Illus.). 128p. (J). (gr. 3-7). pap. 5.99 (*1-56179-882-7*) Bethany Hse. Pubs.

Kershaw, F. M. Heaven's Above. 1993. (J). 13.95 o.p. (*0-533-10231-6*) Vantage Pr., Inc.

Kidd, Pennie. Sleepy Jesus. 2002. (Illus.). 28p. 6.95 (*0-7459-4792-1*) Lion Publishing PLC GBR. *Dist:* Trafalgar Square.

Laughlin, Michael L. The Thornbush. 2000. (Illus.). 32p. (J). (ps-2). 12.99 (*0-8499-5968-3*) Nelson, Tommy.

Le Tord, Bijou. The Little Hills of Nazareth. 1994. (Illus.). 32p. (J). (ps-k). pap. 5.99 o.s.i (*0-440-40997-7*) Dell Publishing.

Letwenko, Edward. Jeremy & the Life of Jesus. 1996. (Jeremy the Bible Bookworm Ser.). (J). (ps-3). pap. 3.95 (*0-88271-313-2*) Regina Pr., Malhame & Co.

—Jeremy & the Nativity. 1996. (Jeremy the Bible Bookworm Ser.). (J). pap. 3.95 (*0-88271-312-4*) Regina Pr., Malhame & Co.

—Jeremy & the Parables. 1996. (Jeremy the Bible Bookworm Ser.). (Illus.). 31p. (J). (ps-3). pap. 3.95 (*0-88271-465-1*) Regina Pr., Malhame & Co.

Lies, Jalon E. Jesus, Vol. 2, Bk. 1. Holland, David, ed. 1996. (Illus.). (J). (ps-2). 7.50 (*1-889994-02-2*) For His Kingdom.

Lisa, Nikola. Hallelujah! A Christmas Celebration. 2000. (Illus.). 32p. (J). (ps-3). 16.00 o.s.i (*0-689-81673-1*, Atheneum) Simon & Schuster Children's Publishing.

Lomasney, Eileen. Two Children Who Knew Jesus: The Apple of Her Father's Eye & The Boy with the Picnic Lunch. 1994. (Illus.). 32p. (Orig.). (J). (gr. k-4). pap. 6.95 (*0-9641725-0-X*) Canticle Pr., Inc.

Lucado, Max. The Crippled Lamb. 1994. (Illus.). 32p. (J). (ps-2). 14.99 (*0-8499-1005-6*) Nelson, Tommy.

—Small Gifts in God's Hands. 2000. (Illus.). 32p. (J). (ps-2). 15.99 (*0-8499-5842-3*) Nelson, Tommy.

Lucado, Max, et al. The Crippled Lamb. 1999. (Illus.). 32p. (J). (ps-2). 5.99 (*0-8499-7502-6*); 5th anniv. collector's ed. 17.99 incl. audio compact disk (*0-8499-5979-9*) Nelson, Tommy.

Lussert, Anneliese. The Christmas Visitor. Lanning, Rosemary, tr. from GER. 1995. Tr. of Simons Weihnacht. (Illus.). 32p. (J). (gr. k-3). 15.95 o.p. (*1-55858-449-8*) North-South Bks., Inc.

Maccabe, Catherine. Teddy Bear, Piglet, Kitten & Me. 2004. (Illus.). 28p. (J). 11.99 (*0-8066-4148-7*, Augsburg Bks.) Augsburg Fortress, Pubs.

Machle, Rick. Ester's Easter Tale: How the Easter Bunny Came to Be. 1999. (Illus.). 36p. (J). pap. 7.99 (*0-9670375-0-6*) Growing Ideas, L.L.C.

Mackall, Dandi Daley. An Ali Cat Christmas. 1991. (Happy Day Bks.). (Illus.). 28p. (J). (gr. k-2). 2.50 o.p. (*0-87403-822-7*, 24-03922) Standard Publishing.

—Go, Go, Fish! 2002. (I'm Not Afraid Ser.). (Illus.). 24p. (J). (ps-2). 6.99 (*0-8499-7751-7*) Nelson, Tommy.

—Journey, Easter Journey. 2004. (J). pap. 9.99 (*1-4003-0373-7*) Nelson, Tommy.

Marsh, Carole. The Legend of the Candy Cane. (J). pap. 2.95 (*0-635-02124-2*, Marsh, Carole Bks.) Gallopade International.

Marvel Comics: The Easter Story. 1994. (Marvel Comics Ser.). (J). pap. 2.99 o.p. (*0-8407-7806-6*) Nelson, Thomas Inc.

Mathews, Nancy M. Friends of Jesus: The Animals Tell Their Stories. 1991. (Illus.). 24p. (J). (gr. 2-3). 9.99 o.p. (*0-8407-9609-9*) Nelson, Thomas Inc.

McGee, Marni. The Colt & the King. 2002. (Illus.). 32p. (J). (gr. k-3). tchr. ed. 16.95 (*0-8234-1695-X*) Holiday Hse., Inc.

Mills. La Estrella de Belen - Start of Bethlehem. 1995. (Libros Ventanitas - Windows Bks.). (SPA.). 8p. (J). (*1-56063-830-3*) Editorial Unilit.

Mills, Claudia. One Small Lost Sheep, RS. 1997. (Illus.). 32p. (J). (ps-3). 16.00 o.p. (*0-374-35649-1*, Farrar, Straus & Giroux (BYR)) Farrar, Straus & Giroux.

Morris, Joshua Packager Staff. The Very First Christmas: The Story of Jesus' Birth. 1995. (Illus.). 16p. (J). pap. 4.99 o.s.i (*0-679-87479-8*) Random Hse., Inc.

Moser, Barry, illus. The Other Wise Man. 1993. (J). 16.95 o.p. (*0-88708-329-3*, Simon & Schuster Children's Publishing) Simon & Schuster Children's Publishing.

Munger, Robert B. & Nystrom, Carolyn. My Heart - Christ's Home: Retold for Children. 1997. (Illus.). 32p. (J). (ps-3). 17.00 (*0-8308-1907-X*, 1907) InterVarsity Pr.

Napoli, Donna Jo. Song of the Magdalene: A Novel. 256p. (gr. 7-12). 1998. (YA). mass mkt. 4.99 (*0-590-93706-5*, Scholastic Paperbacks); 1996. (J). pap. 15.95 (*0-590-93705-7*) Scholastic, Inc.

—Song of the Magdalene: A Novel. 1998. (J). 11.04 (*0-606-13789-0*) Turtleback Bks.

The Newborn King. 2002. (Illus.). 13p. (J). (ps-1). bds. 5.99 (*1-57759-837-7*) Dalmatian Pr.

Nystrom, Carolyn. Growing Jesus' Way. 1982. (Children's Bible Basics Ser.). (J). (ps-2). 4.99 o.p. (*0-8024-6151-4*) Moody Pr.

Oxley, A. T. Nathan the Littlest Disciple. 2000. (Illus.). pap. 12.00 o.p. (*0-8059-5044-3*) Dorrance Publishing Co., Inc.

Pfister, Marcus. Der Weihnachtsstern. 1995. Tr. of Christmas Star. (GER., Illus.). (J). (gr. k-3). 18.95 (*3-314-00601-2*) North-South Bks., Inc.

Pingry, Patricia A. A Child's Easter. 2001. (Illus.). 32p. (J). (ps-3). 12.95 (*0-8249-4197-7*, Candy Cane Pr.) Ideals Pubns.

Ranger, Mary. Daniel's Star. 1977. (Starlight Ser.). (Illus.). (J). (gr. 5-8). pap. 2.25 o.p. (*0-570-03614-3*, 39-1102) Concordia Publishing Hse.

Roche, Luane. Proud Tree. 1995. (Illus.). 48p. 14.95 o.p. (*0-89243-768-5*) Liguori Pubns.

—The Proud Tree. (J). 1999. (Illus.). 48p. (gr. 1-5). pap. 11.95 (*0-7648-0377-8*); 1981. 64p. (gr. 2-6). pap. 3.95 o.p. (*0-89243-146-6*) Liguori Pubns.

—Proud Tree. rev. ed. 1995. (Illus.). 64p. (J). (gr. 1-4). pap. 3.95 (*0-89243-769-3*, 57225) Liguori Pubns.

Rowlands, Avril. The Christmas Sheep: And Other Stories. 2001. (Illus.). 48p. (J). (ps-3). 16.00 (*1-56148-336-2*) Good Bks.

Saloff-Astakhoff, N. I. Willie's Acquaintance with Christ. Patzon, Flora, tr. 1997. Tr. of Guillermo llega a Conocer a Cristo. (SPA., Illus.). 77p. pap. 3.85 (*0-7399-0292-X*, 2473.1) Rod & Staff Pubs., Inc.

Sample, Lempi. The Life of Jesus: As Seen Through the Eyes of a Shepherd Boy. Lt. ed. 1999. (Illus.). 67p. 9.95 (*1-55967-234-X*) Triune Biblical Univ.

Sanchez-Silva, Jose Maria. The Miracle of Marcelino. 1997. (SPA., Illus.). 123p. (Orig.). (J). (gr. 1-6). pap. 2.95 o.p. (*0-933932-28-6*) Scepter Pubs., Inc.

Sarlas-Fontana, Jane. The Adventures of Spero the Orthodox Church Mouse: The Nativity of Our Lord Christ's Birth. 1992. (Illus.). 20p. (J). (ps-4). pap. 8.95 (*0-937032-91-3*) Light & Life Publishing Co.

Savitz, Harriet May & Syring, K. Michael. The Pail of Nails. 1990. (Illus.). (J). (gr. 3 up). pap. text 3.29 o.p. (*0-687-29974-8*) Abingdon Pr.

Sawyer, Denise. My Name Is Mary: The Story of the Mother of Jesus. 2002. 96p. (J). (gr. 5 up). 12.95 (*0-9714276-4-X*) Still Waters Pubs.

Scheidl, Gerda Marie. El Burrito de Belen. 1998. (SPA., Illus.). 32p. (J). (gr. k-3). pap. 6.95 (*0-7358-1001-X*, NS8815) North-South Bks., Inc.

—El Burrito de Belen. 1998. 13.10 (*0-606-16021-3*) Turtleback Bks.

Schrecker, Judie. Santa's New Reindeer. 1996. (Illus.). 39p. (J). (ps up). 17.95 (*1-880664-18-6*) E. M. Productions.

Shaw, Sandra Anne. Jonathan Rabbit: A Story of Jesus. Lt. ed. 1996. (Illus.). 36p. (J). (gr. k-6). pap. 10.00 (*0-9668891-0-X*) Teach My Children Pubns.

Simmons, Diane. Joanna, the Crowing Hen of Bethel. 1979. (J). pap. 2.25 o.p. (*0-570-07976-4*, 39-1116) Concordia Publishing Hse.

Simon, Mary Manz. Noel's Almost-Perfect Just-about-Wonderful Christmas. 1994. (Illus.). 32p. (J). (ps-3). 4.99 o.p. (*0-7852-8194-0*) Nelson, Tommy.

Skeie, Eyvind. Summerland. Durnbaugh, Hedwig T., tr. from NOR. 1989. Orig. Title: Summerlandet. (Illus.). 48p. (J). pap. 6.95 (*0-87178-824-1*, 8241) Brethren Pr.

Skevington, Andrea. The Little Christmas Tree. 2003. (Illus.). 32p. (J). (gr. k-2). pap. 8.95 (*0-7459-4588-0*) Lion Publishing PLC GBR. *Dist:* Trafalgar Square.

Smith, Kathryn. Little Lamb's Christmas Story. 2002. (Snuffleheads Ser.). (Illus.). 14p. (J). (gr. k-3). 7.99 (*1-85985-442-7*); 7.99 (*0-8254-7253-9*) Kregel Pubns.

Smith, Sally A. Candle, a Story of Love & Faith. Luther, Luana, ed. 1991. (Illus.). 35p. (J). (gr. 4-7). pap. 5.95 (*0-944875-22-X*) Doral Publishing, Inc.

Spang, Gunter. The Ox & the Donkey: A Christmas Story. Martens, Marianne, tr. from GER. 2001. (Illus.). 32p. (J). (gr. k-2). 15.95 (*0-7358-1515-1*); lib. bdg. 16.50 (*0-7358-1516-X*) North-South Bks., Inc.

Sparks, Judy, ed. Baby Jesus ABC Storybook. 1979. (Happy Day Bks.). (Illus.). 24p. (J). (gr. k-3). 1.59 o.p. (*0-87239-354-2*, 3624) Standard Publishing.

Speare, Elizabeth George. Bronze Bow, 001. 1961. 255p. (YA). (gr. 6 up). 16.00 o.p. (*0-395-07113-5*) Houghton Mifflin Co.

Speirs, John. The Little Boy's Christmas Gift. 2001. (Illus.). 32p. (J). (ps-3). 16.95 (*0-8109-4399-9*) Abrams, Harry N., Inc.

Spence, Eleanor. Me & Jeshua. 2000. (StarMaker Bks.). 165p. (YA). pap. 5.50 (*0-88489-671-4*) St. Mary's Pr.

Summers, Susan & Van Dyke. The Fourth Wise Man. 1998. (Illus.). 40p. (J). (gr. k-4). 17.99 (*0-8037-2312-1*, Dial Bks. for Young Readers) Penguin Putnam Bks. for Young Readers.

Tafuri, Nancy. The Donkey's Christmas Song. 2002. (Illus.). 32p. (J). (ps-k). pap. 16.95 (*0-439-27313-7*, Scholastic Pr.) Scholastic, Inc.

—The Donkey's Christmas Welcome. 2002. (Illus.). (J). pap. (*0-439-27314-5*) Scholastic, Inc.

Tangvald, Christine Harder. The Best Thing about Easter. 2003. (Illus.). 28p. (J). (ps-2). 6.99 (*0-7847-1285-9*) Standard Publishing.

Tatum, Gwen. K. C.'s Light: I Was Born from a Light. 1999. (Illus.). 32p. (J). pap. 8.00 (*0-8059-4728-0*) Dorrance Publishing Co., Inc.

—K. C.'s Light: I Was Born from a Light. 1998. (Illus.). 32p. (J). (gr. k-6). pap. 9.95 (*0-9664727-0-5*) TNT Publishing.

Taylor, Shirley A. The Cross in the Egg. (Illus.). (J). (ps-2). 1999. 32p. 15.95 (*0-87483-549-6*); 1998. 15.95 o.p. (*0-87483-516-X*) August Hse. Pubs., Inc.

Tharlet, Eve, pseud. Simon & the Holy Night. 1993. (Pixies Ser.: Vol. 26). (Illus.). (J). 4.95 (*0-88708-324-2*, Simon & Schuster Children's Publishing) Simon & Schuster Children's Publishing.

—Simon & the Holy Night. Clements, Andrew, tr. 1991. (Illus.). 28p. (J). (ps up). pap. 14.95 (*0-88708-185-1*, Simon & Schuster Children's Publishing) Simon & Schuster Children's Publishing.

Thomas, Mack. Through the Eyes of Jesus. 1995. (Illus.). 64p. 14.99 o.p. (*0-88070-803-4*) Zonderkidz.

Tigner, Marcy. Little Marcy Loves Jesus. 1980. (J). pap. 1.25 o.p. (*0-89081-227-6*) Harvest Hse. Pubs.

Tolan, Stephanie S. Bartholomew's Blessing. 2003. (Illus.). (J). 15.99 (*0-06-001197-1*) HarperCollins Pubs.

Tommy Nelson Publishing Staff. The Easter Promise. 1998. (Illus.). 36p. (J). (ps-3). 7.99 (*0-8499-5827-X*) Nelson, Tommy.

Underhill, Marjorie Fay. Jeremiah. Garrett, Caroline S., tr. & illus. by. 2003. (J). (*1-887905-75-8*) Parkway Pubs., Inc.

Van DeWeyer, Robert & Spenceley, Annabel. The Shepherd's Son. 1993. 24p. (J). (gr. k-3). 10.00 o.p. (*0-8170-1188-9*) Judson Pr.

Van Dyke, Henry Jackson. The Story of the Other Wise Man. abr. ed. 2000. (Illus.). 96p. (J). 9.95 (*0-7407-1168-7*) Andrews McMeel Publishing.

—The Story of the Other Wise Man. 1996. 112p. pap. 7.95 (*0-345-40695-8*); 1984. mass mkt. 3.95 o.s.i (*0-345-31882-X*, Ballantine Bks.) Ballantine Bks.

—The Story of the Other Wise Man. 1992. 92p. reprint ed. lib. bdg. 15.95 (*0-89968-316-9*, Lightyear Pr.) Buccaneer Bks., Inc.

—The Story of the Other Wise Man. 1985. 98p. reprint ed. pap. 3.95 o.p. (*0-89783-040-7*) Cherokee Publishing Co.

—The Story of the Other Wise Man. 1983. (Illus.). 96p. 10.95 o.p. (*0-06-068855-6*) HarperSanFrancisco.

—The Story of the Other Wise Man. 1984. (Illus.). 87p. pap. 10.95 (*0-941478-33-5*, 930-010) Paraclete Pr., Inc.

—The Story of the Other Wise Man. 1995. (Illus.). 96p. (J). 9.99 o.s.i (*0-517-12277-4*) Random Hse. Value Publishing.

VandenBosch, Lori Walburg. The Legend of the Candy Cane: The Inspirational Story of Our Favorite Christmas Candy. 1997. (Illus.). 32p. (J). (ps-3). 14.99 (*0-310-21247-2*) Zondervan.

—The Legend of the Easter Egg. 1999. 32p. (J). 14.99 (*0-310-22447-0*) Zondervan.

VandenBosch, Lori Walburg, ed. The Legend of the Easter Egg. 2004. (Illus.). 26p. 6.99 (*0-310-70785-4*) Zondervan.

Walburg, Lori. The Legend of the Easter Egg Game. 9999. (J). 14.99 o.p. (*0-310-22741-0*) Zondervan.

Wallace, Lew. Ben Hur. 1965. (Airmont Classics Ser.). (YA). (gr. 9 up). mass mkt. 2.95 o.p. (*0-8049-0074-4*, CL-74) Airmont Publishing Co., Inc.

Wangerin, Walter, Jr. Probity Jones & the Fear Not Angel. 1996. (Illus.). 32p. (J). (gr. 1-4). 16.99 (*0-8066-2992-4*, 9-2992, Augsburg Bks.) Augsburg Fortress, Pubs.

Ward, Helen. The Animals' Christmas Carol. 2001. (Illus.). 40p. (J). 17.95 (*0-7613-1496-2*); lib. bdg. 24.90 (*0-7613-2408-9*) Millbrook Pr., Inc.

Ware, Jim. Dangerous Dreams. 2001. (Kidwitness Tales Ser.). (Illus.). 128p. (J). (gr. 4-7). pap. 5.99 (*1-56179-956-4*) Focus on the Family Publishing.

Watts, Bernadette. The Christmas Bird. 1996. (Illus.). 32p. (J). (gr. k-3). 15.95 o.p. (*1-55858-603-2*); 16.50 o.p. (*1-55858-604-0*) North-South Bks., Inc.

Wedeven, Carol S. The Christmas Crib That Zack Built. 1989. (Illus.). (J). 10.95 o.p. (*0-687-07816-4*) Abingdon Pr.

Wehrheim, Carol A. Good News for Jesus' Friends. 1997. (Illus.). 12p. (J). (ps). bds. 4.95 (*0-8298-1195-8*) Pilgrim Pr., The/United Church Pr.

—Jesus Visits Zacchaeus. 1997. (Illus.). 12p. (J). (ps). bds. 4.95 (*0-8298-1193-1*) Pilgrim Pr., The/United Church Pr.

—Three Visitors for Jesus. 1997. (Illus.). 12p. (J). (ps). bds. 4.95 (*0-8298-1194-X*) Pilgrim Pr., The/United Church Pr.

—Welcome Jesus! 1997. (Illus.). 12p. (J). (ps). bds. 4.95 (*0-8298-1227-X*) Pilgrim Pr., The/United Church Pr.

Weil, Lisl. The Story of the Wise Men & the Child. 1981. (Illus.). 32p. (J). (ps-2). 9.95 o.s.i (*0-689-30860-4*, Atheneum) Simon & Schuster Children's Publishing.

Westall, Robert. The Witness. 1994. (Illus.). 32p. (J). 14.99 o.s.i (*0-525-45331-8*, Dutton Children's Bks.) Penguin Putnam Bks. for Young Readers.

Whetstone, Gary L. The Missing Jesus: A Christmas Story. 1998. (Illus.). 24p. (J). (gr. 2-4). pap. 5.00 (*0-937739-33-2*) Roman, Inc.

Wilhelm, Hans. Waldo, Tell Me about Jesus. 1996. (Waldo, Tell Me about Ser.). (Illus.). 40p. (J). (ps-3). 5.95 (*0-88271-470-8*) Regina Pr., Malhame & Co.

Wilson, Karma. Mortimer's Manger. 2003. (Illus.). (J). 17.95 (*0-689-85511-7*, McElderry, Margaret K.) Simon & Schuster Children's Publishing.

Yeo, Bruce. Captain Salvation: Jesus the Light of the World. 1994. 32p. (J). (gr. 4-12). pap. 1.95 (*0-9644578-0-6*) Streetlight Christian Comics Pubns., The.

JOAN, OF ARC, SAINT, 1412-1431—FICTION

Dana, Barbara. Young Joan. 1997. (Illus.). 352p. (J). (gr. 5 up). pap. 6.99 (*0-06-440661-X*, Harper Trophy); 1991. 384p. (YA). (gr. 7 up). 17.95 (*0-06-021422-8*); 1991. 384p. (YA). (gr. 7 up). lib. bdg. 17.89 o.p. (*0-06-021423-6*) HarperCollins Children's Bk. Group.

—Young Joan. 1997. 12.00 (*0-606-12125-0*) Turtleback Bks.

Garden, Nancy. Dove & Sword. 1997. (J). mass mkt. 4.99 (*0-590-92949-6*) Scholastic, Inc.

—Dove & Sword: A Novel of Joan of Arc, RS. 1995. 304p. (YA). (gr. 7 up). 17.00 o.p. (*0-374-34476-0*, Farrar, Straus & Giroux (BYR)) Farrar, Straus & Giroux.

—Dove & Sword: A Novel of Joan of Arc. 1997. (Point Signature Ser.). 11.04 (*0-606-11274-X*) Turtleback Bks.

Goodwin, Marie. Where the Towers Pierce the Sky. 1989. 192p. (YA). (gr. 7 up). 14.95 o.p. (*0-02-736871-8*, Simon & Schuster Children's Publishing) Simon & Schuster Children's Publishing.

Sachs, Marilyn. A December Tale. 1976. (gr. 5-9). lib. bdg. 7.95 o.p. (*0-385-12315-9*) Doubleday Publishing.

Twain, Mark. Historical Romances: The Prince & the Pauper; A Connecticut Yankee in King Arthur's Court; Personal Recollections of Joan of Arc. Harris, Susan K., ed. 1994. (Library of America: Vol. 71). 1050p. 35.00 (*0-940450-82-8*) Library of America, The.

—Joan of Arc. 1999. (YA). reprint ed. pap. text 28.00 (*1-4047-1122-8*); pap. text 28.00 (*1-4047-1123-6*) Classic Textbooks.

—Joan of Arc. 1996. (Wishbone Classics Ser.: No. 4). (J). (gr. 3-7). 10.04 (*0-606-10367-8*) Turtleback Bks.

Twain, Mark, et al. Joan of Arc. 1996. (Wishbone Classics Ser.: No. 4). (Illus.). 128p. (gr. 3-7). mass mkt. 3.99 (*0-06-106418-1*, HarperEntertainment) Morrow/Avon.

JONES, HERCULEAH (FICTITIOUS CHARACTER)—FICTION

Byars, Betsy C. The Dark Stairs: A Herculeah Jones Mystery. 1995. (Illus.). (J). 16.95 o.p. (*0-7451-3091-7*, Galaxy Children's Large Print) BBC Audiobooks America.

—The Dark Stairs: A Herculeah Jones Mystery. unabr. ed. 1999. (YA). audio 16.98 Highsmith Inc.

—The Dark Stairs: A Herculeah Jones Mystery. (Herculeah Jones Mystery Ser.). (J). (gr. 3-7). 1994. 144p. text 14.99 o.s.i (*0-670-85487-5*, Viking Children's Bks.); No. 1. 1997. (Illus.). 160p. pap. 5.99 (*0-14-036996-1*, Viking) Penguin Putnam Bks. for Young Readers.

—The Dark Stairs: A Herculeah Jones Mystery. unabr. ed. 1995. (J). (gr. 3-5). 160p. pap. 28.00 incl. audio (*0-8072-7572-7*, YA883SP); audio 23.00 (*0-8072-7571-9*, YA883CX) Random Hse. Audio Publishing Group. (Listening Library).

—The Dark Stairs: A Herculeah Jones Mystery. 1997. (Herculeah Jones Mystery Ser.). (J). 11.04 (*0-606-12670-8*) Turtleback Bks.

—Death's Door: A Herculeah Jones Mystery. (Herculeah Jones Mystery Ser.). 144p. (gr. 3-7). 1999. pap. 5.99 (*0-14-130288-7*, Puffin Bks.); 1997. (J). 14.99 (*0-670-87423-X*, Viking) Penguin Putnam Bks. for Young Readers.

—Death's Door: A Herculeah Jones Mystery. 2000. (Illus.). (J). 11.04 (*0-606-18400-7*) Turtleback Bks.

—Disappearing Acts. (Herculeah Jones Mystery Ser.). 128p. (gr. 3-7). 2000. pap. 4.99 (*0-14-130287-9*, Puffin Bks.); 1998. (J). 15.99 (*0-670-87735-2*, Viking Children's Bks.) Penguin Putnam Bks. for Young Readers.

—Disappearing Acts. 1999. (Herculeah Jones Mystery Ser.). (Illus.). (J). 11.04 (*0-606-18401-5*) Turtleback Bks.

—Tarot Says Beware. l.t. ed. (J). 1996. 16.95 o.p. (*0-7451-4733-X*, Galaxy Children's Large Print); 1999. (gr. 1-8). audio 23.00 BBC Audiobooks America.

—Tarot Says Beware, Set. unabr. ed. 1999. (YA). audio 16.98 Highsmith Inc.

—Tarot Says Beware. (Herculeah Jones Mystery Ser.). (Illus.). (J). (gr. 3-7). 1997. 128p. pap. 4.99 (*0-14-036997-X*); 1995. 160p. 14.99 o.s.i (*0-670-85575-8*, Viking) Penguin Putnam Bks. for Young Readers.

—Tarot Says Beware. unabr. ed. 1996. (Herculeah Jones Mystery Ser.: No. 2). (J). (gr. 3-5). pap. 23.00 incl. audio (*0-8072-7754-1*, YA913SP); audio 18.00 (*0-8072-7753-3*, YA913CX) Random Hse. Audio Publishing Group. (Listening Library).

—Tarot Says Beware. 1997. (Herculeah Jones Mystery Ser.). (J). 10.04 (*0-606-12822-0*) Turtleback Bks.

JONES, INDIANA (FICTITIOUS CHARACTER)—FICTION

Bell, Sally. Young Indiana Jones: Safari in Africa. 1993. (Young Indiana Jones Chronicles: No. 2). (Illus.). 48p. (J). (gr. 2-4). pap. 3.25 o.s.i (*0-307-11470-8*, 11470, Golden Bks.) Random Hse. Children's Bks.

Brightfield, Richard. African Safari. 1993. (Young Indiana Jones Chronicles Choose Your Own Adventure Ser.: No. 5). 128p. (YA). (gr. 5-8). mass mkt. 3.25 o.p. (*0-553-29953-0*) Bantam Bks.

—African Safari. 1993. (Young Indiana Jones Chronicles Choose Your Own Adventure Ser.: No. 5). (YA). (gr. 5-8). 8.35 o.p. (*0-606-03004-2*) Turtleback Bks.

—Behind the Great Wall. 1993. (Young Indiana Jones Chronicles Choose Your Own Adventure Ser.: No. 6). 144p. (YA). (gr. 5-8). mass mkt. 3.25 o.s.i (*0-553-56103-0*) Bantam Bks.

—The Irish Rebellion. 1993. (Young Indiana Jones Chronicles Choose Your Own Adventure Ser.: No.8). 144p. (YA). (gr. 5-8). pap. 3.25 o.s.i (*0-553-56349-1*) Bantam Bks.

—Masters of the Louvre. 1992. (Young Indiana Jones Chronicles Choose Your Own Adventure Ser.: No. 4). 128p. (YA). (gr. 5-8). mass mkt. 3.25 o.s.i (*0-553-29969-7*) Bantam Bks.

—Revolution in Russia. 1992. (Young Indiana Jones Chronicles Choose Your Own Adventure Ser.: No. 3). 128p. (YA). (gr. 5-8). mass mkt. 3.25 o.s.i (*0-553-29784-8*) Bantam Bks.

—The Roaring Twenties. 1993. (Young Indiana Jones Chronicles Choose Your Own Adventure Ser.: No. 7). 144p. (YA). (gr. 5-8). pap. 3.25 o.s.i (*0-553-56348-3*) Bantam Bks.

—South of the Border. 1992. (Young Indiana Jones Chronicles Choose Your Own Adventure Ser.: No. 2). 128p. (YA). (gr. 5-8). mass mkt. 3.25 o.p. (*0-553-29757-0*, Starfire) Random Hse. Children's Bks.

—The Valley of the Kings. 1992. (Young Indiana Jones Chronicles Choose Your Own Adventure Ser.: No. 1). 144p. (YA). (gr. 5-8). mass mkt. 3.25 o.s.i (*0-553-29756-2*, Starfire) Random Hse. Children's Bks.

Crown. Indiana Jones & the Temple of Doom. 1984. (Marvel Bks.). (J). (gr. k up). 1.00 o.s.i (*0-517-55504-2*, Random Hse. Bks. for Young Readers) Random Hse. Children's Bks.

Estes, Rose. Indiana Jones & the Lost Treasure of Sheba. 1987. (Find Your Fate Adventure Ser.: No. 2). (Illus.). 115p. (J). mass mkt. 3.50 o.s.i (*0-345-34169-4*) Ballantine Bks.

French, Michael, adapted by. Indiana Jones & the Temple of Doom: The Storybook Based on the Movie. 1984. (Illus.). 64p. (J). (gr. 3-7). 7.99 o.s.i (*0-394-96387-3*, Random Hse. Bks. for Young Readers) Random Hse. Children's Bks.

Luceno, James. The Mata Hari Affair. 1992. (Young Indiana Jones Chronicles). 226p. (J). (gr. 4-6). mass mkt. 4.99 o.s.i (*0-345-38009-6*) Ballantine Bks.

Malam, John. Indiana Jones Explores Ancient Rome. 1996. (Illus.). 47p. (J). (gr. 5-8). 22.95 (*0-237-51223-8*) Evans Brothers, Ltd. GBR. *Dist:* Trafalgar Square.

—Indiana Jones Explores Egypt. 1992. (Illus.). 48p. (J). (gr. 3-7). 13.95 o.p. (*1-55970-183-8*) Arcade Publishing, Inc.

—Indiana Jones Explores the Aztecs. 1996. (Illus.). 47p. (J). (gr. 5-8). 19.95 o.p. (*0-237-51219-X*) Evans Brothers, Ltd. GBR. *Dist:* Trafalgar Square.

—Indiana Jones Explores the Incas. 1993. (Indiana Jones Ser.). (Illus.). 48p. (gr. 3-7). 14.95 (*1-55970-199-4*) Arcade Publishing, Inc.

—Indiana Jones Explores the Vikings. 1996. (Illus.). 47p. (J). (gr. 5-8). 22.95 (*0-237-51222-X*) Evans Brothers, Ltd. GBR. *Dist:* Trafalgar Square.

Martin, Les. Trek of Doom. 1992. (Young Indiana Jones Chronicles: No. 5). (J). (gr. 4-6). lib. bdg. 6.99 o.p. (*0-679-93237-2*, Random Hse. Bks. for Young Readers) Random Hse. Children's Bks.

—Young Indiana Jones & the Gypsy Revenge, No. 6. 1992. (Young Indiana Jones Ser.: No. 6). (Illus.). (J). (gr. 4-6). 2.99 o.p. (*0-517-08737-5*) Random Hse. Value Publishing.

—Young Indiana Jones & the Princess of Peril. 1991. (Young Indiana Jones Ser.: No. 5). 128p. (J). (gr. 4-6). pap. 2.95 o.s.i (*0-679-81178-8*, Random Hse. Bks. for Young Readers) Random Hse. Children's Bks.

—Young Indiana Jones & the Titanic Adventure. 1993. (Young Indiana Jones Ser.: No. 9). 132p. (Orig.). (J). (gr. 4-6). pap. 3.50 o.s.i (*0-679-84925-4*, Random Hse. Bks. for Young Readers) Random Hse. Children's Bks.

—Young Indiana Jones & the Tomb of Terror. 1990. (Young Indiana Jones Ser.: No. 2). 112p. (J). (gr. 4-6). pap. 3.99 (*0-679-80581-8*, Random Hse. Bks. for Young Readers) Random Hse. Children's Bks.

—Young Indiana Jones & the Tomb of Terror. 1992. (Illus.). (J). 2.99 o.p. (*0-517-08942-4*) Random Hse. Value Publishing.

Martin, Les, adapted by. Prisoner of War. 1993. (Young Indiana Jones Chronicles: No. 8). (Illus.). 136p. (Orig.). (J). (gr. 4-6). pap. 3.50 o.s.i (*0-679-84389-2*, Random Hse. Bks. for Young Readers) Random Hse. Children's Bks.

Martin, Les & Schulman, Lester M. Young Indiana Jones & the Gypsy Revenge. 1991. (Young Indiana Jones Ser.: No. 6). 128p. (J). (gr. 4-6). pap. 2.95 o.s.i (*0-679-81179-6*, Random Hse. Bks. for Young Readers) Random Hse. Children's Bks.

—Young Indiana Jones & the Secret City. 1990. (Young Indiana Jones Ser.: No. 4). 112p. (J). (gr. 4-6). pap. 2.95 o.s.i (*0-679-80580-X*, Random Hse. Bks. for Young Readers) Random Hse. Children's Bks.

William, McCay. Young Indiana Jones & the Mask of the Madman. 1998. (Young Indiana Jones Ser.: No. 18). (J). (gr. 4-6). pap. 3.99 (*0-679-87907-2*, Random Hse. Bks. for Young Readers) Random Hse. Children's Bks.

William, McCay. Young Indiana Jones & the Circle of Death. 1990. (Young Indiana Jones Ser.: No. 3). 112p. (J). (gr. 4-6). pap. 2.95 (*0-679-80578-8*, Random Hse. Bks. for Young Readers) Random Hse. Children's Bks.

—Young Indiana Jones & the Curse of the Ruby Cross. 1991. (Young Indiana Jones Ser.: No. 8). 128p. (J). (gr. 4-6). pap. 2.95 o.s.i (*0-679-81181-8*, Random Hse. Bks. for Young Readers) Random Hse. Children's Bks.

—Young Indiana Jones & the Curse of the Ruby Cross. 1992. (Young Indiana Jones Ser.: No. 8). (Illus.). (J). (gr. 4-6). 2.99 o.p. (*0-517-08736-7*) Random Hse. Value Publishing.

—Young Indiana Jones & the Face of the Dragon. 1994. (Young Indiana Jones Ser.: No. 11). 132p. (J). (gr. 4-6). pap. 3.50 o.s.i (*0-679-85092-9*, Random Hse. Bks. for Young Readers) Random Hse. Children's Bks.

—Young Indiana Jones & the Plantation Treasure. 1990. (Young Indiana Jones Ser.: No. 1). 112p. (J). (gr. 4-6). pap. 3.99 (*0-679-80579-6*, Random Hse. Bks. for Young Readers) Random Hse. Children's Bks.

—Young Indiana Jones & the Plantation Treasure. 1992. (Young Indiana Jones Ser.: No. 1). (Illus.). (J). (gr. 4-6). 2.99 o.p. (*0-517-08941-6*) Random Hse. Value Publishing.

McCay, William & Martin, Les. Young Indiana Jones Boxed Set: Young Indiana Jones & the Plantation Treasure; Young Indiana Jones & the Tomb of Terror; Young Indiana Jones & the Gypsy Revenge; Young Indiana Jones & the Ghostly Riders. 1992. (Young Indiana Jones Ser.: Bks. 1, 2, 6, 7). (J). (gr. 4-6). pap. 11.80 o.s.i (*0-679-83866-X*, Random Hse. Bks. for Young Readers) Random Hse. Children's Bks.

Scott, Gavin, adapted by. Revolution! 1992. (Young Indiana Jones Chronicles: No. 6). (J). (gr. 4-6). lib. bdg. 6.99 o.p. (*0-679-93238-0*, Random Hse. Bks. for Young Readers) Random Hse. Children's Bks.

Smith, Parker. The Mummy's Curse. 1992. (Young Indiana Jones Chronicles: No. 1). (Illus.). 24p. (J). (gr. 2-4). pap. 3.29 o.s.i (*0-307-12689-7*, 12689, Golden Bks.) Random Hse. Children's Bks.

Stine, H. William, ed. The Mummy's Curse. 1992. (Young Indiana Jones Chronicles: No. 1). (Illus.). 136p. (J). (gr. 4-6). pap. 3.50 o.s.i (*0-679-82774-9*, Random Hse. Bks. for Young Readers) Random Hse. Children's Bks.

Stine, Megan & Stine, H. William. Indiana Jones & the Dragon of Vengeance. 1985. (Find Your Fate Adventure Ser.: No. 8). (J). mass mkt. 1.95 o.p. (*0-345-32320-3*) Ballantine Bks.

—Young Indiana Jones & the Lost Gold of Durango. 1993. (Young Indiana Jones Ser.: No. 10). 132p. (Orig.). (J). (gr. 4-6). pap. 3.50 o.s.i (*0-679-84926-2*, Random Hse. Bks. for Young Readers) Random Hse. Children's Bks.

—Young Indiana Jones & the Mask of the Madman. 1995. (Young Indiana Jones Ser.: No. 18). 132p. (J). (gr. 4-6). 3.99 (*0-679-87037-7*, Random Hse. Bks. for Young Readers) Random Hse. Children's Bks.

Stine, Megan & H. William. Young Indiana Jones & the Ring of Power. 1999. (Young Indiana Jones Ser.). (J). (gr. 4-6). pap. 3.99 (*0-679-89049-1*); lib. bdg. 11.99 (*0-679-99049-6*) Random Hse. Children's Bks. (Random Hse. Bks. for Young Readers).

Stine, R. L. Indiana Jones & the Ape Slaves of Howling Island. 1986. (Find Your Fate Adventure Ser.: No. 10). (Orig.). (J). (gr. 7 up). mass mkt. 4.50 o.s.i (*0-345-33882-0*) Ballantine Bks.

—Indiana Jones & the Cult of the Mummy's Crypt. 1986. (Find Your Fate Adventure Ser.: No. 7). (J). mass mkt. 4.50 o.s.i (*0-345-33869-3*) Ballantine Bks.

—Indiana Jones & the Curse of Horror Island. 1987. (Find Your Fate Adventure Ser.: No. 1). (Illus.). 118p. (J). (gr. 7 up). mass mkt. 3.50 o.s.i (*0-345-33605-4*); 1984. mass mkt. 1.95 o.p. (*0-345-31665-7*) Ballantine Bks.

—Indiana Jones & the Dragon with Vengeance. 9999. (J). mass mkt. o.s.i (*0-345-39211-6*) Ballantine Bks.

—Indiana Jones & the Giants of the Silver Tower. 1984. (Find Your Fate Adventure Ser.: No. 3). 128p. (J). (gr. 7 up). mass mkt. 3.50 o.s.i (*0-345-31715-7*, Ballantine Bks.) Ballantine Bks.

Super Q. Indiana Jones - His Life of Adventure. 1989. (Super Q Ser.). (J). 5.95 o.p. (*0-8431-3195-0*, Price Stern Sloan) Penguin Putnam Bks. for Young Readers.

Weiss, Ellen. Indiana Jones & the Gold of Genghis. 1985. (Find Your Fate Adventure Ser.: No. 9). (J). mass mkt. 1.95 o.p. (*0-345-32409-9*) Ballantine Bks.

Wenk, Richard. Indiana Jones & the Eye of the Fates. 1984. (Find Your Fate Adventure Ser.: No. 4). 128p. (Orig.). (J). mass mkt. 1.95 o.s.i (*0-345-31716-5*, Ballantine Bks.) Ballantine Bks.

—Indiana Jones & the Legion of Death. 1984. (Find Your Fate Adventure Ser.: No. 6). 128p. (Orig.). (J). mass mkt. 1.95 o.s.i (*0-345-31904-4*) Ballantine Bks.

JONES, JIGSAW (FICTITIOUS CHARACTER)—FICTION

Preller, James. The Case of Hermie the Missing Hamster. 2001. (Jigsaw Jones Mystery Ser.: No. 1). (Illus.). 80p. (J). (gr. 1-4). mass mkt. 3.99 (*0-590-69125-2*) Scholastic, Inc.

—The Case of Hermie the Missing Hamster. 1998. (Jigsaw Jones Mystery Ser.: No. 1). (J). (gr. 1-4). 10.14 (*0-606-15966-5*) Turtleback Bks.

—The Case of the Bicycle Bandit. 2001. (Jigsaw Jones Mystery Ser.). (Illus.). (J). 10.14 (*0-606-21268-X*) Turtleback Bks.

—The Case of the Christmas Snowman. 1998. (Jigsaw Jones Mystery Ser.: No. 2). (Illus.). 80p. (J). (gr. 1-4). mass mkt. 3.99 (*0-590-69126-0*) Scholastic, Inc.

—The Case of the Christmas Snowman. 1998. (Jigsaw Jones Mystery Ser.: No. 2). (J). (gr. 1-4). 10.14 (*0-606-15985-1*) Turtleback Bks.

—The Case of the Class Clown, No. 12. 2001. (Jigsaw Jones Mystery Ser.: No. 12). 80p. (J). (gr. 1-4). mass mkt. 3.99 (*0-439-18474-6*) Scholastic, Inc.

—The Case of the Class Clown. 2001. (Jigsaw Jones Mystery Ser.). (Illus.). (J). 10.14 (*0-606-20742-2*) Turtleback Bks.

—The Case of the Disappearing Dinosaur. 2002. (Jigsaw Jones Mystery Ser.: No. 17). (Illus.). 80p. (J). mass mkt. 3.99 (*0-439-30639-6*) Scholastic, Inc.

—Case of the Ghost Writer. 2001. (Jigsaw Jones Mystery Ser.). (Illus.). (J). 10.14 (*0-606-20740-6*) Turtleback Bks.

—The Case of the Ghostwriter. 2001. (Jigsaw Jones Mystery Ser.: No. 10). 80p. (J). (gr. 1-4). mass mkt. 3.99 o.s.i (*0-439-11429-2*) Scholastic, Inc.

—The Case of the Golden Key. 2002. (Jigsaw Jones Mystery Ser.: No. 19). (Illus.). 96p. (J). mass mkt. 3.99 (*0-439-42628-6*, Scholastic Paperbacks) Scholastic, Inc.

—The Case of the Great Sled Race. 2001. (Jigsaw Jones Mystery Ser.: No. 8). (Illus.). 80p. (J). (gr. 1-4). mass mkt. 3.99 (*0-439-11427-6*, Scholastic Paperbacks) Scholastic, Inc.

—The Case of the Great Sled Race. 1999. (Jigsaw Jones Mystery Ser.: No. 8). (Illus.). (J). (gr. 1-4). 10.14 (*0-606-18527-5*) Turtleback Bks.

—The Case of the Marshmallow Monster. 2001. (Jigsaw Jones Mystery Ser.: No. 11). 80p. (J). (gr. 1-4). mass mkt. 3.99 (*0-439-18473-8*) Scholastic, Inc.

—The Case of the Marshmallow Monster. 2001. (Jigsaw Jones Mystery Ser.). (Illus.). (J). 10.14 (*0-606-20741-4*) Turtleback Bks.

—The Case of the Mummy Mystery. 2001. (Jigsaw Jones Mystery Ser.: No. 6). (Illus.). 80p. (J). (gr. 1-4). mass mkt. 3.99 (*0-439-08094-0*) Scholastic, Inc.

—The Case of the Mummy Mystery. 2000. (Jigsaw Jones Mystery Ser.: No. 6). (Illus.). (J). (gr. 1-4). 10.14 (*0-606-18528-3*) Turtleback Bks.

—The Case of the Rainy Day Mystery. 2003. (Jigsaw Jones Mystery Ser.: No. 21). 80p. (J). mass mkt. 3.99 (*0-439-42631-6*, Scholastic Paperbacks) Scholastic, Inc.

—The Case of the Runaway Dog. 2001. (Jigsaw Jones Mystery Ser.: No. 7). (Illus.). 74p. (J). (gr. 1-4). mass mkt. 3.99 (*0-439-11426-8*) Scholastic, Inc.

—The Case of the Runaway Dog. 1999. (Jigsaw Jones Mystery Ser.: No. 7). (Illus.). (J). (gr. 1-4). 10.14 (*0-606-18529-1*) Turtleback Bks.

—The Case of the Secret Valentine. 1999. (Jigsaw Jones Mystery Ser.: No. 3). (Illus.). 80p. (gr. 1-4). mass mkt. 3.99 (*0-590-69127-9*) Scholastic, Inc.

—The Case of the Secret Valentine. 1999. (Jigsaw Jones Mystery Ser.: No. 3). (J). (gr. 1-4). 10.14 (*0-606-15986-X*) Turtleback Bks.

—The Case of the Spooky Sleepover. 2001. (Jigsaw Jones Mystery Ser.: No. 4). (Illus.). 64p. (J). (gr. 1-4). mass mkt. 3.99 (*0-590-69129-5*) Scholastic, Inc.

—The Case of the Spooky Sleepover. 1999. (Jigsaw Jones Mystery Ser.: No. 4). (Illus.). (J). (gr. 1-4). 10.14 (*0-606-16586-X*) Turtleback Bks.

—The Case of the Stinky Science Project. 2001. (Jigsaw Jones Mystery Ser.: No. 9). (Illus.). 144p. (J). (gr. 1-4). mass mkt. 3.99 (*0-439-11428-4*) Scholastic, Inc.

—The Case of the Stinky Science Project. 2000. (Jigsaw Jones Mystery Ser.: No. 9). (Illus.). (J). (gr. 1-4). 10.14 (*0-606-18530-5*) Turtleback Bks.

—The Case of the Stolen Baseball Card. 2001. (Jigsaw Jones Mystery Ser.: No. 5). (Illus.). 80p. (J). (gr. 1-4). mass mkt. 3.99 (*0-439-08083-5*) Scholastic, Inc.

—The Case of the Stolen Baseball Card. 1999. (Jigsaw Jones Mystery Ser.: No. 5). (J). (gr. 1-4). 10.14 (*0-606-16933-4*) Turtleback Bks.

—Jigsaw Jones, 5 bks., Set. 2003. (Jigsaw Jones Ser.). (J). (gr. 1-3). pap. 15.96 (*0-439-43837-3*, Scholastic Paperbacks) Scholastic, Inc.

—The Race Against Time. 2003. (Jigsaw Jones Mystery Ser.: No. 20). (Illus.). 96p. (J). mass mkt. 3.99 o.s.i (*0-439-42630-8*, Scholastic Paperbacks) Scholastic, Inc.

Schade, Susan & Buller, Jon. Back to the Bayou. 2003. (Danger Joe Show Ser.: No. 4). 112p. (J). mass mkt. 3.99 (*0-439-40978-0*, Scholastic Paperbacks) Scholastic, Inc.

JONES, JULIET (FICTITIOUS CHARACTER)—FICTION

Morris, Gilbert. Too Smart Jones & the Buried Jewels: A Gilbert Morris Mystery. 1999. (Gilbert Morris Mysteries Ser.: Vol. 2). (Illus.). 125p. (J). (gr. 2-7). pap. 5.99 (*0-8024-4026-6*) Moody Pr.

—Too Smart Jones & the Cat's Secret: A Gilbert Morris Mystery. 2000. (Gilbert Morris Mysteries Ser.: Vol. 6). (Illus.). 124p. (J). (gr. 2-7). pap. 5.99 (*0-8024-4030-4*) Moody Pr.

—Too Smart Jones & the Dangerous Woman: A Gilbert Morris Mystery. 2000. (Gilbert Morris Mysteries Ser.: Vol. 4). (Illus.). 112p. (J). (gr. 4-7). pap. 5.99 (*0-8024-4028-2*) Moody Pr.

—Too Smart Jones & the Disappearing Dogs: A Gilbert Morris Mystery. 2000. (Gilbert Morris Mysteries Ser.: Vol. 3). (Illus.). 128p. (J). (gr. 4-7). pap. 5.99 (*0-8024-4027-4*) Moody Pr.

—Too Smart Jones & the Pool Party Thief: A Gilbert Morris Mystery. 1999. (Gilbert Morris Mysteries Ser.: Vol. 1). (Illus.). 115p. (J). (gr. 2-7). pap. 5.99 (*0-8024-4025-8*) Moody Pr.

—Too Smart Jones & the Stolen Bicycle: A Gilbert Morris Mystery. 2000. (Gilbert Morris Mysteries Ser.: Vol. 9). (Illus.). 133p. (J). (gr. 4-7). pap. 5.99 (*0-8024-4031-2*) Moody Pr.

—Too Smart Jones & the Stranger in the Cave: A Gilbert Morris Mystery. 2000. (Gilbert Morris Mysteries Ser.: Vol. 5). (Illus.). 118p. (J). (gr. 2-7). pap. 5.99 (*0-8024-4029-0*) Moody Pr.

—Too Smart Jones & the Wilderness Mystery: A Gilbert Morris Mystery. 2000. (Gilbert Morris Mysteries Ser.: Vol. 10). (Illus.). 142p. (J). (gr. 4-7). pap. 5.99 (*0-8024-4032-0*) Moody Pr.

JONES, JUNIE B. (FICTITIOUS CHARACTER)—FICTION

Osborne, Mary Pope. The Magic Tree House. Bks. 1-8. gif. unabr. ed. 2001. audio compact disk 30.00 (*0-8072-0612-1*); Vol. 9-12. unabr. ed. 2001. (J). audio 18.00 (*0-8072-0470-6*); Vols. 1-4. unabr. ed. 2000. (J). audio 18.00 (*0-8072-6164-5*); Vols. 5-8. 2nd unabr. ed. 2001. (J). audio 18.00 (*0-8072-6184-X*) Random Hse. Audio Publishing Group. (Listening Library).

—The Magic Tree House, Bks. 5-8. 2002. (Illus.). (J). (ps-3). 15.96 (*0-375-82266-6*) Random Hse., Inc.

Park, Barbara. Junie B., First Grader. 2003. (Illus.). 96p. (J). (gr. 1-4). lib. bdg. 11.99 (*0-375-90294-5*, Golden Bks.) Random Hse. Children's Bks.

—Junie B., First Grader: Cheater Pants. 2003. (Illus.). 96p. (J). (gr. 1-4). 11.95 (*0-375-82301-8*); lib. bdg. 13.99 (*0-375-92301-2*) Random Hse. Children's Bks. (Random Hse. Bks. for Young Readers).

—Junie B., First Grader: Cheater Pants. Brunkus, Denise, tr. & illus. by. 2004. 96p. (J). (gr. 1-4). pap. 3.99 (*0-375-82302-6*) Random Hse., Inc.

—Junie B., First Grader: One Man Band. 2003. (Junie B. Jones Ser.). (Illus.). 96p. (J). (gr. 1-4). lib. bdg. 13.99 (*0-375-92522-8*) Random Hse. Children's Bks.

—Junie B., First Grader: Shipwrecked. 2004. (Illus.). 96p. (J). (gr. 1-4). 11.95 (*0-375-82804-4*); lib. bdg. 13.99 (*0-375-92804-9*) Random Hse. Children's Bks. (Random Hse. Bks. for Young Readers).

—Junie B., First Grader: Shipwrecked. 2004. (J). pap. (*0-375-82805-2*) Random Hse., Inc.

—Junie B., First Grader: Toothless Wonder. (Illus.). 96p. (J). (gr. 1-4). 2003. pap. 3.99 (*0-375-82223-2*); 2002. 11.95 (*0-375-80295-9*) Random Hse., Inc.

—Junie B., First Grader (at Last!) (Junie B. Jones Ser.: No. 18). (Illus.). 96p. (J). (gr. 1-4). 2002. pap. 3.99 (*0-375-81516-3*); 2001. lib. bdg. 13.99 (*0-375-90293-7*) Random Hse. Children's Bks. (Random Hse. Bks. for Young Readers).

—Junie B., First Grader (at Last!) 2001. (Junie B. Jones Ser.: No. 18). (Illus.). 96p. (J). (gr. 1-4). 11.95 (*0-375-80293-2*) Random Hse., Inc.

—Junie B. Jones: One Man Band. 2003. (Junie B. Jones Ser.). (Illus.). 96p. (J). (gr. 1-4). 11.95 (*0-375-82522-3*) Random Hse. Children's Bks.

—Junie B. Jones & a Little Monkey Business. unabr. ed. 2002. (Junie B. Jones Ser.: Vol. 2). 68p. (J). (gr. k-4). pap. 17.00 incl. audio (*0-8072-0779-9*, LFTR 238 SP, Listening Library) Random Hse. Audio Publishing Group.

—Junie B. Jones & a Little Monkey Business. 1993. (Junie B. Jones Ser.: No. 2). (Illus.). 80p. (gr. k-2). lib. bdg. 11.99 (*0-679-93886-9*); pap. 3.99 (*0-679-83886-4*) Random Hse. Children's Bks. (Random Hse. Bks. for Young Readers).

—Junie B. Jones & a Little Monkey Business. unabr. ed. 1998. (Junie B. Jones Ser.: No. 2). (J). (gr. k-2). audio 11.00 (*0-7887-2617-X*, 95621E7) Recorded Bks., LLC.

—Junie B. Jones & a Little Monkey Business. 1993. (Junie B. Jones Ser.: No. 2). (Illus.). (J). (gr. k-2). 10.14 (*0-606-09498-9*) Turtleback Bks.

—Junie B. Jones & Her Big Fat Mouth. 1993. (Junie B. Jones Ser.: No. 3). (Illus.). 80p. (gr. k-2). lib. bdg. 11.99 (*0-679-94407-9*); pap. 3.99 (*0-679-84407-4*) Random Hse. Children's Bks. (Random Hse. Bks. for Young Readers).

—Junie B. Jones & Her Big Fat Mouth. 1999. (Junie B. Jones Ser.: No. 3). (J). (gr. k-2). pap., stu. ed. 24.24 incl. audio (*0-7887-2982-9*, 40864); pap., stu. ed. 24.24 incl. audio (*0-7887-2982-9*, 40864); audio 12.00 (*0-7887-2952-7*, 95653E7);Class set. audio 72.70 (*0-7887-3012-6*, 46829) Recorded Bks., LLC.

—Junie B. Jones & Her Big Fat Mouth. 1993. (Junie B. Jones Ser.: No. 3). (Illus.). (J). (gr. k-2). 10.14 (*0-606-05896-6*) Turtleback Bks.

—Junie B. Jones & Some Sneaky Peeky Spying. 1994. (Junie B. Jones Ser.: No. 4). (Illus.). 80p. (gr. k-2). (J). 11.99 o.s.i (*0-679-95101-6*); pap. 3.99 (*0-679-85101-1*) Random Hse. Children's Bks. (Random Hse. Bks. for Young Readers).

—Junie B. Jones & Some Sneaky Peeky Spying. (Junie B. Jones Ser.: No. 4). (J). (gr. k-2). 1999. pap., stu. ed. 23.24 incl. audio (*0-7887-3169-6*, 40904X4); 2000. audio 11.00 (*0-7887-3203-X*, 95652E7); Class set. 1999. stu. ed. 71.70 incl. audio (*0-7887-3215-3*, 46871) Recorded Bks., LLC.

—Junie B. Jones & Some Sneaky Peeky Spying. 1994. (Junie B. Jones Ser.: No. 4). (Illus.). (J). (gr. k-2). 10.14 (*0-606-07018-4*) Turtleback Bks.

—Junie B. Jones & That Meanie Jim's Birthday. 1996. (Junie B. Jones Ser.: No. 6). (Illus.). 96p. (gr. k-2). lib. bdg. 11.99 (*0-679-96695-1*); pap. 3.99 (*0-679-86695-7*) Random Hse., Inc.

—Junie B. Jones & That Meanie Jim's Birthday. 1996. (Junie B. Jones Ser.: No. 6). (Illus.). (J). (gr. k-2). 10.04 (*0-606-09499-7*) Turtleback Bks.

—Junie B. Jones & the Mushy Gushy Valentine. 1999. (Junie B. Jones Ser.: No. 14). (Illus.). 80p. (J). (gr. 1-4). pap. 3.99 (*0-375-80039-5*); lib. bdg. 11.99 (*0-375-90039-X*) Random Hse. Children's Bks. (Random Hse. Bks. for Young Readers).

—Junie B. Jones & the Mushy Gushy Valentine. 1999. (Junie B. Jones Ser.: No. 14). (J). (gr. k-2). 10.14 (*0-606-19516-5*) Turtleback Bks.

—Junie B. Jones & the Stupid Smelly Bus. unabr. ed. 2002. (Junie B. Jones Ser.: Vol. 1). 69p. (J). (gr. k-4). pap. 17.00 incl. audio (*0-8072-0778-0*, LFTR 237 SP, Listening Library) Random Hse. Audio Publishing Group.

—Junie B. Jones & the Stupid Smelly Bus. (Junie B. Jones Ser.: No. 1). (gr. k-2). 2001. (J). 14.99 (*0-375-81462-0*); 1992. (Illus.). 80p. (J). pap. 3.99 (*0-679-82642-4*); 1992. (Illus.). 80p. lib. bdg. 11.99 (*0-679-92642-9*) Random Hse. Children's Bks. (Random Hse. Bks. for Young Readers).

—Junie B. Jones & the Stupid Smelly Bus. 1999. (Junie B. Jones Ser.: No. 1). (Illus.). (J). (gr. k-2). 80p. pap. 1.99 o.s.i (*0-375-80599-0*); pap. 0.99 o.s.i (*0-375-80173-1*) Random Hse., Inc.

—Junie B. Jones & the Stupid Smelly Bus. unabr. ed. (Junie B. Jones Ser.: No. 1). (J). (gr. k-2). audio compact disk 12.00 (*0-7887-4940-4*, C1303E7); 1998. audio 10.00 (*0-7887-2267-0*, 95529E7) Recorded Bks., LLC.

—Junie B. Jones & the Stupid Smelly Bus. 1992. (Junie B. Jones Ser.: No. 1). (Illus.). (J). (gr. k-2). 10.14 (*0-606-02321-6*) Turtleback Bks.

—Junie B. Jones & the Yucky Blucky Fruitcake. 1995. (Junie B. Jones Ser.: No. 5). (Illus.). 80p. (gr. k-2). lib. bdg. 11.99 (*0-679-96694-3*, Random Hse. Bks. for Young Readers) Random Hse. Children's Bks.

—Junie B. Jones & the Yucky Blucky Fruitcake. 1995. (Junie B. Jones Ser.: No. 5). (Illus.). (J). (gr. k-2). 10.14 (*0-606-08557-2*) Turtleback Bks.

—Junie B. Jones Collection. unabr. ed. (ps-3). Bks. 1-4. 2002. (J). audio 18.00 (*0-8072-0682-2*); Bks. 5-8. 2001. (YA). audio 18.00 (*0-8072-0601-6*); Bks. 9-12. 2001. (J). audio 18.00 (*0-8072-0467-6*, LL0220); Bks. 13-16. 2001. (J). audio 23.00 (*0-8072-8840-3*, LL0221) Random Hse. Audio Publishing Group. (Listening Library).

—The Junie B. Jones Collection, Bks. 13-16. unabr. ed. 2001. (Junie B. Jones Ser.: Nos. 13-16). (J). (gr. k-2). audio 18.00 (*0-8072-6183-1*, LL0221, Listening Library) Random Hse. Audio Publishing Group.

—Junie B. Jones Collection. abr. ed. 2002. Bks. 17-20. (J). pap. 23.00 incl. audio (*0-8072-0965-1*); Nos. 17-20. (YA). audio 18.00 (*0-8072-0964-3*) Random Hse. Audio Publishing Group. (Listening Library).

—Junie B. Jones Collection Bks. 9-12, unabr. ed. 2001. (J). (gr. k-4). audio 23.00 (*0-8072-0524-9*, LL0220, Listening Library) Random Hse. Audio Publishing Group.

—Junie B. Jones Has a Monster under Her Bed. unabr. ed. 2001. (Junie B. Jones Ser.: No. 8). 69p. (J). (gr. k-4). pap. 17.00 incl. audio (*0-8072-0644-X*, Listening Library) Random Hse. Audio Publishing Group.

—Junie B. Jones Has a Monster under Her Bed. 2003. 31.92 o.s.i (*0-375-88380-0*, Golden Bks.) Random Hse. Children's Bks.

—Junie B. Jones Has a Monster under Her Bed. 1997. (Junie B. Jones Ser.: No. 8). (Illus.). 80p. (gr. k-2). lib. bdg. 11.99 (*0-679-96697-8*) Random Hse., Inc.

—Junie B. Jones Has a Monster under Her Bed. 1997. (Junie B. Jones Ser.: No. 8). (Illus.). (J). (gr. k-2). 10.14 (*0-606-11529-3*) Turtleback Bks.

—Junie B. Jones Has a Peep in Her Pocket. 2000. (Junie B. Jones Ser.: No. 15). (Illus.). 80p. (J). (gr. 1-4). lib. bdg. 11.99 (*0-375-90040-3*); (gr. k-2). pap. 3.99 (*0-375-80040-9*) Random Hse. Children's Bks. (Random Hse. Bks. for Young Readers).

—Junie B. Jones Has a Peep in Her Pocket. 2000. (Junie B. Jones Ser.: No. 15). (Illus.). (J). (gr. k-2). 10.14 (*0-606-18499-6*) Turtleback Bks.

—Junie B. Jones Is a Beauty Shop Guy. 1998. (Junie B. Jones Ser.: No. 11). (Illus.). 80p. (gr. k-2). (J). lib. bdg. 11.99 (*0-679-98931-5*); pap. 3.99 (*0-679-88931-0*) Random Hse. Children's Bks. (Random Hse. Bks. for Young Readers).

—Junie B. Jones Is a Beauty Shop Guy. 1998. (Junie B. Jones Ser.: No. 11). (Illus.). (J). (gr. k-2). 10.14 (*0-606-13963-X*) Turtleback Bks.

—Junie B. Jones Is a Graduation Girl. 2001. (Junie B. Jones Ser.: No. 17). (Illus.). 80p. (J). (gr. k-2). pap. 3.99 (*0-375-80292-4*, Random Hse. Bks. for Young Readers) Random Hse. Children's Bks.

—Junie B. Jones Is a Party Animal. 1997. (Junie B. Jones Ser.: No. 10). (Illus.). 80p. (gr. k-2). lib. bdg. 11.99 (*0-679-98663-4*); (J). pap. 3.99 (*0-679-88663-X*) Random Hse. Children's Bks. (Random Hse. Bks. for Young Readers).

—Junie B. Jones Is a Party Animal. 1997. (Junie B. Jones Ser.: No. 10). (Illus.). 80p. (J). (gr. k-2). pap. 3.99 (*0-679-86697-3*) Random Hse., Inc.

—Junie B. Jones Is a Party Animal. 1997. (Junie B. Jones Ser.: No. 10). (Illus.). (J). (gr. k-2). 10.14 (*0-606-12747-X*) Turtleback Bks.

—Junie B. Jones Is (Almost) a Flower Girl. 1999. (Junie B. Jones Ser.: No. 13). (Illus.). 80p. (gr. 1-4). lib. bdg. 11.99 (*0-375-90038-1*, Random Hse. Bks. for Young Readers) Random Hse. Children's Bks.

—Junie B. Jones Is (Almost) a Flower Girl. 1999. (Junie B. Jones Ser.: No. 13). (Illus.). 80p. (J). (gr. k-2). pap. 3.99 (*0-375-80038-7*) Random Hse., Inc.

—Junie B. Jones Is (Almost) a Flower Girl. 1999. (Junie B. Jones Ser.: No. 13). (J). (gr. k-2). 10.14 (*0-606-16840-0*) Turtleback Bks.

—Junie B. Jones Is Captain Field Day. 2001. (Junie B. Jones Ser.: No. 16). (Illus.). 80p. (J). (gr. 1-4). lib. bdg. 11.99 (*0-375-90291-0*); 16th ed. (gr. k-2). pap. 3.99 (*0-375-80291-6*) Random Hse. Children's Bks. (Random Hse. Bks. for Young Readers).

—Junie B. Jones Is Captain Field Day. 2000. (Junie B. Jones Ser.: No. 16). (J). (gr. k-2). 10.14 (*0-606-19899-7*) Turtleback Bks.

—Junie B. Jones Is Not a Crook. 1997. (Junie B. Jones Ser.: No. 9). (Illus.). 80p. (gr. k-2). lib. bdg. 11.99 (*0-679-98342-2*); pap. 3.99 (*0-679-88342-8*) Random Hse. Children's Bks. (Random Hse. Bks. for Young Readers).

—Junie B. Jones Is Not a Crook. 1997. (Junie B. Jones Ser.: No. 9). (Illus.). (J). (gr. k-2). 10.14 (*0-606-11530-7*) Turtleback Bks.

—Junie B. Jones Loves Handsome Warren. 1996. (Junie B. Jones Ser.: No. 7). (Illus.). 80p. (gr. k-2). lib. bdg. 11.99 (*0-679-96696-X*) Random Hse., Inc.

—Junie B. Jones Loves Handsome Warren. 1996. (Junie B. Jones Ser.: No. 7). (Illus.). (J). (gr. k-2). 10.14 (*0-606-10855-6*) Turtleback Bks.

—Junie B. Jones Second Boxed Set Ever!, Bks. 5-8. 2002. (J). (ps-3). 15.96 (*0-375-82265-8*) Random Hse., Inc.

—Junie B. Jones Smells Something Fishy. 1998. (Junie B. Jones Ser.: No. 12). (Illus.). 80p. (J). (gr. 1-4). lib. bdg. 11.99 (*0-679-99130-1*, Random Hse. Bks. for Young Readers) Random Hse. Children's Bks.

—Junie B. Jones Smells Something Fishy. 1998. (Junie B. Jones Ser.: No. 12). (Illus.). 80p. (J). (gr. k-2). pap. 3.99 (*0-679-89130-7*) Random Hse., Inc.

—Junie B. Jones Smells Something Fishy. 1998. (Junie B. Jones Ser.: No. 12). (J). (gr. k-2). 10.14 (*0-606-15598-8*) Turtleback Bks.

—Junie B. Jones's First Boxed Set Ever!, 4 bks., Set. 2001. (Junie B. Jones Ser.). (Illus.). (J). (gr. k-2). 15.96 (*0-375-81361-6*, Random Hse. Bks. for Young Readers) Random Hse. Children's Bks.

Park, Barbara, et al. Junie B. Jones & the Yucky Blucky Fruitcake. 1995. (Junie B. Jones Ser.: No. 5). (Illus.). 80p. (gr. k-2). pap. 3.99 (*0-679-86694-9*, Random Hse. Bks. for Young Readers) Random Hse. Children's Bks.

—Junie B. Jones Loves Handsome Warren. 1996. (Junie B. Jones Ser.: No. 7). (Illus.). 80p. (J). (gr. k-2). pap. 3.99 (*0-679-86696-5*) Random Hse., Inc.

K

KENOBI, OBI-WAN (FICTITIOUS CHARACTER)—FICTION

Covey, Stephen R. Star Wars. 1999. (Star Wars Ser.). 12p. pap. 1.79 o.s.i (*0-307-02223-4*, Golden Bks.) Random Hse. Children's Bks.

Davids, Paul & Davids, Hollace. Star Wars, 3 bks. l.t. ed. Incl. Prophets of the Dark Side. lib. bdg. 22.60 (*0-8368-1994-2*); Queen of the Empire. lib. bdg. 22.60 (*0-8368-1993-4*); Zorba the Hutt's Revenge. lib. bdg. 22.60 (*0-8368-1991-8*); 112p. (J). (gr. 4 up). 1997. Set lib. bdg. 67.80 (*0-8368-1988-8*) Stevens, Gareth Inc.

Disney Staff, ed. Star Wars: A New Hope: A Flip Book. 1997. (Star Wars Ser.). 40p. (J). 2.98 o.s.i (*1-57082-577-7*) Mouse Works.

Disney Staff & Steacy, Ken. Star Wars. 1997. (Star Wars Ser.). 24p. (J). 8.98 o.s.i (*1-57082-567-X*) Mouse Works.

Golden Books Staff. Star Wars: A New Hope. 1999. (Star Wars Ser.). 16p. (J). pap. 2.99 o.s.i (*0-307-10577-6*, Golden Bks.) Random Hse. Children's Bks.

—Star Wars: A New Hope: With Tattoos. 1999. (Star Wars Ser.). (Illus.). 24p. pap. 3.99 o.s.i (*0-307-13067-3*, Golden Bks.) Random Hse. Children's Bks.

Hildebrandt, Greg, et al, illus. Star Wars: Episode I:The Phantom Menace: Great Big Flap Book. 1999. 10p. (J). (ps-3). bds. 12.99 o.s.i (*0-375-80010-7*) Random Hse., Inc.

Lucas, George. The Phantom Menace Movie Storybook. 1999. (Star Wars). (Illus.). 64p. (J). (gr. k-3). pap. 7.99 o.s.i (*0-375-80009-3*) Random Hse., Inc.

Random House Staff. The Phantom Menace Movie Storybook. 1999. (Star Wars Episode I Ser.). (Illus.). 64p. (YA). (gr. k up). 11.99 o.s.i (*0-375-90009-8*, Random Hse. Bks. for Young Readers) Random Hse. Children's Bks.

Snyder, Margaret. Star Wars: A More Wretched Hive. 1999. (Star Wars Ser.). 32p. (J). (ps-3). pap. 4.99 o.s.i (*0-307-13552-7*, Golden Bks.) Random Hse. Children's Bks.

Thomas, Jim K. Star Wars: Luke's Fate. 1996. (Step into Reading Ser.). (Illus.). 48p. (J). (gr. 2-3). pap. 3.99 (*0-679-85855-5*) Random Hse., Inc.

Watson, Jude. Captive Temple. 2000. (Star Wars Ser.: Bk. 7). (Illus.). 144p. (J). (gr. 4-7). mass mkt. 4.99 (*0-590-51970-0*) Scholastic, Inc.

—Captive Temple. 2000. (Star Wars Ser.: Bk. 7). (J). (gr. 4-7). 11.04 (*0-606-19619-6*) Turtleback Bks.

—The Dangerous Games. unabr. ed. 2003. (star wars: No. 3). (J). (gr. 3). audio compact disk 19.99 (*0-8072-1043-9*, RH Audio) Random Hse. Audio Publishing Group.

—The Dangerous Games. 2002. (Star Wars Ser.: No. 3). 144p. (YA). mass mkt. 4.99 (*0-439-33919-7*) Scholastic, Inc.

—The Dark Rival. 1999. (Star Wars Ser.: Bk. 2). 122p. (J). (gr. 4-7). mass mkt. 4.99 o.s.i (*0-590-51925-5*) Scholastic, Inc.

—The Day of Reckoning. 2000. (Star Wars Ser.: Bk. 8). (Illus.). 144p. (J). (gr. 4-7). mass mkt. 4.99 (*0-590-52079-2*) Scholastic, Inc.

—The Defenders of the Dead. 1999. (Star Wars Ser.: Bk. 5). 140p. (J). (gr. 4-7). mass mkt. 4.99 (*0-590-51956-5*) Scholastic, Inc.

—The Fight for Truth. 2000. (Star Wars Ser.: Bk. 9). (Illus.). 144p. (J). (gr. 4-7). mass mkt. 4.99 (*0-590-52080-6*) Scholastic, Inc.

—The Fight for Truth. 2000. (Star Wars: Bk. 9). (J). (gr. 4-7). 11.04 (*0-606-19621-8*) Turtleback Bks.

—The Hidden Past. 1999. (Star Wars Ser.: Bk. 3). (Illus.). 138p. (J). (gr. 4-7). mass mkt. 4.99 (*0-590-51933-6*) Scholastic, Inc.

—The Hidden Past. 1999. (Star Wars: No. 3). (J). (gr. 4-7). 11.04 (*0-606-17040-5*) Turtleback Bks.

—Mark of the Crown. 1999. (Star Wars Ser.: Bk. 4). 131p. (J). (gr. 4-7). mass mkt. 4.99 (*0-590-51934-4*) Scholastic, Inc.

—Mark of the Crown. 1999. (Star Wars: Bk. 4). (J). (gr. 4-7). 11.04 (*0-606-19617-X*) Turtleback Bks.

—The Shattered Peace. 2000. (Star Wars Ser.: Bk. 10). (Illus.). 144p. (J). (gr. 3-7). mass mkt. 4.99 (*0-590-52084-9*) Scholastic, Inc.

—The Shattered Peace. 2000. (Star Wars: Bk. 10). (J). (gr. 4-7). 11.04 (*0-606-19615-3*) Turtleback Bks.

—The Uncertain Path. 2000. (Star Wars Ser.: Bk. 6). (Illus.). 144p. (J). (gr. 4-7). mass mkt. 4.99 (*0-590-51969-7*) Scholastic, Inc.

—The Uncertain Path. 2000. (Star Wars: Bk. 6). (J). (gr. 4-7). 11.04 (*0-606-19618-8*) Turtleback Bks.

Wolverton, Dave. The Rising Force. 1999. (Star Wars Ser.: Bk. 1). 171p. (J). (gr. 4-7). mass mkt. 4.99 (*0-590-51922-0*) Scholastic, Inc.

—The Rising Force. 1999. (Star Wars: No. 1). (J). (gr. 4-7). 11.04 (*0-606-16649-1*) Turtleback Bks.

Wrede, Patricia C. Star Wars: Episode I: The Phantom Menace. 1999. (J). (Illus.). 178p. (gr. 3-7). mass mkt. 5.99 (*0-590-01089-1*); mass mkt. 9.95 (*0-439-08706-6*) Scholastic, Inc.

KEY, FRANCIS SCOTT, 1779-1843—FICTION

Mandrell, Louise & Collins, Ace. Sunrise over the Harbor: A Story about the Meaning of Independence Day. 1993. (Children's Holiday Adventure Ser.: Vol. 16). (Illus.). 32p. (J). (ps-3). 12.95 o.p. (*1-56530-040-8*) Summit Publishing Group - Legacy Bks.

Sargent, Dave & Sargent, Pat. Chet (chestnut) Be Optimistic #15. 2001. (Saddle Up Ser.). 36p. (J). pap. 6.95 (*1-56763-610-1*); lib. bdg. 22.60 (*1-56763-609-8*) Ozark Publishing.

Winstead, Amy. The Star-Spangled Banner. Dacey, Bob & Bandelin, Debra, trs. 2003. (Illus.). 32p. (J). 16.95 (*0-8249-5462-9*, Ideals Pr.) Ideals Pubns.

KIDD, WILLIAM, D. 1701—FICTION

Lawson, Robert. Captain Kidd's Cat. 1984. (Illus.). (J). (gr. 2-4). mass mkt. 7.95 (*0-316-51735-6*) Little Brown & Co.

Lourie, Peter. The Lost Treasure of Captain Kidd. 2003. (Illus.). 96p. (J). (gr. 4-7). pap. 8.95 (*1-56397-851-2*) Boyds Mills Pr.

—The Lost Treasure of Captain Kidd. 1996. (Illus.). 157p. (J). (gr. 3 up). pap. 10.95 (*1-885482-03-5*) Shawangunk Pr., Inc.

KIPPER (FICTITIOUS CHARACTER)—FICTION

Inkpen, Mick. Hissss! 2000. (Kipper Ser.). (Illus.). 24p. (J). (ps-2). pap. 4.95 (*0-15-202415-8*, Red Wagon Bks.) Harcourt Children's Bks.

—Kipper. 2002. (Illus.). (J). 13.15 (*0-7587-6464-2*) Book Wholesalers, Inc.

—Kipper. 1999. (Kipper Ser.). (Illus.). 32p. (J). (ps-3). pap. 5.95 (*0-15-202294-5*, Red Wagon Bks.) Harcourt Children's Bks.

—Kipper. 1992. (J). (ps-3). 14.95 o.p. (*0-316-41883-8*) Little Brown & Co.

—Kipper. 1995. (Illus.). 32p. (J). (*1-85430-331-7*); (*1-85430-328-7*) Magi Multicultural Bks.

—Kipper. (Illus.). (J). (ENG & FRE.). 32p. (*1-85430-330-9*, 93450); (CHI & ENG., 43p. o.p. (*1-85430-329-5*, 93449); (ENG & VIE., 32p. (*1-85430-333-3*, 93451) Magi Pubns.

—Kipper. 1999. 12.10 (*0-606-17487-7*) Turtleback Bks.

—Kipper Books, 4 bks., set. 1995. 24.00 (*0-15-201273-7*) Harcourt Trade Pubs.

—Kipper Has a Party. 2000. (Kipper Ser.). (Illus.). 12p. (J). (ps-3). pap. 4.95 (*0-15-202697-5*, Red Wagon Bks.) Harcourt Children's Bks.

—Kipper in the Snow. 2000. (Kipper Ser.). (Illus.). 12p. (J). (ps-3). pap. 4.95 (*0-15-202400-X*, Red Wagon Bks.) Harcourt Children's Bks.

—Kipper Plush Toy. 1995. (J). (ps-3). 13.95 (*0-15-200546-3*, Red Wagon Bks.) Harcourt Children's Bks.

—Kipper's A to Z. 2001. (Kipper Ser.). (Illus.). 64p. (J). (ps-2). 16.95 (*0-15-202594-4*, Red Wagon Bks.) Harcourt Children's Bks.

—Kipper's Bathtime. 2000. (Kipper Ser.). (Illus.). 12p. (J). (ps). bds. 7.95 (*0-15-202694-0*, Red Wagon Bks.) Harcourt Children's Bks.

—Kipper's Bedtime. 2000. (Kipper Ser.). (Illus.). 12p. (J). (ps). bds. 7.95 (*0-15-202403-4*, Red Wagon Bks.) Harcourt Children's Bks.

—Kipper's Birthday. (Kipper Ser.). (Illus.). 28p. (ps-2). 2000. (J). pap. 5.95 (*0-15-202397-6*, Red Wagon Bks.); 1993. (C). 13.95 o.s.i (*0-15-200503-X*, Gulliver Bks.) Harcourt Children's Bks.

—Kipper's Birthday. 2000. (Illus.). (J). 12.10 (*0-606-18181-4*) Turtleback Bks.

—Kipper's Book of Colors. (Kipper Ser.). (Illus.). (J). (ps). 1999. 20p. bds. 4.95 (*0-15-202285-6*); 1995. 28p. 6.00 o.s.i (*0-15-200647-8*) Harcourt Children's Bks. (Red Wagon Bks.).

—Kipper's Book of Numbers. 2002. (Kipper Ser.). (Illus.). (J). 13.19 (*0-7587-6465-0*) Book Wholesalers, Inc.

—Kipper's Book of Numbers. (Kipper Ser.). (Illus.). (J). (ps). 1999. 20p. bds. 4.95 (*0-15-202286-4*); 1995. 28p. 6.00 o.s.i (*0-15-200646-X*) Harcourt Children's Bks. (Red Wagon Bks.).

—Kipper's Book of Opposites. 2002. (Kipper Ser.). (Illus.). (J). 13.19 (*0-7587-6466-9*) Book Wholesalers, Inc.

—Kipper's Book of Opposites. (Kipper Ser.). (Illus.). (J). (ps-k). 1999. 16p. bds. 4.95 (*0-15-202297-X*); 1995. 28p. 6.00 o.s.i (*0-15-200668-0*) Harcourt Children's Bks. (Red Wagon Bks.).

—Kipper's Book of Weather. (Kipper Ser.). (Illus.). (J). (ps-k). 1999. 16p. bds. 4.95 (*0-15-202295-3*); 1995. 24p. 6.00 o.s.i (*0-15-200644-3*) Harcourt Children's Bks. (Red Wagon Bks.).

—Kipper's Christmas Eve. 2000. (Kipper Ser.). (Illus.). 32p. (J). (ps-3). 13.95 (*0-15-202660-6*, Red Wagon Bks.) Harcourt Children's Bks.

—Kipper's Kite. 2002. (Kipper Ser.). (Illus.). 10p. (J). bds. 7.95 (*0-15-216607-6*, Red Wagon Bks.) Harcourt Children's Bks.

—Kipper's Playtime. 2000. (Kipper Ser.). (Illus.). 12p. (J). (ps). bds. 7.95 (*0-15-202421-2*, Red Wagon Bks.) Harcourt Children's Bks.

—Kipper's Rainy Day. 2001. (Kipper Ser.). (Illus.). 12p. (J). (ps-k). bds. 5.95 (*0-15-216351-4*, Red Wagon Bks.) Harcourt Children's Bks.

—Kipper's Snacktime. 2000. (Kipper Ser.). (Illus.). 12p. (J). (ps). bds. 7.95 (*0-15-202433-6*, Red Wagon Bks.) Harcourt Children's Bks.

—Kipper's Snowy Day. 2002. (Kipper Ser.). (Illus.). (J). 13.15 (*0-7587-2935-9*) Book Wholesalers, Inc.

—Kipper's Snowy Day. (Kipper Ser.). (Illus.). 32p. (J). (ps-3). 1999. pap. 5.95 (*0-15-202303-8*, Red Wagon Bks.); 1996. 14.00 (*0-15-201362-8*) Harcourt Children's Bks.

—Kipper's Snowy Day. 1996. (BEN, CHI, ENG, FRE & PAN., Illus.). 32p. (J). (*1-85430-513-1*); (*1-85430-512-3*); (*1-85430-514-X*); (*1-85430-516-6*); (*1-85430-517-4*); (*1-85430-515-8*) Magi Pubns.

—Kipper's Snowy Day. 1999. 12.10 (*0-606-17488-5*) Turtleback Bks.

—Kipper's Sunny Day. 2001. (Kipper Ser.). (Illus.). 12p. (J). (ps-k). bds. 5.95 (*0-15-216357-3*, Red Wagon Bks.) Harcourt Children's Bks.

—Kipper's Surprise. 2002. (Kipper Ser.). (Illus.). 10p. (J). bds. 7.95 (*0-15-216615-7*, Red Wagon Bks.) Harcourt Children's Bks.

—Kipper's Toybox. 2002. (Kipper Ser.). (Illus.). (J). 13.15 (*0-7587-6467-7*) Book Wholesalers, Inc.

—Kipper's Toybox. (Kipper Ser.). (Illus.). 28p. (J). (ps-2). 2000. pap. 5.95 (*0-15-202427-1*, Red Wagon Bks.); 1992. 13.95 o.s.i (*0-15-200501-3*, Gulliver Bks.) Harcourt Children's Bks.

—Kipper's Toybox. (BEN, CHI, ENG, FRE & PAN., Illus.). 25p. (J). 1995. (*1-85430-349-X*); 1995. o.p. (*1-85430-353-8*); o.p. (*1-85430-352-X*); (*1-85430-351-1*, 93453); (*1-85430-350-3*, 93452) Magi Pubns.

—Kipper's Toybox. 1997. (BEN, CHI, ENG, FRE & PAN., Illus.). 25p. (J). 34.20 (*1-85430-354-6*, 93454) Magi Pubns. GBR. *Dist:* Midpoint Trade Bks., Inc.

—Kipper's Toybox. 2000. (Illus.). (J). 12.10 (*0-606-18182-2*) Turtleback Bks.

—Swing. 2000. (Kipper Ser.). (Illus.). 24p. (J). (ps-3). pap. 4.95 (*0-15-202672-X*, Red Wagon Bks.) Harcourt Children's Bks.

—Where, Oh Where, Is Kipper's Bear? 1995. (Illus.). 16p. (J). (ps-k). 15.95 (*0-15-200394-0*, Red Wagon Bks.) Harcourt Children's Bks.

—Where, Oh Where, Is Kipper's Bear? (C). 1997. 16.00 o.s.i (*0-15-201807-7*); 1995. 16.00 o.s.i (*0-15-202688-6*) Harcourt Trade Pubs.

KUBLAI KHAN, 1216-1294—FICTION

McCaughrean, Geraldine. The Kite Rider. (J). (gr. 7 up). 2003. (Illus.). 320p. pap. 6.99 (*0-06-441091-9*); 2002. 288p. lib. bdg. 16.89 (*0-06-623875-7*) HarperCollins Children's Bk. Group.

—The Kite Rider. 2002. (Illus.). 288p. (J). (gr. 7 up). 15.95 (*0-06-623874-9*) HarperCollins Pubs.

L

LAFITTE, JEAN, 1782-1854—FICTION

Dewey, Ariane. Lafitte, the Pirate. 1993. (Illus.). 48p. (J). (gr. 1 up). pap. 4.95 o.p. (*0-688-04578-2*, Morrow, William & Co.) Morrow/Avon.

Fox, Frank G. Jean Laffite & the Big Ol' Whale, RS. 2003. (Illus.). 32p. (J). 16.00 (*0-374-33669-5*, Farrar, Straus & Giroux (BYR)) Farrar, Straus & Giroux.

LA FORGE, GEORDI (FICTITIOUS CHARACTER)—FICTION

Ferguson, Brad. The Haunted Spaceship. 1999. (Star Trek, The Next Generation: No. 13). (J). (gr. 3-6). (*0-613-10125-1*) Econo-Clad Bks.

—The Haunted Spaceship. 1997. (Star Trek Ser.: No. 13). (Illus.). 128p. (J). (gr. 3-6). pap. 3.99 (*0-671-01432-3*, Aladdin) Simon & Schuster Children's Publishing.

Mitchell, V. E. Atlantis Station. 1994. (Star Trek, The Next Generation: No. 5). 128p. (J). (gr. 4-7). per. 3.99 (*0-671-88449-2*, Aladdin) Simon & Schuster Children's Publishing.

—Atlantis Station. 1994. (Star Trek, The Next Generation: No. 5). (J). (gr. 3-6). 9.09 o.p. (*0-606-11904-3*) Turtleback Bks.

Vornholt, John. Capture the Flag. Clancy, Lisa, ed. 1994. (Star Trek Ser.: No. 4). (Illus.). 128p. (J). (gr. 4-7). pap. 3.99 (*0-671-87998-7*, Aladdin) Simon & Schuster Children's Publishing.

—Capture the Flag. 1994. (Star Trek, The Next Generation: No. 4). (J). (gr. 3-6). 10.04 (*0-606-11903-5*) Turtleback Bks.

—Crossfire. 1996. (Star Trek, The Next Generation: No. 11). (J). (gr. 3-6). 9.09 o.p. (*0-606-11901-9*) Turtleback Bks.

—First Contact. 1996. (Star Trek Ser.: No. 8). (J). (ps-3). 10.04 (*0-606-11883-7*) Turtleback Bks.

Vornholt, John, et al. First Contact. 1996. (Star Trek Ser.: No. 8). (Illus.). 128p. (J). (gr. 8 up). per. 3.99 (*0-671-00128-0*, Aladdin) Simon & Schuster Children's Publishing.

LEIA, PRINCESS (FICTITIOUS CHARACTER)—FICTION

Covey, Stephen R. Star Wars. 1999. (Star Wars Ser.). 12p. pap. 1.79 o.s.i (*0-307-02223-4*, Golden Bks.) Random Hse. Children's Bks.

Dana, Michael. Star Wars: The Greatest Battles. 1999. (Star Wars Ser.). (Illus.). 16p. (J). pap. 3.99 o.s.i (*0-307-14656-1*, Golden Bks.) Random Hse. Children's Bks.

Davids, Paul. The Adventure Continues Boxed Set: The Glove of Darth Vader; the Lost City of the Jedi; Zorba the Hutt's Revenge. 1997. (Star Wars: Nos. 1-3). (J). (gr. 2-8). 12.48 o.s.i (*0-553-62866-6*, Dell Books for Young Readers) Random Hse. Children's Bks.

—The Glove of Darth Vader. 1996. (Star Wars: Bk. 1). (J). (gr. 4-7). pap. 4.99 (*0-553-54282-6*, Dell Books for Young Readers) Random Hse. Children's Bks.

—The Glove of Darth Vader. 1992. (Star Wars: Bk. 1). (J). (gr. 4-7). 9.09 o.p. (*0-606-00535-8*) Turtleback Bks.

—Mission from Mount Yoda. 1999. (Star Wars: Bk. 4). (J). (gr. 4-7). pap. 9.50 o.p. (*0-7607-0447-3*) Barnes & Noble, Inc.

—The Mission from Mount Yoda. 1993. (Star Wars Ser.: Bk. 4). 128p. (YA). (gr. 4-7). pap. 4.50 o.s.i (*0-553-15890-2*) Bantam Bks.

—Prophets of the Dark Side. 1993. (Star Wars: Bk. 6). 128p. (gr. 4-7). pap. text 4.50 (*0-553-15892-9*) Bantam Bks.

—The Queen of the Empire. 1993. (Star Wars: Bk. 5). 128p. (YA). (gr. 4-7). pap. 4.50 o.s.i (*0-553-15891-0*) Bantam Bks.

Davids, Paul & Davids, Hollace. The Glove of Darth Vader. 1992. (Star Wars: Bk. 1). (Illus.). 128p. (gr. 4-7). pap. text 4.50 (*0-553-15887-2*, Starfire) Random Hse. Children's Bks.

—The Glove of Darth Vader. l.t. ed. 1997. 112p. (J). (gr. 4 up). lib. bdg. 22.60 o.p. (*0-8368-1989-6*) Stevens, Gareth Inc.

—The Glove of Darth Vader. 1992. 10.04 (*0-606-14216-9*) Turtleback Bks.

—The Lost City of the Jedi. 1999. (Star Wars Ser.: Bk. 2). (Illus.). 94p. (J). (gr. 4-7). reprint ed. pap. 10.00 (*0-7881-6480-5*) DIANE Publishing Co.

—The Lost City of the Jedi. 1992. (Star Wars: Bk. 2). 128p. (gr. 4-7). pap. text 4.50 (*0-553-15888-0*, Starfire) Random Hse. Children's Bks.

—The Lost City of the Jedi. l.t. ed. 1997. 112p. (J). (gr. 4 up). lib. bdg. 22.60 o.p. (*0-8368-1990-X*) Stevens, Gareth Inc.

—The Lost City of the Jedi. 1992. (Star Wars: Bk. 2). (J). (gr. 4-7). 10.55 (*0-606-00543-9*) Turtleback Bks.

—Mission from Mount Yoda. l.t. ed. 1997. 112p. (J). (gr. 4 up). lib. bdg. 22.60 o.p. (*0-8368-1992-6*) Stevens, Gareth Inc.

—Mission from Mount Yoda. 1993. (Star Wars: Bk. 4). (J). (gr. 4-7). 10.55 (*0-606-02755-6*) Turtleback Bks.

—Prophets of the Dark Side. l.t. ed. 1997. (Star Wars Ser.: No. 6). 112p. (J). (gr. 4 up). lib. bdg. 22.60 (*0-8368-1994-2*) Stevens, Gareth Inc.

—Prophets of the Dark Side. 1993. (Star Wars: Bk. 6). (J). (gr. 4-7). 10.55 (*0-606-05557-6*) Turtleback Bks.

—Queen of the Empire. l.t. ed. 1997. (Star Wars Ser.: No. 5). 112p. (J). (gr. 4 up). lib. bdg. 22.60 (*0-8368-1993-4*) Stevens, Gareth Inc.

—Queen of the Empire. 1993. (Star Wars: Bk. 5). (J). (gr. 4-7). 10.55 (*0-606-02849-8*) Turtleback Bks.

—Star Wars, 3 bks. l.t. ed. Incl. Prophets of the Dark Side. lib. bdg. 22.60 (*0-8368-1994-2*); Queen of the Empire. lib. bdg. 22.60 (*0-8368-1993-4*); Zorba the Hutt's Revenge. lib. bdg. 22.60 (*0-8368-1991-8*); 112p. (J). (gr. 4 up). 1997. Set lib. bdg. 67.80 (*0-8368-1988-8*) Stevens, Gareth Inc.

—Zorba the Hutt's Revenge. 1992. (Star Wars: Bk. 3). 128p. (gr. 4-7). pap. text 4.50 (*0-553-15889-9*) Bantam Bks.

—Zorba the Hutt's Revenge. l.t. ed. 1997. (Star Wars Ser.: No. 3). 112p. (J). (gr. 4 up). lib. bdg. 22.60 (*0-8368-1991-8*) Stevens, Gareth Inc.

—Zorba the Hutt's Revenge. 1992. (Star Wars: Bk. 3). (J). (gr. 4-7). 10.55 (*0-606-00544-7*) Turtleback Bks.

Disney Staff, ed. The Empire Strikes Back. (Read Along Star Wars Ser.). (J). 7.99 incl. audio (*0-7634-0194-3*) Walt Disney Records.

—The Empire Strikes Back: A Flip Book. 1997. 40p. (J). 2.98 o.s.i (*1-57082-578-5*) Mouse Works.

—Return of the Jedi. (Read Along Star Wars Ser.). (J). 7.99 incl. audio (*0-7634-0193-5*); 14.99 incl. audio (*0-7634-0196-X*) Walt Disney Records.

—Star Wars: A New Hope: A Flip Book. 1997. (Star Wars Ser.). 40p. (J). 2.98 o.s.i (*1-57082-577-7*) Mouse Works.

Disney Staff & Steacy, Ken. Star Wars. 1997. (Star Wars Ser.). 24p. (J). 8.98 o.s.i (*1-57082-567-X*) Mouse Works.

Gardner, J. J. Return of the Jedi Storybook. 1997. (Illus.). (J). (gr. 5-7). mass mkt. 5.99 (*0-590-06659-5*) Scholastic, Inc.

Golden Books Staff. The Empire Strikes Back: With Tattoos. 1999. (Star Wars Ser.). (Illus.). 24p. pap. 3.99 o.s.i (*0-307-13068-1*, Golden Bks.) Random Hse. Children's Bks.

—Star Wars: A New Hope. 1999. (Star Wars Ser.). 16p. (J). pap. 2.99 o.s.i (*0-307-10577-6*, Golden Bks.) Random Hse. Children's Bks.

—Star Wars: Battling the Empire. 1997. (Extra Smart Pages Ser.). 14p. (J). o.p. (*0-307-75704-8*, Golden Bks.) Random Hse. Children's Bks.

—Star Wars: A New Hope: With Tattoos. 1999. (Star Wars Ser.). (Illus.). 24p. pap. 3.99 o.s.i (*0-307-13067-3*, Golden Bks.) Random Hse. Children's Bks.

Golden, Christopher. The Empire Strikes Back. 1998. (Choose Your Own Star Wars Adventure Ser.). 128p. (gr. 4-8). pap. text 4.50 o.s.i (*0-553-48652-7*, Dell Books for Young Readers) Random Hse. Children's Bks.

Lakin, Patty & Golden Books Staff. Princess Leia's Escape from the Death Star: Star Wars Spelling Story Workbook. 1999. (Star Wars Ser.). 48p. (J). pap., wbk. ed. 3.99 o.s.i (*0-307-21304-8*, Golden Bks.) Random Hse. Children's Bks.

Levy, Elizabeth, ed. Return of the Jedi Step-Up Movie Adventure. 1983. (Star Wars Ser.). (Illus.). 72p. (J). (gr. 1-3). 8.99 o.s.i (*0-394-96117-X*, Random Hse. Bks. for Young Readers) Random Hse. Children's Bks.

Lucas, George. The Empire Strikes Back Adventures. abr. ed. 1994. (J). (gr. k-3). audio 8.98 o.p. Time Warner AudioBooks.

—Return of the Jedi: A Flip Book. 1997. (Star Wars Ser.). 40p. (J). 2.98 o.s.i (*1-57082-579-3*) Mouse Works.

Scholastic, Inc. Staff, ed. The Empire Strikes Back. 9999. (J). pap. 2.50 o.s.i (*0-590-31791-1*) Scholastic, Inc.

—Return of the Jedi. 9999. (J). pap. 2.95 o.s.i (*0-590-32929-4*) Scholastic, Inc.

Steacy, Ken. Princess Leia, Rebel Leader. 1999. (Star Wars Ser.). 24p. (J). pap. 3.29 o.s.i (*0-307-10105-3*, Golden Bks.) Random Hse. Children's Bks.

Vaz, Mark Cotta. The Star Wars Trilogy Scrapbook: The Rebel Alliance. 1997. 48p. (gr. 4-7). mass mkt. 6.99 (*0-590-12051-4*) Scholastic, Inc.

Vinge, Joan D., adapted by. Return of the Jedi: The Storybook Based on the Movie. 1983. (Storybook Based on the Movie Ser.). (Illus.). 64p. (J). (gr. 3-8). 7.99 o.p. (*0-394-95624-9*, Random Hse. Bks. for Young Readers) Random Hse. Children's Bks.

Whitman, John. Return of the Jedi. 1996. (Mighty Chronicles Ser.). (Illus.). 316p. (gr. 4-7). 9.95 o.s.i (*0-8118-1494-7*) Chronicle Bks. LLC.

Whitman, John, adapted by. The Empire Strikes Back. 1996. (Mighty Chronicles Ser.). (Illus.). 432p. (gr. 4-7). 9.95 o.s.i (*0-8118-1482-3*) Chronicle Bks. LLC.

LEONARDO, DA VINCI, 1452-1519—FICTION

Anholt, Laurence. Leonardo & the Flying Boy: A Story about Leonardo da Vinci. 2000. (Illus.). 32p. (J). (ps-2). pap. 14.95 (*0-7641-5225-4*) Barron's Educational Series, Inc.

Bradford, Emma. Kat & the Missing Notebooks. 1999. (Stardust Classics: No. 4). (Illus.). 119p. (J). (gr. 2-5). 12.95 (*1-889514-27-6*); pap. 5.95 (*1-889514-28-4*) Dolls Corp.

Konigsburg, E. L. The Second Mrs. Giaconda. 3rd ed. (J). pap. text 4.95 (*0-13-800061-1*) Prentice Hall (Schl. Div.).

—The Second Mrs. Giaconda. 160p. (J). (gr. 5-9). 1998. pap. 4.99 (*0-689-82121-2*); 1978. (Illus.). pap. 5.95 (*0-689-70450-X*) Simon & Schuster Children's Publishing. (Aladdin).

—The Second Mrs. Giaconda. 1998. 11.04 (*0-606-16213-5*) Turtleback Bks.

Mayhew, James. Katie & the Mona Lisa. 1999. (Illus.). 32p. (J). (ps-2). pap. 15.95 (*0-531-30177-X*, Orchard Bks.) Scholastic, Inc.

Sabuda, Robert. Uh Oh Leonardo. 2003. (Illus.). 48p. (J). 16.95 (*0-689-81160-8*, Atheneum) Simon & Schuster Children's Publishing.

Woodruff, Elvira. The Disappearing Bike Shop. 1994. 176p. (J). (gr. 4-7). pap. 3.99 o.s.i (*0-440-40938-1*) Dell Publishing.

—The Disappearing Bike Shop. 1992. 176p. (J). (gr. 3-7). 13.95 o.p. (*0-8234-0933-3*) Holiday Hse., Inc.

LINCOLN, ABRAHAM, 1809-1865—FICTION

Abe Lincoln & the Colonel. 1992. (Teddy Ser.). (J). (gr. 1-2). pap. text 2.95 (*0-9636154-1-6*) Teddy & Friends.

Borden, Louise. A. Lincoln & Me. 1999. (Illus.). 32p. (J). (ps-3). pap. 15.95 (*0-590-45714-4*) Scholastic, Inc.

Brenner, Martha. Abe Lincoln's Hat. 1994. (Step into Reading Step 2 Bks.). (J). (gr. 1-3). 10.14 (*0-606-06909-7*) Turtleback Bks.

Caseley, Judith. Praying to A. L. 2000. 64p. (J). (gr. 5 up). 15.95 (*0-688-15934-6*, Greenwillow Bks.) HarperCollins Children's Bk. Group.

Dunn, Anne M. Grandmother's Gift: Stories from the Anishinabeg. 1997. 160p. (J). pap. text 12.95 (*0-930100-72-7*) Holy Cow! Pr.

Fife, Dale. Who's in Charge of Lincoln? 1965. (Illus.). 61p. (J). (gr. 2-4). 5.99 o.p. (*0-698-30406-3*) Putnam Publishing Group, The.

Gormley, Beatrice. Back to the Day Lincoln Was Shot. 1996. (Travelers Through Time Ser.: No. 3). (J). (gr. 3-7). mass mkt. 4.50 (*0-590-46228-8*) Scholastic, Inc.

—Back to the Day Lincoln Was Shot. 1996. (Travelers Through Time Ser.). (J). 10.04 (*0-606-09986-7*) Turtleback Bks.

Lewis, Catherine. Postcards to Father Abraham. 2000. (Illus.). 304p. (YA). (gr. 7-12). 17.95 (*0-689-82852-7*, Atheneum) Simon & Schuster Children's Publishing.

McGovern, Ann. If You Grew up with Abraham Lincoln. 1992. (SPA., Illus.). 80p. (J). (gr. 4-7). pap. 5.99 (*0-590-45154-5*) Scholastic, Inc.

Osborne, Mary Pope. After the Rain: Virginia's Civil War Diary, Bk. 2. 2002. (My America Ser.). 112p. (J). (gr. 2-5). pap. 8.95 o.s.i (*0-439-20138-1*); (Illus.). mass mkt. 4.99 (*0-439-36904-5*) Scholastic, Inc. (Scholastic Pr.).

Pinkney, Andrea Davis. Abraham Lincoln: Letters from a Young Slave Girl. 2001. (Dear Mr. President Ser.). (Illus.). 136p. (J). (gr. 4-7). 8.95 (*1-890817-60-0*) Winslow Pr.

Porter, Connie Rose. Addy Studies Freedom. 2002. (American Girls Short Stories Ser.). (Illus.). 64p. (J). 4.95 (*1-58485-480-4*, American Girl) Pleasant Co. Pubns.

Rinaldi, Ann. An Acquaintance with Darkness. 1997. (Great Episodes Ser.). 304p. (YA). (gr. 7 up). 16.00 (*0-15-201294-X*, Gulliver Bks.) Harcourt Children's Bks.

Robinet, Harriette Gillem. If You Please, President Lincoln! 1995. 160p. (J). (gr. 4-7). 16.00 o.s.i (*0-689-31969-X*, Atheneum) Simon & Schuster Children's Publishing.

Sandburg, Carl. Abe Lincoln Grows Up. 1975. (Voyager Bks.). (J). 13.05 (*0-606-01801-8*) Turtleback Bks.

Sargent, Dave & Sargent, Pat. Cassidy (Dark Buckskin) Equal Rights for All #11. 2001. 36p. (J). pap. (*1-56763-670-5*); lib. bdg. 22.60 (*1-56763-669-1*) Ozark Publishing.

Stevenson, Augusta. George Washington & Abraham Lincoln. 2003. (Childhood of Famous Americans Ser.). (Illus.). 384p. (J). pap. 6.99 (*0-689-85624-5*, Aladdin) Simon & Schuster Children's Publishing.

Waber, Bernard. Just Like Abraham Lincoln, 001. 1974. (Illus.). (J). (gr. 1-5). 6.95 o.p. (*0-395-20107-1*) Houghton Mifflin Co.

Walters, Helen B. No Luck for Lincoln. 1981. 160p. (J). (gr. 3-4). 8.75 o.p. (*0-687-28030-3*) Abingdon Pr.

Winnick, Karen B. Mr. Lincoln's Whiskers. 2003. (Illus.). 32p. (J). (gr. k-3). 8.95 (*1-56397-805-9*); pap. 15.95 (*1-56397-485-1*) Boyds Mills Pr.

—Mr. Lincoln's Whiskers. 1998. 14.10 (*0-606-17334-X*) Turtleback Bks.

LINCOLN, NANCY (HANKS), 1784-1818—FICTION

Le Sueur, Meridel. Nancy Hanks of Wilderness Road: A Story of Abraham Lincoln's Mother. 2004. 80p. (J). (gr. 5-7). pap. 7.95 (*0-930100-73-5*) Holy Cow! Pr.

—Nancy Hanks of Wilderness Road: A Story of Abraham Lincoln's Mother. 1967. (Illus.). (J). (gr. 3-7). lib. bdg. 5.39 o.p. (*0-394-91445-7*, Knopf Bks. for Young Readers) Random Hse. Children's Bks.

LITTLE, STUART (FICTITIOUS CHARACTER)—FICTION

Downes, Alice. Soccer Season. 2002. (Stuart-Little Ser.). (Illus.). 24p. (J). (ps-2). pap. 3.25 (*0-06-000185-2*) HarperCollins Children's Bk. Group.

Driscoll, Laura. Stuart Little: A Little Too Fast. 2004. (Festival Reader Ser.). (Illus.). 32p. (J). pap. 3.99 (*0-06-000752-4*, Harper Festival) HarperCollins Children's Bk. Group.

Hill, Susan. Stuart Little. 2003. (Illus.). (J). (gr. k-3). pap. 11.97 (*0-06-053915-1*) HarperCollins Children's Bk. Group.

Richardson, Julia. Stuart Little 2: Stuart Little's Big Adventures. 2002. (Stuart-Little Ser.). (Illus.). 24p. (J). (ps-2). pap. 3.25 (*0-06-000186-0*) HarperCollins Children's Bk. Group.

Stuart Little 2. novel ed. 2002. (Illus.). 64p. (J). (ps-3). pap. 7.99 o.s.i (*0-06-000184-4*) HarperCollins Children's Bk. Group.

White, E. B. My Family Album. 1999. (Stuart Little Tie-In Ser.). (Illus.). 24p. (J). (ps-1). pap. 3.25 (*0-694-01416-8*, Harper Festival) HarperCollins Children's Bk. Group.

—Stuart Little. 2001. (SPA., Illus.). 144p. (J). (gr. 3-5). 11.95 (*84-204-4669-6*) Alfaguara, Ediciones, S.A.- Grupo Santillana ESP. *Dist:* Santillana USA Publishing Co., Inc.

—Stuart Little. Date not set. 141p. 18.95 (*0-8488-2602-7*) Amereon, Ltd.

—Stuart Little. 2000. (J). audio 18.00 (*0-7366-9070-0*); audio compact disk 22.00 (*0-7366-9071-9*) Books on Tape, Inc.

—Stuart Little. l.t. unabr. ed. 1988. (Illus.). 176p. (J). (gr. 3-7). 13.95 o.p. (*0-8161-4490-7*, Macmillan Reference USA) Gale Group.

—Stuart Little. (Illus.). 144p. (J). 2001. (gr. 5 up). pap. 8.99 (*0-06-441092-7*); 1974. (gr. 3-7). pap. 5.99 (*0-06-440056-5*, Harper Trophy); 1945. (ps-k). 16.99 (*0-06-026395-4*); 1945. (gr. 4-7). lib. bdg. 18.89 (*0-06-026396-2*); 1999. (gr. 4-7). 24.95 (*0-06-028297-5*) HarperCollins Children's Bk. Group.

—Stuart Little. l.t. ed. 2000. (LRS Large Print Cornerstone Ser.). (Illus.). 175p. (J). (gr. 2-8). lib. bdg. 27.95 (*1-58118-064-0*, 23655) LRS.

—Stuart Little. 1990. (Illus.). (J). pap. 3.50 (*0-06-107009-2*, HarperTorch) Morrow/Avon.

—Stuart Little. 131p. pap. 5.95 (*0-8072-8333-9*); 2003. (YA). (gr. 4-7). audio 9.99 (*0-8072-8288-X*); 2000. (J). (gr. 3-7). audio 23.00 (*0-8072-8331-2*, LL0173); 2000. 131p. pap. 28.00 incl. audio (*0-8072-8332-0*, YA165SP); 1999. (J). (gr. 4-7). audio 18.00 (*0-553-47051-5*, 21614) Random Hse. Audio Publishing Group. (Listening Library).

—Stuart Little. 1990. 14.05 o.p. (*0-606-10511-5*); 1973. 12.00 (*0-606-05062-0*) Turtleback Bks.

—Stuart Little: Search & Find. 1999. (Stuart-Little Ser.). (Illus.). 24p. (J). (ps-3). pap. 5.99 o.s.i (*0-694-01417-6*) HarperCollins Children's Bk. Group.

—Stuart Little Special Read-Aloud Edition. 1999. (Illus.). 144p. (J). (gr. 7 up). 19.95 (*0-06-028334-3*) HarperCollins Children's Bk. Group.

—Stuart Little's Very Big House. 2000. (Stuart-Little Ser.). (Illus.). 32p. (J). (ps-2). pap. 3.99 (*0-06-444289-6*, Avon) HarperCollins Children's Bk. Group.

—Stuart's New Brother, No. 2. 2000. (Stuart-Little Ser.). (Illus.). 32p. (J). (ps-2). pap. 3.99 (*0-06-444290-X*, Avon) HarperCollins Children's Bk. Group.

LITTLE BEAR (FICTITIOUS CHARACTER: LANGREUTER)—FICTION

Langreuter, Jutta. Little Bear & the Big Fight. 1998. (Little Bear Collection). (Illus.). 32p. (ps-k). 22.90 o.p. (*0-7613-0403-7*); pap. 6.95 o.p. (*0-7613-0375-8*) Millbrook Pr., Inc.

—Little Bear Brushes His Teeth. 1997. (Little Bear Collection). (Illus.). 32p. (J). (ps-k). 22.90 (*0-7613-0190-9*); pap. 7.95 (*0-7613-0230-1*) Millbrook Pr., Inc.

—Little Bear Goes to Kindergarten. 1997. (Little Bear Collection). (Illus.). 32p. (ps-k). (J). 22.40 (*0-7613-0191-7*); pap. 7.95 o.p. (*0-7613-0231-X*) Millbrook Pr., Inc.

—Little Bear Is a Big Brother. 1998. (Little Bear Collection). (Illus.). 32p. (ps-k). 22.90 o.p. (*0-7613-0404-5*); pap. 7.95 o.p. (*0-7613-0376-6*) Millbrook Pr., Inc.

—Little Bear Won't Go to Bed. 2000. (Little Bear Collection). (Illus.). 32p. (ps-k). 22.90 o.p. (*0-7613-1872-0*); pap. 7.95 o.p. (*0-7613-1395-8*) Millbrook Pr., Inc.

LITTLE BEAR (FICTITIOUS CHARACTER: MINARIK)—FICTION

Little Bear. 2003. (Goodnight Mr. Moon Ser.). (Illus.). (J). bds. 2.98 (*0-7525-4740-2*) Parragon, Inc.

Little Bear. 1999. (I Can Read Bks.). (J). (ps-1). pap. 1.95 (*0-590-31967-1*) Scholastic, Inc.

Minarik, Else Holmelund. The Adventures of Little Bear. 1998. (Illus.). (J). 12.95 (*0-06-028044-1*) HarperCollins Pubs.

—Los Amigos de Osito. 1981. 15.15 o.p. (*0-606-10479-8*) Turtleback Bks.

—Father Bear Comes Home. (I Can Read Bks.). (Illus.). 64p. (J). (gr. k-3). 1978. pap. 3.99 (*0-06-444014-1*, Harper Trophy); 1959. lib. bdg. 15.89 (*0-06-024231-0*) HarperCollins Children's Bk. Group.

—Father Bear Comes Home. 1959. (I Can Read Bks.). (Illus.). 64p. (J). (gr. k-3). 15.95 (*0-06-024230-2*) HarperCollins Children's Bk. Group.

—Father Bear Comes Home. 1959. (I Can Read Bks.). (J). (ps-1). 10.10 (*0-606-02113-2*) Turtleback Bks.

—Father Bear Comes Home. unabr. ed. 1995. (I Can Read Bks.). (Illus.). 64p. (J). (gr. k-3). 8.99 incl. audio (*0-694-70010-X*, HarperAudio) HarperTrade.

—Get Well Soon, Little Bear. 2002. (Maurice Sendak's Little Bear Ser.). (Illus.). 16p. (J). (ps up). bds. 5.99 (*0-694-01702-7*) HarperCollins Children's Bk. Group.

—A Kiss for Little Bear. (I Can Read Bks.). (Illus.). 32p. (J). (ps-2). 1984. pap. 3.99 (*0-06-444050-8*, Harper Trophy); 1968. 15.99 (*0-06-024298-1*); 1968. lib. bdg. 16.89 (*0-06-024299-X*) HarperCollins Children's Bk. Group.

—A Kiss for Little Bear. 1984. (I Can Read Bks.). (J). (ps-1). 10.10 (*0-606-03383-1*) Turtleback Bks.

—A Kiss for Little Bear. (I Can Read Bks.). (J). (ps-1). pap. text 12.95 incl. audio. (Illus.). pap. 12.95 incl. audio Weston Woods Studios, Inc.

—Little Bear. 1957. (I Can Read Bks.). (Illus.). 64p. (J). (gr. k-3). 15.99 (*0-06-024240-X*); lib. bdg. 16.89 (*0-06-024241-8*) HarperCollins Children's Bk. Group.

—Little Bear. 1978. (I Can Read Bks.). (Illus.). 64p. (J). (gr. k-3). pap. 3.99 (*0-06-444004-4*, Harper Trophy) HarperCollins Children's Bk. Group.

—Little Bear. 1978. (I Can Read Bks.). (J). (ps-1). 10.10 (*0-606-01530-2*) Turtleback Bks.

—Little Bear. unabr. ed. 1990. (I Can Read Bks.). (Illus.). 64p. (J). (gr. k-3). pap. 8.99 incl. audio (*1-55994-234-7*, HarperAudio) HarperTrade.

—Little Bear, Level 1. 1986. (I Can Read Bks.). (Illus.). 64p. (J). (ps-1). 5.98 o.p. incl. audio (*0-694-00113-9*, JC-068, Harper Trophy) HarperCollins Children's Bk. Group.

—Little Bear, 3 bks., Set. 1992. (I Can Read Bks.). (Illus.). 160p. (J). (gr. k-3). pap. 11.97 (*0-06-444197-0*, Harper Trophy) HarperCollins Children's Bk. Group.

—Little Bear & the Missing Pie. 2002. (Maurice Sendak's Little Bear Ser.). 32p. (J). (ps-2). pap. 3.99 (*0-694-01705-1*) HarperCollins Children's Bk. Group.

—Little Bear Audio Collection. unabr. ed. 1992. (I Can Read Bks.). (ps-3). audio 11.95 (*1-55994-543-5*, HarperAudio) HarperTrade.

—Little Bear Makes a Scarecrow. 2002. (Maurice Sendak's Little Bear Ser.). (Illus.). 14p. (J). (ps up). bds. 5.99 (*0-694-01686-1*, Harper Festival) HarperCollins Children's Bk. Group.

—Little Bear's Friend. (I Can Read Bks.). (Illus.). 64p. (J). (gr. k-3). 1984. mass mkt. 3.99 (*0-06-444051-6*, Harper Trophy); 1960. lib. bdg. 15.89 (*0-06-024256-6*) HarperCollins Children's Bk. Group.

—Little Bear's Friend. 1984. (I Can Read Bks.). (J). (ps-1). 10.10 (*0-606-03384-X*) Turtleback Bks.

—Little Bear's Friend. unabr. ed. 1990. (I Can Read Bks.). (Illus.). 64p. (J). (gr. k-3). pap. 8.95 incl. audio (*1-55994-235-5*, HarperAudio) HarperTrade.

—Little Bear's Friend, Level 1. 1985. (I Can Read Bks.). (Illus.). 64p. (J). (ps-1). 5.98 o.p. incl. audio (*0-694-00031-0*, Harper Trophy) HarperCollins Children's Bk. Group.

—Little Bear's Friends - Los Amigos de Osito. (SPA.). 64p. (J). 7.95 (*84-204-3049-8*) Santillana USA Publishing Co., Inc.

—Little Bear's Scary Night. 2002. (Maurice Sendak's Little Bear Ser.). (Illus.). 14p. (J). (ps up). bds. 5.99 (*0-694-01685-3*, Harper Festival) HarperCollins Children's Bk. Group.

—Little Bear's Visit. (I Can Read Bks.). (Illus.). 64p. (J). (ps-1). 1985. 5.98 incl. audio (*0-694-00032-9*, JC-023, Harper Trophy); 1979. pap. 3.99 (*0-06-444023-0*, Harper Trophy); 1961. 15.99 (*0-06-024265-5*); 1961. lib. bdg. 16.89 (*0-06-024266-3*) HarperCollins Children's Bk. Group.

—Little Bear's Visit. unabr. ed. 1990. (I Can Read Bks.). (Illus.). 64p. (J). (gr. k-3). pap. 8.99 incl. audio (*1-55994-236-3*, HarperAudio) HarperTrade.

—Little Bear's Visit. 1971. (I Can Read Bks.). (J). (ps-1). 10.10 (*0-606-02159-0*) Turtleback Bks.

—Little Bear's Visit. (Illus.). (J). pap. 12.95 incl. audio. pap. 12.95 incl. audio. audio 6.95 (*0-7882-0089-5*) Weston Woods Studios, Inc.

—Osito. 1995. (SPA., Illus.). 64p. (J). (ps-3). 11.95 (*84-204-3044-7*, AF1346) Alfaguara, Ediciones, S.A.- Grupo Santillana ESP. *Dist:* Lectorum Pubns., Inc., Santillana USA Publishing Co., Inc.

—Papa Oso Vuele a Casa. 1995. (Osito Ser.). (SPA., Illus.). (J). (ps-3). pap. (*84-204-3048-X*, AF1359) Alfaguara, Ediciones, S.A.- Grupo Santillana ESP. *Dist:* Lectorum Pubns., Inc.

—Papa Oso Vuelve a Casa. 1981. Tr. of Father Bear Comes Home. 15.10 (*0-606-10489-5*) Turtleback Bks.

—La Visita de Osito. 1995. (SPA., Illus.). (J). (ps-3). lib. bdg. 15.95 (*84-204-3051-X*) Alfaguara, Ediciones, S.A.- Grupo Santillana ESP. *Dist:* Santillana USA Publishing Co., Inc.

—La Visita de Osito. 2002. (SPA., Illus.). 64p. (J). (gr. k-3). pap. 11.95 (*968-19-0623-3*, AF1060) Aguilar Editorial MEX. *Dist:* Lectorum Pubns., Inc., Santillana USA Publishing Co., Inc.

—La Visita de Osito. 1982. 15.10 (*0-606-10446-1*) Turtleback Bks.

Minarik, Else Holmelund & Sendak, Maurice. Little Bear Audio Collection. anniv. unabr. ed. 1999. (J). audio 11.98 Random Hse. Audio Publishing Group.

Sendak, Maurice, illus. Father Bear Comes Home. 2002. (Little Bear Ser.). (J). 12.34 (*0-7587-6089-2*) Book Wholesalers, Inc.

—A Kiss for Little Bear. 2002. (Little Bear Ser.). (J). 12.34 (*0-7587-6175-9*) Book Wholesalers, Inc.

—Little Bear's Friend. 2002. (Little Bear Ser.). (J). 12.34 (*0-7587-6185-6*) Book Wholesalers, Inc.

Sendak, Maurice & Minarik, Else Holmelund. A Kiss for Little Bear. abr. ed. 1991. (I Can Read Bks.). (Illus.). 32p. (J). (ps-2). pap. 8.99 incl. audio (*1-55994-263-0*, TBC 2630, HarperAudio) HarperTrade.

—Little Bear's Friend. 1960. (I Can Read Bks.). (Illus.). 64p. (J). (gr. k-3). 15.95 (*0-06-024255-8*) HarperCollins Children's Bk. Group.

LITTLE BEAR (FICTITIOUS CHARACTER: WADDELL)—FICTION

Waddell, Martin. Can't You Sleep, Little Bear? (Little Book Cards Ser.). 32p. (J). 1997. (gr. 1-4). bds. 3.29 o.p. (*0-7636-0215-9*); 1995. (Illus.). (ps-3). bds. 19.99 (*1-56402-555-1*); 1994. (Illus.). (ps-3). bds. 5.99 (*1-56402-262-5*); 1992. (Illus.). (ps-3). 15.99 (*1-56402-007-X*) Candlewick Pr.

—Can't You Sleep, Little Bear? (J). (CHI & ENG.). (*1-85430-315-5*, 93445); 1995. (PAN.). (*1-85430-314-7*); 1995. (URD.). (*1-85430-312-0*); 1995. (BEN.). (*1-85430-313-9*) Magi Pubns.

—Can't You Sleep, Little Bear? 1997. (ENG & VIE.). (J). 36.40 (*1-85430-311-2*, 93446) Magi Pubns. GBR. *Dist:* Midpoint Trade Bks., Inc.

—Can't You Sleep, Little Bear? 1994. (J). 12.14 (*0-606-05779-X*) Turtleback Bks.

—Can't You Sleep, Little Bear? Book & Play Set. 1995. (Illus.). 32p. (YA). (ps up). 14.95 o.p. (*1-56402-643-4*) Candlewick Pr.

—Can't You Sleep, Little Bear? Mini Book. 1993. (Illus.). 32p. (J). (ps up). 4.95 o.p. (*1-56402-254-4*) Candlewick Pr.

—Good Job, Little Bear. 1999. (Illus.). 32p. (J). (ps-1). 15.99 (*0-7636-0736-3*) Candlewick Pr.

—Let's Go Home, Little Bear. ed. 2000. (J). (gr. 1). spiral bd. (*0-616-01804-5*); (gr. 2). spiral bd. (*0-616-01805-3*) Canadian National Institute for the Blind/Institut National Canadien pour les Aveugles.

—Let's Go Home, Little Bear. (Little Book Cards Ser.). 32p. (J). 1997. (gr. 1-4). bds. 3.29 o.p. (*0-7636-0216-7*); 1995. (Illus.). (ps up). bds. 5.99 (*1-56402-447-4*); 1993. (Illus.). (ps-3). 15.99 o.s.i (*1-56402-131-9*) Candlewick Pr.

—Let's Go Home, Little Bear. 1995. 12.14 (*0-606-08797-4*) Turtleback Bks.

—No Duermes, Osito? 3rd ed. 1996. (SPA., Illus.). 124p. (J). (ps-3). 13.56 net. (*84-88342-04-7*) Lectorum Pubns., Inc.

—Tu y Yo, Osito. Roehrich-Rubio, Esther, tr. from ENG. 1997. (SPA., Illus.). 34p. (J). (gr. k-2). 13.56 net. (*84-88342-09-8*, KK2601) Lectorum Pubns., Inc.

—You & Me, Little Bear. ed. 1999. (J). (gr. 1). spiral bd. (*0-616-01802-9*); (gr. 2). spiral bd. (*0-616-01803-7*) Canadian National Institute for the Blind/Institut National Canadien pour les Aveugles.

—You & Me, Little Bear. (Illus.). 32p. (J). (ps-k). 1998. bds. 6.99 (*0-7636-0574-3*); 1996. 15.99 (*1-56402-879-8*) Candlewick Pr.

—You & Me, Little Bear. 1996. (BEN, CHI, ENG, PAN & SOM., Illus.). 32p. (J). (*1-85430-519-0*); (*1-85430-521-2*); (*1-85430-523-9*); (*1-85430-522-0*); (*1-85430-520-4*); (*1-85430-518-2*) Magi Pubns.

LITTLE WHISTLE (FICTITIOUS CHARACTER)—FICTION

Rylant, Cynthia. Little Whistle. (Little Whistle Ser.). (Illus.). 32p. (J). 2003. pap. 6.00 (*0-15-204762-X*, Voyager Bks./Libros Viajeros); 2001. 14.00 (*0-15-201087-4*) Harcourt Children's Bks.

—Little Whistle's Christmas. 2003. (Little Whistle Ser.). (Illus.). 32p. (J). 16.00 (*0-15-204590-2*) Harcourt Children's Bks.

—Little Whistle's Dinner Party. 2001. (Little Whistle Ser.). (Illus.). 32p. (J). (gr. k-2). 14.00 (*0-15-201079-3*) Harcourt Children's Bks.

—Little Whistle's Medicine. 2002. (Little Whistle Ser.). (Illus.). 32p. (J). (ps-2). 15.00 (*0-15-201086-6*) Harcourt Children's Bks.

LOCKHART, SALLY (FICTITIOUS CHARACTER)—FICTION

Pullman, Philip. The Ruby in the Smoke. 1987. 208p. (YA). (gr. 7 up). 11.95 o.s.i (*0-394-88826-X*); 1987. 208p. (YA). (gr. 7 up). 11.99 o.s.i (*0-394-98826-4*); 1988. 240p. (gr. 5-8). reprint ed. mass mkt. 5.50 (*0-394-89589-4*) Random Hse. Children's Bks. (Knopf Bks. for Young Readers).

—The Ruby in the Smoke. 2002. (YA). 20.50 (*0-8446-7230-0*) Smith, Peter Pub., Inc.

—The Ruby in the Smoke. 1985. (J). 11.04 (*0-606-04047-1*) Turtleback Bks.

—The Ruby in the Smoke: A Sally Lockhart Mystery. 2003. (Illus.). (J). pap. 9.95 (*0-375-82545-2*, Knopf Bks. for Young Readers) Random Hse. Children's Bks.

—Shadow in the North. 1988. 320p. (YA). (gr. 7 up). 12.95 o.s.i (*0-394-89453-7*, Knopf Bks. for Young Readers) Random Hse. Children's Bks.

—Shadow in the North. 1988. (YA). 11.04 (*0-606-04320-9*) Turtleback Bks.

—The Shadow in the North: A Sally Lockhart Mystery. 2003. (Illus.). (J). pap. 9.95 (*0-375-82546-0*, Knopf Bks. for Young Readers) Random Hse. Children's Bks.

—The Tiger in the Well. 1996. (YA). 11.04 (*0-606-09969-7*) Turtleback Bks.

—The Tiger in the Well: A Sally Lockhart Mystery. 2003. (Illus.). (J). pap. 9.95 (*0-375-82547-9*) Random Hse. Children's Bks.

LONGSTOCKING, PIPPI (FICTITIOUS CHARACTER)—FICTION

Levine, Gloria. Pippi Longstocking, Level 4. 1989. (Novel-Ties Ser.). (J). (gr. 4). pap., stu. ed. 15.95 (*0-88122-050-7*, S0563) Learning Links, Inc.

Lindgren, Astrid. Do You Know Pippi Longstocking? Dyssegaard, Elisabeth Kallick, tr. from SWE. 1999. (Pippi Longstocking Storybooks). (Illus.). 32p. (J). (gr. k-2). 9.95 (*91-29-64661-8*) R & S Bks. SWE. *Dist:* Holtzbrinck Pubs.

—The New Adventures of Pippi Longstocking. (Pippi Longstocking Ser.). (Illus.). (J). (gr. 3-5). 1997. 304p. 30.00 (*0-670-87612-7*, Viking); 1988. 60p. 7.95 o.p. (*0-670-82260-4*, Viking Children's Bks.) Penguin Putnam Bks. for Young Readers.

—The New Adventures of Pippi Longstocking Activity Book. 1988. (Pippi Longstocking Ser.). (Orig.). (J). (gr. 3-5). pap. 2.95 o.p. (*0-14-050889-9*, Puffin Bks.) Penguin Putnam Bks. for Young Readers.

—Pippa Mediaslargas. (Pippi Longstocking Ser.).Tr. of Pippi Longstocking. (SPA.). (J). (gr. 3-5). pap. 9.95 (*84-261-2304-X*, JV304X) Juventud, Editorial ESP. *Dist:* Continental Bk. Co., Inc., Lectorum Pubns., Inc.

—Pippi Goes on Board. (Pippi Longstocking Ser.). (J). (gr. 3-5). 1980. 172p. lib. bdg. 13.95 (*0-89967-014-8*, Harmony Raine & Co.); 1981. 192p. reprint ed. lib. bdg. 25.95 o.p. (*0-89966-339-7*) Buccaneer Bks., Inc.

—Pippi Goes on Board. (Pippi Longstocking Ser.). (J). (gr. 3-5). 1988. pap. 3.95 o.p. (*0-14-032774-6*, Puffin Bks.); 1977. 144p. pap. 4.99 (*0-14-030959-4*, Puffin Bks.); 1957. (Illus.). 144p. text 14.99 (*0-670-55677-7*, Viking Children's Bks.) Penguin Putnam Bks. for Young Readers.

—Pippi Goes on Board. (Pippi Longstocking Ser.). (J). (gr. 3-5). 140p. pap. 3.99 (*0-8072-1401-9*); 1980. audio 15.98 (*0-8072-1054-4*, SWR 3 SP); 1980. audio Random Hse. Audio Publishing Group.

—Pippi Goes on Board. 1970. (Pippi Longstocking Ser.). (J). (gr. 3-5). 9.09 o.p. (*0-606-04316-0*) Turtleback Bks.

—Pippi Goes to School. 1999. (Pippi Longstocking Storybooks). (Illus.). 64p. (J). (gr. k-2). pap. 5.99 (*0-14-130236-4*) Penguin Putnam Bks. for Young Readers.

—Pippi Goes to School. Lamborn, Frances, tr. 1998. (Pippi Longstocking Ser.). (Illus.). 32p. (J). (gr. k-2). 14.99 (*0-670-88075-2*) Penguin Putnam Bks. for Young Readers.

—Pippi Goes to School. 1999. (Pippi Longstocking Storybooks). (J). (gr. k-2). 12.14 (*0-606-18446-5*) Turtleback Bks.

—Pippi Goes to the Circus. 2000. (Pippi Longstocking Storybooks). (Illus.). 32p. (J). (gr. k-2). pap. 5.99 (*0-14-130243-7*, Puffin Bks.) Penguin Putnam Bks. for Young Readers.

—Pippi Goes to the Circus. 2000. (Pippi Longstocking Storybooks). (J). (gr. k-2). 12.14 (*0-606-18843-6*) Turtleback Bks.

—Pippi in the South Seas. 1988. (Pippi Longstocking Ser.). (J). (gr. 3-5). pap. 3.95 o.p. (*0-14-032773-8*, Puffin Bks.) Penguin Putnam Bks. for Young Readers.

—Pippi in the South Seas. Bothmer, Gerry, tr. (Pippi Longstocking Ser.). (Illus.). 128p. (J). (gr. 3-5). 1977. pap. 4.99 (*0-14-030958-6*, Puffin Bks.); 1959. 15.99 (*0-670-55711-0*, Viking Children's Bks.) Penguin Putnam Bks. for Young Readers.

—Pippi in the South Seas. (Pippi Longstocking Ser.). (J). (gr. 3-5). 125p. pap. 3.99 (*0-8072-1392-6*); 1980. audio 15.98 (*0-8072-1052-8*, SWR 2 SP); 1980. audio Random Hse. Audio Publishing Group.

—Pippi in the South Seas. 1998. (Pippi Longstocking Ser.). (J). (gr. 3-5). 20.25 (*0-8446-6974-1*) Smith, Peter Pub., Inc.

—Pippi in the South Seas. 1977. (Pippi Longstocking Ser.). (J). (gr. 3-5). 11.04 (*0-606-04317-9*) Turtleback Bks.

—Pippi Longstocking. unabr. ed. 1999. (Pippi Longstocking Ser.). (J). (gr. 3-5). audio 23.00 BBC Audiobooks America.

—Pippi Longstocking. unabr. ed. 1999. (Pippi Longstocking Ser.). (J). (gr. 3-5). audio 17.95 Blackstone Audio Bks., Inc.

—Pippi Longstocking. (Pippi Longstocking Ser.). 192p. (J). (gr. 3-5). reprint ed. 1981. lib. bdg. 25.95 o.p. (*0-89966-338-9*); 1980. lib. bdg. 25.95 (*0-89967-013-X*, Harmony Raine & Co.) Buccaneer Bks., Inc.

—Pippi Longstocking. abr. ed. 1973. (Pippi Longstocking Ser.). (J). (gr. 3-5). 24.95 incl. audio (*0-670-55744-7*); pap. 15.95 incl. audio (*0-670-55743-9*); audio 9.95 (*0-670-55748-X*) Live Oak Media.

—Pippi Longstocking. l.t. ed. 1989. (Pippi Longstocking Ser.). 127p. (J). (gr. 3-5). reprint ed. lib. bdg. 16.95 o.s.i (*1-55736-152-5*, Cornerstone Bks.) Pages, Inc.

—Pippi Longstocking. 1988. (Pippi Longstocking Ser.). 160p. (J). (gr. 3-5). pap. 3.95 o.p. (*0-14-032772-X*, Puffin Bks.) Penguin Putnam Bks. for Young Readers.

—Pippi Longstocking. Lamborn, Florence, tr. (Pippi Longstocking Ser.). (Illus.). (J). (gr. 3-5). 1977. 158p. 4.99 (*0-14-030957-8*, Puffin Bks.); 1950. 160p. 15.99 (*0-670-55745-5*, Viking Children's Bks.) Penguin Putnam Bks. for Young Readers.

—Pippi Longstocking. (Pippi Longstocking Ser.). (J). (gr. 3-5). 160p. pap. 4.99 (*0-8072-1431-0*); 1990. 160p. pap. 28.00 incl. audio (*0-8072-7307-4*, YA807SP); 1990. 160p. pap. 28.00 incl. audio (*0-8072-7307-4*, YA807SP); 1990. audio 15.95 (*0-8072-7388-0*, YA 807 CXR); 1990. audio 23.00 (*0-8072-7214-0*, TYA 807 CX) Random Hse. Audio Publishing Group. (Listening Library).

—Pippi Longstocking. unabr. ed. 1998. (Pippi Longstocking Ser.). (J). (gr. 3-5). audio 31.24 (*0-7887-1939-4*, 40646); audio 19.00 (*0-7887-1911-4*, 95332E7) Recorded Bks., LLC.

—Pippi Longstocking. 1969. (Pippi Longstocking Ser.). (J). (gr. 3-5). 11.04 (*0-606-04318-7*) Turtleback Bks.

—Pippi Longstocking Boxed Set. 1997. (Pippi Longstocking Ser.). (J). (gr. 3-5). 100.00 o.s.i (*0-670-78142-8*) Penguin Putnam Bks. for Young Readers.

—Pippi Longstocking in the Park. Dyssegaard, Elisabeth Kallick, tr. from SWE. 2001. (Pippi Longstocking Storybooks). (Illus.). 20p. (J). (gr. k-2). 9.95 (*91-29-65307-X*) R & S Bks. SWE. *Dist:* Farrar, Straus & Giroux, Holtzbrinck Pubs.

—Pippi Longstocking's After-Christmas Party. (Pippi Longstocking Storybooks). (Illus.). 32p. (J). (gr. k-2). 1998. pap. 5.99 (*0-14-056425-X*, Puffin Bks.); 1996. 13.99 o.s.i (*0-670-86790-X*) Penguin Putnam Bks. for Young Readers.

—Pippi Longstocking's After-Christmas Party. Keeler, Stephen, tr. from SWE. 1996. (Pippi Longstocking Ser.). (Illus.). 64p. (J). (gr. k-2). text o.s.i (*0-670-86465-X*, Viking) Viking Penguin.

—Pippi on the Run. 1976. (Pippi Longstocking Storybooks). (Illus.). 48p. (J). (gr. k-2). 10.95 o.p. (*0-670-55751-X*, Viking Children's Bks.) Penguin Putnam Bks. for Young Readers.

—Pippi to the Rescue. 2000. (Pippi Longstocking Storybooks). (Illus.). 64p. (J). (gr. k-2). 13.99 (*0-670-88074-4*, Viking Children's Bks.) Penguin Putnam Bks. for Young Readers.

—Pippi's Extraordinary Ordinary Day. (Pippi Longstocking Storybooks). (Illus.). (J). (gr. k-2). 2001. 32p. pap. 5.99 (*0-14-056841-7*); 1999. 64p. pap. 14.99 (*0-670-88073-6*, Viking Children's Bks.) Penguin Putnam Bks. for Young Readers.

Lindgren, Astrid & Lamborn, Florence. Pippi Goes to the Circus. 1999. (Pippi Longstocking Ser.). (Illus.). 32p. (J). (gr. k-2). 13.99 o.s.i (*0-670-88070-1*) Penguin Putnam Bks. for Young Readers.

LUKE, SAINT—FICTION

Brown, Robert. Luke: Doctor-Writer. 1977. (BibLearn Ser.). (Illus.). (J). (gr. 1-6). bds. 5.99 o.p. (*0-8054-4233-2*, 4242-33) Broadman & Holman Pubs.

LYLE THE CROCODILE (FICTITIOUS CHARACTER)—FICTION

Lyle, Lyle, Crocodile Audio Collection. abr. ed. Incl. House on East Eighty-Eighth Street. Weber, Bernard. audio Lovable Lyle. Waber, Bernard. audio Lyle & the Birthday Party. Waber, Bernard. audio (J). (ps-3). 1989. (Lyle Ser.). 1989. Set audio 11.95 o.p. (*0-89845-864-1*, CPN 1350, Caedmon) HarperTrade.

Waber, Bernard. Funny, Funny Lyle. 2002. (Lyle the Crocodile Ser.). (Illus.). (J). 14.74 (*0-7587-2559-0*) Book Wholesalers, Inc.

—Funny, Funny Lyle. 1987. (Lyle Ser.). (Illus.). 40p. (J). (ps-3). lib. bdg., tchr. ed. 16.00 (*0-395-43619-2*) Houghton Mifflin Co.

—Funny, Funny Lyle. 1991. (Lyle Ser.). (Illus.). 40p. (J). (ps-3). pap. 6.95 (*0-395-60287-4*) Houghton Mifflin Co. Trade & Reference Div.

—Funny, Funny Lyle. 1987. (Lyle Ser.). (J). (ps-3). 12.10 (*0-606-16122-8*) Turtleback Bks.

—Lovable Lyle. 2002. (Lyle the Crocodile Ser.). (Illus.). (J). 14.74 (*0-7587-3043-8*) Book Wholesalers, Inc.

—Lovable Lyle. (Lyle Ser.). (Illus.). 48p. (J). (ps-3). 1977. pap. 6.95 (*0-395-25378-0*); 1969. lib. bdg., tchr. ed. 17.00 (*0-395-19858-5*) Houghton Mifflin Co.

—Lovable Lyle. 1979. (Lyle Ser.). (J). (ps-3). 12.10 (*0-606-00908-6*) Turtleback Bks.

—Lyle & the Birthday Party. 1966. (Lyle Ser.). (Illus.). 48p. (J). (ps-3). lib. bdg., tchr. ed. 16.00 (*0-395-15080-9*) Houghton Mifflin Co.

—Lyle & the Birthday Party. 1973. (Lyle Ser.). (Illus.). 48p. (J). (ps-3). reprint ed. pap. 6.95 (*0-395-17451-1*, 4-97508) Houghton Mifflin Co. Trade & Reference Div.

—Lyle & the Birthday Party. 1966. (Lyle Ser.). (J). (ps-3). 13.10 (*0-606-00910-8*) Turtleback Bks.

—Lyle at Christmas. 2002. (Lyle the Crocodile Ser.). (Illus.). (J). 23.40 (*0-7587-3058-6*) Book Wholesalers, Inc.

—Lyle at Christmas. 1998. (Lyle Ser.). (Illus.). 48p. (J). (ps-3). tchr. ed. 16.00 (*0-395-91304-7*) Houghton Mifflin Co.

—Lyle at Christmas. 2003. (Lyle Ser.). (Illus.). 48p. (J). (ps-3). pap. 5.95 (*0-618-38002-7*, Lorraine, A. Walter) Houghton Mifflin Co. Trade & Reference Div.

—Lyle at the Office. 2002. (Lyle the Crocodile Ser.). (Illus.). (J). 13.79 (*0-7587-3059-4*) Book Wholesalers, Inc.

—Lyle at the Office. (Lyle Ser.). (Illus.). 48p. (J). (ps-3). 1996. pap. 5.95 (*0-395-82743-4*); 1994. lib. bdg., tchr. ed. 16.00 (*0-395-70563-0*) Houghton Mifflin Co.

—Lyle at the Office. 1994. (Lyle Ser.). (J). (ps-3). 12.10 (*0-606-10863-7*) Turtleback Bks.

—Lyle Finds His Mother. 2002. (Lyle the Crocodile Ser.). (Illus.). (J). 14.74 (*0-7587-3060-8*) Book Wholesalers, Inc.

—Lyle Finds His Mother. (Lyle Ser.). (Illus.). 48p. (J). (ps-3). 1978. pap. 6.95 (*0-395-27398-6*); 1974. lib. bdg., tchr. ed. 16.00 (*0-395-19489-X*) Houghton Mifflin Co.

—Lyle Finds His Mother. 1974. (Lyle Ser.). (J). (ps-3). 12.10 (*0-606-01533-7*) Turtleback Bks.

—Lyle, Lyle Crocodile. 1987. (Lyle Ser.). (J). (ps-3). pap. 7.95 o.p. (*0-395-45742-4*) Houghton Mifflin Co.

—Lyle, Lyle Crocodile. 1999. (Lyle Ser.). (J). (ps-3). 9.95 (*1-56137-327-3*) Novel Units, Inc.

—Lyle, Lyle, Crocodile. 2002. (Lyle the Crocodile Ser.). (Illus.). (J). 14.74 (*0-7587-3061-6*) Book Wholesalers, Inc.

—Lyle, Lyle, Crocodile. (Lyle Ser.). (J). (ps-3). 1987. 48p. pap. 6.95 (*0-395-13720-9*); 1973. (Illus.). 48p. lib. bdg., tchr. ed. 16.00 (*0-395-16995-X*); 1993. 1p. pap. 9.95 incl. audio (*0-395-66502-7*, 497530) Houghton Mifflin Co.

—Lyle, Lyle, Crocodile. 1965. (Lyle Ser.). (J). (ps-3). 12.10 (*0-606-01005-X*) Turtleback Bks.

M

MACCAULEY, TYLER (FICTITIOUS CHARACTER)—FICTION

DeFelice, Cynthia C. Lostman's River. 1995. 160p. (J). (gr. 4-7). pap. 4.95 (*0-380-72396-4*, Avon Bks.) Morrow/Avon.

—Lostman's River. 1994. 160p. (YA). (gr. 7 up). lib. bdg. 15.00 (*0-02-726466-1*, Atheneum) Simon & Schuster Children's Publishing.

—Lostman's River. 1995. (J). 10.55 (*0-606-07810-X*) Turtleback Bks.

MCCLOY, BRANDT (FICTITIOUS CHARACTER)—FICTION

Stine, R. L. The First Horror. 1994. (99 Fear Street: No. 1). 160p. (YA). (gr. 7 up). pap. 4.99 (*0-671-88562-6*, Simon Pulse) Simon & Schuster Children's Publishing.

—The First Horror. 1994. (99 Fear Street: No. 1). (YA). (gr. 7 up). 9.09 o.p. (*0-606-06154-1*) Turtleback Bks.

—The Second Horror. MacDonald, Patricia, ed. 1994. (99 Fear Street: No. 2). 160p. (YA). (gr. 7 up). pap. 3.99 (*0-671-88563-4*, Simon Pulse) Simon & Schuster Children's Publishing.

—The Second Horror. 1994. (99 Fear Street: No. 2). (YA). (gr. 7 up). 9.09 o.p. (*0-606-06155-X*) Turtleback Bks.

—The Third Horror. 1994. (99 Fear Street: No. 3). 176p. (YA). (gr. 7 up). pap. 4.99 (*0-671-88564-2*, Simon Pulse) Simon & Schuster Children's Publishing.

—The Third Horror. 1994. (99 Fear Street: No. 3). (YA). (gr. 7 up). 10.04 (*0-606-06908-9*) Turtleback Bks.

MCDUCK, SCROOGE (FICTITIOUS CHARACTER)—FICTION

Barks, Carl. Uncle Scrooge McDuck: His Life & Times. Summer, Edward, ed. 1995. (Illus.). 376p. (J). (ps-3). 59.95 o.s.i (*0-89087-511-1*) Celestial Arts Publishing Co.

Summer, Edward, ed. Uncle Scrooge McDuck: His Life & Times. 1987. (Illus.). 376p. (J). (ps-3). pap. 34.95 o.p. (*0-89087-510-3*) Celestial Arts Publishing Co.

MCGRADY, JENNIE (FICTITIOUS CHARACTER)—FICTION

Rushford, Patricia H. Abandoned. 1999. (Jennie McGrady Mysteries Ser.: No. 12). 176p. (J). (gr. 4-7). pap. 4.99 (*0-7642-2120-5*) Bethany Hse. Pubs.

—Betrayed. 1996. (Jennie McGrady Mysteries Ser.: No. 7). 192p. (Orig.). (J). (gr. 4-7). pap. 4.99 (*1-55661-560-4*, Bethany Backyard) Bethany Hse. Pubs.

—Deceived. 1994. (Jennie McGrady Mysteries Ser.: No. 4). 192p. (J). (gr. 4-7). pap. 4.99 (*1-55661-334-2*) Bethany Hse. Pubs.

—Desperate Measures. 1998. (Jennie McGrady Mysteries Ser.: No. 11). 192p. (J). (gr. 4-7). pap. 4.99 (*0-7642-2080-2*, 202080) Bethany Hse. Pubs.

—Desperate Measures. l.t. ed. 2000. (Jennie McGrady Mysteries Ser.: No. 11). 333p. (J). (gr. 4-7). 23.95 (*0-7862-2374-X*) Thorndike Pr.

—Dying to Win, 1995. (Jennie McGrady Mysteries Ser.: No. 6). 192p. (J). (gr. 4-7). pap. 4.99 (*1-55661-559-0*) Bethany Hse. Pubs.

—Forgotten. 2000. (Jennie McGrady Mysteries Ser.: No. 13). 192p. (J). (gr. 4-7). pap. 4.99 (*0-7642-2121-3*) Bethany Hse. Pubs.

—From the Ashes, 1997. (Jennie McGrady Mysteries Ser.: No. 10). 192p. (J). (gr. 4-7). pap. 4.99 (*1-55661-563-9*) Bethany Hse. Pubs.

—Grave Matters. 2002. (Jennie McGrady Mysteries Ser.). 208p. (J). pap. 4.99 (*0-7642-2123-X*) Bethany Hse. Pubs.

—In Too Deep. 1996. (Jennie McGrady Mysteries Ser.: No. 8). 208p. (J). (gr. 4-7). pap. 4.99 (*1-55661-561-2*) Bethany Hse. Pubs.

—Jennie McGrady Mysteries Boxed Set: Dying to Win; Betrayed; In Too Deep; Over the Edge; From the Ashes, 1997. (Jennie McGrady Mysteries Ser.: Nos. 6-10). (J). (gr. 4-7). pap. 24.99 (*0-7642-8196-8*, 258196) Bethany Hse. Pubs.

—Jennie McGrady Mysteries Boxed Set: Too Many Secrets; Silent Witness; Pursued; Deceived; Without a Trace, 1995. (Jennie McGrady Mysteries Ser.: Nos. 1-5). (J). (gr. 4-7). pap. 24.99 (*1-55661-799-2*, 252799) Bethany Hse. Pubs.

—Over the Edge, 1997. (Jennie McGrady Mysteries Ser.: No. 9). 160p. (J). (gr. 4-7). pap. 4.99 (*1-55661-562-0*) Bethany Hse. Pubs.

—Pursued. 1994. (Jennie McGrady Mysteries Ser.: No. 3). 176p. (J). (gr. 4-7). pap. 4.99 (*1-55661-333-4*) Bethany Hse. Pubs.

—Silent Witness. 1993. (Jennie McGrady Mysteries Ser.: No. 2). 176p. (J). (gr. 4-7). pap. 4.99 (*1-55661-332-6*) Bethany Hse. Pubs.

—Stranded. 2001. (Jennie McGrady Mysteries Ser.: No. 14). 176p. (J). (gr. 4-7). pap. 4.99 (*0-7642-2122-1*) Bethany Hse. Pubs.

—Too Many Secrets. 1993. (Jennie McGrady Mysteries Ser.: No. 1). 176p. (J). (gr. 4-7). pap. 4.99 (*1-55661-331-8*) Bethany Hse. Pubs.

—Without a Trace. 1995. (Jennie McGrady Mysteries Ser.: No. 5). 192p. (J). (gr. 4-7). pap. 4.99 (*1-55661-558-2*) Bethany Hse. Pubs.

MCGUIRE, LIZZIE (FICTITIOUS CHARACTER)—FICTION

Alfonsi, Alice. The Orchids & Gumbo Poker Club. Date not set. (Lizzie McGuire Ser.). (Illus.). (J). pap. 4.99 (*0-7868-4646-1*) Disney Pr.

Alfonsi, Alice, ed. Mirror Mirror. 2004. (Lizzie McGuire Ser.: No. 14). (Illus.). (J). (gr. 3-7). pap. 4.99 (*0-7868-4551-1*) Disney Pr.

Broken Hearts, No. 7. 2003. (Lizzie McGuire Ser.). 128p. (J). pap. 4.99 (*0-7868-4545-7*) Disney Pr.

Don't Even Go There! A Little Book of Lizzie-isms. 2003. (Lizzie McGuire Ser.). (Illus.). 64p. (J). pap. 3.99 (*0-7868-3460-9*) Disney Pr.

Head over Heels. 2004. (Lizzie McGuire Ser.: No. 12). (Illus.). 128p. (J). pap. 4.99 (*0-7868-4618-6*) Disney Pr.

Jansen, Susan Estelle. The Lizzie McGuire Movie. novel ed. 2003. (Illus.). 48p. (J). (gr. 3-6). pap. 4.99 (*0-7868-4584-8*) Disney Pr.

Larsen, Kirsten. Lizzie Goes Wild. 2002. (Lizzie McGuire - Jr. Novel Ser.: No. 3). 128p. (J). (gr. 3-7). mass mkt. 4.99 (*0-7868-4540-6*) Disney Pr.

—The Rise & Fall of the Kate Empire. 2002. (Lizzie McGuire - Jr. Novel Ser.: No. 4). 128p. (J). (gr. 3-7). pap. 4.99 (*0-7868-4541-4*) Disney Pr.

Lizzie McGuire: Lizzie Loves Ethan, No. 9. 2004. (J). pap. 4.99 (*0-7868-4549-X*) Hyperion Pr.

Lizzie McGuire Valentine Book. 2003. (Illus.). (J). pap. 4.99 (*0-7868-4613-5*) Disney Pr.

Minsky, Terri, creator. Lizzie McGuire Vol. 1: Pool Party & Picture Day. 2003. (Illus.). 144p. (YA). (gr. 2 up). pap. 7.99 (*1-59182-147-9*) TOKYOPOP, Inc.

—Lizzie McGuire Vol. 2: Rumors & I've Got Rhythmic. 2003. (Illus.). 144p. (YA). (gr. 2 up). pap. 7.99 (*1-59182-148-7*) TOKYOPOP, Inc.

—Lizzie McGuire Vol. 3: When Moms Attack & Misadventures in Babysitting. 2003. (Illus.). 192p. (J). pap. 7.99 (*1-59182-245-9*) TOKYOPOP, Inc.

—Lizzie McGuire Vol. 4: I Do, I Don't & Come Fly with Me. 2003. (Illus.). 192p. (J). pap. 7.99 (*1-59182-246-7*) TOKYOPOP, Inc.

—Lizzie McGuire Vol. 5: Lizzie's Nightmare & Sibling Bonding. 2004. (Illus.). 96p. (YA). pap. 7.99 (*1-59182-571-7*) TOKYOPOP, Inc.

My Secret Journal. 2003. (Illus.). 48p. (J). pap. 6.99 (*0-7868-3432-3*) Disney Pr.

New Kid in School, No. 6. 2003. (Lizzie McGuire - Jr. Novel Ser.: Vol. 6). (Illus.). (J). pap. 4.99 (*0-7868-4543-0*) Disney Pr.

Ostrow, Kim & McGuire, Lizzie. When Moms Attack. 2002. (Lizzie McGuire Ser.). 128p. (J). (gr. 3-7). mass mkt. 4.99 (*0-7868-4538-4*) Disney Pr.

Papademetriou, Lisa. On the Job. (Illus.). (J). 83.70 (*0-7910-7408-0*, Chelsea Clubhouse) Chelsea Hse. Pubs.

—On the Job. Alfonsi, Alice, ed. 10th ed. 2004. (Lizzie McQuire Ser.: No. 10). (J). pap. 4.99 (*0-7868-4550-3*) Hyperion Bks. for Children.

—A Very Lizzie Christmas. 2003. (Lizzie McGuire Ser.: No. 8). (Illus.). 128p. (J). pap. 4.99 (*0-7868-4617-8*) Disney Pr.

Thorpe, Kiki. Totally Crushed. 2002. (Lizzie McGuire Ser.). 128p. (J). (gr. 3-7). mass mkt. 4.99 (*0-7868-4539-2*) Disney Pr.

Thorpe, Kiki & Jones, Jasmine. Picture This. 2003. (Lizzie McGuire - Jr. Novel Ser.: No. 5). 128p. (J). (gr. 3-7). mass mkt. 4.99 (*0-7868-4542-2*) Disney Pr.

Thorpe, Kiki & Papademetriou, Lisa. Lizzie McGuire: Just Like Lizzie, Vol. 9. 2003. 160p. (J). pap. 4.99 (*0-7868-4546-5*) Hyperion Pr.

MACK, ALEX (FICTITIOUS CHARACTER)—FICTION

Barnes-Svarney, Patricia L. Computer Crunch! 1998. (Secret World of Alex Mack Ser.: No. 24). 144p. (J). (gr. 4-7). pap. 3.99 (*0-671-01884-1*, Aladdin) Simon & Schuster Children's Publishing.

—High Flyer! 1997. (Secret World of Alex Mack Ser.: No. 14). 144p. (J). (gr. 4-7). pap. 3.99 (*0-671-00449-2*, Aladdin) Simon & Schuster Children's Publishing.

—Junkyard Jitters! 1997. (Secret World of Alex Mack Ser.: No. 11). 144p. (J). (gr. 4-7). per. 3.99 (*0-671-00367-4*, Aladdin) Simon & Schuster Children's Publishing.

Dubowski, Cathy. Bonjour Alex! 1997. (Secret World of Alex Mack Ser.: No. 17). 160p. (J). (gr. 4-7). pap. 3.99 (*0-671-01373-4*, Aladdin) Simon & Schuster Children's Publishing.

—Clean-Up Catastrophe! 1996. (Secret World of Alex Mack Ser.: No. 6). 144p. (J). (gr. 4-7). pap. 3.99 (*0-671-56308-4*, Aladdin) Simon & Schuster Children's Publishing.

—Sink or Swim! 1998. (Secret World of Alex Mack Ser.: No. 29). 144p. (J). (gr. 4-7). pap. 3.99 (*0-671-02108-7*, Aladdin) Simon & Schuster Children's Publishing.

—Take a Hike! 1996. (Secret World of Alex Mack Ser.: No. 7). 144p. (J). (gr. 4-7). pap. 3.99 (*0-671-56309-2*, Aladdin) Simon & Schuster Children's Publishing.

—Truth Trap! 1997. (Secret World of Alex Mack Ser.: No. 21). 144p. (J). (gr. 4-7). pap. 3.99 (*0-671-01157-X*, Aladdin) Simon & Schuster Children's Publishing.

Emery, Clayton. Father-Daughter Disaster! 1997. (Secret World of Alex Mack Ser.: No. 16). 128p. (J). (gr. 4-7). pap. 3.99 (*0-671-01372-6*, Aladdin) Simon & Schuster Children's Publishing.

Gallagher, Diana G. Alex, You're Glowing! 1995. (Secret World of Alex Mack Ser.: No. 1). 144p. (Orig.). (J). (gr. 4-7). pap. 3.99 (*0-671-52599-9*, Aladdin) Simon & Schuster Children's Publishing.

—Bet You Can't! 1995. (Secret World of Alex Mack Ser.: No. 2). 144p. (Orig.). (J). (gr. 4-7). pap. 3.99 (*0-671-53300-2*, Aladdin) Simon & Schuster Children's Publishing.

—Canine Caper! 1998. (Secret World of Alex Mack Ser.: No. 26). 144p. (J). (gr. 4-7). pap. 3.99 (*0-671-00690-8*, Aladdin) Simon & Schuster Children's Publishing.

—Frozen Stiff! 1997. (Secret World of Alex Mack Ser.: No. 12). 144p. (J). (gr. 4-7). pap. 3.99 (*0-671-00281-3*, Aladdin) Simon & Schuster Children's Publishing.

—Go for the Gold! 1996. (Secret World of Alex Mack Ser.: No. 8). 144p. (Orig.). (J). (gr. 4-7). pap. 3.99 (*0-671-55862-5*, Aladdin) Simon & Schuster Children's Publishing.

—Gold Rush Fever! 1998. (Secret World of Alex Mack Ser.: No. 30). 144p. (J). (gr. 4-7). pap. 3.99 (*0-671-00703-3*, Aladdin) Simon & Schuster Children's Publishing.

—Milady Alex! 1997. (Secret World of Alex Mack Ser.: No. 15). 144p. (Orig.). (J). (gr. 4-7). pap. 3.99 (*0-671-00684-3*, Aladdin) Simon & Schuster Children's Publishing.

—Mistaken Identity! 1996. (Secret World of Alex Mack Ser.: No. 5). 144p. (J). (gr. 4-7). pap. 3.99 (*0-671-55778-5*, Aladdin) Simon & Schuster Children's Publishing.

—New Year's Revolution! 1997. (Secret World of Alex Mack Ser.: No. 22). 192p. (J). (gr. 4-7). pap. 3.99 (*0-671-01555-9*, Aladdin) Simon & Schuster Children's Publishing.

—Paradise Lost, Paradise Regained! 1998. (Secret World of Alex Mack Ser.: No. 34). 176p. (J). (gr. 4-7). pap. 4.50 (*0-671-02111-7*, Aladdin) Simon & Schuster Children's Publishing.

—Poison in Paradise! 1996. (Secret World of Alex Mack Ser.: No. 9). 144p. (J). (gr. 4-7). pap. 3.99 (*0-671-00083-7*, Aladdin) Simon & Schuster Children's Publishing.

—Witch Hunt! (Secret World of Alex Mack Ser.: No. 4). (J). (gr. 4-7). 1995. 144p. pap. 3.99 (*0-671-53301-0*); 1900. per. 1.99 (*0-671-01126-X*) Simon & Schuster Children's Publishing. (Aladdin).

—Zappy Holidays! 1996. (Secret World of Alex Mack Ser.: No. 10). 192p. (J). (gr. 4-7). pap. 3.99 (*0-671-00084-5*, Aladdin) Simon & Schuster Children's Publishing.

Garton, Ray. Lights, Camera, Action! 1998. (Secret World of Alex Mack Ser.: No. 33). 144p. (J). (gr. 4-7). pap. 3.99 (*0-671-02109-5*, Aladdin) Simon & Schuster Children's Publishing.

Lipman, Ken. Bad News Babysitting! 1995. (Secret World of Alex Mack Ser.: No. 3). 144p. (J). (gr. 4-7). pap. 3.99 (*0-671-53446-7*, Aladdin) Simon & Schuster Children's Publishing.

Locke, Joseph. Hocus Pocus! 1997. (Secret World of Alex Mack Ser.: No. 19). 144p. (J). (gr. 4-7). pap. 3.99 (*0-671-00707-6*, Aladdin) Simon & Schuster Children's Publishing.

Mitchell, V. E. Pool Party Panic! 1998. (Secret World of Alex Mack Ser.: No. 28). 144p. (J). (gr. 4-7). pap. 3.99 (*0-671-01428-5*, Aladdin) Simon & Schuster Children's Publishing.

Odom, Mel. In Hot Pursuit! 1998. (Secret World of Alex Mack Ser.: No. 25). 144p. (J). (gr. 4-7). pap. 3.99 (*0-671-01892-2*, Aladdin) Simon & Schuster Children's Publishing.

Pass, Erica. New York Nightmare! 1998. (Secret World of Alex Mack Ser.: No. 31). 144p. (J). (gr. 4-7). pap. 3.99 (*0-671-01957-0*, Aladdin) Simon & Schuster Children's Publishing.

Peel, John. I Spy! 1997. (Secret World of Alex Mack Ser.: No. 13). 144p. (J). (gr. 4-7). pap. 3.99 (*0-671-00356-9*, Aladdin) Simon & Schuster Children's Publishing.

—Lost in Vegas! 1998. (Secret World of Alex Mack Ser.: No. 23). 144p. (J). (gr. 4-7). pap. 3.99 (*0-671-00710-6*, Aladdin) Simon & Schuster Children's Publishing.

The Secret World of Alex Mack. 1900. (Secret World of Alex Mack Ser.). (J). (gr. 4-7). mass mkt. (*0-671-00715-7*, Aladdin) Simon & Schuster Children's Publishing.

Stone, Bonnie D. Civil War in Paradise! 1998. (Secret World of Alex Mack Ser.: No. 27). 144p. (J). (gr. 4-7). pap. 3.99 (*0-671-01891-4*, Aladdin) Simon & Schuster Children's Publishing.

Vornholt, John. Halloween Invaders! 1997. (Secret World of Alex Mack Ser.: No. 20). 144p. (J). (gr. 4-7). pap. 3.99 (*0-671-00708-4*, Aladdin) Simon & Schuster Children's Publishing.

—Haunted House Hijinks! 1998. (Secret World of Alex Mack Ser.: No. 32). 144p. (J). (gr. 4-7). pap. 3.99 (*0-671-02110-9*, Aladdin) Simon & Schuster Children's Publishing.

Weiss, David Cody, et al. Close Encounters! 1997. (Secret World of Alex Mack Ser.: No.18). 144p. (J). (gr. 4-7). pap. 3.99 (*0-671-00706-8*, Aladdin) Simon & Schuster Children's Publishing.

MACKENZIE WOMEN (FICTITIOUS CHARACTERS)—FICTION

Armstrong, Jennifer. Ann of the Wild Rose 1774. 1994. (Wild Rose Inn Ser.: No. 2). 192p. (YA). mass mkt. 3.99 o.s.i (*0-553-29867-4*) Bantam Bks.

—Bridie of the Wild Rose Inn 1695. 1994. (Wild Rose Inn Ser.: No. 1). 192p. (YA). mass mkt. 3.99 o.s.i (*0-553-29866-6*) Bantam Bks.

—Claire of the Wild Rose Inn 1928. 1994. (Wild Rose Inn Ser.: No. 5). 192p. (YA). mass mkt. 3.99 o.s.i (*0-553-29911-5*) Bantam Bks.

—Emily of the Wild Rose Inn 1858. 1994. (Wild Rose Inn Ser.: No. 3). 192p. (YA). (gr. 7 up). mass mkt. 3.99 o.s.i (*0-553-29909-3*) Bantam Bks.

—Grace of the Wild Rose Inn, 1944. 1994. (Wild Rose Inn Ser.: No. 6). 192p. (YA). mass mkt. 3.99 o.p. (*0-553-29912-3*) Bantam Bks.

—Laura of the Wild Rose Inn 1895. 1994. (Wild Rose Inn Ser.: No. 4). 176p. (YA). mass mkt. 3.99 o.s.i (*0-553-29910-7*) Bantam Bks.

—Wild Rose Inn. 1994. (J). mass mkt. 3.95 (*0-553-54154-4*);Vol. 2. mass mkt. o.s.i (*0-553-54155-2*) Random Hse. Children's Bks. (Dell Books for Young Readers).

MCLAUGHLIN, KEN (FICTITIOUS CHARACTER)—FICTION

O'Hara, Mary. My Friend Flicka. unabr. ed. 1988. (J). audio 56.00 (*0-7366-1427-3*, 2313) Books on Tape, Inc.

—My Friend Flicka. 1999. (Illus.). 320p. (YA). (gr. 4-7). reprint ed. 37.95 (*1-56849-725-3*) Buccaneer Bks., Inc.

—My Friend Flicka. 2003. (Charming Classics Ser.). (Illus.). 352p. (J). pap. 6.99 (*0-06-052429-4*) HarperCollins Children's Bk. Group.

—My Friend Flicka. 1988. 304p. (gr. 4-7). reprint ed. pap. 6.00 (*0-06-080902-7*, P-902, Perennial) HarperTrade.

—My Friend Flicka. rev. ed. 1973. (Illus.). 272p. (gr. 7-9). (J). text o.p. (*0-397-00008-1*); (YA). 15.95 (*0-397-00981-X*) Lippincott Williams & Wilkins. (Lippincott).

—My Friend Flicka. 1988. (J). 12.05 (*0-606-02855-2*) Turtleback Bks.

—Thunderhead. 1988. 384p. (gr. 4-7). reprint ed. pap. 7.50 (*0-06-080903-5*, P-903, Perennial) HarperTrade.

—Thunderhead. 1967. 320p. (YA). (gr. 5-9). pap. 1.75 o.s.i (*0-440-98875-6*, Laurel Leaf) Random Hse. Children's Bks.

—Thunderhead. 1971. (J). 12.60 o.p. (*0-606-02864-1*) Turtleback Bks.

MADELINE (FICTITIOUS CHARACTER)—FICTION

Bagwell, Stella. Madeline's Song. 1987. (Harlequin Romance Ser.). pap. (*0-373-08543-5*, Silhouette) Harlequin Enterprises, Ltd.

Bemelmans, Ludwig. Mad about Madeline: The Complete Tales. (Madeline Ser.). (J). (ps-3). 2001. 352p. 35.00 (*0-670-88816-8*); 1993. (Illus.). 32p. 35.00 o.s.i (*0-670-85187-6*, Viking Children's Bks.) Penguin Putnam Bks. for Young Readers.

—Mad about Madeline: The Complete Tales. 1999. (Madeline Ser.). (J). (ps-3). pap. 35.00 (*0-670-85297-X*) Viking Penguin.

—Madeline. 2000. (Madeline Ser.). (J). (ps-3). pap. 19.97 incl. audio (*0-7366-9200-2*); pap. 19.97 incl. audio (*0-7366-9200-2*) Books on Tape, Inc.

—Madeline. 1995. (Madeline Ser.). (J). (ps-3). reprint ed. lib. bdg. 25.95 (*1-56849-657-5*) Buccaneer Bks., Inc.

—Madeline. ed. 1988. (J). (gr. 2). spiral bd. (*0-616-01540-2*) Canadian National Institute for the Blind/Institut National Canadien pour les Aveugles.

—Madeline. 2003. (SPA., Illus.). (J). (gr. k-2). (*84-397-1070-4*, MO5057) Grijalbo Mondadori, S.A.-Junior ESP. *Dist:* Lectorum Pubns., Inc.

—Madeline. 1975. (Madeline Ser.). (Illus.). (J). (ps-3). pap., tchr. ed. 33.95 incl. audio (*0-670-44582-7*) Live Oak Media.

—Madeline, 2 bks. Grosman, Ernesto Livon, tr. from ENG. unabr. ed. 1999. (Madeline Ser.). (SPA., Illus.). (J). (ps-3). pap. 29.95 incl. audio (*0-87499-570-1*) Live Oak Media.

—Madeline. unabr. ed. (Madeline Ser.). (J). (ps-3). 1997. (SPA., Illus.). 24.95 incl. audio (*0-87499-409-8*); 1997. (SPA., Illus.). 24.95 incl. audio (*0-87499-409-8*); 1997. (SPA., Illus.). pap. 15.95 incl. audio (*0-87499-408-X*, LK7307); 1997. (SPA., Illus.). pap. 15.95 incl. audio (*0-87499-408-X*, LK7307); 1975. audio 9.95; 1975. (Illus.). 24.95 incl. audio (*0-670-44585-1*); 1975. (Illus.). pap. 15.95 incl. audio (*0-670-44588-6*) Live Oak Media.

—Madeline. (Madeline Ser.). (Illus.). (J). (ps-3). 2000. 48p. pap. 6.99 (*0-14-056439-X*); 1999. 8.10 o.p. (*0-14-095120-2*) Penguin Putnam Bks. for Young Readers. (Puffin Bks.).

—Madeline. Grosman, Ernesto L., tr. 1996. (Madeline Ser.). (SPA., Illus.). 48p. (J). (ps-3). pap. 6.99 (*0-14-055761-X*, VK1051) Penguin Putnam Bks. for Young Readers.

—Madeline. 1993. (Madeline Ser.). (Illus.). 1p. (J). (ps-3). 9.99 (*0-14-095121-0*) Penguin Putnam Bks. for Young Readers.

—Madeline. Grosman, Ernesto L., tr. 1993. (Madeline Ser.). (SPA., Illus.). 64p. (J). (ps-3). 16.99 (*0-670-85154-X*, PG54X, Viking Children's Bks.) Penguin Putnam Bks. for Young Readers.

—Madeline. (Madeline Ser.). (Illus.). (J). (ps-3). 1993. 32p. pap. 19.99 o.s.i (*0-14-054845-9*, Puffin Bks.); 1977. 48p. pap. 5.99 o.s.i (*0-14-050198-3*, Puffin Bks.); 1958. 48p. 16.99 (*0-670-44580-0*, Viking Children's Bks.) Penguin Putnam Bks. for Young Readers.

—Madeline. (Madeline Ser.). (J). (ps-3). 2000. (Illus.). 13.14 (*0-606-18426-0*); 1996. 12.14 (*0-606-08812-1*); 1977. 10.19 o.p. (*0-606-03874-4*) Turtleback Bks.

—Madeline: A Pop-Up Book. 1987. (Madeline Ser.). (Illus.). 12p. (J). (ps-3). 17.99 (*0-670-81667-1*, Viking Children's Bks.) Penguin Putnam Bks. for Young Readers.

—Madeline: A Pop-Up Carousel. 1994. (Madeline Ser.). (Illus.). 5p. (J). (ps-3). 10.99 o.s.i (*0-670-85602-9*) Penguin Putnam Bks. for Young Readers.

—Madeline & Other Bemelmans. unabr. ed. 1992. (Stand Alone Ser.). (J). (ps-3). audio 11.95 (*1-55994-654-7*) HarperChildren's Audio.

—Madeline & Other Bemelmans. abr. ed. Incl. Fifi. audio Happy Place. audio Madeline & the Bad Hat. audio Madeline's Rescue. audio (J). (ps-3). (Madeline Ser.). 1984. Set audio 9.95 (*0-89845-820-X*, CPN 1113, Caedmon) HarperTrade.

—Madeline & the Bad Hat. 2002. (Madeline Ser.). (Illus.). (J). 14.04 (*0-7587-4084-0*) Book Wholesalers, Inc.

—Madeline & the Bad Hat. ed. 1988. (J). (gr. 1). spiral bd. (*0-616-07214-7*); (gr. 2). spiral bd. (*0-616-07215-5*) Canadian National Institute for the Blind/Institut National Canadien pour les Aveugles.

—Madeline & the Bad Hat. (Madeline Ser.). (J). (ps-3). audio HarperTrade.

—Madeline & the Bad Hat. 1975. (Madeline Ser.). (Illus.). (J). (ps-3). pap., tchr. ed. 33.95 incl. audio (*0-670-44616-5*); 24.95 incl. audio (*0-670-44620-3*); pap. 15.95 incl. audio (*0-670-44621-1*) Live Oak Media.

—Madeline & the Bad Hat. (Madeline Ser.). (Illus.). 64p. (J). (ps-3). 2000. pap. 6.99 (*0-14-056648-1*); 1977. pap. 5.99 o.s.i (*0-14-050206-8*) Penguin Putnam Bks. for Young Readers. (Puffin Bks.).

—Madeline & the Bad Hat. 2000. (Madeline Ser.). (Illus.). (J). (ps-3). 13.14 (*0-606-18427-9*) Turtleback Bks.

—Madeline & the Gypsies. (Madeline Ser.). (J). (ps-3). audio o.p. HarperTrade.

—Madeline & the Gypsies. 1980. (Madeline Ser.). (Illus.). (J). (ps-3). pap., tchr. ed. 33.95 incl. audio (*0-670-44684-X*); 24.95 incl. audio (*0-670-44689-0*); pap. 15.95 incl. audio (*0-670-44688-2*) Live Oak Media.

—Madeline & the Gypsies. (Madeline Ser.). (Illus.). (J). (ps-3). 2000. 64p. pap. 6.99 (*0-14-056647-3*, Puffin Bks.); 1977. 64p. pap. 5.99 o.s.i (*0-14-050261-0*, Puffin Bks.); 1959. 56p. 16.99 (*0-670-44682-3*, Viking Children's Bks.) Penguin Putnam Bks. for Young Readers.

—Madeline & the Gypsies. (Madeline Ser.). (J). (ps-3). 2000. (Illus.). 13.14 (*0-606-18428-7*); 1959. 10.19 o.p. (*0-606-01010-6*) Turtleback Bks.

—Madeline & the Gypsies & Other Stories. unabr. ed. Incl. Castle Number Nine. audio o.p. Madeline & the Gypsies. audio o.p. Madeline in London. audio o.p. Quito Express. audio o.p. (J). (Madeline Ser.). Set audio 9.95 o.p. (*0-694-50686-9*, CDL5 1304, Caedmon) HarperTrade.

—Madeline Book & Toy Box. 1991. (Madeline Ser.). 64p. (J). (ps-3). 24.99 (*0-14-034880-8*, Puffin Bks.) Penguin Putnam Bks. for Young Readers.

—Madeline, Grades Preschool-3. 1997. (Madeline Ser.). (SPA., Illus.). pap., tchr. ed. 31.95 incl. audio (*0-87499-410-1*) Live Oak Media.

—Madeline in America & Other Holiday Tales. 2002. (Madeline Ser.). (Illus.). (J). 18.68 (*0-7587-4186-3*) Book Wholesalers, Inc.

—Madeline in America & Other Holiday Tales. 1999. (Madeline Ser.). (J). (ps-3). (Illus.). 111p. pap. 19.95 o.s.i (*0-590-03910-5*, Levine, Arthur A. Bks.); pap. 125.00 (*0-439-09633-2*) Scholastic, Inc.

—Madeline in London. 2002. (Madeline Ser.). (Illus.). (J). 14.04 (*0-7587-5002-1*) Book Wholesalers, Inc.

—Madeline in London. ed. 1998. (J). (gr. 2). spiral bd. (*0-616-01545-3*) Canadian National Institute for the Blind/Institut National Canadien pour les Aveugles.

—Madeline in London. (Madeline Ser.). (J). (ps-3). audio o.p. HarperTrade.

—Madeline in London. (Madeline Ser.). (Illus.). (J). (ps-3). 1978. pap., tchr. ed. 33.95 incl. audio (*0-670-44650-5*); 1995. pap. 15.95 incl. audio (*0-670-44655-6*); 1978. 24.95 incl. audio (*0-670-44651-3*) Live Oak Media.

—Madeline in London. (Madeline Ser.). (Illus.). 64p. (J). (ps-3). 2000. pap. 6.99 (*0-14-056649-X*, Puffin Bks.); 1977. pap. 5.99 o.s.i (*0-14-050199-1*, Puffin Bks.); 1961. 16.99 (*0-670-44648-3*, Viking Children's Bks.) Penguin Putnam Bks. for Young Readers.

—Madeline in London. (Madeline Ser.). (J). (ps-3). 2000. (Illus.). 13.14 (*0-606-18429-5*); 1978. 10.19 o.p. (*0-606-03875-2*) Turtleback Bks.

—Madeline Playtime Activity Book. 1997. (Madeline Ser.). (Illus.). 16p. (J). (ps-3). pap. 7.99 (*0-670-87464-7*) Penguin Putnam Bks. for Young Readers.

—Madeline Storybook Collection Snap & Fold Away. 1994. (J). 14.98 (*0-670-77188-0*) Penguin Putnam Bks. for Young Readers.

—Madeline's Christmas. 2002. (Madeline Ser.). (Illus.). (J). 14.04 (*0-7587-5650-X*) Book Wholesalers, Inc.

—Madeline's Christmas. ed. 1998. (J). (gr. 1). spiral bd. (*0-616-01547-X*); (gr. 2). spiral bd. (*0-616-01548-8*) Canadian National Institute for the Blind/Institut National Canadien pour les Aveugles.

—Madeline's Christmas. (Madeline Ser.). 32p. (J). (ps-3). 2000. (Illus.). pap. 6.99 (*0-14-056650-3*, Puffin Bks.); 1993. (Illus.). pap. 9.99 incl. audio (*0-14-095108-3*, Puffin Bks.); 1988. pap. 5.99 o.s.i

(*0-14-050666-7*, Puffin Bks.); 1985. (Illus.). 15.99 (*0-670-80666-8*, Viking Children's Bks.) Penguin Putnam Bks. for Young Readers.

—Madeline's Christmas. 1984. (Madeline Ser.). (J). (ps-3). 12.14 (*0-606-03983-X*) Turtleback Bks.

—Madeline's Christmas Book: With Doll. 2002. (Illus.). (J). (ps-3). 21.99 (*0-670-03595-5*) Penguin Putnam Bks. for Young Readers.

—Madeline's House: Madeline; Madeline's Rescue; Madeline & the Bad Hat. 1989. (Madeline Ser.). (Illus.). (J). (ps-3). pap. 12.99 (*0-14-095028-1*) Penguin Putnam Bks. for Young Readers.

—Madeline's Rescue. 2002. (Madeline Ser.). (Illus.). (J). 14.04 (*0-7587-4085-9*) Book Wholesalers, Inc.

—Madeline's Rescue. ed. 1998. (J). (gr. 2). spiral bd. (*0-616-01546-1*) Canadian National Institute for the Blind/Institut National Canadien pour les Aveugles.

—Madeline's Rescue. (Madeline Ser.). (J). (ps-3). 14.95 o.p. incl. audio Kimbo Educational.

—Madeline's Rescue. 1978. (Madeline Ser.). (J). (ps-3). audio 9.95. (Illus.). 24.95 incl. audio (*0-670-44719-6*); (Illus.). pap., tchr. ed. 33.95 incl. audio (*0-670-44718-8*); (Illus.). pap. 15.95 incl. audio (*0-670-44723-4*) Live Oak Media.

—Madeline's Rescue. (Madeline Ser.). (J). (ps-3). 2000. (Illus.). 64p. pap. 6.99 (*0-14-056651-1*, Puffin Bks.); 1993. (Illus.). 9.99 (*0-14-095122-9*, Puffin Bks.); 1993. (Illus.). 9.99 (*0-14-095122-9*, Puffin Bks.); 1989. 6.95 o.p. (*0-14-095034-6*, Puffin Bks.); 1977. (Illus.). 64p. pap. 5.99 o.s.i (*0-14-050207-6*, Puffin Bks.); 1953. (Illus.). 56p. 16.99 (*0-670-44716-1*, Viking Children's Bks.) Penguin Putnam Bks. for Young Readers.

—Madeline's Rescue. (Madeline Ser.). (J). (ps-3). 2000. 13.14 (*0-606-17822-8*); 1977. 10.19 o.p. (*0-606-03876-0*) Turtleback Bks.

—Madeline's Rescue. (Madeline Ser.). (J). (ps-3). 24.95 incl. audio. pap. 32.75 incl. audio. pap. 15.95 incl. audio Weston Woods Studios, Inc.

—Madeline's Velcro. 1997. (Madeline Ser.). (J). (ps-3). pap. 14.98 (*0-670-78126-6*) NAL.

Bemelmans, Ludwig, illus. Madeline. 2001. (Early Readers Ser.: Vol. 1). (J). lib. bdg. (*1-59054-454-4*) Fitzgerald Bks.

—Madeline & the Gypsies. 2001. (First Readers Ser.: Vol. 4). lib. bdg. (*1-59054-455-2*) Fitzgerald Bks.

Bemelmans, Ludwig & Barrett, Judith. Madeline's Rescue. 2000. (Madeline Ser.). (J). (ps-3). pap. 19.97 incl. audio (*0-7366-9205-3*) Books on Tape, Inc.

Bemelmans, Ludwig & Outlet Book Company Staff. Madeline & the Bad Hat. 1988. (Madeline Ser.). (J). (ps-3). 0.75 o.s.i (*0-517-18388-9*) Random Hse. Value Publishing.

Jones, Rebecca C. Madeline & the Great (Old) Escape Artist. 1983. (Madeline Ser.). 112p. (J). (ps-3). 9.95 o.p. (*0-525-44074-7*, 0966-290, Dutton) Dutton/Plume.

Madeline's Christmas. 2001. (First Readers Ser.: Vol. 2). (J). lib. bdg. (*1-59054-527-3*) Fitzgerald Bks.

Marciano, John Bemelmans. Madeline Says Merci: The Always Be Polite Book. 2001. (Madeline Ser.). (Illus.). 48p. (J). (ps-3). 11.99 (*0-670-03505-X*, Viking Children's Bks.) Penguin Putnam Bks. for Young Readers.

Wheeler, Jody. Madeline Christmas Activity Book: With Reusable Vinyl Stickers. 1998. (Madeline Ser.). (Illus.). 16p. (J). (ps-3). 7.99 (*0-670-88204-6*, Viking Children's Bks.) Penguin Putnam Bks. for Young Readers.

—Madeline Paper Dolls. 1994. (Madeline Ser.). (Illus.). 24p. (J). (ps-3). 6.99 (*0-670-85601-0*) Penguin Putnam Bks. for Young Readers.

—Madeline's Birthday Activity Book. 1999. (Madeline Ser.). (Illus.). 16p. (J). (ps-3). pap. 7.99 (*0-670-88767-6*, Viking Children's Bks.) Penguin Putnam Bks. for Young Readers.

MAGALHAES, FERNAO DE, D. 1521—FICTION

Torrey, Michele. To the Edge of the World. 2003. (Illus.). 240p. (J). (gr. 7). 15.95 (*0-375-82338-7*); lib. bdg. 17.99 (*0-375-92338-1*) Knopf, Alfred A. Inc.

MAGRUDER, BERNIE (FICTITIOUS CHARACTER)—FICTION

Naylor, Phyllis Reynolds. Bernie Magruder & the Haunted Hotel. 2001. (Bernie Magruder Ser.). (Illus.). 176p. (J). (gr. 3-7). pap. 4.99 (*0-689-84126-4*, Aladdin) Simon & Schuster Children's Publishing.

—Bernie Magruder & the Haunted Hotel. l.t. ed. 2001. 127p. (J). 20.95 (*0-7862-3600-0*) Thorndike Pr.

—The Bodies in the Bessledorf Hotel. 1988. pap. 2.99 (*0-380-70485-4*, Avon Bks.) Morrow/Avon.

—The Bodies in the Bessledorf Hotel. 1986. 144p. (J). (gr. 3-7). lib. bdg. 15.00 (*0-689-31304-7*, Atheneum) Simon & Schuster Children's Publishing.

MAISY (FICTITIOUS CHARACTER)—FICTION

Cousins, Lucy. Los Amigos de Maisy. 2000. (Maisy Bks.).Tr. of Maisy's Friends. (SPA., Illus.). 16p. (J). (ps). 8.95 (*84-95040-11-5*) Lectorum Pubns., Inc.

—El Autobus de Maisy. 2000. (Maisy Bks.). (CAT., Illus.). 24p. (J). (ps). 10.95 (*84-95040-70-0*) Serres, Ediciones, S. L. ESP. *Dist:* Lectorum Pubns., Inc.

—Bathtime, Maisy! 2001. (Maisy Bks.). (Illus.). 6p. (J). (ps). bds. 6.99 (*0-7636-1600-1*) Candlewick Pr.

—Bedtime, Maisy! 2001. (Maisy Bks.). (Illus.). 6p. (J). (ps). bds. 6.99 (*0-7636-1601-X*) Candlewick Pr.

—El Carnaval de Maisy. 2000. (Maisy Bks.). (Illus.). 24p. (J). (ps). (CAT.). 10.95 (*84-95040-41-7*); (SPA., 10.95 (*84-95040-40-9*, RR1669) Serres, Ediciones, S. L. ESP. *Dist:* Lectorum Pubns., Inc.

—Los Colores de Maisy. 2000. (Maisy Bks.). (SPA.). 24p. (J). (ps). (*84-88061-63-3*) Lectorum Pubns., Inc.

—Los Colores de Maisy. 2001. (Illus.). (J). (ps). (CAT.). 16p. 10.95 (*84-95040-60-3*); (SPA., 24p. 15.95 (*84-95040-75-1*, RR7142) Serres, Ediciones, S. L. ESP. *Dist:* Lectorum Pubns., Inc., Lectorum Pubns., Inc., Libros Sin Fronteras.

—Las Cosas Favoritas de Maisy. 2000. (Maisy Bks.).Tr. of Maisy's Favorite Things. (SPA., Illus.). 16p. (J). (ps). 8.95 (*84-95040-12-3*) Lectorum Pubns., Inc.

—Count with Maisy. (Maisy Bks.). (Illus.). (J). (ps). 1997. 24p. bds. 8.99 o.p. (*0-7636-0156-X*); 1996. 4.99 (*0-7636-0166-7*); 2nd ed. 1999. 24p. bds. 5.99 (*0-7636-0234-5*) Candlewick Pr.

—Cuenta con Maisy. 2000. (Maisy Bks.). (SPA.). 24p. (J). (ps). 11.95 (*84-88061-62-5*) Lectorum Pubns., Inc.

—Cuenta con Maisy. 2001. (Illus.). (J). (CAT.). 16p. 10.95 (*84-95040-74-3*); (SPA., 24p. 10.95 (*84-95040-73-5*, RR6313) Serres, Ediciones, S. L. ESP. *Dist:* Lectorum Pubns., Inc.

—Un Dia con Maisy. 2000. (Maisy Bks.). (SPA., Illus.). 16p. (J). (ps). 10.50 (*84-95040-09-3*) Lectorum Pubns., Inc.

—Los Disfraces de Maisy. 2000. (Maisy Bks.). (SPA., Illus.). 16p. (J). (ps). 13.95 (*84-95040-19-0*) Lectorum Pubns., Inc.

—Doctor Maisy. 2001. (Maisy Bks.). (Illus.). 24p. (J). (ps). 9.99 o.s.i (*0-7636-1612-5*); bds. 3.29 (*0-7636-1613-3*) Candlewick Pr.

—Donde Esta el Panda de Maisy? 1999. (Maisy Bks.). (Illus.). 16p. (J). (ps). (CAT.). 10.95 (*84-95040-08-5*); (SPA., 10.95 (*84-95040-07-7*, RR4459) Serres, Ediciones, S. L. ESP. *Dist:* Lectorum Pubns., Inc.

—Donde Se Esconde Maisy? 1999. (Maisy Bks.). (Illus.). 16p. (J). (ps). (CAT.). 10.95 (*84-95040-06-9*); (SPA., 10.95 (*84-95040-05-0*, RR4499) Serres, Ediciones, S. L. ESP. *Dist:* Lectorum Pubns., Inc.

—Donde Vive Maisy? 2000. (Maisy Bks.). (Illus.). 16p. (J). (ps). (CAT.). 10.95 (*84-95040-47-6*); (SPA., 10.95 (*84-95040-46-8*) Serres, Ediciones, S. L. ESP. *Dist:* Lectorum Pubns., Inc.

—Dress Maisy: Sticker Book. 1999. (Maisy Bks.). (Illus.). 16p. (J). (ps). bds. 3.99 (*0-7636-0749-5*) Candlewick Pr.

—Feliz Cumpleanos, Maisy. 1999. (Maisy Bks.). (Illus.). 16p. (J). (ps). (CAT.). 16.95 (*84-88061-95-1*); (SPA., 16.95 (*84-88061-96-X*, RR3371) Serres, Ediciones, S. L. ESP. *Dist:* Lectorum Pubns., Inc.

—Feliz Navidad, Maisy! 2000. (Maisy Bks.). (Illus.). (J). (ps). (CAT.). 18p. 19.95 (*84-95040-62-X*); (SPA., 316p. 19.95 (*84-95040-61-1*, RR1434) Serres, Ediciones, S. L. ESP. *Dist:* Lectorum Pubns., Inc.

—Fun with Maisy. 2002. (Illus.). 16p. (J). (ps-k). pap. 3.99 (*0-7636-1841-1*) Candlewick Pr.

—Go, Maisy, Go! 2003. (Illus.). 10p. (J). bds. 8.99 (*0-7636-2118-8*) Candlewick Pr.

—Good Morning Maisy. 2003. (Backpack Pals Book & Toy Ser.). (Illus.). 14p. bds. 6.99 (*0-7636-2080-7*) Candlewick Pr.

—Happy Birthday, Maisy. (J). 2004. 14p. pap. 4.99 (*0-7636-2454-3*); 1998. (Illus.). 16p. 13.99 (*0-7636-0577-8*) Candlewick Pr.

—Maisy & Her Friends. 1999. (Maisy Bks.). (J). (ps). bds. 1.49 (*0-7636-0821-1*) Candlewick Pr.

—Maisy at the Beach: Sticker Book. 2001. (Maisy Bks.). (Illus.). 16p. (J). (ps). bds. 3.99 (*0-7636-1504-8*) Candlewick Pr.

—Maisy at the Fair. 2001. (Maisy Bks.). (Illus.). 24p. (J). (ps). 9.99 (*0-7636-1500-5*); bds. 3.29 (*0-7636-1502-1*) Candlewick Pr.

—Maisy at the Farm. 1998. (Maisy Bks.). (Illus.). 16p. (J). (ps). 13.99 (*0-7636-0576-X*) Candlewick Pr.

—Maisy Dresses Up. 1999. (Maisy Bks.). (Illus.). 24p. (J). (ps). 9.99 (*0-7636-0885-8*); bds. 3.29 (*0-7636-0909-9*) Candlewick Pr.

—Maisy Drives the Bus. (Maisy Bks.). (Illus.). (J). (ps). 2001. 16p. bds. 4.99 (*0-7636-1463-7*); 2000. 24p. 9.99 o.s.i (*0-7636-1083-6*); 2000. 24p. bds. 3.29 (*0-7636-1085-2*) Candlewick Pr.

—Maisy en la Granja. 1999. (Maisy Bks.). (Illus.). (J). (ps). (CAT.). 16p. 16.95 (*84-88061-94-3*); (SPA., 24p. 16.95 (*84-88061-97-8*, RR3457) Serres, Ediciones, S. L. ESP. *Dist:* Lectorum Pubns., Inc.

—Maisy Goes Shopping. (Backpack Pals Book & Toy Ser.). 2003. 14p. bds. 6.99 (*0-7636-2081-5*); 2001. (Illus.). 24p. (J). 9.99 (*0-7636-1501-3*); 2001. (Illus.). 24p. (J). bds. 3.29 (*0-7636-1503-X*) Candlewick Pr.

—Maisy Goes Swimming. 1990. (Maisy Bks.). 16p. (J). (ps). 13.95 (*0-316-15834-8*) Little Brown Children's Bks.

—Maisy Goes to Bed. 1990. (Maisy Bks.). (Illus.). 1p. (J). (ps). 13.95 (*0-316-15832-1*) Little Brown Children's Bks.

—Maisy Goes to School. 1992. (Maisy Bks.). (Illus.). 16p. (J). (ps). 13.99 (*1-56402-085-1*) Candlewick Pr.

—Maisy Goes to the Playground. 1992. (Maisy Bks.). (Illus.). 16p. (J). (ps). 13.99 (*1-56402-084-3*) Candlewick Pr.

—Maisy Goes to Work. 2002. (Illus.). 16p. (J). (ps-k). bds. 3.99 (*0-7636-1840-3*) Candlewick Pr.

—Maisy Likes Dancing. 2003. (Illus.). 12p. (J). bds. 6.99 (*0-7636-1916-7*) Candlewick Pr.

—Maisy Likes Music. 2002. (Illus.). 12p. (J). (ps-k). bds. 6.99 (*0-7636-1915-9*) Candlewick Pr.

—Maisy Loves You. 2003. (Illus.). 10p. bds. 5.99 (*0-7636-2065-3*) Candlewick Pr.

—Maisy Makes Gingerbread. 1999. (Maisy Bks.). (Illus.). 24p. (J). (ps). 9.99 (*0-7636-0887-4*); bds. 3.29 (*0-7636-0910-2*) Candlewick Pr.

—Maisy Makes Lemonade. 2002. (Illus.). 24p. (J). (ps-k). 9.99 (*0-7636-1728-8*); bds. 3.29 (*0-7636-1729-6*) Candlewick Pr.

—Maisy Plays. 2001. (Maisy Bks.). (Illus.). 16p. (J). (ps). bds. 4.99 (*0-7636-1462-9*) Candlewick Pr.

—Maisy Se Va a la Cama. 2000. (Maisy Bks.). (Illus.). 16p. (J). (ps). (CAT.). 16.95 (*84-88061-50-1*); (SPA., 16.95 (*84-88061-33-1*, RR7051) Serres, Ediciones, S. L. ESP. *Dist:* Lectorum Pubns., Inc., Lectorum Pubns., Inc., Libros Sin Fronteras.

—Maisy Se Va a la Guarderia. 1997. (Maisy Bks.). (Illus.). 16p. (J). (ps). (SPA.). 16.95 (*84-88061-45-5*, RR7148); (CAT., 16.95 (*84-88061-49-8*) Serres, Ediciones, S. L. ESP. *Dist:* Lectorum Pubns., Inc.

—Maisy Se Va a Nadar. 2000. (Maisy Bks.). (Illus.). (J). (ps). (SPA.). 24p. 16.95 (*84-88061-32-3*, RR7052); (CAT & SPA., 16p. 16.95 (*84-88061-47-1*) Serres, Ediciones, S. L. ESP. *Dist:* Lectorum Pubns., Inc.

—Maisy Takes a Bath. 2000. (Maisy Bks.). (Illus.). (J). (ps). 9.99 (*0-7636-0182-9*); 24p. bds. 3.29 (*0-7636-1084-4*); 24p. 9.99 o.s.i (*0-7636-1082-8*) Candlewick Pr.

—Maisy y Sus Amigos. 1999. (Maisy Bks.). (Illus.). 16p. (J). (ps). (CAT & SPA.). 16.95 (*84-95040-03-4*); (SPA., 16.95 (*84-95040-02-6*, RR2456) Serres, Ediciones, S. L. ESP. *Dist:* Lectorum Pubns., Inc.

—Maisy's ABC. 1995. (Maisy Bks.). (Illus.). 16p. (J). (ps). 13.99 (*1-56402-419-9*) Candlewick Pr.

—Maisy's Bedtime. 1999. (Maisy Bks.). (Illus.). 24p. (J). (ps). 9.99 o.s.i (*0-7636-0884-X*); bds. 3.29 (*0-7636-0908-0*) Candlewick Pr.

—Maisy's Bedtime Board Book & Doll Gift Box. gif. ed. 2002. (Illus.). 14p. (J). 12.99 (*0-7636-1943-4*) Candlewick Pr.

—Maisy's Best Friends. 2003. (Illus.). 10p. (J). bds. 5.99 (*0-7636-2128-5*) Candlewick Pr.

—Maisy's Big Flap Book. 2001. (Maisy Bks.). (Illus.). 10p. (J). (ps). bds. 8.99 (*0-7636-1189-1*) Candlewick Pr.

—Maisy's Busy Book. 1999. (Maisy Bks.). (Illus.). 16p. (J). (ps). bds. 4.99 (*0-7636-0927-7*) Candlewick Pr.

—Maisy's Colors. (Maisy Bks.). (Illus.). 24p. (J). (ps). 1997. bds. 8.99 o.p. (*0-7636-0159-4*); 2nd ed. 1999. bds. 5.99 (*0-7636-0237-X*) Candlewick Pr.

—Maisy's Day. 1999. (Maisy Bks.). (Illus.). (J). (ps). bds. 3.99 (*0-7636-0750-9*) Candlewick Pr.

—Maisy's Farm: A Pop-Up & Play Book. 2001. (Maisy Bks.). (Illus.). 8p. (J). (ps). 16.99 (*0-7636-1294-4*) Candlewick Pr.

—Maisy's Favorite Animals. 2001. (Maisy Bks.). (Illus.). 22p. (J). (ps). bds. 3.99 (*0-7636-1572-2*) Candlewick Pr.

—Maisy's Favorite Clothes. 2001. (Maisy Bks.). (Illus.). 22p. (J). (ps). bds. 3.99 (*0-7636-1573-0*) Candlewick Pr.

—Maisy's Favorite Things. (Maisy Bks.). (Illus.). (J). (ps). 2001. 22p. bds. 3.99 (*0-7636-1574-9*); 1999. 24p. bds. 1.49 o.p. (*0-7636-0820-3*) Candlewick Pr.

—Maisy's Favorite Toys. 2001. (Maisy Bks.). (Illus.). 22p. (J). (ps). bds. 3.99 (*0-7636-1571-4*) Candlewick Pr.

—Maisy's Fire Engine. 2002. (Maisy Bks.). (Illus.). 16p. (J). (ps-k). bds. 4.99 (*0-7636-1780-6*) Candlewick Pr.

—Maisy's Garden: Sticker Book. 2001. (Maisy Bks.). (Illus.). 16p. (J). (ps). bds. 3.99 (*0-7636-1505-6*) Candlewick Pr.

—Maisy's Morning on the Farm. 2001. (Maisy Bks.). (Illus.). 24p. (J). (ps). 9.99 o.s.i (*0-7636-1610-9*); bds. 3.29 (*0-7636-1611-7*) Candlewick Pr.

—Maisy's Noisy Day. 2003. (Illus.). 12p. (J). (ps-k). bds. 6.99 (*0-7636-1917-5*) Candlewick Pr.

—Maisy's Party Book. 1999. (Maisy Bks.). (Illus.). 16p. (J). (ps). bds. 4.99 (*0-7636-0926-9*) Candlewick Pr.

—Maisy's Pool. 1999. (Maisy Bks.). (Illus.). 24p. (J). (ps). 9.99 (*0-7636-0886-6*); bds. 3.29 (*0-7636-0907-2*) Candlewick Pr.

—Maisy's Pop-Up Playhouse. 1995. (Maisy Bks.). (Illus.). 8p. (J). (ps). 16.99 (*1-56402-635-3*) Candlewick Pr.

—Maisy's Seasons. 2002. (Illus.). 12p. (J). (ps-k). bds. 8.99 (*0-7636-1914-0*) Candlewick Pr.

—Maisy's Train. 2002. (Maisy Noisy Board Bks.). (Illus.). 16p. (J). (ps-k). bds. 4.99 (*0-7636-1781-4*) Candlewick Pr.

—Merry Christmas, Maisy. (Illus.). 2003. 16p. 4.99 (*0-7636-2241-9*); 2000. 24p. (J). 12.99 (*0-7636-1279-0*) Candlewick Pr.

—Playtime, Maisy! 2001. (Maisy Bks.). (Illus.). 6p. (J). (ps). bds. 6.99 (*0-7636-1602-8*) Candlewick Pr.

—Snacktime, Maisy! 2001. (Maisy Bks.). (Illus.). 6p. (J). (ps). bds. 6.99 (*0-7636-1603-6*) Candlewick Pr.

—Squeak, Squeak, Maisy! 2002. (Illus.). 12p. (J). (ps-k). bds. 6.99 (*0-7636-1918-3*) Candlewick Pr.

—Where Are Maisy's Friends? A Lift-The-Flap Book. 2000. (Maisy Bks.). (Illus.). 12p. (J). (ps). bds. 4.99 (*0-7636-1119-0*) Candlewick Pr.

—Where Does Maisy Live? A Lift-The-Flap Book. 2000. (Maisy Bks.). (Illus.). 12p. (J). (ps). bds. 4.99 (*0-7636-1163-8*) Candlewick Pr.

—Where Is Maisy? A Lift-The-Flap Book. 1999. (Maisy Bks.). (Illus.). 14p. (J). (ps). bds. 4.99 (*0-7636-0752-5*) Candlewick Pr.

—Where Is Maisy's Panda? A Lift-The-Flap Book. 1999. (Maisy Bks.). (Illus.). 14p. (J). (ps). bds. 4.99 (*0-7636-0753-3*) Candlewick Pr.

MARCH FAMILY (FICTITIOUS CHARACTERS)—FICTION

Alcott, Louisa May. Jo's Boys. 1988. (J). 23.95 (*0-8488-0411-2*) Amereon, Ltd.

—Jo's Boys. 1995. 336p. mass mkt. 4.95 (*0-553-21449-7*) Bantam Bks.

—Jo's Boys. 1999. (Children's Thrift Classics Ser.). (Illus.). 80p. (J). pap. 1.00 (*0-486-40789-6*) Dover Pubns., Inc.

—Jo's Boys. 1987. 304p. (YA). (gr. 7-12). mass mkt. 2.25 o.p. (*0-451-52089-0*, Signet Classics) NAL.

—Jo's Boys. (gr. 4-7). 1996. (Illus.). 350p. (YA). 4.99 (*0-14-036714-4*); 1984. 352p. (J). pap. 3.99 o.p. (*0-14-035015-2*, Puffin Bks.) Penguin Putnam Bks. for Young Readers.

—Jo's Boys. 1949. (Illustrated Junior Library). (J). (gr. 4-6). 5.95 o.p. (*0-448-05813-8*); 8.95 o.p. (*0-448-06013-2*) Putnam Publishing Group, The.

—Jo's Boys. 1994. 320p. (J). (gr. 4-8). 8.99 o.s.i (*0-517-11830-0*) Random Hse. Value Publishing.

—Jo's Boys. 1989. (Works of Louisa May Alcott). (J). reprint ed. lib. bdg. 79.00 (*0-7812-1642-7*) Reprint Services Corp.

—Jo's Boys. 1992. 344p. (J). mass mkt. 3.25 o.p. (*0-590-45178-2*, Scholastic Paperbacks) Scholastic, Inc.

—Jo's Boys & How They Turned Out. 2000. 252p. (J). pap. 9.95 (*0-594-05147-9*); E-Book 3.95 (*0-594-05150-9*) 1873 Pr.

—Jo's Boys & How They Turned Out. 1994. 336p. (J). (gr. 4-7). pap. 8.95 (*0-316-03103-8*); 1994. 316p. (J). (gr. 7-10). 16.95 o.p. (*0-316-03110-0*); 1986. (YA). (gr. 7 up). 19.95 o.s.i (*0-316-03093-7*) Little Brown & Co.

—Little Men: Life at Plumfield with Jo's Boys. unabr. ed. 1991. (YA). (gr. 4-7). audio 53.95 (*1-55685-200-2*) Audio Bk. Contractors, Inc.

—Little Women. 1998. (Keepsake Collection Bks.). (J). 3.99 o.p. (*1-57145-101-3*, Thunder Bay Pr.) Advantage Pubs. Group.

—Little Women. 1966. (Airmont Classics Ser.). (Illus.). (YA). (gr. 6 up). pap. 2.95 o.p. (*0-8049-0106-6*, CL-106) Airmont Publishing Co., Inc.

—Little Women. 1996. (Andre Deutsch Classics). 264p. (J). (gr. 5-8). 11.95 (*0-233-99040-2*) Andre Deutsch GBR. *Dist:* Trafalgar Square, Trans-Atlantic Pubns., Inc.

—Little Women. 1983. 480p. (ps up). mass mkt. 3.95 (*0-553-21275-3*, Bantam Classics) Bantam Bks.

—Little Women. 1998. (Young Reader's Christian Library). (Illus.). 192p. (J). (gr. 3-7). pap. 1.39 o.p. (*1-57748-229-8*) Barbour Publishing, Inc.

—Little Women. (Paperback Classics Ser.). (J). 1995. 294p. pap. 2.95 o.p. (*0-681-10333-7*); 1994. (Illus.). 10.95 o.p. (*0-681-00767-2*); 1986. (Illus.). 388p. (gr. 4 up). 12.95 o.p. (*0-681-40055-2*) Borders Pr.

—Little Women. 1995. (Illus.). 93p. (J). 7.98 o.p. (*1-85854-176-X*) Brimax Bks., Ltd.

—Little Women. 1987. 608p. (gr. k-6). pap. text 4.99 o.s.i (*0-440-44768-2*) Dell Publishing.

—Little Women. Gerver, Jane E., ed. 1999. (Eyewitness Classics Ser.). (Illus.). 64p. (J). (gr. 2 up). pap. 14.95 (*0-7894-4767-3*, D K Ink) Dorling Kindersley Publishing, Inc.

—Little Women. 2000. (Juvenile Classics). (Illus.). 608p. (J). pap. 3.00 (*0-486-41023-4*) Dover Pubns., Inc.

—Little Women. 1999. (Focus on the Family Great Stories Ser.). (Illus.). 576p. (J). pap. 9.99 o.p. (*1-56179-744-8*) Focus on the Family Publishing.

—Little Women. 2001. (Young Reader's Classics Ser.). 94p. (J). pap. 9.95 (*1-55013-783-2*, Key Porter kids) Key Porter Bks. CAN. *Dist:* Firefly Bks., Ltd.

—Little Women. (Illus.). 192p. (J). 9.95 (*1-56156-371-4*) Kidsbooks, Inc.

—Little Women. 1994. (Everyman's Library Children's Classics Ser.). 530p. (gr. 4 up). 14.95 (*0-679-43642-1*, Everyman's Library) Knopf Publishing Group.

—Little Women. 1988. (Knopf Book & Cassette Classics Ser.). (Illus.). 512p. (J). 18.95 o.s.i (*0-394-56279-8*) Knopf, Alfred A. Inc.

—Little Women. 1994. 512p. (J). (gr. 4-7). 19.95 (*0-316-03107-0*); 1994. 512p. (J). (gr. 4-7). pap. 9.99 (*0-316-03105-4*); 1968. (Illus.). 524p. (YA). (gr. 7 up). 19.95 (*0-316-03095-3*) Little Brown & Co.

—Little Women. (J). E-Book 1.95 (*1-58515-196-3*) MesaView, Inc.

—Little Women. 1924. (Books of Wonder). (J). 22.99 o.s.i (*0-688-14090-4*, Morrow, William & Co.) Morrow/Avon.

—Little Women. 1983. 480p. (J). (gr. 3 up). mass mkt. 3.95 (*0-451-52341-5*, Signet Classics) NAL.

—Little Women. Bassett, Jennifer, ed. 1995. (Illus.). 78p. (J). pap. text 5.95 o.p. (*0-19-422756-1*) Oxford Univ. Pr., Inc.

—Little Women. 1982. (Oxford Graded Readers Ser.). (Illus.). 48p. (YA). (gr. 7-12). pap. text 3.25 o.p. (*0-19-421804-X*) Oxford Univ. Pr., Inc.

—Little Women. Lindskoog, Kathryn, ed. 2003. (Classics for Young Readers Ser.). (Illus.). 432p. (J). per. 12.99 (*0-87552-734-5*) P&R Publishing.

—Little Women. 9999. (Children's Classics Ser.: No. 740-25). (Illus.). (J). (gr. 3-5). 3.50 o.p. (*0-7214-5005-9*, Ladybird Bks.) Penguin Group (USA) Inc.

—Little Women. (Whole Story Ser.). 1997. 288p. (J). (gr. 7-12). 23.99 o.s.i (*0-670-87705-0*, Viking Children's Bks.); 1997. (Illus.). 696p. (J). (gr. 5-9). pap. 6.99 (*0-14-038022-1*, Puffin Bks.); 1995. (Illus.). 336p. (YA). (gr. 5 up). pap. 4.99 o.p. (*0-14-036668-7*); 1983. 304p. (J). (gr. 3-7). pap. 3.50 o.p. (*0-14-035008-X*, Puffin Bks.); 1981. (Illus.). (J). (gr. 4-6). 9.95 o.s.i (*0-448-11019-9*, Grosset & Dunlap); 1963. (Illus.). (J). (gr. 4-6). 3.95 o.p. (*0-448-05466-3*, Grosset & Dunlap) Penguin Putnam Bks. for Young Readers.

—Little Women. Vogel, Malvina, ed. 1989. (Great Illustrated Classics Ser.: Vol. 4). (Illus.). 240p. (J). (gr. 3-6). 9.95 (*0-86611-955-8*) Playmore, Inc., Pubs.

—Little Women. (Louisa May Alcott Library). (J). 1971. (gr. 4-6). 5.95 o.p. (*0-448-02364-4*); 1969. (Illus.). (gr. 5 up). 15.00 o.s.i (*0-529-00529-8*) Putnam Publishing Group, The.

—Little Women. 2001. (Classics Ser.). (Illus.). 528p. pap. 7.95 (*0-375-75672-8*, Modern Library) Random House Adult Trade Publishing Group.

—Little Women. 1994. (Step into Classics Ser.). 112p. (J). (gr. 3-5). pap. 3.99 (*0-679-86175-0*, Random Hse. Bks. for Young Readers) Random Hse. Children's Bks.

—Little Women. (Children's Classics Ser.). (J). 1998. (Illus.). 400p. 5.99 (*0-517-18954-2*); 1995. 4.99 o.s.i (*0-517-14144-2*); 1995. (Illus.). 16.98 o.s.i (*0-517-15116-2*, Gramercy); 1988. (Illus.). 400p. (gr. 2 up). 12.99 o.s.i (*0-517-63489-9*) Random Hse. Value Publishing.

—Little Women. 1985. (Illus.). 432p. (J). (gr. 4-12). 12.95 o.p. (*0-89577-209-4*) Reader's Digest Assn., Inc., The.

—Little Women. 1999. (Giant Courage Classics Ser.). 688p. (YA). 9.00 o.p. (*0-7624-0565-1*, Courage Bks.) Running Pr. Bk. Pubs.

—Little Women. 1996. (YA). 37.50 (*0-87557-135-2*) Saphrograph Corp.

—Little Women. 9999. (Illus.). (J). pap. 19.95 o.p. (*0-590-74470-4*); 2000. 608p. (gr. 4-7). mass mkt. 6.99 (*0-439-10136-0*); 1994. 510p. (J). (gr. 4-7). mass mkt. 4.50 o.s.i (*0-590-20350-9*); 1994. 32p. (J). (ps-3). mass mkt. 2.95 o.s.i (*0-590-22537-5*); 1986. 256p. (J). (gr. 3-7). pap. 2.50 o.p. (*0-590-40498-9*, Scholastic Paperbacks) Scholastic, Inc.

—Little Women. 1988. (Illustrated Classics Ser.). (J). 2.98 (*0-671-09222-7*) Simon & Schuster.

—Little Women. 2000. (Classics Ser.). 704p. (J). (gr. 4-7). pap. 5.99 (*0-689-83531-0*, Aladdin) Simon & Schuster Children's Publishing.

—Little Women. Barish, Wendy, ed. 1982. (Illus.). 576p. (J). 15.95 o.p. (*0-671-44447-6*, Atheneum) Simon & Schuster Children's Publishing.

—Little Women. 1998. (Children's Classics Ser.). (J). (gr. 4-7). audio 13.95 (*1-55935-188-8*) Soundelux Audio Publishing.

—Little Women. Showalter, Elaine, ed. & intro. by. 1989. (Classics Ser.). 544p. (J). pap. 7.95 (*0-14-039069-3*, Penguin Classics) Viking Penguin.

—Little Women. 1998. (Children's Classics). 224p. (J). (gr. 4-7). pap. 3.95 (*1-85326-116-5*, 1165WW) Wordsworth Editions, Ltd. GBR. *Dist:* Advanced Global Distribution Services.

—Little Women. 1994. 144p. (YA). pap. 3.99 (*0-671-51902-6*, Aladdin) Simon & Schuster Children's Publishing.

—Little Women. unabr. ed. 1985. (J). audio 77.95 (*1-55685-061-1*) Audio Bk. Contractors, Inc.

—Little Women. adapted ed. 1997. (Living Classics Ser.). (Illus.). 32p. (J). (gr. 3-7). 14.95 (*0-7641-7047-3*) Barron's Educational Series, Inc.

—Little Women. unabr. ed. (J). audio 64.95 (*1-55686-149-4*, 149) Books in Motion.

—Little Women. unabr. ed. 2002. (J). audio compact disk 128.00 (*0-7366-8609-6*) Books on Tape, Inc.

—Little Women. 1983. (YA). (gr. 6 up). reprint ed. lib. bdg. 18.95 (*0-89966-408-3*) Buccaneer Bks., Inc.

—Little Women. 1997. (Children's Thrift Classics Ser.). (Illus.). 96p. (J). reprint ed. pap. text 1.00 (*0-486-29634-2*) Dover Pubns., Inc.

—Little Women. abr. ed. (J). 1994. (gr. 5-7). pap. 19.95 incl. audio (*0-88646-835-3*, LSR 7315); 1982. audio 15.95 o.p. (*0-88646-062-X*, TC-LFP 7080) Durkin Hayes Publishing Ltd.

—Little Women. 1993. (Illus.). 352p. (J). reprint ed. 25.00 (*0-88363-203-9*) Levin, Hugh Lauter Assocs.

—Little Women. abr. l.t. ed. 1995. (Illus.). 32p. (J). (gr. k up). pap. 14.95 (*1-886201-05-6*) Nana Banana Classics.

—Little Women. abr. ed. 2000. (YA). audio 17.98 (*962-634-694-9*, NA319414); audio compact disk 19.98 (*962-634-194-7*, NA319412, Naxos AudioBooks) Naxos of America, Inc.

—Little Women. 1998. 559p. (J). reprint ed. lib. bdg. 25.00 (*1-58287-046-2*) North Bks.

—Little Women. 2nd ed. 1993. (Illus.). 62p. pap. text 5.95 (*0-19-585271-0*) Oxford Univ. Pr., Inc.

—Little Women, Level 4. Hedge, Tricia, ed. 2000. (Bookworms Ser.). (Illus.). 96p. (J). pap. text 5.95 (*0-19-423036-8*) Oxford Univ. Pr., Inc.

—Little Women. deluxe ed. (Whole Story Ser.). (Illus.). 288p. (J). 1997. (gr. 7-12). pap. 18.99 (*0-670-87706-9*, Viking Children's Bks.); 1947. (gr. 2 up). 19.99 (*0-448-06019-1*, Grosset & Dunlap) Penguin Putnam Bks. for Young Readers.

—Little Women. abr. ed. (Everyman's Library Children's Classics Ser.). 1994. (J). audio 11.00 o.s.i (*0-679-43757-6*, RH Audio); 1986. (J). audio 16.00 o.s.i (*0-394-55856-1*, RH Audio); 1998. (YA). (gr. 4-7). audio 25.00 o.s.i (*0-553-52543-5*, Listening Library) Random Hse. Audio Publishing Group.

—Little Women, unabr. ed. 1997. (YA). (gr. 7). audio 112.00 (*0-7887-0327-7*, 94519E7) Recorded Bks., LLC.

—Little Women. 1989. (Works of Louisa May Alcott). (J). reprint ed. lib. bdg. 79.00 (*0-7812-1627-3*) Reprint Services Corp.

—Little Women. abr. ed. 1986. 256p. (J). (gr. 4-7). mass mkt. 4.50 (*0-590-43797-6*, Scholastic Paperbacks) Scholastic, Inc.

—Little Women. abr. ed. 1979. (J). pap. 11.95 o.p. incl. audio (*0-88142-372-6*, 391079) Soundelux Audio Publishing.

—Little Women. l.t. ed. 1987. (Charnwood Large Print Ser.). 400p. 29.99 o.p. (*0-7089-8384-7*, Charnwood) Thorpe, F. A. Pubs. GBR. *Dist:* Ulverscroft Large Print Bks., Ltd., Ulverscroft Large Print Canada, Ltd.

—Little Women. abr. ed. 1997. (Good Wives Collection). (J). audio 19.95 (*1-85998-326-X*); audio 13.95 o.p. (*1-85998-324-3*) Trafalgar Square.

—Little Women: Book & Charm. 2003. (Charming Classics Ser.). (Illus.). 384p. (J). pap. 6.99 (*0-06-051180-X*, Harper Festival) HarperCollins Children's Bk. Group.

—Little Women: Book & Charm Keepsake. 1994. 48p. (J). (gr. 4-7). pap. 12.95 (*0-590-22538-3*) Scholastic, Inc.

—Little Women: Four Funny Sisters. Lindskoog, Kathryn, ed. 1991. (Young Reader's Library). (Illus.). (J). (gr. 3-7). pap. 12.99 o.p. (*0-88070-437-3*) Zonderkidz.

—Little Women: The Children's Picture Book. 1995. (Illus.). 96p. (J). (gr. 2 up). pap. 9.95 o.p. (*1-55704-252-7*) Newmarket Pr.

—Little Women Vol. 2: The Sisters Grow Up. Lindskoog, Kathryn, ed. 1991. (Illus.). (J). (gr. 3-7). pap. 4.99 o.p. (*0-88070-463-2*) Zonderkidz.

—Mujercitas. (SPA., Illus.). 192p. (YA). 11.95 (*84-7281-101-8*, AF1101) Auriga, Ediciones S.A. ESP. *Dist:* Continental Bk. Co., Inc.

—Mujercitas. 2002. (Classics for Young Readers Ser.). (SPA.). (YA). 14.95 (*84-392-0901-0*, EV30608) Lectorum Pubns., Inc.

—Mujercitas. 1998. (SPA., Illus.). 304p. (J). (*84-01-46257-6*) Plaza & Janés Editories, S.A.

—Mujercitas. (Coleccion Estrella). (SPA., Illus.). 64p. 14.95 (*950-11-0010-3*, SGM010) Sigmar ARG. *Dist:* Continental Bk. Co., Inc.

—Mujercitas. 1999. (Coleccion "Clasicos Juveniles" Ser.). (SPA., Illus.). 290p. (J). (gr. 4-7). pap. 12.95 (*1-58348-784-0*) iUniverse, Inc.

Alcott, Louisa May, photos by. Little Men: Life at Plumfield with Jo's Boys. unabr. ed. 1998. (J). (gr. 6). audio 69.00 (*0-7887-2640-4*, 95641E7) Recorded Bks., LLC.

Alcott, Louisa May & Golden Books Staff. Little Women. 1987. (Golden Classics Ser.). (Illus.). 128p. (J). (gr. 3-7). pap. 8.95 o.s.i (*0-307-17116-7*, Golden Bks.) Random Hse. Children's Bks.

Alcott, Louisa May & Montgomery, L. M. Anne of Green Gables & Little Women. l.t. ed. 1999. E-Book 24.95 incl. cd-rom (*1-929077-40-8*, Books OnScreen) PageFree Publishing, Inc.

Alcott, Louisa May & Thorne, Jenny. Little Women. 1978. (Illustrated Classics). (J). (*0-8393-6210-2*) Raintree Pubs.

Alcott, Louisa May, et al. Mujercitas. Prunier, James, tr. 2002. (SPA., Illus.). 268p. (J). 29.95 (*84-348-5324-8*) SM Ediciones ESP. *Dist:* AIMS International Bks., Inc.

Blaisdell, Robert. Little Men: Life at Plumfield with Jo's Boys. 1997. (Children's Thrift Classics Ser.). (Illus.). (J). pap. 1.00 (*0-486-29805-1*) Dover Pubns., Inc.

Glencoe McGraw-Hill Staff. Topics from the Restless, Bk. 1. unabr. ed. 1999. (Wordsworth Classics Ser.). (YA). (gr. 10 up). pap. 21.00 (*0-89061-116-5*, R1165WW) Jamestown.

Little Women. abr. ed. Incl. First Wedding. audio Gossip. audio Merry Christmas. audio (J). (gr. 4-6). 1991. 1991. Set audio 11.00 (*1-55994-371-8*, CPN 1470, Caedmon) HarperTrade.

Swicord, Robin. Little Women: The Children's Picture Book. 2004. (Illus.). 96p. (gr. 2 up). 15.95 (*1-55704-216-0*) Newmarket Pr.

MARGARET, SAINT, QUEEN OF SCOTLAND, D. 1093—FICTION

Johnson, Jan. Margaret, the Good Queen: A Story about Queen Margaret of Scotland. 1979. (Stories About Christian Heroes Ser.). (J). (gr. 1-5). 0.95 o.p. (*0-03-022116-1*) HarperSanFrancisco.

MARIE ANTOINETTE, QUEEN, CONSORT OF LOUIS XVI, KING OF FRANCE, 1755-1793—FICTION

Davis, Kathryn. Versailles. l.t. ed. 2003. 25.95 (*1-58724-394-6*, Wheeler Publishing, Inc.) Gale Group.

—Versailles. 2003. 240p. pap. 13.95 (*0-316-73761-5*, Back Bay) Little Brown & Co.

Lasky, Kathryn. Marie Antoinette: Princess of Versailles, Austria-France, 1544. 2000. (Royal Diaries Ser.). (Illus.). 236p. (J). (gr. 4-8). 10.95 (*0-439-07666-8*) Scholastic, Inc.

MARTIN, DANIEL (FICTITIOUS CHARACTER)—FICTION

Paulsen, Gary. Danger on Midnight River. 1995. (World of Adventure Ser.). 80p. (gr. 4-7). pap. text 3.99 (*0-440-41028-2*) Dell Publishing.

—Danger on Midnight River. 1995. (Gary Paulsen's World of Adventure Ser.). (J). 10.14 (*0-606-07411-2*) Turtleback Bks.

MARTY (FICTITIOUS CHARACTER)—FICTION

Dadey, Debbie. Marty the Maniac. 1996. (Marty Ser.). (J). (gr. 2-4). pap. 2.99 o.p. (*0-87406-772-3*) Darby Creek Publishing.

—Marty the Millionaire. 1997. (Marty Ser.). 80p. (J). (gr. 2-4). pap. 3.99 (*0-87406-865-7*, Willowisp Pr.) Darby Creek Publishing.

—Marty the Mudwrestler. 1997. (Marty Ser.). (Illus.). 80p. (J). (gr. 2-4). pap. 3.99 (*0-87406-848-7*, Willowisp Pr.) Darby Creek Publishing.

Davies, Bettilu D. Marty's Double Life. 1983. (Marty Ser.). (Orig.). (J). (gr. 6). pap. 3.95 o.p. (*0-8024-0272-0*) Moody Pr.

—Tall Trouble. 1981. (Marty Ser.). 160p. (J). (gr. 6). pap. 2.95 o.p. (*0-8024-8112-4*) Moody Pr.

MARY, QUEEN OF SCOTS, 1542-1587—FICTION

Hunter, Mollie. You Never Knew Her As I Did! 1981. 224p. (YA). (gr. 7 up). 13.95 (*0-06-022678-1*) HarperCollins Children's Bk. Group.

Lasky, Kathryn. Mary, Queen of Scots: Queen Without a Country, France, 1553. 2002. (Royal Diaries Ser.). (Illus.). 208p. (J). (gr. 4-8). 10.95 (*0-439-19404-0*, Scholastic Pr.) Scholastic, Inc.

Ross, Stewart. Long Live Mary, Queen of Scots! 1998. (Coming Alive Ser.). (Illus.). 62p. (J). (gr. 3-5). 17.95 (*0-237-51787-6*) Evans Brothers, Ltd. GBR. *Dist:* Trafalgar Square.

Yolen, Jane & Harris, Robert J. The Queen's Own Fool. 2000. (Illus.). viii, 390p. (J). (gr. 5-9). 19.99 (*0-399-23380-6*, Philomel) Penguin Putnam Bks. for Young Readers.

MEDEA (GREEK MYTHOLOGY)—FICTION

Greenwood, Kerry, contrib. by. Medea. 1997. (Illus.). (*1-86330-491-6*) Mandarin Australia.

MEENOM, PLESKIT (FICTITIOUS CHARACTER)—FICTION

Abbott, Tony & Coville, Bruce. There's an Alien in My Backpack! 2000. (I Was a Sixth Grade Alien Ser.: Vol. 9). (Illus.). 160p. (J). (gr. 3-6). pap. 3.99 (*0-671-02658-5*, Aladdin) Simon & Schuster Children's Publishing.

Coville, Bruce. The Attack of the Two-Inch Teacher. unabr. ed. 2000. (I Was a Sixth Grade Alien Ser.). (J). (gr. 3-5). 165p. pap. 28.00 incl. audio (*0-8072-8354-1*, YA170SP); audio 23.00 (*0-8072-8353-3*, YA170CX) Random Hse. Audio Publishing Group. (Listening Library).

—The Attack of the Two-Inch Teacher. 1999. (I Was a Sixth Grade Alien Ser.: Vol. 2). 176p. (J). (gr. 3-6). pap. 3.99 (*0-671-02651-8*, Aladdin) Simon & Schuster Children's Publishing.

—The Attack of the Two-Inch Teacher. 1999. (I Was a Sixth Grade Alien Ser.). (Illus.). (J). 10.04 (*0-606-18374-4*) Turtleback Bks.

—Don't Fry My Veeblax! 2000. (Sixth Grade Alien Ser.: Vol. 6). (Illus.). 160p. (J). (gr. 3-6). pap. 3.99 (*0-671-02655-0*, Aladdin) Simon & Schuster Children's Publishing.

—I Lost My Grandfather's Brain. unabr. ed. 2000. (I Was a Sixth Grade Alien Ser.). (J). 160p. (gr. 3-5). pap. 28.00 incl. audio (*0-8072-8385-1*, YA180SP); (gr. 4-6). audio 23.00 (*0-8072-8384-3*, YA180CX) Random Hse. Audio Publishing Group. (Listening Library).

—I Lost My Grandfather's Brain. 1999. (I Was a Sixth Grade Alien Ser.: Vol. 3). 176p. (J). (gr. 3-7). pap. 3.99 (*0-671-02652-6*, Aladdin) Simon & Schuster Children's Publishing.

—I Was a Sixth Grade Alien. 2000. (J). audio 18.00 (*0-7366-9014-X*) Books on Tape, Inc.

—I Was a Sixth Grade Alien. (I Was a Sixth Grade Alien Ser.). 170p. (J). (gr. 4-6). pap. 3.99 (*0-8072-8202-2*); 2000. (gr. 3-5). pap. 23.00 incl. audio (*0-8072-8201-4*, YYA138SP) Random Hse. Audio Publishing Group. (Listening Library).

—I Was a Sixth Grade Alien. 1999. (I Was a Sixth Grade Alien Ser.: Vol. 1). 192p. (J). (gr. 3-6). pap. 3.99 (*0-671-02650-X*, Aladdin); (Illus.). 16.00 (*0-671-03651-3*, Simon & Schuster Children's Publishing) Simon & Schuster Children's Publishing.

—I Was a Sixth Grade Alien. 1999. (I Was a Sixth Grade Alien Ser.). 10.04 (*0-606-17089-8*) Turtleback Bks.

—Peanut Butter Lover Boy. 2000. (I Was a Sixth Grade Alien Ser.: Vol. 4). (Illus.). 160p. (J). (gr. 3-6). pap. 3.99 (*0-671-02653-4*, Aladdin) Simon & Schuster Children's Publishing.

—Peanut Butter Lover Boy. 2000. (I Was a Sixth Grade Alien Ser.). (Illus.). (J). 10.04 (*0-606-18307-8*) Turtleback Bks.

—Snatched from Earth! 2000. (I Was a Sixth Grade Alien Ser.: Vol. 8). (Illus.). 208p. (J). (gr. 3-6). pap. 3.99 (*0-671-02657-7*, Aladdin) Simon & Schuster Children's Publishing.

—Too Many Aliens! 2000. (I Was a Sixth Grade Alien Ser.: Vol. 7). (Illus.). 176p. (YA). (gr. 3-6). pap. 3.99 (*0-671-02656-9*, Aladdin) Simon & Schuster Children's Publishing.

—Zombies of the Science Fair. 5th ed. 2000. (I Was a Sixth Grade Alien Ser.: Vol. 5). (Illus.). 160p. (J). (gr. 3-6). pap. 3.99 (*0-671-02654-2*, Aladdin) Simon & Schuster Children's Publishing.

—Zombies of the Science Fair. 2000. (I Was a Sixth Grade Alien Ser.). (Illus.). (J). 10.04 (*0-606-18308-6*) Turtleback Bks.

MERLIN (LEGENDARY CHARACTER)—FICTION

Barron, T. A. The Fires of Merlin. 1998. (Lost Years of Merlin Ser.: Vol. 3). (Illus.). 272p. (YA). (gr. 5-9). 19.99 (*0-399-23020-3*, Philomel) Penguin Putnam Bks. for Young Readers.

—The Fires of Merlin Bk. 3. 2000. (Lost Years of Merlin Ser.: Vol. 3). (Illus.). 304p. (J). (gr. 4-7). reprint ed. mass mkt. 6.99 (*0-441-00713-9*) Ace Bks.

—The Lost Years of Merlin, Bk. 1. 1999. (Lost Years of Merlin Ser.). 304p. (J). (gr. 4-7). reprint ed. mass mkt. 6.99 (*0-441-00668-X*) Ace Bks.

—The Lost Years of Merlin. 1998. (J). (gr. 4-7). mass mkt. 4.99 (*0-8125-7777-9*, Tor Bks.) Doherty, Tom Assocs., LLC.

—The Lost Years of Merlin. 1996. (Lost Years of Merlin Ser.: No. 1). 336p. (J). (gr. 5-9). 19.99 (*0-399-23018-1*, Philomel) Penguin Putnam Bks. for Young Readers.

—The Seven Songs of Merlin. 1997. (Lost Years of Merlin Ser.: Bk. 2). 320p. (J). (gr. 5-9). 19.99 (*0-399-23019-X*, Philomel) Penguin Putnam Bks. for Young Readers.

—The Seven Songs of Merlin. unabr. ed. 2002. (J). (gr. 4-7). audio 30.00 (*0-8072-0958-9*, Listening Library) Random Hse. Audio Publishing Group.

—The Seven Songs of Merlin Bk. 2. 2000. (Lost Years of Merlin Ser.: Vol. 2). (Illus.). 304p. (YA). (gr. 5-9). reprint ed. mass mkt. 6.99 (*0-441-00701-5*) Ace Bks.

—A T. A. Barron Collection: The Lost Years of Merlin; The Seven Songs of Merlin; The Fires of Merlin, 3 bks. in 1. 2001. (Illus.). (J). 14.98 (*0-399-23734-8*, Philomel) Penguin Putnam Bks. for Young Readers.

—Wings of Merlin. 2000. (Lost Years of Merlin Ser.: Vol. 5). (Illus.). 272p. (J). (gr. 6-9). 19.99 (*0-399-23456-X*, Philomel) Penguin Putnam Bks. for Young Readers.

Littler, Keith. Merlin & the Big Top. 2002. (Illus.). 24p. pap. 6.95 (*1-84222-618-5*) Carlton Bks., Ltd. GBR. *Dist:* Trafalgar Square.

—Merlin, King of the Castle. 2002. (Illus.). 24p. pap. 6.95 (*1-84222-617-7*) Carlton Bks., Ltd. GBR. *Dist:* Trafalgar Square.

—Merlin the Magical Puppy on Ice. 2002. (Illus.). 24p. pap. 6.95 (*1-84222-616-9*) Carlton Bks., Ltd. GBR. *Dist:* Trafalgar Square.

Mayer, Marianna. Merlin. 2015. (J). 15.99 (*0-8037-2187-0*, Dial Bks. for Young Readers) Penguin Putnam Bks. for Young Readers.

Newman, Robert. Merlin's Mistake. 2001. (Lost Treasures Ser.: No. 5). (Illus.). 352p. (J). pap. 4.99 (*0-7868-1546-9*); (gr. 3-7). pap. 1.99 (*0-7868-1545-0*) Hyperion Bks. for Children. (Volo).

—Merlin's Mistake. 1990. (Illus.). (J). (gr. 5-9). 18.75 (*0-8446-6187-2*) Smith, Peter Pub., Inc.

MICHELANGELO BUONARROTI, 1475-1564—FICTION

Parillo, Tony. Michelangelo's Surprise, RS. 1998. 32p. (YA). (ps-3). 16.00 o.p. (*0-374-34961-4*, Farrar, Straus & Giroux (BYR)) Farrar, Straus & Giroux.

Ventura, Piero. Michelangelo's World. 1989. (Illus.). 48p. (YA). (gr. 9-12). 13.95 o.s.i (*0-399-21593-X*, G. P. Putnam's Sons) Penguin Putnam Bks. for Young Readers.

MICKEY MOUSE (FICTITIOUS CHARACTER)—FICTION

Abracadabra. 2001. (Mickey Mysteries Ser.: No. 4). (Illus.). 96p. (J). pap. 4.99 (*0-7868-4452-3*) Disney Pr.

De la Paz, Orlando. El Libro de Camiones de Mickey. 2002. (SPA., Illus.). 12p. (J). bds. 3.99 (*0-7364-2059-2*, RH/Disney) Random Hse. Children's Bks.

Disney Staff. Donald Duck Directs, Vol. 14. 1997. (Illus.). 44p. (J). (gr. 1-6). 3.49 o.p. (*1-885222-89-0*) Advance Pubs. LLC.

—Mickey Mouse & Minnie Mouse Pop-Up Boxed Collector's Set. deluxe ed. 1999. (Illus.). 32p. (J). reprint ed. 100.00 (*1-55709-215-X*) Applewood Bks.

—Mickey Mouse Stories: Disney. 1989. (Illus.). (J). (ps-1). reprint ed. o.p. (*0-307-15751-2*, Golden Bks.) Random Hse. Children's Bks.

—Mickey Mouse Waddle Book. 1992. (Illus.). 32p. reprint ed. 19.95 o.p. (*1-55709-187-0*) Applewood Bks.

—Mickey's Alphabet Soup, Vol. 1. 1997. (Illus.). 44p. (J). (gr. 1-6). 3.49 o.p. (*1-885222-76-9*) Advance Pubs. LLC.

—Mickey's Book of Trucks. 2001. (Illus.). 10p. (J). bds. 3.99 (*0-7364-1111-9*, RH/Disney) Random Hse. Children's Bks.

—Mickey's Weather Machine, Vol. 13. 1997. (Illus.). 44p. (J). (gr. 1-6). 3.49 o.p. (*1-885222-88-2*) Advance Pubs. LLC.

—Minnie's Surprise Trip, Vol. 15. 1997. (Illus.). 44p. (J). (gr. 1-6). 3.49 o.p. (*1-885222-90-4*) Advance Pubs. LLC.

—Perils of Mickey: The Mail Must Go Through. 1993. (Puppet Book). (J). (ps-3). 1.10 o.p. (*0-453-03096-3*) Mouse Works.

—The Pop-up Mickey Mouse: Story & Illustrations. 1993. (Illus.). 32p. (J). (ps-3). reprint ed. 9.95 o.p. (*1-55709-210-9*) Applewood Bks.

Dubowski, Cathy. Goofy Visits Pluto: A Book about the Planets. 1995. (Illus.). 32p. (J). (ps-2). 12.95 (*0-7868-3024-7*) Disney Pr.

Golden Press Staff. Mickey Mouse. 1996. (J). o.p. (*0-307-30053-6*, Golden Bks.) Random Hse. Children's Bks.

Gottfredson, Floyd, intro. Mickey Mouse. 1983. (Walt Disney Best Comics Ser.). (Illus.). 204p. (YA). (gr. 7 up). 25.00 o.p. (*0-89659-005-4*) Abbeville Pr., Inc.

Gutman, Dan. Mickey & Me. 2003. (Baseball Card Adventures Ser.). (Illus.). 160p. (J). (gr. 4-6). lib. bdg. 16.89 (*0-06-029248-2*) HarperCollins Children's Bk. Group.

—Mickey & Me: A Baseball Card Adventure. 2003. (Baseball Card Adventures Ser.). (Illus.). 160p. (J). (gr. 4-6). 15.99 (*0-06-029247-4*) HarperCollins Children's Bk. Group.

Italia, Bob. Mickey Mouse. Wallner, Rosemary, ed. 1991. (Behind the Creation of Ser.). 202p. (J). lib. bdg. 13.95 (*1-56239-053-8*) ABDO Publishing Co.

McCafferty, Catherine. Picture Me on Vacation with Mickey Mouse. 1997. (Picture Me Disney Ser.). (Illus.). 8p. (J). (ps-3). bds. 6.99 o.p. (*1-57151-539-9*) Playhouse Publishing.

Michaels, Kay. Christmas Is Coming: A Fold-Around Pop-up Book Featuring Mickey Mouse & Friends. 1995. (Illus.). 10p. (J). 11.95 (*0-7868-3039-5*) Disney Pr.

Mickey: My Coloring Book. (Disney Ser.). (J). 9.98 o.p. (*0-307-08673-9*, 08673, Golden Bks.) Random Hse. Children's Bks.

Mickey & Goofy: My Coloring Book. (Disney Ser.). (J). 9.95 o.p. (*0-307-08670-4*, 08670, Golden Bks.) Random Hse. Children's Bks.

Mickey Mouse. 1996. (Squeeze Me Bks.). (J). 6.98 o.p. (*1-57082-385-5*) Mouse Works.

Mickey Mouse & Friends. (Illus.). (J). (ps-3). 9999. pap. o.p. (*0-307-02387-7*); 1990. o.p. (*0-307-15535-8*) Random Hse. Children's Bks. (Golden Bks.).

Mickey Mouse's Telling Time. 1994. (Clock Book Ser.). (Illus.). 24p. (J). (ps-1). 8.98 o.p. (*1-57082-155-0*) Mouse Works.

Mouse Works Staff. Go Go Mickey. 1996. (J). 8.98 o.p. (*1-57082-326-X*); 8.98 o.p. (*1-57082-325-1*) Mouse Works.

—Goofy. 1998. (Friendly Tales Ser.). (Illus.). 10p. (J). (ps). 6.99 (*1-57082-928-4*) Mouse Works.

—Mickey Mouse's Xmas Carol. 1997. (J). 7.98 (*1-57082-799-0*) Mouse Works.

—Play Ball, Mickey Mouse. 1995. (Illus.). (J). 7.98 o.p. (*1-57082-228-X*) Mouse Works.

Mystery in Midair. 2001. (Mickey Mysteries Ser.: No. 1). (Illus.). 96p. (J). (gr. 2-5). reprint ed. pap. 4.99 (*0-7868-4449-3*) Disney Pr.

Mystery of the Garbage Gang. 3rd ed. 2001. (Mickey Mysteries Ser.: No. 3). (Illus.). 96p. (J). pap. 4.99 (*0-7868-4451-5*) Disney Pr.

Mystery of the Secret Treasure. 2001. (Mickey Mysteries Ser.: No. 2). (Illus.). 96p. (J). (gr. 2-5). reprint ed. pap. 4.99 (*0-7868-4450-7*) Disney Pr.

Onish, Liane B. Disney's Mickey Mouse Stories. 2001. (Illus.). (J). 12.99 (*0-7868-3326-2*) Disney Pr.

Outlet Book Company Staff. Mickey Mouse & Walt Disney. 1989. (Walt Disney's Best Comics Ser.). (Illus.). 204p. (J). 17.99 o.p. (*0-517-69715-7*) Random Hse. Value Publishing.

Packard, Mary. Mickey Mouse & the Pet Shop. 1996. (Super Shape Bks.). (Illus.). 24p. (J). (ps-3). pap. text 9.99 o.p. (*0-307-10008-1*, 10008, Golden Bks.) Random Hse. Children's Bks.

Paint & Water Books Staff. Mickey Mouse. 9999. (J). o.p. (*0-307-02821-6*, Golden Bks.) Random Hse. Children's Bks.

Santacruz, Daniel M., tr. One Mickey Mouse Un Raton Mickey: Un Libro Disney de Numeros (A Disney Book of Numbers) 1993. (Libros Buena Vista Ser.). (SPA., Illus.). 12p. (J). 5.95 o.s.i (*1-56282-460-0*) Disney Pr.

Walt Disney Productions Staff. The Sorcerer's Apprentice. 1974. (Illus.). 48p. (J). (ps-2). 4.99 o.s.i (*0-394-92551-3*); 6.95 o.s.i (*0-394-82551-9*) Random Hse. Children's Bks. (Random Hse. Bks. for Young Readers).

Walt Disney's the Mickey Mouse Book. 1965. (Golden Super Shape Book Ser.). (Illus.). 24p. (J). (ps). pap. o.p. (*0-307-10077-4*, Golden Bks.) Random Hse. Children's Bks.

Weiss, Ellen. Mickey's Millennium Mystery. 1999. (Illus.). 32p. (J). (ps-3). 9.99 o.p. (*0-7364-1022-8*) Mouse Works.

West, Cindy. Happy Sailing Mickey Mouse. 1989. (Golden Little Look-Look Bks.). (Illus.). (J). (ps-3). pap. o.p. (*0-307-11755-3*, Golden Bks.) Random Hse. Children's Bks.

West, Cyndy. I Am Mickey Mouse. 1991. (Golden Sturdy Bks.). (Illus.). (J). (ps-3). o.p. (*0-307-12166-6*, Golden Bks.) Random Hse. Children's Bks.

MISS NELSON (FICTITIOUS CHARACTER)—FICTION

Allard, Harry G. Miss Nelson Has a Field Day. 1985. (Miss Nelson Ser.). (Illus.). 32p. (J). (ps-3). lib. bdg., tchr. ed. 16.00 (*0-395-36690-9*) Houghton Mifflin Co.

—Miss Nelson Has a Field Day. 1988. (Miss Nelson Ser.). (Illus.). 32p. (J). (ps-3). pap. 5.95 (*0-395-48654-8*) Houghton Mifflin Co. Trade & Reference Div.

—Miss Nelson Has a Field Day. 1985. (Miss Nelson Ser.). (Illus.). (J). (ps-3). 12.10 (*0-606-04276-8*) Turtleback Bks.

—Miss Nelson Is Back. (Miss Nelson Ser.). (Illus.). 32p. (J). (ps-3). 1986. pap. 5.95 (*0-395-41668-X*); 1982. lib. bdg., tchr. ed. 16.00 (*0-395-32956-6*) Houghton Mifflin Co.

—Miss Nelson Is Missing! (Miss Nelson Ser.). (Illus.). (J). (ps-3). 1987. pap. 7.95 o.p. incl. audio (*0-395-45737-8*); 1985. 32p. pap. 5.95 (*0-395-40146-1*) Houghton Mifflin Co.

—Miss Nelson Is Missing! 1978. (Miss Nelson Ser.). (Illus.). (J). (ps-3). pap. 1.95 o.p. (*0-590-11877-3*) Scholastic, Inc.

—Miss Nelson Is Missing! 1977. (Miss Nelson Ser.). (Illus.). (J). (ps-3). 12.10 (*0-606-04400-0*) Turtleback Bks.

—Miss Nelson Is Missing! 2000. (Miss Nelson Ser.). (Illus.). (J). (ps-3). pap. 12.95 incl. audio Weston Woods Studios, Inc.

—Miss Nelson Is Missing. (Miss Nelson Ser.). (J). (ps-3). audio 8.95 Weston Woods Studios, Inc.

—La Senorita Nelson Ha Desaparecido! 1998. (Miss Nelson Ser.). (SPA., Illus.). 32p. (J). (ps-3). lib. bdg. 16.00 (*0-395-90009-3*) Houghton Mifflin Co.

Allard, Harry G., ed. Miss Nelson Is Back. 1988. (Miss Nelson Ser.). (Illus.). 1p. (J). (ps-3). pap. 9.95 incl. audio (*0-395-48872-9*, 480436) Houghton Mifflin Co.

—Miss Nelson Is Back. 1982. (Miss Nelson Ser.). (Illus.). (J). (ps-3). 12.10 (*0-606-02538-3*) Turtleback Bks.

Allard, Harry G. & Marshall, James. Miss Nelson Is Missing! 1977. (Miss Nelson Ser.). (Illus.). 32p. (J). (ps-3). lib. bdg., tchr. ed. 16.00 (*0-395-25296-2*) Houghton Mifflin Co.

MISS SPIDER (FICTITIOUS CHARACTER)—FICTION

Kirk, David. Little Miss Spider. (Miss Spider Ser.). (J). 2003. (Illus.). 32p. pap. 5.99 (*0-439-54315-0*); 1999. 155.40 (*0-439-11737-2*); 1999. (Illus.). 32p. pap. 12.95 (*0-439-08389-3*) Scholastic, Inc.

—Little Miss Spider: A Christmas Wish. 2001. (Miss Spider Ser.). (Illus.). 32p. (J). (ps-2). pap. 12.95 (*0-439-31463-1*, Levine, Arthur A. Bks.) Scholastic, Inc.

—Little Miss Spider at Sunnypatch School. 2002. (Little Miss Spider Ser.). (Illus.). (J). 21.85 (*0-7587-3008-X*) Book Wholesalers, Inc.

—Little Miss Spider at Sunnypatch School. (Miss Spider Ser.). (Illus.). 32p. (J). 2003. pap. 5.99 (*0-439-54316-9*); 2000. pap. 12.95 (*0-439-08727-9*) Scholastic, Inc.

—Miss Spider. 2003. (J). 12.95 (*0-439-54317-7*) Scholastic, Inc.

—Miss Spider's ABC: New Board Book Edition. (Miss Spider Ser.). (Illus.). 32p. (J). (ps-2). 2000. bds. 8.95 (*0-439-13747-0*, Scholastic Reference); 1998. pap. 16.95 o.s.i (*0-590-28279-4*) Scholastic, Inc.

—Miss Spider's Mobile. 1994. (Miss Spider Ser.). (J). (ps-2). pap. o.s.i (*0-590-50440-1*) Scholastic, Inc.

—Miss Spider's New Car. 1997. (Miss Spider Ser.). (Illus.). 32p. (J). (ps-2). pap. 16.95 (*0-590-30713-4*) Scholastic, Inc.

—Miss Spider's Sunny Patch Kids. 2004. (Illus.). 40p. (J). 14.95 (*0-439-40870-9*) Scholastic, Inc.

—Miss Spider's Tea Party. 1998. (Miss Spider Ser.). (Illus.). (J). (ps-2). 14.95 o.s.i (*0-590-12994-5*) Scholastic, Inc.

—Miss Spider's Tea Party. White, Antoinette, ed. 1994. (Miss Spider Ser.). (Illus.). 31p. (J). (ps-2). pap. 15.95 (*0-590-47724-2*) Scholastic, Inc.

—Miss Spider's Tea Party: The Counting Book. White, Antoinette, ed. 1997. (Miss Spider Ser.). (Illus.). 34p. (J). (ps-2). bds. 8.95 (*0-590-06519-X*) Scholastic, Inc.

—Miss Spider's Tea Party: With Plush Toy. 1996. (Miss Spider Ser.). (Illus.). 31p. (J). (ps-2). 29.95 o.p. (*0-590-69782-X*) Scholastic, Inc.

—Miss Spider's Wedding. White, Antoinette, ed. 1995. (Miss Spider Ser.). (Illus.). 32p. (J). (ps-2). pap. 16.95 o.s.i (*0-590-56866-3*) Scholastic, Inc.

MOESHA (FICTITIOUS CHARACTER: SCOTT)—FICTION

Reed, Teresa. What's up, Brother? 1998. (Moesha Ser.). 160p. (YA). (gr. 7 up). pap. 4.50 (*0-671-02592-9*, Simon Pulse) Simon & Schuster Children's Publishing.

Scott, Stefanie. Everybody Say Moesha! 1997. (Moesha Ser.). 160p. (YA). (gr. 7 up). per. 3.99 (*0-671-01147-2*, Simon Pulse) Simon & Schuster Children's Publishing.

—Hollywood Hook-Up. 1998. (Moesha Ser.). 176p. (YA). (gr. 7 up). per. 3.99 (*0-671-01151-0*, Simon Pulse) Simon & Schuster Children's Publishing.

—House Party! 1998. (Moesha Ser.:). 176p. (YA). (gr. 7 up). mass mkt. 4.50 (*0-671-02593-7*, Simon Pulse) Simon & Schuster Children's Publishing.

—Keeping It Real. 1997. (Moesha Ser.). 160p. (YA). (gr. 7 up). per. 3.99 (*0-671-01148-0*, Simon Pulse) Simon & Schuster Children's Publishing.

—Trippin' Out. 1997. (Moesha Ser.). 160p. (YA). (gr. 7 up). pap. 3.99 (*0-671-01149-9*, Simon Pulse) Simon & Schuster Children's Publishing.

MONDAY, ANTHONY (FICTITIOUS CHARACTER)—FICTION

Bellairs, John. The Dark Secret of Weatherend. 1986. 192p. (J). pap. 3.50 o.s.i (*0-553-15621-7*) Bantam Bks.

—The Dark Secret of Weatherend. (Anthony Monday Mystery Ser.). 1997. 192p. (J). (gr. 3-7). pap. 3.99 o.p. (*0-14-038006-X*); 1984. (Illus.). 208p. (YA). (gr. 5 up). 13.89 o.p. (*0-8037-0074-1*, Dial Bks. for Young Readers); 1984. (Illus.). 208p. (YA). (gr. 5 up). 13.95 o.p. (*0-8037-0072-5*, Dial Bks. for Young Readers) Penguin Putnam Bks. for Young Readers.

—The Dark Secret of Weatherend. 1986. 192p. (J). pap. 2.50 o.s.i (*0-553-15375-7*, Skylark) Random Hse. Children's Bks.

—The Dark Secret of Weatherend. 1997. (Anthony Monday Mystery Ser.). 9.09 (*0-606-11238-3*) Turtleback Bks.

—The Lamp from the Warlock's Tomb. (Anthony Monday Mystery Ser.). 1999. 168p. (J). (gr. 3-7). pap. 4.99 o.s.i (*0-14-130077-9*, Puffin Bks.); 1988. 176p. (YA). (gr. 5 up). 12.95 o.p. (*0-8037-0512-3*, Dial Bks. for Young Readers); 1988. 176p. (YA). (gr. 5 up). 12.89 o.p. (*0-8037-0535-2*, Dial Bks. for Young Readers) Penguin Putnam Bks. for Young Readers.

—The Lamp from the Warlock's Tomb. 1989. 176p. (J). (gr. 4-8). pap. 3.99 o.s.i (*0-553-15697-7*, Skylark) Random Hse. Children's Bks.

—The Lamp from the Warlock's Tomb, unabr. ed. 1992. (J). (gr. 5). audio 27.00 (*1-55690-607-2*, 92212E7) Recorded Bks., LLC.

—The Mansion in the Mist. (Anthony Monday Mystery Ser.). 176p. (YA). 1993. (Illus.). (gr. 3-7). pap. 5.99 (*0-14-034933-2*, Puffin Bks.); 1992. (gr. 5 up). 15.00 o.p. (*0-8037-0845-9*, Dial Bks. for Young Readers); 1992. (gr. 5 up). 14.89 o.p. (*0-8037-0846-7*, Dial Bks. for Young Readers) Penguin Putnam Bks. for Young Readers.

—The Mansion in the Mist, unabr. ed. 1994. (J). (gr. 5). audio 35.00 (*0-7887-0175-4*, 94400E7) Recorded Bks., LLC.

—The Mansion in the Mist. 1993. (J). 11.04 (*0-606-05450-2*) Turtleback Bks.

—The Treasure of Alpheus Winterborn. 1978. (Illus.). (J). (gr. 5-7). 7.95 o.p. (*0-15-289936-7*) Harcourt Children's Bks.

—The Treasure of Alpheus Winterborn. 1997. (Anthony Monday Mystery Ser.). (Illus.). 192p. (J). (gr. 3-7). pap. 5.99 (*0-14-038009-4*, Puffin Bks.) Penguin Putnam Bks. for Young Readers.

—The Treasure of Alpheus Winterborn. 1985. 192p. (J). (gr. 3-8). pap. 2.75 o.s.i (*0-553-15527-X*, Skylark) Random Hse. Children's Bks.

—The Treasure of Alpheus Winterborn. 1997. (Anthony Monday Mystery Ser.). (J). 10.04 (*0-606-12003-3*) Turtleback Bks.

MONET, CLAUDE, 1840-1926—FICTION

Anholt, Laurence. The Magical Garden of Claude Monet. 2003. (Illus.). 32p. (J). 14.95 (*0-7641-5574-1*) Barron's Educational Series, Inc.

Sweeney, Joan. Once upon a Lily Pad: Froggy Love in Monet's Garden. 1995. (Illus.). 32p. (J). (ps-1). 9.95 (*0-8118-0868-8*) Chronicle Bks. LLC.

Yarbro, Chelsea Quinn. Monet's Ghost. 1997. (Dragonflight Ser.: No. 12). (Illus.). 160p. (YA). (gr. 7-12). 17.00 (*0-689-80732-5*, Atheneum) Simon & Schuster Children's Publishing.

MOODY, JUDY (FICTITIOUS CHARACTER)—FICTION

McDonald, Megan. Judy Moody. (Illus.). (J). (gr. 1-5). 2002. 160p. pap. 5.99 (*0-7636-1231-6*); 2000. 196p. 15.99 (*0-7636-0685-5*) Candlewick Pr.

—Judy Moody. unabr. ed. 2001. (J). (gr. 2-4). audio 19.00 (*0-7887-5353-3*, 96575E7); (gr. 3-5). audio compact disk 22.00 Recorded Bks., LLC.

—Judy Moody Gets Famous! (Illus.). 144p. (J). (gr. 1-5). 2003. pap. 5.99 (*0-7636-1931-0*); 2001. 15.99 (*0-7636-0849-1*) Candlewick Pr.

—Judy Moody Gets Famous! abr. ed. 2002. (J). (gr. k-3). 10.00 (*1-4025-2020-4*) Recorded Bks., LLC.

—The Judy Moody Mood Journal. 2003. (Illus.). 128p. (J). 9.99 (*0-7636-2236-2*) Candlewick Pr.

—Judy Moody Predicts the Future. 2003. (Illus.). 160p. (J). 15.99 (*0-7636-1792-X*) Candlewick Pr.

—Judy Moody Saves the World. (Illus.). 160p. (J). 2004. pap. 5.99 (*0-7636-2087-4*); 2002. (gr. 1-5). 15.99 (*0-7636-1446-7*) Candlewick Pr.

MOONBEAR (FICTITIOUS CHARACTER)—FICTION

Asch, Frank. Happy Birthday, Moon. 2002. (Moonbear Ser.). (Illus.). (J). 15.53 (*0-7587-2686-4*) Book Wholesalers, Inc.

—Happy Birthday, Moon. (Illus.). 32p. (J). (gr. k-3). 1985. 4.95 o.s.i (*0-13-383696-7*); 1982. 10.95 o.s.i (*0-13-383687-8*) Prentice Hall PTR.

—Happy Birthday, Moon. (Illus.). 32p. (J). (ps-k). 2000. pap. 6.99 (*0-689-83544-2*, Aladdin); 2000. 16.00 (*0-689-83543-4*, Simon & Schuster Children's Publishing); 1988. 7.95 o.s.i incl. audio (*0-671-67145-6*, Little Simon); 1985. pap. 4.95 (*0-671-66455-7*, Aladdin); 1982. pap. 15.00 (*0-671-66454-9*, Simon & Schuster Children's Publishing) Simon & Schuster Children's Publishing.

—Happy Birthday, Moon. 1982. (J). 12.14 (*0-606-00658-3*) Turtleback Bks.

—Happy Birthday, Moon. 1990. (J). (ps-4). audio 8.95 (*1-56008-107-4*, RAC281); (Illus.). pap. 12.95 incl. audio (*1-56008-032-9*, PRA281) Weston Woods Studios, Inc.

—Moonbear Book & Bear. 1994. (Moonbear Ser.). (Illus.). (J). (ps-k). 16.95 (*0-671-89555-9*, Little Simon) Simon & Schuster Children's Publishing.

—Moonbear's Bargain. 2002. (Moonbear Ser.). (Illus.). (YA). 14.47 (*1-4046-0166-X*) Book Wholesalers, Inc.

—Moonbear's Bargain. 2000. (Moonbear Ser.). 32p. (J). (ps-k). pap. 5.99 (*0-689-83516-7*, Aladdin) Simon & Schuster Children's Publishing.

—Moonbear's Bargain. 2000. (Moonbear Ser.). (J). (ps-k). 12.14 (*0-606-18624-7*) Turtleback Bks.

—Moonbear's Books. 1993. (Moonbear Ser.). (Illus.). 14p. (J). (ps-k). 3.95 (*0-671-86744-X*, Little Simon) Simon & Schuster Children's Publishing.

—Moonbear's Canoe. 1993. (Moonbear Ser.). (Illus.). 14p. (J). (ps-k). pap. 3.95 (*0-671-86745-8*, Little Simon) Simon & Schuster Children's Publishing.

—Moonbear's Dream. (Illus.). 32p. (J). (ps-1). 2002. pap. 6.99 (*0-689-85310-6*, Aladdin); 1999. 15.00 (*0-689-82244-8*, Simon & Schuster Children's Publishing) Simon & Schuster Children's Publishing.

—Moonbear's Friend. 1993. (Moonbear Ser.). (Illus.). 14p. (J). (ps-k). pap. 4.99 (*0-671-86746-6*, Little Simon) Simon & Schuster Children's Publishing.

—Moonbear's Pet. 2002. (Moonbear Ser.). (Illus.). (J). 14.47 (*1-4046-0167-8*) Book Wholesalers, Inc.

—Moonbear's Pet. (Moonbear Ser.). (Illus.). 32p. (J). (ps-k). 2000. pap. 4.99 o.s.i (*0-689-82094-1*, Aladdin); 2000. pap. 5.99 (*0-689-83580-9*, Aladdin); 1997. 15.00 o.s.i (*0-689-80794-5*, Simon & Schuster Children's Publishing) Simon & Schuster Children's Publishing.

—Moonbear's Pet. 1998. (Moonbear Ser.). (J). (ps-k). 12.14 (*0-606-15637-2*) Turtleback Bks.

—Moonbear's Shadow. 2002. (Moonbear Ser.). (Illus.). (J). 14.47 (*0-7587-6647-5*) Book Wholesalers, Inc.

—Moonbear's Shadow. 2000. (Moonbear Ser.). 32p. (J). (ps-k). pap. 5.99 (*0-689-83519-1*, Aladdin) Simon & Schuster Children's Publishing.

—Moonbear's Shadow. 2000. 12.14 (*0-606-18625-5*) Turtleback Bks.

—Moonbear's Skyfire. 2000. (Moonbear Ser.). 32p. (J). (ps-k). pap. 5.99 (*0-689-83545-0*, Aladdin) Simon & Schuster Children's Publishing.

—Mooncake. 2002. (Moonbear Ser.). (Illus.). (J). 14.47 (*0-7587-6749-8*) Book Wholesalers, Inc.

—Mooncake. 1983. (Moonbear Ser.). (Illus.). 28p. (J). (ps-k). 11.95 o.s.i (*0-13-601013-X*) Prentice Hall PTR.

—Mooncake. (Moonbear Ser.). 32p. (J). (ps-k). 2000. pap. 5.99 (*0-689-83517-5*); 1986. (Illus.). pap. 4.95 (*0-671-66451-4*) Simon & Schuster Children's Publishing. (Aladdin).

—Mooncake. 1983. (Moonbear Ser.). (J). (ps-k). 12.14 (*0-606-02840-4*) Turtleback Bks.

—Moondance. 2002. (Moonbear Ser.). (Illus.). 13.83 (*1-4046-0169-4*) Book Wholesalers, Inc.

—Moondance. 1999. (Moonbear Ser.). (Illus.). (J). (ps-k). pap. 12.25 (*0-7857-3558-5*) Econo-Clad Bks.

—Moondance. 1994. (Moonbear Ser.). (Illus.). 32p. (J). (ps-1). mass mkt. 5.99 (*0-590-45488-9*) Scholastic, Inc.

—Moondance. 1993. (Moonbear Ser.). (J). (ps-k). 11.14 (*0-606-06578-4*) Turtleback Bks.

—Moongame. 2002. (Moonbear Ser.). (Illus.). (J). 14.47 (*0-7587-6424-3*) Book Wholesalers, Inc.

—Moongame. 1999. (Moonbear Ser.). (Illus.). (J). (ps-k). pap. 12.20 (*0-8085-9171-1*) Econo-Clad Bks.

—Moongame. (Moonbear Ser.). (J). (ps-k). 1987. 4.95 o.s.i (*0-13-601055-5*); 1984. (Illus.). 32p. 11.95 o.s.i (*0-13-600503-9*) Prentice Hall PTR.

—Moongame. 1992. (Moonbear Ser.). (J). (ps-k). 19.95 (*0-590-72624-2*) Scholastic, Inc.

—Moongame. (Moonbear Ser.). (Illus.). 32p. (J). (ps-k). 2000. pap. 5.99 (*0-689-83518-3*, Aladdin); 1987. pap. 4.95 (*0-671-66453-0*, Aladdin); 1984. pap. 14.00 o.s.i (*0-671-66452-2*, Simon & Schuster Children's Publishing) Simon & Schuster Children's Publishing.

—Moongame. 2000. (Moonbear Ser.). (J). (ps-k). 12.14 (*0-606-18896-7*) Turtleback Bks.

MOWGLI (FICTITIOUS CHARACTER)—FICTION

Golden Books Family Entertainment Staff. Walt Disney's Jungle Book. (Illus.). (J). o.p. (*0-307-01138-0*, Golden Bks.) Random Hse. Children's Bks.

Kipling, Rudyard. The Jungle Book. 1999. (Classics Ser.). (Illus.). 160p. (J). 12.95 (*0-7892-0558-0*); pap. 7.95 (*0-7892-0548-3*) Abbeville Pr., Inc. (Abbeville Kids).

—The Jungle Book. 2000. (Juvenile Classics). 160p. (J). pap. 2.00 (*0-486-41024-2*) Dover Pubns., Inc.

—The Jungle Book. 1994. 28p. (J). (gr. 2-8). pap. 4.00 (*1-57514-250-3*, 1163) Encore Performance Publishing.

—The Jungle Book. 1995. (Books of Wonder: Vol. 1). (Illus.). 272p. (J). (ps-3). 24.99 (*0-688-09979-3*) HarperCollins Children's Bk. Group.

—The Jungle Book. 1984. (Illus.). 224p. (J). (gr. 2-9). 12.95 o.s.i (*0-8052-3906-5*, Schocken) Knopf Publishing Group.

—The Jungle Book. 1994. (Everyman's Library Children's Classics Ser.). (Illus.). 272p. (J). (gr. 2 up). 14.95 (*0-679-43637-5*) Knopf, Alfred A. Inc.

—The Jungle Book. 1995. (Classics Ser.). (Illus.). (YA). pap. text 7.87 (*0-582-03587-2*) Longman Publishing Group.

—The Jungle Book. Robson, W. W., ed. & intro. by. 1992. (Oxford World's Classics Ser.). 420p. (J). pap. 5.95 o.p. (*0-19-282901-7*) Oxford Univ. Pr., Inc.

—The Jungle Book. (Whole Story Ser.). (Illus.). 1996. 216p. (YA). (gr. 7-12). 22.99 o.s.i (*0-670-86919-8*, Viking Children's Bks.); 1995. 294p. (J). 16.99 (*0-448-40948-8*, Grosset & Dunlap); 1995. 224p. (YA). (gr. 4-7). pap. 3.99 (*0-14-036686-5*, Puffin Bks.); 1987. 176p. (J). (gr. 5-9). 16.00 o.p. (*0-670-80241-7*, Viking Children's Bks.) Penguin Putnam Bks. for Young Readers.

—The Jungle Book. Hanft, Joshua, ed. 1994. (Great Illustrated Classics Ser.: Vol. 37). (Illus.). 240p. (J). (gr. 3-6). 9.95 (*0-86611-988-4*) Playmore, Inc., Pubs.

—The Jungle Book. (Children's Classics Ser.). (Illus.). (J). 1989. xv, 303p. 12.99 o.s.i (*0-517-67902-7*); 1988. 48p. 5.99 o.p. (*0-517-67006-2*) Random Hse. Value Publishing.

—The Jungle Book. 1995. (J). mass mkt. 3.50 (*0-590-50323-5*, Scholastic Paperbacks) Scholastic, Inc.

—The Jungle Book. 1995. (J). 7.98 o.p. (*0-8317-0747-X*) Smithmark Pubs., Inc.

—The Jungle Book. 1998. (Children's Classics). 192p. (J). (gr. 4-7). pap. 3.95 (*1-85326-119-X*, 119XWW) Wordsworth Editions, Ltd. GBR. *Dist:* Advanced Global Distribution Services.

—The Jungle Book. 1996. (Little Golden Bks.). (Illus.). 24p. (J). (ps-3). bds. 2.99 (*0-307-00326-4*, Golden Bks.) Random Hse. Children's Bks.

—The Jungle Book. 2001. (Young Classics Ser.). (Illus.). 48p. (J). (gr. 1-3). pap. 9.95 o.p. (*0-7894-4944-7*) Dorling Kindersley Publishing, Inc.

—The Jungle Book. l.t. ed. 240p. pap. 24.46 (*0-7583-1258-X*); 175p. pap. 19.88 (*0-7583-1257-1*); 140p. pap. 17.41 (*0-7583-1256-3*); 307p. pap. 29.21 (*0-7583-1259-8*); 393p. pap. 35.29 (*0-7583-1260-1*); 689p. pap. 56.27 (*0-7583-1263-6*); 140p. lib. bdg. 24.06 (*0-7583-1248-2*); 689p. lib. bdg. 67.52 (*0-7583-1255-5*); 240p. lib. bdg. 33.48 (*0-7583-1250-4*); 393p. lib. bdg. 46.54 (*0-7583-1252-0*); 483p. lib. bdg. 52.93 (*0-7583-1253-9*); 594p. lib. bdg. 60.80 (*0-7583-1254-7*); 307p. lib. bdg. 40.18 (*0-7583-1251-2*); 175p. lib. bdg. 27.90 (*0-7583-1249-0*) Huge Print Pr.

—The Jungle Book. l.t. ed. 1997. (Large Print Heritage Ser.). 240p. (YA). (gr. 7-12). lib. bdg. 28.95 (*1-58118-006-3*, 21966) LRS.

—The Jungle Book. l.t. ed. 1998. (Large Print Ser.). 265p. lib. bdg. 25.00 (*0-939495-58-9*) North Bks.

—The Jungle Book. deluxe ed. 1996. (Whole Story Ser.). (Illus.). 45p. (YA). (gr. 7-12). pap. 18.99 o.p. (*0-670-86797-7*, Viking Children's Bks.) Penguin Putnam Bks. for Young Readers.

—The Jungle Book. l.t. ed. 1999. (Classics for Children 8 & Younger Ser.). (Illus.). 48p. (J). (ps-3). (*1-85854-684-2*) Brimax Bks., Ltd.

—The Jungle Book. (J). reprint ed. lib. bdg. 24.95 (*0-88411-819-3*) Amereon, Ltd.

—The Jungle Book. unabr. ed. 1982. (J). audio 29.95 o.p. (*0-7861-0510-0*, 2010) Blackstone Audio Bks., Inc.

—The Jungle Book. unabr. ed. 1990. (J). audio 16.99 (*0-88646-375-0*, 7375) Durkin Hayes Publishing Ltd.

—The Jungle Book, Level 2. Hedge, Tricia, ed. 2000. (Bookworms Ser.). (Illus.). 64p. (J). pap. text 5.95 (*0-19-422977-7*) Oxford Univ. Pr., Inc.

—The Jungle Book: A Young Reader's Edition of the Classic Story. 1994. (Illus.). 56p. (J). (ps up). 9.98 (*1-56138-475-5*, Courage Bks.) Running Pr. Bk. Pubs.

—The Jungle Book: BBC. abr. ed. 1996. (BBC Radio Presents Ser.). (J). audio 16.99 o.s.i (*0-553-47799-4*, 394319, Listening Library) Random Hse. Audio Publishing Group.

—The Jungle Book I. 1994. 400p. mass mkt. 4.99 o.s.i (*0-06-106286-3*) HarperCollins Pubs.

—The Jungle Book I. 1950. (Illus.). 294p. (J). (gr. 4-6). 12.95 o.s.i (*0-448-06014-0*) Putnam Publishing Group, The.

—The Jungle Book I. 1987. 8.98 (*0-671-09226-X*) Simon & Schuster.

—The Jungle Book I. l.t. ed. 1987. (Illus.). 202p. (J). (gr. 3-7). lib. bdg. 13.95 o.p. (*1-85089-904-5*) Transaction Pubs.

—The Jungle Book II. 1995. 177p. (YA). mass mkt. 2.99 (*0-8125-2278-8*, Tor Classics) Doherty, Tom Assocs., LLC.

—The Jungle Books. abr. ed. 1995. (J). (gr. 4-7). audio 17.98 (*962-634-535-7*, NA303514); audio compact disk 19.98 (*962-634-035-5*, NA303512) Naxos of America, Inc. (Naxos AudioBooks).

—Mowgli Stories. unabr. ed. 1997. (J). (gr. 1-8). audio 18.95 (*1-85549-762-X*, CTC 081, Chivers Children's Audio Bks.) BBC Audiobooks America.

—Mowgli Stories. 1994. (Illus.). 128p. (J). pap. 1.00 (*0-486-28030-6*) Dover Pubns., Inc.

—Mowgli's Brothers. (Illus.). (YA). (gr. 5-9). 1994. 64p. lib. bdg. 19.95 (*1-56846-004-X*, Creative Editions); 1992. 62p. lib. bdg. 17.95 o.p. (*0-88682-488-5*, Creative Education) Creative Co., The.

—Mowgli's Brothers. 1995. (Illus.). 64p. (J). (gr. 1-5). 19.95 o.p. (*0-15-200933-7*) Harcourt Trade Pubs.

—Mowgli's Brothers. 1985. (Illus.). 48p. (J). (gr. k-6). 5.95 o.p. (*0-8249-8094-8*) Ideals Pubns.

—Mowgli's Brothers. unabr. ed. 1979. (J). audio 7.95 Jimcin Recordings.

—Mowgli's Brothers. 1985. (J). 13.27 o.p. (*0-516-09163-8*, Children's Pr.) Scholastic Library Publishing.

—Mowgli's Brothers, unabr. ed. 1994. 16.95 incl. audio (*1-883049-09-1*, 391214, Commuters Library) Sound Room Pubs., Inc.

—Mowgli's Brothers: Library Edition. unabr. ed. 1994. lib. bdg. 18.95 incl. audio (*1-883049-28-8*) Sound Room Pubs., Inc.

Mouse Works Staff. El Libro de la Selva. 1996. (Spanish Classics Ser.).Tr. of Jungle Book. (SPA.). 96p. (J). 7.98 o.p. (*1-57082-511-4*) Mouse Works.

—El Libro de la Selva (The Jungle Book) 1995. (SPA., Illus.). 96p. (J). 7.98 o.p. (*1-57082-223-9*) Mouse Works.

MOZART, WOLFGANG AMADEUS, 1756-1791—FICTION

Costanza, Stephen. Mozart & Miss Bimbes. 2004. (J). 17.00 (*0-8050-6627-6*, Holt, Henry & Co. Bks. For Young Readers) Holt, Henry & Co.

MUDGE (FICTITIOUS CHARACTER)—FICTION

Rylant, Cynthia. Henry & Mudge: The First Book of Their Adventures. (Henry & Mudge Ser.). (J). (gr. k-3). 1992. pap. 9.48 (*0-395-61769-3*); 1990. pap. 9.48 (*0-395-55143-9*) Houghton Mifflin Co.

—Henry & Mudge: The First Book of Their Adventures. unabr. ed. 1997. (Henry & Mudge Ser.). (J). (gr. k-3). audio 10.00 (*0-7887-0902-X*, 95040E7) Recorded Bks., LLC.

—Henry & Mudge: The First Book of Their Adventures. (Henry & Mudge Ser.). (J). (gr. k-3). 1992. 79.80 (*0-689-71659-1*, Little Simon); 1987. (Illus.). 40p. text 13.00 o.p. (*0-02-778001-5*, Atheneum/Richard Jackson Bks.); 1990. (Illus.). 48p. reprint ed. pap. 3.95 o.s.i (*0-689-71399-1*, Aladdin); 1996. (Illus.). 40p. 15.00 (*0-689-81004-0*, Atheneum/Richard Jackson Bks.) Simon & Schuster Children's Publishing.

—Henry & Mudge: The First Book of Their Adventures. 1990. (Henry & Mudge Ser.). (J). (gr. k-3). 10.14 (*0-606-03444-7*) Turtleback Bks.

—Henry & Mudge & a Very Merry Christmas. 2000. (Henry & Mudge Ser.). (J). (gr. k-3). 14.00 (*0-689-81168-3*, Simon & Schuster Children's Publishing) Simon & Schuster Children's Publishing.

—Henry & Mudge & Annie's Good Move. 2002. (J). (ps-3). pap., tchr.'s planning gde. ed. 29.95 incl. audio (*0-87499-966-9*); pap., tchr.'s planning gde. ed. 29.95 incl. audio (*0-87499-966-9*) Live Oak Media.

—Henry & Mudge & Annie's Good Move. (Henry & Mudge Ser.). (Illus.). (J). (gr. k-3). 2000. 48p. pap. 3.99 (*0-689-83284-2*, Aladdin); 1998. 40p. 15.00 (*0-689-81174-8*, Simon & Schuster Children's Publishing) Simon & Schuster Children's Publishing.

—Henry & Mudge & Annie's Good Move. 2000. (Henry & Mudge Ser.). (J). (gr. k-3). 10.14 (*0-606-17826-0*) Turtleback Bks.

—Henry & Mudge & Annie's Perfect Pet. (Henry & Mudge Ser.). (Illus.). (J). (gr. k-3). 2001. 40p. pap. 3.99 (*0-689-83443-8*, Aladdin); 2000. 48p. 15.00 (*0-689-81177-2*, Simon & Schuster Children's Publishing) Simon & Schuster Children's Publishing.

—Henry & Mudge & Mrs. Hopper's House. (Henry & Mudge Ser.). (J). 2004. 40p. pap. 3.99 (*0-689-83446-2*, Aladdin); 2003. (Illus.). 40p. 14.95 (*0-689-81153-5*, Simon & Schuster Children's Publishing); 1999. 12.95 (*0-689-81320-1*, Simon & Schuster Children's Publishing) Simon & Schuster Children's Publishing.

—Henry & Mudge & the Bedtime Thumps. unabr. ed. 1997. (Henry & Mudge Ser.). (J). (gr. k-3). audio 10.00 (*0-7887-1113-X*, 95107E7) Recorded Bks., LLC.

—Henry & Mudge & the Bedtime Thumps. (Henry & Mudge Ser.). (Illus.). 40p. (J). (gr. k-3). 1996. 15.00 (*0-689-81011-3*, Simon & Schuster Children's Publishing); 1996. pap. 3.99 (*0-689-80162-9*, Aladdin); 1991. text 14.00 o.s.i (*0-02-778006-6*, Simon & Schuster Children's Publishing) Simon & Schuster Children's Publishing.

—Henry & Mudge & the Bedtime Thumps. 1996. (Henry & Mudge Ser.). (J). (gr. k-3). 10.14 (*0-606-09403-2*) Turtleback Bks.

—Henry & Mudge & the Best Day of All. unabr. ed. (Henry & Mudge Ser.). (J). (gr. k-3). audio 10.00 (*0-7887-1787-1*, 95258E7); 1997. 22.24 incl. audio (*0-7887-1820-7*, 40600) Recorded Bks., LLC.

—Henry & Mudge & the Best Day of All. (Henry & Mudge Ser.). (Illus.). 40p. (J). (gr. k-3). 1997. pap. 3.99 (*0-689-81385-6*, Aladdin); 1997. (SPA., pap. 5.99 (*0-689-81469-0*, Aladdin); 1996. 15.00 (*0-689-81006-7*, Simon & Schuster Children's Publishing); 1995. text 14.00 o.s.i (*0-02-778012-0*, Simon & Schuster Children's Publishing) Simon & Schuster Children's Publishing.

—Henry & Mudge & the Best Day of All. 1997. (Henry & Mudge Ser.). (J). (gr. k-3). 10.14 (*0-606-12723-2*) Turtleback Bks.

—Henry & Mudge & the Big Sleep Over. 2006. (Henry & Mudge Ser.: Vol. 23). (J). (gr. k-3). 14.00 (*0-689-81171-3*, Simon & Schuster Children's Publishing) Simon & Schuster Children's Publishing.

—Henry & Mudge & the Careful Cousin. 2000. (Henry & Mudge Ser.). (J). (gr. k-3). pap. 19.97 incl. audio (*0-7366-9183-9*) Books on Tape, Inc.

—Henry & Mudge & the Careful Cousin. 2001. (Henry & Mudge Ser.). (J). (gr. k-3). pap. 15.95 incl. audio Kimbo Educational.

—Henry & Mudge & the Careful Cousin. unabr. ed. 1999. (Henry & Mudge Ser.). (Illus.). (J). pap. 29.95 incl. audio (*0-87499-530-2*); 24.95 incl. audio (*0-87499-529-9*); 24.95 incl. audio (*0-87499-529-9*); pap. 15.95 incl. audio (*0-87499-528-0*); pap. 15.95 incl. audio (*0-87499-528-0*) Live Oak Media.

—Henry & Mudge & the Careful Cousin. 2000. (Henry & Mudge Ser.). (J). (gr. k-3). pap. 15.98 incl. audio Random Hse. Audio Publishing Group.

—Henry & Mudge & the Careful Cousin. (Henry & Mudge Ser.). (Illus.). 48p. (J). (gr. k-3). 1999. 15.00 (*0-689-81007-5*, Simon & Schuster Children's Publishing); 1997. pap. 3.99 (*0-689-81386-4*, Aladdin); 1994. text 14.00 (*0-02-778021-X*, Simon & Schuster Children's Publishing) Simon & Schuster Children's Publishing.

—Henry & Mudge & the Careful Cousin. 1997. (Henry & Mudge Ser.). (J). (gr. k-3). 10.14 (*0-606-11456-4*) Turtleback Bks.

—Henry & Mudge & the Forever Sea. 2000. (Henry & Mudge Ser.). (J). (gr. k-3). pap. 19.97 incl. audio (*0-7366-9187-1*); pap. 19.97 incl. audio (*0-7366-9187-1*) Books on Tape, Inc.

—Henry & Mudge & the Forever Sea. 2001. (Henry & Mudge Ser.). (J). (gr. k-3). pap. 15.95 incl. audio Kimbo Educational.

—Henry & Mudge & the Forever Sea. 2000. (Henry & Mudge Ser.). (J). (gr. k-3). pap., tchr. ed. 29.95 incl. audio (*0-87499-607-4*); (Illus.). 24.95 incl. audio (*0-87499-606-6*); (Illus.). pap. 15.95 incl. audio (*0-87499-605-8*) Live Oak Media.

—Henry & Mudge & the Forever Sea. (Henry & Mudge Ser.). (Illus.). 48p. (J). (gr. k-3). 1997. pap. 3.99 (*0-689-81017-2*, Aladdin); 1996. 15.00 (*0-689-81016-4*, Simon & Schuster Children's Publishing); 1989. text 12.95 o.s.i (*0-02-778007-4*, Simon & Schuster Children's Publishing); 1993. reprint ed. pap. 3.95 (*0-689-71701-6*, Aladdin) Simon & Schuster Children's Publishing.

—Henry & Mudge & the Forever Sea. 1993. (Henry & Mudge Ser.). (J). (gr. k-3). 10.14 (*0-606-02669-X*) Turtleback Bks.

—Henry & Mudge & the Funny Lunch. 2004. (Henry & Mudge Ser.). (Illus.). 40p. (J). (gr. k-3). 14.95 (*0-689-81178-0*, Simon & Schuster Children's Publishing) Simon & Schuster Children's Publishing.

—Henry & Mudge & the Great Grandpas. 2005. (Henry & Mudge Ser.). (J). (gr. k-3). 14.00 (*0-689-81170-5*, Simon & Schuster Children's Publishing) Simon & Schuster Children's Publishing.

—Henry & Mudge & the Happy Cat. unabr. ed. 1997. (Henry & Mudge Ser.). (J). (gr. k-3). audio 10.00 (*0-7887-1340-X*, 95189E7) Recorded Bks., LLC.

—Henry & Mudge & the Happy Cat. (Henry & Mudge Ser.). (Illus.). 48p. (J). (gr. k-3). 1997. 15.00 (*0-689-81012-1*, Simon & Schuster Children's Publishing); 1996. pap. 3.99 (*0-689-81013-X*, Aladdin); 1990. text 14.00 o.s.i (*0-02-778008-2*, Atheneum/Richard Jackson Bks.); 1994. reprint ed. pap. 3.95 o.s.i (*0-689-71791-1*, Aladdin) Simon & Schuster Children's Publishing.

—Henry & Mudge & the Happy Cat. 1994. (Henry & Mudge Ser.). (J). (gr. k-3). 10.14 (*0-606-05870-2*) Turtleback Bks.

—Henry & Mudge & the Long Weekend. 2001. (Henry & Mudge Ser.). (J). (gr. k-3). pap. 15.95 incl. audio Kimbo Educational.

—Henry & Mudge & the Long Weekend. unabr. ed. 2000. (Henry & Mudge Ser.). (Illus.). pap. 29.95 incl. audio (*0-87499-603-1*); (J). 24.95 incl. audio (*0-87499-602-3*); (J). pap. 15.95 incl. audio (*0-87499-601-5*) Live Oak Media.

—Henry & Mudge & the Long Weekend. (Henry & Mudge Ser.). (Illus.). 40p. (J). (gr. k-3). 1992. 13.00 (*0-02-778013-9*, Simon & Schuster Children's Publishing); 1997. 15.00 (*0-689-81009-1*, Simon & Schuster Children's Publishing); 1996. pap. 3.99 (*0-689-80885-2*, Aladdin) Simon & Schuster Children's Publishing.

—Henry & Mudge & the Long Weekend. 1996. (Henry & Mudge Ser.). (J). (gr. k-3). 10.14 (*0-606-10840-8*) Turtleback Bks.

—Henry & Mudge & the Sneaky Crackers. 2002. (J). pap., tchr.'s planning gde. ed. 29.95 incl. audio (*0-87499-958-8*); pap., tchr.'s planning gde. ed. 29.95 incl. audio (*0-87499-958-8*); pap. 16.95 incl. audio (*0-87499-956-1*) Live Oak Media.

—Henry & Mudge & the Sneaky Crackers. (Henry & Mudge Ser.). (Illus.). (J). (gr. k-3). 1999. 48p. pap. 3.99 (*0-689-82525-0*, Aladdin); 1998. 40p. 15.00 (*0-689-81176-4*, Simon & Schuster Children's Publishing) Simon & Schuster Children's Publishing.

—Henry & Mudge & the Sneaky Crackers. 1999. (Henry & Mudge Ser.). (J). (gr. k-3). 10.14 (*0-606-15925-8*) Turtleback Bks.

—Henry & Mudge & the Snowman Plan. 2002. (J). pap., tchr.'s planning gde. ed. 29.95 incl. audio (*0-87499-970-7*); pap., tchr.'s planning gde. ed. 29.95 incl. audio (*0-87499-970-7*); 25.95 incl. audio (*0-87499-969-3*); pap. 16.95 incl. audio (*0-87499-968-5*) Live Oak Media.

—Henry & Mudge & the Snowman Plan. (Henry & Mudge Ser.). (Illus.). 40p. (J). (gr. k-3). 2000. pap. 3.99 (*0-689-83449-7*, Aladdin); 1999. 15.00 (*0-689-81169-1*, Simon & Schuster Children's Publishing) Simon & Schuster Children's Publishing.

—Henry & Mudge & the Snowman Plan. 2000. (Henry & Mudge Ser.). (J). (gr. k-3). 10.14 (*0-606-19711-7*) Turtleback Bks.

—Henry & Mudge & the Starry Night. abr. ed. 2002. (J). 25.95 incl. audio (*0-87499-961-8*); 25.95 incl. audio (*0-87499-961-8*); pap. 16.95 incl. audio (*0-87499-960-X*); pap. 16.95 incl. audio (*0-87499-960-X*); pap., tchr.'s planning gde. ed. 29.95 incl. audio (*0-87499-962-6*); pap., tchr.'s planning gde. ed. 29.95 incl. audio (*0-87499-962-6*) Live Oak Media.

—Henry & Mudge & the Starry Night. abr. ed. 2002. (J). (gr. k-2). 10.00 (*0-7887-9978-9*) Recorded Bks., LLC.

—Henry & Mudge & the Starry Night. (Henry & Mudge Ser.). (Illus.). 48p. (J). (gr. k-3). 1999. pap. 3.99 (*0-689-82586-2*, 076714003996, Aladdin); 1998. 15.00 (*0-689-81175-6*, Simon & Schuster Children's Publishing) Simon & Schuster Children's Publishing.

—Henry & Mudge & the Starry Night. 1999. (Henry & Mudge Ser.). (J). (gr. k-3). 10.14 (*0-606-16305-0*) Turtleback Bks.

—Henry & Mudge & the Tall Tree House. 2002. (Henry & Mudge Ser.). (Illus.). 40p. (J). (gr. k-3). 14.95 (*0-689-81173-X*, Simon & Schuster Children's Publishing) Simon & Schuster Children's Publishing.

—Henry & Mudge & the Tumbling Trip. 2002. (Henry & Mudge Ser.). (J). (gr. k-3). 14.00 (*0-689-81180-2*, Simon & Schuster Children's Publishing) Simon & Schuster Children's Publishing.

—Henry & Mudge & the Wild Goose Chase. 2003. (Henry & Mudge Ser.). (Illus.). 40p. (J). (gr. k-3). 14.95 (*0-689-81172-1*, Simon & Schuster Children's Publishing) Simon & Schuster Children's Publishing.

—Henry & Mudge & the Wild Wind. unabr. ed. 1998. (Henry & Mudge Ser.). (J). (gr. k-3). audio 10.00 (*0-7887-2214-X*, 95513E7) Recorded Bks., LLC.

—Henry & Mudge & the Wild Wind. (Henry & Mudge Ser.). (Illus.). 40p. (J). (gr. k-3). 2000. 15.00 (*0-689-81008-3*, Simon & Schuster Children's Publishing); 1996. pap. 3.99 (*0-689-80838-0*, Aladdin); 1993. pap. 13.00 (*0-02-778014-7*, Simon & Schuster Children's Publishing) Simon & Schuster Children's Publishing.

—Henry & Mudge & the Wild Wind. 1996. (Henry & Mudge Ser.). (J). (gr. k-3). 10.14 (*0-606-09404-0*) Turtleback Bks.

—Henry & Mudge Book & Toy. 1992. (Henry & Mudge Ser.). (Illus.). 48p. (J). (gr. k-3). pap. 19.95 o.s.i (*0-689-71648-6*, Little Simon) Simon & Schuster Children's Publishing.

—Henry & Mudge Get the Cold Shivers. 2000. (Henry & Mudge Ser.). (J). (gr. k-3). pap. 19.97 incl. audio (*0-7366-9186-3*); pap. 19.97 incl. audio (*0-7366-9186-3*) Books on Tape, Inc.

—Henry & Mudge Get the Cold Shivers. 2001. (Henry & Mudge Ser.). (J). (gr. k-3). pap. 15.95 incl. audio Kimbo Educational.

—Henry & Mudge Get the Cold Shivers. unabr. ed. 1999. (Henry & Mudge Ser.). (Illus.). pap. 29.95 incl. audio (*0-87499-526-4*); pap. 29.95 incl. audio (*0-87499-526-4*); (J). 24.95 incl. audio (*0-87499-525-6*); (J). pap. 15.95 incl. audio (*0-87499-524-8*) Live Oak Media.

—Henry & Mudge Get the Cold Shivers. unabr. ed. 2000. (Henry & Mudge Ser.). (J). (gr. k-3). pap. 15.98 incl. audio Random Hse. Audio Publishing Group.

—Henry & Mudge Get the Cold Shivers. (Henry & Mudge Ser.). (Illus.). 48p. (J). (ps-3). 1996. 15.00 (*0-689-81014-8*, Simon & Schuster Children's Publishing); 1996. pap. 3.99 (*0-689-81015-6*, Aladdin); 1994. pap. 3.95 o.s.i (*0-689-71849-7*, Aladdin); 1989. text 12.95 o.s.i (*0-02-778011-2*, Simon & Schuster Children's Publishing) Simon & Schuster Children's Publishing.

—Henry & Mudge in Puddle Trouble. 2000. (Henry & Mudge Ser.). (J). (gr. k-3). pap. 19.97 incl. audio (*0-7366-9192-8*) Books on Tape, Inc.

—Henry & Mudge in Puddle Trouble. 2001. (Henry & Mudge Ser.). (J). (gr. k-3). pap. 15.95 incl. audio Kimbo Educational.

—Henry & Mudge in Puddle Trouble. unabr. ed. 1998. (Henry & Mudge Ser.). (Illus.). pap. 29.95 incl. audio (*0-87499-443-8*); (J). 24.95 incl. audio (*0-87499-442-X*); (J). 24.95 incl. audio (*0-87499-442-X*); (J). pap. 15.95 incl. audio (*0-87499-441-1*); (J). pap. 15.95 incl. audio (*0-87499-441-1*) Live Oak Media.

—Henry & Mudge in Puddle Trouble. (Henry & Mudge Ser.). (Illus.). 48p. (J). (ps-3). 1996. pap. 3.99 (*0-689-81003-2*, Aladdin); 1990. pap. 3.95 o.s.i (*0-689-71400-9*, Aladdin); 1987. text 12.95 o.s.i (*0-02-778002-3*, Atheneum/Richard Jackson Bks.); 1996. 15.00 (*0-689-81002-4*, Atheneum/Richard Jackson Bks.) Simon & Schuster Children's Publishing.

—Henry & Mudge in Puddle Trouble. 1987. (Henry & Mudge Ser.). (J). (gr. k-3). 10.14 (*0-606-03443-9*) Turtleback Bks.

—Henry & Mudge in the Family Trees. (Henry & Mudge Ser.). (Illus.). 48p. (J). (gr. k-3). 1998. pap. 3.99 (*0-689-82317-7*, Aladdin); 1997. 15.00 (*0-689-81179-9*, Simon & Schuster Children's Publishing) Simon & Schuster Children's Publishing.

—Henry & Mudge in the Family Trees. 1998. (Henry & Mudge Ser.). (J). (gr. k-3). 10.14 (*0-606-15567-8*) Turtleback Bks.

—Henry & Mudge in the Green Time. 2000. (Henry & Mudge Ser.). (J). (gr. k-3). pap. 19.97 incl. audio (*0-7366-9191-X*); pap. 19.97 incl. audio (*0-7366-9191-X*) Books on Tape, Inc.

—Henry & Mudge in the Green Time. unabr. ed. 2001. (Henry & Mudge Ser.). (J). (gr. k-3). pap. 15.95 incl. audio Kimbo Educational.

—Henry & Mudge in the Green Time. 1999. (Henry & Mudge Ser.). (Illus.). (J). (gr. k-3). pap., tchr. ed. 29.95 incl. audio (*0-87499-423-3*); pap., tchr. ed. 29.95 incl. audio (*0-87499-423-3*); 24.95 incl. audio (*0-87499-422-5*); pap. 15.95 incl. audio (*0-87499-421-7*) Live Oak Media.

—Henry & Mudge in the Green Time. unabr. ed. 2000. (Henry & Mudge Ser.). (J). (gr. k-3). pap. 15.98 incl. audio Random Hse. Audio Publishing Group.

—Henry & Mudge in the Green Time. 1988. (Henry & Mudge Ser.). (J). (gr. k-3). 30.66 incl. audio (*0-676-87199-2*) SRA/McGraw-Hill.

—Henry & Mudge in the Green Time. (Henry & Mudge Ser.). (Illus.). 48p. (J). (gr. k-3). 1998. 15.00 (*0-689-81000-8*, Simon & Schuster Children's Publishing); 1996. pap. 3.99 (*0-689-81001-6*, Aladdin); 1987. text 12.95 (*0-02-778003-1*, Simon & Schuster Children's Publishing); 1992. reprint ed. pap. 3.95 o.s.i (*0-689-71582-X*, Aladdin) Simon & Schuster Children's Publishing.

—Henry & Mudge in the Green Time. 1992. (Henry & Mudge Ser.). (J). (gr. k-3). 10.14 (*0-606-01591-4*) Turtleback Bks.

—Henry & Mudge in the Sparkle Days. 2000. (Henry & Mudge Ser.). (J). (gr. k-3). pap. 19.97 incl. audio (*0-7366-9185-5*); pap. 19.97 incl. audio (*0-7366-9185-5*) Books on Tape, Inc.

—Henry & Mudge in the Sparkle Days. 2001. (Henry & Mudge Ser.). (J). (gr. k-3). pap. 15.95 incl. audio Kimbo Educational.

—Henry & Mudge in the Sparkle Days. unabr. ed. 1999. (Henry & Mudge Ser.). (Illus.). pap. 29.95 incl. audio (*0-87499-501-9*); pap. 29.95 incl. audio (*0-87499-501-9*); (J). 24.95 incl. audio (*0-87499-500-0*); (J). pap. 15.95 incl. audio (*0-87499-499-3*) Live Oak Media.

—Henry & Mudge in the Sparkle Days. unabr. ed. 2000. (Henry & Mudge Ser.). (J). (gr. k-3). pap. 15.98 incl. audio Random Hse. Audio Publishing Group.

—Henry & Mudge in the Sparkle Days. (Henry & Mudge Ser.). (Illus.). (J). (ps-3). 1997. 48p. pap. 3.99 (*0-689-81019-9*, Aladdin); 1996. 48p. 15.00 (*0-689-81018-0*, Atheneum/Richard Jackson Bks.); 1988. 40p. text 12.95 o.s.i (*0-02-778005-8*, Atheneum/Richard Jackson Bks.); 1993. 48p. reprint ed. pap. 3.95 o.s.i (*0-689-71752-0*, Aladdin) Simon & Schuster Children's Publishing.

—Henry & Mudge in the Sparkle Days. 1993. (Henry & Mudge Ser.). (J). (gr. k-3). 10.14 (*0-606-05871-0*) Turtleback Bks.

—Henry & Mudge Take the Big Test. unabr. ed. 1997. (Henry & Mudge Ser.). (J). (gr. k-3). audio 10.00 (*0-7887-0744-2*, 94921E7) Recorded Bks., LLC.

—Henry & Mudge Take the Big Test. (Henry & Mudge Ser.). (Illus.). 40p. (J). (ps-3). 1997. 15.00 (*0-689-81010-5*, Simon & Schuster Children's Publishing); 1996. pap. 3.99 (*0-689-80886-0*, Aladdin); 1991. text 12.95 o.s.i (*0-02-778009-0*, Simon & Schuster Children's Publishing) Simon & Schuster Children's Publishing.

—Henry & Mudge Take the Big Test. 1996. (Henry & Mudge Ser.). (J). (gr. k-3). 10.14 (*0-606-10841-6*) Turtleback Bks.

—Henry & Mudge under the Yellow Moon. 2000. (Henry & Mudge Ser.). (J). (gr. k-3). pap. 19.97 incl. audio (*0-7366-9184-7*); pap. 19.97 incl. audio (*0-7366-9184-7*) Books on Tape, Inc.

—Henry & Mudge under the Yellow Moon. 2001. (Henry & Mudge Ser.). (J). (gr. k-3). pap. 15.95 incl. audio Kimbo Educational.

—Henry & Mudge under the Yellow Moon. 1998. (Henry & Mudge Ser.). (Illus.). (J). (gr. k-3). pap., tchr. ed. 29.95 incl. audio (*0-87499-447-0*); pap., tchr. ed. 29.95 incl. audio (*0-87499-447-0*); 24.95 incl. audio (*0-87499-446-2*); pap. 15.95 incl. audio (*0-87499-445-4*) Live Oak Media.

—Henry & Mudge under the Yellow Moon. unabr. ed. 1999. (Henry & Mudge Ser.). (J). (gr. k-3). pap. 15.98 incl. audio Random Hse. Audio Publishing Group.

—Henry & Mudge under the Yellow Moon. (Henry & Mudge Ser.). 48p. (J). (gr. k-3). 1996. (Illus.). pap. 3.99 (*0-689-81021-0*, Aladdin); 1987. (Illus.). text 12.95 (*0-02-778004-X*, Simon & Schuster Children's Publishing); 1992. (Illus.). reprint ed. pap. 3.95 o.s.i (*0-689-71580-3*, Aladdin); 1997. 15.00 (*0-689-81020-2*, Simon & Schuster Children's Publishing) Simon & Schuster Children's Publishing.

—Henry & Mudge under the Yellow Moon. 1992. (Henry & Mudge Ser.). (J). (gr. k-3). 10.14 (*0-606-01592-2*) Turtleback Bks.

—Henry y Mudge: El Primer Libro de Sus Aventuras. 1999. (Henry & Mudge Ser.). (SPA., Illus.). (J). (gr. k-3). 13.00 (*0-689-80685-X*, Atheneum) Simon & Schuster Children's Publishing.

—Henry y Mudge: El Primer Libro de Sus Aventuras. Ada, Alma Flor, tr. from ENG. 1996. (Henry & Mudge Ser.). (SPA., Illus.). 40p. (J). (gr. k-3). mass mkt. 3.99 (*0-689-80684-1*, Aladdin) Simon & Schuster Children's Publishing.

—Henry y Mudge: El Primer Libro de Sus Aventuras. 1996. (Henry & Mudge Ser.). (SPA.). (J). (gr. k-3). 9.19 o.p. (*0-606-09406-7*) Turtleback Bks.

—Henry y Mudge con Barro Hasta el Rabo. (Henry & Mudge Ser.).Tr. of Henry & Mudge in Puddle Trouble. (SPA.). (J). (gr. k-3). 1998. 13.00 (*0-689-80686-8*, Atheneum); 1996. (Illus.). 48p. mass mkt. 5.99 (*0-689-80687-6*, Aladdin) Simon & Schuster Children's Publishing.

—Henry y Mudge con Barro Hasta el Rabo. 1996. (Henry & Mudge Ser.).Tr. of Henry & Mudge in Puddle Trouble. (SPA.). (J). (gr. k-3). 12.14 (*0-606-10427-5*) Turtleback Bks.

—Henry y Mudge y el Mejor Dia del Ano. 1997. (Henry & Mudge Ser.).Tr. of Henry & Mudge & the Best Day of All. (SPA.). (J). (gr. k-3). 12.14 (*0-606-12724-0*) Turtleback Bks.

Rylant, Cynthia & Stevenson, Sucie. Henry & Mudge: The First Book of Their Adventures. 1996. (Henry & Mudge Ser.). (Illus.). 40p. (J). (ps-3). pap. 3.99 (*0-689-81005-9*, Aladdin) Simon & Schuster Children's Publishing.

MULDER, FOX (FICTITIOUS CHARACTER)—FICTION

Bisson, Terry. Miracle Man. 2000. (X-Files Young Adult Ser.: No. 16). 128p. (gr. 4-7). mass mkt. 4.50 (*0-06-106617-6*, HarperEntertainment) Morrow/Avon.

Martin, Les. Darkness Falls, No. 2. 1995. (X-Files Ser.). 112p. (gr. 5 up). pap. 4.50 (*0-06-440614-8*, HarperEntertainment) Morrow/Avon.

—E. B. E. A Novel. 1996. (X-Files Ser.: No. 9). 112p. (YA). (gr. 5 up). pap. 4.50 (*0-06-440653-9*, Harper Trophy) HarperCollins Children's Bk. Group.

—E.B.E. 1996. (X-Files Ser.: No. 9). 10.55 (*0-606-10978-1*) Turtleback Bks.

—Fear, No. 7. 1996. (X-Files Ser.). 112p. (J). (gr. 5 up). pap. 3.95 (*0-06-440642-3*, HarperEntertainment) Morrow/Avon.

—Ghost in the Machine, No. 11. 1997. (X-Files Ser.). 112p. (YA). (gr. 5 up). pap. 4.50 (*0-06-440678-4*, HarperEntertainment) Morrow/Avon.

—Humbug, No. 5. 1996. (X-Files Ser.). 128p. (YA). (gr. 5 up). pap. 3.95 (*0-06-440627-X*, HarperEntertainment) Morrow/Avon.

—Quarantine, No. 13. 1999. (X-Files Young Adult Ser.: No. 13). 128p. (J). (gr. 7 up). mass mkt. 4.50 (*0-06-447189-6*, HarperEntertainment) Morrow/Avon.

—Tiger, Tiger. 1995. 112p. (YA). (gr. 5 up). pap. 4.50 o.s.i (*0-06-440626-1*, Harper Trophy) HarperCollins Children's Bk. Group.

—X Marks the Spot, No. 1. 1995. (X Files Middle Grade Ser.). 128p. (gr. 5 up). pap. 4.50 (*0-06-440613-X*, HarperEntertainment) Morrow/Avon.

Mezrich, Ben. Skin, abr. ed. 1999. audio 18.00 (*0-694-51913-8*, 393578, HarperAudio) HarperTrade.

Owens, Everett. Regeneration, Vol. 14. 2000. (X-Files Young Adult Ser.: No. 14). 128p. (gr. 7-12). mass mkt. 4.50 (*0-06-106619-2*, HarperEntertainment) Morrow/Avon.

Steiber, Ellen. Haunted. 2000. (X-Files Young Adult Ser.: No. 15). (Illus.). 144p. (J). (gr. 4-7). mass mkt. 4.50 (*0-06-106618-4*, HarperEntertainment) Morrow/Avon.

MURRY FAMILY (FICTITIOUS CHARACTER)—FICTION

L'Engle, Madeleine. Many Waters. 2002. (Illus.). (J). 15.00 (*0-7587-9605-6*) Book Wholesalers, Inc.

—Many Waters. (J). 1991. mass mkt. 4.99 (*0-440-80265-2*); 1987. 336p. (gr. 5-9). pap. text 6.50 (*0-440-40548-3*) Dell Publishing.

—Many Waters, RS. (J). 1987. 310p. (gr. 4 up). 50.00 o.p. (*0-374-34797-2*); 1986. 320p. (gr. 8-12). 18.00 (*0-374-34796-4*) Farrar, Straus & Giroux. (Farrar, Straus & Giroux (BYR)).

—Many Waters. 1987. 320p. (J). (gr. k-12). mass mkt. 3.50 o.s.i (*0-440-95252-2*, Laurel Leaf); 1998. (Illus.). 336p. (YA). (gr. 5-8). mass mkt. 5.99 (*0-440-22770-4*, Dell Books for Young Readers) Random Hse. Children's Bks.

—Many Waters. (J). 1998. 12.04 (*0-606-13596-0*); 1986. 12.04 (*0-606-05091-4*) Turtleback Bks.

—A Swiftly Tilting Planet. unabr. ed. 1997. (Wrinkle in Time Trilogy: Vol. 2). audio 40.00 BBC Audiobooks America.

—A Swiftly Tilting Planet. unabr. ed. 1999. (YA). audio 44.95 Blackstone Audio Bks., Inc.

—A Swiftly Tilting Planet. 1986. o.p.; 1980. 304p. (J). (gr. 5-9). pap. text 6.50 (*0-440-40158-5*) Dell Publishing.

—A Swiftly Tilting Planet, RS. 1978. 288p. (J). (gr. 4-7). 17.00 (*0-374-37362-0*, Farrar, Straus & Giroux (BYR)) Farrar, Straus & Giroux.

—A Swiftly Tilting Planet, Set. unabr. ed. 1999. (YA). audio 37.98 Highsmith Inc.

—A Swiftly Tilting Planet. 228p. (YA). (gr. 5 up). pap. 5.50 (*0-8072-1495-7*); 2002. (J). (gr. 4-7). audio 30.00 (*0-8072-0916-3*); 2002. (J). (gr. 4-7). audio 30.00 (*0-8072-0916-3*); 1996. 228p. (J). (gr. 5 up). pap. 46.00 incl. audio (*0-8072-7757-6*, YA910SP) Random Hse. Audio Publishing Group. (Listening Library).

—A Swiftly Tilting Planet. 1979. 272p. (YA). (gr. 5-9). mass mkt. 5.99 (*0-440-90158-8*, Laurel Leaf) Random Hse. Children's Bks.

—A Swiftly Tilting Planet. 1978. 11.55 (*0-606-01841-7*) Turtleback Bks.

—A Swiftly Tilting Planet: Digest Edition. 1998. 12.04 (*0-606-13831-5*) Turtleback Bks.

—A Swiftly Tilting Planet: Library Edition. unabr. ed. 1996. (YA). (gr. 5-9). audio 40.00 (*0-8072-7756-8*, YA910CX, Listening Library) Random Hse. Audio Publishing Group.

—A Wind in the Door. unabr. ed. 1999. (J). audio 32.95 Blackstone Audio Bks., Inc.

—A Wind in the Door. 1986. o.p.; 1974. 240p. (J). (gr. 4-7). pap. text 6.50 (*0-440-48761-7*) Dell Publishing.

—A Wind in the Door, RS. 1973. 224p. (J). (gr. 4-7). 17.00 (*0-374-38443-6*, Farrar, Straus & Giroux (BYR)) Farrar, Straus & Giroux.

—A Wind in the Door. unabr. ed. 1999. (YA). audio 29.98 Highsmith Inc.

—A Wind in the Door. (gr. 5 up). 211p. (YA). pap. 5.50 (*0-8072-1466-3*); 2002. (YA). audio 26.00 (*0-8072-0694-6*); 1994. 211p. (J). pap. 37.00 incl. audio (*0-8072-7507-7*, YA864SP) Random Hse. Audio Publishing Group. (Listening Library).

—A Wind in the Door. 1991. (J). mass mkt. o.s.i (*0-440-80253-9*, Dell Books for Young Readers); 1976. 224p. (YA). (gr. 4-7). mass mkt. 5.99 (*0-440-98761-X*, Laurel Leaf) Random Hse. Children's Bks.

—A Wind in the Door. 1979. (J). 12.04 (*0-606-13920-6*); 1973. 11.55 (*0-606-05084-1*) Turtleback Bks.

—A Wind in the Door: Library Edition. unabr. ed. 2002. (YA). (gr. 5 up). audio 32.00 (*0-8072-7506-9*, YA864CX, Listening Library) Random Hse. Audio Publishing Group.

—A Wrinkle in Time. 1999. 224p. mass mkt. 2.99 o.s.i (*0-440-22839-5*) Bantam Bks.

—A Wrinkle in Time. unabr. ed. 1999. (YA). audio 32.95 Blackstone Audio Bks., Inc.

—A Wrinkle in Time. 2002. (J). 15.00 (*0-7587-6754-4*) Book Wholesalers, Inc.

—A Wrinkle in Time. 1997. mass mkt. 2.69 o.p. (*0-440-22715-1*); 1996. 224p. mass mkt. 2.49 o.s.i (*0-440-22039-4*); 1988. (J). mass mkt. o.p. (*0-440-80054-4*) Dell Publishing.

—A Wrinkle in Time, RS. 224p. (J). (gr. 4). 1988. 50.00 o.p. (*0-374-38614-5*); 1962. 17.00 (*0-374-38613-7*) Farrar, Straus & Giroux. (Farrar, Straus & Giroux (BYR)).

—A Wrinkle in Time. unabr. ed. 1999. (YA). audio 29.98 Highsmith Inc.

—A Wrinkle in Time, 2 vols., Set. 20.00 (*0-89064-014-9*) National Assn. for Visually Handicapped.

—A Wrinkle in Time. l.t. ed. 1987. 216p. reprint ed. lib. bdg. 16.95 o.s.i (*1-55736-059-6*, Cornerstone Bks.) Pages, Inc.

—A Wrinkle in Time. 211p. (YA). (gr. 5 up). pap. 5.99 (*0-8072-1460-4*); 2000. (J). audio 26.00 (*0-8072-7587-5*, 593911); 2000. (J). audio 26.00 (*0-8072-7587-5*, 593911); 1993. 45p. (YA). (gr. 4-7). audio 32.00 (*0-8072-7412-7*, YA854CX); 1993. 211p. (YA). (gr. 5 up). pap. 37.00 incl. audio (*0-8072-7413-5*, YA854SP); 1993. 211p. (YA). (gr. 5 up). pap. 37.00 incl. audio (*0-8072-7413-5*, YA854SP) Random Hse. Audio Publishing Group. (Listening Library).

—A Wrinkle in Time. (gr. 4-7). 1998. (Illus.). 240p. pap. 6.50 (*0-440-49805-8*, Yearling); 1976. 224p. (YA). mass mkt. 6.50 (*0-440-99805-0*, Laurel Leaf) Random Hse. Children's Bks.

—A Wrinkle in Time. unabr. ed. 1994. (J). (gr. 5). audio 46.00 (*0-7887-0137-1*, 94362E7) Recorded Bks., LLC.

—A Wrinkle in Time. 1997. (Literature Guide Ser.). 16p. (J). mass mkt. 3.95 (*0-590-37360-9*) Scholastic, Inc.

—A Wrinkle in Time. l.t. ed. 1998. (Perennial Bestsellers Ser.). 208p. (J). (gr. 4-7). 24.95 (*0-7838-8371-4*) Thorndike Pr.

—A Wrinkle in Time. 1976. (J). 12.55 (*0-606-13931-1*); 1962. 12.55 (*0-606-05085-X*) Turtleback Bks.

—A Wrinkle in Time Series, unabr. ed. 1996. (J). (gr. 4-7). audio 52.00 (*0-7366-3437-1*, 4081) Books on Tape, Inc.

MUSA, SULTAN OF MALI, FL. 1324—FICTION

Burns, Khephra. Mansa Musa: The Lion of Mali. 2001. (Illus.). 56p. (J). (gr. 3-5). 18.00 (*0-15-200375-4*, Gulliver Bks.) Harcourt Children's Bks.

MYERS, MICHAEL (FICTITIOUS CHARACTER)—FICTION

O'Rourke, Kelly. The Mad House. 1998. (Halloween Ser.: Vol. 3). 160p. (YA). (gr. 7-12). mass mkt. 4.50 o.s.i (*1-57297-342-0*) Boulevard Bks.

—The Old Myers Place. 1997. (Halloween Ser.: No. 2). 160p. (YA). mass mkt. 4.50 o.s.i (*1-57297-341-2*) Boulevard Bks.

O'Rourke, Michael. The Scream Factory. 1997. (Halloween Ser.: No. 1). 160p. (YA). (gr. 5-11). mass mkt. 4.50 o.s.i (*1-57297-298-X*) Boulevard Bks.

N

NAPOLEON I, EMPEROR OF THE FRENCH, 1769-1821—FICTION

Brighton, Catherine. My Napoleon. 1997. 4. (Illus.). 32p. (gr. k-5). pap. 16.95 o.p. (*0-7613-0106-2*) Millbrook Pr., Inc.

Marcellino, Fred. I, Crocodile. (Illus.). 32p. (J). 2002. (ps-3). pap. 6.99 (*0-06-008859-1*, Harper Trophy); 1999. (gr. 1-3). lib. bdg. 15.89 (*0-06-205199-7*); 1999. (gr. k-3). 15.95 (*0-06-205168-7*) HarperCollins Children's Bk. Group.

—I, Crocodile. (J). (gr. 1-2). 6.95 net. (*1-55592-982-6*) Weston Woods Studios, Inc.

Robbins, Ruth. The Emperor & the Drummer Boy. 1962. (Illus.). (J). (gr. 2-6). 4.95 o.p. (*0-87466-043-2*); lib. bdg. 5.38 o.p. (*0-87466-011-4*) Houghton Mifflin Co.

Woodruff, Elvira. Dear Napoleon, I Know You're Dead, But... 1994. 224p. (gr. 4-7). pap. text 4.99 (*0-440-40907-1*) Dell Publishing.

—Dear Napoleon, I Know You're Dead, But... 1992. 128p. (J). (gr. 4-7). tchr. ed. 16.95 (*0-8234-0962-7*) Holiday Hse., Inc.

—Dear Napoleon, I Know You're Dead, But... (J). 1996. pap. 4.50 (*0-440-91110-9*); 1994. pap. o.p. (*0-440-90078-6*) Random Hse. Children's Bks. (Dell Books for Young Readers).

—Dear Napoleon, I Know You're Dead, But... 1992. (J). 10.04 (*0-606-06965-8*) Turtleback Bks.

NATE THE GREAT (FICTITIOUS CHARACTER)—FICTION

Bolte, Mary. Nate the Great: A Classroom Guide. 1998. (Literature Unit Ser.). (Illus.). 48p. (gr. k-3). pap., tchr. ed. 7.99 (*1-57690-346-X*, TCA2346) Teacher Created Materials, Inc.

Diamond, Laurie. Nate the Great & the Musical Note, Level 2. Friedland, J. & Kessler, Rikki, eds. 1992. (Novel-Ties Ser.). (Illus.). (J). (gr. 2). pap., stu. ed. 15.95 (*0-88122-726-9*, S1403) Learning Links, Inc.

Searl, Duncan. Nate the Great, Level 2. Friedland, J. & Kessler, Rikki, eds. 1996. (Novel-Ties Ser.). (Illus.). 18p. (J). (gr. 2). pap., stu. ed. 15.95 (*1-56982-602-1*, S0602) Learning Links, Inc.

Sharmat, Marjorie Weinman. Nate the Great. 1986. (Nate the Great Ser.). (Illus.). (J). (gr. 1-4). 16.99 o.p. (*0-399-23239-7*) Penguin Group (USA) Inc.

—Nate the Great. (Nate the Great Ser.). (Illus.). (J). (gr. 1-4). 1986. 48p. 14.95 o.p. (*0-698-20627-4*); 1972. 64p. 8.99 o.p. (*0-698-30444-6*) Putnam Publishing Group, The. (Coward-McCann).

—Nate the Great. (Nate the Great Ser.). (Illus.). 48p. (J). (gr. 1-4). pap. 4.50 (*0-8072-1351-9*, Listening Library) Random Hse. Audio Publishing Group.

—Nate the Great. 1977. (Nate the Great Ser.). (Illus.). 64p. (gr. 1-4). pap. text 4.50 (*0-440-46126-X*, Yearling) Random Hse. Children's Bks.

—Nate the Great. anniv. ed. 2002. 64p. (gr. 1-4). text 13.95 (*0-385-73017-9*); lib. bdg. 15.99 (*0-385-90068-6*) Random Hse., Inc.

—Nate the Great. 1972. (Nate the Great Ser.). (Illus.). (J). (gr. 1-4). 10.65 (*0-606-01256-7*) Turtleback Bks.

—Nate the Great & Me: The Case of the Fleeing Fang. 1998. (Nate the Great Ser.). (Illus.). 64p. (gr. 1-4). text 9.95 o.s.i (*0-385-32601-7*, Delacorte Pr.) Dell Publishing.

—Nate the Great & Me: The Case of the Fleeing Fang. 2000. (Nate the Great Ser.). (Illus.). 64p. (J). (gr. 1-4). pap. 4.50 (*0-440-41381-8*, Dell Books for Young Readers) Random Hse. Children's Bks.

—Nate the Great & the Big Sniff. (Illus.). 48p. (gr. 1-4). 2003. pap. text 4.50 (*0-440-41502-0*, Yearling); 2001. lib. bdg. 15.99 (*0-385-90020-1*, Dell Books for Young Readers) Random Hse. Children's Bks.

—Nate the Great & the Boring Beach Bag. 1987. (Nate the Great Ser.). (Illus.). (J). (gr. 1-4). 16.99 o.p. (*0-399-23238-9*) Penguin Group (USA) Inc.

—Nate the Great & the Boring Beach Bag. 1987. (Nate the Great Ser.). (Illus.). 48p. (J). (gr. 1-4). 14.95 o.p. (*0-698-20631-2*, Coward-McCann) Putnam Publishing Group, The.

—Nate the Great & the Boring Beach Bag. 1989. (Nate the Great Ser.). (Illus.). 48p. (gr. 1-4). pap. text 4.50 (*0-440-40168-2*, Yearling) Random Hse. Children's Bks.

—Nate the Great & the Boring Beach Bag. 1987. (Nate the Great Ser.). (Illus.). (J). (gr. 1-4). 10.65 (*0-606-04281-4*) Turtleback Bks.

—Nate the Great & the Crunchy Christmas. 1997. (Nate the Great Ser.). (J). (gr. 1-4). 10.65 (*0-606-12779-8*) Turtleback Bks.

—Nate the Great & the Fishy Prize. (Nate the Great Ser.). (Illus.). 48p. (J). (gr. 1-4). 1988. 11.95 o.p. (*0-698-20639-8*); 1985. 9.99 o.p. (*0-698-30745-3*) Putnam Publishing Group, The. (Coward-McCann).

—Nate the Great & the Fishy Prize. 1988. (Nate the Great Ser.). (Illus.). 48p. (gr. 1-4). pap. text 4.50 (*0-440-40039-2*, Yearling) Random Hse. Children's Bks.

—Nate the Great & the Fishy Prize. 1985. (Nate the Great Ser.). (J). (gr. 1-4). 10.65 (*0-606-03869-8*) Turtleback Bks.

—Nate the Great & the Halloween Hunt. 1989. (Nate the Great Ser.). (Illus.). 48p. (J). (gr. 1-4). 12.95 o.p. (*0-698-20635-5*, Coward-McCann) Putnam Publishing Group, The.

—Nate the Great & the Halloween Hunt. (Nate the Great Ser.). (J). (Illus.). 48p. (gr. 1-4). pap. 4.50 (*0-8072-1283-0*); 2003. audio 17.00 (*0-8072-1935-5*); 1994. 48p. (gr. 1-4). pap. 17.00 incl. audio (*0-8072-0198-7*, FTR170SP) Random Hse. Audio Publishing Group. (Listening Library).

—Nate the Great & the Halloween Hunt. 1990. (Nate the Great Ser.). (Illus.). 48p. (gr. 1-4). pap. text 4.50 (*0-440-40341-3*, Yearling) Random Hse. Children's Bks.

—Nate the Great & the Halloween Hunt. 1989. (Nate the Great Ser.). (J). (gr. 1-4). 10.65 (*0-606-04487-6*) Turtleback Bks.

—Nate the Great & the Lost List. (Nate the Great Ser.). (Illus.). (J). (gr. 1-4). 1989. 48p. 13.95 o.p. (*0-698-20646-0*); 1975. 9.99 o.p. (*0-698-30593-0*) Putnam Publishing Group, The. (Coward-McCann).

—Nate the Great & the Lost List. 1991. (Nate the Great Ser.). (Illus.). 48p. (gr. 1-4). pap. text 4.50 (*0-440-46282-7*, Yearling) Random Hse. Children's Bks.

—Nate the Great & the Lost List. 1975. (Nate the Great Ser.). (Illus.). (J). (gr. 1-4). 10.65 (*0-606-02204-X*) Turtleback Bks.

—Nate the Great & the Missing Key. (Nate the Great Ser.). (J). (gr. 1-4). 15.98 o.p. incl. audio Kimbo Educational.

—Nate the Great & the Missing Key. (Nate the Great Ser.). (Illus.). 48p. (J). (gr. 1-4). 1987. 11.95 o.p. (*0-698-20630-4*); 1981. 8.99 o.p. (*0-698-30726-7*) Putnam Publishing Group, The. (Coward-McCann).

—Nate the Great & the Missing Key. (Nate the Great Ser.). (J). (Illus.). 48p. (gr. 1-4). pap. 4.50 (*0-8072-1335-7*); 2003. audio 17.00 (*0-8072-1936-3*); 1984. 48p. (gr. 1-4). pap. 17.00 incl. audio (*0-8072-0040-9*, FTR 75 SP); 1984. (gr. 1-4). audio Random Hse. Audio Publishing Group.

—Nate the Great & the Missing Key. 1982. (Nate the Great Ser.). (Illus.). 48p. (gr. 1-4). pap. text 4.50 (*0-440-46191-X*, Yearling) Random Hse. Children's Bks.

—Nate the Great & the Missing Key. 1981. (Nate the Great Ser.). (Illus.). (J). (gr. 1-4). 10.65 (*0-606-00708-3*) Turtleback Bks.

—Nate the Great & the Monster Mess. 1999. (Nate the Great Ser.). (Illus.). 48p. (gr. 1-4). text 14.95 (*0-385-32114-7*, Delacorte Pr.) Dell Publishing.

—Nate the Great & the Monster Mess. 2001. (Nate the Great Ser.). (Illus.). 48p. (gr. 1-4). pap. text 4.50 (*0-440-41662-0*, Dell Books for Young Readers) Random Hse. Children's Bks.

—Nate the Great & the Monster Mess. 2001. 10.65 (*0-606-22399-1*) Turtleback Bks.

—Nate the Great & the Mushy Valentine. (Nate the Great Ser.). (Illus.). 48p. (J). (gr. 1-4). 1995. pap. 4.50 (*0-440-41013-4*); 1994. 12.95 o.s.i (*0-385-31166-4*, Delacorte Pr.) Dell Publishing.

—Nate the Great & the Mushy Valentine. 1993. (Nate the Great Ser.). (J). (gr. 1-4). o.s.i (*0-385-44603-9*, Dell Books for Young Readers) Random Hse. Children's Bks.

—Nate the Great & the Mushy Valentine. 1995. (Nate the Great Ser.). (Illus.). (J). (gr. 1-4). 10.65 (*0-606-07938-6*) Turtleback Bks.

—Nate the Great & the Musical Note. 1991. (Nate the Great Ser.). (Illus.). 48p. (J). (gr. 1-4). pap. text 4.50 (*0-440-40466-5*) Dell Publishing.

—Nate the Great & the Musical Note. 1990. (Nate the Great Ser.). (Illus.). 48p. (J). (gr. 1-4). 13.95 o.p. (*0-698-20645-2*, Coward-McCann) Putnam Publishing Group, The.

—Nate the Great & the Musical Note. 1990. (Nate the Great Ser.). (Illus.). (J). (gr. 1-4). 10.65 (*0-606-04989-4*) Turtleback Bks.

—Nate the Great & the Phony Clue. 1999. (Nate the Great Ser.). (Illus.). (J). (gr. 1-4). pap. 11.70 (*0-8085-3753-9*) Econo-Clad Bks.

—Nate the Great & the Phony Clue. (Nate the Great Ser.). (Illus.). 48p. (J). (gr. 1-4). 1988. 11.95 o.p. (*0-698-20638-X*); 1977. 9.99 o.p. (*0-698-30650-3*) Putnam Publishing Group, The. (Coward-McCann).

—Nate the Great & the Phony Clue. 1982. (Nate the Great Ser.). (Illus.). 48p. (gr. 1-4). pap. text 4.50 (*0-440-46300-9*, Yearling) Random Hse. Children's Bks.

—Nate the Great & the Phony Clue. 1977. (Nate the Great Ser.). (Illus.). (J). (gr. 1-4). 10.65 (*0-606-02205-8*) Turtleback Bks.

—Nate the Great & the Snowy Trail. 1987. (Nate the Great Ser.). (Illus.). 48p. (J). (gr. 1-4). 11.95 o.p. (*0-698-20628-2*, Coward-McCann) Putnam Publishing Group, The.

—Nate the Great & the Snowy Trail. 1983. (Nate the Great Ser.). (Illus.). 48p. (gr. 1-4). pap. text 4.50 (*0-440-46276-2*, Yearling) Random Hse. Children's Bks.

—Nate the Great & the Snowy Trail. 1982. (Nate the Great Ser.). (Illus.). (J). (gr. 1-4). 10.65 (*0-606-02977-X*) Turtleback Bks.

—Nate the Great & the Sticky Case. 1981. (Nate the Great Ser.). (Illus.). 48p. (J). (gr. 1-4). pap. text 4.50 (*0-440-46289-4*) Dell Publishing.

—Nate the Great & the Sticky Case. 1999. (Nate the Great Ser.). (Illus.). (J). (gr. 1-4). pap. 11.70 (*0-8085-3755-5*) Econo-Clad Bks.

—Nate the Great & the Sticky Case. 1999. (Nate the Great Ser.). (Illus.). (J). (gr. 1-4). 9.95 (*1-56137-263-3*) Novel Units, Inc.

—Nate the Great & the Sticky Case. (Nate the Great Ser.). (Illus.). (J). (gr. 1-4). 1987. 11.95 o.p. (*0-698-20629-0*); 1978. 8.99 o.p. (*0-698-30697-X*) Putnam Publishing Group, The. (Coward-McCann).

—Nate the Great & the Sticky Case. 1978. (Nate the Great Ser.). (Illus.). (J). (gr. 1-4). 10.65 (*0-606-02206-6*) Turtleback Bks.

—Nate the Great & the Stolen Base. 1994. (Nate the Great Ser.). (Illus.). 48p. (J). (gr. 1-4). pap. text 4.50 (*0-440-40932-2*) Dell Publishing.

—Nate the Great & the Stolen Base. 1992. (Nate the Great Ser.). (Illus.). (J). (gr. 1-4). 16.99 o.p. (*0-399-23240-0*, G. P. Putnam's Sons); 48p. 14.95 o.p. (*0-698-20708-4*, Coward-McCann) Penguin Group (USA) Inc.

—Nate the Great & the Stolen Base. 1992. (Nate the Great Ser.). (Illus.). (J). (gr. 1-4). 10.65 (*0-606-05950-4*) Turtleback Bks.

—Nate the Great & the Tardy Tortoise. (Nate the Great Ser.). (Illus.). 48p. (J). (gr. 1-4). 1996. pap. text 4.50 (*0-440-41269-2*); 1995. 13.95 (*0-385-32111-2*, Delacorte Pr.) Dell Publishing.

—Nate the Great & the Tardy Tortoise. (Nate the Great Ser.). (Illus.). (J). (gr. 1-4). 1996. pap. 4.99 (*0-440-91264-4*); 1995. pap. 19.95 (*0-385-31010-2*) Random Hse. Children's Bks. (Dell Books for Young Readers).

—Nate the Great & the Tardy Tortoise. 1997. (Nate the Great Ser.). (Illus.). (J). (gr. 1-4). 10.65 (*0-606-10891-2*) Turtleback Bks.

—Nate the Great Goes Down in the Dumps. 1989. (Nate the Great Ser.). (Illus.). 48p. (J). (gr. 1-4). 13.95 o.p. (*0-698-20636-3*, Coward-McCann) Putnam Publishing Group, The.

—Nate the Great Goes down in the Dumps. 1991. (Nate the Great Ser.). (Illus.). 48p. (J). (gr. 1-4). pap. text 4.50 (*0-440-40438-X*) Dell Publishing.

—Nate the Great Goes down in the Dumps. 1989. (Nate the Great Ser.). (Illus.). (J). (gr. 1-4). 10.65 (*0-606-04990-8*) Turtleback Bks.

—Nate the Great Goes Undercover. (Nate the Great Ser.). (Illus.). (J). (gr. 1-4). 10.95 (*0-698-20632-0*, Coward-McCann); 1989. 48p. 14.95 o.p. (*0-698-20643-6*, Coward-McCann); 1974. 48p. 16.99 o.p. (*0-399-23234-6*, G. P. Putnam's Sons) Penguin Group (USA) Inc.

—Nate the Great Goes Undercover. 1974. (Nate the Great Ser.). (Illus.). 48p. (J). (gr. 1-4). 9.99 o.p. (*0-698-30547-7*, Coward-McCann) Putnam Publishing Group, The.

—Nate the Great Goes Undercover. (Nate the Great Ser.). (J). (Illus.). 48p. (gr. 1-4). pap. 4.50 (*0-8072-1284-9*); 2003. audio 17.00 (*0-8072-1934-7*); 2001. (Illus.). 48p. (gr. 1-4). pap. text 17.00 incl. audio (*0-8072-0201-0*, FTR172SP); 1985. (gr. 1-4). pap. 17.00 incl. audio (*0-8072-0076-X*, FTR93SP) Random Hse. Audio Publishing Group. (Listening Library).

—Nate the Great Goes Undercover. 1978. (Nate the Great Ser.). (Illus.). 48p. (gr. 1-4). pap. text 4.50 (*0-440-46302-5*, Yearling) Random Hse. Children's Bks.

—Nate the Great Goes Undercover. 1974. (Nate the Great Ser.). (Illus.). (J). (gr. 1-4). 10.65 (*0-606-02563-4*) Turtleback Bks.

—Nate the Great, San Francisco Detective. 2002. (Nate the Great Ser.). 48p. (gr. 1-4). pap. text 4.50 (*0-440-41821-6*, Yearling) Random Hse. Children's Bks.

—Nate the Great Saves the King of Sweden. 1997. (Nate the Great Ser.). (Illus.). 48p. (gr. 1-4). text 14.95 o.s.i (*0-385-32120-1*, Delacorte Pr.) Dell Publishing.

—Nate the Great Saves the King of Sweden. 1999. (Nate the Great Ser.). (Illus.). 48p. (gr. 1-4). pap. text 4.50 (*0-440-41302-8*, Dell Books for Young Readers) Random Hse. Children's Bks.

—Nate the Great Saves the King of Sweden. 1999. (Nate the Great Ser.). (J). (gr. 1-4). 10.65 (*0-606-16583-5*) Turtleback Bks.

—Nate the Great Stalks Stupidweed. 1986. (Nate the Great Ser.). (Illus.). 48p. (J). (gr. 1-4). 11.95 o.p. (*0-698-20626-6*, Coward-McCann) Putnam Publishing Group, The.

—Nate the Great Stalks Stupidweed. 1989. (Nate the Great Ser.). (Illus.). 48p. (gr. 1-4). pap. text 4.50 (*0-440-40150-X*, Yearling) Random Hse. Children's Bks.

—Nate the Great Stalks Stupidweed. 1986. (Nate the Great Ser.). (Illus.). (J). (gr. 1-4). 10.65 (*0-606-04282-2*) Turtleback Bks.

Sharmat, Marjorie Weinman & Gannett, Ruth Stiles. Nate the Great Goes Undercover. unabr. ed. 1997. (Nate the Great Ser.). 87p. (J). (gr. 1-4). pap. 17.00 incl. audio (*0-8072-0229-0*, FTR176SP, Listening Library) Random Hse. Audio Publishing Group.

Sharmat, Marjorie Weinman & Sharmat, Craig. Nate the Great & the Crunchy Christmas. 1997. (Nate the Great Ser.). (Illus.). 48p. (gr. 1-4). pap. text 4.50 (*0-440-41299-4*, Dell Books for Young Readers) Random Hse. Children's Bks.

Sharmat, Marjorie Weinman & Simont, Marc. Nate the Great. 1999. (Nate the Great Ser.). (Illus.). 64p. (gr. 1-4). pap. text 1.99 o.s.i (*0-375-80604-0*) Random Hse., Inc.

—Nate the Great & the Big Sniff. 2001. (Nate the Great Ser.). (Illus.). 48p. (gr. 1-4). text 13.95 (*0-385-32604-1*, Delacorte Pr.) Dell Publishing.

Sharmat, Marjorie Weinman & Weinman, Rosalind. Nate the Great & the Pillowcase. 1993. (Nate the Great Ser.). (Illus.). 48p. (J). (gr. 1-4). 12.95 o.p. (*0-385-31051-X*, Delacorte Pr.) Dell Publishing.

—Nate the Great & the Pillowcase. 1995. (Nate the Great Ser.). (Illus.). 48p. (gr. 1-4). pap. text 4.50 (*0-440-41015-0*, Yearling) Random Hse. Children's Bks.

—Nate the Great & the Pillowcase. 1995. (Nate the Great Ser.). (Illus.). (J). (gr. 1-4). 10.65 (*0-606-08581-5*) Turtleback Bks.

Sharmat, Marjorie Weinman, et al. Nate the Great, San Francisco Detective. Bui, Francoise, ed. 2000. (Nate the Great Ser.). (Illus.). 48p. (gr. 1-4). text 13.95 (*0-385-32605-X*); lib. bdg. 15.99 (*0-385-90000-7*) Random Hse. Children's Bks. (Delacorte Bks. for Young Readers).

Sheff, Alice. Nate the Great & the Missing Key, Level 2. 1987. (Novel-Ties Ser.). (J). (gr. 2). pap., stu. ed. 15.95 (*0-88122-070-1*, S0267) Learning Links, Inc.

NELSON, HORATIO NELSON, VISCOUNT, 1758-1805—FICTION

Henty, G. A. By Conduct & Courage: A Story of Nelson's Day. 2000. 252p. (J). E-Book 3.95 (*0-594-02369-6*) 1873 Pr.

NEUTRON, JIMMY (FICTITIOUS CHARACTER)—FICTION

Banks, Steven. When Pants Attack. 2003. (Jimmy Neutron Boy Genius Ser.). (Illus.). 24p. (J). pap. 3.50 (*0-689-85465-X*, Simon Spotlight/ Nickelodeon) Simon & Schuster Children's Publishing.

Banks, Steven & Siciliano, John. Sick Day: Jimmie Neutron. 2003. (Jimmy Neutron Boy Genius Ser.). (Illus.). 24p. (J). pap. 3.50 (*0-689-85848-5*, Simon Spotlight/Nickelodeon) Simon & Schuster Children's Publishing.

Beechen, Adam. Holly Jolly Jimmy. 2003. (Jimmy Neutron Boy Genius Ser.). (Illus.). 32p. (J). pap. 5.99 (*0-689-85846-9*, Simon Spotlight/ Nickelodeon) Simon & Schuster Children's Publishing.

—Jimmy on Ice. 2003. (Jimmy Neutron Ser.). (Illus.). 32p. (J). pap. 3.99 (*0-689-85294-0*, Simon Spotlight/Nickelodeon) Simon & Schuster Children's Publishing.

Cerasini, Marc. Boy Genius. novel ed. 2001. (Jimmy Neutron Boy Genius Ser.). (Illus.). 144p. (J). (gr. 4-7). pap. 4.99 (*0-689-84542-1*, Simon Spotlight) Simon & Schuster Children's Publishing.

Collins, Terry. Boy Genius: Movie Storybook. 2001. (Jimmy Neutron Boy Genius Ser.). (Illus.). 32p. (J). (gr. 4-7). 8.99 (*0-689-84552-9*, Simon Spotlight/Nickelodeon) Simon & Schuster Children's Publishing.

—Canine Catastrophe! 2003. (Jimmy Neutron Boy Genius Ser.). (Illus.). 24p. (J). pap. 3.50 (*0-689-85464-1*, Simon Spotlight/Nickelodeon) Simon & Schuster Children's Publishing.

DNA Productions Staff, ed. Jimmy Neutron. 2003. (Illus.). 96p. (J). pap. 7.99 (*1-59182-401-X*) TOKYOPOP, Inc.

Golden Books Staff. Off the Deep End! 2004. (Illus.). (J). pap. 4.99 (*0-375-82662-9*, Golden Bks.) Random Hse. Children's Bks.

Koeppel, Ruth. Jimmy Neutron Come Home. 2003. (Ready-to-Read Ser.: Vol. 4). (Illus.). 32p. (J). pap. 3.99 (*0-689-85625-3*, Simon Spotlight/ Nickelodeon) Simon & Schuster Children's Publishing.

—The Time Pincher. 2003. (Jimmy Neutron Boy Genius Ser.: Vol. 1). (Illus.). 32p. (J). pap. 3.99 (*0-689-85293-2*, Simon Spotlight/Nickelodeon) Simon & Schuster Children's Publishing.

Miglis, Jenny & Siciliano, John. Return of the Pumpkin Head. 2003. (Jimmy Neutron Boy Genius Ser.). (Illus.). 24p. (J). pap. 3.99 (*0-689-85847-7*, Simon Spotlight/Nickelodeon) Simon & Schuster Children's Publishing.

Redeker, Kent. Jimmy Neutron 101 Exploring My World. 2003. (Jimmy Neutron Boy Genius Ser.). 24p. pap. 5.99 (*0-689-85301-7*, Simon Spotlight/ Nickelodeon) Simon & Schuster Children's Publishing.

Siciliano, John & Banks, Steven. Jimmy Neutron of the Band. 2003. (Jimmy Neutron Boy Genius Ser.). (Illus.). 24p. pap. 3.50 (*0-689-85299-1*, Simon Spotlight/Nickelodeon) Simon & Schuster Children's Publishing.

Siciliano, John & Collins, Terry. Jimmy Neutron This. 2003. (Jimmy Neutron Boy Genius Ser.). (Illus.). 24p. pap. 3.50 (*0-689-85300-9*, Simon Spotlight/ Nickelodeon) Simon & Schuster Children's Publishing.

NICHOLAS, SAINT, BISHOP OF MYRA—FICTION

CCC of America Staff. Nicholas: The Boy Who Became Santa. 1989. (Illus.). 35p. (J). (ps-4). 14.99 incl. VHS (*1-56814-003-7*) CCC of America.

NIGHTINGALE, FLORENCE, 1820-1910—FICTION

Jackson, Dave & Jackson, Neta. The Drummer Boy's Battle: Florence Nightingale. 1997. (Trailblazer Bks.: Vol. 21). (Illus.). 144p. (J). (gr. 3-7). pap. 5.99 (*1-55661-740-2*) Bethany Hse. Pubs.

Ross, Stewart. Please Help, Miss Nightingale! 1998. (Coming Alive Ser.). (Illus.). 62p. (J). (ps-4). 17.95 (*0-237-51749-3*) Evans Brothers, Ltd. GBR. *Dist:* Trafalgar Square.

NOG (FICTITIOUS CHARACTER)—FICTION

Antilles, Kem. Highest Score. 1996. (Star Trek Ser.: No. 8). (Illus.). 128p. (J). (gr. 4-7). pap. 3.99 (*0-671-89936-8*, Aladdin) Simon & Schuster Children's Publishing.

Gallagher, Diana G. Arcade. 1995. (Star Trek Ser.: No. 5). (Illus.). 112p. (J). (gr. 4-7). pap. 3.99 o.s.i (*0-671-89678-4*, Aladdin) Simon & Schuster Children's Publishing.

—Arcade. 1995. 10.04 (*0-606-14155-3*) Turtleback Bks.

Gilden, Mel. Cardassian Imps. 1997. (Star Trek Ser.: No. 9). (Illus.). 128p. (J). (gr. 3-6). pap. 3.99 (*0-671-51116-5*, Aladdin) Simon & Schuster Children's Publishing.

—Cardassian Imps. 1997. 10.04 (*0-606-14175-8*) Turtleback Bks.

Gilden, Mel & Pedersen, Ted. The Pet. Clancy, Lisa, ed. 1994. (Star Trek Ser.: No. 4). (Illus.). 128p. (J). (gr. 4-7). pap. 3.99 (*0-671-88352-6*, Aladdin) Simon & Schuster Children's Publishing.

Pedersen, Ted. Gypsy World. 1996. (Star Trek Ser.: No. 7). (Illus.). 128p. (J). (gr. 4-7). pap. 3.99 (*0-671-51115-7*, Aladdin) Simon & Schuster Children's Publishing.

—Gypsy World. 1996. 10.04 (*0-606-14221-5*) Turtleback Bks.

—Space Camp. 1997. 10.04 (*0-606-14319-X*) Turtleback Bks.

—Trapped in Time. 1998. (Star Trek Deep Space Nine Ser.: No. 12). (Illus.). 128p. (J). (gr. 4-7). pap. 3.99 (*0-671-01440-4*, Aladdin) Simon & Schuster Children's Publishing.

Pedersen, Ted & Neuville, H. Richmond. Space Camp. 1997. (Star Trek Deep Space Nine Ser.: No. 10). (Illus.). 128p. (J). (gr. 3-6). pap. 3.99 (*0-671-00730-0*, Aladdin) Simon & Schuster Children's Publishing.

Peel, John. Field Trip. 1995. (Star Trek Ser.: No. 6). (Illus.). 128p. (J). (gr. 4-7). pap. 3.99 (*0-671-88287-2*, Aladdin) Simon & Schuster Children's Publishing.

—Prisoners of Peace. Clancy, Lisa, ed. 1994. (Star Trek Deep Space Nine Ser.: No. 3). (Illus.). 128p. (J). (gr. 4-7). pap. 3.99 (*0-671-88288-0*, Aladdin) Simon & Schuster Children's Publishing.

—Prisoners of Peace. 1994. 10.04 (*0-606-14295-9*) Turtleback Bks.

Strickland, Brad. The Star Ghost. Clancy, Lisa, ed. 1994. (Star Trek Ser.: No. 1). (Illus.). 128p. (J). (gr. 4-7). 3.99 (*0-671-87999-5*, Aladdin) Simon & Schuster Children's Publishing.

—The Star Ghost. 1994. 10.04 (*0-606-14322-X*) Turtleback Bks.

—Stowaways. 1994. (Star Trek Deep Space Nine Ser.: No. 2). (Illus.). 128p. (J). (gr. 3-6). pap. 3.99 (*0-671-88000-4*, Aladdin) Simon & Schuster Children's Publishing.

NORBY THE ROBOT (FICTITIOUS CHARACTER)—FICTION

Asimov, Isaac & Asimov, Janet. Norby: Robot for Hire. 1987. (Norby Chronicles Ser.: Bk. II). 208p. mass mkt. 3.95 o.s.i (*0-441-58635-X*) Ace Bks.

—Norby & the Lost Princess. 129p. (J). lib. bdg. 20.90 (*0-8027-6593-9*); 1985. 10.95 o.p. (*0-8027-6583-1*) Walker & Co.

—Norby Through Time & Space. 1988. (J). mass mkt. 2.95 o.s.i (*0-441-58637-6*) Ace Bks.

Asimov, Janet. Norby & the Terrified Taxi. 1997. (Norby Ser.). 125p. (J). (gr. 3-7). 15.95 (*0-8027-8642-1*) Walker & Co.

Asimov, Janet & Asimov, Isaac. Norby & the Court Jester. 1996. 192p. mass mkt. 5.50 o.s.i (*0-441-00341-9*) Ace Bks.

—Norby & the Court Jester. l.t. ed. 1999. (Science Fiction Ser.). 168p. 24.95 (*0-7838-8610-1*) Thorndike Pr.

—Norby & the Court Jester. 1991. (Norby Ser.). 128p. (J). (gr. 3-7). 14.95 (*0-8027-8131-4*); (gr. 7 up). lib. bdg. 15.85 (*0-8027-8132-2*) Walker & Co.

—Norby & the Invaders. 1985. (Norby Ser.). 138p. (J). (gr. 3-5). 10.95 (*0-8027-6599-8*); lib. bdg. 10.85 (*0-8027-6607-2*) Walker & Co.

—Norby & the Oldest Dragon. 1993. 160p. (J). mass mkt. 4.50 o.s.i (*0-441-58632-5*) Ace Bks.

—Norby & the Oldest Dragon. 1990. (Norby Ser.). (J). (gr. 4-9). 14.95 (*0-8027-6909-8*); lib. bdg. 15.85 (*0-8027-6910-1*) Walker & Co.

—Norby & the Queen's Necklace. 1986. (Norby Ser.). 144p. (J). (gr. 4-9). 11.95 (*0-8027-6659-5*); lib. bdg. 12.85 (*0-8027-6660-9*) Walker & Co.

—Norby & Yobo's Great Adventure. 1991. (J). mass mkt. 3.95 o.s.i (*0-441-58638-4*) Ace Bks.

—Norby & Yobo's Great Adventure. 1989. (Norby Ser.). 224p. (J). (gr. 4-9). 12.95 (*0-8027-6893-8*); lib. bdg. 13.85 (*0-8027-6894-6*) Walker & Co.

—The Norby Chronicles. 1986. (J). mass mkt. 3.50 o.s.i (*0-441-58634-1*); 192p. mass mkt. 2.95 o.s.i (*0-441-58633-3*) Ace Bks.

—Norby down to Earth. 1991. (Norby Chronicles Ser.). mass mkt. 3.99 o.s.i (*0-441-58607-4*) Ace Bks.

—Norby down to Earth. 1989. (Norby Ser.). (Illus.). (J). (gr. 4-9). lib. bdg. 13.85 o.p. (*0-8027-6867-9*) Walker & Co.

—Norby Finds a Villain. 1987. 102p. (J). (gr. 4-9). 12.95 (*0-8027-6710-9*); lib. bdg. 13.85 (*0-8027-6711-7*) Walker & Co.

—Norby, the Mixed up Robot. unabr. ed. 1986. (J). (gr. 1-5). pap. 10.50 o.s.i incl. audio (*0-89845-634-7*, CP 1792, Caedmon) HarperTrade.

—Norby, the Mixed up Robot. (J). 1985. 9.95 o.p. (*0-8027-6495-9*); 1983. 96p. (gr. 5-7). lib. bdg. 10.85 (*0-8027-6496-7*) Walker & Co.

—Norby's Other Secret. 1984. 138p. (J). 10.95 (*0-8027-6525-4*) Walker & Co.

Asimov, Janet, et al. Norby down to Earth. 1989. (Norby Ser.). (Illus.). 107p. (J). (gr. 7 up). 12.95 o.p. (*0-8027-6866-0*) Walker & Co.

O

OAKLEY, ANNIE, 1860-1926—FICTION

Fontes, Ron & Fontes, Justine. Annie Oakley in the Wild West Extravaganza! 1993. (American Frontier Ser.: Bk. 9). (Illus.). 80p. (J). (gr. 1-4). lib. bdg. 12.89 o.s.i (*1-56282-492-9*); pap. 3.50 (*1-56282-491-0*) Disney Pr.

Klass, Sheila S. A Shooting Star: A Novel about Annie Oakley. 440th ed. 1998. 176p. (gr. 4-7). pap. text 4.50 o.s.i (*0-440-41493-8*, Dell Books for Young Readers) Random Hse. Children's Bks.

—A Shooting Star: A Novel about Annie Oakley. 1998. 10.55 (*0-606-15702-6*) Turtleback Bks.

Kunstler, James H. Annie Oakley. 1993. (Illus.). (J). 14.95 (*0-88708-338-2*); pap. 19.95 incl. audio (*0-88708-337-4*) Simon & Schuster Children's Publishing. (Simon & Schuster Children's Publishing).

Kunstler, James Howard & Warter, Fred. Annie Oakley. 1996. (Illus.). 40p. (J). (ps-3). pap. 19.95 o.p. incl. audio (*0-689-80605-1*, Simon & Schuster Children's Publishing) Simon & Schuster Children's Publishing.

Sargent, Dave & Sargent, Pat. Cactus (Smoky Black) Competition Is Good #10. 2001. (Saddle Up Ser.). 36p. (J). lib. bdg. 22.60 (*1-56763-671-3*) Ozark Publishing.

—Cactus (Smoky Black) Competition Is Good #10: Competition Is Good #10. 2001. (Saddle Up Ser.). 36p. (J). pap. (*1-56763-672-1*) Ozark Publishing.

OBI-WAN KENOBI (FICTITIOUS CHARACTER)—FICTION

see Kenobi, Obi-Wan (Fictitious Character)—Fiction

OLIVIA (FICTITIOUS CHARACTER)—FICTION

Falconer, Ian. Olivia. 2002. (YA). 26.13 (*1-4046-0034-5*) Book Wholesalers, Inc.

—Olivia. ed. 2003. (gr. 1). spiral bd. (*0-616-14599-3*); 2001. (J). (gr. 1). spiral bd. (*0-616-07232-5*); 2001. (J). (gr. 2). spiral bd. (*0-616-07233-3*) Canadian National Institute for the Blind/Institut National Canadien pour les Aveugles.

—Olivia. 2001. (Illus.). (J). (CAT.). 40p. (*84-8488-017-6*); (SPA., 146p. (*84-8488-016-8*) Serres, Ediciones, S. L. ESP. *Dist:* Lectorum Pubns., Inc.

—Olivia. 2000. (Illus.). 40p. (J). (ps-3). 16.95 (*0-689-82953-1*, Atheneum/Anne Schwartz Bks.) Simon & Schuster Children's Publishing.

—Olivia... & the Missing Toy. 2003. (Illus.). 42p. (J). (gr. k-3). 16.95 (*0-689-85291-6*, Atheneum/Anne Schwartz Bks.) Simon & Schuster Children's Publishing.

—Olivia Counts. 2002. bds. 6.99 (*0-689-85447-1*); (Illus.). 12p. (J). bds. 6.99 (*0-689-85087-5*) Simon & Schuster Children's Publishing. (Atheneum).

—Olivia, la Reina del Circo. Mlawer, Teresa, tr. (SPA., Illus.). (J). (gr. k-2). 16.00 (*1-930332-20-3*, LC5675); 2002. 16.00 (*1-930332-08-4*, LC30181) Lectorum Pubns., Inc.

—Olivia Saves the Circus. ed. 2001. (YA). (gr. 1 up). spiral bd. (*0-616-11110-X*); (gr. 2 up). spiral bd. (*0-616-11111-8*) Canadian National Institute for the Blind/Institut National Canadien pour les Aveugles.

—Olivia Saves the Circus. (Illus.). 44p. (J). (ps-2). 2001. 16.95 (*0-689-82954-X*, Atheneum/Anne Schwartz Bks.); 2002. 150.00 (*0-689-85039-5*, Atheneum) Simon & Schuster Children's Publishing.

—Olivia's Opposites. 2002. (J). bds. 6.99 (*0-689-85448-X*); (Illus.). 12p. bds. 6.99 (*0-689-85088-3*) Simon & Schuster Children's Publishing. (Atheneum).

—Presenting Olivia. 2002. (Illus.). (J). (ps-2). 33.95 (*0-689-85389-0*, Atheneum/Anne Schwartz Bks.) Simon & Schuster Children's Publishing.

OLSEN TWINS (FICTITIOUS CHARACTERS)—FICTION

Aber, Linda Williams. Super Secret Detective Kit: Become a Super Detective-Just Like the Trench-coat Twins. 1999. (J). (gr. 1-3). 7.95 o.p. (*0-590-29396-6*) Scholastic, Inc.

Alexander, Nina. The Case of the Haunted Camp. 1998. (New Adventures of Mary-Kate & Ashley Ser.). (Illus.). 85p. (J). (gr. 2-7). mass mkt. 3.99 (*0-590-29397-4*) Scholastic, Inc.

—The Case of the 202 Clues. 1998. (New Adventures of Mary-Kate & Ashley Ser.). (Illus.). 87p. (J). (gr. 2-7). mass mkt. 3.99 (*0-590-29307-9*) Scholastic, Inc.

—The Case of Thorn Mansion. 1997. (Adventures of Mary-Kate & Ashley Ser.). (J). (gr. 2-7). mass mkt. 3.99 (*0-590-88016-0*) Scholastic, Inc.

Banim, Lisa, et al. Winner Take All. 2000. (Two of a Kind Ser.: No. 10). (Illus.). 112p. (gr. 3-7). mass mkt. 4.99 (*0-06-106580-3*, HarperEntertainment) Morrow/Avon.

Butcher, Nancy. It's Snow Problem. 2001. (Two of a Kind Ser.: No. 15). (Illus.). 128p. (gr. 3-7). mass mkt. 4.99 (*0-06-106655-9*, HarperEntertainment) Morrow/Avon.

Carr, Jan. Ballet Party! 1998. (You're Invited to Mary-Kate & Ashley's Ser.). (J). (gr. 2-4). audio 8.98 (*1-56896-314-9*); audio compact disk 15.98 (*1-56896-313-0*) Lightyear Entertainment, L.P.

—Ballet Party! 1998. (You're Invited to Mary-Kate & Ashley's Ser.). (Illus.). 48p. (J). (gr. 2-4). pap. 12.95 (*0-590-29399-0*) Scholastic, Inc.

Charbonnet, Gabrielle. Once upon a Time with Mary-Kate & Ashley: A Disney Princess Story & Activity Collection. 1998. (Mary-Kate & Ashley Ser.). (Illus.). 96p. (J). (gr. 2-4). 16.95 (*0-7868-3189-8*) Disney Pr.

Charbonnet, Gabrielle, et al. Once upon a Time with Mary-Kate & Ashley: A Disney Princess Story & Activity Collection. 1999. (Mary-Kate & Ashley Ser.). 96p. (J). (gr. 2-4). pap. 9.99 (*0-7868-4343-8*) Hyperion Pr.

Doolittle, June, et al. The Case of the Great Elephant Escape. 1999. (New Adventures of Mary-Kate & Ashley Ser.). (Illus.). 96p. (gr. 2-7). mass mkt. 4.50 (*0-06-106583-8*, HarperEntertainment) Morrow/Avon.

Dubowski, Cathy. The Case of the High Seas Secret. 2001. (New Adventures of Mary-Kate & Ashley Ser.). 96p. (gr. 2-7). mass mkt. 4.50 (*0-06-106644-3*, HarperEntertainment) Morrow/Avon.

—The Case of the Sea World Adventure. 1996. (Adventures of Mary-Kate & Ashley Ser.). (Illus.). 80p. (J). (gr. 2-7). mass mkt. 3.99 (*0-590-86369-X*) Scholastic, Inc.

—The Case of the Slam Dunk Mystery. 15th ed. 2000. (New Adventures of Mary-Kate & Ashley Ser.). (Illus.). 96p. (gr. 2-7). mass mkt. 4.50 (*0-06-106588-9*, HarperEntertainment) Morrow/Avon.

—The Case of the Surfing Secret. 1999. (New Adventures of Mary-Kate & Ashley Ser.). (Illus.). 96p. (gr. 2-7). mass mkt. 4.50 (*0-06-106585-4*) HarperCollins Pubs.

Eisenberg, Lisa. The Case of the Rock & Roll Mystery. 1998. (New Adventures of Mary-Kate & Ashley Ser.). 87p. (J). (gr. 2-7). mass mkt. 3.99 (*0-590-29402-4*) Scholastic, Inc.

Eisenberg, Lisa, et al. The Case of the Disappearing Princess. 1999. (New Adventures of Mary-Kate & Ashley Ser.). 85p. (J). (gr. 2-7). mass mkt. 3.99 (*0-439-06043-5*) Scholastic, Inc.

Ellis, Ann. Sleepover Party. 1996. (You're Invited to Mary-Kate & Ashley's Ser.). 48p. (J). (gr. 2-4). pap. 12.95 (*0-590-88007-1*) Scholastic, Inc.

Ellis, Carol. The Case of the Big Scare Mountain Mystery. 1999. (New Adventures of Mary-Kate & Ashley Ser.). (Illus.). 96p. (gr. 2-7). mass mkt. 4.50 (*0-06-106587-0*, HarperEntertainment) Morrow/Avon.

—The Case of the Green Ghost. 13th ed. 1999. (New Adventures of Mary-Kate & Ashley Ser.). (Illus.). 96p. (gr. 2-7). mass mkt. 4.50 (*0-06-106586-2*, HarperEntertainment) Morrow/Avon.

Fiedler, Lisa. The Case of the Cheerleading Camp Mystery. 17th ed. 2000. (New Adventures of Mary-Kate & Ashley Ser.). (Illus.). 96p. (gr. 2-7). mass mkt. 4.50 (*0-06-106590-0*, HarperEntertainment) Morrow/Avon.

HarperCollins Staff. Mary-Kate & Ashley Be My Valentine: Cards for You to Make. 2000. (Illus.). 24p. (J). (gr. 2-5). mass mkt. 10.99 o.s.i (*0-06-107568-X*) HarperCollins Children's Bk. Group.

HarperEntertainment Staff. Bye-Bye Boyfriend. 2000. (Two of a Kind Ser.: No. 14). 112p. (gr. 3-7). mass mkt. 4.99 (*0-06-106637-0*, HarperEntertainment) Morrow/Avon.

—My Mary-Kate & Ashley Diary: For All My Words. 1999. (Illus.). 128p. (gr. 2-7). 12.99 (*0-06-107567-1*, HarperEntertainment) Morrow/Avon.

—War of the Wardrobes. 2000. (Two of a Kind Ser.: No. 13). (Illus.). 112p. (gr. 3-7). mass mkt. 4.99 (*0-06-106636-2*, HarperEntertainment) Morrow/ Avon.

Harrison, Emma. Never Been Kissed. 2002. (Mary-Kate & Ashley Sweet 16 Ser.: Vol. 1). 144p. mass mkt. 4.99 (*0-06-009209-2*) HarperCollins Children's Bk. Group.

Katschke, Judy. The Case of the Creepy Castle. 2000. (New Adventures of Mary-Kate & Ashley Ser.). 96p. (gr. 2-7). mass mkt. 4.50 (*0-06-106592-7*, HarperEntertainment) Morrow/Avon.

—The Case of the Dog Camp Mystery. 2001. (New Adventures of Mary-Kate & Ashley Ser.). (Illus.). 96p. (gr. 2-7). mass mkt. 4.99 (*0-06-106646-X*, HarperEntertainment) Morrow/Avon.

—The Case of the Flapper 'Napper. 2001. (New Adventures of Mary-Kate & Ashley Ser.: V). 96p. (gr. 2-7). mass mkt. 4.50 (*0-06-106594-3*, HarperEntertainment) Morrow/Avon.

—The Case of the Screaming Scarecrow. 2001. (New Adventures of Mary-Kate & Ashley Ser.). (Illus.). 96p. (gr. 4-7). mass mkt. 4.50 (*0-06-106647-8*, HarperEntertainment) Morrow/Avon.

—The Case of the Summer Camp Caper. 1999. (New Adventures of Mary-Kate & Ashley Ser.). (Illus.). 96p. (gr. 2-7). mass mkt. 4.50 (*0-06-106584-6*, HarperEntertainment) Morrow/Avon.

—The Case of the Wild Wolf River. 1998. (New Adventures of Mary-Kate & Ashley Ser.). 87p. (J). (gr. 2-7). mass mkt. 3.99 (*0-590-29401-6*) Scholastic, Inc.

—It's a Twin Thing. 1999. (Two of a Kind Ser.: No. 1). (Illus.). 112p. (gr. 3-7). mass mkt. 4.99 (*0-06-106571-4*) HarperCollins Pubs.

—Let's Party! 8th ed. 1999. (Two of a Kind Ser.: No. 8). 112p. (gr. 3-7). mass mkt. 4.99 (*0-06-106578-1*, HarperEntertainment) Morrow/Avon.

—Shore Thing. 2001. (Two of a Kind Ser.: No. 17). (Illus.). 112p. (gr. 3-7). mass mkt. 4.99 (*0-06-106657-5*, HarperEntertainment) Morrow/Avon.

—The Sleepover Secret. 1999. (Two of a Kind Ser.: No. 3). (Illus.). 112p. (gr. 3-7). mass mkt. 4.99 (*0-06-106573-0*, HarperEntertainment) Morrow/Avon.

—To Snoop or Not to Snoop. 1999. (Two of a Kind Ser.: No. 5). 112p. (gr. 3-7). mass mkt. 4.99 (*0-06-106575-7*, HarperEntertainment) Morrow/Avon.

—Two's a Crowd. 7th ed. 1999. (Two of a Kind Ser.: No. 7). (Illus.). 112p. (Orig.). (gr. 3-7). mass mkt. 4.25 (*0-06-106577-3*, HarperEntertainment) Morrow/Avon.

Katschke, Judy, et al. Calling All Boys. 2000. (Two of a Kind Ser.: No. 9). (Illus.). 112p. (gr. 2-7). mass mkt. 4.99 (*0-06-106579-X*, HarperEntertainment) Morrow/Avon.

Krulik, Nancy E. The Case of the Fun House Mystery. 1996. (Adventures of Mary-Kate & Ashley Ser.). (Illus.). 80p. (J). (gr. 2-7). mass mkt. 3.99 (*0-590-86231-6*) Scholastic, Inc.

—The Case of the Shark Encounter. 1997. (Adventures of Mary-Kate & Ashley Ser.). 64p. (J). (gr. 2-7). mass mkt. 3.99 (*0-590-88010-1*) Scholastic, Inc.

Krulik, Nancy E., et al. Hawaiian Beach Party. 1997. (You're Invited to Mary-Kate & Ashley's Ser.). 48p. (J). (gr. 2-4). pap. 12.95 (*0-590-88012-8*) Scholastic, Inc.

—Mary-Kate & Ashley's Adventure at Walt Disney World. 1998. (Mary-Kate & Ashley Ser.). (Illus.). 64p. (J). (gr. 2-4). 9.95 o.p. (*0-7868-3205-3*) Hyperion Pr.

Lantz, Francess L. The Case of the Missing Mummy. 1998. (New Adventures of Mary-Kate & Ashley Ser.). (Illus.). 82p. (J). (gr. 2-7). mass mkt. 3.99 (*0-590-29404-0*) Scholastic, Inc.

Metz, Melinda. The Case of the Flying Phantom. 2000. (New Adventures of Mary-Kate & Ashley Ser.). (Illus.). 96p. (gr. 2-7). mass mkt. 4.25 (*0-06-106591-9*) HarperCollins Children's Bk. Group.

—The Case of the Golden Slipper. 20th ed. 2000. (New Adventures of Mary-Kate & Ashley Ser.). 96p. (gr. 2-7). mass mkt. 4.50 (*0-06-106593-5*, HarperEntertainment) Morrow/Avon.

—The Case of the Golden Slipper. 2000. (New Adventures of Mary Kate & Ashley Ser.). (Illus.). (J). 10.30 (*0-606-21918-8*) Turtleback Bks.

—The Case of the Rock Star's Secret. 2000. (New Adventures of Mary-Kate & Ashley Ser.). (Illus.). 96p. (gr. 2-7). mass mkt. 4.50 (*0-06-106589-7*, HarperEntertainment) Morrow/Avon.

—The Case of the Surprise Call. 1999. (New Adventures of Mary-Kate & Ashley Ser.). 86p. (J). (gr. 2-7). mass mkt. 3.99 (*0-590-29403-2*) Scholastic, Inc.

Older, Effin. Birthday Party. (You're Invited to Mary-Kate & Ashley's Ser.). (J). (gr. 2-4). audio 7.18. audio compact disk 12.78 NewSound, LLC.

—Birthday Party. 1998. (You're Invited to Mary-Kate & Ashley's Ser.). (Illus.). 48p. (J). (gr. 2-4). pap. 12.95 (*0-590-22593-6*) Scholastic, Inc.

Olsen, Mary-Kate & Olsen, Ashley. April Fools' Rules! 2002. (Two of a Kind Ser.: Vol. 22). (Illus.). 112p. mass mkt. 4.99 (*0-06-106662-1*) HarperCollins Pubs.

—The Case of Camp Crooked Lake. 2002. (New Adventures of Mary-Kate & Ashley Ser.: 30). 96p. (gr. 1-5). mass mkt. 4.50 (*0-06-106652-4*) HarperCollins Pubs.

—The Case of Clue's Circus Caper, No. 35. 2003. (New Adventures of Mary-Kate & Ashley Ser.). (Illus.). 96p. mass mkt. 4.50 (*0-06-009333-1*, HarperEntertainment) Morrow/Avon.

—The Case of the Weird Science Mystery. 2002. (New Adventures of Mary-Kate & Ashley Ser.: 29). 96p. (gr. 1-5). mass mkt. 4.50 (*0-06-106651-6*) HarperCollins Pubs.

—The Cool Club. 2000. (Two of a Kind Ser.: No. 12). (Illus.). 112p. (gr. 3-7). mass mkt. 4.99 (*0-06-106582-X*, HarperEntertainment) Morrow/Avon.

—Dating Game, No. 9. 2003. (So Little Time Ser.). 128p. mass mkt. 4.99 (*0-06-009313-7*, HarperEntertainment) Morrow/Avon.

—A Girls Guide to Guys. 2003. (So Little Time Ser.: No. 10). (Illus.). 128p. mass mkt. 4.99 (*0-06-009314-5*, HarperEntertainment) Morrow/Avon.

—How to Flunk Your First Date. 1999. (Two of a Kind Ser.: No. 2). (Illus.). 112p. (gr. 3-7). mass mkt. 4.99 (*0-06-106572-2*, HarperEntertainment) Morrow/Avon.

—I Am the Cute One. (J). audio 7.18. audio compact disk 12.78 NewSound, LLC.

—Island Girls. 2002. (Two of a Kind Ser.: 23). 112p. (gr. 3-7). mass mkt. 4.99 (*0-06-106663-X*) HarperCollins Pubs.

—Mary-Kate & Ashley Grad. 2004. 144p. No. 1. mass mkt. 4.99 (*0-06-072282-7*); No. 2. pap. 4.99 (*0-06-072283-5*) Morrow/Avon. (HarperEntertainment).

—Mary-Kate & Ashley Our Story: Mary-Kate & Ashley Olsen's Official Biography. 2000. (Illus.). 96p. (J). (gr. 3-7). mass mkt. 4.99 (*0-06-107569-8*) HarperCollins Pubs.

—Mary-Kate & Ashley Starring in... 2002. (Illus.). (J). mass mkt. 19.96 (*0-06-052110-4*, HarperEntertainment) Morrow/Avon.

—Mary-Kate & Ashley Sweet 16. 2002. (J). (Sweet Sixteen Ser.: No. 6). (Illus.). mass mkt. 4.99 (*0-06-052812-5*); mass mkt. 19.96 (*0-06-052112-0*); No. 5. (Sweet Sixteen Ser.: No. 5). (Illus.). mass mkt. 4.99 (*0-06-052811-7*) Morrow/Avon. (HarperEntertainment).

—Mary-Kate & Ashley Sweet 16: Getting There, No. 4. 2002. 144p. mass mkt. 4.99 (*0-06-051595-3*, HarperEntertainment) Morrow/Avon.

—New Adventures of Mary-Kate & Ashley. 2001. pap. text 17.00 (*0-06-009013-8*) HarperCollins Children's Bk. Group.

—New Adventures of Mary-Kate & Ashley. 2002. (Illus.). (J). mass mkt. 18.00 (*0-06-052114-7*, HarperEntertainment) Morrow/Avon.

—P. S. Wish You Were Here. 2000. (Two of a Kind Ser.: No. 11). (Illus.). 112p. (gr. 3-7). mass mkt. 4.25 (*0-06-106581-1*, HarperEntertainment) Morrow/Avon.

—School Dance Party. 2001. (Mary-Kate & Ashley Starring In Ser.: No. 3). (Illus.). 96p. mass mkt. 4.99 (*0-06-106667-2*) HarperCollins Pubs.

—So Little Time. 2002. (Illus.). (J). mass mkt. 19.96 (*0-06-052095-7*, HarperEntertainment) Morrow/Avon.

—Switching Goals. 2000. (Mary-Kate & Ashley Ser.). 128p. (gr. 2-4). mass mkt. 4.99 (*0-06-107603-1*, HarperEntertainment) Morrow/Avon.

—Two for the Road. 2001. (Two of a Kind Ser.: No. 18). 112p. (gr. 3-7). mass mkt. 4.99 (*0-06-106658-3*) HarperCollins Pubs.

—Winning London. 2001. (Mary-Kate & Ashley Starring in Ser.: Vol. 2). (Illus.). 96p. (gr. 2-4). mass mkt. 4.99 (*0-06-106666-4*, HarperEntertainment) Morrow/Avon.

—Wish Come True. 2002. (Mary-Kate & Ashley Sweet 16 Ser.: Vol. 2). 144p. mass mkt. 4.99 (*0-06-009210-6*) HarperCollins Children's Bk. Group.

O'Neil, Laura. The Case of the Ballet Bandit. 1998. (New Adventures of Mary-Kate & Ashley Ser.). (Illus.). 87p. (J). (gr. 2-7). mass mkt. 3.99 (*0-590-29542-X*) Scholastic, Inc.

—The Case of the Hotel Who-Done-It. 1997. (Adventures of Mary-Kate & Ashley Ser.). 88p. (J). (gr. 2-7). mass mkt. 3.99 (*0-590-88013-6*) Scholastic, Inc.

Perlberg, Deborah. The Case of the U. S. Navy Adventure. 1997. (Adventures of Mary-Kate & Ashley Ser.). (J). (gr. 2-7). mass mkt. 3.99 (*0-590-88015-2*) Scholastic, Inc.

Preiss, Pauline. The Case of the Logical I Ranch. 2001. (New Adventures of Mary-Kate & Ashley Ser.). (Illus.). 96p. (gr. 2-7). mass mkt. 4.50 (*0-06-106645-1*, HarperEntertainment) Morrow/Avon.

—The Case of the Logical I Ranch. 2001. (New Adventures of Mary Kate & Ashley Ser.). (Illus.). (J). 10.30 (*0-606-21920-X*) Turtleback Bks.

Reymes, Ellen. Christmas Party. 1997. (You're Invited to Mary-Kate & Ashley's Ser.). 48p. (J). (gr. 2-4). pap. 12.95 (*0-590-76958-8*) Scholastic, Inc.

Scholastic, Inc. Staff. The Case of the Missing Mummy. 1998. pap. text 71.82 (*0-590-63041-5*) Scholastic, Inc.

Stine, Megan. Likes Me, Likes Me Not. 2001. (Two of a Kind Ser.: No. 16). 112p. (gr. 3-7). mass mkt. 4.25 (*0-06-106656-7*, HarperEntertainment) Morrow/Avon.

—My Sister the Supermodel. 1999. (Two of a Kind Ser.: No. 6). (Illus.). 112p. (gr. 3-7). mass mkt. 4.99 (*0-06-106576-5*, HarperEntertainment) Morrow/Avon.

—One Twin Too Many. 1999. (Two of a Kind Ser.: No. 4). (Illus.). 112p. (gr. 3-7). mass mkt. 4.99 (*0-06-106574-9*, HarperEntertainment) Morrow/Avon.

—Surprise, Surprise. 2001. (Two of a Kind Ser.: No. 19). (Illus.). 112p. (gr. 3-7). mass mkt. 4.99 (*0-06-106659-1*, HarperEntertainment) Morrow/Avon.

Swobud, I. K. The Case of the Blue-Ribbon-Horse. 1998. (New Adventures of Mary-Kate & Ashley Ser.). 86p. (J). (gr. 2-7). mass mkt. 3.99 (*0-590-29309-5*) Scholastic, Inc.

Thompson, Carol. The Case of the Mystery Cruise. 1996. (Adventures of Mary-Kate & Ashley Ser.). 64p. (J). (gr. 2-7). mass mkt. 3.99 (*0-590-86370-3*) Scholastic, Inc.

—The Case of the U. S. Space Camp Mission. 1996. (Adventures of Mary-Kate & Ashley Ser.). (J). (gr. 2-7). mass mkt. 3.99 (*0-590-88008-X*) Scholastic, Inc.

—The Case of the Volcano Mystery. 1997. (Adventures of Mary-Kate & Ashley Ser.). 64p. (J). (gr. 2-7). mass mkt. 3.99 (*0-590-88014-4*, Scholastic Paperbacks) Scholastic, Inc.

Waricha, Jean. The Case of the Christmas Caper. 1996. (Adventures of Mary-Kate & Ashley Ser.). (Illus.). (J). (gr. 2-7). mass mkt. 3.99 (*0-590-88009-8*) Scholastic, Inc.

Willard, Eliza. Holiday in the Sun. 2001. (Mary-Kate & Ashley Starring in Ser.: Vol. 4). (Illus.). 96p. (gr. 3-6). mass mkt. 4.99 (*0-06-106668-0*, HarperEntertainment) Morrow/Avon.

—Our Lips Are Sealed. 2001. (Mary-Kate & Ashley Starring in Ser.: Vol. 1). (Illus.). 96p. (gr. 2-4). mass mkt. 4.99 (*0-06-106665-6*, HarperEntertainment) Morrow/Avon.

P

PADDINGTON BEAR (FICTITIOUS CHARACTER)—FICTION

Bond, Michael. A Bear Called Paddington. 1986. (Paddington Ser.). (Illus.). (J). (ps-3). Dell Publishing.

—A Bear Called Paddington. abr. ed. 1992. (Paddington Ser.). (J). (ps-3). audio 11.00 (*1-55994-653-9*) HarperChildren's Audio.

—A Bear Called Paddington. 1986. (Paddington Ser.). (J). (ps-3). audio 9.95 o.p. (*0-89845-722-X*, CPN 1589, Caedmon) HarperTrade.

—A Bear Called Paddington, (Paddington Ser.). (Illus.). (J). 1960. 128p. (ps-3). 14.95 o.p. (*0-395-06636-0*); 1998. (SPA., 144p. (gr. 4-6). 15.00 (*0-395-92951-2*) Houghton Mifflin Co.

—A Bear Called Paddington. (Paddington Ser.). (Illus.). (ps-3). 1993. (J). pap. o.s.i (*0-440-80357-8*, Dell Books for Young Readers); 1968. 128p. pap. text 4.99 o.s.i (*0-440-40483-5*, Yearling) Random Hse. Children's Bks.

—A Bear Called Paddington. 1958. (Paddington Ser.). (Illus.). (J). (ps-3). 9.60 (*0-606-02273-2*) Turtleback Bks.

—The Hilarious Adventures of Paddington, 5 bks., Set. Incl. Bear Called Paddington. More about Paddington. Paddington at Large. Paddington at Work. Paddington Helps Out. (J). (ps-3). (Illus.). 1986. 14.75 (*0-440-43668-0*) Dell Publishing.

—My Scrapbook. 1999. (Paddington Ser.). (Illus.). 20p. (J). (ps-3). 12.95 (*0-694-00886-9*, Harper Festival) HarperCollins Children's Bk. Group.

—Un Oso Llamado Paddington. 4th ed. 1996. (SPA., Illus.). 128p. (J). (gr. 4-7). 8.95 (*84-279-3701-6*, NG3465) Noguer y Caralt Editores, S. A. ESP. *Dist:* Continental Bk. Co., Inc., Lectorum Pubns., Inc.

—Paddington & the Christmas Shopping. unabr. ed. (Paddington Ser.). (J). (ps-3). 9.95 o.p. incl. audio (*0-89845-621-5*, TBC 6215, Caedmon) HarperTrade.

—Paddington Bear. (Paddington Ser.). (Illus.). (J). (ps-3). 1995. 16p. 11.95 o.p. (*0-694-00838-9*, Harper Festival); 1992. 32p. 8.95 o.p. (*0-694-00394-8*); 1998. 40p. 13.95 (*0-06-027854-4*) HarperCollins Children's Bk. Group.

—Paddington Bear. 1973. (Paddington Ser.). (Illus.). (J). (ps-3). 5.95 o.s.i (*0-394-82642-6*); 5.99 o.s.i (*0-394-92642-0*) Random Hse. Children's Bks. (Random Hse. Bks. for Young Readers).

—Paddington Bear. unabr. ed. Incl. Paddington Bear: Something Nasty in the Kitchen. audio Paddington Bear & a Visit to the Dentist. audio (J). (ps-3). (Paddington Ser.). 1985. Set audio 8.98 (*0-89845-410-7*, CP 1773, Caedmon) HarperTrade.

—Paddington Bear: Something Nasty in the Kitchen. (Paddington Ser.). (J). (ps-3). audio HarperTrade.

—Paddington Bear: Trouble at the Airport; Paddington Prepares; Pantomime Time. unabr. ed. (Paddington Ser.). (Illus.). (J). (ps-3). audio 8.98 o.p. (*0-89845-538-3*, CP 1780, Caedmon) HarperTrade.

—Paddington Bear All Day. braille ed. 2000. (J). (gr. 1). bds. (*0-616-01860-6*) Canadian National Institute for the Blind/Institut National Canadien pour les Aveugles.

—Paddington Bear All Day. 1998. (Paddington Ser.). (Illus.). 7p. (J). (ps up). 5.95 (*0-694-00893-1*, Harper Festival) HarperCollins Children's Bk. Group.

—Paddington Bear & a Visit to the Dentist. (Paddington Ser.). (J). (ps-3). audio HarperTrade.

—Paddington Bear & the Busy Bee Carnival. 1998. (Paddington Ser.). (Illus.). 40p. (J). (ps-3). 13.95 (*0-06-027765-3*) HarperCollins Children's Bk. Group.

—Paddington Bear & the Christmas Surprise. (Paddington Ser.). (Illus.). (J). (ps-1). 1999. 32p. pap. 5.95 (*0-06-443595-4*, Harper Trophy); 1997. 40p. 11.95 (*0-694-00897-4*, Harper Festival); 1997. 32p. 12.95 (*0-06-027766-1*) HarperCollins Children's Bk. Group.

—Paddington Bear & the Christmas Surprise. 1999. (Paddington Ser.). (J). (ps-3). 12.10 (*0-606-17305-6*) Turtleback Bks.

—Paddington Bear at the Circus. (Paddington Ser.). (Illus.). (J). (ps-3). 2000. 40p. 12.95 (*0-06-028213-4*); 1992. 32p. 8.95 o.p. (*0-694-00415-4*, Harper Festival) HarperCollins Children's Bk. Group.

—Paddington Bear at the Circus. 1974. (Paddington Ser.). (Illus.). 36p. (J). (ps-3). 4.99 o.s.i (*0-394-92918-7*); 3.95 o.s.i (*0-394-82918-2*) Random Hse. Children's Bks. (Random Hse. Bks. for Young Readers).

—Paddington Bear Gift Set Paddington Bear All Day. 1999. (Paddington Bear Ser.). (Illus.). 14p. (J). (ps up). 15.95 (*0-694-00887-7*, Harper Festival) HarperCollins Children's Bk. Group.

—Paddington Bear Goes to Market. 1998. (Paddington Ser.). (Illus.). 7p. (J). (ps up). 5.95 (*0-694-00891-5*, Harper Festival) HarperCollins Children's Bk. Group.

—Paddington Bear in the Garden. 2002. (Paddington Bear Ser.). (Illus.). 40p. (J). (ps-3). 12.95 (*0-06-029696-8*) HarperCollins Children's Bk. Group.

—Paddington Goes to School. unabr. ed. (Paddington Ser.). (J). (ps-3). 9.95 o.p. incl. audio (*0-89845-622-3*, TBC 6223, Caedmon) HarperTrade.

—Paddington Goes to Town. l.t. ed. 1994. (Paddington Ser.). (Illus.). (J). (ps-3). 16.95 o.p. (*0-7451-2649-9*) Chivers Large Print GBR. *Dist:* BBC Audiobooks America.

—Paddington Goes to Town. unabr. ed. (Paddington Ser.). (J). (ps-3). 9.95 o.p. incl. audio (*0-89845-623-1*, TBC 6231, Caedmon) HarperTrade.

—Paddington Goes to Town, 001. 1977. (Paddington Ser.). (Illus.). 128p. (J). (ps-3). 15.00 o.p. (*0-395-06635-2*) Houghton Mifflin Co.

—Paddington Goes to Town. 1972. (Paddington Ser.). (Illus.). 128p. (J). (ps-3). pap. 0.75 o.s.i (*0-440-46793-4*, Yearling) Random Hse. Children's Bks.

—Paddington Takes the Air. 2003. (Illus.). 144p. (J). (gr. 4-6). 15.00 (*0-618-33141-7*) Houghton Mifflin Co.

—Paddington Takes the Test. (Illus.). (J). 2002. 144p. 15.00 (*0-618-18384-1*); 1980. 128p. 15.00 o.p. (*0-395-29519-X*) Houghton Mifflin Co.

—Paddington Takes the Test. 1982. (Paddington Ser.). (Illus.). 128p. (J). (ps-3). pap. 1.95 o.s.i (*0-440-47021-8*, Yearling) Random Hse. Children's Bks.

—Paddington's Birthday Treat. abr. ed. (Paddington Ser.). (J). (ps-3). audio 8.98 o.p. (*0-89845-361-5*, CP 1767, HarperAudio) HarperTrade.

—Please Look after This Bear. unabr. ed. (Paddington Ser.). (J). (ps-3). 9.95 o.p. incl. audio (*0-89845-620-7*, TBC 6207, Caedmon) HarperTrade.

Bond, Michael & Jankel, Karen. Paddington Bear Goes to the Hospital. 2001. (Paddington Ser.). (Illus.). 40p. (J). (ps-3). 12.95 (*0-694-01563-6*) HarperCollins Children's Bk. Group.

PAJAMA SAM (FICTITIOUS CHARACTER)—FICTION

Greenfield, N. S., illus. Pajama Sam Mission to the Moon. 2000. 24p. (J). (ps-2). pap. 3.99 o.p. (*1-57064-950-2*, 73117, Humongous Bks.) Lyrick Publishing.

—Pajama Sam the Magic Hat Tree. 2000. 14p. (J). (ps-k). 7.99 o.p. (*1-57064-951-0*, Humongous Bks.) Lyrick Publishing.

Pajama Sam in There's No Need to Hide When It's Dark Outside. 1996. (J). sl. 37.85 o.s.i (*1-56893-321-5*) Random Hse., Inc.

PAREJA, JUAN DE, 1606-1670—FICTION

de Trevino, Elizabeth Borton. I, Juan de Pareja, RS. 1987. (Sunburst Ser.). 192p. (YA). (gr. 3-7). pap. 5.95 (*0-374-43525-1*, Sunburst) Farrar, Straus & Giroux.

de Trevino, Elizabeth Borton, et al. I, Juan De Pareja, RS. 1965. (Sunburst Ser.). 192p. (YA). (ps-3). 17.00 (*0-374-33531-1*, Farrar, Straus & Giroux (BYR)) Farrar, Straus & Giroux.

I, Juan de Pareja. 3rd ed. (J). pap. text, stu. ed. (*0-13-667452-6*) Prentice Hall (Schl. Div.).

PATRICK, SAINT, 373?-463?—FICTION

Dunlop, Eileen. Tales of St. Patrick. 1996. 144p. (J). (gr. 4-7). tchr. ed. 15.95 (*0-8234-1218-0*) Holiday Hse., Inc.

PAUL, THE APOSTLE, SAINT—FICTION

Hernandez, David. The Mighty Armor. 2003. (Adventures of Toby Digz Ser.). (Illus.). 96p. (J). 5.99 (*1-4003-0196-3*) Nelson, Tommy.

Hostetler, Marian. We Knew Paul. 1992. 128p. (Orig.). (J). (gr. 4-7). pap. 5.99 (*0-8361-3589-X*) Herald Pr.

PENN, WILLIAM, 1644-1718—FICTION

Jackson, Dave & Jackson, Neta. Hostage on the Nighthawk: William Penn. 2000. (Trailblazer Bks.: Vol. 32). (Illus.). 144p. (J). (gr. 3-7). pap. 5.99 (*0-7642-2265-1*) Bethany Hse. Pubs.

PETER PAN (FICTITIOUS CHARACTER)—FICTION

Barrie, J. M. Peter Pan. 1994. (Illus.). 96p. (J). 14.95 o.p. (*1-56282-638-7*); lib. bdg. 15.49 o.p. (*1-56282-639-5*) Disney Pr.

—Peter Pan. 1998. (Illus.). 144p. (J). 19.95 (*1-85149-702-1*) Antique Collectors' Club.

—Peter Pan. 1985. (Bantam Classics Ser.). 176p. (gr. 4-7). mass mkt. 4.95 (*0-553-21178-1*, Bantam Classics) Bantam Bks.

—Peter Pan. 1994. (Classics for Young Readers Ser.). (J). 64p. 5.98 o.p. (*0-86112-822-2*); 112p. 9.98 o.p. (*0-86112-648-3*) Brimax Bks., Ltd.

—Peter Pan. 1984. (Great 3-D Fairy Tale Bks.). (Illus.). (J). 2.99 o.s.i (*0-517-45984-1*) Crown Publishing Group.

—Peter Pan. 2003. (Illus.). 224p. (J). mass mkt. 5.99 (*0-7653-4719-9*, Starscape) Doherty, Tom Assocs., LLC.

—Peter Pan. 1999. (Illus.). 176p. (J). pap. text 2.00 (*0-486-40783-7*) Dover Pubns., Inc.

—Peter Pan. (ACE.). (YA). E-Book 2.49 (*1-58627-197-0*) Electric Umbrella Publishing.

—Peter Pan. 1995. (Illus.). (J). mass mkt. 8.95 (*0-340-62664-X*) Hodder & Stoughton, Ltd. GBR. *Dist:* Lubrecht & Cramer, Ltd., Trafalgar Square.

—Peter Pan. 1987. (J). audio 28.00 Jimcin Recordings.

—Peter Pan. 1991. (Illustrated Classics Ser.). (Illus.). 128p. (J). pap. 2.95 o.p. (*1-56156-029-4*) Kidsbooks, Inc.

—Peter Pan. 1992. (Everyman's Library Children's Classics Ser.). (Illus.). 240p. (ps-3). 12.95 (*0-679-41792-3*, Everyman's Library) Knopf Publishing Group.

—Peter Pan. 1987. 208p. (J). mass mkt. 4.95 (*0-451-52088-2*, Signet Classics) NAL.

—Peter Pan. (Classic Ser.). (J). 1997. 56p. (gr. 3-6). 2.99 o.s.i (*0-7214-5681-2*); 1994. (Illus.). 52p. text 3.50 o.p. (*0-7214-1659-4*) Penguin Group (USA) Inc. (Ladybird Bks.).

—Peter Pan. 1996. (Illus.). 256p. (YA). (gr. 5-9). pap. 3.99 (*0-14-036674-1*, Puffin Bks.); 1993. (Illus.). 208p. (J). (gr. 5 up). pap. 3.99 o.p. (*0-14-032007-5*, Puffin Bks.); 1991. (Illus.). 192p. (J). (gr. 4-7). 24.99 (*0-670-84180-3*, Viking Children's Bks.); 1987. (Illus.). (J). (gr. 5 up). 12.95 o.p. (*0-670-80862-8*, Viking Children's Bks.); 1987. (Illus.). 224p. (J). (gr. 4 up). 13.95 o.s.i (*0-448-06033-7*, Grosset & Dunlap); 1987. (J). 10.95 o.p. (*0-448-19209-8*, Platt & Munk); 1986. 224p. (J). pap. 3.50 o.p. (*0-14-035066-7*, Puffin Bks.) Penguin Putnam Bks. for Young Readers.

—Peter Pan. Hanft, Joshua, ed. 1995. (Great Illustrated Classics Ser.: Vol. 46). (Illus.). 240p. (J). (gr. 3-6). 9.95 (*0-86611-997-3*) Playmore, Inc., Pubs.

—Peter Pan. 1970. (Silver Dollar Library Ser.). (Illus.). (J). (gr. 2-6). 1.95 o.p. (*0-448-02137-4*) Putnam Publishing Group, The.

—Peter Pan. (Book & Cassette Classics Ser.). (Illus.). (J). (ps-5). 1987. 72p. 15.95 o.s.i (*0-394-89226-7*); 1985. 1.00 o.s.i (*0-517-48144-8*); 1983. 72p. 8.95 o.s.i (*0-394-85717-8*); 1983. 72p. 8.99 o.s.i (*0-394-95717-2*) Random Hse. Children's Bks. (Random Hse. Bks. for Young Readers).

—Peter Pan. (Children's Classics Ser.). (J). 1999. (Illus.). 304p. (gr. 4-7). 6.99 (*0-517-20577-7*); 1996. 1.10 o.s.i (*0-517-14151-5*) Random Hse. Value Publishing.

—Peter Pan. 1988. (Folio - Junior Ser.: No. 411). (FRE., Illus.). 239p. (J). (gr. 5-10). pap. 9.95 (*2-07-033411-2*) Schoenhof's Foreign Bks., Inc.

—Peter Pan. (Classics Ser.). 2002. (Illus.). 224p. (YA). (gr. 4 up). mass mkt. 3.99 (*0-439-29133-X*); 1993. 208p. (J). (gr. 4-7). mass mkt. 3.25 (*0-590-46735-2*, Scholastic Paperbacks); 1978. (J). pap. 1.95 (*0-590-30054-7*) Scholastic, Inc.

—Peter Pan. 1988. 2.98 (*0-671-10162-5*, Fireside) Simon & Schuster.

—Peter Pan. (J). (gr. k up). 1980. (Illus.). 192p. lib. bdg. 19.95 o.s.i (*0-684-16611-9*); 1972. 12.95 o.s.i (*0-684-13214-1*) Simon & Schuster Children's Publishing. (Atheneum).

—Peter Pan. 2000. (Illus.). 134p. (J). 24.95 (*1-58479-029-6*) Stewart, Tabori & Chang.

—Peter Pan. 1999. (J). E-Book 3.25 (*1-58505-994-3*) Treeless Pr.

—Peter Pan. (J). 1990. 16.10 (*0-606-00686-9*); 1985. 11.00 (*0-606-02465-4*) Turtleback Bks.

—Peter Pan. (J). (ps-5). 1988. 5.95 o.p. (*0-88101-080-4*); 1987. 16.95 o.p. (*0-88101-069-3*); 1987. (Illus.). 160p. 14.95 o.p. (*0-88101-270-X*) Unicorn Publishing Hse., Inc., The.

—Peter Pan. 1970. (J). pap. 1.50 o.p. (*0-14-030298-0*) Viking Penguin.

—Peter Pan. 1998. (Children's Classics). 176p. (J). (gr. 4-7). pap. 3.95 (*1-85326-120-3*, 1203WW) Wordsworth Editions, Ltd. GBR. *Dist:* Advanced Global Distribution Services.

—Peter Pan. (Step-up Classic Chillers Ser.). (Illus.). 96p. (J). 2003. (gr. 1-4). 11.99 (*0-679-91044-1*); 1991. (gr. 2-7). pap. 3.99 (*0-679-81044-7*) Random Hse. Children's Bks. (Random Hse. Bks. for Young Readers).

—Peter Pan. abr. ed. 1982. (J). audio 15.95 o.p. (*0-88646-067-0*, TC-LFP 7086) Durkin Hayes Publishing Ltd.

—Peter Pan. abr. ed. 1999. (Story Theatre for Young Readers Ser.). (J). (gr. 4-7). audio 16.95 (*1-56994-518-7*, 337354, Monterey SoundWorks) Monterey Media, Inc.

—Peter Pan. abr. ed. 1996. (Illus.). (J). audio 13.98 (*962-634-602-7*, NA210214); (gr. 4-7). audio compact disk 15.98 (*962-634-102-5*, NA210212) Naxos of America, Inc. (Naxos AudioBooks).

—Peter Pan. abr. ed. 1993. (J). (ps-6). audio 10.95 o.p. (*1-55800-121-2*, 30080, Dove Audio) NewStar Media, Inc.

—Peter Pan. abr. ed. (J). 1999. (gr. 4-7). audio 18.00 o.s.i (*0-553-47771-4*, 396218, Listening Library); 1993. audio 11.00 o.s.i (*0-679-42949-2*, RH Audio) Random Hse. Audio Publishing Group.

—Peter Pan. abr. ed. (Illus.). (J). (gr. 1-4). 1965. 4.79 o.s.i (*0-394-90749-3*); 1957. 3.95 o.s.i (*0-394-80749-9*) Random Hse. Children's Bks. (Random Hse. Bks. for Young Readers).

—Peter Pan, 2 cass. abr. ed. 1979. (J). pap. 11.95 o.p. incl. audio (*0-88142-328-9*); pap. 11.95 o.p. incl. audio (*0-88142-328-9*) Soundelux Audio Publishing.

—Peter Pan. l.t. ed. 2003. (Perennial Bestsellers Ser.). (J). 28.95 (*0-7862-5263-4*) Thorndike Pr.

—Peter Pan. abr. ed. (Children's Classics Ser.). (J). 1998. pap. 16.95 o.p. incl. audio (*1-85998-588-2*); 1998. pap. 16.95 o.p. incl. audio (*1-85998-588-2*); 1997. audio 14.95 (*1-85998-338-3*) Trafalgar Square.

—Peter Pan. abr. ed. 1997. (Classic Ser.). (J). 10.95 o.s.i incl. audio (*0-14-086460-1*); 10.95 o.s.i incl. audio (*0-14-086460-1*) Viking Penguin. (Penguin AudioBooks).

—Peter Pan. l.t. ed. 1999. (Classics for Children 8 & Younger Ser.). (Illus.). 48p. (J). (ps-3). (*1-85854-603-6*) Brimax Bks., Ltd.

—Peter Pan, Set. unabr. ed. 1987. (J). (gr. 3-5). audio 29.95 (*1-55685-075-1*) Audio Bk. Contractors, Inc.

—Peter Pan. unabr. ed. (J). audio 26.95 o.p. (*1-55656-093-1*, DAB 002) BBC Audiobooks America.

—Peter Pan. unabr. ed. 1987. (J). audio 32.95 (*0-7861-0607-7*, 2585) Blackstone Audio Bks., Inc.

—Peter Pan. unabr. ed. 1992. (J). audio 26.95 (*1-55686-439-6*, 439) Books in Motion.

—Peter Pan. unabr. collector's ed. 1993. (J). audio 30.00 (*0-7366-2537-2*, 3289) Books on Tape, Inc.

—Peter Pan. unabr. ed. (J). audio 21.95 o.s.i (*1-55656-042-7*); 1997. pap. 21.95 incl. audio (*1-55656-201-2*) Dercum Audio.

—Peter Pan, ERS. 1987. (Illus.). 144p. (YA). (gr. 2 up). 19.95 o.s.i (*0-8050-0276-6*, Holt, Henry & Co. Bks. For Young Readers) Holt, Henry & Co.

—Peter Pan, Set. 1992. 35.95 incl. audio Olivia & Hill Pr., The.

—Peter Pan. 1988. (Children's Classics Ser.). (Illus.). 304p. (J). (gr. k-5). reprint ed. 12.99 o.s.i (*0-517-63222-5*) Random Hse. Value Publishing.

—Peter Pan, unabr. ed. 1991. (J). (gr. 4). audio 44.00 (*1-55690-409-6*, 91105E7) Recorded Bks., LLC.

—Peter Pan: A Changing Picture & Lift-the-Flap Book. abr. ed. 1992. (Illus.). 320p. (J). (ps-3). 15.95 o.p. (*0-670-83608-7*, Viking Children's Bks.) Penguin Putnam Bks. for Young Readers.

—Peter Pan: Fairy Tales. Tallarico, Tony, ed. 1987. (Tuffy Story Bks.). (Illus.). 32p. (J). (ps-3). 1.95 (*0-89828-339-6*, 83396, Tuffy Bks.) Putnam Publishing Group, The.

—Peter Pan: The Complete Book. 1988. (Illus.). 180p. (J). (gr. 4 up). reprint ed. pap. 4.95 o.p. (*0-88776-206-9*) Tundra Bks. of Northern New York.

—Peter Pan: The Complete Play. 1988. 136p. (J). (gr. 4 up). pap. 4.95 o.p. (*0-88776-207-7*) Tundra Bks. of Northern New York.

—Peter Pan: 100th Anniversary Edition, ERS. 2003. (Illus.). 176p. (J). 19.95 (*0-8050-7245-4*, Holt, Henry & Co. Bks. For Young Readers) Holt, Henry & Co.

—Peter Pan & Other Plays: The Admirable Crichton; Peter Pan; When Wendy Grew Up; What Every Woman Knows; Mary Rose. Hollindale, Peter, ed. & intro. by. 1999. (Oxford World's Classics Ser.). 384p. (J). pap. 14.95 (*0-19-283919-5*) Oxford Univ. Pr., Inc.

—Peter Pan & Other Plays: The Admirable Crichton; Peter Pan; When Wendy Grew Up; What Every Woman Knows; Mary Rose, Vol. 10. reprint ed. 57.50 (*0-404-08790-6*) AMS Pr., Inc.

—Peter Pan & Other Plays: The Admirable Crichton; Peter Pan; When Wendy Grew Up; What Every Woman Knows; Mary Rose. Hollindale, Peter, ed. 1995. (Oxford World's Classics Ser.). 374p. pap. 13.95 o.p. (*0-19-282572-0*); 376p. text 80.00 (*0-19-812162-8*) Oxford Univ. Pr., Inc.

—Peter Pan & Wendy. 1999. (Abbeville Classics Ser.). (Illus.). 176p. (J). 12.95 (*0-7892-0560-2*); pap. 7.95 (*0-7892-0550-5*) Abbeville Pr., Inc. (Abbeville Kids).

—Peter Pan & Wendy. 1988. (Illus.). 160p. (J). (gr. 4-6). 12.95 o.s.i (*0-517-56837-3*, Clarkson Potter) Crown Publishing Group.

—Peter Pan & Wendy. Carruth, Jane, ed. 2000. (Illus.). 92p. (J). (gr. 4-6). reprint ed. 25.00 (*0-7881-9230-2*) DIANE Publishing Co.

—Peter Pan & Wendy. (Illus.). 2000. 176p. pap. 8.95 (*1-85793-909-3*); 1992. 160p. (J). (gr. 3-6). 24.95 o.p. (*1-85145-179-X*); 1992. 160p. (J). (gr. 3-6). pap. 17.95 (*1-85145-449-7*) Pavilion Bks., Ltd. GBR. *Dist:* Trafalgar Square.

—Peter Pan & Wendy. 1988. (J). 7.99 o.s.i (*0-517-66189-6*) Random Hse. Value Publishing.

—Peter Pan Book: Includes Tinker Bell Charm & Necklace. 2000. (Charming Classic Bks.). 240p. (J). (gr. 4-7). pap. 6.99 (*0-694-01318-8*, Harper Festival) HarperCollins Children's Bk. Group.

—Peter Pan Deluxe Book & Charm. 2003. (Charming Classics Ser.). (Illus.). 240p. (J). 9.99 (*0-06-055412-6*, Harper Festival) HarperCollins Children's Bk. Group.

—Peter Pan in Kensington Gardens. (J). 18.95 (*0-8488-0427-9*) Amereon, Ltd.

—Peter Pan in Kensington Gardens. unabr. ed. 1994. (J). (gr. 1 up). audio 19.95 (*1-55685-337-8*) Audio Bk. Contractors, Inc.

—Peter Pan in Kensington Gardens. (J). reprint ed. 1981. 175p. lib. bdg. 16.95 (*0-89966-328-1*); 1980. 150p. lib. bdg. 16.95 (*0-89967-006-7*, Harmony Raine & Co.) Buccaneer Bks., Inc.

—Peter Pan in Kensington Gardens. (YA). E-Book 2.49 (*1-58627-198-9*) Electric Umbrella Publishing.

—Peter Pan in Kensington Gardens. 1995. 64p. (J). pap. 0.95 o.p. (*0-14-600077-3*) Penguin Group (USA) Inc.

—Peter Pan in Kensington Gardens & Peter & Wendy. Hollingdale, Peter, ed. 1999. (Oxford World's Classics Ser.). (Illus.). 288p. (J). pap. 8.95 (*0-19-283929-2*) Oxford Univ. Pr., Inc.

—Peter Pan in Kensington Gardens & Peter & Wendy. 1991. (Oxford World's Classics Ser.). (Illus.). 276p. (J). pap. 7.95 o.p. (*0-19-282593-3*) Oxford Univ. Pr., Inc.

—Peter Pan in Neverland. 1995. (Illus.). 58p. pap. 4.50 (*0-88680-414-0*) Clark, I. E. Pubns.

—Peter Pan: or The Boy Who Would Not Grow Up. adapted ed. 1994. per. 6.50 (*0-8222-1345-1*) Dramatists Play Service, Inc.

—Peter Pan: or The Boy Who Would Not Grow Up. 1982. 208p. (J). (gr. k up). pap. 2.95 o.p. (*0-380-57752-6*, Avon Bks.) Morrow/Avon.

Barrie, J. M., et al. Peter Pan: A Classic Illustrated Edition. 2000. (Illus.). 176p. (J). (gr. 4-7). 19.95 (*0-8118-2297-4*) Chronicle Bks. LLC.

Birkin. J. M. Barrie & the Lost Boys. o.p. (*0-09-462000-8*) Hutchinson.

Disney Staff. Peter Pan. 2002. (Illus.). 24p. (J). (gr. k-3). pap. 3.25 (*0-7364-1295-6*, RH/Disney) Random Hse. Children's Bks.

—Peter Pan: Friends Ahoy! 1997. (Disney's "Storytime Treasures" Library: Vol. 18). (Illus.). 44p. (J). (gr. 1-6). 3.49 o.p. (*1-57973-014-0*) Advance Pubs. LLC.

—Return to Neverland. movie tie-in ed. 2002. (Illus.). 24p. (J). (ps-3). pap. 3.25 (*0-7364-1306-5*, RH/Disney) Random Hse. Children's Bks.

Golden Staff. Peter Pan. 1997. (J). (ps-4). 12.95 o.p. (*0-307-08657-7*, 08657, Golden Bks.) Random Hse. Children's Bks.

Granowsky, Alvin. Peter Pan - Grow up, Peter Pan! 1993. (Steck-Vaughn Point of View Stories Ser.). (Illus.). 48p. (J). (gr. 4-7). pap. 4.40 (*0-8114-2216-X*) Raintree Pubs.

Harris, Sarah, adapted by. Peter Pan. 1995. (Comes to Life Bks.). 16p. (J). (ps-2). (ENG & FRE.). (*1-57234-044-4*); (DUT & ENG.). (*1-57234-035-5*) YES! Entertainment Corp.

Johnstone, Michael & Barrie, J. M. Peter Pan. 2001. (Young Classics Ser.). (Illus.). 48p. (J). (gr. 1-3). pap. 9.95 o.p. (*0-7894-3796-1*) Dorling Kindersley Publishing, Inc.

Johnstone, Michael, et al. Peter Pan. 2001. (Read & Listen Ser.). (Illus.). 64p. (J). (gr. 4-7). pap. 9.99 incl. audio (*0-7894-6199-4*, D K Ink) Dorling Kindersley Publishing, Inc.

Martin, Mary. Peter Pan. (J). (ps up). audio 9.98 Music for Little People, Inc.

Peter Pan. 2003. (Illus.). 12.99 (*0-7868-3479-X*) Disney Pr.

Peter Pantm. 2003. (J). 173.68 (*0-06-056911-5*) HarperCollins Children's Bk. Group.

Peterson. Peter Pan. 2002. (Walt Disney Classics Ser.). (Illus.). 32p. 14.99 (*0-7868-5330-1*, Disney Editions) Disney Pr.

Strasser, Todd & Barrie, J. M. Peter Pan: Junior Novelization. 1994. (Illus.). 80p. (J). (gr. 2-6). pap. 3.50 o.p. (*1-56282-640-9*) Disney Pr.

TBD Staff. Peter Pan the Movie Storybook. 2003. (Peter Pan Ser.). (Illus.). 48p. (J). 7.99 (*0-06-056302-8*, Harper Festival) HarperCollins Children's Bk. Group.

PETER RABBIT (FICTITIOUS CHARACTER)—FICTION

Ada, Alma Flor. Dear Peter Rabbit. (Illus.). 32p. (gr. k-3). 1997. pap. 5.99 (*0-689-81289-2*, Aladdin); 1997. (SPA., (J). pap. 6.99 (*0-689-80879-8*, Aladdin); 1994. (J). 16.95 (*0-689-31850-2*, Atheneum) Simon & Schuster Children's Publishing.

—Dear Peter Rabbit. 1997. (J). 12.14 (*0-606-11246-4*) Turtleback Bks.

—Dear Peter Rabbit: Querido Pedrin. Zubizarreta, Rosa, tr. 1994. (Illus.). 40p. (J). (ps-3). lib. bdg. 14.95 (*0-689-31915-0*, Atheneum) Simon & Schuster Children's Publishing.

Akmon, Nancy C. Peter Rabbit Celebrates Christmas. Akmon, Roni, ed. 1999. (Illus.). 48p. (J). 8.95 (*1-884807-45-3*, EC745) Blushing Rose Publishing.

Bolinske, Janet L., ed. The Tale of Peter Rabbit. 1987. (Children's Classics Ser.). (Illus.). 32p. (J). (gr. 1-3). text 8.95 o.p. (*0-88335-552-3*); pap. text 4.95 (*0-88335-572-8*); spiral bd. 14.95 o.p. (*0-88335-542-6*) Milliken Publishing Co.

Bornstein, Harry. The Tale of Peter Rabbit: A Coloring Book in Signed English. 1986. (Signed English Ser.). (Illus.). 64p. (J). (ps-2). pap. 4.95 o.p. (*0-930323-29-7*) Kendall Green Pubns.

Bracken, Carolyn. Peter Rabbit's Pockets. 1982. (Illus.). 8p. (J). (ps). pap. 3.95 o.s.i (*0-671-44528-6*, Little Simon) Simon & Schuster Children's Publishing.

Carlson, David, illus. Peter Rabbit & His Friends. 1982. (Beatrix Potter Board Bks.). 14p. (J). (ps). 3.50 o.p. (*0-671-44519-7*, Atheneum) Simon & Schuster Children's Publishing.

Dobrin, Arnold. Peter Rabbit's Natural Foods Cookbook. 1977. (Illus.). (J). 10.95 o.p. (*0-7232-6142-3*, Warne, Frederick) Penguin Putnam Bks. for Young Readers.

Douglis, Marjie. Peter Rabbit & His Friends Dolls to Crochet: Complete Instructions for 11 Projects. 1986. (Illus.). 48p. (Orig.). pap. 3.50 o.p. (*0-486-25122-5*) Dover Pubns., Inc.

Dykstra, Brian. Peter Rabbit Plays Piano: Fun Songs for Children Playing Piano. 1988. 46p. pap. text 7.95 (*0-931759-29-3*) Centerstream Publishing.

Emerson, Anne. Peter Rabbit's Cookery Book. 1986. (Non-Fiction Ser.). (Illus.). 48p. (J). (gr. k-3). 6.95 o.p. (*0-7232-3328-4*, Warne, Frederick) Penguin Putnam Bks. for Young Readers.

Frederick, Warne. Peter Rabbit's Little Guide to Life. 1998. (World of Beatrix Potter Ser.). (Illus.). 48p. (J). (ps up). 8.99 o.s.i (*0-7232-4444-8*, Warne, Frederick) Penguin Putnam Bks. for Young Readers.

Frederick, Warne & Potter, Beatrix. What Time Is It, Peter Rabbit? 1998. (World of Beatrix Potter Ser.). (Illus.). 20p. (J). (ps-3). 9.99 (*0-7232-4431-6*, Warne, Frederick) Penguin Putnam Bks. for Young Readers.

Frederick Warne Publishing Staff. Peter Rabbit's Words, Colors & Numbers. 1996. (Illus.). 24p. (J). (ps-1). 9.99 o.s.i (*0-7232-4264-X*, Warne, Frederick) Penguin Putnam Bks. for Young Readers.

Galland, Sarah. Peter Rabbit's Gardening Book. 1983. (Illus.). 48p. (J). (gr. 5-9). 6.95 o.p. (*0-7232-2994-5*, Warne, Frederick) Penguin Putnam Bks. for Young Readers.

Gerver, Jane E. Peter Rabbit's Sniffy Adventure. 1984. (Sniffy Bks.). (Illus.). 24p. (J). (gr. k-2). 3.95 o.s.i (*0-394-86352-6*, Random Hse. Bks. for Young Readers) Random Hse. Children's Bks.

Harris, Aurand. Peter Rabbit & Me: Playscript. 1994. 52p. (J). 6.00 (*0-87602-326-X*) Anchorage Pr.

Holland, Sharon. Peter Rabbit. 96p. mass mkt. 2.99 o.s.i (*0-06-106330-4*, HarperTorch) Morrow/Avon.

Labelle, Susan Whited, illus. Peter Rabbit Postcards in Full Color. 1984. 12p. (J). pap. 4.50 (*0-486-24617-5*) Dover Pubns., Inc.

Lapin, Pierre. The Tale of Peter Rabbit. 1973. (Potter 23 Tales Ser.). (FRE.). 64p. (J). 5.95 o.s.i (*0-7232-3673-9*, Warne, Frederick) Penguin Putnam Bks. for Young Readers.

Leigh, Vivien, reader. The Tale of Peter Rabbit. (Playtape Ser.). (J). (gr. 3-7). audio 2.98 o.p. (*1-55886-047-9*) Smarty Pants.

Linder, Leslie L. The History of the Tale of Peter Rabbit. Emerson, Anne, ed. 1976. (Illus.). 64p. 7.95 o.p. (*0-7232-1988-5*, Warne, Frederick) Penguin Putnam Bks. for Young Readers.

Outlet Book Company Staff. Peter Rabbit & Friends Sticker Book. 1989. (J). 2.99 o.p. (*0-517-02032-7*, Random Hse. Bks. for Young Readers) Random Hse. Children's Bks.

Peter Rabbit. audio Audio Bk. Co.

Peter Rabbit. 1987. (J). (gr. k-3). 4.95 o.p. (*0-932715-05-2*) Evans Pubns.

Peter Rabbit. 1993. (Classic Tales Ser.). (Illus.). 24p. (J). 4.98 (*1-56173-474-8*); 7.98 (*1-56173-417-9*) Publications International, Ltd.

Peter Rabbit & Friends. 1990. (Peter Rabbit Coloring & Activity Bks.). (Illus.). 48p. (J). (ps-2). pap. 1.29 o.s.i (*0-87449-946-1*) Modern Publishing.

Peter Rabbit Treasury, 12 bks. 1993. (Illus.). 24p. (J). 19.98 (*0-7853-0012-0*) Publications International, Ltd.

Pomaska, Anna. Peter Rabbit Bookmarks. 1989. (J). (ps up). pap. 3.95 (*0-486-25444-5*) Dover Pubns., Inc.

Potter, Beatrix. The Adventure of Peter Rabbit & Other Favourite Tales. abr. ed. 1998. (World of Beatrix Potter Ser.). 2p. (ps-3). audio compact disk 12.95 o.s.i (*0-14-086705-8*, Warne, Frederick) Viking Penguin.

—The Adventures of Peter Rabbit. 1990. (Peter Rabbit Coloring & Activity Bks.). (Illus.). 48p. (J). (ps-2). pap. 1.29 o.s.i (*0-87449-947-X*) Modern Publishing.

—The Adventures of Peter Rabbit: And Other Favourite Tales. abr. unabr. ed. 1997. (Classic Ser.). 2p. (J). pap. 10.95 o.s.i incl. audio (*0-14-086016-9*, Penguin AudioBooks) Viking Penguin.

—The Adventures of Peter Rabbit & His Friends. 1994. pap. 5.60 (*0-87129-356-0*, A53) Dramatic Publishing Co.

—Baby Grows up with Peter Rabbit: A Record of Babies First Year. 2002. (Illus.). (J). 9.99 (*0-7232-4802-8*, Warne, Frederick) Penguin Putnam Bks. for Young Readers.

—Beatrix Potter & Peter Rabbit Classic Treasury. 1988. (J). 9.99 o.s.i (*0-517-67150-6*) Random Hse. Value Publishing.

—Beatrix Potter's Peter Rabbit: A Lift-the-Flap Rebus Book. 1991. (Lift-the-Flap Ser.). 16p. (J). (ps-3). 12.99 o.s.i (*0-7232-3798-0*, Warne, Frederick) Penguin Putnam Bks. for Young Readers.

—Beatrix Potter's Peter Rabbit Tales. 1995. (Illus.). 80p. (J). (ps-3). pap. 6.99 o.s.i (*0-7232-3665-8*, Warne, Frederick) Penguin Putnam Bks. for Young Readers.

—Benjamin Bunny Visits Peter Rabbit. 1988. (J). 2.99 o.s.i (*0-517-60594-5*) Random Hse. Value Publishing.

—Big Big Book of Peter Rabbit & His Friends. 1988. (J). 5.99 o.s.i (*0-517-64374-X*) Random Hse. Value Publishing.

—The Big Peter Rabbit Book. 1987. (Frederick Warne Picture Bks.). 64p. (J). (gr. 1-3). 8.95 o.p. (*0-7232-3409-4*, Warne, Frederick) Penguin Putnam Bks. for Young Readers.

—The Big Peter Rabbit Coloring Book. 1995. (Illus.). 64p. (J). (ps-3). pap. 4.99 o.s.i (*0-7232-4263-1*, Warne, Frederick) Penguin Putnam Bks. for Young Readers.

—Bunnies Peek Through: Peter Rabbit Peek-Through Board Book. 1996. (Illus.). 12p. (J). (ps). bds. 4.99 o.s.i (*0-7232-4308-5*, Warne, Frederick) Penguin Putnam Bks. for Young Readers.

—The Complete Adventures of Peter Rabbit. 80p. (J). 2003. (Illus.). 14.99 (*0-7232-4734-X*, Warne, Frederick); 1987. (Illus.). 14.99 (*0-7232-2951-1*, Warne, Frederick); 1984. pap. 7.99 (*0-14-050444-3*, Puffin Bks.) Penguin Putnam Bks. for Young Readers.

—The Complete Tales of Peter Rabbit: And Other Favorite Stories. (Illus.). 2000. 56p. (J). text 9.98 (*0-7624-1271-2*); 2000. 32p. (J). (gr. k-5). text 20.00 o.p. (*0-7624-0304-7*, Courage Bks.); 2000. 56p. (J). text 19.98 (*0-7624-1272-0*); 1990. 56p. (J). (gr. 2 up). text 5.95 o.p. (*0-89471-855-X*); 1986. 56p. (YA). (gr. k up). 9.98 (*0-89471-460-0*, Courage Bks.); 1986. 56p. (J). (gr. k up). 11.49 o.p. (*0-89471-488-0*, Courage Bks.) Running Pr. Bk. Pubs.

—Create Your Own Peter Rabbit Nursery. 1999. (Peter Rabbit Bks.). (Illus.). 48p. 11.99 o.s.i (*0-7232-4487-1*, Warne, Frederick) Penguin Putnam Bks. for Young Readers.

—El Cuento de Pedrito Conejo. Marcuse, Aida E., tr. 1993. (Mariposa Scholastic en Espanol Ser.). (SPA., Illus.). 32p. (J). (ps-3). pap. 3.50 (*0-590-46475-2*, SO4935) Scholastic, Inc.

—El Cuento de Pedrito Conejo. 1993. (Mariposa Scholastica en Espanol Ser.). (SPA.). (J). 9.40 (*0-606-02622-3*) Turtleback Bks.

—El Cuento de Pedro, el Conejo. 1998. Orig. Title: The Tales of Peter Rabbit. (J). (ps-3). pap. 2.95 (*0-486-27995-2*) Dover Pubns., Inc.

—El Cuento de Pedro, el Conejo, y Otros Once Cuentos de Beatrix Potter: 11 Stories. DeZardain, Paul F. & Saludes, Esperanza G., trs. 1995. (SPA., Illus.). 96p. (J). pap. text 1.00 (*0-486-28566-9*) Dover Pubns., Inc.

—El Cuento de Perico el Conejo Travieso. unabr. ed. 1991. (SPA., Illus.). (J). (gr. k-3). pap. 13.95 o.p. incl. audio (*0-87499-225-7*); pap. 29.95 o.p. incl. audio (*0-87499-226-5*); pap. 13.95 o.p. incl. audio (*0-87499-225-7*); pap. 29.95 o.p. incl. audio (*0-87499-226-5*) Live Oak Media.

—El Cuento de Perico el Conejo Travieso. 1988. (Original Peter Rabbit Bks.). (SPA., Illus.). 64p. (J). 5.95 o.p. (*0-7232-3556-2*, Warne, Frederick) Penguin Putnam Bks. for Young Readers.

—El Cuento del Conejo Pedrin. 1995. (Pudgy Pal Board Bks.). Orig. Title: The Tale of Peter Rabbit. (SPA., Illus.). 18p. (J). (ps). 3.95 o.p. (*0-448-40847-3*, Grosset & Dunlap) Penguin Putnam Bks. for Young Readers.

—Dear Peter Rabbit: A Beatrix Potter Mini Letters Book. 1995. (Illus.). 24p. (J). (ps-3). 10.99 o.s.i (*0-7232-4139-2*, Warne, Frederick) Penguin Putnam Bks. for Young Readers.

—Easter Fun with Peter Rabbit. 2003. (Illus.). 28p. (J). 4.99 (*0-7232-4896-6*, Warne, Frederick) Penguin Putnam Bks. for Young Readers.

—Fabula Petro Cuniculo: Peter Rabbit. 1962. (Potter 23 Tales Ser.). (LAT.). (J). (gr. 3-7). 5.00 o.p. (*0-7232-0648-1*, Warne, Frederick) Penguin Putnam Bks. for Young Readers.

—A First Peter Rabbit Book: A Learning Book for Young Children. 1997. (Illus.). 48p. (J). 9.99 o.s.i (*0-7232-4327-1*, Warne, Frederick) Penguin Putnam Bks. for Young Readers.

—Further Adventures of Peter Rabbit. 1989. (J). 6.99 o.s.i (*0-517-68371-7*) Random Hse. Value Publishing.

—Die Geschichte von Peterchen Hase: Ein Buntes Marchenbuch. 1995. Tr. of Peter Rabbit. (GER., Illus.). 32p. (J). pap. text 1.00 (*0-486-28557-X*, 28557-X) Dover Pubns., Inc.

—Giant Treasury of Peter Rabbit. 1989. (Illus.). 96p. (J). (gr. k-6). 6.99 (*0-517-31687-0*) Random Hse. Value Publishing.

—Learn with Peter Rabbit: Book of Numbers. 1993. (Beatrix Potter Learning Board Bks.). (Illus.). 12p. (J). 2.99 o.s.i (*0-517-07697-7*) Random Hse. Value Publishing.

—Listen & Read the Tale of Peter Rabbit & Other Favorite Stories. 1996. (Illus.). 96p. (Orig.). (J). pap. text 5.95 incl. audio (*0-486-29299-1*) Dover Pubns., Inc.

—Look! Peter Rabbit. 2002. (Illus.). 22p. (J). bds. 5.99 (*0-7232-4825-7*, Warne, Frederick) Penguin Putnam Bks. for Young Readers.

—Meet Peter Rabbit. 1986. (Board Bks.). (Illus.). 12p. (J). (ps). bds. 3.50 o.s.i (*0-7232-3418-3*, Warne, Frederick) Penguin Putnam Bks. for Young Readers.

—Meet Peter Rabbit. 1988. 2.99 o.s.i (*0-517-60595-3*) Random Hse. Value Publishing.

—Meet Peter Rabbit: Peter Rabbit Seedlings. 2003. (Illus.). 20p. (J). bds. 2.99 (*0-7232-4889-3*, Warne, Frederick) Penguin Putnam Bks. for Young Readers.

—Merry Christmas. 2003. (Illus.). 12p. bds. 6.99 (*0-7232-4925-3*, Warne, Frederick) Penguin Putnam Bks. for Young Readers.

—Mini Peter Rabbit Bookshop, 23 bks., Set. 1993. (Illus.). (J). (ps-3). 35.00 o.p. (*0-7232-3989-4*, Warne, Frederick) Penguin Putnam Bks. for Young Readers.

—The Miniature World of Peter Rabbit. 1989. 64p. 18.50 o.s.i (*0-7232-3988-6*, Warne, Frederick) Penguin Putnam Bks. for Young Readers.

—Munch Munch. 2003. 12p. 6.99 (*0-7232-4944-X*, Warne, Frederick) Penguin Putnam Bks. for Young Readers.

—My Peter Rabbit Book & Toy Box. 1989. (J). 22.95 o.p. (*0-7232-3667-4*, Warne, Frederick) Penguin Putnam Bks. for Young Readers.

—My Peter Rabbit Cloth Book. 1994. (Illus.). 10p. (J). (ps). 4.99 (*0-7232-0020-3*, Warne, Frederick) Penguin Putnam Bks. for Young Readers.

—My Peter Rabbit Diary. 1987. 80p. 6.95 o.p. (*0-7232-3443-4*, Warne, Frederick) Penguin Putnam Bks. for Young Readers.

—My Peter Rabbit Learning Box: Peter Rabbit's 123 & Peter Rabbit's ABC, Set. 1988. (Potter Original Ser.). (J). (ps-3). 13.95 o.p. (*0-7232-5168-1*, Warne, Frederick) Penguin Putnam Bks. for Young Readers.

—My Peter Rabbit Playbox. 1991. (J). 14.95 o.p. incl. audio (*0-7232-3794-8*, Warne, Frederick) Penguin Putnam Bks. for Young Readers.

—The New Adventures of Peter Rabbit. 1986. 7.98 o.p. (*0-8317-6797-9*) Smithmark Pubs., Inc.

—Original Peter Rabbit: Tales of Peter Rabbit, Tales of Squirrel Nutkin, Tailor of Gloucester. 1987. 70.00 o.p. (*0-7232-5166-5*, Warne, Frederick) Penguin Putnam Bks. for Young Readers.

—The Original Peter Rabbit Books. (J). E-Book 2.49 (*1-58627-757-X*) Electric Umbrella Publishing.

—The Original Peter Rabbit Books, 23 bks., Set. 1986. 135.00 o.s.i (*0-7232-5162-2*, Warne, Frederick) Penguin Putnam Bks. for Young Readers.

—The Original Peter Rabbit Miniature Collection. 1986. (Mini-Pack Ser.). (Illus.). pap. 4.95 o.p. (*0-7232-5022-7*) Penguin Putnam Bks. for Young Readers.

—Original Peter Rabbit Miniature Collection. 1989. (Illus.). (J). 14.95 o.p. (*0-7232-5173-8*, Warne, Frederick) Penguin Putnam Bks. for Young Readers.

—The Original Peter Rabbit Miniature Collection. (Original Peter Rabbit Miniature Collection: Vol. I). (Illus.). 64p. (J). (ps-3). No. I. 1991. 5.99 o.s.i (*0-7232-3982-7*); No. III. 1989. 5.95 o.s.i (*0-7232-3984-3*) Penguin Putnam Bks. for Young Readers. (Warne, Frederick).

—Original Peter Rabbit Miniature Collection, No. IV. 1990. (Mini-Pack Ser.). (J). (ps-3). 4.95 o.p. (*0-7232-5076-6*, Warne, Frederick) Penguin Putnam Bks. for Young Readers.

—The Original Peter Rabbit Miniature Collection. (ps-3). Vol. II. 1988. (Original Peter Rabbit Miniature Collection: Vol. II). 64p. (J). 5.95 o.s.i (*0-7232-3983-5*, Warne, Frederick); Vol. 2. 1988. (Mini-Pack Ser.). (Illus.). pap. 4.95 o.p. (*0-7232-5023-5*); Vol. 3. 1989. (Mini-Pack Ser.). (Illus.). 4.95 o.p. (*0-7232-5070-7*); Vol. 5. 1991. (Mini-Pack Ser.). (Illus.). 64p. (J). pap. 4.95 o.p. (*0-7232-3986-X*, Warne, Frederick); Vol. V. 1990. (Mini-Pack Ser.). (J). 4.95 o.p. (*0-7232-5078-2*, Warne, Frederick); Vol. VI. 1991. (Mini-Pack Ser.). (Illus.). 64p. (J). pap. 4.95 o.p. (*0-7232-3987-8*, Warne, Frederick); Vol. VI. 1991. (Mini-Pack Ser.). (Illus.). (J). 4.95 o.p. (*0-7232-5079-0*, Warne, Frederick) Penguin Putnam Bks. for Young Readers.

—The Original Peter Rabbit Miniature Collection: The Tale of Timmy Tiptoes; The Tale of Mrs. Tittlemouse; The Tale of Samuel Whiskers; The Story of Miss Moppet, 4 bks. 1989. (Mini-Pack Ser.). 5.95 o.s.i (*0-7232-3985-1*, Warne, Frederick) Penguin Putnam Bks. for Young Readers.

—The Original Pop-Up Tale of Peter Rabbit. 1996. (Illus.). 12p. (J). (ps-2). 13.99 (*0-7232-4280-1*, Warne, Frederick) Penguin Putnam Bks. for Young Readers.

—Pedrin, el Conejo Travieso: Peter Rabbit. 1931. (SPA., Illus.). 64p. (J). (gr. 3-7). 5.00 o.p. (*0-7232-1797-1*, Warne, Frederick) Penguin Putnam Bks. for Young Readers.

—Peter Rabbit. 1989. (Allen D. Bragdon Bedtime Classics Library). (Illus.). 64p. (J). (gr. k-5). 11.95 o.p. (*0-916410-24-2*) Bragdon, Allen D. Pubs., Inc.

—Peter Rabbit. 1986. (Illus.). 24p. (J). (gr. k-6). pap. 2.95 o.p. (*0-8249-8110-3*) Ideals Pubns.

—Peter Rabbit. (J). (ps-2). 1989. (Beatrix Potter Coloring Bks.: No. S884-1). (Illus.). pap. 1.95 o.p. (*0-7214-5138-1*); 1988. (Beatrix Potter Ser.: No. S880-1). pap. 3.95 o.p. (*0-7214-5044-X*) Penguin Group (USA) Inc. (Ladybird Bks.).

—Peter Rabbit. (Little Hide-and-Seek Bks.). (J). (ps-3). 1994. (Illus.). 10p. 3.99 o.s.i (*0-7232-4105-8*, Warne, Frederick); 1992. (Illus.). 12p. 5.99 o.s.i (*0-7232-3997-5*, Warne, Frederick); 1981. (Illus.). 18p. 3.95 o.s.i (*0-448-09755-9*, Grosset & Dunlap); 1979. 7.00 o.p. (*0-7232-2334-3*, Warne, Frederick); 1978. (Illus.). 18p. 2.29 o.p. (*0-448-13084-X*, Grosset & Dunlap) Penguin Putnam Bks. for Young Readers.

—Peter Rabbit. 1998. (Illus.). (J). (*0-7853-2634-0*) Publications International, Ltd.

—Peter Rabbit. 1962. (Nursery Treasure Books Ser.). (Illus.). (J). 1.50 o.p. (*0-448-04203-7*) Putnam Publishing Group, The.

—Peter Rabbit. 1993. (Rabbit Ears Family Classics Ser.). (Illus.). 24p. (J). (ps-3). 12.95 o.s.i (*0-307-12349-9*, 12349, Golden Bks.) Random Hse. Children's Bks.

—Peter Rabbit: Beatrix Potter Deluxe Pop Up. 1992. (Illus.). (J). 4.99 o.p. (*0-517-07000-6*) Random Hse. Value Publishing.

—Peter Rabbit: Story Pak. 1992. (Graphic Learning Literature Program Ser.). (ENG & SPA., Illus.). (J). (gr. k-3). 45.00 (*0-87746-231-3*) Graphic Learning.

—The Peter Rabbit Address Book. 1987. 160p. (gr. 2 up). 6.95 o.s.i (*0-7232-3524-4*, Warne, Frederick) Penguin Putnam Bks. for Young Readers.

—The Peter Rabbit & Benjamin Bunny Coloring Book. 1987. (Illus.). (J). (gr. 1 up). pap. 1.49 (*0-671-62987-5*, Little Simon) Simon & Schuster Children's Publishing.

—Peter Rabbit & Friends. 1992. (Potter Original Ser.). (Illus.). (J). 14.00 o.p. (*0-7232-5210-6*, Warne, Frederick) Penguin Putnam Bks. for Young Readers.

—Peter Rabbit & Friends. 1986. (Picture Book Parade Ser.). (J). (ps-4). audio 16.95 (*0-89719-930-8*, WW733C) Weston Woods Studios, Inc.

—Peter Rabbit & Friends: A Stand-Up Story Book. 1998. (Illus.). 10p. (J). (ps-3). 14.99 o.s.i (*0-7232-4343-3*, Warne, Frederick) Penguin Putnam Bks. for Young Readers.

—Peter Rabbit & Friends: Changing Pictures. 2004. (Illus.). 12p. (J). 5.99 (*0-7232-4915-6*, Warne, Frederick) Penguin Putnam Bks. for Young Readers.

—Peter Rabbit & Friends: Three Complete Tales, 3 vols. 1985. (Illus.). 178p. (J). (gr. 2 up). pap. 5.25 o.p. (*0-486-24772-4*) Dover Pubns., Inc.

—The Peter Rabbit & Friends Cookbook. 1994. (Illus.). 48p. (J). (ps-3). 6.99 o.s.i (*0-7232-4146-5*, Warne, Frederick) Penguin Putnam Bks. for Young Readers.

—The Peter Rabbit & Friends Poster Activity Book. 1995. (Illus.). 24p. (J). (ps-3). pap. 6.99 o.p. (*0-7232-4088-4*, Warne, Frederick) Penguin Putnam Bks. for Young Readers.

—Peter Rabbit & Friends Sticker Activity Book. 2000. (Illus.). 18p. (J). (ps-3). 7.99 o.p. (*0-7232-4681-5*, Warne, Frederick) Penguin Putnam Bks. for Young Readers.

—The Peter Rabbit & Friends Treasury. 1999. (Potter Original Ser.). (Illus.). 240p. (J). (ps-3). 19.99 o.p. (*0-7232-4576-2*, Warne, Frederick) Penguin Putnam Bks. for Young Readers.

—Peter Rabbit & His Friends. 1994. (Illus.). 24p. (J). (ps). bds. 2.99 o.p. (*0-7232-4093-0*, Warne, Frederick) Penguin Putnam Bks. for Young Readers.

—Peter Rabbit & His Friends, 6 vols. 1994. (Little Books of Beatrix Potter). (Illus.). (J). 5.99 o.s.i (*0-517-10084-3*) Random Hse. Value Publishing.

—Peter Rabbit & His Friends. 1985. (Chubby Board Bks.). (Illus.). 16p. (YA). (ps up). bds. 3.95 (*0-671-52698-7*, Little Simon) Simon & Schuster Children's Publishing.

—The Peter Rabbit & His Friends Sticker Book. 1988. 36p. (J). pap. 5.95 o.p. (*0-7232-3537-6*, Warne, Frederick) Penguin Putnam Bks. for Young Readers.

—Peter Rabbit & His Friends Word Book. 1989. (J). 7.99 o.p. (*0-517-64156-9*) Random Hse. Value Publishing.

—Peter Rabbit & Other Stories. 1993. (J). 4.98 (*0-89009-187-0*) Book Sales, Inc.

—Peter Rabbit & Other Stories. abr. ed. 1997. (J). audio 6.95 (*0-7871-0925-8*, Dove Audio) NewStar Media, Inc.

—Peter Rabbit & Other Stories. unabr. ed. 2002. (J). audio compact disk 18.95 (*1-58472-302-5*, 064); pap. incl. audio compact disk (*1-58472-304-1*) Sound Room Pubs., Inc. (In Audio).

—Peter Rabbit Bath Book. 1989. (Illus.). 12p. (J). (ps-k). 3.99 (*0-7232-3584-8*, Warne, Frederick) Penguin Putnam Bks. for Young Readers.

—The Peter Rabbit Bedtime Box. 1995. (Illus.). 32p. (J). (gr. k-3). 25.00 o.p. (*0-7232-5453-2*, Warne, Frederick) Penguin Putnam Bks. for Young Readers.

—Peter Rabbit Birthday Book. 1987. 160p. (J). (ps-3). 6.95 o.p. (*0-7232-3523-6*, Warne, Frederick) Penguin Putnam Bks. for Young Readers.

—Peter Rabbit Comes Home. 1988. (J). 2.99 o.s.i (*0-517-60596-1*) Random Hse. Value Publishing.

—The Peter Rabbit Cut-Out Book. 1986. (Activity Bks.). (Illus.). 24p. (J). (ps-3). pap. 3.95 o.p. (*0-7232-3331-4*, Warne, Frederick) Penguin Putnam Bks. for Young Readers.

—The Peter Rabbit Diary. 1982. (Illus.). 90p. (J). 3.95 o.p. (*0-7232-2982-1*, Warne, Frederick) Penguin Putnam Bks. for Young Readers.

—Peter Rabbit Diary for Any Year. 1991. 80p. (J). 6.95 o.p. (*0-7232-3993-2*, Warne, Frederick) Penguin Putnam Bks. for Young Readers.

—Peter Rabbit Finger Puppet Book. 2004. (Illus.). 16p. bds. 10.99 (*0-7232-4942-3*, Warne, Frederick) Penguin Putnam Bks. for Young Readers.

—Peter Rabbit in Mr. McGregor's Garden. 1988. (J). 2.99 o.s.i (*0-517-60597-X*) Random Hse. Value Publishing.

—The Peter Rabbit Make-a-Mobile Book. (J). 1991. 16p. pap. 5.95 o.p. (*0-7232-3764-6*); 1987. 3.95 o.p. (*0-7232-3426-4*) Penguin Putnam Bks. for Young Readers. (Warne, Frederick).

—Peter Rabbit Miniature Library. 32p. 2002. 10.00 o.p. (*0-7232-4359-X*); 1998. (Illus.). (J). 12.00 o.s.i (*0-7232-8286-2*, Warne, Frederick) Penguin Putnam Bks. for Young Readers.

—The Peter Rabbit Nursery Book & Toy. 1997. (Illus.). 48p. (J). (ps-k). 21.99 o.s.i (*0-7232-4413-8*, Warne, Frederick) Penguin Putnam Bks. for Young Readers.

—The World of Peter Rabbit Sticker Book. 1990. (Rebus Sticker Storybooks Ser.). (Illus.). 24p. (J). (ps-3). pap. 6.99 o.s.i (*0-7232-3645-3*, Warne, Frederick) Penguin Putnam Bks. for Young Readers.

—Yours Affectionately, Peter Rabbit. 1983. (Illus.). 96p. (J). 6.95 o.p. (*0-7232-3178-8*, Warne, Frederick) Penguin Putnam Bks. for Young Readers.

Potter, Beatrix, illus. Little Treasury of Peter Rabbit, 6 vols. 1988. (J). (ps). 5.99 o.s.i (*0-517-41069-9*) Random Hse. Value Publishing.

—Meet Peter Rabbit. 1996. (First Board Book Ser.). 12p. (J). (ps-k). bds. 4.99 (*0-7232-4322-0*, Warne, Frederick) Penguin Putnam Bks. for Young Readers.

—My Peter Rabbit Keepsake: A Photograph Album. 1994. 32p. (J). 9.95 o.s.i (*0-7232-4121-X*, Warne, Frederick) Penguin Putnam Bks. for Young Readers.

—The Peter Rabbit Make-&-Play Book. 1992. 32p. (J). (ps-5). pap. 6.99 o.s.i (*0-7232-3991-6*, Warne, Frederick) Penguin Putnam Bks. for Young Readers.

—The Peter Rabbit Sticker Book. rev. ed. 1991. 24p. (J). (ps-3). pap. 6.99 o.p. (*0-7232-3979-7*, Warne, Frederick) Penguin Putnam Bks. for Young Readers.

—The Peter Rabbit Theatre. 1983. 12p. (J). (gr. k-5). 5.00 o.p. (*0-7232-3180-X*, Warne, Frederick) Penguin Putnam Bks. for Young Readers.

—Peter Rabbit's Counting Book. 1999. (World of Beatrix Potter Ser.). 20p. (YA). (ps-3). 9.99 (*0-7232-4485-5*, Warne, Frederick) Penguin Putnam Bks. for Young Readers.

—Peter Rabbit's Easter Activity Book. 1999. (World of Beatrix Potter Ser.). 24p. pap. 4.99 (*0-7232-4486-3*, Warne, Frederick) Penguin Putnam Bks. for Young Readers.

—The Tale of Peter Rabbit. 1999. 12p. (J). (ps-k). bds. 6.99 (*0-7232-4432-4*, Warne, Frederick) Penguin Putnam Bks. for Young Readers.

Potter, Beatrix & Burgess, Thornton W. The Tale of Peter Rabbit & Other Stories. unabr. collector's ed. 1997. (J). (ps-3). audio 30.00 (*0-7366-3580-7*, 4233) Books on Tape, Inc.

Potter, Beatrix & Golden Books Staff. The Tale of Peter Rabbit. (Little Golden Bks.). (Illus.). (J). (ps-2). 2001. 24p. 2.99 (*0-307-03071-7*, 98039); 1998. 72p. pap. 2.22 o.s.i (*0-307-11950-5*) Random Hse. Children's Bks. (Golden Bks.).

Potter, Beatrix & Pomaska, Anna. El Cuento de Pedro, el Conejo: Libro de Cuentos en Colores - Por Beatrix Potter, Ilustrato Por Anna Pomaska. 1995. (Little Activity Bks.).Tr. of Tale of Peter Rabbit. (SPA., Illus.). 32p. (J). pap. text 1.50 (*0-486-28539-1*, 28539-1) Dover Pubns., Inc.

—L' Histoire de Pierre Lapin: Livre d'Histoires en Couleurs. 1995. Tr. of Peter Rabbit. (FRE., Illus.). 32p. (J). pap. text 1.00 (*0-486-28540-5*, 28540-5) Dover Pubns., Inc.

—Peter Rabbit & Friends, 10 bks., Set, incl. stickers. 1999. (Illus.). (J). pap. 10.00 (*0-486-29463-3*) Dover Pubns., Inc.

—Skazka O Zaichonke Pete (The Tale of Peter Rabbit) Maler, Elvira, tr. 1996. (RUS., Illus.). 32p. (J). reprint ed. pap. text 1.00 (*0-486-28717-3*, 28717-3) Dover Pubns., Inc.

—La Storia del Coniglietto Pietro: Libro Di Racconti in Colore. Vettori, Alessandro, tr. 1995. Tr. of Peter Rabbit. (ITA., Illus.). 32p. (J). reprint ed. pap. text 1.00 o.p. (*0-486-28558-8*) Dover Pubns., Inc.

—The Tale of Peter Rabbit: Full-Color Storybook. 1995. (Little Activity Bks.). 32p. (Orig.). (J). pap. text 1.00 (*0-486-28541-3*) Dover Pubns., Inc.

—The Tale of Peter Rabbit Sticker Storybook. 1996. (Illus.). 16p. (Orig.). (J). pap. text 1.00 (*0-486-29087-5*) Dover Pubns., Inc.

Potter, Beatrix & Random House Value Publishing Staff. The Tale of Peter Rabbit. 1996. (Illus.). 16p. (J). 2.99 o.s.i (*0-517-15989-9*) Random Hse. Value Publishing.

Potter, Beatrix, et al. Easter Twin Pack: Peter Rabbit & Peter Cottontail, 2 bks. 1989. (Illus.). (J). (ps-3). pap. 7.95 o.p. (*0-8249-7221-X*) Ideals Pubns.

Schoonover, Pat & Nelson, Anita, illus. Peter Rabbit. 1992. (Classic Tales Ser.). 24p. (J). (gr. 2-4). lib. bdg. 11.95 (*1-56674-008-8*, HTS Bks.) Forest Hse. Publishing Co., Inc.

Seafarer Staff. The Peter Rabbit Puzzle Play Book. 1994. 10p. 5.98 o.p. (*0-8289-0839-7*) Greene, Stephen Pr., The.

Searcy, David. Peter Rabbit's Trick. 1980. (Lucky Heart Book Ser.). 24p. reprint ed. pap. 30.00 (*0-7837-9151-8*, 204985100003) Bks. on Demand.

Sharp, Vera. Peter Rabbit's Second Tale. (J). audio. 1996. 49.00 (*0-9616987-1-3*) Sharp, Vera.

Smith, Debbie. The Peter Rabbit Craft Book. 1988. (Illus.). 32p. (J). (gr. k-5). 7.95 o.p. (*0-7232-3440-X*, Warne, Frederick) Penguin Putnam Bks. for Young Readers.

Sternhagen, Frances, reader. The Tale of Peter Rabbit. unabr. ed. 1987. (Coloring Book Readalongs Ser.). (J). audio 13.95 Spoken Arts, Inc.

Stewart, Pat Ronson & Potter, Beatrix. Peter Rabbit & Eleven Other Favorite Tales. 1993. (Children's Thrift Classics Ser.). (Illus.). 96p. (J). reprint ed. pap. 1.00 (*0-486-27845-X*) Dover Pubns., Inc.

Stott, Philip. The Peter Rabbit Recorder Book. 1984. (Illus.). 24p. (J). (gr. 3-9). pap. 4.95 o.p. (*0-7232-3179-6*, Warne, Frederick) Penguin Putnam Bks. for Young Readers.

The Tale of Peter Rabbit. 1986. (Talking Bear Tapes Ser.). (J). audio 4.95 (*0-89926-202-3*, 915D) Audio Bk. Co.

The Tale of Peter Rabbit. (Easy-to-Read Folktales Ser.). (J). audio 5.95 (*0-590-63104-7*) Scholastic, Inc.

The Tale of Peter Rabbit. (J). audio 3.98 (*1-55886-070-3*, GDP 401) Smarty Pants.

The Tale of Peter Rabbit. (J). 14.00 incl. audio Windham Hill Productions.

The Tale of Peter Rabbit & Other Stories. Incl. Tale of Benjamin Bunny. audio o.p. Tale of Mr. Jeremy Fisher. audio o.p. Tale of Mrs. Tiggy-Winkle. audio o.p. Tale of Two Bad Mice. audio o.p. (J). (ps-1). 1984. 1984. Set audio 9.95 o.p. (*0-89845-575-8*, CPN 1760, Caedmon) HarperTrade.

Tallarico, Tony, illus. Meet Peter Rabbit. 1988. (Tote Bks.). 12p. (J). (ps-1). 3.95 o.s.i (*0-89828-321-3*, Tuffy Bks.) Putnam Publishing Group, The.

—Peter Rabbit's Big Adventure. 1988. (Tote Bks.). 12p. (J). (ps-1). 3.95 o.s.i (*0-89828-324-8*, Tuffy Bks.) Putnam Publishing Group, The.

—Peter Rabbit's Family. 1988. (Tote Bks.). 12p. (J). (ps-1). 3.95 o.s.i (*0-89828-312-4*, Tuffy Bks.) Putnam Publishing Group, The.

—A Tale of Peter Rabbit. 1988. (Tote Bks.). 12p. (J). (ps-1). 3.95 o.s.i (*0-89828-322-1*, Tuffy Bks.) Putnam Publishing Group, The.

Terrio, Bob, illus. Peter Rabbit & His Friends. 1995. (Look & Find Ser.). 24p. (J). (gr. k-6). lib. bdg. 13.95 o.p. (*1-56674-097-5*, HTS Bks.) Forest Hse. Publishing Co., Inc.

Unknown. Peter Rabbit. 1985. (J). (gr. k-3). 185.00 o.s.i (*0-8431-4171-9*, Price Stern Sloan) Penguin Putnam Bks. for Young Readers.

Walters, Jennie. Gardening with Peter Rabbit. 1992. (Illus.). 48p. (J). (gr. k-4). 9.00 o.p. (*0-7232-3998-3*, Warne, Frederick) Penguin Putnam Bks. for Young Readers.

—Gardening with Peter Rabbit: A Gardening Kit. 1992. (Illus.). 48p. (J). (gr. k-4). 14.50 o.p. (*0-7232-4024-8*, Warne, Frederick) Penguin Putnam Bks. for Young Readers.

Ward, Ann. Peter Rabbit & Friends: Study Guide for Children for the Works of Beatrix Potter. 1993. 95p. pap. text 10.00 o.p. (*0-923463-96-8*) Noble Publishing Assocs.

Warne, Frederick. Be My Valentine, Peter Rabbit. 2002. (Illus.). 10p. (J). bds. 5.99 (*0-7232-4864-8*, Warne, Frederick) Penguin Putnam Bks. for Young Readers.

Wheeler, Jody. The Tale of Peter Rabbit. 1995. (Take-a-Look Bks.). (Illus.). 14p. (J). (ps-3). pap. 3.49 o.s.i (*0-307-12473-8*, Golden Bks.) Random Hse. Children's Bks.

The World of Peter Rabbit & Friends: Posters. 1994. (Illus.). (J). pap. 7.95 o.p. (*0-7232-4129-5*, Warne, Frederick) Penguin Putnam Bks. for Young Readers.

PHANTOM OF THE OPERA (FICTITIOUS CHARACTER)—FICTION

Aurum Press & Van der Meer, Frank. The Phantom of the Opera Pop-Up Book. 1989. 19.95 o.p. (*0-06-016012-8*) HarperTrade.

Leroux, Gaston. The Phantom of the Opera. l.t. ed. 1999. (Large Print Heritage Ser.). 420p. (J). (gr. 7-12). lib. bdg. 35.95 (*1-58118-043-8*, 22512) LRS.

—The Phantom of the Opera. 1994. (Classics for Young Readers Ser.). (Illus.). 336p. (YA). (gr. 4-7). pap. 4.99 (*0-14-036813-2*, Puffin Bks.) Penguin Putnam Bks. for Young Readers.

—The Phantom of the Opera. 1989. (Step-up Classic Chillers Ser.). (Illus.). 96p. (J). (gr. 2-5). pap. 3.99 (*0-394-83847-5*, Random Hse. Bks. for Young Readers) Random Hse. Children's Bks.

—The Phantom of the Opera. Bair, Lowell, tr. abr. ed. 1998. 336p. (YA). (gr. 7-12). mass mkt. 3.99 (*0-440-22774-7*, Dell Books for Young Readers) Random Hse. Children's Bks.

—The Phantom of the Opera. abr. ed. 1998. 10.04 (*0-606-15677-1*) Turtleback Bks.

—The Phantom of the Opera. 1988. (Illus.). (J). (gr. 4 up). 14.95 o.p. (*0-88101-082-0*); 208p. (YA). (gr. 7 up). 9.95 o.p. (*0-88101-121-5*) Unicorn Publishing Hse., Inc., The.

Neumeyer, Peter. The Phantom of the Opera. abr. ed. 1988. (Illus.). 48p. (J). 14.95 o.p. (*0-87905-330-5*) Smith, Gibbs Pub.

Weinberg, Larry. Universal Monsters: The Phantom of the Opera. 1993. (J). (gr. 4-7). pap. o.p. (*0-307-22334-5*, Golden Bks.) Random Hse. Children's Bks.

PICARD, JEAN-LUC (FICTITIOUS CHARACTER)—FICTION

Mason, Jane B. First Contact: The Movie Storybook. 1996. (Star Trek Ser.). (Illus.). 32p. (J). (ps-3). pap. 9.99 (*0-689-80899-2*, Simon Spotlight) Simon & Schuster Children's Publishing.

Strickland, Brad & Strickland, Barbara. Nova Command. 1995. (Star Trek, The Next Generation: No. 9). (Illus.). 128p. (J). (gr. 4-7). pap. 3.99 (*0-671-51009-6*, Aladdin) Simon & Schuster Children's Publishing.

—Nova Command. 1995. (Star Trek, The Next Generation: No. 9). (J). (gr. 3-6). 9.09 (*0-606-08617-X*) Turtleback Bks.

—Starfall. 1995. (Star Trek Ser.: No. 8). (Illus.). 128p. (J). (gr. 4-7). pap. 3.99 (*0-671-51010-X*, Aladdin) Simon & Schuster Children's Publishing.

—Starfall. 1995. (Star Trek, The Next Generation: No. 8). (J). (gr. 3-6). 10.04 (*0-606-08616-1*) Turtleback Bks.

Vornholt, John. First Contact. 1996. (Star Trek Ser.: No. 8). (J). (ps-3). 10.04 (*0-606-11883-7*) Turtleback Bks.

—Generations. 1994. (Star Trek Ser.: No. 7). 128p. (J). (gr. 4-7). pap. 3.99 (*0-671-51901-8*, Aladdin) Simon & Schuster Children's Publishing.

—Insurrection. 1998. (Star Trek Ser.). (Illus.). 128p. (J). (gr. 3-6). pap. 4.50 (*0-671-02107-9*, Aladdin) Simon & Schuster Children's Publishing.

Vornholt, John, et al. First Contact. 1996. (Star Trek Ser.: No. 8). (Illus.). 128p. (J). (gr. 8 up). per. 3.99 (*0-671-00128-0*, Aladdin) Simon & Schuster Children's Publishing.

PICASSO, PABLO, 1881-1973—FICTION

Anholt, Laurence. Picasso & the Girl with a Ponytail. 1998. (Illus.). 32p. (J). (ps-2). 14.95 (*0-7641-5031-6*) Barron's Educational Series, Inc.

—Picasso y Sylvette: Un Cuento Sobre Pablo Picasso. 2000. (Illus.). (J). (gr. 3-5). (CAT.). 32p. 14.95 (*84-8488-003-6*); (SPA., 200p. 14.95 (*84-95040-01-8*) Serres, Ediciones, S. L. ESP. *Dist:* Lectorum Pubns., Inc.

Antoine, Veronique. Picasso: A Day in His Studio. 1994. (Art for Children Ser.). (Illus.). 64p. (J). (gr. 4-7). lib. bdg. 15.95 (*0-7910-2815-1*) Chelsea Hse. Pubs.

PIGGLE-WIGGLE, MRS. (FICTITIOUS CHARACTER)—FICTION

MacDonald, Betty. Hello, Mrs. Piggle-Wiggle. 1985. (Trophy Bk.). (Illus.). 128p. (J). (gr. 5 up). pap. 4.99 (*0-06-440149-9*, Harper Trophy) HarperCollins Children's Bk. Group.

—Mrs. Piggle-Wiggle. 2002. (Illus.). (J). 13.40 (*0-7587-6605-X*) Book Wholesalers, Inc.

—Mrs. Piggle-Wiggle. rev. ed. 1985. (Trophy Bk.). (Illus.). 128p. (J). (gr. 1-5). pap. 4.99 (*0-06-440148-0*, Harper Trophy) HarperCollins Children's Bk. Group.

—Mrs. Piggle-Wiggle's Farm. 1985. (Trophy Bk.). (Illus.). 128p. (J). (gr. 1-5). pap. 4.99 (*0-06-440150-2*, Harper Trophy) HarperCollins Children's Bk. Group.

—Mrs. Piggle-Wiggle's Magic. 1985. (Trophy Bk.). (Illus.). 144p. (J). (gr. 1-5). pap. 5.99 (*0-06-440151-0*, Harper Trophy) HarperCollins Children's Bk. Group.

—The Won't-Pick-up-Toys Cure. 1998. (Mrs. Piggle-Wiggle Adventure Ser.). (Illus.). (J). lib. bdg. (*0-06-027629-0*) HarperCollins Children's Bk. Group.

—The Won't-Take-a-Bath-Cure. 1998. (Mrs. Piggle-Wiggle Adventure Ser.). (Illus.). 40p. (J). (ps-2). lib. bdg. 14.89 (*0-06-027631-2*) HarperCollins Children's Bk. Group.

MacDonald, Betty, ed. Mrs. Piggle-Wiggle's Bad Table-Manners Cure. 2000. (Mrs. Piggle-Wiggle Adventure Ser.). (Illus.). (J). lib. bdg. 12.89 (*0-06-027633-9*) HarperCollins Children's Bk. Group.

MacDonald, Betty Bard. Hello, Mrs. Piggle-Wiggle. 1957. (Illus.). 132p. (J). (gr. 1-5). 15.99 (*0-397-31715-8*) HarperCollins Children's Bk. Group.

—Hello, Mrs. Piggle-Wiggle. 2000. (YA). pap. 40.20 incl. audio (*0-7887-4171-3*, 41089); pap. 40.20 incl. audio (*0-7887-4171-3*, 41089) Recorded Bks., LLC.

—Hello, Mrs. Piggle-Wiggle. 1985. (J). 11.00 (*0-606-07636-0*) Turtleback Bks.

—Mrs. Piggle-Wiggle. rev. ed. (J). (gr. k-3). 1957. (Illus.). 128p. 15.99 (*0-397-31712-3*); Set. 1986. pap. 11.80 o.p. (*0-06-440152-9*, Harper Trophy) HarperCollins Children's Bk. Group.

—Mrs. Piggle-Wiggle. 1999. (J). (gr. 1 up). pap., stu. ed. 32.20 incl. audio (*0-7887-3851-8*, 41049X4) Recorded Bks., LLC.

—Mrs. Piggle-Wiggle. 1957. (J). 11.00 (*0-606-00728-8*) Turtleback Bks.

—The Mrs. Piggle-Wiggle Treasury. 1995. (Illus.). 368p. (J). 4.75 o.s.i (*0-06-024812-2*) HarperCollins Children's Bk. Group.

—Mrs. Piggle-Wiggle's Farm. (Illus.). (J). 1996. (gr. 2-6). 14.95 o.p. (*0-397-30273-8*, 592801); 1954. 132p. (gr. 7 up). 15.99 (*0-397-31713-1*) HarperCollins Children's Bk. Group.

—Mrs. Piggle-Wiggle's Farm. 1985. (J). 11.00 (*0-606-00729-6*) Turtleback Bks.

—Mrs. Piggle-Wiggle's Magic. 1976. 136p. (J). 17.95 (*0-8488-1087-2*) Amereon, Ltd.

—Mrs. Piggle-Wiggle's Magic. 1957. (Illus.). 144p. (J). (ps-3). 15.99 (*0-397-31714-X*) HarperCollins Children's Bk. Group.

—Mrs. Piggle-Wiggle's Magic. 2000. (J). pap., stu. ed. 51.95 incl. audio (*0-7887-4343-0*, 41137); pap., stu. ed. 51.95 incl. audio (*0-7887-4343-0*, 41137); (gr. 1 up). stu. ed. 196.80 incl. audio (*0-7887-4443-7*, 47134) Recorded Bks., LLC.

—Mrs. Piggle-Wiggle's Magic. 1957. (J). 11.00 (*0-606-00731-8*) Turtleback Bks.

—The Won't-Pick-up-Toys Cure. 1997. (Mrs. Piggle-Wiggle Adventure Ser.). (Illus.). 40p. (J). (ps-2). 12.95 o.p. (*0-06-027628-2*) HarperCollins Children's Bk. Group.

MacDonald, Betty Bard, ed. Mrs. Piggle-Wiggle's Bad Table-Manners Cure. 2000. (Mrs. Piggle-Wiggle Adventure Ser.). (Illus.). (J). 12.95 (*0-06-027632-0*) HarperCollins Children's Bk. Group.

PIGLET (FICTITIOUS CHARACTER)—FICTION

Biglet: Book of Pooh. 2002. (Illus.). 32p. (J). (ps-1). 5.99 (*0-7868-3363-7*) Disney Pr.

Disney Staff. The Piglet Movie. 2003. (Illus.). 24p. (J). pap. 3.25 (*0-7364-2111-4*, RH/Disney) Random Hse. Children's Bks.

—The Piglet Movie: A Read-Aloud Story Book. 2003. (Illus.). 72p. (J). 8.99 (*0-7364-2090-8*, RH/Disney) Random Hse. Children's Bks.

—Piglet's Picnic. 2001. (Illus.). 12p. (J). bds. 7.99 (*0-7364-1204-2*, RH/Disney) Random Hse. Children's Bks.

Liberts, Jennifer & Milne, A. A. Piglet Feels Small. 2002. (Early Step into Reading Ser.). (Illus.). 32p. (J). pap. 3.99 (*0-7364-1226-3*, RH/Disney) Random Hse. Children's Bks.

Milne, A. A., pseud. Piglet. 2000. (Pooh Giant Shaped Board Bks.). (Illus.). 10p. (YA). (ps up). bds. 7.99 (*0-525-46334-8*, Dutton Children's Bks.) Penguin Putnam Bks. for Young Readers.

—Piglet Clip & Read Book. abr. ed. 1999. (Illus.). 24p. (J). (ps-3). bds. 2.99 o.s.i (*0-525-46205-8*, Dutton Children's Bks.) Penguin Putnam Bks. for Young Readers.

—Piglet Has a Bath. 1998. (Winnie-the-Pooh Collections). (Illus.). 12p. (J). 5.99 o.s.i (*0-525-46092-6*, Dutton Children's Bks.) Penguin Putnam Bks. for Young Readers.

—Piglet Is Entirely Surrounded by Water. 1991. (Pop-Up Storybook). (Illus.). 16p. (J). (ps up). 7.95 o.p. (*0-525-44784-9*, Dutton Children's Bks.) Penguin Putnam Bks. for Young Readers.

—Piglet Is Entirely Surrounded by Water. Bonnell, J., ed. abr. ed. 2001. (Pooh Read-Along Ser.). (Illus.). 32p. (J). (ps-3). pap. 9.99 o.s.i incl. audio (*0-14-090420-4*, Puffin Bks.) Penguin Putnam Bks. for Young Readers.

—Piglet Is Entirely Surrounded by Water: A Winnie the Pooh Storybook. 1993. (Pooh Storybook Ser.). (Illus.). 32p. (J). 4.99 o.s.i (*0-525-45143-9*, Dutton Children's Bks.) Penguin Putnam Bks. for Young Readers.

—Piglet Is Entirely Surrounded by Water Puzzle. 1999. (Illus.). 14p. (J). (ps-3). 7.99 o.s.i (*0-525-46273-2*, Dutton) Penguin Putnam Bks. for Young Readers.

—Piglet Meets a Heffalump & Other Stories. abr. ed. 1998. (J). mass mkt. 7.95 incl. audio (*1-84032-052-4*) Hodder Headline Audiobooks GBR. *Dist:* Trafalgar Square, Ulverscroft Large Print Bks., Ltd.

—Piglet Meets a Heffalump & Other Stories. 1993. (Pooh Storybook Ser.). (Illus.). 32p. (J). (gr. 2 up). 4.99 o.s.i (*0-525-45042-4*, Dutton Children's Bks.) Penguin Putnam Bks. for Young Readers.

—Pooh & Piglet Giant Shaped Board Book. 2002. (Illus.). 10p. bds. 7.99 (*0-525-46845-5*, Dutton Children's Bks.) Penguin Putnam Bks. for Young Readers.

PINOCCHIO (FICTITIOUS CHARACTER)—FICTION

Abiuso, G. & Giglio, M., adapted by. Le Avventure di Pinocchio: Beginning Through Intermediate. 2001. (ENG & ITA., Illus.). 88p. (C). pap. 9.95 (*0-8442-8023-2*, X8023-2) McGraw-Hill/Contemporary.

Alvin S. White Studio Staff, illus. Walt Disney's Pinocchio: A Pop-Up Book. 1992. 12p. (J). (ps-3). 11.95 o.p. (*1-56282-172-5*) Disney Pr.

Brown, Kay & Collodi, Carlo. Pinocchio. 1988. (Derrydale Fairytale Library). (Illus.). (J). (ps-3). 1.99 o.s.i (*0-517-28809-5*) Random Hse. Value Publishing.

Carlin, Dan. The Pinocchio Effect: More Rights & Less Liberty in the 21st Century. 1999. 264p. 25.95 (*1-58112-841-X*) Upublish.com.

Carr, M. J. Carlo Collodi's Pinocchio: Picture Story Book. 1996. (J). (gr. 7-10). mass mkt. 2.99 o.p. (*0-590-92263-7*) Scholastic, Inc.

Carroll, Lewis, pseud & Collodi, Carlo. Pinocchio & The Hunting of the Snark. unabr. ed. 1985. (J). audio 24.95 (*1-55685-064-6*) Audio Bk. Contractors, Inc.

Charyn, Jerome. Pinocchio's Nose. 1983. 15.95 o.p. (*0-87795-438-0*); 1982. 320p. 16.95 o.p. (*0-87795-303-1*) Morrow/Avon. (Morrow, William & Co.).

Collodi, Carlo. The Adventures of Pinocchio. unabr. ed. (J). audio 29.75. audio 6.95 Audio Bk. Co.

—The Adventures of Pinocchio. (J). 2000. per. 9.90 (*1-891355-71-6*); 2001. per. 15.50 (*1-58396-237-9*) Blue Unicorn Editions.

—The Adventures of Pinocchio. 1984. 256p. (J). lib. bdg. 25.95 o.s.i (*0-89968-257-X*, Lightyear Pr.) Buccaneer Bks., Inc.

—The Adventures of Pinocchio. 1988. (Roberto Innocenti Ser.). (Illus.). 144p. (J). (gr. 1-12). lib. bdg. 19.95 o.p. (*0-8211-0394-6*, 97080-098, Creative Education) Creative Co., The.

—The Adventures of Pinocchio. (J). E-Book 2.49 (*0-7574-0328-X*) Electric Umbrella Publishing.

—The Adventures of Pinocchio. Rosenthal, M. L., tr. 1983. (Illus.). 256p. (J). (gr. 3 up). 17.50 o.p. (*0-688-02267-7*) HarperCollins Children's Bk. Group.

—The Adventures of Pinocchio, ERS. Wainwright, Francis, tr. & illus. by. 1986. 96p. (J). (gr. 2-4). o.p. (*0-8050-0027-5*, Holt, Henry & Co. Bks. For Young Readers) Holt, Henry & Co.

—The Adventures of Pinocchio. Chiesa, Carol Delia, tr. 2001. (gr. 4-7). 168p. 17.99 (*1-58827-400-4*); 180p. 123.99 (*1-58827-932-4*); 168p. 23.99 (*1-58827-398-9*); 180p. 23.99 (*1-58827-396-2*); 168p. 123.99 (*1-58827-934-0*); 168p. per. 12.99 (*1-58827-401-2*); 180p. per. 119.99 (*1-58827-933-2*); 168p. per. 18.99 (*1-58827-399-7*); 168p. per. 118.99 (*1-58827-935-9*); 180p. per. 19.99 (*1-58827-397-0*) IndyPublish.com.

—The Adventures of Pinocchio. unabr. ed. 1985. (J). audio 21.00 Jimcin Recordings.

—The Adventures of Pinocchio. (J). E-Book 1.95 (*1-57799-814-6*) Logos Research Systems, Inc.

—The Adventures of Pinocchio. E-Book 1.95 (*1-58515-050-9*) MesaView, Inc.

—The Adventures of Pinocchio. 2003. (Twelve-Point Ser.). (J). lib. bdg. 25.00 (*1-58287-248-1*); lib. bdg. 25.00 (*1-58287-732-7*) North Bks.

—The Adventures of Pinocchio. Lucas, Ann Lawson, tr. 2002. (Oxford World's Classics Ser.). (Illus.). 192p. (J). pap. 8.95 (*0-19-280150-3*) Oxford Univ. Pr., Inc.

—The Adventures of Pinocchio. Lucas, Ann L., tr. from ITA. & intro. by. 1996. (World's Classics Ser.). (Illus.). 248p. (J). pap. 8.95 o.p. (*0-19-282340-X*) Oxford Univ. Pr., Inc.

—The Adventures of Pinocchio. (Illustrated Junior Library). (Illus.). 1996. 272p. (YA). 15.95 o.s.i (*0-448-41479-1*); 1965. (J). (gr. 4-6). 2.95 o.p. (*0-448-05471-X*); 1946. 272p. (J). (gr. 4-6). 12.95 o.s.i (*0-448-06001-9*) Penguin Putnam Bks. for Young Readers. (Grosset & Dunlap).

—The Adventures of Pinocchio. 1982. (Illustrated Junior Library). (Illus.). 272p. (J). 5.95 o.p. (*0-448-11001-6*) Putnam Publishing Group, The.

—The Adventures of Pinocchio. 1992. (Pictureback Ser.). (Illus.). 32p. (J). (ps-3). pap. 3.25 o.s.i (*0-679-83466-4*, Random Hse. Bks. for Young Readers) Random Hse. Children's Bks.

—The Adventures of Pinocchio. Harden, E., tr. from ITA. 1988. (Illus.). 144p. (J). (ps up). 18.95 o.s.i (*0-394-82110-6*, Knopf Bks. for Young Readers) Random Hse. Children's Bks.

—The Adventures of Pinocchio. 1990. 6.99 o.p. incl. audio (*0-517-05562-7*) Random Hse. Value Publishing.

—The Adventures of Pinocchio. Chiesa, Carol D., tr. from ITA. 1989. (Illus.). 280p. (J). (gr. 3 up). lib. bdg. 24.95 o.s.i (*0-02-722821-5*, Simon & Schuster Children's Publishing) Simon & Schuster Children's Publishing.

—The Adventures of Pinocchio. Mayer, Marianna, tr. from ITA. 1984. (Illus.). 128p. (J). (gr. 3-6). 14.95 o.p. (*0-02-765310-2*, Simon & Schuster Children's Publishing) Simon & Schuster Children's Publishing.

—The Adventures of Pinocchio. unabr. ed. 2002. (Illus.). 160p. (*0-9688768-0-3*) Simply Read Bks.

—The Adventures of Pinocchio. Canepa, Nancy L., tr. from ITA. 2002. (Illus.). 210p. (J). reprint ed. pap. 12.95 (*1-58642-052-6*, Steerforth Italia) Steerforth Pr.

—The Adventures of Pinocchio. Perella, Nicolas J., tr. & intro. by. 1997. reprint ed. pap. text 19.95 (*0-520-07782-2*) Univ. of California Pr.

—Las Aventuras de Pinocho. (SPA., Illus.). 160p. (YA). 14.95 (*84-7281-190-5*, AF1905) Auriga, Ediciones S.A. ESP. *Dist:* Continental Bk. Co., Inc.

—Las Aventuras de Pinocho. 1995. (SPA.). 196p. (gr. 4-7). per. (*950-581-271-X*) Colihue.

—Las Aventuras de Pinocho. (Coleccion Cuentos Universales). (SPA.). (YA). (gr. 4 up). (*84-261-3145-X*, JV30301) Juventud, Editorial ESP. *Dist:* Lectorum Pubns., Inc.

—Las Aventuras de Pinocho. 2002. (Classics for Young Readers Ser.). (SPA.). (YA). 14.95 (*84-392-0916-9*, EV30602) Lectorum Pubns., Inc.

—Le Avventure di Pinocchio, Level B. (ITA.). pap. 8.95 (*0-88436-050-4*, 55254) EMC/Paradigm Publishing.

—Le Avventure di Pinocchio. Perella, Nicolas J., tr. 1986. (Biblioteca Italiana Ser.: No. 5). 500p. 70.00 o.p. (*0-520-05404-0*) Univ. of California Pr.

—The Commedia Pinocchio. 1989. (Commedia Plays Ser.). 31p. (J). (gr. 1-9). pap. 4.00 (*1-57514-213-9*, 1030) Encore Performance Publishing.

—Pinocchio. 1989. (Illus.). 80p. (J). 19.95 o.p. (*0-8109-1467-0*) Abrams, Harry N. , Inc.

—Pinocchio. 1966. (Airmont Classics Ser.). (Illus.). (J). (gr. 4 up). mass mkt. 1.75 o.p. (*0-8049-0101-5*, CL-101) Airmont Publishing Co., Inc.

—Pinocchio. 22.95 (*0-88411-249-7*) Amereon, Ltd.

—Pinocchio. abr. ed. (J). audio 12.95 (*0-89926-134-5*, 822) Audio Bk. Co.

—Pinocchio. 1975. (Dent's Illustrated Children's Classics Ser.). (Illus.). (J). reprint ed. 5.50 o.p. (*0-460-06923-3*) Biblio Distribution.

—Pinocchio. unabr. ed. (J). 1997. audio 23.95 (*0-7861-1180-1*, 1939); 1989. audio 23.95 (*0-7861-0504-6*, 2004) Blackstone Audio Bks., Inc.

—Pinocchio. unabr. ed. 1991. (J). (gr. 2-7). audio 26.95 (*1-55686-350-0*, 350) Books in Motion.

—Pinocchio. unabr. ed. (Jimcin Recording Ser.). audio 22.00 o.p. 1996. (J). audio 24.00 (*0-7366-3369-3*, 4019) Books on Tape, Inc.

—Pinocchio. 1987. (Children's Classics Ser.). (Illus.). 258p. (J). (gr. 4 up). 10.95 o.p. (*0-681-40315-2*) Borders Pr.

—Pinocchio. abr. ed. (J). audio 12.00 (*1-878427-48-2*, XC448) Cimino Publishing Group.

—Pinocchio. 1996. 171p. (J). (gr. 4-7). mass mkt. 2.99 (*0-8125-6702-1*, Tor Classics) Doherty, Tom Assocs., LLC.

—Pinocchio. 2001. (Young Classics Ser.). (Illus.). 48p. (J). (gr. 1-3). pap. 9.95 (*0-7894-4443-7*, D K Ink) Dorling Kindersley Publishing, Inc.

—Pinocchio. 1998. (Illus.). (J). pap. 1.00 (*0-486-40090-5*) Dover Pubns., Inc.

—Pinocchio. abr. ed. (J). 1986. (gr. 4-6). audio 29.95 o.p. (*0-88646-820-5*, R 7152); 1986. audio 15.95 o.p. (*0-88646-151-0*, 7152); 1992. audio 4.99 (*0-88646-644-X*) Durkin Hayes Publishing Ltd.

—Pinocchio. 2000. (ITA.). (J). pap. 15.95 (*88-452-4182-3*) Fabbri - RCS Libri ITA. *Dist:* Distribooks, Inc.

—Pinocchio. 1993. (Illus.). (J). (gr. 2 up). 15.00 o.p. (*0-688-12450-X*); lib. bdg. 14.93 o.p. (*0-688-12451-8*) HarperCollins Children's Bk. Group.

—Pinocchio. (J). audio 9.95 o.p. (*0-694-50690-7*, CDL5 1262, Caedmon) HarperTrade.

—Pinocchio. 1996. 240p. mass mkt. 4.95 o.s.i (*0-451-52637-6*); 1986. pap. 2.50 (*0-451-51986-8*, Signet Classics) NAL.

—Pinocchio. abr. ed. 1997. (J). audio compact disk 15.98 (*962-634-119-X*, NA211912); audio 13.98 (*962-634-619-1*, NA211914) Naxos of America, Inc. (Naxos AudioBooks).

—Pinocchio. abr. ed. 1996. (Children's Classics Ser.). (J). (ps-3). 6.95 o.p. (*0-7871-1167-8*) NewStar Media, Inc.

—Pinocchio. 1996. (Oxford Illustrated Classics Ser.). (Illus.). 96p. (YA). (gr. 3 up). pap. 11.95 o.p. (*0-19-272287-5*) Oxford Univ. Pr., Inc.

—Pinocchio. l.t. ed. 1999. (J). E-Book 14.99 incl. cd-rom (*1-929077-74-2*, Books OnScreen) PageFree Publishing, Inc.

—Pinocchio. 1996. (Illus.). 48p. (J). (ps-3). 18.95 (*0-399-22941-8*, Philomel); 1996. 272p. pap. 3.99 o.s.i (*0-14-038262-3*, Puffin Bks.); 1996. (Illus.). 272p. (YA). (gr. 4-7). 4.99 (*0-14-036708-X*, Puffin Bks.); 1985. 240p. (J). (gr. 4-6). pap. 3.50 o.p. (*0-14-035037-3*, Puffin Bks.) Penguin Putnam Bks. for Young Readers.

—Pinocchio. 1988. (J). 10.99 o.s.i (*0-517-61815-X*) Random Hse. Value Publishing.

—Pinocchio. 1996. (Bullseye Step into Classics Ser.). (Illus.). 108p. (J). (gr. 2-6). pap. 3.99 o.s.i (*0-679-88071-2*) Random Hse., Inc.

—Pinocchio. unabr. ed. 1991. (J). (gr. 4). audio 35.00 (*1-55690-415-0*, 91221E7) Recorded Bks., LLC.

—Pinocchio. 1985. (Folio - Junior Ser.: No. 283). (FRE., Illus.). 235p. (J). (gr. 5-10). pap. 10.95 (*2-07-033283-7*) Schoenhof's Foreign Bks., Inc.

—Pinocchio. 1997. (Illus.). 60p. (J). 7.98 o.p. (*0-7651-9187-3*) Smithmark Pubs., Inc.

—Pinocchio. unabr. ed. 2002. (J). audio compact disk 26.95 (*1-58472-306-8*, 068, In Audio) Sound Room Pubs., Inc.

—Pinocchio. (Children's Classics Ser.). (J). (ps-3). 1998. audio 13.95 o.p. (*1-55935-190-X*); 1979. pap. 11.95 o.p. incl. audio (*0-88142-377-7*); 1979. pap. 11.95 o.p. incl. audio (*0-88142-377-7*) Soundelux Audio Publishing.

—Pinocchio. 1996. 9.04 (*0-606-11750-4*); 11.04 (*0-606-19880-6*) Turtleback Bks.

—Pinocchio. 1986. (J). (ps up). 16.95 o.p. (*0-88101-058-8*); (Illus.). 160p. 14.95 o.p. (*0-88101-271-8*) Unicorn Publishing Hse., Inc., The.

—Pinocchio. abr. ed. 1996. (Classic Ser.). (J). pap. 10.95 o.s.i incl. audio (*0-14-086242-0*); pap. 10.95 o.s.i incl. audio (*0-14-086242-0*) Viking Penguin. (Penguin AudioBooks).

—Pinocchio. 1998. (Children's Classics). 192p. (J). (gr. 4-7). pap. 3.95 (*1-85326-160-2*, 1602WW) Wordsworth Editions, Ltd. GBR. *Dist:* Advanced Global Distribution Services.

—Pinocchio: A Classic Tale. Moncure, Jane Belk, tr. from SPA. 1988. (Classic Tales Ser.).Tr. of Pinocho. (Illus.). 32p. (J). (ps-3). lib. bdg. 19.93 o.p. (*0-89565-458-X*) Child's World, Inc.

—Pinocchio: Fairy Tales. Tallarico, Tony, ed. 1987. (Tuffy Story Bks.). (Illus.). 32p. (J). (ps-3). 2.95 (*0-89828-334-5*, 83325, Tuffy Bks.) Putnam Publishing Group, The.

—Pinocchio: Storia di un Burattino. 1997. (ITA.). 70p. pap. text 19.50 o.p. (*1-58085-003-0*) Interlingua Foreign Language AudioBooks.

—Pinocchio: Storia di un Burattino. Gibson, Dick, tr. 1997. (ENG & ITA.). 140p. pap. text 29.50 o.p. (*1-58085-004-9*) Interlingua Foreign Language AudioBooks.

—Pinocchio: Storia di un Burattino. 1996. (ITA.). pap. 79.50 incl. audio (*1-58085-451-6*) Interlingua Foreign Language AudioBooks.

—Pinocchio Coloring Book. 1994. (Illus.). (J). (gr. k-3). pap. 2.95 (*0-486-28003-9*) Dover Pubns., Inc.

—Pinocho - La Historica de un Muneco: Pinocchio - Story of a Puppet. (J). (SPA.). pap. 69.50 incl. audio (*1-58085-260-2*); (SPA.). pap. 79.50 incl. audio (*1-58085-261-0*); 1998. (ENG & SPA.). 220p. 29.50 o.p. (*1-58085-015-4*); 1998. 110p. pap. 19.50 o.p. (*1-58085-014-6*) Interlingua Foreign Language AudioBooks.

Collodi, Carlo, contrib. by. Adventures of Pinocchio. 2004. 56p. (J). 9.98 (*0-7624-1713-7*) Running Pr. Bk. Pubs.

Collodi, Carlo & Ajhar, Brian. Pinocchio. unabr. ed. 1996. (Illus.). 40p. (J). (ps-3). per. 19.95 o.p. incl. audio (*0-689-80230-7*, Simon & Schuster Children's Publishing) Simon & Schuster Children's Publishing.

Collodi, Carlo & Blaisdell, Bob. The Adventures of Pinocchio. unabr. ed. 1995. (Children's Thrift Classics Ser.). (Illus.). 96p. (J). reprint ed. pap. text 1.00 (*0-486-28840-4*) Dover Pubns., Inc.

Collodi, Carlo & Mattotti, Lorenzo. Pinocchio. (Illus.). 34p. (J). 3.98 o.p. (*0-8317-3065-X*) Smithmark Pubs., Inc.

Collodi, Carlo, et al. Pinocchio. 1998. (Pair-it Bks.). 32 p. 30.00 (*0-8172-7290-9*) Raintree Pubs.

Coover, Robert. Pinocchio in Venice. 1997. 336p. reprint ed. pap. 13.50 (*0-8021-3485-8*, Grove Pr.) Grove/Atlantic, Inc.

Daly-Weir, Catherine. Pinocchio. 1996. (Illus.). o.p. (*0-679-88058-5*) Random Hse., Inc.

Daughters of St. Paul Staff. Pinocchio. 1976. pap. 1.75 o.s.i (*0-8198-0449-5*) Pauline Bks. & Media.

DiCicco, Gil, illus. Walt Disney's Pinocchio. 1992. (Illustrated Classics Ser.). 96p. (J). 14.95 o.p. (*1-56282-136-9*); lib. bdg. 14.89 o.s.i (*1-56282-137-7*) Disney Pr.

Disney Staff. Pinocchio: Nose for Trouble. 1997. (Disney's "Storytime Treasures" Library: Vol. 13). (Illus.). 44p. (J). (gr. 1-6). 3.49 o.p. (*1-57973-009-4*) Advance Pubs. LLC.

—Pinocchio & the Puppet Theater. 1977. (J). (ps-1). 1.50 o.p. (*0-525-61551-2*, Dutton) Dutton/Plume.

—Pinocchio Bath Book. 1992. (Penguin-Disney Ser.). (J). (ps). 5.98 (*0-453-03028-9*) Viking Penguin.

—Pinocchio Little Library. 1992. (Penguin-Disney Ser.). (J). (ps-3). 5.98 o.p. (*0-453-03027-0*) Viking Penguin.

—Pinocchio on Pleasure Island. 1988. (J). bds. 5.98 o.p. (*0-8317-6880-0*) Smithmark Pubs., Inc.

Disney, Walter Elias. Pinocchio. 1982. (Disney Ser.). (Illus.). 10p. (J). (ps-3). bds. 8.95 o.s.i (*0-671-44899-4*, Golden Bks.) Random Hse. Children's Bks.

Doty, Roy. Gunga Your Din-Din is Ready: Pinocchio was Nosey. 1978. (Illus.). (J). (gr. 3-5). pap. (*0-671-29856-9*, Simon Pulse) Simon & Schuster Children's Publishing.

—Pinocchio Was Nosy: Grandson of Puns, Gags, Quips & Riddles. 1977. (Illus.). (gr. 4-6). lib. bdg. 5.95 o.p. (*0-385-12920-3*) Doubleday Publishing.

Fanelli, Sara. Pinocchio: Picture Box. 1996. (Illus.). 8p. (J). (ps-1). 9.95 o.p. (*0-694-00829-X*, Harper Festival) HarperCollins Children's Bk. Group.

Fior, Jane, et al. Pinocchio. 2001. (Read & Listen Ser.). (Illus.). 32p. (J). (gr. 4-7). pap. 9.99 (*0-7894-6112-9*, D K Ink) Dorling Kindersley Publishing, Inc.

First Little Golden Book Staff. Pinocchio. 9999. (J). o.p. (*0-307-10189-4*, Golden Bks.) Random Hse. Children's Bks.

Fletcher, Steffi. Pinocchio. 2002. (Illus.). 24p. (J). 2.99 (*0-7364-2152-1*, RH/Disney) Random Hse. Children's Bks.

Gardner, J. J. Carlo Collodi's Pinocchio: Digest. 1996. (J). (gr. 4-7). mass mkt. 3.99 (*0-590-92264-5*) Scholastic, Inc.

Gave, Marc. Walt Disney's Pinocchio Fun with Shapes & Sizes. 1992. (Golden Sturdy Bks.). (Illus.). 14p. (J). (ps). bds. o.p. (*0-307-12332-4*, 12332, Golden Bks.) Random Hse. Children's Bks.

Gaylin, Willard. Adam & Eve & Pinocchio: On Being & Becoming Human. 1990. 304p. 18.95 o.p. (*0-670-82601-4*, Viking) Viking Penguin.

Hildebrandt, Greg. Pinocchio. 1988. (J). (ps-3). 5.95 o.p. (*0-88101-078-2*) Unicorn Publishing Hse., Inc., The.

Hildebrandt, Greg, illus. Pinocchio. 1992. (Gateway Classic Ser.). 48p. (J). (gr. 2-5). 6.95 o.p. (*0-88101-267-X*) Unicorn Publishing Hse., Inc., The.

Hillert, Margaret. Pinocchio. 2001. (Margaret Hillerts Fabulous Firsts Ser.). (J). lib. bdg. (*1-59054-166-9*) Fitzgerald Bks.

—Pinocchio. (J). 1985. 4.95 (*0-87895-684-0*); 1981. (Illus.). pap. 5.10 (*0-8136-5603-6*, TK2173); 1981. (Illus.). lib. bdg. 7.95 (*0-8136-5103-4*, TK2172) Modern Curriculum Pr.

Ingoglia, Gina. Pinocchio & the Whale: Walt Disney. (Illus.). (J). (ps-3). 1993. (Very Easy Readers Ser.). 32p. pap. o.p. (*0-307-15975-2*, 15975); 1992. (Golden Book Ser.: Level 1). 40p. o.p. (*0-307-11583-6*, 11583) Random Hse. Children's Bks. (Golden Bks.).

Ingoglia, Gina, adapted by. Walt Disney's Pinocchio. 1992. (Junior Novelization Ser.). (Illus.). 64p. (J). (gr. 2-6). pap. 3.50 o.p. (*1-56282-033-8*) Disney Pr.

Jackson, R. Eugene. Pinocchio: Musical Dramatization of Carlo Collodi's Tale. 1985. (Illus.). 36p. (J). (gr. k-12). pap. 4.50 (*0-88680-245-8*) Clark, I. E. Pubns.

Jennings, Linda M. Pinocchio. 1994. (Favorite Tales Ser.). (Illus.). 28p. (J). 2.99 (*0-7214-5449-6*, Ladybird Bks.) Penguin Group (USA) Inc.

Jones, Claire & Varga, Bob. A Present from Pinocchio. 1995. 35p. (J). (gr. k-5). mass mkt. 4.00 (*1-58193-172-7*) Brown Bag Productions.

Kuglen, Sam. Pinocchio: A Play. 1999. pap. 4.50 (*1-57514-338-0*, 1134) Encore Performance Publishing.

Kunhardt, Dorothy. Rub-a-Dub Bunny. 2003. (Pat the Bunny Ser.). (Illus.). 10p. (J). (ps). vinyl bd. 4.99 (*0-307-10580-6*, Golden Bks.) Random Hse. Children's Bks.

Kunhardt, Dorothy, ed. Pinocchio. deluxe ed. 1999. (J). 100.00 (*1-55709-341-5*) Applewood Bks.

—Pinocchio. 1980. (Illus.). (J). (ps). 1.95 o.p. (*0-525-69521-4*, Dutton) Dutton/Plume.

—Pinocchio. (FRE.). 96p. (J). (gr. k-5). pap. 9.95 (*0-7859-8845-9*) French & European Pubns., Inc.

—Pinocchio. 1987. (Penguin-Disney Ser.). (J). 6.98 o.p. (*0-8317-6889-4*, Viking Children's Bks.) Penguin Putnam Bks. for Young Readers.

—Pinocchio. (Illus.). (J). 2002. lib. bdg. 14.99 (*0-7364-8019-6*, RH/Disney); 1986. o.p. (*0-307-10381-1*, Golden Bks.) Random Hse. Children's Bks.

—Pinocchio. 1988. (Disney Animated Ser.). (J). 5.99 o.p. (*0-517-66198-5*) Random Hse., Inc.

—Pinocchio. 1992. (Penguin-Disney Ser.). (Illus.). 96p. (J). (ps-4). 6.98 o.p. (*0-453-03026-2*) Viking Penguin.

Ladybird Books Staff. Pinocchio. 1997. (Favorite Tale Ser.). (Illus.). 30p. 2.50 o.s.i (*0-7214-5711-8*) Penguin Group (USA) Inc.

Lancy, Michael. Pinocchio II: One Little Puppet. 1983. 68p. pap. 5.00 (*1-890298-36-0*) Centerstage Pr., Inc.

Lipton, Alfred. Pinocchio, Vol. 516. Caban, Janice, ed. & illus. by. rev. ed. 1989. (Once upon a Tale Ser.). 10p. (J). pap. 2.00 (*1-878501-03-8*) Natural Science Industries, Ltd.

Little Golden Books Staff. Pinocchio with 16 Crayons. 9999. (J). (ps-2). pap. o.p. (*0-307-04964-7*, Golden Bks.) Random Hse. Children's Bks.

Lockman, Vic, illus. Pinocchio's Quest: Coloring Book. 2000. 40p. (J). (gr. 2-6). pap. text 2.00 (*1-930367-40-6*, CLP 29650) Christian Liberty Pr.

Malerba, Luigi. Pinocho Con Botas (Pinocchio with Boots) Morábito, Fabio, tr. 1992. (SPA., Illus.). 68p. (J). (gr. 5-6). pap. 5.99 (*968-16-3913-8*) Fondo de Cultura Economica MEX. *Dist:* Continental Bk. Co., Inc.

Marvin, Fred, illus. Pinocchio: Geppetto's Surprise. 1993. (Tiny Changing Pictures Bk.). 10p. (J). (ps). 4.95 (*1-56282-397-3*) Disney Pr.

—Walt Disney's Pinocchio. 1992. (Little Nugget Bks.). 28p. (J). (ps). bds. o.p. (*0-307-12532-7*, 12532, Golden Bks.) Random Hse. Children's Bks.

McEwan, Chris. Pinocchio. 1990. 32p. (J). 14.99 o.s.i (*0-385-41328-9*); 14.95 o.s.i (*0-385-41327-0*) Doubleday Publishing.

Miller, Madge. Pinocchio. 1954. (J). 6.00 (*0-87602-175-5*) Anchorage Pr.

Morris, Neil & Morris, Ting. Pinocchio. 1991. (Evans Illustrated Stories Ser.). (Illus.). 48p. (J). (gr. 2-5). 13.95 o.p. (*0-237-50974-1*) Evans Brothers, Ltd. GBR. *Dist:* Trafalgar Square.

Mouse Works Staff. Pinocchio. 1997. (Illus.). (J). 7.98 (*1-57082-806-7*) Mouse Works.

—Pinocchio - Toy Story, 2. 75th anniv. ed. 1998. 9.99 (*0-7364-0088-5*) Mouse Works.

Nickel. Pinocchio. Date not set. (J). 4.99 (*0-7214-5404-6*) Nickel Pr.

Nuebacher, G. Pinocchio. 1989. (Traditional Fairy Tales Ser.). (Illus.). 32p. (J). (gr. 1-4). 6.95 o.p. (*0-88625-218-0*) Durkin Hayes Publishing Ltd.

Outlet Book Company Staff. Pinocchio. 1987. o.s.i (*0-517-64691-9*) Crown Publishing Group.

—Pinocchio. 1992. (J). 2.99 o.p. (*0-517-08666-2*) Random Hse. Value Publishing.

—Pinocchio-Sticker Book. 1990. 3.99 o.s.i (*0-517-69694-0*) Random Hse. Value Publishing.

Parsons, Virginia. Pinocchio & Geppetto. 1979. (J). (ps-2). o.s.i (*0-07-048531-3*) McGraw-Hill Cos., The.

—Pinocchio & the Money Tree. 1979. (J). (ps-2). text 6.95 o.p. (*0-07-048533-X*) McGraw-Hill Cos., The.

—Pinocchio Goes on Stage. 1979. (J). (ps-2). 4.95 o.s.i (*0-07-048532-1*) McGraw-Hill Cos., The.

—Pinocchio Plays Truant. 1979. (J). (ps-2). 4.95 o.s.i (*0-07-048530-5*) McGraw-Hill Cos., The.

Patri, Angelo. Pinocchio in Africa: Cherubini, 1911. 1995. Orig. Title: Cherubini. (Illus.). 150p. (J). pap. 25.00 (*0-87556-781-9*) Saifer, Albert Pub.

Pearson Education. Pinocchio. 2000. (Penguin Young Reader Ser.). (C). pap. 8.33 (*0-582-42864-5*) Longman Publishing Group.

Pinocchio. 1986. (Talking Bear Tape Ser.). (J). audio 4.95 (*0-89926-205-8*, 918-D) Audio Bk. Co.

Pinocchio. 2002. (Puppy Tales Ser.). (Illus.). 24p. (J). (gr. k-3). 1.49 (*1-57759-260-3*) Dalmatian Pr.

Pinocchio. 2003. (Illus.). 12.99 (*0-7868-3480-3*) Disney Pr.

Pinocchio. 1999. (ITA., Illus.). 24p. (J). (ps-3). pap. 7.95 (*88-8148-258-4*) European Language Institute ITA. *Dist:* Distribooks, Inc., Midwest European Pubns.

Pinocchio. 1992. (Recorder Fun! Ser.). (Illus.). 256p. (J). pap. 9.95 (*0-7935-1659-5*, 00710363) Leonard, Hal Corp.

Pinocchio. (Treasury of Fairy Tales Ser.). (Illus.). (J). 1993. 24p. (gr. 2-5). pap. 3.95 (*1-56144-361-1*); 1992. 32p. (gr. k-2). pap. 1.95 o.s.i (*1-56144-141-4*) Modern Publishing. (Honey Bear Bks.).

Pinocchio. 1997. (Classic Storybook Ser.). (Illus.). 96p. (J). (ps-4). 7.98 o.s.i (*1-57082-047-3*) Mouse Works.

Pinocchio, , 1985. (ITA.). 202p. (YA). pap. 79.50 incl. audio (*1-57970-006-3*, SIT100); pap. 79.50 incl. audio (*1-57970-006-3*, SIT100) Norton Pubs., Inc., Jeffrey /Audio-Forum.

Pinocchio. (FRE.). (J). 15.95 o.p. incl. audio Olivia & Hill Pr., The.

Pinocchio. 9999. (Illus.). (J). (gr. 2-4). (Well-Loved Tales Ser.: Level 2, No. 606D-9). 3.50 o.p. (*0-7214-0589-4*); (French Language Editions Ser.: No. 600-2). (FRE., 3.50 o.p. (*0-7214-1281-5*) Penguin Group (USA) Inc. (Ladybird Bks.).

Pinocchio. 1978. (Three Dimensional Bks.). (J). (gr. 1-4). 5.95 o.p. (*0-8431-0959-9*, Price Stern Sloan) Penguin Putnam Bks. for Young Readers.

Pinocchio. 2004. (J). bds. (*1-4127-0333-6*, 7217811) Publications International, Ltd.

Pinocchio. (J). 1982. (Illus.). (gr. 3-8). 3.95 o.p. (*0-399-20892-5*); 1974. (Illus.). 6p. (gr. k-2). 2.50 o.p. (*0-448-11794-0*); 1973. (gr. k-3). 1.50 o.p. (*0-448-04274-6*) Putnam Publishing Group, The.

Pinocchio. (Little Golden Bks.). (J). 1997. o.p. (*0-307-09340-9*); 1995. (Illus.). 14p. bds. o.p. (*0-307-72332-1*); 1995. (Illus.). 24p. bds. 3.99 o.p. (*0-307-02185-8*, 98066) Random Hse. Children's Bks. (Golden Bks.).

Pinocchio. unabr. ed. 2002. (J). audio compact disk 43.00 (*1-58472-151-0*, Commuters Library) Sound Room Pubs., Inc.

Pinocchio. (J). audio o.p. Soundelux Audio Publishing.

Pinocchio. (J). audio 11.99 (*1-55723-330-6*); audio 11.99 (*1-55723-329-2*); audio compact disk 19.99 (*1-55723-331-4*); audio compact disk 19.99 (*1-55723-439-6*); 1993. 7.99 incl. audio (*1-55723-363-2*); 1992. 14.98 o.p. incl. audio (*1-55723-324-1*) Walt Disney Records.

Pinocchio: Deluxe Read-along with Pop-Ups. (J). 15.98 o.p. incl. audio (*1-55723-325-X*) Walt Disney Records.

Pinocchio: My Coloring Book. (J). 9.98 o.p. (*0-307-08675-5*, 08675, Golden Bks.) Random Hse. Children's Bks.

Pinocchio: The Human Body, Sea Life, The Bedroom. 1999. (ENG & FRE., Illus.). 24p. (J). (ps-5). pap., stu. ed. 4.95 (*88-8148-243-6*) European Language Institute ITA. *Dist:* Midwest European Pubns.

Pinocchio: The Human Body; Sea Life; The Bedroom. 1999. (Lesen Leicht Gemacht Ser.). (ENG & GER., Illus.). 24p. (J). (ps-5). pap. 4.95 (*88-8148-248-7*) European Language Institute ITA. *Dist:* Midwest European Pubns.

Pinocchio: The Story Teller. audio 24.95 (*0-8442-6837-2*, National Textbook Co.) McGraw-Hill/ Contemporary.

Pinocchio: Walt Disney. (Golden Sound Story Bks.). (Illus.). (J). (ps-3). 1992. 24p. o.p. (*0-307-74025-0*, 64025); 1990. o.p. (*0-307-12109-7*); 1988. 24p. pap. o.p. (*0-307-10093-6*); 1988. 36p. pap. o.p. (*0-307-11054-0*) Random Hse. Children's Bks. (Golden Bks.).

Pinocchio Learns the Truth: A Book about Honesty. 1987. (Disney Ser.). (Illus.). 32p. (J). (ps-2). o.p. (*0-307-11670-0*, Golden Bks.) Random Hse. Children's Bks.

Pinocho: The Human Body, Sea Life, the Bedroom. 1999. Tr. of Pinocchio. (ENG & SPA., Illus.). (J). (ps-5). pap. 4.95 (*88-8148-253-3*) European Language Institute ITA. *Dist:* Midwest European Pubns.

Random House Disney Staff. Pinocchio. 2002. (Illus.). (J). 2.99 (*0-7364-2075-4*, RH/Disney) Random Hse. Children's Bks.

—Pinocchio's Nose Grows. 2002. (Step into Reading Bks.). (Illus.). 32p. (J). (gr. k-2). lib. bdg. 11.99 (*0-7364-8001-3*, RH/Disney) Random Hse. Children's Bks.

Riordan, James. Pinocchio. 1988. (Illus.). 96p. (J). (gr. 3 up). 18.95 o.p. (*0-19-279855-3*) Oxford Univ. Pr., Inc.

River, Chatham. Make a Pinocchio String Puppet. 1989. (Make a Model Ser.). (J). 4.99 o.s.i (*0-517-69513-8*) Random Hse. Value Publishing.

Rogland, Robert. Pinocchio's Quest. 2000. (Illus.). 216p. (J). (gr. 4-6). pap. text 8.95 (*1-930367-39-2*, CLP 29650); text 12.95 (*1-930367-55-4*, CLP29651) Christian Liberty Pr.

Slepian, Jan. Pinocchio's Sister. 1995. 122p. (J). (gr. 3-7). 14.95 o.p. (*0-399-22811-X*, Philomel) Penguin Putnam Bks. for Young Readers.

Smith, Maggie, reader. Pinocchio. (J). (ps-2). audio 2.98 (*1-55886-021-5*); audio 3.98 (*1-55886-025-8*) Smarty Pants.

Stone, Dorothy D., adapted by. Pinocchio. 1974. 3.60 (*0-87129-266-1*, P27) Dramatic Publishing Co.

Tyrrell, Melissa. Pinocchio. 2001. (Fairytale Friends Ser.: Vol. 7). (Illus.). 12p. (J). (ps-k). bds. 5.95 (*1-58117-151-X*, Piggy Toes Pr.) Intervisual Bks., Inc.

Walt Disney Productions Staff. Pinocchio's Promise. 1986. (Walt Disney's Fun-to-Read Library Ser.: Vol. 3). (Illus.). 44p. (J). (gr. 1-6). reprint ed. 3.49 o.p. (*1-885222-15-7*) Advance Pubs. LLC.

—Walt Disney's Pinocchio. 1973. (Disney's Wonderful World of Reading Ser.: No. 10). (Illus.). (J). (ps-3). 4.99 o.s.i (*0-394-92626-9*, Random Hse. Bks. for Young Readers) Random Hse. Children's Bks.

Walt Disney's Pinocchio. 2002. (J). spiral bd. (*0-9720651-2-1*) Story Reader, Inc.

Weir, Catherine Daly. Pinocchio. 1996. (Bullseye Step into Classics Ser.). (J). 9.09 o.p. (*0-606-09753-8*) Turtleback Bks.

Wengrow, Arnold & Collodi, Carlo. Pinocchio. 1992. (J). pap. 6.00 (*0-87602-298-0*) Anchorage Pr.

Wunderlich, Richard. The Pinocchio Catalogue: Being a Descriptive Bibliography & Printing History of English Language Translations & Other Renditions Appearing in the United States, 1892-1987, 16. 1988. (Bibliographies & Indexes in World Literature Ser.). 241p. (C). text 78.95 (*0-313-26334-5*, WUP) Greenwood Publishing Group, Inc.

PLUTO (FICTITIOUS CHARACTER)—FICTION

Disney Staff. Detective Pluto. 1989. (J). bds. 5.98 o.p. (*0-8317-2330-0*) Smithmark Pubs., Inc.

Pluto's Big Race. 1990. 48p. (J). pap. 2.24 o.p. incl. audio (*0-553-05627-1*) Bantam Bks.

Walt Disney Productions Staff. Pluto & the Big Race. 1990. (Mickey's Young Readers Library Ser.: Vol. 12). (Illus.). (J). (gr. 1-6). reprint ed. 3.49 o.p. (*1-885222-45-9*) Advance Pubs. LLC.

POCAHONTAS, D. 1617—FICTION

Bulla, Clyde Robert. Pocahontas & the Strangers. 1988. (Illus.). 176p. (J). (gr. 2-6). pap. 2.50 o.p. (*0-590-41711-8*) Scholastic, Inc.

—Pocahontas & the Strangers. 1971. (J). 10.55 (*0-606-03892-2*) Turtleback Bks.

Destiny Calls - Pocahontas. 1995. (Picture Window Ser.). (Illus.). 30p. (J). (ps-4). 9.98 o.p. (*1-57082-241-7*) Mouse Works.

Fontes, Justine. Pocahontas: Disney. 1995. (Big Golden Bks.). (Illus.). 24p. (J). (ps-3). 3.50 o.p. (*0-307-12378-2*, Golden Bks.) Random Hse. Children's Bks.

Gleiter, Jan & Thompson, Kathleen. Pocahontas. 1984. (Story Clippers Ser.). (Illus.). 32p. (J). (gr. 2-5). 32.10 o.p. incl. audio (*0-8172-2240-5*); pap. 9.27 o.p. (*0-8172-2261-8*); pap. 23.95 o.p. (*0-8172-2271-5*); lib. bdg. 19.97 o.p. (*0-8172-2118-2*) Raintree Pubs.

Golden Books Staff. Pocahontas Little Golden Book. 1995. (Illus.). (J). (ps-3). pap. o.p. (*0-307-30282-2*, Golden Bks.) Random Hse. Children's Bks.

Hide & Squeak, Meeko. 1995. (Squeeze Me Bks.). (Illus.). 10p. (J). (ps-1). 6.98 o.p. (*1-57082-100-3*) Mouse Works.

Ingoglia, Gina. Pocahontas. 1997. (Wonderful World of Disney Ser.). (Illus.). 80p. (J). (gr. 3-7). pap. 3.25 (*0-7868-4216-4*) Disney Pr.

—Pocahontas: Illustrated Classic. 1996. (Illus.). 96p. (J). pap. 5.95 o.p. (*0-7868-4050-1*) Disney Pr.

—Pocahontas Illustrated Classic. 1995. (Illustrated Classics Ser.). (Illus.). 96p. (J). 14.95 o.p. (*0-7868-3042-5*); lib. bdg. 15.49 (*0-7868-5023-X*) Disney Pr.

—Pocahontas Junior Novelization. 1995. (Junior Novelization Ser.). (Illus.). 80p. (J). (gr. 2-6). pap. 3.50 o.p. (*0-7868-4036-6*) Disney Pr.

Ingoglia, Gina, tr. Pocahontas Junior Novelization. 1995. (Junior Novelization Ser.). (SPA., Illus.). 80p. (J). (gr. 2-6). pap. 3.50 o.p. (*0-7868-4046-3*) Disney Pr.

Lundell, Margo. Disney's If You Met Pocahontas. 1996. (Golden Look-Look Bks.). (Illus.). 24p. (J). (ps-3). pap. text o.p. (*0-307-12923-3*, Golden Bks.) Random Hse. Children's Bks.

—Hello, Funny Face: Pocahontas. 1995. (Golden Look-Look Bks.). (Illus.). 24p. (J). (ps-3). pap. text o.p. (*0-307-12916-0*, Golden Bks.) Random Hse. Children's Bks.

—Pocahontas: Disney. 1995. (Golden Look-Look Bks.). (Illus.). 24p. (J). (ps-3). pap. o.p. (*0-307-12886-5*, Golden Bks.) Random Hse. Children's Bks.

Marsh, Carole. Pocahontas. 2002. (One Thousand Readers Ser.). (Illus.). 12p. (J). (gr. 2-6). pap. 2.95 (*0-635-01506-4*, 15064) Gallopade International.

—Pocahontas. 1995. (Spanish Classics Ser.). (Illus.). (ps-4). (SPA.). 96p. (J). 7.98 o.p. (*1-57082-116-X*); 96p. (J). 7.98 o.p. (*1-57082-114-3*); 40p. (YA). 5.98 o.p. (*1-57082-115-1*) Mouse Works.

—Pocahontas. (Biographical Stories Ser.). (J). (gr. 1-5). pap. 5.72 o.p. (*0-8114-8304-5*); audio 8.49 o.p. (*0-8114-8339-8*) Raintree Pubs.

—Pocahontas. (Read-Along Ser.). (J). 7.99 incl. audio (*1-55723-739-5*); 7.99 incl. audio (*1-55723-739-5*); audio 11.99 (*1-55723-741-7*); audio compact disk 19.99 (*1-55723-743-3*); 1995. 11.99 incl. audio (*1-55723-745-X*); 1995. audio 11.99 (*1-55723-740-9*); 1995. audio compact disk 19.99 (*1-55723-742-5*) Walt Disney Records.

Mones, Isidre, illus. Pocahontas: Looking for Meeko. 1996. (Follow the Tracks Bk.). 16p. (J). (ps-k). 12.95 (*0-7868-3094-8*) Disney Pr.

O'Dell, Scott. The Serpent Never Sleeps: A Novel of Jamestown & Pocahontas. 1988. 192p. (gr. 7 up). mass mkt. 6.50 (*0-449-70328-2*, Fawcett) Ballantine Bks.

Packard, Mary. Pocahontas - Disney's: Into the Forest. 1995. (Golden Sturdy Bks.). (Illus.). (J). (ps-3). bds. o.p. (*0-307-12474-6*, Golden Bks.) Random Hse. Children's Bks.

Pocahontas: Deluxe Coloring Book. 1995. (J). pap. o.p. (*0-307-05583-3*, Golden Bks.) Random Hse. Children's Bks.

Pocahontas: Giant Coloring Book. 1995. (J). 72p. pap. o.p. (*0-307-08281-4*); pap. o.p. (*0-307-08282-2*) Random Hse. Children's Bks. (Golden Bks.).

Pocahontas: Trace & Color. 1995. (J). pap. o.p. (*0-307-02460-1*, Golden Bks.) Random Hse. Children's Bks.

Pocahontas Little Golden Book. 1995. (Illus.). (J). (ps-3). pap. text 1.99 o.p. (*0-307-30200-8*, Golden Bks.) Random Hse. Children's Bks.

Pocahontas Play-Along. 1995. (J). (ps-3). 22.78 incl. audio (*1-55723-744-1*) Walt Disney Records.

Rebello, Stephen. Art of Pocahontas: A Disney Miniature. 1996. (Disney Miniatures Ser.). (Illus.). 192p. (J). 10.95 o.p. (*0-7868-6211-4*) Hyperion Bks. for Children.

Reece, Colleen L. Pocahontas. unabr. ed. 1996. (Young Reader's Christian Library). (Illus.). 224p. (J). (gr. 3-7). pap. 1.39 o.p. (*1-55748-798-7*) Barbour Publishing, Inc.

Slater, Teddy. Pocahontas: Painting with the Wind: A Book about Colors. 1995. (Illus.). 24p. (J). (ps-k). lib. bdg. 13.49 (*0-7868-5031-0*) Disney Pr.

The Sparkling River. 1995. (Shimmer Book Ser.). 24p. (J). 8.98 o.p. (*1-57082-245-X*) Mouse Works.

Walt Disney's Feature Animation Department Staff. Pocahontas: An Animated Flip Book. 1995. (Illus.). 96p. pap. 3.95 (*0-7868-8061-9*) Hyperion Pr.

POE, EDGAR ALLAN, 1809-1849—FICTION

Avi. The Man Who Was Poe. 1989. 224p. (J). (gr. 6-8). 13.95 o.p. (*0-531-05833-6*); mass mkt. 13.99 o.p. (*0-531-08433-7*) Scholastic, Inc. (Orchard Bks.).

—The Man Who Was Poe. 1997. (J). 11.04 (*0-606-11595-1*) Turtleback Bks.

POKEMON (FICTITIOUS CHARACTERS)—FICTION

Aoki, Toshinao. Pikachu's Day. 1999. (Pokemon Tales Ser.: No. 4). (Illus.). 18p. (YA). (ps-k). bds. 4.95 (*1-56931-386-5*) Viz Communications, Inc.

The Art of Pokemon: The Third Movie. 2001. (Illus.). 64p. (gr. 4-7). pap. 12.95 (*1-56931-633-3*) Viz Communications, Inc.

Brymer, Mark. Pokemon - Showtrax. 2000. audio compact disk 19.95 Leonard, Hal Corp.

Dewin, Howard. Pokemon 4Ever: The Voice of the Forest. 2002. (Pokemon Ser.). (Illus.). 96p. (J). (gr. 2-7). mass mkt. 4.99 (*0-439-38919-4*) Scholastic, Inc.

Dewin, Howie. Mewtwo Returns. movie tie-in ed. 2002. (Pokemon Ser.). (Illus.). 80p. (J). mass mkt. 4.50 (*0-439-38564-4*) Scholastic, Inc.

Golden Books Staff. Mewtwo Strikes Back. 1999. (Illus.). 24p. (J). (ps-3). 2.29 o.s.i (*0-307-98916-X*, Golden Bks.) Random Hse. Children's Bks.

—Mile 3: Next Stop, Orange Islands. 2000. (Pokemon Ser.). (Illus.). 48p. (J). (ps-3). pap. 3.99 o.s.i (*0-307-45412-6*, 45412, Golden Bks.) Random Hse. Children's Bks.

—Where Are You Pikachu? 2000. (Pokemon Ser.). (Illus.). 4p. (J). (ps-3). bds. 12.99 o.s.i (*0-307-33237-3*, 33237, Golden Bks.) Random Hse. Children's Bks.

Golden Books Staff & Muldrow, Diane. Attack of the Prehistoric Pokemon. 1999. (Pokemon Adventure Ser.: No. 2). (Illus.). 24p. (J). (ps-3). pap. 3.99 o.s.i (*0-307-13267-6*, Golden Bks.) Random Hse. Children's Bks.

—Bye, Bye, Butterfree. 1999. (Pokemon Adventure Ser.: No. 1). (Illus.). 24p. (J). (ps-3). pap. 3.99 o.s.i (*0-307-13266-8*, Golden Bks.) Random Hse. Children's Bks.

—Electric Shock Showdown. 2000. (Pokemon Adventure Ser.: No. 3). (Illus.). 24p. (J). (ps-3). pap. 3.99 o.s.i (*0-307-20125-2*, 20125, Golden Bks.) Random Hse. Children's Bks.

Hayahibara, Megumi. Jigglypuff's Magic Lullaby. 2000. (Pokemon Tales Ser.: No. 11). (Illus.). 18p. (YA). (ps-k). bds. 4.95 (*1-56931-442-X*) Viz Communications, Inc.

Heller, Sarah E. Bellossom's Big Battle. 2001. (Pokemon Junior Chapter Bks.: No. 11). (Illus.). 48p. (J). (ps-3). mass mkt. 3.99 (*0-439-23400-X*) Scholastic, Inc.

—A Pokemon Snow-Down. 2001. (Pokemon Junior Chapter Bks.: No. 8). (Illus.). 48p. (J). (ps-3). mass mkt. 3.99 (*0-439-20097-0*) Scholastic, Inc.

—Snorlax Takes a Stand. 2001. (Pokemon Junior Chapter Bks.: No. 9). 48p. (J). (ps-3). mass mkt. 3.99 (*0-439-20098-9*) Scholastic, Inc.

—The Snubbull Blues. 2001. (Pokemon Junior Chapter Bks.: No. 12). (Illus.). 48p. (J). (ps-3). mass mkt. 3.99 (*0-439-23401-8*, Cartwheel Bks.) Scholastic, Inc.

—Two of a Kind. 2000. (Pokemon Junior Chapter Bks.: No. 5). (Illus.). 112p. (J). (ps-3). mass mkt. 3.99 (*0-439-15431-6*) Scholastic, Inc.

Heller, Sarah E. & Batcheller, Keith. Pikachu & Pichu: Pikachu's Apple Company. 2002. (Pokemon Junior Chapter Bks.: No. 14). (Illus.). 48p. (J). (ps-3). mass mkt. 3.99 (*0-439-37212-7*) Scholastic, Inc.

Imakuni, Tomoaki. Come Out, Squirtle! 1999. (Pokemon Tales Ser.: No. 2). (Illus.). 18p. (YA). (ps-k). bds. 4.95 (*1-56931-384-9*) Viz Communications, Inc.

Johnson, Jennifer. All Fired Up: Pokemon the Johto Journeys. 2001. (Pokemon Chapter Bks.: Vol. 22). (Illus.). 96p. (J). (gr. 2-7). mass mkt. 4.50 o.s.i (*0-439-22114-5*) Scholastic, Inc.

—Secrets of the GS Ball. 2001. (Pokemon Chapter Bks.: Vol. 24). 96p. (J). (gr. 2-5). mass mkt. 4.50 (*0-439-22091-2*) Scholastic, Inc.

Kawamura, Kunimi. Lapras Makes a Friend. 2000. (Pokemon Tales Ser.: No. 12). (Illus.). 18p. (YA). (ps-k). bds. 4.95 (*1-56931-443-8*) Viz Communications, Inc.

Kinebuchi, Keiji & Namazaki, Yachiyo. Magnemite's Missions. 2001. (Pokemon Tales Ser.: No. 18). (Illus.). 18p. (J). (ps-k). bds. 4.95 (*1-56931-534-5*, Cadence Bks.) Viz Communications, Inc.

Kizuki, Sumiyashi. Snorlax's Snack. 2000. (Pokemon Tales Ser.: No. 10). (Illus.). 18p. (YA). (ps-k). bds. 4.95 (*1-56931-441-1*) Viz Communications, Inc.

Kusaka, Hidenori. Desperado Pikachu. 2000. (Pokemon Adventures Ser.: Vol. 1). (Illus.). 208p. (J). (gr. 4-7). pap. 13.95 (*1-56931-507-8*, Viz Comics) Viz Communications, Inc.

—The Ghastly Ghosts. 2000. (Pokemon Adventures Ser.: No. 5). (Illus.). 48p. (YA). (gr. 4-7). pap. 5.95 (*1-56931-409-8*, Cadence Bks.) Viz Communications, Inc.

—Legendary Pokemon. 2000. (Pokemon Adventures Ser.: Vol. 2). (Illus.). 208p. (J). (gr. 4-7). pap. 14.95 (*1-56931-508-6*, Viz Comics) Viz Communications, Inc.

—Mysterious Mew. 1999. (Pokemon Adventures Ser.: No. 1). (Illus.). 48p. (YA). (gr. 4-7). pap. 5.95 (*1-56931-387-3*) Viz Communications, Inc.
—Pokemon Adventures: Saffron City Siege. 2001. (Pokemon Chapter Bks.). (Illus.). (J). 20.00 (*0-606-22062-3*) Turtleback Bks.
—The Snorlax Stop. 2000. (Pokemon Adventures Ser.: No. 4). (Illus.). 48p. (YA). (gr. 4-7). pap. 5.95 (*1-56931-408-X*) Viz Communications, Inc.
—Starmie Surprise. 1999. (Pokemon Adventures Ser.: No. 3). (Illus.). 48p. (YA). (gr. 4-7). pap. 5.95 (*1-56931-389-X*) Viz Communications, Inc.
—Wanted: Pikachu. 1999. (Pokemon Adventures Ser.: No. 2). (Illus.). 48p. (YA). (gr. 4-7). pap. 5.95 (*1-56931-388-1*) Viz Communications, Inc.
—Yellow Caballero: A Trainer in Yellow. 2002. (Pokemon Adventures Ser.: Vol. 4). 200p. pap. 13.95 (*1-56931-710-0*) Viz Communications, Inc.
—Yellow Caballero: Dratini of the Deep. 2002. (Pokemon Adventures Ser.: Vol. 4). 48p. pap. 4.95 (*1-56931-725-9*) Viz Communications, Inc.
—Yellow Caballero: Evolution Action. 2002. (Pokemon Adventures Ser.: Vol. 3). 48p. pap. 4.95 (*1-56931-724-0*) Viz Communications, Inc.
—Yellow Caballero: Pikachu's New Partner. 2001. (Pokemon Adventures Ser.). (Illus.). 48p. (gr. 4-7). pap. 2.95 (*1-56931-561-2*) Viz Communications, Inc.
—Yellow Caballero: The Cave Campaign. 2002. (Pokemon Adventures Ser.: No. 6). (Illus.). 192p. pap. 13.95 (*1-59116-028-6*) Viz Communications, Inc.
—Yellow Caballero: The Ice Cage. 2001. (Pokemon Adventures Ser.). (Illus.). 48p. (gr. 4-7). pap. 3.95 (*1-56931-562-0*) Viz Communications, Inc.
—Yellow Caballero: The S. S. Ann Adventure. 2002. (Pokemon Adventures Ser.: Vol. 2). 48p. pap. 4.95 (*1-56931-723-2*) Viz Communications, Inc.
—Yellow Caballero: To Catch a Caterpie. 2002. (Pokemon Adventures Ser.: Vol. 1). 48p. pap. 4.95 (*1-56931-679-1*) Viz Communications, Inc.
Levithan, David. Journey Through the Lost Canyon. 2000. (Pokemon Challenge Ser.: No. 1). 128p. (gr. 4-7). pap. 5.99 (*0-439-15407-3*) Scholastic, Inc.
Michaels, Bill. Meowth, the Big Mouth. 2000. (Pokemon Junior Chapter Bks.: No. 2). (Illus.). 48p. (J). (ps-3). mass mkt. 3.99 (*0-439-15417-0*) Scholastic, Inc.
—Surf's up, Pikachu! 2000. (Pokemon Junior Chapter Bks.: No. 1). (Illus.). 48p. (J). (ps-3). mass mkt. 3.99 (*0-439-15405-7*) Scholastic, Inc.
Michaels, Bill & West, Tracey. Bulbasaur's Bad Day. 2000. (Pokemon Junior Chapter Bks.: No. 4). (Illus.). 112p. (J). (ps-3). mass mkt. 3.99 (*0-439-15427-8*) Scholastic, Inc.
Ono, Toshihiro. Electric Pikachu Boogaloo. 2000. (Pokemon Ser.). (Illus.). 168p. (YA). (gr. 4-7). pap. 12.95 (*1-56931-436-5*) Viz Communications, Inc.
—The Electric Tale of Pikachu! 1999. (Pokemon Ser.). (Illus.). 160p. (YA). (gr. 4-7). pap. 12.95 (*1-56931-378-4*) Viz Communications, Inc.
—Pikachu Shocks Back. 1999. (Pokemon Ser.). (Illus.). 160p. (YA). (gr. 4-7). pap. 12.95 (*1-56931-411-X*, Viz Comics) Viz Communications, Inc.
—Surf's up, Pikachu! 2000. (Pokemon Ser.). (Illus.). 160p. (J). (ps-3). pap. 12.95 (*1-56931-494-2*, Viz Comics) Viz Communications, Inc.
Sacon, Gregg. Good-Bye Lapras. 2001. (Pokemon Junior Chapter Bks.: No. 10). (Illus.). 48p. (J). (ps-3). mass mkt. 3.99 (*0-439-23399-2*) Scholastic, Inc.
—Nidoran's New Friend. 2000. (Pokemon Junior Chapter Bks.: No. 7). (Illus.). 48p. (J). (ps-3). mass mkt. 3.99 (*0-439-20096-2*) Scholastic, Inc.
Shudo, Takeshi. Mewtwo Strikes Back. 1999. (Pokemon Ser.). (Illus.). 109p. (gr. 3-7). mass mkt. 4.99 (*0-439-13741-1*) Scholastic, Inc.
—Mewtwo Strikes Back. 2000. (Pokemon Ser.). (Illus.). 208p. (YA). (gr. 4-7). pap. 15.95 (*1-56931-505-1*, Viz Comics) Viz Communications, Inc.
—Pokemon the Movie 2000: The Power of One. 2001. (Illus.). 208p. (gr. 4-7). pap. 15.95 (*1-56931-572-8*, Cadence Bks.) Viz Communications, Inc.
Sweeny, Sheila. Prize Pokemon. 2001. (Pokemon Chapter Bks.: No. 25). (Illus.). 96p. (J). (gr. 2-7). mass mkt. 4.50 (*0-439-20276-0*) Scholastic, Inc.
—Scyther, Heart of a Champion. 2000. (Pokemon Chapter Bks.: No.12). (Illus.). (J). (gr. 2-7). pap. text 128.88 (*0-439-21190-5*);No. 12. 96p. mass mkt. 4.50 (*0-439-16945-3*) Scholastic, Inc.
Tajin, Satoshi. I Choose You! 1999. (Pokemon Ser.). (Illus.). 128p. (J). (gr. 2-7). pap. 10.95 (*1-56931-455-1*) Viz Communications, Inc.
Takashi, Toshiko. Fly on, Butterfree. 1999. (Pokemon Tales Ser.: No. 7). (Illus.). 18p. (YA). (ps-k). bds. 4.95 (*1-56931-420-9*, Cadence Bks.) Viz Communications, Inc.
Toda, Akihito. Bulbasaur's Trouble. 1999. (Pokemon Tales Ser.: No. 3). (Illus.). 18p. (YA). (ps-k). bds. 4.95 (*1-56931-385-7*) Viz Communications, Inc.
—Charmander Sees a Ghost. 1999. (Pokemon Tales Ser.: No. 1). (Illus.). 18p. (YA). (ps-k). bds. 4.95 (*1-56931-383-0*) Viz Communications, Inc.
—Cyndaquil & the Mystery Hole Vol. 2: Pokemon Gold & Silver Tales. 2002. (Illus.). 18p. pap. 5.50 (*1-56931-658-9*, Viz Comics) Viz Communications, Inc.
—Detective Chikorita Vol. 1: Pokemon Gold & Silver Tales. 2002. (Illus.). 18p. bds. 5.50 (*1-56931-657-0*, Viz Comics) Viz Communications, Inc.
—Meet Mew! 2000. (Pokemon Tales Ser.: No. 9). (Illus.). 18p. (YA). (ps-k). bds. 4.95 (*1-56931-440-3*) Viz Communications, Inc.
—Mewtwo's Watching You! 2001. (Pokemon Tales Ser.: No. 17). (Illus.). 18p. (J). (ps-k). bds. 4.95 (*1-56931-533-7*, Cadence Bks.) Viz Communications, Inc.
—A Star for Tauros. 2001. (Pokemon Tales Ser.: No. 22). (Illus.). 18p. (J). pap. 4.95 (*1-56931-652-X*) Viz Communications, Inc.
—Totodile's One Gulp Vol. 3: Pokemon Gold & Silver Tales. 2002. (Illus.). 18p. bds. 5.50 (*1-56931-729-1*, Viz Comics) Viz Communications, Inc.
Toriyama, Akira. Dragon Ball. (Illus.). 192p. Vol. 6. 2001. (J). pap. 12.95 (*1-56931-637-6*); Vol. 8. 2002. pap. 12.95 (*1-59116-005-7*) Viz Communications, Inc.
—Dragon Ball Z, Vol. 6. 2001. (Illus.). 184p. (J). pap. 12.95 (*1-56931-638-4*) Viz Communications, Inc.
Tsukirino, Yumi. Abra & Kadabra Magic. 2001. (Magical Pokemon Journey Ser.: Bk. 3). (Illus.). 176p. (J). pap. 13.95 (*1-56931-644-9*) Viz Communications, Inc.
—Bulbasaur's Beau. 2001. (Magical Pokemon Journey Ser.: Pt. 4, No. 1). (Illus.). 40p. (J). pap. 4.95 (*1-56931-666-X*) Viz Communications, Inc.
—Cooking with Jigglypuff. 2000. (Magical Pokemon Journey Ser.: No. 2). (Illus.). 40p. (J). (ps-3). pap. 4.95 (*1-56931-456-X*) Viz Communications, Inc.
—Friends & Families. 2001. (Magical Pokemon Journey Ser.: Bk. 4). (Illus.). 176p. (J). pap. 13.95 (*1-56931-645-7*) Viz Communications, Inc.
—How Do You Do, Pikachu? 2000. (Magical Pokemon Journey Ser.: No. 1). (Illus.). 40p. (YA). (ps-3). pap. 4.95 (*1-56931-446-2*) Viz Communications, Inc.
—Love Potion Pursuit. 2001. (Magical Pokemon Journey Ser.: Pt. 4, No. 2). (Illus.). 40p. (J). pap. 4.95 (*1-56931-675-9*) Viz Communications, Inc.
—Magical Pokemon Journey Pt. 5, No. 1: A Date with Wigglytuff. 2002. 48p. pap. 4.95 (*1-56931-678-3*, Viz Comics) Viz Communications, Inc.
—Magical Pokemon Journey Pt. 5, No. 2: Hypnotism. 2nd ed. 2002. 48p. pap. 4.95 (*1-56931-704-6*, Viz Comics) Viz Communications, Inc.
—Magical Pokemon Journey Pt. 5, No. 3: Hazel's Holiday. 3rd ed. 2002. 48p. pap. 4.95 (*1-56931-705-4*, Viz Comics) Viz Communications, Inc.
—Magical Pokemon Journey Pt. 5, No. 4: Magikarp Journey. 2002. 48p. pap. 4.95 (*1-56931-706-2*, Viz Comics) Viz Communications, Inc.
—Magical Pokemon Journey Pt. 5 No. 5: Going Coconuts. 2002. 160p. pap. 13.95 (*1-56931-707-0*, Viz Comics) Viz Communications, Inc.
—One Lone Pikachu. 2001. (Magical Pokemon Journey, Part 3 Ser.: No. 1). (Illus.). 40p. (J). (ps-3). pap. 4.95 (*1-56931-547-7*) Viz Communications, Inc.
—Pokemon Holiday. 2000. (Magical Pokemon Journey Ser.: No. 3). (Illus.). 40p. (J). (ps-3). pap. 4.95 (*1-56931-457-8*) Viz Communications, Inc.
—Pokemon Matchmakers. 2001. (Magical Pokemon Journey Part 2 Ser.). (Illus.). 168p. (gr. 4-7). pap. 13.95 (*1-56931-554-X*) Viz Communications, Inc.
—Pokemon Sleepover. 2001. (Magical Pokemon Journey Ser.: Pt. 4, No. 4). (Illus.). 40p. (J). pap. 4.95 (*1-56931-677-5*) Viz Communications, Inc.
Viz Comics Staff. Pokemon Tales Gift Box: Charmander Sees a Ghost; Come Out, Squirtle; Bulbasaur's Trouble; Pikachu's Day, Set 1. 2000. (Pokemon Tales Ser.: Nos. 1-4). (Illus.). (J). (ps-k). pap. 19.95 (*1-56931-525-6*, Viz Comics) Viz Communications, Inc.
—Pokemon Tales Gift Box: Psyduck's Tongue Twisters; Where's Clefairy's Voice?; Fly on, Butterfree; Dragonite's Christmas, Set 2. 2000. (Pokemon Tales Ser.: Nos. 5-8). (Illus.). (J). (ps-k). pap. 19.95 (*1-56931-526-4*, Viz Comics) Viz Communications, Inc.
Wada, Junko. Diglett's Birthday Party. 2000. (Pokemon Tales Ser.: No. 14). (Illus.). 18p. (J). (ps-k). bds. 4.95 (*1-56931-487-X*) Viz Communications, Inc.
—Dragonite's Christmas. 1999. (Pokemon Tales Ser.: No. 8). (Illus.). 18p. (YA). (ps-k). bds. 4.95 (*1-56931-421-7*, Cadence Bks.) Viz Communications, Inc.
—Eevee's Weather Report. 2000. (Pokemon Tales Ser.: No. 13). (Illus.). 18p. (J). (ps-k). bds. 4.95 (*1-56931-486-1*) Viz Communications, Inc.
—I'm Not Pikachu! 1999. (Pokemon Tales Movie Special Ser.: No. 1). (Illus.). 18p. (YA). (ps-k). bds. 4.95 (*1-56931-422-5*) Viz Communications, Inc.
—Pikachu's Unparalleled Adventure. 2000. (Pokemon Tales Movie Special Ser.: No. 2). (Illus.). 18p. (YA). (ps-k). bds. 4.95 (*1-56931-485-3*) Viz Communications, Inc.
West, Terry M. The Legend of the Ghost Pokemon. 2000. (Pokemon Challenge Ser.: No. 2). (Illus.). 128p. (YA). (gr. 4-7). pap. 5.99 (*0-439-15419-7*) Scholastic, Inc.
West, Tracey. Ash to the Rescue. 2001. (Pokemon Chapter Bks.: No. 23). 96p. (J). (gr. 2-7). mass mkt. 4.50 (*0-439-22092-0*) Scholastic, Inc.
—Attack of the Prehistoric Pokemon. 1999. (Pokemon Chapter Bks.: No. 3). (J). (gr. 2-7). 10.55 (*0-606-19535-1*) Turtleback Bks.
—Charizard, Go! 2000. (Pokemon Chapter Bks.: No. 6). (Illus.). 96p. (J). (gr. 2-7). mass mkt. 4.50 (*0-439-15421-9*) Scholastic, Inc.
—The Four-Star Challenge. 2000. (Pokemon Chapter Bks.: No. 11). (Illus.). 80p. (J). (gr. 2-7). mass mkt. 4.50 (*0-439-16944-5*) Scholastic, Inc.
—Get Well Pikachu. 2004. (Pokemon Readers Ser.: No. 6). (J). mass mkt. 3.99 (*0-439-55991-X*) Scholastic, Inc.
—The Haunted Gym. 2003. (Pokemon Readers Ser.: No. 3). 32p. (J). mass mkt. 3.99 (*0-439-42988-9*) Scholastic, Inc.
—Hoothoot's Haunted Forest. 2001. (Pokemon Junior Chapter Bks.: No. 13). (Illus.). 48p. (J). (gr. k-4). pap. 3.99 (*0-439-32066-6*) Scholastic, Inc.
—I Choose You! 1999. (Pokemon Chapter Bks.: No. 1). (J). (gr. 2-7). 10.65 (*0-606-19568-8*) Turtleback Bks.
—Island of the Giant Pokeman, 1 vol. 1999. (Pokemon Chapter Bks.: Vol. 2). (Illus.). 85p. (J). (gr. 2-5). mass mkt. 4.50 (*0-439-10466-1*) Scholastic, Inc.
—Island of the Giant Pokemon. 1999. (Pokemon Chapter Bks.: No. 2). (Illus.). (J). (gr. 2-7). pap. 11.70 (*0-613-17920-X*) Econo-Clad Bks.
—Island of the Giant Pokemon. 1999. (Pokemon Chapter Bks.: No. 2). (J). (gr. 2-7). 10.55 (*0-606-19570-X*) Turtleback Bks.
—Journey to the Orange Islands. 2000. (Pokemon Chapter Bks.: No. 9). (Illus.). 96p. (J). (gr. 2-7). mass mkt. 4.50 (*0-439-16942-9*) Scholastic, Inc.
—Let It Snow! 2003. (Pokemon Readers Ser.: No. 4). 32p. (J). mass mkt. 3.99 (*0-439-42989-7*) Scholastic, Inc.
—Night in the Haunted Tower. 1999. (Pokemon Chapter Bks.: No. 4). (Illus.). 70p. (J). (gr. 2-7). mass mkt. 4.50 (*0-439-13742-X*) Scholastic, Inc.
—Night in the Haunted Tower. 1999. (Pokemon Chapter Bks.: No. 4). (J). (gr. 2-7). 10.55 (*0-606-19585-8*) Turtleback Bks.
—Pikachu & Pichu in the City, No. 3. 2001. (Pokemon Ser.). (Illus.). 64p. (J). (gr. 1-3). mass mkt. 4.50 (*0-439-29488-6*) Scholastic, Inc.
—Pikachu in Love. 2003. (Pokemon Readers Ser.). (Illus.). 32p. (J). (gr. k-2). mass mkt. 3.99 (*0-439-42990-0*) Scholastic, Inc.
—Pikachu's Rescue Adventure. 2000. (Pokemon Ser.). (Illus.). 64p. (YA). (gr. 4-7). mass mkt. 4.50 (*0-439-19969-7*) Scholastic, Inc.
—Pikachu's Vacation. 1999. (Pokemon Ser.). (Illus.). 65p. (YA). (gr. k-4). mass mkt. 4.50 (*0-439-15986-5*) Scholastic, Inc.
—Pokemon the Movie 2000. 2000. (Pokemon Ser.). (Illus.). 94p. (YA). (gr. 3-7). mass mkt. 4.99 (*0-439-19968-9*) Scholastic, Inc.
—Pokemon 4Ever: The Voice of the Forest Sticker Storybook. 2002. (Pokemon Ser.). (Illus.). 32p. (J). (gr. 1-3). mass mkt. 5.99 (*0-439-38920-8*) Scholastic, Inc.
—Psyduck Ducks Out. 2000. (Pokemon Chapter Bks.: Vol. 15). (Illus.). 96p. (J). (gr. 2-7). mass mkt. 4.50 (*0-439-20091-1*) Scholastic, Inc.
—Race to Danger. 2000. (Pokemon Chapter Bks.: Vol. 13). (Illus.). 96p. (J). (gr. 2-7). mass mkt. 4.50 (*0-439-20089-X*) Scholastic, Inc.
—Return of the Squirtle Squad. 2000. (Pokemon Chapter Bks.: No. 8). (Illus.). 96p. (J). (gr. 2-7). mass mkt. 4.50 (*0-439-15429-4*) Scholastic, Inc.
—Secret of the Pink Pokemon. 2000. (Pokemon Chapter Bks.: No. 10). (Illus.). 96p. (J). (gr. 2-7). mass mkt. 4.50 (*0-439-16943-7*) Scholastic, Inc.
—Splashdown in Cerulean City. 2000. (Pokemon Chapter Bks.: No. 7). (Illus.). 96p. (J). (gr. 2-7). mass mkt. 4.50 (*0-439-15426-X*) Scholastic, Inc.
—Talent Showdown. 2000. (Pokemon Chapter Bks.: Vol. 14). (Illus.). 96p. (J). (gr. 2-7). mass mkt. 4.50 (*0-439-20090-3*) Scholastic, Inc.
—Team Rocket Blasts Off. 2000. (Pokemon Chapter Bks.: No. 5). (Illus.). 96p. (J). (gr. 2-7). mass mkt. 4.50 (*0-439-15418-9*) Scholastic, Inc.
—Teaming up with Totodile. 2001. (Pokemon Chapter Bks.: No. 26). (Illus.). 96p. (J). (gr. 2-7). mass mkt. 4.50 (*0-439-29574-2*, Cartwheel Bks.) Scholastic, Inc.
—Togepi Springs to Action! 2003. (Pokemon Readers Ser.: No. 2). (Illus.). 32p. (J). (gr. k-2). mass mkt. 3.99 (*0-439-42991-9*) Scholastic, Inc.
—Tough Enough. 2002. (Pokemon Chapter Bks.: No. 27). (Illus.). 96p. (J). (gr. 2-7). mass mkt. 4.50 (*0-439-35801-9*) Scholastic, Inc.
—Winner Takes All. 2002. (Pokemon Chapter Bks.: Vol. 28). (Illus.). 96p. (J). (gr. 4-6). mass mkt. 4.50 (*0-439-35802-7*) Scholastic, Inc.
West, Tracey, adapted by. Ash Ketchum, Pokemon Detective. 2001. (Pokemon Chapter Bks.: Vol. 18). (Illus.). 96p. (J). (gr. 2-7). mass mkt. 4.50 (*0-439-20094-6*) Scholastic, Inc.
—Attack of the Prehistoric Pokemon. 1999. (Pokemon Chapter Bks.: No. 3). (Illus.). 71p. (J). (gr. 2-7). mass mkt. 4.50 (*0-439-13550-8*) Scholastic, Inc.
—Catch That Wobbuffet! 2003. (Pokemon Readers Ser.: No. 5). (Illus.). 32p. (J). mass mkt. 3.99 (*0-439-53051-2*) Scholastic, Inc.
—I Choose You! 1999. (Pokemon Chapter Bks.: No. 1). (Illus.). 87p. (J). (gr. 2-7). mass mkt. 4.50 (*0-439-10464-5*) Scholastic, Inc.
West, Tracey & Golden Books Staff. Pikachu's Vacation. 1999. (Pokemon Ser.). (Illus.). 24p. (YA). (ps-3). pap. 3.99 o.s.i (*0-307-13271-4*, Golden Bks.) Random Hse. Children's Bks.
West, Tracey & Michaels, Bill. Save Our Squirtle! 2000. (Pokemon Junior Chapter Bks.: No. 3). (Illus.). 80p. (J). (ps-3). mass mkt. 3.99 (*0-439-15420-0*) Scholastic, Inc.
Yamamoto, Kazuyuki. First Prize for Starmie. 2000. (Pokemon Tales Ser.: No. 15). (Illus.). 18p. (J). (ps-k). bds. 4.95 (*1-56931-489-6*) Viz Communications, Inc.
—Seel to the Rescue. 2000. (Pokemon Tales Ser.: No. 16). (Illus.). 18p. (J). (ps-k). bds. 4.95 (*1-56931-488-8*) Viz Communications, Inc.
Yume, Hajime. Psyduck's Tongue Twisters. 1999. (Pokemon Tales Ser.: No. 5). (Illus.). 18p. (YA). (ps-k). bds. 4.95 (*1-56931-418-7*) Viz Communications, Inc.
—Togepi's Tears. 2001. (Pokemon Tales Ser.: No. 21). (Illus.). 18p. (J). pap. 4.95 (*1-56931-651-1*) Viz Communications, Inc.
—Where's Clefairy's Voice? 1999. (Pokemon Tales Ser.: No. 6). (Illus.). 18p. (YA). (ps-k). bds. 4.95 (*1-56931-419-5*) Viz Communications, Inc.

POLTORATZKY, MARK, 1726?-1789—FICTION

Almedingen, E. M. Young Mark, RS. 1968. (Illus.). (J). (gr. 7 up). 3.75 o.p. (*0-374-38745-1*, Farrar, Straus & Giroux (BYR)) Farrar, Straus & Giroux.

POOH (FICTITIOUS CHARACTER)—FICTION

see Winnie-the-Pooh (Fictitious Character)—Fiction

POPEYE (FICTITIOUS CHARACTER)—FICTION

King Features Syndicate. Popeye & the Magic Flute. 1981. (Little Pops Ser.). (Illus.). 12p. (J). (ps-3). 2.50 o.p. (*0-394-84867-5*) Random Hse., Inc.
—Popeye & the Treasure Hunt. 1981. (Little Pops Ser.). (Illus.). 12p. (J). (ps-3). 2.50 o.p. (*0-394-84864-0*) Random Hse., Inc.
Pearson, Bill. Popeye & His Pals Stay in Shape. Mann, Philip, ed. 1980. (Shape Board Play Bks.). (Illus.). 14p. (J). (gr. k-3). spiral bd. 3.50 o.p. (*0-89828-125-3*, 06007, Tuffy Bks.) Putnam Publishing Group, The.
Penick, Ib. Popeye: A Pop-Up Book. 1981. (Pop-up Books Ser. No. 42). (Illus.). 16p. (J). (ps-3). bds. 5.95 o.s.i (*0-394-84584-6*) Random Hse., Inc.
Sagendorf, Bud. Popeye on Spook Island. 1982. 128p. (J). mass mkt. 1.75 (*0-523-49011-9*, Tor Bks.) Doherty, Tom Assocs., LLC.
Spinner, Stephanie, adapted by. Popeye: A Photo-Storybook Based on the Movie. 1981. (Movie Storybooks Ser.). (Illus.). 64p. (J). (gr. 6-9). lib. bdg. 6.99 o.p. (*0-394-94668-5*); bds. 5.95 o.p. (*0-394-84668-0*) Random Hse. Children's Bks. (Random Hse. Bks. for Young Readers).
Unauthored. Popeye & the Haunted House. 1983. (J). (gr. k-3). 0.99 o.s.i (*0-8431-4132-8*, Price Stern Sloan) Penguin Putnam Bks. for Young Readers.
—Popeye Climbs a Mountain. 1983. (J). (gr. k-3). 0.99 o.p. (*0-8431-4129-8*, Price Stern Sloan) Penguin Putnam Bks. for Young Readers.
Verral, Charles S. Popeye Goes Fishing. 1983. (Warner Brothers Ser.). (J). (gr. k-3). 0.99 o.s.i (*0-8431-4130-1*, Price Stern Sloan) Penguin Putnam Bks. for Young Readers.
Waring, Barbara. Popeye's Big Surprise. 1983. (Warner Brothers Ser.). (J). (gr. k-3). 0.99 o.s.i (*0-8431-4128-X*, Price Stern Sloan) Penguin Putnam Bks. for Young Readers.
Wildman, George, illus. The Popeye Mix or Match Storybook. 1981. (Mix or Match Ser.). 9p. (J). (ps-3). spiral bd. 3.50 o.p. (*0-394-84585-4*) Random Hse., Inc.

POPPLETON (FICTITIOUS CHARACTER)—FICTION

Rylant, Cynthia. Poppleton. ed. 1998. (J). (gr. 1). spiral bd. (*0-616-01776-6*); (gr. 2). spiral bd. (*0-616-01777-4*) Canadian National Institute for the Blind/Institut National Canadien pour les Aveugles.
—Poppleton. 1997. (Poppleton Ser.). (Illus.). (J). (gr. k-3). 56p. pap. 14.95 (*0-590-84782-1*); 72p. mass mkt. 3.99 (*0-590-84783-X*) Scholastic, Inc. (Blue Sky Pr., The).

—Poppleton. 1997. (Poppleton Ser.). (J). (gr. k-3). 10.14 (*0-606-11760-1*) Turtleback Bks.

—Poppleton & Friends. 1997. (Poppleton Ser.). (Illus.). (J). (ps-2). 56p. pap. 15.95 (*0-590-84786-4*); 48p. mass mkt. 3.99 (*0-590-84788-0*) Scholastic, Inc. (Blue Sky Pr., The).

—Poppleton & Friends. 1998. (Poppleton Ser.). (J). (gr. k-3). 10.14 (*0-606-13716-5*) Turtleback Bks.

—Poppleton Everyday. 1998. (Poppleton Ser.). (Illus.). 48p. (J). (gr. k-3). pap. 15.95 (*0-590-84845-3*, Blue Sky Pr., The); mass mkt. 3.99 (*0-590-84853-4*) Scholastic, Inc.

—Poppleton Everyday. 1998. (Poppleton Ser.). (J). (gr. k-3). 10.14 (*0-606-13717-3*) Turtleback Bks.

—Poppleton Forever. 1998. (Poppleton Ser.). (Illus.). 56p. (J). (gr. k-3). pap. 15.95 (*0-590-84843-7*, Blue Sky Pr., The); mass mkt. 3.99 (*0-590-84844-5*) Scholastic, Inc.

—Poppleton Forever. 1998. (Poppleton Ser.). (J). (gr. k-3). 10.14 (*0-606-13718-1*) Turtleback Bks.

—Poppleton in Fall. 1999. (Poppleton Ser.). (Illus.). 56p. (J). (gr. k-3). pap. 15.95 (*0-590-84789-9*); mass mkt. 3.99 (*0-590-84794-5*) Scholastic, Inc. (Blue Sky Pr., The).

—Poppleton in Fall. 1999. (J). (gr. k-3). 10.14 (*0-606-17273-4*) Turtleback Bks.

—Poppleton in Spring. 1999. (Poppleton Ser.). (Illus.). 48p. (J). (gr. k-3). mass mkt. 3.99 (*0-590-84822-4*); pap. 15.95 (*0-590-84818-6*, Blue Sky Pr., The) Scholastic, Inc.

—Poppleton in Spring. 1999. (J). (gr. k-3). 10.14 (*0-606-16594-0*) Turtleback Bks.

—Poppleton in Winter. 2001. (Poppleton Ser.). (Illus.). 56p. (J). mass mkt. 3.99 (*0-590-84838-0*, Blue Sky Pr., The) Scholastic, Inc.

Rylant, Cynthia & Teague, Mark, illus. Poppleton Through & Through. 2000. (Poppleton Ser.). 52p. (J). (gr. k-3). pap. 15.95 (*0-590-84839-9*) Scholastic, Inc.

POPPINS, MARY (FICTITIOUS CHARACTER)—FICTION

Mary Poppins. 1997. (Classic Soundtrack Ser.). (J). (gr. k up). audio 11.99 (*0-7634-0295-8*); audio 11.99 (*0-7634-0294-X*); audio compact disk 19.99 (*0-7634-0297-4*); audio compact disk 19.99 (*0-7634-0296-6*) Walt Disney Records.

Travers, Pamela L. The Complete Mary Poppins, 4 vols. 1976. (Illus.). (J). pap. 17.25 o.p. (*0-15-619810-X*, Voyager Bks./Libros Viajeros) Harcourt Children's Bks.

—Maria Poppina AB ad ZA. Lyne, G. M., tr. 1968. (LAT., Illus.). (YA). (gr. 6 up). 4.95 o.p. (*0-15-252087-2*) Harcourt Children's Bks.

—Mary Poppins. 1981. (J). (gr. 4-7). reprint ed. lib. bdg. 27.95 (*0-89966-390-7*) Buccaneer Bks., Inc.

—Mary Poppins. rev. ed. 1991. 224p. (J). (gr. 4-7). pap. 4.50 o.s.i (*0-440-40406-1*) Dell Publishing.

—Mary Poppins. 1972. (J). pap. 2.25 o.p. (*0-15-657680-5*); 1934. (J). 9.95 o.p. (*0-15-252410-X*); rev. ed. 1997. (Illus.). 224p. (YA). (gr. 3-7). 18.00 (*0-15-252595-5*); 2nd rev. ed. 1997. (Illus.). 224p. (YA). (gr. 3-7). pap. 6.00 (*0-15-201717-8*, Odyssey Classics) Harcourt Children's Bks.

—Mary Poppins. 1997. (J). 100.00 o.s.i (*0-15-252596-3*); 1985. pap. 4.95 o.s.i (*0-15-252409-6*); 1981. (Illus.). 206p. (J). (gr. 3-7). 14.95 (*0-15-252408-8*) Harcourt Trade Pubs.

—Mary Poppins. 1992. (J). (ps-3). audio 11.00 (*1-55994-657-1*) HarperChildren's Audio.

—Mary Poppins. 202p. (J). (gr. 3-5). pap. 6.00 (*0-8072-1536-8*); 2000. (YA). (gr. 3-7). audio 25.00 (*0-8072-8106-9*, YA997CXR); 1999. 202p. (J). (gr. 3-7). pap. 35.00 incl. audio (*0-8072-8082-8*, YA997SP); 1999. 202p. (J). (gr. 3-7). pap. 35.00 incl. audio (*0-8072-8082-8*, YA997SP); 1999. (J). (gr. 4-7). audio 30.00 (*0-8072-8081-X*, YA997CX) Random Hse. Audio Publishing Group. (Listening Library).

—Mary Poppins. 1997. 12.05 (*0-606-12418-7*) Turtleback Bks.

—Mary Poppins & Mary Poppins Comes Back. 1964. (Illus.). (J). (gr. 4-6). 7.50 o.p. (*0-15-252415-0*) Harcourt Children's Bks.

—Mary Poppins & the House Next Door. 1992. (Illus.). 96p. (J). (gr. 4-7). pap. 3.50 o.s.i (*0-440-40656-0*, Yearling) Random Hse. Children's Bks.

—Mary Poppins Comes Back. 1981. (J). reprint ed. lib. bdg. 17.95 (*0-89966-392-3*) Buccaneer Bks., Inc.

—Mary Poppins Comes Back. 1991. 288p. (J). (gr. 4-7). pap. 3.50 o.s.i (*0-440-40418-5*) Dell Publishing.

—Mary Poppins Comes Back. (Illus.). (J). (gr. 3-7). 1997. 320p. 18.00 (*0-15-201718-6*); 1997. 320p. pap. 6.00 (*0-15-201719-4*, Odyssey Classics); 1985. 288p. reprint ed. pap. 5.95 o.s.i (*0-15-657683-X*, Voyager Bks./Libros Viajeros) Harcourt Children's Bks.

—Mary Poppins from A to Z. 1962. (Illus.). (J). (gr. 1-4). 56p. 10.95 o.s.i (*0-15-252590-4*); 4.50 o.p. (*0-15-252591-2*) Harcourt Children's Bks.

—Mary Poppins from A to Z. 1991. 64p. (J). (gr. 4-7). pap. 3.50 o.s.i (*0-440-40526-2*, Yearling) Random Hse. Children's Bks.

—Mary Poppins in Cherry Tree Lane. 1982. (J). 10.95 (*0-440-05137-1*, Delacorte Pr.) Dell Publishing.

—Mary Poppins in Cherry Tree Lane. 1992. 96p. (J). (gr. 3-7). pap. 3.50 o.s.i (*0-440-40637-4*, Yearling) Random Hse. Children's Bks.

—Mary Poppins in the Kitchen: A Cookery Book with a Story. 1991. 128p. (J). (gr. 4-7). pap. 3.50 o.s.i (*0-440-40527-0*, Yearling) Random Hse. Children's Bks.

—Mary Poppins in the Park. 1991. 256p. (J). (gr. 4-7). pap. 3.50 o.s.i (*0-440-40452-5*) Dell Publishing.

—Mary Poppins in the Park. (Illus.). (J). 1997. 288p. (gr. 3-7). 18.00 (*0-15-201716-X*); 1952. 265 p. 11.95 (*0-15-252947-0*); 1985. 235p. (gr. 3-7). reprint ed. pap. 4.95 o.s.i (*0-15-657690-2*, Voyager Bks./Libros Viajeros); 2nd ed. 1997. 288p. (gr. 3-7). pap. 6.00 (*0-15-201721-6*, Odyssey Classics) Harcourt Children's Bks.

—Mary Poppins in the Park. 1988. (Illus.). (J). (gr. 3-7). 16.00 o.p. (*0-8446-6355-7*) Smith, Peter Pub., Inc.

—Mary Poppins Opens the Door. 1981. (J). reprint ed. lib. bdg. 27.95 (*0-89966-391-5*) Buccaneer Bks., Inc.

—Mary Poppins Opens the Door. 1991. 256p. (J). (gr. 4-7). pap. 3.50 o.s.i (*0-440-40432-0*) Dell Publishing.

—Mary Poppins Opens the Door. (Illus.). (gr. 3-7). 1997. 272p. (YA). 18.00 (*0-15-201720-8*); 1985. 288p. (J). reprint ed. pap. 4.95 o.s.i (*0-15-657692-9*, Voyager Bks./Libros Viajeros); 2nd ed. 1997. 272p. (YA). pap. 6.00 (*0-15-201722-4*, Odyssey Classics) Harcourt Children's Bks.

Travers, Pamela L. & Moore-Betty, Maurice. Mary Poppins in the Kitchen: A Cookery Book with a Story. (Illus.). (J). 1978. (gr. 1 up). pap. 4.95 o.s.i (*0-15-657688-0*, Voyager Bks./Libros Viajeros); 1975. 128p. (gr. k up). 6.95 o.s.i (*0-15-252898-9*) Harcourt Children's Bks.

Walt Disney Productions Staff, prod. Let's Fly with Mary Poppins. 1998. (Archive Collections). (J). (ps-3). audio 22.50 (*0-7634-0397-0*) Walt Disney Records.

PORKY PIG (FICTITIOUS CHARACTER)—FICTION

Brosk, Bernie & Golden Books Staff. The Porky Pig's Counting Book. 1990. (Golden Super Shape Book Ser.). (Illus.). 24p. (J). (ps). pap. 3.29 o.s.i (*0-307-10075-8*, Golden Bks.) Random Hse. Children's Bks.

Gilchrist, Brad. You're Too Big, Porky Pig! 1990. (J). 4.98 o.p. (*1-55521-685-4*) Book Sales, Inc.

—You're Too Big, Porky Pig! 1990. (Looney Tunes Library). (Illus.). 12p. (J). (gr. 1-3). 4.95 o.p. (*0-681-40554-6*) Borders Pr.

Robinson, Connie. Porky & the Gasto. l.t. ed. 2001. (Illus.). 30p. (J). (gr. k-3). pap. 7.95 (*1-928632-55-6*) Writers Marketplace:Consulting, Critiquing & Publishing.

POTTER, HARRY (FICTITIOUS CHARACTER)—FICTION

Harry's Glasses, Vol. 7. 2001. (Harry Potter Ser.). 29.94 (*0-439-32358-4*) Scholastic, Inc.

Hedwig the Owl: Harry Potter Journal, Vol. 2. 2000. 144p. (J). pap. 8.99 (*0-439-23654-1*) Scholastic, Inc.

Hogwarts Express, Vol. 8. 2001. (Harry Potter Ser.). 29.94 (*0-439-32359-2*) Scholastic, Inc.

Hogwarts Journal. deluxe ed. 2000. 64p. (J). pap. 12.95 (*0-439-23653-3*) Scholastic, Inc.

Houghton, John. A Closer Look at Harry Potter. 2001. pap. 7.99 o.p. (*0-85476-941-2*) Cook Communications Ministries.

Lightning Bolt, Vol. 6. 2001. (Harry Potter Ser.: 6). 29.94 (*0-439-32357-6*) Scholastic, Inc.

Magical Movie Scenes from Harry Potter & the Sorcerer's Stone: A Poster Book. movie tie-in ed. 2001. (Illus.). 32p. (YA). (gr. 1 up). mass mkt. 6.99 (*0-439-34256-2*) Scholastic, Inc.

Nimbus Two Thousand, Vol. 5. 2001. (Harry Potter Ser.: No. 5). 29.94 (*0-439-32356-8*) Scholastic, Inc.

Rowling, J. K. Harri Potter Maen yr Athronydd. 2003. (WEL.). 300p. (J). pap. 21.95 (*1-58234-827-8*, Bloomsbury Children) Bloomsbury Publishing.

—Harrius Potter et Philosophi Lapis. 2003. (Harry Potter Ser.: Year 1). (LAT., Illus.). 300p. (J). 26.95 o.s.i (*1-58234-825-1*, Bloomsbury Children) Bloomsbury Publishing.

—Harry Potter & the Chamber of Secrets. collector's ed. (Harry Potter Ser.: Year 2). (YA). (gr. 3 up). 1999. audio 38.00 (*0-7366-9130-8*); 2000. audio compact disk 60.00 (*0-7366-5091-1*) Books on Tape, Inc.

—Harry Potter & the Chamber of Secrets. 2003. 464p. (J). pap. 13.95 (*1-59413-001-9*, Wheeler Publishing, Inc.) Gale Group.

—Harry Potter & the Chamber of Secrets. braille ed. 1999. (Harry Potter Ser.: Year 2). 520p. (YA). (gr. 3 up). pap. 17.99 (*0-939173-35-2*) National Braille Pr.

—Harry Potter & the Chamber of Secrets. unabr. ed. (Harry Potter Ser.: Year 2). (gr. 3 up). 2001. (YA). audio compact disk 60.00 (*0-8072-8601-X*); 2000. (YA). audio 44.00 (*0-8072-8207-3*, YA137SP); 2000. (YA). audio 40.00 (*0-8072-8206-5*, LL0160); 1999. (J). audio 35.00 (*0-8072-8191-3*); 1999. (J). audio compact disk 49.95 (*0-8072-8194-8*) Random Hse. Audio Publishing Group. (Listening Library).

—Harry Potter & the Chamber of Secrets. (Harry Potter Ser.). 2003. 352p. (J). 24.95 (*0-439-55489-6*, Levine, Arthur A. Bks.); 2002. (Illus.). 352p. (J). pap. 6.99 (*0-439-42010-5*, Levine, Arthur A. Bks.); 2000. (Illus.). 352p. (YA). (gr. 3 up). pap. 6.99 (*0-439-06487-2*); 1999. (Illus.). viii, 341p. (J). (gr. 3 up). 19.95 (*0-439-06486-4*, Levine, Arthur A. Bks.); 2002. (Illus.). 352p. (J). 75.00 (*0-439-20353-8*, Levine, Arthur A. Bks.) Scholastic, Inc.

—Harry Potter & the Chamber of Secrets. l.t. ed. 2000. (Harry Potter Ser.: Year 2). (Illus.). 464p. (J). (gr. 3 up). 24.95 (*0-7862-2273-5*) Thorndike Pr.

—Harry Potter & the Chamber of Secrets. 2000. (Harry Potter Ser.: Year 2). (YA). (gr. 3 up). 13.04 (*0-606-19181-X*) Turtleback Bks.

—Harry Potter & the Chamber of Secrets with Poster. 2000. (Harry Potter Ser.: Year 2). (Illus.). 16p. (YA). (gr. 3 up). pap. 5.95 (*0-439-21114-X*) Scholastic, Inc.

—Harry Potter & the Goblet of Fire. unabr. ed. 2000. (Harry Potter Ser.: Year 4). (YA). (gr. 3 up). audio 60.00 Blackstone Audio Bks., Inc.

—Harry Potter & the Goblet of Fire. collector's ed. 2000. (Harry Potter Ser.: Year 4). (YA). (gr. 3 up). audio 39.95 (*0-7366-5519-0*); audio 36.00 (*0-7366-5847-5*); audio compact disk 33.95 (*0-7366-5848-3*) Books on Tape, Inc.

—Harry Potter & the Goblet of Fire. 2003. 936p. pap. 14.95 (*1-59413-003-5*, Wheeler Publishing, Inc.) Gale Group.

—Harry Potter & the Goblet of Fire. braille ed. 2000. (Harry Potter Ser.: Year 4). 650p. (YA). (gr. 3 up). pap. 25.95 (*0-939173-37-9*) National Braille Pr.

—Harry Potter & the Goblet of Fire. unabr. ed. (Harry Potter Ser.: Year 4). (gr. 3 up). 2001. (YA). audio compact disk 80.00 (*0-8072-8603-6*); 2000. (J). audio compact disk 69.95 (*0-8072-8259-6*); 2000. (YA). audio 39.95 (*0-8072-8258-8*); 2000. (YA). audio 55.00 (*0-8072-8793-8*, LL0190) Random Hse. Audio Publishing Group. (Listening Library).

—Harry Potter & the Goblet of Fire. (Harry Potter Ser.). 2003. 752p. (J). 30.95 (*0-439-55490-X*, Levine, Arthur A. Bks.); 2002. 752p. (J). (gr. 3 up). pap. 8.99 (*0-439-13960-0*, Levine, Arthur A. Bks.); 2000. (Illus.). 24p. (YA). (gr. 3 up). pap. 5.95 (*0-439-23194-9*); 2000. (Illus.). xi, 734p. (YA). (gr. 3 up). 25.95 (*0-439-13959-7*, Levine, Arthur A. Bks.) Scholastic, Inc.

—Harry Potter & the Goblet of Fire. l.t. ed. 2000. (Harry Potter Ser.: Year 4). (Illus.). 936p. (J). (gr. 3 up). 25.95 (*0-7862-2927-6*) Thorndike Pr.

—Harry Potter & the Order of the Phoenix, 13 vols. braille ed. 2003. (Harry Potter Ser.: 5). (YA). 29.99 (*0-939173-38-7*) National Braille Pr.

—Harry Potter & the Order of the Phoenix. unabr. ed. 2003. audio 45.00 (*0-8072-2030-2*); (J). audio compact disk 90.00 (*0-8072-2031-0*, Listening Library); (Harry Potter Ser.: Year 5). (J). audio 45.00 (*0-8072-2028-0*, Listening Library); (Harry Potter Ser.: Year 5). (J). audio compact disk 75.00 (*0-8072-2029-9*, Listening Library) Random Hse. Audio Publishing Group.

—Harry Potter & the Order of the Phoenix. 2003. (Harry Potter Ser.: Year 5). (Illus.). 896p. (J). (gr. 3-6). 34.99 (*0-439-56761-0*); 29.99 (*0-439-35806-X*); 60.00 (*0-439-56762-9*) Scholastic, Inc.

—Harry Potter & the Order of the Phoenix. l.t. ed. 2003. (Sequel to Harry Potter & the Goblet of Fire Ser.). 1093p. 29.95 (*0-7862-5778-4*) Thorndike Pr.

—Harry Potter & the Prisoner of Azkaban. unabr. ed. 2000. (Harry Potter Ser.: Year 3). (YA). (gr. 3 up). audio 38.00 Blackstone Audio Bks., Inc.

—Harry Potter & the Prisoner of Azkaban. unabr. ed. 2000. (Harry Potter Ser.: Year 3). (YA). (gr. 3 up). audio compact disk 49.46 (*0-7366-5096-2*); audio 31.50 (*0-7366-9131-6*) Books on Tape, Inc.

—Harry Potter & the Prisoner of Azkaban. 2003. 592p. (J). pap. 13.95 (*1-59413-002-7*, Wheeler Publishing, Inc.) Gale Group.

—Harry Potter & the Prisoner of Azkaban. braille ed. 1999. (Harry Potter Ser.: Year 3). (YA). (gr. 3 up). pap. 19.95 (*0-939173-36-0*) National Braille Pr.

—Harry Potter & the Prisoner of Azkaban. 2000. tchr. ed. 9.95 (*1-58130-656-3*); stu. ed. 11.95 (*1-58130-657-1*) Novel Units, Inc.

—Harry Potter & the Prisoner of Azkaban. unabr. ed. (Harry Potter Ser.: Vol. 3). 2002. 448p. audio 52.00 (*0-8072-8316-9*, LYA 160 SP); 2001. (YA). (gr. 3 up). audio compact disk 65.00 (*0-8072-8602-8*); 2000. (YA). (gr. 3 up). audio 46.00 (*0-8072-8315-0*, LL0164); 2000. (YA). (gr. 3 up). audio compact disk 54.95 (*0-8072-8232-4*); 2000. (YA). (gr. 3 up). audio 35.00 (*0-8072-8231-6*) Random Hse. Audio Publishing Group. (Listening Library).

—Harry Potter & the Prisoner of Azkaban. (Harry Potter Ser.). (J). 2003. 448p. 24.95 (*0-439-55492-6*, Levine, Arthur A. Bks.); 2001. (Illus.). 448p. (gr. 3 up). pap. 7.99 (*0-439-13636-9*, Levine, Arthur A. Bks.); 1999. (Illus.). ix, 435p. (gr. 3 up). 19.95 (*0-439-13635-0*) Scholastic, Inc.

—Harry Potter & the Prisoner of Azkaban. l.t. ed. 2000. (Harry Potter Ser.: Year 3). (Illus.). 592p. (YA). (gr. 3 up). 24.95 (*0-7862-2274-3*) Thorndike Pr.

—Harry Potter & the Prisoner of Azkaban. 2001. (Illus.). (J). 13.04 (*0-606-21584-0*) Turtleback Bks.

—Harry Potter & the Sorcerer's Stone. unabr. ed. 1999. (Harry Potter Ser.: Year 1). (YA). (gr. 3 up). audio 37.98 BBC Audiobooks America.

—Harry Potter & the Sorcerer's Stone. unabr. ed. 2000. (Harry Potter Ser.: Year 1). (YA). (gr. 3 up). audio 38.00 Blackstone Audio Bks., Inc.

—Harry Potter & the Sorcerer's Stone. 1997. (Harry Potter Ser.: Year 1). (Illus.). 223p. (YA). (gr. 3 up). pap. (*0-7475-3274-5*) Bloomsbury Publishing, Ltd. GBR. *Dist:* Raincoast Bk. Distribution.

—Harry Potter & the Sorcerer's Stone. unabr. ed. (Harry Potter Ser.: Year 1). (YA). (gr. 3 up). 2000. audio compact disk 49.95 (*0-7366-5092-X*); 1999. audio 33.95 (*0-7366-9000-X*, 4195) Books on Tape, Inc.

—Harry Potter & the Sorcerer's Stone. 2003. 423p. pap. 13.95 (*1-59413-000-0*, Wheeler Publishing, Inc.) Gale Group.

—Harry Potter & the Sorcerer's Stone. unabr. ed. 1999. (Harry Potter Ser.: Year 1). (YA). (gr. 3 up). audio 37.98 Highsmith Inc.

—Harry Potter & the Sorcerer's Stone. unabr. ed. (Harry Potter Ser.: Year 1). 320p. (YA). (gr. 3 up). pap. 62.00 incl. audio (*0-8072-1547-3*); 2001. (Harry Potter Ser.: Year 1). (YA). (gr. 3 up). audio compact disk 60.00 (*0-8072-8600-1*); 2000. (Harry Potter Ser.: Year 1). (YA). (gr. 3 up). pap. 44.00 incl. audio (*0-8072-8119-0*, YYA108SP); 2000. (Harry Potter Ser.: Year 1). (YA). (gr. 3 up). pap. 44.00 incl. audio (*0-8072-8119-0*, YYA108SP); 1999. (J). audio 33.00 o.s.i (*0-8072-8161-1*); 1999. (Harry Potter Ser.: Year 1). (J). (gr. 3 up). audio compact disk 49.95 (*0-8072-8195-6*); 1999. (Harry Potter Ser.: Year 1). (J). (gr. 3 up). audio 35.00 (*0-8072-8175-1*, YA108CXR); 1999. (Harry Potter Ser.: Year 1). (YA). (gr. 3 up). audio 40.00 (*0-8072-8118-2*, LL0146) Random Hse. Audio Publishing Group. (Listening Library).

—Harry Potter & the Sorcerer's Stone. (Harry Potter Ser.). 2003. 320p. (J). 24.95 (*0-439-55493-4*, Levine, Arthur A. Bks.); 2001. 384p. (YA). (gr. 3 up). mass mkt. 6.99 (*0-439-36213-X*); 2000. (Illus.). 16p. (YA). (gr. 3 up). pap. 5.95 (*0-439-21116-6*); 1999. (Illus.). 312p. (YA). (gr. 3 up). pap. 6.99 (*0-590-35342-X*); 1998. (Illus.). 320p. (YA). (gr. 3 up). 19.95 (*0-590-35340-3*, Levine, Arthur A. Bks.); 2000. 320p. (YA). (gr. 3 up). 75.00 (*0-439-20352-X*) Scholastic, Inc.

—Harry Potter & the Sorcerer's Stone. l.t. ed. 1999. (Harry Potter Ser.: Year 1). (Illus.). 422p. (YA). (gr. 3 up). 24.95 (*0-7862-2272-7*) Thorndike Pr.

—Harry Potter & the Sorcerer's Stone. 2001. (Illus.). (J). 13.04 (*0-606-21606-5*); 1999. (Harry Potter Ser.: Year 1). (Illus.). (YA). (gr. 3 up). 12.95 o.p. (*0-606-17233-5*); 1998. (Harry Potter Ser.: Year 1). (YA). (gr. 3 up). 13.04 (*0-606-17097-9*) Turtleback Bks.

—Harry Potter Aur Azkaban Ka Qaidi. Khokhar, Darakhshanda Asghar, tr. 2003. 372p. 12.95 (*0-19-579915-1*) Oxford Univ. Pr., Inc.

—Harry Potter Boxed Set: Harry Potter & the Sorcerer's Stone; Harry Potter & the Chamber of Secrets; Harry Potter & the Prisoner of Azkaban, 3 vols. (Harry Potter Ser.: Years 1-3). (Illus.). (YA). 2002. pap. 21.97 (*0-439-32466-1*); 1999. (gr. 3 up). 55.85 (*0-439-13316-5*) Scholastic, Inc. (Levine, Arthur A. Bks.).

—Harry Potter Boxed Set: Harry Potter & the Sorcerer's Stone; Harry Potter & the Chamber of Secrets; Harry Potter & the Prisoner of Azkaban; Harry Potter & the Goblet of Fire, 4 vols. (Harry Potter Ser.: Years 1-4). 2002. 752p. (YA). (gr. 3 up). pap. 30.96 (*0-439-43486-6*, Levine, Arthur A. Bks.); 2001. 85.80 (*0-439-24954-6*); 2000. (YA). (gr. 3 up). 85.80 (*0-641-06631-7*, Levine, Arthur A. Bks.) Scholastic, Inc.

—Harry Potter Boxed Set: Harry Potter & the Sorcerer's Stone; Harry Potter & the Chamber of Secrets; Harry Potter & the Prisoner of Azkaban; Harry Potter & the Goblet of Fire; Harry Potter & the Order of the Phoenix, 5 vols. ltd. ed. 2003. (Harry Potter Ser.). 2000p. (J). 99.95 (*0-439-61255-1*) Scholastic, Inc.

—Harry Potter Coffret: Harry Potter a l'Ecole des Sorciers; Harry Potter et la Chambre des Secrets; Harry Potter et le Prisonnier d'Azkaban. 1999. (Harry Potter Ser.: Years 1-3). Tr. of Harry Potter

POTTINGER, ROSE RITA (FICTITIOUS CHARACTER)—FICTION

POWERPUFF GIRLS (FICTITIOUS CHARACTERS)—FICTION

Q

QUASIMODO (FICTITIOUS CHARACTER)—FICTION

Bollinger, Marilyn. The Hunchback of Notre Dame: Quasimodo Finds a Friend. 1996. (Magic Touch Talking Bks.). (Illus.). 22p. (J). (ps-2). 19.99 (*1-888208-16-3*) Hasbro, Inc.

Carr, Jan. The Hunchback of Notre Dame: Upside Down & Topsy-Turvy. 1996. (Illus.). 24p. (J). (gr. k-3). 12.89 o.p. (*0-7868-5040-X*); 12.95 o.p. (*0-7868-3090-5*) Disney Pr.

Cuddy, Robbin, illus. The Hunchback of Notre Dame Illustrated Classic. 1996. 96p. (J). 14.95 (*0-7868-3089-1*) Disney Pr.

Disney Staff. The Hunchback of Notre Dame: The Hidden Hero. 1997. (Disney's "Storytime Treasures" Library: Vol. 16). (Illus.). 44p. (J). (gr. 1-6). 3.49 o.p. (*1-57973-012-4*) Advance Pubs. LLC.

Disney Staff, illus. The Hunchback of Notre Dame: An Animated Flip Book. 1996. 96p. (Orig.). pap. 3.95 (*0-7868-8160-7*) Hyperion Pr.

Fontes, Justine. The Hunchback of Notre Dame: Big Golden Book. 1996. (Illus.). 24p. (J). (ps-3). o.p. (*0-307-10378-1*, Golden Bks.) Random Hse. Children's Bks.

Friedman, Michael Jan. Hunchdog of Notre Dame. 1997. (Adventures of Wishbone Ser.: No. 5). (Illus.). 144p. (J). (gr. 2-5). mass mkt. 3.99 o.p. (*1-57064-270-2*, Big Red Chair Bks.) Lyrick Publishing.

—Hunchdog of Notre Dame. l.t. ed. 1999. (Adventures of Wishbone Ser.: No. 5). (Illus.). 139p. (J). (gr. 4 up). lib. bdg. 22.60 (*0-8368-2301-X*) Stevens, Gareth Inc.

Golden Books Staff. The Hunchback of Notre Dame. 1999. (Song Book & Tape Ser.). (J). (ps-3). pap. 6.98 o.p. incl. audio (*0-307-47720-7*, Golden Bks.) Random Hse. Children's Bks.

Harchy, Philippe, illus. The Hunchback of Notre Dame Pop-up Book. 1996. 12p. (J). (gr. k-3). 12.95 o.p. (*0-7868-3091-3*) Disney Pr.

Hugo, Victor. The Hunchback of Notre-Dame. 2000. (Giant Courage Classics Ser.). 704p. (YA). 9.00 o.p. (*0-7624-0563-5*, Courage Bks.) Running Pr. Bk. Pubs.

—The Hunchback of Notre Dame. 1968. (Airmont Classics Ser.). (YA). (gr. 11 up). mass mkt. 2.25 (*0-8049-0162-7*, CL-162) Airmont Publishing Co., Inc.

—The Hunchback of Notre Dame. 1998. (Illustrated Classic Book Ser.). (Illus.). 61p. (J). (gr. 3 up). pap. text 4.95 (*1-56767-247-7*) Educational Insights, Inc.

—The Hunchback of Notre Dame. (Young Collector's Illustrated Classics Ser.). (Illus.). 192p. (J). (gr. 3-7). 9.95 (*1-56156-458-3*) Kidsbooks, Inc.

—The Hunchback of Notre Dame. Hanft, Joshua, ed. 1994. (Great Illustrated Classics Ser.: Vol. 36). (Illus.). 240p. (J). (gr. 3-6). 9.95 (*0-86611-987-6*) Playmore, Inc., Pubs.

—The Hunchback of Notre Dame. 1987. (Regents Illustrated Classics Ser.). 62p. (YA). (gr. 7-12). pap. text 3.75 o.p. (*0-13-448085-6*, 20519) Prentice Hall, ESL Dept.

—The Hunchback of Notre Dame. (Short Classics Ser.). (Illus.). 48p. (J). (gr. 4 up). 1983. pap. 9.27 o.p. (*0-8172-2010-0*); 1981. lib. bdg. 24.26 o.p. (*0-8172-1671-5*) Raintree Pubs.

—The Hunchback of Notre Dame. 1995. (Illus.). 416p. (J). 12.99 o.s.i (*0-517-12375-4*) Random Hse. Value Publishing.

—The Hunchback of Notre Dame. 1995. (Step into Classics Ser.). 112p. (J). (gr. 3-5). pap. 3.99 (*0-679-87429-1*) Random Hse., Inc.

—The Hunchback of Notre Dame. (gr. k-3). 1997. (Illus.). 40p. (J). pap. 15.95 (*0-531-30055-2*, Orchard Bks.); 1996. (YA). mass mkt. 4.50 (*0-590-93808-8*, Scholastic Paperbacks) Scholastic, Inc.

—The Hunchback of Notre Dame. 1996. 112p. (J). (gr. 4-7). per. 4.50 (*0-689-81027-X*, Aladdin) Simon & Schuster Children's Publishing.

—Hunchback of Notre Dame. 2002. (Great Illustrated Classics). (Illus.). 240p. (J). (gr. 3-8). lib. bdg. 21.35 (*1-57765-813-2*, ABDO & Daughters) ABDO Publishing Co.

—The Hunchback of Notre Dame. unabr. ed. 1998. (Wordsworth Classics Ser.). (YA). (gr. 6-12). 5.27 (*0-89061-068-1*, R0681WW) Jamestown.

—The Hunchback of Notre Dame. abr. ed. 2001. (YA). (gr. 5-12). audio 16.95 (*1-56994-529-2*) Monterey Media, Inc.

—The Hunchback of Notre Dame. abr. ed. 1996. (J). 12.98 o.p. (*0-7871-1081-7*); (gr. 4-7). audio 6.95 o.p. (*0-7871-0992-4*, 628697) NewStar Media, Inc.

—The Hunchback of Notre Dame. abr. ed. 1997. (Puffin Classics Ser.). (Illus.). 320p. (YA). (gr. 5-9). pap. 4.99 (*0-14-038253-4*) Penguin Putnam Bks. for Young Readers.

—The Hunchback of Notre Dame. abr. ed. 1996. 288p. (YA). mass mkt. 4.50 o.s.i (*0-440-22675-9*, Dell Books for Young Readers) Random Hse. Children's Bks.

—The Hunchback of Notre Dame Readalong. 1994. (Illustrated Classics Collection). 64p. pap. 14.95 incl. audio (*0-7854-0683-2*, 40399); pap. 13.50 o.p. incl. audio (*1-56103-487-8*) American Guidance Service, Inc.

Hugo, Victor, et al. The Hunchback of Notre Dame. 1997. (Eyewitness Classics Ser.). (Illus.). 64p. (J). (gr. 3-6). pap. 14.95 o.p. (*0-7894-1491-0*) Dorling Kindersley Publishing, Inc.

The Hunchback of Notre Dame. 1996. 96p. pap. 14.95 (*0-7935-6655-X*) Leonard, Hal Corp.

The Hunchback of Notre Dame. 1991. (Short Classics Ser.). 48p. (J). pap. 34.00 (*0-8114-6963-8*) Raintree Pubs.

The Hunchback of Notre Dame. (Read-Along Ser.). (J). 7.99 incl. audio (*1-55723-992-4*); audio 11.99 (*1-55723-986-X*); audio compact disk 19.99 (*1-55723-989-4*); 1996. audio 11.99 (*1-55723-987-8*); 1996. audio compact disk 19.99 (*1-55723-988-6*) Walt Disney Records.

The Hunchback of Notre Dame: My First Read along. 1996. (J). audio 6.98 (*1-55723-999-1*) Walt Disney Records.

The Hunchback of Notre Dame Read-Along. 1996. (J). (*1-55723-993-2*) Walt Disney Records.

Ingoglia, Gina. The Hunchback of Notre Dame. 1996. (Illus.). 96p. (J). lib. bdg. 15.49 (*0-7868-5034-5*) Disney Pr.

—The Hunchback of Notre Dame Junior Novelization. 1996. 96p. (J). (gr. 2-6). pap. 3.95 o.p. (*0-7868-4062-5*) Disney Pr.

Mouse Works Staff. The Hunchback of Notre Dame. 1996. (J). 5.98 o.p. (*1-57082-279-4*); 8p. 5.98 o.p. (*1-57082-273-5*); 96p. 7.98 o.p. (*1-57082-173-9*) Mouse Works.

Sohl, Marcia & Dackerman, Gerald. The Hunchback of Notre Dame: Student Activity Book. 1976. (Now Age Illustrated Ser.). (Illus.). (J). (gr. 4-10). stu. ed. 1.25 (*0-88301-189-1*) Pendulum Pr., Inc.

Van Gool Studio Staff, illus. The Hunchback of Notre Dame. 1995. (Classic Ser.). 64p. (J). (ps-1). 4.98 o.p. (*0-8317-1653-3*) Smithmark Pubs., Inc.

Walt Disney's Feature Animation Department Staff, illus. The Hunchback of Notre Dame Postcard Book. 1996. 64p. (Orig.). pap. 8.95 (*0-7868-8161-5*) Hyperion Pr.

Weingartner, Amy. The Hunchback of Notre Dame. 1996. (Illus.). 48p. pap. text 4.95 o.p. (*0-7851-0225-6*) Marvel Enterprises.

QUI-GON JINN (FICTITIOUS CHARACTER)—FICTION

Cerasini, Marc A. I am a Jedi. 1999. (Star Wars Ser.). (Illus.). (J). (ps-3). pap. 3.99 o.s.i (*0-375-80026-3*) Random Hse., Inc.

Hildebrandt, Greg, et al, illus. Star Wars: Episode I:The Phantom Menace: Great Big Flap Book. 1999. 10p. (J). (ps-3). bds. 12.99 o.s.i (*0-375-80010-7*) Random Hse., Inc.

Lucas, George. The Phantom Menace Movie Storybook. 1999. (Star Wars). (Illus.). 64p. (J). (gr. k-3). pap. 7.99 o.s.i (*0-375-80009-3*) Random Hse., Inc.

Random House Staff. The Phantom Menace Movie Storybook. 1999. (Star Wars Episode I Ser.). (Illus.). 64p. (YA). (gr. k up). 11.99 o.s.i (*0-375-90009-8*, Random Hse. Bks. for Young Readers) Random Hse. Children's Bks.

Venn, Cecilia. Anakin to the Rescue. 1999. (Star Wars). (Illus.). 48p. (J). (gr. 1-3). pap. 4.99 o.s.i (*0-375-80001-8*) Random Hse., Inc.

Venn, Cecilia & Keenan, Sheila. Anakin to the Rescue. 1999. (Star Wars: Step. 2). (Illus.). (J). (gr. 1-3). 11.99 o.s.i (*0-375-90001-2*) Random Hse., Inc.

Watson, Jude. Captive Temple. 2000. (Star Wars Ser.: Bk. 7). (Illus.). 144p. (J). (gr. 4-7). mass mkt. 4.99 (*0-590-51970-0*) Scholastic, Inc.

—Captive Temple. 2000. (Star Wars: Bk. 7). (J). (gr. 4-7). 11.04 (*0-606-19619-6*) Turtleback Bks.

—The Dark Rival. 1999. (Star Wars Ser.: Bk. 2). 122p. (J). (gr. 4-7). mass mkt. 4.99 o.s.i (*0-590-51925-5*) Scholastic, Inc.

—The Day of Reckoning. 2000. (Star Wars Ser.: Bk. 8). (Illus.). 144p. (J). (gr. 4-7). mass mkt. 4.99 (*0-590-52079-2*) Scholastic, Inc.

—The Defenders of the Dead. 1999. (Star Wars Ser.: Bk. 5). 140p. (J). (gr. 4-7). mass mkt. 4.99 (*0-590-51956-5*) Scholastic, Inc.

—The Fight for Truth. 2000. (Star Wars Ser.: Bk. 9). (Illus.). 144p. (J). (gr. 4-7). mass mkt. 4.99 (*0-590-52080-6*) Scholastic, Inc.

—The Fight for Truth. 2000. (Star Wars: Bk. 9). (J). (gr. 4-7). 11.04 (*0-606-19621-8*) Turtleback Bks.

—The Hidden Past. 1999. (Star Wars Ser.: Bk. 3). (Illus.). 138p. (J). (gr. 4-7). mass mkt. 4.99 (*0-590-51933-6*) Scholastic, Inc.

—The Hidden Past. 1999. (Star Wars: No. 3). (J). (gr. 4-7). 11.04 (*0-606-17040-5*) Turtleback Bks.

—Mark of the Crown. 1999. (Star Wars Ser.: Bk. 4). 131p. (J). (gr. 4-7). mass mkt. 4.99 (*0-590-51934-4*) Scholastic, Inc.

—Mark of the Crown. 1999. (Star Wars: Bk. 4). (J). (gr. 4-7). 11.04 (*0-606-19617-X*) Turtleback Bks.

—The Shattered Peace. 2000. (Star Wars Ser.: Bk. 10). (Illus.). 144p. (J). (gr. 3-7). mass mkt. 4.99 (*0-590-52084-9*) Scholastic, Inc.

—The Shattered Peace. 2000. (Star Wars: Bk. 10). (J). (gr. 4-7). 11.04 (*0-606-19615-3*) Turtleback Bks.

—The Uncertain Path. 2000. (Star Wars Ser.: Bk. 6). (Illus.). 144p. (J). (gr. 4-7). mass mkt. 4.99 (*0-590-51969-7*) Scholastic, Inc.

—The Uncertain Path. 2000. (Star Wars: Bk. 6). (J). (gr. 4-7). 11.04 (*0-606-19618-8*) Turtleback Bks.

Wolverton, Dave. The Rising Force. 1999. (Star Wars Ser.: Bk. 1). 171p. (J). (gr. 4-7). mass mkt. 4.99 (*0-590-51922-0*) Scholastic, Inc.

—The Rising Force. 1999. (Star Wars: No. 1). (J). (gr. 4-7). 11.04 (*0-606-16649-1*) Turtleback Bks.

Wrede, Patricia C. Star Wars: Episode I: The Phantom Menace. 1999. (J). (Illus.). 178p. (gr. 3-7). mass mkt. 5.99 (*0-590-01089-1*); mass mkt. 9.95 (*0-439-08706-6*) Scholastic, Inc.

QUIMBY, RAMONA (FICTITIOUS CHARACTER)—FICTION

Cleary, Beverly. Beezus & Ramona. unabr. ed. 1999. (Ramona Ser.). (J). (gr. 3-5). audio 23.00 BBC Audiobooks America.

—Beezus & Ramona. unabr. ed. 1996. (Ramona Ser.). (J). (gr. 3-5). audio 17.95 Blackstone Audio Bks., Inc.

—Beezus & Ramona. 1989. (Ramona Ser.). (J). (gr. 3-5). mass mkt. o.p. (*0-440-80144-3*) Dell Publishing.

—Beezus & Ramona. 1988. (Ramona Ser.). (J). (gr. 3-5). mass mkt. o.s.i (*0-440-80009-9*) Doubleday Publishing.

—Beezus & Ramona. 1955. (Ramona Ser.). (Illus.). 160p. (J). (gr. 4-7). 15.95 (*0-688-21076-7*); lib. bdg. 16.89 (*0-688-31076-1*) HarperCollins Children's Bk. Group.

—Beezus & Ramona. 1990. (Ramona Ser.). (Illus.). 176p. (J). (gr. 3-7). pap. 5.99 (*0-380-70918-X*, Avon Bks.) Morrow/Avon.

—Beezus & Ramona. (Ramona Ser.). 142p. (J). (gr. 3-5). pap. 4.99 (*0-8072-1441-8*); 2000. (J). (gr. 3-5). audio 23.00 o.s.i (*0-8072-7280-9*, YA 822 CX); 2000. (YA). (gr. 4-7). audio 18.00 (*0-8072-7385-6*, TA 822 CXR); 1990. 142p. (J). (gr. 3-5). pap. 28.00 incl. audio (*0-8072-7317-1*, YA 822 SP) Random Hse. Audio Publishing Group. (Listening Library).

—Beezus & Ramona. 1979. (Ramona Ser.). (J). (gr. 3-5). pap. 3.25 o.s.i (*0-440-70665-3*, Dell Books for Young Readers); (Illus.). 160p. pap. 1.75 o.s.i (*0-440-40665-X*, Yearling) Random Hse. Children's Bks.

—Beezus & Ramona. 1995. (Ramona Ser.). (J). (gr. 3-5). audio 21.33 (*0-394-64514-6*) SRA/McGraw-Hill.

—Beezus & Ramona. 9999. (Ramona Ser.). (J). (gr. 3-5). pap. 1.95 o.s.i (*0-590-11828-5*) Scholastic, Inc.

—Beezus & Ramona. 1955. (Ramona Ser.). (J). (gr. 3-5). 11.04 (*0-606-03061-1*) Turtleback Bks.

—The Beezus & Ramona Diary. 1986. (Ramona Ser.). (Illus.). 224p. (J). (gr. 3-5). pap. 11.95 (*0-688-06353-5*, Morrow, William & Co.) Morrow/Avon.

—Ramona & Her Family. (J). Dell Publishing.

—Ramona & Her Father. unabr. ed. 1999. (Ramona Ser.). (J). (gr. 3-5). audio 23.00 BBC Audiobooks America.

—Ramona & Her Father. unabr. ed. 1999. (Ramona Ser.). (J). (gr. 3-5). audio 17.95 Blackstone Audio Bks., Inc.

—Ramona & Her Father. 2002. (Illus.). (J). 13.83 (*0-7587-5636-4*) Book Wholesalers, Inc.

—Ramona & Her Father. (Ramona Ser.). (J). (gr. 3-5). 1983. pap.; 1923. pap. 2.95 o.s.i (*0-440-77241-9*) Dell Publishing.

—Ramona & Her Father. 1977. (Ramona Ser.). (Illus.). 192p. (J). (gr. 3-5). 15.95 (*0-688-22114-9*); lib. bdg. 16.89 (*0-688-32114-3*) HarperCollins Children's Bk. Group.

—Ramona & Her Father. 1990. (Ramona Ser.). (Illus.). 208p. (J). (gr. 3-5). pap. 5.99 (*0-380-70916-3*, Avon Bks.) Morrow/Avon.

—Ramona & Her Father. l.t. ed. 1988. (Ramona Ser.). 155p. (J). (gr. 3-5). reprint ed. lib. bdg. 16.95 o.s.i (*1-55736-076-6*, Cornerstone Bks.) Pages, Inc.

—Ramona & Her Father. (Ramona Ser.). (J). 186p. (gr. 3-5). pap. 4.99 (*0-8072-1439-6*); 2003. (gr. 2). audio 18.00 (*0-8072-1032-3*); 1990. (gr. 4-7). audio 23.00 (*0-8072-7274-4*, YA 820 CX) Random Hse. Audio Publishing Group. (Listening Library).

—Ramona & Her Father. 1979. (Ramona Ser.). (Illus.). 196p. (J). (gr. 3-5). pap. 1.75 o.s.i (*0-440-47241-5*, Yearling) Random Hse. Children's Bks.

—Ramona & Her Father. 1992. (Ramona Ser.). (J). (gr. 3-5). audio 15.95 o.p. (*0-8161-9281-2*) Thorndike Pr.

—Ramona & Her Father. 1977. (Ramona Ser.). (J). (gr. 3-5). 11.00 (*0-606-04522-8*) Turtleback Bks.

—Ramona & Her Mother. unabr. ed. 1999. (Ramona Ser.). (J). (gr. 3-5). audio 23.00 BBC Audiobooks America.

—Ramona & Her Mother. unabr. ed. 1999. (Ramona Ser.). (J). (gr. 3-5). audio 17.95 Blackstone Audio Bks., Inc.

—Ramona & Her Mother. (Ramona Ser.). (J). (gr. 3-5). 1988. pap. o.p. (*0-440-80004-8*); 1980. 208p. pap. 3.25 o.s.i (*0-440-47243-1*); 1923. pap. 3.25 o.s.i (*0-440-77243-5*) Dell Publishing.

—Ramona & Her Mother. 1979. (Ramona Ser.). (Illus.). 208p. (J). (gr. 3-5). 16.99 (*0-688-22195-5*); (ps-3). lib. bdg. 17.89 (*0-688-32195-X*) HarperCollins Children's Bk. Group.

—Ramona & Her Mother. 1990. (Ramona Ser.). (Illus.). 224p. (J). (gr. 3-5). reprint ed. pap. 5.99 (*0-380-70952-X*) Morrow/Avon.

—Ramona & Her Mother. (Ramona Ser.). (J). 208p. (gr. 3-5). pap. 4.99 (*0-8072-1435-3*); 2003. (gr. 2). audio 18.00 (*0-8072-1030-7*); 1990. 186p. (gr. 3-5). pap. 28.00 incl. audio (*0-8072-7314-7*, YA 820 SP); 1989. (gr. 4-7). tchr.'s assessmt. gde. ed. 23.00 incl. audio (*0-8072-7259-0*, YA 815 CX) Random Hse. Audio Publishing Group. (Listening Library).

—Ramona & Her Mother. 1980. (Ramona Ser.). (J). (gr. 3-5). pap. 4.50 (*0-440-70007-8*, Dell Books for Young Readers) Random Hse. Children's Bks.

—Ramona & Her Mother. 1979. (Ramona Ser.). (J). (gr. 3-5). audio 21.33 (*0-394-66099-4*) SRA/McGraw-Hill.

—Ramona & Her Mother. 1979. (Ramona Ser.). (J). (gr. 3-5). 11.00 (*0-606-04781-6*) Turtleback Bks.

—The Ramona Collection, Vol. 2. 2002. pap. 23.96 (*0-06-441006-4*) HarperCollins Children's Bk. Group.

—Ramona Empieza el Curso. 1996. (Ramona Ser.). (SPA.). 176p. (J). (gr. 3-5). 9.95 o.p. (*84-239-2791-1*) Espasa Calpe, S.A. ESP. *Dist:* AIMS International Bks., Inc.

—Ramona Empieza el Curso. 1997. (Ramona Ser.). (SPA., Illus.). 192p. (J). (gr. 3-7). 15.00 (*0-688-15467-0*, MR7552, Greenwillow Bks.) HarperCollins Children's Bk. Group.

—Ramona Empieza el Curso. Bustelo, Gabriela, tr. 1997. (Ramona Ser.). (SPA., Illus.). 224p. (J). (gr. 2-6). pap. 6.99 (*0-688-15487-5*, MR7554, Morrow, William & Co.) Morrow/Avon.

—Ramona Empieza el Curso. 1997. (J). 13.00 (*0-606-11779-2*) Turtleback Bks.

—Ramona Forever. unabr. ed. 1999. (Ramona Ser.). (J). (gr. 3-5). audio 23.00 BBC Audiobooks America.

—Ramona Forever. unabr. ed. 1999. (Ramona Ser.). (J). (gr. 3-5). audio 17.95 Blackstone Audio Bks., Inc.

—Ramona Forever. (Ramona Ser.). (J). (gr. 3-5). 1994. 192p. pap. 1.99 o.s.i (*0-440-21937-X*); 1993. 192p. pap. 1.99 o.s.i (*0-440-21616-8*); 1985. pap. 2.95 o.s.i (*0-440-77210-9*) Dell Publishing.

—Ramona Forever. (Ramona Ser.). (Illus.). (J). 1984. 192p. (gr. 3-5). lib. bdg. 16.89 (*0-688-03786-0*); 1984. 192p. (ps-3). 15.99 (*0-688-03785-2*); 1995. 208p. (gr. 3-5). reprint ed. pap. 5.99 (*0-380-70960-0*, Harper Trophy) HarperCollins Children's Bk. Group.

—Ramona Forever. 1996. (Ramona Ser.). (J). (gr. 3-5). pap. 4.50 (*0-380-72801-X*, Avon Bks.) Morrow/Avon.

—Ramona Forever. 2001. (Ramona Ser.). (J). (gr. 3-5). pap., wbk. ed. (*1-58130-691-1*); pap., wbk. ed. (*1-58130-690-3*) Novel Units, Inc.

—Ramona Forever. l.t. ed. 1989. (Ramona Ser.). 192p. (J). (gr. 3-5). reprint ed. lib. bdg. 16.95 o.s.i (*1-55736-139-8*, Cornerstone Bks.) Pages, Inc.

—Ramona Forever. (Ramona Ser.). (J). 182p. (gr. 3-5). pap. 4.99 (*0-8072-1437-X*); 2003. (gr. 2). audio 18.00 (*0-8072-1028-5*); 1988. 182p. (gr. 3-5). pap. 28.00 incl. audio (*0-8072-7318-X*, YA817SP); 1988. 182p. (gr. 3-5). pap. 28.00 incl. audio (*0-8072-7318-X*, YA817SP); 1988. (gr. 3-5). audio 23.00 (*0-8072-7265-5*, YA 817 CX) Random Hse. Audio Publishing Group. (Listening Library).

—Ramona Forever. (Ramona Ser.). (J). (gr. 3-5). 1988. pap. o.s.i (*0-440-80005-6*, Dell Books for Young Readers); 1985. 192p. pap. 4.50 o.p. (*0-440-47210-5*, Yearling) Random Hse. Children's Bks.

—Ramona Forever. (Ramona Ser.). (J). (gr. 3-5). 1996. 8.60 o.p. (*0-606-09778-3*); 1995. 11.00 (*0-606-08054-6*) Turtleback Bks.

—Ramona la Chinche. 1996. Tr. of Ramona the Pest. (SPA., Illus.). 192p. (J). (ps-3). pap. 5.99 (*0-688-14888-3*, MR2295, Rayo) HarperTrade.

—Ramona la Chinche. Palacios, Argentina, tr. 1984. Tr. of Ramona the Pest. (SPA., Illus.). 192p. (J). (ps-3). 16.95 (*0-688-02783-0*, MR1442, Rayo) HarperTrade.

—Ramona la Chinche. 1996. Tr. of Ramona the Pest. 12.00 (*0-606-10495-X*) Turtleback Bks.

—Ramona la Valiente. 2000. (SPA., Illus.). 124p. pap. 9.95 (*84-239-7099-X*, AV2133) Espasa Calpe, S.A. ESP. *Dist:* Libros Sin Fronteras.
—Ramona Quimby, 4 vols., Set. 1993. (Ramona Ser.). (J). (gr. 3-5). pap. 19.96 (*0-380-72123-6*, Avon Bks.) Morrow/Avon.
—Ramona Quimby, Age 8. l.t. ed. 1987. (Ramona Ser.). (Illus.). 142p. (J). (gr. 3-5). reprint ed. lib. bdg. 14.95 o.p. (*1-55736-000-6*) Bantam Doubleday Dell Large Print Group, Inc.
—Ramona Quimby, Age 8. unabr. ed. 1999. (Ramona Ser.). (J). (gr. 3-5). audio 17.95 Blackstone Audio Bks., Inc.
—Ramona Quimby, Age 8. (Ramona Ser.). (J). (gr. 3-5). 1983. pap. Dell Publishing.
—Ramona Quimby, Age 8. 1988. (Ramona Ser.). (J). (gr. 3-5). pap. o.s.i (*0-440-80012-9*) Doubleday Publishing.
—Ramona Quimby, Age 8. 1994. (Ramona Ser.). (J). (gr. 3-5). pap. 5.60 (*0-87129-330-7*, R54) Dramatic Publishing Co.
—Ramona Quimby, Age 8. 95th ed. 1995. (Ramona Ser.). (J). (gr. 3-5). lib. bdg. 13.25 (*0-15-305205-8*) Harcourt College Pubs.
—Ramona Quimby, Age 8, 4 vols. (Ramona Ser.). (gr. 3-7). 1999. 19.80 (*0-380-81468-4*); 1992. (Illus.). 208p. (J). pap. 5.99 (*0-380-70956-2*, Avon Bks.); 1981. (Illus.). 192p. (J). 16.99 (*0-688-00477-6*, Morrow, William & Co.); 1981. (Illus.). 192p. (J). lib. bdg. 16.89 (*0-688-00478-4*, Morrow, William & Co.) Morrow/Avon.
—Ramona Quimby, Age 8. (Ramona Ser.). (J). (gr. 3-5). 1999. 9.95 (*1-56137-448-2*); 1998. 44p. 11.95 (*1-56137-708-2*, NU7082SP) Novel Units, Inc.
—Ramona Quimby, Age 8. (Ramona Ser.). (J). (gr. 3-5). 190p. pap. 4.99 (*0-8072-1436-1*); 2000. audio 18.00 (*0-8072-7403-8*); 2000. audio 18.00 (*0-8072-7403-8*); 1990. audio 15.95. 1990. audio 23.00 (*0-8072-7262-0*, YA 816 CX); 1989. 190p. pap. 28.00 incl. audio (*0-8072-7320-1*, YA816SP); 1989. 190p. pap. 28.00 incl. audio (*0-8072-7320-1*, YA816SP) Random Hse. Audio Publishing Group. (Listening Library).
—Ramona Quimby, Age 8. 1992. (Ramona Ser.). (J). (gr. 3-5). audio 15.95 o.p. (*0-8161-9280-4*) Thorndike Pr.
—Ramona Quimby, Age 8. 1981. (Ramona Ser.). (J). (gr. 3-5). 11.00 (*0-606-01002-5*) Turtleback Bks.
—Ramona Quimby Boxed Set. 1995. (Ramona Ser.). (Illus.). (J). (gr. 3-7). pap. 19.96 (*0-380-72654-8*, Avon Bks.) Morrow/Avon.
—Ramona Quimby Diary. 1970. (J). pap. 7.95 o.p. (*0-688-06778-6*, Morrow, William & Co.) Morrow/Avon.
—Ramona Quimby Series. unabr. ed. 1996. (J). (gr. 4-7). audio 45.00 (*0-7366-3426-6*, 4071) Books on Tape, Inc.
—Ramona the Brave. unabr. ed. 1997. (Ramona Ser.). (J). (gr. 3-5). audio 23.00 BBC Audiobooks America.
—Ramona the Brave. unabr. ed. 1999. (Ramona Ser.). (J). (gr. 3-5). audio 17.95 Blackstone Audio Bks., Inc.
—Ramona the Brave. 1984. (Ramona Ser.). (J). (gr. 3-5). pap. 2.95 o.s.i (*0-440-77351-2*) Dell Publishing.
—Ramona the Brave. (Ramona Ser.). (Illus.). 192p. (J). (gr. 3-5). 1995. pap. 5.99 (*0-380-70959-7*, Harper Trophy); 1975. 15.99 (*0-688-22015-0*); 1975. lib. bdg. 17.89 (*0-688-32015-5*) HarperCollins Children's Bk. Group.
—Ramona the Brave. 2000. (Ramona Ser.). (J). (gr. 3-5). 9.95 (*1-56137-444-X*) Novel Units, Inc.
—Ramona the Brave. l.t. ed. 1989. (Ramona Ser.). (Illus.). 143p. (J). (gr. 3-5). reprint ed. lib. bdg. 16.95 o.s.i (*1-55736-159-2*, Cornerstone Bks.) Pages, Inc.
—Ramona the Brave. (Ramona Ser.). (J). (gr. 3-5). 190p. pap. 4.99 (*0-8072-1440-X*); 2000. audio 18.00 (*0-8072-7418-6*, YA 821 CXR); 2000. audio 18.00 (*0-8072-7418-6*, YA 821 CXR); 1990. pap. 28.00 incl. audio (*0-8072-7315-5*, YA 821 SP); 1990. audio 23.00 (*0-8072-7277-9*, YA 821 CX) Random Hse. Audio Publishing Group. (Listening Library).
—Ramona the Brave. 1995. (Ramona Ser.). (J). (gr. 3-5). 11.00 (*0-606-08055-4*) Turtleback Bks.
—Ramona the Pest. unabr. ed. 1997. (Ramona Ser.). (J). (gr. 3-5). audio 23.00 BBC Audiobooks America.
—Ramona the Pest. unabr. ed. 1999. (Ramona Ser.). (J). (gr. 3-5). audio 17.95 Blackstone Audio Bks., Inc.
—Ramona the Pest. (Ramona Ser.). (J). (gr. 3-5). 1988. pap. o.p. (*0-440-80051-X*); 1983. pap. 1923. pap. 2.25 o.s.i (*0-440-77209-5*) Dell Publishing.
—Ramona the Pest. 1968. (Ramona Ser.). (Illus.). 192p. (J). (gr. 3-5). 15.99 (*0-688-21721-4*); lib. bdg. 16.89 (*0-688-31721-9*) HarperCollins Children's Bk. Group.
—Ramona the Pest. 1992. (Ramona Ser.). (Illus.). 192p. (J). (gr. 3-5). pap. 5.99 (*0-380-70954-6*, Avon Bks.) Morrow/Avon.
—Ramona the Pest. l.t. ed. 1990. (Ramona Ser.). (Illus.). 175p. (J). (gr. 3-5). reprint ed. lib. bdg. 16.95 o.s.i (*1-55736-158-4*, Cornerstone Bks.) Pages, Inc.
—Ramona the Pest. (Ramona Ser.). (J). (gr. 3-5). 192p. pap. 4.99 (*0-8072-1438-8*); 2000. audio 23.00 o.s.i (*0-8072-7271-X*, YA819CX); 2000. audio 18.00 (*0-8072-7394-5*, YA819); 2000. audio 18.00 (*0-8072-7394-5*, YA819); 1991. 192p. pap. 28.00 incl. audio (*0-8072-7316-3*, YA 819SP) Random Hse. Audio Publishing Group. (Listening Library).
—Ramona the Pest. 1968. (Ramona Ser.). (J). (gr. 3-5). 11.04 (*0-606-00711-3*) Turtleback Bks.
—Ramona y Su Madre. 1996. (Ramona Ser.). (SPA.). 184p. (J). (gr. 4-7). 9.95 (*84-239-2803-9*) Espasa Calpe, S.A. ESP. *Dist:* AIMS International Bks., Inc.
—Ramona y su Madre. 1997. Orig. Title: Ramona & Her Mother. (SPA., Illus.). 184p. (J). (gr. 2-6). pap. 5.95 (*0-688-15486-7*, Morrow, William & Co.) Morrow/Avon.
—Ramona y Su Padre. 10th ed. (SPA., Illus.). 136p. (J). (gr. 3-5). 9.95 (*84-239-9020-6*, EC1443) Espasa Calpe, S.A. ESP. *Dist:* Lectorum Pubns., Inc., Planeta Publishing Corp.
—Ramona y Su Padre. 1996. (SPA.). 160p. (J). (gr. 4-7). 8.95 o.p. (*84-239-2770-9*) Lectorum Pubns., Inc.
—Ramona y Su Padre. 1987. (J). 14.05 o.p. (*0-606-10497-6*) Turtleback Bks.
—Ramona's World. unabr. ed. 1999. (Ramona Ser.). (J). (gr. 3-5). audio 23.00 BBC Audiobooks America.
—Ramona's World. (Ramona Ser.). (J). (gr. 3-5). 2000. audio 18.00; 1999. audio 18.00 (*0-7366-9003-4*) Books on Tape, Inc.
—Ramona's World. 1999. (Ramona Ser.). (Illus.). 192p. (J). (gr. 3-5). lib. bdg. 15.89 (*0-688-16818-3*); lib. bdg. 15.89 (*0-688-16818-3*) HarperCollins Children's Bk. Group.
—Ramona's World. (Ramona Ser.). (Illus.). (J). (gr. 3-5). 2001. 208p. pap. 5.99 (*0-380-73272-6*); 1999. 192p. 15.99 (*0-688-16816-7*, Morrow, William & Co.) Morrow/Avon.
—Ramona's World. (Ramona Ser.). (J). (gr. 3-5). 2001. audio compact disk 28.00 (*0-8072-0509-5*); 2001. audio compact disk 23.00 (*0-8072-0473-0*); 1999. audio 18.00 (*0-8072-8173-5*, YA123CXR); 1999. audio 18.00 (*0-8072-8173-5*, YA123CXR); 1999. 194p. pap. 28.00 incl. audio (*0-8072-8169-7*); 1999. audio 23.00 (*0-8072-8168-9*, YA123CX) Random Hse. Audio Publishing Group. (Listening Library).
—Viva Ramona. 1996. (Ramona Ser). (SPA.). 192p. (J). (gr. 4-7). 11.95 (*84-239-7120-1*) Espasa Calpe, S.A. ESP. *Dist:* AIMS International Bks., Inc.

R

RAFFERTY, MARY ELIZABETH (FICTITIOUS CHARACTER)—FICTION

Nixon, Joan Lowery. The Dark & Deadly Pool. 1993. (J). mass mkt. 3.99 (*0-440-90036-0*) Dell Publishing.
—The Dark & Deadly Pool. 192p. (YA). 2003. (Illus.). (gr. 5). pap. 4.99 (*0-440-41981-6*, Dell Books for Young Readers); 1989. (gr. 7 up). mass mkt. 4.99 (*0-440-20348-1*, Laurel Leaf) Random Hse. Children's Bks.
—The Dark & Deadly Pool. 1987. (Laurel-Leaf Suspense Ser.). (J). 10.55 (*0-606-04194-X*) Turtleback Bks.
—The Weekend Was Murder. 1994. (Law at Work Ser.). 208p. (YA). (gr. 7 up). mass mkt. 4.99 (*0-440-21901-9*) Dell Publishing.
—The Weekend Was Murder. (J). 1993. mass mkt. o.p. (*0-440-90060-3*); 1991. o.s.i (*0-385-30567-2*) Random Hse. Children's Bks. (Dell Books for Young Readers).
—The Weekend Was Murder. 1992. 11.04 (*0-606-06085-5*) Turtleback Bks.
—The Weekend Was Murder! 2003. 208p. (gr. 5). pap. text 4.99 (*0-440-41983-2*, Dell Books for Young Readers) Random Hse. Children's Bks.

REMUS, UNCLE (FICTITIOUS CHARACTER)—FICTION

Frost, A. B., illus. Brer Rabbit: Stories from Uncle Remus. 1941. (J). (gr. 1-5). lib. bdg. 8.79 o.p. (*0-06-020876-7*) HarperCollins Pubs.
Harris, Joel Chandler. Daddy Jake, the Runaway: And Short Stories Told after Dark by Uncle Remus. 1977. (Short Story Index Reprint Ser.). reprint ed. 19.95 (*0-8369-4104-7*) Ayer Co. Pubs., Inc.
—The Favorite Uncle Remus. Van Santvoord, George & Coolidge, Archibald C., eds. 1973. (Illus.). 320p. (J). (gr. 4-6). tchr. ed. 20.00 (*0-395-06800-2*) Houghton Mifflin Co.
—Uncle Remus. 1987. (Illus.). (J). (gr. 3 up). pap. 6.95 o.s.i (*0-8052-0101-7*); 12.95 o.p. (*0-8052-3273-7*) Knopf Publishing Group. (Schocken).
—Uncle Remus: His Songs & His Sayings. Date not set. (J). lib. bdg. 24.95 (*0-8488-0711-1*) Amereon, Ltd.
—Uncle Remus: His Songs & His Sayings. 265p. (J). 18.00 (*0-9645990-0-7*) Historic Pr.-South.
—Uncle Remus: His Songs & His Sayings. 1956. (Thrushwood Bks.). (Illus.). 288p. (J). (gr. 3-9). reprint ed. 3.95 o.p. (*0-448-02382-2*) Putnam Publishing Group, The.
—Uncle Remus: His Songs & His Sayings. Hemenway, Robert, ed. & intro. by. 1982. (American Library). 224p. (J). 10.95 (*0-14-039014-6*, Penguin Classics) Viking Penguin.
—Uncle Remus: Tales. (Illus.). (J). 1992. 207p. 20.00 o.p. (*0-88322-011-3*); 1999. 234p. reprint ed. 30.00 (*0-88322-041-5*) Beehive Pr., The.
—Uncle Remus & Brer Rabbit. 1998. (Illus.). 64p. (J). (gr. 4-7). reprint ed. 19.95 (*1-55709-491-8*) Applewood Bks.
—Uncle Remus & Brer Rabbit. 1986. (J). reprint ed. lib. bdg. 17.95 (*0-89966-540-3*) Buccaneer Bks., Inc.
—Uncle Remus Stories. (J). (gr. 5-6). 24.95 (*0-89190-311-9*) Amereon, Ltd.
—Uncle Remus Stories. 1960. (Illus.). (J). (gr. 3 up). 5.95 o.p. (*0-00-138187-3*) Penguin Group (USA) Inc.
Harris, Joel Chandler & Burgess, Thornton W. Uncle Remus: The Adventures of Grandfather Frog, Set. unabr. ed. 1998. (J). 20.95 incl. audio (*1-55685-616-4*) Audio Bk. Co.
Harris, Joel Chandler & Golden Books Staff. Uncle Remus Stories. Palmer, Marion, ed. 1986. (Walt Disney's Ser.). (Illus.). (J). (gr. 3-5). 2.22 o.s.i (*0-307-15551-X*, Golden Bks.) Random Hse. Children's Bks.
Lester, Julius. The Tales of Uncle Remus: The Adventures of Brer Rabbit. 1999. (Illus.). 160p. (J). (gr. 3-7). pap. 8.99 (*0-14-130347-6*, Puffin Bks.) Penguin Putnam Bks. for Young Readers.
—Uncle Remus: The Complete Tales. Fogelman, Phyllis, ed. 1999. (Illus.). 688p. (J). (ps-3). 35.00 (*0-8037-2451-9*, Dial Bks. for Young Readers) Penguin Putnam Bks. for Young Readers.
Pinkney, Jerry, illus. The Last Tales of Uncle Remus. 1994. 176p. (J). (gr. 2 up). 18.99 o.p. (*0-8037-1303-7*); (ps-4). 18.89 o.s.i (*0-8037-1304-5*) Penguin Putnam Bks. for Young Readers. (Dial Bks. for Young Readers).
—More Tales of Uncle Remus: Further Adventures of Brer Rabbit, His Friends, Enemies & Others. 1988. 160p. (J). (gr. 2 up). 18.99 o.p. (*0-8037-0419-4*); (ps up). 15.89 o.p. (*0-8037-0420-8*) Penguin Putnam Bks. for Young Readers. (Dial Bks. for Young Readers).
—The Tales of Uncle Remus: The Adventures of Brer Rabbit. 1987. (Tales of Uncle Remus Ser.: Vol. I). 176p. (J). (gr. 3-7). 19.99 (*0-8037-0271-X*, Dial Bks. for Young Readers) Penguin Putnam Bks. for Young Readers.
—The Tales of Uncle Remus Vol. I: The Adventures of Brer Rabbit. 1987. 176p. (YA). (ps up). 16.89 o.p. (*0-8037-0272-8*, Dial Bks. for Young Readers) Penguin Putnam Bks. for Young Readers.
Uncle Remus Tales. audio Audio Bk. Co.

REVERE, PAUL, 1735-1818—FICTION

Dell, Pamela. Freedom's Light: A Story about Paul Revere's Midnight Ride. 2002. (Illus.). 48p. (J). lib. bdg. 27.07 (*1-59187-016-X*) Child's World, Inc.
Gormley, Beatrice. Back to Paul Revere. 1994. (Travelers Through Time Ser.: No. 02). 160p. (J). (gr. 4-7). mass mkt. 3.25 o.p. (*0-590-46227-X*) Scholastic, Inc.
Lawson, Robert. Mr. Revere & I. (Illus.). (J). 1988. 152p. (gr. 4-7). pap. 6.99 (*0-316-51729-1*); 1953. (gr. 7-10). 16.95 o.p. (*0-316-51739-9*) Little Brown & Co.
—Mr. Revere & I. 1973. (J). (gr. 3-6). pap. 2.95 o.s.i (*0-440-45897-8*, Yearling) Random Hse. Children's Bks.
Rinaldi, Ann. The Secret of Sarah Revere. (Great Episodes Ser.). 336p. (YA). 2003. pap. 6.95 (*0-15-204684-4*); 1995. (gr. 7 up). 13.00 (*0-15-200393-2*, Gulliver Bks.); 1995. (gr. 7 up). pap. 6.00 o.s.i (*0-15-200392-4*, Gulliver Bks.) Harcourt Children's Bks.
Sargent, Dave & Sargent, Pat. Dan (Dappled Mahogany Bay) Determination #21. 2001. (Saddle Up Ser.). 36p. (J). pap. 6.95 (*1-56763-652-7*); lib. bdg. 22.60 (*1-56763-651-9*) Ozark Publishing.

RICHARD I, KING OF ENGLAND, 1157-1199—FICTION

Blaisdell, Robert & Scott, Walter, Sr. Ivanhoe. 1998. (Children's Thrift Classics). (Illus.). (J). pap. 1.00 (*0-486-40143-X*) Dover Pubns., Inc.
Cadnum, Michael. Forbidden Forest: The Story of Little John & the Robin Hood. 2002. 224p. (J). (gr. 7 up). pap. 17.95 (*0-439-31774-6*, Orchard Bks.) Scholastic, Inc.
Scott, Walter, Sr. Ivanhoe. 1977. (McKay Illustrated Classics Ser.). (gr. 7 up). 7.95 o.p. (*0-679-20394-X*) McKay, David Co., Inc.
—Ivanhoe. 1978. (Illus.). (J). (gr. 4-12). text 7.50 o.p. (*0-88301-327-4*) Pendulum Pr., Inc.
—Ivanhoe. Farr, Naunerle C., ed. 1978. (Now Age Illustrated III Ser.). (Illus.). (J). (gr. 4-12). stu. ed. 1.25 (*0-88301-339-8*); pap. text 2.95 (*0-88301-315-0*) Pendulum Pr., Inc.
—Ivanhoe. Hanft, Josua, ed. 1994. (Great Illustrated Classics Ser.: Vol. 35). (Illus.). 240p. (J). (gr. 3-6). 9.95 (*0-86611-986-8*) Playmore, Inc., Pubs.
—Ivanhoe. 1988. (Short Classics Ser.). (Illus.). 48p. (J). (gr. 4 up). lib. bdg. 24.26 o.p. (*0-8172-2765-2*) Raintree Pubs.
—Ivanhoe. (J). 1997. (Wishbone Classics Ser.: No. 12). (gr. 2-5). 10.04 (*0-606-12105-6*); 1962. 12.00 (*0-606-02708-4*) Turtleback Bks.
—Ivanhoe Readalong. 1994. (Illustrated Classics Collection). 64p. pap. 14.95 incl. audio (*0-7854-0765-0*, 40502) American Guidance Service, Inc.
Scott, Walter, Sr. & Wright, Robin S. Ivanhoe. 1972. 128 P.p. (*0-8212-0471-8*) Little Brown & Co.
Scott, Walter, Sr., et al. Ivanhoe. (Classics Illustrated Ser.). (Illus.). 52p. (YA). pap. 4.95 (*1-57209-023-5*) Classics International Entertainment, Inc.
Tarr, Judith. Pride of Kings. 2001. 464p. pap. 14.95 (*0-451-45847-8*, ROC) NAL.

RICOTTA, RICKY (FICTITIOUS CHARACTER)—FICTION

Pilkey, Dav. Ricky Ricotta's Giant Robot. 2000. (Ricky Ricotta Ser.: No. 1). (Illus.). (J). (ps-3). 112p. pap. 3.99 (*0-590-30720-7*); 111p. pap. 16.95 (*0-590-30719-3*) Scholastic, Inc. (Blue Sky Pr., The).
—Ricky Ricotta's Giant Robot. 2000. (Ricky Ricotta Ser.: No. 1). (J). (ps-3). 10.04 (*0-606-18592-5*) Turtleback Bks.
—Ricky Ricotta's Giant Robot vs. the Mutant Mosquitos from Mercury. 2000. (Ricky Ricotta Ser.: No. 2). (Illus.). (J). (ps-3). 127p. pap. 16.95 (*0-590-30721-5*, Blue Sky Pr., The); 128p. pap. 3.99 (*0-590-30722-3*, Blue Sky Pr., The); pap. text 47.88 (*0-439-21522-6*) Scholastic, Inc.
—Ricky Ricotta's Giant Robot vs. the Mutant Mosquitos from Mercury. 2000. (Ricky Ricotta Ser.: No. 2). (J). (ps-3). 10.04 (*0-606-19604-8*) Turtleback Bks.
—Ricky Ricotta's Giant Robot vs. the Voodoo Vultures from Venus. 2001. (Ricky Ricotta Ser.: No. 3). (Illus.). 112p. (J). (ps-3). pap. 3.99 (*0-439-23625-8*);No. 3. pap. 16.95 (*0-439-23624-X*) Scholastic, Inc.
—Ricky Ricotta's Giant Robot vs. the Voodoo Vultures from Venus. 2001. (Ricky Ricotta Ser.: No. 3). (J). (ps-3). 10.04 (*0-606-20065-7*) Turtleback Bks.
—Ricky Ricotta's Mighty Robot vs. the Jurassic Jackrabbits from Jupiter. 2002. (Ricky Ricotta's Mighty Robot Ser.). (Illus.). 144p. (J). (ps-3). pap. 16.95 (*0-439-37642-4*); pap. 3.99 (*0-439-37643-2*) Scholastic, Inc. (Blue Sky Pr., The).
—Ricky Ricotta's Mighty Robot vs. the Mecha-Monkeys from Mars. 2002. (Ricky Ricotta Ser.: No. 4). (Illus.). 144p. (J). (gr. 2-4). pap. 3.99 (*0-439-25296-2*); (ps-3). pap. 16.95 (*0-439-25295-4*) Scholastic, Inc. (Blue Sky Pr., The).
—Ricky Ricotta's Mighty Robot vs. the Stupid Stinkbugs from Saturn. 2003. (Ricky Ricotta Ser.). 128p. (J). pap. 3.99 (*0-439-37645-9*, Blue Sky Pr., The) Scholastic, Inc.

RIKER, WILLIAM THOMAS (FICTITIOUS CHARACTER)—FICTION

Mason, Jane B. First Contact: The Movie Storybook. 1996. (Star Trek Ser.). (Illus.). 32p. (J). (ps-3). pap. 9.99 (*0-689-80899-2*, Simon Spotlight) Simon & Schuster Children's Publishing.
Vornholt, John. Crossfire. 1996. (Star Trek, The Next Generation: No. 11). (J). (gr. 3-6). 9.09 o.p. (*0-606-11901-9*) Turtleback Bks.
—First Contact. 1996. (Star Trek Ser.: No. 8). (J). (ps-3). 10.04 (*0-606-11883-7*) Turtleback Bks.
Vornholt, John, et al. First Contact. 1996. (Star Trek Ser.: No. 8). (Illus.). 128p. (J). (gr. 8 up). per. 3.99 (*0-671-00128-0*, Aladdin) Simon & Schuster Children's Publishing.

ROBERT I, KING OF SCOTS, 1274-1329—FICTION

Hunter, Mollie. The King's Swift Rider: A Novel on Robert the Bruce. 2000. (Illus.). 336p. (J). (gr. 7 up). pap. 5.95 (*0-06-447216-7*, Harper Trophy) HarperCollins Children's Bk. Group.
—The King's Swift Rider: A Novel on Robert the Bruce. 1998. 256p. (J). (gr. 7 up). 16.95 (*0-06-027186-8*) HarperCollins Pubs.
—The King's Swift Rider: A Novel on Robert the Bruce. 2000. (Illus.). (J). 12.00 (*0-606-18701-4*) Turtleback Bks.

ROBINSON, JACKIE, 1919-1972—FICTION

Cohen, Barbara. Thank You, Jackie Robinson. annuals (Illus.). 128p. (J). 1997. (ps-3). pap. 4.99 (*0-688-15293-7*, Harper Trophy); 1988. (gr. 3-6). 15.00 o.p. (*0-688-07909-1*) HarperCollins Children's Bk. Group.

—Thank You, Jackie Robinson. 1989. 128p. (J). (gr. 3-7). pap. 3.99 (*0-590-42378-9*) Scholastic, Inc.

—Thank You, Jackie Robinson. 1997. 11.00 (*0-606-18309-4*) Turtleback Bks.

Gutman, Dan. Jackie & Me. 1999. (Avon Camelot Bks.). (Illus.). 160p. (J). (gr. 4-7). 15.99 (*0-380-97685-4*) HarperCollins Children's Bk. Group.

—Jackie & Me. 2000. (Avon Camelot Bks.). 160p. (J). (gr. 3-7). pap. 5.99 (*0-380-80084-5*, Avon Bks.) Morrow/Avon.

—Jackie & Me. 2000. (Illus.). (J). 11.04 (*0-606-17974-7*) Turtleback Bks.

ROGERS, BUCK (FICTITIOUS CHARACTER)—FICTION

Doyle, Arthur Conan. The Hound of the Baskervilles. 1996. (Andre Deutsch Classics). 204p. (J). (gr. 5-8). 11.95 (*0-233-99035-6*) Andre Deutsch GBR. *Dist:* Trafalgar Square, Trans-Atlantic Pubns., Inc.

—The Hound of the Baskervilles. unabr. ed. 1994. (Thrift Editions Ser.). 128p. (J). pap. 1.50 (*0-486-28214-7*) Dover Pubns., Inc.

—The Hound of the Baskervilles. 2nd ed. 1993. (Illus.). 94p. pap. text 5.95 (*0-19-585432-2*) Oxford Univ. Pr., Inc.

—The Hound of the Baskervilles. 2000. (Aladdin Classics Ser.). 256p. (J). (gr. 4-11). pap. 3.99 (*0-689-83571-X*, Aladdin) Simon & Schuster Children's Publishing.

Nowlan, Phil & Calkins, Dick. Buck Rogers in the 25th Century. 1994. 32p. (J). pap. 4.95 (*0-9647830-0-2*) EKTEK, Inc.

ROOSEVELT, ELEANOR, 1884-1962—FICTION

Coleman, Evelyn. Circle of Fire. 2001. (American Girl Collection: Bk. 14). (Illus.). 160p. (J). 9.95 o.p. (*1-58485-340-9*); pap. 5.95 (*1-58485-339-5*) Pleasant Co. Pubns. (American Girl).

—Circle of Fire. 2001. (American Girl Collection). (Illus.). (J). 12.00 (*0-606-21249-3*) Turtleback Bks.

De Young, C. Coco. A Letter to Mrs. Roosevelt. 2000. 112p. (gr. 3-7). pap. text 4.50 (*0-440-41529-2*, Yearling) Random Hse. Children's Bks.

Ryan, Pam Muñoz. Amelia & Eleanor Go for a Ride. 1999. (Illus.). 40p. (J). (gr. k-4). pap. 16.95 (*0-590-96075-X*) Scholastic, Inc.

ROOSEVELT, FRANKLIN D. (FRANKLIN DELANO), 1882-1945—FICTION

Kirk, Daniel. Breakfast at the Liberty Diner. 1997. (Illus.). 32p. (J). (ps-3). lib. bdg. 15.49 (*0-7868-2243-0*);Vol. 1. 14.95 (*0-7868-0303-7*) Hyperion Bks. for Children.

Winthrop, Elizabeth. Franklin Delano Roosevelt: Letters from a Mill Town Girl. 2001. (Dear Mr. President Ser.). (Illus.). 128p. (J). (gr. 4-6). 9.95 (*1-890817-61-9*) Winslow Pr.

ROOSEVELT, THEODORE, 1858-1919—FICTION

Armstrong, Jennifer. Theodore Roosevelt: Letters from a Young Coal Miner. 2001. (Dear Mr. President Ser.: Vol. 1). (Illus.). 118p. (J). (gr. 4-7). 8.95 (*1-890817-27-9*) Winslow Pr.

Fritz, Jean. Bully for You, Teddy Roosevelt! 1997. 12.04 (*0-606-11174-3*) Turtleback Bks.

Henry, Will. San Juan Hill. 1996. E-Book 9.95 (*0-585-25332-3*) netLibrary, Inc.

Hines, Gary. A Christmas Tree in the White House, ERS. (Illus.). 32p. (J). (ps-3). 2001. pap. 6.95 (*0-8050-6768-X*); 1998. 15.95 o.s.i (*0-8050-5076-0*) Holt, Henry & Co. (Holt, Henry & Co. Bks. For Young Readers).

Kay, Helen. The First Teddy Bear. 1985. (Illus.). 40p. (J). (gr. 2 up). 14.95 (*0-88045-042-8*) Stemmer Hse. Pubs., Inc.

Monjo, F. N. The One Bad Thing about Father. 1987. (I Can Read Bks.). (Illus.). 64p. (J). (gr. 2-4). pap. 3.75 o.p. (*0-06-444110-5*, Harper Trophy) HarperCollins Children's Bk. Group.

Quackenbush, Robert. Don't You Dare Shoot That Bear! A Story of Theodore Roosevelt. 1984. (Illus.). 40p. (J). (gr. 1-5). 9.95 o.s.i (*0-13-218496-6*) Prentice Hall PTR.

Sargent, Dave & Sargent, Pat. Buckshot (Blue Eyed Chestnet) Mind Your Manners #8. 2001. (Saddle Up Ser.). 36p. (J). pap. (*1-56763-674-8*) Ozark Publishing.

—Buckshot (Blue Eyed Chestnut) Mind Your Manners #8. 2001. (Saddle Up Ser.). 36p. (J). lib. bdg. 22.60 (*1-56763-673-X*) Ozark Publishing.

ROOSEVELT FAMILY—FICTION

Buckley, Anne. The Day Mrs. Roosevelt Came to Town. Kemnitz, Myrna, ed. 2000. 186p. (YA). (gr. 6 up). pap. 9.99 (*0-88092-458-6*) Royal Fireworks Publishing Co.

ROWAN (FICTITIOUS CHARACTER)—FICTION

Rodda, Emily. Rowan & the Ice Creepers. 2003. (Rowan of Rin Ser.). 272p. (J). (gr. 2 up). 15.99 (*0-06-029780-8*); lib. bdg. 16.89 (*0-06-029781-6*) HarperCollins Children's Bk. Group. (Greenwillow Bks.).

—Rowan & the Keeper of the Crystal. 2002. (Rowan of Rin Ser.). 208p. (J). (gr. 2 up). pap. 5.99 (*0-06-441025-0*); 15.95 (*0-06-029776-X*, Greenwillow Bks.); (Illus.). lib. bdg. 15.89 (*0-06-029777-8*, Greenwillow Bks.) HarperCollins Children's Bk. Group.

—Rowan & the Travelers. (Rowan of Rin Ser.). 176p. (J). (gr. 2 up). 2002. pap. 5.95 (*0-06-441026-9*, Harper Trophy); 2001. 15.95 (*0-06-029775-1*, Greenwillow Bks.); 2001. (Illus.). lib. bdg. 16.89 (*0-06-029774-3*, Greenwillow Bks.) HarperCollins Children's Bk. Group.

—Rowan & the Travelers. 2004. (Rowan of Rin Ser.). 192p. (J). pap. 5.99 (*0-06-056072-X*, Avon Bks.) Morrow/Avon.

—Rowan & the Zebak. (Rowan of Rin Ser.). 208p. (J). (gr. 2 up). 2003. (Illus.). pap. 5.99 (*0-06-441024-2*, Harper Trophy); 2002. 15.95 (*0-06-029778-6*, Greenwillow Bks.); 2002. lib. bdg. 16.89 (*0-06-029779-4*, Greenwillow Bks.) HarperCollins Children's Bk. Group.

—Rowan of Rin. (Rowan of Rin Ser.). 160p. (J). (gr. 2 up). 2002. pap. 5.95 (*0-06-441019-6*, Harper Trophy); 2001. (Illus.). 15.99 (*0-06-029707-7*, Greenwillow Bks.); 2001. (Illus.). lib. bdg. 15.89 (*0-06-029708-5*, Greenwillow Bks.) HarperCollins Children's Bk. Group.

—Rowan of Rin. 2004. (Rowan of Rin Ser.). 176p. (J). pap. 5.99 (*0-06-056071-1*, Avon Bks.) Morrow/Avon.

RUGRATS (FICTITIOUS CHARACTERS)—FICTION

Albee, Sarah. Space Invaders! 1998. (Ready-to-Read Ser.). (Illus.). 32p. (J). (ps-3). pap. 3.99 (*0-689-82130-1*, Simon Spotlight/Nickelodeon) Simon & Schuster Children's Publishing.

Angelica's Backpack Book. 2003. (Rugrats Ser.). (Illus.). 16p. (J). 6.99 (*0-689-86181-8*, Simon Spotlight/Nickelodeon) Simon & Schuster Children's Publishing.

Banks, Steven. In Search of Reptar: A Time Travel Adventure. 2002. (Rugrats Files: Bk. 5). (Illus.). 96p. (J). (gr. 3-7). pap. 3.99 (*0-689-84609-6*, Simon Spotlight) Simon & Schuster Children's Publishing.

Barkan, Joanne. Riddle of the Lost Lake. 2000. (Wishbone Super Mysteries Ser.: No. 4). (Illus.). 256p. (J). (gr. 2-5). mass mkt. 3.99 o.p. (*1-57064-540-X*, Big Red Chair Bks.) Lyrick Publishing.

Bergen, Lara. Angelica & the Island Princess. 2003. (Rugrats Ser.). (Illus.). 24p. (J). pap. 3.99 (*0-689-85450-1*, 53497522, Simon Spotlight/Nickelodeon) Simon & Schuster Children's Publishing.

Bergen, Lara Rice. Ultimate Rugrats Trivia Sticker Book. 1999. (Rugrats Ser.). (J). pap. 5.99 (*0-689-82892-6*, Little Simon) Simon & Schuster Children's Publishing.

Breslauer, Jan. The Making of the Rugrats Movie: Behind the Scences at Klasky Csupo. 1998. (Rugrats Ser.). (Illus.). 144p. (J). (ps-3). 25.00 (*0-671-02809-X*, MSG) Simon & Schuster.

Capeci, Anne. The Halloween Joker. Ryan, Kevin, ed. 1998. (Wishbone Super Mysteries Ser.: No. 1). (Illus.). 255p. (J). (gr. 2-5). mass mkt. 3.99 o.p. (*1-57064-338-5*) Scholastic, Inc.

—The Halloween Joker. 1998. (Wishbone Super Mysteries Ser.: No. 1). (J). (gr. 2-5). 10.04 (*0-606-17162-2*) Turtleback Bks.

—Key to the Golden Dog. 1998. (Wishbone Mysteries Ser.: No. 8). (Illus.). 144p. (J). (gr. 2-5). mass mkt. 3.99 o.p. (*1-57064-284-2*, Big Red Chair Bks.) Lyrick Publishing.

—Key to the Golden Dog. l.t. ed. 1999. (Wishbone Mysteries Ser.: No. 8). 144p. (J). (gr. 4 up). lib. bdg. 22.60 (*0-8368-2389-3*) Stevens, Gareth Inc.

—Key to the Golden Dog. 1998. (Wishbone Mysteries Ser.: No. 8). (J). (gr. 2-5). 10.04 (*0-606-15888-X*) Turtleback Bks.

—The Maltese Dog. l.t. ed. 1999. (Wishbone Mysteries Ser.: No. 6). 144p. (J). (gr. 4 up). lib. bdg. 22.60 (*0-8368-2387-7*) Stevens, Gareth Inc.

—The Maltese Dog. 1998. (Wishbone Mysteries Ser.: No. 6). (J). (gr. 2-5). 10.04 (*0-606-15886-3*) Turtleback Bks.

Cassity, Don, illus. Discovering America. 2000. (Rugrats Ser.). Orig. Title: Rugrats Discover America. 32p. (J). (ps-2). pap. 5.99 (*0-689-83272-9*, Simon Spotlight/Nickelodeon) Simon & Schuster Children's Publishing.

Chevat, Richie. Rugrats Over. 2003. (Rugrats Ser.). (Illus.). 24p. (J). pap. 3.50 (*0-689-85232-0*, Simon Spotlight/Nickelodeon) Simon & Schuster Children's Publishing.

Collins, Terry. Spike Speaks. 2003. (Rugrats Ser.). (Illus.). 24p. (J). pap. 3.99 (*0-689-85451-X*, 53497313, Simon Spotlight/Nickelodeon) Simon & Schuster Children's Publishing.

Craig, Karen. Rugrats 1: Super Coloring Book. 2000. (Rugrats Ser.). (Illus.). 64p. (J). (ps-2). pap. 1.99 o.s.i (*0-307-40503-6*, Golden Bks.) Random Hse. Children's Bks.

Daly, Catherine. At the Movies. 1992. (Rugrats Ser.). (Illus.). (J). (ps-2). 2.25 o.p. (*0-448-40500-8*, Grosset & Dunlap) Penguin Putnam Bks. for Young Readers.

David, Luke. Chuckie Visits the Eye Doctor. 1999. (Rugrats Ser.). (Illus.). 24p. (J). (ps-2). pap. 3.50 (*0-689-82670-2*, 076714003507, Simon Spotlight/Nickelodeon) Simon & Schuster Children's Publishing.

—Oh, Brother! 1999. (Rugrats Ser.). (Illus.). 24p. (J). (ps-2). pap. 3.50 (*0-689-82440-8*, 076714003507, Simon Spotlight/Nickelodeon) Simon & Schuster Children's Publishing.

—Rugrats vs. the Monkeys. 1998. (Rugrats Ser.). (Illus.). 24p. (J). (ps-2). pap. 3.50 (*0-689-82142-5*, Simon Spotlight/Nickelodeon) Simon & Schuster Children's Publishing.

—Sight for Sore Eyes. Goldberg, Barry, tr. & illus. by. 1999. (Rugrats Ser.). 32p. (J). (ps-3). per. 3.50 (*0-671-02866-9*, Simon & Schuster Children's Publishing) Simon & Schuster Children's Publishing.

—Sight for Sore Eyes. 1999. (Rugrats Ser.). (Illus.). 24p. (J). (ps-2). pap. 3.50 (*0-689-82262-6*, Simon Spotlight/Nickelodeon) Simon & Schuster Children's Publishing.

—Tommy's New Playmate. 1998. (Rugrats Ser.). (Illus.). 24p. (J). (ps-2). pap. 3.50 (*0-689-82141-7*, Simon Spotlight/Nickelodeon) Simon & Schuster Children's Publishing.

—Twin Trouble. 1999. (Rugrats Ser.). (Illus.). 24p. (J). (ps-2). pap. 3.50 (*0-689-82624-9*, 076714003507, Simon Spotlight/Nickelodeon) Simon & Schuster Children's Publishing.

David, Luke & Cardona, Jose M. Bonjour, Babies! 1999. (Rugrats Chapter Bks.: No. 4). (Illus.). 64p. (J). (gr. 1-4). pap. 3.99 (*0-689-82894-2*, Simon Spotlight) Simon & Schuster Children's Publishing.

Dubowski, Cathy. The Rugrats Meet the Thornberrys. 2003. (Rugrats Ser.). (Illus.). 144p. (J). pap. 4.99 (*0-689-85431-5*, 53497521, Simon Spotlight) Simon & Schuster Children's Publishing.

Dubowski, Cathy & Dubowski, Mark. Rugrats in Paris: The Movie. movie tie-in ed. 2000. (Rugrats Ser.). (Illus.). 144p. (J). (ps-2). pap. 4.99 (*0-689-83394-6*, Simon Spotlight) Simon & Schuster Children's Publishing.

—The Rugrats Movie. 1998. (Rugrats Ser.). (Illus.). 144p. (J). (ps-2). pap. 3.99 (*0-671-02106-0*, Aladdin) Simon & Schuster Children's Publishing.

—The Rugrats Movie Music Book. 1999. (Rugrats Ser.). (Illus.). 72p. (J). (ps-2). otabind 14.95 (*0-634-00514-6*) Leonard, Hal Corp.

Dubowski, Cathy & Rosado, Maria. It Takes Two. 2000. (Rugrats Chapter Bks.: No. 9). (Illus.). 64p. (J). (gr. 1-4). pap. 3.99 (*0-689-83169-2*, Simon Spotlight) Simon & Schuster Children's Publishing.

Dubowski, Cathy, et al. Chuckie's Big Wish. 1999. (Rugrats Chapter Bks.: No. 5). (Illus.). 64p. (J). (gr. 1-4). pap. 3.99 (*0-689-82895-0*, Simon Spotlight) Simon & Schuster Children's Publishing.

Gallegly, Kevin, illus. Angelica's Sassy Styles. 2002. (Rugrats Ser.). 20p. (J). (ps-2). mass mkt. 7.99 (*0-689-84841-2*, Simon Spotlight/Nickelodeon) Simon & Schuster Children's Publishing.

Giarrano, Vincent, illus. No Place Like Home. 2000. (Rugrats Ser.). 32p. (J). (ps-2). pap. 5.99 (*0-689-83170-6*, Simon Spotlight/Nickelodeon) Simon & Schuster Children's Publishing.

Gold, Becky. Babies in Reptarland. 2000. (Rugrats Ser.). (Illus.). 32p. (J). (ps-2). pap. 5.99 (*0-689-83337-7*, Simon Spotlight/Nickelodeon) Simon & Schuster Children's Publishing.

—The Phil & Lil Go to the Doctor. 2001. (Rugrats Ser.). (Illus.). 24p. (J). (ps-2). pap. 3.50 (*0-689-83167-6*, Simon Spotlight/Nickelodeon) Simon & Schuster Children's Publishing.

—Tommy's Bestest Adventure. 2000. (Rugrats Ser.). (Illus.). 24p. (J). (ps-2). pap. 3.50 (*0-689-83426-8*, Simon Spotlight/Nickelodeon) Simon & Schuster Children's Publishing.

—Tommy's Bestest Adventure. 2000. (Rugrats Chapter Bks.). (Illus.). (J). 9.65 (*0-606-20948-4*) Turtleback Bks.

Gold, Rebecca. Camp Out. 1999. (Ready-to-Read Ser.). (Illus.). 32p. (J). (ps-3). pap. 3.99 (*0-689-82390-8*, Simon Spotlight/Nickelodeon) Simon & Schuster Children's Publishing.

—Camp Out. 1999. (Ready-to-Read Ser.). (J). (ps-3). 10.14 (*0-606-17786-8*) Turtleback Bks.

—Surprise, Angelica! 2000. (Ready-to-Read Ser.). (Illus.). 32p. (J). (ps-3). pap. 3.99 o.s.i (*0-689-82829-2*, Simon Spotlight/Nickelodeon) Simon & Schuster Children's Publishing.

—Take a Bow, Babies! 2000. (Ready-to-Read Ser.). (Illus.). 32p. (J). (ps-3). per. (*0-7434-0854-3*, Simon & Schuster Children's Publishing); pap. 3.99 (*0-689-82830-6*, Simon Spotlight/Nickelodeon) Simon & Schuster Children's Publishing.

Golden Books Staff. Best Buddies. 2002. (Illus.). 48p. (J). pap. 3.99 (*0-307-10854-6*, Golden Bks.) Random Hse. Children's Bks.

—Christmas Angels. 2001. (Rugrats Ser.). 56p. (J). (ps-2). pap. 4.99 o.p. (*0-307-27625-2*, Golden Bks.) Random Hse. Children's Bks.

—C'mon, Let's Play. 2001. (Rugrats Ser.). 32p. (J). (ps-2). pap. 3.99 (*0-307-10437-0*, Golden Bks.) Random Hse. Children's Bks.

—Here Comes Trouble. 2001. (Rugrats Ser.). 96p. (J). (ps-2). pap. 3.99 (*0-307-25405-4*, Golden Bks.) Random Hse. Children's Bks.

—Let's Party. 2002. (Illus.). 16p. (J). pap. 3.99 (*0-307-25303-1*, Golden Bks.) Random Hse. Children's Bks.

—My Favorite Things. 2002. (Illus.). 32p. (J). pap. 3.99 (*0-307-20218-6*, Golden Bks.) Random Hse. Children's Bks.

—Opposites Attract. 2001. (Rugrats Ser.). 56p. (J). (ps-2). pap. 4.99 (*0-307-27624-4*, Golden Bks.) Random Hse. Children's Bks.

—Ready, Set, Write. 2001. (Rugrats Ser.). 16p. (J). (ps-2). pap. 4.99 (*0-307-12863-6*, Golden Bks.) Random Hse. Children's Bks.

—Rugrats: Paint with Water. 2000. (Rugrats Ser.). (Illus.). 32p. (J). (ps-2). pap. 2.49 (*0-307-40304-1*, Golden Bks.) Random Hse. Children's Bks.

—Rugrats: Sticker Book. 2000. (Rugrats Ser.). (Illus.). (J). (ps-2). pap. 1.99 o.s.i (*0-307-40402-1*, Golden Bks.) Random Hse. Children's Bks.

—Rugrats 2: Super Coloring Book. 2000. (Rugrats Ser.). (Illus.). 64p. (J). (ps-2). pap. 1.99 o.s.i (*0-307-40504-4*, Golden Bks.) Random Hse. Children's Bks.

—Uneasy Rider. 2004. (Illus.). (J). pap. 2.99 (*0-375-82659-9*, Golden Bks.) Random Hse. Children's Bks.

Gorey, Jill & Herndon, Barbara. Mine! 1999. (Rugrats Books for Parents Ser.). (Illus.). 64p. (J). pap. 6.99 (*0-671-02638-0*, Simon Pulse) Simon & Schuster Children's Publishing.

Gorey, Jill, et al. What to Explain When You're Expecting. 1999. (Rugrats Books for Parents Ser.). (Illus.). 64p. (YA). pap. 6.99 (*0-671-02639-9*, Simon Pulse) Simon & Schuster Children's Publishing.

Graham, Jefferson. The Ultimate Rugrats Fan Book. 1998. (Rugrats Ser.). (Illus.). 64p. (J). (ps-2). pap. 8.99 (*0-689-81678-2*, Simon Spotlight/Nickelodeon) Simon & Schuster Children's Publishing.

Greene, Stephanie. The Rugrats First Kwanzaa. 2001. (Rugrats Ser.). (Illus.). 32p. (J). (ps-2). pap. 5.99 (*0-689-84191-4*, Simon Spotlight/Nickelodeon) Simon & Schuster Children's Publishing.

Herman, Gail. Pizza Cats. (Ready-to-Read Ser.). (Illus.). (J). (ps-3). 2000. 31p. per. (*0-671-77316-X*, Simon & Schuster Children's Publishing); 1999. 32p. pap. 3.99 (*0-689-82391-6*, Simon Spotlight/Nickelodeon) Simon & Schuster Children's Publishing.

—Pizza Cats. 1999. (Ready-to-Read Ser.). (J). (ps-3). 10.14 (*0-606-17785-X*) Turtleback Bks.

Herndon, Barbara & Gorey, Jill. No Place Like Home. 2000. (Rugrats Ser.). (Illus.). 30p. (J). (ps-3). per. (*0-7434-0853-5*, Simon & Schuster Children's Publishing) Simon & Schuster Children's Publishing.

Hood, Susan. The Bestest Mom. 1998. (Rugrats Ser.). (Illus.). 32p. (J). (ps-2). pap. 5.99 (*0-689-82047-X*, Simon Spotlight/Nickelodeon) Simon & Schuster Children's Publishing.

Hughes, Francesca. Monster in the Garage. 1992. (Rugrats Ser.). (Illus.). (J). (ps-2). 2.25 o.p. (*0-448-40501-6*, Grosset & Dunlap) Penguin Putnam Bks. for Young Readers.

In Search of the Mighty Reptar: Songs & Stories. (Rugrats Ser.). (J). audio 6.38. audio compact disk 9.58 NewSound, LLC.

Inches, Alison. How to Be a Princess by Angelica Pickles. 2000. (Rugrats Ser.). (Illus.). 20p. (J). (ps-2). pap. 9.99 (*0-689-83481-0*, Simon Spotlight/Nickelodeon) Simon & Schuster Children's Publishing.

Inches, Alison & Cardona, Jose Maria. Planet Reptar. 2001. (Rugrats Ser.). (Illus.). 12p. (J). (ps-2). bds. 10.95 (*0-689-82853-5*, Simon Spotlight/Nickelodeon) Simon & Schuster Children's Publishing.

Jablonski, Carla. Twenty Thousand Wags under the Sea. 2000. (Adventures of Wishbone Ser.: No. 22). (Illus.). 144p. (J). (gr. 2-5). pap. 3.99 o.p. (*1-57064-387-3*, Big Red Chair Bks.) Lyrick Publishing.

—Sweet Victory. 1998. (Rugrats Ser.). (Illus.). 14p. (J). (ps-2). bds. 4.99 (*0-689-81989-7*, Simon Spotlight/ Nickelodeon) Simon & Schuster Children's Publishing.

—Tommy & Chuckie on the Go! 1997. (Rugrats Ser.). (Illus.). 6p. (J). (ps-2). bds. 4.99 (*0-689-81642-1*, Simon Spotlight/Nickelodeon) Simon & Schuster Children's Publishing.

—Up & Away, Reptar! (Ready-to-Read Ser.). (Illus.). 32p. (J). (ps-3). 2000. per. 3.99 (*0-671-77315-1*, Simon & Schuster Children's Publishing); 1999. pap. 3.99 (*0-689-82631-1*, 076714003996, Simon Spotlight/Nickelodeon) Simon & Schuster Children's Publishing.

Wilson, Sarah. Chuckie Meets the Beastie Bunny. 2000. (Rugrats Ser.). (Illus.). 24p. (J). (ps-2). pap. 3.50 (*0-689-83066-1*, Simon Spotlight/ Nickelodeon) Simon & Schuster Children's Publishing.

—Chuckie Meets the Beastie Bunny. 2000. (Rugrats Chapter Bks.). (Illus.). (J). 9.65 (*0-606-20604-3*) Turtleback Bks.

—Prince Chuckie. 2001. (Rugrats Chapter Bks.: No. 12). (Illus.). 64p. (J). (gr. 1-4). pap. 3.99 (*0-689-84060-8*, Simon Spotlight) Simon & Schuster Children's Publishing.

—Tommy Catches a Cold. 1998. (Rugrats Ser.). (Illus.). 24p. (Orig.). (J). (ps-2). pap. 3.50 (*0-689-82126-3*, Simon Spotlight/Nickelodeon) Simon & Schuster Children's Publishing.

—Tricked for Treats: A Rugrats Halloween. 1999. (Rugrats Ser.). (Illus.). 32p. (J). (ps-2). pap. 5.99 (*0-689-82572-2*, Simon Spotlight/Nickelodeon) Simon & Schuster Children's Publishing.

Zalme, Ron. Space Invaders! 1998. (Ready-to-Read Ser.). (J). (ps-3). 10.14 (*0-606-17788-4*) Turtleback Bks.

RUTH (BIBLICAL CHARACTER)—FICTION

Pakulak, Eric. At the Side of Ruth: A Multiple-Ending Bible Adventure. 2001. (Illus.). 74p. (J). pap. 6.95 (*0-8198-0771-0*) Pauline Bks. & Media.

Petersham, Maud. The Story of Ruth & the Story of David. 1900. (J). per. 5.99 (*0-689-81399-6*, Aladdin) Simon & Schuster Children's Publishing.

S

SABRINA, THE TEENAGE WITCH (FICTITIOUS CHARACTER)—FICTION

Barnes-Svarney, Patricia L. Sabrina the Teenage Witch Magic Handbook. 1998. (Sabrina, the Teenage Witch Ser.). 96p. (YA). (gr. 5 up). mass mkt. 6.99 (*0-671-02427-2*, Simon Pulse) Simon & Schuster Children's Publishing.

—Sabrina's Guide to the Universe. 1999. (Sabrina, the Teenage Witch Ser.). (Illus.). 96p. (YA). (gr. 5 up). pap. 6.99 (*0-671-03641-6*, Simon Pulse) Simon & Schuster Children's Publishing.

—Teacher's Pet. 1998. (Sabrina, the Teenage Witch: No. 2). (Illus.). 96p. (J). (gr. 2-5). pap. 3.99 (*0-671-02381-0*, Simon Pulse) Simon & Schuster Children's Publishing.

Batrae, Margot. Switcheroo. 2000. (Sabrina, the Teenage Witch Ser.: No. 30). 160p. (YA). (gr. 5 up). mass mkt. 4.50 (*0-671-04067-7*, Simon Pulse) Simon & Schuster Children's Publishing.

—Switcheroo. 2000. (Sabrina, the Teenage Witch Ser.: No. 30). (YA). (gr. 5 up). 10.55 (*0-606-18380-9*) Turtleback Bks.

—While the Cat's Away. 1999. (Sabrina, the Teenage Witch Ser.: No. 25). 144p. (YA). (gr. 5 up). mass mkt. 4.99 (*0-671-02821-9*, Simon Pulse) Simon & Schuster Children's Publishing.

Berney, Sarah J. Cat by the Tail. 1999. (Sabrina, the Teenage Witch: No. 7). 96p. (J). (gr. 2-5). pap. 3.99 (*0-671-02383-7*, Simon Pulse) Simon & Schuster Children's Publishing.

Canning, Shelagh. Becoming a Witch. (Sabrina, the Teenage Witch Ser.: No. 1). (J). (gr. 2-4). 1998. 30p. pap. 3.99 (*0-689-82123-9*); 1997. (Illus.). 32p. pap. text 4.99 (*0-689-81743-6*) Simon & Schuster Children's Publishing. (Simon Pulse).

Dubowski, Cathy. Cat Showdown! 1998. (Sabrina, the Teenage Witch Ser.: No. 3). (Illus.). 32p. (J). (gr. 2-4). pap. 3.99 (*0-689-81878-5*, Simon Pulse) Simon & Schuster Children's Publishing.

—A Dog's Life. 1998. (Sabrina, the Teenage Witch Ser.: No. 9). 160p. (YA). (gr. 5 up). pap. 4.50 (*0-671-01979-1*, Simon Pulse) Simon & Schuster Children's Publishing.

—A Doll's Story. 1998. (Sabrina, the Teenage Witch Ser.: No. 6). (Illus.). 32p. (J). (gr. 2-4). pap. 3.99 (*0-689-81879-3*, Simon Pulse) Simon & Schuster Children's Publishing.

—Fortune Cookie Fox. 1999. (Sabrina, the Teenage Witch Ser.: No. 26). 128p. (YA). (gr. 5 up). pap. 4.50 (*0-671-02817-0*, Simon Pulse) Simon & Schuster Children's Publishing.

—It's a Miserable Life! 2000. (Sabrina, the Teenage Witch Ser.: No. 34). 144p. (YA). (gr. 5 up). pap. 4.99 (*0-671-04071-5*, Simon Pulse) Simon & Schuster Children's Publishing.

—Milady's Dragon. 2001. (Sabrina, the Teenage Witch Ser.: Bk. 38). (Illus.). 128p. (YA). (gr. 5 up). pap. 4.99 (*0-7434-1809-3*, Simon Pulse) Simon & Schuster Children's Publishing.

—Psychic Kitty. 1999. (Sabrina, the Teenage Witch: No. 6). 96p. (J). (gr. 2-5). pap. 3.99 (*0-671-02382-9*, Simon Pulse) Simon & Schuster Children's Publishing.

—Santa's Little Helper. 1997. (Sabrina, the Teenage Witch Ser.: No. 5). 160p. (YA). (gr. 5 up). per. 4.50 (*0-671-01519-2*, Simon Pulse) Simon & Schuster Children's Publishing.

Dubowski, Mark. The King of Cats. 1999. (Sabrina, the Teenage Witch: No. 4). 96p. (J). (gr. 2-5). pap. 3.99 (*0-671-02105-2*, Simon Pulse) Simon & Schuster Children's Publishing.

Dubowski, Mark & Dubowski, Cathy. Cat-TV. 1998. (Sabrina, the Teenage Witch: No. 1). (Illus.). 96p. (J). (gr. 2-5). pap. 3.99 (*0-671-02102-8*, Simon Pulse) Simon & Schuster Children's Publishing.

Fiedler, Lisa. Know-It-All. 2002. (Sabrina, the Teenage Witch Ser.: Bk. = 43). (Illus.). 144p. (J). (gr. 5 up). pap. 4.99 (*0-7434-4239-3*, Simon Pulse) Simon & Schuster Children's Publishing.

Gallagher, Diana G. Bridal Bedlam. 1999. (Sabrina, the Teenage Witch Ser.: No. 23). 176p. (YA). (gr. 5 up). mass mkt. 4.50 (*0-671-02818-9*, Simon Pulse) Simon & Schuster Children's Publishing.

—Dog Day Afternoon. 1999. (Sabrina, the Teenage Witch: No. 5). (Illus.). 96p. (J). (gr. 2-5). mass mkt. 3.99 (*0-671-02103-6*, Simon Pulse) Simon & Schuster Children's Publishing.

—From the Horse's Mouth. 2001. (Sabrina, the Teenage Witch Ser.: Bk. 39). 176p. (YA). (gr. 5 up). mass mkt. 4.99 (*0-7434-1811-5*, Simon Pulse) Simon & Schuster Children's Publishing.

—Halloween Havoc. 1997. (Sabrina, the Teenage Witch Ser.: No. 4). 192p. (YA). (gr. 5 up). per. 4.50 (*0-671-01436-6*, Simon Pulse) Simon & Schuster Children's Publishing.

—Lotsa Luck. 1998. (Sabrina, the Teenage Witch Ser.: No. 10). 176p. (YA). (gr. 5 up). per. 4.99 (*0-671-01980-5*, Simon Pulse) Simon & Schuster Children's Publishing.

—Now You See Her, Now You Don't. 1998. (Sabrina, the Teenage Witch Ser.: No. 16). 176p. (YA). (gr. 5 up). per. 4.50 (*0-671-02120-6*, Simon Pulse) Simon & Schuster Children's Publishing.

—Shamrock Shenanigans. 1999. (Sabrina, the Teenage Witch Ser.: No. 19). 176p. (YA). (gr. 5 up). pap. 4.50 (*0-671-02780-8*, Simon Pulse) Simon & Schuster Children's Publishing.

—Showdown at the Mall. 1997. (Sabrina, the Teenage Witch Ser.: No. 2). 160p. (YA). (gr. 5 up). pap. 4.99 (*0-671-01434-X*, Simon Pulse) Simon & Schuster Children's Publishing.

—Wake-Up Call. 2001. (Sabrina, the Teenage Witch Ser.: No. 36). (Illus.). 160p. (YA). (gr. 5 up). mass mkt. 4.99 (*0-7434-1750-X*, Simon Pulse) Simon & Schuster Children's Publishing.

—Worth a Shot. 2000. (Sabrina, the Teenage Witch: No. 11). (J). (gr. 2-5). 81p. per. (*0-671-77334-8*, Simon & Schuster Children's Publishing); 96p. pap. 3.99 (*0-671-03834-6*, Simon Pulse) Simon & Schuster Children's Publishing.

Garton, Ray. All That Glitters. 1998. (Sabrina, the Teenage Witch Ser.: No. 12). 176p. (YA). (gr. 5 up). pap. 4.99 (*0-671-02116-8*, Simon Pulse) Simon & Schuster Children's Publishing.

Goldman, Leslie. The Truth Hurts. 2003. (Sabrina, the Teenage Witch Ser.). (Illus.). 160p. (J). pap. 4.99 (*0-689-85579-6*, Simon Pulse) Simon & Schuster Children's Publishing.

—Witch Glitch. 2003. (Sabrina, the Teenage Witch Ser.). (Illus.). 160p. (J). pap. 4.99 (*0-689-85578-8*, Simon Pulse) Simon & Schuster Children's Publishing.

Herman, Gail. Sabrina, the Teenage Boy. 1998. (Sabrina, the Teenage Witch Ser.: No. 5). (Illus.). 32p. (J). (gr. 2-4). pap. 3.99 (*0-689-81881-5*, Simon Pulse) Simon & Schuster Children's Publishing.

Holder, Nancy. Eight Spells a Week: Super Edition. 1998. (Sabrina, the Teenage Witch Ser.: No. 17). 272p. (YA). (gr. 5 up). pap. 4.99 (*0-671-02121-4*, Simon Pulse) Simon & Schuster Children's Publishing.

—Feline Felon. 1999. (Sabrina, the Teenage Witch: No. 8). 96p. (J). (gr. 2-5). pap. 3.99 (*0-671-02384-5*, Simon Pulse) Simon & Schuster Children's Publishing.

—Scarabian Nights. 1999. (Sabrina, the Teenage Witch Ser.: No. 24). 176p. (YA). (gr. 5 up). mass mkt. 4.50 (*0-671-02804-9*, Simon Pulse) Simon & Schuster Children's Publishing.

—Spying Eyes. 1998. (Sabrina, the Teenage Witch Ser.: No. 14). 160p. (YA). (gr. 5 up). pap. 4.99 (*0-671-02118-4*, Simon Pulse) Simon & Schuster Children's Publishing.

—Up, up & Away! 1999. (Sabrina, the Teenage Witch Ser.: No. 28). 144p. (YA). (gr. 5 up). pap. 4.50 (*0-671-02805-7*, Simon Pulse) Simon & Schuster Children's Publishing.

—Up, up & Away! 1999. (Sabrina, the Teenage Witch Ser.: No. 28). (YA). (gr. 5 up). 10.55 (*0-606-18381-7*) Turtleback Bks.

Krulik, Nancy E. Christmas Crisis. 2003. (Sabrina, the Teenage Witch Ser.). (Illus.). 160p. (J). mass mkt. 4.99 (*0-689-85582-6*, Simon Pulse) Simon & Schuster Children's Publishing.

—Happily Ever After. 1999. (Sabrina, the Teenage Witch Ser.: No. 9). 96p. (J). (gr. 2-5). pap. 3.99 (*0-671-03832-X*, Simon Pulse) Simon & Schuster Children's Publishing.

—Rulin' the School. 2000. (Sabrina, the Teenage Witch: No. 12). (J). (gr. 2-5). 85p. per. (*0-671-77335-6*, Simon & Schuster Children's Publishing); (Illus.). 96p. pap. 3.99 (*0-671-03835-4*, Simon Pulse) Simon & Schuster Children's Publishing.

—What a Doll! 2003. (Sabrina, the Teenage Witch Ser.). (Illus.). 160p. (J). mass mkt. 4.99 (*0-689-85580-X*, Simon Pulse) Simon & Schuster Children's Publishing.

—The Witch That Launched a Thousand Ships. 2002. (Sabrina, the Teenage Witch Ser.: Bk. 42). 160p. (YA). (gr. 5 up). pap. 4.99 (*0-7434-4238-5*, Simon Pulse) Simon & Schuster Children's Publishing.

Locke, Joseph. Ben There, Done That. 1998. (Sabrina, the Teenage Witch Ser.: No. 6). 160p. (YA). (gr. 5 up). pap. 4.50 (*0-671-01680-6*, Simon Pulse) Simon & Schuster Children's Publishing.

—The Troll Bride. 1998. (Sabrina, the Teenage Witch Ser.: No. 4). (Illus.). 32p. (J). (gr. 2-4). pap. 3.99 (*0-689-81880-7*, Simon Pulse) Simon & Schuster Children's Publishing.

Lundell, Margo. Dream Date. (Sabrina, the Teenage Witch Ser.: No. 2). (Illus.). 32p. (J). (gr. 2-4). 1998. pap. 3.99 (*0-689-82124-7*); 1997. pap. 4.99 (*0-689-81744-4*) Simon & Schuster Children's Publishing. (Simon Pulse).

Odom, Mel. Dream Boat. 2001. (Sabrina, the Teenage Witch Ser.: Bk. 40). 144p. (YA). (gr. 5 up). pap. 4.99 (*0-7434-1812-3*, Simon Pulse) Simon & Schuster Children's Publishing.

—Harvest Moon. 1998. (Sabrina, the Teenage Witch Ser.: No. 15). 160p. (YA). (gr. 5 up). mass mkt. 4.99 (*0-671-02119-2*, Simon Pulse) Simon & Schuster Children's Publishing.

—I'll Zap Manhattan. 1999. (Sabrina, the Teenage Witch Ser.: No. 18). 176p. (YA). (gr. 5 up). pap. 4.50 (*0-671-02702-6*, Simon Pulse) Simon & Schuster Children's Publishing.

—Mummy Dearest. 2000. (Sabrina, the Teenage Witch Ser.: No. 31). (YA). (gr. 5 up). 161p. per. (*0-671-77324-0*, Simon & Schuster Children's Publishing); (Illus.). 176p. pap. 4.50 (*0-671-04068-5*, Simon Pulse) Simon & Schuster Children's Publishing.

—Pirate Pandemonium. 2001. (Sabrina, the Teenage Witch Ser.: No. 35). 192p. (YA). (gr. 5 up). pap. 4.99 (*0-671-04072-3*, Simon Pulse) Simon & Schuster Children's Publishing.

—Sabrina Goes to Rome. 1998. (Sabrina, the Teenage Witch Ser.). 176p. (YA). (gr. 5 up). mass mkt. 4.50 (*0-671-02772-7*, Simon Pulse) Simon & Schuster Children's Publishing.

—Tiger Tale. 2002. (Sabrina, the Teenage Witch Ser.: Vol. 41). (Illus.). 160p. (YA). (gr. 5 up). pap. 4.99 (*0-7434-2430-1*, Simon Pulse) Simon & Schuster Children's Publishing.

Pocket Books Staff. Millennium Madness: Super Edition. 2000. (Sabrina, the Teenage Witch Ser.: No. 29). 368p. (YA). (gr. 5 up). pap. 5.99 (*0-671-02820-0*, Simon Pulse) Simon & Schuster Children's Publishing.

Reisfeld, Randi. All You Need Is a Love Spell. 1998. (Sabrina, the Teenage Witch Ser.: No. 7). 176p. (YA). (gr. 5 up). pap. 4.99 (*0-671-01695-4*, Simon Pulse) Simon & Schuster Children's Publishing.

Richards, Kitty. Salem's Guide to Life with Sabrina the Teenage Witch: A Spellbinding Trivia Book with Stickers. 1997. (Sabrina, the Teenage Witch Ser.). (Illus.). 24p. (YA). (gr. 5 up). pap. text 6.99 (*0-689-81745-2*, Simon Pulse) Simon & Schuster Children's Publishing.

Ruditis, Paul. Sabrina the Teenage Witch: The Official Episode Guide. 2002. (Illus.). 192p. (J). pap. 22.50 (*0-7522-6493-1*) Boxtree, Ltd. GBR. *Dist:* Trans-Atlantic Pubns., Inc.

—Topsy Turvy. 2002. (Sabrina, the Teenage Witch Ser.: Bk. 44). (Illus.). 160p. (J). (gr. 5 up). pap. 4.99 (*0-7434-4240-7*, Simon Pulse) Simon & Schuster Children's Publishing.

—Where in the World Is Sabrina Spellman? 2003. (Sabrina, the Teenage Witch Ser.). (Illus.). 160p. (J). pap. 4.99 (*0-7434-4243-1*, Simon Pulse) Simon & Schuster Children's Publishing.

—Witch Way Did She Go? 2001. (Sabrina, the Teenage Witch Ser.: No. 37). 160p. (J). (gr. 5 up). pap. 4.99 (*0-7434-1810-7*, Simon Pulse) Simon & Schuster Children's Publishing.

Strickland, Brad & Strickland, Barbara. You're History. 1998. (Sabrina, the Teenage Witch: No. 3). (Illus.). 96p. (J). (gr. 2-5). pap. 3.99 (*0-671-02104-4*, Simon Pulse) Simon & Schuster Children's Publishing.

Titlebaum, Ellen. Sabrina down Under. 1999. (Sabrina, the Teenage Witch Ser.). 160p. (YA). (gr. 5 up). pap. 4.99 (*0-671-04752-3*, Simon Pulse) Simon & Schuster Children's Publishing.

Vornholt, John. Gone Fishin' 2000. (Sabrina, the Teenage Witch: No. 10). 80p. (J). (gr. 2-5). pap. 3.99 (*0-671-03833-8*, Aladdin) Simon & Schuster Children's Publishing.

—Haunts in the House. 1999. (Sabrina, the Teenage Witch Ser.: No. 27). 144p. (YA). (gr. 5 up). mass mkt. 4.50 (*0-671-02819-7*, Simon Pulse) Simon & Schuster Children's Publishing.

—Knock on Wood. 2000. (Sabrina, the Teenage Witch Ser.: No. 33). 128p. (YA). (gr. 5 up). mass mkt. 4.99 (*0-671-04070-7*, Simon Pulse) Simon & Schuster Children's Publishing.

—Mascot Mayhem. 2000. (Sabrina, the Teenage Witch Ser.: No. 14). (Illus.). 96p. (J). (gr. 2-5). pap. 3.99 (*0-671-03837-0*, Simon Pulse) Simon & Schuster Children's Publishing.

—Prisoner of Cabin 13. 1998. (Sabrina, the Teenage Witch Ser.: No. 11). 176p. (YA). (gr. 5 up). pap. 4.99 (*0-671-02115-X*, Simon Pulse) Simon & Schuster Children's Publishing.

—Witchopoly. 1999. (Sabrina, the Teenage Witch Ser.: No. 22). 160p. (YA). (gr. 5 up). pap. 4.99 (*0-671-02806-5*, Simon Pulse) Simon & Schuster Children's Publishing.

Weiss, Bobbi J. G. & Weiss, David Cody. The Age of Aquariums. 1999. (Sabrina, the Teenage Witch Ser.: No. 20). 176p. (YA). (gr. 5 up). mass mkt. 4.99 (*0-671-02676-3*, Simon Pulse) Simon & Schuster Children's Publishing.

—Go Fetch! 1998. (Sabrina, the Teenage Witch Ser.: No. 13). 176p. (YA). (gr. 5 up). per. 4.50 (*0-671-02117-6*, Simon Pulse) Simon & Schuster Children's Publishing.

—Prom Time. 1999. (Sabrina, the Teenage Witch Ser.: No. 21). 176p. (YA). (gr. 5 up). mass mkt. 4.99 (*0-671-02816-2*, Simon Pulse) Simon & Schuster Children's Publishing.

Weiss, David Cody. Kitty Cornered. 2000. (Sabrina, the Teenage Witch: No. 13). 64p. (J). (gr. 2-5). per. (*0-671-77336-4*, Simon & Schuster Children's Publishing) Simon & Schuster Children's Publishing.

Weiss, David Cody & Weiss, Bobbi J. G. Good Switch, Bad Switch. 1997. (Sabrina, the Teenage Witch Ser.: No. 3). 176p. (YA). (gr. 5 up). mass mkt. 4.99 (*0-671-01435-8*, Simon Pulse) Simon & Schuster Children's Publishing.

—Kitty Cornered. 2000. (Sabrina, the Teenage Witch Ser.: No. 13). (Illus.). 80p. (J). (gr. 2-5). pap. 3.99 (*0-671-03836-2*, Simon Pulse) Simon & Schuster Children's Publishing.

—Now & Again. 2003. (Sabrina, the Teenage Witch Ser.). (Illus.). 160p. (J). mass mkt. 4.99 (*0-689-85581-8*, Simon Pulse) Simon & Schuster Children's Publishing.

—Sabrina, the Teenage Witch. 1997. (Sabrina, the Teenage Witch Ser.: No. 1). 160p. (YA). (gr. 5 up). pap. 4.99 (*0-671-01433-1*, Simon Pulse) Simon & Schuster Children's Publishing.

—Salem on Trial. 1998. (Sabrina, the Teenage Witch Ser.: No. 8). 160p. (YA). (gr. 5 up). per. 4.99 (*0-671-01757-8*, Simon Pulse) Simon & Schuster Children's Publishing.

SAGWA, THE CHINESE SIAMESE CAT (FICTITIOUS CHARACTER)—FICTION

Benjamin, Cynthia. Firefly Nights. 2003. (Sagwa, the Chinese Siamese Cat Ser.). (Illus.). 64p. (J). (ps-3). pap. 2.99 (*0-439-45182-5*) Scholastic, Inc.

—Treasure Hunters. 2003. (Sagwa, the Chinese Siamese Cat Ser.). (Illus.). 32p. (J). (ps-3). pap. 3.99 (*0-439-45180-9*) Scholastic, Inc.

Daugherty, George. Bow Wow Meow. 2003. (Sagwa, the Chinese Siamese Cat Ser.). 24p. (J). mass mkt. 3.50 (*0-439-45599-5*) Scholastic, Inc.

—Cat & Mouse. 2003. (Sagwa, the Chinese Siamese Cat Ser.). 24p. (J). mass mkt. 3.50 (*0-439-45598-7*) Scholastic, Inc.

—New Year's Cleanup. 2004. (Sagwa Ser.). (Illus.). 32p. (J). mass mkt. 3.99 (*0-439-55734-8*, Scholastic Paperbacks) Scholastic, Inc.

Sander, Sonia. Festival of Lanterns. 2003. (Sagwa, the Chinese Siamese Cat Ser.). (Illus.). 32p. (J). (ps-3). pap. 3.99 (*0-439-45179-5*) Scholastic, Inc.

—Sagwa's Lucky Bat. 2003. (Sagwa, the Chinese Siamese Cat Ser.). (Illus.). 64p. (J). (ps-3). pap. 2.99 (*0-439-45181-7*) Scholastic, Inc.

Scholastic, Inc. Staff. Acrobat Cats. 2002. (Sagwa, the Chinese Siamese Cat Ser.: No. 1). (Illus.). 32p. (J). (ps-3). mass mkt. 3.99 (*0-439-42873-4*) Scholastic, Inc.

—Princess Sheegwa. 2002. (Sagwa, the Chinese Siamese Cat Ser.: No. 2). (Illus.). 32p. (J). mass mkt. 3.99 (*0-439-42880-7*) Scholastic, Inc.

Tan, Amy. Sagwa: The Chinese Siamese Cat. 2001. (Illus.). 40p. (J). pap. 6.99 (*0-689-84617-7*, Aladdin) Simon & Schuster Children's Publishing.
—Sagwa: The Chinese Siamese Cat. 2001. 13.14 (*0-606-22103-4*) Turtleback Bks.

SAILOR MOON (FICTITIOUS CHARACTER)—FICTION

Mixx Entertainment Inc., Staff. Meet Sailor Jupiter-Thunder. 2000. (Sailor Moon Scout Guides). (Illus.). 96p. (J). (gr. 4-7). pap. 12.95 (*1-892213-30-3*) Mixx Entertainment, Inc.
—Meet Sailor Mars - Fire. 2000. (Sailor Moon Scout Guides). (Illus.). 96p. (gr. 4-7). pap. 12.99 (*1-892213-28-1*) Mixx Entertainment, Inc.
—Meet Sailor Mercury - Ice. 2000. (Sailor Moon Scout Guides). (Illus.). 96p. (J). (gr. 4-7). pap. 12.95 (*1-892213-31-1*) Mixx Entertainment, Inc.
—Meet Sailor Moon - Crystal. 2000. (Sailor Moon Scout Guides). (Illus.). 96p. (J). (gr. 4-7). pap. 12.95 (*1-892213-32-X*) Mixx Entertainment, Inc.
—Meet Sailor Venus - Love. 2000. (Sailor Moon Scout Guides). (Illus.). 96p. (J). (gr. 4-7). pap. 12.95 (*1-892213-29-X*) Mixx Entertainment, Inc.
Rhino Records Staff. Sailor Moon: Songs from the Hit TV Series with Other. 1998. (J). (ps-3). audio compact disk 16.98 (*1-56826-638-3*, 72267) Rhino Entertainment.
—Sailor Moon: Unnatural Phenomena. 1998. (ps-3). audio 7.99 (*1-56826-628-6*) Rhino Entertainment.
Takeuchi, Naoko. Eternal Sleep. 2000. (Sailor Moon the Novel Ser.: Vol. 5). (Illus.). 120p. (gr. 7-12). pap. 4.99 (*1-892213-33-8*) Mixx Entertainment, Inc.
—Sailor Moon. (Illus.). 192p. Bk. 4. 1999. (Sailor Moon Ser.: Vol. 4). (YA). (gr. 7-12). mass mkt. 9.95 (*1-892213-15-X*, Pocket Mixx); Bk. 5. 1999. (Sailor Moon Ser.: Vol. 5). (J). (gr. 7-12). mass mkt. 9.95 (*1-892213-20-6*, Pocket Mixx); Vol. 1. 1998. (YA). (gr. 8-12). mass mkt. 11.95 (*1-892213-01-X*, Mixx Special Editions) Mixx Entertainment, Inc.
—Sailor Moon. (Illus.). (YA). (gr. 7-12). No. 3 1999. 191p. mass mkt. 9.99 (*1-892213-06-0*); Vol. 2. 2003. (Sailor Moon Ser.: Vol. 2). 192p. mass mkt. 9.99 (*1-892213-05-2*) TOKYOPOP, Inc.
—Sailor Moon: Friends & Foes. Noma, Chikako, ed. 1995. (Illus.). 16p. (J). (ps-3). pap. 5.95 o.s.i (*1-56836-118-1*) Kodansha America, Inc.
—Sailor Moon Supers. 1999. (Sailor Moon Supers Ser.: Vol. 1). (Illus.). (gr. 7-12). No. 1 182p. mass mkt. 9.95 (*1-892213-12-5*); No. 2. 184p. (YA). mass mkt. 9.99 (*1-892213-24-9*) Mixx Entertainment, Inc. (Pocket Mixx).
—Sailor Moon Supers, No. 3. 2000. (Illus.). 184p. (J). (gr. 7-12). mass mkt. 9.99 (*1-892213-26-5*) TOKYOPOP, Inc.
—Scouts on Film. 2000. (Sailor Moon the Novel Ser.: Vol. 6). 120p. (gr. 7-12). pap. text 4.99 (*1-892213-37-0*) Mixx Entertainment, Inc.
West, Tracey. The Doom Tree. 2002. (Sailor Moon Junior Chapter Bks.: Vol. 4). (Illus.). 48p. (J). (gr. 4-6). mass mkt. 3.99 (*0-439-22440-3*) Scholastic, Inc.

SALEM (FICTITIOUS CHARACTER)—FICTION

Barnes-Svarney, Patricia L. Teacher's Pet. 1998. (Sabrina, the Teenage Witch: No. 2). (Illus.). 96p. (J). (gr. 2-5). pap. 3.99 (*0-671-02381-0*, Simon Pulse) Simon & Schuster Children's Publishing.
Berney, Sarah J. Cat by the Tail. 1999. (Sabrina, the Teenage Witch: No. 7). 96p. (J). (gr. 2-5). pap. 3.99 (*0-671-02383-7*, Simon Pulse) Simon & Schuster Children's Publishing.
Dubowski, Cathy. Psychic Kitty. 1999. (Sabrina, the Teenage Witch: No. 6). 96p. (J). (gr. 2-5). pap. 3.99 (*0-671-02382-9*, Simon Pulse) Simon & Schuster Children's Publishing.
Dubowski, Mark. The King of Cats. 1999. (Sabrina, the Teenage Witch: No. 4). 96p. (J). (gr. 2-5). pap. 3.99 (*0-671-02105-2*, Simon Pulse) Simon & Schuster Children's Publishing.
Dubowski, Mark & Dubowski, Cathy. Cat-TV, 1998. (Sabrina, the Teenage Witch: No. 1). (Illus.). 96p. (J). (gr. 2-5). pap. 3.99 (*0-671-02102-8*, Simon Pulse) Simon & Schuster Children's Publishing.
Gallagher, Diana G. Dog Day Afternoon. 1999. (Sabrina, the Teenage Witch: No. 5). (Illus.). 96p. (J). (gr. 2-5). mass mkt. 3.99 (*0-671-02103-6*, Simon Pulse) Simon & Schuster Children's Publishing.
—Worth a Shot. 2000. (Sabrina, the Teenage Witch: No. 11). (J). (gr. 2-5). 81p. per. (*0-671-77334-8*, Simon & Schuster Children's Publishing); 96p. pap. 3.99 (*0-671-03834-6*, Simon Pulse) Simon & Schuster Children's Publishing.
Holder, Nancy. Feline Felon. 1999. (Sabrina, the Teenage Witch: No. 8). 96p. (J). (gr. 2-5). pap. 3.99 (*0-671-02384-5*, Simon Pulse) Simon & Schuster Children's Publishing.
Krulik, Nancy E. Happily Ever After. 1999. (Sabrina, the Teenage Witch Ser.: No. 9). 96p. (J). (gr. 2-5). pap. 3.99 (*0-671-03832-X*, Simon Pulse) Simon & Schuster Children's Publishing.
—Rulin' the School. 2000. (Sabrina, the Teenage Witch: No. 12). (J). (gr. 2-5). 85p. per. (*0-671-77335-6*, Simon & Schuster Children's Publishing); (Illus.). 96p. pap. 3.99 (*0-671-03835-4*, Simon Pulse) Simon & Schuster Children's Publishing.
Richards, Kitty. Salem's Guide to Life with Sabrina the Teenage Witch: A Spellbinding Trivia Book with Stickers. 1997. (Sabrina, the Teenage Witch Ser.). (Illus.). 24p. (YA). (gr. 5 up). pap. text 6.99 (*0-689-81745-2*, Simon Pulse) Simon & Schuster Children's Publishing.
Strickland, Brad & Strickland, Barbara. You're History, 1998. (Sabrina, the Teenage Witch: No. 3). (Illus.). 96p. (J). (gr. 2-5). pap. 3.99 (*0-671-02104-4*, Simon Pulse) Simon & Schuster Children's Publishing.
Vornholt, John. Mascot Mayhem. 2000. (Sabrina, the Teenage Witch Ser.: No. 14). (Illus.). 96p. (J). (gr. 2-5). pap. 3.99 (*0-671-03837-0*, Simon Pulse) Simon & Schuster Children's Publishing.
Weiss, David Cody. Kitty Cornered. 2000. (Sabrina, the Teenage Witch: No. 13). 64p. (J). (gr. 2-5). per. (*0-671-77336-4*, Simon & Schuster Children's Publishing) Simon & Schuster Children's Publishing.
Weiss, David Cody & Weiss, Bobbi J. G. Kitty Cornered. 2000. (Sabrina, the Teenage Witch Ser.: No. 13). (Illus.). 80p. (J). (gr. 2-5). pap. 3.99 (*0-671-03836-2*, Simon Pulse) Simon & Schuster Children's Publishing.
—Salem on Trial. 1998. (Sabrina, the Teenage Witch Ser.: No. 8). 160p. (YA). (gr. 5 up). per. 4.99 (*0-671-01757-8*, Simon Pulse) Simon & Schuster Children's Publishing.

SAMSON (BIBLICAL JUDGE)—FICTION

Larsen, Chris & Kolbrek, Loyal A. Samson's Secret. 1970. (Arch Bks.). (Orig.). (J). (ps-4). pap. 1.99 o.s.i (*0-570-06052-4*, 59-1168) Concordia Publishing Hse.

SAMURAI JACK (FICTITIOUS CHARACTER)—FICTION

Siefken, Paul, et al. Fighting Blind. 2003. (Samurai Jack Chapter Bks.: No. 4). 80p. (J). mass mkt. 4.50 (*0-439-44920-0*) Scholastic, Inc.
Teitelbaum, Michael. The Legend Begins. 2002. (Samurai Jack Ser.). (Illus.). 32p. (J). (gr. 3-7). mass mkt. 4.50 (*0-439-40972-1*) Scholastic, Inc.
West, Tracey. Code of the Samurai. 2003. (Samurai Jack Ser.). 48p. (J). mass mkt. 5.99 (*0-439-45555-3*) Scholastic, Inc.
—Jack & the Wanderers. 2004. (Samurai Jack Ser.). (Illus.). 80p. (J). mass mkt. 4.50 (*0-439-44945-6*, Scholastic Paperbacks) Scholastic, Inc.
—Journey to the Impossible Islands. 2003. (Samurai Jack Chapter Bks.: No. 3). 80p. (J). mass mkt. 4.50 (*0-439-45554-5*) Scholastic, Inc.
—Mountain of Mayhem. 2002. (Samurai Jack Chapter Bks.: No. 1). 80p. (J). (gr. 3-7). mass mkt. 3.99 (*0-439-40975-6*) Scholastic, Inc.
—The Seven Labors of Jack. 2003. (Samurai Jack Chapter Bks.: No. 2). (Illus.). 80p. (J). (gr. 3-7). mass mkt. 4.50 (*0-439-40974-8*) Scholastic, Inc.

SANDIEGO, CARMEN (FICTITIOUS CHARACTER)—FICTION

Bader, Bonnie. Highway Robbery. 1997. (Carmen Sandiego Mystery Ser.). (J). (gr. 4-6). 9.60 o.p. (*0-606-11193-X*) Turtleback Bks.
—One T. Rex over Easy. 1997. (Carmen Sandiego Mystery Ser.). (Illus.). 144p. (J). (gr. 4-6). pap. 4.50 o.p. (*0-06-440679-2*, Harper Trophy) HarperCollins Children's Bk. Group.
—One T. Rex over Easy. 1997. (Carmen Sandiego Mystery Ser.). (J). (gr. 4-6). 9.60 o.p. (*0-606-11190-5*) Turtleback Bks.
Bader, Bonnie & West, Tracey. Highway Robbery. 1997. (Carmen Sandiego Mystery Ser.). (Illus.). 144p. (J). (gr. 4-6). pap. 4.50 o.s.i (*0-06-440685-7*, Harper Trophy) HarperCollins Children's Bk. Group.
DeMaria, Rusel. The Official Carmen Sandiego Clue Book: The Complete Guide to "Where in the World Is Carmen Sandiego?" & "Where in the U. S. A. is Carmen Sandiego?" 1996. (Illus.). 80p. (YA). (gr. 1 up). pap. 11.95 o.p. (*0-06-446193-9*, Harper Trophy) HarperCollins Children's Bk. Group.
—Official Where in the U. S. A. Is Carmen Sandiego? Clue Book. 1997. (Illus.). 80p. (J). pap. 11.95 o.p. (*0-06-446197-1*) HarperCollins Children's Bk. Group.
Golden Books Staff. Where in Europe Is Carmen Sandiego? 1993. (Carmen Sandiego). (Illus.). 96p. (J). (gr. 4-6). pap. 3.25 o.s.i (*0-307-22203-9*, 22203, Golden Bks.) Random Hse. Children's Bks.
—Where in the U. S. A. Is Carmen Sandiego? 1993. (Carmen Sandiego). (Illus.). 96p. (J). (gr. 3-7). pap. 3.25 o.s.i (*0-307-22202-0*, 22202, Golden Bks.) Random Hse. Children's Bks.
Peel, John. Carmen Sandiego: Golden Mini Play Lights. 1994. (Carmen Sandiego). (Illus.). 14p. (J). (gr. 4-6). pap. 10.95 o.s.i (*0-307-75403-0*, Golden Bks.) Random Hse. Children's Bks.
—Where in the U. S. A. Is Carmen Sandiego? 1994. (Carmen Sandiego). 96p. (J). (gr. 4-6). pap. 3.25 o.s.i (*0-307-22208-X*, Golden Bks.) Random Hse. Children's Bks.
—Where in Time Is Carmen Sandiego? Part II. 1993. (Carmen Sandiego). (Illus.). 96p. (J). (gr. 4-6). pap. 3.25 o.s.i (*0-307-22206-3*, 22206-00, Golden Bks.) Random Hse. Children's Bks.
Peel, John & Golden Books Staff. Where in America's Past Is Carmen Sandiego? 1994. (Carmen Sandiego). (Illus.). 96p. (J). (gr. 4-6). pap. 3.25 o.s.i (*0-307-22205-5*, 22205, Golden Bks.) Random Hse. Children's Bks.
—Where in Space Is Carmen Sandiego? 1994. (Carmen Sandiego). (J). (gr. 4-6). pap. 3.95 o.s.i (*0-307-22305-1*, Golden Bks.) Random Hse. Children's Bks.
—Where in the U. S. A. Is Carmen Sandiego? 1993. (J). (gr. 4-7). pap. 3.95 o.s.i (*0-307-22304-3*, Golden Bks.) Random Hse. Children's Bks.
—Where in the World Is Carmen Sandiego? 1991. (Carmen Sandiego). 48p. (J). (gr. 4-6). pap. 3.95 o.s.i (*0-307-22301-9*, 22301, Golden Bks.) Random Hse. Children's Bks.
—Where in Time Is Carmen Sandiego? (Carmen Sandiego). (J). (gr. 4-6). 1996. 48p. pap. 3.95 o.s.i (*0-307-22302-7*, 22302); 1993. (Illus.). 96p. pap. 3.25 o.s.i (*0-307-22204-7*, 22204) Random Hse. Children's Bks. (Golden Bks.).
Peel, John & Neuwirth, Allan. Where in America Is Carmen Sandiego? 1992. (Golden Favorites Ser.). (Illus.). 32p. (J). (gr. 2-5). pap. 8.99 o.s.i (*0-307-15859-4*, 15859, Golden Bks.) Random Hse. Children's Bks.
Peel, John & Nez, John. Where in Space Is Carmen Sandiego? 1993. (Carmen Sandiego). (Illus.). 96p. (J). (gr. 4-6). pap. 3.25 o.s.i (*0-307-22207-1*, Golden Bks.) Random Hse. Children's Bks.
—Where in the World Is Carmen Sandiego? 1991. (Carmen Sandiego). (Illus.). 96p. (J). (gr. 4-6). pap. 3.25 o.s.i (*0-307-22201-2*, 22201, Golden Bks.) Random Hse. Children's Bks.
Peterson, Melissa. The Cocoa Commotion. 1997. (Carmen Sandiego Mystery Ser.). (Illus.). 144p. (J). (gr. 4-6). pap. 4.50 (*0-06-440666-0*, Harper Trophy) HarperCollins Children's Bk. Group.
—The Cocoa Commotion. 1997. (Carmen Sandiego Mystery Ser.). (J). (gr. 4-6). 10.55 (*0-606-11191-3*) Turtleback Bks.
—Hasta la Vista, Blarney. 1997. (Carmen Sandiego Mystery Ser.). (Illus.). 144p. (J). (gr. 4-6). pap. 4.50 o.p. (*0-06-440665-2*, Harper Trophy) HarperCollins Children's Bk. Group.
—Hasta la Vista, Blarney. 1997. (Carmen Sandiego Mystery Ser.). (J). (gr. 4-6). 10.55 (*0-606-11189-1*) Turtleback Bks.
Rieman, Barbara & Rieman, Roy. Where in America's Past Is Carmen Sandiego? 1992. (Carmen Sandiego). (Illus.). (J). (gr. 4-6). 14.95 o.p. (*0-672-48527-3*, Hayden) New Riders Publishing.
—Where in the U. S. A. Is Carmen Sandiego? Book. 1992. (Illus.). 14.95 o.p. (*0-672-48528-1*, Hayden) New Riders Publishing.
—Where in the World Is Carmen Sandiego? 1992. (Carmen Sandiego). (Illus.). (J). (gr. 4-6). 14.95 o.p. (*0-672-48525-7*, Hayden) New Riders Publishing.
—Where in Time Is Carmen Sandiego? 1992. (Carmen Sandiego). (Illus.). (J). (gr. 4-6). 14.95 o.p. (*0-672-48524-9*, Hayden) New Riders Publishing.
Weiss, Ellen. Color Me Criminal. 1997. (Carmen Sandiego Mystery Ser.). (J). (gr. 4-6). 10.55 (*0-606-11188-3*) Turtleback Bks.
—Take the Mummy & Run. 1997. (Carmen Sandiego Mystery Ser.). (J). (gr. 4-6). 9.60 o.p. (*0-606-11192-1*) Turtleback Bks.
Weiss, Ellen & Friedman, Mel. Color Me Criminal. 1997. (Carmen Sandiego Mystery Ser.). (Illus.). 144p. (J). (gr. 4-6). pap. 4.50 o.s.i (*0-06-440663-6*, Harper Trophy) HarperCollins Children's Bk. Group.
—Take the Mummy & Run. 1997. (Carmen Sandiego Mystery Ser.). (Illus.). 160p. (J). (gr. 4-6). pap. 4.50 o.s.i (*0-06-440664-4*, Harper Trophy) HarperCollins Children's Bk. Group.

SANTA CLAUS—FICTION

Alavezos, Gus, illus. Christmas at Santa's. 1994. (Read & Play Board Bks.). 8p. (J). (ps-2). 5.95 o.p. (*0-8431-3732-0*, Price Stern Sloan) Penguin Putnam Bks. for Young Readers.
Albertson, Bernard. So You Think There Is No Santa. 2001. 152p. pap. 7.95 (*0-87714-795-7*); 2000. E-Book 6.95 (*0-87714-600-4*) Denlingers Pubs., Ltd.
Alexander, Liza. Big Bird Meets Santa Claus. 1999. (Little Golden Bks.). (Illus.). (J). 2.29 o.s.i (*0-307-98814-7*, Golden Bks.) Random Hse. Children's Bks.
Ambrus, Victor G. & Ambrus, Glenys. Santa Claus Snowed Under. 1995. (Illus.). 32p. (J). (*0-19-279941-X*) Oxford Univ. Pr., Inc.
Amoss, Berthe. What Did You Lose, Santa Claus? 1987. (Illus.). 24p. (J). (ps-1). 3.95 o.p. (*0-694-00197-X*) HarperCollins Children's Bk. Group.
Aoki, Hisako & Gantschev, Ivan. Santa's Favorite Story. 1997. (Illus.). 28p. (J). (ps-3). pap. 5.99 (*0-689-81723-1*, Aladdin) Simon & Schuster Children's Publishing.
Apperley, Dawn. Santa Claus Will Come Tonight. 2002. (Illus.). 24p. (J). (ps-1). pap. 6.95 (*0-439-40449-5*, Cartwheel Bks.) Scholastic, Inc.
Arkadia. Rudolph the Red-Nosed Reindeer. 1999. (Rudolph Ser.). (Illus.). 24p. (J). 3.99 o.s.i (*0-307-16601-5*, Golden Bks.) Random Hse. Children's Bks.
Arnold, Katya R. The Adventures of Snowwoman. 1998. (Illus.). 32p. (J). (ps-3). tchr. ed. 15.95 (*0-8234-1390-X*) Holiday Hse., Inc.
Autry, Gene & Haldeman, Oakley. Here Comes Santa Claus. 2002. (Illus.). 32p. (J). (ps-3). 16.99 (*0-06-028268-1*); lib. bdg. 18.89 (*0-06-028269-X*) HarperCollins Children's Bk. Group.
Babcock, Bruce. The Year Santa Got Sick. unabr. ed. 1998. (Illus.). 32p. (J). (ps-6). pap. 7.95 (*1-892161-02-8*) Babcock Publishing Co.
—The Year Santa Got Sick. 1996. (Illus.). 32p. (J). (gr. 1-3). pap. 7.00 o.p. (*0-8059-3784-6*) Dorrance Publishing Co., Inc.
Bailey, Mary Bryant. Jeoffry's Christmas, RS. 2002. (Illus.). 32p. (J). (gr. k-3). 16.00 (*0-374-33676-8*, Farrar, Straus & Giroux (BYR)) Farrar, Straus & Giroux.
Balian, Lorna. Bah! Humbug? 1982. (Illus.). (J). (gr. k-3). 10.95 o.p. (*0-687-02345-9*) Abingdon Pr.
Barkan, Joanne. A Very Merry Santa Story. 1992. 24p. (J). (ps-3). mass mkt. 3.95 (*0-590-46020-X*, Cartwheel Bks.) Scholastic, Inc.
Baum, L. Frank. The Life & Adventures of Santa Claus. 1988. (J). 16.95 (*0-8488-0428-7*) Amereon, Ltd.
—The Life & Adventures of Santa Claus. 1993. (Illus.). (J). reprint ed. lib. bdg. 18.95 (*1-56849-175-1*) Buccaneer Bks., Inc.
—The Life & Adventures of Santa Claus, ERS. 2003. (Illus.). 192p. (J). 19.95 (*0-8050-3822-1*, Holt, Henry & Co. Bks. For Young Readers) Holt, Henry & Co.
—The Life & Adventures of Santa Claus. 2002. 112p. (ps-3). 92.99 (*1-4043-1252-8*); per. 87.99 (*1-4043-1253-6*) IndyPublish.com.
—The Life & Adventures of Santa Claus. Baisden, Greg S., ed. 1992. (Illus.). 96p. (J). text 24.95 (*1-879450-76-3*) Kitchen Sink Pr., Inc.
—The Life & Adventures of Santa Claus. 1986. (Signet Classics). 160p. (J). (gr. 7-12). mass mkt. 4.95 (*0-451-52064-5*, Signet Classics) NAL.
—The Life & Adventures of Santa Claus. (J). 1999. (Illus.). 224p. (ps up). 6.99 o.s.i (*0-517-20579-3*); 1984. (gr. 2-6). 3.99 o.s.i (*0-517-42062-7*) Random Hse. Value Publishing.
—The Life & Adventures of Santa Claus. 1990. (Illus.). (J). (gr. 3-8). 24.50 (*0-8446-5450-7*) Smith, Peter Pub., Inc.
Benjamin, Alan. Dear Santa Chubby Board Book. 1993. (Chubby Board Bks.). (Illus.). 16p. (J). (ps up). 3.95 (*0-671-87068-8*, Little Simon) Simon & Schuster Children's Publishing.
Bentley, Dawn. Santa's Surprise: A Pop-Up Story Box. 1998. (Illus.). 12p. (YA). (gr. 2 up). 12.95 (*1-58117-018-1*, Piggy Toes Pr.) Intervisual Bks., Inc.
Birchmore, Daniel A. The Reluctant Santa: Christmas Has Been Cancelled. 1997. (Illus.). 32p. (J). (ps-3). 15.95 (*1-887813-00-4*) Cucumber Island Storytellers.
Birenbaum, Barbara. The Cupdeer. 1992. (Illus.). (J). pap. o.p. (*0-935343-02-4*); lib. bdg. o.p. (*0-935343-04-0*) Peartree.
Boniface, William. Santa's Sleigh Is Full. 2002. (Top This! Ser.). (Illus.). 5p. (J). bds. 9.99 (*0-8431-4543-9*, Price Stern Sloan) Penguin Putnam Bks. for Young Readers.
Bonsall, Crosby N. Twelve Bells for Santa. 1977. (I Can Read Bks.). (Illus.). 64p. (J). (ps-3). lib. bdg. 11.89 o.p. (*0-06-020582-2*) HarperCollins Children's Bk. Group.
Bracken, Carolyn, et al. Santa's Workshop. 1997. (Illus.). (J). (ps-3). pap., stu. ed. 2.75 o.s.i (*0-679-88875-6*, Random Hse. Bks. for Young Readers) Random Hse. Children's Bks.
Bradbury. Santa Claus Has a Busy Night. (Christmas Titles Ser.: No. S808-6). (Illus.). (J). 3.95 (*0-7214-5077-6*, Ladybird Bks.) Penguin Group (USA) Inc.
Bratun, Katy. The Gingerbread Mouse. 2003. (Illus.). 32p. (J). 12.99 (*0-06-009080-4*); lib. bdg. 13.89 (*0-06-009081-2*) HarperCollins Pubs.
Braybrooks, Ann. Walt Disney's Santa's Workshop. 1995. (Illus.). 32p. (J). (gr. k-3). 12.95 (*0-7868-3026-3*) Disney Pr.

Breathed, Berkeley. Red Ranger Came Calling. (Illus.). (J). 1994. 16.95 o.p. (*0-316-10881-2*); 1997. 32p. reprint ed. pap. 7.95 (*0-316-10249-0*) Little Brown & Co.

Bridgman, C. A. Santa's Hawaiian Vacation. (J). 14.95 (*0-681-32827-4*) Booklines Hawaii, Ltd.

—Santa's Hawaiian Vacation. 1996. (Illus.). 32p. (J). (ps-4). 14.95 (*0-9659382-0-4*) Immanuel Pr.

Briggs, Raymond. Father Christmas. 1977. (Picture Puffin Ser.). (Illus.). 32p. (J). (gr. k-3). pap. 4.50 o.p. (*0-14-050125-8*, Puffin Bks.) Penguin Putnam Bks. for Young Readers.

—Father Christmas. 1973. (Illus.). 32p. (J). (gr. k-3). 14.95 o.s.i (*0-698-20272-4*, Coward-McCann) Putnam Publishing Group, The.

—Father Christmas. 1997. (J). 18.99 o.s.i (*0-679-88776-8*, Random Hse. Bks. for Young Readers) Random Hse. Children's Bks.

Brooke, Roger. Santa's Christmas Journey. 1984. (Story Clippers Ser.). (Illus.). 32p. (J). (gr. k-5). pap. 9.27 o.p. (*0-8172-2259-6*); pap. 23.95 o.p. (*0-8172-2269-3*); lib. bdg. 19.97 o.p. (*0-8172-2116-6*); lib. bdg. 29.28 o.p. incl. audio (*0-8172-2244-8*) Raintree Pubs.

Brooks, Walter R. Freddy Goes to the North Pole. 2001. (Illus.). 306p. (J). 23.95 (*1-58567-104-5*) Overlook Pr., The.

—Freddy Goes to the North Pole. 2002. (Illus.). 320p. (J). pap. 7.99 (*0-14-230206-6*, Puffin Bks.) Penguin Putnam Bks. for Young Readers.

Brown, Jeff. Stanleys Christmas Adventure. 2003. (Stanley Lambchop Adventure Ser.). (Illus.). 80p. (J). pap. 4.99 (*0-06-442175-9*, Harper Trophy) HarperCollins Children's Bk. Group.

—Stanleys Christmas Adventure. 2003. (Stanley Lambchop Adventure Ser.). 96p. (J). lib. bdg. 15.89 (*0-06-029828-6*) HarperCollins Pubs.

Buckner, Arlene. Elphina. 1998. (Illus.). 32p. (J). (gr. k-2). 17.95 (*1-890309-56-7*) Tem Bk. Co., Inc., The.

Bunsen, Rick. Rudolph the Red-Nosed Reindeer. 2000. (Little Golden Bks.). (Illus.). 24p. (J). (ps-3). 2.99 (*0-307-98829-5*, 98829, Golden Bks.) Random Hse. Children's Bks.

—The Story of Santa Claus. 1994. (Storytime Christmas Bks.). (Illus.). 24p. (J). (ps-2). pap. 1.29 o.p. (*1-56293-496-1*, McClanahan Bk.) Learning Horizons, Inc.

Burningham, John. Harvey Slumfenburger's Christmas Present. (Illus.). (J). (ps-3). 2000. 48p. bds. 6.99 (*0-7636-1378-9*); 1993. 32p. 16.95 o.p. (*1-56402-246-3*); 1996. 48p. reprint ed. bds. 6.99 o.p. (*1-56402-978-6*) Candlewick Pr.

Burton, Terry, illus. Santa's Busy Night. 1996. 20p. (J). (ps). bds. 3.49 (*1-85854-545-5*) Brimax Bks., Ltd.

Bushell, Isobel, illus. Santa Claus Is Coming to Town Board Book. 1993. (Musical Board Bk.). 12p. (J). (ps up). 5.95 (*0-694-00563-0*, Harper Festival) HarperCollins Children's Bk. Group.

Campbell, Louisa. Gargoyles' Christmas. 1994. (Illus.). 32p. (J). 19.95 o.p. (*0-87905-587-1*) Smith, Gibbs Pub.

Catalano, Dominic. Santa & the Three Bears. 2001. (Illus.). 32p. (J). 15.95 (*1-56397-864-4*) Boyds Mills Pr.

CCC of America Staff. Nicholas: The Boy Who Became Santa. 1989. (Illus.). 35p. (J). (ps-4). 14.99 incl. VHS (*1-56814-003-7*) CCC of America.

Chambers, Julie. Santa's Busy Christmas. 1996. (Illus.). 14p. (J). (ps-k). 7.95 o.s.i (*0-694-00905-9*, Harper Festival) HarperCollins Children's Bk. Group.

Charbonnel, Olivier. Santa's Factory. 2000. (Illus.). 12p. (J). pap. 15.95 (*1-902413-51-2*) Van der Meer, a Div. of PHPC GBR. *Dist:* Abbeville Pr., Inc.

Christie, Michael G. Olive the Orphan Reindeer. 2000. (Illus.). 50p. (J). (gr. 4-7). pap. 7.95 (*1-889658-16-2*) New Canaan Publishing Co., Inc.

—The Story of Olive. 1999. (Illus.). 50p. (J). (gr. 4-7). 14.95 (*1-889658-18-9*) New Canaan Publishing Co., Inc.

Civardi, Annie. The Secrets of Santa. 1991. (Illus.). 32p. (J). (ps-1). pap. 13.95 (*0-671-74270-1*, Simon & Schuster Children's Publishing) Simon & Schuster Children's Publishing.

Clements, Andrew. Santa's Secret Helper. 1991. (Illus.). 32p. (J). (gr. k up). pap. 14.95 o.p. (*0-88708-136-3*, Simon & Schuster Children's Publishing) Simon & Schuster Children's Publishing.

Coffey, Tim. Christmas at the Top of the World. 2003. (Illus.). 32p. (J). 15.95 (*0-8075-5762-5*) Whitman, Albert & Co.

Compton, Kenn. Happy Christmas to All! 1991. (Illus.). 32p. (J). (ps-3). lib. bdg. 14.95 o.p. (*0-8234-0890-6*) Holiday Hse., Inc.

Conrad, Pam. The Tub People's Christmas. 1999. (Laura Geringer Bks.). (Illus.). (J). (ps-3). 32p. 15.95 (*0-06-026028-9*); 40p. lib. bdg. 15.89 (*0-06-026029-7*) HarperCollins Children's Bk. Group. (Geringer, Laura Bk.).

Conyers, DeWitt. Santa Claus the Movie: Santa's Sleigh. 1985. (Fast Rolling Bks.). (Illus.). 12p. (J). (ps). 5.95 o.p. (*0-448-10282-X*, Grosset & Dunlap) Penguin Putnam Bks. for Young Readers.

Cornetta, Fred. Holly Snow. 1997. (Illus.). 32p. (Orig.). (J). (ps-6). pap. 5.95 (*0-9658318-2-5*) Icicle Publishing.

Costello, Carol. Santa on My Couch. DHP, Inc. Staff, ed. 1995. (Illus.). 32p. (J). (ps-3). pap. (*1-885531-11-7*) Mess Hall Writers.

Cowley, Stewart. Santa's Littlest Helper. 1996. (Fluffy Tales Ser.). (Illus.). 10p. (J). (ps-k). bds. 4.99 o.p. (*0-88705-964-3*) Reader's Digest Children's Publishing, Inc.

Crespi, Francesca, illus. Santa Claus Is Coming!, ERS. 1987. 8p. (J). (ps-2). pap. 3.95 o.p. (*0-8050-0472-6*, Holt, Henry & Co. Bks. For Young Readers) Holt, Henry & Co.

Currey, Anna. Truffle's Christmas. 2000. (Illus.). (J). (*0-531-30289-X*); 32p. pap. 15.95 (*0-531-30266-0*) Scholastic, Inc. (Orchard Bks.).

Cuyler, Margery. Fat Santa, ERS. 32p. (J). (ps-3). 1989. (Illus.). pap. 4.95 o.s.i (*0-8050-1167-6*); 1987. 14.95 o.p. (*0-8050-0423-8*) Holt, Henry & Co. (Holt, Henry & Co. Bks. For Young Readers).

Dadey, Debbie & Jones, Marcia Thornton. Santa Claus Doesn't Mop Floors. 1991. (Adventures of the Bailey School Kids Ser.: No. 3). 80p. (J). (gr. 2-4). mass mkt. 3.99 (*0-590-44477-8*) Scholastic, Inc.

—Santa Claus Doesn't Mop Floors. 1991. (Adventures of the Bailey School Kids Ser.: No. 3). (J). (gr. 2-4). 10.14 (*0-606-01936-7*) Turtleback Bks.

Daly, Eileen. The Santa Claus Book. 1987. (Golden Super Shape Book Ser.). (Illus.). 24p. (J). (gr. 2-5). reprint ed. pap. 3.29 o.s.i (*0-307-10046-4*, Golden Bks.) Random Hse. Children's Bks.

David, Lawrence. Peter Claus & the Naughty List. Date not set. (Illus.). 32p. (J). pap. 6.99 (*0-440-41575-6*) Dell Bks. for Young Readers CAN. *Dist:* Random Hse. of Canada, Ltd.

—Peter Claus & the Naughty List. 2001. (Illus.). 32p. (J). (ps-2). 15.95 (*0-385-32654-8*, Doubleday Bks. for Young Readers) Random Hse. Children's Bks.

David, Lawrence & Durand, Delphine. Peter Claus & the Naughty List. 2001. (Illus.). 32p. (J). (ps-2). lib. bdg. 17.99 (*0-385-90842-3*, Dell Books for Young Readers) Random Hse. Children's Bks.

Davies, Gill. Santa's Sleigh. 1997. (Christmas Window Bks.). (Illus.). 14p. (J). (ps up). bds. 4.98 (*1-85854-667-2*) Brimax Bks., Ltd.

Davies, Valentine. Miracle on 34th Street. 1996. 76p. pap. 5.60 (*0-87129-707-8*, M96) Dramatic Publishing Co.

—Miracle on 34th Street. 2002. 80p. pap. 6.25 (*0-573-62892-0*) French, Samuel Inc.

—Miracle on 34th Street. fac. ed. 2001. 136p. (YA). 12.95 (*0-15-216377-8*) Harcourt Children's Bks.

—Miracle on 34th Street. gif. ed. 1991. (Illus.). 146p. pap. 9.95 (*0-15-660455-8*, Harvest Bks.) Harcourt Trade Pubs.

—Miracle on 34th Street: (Ornament & Book) gif. ed. 2002. (Illus.). 144p. (J). 16.95 (*0-15-204575-9*) Harcourt Children's Bks.

de Brunhoff, Jean. Babar & Father Christmas. Haas, Merle, tr. from FRE. 2001. Tr. of Babar et le Pere Noel. 48p. (J). (gr. 3). 15.95 (*0-375-81444-2*); (Illus.). (ps-2). lib. bdg. 17.99 (*0-375-91444-7*) Random Hse. Children's Bks. (Random Hse. Bks. for Young Readers).

de Paola, Tomie. Get Dressed, Santa! 1996. (Illus.). 12p. (J). (ps). 4.99 (*0-448-41258-6*, Grosset & Dunlap) Penguin Putnam Bks. for Young Readers.

Demi, Hitz. Santa's Furry Friends, ERS. 1994. (J). 9.95 o.p. (*0-8050-2202-3*, Holt, Henry & Co. Bks. For Young Readers) Holt, Henry & Co.

Dollin, Laura. Santa Claus. 2003. (Illus.). 12p. bds. 5.99 (*0-7636-2144-7*) Candlewick Pr.

Douglas, Vincent. Santa's Little Library of Christmas Stories, 12 bks. 2001. (Illus.). 120p. (J). (ps-k). 3.00 (*1-58845-235-2*) McGraw-Hill Children's Publishing.

—Santa's Workshop, 4 bks., Set. 2003. (My Block Book Schoolhouse Collections). (Illus.). 22p. (J). 12.95 (*1-58845-523-8*) McGraw-Hill Children's Publishing.

Drescher, Henrik. Looking for Santa Claus. 1984. (Illus.). 32p. (J). (ps-1). 12.50 o.p. (*0-688-02997-3*); lib. bdg. 11.47 o.p. (*0-688-02999-X*) HarperCollins Children's Bk. Group.

Drop, Paul A. Santa Goes to Heaven. 1985. 22p. (J). pap. text 6.95 o.p. (*0-9615147-0-1*) Mr. Padco Pubns.

Dubowski, Cathy. The Christmas Santa Almost Missed. 1992. (Storytime Christmas Bks.). (Illus.). 24p. (Orig.). (J). (ps-2). pap. 1.29 o.p. (*1-878624-48-2*, McClanahan Bk.) Learning Horizons, Inc.

Dubowski, Cathy & Lucas, Margeaux. Santa's Biggest Little Helper. 1997. (Scratch & Sniff Bks.). 32p. (J). pap. 4.99 o.s.i (*0-307-13553-5*, Golden Bks.) Random Hse. Children's Bks.

Dupuis, Ann. Santa's Secret: A Gatecrasher Adventure with "All the Rules You Need to Know" 2nd ed. 1998. (Illus.). 24p. pap. 4.95 (*1-887154-05-1*, GGG3003) Grey Ghost Pr., Inc.

Duvoisin, Roger. One Thousand Christmas Beards. 1962. (Illus.). (J). (gr. k-3). lib. bdg. 6.99 o.p. (*0-394-91466-X*, Knopf Bks. for Young Readers) Random Hse. Children's Bks.

Edens, Cooper. Nicholi. (Illus.). (J). (ps-2). 1997. 40p. lib. bdg. 16.00 (*0-689-80495-4*); 1996. 15.00 (*0-671-50545-9*) Simon & Schuster Children's Publishing. (Simon & Schuster Children's Publishing).

Edwards, Julie Andrews & Hamilton, Emma Walton. Dumpy Saves Christmas. 2001. (Dumpy Ser.: No. 3). (Illus.). 32p. (J). 15.99 (*0-7868-0743-1*) Hyperion Bks. for Children.

Egan, Louise B. Santa's Christmas Ride: A Storybook with Real Presents. 1993. (Illus.). 52p. (J). 16.95 (*0-8362-4505-9*) Andrews McMeel Publishing.

Ewing, Juliana H. Old Father Christmas: Based on a Story by Juliana Horatia Ewing. 1993. (Illus.). 42p. (J). (ps-3). 12.95 o.p. (*0-8120-6354-6*) Barron's Educational Series, Inc.

Fass, Bernie & Wolfson, Mack. United Santas of America. 1987. 48p. (J). (gr. 3-12). pap. 16.95 (*0-86704-038-6*); stu. ed. 2.95 (*0-86704-039-4*) Clarus Music, Ltd.

Faulkner, Keith. Charlie Chimp's Christmas: A Pop-Up Extravaganza of Festive Friends. 2002. (Illus.). 16p. (J). (gr. k-3). 9.95 (*0-7641-5556-3*) Barron's Educational Series, Inc.

Fearnley, Jan. Little Robin's Christmas. 1998. (Illus.). 32p. (J). (ps-2). 14.95 (*1-888444-40-1*) Little Tiger Pr.

—Little Robin's Christmas. 2002. 32p. (J). pap. 5.95 (*1-58925-371-X*, Tiger Tales) ME Media LLC.

Fernandes, Kim. A Visit from Saint Nicholas. 1999. 32p. (J). pap. o.s.i (*0-385-25929-8*) Doubleday Canada, Ltd. CAN. *Dist:* Random Hse., Inc.

Fewell, Anne. Merrywinkle: The Adventures of Santa's Big Brother. 1996. (Illus.). 32p. 11.95 (*1-888045-02-7*) Action Publishing, LLC.

Fitzgerald, Clyde C. The Year Santa's Reindeer Went. . . on Strike! 2001. 6.95 (*0-9715874-0-X*) Ira Valley Ideas.

Fitzwater, Ivan W. Cappy the Christmas Woodpecker. 2002. pap. 8.95 (*0-934955-51-4*) Watercress Pr.

Ford, Linda. Santa Claus, Inc. 1998. mass mkt. 3.99 (*0-590-11504-9*) Scholastic, Inc.

Frances, Marian. The Christmas Santa Almost Missed. 1997. (J). 7.95 o.p. (*0-606-19104-6*) Turtleback Bks.

Fulgaro, Elizabeth B. Santa Claus Celebrates Jesus' Birthday. 1994. (Illus.). 32p. (Orig.). (J). (gr. 3-7). pap. 5.95 (*0-9638891-0-9*) Holy Spirit Pr.

Funworks Staff. Santa's Squeaky Boots. 1996. 9p. (J). 6.98 o.s.i (*1-57082-338-3*) Mouse Works.

Gaffington, Urslan J. Silver Berries & Christmas Magic. 1996. (Illus.). 32p. (J). (ps-3). 18.95 (*0-9647811-0-7*) RiverMoon Bks.

Geyer, Waldon M. Santa & Friends. 1991. 32p. (J). 14.95 (*1-880695-01-4*); 23.95 incl. audio (*1-880695-03-0*); 7.95 (*1-880695-00-6*); pap. 15.95 incl. audio (*1-880695-04-9*); pap. 8.95 (*1-880695-02-2*) Santa & Friends.

Gibbons, Gail. Santa Who? 1999. (Illus.). 32p. (J). (gr. k-3). 15.95 (*0-688-15528-6*); 15.89 (*0-688-15529-4*); 15.95 (*0-688-15528-6*) HarperCollins Children's Bk. Group.

Gifford, Christopher. A Present for Santa! 2002. (Dora the Explorer Ser.). (Illus.). 12p. (J). 11.95 (*0-689-84935-4*, Simon Spotlight/Nickelodeon) Simon & Schuster Children's Publishing.

Gifford, Myrna. When Santa Got Stuck in the Chimney. 2001. (Illus.). 16p. (J). 5.95 (*0-9720763-0-1*, PB1) Action Factor, Inc.

Gimbel, Cheryl F. Why Does Santa Celebrate Christmas? Lovelady, Janet, ed. 1990. (Illus.). 36p. (J). (gr. 2 up). 12.95 (*0-915190-67-2*, JP9067-2) Jalmar Pr.

Godwin, Laura. Happy Christmas, Honey! 2002. (Happy Honey Ser.). (Illus.). 32p. (J). pap. 3.99 (*0-689-84764-5*, Aladdin) Simon & Schuster Children's Publishing.

Golden Books Staff. Santa's Big Problem: Christmas Workshop. 2001. 80p. (J). (ps-1). pap. 2.99 (*0-307-25229-9*, Golden Bks.) Random Hse. Children's Bks.

—What's in Santa's Bag? 2002. (Illus.). 12p. (J). bds. 7.99 (*0-307-20070-1*, Golden Bks.) Random Hse. Children's Bks.

Gomi, Taro. Santa Through the Window. 1995. (Single Titles Ser.). (Illus.). 36p. 12.95 o.p. (*1-56294-934-9*); (J). 21.90 (*1-56294-454-1*) Millbrook Pr., Inc.

Graham, Brandon. Perverts of the Unknown. 2003. (Illus.). 56p. pap. 9.95 (*1-56163-374-7*, Amerotica) NBM Publishing Co.

Great Aunt Adeline. The Legend of Sinter Klaas. 1992. (Illus.). 32p. (Orig.). (J). (gr. k-4). pap. text 5.95 (*0-9632863-0-7*) Ebner, Adeline R. & Melissa A. Steffes.

Greenburg, Dan. Young Santa. (Illus.). 80p. (J). 1993. pap. 4.99 o.p. (*0-14-034773-9*, Puffin Bks.); 1991. 13.95 o.p. (*0-670-83905-1*, Viking Children's Bks.) Penguin Putnam Bks. for Young Readers.

Gregory, Dave & Puls, Grace. Theodore Was Here. 1997. (Illus.). 28p. (J). (ps-4). 15.95 (*0-9653798-0-9*) Theodore Publishing, Inc.

Grimsley-Fambro, Sonja. Santa Spent the Night with Me. l.t. ed. 2002. (Illus.). 30p. (J). per. 40.99 (*1-893108-88-0*) Neighborhood Pr. Publishing.

—Santa Spent the Night with Me - Coloring Book. l.t. ed. 2002. (Illus.). 16p. (J). 4.99 (*1-893108-89-9*) Neighborhood Pr. Publishing.

Guinn, Jeff. The Autobiography of Santa Claus: It's Better to Give. Towle, Mike, ed. 1994. (Illus.). 283p. (J). 22.95 o.p. (*1-56530-140-4*) Summit Publishing Group - Legacy Bks.

Haban, Rita. Who Is Santa? 2001. 26p. (J). 7.95 net. (*0-9706654-3-1*) Sprite Pr.

Hader, Bertha. Visit from Saint Nick. 1990. (Hader Illustrated Ser.). (J). 3.98 o.p. (*0-8317-4274-7*) Smithmark Pubs., Inc.

Harper, Stephan J. One Christmas Story. 2003. (Illus.). 32p. lib. bdg. 16.95 (*0-9741800-0-9*) Inspire Press, Inc.

Harrington, D. A. Santa's Marriage. 1997. (Illus.). 24p. (J). pap. 7.00 (*0-8059-4234-3*) Dorrance Publishing Co., Inc.

Hartelius, Margaret A. Is That You, Santa? 1998. (All Aboard Reading Ser.). (Illus.). 32p. (J). (ps-1). 3.99 (*0-448-41849-5*, Platt & Munk) Penguin Putnam Bks. for Young Readers.

Hayes, Sarah. A Bad Start for Santa Claus. 1997. (Illus.). 32p. (J). (ps-1). reprint ed. bds. 3.99 o.s.i (*0-7636-0348-1*) Candlewick Pr.

—A Bad Start for Santa Claus. 1986. (Illus.). 32p. (J). (ps-3). 12.95 o.s.i (*0-316-35183-0*, Joy Street Bks.) Little Brown & Co.

Haywood, Carolyn. How the Reindeer Saved Santa. 1991. (Illus.). 32p. (J). (ps up). reprint ed. pap. 4.95 o.p. (*0-688-11073-8*, Morrow, William & Co.) Morrow/Avon.

—Santa Claus Forever! 1983. (Illus.). 32p. (J). (gr. k-3). lib. bdg. 11.88 o.p. (*0-688-02345-2*); pap. 11.95 o.p. (*0-688-10998-5*) Morrow/Avon. (Morrow, William & Co.).

Hazen, Barbara Shook. Rudolph the Red-Nosed Reindeer. 1997. (Super Shape Bks.). (J). o.p. (*0-307-13012-6*, Golden Bks.) Random Hse. Children's Bks.

Hazen, Barbara Shook & Golden Books Staff. The Story of Santa Claus. 1989. (Big Story Ser.). (Illus.). 32p. (J). (ps up). pap. 5.99 o.s.i (*0-307-12097-X*, Golden Bks.) Random Hse. Children's Bks.

Hegg, Tom. A Silent Night for Peef. 1998. (Illus.). 48p. (J). (ps-3). 15.95 (*0-931674-35-2*) Waldman Hse. Pr., Inc.

Henkel, Donald G. A Legend of Santa & His Brother Fred. 2000. (Illus.). 46p. (J). 20.50 (*0-9673504-0-9*) Quillpen.

Herman, Gail. The Secret Santa Mystery. 2003. (Scooby-Doo! Reader Ser.). 32p. (J). mass mkt. 3.99 (*0-439-45619-3*, Scholastic Paperbacks) Scholastic, Inc.

Heufemann, Danielle. The Secret of the North Pole. 2001. (Illus.). 32p. (J). (gr. k-3). 15.00 (*1-56189-309-9*, American Education Publishing) McGraw-Hill Children's Publishing.

Hill, Laban C. & Johnson, Evelyn. Santa's Surprises, 6 bks., Set. 1994. (Illus.). (J). (gr. k-3). 9.95 o.p. (*0-89577-633-2*) Reader's Digest Assn., Inc., The.

Himmel, Roger J. Lollipop Dragon Helps Santa. Manoni, Mary H., ed. 1978. (Holiday Adventures of the Lollipop Dragon Ser.). (Illus.). (J). (gr. k-3). pap. text 29.95 o.p. (*0-89290-037-7*) S V E & Churchill Media.

Hoff, Syd. Where's Prancer? (Illus.). (J). (ps-2). 1999. 32p. pap. 5.95 (*0-06-443594-6*, Harper Trophy); 1960. lib. bdg. 12.89 o.p. (*0-06-022546-7*); 1997. 32p. 14.95 (*0-06-027600-2*) HarperCollins Children's Bk. Group.

Holmquist, Delano. Santasauras. 2002. (Illus.). 32p. (J). (ps-2). 14.95 (*1-56554-933-3*) Pelican Publishing Co., Inc.

Hover, M. Here Comes Santa Claus. 1996. (Sturdy Shape Bks.). (Illus.). 14p. (J). (ps). bds. 3.99 o.s.i (*0-307-12267-0*, 12267, Golden Bks.) Random Hse. Children's Bks.

Huang, Benrei, illus. Pop-Up Santa's Workshop. 1992. (Christmas Mini Pop-Ups Ser.). 14p. (J). (ps-1). 3.95 o.p. (*0-448-40252-1*, Grosset & Dunlap) Penguin Putnam Bks. for Young Readers.

Hunt, Amber. Santa's Letters: Lift Flap. 1995. (J). 7.98 o.p. (*0-681-10267-5*) Borders Pr.

Hurd, Thacher. Santa Mouse & the Ratdeer. (Illus.). 40p. (J). (ps-1). 2000. pap. 5.95 (*0-06-443709-4*, Harper Trophy); 1998. 14.95 (*0-06-027694-0*) HarperCollins Children's Bk. Group.

—Santa Mouse & the Ratdeer. 2000. (Illus.). (J). 12.10 (*0-606-22063-1*) Turtleback Bks.

Ideals Publications Inc. Staff. Jolly Old Santa Claus. 1988. (Illus.). 24p. (J). (gr. k-6). 10.95 o.p. (*0-8249-7270-8*) Ideals Pubns.

Ives, Penny. Mrs. Santa Claus. 1991. 32p. (J). (ps-3). 14.99 o.s.i (*0-385-30303-3*, Delacorte Pr.) Dell Publishing.

—Mrs. Santa Claus. 1992. (J). o.s.i (*0-385-30708-X*) Doubleday Publishing.

—Santa's Christmas Journey: A Scrolling Picture Book. 1995. (Illus.). (J). (ps-3). 14.95 (*0-7868-0023-2*) Hyperion Bks. for Children.

Jacobs, Edwin. The Eve They Hi-Jacked Santa Claus. Lt. ed. 2001. 47p. (J). 21.95 (*0-9612948-5-X*) Lem Publishing & Production.

James, Emily. Santa's Surprise. 1992. (Watch Me Glow Bks.). (Illus.). (J). (ps). pap. 3.99 o.s.i (*0-553-37117-7*) Bantam Bks.

Janovitz, Marilyn. What Could Be Keeping Santa? 1997. (Illus.). 32p. (J). (ps-1). 15.95 o.p. (*1-55858-819-1*); 16.50 o.p. (*1-55858-820-5*) North-South Bks., Inc.

Johnston, Tony. Clear Moon, Snow Soon. 2001. (Illus.). (J). 15.95 (*0-87358-785-5*, Rising Moon Bks. for Young Readers) Northland Publishing.

—A Kenya Christmas. 2003. (Illus.). (J). (gr. k-3). tchr. ed. 16.95 (*0-8234-1623-2*) Holiday Hse., Inc.

Jones, Ruthie M. Santa Takes a Vacation - The Happy Adventures of Mr. & Mrs. Claus. 1996. (Illus.). 80p. (Orig.). (J). (ps-6). pap. 15.95 (*0-9655010-2-7*) Celebrity Pubs.

Joyce, Jacqueline. Santa Cookie. 1998. (Illus.). 36p. (Orig.). (J). (ps-4). pap. 7.95 (*0-9652211-6-4*, 11133) Bear Path, The.

—Santa Cookie. DelMar Communication International Staff, tr. 1998. (SPA., Illus.). 36p. (Orig.). (J). (ps-4). pap. 7.95 (*0-9652211-7-2*, 11134) Bear Path, The.

Kapraun, Francis. Santa's Red Toy Bag: (How it All Began) 1994. (Illus.). 24p. (J). (*0-9643313-0-6*) Inspired Ink Productions by Kapraun.

Katchke, Judy, et al. How Will Santa Find Me? 2003. (Full House Ser.: No. 2). 96p. mass mkt. 4.99 (*0-06-054084-2*, HarperEntertainment) Morrow/ Avon.

Keller, Dick & Keller, Irene. Santa Claus Visits the Thinggumajigs. 1982. (Illus.). 48p. (J). (gr. k-6). 2.95 o.p. (*0-8249-8045-X*) Ideals Pubns.

Kessler, Leonard. That's Not Santa! (Hello Reader! Ser.). (Illus.). (J). (FRE.). pap. 5.99 (*0-590-24360-8*); 1994. 28p. pap. 3.99 (*0-590-48140-1*) Scholastic, Inc.

Kessler, Leonard P. That's Not Santa! 1994. (Hello Reader! Ser.). 10.14 (*0-606-06801-5*) Turtleback Bks.

King, Joseph P. & Thomas, E. Del. Boofo: The Dog That Goes Where Santa Goes. 1997. (Illus.). 32p. (J). (ps-3). 14.95 (*1-56554-295-9*) Pelican Publishing Co., Inc.

Kirk, Daniel. Santa Claus the Movie: Pop-Up Panorama Book. 1985. (Illus.). 12p. (J). (ps-3). 7.95 o.p. (*0-448-10276-5*, Grosset & Dunlap) Penguin Putnam Bks. for Young Readers.

Knights, Harry. Luigi & the Lost Wish. 2003. (Nicholas Stories : No. 4). (Illus.). 56p. (J). 20.00 (*1-58980-162-8*) Pelican Publishing Co., Inc.

—The Maiden Voyage of Kris Kringle. 2003. (Nicholas Stories : No. 3). (Illus.). 56p. (J). 20.00 (*1-58980-161-X*) Pelican Publishing Co., Inc.

Koontz, Dean. Santa's Twin. 1996. (Illus.). 60p. (J). (gr. 3-6). reprint ed. 20.00 (*0-7567-6681-8*) DIANE Publishing Co.

—Santa's Twin. abr. ed. 1996. (gr. 4-7). audio 8.95 (*0-694-51771-2*, CPN 10098, Caedmon) Harper-Trade.

—Santa's Twin. 1996. (Illus.). 72p. (gr. 4-7). 20.00 (*0-06-105355-4*, Morrow, William & Co.) Morrow/ Avon.

Krasovec, Bernice. A Legend of Saint Nicholas: A Child's Pictorial Legend. 2nd Lt. rev. ed. 1985. (Children's Pictorial Legends Ser.: No. 1). (Illus.). 31p. (J). (gr. k-6). spiral bd. 5.95 (*0-9661627-0-6*) Children's Pictorial Legends.

Krause, Ute, illus. The Santa Clauses. (Pied Piper Paperback Ser.). 28p. (J). (ps-3). 1988. pap. 3.95 o.s.i (*0-8037-0557-3*); 1986. 11.95 o.p. (*0-8037-0266-3*, Dial Bks. for Young Readers) Penguin Putnam Bks. for Young Readers.

Krensky, Stephen. How Santa Got His Job. 2002. (Illus.). (J). 24.04 (*0-7587-2770-4*) Book Wholesalers, Inc.

—How Santa Got His Job. (Illus.). 32p. 2002. pap. 6.99 (*0-689-84668-1*, Aladdin); 1998. (J). 15.00 (*0-689-80697-3*, Simon & Schuster Children's Publishing) Simon & Schuster Children's Publishing.

Kroll, Steven. Santa's Crash-Bang Christmas. 1977. (Illus.). 32p. (J). (ps-3). tchr. ed. 15.95 o.p. (*0-8234-0302-5*); pap. 5.95 o.p. (*0-8234-0621-0*) Holiday Hse., Inc.

Kunnas, Mauri. Santa Claus & His Elves. Robbins, Maria R., tr. from FIN. 1982. (Illus.). 48p. (J). (ps up). 4.95 o.s.i (*0-517-54781-3*, Random Hse. Bks. for Young Readers) Random Hse. Children's Bks.

Lachner, Dorothea. The Gift from Saint Nicholas. James, J. Alison, tr. from GER. 1995. Tr. of Geschenk vom Nikolaus. (Illus.). 32p. (J). (gr. k-3). 15.95 o.p. (*1-55858-456-0*); lib. bdg. 16.50 (*1-55858-457-9*) North-South Bks., Inc.

Landa, Norbert. Where Is Santa Claus? 1989. (Illus.). 32p. (J). (ps). 5.95 o.p. (*0-8249-8299-1*) Ideals Pubns.

Landa, Norbert & Outlet Book Company Staff. Where Is Santa Claus? 1994. (Illus.). 32p. (J). (gr. k-2). 3.99 o.s.i (*0-517-10215-3*) Random Hse. Value Publishing.

Lane, Julie. The Life & Adventures of Santa Claus. rev. ed. 1985. (Illus.). 154p. (J). pap. 10.00 (*0-9615664-1-8*) Parkhurst Brook Pubs.

—The Life & Adventures of Santa Claus: A Keepsake. rev. ed. 1995. (Illus.). (J). (ps-8). 18.95 (*1-56888-149-5*) Tapestry Pr., Ltd.

Lang, Tom. Mrs. Claus: A Story by Tom Lang. 1997. (Illus.). 64p. (J). (gr. 2-12). pap. 5.00 (*0-9649742-0-7*) Boudelang Pr.

Lanning, Rosemary. I'm the Real Santa Claus! Lanning, Rosemary, tr. 1945. (Illus.). 32p. (J). (ps-2). 14.95 o.p. (*1-55858-318-1*) North-South Bks., Inc.

Leeds, Robert X. How Santa's Best Friend Saved Christmas. 1977. (Illus.). (J). 4.95 o.p. (*0-533-02780-2*) Vantage Pr., Inc.

Levine, Joan G. The Santa Claus Mystery. 1975. (Illus.). 48p. (J). (gr. 1-3). 7.50 o.p. (*0-525-38795-1*, Dutton) Dutton/Plume.

Lewis, J. Patrick. Crystal & Ivory: The Snowflake Sisters. 2003. (Illus.). 32p. (J). 16.95 (*0-689-85029-8*, Atheneum/Anne Schwartz Bks.) Simon & Schuster Children's Publishing.

Lippman, Peter. Santa's Workshop. 1993. (Mini House Book Ser.). (Illus.). 20p. (J). (ps-k). pap. 9.95 (*1-56305-499-X*, 3499) Workman Publishing Co., Inc.

Lonergan, Elaine. Bugs Tubes. 2000. (Activity Ser.). (Illus.). (J). (ps-2). bds. 9.99 o.s.i (*0-307-10733-7*, Golden Bks.) Random Hse. Children's Bks.

Lukas, Catherine. Hello, Santa! 2003. (Little Bill Ser.). (Illus.). 20p. (J). 7.99 (*0-689-85850-7*, Simon Spotlight/Nickelodeon) Simon & Schuster Children's Publishing.

Major, Kevin. The Story of the House of Wooden Santas: An Advent Read-Along in 24 Chapters. rev. ed. 1998. (Illus.). 96p. (gr. 4-7). 12.98 (*0-7651-0829-1*) Smithmark Pubs., Inc.

Marsaw, Roy. Swim, Swam, Swum. Nelson, Shanti, ed. 2002. (Illus.). 32p. (J). (ps-3). pap. 9.95 o.p. (*0-9710278-0-3*) All About Kids Publishing.

—Swim, Swam, Swum. 2nd ed. 2003. (Illus.). 32p. (J). pap. 6.95 (*0-9710278-3-8*) All About Kids Publishing.

Marsh, Carole. The Story of Santa Claus. (J). pap. 2.95 (*0-635-02151-X*, Marsh, Carole Bks.) Gallopade International.

Martin, Frances. The Scarecrow & Santa Claus. 1994. (Illus.). 32p. (J). (ps-2). o.p. (*0-370-31895-1*) Random Hse., Inc.

Masurel, Claire. Where's Santa? 1998. (Lift-the-Flap Ser.). 16p. (J). (ps-1). pap. 6.99 o.s.i (*0-14-056322-9*, Puffin Bks.) Penguin Putnam Bks. for Young Readers.

Matsuura, Richard & Matsuura, Ruth. Gift from Santa. (Illus.). (J). 7.95 (*1-887916-06-7*) Orchid Isle Publishing Co.

McGuy, Bruce. Just Ask Santa. 2001. (Santas Ser.: Bk. 4). 56p. pap. 7.95 (*0-9642311-3-1*) Santa's Publishing.

McLendon, Charles H., Jr. Santa's Stories for Children & Adults, Vol. I. collector's ed. 2002. (Illus.). 12p. (J). (ps-6). pap. 19.95 (*0-9723225-0-7*) Christmas City Distribution, Inc.

McMullan, Kate. Fluffy Saves Christmas. 1999. (Hello Reader! Ser.). (Illus.). 40p. (J). (gr. 1-3). mass mkt. 3.99 (*0-590-52308-2*, Cartwheel Bks.) Scholastic, Inc.

—Fluffy Saves Christmas. (Hello Reader! Ser.). 2000. (Illus.). (J). 9.44 o.p. (*0-606-18546-1*); 1998. 10.14 (*0-606-17295-5*) Turtleback Bks.

McPhail, David M. Santa's Book of Names. 1997. (Illus.). 32p. (J). (ps-3). reprint ed. pap. 6.99 (*0-316-11534-7*) Little Brown & Co.

Mercurio, Helen C. The Miracle Santa's Beard. Mercurio, Mary M., ed. 1985. (Illus.). 29p. (J). 12.00 (*0-9616079-0-4*) Tiffany Publishing Co.

Miles, Calvin. Calvin's Christmas Wish. (Illus.). 32p. (J). (ps-3). 1996. pap. 4.99 o.s.i (*0-14-055866-7*); 1993. 13.99 o.p. (*0-670-84295-8*, Viking Children's Bks.) Penguin Putnam Bks. for Young Readers.

—Calvin's Christmas Wish. 1996. 10.19 o.p. (*0-606-10153-5*) Turtleback Bks.

Miller, Daisy. Santa Claus the Movie: Patch & the Evil Toymaker. 1985. (Illus.). 24p. (J). (ps-1). 1.95 o.p. (*0-448-10278-1*, Grosset & Dunlap) Penguin Putnam Bks. for Young Readers.

—Santa's Reindeer: Santa Claus the Movie. 1985. (Pudgy Pal Board Bks.). (Illus.). 16p. (J). (ps). 3.95 o.p. (*0-448-10222-6*, Grosset & Dunlap) Penguin Putnam Bks. for Young Readers.

Miller, Sherry C. Santa's Helper. 1983. (Molly Character - Color Me Ser.: No. 1). (Illus.). 32p. (Orig.). (J). (gr. k-5). pap. 1.95 (*0-913379-00-X*) Double M Publishing Co.

Mitchell, Grace E. How Santa Got His Reindeer. 1987. (J). (gr. 3-5). 4.95 o.p. (*0-533-07198-4*) Vantage Pr., Inc.

Moerbeek, Kees. Oh No, Santa! 1991. (Triangle Pop-up Ser.). (Illus.). 12p. (J). (ps up). 10.95 o.s.i (*0-8431-2984-0*, Price Stern Sloan) Penguin Putnam Bks. for Young Readers.

Moody, Betty G. Magical Wish. 1998. (Illus.). (J). 15.95 (*0-9663522-1-1*) Character Lines Publishing.

Moore, Clement C. Grumpy Santa. 2003. (J). pap. (*0-439-53039-3*, Orchard Bks.) Scholastic, Inc.

Moore, Lorrie. The Forgotten Helper: A Christmas Story. 2000. (Illus.). 96p. (J). (gr. 4-7). 12.95 (*0-385-32791-9*, Dell Books for Young Readers) Random Hse. Children's Bks.

Mora, Emma. Mortimer Visits Santa Claus. 1987. (Illus.). (J). (ps-1). 3.95 o.p. (*0-8120-5808-9*) Barron's Educational Series, Inc.

Morozumi, Atsuko. Santa's Christmas Countdown. 2003. (Illus.). 15.95 (*0-7696-3189-4*) McGraw-Hill Children's Publishing.

Morrissey, Dean. The Christmas Ship. 2000. (Illus.). 40p. (J). (gr. k-4). lib. bdg. 16.89 (*0-06-028576-1*) HarperCollins Children's Bk. Group.

Mosley, Keith. A Busy Day for Santa. 2001. 8p. pap. 10.95 (*1-902413-49-0*) Van der Meer, a Div. of PHPC GBR. *Dist:* Abbeville Pr., Inc.

Mouse Works Staff. Santa's Helpers. 1995. 24p. (J). 5.98 o.p. (*1-57082-321-9*) Mouse Works.

My Santa Claus Coloring Book. 1986. (J). pap. 1.49 o.s.i (*0-671-63136-5*, Little Simon) Simon & Schuster Children's Publishing.

Nagy, Gloria & Chwast, Seymour. The Wizard Who Wanted to Be Santa. 2000. (Illus.). (J). (ps-3). 16.95 (*0-9679436-0-4*) Sheer Bliss Communications, LLC.

Novak, Matt. The Last Christmas Present. 1993. (Illus.). 32p. (J). (ps-1). mass mkt. 15.99 o.p. (*0-531-08645-3*); pap. 15.95 (*0-531-05495-0*) Scholastic, Inc. (Orchard Bks.).

O'Connell, Jennifer Barrett. Ten Timid Ghosts on a Christmas Night. 2002. (Illus.). 32p. (J). mass mkt. 3.25 (*0-439-39553-4*, Cartwheel Bks.) Scholastic, Inc.

Oetting, Rae. Wrongway Santa. 1991. (Illus.). 32p. (J). lib. bdg. 15.95 (*0-87783-254-4*) Oddo Publishing, Inc.

Oliver, Mary. Legend Santa McDonald. (J). (*0-448-18975-5*) Penguin Putnam Bks. for Young Readers.

—Santa Claus the Movie: The Legend of Santa Claus. 1985. (Illus.). 24p. (J). (ps-1). 1.95 o.p. (*0-448-10280-3*, Grosset & Dunlap) Penguin Putnam Bks. for Young Readers.

Ostheeren, Ingrid. I'm the Real Santa Claus! Lanning, Rosemary, tr. 1994. (Illus.). 32p. (J). 14.88 o.p. (*1-55858-319-X*) North-South Bks., Inc.

—I'm the Real Santa Claus! Lanning, Rosemary, tr. from GER. 1996. (Illus.). 32p. (J). (gr. k-3). pap. 6.95 o.p. (*1-55858-616-4*) North-South Bks., Inc.

Ostrow, Kim. A Colorful Christmas. 2003. (Magical Color Bks.). (Illus.). 10p. (J). bds. 5.95 (*1-4027-0991-9*, Sterling/Pinwheel) Sterling Publishing Co., Inc.

—Jingle Santa: A Book to Touch & Feel. 2001. (Jingle Ears Ser.). (Illus.). 12p. (J). bds. 4.99 (*0-689-84281-3*, Little Simon) Simon & Schuster Children's Publishing.

Outlet Book Company Staff. Santa Claus Is Coming to Town: Timeless Tales. 1992. (Illus.). 48p. (J). 3.99 o.s.i (*0-517-06970-9*) Random Hse. Value Publishing.

Packard, Mary. Christmas Kitten. 1994. (My First Reader Ser.). (Illus.). 28p. (J). (ps-2). mass mkt. 16.00 o.p. (*0-516-05364-7*); pap. 3.95 o.p. (*0-516-45364-5*) Scholastic Library Publishing. (Children's Pr.).

Packer, Gita & Bumpass, Gene. The Nick of Time. 1979. 5.95 o.p. (*0-533-03874-X*) Vantage Pr., Inc.

Palatini, Margie. Elf Help: http://www.falala.com. 1997. (Illus.). 32p. (J). (ps-2). 14.95 (*0-7868-0359-2*); lib. bdg. 15.49 (*0-7868-2304-6*) Hyperion Bks. for Children.

Paulsen, Gary. A Christmas Sonata. 1994. 80p. (J). (gr. 3-7). pap. 4.50 (*0-440-40958-6*) Dell Publishing.

—A Christmas Sonata. 1997. (Illus.). 80p. (gr. 3-7). text 14.95 o.s.i (*0-385-30441-2*, Dell Books for Young Readers) Random Hse. Children's Bks.

—Christmas Sonata. 1994. (J). pap. o.p. (*0-440-90082-4*, Dell Books for Young Readers) Random Hse. Children's Bks.

—Christmas Sonata. 1994. 10.65 (*0-606-06958-5*) Turtleback Bks.

Paxton, Tom. The Story of Santa Claus. 1995. (Illus.). 40p. (J). (ps-3). 15.95 (*0-688-11364-8*) HarperCollins Children's Bk. Group.

—The Story of Santa Claus. (Illus.). 40p. (J). (gr. k-3). 1997. mass mkt. 5.95 (*0-688-15475-1*); 1995. lib. bdg. 14.93 o.p. (*0-688-11365-6*) Morrow/Avon. (Morrow, William & Co.).

—The Story of Santa Claus. 1997. (J). 12.10 (*0-606-11921-3*) Turtleback Bks.

Pellegrini, Nina. Charlie Claus: Santa's Best Friend. 1993. (Illus.). 32p. (J). (ps-6). 2.99 o.s.i (*0-517-09309-X*) Random Hse. Value Publishing.

Peterson, Monique. Santa's Toy Shop. 2000. (Walt Disney Classics Ser.). (Illus.). 32p. (ps-3). 14.99 (*0-7868-5313-1*, Disney Editions) Disney Pr.

Peyo & Matagne. The Smurfs & the Toyshop. 1984. (Illus.). 24p. (J). (ps-3). 3.95 o.p. (*0-394-86077-2*) Random Hse., Inc.

Pfister, Marcus. Wake up, Santa Claus! 1996. (Illus.). 32p. (J). (gr. k-3). 15.95 o.p. (*1-55858-605-9*); 16.50 (*1-55858-606-7*) North-South Bks., Inc.

Pickavance, Lynne. Santa's Surprise. 2003. (Illus.). 16p. (J). 12.99 (*0-8037-2903-0*, Dial Bks. for Young Readers) Penguin Putnam Bks. for Young Readers.

Pierce, Anne M. So Many Gifts. Lindquist, Tom, ed. unabr. ed. 1993. (Illus.). 32p. (J). (gr. k-6). reprint ed. 25.00 incl. audio (*0-9623937-0-3*) Forword.

Pingry, Patricia A. & Hinke, George. Jolly Old Santa Claus: A Christmas Classic. 2000. (Illus.). 26p. (J). (ps-3). bds. 6.95 (*0-8249-4182-9*, Candy Cane Pr.) Ideals Pubns.

Piper, Watty. The Little Engine That Could & the Snowy, Blowy Christmas. 1998. (All Aboard Bks.). (Illus.). 24p. (J). (ps-3). 3.49 (*0-448-41850-9*, Grosset & Dunlap) Penguin Putnam Bks. for Young Readers.

Polacco, Patricia. Welcome Comfort. 40p. (J). 2002. pap. 6.99 (*0-698-11965-7*); 1999. (Illus.). 16.99 (*0-399-23169-2*, G. P. Putnam's Sons) Penguin Putnam Bks. for Young Readers.

Porter-Chase, Mary. The Return of Sinta Claus: A Family Winter Solstice Tale. 1991. (Illus.). (Orig.). (J). (gr. 3-12). pap. 6.00 (*0-9630798-0-8*) Samary Pr.

Posner, Andrea. Santa from Head to Toe. 1999. (Golden Book Ser.). (Illus.). 12p. (J). (ps). bds. 3.99 (*0-307-14527-1*, Golden Bks.) Random Hse. Children's Bks.

Primavera, Elise. Auntie Claus. (Illus.). 40p. (J). (ps-3). 1999. 16.00 (*0-15-201909-X*); 2001. 24.95 o.s.i incl. audio compact disk (*0-15-216259-3*) Harcourt Children's Bks. (Silver Whistle).

—Auntie Claus & the Key to Christmas. 2002. (Illus.). 40p. (J). (gr. k-3). 16.00 (*0-15-202441-7*, Silver Whistle) Harcourt Children's Bks.

Public Domain Staff. Santa Claus Is Coming to Town. 2001. (Sing-Along Storybks.). (Illus.). 6p. (J). (ps up). bds. 6.95 (*0-694-01559-8*, Harper Festival) HarperCollins Children's Bk. Group.

Pulver, Robin. Christmas for a Kitten. 2003. (Illus.). 32p. (J). (gr. k-3). 15.95 (*0-8075-1151-X*) Whitman, Albert & Co.

Quackenbush, Robert. The Most Welcome Visitor. 1982. (Illus.). 32p. (J). (gr. 1 up). 7.95 o.p. (*0-671-96201-9*, Atheneum) Simon & Schuster Children's Publishing.

Quattrocki, Carolyn. Santa Claus Is Coming to Town. 1992. (Favorite Christmas Tales Ser.). (Illus.). 24p. (J). (ps-4). lib. bdg. 11.95 (*1-56674-026-6*, HTS Bks.) Forest Hse. Publishing Co., Inc.

Rader, Laura. Who'll Pull Santa's Sleigh Tonight? 2003. (Illus.). 40p. (J). 12.99 (*0-06-008088-4*) HarperCollins Pubs.

Rader, Laura. Santa's New Suit. (Illus.). 40p. (J). (ps-3). 2002. pap. 5.99 (*0-06-443580-6*); 2000. 12.95 (*0-06-028439-0*); 2000. lib. bdg. 12.89 (*0-06-029284-9*) HarperCollins Children's Bk. Group.

—Who'll Pull Santa's Sleigh Tonight? 2003. (Illus.). 40p. (J). lib. bdg. 13.89 (*0-06-008089-2*) HarperCollins Pubs.

Rader, Laura, illus. Santa's Toyshop. 1997. (*0-7853-2463-1*) Publications International, Ltd.

Rapunzel Meets Santa Claus in Hell. 1999. (C). E-Book 6.95 (*1-931090-01-7*) Street Saint Pubns.

Reiss, Mike. How Murray Saved Christmas. 2000. (Illus.). 32p. (J). (ps-3). 10.99 (*0-8431-7610-5*, Price Stern Sloan) Penguin Putnam Bks. for Young Readers.

—Santa Claustrophobia. 2002. (Illus.). 32p. (J). (gr. 2-5). 10.99 (*0-8431-7756-X*, Price Stern Sloan) Penguin Putnam Bks. for Young Readers.

Rex, Michael. Santa's Busy Night. 2002. (Word-by-Word First Reader Ser.). (Illus.). 32p. (J). mass mkt. 3.99 (*0-439-33491-8*, Cartwheel Bks.) Scholastic, Inc.

Rice, James. Gaston the Green-Nosed Alligator. 2nd ed. 1998. (Illus.). 40p. (YA). (ps up). 14.95 (*1-56554-285-1*) Pelican Publishing Co., Inc.

Richter, Konrad. Wipe Your Feet, Santa Claus! (Illus.). (J). (gr. k-3). 1997. 32p. pap. 6.95 o.p. (*1-55858-775-6*); 1945. 24p. 14.95 o.p. (*1-55858-016-6*) North-South Bks., Inc.

Rojany, Lisa. Santa's New Suit! 1993. (Surprise Bks.). (Illus.). 24p. (J). (ps-2). 7.95 o.s.i (*0-8431-3587-5*, Price Stern Sloan) Penguin Putnam Bks. for Young Readers.

Romano, Ralph & Burke, Joe. Elbo Elf. 2nd ed. 2001. 26p. lib. bdg. 19.95 (*0-9704125-1-7*) Elbo Elf, Inc.

—Elbo Elf: The Package Master of Christmas. l.t. ed. 2000. (Illus.). 29p. (J). (gr. 1-5). 19.95 (*0-9704125-0-9*) Elbo Elf, Inc.

Rosenberg, Liz. On Christmas Eve. 2002. (Illus.). 40p. (J). (gr. k-3). 15.95 (*0-7613-1627-2*); 22.90 (*0-7613-2707-X*) Millbrook Pr., Inc. (Roaring Brook Pr.).

Rylant, Cynthia. Little Whistle's Christmas. 2003. (Little Whistle Ser.). (Illus.). 32p. (J). 16.00 (*0-15-204590-2*) Harcourt Children's Bks.

Santa. 2002. (Little Pups Board Bks.). (Illus.). 11p. (J). (ps). bds. 2.99 (*1-57759-999-3*) Dalmatian Pr.

Santa. 2002. 14p. (J). (ps-k). bds. 9.95 (*0-7525-8851-6*) Parragon, Inc.

Santa Claus Is Coming to Town. 1993. (Favorite Christmas Tales Ser.). (Illus.). 24p. (J). 4.98 (*1-56173-715-1*) Publications International, Ltd.

Santa's Big Day. 1989. (J). pap. 3.95 o.p. (*0-02-689341-X*) Checkerboard Pr., Inc.

Santa's Busy Day. 1998. (Wipe-Off Activity Bks.). (Illus.). 16p. (J). (ps-1). wbk. ed. 3.79 (*1-889319-26-0*) Trend Enterprises, Inc.

Santa's Wish List. 2002. (Little Pups Board Bks.). (Illus.). 24p. (J). (gr. k-4). pap. 2.99 (*1-57759-853-9*) Dalmatian Pr.

Sargent, Dave & Sargent, Pat. Sweetpea: Be Happy. 2003. (Saddle Up Ser.: Vol. 58). (Illus.). 42p. (J). pap. 6.95 (*1-56763-816-3*) Ozark Publishing.

—Sweetpea (Purple Corn Welsh) Be Happy. 2003. (Saddle Up Ser.: Vol. 58). (Illus.). 42p. (J). lib. bdg. 22.60 (*1-56763-815-5*) Ozark Publishing.

Scheidl, Gerda M. Can We Help You, Saint Nicholas? Lanning, Rosemary, tr. from GER. 1945. (Illus.). 32p. (J). (gr. k-3). 14.88 o.p. (*1-55858-155-3*); 14.95 o.p. (*1-55858-154-5*) North-South Bks., Inc.

Schmid, Eleonore. Wake up, Dormouse, Santa Claus Is Here. (Illus.). 32p. (J). (gr. k-3). 1994. pap. 5.95 o.p. (*1-55858-355-6*); 1989. 14.95 o.p. (*1-55858-020-4*) North-South Bks., Inc.

Schoberle, Cecile. Santa Claus & the Christmas Fairies. 1999. (Sparkle 'n' Twinkle Ser.). (Illus.). 16p. (J). (ps-2). pap. 4.99 (*0-689-82874-8*, Little Simon) Simon & Schuster Children's Publishing.

Schrecker, Judie. Santa's New Reindeer. 1996. (Illus.). 39p. (J). (ps up). 17.95 (*1-880664-18-6*) E. M. Productions.

Seibold, J. Otto & Walsh, Vivian. Olive, the Other Reindeer. 1997. (Illus.). 40p. (J). (ps-3). 14.95 (*0-8118-1807-1*) Chronicle Bks. LLC.

Shapiro, Arnold. Day Before Christmas. 1997. (Diorama Pop-Up Bks.). (Illus.). 6p. (J). (ps-1). 5.99 (*0-689-81436-4*, Little Simon) Simon & Schuster Children's Publishing.

Sharmat, Marjorie Weinman. I'm Santa Claus & I'm Famous. 1990. (Illus.). 32p. (J). (ps-4). tchr. ed. 15.95 o.p. (*0-8234-0826-4*) Holiday Hse., Inc.

Sharp, Rhonda. The Nine Most Famous Reindeer of All. 2003. (Illus.). 32p. (J). 21.95 (*0-9708666-3-1*) Tea Road Pr.

Sheppard, Dorothy M. & Sheppard, Jack G. Jo Jo the Elf Meets Santa's Enemy. (Illus.). 65p. (J). (gr. 1-6). pap. 7.95 (*0-9634300-0-9*); 1992. lib. bdg. 12.95 (*0-9634300-1-7*) D&J Arts Pubs.

Shoolbred, Catherine. Santas Reindeer. 2003. (Illus.). 12p. bds. 5.99 (*0-7636-2143-9*) Candlewick Pr.

Siegenthaler, Kathrin. Santa Claus & the Woodcutter. Crawford, Elizabeth, tr. from GER. (Illus.). 32p. (J). (gr. k-3). 1995. pap. 6.95 o.p. (*1-55858-505-2*); 1989. pap. 2.95 o.p. (*1-55858-032-8*); 1945. 13.95 o.p. (*1-55858-027-1*) North-South Bks., Inc.

Silbert, Jack. Santa in Space. 2001. 24p. (J). pap. 3.29 o.p. (*0-307-20410-3*, Golden Bks.) Random Hse. Children's Bks.

Sims, J. Michael. Young Claus: The Legend of the Boy Who Became Santa. 1995. 112p. (J). (ps-3). 12.95 (*0-9645976-6-7*) Cygnet Trumpeter Pubs.

Skelton, Peter. Mr. Jimmy Chimney Sweep: The Mystery Elf of Christmas. 2000. (Illus.). 29p. (J). (ps-1). per. (*0-9706099-0-6*) Breckenridge Group & Assocs.

—Twinkle Toes: The Magical Elf of Christmas. 2000. 24p. (J). (ps-1). per. (*0-9706099-1-4*) Breckenridge Group & Assocs.

Skinner, Daphne. Santa Clause Jr. 1994. (J). pap. 1.00 o.p. (*0-7868-1058-0*) Hyperion Bks. for Children.

Skinner, Daphne, adapted by. The Santa Clause. 1994. (Junior Novel Ser.). (Illus.). 80p. (J). (gr. 3-7). pap. 3.95 (*0-7868-1011-4*) Disney Pr.

Smith, George S. The Christmas Eve Cattle Drive. 1991. (Illus.). 32p. (J). (gr. 3-4). pap. 3.95 (*0-89015-820-7*) Eakin Pr.

Solomon, Aubrey. Twentieth Century-Fox: A Corporate & Financial History. rev. ed. 2002. (Illus.). 300p. (J). pap. 32.95 (*0-8108-4244-0*) Scarecrow Pr., Inc.

Solotareff, Gregoire. The Secret Life of Santa Claus. 2001. (Illus.). 250p. (YA). reprint ed. 18.00 (*0-7881-9575-1*) DIANE Publishing Co.

Sorrentino, Scott. 4208. 1997. (Wonderful World of Disney Ser.). (Illus.). 80p. (J). (gr. 3-7). pap. 3.25 (*0-7868-4215-6*) Disney Pr.

Sparkie. Jolly Old Santa Claus. 2nd ed. 1996. (Illus.). 32p. (J). (gr. 1-4). 16.95 (*0-8249-4080-6*, Candy Cane Pr.) Ideals Pubns.

—Jolly Old Santa Claus: Coloring Book. 1998. (Illus.). 48p. (J). pap. 2.49 (*0-8249-4098-9*, Candy Cane Pr.) Ideals Pubns.

Stainton, Sue. Santa's Snow Cat. 2001. (Illus.). 32p. (J). (ps-2). 15.95 (*0-06-623827-7*); lib. bdg. 15.89 (*0-06-623828-5*) HarperCollins Children's Bk. Group.

—Snow Cat: Santa's Littlest Cat. 2000. (Illus.). (J). (*0-7868-4437-X*) Hyperion Bks. for Children.

Steer, Dugald. An Accidental Christmas. 1998. (Illus.). 24p. (ps-2). 14.95 o.p. (*0-7613-0438-X*) Millbrook Pr., Inc.

Steven, Kenneth C. The Bearer of Gifts. 1998. (Illus.). 32p. (J). (gr. 1-3). 12.99 o.p. (*0-8037-2374-1*, Dial Bks. for Young Readers) Penguin Putnam Bks. for Young Readers.

Stevenson, James. The Oldest Elf. 1996. (Illus.). 32p. (J). 15.00 o.s.i (*0-688-13755-5*); lib. bdg. 14.93 o.p. (*0-688-13756-3*) HarperCollins Children's Bk. Group. (Greenwillow Bks.).

Stickland, Henrietta. The Christmas Bear Mini Book. 1993. (Illus.). 32p. (J). (ps-3). 15.99 o.s.i (*0-525-45062-9*, Dutton Children's Bks.) Penguin Putnam Bks. for Young Readers.

Stickland, Paul. Santa's Workshop: A Magical Three-Dimensional Tour. 1995. (Illus.). 8p. (J). (ps-3). 18.99 o.p. (*0-525-45343-1*, Dutton Children's Bks.) Penguin Putnam Bks. for Young Readers.

Stimson, Joan. Kim Meets Santa Claus. 1991. (Illus.). 28p. (J). (ps-1). pap. 3.95 o.p. (*0-7214-9615-6*, S808-24 SER., Ladybird Bks.) Penguin Group (USA) Inc.

Stone, Bev. Santa Plus Martha. 1992. (Illus.). 62p. (J). (gr. k-6). pap. 12.95 (*0-9619791-1-9*) Stone Studios.

—The Secret of Santa Claus: Flower Blue & Snowie Elves Help Santa Meet His Brothers. 1987. (Illus.). 64p. (J). (gr. k-6). pap. 12.95 (*0-9619791-0-0*) Stone Studios.

Stout, Robert T. Children's Favorite Story of Santa Claus. 1982. (Illus.). 32p. (J). (ps-6). 5.95 (*0-911049-08-8*); pap. 3.95 (*0-911049-04-5*) Yuletide International.

—The Original Story of Santa Claus. 1981. (Illus.). 56p. (J). (ps-8). 6.95 (*0-911049-00-2*) Yuletide International.

Strasser, Todd. Help! I'm Trapped in Santa's Body. 1997. (Help! I'm Trapped Ser.). (J). (gr. 4-7). mass mkt. 3.99 (*0-590-02972-X*) Scholastic, Inc.

Strider, Errol. Elfbert, Sant's Reluctant Helper. 1984. (Illus.). 24p. (Orig.). (J). pap. text incl. audio (*1-878868-03-9*) Creative Recovery.

Sullivan, Ellen. How Santa Got His Elves. 1998. (J). (*1-58173-148-5*) Sweetwater Pr.

Sundvall, Viveca L. Santa's Winter Vacation. Board, Kjersti, tr. 1995. (Illus.). 26p. (ps-3). 13.00 o.p. (*91-29-62953-5*) R & S Bks. SWE. *Dist:* Holtzbrinck Pubs.

Sykes, Julie. Careful, Santa! 2002. (Illus.). 32p. (J). (ps-1). tchr. ed. 14.95 (*1-58925-023-0*, Tiger Tales) ME Media LLC.

—Hurry, Santa! 1998. (Illus.). 32p. (J). (ps-2). 14.95 (*1-888444-37-1*) Little Tiger Pr.

Szekeres, Cyndy & Church, Francis P. Yes Virginia, There Is a Santa Claus. 1997. (Illus.). 32p. (J). (ps-1). pap. 5.95 (*0-590-69196-1*) Scholastic, Inc.

Tallarico, Tony. Santa Claus Activity Book. Duenewald, Doris, ed. 1978. (Elephant Books Ser.). (Illus.). (J). (gr. 1-7). 1.25 o.p. (*0-448-16166-4*) Putnam Publishing Group, The.

Tanner, Suzy-Jane. The Great Santa Surprise. 1996. (Lift-the-Flap Book Ser.). (Illus.). 16p. (J). (ps up). 5.95 (*0-694-00706-4*, Harper Festival) HarperCollins Children's Bk. Group.

Ted E. Bear Rescues Santa Claus. 1985. (J). (gr. k-5). 2.95 o.p. (*0-8249-8115-4*) Ideals Pubns.

Teitelbaum, Michael. Santa Claus the Movie: The Boy Who Didn't Believe in Christmas. 1985. (Illus.). 24p. (J). (ps-1). 1.95 o.p. (*0-448-10277-3*, Grosset & Dunlap) Penguin Putnam Bks. for Young Readers.

Thompson, Corrynn. Angel Elf. 1978. (J). 4.50 o.p. (*0-533-03762-X*) Vantage Pr., Inc.

Tiller, Steve. Rudolf the Red Nose Rocket. 2002. (Illus.). 28p. (J). (gr. k-3). 15.95 (*0-9704597-9-3*) MichaelsMind LLC.

Trimble, Marcia. Moonbeams for Santa. 2001. (Illus.). 32p. (J). (ps-4). 15.95 (*1-891577-89-1*) Images Pr.

Trondheim, Lewis. Happy Halloween, Li'l Santa. 2003. (Illus.). 48p. (J). 14.95 (*1-56163-361-5*) NBM Publishing Co.

—Li'l Santa. 2002. (Illus.). 48p. (J). 14.95 (*1-56163-335-6*) NBM Publishing Co.

Tryon, Leslie. Albert's Christmas. (Illus.). 40p. (J). (gr. k-3). 2000. pap. 5.99 (*0-689-83871-9*, Aladdin); 1997. 16.00 o.s.i (*0-689-81034-2*, Atheneum) Simon & Schuster Children's Publishing.

—Albert's Christmas. 2000. 12.14 (*0-606-19247-6*) Turtleback Bks.

Tulip, Jenny, illus. Santa Claus. 1996. 12p. (J). (ps). bds. 4.98 (*1-85854-551-X*) Brimax Bks., Ltd.

Turner, Sandy. Silent Night. 2001. (Illus.). 40p. (J). (gr. 2 up). 16.00 (*0-689-84156-6*, Atheneum) Simon & Schuster Children's Publishing.

Turner, Thomas N. Country Music Night Before Christmas. 2003. (Illus.). 32p. (J). 14.95 (*1-58980-148-2*) Pelican Publishing Co., Inc.

Twenstrup, Norm. A Surprise for Santa. DHP, Inc. Staff, ed. (Illus.). 32p. (J). (ps-3). pap. (*1-885531-12-5*) Mess Hall Writers.

Tyrrell, Melissa. Here Comes Santa! A Little Foil Book. 1998. (Merry Little Foil Bks.). (Illus.). 10p. (YA). (ps up). 2.95 (*1-58117-007-6*, Piggy Toes Pr.) Intervisual Bks., Inc.

Upton, Richard & Fair, Sharon. The Search for the Smell of Christmas. 1992. (Illus.). 32p. (J). 14.95 (*0-9633348-0-8*) Aromatique, Inc.

Van Allsburg, Chris. The Polar Express. 15th anniv. ed. 2000. (Illus.). 32p. (J). (ps-3). tchr. ed. 29.95 (*0-618-07736-7*, Mariner Bks.) Houghton Mifflin Co. Trade & Reference Div.

Vinge, Joan D. The Santa Claus Storybook: Santa Claus the Movie. 1985. (Illus.). 58p. (J). (gr. 3 up). 6.95 o.p. (*0-448-10281-1*, Grosset & Dunlap) Penguin Putnam Bks. for Young Readers.

Walker, David R. Six Months Before Christmas: A Christmas Story in July. 1996. (Illus.). 14.95 o.p. (*1-880092-37-9*) Bright Bks., Inc.

Wallace, Ivy. Pookie Believes in Santa Claus. 2001. (Illus.). 32p. (J). (gr. k-4). 16.95 (*0-00-198380-6*) HarperCollins Pubs. Ltd. GBR. *Dist:* Trafalgar Square.

—Pookie Believes in Santa Claus. 2001. (Illus.). 32p. pap. 8.95 o.p. (*0-00-664734-0*) Trafalgar Square.

Warren, Jean. Huff & Puff's Foggy Christmas: A Totline Teaching Tale. Cubley, Kathleen, ed. 1994. (Huff & Puff Ser.). (Illus.). 32p. (Orig.). (J). (ps-2). pap. 12.95 o.p. (*0-911019-97-9*, WPH 2012); pap. 5.95 o.p. (*0-911019-96-0*, WPH 2011) McGraw-Hill Children's Publishing. (Totline Pubns.).

Waters, Meg. Santa Claus the Movie: The Elves at the Top of the World. 1985. (Illus.). 24p. (J). (ps-1). 1.95 o.p. (*0-448-10279-X*, Grosset & Dunlap) Penguin Putnam Bks. for Young Readers.

Watson, Wendy. Holly's Christmas Eve. 2002. (Illus.). 32p. (J). (ps-3). lib. bdg. 17.89 (*0-688-17653-4*) HarperCollins Children's Bk. Group.

—Holly's Christmas Eve. 2002. (Illus.). 32p. (J). (ps-3). 15.99 (*0-688-17652-6*); 15.99 (*0-688-17652-6*) HarperCollins Pubs.

Weber, Jill. Santa Flip Book. 1991. (J). pap. 2.50 (*1-878689-03-7*) Frajil Farms.

Weil, Lisl. Santa Claus Around the World. 1987. (Illus.). 32p. (J). (ps-3). lib. bdg. 13.95 o.p. (*0-8234-0665-2*) Holiday Hse., Inc.

Weinberg, Larry. Forgetful Bears Help Santa. 1989. (J). (ps-3). pap. 2.50 o.p. (*0-590-40994-8*) Scholastic, Inc.

—The Forgetful Bears Help Santa. 2002. 40p. (J). 12.95 (*0-375-82291-7*); lib. bdg. 14.99 (*0-375-92291-1*) Random Hse., Inc.

Weinberg, Larry. The Forgetful Bears Help Santa. 2001. (Illus.). 40p. (J). (gr. k-2). 9.95 (*0-307-10684-5*, Golden Bks.) Random Hse. Children's Bks.

—The Forgetful Bears Help Santa. 1988. (Illus.). 32p. (J). (ps-3). pap. 11.95 o.p. (*0-590-40993-X*) Scholastic, Inc.

Wells, Rosemary. McDuff's New Friend with Plush Box Set. 2003. (Illus.). 112p. (J). 14.99 (*0-7868-1866-2*, Disney Editions) Disney Pr.

Wells, Rosemary. The McDuff Stories. 2000. (Illus.). 98p. (J). (ps-k). 19.99 (*0-7868-0697-4*) Hyperion Bks. for Children.

—McDuff's New Friend. (Illus.). (J). (ps-k). 2001. 28p. bds. 6.99 (*0-7868-0745-8*); 1998. 24p. lib. bdg. 13.49 (*0-7868-2337-2*); 1998. 24p. 12.95 (*0-7868-0386-X*) Hyperion Bks. for Children.

—McDuff's New Friend: Christmas Bag. 1998. 8.95 (*0-7868-0493-9*) Hyperion Bks. for Children.

—McDuff's New Friend: Includes Stuffed Toy Puppy. 1998. (Illus.). (J). 219.00 (*0-7868-2825-0*) Hyperion Pr.

Weninger, Brigitte, pseud. A Letter to Santa Claus. 2000. (Illus.). 32p. (J). (gr. k-3). 15.95 o.p. (*0-7358-1359-0*); 16.50 (*0-7358-1360-4*) North-South Bks., Inc.

Wild, Margaret. Thank You, Santa. (J). (ps-3). 1994. mass mkt. 4.95 (*0-590-48100-2*); 1992. (Illus.). 32p. pap. 12.95 (*0-590-45805-1*) Scholastic, Inc.

—Thank You, Santa: Written By Margaret Wild; Illustrated By Kerry Argent. 1992. 10.15 o.p. (*0-606-06800-7*) Turtleback Bks.

Willson, Sarah. Santa's Workshop. 2000. (Illus.). 12p. (J). (ps-k). bds. 5.99 (*0-689-83138-2*, Little Simon) Simon & Schuster Children's Publishing.

Wolff, Patricia Rae. A New Improved Santa. 2002. (Illus.). 32p. (J). (gr. k-2). pap. 15.95 (*0-439-35249-5*, Orchard Bks.) Scholastic, Inc.

Wood, Douglas. What Santa Can't Do. 2003. (Illus.). 32p. (J). 15.95 (*0-689-86171-0*, Simon & Schuster Children's Publishing) Simon & Schuster Children's Publishing.

Wright, Cliff. Santa's Ark. 1997. (Illus.). 36p. (ps-2). (Picture Books for Holidays). (J). 23.90 (*0-7613-0314-6*); 2. 16.95 o.p. (*0-7613-0299-9*) Millbrook Pr., Inc.

Yin. Dear Santa, Please Come to the 19th Floor. 2002. (Illus.). 32p. (J). (gr. k-3). 16.99 (*0-399-23636-8*, Philomel) Penguin Putnam Bks. for Young Readers.

Youngs, Robert J. Santa - The Unauthorized Biography. Nosco, Michelle, ed. l.t. ed. 1995. (Illus.). 600p. (J). per. 19.95 (*0-9646561-0-8*) Feathertouch Publishing.

Ziefert, Harriet. Little Mouse Meets Santa. 1995. (Lift-the-Flap Bk.). (Illus.). 16p. (J). (ps-k). 5.95 o.p. (*0-694-00659-9*, Harper Festival) HarperCollins Children's Bk. Group.

—When Will Santa Come? 1991. (Illus.). 16p. (J). (ps-3). mass mkt. 5.95 (*0-06-107440-3*) HarperCollins Children's Bk. Group.

SAWYER, TOM (FICTITIOUS CHARACTER)—FICTION

Abbott, Tony. Mississippi River Blues: The Adventures of Tom Sawyer, Vol. 2. 2002. (Cracked Classics Ser.). (Illus.). 144p. (J). (gr. 3-7). pap. 4.99 (*0-7868-1325-3*, Volo) Hyperion Bks. for Children.

The Adventures of Tom Sawyer. 1987. mass mkt. 1.95 (*0-938819-01-1*, Aerie) Doherty, Tom Assocs., LLC.

The Adventures of Tom Sawyer. 2003. (Classic Retelling Ser.). (J). (*0-618-12053-X*) McDougal Littell Inc.

The Adventures of Tom Sawyer. 1998. 44p. (YA). stu. ed. 11.95 (*1-56137-528-4*, NU5284SP) Novel Units, Inc.

The Adventures of Tom Sawyer. 2004. (Literature Units Ser.). (Illus.). 48p. 7.99 (*1-57690-637-X*) Teacher Created Materials, Inc.

Penguin Books Staff. Adventures of Tom Sawyer & Others. 2001. (Illus.). (J). 28.00 (*0-582-45438-7*); pap. 21.00 (*0-582-45439-5*) Longman Publishing Group.

Twain, Mark. The Adventures of Tom Sawyer. (YA). E-Book 3.95 (*0-594-05730-2*); 2002. (J). E-Book 3.95 (*0-594-09149-7*) 1873 Pr.

—The Adventures of Tom Sawyer. 2002. (Great Illustrated Classics). (Illus.). 240p. (J). (gr. 3-8). lib. bdg. 21.35 (*1-57765-679-2*, ABDO & Daughters) ABDO Publishing Co.

—The Adventures of Tom Sawyer. 1962. (Airmont Classics Ser.). (YA). (gr. 5 up). mass mkt. 2.95 (*0-8049-0006-X*, CL-6) Airmont Publishing Co., Inc.

—The Adventures of Tom Sawyer. 1999. (Andre Deutsch Classics). (Illus.). 272p. (J). 9.95 (*0-233-99242-1*) Andre Deutsch GBR. *Dist:* Trafalgar Square, Trans-Atlantic Pubns., Inc.

—The Adventures of Tom Sawyer, Vol. 1. 1995. (Adventures of Tom Sawyer Ser.: Vol. 1). 224p. mass mkt. 5.50 (*0-553-21128-5*, Bantam Classics) Bantam Bks.

—The Adventures of Tom Sawyer. 2002. 12.17 (*0-7587-7968-2*) Book Wholesalers, Inc.

—The Adventures of Tom Sawyer. 1983. 167p. (J). (gr. 4-7). reprint ed. lib. bdg. 17.95 (*0-89966-467-9*) Buccaneer Bks., Inc.

—The Adventures of Tom Sawyer. 1999. (YA). reprint ed. pap. text 28.00 (*1-4047-1117-1*) Classic Textbooks.

—The Adventures of Tom Sawyer. 2003. 192p. (J). 4.99 (*1-57759-556-4*) Dalmatian Pr.

—The Adventures of Tom Sawyer. 2002. (Kingfisher Classics Ser.). (Illus.). 352p. (J). tchr. ed. 15.95 (*0-7534-5478-5*, Kingfisher) Houghton Mifflin Co. Trade & Reference Div.

—The Adventures of Tom Sawyer. l.t. ed. 256p. pap. 23.48 (*0-7583-0057-3*); 351p. pap. 29.38 (*0-7583-0058-1*); 449p. pap. 36.45 (*0-7583-0059-X*); 869p. pap. 69.01 (*0-7583-0062-X*); 1008p. pap. 79.44 (*0-7583-0063-8*); 575p. pap. 44.94 (*0-7583-0060-3*); 205p. pap. 20.60 (*0-7583-0056-5*); 707p. pap. 53.86 (*0-7583-0061-1*); 869p. lib. bdg. 82.83 (*0-7583-0054-9*); 1008p. lib. bdg. 91.44 (*0-7583-0055-7*); 256p. lib. bdg. 29.48 (*0-7583-0049-2*); 205p. lib. bdg. 26.60 (*0-7583-0048-4*); 449p. lib. bdg. 42.45 (*0-7583-0051-4*); 707p. lib. bdg. 59.86 (*0-7583-0053-0*); 575p. lib. bdg. 50.94 (*0-7583-0052-2*); 351p. lib. bdg. 35.38 (*0-7583-0050-6*) Huge Print Pr.

—The Adventures of Tom Sawyer. (Young Collector's Illustrated Classics Ser.). (Illus.). 192p. (J). (gr. 3-7). 9.95 (*1-56156-453-2*) Kidsbooks, Inc.

—The Adventures of Tom Sawyer. l.t. ed. 1997. (Large Print Heritage Ser.). 357p. (YA). (gr. 7-12). lib. bdg. 30.95 (*1-58118-014-4*, 21488) LRS.

—The Adventures of Tom Sawyer. 1995. (Fiction Ser.). (YA). pap. text 7.88 o.p. (*0-582-09677-4*, 79814) Longman Publishing Group.

—The Adventures of Tom Sawyer. (Illus.). 1997. (Wishbone Classics Ser.: No. 11). 144p. (gr. 3-7). mass mkt. 4.25 (*0-06-106498-X*, HarperEntertainment); 1989. (Books of Wonder). 272p. (J). (gr. 8-12). 24.99 (*0-688-07510-X*, Morrow, William & Co.) Morrow/Avon.

—The Adventures of Tom Sawyer. (J). 2002. (Illus.). 544p. mass mkt. 5.95 (*0-451-52864-6*, Signet Bks.); 1959. 224p. (gr. 7). mass mkt. 3.95 o.p. (*0-451-52355-5*, Signet Classics) NAL.

—The Adventures of Tom Sawyer. abr. ed. 1996. (J). audio 13.98 (*962-634-580-2*, NA208014, Naxos AudioBooks) Naxos of America, Inc.

—The Adventures of Tom Sawyer. 2000. (J). audio 12.95 (*0-19-422879-7*) Oxford Univ. Pr., Inc.

—The Adventures of Tom Sawyer, Level 1. Hedge, Tricia, ed. 2000. (Bookworms Ser.). (Illus.). 57p. (J). pap. text 5.95 (*0-19-422936-X*) Oxford Univ. Pr., Inc.

—The Adventures of Tom Sawyer. (J). (*0-448-41455-4*); 2003. (Illus.). 228p. (J). pap. 3.99 o.p. (*0-14-250097-6*, Puffin Bks.); 1999. (gr. 4-7). pap. 2.99 o.p. (*0-14-130544-4*, Puffin Bks.); 1996. (Illus.). 288p. (YA). (gr. 7-12). 23.99 o.s.i (*0-670-86984-8*); 1995. (Illus.). 304p. (J). (gr. 4-7). pap. 4.99 (*0-14-036673-3*, Puffin Bks.); 1983. 224p. (J). (gr. 3-7). pap. 3.50 o.p. (*0-14-035003-9*, Puffin Bks.); 1996. (Illus.). 288p. (J). (gr. 7-12). 19.99 (*0-670-86985-6*); 1981. (Illus.). (J). (gr. 4-6). reprint ed. 7.95 o.p. (*0-448-11002-4*, Grosset & Dunlap); 1946. (Illus.). 336p. (J). (gr. 4-6). reprint ed. 13.95 o.p. (*0-448-06002-7*, Grosset & Dunlap) Penguin Putnam Bks. for Young Readers.

—The Adventures of Tom Sawyer. Vogel, Malvina, ed. 1989. (Great Illustrated Classics Ser.: Vol. 6). (Illus.). 240p. (J). (gr. 3-6). 9.95 (*0-86611-957-4*) Playmore, Inc., Pubs.

—The Adventures of Tom Sawyer. 1978. (Illus.). (J). (gr. 6-9). 2.95 o.p. (*0-448-14921-4*) Putnam Publishing Group, The.

—The Adventures of Tom Sawyer. 2001. (Paperback Classics Ser.). (Illus.). 304p. pap. 6.95 (*0-375-75681-7*, Modern Library) Random House Adult Trade Publishing Group.

—The Adventures of Tom Sawyer. (Illustrated Library for Children). (Illus.). (J). 2002. 224p. 16.99 (*0-517-22108-X*, Random Hse. Bks. for Young Readers); 1986. 304p. o.p. (*0-307-17110-8*, Golden Bks.) Random Hse. Children's Bks.

—The Adventures of Tom Sawyer. (Children's Library Ser.). (J). 1995. 1.10 o.s.i (*0-517-14155-8*); 1989. (Illus.). 288p. 12.99 o.s.i (*0-517-68813-1*) Random Hse. Value Publishing.

—The Adventures of Tom Sawyer. 1995. (Step into Classics Ser.). (Illus.). 112p. (gr. 2-7). pap. 3.99 (*0-679-88070-4*) Random Hse., Inc.

—The Adventures of Tom Sawyer. 1985. (Illus.). 223p. (YA). (gr. 7-12). 12.95 o.p. (*0-89577-217-5*) Reader's Digest Assn., Inc., The.

—The Adventures of Tom Sawyer. (Literary Classics Ser.). 2002. (Illus.). 176p. 6.00 o.p. (*0-7624-0542-2*); 1987. 160p. (J). (gr. 4 up). pap. 4.95 o.p. (*0-89471-541-0*); 1987. 160p. (J). (gr. 4 up). lib. bdg. 12.90 o.p. (*0-89471-542-9*) Running Pr. Bk. Pubs.

—The Adventures of Tom Sawyer. 1987. 320p. (J). (gr. 4-6). 1.25 o.p. (*0-590-40663-9*); pap. 2.50 o.p. (*0-590-40800-3*); mass mkt. 3.50 (*0-590-43352-0*) Scholastic, Inc. (Scholastic Paperbacks).

—The Adventures of Tom Sawyer. 1982. (Silver Classic Ser.). (Illus.). 246p. (J). (*0-382-03437-6*) Silver, Burdett & Ginn, Inc.

—The Adventures of Tom Sawyer. 1986. (J). 2.98 o.p. (*0-671-08315-5*) Simon & Schuster.

—The Adventures of Tom Sawyer. abr. ed. 2000. (J). audio compact disk 20.00 (*0-7435-0634-0*, Simon & Schuster Audioworks) Simon & Schuster Audio.

—The Adventures of Tom Sawyer. 2001. (Aladdin Classics Ser.). 272p. (J). (gr. 4-7). pap. 3.99 (*0-689-84224-4*, Aladdin) Simon & Schuster Children's Publishing.

—The Adventures of Tom Sawyer. Barish, Wendy, ed. 1982. (Illus.). 279p. (J). 14.50 o.p. (*0-671-43791-7*, Atheneum) Simon & Schuster Children's Publishing.

—The Adventures of Tom Sawyer. rev. ed. 1981. (Illus.). (YA). (gr. 7-12). pap. 2.95 (*0-671-44135-3*, Simon Pulse) Simon & Schuster Children's Publishing.

—The Adventures of Tom Sawyer. l.t. ed. 1996. (Perennial Bestsellers Ser.). 285p. (J). 24.95 (*0-7838-1705-3*) Thorndike Pr.

—The Adventures of Tom Sawyer. 1997. (J). 11.00 (*0-606-01797-6*); (Wishbone Classics Ser.: No. 11). (gr. 3-7). 10.30 (*0-606-12104-8*) Turtleback Bks.

—The Adventures of Tom Sawyer. Gise, Joanne, ed. 1990. (Troll Illustrated Classics). (J). 12.10 (*0-606-00298-7*) Turtleback Bks.

—The Adventures of Tom Sawyer. (Illus.). 292p. pap. 14.95 (*0-520-23575-4*) Univ. of California Pr.

—The Adventures of Tom Sawyer. 2001. 184p. pap. 9.95 (*1-57002-169-4*) University Publishing Hse., Inc.

—Las Aventuras de Tom Sawyer. 2000. (SPA., Illus.). 272p. (J). 7.95 (*84-406-8397-9*) B Ediciones S.A. ESP. *Dist:* Distribooks, Inc.

—Las Aventuras de Tom Sawyer. 2002. (SPA.). (YA). 7.95 (*956-13-1069-4*) Bello, Andres CHL. *Dist:* AIMS International Bks., Inc.

—Las Aventuras de Tom Sawyer. 2002. (Classics for Young Readers Ser.). (SPA.). (YA). 14.95 (*84-392-0908-8*, EV30591) Gaviota Ediciones ESP. *Dist:* Lectorum Pubns., Inc.

—Las Aventuras de Tom Sawyer. (Coleccion Estrella). (SPA., Illus.). 64p. (YA). 14.95 (*950-11-0012-X*, SGM012) Sigmar ARG. *Dist:* Continental Bk. Co., Inc.

—Tom Sawyer. 1997. (Classics Illustrated Study Guides). (Illus.). 64p. (YA). (gr. 7 up). mass mkt., stu. ed. 4.99 (*1-57840-001-5*) Acclaim Bks.

—Tom Sawyer, Set. 1986. (J). (gr. 5-7). audio 35.95 (*1-55685-070-0*) Audio Bk. Contractors, Inc.

—Tom Sawyer. abr. adapted ed. 1998. (Children's Thrift Classics Ser.). (Illus.). 96p. (J). (gr. 1 up). pap. 1.00 (*0-486-29156-1*) Dover Pubns., Inc.

—Tom Sawyer. 2nd ed. 1998. (Illustrated Classic Book Ser.). (Illus.). 61p. (J). (gr. 3 up). reprint ed. pap. text 4.95 (*1-56767-263-9*) Educational Insights, Inc.

—Tom Sawyer. 1992. (Children's Classics Ser.). (Illus.). 272p. (J). (*0-89434-127-8*, Ferguson Publishing Co.) Facts on File Inc.

—Tom Sawyer. adapted ed. (YA). (gr. 5-12). pap. text 9.95 (*0-8359-0212-9*) Globe Fearon Educational Publishing.

—Tom Sawyer. abr. ed. (J). audio 12.95 o.p. (*0-694-50155-7*, SWC 1205, Caedmon) HarperTrade.

—Tom Sawyer. unabr. ed. 1980. (J). audio 34.00 Jimcin Recordings.

—Tom Sawyer. 1998. (Cloth Bound Pocket Ser.). 240p. (J). 7.95 (*3-89508-463-8*, 520258) Konemann.

—Tom Sawyer. (J). (gr. k-7). audio 16.98 Music for Little People, Inc.

—Tom Sawyer. (Coleccion Clasicos de la Juventud). (SPA., Illus.). 220p. (J). 12.95 (*84-7189-029-1*, ORT310) Ortells, Alfredo Editorial S.L. ESP. *Dist:* Continental Bk. Co., Inc.

—Tom Sawyer. Shapiro, Irwin, ed. 1973. (Now Age Illustrated Ser.). (Illus.). 64p. (J). (gr. 5-10). 7.50 o.p. (*0-88301-220-0*); stu. ed. 1.25 (*0-88301-179-4*); pap. 2.95 (*0-88301-103-4*) Pendulum Pr., Inc.

—Tom Sawyer. 9999. (Children's Classics Ser.: No. 740-24). (Illus.). (J). (gr. 3-5). text 3.50 o.p. (*0-7214-0977-6*, Ladybird Bks.) Penguin Group (USA) Inc.

—Tom Sawyer. (American Short Classics Ser.). (J). (gr. 4-7). 1993. 32p. pap. 4.95 o.p. (*0-8114-6843-7*); 1983. (Illus.). 48p. pap. 9.27 o.p. (*0-8172-2025-9*); 1983. (Illus.). 48p. lib. bdg. 24.26 o.p. (*0-8172-1665-0*) Raintree Pubs.

—Tom Sawyer. 1999. (Illus.). 336p. (gr. 4-7). mass mkt. 3.99 (*0-439-09940-4*) Scholastic, Inc.

—Tom Sawyer. 1994. (Classic Story Bks.). (J). 4.98 o.p. (*0-8317-1646-0*) Smithmark Pubs., Inc.

—Tom Sawyer. unabr. ed. 2002. (YA). audio compact disk 37.95 (*1-58472-339-4*, 077); pap. incl. audio compact disk (*1-58472-341-6*) Sound Room Pubs., Inc. (In Audio).

—Tom Sawyer. 1996. 16.00 (*0-606-16016-7*) Turtleback Bks.

—Tom Sawyer Abroad. unabr. collector's ed. 1981. (J). audio 36.00 (*0-7366-0252-6*, 1246) Books on Tape, Inc.

—Tom Sawyer Abroad. 1999. (YA). reprint ed. pap. text 28.00 (*1-4047-1125-2*) Classic Textbooks.

—Tom Sawyer Abroad. 1993. 112p. mass mkt. 2.50 (*0-8125-2334-2*, Tor Classics) Doherty, Tom Assocs., LLC.

—Tom Sawyer Abroad. 1965. (Illus.). (J). (gr. 4-6). 2.95 o.p. (*0-448-05478-7*) Putnam Publishing Group, The.

—Tom Sawyer Abroad. unabr. ed. 1996. (J). audio (gr. 5). audio 27.00 (*0-7887-0597-0*, 94775E7);Set. pap. 46.20 incl. audio (*0-7887-1442-2*, 40272) Recorded Bks., LLC.

—Tom Sawyer Abroad & Tom Sawyer, Detective. 1966. (Classics Ser.). (YA). (gr. 5 up). mass mkt. 1.50 o.s.i (*0-8049-0126-0*, CI-126) Airmont Publishing Co., Inc.

—Tom Sawyer Abroad & Tom Sawyer, Detective. 1985. 224p. (J). (ps-8). mass mkt. 1.95 o.p. (*0-451-51961-2*, Signet Classics) NAL.

—Tom Sawyer Abroad; Tom Sawyer, Detective. l.t. ed. 1999. (Large Print Heritage Ser.). 265p. (YA). (gr. 7-12). lib. bdg. 29.95 (*1-58118-046-2*, 22515) LRS.

—Tom Sawyer & Huckleberry Finn. unabr. ed. 1998. (Wordsworth Classics Ser.). (YA). (gr. 6-12). 5.27 (*0-89061-011-8*, R0118WW) Jamestown.

—Tom Sawyer, Detective. 2002. (Dover Juvenile Classics Ser.). 80p. (YA). pap. 2.00 (*0-486-42109-0*) Dover Pubns., Inc.

—Tom Sawyer, Detective. 1965. (Illus.). (J). (gr. 4-6). 2.95 o.p. (*0-448-05479-5*) Putnam Publishing Group, The.

SCOOBY-DOO (FICTITIOUS CHARACTER)—FICTION

Barbo, Maria S. Catnapped Caper. 2000. (Scooby-Doo! Picture Clue Book Ser.: No. 1). (Illus.). 32p. (ps-3). mass mkt. 3.99 (*0-439-16010-3*) Scholastic, Inc.

—Sled Race Mystery. 2003. (Scooby-Doo! Picture Clue Book Ser.: No. 15). (Illus.). 32p. (J). (ps-2). mass mkt. 3.99 (*0-439-44417-9*) Scholastic, Inc.

—Treasure Hunt. 2002. (Scooby-Doo! Picture Clue Book Ser.: No. 13). 32p. (J). (gr. k-2). mass mkt. 3.99 o.s.i (*0-439-31849-1*) Scholastic, Inc.

Barbo, Maria S. & Sur, Duendes del. Missing Tooth Mystery. 2002. (Scooby-Doo! Picture Clue Book Ser.: Vol. 11). 32p. (J). mass mkt. 3.99 (*0-439-31847-5*) Scholastic, Inc.

Beall, Pamela Conn. Scooby-Doo & the Case of the Count. 1984. (Scooby-Doo Ser.). (J). (ps-3). 9.95 (*0-8431-4133-6*, Grosset & Dunlap) Penguin Putnam Bks. for Young Readers.

—Scooby-Doo & the Haunted Dog House. 1984. (Scooby-Doo Ser.). (J). (ps-3). 9.99 o.s.i (*0-8431-4134-4*, Grosset & Dunlap) Penguin Putnam Bks. for Young Readers.

—Scooby-Doo & the Headless Horseman. 1984. (Scooby-Doo Ser.). (J). (ps-3). 9.95 o.s.i (*0-8431-4135-2*, Grosset & Dunlap) Penguin Putnam Bks. for Young Readers.

—Scooby-Doo & the Ship Mystery. 1984. (Scooby-Doo Ser.). (J). (ps-3). 9.95 o.s.i (*0-8431-4137-9*, Grosset & Dunlap) Penguin Putnam Bks. for Young Readers.

Crime Sniffers. 2001. (Scooby-Doo Ser.). (Illus.). 32p. (ps-3). pap. text 4.99 (*0-307-29905-8*, Golden Bks.) Random Hse. Children's Bks.

Deall, P. Scooby-Doo & the Mystery Monster. 1984. (Scooby-Doo Ser.). (J). (ps-3). 9.95 (*0-8431-4136-0*, Grosset & Dunlap) Penguin Putnam Bks. for Young Readers.

del Sur, Duendes, illus. Baseball Blackout. 2001. (Scooby-Doo! Picture Clue Book Ser.: No. 6). 32p. (J). (ps-3). mass mkt. 3.99 (*0-439-20233-7*) Scholastic, Inc.

—Clues at the Carnival. 2001. (Scooby-Doo! Picture Clue Book Ser.: No. 5). 32p. (J). (ps-3). mass mkt. 3.99 (*0-439-20232-9*) Scholastic, Inc.

—Parade Puzzle. 2001. (Scooby-Doo! Picture Clue Book Ser.: No. 7). 32p. (J). (ps-3). mass mkt. 3.99 (*0-439-24235-5*) Scholastic, Inc.

—Pizza Place Ghost. 2001. (Scooby-Doo! Picture Clue Book Ser.: No. 4). 32p. (J). (gr. 5). mass mkt. 3.99 (*0-439-20495-X*) Scholastic, Inc.

Dewin, Howie. Scooby-Doo's Guide to School. 2003. (Scooby Doo Ser.). (Illus.). 80p. (J). mass mkt. 3.99 (*0-439-43817-9*) Scholastic, Inc.

Dower, Laura. Scooby-Doo's Guide to Life - Just Say "Ruh-Roh!" 1999. (Scooby-Doo Ser.). 80p. (J). (ps-3). mass mkt. 3.99 (*0-590-63109-8*) Scholastic, Inc.

Draw Your Own Scooby-Doo Coloring Clues. 2001. (Scooby-Doo Ser.). (Illus.). 32p. (ps-3). pap. text 4.99 (*0-307-10372-2*, Golden Bks.) Random Hse. Children's Bks.

Erwin, Vicki Berger. Scooby-Doo! The Case of the Spinning Spider. 2001. (Collect the Clues Mystery Ser.). (Illus.). 59p. (J). pap. (*0-439-23167-1*) Scholastic, Inc.

Flatau, Carole, ed. Scooby-Doo's Upbeat Songs: Level Three for Early Intermediate Students. 2000. (Looney Tunes Piano Library). (J). 5.95 (*0-7692-8438-8*) Warner Bros. Pubns.

Gelsey, James. Scooby-Doo & the Bowling Boogeyman. 2002. (Scooby-Doo Mysteries Ser.: Bk. 24). (Illus.). 64p. (J). mass mkt. 3.99 (*0-439-42071-7*) Scholastic, Inc.

—Scooby-Doo & the Carnival Creeper. 1999. (Scooby-Doo Mysteries Ser.: No. 7). (Illus.). 60p. (J). (ps-3). mass mkt. 3.99 (*0-439-11346-6*) Scholastic, Inc.

—Scooby-Doo & the Caveman Caper. 2001. (Scooby-Doo Mysteries Ser.: No. 18). (Illus.). 64p. (J). (ps-3). mass mkt. 3.99 (*0-439-24238-X*) Scholastic, Inc.

—Scooby-Doo & the Deep Sea Diver. 2003. (Scooby-Doo Mysteries Ser.: No. 26). (Illus.). 64p. (J). mass mkt. 3.99 (*0-439-42073-3*, Levine, Arthur A. Bks.) Scholastic, Inc.

—Scooby-Doo & the Fairground Phantom. 2000. (Scooby-Doo Mysteries Ser.: No. 11). (Illus.). 64p. (J). (ps-3). mass mkt. 3.99 (*0-439-10664-8*) Scholastic, Inc.

—Scooby-Doo & the Farmyard Fright. 2001. (Scooby-Doo Mysteries Ser.: No. 17). (Illus.). 64p. (J). (ps-3). mass mkt. 3.99 (*0-439-18881-4*) Scholastic, Inc.

—Scooby-Doo & the Frankenstein Monster. 2000. (Scooby-Doo Mysteries Ser.: No. 12). (Illus.). 64p. (J). (ps-3). mass mkt. 3.99 (*0-439-18876-8*) Scholastic, Inc.

—Scooby-Doo & the Ghostly Gorilla. 2002. (Scooby-Doo Mysteries Ser.: No. 20). (Illus.). 64p. (J). (gr. 1-4). mass mkt. 3.99 (*0-439-28485-6*) Scholastic, Inc.

—Scooby-Doo & the Groovy Ghost. 8th ed. 2000. (Scooby-Doo Mysteries Ser.: No. 8). (Illus.). 64p. (J). (ps-3). mass mkt. 3.99 (*0-439-11347-4*, Scholastic Paperbacks) Scholastic, Inc.

—Scooby-Doo & the Gruesome Goblin. 2004. (Scooby-Doo, Mysteries Ser.). 64p. (J). mass mkt. 3.99 (*0-439-42076-8*, Scholastic Paperbacks) Scholastic, Inc.

—Scooby-Doo & the Haunted Castle. 1998. (Scooby-Doo Mysteries Ser.: No. 1). (Illus.). 64p. (J). (ps-3). mass mkt. 3.99 (*0-590-81909-7*) Scholastic, Inc.

—Scooby-Doo & the Headless Horseman. 2002. (Scooby-Doo Mysteries Ser.: No. 25). 64p. (J). (gr. 1-4). mass mkt. 3.99 (*0-439-42072-5*) Scholastic, Inc.

—Scooby-Doo & the Howling Wolfman. 1999. (Scooby-Doo Mysteries Ser.: No. 5). (Illus.). 59p. (J). (ps-3). mass mkt. 3.99 (*0-439-08095-9*) Scholastic, Inc.

—Scooby-Doo & the Karate Caper. 2002. (Scooby-Doo Mysteries Ser.: No. 23). 64p. (J). (gr. 1-4). mass mkt. 3.99 (*0-439-28489-9*) Scholastic, Inc.

—Scooby-Doo & the Masked Magician. 2001. (Scooby-Doo Mysteries Ser.: No. 14). (Illus.). 64p. (J). (ps-3). mass mkt. 3.99 (*0-439-18878-4*) Scholastic, Inc.

—Scooby-Doo & the Mummy's Curse. 1998. (Scooby-Doo Mysteries Ser.: No. 2). (Illus.). 64p. (J). (ps-3). mass mkt. 3.99 (*0-590-81910-0*) Scholastic, Inc.

—Scooby-Doo & the Phony Fortune-Teller. 2001. (Scooby-Doo Mysteries Ser.: No. 15). (Illus.). 64p. (J). (ps-3). mass mkt. 3.99 (*0-439-18879-2*) Scholastic, Inc.

—Scooby-Doo & the Rowdy Rodeo. 2001. (Scooby-Doo Mysteries Ser.: No. 19). (Illus.). 64p. (J). (ps-3). mass mkt. 3.99 (*0-439-28484-8*) Scholastic, Inc.

—Scooby-Doo & the Runaway Robot. 2000. (Scooby-Doo Mysteries Ser.: No. 13). (Illus.). 64p. (J). (ps-3). mass mkt. 3.99 (*0-439-18877-6*) Scholastic, Inc.

—Scooby-Doo & the Seashore Slimer. 2002. (Scooby-Doo Mysteries Ser.: No. 22). (Illus.). 64p. (J). (gr. 4-6). mass mkt. 3.99 (*0-439-28488-0*) Scholastic, Inc.

—Scooby-Doo & the Snow Monster. 1999. (Scooby-Doo Mysteries Ser.: No. 3). (Illus.). 57p. (J). (ps-3). mass mkt. 3.99 (*0-590-81914-3*, Scholastic Paperbacks) Scholastic, Inc.

—Scooby-Doo & the Spooky Strikeout. 10th ed. 2000. (Scooby-Doo Mysteries Ser.: No. 10). (Illus.). 64p. (J). (ps-3). mass mkt. 3.99 (*0-439-11349-0*) Scholastic, Inc.

—Scooby-Doo & the Sunken Ship. 1999. (Scooby-Doo Mysteries Ser.: No. 4). (Illus.). 57p. (J). (ps-3). mass mkt. 3.99 (*0-590-81917-8*) Scholastic, Inc.

—Scooby-Doo & the Sunken Ship: Scooby-Doo y el Barco Hundido. 2004. (Scooby-Doo Ser.). (ENG & SPA.). 64p. (J). pap. 3.99 (*0-439-55116-1*, Scholastic en Espanola) Scholastic, Inc.

—Scooby-Doo & the Toy Store Terror. 2001. (Scooby-Doo Mysteries Ser.: No. 16). (Illus.). 64p. (J). (ps-3). mass mkt. 3.99 (*0-439-18880-6*) Scholastic, Inc.

—Scooby-Doo & the Vampire's Revenge. 1999. (Scooby-Doo Mysteries Ser.: No. 6). (Illus.). 58p. (J). (ps-3). mass mkt. 3.99 (*0-439-08278-1*) Scholastic, Inc.

—Scooby-Doo & the Vicious Viking. 2002. (Scooby-Doo Mysteries Ser.: No. 21). (Illus.). 64p. (J). mass mkt. 3.99 (*0-439-28486-4*) Scholastic, Inc.

—Scooby-Doo & the Zombie's Treasure. 2000. (Scooby-Doo Mysteries Ser.: No. 9). (Illus.). 64p. (J). (ps-3). mass mkt. 3.99 (*0-439-11348-2*) Scholastic, Inc.

—Scooby-Doo! & You. 2001. (Collect the Clues Mystery Ser.). (Illus.). 60p. (J). (*0-439-23155-8*) Scholastic, Inc.

—Scooby-Doo! & You: The Case of Dr. Jenkins & Mr. Hyde. 2001. (Collect the Clues Mystery Ser.). (Illus.). 60p. pap. (*0-439-23157-4*) Scholastic, Inc.

—Scooby-Doo! & You: The Case of the Seaweed Monster. 2001. (Collect the Clues Mystery Ser.). (Illus.). 60p. (J). pap. (*0-439-23153-1*) Scholastic, Inc.

—Scooby-Doo! & You: The Case of the Singing Ghost. 2001. (Collect the Clues Mystery Ser.). (Illus.). 61p. (J). pap. (*0-439-23163-9*) Scholastic, Inc.

—Scooby-Doo y el Castillo Hechizado. 2002. (Scooby-Doo Mysteries Ser.: No. 1). (SPA., Illus.). 64p. (J). (gr. 2-4). pap. 4.99 (*0-439-40984-5*, Scholastic en Espanola) Scholastic, Inc.

—Scooby-Doo y la Maldicion de la Momia. 2003. (Scooby-Doo Mysteries Ser.: No. 2). (SPA., Illus.). 48p. (J). (gr. 2-4). pap. 3.99 (*0-439-40985-3*, Scholastic en Espanola) Scholastic, Inc.

—Witch Doctor. 2003. (Scooby Doo Mystery Ser.). (Illus.). 64p. (J). (gr. k-3). mass mkt. 3.99 (*0-439-42075-X*, Scholastic Paperbacks) Scholastic, Inc.

Glow in the Dark: Spooky Scooby Doo. 2004. (Ultimate Sticker Books Ser.). 16p. (J). pap. 6.99 (0-7566-0301-3) Dorling Kindersley Publishing, Inc.

Golden Books Staff. The Beast of Blueberry Heights. 2000. (Scooby-Doo Ser.). (Illus.). 12p. (J). (ps-3). pap. 9.99 (0-307-10143-6, 10143, Golden Bks.) Random Hse. Children's Bks.

—Ghoul's Inn. 2000. (Scooby-Doo Ser.). (Illus.). 16p. (J). (ps-3). pap. 3.99 (0-307-15400-9, 15400, Golden Bks.) Random Hse. Children's Bks.

—Jeepers, It's the Creeper! 2000. (Scooby-Doo Ser.). (Illus.). 64p. (J). (ps-3). pap. text 2.99 (0-307-29051-4, 29051, Golden Bks.) Random Hse. Children's Bks.

—Mummy's Tomb Maze Book. 2000. (Scooby-Doo Ser.). (Illus.). 8p. (J). (ps-3). 9.99 (0-307-11127-X, 11127, Golden Bks.) Random Hse. Children's Bks.

—Trouble Ahead. 2000. (Scooby-Doo Ser.). (Illus.). 56p. (J). (ps-3). pap. text 3.99 (0-307-27610-4, 27610, Golden Bks.) Random Hse. Children's Bks.

Golden Books Staff, ed. The Haunted Carnival. 1999. (Scooby-Doo Ser.). (Illus.). 16p. (J). (ps-3). bds. 2.99 (0-307-99504-6, Golden Bks.) Random Hse. Children's Bks.

Herman, Gail. Apple Picking Mystery. 2002. (Scooby-Doo! Reader Ser.: Bk. 13). 32p. (J). mass mkt. 3.99 (0-439-34115-9) Scholastic, Inc.

—Dinosaur Dig. 2000. (Scooby-Doo! Picture Clue Book Ser.: No. 3). (Illus.). 32p. (J). (ps-3). mass mkt. 3.99 (0-439-20231-0) Scholastic, Inc.

—Disappearing Donuts. 2000. (Scooby-Doo! Reader Ser.: No. 2). (Illus.). 32p. (J). (ps-3). mass mkt. 3.99 (0-439-16168-1) Scholastic, Inc.

—Football Fright. 2002. (Scooby-Doo! Reader Ser.: No. 14). (Illus.). 32p. (J). (gr. k-3). mass mkt. 3.99 (0-439-34116-7) Scholastic, Inc.

—Ghost in the Garden. 2001. (Scooby-Doo! Reader Ser.: No. 4). (Illus.). 32p. (J). (gr. 5). mass mkt. 3.99 (0-439-20226-4) Scholastic, Inc.

—The Haunted Pumpkins. 2001. (Scooby-Doo! Picture Clue Book Ser.: No. 8). (Illus.). 32p. (J). (ps-3). mass mkt. 3.99 (0-439-31836-X) Scholastic, Inc.

—Howling on the Playground. 2000. (Scooby-Doo! Reader Ser.: No. 3). (Illus.). 32p. (J). (ps-3). mass mkt. 3.99 (0-439-16169-X) Scholastic, Inc.

—Map in the Mystery Machine. 2000. (Scooby-Doo! Reader Ser.: No. 1). (Illus.). 32p. (J). (ps-3). mass mkt. 3.99 (0-439-16167-3) Scholastic, Inc.

—The Mixed-Up Museum. 2001. (Scooby-Doo! Reader Ser.: No. 6). (Illus.). 32p. (J). (ps-3). mass mkt. 3.99 (0-439-20228-0) Scholastic, Inc.

—Mummies at the Mall. 2002. (Scooby-Doo! Reader Ser.: Vol. 11). (Illus.). 32p. (J). (ps-3). mass mkt. 3.99 (0-439-34114-0) Scholastic, Inc.

—Scooby-Doo & Aliens Too! 2000. (Scooby-Doo Movie Storybooks). (Illus.). 32p. (J). (ps-3). mass mkt. 3.50 (0-439-17701-4) Scholastic, Inc.

—Scooby-Doo & Zombies, Too? Zoinks! 1998. (Scooby-Doo Movie Storybooks). (Illus.). 32p. (J). (ps-3). mass mkt. 3.50 (0-590-38653-0) Scholastic, Inc.

—Scooby-Doo on Zombie Island. 1998. (Scooby-Doo Movie Storybooks). (Illus.). 32p. (J). (ps-3). mass mkt. 3.50 (0-590-38652-2) Scholastic, Inc.

—Sea Monster Scare. 2002. (Scooby-Doo! Reader Ser.: No. 12). 32p. (J). (gr. k-2). mass mkt. 3.99 (0-439-31831-9) Scholastic, Inc.

—The Secret Santa Mystery. 2003. (Scooby-Doo! Reader Ser.). 32p. (J). mass mkt. 3.99 (0-439-45619-3, Scholastic Paperbacks) Scholastic, Inc.

—Shiny Spooky Knights. 2001. (Scooby-Doo! Reader Ser.: No. 5). (Illus.). 32p. (J). (ps-3). mass mkt. 3.99 (0-439-20227-2) Scholastic, Inc.

—Snack Snatcher. 2001. (Scooby-Doo! Reader Ser.: No. 7). (Illus.). 32p. (J). (ps-3). mass mkt. 3.99 (0-439-20229-9) Scholastic, Inc.

Leon McCann, Jesse. Scooby-Doo! & the Trick-or-Treat Thief. 2002. (Scooby Doo Ser.). 32p. (J). mass mkt. 5.99 (0-439-44294-X) Scholastic, Inc.

Markas, Jenny. Scooby Doo & the Legend of Vampire Rock. 2003. (Scooby-Doo Ser.). (Illus.). 64p. (J). mass mkt. 3.99 (0-439-45521-9) Scholastic, Inc.

—Scooby-Doo! & You: The Case of the Headless Henry. 2001. (Collect the Clues Mystery Ser.). (Illus.). 60p. (0-439-23162-0) Scholastic, Inc.

—Scooby-Doo! & You: The Case of the Leaping Lion. 2001. (Collect the Clues Mystery Ser.). (Illus.). 62p. (J). (0-439-23154-X) Scholastic, Inc.

—Scooby-Doo! Monster of Mexico. 2003. (Scooby-Doo Ser.). 80p. (J). mass mkt. 4.99 (0-439-44919-7, Scholastic Paperbacks) Scholastic, Inc.

McCann, Jesse Leon. Scooby-Doo & the Tiki's Curse. 2004. (Scooby-Doo Ser.). 24p. (J). mass mkt. 3.50 (0-439-54604-4, Scholastic Paperbacks) Scholastic, Inc.

McCann, Jesse Leon. Monster of Mexico. 2003. (Scooby-Doo Ser.). 32p. (J). mass mkt. 3.50 (0-439-44946-4, Scholastic Paperbacks) Scholastic, Inc.

—Scooby-Doo & Santa's Bake Shop. 2000. (Scooby-Doo Ser.). (Illus.). 24p. (J). (ps-3). mass mkt. 5.99 (0-439-20999-4) Scholastic, Inc.

—Scooby-Doo & the Alien Invaders. 2000. (Golden Book Ser.). (Illus.). 32p. (J). (ps-3). pap. text 3.99 (0-307-10474-5, 10474, Golden Bks.) Random Hse. Children's Bks.

—Scooby-Doo & the Alien Invaders. 2000. (Scooby-Doo Movie Storybooks). (Illus.). 32p. (J). (ps-3). mass mkt. 3.50 (0-439-17700-6) Scholastic, Inc.

—Scooby-Doo & the Creepy Carnival. 1998. (Scooby-Doo 3-D Storybooks: No. 1). (Illus.). 16p. (J). (ps-3). mass mkt. 5.99 (0-590-38654-9) Scholastic, Inc.

—Scooby-Doo & the Eerie Ice Monster. 2000. (Scooby-Doo Ser.). (Illus.). 24p. (J). (ps-3). mass mkt. 5.99 (0-439-20667-7) Scholastic, Inc.

—Scooby-Doo & the Fantastic Puppet Factory. 2000. (Scooby-Doo Original Titles Ser.: No. 4). (Illus.). 32p. (J). (ps-3). mass mkt. 3.50 (0-439-17254-3) Scholastic, Inc.

—Scooby-Doo & the Halloween Hotel Haunt: A Glow in the Dark Mystery! 1999. (Scooby-Doo Ser.). (Illus.). 24p. (J). (ps-3). mass mkt. 5.99 (0-439-11768-2) Scholastic, Inc.

—Scooby-Doo & the Haunted Lab: Scooby-Doo Decoder Book. 2002. (Scooby-Doo Ser.). (Illus.). 32p. (J). (ps-3). mass mkt. 5.99 (0-439-40789-3) Scholastic, Inc.

—Scooby Doo & the Legend of Vampire Rock. 2003. (Scooby-Doo Ser.). (Illus.). 32p. (J). mass mkt. 3.50 (0-439-45522-7) Scholastic, Inc.

—Scooby-Doo & the Mystery Mall. 1998. (Scooby-Doo 3-D Storybooks: No. 2). (Illus.). 16p. (J). (ps-3). mass mkt. 5.99 (0-590-38656-5) Scholastic, Inc.

—Scooby Doo & the Opera Ogre. 2001. (Scooby-Doo Original Titles Ser.: No. 1). (Illus.). 32p. (ps-3). mass mkt. 3.50 (0-439-26074-4) Scholastic, Inc.

—Scooby-Doo & the Phantom Cowboy. 2002. (Scooby-Doo Ser.). (Illus.). 32p. (J). (ps-3). mass mkt. 3.50 (0-439-36586-4) Scholastic, Inc.

—Scooby-Doo & the Secret Admirer. 2003. (Scooby-Doo Ser.). 32p. (J). mass mkt. 5.99 (0-439-45520-0) Scholastic, Inc.

—Scooby-Doo & the Weird Water Park. 2000. (Scooby-Doo Original Titles Ser.: No. 3). (Illus.). 32p. (J). (ps-3). mass mkt. 3.50 (0-439-17253-5) Scholastic, Inc.

—Scooby-Doo! & You: The Case of the Mad Mermaid. 2001. (Collect the Clues Mystery Ser.). (Illus.). 62p. (J). pap. (0-439-23164-7) Scholastic, Inc.

—Scooby-Doo in Jungle Jeopardy. 2001. (Scooby-Doo Original Titles Ser.: No. 2). (Illus.). 32p. (ps-3). mass mkt. 3.50 (0-439-26075-2) Scholastic, Inc.

McCann, Jesse Leon, et al. Scooby-Doo & the Haunted Halloween Mask. 2003. (Scooby-Doo Ser.). 24p. (J). mass mkt. 5.99 (0-439-44937-5, Scholastic Paperbacks) Scholastic, Inc.

Mystery Adventures. 2001. (Scooby-Doo Ser.). (Illus.). 70p. (ps-3). pap. 2.99 (0-307-33765-0, Golden Bks.) Random Hse. Children's Bks.

The Mystery Machine Adventure. 2001. (Scooby-Doo Ser.). (Illus.). 12p. (J). (ps-3). bds. 5.99 (0-307-20038-8, Golden Bks.) Random Hse. Children's Bks.

Nagler, Michelle H. Big Foot Mystery. 2002. (Scooby-Doo! Picture Clue Book Ser.: No. 12). (Illus.). (J). mass mkt. 3.99 (0-439-31848-3) Scholastic, Inc.

Nagler, Michelle H., contrib. by. The Surf Scare. 2003. (Scooby Doo Ser.). 32p. (J). mass mkt. 3.99 (0-439-44419-5, Scholastic Paperbacks) Scholastic, Inc.

Price, Roger. Scooby-Doo & Scrappy Doo Mad Libs. 1981. (Scooby-Doo Ser.). 48p. (J). (ps-3). pap. 1.75 o.p. (0-8431-0706-5, Price Stern Sloan) Penguin Putnam Bks. for Young Readers.

—Scooby-Doo Movie. 2002. (Mad Libs Ser.). (Illus.). 48p. mass mkt. 3.99 (0-8431-4865-9, Wee Sing Bks.) Putnam Publishing Group, The.

Price, Roger & Stern, Leonard. Scooby-Doo Halloween Mad Libs. 2001. (Scooby-Doo Ser.). (Illus.). 48p. (J). (ps-3). mass mkt. 3.99 (0-8431-7701-2, Price Stern Sloan) Penguin Putnam Bks. for Young Readers.

Scholastic, Inc. Staff. Scooby Doo Storybook Collection. 2003. 14.00 (0-439-55194-3); Set. 2002. (Illus.). 256p. (J). pap. 10.99 (0-439-51320-0) Scholastic, Inc.

Scholastic, Inc. Staff, et al. Scooby-Doo & the Hex Files. 1999. (Scooby-Doo Movie Storybooks). (Illus.). 32p. (J). (ps-3). mass mkt. 3.50 (0-439-08787-2) Scholastic, Inc.

—Scooby-Doo & the Witch's Ghost. 1999. (Scooby-Doo Movie Storybooks). (Illus.). 32p. (J). (ps-3). mass mkt. 3.50 (0-439-08786-4) Scholastic, Inc.

Scooby-Doo! 2000. (Scooby-Doo Ser.). (J). (ps-3). 1.99 (0-307-28915-X, Golden Bks.) Random Hse. Children's Bks.

Scooby Doo - Large Picture Puzzle Board Book (English) 1999. (Scooby-Doo Ser.). (ps-3). bds. (1-58805-002-5) DS-Max USA, Inc.

Scooby-Doo & Scrappy Doo Super Sleuths. 1986. (Scooby-Doo Ser.). 48p. (J). (ps-3). pap. o.s.i (0-8431-0841-X, Price Stern Sloan) Penguin Putnam Bks. for Young Readers.

Scooby-Doo & the Hidden Treasure. 1986. (Scooby-Doo Ser.). 48p. (J). (ps-3). pap. o.p. (0-8431-0840-1, Price Stern Sloan) Penguin Putnam Bks. for Young Readers.

Scooby Doo & the Pirate Ghost. 2001. (Illus.). (J). 15.95 (0-7853-4875-1) Publications International, Ltd.

Scooby-Doo Mad Libs. 1980. (Scooby-Doo Ser.). 48p. (J). pap. 1.75 o.p. (0-8431-0695-6, Price Stern Sloan) Penguin Putnam Bks. for Young Readers.

Scooby-Doo Mystery Mania Box Set with Coloring Books. 2000. (Scooby-Doo Ser.). (J). (ps-3). (1-58805-136-6) DS-Max USA, Inc.

Scooby Doo Where Are You? 2001. (Look & Find Ser.). (J). lib. bdg. 15.95 (1-56674-298-6) Forest Hse. Publishing Co., Inc.

Scooby-Doo's Snack Tracks: The Ultimate Collection. 1998. (Scooby-Doo Ser.). (J). (ps-3). audio 10.98 (1-56826-920-X, R475504); audio compact disk 16.98 (1-56826-921-8, R2 76505) Rhino Entertainment.

Scooby-Doo's Upbeat Songs: Level Three for Early Intermediate Students. 2000. (Looney Tunes Piano Library). 24p. (J). pap. 12.95 incl. disk, audio compact disk (0-7692-9609-2) Warner Bros. Pubns.

Smith, Geof. Scooby-Doo! & the Cyber Chase. 2001. 16p. (J). (ps-3). pap. 3.99 (0-307-25301-5, Golden Bks.) Random Hse. Children's Bks.

Snack-A-Thon! 2001. (Scooby-Doo Ser.). (Illus.). 16p. (ps-3). pap. text 3.99 (0-307-28332-1, Golden Bks.) Random Hse. Children's Bks.

Soderberg, Erin. Spooky Sports Day. 2002. (Scooby-Doo! Picture Clue Book Ser.: No. 14). (Illus.). 32p. (J). (ps-1). mass mkt. 3.99 (0-439-31850-5) Scholastic, Inc.

Tyo, Courtney. Shamrock Scare. 2004. (Scooby-Doo Ser.). 32p. (J). mass mkt. 3.99 (0-439-55715-1, Scholastic Paperbacks) Scholastic, Inc.

Ultimate Sticker Book: Scooby Doo. 2004. (Ultimate Sticker Books Ser.). 16p. (J). pap. 6.99 (0-7566-0302-1) Dorling Kindersley Publishing, Inc.

Wasserman, Robin. Search for Scooby Snacks. 2000. (Scooby-Doo! Picture Clue Book Ser.: No. 2). (Illus.). 32p. (J). (ps-3). mass mkt. 3.99 (0-439-16166-5) Scholastic, Inc.

Wasserman, Robin, et al. Ghost School. 2003. (Scooby-Doo Ser.). 32p. (J). mass mkt. 3.99 (0-439-44227-3, Scholastic Paperbacks) Scholastic, Inc.

Weyn, Suzanne. Scooby-Doo! & You: The Case of the Batty Vampire. 2001. (Collect the Clues Mystery Ser.). (Illus.). 59p. (J). pap. (0-439-23168-X) Scholastic, Inc.

Weyn, Suzanne & Erwin, Vicky Berger. Scooby-Doo's Big Book of Mysteries. 2002. (Scooby-Doo Mysteries Ser.). (Illus.). 144p. (J). mass mkt. 4.50 (0-439-40788-5) Scholastic, Inc.

Wigand, Molly. Scooby-Doo: That's Snow Ghost. 2001. 24p. (J). (ps-k). pap. 2.99 (0-307-96012-9, Golden Bks.) Random Hse. Children's Bks.

SCROOGE, EBENEZER (FICTITIOUS CHARACTER)—FICTION

Dickens, Charles. Children's Classics: A Christmas Carol & Other Christmas Stories. 1990. (J). 12.99 o.s.i (0-517-64126-7) Random Hse. Value Publishing.

—A Christmas Carol. 1963. (YA). (gr. 7 up). mass mkt. 2.25 (0-8049-0026-4, CL-26) Airmont Publishing Co., Inc.

—A Christmas Carol. 1985. (Illus.). 80p. (J). (ps up). 1.50 o.p. (0-8120-5705-8) Barron's Educational Series, Inc.

—A Christmas Carol. 1990. (YA). (gr. 1-12). 3.75 o.s.i (0-425-12334-0, Classics Illustrated) Berkley Publishing Group.

—A Christmas Carol. 2001. (J). audio 28.00 (0-7366-8071-3) Books on Tape, Inc.

—A Christmas Carol. 1993. (Illus.). 48p. (J). (ps-3). 15.95 o.p. (1-56402-204-8) Candlewick Pr.

—A Christmas Carol. (Illus.). (YA). 1990. 152p. (gr. 1 up). lib. bdg. 46.65 (0-88682-327-7, 97200-098, Creative Editions); 1984. 78p. (gr. 4 up). lib. bdg. 13.95 o.p. (0-87191-955-9, Creative Education) Creative Co., The.

—A Christmas Carol. 1990. (Classics Ser.). (Illus.). 128p. (YA). (gr. 2-12). mass mkt. 2.99 (0-8125-0434-8, Tor Classics) Doherty, Tom Assocs., LLC.

—A Christmas Carol. 1996. (Illus.). 152p. (J). lib. bdg. 35.00 (0-15-100200-2, Red Wagon Bks.) Harcourt Children's Bks.

—A Christmas Carol. 2001. (Illus.). 80p. (J). (gr. 1-5). 17.95 (0-06-028577-X); (gr. 2-5). lib. bdg. 17.89 (0-06-028578-8) HarperCollins Children's Bk. Group.

—A Christmas Carol. 1983. (Illus.). 128p. (J). (gr. 2-12). tchr. ed. 18.95 (0-8234-0486-2) Holiday Hse., Inc.

—A Christmas Carol. 1992. (J). pap. 10.95 o.p. (0-395-60726-4) Houghton Mifflin Co.

—A Christmas Carol. 1987. (Illus.). 88p. (J). 6.95 o.p. (0-89783-046-6) Larlin Corp.

—A Christmas Carol. 1985. (J). audio 4.95 (0-913675-40-7) McGraw-Hill Cos., The.

—A Christmas Carol. 1996. (Books of Wonder). (Illus.). 64p. (J). (gr. 4-7). 18.00 (0-688-13606-0, Morrow, William & Co.) Morrow/Avon.

—A Christmas Carol. 1997. 128p. pap. 2.95 (0-89375-356-4) NAL.

—A Christmas Carol. 2001. (Illus.). 72p. (J). (ps up). 19.95 (0-7358-1259-4, Michael Neugebauer Bks.) North-South Bks., Inc.

—A Christmas Carol. 2001. (Illus.). 160p. pap. 8.95 (1-86205-130-5) Pavilion Bks., Ltd. GBR. Dist: Trafalgar Square.

—A Christmas Carol. 1990. (Illus.). 48p. (YA). (gr. 7-12). 14.95 (0-88289-812-4) Pelican Publishing Co., Inc.

—A Christmas Carol. Fagan, Tom, ed. 1978. (Now Age Illustrated IV Ser.). (Illus.). (gr. 4-12). (J). stu. ed. 1.25 (0-88301-337-1); (J). pap. text 2.95 (0-88301-313-4); (YA). text 7.50 o.p. (0-88301-325-8) Pendulum Pr., Inc.

—A Christmas Carol. (Classic Ser.). (Illus.). 56p. (J). 1996. (gr. 2-4). 2.99 o.s.i (0-7214-5677-4); 1994. text 3.50 (0-7214-1729-9) Penguin Group (USA) Inc. (Ladybird Bks.).

—A Christmas Carol. 2001. (Illus.). 144p. (J). pap. 4.99 (0-14-230055-1, Puffin Bks.); 2000. (Illus.). 112p. (YA). (gr. 7-12). pap. 17.99 (0-670-88879-6, Viking Children's Bks.); 1995. (Illus.). 144p. (YA). (gr. 5 up). pap. 3.99 o.p. (0-14-036723-3, Puffin Bks.); 1984. 112p. (J). (gr. 7). pap. 2.99 o.p. (0-14-035027-6, Puffin Bks.); 1983. (Illus.). 128p. (J). (gr. 6). 12.95 o.p. (0-8037-0032-6, Dial Bks. for Young Readers) Penguin Putnam Bks. for Young Readers.

—A Christmas Carol. 1965. 96p. (J). (gr. 6 up). 6.95 o.p. (0-88088-125-9) Peter Pauper Pr. Inc.

—A Christmas Carol. 1997. (Illus.). 144p. (gr. 4-7). pap. text 3.99 (0-440-41421-0, Dell Books for Young Readers) Random Hse. Children's Bks.

—A Christmas Carol. 1993. (Christmas Treasury Pop-Up Ser.). (J). 4.99 o.s.i (0-517-08787-1) Random Hse. Value Publishing.

—A Christmas Carol. (Everyman's Library Children's Classics Ser.). (Illus.). (gr. 2-12). 1994. 180p. 13.95 (0-679-43639-1); 1984. (J). 4.99 o.s.i (0-517-23159-X) Random Hse., Inc.

—A Christmas Carol. 1996. (Illus.). 128p. (J). (gr. 4-7). text 4.95 (0-7624-0831-6) Running Pr. Bk. Pubs.

—A Christmas Carol. (J). (gr. 4-7). 2000. (Illus.). 144p. mass mkt. 2.99 (0-439-10133-6); 1987. (Illus.). 128p. pap. 3.50 (0-590-43527-2, Scholastic Paperbacks); 1986. pap. 1.95 o.p. (0-590-02102-8) Scholastic, Inc.

—A Christmas Carol. 1983. (Illus.). 240p. mass mkt. 3.99 (0-671-47369-7, Pocket) Simon & Schuster.

—A Christmas Carol. (Illus.). (J). 1995. 144p. mass mkt. 19.95 o.s.i (0-689-80213-7, McElderry, Margaret K.); 1995. 68p. 19.95 (0-88708-069-3, Simon & Schuster Children's Publishing); 1983. 128p. pap. 16.00 o.p. (0-671-45599-0, Simon & Schuster Children's Publishing) Simon & Schuster Children's Publishing.

—A Christmas Carol. (J). E-Book 5.00 (0-7410-0516-6) SoftBook Pr.

—A Christmas Carol. (Children's Classics Ser.). (J). 1998. audio 10.95 o.p. (1-55935-212-4); 1972. pap. 5.95 o.p. incl. audio (0-88142-364-5, 364) Soundelux Audio Publishing.

—A Christmas Carol. (Illus.). 1997. 164p. 19.95 (1-55670-648-0); 1990. 152p. (J). 30.00 o.p. (1-55670-161-6) Stewart, Tabori & Chang.

—A Christmas Carol. 1997. 10.04 (0-606-13273-2) Turtleback Bks.

—A Christmas Carol. (Through the Magic Window Ser.). (Illus.). (J). (ps-2). 1991. 48p. 6.95 o.p. (0-88101-160-6); 1990. 11.95 o.p. (0-88101-108-8) Unicorn Publishing Hse., Inc., The.

—A Christmas Carol. 1998. (Children's Classics). (Illus.). 96p. (YA). (ps up). pap. 3.95 (1-85326-121-1, 1211WW) Wordsworth Editions, Ltd. GBR. Dist: Advanced Global Distribution Services.

—A Christmas Carol. 1995. (Illus.). 4p. (J). cd-rom 17.95 (0-7611-0036-9, 10036) Workman Publishing Co., Inc.

—A Christmas Carol. 1986. (Illus.). 48p. (J). (ps up). lib. bdg. 16.95 o.s.i (0-02-730310-1, Simon & Schuster Children's Publishing) Simon & Schuster Children's Publishing.

—A Christmas Carol, Set. unabr. ed. 1984. (J). audio 20.95 (1-55685-048-4) Audio Bk. Contractors, Inc.

—A Christmas Carol. unabr. ed. (J). audio 16.95 (1-55686-138-9, 138) Books in Motion.

—A Christmas Carol. unabr. ed. (J). 2001. audio compact disk 28.00 (0-7366-8273-2); 1979. audio 18.00 (0-7366-0953-9, 1897) Books on Tape, Inc.

—A Christmas Carol. reprint ed. 1981. (Illus.). 191p. (YA). lib. bdg. 15.95 (0-89966-344-3); 1980. 150p. (J). lib. bdg. 15.95 (0-89967-017-2, Harmony Raine & Co.) Buccaneer Bks., Inc.

—A Christmas Carol. 1996. (Illus.). 48p. (J). (gr. 3-7). reprint ed. bds. 6.99 o.p. (*1-56402-977-8*) Candlewick Pr.

—A Christmas Carol. abr. ed. (J). 1992. audio 4.99 (*0-88646-654-7*); 1986. (gr. 5-7). audio 29.95 o.p. (*0-88646-798-5*, R 7051) Durkin Hayes Publishing Ltd.

—A Christmas Carol. 2nd ed. 1998. (Illustrated Classic Book Ser.: Vol. III). (Illus.). 61p. (J). reprint ed. pap. text 4.95 (*1-56767-241-8*) Educational Insights, Inc.

—A Christmas Carol. abr. ed. 1980. (J). audio 8.98 o.p. (*0-89845-103-5*, CP 1657, Caedmon) HarperTrade.

—A Christmas Carol. l.t. ed. 420p. pap. 42.42 (*0-7583-3607-1*); (Illus.). 82p. pap. 15.16 (*0-7583-3600-4*); (Illus.). 187p. pap. 23.63 (*0-7583-3603-9*); (Illus.). 107p. pap. 17.15 (*0-7583-3601-2*); (Illus.). 362p. pap. 37.75 (*0-7583-3606-3*); (Illus.). 294p. pap. 32.29 (*0-7583-3605-5*); (Illus.). 239p. pap. 27.85 (*0-7583-3604-7*); (Illus.). 146p. pap. 20.33 (*0-7583-3602-0*); (Illus.). 362p. lib. bdg. 44.36 (*0-7583-3598-9*); (Illus.). 239p. lib. bdg. 35.68 (*0-7583-3596-2*); (Illus.). 107p. lib. bdg. 25.47 (*0-7583-3593-8*); (Illus.). 146p. lib. bdg. 29.08 (*0-7583-3594-6*); (Illus.). 420p. lib. bdg. 48.46 (*0-7583-3599-7*); (Illus.). 294p. lib. bdg. 39.57 (*0-7583-3597-0*); (Illus.). 187p. lib. bdg. 31.98 (*0-7583-3595-4*); (Illus.). 82p. lib. bdg. 22.64 (*0-7583-3592-X*) Huge Print Pr.

—A Christmas Carol. Stemach, Jerry et al, eds. l.t. ed. (J). 2000. (Start-to-Finish? Books: Vol. 6). 116p. pap. text 65.00 incl. audio, cd-rom (*1-58702-395-4*); Vol. 6. 2002. (Start-to-Finish Books). (gr. 2-3). audio 100.00 (*1-58702-949-9*); Vol. 6. 2000. (Start-to-Finish Books). (gr. 2-3). audio (*1-58702-371-7*, F31K2) Johnston, Don Inc.

—A Christmas Carol. l.t. ed. 1999. (Large Print Heritage Ser.). 140p. (YA). (gr. 7-12). lib. bdg. 24.95 (*1-58118-041-1*, 22510) LRS.

—A Christmas Carol, Level 2. 2001. (Penguin Readers Lv. 2). (Illus.). (J). pap. 7.66 (*0-582-42120-9*) Longman Publishing Group.

—A Christmas Carol. 2nd ed. 1993. (Illus.). 78p. pap. text 5.95 (*0-19-585258-3*) Oxford Univ. Pr., Inc.

—A Christmas Carol, Level 3. Hedge, Tricia, ed. 2000. (Bookworms Ser.). (Illus.). 80p. (J). pap. text 5.95 (*0-19-423000-7*) Oxford Univ. Pr., Inc.

—A Christmas Carol. abr. ed. 1988. (Illus.). (gr. 4-7). audio 9.99 (*0-553-45146-4*, RH Audio) Random Hse. Audio Publishing Group.

—A Christmas Carol, unabr. ed. 1981. (J). (gr. 6 up). audio 18.00 (*1-55690-101-1*, 80200E7) Recorded Bks., LLC.

—A Christmas Carol. 1987. (Illus.). 128p. (J). (gr. 4-6). reprint ed. pap. 2.50 o.p. (*0-590-41293-0*, Scholastic Paperbacks) Scholastic, Inc.

—A Christmas Carol. unabr. ed. 2002. (YA). audio compact disk 22.95 (*1-58472-227-4*, 015); pap. 45.00 incl. audio compact disk (*1-58472-229-0*) Sound Room Pubs., Inc. (In Audio).

—A Christmas Carol. abr. ed. 1997. (J). audio 14.95 o.p. (*1-85998-304-9*) Trafalgar Square.

—A Christmas Carol. Wendt, Michael & Pizar, Kathleen, eds. abr. ed. 1988. (Little Unicorn Classic Ser.). (Illus.). 80p. (J). (gr. 2-5). 5.95 o.p. (*0-88101-087-1*) Unicorn Publishing Hse., Inc., The.

—A Christmas Carol. abr. ed. 1995. 2p. pap. 16.95 incl. audio (*0-14-086178-5*); pap. 16.95 incl. audio (*0-14-086178-5*) Viking Penguin. (Penguin Audio-Books).

—A Christmas Carol: A Changing Picture & Lift-the-Flap Book. 1989. (Illus.). 320p. (J). (ps-3). 14.95 o.p. (*0-670-82694-4*, Viking Children's Bks.) Penguin Putnam Bks. for Young Readers.

—A Christmas Carol: A Young Reader's Edition of the Classic Holiday Tale. 2002. (Illus.). 56p. (J). (gr. 4-7). text 9.98 (*0-7624-0848-0*) Running Pr. Bk. Pubs.

—A Christmas Carol: Charles Dickens' Tale. 1997. (Eyewitness Classics Ser.). (Illus.). 64p. (J). (gr. 3-6). pap. 14.95 (*0-7894-2070-8*, D K Ink) Dorling Kindersley Publishing, Inc.

—A Christmas Carol & Other Christmas Stories. 1984. (Signet Classics). (Illus.). 224p. (YA). mass mkt. 3.95 (*0-451-52283-4*, Signet Classics) NAL.

—A Christmas Carol & Other Christmas Stories. 1984. (Signet Classics Ser.). 10.00 (*0-606-04893-6*) Turtleback Bks.

—A Christmas Carol & The Cricket on the Hearth. 1973. (Dent's Illustrated Children's Classics Ser.). (Illus.). 220p. (J). reprint ed. 9.00 o.p. (*0-460-05059-1*) Biblio Distribution.

—Cuento de Navidad. 2002. (Classics for Young Readers Ser.). (SPA.). (YA). 14.95 (*84-392-0913-4*, EV30594) Gaviota Ediciones ESP. *Dist:* Lectorum Pubns., Inc.

—Whole Story Christmas Carol. 2000. (Whole Story Ser.). (Illus.). 112p. (YA). (gr. 7-12). 25.99 o.s.i (*0-670-88878-8*, Viking Children's Bks.) Penguin Putnam Bks. for Young Readers.

Dickens, Charles & Skarmeas, Nancy J. A Christmas Carol. abr. ed. 1998. (Illus.). 48p. (J). (gr. 4-7). 14.00 (*0-8249-4096-2*, Candy Cane Pr.) Ideals Pubns.

Dickens, Charles & Sweaney, A. A Christmas Carol: Retold by A. Sweaney. 1976. (Oxford Progressive English Readers Ser.). (J). (gr. k-6). pap. text 4.95 o.p. (*0-19-580724-3*) Oxford Univ. Pr., Inc.

Dickens, Charles & Wheatcroft, Andrew. A Christmas Carol. (Classics Ser.). (Illus.). 64p. (J). 2001. pap. 9.99 (*0-7894-6246-X*, D K Ink); 2000. pap. incl. cd-rom (*0-7894-6363-6*) Dorling Kindersley Publishing, Inc.

Dickens, Charles, et al. A Christmas Carol. unabr. ed. 1994. (J). audio 11.00 o.s.i (*0-89845-755-6*, CPN 1135, Caedmon) HarperTrade.

Gikow, Louise. Muppet Christmas Carol. 1993. (Illus.). 24p. (J). (ps-3). pap. 3.29 o.s.i (*0-307-12795-8*, Golden Bks.) Random Hse. Children's Bks.

Golden Books Staff. Muppet's Christmas Carol. 1992. 56p. pap. 1.69 o.s.i (*0-307-30064-1*, Golden Bks.) Random Hse. Children's Bks.

Lillington, Kenneth, text. A Christmas Carol. 1988. (Easy Piano Picture Bks.). (Illus.). 32p. (Orig.). (J). (gr. k up). pap. 9.95 o.p. (*0-571-10093-7*) Faber & Faber, Inc.

The Muppet Christmas Carol. 1992. 64p. per. 14.95 (*0-7935-2007-X*, 00312483) Leonard, Hal Corp.

Okun, Milton, ed. Scrooge Revised Vocal Selections. 1995. 88p. (YA). pap. 19.95 (*0-89524-988-X*) Cherry Lane Music Co.

SCULLY, DANA (FICTITIOUS CHARACTER)—FICTION

Bisson, Terry. Miracle Man. 2000. (X-Files Young Adult Ser.: No. 16). 128p. (gr. 4-7). mass mkt. 4.50 (*0-06-106617-6*, HarperEntertainment) Morrow/Avon.

Martin, Les. Darkness Falls, No. 2. 1995. (X-Files Ser.). 112p. (gr. 5 up). pap. 4.50 (*0-06-440614-8*, HarperEntertainment) Morrow/Avon.

—E. B. E. A Novel. 1996. (X-Files Ser.: No. 9). 112p. (YA). (gr. 5 up). pap. 4.50 (*0-06-440653-9*, Harper Trophy) HarperCollins Children's Bk. Group.

—E.B.E. 1996. (X-Files Ser.: No. 9). 10.55 (*0-606-10978-1*) Turtleback Bks.

—Fear, No. 7. 1996. (X-Files Ser.). 112p. (J). (gr. 5 up). pap. 3.95 (*0-06-440642-3*, HarperEntertainment) Morrow/Avon.

—Ghost in the Machine, No. 11. 1997. (X-Files Ser.). 112p. (YA). (gr. 5 up). pap. 4.50 (*0-06-440678-4*, HarperEntertainment) Morrow/Avon.

—Humbug, No. 5. 1996. (X-Files Ser.). 128p. (YA). (gr. 5 up). pap. 3.95 (*0-06-440627-X*, HarperEntertainment) Morrow/Avon.

—Quarantine, No. 13. 1999. (X-Files Young Adult Ser.: No. 13). 128p. (J). (gr. 7 up). mass mkt. 4.50 (*0-06-447189-6*, HarperEntertainment) Morrow/Avon.

—Tiger, Tiger. 1995. 112p. (YA). (gr. 5 up). pap. 4.50 o.s.i (*0-06-440626-1*, Harper Trophy) HarperCollins Children's Bk. Group.

—X Marks the Spot, No. 1. 1995. (X Files Middle Grade Ser.). 128p. (gr. 5 up). pap. 4.50 (*0-06-440613-X*, HarperEntertainment) Morrow/Avon.

Mezrich, Ben. Skin, abr. ed. 1999. audio 18.00 (*0-694-51913-8*, 393578, HarperAudio) HarperTrade.

Owens, Everett. Regeneration, Vol. 14. 2000. (X-Files Young Adult Ser.: No. 14). 128p. (gr. 7-12). mass mkt. 4.50 (*0-06-106619-2*, HarperEntertainment) Morrow/Avon.

Steiber, Ellen. Haunted. 2000. (X-Files Young Adult Ser.: No. 15). (Illus.). 144p. (J). (gr. 4-7). mass mkt. 4.50 (*0-06-106618-4*, HarperEntertainment) Morrow/Avon.

SHAKESPEARE, WILLIAM, 1564-1616—FICTION

Blackwood, Gary. Shakespeare's Spy. 2003. 280p. (J). 16.99 (*0-525-47145-6*, Dutton Children's Bks.) Penguin Putnam Bks. for Young Readers.

Blackwood, Gary L. The Shakespeare Stealer. (J). (gr. 4-8). 2000. (Illus.). 224p. pap. 5.99 (*0-14-130595-9*, Puffin Bks.); 1998. 208p. 15.99 (*0-525-45863-8*, Dutton Children's Bks.) Penguin Putnam Bks. for Young Readers.

—The Shakespeare Stealer. 2000. 12.04 (*0-606-17870-8*) Turtleback Bks.

—Shakespeare's Scribe. 2002. (Illus.). (YA). 13.19 (*1-4046-0844-3*) Book Wholesalers, Inc.

—Shakespeare's Scribe. 2002. 272p. pap. 5.99 (*0-14-230066-7*, Puffin Bks.); 2000. (Illus.). 224p. (J). (gr. 4-6). 15.99 (*0-525-46444-1*, Dutton Children's Bks.) Penguin Putnam Bks. for Young Readers.

Burdett, Lois. A Child's Portrait of Shakespeare. 1995. (Illus.). 64p. (YA). (gr. 2 up). pap. 8.95 (*0-88753-261-6*); lib. bdg. 19.95 (*0-88753-263-2*) Black Moss Pr. CAN. *Dist:* Firefly Bks., Ltd.

—A Child's Portrait of Shakespeare. 1995. (Shakespeare Can Be Fun! Ser.). 15.10 (*0-606-07364-7*) Turtleback Bks.

Carter, Avis M. One Day in Shakespeare's England. 1974. (Day Book Ser.). (Illus.). 48p. (J). (gr. 3 up). o.p. (*0-200-00135-3*) Criterion Bks., Inc.

Cheaney, Janie B. The True Prince. 352p. (J). (gr. 5). 2004. pap. 5.99 (*0-440-41940-9*, Yearling); 2002. (Illus.). 15.95 (*0-375-81433-7*, Knopf Bks. for Young Readers); 2002. (Illus.). lib. bdg. 17.99 (*0-375-91433-1*, Knopf Bks. for Young Readers) Random Hse. Children's Bks.

Chute, Marchette. The Wonderful Winter. 1954. (J). (gr. 5-9). lib. bdg. 5.95 o.p. (*0-525-43208-6*, Dutton) Dutton/Plume.

—The Wonderful Winter. 2002. 256p. (J). 12.95 (*0-9714612-1-X*) Green Mansion Pr. LLC.

Cooper, Susan. King of Shadows. (Illus.). 192p. (gr. 5-9). 2001. (J). pap. 4.99 (*0-689-84445-X*, Aladdin); 1999. (YA). 16.00 (*0-689-82817-9*, McElderry, Margaret K.) Simon & Schuster Children's Publishing.

—King of Shadows. l.t. ed. 2000. (Thorndike Press Large Print Juvenile Ser.). (Illus.). 246p. (J). (gr. 8-12). 21.95 (*0-7862-2706-0*) Thorndike Pr.

Deary, Terry. Shakespeare Stories. 1999. (Top Ten Ser.). (Illus.). 192p. (gr. 6-12). mass mkt. 4.50 (*0-439-08387-7*) Scholastic, Inc.

Dhondy, Farrukh. Black Swan. 1993. 208p. (YA). (gr. 6 up). 14.95 o.p. (*0-395-66076-9*) Houghton Mifflin Co.

Freeman, Don. Will's Quill. 1975. (Illus.). 32p. (J). (gr. k-3). 12.50 o.p. (*0-670-76922-3*) Viking Penguin.

Hassinger, Peter. Shakespeare's Daughter. 2004. 320p. (J). 15.99 (*0-06-028467-6*, Geringer, Laura Bk.) HarperCollins Children's Bk. Group.

Kositsky, Lynne. A Question of Will. 2001. (Out of This World Ser.). (Illus.). 144p. (YA). (gr. 7 up). pap. 5.95 (*1-896184-66-9*) Roussan Pubs., Inc./Roussan Editeur, Inc. CAN. *Dist:* Orca Bk. Pubs.

Lepscky, Ibi. William Shakespeare. 1989. (Famous People Ser.). (Illus.). 28p. (J). (gr. k-3). 7.95 (*0-8120-6106-3*) Barron's Educational Series, Inc.

MacInnes, Colin. Three Years to Play. 1970. 354p. (J). 6.95 o.p. (*0-374-27681-1*) Farrar, Straus & Giroux.

Random House Value Publishing Staff, ed. Shakespeare, Illustrated Stories for Children. 1999. 6.99 (*0-517-20430-4*) Random Hse. Value Publishing.

Rosen, Michael & Shakespeare, William. Shakespeare's Romeo & Juliet. Ray, Jane, tr. & illus. by. 2003. 80p. (J). 17.99 (*0-7636-2258-3*) Candlewick Pr.

Shakespeare, William. Antony & Cleopatra. Gill, Roma, ed. 2002. (Oxford School Shakespeare Ser.). (Illus.). 224p. pap. text 7.95 (*0-19-832057-4*) Oxford Univ. Pr., Inc.

—Antony & Cleopatra. 2002. (Shakespeare Collection). (Illus.). 46p. (J). 9.95 o.p. (*0-19-521793-4*) Oxford Univ. Pr., Inc.

SHIRLEY, ANNE (FICTITIOUS CHARACTER)—FICTION

see Anne of Green Gables (Fictitious Character)—Fiction

SIMPLE (FICTITIOUS CHARACTER)—FICTION

Hughes, Langston. The Best of Simple. 1990. (Illus.). 245p. (J). (gr. 4-6). pap. 13.00 (*0-374-52133-6*, Hill & Wang) Farrar, Straus & Giroux.

—Simple Speaks His Mind. (J). (gr. 5-6). reprint ed. lib. bdg. 22.95 (*0-88411-061-3*) Amereon, Ltd.

SISKO, BENJAMIN (FICTITIOUS CHARACTER)—FICTION

Gilden, Mel & Pedersen, Ted. The Pet. Clancy, Lisa, ed. 1994. (Star Trek Ser.: No. 4). (Illus.). 128p. (J). (gr. 4-7). pap. 3.99 (*0-671-88352-6*, Aladdin) Simon & Schuster Children's Publishing.

Pedersen, Ted. Gypsy World. 1996. (Star Trek Ser.: No. 7). (Illus.). 128p. (J). (gr. 4-7). pap. 3.99 (*0-671-51115-7*, Aladdin) Simon & Schuster Children's Publishing.

—Gypsy World. 1996. 10.04 (*0-606-14221-5*) Turtleback Bks.

—Space Camp. 1997. 10.04 (*0-606-14319-X*) Turtleback Bks.

Pedersen, Ted & Neuville, H. Richmond. Space Camp. 1997. (Star Trek Deep Space Nine Ser.: No. 10). (Illus.). 128p. (J). (gr. 3-6). pap. 3.99 (*0-671-00730-0*, Aladdin) Simon & Schuster Children's Publishing.

SISKO, JAKE (FICTITIOUS CHARACTER)—FICTION

Antilles, Kem. Highest Score. 1996. (Star Trek Ser.: No. 8). (Illus.). 128p. (J). (gr. 4-7). pap. 3.99 (*0-671-89936-8*, Aladdin) Simon & Schuster Children's Publishing.

Gallagher, Diana G. Arcade. 1995. (Star Trek Ser.: No. 5). (Illus.). 112p. (J). (gr. 4-7). pap. 3.99 o.s.i (*0-671-89678-4*, Aladdin) Simon & Schuster Children's Publishing.

—Arcade. 1995. 10.04 (*0-606-14155-3*) Turtleback Bks.

Gilden, Mel. Cardassian Imps. 1997. (Star Trek Ser.: No. 9). (Illus.). 128p. (J). (gr. 3-6). pap. 3.99 (*0-671-51116-5*, Aladdin) Simon & Schuster Children's Publishing.

—Cardassian Imps. 1997. 10.04 (*0-606-14175-8*) Turtleback Bks.

Gilden, Mel & Pedersen, Ted. The Pet. Clancy, Lisa, ed. 1994. (Star Trek Ser.: No. 4). (Illus.). 128p. (J). (gr. 4-7). pap. 3.99 (*0-671-88352-6*, Aladdin) Simon & Schuster Children's Publishing.

Pedersen, Ted. Gypsy World. 1996. (Star Trek Ser.: No. 7). (Illus.). 128p. (J). (gr. 4-7). pap. 3.99 (*0-671-51115-7*, Aladdin) Simon & Schuster Children's Publishing.

—Gypsy World. 1996. 10.04 (*0-606-14221-5*) Turtleback Bks.

—Space Camp. 1997. 10.04 (*0-606-14319-X*) Turtleback Bks.

—Trapped in Time. 1998. (Star Trek Deep Space Nine Ser.: No. 12). (Illus.). 128p. (J). (gr. 4-7). pap. 3.99 (*0-671-01440-4*, Aladdin) Simon & Schuster Children's Publishing.

Pedersen, Ted & Neuville, H. Richmond. Space Camp. 1997. (Star Trek Deep Space Nine Ser.: No. 10). (Illus.). 128p. (J). (gr. 3-6). pap. 3.99 (*0-671-00730-0*, Aladdin) Simon & Schuster Children's Publishing.

Peel, John. Field Trip. 1995. (Star Trek Ser.: No. 6). (Illus.). 128p. (J). (gr. 4-7). pap. 3.99 (*0-671-88287-2*, Aladdin) Simon & Schuster Children's Publishing.

—Prisoners of Peace. Clancy, Lisa, ed. 1994. (Star Trek Deep Space Nine Ser.: No. 3). (Illus.). 128p. (J). (gr. 4-7). pap. 3.99 (*0-671-88288-0*, Aladdin) Simon & Schuster Children's Publishing.

—Prisoners of Peace. 1994. 10.04 (*0-606-14295-9*) Turtleback Bks.

Strickland, Brad. The Star Ghost. Clancy, Lisa, ed. 1994. (Star Trek Ser.: No. 1). (Illus.). 128p. (J). (gr. 4-7). 3.99 (*0-671-87999-5*, Aladdin) Simon & Schuster Children's Publishing.

—The Star Ghost. 1994. 10.04 (*0-606-14322-X*) Turtleback Bks.

—Stowaways. 1994. (Star Trek Deep Space Nine Ser.: No. 2). (Illus.). 128p. (J). (gr. 3-6). pap. 3.99 (*0-671-88000-4*, Aladdin) Simon & Schuster Children's Publishing.

SKYWALKER, ANAKIN (FICTITIOUS CHARACTER)—FICTION

Alfonsi, Alice. Anakin's Race for Freedom. 1999. (Star Wars Episode I Ser.). (Illus.). 24p. (J). (ps-3). pap. 3.99 (*0-375-80027-1*, Random Hse. Bks. for Young Readers) Random Hse. Children's Bks.

Cerasini, Marc A. Anakin's Fate. 1999. (Star Wars: Step. 4). (Illus.). 48p. (J). (gr. 2-4). pap. 4.99 o.s.i (*0-375-80029-8*) Random Hse., Inc.

Cerasini, Marc A. & Alvin, John. Anakin's Fate. 1999. (Star Wars: Step. 4). (Illus.). (J). (gr. 2-4). 11.99 o.s.i (*0-375-90029-2*) Random Hse., Inc.

Fontes, Justine & Fontes, Ron. Anakin's Pit Droid. 2000. (Star Wars: Step. 2). (Illus.). 48p. (J). (gr. 1-3). lib. bdg. 11.99 o.s.i (*0-375-90431-X*, Random Hse. Bks. for Young Readers) Random Hse. Children's Bks.

Hildebrandt, Greg, et al, illus. Star Wars: Episode I:The Phantom Menace: Great Big Flap Book. 1999. 10p. (J). (ps-3). bds. 12.99 o.s.i (*0-375-80010-7*) Random Hse., Inc.

Lucas, George. The Phantom Menace Movie Storybook. 1999. (Star Wars). (Illus.). 64p. (J). (gr. k-3). pap. 7.99 o.s.i (*0-375-80009-3*) Random Hse., Inc.

Random House Staff. The Phantom Menace Movie Storybook. 1999. (Star Wars Episode I Ser.). (Illus.). 64p. (YA). (gr. k up). 11.99 o.s.i (*0-375-90009-8*, Random Hse. Bks. for Young Readers) Random Hse. Children's Bks.

Strasser, Todd. Anakin Skywalker, Vol. 1. 1999. (Star Wars Ser.). (Illus.). 112p. (J). (gr. 4-7). mass mkt. 5.99 (*0-590-52093-8*) Scholastic, Inc.

Venn, Cecilia. Anakin to the Rescue. 1999. (Star Wars). (Illus.). 48p. (J). (gr. 1-3). pap. 4.99 o.s.i (*0-375-80001-8*) Random Hse., Inc.

Venn, Cecilia & Keenan, Sheila. Anakin to the Rescue. 1999. (Star Wars: Step. 2). (Illus.). (J). (gr. 1-3). 11.99 o.s.i (*0-375-90001-2*) Random Hse., Inc.

Watson, Jude. The Dangerous Games. unabr. ed. 2003. (star wars: No. 3). (J). (gr. 3). audio compact disk 19.99 (*0-8072-1043-9*, RH Audio) Random Hse. Audio Publishing Group.

—The Dangerous Games. 2002. (Star Wars Ser.: No. 3). 144p. (YA). mass mkt. 4.99 (*0-439-33919-7*) Scholastic, Inc.

Wrede, Patricia C. Star Wars: Episode I: The Phantom Menace. 1999. (J). (Illus.). 178p. (gr. 3-7). mass mkt. 5.99 (*0-590-01089-1*); mass mkt. 9.95 (*0-439-08706-6*) Scholastic, Inc.

SKYWALKER, LUKE (FICTITIOUS CHARACTER)—FICTION

Covey, Stephen R. Star Wars. 1999. (Star Wars Ser.). 12p. pap. 1.79 o.s.i (*0-307-02223-4*, Golden Bks.) Random Hse. Children's Bks.

Dana, Michael. Star Wars: The Greatest Battles. 1999. (Star Wars Ser.). (Illus.). 16p. (J). pap. 3.99 o.s.i (*0-307-14656-1*, Golden Bks.) Random Hse. Children's Bks.

Davids, Paul. The Adventure Continues Boxed Set: The Glove of Darth Vader; the Lost City of the Jedi; Zorba the Hutt's Revenge. 1997. (Star Wars: Nos. 1-3). (J). (gr. 2-8). 12.48 o.s.i (0-553-62866-6, Dell Books for Young Readers) Random Hse. Children's Bks.

—The Glove of Darth Vader. 1996. (Star Wars: Bk. 1). (J). (gr. 4-7). pap. 4.99 (0-553-54282-6, Dell Books for Young Readers) Random Hse. Children's Bks.

—The Glove of Darth Vader. 1992. (Star Wars: Bk. 1). (J). (gr. 4-7). 9.09 o.p. (0-606-00535-8) Turtleback Bks.

—Mission from Mount Yoda. 1999. (Star Wars: Bk. 4). (J). (gr. 4-7). pap. 9.50 o.p. (0-7607-0447-3) Barnes & Noble, Inc.

—The Mission from Mount Yoda. 1993. (Star Wars Ser.: Bk. 4). 128p. (YA). (gr. 4-7). pap. 4.50 o.s.i (0-553-15890-2) Bantam Bks.

—Prophets of the Dark Side. 1993. (Star Wars: Bk. 6). 128p. (gr. 4-7). pap. text 4.50 (0-553-15892-9) Bantam Bks.

—The Queen of the Empire. 1993. (Star Wars: Bk. 5). 128p. (YA). (gr. 4-7). pap. 4.50 o.s.i (0-553-15891-0) Bantam Bks.

Davids, Paul & Davids, Hollace. The Glove of Darth Vader. 1992. (Star Wars: Bk. 1). (Illus.). 128p. (gr. 4-7). pap. text 4.50 (0-553-15887-2, Starfire) Random Hse. Children's Bks.

—The Glove of Darth Vader. l.t. ed. 1997. 112p. (J). (gr. 4 up). lib. bdg. 22.60 o.p. (0-8368-1989-6) Stevens, Gareth Inc.

—The Glove of Darth Vader. 1992. 10.04 (0-606-14216-9) Turtleback Bks.

—The Lost City of the Jedi. 1999. (Star Wars Ser.: Bk. 2). (Illus.). 94p. (J). (gr. 4-7). reprint ed. pap. 10.00 (0-7881-6480-5) DIANE Publishing Co.

—The Lost City of the Jedi. 1992. (Star Wars: Bk. 2). 128p. (gr. 4-7). pap. text 4.50 (0-553-15888-0, Starfire) Random Hse. Children's Bks.

—The Lost City of the Jedi. l.t. ed. 1997. 112p. (J). (gr. 4 up). lib. bdg. 22.60 o.p. (0-8368-1990-X) Stevens, Gareth Inc.

—The Lost City of the Jedi. 1992. (Star Wars: Bk. 2). (J). (gr. 4-7). 10.55 (0-606-00543-9) Turtleback Bks.

—Mission from Mount Yoda. l.t. ed. 1997. 112p. (J). (gr. 4 up). lib. bdg. 22.60 o.p. (0-8368-1992-6) Stevens, Gareth Inc.

—Mission from Mount Yoda. 1993. (Star Wars: Bk. 4). (J). (gr. 4-7). 10.55 (0-606-02755-6) Turtleback Bks.

—Prophets of the Dark Side. l.t. ed. 1997. (Star Wars Ser.: No. 6). 112p. (J). (gr. 4 up). lib. bdg. 22.60 (0-8368-1994-2) Stevens, Gareth Inc.

—Prophets of the Dark Side. 1993. (Star Wars: Bk. 6). (J). (gr. 4-7). 10.55 (0-606-05557-6) Turtleback Bks.

—Queen of the Empire. l.t. ed. 1997. (Star Wars Ser.: No. 5). 112p. (J). (gr. 4 up). lib. bdg. 22.60 (0-8368-1993-4) Stevens, Gareth Inc.

—Queen of the Empire. 1993. (Star Wars: Bk. 5). (J). (gr. 4-7). 10.55 (0-606-02849-8) Turtleback Bks.

—Star Wars, 3 bks. l.t. ed. Incl. Prophets of the Dark Side. lib. bdg. 22.60 (0-8368-1994-2); Queen of the Empire. lib. bdg. 22.60 (0-8368-1993-4); Zorba the Hutt's Revenge. lib. bdg. 22.60 (0-8368-1991-8); 112p. (J). (gr. 4 up). 1997. Set lib. bdg. 67.80 (0-8368-1988-8) Stevens, Gareth Inc.

—Zorba the Hutt's Revenge. 1992. (Star Wars: Bk. 3). 128p. (gr. 4-7). pap. text 4.50 (0-553-15889-9) Bantam Bks.

—Zorba the Hutt's Revenge. l.t. ed. 1997. (Star Wars Ser.: No. 3). 112p. (J). (gr. 4 up). lib. bdg. 22.60 (0-8368-1991-8) Stevens, Gareth Inc.

—Zorba the Hutt's Revenge. 1992. (Star Wars: Bk. 3). (J). (gr. 4-7). 10.55 (0-606-00544-7) Turtleback Bks.

Disney Staff, ed. The Empire Strikes Back. (Read Along Star Wars Ser.). (J). 7.99 incl. audio (0-7634-0194-3) Walt Disney Records.

—The Empire Strikes Back: A Flip Book. 1997. 40p. (J). 2.98 o.s.i (1-57082-578-5) Mouse Works.

—Return of the Jedi. (Read Along Star Wars Ser.). (J). 7.99 incl. audio (0-7634-0193-5); 14.99 incl. audio (0-7634-0196-X) Walt Disney Records.

—Star Wars: A New Hope: A Flip Book. 1997. (Star Wars Ser.). 40p. (J). 2.98 o.s.i (1-57082-577-7) Mouse Works.

Disney Staff & Steacy, Ken. Star Wars. 1997. (Star Wars Ser.). 24p. (J). 8.98 o.s.i (1-57082-567-X) Mouse Works.

Gardner, J. J. Return of the Jedi Storybook. 1997. (Illus.). (J). (gr. 5-7). mass mkt. 5.99 (0-590-06659-5) Scholastic, Inc.

Golden Books Staff. The Empire Strikes Back: With Tattoos. 1999. (Star Wars Ser.). (Illus.). 24p. pap. 3.99 o.s.i (0-307-13068-1, Golden Bks.) Random Hse. Children's Bks.

—Invisible Forces: Color Surprise. 1999. (Star Wars Ser.). (Illus.). 32p. (J). pap. 3.99 o.s.i (0-307-15291-X, Golden Bks.) Random Hse. Children's Bks.

—Star Wars: A New Hope. 1999. (Star Wars Ser.). 16p. (J). pap. 2.99 o.s.i (0-307-10577-6, Golden Bks.) Random Hse. Children's Bks.

—Star Wars: Battling the Empire. 1997. (Extra Smart Pages Ser.). 14p. (J). o.p. (0-307-75704-8, Golden Bks.) Random Hse. Children's Bks.

—Star Wars: A New Hope: With Tattoos. 1999. (Star Wars Ser.). (Illus.). 24p. pap. 3.99 o.s.i (0-307-13067-3, Golden Bks.) Random Hse. Children's Bks.

Golden, Christopher. The Empire Strikes Back. 1998. (Choose Your Own Star Wars Adventure Ser.). 128p. (gr. 4-8). pap. text 4.50 o.s.i (0-553-48652-7, Dell Books for Young Readers) Random Hse. Children's Bks.

Levy, Elizabeth, ed. Return of the Jedi Step-Up Movie Adventure. 1983. (Star Wars Ser.). (Illus.). 72p. (J). (gr. 1-3). 8.99 o.s.i (0-394-96117-X, Random Hse. Bks. for Young Readers) Random Hse. Children's Bks.

Lucas, George. The Empire Strikes Back Adventures. abr. ed. 1994. (J). (gr. k-3). audio 8.98 o.p. Time Warner AudioBooks.

—Return of the Jedi: A Flip Book. 1997. (Star Wars Ser.). 40p. (J). 2.98 o.s.i (1-57082-579-3) Mouse Works.

Macan, Darko, et al. Vader's Quest. 1999. (Star Wars Ser.). (Illus.). 96p. (YA). (gr. 7 up). pap. 11.95 (1-56971-415-0) Dark Horse Comics.

Scholastic, Inc. Staff, ed. The Empire Strikes Back. 9999. (J). pap. 2.50 o.s.i (0-590-31791-1) Scholastic, Inc.

—Return of the Jedi. 9999. (J). pap. 2.95 o.s.i (0-590-32929-4) Scholastic, Inc.

Snyder, Margaret. Star Wars: A More Wretched Hive. 1999. (Star Wars Ser.). 32p. (J). (ps-3). pap. 4.99 o.s.i (0-307-13552-7, Golden Bks.) Random Hse. Children's Bks.

Sweeny, Sheila & Golden Books Staff. Luke Skywalker's Battle with Darth Vader: Star Wars Reading Story Workbook. 1999. (Star Wars Ser.). 48p. (J). pap., wbk. ed. 3.99 o.s.i (0-307-21305-6, Golden Bks.) Random Hse. Children's Bks.

Thomas, Jim K. Star Wars: Luke's Fate. 1996. (Step into Reading Ser.). (Illus.). 48p. (J). (gr. 2-3). pap. 3.99 (0-679-85855-5) Random Hse., Inc.

Vaz, Mark Cotta. The Star Wars Trilogy Scrapbook: The Rebel Alliance. 1997. 48p. (gr. 4-7). mass mkt. 6.99 (0-590-12051-4) Scholastic, Inc.

Vinge, Joan D., adapted by. Return of the Jedi: The Storybook Based on the Movie. 1983. (Storybook Based on the Movie Ser.). (Illus.). 64p. (J). (gr. 3-8). 7.99 o.p. (0-394-95624-9, Random Hse. Bks. for Young Readers) Random Hse. Children's Bks.

Whitman, John. Return of the Jedi. 1996. (Mighty Chronicles Ser.). (Illus.). 316p. (gr. 4-7). 9.95 o.s.i (0-8118-1494-7) Chronicle Bks. LLC.

Whitman, John, adapted by. The Empire Strikes Back. 1996. (Mighty Chronicles Ser.). (Illus.). 432p. (gr. 4-7). 9.95 o.s.i (0-8118-1482-3) Chronicle Bks. LLC.

SLEEPING BEAUTY (FICTITIOUS CHARACTER)—FICTION

Disney Staff. The Sleeping Beauty. (FRE.). 96p. (J). (gr. k-5). pap. 9.95 (0-7859-8854-8) French & European Pubns., Inc.

—Sleeping Beauty: A Magic Plan. 1997. (Disney's "Storytime Treasures" Library: Vol. 14). (Illus.). 44p. (J). (gr. 1-6). 3.49 o.p. (1-57973-010-8) Advance Pubs. LLC.

Golden Books Staff. Sleeping Beauty. (Sleeping Beauty Ser.). (ps-3). 1999. (Illus.). 24p. o.p. (0-307-16235-4); 1998. 2.22 o.s.i (0-307-34044-9) Random Hse. Children's Bks. (Golden Bks.).

Heyer, Carol. The Sleeping Beauty in the Wood. 2001. (J). (gr. 4-7). 14.95 (0-8249-5401-7) Ideals Pubns.

RH Disney Staff. The Fairest of the Fall. 2003. (Illus.). 24p. (J). (gr. k-3). pap. 3.25 (0-7364-2148-3, RH/Disney) Random Hse. Children's Bks.

Umansky, Kaye. Sleeping Beauty. 2002. (Curtain Up Ser.). (Illus.). 48p. pap. 15.00 (0-7136-5371-X) A & C Black GBR. *Dist:* Players Pr., Inc.

SMITH, CASEY (FICTITIOUS CHARACTER)—FICTION

Ellerbee, Linda. Ghoul Reporter Digs up Zombies! 2000. (Get Real Ser.: No. 5). 208p. (J). (gr. 3-7). lib. bdg. 14.89 (0-06-028249-5);No. 5. pap. 4.99 (0-06-440759-4, Avon) HarperCollins Children's Bk. Group.

—Girl Reporter Blows Lid off Town! 2000. (Get Real Ser.: No. 1). (Illus.). 208p. (J). (gr. 3-7). lib. bdg. 14.89 (0-06-028245-2);No. 1. pap. 4.99 (0-06-440755-1, Avon) HarperCollins Children's Bk. Group.

—Girl Reporter Bytes Back! 2001. (Get Real Ser.: No. 8). 176p. (J). (gr. 3-7). pap. 4.99 (0-06-440952-X, Avon); lib. bdg. 14.89 (0-06-029258-X) HarperCollins Children's Bk. Group.

—Girl Reporter Gets the Skinny! 2001. (Get Real Ser.: No. 7). (Illus.). 192p. (J). (gr. 3-7). pap. 4.99 (0-06-440951-1, Avon); lib. bdg. 14.89 (0-06-029257-1) HarperCollins Children's Bk. Group.

—Girl Reporter Rocks Polls! 2000. (Get Real Ser.: No. 6). 224p. (J). (gr. 3-7). lib. bdg. 14.89 (0-06-028250-9);No. 6. pap. 4.99 (0-06-440760-8, Avon) HarperCollins Children's Bk. Group.

—Girl Reporter Sinks School! 2000. (Get Real Ser.: No. 2). (Illus.). 176p. (J). (gr. 3-7). lib. bdg. 14.89 (0-06-028246-0);No. 2. pap. 4.50 (0-06-440756-X, Avon) HarperCollins Children's Bk. Group.

—Girl Reporter Snags Crush! 2000. (Get Real Ser.: No. 4). (Illus.). (J). (gr. 3-7). 229p. lib. bdg. 14.89 (0-06-028248-7);No. 4. 240p. pap. 4.50 (0-06-440758-6, Avon) HarperCollins Children's Bk. Group.

—Girl Reporter Stuck in Jam! 2000. (Get Real Ser.: No. 3). (Illus.). 224p. (J). (gr. 3-7). lib. bdg. 14.89 (0-06-028247-9);No. 3. pap. 4.50 (0-06-440757-8, Avon) HarperCollins Children's Bk. Group.

SMITH, JOHN, 1580-1631—FICTION

Foster, Genevieve. World of Captain John Smith. 1999. (Illus.). 416p. (J). (gr. 5-8). pap. 15.95 (1-893103-00-5) Beautiful Feet Bks.

Karwoski, Gail Langer. Surviving Jamestown: The Adventures of Young Sam Collier. 2001. (Illus.). 192p. (J). (gr. 3-7). 14.95 (1-56145-239-4); pap. 8.95 (1-56145-245-9) Peachtree Pubs., Ltd.

SMURFS (FICTITIOUS CHARACTERS)—FICTION

Peyo. Smurf Cake. 1981. (Smurf Mini-Storybooks). (Illus.). 32p. (J). (ps-5). pap. 1.25 o.s.i (0-394-84930-2) Random Hse., Inc.

—A Smurf in the Air. 1981. (Smurf Mini-Storybooks). (Illus.). 32p. (J). (ps-5). pap. 1.25 o.s.i (0-394-84929-9) Random Hse., Inc.

—A Smurf Picnic. 1982. (Smurf Little Pops Ser.). (Illus.). 12p. (J). (ps-3). pap. 2.50 o.s.i (0-394-85172-2) Random Hse., Inc.

—The Smurfic Games & Smurf of One & Smurf a Dozen of the Other. Bell, Anthea & Hockridge, Derek, trs. from FRE. 1983. (Illus.). (J). (ps-5). pap. 2.95 o.p. (0-394-85619-8, Random Hse. Bks. for Young Readers) Random Hse. Children's Bks.

—The Smurfs & the Howlibird. 1983. (Smurf Adventures Ser.). (Illus.). 48p. (J). (gr. 9-12). pap. 2.95 o.p. (0-394-86075-6, Random Hse. Bks. for Young Readers) Random Hse. Children's Bks.

—The Smurfs & the Magic Flute. 1983. (Smurf Adventures Ser.). (Illus.). 64p. (J). pap. 2.95 o.s.i (0-394-86074-8) Random Hse., Inc.

—The Smurfs & Their Woodland Friends. 1983. (Chunky Bks.). (Illus.). 28p. (J). pap. 2.95 o.p. (0-394-85370-9) Random Hse., Inc.

—The Smurf's Apprentice. 1982. (Smurf Mini-Storybooks). (Illus.). 32p. (J). (ps-5). pap. 1.25 o.p. (0-394-85373-3) Random Hse., Inc.

Peyo, illus. Smurf Punch-Out Book. 1982. 32p. (J). (gr. 1-5). pap. 3.95 o.p. (0-394-85415-2) Random Hse., Inc.

Peyo & Matagne. The Smurfs & the Miller. 1984. (Illus.). 24p. (J). (ps-3). 3.95 o.p. (0-394-86076-4) Random Hse., Inc.

—The Smurfs & the Toyshop. 1984. (Illus.). 24p. (J). (ps-3). 3.95 o.p. (0-394-86077-2) Random Hse., Inc.

Peyo & Schwarz, Rae P. The Smurf Activity Book. 1983. (Illus.). 64p. (J). (gr. 1-5). 3.95 o.p. (0-394-85383-0) Random Hse., Inc.

SNOOPY (FICTITIOUS CHARACTER)—FICTION

LoBianco, Peter & LoBianco, Nick, illus. It's Time for School, Charlie Brown. 2002. (Ready-to-Read Ser.). 32p. (J). (gr. 1-4). lib. bdg. 11.89 (0-689-85147-2, Little Simon) Simon & Schuster Children's Publishing.

Schulz, Charles M. Un Beagle Qui a du Chien. 1982. (FRE.). (J). pap. 5.95 o.s.i (0-03-061653-0, Owl Bks.) Holt, Henry & Co.

—Beagle Scout Snoopy: Peanuts Backpack Book. 2004. (Illus.). 14p. (J). mass mkt. 6.99 (0-689-85855-8, Little Simon) Simon & Schuster Children's Publishing.

—Classroom Peanuts. 1982. (Illus.). 208p. (J). (gr. 4-6). 17.00 o.p. (0-03-061529-1) Holt, Henry & Co.

—Friends Forever, Snoopy. 2001. (Ready-to-Read Ser.). (Illus.). 32p. (J). pap. 3.99 (0-689-84597-9, Little Simon) Simon & Schuster Children's Publishing.

—Have No Fear, Snoopy. 1988. (J). mass mkt. 3.99 o.s.i (0-449-21490-7, Fawcett) Ballantine Bks.

—Hello, World! 2003. (Baby Snoopy Ser.). (Illus.). 8p. (J). 7.99 (0-689-86365-9, Little Simon) Simon & Schuster Children's Publishing.

—Inegalable Snoopy. 1990. (Peanuts Ser.). (FRE.). 124p. (J). pap. 10.95 (0-7859-4570-9) French & European Pubns., Inc.

—L' Infaillible Snoopy. 1990. (Peanuts Ser.). (FRE.). 126p. (J). pap. 10.95 (0-7859-4571-7) French & European Pubns., Inc.

—Invincible Snoopy. 1991. (Peanuts Ser.). (FRE.). 123p. (J). pap. 11.95 (0-7859-4573-3) French & European Pubns., Inc.

—It Was a Dark & Stormy Night, Snoopy. 2004. (Illus.). 160p. pap. 11.95 (0-345-44272-5) Ballantine Bks.

—It's Chow Time, Snoopy! Selected Cartoons from Dr. Beagle & Mr. Hyde. 1986. mass mkt. 2.95 o.s.i (0-449-21355-2); 1982. (Illus.). 128p. mass mkt. 1.95 o.p. (0-449-20096-5, Fawcett) Ballantine Bks.

—It's Show Time, Snoopy: Selected Cartoons from "Speak Softly & Carry a Beagle" 1986. mass mkt. 2.25 o.s.i (0-449-21336-6); Vol. 2. 1981. (Illus.). mass mkt. 1.75 o.s.i (0-449-23602-1, Fawcett) Ballantine Bks.

—Sleepy Time. 2003. (Baby Snoopy Ser.). (Illus.). 8p. (J). 7.99 (0-689-86364-0, Little Simon) Simon & Schuster Children's Publishing.

—Snoopy: Not Your Average Dog. 1996. (Illus.). 80p. (J). 19.95 o.s.i (0-00-225188-4) HarperSanFrancisco.

—Snoopy & the Twelve Days of Christmas, ERS. 1985. (J). o.p. (0-03-007527-0, Holt, Henry & Co. Bks. For Young Readers) Holt, Henry & Co.

—Snoopy, Flying Ace to the Rescue. 2002. (Peanuts Ser.). 32p. (J). pap. 3.99 (0-689-85148-0, Little Simon) Simon & Schuster Children's Publishing.

—Snoopy's Doghouse. 2003. (Illus.). 16p. (J). 10.95 (0-689-85854-X, Little Simon) Simon & Schuster Children's Publishing.

—Snoopy's Tennis Book. 1979. (Peanuts Parade Bks.). (Illus.). 104p. (J). pap. 4.95 o.p. (0-03-050585-2, Owl Bks.) Holt, Henry & Co.

—Woodstock: Peanuts Backpack Book. 2003. (Illus.). 14p. (J). mass mkt. 6.99 (0-689-85856-6, Little Simon) Simon & Schuster Children's Publishing.

—You're Not for Real, Snoopy: Selected Cartoons from "Peanuts Every Sunday" 1975. mass mkt. 0.95 o.s.i (0-449-22644-1); Vol. 2. 1981. (Illus.). (J). (gr. 3-7). mass mkt. 1.75 o.s.i (0-449-23879-2, Fawcett) Ballantine Bks.

Schulz, Charles M. & Golden Books Staff. Get in Shape, Snoopy! 1989. (Golden Little Look-Look Bks.). (Illus.). 24p. (J). (ps). pap. 1.79 o.s.i (0-307-11866-5, Golden Bks.) Random Hse. Children's Bks.

Schulz, Charles M. & Mack, Lizzie. Puppy Days. 2003. (Baby Snoopy Ser.). (Illus.). 24p. (J). pap. 3.99 (0-689-85900-7); lib. bdg. 11.89 (0-689-85902-3) Simon & Schuster Children's Publishing. (Little Simon).

SOLO, ANAKIN (FICTITIOUS CHARACTER)—FICTION

Moesta, Rebecca. Anakin's Quest. 1998. (Star Wars Ser.: Bk. 4). (Illus.). 128p. (J). (gr. 4-6). mass mkt. 4.50 (0-425-16824-7) Berkley Publishing Group.

—Anakin's Quest. 1997. (Star Wars: Bk. 4). 128p. (J). (gr. 4-6). mass mkt. 4.50 o.s.i (1-57297-136-3) Boulevard Bks.

—Anakin's Quest. 1997. 10.55 (0-606-14151-0) Turtleback Bks.

—Kenobi's Blade. 1999. (Star Wars Ser.: Bk. 6). 118p. (J). (gr. 4-6). mass mkt. 4.50 (0-425-17315-1) Berkley Publishing Group.

—Kenobi's Blade. 1997. (Star Wars: Bk. 6). 128p. (J). (gr. 4-6). mass mkt. 4.50 o.s.i (1-57297-208-4) Boulevard Bks.

—Vader's Fortress. 1999. (Star Wars Ser.: Bk. 5). 128p. (J). (gr. 4-6). mass mkt. 4.99 (0-425-16956-1) Berkley Publishing Group.

—Vader's Fortress. 1997. (Star Wars: Bk. 5). 128p. (J). (gr. 4-6). mass mkt. 4.50 o.s.i (1-57297-173-8) Boulevard Bks.

—Vader's Fortress. 1999. 10.55 (0-606-14362-9) Turtleback Bks.

Richardson, Nancy A. The Golden Globe. 1998. (Star Wars Ser.: Bk. 1). 128p. (J). (gr. 4-6). mass mkt. 4.99 (0-425-16825-5) Berkley Publishing Group.

—The Golden Globe, No. 1. 1995. (Star Wars: Bk. 1). 128p. (J). (gr. 4-6). mass mkt. 4.50 o.s.i (1-57297-035-9) Boulevard Bks.

—The Golden Globe. 1995. 10.55 (0-606-14217-7) Turtleback Bks.

—Lyric's World. 1999. (Star Wars Ser.: Bk. 2). 128p. (J). (gr. 4-7). mass mkt. 4.99 (0-425-16762-3) Berkley Publishing Group.

—Lyric's World. 1996. (Star Wars: Bk. 2). 128p. (J). (gr. 4-6). mass mkt. 4.50 o.s.i (1-57297-068-5) Boulevard Bks.

—Lyric's World. 1996. (Star Wars Junior Jedi Knights: No. 2). 10.55 (0-606-14324-6) Turtleback Bks.

—Promises. 1999. (Star Wars Ser.: Bk. 3). 128p. (J). (gr. 4-6). mass mkt. 4.50 (0-425-16955-3) Berkley Publishing Group.

—Promises, No. 3. 1996. (Star Wars: Bk. 3). 128p. (J). (gr. 4-6). mass mkt. 4.50 o.s.i (1-57297-097-9) Boulevard Bks.

—Promises. 1996. 10.55 (0-606-14298-3) Turtleback Bks.

SOLO, HAN (FICTITIOUS CHARACTER)—FICTION

Covey, Stephen R. Star Wars. 1999. (Star Wars Ser.). 12p. pap. 1.79 o.s.i (0-307-02223-4, Golden Bks.) Random Hse. Children's Bks.

Dana, Michael. Star Wars: The Greatest Battles. 1999. (Star Wars Ser.). (Illus.). 16p. (J). pap. 3.99 o.s.i (*0-307-14656-1*, Golden Bks.) Random Hse. Children's Bks.

Davids, Paul. The Adventure Continues Boxed Set: The Glove of Darth Vader; the Lost City of the Jedi; Zorba the Hutt's Revenge. 1997. (Star Wars: Nos. 1-3). (J). (gr. 2-8). 12.48 o.s.i (*0-553-62866-6*, Dell Books for Young Readers) Random Hse. Children's Bks.

—The Glove of Darth Vader. 1996. (Star Wars: Bk. 1). (J). (gr. 4-7). pap. 4.99 (*0-553-54282-6*, Dell Books for Young Readers) Random Hse. Children's Bks.

—The Glove of Darth Vader. 1992. (Star Wars: Bk. 1). (J). (gr. 4-7). 9.09 o.p. (*0-606-00535-8*) Turtleback Bks.

—Mission from Mount Yoda. 1999. (Star Wars: Bk. 4). (J). (gr. 4-7). pap. 9.50 o.p. (*0-7607-0447-3*) Barnes & Noble, Inc.

—The Mission from Mount Yoda. 1993. (Star Wars Ser.: Bk. 4). 128p. (YA). (gr. 4-7). pap. 4.50 o.s.i (*0-553-15890-2*) Bantam Bks.

—Prophets of the Dark Side. 1993. (Star Wars: Bk. 6). 128p. (gr. 4-7). pap. text 4.50 (*0-553-15892-9*) Bantam Bks.

—The Queen of the Empire. 1993. (Star Wars: Bk. 5). 128p. (YA). (gr. 4-7). pap. 4.50 o.s.i (*0-553-15891-0*) Bantam Bks.

Davids, Paul & Davids, Hollace. The Glove of Darth Vader. 1992. (Star Wars: Bk. 1). (Illus.). 128p. (gr. 4-7). pap. text 4.50 (*0-553-15887-2*, Starfire) Random Hse. Children's Bks.

—The Glove of Darth Vader. l.t. ed. 1997. 112p. (J). (gr. 4 up). lib. bdg. 22.60 o.p. (*0-8368-1989-6*) Stevens, Gareth Inc.

—The Glove of Darth Vader. 1992. 10.04 (*0-606-14216-9*) Turtleback Bks.

—The Lost City of the Jedi. 1999. (Star Wars Ser.: Bk. 2). (Illus.). 94p. (J). (gr. 4-7). reprint ed. pap. 10.00 (*0-7881-6480-5*) DIANE Publishing Co.

—The Lost City of the Jedi. 1992. (Star Wars: Bk. 2). 128p. (gr. 4-7). pap. text 4.50 (*0-553-15888-0*, Starfire) Random Hse. Children's Bks.

—The Lost City of the Jedi. l.t. ed. 1997. 112p. (J). (gr. 4 up). lib. bdg. 22.60 o.p. (*0-8368-1990-X*) Stevens, Gareth Inc.

—The Lost City of the Jedi. 1992. (Star Wars: Bk. 2). (J). (gr. 4-7). 10.55 (*0-606-00543-9*) Turtleback Bks.

—Mission from Mount Yoda. l.t. ed. 1997. 112p. (J). (gr. 4 up). lib. bdg. 22.60 o.p. (*0-8368-1992-6*) Stevens, Gareth Inc.

—Mission from Mount Yoda. 1993. (Star Wars: Bk. 4). (J). (gr. 4-7). 10.55 (*0-606-02755-6*) Turtleback Bks.

—Prophets of the Dark Side. l.t. ed. 1997. (Star Wars Ser.: No. 6). 112p. (J). (gr. 4 up). lib. bdg. 22.60 (*0-8368-1994-2*) Stevens, Gareth Inc.

—Prophets of the Dark Side. 1993. (Star Wars: Bk. 6). (J). (gr. 4-7). 10.55 (*0-606-05557-6*) Turtleback Bks.

—Queen of the Empire. l.t. ed. 1997. (Star Wars Ser.: No. 5). 112p. (J). (gr. 4 up). lib. bdg. 22.60 (*0-8368-1993-4*) Stevens, Gareth Inc.

—Queen of the Empire. 1993. (Star Wars: Bk. 5). (J). (gr. 4-7). 10.55 (*0-606-02849-8*) Turtleback Bks.

—Star Wars, 3 bks. l.t. ed. Incl. Prophets of the Dark Side. lib. bdg. 22.60 (*0-8368-1994-2*); Queen of the Empire. lib. bdg. 22.60 (*0-8368-1993-4*); Zorba the Hutt's Revenge. lib. bdg. 22.60 (*0-8368-1991-8*); 112p. (J). (gr. 4 up). 1997. Set lib. bdg. 67.80 (*0-8368-1988-8*) Stevens, Gareth Inc.

—Zorba the Hutt's Revenge. 1992. (Star Wars: Bk. 3). 128p. (gr. 4-7). pap. text 4.50 (*0-553-15889-9*) Bantam Bks.

—Zorba the Hutt's Revenge. l.t. ed. 1997. (Star Wars Ser.: No. 3). 112p. (J). (gr. 4 up). lib. bdg. 22.60 (*0-8368-1991-8*) Stevens, Gareth Inc.

—Zorba the Hutt's Revenge. 1992. (Star Wars: Bk. 3). (J). (gr. 4-7). 10.55 (*0-606-00544-7*) Turtleback Bks.

Disney Staff, ed. The Empire Strikes Back. (Read Along Star Wars Ser.). (J). 7.99 incl. audio (*0-7634-0194-3*) Walt Disney Records.

—The Empire Strikes Back: A Flip Book. 1997. 40p. (J). 2.98 o.s.i (*1-57082-578-5*) Mouse Works.

—Return of the Jedi. (Read Along Star Wars Ser.). (J). 7.99 incl. audio (*0-7634-0193-5*); 14.99 incl. audio (*0-7634-0196-X*) Walt Disney Records.

—Star Wars: A New Hope: A Flip Book. 1997. (Star Wars Ser.). 40p. (J). 2.98 o.s.i (*1-57082-577-7*) Mouse Works.

Disney Staff & Steacy, Ken. Star Wars. 1997. (Star Wars Ser.). 24p. (J). 8.98 o.s.i (*1-57082-567-X*) Mouse Works.

Gardner, J. J. Return of the Jedi Storybook. 1997. (Illus.). (J). (gr. 5-7). mass mkt. 5.99 (*0-590-06659-5*) Scholastic, Inc.

Golden Books Staff. The Empire Strikes Back: With Tattoos. 1999. (Star Wars Ser.). (Illus.). 24p. pap. 3.99 o.s.i (*0-307-13068-1*, Golden Bks.) Random Hse. Children's Bks.

—Star Wars: A New Hope. 1999. (Star Wars Ser.). 16p. (J). pap. 2.99 o.s.i (*0-307-10577-6*, Golden Bks.) Random Hse. Children's Bks.

—Star Wars: Battling the Empire. 1997. (Extra Smart Pages Ser.). 14p. (J). o.p. (*0-307-75704-8*, Golden Bks.) Random Hse. Children's Bks.

—Star Wars: A New Hope: With Tattoos. 1999. (Star Wars Ser.). (Illus.). 24p. pap. 3.99 o.s.i (*0-307-13067-3*, Golden Bks.) Random Hse. Children's Bks.

Golden, Christopher. The Empire Strikes Back. 1998. (Choose Your Own Star Wars Adventure Ser.). 128p. (gr. 4-8). pap. text 4.50 o.s.i (*0-553-48652-7*, Dell Books for Young Readers) Random Hse. Children's Bks.

Levy, Elizabeth, ed. Return of the Jedi Step-Up Movie Adventure. 1983. (Star Wars Ser.). (Illus.). 72p. (J). (gr. 1-3). 8.99 o.s.i (*0-394-96117-X*, Random Hse. Bks. for Young Readers) Random Hse. Children's Bks.

Lucas, George. The Empire Strikes Back Adventures. abr. ed. 1994. (J). (gr. k-3). audio 8.98 o.p. Time Warner AudioBooks.

—Return of the Jedi: A Flip Book. 1997. (Star Wars Ser.). 40p. (J). 2.98 o.s.i (*1-57082-579-3*) Mouse Works.

Ruiz, Art. Han Solo, Rebel Hero. 1999. (Star Wars Ser.). (Illus.). 24p. (J). pap. 3.29 o.s.i (*0-307-10346-3*, 10346, Golden Bks.) Random Hse. Children's Bks.

Scholastic, Inc. Staff, ed. The Empire Strikes Back. 9999. (J). pap. 2.50 o.s.i (*0-590-31791-1*) Scholastic, Inc.

—Return of the Jedi. 9999. (J). pap. 2.95 o.s.i (*0-590-32929-4*) Scholastic, Inc.

Vaz, Mark Cotta. The Star Wars Trilogy Scrapbook: The Rebel Alliance. 1997. 48p. (gr. 4-7). mass mkt. 6.99 (*0-590-12051-4*) Scholastic, Inc.

Vinge, Joan D., adapted by. Return of the Jedi: The Storybook Based on the Movie. 1983. (Storybook Based on the Movie Ser.). (Illus.). 64p. (J). (gr. 3-8). 7.99 o.p. (*0-394-95624-9*, Random Hse. Bks. for Young Readers) Random Hse. Children's Bks.

Whitman, John. Return of the Jedi. 1996. (Mighty Chronicles Ser.). (Illus.). 316p. (gr. 4-7). 9.95 o.s.i (*0-8118-1494-7*) Chronicle Bks. LLC.

Whitman, John, adapted by. The Empire Strikes Back. 1996. (Mighty Chronicles Ser.). (Illus.). 432p. (gr. 4-7). 9.95 o.s.i (*0-8118-1482-3*) Chronicle Bks. LLC.

Windham, Ryder. Battle of the Bounty Hunters. unabr. ed. 1996. (Star Wars Ser.). (Illus.). 12p. (J). (ps up). 17.95 (*1-56971-129-1*) Dark Horse Comics.

SOLO, JACEN (FICTITIOUS CHARACTER)—FICTION

Anderson, Kevin J. The Darkest Knight. 1999. (Star Wars Ser.: No. 5). 240p. (YA). (gr. 7-12). mass mkt. 5.99 (*0-425-16950-2*) Berkley Publishing Group.

—The Darkest Knight. 1996. 12.04 (*0-606-14189-8*) Turtleback Bks.

—Delusions of Grandeur. 1999. (Star Wars Ser.: No. 9). 240p. (J). (gr. 8-12). mass mkt. 5.99 (*0-425-17061-6*) Berkley Publishing Group.

—Diversity Alliance, Bk. 8. 1999. (Star Wars Ser.: No. 8). 240p. (J). (gr. 3-6). mass mkt. 5.99 (*0-425-16905-7*) Berkley Publishing Group.

—Diversity Alliance. 1998. 12.04 (*0-606-14194-4*) Turtleback Bks.

—The Emperor's Plague. 1999. (Star Wars Ser.: No. 11). 224p. (J). (gr. 3-5). mass mkt. 5.99 (*0-425-17314-3*) Berkley Publishing Group.

—Heirs of the Force. 1999. (Star Wars Ser.: Vol. 1). 240p. (J). mass mkt. 5.99 (*0-425-16949-9*) Berkley Publishing Group.

—Heirs of the Force. 1995. 12.04 (*0-606-14372-6*) Turtleback Bks.

—Jedi Bounty. 1999. (Star Wars Ser.: No. 10). 240p. (J). (gr. 3-5). mass mkt. 5.99 (*0-425-17313-5*) Berkley Publishing Group.

—Jedi under Siege. 1999. (Star Wars Ser.: No. 6). 240p. (J). (gr. 8-12). mass mkt. 5.99 (*0-425-16633-3*) Berkley Publishing Group.

—Jedi under Siege. 1998. (Star Wars: No. 6). (J). (gr. 3-6). 12.04 (*0-606-14240-1*) Turtleback Bks.

—Lightsabers. 1999. (Star Wars Ser.: No. 4). 240p. (J). (gr. 8-12). mass mkt. 5.99 (*0-425-16951-0*) Berkley Publishing Group.

—The Lost Ones. 1999. (Star Wars Ser.: No. 3). 240p. (J). (gr. 4-7). mass mkt. 5.99 (*0-425-16999-5*) Berkley Publishing Group.

—The Lost Ones. 1995. (Star Wars Ser.). 12.04 (*0-606-14325-4*) Turtleback Bks.

—The Shadow Academy. 1999. (Star Wars Ser.: No. 2). 240p. (J). (gr. 7-12). mass mkt. 5.99 (*0-425-17153-1*) Berkley Publishing Group.

—The Shadow Academy. 1995. 12.04 (*0-606-14312-2*) Turtleback Bks.

—The Shards of Alderaan. 1999. (Star Wars Ser.: No. 7). 240p. (J). (gr. 8-12). mass mkt. 5.99 (*0-425-16952-9*) Berkley Publishing Group.

—The Shards of Alderaan. 1999. 12.04 (*0-606-14313-0*) Turtleback Bks.

Anderson, Kevin J. & Moesta, Rebecca. Crisis at Crystal Reef. 1998. (Star Wars Ser.: No. 14). 224p. (J). (gr. 8-12). pap. 5.99 (*0-425-16519-1*, JAM) Berkley Publishing Group.

—The Darkest Knight. 1996. (Star Wars: No. 5). 240p. (J). (gr. 3-5). mass mkt. 5.99 o.s.i (*1-57297-129-0*) Boulevard Bks.

—Delusions of Grandeur. 1997. (Star Wars: No. 9). 240p. (J). (gr. 3-5). mass mkt. 5.99 o.s.i (*1-57297-272-6*) Boulevard Bks.

—Diversity Alliance. 1997. (Star Wars: No. 8). 240p. (J). (gr. 3-5). mass mkt. 5.99 o.s.i (*1-57297-234-3*) Boulevard Bks.

—The Emperor's Plague, No. 11. 1998. (Star Wars: No. 11). 224p. (J). (gr. 3-5). pap. 5.99 o.s.i (*1-57297-331-5*) Boulevard Bks.

—Heirs of the Force. 1995. (Star Wars: No. 1). 240p. (J). (gr. 3-5). mass mkt. 5.99 o.s.i (*1-57297-066-9*); mass mkt. 4.99 (*1-57297-000-6*) Boulevard Bks.

—Jedi Bounty, No. 10. 1997. (Star Wars: No. 10). 240p. (J). (gr. 4-7). pap. 5.99 o.s.i (*1-57297-297-1*) Boulevard Bks.

—Jedi under Siege. 1996. (Star Wars: No. 6). 230p. (J). (gr. 3-5). mass mkt. 5.99 o.s.i (*1-57297-163-0*) Boulevard Bks.

—Lightsabers, No. 4. 1996. (Star Wars: No. 4). 240p. (J). (gr. 3-5). mass mkt. 5.99 o.s.i (*1-57297-091-X*) Boulevard Bks.

—The Lost Ones, No. 3. 1995. (Star Wars: No. 3). 240p. (YA). (gr. 8-12). pap. 5.99 o.s.i (*1-57297-052-9*) Boulevard Bks.

—Return to Ord Mantell. 1998. (Star Wars Ser.: No. 12). 240p. (J). (gr. 7-12). mass mkt. 5.99 (*0-425-16362-8*, JAM) Berkley Publishing Group.

—The Shadow Academy, Vol. 2. 1995. (Star Wars). 240p. (J). (gr. 3-5). pap. 5.99 o.s.i (*1-57297-025-1*) Boulevard Bks.

—The Shards of Alderaan. 1997. (Star Wars: No. 7). 240p. (J). (gr. 3-5). mass mkt. 5.99 o.s.i (*1-57297-207-6*) Boulevard Bks.

—Trouble on Cloud City. 1998. (Star Wars Ser.: No. 13). 224p. (J). (gr. 8-12). mass mkt. 5.99 (*0-425-16416-0*) Berkley Publishing Group.

Boulevard Books Staff. The Young Jedi Knights, 3 vols., Set. 1997. (Star Wars). (J). (gr. 3-5). 17.97 o.s.i (*1-57297-344-7*) Boulevard Bks.

Whitman, John. Star Wars Fairy Tales: Jaina & the Hanadak. abr. ed. 1995. (Star Wars Ser.). (J). pap. 6.98 o.p. incl. audio (*1-57042-331-8*) Time Warner AudioBooks.

SOLO, JAINA (FICTITIOUS CHARACTER)—FICTION

Anderson, Kevin J. The Darkest Knight. 1999. (Star Wars Ser.: No. 5). 240p. (YA). (gr. 7-12). mass mkt. 5.99 (*0-425-16950-2*) Berkley Publishing Group.

—The Darkest Knight. 1996. 12.04 (*0-606-14189-8*) Turtleback Bks.

—Delusions of Grandeur. 1999. (Star Wars Ser.: No. 9). 240p. (J). (gr. 8-12). mass mkt. 5.99 (*0-425-17061-6*) Berkley Publishing Group.

—Diversity Alliance, Bk. 8. 1999. (Star Wars Ser.: No. 8). 240p. (J). (gr. 3-6). mass mkt. 5.99 (*0-425-16905-7*) Berkley Publishing Group.

—Diversity Alliance. 1998. 12.04 (*0-606-14194-4*) Turtleback Bks.

—The Emperor's Plague. 1999. (Star Wars Ser.: No. 11). 224p. (J). (gr. 3-5). mass mkt. 5.99 (*0-425-17314-3*) Berkley Publishing Group.

—Heirs of the Force. 1999. (Star Wars Ser.: Vol. 1). 240p. (J). mass mkt. 5.99 (*0-425-16949-9*) Berkley Publishing Group.

—Heirs of the Force. 1995. 12.04 (*0-606-14372-6*) Turtleback Bks.

—Jedi Bounty. 1999. (Star Wars Ser.: No. 10). 240p. (J). (gr. 3-5). mass mkt. 5.99 (*0-425-17313-5*) Berkley Publishing Group.

—Jedi under Siege. 1999. (Star Wars Ser.: No. 6). 240p. (J). (gr. 8-12). mass mkt. 5.99 (*0-425-16633-3*) Berkley Publishing Group.

—Jedi under Siege. 1998. (Star Wars: No. 6). (J). (gr. 3-6). 12.04 (*0-606-14240-1*) Turtleback Bks.

—Lightsabers. 1999. (Star Wars Ser.: No. 4). 240p. (J). (gr. 8-12). mass mkt. 5.99 (*0-425-16951-0*) Berkley Publishing Group.

—The Lost Ones. 1999. (Star Wars Ser.: No. 3). 240p. (J). (gr. 4-7). mass mkt. 5.99 (*0-425-16999-5*) Berkley Publishing Group.

—The Lost Ones. 1995. (Star Wars Ser.). 12.04 (*0-606-14325-4*) Turtleback Bks.

—The Shadow Academy. 1999. (Star Wars Ser.: No. 2). 240p. (J). (gr. 7-12). mass mkt. 5.99 (*0-425-17153-1*) Berkley Publishing Group.

—The Shadow Academy. 1995. 12.04 (*0-606-14312-2*) Turtleback Bks.

—The Shards of Alderaan. 1999. (Star Wars Ser.: No. 7). 240p. (J). (gr. 8-12). mass mkt. 5.99 (*0-425-16952-9*) Berkley Publishing Group.

—The Shards of Alderaan. 1999. 12.04 (*0-606-14313-0*) Turtleback Bks.

Anderson, Kevin J. & Moesta, Rebecca. Crisis at Crystal Reef. 1998. (Star Wars Ser.: No. 14). 224p. (J). (gr. 8-12). pap. 5.99 (*0-425-16519-1*, JAM) Berkley Publishing Group.

—The Darkest Knight. 1996. (Star Wars: No. 5). 240p. (J). (gr. 3-5). mass mkt. 5.99 o.s.i (*1-57297-129-0*) Boulevard Bks.

—Delusions of Grandeur. 1997. (Star Wars: No. 9). 240p. (J). (gr. 3-5). mass mkt. 5.99 o.s.i (*1-57297-272-6*) Boulevard Bks.

—Diversity Alliance. 1997. (Star Wars: No. 8). 240p. (J). (gr. 3-5). mass mkt. 5.99 o.s.i (*1-57297-234-3*) Boulevard Bks.

—The Emperor's Plague, No. 11. 1998. (Star Wars: No. 11). 224p. (J). (gr. 3-5). pap. 5.99 o.s.i (*1-57297-331-5*) Boulevard Bks.

—Heirs of the Force. 1995. (Star Wars: No. 1). 240p. (J). (gr. 3-5). mass mkt. 5.99 o.s.i (*1-57297-066-9*); mass mkt. 4.99 (*1-57297-000-6*) Boulevard Bks.

—Jedi Bounty, No. 10. 1997. (Star Wars: No. 10). 240p. (J). (gr. 4-7). pap. 5.99 o.s.i (*1-57297-297-1*) Boulevard Bks.

—Jedi under Siege. 1996. (Star Wars: No. 6). 230p. (J). (gr. 3-5). mass mkt. 5.99 o.s.i (*1-57297-163-0*) Boulevard Bks.

—Lightsabers, No. 4. 1996. (Star Wars: No. 4). 240p. (J). (gr. 3-5). mass mkt. 5.99 o.s.i (*1-57297-091-X*) Boulevard Bks.

—The Lost Ones, No. 3. 1995. (Star Wars: No. 3). 240p. (YA). (gr. 8-12). pap. 5.99 o.s.i (*1-57297-052-9*) Boulevard Bks.

—Return to Ord Mantell. 1998. (Star Wars Ser.: No. 12). 240p. (J). (gr. 7-12). mass mkt. 5.99 (*0-425-16362-8*, JAM) Berkley Publishing Group.

—The Shadow Academy, Vol. 2. 1995. (Star Wars). 240p. (J). (gr. 3-5). pap. 5.99 o.s.i (*1-57297-025-1*) Boulevard Bks.

—The Shards of Alderaan. 1997. (Star Wars: No. 7). 240p. (J). (gr. 3-5). mass mkt. 5.99 o.s.i (*1-57297-207-6*) Boulevard Bks.

—Trouble on Cloud City. 1998. (Star Wars Ser.: No. 13). 224p. (J). (gr. 8-12). mass mkt. 5.99 (*0-425-16416-0*) Berkley Publishing Group.

Boulevard Books Staff. The Young Jedi Knights, 3 vols., Set. 1997. (Star Wars). (J). (gr. 3-5). 17.97 o.s.i (*1-57297-344-7*) Boulevard Bks.

Whitman, John. Star Wars Fairy Tales: Jaina & the Hanadak. abr. ed. 1995. (Star Wars Ser.). (J). pap. 6.98 o.p. incl. audio (*1-57042-331-8*) Time Warner AudioBooks.

SOLOMON, KING OF ISRAEL—FICTION

Biers-Ariel, Matt. Solomon & the Trees. 2000. (Illus.). (J). 12.95 (*0-8074-0749-6*) UAHC Pr.

Borchard, Therese J. Whitney Solves a Dilemma with Solomon: And Learns the Importance of Honesty. 2000. (Emerald Bible Collection). (Illus.). 80p. (J). (gr. 3-7). pap. 5.95 (*0-8091-6668-2*) Paulist Pr.

Haggard, Hider. Las Minas del Rey Salomon. (SPA., Illus.). 184p. (YA). 11.95 (*84-7281-094-1*, AF1094) Auriga, Ediciones S.A. ESP. *Dist:* Continental Bk. Co., Inc.

Marsh, T. F. The Super Secret: A Tale about Wisdom. (Tale Tellers Ser.). (Illus.). 32p. (J). (ps-3). pap. 4.99 (*0-7814-3519-6*) Cook Communications Ministries.

Las Minas del Rey Salomon. 1990. (Spanish Children's Classics Ser.: No. 800-8). (SPA.). (J). 3.50 (*0-7214-1402-8*, Ladybird Bks.) Penguin Group (USA) Inc.

Oberman, Sheldon. The Wisdom Bird: A Tale of Solomon & Sheba. 2003. (Illus.). 32p. (J). (ps-3). 15.95 (*1-56397-816-4*) Boyds Mills Pr.

Sanders, Nancy I. King Solomon: With Envelope Surprises. 2001. (Kingdom Kidz Bible Ser.). (Illus.). 12p. (J). (ps-3). 5.99 (*1-58660-309-4*) Barbour Publishing, Inc.

Wiesel, Elie. King Solomon & His Magic Ring. 1999. (Illus.). 56p. (J). (gr. k-3). 16.00 (*0-688-16959-7*, Greenwillow Bks.) HarperCollins Children's Bk. Group.

SPIDER-MAN (FICTITIOUS CHARACTER)—FICTION

Andrews, Kaare. Spider-Man Legend of the Spider-Clan, 3 vols. 2003. (Mangaverse Ser.: Vol. 3). (Illus.). 128p. (YA). pap. 11.99 (*0-7851-1114-X*) Marvel Enterprises.

Bendis, Brian Michael. Ultimate Spider-Man: Irresponsible, 8 vols. 2003. (Ultimate Spider-man Ser.). (Illus.). 144p. (J). pap. 12.99 (*0-7851-1092-5*) Marvel Enterprises.

Bendis, Brian Michael. Ultimate Spider-Man, 2 vols., Vol. 2. 2003. (Ultimate Spider-man Ser.). (Illus.). 336p. (J). 29.99 (*0-7851-1061-5*) Marvel Enterprises.

—Ultimate Spider-Man Vol. 5: Public Scrutiny, 5 vols. 2003. (Ultimate Spider-man Ser.). (Illus.). 120p. (J). pap. 11.99 (*0-7851-1087-9*) Marvel Enterprises.

Berry, James. Spider-Man Anancy, ERS. 1989. (Illus.). 148p. (J). (gr. 4-6). 13.95 o.p. (*0-8050-1207-9*, Holt, Henry & Co. Bks. For Young Readers) Holt, Henry & Co.

Busiek, Kurt. Goblin Moon. 2000. (Spider-Man Ser.). 288p. (J). mass mkt. 6.99 o.s.i (*0-425-17403-4*) Berkley Publishing Group.

Castro, Adam-Troy. Spider-Man: Secret of the Sinister Six. 2002. (Illus.). 448p. 24.95 (*0-7434-4464-7*) ibooks, Inc.

Chevat, Richie. The Sinister Six: You Are Spider-Man. 1996. (Spider-Man Ser.: No. 1). 144p. (YA). (gr. 7 up). mass mkt. 3.99 (*0-671-00319-4*, Simon Pulse) Simon & Schuster Children's Publishing.

—You Are Spider-Man vs. the Incredible Hulk, Vol. 2. 1997. (Illus.). 144p. (J). (gr. 7 up). pap. 4.99 (*0-671-00797-1*, Simon Pulse) Simon & Schuster Children's Publishing.

Cooke, Darwyn, et al. Spider-Man's Tangled Web, 4 vols., Vol. 4. 2003. (Spider-Man's Tangled Web Ser.). (Illus.). 176p. (YA). pap. 15.99 (*0-7851-1064-X*) Marvel Enterprises.

Dancer's Dream. 1996. (Barbie Ser.). (J). 9.98 o.s.i (*1-57082-379-0*) Mouse Works.

Davis, Alan. Killraven. 2003. (Spider-Man Ser.). (Illus.). 144p. (YA). pap. 16.99 (*0-7851-1083-6*) Marvel Enterprises.

Duey, Kathleen. Spider-Man Ultimate Picture Book, Vol. 1. 2003. (Illus.). 48p. (J). (ps-7). 15.95 (*1-929945-22-1*); pap. 8.95 (*1-929945-25-6*) Big Guy Bks., Inc.

—Ultimate Super Hero Picture Book Gift Set. 2003. (Illus.). 48p. (J). 24.95 (*1-929945-38-8*) Big Guy Bks., Inc.

Fingeroth, Danny. Rampage. 1998. (Spider-Man & the Incredible Hulk Ser.). (Illus.). (YA). mass mkt. 6.99 o.s.i (*0-425-17060-8*) Berkley Publishing Group.

Fingeroth, Danny & Fein, Eric. Rampage Doom. 1996. (Spider-Man & the Incredible Hulk Ser.). 288p. (YA). mass mkt. 6.50 o.s.i (*1-57297-164-9*) Boulevard Bks.

Funworks Staff. Caged Captive. 1996. 16p. (J). (gr. k-5). 8.98 o.s.i (*1-57082-349-9*) Mouse Works.

—Spider-Man. 1996. (J). pap. text 5.98 o.p. (*1-57082-337-5*) Mouse Works.

Geary, Rick. Chase of the Blue Tiger: Spider Man. 1995. (Come to Life Bks.). 16p. (J). (*1-57234-062-2*) YES! Entertainment Corp.

Golden Books Staff. Meet the Amazing Spider-Man. 1999. (Spider-Man Ser.). 32p. pap. 1.09 o.s.i (*0-307-08745-X*, Golden Bks.) Random Hse. Children's Bks.

—Web of Villans. 1999. (Spider-Man Ser.). 40p. (J). pap. 1.09 o.s.i (*0-307-03642-1*, 03642, Golden Bks.) Random Hse. Children's Bks.

Golden Books Staff & Butler, Steven. Spider-Man Caught in the Web. 1997. (Spider-Man Ser.). (Illus.). 24p. pap. 3.29 o.s.i (*0-307-12961-6*, Golden Bks.) Random Hse. Children's Bks.

Goldman, Leslie. Attack of the Green Goblin. 2002. (Spider Man Ser.). 64p. (J). pap. 4.99 (*0-06-442176-7*, Harper Festival) HarperCollins Children's Bk. Group.

How to Draw Spider-Man Kit. 1997. (Snap Pack Ser.). (Illus.). 32p. (YA). (gr. 3 up). 12.95 o.p. (*1-56010-308-6*, M01P) Foster, Walter Publishing, Inc.

Jenkins, Paul. Peter Parker: Trials & Tribulations, 4 vols. 2003. (Spider-Man Ser.: Vol. 4). (Illus.). 144p. (YA). pap. 11.99 (*0-7851-1150-6*) Marvel Enterprises.

—Spectacular Spider-Man Vol. 1: The Hunger. 2004. (Spider-Man Ser.). (Illus.). 120p. (YA). pap. 11.99 (*0-7851-1169-7*) Marvel Enterprises.

Kingore, Bertie. The Amazing Spider-Man in the Skyscraper Caper. 1982. (Texas Instruments Magic Wand Speaking Library). (Illus.). 51p. (J). (ps-3). text 7.30 o.p. (*0-89512-064-X*) Texas Instruments, Inc.

Lee, Stan. The Amazing Spider-Man. 1993. (Look & Find Ser.). (Illus.). 24p. (J). 7.98 (*1-56173-702-X*) Publications International, Ltd.

The Legend Begins - Spiderman. 1995. (Puffy Cover Book). (Illus.). 24p. (J). (ps-3). 6.98 o.p. (*1-57082-247-6*) Mouse Works.

Loeb, Jeph. Spider-Man: Blue. 2003. (Spider-Man Ser.). (Illus.). 160p. (YA). 21.99 (*0-7851-1062-3*) Marvel Enterprises.

Marvel Super Heroes Secret Wars Spider-Man's Stamp Fun. 1985. (Illus.). 32p. (J). pap. 1.49 o.p. (*0-517-55510-7*, Crown) Crown Publishing Group.

Michelinie, David. Spider-Man Legends Vol. 2: Todd McFarlane, 3 vols. 2003. (Spider-Man Legends Ser.). (Illus.). 224p. (YA). pap. 19.99 (*0-7851-1037-2*) Marvel Enterprises.

—Spiderman: Carnage in New York. 1998. (Spider-Man Ser.). 245p. (J). mass mkt. 6.50 o.s.i (*0-425-16703-8*) Berkley Publishing Group.

Redman, Rich. Spider-Man: Mysterio's Ways. 2000. (Marvel Super Heroes Adventures Ser.). (Illus.). 32p. (J). pap. 4.95 (*0-7869-1669-9*) Wizards of the Coast.

Sherlock, Philip K. Anansi, the Spider Man. 1954. (Illus.). 112p. (J). (gr. 3-7). 15.00 o.p. (*0-690-08905-8*) HarperCollins Children's Bk. Group.

Smith, Kevin. Spider-Man/Black Cat: The Evil That Men Do. 2003. (Spider-Man Ser.). (Illus.). 144p. (YA). 20.99 (*0-7851-1095-X*) Marvel Enterprises.

Spider-Man - Hide, Seek & Destroy. 1995. (Open Door Mystery Ser.). (Illus.). 16p. (J). (ps-3). 7.98 o.p. (*1-57082-229-8*) Mouse Works.

Spider-Man - Lizard's Deadly Trap. 1995. (Pop Up Ser.). (Illus.). 12p. (J). (ps-3). 6.98 o.p. (*1-57082-227-1*) Mouse Works.

Spider-Man: Night of the Lizard. 1995. (Favorite Sound Story Bks.). (Illus.). 24p. (J). (ps-3). o.p. (*0-307-70925-6*, Golden Bks.) Random Hse. Children's Bks.

Stern, Roger. Spider-Man: Hobgoblin Lives. 1998. (Illus.). 112p. (YA). (gr. 5-12). pap. 14.95 (*0-7851-0585-9*) Marvel Enterprises.

Stewart, Michael. Spider-Man. 1996. (My Favorite Sound Story Bks.). (Illus.). 32p. (J). o.p. (*0-307-71142-0*, 61142, Golden Bks.) Random Hse. Children's Bks.

Straczynski, J. Michael. Amazing Spider-Man: The Life & Death of Spiders, 4 vols., Vol. 4. 2003. (Amazing Spider-man Ser.). (Illus.). 120p. (YA). pap. 11.99 (*0-7851-1097-6*) Marvel Enterprises.

—The Amazing Spiderman: Until the Stars Turn Cold, No. 3. 2002. (Illus.). 144p. (YA). (gr. 7). per. 12.99 (*0-7851-1075-5*) Marvel Enterprises.

—Best of Spider-Man. Youngquist, Jeff, ed. 2004. (Spider-Man Ser.). (Illus.). 368p. 29.99 (*0-7851-1339-8*) Marvel Enterprises.

Straczynski, J. Michael & Jenkins, Paul. Best of Spider-Man, 2 vols. annuals 2003. (Spider-Man Ser.: Vol. 2). (Illus.). 368p. (YA). 29.99 (*0-7851-1100-X*) Marvel Enterprises.

Teitelbaum, Michael. Spider-Man: The First Adventure. 1996. (Look-Look Bks.). (Illus.). 24p. (J). (ps-3). pap. 3.29 o.s.i (*0-307-12905-5*, Golden Bks.) Random Hse. Children's Bks.

Teitelbaum, Michael & Jarvinen, Kirk. Meet the Amazing Spiderman. 1996. (Illus.). 24p. (J). (ps-3). pap. 12.95 o.s.i (*0-307-10379-X*, Golden Bks.) Random Hse. Children's Bks.

—Spider-Man: Dangerous Dr. Octopus. 1995. (Look-Look Bks.). (Illus.). 24p. (J). (ps-3). pap. 3.29 o.s.i (*0-307-12909-8*, Golden Bks.) Random Hse. Children's Bks.

Vornholt, John. The Valley of the Lizard. 1998. (Spider-Man Ser.). 272p. (J). (gr. 4-7). mass mkt. 6.50 o.s.i (*1-57297-333-1*) Boulevard Bks.

Warner, Rita. The Crazy Spider-Man Hex Game. 1997. (Crazy Games Ser.). (J). (gr. 1 up). 2.95 o.s.i (*0-8431-7985-6*, Price Stern Sloan) Penguin Putnam Bks. for Young Readers.

Youngquist, Jeff & Marvel Staff, eds. Spider-Man, 4 vols., Vol. 4. 2003. (Marvel Encyclopedia Ser.: Vol. 4). (Illus.). 240p. (J). (gr. 7 up). 24.99 (*0-7851-1304-5*) Marvel Enterprises.

SPONGEBOB SQUAREPANTS (FICTITIOUS CHARACTER)—FICTION

Banks, Steven. Dear SpongeBob . . . A Funny Fill-Ins Book. 2003. (Spongebob SquarePants Ser.). (Illus.). 48p. (J). pap. 2.99 (*0-689-85997-X*, Simon Spotlight) Simon & Schuster Children's Publishing.

—The Never-Ending Song. 2004. (Ready-to-Read Ser.: Vol. 4). 32p. (J). pap. 3.99 (*0-689-86528-7*, Simon Spotlight/Nickelodeon) Simon & Schuster Children's Publishing.

Boczkowski, Tricia. Meet Patrick. 2003. (Spongebob SquarePants Ser.). (Illus.). 12p. (J). bds. 7.99 (*0-689-85904-X*, Simon Spotlight/Nickelodeon) Simon & Schuster Children's Publishing.

Bubble Trouble. 2001. (SpongeBob SquarePants Ser.). (Illus.). (J). pap. 3.99 (*0-307-10981-X*, 10981, Golden Bks.) Random Hse. Children's Bks.

Golden Books Staff. Bikini Bottom Confidential. 2003. (Illus.). 32p. (J). (ps-3). pap. 3.99 (*0-307-10455-9*, Golden Bks.) Random Hse. Children's Bks.

—Brush with Greatness. 2002. (Illus.). 32p. (J). pap. 4.99 (*0-307-29958-9*, Golden Bks.) Random Hse. Children's Bks.

—Don't Pencil Me In. 2004. (Illus.). (J). pap. 4.99 (*0-375-82660-2*, Golden Bks.) Random Hse. Children's Bks.

—Sponge on the Run. 2002. (Illus.). 56p. (J). pap. 4.99 (*0-307-12562-9*, Golden Bks.) Random Hse. Children's Bks.

—SpongeBob. 2002. (SpongeBob SquarePants Ser.). (Illus.). 32p. (J). (ps-3). pap. 4.99 (*0-307-27902-2*, Golden Bks.) Random Hse. Children's Bks.

—SpongeBob Square Pants. 2002. (Illus.). 32p. (J). (ps-3). pap. 3.99 (*0-307-20217-8*, Golden Bks.) Random Hse. Children's Bks.

—They Blow up So Fast. 2002. (Illus.). 32p. (J). (ps-3). pap. 4.99 (*0-307-27635-X*, Golden Bks.) Random Hse. Children's Bks.

Golden Books Staff, contrib. by. SpongeBob SquarePants: Blast off, Splash down! 2001. (SpongeBob SquarePants Ser.). (Illus.). 32p. (J). (ps-3). pap. 3.99 (*0-307-21692-6*, Golden Bks.) Random Hse. Children's Bks.

The Greetings from Bikini Bottom. 2003. 32p. mass mkt. 2.64 (*0-689-85651-2*, Simon Spotlight/Nickelodeon) Simon & Schuster Children's Publishing.

Hillenburg, Steven, creator. SpongeBob SquarePants Vol. 1: Krusty Krab Adventures. 2003. (Illus.). 96p. (J). pap. 7.99 (*1-59182-398-6*) TOKYOPOP, Inc.

—SpongeBob SquarePants Vol. 2: Friends Forever. 2003. (Illus.). 96p. (J). pap. 7.99 (*1-59182-399-4*) TOKYOPOP, Inc.

—SpongeBob SquarePants Vol. 3: Tales from Bikini Bottom. 2004. (Illus.). 96p. (J). pap. 7.99 (*1-59182-575-X*) TOKYOPOP, Inc.

—SpongeBob SquarePants Vol. 4: Crime & Funishment. (Illus.). 96p. pap. 7.99 (*1-59182-576-8*) TOKYOPOP, Inc.

Kowitt, Holly. Belly Laughs from Bikini Bottom. 2003. (Spongebob SquarePants Ser.). (Illus.). 48p. (J). pap. 2.99 (*0-689-86165-6*, Simon Spotlight) Simon & Schuster Children's Publishing.

Lewman, David. SpongeBob & the Princess. 2004. (SpongeBob SquarePants 8 X 8 Paperback ; #5 Ser.). (J). pap. (*0-689-86581-3*, Simon Spotlight/Nickelodeon) Simon & Schuster Children's Publishing.

—Spongebob Jokepants. 2003. (Spongebob SquarePants Ser.). (Illus.). 48p. (J). pap. 2.99 (*0-689-85568-0*, Simon Spotlight) Simon & Schuster Children's Publishing.

Miglis, Jenny. New Student Starfish. 2003. (Spongebob SquarePants Ser.). (Illus.). 64p. (J). pap. 3.99 (*0-689-86164-8*, Simon Spotlight) Simon & Schuster Children's Publishing.

Reiss, William & Greenblatt, C. H., illus. SpongeBob's Christmas Wish. 2003. (Spongebob SquarePants Ser.). 32p. (J). pap. 5.99 (*0-689-85878-7*, Simon Spotlight/Nickelodeon) Simon & Schuster Children's Publishing.

Richards, Kitty. SpongeBob Airpants: The Lost Episode. 2003. (Spongebob SquarePants Ser.). (Illus.). 64p. (J). pap. 3.99 (*0-689-86163-X*, Simon Spotlight) Simon & Schuster Children's Publishing.

Spongebob Squarepants. 2001. (Spongebob SquarePants Ser.). (Illus.). 80p. (ps-3). pap. 2.99 (*0-689-84465-4*, Simon Spotlight/Nickelodeon) Simon & Schuster Children's Publishing.

SQUANTO, WAMPANOAG INDIAN, D. 1622—FICTION

Bulla, Clyde Robert. John Billington, Friend of Squanto. 1956. (Illus.). (J). (gr. 2-5). 11.49 o.p. (*0-690-46253-0*) HarperCollins Children's Bk. Group.

STANTON, WILL (FICTITIOUS CHARACTER)—FICTION

Cooper, Susan. The Dark Is Rising. unabr. ed. 1999. (J). (gr. 1-8). audio 40.00 BBC Audiobooks America.

—The Dark Is Rising. 2000. (J). audio 38.00 (*0-7366-5121-7*) Books on Tape, Inc.

—The Dark Is Rising, Set. unabr. ed. 1999. (YA). audio 37.98 Highsmith Inc.

—The Dark Is Rising. 244p. (YA). (gr. 5 up). pap. 4.99 (*0-8072-1533-3*); 2000. (J). (gr. 4-7). audio 30.00 (*0-8072-8274-X*); 2000. (J). (gr. 4-7). audio 30.00 (*0-8072-8274-X*); 1999. (YA). (gr. 4-7). audio 40.00 (*0-8072-8059-3*, YA990CX); 1999. 244p. (YA). (gr. 6 up). pap. 46.00 incl. audio (*0-8072-8060-7*, YA990SP); 1999. 244p. (YA). (gr. 6 up). pap. 46.00 incl. audio (*0-8072-8060-7*, YA990SP) Random Hse. Audio Publishing Group. (Listening Library).

—The Dark Is Rising. (Dark Is Rising Sequence Ser.). 1999. (Illus.). 232p. (J). (gr. 7 up). mass mkt. 4.99 (*0-689-82983-3*, Aladdin); 1999. pap. 2.99 (*0-689-82989-2*, Aladdin); 1976. (YA). (gr. 7 up). pap. 3.95 o.s.i (*0-689-70420-8*, Simon & Schuster Children's Publishing); 1973. (Illus.). 232p. (J). (gr. 5-9). 18.95 (*0-689-30317-3*, McElderry, Margaret K.); 1986. 232p. (J). (gr. 7 up). reprint ed. mass mkt. 4.99 (*0-689-71087-9*, Simon Pulse) Simon & Schuster Children's Publishing.

—The Dark Is Rising. l.t. ed. 2001. 395p. (J). (gr. 4-7). 21.95 (*0-7862-2920-9*) Thorndike Pr.

—The Dark Is Rising. (Dark Is Rising Sequence Ser.). 1986. (J). 11.04 (*0-606-00687-7*); 1973. 11.04 (*0-606-17313-7*) Turtleback Bks.

—The Dark Is Rising. unabr. ed. (YA). pap. 44.00 incl. audio Weston Woods Studios, Inc.

—The Dark Is Rising Sequence: Over Sea, under Stone; The Dark Is Rising; Greenwitch; The Grey King; Silver on the Tree, 5 bks. 2000. (J). (gr. 3-6). reprint ed. pap. 24.95 (*0-02-042565-1*, Simon Pulse) Simon & Schuster Children's Publishing.

—The Dark Is Rising Sequence Box Set, Set. 1987. (Dark Is Rising Sequence Ser.: 4 bks.). 874p. (YA). (gr. 6 up). reprint ed. pap. 15.75 (*0-689-71155-7*, Simon Pulse) Simon & Schuster Children's Publishing.

—Greenwitch. (Dark Is Rising Sequence Ser.). (J). 2000. 144p. (gr. 4-7). pap. 4.99 (*0-689-84034-9*, Aladdin); 1985. (Illus.). 148p. (gr. 4-7). 18.00 (*0-689-30426-9*, McElderry, Margaret K.); 1977. pap. 3.95 o.s.i (*0-689-70431-3*, Simon & Schuster Children's Publishing); 1986. 148p. (gr. 4-7). reprint ed. pap. 4.99 (*0-689-71088-7*, Simon Pulse) Simon & Schuster Children's Publishing.

—Greenwitch. l.t. ed. 2001. (Dark Is Rising Sequence Ser.). 131p. (J). 21.95 (*0-7862-2923-3*) Thorndike Pr.

—Greenwitch. (J). 2000. 11.04 (*0-606-19710-9*); 1974. 9.05 (*0-606-00700-8*) Turtleback Bks.

—The Grey King. unabr. ed. 2001. (YA). (gr. 5 up). audio 32.00 (*0-8072-8877-2*); (Dark Is Rising Ser.: No. 4). (J). (gr. 4-7). audio 25.00 (*0-8072-6196-3*); (Dark Is Rising Ser.: No. 4). (J). (gr. 4-7). audio 25.00 (*0-8072-6196-3*) Random Hse. Audio Publishing Group. (Listening Library).

—The Grey King. 2002. 224p. (J). E-Book 6.99 (*0-689-84783-1*, McElderry, Margaret K.); 1999. (Dark Is Rising Sequence Ser.). (Illus.). 176p. (J). (gr. 4-7). pap. 4.99 (*0-689-82984-1*, Aladdin); 1978. (Dark Is Rising Sequence Ser.). (Illus.). (YA). (gr. 7 up). pap. 3.95 o.s.i (*0-689-70448-8*, Simon & Schuster Children's Publishing); 1975. (Grey King Ser.: Vol. 1). (Illus.). 224p. (J). 18.95 (*0-689-50029-7*, McElderry, Margaret K.); 1986. (Dark Is Rising Sequence Ser.). 224p. (YA). (gr. 4-7). reprint ed. mass mkt. 4.99 (*0-689-71089-5*, Simon Pulse); Vol. 1. 1999. (Dark Is Rising Sequence Ser.). 165p. (gr. 5-9). pap. 2.99 (*0-689-82988-4*, Aladdin) Simon & Schuster Children's Publishing.

—The Grey King. (Dark Is Rising Sequence Ser.). 1986. (J). 11.04 (*0-606-01150-1*); 1975. 11.04 (*0-606-17326-9*) Turtleback Bks.

—Silver on the Tree. l.t. ed. 2002. (Dark Is Rising Sequence Ser.). (Illus.). 430p. (J). 23.95 (*0-7862-2921-7*) Gale Group.

—Silver on the Tree. unabr. ed. 2002. (YA). (gr. 3 up). audio 30.00 (*0-8072-6209-9*, Listening Library) Random Hse. Audio Publishing Group.

—Silver on the Tree. 2000. (Dark Is Rising Sequence Ser.). 288p. (J). (gr. 4-7). pap. 4.99 (*0-689-84033-0*, Aladdin); 1986. (J). pap. 2.95 o.s.i (*0-689-71090-9*, Simon & Schuster Children's Publishing); 1980. (Dark Is Rising Sequence Ser.). 256p. (J). (gr. 4-8). 4.95 o.s.i (*0-689-70467-4*, Simon Pulse); 1977. (Silver on the Tree Ser.: Vol. 1). 256p. (J). (gr. 4-7). 18.00 (*0-689-50088-2*, McElderry, Margaret K.); 1987. (Dark Is Rising Sequence Ser.). 256p. (YA). (gr. 4-7). reprint ed. pap. 4.99 (*0-689-71152-2*, Simon Pulse) Simon & Schuster Children's Publishing.

—Silver on the Tree. 1986. (Dark Is Rising Sequence Ser.). (J). 10.00 (*0-606-02257-0*) Turtleback Bks.

Cooper, Susan & Houghton Mifflin Company Staff. The Dark Is Rising. 1992. (Literature Experience 1993 Ser.). (J). (gr. 8). pap., stu. ed. 11.04 (*0-395-61880-0*) Houghton Mifflin Co.

STARR, EMILY (FICTITIOUS CHARACTER)—FICTION

see Emily (Fictitious Character)—Fiction

STERLING, ERIC (FICTITIOUS CHARACTER)—FICTION

Herndon, Ernest. Deathbird of Paradise. 1997. (Eric Sterling, Secret Agent Ser.: Bk. 7). 128p. (J). (gr. 3-7). pap. 5.99 (*0-310-20732-0*) Zondervan.

—Double-Crossed in Gator Country. 1994. (Eric Sterling, Secret Agent Ser.: Vol. 2). 128p. (J). pap. 5.99 o.p. (*0-310-38261-0*) Zondervan.

—Little People of the Lost Coast. 1997. (Eric Sterling, Secret Agent Ser.: Bk. 8). 128p. (J). (gr. 3-7). pap. 5.99 (*0-310-20733-9*) Zondervan.

—Night of the Jungle Cat. 1994. (Eric Sterling, Secret Agent Ser.: Vol. 3). 128p. (YA). (gr. 5 up). pap. 5.99 o.p. (*0-310-38271-8*) Zondervan.

—The Secret of Lizard Island. 1994. (Eric Sterling, Secret Agent Ser.: Vol. 1). 128p. (J). pap. 5.99 (*0-310-38251-3*) Zondervan.

—Sisters of the Wolf. 1996. (Eric Sterling, Secret Agent Ser.: Bk. 5). 128p. (YA). (gr. 8-12). pap. 5.99 (*0-310-20729-0*) Zondervan.

—Smugglers on Grizzly Mountain. 1994. (Eric Sterling, Secret Agent Ser.: Vol. 4). 128p. (J). pap. 5.99 (*0-310-38281-5*) Zondervan.

—Trouble at Bamboo Bay. 1996. (Eric Sterling, Secret Agent Ser.: Bk. 6). 128p. (YA). (gr. 8-12). pap. 5.99 (*0-310-20730-4*) Zondervan.

STILTON, GERONIMO (FICTITIOUS CHARACTER)—FICTION

Stilton, Geronimo. Cat & Mouse in a Haunted House. 2004. (Geronimo Stilton Ser.: No. 3). (Illus.). 128p. (J). mass mkt. 5.99 (*0-439-55965-0*, Scholastic Paperbacks) Scholastic, Inc.

—The Curse of the Cheese Pyramid. 2004. (Geronimo Stilton Ser.: No. 2). (Illus.). 128p. (J). mass mkt. 5.99 (*0-439-55964-2*) Scholastic, Inc.

—Four Mice Deep in the Jungle. 2004. (Geronimo Stilton Ser.: No. 5). (Illus.). 128p. (J). mass mkt. 5.99 (*0-439-55967-7*, Scholastic Paperbacks) Scholastic, Inc.

—I'm Too Fond of My Fur! 2004. (Illus.). 128p. (J). mass mkt. 5.99 (*0-439-55966-9*, Scholastic Paperbacks) Scholastic, Inc.

—Lost Treasure of the Emerald Eye. 2004. (Geronimo Stilton Ser.: No. 1). (Illus.). 128p. (J). mass mkt. 5.99 (*0-439-55963-4*, Scholastic Paperbacks) Scholastic, Inc.

—Paws Off, Cheddarface. 2004. (Geronimo Stilton Ser.: No. 6). (Illus.). 128p. (J). mass mkt. 5.99 (*0-439-55968-5*) Scholastic, Inc.

—Red Pizzas for Blue Count. 2004. (Geronimo Stilton Ser.: No. 7). (Illus.). 128p. (J). mass mkt. 5.99 (*0-439-55969-3*) Scholastic, Inc.

STRANGE, ALLEN (FICTITIOUS CHARACTER)—FICTION

Dubowski, Cathy & Dubowski, Mark. Split Image. 1999. (Journey of Allen Strange Ser.: No. 3). 160p. (J). (gr. 4-7). pap. 3.99 (*0-671-02510-4*, Aladdin) Simon & Schuster Children's Publishing.

Gallagher, Diana G., et al. Invasion. 1999. (Journey of Allen Strange Ser.: No. 2). 144p. (J). (gr. 4-7). pap. 3.99 (*0-671-02511-2*, Aladdin) Simon & Schuster Children's Publishing.

Odom, Mel. Legacy. 1999. (Journey of Allen Strange Ser.: No. 4). 144p. (J). (gr. 4-7). pap. 3.99 (*0-671-02512-0*, Aladdin) Simon & Schuster Children's Publishing.

Ponti, James. Election Connection. 1999. (Journey of Allen Strange Ser.: No. 7). 144p. (J). (gr. 4-7). pap. 3.99 (*0-671-02514-7*, Aladdin) Simon & Schuster Children's Publishing.

Vornholt, John. The Joyride. 2000. (Journey of Allen Strange Ser.: No. 8). 144p. (J). (gr. 4-7). pap. 3.99 (*0-671-02516-3*, Aladdin) Simon & Schuster Children's Publishing.

Weiss, Bobbi J. G., et al. Alien Vacation. 1999. (Journey of Allen Strange Ser.: No. 6). (Illus.). 144p. (J). (gr. 4-7). pap. 3.99 (*0-671-03642-4*, Simon Pulse) Simon & Schuster Children's Publishing.

Weiss, David Cody & Weiss, Bobbi J. G. The Arrival. 1999. (Journey of Allen Strange Ser.: No. 1). 144p. (J). (gr. 4-7). pap. 3.99 (*0-671-02509-0*, Aladdin) Simon & Schuster Children's Publishing.

SUPERMAN (FICTITIOUS CHARACTER)—FICTION

Boyd, Ron. Superman Animation Cel Painting Kit. 1998. (DC Comics Cel Painting Bks.). (Illus.). 40p. (J). (gr. 3 up). pap. 16.95 o.p. (*1-56010-294-2*, CBC2) Foster, Walter Publishing, Inc.

Byrne, John. Generations: An Imaginary Tale. Crain, Dale, ed. 2000. (Illus.). 191p. pap. 14.95 (*1-56389-605-2*) DC Comics.

Campbell, Tom. Superman: The Lost Son of Krypton. Sahler, John, ed. 1997. (Magic Touch Talking Bks.). (Illus.). (J). (ps-2). 19.99 (*1-888208-36-8*) Hasbro, Inc.

Carlin, Mike, ed. Superman: Panic in the Sky. 1993. (Illus.). 192p. (J). pap. 9.95 (*1-56389-094-1*) DC Comics.

Chaykin, Howard. Son of Superman. 1999. (Illus.). 95p. (YA). 24.95 (*1-56389-595-1*) DC Comics.

DC Comics Staff. Arrival. 2002. (Smallville Ser.: No. 1). 176p. (J). pap. 5.99 (*0-316-17359-2*) Little Brown Children's Bks.

—Superman. novel ed. 2001. 32p. (J). pap. (*0-316-17805-5*) Little Brown Children's Bks.

—Superman: They Saved Luthor's Brain. 2000. (Superman Ser.). (Illus.). 159p. pap. text 14.95 (*1-56389-601-X*) DC Comics.

—Superman: Time & Time Again. Kahan, Bob, ed. 1994. (Illus.). 208p. (J). pap. 7.50 o.p. (*1-56389-129-8*) DC Comics.

—Superman Puzzle & Game Book. 1987. 160p. (YA). (gr. 4-7). pap. text 3.99 (*0-8125-7733-7*, Tor Bks.) Doherty, Tom Assocs., LLC.

Dematteis, J. M. & Barreto, Eduardo. Superman: Speeding Bullet. 1993. (Illus.). 48p. (J). pap. 5.95 (*1-56389-117-4*) DC Comics.

Edkin, Joe & Golden Books Staff. Superman & the Flash: Race Around the World. 1996. (Illus.). 24p. (J). (ps-3). pap. 3.29 o.s.i (*0-307-12931-4*, Golden Bks.) Random Hse. Children's Bks.

Giant Superman Annual #1 (Replica Edition) 1998. (Illus.). 80p. pap. 4.95 (*1-56389-466-1*) DC Comics.

Golden Books Staff. Superman Man of Steel. 1997. 12p. pap. 1.79 o.s.i (*0-307-08467-1*, Golden Bks.) Random Hse. Children's Bks.

—Superman to the Rescue: Puzzles & Mazes. 1999. (Illus.). 40p. pap. 1.09 o.s.i (*0-307-03639-1*, Golden Bks.) Random Hse. Children's Bks.

Jurgens, Dan. Superman / Aliens. unabr. ed. 1996. (Aliens Ser.). (Illus.). 152p. (YA). (gr. 7 up). pap. 14.95 (*1-56971-167-4*) Dark Horse Comics.

Kahan, Bob, ed. The Death of Superman. 1993. (Superman Ser.). (Illus.). 168p. pap. 9.95 (*1-56389-097-6*) DC Comics.

—Superman: The Return of Superman. deluxe ed. 1993. (Superman Ser.). (Illus.). 480p. pap. 14.95 (*1-56389-149-2*) DC Comics.

Lowther, George. The Adventures of Superman. 1995. (Illus.). 228p. (YA). (gr. 5 up). reprint ed. 17.95 (*1-55709-228-1*) Applewood Bks.

Moore, Alan, et al. Superman: Whatever Happened to the Man of Tomorrow? 1997. (Superman Ser.). 64p. pap. 5.95 (*1-56389-315-0*) DC Comics.

Siegel, Jerry. Superman Archives, Vol. 5. 2000. (Superman Archives Ser.: Vol. 5). (Illus.). 224p. 49.95 (*1-56389-602-8*) DC Comics.

Simonson, Louise. Superman: Doomsday. 1993. 144p. (J). pap. 3.99 o.s.i (*0-553-48168-1*) Bantam Bks.

—Wild at Heart, No. 6. abr. ed. 2003. (Justice League Ser.). (J). (gr. 3). audio compact disk 19.99 (*0-8072-1039-0*, Listening Library) Random Hse. Audio Publishing Group.

—Wild at Heart. 2003. (Illus.). 160p. (gr. 3-7). pap. text 4.99 (*0-553-48775-2*, Bantam Bks. for Young Readers) Random Hse. Children's Bks.

Simonson, Louise & Parobeck, Mike. The True Story of Superman. 1995. (Golden Super Shape Book Ser.). (Illus.). 24p. (J). (ps-3). pap. 3.29 o.s.i (*0-307-10005-7*, Golden Bks.) Random Hse. Children's Bks.

Superman. 2001. (Look & Find Ser.). (Illus.). (J). lib. bdg. 15.95 (*1-56674-299-4*) Forest Hse. Publishing Co., Inc.

SWIFT, TOM (FICTITIOUS CHARACTER)—FICTION

Appleton, Victor. The Alien Probe. (Tom Swift Ser.). (J). (gr. 3-7). 20.95 (*0-88411-464-3*) Amereon, Ltd.

—The Alien Probe. 1981. (Tom Swift Ser.). 192p. (J). (gr. 3-7). (*0-671-42538-2*, Simon & Schuster Children's Publishing); pap. 2.65 (*0-671-42578-1*, Aladdin) Simon & Schuster Children's Publishing.

—Ark Two. 1982. (Tom Swift Ser.). (Illus.). 192p. (J). (gr. 3-7). 8.50 o.s.i (*0-671-43952-9*, Simon & Schuster Children's Publishing); pap. 2.65 (*0-671-43953-7*, Aladdin) Simon & Schuster Children's Publishing.

—The Astral Fortress. 1982. (Tom Swift Ser.). 192p. (J). (gr. 3-7). pap. 8.95 (*0-671-43369-5*, Simon & Schuster Children's Publishing); pap. 2.50 (*0-671-43385-7*, Aladdin) Simon & Schuster Children's Publishing.

—The City in the Stars. (Tom Swift Ser.). (J). (gr. 3-7). 20.95 (*0-88411-463-5*) Amereon, Ltd.

—The City in the Stars. 1981. (Tom Swift Ser.). 192p. (J). (gr. 3-7). 7.95 (*0-671-41120-9*, Simon & Schuster Children's Publishing); pap. 3.40 (*0-671-41115-2*, Aladdin) Simon & Schuster Children's Publishing.

—Crater of Mystery. Barish, Wendy, ed. 1983. (Tom Swift Ser.). 192p. (J). (gr. 3-7). pap. 8.50 (*0-671-43954-5*, Simon & Schuster Children's Publishing); pap. 3.80 (*0-671-43955-3*, Aladdin) Simon & Schuster Children's Publishing.

—Gateway to Doom. Barish, Wendy, ed. 1983. (Tom Swift Ser.). 192p. (J). (gr. 3-7). pap. 8.50 (*0-671-43956-1*, Simon & Schuster Children's Publishing); pap. 3.80 (*0-671-43957-X*, Aladdin) Simon & Schuster Children's Publishing.

—The Rescue Mission. (Tom Swift Ser.). (J). (gr. 3-7). 20.95 (*0-88411-458-9*) Amereon, Ltd.

—The Rescue Mission. 1982. (Tom Swift Ser.). 192p. (J). (gr. 3-7). pap. 8.95 (*0-671-43370-9*, Simon & Schuster Children's Publishing); pap. 2.50 (*0-671-43386-5*, Aladdin) Simon & Schuster Children's Publishing.

—Terror on the Moons of Jupiter. (Tom Swift Ser.). (J). (gr. 3-7). 20.95 (*0-88411-460-0*) Amereon, Ltd.

—Tom Swift among the Diamond Makers. (Tom Swift Original Ser.: No. 7). (J). (gr. 3-7). E-Book 2.49 (*1-929120-92-3*) Electric Umbrella Publishing.

—Tom Swift among the Diamond Makers. 1999. (Tom Swift Original Ser.: Vol. No. 7). (J). (gr. 3-7). E-Book 3.99 o.p. incl. cd-rom (*1-57646-026-6*) Quiet Vision Publishing.

—Tom Swift among the Fire Fighters. (Tom Swift Original Ser.: No. 24). (J). (gr. 3-7). E-Book 2.49 (*1-58627-071-0*) Electric Umbrella Publishing.

—Tom Swift among the Fire Fighters. (Tom Swift Original Ser.: No. 24). (J). (gr. 3-7). E-Book 1.95 (*1-57799-871-5*) Logos Research Systems, Inc.

—Tom Swift among the Fire Fighters. 1999. (Tom Swift Original Ser.: Vol. No. 24). (J). (gr. 3-7). E-Book 3.99 o.p. incl. cd-rom (*1-57646-037-1*) Quiet Vision Publishing.

—Tom Swift & His Aerial Warship. (Tom Swift Original Ser.: No. 18). (J). (gr. 3-7). E-Book 2.49 (*1-58627-072-9*) Electric Umbrella Publishing.

—Tom Swift & His Aerial Warship. (Tom Swift Original Ser.: No. 18). (J). (gr. 3-7). E-Book 1.95 (*1-57799-864-2*) Logos Research Systems, Inc.

—Tom Swift & His Aerial Warship. 1999. (Tom Swift Original Ser.: Vol. No. 18). (J). (gr. 3-7). E-Book 3.99 o.p. incl. cd-rom (*1-57646-031-2*) Quiet Vision Publishing.

—Tom Swift & His Air Glider. (Tom Swift Original Ser.: No. 12). (J). (gr. 3-7). E-Book 2.49 (*1-58627-026-5*) Electric Umbrella Publishing.

—Tom Swift & His Air Glider. (Tom Swift Original Ser.: No. 12). (J). (gr. 3-7). E-Book 1.95 (*1-57799-856-1*) Logos Research Systems, Inc.

—Tom Swift & His Air Glider. 1999. (Tom Swift Original Ser.: Vol. No. 12). (J). (gr. 3-7). E-Book 3.99 o.p. incl. cd-rom (*1-57646-028-2*) Quiet Vision Publishing.

—Tom Swift & His Air Scout. (Tom Swift Original Ser.: No. 22). (J). (gr. 3-7). E-Book 2.49 (*1-58627-025-7*) Electric Umbrella Publishing.

—Tom Swift & His Air Scout. (Tom Swift Original Ser.: No. 22). (J). (gr. 3-7). E-Book 1.95 (*1-57799-865-0*) Logos Research Systems, Inc.

—Tom Swift & His Air Scout. 1999. (Tom Swift Original Ser.: Vol. No. 22). (J). (gr. 3-7). E-Book 3.99 o.p. incl. cd-rom (*1-57646-035-5*) Quiet Vision Publishing.

—Tom Swift & His Airship. 2004. (Tom Swift Original Ser.: No. 3). 216p. (J). (gr. 3-7). 17.95 (*1-55709-177-3*) Applewood Bks.

—Tom Swift & His Airship. (Tom Swift Original Ser.: Vol. No. 3). 2000. 120p. (YA). (gr. 3-7). lib. bdg. 20.99 (*1-57646-359-1*); 2000. 120p. (YA). (gr. 3-7). pap. 10.99 (*1-57646-203-X*); 1999. 203p. (J). (gr. 3-7). E-Book 3.99 o.p. incl. audio compact disk (*1-57646-132-7*); 2000. 186p. pap. 14.99 (*1-57646-360-5*); 2000. 186p. (YA). (gr. 3-7). lib. bdg. 25.99 o.p. (*1-57646-361-3*) Quiet Vision Publishing.

—Tom Swift & His Big Tunnel. (Tom Swift Original Ser.: No. 19). (J). (gr. 3-7). E-Book 2.49 (*1-58627-024-9*) Electric Umbrella Publishing.

—Tom Swift & His Big Tunnel. (Tom Swift Original Ser.: No. 19). (J). (gr. 3-7). E-Book 1.95 (*1-57799-866-9*) Logos Research Systems, Inc.

—Tom Swift & His Big Tunnel. 1999. (Tom Swift Original Ser.: Vol. No. 19). (J). (gr. 3-7). E-Book 3.99 o.p. incl. cd-rom (*1-57646-032-0*) Quiet Vision Publishing.

—Tom Swift & His Electric Locomotive. (Tom Swift Original Ser.: No. 25). (J). (gr. 3-7). E-Book 2.49 (*1-58627-070-2*) Electric Umbrella Publishing.

—Tom Swift & His Electric Locomotive. (Tom Swift Original Ser.: No. 25). (J). (gr. 3-7). E-Book 1.95 (*1-57799-867-7*) Logos Research Systems, Inc.

—Tom Swift & His Electric Locomotive. 1999. (Tom Swift Original Ser.: Vol. No. 25). (J). (gr. 3-7). E-Book 3.99 o.p. incl. cd-rom (*1-57646-038-X*) Quiet Vision Publishing.

—Tom Swift & His Electric Rifle. 1999. (Tom Swift Original Ser.: Vol. No. 10). 200p. (J). (gr. 3-7). E-Book 3.99 o.p. incl. audio compact disk (*1-57646-137-8*) Quiet Vision Publishing.

—Tom Swift & His Electric Rifle. 1998. (Tom Swift Original Ser.: No. 10). (J). (gr. 3-7). lib. bdg. 18.95 (*1-56723-020-2*) Yestermorrow, Inc.

—Tom Swift & His Electric Runabout. unabr. ed. 1992. (Tom Swift Original Ser.: No. 5). (J). (gr. 3-7). audio 26.95 (*1-55686-403-5*, 403) Books in Motion.

—Tom Swift & His Electric Runabout. (Tom Swift Original Ser.: No. 5). (J). (gr. 3-7). E-Book 2.49 (*1-58627-074-5*) Electric Umbrella Publishing.

—Tom Swift & His Electric Runabout. (Tom Swift Original Ser.: No. 5). (J). (gr. 3-7). E-Book 1.95 (*1-57799-858-8*) Logos Research Systems, Inc.

—Tom Swift & His Electric Runabout. 1999. (Tom Swift Original Ser.: Vol. No. 5). (J). (gr. 3-7). E-Book 3.99 o.p. incl. cd-rom (*1-57646-025-8*) Quiet Vision Publishing.

—Tom Swift & His Electronic Electroscope. (J). (gr. 5-6). 20.95 (*0-88411-462-7*) Amereon, Ltd.

—Tom Swift & His Giant Cannon. (Tom Swift Original Ser.: No. 16). (J). (gr. 3-7). E-Book 2.49 (*1-929120-93-1*) Electric Umbrella Publishing.

—Tom Swift & His Giant Cannon. (Tom Swift Original Ser.: No. 16). (J). (gr. 3-7). E-Book 1.95 (*1-57799-859-6*) Logos Research Systems, Inc.

—Tom Swift & His Giant Cannon. 1999. (Tom Swift Original Ser.: Vol. No. 16). (J). (gr. 3-7). E-Book 3.99 o.p. incl. cd-rom (*1-57646-030-4*) Quiet Vision Publishing.

—Tom Swift & His Giant Search Light. 1999. (Tom Swift Original Ser.: Vol. No. 15). 221p. (J). (gr. 3-7). E-Book 3.99 o.p. incl. audio compact disk (*1-57646-130-0*) Quiet Vision Publishing.

—Tom Swift & His Motor Boat. 2004. (Tom Swift Original Ser.: No. 2). 212p. (J). (gr. 3-7). 14.95 (*1-55709-176-5*) Applewood Bks.

—Tom Swift & His Motor Boat. (Tom Swift Original Ser.: Vol. No. 2). 2000. 114p. (YA). (gr. 3-7). lib. bdg. 20.99 (*1-57646-356-7*); 2000. 114p. (YA). (gr. 3-7). pap. 10.99 (*1-57646-202-1*); 1999. 205p. (J). (gr. 3-7). E-Book 3.99 o.p. incl. audio compact disk (*1-57646-131-9*); 2000. 182p. pap. 14.99 (*1-57646-357-5*); 2000. 182p. (YA). (gr. 3-7). lib. bdg. 25.99 o.p. (*1-57646-358-3*) Quiet Vision Publishing.

—Tom Swift & His Motor Cycle. 2004. (Tom Swift Original Ser.: No. 1). 206p. (J). (gr. 3-7). 14.95 (*1-55709-175-7*) Applewood Bks.

—Tom Swift & His Motor Cycle. (Tom Swift Original Ser.: Vol. No. 1). 2000. 114p. (YA). (gr. 3-7). lib. bdg. 20.99 (*1-57646-353-2*); 2000. 114p. (YA). (gr. 3-7). pap. 10.99 (*1-57646-201-3*); 1999. (J). (gr. 3-7). E-Book 3.99 o.p. incl. cd-rom (*1-57646-023-1*); 2000. 180p. pap. 14.99 (*1-57646-354-0*); 2000. 180p. (YA). (gr. 3-7). lib. bdg. 24.99 o.p. (*1-57646-355-9*) Quiet Vision Publishing.

—Tom Swift & His Photo Telephone. 1999. (Tom Swift Original Ser.: Vol. No. 17). 206p. (J). (gr. 3-7). E-Book 3.99 o.p. incl. audio compact disk (*1-57646-135-1*) Quiet Vision Publishing.

—Tom Swift & His Photo Telephone. 1998. (Tom Swift Original Ser.: No. 17). (J). (gr. 3-7). lib. bdg. 18.95 (*1-56723-022-9*) Yestermorrow, Inc.

—Tom Swift & His Sky Racer. (Tom Swift Original Ser.: No. 9). (J). (gr. 3-7). E-Book 2.49 (*1-58627-027-3*) Electric Umbrella Publishing.

—Tom Swift & His Sky Racer. (Tom Swift Original Ser.: No. 9). (J). (gr. 3-7). E-Book 1.95 (*1-57799-861-8*) Logos Research Systems, Inc.

—Tom Swift & His Sky Racer. 1999. (Tom Swift Original Ser.: Vol. No. 9). (J). (gr. 3-7). E-Book 3.99 o.p. incl. cd-rom (*1-57646-027-4*) Quiet Vision Publishing.

—Tom Swift & His Submarine Boat. (Tom Swift Original Ser.: No. 4). (J). (gr. 3-7). E-Book 2.49 (*1-58627-023-0*) Electric Umbrella Publishing.

—Tom Swift & His Submarine Boat. (Tom Swift Original Ser.: No. 4). (J). (gr. 3-7). E-Book 1.95 (*1-57799-862-6*) Logos Research Systems, Inc.

—Tom Swift & His Submarine Boat. (Tom Swift Original Ser.: Vol. No. 4). (gr. 3-7). 2000. 114p. (YA). pap. 10.99 (*1-57646-204-8*); 1999. (J). E-Book 3.99 o.p. incl. cd-rom (*1-57646-024-X*) Quiet Vision Publishing.

—Tom Swift & His Triphibian Atomicar. (Tom Swift Ser.). (J). (gr. 5-6). 20.95 (*0-88411-459-7*) Amereon, Ltd.

—Tom Swift & His Undersea Search. (Tom Swift Original Ser.: No. 23). (J). (gr. 3-7). E-Book 2.49 (*1-58627-073-7*) Electric Umbrella Publishing.

—Tom Swift & His Undersea Search. (Tom Swift Original Ser.: No. 23). (J). (gr. 3-7). E-Book 1.95 (*1-57799-868-5*) Logos Research Systems, Inc.

—Tom Swift & His Undersea Search. 1999. (Tom Swift Original Ser.: Vol. No. 23). (J). (gr. 3-7). E-Book 3.99 o.p. incl. cd-rom (*1-57646-036-3*) Quiet Vision Publishing.

—Tom Swift & His War Tank. (Tom Swift Original Ser.: No. 21). (J). (gr. 3-7). E-Book 2.49 (*1-58627-022-2*) Electric Umbrella Publishing.

—Tom Swift & His War Tank. (Tom Swift Original Ser.: No. 21). (J). (gr. 3-7). E-Book 1.95 (*1-57799-869-3*) Logos Research Systems, Inc.

—Tom Swift & His War Tank. 1999. (Tom Swift Original Ser.: Vol. No. 21). (J). (gr. 3-7). E-Book 3.99 o.p. incl. cd-rom (*1-57646-034-7*) Quiet Vision Publishing.

—Tom Swift & His Wireless Message. 1999. (Tom Swift Original Ser.: Vol. No. 6). 299p. (J). (gr. 3-7). E-Book 3.99 o.p. incl. audio compact disk (*1-57646-133-5*) Quiet Vision Publishing.

—Tom Swift & His Wizard Camera. unabr. ed. 1992. (Tom Swift Original Ser.: No. 14). (J). (gr. 3-7). audio 26.95 (*1-55686-405-1*, 405) Books in Motion.

—Tom Swift & His Wizard Camera. (Tom Swift Original Ser.: No. 14). (J). (gr. 3-7). E-Book 2.49 (*1-58627-069-9*) Electric Umbrella Publishing.

—Tom Swift & His Wizard Camera. (Tom Swift Original Ser.: No. 14). (J). (gr. 3-7). E-Book 1.95 (*1-57799-863-4*) Logos Research Systems, Inc.

—Tom Swift & His Wizard Camera. 1999. (Tom Swift Original Ser.: Vol. No. 14). (J). (gr. 3-7). E-Book 3.99 o.p. incl. cd-rom (*1-57646-029-0*) Quiet Vision Publishing.

—Tom Swift in Captivity. 1999. (Tom Swift Original Ser.: Vol. No. 13). 200p. (J). (gr. 3-7). E-Book 3.99 o.p. incl. audio compact disk (*1-57646-138-6*) Quiet Vision Publishing.

—Tom Swift in the Caves of Ice. unabr. ed. 1992. (Tom Swift Original Ser.: No. 8). (J). (gr. 3-7). audio 26.95 (*1-55686-406-X*, 406) Books in Motion.

—Tom Swift in the Caves of Ice. 1998. (Tom Swift Original Ser.: No. 8). (J). (gr. 3-7). lib. bdg. 18.95 (*1-56723-021-0*) Yestermorrow, Inc.

—Tom Swift in the City of Gold. unabr. ed. 1991. (Tom Swift Original Ser.: No. 11). (J). (gr. 3-7). audio 26.95 (*1-55686-388-8*, 388) Books in Motion.

—Tom Swift in the City of Gold. 1999. (Tom Swift Original Ser.: Vol. No. 11). 209p. (J). (gr. 3-7). E-Book 3.99 o.p. incl. audio compact disk (*1-57646-134-3*) Quiet Vision Publishing.

—Tom Swift in the Land of Wonder. (Tom Swift Original Ser.: No. 20). (J). (gr. 3-7). E-Book 2.49 (*1-58627-021-4*) Electric Umbrella Publishing.

—Tom Swift in the Land of Wonder. 1999. (Tom Swift Original Ser.: Vol. No. 20). (J). (gr. 3-7). E-Book 3.99 o.p. incl. cd-rom (*1-57646-033-9*) Quiet Vision Publishing.

—Tom Swift Jr. & His Aquatromic Tracker. 1964. (Tom Swift Jr. Ser.). (J). (gr. 5-9). 2.95 o.p. (*0-448-09123-2*) Putnam Publishing Group, The.

—Tom Swift Jr. & His Flying Lab. 1954. (Tom Swift Jr. Ser.). (J). (gr. 5-9). 2.95 o.p. (*0-448-09101-1*) Putnam Publishing Group, The.

—Tom Swift Jr. & His Jetmarine. 1954. (Tom Swift Jr. Ser.). (J). (gr. 5-9). 2.95 o.p. (*0-448-09102-X*) Putnam Publishing Group, The.

—Tom Swift Jr. & His Polar-Ray Dynasphere. 1964. (Tom Swift Jr. Ser.). (J). (gr. 5-9). 2.95 o.p. (*0-448-09125-9*) Putnam Publishing Group, The.

—Tom Swift Jr. & His Rocket Ship. 1954. (Tom Swift Jr. Ser.). (J). (gr. 5-9). 2.95 o.p. (*0-448-09103-8*) Putnam Publishing Group, The.

—Tom Swift Jr. & the Captive Planetoid. 1967. (Tom Swift Jr. Ser.). (YA). (gr. 5-9). 2.95 o.p. (*0-448-09129-1*) Putnam Publishing Group, The.

—Tom Swift, Land of Wonders. (J). E-Book 1.95 (*1-57799-870-7*) Logos Research Systems, Inc.

—Tom Swift Sr. Collection #1. 1999. (Tom Swift Original Ser.). 1181p. (J). (gr. 3-7). E-Book 19.99 o.p. incl. audio compact disk (*1-57646-139-4*) Quiet Vision Publishing.

—Tom Swift Sr. Collection #2. 1999. (Tom Swift Original Ser.). 1000p. (J). (gr. 3-7). E-Book 19.99 o.p. incl. audio compact disk (*1-57646-140-8*) Quiet Vision Publishing.

—Tom Swift Sr. Collection #3. 1999. (Tom Swift Original Ser.). 1000p. (J). (gr. 3-7). E-Book 19.99 o.p. incl. audio compact disk (*1-57646-141-6*) Quiet Vision Publishing.

—Tom Swift Sr. Collection #4. 1999. (Tom Swift Original Ser.). 1000p. (J). (gr. 3-7). E-Book 19.99 o.p. incl. audio compact disk (*1-57646-142-4*) Quiet Vision Publishing.

—Tom Swift Sr. Collection #5. 1999. (Tom Swift Original Ser.). (J). (gr. 3-7). E-Book 8.99 o.p. incl. cd-rom (*1-57646-064-9*) Quiet Vision Publishing.

—Tom Swift Sr. 25 Book Set. 1999. (Tom Swift Original Ser.). 5000p. (J). (gr. 3-7). E-Book 49.99 incl. audio compact disk (*1-57646-143-2*) Quiet Vision Publishing.

—The War in Outer Space. 1981. (Tom Swift Ser.). 192p. (J). (gr. 3-7). pap. 3.80 (*0-671-42579-X*, Aladdin); 7.95 (*0-671-42539-0*, Simon & Schuster Children's Publishing) Simon & Schuster Children's Publishing.

T

TARZAN (FICTITIOUS CHARACTER)—FICTION

Burroughs, Edgar Rice. Tarzan. 1999. (Illus.). 31p. (J). (gr. k-4). 15.99 (*0-7868-0384-3*) Disney Pr.

—Tarzan. 1998. (Children's Thrift Classics Ser.). (Illus.). 96p. (J). reprint ed. pap. text 1.00 (*0-486-29530-3*) Dover Pubns., Inc.

—Tarzan: Tarzan at the Earth's Core/Tarzan the Invincible. 1997. (Tarzan Ser.: Nos. 13 & 14). 432p. mass mkt. 6.99 o.s.i (*0-345-41349-0*, Del Rey) Ballantine Bks.

—Tarzan of the Apes. 1991. (J). 10.04 (*0-606-12823-9*) Turtleback Bks.

—Tarzan of the Apes: Adapted by Robin Moore from Edgar Rice Burrough's Tarzan of the Apes. abr. ed. 1999. (Illus.). 88p. (J). (gr. 2-5). pap. 3.99 (*0-689-82413-0*, 076714003886, Aladdin) Simon & Schuster Children's Publishing.

Burroughs, Edgar Rice & Green, John. Tarzan Coloring Book. 1998. (Illus.). 48p. (J). pap. 2.50 (*0-486-40359-9*) Dover Pubns., Inc.

Byars, Betsy C. Me Tarzan. 2000. (Illus.). 96p. (J). (ps-1). 14.95 (*0-06-028706-3*); lib. bdg. 15.89 (*0-06-028707-1*) HarperCollins Children's Bk. Group.

—Me Tarzan. 2002. (Illus.). 96p. (J). (gr. 2-5). pap. 4.99 (*0-06-442119-8*) HarperCollins Pubs.

Clarke, Judith, et al, illus. Tarzan. 1999. (Disney Ser.). 24p. (J). (ps-3). 3.99 o.p. (*0-307-16230-3*, Golden Bks.) Random Hse. Children's Bks.

Disney Staff. Tarzan Flip Book. 1999. 96p. (J). (ps-3). pap. (*0-7364-0143-1*) Mouse Works.

—Tarzan, Me & You. 1999. (Illus.). 10p. (J). (ps). 3.99 (*0-7364-0132-6*) Mouse Works.

—Tarzan's Jungle Adventure. 1999. (Giant Lift-the-Flap Ser.). (Illus.). 10p. (J). (ps). 8.99 (*0-7364-0066-4*) Mouse Works.

Golden Books Staff. Always in My Heart. 1999. (Disney Ser.). (Illus.). 16p. (J). (ps-3). pap. text 1.99 o.p. (*0-307-28306-2*, Golden Bks.) Random Hse. Children's Bks.

—Amazing Adventures. 1999. (Disney Ser.). (Illus.). 48p. (J). (ps-3). pap. text 1.95 o.p. (*0-307-25276-0*, Golden Bks.) Random Hse. Children's Bks.

—Best Ape Ever. 1999. (Disney Ser.). (Illus.). 192p. (ps-3). pap. text 1.95 o.p. (*0-307-25250-7*, Golden Bks.) Random Hse. Children's Bks.

—Deep in the Jungle. 1999. (Disney Ser.). (Illus.). 72p. (J). (ps-3). pap. text 6.99 o.p. (*0-307-25720-7*, Golden Bks.) Random Hse. Children's Bks.

—Growing up in the Jungle: Paint Box Book. 1999. (Disney Ser.). (Illus.). 32p. (J). (ps-3). pap. 0.99 o.p. (*0-307-09229-1*, Golden Bks.) Random Hse. Children's Bks.

—Jungle Friends. 1999. (Disney Ser.). (Illus.). 56p. (J). (ps-3). pap. text 3.99 o.p. (*0-307-27614-7*, Golden Bks.) Random Hse. Children's Bks.

—Swing Time. 1999. (Disney Ser.). (Illus.). 84p. (J). (ps-3). pap. text 2.99 o.p. (*0-307-25721-5*, Golden Bks.) Random Hse. Children's Bks.

Katschke, Judy. Tarzan Goes Bananas: Disney First Reader Ser. 1999. (Disney's Tarzan Ser.). (Illus.). 32p. (J). (gr. k-2). pap. text 2.99 (*0-7868-4281-4*) Hyperion Pr.

Manning, Russ & Burroughs, Edgar Rice. Tarzan: The Land That Time Forgot. unabr. ed. 1996. (Illus.). 112p. (YA). (gr. 9 up). pap. 12.95 (*1-56971-151-8*) Dark Horse Comics.

Milnes, Ellen. Tarzan Jungle Jam. 1999. (Chunky Roly-Poly Book Ser.). (Illus.). 16p. (J). 3.50 (*0-7364-0048-6*) Mouse Works.

Mouse Works Staff. Tarzan. 1999. (Spanish Read-Aloud Storybook Classics). (Illus.). 64p. (J). (ps-2). (SPA.). 6.99 (*0-7364-0057-5*); 8.99 (*0-7364-0047-8*) Mouse Works.

Niles, Douglas. Tarzan & the Well of Slaves. 1985. (Endless Quest Bks.). (Illus.). 160p. (J). (gr. 4-7). pap. 2.25 o.p. (*0-394-73968-X*, Random Hse. Bks. for Young Readers) Random Hse. Children's Bks.

Petruccio, Steven James. Tarzan. 1999. (Little Activity Bks.). (Illus.). (J). pap. 1.00 (*0-486-40933-3*) Dover Pubns., Inc.

Schroeder, Russell & Saxon, Victoria. Disney's Tarzan: Special Collector's Edition. 1999. (Illus.). 72p. (J). 17.99 (*0-7868-3221-5*) Disney Pr.

—Tarzan: Special Collector's Edition. 1999. (Illus.). 72p. (J). lib. bdg. 18.49 (*0-7868-5093-0*) Disney Pr.

Suben, Eric. Terk's Tale, SUPSB. 1999. (Disney Ser.). (Illus.). 24p. (J). (ps-k). pap. 3.29 o.p. (*0-307-13324-9*, Golden Bks.) Random Hse. Children's Bks.

Suben, Eric, et al, illus. Tarzan. 1999. (Disney Ser.). 24p. (ps-3). pap. 3.29 (*0-307-13194-7*, Golden Bks.) Random Hse. Children's Bks.

Tarzan Read Along. 1999. (ps-3). pap. 6.98 incl. audio (*0-7634-0530-2*) Walt Disney Records.

Tarzan Read & Sing Along. 1999. (ps-3). pap. 14.48 incl. audio (*0-7634-0525-6*) Walt Disney Records.

Zoehfeld, Kathleen Weidner, adapted by. Tarzan. 1999. (Illus.). 48p. (J). (ps-3). 10.99 o.p. (*0-7868-3220-7*) Disney Pr.

TASSEL, LINDA (FICTITIOUS CHARACTER)—FICTION

Charbonneau, Eileen. The Connor Emerald. 1995. 224p. (J). mass mkt. 3.99 o.p. (*0-8217-4823-8*) Kensington Publishing Corp.

—The Connor Emerald. Williams, Lori, ed. 1999. (YA). 170p. pap. 9.99 (*1-58365-753-3*, Timeless Romance); E-Book 2.99 (*1-58365-754-1*, Timeless Treasures) Sierra Raconteur Publishing.

—Disappearance at Harmony Festivel. 1994. (You-Solve-It Mysteries Ser.: No. 5). 224p. (YA). mass mkt. 3.50 o.s.i (*0-8217-4674-X*) Kensington Publishing Corp.

—The Mound Builders' Secret. 1994. (You-Solve-It Mysteries Ser.: No. 3). 224p. (YA). mass mkt. 3.50 o.s.i (*0-8217-4610-3*) Kensington Publishing Corp.

TEACH, EDWARD, D. 1718—FICTION

Johnson, Charles. Pieces of Eight. 1989. (Footprints in Time Ser.). (Illus.). 110p. (J). (gr. 3-6). 9.95 (*0-944770-00-2*) Discovery Pr., Inc.

Miers, Earl J. Pirate Chase. 1965. (Younger Readers Ser.). (Illus.). (J). (gr. 4-7). 3.95 o.p. (*0-910412-69-3*) Colonial Williamsburg Foundation.

Stahl, Ben. Blackbeard's Ghost. 1965. (Illus.). 192p. (J). (gr. 4-6). 7.95 o.p. (*0-395-07115-1*) Houghton Mifflin Co.

Wechter, Nell W. & Tucker, Bruce. Teach's Light. 1999. (Chapel Hill Book Ser.). (Illus.). 160p. (J). (gr. 4-7). pap. 9.95 (*0-8078-4793-3*) Univ. of North Carolina Pr.

TEENAGE MUTANT NINJA TURTLES (FICTITIOUS CHARACTERS)—FICTION

Brown, Ryan, et al. Teenage Mutant Ninja Turtles, Vol. 1. 1990. (Illus.). 150p. (YA). pap. 9.95 o.p. (*1-879450-00-3*) Kitchen Sink Pr., Inc.

Carlson, Gary. Teenage Mutant Ninja Turtles: A New Beginning. 1997. (Illus.). 112p. pap. 9.95 (*1-887279-56-3*) Image Comics.

Clarke, Catherine. Teenage Mutant Ninja Turtles: The Next Mutation. 1998. (J). 3.99 (*0-679-89302-4*, Random Hse. Bks. for Young Readers) Random Hse. Children's Bks.

Clarrain, Dean & Lawson, Jim. Teenage Mutant Ninja Turtles: The Secret of the Ooze - Movie Adaptation. 1991. (Illus.). 64p. (Orig.). (J). pap. 5.95 (*1-879450-08-9*) Kitchen Sink Pr., Inc.

Fontes, Justine. Teenage Mutant Ninja Turtles: The Movie Sequel Storybook. 1991. (J). pap. 69.50 o.p. (*0-679-81662-3*) Random Hse., Inc.

Hal Leonard Corporation Staff. Teenage Mutant Ninja Turtles. 1990. pap. 12.95 o.p. (*0-7935-0022-2*, HL00490392) Leonard, Hal Corp.

—Teenage Mutant Ninja Turtles: Book & Kazoo Clamshell Package. 1990. pap. 14.95 o.p. (*0-7935-0026-5*, HL00290302) Leonard, Hal Corp.

Hiller, B. B. Teenage Mutant Ninja Turtles. 1990. 96p. (J). pap. 2.95 o.s.i (*0-440-40322-7*) Dell Publishing.

—Teenage Mutant Ninja Turtles II: The Secret of the Ooze. 1991. (Teenage Mutant Ninja Turtles Ser.: No. 2). 112p. (J). (gr. 4-7). pap. 3.50 o.s.i (*0-440-40451-7*) Dell Publishing.

Hudson, Eleanor. Teenage Mutant Ninja Turtles Pizza Party. 1991. (Step into Reading Step 1 Bks.). (Illus.). 32p. (J). (ps-1). 7.99 o.s.i (*0-679-91452-8*, Random Hse. Bks. for Young Readers) Random Hse. Children's Bks.

Italia, Bob. Teenage Mutant Ninja Turtles. Wallner, Rosemary, ed. 1991. (Behind the Creation of Ser.). (J). lib. bdg. 13.95 (*1-56239-050-3*) ABDO Publishing Co.

Kebbe, Jonathan. Shredder. 2004. 64p. (J). (gr. 1). pap. (*0-552-55129-5*, Corgi) Bantam Bks.

Morris, Dave. Teenage Mutant Ninja Turtles, 5 vols. 1990. (J). (gr. 4-7). 14.75 (*0-440-36030-7*) Dell Publishing.

—Teenage Mutant Ninja Turtles: Sixguns & Shuriken. 1990. (J). pap. o.p. (*0-440-80218-0*, Dell Books for Young Readers) Random Hse. Children's Bks.

Random House. Teenage Mutant Ninja Turtles. 1991. pap. 1.28 o.s.i (*0-679-81492-2*, Random Hse. Bks. for Young Readers) Random Hse. Children's Bks.

Robie, Joan H. Teenage Mutant Ninja Turtles Exposed. 1991. 80p. (J). (gr. 4-7). pap. 5.95 (*0-914984-31-4*) Starburst Pubs.

Ross, Katharine. Teenage Mutant Ninja Turtles: The Movie Storybook. 1990. (Illus.). 48p. (J). (gr. 1 up). 6.95 o.s.i (*0-679-80653-9*, Random Hse. Bks. for Young Readers) Random Hse. Children's Bks.

Spaziante, Patrick, illus. Look Out! It's Turtle Titan! 2004. (Teenage Mutant Ninja Turtles Ser.). 24p. (J). pap. 3.99 (*0-689-86900-2*, Simon Spotlight) Simon & Schuster Children's Publishing.

—Meet Casey Jones. 2004. (Teenage Mutant Ninja Turtles Ser.). 24p. (J). pap. 3.99 (*0-689-86899-5*, Simon Spotlight) Simon & Schuster Children's Publishing.

Teenage Mutant Ninja Turtles. 1990. (Easy Piano Ser.). 64p. pap. 12.95 o.p. (*0-7935-0051-6*, 00490399) Leonard, Hal Corp.

Teenage Mutant Ninja Turtles School Friends Album. 1991. (J). (ps-3). pap. 2.25 o.p. (*0-89954-419-3*) Antioch Publishing Co.

Wenzel, Paul. A Visit to Stump Asteroid. 1991. (Teenage Mutant Ninja Turtles Mini-Storybooks Ser.). (Illus.). 48p. (J). (ps-3). 3.99 o.s.i (*0-679-81170-2*, Random Hse. Bks. for Young Readers) Random Hse. Children's Bks.

Wujcik, Erick. Teenage Mutant Ninja Turtles Adventures. Marciniszyn, Alex, ed. 1986. (Teenage Mutant Ninja Turtles RPG Adventures Ser.). (Illus.). 48p. (Orig.). (YA). (gr. 8 up). pap. 7.95 o.p. (*0-916211-16-9*, 504) Palladium Bks., Inc.

—Teenage Mutant Ninja Turtles & Other Strangeness. Marciniszyn, Alex et al, eds. 1985. (Illus.). 112p. (Orig.). (YA). (gr. 8 up). pap. 12.95 o.p. (*0-916211-14-2*, 502) Palladium Bks., Inc.

—Teenage Mutant Ninja Turtles Guide to the Universe. Marciniszyn, Alex & Siembieda, Florence, eds. 1987. (Teenage Mutant Ninja Turtles RPG Adventures Ser.). (Illus.). 48p. (Orig.). (YA). (gr. 8 up). pap. 7.95 o.p. (*0-916211-25-8*, 506) Palladium Bks., Inc.

TELETUBBIES (FICTITIOUS CHARACTERS)—FICTION

Bader, Bonnie. The Magic Pumpkin: A Lift-the-Flap Book. 2000. (Teletubbies Ser.). (Illus.). 12p. (J). (ps). bds. 5.99 (*0-439-15514-2*) Scholastic, Inc.

—The Snow Tubby. 2000. (Teletubbies Ser.). (Illus.). 32p. (J). (ps). mass mkt. 5.99 (*0-439-15510-X*) Scholastic, Inc.

The Butterfly. 2001. (Butterfly). 12p. pap. text 12.00 (*0-9710595-0-0*) Herbert, Jo Lynn.

The Butterfly. 1998. (Teletubbies Ser.). (Illus.). 24p. (J). (ps). pap. (*0-7666-0259-1*, Honey Bear Bks.) Modern Publishing.

Come & Play. 1998. (Teletubbies Ser.). (Illus.). 96p. (J). (ps). pap. (*0-7666-0266-4*, Honey Bear Bks.) Modern Publishing.

Davenport, Andrew. Dancing with the Skirt. 1999. (Teletubbies Ser.). (Illus.). 24p. (J). (ps). mass mkt. 3.50 (*0-590-98294-X*) Scholastic, Inc.

—Here Come the Teletubbies. ed. 2000. (J). (gr. 1). spiral bd. (*0-616-03029-0*); (gr. 2). spiral bd. (*0-616-04551-4*) Canadian National Institute for the Blind/Institut National Canadien pour les Aveugles.

—Here Come the Teletubbies. 1998. (Teletubbies Ser.). (Illus.). 32p. (J). (ps). pap. 9.99 (*0-590-38623-9*) Scholastic, Inc.

—It's Tubby Bedtime. 1999. (Teletubbies Ser.). (Illus.). 24p. (J). (ps). mass mkt. 3.50 (*0-590-98325-3*) Scholastic, Inc.

—Little Lamb. 1999. (Teletubbies Ser.). (Illus.). 24p. (J). (ps). mass mkt. 3.50 (*0-439-10601-X*) Scholastic, Inc.

—Merry Christmas, Teletubbies! 1999. (Teletubbies Ser.). (Illus.). 32p. (J). (ps). pap. 9.99 (*0-439-10596-X*) Scholastic, Inc.

—The Noo-Noo Tidies Up. 1999. (Teletubbies Ser.). (Illus.). 24p. (J). (ps). bds. 6.99 (*0-590-27855-X*) Scholastic, Inc.

—Teletubbies Love to Roll! 1999. (Teletubbies Ser.). (Illus.). 20p. (J). (ps). bds. 4.99 (*0-439-07794-X*) Scholastic, Inc.

—This Little Teletubby. 1999. (Teletubbies Ser.). (Illus.). 24p. (J). (ps). mass mkt. 3.50 (*0-439-10602-8*) Scholastic, Inc.

Dipsy's Day to Dance. 1998. (Teletubbies Ser.). (Illus.). 32p. (J). (ps). pap. (*0-7666-0256-7*, Honey Bear Bks.) Modern Publishing.

Follow the Leader. 2001. (Teletubbies Ser.). (Illus.). 10p. (J). (ps). bds. 5.99 (*0-439-25234-2*) Scholastic, Inc.

A Funny Day. 1998. (Teletubbies Ser.). (Illus.). 32p. (J). (ps). pap. (*0-7666-0264-8*, Honey Bear Bks.) Modern Publishing.

Jacobus, Tim & Ferrigno, Joan, illus. The Happy Day. 1999. (Teletubbies Ser.). 10p. (J). (ps). pap. 11.99 (*0-590-98333-4*) Scholastic, Inc.

Kong, Emilie, illus. The Magic Telescope: A Touch-and-Feel Book. 1999. (Teletubbies Ser.). 12p. (J). (ps). bds. 8.99 (*0-590-98335-0*) Scholastic, Inc.

—Tubby Toast, Tubby Toast! 1999. (Teletubbies Ser.). 11p. (J). (ps). bds. 4.99 (*0-439-10598-6*) Scholastic, Inc.

—Who Spilled the Tubby Custard? 1999. (Teletubbies Ser.). 11p. (J). (ps). bds. 4.99 (*0-439-10597-8*) Scholastic, Inc.

Laa Laa Gets a Guitar. 1998. (Teletubbies Ser.). (Illus.). 32p. (J). (ps). pap. (*0-7666-0257-5*, Honey Bear Bks.) Modern Publishing.

The Magic Cloud. 1998. (Teletubbies Ser.). (Illus.). 24p. (J). (ps). pap. (*0-7666-0260-5*, Honey Bear Bks.) Modern Publishing.

Meet the Teletubbies. 1998. (Teletubbies Ser.). (Illus.). 96p. (J). (ps). pap. (*0-7666-0265-6*, Honey Bear Bks.) Modern Publishing.

Playing Inside the Tubbytronic Superdome. 1999. (Teletubbies Ser.). (Illus.). (J). (ps). 19.99 (*0-439-10603-6*) Scholastic, Inc.

Po Follows a Path. 1998. (Teletubbies Ser.). (Illus.). 32p. (J). (ps). pap. (*0-7666-0258-3*, Honey Bear Bks.) Modern Publishing.

Ready, Set, Go...Touch Toes! 2001. (Teletubbies Ser.). (Illus.). 10p. (J). (ps). mass mkt. 5.99 (*0-439-25235-0*) Scholastic, Inc.

Scholastic, Inc. Staff. Big Hug! 2000. (Teletubbies Ser.). (Illus.). 6p. (J). (ps). bds. 5.99 (*0-439-13854-X*) Scholastic, Inc.

—The Boom-Boom Dance. 2000. (Teletubbies Ser.). (Illus.). 6p. (J). (ps). bds. 11.99 (*0-439-13853-1*) Scholastic, Inc.

—Come & See with Laa-Laa. 1999. (Teletubbies Ser.). (Illus.). (J). (ps). bds. 4.99 o.s.i (*0-590-38626-3*) Scholastic, Inc.

—Dipsy Dances. 1998. (Teletubbies Ser.). (Illus.). 24p. (J). (ps). mass mkt. 3.50 (*0-590-64310-X*) Scholastic, Inc.

—Flying Kites. 2000. (Teletubbies Ser.). (Illus.). 24p. (J). (ps). mass mkt. 3.50 (*0-439-13856-6*) Scholastic, Inc.

—Four Happy Teletubbies. 1998. (Teletubbies Ser.). (Illus.). 24p. (J). (ps). mass mkt. 3.50 (*0-590-38615-8*) Scholastic, Inc.

—Go Po Go! 1998. (Teletubbies Ser.). (Illus.). 22p. (J). (ps). mass mkt. 3.50 (*0-590-64312-6*) Scholastic, Inc.

—Jack & Jill. 2000. (Teletubbies Ser.). (Illus.). 22p. (J). (ps). bds. 3.99 (*0-439-06393-0*) Scholastic, Inc.

—Little Miss Muffet. 2000. (Teletubbies Ser.). (Illus.). 22p. (J). (ps). bds. 3.99 (*0-590-56601-6*) Scholastic, Inc.

—The Little Puffy Cloud. 1998. (Teletubbies Ser.). (Illus.). 14p. (J). (ps). bds. 3.99 (*0-590-64320-7*) Scholastic, Inc.

—Love to Jump! 1999. (Teletubbies Ser.). (Illus.). 20p. (J). (ps). bds. 4.99 (*0-439-07795-8*) Scholastic, Inc.

—The Magic Hat. 2000. (Teletubbies Ser.). (Illus.). 24p. (J). (ps). mass mkt. 3.50 (*0-439-13855-8*) Scholastic, Inc.

—The Magic String. 1998. (Teletubbies Ser.). (Illus.). 14p. (J). (ps). bds. 4.99 (*0-590-64321-5*) Scholastic, Inc.

—Teletubbies Play Hide & Seek! 1998. (Teletubbies Ser.). (Illus.). 12p. (J). (ps). bds. 5.99 (*0-590-38617-4*) Scholastic, Inc.

—Teletubbyland Sticker Storybook. 1999. (Teletubbies Ser.). (Illus.). 15p. (J). (ps). 5.99 (*0-439-10600-1*) Scholastic, Inc.

—Tubby Custard Mess. 1998. (Teletubbies Ser.). (Illus.). 24p. (J). (ps). mass mkt. 3.50 (*0-590-38616-6*) Scholastic, Inc.

—Tubbytronic Superdome Sticker Storybook. 1999. (Teletubbies Ser.). (Illus.). 15p. (J). (ps). 5.99 (*0-439-10599-4*) Scholastic, Inc.

Scholastic, Inc. Staff, ed. Come & See with Dipsy. 1999. (Teletubbies Ser.). (Illus.). (J). (ps). bds. 4.99 (*0-590-38625-5*) Scholastic, Inc.

—Come & See with Po. 1999. (Teletubbies Ser.). (Illus.). (J). (ps). bds. 4.99 (*0-590-38627-1*) Scholastic, Inc.

—Come & See with Tinky Winky. 1999. (Teletubbies Ser.). (Illus.). (J). (ps). bds. 4.99 (*0-590-38624-7*) Scholastic, Inc.

—Po's Magic Watering Can. 1999. (Teletubbies Ser.). (Illus.). 24p. (J). (ps). bds. 6.99 (*0-590-98334-2*) Scholastic, Inc.

Teletubbies' Favorite Things. 1998. (Teletubbies Ser.). (Illus.). 24p. (J). (ps). pap. (*0-7666-0262-1*, Honey Bear Bks.) Modern Publishing.

Teletubbies Happy Time. 2001. (Illus.). (J). 7.95 (*0-7853-4784-4*) Publications International, Ltd.

Teletubbies Super Coloring Activity Book. 1998. (Teletubbies Ser.). (Illus.). 240p. (J). (ps). pap. (*0-7666-0384-9*, Honey Bear Bks.) Modern Publishing.

Thompson, Dana & Thompson, Del, illus. Teletubbies Like to Dance! 1998. (Teletubbies Ser.). 12p. (J). (ps). bds. 5.99 (*0-590-38621-2*) Scholastic, Inc.

Time for a Walk. 1998. (Teletubbies Ser.). (Illus.). 32p. (J). (ps). pap. (*0-7666-0263-X*, Honey Bear Bks.) Modern Publishing.

Time for Tubbyrobies. abr. ed. 1998. (Teletubbies Ser.). (J). (ps). audio 11.25 (*0-563-55855-5*) BBC Bk. Publishing GBR. *Dist:* Ulverscroft Large Print Bks., Ltd.

Tinky-Winky's Tubby Toast. 1998. (Teletubbies Ser.). (Illus.). 32p. (J). (ps). pap. (*0-7666-0255-9*, Honey Bear Bks.) Modern Publishing.

Tubby Custard Mess. 1998. (Teletubbies Ser.). (Illus.). 24p. (J). (ps). pap. (*0-7666-0261-3*, Honey Bear Bks.) Modern Publishing.

THOMAS, THE TANK ENGINE (FICTITIOUS CHARACTER)—FICTION

Allcroft, Britt. The Cranky Day & Other Thomas the Tank Engine Stories. 2001. (Thomas the Tank Engine Ser.). (Illus.). 24p. (J). (ps-3). pap. 8.95 incl. audio (*0-375-81214-8*, Random Hse. Bks. for Young Readers) Random Hse. Children's Bks.

Awdry, Christopher. Learn with Thomas. 1996. (Illus.). 32p. (J). (ps-3). 12.99 o.s.i (*0-679-87951-X*) McKay, David Co., Inc.

—Really Useful Engines. 2001. (Railway Ser.). (Illus.). 64p. (J). (gr. k-3). 6.99 (*0-375-81225-3*, Random Hse. Bks. for Young Readers) Random Hse. Children's Bks.

—Thomas the Tank Engine & the Scrambled Eggs. 1995. (J). 4.50 o.s.i (*0-679-86993-X*) Random Hse., Inc.

—Thomas the Tank Engine Catches a Thief. 1995. (J). 4.50 o.s.i (*0-679-86994-8*) Random Hse., Inc.

—Thomas the Tank Engine's Big Blue Treasury. 1999. (Thomas the Tank Engine Ser.). (Illus.). 80p. (J). (gr. k-3). 7.99 (*0-679-89478-0*, Random Hse. Bks. for Young Readers) Random Hse. Children's Bks.

—Thomas the Tank Engine's Big Yellow Treasury. 1999. (Thomas the Tank Engine Ser.). (Illus.). 80p. (J). (gr. k-3). 7.99 (*0-679-89479-9*, Random Hse. Bks. for Young Readers) Random Hse. Children's Bks.

Awdry, Christopher, ed. Thomas: The Really Useful Engine. 1999. (Thomas the Tank Engine & Friends Ser.). (Illus.). 48p. (J). (ps-3). 11.99 (*0-375-80242-8*, Random Hse. Bks. for Young Readers) Random Hse. Children's Bks.

Awdry, Wilbert V. Bertie the Bus & Thomas the Tank Engine. 1995. (J). 4.50 o.s.i (*0-679-86996-4*) Random Hse., Inc.

—A Better View for Gordon. 2002. (Illus.). 24p. (J). (ps-1). pap. 8.95 incl. audio (*0-375-81546-5*) Random Hse., Inc.

—Breakfast-Time for Thomas. (Thomas the Tank Engine Ser.). (Illus.). (J). (ps-3). 1998. 7.99 o.s.i (*0-679-99237-5*); 1998. 24p. 1.99 o.s.i (*0-679-89237-0*); 1990. 32p. 1.50 o.s.i (*0-679-80409-9*) Random Hse. Children's Bks. (Random Hse. Bks. for Young Readers).

—Catch Me, Catch Me! 1990. (Random House Pictureback Reader Ser.). (Illus.). 24p. (J). (ps-3). pap. 3.25 (*0-679-80485-4*, Random Hse. Bks. for Young Readers) Random Hse. Children's Bks.

—Catch Me, Catch Me! 1990. (Pictureback Reader Ser.). (Illus.). (J). 9.40 (*0-606-12215-X*) Turtleback Bks.

—Choo-Choo, Peek-a-Boo. 1992. (Peek-A-Board Book Ser.). (Illus.). 14p. (ps). bds. 4.99 (*0-679-82262-3*, Random Hse. Bks. for Young Readers) Random Hse. Children's Bks.

—A Cow on the Line & Other Thomas the Tank Engine Stories. Starr, Ringo, ed. 1992. (Thomas the Tank Engine & Friends Ser.). (Illus.). 32p. (ps-3). 8.95 incl. audio (*0-679-83476-1*, Random Hse. Bks. for Young Readers) Random Hse. Children's Bks.

—A Cow on the Line & Other Thomas the Tank Engine Stories. 1992. (Random House Picturebacks Ser.). (Illus.). 32p. (J). (ps-3). pap. 3.25 (*0-679-81977-0*, Random Hse. Bks. for Young Readers) Random Hse. Children's Bks.

—A Crack in the Track. 2004. (Illus.). 24p. (J). bds. 4.99 (*0-375-82755-2*) Random Hse. Children's Bks.

—A Crack in the Track. 2001. (Beginner Bks.). (Illus.). 48p. (J). (ps-3). 8.99 (*0-375-81246-6*, Random Hse. Bks. for Young Readers) Random Hse. Children's Bks.

—Diesel's Devious Deed & Other Thomas the Tank Engine Stories. Starr, Ringo, ed. 1992. (Thomas the Tank Engine & Friends Ser.). (Illus.). 32p. (J). (ps-3). pap. 8.95 incl. audio (*0-679-83474-5*); pap. 8.95 incl. audio (*0-679-83474-5*) Random Hse. Children's Bks. (Random Hse. Bks. for Young Readers).

—Diesel's Devious Deed & Other Thomas the Tank Engine Stories. (Random House Picturebacks Ser.). (ps-3). 1992. (Illus.). 32p. (J). pap. 3.25 (*0-679-81976-2*); 1991. o.s.i (*0-679-83473-7*) Random Hse. Children's Bks. (Random Hse. Bks. for Young Readers).

—Edward, Trevor, & the Really Useful Party. 1994. (Thomas the Tank Engine Photographic Board Bks.). (Illus.). 16p. (J). (ps-k). 3.99 o.s.i (*0-679-86186-6*, Random Hse. Bks. for Young Readers) Random Hse. Children's Bks.

—Gordon & the Famous Visitor. 1993. (Illus.). (J). o.s.i (*0-679-86205-6*) Random Hse. Children's Bks.

—Gordon's Trouble with Mud. 1994. (Thomas the Tank Engine Photographic Board Bks.). (Illus.). 16p. (J). (ps). 3.99 o.s.i (*0-679-86185-8*, Random Hse. Bks. for Young Readers) Random Hse. Children's Bks.

—Henry & the Elephant. (Jellybean Bks.). (Illus.). (J). (ps-3). 1999. 24p. 7.99 o.s.i (*0-679-99414-9*); 1999. 24p. 1.99 o.s.i (*0-679-89414-4*); 1990. 32p. 1.50 o.s.i (*0-679-80408-0*) Random Hse. Children's Bks. (Random Hse. Bks. for Young Readers).

—Henry the Green Engine & the Tunnel. 1997. (My First Thomas Ser.). (Illus.). 16p. (ps-k). 5.99 o.s.i (*0-679-88679-6*, Random Hse. Bks. for Young Readers) Random Hse. Children's Bks.

—Henry's Forest. 1994. (Thomas the Tank Engine Photographic Board Bks.). (Illus.). 16p. (J). (ps). 3.99 o.s.i (*0-679-86184-X*, Random Hse. Bks. for Young Readers) Random Hse. Children's Bks.

—James & the Foolish Freight Cars. (Illus.). (J). 1993. o.s.i (*0-679-86209-9*); 1991. 32p. 3.50 o.s.i (*0-679-82086-8*, Random Hse. Bks. for Young Readers) Random Hse. Children's Bks.

—James & the Trucks. 1997. (Illus.). 16p. (ps-k). bds. 5.99 o.s.i (*0-679-88680-X*, Random Hse. Bks. for Young Readers) Random Hse. Children's Bks.

—Meet Thomas the Tank Engine & His Friends. 1989. (Illus.). 32p. (J). (ps-1). 6.95 o.s.i (*0-679-80102-2*, Random Hse. Bks. for Young Readers) Random Hse. Children's Bks.

—The Midnight Ride of Thomas the Tank Engine. 1994. (Glow-Backs Ser.). (Illus.). 16p. (J). (ps-3). pap. 5.99 o.s.i (*0-679-85643-9*, Random Hse. Bks. for Young Readers) Random Hse. Children's Bks.

—One Blue Engine. 1995. (Magic Window Bks.). (Illus.). 9p. (J). (ps). 6.99 o.s.i (*0-679-85310-3*, Random Hse. Bks. for Young Readers) Random Hse. Children's Bks.

—Para, Trencito, Para! 2001. (Illus.). 24p. (J). bds. 4.99 (*0-375-81502-3*) Random Hse. Children's Bks.

—Percy Runs Away. 1993. (J). (gr. 2 up). o.s.i (*0-679-86208-0*, Random Hse. Bks. for Young Readers) Random Hse. Children's Bks.

—The Special Delivery. 2002. (Jellybean Bks.). 24p. (J). pap. 3.25 (*0-375-81494-9*, Random Hse. Bks. for Young Readers) Random Hse. Children's Bks.

—Stop, Train, Stop! 1998. (Thomas the Tank Engine Picturebacks Ser.). (Illus.). 12p. (J). (ps). bds. 4.99 (*0-679-89273-7*, Random Hse. Bks. for Young Readers) Random Hse. Children's Bks.

—Tank Engine Thomas Again. 2000. (Thomas the Tank Engine & Friends Ser.). (Illus.). 72p. (J). (gr. k-3). 6.99 (*0-375-80532-X*, Random Hse. Bks. for Young Readers) Random Hse. Children's Bks.

—Tank Engine Thomas Again. 1985. (Railway Ser.). (Illus.). 64p. (J). (gr. k-2). reprint ed. 6.95 o.p. (*0-7182-0003-9*) Trafalgar Square.

—Thomas & the Hide-&-Seek Animals. 1991. (Flap Bks.). (Illus.). 24p. (ps-3). 10.95 o.s.i (*0-679-81316-0*, Random Hse. Bks. for Young Readers) Random Hse. Children's Bks.

—Thomas & the Shooting Star. 2002. (Thomas & Friends Ser.). (Illus.). 32p. (J). (ps-2). 8.99 (*0-375-81523-6*) Random Hse., Inc.

—Thomas Gets Bumped. 1994. (Thomas the Tank Engine & Friends Ser.). (Illus.). 32p. (J). (ps-3). 3.50 o.s.i (*0-679-86045-2*, Random Hse. Bks. for Young Readers) Random Hse. Children's Bks.

—Thomas Gets Tricked & Other Stories. (Thomas the Tank Engine & Friends Book & Cassette Ser.). (Illus.). 32p. (ps-2). 1991. 8.95 incl. audio (*0-679-80108-1*); 1989. pap. 3.25 (*0-679-80100-6*) Random Hse. Children's Bks. (Random Hse. Bks. for Young Readers).

—Thomas, Percy, & the Dragon. 1994. (Thomas the Tank Engine Photographic Board Bks.). (Illus.). 16p. (J). (ps). 3.99 o.s.i (*0-679-86183-1*, Random Hse. Bks. for Young Readers) Random Hse. Children's Bks.

—Thomas the Really Useful Engine. 1999. (Illus.). 48p. (J). (ps-3). lib. bdg. 13.99 o.s.i (*0-375-90242-2*) Random Hse., Inc.

—Thomas the Tank Engine. (Thomas the Tank Engine & Friends Ser.). (Illus.). (J). (gr. k-3). 2000. 72p. 6.99 (*0-375-80533-8*); 1999. 6p. bds. 6.99 (*0-679-89388-1*) Random Hse., Inc.

—Thomas the Tank Engine. 1985. (Railway Ser.). (Illus.). 64p. (J). (gr. k-2). reprint ed. 6.95 o.p. (*0-7182-0001-2*) Trafalgar Square.

—Thomas the Tank Engine: Cranky Bug. 2000. (Random House Picturebacks Ser.). (Illus.). 24p. (J). (gr. k-3). pap. 3.25 (*0-375-80246-0*) Random Hse., Inc.

—Thomas the Tank Engine ABC: Just Right for 2's & 3's. 1990. (Just Right Bks.). (Illus.). 24p. (J). (ps). 6.99 o.s.i (*0-679-80362-9*, Random Hse. Bks. for Young Readers) Random Hse. Children's Bks.

—Thomas the Tank Engine & the Great Race. 1989. (Illus.). 7p. (J). (ps). 7.00 o.s.i (*0-679-80000-X*, Random Hse. Bks. for Young Readers) Random Hse. Children's Bks.

—Thomas the Tank Engine & the School Trip. 2003. (Step into Reading Step 1 Bks.). (Illus.). 32p. (J). (ps-1). lib. bdg. 11.99 (*0-679-94365-X*, Random Hse. Bks. for Young Readers) Random Hse. Children's Bks.

—Thomas the Tank Engine & the Tractor. 1992. (Thomas the Tank Engine Little Pops Ser.). (Illus.). 12p. (J). (ps-1). 3.99 o.s.i (*0-679-83452-4*, Random Hse. Bks. for Young Readers) Random Hse. Children's Bks.

—The Thomas the Tank Engine Collector's Box, Set. 2003. (Illus.). 64p. (J). 39.95 (*0-375-82743-9*) Random Hse. Children's Bks.

—Thomas the Tank Engine Starter Library, 4 bks., Set. 1990. (Illus.). (J). (gr. 1-5). reprint ed. 19.95 o.s.i (*0-679-80792-6*, Random Hse. Bks. for Young Readers) Random Hse. Children's Bks.

—Thomas the Tank Engine Take-Along Library, 5 bks., Set. 1992. (Illus.). (J). (ps-3). 11.50 o.s.i (*0-679-83840-6*, Random Hse. Bks. for Young Readers) Random Hse. Children's Bks.

—Thomas the Tank Engine's Hidden Surprises. 1999. (Let's Go Lift & Peek Bks.). (Illus.). 14p. (J). (ps). bds. 4.99 (*0-679-89482-9*, Random Hse. Bks. for Young Readers) Random Hse. Children's Bks.

—Thomas the Tank Engine's Noisy Trip. 1989. (Chunky Book Ser.). (Illus.). 14p. bds. 3.99 (*0-679-80083-2*, Random Hse. Bks. for Young Readers) Random Hse. Children's Bks.

—Toby the Tram Engine. 1991. (Thomas the Tank Engine & Friends Ser.). (Illus.). 32p. (J). (ps-2). 3.50 o.s.i (*0-679-82095-7*, Random Hse. Bks. for Young Readers) Random Hse. Children's Bks.

—Toby the Tram Engine. 1985. (Railway Ser.). (Illus.). 64p. (J). (gr. k-2). reprint ed. 6.95 o.p. (*0-7182-0006-3*) Trafalgar Square.

—Tracking Thomas the Tank Engine & His Friends: A Book with Finger Tabs. 1992. (Illus.). 16p. (J). (ps-1). 8.99 o.s.i (*0-679-83458-3*, Random Hse. Bks. for Young Readers) Random Hse. Children's Bks.

—Trouble for Thomas & Other Stories. (Random House Picturebacks Ser.). (Illus.). 32p. (ps-3). 1989. pap. 3.25 (*0-679-80101-4*); 1991. 8.95 incl. audio (*0-679-80106-5*) Random Hse. Children's Bks. (Random Hse. Bks. for Young Readers).

Baldwin, Alec, contrib. by. Percy's Chocolate Crunch. 2004. (Thomas the Tank Engine Ser.). 24p. (J). pap. 8.95 incl. audio (*0-375-82724-2*, Golden Bks.) Random Hse. Children's Bks.

Bell, Owain. Stop, Train, Stop! A Thomas the Tank Engine Story. 1995. (J). (gr. 1 up). 11.99 o.s.i (*0-679-95806-1*); (Illus.). 48p. (ps-3). 8.99 (*0-679-85806-7*) Beginner Bks.

Borgo, Deborah C., illus. Thomas the Tank Engine Counts to Ten. 1991. (Thomas the Tank Engine Toddler Board Bks.). 14p. (J). (ps). 2.50 o.s.i (*0-679-81644-5*, Random Hse. Bks. for Young Readers) Random Hse. Children's Bks.

Catch Me Catch Me: A Thomas the Tank Engine Story. 2001. (First Readers Ser.: Vol. 2). (J). lib. bdg. (*1-59054-391-2*) Fitzgerald Bks.

Courtney, Richard. Thomas Tells a Lie. 2001. (Jellybean Bks.). (Illus.). 32p. (J). (ps-k). 3.99 o.s.i (*0-375-81306-3*, Random Hse. Bks. for Young Readers) Random Hse. Children's Bks.

Davies, Robin & Awdry, Wilbert V. Henry the Green Engine & the Tunnel. 1997. (My First Thomas Ser.). (Illus.). 16p. (J). (*0-434-80116-X*, Butterworth-Heinemann) Elsevier Science & Technology Bks.

Gerver, Jane E. A Crack in the Track: A Thomas the Tank Engine Story. 2001. (Beginner Bks.). (Illus.). 48p. (J). (ps-3). lib. bdg. 11.99 (*0-375-91246-0*, Random Hse. Bks. for Young Readers) Random Hse. Children's Bks.

Golden Books Staff. All Aboard! 2004. (Illus.). 32p. (J). pap. 4.99 (*0-375-82652-1*, Golden Bks.) Random Hse. Children's Bks.

—Count along with Thomas. 2000. (Thomas the Tank Engine Ser.). (ps-3). bds. 12.99 (*0-307-71308-3*, Golden Bks.) Random Hse. Children's Bks.

—One Stop Color & Match. 2004. (Illus.). 32p. (J). pap. 4.99 (*0-375-82653-X*, Golden Bks.) Random Hse. Children's Bks.

Mitton, David, et al, photos by. James in a Mess & Other Thomas the Tank Engine Stories. 1993. (Random House Picturebacks Ser.). (Illus.). 32p. (J). (ps-3). pap. 3.25 (*0-679-83895-3*, Random Hse. Bks. for Young Readers) Random Hse. Children's Bks.

Mitton, David & Permane, Terry, photos by. Edward's Exploit & Other Thomas the Tank Engine Stories. 1993. (Random House Picturebacks Ser.). (Illus.). 32p. (J). (ps-3). pap. 3.25 (*0-679-83896-1*, Random Hse. Bks. for Young Readers) Random Hse. Children's Bks.

—Thomas the Tank Engine Storybook. 1993. (Illus.). (J). 8.00 o.s.i (*0-679-84465-1*, Random Hse. Bks. for Young Readers) Random Hse. Children's Bks.

Random House Staff. Little Engines Can Do Big Things. 2000. (Thomas & the Magic Railroad Ser.). (Illus.). 24p. (J). (ps-1). pap. 3.25 (*0-375-80553-2*, Random Hse. Bks. for Young Readers) Random Hse. Children's Bks.

—Thomas the Tank Engine Coming & Going. 1997. (Board Bks.). (J). (ps). pap. 2.50 o.s.i (*0-679-88880-2*, Random Hse. Bks. for Young Readers) Random Hse. Children's Bks.

Surprise for Thomas. 2001. (Illus.). (J). 7.95 (*0-7853-4789-5*) Publications International, Ltd.

Thomas & Friends Picture Day. 2001. (Illus.). (J). 7.95 (*0-7853-4782-8*) Publications International, Ltd.

Thomas the Tank Engine & Friends. abr. ed. 1999. audio 7.50 (*1-86117-147-1*) Ulverscroft Audio (U.S.A.).

THOMAS, A BECKET, SAINT, 1118?-1170—FICTION

Willard, Barbara. If All the Swords in England. 2000. (Living History Library). (Illus.). x, 181p. (J). (gr. 8-12). reprint ed. pap. 12.95 (*1-883937-49-3*, 49-3) Bethlehem Bks.

THREE MUSKETEERS (FICTITIOUS CHARACTERS)—FICTION

Dumas, Alexandre. The Man in the Iron Mask. 1967. (Airmont Classics Ser.). (YA). (gr. 9 up). mass mkt. 2.75 o.p. (*0-8049-0150-3*, CL-150) Airmont Publishing Co., Inc.

—The Man in the Iron Mask. 1994. (Illustrated Classics Collection). 64p. pap. 3.60 o.p. (*1-56103-591-2*) American Guidance Service, Inc.

—The Man in the Iron Mask. Farr, Naunerle C., ed. 1978. (Now Age Illustrated IV Ser.). (Illus.). (J). (gr. 4-12). stu. ed. 1.25 (*0-88301-340-1*); text 7.50 o.p. (*0-88301-328-2*); pap. text 2.95 (*0-88301-316-9*) Pendulum Pr., Inc.

—The Man in the Iron Mask. 1998. (Bullseye Step into Classics Ser.). (Illus.). 128p. (J). (gr. 3-5). pap. 3.99 (*0-679-89433-0*, Random Hse. Bks. for Young Readers) Random Hse. Children's Bks.

—The Man in the Iron Mask. 1998. 11.04 (*0-606-13594-4*) Turtleback Bks.

—The Man in the Iron Mask Readalong. 1994. (Illustrated Classics Collection). 64p. pap. 14.95 incl. audio (*0-7854-0766-9*, 40505); pap. 13.50 o.p. incl. audio (*1-56103-593-9*) American Guidance Service, Inc.

—The Three Musketeers. 1966. (Airmont Classics Ser.). (YA). (gr. 8 up). mass mkt. 3.95 o.p. (*0-8049-0127-9*, CL-127) Airmont Publishing Co., Inc.

—The Three Musketeers. abr. ed. (Classics Illustrated Bks.). (J). audio 5.95. (Illus.). audio Audio Bk. Co.

—The Three Musketeers. 1993. (Junior Novelization Ser.). (Illus.). (J). (gr. 4-7). pap. 3.50 o.p. (*1-56282-590-9*) Disney Pr.

—The Three Musketeers. 2nd ed. 1998. (Illustrated Classic Book Ser.). (Illus.). 61p. (J). (gr. 3 up). reprint ed. pap. text 4.95 (*1-56767-251-5*) Educational Insights, Inc.

—The Three Musketeers. Bair, Lowell, tr. 1998. (Books of Wonder). (Illus.). 656p. (J). (gr. 4-7). 25.00 (*0-688-14583-3*, Morrow, William & Co.) Morrow/Avon.

—The Three Musketeers. (Classics Ser.). 56p. (J). text 3.50 (*0-7214-1753-1*, Ladybird Bks.) Penguin Group (USA) Inc.

—The Three Musketeers. 9999. (Children's Classics Ser.: No. 740-5). (Illus.). (J). (gr. 3-5). pap. 3.50 o.p. (0-7214-0633-5, Ladybird Bks.) Penguin Group (USA) Inc.

—The Three Musketeers. 1996. (Classic Ser.). (Illus.). 56p. (J). (gr. 2-4). 2.99 o.s.i (0-7214-5610-3, Ladybird Bks.) Penguin Group (USA) Inc.

—The Three Musketeers. (Illustrated Junior Library). (Illus.). (gr. 4-6). 1982. (J). 6.95 o.p. (0-448-11024-5, Grosset & Dunlap); 1953. 320p. (J). 16.99 (0-448-06024-8, Grosset & Dunlap); 1995. 464p. (YA). pap. 4.99 (0-14-036747-0, Puffin Bks.) Penguin Putnam Bks. for Young Readers.

—The Three Musketeers. Vogel, Malvina, ed. 1990. (Great Illustrated Classics Ser.: Vol. 15). (Illus.). 240p. (J). (ps up). 9.95 (0-86611-966-3) Playmore, Inc., Pubs.

—The Three Musketeers. Le Clercq, Jacques, tr. from ENG. 1999. (Modern Library Ser.). 624p. (gr. 4-11). 24.95 (0-679-60332-8) Random Hse., Inc.

—The Three Musketeers Readalong. 1994. (Illustrated Classics Collection). 64p. pap. 13.50 o.p. incl. audio (1-56103-511-4); pap. 14.95 incl. audio (0-7854-0691-3, 40423) American Guidance Service, Inc.

—Los Tres Mosqueteros. (SPA.). (J). 2.49 (968-890-125-3) Editorial Diana, S.A. MEX. Dist: Continental Bk. Co., Inc.

—Los Tres Mosqueteros. 2002. (Classics for Young Readers Ser.). (SPA.). (YA). 14.95 (84-392-0928-2, EV30622) Lectorum Pubns., Inc.

Ladybird Books Staff, ed. Three Musketeers. 1998. (Ladybird Picture Classics Ser.). (Illus.). 32p. (J). (gr. 2 up). pap. 4.99 o.p. (0-7214-7383-0, Ladybird Bks.) Penguin Group (USA) Inc.

Leitch, Michael & Dumas, Alexandre, contrib. by. The Three Musketeers. 2000. (Dorling Kindersley Classics Ser.). (Illus.). 64p. (J). (gr. 2-5). pap. 14.95 o.p. (0-7894-5456-4) Dorling Kindersley Publishing, Inc.

Mantell, Paul. The Man in the Iron Mask. 1998. (Bullseye Step into Classics Ser.). (J). 10.04 (0-606-13965-6) Turtleback Bks.

Storr, Catherine, as told by. The Three Musketeers. 1985. (Legends & Folktales Ser.). (Illus.). 32p. (J). (gr. k-5). pap. 9.27 o.p. (0-8172-2508-0); lib. bdg. 19.97 o.p. (0-8172-2500-5) Raintree Pubs.

Weiss, Jim, reader. Three Musketeers. (J). audio NewSound, LLC.

TINTIN (FICTITIOUS CHARACTER)—FICTION

Hergé. The Adventures of Tintin. 192p. (J). Vol. 1. 1994. (Adventures of Tintin Ser.: Vol. 1). (gr. 3-7). 17.95 (0-316-35940-8); Vol. 2. 1994. (gr. 4-7). 17.95 (0-316-35942-4); Vol. 3. 1994. (Adventures of Tintin Ser.: Vol. 3). (gr. 4-7). 17.95 (0-316-35944-0); Vol. 4. 1995. (Tintin Three-In-One Ser.: Vol. 1-). (Illus.). (ps-3). 17.95 (0-316-35814-2); Vol. 5. 1995. (Tintin Three-In-One Ser.: Vol. 1-). (Illus.). (gr. 4-7). 17.95 (0-316-35816-9); Vol. 6. 1997. (Tintin Ser.: Vol. 6). (gr. 3 up). 17.95 (0-316-35724-3); Vol. 7. 1997. (Tintin Ser.: Vol. 7). (gr. 4-7). 17.95 (0-316-35727-8) Little Brown & Co.

—L' Affaire Tournesol. 1999. (Tintin Ser.).Tr. of Calculus Affair. (FRE.). (gr. 4-7). 19.95 (2-203-00117-8) Casterman, Editions FRA. Dist: Distribooks, Inc.

—L' Affaire Tournesol.Tr. of Calculus Affair. (FRE., Illus.). (J). (gr. 7-9). lib. bdg. 19.95 o.p. (0-8288-6087-4, FC867) French & European Pubns., Inc.

—Les Bijoux de la Castafiore. 1999. (Tintin Ser.).Tr. of Castafiore Emerald. (FRE.). (gr. 4-7). 19.95 (2-203-00120-8) Casterman, Editions FRA. Dist: Distribooks, Inc.

—Les Bijoux de la Castafiore.Tr. of Castafiore Emerald. (FRE., Illus.). 62p. (J). (gr. 7-9). ring bd. 19.95 o.p. (0-8288-5011-9) French & European Pubns., Inc.

—The Black Island. (Illus.). 62p. (J). 19.95 (0-8288-5012-7); pap. 4.95 o.p. (0-416-24040-2) French & European Pubns., Inc.

—The Black Island. 1975. (Adventures of Tintin Ser.). 62p. (J). (gr. 4-7). pap. 9.99 (0-316-35835-5, Joy Street Bks.) Little Brown & Co.

—The Black Island. 1975. 27.71 (0-416-92640-1) Routledge.

—The Blue Lotus. (Illus.). (J). 19.95 (0-8288-5480-7) French & European Pubns., Inc.

—The Blue Lotus. (Adventures of Tintin Ser.). (Illus.). (J). 1992. 64p. 12.95 o.p. (0-316-35891-6); 1984. 62p. (gr. 2 up). pap. 9.99 (0-316-35856-8) Little Brown & Co. (Joy Street Bks.).

—The Broken Ear. (Illus.). 62p. (J). 24.95 (0-8288-5086-0); pap. 4.95 o.p. (0-416-57030-5) French & European Pubns., Inc.

—The Broken Ear. 1978. (Adventures of Tintin Ser.). 62p. (J). (gr. 2 up). pap. 9.99 (0-316-35850-9, Joy Street Bks.) Little Brown & Co.

—The Broken Ear. 1993. 27.71 (0-416-14872-7); 1985. 10.95 (0-416-83450-7) Routledge.

—The Calculus Affair. (Illus.). 62p. (J). 19.95 (0-8288-5014-3); pap. 4.95 o.p. (0-416-77390-7) French & European Pubns., Inc.

—The Calculus Affair. 1976. (Adventures of Tintin Ser.). 62p. (J). (gr. 2 up). pap. 9.99 (0-316-35847-9, Joy Street Bks.) Little Brown & Co.

—The Castafiore Emerald. (Illus.). 62p. (J). 19.95 (0-8288-5016-X); pap. 4.95 o.p. (0-416-77400-8) French & European Pubns., Inc.

—The Castafiore Emerald. 1975. (Adventures of Tintin Ser.). 62p. (J). (gr. 2 up). pap. 9.99 (0-316-35842-8, Joy Street Bks.) Little Brown & Co.

—Les Cigares du Pharaon. 1999. (Tintin Ser.).Tr. of Cigars of the Pharaoh. (FRE.). (gr. 4-7). 19.95 (2-203-00103-8) Casterman, Editions FRA. Dist: Distribooks, Inc.

—Les Cigares du Pharaon.Tr. of Cigars of the Pharaoh. (FRE.). (J). (gr. 7-9). ring bd. 19.95 o.p. (0-8288-5018-6); 1992. 64p. reprint ed. (0-7859-4560-1) French & European Pubns., Inc.

—Cigars of the Pharaoh.Tr. of Cigares du Pharoan. (Illus.). 62p. (J). 19.95 (0-8288-5021-6); pap. 4.95 o.p. (0-416-83610-0) French & European Pubns., Inc.

—Cigars of the Pharaoh. 1975. (Adventures of Tintin Ser.).Tr. of Cigares du Pharoan. 62p. (J). (gr. 2 up). pap. 9.99 (0-316-35836-3, Joy Street Bks.) Little Brown & Co.

—Coke en Stock. 1999. (Tintin Ser.). (FRE.). (gr. 4-7). 19.95 (2-203-00118-6) Casterman, Editions FRA. Dist: Distribooks, Inc.

—Coke en Stock. (FRE., Illus.). (J). (gr. 7-9). ring bd. 19.95 o.p. (0-8288-5022-4); 1992. 64p. reprint ed. (0-7859-4563-6) French & European Pubns., Inc.

—The Crab with the Golden Claws. (Illus.). 62p. (J). (gr. 3-8). 19.95 (0-8288-5023-2); pap. 4.95 o.p. (0-416-24050-X) French & European Pubns., Inc.

—The Crab with the Golden Claws. 1974. (Adventures of Tintin Ser.). (Illus.). 62p. (J). (gr. 2 up). reprint ed. pap. 9.99 (0-316-35833-9, Joy Street Bks.) Little Brown & Co.

—The Crab with the Golden Claws. 1986. 7.95 (0-416-60500-1) Routledge.

—Le Crabe aux Pinces d'Or. 1999. (Tintin Ser.).Tr. of Crab with the Golden Claws. (FRE.). (gr. 4-7). 19.95 (2-203-00108-9) Casterman, Editions FRA. Dist: Distribooks, Inc.

—Le Crabe aux Pinces d'Or.Tr. of Crab with the Golden Claws. (FRE., Illus.). (J). 62p. 19.95 o.p. (0-8288-5024-0); (gr. 7-9). ring bd. 19.95 (0-8288-5025-9); 1992. 64p. reprint ed. 19.95 (0-7859-4561-X) French & European Pubns., Inc.

—Destination Moon.Tr. of Objectif Lune. (J). (gr. 3-8). ring bd. 19.95 (0-8288-5026-7); (Illus.). 62p. 19.95 (0-8288-5027-5); (Illus.). 62p. pap. 4.95 o.p. (0-416-80030-0) French & European Pubns., Inc.

—Destination Moon. 1976. (Adventures of Tintin Ser.).Tr. of Objectif Lune. 62p. (J). (gr. 2 up). pap. 9.99 (0-316-35845-2, Joy Street Bks.) Little Brown & Co.

—Destination Moon. 1940. Tr. of Objectif Lune. 27.71 (0-416-92550-2) Routledge.

—L' Etoile Mysterieuse. 1999. (Tintin Ser.).Tr. of Mysterious Star. (FRE.). (gr. 4-7). 19.95 (2-203-00109-7) Casterman, Editions FRA. Dist: Distribooks, Inc.

—Explorers on the Moon. 1970. Tr. of On a Marche Sur la Lune. (J). (gr. 3-8). 19.95 o.p. (0-8288-5032-1) French & European Pubns., Inc.

—Explorers on the Moon. (Pop-up Book Ser.).Tr. of On a Marche Sur la Lune. (J). 1992. (Illus.). 24p. (ps-3). 16.95 o.p. (0-316-35860-6, Joy Street Bks.); 1976. 62p. (gr. 2 up). pap. 9.99 (0-316-35846-0) Little Brown & Co.

—Explorers on the Moon. 1986. Tr. of On a Marche Sur la Lune. 7.95 (0-416-92560-X) Routledge.

—Flight 714. (Illus.). 62p. (J). 19.95 (0-8288-5034-8); pap. 4.95 o.p. (0-416-77420-2) French & European Pubns., Inc.

—Flight 714. 1975. (Adventures of Tintin Ser.). 62p. (J). (gr. 2 up). pap. 9.95 (0-316-35837-1, Joy Street Bks.) Little Brown & Co.

—L' Ile Noire. 1999. (Tintin Ser.).Tr. of Black Island. (FRE.). (gr. 4-7). 19.95 (2-203-00106-2) Casterman, Editions FRA. Dist: Distribooks, Inc.

—L' Ile Noire.Tr. of Black Island. (FRE., Illus.). (J). (gr. 7-9). ring bd. 19.95 (0-8288-5039-9) French & European Pubns., Inc.

—King Ottokar's Sceptre. Orig. Title: Sceptre d'Ottokar. (Illus.). 62p. (J). 19.95 (0-8288-5044-5); pap. 4.95 o.p. (0-416-24060-7) French & European Pubns., Inc.

—King Ottokar's Sceptre. 1974. (Adventures of Tintin Ser.). Orig. Title: Sceptre d'Ottokar. (Illus.). 62p. (J). (gr. 2 up). pap. 9.95 (0-316-35831-2, Joy Street Bks.) Little Brown & Co.

—Land of Black Gold. Orig. Title: Tintin au Pays de l'Or Noir. (Illus.). 62p. (J). 19.95 (0-8288-5048-8); pap. 4.95 o.p. (0-416-83620-8) French & European Pubns., Inc.

—Land of Black Gold. 1975. (Adventures of Tintin Ser.). Orig. Title: Tintin au Pays de l'Or Noir. (Illus.). 62p. (J). (gr. 2 up). pap. 9.99 (0-316-35844-4, Joy Street Bks.) Little Brown & Co.

—El Loto Azul.Tr. of Blue Lotus. (SPA., Illus.). 62p. (J). 19.95 (0-8288-5049-6) French & European Pubns., Inc.

—El Loto Azul. (Tintin Ser.).Tr. of Blue Lotus. (SPA.). 64p. (J). 14.95 (84-261-1418-0) Juventud, Editorial ESP. Dist: Distribooks, Inc.

—Le Lotus Bleu. 1999. (Tintin Ser.).Tr. of Blue Lotus. (FRE.). (gr. 4-7). 19.95 (2-203-00104-6) Casterman, Editions FRA. Dist: Distribooks, Inc.

—Le Lotus Bleu.Tr. of Blue Lotus. (FRE.). (J). (gr. 2-9). 19.95 (0-8288-5050-X) French & European Pubns., Inc.

—Objectif Lune. 1999. (Tintin Ser.).Tr. of Destination Moon. (FRE.). (gr. 4-7). 19.95 (2-203-00115-1) Casterman, Editions FRA. Dist: Distribooks, Inc.

—Objectif Lune.Tr. of Destination Moon. (FRE., Illus.). (J). (gr. 7-9). ring bd. 19.95 (0-8288-5051-8) French & European Pubns., Inc.

—On a Marche sur la Lune. (Tintin Ser.).Tr. of Explorers on the Moon. (FRE.). (J). pap. 19.95 (2-203-00116-X) Casterman, Editions FRA. Dist: Distribooks, Inc.

—On a Marche sur la Lune.Tr. of Explorers on the Moon. (FRE., Illus.). (J). (gr. 7-9). ring bd. 19.95 (0-8288-5053-4) French & European Pubns., Inc.

—L' Oreille Cassee. 1999. (Tintin Ser.).Tr. of Broken Ear. (FRE.). (gr. 4-7). 19.95 (2-203-00105-4) Casterman, Editions FRA. Dist: Distribooks, Inc.

—L' Oreille Cassee.Tr. of Broken Ear. (FRE., Illus.). 62p. (J). 19.95 (0-8288-5054-2) French & European Pubns., Inc.

—Prisoners of the Sun. (Illus.). 62p. (J). 24.95 (0-8288-5056-9); pap. 4.95 o.p. (0-416-77410-5) French & European Pubns., Inc.

—Prisoners of the Sun. 1975. (Adventures of Tintin Ser.). 62p. (J). (gr. 2 up). pap. 9.99 (0-316-35843-6, Joy Street Bks.) Little Brown & Co.

—Prisoners of the Sun. 1986. (J). 1.00 (0-416-92620-7) Routledge.

—Red Rackham's Treasure. Orig. Title: Tresor de Rackham le Rouge. (Illus.). 62p. (J). 24.95 (0-8288-5057-7); pap. 4.95 o.p. (0-416-80010-6) French & European Pubns., Inc.

—Red Rackham's Treasure. (Adventures of Tintin Ser.). Orig. Title: Tresor de Rackham le Rouge. (Illus.). (J). 1992. 64p. 12.95 o.p. (0-316-35893-2); 1974. 62p. (gr. 2 up). reprint ed. pap. 9.99 (0-316-35834-7) Little Brown & Co. (Joy Street Bks.).

—Red Rackham's Treasure. 1984. Orig. Title: Tresor de Rackham le Rouge. 24.95 (0-416-92540-5) Routledge.

—The Red Sea Sharks. (Illus.). (J). 62p. 15.95 o.p. (0-416-60570-2); 62p. pap. 4.95 o.p. (0-416-24070-4); (gr. 3-8). 24.95 (0-8288-5058-5) French & European Pubns., Inc.

—The Red Sea Sharks. 1976. (Adventures of Tintin Ser.). 62p. (J). (gr. 2 up). pap. 9.99 (0-316-35848-7, Joy Street Bks.) Little Brown & Co.

—Le Sceptre d'Ottokar. 1999. (Tintin Ser.).Tr. of King Ottokar's Sceptre. (FRE.). (gr. 4-7). 19.95 (2-203-00107-0) Casterman, Editions FRA. Dist: Distribooks, Inc.

—Secret de la Licorne.Tr. of Secret of the Unicorn. (FRE., Illus.). (J). (gr. 7-9). 24.95 (0-8288-5065-8) French & European Pubns., Inc.

—La Secret de la Licorne. 1999. (Tintin Ser.).Tr. of Secret of the Unicorn. (FRE.). (gr. 4-7). 19.95 (2-203-00110-0) Casterman, Editions FRA. Dist: Distribooks, Inc.

—The Secret of the Unicorn. Orig. Title: Secret de la Licorne. (Illus.). 62p. (J). 24.95 (0-8288-5066-6); pap. 4.95 o.p. (0-416-80020-3) French & European Pubns., Inc.

—The Secret of the Unicorn. (Adventures of Tintin Ser.). Orig. Title: Secret de la Licorne. (Illus.). (J). 1992. 64p. 12.95 o.p. (0-316-35902-5); 1974. 62p. (gr. 2 up). reprint ed. pap. 9.99 (0-316-35832-0) Little Brown & Co. (Joy Street Bks.).

—Sept Boules de Cristal. (FRE., Illus.). (J). (gr. 7-9). 24.95 (0-8288-5069-0) French & European Pubns., Inc.

—Les Sept Boules de Cristal. 1999. (Tintin Ser.). (FRE.). (gr. 4-7). 19.95 (2-203-00112-7) Casterman, Editions FRA. Dist: Distribooks, Inc.

—The Seven Crystal Balls. (Illus.). 62p. (J). (gr. 3-8). 24.95 (0-8288-5071-2); pap. 4.95 o.p. (0-416-78000-8) French & European Pubns., Inc.

—The Seven Crystal Balls. 1975. (Adventures of Tintin Ser.). (Illus.). 62p. (J). (gr. 2 up). pap. 9.99 (0-316-35840-1, Joy Street Bks.) Little Brown & Co.

—The Shooting Star. (Illus.). (J). 62p. 15.95 o.p. (0-416-60580-X); 62p. pap. 4.95 o.p. (0-416-24080-1); (gr. 3-8). ring bd. 24.95 (0-8288-5073-9) French & European Pubns., Inc.

—The Shooting Star. 1978. (Adventures of Tintin Ser.). 62p. (J). (gr. 2 up). pap. 9.99 (0-316-35851-7, Joy Street Bks.) Little Brown & Co.

—Six Adventures of Tintin, Vol. 1. unabr. ed. 1999. (J). (gr. 1-8). audio 23.00 BBC Audiobooks America.

—Six Adventures of Tintin, Vol. 1. unabr. ed. (gr. 4-7). 2000. (YA). audio 18.00 (0-8072-8103-4, YA999CXR); 1999. (J). audio 23.00 (0-8072-8087-9, YA999CX) Random Hse. Audio Publishing Group. (Listening Library).

—Le Temple du Soleil. 1999. (Tintin Ser.). (FRE.). (gr. 4-7). 19.95 (2-203-00113-5) Casterman, Editions FRA. Dist: Distribooks, Inc.

—The Tintin Adventure Series. 1991. (Illus.). (J). pap. 222.60 o.s.i (0-316-35859-2) Little Brown & Co.

—Tintin & the Golden Fleece. (J). (gr. 3-8). 24.95 (0-8288-5087-9) French & European Pubns., Inc.

—Tintin & the Lake of Sharks. (Illus.). 62p. (J). 24.95 (0-416-78950-1); pap. 4.95 o.p. (0-8288-5088-7) French & European Pubns., Inc.

—Tintin & the Picaros. Orig. Title: Tintin et les Picaros. (Illus.). 62p. (J). 24.95 (0-8288-5089-5); pap. 4.95 o.p. (0-416-57990-6) French & European Pubns., Inc.

—Tintin & the Picaros. 1978. (Adventures of Tintin Ser.). Orig. Title: Tintin et les Picaros. 62p. (J). (gr. 2 up). pap. 9.99 (0-316-35849-5, Joy Street Bks.) Little Brown & Co.

—Tintin au Congo. 1999. (Tintin Ser.). (FRE.). (gr. 4-7). 19.95 (2-203-00101-1) Casterman, Editions FRA. Dist: Distribooks, Inc.

—Tintin au Congo. (FRE., Illus.). (J). (gr. 7-9). 24.95 (0-8288-5090-9) French & European Pubns., Inc.

—Tintin au Pays de l'Or Noir. 1999. (Tintin Ser.).Tr. of Land of Black Gold. (FRE.). (gr. 4-7). 19.95 (2-203-00114-3) Casterman, Editions FRA. Dist: Distribooks, Inc.

—Tintin au Pays de l'Or Noir.Tr. of Land of Black Gold. (FRE.). (J). (gr. 7-9). 24.95 (0-8288-5091-7) French & European Pubns., Inc.

—Tintin au Pays des Soviets. 1999. (Tintin Ser.). (FRE.). (gr. 4-7). 19.95 (2-203-01101-7) Midwest European Pubns.

—Tintin au Tibet. 1999. (Tintin Ser.).Tr. of Tintin in Tibet. (FRE.). (gr. 4-7). 19.95 (2-203-00119-4) Casterman, Editions FRA. Dist: Distribooks, Inc.

—Tintin au Tibet.Tr. of Tintin in Tibet. (J). (gr. 7-9). ring bd. 24.95 (0-8288-5092-5) French & European Pubns., Inc.

—Tintin en Amerique. 1999. (Tintin Ser.). Orig. Title: Tintin in America. (FRE.). (gr. 4-7). 19.95 (2-203-00102-X) Casterman, Editions FRA. Dist: Distribooks, Inc.

—Tintin en Amerique. Orig. Title: Tintin in America. (Illus.). 62p. (J). (SPA.). 24.95 (0-8288-5094-1); (FRE., 24.95 (0-8288-5093-3) French & European Pubns., Inc.

—Tintin en Amerique. (Tintin Ser.). Orig. Title: Tintin in America. (SPA.). 64p. (J). 14.95 (84-261-1400-8) Juventud, Editorial ESP. Dist: Distribooks, Inc.

—Tintin en el Congo. (SPA., Illus.). 62p. (J). 24.95 (0-8288-5095-X) French & European Pubns., Inc.

—Tintin en el Congo. (Tintin Ser.). (SPA.). 64p. (J). 14.95 (84-261-1401-6) Juventud, Editorial ESP. Dist: Distribooks, Inc.

—Tintin en el Pais del Oro Negro.Tr. of Land of Black Gold. (SPA., Illus.). 62p. (J). 24.95 (0-8288-4995-1) French & European Pubns., Inc.

—Tintin en Tibet. (SPA., Illus.). 62p. (J). 24.95 (0-8288-4996-X) French & European Pubns., Inc.

—Tintin en Tibet. (Tintin Ser.). (SPA.). 64p. (J). 14.95 (84-261-1403-2) Juventud, Editorial ESP. Dist: Distribooks, Inc.

—Tintin et les Picaros. 1999. (Tintin Ser.).Tr. of Tintin & the Picaros. (FRE.). (gr. 4-7). 19.95 (2-203-00123-2) Casterman, Editions FRA. Dist: Distribooks, Inc.

—Tintin et les Picaros.Tr. of Tintin & the Picaros. (FRE., Illus.). 62p. (J). 24.95 (0-8288-4997-8) French & European Pubns., Inc.

—Tintin Games Book, Vol. 1. 1990. (J). pap. 6.95 o.p. (0-316-35858-4) Little Brown & Co.

—Tintin im Amerika.Tr. of Tintin in America. (GER., Illus.). 62p. (J). pap. 24.95 (0-8288-4999-4) French & European Pubns., Inc.

—Tintin im Kongo. (GER., Illus.). 62p. (J). pap. 24.95 (0-8288-4998-6) French & European Pubns., Inc.

—Tintin in America. Orig. Title: Tintin en Amerique. (Illus.). 62p. (J). 24.95 (0-8288-5000-3) French & European Pubns., Inc.

—Tintin in America. 1979. (Adventures of Tintin Ser.). Orig. Title: Tintin en Amerique. 62p. (J). (gr. 2 up). pap. 9.99 (0-316-35852-5) Little Brown & Co.

—Tintin in the Land of the Soviets. 1992. 116p. (J). 39.95 (0-7859-0978-8, 2203020016) French & European Pubns., Inc.

—Tintin in the Land of the Soviets. fac. ed. 2003. 128p. (J). reprint ed. 19.95 (0-86719-903-2) Last Gasp Eco-Funnies, Inc.

—Tintin in Tibet. Orig. Title: Tintin au Tibet. (Illus.). 62p. (J). 24.95 (0-8288-5001-1); pap. 4.95 o.p. (0-416-24090-9) French & European Pubns., Inc.

—Tintin in Tibet. (Adventures of Tintin Ser.). Orig. Title: Tintin au Tibet. (J). 1992. (Illus.). 64p. 12.95 o.p. (*0-316-35863-0*); 1975. 62p. (gr. 2 up). pap. 9.99 (*0-316-35839-8*) Little Brown & Co. (Joy Street Bks.).

—Tintin y los Picaros. (SPA., Illus.). 62p. (J). 24.95 (*0-8288-5002-X*) French & European Pubns., Inc.

—Tintin y los Picaros. (Tintin Ser.). (SPA.). 64p. (J). 14.95 (*84-261-1389-3*) Juventud, Editorial ESP. *Dist:* Distribooks, Inc.

—Tresor de Rackham le Rouge.Tr. of Red Rackham's Treasure. (FRE., Illus.). 62p. (J). (gr. 7-9). 24.95 (*0-8288-5003-8*) French & European Pubns., Inc.

TRANSFORMERS (FICTITIOUS CHARACTERS)—FICTION

Autobots' Advantage. 1993. (Transformers Generation Two Coloring & Activity Bks.). (Illus.). 32p. (Orig.). (J). (gr. 1-3). pap. 1.29 o.s.i (*1-56144-342-5*, Honey Bear Bks.) Modern Publishing.

Autobots on Patrol. 1993. (Transformers Generation Two Flip 'n' Fun Activity Pads Ser.). (Illus.). 80p. (Orig.). (J). (gr. 1-3). pap. 2.95 o.s.i (*1-56144-347-6*, Honey Bear Bks.) Modern Publishing.

Beach, Lynn. Attack of the Insecticons. 1985. (Transformers Find Your Fate Junior Ser.: No. 3). 80p. (Orig.). (J). (gr. 4 up). pap. 1.95 o.p. (*0-345-32671-7*) Ballantine Bks.

Casey, Todd. Dinobots Strike Back. (Transformers Find Your Fate Junior Ser.: No. 1). 80p. (J). (gr. 4 up). 1986. pap. 2.50 o.s.i (*0-345-34150-3*); 1985. pap. 1.95 o.p. (*0-345-32669-5*) Ballantine Bks.

Crown. The Battle for Cybertron. 1986. (Transformers Coloring & Activity Bks.). 32p. (J). (gr. k up). 1.50 o.s.i (*0-517-55511-5*, Random Hse. Bks. for Young Readers) Random Hse. Children's Bks.

Decepticon Danger. 1993. (Transformers Generation Two Coloring & Activity Bks.). (Illus.). 32p. (Orig.). (J). (gr. 1-3). pap. 1.29 o.s.i (*1-56144-343-3*, Honey Bear Bks.) Modern Publishing.

Decepticon Madness. 1993. (Transformers Generation Two Flip 'n' Fun Activity Pads Ser.). (Illus.). 80p. (Orig.). (J). (gr. 1-3). pap. 2.95 o.s.i (*1-56144-346-8*, Honey Bear Bks.) Modern Publishing.

Dinobots vs. Constructicons. 1993. (Transformers Generation Two Coloring & Activity Bks.). (Illus.). 32p. (Orig.). (J). (gr. 1-3). pap. 1.29 o.s.i (*1-56144-344-1*, Honey Bear Bks.) Modern Publishing.

Matthews, Ann. Earthquake. 1986. (Transformers Find Your Fate Junior Ser.: No. 4). (Orig.). (J). (gr. 4 up). pap. 2.50 o.s.i (*0-345-33071-4*) Ballantine Bks.

Outlet Book Company Staff. Decepticon Patrol. 1985. (Transformers Coloring & Activity Bks.). (Illus.). 48p. (J). 0.50 o.p. (*0-517-55642-1*) Random Hse. Value Publishing.

—The Great Car Rally. 1986. (Transformers Ser.). (Illus.). 32p. (J). 0.79 o.p. (*0-517-55512-3*) Random Hse. Value Publishing.

Razzi, Jim. Desert Flight. 1986. (Transformers Find Your Fate Junior Ser.: No. 5). (Orig.). (J). (gr. 4 up). pap. 2.50 o.p. (*0-345-33072-2*) Ballantine Bks.

Reader's Digest Editors. The Autobots Strike Back. 2004. (Transformers Armada Chapter Bks.: No. 4). (Illus.). 64p. (J). pap. 3.99 (*0-7944-0382-4*, Reader's Digest Children's Bks.) Reader's Digest Children's Publishing, Inc.

Search & Rescue Mission. 1993. (Transformers Generation Two Coloring & Activity Bks.). (Illus.). 32p. (Orig.). (J). (gr. 1-3). pap. 1.29 o.s.i (*1-56144-345-X*, Honey Bear Bks.) Modern Publishing.

Siegel, Barbara & Siegel, Scott. Battle Drive. 1985. (Transformers Find Your Fate Junior Ser.: No. 2). 80p. (Orig.). (J). (gr. 4 up). pap. 1.95 o.p. (*0-345-32670-9*) Ballantine Bks.

Stamper, Judith Bauer. Autobot Alert! 1986. (Transformers Find Your Fate Junior Ser.: No. 7). (Orig.). (J). (gr. 4 up). pap. 2.50 o.p. (*0-345-33388-8*) Ballantine Bks.

—Decepticon Poison. 1986. (Transformers Find Your Fate Junior Ser.: No. 6). (Orig.). (J). (gr. 4 up). pap. 2.50 o.p. (*0-345-33073-0*) Ballantine Bks.

Transformers Autobots. 1986. (Illus.). (J). pap. 1.25 o.s.i (*0-440-82076-6*) Dell Publishing.

Transformers Project BR. 1986. (Illus.). (J). pap. 1.25 o.s.i (*0-440-82136-3*) Dell Publishing.

TROI, DEANNA (FICTITIOUS CHARACTER)—FICTION

Vornholt, John. First Contact. 1996. (Star Trek Ser.: No. 8). (J). (ps-3). 10.04 (*0-606-11883-7*) Turtleback Bks.

Vornholt, John, et al. First Contact. 1996. (Star Trek Ser.: No. 8). (Illus.). 128p. (J). (gr. 8 up). per. 3.99 (*0-671-00128-0*, Aladdin) Simon & Schuster Children's Publishing.

Weiss, Bobbi J. G. & Weiss, David Cody. Breakaway. 1997. (Star Trek Ser.: No. 12). (Illus.). 128p. (J). (gr. 3-6). per. 3.99 (*0-671-00226-0*, Aladdin) Simon & Schuster Children's Publishing.

—Breakaway. 1997. (Star Trek, The Next Generation: No. 12). (J). (gr. 3-6). 10.04 (*0-606-11902-7*) Turtleback Bks.

TUBMAN, HARRIET, 1820?-1913—FICTION

Childress, Alice. When the Rattlesnake Sounds: A Play about Harriet Tubman. 1975. (Illus.). 32p. (J). (gr. 7-11). 6.95 o.p. (*0-698-20342-9*) Putnam Publishing Group, The.

Hedstrom, Deborah. From Settlement to City with Benjamin Franklin. 1997. (My American Journey Ser.). (Illus.). 19.99 o.p. (*1-57673-164-2*) Multnomah Pubs., Inc.

Lawrence. Harriet & the Promise Land. 1998. (J). pap. 5.99 (*0-87628-392-X*) Ctr. for Applied Research in Education, The.

Ringgold, Faith. Aunt Harriet's Underground Railroad in the Sky. 1995. (Illus.). 32p. (ps-3). pap. 6.99 (*0-517-88543-3*) Crown Publishing Group.

—Aunt Harriet's Underground Railroad in the Sky. 1992. (Illus.). 32p. (J). (ps-3). lib. bdg. 17.99 o.s.i (*0-517-58768-8*); 16.00 o.s.i (*0-517-58767-X*) Random Hse. Children's Bks. (Random Hse. Bks. for Young Readers).

—Aunt Harriet's Underground Railroad in the Sky. 1995. (J). 13.14 (*0-606-08478-9*) Turtleback Bks.

TUROK (FICTITIOUS CHARACTER)—FICTION

Teitelbaum, Michael. Arena of Doom: Turok, No. 3. 1998. (Turok Ser.: Vol. 3). 176p. (YA). (gr. 7-12). pap. 3.99 o.s.i (*0-307-16282-6*, Golden Bks.) Random Hse. Children's Bks.

—Path of Destruction: Turok, No. 4. 1998. (Turok Ser.: Vol. 4). 176p. (YA). (gr. 7-12). pap. 3.99 o.s.i (*0-307-16283-4*, Golden Bks.) Random Hse. Children's Bks.

—Seeds of Evil. 1998. (Turok Ser.: Vol. 2). 176p. (YA). (gr. 7-12). pap. 3.99 o.s.i (*0-307-16281-8*, 16281, Golden Bks.) Random Hse. Children's Bks.

—Way of the Warrior. 1998. (Turok Ser.: Vol. 1). 176p. (YA). (gr. 7-12). pap. 3.99 o.s.i (*0-307-16280-X*, 16280, Golden Bks.) Random Hse. Children's Bks.

TWAIN, MARK, 1835-1910—FICTION

Lasky, Kathryn. Alice Rose & Sam. 1999. 208p. (J). (gr. 3-7). pap. 5.99 (*0-7868-1222-2*) Disney Pr.

—Alice Rose & Sam. 1998. (Illus.). 208p. (J). (gr. 3-7). 15.95 (*0-7868-0336-3*); lib. bdg. 16.49 (*0-7868-2277-5*) Hyperion Bks. for Children.

—Alice Rose & Sam. 1999. 12.04 (*0-606-17380-3*) Turtleback Bks.

Miller, Albert G. Mark Twain in Love. 1973. (J). (gr. 7 up). 5.95 o.p. (*0-15-230295-6*) Harcourt Children's Bks.

Quackenbush, Robert. Mark Twain? What Kind of Name Is That? A Story of Samuel Langhorne Clemens. 1984. (Illus.). 32p. (J). (gr. 1-5). 10.95 o.s.i (*0-13-557000-X*) Prentice Hall PTR.

Sargent, Dave & Sargent, Pat. Charcoal (Charcoal Grey) Be Decisive #13. 2001. (Saddle Up Ser.). 36p. (J). pap. 6.95 (*1-56763-606-3*); lib. bdg. 22.60 (*1-56763-605-5*) Ozark Publishing.

V

VAN WINKLE, RIP (FICTITIOUS CHARACTER)—FICTION

Irving, Washington. Rip Van Winkle. (J). audio Audio Bk. Co.

—Rip Van Winkle. 1993. (Illus.). 64p. (YA). (gr. 4-7). 21.95 (*1-56846-082-1*, Creative Editions); 62p. (J). lib. bdg. 17.95 o.p. (*0-88682-631-4*, Creative Education) Creative Co., The.

—Rip Van Winkle. 1995. (Illus.). 64p. (J). 21.95 o.p. (*0-15-200927-2*) Harcourt Trade Pubs.

—Rip Van Winkle. (Books of Wonder). (Illus.). (J). 1987. 104p. (gr. 2 up). 22.95 (*0-688-07459-6*); 1967. (gr. 4-6). o.p. (*0-397-30981-3*) HarperCollins Children's Bk. Group.

—Rip Van Winkle. (Illus.). (J). (ps-3). 1991. mass mkt. 5.95 (*0-316-37584-5*); 1988. 14.95 o.p. (*0-316-37578-0*) Little Brown & Co.

—Rip Van Winkle. 2000. (Books of Wonder). (Illus.). 109p. (J). 19.95 (*1-58717-039-6*) North-South Bks., Inc.

—Rip Van Winkle. (Illus.). (J). 1999. 48p. (ps-3). 16.99 (*0-399-23152-8*); 1992. 128p. (gr. 1). 19.00 o.p. (*0-8037-1264-2*, Dial Bks. for Young Readers) Penguin Putnam Bks. for Young Readers.

—Rip Van Winkle. 1979. audio Random Hse. Audio Publishing Group.

—Rip Van Winkle. 1967. (Peter Possum Paperbacks Ser.). (J). pap. 0.95 o.p. (*0-531-05127-7*, Watts, Franklin) Scholastic Library Publishing.

—Rip Van Winkle. Saunders, Sandra, ed. 9999. (Illus.). 80p. (J). (gr. 4-7). pap. 1.95 o.p. (*0-590-40110-6*) Scholastic, Inc.

—Rip Van Winkle. (J). audio 10.95 (*0-8045-0997-2*, SAC 7023) Spoken Arts, Inc.

—Rip Van Winkle. 1984. (Story Clippers Ser.). (Illus.). 32p. (J). (gr. k-5). lib. bdg. 19.97 o.p. (*0-8172-2108-5*) Raintree Pubs.

—Rip Van Winkle. 1988. (Illus.). 32p. (J). (ps up). 15.89 o.p. (*0-8037-0521-2*, Dial Bks. for Young Readers) Penguin Putnam Bks. for Young Readers.

—Rip Van Winkle. 1988. (Derrydale Fairytale Library). (Illus.). (J). (ps-3). 2.99 o.s.i (*0-517-28806-0*) Random Hse. Value Publishing.

—Rip Van Winkle. abr. ed. (J). audio 12.95 (*0-89926-131-0*, 819) Audio Bk. Co.

—Rip Van Winkle. abr. ed. 1970. (J). audio 11.00 o.s.i (*0-694-50673-7*, CDL5 1241, Caedmon) HarperTrade.

—Rip Van Winkle. adapted ed. 1995. (Illus.). 40p. (J). (gr. k-3). 19.95 o.p. incl. audio (*0-689-80193-9*, Simon & Schuster Children's Publishing) Simon & Schuster Children's Publishing.

—Rip Van Winkle: The Mountain Top Edition. Oakes, Donald T., ed. rev. ed. 1989. (Illus.). 92p. (J). (gr. 9). pap. (*0-9624216-0-X*) Mountain Top Historical Society, Inc.

—Rip Van Winkle & Other Stories. 1996. (Illus.). 192p. (YA). (gr. 7 up). pap. 5.99 (*0-14-036771-3*); 1987. 160p. (J). pap. 3.50 o.p. (*0-14-035051-9*) Penguin Putnam Bks. for Young Readers. (Puffin Bks.).

—Rip Van Winkle & the Legend of Sleepy Hollow. unabr. ed. 1986. (J). audio 20.95 (*1-55685-066-2*) Audio Bk. Contractors, Inc.

—Rip Van Winkle & the Legend of Sleepy Hollow. unabr. ed. 1990. audio 17.95 (*0-7861-0204-7*, 1179) Blackstone Audio Bks., Inc.

—Rip Van Winkle & the Legend of Sleepy Hollow. 1967. (Companion Library Ser.). (Illus.). (J). (gr. 6 up). 2.95 o.p. (*0-448-05482-5*) Putnam Publishing Group, The.

—Rip Van Winkle & the Legend of Sleepy Hollow. unabr. ed. (J). 1999. (gr. 4). audio 18.00 (*1-55690-915-2*, 93411E7); 1997. (gr. 2). audio 3.00 o.p. (*1-55690-445-2*, T81100G) Recorded Bks., LLC.

—Rip Van Winkle Coloring Book. 1983. (Illus.). (J). pap. 2.95 (*0-486-24479-2*) Dover Pubns., Inc.

—Wake up, Rip Van Winkle. 1993. (Steck-Vaughn Point of View Stories Ser.). 48p. (J). (gr. 4-7). pap. 4.95 (*0-8114-2222-4*) Raintree Pubs.

Irving, Washington & Busch, Jeffrey. Rip Van Winkle. (Classics Illustrated Ser.). (Illus.). 52p. (YA). pap. 4.95 (*1-57209-009-X*) Classics International Entertainment, Inc.

Littledale, Freya & Irving, Washington. Rip Van Winkle. 1991. (Illus.). 40p. (J). (gr. 1-4). mass mkt. 3.95 o.p. (*0-590-43113-7*) Scholastic, Inc.

Storr, Catherine. Rip Van Winkle. 1995. (J). (gr. 4-7). pap. 4.95 o.p. (*0-8114-8354-1*) Raintree Pubs.

VELAZQUEZ, DIEGO RODRIQUEZ DE SILVA Y, 1599-1660—FICTION

de Trevino, Elizabeth Borton. I, Juan de Pareja, RS. 1987. (Sunburst Ser.). 192p. (YA). (gr. 3-7). pap. 5.95 (*0-374-43525-1*, Sunburst) Farrar, Straus & Giroux.

de Trevino, Elizabeth Borton, et al. I, Juan De Pareja, RS. 1965. (Sunburst Ser.). 192p. (YA). (ps-3). 17.00 (*0-374-33531-1*, Farrar, Straus & Giroux (BYR)) Farrar, Straus & Giroux.

I, Juan de Pareja. 3rd ed. (J). pap. text, stu. ed. (*0-13-667452-6*) Prentice Hall (Schl. Div.).

Johnson, Jane. The Princess & the Painter, RS. 1994. 32p. (J). (ps-3). 15.00 o.p. (*0-374-36118-5*, Farrar, Straus & Giroux (BYR)) Farrar, Straus & Giroux.

W

WALLACE AND GROMIT (FICTITIOUS CHARACTERS)—FICTION

Davies, Tristan. Anoraknophobia. 1999. (Illus.). 48p. (J). pap. 8.95 (*0-340-72834-5*) Hodder & Stoughton, Ltd. GBR. *Dist:* Lubrecht & Cramer, Ltd., Trafalgar Square.

—Wallace & Gromit: The Lost Slipper & The Curse of the Ramsbottoms. 1997. (Wallace & Gromit Comic Strip Bks.). (Illus.). 44p. (J). 5.95 (*0-8417-2026-6*) Adler's Foreign Bks., Inc.

—Wallace & Gromit: The Lost Slipper & The Curse of the Ramsbottoms. 1998. (Wallace & Gromit Comic Strip Bks.). (J). (ps-3). pap. text 9.95 (*0-8417-3035-0*) Adventure Medical Kits.

Davies, Tristan & Newman, Nick. The Lost Slipper. abr. ed. 2000. pap. 10.95 incl. audio (*1-85998-903-9*) Hodder Headline Audiobooks GBR. *Dist:* Ulverscroft Large Print Bks., Ltd.

—Wallace & Gromit: Anoraknophobia. 1998. (Wallace & Gromit Comic Strip Bks.). (Illus.). 48p. (J). 9.95 (*0-8417-2031-2*) Adler's Foreign Bks., Inc.

Davies, Tristan, et al. Crackers in Space. 2000. (Illus.). 48p. (J). mass mkt. 8.95 (*0-340-71290-2*); 15.95 (*0-340-71289-9*) Hodder & Stoughton, Ltd. GBR. *Dist:* Lubrecht & Cramer, Ltd., Trafalgar Square.

Park, Nick. The Complete Wallace & Gromit. 1997. audio 16.99 o.s.i (*1-55853-570-5*) Rutledge Hill Pr.

—Wallace & Gromit: A Close Shave. 1996. 48p. (J). pap. 0.99 o.s.i (*0-385-32321-2*, Doubleday Bks. for Young Readers) Random Hse. Children's Bks.

—Wallace & Gromit: Cheese Lover's Yearbook. 1997. (J). pap. text 10.95 o.p. (*0-8362-5292-6*) Andrews McMeel Publishing.

—Wallace & Gromit: The Wrong Trousers. 1996. (J). pap. 7.99 o.p. (*0-385-32320-4*, Doubleday Bks. for Young Readers) Random Hse. Children's Bks.

—Wallace & Gromit Postcard Book. 1996. (Illus.). (J). pap. 6.99 o.s.i (*0-385-32322-0*, Doubleday Bks. for Young Readers) Random Hse. Children's Bks.

Rimmer, Ian. Wallace & Gromit: Catch of the Day. 2002. (Illus.). 48p. (J). (gr. 2-7). pap. 12.95 (*1-84023-495-4*) Titan Bks. Ltd. GBR. *Dist:* Client Distribution Services.

Sallis, Peter & Armstrong, Gareth, readers. Araknophobia. abr. ed. 1998. (J). pap. 16.95 incl. audio (*1-84032-171-7*) Hodder Headline Audiobooks GBR. *Dist:* Trafalgar Square, Ulverscroft Large Print Bks., Ltd.

Wallace & Gromit: Miniature Portrait. 1997. (J). pap. 6.99 o.p. (*1-55853-524-1*) Rutledge Hill Pr.

WASHINGTON, GEORGE, 1732-1799—FICTION

Barton, David. The Bulletproof George Washington. 3rd ed. 1990. (Illus.). 59p. (Orig.). (YA). (gr. 8-12). pap. 5.95 (*0-925279-14-5*) WallBuilders, Inc.

Bennett, William J. Book of Virtues: Honesty: Zach's Tall Tale. 1996. (Adventures from the Book of Virtues Ser.: Vol. 1). 24p. (J). (ps-2). pap. 3.25 (*0-689-80902-6*, Simon Spotlight) Simon & Schuster Children's Publishing.

Fleming, Alice. George Washington Wasn't Always Old. 1991. (J). (gr. 4-7). 11.95 o.s.i (*0-671-69557-6*, Simon & Schuster Children's Publishing) Simon & Schuster Children's Publishing.

Fritz, Jean. George Washington's Breakfast. (Illus.). 43p. (J). (gr. 2-6). 1984. 7.95 o.s.i (*0-698-20616-9*); 1969. 10.99 o.p. (*0-698-30099-8*) Putnam Publishing Group, The. (Coward-McCann).

—George Washington's Breakfast. 1998. 13.14 (*0-606-13418-2*) Turtleback Bks.

—George Washington's Mother. 1992. (All Aboard Reading Ser.). (Illus.). (J). (ps-3). 32p. 7.99 o.s.i (*0-448-40385-4*); 48p. 3.99 (*0-448-40384-6*) Penguin Putnam Bks. for Young Readers. (Grosset & Dunlap).

—George Washington's Mother. 1992. (All Aboard Reading Ser.). (J). 10.14 (*0-606-02343-7*) Turtleback Bks.

—George Washington's Mother. 2000. (Illus.). (J). (gr. k-5). pap. 12.95 incl. audio (*1-55592-065-9*, QPRA433) Weston Woods Studios, Inc.

Griffin, Judith Berry. Phoebe, the Spy. 2002. (Illus.). 48p. (J). pap. 6.99 (*0-698-11956-8*, PaperStar) Penguin Putnam Bks. for Young Readers.

Gross, Ruth Belov. If You Grew up with George Washington. 1993. 64p. (J). (gr. 4-7). pap. 5.99 (*0-590-45155-3*) Scholastic, Inc.

Hedstrom, Deborah. From Colonies to Country with George Washington. 1997. (My American Journey Ser.). 45p. (J). (gr. 4-7). 19.99 (*1-57673-155-3*) Questar, Inc.

Johnston, Johanna. A Birthday for General Washington. 1976. (Holiday Play Bks.). (Illus.). 32p. (J). (gr. k-4). lib. bdg. 15.93 o.p. (*0-516-08881-5*, Children's Pr.) Scholastic Library Publishing.

Meadowcroft, Enid L. Silver for General Washington: A Story of Valley Forge. rev. ed. 1967. (Illus.). (J). (gr. 3-7). o.p. (*0-690-73731-9*) HarperCollins Children's Bk. Group.

Morris, Gilbert. Vanishing Clues. 1996. (Time Navigators Ser.: Vol. 2). 144p. (J). (gr. 4-7). pap. 5.99 o.p. (*1-55661-396-2*) Bethany Hse. Pubs.

Osborne, Mary Pope. Revolutionary War on Wednesday. Loehr, Mallory, ed. 2000. (Magic Tree House Ser.: No. 22). (Illus.). 96p. (J). (gr. k-3). lib. bdg. 11.99 (*0-679-99068-2*); pap. 3.99 (*0-679-89068-8*) Random Hse. Children's Bks. (Random Hse. Bks. for Young Readers).

—Revolutionary War on Wednesday. 2000. (Magic Tree House Ser.: No. 22). (J). (gr. k-3). 10.04 (*0-606-19907-1*) Turtleback Bks.

Quackenbush, Robert. I Did It with My Hatchet: A Story of George Washington. 1989. (Illus.). 32p. (J). (gr. 2-6). 14.95 (*0-945912-04-8*) Pippin Pr.

Richards, Kitty. Star-Spangled Babies. 1999. (Rugrats Chapter Bks.: No. 3). (Illus.). 64p. (J). (gr. 1-4). pap. 3.99 (*0-689-82891-8*, Simon Spotlight) Simon & Schuster Children's Publishing.

Rinaldi, Ann. Taking Liberty: The Story of Oney Judge, George Washington's Runaway Slave. 272p. (YA). 2004. (Illus.). mass mkt. 5.99 (*0-689-85188-X*, Simon Pulse); 2002. (gr. 7 up). 16.95 (*0-689-85187-1*, Simon & Schuster Children's Publishing) Simon & Schuster Children's Publishing.

—Taking Liberty: The Story of Oney Judge, George Washington's Runaway Slave. 2003. (Young Adult Ser.). 277p. (J). 24.95 (*0-7862-5557-9*) Thorndike Pr.

Rosenburg, John M. First in War: George Washington in the American Revolution. 1998. (Single Titles Ser.: up). (Illus.). 256p. (gr. 7-12). 25.90 (*0-7613-0311-1*) Millbrook Pr., Inc.

Sargent, Dave & Sargent, Pat. Biscuit (skewbald) Follow Rules #3. 2001. (Saddle Up Ser.). 36p. (J). pap. 6.95 (*1-56763-676-4*); lib. bdg. 22.60 (*1-56763-675-6*) Ozark Publishing.

Small, David. George Washington's Cows, RS. 40p. (J). (ps-13). 1997. (Illus.). pap. 6.95 (*0-374-42534-5*, Sunburst); 1994. 16.00 (*0-374-32535-9*, Farrar, Straus & Giroux (BYR)) Farrar, Straus & Giroux.

—George Washington's Cows. 1997. 11.10 (*0-606-11364-9*) Turtleback Bks.

Stevenson, Augusta. George Washington & Abraham Lincoln. 2003. (Childhood of Famous Americans Ser.). (Illus.). 384p. (J). pap. 6.99 (*0-689-85624-5*, Aladdin) Simon & Schuster Children's Publishing.

Tripp, Valerie. Molly's A+ Partner. 2002. (American Girls Short Stories Ser.). (Illus.). 56p. (J). 4.95 (*1-58485-483-9*, American Girl) Pleasant Co. Pubns.

Tunnell, Michael O. The Joke's on George. 2003. (Illus.). 32p. (J). (gr. 1-3). 9.95 (*1-56397-970-5*) Boyds Mills Pr.

—The Joke's on George. 1993. (Illus.). 32p. (J). (gr. k up). 14.00 o.p. (*0-688-11758-9*); lib. bdg. 13.93 o.p. (*0-688-11759-7*) Morrow/Avon. (Morrow, William & Co.).

—The Joke's on George. 1995. 4.99 (*5-551-24172-6*) World Pr., Ltd.

Woodruff, Elvira. George Washington's Socks. 1999. (YA). pap. 40.75 incl. audio (*0-7887-2995-0*, 40877) Recorded Bks., LLC.

—George Washington's Socks. 1993. 176p. (J). (gr. 4-7). 4.50 (*0-590-44036-5*) Scholastic, Inc.

—George Washington's Socks. 1991. (J). 10.55 (*0-606-02650-9*) Turtleback Bks.

—In George Washington's Socks. 1991. 176p. (J). 13.95 o.p. (*0-590-44035-7*) Scholastic, Inc.

WATIE, STAND, 1806-1871—FICTION

Keith, Harold. Rifles for Watie. (gr. 7 up). 1991. 352p. (J). lib. bdg. 16.89 (*0-690-04907-2*); 1987. 352p. (J). mass mkt. 5.99 (*0-06-447030-X*, Harper Trophy); 1957. 322p. (YA). 14.95 o.p. (*0-690-70181-0*) HarperCollins Children's Bk. Group.

—Rifles for Watie. 1987. (J). 12.00 (*0-606-03520-6*) Turtleback Bks.

Rifles for Watie. 1999. (YA). 9.95 (*1-56137-598-5*) Novel Units, Inc.

WEBSTER, DANIEL, 1782-1852—FICTION

Gibbons, Ted. Daniel Webster & the Blacksmith's Fee. 1988. (Keepsake Bookcards Ser.). 8p. (Orig.). (YA). pap. 1.95 o.p. (*0-929985-03-6*) Jackman Publishing.

WELLS, JEFF (FICTITIOUS CHARACTER)—FICTION

Asimov, Isaac & Asimov, Janet. Norby: Robot for Hire. 1987. (Norby Chronicles Ser.: Bk. II). 208p. mass mkt. 3.95 o.s.i (*0-441-58635-X*) Ace Bks.

—Norby & the Lost Princess. 129p. (J). lib. bdg. 20.90 (*0-8027-6593-9*); 1985. 10.95 o.p. (*0-8027-6583-1*) Walker & Co.

—Norby Through Time & Space. 1988. (J). mass mkt. 2.95 o.s.i (*0-441-58637-6*) Ace Bks.

Asimov, Janet. Norby & the Terrified Taxi. 1997. (Norby Ser.). 125p. (J). (gr. 3-7). 15.95 (*0-8027-8642-1*) Walker & Co.

Asimov, Janet & Asimov, Isaac. Norby & the Court Jester. 1996. 192p. mass mkt. 5.50 o.s.i (*0-441-00341-9*) Ace Bks.

—Norby & the Court Jester. l.t. ed. 1999. (Science Fiction Ser.). 168p. 24.95 (*0-7838-8610-1*) Thorndike Pr.

—Norby & the Court Jester. 1991. (Norby Ser.). 128p. (J). (gr. 3-7). 14.95 (*0-8027-8131-4*); (gr. 7 up). lib. bdg. 15.85 (*0-8027-8132-2*) Walker & Co.

—Norby & the Invaders. 1985. (Norby Ser.). 138p. (J). (gr. 3-5). 10.95 (*0-8027-6599-8*); lib. bdg. 10.85 (*0-8027-6607-2*) Walker & Co.

—Norby & the Oldest Dragon. 1993. 160p. (J). mass mkt. 4.50 o.s.i (*0-441-58632-5*) Ace Bks.

—Norby & the Oldest Dragon. 1990. (Norby Ser.). (J). (gr. 4-9). 14.95 (*0-8027-6909-8*); lib. bdg. 15.85 (*0-8027-6910-1*) Walker & Co.

—Norby & the Queen's Necklace. 1986. (Norby Ser.). 144p. (J). (gr. 4-9). 11.95 (*0-8027-6659-5*); lib. bdg. 12.85 (*0-8027-6660-9*) Walker & Co.

—Norby & Yobo's Great Adventure. 1991. (J). mass mkt. 3.95 o.s.i (*0-441-58638-4*) Ace Bks.

—Norby & Yobo's Great Adventure. 1989. (Norby Ser.). 224p. (J). (gr. 4-9). 12.95 (*0-8027-6893-8*); lib. bdg. 13.85 (*0-8027-6894-6*) Walker & Co.

—The Norby Chronicles. 1986. (J). mass mkt. 3.50 o.s.i (*0-441-58634-1*); 192p. mass mkt. 2.95 o.s.i (*0-441-58633-3*) Ace Bks.

—Norby down to Earth. 1991. (Norby Chronicles Ser.). mass mkt. 3.99 o.s.i (*0-441-58607-4*) Ace Bks.

—Norby down to Earth. 1989. (Norby Ser.). (Illus.). (J). (gr. 4-9). lib. bdg. 13.85 o.p. (*0-8027-6867-9*) Walker & Co.

—Norby Finds a Villain. 1987. 102p. (J). (gr. 4-9). 12.95 (*0-8027-6710-9*); lib. bdg. 13.85 (*0-8027-6711-7*) Walker & Co.

—Norby, the Mixed up Robot. unabr. ed. 1986. (J). (gr. 1-5). pap. 10.50 o.s.i incl. audio (*0-89845-634-7*, CP 1792, Caedmon) HarperTrade.

—Norby, the Mixed up Robot. (J). 1985. 9.95 o.p. (*0-8027-6495-9*); 1983. 96p. (gr. 5-7). lib. bdg. 10.85 (*0-8027-6496-7*) Walker & Co.

—Norby's Other Secret. 1984. 138p. (J). 10.95 (*0-8027-6525-4*) Walker & Co.

Asimov, Janet, et al. Norby down to Earth. 1989. (Norby Ser.). (Illus.). 107p. (J). (gr. 7 up). 12.95 o.p. (*0-8027-6866-0*) Walker & Co.

WHITMAN, MARCUS, 1802-1847—FICTION

Allen, T. D. Doctor in Buckskin. 1951. lib. bdg. 9.87 o.p. (*0-06-010096-6*) HarperCollins Pubs.

Frazier, Neta L. Stout-Hearted Seven. 1973. (J). (gr. 4-6). 5.95 o.p. (*0-15-281450-7*) Harcourt Children's Bks.

WINNIE-THE-POOH (FICTITIOUS CHARACTER)—FICTION

Alexander, Liza. Winnie the Pooh & Valentines, Too. 1998. (Pooh Ser.). (Illus.). 32p. (J). (ps-3). 12.95 (*0-7868-3217-7*) Disney Pr.

Allen, Roger E. Winnie the Pooh on Success. 2015. 160p. pap. 9.95 o.s.i (*0-452-27814-7*) Dutton/Plume.

American Education Publishing Staff. Pooh's Number Game. 2001. (Illus.). 36p. (J). suppl. ed. 2.99 (*1-56189-537-7*, 31230, American Education Publishing) McGraw-Hill Children's Publishing.

Benedictus, David, et al. Winnie the Pooh. 1999. (J). (ps-3). audio 14.95 (*1-85998-650-1*) Trafalgar Square.

Birney, Betty. Winnie the Pooh: The Merry Christmas Mystery. 1993. (Look-Look Bks.). (J). (ps-3). pap. 4.99 o.p. (*0-307-12774-5*, 12774, Golden Bks.) Random Hse. Children's Bks.

—Winnie the Pooh & the Little Lost Bird: A Big Golden Book. 1993. (J). (ps-3). o.p. (*0-307-12369-3*, Golden Bks.) Random Hse. Children's Bks.

—Winnie the Pooh & the Missing Pots. 1992. (Big Golden Bks.). (Illus.). 24p. (J). (ps-2). o.p. (*0-307-12337-5*, 12337, Golden Bks.) Random Hse. Children's Bks.

The Book of Boo! 2002. (Illus.). 32p. (J). (ps-1). 5.99 (*0-7868-3364-5*) Disney Pr.

Book of Pooh No. 2: This Is the Honey That Pooh Ate. 2002. 14p. (J). bds. 7.74 (*0-7868-3358-0*) Time Warner Bk. Group.

Book of Pooh Tabbed Board Book, No. 1. 2002. 14p. (J). bds. 7.74 (*0-7868-3357-2*) Time Warner Bk. Group.

Braybooks, Ann. The Very Best Easter Bunny. 2000. (Pooh Ser.). (Illus.). 24p. (J). (ps-k). 11.99 o.p. (*0-307-16604-X*, Golden Bks.) Random Hse. Children's Bks.

Braybrooks, Ann. Tiggers Hate to Lose. 1999. (Winnie the Pooh First Readers Ser.: No. 8). (Illus.). 40p. (J). (gr. k-3). pap. 3.99 (*0-7868-4266-0*) Disney Pr.

Calmenson, Stephanie. Winnie the Pooh & Tigger Too. 1994. (Many Adventures of Winnie the Pooh Ser.). (Illus.). 48p. (J). (ps-4). 12.95 (*1-56282-630-1*) Disney Pr.

Channing, Carol, reader. Winnie the Pooh & Eeyore. abr. ed. 1984. (J). (ps-3). audio 8.98 o.p. (*0-89845-886-2*, CPN 1747, Caedmon) HarperTrade.

Connolly, Paula T. Winnie the Pooh & the House at Pooh Corner: Recovering Arcadia. 1994. (Twayne's Masterwork Studies). 160p. (J). 30.00 (*0-8057-8810-7*); (Illus.). per. 16.00 (*0-8057-8811-5*) Gale Group. (Macmillan Reference USA).

Craig, Petra. Winnie the Pooh Mask Book. 1995. (Illus.). 26p. (J). (ps-3). pap. 12.95 (*0-7868-4033-1*) Disney Pr.

Daly, C., ed. Pooh's Magic Wishes. 2001. (Learn to Read Ser.). (Illus.). 32p. (J). (ps-1). 5.99 (*0-7868-3345-9*) Disney Pr.

Delton, Judy. Disney's Winnie the Pooh's Book of Manners. 2000. (Illus.). 48p. lib. bdg. 13.49 (*0-7868-5083-3*) Disney Pr.

Delton, Judy & Hogan, Mary. Disney's Winnie the Pooh's Book of Manners. 2000. (Illus.). 176p. (J). (gr. 3-7). 13.99 (*0-7868-3206-1*) Disney Pr.

Disney. Sweet Dreams, Pooh! Including 3 Plush Characters, 3 bks. 2002. (Illus.). 16p. (J). (ps-1). bds. 24.99 (*0-7944-0018-3*, Reader's Digest Children's Bks.) Reader's Digest Children's Publishing, Inc.

Disney Staff. A Bear-y Good Neighbor. 2001. (Disney's Winnie the Pooh Ser.). (Illus.). 24p. (J). (gr. k-3). pap. 3.25 (*0-7364-1108-9*, RH/Disney) Random Hse. Children's Bks.

—The Big, Fat Bee. 1994. (Winnie the Pooh Ser.). (Illus.). (J). (ps-3). 6.98 o.p. (*1-57082-098-8*) Mouse Works.

—Colors. 2001. (Disney's Winnie the Pooh Ser.). (Illus.). 12p. (J). bds. 4.99 (*0-7364-1088-0*, RH/Disney) Random Hse. Children's Bks.

—Eeyore's Backpack. 2002. (J). bds. 7.99 (*0-7364-1255-7*, RH/Disney) Random Hse. Children's Bks.

—Knock, Knock! It's Pooh. 2001. (Illus.). 14p. (J). bds. 7.99 o.s.i (*0-7364-1245-X*, RH/Disney) Random Hse. Children's Bks.

—The Many Adventures of Winnie the Pooh: A Classic Disney Treasury. 1997. (Classic Disney Treasury Ser.). (Illus.). 192p. (J). (ps-2). 19.95 o.s.i (*0-7868-3138-3*) Disney Pr.

—Opposites. 2001. (Disney's Winnie the Pooh Ser.). (Illus.). 12p. (J). bds. 4.99 (*0-7364-1089-9*, RH/Disney) Random Hse. Children's Bks.

—Piglet's Backpack. 2002. 16p. (J). bds. 7.99 (*0-7364-1254-9*, RH/Disney) Random Hse. Children's Bks.

—Pooh Goes Fast & Slow. 2001. (Illus.). 14p. (J). bds. 7.99 (*0-7364-1244-1*, RH/Disney) Random Hse. Children's Bks.

—Pooh Goes Fast & Slow: Busy Book, No. 8. 2000. (Winnie the Pooh Ser.). (Illus.). 12p. (J). (ps). bds. 6.99 (*0-7364-1005-8*) Mouse Works.

—Pooh Loves You. 2002. (Disney Winnie the Pooh Ser.). (Illus.). 24p. (J). pap. 3.25 (*0-7364-1305-7*, RH/Disney) Random Hse. Children's Bks.

—Pooh Says Please! Chunky Roly Poly Book. 1999. (Learn & Grow Ser.). (Illus.). 18p. (J). (ps-k). bds. 3.50 (*0-7364-0150-4*) Mouse Works.

—Pooh Va Al Doctor. 2002. 24p. (J). pap. 3.25 (*0-7364-2060-6*, RH/Disney) Random Hse. Children's Bks.

—Pooh's Backpack. 2002. 16p. (J). bds. 7.99 (*0-7364-1253-0*, RH/Disney) Random Hse. Children's Bks.

—Pooh's Basket of Surprises. 2001. (Disney's Winnie the Pooh Ser.). (Illus.). 32p. (J). 3.99 (*0-7364-1105-4*, RH/Disney) Random Hse. Children's Bks.

—Pooh's Five Little Honey Pots. 2001. (Illus.). 14p. (J). bds. 7.99 (*0-7364-1243-3*, RH/Disney) Random Hse. Children's Bks.

—Pooh's Fuzzy Friends. 2002. (Illus.). 20p. (J). bds. 11.99 (*0-7364-2051-7*, RH/Disney) Random Hse. Children's Bks.

—Pooh's Garden. 1999. (Pooh's Learn & Grow Ser.: Vol. 11). (Illus.). 12p. (J). 3.49 (*1-57973-045-0*) Advance Pubs. LLC.

—Pooh's Hero Party, No. 12. 1999. (Winnie the Pooh First Readers Ser.: No. 12). (Illus.). 37p. (J). (gr. k-3). pap. 3.99 (*0-7868-4270-9*) Disney Pr.

—Pooh's Perfect Presents. 2001. (Illus.). 12p. (J). bds. 7.99 o.s.i (*0-7364-1203-4*, RH/Disney) Random Hse. Children's Bks.

—Pooh's Pitter Patter Splash. 2001. (Illus.). 14p. (J). bds. 7.99 o.s.i (*0-7364-1241-7*, RH/Disney) Random Hse. Children's Bks.

—Pooh's Rainy Day. 1999. (Pooh's Learn & Grow Ser.: Vol. 10). (Illus.). 12p. (J). 3.49 (*1-57973-044-2*) Advance Pubs. LLC.

—Pooh's Tunes-Day Parade. 2001. (Illus.). 14p. (J). bds. 7.99 (*0-7364-1248-4*, RH/Disney) Random Hse. Children's Bks.

—A Pumpkin for Pooh. 2002. (Illus.). 12p. (J). bds. 3.99 (*0-7364-1359-6*, RH/Disney) Random Hse. Children's Bks.

—Seasons. 2001. (Disney's Winnie the Pooh Ser.). (Illus.). 12p. (J). bds. 4.99 (*0-7364-1090-2*, RH/Disney) Random Hse. Children's Bks.

—Shapes. 2001. (Disney's Winnie the Pooh Ser.). (Illus.). 12p. (J). bds. 4.99 (*0-7364-1091-0*, RH/Disney) Random Hse. Children's Bks.

—Sunny Day in the Hundred-Acre Wood. 2001. (Illus.). 14p. (J). bds. 7.99 (*0-7364-1132-1*, RH/Disney) Random Hse. Children's Bks.

—Tick-Tock, Pooh's Clock. 2001. (Illus.). 14p. (J). bds. 7.99 (*0-7364-1247-6*, RH/Disney) Random Hse. Children's Bks.

—What to Do wth Winnie the Pooh. 2002. (J). pap. 2.99 (*0-7364-2115-7*, RH/Disney) Random Hse. Children's Bks.

—Whose Face? Pooh's Face. 2001. (Illus.). 14p. (J). bds. 7.99 (*0-7364-1246-8*, RH/Disney) Random Hse. Children's Bks.

—Winnie the Pooh. 1980. (Illus.). (J). (ps). 1.95 o.p. (*0-525-69513-3*, Dutton) Dutton/Plume.

—Winnie the Pooh. (FRE.). 96p. (J). (gr. k-5). pap. 9.95 (*0-7859-8848-3*) French & European Pubns., Inc.

—Winnie the Pooh. 1990. (Penguin-Disney Ser.). (J). 7.98 o.p. (*0-453-03014-9*) Mouse Works.

—Winnie the Pooh: Sleepytime Set, Incl. plush Pooh. 1996. (Illus.). 32p. (J). pap. 19.95 (*0-7868-4121-4*) Disney Pr.

—Winnie the Pooh Treasury Collection, 3 bks., Ea. 1994. (Illus.). 32p. (J). (ps-3). 7.98 o.p. (*1-57082-016-3*) Mouse Works.

Disney Staff, illus. Walt Disney's Winnie the Pooh Storybook. 1989. 128p. 24.95 o.p. (*0-8109-1129-9*) Abrams, Harry N. , Inc.

Disney, Walter Elias. Pooh's Adventures with Words. 1981. (Illus.). 6.95 o.p. (*0-525-69690-3*, Dutton) Dutton/Plume.

—Winnie the Pooh. 1988. (Disney Animated Ser.). (Illus.). 48p. (J). (ps-6). 5.99 o.p. (*0-517-67005-4*) Random Hse. Value Publishing.

Disney's Winnie the Pooh Busy Book. 2001. (Illus.). 10p. (J). 15.99 (*0-7868-3302-5*) Disney Pr.

Disney's Winnie the Pooh Christmas Treasury. 2002. (Illus.). 160p. (J). (ps-2). 14.99 (*0-7868-3400-5*) Disney Pr.

Disney's Winnie the Pooh Shapes. 2002. (Wonderful World of Disney Ser.). (J). 14.99 (*0-7868-3371-8*) Disney Pr.

Doering, Andrea. Winnie the Pooh's Colors. 1999. (Learn & Grow Ser.). (Illus.). 20p. (J). (ps). bds. 4.99 (*0-7364-0119-9*, RH/Disney) Random Hse. Children's Bks.

—Winnie the Pooh's Shapes. 1999. (Learn & Grow Ser.). (Illus.). 18p. (J). (ps-3). bds. 4.99 (*0-7364-0118-0*) Mouse Works.

Douglas, Vincent. The Blustery Day. 2001. (Illus.). 32p. (J). (ps-k). pap. 4.99 (*1-57768-730-2*) McGraw-Hill Children's Publishing.

—Pooh Helps Out. 2001. (Illus.). 32p. (J). (ps-k). pap. 4.99 (*1-57768-731-0*) McGraw-Hill Children's Publishing.

Driscoll, Laura. Disney's 5 Minute Winnie the Pooh Stories. Date not set. (Illus.). (J). 12.99 (*0-7868-3482-X*) Disney Pr.

Du Rand, Le Clanche. Winnie the Pooh: Small Cast Musical. 1992. pap. 5.95 (*0-87129-182-7*, W72) Dramatic Publishing Co.

Edgar, Amy. Winnie the Pooh's Bedtime Hummables. 2000. (Winnie the Pooh Ser.). (Illus.). 14p. (J). (ps-k). bds. 7.99 (*0-7364-1020-1*) Mouse Works.

Ellison, Virginia H. The Pooh Cook Book. 1969. (Illus.). (J). (gr. 4-7). 6.95 o.p. (*0-525-37404-3*, Dutton) Dutton/Plume.

Ferguson, Don. Winnie the Pooh's A to Zzzz. Date not set. (Illus.). 32p. (J). pap. 4.99 (*0-7868-4094-3*) Disney Pr.

—Winnie the Pooh's A to Zzzz: Miniature Edition. (Illus.). 32p. (J). (ps-k). 1994. 5.95 o.p. (*0-7868-3009-3*); 1992. lib. bdg. 12.89 o.p. (*1-56282-142-3*); 1992. 12.95 o.p. (*1-56282-015-X*) Disney Pr.

Finch, Christopher. Winnie the Pooh: A Celebration of the Silly Old Bear. 2002. (Illus.). 176p. (J). pap. 20.00 (*0-7868-5344-1*, Disney Editions) Disney Pr.

Friedrichson, Carol. Pooh Craft Book. 1976. (Illus.). (J). (gr. 4 up). 6.95 o.p. (*0-525-37410-8*, Dutton) Dutton/Plume.

Gaines, Isabel. Be Quiet, Pooh! 1999. 40p. (J). pap. 3.99 (*0-7868-4385-3*) Disney Pr.

—Disney's Winnie the Pooh Easy-to-Read Stories. 2001. (Winnie the Pooh Ser.). (Illus.). 192p. (J). (ps-3). 9.99 (*0-7868-3317-3*) Disney Pr.

—Giving Bear. 9th ed. 1999. 40p. (J). pap. 3.99 o.s.i (*0-7868-4404-3*) Little Brown & Co.

—Giving Bear. 2001. (Winnie the Pooh First Readers Ser.). (Illus.). (J). 10.14 (*0-606-21649-9*) Turtleback Bks.

—Happy Birthday, Eeyore! 2001. (Winnie the Pooh First Readers Ser.). (Illus.). (J). 10.14 (*0-606-21650-2*) Turtleback Bks.

—Happy Valentine's Day, Pooh. 2000. (Winnie the Pooh Ser.: Vol. 25). (Illus.). 37p. (J). pap. 3.99 (*0-7868-4372-1*) Disney Pr.

—Pooh & the Storm That Sparkled. 2001. (Winnie the Pooh First Readers Ser.). (Illus.). (J). 10.14 (*0-606-21651-0*) Turtleback Bks.

—Pooh Gets Stuck. (Winnie the Pooh First Readers Ser.: No. 1). 48p. (J). 1999. pap. 3.95 o.s.i (*0-7868-4361-6*); No. 1. 1998. (Illus.). pap. 3.95 (*0-7868-4184-2*) Disney Pr.

—Pooh's Christmas Gift. 1999. 40p. (J). pap. 3.99 (*0-7868-4402-7*) Disney Pr.

—Pooh's Christmas Gifts. 2001. (Winnie the Pooh First Readers Ser.). (Illus.). (J). 10.14 (*0-606-21653-7*) Turtleback Bks.

—Pooh's Easter Egg Hunt. 1999. (Winnie the Pooh First Readers Ser.: No. 10). (Illus.). 40p. (J). (gr. k-3). pap. 3.99 (*0-7868-4268-7*) Disney Pr.

—Pooh's Fall Harvest. 2000. (Winnie the Pooh First Readers Ser.: No. 23). (Illus.). 35p. (J). (ps-3). pap. 3.99 (*0-7868-4370-5*) Disney Pr.

—Pooh's Graduation. 2000. (Winnie the Pooh Ser.). 40p. (J). (gr. k-3). pap. 3.99 (*0-7364-1157-7*, RH/Disney) Random Hse. Children's Bks.

—Pooh's Graduation. 2001. (Winnie the Pooh First Readers Ser.). (Illus.). (J). 10.14 (*0-606-21655-3*) Turtleback Bks.

—Pooh's Halloween Parade. 2001. (Winnie the Pooh First Readers Ser.). (Illus.). (J). 10.14 (*0-606-21656-1*) Turtleback Bks.

—Pooh's Halloween Pumpkin. 2003. (Disney Winnie the Pooh Ser.). (Illus.). 32p. (J). (ps-2). pap. 3.99 (*0-7364-2160-2*); lib. bdg. 11.99 (*0-7364-8023-4*) Random Hse., Inc.

—Pooh's Leaf Pile. 2001. (Winnie the Pooh First Readers Ser.). (Illus.). (J). 10.14 (*0-606-21659-6*) Turtleback Bks.

—Pooh's Pumpkin. 2001. (Winnie the Pooh First Readers Ser.). (Illus.). (J). 10.14 (*0-606-21660-X*) Turtleback Bks.

—Pooh's Scavenger Hunt. 2001. (Winnie the Pooh First Readers Ser.). (Illus.). (J). 10.14 (*0-606-21661-8*) Turtleback Bks.

—Pooh's Sled Ride. 2000. (Winnie the Pooh First Readers Ser.: No. 24). (Illus.). 34p. (J). (ps-3). pap. 3.99 (*0-7868-4371-3*) Disney Pr.

—Pooh's Sled Ride. 2000. (Winnie the Pooh First Readers Ser.: Vol. 24). 40p. (J). (ps-3). pap. 3.99 (*0-7364-1159-3*, RH/Disney) Random Hse. Children's Bks.

—Pooh's Surprise Basket. 2001. (Winnie the Pooh First Readers Ser.). (Illus.). (J). 10.14 (*0-606-21662-6*) Turtleback Bks.

—Presents from Pooh. 2001. (Disney's Winnie the Pooh Ser.). (Illus.). 32p. (J). 3.99 o.s.i (*0-7364-1106-2*, RH/Disney) Random Hse. Children's Bks.

—Rabbit Gets Lost. 2001. (Winnie the Pooh First Readers Ser.). (Illus.). (J). 10.14 (*0-606-21663-4*) Turtleback Bks.

—Sing a Song with Pooh. 2001. (Illus.). 32p. (J). (ps-k). 3.99 o.s.i (*0-7364-1171-2*, RH/Disney) Random Hse. Children's Bks.

—Tiggers Hate to Lose. 1999. 40p. (J). pap. 3.99 (*0-7868-4389-6*) Disney Pr.

—Tiggers Hate to Lose. 2001. (Winnie the Pooh First Readers Ser.). (Illus.). (J). 10.14 (*0-606-21664-2*) Turtleback Bks.

Gaines, Isabel, et al. The Giving Bear. 1999. (Winnie the Pooh First Readers Ser.: No. 9). (Illus.). 37p. (J). (gr. k-3). pap. 3.99 (*0-7868-4267-9*) Disney Pr.

Gardening with Pooh: Cheerful Poems Plus Planting Pointers. 1997. 24p. (J). (ps-3). 9.98 (*1-57082-426-6*) Mouse Works.

Glasscock, Jessica. Mind Your Manners, Pooh! 2001. (Disney's Winnie the Pooh Ser.). (Illus.). 12p. (J). bds. 7.99 (*0-7364-1131-3*, RH/Disney) Random Hse. Children's Bks.

Golden Books Staff. Pooh: Coloring, Paint with Water, Activities. 2000. (Disney Ser.). (Illus.). 96p. (J). (ps-3). pap. text 3.99 (*0-307-25401-1*, Golden Bks.) Random Hse. Children's Bks.

—Winnie the Boo! 1998. (Disney Ser.). pap. o.p. (*0-307-15294-4*, Golden Bks.) Random Hse. Children's Bks.

—Winnie the Pooh. 2000. (J). (ps-3). pap. text 2.99 (*0-307-05545-0*, 05545, Golden Bks.) Random Hse. Children's Bks.

—Winnie the Pooh. 1997. 48p. pap. 2.22 o.s.i (*0-307-02910-7*) Random Hse., Inc.

Goodnight Pooh. 2001. (Illus.). (J). 7.95 (*0-7853-4788-7*) Publications International, Ltd.

Hal Leonard Corporation Staff. Winnie the Pooh. 1998. 40p. (ps-3). pap. 10.95 (*0-7935-8754-9*) Leonard, Hal Corp.

Halfmann, Janet. Fun with Opposites. 2001. (Disney's Winnie the Pooh Ser.). (Illus.). 48p. (J). (ps-1). pap. 2.99 (*0-7364-1097-X*) Mouse Works.

—How Does Your Garden Grow? 2001. (Disney's Winnie the Pooh Ser.). (Illus.). 48p. (J). (ps-3). pap. 2.99 o.s.i (*0-7364-1099-6*, RH/Disney) Random Hse. Children's Bks.

Happy Birthday to You! 2002. (Winnie the Pooh Ser.). (Illus.). 10p. (J). bds. 15.99 (*0-7868-3360-2*) Disney Pr.

I Can Learn with Pooh. 2002. 32p. pap. 83.76 (*1-56189-818-X*, American Education Publishing) McGraw-Hill Children's Publishing.

Kenneth, Caroline. Disney's Pooh: I Can Share Too! 1997. (Sturdy Shape Bks.). (Illus.). (J). o.p. (*0-307-12409-6*, Golden Bks.) Random Hse. Children's Bks.

Krulik, Nancy E. Puzzlers. 1999. (My Very First Winnie the Pooh Ser.). (Illus.). 64p. (J). (ps-1). pap. 4.99 (*0-7868-4344-6*) Disney Pr.

Kurtz, John, illus. Winnie the Pooh & the Honey Tree. 1993. (Many Adventures of Winnie the Pooh Ser.). 48p. (J). (ps-4). 12.95 o.p. (*1-56282-379-5*) Disney Pr.

Liberts, Jennifer. Pooh's This & That. 2001. (Disney's Winnie the Pooh Ser.). (Illus.). 12p. (J). bds. 7.99 (*0-7364-1092-9*, RH/Disney) Random Hse. Children's Bks.

Little Golden Books Staff. Walt Disney's Winnie the Pooh & the Pebble Hunt. 9999. (J). o.p. (*0-307-68121-1*, Golden Bks.) Random Hse. Children's Bks.

Little Red Riding Pooh: A Fairy Tale Friend a Board Book & Plush Figure. 2004. (Pooh's Fairy Tale Theater Ser.). 12p. (J). 6.99 (*0-7364-2239-0*, RH/Disney) Random Hse. Children's Bks.

Little Studios, illus. Winnie the Pooh & Piglet's Book of Opposites. 1984. (Disney Ser.). (J). (ps). o.p. (*0-307-06043-8*, 6092, Golden Bks.) Random Hse. Children's Bks.

The Many Adventures of Winnie the Pooh. abr. ed. 1990. (J). audio 9.95 (*1-55800-178-6*, Dove Audio) NewStar Media, Inc.

Marshall, Hallie. Disney's Winnie the Pooh's Telling Time: Book & Watch Set. 2000. (Illus.). 24p. (J). (ps-3). 9.99 (*0-7364-1028-7*) Mouse Works.

—Oh Brother! Pooh's Book about Trying New Things. 2001. (Illus.). 176p. (J). (ps-2). 14.99 (*0-7868-3279-7*) Disney Pr.

Melrose, A. R., ed. The Pooh Bedside Reader. 1996. (Illus.). 174p. (J). (ps up). 25.00 o.s.i (*0-525-45600-7*) Penguin Putnam Bks. for Young Readers.

Milne, A. A., pseud. Bedtime with Winnie the Pooh. 2003. (Illus.). 22p. 9.99 (*0-525-47148-0*) Penguin Group (USA) Inc.

—Christopher Robin & Pooh Giant Board Book. 2002. (Illus.). 10p. bds. 7.99 (*0-525-46846-3*, Dutton Children's Bks.) Penguin Putnam Bks. for Young Readers.

—Christopher Robin Leads an Expedition. 2003. (Winnie the Pooh Easy Reader Ser.). (Illus.). 48p. 13.99 (*0-525-46824-2*, Dutton Children's Bks.); (J). pap. 3.99 (*0-14-250007-0*, Puffin Bks.) Penguin Putnam Bks. for Young Readers.

—Christopher Robin Leads an Expedition: A Winnie the Pooh Storybook. 1993. (Pooh Storybook Ser.). (Illus.). 32p. (J). (gr. 2 up). 4.99 o.s.i (*0-525-45142-0*, Dutton Children's Bks.) Penguin Putnam Bks. for Young Readers.

—Christopher Robin Story Book. 1966. (Pooh Storybook Ser.). (Illus.). (J). (ps-3). 7.95 o.p. (*0-525-27933-4*, Dutton) Dutton/Plume.

—The Classic Pooh Treasury Vol. 3: The House At Pooh Corner, Set. 1997. (Illus.). (J). incl. audio (*1-57375-465-X*) Audioscope.

—The Complete Tales of Winnie the Pooh. (Illus.). 344p. (J). 1996. (ps-3). 35.00 (*0-525-45723-2*); 70th ed. 1999. (gr. 4-7). 40.00 (*0-525-45060-2*, Dutton Children's Bks.) Penguin Putnam Bks. for Young Readers.

—Disney's Winnie the Pooh: A Very Merry Christmas. 1998. (Winnie the Pooh Ser.). (Illus.). 10p. (J). (ps-k). bds. 9.99 (*1-57082-965-9*) Mouse Works.

—Eeyore Loses a Tail. 1993. (Winnie-the-Pooh Story Bks.). (Illus.). 32p. (J). 4.99 o.p. (*0-525-45137-4*); 13.99 o.p. (*0-525-45045-9*) Penguin Putnam Bks. for Young Readers. (Dutton Children's Bks.).

—Eeyore's (Mis) Adventures. 2003. (Winnie-the-Pooh Collections). (Illus.). 64p. (J). 15.99 (*0-525-47070-0*, Dutton Children's Bks.) Penguin Putnam Bks. for Young Readers.

—The House at Pooh Corner: 75th Anniversary Edition. anniv. ed. 2001. (Illus.). 192p. 14.99 o.s.i (*0-525-46758-0*, Dutton Children's Bks.) Penguin Putnam Bks. for Young Readers.

—Little Big Book of Pooh. 2004. (Illus.). 14.99 (*0-525-47142-1*, Dutton Children's Bks.) Penguin Putnam Bks. for Young Readers.

—Love, Pooh. 2003. (Illus.). 24p. 4.99 (*0-525-47237-1*, Dutton Children's Bks.) Penguin Putnam Bks. for Young Readers.

—The Magical World of Winnie-the-Pooh. 2003. (Illus.). 5p. 24.99 (*0-525-47141-3*, Dutton Children's Bks.) Penguin Putnam Bks. for Young Readers.

—My Very First Winnie-the-Pooh. 2002. (Illus.). 22p. 9.99 (*0-525-46838-2*, Dutton Children's Bks.) Penguin Putnam Bks. for Young Readers.

—Peek-a-Pooh. Ketchersid, Sarah, ed. 2001. (Illus.). 14p. (J). (ps-k). 9.99 o.s.i (*0-525-46541-3*, Dutton Children's Bks.) Penguin Putnam Bks. for Young Readers.

—Piglet Has a Bath. 1998. (Winnie-the-Pooh Collections). (Illus.). 12p. (J). 5.99 o.s.i (*0-525-46092-6*, Dutton Children's Bks.) Penguin Putnam Bks. for Young Readers.

—Pooh & Friends. 2004. (Illus.). 16p. bds. 7.99 (*0-525-47253-3*, Dutton Children's Bks.) Penguin Putnam Bks. for Young Readers.

—Pooh & Piglet Find a Heffalump. Ketchersid, Sarah, ed. abr. ed. 2001. (Illus.). 12p. (J). (ps-k). 6.99 o.s.i (*0-525-46702-5*, Dutton Children's Bks.) Penguin Putnam Bks. for Young Readers.

—Pooh & Piglet Giant Shaped Board Book. 2002. (Illus.). 10p. bds. 7.99 (*0-525-46845-5*, Dutton Children's Bks.) Penguin Putnam Bks. for Young Readers.

—Pooh Goes Visiting. (gr. k-2). 2002. (Easy-to-Read Ser.). (Illus.). 48p. (J). 13.99 (*0-525-46821-8*); 2001. (Book-in-a-Book Ser.). (Illus.). 10p. 7.99 (*0-525-46733-5*, Dutton Children's Bks.); 2000. (Winnie-the-Pooh Deluxe Picture Bks.: Vol. II). (Illus.). 32p. (J). 9.99 o.s.i (*0-525-46457-3*, Dutton Children's Bks.); 1996. (Illus.). 26p. (J). bds. 3.99 (*0-525-45527-2*, Dutton Children's Bks.); 1993. (Winnie-the-Pooh Story Bks.). (Illus.). 32p. (J). 4.99 o.p. (*0-525-45040-8*, Dutton Children's Bks.); 1990. 4.95 o.p. (*0-525-44707-5*, Dutton Children's Bks.); 1987. (Illus.). 10p. (J). 7.95 o.p. (*0-525-44337-1*, 0674-210, Dutton Children's Bks.); Vol. 2. 2002. (Puffin Easy-to-Read Ser.). (Illus.). 48p. (J). pap. 3.99 (*0-14-230184-1*, Puffin Bks.) Penguin Putnam Bks. for Young Readers.

—Pooh Goes Visiting & Other Stories. 1998. (J). mass mkt. 7.95 incl. audio (*1-84032-047-8*) Hodder Headline Audiobooks GBR. *Dist:* Trafalgar Square.

—Pooh Goes Visiting Puzzle. 1999. (Illus.). 14p. (J). (ps-3). 7.99 o.s.i (*0-525-46272-4*, Dutton) Penguin Putnam Bks. for Young Readers.

—Pooh Song Book. 1961. (J). (gr. 1-4). 7.95 o.p. (*0-525-37489-2*, Dutton) Dutton/Plume.

—The Pooh Song Book. abr. ed. (J). audio 8.98 o.p. (*0-89845-064-0*, CP 1686, HarperAudio) HarperTrade.

—Pooh Touch & Feel. abr. ed. 1998. (Illus.). 12p. (J). (ps). 9.99 (*0-525-45830-1*) Penguin Putnam Bks. for Young Readers.

—Pooh's First Clock. 1998. (Illus.). 12p. (J). (ps-3). bds. 12.99 (*0-525-45983-9*, Dutton Children's Bks.) Penguin Putnam Bks. for Young Readers.

—Pooh's Grand Adventure. 1997. (Illus.). 24p. (J). (ps-3). 6.98 o.s.i (*1-57082-671-4*) Mouse Works.

—Pooh's House, 3 bks., Set. 2002. (Illus.). 40p. 12.99 (*0-525-46985-0*) Penguin Putnam Bks. for Young Readers.

—Pooh's Library, 4 bks., Set. (Pooh Original Edition Ser.). (Illus.). (J). 1992. 48p. (gr. 2 up). 19.99 (*0-14-095560-7*, Puffin Bks.); 1988. (ps-3). 44.00 (*0-525-44451-3*, Dutton Children's Bks.) Penguin Putnam Bks. for Young Readers.

—Pooh's Library, 4 bks. Incl. Now We Are Six. (Illus.). 1961. (Illus.). 1961. 39.80 o.p. (*0-525-37461-2*, 02718-820, Dutton) Dutton/Plume.

—Pooh's Quiz Book. Shepard, Ernest H., tr. 1977. (J). 3.95 o.p. (*0-525-37485-X*, Dutton) Dutton/Plume.

—Slide & Seek Alphabet: A Sliding Window Book. 1999. (Illus.). 8p. (J). 10.99 (*0-7868-3240-1*) Disney Pr.

—Slide & Seek Numbers: A Sliding Window Book. 1999. (Illus.). 8p. (J). 10.99 (*0-7868-3241-X*) Disney Pr.

—The Smackerel of Pooh. 2003. (Illus.). 80p. 15.99 (*0-525-47037-9*, Dutton Children's Bks.) Penguin Putnam Bks. for Young Readers.

—Where Is Poohs Honey: Slide & Find Books. 2001. (Illus.). 8p. (J). (ps-k). 6.99 (*0-525-46539-1*, Dutton Children's Bks.) Penguin Putnam Bks. for Young Readers.

—Winnie Ille Pu Semper Ludet. Staples, Brian, tr. 1998. (Winnie-the-Pooh Collections). (LAT., Illus.). 160p. (YA). (gr. 7-12). 17.99 (*0-525-46091-8*, Dutton Children's Bks.) Penguin Putnam Bks. for Young Readers.

—Winnie the Pooh. 1991. 176p. (J). (gr. k-6). pap. 4.99 o.s.i (*0-440-40116-X*) Dell Publishing.

—Winnie the Pooh. (Illus.). (J). 1999. 176p. pap. 7.95 (*0-452-27764-7*, Plume); 1961. (gr. 1-5). 9.95 o.p. (*0-525-43035-0*, Dutton) Dutton/Plume.

—Winnie the Pooh. 1998. (E-Z Play Today Ser.: Vol. #282). 48p. pap. 6.95 (*0-7935-8967-3*) Leonard, Hal Corp.

—Winnie the Pooh. (J). audio 13.58 NewSound, LLC.

—Winnie the Pooh. 1995. 96p. (J). pap. 0.95 o.p. (*0-14-600104-4*) Penguin Group (USA) Inc.

—Winnie the Pooh. (Illus.). 2002. 10p. (J). 12.99 (*0-525-47007-7*); 1993. (J). 49.90 o.p. (*0-525-45378-4*, Dutton Children's Bks.); 1992. 176p. (J). (gr. 4-7). pap. 4.99 (*0-14-036121-9*, Puffin Bks.); 1988. 176p. (YA). (gr. 4-7). 10.99 (*0-525-44443-2*, Dutton Children's Bks.) Penguin Putnam Bks. for Young Readers.

—Winnie the Pooh. 1981. (Illus.). 176p. (J). (gr. 3-7). pap. 0.75 o.s.i (*0-440-49571-7*, Yearling) Random Hse. Children's Bks.

—Winnie the Pooh. 1992. 11.04 (*0-606-08938-1*) Turtleback Bks.

—Winnie the Pooh. 1998. (Winnie the Pooh Ser.). 3p. 49.95 o.p. incl. audio (*0-14-086812-7*, Penguin AudioBooks) Viking Penguin.

—The Winnie-the-Pooh. 2003. audio compact disk 22.00 (*0-06-056627-2*) HarperCollins Children's Bk. Group.

—Winnie the Pooh. unabr. ed. 2002. (J). audio 20.95 (*1-55685-635-0*) Audio Bk. Contractors, Inc.

—Winnie the Pooh. abr. ed. (J). audio 15.95 o.p. (*0-88646-036-0*, 7052) Durkin Hayes Publishing Ltd.

—Winnie the Pooh. deluxe ed. (Pooh Color Edition Ser.). (Illus.). (J). 1991. 176p. (ps up). 22.50 (*0-525-44776-8*); Set. 1992. (gr. 2 up). 90.00 o.s.i (*0-525-45004-1*) Penguin Putnam Bks. for Young Readers. (Dutton Children's Bks.).

—Winnie the Pooh. abr. ed. (J). 1997. 22.00 o.s.i incl. audio (*0-553-47866-4*); 1998. audio 16.98 Random Hse. Audio Publishing Group.

—Winnie the Pooh. abr. ed. (Classic Ser.). (J). 1996. audio 10.95 o.s.i (*0-14-086267-6*); 1997. audio 16.95 o.p. (*0-14-086682-5*) Viking Penguin. (Penguin AudioBooks).

—Winnie the Pooh: A Pop-Up Book. 1984. (Illus.). 1p. (J). (ps up). 13.00 o.s.i (*0-525-44119-0*, Dutton Children's Bks.) Penguin Putnam Bks. for Young Readers.

—Winnie the Pooh: A Reproduction of the Original Manuscript. 1971. (J). (gr. k up). 25.00 o.p. (*0-525-43040-7*, Dutton) Dutton/Plume.

—Winnie the Pooh: Colored Ed. 1974. (J). (gr. 1-5). 8.95 o.p. (*0-525-43034-2*, Dutton) Dutton/Plume.

—Winnie the Pooh: Full Musical. 1964. 5.95 (*0-87129-364-1*, W01) Dramatic Publishing Co.

—Winnie the Pooh: 75th Anniversary Edition. anniv. ed. 2001. (Illus.). 176p. 14.99 (*0-525-46756-4*, Dutton Children's Bks.) Penguin Putnam Bks. for Young Readers.

—Winnie the Pooh & Some Bees. 2001. (Illus.). 48p. (J). 13.99 o.s.i (*0-525-46781-5*, Dutton Children's Bks.) Penguin Putnam Bks. for Young Readers.

—Winnie the Pooh & Some Bees. (Easy-to-Read Ser.). (Illus.). 2001. 48p. (J). pap. 3.99 (*0-14-230041-1*, Puffin Bks.); 1999. 32p. (J). 9.99 o.s.i (*0-525-46270-8*, Dutton); 1993. 32p. (J). 4.99 o.p. (*0-525-45443-8*, Dutton Children's Bks.); 1993. 32p. (J). 14.99 o.s.i (*0-525-45044-0*, Dutton Children's Bks.); 2000. 32p. pap. 9.99 incl. audio (*0-14-095450-3*, Puffin Bks.) Penguin Putnam Bks. for Young Readers.

—Winnie the Pooh & Some Bees Storybooks. (Pooh Storybook Ser.). (J). 1993. (Illus.). 32p. (gr. 2 up). 4.99 o.s.i (*0-525-45033-5*); 1973. 128p. (ps-2). 6.95 o.p. (*0-525-38285-2*) Penguin Putnam Bks. for Young Readers. (Dutton Children's Bks.).

—Winnie the Pooh & the House Around the Corner. abr. ed. 1995. (Napier & Judd Ser.). (J). (gr. 4-7). audio 16.99 o.s.i (*0-553-47433-2*, Listening Library) Random Hse. Audio Publishing Group.

—Winnie the Pooh & the House at Pooh Corner. unabr. ed. 1997. audio 16.95 Viking Penguin.

—Winnie the Pooh & When We Were Young. (J). Boxed set. 32p. pap. incl. audio compact disk (*1-57375-583-4*, 71512); Set. 1998. audio 29.98; Set. 32p. pap. incl. audio (*1-57375-652-0*, 71514) Audioscope.

—Winnie the Pooh & When We Were Young. unabr. ed. (J). 1998. audio 26.95; 1998. audio 22.95 (*1-55935-243-4*); Set. 1995. (gr. 4-7). 26.95 incl. audio (*1-55935-124-1*, 492024) Soundelux Audio Publishing.

—Winnie the Pooh at Pooh Corner & Now We Are Six, Set. 1998. (J). 29.98 incl. audio Audioscope.

—Winnie the Pooh Collection. abr. ed. 1998. (J). audio 29.95 o.p. (*1-85998-887-3*) Trafalgar Square.

—Winnie the Pooh Goes Exploring. 1986. (Pooh Sticker Bks.). (Illus.). (J). (ps-4). 2.98 o.p. (*0-525-44269-3*, Dutton Children's Bks.) Penguin Putnam Bks. for Young Readers.

—The Winnie the Pooh Journal. 1986. (Illus.). 6p. (J). (ps up). 7.99 o.s.i (*0-525-44237-5*, Dutton Children's Bks.) Penguin Putnam Bks. for Young Readers.

—Winnie the Pooh Lift-the-Flap Rebus Book. 1992. (Illus.). 160p. (J). (ps-3). 13.99 o.s.i (*0-525-44987-6*, Dutton Children's Bks.) Penguin Putnam Bks. for Young Readers.

—Winnie the Pooh Read Aloud Collection, 3 vols., Set. 1998. (Illus.). 32p. (J). (ps-3). pap. 21.99 o.p. incl. audio (*0-525-46111-6*, Dutton Children's Bks.) Penguin Putnam Bks. for Young Readers.

—Winnie the Pooh Tells Time. (Winnie-the-Pooh Sticker Storybooks Ser.). (Illus.). (J). 2000. 16p. (ps-3). 5.99 o.s.i (*0-525-46336-4*, Dutton Children's Bks.); 1997. 28p. (gr. 1-4). 9.99 o.s.i (*0-525-45535-3*) Penguin Putnam Bks. for Young Readers.

—Winnie the Pooh's ABC Sticker Storybook. 1999. (Illus.). (J). (ps-3). 5.99 o.s.i (*0-525-46275-9*) Penguin Putnam Bks. for Young Readers.

—Winnie the Pooh's Baby Book. 1994. (Illus.). 32p. (J). (gr. k up). 15.99 (*0-525-45298-2*, Dutton Children's Bks.) Penguin Putnam Bks. for Young Readers.

—Winnie the Pooh's Book & Toy Box. 1994. (Illus.). 32p. (J). (gr. k up). 29.99 o.s.i (*0-525-45342-3*, Dutton Children's Bks.) Penguin Putnam Bks. for Young Readers.

—Winnie the Pooh's Book of Spring. 2002. (Illus.). 48p. (J). 8.99 (*0-525-46819-6*, Dutton Children's Bks.) Penguin Putnam Bks. for Young Readers.

—Winnie the Pooh's Colors. 1995. (Illus.). 32p. (J). (ps-3). 9.99 o.s.i (*0-525-45428-4*, Dutton Children's Bks.) Penguin Putnam Bks. for Young Readers.

—Winnie the Pooh's Cookie Book. 1996. (Illus.). 64p. (J). (ps-3). 8.99 o.s.i (*0-525-45688-0*) Penguin Putnam Bks. for Young Readers.

—Winnie the Pooh's Friendship Book. 1994. (Illus.). 48p. (J). (ps-3). 8.99 o.s.i (*0-525-45204-4*, Dutton Children's Bks.) Penguin Putnam Bks. for Young Readers.

—Winnie the Pooh's Giant Lift-the-Flap Book. 1997. (Illus.). 12p. (J). (ps-2). 9.99 (*0-525-45841-7*) Penguin Putnam Bks. for Young Readers.

—Winnie the Pooh's Hundred Acre Wood: A Press-Out Model Book. 1994. (Illus.). 40p. (J). (gr. k up). pap. 9.99 o.s.i (*0-525-45341-5*, Dutton Children's Bks.) Penguin Putnam Bks. for Young Readers.

—Winnie the Pooh's Little Book about Food. 1992. (Illus.). 10p. (J). (ps up). 4.95 o.s.i (*0-525-44875-6*, Dutton Children's Bks.) Penguin Putnam Bks. for Young Readers.

—Winnie the Pooh's Little Book about Friends. 1992. (Illus.). 10p. (J). (ps up). 4.95 o.s.i (*0-525-44874-8*, Dutton Children's Bks.) Penguin Putnam Bks. for Young Readers.

—Winnie the Pooh's Little Book about Parties. 1992. (Illus.). 10p. (J). (ps up). 4.95 o.s.i (*0-525-44876-4*, Dutton Children's Bks.) Penguin Putnam Bks. for Young Readers.

—Winnie the Pooh's Little Book about the Weather. 1992. (Illus.). 10p. (J). (ps up). 4.95 o.s.i (*0-525-44877-2*, Dutton Children's Bks.) Penguin Putnam Bks. for Young Readers.

—Winnie the Pooh's Opposites. 1995. (Illus.). 32p. (J). (ps-3). bds. 9.99 o.s.i (*0-525-45429-2*, Dutton Children's Bks.) Penguin Putnam Bks. for Young Readers.

—Winnie the Pooh's Picnic Cookbook. 1997. (Illus.). 64p. (J). (gr. 1-4). 8.99 o.s.i (*0-525-45533-7*) Penguin Putnam Bks. for Young Readers.

—Winnie the Pooh's Pop-Up Theater Book. 1993. (Illus.). 12p. (J). (ps-3). 15.99 o.p. (*0-525-44990-6*, Dutton Children's Bks.) Penguin Putnam Bks. for Young Readers.

—Winnie the Pooh's Revolving Picture Book. 1990. (Illus.). 1p. (J). (ps up). 13.99 o.p. (*0-525-44645-1*, Dutton Children's Bks.) Penguin Putnam Bks. for Young Readers.

—Winnie the Pooh's Shapes & Colors. 2000. (Winnie-the-Pooh Sticker Storybooks Ser.). (Illus.). 16p. (J). (ps-k). 5.99 o.s.i (*0-525-46337-2*, Dutton Children's Bks.) Penguin Putnam Bks. for Young Readers.

—Winnie the Pooh's Story Box, 10 bks., Set. 1993. (Illus.). (J). 49.90 o.s.i (*0-525-45168-4*, Dutton Children's Bks.) Penguin Putnam Bks. for Young Readers.

—Winnie-the-Pooh's Storybook Set. 2003. (Illus.). 60p. 10.99 (*0-525-47048-4*, Dutton Children's Bks.) Penguin Putnam Bks. for Young Readers.

—Winnie the Pooh's Teatime Cookbook. 1993. (Illus.). 64p. (J). (gr. 2 up). 10.99 o.p. (*0-525-45135-8*, Dutton Children's Bks.) Penguin Putnam Bks. for Young Readers.

—Winnie the Pooh's Trivia Quiz Book. 1994. (Illus.). 48p. (J). (gr. 2 up). 9.99 o.s.i (*0-525-45265-6*, Dutton Children's Bks.) Penguin Putnam Bks. for Young Readers.

—Winnie the Pooh's Visitors Book. 1994. (Illus.). 128p. (J). 13.99 o.p. (*0-525-45217-6*, Dutton Children's Bks.) Penguin Putnam Bks. for Young Readers.

—Winnie the Pooh's 1-2-3. 2015. (Illus.). 32p. (J). pap. 4.99 (*0-14-056506-X*, Puffin Bks.) Penguin Putnam Bks. for Young Readers.

—Winnie the Pooh's 1-2-3. 1996. (Illus.). 32p. (J). (ps-3). 9.99 o.s.i (*0-525-45534-5*) Penguin Putnam Bks. for Young Readers.

—Winnie the Pooh's 1-2-3 Sticker Storybook. (Illus.). 2002. mass mkt. 5.99 (*0-525-47011-5*); 1999. 16p. (J). pap. 5.99 o.s.i (*0-525-46274-0*) Penguin Putnam Bks. for Young Readers.

—The World of Pooh. 1957. (Illus.). (J). (gr. 1-4). 13.95 o.p. (*0-525-43320-1*, 01258-370, Dutton) Dutton/Plume.

—The World of Pooh. 1988. (Pooh Original Edition Ser.). (Illus.). 32p. (J). (ps-3). 21.99 (*0-525-44447-5*, Dutton Children's Bks.) Penguin Putnam Bks. for Young Readers.

Milne, A. A., pseud & Fraser-Simon, H. The Pooh Song Book. 1985. (Illus.). 154p. (J). pap. 8.95 o.p. (*0-87923-557-8*) Godine, David R. Pub.

Milnes, Ellen. Winnie the Pooh's School Days. 2000. (Winnie the Pooh Ser.). (Illus.). 10p. (J). (ps-k). bds. 9.99 (*0-7364-1034-1*) Mouse Works.

Moore, Sparky, et al. Pooh Christmas Days. 1996. (J). (*0-7853-1784-8*) Publications International, Ltd.

Mordden, Ethan. Pooh's Workout Book. 1984. (Illus.). 160p. 10.95 o.p. (*0-525-24276-7*, Dutton) Dutton/Plume.

—Pooh's Workout Book. 1985. 180p. pap. 5.95 o.p. (*0-14-008304-9*, Penguin Bks.) Viking Penguin.

Mouse Works Staff. Pooh. 1999. (My Very First Cloth Book Ser.). (J). 6.99 (*0-7364-0177-6*) Disney Pr.

—Pooh. 1998. 10p. (J). 6.99 (*0-7364-0019-2*) Mouse Works.

—Pooh Cuddler. 2001. 6p. (J). 2.10 (*0-7364-0234-9*) Mouse Works.

—Pooh's A-B-C Learn & Grow. 1998. (Winnie the Pooh Ser.). (Illus.). 18p. (J). (ps). bds. 4.99 (*1-57082-779-6*) Mouse Works.

—Pooh's Pitter Patter Splash. 1999. (Pooh Busy Bks.). (Illus.). 12p. (J). (ps-k). bds. 6.99 (*1-57082-943-8*) Mouse Works.

—Pooh's Tree House. 2001. (Illus.). 12p. (J). bds. 8.99 o.s.i (*0-7364-1211-5*, RH/Disney) Random Hse. Children's Bks.

—Pooh's 1-2-3 Learn & Grow. 1998. (Winnie the Pooh Ser.). (Illus.). 20p. (J). bds. 4.99 (*1-57082-789-3*) Mouse Works.

—Santa Roo: Peek-a-Pooh. 1996. 10p. (J). 6.98 (*1-57082-331-6*) Mouse Works.

—Tigger Cuddler. 2001. 6p. (J). 2.10 (*0-7364-0235-7*) Mouse Works.

—Where's Piglet? 1995. (Winnie the Pooh Ser.). (Illus.). 12p. (J). (ps-k). 6.98 (*1-57082-262-X*) Mouse Works.

—Winnie the Pooh First Reader Collection: Storybook Collect. 2000. (Storybook Collection Ser.). (Illus.). 192p. (J). (ps-3). 9.99 o.s.i (*0-7364-1050-3*) Mouse Works.

—Winnie the Pooh Spanish Read. 1999. 48p. (J). pap. 4.99 (*0-7364-0108-3*) Mouse Works.

—Winnie the Pooh's Big Book of First Words, Vol. 1. 1999. (Learn & Grow Ser.). (Illus.). 48p. (J). (ps-k). 12.99 o.s.i (*0-7364-0142-3*) Mouse Works.

—Winnie the Pooh's Christmas Stories: Winnie-the-Pooh & Some Bees - Eeyore Has a Birthday - Piglet Is Entirely Surrounded by Water. 1999. (Learn & Grow Ser.). (Illus.). 48p. (J). (ps-2). 12.99 o.s.i (*0-7364-0109-1*) Mouse Works.

—Winnie the Pooh's Friendly Adventures. 1999. (Disney's Read-Aloud Storybooks Ser.). (Illus.). 64p. (J). (ps-2). 8.99 (*0-7364-0107-5*) Mouse Works.

—Winnie the Pooh's Holiday Hummables. 2000. (Tab Board Bks.). 14p. (J). (ps-k). bds. 7.99 (*0-7364-1060-0*) Mouse Works.

—Winnie the Pooh's Sweet Dreams Set: One, Two, Pooh's Looking for You, 4 vol., set. 1999. (Learn & Grow Ser.). (Illus.). 10p. (J). (ps-k). bds. 9.99 (*0-7364-0145-8*) Mouse Works.

—Winnie the Pooh's Touch & Feel Book. 2nd ed. 2005. 10p. (J). 6.99 (*0-7364-1021-X*) Hyperion Pr.

My Name Is Pooh! 2004. (Bath Books with Crayon Ser.). 6p. (J). 5.99 (*0-7364-2195-5*, RH/Disney) Random Hse. Children's Bks.

My Very First Winnie the Pooh. 2000. 192p. (J). 14.99 (*0-7868-3271-1*) Disney Pr.

Nal-Dutton Staff. Winnie the Pooh Engagement. 1999. (Illus.). 112p. 12.99 o.p. (*0-525-46210-4*) Penguin Putnam Bks. for Young Readers.

Opposites: Book of Pooh. 2002. (Illus.). 10p. (J). (ps-k). bds. 5.99 (*0-7868-3355-6*) Disney Pr.

Parent, Nancy. Pooh Says Boo. 1998. (Pooh Ser.). (Illus.). 10p. (J). (ps). 4.99 (*1-57082-752-4*) Mouse Works.

Pooh: Tricks & Treats. 2001. 16p. (J). pap. 2.99 (*0-7364-1191-7*, RH/Disney) Random Hse. Children's Bks.

Pooh Busca Numeros Number Hunt. 2001. (Illus.). (J). 12.98 (*0-7853-5351-8*) Publications International, Ltd.

Pooh Dulces Suenos. 2001. (SPA., Illus.). (J). 7.95 (*0-7853-5227-9*) Publications International, Ltd.

Pooh Gets Stuck. 1999. (J). pap. 3.95 o.s.i (*0-7364-0915-7*) Mouse Works.

Pooh Hello Friend Book & Box. 2002. (Illus.). (J). pap. 9.98 (*0-7853-5251-1*) Publications International, Ltd.

Pooh Juegos y Fiestas. 2001. (SPA., Illus.). (J). (*0-7853-5228-7*) Publications International, Ltd.

Pooh Time for School. 2001. (Illus.). (J). 7.95 (*0-7853-4790-9*) Publications International, Ltd.

Pooh's Perfect Day. 2000. (Giant Pooh Book Ends Ser.). (Illus.). 10p. (J). (ps). (*1-57584-807-4*) Reader's Digest Children's Publishing, Inc.

Pooh's Perfect Picnic. 2001. (Learn to Read Ser.). (Illus.). 18p. (J). bds. 5.99 (*0-7868-3351-3*) Disney Pr.

Randall, Ronne. Disney's Pooh: Thank You, Pooh! 1996. (Illus.). 24p. (J). pap. text o.p. (*0-307-98756-6*, Golden Bks.) Random Hse. Children's Bks.

Random House Books for Young Readers Staff. Pooh's Search for Honey. 2003. (Illus.). 12p. (J). bds. 6.99 (*0-7364-2052-5*, RH/Disney) Random Hse. Children's Bks.

Random House Disney Staff. Eeyore's Not-So-Gloomy Day. 2003. (Illus.). 12p. (J). bds. 6.99 (*0-7364-2055-X*, RH/Disney) Random Hse. Children's Bks.

—Little Red Riding Pooh. 2004. (J). (*0-7364-2216-1*, RH/Disney) Random Hse. Children's Bks.

—Piglet's New Friend. 2003. (Illus.). 12p. (J). bds. 6.99 (*0-7364-2053-3*, RH/Disney) Random Hse. Children's Bks.

—Playfully Pooh. 2003. (J). pap. 3.99 (*0-7364-2124-6*, RH/Disney) Random Hse. Children's Bks.

—Pooh's Christmas Sled Ride. 2003. (Illus.). 32p. (J). pap. 3.99 (*0-7364-2165-3*, RH/Disney) Random Hse. Children's Bks.

—Pooh's Easter Egg Hunt. 2003. (Step into Reading Ser.). 32p. (J). lib. bdg. 11.99 (*0-7364-8005-6*, RH/Disney) Random Hse. Children's Bks.

—What Tigger's Do Best. 2003. (Illus.). 12p. (J). bds. 6.99 (*0-7364-2054-1*, RH/Disney) Random Hse. Children's Bks.

RH Disney Staff. Giggle with Tigger. 2003. (Illus.). 16p. (J). 3.99 (*0-7364-2182-3*, RH/Disney) Random Hse. Children's Bks.

—Graduation Pooh. 2004. (Illus.). bds. 6.99 (*0-7364-2261-7*, RH/Disney) Random Hse. Children's Bks.

—Playtime with Pooh. 2003. (Illus.). 16p. (J). 3.99 (*0-7364-2183-1*, RH/Disney) Random Hse. Children's Bks.

—Pooh's Christmas Sled Ride. 2003. (Illus.). 32p. (J). lib. bdg. 11.99 (*0-7364-8024-2*, RH/Disney) Random Hse. Children's Bks.

—Pooh's Colourful Garden. 2003. (Pooh's Wheel Bks.). (Illus.). 6p. (J). (ps-k). bds. 5.99 (*0-7364-2133-5*, RH/Disney) Random Hse. Children's Bks.

—Pooh's Happy Halloween. 2003. (Illus.). 24p. (J). (gr. k-3). pap. 3.25 (*0-7364-1329-4*, RH/Disney) Random Hse. Children's Bks.

Rodgers, James W. A Winnie the Pooh Christmas Tail: Christmas Musical. 1994. pap. 5.95 (*0-87129-225-4*, W03) Dramatic Publishing Co.

Sergel, Kristin. Winnie the Pooh: Straight Version. rev. ed. 1992. pap. 5.95 (*0-87129-194-0*, W37) Dramatic Publishing Co.

Shealy, Dennis R. Winnie the Pooh's Great Big Flap Book. 2001. (Disney's Winnie the Pooh Ser.). (Illus.). 12p. (J). bds. 11.99 o.s.i (*0-7364-1094-5*, RH/Disney) Random Hse. Children's Bks.

Shepard, Ernest H., illus. The Pooh Sketchbook. 1984. 96p. (YA). (gr. 3 up). 14.95 o.p. (*0-525-44084-4*) NAL.

—Pooh's Etiquette Book. 1995. 96p. (J). (ps up). 8.99 o.s.i (*0-525-45501-9*, Dutton Children's Bks.) Penguin Putnam Bks. for Young Readers.

—Winnie the Pooh's ABC. 1995. (Winnie-the-Pooh Collections). 32p. (J). (ps-2). 9.99 o.s.i (*0-525-45365-2*, Dutton Children's Bks.) Penguin Putnam Bks. for Young Readers.

—Winnie the Pooh's Birthday Book. 1993. 128p. (J). (ps-3). 12.99 o.p. (*0-525-45061-0*, Dutton Children's Bks.) Penguin Putnam Bks. for Young Readers.

Sherman, Richard. Pooh: Songs from Classic "Winnie the Pooh" Featurettes. 1995. (Illus.). 40p. (gr. 1-3). pap. 10.95 (*0-7935-4058-5*) Leonard, Hal Corp.

Slater, Teddy. Winnie the Pooh & a Day for Eeyore. 1994. (Illus.). 48p. (J). (ps-4). 12.95 o.p. (*1-56282-657-3*) Disney Pr.

—Winnie the Pooh & the Blustery Day. 1993. (Many Adventures of Winnie the Pooh Ser.). (Illus.). 48p. (J). (ps-4). 12.95 (*1-56282-488-0*) Disney Pr.

Talkington, Bruce. Disney's Winnie the Pooh's Halloween. 1993. (Illus.). 32p. (J). (ps-4). 11.95 (*1-56282-540-2*) Disney Pr.

—Happy Birthday, Pooh! 1999. (Pooh Ser.). (Illus.). 32p. (J). (ps-2). 12.99 (*0-7868-3218-5*) Disney Pr.

—Pooh's Grand Adventure: The Search for Christopher Robin, Vol. 1. 1997. (Pooh's Grand Adventure Ser.: Vol. 1). (Illus.). 32p. (J). (gr. k-2). 12.95 (*0-7868-3135-9*) Disney Pr.

—Pooh's Wishing Star. 1998. (Winnie the Pooh Ser.). (Illus.). 32p. (J). (ps-2). 12.95 o.s.i (*0-7868-3176-6*) Little Brown & Co.

—Winnie the Pooh & the Bumble Bee Chase. rev. ed. 1998. 14p. (J). 11.95 (*0-7868-3228-2*) Disney Pr.

—Winnie the Pooh & the Bumble Bee Chase: A Turn-the-Wheel Storybook. 1995. (Illus.). 14p. (J). (ps-k). text 11.95 (*0-7868-3022-0*, Irwin Professional Publishing) McGraw-Hill School Education Group.

—Winnie the Pooh & the Perfect Christmas Tree: A Pop-Up Book. 1994. (Illus.). 12p. (J). (ps-3). 11.95 o.p. (*1-56282-649-2*) Disney Pr.

—Winnie the Pooh's Bedtime Stories. 1994. (Illus.). 96p. (J). (ps-3). 14.95 (*1-56282-646-8*) Disney Pr.

—Winnie the Pooh's Easter. (Winnie the Pooh Ser.). (Illus.). 32p. (J). (ps-1). 1998. 5.95 (*0-7868-3191-X*); 1996. pap. 5.95 (*0-7868-4065-X*); 1993. 12.95 (*1-56282-377-9*) Disney Pr.

—Winnie the Pooh's Easter. 1998. 32p. (J). 5.95 (*0-7868-3202-9*) Hyperion Bks. for Children.

—Winnie the Pooh's Nightmare: A Pop-Up Book. 1995. (Illus.). 12p. (J). (ps-3). 12.95 (*0-7868-3019-0*) Disney Pr.

—Winnie the Pooh's Silly Day. (Pooh Ser.). (Illus.). 32p. (J). (ps-2). 1999. pap. 4.99 (*0-7868-4334-9*); 1996. 11.95 o.p. (*0-7868-3069-7*) Disney Pr.

—Winnie the Pooh's Stories for Christmas. 1996. (Illus.). 80p. (J). (ps-3). 14.95 (*0-7868-3107-3*) Disney Pr.

—Winnie the Pooh's Thanksgiving. (Pooh Ser.). (Illus.). 32p. (J). (ps-4). 1998. pap. 4.95 (*0-7868-4293-8*); 1995. 11.95 (*0-7868-3053-0*) Disney Pr.

—Winnie the Pooh's Valentine Kit. (Winnie the Pooh Ser.). (Illus.). 32p. (J). (ps-3). 1996. pap. 4.95 (*0-7868-4111-7*); 1995. 11.95 (*0-7868-3017-4*) Disney Pr.

—Winnie the Pooh's Valentine Mini. 1998. (Illus.). 32p. (J). 11.95 (*0-7868-3201-0*) Disney Pr.

Talkington, Bruce & Langley, Bill. Winnie the Pooh's Easter Egg Decorating Kit: Everything You Need to Decorate Adorable Eggs for Easter. 1997. (Illus.). 32p. (J). (ps-2). 9.95 (*0-7868-4127-3*, 715169) Disney Pr.

Talkington, Bruce & Milne, A. A. Spooking Pooh. 1998. (Pooh Ser.). (Illus.). 32p. (J). (ps). 12.95 o.s.i (*0-7868-3177-4*) Little Brown & Co.

Tallarico, Tony, illus. Winnie the Pooh: Punch Out & Stencil Books. 1987. (Disney Ser.). 24p. (J). (ps-5). 6.95 o.s.i (*0-89828-352-3*, 83523, Tuffy Bks.) Putnam Publishing Group, The.

Templar Publishing Staff. Winnie the Pooh: Winnie's Hologram Book. Date not set. (Illus.). 32p. (J). pap. 11.99 (*0-7868-4162-1*) Disney Pr.

Titlebaum, Ellen. The Tigger Movie: Disney's Winnie the Pooh & the Family Tree. 2000. (Read-Aloud Storybook Ser.). (Illus.). 72p. (J). (ps-2). 6.99 (*0-7364-1002-3*) Mouse Works.

Vaccaro Associates, contrib. by. Pooh's Big & Little Book. 1994. (Pull a Page Ser.). (Illus.). 6p. (J). (ps-1). 9.98 (*1-57082-147-X*) Mouse Works.

Walt Disney's Winnie the Pooh & the Pebble Hunt. 1982. (J). o.p. (*0-307-10121-5*, Golden Bks.) Random Hse. Children's Bks.

Williams, Bill, illus. Walt Disney's Winnie the Pooh All Year Long. 1995. (Golden Sturdy Bks.). 14p. (J). (ps). bds. 3.29 o.p. (*0-307-12260-3*, Golden Bks.) Random Hse. Children's Bks.

Winnie the Pooh. Date not set. (Pop-Up Bks.). (Illus.). 24p. (J). 15.99 (*0-7868-3162-6*) Disney Pr.

Winnie the Pooh. 2004. (Ultimate Sticker Books Ser.). 16p. (J). pap. 6.99 (*0-7894-9996-7*) Dorling Kindersley Publishing, Inc.

Winnie the Pooh. 1994. (Classics Ser.). (Illus.). 96p. (J). 7.98 (*1-57082-053-8*) Mouse Works.

Winnie the Pooh. (J). 9999. pap. o.p. (*0-307-04040-2*); 1991. (Illus.). 24p. o.p. (*0-307-74019-6*) Random Hse. Children's Bks. (Golden Bks.).

Winnie the Pooh. (Play Packs Ser.). (J). 14.99 incl. audio (*0-7634-0200-1*); 11.99 incl. audio (*1-55723-933-9*); 11.99 incl. audio (*1-55723-933-9*); audio compact disk 12.99 (*0-7634-0392-X*) Walt Disney Records.

Winnie the Pooh. unabr. ed. Incl. Winnie the Pooh: In Which Eeyore Loses a Tail & Pooh Finds One. audio o.p. Winnie the Pooh: In Which Piglet Meets a Heffalump. audio o.p. Winnie the Pooh: In Which Pooh Goes Visiting & Gets Stuck into a Tight Place. audio o.p. (J). (ps-3). 1972. 1972. Set audio 11.00 o.p. (*0-89845-094-2*, CPN 1408, Caedmon) HarperTrade.

Winnie the Pooh: In Which Eeyore Loses a Tail & Pooh Finds One. 1972. (J). (ps-3). audio o.p. HarperTrade.

Winnie the Pooh: In Which Piglet Meets a Heffalump. 1972. (J). (ps-3). audio o.p. HarperTrade.

Winnie the Pooh: In Which Pooh Goes Visiting & Gets Stuck into a Tight Place. 1972. (J). (ps-3). audio o.p. HarperTrade.

Winnie the Pooh: Storybook Collection Edition. 2003. 320p. (J). 15.99 (*0-7868-3444-7*) Disney Pr.

Winnie the Pooh: Take My Hand. (Classic Collections). (J). audio 10.99 (*1-55723-626-7*); audio compact disk 16.99 (*1-55723-628-3*); audio compact disk 16.99 (*1-55723-627-5*); 1995. audio 10.99 (*1-55723-625-9*) Walt Disney Records.

Winnie the Pooh: 6 Wonderful Stories. (Little Golden Bks.). (J). 0.99 o.p. (*0-307-15888-8*, 15888, Golden Bks.) Random Hse. Children's Bks.

Winnie the Pooh & a Day for Eeyore. (Read-Along Ser.). (J). 7.99 incl. audio (*1-55723-176-1*) Walt Disney Records.

Winnie the Pooh & Christopher Robin. abr. ed. Incl. Winnie the Pooh & Christopher Robin: A Search Is Organized & Piglet Nearly Meets the Heffalump Again. audio o.p. Winnie the Pooh & Christopher Robin: Christopher Robin Leads An Expedition to the North Pole. audio o.p. Winnie the Pooh & Christopher Robin: Pooh & Piglet Go Hunting & Nearly Catch a Woozle. audio o.p. Winnie the Pooh & Christopher Robin: Rabbit Has a Busy Day & We Learn What Christopher Robin Does in the Morning. audio o.p. (J). Set audio 8.98 o.p. (*0-89845-265-1*, CP 1744, Caedmon) HarperTrade.

Winnie the Pooh & Christopher Robin: A Search Is Organized & Piglet Nearly Meets the Heffalump Again. (J). audio o.p. HarperTrade.

Winnie the Pooh & Christopher Robin: Christopher Robin Leads An Expedition to the North Pole. (J). audio o.p. HarperTrade.

Winnie the Pooh & Christopher Robin: Pooh & Piglet Go Hunting & Nearly Catch a Woozle. (J). audio o.p. HarperTrade.

Winnie the Pooh & Christopher Robin: Rabbit Has a Busy Day & We Learn What Christopher Robin Does in the Morning. (J). audio o.p. HarperTrade.

Winnie the Pooh & Kanga & Roo. abr. ed. Incl. Winnie the Pooh & Kanga & Roo: Christopher Robin & Pooh Come to an Enchanted Place & We Leave Them There. audio o.p. Winnie the Pooh & Kanga & Roo: Kanga & Baby Roo Come to the Forest & Piglet Has a Bath. audio o.p. Winnie the Pooh & Kanga & Roo: Piglet Is Entirely Surrounded by Water. audio o.p. (J). Set audio 8.98 o.p. (*0-89845-062-4*, CP 1685, Caedmon) HarperTrade.

Winnie the Pooh & Kanga & Roo: Christopher Robin & Pooh Come to an Enchanted Place & We Leave Them There. (J). audio o.p. HarperTrade.

Winnie the Pooh & Kanga & Roo: Kanga & Baby Roo Come to the Forest & Piglet Has a Bath. (J). audio o.p. HarperTrade.

Winnie the Pooh & Kanga & Roo: Piglet Is Entirely Surrounded by Water. (J). audio o.p. HarperTrade.

Winnie the Pooh & the Blustery Day. 1999. (Disney Ser.). (Illus.). 56p. (ps-3). pap. text 2.99 (*0-307-28029-2*, Golden Bks.) Random Hse. Children's Bks.

Winnie the Pooh & the Blustery Day. 1991. (Read-Along Ser.). (J). (ps-3). 7.99 incl. audio (*1-55723-174-5*) Walt Disney Records.

Winnie the Pooh & the Hanukkah Dreidel. 1998. (Winnie the Pooh Ser.). (Illus.). 8p. (J). (ps-1). 2.99 (*1-57082-994-2*) Mouse Works.

Winnie the Pooh & the Honey Tree. 1994. (Little Golden Bks.). (Illus.). 24p. (J). (ps-2). bds. 2.99 o.p. (0-307-30201-6, 98267, Golden Bks.) Random Hse. Children's Bks.
Winnie the Pooh & the Honey Tree. 1991. (Read-Along Ser.). (J). (ps-3). 7.99 incl. audio (1-55723-173-7) Walt Disney Records.
Winnie the Pooh & Tigger. unabr. ed. Incl. Winnie the Pooh & Tigger: It Is Shown That Tiggers Don't Climb Trees. audio o.p. Winnie the Pooh & Tigger: Tigger Comes to the Forest & Has Breakfast. audio o.p. Winnie the Pooh & Tigger: Tigger Is Unbounced. audio o.p. (J). Set audio 9.95 o.p. (0-89845-806-4, CPN 1696, Caedmon) HarperTrade.
Winnie the Pooh & Tigger: It Is Shown That Tiggers Don't Climb Trees. (J). audio o.p. HarperTrade.
Winnie the Pooh & Tigger: Tigger Comes to the Forest & Has Breakfast. (J). audio o.p. HarperTrade.
Winnie the Pooh & Tigger: Tigger Is Unbounced. (J). audio o.p. HarperTrade.
Winnie the Pooh & Tigger Too. 1991. (Disney Learn to Draw Ser.). (Illus.). (J). 32p. pap. 6.95 o.p. (1-56010-096-6, DS05-H); 28p. pap. 6.95 o.p. (1-56010-090-7, DS05) Foster, Walter Publishing, Inc.
Winnie the Pooh & Tigger Too. 1991. (Read-Along Ser.). (J). (ps-3). 7.99 incl. audio (1-55723-175-3) Walt Disney Records.
Winnie the Pooh Box Set, TC. 1995. pap. text 2.49 o.p. (0-307-82117-X, Golden Bks.) Random Hse. Children's Bks.
Winnie the Pooh Friends Forever. (Classic Collections). (J). audio 11.99 (0-7634-0394-6); audio 11.99 (0-7634-0393-8); audio compact disk 19.99 (0-7634-0396-2); 1998. audio compact disk 19.99 (0-7634-0395-4) Walt Disney Records.
Winnie the Pooh Helping Hands. 1995. (Golden Look-Look Bks.). (Illus.). (J). (ps-3). pap. o.p. (0-307-16207-9, Golden Bks.) Random Hse. Children's Bks.
Winnie the Pooh Storytime: Fun Friendship Book. 1999. (J). 9.99 o.s.i (0-7364-1029-5) Mouse Works.
Winnie the Pooh, Whose Egg Are You? 1995. (Motion Picture Book Ser.). (Illus.). 12p. (J). (ps-3). pap. 7.98 o.p. (1-57082-127-5) Mouse Works.
XYZ Group Staff. Winnie the Pooh: The First Get Dressed Book. 1998. (Disney Cloth Book Ser.). (Illus.). (J). (ps-2). text 19.95 o.p. (1-879332-88-4) Futech Interactive Products, Inc.
Zoehfeld, Kathleen Weidner. Be Patient, Pooh. 2000. (Illus.). 32p. (J). (ps-k). 12.99 (0-7868-3250-9) Disney Pr.
—Disney's Pooh's Christmas Box. 1997. (Illus.). 24p. (J). (ps-2). 9.95 (0-7868-3156-1) Disney Pr.
—Don't Talk to Strangers, Pooh. 2000. (My Very First Winnie the Pooh Ser.). (Illus.). 32p. (J). (ps-k). pap. 4.99 (0-7868-4378-0) Disney Pr.
—Growing up Stories. 1999. (My Very First Winnie the Pooh Ser.). (Illus.). 192p. (J). (ps-k). 15.99 (0-7868-3238-X) Disney Pr.
—Happy New Year, Pooh! (My Very First Winnie the Pooh Ser.). (Illus.). 32p. (J). (ps-k). 2000. pap. 4.99 (0-7868-4418-3); 1997. 11.95 o.p. (0-7868-3144-8) Disney Pr.
—Hello, Spring! 2001. (Disney's Winnie the Pooh Ser.). (Illus.). 24p. (J). (ps-k). pap. 3.25 o.s.i (0-7364-1109-7, RH/Disney) Random Hse. Children's Bks.
—More Growing up Stories. 2001. (My Very First Winnie the Pooh Ser.). (Illus.). 192p. (J). (ps-k). 15.99 (0-7868-3310-6) Disney Pr.
—Pooh Welcomes Winter. 1997. (My Very First Winnie the Pooh Ser.). (Illus.). 32p. (J). (ps). 11.95 (0-7868-3146-4) Disney Pr.
—Pooh's Bad Dream. 2000. (My Very First Winnie the Pooh Ser.). (Illus.). 32p. (J). (ps-k). pap. 4.99 (0-7868-4377-2) Disney Pr.
—Pooh's Jingle Bells. (Illus.). 32p. (J). (ps-k). 2000. pap. 4.99 o.p. (0-7868-4419-1); 1998. 11.95 (0-7868-3204-5) Disney Pr.
—Pooh's Mailbox. 1998. (Winnie the Pooh Ser.). (Illus.). 32p. (J). (ps-2). 12.95 (0-7868-3154-5) Disney Pr.
—Roo's New Babysitter. 1999. (My Very First Winnie the Pooh Ser.). (Illus.). 32p. (J). (ps-k). 11.99 (0-7868-3215-0) Disney Pr.
—Winnie Pooh's Honey Adventure. 1999. (Disney's Read-Aloud Storybooks Ser.). (Illus.). 64p. (J). (ps-2). 6.99 (0-7364-0133-4) Mouse Works.
—Winnie the Pooh Christmas Book & Plush. 2001. 32p. (J). pap. 11.99 (0-7868-4163-X) Hyperion Pr.
—Winnie the Pooh's Honey Adventures. 1999. 64p. (J). 6.99 (0-7364-0139-3) Mouse Works.
Zoehfeld, Kathleen Weidner & Milne, A. A. Don't Talk to Strangers, Pooh! 1998. (My Very First Winnie the Pooh Ser.). (Illus.). 32p. (J). (ps). pap. 11.95 (0-7868-3145-6) Disney Pr.
Zolotow, Charlotte. Growing up Stories. Date not set. 114p. 20.49 (0-7868-2456-5) Hyperion Bks. for Children.
—Growing up Stories for 5-6 Grade. Date not set. 114p. pap. 19.99 (0-7868-0519-6) Disney Pr.

WISHBONE (FICTITIOUS CHARACTER)—FICTION

The Adventures of Wishbone, 18 bks. l.t. ed. Incl. Be a Wolf! Strickland, Brad. 144p. (gr. 4 up). lib. bdg. 22.60 (0-8368-2297-8); Digging to the Center of the Earth. Steele, Michael Anthony. (gr. 4 up). lib. bdg. 22.60 (0-8368-2595-0); Digging up the Past. Sathre, Vivian. 144p. (gr. 4 up). lib. bdg. 22.60 (0-8368-2302-8); Dog Overboard! Sathre, Vivian. (gr. 4 up). lib. bdg. 22.60 (0-8368-2590-X); Dr. Jekyll & Mr. Dog. Butcher, Nancy. (gr. 4 up). lib. bdg. 22.60 (0-8368-2592-6); Gullifur's Travels. Strickland, Brad & Strickland, Barbara. (gr. 4 up). lib. bdg. 22.60 (0-8368-2596-9); Homer Sweet Homer. Jablonski, Carla. (gr. 4 up). lib. bdg. 22.60 (0-8368-2591-8); Hunchdog of Notre Dame. Friedman, Michael Jan. 139p. (gr. 4 up). lib. bdg. 22.60 (0-8368-2301-X); Last of the Breed. Steele, Alexander. 163p. (gr. 4 up). lib. bdg. 22.60 (0-8368-2594-2); Moby Dog. Steele, Alexander. 144p. (gr. 4 up). lib. bdg. 22.60 (0-8368-2306-0); Mutt in the Iron Muzzle. Friedman, Michael Jan. 144p. (gr. 4 up). lib. bdg. 22.60 (0-8368-2303-6); Muttketeer! Crider, Bill. 144p. (gr. 4 up). lib. bdg. 22.60 (0-8368-2304-4); Pawloined Paper. Litowinski, Olga. (gr. 4 up). lib. bdg. 22.60 (0-8368-2589-6); Prince & the Pooch. Leavitt, Caroline. 144p. (gr. 4 up). lib. bdg. 22.60 (0-8368-2299-4); Pup in King Arthur's Court. Barkan, Joanne. 164p. (gr. 2-5). lib. bdg. 22.60 (0-8368-2593-4); Robinhound Crusoe. Leavitt, Caroline. 144p. (gr. 4 up). lib. bdg. 22.60 (0-8368-2300-1); Salty Dog. Strickland, Brad. 140p. (gr. 4 up). lib. bdg. 22.60 (0-8368-2298-6); Tale of Two Sitters. Barkan, Joanne. 144p. (gr. 4 up). lib. bdg. 22.60 (0-8368-2305-2); (J). 1999. (Illus.). 1999. Set lib. bdg. 406.80 (0-8368-2654-X) Stevens, Gareth Inc.
Barkan, Joanne. A Pup in King Arthur's Court. 1998. (Adventures of Wishbone Ser.: No. 15). (Illus.). 164p. (J). (gr. 2-5). pap. 3.99 o.p. (1-57064-325-3) Lyrick Publishing.
—A Pup in King Arthur's Court. l.t. ed. 1999. (Adventures of Wishbone Ser.: No. 15). (Illus.). 164p. (J). (gr. 2-5). lib. bdg. 22.60 (0-8368-2593-4) Stevens, Gareth Inc.
—A Pup in King Arthur's Court. 1999. (Adventures of Wishbone Ser.: No. 15). (J). (gr. 2-5). 10.04 (0-606-17609-8) Turtleback Bks.
—A Tale of Two Sitters. 1998. (Adventures of Wishbone Ser.: No. 9). (Illus.). 144p. (J). (gr. 2-5). mass mkt. 3.99 o.p. (1-57064-277-X, Big Red Chair Bks.) Lyrick Publishing.
—A Tale of Two Sitters. l.t. ed. 1999. (Adventures of Wishbone Ser.: No. 9). (Illus.). 144p. (J). (gr. 4 up). lib. bdg. 22.60 (0-8368-2305-2) Stevens, Gareth Inc.
—A Tale of Two Sitters. 1998. (Adventures of Wishbone Ser.: No. 9). (J). (gr. 2-5). 10.04 (0-606-19461-4) Turtleback Bks.
Butcher, Nancy. Dr. Jekyll & Mr. Dog. 1998. (Adventures of Wishbone Ser.: No. 14). (Illus.). 143p. (J). (gr. 2-5). pap. 3.99 o.p. (1-57064-388-1, Big Red Chair Bks.) Lyrick Publishing.
—Dr. Jekyll & Mr. Dog. l.t. ed. 1999. (Adventures of Wishbone Ser.: No. 14). (Illus.). (J). (gr. 4 up). lib. bdg. 22.60 (0-8368-2592-6) Stevens, Gareth Inc.
—Dr. Jekyll & Mr. Dog. 1998. (Adventures of Wishbone Ser.: No. 14). (J). (gr. 2-5). 10.04 (0-606-19455-X) Turtleback Bks.
—Lights! Camera! Action Dog!, 1999. (Wishbone Mysteries Ser.: No. 11). (J). (gr. 2-5). pap. text 1.99 o.p. (1-57064-762-3) Lyrick Publishing.
—Lights! Camera! Action Dog! Ryan, Kevin, ed. 1998. (Wishbone Mysteries Ser.: No. 11). (Illus.). 144p. (J). (gr. 2-5). mass mkt. 3.99 o.p. (1-57064-289-3) Scholastic, Inc.
—Lights! Camera! Action Dog! l.t. ed. 2000. (Wishbone Mysteries Ser.: No. 11). 139p. (J). (gr. 4 up). lib. bdg. 22.60 (0-8368-2694-9) Stevens, Gareth Inc.
—Lights! Camera! Action Dog! 1998. (Wishbone Mysteries Ser.: No. 11). (J). (gr. 2-5). 10.04 (0-606-15891-X) Turtleback Bks.
Capeci, Anne. The Case of the Cyber-Hacker. Ryan, Kevin, ed. 2000. (Wishbone Mysteries Ser.: No. 19). (Illus.). 144p. (J). (gr. 2-5). mass mkt. 3.99 o.p. (1-57064-773-9, Big Red Chair Bks.) Lyrick Publishing.
—Case of the Cyber-Hacker. l.t. ed. 2000. (Wishbone Mysteries Ser.: No. 19). 141p. (J). (gr. 4 up). lib. bdg. 22.60 (0-8368-2702-3) Stevens, Gareth Inc.
Cervantes Saavedra, Miguel de. Don Quixote: Wishbone Classics. 1996. (Wishbone Classics Ser.: No. 1). (Illus.). 128p. (gr. 3-7). mass mkt. 4.25 (0-06-106416-5, HarperEntertainment) Morrow/Avon.
—Don Quixote: Wishbone Classics. 1996. (Wishbone Classics Ser.: No. 1). (J). (gr. 3-7). 10.30 (0-606-10364-3) Turtleback Bks.
Crider, Bill. Muttketeer! 1997. (Adventures of Wishbone Ser.: No. 8). (Illus.). 144p. (J). (gr. 2-5). mass mkt. 3.99 o.p. (1-57064-272-9, Big Red Chair Bks.) Lyrick Publishing.
—Muttketeer! l.t. ed. 1999. (Adventures of Wishbone Ser.: No. 8). (Illus.). 144p. (J). (gr. 4 up). lib. bdg. 22.60 (0-8368-2304-4) Stevens, Gareth Inc.
—Muttketeer! 1997. (Adventures of Wishbone Ser.: No. 8). (J). (gr. 2-5). 10.04 (0-606-19460-6) Turtleback Bks.
Francis, A. D. Curse of Gold. 2000. (Adventures of Wishbone Ser.: No. 23). (Illus.). 144p. (J). (gr. 2-5). mass mkt. 3.99 o.p. (1-57064-432-2, Big Red Chair Bks.) Lyrick Publishing.
Friedman, Michael Jan. Hunchdog of Notre Dame. 1997. (Adventures of Wishbone Ser.: No. 5). (Illus.). 144p. (J). (gr. 2-5). mass mkt. 3.99 o.p. (1-57064-270-2, Big Red Chair Bks.) Lyrick Publishing.
—Hunchdog of Notre Dame. l.t. ed. 1999. (Adventures of Wishbone Ser.: No. 5). (Illus.). 139p. (J). (gr. 4 up). lib. bdg. 22.60 (0-8368-2301-X) Stevens, Gareth Inc.
—Hunchdog of Notre Dame. 1997. (Adventures of Wishbone Ser.: No. 5). (J). (gr. 2-5). 11.04 (0-606-18274-8) Turtleback Bks.
—The Mutt in the Iron Muzzle. 1997. (Adventures of Wishbone Ser.: No. 7). (Illus.). 141p. (J). (gr. 2-5). mass mkt. 3.99 o.p. (1-57064-274-5, Big Red Chair Bks.) Lyrick Publishing.
—The Mutt in the Iron Muzzle. 1997. (Adventures of Wishbone Ser.: No. 7). (J). (gr. 2-5). 10.04 (0-606-19459-2) Turtleback Bks.
—The Sirian Conspiracy. 1999. (Wishbone Mysteries Ser.: No. 16). (J). (gr. 2-5). 10.04 (0-606-17768-X) Turtleback Bks.
—The Stolen Trophy. 1998. (Wishbone Mysteries Ser.: No. 5). (Illus.). 144p. (J). (gr. 2-5). mass mkt. 3.99 o.p. (1-57064-286-9, Big Red Chair Bks.) Lyrick Publishing.
—The Stolen Trophy. l.t. ed. 1999. (Wishbone Mysteries Ser.: No. 5). 144p. (J). (gr. 4 up). lib. bdg. 22.60 (0-8368-2386-9) Stevens, Gareth Inc.
—The Stolen Trophy, 1998. (Wishbone Mysteries Ser.: No. 5). (J). (gr. 2-5). 10.04 (0-606-12859-X) Turtleback Bks.
Friedman, Michael Jan & Kupperberg, Paul. The Sirian Conspiracy. Ryan, Kevin, ed. 1999. (Wishbone Mysteries Ser.: Vol. No. 16). (Illus.). 144p. (J). (gr. 3-7). pap. 3.99 o.p. (1-57064-588-4) Lyrick Publishing.
Friedman, Michael Jan, et al. The Sirian Conspiracy. l.t. ed. 2000. (Wishbone Mysteries Ser.: No. 16). 141p. (J). (gr. 4 up). lib. bdg. 22.60 (0-8368-2699-X) Stevens, Gareth Inc.
Gantt, Leticia. Phantom of the Video Store. Ryan, Kevin, ed. 1999. (Wishbone Mysteries Ser.: No. 18). (Illus.). 144p. (J). (gr. 2-5). mass mkt. 3.99 o.p. (1-57064-587-6, Big Red Chair Bks.) Lyrick Publishing.
—Phantom of the Video Store. l.t. ed. 2000. (Wishbone Mysteries Ser.: No. 18). 141p. (J). (gr. 4 up). lib. bdg. 22.60 (0-8368-2701-5) Stevens, Gareth Inc.
—Phantom of the Video Store. 1999. E-Book (1-58824-427-X); E-Book (1-58824-396-6) ipicturebooks, LLC.
Holder, Nancy. Ivanhound. Ryan, Kevin, ed. 2000. Vol. No. 20. (Illus.). 144p. (J). (gr. 3-7). mass mkt. 3.99 o.p. (1-57064-431-4, Big Red Chair Bks.) Lyrick Publishing.
—Ivanhound. 2000. E-Book (1-58824-425-3); E-Book (1-58824-401-6) ipicturebooks, LLC.
Jablonski, Carla. Homer Sweet Homer. 1998. (Adventures of Wishbone Ser.: No. 13). (Illus.). 143p. (J). (gr. 2-5). pap. 3.99 o.p. (1-57064-392-X, Big Red Chair Bks.) Lyrick Publishing.
—Homer Sweet Homer. l.t. ed. 1999. (Adventures of Wishbone Ser.: No. 13). (Illus.). (J). (gr. 4 up). lib. bdg. 22.60 (0-8368-2591-8) Stevens, Gareth Inc.
—Homer Sweet Homer. 1998. (Adventures of Wishbone Ser.: No. 13). (J). (gr. 2-5). 10.04 (0-606-19454-1) Turtleback Bks.
—Legend of Sleepy Hollow. Ryan, Kevin, ed. 1998. (Super Adventures of Wishbone Ser.: No. 2). (Illus.). 233p. (J). (gr. 4-7). pap. 3.99 o.p. (1-57064-374-1, Big Red Chair Bks.) Lyrick Publishing.
—Legend of Sleepy Hollow. 1998. (Super Adventures of Wishbone Ser.: No. 2). (J). (gr. 4-7). 10.04 (0-606-17156-8) Turtleback Bks.
—Twenty Thousand Wags under the Sea. 2000. (Adventures of Wishbone Ser.: No. 22). (Illus.). 144p. (J). (gr. 2-5). pap. 3.99 o.p. (1-57064-387-3, Big Red Chair Bks.) Lyrick Publishing.
Leavitt, Caroline. The Prince & the Pooch. 1997. (Adventures of Wishbone Ser.: No. 3). (Illus.). 128p. (J). (gr. 2-5). mass mkt. 3.99 o.p. (1-57064-196-X, Big Red Chair Bks.) Lyrick Publishing.
—The Prince & the Pooch. l.t. ed. 1999. (Adventures of Wishbone Ser.: No. 3). (Illus.). 144p. (J). (gr. 4 up). lib. bdg. 22.60 (0-8368-2299-4) Stevens, Gareth Inc.
—The Prince & the Pooch. 1997. (Adventures of Wishbone Ser.: No. 3). (Illus.). (J). (gr. 2-5). 11.04 (0-606-18272-1) Turtleback Bks.
—Robinhound Crusoe. 1997. (Adventures of Wishbone Ser.: No. 4). (Illus.). 144p. (J). (gr. 2-5). mass mkt. 3.99 o.p. (1-57064-271-0, Big Red Chair Bks.) Lyrick Publishing.
—Robinhound Crusoe. l.t. ed. 1999. (Adventures of Wishbone Ser.: No. 4). (Illus.). 144p. (J). (gr. 4 up). lib. bdg. 22.60 (0-8368-2300-1) Stevens, Gareth Inc.
—Robinhound Crusoe. 1997. (Adventures of Wishbone Ser.: No. 4). (Illus.). (J). (gr. 2-5). 11.04 (0-606-18273-X) Turtleback Bks.
Litowinski, Olga. The Pawloined Paper. 1998. (Adventures of Wishbone Ser.: No. 11). (Illus.). 137p. (J). (gr. 2-5). pap. 3.99 o.p. (1-57064-276-1, Big Red Chair Bks.) Lyrick Publishing.
—The Pawloined Paper. l.t. ed. 1999. (Adventures of Wishbone Ser.: No. 11). (Illus.). (J). (gr. 4 up). lib. bdg. 22.60 (0-8368-2589-6) Stevens, Gareth Inc.
Lyrick Studios Staff. The Wishbone Mystery Pack. 1999. (Wishbone Mysteries Ser.). (Illus.). (J). (gr. 2-5). mass mkt. 11.97 o.p. (1-57064-756-9, Big Red Chair Bks.) Lyrick Publishing.
Mattern, Joanne. The Adventures of Robin Hood. 1996. (Wishbone Classics Ser.: No. 6). (J). (gr. 3-7). 10.04 (0-606-10369-4) Turtleback Bks.
Night of Three Ghosts. 2000. (Wishbone Adventures Ser.: No. 25). (Illus.). 144p. (J). (gr. 2-5). mass mkt. 3.99 o.p. (1-57064-391-1, Big Red Chair Bks.) Lyrick Publishing.
Orr, Wendy. Ark in the Park, ERS. 2000. (Redfeather Book Ser.). (Illus.). 78p. (J). (gr. k-5). 15.95 (0-8050-6221-1, Holt, Henry & Co. Bks. For Young Readers) Holt, Henry & Co.
Ryan, Kevin. Unleashed in Space. 2000. (Illus.). (J). (gr. 4-7). pap. text 3.99 o.p. (1-57064-968-5) Lyrick Publishing.
Sathre, Vivian. Digging up the Past. l.t. ed. 1999. (Adventures of Wishbone Ser.: No. 6). (Illus.). 144p. (J). (gr. 4 up). lib. bdg. 22.60 (0-8368-2302-8) Stevens, Gareth Inc.
—Digging up the Past. 1997. (Adventures of Wishbone Ser.: No. 6). (J). (gr. 2-5). 11.04 (0-606-18275-6) Turtleback Bks.
—Dog Days of the West. (Super Adventures of Wishbone Ser.: No. 1). (J). (gr. 4-7). 2000. pap. text 3.99 o.p. (1-57064-966-9); 1998. (Illus.). 256p. mass mkt. 3.99 o.p. (1-57064-336-9) Lyrick Publishing.
—Dog Days of the West. 1998. (Super Adventures of Wishbone Ser.: No. 1). (J). (gr. 4-7). 10.04 (0-606-17155-X) Turtleback Bks.
—Dog Overboard! 1998. (Adventures of Wishbone Ser.: No. 12). (Illus.). 144p. (J). (gr. 2-5). mass mkt. 3.99 o.p. (1-57064-367-9, Big Red Chair Bks.) Lyrick Publishing.
—Dog Overboard! l.t. ed. 1999. (Adventures of Wishbone Ser.: No. 12). (Illus.). (J). (gr. 4 up). lib. bdg. 22.60 (0-8368-2590-X) Stevens, Gareth Inc.
—Dog Overboard! 1998. (Adventures of Wishbone Ser.: No. 12). (J). (gr. 2-5). 10.04 (0-606-19453-3) Turtleback Bks.
—Stage Invader, 1999. (Wishbone Mysteries Ser.: No. 15). (J). (gr. 2-5). pap. 1.99 o.p. (1-57064-765-8) Lyrick Publishing.
—Stage Invader. Pollack, Pam, ed. 1999. (Wishbone Mysteries Ser.: No. 15). (Illus.). 144p. (J). (gr. 2-5). mass mkt. 3.99 o.p. (1-57064-563-9) Lyrick Publishing.
—Stage Invader. l.t. ed. 2000. (Wishbone Mysteries Ser.: No. 15). 140p. (J). (gr. 4 up). lib. bdg. 22.60 (0-8368-2698-1) Stevens, Gareth Inc.
—Stage Invader. 1999. (Wishbone Mysteries Ser.: No. 15). (J). (gr. 2-5). 10.04 (0-606-15826-X) Turtleback Bks.
Scent of a Vampire. 2000. (Adventures of Wishbone Ser.: No. 24). (Illus.). 144p. (J). (gr. 2-5). mass mkt. 3.99 o.p. (1-57064-390-3, Big Red Chair Bks.) Lyrick Publishing.
Scott, Walter, Sr. Ivanhoe. 1997. (Wishbone Classics Ser.: No. 12). (Illus.). 128p. (gr. 3-7). mass mkt. 3.99 (0-06-106499-8, HarperEntertainment) Morrow/Avon.
Shelley, Mary Wollstonecraft. Frankenstein. 1996. (Wishbone Classics Ser.: No. 7). (Illus.). 128p. (gr. 3-7). mass mkt. 3.99 (0-06-106417-3, HarperEntertainment) Morrow/Avon.
—Frankenstein. 1996. (Wishbone Classics Ser.: No.7). (J). (gr. 3-7). 10.04 (0-606-10370-8) Turtleback Bks.
Steele, Alexander. Case of the Breaking Story. 2000. (Wishbone Mysteries Ser.: No. 20). (Illus.). 144p. (J). (gr. 2-5). mass mkt. 3.99 o.p. (1-57064-771-2, Big Red Chair Bks.) Lyrick Publishing.
—Case of the Breaking Story. l.t. ed. 2000. (Wishbone Mysteries Ser.: No. 20). 144p. (J). (gr. 4 up). lib. bdg. 22.60 (0-8368-2703-1) Stevens, Gareth Inc.
—Case of the Unsolved Case, 1999. (Wishbone Mysteries Ser.: No. 13). (J). (gr. 2-5). pap. text 1.99 o.p. (1-57064-760-7) Lyrick Publishing.

—Case of the Unsolved Case. Ryan, Kevin, ed. 1998. (Wishbone Mysteries Ser.: No. 13). (Illus.). 144p. (J). (gr. 2-5). mass mkt. 3.99 o.p. (*1-57064-287-7*, Big Red Chair Bks.) Lyrick Publishing.

—Case of the Unsolved Case. l.t. ed. 2000. (Wishbone Mysteries Ser.: No. 13). 139p. (J). (gr. 4 up). lib. bdg. 22.60 (*0-8368-2696-5*) Stevens, Gareth Inc.

—Case of the Unsolved Case. 1998. (Wishbone Mysteries Ser.: No. 13). (J). (gr. 2-5). 10.04 (*0-606-15893-6*) Turtleback Bks.

—The Haunting of Hathaway House. 2000. (Wishbone Super Mysteries Ser.: No. 3). (Illus.). (J). (gr. 2-5). pap. text 3.99 o.p. (*1-57064-971-5*) Lyrick Publishing.

—The Haunting of Hathaway House. Ryan, Kevin, ed. 1999. (Wishbone Super Mysteries Ser.: No. 3). (Illus.). 251p. (J). (gr. 2-5). mass mkt. 3.99 o.p. (*1-57064-590-6*, Big Red Chair Bks.) Lyrick Publishing.

—Huckleberry Dog. 2000. (Adventures of Wishbone Ser.: No. 21). (Illus.). 144p. (J). (gr. 2-5). pap. 3.99 o.p. (*1-57064-389-X*) Lyrick Publishing.

—Huckleberry Dog. 2000. E-Book (*1-58824-397-4*); E-Book (*1-58824-428-8*) ipicturebooks, LLC.

—The Last of the Breed. Ryan, Kevin, ed. 1999. (Adventures of Wishbone Ser.: No. 16). (Illus.). 163p. (J). (gr. 2-5). pap. 3.99 o.p. (*1-57064-273-7*, Big Red Chair Bks.) Lyrick Publishing.

—The Last of the Breed. l.t. ed. 1999. (Adventures of Wishbone Ser.: No. 16). (Illus.). 163p. (J). (gr. 4 up). lib. bdg. 22.60 (*0-8368-2594-2*) Stevens, Gareth Inc.

—The Last of the Breed. 1999. (Adventures of Wishbone Ser.: No. 16). (J). (gr. 2-5). 10.04 (*0-606-17610-1*) Turtleback Bks.

—Moby Dog. 1998. (Adventures of Wishbone Ser.: No. 10). (Illus.). 144p. (J). (gr. 2-5). mass mkt. 3.99 o.p. (*1-57064-305-9*, Big Red Chair Bks.) Lyrick Publishing.

—Moby Dog. l.t. ed. 1999. (Adventures of Wishbone Ser.: No. 10). (Illus.). 144p. (J). (gr. 4 up). lib. bdg. 22.60 (*0-8368-2306-0*) Stevens, Gareth Inc.

—Moby Dog. 1998. (Adventures of Wishbone Ser.: No. 10). (J). (gr. 2-5). 10.04 (*0-606-19451-7*) Turtleback Bks.

—Tale of the Missing Mascot. 1998. (Wishbone Mysteries Ser.: No. 4). (Illus.). 144p. (J). (gr. 2-5). mass mkt. 3.99 o.p. (*1-57064-283-4*, Big Red Chair Bks.) Lyrick Publishing.

—Tale of the Missing Mascot. l.t. ed. 1999. (Wishbone Mysteries Ser.: No. 4). 144p. (J). (gr. 4 up). lib. bdg. 22.60 (*0-8368-2385-0*) Stevens, Gareth Inc.

—Unleashed in Space. Ryan, Kevin, ed. 1999. (Super Adventures of Wishbone Ser.: Vol. No. 3). (Illus.). 252p. (J). (ps-3). pap. 3.99 o.p. (*1-57064-329-6*) Lyrick Publishing.

Steele, Michael Anthony. Case of the Impounded Hounds. Ryan, Kevin, ed. 1999. (Wishbone Mysteries Ser.: No. 17). (Illus.). 144p. (J). (gr. 2-5). mass mkt. 3.99 o.p. (*1-57064-586-8*, Big Red Chair Bks.) Lyrick Publishing.

—Case of the Impounded Hounds. l.t. ed. 2000. (Wishbone Mysteries Ser.: No. 17). 138p. (J). (gr. 4 up). lib. bdg. 22.60 (*0-8368-2700-7*) Stevens, Gareth Inc.

—Case of the Impounded Hounds. 1999. (Wishbone Mysteries Ser.: No. 17). 10.04 (*0-606-17769-8*) Turtleback Bks.

—Case of the Impounded Hounds. 1999. E-Book (*1-58824-402-4*) ipicturebooks, LLC.

—Digging to the Center of the Earth. Ryan, Kevin, ed. 1999. (Adventures of Wishbone Ser.: No. 17). (Illus.). 141p. (J). (gr. 2-5). pap. 3.99 o.p. (*1-57064-393-8*) Lyrick Publishing.

—Digging to the Center of the Earth. l.t. ed. 1999. (Adventures of Wishbone Ser.: No. 17). (Illus.). (J). (gr. 4 up). lib. bdg. 22.60 (*0-8368-2595-0*) Stevens, Gareth Inc.

—Digging to the Center of the Earth. 1999. (Adventures of Wishbone Ser.: No. 17). (J). (gr. 2-5). 10.04 (*0-606-17611-X*) Turtleback Bks.

—Forgotten Heroes. Ryan, Kevin, ed. 1998. Vol. No. 12. (Illus.). 139p. (J). (gr. 4-7). pap. 3.99 o.p. (*1-57064-288-5*, Big Red Chair Bks.) Lyrick Publishing.

—Forgotten Heroes. l.t. ed. 2000. (Wishbone Mysteries Ser.: No. 12). 139p. (J). (gr. 4 up). lib. bdg. 22.60 (*0-8368-2695-7*) Stevens, Gareth Inc.

—The Ghost of Camp Ka Nowato. 2000. (Wishbone Super Mysteries Ser.: No. 2). (Illus.). (J). (gr. 2-5). pap. text 3.99 o.p. (*1-57064-970-7*) Lyrick Publishing.

—The Ghost of Camp Ka Nowato. Ryan, Kevin, ed. 1999. (Wishbone Super Mysteries Ser.: No. 2). (Illus.). 256p. (J). (gr. 2-5). mass mkt. 3.99 o.p. (*1-57064-630-9*, Big Red Chair Bks.) Lyrick Publishing.

—The Ghost of Camp Ka Nowato. 1999. (Wishbone Super Mysteries Ser.: No. 2). (J). (gr. 2-5). 10.04 (*0-606-19033-3*) Turtleback Bks.

Strickland, Brad. Be a Wolf! 1997. (Adventures of Wishbone Ser.: No. 1). (Illus.). 142p. (J). (gr. 2-5). pap. 3.99 o.p. (*1-57064-195-1*, Big Red Chair Bks.) Lyrick Publishing.

—Be a Wolf! l.t. ed. 1999. (Adventures of Wishbone Ser.: No. 1). (Illus.). 144p. (J). (gr. 4 up). lib. bdg. 22.60 (*0-8368-2297-8*) Stevens, Gareth Inc.

—Be a Wolf! 1997. (Adventures of Wishbone Ser.: No. 1). (Illus.). (J). (gr. 2-5). 11.04 (*0-606-18270-5*) Turtleback Bks.

—Be a Wolf! 1997. E-Book (*1-58824-426-1*); E-Book (*1-58824-400-8*) ipicturebooks, LLC.

—Disoriented Express, 1999. (Wishbone Mysteries Ser.: No. 14). (J). (gr. 2-5). pap. text 1.99 o.p. (*1-57064-764-X*) Lyrick Publishing.

—Gullifur's Travels. 1999. (Adventures of Wishbone Ser.: No. 18). (J). (gr. 2-5). 10.04 (*0-606-19456-8*) Turtleback Bks.

—Salty Dog. 1997. (Adventures of Wishbone Ser.: No. 2). (Illus.). 144p. (J). (gr. 2-5). mass mkt. 3.99 o.p. (*1-57064-194-3*, Big Red Chair Bks.) Lyrick Publishing.

—Salty Dog. l.t. ed. 1999. (Adventures of Wishbone Ser.: No. 2). (Illus.). 140p. (J). (gr. 4 up). lib. bdg. 22.60 (*0-8368-2298-6*) Stevens, Gareth Inc.

—Salty Dog. 1997. E-Book (*1-58824-399-0*); E-Book (*1-58824-430-X*) ipicturebooks, LLC.

—Terrier of the Lost Mines. 1999. (Adventures of Wishbone Ser.: No. 19). (J). (gr. 2-5). 10.04 (*0-606-19457-6*) Turtleback Bks.

Strickland, Brad & Fuller, Thomas. Disoriented Express. Ryan, Kevin, ed. 1998. (Wishbone Mysteries Ser.: No. 14). (Illus.). 144p. (J). (gr. 2-5). mass mkt. 3.99 o.p. (*1-57064-502-7*, Big Red Chair Bks.) Lyrick Publishing.

—Terrier of the Lost Mines. Ryan, Kevin, ed. 1999. (Adventures of Wishbone Ser.: No. 19). (Illus.). 144p. (J). (gr. 2-5). pap. 3.99 o.p. (*1-57064-278-8*, Big Red Chair Bks.) Lyrick Publishing.

Strickland, Brad & Fuller, Thomas E. Disoriented Express. 1998. (Wishbone Mysteries Ser.: No. 14). (J). (gr. 2-5). 10.04 (*0-606-15894-4*) Turtleback Bks.

Strickland, Brad & Strickland, Barbara. Gullifur's Travels. Ryan, Kevin, ed. 1999. (Adventures of Wishbone Ser.: No. 18). (Illus.). 144p. (J). (gr. 2-5). mass mkt. 3.99 o.p. (*1-57064-403-9*, Big Red Chair Bks.) Lyrick Publishing.

—Gullifur's Travels. l.t. ed. 1999. (Adventures of Wishbone Ser.: No. 18). (Illus.). (J). (gr. 4 up). lib. bdg. 22.60 (*0-8368-2596-9*) Stevens, Gareth Inc.

Strickland, Brad, et al. Disoriented Express. l.t. ed. 2000. (Wishbone Mysteries Ser.: No. 14). 167p. (J). (gr. 4 up). lib. bdg. 22.60 (*0-8368-2697-3*) Stevens, Gareth Inc.

Twain, Mark. Joan of Arc. 1999. (YA). reprint ed. pap. text 28.00 (*1-4047-1122-8*); pap. text 28.00 (*1-4047-1123-6*) Classic Textbooks.

—Joan of Arc. 1996. (Wishbone Classics Ser.: No. 4). (J). (gr. 3-7). 10.04 (*0-606-10367-8*) Turtleback Bks.

Verne, Jules. Journey to the Center of the Earth. 1996. (J). (gr. 2-5). 10.04 (*0-606-10975-7*) Turtleback Bks.

The Wishbone Mysteries, 20 bks. l.t. ed. Incl. Case of the Breaking Story. Steele, Alexander. 144p. 2000. lib. bdg. 22.60 (*0-8368-2703-1*); Case of the Cyber-Hacker. Capeci, Anne. 141p. 2000. lib. bdg. 22.60 (*0-8368-2702-3*); Case of the Impounded Hounds. Steele, Michael Anthony. 138p. 2000. lib. bdg. 22.60 (*0-8368-2700-7*); Case of the On-Line Alien. Steele, Alexander. 144p. 1999. lib. bdg. 22.60 (*0-8368-2449-0*); Case of the Unsolved Case. Steele, Alexander. 139p. 2000. lib. bdg. 22.60 (*0-8368-2696-5*); Disappearing Dinosaurs. Strickland, Brad & Fuller, Thomas E. 144p. 1999. lib. bdg. 22.60 (*0-8368-2450-4*); Disoriented Express. Strickland, Brad. 167p. 2000. lib. bdg. 22.60 (*0-8368-2697-3*); Drive-In of Doom. Strickland, Brad & Fuller, Thomas E. 144p. 1999. lib. bdg. 22.60 (*0-8368-2388-5*); Forgotten Heroes. Steele, Michael Anthony. 139p. 2000. lib. bdg. 22.60 (*0-8368-2695-7*); Haunted Clubhouse. Leavitt, Caroline. 144p. 1999. lib. bdg. 22.60 (*0-8368-2383-4*); Key to the Golden Dog. Capeci, Anne. 144p. 1999. lib. bdg. 22.60 (*0-8368-2389-3*); Lights! Camera! Action Dog! Butcher, Nancy. 139p. 2000. lib. bdg. 22.60 (*0-8368-2694-9*); Maltese Dog. Capeci, Anne. 144p. 1999. lib. bdg. 22.60 (*0-8368-2387-7*); Phantom of the Video Store. Gantt, Leticia. 141p. 2000. lib. bdg. 22.60 (*0-8368-2701-5*); Riddle of the Wayward Books. Strickland, Brad & Fuller, Thomas E. 144p. 1999. lib. bdg. 22.60 (*0-8368-2384-2*); Sirian Conspiracy. Friedman, Michael Jan. 141p. 2000. lib. bdg. 22.60 (*0-8368-2699-X*); Stage Invader. Sathre, Vivian. 140p. 2000. lib. bdg. 22.60 (*0-8368-2698-1*); Stolen Trophy. Friedman, Michael Jan. 144p. 1999. lib. bdg. 22.60 (*0-8368-2386-9*); Tale of the Missing Mascot. Steele, Alexander. 144p. 1999. lib. bdg. 22.60 (*0-8368-2385-0*); Treasure of Skeleton Reef. Strickland, Brad & Fuller, Thomas E. 144p. 1999. lib. bdg. 22.60 (*0-8368-2382-6*); (J). (gr. 4 up). Set lib. bdg. 452.00 (*0-8368-2752-X*) Stevens, Gareth Inc.

Wonders Never Cease. 2000. (Adventures of Wishbone Ser.: No. 26). (Illus.). 144p. (J). (gr. 2-5). mass mkt. 3.99 o.p. (*1-57064-998-7*, Big Red Chair Bks.) Lyrick Publishing.

WOLFE, JAMES, 1727-1759—FICTION

Henty, G. A. With Wolfe in Canada: The Winning of a Continent. 2001. (Illus.). 353p. (J). pap. 13.99 (*0-921100-87-6*); text 19.99 (*0-921100-86-8*) Inheritance Pubns.

—With Wolfe in Canada: The Winning of a Continent. (Illus.). 353p. 2000. (gr. 8-12). pap. 14.99 (*1-887159-30-4*); 1998. (J). lib. bdg. 20.99 (*1-887159-18-5*) Preston-Speed Pubns.

WONDER WOMAN (FICTITIOUS CHARACTER)—FICTION

Jaffe, Nina. Wonder Woman Chapter Book & Charm. 2004. (Wonder Woman Ser.). (Illus.). 64p. (J). pap. 4.99 (*0-06-056521-7*);No. 2. pap. 4.99 (*0-06-056522-5*) HarperCollins Children's Bk. Group. (Harper Festival).

—Wonder Woman Festival Reader. 2004. (Festival Reader Ser.). (Illus.). 32p. (J). No. 1. pap. 3.99 (*0-06-056517-9*); No. 2. pap. 3.99 (*0-06-056518-7*) HarperCollins Children's Bk. Group. (Harper Festival).

Simonson, Louise & Golden Books Staff. The True Story of Wonder Woman. 1995. (Golden Super Shape Book Ser.). (Illus.). 24p. (J). (ps-3). pap. 3.29 o.s.i (*0-307-10006-5*, Golden Bks.) Random Hse. Children's Bks.

WOO, SHELBY (FICTITIOUS CHARACTER)—FICTION

Collins, Suzanne. Fire Proof. 1999. (Mystery Files of Shelby Woo Ser.: No. 11). 144p. (J). (gr. 4-6). pap. 3.99 (*0-671-02695-X*, Aladdin) Simon & Schuster Children's Publishing.

Dubowski, Cathy & Dubowski, Mark. Comic Book Criminal. 1998. (Mystery Files of Shelby Woo Ser.: No. 7). 144p. (J). (gr. 4-6). pap. 3.99 (*0-671-02007-2*, Aladdin) Simon & Schuster Children's Publishing.

—High Wire. 1998. (Mystery Files of Shelby Woo Ser.: No. 10). 144p. (J). (gr. 4-6). pap. 4.50 (*0-671-02694-1*, Aladdin) Simon & Schuster Children's Publishing.

Erwin, Vicki B. Ski Slope Sabotage. 1999. (Mystery Files of Shelby Woo Ser.: No. 15). (J). (gr. 4-6). pap. 3.99 (*0-671-03460-X*, Aladdin) Simon & Schuster Children's Publishing.

Gallagher, Diana G. Cut & Run. 1998. (Mystery Files of Shelby Woo Ser.: No. 5). 144p. (J). (gr. 4-6). pap. 3.99 (*0-671-02004-8*, Aladdin) Simon & Schuster Children's Publishing.

—Takeout Stakeout. 1997. (Mystery Files of Shelby Woo Ser.: No.2). 128p. (J). (gr. 4-6). pap. 3.99 (*0-671-01152-9*, Aladdin) Simon & Schuster Children's Publishing.

Goodman, Alan. A Slash in the Night. 1997. (Mystery Files of Shelby Woo Ser.: No. 1). 128p. (J). (gr. 4-6). pap. 3.99 (*0-671-01153-7*, Aladdin) Simon & Schuster Children's Publishing.

Marano, Lydia C. House Arrest. 1998. (Mystery Files of Shelby Woo Ser.: No. 6). 144p. (J). (gr. 4-6). pap. 3.99 (*0-671-02006-4*, Aladdin) Simon & Schuster Children's Publishing.

—Rock 'n' Roll Robbery. 1997. (Mystery Files of Shelby Woo Ser.: No. 4). 144p. (J). (gr. 4-6). pap. 3.99 (*0-671-01155-3*, Aladdin) Simon & Schuster Children's Publishing.

Peel, John. Hot Rock. 1997. (Mystery Files of Shelby Woo Ser.: No. 3). 144p. (J). (gr. 4-6). pap. 3.99 (*0-671-01154-5*, Aladdin) Simon & Schuster Children's Publishing.

Ponti, James. Friends in Need. 1999. (Mystery Files of Shelby Woo Ser.: No. 14). 144p. (J). (gr. 4-6). pap. 3.99 (*0-671-03465-0*, Aladdin) Simon & Schuster Children's Publishing.

—The Green Monster. 1999. (Mystery Files of Shelby Woo Ser.: No. 12). 144p. (J). (gr. 4-6). pap. 3.99 (*0-671-02696-8*, Aladdin) Simon & Schuster Children's Publishing.

—History Mystery. 1998. (Mystery Files of Shelby Woo Ser.: No. 9). 144p. (J). (gr. 4-6). pap. 3.99 (*0-671-02009-9*, Aladdin) Simon & Schuster Children's Publishing.

Strickland, Brad & Strickland, Barbara. Frame-Up. 1998. (Mystery Files of Shelby Woo Ser.: No. 8). 144p. (J). (gr. 4-6). pap. 3.99 (*0-671-02008-0*, Aladdin) Simon & Schuster Children's Publishing.

—Man Overboard. 1999. (Mystery Files of Shelby Woo Ser.: No. 13). 144p. (J). (gr. 4-6). pap. 3.99 (*0-671-02697-6*, Aladdin) Simon & Schuster Children's Publishing.

WORF (FICTITIOUS CHARACTER)—FICTION

David, Peter. Line of Fire. 1999. (Star Trek, The Next Generation: No. 2). (J). (gr. 3-6). (*0-7857-1333-6*) Econo-Clad Bks.

—Line of Fire. 1993. (Star Trek Ser.: No. 2). 128p. (J). (gr. 4-7). mass mkt. 3.99 (*0-671-87085-8*, Aladdin) Simon & Schuster Children's Publishing.

—Line of Fire. 1993. (Star Trek, The Next Generation: No. 2). (J). (gr. 3-6). 10.04 (*0-606-05622-X*) Turtleback Bks.

—Survival. 1993. (Star Trek Ser.: No. 3). (Illus.). 128p. (J). (gr. 4-7). mass mkt. 3.99 (*0-671-87086-6*, Aladdin) Simon & Schuster Children's Publishing.

—Survival. 1993. (Star Trek, The Next Generation: No. 3). (J). (gr. 3-6). 10.04 (*0-606-06019-7*) Turtleback Bks.

—Worf's First Adventure. 1993. (Star Trek Ser.: No. 1). 128p. (J). (gr. 4-7). pap. 3.99 (*0-671-87084-X*, Aladdin) Simon & Schuster Children's Publishing.

—Worf's First Adventure. 1993. (Star Trek, The Next Generation: No. 1). (J). (gr. 3-6). 10.04 (*0-606-05621-1*) Turtleback Bks.

Gallagher, Diana G. Day of Honor No. 5: Honor Bound. 1997. (Star Trek Deep Space Nine Ser.: No. 11). 128p. (J). (gr. 3-6). pap. 3.99 (*0-671-01452-8*, Aladdin) Simon & Schuster Children's Publishing.

WRIGHT, WILBUR, 1867-1912—FICTION

Gaffney, Timothy R. The Mouse & the Wright Brothers. 2004. (J). 16.95 (*0-8050-7172-5*, Holt, Henry & Co. Bks. For Young Readers) Holt, Henry & Co.

Gutman, Dan. Race for the Sky: The Kitty Hawk Diaries of Johnny Moore. 2003. (Illus.). 192p. (J). (gr. 3-6). 15.95 (*0-689-84554-5*, Simon & Schuster Children's Publishing) Simon & Schuster Children's Publishing.

Hedstrom, Deborah. From Ground to Air with the Wright Brothers. 1998. (My American Journey Ser.: No. 5). 19.99 o.p. (*1-57673-258-4*) Multnomah Pubs., Inc.

Rigsby, Annelle & Raffa, Edwina. Race to Kitty Hawk. 2003. (Adventures in America Ser.). (J). 14.95 (*1-893110-33-8*) Silver Moon Pr.

Schultz, Walter A. Will & Orv. 1991. (On My Own History Ser.). (Illus.). 48p. (J). (gr. 1-3). pap. 6.95 (*0-87614-568-3*, Carolrhoda Bks.) Lerner Publishing Group.

Schulz, Walter A. Will & Orv. 1995. (Illus.). (J). (gr. 3). 8.60 (*0-395-73236-0*) Houghton Mifflin Co.

—Will & Orv. 1991. (On My Own History Ser.). (Illus.). 48p. (J). (gr. 1-3). lib. bdg. 21.27 (*0-87614-669-8*, Carolrhoda Bks.) Lerner Publishing Group.

X

X-MEN (FICTITIOUS CHARACTERS)—FICTION

Austen, Chuck. Uncanny X-Men Vol. 1: Hope, 2 vols. 2003. (Uncanny X-men Ser.). (Illus.). 144p. (YA). pap. 12.99 (*0-7851-1060-7*) Marvel Enterprises.

—Uncanny X-Men Vol. 2: Dominant Species, 2 vols. 2003. (Uncanny X-men Ser.). (Illus.). 128p. (YA). pap. 11.99 (*0-7851-1132-8*) Marvel Enterprises.

Bergen, Lara Rice. X-Men. 2000. (Illus.). 176p. (gr. 4-7). pap. text 4.99 (*0-440-41712-0*, Yearling) Random Hse. Children's Bks.

Brady Games Staff, et al. X-Men Official Strategy Guide. 2000. (BradyGames Strategy Guides). (Illus.). 128p. pap., stu. ed. 12.99 (*1-56686-880-7*) Brady Publishing.

Conner, Ted. X-Men 2. 2003. (Illus.). 160p. (gr. 4). pap. text 5.50 (*0-553-48776-0*) Random Hse., Inc.

Dorling Kindersley Publishing Staff, et al. Ultimate X-Men. 2003. (Readers Ser.). (Illus.). 176p. (J). (gr. 4-7). pap. 19.99 (*0-7894-6693-7*) Dorling Kindersley Publishing, Inc.

Duey, Kathleen. Ultimate Super Hero Picture Book Gift Set. 2003. (Illus.). 48p. (J). 24.95 (*1-929945-38-8*) Big Guy Bks., Inc.

—X-Men Ultimate Picture Book. 2003. (Illus.). 48p. (J). 15.95 (*1-929945-24-8*); pap. 8.95 (*1-929945-26-4*) Big Guy Bks., Inc.

Fontes, Justine. The Xavier Files. 1994. (X-Men Digest Novels Ser.). (Illus.). 108p. (Orig.). (J). (gr. 2 up). pap. 3.50 o.s.i (*0-679-86177-7*, Random Hse. Bks. for Young Readers) Random Hse. Children's Bks.

Gallagher, Michael. X-Men, Magneto's Master Plan. (Illus.). 24p. (YA). (gr. k up). text 12.95 (*0-9627001-6-9*) Futech Educational Products, Inc.

—X-Men, Scourge of the Savage Land. (Illus.). 24p. (YA). (gr. k up). text 12.95 (*0-9627001-7-7*) Futech Educational Products, Inc.

Hart, Avery, ed. Second Genesis. 1994. (X-Men Digest Novels Ser.). (Illus.). 108p. (Orig.). (J). (gr. 2 up). pap. 3.50 o.s.i (*0-679-86012-6*, Random Hse. Bks. for Young Readers) Random Hse. Children's Bks.

Herman, Gail & Hughes, Francine. Wolverine: Top Secret. 1994. (X-Men Digest Novels Ser.). (Illus.). 108p. (Orig.). (J). (gr. 2 up). pap. 3.50 o.s.i (*0-679-86004-5*, Random Hse. Bks. for Young Readers) Random Hse. Children's Bks.

How to Draw X-Men. 1997. (Marvel Super Heroes Ser.). 40p. (YA). (gr. 3 up). pap. 8.95 o.p. (*1-56010-206-3*, M04) Foster, Walter Publishing, Inc.

How to Draw X-Men Kit. 1997. (Snap Pack Ser.). (Illus.). 40p. (YA). (gr. 3 up). o.p. (*1-56010-344-2*, M04P) Foster, Walter Publishing, Inc.

Hughes, Francine. Wolverine: Duty & Honor. 1994. (X-Men Digest Novels Ser.). (Illus.). 112p. (Orig.). (J). (gr. 2 up). pap. 3.50 o.s.i (*0-679-86154-8*, Random Hse. Bks. for Young Readers) Random Hse. Children's Bks.

Jenson, Jeff. X-Factor. 2003. (X-Men Ser.: Vol. 1). (Illus.). 96p. (YA). pap. 9.99 (*0-7851-1016-X*) Marvel Enterprises.

Kamida, Vicki. X-Tinction Agenda. 1994. (X-Men Digest Novels Ser.). (Illus.). 112p. (Orig.). (J). (gr. 2 up). pap. 3.50 o.s.i (*0-679-86567-5*, Random Hse. Bks. for Young Readers) Random Hse. Children's Bks.

Knowledge Adventures Staff. X-Men Cartoon Maker. 1995. (J). 16.00 net. (*1-56997-190-0*) Knowledge Adventure, Inc.

Lobdell, Scott & Robinson, James. X-Men: Zero Tolerance. 2000. (Marvels Finest Ser.). (Illus.). 336p. pap. 24.95 (*0-7851-0738-X*, Marvel's Finest) Marvel Enterprises.

Marvel Comics Staff. Night of the Sentinels Pt. 1: Meet the X-Men. 1994. (J). (gr. 4-7). 2.50 o.s.i (*0-679-85707-9*, Random Hse. Bks. for Young Readers) Random Hse. Children's Bks.

—X-Men: Beginnings. 2000. (Illus.). (J). pap. 14.95 (*0-7851-0750-9*) Marvel Enterprises.

—X-Men: The Movie. 2000. (Illus.). (J). pap. 14.95 (*0-7851-0749-5*) Marvel Enterprises.

Millar, Mark. Hellfire & Brimstone, 4 vols. 2003. (Ultimate X-Men Ser.: Vol. 4). (Illus.). 144p. (J). pap. 12.99 (*0-7851-1089-5*) Marvel Enterprises.

—Ultimate War: X-Men, 6 vols., Vol. 5. 2003. (Ultimate X-Men Ser.: Vol. 5). (Illus.). 112p. (J). pap. 10.99 (*0-7851-1129-8*) Marvel Enterprises.

—Ultimate X-Men, Vol. 3. 2004. (Ultimate X-men Ser.). (Illus.). 312p. (J). 29.99 (*0-7851-1131-X*) Marvel Enterprises.

—Ultimate X-Men: Return of the King, 7 vols. 2003. (Ultimate X-men Ser.). (Illus.). 192p. (J). pap. 16.99 (*0-7851-1091-7*) Marvel Enterprises.

Millar, Mark & Austen, Chuck. Ultimate X-Men, 2 vols., Vol. 2. 2003. (Ultimate X-men Ser.). (Illus.). 336p. (J). 29.99 (*0-7851-1130-1*) Marvel Enterprises.

Milligan, Peter. Good Omens. 2003. (X-Statix Ser.). (Illus.). 128p. (YA). pap. 11.99 (*0-7851-1059-3*) Marvel Enterprises.

—X-Force: Famous, Mutant & Mortal. 2003. (X-Statix Ser.). (Illus.). 352p. (YA). 29.99 (*0-7851-1023-2*) Marvel Enterprises.

—X-Statix, 2 vols., Vol. 2. 2003. (X-Statix Ser.). (Illus.). 176p. (YA). pap. 15.99 (*0-7851-1139-5*) Marvel Enterprises.

Morrison, Grant. New X-Men Vol. 3: New Worlds. 2002. (Illus.). 176p. (YA). (gr. 8 up). per. 14.99 (*0-7851-0976-5*) Marvel Enterprises.

Rodi, Robert. Elektra Vol. 3: Relentless. 2004. (Illus.). 144p. (YA). pap. 14.99 (*0-7851-1222-7*) Marvel Enterprises.

Roman, Steven A. X-Men: Red Skull, 2000. (Chaos Engine Trilogy Ser.: Bk. 3). 384p. pap. 14.95 (*0-7434-0723-7*) ibooks, Inc.

Roman, Steven A. & Timmons, Stan. X-Men: Doctor Doom, 2000. (Chaos Engine Trilogy Ser.: Vol. 1). 384p. (gr. 4-7). pap. 14.95 (*0-7434-0019-4*) ibooks, Inc.

—X-Men: Magneto. 2002. (Chaos Engine Ser.: Bk. 2). 320p. (gr. 4-7). pap. 14.95 (*0-7434-0023-2*) ibooks, Inc.

Rucka, Greg. Wolverine Vol. 1: The Brotherhood. 2004. (Wolverine Ser.). (Illus.). 144p. (YA). (ps). pap. 12.99 (*0-7851-1136-0*) Marvel Enterprises.

Ruiz, Aristides, illus. Days of Future Past. adapted ed. 1994. (X-Men Digest Novels Ser.). 108p. (Orig.). (J). (gr. 2 up). pap. 3.50 o.s.i (*0-679-86181-5*, Random Hse. Bks. for Young Readers) Random Hse. Children's Bks.

Stern, Roger. X-Men: Phoenix Rising. 1999. (Marvel's Finest' Collection). 96p. pap. 14.95 (*0-7851-0711-8*) Marvel Enterprises.

Teitelbaum, Michael. The Story of the X-Men: How It All Began. 2000. (Dorling Kindersley Readers Ser.). (Illus.). 32p. (J). (gr. 4-7). pap. 12.95 (*0-7894-6696-1*); pap. 3.99 (*0-7894-6697-X*) Dorling Kindersley Publishing, Inc.

—The Story of the X-Men: How It All Began. 2000. 10.10 (*0-606-22326-6*) Turtleback Bks.

Tiere, Frank. Weapon X: The Draft. 2003. (Wolverine Ser.: Vol. 1). (Illus.). 248p. (YA). pap. 21.99 (*0-7851-1148-4*) Marvel Enterprises.

Warner, Rita. Crazy X-Men Hex Game. 1997. (Crazy Games Ser.). (J). (gr. 1 up). 2.95 o.s.i (*0-8431-7986-4*, Price Stern Sloan) Penguin Putnam Bks. for Young Readers.

X-Men. 1993. (Look & Find Ser.). (Illus.). 24p. (J). 7.98 (*1-56173-703-8*) Publications International, Ltd.

X-Men: Repo Man. 1995. (Favorite Sound Story Bks.). (Illus.). 20p. (J). (ps). o.p. (*0-307-70931-0*, Golden Bks.) Random Hse. Children's Bks.

XYZ Group Staff. X-Men: Beware of the Blob (Includes Sound Stix) 1995. (Sound Stix Ser.). (Illus.). 24p. (J). (ps-2). pap. text 12.95 o.p. (*1-879332-40-X*) Futech Interactive Products, Inc.

XENA (FICTITIOUS CHARACTER)—FICTION

Kennedy, Hunter. Xena & the Magic Arrow of Myx. 1999. (Xena, Warrior Princess Ser.). 112p. (Orig.). (gr. 4-7). mass mkt. 4.50 o.s.i (*0-425-16776-3*) Berkley Publishing Group.

Milliron, Kerry. Xena Warrior Princess: Princess in Peril. 1996. (Random House Picturebacks Ser.). (J). (ps-3). pap. 3.25 o.s.i (*0-679-88259-6*) Random Hse., Inc.

Whitman, John. Xena: Warrior Princess. 1998. (Mighty Chronicles Ser.). (Illus.). 320p. (J). (gr. 3-7). 9.95 o.p. (*0-8118-2207-9*) Chronicle Bks. LLC.

Z

ZANE, ELIZABETH, 1759?-1847?—FICTION

Durrant, Linda. Betsy Zane, the Rose of Fort Henry. 2000. 176p. (J). (gr. 5-9). tchr. ed. 15.00 (*0-395-97899-8*, Clarion Bks.) Houghton Mifflin Co. Trade & Reference Div.

ZENAS, NIKKI (FICTITIOUS CHARACTER)—FICTION

Wolfe, Hillary. Dead Asleep. 1994. (You-Solve-It Mysteries Ser.: No. 2). 224p. (YA). mass mkt. 3.50 o.s.i (*0-8217-4581-6*) Kensington Publishing Corp.

—Death Spirit. 1994. (You-Solve-It Mysteries Ser.: No. 8). 224p. (YA). mass mkt. 3.50 (*0-8217-4766-5*, Zebra Bks.) Kensington Publishing Corp.

—Raven's Blood. 1996. (YA). mass mkt. 3.99 o.s.i (*0-8217-5152-2*) Kensington Publishing Corp.

—Threads of Death. 1995. (You-Solve-It Mysteries Ser.). 224p. (YA). mass mkt. 3.99 o.s.i (*0-8217-4850-5*) Kensington Publishing Corp.

ZOMO, THE RABBIT (FICTITIOUS CHARACTER)—FICTION

McDermott, Gerald. Zomo the Rabbit: A Trickster Tale from West Africa. (Illus.). 32p. (J). (ps-3). 1992. 14.95 (*0-15-299967-1*); 1996. pap. 7.00 (*0-15-201010-6*, Harcourt Paperbacks) Harcourt Children's Bks.

—Zomo the Rabbit: A Trickster Tale from West Africa. (Illus.). (J). (ps-3). 1996. 32p. pap. 22.00 (*0-15-201011-4*); 1992. 6.75 o.p. (*0-15-200739-3*) Harcourt Trade Pubs.

—Zomo the Rabbit: A Trickster Tale from West Africa. 9999. (J). 12.15 (*0-606-10107-1*) Turtleback Bks.

ETHNIC GROUPS

A

AFRO-AMERICANS—CIVIL RIGHTS—FICTION

Moore, Yvette. Freedom Songs. 1992. 176p. (YA). (gr. 7 up). pap. 5.99 (*0-14-036017-4*, Puffin Bks.) Penguin Putnam Bks. for Young Readers.

—Freedom Songs. 1991. 176p. (YA). (gr. 7 up). mass mkt. 15.99 o.p. (*0-531-08412-4*); mass mkt. 15.95 o.p. (*0-531-05812-3*) Scholastic, Inc. (Orchard Bks.).

—Freedom Songs. 1992. (J). 12.04 (*0-606-01693-7*) Turtleback Bks.

Schotter, Roni. Northern Fried Chicken. 1983. (J). (gr. 6-9). 10.95 o.p. (*0-399-20920-4*, Philomel) Penguin Putnam Bks. for Young Readers.

AFRO-AMERICANS—EDUCATION—FICTION

Bauldock, Gerald, Sr. Reaching for the Moon. 1989. 303p. (Orig.). (YA). (gr. 7-12). pap. text 14.95 (*0-9621728-0-4*) B-Dock Pr.

Clifton, Fred. Darl. 1973. (Illus.). 104p. (J). (gr. 2-6). 12.00 (*0-89388-098-1*) Okpaku Communications Corp.

De Gree, Melvin. Brickhouse Dreams: Young Benjamin E. Mays. 1992. (Illus.). 140p. (Orig.). (J). (gr. 3-10). pap. 11.95 (*0-9632895-0-0*) Trail of Success Pubs.

Newell, Hope. Cap for Mary Ellis. 1953. (YA). (gr. 7 up). lib. bdg. 12.89 o.p. (*0-06-024526-3*) Harper-Collins Children's Bk. Group.

Waldron, Ann. The Integration of Mary-Larkin Thornhill. 1985. 144p. (J). (gr. 5 up). 8.95 o.p. (*0-525-32580-8*, Dutton) Dutton/Plume.

Yates, Elizabeth. Prudence Crandall: Woman of Courage. 1955. (Illus.). (J). (gr. 7 up). 8.50 o.p. (*0-525-37883-9*, Dutton) Dutton/Plume.

AFRO-AMERICANS—FICTION

Ackerman, Karen. By the Dawn's Early Light. 1999. (Illus.). 32p. (J). (ps-3). pap. 5.99 (*0-689-82481-5*, Aladdin) Simon & Schuster Children's Publishing.

—By the Dawn's Early Light. 1999. 12.14 (*0-606-15924-X*) Turtleback Bks.

—By the Dawn's Early Light: Al Amanecer. Ada, Alma Flor, tr. 1994. (ENG & SPA., Illus.). 32p. (J). (ps-3). 16.00 (*0-689-31788-3*); 14.95 (*0-689-31917-7*) Simon & Schuster Children's Publishing. (Atheneum).

Adebayo, Yinka. Age Ain't Nothin' but a Number. 1998. (Drummond Hill Crew Ser.). 144p. (J). mass mkt. 5.99 (*1-874509-33-6*) X Pr., The GBR. *Dist:* LPC Group.

—Livin' Large. 1998. 144p. (J). mass mkt. 5.99 (*1-874509-34-4*) X Pr., The GBR. *Dist:* LPC Group.

Adlerman, Daniel, ed. Africa Calling, Nighttime Falling. 2001. (J). 13.10 (*0-606-20533-0*) Turtleback Bks.

Adoff, Arnold. Big Sister Tells Me That I'm Black, ERS. 1976. (Illus.). 32p. (J). (gr. k-4). o.p. (*0-03-014546-5*, Holt, Henry & Co. Bks. For Young Readers) Holt, Henry & Co.

Ain't No Mountain High Enough: Motown, Vol. 5. 2002. (Illus.). 24p. (J). bds. 6.99 (*0-7868-0786-5*, Jump at the Sun) Hyperion Bks. for Children.

Albee, Sarah. Mr. Ron's Favorite Animals. 1997. (Peek 'n' Seek Board Bks.). (Illus.). 14p. (J). (ps-k). bds. 4.99 (*0-689-81301-5*, Simon Spotlight/ Nickelodeon) Simon & Schuster Children's Publishing.

Albert, Burton. Where Does the Trail Lead? (Illus.). 40p. (J). (ps-3). 1993. pap. 5.95 (*0-671-79617-8*, Aladdin); 1991. pap. 16.00 o.s.i (*0-671-73409-1*, Simon & Schuster Children's Publishing) Simon & Schuster Children's Publishing.

Altman, Linda Jacobs. The Legend of Freedom Hill. (Illus.). (J). 2003. pap. (*1-58430-169-4*); 2000. 32p. 15.95 (*1-58430-003-5*) Lee & Low Bks., Inc.

—Singin' with Momma Lou. 2002. (Illus.). 32p. (J). (gr. 1-5). 16.95 (*1-58430-040-X*) Lee & Low Bks., Inc.

Anderson, Janet. The Key into Winter. 1993. (Illus.). (YA). lib. bdg. 15.95 o.p. (*0-8075-4170-2*) Whitman, Albert & Co.

Anderson, Launi K. Janey's Own. 1997. (Latter-Day Daughters Ser.). (J). pap. o.p. (*1-57345-319-6*, Cinnamon Tree) Deseret Bk. Co.

Anderson, Susan. Flowers for Mommy. 1995. (J). (ps-3). pap. 8.95 (*0-86543-453-0*); (Illus.). 16.95 (*0-86543-452-2*) Africa World Pr.

Andrews, V. C. Star. l.t. ed. 1999. (Core Ser.). 161p. (YA). 28.95 o.p. (*0-7838-8803-1*, Macmillan Reference USA) Gale Group.

—Star. 1999. (Wildflowers Ser.: No. 2). 176p. pap. 3.99 o.s.i (*0-671-02801-4*, Pocket) Simon & Schuster.

—Star. 1999. 10.04 (*0-606-17533-4*) Turtleback Bks.

Armistead, John. The Return of Gabriel. 2002. (Illus.). 240p. (J). (gr. 3-8). 17.95 (*1-57131-637-X*); pap. 6.95 (*1-57131-638-8*) Milkweed Editions.

Armstrong, Jennifer. Steal Away. 224p. 1993. (J). (gr. 3-7). pap. 4.50 (*0-590-46921-5*, Scholastic Paperbacks); 1992. (YA). (gr. 6 up). mass mkt. 16.99 o.p. (*0-531-08583-X*, Orchard Bks.); 1992. (YA). (gr. 6 up). 15.95 o.p. (*0-531-05983-9*, Orchard Bks.) Scholastic, Inc.

—Steal Away. 1992. (J). 10.55 (*0-606-05623-8*) Turtleback Bks.

Armstrong, Robb. Drew & the Bub Daddy Showdown. 1996. (Trophy Chapter Bks.). (Illus.). (J). (gr. 2-5). 64p. pap. 4.25 o.p. (*0-06-442030-2*, Harper Trophy); 96p. lib. bdg. 13.89 o.p. (*0-06-027275-9*) HarperCollins Children's Bk. Group.

—Drew & the Bub Daddy Showdown. 1996. 9.15 o.p. (*0-606-09217-X*) Turtleback Bks.

—Drew & the Homeboy Question. 1997. (Illus.). (J). (gr. 2-5). 64p. pap. 4.25 (*0-06-442047-7*, Harper Trophy); 80p. lib. bdg. 14.89 o.p. (*0-06-027527-8*) HarperCollins Children's Bk. Group.

—Drew & the Homeboy Question. 1997. 10.10 (*0-606-11282-0*) Turtleback Bks.

—Stuffin' It! 1998. (Patrick's Pals Ser.: No. 4). (Illus.). 96p. (J). (gr. 2-7). mass mkt. 3.99 o.s.i (*0-06-107070-X*) HarperCollins Pubs.

Armstrong, William H. Sounder. (Trophy Bk.). (Illus.). 128p. 1996. (YA). (gr. 7 up). pap. 2.25 o.p. (*0-06-447153-5*, Harper Trophy); 1969. (J). (gr. 5 up). 15.99 (*0-06-020143-6*); 1969. (J). (gr. 5 up). lib. bdg. 16.89 (*0-06-020144-4*); 1972. (J). (gr. 5 up). reprint ed. pap. 5.99 (*0-06-440020-4*, Harper Trophy) HarperCollins Children's Bk. Group.

—Sounder. (Perennial Classics Ser.). 2001. 96p. (gr. 4-7). pap. 7.00 (*0-06-093548-0*); 1978. pap. 4.50 o.p. (*0-06-080379-7*, P379) HarperTrade. (Perennial).

—Sounder. l.t. ed. 1999. (LRS Large Print Cornerstone Ser.). (Illus.). 230p. (YA). (gr. 6-12). lib. bdg. 27.95 (*1-58118-054-3*, 22768) LRS.

—Sounder. l.t. ed. 1987. (Illus.). 99p. (J). (gr. 2-6). reprint ed. lib. bdg. 16.95 o.s.i (*1-55736-003-0*, Cornerstone Bks.) Pages, Inc.

—Sounder. 9999. 116p. (YA). (gr. 7 up). pap. 2.50 o.p. (*0-590-40212-9*) Scholastic, Inc.

—Sounder. 1972. (J). 12.00 (*0-606-04962-2*) Turtleback Bks.

—Sounder Ri. 1989. 128p. (YA). (gr. 4-7). reprint ed. pap. 6.00 (*0-06-080975-2*, P 975, Perennial) HarperTrade.

—Trueno. 2nd ed. 1996. (SPA., Illus.). 104p. (YA). (gr. 5-8). 9.95 (*84-241-3187-8*, EV5672) Everest de Ediciones y Distribucion, S.L. ESP. *Dist:* Lectorum Pubns., Inc.

Aston, Dianna Hutts. When You Were Born. 2004. (J). (*0-7636-1438-6*) Candlewick Pr.

Bahr, Howard. Home for Christmas. 1997. (J). 9.95 (*1-877853-51-8*) Nautical & Aviation Publishing Co. of America, Inc., The.

Baicker, Karen. I Can Do It Too! 2003. 24p. (J). 13.95 (*1-929766-83-1*) Handprint Bks.

Bailey, Barbara. When I Get Older I'll Understand. 2000. 192p. (YA). (gr. 7-12). pap. 7.95 (*1-56315-211-8*) SterlingHouse Pubs., Inc.

Bailey-Williams, Nicole. A Little Piece of Sky. 2000. 110p. pap. 8.95 o.p. (*0-9700186-0-6*) Sugarene's Pr.

Baker. Gullah. 1997. (Gullah Gullah Island Ser.: No. 8). (Illus.). 24p. (J). (ps-1). mass mkt. 3.25 o.s.i (*0-689-81243-4*, Simon Spotlight/Nickelodeon) Simon & Schuster Children's Publishing.

Baker, Carin G. Families, Phooey! No. 6. 1996. (Gullah Gullah Island Ser.). (Illus.). 24p. (ps-3). mass mkt. 3.25 (*0-689-80826-7*, Simon Spotlight/ Nickelodeon) Simon & Schuster Children's Publishing.

Baldwin, James. Sonny's Blues. 1993. (J). o.p. (*0-88682-589-X*, Creative Education) Creative Co., The.

Ball, Dorothy W. Don't Drive up a Dirt Road. 1969. (J). (gr. 5-9). lib. bdg. 6.87 o.p. (*0-87460-144-4*) Lion Bks.

Balter, Lawrence. Alfred Goes to the Hospital. 1990. (Stepping Stone Stories Ser.). (Illus.). 40p. (J). (gr. 3-7). 5.95 o.p. (*0-8120-6150-0*) Barron's Educational Series, Inc.

Bambara, Toni Cade. Raymond's Run. 1993. (Short Stories Ser.). 32p. (YA). (gr. 5 up). lib. bdg. 18.60 (*0-88682-351-X*, 97222-098, Creative Education) Creative Co., The.

Bancroft, Bronwyn, illus. Dreamtime: Aboriginal Stories. 1994. 96p. (J). (gr. 4-7). 16.00 (*0-688-13296-0*) HarperCollins Children's Bk. Group.

Bang, Molly Garrett. One Fall Day. 1994. (Illus.). 24p. (J). lib. bdg. 14.93 o.p. (*0-688-07016-7*); 15.00 (*0-688-07015-9*) HarperCollins Children's Bk. Group. (Greenwillow Bks.).

Banks, Jacqueline Turner. Egg-Drop Blues. 128p. (J). 2003. pap. 4.95 (*0-618-25080-8*); 2003. (gr. 4-6). 15.00 (*0-618-34885-9*); 1995. (gr. 4-6). tchr. ed. 15.00 o.s.i (*0-395-70931-8*) Houghton Mifflin Co.

—The New One. 1994. 112p. (J). (gr. 4-6). 15.00 (*0-395-66610-4*) Houghton Mifflin Co.

—Project Wheels. 1993. 112p. (J). (gr. 3-6). 13.95 o.p. (*0-395-64378-3*) Houghton Mifflin Co.

Banks, Sarah Harrell. A Net to Catch Time. 1996. (Illus.). 32p. (J). (ps-3). 17.99 o.s.i (*0-679-96673-0*) Random Hse., Inc.

Bantam Books Inc. Editors. Cop & a Half. 1993. 144p. (J). (gr. 4-6). mass mkt. 3.50 o.s.i (*0-553-48138-X*) Bantam Bks.

Barber, Barbara E. Allie's Basketball Dream. (Illus.). 32p. (J). (ps-5). 1998. pap. 6.95 (*1-880000-72-5*); 1996. 15.95 (*1-880000-38-5*) Lee & Low Bks., Inc.

—Allie's Basketball Dream. 1996. 13.10 (*0-606-15431-0*) Turtleback Bks.

—Saturday at the New You. 2002. (Illus.). (J). 14.66 (*0-7587-3566-9*) Book Wholesalers, Inc.

—Saturday at the New You. (Illus.). 32p. (J). (ps up). 1994. 14.95 (*1-880000-06-7*); 1996. reprint ed. pap. 6.95 (*1-880000-43-1*) Lee & Low Bks., Inc.

—Saturday at the New You. 1994. (J). 13.10 (*0-606-09819-4*) Turtleback Bks.

Bargar, Gary W. Life Is Not Fair. 1984. 180p. (J). (gr. 4-7). 13.95 o.p. (*0-89919-218-1*, Clarion Bks.) Houghton Mifflin Co. Trade & Reference Div.

Barnes, Joyce Annette. The Baby Grand, the Moon in July, & Me. 1998. 10.09 o.p. (*0-606-13157-4*) Turtleback Bks.

—The Baby Grand, the Moon in July & Me. 144p. (J). (gr. 3-7). 1998. (Illus.). pap. 4.99 o.s.i (*0-14-130061-2*, Puffin Bks.); 1994. 15.99 o.s.i (*0-8037-1586-2*, Dial Bks. for Young Readers); 1994. 14.89 o.p. (*0-8037-1600-1*, Dial Bks. for Young Readers) Penguin Putnam Bks. for Young Readers.

—Promise Me the Moon. 1999. (YA). pap. 14.89 (0-8037-1799-7, Dial Bks. for Young Readers); 1999. 176p. (J). (gr. 3-7). pap. 4.99 o.p. (0-14-038040-X); 1997. 176p. (YA). (gr. 5-9). 15.99 o.s.i (0-8037-1798-9, Dial Bks. for Young Readers) Penguin Putnam Bks. for Young Readers.

—Promise Me the Moon. 1999. 11.04 (0-606-14297-5) Turtleback Bks.

Barnwell, Ysaye M. No Mirrors in My Nana's House. 1998. (Illus.). 32p. (J). (gr. k-3). 18.00 incl. audio compact disk (0-15-201825-5) Harcourt Children's Bks.

Barrett, Anna Pearl. The Middlebatchers: Throw a Party for the Marriage of Hetty Wish & Lester Leg, Vol. 1. Darst, Shelia S., ed. 1984. (Illus.). 118p. (Orig.). (J). (gr. 3-7). pap. 7.95 (0-89896-105-X) Larksdale.

Barrett, Mary Brigid. Sing to the Stars. 1994. (Illus.). (J). 15.95 o.p. (0-316-08224-4) Little Brown & Co.

Barrett, William E. The Lilies of the Field. 1967. (Illus.). (YA). (gr. 7 up). pap. 3.95 o.s.i (0-385-07246-5, Image) Doubleday Publishing.

Barwick, Mary. The Alabama Angels. 1993. (Illus.). 64p. 15.00 o.s.i (0-345-38574-8) Ballantine Bks.

—The Alabama Angels. 3rd ed. 1989. (Illus.). 28p. (J). pap. 8.95 o.p. (0-9622815-1-4, Black Belt Pr.) River City Publishing.

Battle-Lavert, Gwendolyn. The Barber's Cutting Edge. 1994. (Illus.). 32p. (J). (gr. 1 up). 14.95 (0-89239-127-8) Children's Bk. Pr.

—The Music in Derrick's Heart. 2000. (Illus.). 32p. (J). (ps-3). tchr. ed. 16.95 (0-8234-1353-5) Holiday Hse., Inc.

—Off to School. 1995. (Illus.). 32p. (J). (ps-3). 15.95 (0-8234-1185-0) Holiday Hse., Inc.

—Papa's Mark. 2003. (Illus.). (J). (gr. k-3). tchr. ed. 16.95 (0-8234-1650-X) Holiday Hse., Inc.

Baum, Betty. New Home for Theresa. 1968. (Illus.). (J). (gr. 4-8). lib. bdg. 5.39 o.p. (0-394-91472-4, Knopf Bks. for Young Readers) Random Hse. Children's Bks.

Bearden, Romare. Li'l Dan the Drummer Boy: A Civil War Story. 2003. (Illus.). 40p. (J). 18.95 incl. audio compact disk (0-689-86237-7, Simon & Schuster Children's Publishing) Simon & Schuster Children's Publishing.

Belton, Sandra. Beauty, Her Basket. 2004. 32p. (J). 15.99 (0-688-17821-9); lib. bdg. 16.89 (0-688-17822-7) HarperCollins Children's Bk. Group. (Greenwillow Bks.).

—Ernestine & Amanda. (Ernestine & Amanda Ser.: Vol. 1). 160p. (J). 1996. (gr. 4-7). 16.00 o.p. (0-689-80848-8, Simon & Schuster Children's Publishing); Bk. 1. 1998. (gr. 3-7). pap. 4.50 (0-689-80847-X, Aladdin) Simon & Schuster Children's Publishing.

—Ernestine & Amanda: Mysteries on Monroe Street. 1998. (Ernestine & Amanda Ser.). 176p. (J). (gr. 3-7). 16.00 (0-689-81612-X, Simon & Schuster Children's Publishing) Simon & Schuster Children's Publishing.

—Ernestine & Amanda: Summer Camp Ready or Not!, No. 2. (Ernestine & Amanda Ser.: Vol. 2). 176p. (J). (gr. 3-7). 1998. bds. 3.99 o.p. (0-689-80845-3, Aladdin); 1997. 16.00 o.p. (0-689-80846-1, Simon & Schuster Children's Publishing) Simon & Schuster Children's Publishing.

—From Miss Ida's Porch. (Illus.). 40p. (J). (gr. 2-5). 1998. pap. 5.99 (0-689-81802-5, Aladdin); 11th ed. 1993. lib. bdg. 14.95 o.s.i (0-02-708915-0, Simon & Schuster Children's Publishing) Simon & Schuster Children's Publishing.

—From Miss Ida's Porch. 1998. (J). 12.14 (0-606-12940-5) Turtleback Bks.

—May'naise Sandwiches & Sunshine Tea. 1994. (Illus.). 32p. (J). (ps-4). mass mkt. 14.95 o.p. (0-02-709035-3, Simon & Schuster Children's Publishing) Simon & Schuster Children's Publishing.

—McKendree. 2000. 272p. (J). (gr. 5 up). 16.99 (0-688-15950-8, Greenwillow Bks.) HarperCollins Children's Bk. Group.

—Members of the C. L. U. B. (Ernestine & Amanda Ser.). 176p. (J). (gr. 3-7). 1998. pap. 4.50 (0-689-81661-8, Aladdin); 1997. lib. bdg. 16.00 o.p. (0-689-81611-1, Simon & Schuster Children's Publishing) Simon & Schuster Children's Publishing.

—Pictures for Miss Josie. 2003. (Illus.). 40p. (J). (gr. k-3). 16.99 (0-688-17480-9); (gr. 5 up). lib. bdg. 17.89 (0-688-17481-7) HarperCollins Children's Bk. Group. (Greenwillow Bks.).

Belton, Sandra & Carpenter, Nancy. Ernestine & Amanda: Mysteries on Monroe Street. 1999. (Ernestine & Amanda Ser.: No. 4). 176p. (J). (gr. 4-7). mass mkt. 4.50 o.p. (0-689-81662-6, 076714004504, Aladdin) Simon & Schuster Children's Publishing.

Ben-Moring, Alvin L. Quadrus & Goliath. 1976. (Illus.). (J). (gr. 6-9). 6.95 o.p. (0-664-32590-4) Westminster John Knox Pr.

Binch, Caroline. Gregory Cool. 1994. 32p. (J). 14.99 o.s.i (0-8037-1577-3, Dial Bks. for Young Readers) Penguin Putnam Bks. for Young Readers.

Blackburn, Joyce K. Suki & the Magic Sand Dollar. rev. ed. 1996. (Suki Ser.). (Illus.). 64p. (J). (ps-3). 14.95 (1-881576-70-1) Providence Hse. Pubs.

Blackman, Malorie. A New Dress for Maya. 1993. (Illus.). 32p. (J). (ps-3). lib. bdg. 19.93 o.p. (0-8368-0713-8) Stevens, Gareth Inc.

Blakeslee, Ann R. Summer Battles. 2000. (Illus.). 128p. (YA). (gr. 5-9). 14.95 (0-7614-5064-5, Cavendish Children's Bks.) Cavendish, Marshall Corp.

Bland, Celia. The Conspiracy of the Secret Nine. 1995. (Mysteries in Time Ser.). (Illus.). 90p. (J). (gr. 4-7). text 14.95 (1-881889-67-X) Silver Moon Pr.

Blaton, Catherine. Hold Fast to Your Dreams. 1969. (J). (gr. 6-9). lib. bdg. 4.29 o.s.i (0-671-32055-6, Archway Paperbacks) Pocket Bks.

Bledsoe, Lucy Jane. The Big Bike Race. 1997. (Illus.). 96p. (J). (gr. 3). pap. 4.95 (0-380-72830-3, Harper Trophy) HarperCollins Children's Bk. Group.

—The Big Bike Race. 1995. (Illus.). 96p. (J). (gr. 4-5). 15.95 (0-8234-1206-7) Holiday Hse., Inc.

—The Big Bike Race. 1997. 11.10 (0-606-10996-X) Turtleback Bks.

Boelts, Meribeth. With My Mom - With My Dad. 1992. (Sunshine Ser.). 32p. (J). pap. 0.97 o.p. (0-8163-1060-2) Pacific Pr. Publishing Assn.

Bolden, Tonya. Just Family. 1996. 160p. (J). (gr. 4-7). 14.99 o.s.i (0-525-65192-6, Dutton Children's Bks.) Penguin Putnam Bks. for Young Readers.

—Rites of Passage: Stories about Growing up by Black Writers from Around the World. 1995. 12.80 o.p. (0-606-08858-X) Turtleback Bks.

—Through Loona's Door: A Tammy & Owen Adventure with Carter G. Woodson. 1997. (America's Family Bks.). (Illus.). 48p. (J). (gr. k-5). 15.95 (1-885053-00-2) Corporation for Cultural Literacy.

Bolden, Tonya, ed. Rites of Passage: Stories about Growing up by Black Writers from Around the World. 1994. 240p. (J). (gr. 5 up). 16.95 (1-56282-688-3) Hyperion Bks. for Children.

Bond, Adrienne. Sugarcane House: And Other Stories about Mr. Fat. 1997. (Illus.). 96p. (J). (gr. 3-7). 16.00 (0-15-201446-2) Harcourt Children's Bks.

Bond, Adrienne Moore. Sugarcane House. 1997. pap. 5.00 (0-15-201447-0) Harcourt Trade Pubs.

Bond, Katherine Grace & Tate, Don, II. The Legend of the Valentine: An Inspirational Story of Love & Forgiveness. 2002. (Illus.). 32p. (J). 14.99 (0-310-70039-6) Zondervan.

Bonham, Frank. Durango Street. 1999. 192p. (J). (gr. 7-12). pap. 5.99 (0-14-130309-3, Puffin Bks.) Penguin Putnam Bks. for Young Readers.

—Hey, Big Spender. 1972. 176p. (J). (gr. 6 up). 8.95 o.p. (0-525-31855-0, Dutton) Dutton/Plume.

—Mystery of the Fat Cat. 1968. (Illus.). (J). (gr. 5-9). lib. bdg. 7.95 o.p. (0-525-35588-X, Dutton) Dutton/Plume.

—Mystery of the Fat Cat. 1971. (Illus.). 160p. (J). (gr. 5-9). pap. 2.75 o.s.i (0-440-46226-6, Yearling) Random Hse. Children's Bks.

—Nitty Gritty. 1968. (Illus.). (J). (gr. 5 up). 8.95 o.p. (0-525-35957-5, Dutton) Dutton/Plume.

Bontemps, Arna. Bubber Goes to Heaven. 1998. (Iona & Peter Opie Library of Children's Literature). (Illus.). 96p. (J). (gr. 1-7). 17.95 o.p. (0-19-512365-4) Oxford Univ. Pr., Inc.

—Chariot in the Sky: A Story of the Jubilee Singers. 2002. (Illus.). 240p. (J). 21.95 (0-19-515658-7) Oxford Univ. Pr., Inc.

—Lonesome Boy. 1988. (Night Lights Ser.). (Illus.). 32p. (J). (gr. k-3). reprint ed. pap. 4.95 o.p. (0-8070-8307-0, NL 2); lib. bdg. 12.95 o.p. (0-8070-8306-2) Beacon Pr.

Bontemps, Arna W. & Hughes, Langston. Popo & Fifina. 1993. (Iona & Peter Opie Library of Children's Literature). (Illus.). 128p. (YA). (gr. 3 up). 16.95 o.p. (0-19-508765-8) Oxford Univ. Pr., Inc.

Booth, Coleen E. Going Live. 1994. 192p. (J). pap. 3.50 (0-380-72039-6, Avon Bks.) Morrow/Avon.

—Going Live. 1992. 192p. (J). (gr. 5-7). lib. bdg. 14.95 o.p. (0-684-19392-2, Atheneum) Simon & Schuster Children's Publishing.

Boyd, Candy Dawson. Charlie Pippin. 1988. 192p. (J). (gr. 4-7). pap. 5.99 (0-14-032587-5, Puffin Bks.) Penguin Putnam Bks. for Young Readers.

—Charlie Pippin. 1987. 192p. (J). (gr. 3-7). lib. bdg. 14.95 o.s.i (0-02-726350-9, Simon & Schuster Children's Publishing) Simon & Schuster Children's Publishing.

—Charlie Pippin. 1987. (J). 11.04 (0-606-03752-7) Turtleback Bks.

—Chevrolet Saturdays. 1995. 192p. (J). (gr. 3-7). pap. 5.99 (0-14-036859-0, Puffin Bks.) Penguin Putnam Bks. for Young Readers.

—Chevrolet Saturdays. 1993. 192p. (J). (gr. 3-7). 16.00 (0-02-711765-0, Simon & Schuster Children's Publishing) Simon & Schuster Children's Publishing.

—Chevrolet Saturdays. 1995. (J). 11.04 (0-606-07361-2) Turtleback Bks.

—A Different Beat. 1996. 192p. (J). (gr. 3-7). pap. 4.99 o.s.i (0-14-036582-6, Puffin Bks.) Penguin Putnam Bks. for Young Readers.

—Fall Secrets. 1994. (Seasons Ser.). 224p. (J). (gr. 3-7). pap. 3.99 o.s.i (0-14-036583-4, Puffin Bks.) Penguin Putnam Bks. for Young Readers.

—Forever Friends. 1986. (Novels Ser.). 224p. (J). (gr. 7 up). pap. 4.99 o.s.i (0-14-032077-6, Puffin Bks.) Penguin Putnam Bks. for Young Readers.

—Forever Friends. 1992. (J). (gr. 4-8). 17.75 o.p. (0-8446-6571-1) Smith, Peter Pub., Inc.

Boyd, Patti. My Doctor Bag. 1994. (Tote-Along Board Bks.). (Illus.). 10p. (J). (ps). 3.95 o.p. (0-8431-3741-X, Price Stern Sloan) Penguin Putnam Bks. for Young Readers.

Braby, Marie. The Longest Wait. 1995. (Illus.). 32p. (J). (ps-2). pap. 15.95 o.p. (0-531-06871-4); lib. bdg. 16.99 o.p. (0-531-08721-2) Scholastic, Inc. (Orchard Bks.).

Bradbury, Ray. The Other Foot. 1993. (Creative Short Stories Ser.). (Illus.). 39p. (YA). (gr. 3-12). lib. bdg. 18.60 (0-88682-106-1, Creative Education) Creative Co., The.

Bradby, Marie. Momma, Where Are You From? 2000. (Illus.). 32p. (J). (ps-2). pap. 16.95 (0-531-30105-2, Orchard Bks.) Scholastic, Inc.

—More Than Anything Else. 1996. (Illus.). 32p. (J). (ps-3). pap. 15.95 o.s.i (0-531-09464-2); lib. bdg. 16.99 (0-531-08764-6) Scholastic, Inc. (Orchard Bks.).

Bradford, Clare. Birthday Wishes. 1994. (Illus.). (J). 4.25 (0-383-03737-9) SRA/McGraw-Hill.

Bray, Jeannine D. Superfro. Kenyatta, Imani, ed. 1998. (Illus.). 72p. (J). (gr. k-6). 14.95 (1-886580-10-3) Pinnacle-Syatt Pubns.

Breeze, Lynn, illus. This Little Baby Goes Out. 1993. (J). (ps). 5.95 o.p. (0-316-10854-5) Little Brown & Co.

Brenaman, Miriam. Evvy's Civil War. 2002. 224p. (J). (gr. 7-10). 18.99 (0-399-23713-5) Penguin Group (USA) Inc.

—Evvy's Civil War. 2004. (Illus.). 224p. pap. 6.99 (0-14-240039-4, Puffin Bks.) Penguin Putnam Bks. for Young Readers.

Brenner, Barbara. Wagon Wheels. (I Can Read Bks.). (Illus.). 64p. (J). (gr. k-3). 1978. 15.95 (0-06-020668-3); 1978. lib. bdg. 15.89 (0-06-020669-1); unabr. ed. 1995. pap. 8.99 incl. audio (0-694-70001-0); 97th ed. 1997. pap. 3.99 (0-06-444052-4, Harper Trophy) HarperCollins Children's Bk. Group.

—Wagon Wheels. 1978. (I Can Read Bks.). (J). (gr. 2-4). 10.10 (0-606-02372-0) Turtleback Bks.

Brooks, Bruce. The Moves Make the Man. (Trophy Bk.). (gr. 7 up). 1996. 288p. (J). pap. 5.99 (0-06-440564-8, Harper Trophy); 1987. 256p. (J). pap. 6.99 (0-06-447022-9, Harper Trophy); 1984. 208p. (J). lib. bdg. 16.89 (0-06-020698-5); 1984. 320p. (YA). 15.00 o.s.i (0-06-020679-9) HarperCollins Children's Bk. Group.

—The Moves Make the Man. 1987. 12.00 (0-606-09638-8) Turtleback Bks.

—Prince. 1998. (Wolfbay Wings Ser.: No. 5). (Illus.). (J). 144p. (gr. 4-7). pap. 4.50 (0-06-440600-8); 40p. (ps-k). lib. bdg. 14.89 o.s.i (0-06-027542-1) HarperCollins Pubs.

—Prince. 1998. (Wolfbay Wings Ser.: No. 5). (J). (gr. 4-7). 10.55 (0-606-13925-7) Turtleback Bks.

Brown, Kay. Willy's Summer Dream. 1989. 144p. (YA). (gr. 7 up). 13.95 (0-15-200645-1, Gulliver Bks.) Harcourt Children's Bks.

Brown, Margery W. Afro-Bets Book of Colors. 1991. (Illus.). 24p. (J). (ps-1). pap. 3.95 o.p. (0-940975-28-9) Just Us Bks., Inc.

—Baby Jesus Like My Brother. 1995. (Illus.). 32p. (J). (ps-3). 15.95 (0-940975-53-X); pap. 7.95 (0-940975-54-8) Just Us Bks., Inc.

—Baby Jesus Like My Brother. 1995. (J). 13.20 o.p. (0-606-09028-2) Turtleback Bks.

—Baby Jesus Like My Brother. (Illus.). 2001. (J). E-Book (1-59019-146-3); 1995. E-Book (1-59019-147-1); 1995. E-Book 5.99 (1-59019-148-X) ipicturebooks, LLC.

Bryant, Louella. The Black Bonnet. 1996. (YA). (gr. 5 up). pap. 12.95 (1-881535-22-3) New England Pr., Inc., The.

Bryant, Sara Cone. Epaminondas & His Auntie. 1986. (Illus.). 16p. (J). (ps-3). reprint ed. pap. 8.95 (0-89966-556-X) Buccaneer Bks., Inc.

Buckley, Helen E. Grandfather & I. (Illus.). 24p. (J). (ps-3). 2000. pap. 5.95 (0-688-17526-0, Harper Trophy); 1994. 15.89 (0-688-12534-4); 1994. 15.95 (0-688-12533-6) HarperCollins Children's Bk. Group.

—Grandmother & I. (Illus.). 24p. (J). 2000. (ps-3). pap. 5.99 (0-688-17525-2, Harper Trophy); 1994. (ps-3). 16.99 (0-688-12531-X); 1994. (gr. 3 up). lib. bdg. 15.93 o.p. (0-688-12532-8) HarperCollins Children's Bk. Group.

Bunney, Ron. Eye of the Eagle. 1995. 156p. (YA). pap. 9.95 (1-86368-126-4) Fremantle Arts Centre Pr. AUS. *Dist:* International Specialized Bk. Services.

Bunting, Eve. The Blue & the Gray. 1996. (Illus.). 32p. (J). pap. 14.95 (0-590-60197-0) Scholastic, Inc.

—Face at the Edge of the World. (gr. 7 up). 1988. 168p. (YA). pap. 6.95 (0-89919-800-7); 1985. 192p. (J). 13.95 o.p. (0-89919-399-4) Houghton Mifflin Co. Trade & Reference Div. (Clarion Bks.).

—Face at the Edge of the World. 1988. 13.00 (0-606-12282-6) Turtleback Bks.

—Flower Garden. 2002. (Illus.). (J). 13.19 (0-7587-2519-1) Book Wholesalers, Inc.

—Flower Garden. (Illus.). 32p. (J). (ps-3). 2000. pap. 6.00 (0-15-202372-0); 1994. 16.00 (0-15-228776-0) Harcourt Children's Bks.

—Flower Garden. 1999. (Illus.). 32p. (J). (ps-3). pap. 25.95 (0-15-201968-5) Harcourt Trade Pubs.

—Flower Garden. 2000. 12.15 (0-606-17842-2) Turtleback Bks.

—Two Different Girls. 1992. (Eve Bunting Collection Ser.). (Illus.). 48p. (J). (gr. 2-6). lib. bdg. 12.79 o.p. (0-89565-772-4) Child's World, Inc.

—Two Different Girls. 1978. (Young Romance Ser.). (Illus.). (J). (gr. 3-9). pap. 3.25 o.p. (0-89812-067-5); lib. bdg. 7.95 o.p. (0-87191-637-1) Creative Co., The. (Creative Education).

—Two Different Girls. 2001. 32p. (YA). (gr. 6-12). pap. (0-8224-3535-7) Globe Fearon Educational Publishing.

—Your Move. 1998. (Illus.). 32p. (J). (gr. 1-5). 16.00 (0-15-200181-6) Harcourt Children's Bks.

Burden-Patmon, Denise. Imani's Gift at Kwanzaa. 48.95 (0-8136-2248-4) Modern Curriculum Pr.

—Imani's Gift at Kwanzaa. 1993. (Illus.). 32p. (J). (ps-3). pap. 4.95 (0-671-79841-3, Aladdin) Simon & Schuster Children's Publishing.

—Imani's Gift at Kwanzaa. 1993. (J). 11.10 (0-606-05372-7) Turtleback Bks.

Burgess, Barbara H. The Fred Field. 1995. 192p. (J). pap. 3.99 o.s.i (0-440-41067-3) Dell Publishing.

—Oren Bell. 192p. (J). (ps-3). 1992. pap. 3.50 o.s.i (0-440-40747-8); 1991. 15.00 o.s.i (0-385-30325-4, Delacorte Pr.) Dell Publishing.

Burleigh, Robert. Lookin' for Bird in the Big City. 2001. (Illus.). 32p. (J). (gr. 1-4). 16.00 (0-15-202031-4, Silver Whistle) Harcourt Children's Bks.

Burt, Barbara Swett. Measuring. 1998. (J). (0-8172-7268-2) Raintree Pubs.

Burton, Elizabeth. Mean Mean Madeleen - Sweet Sweet Angeleen. Caso, Adolph, ed. unabr. ed. 1997. (Illus.). 32p. (J). (gr. 2-6). pap. 12.95 (0-8283-2043-8) Branden Bks.

Byars, Betsy C. The Burning Questions of Bingo Brown. l.t. ed. 1989. (G. K. Hall Large Print Book Ser.). 232p. (J). (gr. 3-7). lib. bdg. 14.95 o.p. (0-8161-4770-1, Macmillan Reference USA) Gale Group.

—The Burning Questions of Bingo Brown. (Bingo Brown Ser.). (J). 1990. (Illus.). 176p. (gr. 4-7). pap. 5.99 (0-14-032479-8, Puffin Bks.); 1988. 160p. (gr. 5-9). 15.99 o.p. (0-670-81932-8, Viking Children's Bks.) Penguin Putnam Bks. for Young Readers.

Caines, Jeannette F. I Need a Lunch Box. (Trophy Picture Bk.). (Illus.). 32p. (J). (ps-1). 1993. pap. 5.99 (0-06-443341-2, Harper Trophy); 1993. 15.00 o.p. (0-06-020984-4); 1988. lib. bdg. 16.89 (0-06-020985-2) HarperCollins Children's Bk. Group.

Cameron, Ann. Gloria, Rising, RS. 2002. (Illus.). 112p. (J). (gr. 2-5). 15.00 (0-374-32675-4, Farrar, Straus & Giroux (BYR)) Farrar, Straus & Giroux.

—Gloria's Way. 2002. (Illus.). 12.34 (1-4046-0952-0) Book Wholesalers, Inc.

—Gloria's Way, RS. 2000. (Illus.). 96p. (J). (ps-3). 15.00 (0-374-32670-3, Farrar, Straus & Giroux (BYR)) Farrar, Straus & Giroux.

—Gloria's Way. 2001. (Chapter Ser.). (Illus.). 112p. (J). pap. 4.99 (0-14-230023-3, Puffin Bks.) Penguin Putnam Bks. for Young Readers.

—Julian, Dream Doctor. 2002. (J). 12.32 (0-7587-6155-4) Book Wholesalers, Inc.

—Julian, Dream Doctor. 1995. (Illus.). (J). (gr. 3). 8.60 (0-395-73237-9) Houghton Mifflin Co.

—Julian, Dream Doctor. (Stepping Stone Bks.). (Illus.). 64p. 1993. (J). (gr. 4-7). pap. 4.50 (0-679-80524-9); 1990. (ps-3). lib. bdg. 11.99 (0-679-90524-3) Random Hse. Children's Bks. (Random Hse. Bks. for Young Readers).

—Julian, Dream Doctor. 1990. (Stepping Stone Bks.). 10.14 (0-606-09497-0) Turtleback Bks.

—Julian, Secret Agent. 2002. (Illus.). (J). 12.87 (0-7587-1353-3) Book Wholesalers, Inc.

—Julian, Secret Agent. 1988. (Stepping Stone Bks.). (Illus.). 64p. (J). (gr. 2-4). 6.99 o.s.i (0-394-91949-1, Random Hse. Bks. for Young Readers); (gr. 4-7). pap. 4.50 (0-394-81949-7) Random Hse. Children's Bks.

—Julian, Secret Agent. 1988. (Stepping Stone Bks.). (J). 10.14 (0-606-03835-3) Turtleback Bks.

—Julian's Glorious Summer. 2002. (Illus.). (J). 12.87 (0-7587-1354-1) Book Wholesalers, Inc.

—Julian's Glorious Summer. 1987. (Stepping Stone Bks.). (Illus.). 64p. (J). (ps-3). pap. 4.50 (0-394-89117-1, Random Hse. Bks. for Young Readers) Random Hse. Children's Bks.

—Julian's Glorious Summer. 1987. (Stepping Stone Bks.). 10.14 (*0-606-10235-3*) Turtleback Bks.

—More Stories Huey Tells, RS. 1997. (Illus.). 128p. (J). (gr. 3-5). 14.00 (*0-374-35065-5*, Farrar, Straus & Giroux (BYR)) Farrar, Straus & Giroux.

—More Stories Huey Tells. 1999. (Illus.). 128p. (J). (gr. k-4). pap. 4.99 (*0-679-88363-0*) Knopf, Alfred A. Inc.

—More Stories Huey Tells. 1998. (J). pap. 4.99 (*0-679-88576-5*, Knopf Bks. for Young Readers) Random Hse. Children's Bks.

—More Stories Huey Tells. 1999. 11.04 (*0-606-16567-3*) Turtleback Bks.

—More Stories Julian Tells. (Illus.). 96p. (J). (gr. k-4). 1986. 13.95 o.s.i (*0-394-86969-9*); 1986. 14.99 o.s.i (*0-394-96969-3*); 1989. reprint ed. pap. 4.99 (*0-394-82454-7*) Random Hse. Children's Bks. (Knopf Bks. for Young Readers).

—More Stories Julian Tells. 1986. (J). 11.04 (*0-606-04278-4*) Turtleback Bks.

—The Stories Huey Tells. (Illus.). 112p. (J). 1995. (gr. k-4). 17.99 o.s.i (*0-679-96732-X*); 1995. (gr. 3-5). 16.00 o.s.i (*0-679-86732-5*); 1997. (gr. k-4). reprint ed. pap. 4.99 (*0-679-88559-5*) Random Hse. Children's Bks. (Knopf Bks. for Young Readers).

—The Stories Huey Tells. 1997. 11.04 (*0-606-13042-X*) Turtleback Bks.

—The Stories Julian Tells. 1995. (J). pap. text 15.40 (*0-15-305580-4*) Harcourt Trade Pubs.

—The Stories Julian Tells. 1999. (J). 9.95 (*1-56137-671-X*) Novel Units, Inc.

—The Stories Julian Tells. (J). 1996. pap. 3.99 o.p. (*0-679-88125-5*, Random Hse. Bks. for Young Readers); 1989. (Illus.). 80p. reprint ed. pap. 4.99 (*0-394-82892-5*, Knopf Bks. for Young Readers) Random Hse. Children's Bks.

—The Stories Julian Tells. 1981. (J). 11.14 (*0-606-03480-3*) Turtleback Bks.

Cameron, Ann & Strugnell, Ann. The Stories Julian Tells. 1981. (Illus.). 96p. (J). (gr. k-5). 15.99 o.s.i (*0-394-94301-5*, Pantheon) Knopf Publishing Group.

Campbell, Bebe Moore. Sometimes My Mommy Gets Angry. 2003. (Illus.). 32p. (J). 16.99 (*0-399-23972-3*, G. P. Putnam's Sons) Penguin Putnam Bks. for Young Readers.

Campbell, Tammie L. Honey Brown in Search of Her Identity, Vol. 1. 1990. (Illus.). 24p. (Orig.). (J). (gr. k-5). pap. 4.95 (*0-9623947-0-X*) Campbell, Tammie Lang.

Capizzi, Michael. Getting It All Together. 1972. (Illus.). 128p. (J). (gr. 5-9). 5.95 o.p. (*0-440-03050-1*, Delacorte Pr.) Dell Publishing.

Carbone, Elisa L. The Surfmen of Pea Island. 2001. 176p. (gr. 5-8). lib. bdg. 18.99 (*0-375-90664-9*) Random Hse., Inc.

Carbone, Elisa L. Stealing Freedom. 2002. (EMC Masterpiece Series Access Editions). (Illus.). xix, 284p. (J). 14.60 (*0-8219-2507-5*) EMC/Paradigm Publishing.

Carlson, Margaret. The Canning Season. 1999. (First Person Ser.). (Illus.). (J). (gr. 2-4). 32p. pap. 7.95 (*1-57505-283-0*, Carolrhoda Bks.); 40p. lib. bdg. 19.93 o.s.i (*1-57505-260-1*) Lerner Publishing Group.

Carr, Pat M. If We Must Die: A Novel. 2002. (Chaparral Book for Young Readers Ser.). 168p. (J). 15.95 (*0-87565-262-X*) Texas Christian Univ. Pr.

Carter, Dorothy. Bye, Mis' Lela, RS. 1998. (Frances Foster Bks.). (Illus.). 32p. (J). (gr. k-3). 16.00 (*0-374-31013-0*, Farrar, Straus & Giroux (BYR)) Farrar, Straus & Giroux.

—Grandma's General Store: The Ark, RS. 2004. (J). (*0-374-32766-1*, Farrar, Straus & Giroux (BYR)) Farrar, Straus & Giroux.

Carter, Madeline. Look at You, Baby Face! 1998. (Super Shape Bks.). (Illus.). 24p. (J). (ps-k). pap. 3.29 o.s.i (*0-307-10004-9*, Golden Bks.) Random Hse. Children's Bks.

Case, Dianne. Ninety-Two Queens Road, RS. 1995. 176p. (J). (gr. 4-7). 16.00 o.p. (*0-374-35518-5*, Farrar, Straus & Giroux (BYR)) Farrar, Straus & Giroux.

Ceasor, Frank, Sr. & Gaines, Edith M. Can You Count?; Carpetbaggers in Action; Mr. Impossible. McCluskey, John A., ed. 2nd ed. 1993. (Stories from Black History Series II: Vol. 3). (Illus.). (J). (gr. 4-7). pap. 2.00 (*0-913678-27-9*) New Day Pr.

Chang, Heidi, illus. Saturday Sandwiches. 1997. (J). (*0-7802-8024-5*) Wright Group, The.

Chapman, Cheryl. Snow on Snow on Snow. 1994. (Illus.). 32p. (J). (ps-3). 14.99 o.s.i (*0-8037-1456-4*); 14.89 o.s.i (*0-8037-1457-2*) Penguin Putnam Bks. for Young Readers. (Dial Bks. for Young Readers).

Chapman, Christina. Treasure in the Attic. 1992. (Publish-a-Book Contest Ser.). (Illus.). 32p. (J). (gr. 1-6). lib. bdg. 22.83 o.p. (*0-8114-3582-2*) Raintree Pubs.

Charbonnet, Gabrielle. Attack of the Beast. 1998. (Disney Girls Ser.: Vol. 2). 96p. (J). (gr. 2-5). pap. 3.95 (*0-7868-4160-5*) Disney Pr.

Cheatham, K. Follis. The Best Way Out. 1982. 168p. (J). 9.95 o.p. (*0-15-206741-8*) Harcourt Children's Bks.

Childress, Alice. A Hero Ain't Nothin' but a Sandwich. 1977. 128p. (YA). (gr. 7 up). pap. 4.50 o.p. (*0-380-00132-2*, Avon Bks.) Morrow/Avon.

—A Hero Ain't Nothin' but a Sandwich. l.t. ed. 1989. 144p. (J). lib. bdg. 16.95 o.s.i (*1-55736-112-6*, Cornerstone Bks.) Pages, Inc.

—A Hero Ain't Nothin' but a Sandwich. 2000. 128p. (J). (gr. 7-12). pap. 5.99 (*0-698-11854-5*) Penguin Putnam Bks. for Young Readers.

—A Hero Ain't Nothin' but a Sandwich. 1973. 128p. (YA). (gr. 5-9). 15.95 o.p. (*0-698-20278-3*, Coward-McCann) Putnam Publishing Group, The.

—A Hero Ain't Nothin' but a Sandwich. 2000. 11.04 (Illus.). (*0-606-17821-X*); 1973. (YA). 9.60 o.p. (*0-606-03528-1*) Turtleback Bks.

—Rainbow Jordan. 1982. 128p. (J). (gr. 7-12). pap. 4.99 (*0-380-58974-5*, Avon Bks.) Morrow/Avon.

—Rainbow Jordan. 1981. (Illus.). 182p. (J). (gr. 7 up). 14.99 o.s.i (*0-698-32500-1*, Coward-McCann) Penguin Group (USA) Inc.

—Rainbow Jordan. 1981. (J). 13.95 o.s.i (*0-698-20531-6*) Putnam Publishing Group, The.

—Rainbow Jordan. 1998. (YA). 20.25 (*0-8446-6966-0*) Smith, Peter Pub., Inc.

—Rainbow Jordan. 1981. 10.04 (*0-606-00560-9*) Turtleback Bks.

—Those Other People. 1989. 144p. (YA). (gr. 8 up). 14.95 o.s.i (*0-399-21510-7*, G. P. Putnam's Sons) Penguin Putnam Bks. for Young Readers.

Chocolate, Deborah M. Newton. Elizabeth's Wish. 1994. (Neate Ser.: Bk. 2). (Illus.). 96p. (YA). (gr. 3-7). pap. 3.95 (*0-940975-45-9*) Just Us Bks., Inc.

—Elizabeth's Wish. 1994. E-Book (*1-59019-157-9*); (Neate Ser.: Bk. 2). E-Book (*1-59019-156-0*); (Neate Ser.: Vol. 2). E-Book (*1-59019-158-7*) ipicturebooks, LLC.

—On the Day I Was Born. 1995. (Illus.). 32p. (J). (gr. k-4). pap. 12.95 o.p. (*0-590-47609-2*, Cartwheel Bks.) Scholastic, Inc.

—The Piano Man. 1998. (Illus.). 32p. (J). (gr. k-3). 15.95 (*0-8027-8646-4*); lib. bdg. 16.85 (*0-8027-8647-2*) Walker & Co.

Chocolate, Deborah M. Newton & Hudson, Wade. Neate to the Rescue! 1992. (Neate Ser.). (Illus.). 112p. (YA). (gr. 3-7). pap. 3.95 (*0-940975-42-4*) Just Us Bks., Inc.

Clary, Margie Willis. A Sweet, Sweet Basket. Stone, Barbara, ed. 1995. (Illus.). 40p. (J). (gr. k-7). 15.95 (*0-87844-127-1*) Sandlapper Publishing Co., Inc.

Cleary, Brian P. You Never Sausage Love. 1996. (It Could Be Verse Ser.). (Illus.). 32p. (J). (gr. 3-6). lib. bdg. 12.95 (*0-8225-2115-6*) Lerner Publishing Group.

Clifton, Lucille. All Us Come Cross the Water. 1973. (Illus.). 32p. (gr. k-4). 5.95 o.p. (*0-03-089262-7*) Holt, Henry & Co.

—Everett Anderson's Christmas Coming, ERS. (Illus.). 32p. (J). (ps-3). 1993. pap. 4.95 o.s.i (*0-8050-2949-4*); 1991. 14.95 (*0-8050-1549-3*) Holt, Henry & Co. (Holt, Henry & Co. Bks. For Young Readers).

—Everett Anderson's Christmas Coming. 1991. 11.10 (*0-606-16135-X*) Turtleback Bks.

—Everett Anderson's Year, ERS. rev. ed. 1992. (Illus.). 32p. (J). (ps-3). 14.95 o.s.i (*0-8050-2247-3*, Holt, Henry & Co. Bks. For Young Readers) Holt, Henry & Co.

—Everett Anderson's 1-2-3, ERS. (Illus.). (J). (gr. k-3). 1977. o.p. (*0-03-017441-4*); 1992. 32p. 16.95 (*0-8050-2310-0*) Holt, Henry & Co. (Holt, Henry & Co. Bks. For Young Readers).

—One of the Problems of Everett Anderson, ERS. 2001. (Illus.). 32p. (J). (gr. k-3). 16.95 (*0-8050-5201-1*, Holt, Henry & Co. Bks. For Young Readers) Holt, Henry & Co.

—The Times They Used to Be. 1976. pap. 0.95 o.p. (*0-440-48703-X*) Dell Publishing.

—The Times They Used to Be, ERS. 1974. (Illus.). 64p. (J). (gr. 3-7). o.p. (*0-03-012171-X*, Holt, Henry & Co. Bks. For Young Readers) Holt, Henry & Co.

—The Times They Used to Be. 2002. (Illus.). 48p. (YA). (gr. 5). pap. 4.99 (*0-440-41867-4*, Laurel Leaf) Random Hse. Children's Bks.

Clovis, Donna L. Locket of Dreams: A Modern African American Fairy Tale. 1999. (Illus.). 24p. (J). (gr. 3-8). pap. text 9.95 (*1-58521-001-3*) Books for Black Children, Inc.

Codell, Esme Raji. Sahara Special. 2003. (J). pap. (*0-7868-1611-2*); (Illus.). 177p. 15.99 (*0-7868-0793-8*); (Illus.). 208p. lib. bdg. 16.49 (*0-7868-2627-4*) Hyperion Bks. for Children.

Cohen, Barbara. Two Hundred Thirteen Valentines, ERS. (Redfeather Bks.). (Illus.). 64p. (J). (gr. 2-4). 1993. pap. 7.95 (*0-8050-2627-4*); 1991. 13.95 o.p. (*0-8050-1536-1*) Holt, Henry & Co. (Holt, Henry & Co. Bks. For Young Readers).

Coker, Deborah C. Aunt Mattie's Present. 1998. (Illus.). (J). (*0-316-23498-2*) Little Brown & Co.

Coker, Deborah Connor. I Like Me! 1999. (Illus.). 36p. (J). (ps-3). pap. 5.49 o.s.i (*0-307-11438-4*, Golden Bks.) Random Hse. Children's Bks.

Coker, Deborah Connor. I Like Me! 1998. (Little Golden Storybook Ser.). (Illus.). 24p. (J). (ps-3). 3.99 o.s.i (*0-307-16187-0*, Golden Bks.) Random Hse. Children's Bks.

Cole, Kenneth. No Bad News. 2001. (Concept Book Ser.). (Illus.). 40p. (J). (gr. 1-4). 15.95 (*0-8075-4743-3*) Whitman, Albert & Co.

Coleman, Evelyn. Born in Sin. (YA). (gr. 7 up). 2003. 272p. mass mkt. 5.99 (*0-689-85552-4*, Simon Pulse); 2001. (Illus.). 240p. 16.00 (*0-689-83833-6*, Atheneum/Richard Jackson Bks.) Simon & Schuster Children's Publishing.

—Circle of Fire. 2001. (American Girl Collection: Bk. 14). (Illus.). 160p. (J). 9.95 o.p. (*1-58485-340-9*); pap. 5.95 (*1-58485-339-5*) Pleasant Co. Pubns. (American Girl).

—Circle of Fire. 2001. (American Girl Collection). (Illus.). (J). 12.00 (*0-606-21249-3*) Turtleback Bks.

—The Foot Warmer & the Black Crow. 1994. (Illus.). 32p. (J). (gr. 1 up). mass mkt. 14.95 o.s.i (*0-02-722816-9*, Simon & Schuster Children's Publishing) Simon & Schuster Children's Publishing.

—The Glass Bottle Tree. 1996. (Illus.). 32p. (J). (ps-3). pap. 15.95 (*0-531-09467-7*); lib. bdg. 16.99 (*0-531-08767-0*) Scholastic, Inc. (Orchard Bks.).

—Mystery of the Dark Tower. 2000. (American Girl Collection: Bk. 6). (Illus.). 160p. (J). (gr. 5-9). pap. 5.95 (*1-58485-084-1*); 9.95 (*1-58485-085-X*) Pleasant Co. Pubns. (American Girl).

—Mystery of the Dark Tower. 2000. (History Mysteries Ser.). 12.00 (*0-606-18356-6*) Turtleback Bks.

—To Be a Drum. 1998. (Illus.). 32p. (YA). (gr. k-3). lib. bdg. 16.95 (*0-8075-8006-6*) Whitman, Albert & Co.

—White Socks Only. (Prairie Paperback Bks.). (Illus.). 32p. (J). (gr. k-4). 1999. pap. 6.95 (*0-8075-8956-X*); 1996. lib. bdg. 15.95 (*0-8075-8955-1*) Whitman, Albert & Co.

Collier, Bryan. Uptown, ERS. (Illus.). 32p. (J). 2004. pap. 6.95 (*0-8050-7399-X*); 2000. 16.95 (*0-8050-5721-8*) Holt, Henry & Co. (Holt, Henry & Co. Bks. For Young Readers).

Collier, James Lincoln, Christopher. Who Is Carrie? 2001. 176p. (gr. 5-7). pap. text 12.00 (*0-375-89503-5*) Random Hse., Inc.

Collier, James Lincoln. Jump Ship to Freedom. 1996. (J). pap. 5.99 (*0-440-91158-3*, Dell Books for Young Readers) Random Hse. Children's Bks.

—Jump Ship to Freedom. 1987. (Arabus Family Saga Ser.). (J). 11.55 (*0-606-02265-1*) Turtleback Bks.

—War Comes to Willy Freeman. 1983. (J). 12.95 (*0-440-09642-1*) Dell Publishing.

—War Comes to Willy Freeman. 1987. (Arabus Family Saga Ser.). (J). 11.55 (*0-606-03076-X*) Turtleback Bks.

Collier, James Lincoln & Collier, Christopher. Jump Ship to Freedom. 1981. 192p. (J). (gr. 4-6). pap. 13.95 o.s.i (*0-385-28484-5*, Delacorte Pr.) Dell Publishing.

—Jump Ship to Freedom. 1987. (Arabus Family Saga Ser.: Vol. 2). 208p. (gr. 4-7). pap. text 5.50 (*0-440-44323-7*, Yearling) Random Hse. Children's Bks.

—War Comes to Willy Freeman. 1987. (Arabus Family Saga Ser.: Vol. 1). 192p. (gr. 4-7). pap. text 5.50 (*0-440-49504-0*, Yearling) Random Hse. Children's Bks.

—War Comes to Willy Freeman. 1992. (J). (gr. 4-6). 17.25 o.p. (*0-8446-6596-7*) Smith, Peter Pub., Inc.

—Who Is Carrie? 1984. 192p. (J). (gr. 4-6). 14.95 o.s.i (*0-385-29295-3*, Delacorte Pr.) Dell Publishing.

—Who Is Carrie? 1987. (Arabus Family Saga Ser.: Vol. 3). 176p. (gr. 5-7). pap. text 4.99 o.s.i (*0-440-49536-9*, Yearling) Random Hse. Children's Bks.

—Who Is Carrie? 1987. (Arabus Family Saga Ser.). (J). 11.04 (*0-606-03505-2*) Turtleback Bks.

—With Every Drop of Blood. 1994. 256p. (J). 16.95 o.s.i (*0-385-32028-0*, Delacorte Pr.) Dell Publishing.

Condon, Bill. Holly & Mac. 1999. (Supa Doopers Ser.). (Illus.). 64p. (J). (*0-7608-1924-6*) Sundance Publishing.

Connelly, Bernardine. Follow the Drinking Gourd. 1993. (Illus.). (J). 14.95 (*0-88708-336-6*); 19.95 incl. audio (*0-88708-335-8*) Simon & Schuster Children's Publishing. (Simon & Schuster Children's Publishing).

Conover, K. Scott. Can I Play, Too? 1998. (Illus.). 70p. (J). (gr. 4-8). pap. 9.95 (*1-882792-69-6*) Proctor Pubns.

Cooke, Trish. Full, Full, Full of Love. 2003. (Illus.). 32p. (YA). 15.99 (*0-7636-1851-9*) Candlewick Pr.

—Mr. Pam Pam & the Hullabazoo. 1994. (Illus.). 32p. (J). (ps up). 14.95 o.p. (*1-56402-411-3*) Candlewick Pr.

Cooney, Caroline B. Burning Up. 1999. (YA). pap., stu. ed. 68.99 incl. audio (*0-7887-3190-4*, 40925); pap., stu. ed. 68.99 incl. audio (*0-7887-3190-4*, 40925) Recorded Bks., LLC.

—Burning Up. 2001. (YA). 11.55 (*0-606-20585-3*) Turtleback Bks.

Cooper, Floyd, illus. Rites of Passage: Stories about Growing up by Black Writers from Around the World. 1995. 240p. (YA). (gr. 5 up). pap. 7.95 o.p. (*0-7868-1076-9*) Hyperion Paperbacks for Children.

Cooper, Melrose. Gettin' Through Thursday. 2000. (Illus.). 32p. (J). (ps-5). 15.95 (*1-880000-67-9*); pap. 6.95 (*1-58430-014-0*) Lee & Low Bks., Inc.

—Life Magic, ERS. 1996. 128p. (J). (gr. 4-7). 14.95 o.p. (*0-8050-4114-1*, Holt, Henry & Co. Bks. For Young Readers) Holt, Henry & Co.

—Life Riddles. 1995. mass mkt. 4.50 o.s.i (*0-449-70446-7*, Fawcett) Ballantine Bks.

—Life Riddles, ERS. 1994. 88p. (J). (gr. 5-7). 14.95 o.p. (*0-8050-2613-4*, Holt, Henry & Co. Bks. For Young Readers) Holt, Henry & Co.

Corey, Dorothy. Will There Be a Lap for Me? Levine, Abby, ed. 1992. (Illus.). 24p. (J). (gr. k-2). lib. bdg. 13.95 (*0-8075-9109-2*); pap. 5.95 (*0-8075-9110-6*) Whitman, Albert & Co.

Cosby, Bill. The Best Way to Play. 1997. (Little Bill Books for Beginning Readers Ser.). (Illus.). 40p. (J). (gr. k-3). pap. 13.95 (*0-590-13756-5*); mass mkt. 3.99 (*0-590-95617-5*, Cartwheel Bks.) Scholastic, Inc.

—The Best Way to Play. 1997. (Little Bill Books for Beginning Readers Ser.). (J). (gr. k-3). 10.14 (*0-606-11116-6*) Turtleback Bks.

—The Day I Saw My Father Cry. 2000. (Little Bill Books for Beginning Readers Ser.). (Illus.). 40p. (J). (gr. k-3). pap. 15.95 (*0-590-52197-7*); mass mkt. 3.99 (*0-590-52199-3*) Scholastic, Inc.

—The Day I Saw My Father Cry. 2000. (Little Bill Books for Beginning Readers Ser.). (Illus.). (J). 10.14 (*0-606-20470-9*) Turtleback Bks.

—Money Troubles. 1998. (Little Bill Books for Beginning Readers Ser.). (Illus.). 40p. (J). (gr. k-3). pap. 13.95 (*0-590-16402-3*); mass mkt. 3.99 (*0-590-95623-X*) Scholastic, Inc.

—Money Troubles. 1998. (Little Bill Books for Beginning Readers Ser.). (J). (gr. k-3). 10.14 (*0-606-13615-0*) Turtleback Bks.

—My Big Lie. 1999. (Little Bill Books for Beginning Readers Ser.). (Illus.). 40p. (J). (gr. k-3). pap. 15.95 (*0-590-52160-8*); (gr. 1-5). mass mkt. 3.99 (*0-590-52161-6*) Scholastic, Inc.

—My Big Lie. 1999. (Little Bill Books for Beginning Readers Ser.). (J). (gr. k-3). 10.14 (*0-606-16631-9*) Turtleback Bks.

—One Dark & Scary Night. 1999. (Little Bill Books for Beginning Readers Ser.). (J). (gr. k-3). pap. text 47.88 (*0-439-04655-6*, Cartwheel Bks.); (Illus.). pap. 15.95 (*0-590-51475-X*); (Illus.). 40p. mass mkt. 3.99 (*0-590-51476-8*) Scholastic, Inc.

—One Dark & Scary Night. 1999. (Little Bill Books for Beginning Readers Ser.). (J). (gr. k-3). 10.14 (*0-606-15831-6*) Turtleback Bks.

—Shipwreck Saturday. 1998. (Little Bill Books for Beginning Readers Ser.). (Illus.). 40p. (J). (gr. k-3). pap. 13.95 (*0-590-16400-7*); mass mkt. 3.99 o.s.i (*0-590-95620-5*) Scholastic, Inc.

—The Treasure Hunt. 1997. (Little Bill Books for Beginning Readers Ser.). (Illus.). 40p. (J). (gr. k-3). pap. 13.95 (*0-590-16399-X*); (gr. 1-5). mass mkt. 3.99 (*0-590-95618-3*) Scholastic, Inc.

—The Treasure Hunt. 1997. (Little Bill Books for Beginning Readers Ser.). (J). (gr. k-3). 10.14 (*0-606-12002-5*) Turtleback Bks.

—The Worst Day of My Life. 1999. (Little Bill Books for Beginning Readers Ser.). (Illus.). 40p. (J). (gr. k-3). mass mkt. 15.95 (*0-590-52190-X*, Cartwheel Bks.) Scholastic, Inc.

Cosby, Bill & Honeywood, Varnette P. Hooray for the Dandelion Warriors! 1999. (Little Bill Books for Beginning Readers Ser.). (Illus.). 40p. (J). (gr. 1-5). mass mkt. 3.99 (*0-590-52194-2*, Cartwheel Bks.) Scholastic, Inc.

Cossi, Olga. The Great Getaway. 1991. (People Who Have Helped the World Ser.). 32p. (J). (gr. 1-2). lib. bdg. 18.60 o.p. (*0-8368-0107-5*); (Illus.). o.p. (*0-8368-0833-9*) Stevens, Gareth Inc.

—The Great Getaway. (Illus.). 2002. (J). E-Book (*1-59019-741-0*); 1991. E-Book (*1-59019-742-9*) ipicturebooks, LLC.

Cottonwood, Joe. Babcock. 1996. 240p. (YA). (gr. 4-7). pap. 15.95 (*0-590-22221-X*) Scholastic, Inc.

Cousain, Hattie M. When I Was Little. (J). 8.95 (*0-9640459-0-7*) Cole's, C. Consultant & Pubns.

Cowley, Joy. Singing down the Rain. 1997. (Illus.). 32p. (J). (gr. 1-4). 15.99 (*0-06-027602-9*); lib. bdg. 14.89 (*0-06-027603-7*) HarperCollins Children's Bk. Group.

—Singing down the Rain. 1997. (Illus.). (J). (*0-590-52701-0*) Scholastic, Inc.

Coy, John, et al. Directo Al Aro. 2002. (Illus.). (J). (ENG & SPA.). 16.95 (*1-58430-082-5*); (SPA., pap. 6.95 (*1-58430-083-3*) Lee & Low Bks., Inc.

Crespo, Beverly. Melanin 'n Me. Taylor, Maxwell, ed. 1996. (Illus.). 32p. (J). (gr. 1-3). pap. 6.95 (*1-881316-46-7*) A & B Distributors & Pubs. Group.

Ethnic Groups

Crews, Donald. Shortcut. (Illus.). (J). (ps-3). 1996. 40p. pap. 5.99 (*0-688-13576-5*, Harper Trophy); 1992. 32p. 16.99 (*0-688-06436-1*, Greenwillow Bks.); 1992. 32p. lib. bdg. 17.89 (*0-688-06437-X*, Greenwillow Bks.) HarperCollins Children's Bk. Group.

—Shortcut. 1996. 12.10 (*0-606-11840-3*) Turtleback Bks.

Crews, Nina. You Are Here. 1998. (Illus.). 32p. (J). (gr. k-3). lib. bdg. 15.89 o.p. (*0-688-15754-8*); 16.00 (*0-688-15753-X*) HarperCollins Children's Bk. Group. (Greenwillow Bks.).

Cromer, Mary L. Stories for Jason. 1993. 110p. (J). pap. 9.00 (*0-944350-28-3*) Friends United Pr.

Crowe, Chris. The Mississippi Trial, 1955. 2003. 240p. pap. 5.99 (*0-14-250192-1*, Puffin Bks.) Penguin Putnam Bks. for Young Readers.

Crutcher, Chris. The Crazy Horse Electric Game. 1988. (Laurel-Leaf Contemporary Fiction Ser.). 224p. (YA). (gr. 7 up). reprint ed. mass mkt. 5.50 o.s.i (*0-440-20094-6*) Dell Publishing.

—The Crazy Horse Electric Game. 1987. 224p. (J). (gr. 7 up). 16.99 (*0-688-06683-6*, Greenwillow Bks.) HarperCollins Children's Bk. Group.

Cummings, Pat. Angel Baby. 2000. (Illus.). 24p. (J). (gr. k-2). 15.89 (*0-688-14822-0*) HarperCollins Children's Bk. Group.

—Angel Baby. 2000. (Illus.). 24p. (J). (ps-3). 15.95 (*0-688-14821-2*) Morrow/Avon.

—Clean Your Room, Harvey Moon! 2002. (Illus.). (J). 14.47 (*0-7587-2248-6*) Book Wholesalers, Inc.

—Clean Your Room, Harvey Moon! 1998. (J). pap. 4.95 (*0-87628-335-0*) Ctr. for Applied Research in Education, The.

—Clean Your Room, Harvey Moon! 32p. (J). (ps-3). 1991. lib. bdg. 16.95 (*0-02-725511-5*, Simon & Schuster Children's Publishing); 1994. (Illus.). reprint ed. pap. 5.99 (*0-689-71798-9*, Aladdin) Simon & Schuster Children's Publishing.

—Clean Your Room, Harvey Moon! unabr. ed. 1993. (J). (gr. k-3). pap. 16.95 incl. audio (*0-8045-6667-4*, 6667) Spoken Arts, Inc.

—Clean Your Room, Harvey Moon! 1994. (J). 12.14 (*0-606-05789-7*) Turtleback Bks.

—Jimmy Lee Did It. (Trophy Picture Bk.). (Illus.). (J). (ps-3). 1994. 32p. pap. 4.95 o.p. (*0-06-443357-9*, Harper Trophy); 1985. 16.00 o.p. (*0-688-04632-0*); 1985. lib. bdg. 15.93 o.p. (*0-688-04633-9*) HarperCollins Children's Bk. Group.

—My Aunt Came Back. 1998. (Growing Tree Ser.). (Illus.). 14p. (J). (ps up). 6.99 (*0-694-01059-6*, Harper Festival) HarperCollins Children's Bk. Group.

—Purrrr. 1999. (Growing Tree Ser.). (Illus.). 14p. (J). (ps up). 5.95 (*0-694-01056-1*, Harper Festival) HarperCollins Children's Bk. Group.

Curtis, Christopher Paul. Bud, Not Buddy. 2002. (Illus.). 14.47 (*1-4046-1884-8*) Book Wholesalers, Inc.

—Bud, Not Buddy. 1999. (Illus.). 256p. (gr. 4-7). text 16.95 (*0-385-32306-9*, Delacorte Pr.) Dell Publishing.

—Bud, Not Buddy. unabr. ed. 2000. (YA). (gr. 4-7). audio 22.00 (*0-553-52675-8*, Listening Library) Random Hse. Audio Publishing Group.

—Bud, Not Buddy. l.t. ed. 2000. (Young Adult Ser.). (Illus.). 279p. (J). (gr. 8-12). 22.95 (*0-7862-2574-2*) Thorndike Pr.

—The Watsons Go to Birmingham - 1963. 1999. 240p. (gr. 5-8). mass mkt. 2.99 o.s.i (*0-440-22836-0*) Bantam Bks.

—The Watsons Go to Birmingham - 1963. 1998. 15p. pap., stu. ed., tchr.'s training gde. ed. 15.95 (*1-58303-068-9*) Pathways Publishing.

—The Watsons Go to Birmingham - 1963. 210p. (YA). (gr. 5 up). pap. 5.50 (*0-8072-8336-3*); 2000. (J). pap. 37.00 incl. audio (*0-8072-8335-5*, YA166SP) Random Hse. Audio Publishing Group. (Listening Library).

—The Watsons Go to Birmingham - 1963. 2000. 224p. (YA). (gr. 5-7). mass mkt. 5.99 (*0-440-22800-X*, Laurel Leaf); 1997. 224p. (gr. 4-10). pap. text 6.50 (*0-440-41412-1*, Dell Books for Young Readers); 1997. (YA). pap. o.s.i (*0-440-41431-8*, Dell Books for Young Readers) Random Hse. Children's Bks.

—The Watsons Go to Birmingham - 1963. l.t. ed. 2000. (Illus.). 260p. (J). (ps up). 22.95 (*0-7862-2741-9*) Thorndike Pr.

—The Watsons Go to Birmingham - 1963. 1997. (YA). 12.04 (*0-606-10993-5*) Turtleback Bks.

—The Watsons Go to Birmingham—1963. 1995. 224p. (gr. 4-7). text 16.95 (*0-385-32175-9*, Dell Books for Young Readers) Random Hse. Children's Bks.

Curtis, Gavin. The Bat Boy & His Violin. (J). (ps-3). 2001. (Illus.). 32p. pap. 6.99 (*0-689-84115-9*, Aladdin); 1999. mass mkt. 6.99 (*0-689-83012-2*, Aladdin); 1998. (Illus.). 32p. 16.95 (*0-689-80099-1*, Simon & Schuster Children's Publishing) Simon & Schuster Children's Publishing.

—Grandma's Baseball. 1992. (Illus.). (J). 3.99 o.p. (*0-517-08302-7*) Random Hse. Value Publishing.

Curtis, Matt. Six Empty Pockets. (Rookie Readers Ser.). (Illus.). 32p. (J). (gr. 1-2). 1998. pap. 4.95 (*0-516-26253-X*); 1997. lib. bdg. 19.00 (*0-516-20399-1*) Scholastic Library Publishing. (Children's Pr.).

Daise, Natalie E. Gullah. 1997. (Gullah Gullah Island Ser.: No. 7). (Illus.). 24p. (J). (ps-k). mass mkt. 3.25 o.s.i (*0-689-81242-6*, Simon Spotlight/ Nickelodeon) Simon & Schuster Children's Publishing.

Dale, Penny. Bet You Can't. 1988. (Illus.). 32p. (J). (ps-1). 12.95 (*0-397-32235-6*); lib. bdg. 12.89 (*0-397-32256-9*) HarperCollins Children's Bk. Group.

—Bet You Can't. 1991. 3.99 o.p. (*0-517-07099-5*); 3.99 o.p. (*0-517-07100-2*) Random Hse. Value Publishing.

Davis, Ossie. Just Like Martin. 2001. (J). pap. (*0-7868-1642-2*); 176p. lib. bdg. 16.49 (*0-7868-2632-0*) Hyperion Bks. for Children. (Jump at the Sun).

—Just Like Martin. 1995. 224p. (YA). (gr. 5-9). pap. 5.99 (*0-14-037095-1*, Puffin Bks.) Penguin Putnam Bks. for Young Readers.

—Just Like Martin. 1992. 208p. (YA). (gr. 5-9). pap. 15.00 (*0-671-73202-1*, Simon & Schuster Children's Publishing) Simon & Schuster Children's Publishing.

—Just Like Martin. 1996. (J). (gr. 5-9). 19.50 o.p. (*0-8446-6897-4*) Smith, Peter Pub., Inc.

—Just Like Martin. 1995. (YA). 12.04 (*0-606-07756-1*) Turtleback Bks.

De Veaux, Alexis. An Enchanted Hair Tale. (Trophy Picture Bk.). (Illus.). (J). (gr. k-3). 1991. 48p. pap. 4.95 o.p. (*0-06-443271-8*, Harper Trophy); 1987. 40p. lib. bdg. 14.89 (*0-06-021624-7*) HarperCollins Children's Bk. Group.

DeFelice, Cynthia C. Willy's Silly Grandma. 1997. (Illus.). 32p. (J). (ps-2). pap. 15.95 (*0-531-30012-9*); lib. bdg. 16.99 (*0-531-33012-5*) Scholastic, Inc. (Orchard Bks.).

Dennis-Wyeth, Sharon. Something Beautiful. 2002. 32p. (J). pap. 6.99 (*0-440-41210-2*, Random Hse. Bks. for Young Readers) Random Hse. Children's Bks.

Derby, Sally. Mi Escalera. de la Vega, Eida, tr. from SPA. 1998. (ENG & SPA., Illus.). 32p. (J). (ps-3). 15.95 (*1-880000-74-1*, LW7547); pap. 6.95 (*1-880000-75-X*, LW7771) Lee & Low Bks., Inc.

—My Steps. 1999. (Illus.). 32p. (J). (gr. 1-4). pap. 6.95 (*1-880000-84-9*); (ps-4). 15.95 (*1-880000-40-7*) Lee & Low Bks., Inc.

—My Steps. 1996. 13.10 (*0-606-17078-2*) Turtleback Bks.

Devore, Cynthia D. The Wind Before It Blows. 1993. (Children of Courage Ser.). (Illus.). (J). lib. bdg. 21.95 (*1-56239-247-6*) ABDO Publishing Co.

Dickey, Eric Jerome. The Liar's Game. 2002. 400p. pap. 13.95 (*0-451-20593-6*) NAL.

Dickinson, Peter. AK. 1993. 240p. (YA). mass mkt. 3.99 o.s.i (*0-440-21897-7*) Dell Publishing.

—AK. 1992. (J). 9.09 o.p. (*0-606-05727-7*) Turtleback Bks.

Dike, Tina. His Greatest Challenge. Schulman, Cory & Johnstone, Sandy, eds. 2000. 125p. (YA). (gr. 7-9). pap. 9.95 (*0-9642997-1-2*) Best Seller Pubns., Inc.

Dillon, Leo & Dillon, Diane. Rap a Tap Tap: Here's Bojangles - Think of That! 2002. (Illus.). 32p. (J). pap. 15.95 (*0-590-47883-4*, Blue Sky Pr., The) Scholastic, Inc.

Dionne, Wanda. The Couturiere of Galvez. 1993. (Illus.). (J). (gr. 6-7). 176p. 15.95 o.p. (*0-89015-860-6*); pap. 9.95 (*1-57168-161-2*) Eakin Pr.

—The Couturiere of Galvez. 1993. E-Book 9.95 (*0-585-23700-X*) netLibrary, Inc.

—A Yank among Us. 1997. 176p. (J). (gr. 6). pap. 12.95 (*1-57168-108-6*) Eakin Pr.

Dixon, Sylvia W. Sug Learns How to Cook. Angaza, Mai T., ed. 1991. (Illus.). 28p. (Orig.). (J). (gr. 3-10). pap. 5.00 (*0-9652951-0-9*) Dixon, S. W.

Dobkin, Bonnie. Everybody Says. 1993. (Rookie Readers Ser.). (Illus.). 32p. (J). (ps-2). mass mkt. 4.95 (*0-516-42019-4*); (gr. 1-2). lib. bdg. 19.00 (*0-516-02019-6*) Scholastic Library Publishing. (Children's Pr.).

Douglas, Marjory S. Freedom River. 1994. (Illus.). 240p. (J). (gr. 4 up). 19.95 (*0-9633461-4-8*); pap. 14.95 (*0-9633461-5-6*) Valiant Pr., Inc.

Draper, Sharon M. Darkness Before Dawn. (Hazelwood High Trilogy: Bk. 3). (J). (gr. 7 up). 2002. 288p. mass mkt. 5.99 (*0-689-85134-0*, Simon Pulse); 2001. 240p. 16.95 (*0-689-83080-7*, Atheneum) Simon & Schuster Children's Publishing.

—Double Dutch. 192p. (J). 2004. pap. 4.99 (*0-689-84231-7*, Aladdin); 2002. (gr. 7 up). 16.00 (*0-689-84230-9*, Atheneum) Simon & Schuster Children's Publishing.

—Forged by Fire. 2002. (Illus.). (J). 13.40 (*0-7587-0354-6*) Book Wholesalers, Inc.

—Forged by Fire. (Hazelwood High Trilogy: Bk. 2). 160p. (YA). (gr. 7 up). 1998. mass mkt. 4.99 (*0-689-81851-3*, Simon Pulse); 1997. 16.95 (*0-689-80699-X*, Atheneum) Simon & Schuster Children's Publishing.

—Forged by Fire. 1998. 11.04 (*0-606-13397-6*) Turtleback Bks.

—Jazz Imagination: A Journal to Read & Write. 2000. 81p. (J). (gr. 3-7). mass mkt. 12.95 (*0-439-06130-X*) Scholastic, Inc.

—Jazzimagination: A Journal to Read & Write. 2002. 128p. (J). pap. 4.50 (*0-439-26577-0*) Scholastic, Inc.

—Romiette & Julio. (YA). (gr. 7-12). 2001. 336p. mass mkt. 4.99 (*0-689-84209-0*, Simon Pulse); 1999. (Illus.). 240p. 16.00 (*0-689-82180-8*, Atheneum) Simon & Schuster Children's Publishing.

—Tears of a Tiger. (Hazelwood High Trilogy: Bk. 1). 192p. (YA). (gr. 7-12). 1996. mass mkt. 4.99 (*0-689-80698-1*, Simon Pulse); 1994. 16.95 (*0-689-31878-2*, Atheneum) Simon & Schuster Children's Publishing.

—Tears of a Tiger. 1996. 11.04 (*0-606-09952-2*) Turtleback Bks.

—Ziggy & the Black Dinosaurs. 1994. (Ziggy & the Black Dinosaurs Ser.: Vol. 1). (Illus.). 96p. (J). (gr. 4-7). pap. 6.00 (*0-940975-48-3*) Just Us Bks., Inc.

—Ziggy & the Black Dinosaurs: Lost in the Tunnel of Time. (Ziggy & the Black Dinosaurs Ser.: No. 2). (Illus.). 96p. (J). (gr. 3-7). 1996. pap. 6.00 (*0-940975-63-7*); 1994. 14.00 o.p. (*0-940975-47-5*) Just Us Bks., Inc.

—Ziggy & the Black Dinosaurs: Shadows of Caesar's Creek. 1997. (Ziggy & the Black Dinosaurs Ser.: No. 3). (J). (gr. 3-7). 96p. 15.95 o.p. (*0-940975-78-5*); 91p. pap. text 6.00 (*0-940975-76-9*) Just Us Bks., Inc.

Duey, Kathleen. Evie Peach: St. Louis, 1857. 1997. (American Diaries Ser.: No. 8). 144p. (J). (gr. 3-7). pap. 4.99 (*0-689-81621-9*, Simon Pulse) Simon & Schuster Children's Publishing.

—Evie Peach: St. Louis, 1857. 1997. (American Diaries Ser.: No. 8). (J). (gr. 3-7). 10.55 (*0-606-12615-5*) Turtleback Bks.

Duey, Kathleen & Bale, Karen A. Flood, Mississippi, 1927. 1998. (Survival! Ser.: No. 5). (J). (gr. 4-7). 10.04 (*0-606-13829-3*) Turtleback Bks.

—Flood, Mississippi 1927. 1998. (Survival! Ser.: No. 5). 176p. (J). (gr. 4-7). pap. 3.99 (*0-689-82116-6*, Aladdin) Simon & Schuster Children's Publishing.

Duffy, James. Uncle Shamus. 1992. 144p. (J). (gr. 4-6). lib. bdg. 13.95 (*0-684-19434-1*, Atheneum) Simon & Schuster Children's Publishing.

Dugdale, John, concept. The Jump at the Sun Treasury: An African American Storybook Treasury. 2001. (Illus.). 208p. (J). (ps up). 15.99 (*0-7868-0754-7*, Jump at the Sun) Hyperion Bks. for Children.

Duncan, Alice F. Miss Viola & Uncle Ed Lee. 1999. (Illus.). 40p. (J). (gr. k-3). 16.00 (*0-689-80476-8*, Atheneum) Simon & Schuster Children's Publishing.

—Willie Jerome. 1995. (Illus.). 32p. (J). (ps-3). 15.00 o.p. (*0-02-733208-X*, Atheneum) Simon & Schuster Children's Publishing.

Dupre, Rick. The Wishing Chair. 1993. (Illus.). 32p. (J). (ps-3). lib. bdg. 14.95 (*0-87614-774-0*, Carolrhoda Bks.) Lerner Publishing Group.

Edwards, Pamela Duncan. Barefoot: Escape on the Underground Railroad. 1997. (Illus.). 32p. (J). (gr. k-4). 15.99 (*0-06-027137-X*); lib. bdg. 15.89 (*0-06-027138-8*) HarperCollins Children's Bk. Group.

—Barefoot: Escape on the Underground Railroad. 1998. 12.10 (*0-606-15847-2*) Turtleback Bks.

Edwards, Pat. Little John & Plutie. 1988. 180p. (J). (gr. 3-7). 13.95 o.p. (*0-395-48223-2*) Houghton Mifflin Co.

Edwards, Roberta. Don't Cry, Leon. 1996. (Puzzle Place Ser.). (Illus.). 32p. (J). 13.99 o.s.i (*0-448-41331-0*); 4.95 o.s.i (*0-448-41288-8*) Penguin Putnam Bks. for Young Readers. (Grosset & Dunlap).

Eisenberg, Phyllis R. You're My Nikki. (Illus.). 32p. (J). (ps-3). 1995. pap. 5.99 o.s.i (*0-14-055463-7*, Puffin Bks.); 1992. 13.89 o.s.i (*0-8037-1129-8*, Dial Bks. for Young Readers); 1992. 14.00 o.s.i (*0-8037-1127-1*, Dial Bks. for Young Readers) Penguin Putnam Bks. for Young Readers.

Eitzen, Stanley D., et al. Mr. Bradley's Day of Surprises. 1996. (Gullah Gullah Island Ser.). 24p. (J). (ps-3). mass mkt. 4.99 (*0-689-80423-7*, Simon Spotlight/Nickelodeon) Simon & Schuster Children's Publishing.

Ellis, Veronica F. Land of the Four Winds. 1993. (Illus.). 32p. (J). (gr. 1-4). 14.95 (*0-940975-38-6*); (ps-3). pap. 6.95 (*0-940975-39-4*) Just Us Bks., Inc.

Elster, Jean Alicia. I Have a Dream, Too! 2002. (Joe Joe in the City Ser.: No. 2). (Illus.). 32p. (J). (gr. 1-5). 12.00 (*0-8170-1397-0*) Judson Pr.

—I'll Do the Right Thing. 2003. (Joe Joe in the City Ser.). (Illus.). 32p. (J). (gr. 1-5). 12.00 (*0-8170-1408-X*) Judson Pr.

—I'll Fly My Own Plane. 2002. (Joe Joe in the City Ser.: 3). (Illus.). 32p. (J). 12.00 (*0-8170-1407-1*) Judson Pr.

—Just Call Me Joe Joe. 2001. (Illus.). 32p. (J). (gr. 1-5). 12.00 (*0-8170-1398-9*) Judson Pr.

Engel, Diana. Fishing. 1993. (Illus.). 32p. (J). (gr. k-3). 14.95 o.p. (*0-02-733463-5*, Simon & Schuster Children's Publishing) Simon & Schuster Children's Publishing.

—Fishing. (Illus.). 32p. (J). 4.98 o.p. (*0-7651-0068-1*) Smithmark Pubs., Inc.

England, Linda. The Old Cotton Blues. 1998. (Illus.). 32p. (J). (ps-2). 16.00 (*0-689-81074-1*, McElderry, Margaret K.) Simon & Schuster Children's Publishing.

English, Karen. Francie. 2002. (Illus.). (J). 25.45 (*0-7587-0355-4*) Book Wholesalers, Inc.

—Francie, RS. 2002. 208p. (J). pap. 5.95 (*0-374-42459-4*, Sunburst) Farrar, Straus & Giroux.

—Francie. l.t. ed. 2002. 220p. (J). 21.95 (*0-7862-3717-1*) Gale Group.

—Hot Day on Abbott Avenue. 2004. (Illus.). 32p. (J). 15.00 (*0-395-98527-7*, Clarion Bks.) Houghton Mifflin Co. Trade & Reference Div.

—Just Right Stew. (Illus.). 32p. (J). pap. 8.95 (*1-59078-168-6*); 2003. 15.95 (*1-56397-487-8*) Boyds Mills Pr.

—Neeny Coming, Neeny Going. 1998. 12.10 (*0-606-13656-8*) Turtleback Bks.

—Strawberry Moon, RS. 2001. 128p. (J). (gr. 4-6). 16.00 (*0-374-47122-3*, Farrar, Straus & Giroux (BYR)) Farrar, Straus & Giroux.

—Sweet Little Baby. 2005. (J). (*0-374-37361-2*, Farrar, Straus & Giroux (BYR)) Farrar, Straus & Giroux.

Epaminondas. 1989. (Read Along With Me Ser.). (Illus.). 24p. (J). (ps-3). 2.25 (*1-56288-163-9*) Checkerboard Pr., Inc.

Eskridge, Ann E. The Sanctuary. 1994. 144p. (J). (gr. 4 up). 13.99 o.p. (*0-525-65168-3*, Dutton Children's Bks.) Penguin Putnam Bks. for Young Readers.

Eubanks, Toni. Journey Home: Passage to Womanhood. 1996. 158 p. (J). 11.99 (*1-56256-413-7*) Peoples Publishing Group, Inc., The.

Evans, Freddi Williams. A Bus of Our Own. (Illus.). 32p. (J). 2003. pap. 6.95 (*0-8075-0971-X*); 2001. lib. bdg. 15.95 (*0-8075-0970-1*) Whitman, Albert & Co.

Evans, Karen L. & Dade, Pat. You Must Remember This. 1997. 144p. (J). (gr. 3-7). lib. bdg. 14.49 (*0-7868-2075-6*); 13.95 (*0-7868-0090-9*) Hyperion Bks. for Children.

Evans, Mari. Jd. 1982. (Illus.). (J). (gr. 3-5). pap. 0.95 o.p. (*0-380-00348-1*, 25668, Avon Bks.) Morrow/ Avon.

Falwell, Cathryn. David's Drawings. 2001. (Illus.). 32p. (J). (ps-3). 16.00 (*1-58430-031-0*) Lee & Low Bks., Inc.

—Feast for Ten. 1995. (J). pap. text 5.95 o.p. (*0-590-48466-4*) Scholastic, Inc.

—Feast for 10. 2002. (Illus.). (J). 14.74 (*0-7587-2485-3*) Book Wholesalers, Inc.

—Feast for 10. (Illus.). (J). 2003. 30p. bds. 4.95 (*0-618-38226-7*); 1996. 1p. pap. 9.95 incl. audio (*0-395-72082-6*, 1-11762); 1995. 32p. pap. 6.95 (*0-395-72081-8*); 1993. 32p. lib. bdg., tchr. ed. 16.00 (*0-395-62037-6*) Houghton Mifflin Co. Trade & Reference Div. (Clarion Bks.).

Faux, Ruth. Golden Dawn. 1994. (Illus.). 192p. (Orig.). (YA). (gr. 7 up). pap. 6.95 o.p. (*1-878893-43-2*) Telcraft Bks.

Felder, Pamela T. I'm Black & I'm Beautiful. Slade, John, ed. 1993. (Illus.). 14p. (Orig.). (J). pap. 3.50 (*0-9638310-0-3*) Pam's Unique Technique.

Fenner, Carol. Yolonda's Genius. 2002. (Illus.). (J). 14.47 (*0-7587-0333-3*) Book Wholesalers, Inc.

—Yolonda's Genius. (J). 2002. 224p. E-Book 6.99 (*0-689-84785-8*, McElderry, Margaret K.); 1998. pap. 2.65 (*0-689-82172-7*, Aladdin); 1997. 224p. (gr. 3-7). pap. 5.99 (*0-689-81327-9*, Aladdin); 1995. 224p. (gr. 3-7). 17.00 (*0-689-80001-0*, McElderry, Margaret K.) Simon & Schuster Children's Publishing.

—Yolonda's Genius. 1997. (J). 12.04 (*0-606-12122-6*) Turtleback Bks.

Ferguson, A. Dwayne. The Case of the Missing Anhk. 1996. (Kid Caramel, Private Investigator Ser.: Vol. 1). (Illus.). 48p. (J). (gr. 4-7). pap. 4.50 (*0-940975-71-8*) Just Us Bks., Inc.

Ferguson, Dwayne J. The Werewolf of PS 40. 1998. (Kid Caramel, Private Investigator Ser.: Vol. 2). 68p. (J). (gr. 4-7). pap. 4.50 (*0-940975-82-3*) Just Us Bks., Inc.

—The Werewolf of PS 40. 1998. (Kid Caramel, Private Investigator Ser.: Vol. 2). E-Book (*1-59019-132-3*); E-Book (*1-59019-130-7*); E-Book (*1-59019-131-5*) ipicturebooks, LLC.

Flake, Sharon G. Money Hungry. (J). 2003. 208p. pap. 5.99 (*0-7868-1503-5*); 2001. 192p. (gr. 3-7). 15.99 (*0-7868-0548-X*); 2001. 192p. (gr. 3-7). lib. bdg. 16.49 (*0-7868-2476-X*) Hyperion Bks. for Children. (Jump at the Sun).

—The Skin I'm In. 1999. 192p. (J). pap. 7.99 (*0-7868-1307-5*); 1998. 171p. (J). 14.95 (*0-7868-0444-0*); 1998. 171p. (YA). pap. 15.49 (*0-7868-2392-5*) Hyperion Pr.

—The Skin I'm In. l.t. ed. 1999. (Young Adult Ser.). 173p. (J). (gr. 7-12). 20.95 (*0-7862-2179-8*) Thorndike Pr.

—The Skin I'm In. 2000. 12.04 (*0-606-17605-5*) Turtleback Bks.

Flood, Pansie Hart. Secret Holes. 2003. (Illus.). 122p. (J). 15.95 (*0-87614-923-9*, Carolrhoda Bks.) Lerner Publishing Group.

—Sylvia & Miz Lula Maye. 2002. (Middle Grade Fiction Ser.). (Illus.). 120p. (J). (gr. 3-6). lib. bdg. 15.95 (*0-87614-204-8*, Carolrhoda Bks.) Lerner Publishing Group.

Flournoy, Valerie. The Patchwork Quilt. 1985. (Illus.). 32p. (J). (gr. 4-8). 14.89 o.p. (*0-8037-0098-9*); (ps-3). 16.99 (*0-8037-0097-0*) Penguin Putnam Bks. for Young Readers. (Dial Bks. for Young Readers).

—The Twins Strike Back. 1994. (Illus.). 32p. (J). (gr. 2 up). 13.00 o.p. (*0-940975-51-3*); (gr. 4-7). pap. 5.00 (*0-940975-52-1*) Just Us Bks., Inc.

—The Twins Strike Back. 1980. (Illus.). (J). (ps-4). 7.45 o.p. (*0-8037-8692-1*); 7.95 o.p. (*0-8037-8691-3*) Penguin Putnam Bks. for Young Readers. (Dial Bks. for Young Readers).

Flournoy, Vanessa & Flournoy, Valerie. Celie & the Harvest Fiddle. 1995. (Illus.). 32p. (J). (gr. k up). 15.00 (*0-688-11457-1*, Morrow, William & Co.) Morrow/Avon.

—Celie & the Harvest Fiddler. 1995. (Illus.). 32p. (J). (gr. k up). lib. bdg. 14.93 o.p. (*0-688-11458-X*, Morrow, William & Co.) Morrow/Avon.

Fogelin, Adrian. Crossing Jordan. 2000. (Illus.). 140p. (J). (gr. 3-7). 14.95 (*1-56145-215-7*) Peachtree Pubs., Ltd.

Fogelman, Phyllis J., ed. Further Tales of Uncle Remus: The Misadventures of Brer Rabbit, Brer Fox, Brer Wolf, the Doodang, & All the Other Creatures. 1990. (Illus.). 16p. (J). (gr. 2 up). 18.99 o.s.i (*0-8037-0610-3*); (ps up). 14.89 o.p. (*0-8037-0611-1*) Penguin Putnam Bks. for Young Readers. (Dial Bks. for Young Readers).

Ford, Carolyn. Nothing in the Mailbox. 1996. (Books for Young Learners). (Illus.). 12p. (J). (gr. k-2). pap. text 5.00 (*1-57274-022-1*, A2483) Owen, Richard C. Pubs., Inc.

Ford, Juwanda G. Kente Dress for Kenya. 1996. (Illus.). 32p. pap. 3.25 (*0-590-53735-0*, Cartwheel Bks.) Scholastic, Inc.

—Kente Dress for Kenya. 1996. 9.40 (*0-606-09510-1*) Turtleback Bks.

—Kenya's Family Reunion. 1996. (Illus.). 32p. (J). mass mkt. 2.99 (*0-590-53736-9*) Scholastic, Inc.

—Kenya's Family Reunion. 1996. 8.19 o.p. (*0-606-09511-X*) Turtleback Bks.

Forrester, Sandra. My Home Is over Jordan: Sequel to "Sound the Jubilee" 1997. Orig. Title: Fire & Shadow. 160p. (J). (gr. 5-9). 15.99 o.s.i (*0-525-67568-X*, Dutton Children's Bks.) Penguin Putnam Bks. for Young Readers.

Fox, Mem. Sophie. abr. ed. (Illus.). 32p. (J). (ps-3). 1994. 15.00 (*0-15-277160-3*); 1997. reprint ed. pap. 6.00 (*0-15-201598-1*, Harcourt Paperbacks) Harcourt Children's Bks.

Frame, Jeron Ashford. Yesterday I Had the Blues. 2003. (Illus.). 30p. (J). (gr. k-3). 14.95 (*1-58246-084-1*) Tricycle Pr.

Frankel, Julie E. Oh No, Otis! 1991. (Rookie Readers Ser.). (Illus.). 32p. (J). mass mkt. 4.95 o.p. (*0-516-42009-7*); mass mkt. 17.00 o.p. (*0-516-02009-9*) Scholastic Library Publishing. (Children's Pr.).

Fraser, Julia. Musical Discoveries: A Story about Music, History & Friendship, Bk. 1. 1995. (Grammy Musical Discoveries Ser.: Bk. 1). (Illus.). (J). (gr. 6-8). 6.95 (*0-88284-656-6*, 4707) Alfred Publishing Co., Inc.

Fraser, Kathleen & Levy, Miriam. Adam's World: San Francisco. 1971. (Illus.). (J). (gr. k-2). 5.75 o.p. (*0-8075-0174-3*) Whitman, Albert & Co.

Fraser, Sheila. I Can Roller Skate. 1991. (I Can Read Bks.). (Illus.). 24p. (J). (ps-3). 5.95 o.p. (*0-8120-6228-0*) Barron's Educational Series, Inc.

Fremont, Eleanor. The Big Day at School. 2003. (Little Bill Ser.). (Illus.). 24p. (J). pap. 3.50 (*0-689-85497-8*, Simon Spotlight/Nickelodeon) Simon & Schuster Children's Publishing.

Fuqua, Jonathon Scott. Darby. 2002. 256p. (J). (gr. 5 up). 15.99 (*0-7636-1417-3*) Candlewick Pr.

—The Reappearance of Sam Webber. 1999. (Illus.). 232p. (YA). 23.95 (*1-890862-03-7*) Bancroft Pr.

—The Reappearance of Sam Webber. 2001. (Illus.). 288p. (J). reprint ed. bds. 9.99 (*0-7636-1424-6*) Candlewick Pr.

Gaines, Ernest J. Long Day in November. (Illus.). (J). (gr. 4-6). 1985. 7.89 o.p. (*0-8037-4938-4*); 1971. 5.95 o.s.i (*0-8037-4937-6*) Penguin Putnam Bks. for Young Readers. (Dial Bks. for Young Readers).

—The Sky Is Gray. 1993. (J). (gr. 4 up). o.p. (*0-88682-582-2*, Creative Education) Creative Co., The.

Gaudissart, Martine. Kanyon & the Rainbow Stone. 2000. (Illus.). 64p. (J). (gr. k-3). 17.95 (*0-9677547-0-4*) Black Orb.

Gayle, Sharon Shavers. Emma's Escape: A Story of America's Underground Railroad. 2003. (J). pap. 3.95 (*1-59249-021-2*) Soundprints.

Gee, Maurice. The Champion. 1993. (Illus.). 176p. (J). (gr. 5-9). pap. 16.00 (*0-671-86561-7*, Simon & Schuster Children's Publishing) Simon & Schuster Children's Publishing.

Gershator, Phillis. Someday Cyril. 2000. (MONDO Chapter Books). (Illus.). 46p. (J). (*1-57255-748-6*) Mondo Publishing.

Gilchrist, Jan Spivey. Madelia. 1997. (Illus.). 32p. (J). (ps-3). 14.99 o.s.i (*0-8037-2052-1*); 14.89 o.s.i (*0-8037-2054-8*) Penguin Putnam Bks. for Young Readers. (Dial Bks. for Young Readers).

Glaser, Linda. Stop That Garbage Truck! 1993. (Illus.). 32p. (J). (ps-2). lib. bdg. 14.95 o.p. (*0-8075-7626-3*) Whitman, Albert & Co.

Goggins, Alfonza R. & Lamar, Angela M. Father Kwanzaa Vol. I: The Spirit of Kwanzaa. Spenser, Delores, ed. 1997. (Illus.). (J). (gr. 4 up). pap. 9.95 (*0-9654203-0-2*) Spiritual Moon Publishing, Ltd.

—Father Kwanzaa Vol. II: The Intent of Kwanzaa. Spenser, Delores, ed. 1997. (Illus.). (YA). pap. 9.95 (*0-9654203-1-0*) Spiritual Moon Publishing, Ltd.

—Father Kwanzaa Vol. III: The Faith of Kwanzaa. Spenser, Delores, ed. 1997. (Illus.). (YA). pap. 9.95 (*0-9654203-2-9*) Spiritual Moon Publishing, Ltd.

Graham, Lorenz. Return to South Town. 2003. 240p. (YA). (gr. 7 up). 16.95 (*1-59078-164-3*) Boyds Mills Pr.

—Return to South Town. 1976. (J). (gr. 7 up). 11.49 o.p. (*0-690-01081-8*) HarperCollins Children's Bk. Group.

—South Town. 2003. 188p. (YA). (gr. 7 up). 16.95 (*1-59078-161-9*) Boyds Mills Pr.

—South Town. 1970. mass mkt. 0.60 o.p. (*0-451-04409-6*); 1965. mass mkt. 0.95 o.p. (*0-451-06244-2*); 1965. mass mkt. 1.25 o.p. (*0-451-07915-9*); 1965. (J). (gr. 6). mass mkt. 1.75 o.p. (*0-451-11483-3*, AE1483) NAL. (Signet Bks.).

Graham, Wendy. My Weird Mother. 1999. (Supa Doopers Ser.). (Illus.). 56p. (J). (*0-7608-1921-1*) Sundance Publishing.

Grant, Larry. Hewie Goes to the Million Man March. 1998. (Illus.). 48p. (Orig.). (J). (gr. 1-5). pap. 8.95 (*1-889851-05-1*) SolidGumboWorks.

Gray, Libba Moore. Dear Willie Rudd. 1993. (Illus.). 40p. (YA). (ps-1). mass mkt. 14.00 (*0-671-79774-3*, Simon & Schuster Children's Publishing) Simon & Schuster Children's Publishing.

—Little Lil & the Swing-Singing Sax. 1996. (Illus.). 32p. (J). (gr. k-2). 16.00 o.p. (*0-689-80681-7*, Simon & Schuster Children's Publishing) Simon & Schuster Children's Publishing.

—Miss Tizzy. (Illus.). 40p. (J). (ps-3). 1998. pap. 6.99 (*0-689-81897-1*, Aladdin); 1993. 15.00 (*0-671-77590-1*, Simon & Schuster Children's Publishing) Simon & Schuster Children's Publishing.

—Miss Tizzy. 1998. 12.14 (*0-606-13611-8*) Turtleback Bks.

Greenberg, Polly. Oh Lord, I Wish I Was a Buzzard. (Illus.). 32p. (J). (gr. k-3). 2003. pap. 5.95 (*1-58717-220-8*); 2002. 15.95 (*1-58717-122-8*); 2002. lib. bdg. 16.50 (*1-58717-123-6*) North-South Bks., Inc.

Greene, Bette. I've Already Forgotten Your Name. 2004. 176p. (J). lib. bdg. 16.89 (*0-06-051836-7*) HarperCollins Pubs.

Greene, Patricia B. The Sabbath Garden. 1993. (Illus.). 224p. (YA). (gr. 7 up). 15.99 o.p. (*0-525-67430-6*, Dutton Children's Bks.) Penguin Putnam Bks. for Young Readers.

Greenfield, Eloise. Easter Parade. 1998. (Illus.). 64p. (J). (gr. 1-5). 13.95 (*0-7868-0326-6*); lib. bdg. 14.49 (*0-7868-2271-6*) Hyperion Bks. for Children.

—First Pink Light. 1976. (Illus.). 40p. (J). (gr. k-3). lib. bdg. 7.89 o.p. (*0-690-01087-7*) HarperCollins Children's Bk. Group.

—First Pink Light. 1979. (J). pap. 1.50 o.p. (*0-590-12083-2*) Scholastic, Inc.

—First Pink Light. (Illus.). 32p. (J). (ps-4). 1993. pap. 6.95 (*0-86316-212-6*); 1991. 13.95 (*0-86316-207-X*) Writers & Readers Publishing, Inc.

—Grandmama's Joy. 1999. (Illus.). 32p. (ps-3). pap. 5.99 o.p. (*0-698-11754-9*, PaperStar); 1988. (Illus.). 32p. (J). (ps-3). 16.99 o.p. (*0-399-21064-4*, Philomel); 1980. (J). 8.95 o.p. (*0-529-05536-8*); 1980. (Illus.). 32p. (J). (gr. 2-5). 8.99 o.p. (*0-529-05537-6*, Philomel) Penguin Putnam Bks. for Young Readers.

—Grandmama's Joy. 1999. 12.14 (*0-606-16847-8*) Turtleback Bks.

—Grandpa's Face. 1992. (Illus.). (J). o.p. (*0-09-174177-7*) Hutchinson Children's Bks, Ltd. GBR. *Dist:* Random Hse. of Canada, Ltd.

—Grandpa's Face. (Illus.). 32p. (J). (ps-3). 1996. pap. 6.99 (*0-698-11381-0*, PaperStar); 1993. (SPA., 5.95 o.p. (*0-399-22511-0*, Philomel); 1991. 5.95 o.s.i (*0-399-22106-9*, Sandcastle Bks.); 1988. 16.99 (*0-399-21525-5*, Philomel) Penguin Putnam Bks. for Young Readers.

—Grandpa's Face. 1996. 13.14 (*0-606-09349-4*) Turtleback Bks.

—Kia Tanisha, Bk. 1. 1996. (Illus.). 12p. (J). (ps). 5.95 o.p. (*0-694-00847-8*) HarperCollins Children's Bk. Group.

—Kia Tanisha Drives Her Car, Bk. 2. 1996. (Illus.). 12p. (J). (ps). 5.95 o.p. (*0-694-00848-6*) HarperCollins Children's Bk. Group.

—Koya DeLaney & the Good Girl Blues. 128p. (J). 1995. (gr. 4-7). mass mkt. 2.95 (*0-590-43299-0*); 1992. (gr. 3-7). pap. 13.95 o.p. (*0-590-43300-8*) Scholastic, Inc.

—Me & Neesie. (Trophy Picture Bk.). (Illus.). (J). 1984. 80p. (gr. k-3). pap. 4.95 o.p. (*0-06-443057-X*, Harper Trophy); 1975. 40p. (gr. 1-4). lib. bdg. 14.89 o.p. (*0-690-00715-9*) HarperCollins Children's Bk. Group.

—Me & Neesie. 2004. (J). (*0-06-000701-X*); (Illus.). lib. bdg. (*0-06-000702-8*) HarperCollins Pubs.

—My Daddy & I... 1991. (Illus.). 12p. (J). bds. 5.95 (*0-86316-206-1*) Writers & Readers Publishing, Inc.

—On My Horse. 1994. (Let's Read Aloud Ser.). (Illus.). 20p. (J). (ps). 7.95 o.p. (*0-694-00583-5*, Harper Festival) HarperCollins Children's Bk. Group.

—Sweet Baby Coming. 1994. (Illus.). 14p. (J). (ps). 5.95 o.p. (*0-694-00578-9*, Harper Festival) HarperCollins Children's Bk. Group.

—William & the Good Old Days. 1993. (Illus.). 32p. (J). (gr. k-3). 15.00 o.p. (*0-06-021093-1*); lib. bdg. 15.89 (*0-06-021094-X*) HarperCollins Children's Bk. Group.

—William & the Good Old Days. Date not set. (Illus.). 32p. (J). (gr. k-3). pap. 4.99 (*0-06-443453-2*) HarperCollins Pubs.

Greenfield, Monica. Baby. 1994. (Illus.). 80p. (J). (ps). 5.95 o.p. (*0-694-00577-0*, Harper Festival) HarperCollins Children's Bk. Group.

Gregory, Deborah. The Cheetah Girls No. 2: Supa Dupa Sparkle. 2003. 544p. (J). pap. 9.99 (*0-7868-1790-9*, Jump at the Sun) Hyperion Bks. for Children.

—Dorinda's Secret. 2000. (Cheetah Girls Ser.: No. 7). 141p. (J). (gr. 3-7). pap. 3.99 (*0-7868-1426-8*, Jump at the Sun) Hyperion Bks. for Children.

—Growl Power. 2000. (Cheetah Girls Ser.: No. 8). 143p. (J). (gr. 3-7). pap. 3.99 (*0-7868-1427-6*, Jump at the Sun) Hyperion Bks. for Children.

—It's Raining Benjamins! 2000. (Cheetah Girls Ser.: No. 6). 150p. (J). (gr. 3-7). pap. 3.99 (*0-7868-1425-X*) Disney Pr.

—Oops, Doggy Dog! 2002. (Cheetah Girls Ser.: Bk. 13). 160p. (J). (gr. 3-7). pap. 3.99 (*0-7868-1484-5*) Disney Pr.

—Showdown at the Okie-Dokie. 2000. (Cheetah Girls Ser.: Vol. 9). 96p. (J). (gr. 3-7). pap. 3.99 (*0-7868-1475-6*, Jump at the Sun) Hyperion Bks. for Children.

—Who's 'Bout to Bounce? 1999. (Cheetah Girls Ser.: No. 3). 142p. (J). (gr. 3-7). pap. text 3.99 (*0-7868-1386-5*) Disney Pr.

—Woof, There It Is!, 2000. (Cheetah Girls Ser.: No. 5). 144p. (J). (gr. 3-7). pap. 3.99 (*0-7868-1424-1*) Disney Pr.

Grifalconi, Ann. Electric Yancy. 1924. (Illus.). 32p. (J). (ps up). 16.00 o.s.i (*0-688-13187-5*); lib. bdg. 15.93 o.s.i (*0-688-13188-3*) HarperCollins Children's Bk. Group.

—Kinda Blue. 1993. (Illus.). 32p. (J). (ps-3). 15.95 o.p. (*0-316-32869-3*) Little Brown & Co.

—Not Home: Somehow, Somewhere, There Must Be Love: A Novel. 1995. (J). 15.95 o.p. (*0-316-32905-3*) Little Brown & Co.

—Tiny's Hat. (Illus.). 32p. (J). (gr. k-3). 1999. lib. bdg. 14.89 (*0-06-027655-X*); 1998. 14.95 o.p. (*0-06-027654-1*) HarperCollins Children's Bk. Group.

Griffen, Peni R. Margo's House. 1996. 128p. (J). (gr. 7 up). 16.00 (*0-689-80944-1*, McElderry, Margaret K.) Simon & Schuster Children's Publishing.

Grimes, Nikki. Bronx Masquerade. 176p. (J). 2003. pap. 5.99 (*0-14-250189-1*, Puffin Bks.); 2001. (Illus.). (gr. 8 up). 16.99 (*0-8037-2569-8*, Dial Bks. for Young Readers) Penguin Putnam Bks. for Young Readers.

—Growin' 6.95 o.p. (*0-8037-3272-4*, Dial Bks. for Young Readers); 6.46 o.p. (*0-8037-3273-2*, Dial Bks. for Young Readers); 1995. 112p. (J). pap. 5.99 o.p. (*0-14-037066-8*, Puffin Bks.) Penguin Putnam Bks. for Young Readers.

—Growin' 1995. 9.09 o.p. (*0-606-07603-4*) Turtleback Bks.

—Jazmin's Notebook. 2002. (Illus.). (J). 12.34 (*0-7587-0368-6*) Book Wholesalers, Inc.

—Jazmin's Notebook. 112p. (YA). 1998. (gr. 8-12). 15.99 (*0-8037-2224-9*, Dial Bks. for Young Readers); 2000. (gr. 5-9). reprint ed. pap. 5.99 (*0-14-130702-1*, Puffin Bks.) Penguin Putnam Bks. for Young Readers.

—Jazmin's Notebook. 2000. (Illus.). (J). 11.04 (*0-606-18414-7*) Turtleback Bks.

—Wild, Wild Hair. 2002. (Illus.). (J). 11.91 (*0-7587-1855-1*) Book Wholesalers, Inc.

—Wild, Wild Hair. 1997. (Hello Reader! Ser.). (Illus.). (J). (ps-k). 3.50 (*0-590-25690-4*, Cartwheel Bks.); 32p. (gr. 1-3). pap. 3.99 (*0-590-26590-3*) Scholastic, Inc.

—Wild, Wild Hair. 1997. (Hello Reader! Ser.). (J). 10.14 (*0-606-12096-3*) Turtleback Bks.

Grove, Vicki. The Starplace. 1999. 214p. (YA). (gr. 5-9). 17.99 (*0-399-23207-9*) Penguin Group (USA) Inc.

—The Starplace. 2000. (Illus.). 224p. (J). (gr. 5-9). pap. 5.99 (*0-698-11868-5*, Puffin Bks.) Penguin Putnam Bks. for Young Readers.

—The Starplace. 2000. 12.04 (*0-606-20373-7*); (J). 12.04 (*0-606-20257-9*) Turtleback Bks.

Guccione, Leslie Davis. Come Morning. (Adventures in Time Ser.). 120p. (J). (gr. 4-7). 1995. lib. bdg. 15.95 (*0-87614-892-5*); 1997. (Illus.). reprint ed. pap. 6.95 (*1-57505-228-8*) Lerner Publishing Group. (Carolrhoda Bks.).

Guthrie, Donna. A Rose for Abby. (Illus.). (J). 1997. 32p. (gr. k-3). pap. text 7.00 (*0-687-06080-X*); 1988. (gr. 2 up). 6.48 o.p. (*0-687-36586-4*) Abingdon Pr.

Gutman, Dan. Jackie & Me. 1999. (Avon Camelot Bks.). (Illus.). 160p. (J). (gr. 4-7). 15.99 (*0-380-97685-4*); 15.99 (*0-380-97685-4*) HarperCollins Children's Bk. Group.

—Jackie & Me. 2000. (Avon Camelot Bks.). 160p. (J). (gr. 3-7). pap. 5.99 (*0-380-80084-5*, Avon Bks.) Morrow/Avon.

—Jackie & Me. 2000. (Illus.). (J). 11.04 (*0-606-17974-7*) Turtleback Bks.

Guy, Rosa. And I Heard a Bird Sing. 1988. 240p. (J). reprint ed. mass mkt. 3.25 o.s.i (*0-440-20152-7*) Dell Publishing.

—Billy the Great. 1994. (Illus.). 32p. (J). (ps-3). pap. 4.99 o.s.i (*0-440-40920-9*) Dell Publishing.

—Edith Jackson. 1981. 192p. pap. 1.95 o.p. (*0-553-20109-3*) Bantam Bks.

—Edith Jackson. 1992. 192p. (YA). (gr. 7 up). mass mkt. 3.50 o.s.i (*0-440-21137-9*) Dell Publishing.

—Edith Jackson. 1993. (J). (gr. 7 up). 17.00 o.p. (*0-8446-6690-4*) Smith, Peter Pub., Inc.

—Edith Jackson. 1978. 180p. (J). (gr. 7 up). 11.50 o.p. (*0-670-28906-X*) Viking Penguin.

—The Music of Summer. 1992. 12.95 (*0-385-30704-7*) Doubleday Publishing.

—New Guys Around the Block. 1983. 192p. (J). (gr. 7 up). 11.95 o.s.i (*0-385-29247-3*, Delacorte Pr.) Dell Publishing.

—New Guys Around the Block. 1987. 208p. (J). (gr. k-12). mass mkt. 2.95 o.s.i (*0-440-95888-1*, Laurel Leaf) Random Hse. Children's Bks.

—Paris, Pee Wee & Big Dog. 1988. 112p. (J). (gr. 3 up). pap. 2.95 o.s.i (*0-440-40072-4*) Dell Publishing.

—The Ups & Downs of Carl Davis III. 1992. 128p. (J). (gr. 4-7). pap. 3.50 o.s.i (*0-440-40744-3*) Dell Publishing.

Hahn, Harriet. The Plantain Season. 1976. 207p. 6.95 o.p. (*0-393-08729-8*) Norton, W. W. & Co., Inc.

Hahn, Mary Downing. Promises to the Dead. 2002. 208p. (J). (gr. 3 up). pap. 5.95 (*0-06-440982-1*, Harper Trophy) HarperCollins Children's Bk. Group.

—Promises to the Dead. 2000. 208p. (J). (gr. 5-9). tchr. ed. 15.00 (*0-395-96394-X*, Clarion Bks.) Houghton Mifflin Co. Trade & Reference Div.

Haines, Sandra. Donnie Makes a Difference. (Illus.). (Orig.). (J). (gr. k-5). 1994. 32p. pap. 6.99 (*1-885101-06-6*); Large Class Set. 1994. pap. 209.65 o.p. (*1-885101-32-5*); Resource Center Set. pap. 59.90 o.p. (*1-885101-30-9*); Small Class Set. 1994. pap. 149.75 o.p. (*1-885101-31-7*) Writers Pr., Inc.

Haislip, Phyllis Hall. Lottie's Courage: A Contraband Slave's Story. 2003. (Illus.). 120p. (J). pap. 7.95 (*1-57249-311-9*, WM Kids) White Mane Publishing Co., Inc.

Hall, Monica, et al. Fear Not: A Story of Hope. 1998. (Touched by an Angel Ser.). (Illus.). 32p. (J). (gr. 4-7). 14.99 (*0-8499-5800-8*) Nelson, Tommy.

Hamanaka, Sheila. Peace Crane. 1995. (Illus.). 40p. (J). (ps-3). 16.95 (*0-688-13815-2*) HarperCollins Children's Bk. Group.

—Peace Crane. 1995. (Illus.). 40p. (J). lib. bdg. 15.93 o.p. (*0-688-13816-0*, Morrow, William & Co.) Morrow/Avon.

Hamilton, Dorothy. Linda's Rain Tree. 1975. (Illus.). 120p. (J). (gr. 4-8). 4.95 o.p. (*0-8361-1777-8*); pap. 3.95 o.p. (*0-8361-1778-6*) Herald Pr.

Hamilton, Patricia Birdsong. Mommy & Baby Jasmine. 1996. (Shades of Black Ser.). (Illus.). 10p. (Orig.). (J). (ps-k). pap. text 5.95 (*1-889826-05-7*) Scripts Publishing.

Hamilton, Virginia. The Bells of Christmas. (Illus.). 64p. 1997. (J). (gr. 4-7). pap. 10.00 (*0-15-201550-7*, Harcourt Paperbacks); 1989. (YA). (gr. 2 up). 19.00 (*0-15-206450-8*) Harcourt Children's Bks.

—The Bells of Christmas. 1997. 14.15 (*0-606-12185-4*) Turtleback Bks.

—Bluish: A Novel. 1999. 127p. (YA). (gr. 4-9). pap. 15.95 (*0-590-28879-2*, Blue Sky Pr., The) Scholastic, Inc.

—Drylongso. (Illus.). 64p. (J). 1997. (ps-3). pap. 10.00 (*0-15-201587-6*, Harcourt Paperbacks); 1992. (gr. 3-7). 18.95 (*0-15-224241-4*) Harcourt Children's Bks.

—Drylongso. 1992. 15.15 (*0-606-11283-9*) Turtleback Bks.

—Dustland. 1989. (Justice Cycle Ser.: Vol. 2). 224p. (YA). (gr. 7 up). pap. 3.95 o.p. (*0-15-224315-1*, Odyssey Classics) Harcourt Children's Bks.

—Dustland. 1980. (Justice Cycle Ser.: Vol. 2). 192p. (J). (gr. 7 up). 13.00 o.p. (*0-688-80228-1*); lib. bdg. 12.88 o.p. (*0-688-84228-3*) HarperCollins Children's Bk. Group. (Greenwillow Bks.).

—Dustland. 1985. (J). pap. 1.95 o.p. (*0-380-56127-1*, 56127-1, Avon Bks.) Morrow/Avon.

—Dustland. 1998. (Justice Cycle Ser.: Bk. 2). 214p. (YA). (gr. 6-12). mass mkt. 4.50 (*0-590-36217-8*) Scholastic, Inc.

—Dustland. (Justice Cycle Ser.). 1998. 10.55 (*0-606-12927-8*); 1989. 9.05 o.p. (*0-606-00822-5*) Turtleback Bks.

—The Gathering. 1981. (Justice Cycle Ser.: Vol. 3). 192p. (J). (gr. 7 up). 12.95 o.p. (*0-688-80269-9*); lib. bdg. 12.88 o.p. (*0-688-84269-0*) HarperCollins Children's Bk. Group. (Greenwillow Bks.).

—The Gathering. 1985. 160p. pap. 1.95 o.p. (*0-380-56135-2*, 56135-2, Avon Bks.) Morrow/Avon.

—The Gathering. 1998. (Justice Cycle Ser.: Bk. 3). 214p. (J). (gr. 6-12). mass mkt. 4.50 (*0-590-36216-X*) Scholastic, Inc.

—The Gathering. (Justice Cycle Ser.). 1998. 10.55 (*0-606-13414-X*); 1989. (J). 9.05 o.p. (*0-606-01140-4*) Turtleback Bks.

—The Gathering Bk. 3. 1989. (Justice Cycle Ser.: Vol. 3). 224p. (YA). (gr. 7 up). pap. 3.95 o.p. (*0-15-230592-0*, Odyssey Classics) Harcourt Children's Bks.

—The Great M. C. Higgins, 6 vols. 3rd ed. (J). pap. text 23.70 (*0-13-620220-9*); pap. text 3.95 (*0-13-800137-5*) Prentice Hall (Schl. Div.).

—The House of Dies Drear, l.t. ed. 2001. 305p. lib. bdg. 29.95 (*1-58118-087-X*) LRS.

—The House of Dies Drear. 1998. 32p. 9.95 (*1-56137-516-0*, NU5168) Novel Units, Inc.

—The House of Dies Drear. 2001. (Assessment Packs Ser.). 15p. pap. text 15.95 (*1-58303-122-7*) Pathways Publishing.

—The House of Dies Drear. 8.97 (*0-13-437491-6*) Prentice Hall PTR.

—The House of Dies Drear. (Illus.). 256p. (YA). 1984. (gr. 7 up). mass mkt. 5.99 (*0-02-043520-7*, Simon Pulse); 1968. (gr. 4-7). 18.95 (*0-02-742500-2*, Simon & Schuster Children's Publishing) Simon & Schuster Children's Publishing.

—The House of Dies Drear. 1984. (Dies Drear Chronicle Ser.). (J). 11.04 (*0-606-03314-9*) Turtleback Bks.

—Justice & Her Brothers. 1989. (Justice Cycle Ser.: Vol. 1). 290p. (YA). (gr. 7 up). pap. 3.95 o.p. (*0-15-241640-4*, Odyssey Classics) Harcourt Children's Bks.

—Justice & Her Brothers. 1978. (Justice Cycle Ser.: Vol. 1). 224p. (J). (gr. 7 up). lib. bdg. 12.88 o.p. (*0-688-84182-1*, Greenwillow Bks.) HarperCollins Children's Bk. Group.

—Justice & Her Brothers. 1985. pap. 1.95 o.p. (*0-380-56119-0*, 56119-0, Avon Bks.) Morrow/Avon.

—Justice & Her Brothers. 1998. (Justice Cycle Ser.: Vol. 1). 214p. (J). (gr. 6-12). mass mkt. 4.99 (*0-590-36214-3*, Scholastic Paperbacks) Scholastic, Inc.

—Justice & Her Brothers. 1992. (J). (gr. 4-7). 17.55 o.p. (*0-8446-6577-0*) Smith, Peter Pub., Inc.

—Justice & Her Brothers. (Justice Cycle Ser.: Vol. 1). 1998. 11.04 (*0-606-12973-1*); 1989. 9.05 o.p. (*0-606-01602-3*) Turtleback Bks.

—A Little Love. 1985. 2.50 o.p. (*0-425-08424-8*) Berkley Publishing Group.

—A Little Love. 1984. 192p. (J). 12.95 o.s.i (*0-399-21046-6*, Philomel) Penguin Putnam Bks. for Young Readers.

—M. C. Higgins, the Great. l.t. ed. 1988. 320p. (J). (gr. 3-7). reprint ed. lib. bdg. 15.95 o.p. (*1-55736-075-8*) Bantam Doubleday Dell Large Print Group, Inc.

—M. C. Higgins, the Great. 1998. (J). pap. 4.50 (*0-87628-568-X*) Ctr. for Applied Research in Education, The.

—M. C. Higgins, the Great. l.t. ed. 1976. 400 p. lib. bdg. 10.95 o.p. (*0-8161-6356-1*, Macmillan Reference USA) Gale Group.

—M. C. Higgins, the Great. pap. text, stu. ed. (*0-13-620246-2*) Prentice Hall (Schl. Div.).

—M. C. Higgins, the Great. 1976. 240p. (J). (gr. 7 up). pap. 2.50 o.s.i (*0-440-95598-X*, Laurel Leaf) Random Hse. Children's Bks.

—M. C. Higgins, the Great. 2003. (J). E-Book 6.99 (*0-689-84806-4*, Simon & Schuster Children's Publishing); 1998. (J). pap. 2.65 o.p. (*0-689-82168-9*, Aladdin); 1974. 288p. (YA). (gr. 7 up). lib. bdg. 17.00 (*0-02-742480-4*, Simon & Schuster Children's Publishing); 1987. 288p. (YA). (gr. 5-9). reprint ed. pap. 4.99 (*0-02-043490-1*, Simon Pulse); 2nd ed. 1993. 288p. (J). (gr. 4-7). reprint ed. mass mkt. 4.99 (*0-689-71694-X*, Simon Pulse); 25th anniv. ed. 1999. (Illus.). 240p. (J). (gr. 7). 18.00 (*0-689-83074-2*, Simon & Schuster Children's Publishing) Simon & Schuster Children's Publishing.

—M. C. Higgins, the Great. 1987. (J). 11.04 (*0-606-02497-2*) Turtleback Bks.

—M. C. Higgins, the Great & Newbery Summer. 2003. 288p. (J). pap. 2.99 (*0-689-86228-8*, Aladdin) Simon & Schuster Children's Publishing.

—The Magical Adventures of Pretty Pearl. (Harper Trophy Bks.). 320p. 1986. (Illus.). (J). (gr. 6 up). pap. 7.95 (*0-06-440178-2*, Harper Trophy); 1983. (YA). (gr. 7 up). 12.95 o.p. (*0-06-022186-0*); 1983. (YA). (gr. 7 up). lib. bdg. 17.89 o.p. (*0-06-022187-9*) HarperCollins Children's Bk. Group.

—The Magical Adventures of Pretty Pearl. 1999. (J). (gr. 5 up). 21.50 (*0-8446-6998-9*) Smith, Peter Pub., Inc.

—The Magical Adventures of Pretty Pearl. 1986. (J). 14.00 (*0-606-03253-3*) Turtleback Bks.

—The Mystery of Drear House. 1987. 224p. (J). (gr. 3 up). 16.95 (*0-688-04026-8*, Greenwillow Bks.) HarperCollins Children's Bk. Group.

—The Mystery of Drear House. 1997. mass mkt. 4.50 (*0-590-95627-2*) Scholastic, Inc.

—The Mystery of Drear House. 1997. (Apple Signature Edition Ser.). (J). 11.04 (*0-606-12775-5*) Turtleback Bks.

—Plain City. (Barco de Vapor). (SPA.). 176p. (YA). (gr. 5-8). 6.95 (*84-348-4686-1*, LEC6861) SM Ediciones ESP. *Dist:* Continental Bk. Co., Inc.

—Plain City. (J). 2003. 208p. (gr. 4-7). mass mkt. 5.99 (*0-590-47365-4*, Scholastic Paperbacks); 1993. 176p. (gr. 3-7). pap. 13.95 (*0-590-47364-6*) Scholastic, Inc.

—Plain City. 1993. (J). 11.04 (*0-606-08020-1*) Turtleback Bks.

—The Planet of Junior Brown. 1998. (J). pap. 4.50 (*0-87628-347-4*) Ctr. for Applied Research in Education, The.

—The Planet of Junior Brown. l.t. unabr. ed. 1988. 400p. (YA). (gr. 5 up). 13.95 o.p. (*0-8161-4642-X*, Macmillan Reference USA) Gale Group.

—The Planet of Junior Brown. 240p. 2002. (J). E-Book 6.99 (*0-689-84805-6*, Simon & Schuster Children's Publishing); 1971. (YA). (gr. 5-9). 18.00 (*0-02-742510-X*, Simon & Schuster Children's Publishing); 2nd ed. 1993. (YA). (gr. 5-9). reprint ed. mass mkt. 4.99 (*0-689-71721-0*, Simon Pulse); 3rd ed. 1986. (Illus.). (YA). (gr. 5-9). mass mkt. 4.99 (*0-02-043540-1*, Simon Pulse) Simon & Schuster Children's Publishing.

—The Planet of Junior Brown. 1993. (YA). 11.04 (*0-606-05975-X*) Turtleback Bks.

—Sweet Whispers, Brother Rush. 1999. (gr. 4-7). pap. 12.25 (*0-88103-610-2*) Econo-Clad Bks.

—Sweet Whispers, Brother Rush. 1983. (Amistad Ser.). 224p. (J). (gr. 7 up). pap. 5.99 (*0-380-65193-9*, Amistad Pr.) HarperTrade.

—Sweet Whispers, Brother Rush. 1983. 220p. (J). (gr. 5 up). pap. 2.25 o.p. (*0-380-64824-5*, Avon Bks.) Morrow/Avon.

—Sweet Whispers, Brother Rush. 1982. 224p. (J). (gr. 7 up). 21.99 (*0-399-20894-1*, Philomel) Penguin Putnam Bks. for Young Readers.

—Sweet Whispers, Brother Rush. 1983. 12.00 (*0-606-02885-4*) Turtleback Bks.

—A White Romance. 1989. 240p. (YA). (gr. 7 up). pap. 3.95 o.p. (*0-15-295888-6*, Odyssey Classics) Harcourt Children's Bks.

—A White Romance. 1987. 200p. (YA). (gr. 8 up). 14.95 o.s.i (*0-399-21213-2*, Philomel) Penguin Putnam Bks. for Young Readers.

—A White Romance. 1998. (Point Signature Ser.). 4.50p. (YA). (gr. 8-12). mass mkt. 4.50 (*0-590-13005-6*) Scholastic, Inc.

—A White Romance. 1998. 10.09 o.p. (*0-606-13912-5*); 1987. (J). 10.00 (*0-606-04421-3*) Turtleback Bks.

—Willie Bea & the Time the Martians Landed. 1983. 224p. (J). (gr. 5-9). 16.00 o.s.i (*0-688-02390-8*, Greenwillow Bks.) HarperCollins Children's Bk. Group.

—Willie Bea & the Time the Martians Landed. 1989. 224p. (J). (gr. 4-7). reprint ed. pap. 3.95 o.p. (*0-689-71328-2*, Simon Pulse) Simon & Schuster Children's Publishing.

—Zeely. 93rd ed. 1993. pap. text 17.40 (*0-15-300358-8*) Harcourt Children's Bks.

—Zeely. 1998. (C). pap. 3.95 (*0-87628-345-8*) Simon & Schuster.

—Zeely. (Illus.). 128p. (J). 1968. (gr. 4-7). 17.95 (*0-02-742470-7*, Simon & Schuster Children's Publishing); 1987. (gr. 5-7). reprint ed. pap. 3.95 o.s.i (*0-689-71110-7*, Aladdin); 2nd ed. 1993. (gr. 4-7). reprint ed. pap. 4.99 (*0-689-71695-8*, Aladdin) Simon & Schuster Children's Publishing.

—Zeely. 1986. 11.04 (*0-606-03513-3*) Turtleback Bks.

Hansen, Joyce. The Gift-Giver. 128p. (J). (gr. 4-6). 1989. pap. 6.95 (*0-89919-852-X*); 1980. 14.95 o.p. (*0-395-29433-9*) Houghton Mifflin Co. Trade & Reference Div. (Clarion Bks.).

—The Heart Calls Home. 2002. 256p. (J). (gr. 7 up). pap. 5.95 (*0-380-73294-7*, Harper Trophy) HarperCollins Children's Bk. Group.

—The Heart Calls Home. 1999. viii, 175p. (J). (gr. 7-12). 16.95 (*0-8027-8636-7*) Walker & Co.

—I Thought My Soul Would Rise & Fly: The Diary of Patsy, a Freed Girl, Mars Bluff, South Carolina, 1865. 1997. (Dear America Ser.). (Illus.). 202p. (J). (gr. 4-9). pap. 10.95 (*0-590-84913-1*) Scholastic, Inc.

—Out from This Place. 1988. 10.55 (*0-606-00682-6*) Turtleback Bks.

—Out from This Place. 1988. 13.95 (*0-8027-6816-4*) Walker & Co.

—Out from this Place. 1992. 144p. (J). (gr. 4-7). pap. 5.99 (*0-380-71409-4*, Avon Bks.) Morrow/Avon.

—Yellow Bird & Me. (J). 1986. (gr. 3-7). 13.95 o.p. (*0-89919-335-8*); 1991. 168p. (gr. 4-6). reprint ed. pap. 6.95 (*0-395-55388-1*) Houghton Mifflin Co. Trade & Reference Div. (Clarion Bks.).

—Yellow Bird & Me. 1986. 13.00 (*0-606-05050-7*) Turtleback Bks.

Hanson, Harvey. Game Time. 1975. (Illus.). 128p. (gr. 6-10). 5.90 o.p. (*0-531-02831-3*, Watts, Franklin) Scholastic Library Publishing.

Harding, Donal. The Leaving Summer. 1996. 192p. (YA). (gr. 5 up). 15.00 (*0-688-13893-4*, Morrow, William & Co.) Morrow/Avon.

—The Leaving Summer. 1998. 9.09 o.p. (*0-606-13566-9*) Turtleback Bks.

Harper, Donna A., ed. The Later Simple Stories. 2002. (Collected Works of Langston Hughes: Vol. 8). 384p. 34.95 (*0-8262-1409-6*) Univ. of Missouri Pr.

Harrington, Janice N. Going North, RS. 2004. (J). (*0-374-32681-9*, Farrar, Straus & Giroux (BYR)) Farrar, Straus & Giroux.

Hart, Alison. Jina Rides to Win, 1994. (Riding Academy Ser.: No. 3). 132p. (Orig.). (YA). (gr. 5-8). pap. 3.50 o.s.i (*0-679-85694-3*, Random Hse. Bks. for Young Readers) Random Hse. Children's Bks.

Haskins, Francine. Things I Like about Grandma. 32p. (gr. 1 up). 1994. (J). pap. 7.95 (*0-89239-123-5*); 1992. (Illus.). (YA). 14.95 o.p. (*0-89239-107-3*) Children's Bk. Pr.

Haskins, James. The March on Washington. 2003. 192p. (YA). (gr. 5 up). pap. 10.95 (*0-940975-93-9*) Just Us Bks., Inc.

Hathorn, Libby. Sky Sash So Blue. 1998. (Illus.). 32p. (J). (gr. k-3). 16.00 (*0-689-81090-3*, Simon & Schuster Children's Publishing) Simon & Schuster Children's Publishing.

Havill, Juanita. Jamaica & Brianna. 1993. (Illus.). 32p. (J). (ps-3). lib. bdg., tchr. ed. 16.00 (*0-395-64489-5*) Houghton Mifflin Co.

—Jamaica & Brianna. 1996. (Illus.). 32p. (J). (ps-3). pap. 5.95 (*0-395-77939-1*) Houghton Mifflin Co. Trade & Reference Div.

—Jamaica & Brianna. 1993. 11.15 o.p. (*0-606-08785-0*) Turtleback Bks.

—Jamaica Tag-Along. (Carry-Along Book & Cassette Favorites Ser.). (J). 1996. (Illus.). 1p. (ps-3). pap. 9.95 incl. audio (*0-395-77941-3*, 4-95859); 1996. (Illus.). 1p. (ps-3). pap. 9.95 incl. audio (*0-395-77941-3*, 4-95859); 1994. pap. 44.32 (*0-395-70375-1*); 1992. (gr. 1). pap. 8.72 (*0-395-61768-5*); 1990. (Illus.). 32p. (ps-3). pap. 6.95 (*0-395-54949-3*); 1989. (Illus.). 32p. (ps-3). lib. bdg., tchr. ed. 16.00 (*0-395-49602-0*) Houghton Mifflin Co.

—Jamaica Tag-Along. 1990. 12.10 (*0-606-17136-3*) Turtleback Bks.

—Jamaica's Blue Marker. (Illus.). 32p. (J). (ps-3). 2003. pap. 5.95 (*0-618-36917-1*); 1995. lib. bdg. 16.00 (*0-395-72036-2*) Houghton Mifflin Co.

—Jamaica's Find. (Carry-Along Book & Cassette Favorites Ser.). (J). (ps-3). 1993. 1p. pap. 9.95 incl. audio (*0-395-66489-6*, 4-87433); 1993. 1p. pap. 9.95 incl. audio (*0-395-66489-6*, 4-87433); 1987. (Illus.). 32p. pap. 5.95 (*0-395-45357-7*); 1986. (Illus.). 32p. lib. bdg., tchr. ed. 16.00 (*0-395-39376-0*) Houghton Mifflin Co.

—Jamaica's Find. 1986. 12.10 (*0-606-02973-7*) Turtleback Bks.

Hayes, Sarah. Eat up, Gemma. 93rd ed. 1999. pap. text 11.70 (*0-15-300315-4*) Harcourt Children's Bks.

—Eat up, Gemma. 1988. (Illus.). 32p. (J). (ps-3). 16.00 (*0-688-08149-5*) HarperCollins Children's Bk. Group.

—Eat up, Gemma. Cohn, Amy, ed. 1994. (Illus.). 32p. (J). (ps-3). reprint ed. mass mkt. 5.95 (*0-688-13638-9*, Harper Trophy) HarperCollins Children's Bk. Group.

—Eat up, Gemma. 1994. 12.10 (*0-606-06346-3*) Turtleback Bks.

—Happy Christmas, Gemma. 1986. (Illus.). 32p. (J). (ps-1). 16.00 (*0-688-06508-2*) HarperCollins Children's Bk. Group.

—Happy Christmas, Gemma. ALC Staff, ed. 1992. (Illus.). 32p. (J). (ps up). pap. 4.95 o.p. (*0-688-11702-3*, Morrow, William & Co.) Morrow/Avon.

Haynes, David. The Gumma Wars. 1997. (West 7th Wildcats Ser.). (Illus.). 128p. (J). (gr. 2-6). pap. 6.95 o.p. (*1-57131-610-8*) Milkweed Editions.

Haynes, Henry L. If I Grow Up. 1999. (Illus.). 150p. pap. text 10.95 (*1-58521-004-8*) Books for Black Children, Inc.

Hazen, Barbara Shook & Golden Books Staff. Why Are People Different? A Book about Prejudice. 1985. (Golden Learn About Living Bks.). (Illus.). 72p. (J). (gr. k-3). pap. 3.99 o.s.i (*0-307-12485-1*, 12485, Golden Bks.) Random Hse. Children's Bks.

Heath, Amy. Sofie's Role. 1992. (Illus.). 40p. (J). (ps-2). 14.95 (*0-02-743505-9*, Simon & Schuster Children's Publishing) Simon & Schuster Children's Publishing.

Hedstrom, Deborah. From Settlement to City with Benjamin Franklin. 1997. (My American Journey Ser.). (Illus.). 19.99 o.p. (*1-57673-164-2*) Multnomah Pubs., Inc.

Hentoff, Nat. Jazz Country. 1965. 160p. (YA). (gr. 7 up). lib. bdg. 12.89 o.p. (*0-06-022306-5*) HarperCollins Children's Bk. Group.

—Jazz Country. 1976. (J). (gr. 7-12). pap. 1.25 o.p. (*0-06-080355-X*, P355) HarperCollins Pubs.

—Jazz Country. 1983. 144p. (YA). (gr. 7 up). mass mkt. 2.25 o.s.i (*0-440-94203-9*, Laurel Leaf) Random Hse. Children's Bks.

Heo, Yumi. Father's Rubber Shoes. 1996. (Illus.). 32p. (J). (ps-3). pap. 15.95 (*0-531-06873-0*); lib. bdg. 16.99 (*0-531-08723-9*) Scholastic, Inc. (Orchard Bks.).

Hering, Marianne. The Secret of the Missing Teacup. (White House Adventures Ser.: Vol. 2). 64p. (J). (gr. 2-5). pap. 4.99 (*0-7814-3064-X*) Cook Communications Ministries.

Hermes, Patricia. On Winter's Wind. 1995. 176p. (J). (gr. 3-7). 15.95 o.p. (*0-316-35978-5*) Little Brown & Co.

Herron, Carolivia. Nappy Hair. (Illus.). (J). (gr. k-3). 1998. 32p. pap. 6.99 (*0-679-89445-4*, Random Hse. Bks. for Young Readers); 1997. 32p. 17.00 (*0-679-87937-4*, Knopf Bks. for Young Readers); 1997. 18.99 o.s.i (*0-679-97937-9*, Random Hse. Bks. for Young Readers) Random Hse. Children's Bks.

—Nappy Hair. 1999. 13.14 (*0-606-16082-5*) Turtleback Bks.

Herschler, Mildred Barger. The Darkest Corner. 2000. 240p. (J). (gr. 7-12). 16.95 (*1-886910-54-5*, Front Street) Front Street, Inc.

Hess, Donna Lynn. Dust of the Earth. 1994. (Illus.). 198p. (YA). (gr. 7 up). pap. 6.49 (*0-89084-763-0*, 080572) Jones, Bob Univ. Pr.

Hest, Amy. Jamaica Louise James. (Illus.). 32p. (J). (ps-3). 1996. 15.99 o.s.i (*1-56402-348-6*); 1997. reprint ed. bds. 5.99 (*0-7636-0284-1*) Candlewick Pr.

—Jamaica Louise James. 1997. (J). 12.14 (*0-606-12745-3*) Turtleback Bks.

—Mr. Joe Baker. 2003. (J). (*0-7636-1233-2*) Candlewick Pr.

Hewett, Lorri. Dancer: Everybody Has a Dream. 2001. 224p. (YA). (gr. 8-12). pap. 5.99 (*0-14-131085-5*) Penguin Putnam Bks. for Young Readers.

—Lives of Our Own. (gr. 7-12). 1998. 192p. (J). 15.99 (*0-525-45959-6*); 2000. (Illus.). 196p. (YA). reprint ed. pap. 5.99 o.s.i (*0-14-130589-4*, Puffin Bks.) Penguin Putnam Bks. for Young Readers.

—Lives of Our Own. 2000. 12.04 (*0-606-19695-1*) Turtleback Bks.

—Soulfire. 240p. (gr. 7-12). 1998. pap. 5.99 o.s.i (*0-14-038960-1*, Puffin Bks.); 1996. (YA). 15.99 o.p. (*0-525-45559-0*, Dutton Children's Bks.) Penguin Putnam Bks. for Young Readers.

Higginsen, Vy & Bolden, Tonya. Mama, I Want to Sing. 192p. (YA). (gr. 7-9). 1995. mass mkt. 3.25 (*0-590-44202-3*); 1992. pap. 13.95 o.p. (*0-590-44201-5*) Scholastic, Inc.

Hill, Elizabeth S. Evan's Corner. (J). (ps-3). 1991. 320p. 13.99 o.s.i (*0-670-82830-0*, Viking Children's Bks.); 1993. (Illus.). 32p. reprint ed. pap. 5.99 o.s.i (*0-14-054406-2*, Puffin Bks.) Penguin Putnam Bks. for Young Readers.

—Evan's Corner. 1993. (Picture Puffin Ser.). (Illus.). (J). 10.19 o.p. (*0-606-02635-5*) Turtleback Bks.

Hill, Pamela Smith. A Voice from the Border. 1998. 320p. (YA). (gr. 7-12). tchr. ed. 16.95 (*0-8234-1356-X*) Holiday Hse., Inc.

Hilliard-Nunn, Nefertari Patricia. Foluke: The Afro Queen. 1997. (Illus.). 16p. (Orig.). (J). (ps-2). pap. 6.95 (*0-9655402-2-7*) Makare Publishing Co.

Hinds, P. Mignon & Golden Books Staff. What I Want to Be. 1998. 24p. (J). 3.99 o.s.i (*0-307-16168-4*, Golden Bks.) Random Hse. Children's Bks.

Hinds, Patricia Mignon. My Best Friend. 1998. (Illus.). 36p. (J). pap. 5.49 o.s.i (*0-307-11441-4*, Golden Bks.) Random Hse. Children's Bks.

—What I Want to Be. 1998. (Illus.). 36p. (J). (gr. k-3). pap. 5.49 o.s.i (*0-307-11439-2*, Golden Bks.) Random Hse. Children's Bks.

Hinson, Robert. Of Fairfield Plantation. 1997. 64p. (YA). (gr. 7-12). pap. 5.95 (*1-890424-00-5*) D-N Publishing.

Hoffman, Mary. Amazing Grace. 32p. (J). (ARA & ENG.). (*1-85430-334-1*, 93433); (ENG & VIE., Illus.). (*1-85430-340-6*, 93435); 1998. (Illus.). (*1-85430-338-4*); 1995. o.p. (*1-85430-341-4*); 1994. (*1-85430-336-8*, 93434) Magi Pubns.

—Amazing Grace. (gr. k-3). 1998. 24p. pap. 6.99 o.s.i (*0-8037-2297-4*); 1991. (Illus.). 32p. (J). 16.99 (*0-8037-1040-2*) Penguin Putnam Bks. for Young Readers. (Dial Bks. for Young Readers).

—Amazing Grace. 1999. (YA). pap. 32.99 incl. audio (*0-7887-4097-0*, 41103); pap. 32.99 incl. audio (*0-7887-4097-0*, 41103) Recorded Bks., LLC.

—The Amazing Grace Doll & Book Set. 1994. (Illus.). 32p. (J). (ps-4). 19.95 o.p. (*0-8037-1726-1*, Dial Bks. for Young Readers) Penguin Putnam Bks. for Young Readers.

—An Angel Just Like Me. 1997. (Illus.). 32p. (J). (ps-3). 14.99 o.p. (*0-8037-2265-6*, Dial Bks. for Young Readers) Penguin Putnam Bks. for Young Readers.

—La Asombrosa Graciela. 1996. (SPA., Illus.). 32p. (J). (gr. k-3). 16.99 (*0-8037-1938-8*, VK0996, Dial Bks. for Young Readers) Penguin Putnam Bks. for Young Readers.

—Boundless Grace. 2002. (Illus.). (J). 25.45 (*0-7587-2139-0*) Book Wholesalers, Inc.

—Boundless Grace. (Illus.). 32p. (J). (ps-3). 2000. pap. 5.99 (*0-14-055667-2*, Puffin Bks.); 1995. 16.99 (*0-8037-1715-6*, Dial Bks. for Young Readers) Penguin Putnam Bks. for Young Readers.

—Boundless Grace. 2000. 12.14 (*0-606-20350-8*); 12.14 (*0-606-20224-2*) Turtleback Bks.

—Starring Grace. (Chapters Ser.). (Illus.). 96p. (J). 2001. (gr. 2-6). pap. 4.99 (*0-14-230022-5*, Puffin Bks.); 2000. (gr. k-4). 14.99 (*0-8037-2559-0*, Dial Bks. for Young Readers) Penguin Putnam Bks. for Young Readers.

Hoffman, Mary & Youngblood, Shay. Amazing Grace. 1998. 44p. pap. 5.60 (*0-87129-809-0*, A64) Dramatic Publishing Co.

Holland, Isabelle. Behind the Lines. (Point Ser.). (gr. 7 up). 1997. 208p. (J). mass mkt. 4.50 (*0-590-45114-6*); 1994. (Illus.). 240p. (YA). pap. 13.95 (*0-590-45113-8*) Scholastic, Inc.

—Behind the Lines. 1997. (Point Ser.). 10.55 (*0-606-11104-2*) Turtleback Bks.

Holley, Juliette A. Jamie Lemme See. 1975. 113p. (J). 5.95 o.p. (*0-89227-016-0*) Commonwealth Pr., Inc.

Holman, Sandy Lynne. Grandpa, Is Everything Black Bad? Holman, Sandy Lynne, ed. 1998. (Illus.). 32p. (J). (gr. 2-6). lib. bdg. 18.95 (*0-9644655-0-7*) Culture C.O.-O.P., The.

Holmes, Mary Z. See You in Heaven. 1992. (History's Children Ser.). (Illus.). 48p. (J). (gr. 4-5). pap. o.p. (*0-8114-6427-X*); lib. bdg. 21.36 o.p. (*0-8114-3502-4*) Raintree Pubs.

Holt, Kimberly Willis. Mister & Me. 1998. (Illus.). 80p. (J). (gr. 2-6). 13.99 (*0-399-23215-X*) Penguin Group (USA) Inc.

Hoobler, Dorothy & Hoobler, Thomas. The 1920s: Luck. 2000. (Century Kids Ser.). (Illus.). 160p. (YA). (gr. 5-8). 22.90 (*0-7613-1602-7*) Millbrook Pr., Inc.

—The 1950s: Music. 2001. (Century Kids Ser.). (Illus.). 160p. (J). (gr. 5-8). 22.90 (*0-7613-1605-1*) Millbrook Pr., Inc.

—The 1960s: Rebels, 2001. (Century Kids Ser.). (Illus.). 160p. (J). (gr. 5-8). 22.90 (*0-7613-1606-X*) Millbrook Pr., Inc.

Hood, Susan. Look! I Can Read! 2000. (All Aboard Reading Ser.). (Illus.). 32p. (J). (ps-3). 13.89 o.s.i (*0-448-42282-4*); mass mkt. 3.99 (*0-448-41967-X*) Penguin Putnam Bks. for Young Readers. (Grosset & Dunlap).

—Look! I Can Read!, field. 2000. (All Aboard Reading Ser.). (Illus.). (J). 10.14 (*0-606-18470-8*) Turtleback Bks.

hooks, bell. Be Boy Buzz. Raschka, Christopher, tr. & illus. by. 2002. (J). pap. (*0-7868-1643-0*) Hyperion Bks. for Children.

—Be Boy Buzz. 2002. (Illus.). 32p. (J). (ps-3). 16.99 (*0-7868-0814-4*, Jump at the Sun) Hyperion Bks. for Children.

—Be Boy Buzz. Raschka, Christopher, tr. & illus. by. 2002. (J). lib. bdg. (*0-7868-2633-9*) Hyperion Bks. for Children.

—Happy to Be Nappy. 1999. (Jump at the Sun Ser.). (Illus.). 32p. (J). (ps-3). 14.99 (*0-7868-0427-0*); lib. bdg. 15.49 (*0-7868-2377-1*) Hyperion Bks. for Children.

—Homemade Love. 2002. (Illus.). (J). (gr. k-3). 16.99 (*0-7868-0643-5*, Jump at the Sun) Hyperion Bks. for Children.

hooks, bell & Raschka, Chris. Happy to Be Nappy. 2001. (Illus.). 16p. (J). bds. 6.99 (*0-7868-0756-3*, Jump at the Sun) Hyperion Bks. for Children.

Hooks, William H. Freedom's Fruit. 1995. (Illus.). (J). (ps-3). 16.00 o.s.i (*0-679-82438-3*); 17.99 o.s.i (*0-679-92438-8*) Knopf, Alfred A. Inc.

Hopkins, Lila. Talking Turkey. (J). 1990. 128p. (gr. 7-9). 21.10 o.p. (*0-531-10797-3*); 1989. 13.95 o.p. (*0-531-15119-0*) Scholastic Library Publishing. (Watts, Franklin).

Hopkinson, Deborah. A Band of Angels: A Story Inspired by the Jubilee Singers. 1999. (Anne Schwartz Bks.). (Illus.). 40p. (J). (gr. 1-4). 16.00 (*0-689-81062-8*, Atheneum/Anne Schwartz Bks.) Simon & Schuster Children's Publishing.

—Under the Quilt of Night. 2002. (Illus.). 40p. (J). 16.00 (*0-689-82227-8*, Atheneum/Anne Schwartz Bks.) Simon & Schuster Children's Publishing.

Houghton Mifflin Company Staff. Flossie & the Fox. 1992. (Literature Experience 1993 Ser.). (J). (gr. 4). pap. 10.24 (*0-395-61797-9*) Houghton Mifflin Co.

Houston, Gloria M. Bright Freedom's Song: A Story of the Underground Railroad. 1998. (Illus.). 160p. (YA). (gr. 5 up). 16.00 (*0-15-201812-3*, Silver Whistle) Harcourt Children's Bks.

Howard-Douglas, Daisy. Jad & Old Ananias. 1999. (Illus.). (J). (gr. 3-6). 12.95 o.p. (*0-533-13028-X*) Vantage Pr., Inc.

Howard, Elizabeth Fitzgerald. Aunt Flossie's Hats (& Crab Cakes Later) 1991. (Illus.). 32p. (J). (ps-1). tchr. ed. 16.00 o.s.i (*0-395-54682-6*) Houghton Mifflin Co.

—Aunt Flossie's Hats (& Crab Cakes Later) 1991. 13.10 (*0-606-07214-4*) Turtleback Bks.

—Aunt Flossie's Hats (And Crab Cakes Later) 1995. (Illus.). 32p. (J). (ps-3). pap. 6.95 (*0-395-72077-X*, Clarion Bks.) Houghton Mifflin Co. Trade & Reference Div.

—Aunt Flossie's Hats (and Crab Cakes Later) 10th anniv. ed. 2001. (Illus.). 40p. (J). (ps-3). lib. bdg., tchr. ed. 16.00 (*0-618-12038-6*, Clarion Bks.) Houghton Mifflin Co. Trade & Reference Div.

—Chita's Christmas Tree. (Illus.). 32p. (J). (ps-2). 1989. lib. bdg. 14.95 (*0-02-744621-2*, Simon & Schuster Children's Publishing); 1993. reprint ed. pap. 5.99 (*0-689-71739-3*, Aladdin) Simon & Schuster Children's Publishing.

—Mac & Marie & the Train Toss Surprise. 1993. (Illus.). 32p. (J). (ps-2). 14.95 o.s.i (*0-02-744640-9*, Simon & Schuster Children's Publishing) Simon & Schuster Children's Publishing.

—Papa Tells Chita a Story. (Illus.). 32p. (J). (ps-2). 1998. pap. 5.99 (*0-689-82220-0*, Aladdin); 1995. 15.00 (*0-02-744623-9*, Simon & Schuster Children's Publishing) Simon & Schuster Children's Publishing.

—Papa Tells Chita a Story. 1998. 12.14 (*0-606-15670-4*) Turtleback Bks.

—The Train to Lulu's. 1998. (J). pap. 4.95 (*0-87628-336-9*) Simon & Schuster.

—The Train to Lulu's. (Illus.). 32p. (J). (ps-2). 1988. lib. bdg. 14.95 o.s.i (*0-02-744620-4*, Atheneum/Richard Jackson Bks.); 1994. reprint ed. pap. 4.95 (*0-689-71797-0*, Aladdin) Simon & Schuster Children's Publishing.

—The Train to Lulu's. 1994. 10.40 o.p. (*0-606-18946-7*); (J). 10.15 o.p. (*0-606-06064-2*) Turtleback Bks.

—Virgie Goes to School with Us Boys. 2002. (Illus.). (J). 25.11 (*0-7587-3907-9*) Book Wholesalers, Inc.

—Virgie Goes to School with Us Boys. 2000. (Illus.). 32p. (J). (gr. k-3). 16.00 (*0-689-80076-2*, Simon & Schuster Children's Publishing) Simon & Schuster Children's Publishing.

—What's in Aunt Mary's Room? 2002. (Illus.). 32p. (J). (ps-3). pap. 5.95 (*0-618-24621-5*, Clarion Bks.) Houghton Mifflin Co. Trade & Reference Div.

—When Will Sarah Come. 1999. (Illus.). 24p. (J). (ps-3). 16.00 (*0-688-16180-4*); lib. bdg. 15.89 (*0-688-16181-2*) HarperCollins Children's Bk. Group. (Greenwillow Bks.).

Howard, Elizabeth Fitzgerald & Lucas, Cedric. What's in Aunt Mary's Room? 1996. (Illus.). 32p. (J). (ps-3). lib. bdg., tchr. ed. 16.00 (*0-395-69845-6*, Clarion Bks.) Houghton Mifflin Co. Trade & Reference Div.

Howe, Fanny. Radio City. 1984. 128p. (YA). (gr. 7 up). pap. 2.25 o.p. (*0-380-86025-2*, 86025, Avon Bks.) Morrow/Avon.

Howe, Quincy. StreetSmart. 1993. (Illus.). 106p. (YA). (gr. 7-12). pap. 6.95 o.p. (*0-932765-42-4*, 1325-93) Close Up Foundation.

Hru, Dakari. Joshua's Masai Mask. (Illus.). 32p. (J). (ps-5). 1996. pap. 6.95 (*1-880000-32-6*); 1993. 15.95 (*1-880000-02-4*) Lee & Low Bks., Inc.

—Joshua's Masai Mask. 1993. 13.10 (*0-606-09495-4*) Turtleback Bks.

—The Magic Moonberry Jump Ropes. 1996. (Illus.). 32p. (J). (ps-3). 14.99 o.p. (*0-8037-1754-7*); 14.89 o.p. (*0-8037-1755-5*) Penguin Putnam Bks. for Young Readers. (Dial Bks. for Young Readers).

Hubbell, Patricia. Black All Around! 2003. (Illus.). 32p. (J). 16.95 (*1-58430-048-5*) Lee & Low Bks., Inc.

Hudson, Cheryl Willis. Animal Sounds for Baby. (Illus.). 10p. 1997. bds. 4.95 (*0-590-94919-5*); 1995. (J). bds. 5.95 (*0-590-48029-4*) Scholastic, Inc. (Cartwheel Bks.).

—Bright Eyes, Brown Skin. 1990. (Feeling Good Ser.). (J). 12.15 o.p. (*0-606-08705-2*) Turtleback Bks.

—Good Morning, Baby. (Illus.). 10p. 1995. bds. 4.95 (*0-590-94918-7*); 1992. (J). bds. 5.95 (*0-590-45760-8*) Scholastic, Inc. (Cartwheel Bks.).

—Good Night, Baby. (Illus.). 10p. 1997. bds. 4.95 (*0-590-94942-X*); 1992. (J). bds. 5.95 (*0-590-45761-6*) Scholastic, Inc. (Cartwheel Bks.).

—Let's Count, Baby. 1995. (Illus.). 10p. (J). (ps). bds. 4.95 (*0-590-94922-5*); bds. 5.95 o.p. (*0-590-48028-6*) Scholastic, Inc. (Cartwheel Bks.).

Hudson, Cheryl Willis & Ford, Bernette. Bright Eyes, Brown Skin. 1990. (Illus.). E-Book (*1-59019-140-4*) ipicturebooks, LLC.

Hudson, Cheryl Willis & Ford, Bernette G. Bright Eyes, Brown Skin. 1990. (Illus.). 24p. (J). (ps-2). 12.95 (*0-940975-10-6*); pap. 6.95 (*0-940975-23-8*) Just Us Bks., Inc.

—Bright Eyes, Brown Skin. 1993. (Illus.). (J). (gr. k-2). pap. 8.95 o.p. incl. audio (*0-7608-0483-4*); pap. 4.95 o.p. (*0-88741-905-4*);Big bk. pap. 17.95 o.p. (*0-88741-904-6*, 04271) Sundance Publishing.

—Bright Eyes, Brown Skin. (Illus.). 2001. (J). E-Book (*1-59019-139-0*); 1990. E-Book 5.99 (*1-59019-141-2*) ipicturebooks, LLC.

Hudson, Wade. I Love My Family: An African-American Family Reunion. (Illus.). 32p. (J). (ps-2). 1995. mass mkt. 4.95 (*0-590-47325-5*); 1993. pap. 12.95 o.p. (*0-590-45763-2*) Scholastic, Inc.

—I'm Gonna Be! 1992. (Afro-Bets Ser.). (Illus.). 32p. (J). (ps-3). pap. 6.95 (*0-940975-40-8*) Just Us Bks., Inc.

—I'm Gonna Be! (Afro Bets Kids Ser.). 2001. (Illus.). (J). E-Book (*1-59019-133-1*); 1992. E-Book 5.99 (*1-59019-135-8*); 1992. E-Book (*1-59019-134-X*) ipicturebooks, LLC.

—Jamal's Busy Day. 1991. (Feeling Good Ser.). (J). 12.15 o.p. (*0-606-08786-9*) Turtleback Bks.

—Jamal's Busy Day. (Illus.). 2001. (J). E-Book (*1-59019-136-6*); 1991. E-Book (*1-59019-137-4*); 1991. E-Book (*1-59019-138-2*) ipicturebooks, LLC.

Hudson, Wade, et al. Jamal's Busy Day. 1991. (Feeling Good Ser.). (Illus.). (J). (ps-3). 28p. pap. 6.95 (*0-940975-24-6*); 24p. lib. bdg. 12.95 (*0-940975-21-1*) Just Us Bks., Inc.

Hughes, Langston. The Best of Simple. 1990. (Illus.). 245p. (J). (gr. 4-6). pap. 13.00 (*0-374-52133-6*, Hill & Wang) Farrar, Straus & Giroux.

—Simple Speaks His Mind. (J). (gr. 5-6). reprint ed. lib. bdg. 22.95 (*0-88411-061-3*) Amereon, Ltd.

—Thank You, M'am. 1993. (Creative Short Stories Ser.). 32p. (YA). (gr. 3-12). lib. bdg. 18.60 (*0-88682-478-8*, Creative Education) Creative Co., The.

Hulbert, Jay & Kantor, Sid. Armando Asked "Why?" 1990. (Ready-Set-Read Ser.). (Illus.). (J). (ps-2). 24p. pap. 4.95 o.p. (*0-8114-6739-2*); 32p. lib. bdg. 21.40 o.p. (*0-8172-3576-0*) Raintree Pubs.

Humphrey, Margo. The River That Gave Gifts: An Afro American Story. 1987. (J). 13.95 o.p. (*0-89239-019-0*); (Illus.). 24p. (gr. 1 up). 14.95 (*0-89239-027-1*); (Illus.). 24p. (gr. 1 up). pap. 6.95 (*0-89239-128-6*) Children's Bk. Pr.

—The River That Gave Gifts: An Afro American Story. 1987. (Fifth World Tales Ser.). 12.15 o.p. (*0-606-09792-9*) Turtleback Bks.

Hunt, Irene. William. 1977. (J). (gr. 5 up). 11.95 o.s.i (*0-684-14902-8*, Atheneum) Simon & Schuster Children's Publishing.

Hunter, Kristin. Boss Cat. 1981. (J). (gr. 2-5). pap. 0.95 o.p. (*0-380-00196-9*, 21873, Avon Bks.) Morrow/Avon.

—Guests in the Promised Land. 1976. (gr. 7 up). pap. 1.50 o.p. (*0-380-00515-8*, 44891-2, Avon Bks.) Morrow/Avon.

—The Soul Brothers & Sister Lou. 1976. (YA). (gr. 7 up). pap. 1.75 o.p. (*0-380-00686-3*, 59717-9, Avon Bks.) Morrow/Avon.

—The Soul Brothers & Sister Lou. 1997. 249p. (J). (gr. 5-9). pap. 11.95 (*0-7043-4900-0*) Women's Pr., Ltd., The GBR. *Dist:* Trafalgar Square.

Hutchins, Pat. My Best Friend. 1993. (Illus.). 32p. (J). (ps-3). 16.99 (*0-688-11485-7*); lib. bdg. 15.93 o.p. (*0-688-11486-5*) HarperCollins Children's Bk. Group. (Greenwillow Bks.).

Hyppolite, Joanne. Ola Shakes It Up. 1998. (Illus.). 176p. (gr. 2-6). text 14.95 o.s.i (*0-385-32235-6*, Delacorte Pr.) Dell Publishing.

—Ola Shakes It Up. 1999. (Illus.). 176p. (gr. 4-7). pap. text 4.50 o.s.i (*0-440-41204-8*, Dell Books for Young Readers) Random Hse. Children's Bks.

Igus, Toyomi. Two Mrs. Gibsons. 1996. (Illus.). 32p. (J). (gr. 2-4). lib. bdg. 19.90 (*0-516-20001-1*, Children's Pr.) Scholastic Library Publishing.

—When I Was Little. 1992. (Illus.). 32p. (J). (ps-3). 14.95 (*0-940975-32-7*); pap. 6.95 (*0-940975-33-5*) Just Us Bks., Inc.

—When I Was Little. 1992. (J). 12.15 o.p. (*0-606-08900-4*) Turtleback Bks.

—When I Was Little. 2001. (J). E-Book (*1-59019-149-8*); 1992. E-Book (*1-59019-150-1*) ipicturebooks, LLC.

Irwin, Hadley. Be Somebody. 1988. 160p. mass mkt. 2.50 o.p. (*0-451-15303-0*, Signet Bks.) NAL.

—Be Somebody. 1984. 180p. (J). (gr. 4-7). 13.95 o.s.i (*0-689-50308-3*, McElderry, Margaret K.) Simon & Schuster Children's Publishing.

Isadora, Rachel. Bring on That Beat. 2002. (Illus.). 32p. (J). (ps-3). 14.99 (*0-399-23232-X*) Penguin Group (USA) Inc.

—Peekaboo Morning. 2002. (Illus.). 32p. (J). (ps-1). 15.99 (*0-399-23602-3*) Penguin Group (USA) Inc.

Jackson, Dave & Jackson, Neta. Defeat of the Ghost Riders: Mary McLeod Bethune. 1997. (Trailblazer Bks.: Vol. 23). 144p. (J). (gr. 3-7). pap. 5.99 (*1-55661-742-9*) Bethany Hse. Pubs.

—The Forty-Acre Swindle: George Washington Carver. 2000. (Trailblazer Bks.: Vol. 31). (Illus.). 144p. (J). (gr. 3-7). pap. 5.99 (*0-7642-2264-3*) Bethany Hse. Pubs.

—Journey to the End of the Earth: William Seymour. 2000. (Trailblazer Bks.: Vol. 33). (Illus.). 160p. (J). (gr. 3-7). pap. 5.99 (*0-7642-2266-X*) Bethany Hse. Pubs.

Jackson, Isaac. Somebody's New Pajamas. 1996. (Illus.). 32p. (J). (gr. 1-5). 14.89 o.s.i (*0-8037-1549-8*); (ps-3). 14.99 o.s.i (*0-8037-1570-6*) Penguin Putnam Bks. for Young Readers. (Dial Bks. for Young Readers).

Javernick, Ellen. Ms. Pollywog's Problem-Solving Service. 1995. (Ready, Set, Read!). (Illus.). 64p. (J). (gr. 2-5). pap. 4.99 (*0-8066-2813-8*, 9-2813) Augsburg Fortress, Pubs.

Johnson, Angela. Daddy Calls Me Man. 1997. (Illus.). 32p. (J). (ps-k). pap. 15.95 (*0-531-30042-0*); lib. bdg. 16.99 o.p. (*0-531-33042-7*) Scholastic, Inc. (Orchard Bks.).

—Do Like Kyla. (Illus.). 32p. (J). (ps-3). 1993. mass mkt. 6.95 (*0-531-07040-9*); 1990. mass mkt. 16.99 o.p. (*0-531-08452-3*); 1990. pap. 15.95 (*0-531-05852-2*) Scholastic, Inc. (Orchard Bks.).

—Do Like Kyla. 1993. (J). 13.10 (*0-606-05810-9*) Turtleback Bks.

—The First Part Last. 2003. (Illus.). 144p. (YA). (gr. 6 up). 15.95 (*0-689-84922-2*, Simon & Schuster Children's Publishing) Simon & Schuster Children's Publishing.

—The Girl Who Wore Snakes. 1993. (Illus.). 32p. (J). (ps-2). pap. 15.95 o.p. (*0-531-05491-8*); lib. bdg. 16.99 o.p. (*0-531-08641-0*) Scholastic, Inc. (Orchard Bks.).

—Heaven. 2002. (Illus.). 13.40 (*0-7587-0359-7*) Book Wholesalers, Inc.

—Heaven. 2001. (YA). pap., stu. ed. 40.24 incl. audio. (gr. 7). audio 26.00 (*0-7887-4563-8*, 96334E7) Recorded Bks., LLC.

—Heaven. 144p. (YA). 2000. (Illus.). (gr. 8-12). mass mkt. 4.99 (*0-689-82290-1*, Simon Pulse); 1998. (gr. 7-12). 16.00 (*0-689-82229-4*, Simon & Schuster Children's Publishing) Simon & Schuster Children's Publishing.

—Heaven. l.t. ed. 2000. (Young Adult Ser.). 157p. (J). (gr. 7-12). 20.95 (*0-7862-2463-0*) Thorndike Pr.

—Heaven. 2000. (Illus.). (YA). 11.04 (*0-606-18799-5*) Turtleback Bks.

—Joshua by the Sea. 1994. (Illus.). 12p. (J). (ps). pap. 4.95 (*0-531-06846-3*, Orchard Bks.) Scholastic, Inc.

—Joshua's Night Whispers. 1994. (Illus.). 12p. (J). (ps). mass mkt. 4.95 o.p. (*0-531-06847-1*, Orchard Bks.) Scholastic, Inc.

—Just Like Josh Gibson. 2003. (Illus.). 32p. (J). 15.95 (*0-689-82628-1*, Simon & Schuster Children's Publishing) Simon & Schuster Children's Publishing.

—The Leaving Morning. (Illus.). 32p. (J). (ps-3). 1996. mass mkt. 5.95 (*0-531-07072-7*); 1992. 14.95 o.p. (*0-531-05992-8*); 1992. mass mkt. 15.99 o.p. (*0-531-08592-9*) Scholastic, Inc. (Orchard Bks.).

—The Leaving Morning. 1996. 12.10 (*0-606-09532-2*) Turtleback Bks.

—Looking for Red. 128p. 2003. (Illus.). (YA). mass mkt. 4.99 (*0-689-86388-8*, Simon Pulse); 2002. (J). (gr. 7 up). 15.95 (*0-689-83253-2*, Simon & Schuster Children's Publishing) Simon & Schuster Children's Publishing.

—Looking for Red. l.t. ed. 2003. 117p. (J). 24.95 (*0-7862-5603-6*) Thorndike Pr.

—Mama Bird, Baby Birds. 1994. (Illus.). 12p. (J). (ps). mass mkt. 4.95 o.p. (0-531-06848-X, Orchard Bks.) Scholastic, Inc.

—Rain Feet. 1994. (Illus.). 12p. (J). (ps). pap. 4.95 (0-531-06849-8, Orchard Bks.) Scholastic, Inc.

—The Rolling Store. 1997. (Illus.). 32p. (J). (ps-2). pap. 15.95 (0-531-30015-3); lib. bdg. 16.99 (0-531-33015-X) Scholastic, Inc. (Orchard Bks.).

—Shoes Like Miss Alice's. 1995. (Illus.). 32p. (J). (ps-3). pap. 15.95 (0-531-06814-5); lib. bdg. 16.99 (0-531-08664-X) Scholastic, Inc. (Orchard Bks.).

—Songs of Faith. (YA). (gr. 5-8). 2001. 112p. mass mkt. 4.99 (0-440-22944-8, Dell Books for Young Readers); 1999. 108p. reprint ed. pap. 4.99 (0-679-89488-8, Knopf Bks. for Young Readers) Random Hse. Children's Bks.

—Songs of Faith. 1998. (Illus.). 112p. (J). (gr. 3-7). pap. 15.95 (0-531-30023-4); lib. bdg. 16.99 (0-531-33023-0) Scholastic, Inc. (Orchard Bks.).

—Songs of Faith. 1999. 11.04 (0-606-17374-9) Turtleback Bks.

—Tell Me a Story, Mama. (Illus.). 32p. (J). (ps-3). 1992. mass mkt. 6.95 (0-531-07032-8); 1989. pap. 15.95 (0-531-05794-1); 1989. mass mkt. 16.99 o.p. (0-531-08394-2) Scholastic, Inc. (Orchard Bks.).

—Tell Me a Story, Mama. 1992. (J). 11.15 o.p. (0-606-02944-3) Turtleback Bks.

—Toning the Sweep. 2002. (J). 13.19 (0-7587-0401-1) Book Wholesalers, Inc.

—Toning the Sweep. 112p. 2003. (J). (gr. 7 up). mass mkt. 5.99 (0-590-48142-8, Scholastic Paperbacks); 1993. (YA). (gr. 6 up). mass mkt. 15.99 o.p. (0-531-08626-7, Orchard Bks.); 1993. (YA). (gr. 6 up). pap. 15.95 (0-531-05476-4, Orchard Bks.) Scholastic, Inc.

—Toning The Sweep. 1993. (Point Signature Ser.). 11.04 (0-606-06817-1) Turtleback Bks.

—The Wedding. 1999. (Illus.). 32p. (J). (ps-2). pap. 16.95 (0-531-30139-7); lib. bdg. 17.99 (0-531-33139-3) Scholastic, Inc. (Orchard Bks.).

—When I Am Old with You. (Illus.). 32p. (J). (ps-3). 1993. mass mkt. 6.95 (0-531-07035-2); 1990. pap. 15.95 (0-531-05884-0); 1990. lib. bdg. 16.99 (0-531-08484-1) Scholastic, Inc. (Orchard Bks.).

—When I Am Old with You. 1993. (J). 13.10 (0-606-05696-3) Turtleback Bks.

Johnson, Dinah. Quinnie Blue, ERS. 2000. (Illus.). 32p. (J). (ps-2). 16.95 (0-8050-4378-0, Holt, Henry & Co. Bks. For Young Readers) Holt, Henry & Co.

—Sunday Week, ERS. 1999. (Illus.). 32p. (J). (ps-2). 15.95 (0-8050-4911-8, Holt, Henry & Co. Bks. For Young Readers) Holt, Henry & Co.

Johnson, Dolores. Now Let Me Fly: The Story of a Slave Family. 1998. pap. 5.99 (0-87628-977-4) Ctr. for Applied Research in Education, The.

—Now Let Me Fly: The Story of a Slave Family. 32p. (ps-3). 1997. pap. 6.99 (0-689-80966-2, Aladdin); 1993. (Illus.). (J). lib. bdg. 15.00 (0-02-747699-5, Atheneum) Simon & Schuster Children's Publishing.

—Now Let Me Fly: The Story of a Slave Family. 1997. 12.14 (0-606-11692-3) Turtleback Bks.

—Papa's Stories. 1994. (Illus.). 32p. (J). (gr. k-3). lib. bdg. 14.95 (0-02-747847-5, Atheneum) Simon & Schuster Children's Publishing.

—What Kind of Baby-Sitter Is This? 1991. (Illus.). 32p. (J). (gr. k-3). lib. bdg. 15.00 (0-02-747846-7, Atheneum) Simon & Schuster Children's Publishing.

—What Will Mommy Do When I'm at School? 1990. (Illus.). 32p. (J). (ps-1). lib. bdg. 15.00 (0-02-747845-9, Atheneum) Simon & Schuster Children's Publishing.

—Your Dad Was Just Like You. 1993. (Illus.). 32p. (J). (gr. k-3). text 13.95 (0-02-747838-6, Atheneum) Simon & Schuster Children's Publishing.

Johnson, Dolores, illus. Grandma's Hands. 1998. (Accelerated Reader Bks.). 32p. (J). (gr. 1-4). 15.95 (0-7614-5025-4, Cavendish Children's Bks.) Cavendish, Marshall Corp.

Johnson-Feelings, Dianne. The Painter Man. 1993. (Illus.). (J). 14.95 o.p. (0-89334-220-3) Humanics Publishing Group.

Johnson, Herschel. A Visit to the Country. 1989. (Illus.). 32p. (J). (ps-3). 13.95 (0-06-022849-0); lib. bdg. 13.89 o.p. (0-06-022854-7) HarperCollins Children's Bk. Group.

Johnson, Lois Walfrid. Escape into the Night. 1995. (Riverboat Adventures Ser.: Vol. 1). (Illus.). 176p. (J). (gr. 4-7). pap. 5.99 (1-55661-351-2) Bethany Hse. Pubs.

Johnston, Tony. Angel City. 2002. (Illus.). (J). (0-399-23405-5, Philomel) Penguin Putnam Bks. for Young Readers.

—The Wagon. (Illus.). 40p. (J). (ps-3). 1999. mass mkt. 5.95 (0-688-16694-6, Morrow, William & Co.); 1996. lib. bdg. 15.89 o.s.i (0-688-13537-4); 1996. 17.00 (0-688-13457-2, Morrow, William & Co.) Morrow/Avon.

Jonas, Ann. The Quilt. 2002. (Illus.). (J). 13.19 (0-7587-3478-6) Book Wholesalers, Inc.

—The Quilt. 1984. (Illus.). (J). 32p. lib. bdg. 15.93 o.p. (0-688-03826-3); 40p. 16.95 (0-688-03825-5) HarperCollins Children's Bk. Group. (Greenwillow Bks.).

—The Quilt. 1994. (Picture Puffins Ser.). (Illus.). 40p. (J). (ps-3). pap. 5.99 (0-14-055308-8, Puffin Bks.) Penguin Putnam Bks. for Young Readers.

Jones, Hettie. Spooky Tales from Gullah Gullah Island: A Glow-in-the-Dark Book. 1996. (Illus.). 24p. (J). (ps-3). pap. 11.95 (0-689-80829-1, Simon Spotlight/Nickelodeon) Simon & Schuster Children's Publishing.

Jones, Joy. Tambourine Moon. 1999. (Illus.). 32p. (J). (ps-3). 16.00 (0-689-80648-5, Simon & Schuster Children's Publishing) Simon & Schuster Children's Publishing.

Jones, Kathryn. Happy Birthday, Dr. King! 1994. (J). (gr. 4-7). pap. 4.95 o.s.i (0-671-87523-X, Aladdin) Simon & Schuster Children's Publishing.

Joosse, Barbara M. Hot City. Gauch, Patricia Lee, ed. 2004. (Illus.). (J). 16.99 (0-399-23640-6, Philomel) Penguin Putnam Bks. for Young Readers.

—Snow Day! (Illus.). 32p. (J). (ps-3). 1999. pap. 5.95 (0-395-96890-9); 1993. lib. bdg. 14.95 (0-395-66588-4) Houghton Mifflin Co. Trade & Reference Div. (Clarion Bks.).

—Snow Day! 1995. 12.10 (0-606-17342-0) Turtleback Bks.

—Stars in the Darkness. 2001. (Illus.). 36p. (J). (gr. k-3). 14.95 (0-8118-2168-4) Chronicle Bks. LLC.

The Journal of Biddy Owens: The Negro Leagues. 2003. (J). lib. bdg. 12.95 (0-439-55499-3) Scholastic, Inc.

Justus, Adalu. The Storyteller House. 1999. 180p. (YA). (gr. 5-12). per. (0-937109-11-8) Ike, J. Bks.

Justus, May. New Boy in School. 1963. (Illus.). (J). (gr. 1-4). lib. bdg. 5.95 o.p. (0-8038-5011-5) Hastings Hse. Daytrips Pubs.

Kabel, Larassa, illus. Holding the Yellow Rabbit. 1998. (Cover-to-Cover Bks.). (J). (0-7807-6784-5) Perfection Learning Corp.

Katz, Karen. My First Kwanzaa, ERS. 2003. (Illus.). 32p. (J). 14.95 (0-8050-7077-X, Holt, Henry & Co. Bks. For Young Readers) Holt, Henry & Co.

Kay, Alan N. Send 'Em South. 2001. (Young Heroes of History Ser.: Vol. 1). (Illus.). 145p. (J). (gr. 3-6). pap. 5.95 (1-57249-208-2, WM Kids) White Mane Publishing Co., Inc.

Keats, Ezra Jack. Goggles. 1998. (Illus.). 40p. (J). 15.99 (0-670-88062-0); pap. 6.99 (0-14-056440-3, Puffin Bks.) Penguin Putnam Bks. for Young Readers.

—Goggles. 1987. (Illus.). 40p. (J). (gr. k-3). reprint ed. pap. 4.95 (0-689-71157-3, Aladdin) Simon & Schuster Children's Publishing.

—Goggles. 1998. (Illus.). (J). 12.14 (0-606-21779-7) Turtleback Bks.

—Hi, Cat! 2002. (Illus.). (J). 22.72 (0-7587-6792-7) Book Wholesalers, Inc.

—Hi, Cat! (J). (gr. k-3). 1990. pap. 9.95 incl. audio (0-87499-179-X); 1990. pap. 9.95 incl. audio (0-87499-179-X); 1998. (Illus.). 24.95 incl. audio (0-87499-180-3); Set. 1990. stu. ed. 33.95 incl. audio (0-87499-181-1) Live Oak Media.

—Hi, Cat! 1999. (Illus.). (J). pap. 5.99 (0-14-056568-X, Puffin Bks.); 32p. 15.99 (0-670-88546-0) Penguin Putnam Bks. for Young Readers.

—Hi, Cat! 2nd ed. 1988. (Illus.). 32p. (J). (gr. k-3). mass mkt. 5.99 o.s.i (0-689-71258-8, Aladdin) Simon & Schuster Children's Publishing.

—Hi, Cat! 1988. (Illus.). 11.19 o.p. (0-606-00797-0) Turtleback Bks.

—Pet Show! 1987. (Reading Rainbow Book Ser.). (Illus.). 32p. (J). (ps-3). reprint ed. mass mkt. 5.99 (0-689-71159-X, Aladdin) Simon & Schuster Children's Publishing.

—Pet Show! 2001. 13.14 (0-606-22504-8); 1974. (Illus.). 12.14 (0-606-01233-8) Turtleback Bks.

—Silba por Willie. 1992. (SPA., Illus.). 32p. (J). (gr. k-3). 15.99 o.s.i (0-670-84395-4, VK4607, Viking Children's Bks.) Penguin Putnam Bks. for Young Readers.

—Silbale a Willie. Grosman, Ernesto L., tr. 1996. (SPA., Illus.). 32p. (J). (gr. k-2). pap. 5.99 (0-14-055766-0, VK0987) Penguin Putnam Bks. for Young Readers.

—Silbale a Willie. 1996. (Illus.). 12.14 (0-606-08872-5) Turtleback Bks.

—The Snowy Day. 2002. (Illus.). (J). 12.40 (0-7587-0027-X) Book Wholesalers, Inc.

—The Snowy Day. 2000. (J). pap. 19.97 incl. audio (0-7366-9215-0); pap. 19.97 incl. audio (0-7366-9215-0) Books on Tape, Inc.

—The Snowy Day. 1974. (Illus.). (J). (gr. k-3). pap., tchr. ed. 33.95 incl. audio (0-670-65402-7); 24.95 incl. audio (0-670-65405-1); 24.95 incl. audio (0-670-65405-1); pap. 15.95 incl. audio (0-670-65408-6) Live Oak Media.

—The Snowy Day. (ps-k). 1996. (Illus.). 28p. (J). bds. 6.99 (0-670-86733-0, Viking Children's Bks.); 1976. (Illus.). 40p. (J). pap. 5.99 (0-14-050182-7, Puffin Bks.); 1972. pap. 0.95 o.p. (0-670-05061-X, Dutton Children's Bks.); 1962. (Illus.). 32p. (J). 15.99 (0-670-65400-0, Viking Children's Bks.) Penguin Putnam Bks. for Young Readers.

—The Snowy Day. 1992. o.p. (0-370-00776-X) Random Hse., Inc.

—The Snowy Day. (Illus.). (J). 9999. pap. 1.95 o.s.i (0-590-03031-0); 1993. 31p. pap. 19.95 (0-590-73323-0); 1993. (SPA., pap. 19.95 o.p. (0-590-72632-3) Scholastic, Inc.

—The Snowy Day. 1962. 3.37 o.p. (0-670-65401-9, Viking) Viking Penguin.

—Whistle for Willie. 2002. (Illus.). (J). 13.19 (0-7587-4003-4) Book Wholesalers, Inc.

—Whistle for Willie. 2000. (J). pap. 19.97 incl. audio (0-7366-9211-8); pap. 19.97 incl. audio (0-7366-9211-8) Books on Tape, Inc.

—Whistle for Willie. 1992. o.p. (1-85681-134-4) MacRae, Julia GBR. *Dist:* Random Hse. of Canada, Ltd., Trafalgar Square.

—Whistle for Willie. (ps-k). 1998. (Illus.). 32p. (J). bds. 7.99 (0-670-88046-9); 1977. (Illus.). 32p. (J). pap. 6.99 (0-14-050202-5, Puffin Bks.); 1969. pap. 0.95 o.p. (0-670-05016-4, Dutton Children's Bks.); 1964. (Illus.). 32p. (J). 15.99 (0-670-76240-7, Viking Children's Bks.) Penguin Putnam Bks. for Young Readers.

—Whistle for Willie. 1977. (Picture Puffin Ser.). (Illus.). 12.14 (0-606-05082-5) Turtleback Bks.

—Whistle for Willie. 1964. 3.37 o.p. (0-670-76241-5, Viking) Viking Penguin.

Kelly, Keith. Basketball Jones. unabr. ed. 1990. (Illus.). 32p. (Orig.). (J). (gr. 1-6). pap. 3.00 (1-56411-114-8) Conquering Bks.

Ketteman, Helen. Not Yet, Yvette. 1995. (J). (ps-3). pap. 4.95 (0-8075-5772-2) Whitman, Albert & Co.

—Not Yet, Yvette. Mathews, Judith, ed. 1992. (Illus.). 24p. (J). (ps-2). lib. bdg. 12.95 o.p. (0-8075-5771-4) Whitman, Albert & Co.

Kirby, Lynn. Dreams of Gold. 1998. (Winning Edge Ser.: Vol. 3). 128p. (J). (gr. 5-9). pap. 5.99 (0-8499-5837-7) Nelson, Tommy.

Klaperman, Libby M. Different Girl. 1969. (Illus.). (J). (gr. 5-9). lib. bdg. 6.87 o.p. (0-87460-127-4) Lion Bks.

Klass, David. Danger Zone. (Point Signature Ser.). 240p. (YA). (gr. 7-12). 1998. mass mkt. 4.99 (0-590-48591-1); 1996. pap. 16.95 (0-590-48590-3) Scholastic, Inc.

—Danger Zone. 1998. (J). 11.04 (0-606-13080-2) Turtleback Bks.

Knight, Ginny. Jessie Helps a Wish. 1991. (Illus.). (J). 3.00 (0-940248-82-4) Guild Pr.

Knox, Jeri A. Introducing Nikki & Kiana. 1993. 82p. (Orig.). (J). (gr. 6-10). pap. text 7.00 (1-880679-03-5) Mountaintop Bks., Inc.

Koertge, Ronald. The Heart of the City. 1998. (J). (gr. 3-7). 144p. pap. 15.95 (0-531-30078-1); 128p. lib. bdg. 16.99 (0-531-33078-8) Scholastic, Inc. (Orchard Bks.).

Koller, Jackie French. A Place to Call Home. 208p. (YA). (gr. 7-12). 1997. mass mkt. 4.99 (0-689-81395-3, Simon Pulse); 1995. 16.00 (0-689-80024-X, Atheneum) Simon & Schuster Children's Publishing.

—A Place to Call Home. 1997. (YA). 11.04 (0-606-11754-7) Turtleback Bks.

Konigsburg, E. L. Jennifer, Hecate, MacBeth, William McKinley & Me, Elizabeth. 117p. (J). (gr. 3-6). pap. 4.99 (0-8072-1417-5, Listening Library) Random Hse. Audio Publishing Group.

—Jennifer, Hecate, Macbeth, William McKinley & Me, Elizabeth. 1999. 144p. mass mkt. 2.99 o.s.i (0-440-22824-7) Bantam Bks.

—Jennifer, Hecate, Macbeth, William McKinley & Me, Elizabeth. 1984. 128p. (gr. 4-7). pap. text 5.50 (0-440-44162-5, Yearling) Random Hse. Children's Bks.

—Jennifer, Hecate, Macbeth, William McKinley & Me, Elizabeth. 1971. (Illus.). 128p. (J). (gr. 3-5). 16.95 (0-689-30007-7, Atheneum) Simon & Schuster Children's Publishing.

—Jennifer, Hecate, Macbeth, William McKinley & Me, Elizabeth. 1985. (J). 11.55 (0-606-03672-5) Turtleback Bks.

—Jennifer, Hecate, Macbeth, William Mckinley & Me, Elizabeth. 2001. (Illus.). 128p. (J). pap. 4.99 (0-689-84625-8, Aladdin) Simon & Schuster Children's Publishing.

—Jennifer, Hecate, Macbeth, William McKinley & Me, Elizabeth. l.t. ed. 1989. (J). (gr. 3-7). reprint ed. lib. bdg. 16.95 o.s.i (1-55736-143-6, Cornerstone Bks.) Pages, Inc.

—Jennifer, Hecate, MacBeth, William McKinley & Me, Elizabeth. unabr. ed. 1998. 177p. (J). (gr. 3-6). pap. 28.00 incl. audio (0-8072-8001-1, YA963SP, Listening Library) Random Hse. Audio Publishing Group.

Kroll, Virginia K. Faraway Drums. 1998. (Illus.). 32p. (J). (ps-3). 14.95 o.p. (0-316-50449-1) Little Brown & Co.

Kroll, Virginia L. Africa Brothers & Sisters. (Illus.). 32p. (J). (ps-2). 1998. pap. 5.99 o.s.i (0-689-81816-5, Aladdin); 1993. lib. bdg. 15.00 (0-02-751166-9, Simon & Schuster Children's Publishing) Simon & Schuster Children's Publishing.

—Africa Brothers & Sisters. 1998. 12.14 (0-606-12870-0) Turtleback Bks.

—Can You Dance, Dalila? 1996. (Illus.). 32p. (J). (ps-3). 15.00 (0-689-80551-9, Simon & Schuster Children's Publishing) Simon & Schuster Children's Publishing.

—Masai & I. 32p. (J). (ps-2). 1997. pap. 5.99 (0-689-80454-7, Aladdin); 1992. (Illus.). lib. bdg. 16.00 (0-02-751165-0, Simon & Schuster Children's Publishing) Simon & Schuster Children's Publishing.

—Masai & I. 1997. 12.14 (0-606-11601-X) Turtleback Bks.

—Pink Paper Swans. 1994. (Illus.). 32p. (J). (gr. k-5). 15.00 (0-8028-5081-2, Eerdmans Bks For Young Readers) Eerdmans, William B. Publishing Co.

—Sweet Magnolia. 1995. (Illus.). 32p. (J). (ps-3). 15.95 (0-88106-415-7, Talewinds); pap. 6.95 (0-88106-414-9, Talewinds); lib. bdg. 15.88 o.p. (0-88106-416-5) Charlesbridge Publishing, Inc.

—Sweet Magnolia. 1995. (J). 13.10 (0-606-09919-0) Turtleback Bks.

—Wood-Hoopoe Willie. (Illus.). 32p. (J). (ps-3). 1995. pap. 6.95 (0-88106-408-4, Talewinds); 1993. 14.95 (0-88106-409-2, Talewinds); 1993. lib. bdg. 15.88 o.p. (0-88106-410-6) Charlesbridge Publishing, Inc.

—Wood-Hoopoe Willie. 1992. (J). 13.10 (0-606-08396-0) Turtleback Bks.

Kuklin, Susan & Byrd, Donald. Harlem Nutcracker. 2001. (Illus.). 48p. (J). 19.99 (0-7868-0633-8) Disney Pr.

Kurtz, Jane. Faraway Home. 2000. (Illus.). 32p. (J). (gr. 1-5). 16.00 (0-15-200036-4, Gulliver Bks.) Harcourt Children's Bks.

—The Storyteller's Beads. Van Doren, Liz, ed. 1998. (Illus.). 160p. (J). (gr. 3-7). 15.00 (0-15-201074-2, Gulliver Bks.) Harcourt Children's Bks.

Ladwig, Tim, illus. Psalm Twenty-Three. 1997. (J). (ps-3). 40p. 16.00 (0-8028-5160-6); 32p. pap. 8.00 (0-8028-5163-0) Eerdmans, William B. Publishing Co. (Eerdmans Bks For Young Readers).

Lasky, Kathryn. True North: A Novel of the Underground Railroad. 208p. 1998. (J). (gr. 5-9). mass mkt. 4.99 (0-590-20524-2); 1996. (YA). (gr. 7 up). pap. 15.95 (0-590-20523-4) Scholastic, Inc. (Blue Sky Pr., The).

—True North: A Novel of the Underground Railroad. 1998. (J). 11.04 (0-606-13874-9) Turtleback Bks.

Lawlor, Laurie. Old Crump: The True Story of a Trip West. 2002. (Illus.). 32p. (J). (gr. 2-4). tchr. ed. 16.95 (0-8234-1608-9) Holiday Hse., Inc.

Lee, Spike & Lee, Tonya Lewis. Please, Baby, Please. 2002. (Illus.). 32p. (J). 16.95 (0-689-83233-8, Simon & Schuster Children's Publishing) Simon & Schuster Children's Publishing.

Lehne, Judith Logan. When the Ragman Sings. 1993. 128p. (J). (gr. 3-7). 14.00 (0-06-023316-8); lib. bdg. 13.89 (0-06-023317-6) HarperCollins Children's Bk. Group.

Leigh, Peter. A Different Kind of Hero. 1998. (Livewire Kaleidoscope Ser.). 44 p. (J). (0-89061-620-5) McGraw-Hill/Contemporary.

—A Different Kind of Hero: Livewire Fiction. 2003. (Illus.). 48p. (J). pap. text (0-340-69697-4) Hodder Arnold GBR. *Dist:* Oxford Univ. Pr., Inc.

Leonard, Marcia. My Camp-Out. 1999. (Real Kids Readers Ser.). (Illus.). 32p. (J). (ps-1). 18.90 (0-7613-2052-0); pap. 4.99 (0-7613-2077-6) Millbrook Pr., Inc.

—My Camp-Out. 1999. (J). 10.14 (0-606-19165-8) Turtleback Bks.

—My Camp-Out. 1999. E-Book (1-58824-728-7); E-Book (1-58824-811-9); E-Book (1-58824-480-6) ipicturebooks, LLC.

Lester, Julius. Black Cowboy Wild Horses. 1998. (Illus.). 32p. (J). (gr. k-3). 18.99 (0-8037-1787-3, Dial Bks. for Young Readers) Penguin Putnam Bks. for Young Readers.

—The Long Journey Home: Stories from Black History. annuals 160p. 1998. (YA). (gr. 5-9). pap. 5.99 (0-14-038981-4, Puffin Bks.); 1985. (J). (gr. 6 up). 14.99 o.s.i (0-8037-4953-8, Dial Bks. for Young Readers) Penguin Putnam Bks. for Young Readers.

—The Long Journey Home: Stories from Black History. 1988. 160p. (J). (gr. 7-9). reprint ed. mass mkt. 3.50 o.p. (0-590-41433-X, Scholastic Paperbacks) Scholastic, Inc.

—The Long Journey Home: Stories from Black History. 1998. (J). 11.04 (0-606-12987-1) Turtleback Bks.

—The Man Who Was Horse. 1998. (Illus.). 40p. (J). (gr. k-3). 16.89 o.s.i (0-8037-1788-1, Dial Bks. for Young Readers) Penguin Putnam Bks. for Young Readers.

—This Strange New Feeling. 1982. 16p. (J). (gr. 7 up). 14.95 o.p. (*0-8037-8491-0*, Dial Bks. for Young Readers) Penguin Putnam Bks. for Young Readers.

—This Strange New Feeling. 1985. (gr. 7 up). 172p. (YA). pap. 4.50 (*0-590-44047-0*); 164p. (J). reprint ed. 1.25 o.p. (*0-590-40681-7*, Scholastic Paperbacks); 164p. (J). reprint ed. pap. 2.50 o.p. (*0-590-41061-X*, Scholastic Paperbacks) Scholastic, Inc.

—What a Truly Cool World! 1997. (Illus.). 40p. (J). (ps-2). pap. 15.95 (*0-590-86468-8*) Scholastic, Inc.

—Why Heaven Is Far Away. 2002. (Illus.). 40p. (J). (gr. 1-3). pap. 16.95 (*0-439-17871-1*, Scholastic Pr.) Scholastic, Inc.

Levy, Marilyn. Run for Your Life. 1996. (Illus.). 224p. (YA). (gr. 7-7). tchr. ed. 15.00 (*0-395-74520-9*) Houghton Mifflin Co.

—Run for Your Life. 1997. 224p. (J). (gr. 5-9). pap. 5.99 (*0-698-11608-9*, PaperStar) Penguin Putnam Bks. for Young Readers.

—Run for Your Life. 1997. 12.04 (*0-606-12802-6*) Turtleback Bks.

Lewis, Zoe. Keisha Discovers Harlem. 1998. (Magic Attic Club Ser.). (Illus.). 80p. (gr. 2-6). 18.90 (*1-57513-144-7*, Magic Attic Pr.) Millbrook Pr., Inc.

—Keisha Discovers Harlem. Bodnar, Judit, ed. 1998. (Magic Attic Club Ser.). (Illus.). 80p. (gr. 2-6). (J). 13.95 (*1-57513-130-7*); pap. 5.95 o.p. (*1-57513-129-3*) Millbrook Pr., Inc. (Magic Attic Pr.).

—Keisha Discovers Harlem. 1998. (Magic Attic Club Ser.). (J). (gr. 2-6). 12.10 (*0-606-16855-9*) Turtleback Bks.

Lexau, Joan M. Me Day. (Illus.). (J). (ps-3). 1985. 7.45 o.p. (*0-8037-5573-2*); 1971. 4.95 o.p. (*0-8037-5572-4*) Penguin Putnam Bks. for Young Readers. (Dial Bks. for Young Readers).

—Striped Ice Cream. 1968. (Illus.). 96p. (J). (gr. k-3). 15.89 (*0-397-31047-1*) HarperCollins Children's Bk. Group.

—Striped Ice Cream. 1968. (J). (gr. 1-6). 12.89 o.p. (*0-397-31046-3*) HarperCollins Pubs.

—Striped Ice Cream. (J). (gr. 2-5). 1992. 128p. 3.99 (*0-590-45729-2*, Scholastic Paperbacks); 1985. 128p. pap. 2.75 o.p. (*0-590-42903-5*); 1971. (Illus.). pap. 2.50 o.p. (*0-590-41307-4*) Scholastic, Inc.

—Striped Ice Cream. 1968. (J). 10.04 (*0-606-04060-9*) Turtleback Bks.

Liddell, Janice. Imani & the Flying Africans. 1993. (Illus.). 32p. (J). (gr. 3-8). 14.95 (*0-86543-365-8*); (ps-3). pap. 6.95 (*0-86543-366-6*) Africa World Pr.

Lieurance, Suzanne. Shoelaces. 2000. (Rookie Readers Ser.). (Illus.). 32p. (J). (gr. 1-2). pap. 4.95 (*0-516-26546-6*); lib. bdg. 19.00 (*0-516-21613-9*) Scholastic Library Publishing. (Children's Pr.).

Lindbergh, Reeve. Nobody Owns the Sky: The Story of "Brave Bessie" Coleman. (Illus.). 32p. (J). (gr. 1-4). 1996. 15.99 o.s.i (*1-56402-533-0*); 1998. reprint ed. bds. 5.99 (*0-7636-0361-9*) Candlewick Pr.

—Nobody Owns the Sky: The Story of "Brave Bessie" Coleman. 1998. (J). 12.14 (*0-606-13668-1*) Turtleback Bks.

Lindsey, Kathleen D. Sweet Potato Pie. 2003. (Illus.). (J). 16.95 (*1-58430-061-2*) Lee & Low Bks., Inc.

Lipsyte, Robert. The Brave. (Charlotte Zolotow Bk.). (gr. 7 up). 1993. 240p. (J). pap. 5.99 (*0-06-447079-2*, Harper Trophy); 1991. 208p. (YA). 15.00 o.p. (*0-06-023915-8*); 1991. 208p. (YA). lib. bdg. 14.89 o.p. (*0-06-023916-6*) HarperCollins Children's Bk. Group.

—Brave. 1993. (J). 11.00 (*0-606-02539-1*) Turtleback Bks.

—The Contender. 1969. (YA). (gr. 7 up). pap. 2.50 o.p. (*0-553-24071-4*) Bantam Bks.

—The Contender. (Trophy Bk.). 1996. 190p. (YA). pap. 2.25 o.p. (*0-06-447152-7*); 1987. (YA). 2.95 o.p. (*0-694-05602-2*, Harper Festival); 1987. 240p. (J). (gr. 7 up). pap. 5.99 (*0-06-447039-3*, Harper Trophy); 1967. 192p. (J). (gr. 7 up). lib. bdg. 16.89 (*0-06-023920-4*); 1967. 190p. (YA). (gr. 7 up). pap. 15.00 o.p. (*0-06-023919-0*) HarperCollins Children's Bk. Group.

—The Contender. l.t. ed. 1987. 232p. (J). (gr. 2-7). reprint ed. lib. bdg. 16.95 o.s.i (*1-55736-024-3*, Cornerstone Bks.) Pages, Inc.

—The Contender. 1987. (YA). 11.00 (*0-606-02525-1*) Turtleback Bks.

Littlesugar, Amy. Jonkonnu: A Story from the Sketch-book of Winslow Homer. 1997. (Illus.). 32p. (J). (ps-3). 15.95 o.s.i (*0-399-22831-4*, Philomel) Penguin Putnam Bks. for Young Readers.

—Tree of Hope. 1999. (Illus.). 40p. (J). (ps-3). 16.99 o.s.i (*0-399-23300-8*, Philomel) Penguin Putnam Bks. for Young Readers.

—The Tree of Hope. 2001. (Illus.). 40p. (J). pap. 6.99 (*0-698-11903-7*, Puffin Bks.) Penguin Putnam Bks. for Young Readers.

Littleton, Mark. Friends No Matter What. 1995. (Crista Chronicles Ser.: No. 6). (Orig.). (YA). mass mkt. 3.99 o.p. (*1-56507-256-1*) Harvest Hse. Pubs.

Littleton, Mark R. Trouble down the Creek. Norton, LoraBeth, ed. 1994. 208p. (J). (gr. 4-6). pap. 5.99 (*0-7814-0082-1*) Cook Communications Ministries.

Littlewood, Karin, illus. I Say a Little Prayer for You. 2002. 32p. (J). pap. 16.95 (*0-439-29658-7*, Chicken Hse., The) Scholastic, Inc.

Lorbiecki, Marybeth. Just One Flick of a Finger. 1996. (Illus.). (J). (gr. 3 up). 40p. 14.99 o.s.i (*0-8037-1948-5*); 36p. 14.89 o.s.i (*0-8037-1949-3*) Penguin Putnam Bks. for Young Readers. (Dial Bks. for Young Readers).

—Sister Anne's Hands. 1998. (Illus.). 40p. (J). (ps-3). 16.99 (*0-8037-2038-6*); 15.89 o.s.i (*0-8037-2039-4*) Penguin Putnam Bks. for Young Readers. (Dial Bks. for Young Readers).

Lotz, Karen E. Can't Sit Still. (Picture Puffins Ser.). (Illus.). (J). (ps-3). 1998. 40p. pap. 5.99 o.p. (*0-14-056361-X*); 1993. 480p. 13.99 o.p. (*0-525-45066-1*, Dutton Children's Bks.) Penguin Putnam Bks. for Young Readers.

Love, Judith DuFour, illus. The Missing Pet. 1998. pap. 5.18 (*0-8172-7254-2*) Raintree Pubs.

Lukas, Catherine. Hello, Santa! 2003. (Little Bill Ser.). (Illus.). 20p. (J). 7.99 (*0-689-85850-7*, Simon Spotlight/Nickelodeon) Simon & Schuster Children's Publishing.

—Little Bill Mothers Day. 2003. (Little Bill Ser.). (Illus.). 32p. (J). pap. 5.99 (*0-689-85241-X*, Simon Spotlight/Nickelodeon) Simon & Schuster Children's Publishing.

Lutz, Norma Jean. Escape from Slavery: A Family's Fight for Freedom. 1999. (American Adventure Ser.: No. 16). 144p. (J). (gr. 3-7). lib. bdg. 15.95 (*0-7910-5590-6*) Chelsea Hse. Pubs.

Lynch, Marcia. United in Freedom. 2000. (Cover-to-Cover Bks.). (Illus.). 92p. (J). (*0-7807-9068-5*); pap. (*0-7891-5102-2*) Perfection Learning Corp.

Lyons, Mary E. Letters from a Slave Girl: The Story of Harriet Jacobs. 176p. 1996. (J). (gr. 4-7). mass mkt. 4.99 (*0-689-80015-0*, Simon Pulse); 1992. (Illus.). (YA). (gr. 7 up). 16.00 (*0-684-19446-5*, Atheneum) Simon & Schuster Children's Publishing.

—Letters from a Slave Girl: The Story of Harriet Jacobs. 1996. 11.04 (*0-606-09551-9*) Turtleback Bks.

—The Poison Palace. 1997. (Illus.). 160p. (J). (gr. 7 up). 16.00 (*0-689-81146-2*, Atheneum) Simon & Schuster Children's Publishing.

MacKinnon, Bernie. The Meantime. 1992. (YA). pap. 4.95 o.p. (*0-395-61622-0*); 1984. 192p. (J). (gr. 7 up). 13.95 o.p. (*0-395-35387-4*) Houghton Mifflin Co.

Magnet Magic. 1991. (Illus.). (J). (ps-2). pap. 5.10 (*0-8136-5693-1*); lib. bdg. 7.95 (*0-8136-5193-X*) Modern Curriculum Pr.

Mahony, Mary. Stand Tall, Harry. Pasternack, Susan, ed. 2002. (Illus.). 200p. (J). (gr. 4). pap. 14.95 (*0-9658879-2-8*) Redding Pr.

Manson, William R. Bay. 2nd ed. 1997. 197p. (YA). (gr. 6-12). pap. 8.00 (*0-9660099-0-8*) CC Pubs.

Marino, Jan. The Day That Elvis Came to Town. 1993. 208p. (J). (gr. 5). reprint ed. pap. 3.50 (*0-380-71672-0*, Avon Bks.) Morrow/Avon.

—Day That Elvis Came to Town, Vol. 1. 1991. (YA). (gr. 9-12). 15.95 o.p. (*0-316-54618-6*) Little Brown & Co.

Markman, Michael. The Path: An Adventure in African History. Gift, Wendy, ed. 1997. (Illus.). 32p. (J). (gr. 1-5). 7.95 (*1-881316-19-X*); (gr. 2-9). pap. 8.95 (*1-881316-35-1*) A & B Distributors & Pubs. Group.

Marshall, Catherine. Family Secrets. 1996. (Christy Fiction Ser.: No. 8). (Illus.). 128p. (Orig.). (J). (gr. 4-8). mass mkt. 4.99 (*0-8499-3959-3*) Nelson, Tommy.

Marshall, Felicia. Willa Mae Johnson & the Fayette County Market. 1998. (J). 16.00 (*0-689-80855-0*, Atheneum) Simon & Schuster Children's Publishing.

Martin, Ann M. Belle Teal. 2001. 256p. (YA). (gr. 5-9). pap. 15.95 (*0-439-09823-8*) Scholastic, Inc.

—Claudia & Crazy Peaches. (Baby-Sitters Club Ser.: No. 78). (J). (gr. 3-7). 1999. 138p. pap. 3.99 (*0-590-92610-1*); 1994. 192p. mass mkt. 3.50 (*0-590-48222-X*) Scholastic, Inc.

—Claudia & Crazy Peaches. 1994. (Baby-Sitters Club Ser.: No. 78). (J). (gr. 3-7). 10.04 (*0-606-06204-1*) Turtleback Bks.

—Claudia & Crazy Peaches. 1995. (Baby-Sitters Club Ser.: No. 78). (J). (gr. 3-7). 7.98 (*1-57042-367-9*) Warner Bks., Inc.

—Claudia & Mean Janine. l.t. ed. 1988. (Baby-Sitters Club Ser.: No. 7). 145p. (J). (gr. 3-7). reprint ed. 9.50 o.p. (*0-942545-68-0*); lib. bdg. 10.50 o.p. (*0-942545-78-8*) Grey Castle Pr.

—Claudia & Mean Janine. (Baby-Sitters Club Ser.: No. 7). (J). (gr. 3-7). 1995. mass mkt. 3.99 (*0-590-25162-7*); 1987. 160p. pap. 2.75 o.p. (*0-590-41041-5*, Scholastic Paperbacks); 1987. 192p. mass mkt. 3.50 (*0-590-43719-4*) Scholastic, Inc.

—Claudia & Mean Janine. 1995. (Baby-Sitters Club Ser.: No. 7). 176p. (J). (gr. 3-7). lib. bdg. 21.27 o.p. (*0-8368-1320-0*) Stevens, Gareth Inc.

—Claudia & Mean Janine. 1987. (Baby-Sitters Club Ser.: No. 7). (J). (gr. 3-7). 10.04 (*0-606-00551-X*) Turtleback Bks.

—Claudia & the Bad Joke. (Baby-Sitters Club Ser.: No. 19). (J). (gr. 3-7). 1996. mass mkt. 3.99 (*0-590-60671-9*); 1988. 192p. mass mkt. 3.50 (*0-590-43510-8*) Scholastic, Inc.

—Claudia & the Bad Joke. l.t. ed. 1993. (Baby-Sitters Club Ser.: No. 19). 176p. (J). (gr. 3-7). lib. bdg. 19.93 o.p. (*0-8368-1023-6*) Stevens, Gareth Inc.

—Claudia & the Bad Joke. 1988. (Baby-Sitters Club Ser.: No. 19). (J). (gr. 3-7). 10.04 (*0-606-04084-6*) Turtleback Bks.

—Claudia & the Clue in the Photograph. 1994. (Baby-Sitters Club Mystery Ser.: No. 16). 176p. (J). (gr. 3-7). mass mkt. 3.99 (*0-590-47054-X*) Scholastic, Inc.

—Claudia & the Clue in the Photograph. 1994. (Baby-Sitters Club Mystery Ser.: No. 16). (J). (gr. 3-7). 10.04 (*0-606-06208-4*) Turtleback Bks.

—Claudia & the First Thanksgiving. 1995. (Baby-Sitters Club Ser.: No. 91). (J). (gr. 3-7). mass mkt. 3.50 (*0-590-22875-7*) Scholastic, Inc.

—Claudia & the First Thanksgiving. 1995. (Baby-Sitters Club Ser.: No. 91). (J). (gr. 3-7). 8.60 o.p. (*0-606-08480-0*) Turtleback Bks.

—Claudia & the Genius of Elm Street. 1996. (Baby-Sitters Club Ser.: No. 49). (J). (gr. 3-7). lib. bdg. 21.27 o.p. (*0-8368-1573-4*) Stevens, Gareth Inc.

—Claudia & the Genius of Elm Street. 1991. (Baby-Sitters Club Ser.: No. 49). (J). (gr. 3-7). 9.30 (*0-606-00357-6*) Turtleback Bks.

—Claudia & the Great Search. 1990. (Baby-Sitters Club Ser.: No. 33). 192p. (J). (gr. 3-7). mass mkt. 3.25 (*0-590-42495-5*); mass mkt. 3.99 (*0-590-73190-4*) Scholastic, Inc.

—Claudia & the Great Search. l.t. ed. 1995. (Baby-Sitters Club Ser.: No. 33). 147p. (J). (gr. 3-7). lib. bdg. 21.27 o.p. (*0-8368-1413-4*) Stevens, Gareth Inc.

—Claudia & the Great Search. 1990. (Baby-Sitters Club Ser.: No. 33). (J). (gr. 3-7). 10.04 (*0-606-03158-8*) Turtleback Bks.

—Claudia & the Lighthouse Ghost. 1996. (Baby-Sitters Club Mystery Ser.: No. 27). 154p. (J). (gr. 3-7). mass mkt. 3.99 (*0-590-69175-9*) Scholastic, Inc.

—Claudia & the Lighthouse Ghost. 1996. (Baby-Sitters Club Mystery Ser.: No. 27). (J). (gr. 3-7). 10.04 (*0-606-10134-9*) Turtleback Bks.

—Claudia & the Little Liar. 1999. (Baby-Sitters Club Ser.: No. 128). 114p. (J). (gr. 3-7). mass mkt. 4.50 (*0-590-50351-0*) Scholastic, Inc.

—Claudia & the Middle School Mystery. 1991. (Baby-Sitters Club Ser.: No. 40). 192p. (J). (gr. 3-7). mass mkt. 3.25 (*0-590-44082-9*) Scholastic, Inc.

—Claudia & the Middle School Mystery. l.t. ed. 1995. (Baby-Sitters Club Ser.: No. 40). 176p. (J). (gr. 3-7). lib. bdg. 21.27 o.p. (*0-8368-1420-7*) Stevens, Gareth Inc.

—Claudia & the Middle School Mystery. 1991. (Baby-Sitters Club Ser.: No. 40). (J). (gr. 3-7). 10.04 (*0-606-04637-2*) Turtleback Bks.

—Claudia & the Mystery at the Museum. 1993. (Baby-Sitters Club Mystery Ser.: No. 11). 176p. (J). (gr. 3-7). mass mkt. 3.50 (*0-590-47049-3*) Scholastic, Inc.

—Claudia & the Mystery at the Museum. 1993. (Baby-Sitters Club Mystery Ser.: No. 11). (J). (gr. 3-7). 9.55 (*0-606-05142-2*) Turtleback Bks.

—Claudia & the Mystery in the Painting. 1997. (Baby-Sitters Club Mystery Ser.: No. 32). 144p. (J). (gr. 3-7). mass mkt. 3.99 (*0-590-05972-6*) Scholastic, Inc.

—Claudia & the Mystery in the Painting. 1997. (Baby-Sitters Club Mystery Ser.: No. 32). (J). (gr. 3-7). 10.04 (*0-606-11076-3*) Turtleback Bks.

—Claudia & the New Girl. (Baby-Sitters Club Ser.: No. 12). (J). (gr. 3-7). 1988. 160p. pap. 2.75 o.p. (*0-590-41126-8*, Scholastic Paperbacks); 1988. 192p. mass mkt. 3.50 (*0-590-43721-6*); 1996. 160p. mass mkt. 3.99 (*0-590-25167-8*) Scholastic, Inc.

—Claudia & the New Girl. l.t. ed. 1993. (Baby-Sitters Club Ser.: No. 12). 176p. (J). (gr. 3-7). lib. bdg. 21.27 o.p. (*0-8368-1016-3*) Stevens, Gareth Inc.

—Claudia & the New Girl. 1989. (Baby-Sitters Club Ser.: No. 12). (J). (gr. 3-7). 10.04 (*0-606-03758-6*) Turtleback Bks.

—Claudia & the Perfect Boy. 1994. (Baby-Sitters Club Ser.: No. 71). 192p. (J). (gr. 3-7). mass mkt. 3.99 (*0-590-47009-4*) Scholastic, Inc.

—Claudia & the Perfect Boy. 1994. (Baby-Sitters Club Ser.: No. 71). (J). (gr. 3-7). 10.04 (*0-606-05736-6*) Turtleback Bks.

—Claudia & the Phantom Phone Calls. l.t. ed. 1988. (Baby-Sitters Club Ser.: No. 2). 153p. (J). (gr. 3-7). reprint ed. 9.50 o.p. (*0-942545-63-X*); lib. bdg. 10.50 o.p. (*0-942545-73-7*) Grey Castle Pr.

—Claudia & the Phantom Phone Calls. (Baby-Sitters Club Ser.: No. 2). (J). (gr. 3-7). 1986. 160p. mass mkt. 3.50 (*0-590-43513-2*); 1995. 192p. mass mkt. 3.99 (*0-590-22763-7*) Scholastic, Inc.

—Claudia & the Phantom Phone Calls. l.t. ed. 1995. (Baby-Sitters Club Ser.: No. 2). 153p. (J). (gr. 3-5). lib. bdg. 21.27 o.p. (*0-8368-1315-4*) Stevens, Gareth Inc.

—Claudia & the Phantom Phone Calls. 1986. (Baby-Sitters Club Ser.: No. 2). (J). (gr. 3-7). 10.04 (*0-606-03083-2*) Turtleback Bks.

—Claudia & the Recipe for Danger. 1995. (Baby-Sitters Club Mystery Ser.: No. 21). 176p. (J). (gr. 3-7). mass mkt. 3.50 (*0-590-48310-2*) Scholastic, Inc.

—Claudia & the Recipe for Danger. 1995. (Baby-Sitters Club Mystery Ser.: No. 21). (J). (gr. 3-7). 9.55 (*0-606-07235-7*) Turtleback Bks.

—Claudia & the Sad Good-Bye. (Baby-Sitters Club Ser.: No. 26). (J). (gr. 3-7). 1997. mass mkt. 3.99 (*0-590-67394-7*); 1989. 192p. mass mkt. 3.50 (*0-590-42503-X*) Scholastic, Inc.

—Claudia & the Sad Good-Bye. l.t. ed. 1994. (Baby-Sitters Club Ser.: No. 26). 176p. (J). (gr. 3-7). lib. bdg. 21.27 o.p. (*0-8368-1247-6*) Stevens, Gareth Inc.

—Claudia & the Sad Good-Bye. 1989. (Baby-Sitters Club Ser.: No. 26). (J). (gr. 3-7). 10.04 (*0-606-04187-7*) Turtleback Bks.

—Claudia & the Terrible Truth. 1998. (Baby-Sitters Club Ser.: No. 117). (J). (gr. 3-7). mass mkt. 4.50 (*0-590-05995-5*, Scholastic Paperbacks) Scholastic, Inc.

—Claudia & the World's Cutest Baby. 1996. (Baby-Sitters Club Ser.: No. 97). (J). (gr. 3-7). mass mkt. 3.99 (*0-590-22881-1*) Scholastic, Inc.

—Claudia & the World's Cutest Baby. 1996. (Baby-Sitters Club Ser.: No. 97). (J). (gr. 3-7). 9.09 o.p. (*0-606-09033-9*) Turtleback Bks.

—Claudia Kishi, Live from WSTO! 1995. (Baby-Sitters Club Ser.: No. 85). (J). (gr. 3-7). pap. text 3.99 (*0-590-94784-2*) Scholastic, Inc.

—Claudia, Queen of the Seventh Grade. 1997. (Baby-Sitters Club Ser.: No. 106). (J). (gr. 3-7). mass mkt. 3.99 (*0-590-69212-7*) Scholastic, Inc.

—Jessi & the Dance School Phantom. 1996. (Baby-Sitters Club Ser.: No. 42). 144p. (J). (gr. 3-7). lib. bdg. 21.27 o.p. (*0-8368-1566-1*) Stevens, Gareth Inc.

—Jessi's Secret Language. l.t. ed. 1993. (Baby-Sitters Club Ser.: No. 16). 176p. (J). (gr. 3-7). lib. bdg. 21.27 o.p. (*0-8368-1020-1*) Stevens, Gareth Inc.

—Jessi's Wish. 1991. (Baby-Sitters Club Ser.: No. 48). 192p. (J). (gr. 3-7). mass mkt. 3.50 (*0-590-43571-X*) Scholastic, Inc.

—Jessi's Wish. 1996. (Baby-Sitters Club Ser.: No. 48). 144p. (J). (gr. 3-7). lib. bdg. 21.27 o.p. (*0-8368-1572-6*) Stevens, Gareth Inc.

—Kristy & Mr. Mom. 1995. (Baby-Sitters Club Ser.: No. 81). 192p. (J). (gr. 3-7). mass mkt. 3.50 (*0-590-48225-4*) Scholastic, Inc.

—Kristy & Mr. Mom. 1995. (Baby-Sitters Club Ser.: No. 81). (J). (gr. 3-7). 8.60 (*0-606-07223-3*) Turtleback Bks.

—Kristy & Mr. Mom. 1995. (Baby-Sitters Club Ser.: No. 81). (J). (gr. 3-7). 7.98 (*1-57042-368-7*) Warner Bks., Inc.

—Kristy & the Baby Parade. 1991. (Baby-Sitters Club Ser.: No. 45). 192p. (J). (gr. 3-7). mass mkt. 3.50 (*0-590-43574-4*) Scholastic, Inc.

—Kristy & the Baby Parade. 1996. (Baby-Sitters Club Ser.: No. 45). 176p. (J). (gr. 3-7). lib. bdg. 21.27 o.p. (*0-8368-1569-6*) Stevens, Gareth Inc.

—Kristy & the Baby Parade. 1991. (Baby-Sitters Club Ser.: No. 45). (J). (gr. 3-7). 9.55 (*0-606-04960-6*) Turtleback Bks.

—Kristy & the Cat Burglar. 1998. (Baby-Sitters Club Mystery Ser.: No. 36). (J). (gr. 3-7). mass mkt. 4.50 (*0-590-05976-9*, Scholastic Paperbacks) Scholastic, Inc.

—Kristy & the Copycat. 1994. (Baby-Sitters Club Ser.: No. 74). 192p. (J). (gr. 3-7). mass mkt. 3.99 (*0-590-47012-4*) Scholastic, Inc.

—Kristy & the Copycat. 1994. (Baby-Sitters Club Ser.: No. 74). (J). (gr. 3-7). 9.09 o.p. (*0-606-06200-9*) Turtleback Bks.

—Kristy & the Dirty Diapers. 1995. (Baby-Sitters Club Ser.: No. 89). 192p. (gr. 3-7). mass mkt. 3.50 (*0-590-22873-0*) Scholastic, Inc.

—Kristy & the Dirty Diapers. 1995. (Baby-Sitters Club Ser.: No. 89). (J). (gr. 3-7). 8.60 o.p. (*0-606-07231-4*) Turtleback Bks.

—Kristy & the Haunted Mansion. 1993. (Baby-Sitters Club Mystery Ser.: No. 9). 176p. (J). (gr. 3-7). mass mkt. 3.50 (*0-590-44958-3*) Scholastic, Inc.

—Kristy & the Haunted Mansion. 1993. (Baby-Sitters Club Mystery Ser.: No. 9). (J). (gr. 3-7). 8.60 o.p. (*0-606-05144-9*) Turtleback Bks.

—Kristy & the Middle School Vandal. 1996. (Baby-Sitters Club Mystery Ser.: No. 25). (J). (gr. 3-7). mass mkt. 3.99 (*0-590-22869-2*) Scholastic, Inc.

—Kristy & the Middle School Vandal. 1996. (Baby-Sitters Club Mystery Ser.: No. 25). (J). (gr. 3-7). 9.09 o.p. (*0-606-09039-8*) Turtleback Bks.

—Kristy & the Missing Child. 1992. (Baby-Sitters Club Mystery Ser.: No. 4). 176p. (J). (gr. 3-7). mass mkt. 3.99 (*0-590-44800-5*) Scholastic, Inc.

—Kristy & the Missing Child. 1992. (Baby-Sitters Club Mystery Ser.: No. 4). (J). (gr. 3-7). 9.55 (*0-606-01879-4*) Turtleback Bks.

—Kristy & the Missing Fortune. 1995. (Baby-Sitters Club Mystery Ser.: No. 19). 176p. (J). (gr. 3-7). mass mkt. 3.50 (*0-590-48234-3*) Scholastic, Inc.

—Kristy & the Missing Fortune. 1995. (Baby-Sitters Club Mystery Ser.: No. 19). (J). (gr. 3-7). 8.60 (*0-606-07233-0*) Turtleback Bks.

—Kristy & the Mother's Day Surprise. (Baby-Sitters Club Ser.: No. 24). (J). (gr. 3-7). 1997. 160p. mass mkt. 3.99 (*0-590-67392-0*); 1989. 192p. pap. 3.50 (*0-590-43506-X*); 1989. mass mkt. 2.75 o.p. (*0-590-42002-X*) Scholastic, Inc.

—Kristy & the Mother's Day Surprise. l.t. ed. 1994. (Baby-Sitters Club Ser.: No. 24). 176p. (J). (gr. 3-7). lib. bdg. 21.27 o.p. (*0-8368-1245-X*) Stevens, Gareth Inc.

—Kristy & the Mother's Day Surprise. 1989. (Baby-Sitters Club Ser.: No. 24). (J). (gr. 3-7). 10.04 (*0-606-04260-1*) Turtleback Bks.

—Kristy & the Mystery Train. 1997. (Baby-Sitters Club Mystery Ser.: No. 30). 160p. (J). (gr. 3-7). mass mkt. 3.99 (*0-590-69178-3*, Scholastic Paperbacks) Scholastic, Inc.

—Kristy & the Mystery Train. 1997. (Baby-Sitters Club Mystery Ser.: No. 30). (J). (gr. 3-7). 10.04 (*0-606-11074-7*) Turtleback Bks.

—Kristy & the Secret of Susan. 1990. (Baby-Sitters Club Ser.: No. 32). 192p. (J). (gr. 3-7). mass mkt. 3.50 (*0-590-42496-3*) Scholastic, Inc.

—Kristy & the Secret of Susan. 1995. (Baby-Sitters Club Ser.: No. 32). 144p. (J). (gr. 3-7). lib. bdg. 21.27 o.p. (*0-8368-1412-6*) Stevens, Gareth Inc.

—Kristy & the Secret of Susan. 1990. (Baby-Sitters Club Ser.: No. 32). (J). (gr. 3-7). 10.04 (*0-606-04462-0*) Turtleback Bks.

—Kristy & the Sister War. 1997. (Baby-Sitters Club Ser.: No. 112). 160p. (J). (gr. 3-7). mass mkt. 3.99 (*0-590-05990-4*) Scholastic, Inc.

—Kristy & the Sister War. 1997. (Baby-Sitters Club Ser.: No. 112). (J). (gr. 3-7). 10.04 (*0-606-11072-0*) Turtleback Bks.

—Kristy & the Snobs. (Baby-Sitters Club Ser.: No. 11). (J). (gr. 3-7). 1996. 176p. mass mkt. 3.99 (*0-590-25166-X*); 1988. 160p. pap. 2.75 o.p. (*0-590-41125-X*, Scholastic Paperbacks); 1988. 192p. mass mkt. 3.50 (*0-590-43660-0*) Scholastic, Inc.

—Kristy & the Snobs. l.t. ed. 1993. (Baby-Sitters Club Ser.: No. 11). 176p. (J). (gr. 3-7). lib. bdg. 19.93 o.p. (*0-8368-1015-5*) Stevens, Gareth Inc.

—Kristy & the Snobs. 1988. (Baby-Sitters Club Ser.: No. 11). (J). (gr. 3-7). 10.55 (*0-606-03547-8*) Turtleback Bks.

—Kristy & the Vampires. 1994. (Baby-Sitters Club Mystery Ser.: No. 15). 176p. (J). (gr. 3-7). mass mkt. 3.50 (*0-590-47053-1*) Scholastic, Inc.

—Kristy & the Vampires. 1994. (Baby-Sitters Club Mystery Ser.: No. 14). (J). (gr. 3-7). 10.04 (*0-606-06207-6*) Turtleback Bks.

—Kristy & the Walking Disaster. (Baby-Sitters Club Ser.: No. 20). (J). (gr. 3-7). 1996. mass mkt. 3.99 (*0-590-60692-1*); 1989. 160p. pap. 2.75 o.p. (*0-590-42004-6*, Scholastic Paperbacks); 1989. 192p. mass mkt. 3.50 (*0-590-43722-4*) Scholastic, Inc.

—Kristy & the Walking Disaster. l.t. ed. 1993. (Baby-Sitters Club Ser.: No. 20). 176p. (J). (gr. 3-7). lib. bdg. 21.27 o.p. (*0-8368-1024-4*) Stevens, Gareth Inc.

—Kristy & the Walking Disaster. 1989. (Baby-Sitters Club Ser.: No. 20). (J). (gr. 3-7). 9.09 o.p. (*0-606-04088-9*) Turtleback Bks.

—Kristy & the Worst Kid Ever. 1993. (Baby-Sitters Club Ser.: No. 62). 192p. (J). (gr. 3-7). mass mkt. 3.50 (*0-590-45664-4*) Scholastic, Inc.

—Kristy & the Worst Kid Ever. 1993. (Baby-Sitters Club Ser.: No. 62). (J). (gr. 3-7). 9.55 (*0-606-02500-6*) Turtleback Bks.

—Mallory & the Dream Horse. 1992. (Baby-Sitters Club Ser.: No. 54). 192p. (J). (gr. 3-7). mass mkt. 3.25 (*0-590-44965-6*) Scholastic, Inc.

—Mallory & the Dream Horse. 1992. (Baby-Sitters Club Ser.: No. 54). (J). (gr. 3-7). 8.35 o.p. (*0-606-01896-4*) Turtleback Bks.

—Mallory & the Ghost Cat. 1992. (Baby-Sitters Club Mystery Ser.: No. 3). (J). (gr. 3-7). pap. 117.00 o.p. (*0-590-66038-1*); 160p. mass mkt. 3.50 (*0-590-44799-8*) Scholastic, Inc.

—Mallory & the Ghost Cat. 1992. (Baby-Sitters Club Mystery Ser.: No. 3). (J). (gr. 3-7). 8.35 o.p. (*0-606-02501-4*) Turtleback Bks.

—Mallory & the Mystery Diary. 1989. (Baby-Sitters Club Ser.: No. 29). (gr. 3-7). 192p. (J). mass mkt. 3.50 (*0-590-42500-5*, Scholastic Paperbacks); mass mkt. 3.99 (*0-590-67397-1*) Scholastic, Inc.

—Mallory & the Mystery Diary. l.t. ed. 1994. (Baby-Sitters Club Ser.: No. 29). 176p. (J). (gr. 3-7). lib. bdg. 21.27 o.p. (*0-8368-1250-6*) Stevens, Gareth Inc.

—Mallory & the Mystery Diary. 1989. (Baby-Sitters Club Ser.: No. 29). (J). (gr. 3-7). 10.04 (*0-606-01845-X*) Turtleback Bks.

—Mallory & the Trouble with Twins. (Baby-Sitters Club Ser.: No. 21). (J). (gr. 3-7). 1997. mass mkt. 3.99 (*0-590-67389-0*); 1989. 160p. pap. 2.75 o.p. (*0-590-42005-4*, Scholastic Paperbacks); 1989. mass mkt. 3.50 (*0-590-43507-8*) Scholastic, Inc.

—Mallory & the Trouble with Twins. l.t. ed. 1994. (Baby-Sitters Club Ser.: No. 21). 176p. (J). (gr. 3-7). lib. bdg. 19.93 o.p. (*0-8368-1242-5*) Stevens, Gareth Inc.

—Mallory & the Trouble with Twins. 1989. (Baby-Sitters Club Ser.: No. 21). (J). (gr. 3-7). 10.04 (*0-606-04089-7*) Turtleback Bks.

—Mallory Hates Boys (and Gym) 1992. (Baby-Sitters Club Ser.: No. 59). 192p. (J). (gr. 3-7). mass mkt. 3.50 (*0-590-45660-1*) Scholastic, Inc.

—Mallory on Strike. 1991. (Baby-Sitters Club Ser.: No. 47). 192p. (J). (gr. 3-7). mass mkt. 3.25 (*0-590-44971-0*) Scholastic, Inc.

—Mallory on Strike. 1996. (Baby-Sitters Club Ser.: No. 47). 144p. (J). (gr. 3-7). lib. bdg. 21.27 o.p. (*0-8368-1571-8*) Stevens, Gareth Inc.

—Mallory on Strike. 1991. (Baby-Sitters Club Ser.: No. 47). (J). (gr. 3-7). 8.35 o.p. (*0-606-00586-2*) Turtleback Bks.

—Mallory Pike, #1 Fan. 1994. (Baby-Sitters Club Ser.: No. 80). 192p. (J). (gr. 3-7). mass mkt. 3.99 (*0-590-48224-6*) Scholastic, Inc.

—Mallory Pike, #1 Fan. 1994. (Baby-Sitters Club Ser.: No. 80). (J). (gr. 3-7). 9.09 o.p. (*0-606-06920-8*) Turtleback Bks.

—Mallory y el Gato Fantasma. 1995. 16.00 (*0-606-10396-1*) Turtleback Bks.

—Mallory's Christmas Wish. 1995. (Baby-Sitters Club Ser.: No. 92). (J). (gr. 3-7). mass mkt. 3.50 (*0-590-22876-5*) Scholastic, Inc.

—Mallory's Christmas Wish. 1995. (Baby-Sitters Club Ser.: No. 92). (J). (gr. 3-7). 8.60 o.p. (*0-606-08481-9*) Turtleback Bks.

—Mary Anne & Camp BSC. 1995. (Baby-Sitters Club Ser.: No. 86). 192p. (gr. 3-7). mass mkt. 3.50 (*0-590-48227-0*) Scholastic, Inc.

—Mary Anne & Camp BSC. 1995. (Baby-Sitters Club Ser.: No. 86). (J). (gr. 3-7). 8.60 o.p. (*0-606-07228-4*) Turtleback Bks.

—Mary Anne & Miss Priss. 1994. (Baby-Sitters Club Ser.: No. 73). 192p. (J). (gr. 3-7). mass mkt. 3.99 (*0-590-47011-6*) Scholastic, Inc.

—Mary Anne & Miss Priss. 1994. (Baby-Sitters Club Ser.: No. 73). (J). (gr. 3-7). 10.04 (*0-606-05738-2*) Turtleback Bks.

—Mary Anne & the Great Romance. (Baby-Sitters Club Ser.: No. 30). (J). (gr. 3-7). 1997. 160p. mass mkt. 3.99 (*0-590-67398-X*); 1990. 192p. mass mkt. 3.50 (*0-590-42498-X*) Scholastic, Inc.

—Mary Anne & the Great Romance. l.t. ed. 1994. (Baby-Sitters Club Ser.: No. 30). 176p. (J). (gr. 3-7). lib. bdg. 21.27 o.p. (*0-8368-1251-4*) Stevens, Gareth Inc.

—Mary Anne & the Great Romance. 1990. (Baby-Sitters Club Ser.: No. 30). (J). (gr. 3-7). 10.04 (*0-606-01876-X*) Turtleback Bks.

—Mary Anne & the Haunted Bookstore. 1998. (Baby-Sitters Club Mystery Ser.: No. 34). (J). (gr. 3-7). mass mkt. 3.99 (*0-590-05974-2*, Scholastic Paperbacks) Scholastic, Inc.

—Mary Anne & the Library Mystery. 1994. (Baby-Sitters Club Mystery Ser.: No. 13). 176p. (J). (gr. 3-7). mass mkt. 3.50 (*0-590-47051-5*) Scholastic, Inc.

—Mary Anne & the Library Mystery. 1994. (Baby-Sitters Club Mystery Ser.: No. 13). (J). (gr. 3-7). 9.55 (*0-606-05740-4*) Turtleback Bks.

—Mary Anne & the Little Princess. 1996. (Baby-Sitters Club Ser.: No. 102). 142p. (J). (gr. 3-7). mass mkt. 3.99 (*0-590-69208-9*) Scholastic, Inc.

—Mary Anne & the Little Princess. 1996. (Baby-Sitters Club Ser.: No. 102). (J). (gr. 3-7). 10.04 (*0-606-10132-2*) Turtleback Bks.

—Mary Anne & the Memory Garden. 1996. (Baby-Sitters Club Ser.: No. 93). (J). (gr. 3-7). mass mkt. 3.99 (*0-590-22877-3*) Scholastic, Inc.

—Mary Anne & the Memory Garden. 1996. (Baby-Sitters Club Ser.: No. 93). (J). (gr. 3-7). 9.09 o.p. (*0-606-08482-7*) Turtleback Bks.

—Mary Anne & the Music Box Secret. 1997. (Baby-Sitters Club Mystery Ser.: No. 31). 144p. (J). (gr. 3-7). mass mkt. 3.99 (*0-590-69179-1*) Scholastic, Inc.

—Mary Anne & the Music Box Secret. 1997. (Baby-Sitters Club Mystery Ser.: No. 31). (J). (gr. 3-7). 10.04 (*0-606-11075-5*) Turtleback Bks.

—Mary Anne & the Playground Fight. 1998. (Baby-Sitters Club Ser.: No. 120). (J). (gr. 3-7). mass mkt. 3.99 (*0-590-05998-X*, Scholastic Paperbacks) Scholastic, Inc.

—Mary Anne & the Playground Fight. 1998. (Baby-Sitters Club Ser.: No. 120). (J). (gr. 3-7). 10.04 (*0-606-13164-7*) Turtleback Bks.

—Mary Anne & the Search for Tigger. (Baby-Sitters Club Ser.: No. 25). (J). (gr. 3-7). 1997. 160p. mass mkt. 3.99 (*0-590-67393-9*, Scholastic Paperbacks); 1989. pap. 2.75 o.p. (*0-590-42003-8*); 1989. 192p. mass mkt. 3.50 (*0-590-43347-4*) Scholastic, Inc.

—Mary Anne & the Search for Tigger. l.t. ed. 1994. (Baby-Sitters Club Ser.: No. 25). 176p. (J). (gr. 3-7). lib. bdg. 23.95 o.p. (*0-8368-1246-8*) Stevens, Gareth Inc.

—Mary Anne & the Search for Tigger. 1989. (Baby-Sitters Club Ser.: No. 25). (J). (gr. 3-7). 10.04 (*0-606-04272-5*) Turtleback Bks.

—Mary Anne & the Secret in the Attic. 1992. (Baby-Sitters Club Mystery Ser.: No. 5). 176p. (J). (gr. 3-7). mass mkt. 3.50 (*0-590-44801-3*, Scholastic Paperbacks) Scholastic, Inc.

—Mary Anne & the Silent Witness. 1996. (Baby-Sitters Club Mystery Ser.: No. 24). (J). (gr. 3-7). mass mkt. 4.50 (*0-590-22868-4*) Scholastic, Inc.

—Mary Anne & the Silent Witness. 1996. (Baby-Sitters Club Mystery Ser.: No. 24). (J). (gr. 3-7). 9.09 o.p. (*0-606-09038-X*) Turtleback Bks.

—Mary Anne & the Zoo Mystery. 1995. (Baby-Sitters Club Mystery Ser.: No. 20). 176p. (J). (gr. 3-7). mass mkt. 3.50 (*0-590-48309-9*) Scholastic, Inc.

—Mary Anne & the Zoo Mystery. 1995. (Baby-Sitters Club Mystery Ser.: No. 20). (J). (gr. 3-7). 9.55 (*0-606-07234-9*) Turtleback Bks.

—Mary Anne & Too Many Boys. 1990. (Baby-Sitters Club Ser.: No. 34). (J). (gr. 3-7). mass mkt. 3.99 (*0-590-73283-8*); 192p. mass mkt. 3.50 (*0-590-42494-7*) Scholastic, Inc.

—Mary Anne & Too Many Boys. l.t. ed. 1995. (Baby-Sitters Club Ser.: No. 34). 144p. (J). (gr. 3-7). lib. bdg. 21.27 o.p. (*0-8368-1414-2*) Stevens, Gareth Inc.

—Mary Anne & Too Many Boys. 1990. (Baby-Sitters Club Ser.: No. 34). (J). (gr. 3-7). 8.60 (*0-606-04475-2*) Turtleback Bks.

—Mary Anne & 2 Many Babies. (Baby-Sitters Club Ser.: No. 52). (J). (gr. 3-7). 1992. 192p. mass mkt. 3.50 (*0-590-44966-4*); 1948. mass mkt. 3.99 (*0-590-92577-6*) Scholastic, Inc.

—Mary Anne & 2 Many Babies. 1992. (Baby-Sitters Club Ser.: No. 52). (J). (gr. 3-7). 9.09 o.p. (*0-606-01897-2*) Turtleback Bks.

—Mary Anne Breaks the Rules. 1994. (Baby-Sitters Club Ser.: No. 79). 192p. (J). (gr. 3-7). mass mkt. 3.50 (*0-590-48223-8*) Scholastic, Inc.

—Mary Anne Breaks the Rules. 1994. (Baby-Sitters Club Ser.: No. 79). (J). (gr. 3-7). 8.60 o.p. (*0-606-06205-X*) Turtleback Bks.

—Mary Anne in the Middle. 1998. (Baby-Sitters Club Ser.: No. 125). (Illus.). 121p. (J). (gr. 3-7). mass mkt. 3.99 (*0-590-50179-8*) Scholastic, Inc.

—Mary Anne Misses Logan. 1991. (Baby-Sitters Club Ser.: No. 46). 192p. (J). (gr. 3-7). mass mkt. 3.50 (*0-590-43569-8*) Scholastic, Inc.

—Mary Anne Misses Logan. 1996. (Baby-Sitters Club Ser.: No. 46). 144p. (J). (gr. 3-7). lib. bdg. 21.27 o.p. (*0-8368-1570-X*) Stevens, Gareth Inc.

—Mary Anne to the Rescue. 1997. (Baby-Sitters Club Ser.: No. 109). (J). (gr. 3-7). mass mkt. 3.99 (*0-590-69215-1*, Scholastic Paperbacks) Scholastic, Inc.

—Mary Anne vs. Logan. (Baby-Sitters Club Ser.: No. 41). (J). (gr. 3-7). 1997. mass mkt. 3.99 (*0-590-74241-8*, Scholastic Reference); 1991. 192p. mass mkt. 3.50 (*0-590-43570-1*) Scholastic, Inc.

—Mary Anne vs. Logan. 1996. (Baby-Sitters Club Ser.: No. 41). 176p. (J). (gr. 3-7). lib. bdg. 21.27 o.p. (*0-8368-1565-3*) Stevens, Gareth Inc.

—Mary Anne vs. Logan. 1991. (Baby-Sitters Club Ser.: No. 41). (J). (gr. 3-7). 10.04 (*0-606-04743-3*) Turtleback Bks.

—Rachel Parker, Kindergarten Show-Off. 1992. (Illus.). 40p. (J). (ps-3). tchr. ed. 16.95 o.p. (*0-8234-0935-X*); pap. 6.95 (*0-8234-1067-6*) Holiday Hse., Inc.

Martin, Juliet. A Puzzle. 1994. (Illus.). (J). 9.70 (*0-383-03710-7*) SRA/McGraw-Hill.

Martini, Teri. Christmas for Andy. 1991. (J). (gr. 3 up). pap. 3.95 (*0-8091-6603-8*) Paulist Pr.

Marzolla, Jean. Shanna's Princess Show. 2001. (Illus.). 24p. (J). (ps-2). 12.99 (*0-7868-0631-1*, Jump at the Sun) Hyperion Bks. for Children.

Marzollo, Jean. Shanna's Doctor Show: Picture Book. 2001. (Illus.). 24p. (J). (ps-2). 12.99 (*0-7868-0636-2*, Jump at the Sun) Hyperion Bks. for Children.

—Shanna's Reading Show: Level 1: Shanna's Animal Riddles. 2004. (Shanna Show! Ser.). (Illus.). (J). (ps-1). pap. 3.99 (*0-7868-1827-1*) Hyperion Bks. for Children.

—Shanna's Reading Show: Level 1: Shanna's Bear Hunt. 2004. (Shanna Show! Ser.). (Illus.). (J). pap. 3.99 (*0-7868-1829-8*) Hyperion Bks. for Children.

—Shanna's Reading Show: Level 1: Shanna's Hip Hop Hooray! 2004. (Shanna Show! Ser.). (Illus.). (J). pap. 3.99 (*0-7868-1830-1*) Hyperion Bks. for Children.

—Shanna's Reading Show: Level 1: Shanna's Party Surprise. 2004. (Shanna Show! Ser.). (Illus.). (J). pap. 3.99 (*0-7868-1828-X*) Hyperion Bks. for Children.

Masters, Susan Rowan. Night Journey to Vicksburg. Killcoyne, Hope L., ed. 2003. (J). 14.95 (*1-893110-30-3*) Silver Moon Pr.

Mather, Melissa. One Summer in Between. 1967. 9.95 o.p. (*0-06-012837-2*) HarperCollins Pubs.

—One Summer in Between. 2000. 228p. pap. 14.95 (*0-595-09384-1*, Backinprint.com) iUniverse, Inc.

Mathis, Sharon Bell. Listen for the Fig Tree. 1990. 176p. (J). (gr. 7 up). pap. 4.99 o.s.i (*0-14-034364-4*, Puffin Bks.) Penguin Putnam Bks. for Young Readers.

—Listen for the Fig Tree. 1974. 176p. (J). (gr. 7 up). 9.95 o.p. (*0-670-43016-1*) Viking Penguin.

—Running Girl: The Diary of Ebonee Rose. 1997. (Illus.). 64p. (J). (gr. 3-7). 17.00 o.s.i (*0-15-200674-5*) Harcourt Trade Pubs.

—Sidewalk Story. 1981. (J). (gr. 2-4). pap. 0.95 o.p. (*0-380-00851-3*, 31146, Avon Bks.) Morrow/Avon.

—Sidewalk Story. 1986. (Novels Ser.). 64p. (J). (gr. 4-7). pap. 4.99 (*0-14-032165-9*, Puffin Bks.) Penguin Putnam Bks. for Young Readers.

—Sidewalk Story. 1986. 10.14 (*0-606-12514-0*) Turtleback Bks.

—Teacup Full of Roses. l.t. ed. 1973. (J). lib. bdg. 5.95 o.p. (*0-8161-6121-6*, Macmillan Reference USA) Gale Group.

—Teacup Full of Roses. 1979. (YA). (gr. 7 up). pap. 1.50 o.p. (*0-380-00780-0*, 54312, Avon Bks.) Morrow/Avon.

—Teacup Full of Roses. 1987. (Novels Ser.). 128p. (J). (gr. 4-7). pap. 4.99 (*0-14-032328-7*, Puffin Bks.) Penguin Putnam Bks. for Young Readers.

—Teacup Full of Roses. 9999. pap. 1.75 o.s.i (*0-590-03178-3*) Scholastic, Inc.

—Teacup Full of Roses. 1993. (J). (gr. 5-9). 17.05 o.p. (*0-8446-6650-5*) Smith, Peter Pub., Inc.

—Teacup Full of Roses. 1987. 11.04 (*0-606-03482-X*) Turtleback Bks.

—Teacup Full of Roses. 1972. 128p. (YA). (gr. 7 up). 10.95 o.p. (*0-670-69434-7*) Viking Penguin.

McConduit, Denise W. D. J. & the Jazz Fest. 1997. (Illus.). 32p. (J). 14.95 (*1-56554-239-8*) Pelican Publishing Co., Inc.

—D. J. & the Zulu Parade. 1994. (Illus.). 32p. (J). (ps-3). 8.95 (*1-56554-063-8*) Pelican Publishing Co., Inc.

McCurty, Darlene M. I'm Special Too. 1992. 55p. (J). (gr. 4-8). pap. 6.95 (*0-913543-27-6*) African American Images.

McDaniel, Becky Bring. Larry & the Cookie. 1993. (Rookie Readers Ser.). (Illus.). 32p. (J). (gr. 1-2). lib. bdg. 19.00 (*0-516-02014-5*, Children's Pr.) Scholastic Library Publishing.

McDaniel, Becky Bring, ed. Larry & the Cookie. 1993. (Rookie Readers Ser.). (Illus.). 32p. (J). (ps-2). mass mkt. 4.95 o.p. (*0-516-42014-3*, Children's Pr.) Scholastic Library Publishing.

McDaniel, Lurlene. Please Don't Die. 1993. (J). mass mkt. o.s.i (*0-553-54126-9*, Dell Books for Young Readers) Random Hse. Children's Bks.

—Please Don't Die. 1993. 9.60 o.p. (*0-606-07972-6*); 10.55 (*0-606-18965-3*) Turtleback Bks.

McDaniels, William. Abdul & the Designer Tennis Shoes. 1997. (Illus.). 33p. (YA). (gr. 2-12). pap. 6.95 (*0-913543-15-2*) African American Images.

McDonald, Janet. Chill Wind, RS. 2002. 144p. (YA). (gr. 7 up). 16.00 (*0-374-39958-1*, Farrar, Straus & Giroux (BYR)) Farrar, Straus & Giroux.

—Chill Wind. 2003. 165p. (J). 24.95 (*0-7862-5502-1*) Thorndike Pr.

—Spellbound. l.t. ed. 2002. (Young Adult Ser.). 176p. 23.95 (*0-7862-4784-3*) Thorndike Pr.

—Twists & Turns, RS. 2003. 144p. (YA). 16.00 (*0-374-39955-7*, Farrar, Straus & Giroux (BYR)) Farrar, Straus & Giroux.

McDonnell, Janet. Victor's Adventure in Alphabet Town. 1992. (Read Around Alphabet Town Ser.). (Illus.). 32p. (J). mass mkt. 19.00 o.p. (*0-516-05422-8*, Children's Pr.) Scholastic Library Publishing.

McGuigan, Mary Ann. Where You Belong. (J). (gr. 5-9). 1998. 192p. per. 4.50 (*0-689-82318-5*, Simon Pulse); 1997. 176p. 16.95 (*0-689-81250-7*, Atheneum) Simon & Schuster Children's Publishing.

—Where You Belong. 1998. 10.55 (*0-606-15763-8*) Turtleback Bks.

McKay, Kathleen C. Hearts of Rosewood: A Novel. unabr. ed. 1997. 122p. (J). (gr. 5-12). 18.95 o.p. (*0-936389-46-X*) Tudor Pubs., Inc.

McKissack, Patricia C. Color Me Dark: The Diary of Nellie Lee Love, the Great Migration North, Chicago, Illinois, 1919. 2000. (Dear America Ser.). (Illus.). 218p. (J). (gr. 4-9). pap. 10.95 (*0-590-51159-9*, Scholastic Pr.) Scholastic, Inc.

—The Dark-Thirty: Southern Tales of the Supernatural. (Illus.). 1998. 176p. (YA). (gr. 5). pap. 5.50 (*0-679-89006-8*, Random Hse. Bks. for Young Readers); 1992. 128p. (J). (gr. 4-7). 17.99 o.s.i

(0-679-91863-9, Knopf Bks. for Young Readers); 1992. 128p. (YA). 16.00 o.s.i (0-679-81863-4, Knopf Bks. for Young Readers) Random Hse. Children's Bks.

—The Dark-Thirty: Southern Tales of the Supernatural. 1998. 11.55 (0-606-15884-7); 1992. (YA). 18.05 (0-606-10779-7) Turtleback Bks.

—Flossie & the Fox. 1986. (Illus.). 32p. (J). (ps-3). 15.99 (0-8037-0250-7); 13.89 o.p. (0-8037-0251-5) Penguin Putnam Bks. for Young Readers. (Dial Bks. for Young Readers).

—Goin' Someplace Special. 2001. (Illus.). 40p. (J). (ps-3). 16.00 (0-689-81885-8, Atheneum/Anne Schwartz Bks.) Simon & Schuster Children's Publishing.

—The Honest-to-Goodness Truth. (Illus.). 40p. (J). (ps-3). 2003. pap. 6.99 (0-689-85395-5, Aladdin); 2000. 16.00 (0-689-82668-0, Atheneum/Anne Schwartz Bks.) Simon & Schuster Children's Publishing.

—Ma Dear's Aprons. 1997. (Illus.). (J). lib. bdg. 16.99 (0-679-95099-0, Knopf Bks. for Young Readers) Random Hse. Children's Bks.

—Ma Dear's Aprons. (Illus.). 32p. (J). (ps-3). 1997. 16.00 (0-689-81051-2, Atheneum/Anne Schwartz Bks.); 2000. reprint ed. pap. 5.99 (0-689-83262-1, Aladdin) Simon & Schuster Children's Publishing.

—Ma Dear's Aprons. 2000. (Illus.). (J). 12.14 (0-606-17928-3) Turtleback Bks.

—Miami Gets It Straight. 2000. (Road to Reading Ser.). (Illus.). (J). 10.14 (0-606-20444-X) Turtleback Bks.

—Mirandy & Brother Wind. (Dragon Tales Ser.). (Illus.). 32p. (ps-3). 1997. (J). pap. 6.99 (0-679-88333-9, Random Hse. Bks. for Young Readers); 1988. (J). 18.99 o.s.i (0-394-98765-9, Knopf Bks. for Young Readers); 1988. 17.00 (0-394-88765-4, Knopf Bks. for Young Readers) Random Hse. Children's Bks.

—Mirandy & Brother Wind. 1996. (J). 13.14 (0-606-10877-7) Turtleback Bks.

McKissack, Patricia C. & McKissack, Fredrick L. Christmas in the Big House, Christmas in the Quarters. (Illus.). 80p. (J). 2002. pap. 6.99 (0-590-43028-9); 1994. (gr. 3-8). pap. 17.95 (0-590-43027-0) Scholastic, Inc.

—Let My People Go: Bible Stories Told by a Freeman of Color. 1998. (Illus.). 144p. (J). (gr. 4-7). 20.00 (0-689-80856-9, Atheneum/Anne Schwartz Bks.) Simon & Schuster Children's Publishing.

—Messy Bessey & the Birthday Overnight. 1998. (Rookie Readers Ser.). (Illus.). 32p. (J). (gr. 1-2). lib. bdg. 19.00 (0-516-20828-4, Children's Pr.) Scholastic Library Publishing.

—Messy Bessey's Garden. (Rookie Readers Ser.). (Illus.). 32p. (J). 1992. (ps-3). mass mkt. 4.95 (0-516-42008-9); 1991. (gr. 1-2). lib. bdg. 19.00 (0-516-02008-0); 2002. pap. 4.95 (0-516-27386-8) Scholastic Library Publishing. (Children's Pr.).

—Messy Bessey's Garden Level C. rev. ed. 2002. (Rookie Readers Ser.). (Illus.). 32p. (J). (gr. 1-2). lib. bdg. 19.00 (0-516-22491-3, Children's Pr.) Scholastic Library Publishing.

—Miami Gets It Straight. (Road to Reading Ser.). (Illus.). (J). (gr. 4-7). 2000. 80p. lib. bdg. 11.99 o.p. (0-307-46501-2); 1999. 96p. pap. 3.99 (0-307-26501-3) Random Hse. Children's Bks. (Golden Bks.).

—Miami Makes the Play. 2001. (Road to Reading Ser.). (Illus.). 80p. (J). (gr. 4-7). pap. 3.99 (0-307-26505-6, Golden Bks.) Random Hse. Children's Bks.

—Miami Sees It Through. 2002. (Road to Reading Ser.). (Illus.). 96p. (J). (gr. 2-4). pap. 3.99 (0-307-26513-7); lib. bdg. 11.99 (0-307-46513-6) Random Hse. Children's Bks. (Golden Bks.).

McKissack, Patricia C. & Moss, Onawumi Jean. Li'l Sis & the Booga-She. 2003. (Illus.). (J). 16.00 (0-689-85194-4, Atheneum/Anne Schwartz Bks.) Simon & Schuster Children's Publishing.

McKissack, Patricia C., et al. Miami Makes the Play. 2001. (Road to Reading Ser.). (Illus.). 80p. (J). (ps up). lib. bdg. 11.99 (0-307-46505-5, Golden Bks.) Random Hse. Children's Bks.

McMillan, Naomi. Busy Baby. 1998. (Golden Super Shape Book Ser.). (Illus.). 24p. (J). (ps-3). pap. 3.29 o.s.i (0-307-10003-0, Golden Bks.) Random Hse. Children's Bks.

McMillan, Naomi & Grimes, Nikki. Baby's Bedtime. 1999. (Essence Ser.). (Illus.). 12p. (J). (ps). bds. 3.49 o.s.i (0-307-12872-5, Golden Bks.) Random Hse. Children's Bks.

McMillan, Naomi & Mellage, Nanette. Baby's Colors. 1998. (Essence Ser.). (Illus.). 16p. (J). (ps-3). bds. 3.49 o.s.i (0-307-12873-3, Golden Bks.) Random Hse. Children's Bks.

McMillan, Rosalyn. This Side of Eternity. 2002. 464p. reprint ed. pap. 6.99 (0-671-03436-7, Pocket) Simon & Schuster.

Mead, Alice. Junebug. RS. 1995. 112p. (J). (gr. 3-7). 16.00 (0-374-33964-3, Farrar, Straus & Giroux (BYR)) Farrar, Straus & Giroux.

—Junebug. 1997. 112p. (gr. 3-7). pap. text 4.50 (0-440-41245-5, Yearling); 1996. (J). pap. 4.99 (0-440-91275-X, Dell Books for Young Readers) Random Hse. Children's Bks.

—Junebug. 1997. (J). 10.55 (0-606-11528-5) Turtleback Bks.

—Junebug & the Reverend. 2002. (Illus.). (J). 13.40 (0-7587-6518-5) Book Wholesalers, Inc.

—Junebug & the Reverend, RS. 1998. 192p. (J). (gr. 3-7). 16.00 (0-374-33965-1, Farrar, Straus & Giroux (BYR)) Farrar, Straus & Giroux.

—Junebug & the Reverend. 2000. (Illus.). 192p. (gr. 4-7). pap. text 4.99 (0-440-41571-3, Yearling) Random Hse. Children's Bks.

—Junebug & the Reverend. 2000. (Illus.). (J). 10.55 (0-606-18785-5) Turtleback Bks.

—Junebug in Trouble, RS. 2002. 144p. (J). (gr. 4-7). 16.00 (0-374-33969-4, Farrar, Straus & Giroux (BYR)) Farrar, Straus & Giroux.

—Junebug in Trouble. 2003. (Illus.). 144p. (gr. 4-7). pap. text 4.99 (0-440-41937-9, Dell Books for Young Readers) Random Hse. Children's Bks.

Means, Florence C. Reach for a Star, 001. 1957. (Illus.). (J). (gr. 7 up). 7.95 o.p. (0-395-06934-3) Houghton Mifflin Co.

—Shuttered Windows, 001. 9999. (Illus.). (J). (gr. 7-9). 6.95 o.p. (0-395-06936-X) Houghton Mifflin Co.

Medearis, Angela Shelf. Annie's Gifts. 1994. (Feeling Good Ser.). (Illus.). 32p. (J). (gr. 1-4). 14.95 (0-940975-30-0); (ps-3). pap. 6.95 (0-940975-31-9) Just Us Bks., Inc.

—Annie's Gifts. 1994. 13.10 (0-606-08690-0) Turtleback Bks.

—Annie's Gifts. 1994. E-Book (1-59019-143-9); (Illus.). E-Book (1-59019-142-0) ipicturebooks, LLC.

—Dancing with the Indians. 1991. (Illus.). (J). (ps-3). 32p. tchr. ed. 16.95 (0-8234-0893-0); reprint ed. pap. 6.95 (0-8234-1023-4) Holiday Hse., Inc.

—Dancing with the Indians. 2000. (Illus.). (J). (gr. 1-6). 24.95 incl. audio (0-87499-333-4); pap. 15.95 incl. audio (0-87499-332-6) Live Oak Media.

—Dancing with the Indians, Grades 1-6. 2000. (Illus.). (J). pap., tchr. ed. 37.95 incl. audio (0-87499-334-2) Live Oak Media.

—The Ghost of Sifty-Sifty Sam. 1997. (Illus.). (J). (gr. k-4). 32p. pap. 14.95 (0-590-48290-4); pap. (0-590-48291-2) Scholastic, Inc.

—Poppa's New Pants. 1995. (Illus.). 32p. (J). (ps-3). tchr. ed. 15.95 (0-8234-1155-9) Holiday Hse., Inc.

—Treemonisha, ERS. 1995. (Illus.). 40p. (J). (ps-3). 15.95 o.s.i (0-8050-1748-8, Holt, Henry & Co. Bks. For Young Readers) Holt, Henry & Co.

Medearis, Michael & Medearis, Angela Shelf. Daisy & the Doll. 2000. (Family Heritage Ser.). (Illus.). 32p. (J). (gr. 1-5). text 14.95 (0-916718-15-8) Vermont Folklife Ctr.

Medina, Tony. Christmas Makes Me Think. 2001. (Illus.). 32p. (J). (gr. 1-7). 16.95 (1-58430-024-8) Lee & Low Bks., Inc.

Mellage, Nanette. See Me Grow, Head to Toe. 1998. (Illus.). 24p. (J). pap. 3.29 o.s.i (0-307-10036-7, Golden Bks.) Random Hse. Children's Bks.

Mendez, Phil. The Black Snowman. (Illus.). 48p. (J). 1991. (gr. 4-7). mass mkt. 5.99 (0-590-44873-0, Scholastic Paperbacks); 1989. (gr. 2-5). pap. 15.95 (0-590-40552-7) Scholastic, Inc.

—The Black Snowman. 1989. 12.14 (0-606-00318-5) Turtleback Bks.

Mennen, Ingrid. One Round Moon & a Star for Me. 1994. (Illus.). 32p. (J). (ps-2). pap. 15.95 (0-531-06804-8); lib. bdg. 16.99 (0-531-08654-2) Scholastic, Inc. (Orchard Bks.).

Meyer, Carolyn. Denny's Tapes. 1987. 224p. (YA). (gr. 9 up). lib. bdg. 14.95 o.s.i (0-689-50413-6, McElderry, Margaret K.) Simon & Schuster Children's Publishing.

—Jubilee Journey. 1997. 288p. (YA). (gr. 5-9). 13.00 (0-15-201377-6); pap. 6.00 (0-15-201591-4) Harcourt Children's Bks. (Gulliver Bks.).

—Jubilee Journey. 1997. 12.05 (0-606-14244-4) Turtleback Bks.

—White Lilacs. 1993. (Illus.). 256p. (J). (gr. 4-7). pap. 6.00 (0-15-295876-2); (YA). (gr. 5-9). 13.00 (0-15-200641-9) Harcourt Children's Bks. (Gulliver Bks.).

—White Lilacs. 1993. 12.05 (0-606-17360-9) Turtleback Bks.

Micklish, Rita. Sugar Bee. 1972. (J). (gr. 3-7). 5.95 o.p. (0-440-08358-3); lib. bdg. 5.47 o.p. (0-440-08350-8) Dell Publishing. (Delacorte Pr.).

Miles, Betty. Sink or Swim. 1987. 208p. (YA). (gr. 3-7). pap. 2.95 (0-380-69913-3, Avon Bks.) Morrow/Avon.

Miles, Calvin. Calvin's Christmas Wish. (Illus.). 32p. (J). (ps-3). 1996. pap. 4.99 o.s.i (0-14-055866-7); 1993. 13.99 o.p. (0-670-84295-8, Viking Children's Bks.) Penguin Putnam Bks. for Young Readers.

—Calvin's Christmas Wish. 1996. 10.19 o.p. (0-606-10153-5) Turtleback Bks.

Milich, Melissa. Miz Fannie Mae's Fine New Easter Hat. 1997. (Illus.). 32p. (J). (ps-3). 14.95 o.p. (0-316-57159-8) Little Brown & Co.

Miller, William. The Bus Ride. (Illus.). 32p. (YA). (gr. k up). 1998. 15.95 (1-880000-60-1); 2001. reprint ed. pap. 6.95 (1-58430-026-4) Lee & Low Bks., Inc.

—The Bus Ride. 2001. (J). 13.10 (0-606-21094-6) Turtleback Bks.

—The Conjure Woman: Madame Zina. 1996. (Illus.). 32p. (J). (gr. k-3). 15.00 o.s.i (0-689-31962-2, Atheneum) Simon & Schuster Children's Publishing.

—A House by the River. 1997. (Illus.). 32p. (J). (ps up). 15.95 (1-880000-48-2) Lee & Low Bks., Inc.

—Joe Louis, My Champion. Pate, Rodney, tr. & illus. by. 2004. (J). 16.95 (1-58430-161-9) Lee & Low Bks., Inc.

—Night Golf. (Illus.). 32p. 2002. (YA). pap. 6.95 (1-58430-056-6); 1999. (J). (gr. 1-4). 15.95 (1-880000-79-2) Lee & Low Bks., Inc.

—The Piano. 2000. (Illus.). 32p. (J). (ps up). 15.95 (1-880000-98-9) Lee & Low Bks., Inc.

—Rent Party Jazz. 2001. (Illus.). 32p. (J). (gr. 1-5). 16.95 (1-58430-025-6) Lee & Low Bks., Inc.

—Richard Wright & the Library Card. (Illus.). 32p. 1999. (J). (gr. k up). pap. 6.95 (1-880000-88-1); 1997. (YA). (gr. 1 up). 16.95 (1-880000-57-1) Lee & Low Bks., Inc.

—Richard Wright & the Library Card. 1997. 13.10 (0-606-17379-X) Turtleback Bks.

—Richard Wright y el Carne de Biblioteca. 2003. (SPA.). (J). 32p. 16.95 (1-58430-180-5); pap. 6.95 (1-58430-181-3) Lee & Low Bks., Inc.

Mills, Charles. Stranger in the Shadows. 1998. (Shadow Creek Ranch Ser.: Vol. 11). 151p. (Orig.). (J). (gr. 4-7). pap. 5.99 (0-8280-1316-0) Review & Herald Publishing Assn.

Milstein, Linda B. Coconut Mon. 1995. (Illus.). 32p. (J). (ps up). 16.00 o.p. (0-688-12862-9); lib. bdg. 15.93 o.p. (0-688-12863-7) Morrow/Avon. (Morrow, William & Co.).

Mitchell, Margaree K. Uncle Jed's Barbershop. 1998. (J). pap. 5.99 (0-87628-331-8) Ctr. for Applied Research in Education, The.

—Uncle Jed's Barbershop. 1995. (Illus.). (J). (gr. 4). 9.00 (0-395-73246-8) Houghton Mifflin Co.

—Uncle Jed's Barbershop. (Illus.). 40p. (J). (ps-2). 1998. pap. 6.99 (0-689-81913-7, Aladdin); 1993. pap. 17.00 (0-671-76969-3, Simon & Schuster Children's Publishing) Simon & Schuster Children's Publishing.

—Uncle Jed's Barbershop. 1998. (J). 13.14 (0-606-13060-8) Turtleback Bks.

Molnar, James. Otto's Box of Bad Feelings. 1995. (Kid Safe Ser.). (Illus.). (Orig.). (J). (ps-3). pap. 5.00 (0-9644142-1-X) Open Bk. Publishing Hse.

Monjo, F. N. La Osa Menor: Una Historia del Ferrocarril Subterraneo. Mlawer, Teresa, tr. 1997. (Ya Se Leer Ser.). (SPA., Illus.). 64p. (J). (gr. k-3). pap. 4.95 o.p. (0-06-444217-9) HarperCollins Children's Bk. Group.

Moore, Dessie. Good Morning. 1994. (Jump at the Sun Board Bks.). (Illus.). 16p. (J). (ps). 5.95 o.p. (0-694-00593-2, Harper Festival) HarperCollins Children's Bk. Group.

—Let's Pretend. 1994. (Jump at the Sun Board Bks.). (Illus.). 16p. (YA). (ps up). 5.95 o.p. (0-694-00591-6) HarperCollins Children's Bk. Group.

Moore, Emily. Whose Side Are You On?, RS. 128p. (J). (gr. 4-7). 1990. pap. 5.95 (0-374-48373-6, Sunburst); 1988. 14.00 o.p. (0-374-38409-6, Farrar, Straus & Giroux (BYR)) Farrar, Straus & Giroux.

Moore, Johnny Ray. But Still, We Dream. 1999. (Illus.). 36p. pap. text 7.95 (1-58521-006-4) Books for Black Children, Inc.

—Talking Tyrone Said It. 1999. (Illus.). 60p. pap. text 6.95 (1-58521-007-2) Books for Black Children, Inc.

Moore, Miriam. The Kwanzaa Contest. 1996. (Hyperion Chapters Ser.). (Illus.). 64p. (J). (gr. 4-7). pap. 3.95 (0-7868-1122-6) Disney Pr.

—The Kwanzaa Contest. 1996. 10.10 (0-606-10245-0) Turtleback Bks.

Moore, Miriam & Taylor, Penny. The Kwanzaa Contest. 1997. (Illus.). 64p. (J). lib. bdg. 14.49 (0-7868-2336-4) Disney Pr.

—The Kwanzaa Contest. 1996. (Illus.). 64p. (J). (gr. 3-4). 13.95 (0-7868-0261-8) Hyperion Bks. for Children.

Moore, Stephanie Perry. Saved Race. 2001. (Payton Skky Ser.). 159p. (J). (gr. 7-13). pap. 8.99 (0-8024-4238-2) Moody Pr.

Morninghouse, Sundaira. Habari Gani? What's the News? 1992. (Illus.). 32p. (J). (gr. k-4). 14.95 (0-940880-39-3) Open Hand Publishing, LLC.

Morris, Judy K. Nightwalkers. 1996. (Illus.). 144p. (J). (gr. 3-7). 14.95 o.s.i (0-06-027200-7) HarperCollins Children's Bk. Group.

Moses, Amy. I Am an Explorer. 1990. (Rookie Readers Ser.). (Illus.). 32p. (J). (ps-2). mass mkt. 16.00 o.p. (0-516-02059-5); mass mkt. 4.95 o.p. (0-516-42059-3) Scholastic Library Publishing. (Children's Pr.).

Moses, Shelia P. The Legend of Buddy Bush. 2004. (Illus.). 224p. (YA). 15.95 (0-689-85839-6, McElderry, Margaret K.) Simon & Schuster Children's Publishing.

Moss, Thylias. I Want to Be. (Illus.). 32p. (J). (ps-3). 1998. pap. 5.99 o.p. (0-14-056286-9, Puffin Bks.); 1993. 16.99 o.s.i (0-8037-1286-3, Dial Bks. for Young Readers); 1993. 14.89 o.p. (0-8037-1287-1, Dial Bks. for Young Readers) Penguin Putnam Bks. for Young Readers.

—I Want to Be. 1998. 12.14 (0-606-13511-1) Turtleback Bks.

Mowry, Jess. Babylon Boyz. 192p. (J). 1999. (gr. 8-12). pap. 8.00 (0-689-82592-7, 076714008007, Simon Pulse); 1997. (Illus.). (gr. 7 up). pap. 16.00 (0-689-80839-9, Simon & Schuster Children's Publishing) Simon & Schuster Children's Publishing.

—Babylon Boyz. 1999. 14.05 (0-606-16318-2) Turtleback Bks.

—Ghost Train, ERS. 1996. 128p. (YA). (gr. 4-7). 14.95 (0-8050-4440-X, Holt, Henry & Co. Bks. For Young Readers) Holt, Henry & Co.

Mungin, Horace. Sleepy Willie. Orange, Charlotte, ed. 1991. 128p. (Orig.). (YA). (gr. 8-12). pap. 8.95 (0-936026-24-3) R&M Publishing Co.

Murphy, Elspeth Campbell. Curtis Anderson. 1986. (Apple Street Church Ser.). (Illus.). 120p. (J). (gr. 3-7). pap. 4.49 o.p. (1-55513-027-5) Cook Communications Ministries.

Murphy, Rita. Black Angels. 2002. 176p. (gr. 4). pap. text 4.99 (0-440-22934-0) Random Hse., Inc.

Murray, Michele. Nellie Cameron, 001. 1979. (Illus.). 160p. (J). (gr. 3-6). 6.95 o.p. (0-395-28867-3, Clarion Bks.) Houghton Mifflin Co. Trade & Reference Div.

Myers, Christopher. Fly! 2001. (Illus.). 32p. (J). 15.99 (0-7868-0652-4) Disney Pr.

—Fly! 2001. (Illus.). 32p. (J). 16.49 (0-7868-2373-9, Jump at the Sun) Hyperion Bks. for Children.

Myers, Roy J. & Myers, Stephanie E. The Rescue of Robby Robo. 1995. (Robby Robo Ser.: No. 1). (Illus.). 20p. (Orig.). (J). (gr. k-6). pap. (1-884108-00-8) Myers, R.J. Publishing Co.

Myers, Walter Dean. Bearer Of Dreams. 2003. 192p. (J). (gr. 5 up). lib. bdg. 16.89 (0-06-029522-8, Amistad Pr.) HarperTrade.

—Beast. 2003. 224p. (J). pap. 16.95 (0-439-36841-3) Scholastic, Inc.

—Crystal. 2002. 208p. (J). (gr. 7 up). lib. bdg. 15.89 (0-06-008350-6); reprint ed. pap. 5.95 (0-06-447312-0) HarperCollins Children's Bk. Group. (Harper Trophy).

—Crystal. 1987. (J). (gr. 5-9). 14.95 o.p. (0-670-80426-6, Viking Children's Bks.) Penguin Putnam Bks. for Young Readers.

—Crystal. (J). 1990. (Illus.). mass mkt. 5.95 (0-440-80157-5, Dell Books for Young Readers); 1989. 208p. mass mkt. 3.25 o.s.i (0-440-20538-7, Laurel Leaf) Random Hse. Children's Bks.

—Darnell Rock Reporting. 1994. 144p. (J). 14.95 o.s.i (0-385-32096-5, Delacorte Pr.) Dell Publishing.

—The Dream Bearer. 2003. 192p. (J). (gr. 5 up). 15.99 (0-06-029521-X, Amistad Pr.) HarperTrade.

—The Dream Bearer. l.t. ed. 2003. 207p. (J). 25.95 (0-7862-5923-X) Thorndike Pr.

—Fallen Angels. 2002. (Illus.). (J). 13.19 (0-7587-0353-8) Book Wholesalers, Inc.

—Fallen Angels. 320p. (gr. 7-12). 2003. (J). mass mkt. 5.95 (0-590-40943-3, Scholastic Paperbacks); 1988. (YA). pap. 16.95 (0-590-40942-5) Scholastic, Inc.

—Fallen Angels. 1988. (J). 11.04 (0-606-04220-2) Turtleback Bks.

—The Glory Field. 1999. 420p. (J). 15.60 (0-03-054616-8) Holt, Rinehart & Winston.

—The Glory Field. 288p. (gr. 7-12). 1996. (YA). mass mkt. 4.99 (0-590-45898-1); 1994. (J). pap. 14.95 (0-590-45897-3) Scholastic, Inc.

—The Glory Field. 1994. (J). 11.04 (0-606-08527-0) Turtleback Bks.

—Handbook for Boys: A Novel. 2002. (Illus.). 192p. (J). (gr. 5 up). 15.95 (0-06-029146-X); lib. bdg. 15.89 (0-06-029147-8) HarperCollins Children's Bk. Group.

—Handbook for Boys: A Novel. 2003. (Amistad Ser.). 224p. (J). (gr. 5 up). pap. 5.99 (0-06-440930-9) HarperCollins Pubs.

—Handbook for Boys: A Novel. unabr. ed. 2002. (gr. 5 up). pap. 24.00 incl. audio (0-06-008968-7, HarperAudio) HarperTrade.

—The Journal of Biddy Owens: The Negro Leagues. 2001. (My Name Is America Ser.). (Illus.). 144p. (J). (gr. 4-8). pap. 10.95 (0-439-09503-4) Scholastic, Inc.

—The Journal of Biddy Owens: The Negro Leagues. 2001. 17.00 (0-606-22807-1) Turtleback Bks.

Ethnic Groups

—The Journal of Joshua Loper: A Black Cowboy: The Chisholm Trail, 1871. 1999. (My Name Is America Ser.). (Illus.). 158p. (J). (gr. 4-8). pap. 10.95 (*0-590-02691-7*) Scholastic, Inc.

—Me, Mop & the Moondance Kid. 1990. (J). pap. o.s.i (*0-440-80215-6*) Bantam Bks.

—Me, Mop & the Moondance Kid. Foresmman, Scoot, ed. 1994. 160p. (J). pap. 3.50 (*0-440-91005-6*) Dell Publishing.

—Me, Mop & the Moondance Kid. 1988. (Illus.). 128p. (J). (gr. 3-7). 13.95 o.s.i (*0-440-50065-6*, Delacorte Pr.); 1990. 160p. (gr. 4-7). reprint ed. pap. text 4.99 (*0-440-40396-0*) Dell Publishing.

—Me, Mop & the Moondance Kid. 1988. 160p. (J). (gr. 4-7). 13.95 o.s.i (*0-385-30147-2*) Doubleday Publishing.

—Me, Mop & the Moondance Kid. (J). 1996. pap. 4.99 (*0-440-91093-5*); 1995. pap. 4.99 (*0-440-91071-4*) Random Hse. Children's Bks. (Dell Books for Young Readers).

—Me, Mop & the Moondance Kid. 1988. (J). 11.04 (*0-606-04745-X*) Turtleback Bks.

—Monster. 1999. (Amistad Ser.). (Illus.). 288p. (J). (gr. 7 up). 15.95 (*0-06-028077-8*); lib. bdg. 15.89 (*0-06-028078-6*) HarperCollins Children's Bk. Group.

—Mop, Moondance & the Nagasaki Knights. 1993. 160p. (J). (gr. 4-7). pap. 3.50 o.s.i (*0-440-40914-4*) Dell Publishing.

—Mop, Moondance & the Nagasaki Knights. 1995. (J). (gr. 6). 9.28 (*0-395-73269-7*) Houghton Mifflin Co.

—Motown & Didi: A Love Story. 2002. (Illus.). (J). 13.40 (*0-7587-0384-8*) Book Wholesalers, Inc.

—Motown & Didi: A Love Story. 1984. 192p. (YA). (gr. 7 up). 14.95 o.p. (*0-670-49062-8*, Viking Children's Bks.) Penguin Putnam Bks. for Young Readers.

—Motown & Didi: A Love Story. 1987. (Laurel-Leaf Contemporary Fiction Ser.). 176p. (YA). (gr. 7 up). mass mkt. 4.99 o.s.i (*0-440-95762-1*, Laurel Leaf) Random Hse. Children's Bks.

—Motown & Didi: A Love Story. 1987. (Laurel-Leaf Contemporary Fiction Ser.). (J). 11.04 (*0-606-03623-7*) Turtleback Bks.

—The Mouse Rap. Bacha, Andy, ed. & contrib. by by. 1992. (Trophy Bk.). 192p. (J). (gr. 5-9). pap. 5.99 (*0-06-440356-4*, Harper Trophy) HarperCollins Children's Bk. Group.

—The Mouse Rap. 1990. 192p. (J). (gr. 5-9). 14.95 o.p. (*0-06-024343-0*); lib. bdg. 14.89 o.s.i (*0-06-024344-9*) HarperCollins Children's Bk. Group.

—The Mouse Rap. 3rd ed. pap. text 3.95 (*0-13-800087-5*) Prentice Hall (Schl. Div.).

—The Outside Shot. 1984. 192p. (J). (gr. 7 up). 14.95 o.p. (*0-385-29353-4*, Delacorte Pr.) Dell Publishing.

—The Outside Shot. 1986. 192p. (YA). (gr. 7 up). reprint ed. mass mkt. 5.50 (*0-440-96784-8*, Laurel Leaf) Random Hse. Children's Bks.

—The Outside Shot. 1993. (YA). (gr. 7 up). 17.25 o.p. (*0-8446-6674-2*) Smith, Peter Pub., Inc.

—The Outside Shot. 1987. (J). 10.55 (*0-606-03069-7*) Turtleback Bks.

—The Righteous Revenge of Artemis Bonner. (Trophy Bk.). 144p. (J). (gr. 5 up). 1994. (Illus.). pap. 5.99 (*0-06-440462-5*, Harper Trophy); 1992. 14.95 o.p. (*0-06-020844-9*); 1992. lib. bdg. 14.89 o.p. (*0-06-020846-5*) HarperCollins Children's Bk. Group.

—The Righteous Revenge of Artemis Bonner. 1994. (YA). 11.00 (*0-606-06698-5*) Turtleback Bks.

—Scorpions. (Trophy Bk.). 224p. (J). (gr. 7 up). 1996. pap. 5.99 (*0-06-440623-7*, Harper Trophy); 1990. pap. 5.99 (*0-06-447066-0*, Harper Trophy); 1988. 16.99 (*0-06-024364-3*); 1988. (Illus.). lib. bdg. 16.89 (*0-06-024365-1*) HarperCollins Children's Bk. Group.

—Scorpions. unabr. ed. 1997. (J). Class Set. 105.30 incl. audio (*0-7887-2585-8*, 46431); Homework Set. 48.20 incl. audio (*0-7887-1599-2*, 40630) Recorded Bks., LLC.

—Scorpions. 1990. 12.00 (*0-606-09833-X*); (J). 12.00 (*0-606-04533-3*) Turtleback Bks.

—Slam! (Point Signature Ser.). (YA). (gr. 7-12). 2003. 272p. mass mkt. 5.99 (*0-590-48668-3*, Scholastic Paperbacks); 1996. 240p. pap. 15.95 (*0-590-48667-5*) Scholastic, Inc.

—Slam! 1996. 11.04 (*0-606-15706-9*) Turtleback Bks.

—Smiffy Blue, Ace Crime Detective: The Case of the Missing Ruby & Other Stories. 1996. (Illus.). 96p. (J). (gr. 3-6). pap. 14.95 o.p. (*0-590-67665-2*) Scholastic, Inc.

—145th Street: Short Stories. 2000. 160p. (YA). (gr. 7-12). 15.95 (*0-385-32137-6*, Delacorte Pr.) Dell Publishing.

—145th Street: Short Stories. 2001. 160p. (YA). (gr. 7 up). mass mkt. 5.50 (*0-440-22916-2*, Laurel Leaf) Random Hse. Children's Bks.

—145th Street: Short Stories. 2001. 11.55 (*0-606-22414-9*) Turtleback Bks.

Myers, Walter Dean & Myers, Christopher A. Monster. 2001. (Amistad Ser.). (Illus.). 288p. (J). (gr. 7 up). reprint ed. pap. 6.99 (*0-06-440731-4*, Amistad Pr.) HarperTrade.

Nash, Alissa. Markita. 1997. (Illus.). 35p. (J). (gr. k-3). pap. 7.95 (*0-913543-39-X*) African American Images.

Neasi, Barbara J. Escucheme. 2002. (Spanish Rookie Readers Ser.). (Illus.). (J). (gr. k-2). pap. 4.95 (*0-516-26314-5*, Children's Pr.) Scholastic Library Publishing.

—Escucheme. 2001. (Rookie Espanol Ser.). (SPA., Illus.). 32p. (J). (gr. k-2). lib. bdg. 15.00 (*0-516-22358-5*, Children's Pr.) Scholastic Library Publishing.

—Listen to Me. (Rookie Readers Ser.). (Illus.). 32p. (J). (gr. 1-2). rev. ed. 1986. lib. bdg. 19.00 (*0-516-02072-2*); 2nd rev. ed. 2001. pap. 4.95 (*0-516-25970-9*) Scholastic Library Publishing. (Children's Pr.).

—Listen to Me Level C. rev. ed. 2001. (Rookie Readers Ser.). (Illus.). 32p. (J). (gr. 1-2). lib. bdg. 19.00 (*0-516-22154-X*, Children's Pr.) Scholastic Library Publishing.

Nelson, Vaunda M. Beyond Mayfield. 1999. 144p. (J). (gr. 5-9). 15.99 (*0-399-23355-5*, G. P. Putnam's Sons) Penguin Group (USA) Inc.

Nelson, Vaunda Micheaux. Almost to Freedom. 2003. (Carolrhoda Picture Books Ser.). (Illus.). 40p. (J). (gr. 1-5). 15.95 (*1-57505-342-X*, Carolrhoda Bks.) Lerner Publishing Group.

—Mayfield Crossing. 2002. 96p. (J). pap. 5.99 (*0-698-11930-4*, Puffin Bks.) Penguin Putnam Bks. for Young Readers.

—Possibles. 1995. 192p. (J). (gr. 3-7). 15.95 o.s.i (*0-399-22823-3*, G. P. Putnam's Sons) Penguin Group (USA) Inc.

—Possibles. 1997. (Illus.). 192p. (YA). (gr. 5-9). pap. 5.99 o.p. (*0-698-11551-1*, PaperStar) Penguin Putnam Bks. for Young Readers.

—Possibles. 1997. (J). 12.04 (*0-606-10989-7*) Turtleback Bks.

Netzarel, Orly. Yellow, Yellow-Brown, Yellow-Brown & Black. 2001. 160p. pap. 11.95 (*0-595-18742-0*, Writers Club Pr.) iUniverse, Inc.

Nicholas, Evangeline. These Old Rags. 1997. (Illus.). (J). (*0-7802-8021-0*) Wright Group, The.

Nichols, Joan K. All but the Right Folks. 1985. 144p. (J). (gr. 3 up). lib. bdg. 11.95 o.p. (*0-88045-065-7*) Stemmer Hse. Pubs., Inc.

Nikola-Lisa, W. Summer Sun Risin' 2002. (Illus.). 32p. (J). (ps-1). 16.95 (*1-58430-034-5*) Lee & Low Bks., Inc.

Nixon, Joan Lowery. David's Search. 1998. (Orphan Train Children Ser.: No. 4). 144p. (gr. 2-6). text 9.95 o.s.i (*0-385-32296-8*, Delacorte Pr.) Dell Publishing.

Nolen, Jerdine. Big Jabe. 2000. (Illus.). 32p. (J). (gr. 1 up). lib. bdg. 16.89 (*0-688-13663-X*) HarperCollins Children's Bk. Group.

—Big Jabe. 2000. (Illus.). 32p. (J). (gr. 1 up). 15.99 (*0-688-13662-1*); 15.99 (*0-688-13662-1*) HarperCollins Pubs.

—Big Jabe. 2004. (Illus.). 32p. (J). pap. 6.99 (*0-06-054061-3*, Amistad Pr.) HarperTrade.

—In My Momma's Kitchen. 2001. (Illus.). (J). 12.10 (*0-606-21246-9*) Turtleback Bks.

Ochs, Carol P. When I'm Alone. 1993. (Illus.). 32p. (J). (ps-3). pap. 6.95 (*0-87614-620-5*); lib. bdg. 14.95 (*0-87614-752-X*) Lerner Publishing Group. (Carolrhoda Bks.).

Olswanger, Anna. Sweet Potato Pudding. 1999. (Illus.). 60p. pap. text 6.95 (*1-58521-008-0*) Books for Black Children, Inc.

Oppenheim, Shulamith Levey. Fireflies for Nathan. 1994. (Illus.). (J). 16.00 (*0-688-12147-0*); lib. bdg. 15.93 o.p. (*0-688-12148-9*) Morrow/Avon. (Morrow, William & Co.).

—Fireflies for Nathan. 1996. (Picture Puffin Bks.). (Illus.). 32p. (J). (ps-3). pap. 4.99 o.p. (*0-14-055782-2*, Puffin Bks.) Penguin Putnam Bks. for Young Readers.

Ormerod, Jan. Young Joe. 1986. (Illus.). 24p. (J). (ps). pap. 4.95 o.p. (*0-688-04210-4*) HarperCollins Children's Bk. Group.

O'Shea, Robbie. I'm Brown & My Sister Isn't. 2002. (Illus.). 20p. (J). (ps-5). pap. 13.95 (*0-9718034-0-4*, 9718034) RKO Enterprises.

Owens, Tom. Free to Learn. 2000. (Cover-to-Cover Bks.). (Illus.). 55p. (J). 15.95 (*0-7807-9314-5*); pap. (*0-7891-5164-2*) Perfection Learning Corp.

Owens, Vivian. I Met a Great Lady: Ivy Meets Mary McLeod Bethune. Maxwell, Carolyn, ed. unabr. ed. 1998. (Illus.). 80p. (J). (gr. 4-11). pap. 8.95 (*0-9623839-5-3*) Eschar Pubns.

—I Met a Great Man: John Meets Dr. Carver of Tuskegee. Owens, April, ed. unabr. ed. 1998. (Illus.). 64p. (J). (gr. 4-10). pap. 8.95 (*0-9623839-6-1*) Eschar Pubns.

Owens, Vivian W. Nadanda, the Wordmaker: Hide the Doll. Maxwell, Carolyn, ed. 1994. (Illus.). 246p. (YA). (gr. 5 up). 16.95 (*0-9623839-3-7*) Eschar Pubns.

—The Rosebush Witch. 1996. (Illus.). 96p. (J). (gr. 3-9). pap. 8.95 (*0-9623839-4-5*) Eschar Pubns.

Pace, Lorenzo. Jalani & the Lock. 2001. (Illus.). 48p. (J). lib. bdg. 17.95 (*0-8239-9700-6*, PowerKids Pr.) Rosen Publishing Group, Inc., The.

Paley, Nina, illus. Inside-Out Feelings. 1993. (Contemporary Health Ser.). (J). 3.00 (*1-56071-315-1*) ETR Assocs.

Parker, Carol. Why Do You Call Me Chocolate Boy? 1993. (Illus.). 28p. (Orig.). (J). (gr. 2-6). pap. 7.95 (*0-9637267-0-6*) Gull Crest Publishing.

Parker, Toni Trent. Snowflake Kisses & Gingerbread Smiles. 2002. (Illus.). 16p. (J). mass mkt. 6.95 (*0-439-33872-7*, Cartwheel Bks.) Scholastic, Inc.

—Sweets & Treats. 2002. (Illus.). 16p. (J). pap. 6.95 (*0-439-33871-9*, Cartwheel Bks.) Scholastic, Inc.

Partridge, Elizabeth. Clara & the Hoodoo Man. 176p. (gr. 3-7). 1998. pap. 4.99 o.s.i (*0-14-038348-4*); 1996. (J). 14.99 o.s.i (*0-525-45403-9*, Dutton Children's Bks.) Penguin Putnam Bks. for Young Readers.

Patrick, Denise L. I Can Count. 1999. (Illus.). 12p. (J). bds. 3.49 o.s.i (*0-307-12207-5*, Golden Bks.) Random Hse. Children's Bks.

—No Diapers for Baby! 1998. (Essence Ser.). (Illus.). 12p. (J). (ps). bds. 3.49 o.s.i (*0-307-12870-9*, Golden Bks.) Random Hse. Children's Bks.

—Peekaboo, Baby! 1998. (Essence Ser.). (Illus.). 16p. (J). (ps-3). bds. 3.49 o.s.i (*0-307-12871-7*, Golden Bks.) Random Hse. Children's Bks.

—See What Baby Can Do! 1998. (Illus.). 12p. (J). bds. 3.49 o.s.i (*0-307-12208-5*, Golden Bks.) Random Hse. Children's Bks.

Patrick, Denise Lewis. The Adventures of Midnight Son, ERS. 1997. 128p. (J). (gr. 4-7). 16.00 (*0-8050-4714-X*, Holt, Henry & Co. Bks. For Young Readers) Holt, Henry & Co.

—The Car Washing Street. 1993. (Illus.). 32p. (J). (ps up). 14.00 o.p. (*0-688-11452-0*); lib. bdg. 13.93 o.p. (*0-688-11453-9*) Morrow/Avon. (Morrow, William & Co.).

—Case of the Missing Cookies. 1996. (Gullah Gullah Island Ser.: Vol. 4). 24p. (J). (ps-3). mass mkt. 3.25 (*0-689-80398-2*, Simon Spotlight/Nickelodeon) Simon & Schuster Children's Publishing.

—Red Dancing Shoes. 1998. (Illus.). 32p. (J). (ps-3). pap. 5.99 (*0-688-15850-1*, Harper Trophy) HarperCollins Children's Bk. Group.

—Red Dancing Shoes. 1993. (Illus.). 32p. (J). (ps-3). 16.00 o.s.i (*0-688-10392-8*); 15.89 (*0-688-10393-6*) Morrow/Avon. (Morrow, William & Co.).

—Red Dancing Shoes. 1998. 11.10 (*0-606-13023-3*) Turtleback Bks.

—Shaina's Garden. 3rd ed. 1996. (Gullah Gullah Island Ser.: 3). 24p. (ps-3). pap. 3.25 (*0-689-80397-4*, Simon Spotlight/Nickelodeon) Simon & Schuster Children's Publishing.

Paulsen, Gary. Sarny: A Life Remembered. 1997. 192p. (YA). (gr. 7-12). 15.95 o.s.i (*0-385-32195-3*, Delacorte Pr.) Dell Publishing.

—Sarny: A Life Remembered. 1999. 192p. (YA). (gr. 7-12). mass mkt. 5.50 (*0-440-21973-6*, Dell Books for Young Readers) Random Hse. Children's Bks.

—Sarny: A Life Remembered. 1999. 11.04 (*0-606-16454-5*) Turtleback Bks.

Peacock, Nancy. R U 4 Real? 2000. (TodaysGirls.com Ser.: Vol. 4). 144p. (J). (gr. 5-9). pap. 5.99 o.s.i (*0-8499-7563-8*) Nelson, Tommy.

Pearsall, Shelley. Trouble Don't Last. 256p. 2003. (gr. 3-7). pap. text 5.50 (*0-440-41811-9*, Dell Books for Young Readers); 2002. (Illus.). (gr. 4-8). text 14.95 (*0-375-81490-6*, Random Hse. Bks. for Young Readers); 2002. (Illus.). (gr. 4-8). lib. bdg. 16.99 (*0-375-91490-0*, Random Hse. Bks. for Young Readers) Random Hse. Children's Bks.

Pegram, Laura. Daughter's Day Blues. (Illus.). 32p. 2002. pap. 6.99 (*0-14-056187-0*); 2000. (J). 15.99 o.s.i (*0-8037-1557-9*, Dial Bks. for Young Readers) Penguin Putnam Bks. for Young Readers.

—Windy Day. 1994. (Illus.). 12p. (J). (ps). bds. 5.95 (*0-86316-218-5*) Writers & Readers Publishing, Inc.

Pepper Bird Staff. Copasetic: Adventures of Bojangles Robinson. 1993. (Multicultural Historical Fiction Ser.). (Illus.). 48p. (Orig.). (J). (gr. 4-7). pap. 3.95 (*1-56817-000-9*) Pepper Bird Publishing.

Perkins, Charles D. Swinging on a Rainbow. 1992. (Illus.). 32p. (J). (gr. 1-4). 14.95 (*0-86543-286-4*); (ps-3). pap. 6.95 (*0-86543-287-2*) Africa World Pr.

Peterson, Jeanne W. My Mama Sings. 1994. (Illus.). 32p. (J). (ps-3). lib. bdg. 15.89 o.p. (*0-06-023859-3*); 15.00 o.p. (*0-06-023854-2*) HarperCollins Children's Bk. Group.

Petry, Ann. Tituba of Salem Village. (Trophy Bk.). (YA). 1991. 272p. (gr. 5 up). pap. 5.99 (*0-06-440403-X*, Harper Trophy); 1964. (gr. 7-11). 14.95 (*0-690-82677-X*) HarperCollins Children's Bk. Group.

Pickhardt, Carl E. The Case of the Scary Divorce. 1997. (Jackson Skye Mystery Ser.). (Illus.). 96p. (YA). (gr. 3-10). pap. 14.95 o.p. (*0-945354-80-0*) American Psychological Assn.

Pinkney, Gloria J. The Sunday Outing. 1994. (Illus.). 32p. (J). (gr. k-4). 16.99 (*0-8037-1198-0*); 14.89 o.s.i (*0-8037-1199-9*) Penguin Putnam Bks. for Young Readers. (Dial Bks. for Young Readers).

Piercy, Patricia A. The Great Encounter: A Special Meeting Before Columbus. 1991. (Illus.). 41p. (J). (gr. 2-5). pap. 6.95 (*0-913543-26-8*) African American Images.

Pinkney, Andrea Davis. Fishing Day. 2003. (J). lib. bdg. (*0-7868-2614-2*, Jump at the Sun) Hyperion Bks. for Children.

—Fishing Day. 2003. (Illus.). 32p. (J). 15.99 (*0-7868-0766-0*) Hyperion Pr.

—Hold Fast to Dreams. 1996. (Illus.). 112p. (J). (gr. 5-9). pap. 4.50 o.s.i (*0-7868-1125-0*) Disney Pr.

—Hold Fast to Dreams. 1995. (Illus.). 112p. (YA). (gr. 5 up). 16.00 (*0-688-12832-7*, Morrow, William & Co.) Morrow/Avon.

—Hold Fast to Dreams. 1996. 9.60 o.p. (*0-606-11469-6*) Turtleback Bks.

—I Smell Honey. 1997. (Illus.). 16p. (J). (ps). bds. 5.95 (*0-15-200640-0*, Red Wagon Bks.) Harcourt Children's Bks.

—Mim's Christmas Jam. 2001. (Illus.). 32p. (J). (ps-2). 16.00 (*0-15-201918-9*, Gulliver Bks.) Harcourt Children's Bks.

—Pretty Brown Face. 1997. (Illus.). 8p. (J). (ps). bds. 5.95 (*0-15-200643-5*, Red Wagon Bks.) Harcourt Children's Bks.

—Raven in a Dove House. 1998. 224p. (J). (gr. 6). 16.00 o.s.i (*0-15-201461-6*, Gulliver Bks.) Harcourt Children's Bks.

—Raven in a Dove House. 1999. 208p. (J). pap. 6.99 (*0-7868-1349-0*) Hyperion Bks. for Children.

—Raven in a Dove House. 1999. 13.04 (*0-606-17789-2*) Turtleback Bks.

—Shake Shake Shake. 1997. (Illus.). 16p. (J). (ps). bds. 5.95 (*0-15-200632-X*, Red Wagon Bks.) Harcourt Children's Bks.

—Silent Thunder: A Civil War Story. 2001. 224p. (J). (gr. 3-7). pap. 5.99 (*0-7868-1569-8*, Jump at the Sun); 1999. (Illus.). 208p. (J). (gr. 4-7). 15.99 (*0-7868-0439-4*); 1999. (Illus.). 208p. (YA). (gr. 4-7). lib. bdg. 16.49 (*0-7868-2388-7*) Hyperion Bks. for Children.

—Silent Thunder: A Civil War Story. 2001. (J). 12.04 (*0-606-21434-8*) Turtleback Bks.

—Solo Girl. 1997. (Hyperion Chapters Ser.: Vol. 1). (Illus.). 64p. (J). (gr. 2-4). pap. 3.95 (*0-7868-1216-8*) Disney Pr.

—Solo Girl. 1997. (Hyperion Chapters Ser.: Vol. 1). (Illus.). 64p. (J). (gr. 2-4). lib. bdg. 14.49 (*0-7868-2265-1*) Hyperion Bks. for Children.

Pinkney, Brian. The Adventures of Sparrowboy. 2002. (Illus.). (J). 14.47 (*0-7587-1906-X*) Book Wholesalers, Inc.

—The Adventures of Sparrowboy. (Illus.). 40p. (J). (ps-3). 2000. pap. 5.99 (*0-689-83534-5*, Aladdin); 1997. 16.00 (*0-689-81071-7*, Simon & Schuster Children's Publishing) Simon & Schuster Children's Publishing.

—Jojo's Flying Side Kick. 1998. (Illus.). (gr. k-4). 13.40 (*0-613-10514-1*) Econo-Clad Bks.

—Jojo's Flying Side Kick. 1995. (J). 14.00 (*0-671-88111-6*); (Illus.). 32p. 15.00 (*0-689-80283-8*) Simon & Schuster Children's Publishing. (Simon & Schuster Children's Publishing).

—Jojo's Flying Side Kick. 1998. 12.14 (*0-606-15874-X*) Turtleback Bks.

—Jojo's Flying Sidekick. 1998. (Illus.). 32p. (J). (gr. k-3). pap. 6.99 (*0-689-82192-1*, Aladdin) Simon & Schuster Children's Publishing.

—Max Found Two Sticks. 2002. (Illus.). (J). 15.53 (*0-7587-3106-X*) Book Wholesalers, Inc.

—Max Found Two Sticks. 40p. (J). (gr. k-3). 1997. pap. 6.99 (*0-689-81593-X*, Aladdin); 1994. (Illus.). pap. 17.00 (*0-671-78776-4*, Simon & Schuster Children's Publishing) Simon & Schuster Children's Publishing.

—Max Found Two Sticks. 1997. 12.14 (*0-606-11605-2*) Turtleback Bks.

Pinkney, Gloria J. Back Home. 1992. (Illus.). (J). (gr. k-4). 400p. 14.89 o.p. (*0-8037-1169-7*); 40p. 16.99 (*0-8037-1168-9*) Penguin Putnam Bks. for Young Readers. (Dial Bks. for Young Readers).

—Back Home. 1999. 13.14 (*0-606-16773-0*) Turtleback Bks.

Pinkney, Sandra L. Shades of Black: A Celebration of Our Children. 2000. (Illus.). 40p. (J). (ps-3). pap. 14.95 o.s.i (*0-439-14892-8*) Scholastic, Inc.

Pisano, Mary B. Going to New Orleans to Visit Weezie Anna. 1994. (Illus.). 24p. (J). (ps-3). 8.95 o.p. (*0-937552-52-6*) Quail Ridge Pr., Inc.

Polacco, Patricia. Mrs. Katz & Tush. 1993. pap. 19.95 o.s.i incl. audio (*0-553-45913-9*); pap. 19.95 o.s.i incl. audio (*0-553-45913-9*) Bantam Bks.

—Mrs. Katz & Tush. 2002. (Illus.). (J). 14.79 (*0-7587-3191-4*) Book Wholesalers, Inc.

—Mrs. Katz & Tush. ed. 1994. (J). (gr. 2). spiral bd. (*0-616-01760-X*) Canadian National Institute for the Blind/Institut National Canadien pour les Aveugles.

Ethnic Groups

—Mrs. Katz & Tush. 1994. (Picture Yearling Ser.). (Illus.). 32p. (ps-3). pap. text 6.99 (*0-440-40936-5*) Dell Publishing.

—Mrs. Katz & Tush. (J). 1993. mass mkt. o.p. (*0-440-90065-4*); 1992. (Illus.). 15.00 (*0-553-08122-5*); 1991. mass mkt. o.s.i (*0-553-53092-5*) Random Hse. Children's Bks. (Dell Books for Young Readers).

—Mrs. Katz & Tush. 1994. 13.14 (*0-606-05930-X*) Turtleback Bks.

Porte, Barbara Ann. I Only Made up the Roses. 1987. 128p. (YA). (gr. 7 up). 15.00 o.p. (*0-688-05216-9*, Greenwillow Bks.) HarperCollins Children's Bk. Group.

Porter. Addy's Short Story Set: High Hopes for Addy; Addy's Little Brother; Addy Studies Freedom, 3 vols. 2002. (American Girls Short Stories Ser.). (Illus.). (YA). (gr. 2). 11.95 (*1-58485-497-9*, American Girl) Pleasant Co. Pubns.

Porter, Connie Rose. Addy Learns a Lesson: A School Story. Johnson, Roberta, ed. 1993. (American Girls Collection: Bk. 2). (Illus.). 80p. (J). (gr. 2 up). 12.95 (*1-56247-078-7*); pap. 5.95 (*1-56247-077-9*) Pleasant Co. Pubns. (American Girl).

—Addy Learns a Lesson: A School Story. 1993. (American Girls Collection: Bk. 2). (Illus.). (YA). (gr. 2 up). 12.10 (*0-606-05103-1*) Turtleback Bks.

—Addy Saves the Day: A Summer Story. Johnson, Roberta, ed. 1993. (American Girls Collection: Bk. 5). (Illus.). 80p. (YA). (gr. 2 up). 12.95 (*1-56247-084-1*); pap. 5.95 (*1-56247-083-3*) Pleasant Co. Pubns. (American Girl).

—Addy Saves the Day: A Summer Story. Johnson, Roberta, ed. 1993. (American Girls Collection: Bk. 5). (Illus.). (YA). (gr. 2 up). 12.10 (*0-606-06160-6*) Turtleback Bks.

—Addy Studies Freedom. 2002. (American Girls Short Stories Ser.). (Illus.). 64p. (J). 4.95 (*1-58485-480-4*, American Girl) Pleasant Co. Pubns.

—Addy's Boxed Set: Meet Addy; Addy Learns a Lesson; Addy's Surprise; Happy Birthday, Addy!; Addy Saves the Day; Changes for Addy, 6 bks. Johnson, Roberta, ed. 1994. (American Girls Collection: Bks. 1-6). (Illus.). 392p. (YA). pap. 34.95 (*1-56247-087-6*); (gr. 2 up). 74.95 (*1-56247-088-4*) Pleasant Co. Pubns. (American Girl).

—Addy's Little Brother. 2000. (American Girls Short Stories Ser.). (Illus.). 56p. (YA). (gr. 2 up). 3.95 (*1-58485-033-7*, American Girl) Pleasant Co. Pubns.

—Addy's Story Collection. 2001. (American Girls Collection). (Illus.). 370p. (J). (gr. 2 up). 29.95 (*1-58485-444-8*, American Girl) Pleasant Co. Pubns.

—Addy's Summer Place. 2003. (American Girls Collection). (Illus.). 38p. (J). pap. 4.95 (*1-58485-697-1*, American Girl) Pleasant Co. Pubns.

—Addy's Surprise: A Christmas Story. Johnson, Roberta, ed. 1993. (American Girls Collection: Bk. 3). (Illus.). 80p. (J). (gr. 2 up). 12.95 (*1-56247-080-9*); pap. 5.95 (*1-56247-079-5*) Pleasant Co. Pubns. (American Girl).

—Addy's Surprise: A Christmas Story. 1993. (American Girls Collection: Bk. 3). (Illus.). (YA). (gr. 2 up). 12.10 (*0-606-05104-X*) Turtleback Bks.

—Changes for Addy: A Winter Story. Johnson, Roberta, ed. 1994. (American Girls Collection: Bk. 6). (Illus.). 72p. (YA). (gr. 2 up). 12.95 (*1-56247-086-8*); pap. 5.95 (*1-56247-085-X*) Pleasant Co. Pubns. (American Girl).

—Changes for Addy: A Winter Story. 1994. (American Girls Collection: Bk. 6). (Illus.). (YA). (gr. 2 up). 12.10 (*0-606-06272-6*) Turtleback Bks.

—Happy Birthday, Addy! A Springtime Story. 1993. (American Girls Collection: Bk. 4). (Illus.). 72p. (YA). (gr. 2 up). 12.95 (*1-56247-082-5*, American Girl) Pleasant Co. Pubns.

—Happy Birthday, Addy! A Springtime Story. Johnson, Roberta, ed. 1993. (American Girls Collection: Bk. 4). (Illus.). 72p. (YA). (gr. 2 up). pap. 5.95 (*1-56247-081-7*, American Girl) Pleasant Co. Pubns.

—Happy Birthday, Addy! A Springtime Story. 1994. (American Girls Collection: Bk. 4). (Illus.). (YA). (gr. 2 up). 12.10 (*0-606-06439-7*) Turtleback Bks.

—High Hopes for Addy. 1999. (American Girls Short Stories Ser.). (Illus.). 56p. (YA). (gr. 2 up). 3.95 (*1-56247-765-X*, American Girl) Pleasant Co. Pubns.

—Meet Addy: An American Girl. Johnson, Roberta, ed. 1993. (American Girls Collection: Bk. 1). (Illus.). 80p. (J). (gr. 2 up). pap. 5.95 (*1-56247-075-2*); lib. bdg. 12.95 (*1-56247-076-0*) Pleasant Co. Pubns. (American Girl).

—Meet Addy: An American Girl. 1993. (American Girls Collection: Bk. 1). (Illus.). (YA). (gr. 2 up). 12.10 (*0-606-05459-6*) Turtleback Bks.

Porter, Connie Rose & McAliley, Susan. Addy's Wedding Quilt. 2001. (American Girls Short Stories Ser.). (Illus.). 64p. (J). (gr. 2 up). 3.95 (*1-58485-274-7*, American Girl) Pleasant Co. Pubns.

Poydar, Nancy. Busy Bea. 1994. (Illus.). 32p. (J). (ps-2). 14.95 (*0-689-50592-2*, McElderry, Margaret K.) Simon & Schuster Children's Publishing.

Prather, Ray. Fish & Bones. 1992. 272p. (J). (gr. 5-9). 14.00 o.p. (*0-06-025121-2*); lib. bdg. 14.89 o.p. (*0-06-025122-0*) HarperCollins Children's Bk. Group.

Price, Hope Lynne. These Hands. 1999. (Jump at the Sun Ser.). (Illus.). 24p. (J). 14.99 (*0-7868-0370-3*) Hyperion Bks. for Children.

—These Hands. 1999. (Jump at the Sun Ser.). (Illus.). 24p. (J). lib. bdg. 15.49 (*0-7868-2320-8*) Hyperion Pr.

Pruitt, Pamela, et al. Henry Box Brown; Struggle for Freedom; Wildfire. McCluskey, John A., ed. 2nd ed. 1993. (Stories from Black History Series II: Vol. 1). (Illus.). (Orig.). (J). (gr. 4-7). pap. 2.00 (*0-913678-25-2*) New Day Pr.

Quattlebaum, Mary. Jackson Jones & the Puddle of Thorns. 1995. (Illus.). 128p. (J). (gr. 3-7). pap. 4.50 (*0-440-41066-5*) Dell Publishing.

—Jackson Jones & the Puddle of Thorns. 1995. (J). 10.55 (*0-606-07725-1*) Turtleback Bks.

Quigley, Martin. The Original Colored House of David. 1981. (J). (gr. 7 up). 8.95 o.p. (*0-395-31608-1*) Houghton Mifflin Co.

Rahaman, Vashanti. Read for Me, Mama. 2003. (Illus.). 32p. (J). (gr. 1). 15.95 (*1-56397-313-8*) Boyds Mills Pr.

Raintree Steck-Vaughn Staff. The River That Gave Gifts. 1992. 24p. 5.00 (*0-8172-6727-1*) Raintree Pubs.

Randall, Florence E. The Almost Year. 1975. (J). pap. 1.50 o.p. (*0-590-05209-8*) Scholastic, Inc.

Ransom, Candice F. Liberty Street. 2003. (J). lib. bdg. 17.85 (*0-8027-8871-8*); (Illus.). 16.95 (*0-8027-8869-6*) Walker & Co.

—Rescue on the Outer Banks. 2002. (On My Own History Ser.). (Illus.). 48p. (J). (gr. 1-3). lib. bdg. 21.27 (*0-87614-460-1*, Carolrhoda Bks.) Lerner Publishing Group.

Raschka, Chris. Yo! Yes? (Illus.). 32p. (J). (ps-1). 1998. mass mkt. 6.95 (*0-531-07108-1*); 1993. pap. 15.95 (*0-531-05469-1*); 1993. lib. bdg. 16.99 (*0-531-08619-4*) Scholastic, Inc. (Orchard Bks.).

—Yo! Yes? (J). (ps-5). 2001. 24.95 incl. audio (*1-55592-066-7*); 2001. 24.95 incl. audio (*1-55592-066-7*); 2000. pap. 12.95 incl. audio (*1-55592-067-5*, QPRA566); 2000. pap. 12.95 incl. audio (*1-55592-067-5*, QPRA566) Weston Woods Studios, Inc.

Raven, Margot T. Circle Unbroken: The Story of the Sweetgrass Basket, RS. 2004. 16.00 (*0-374-31289-3*, Farrar, Straus & Giroux (BYR)) Farrar, Straus & Giroux.

Reed, Teresa. Rain, Rain Go Away. 1996. (Gullah Gullah Island Ser.). 24p. (J). (ps-3). mass mkt. 3.25 (*0-689-80395-8*, Simon Spotlight/Nickelodeon) Simon & Schuster Children's Publishing.

Rees, Douglas. Lightning Time. 1997. (Illus.). 172p. (J). (gr. 5-9). pap. 15.95 o.p. (*0-7894-2458-4*) Dorling Kindersley Publishing, Inc.

—Lightning Time. 1999. 176p. (J). (gr. 5-9). pap. 4.99 (*0-14-130317-4*, Puffin Bks.) Penguin Putnam Bks. for Young Readers.

—Lightning Time. 1999. 11.04 (*0-606-19069-4*) Turtleback Bks.

Reese, Della. God Inside of Me. 32p. (ps-3). Date not set. (J). pap. 15.99 (*0-7868-1311-3*); 1999. (Illus.). lib. bdg. 16.49 (*0-7868-2395-X*); 1999. (Illus.). (J). 16.99 (*0-7868-0434-3*) Hyperion Bks. for Children. (Jump at the Sun).

Reeves, Adrienne E. Willie & the Number Three Door & Other Adventures. 1991. (Illus.). 120p. (Orig.). (J). (gr. 1-3). pap. 8.95 o.s.i (*0-87743-703-3*) Baha'i Distribution Service.

Reid, Robin. Thank You, Dr. King. 2003. (Nick Jr. Ser.). (Illus.). 24p. (J). (gr. k-3). pap. 3.50 (*0-689-85242-8*, Simon Spotlight/Nickelodeon) Simon & Schuster Children's Publishing.

Rhone, Alexus D. Premature Pleasures. 2001. 224p. (YA). (gr. 6 up). 16.95 (*0-9708688-0-4*) Unshackled Publishing.

Richemont, Enid. The Magic Skateboard. (Illus.). (J). 1995. bds. 3.99 o.p. (*1-56402-449-0*); 1993. 80p. (gr. 3-6). 14.95 o.p. (*1-56402-132-7*) Candlewick Pr.

Riggio, Anita. Secret Signs: Along the Underground Railroad. 2003. (Illus.). 32p. (J). (gr. k-3). 15.95 (*1-56397-555-6*) Boyds Mills Pr.

Rinaldi, Ann. The Education of Mary: A Little Miss of Color, 1832. 2000. 256p. (J). (gr. 6-8). 15.99 (*0-7868-0532-3*, Jump at the Sun) Hyperion Bks. for Children.

—The Education of Mary: A Little Miss of Color, 1832. 2000. 254p. (J). pap. (*0-7868-1377-6*) Hyperion Pr.

—Hang a Thousand Trees with Ribbons: The Story of Phillis Wheatley. 1996. (Great Episodes Ser.). 352p. (YA). (gr. 7-12). pap. 6.00 (*0-15-200877-2*); 14.00 (*0-15-200876-4*) Harcourt Children's Bks. (Gulliver Bks.).

—Hang a Thousand Trees with Ribbons: The Story of Phillis Wheatley. 1996. 12.05 (*0-606-10834-3*) Turtleback Bks.

—Numbering All the Bones. 2002. (Illus.). 176p. (J). (gr. 5-9). 15.99 (*0-7868-0533-1*, Jump at the Sun) Hyperion Bks. for Children.

—Taking Liberty: The Story of Oney Judge, George Washington's Runaway Slave. 272p. (YA). 2004. (Illus.). mass mkt. 5.99 (*0-689-85188-X*, Simon Pulse); 2002. (gr. 7 up). 16.95 (*0-689-85187-1*, Simon & Schuster Children's Publishing) Simon & Schuster Children's Publishing.

—Taking Liberty: The Story of Oney Judge, George Washington's Runaway Slave. 2003. (Young Adult Ser.). 277p. (J). 24.95 (*0-7862-5557-9*) Thorndike Pr.

—Wolf by the Ears. (Point Ser.). 272p. (gr. 7-12). 1993. (YA). mass mkt. 4.99 (*0-590-43412-8*); 1991. (J). 13.95 (*0-590-43413-6*) Scholastic, Inc.

—Wolf by the Ears. 1991. (Point Ser.). (J). 11.04 (*0-606-02993-1*) Turtleback Bks.

Ringgold, Faith. Aunt Harriet's Underground Railroad in the Sky. 1995. (Illus.). 32p. (ps-3). pap. 6.99 (*0-517-88543-3*) Crown Publishing Group.

—Aunt Harriet's Underground Railroad in the Sky. 1992. (Illus.). 32p. (J). (ps-3). lib. bdg. 17.99 o.s.i (*0-517-58768-8*); 16.00 o.s.i (*0-517-58767-X*) Random Hse. Children's Bks. (Random Hse. Bks. for Young Readers).

—Aunt Harriet's Underground Railroad in the Sky. 1995. (J). 13.14 (*0-606-08478-9*) Turtleback Bks.

—Bonjour, Lonnie. 1996. (Illus.). 32p. (J). (gr. k-4). 15.95 (*0-7868-0076-3*); (gr. 4-7). lib. bdg. 16.49 (*0-7868-2062-4*) Hyperion Bks. for Children.

—Cassie's Word Quilt. (Illus.). 32p. (J). 2004. pap. 6.99 (*0-553-11233-3*, Dragonfly Bks.); 2002. lib. bdg. 15.99 (*0-375-91200-2*, Knopf Bks. for Young Readers); 2002. 13.95 (*0-375-81200-8*, Random Hse. Bks. for Young Readers) Random Hse. Children's Bks.

—Dinner at Aunt Connie's House. 1996. (Illus.). 32p. (J). (ps-3). pap. 4.95 (*0-7868-1150-1*) Disney Pr.

—Dinner at Aunt Connie's House. 1993. (Illus.). 32p. (J). (gr. k-4). 16.95 (*1-56282-425-2*); lib. bdg. 15.49 (*1-56282-426-0*) Hyperion Bks. for Children.

—Dinner at Aunt Connie's House. 1996. (J). 11.10 (*0-606-10782-7*) Turtleback Bks.

—The Invisible Princess. 2001. (Illus.). 32p. (J). (gr. 1-5). pap. 6.99 (*0-440-41735-X*, Dell Books for Young Readers) Random Hse. Children's Bks.

—The Invisible Princess. 2001. 13.14 (*0-606-20729-5*) Turtleback Bks.

—Tar Beach. 2002. (Illus.). (J). 14.79 (*0-7587-5352-7*) Book Wholesalers, Inc.

—Tar Beach. (Book & Doll Packages Ser.). (Illus.). 32p. (ps-4). 1994. (J). 10.00 o.s.i (*0-517-59961-9*, Random Hse. Bks. for Young Readers); 1991. (J). lib. bdg. 18.99 (*0-517-58031-4*, Knopf Bks. for Young Readers); 1991. 18.00 (*0-517-58030-6*, Random Hse. Bks. for Young Readers) Random Hse. Children's Bks.

—Tar Beach. 1996. (ps-3). (Illus.). 32p. pap. 6.99 (*0-517-88544-1*); (J). 5.99 o.s.i (*0-517-58984-2*) Random Hse. Value Publishing.

—Tar Beach. 1996. (J). 13.14 (*0-606-10950-1*) Turtleback Bks.

Roberts, Brenda C. Jazzy Miz Mozetta, RS. 2004. (J). (*0-374-33674-1*, Farrar, Straus & Giroux (BYR)) Farrar, Straus & Giroux.

—Sticks & Stones, Bobbie Bones. 1993. 96p. (J). (gr. 4-6). mass mkt. 2.99 o.p. (*0-590-46518-X*) Scholastic, Inc.

Robinet, Harriette Gillem. Forty Acres & Maybe a Mule. 2000. (YA). (gr. 3 up). pap. 52.00 incl. audio (*0-7887-4332-5*, 41127); pap. 52.00 incl. audio (*0-7887-4332-5*, 41127) Recorded Bks., LLC.

—Forty Acres & Maybe a Mule. (Jean Karl Bks.). 144p. (J). (gr. 3-7). 1998. (Illus.). 16.95 (*0-689-82078-X*, Atheneum); 2000. reprint ed. pap. 4.99 (*0-689-83317-2*, Aladdin) Simon & Schuster Children's Publishing.

—Forty Acres & Maybe a Mule. l.t. ed. 2001. (Illus.). 184p. (J). (gr. 4-7). 21.95 (*0-7862-2704-4*) Thorndike Pr.

—Forty Acres & Maybe a Mule. 2000. 11.04 (*0-606-17824-4*) Turtleback Bks.

—If You Please, President Lincoln! 1995. 160p. (J). (gr. 4-7). 16.00 o.s.i (*0-689-31969-X*, Atheneum) Simon & Schuster Children's Publishing.

—Mississippi Chariot. 128p. (J). (gr. 4-7). 1997. per. 3.99 (*0-689-80632-9*, Aladdin); 1994. 14.95 (*0-689-31960-6*, Atheneum) Simon & Schuster Children's Publishing.

—Twelve Travelers, Twenty Horses. 2003. (Illus.). 208p. (J). 16.95 (*0-689-84561-8*, Atheneum) Simon & Schuster Children's Publishing.

—The Twins, the Pirates & the Battle of New Orleans. 1997. 144p. (J). (gr. 3-7). 15.00 o.s.i (*0-689-81208-6*, Atheneum) Simon & Schuster Children's Publishing.

—Walking to the Bus Rider Blues. 2000. (Illus.). 146p. (J). (gr. 4-7). 16.00 (*0-689-83191-9*, Atheneum) Simon & Schuster Children's Publishing.

Robinson, Glen. The Clue in the Secret Passage. 1997. (Shoebox Kids Ser.: Vol. 7). (Illus.). 96p. (J). (gr. 2-5). pap. 6.99 (*0-8163-1386-5*) Pacific Pr. Publishing Assn.

Rochelle, Belinda. Jewels. 1998. (Illus.). 32p. (J). (gr. k-3). 15.99 o.s.i (*0-525-67502-7*, Dutton Children's Bks.) Penguin Putnam Bks. for Young Readers.

—When Jo Louis Won the Title. (Illus.). 32p. (J). (ps-3). 1996. pap. 6.95 (*0-395-81657-2*); 1994. tchr. ed. 14.95 o.p. (*0-395-66614-7*) Houghton Mifflin Co.

—When Jo Louis Won the Title. 1994. 12.10 (*0-606-10968-4*) Turtleback Bks.

Roddy, Lee. Risking the Dream. 2000. (Between Two Flags Ser.: Vol. 6). (Illus.). 176p. (J). (gr. 6-9). pap. 5.99 o.p. (*0-7642-2030-6*) Bethany Hse. Pubs.

Rodman, Mary Ann. Yankee Girl, RS. 2004. (J). 16.00 (*0-374-38661-7*, Farrar, Straus & Giroux (BYR)) Farrar, Straus & Giroux.

Rodriguez, Anita. Jamal & the Angel. 1992. (Illus.). 32p. (J). (ps-2). 14.00 o.s.i (*0-517-58601-0*, Random Hse. Bks. for Young Readers) Random Hse. Children's Bks.

Rollins, A. Shelton. Nobody Knows. 2003. (Illus.). 16p. (J). 6.99 (*0-8024-2920-3*) Moody Pr.

Romain, Trevor. Jemma's Journey. 2003. (Illus.). 32p. (J). (gr. k-3). 15.95 (*1-56397-937-3*) Boyds Mills Pr.

Rosado, Maria. Armando's Great Big Surprise No. 5. 1996. (Gullah Gullah Island Ser.). (Illus.). 24p. (ps-3). mass mkt. 3.25 (*0-689-80825-9*, Simon Spotlight/Nickelodeon) Simon & Schuster Children's Publishing.

Rosales, Melodye. The Adventures of Minnie, Bk. 2. 2003. (J). (*0-316-75688-1*) Little Brown Children's Bks.

—The Adventures of Minny, Bk. 3. 2000. (J). (*0-316-75633-4*) Little Brown & Co.

Rosales, Melodye Benson. Minnie Saves the Day! 2001. (Adventures of Minnie Merriweather Ser.). (Illus.). 96p. (J). (gr. 1-4). 12.95 (*0-316-75605-9*) Little Brown Children's Bks.

Rosen, Michael J. Elijah's Angel: A Story for Chanukah & Christmas. (Illus.). 32p. (J). (gr. k up). 1992. 16.00 (*0-15-225394-7*); 1997. reprint ed. pap. 7.00 (*0-15-201558-2*, Harcourt Paperbacks) Harcourt Children's Bks.

—Elijah's Angel: A Story for Chanukah & Christmas. 1997. (J). 12.15 (*0-606-12276-1*) Turtleback Bks.

—A School for Pompey Walker. 1995. (Illus.). 48p. (J). (gr. 4-7). 16.00 (*0-15-200114-X*) Harcourt Children's Bks.

Ross, Andrea. Littlest Ballerina. 1996. (Illus.). 23p. (J). (gr. k-3). 7.95 (*1-887683-13-5*) Storybook Pr. & Productions.

—To Touch the Sun. Davenport, May, ed. l.t. ed. 2000. 195p. (YA). (gr. 9-12). pap. text 15.95 (*0-943864-99-2*) Davenport, May Pubs.

Ross, Kent & Ross, Alice. Jezebel's Spooky Spot. 1999. (Illus.). 32p. (J). (gr. 1-4). 15.99 o.p. (*0-525-45448-9*, Dutton Children's Bks.) Penguin Putnam Bks. for Young Readers.

Rountree, Wendy. Lost Soul. 2003. 87p. (J). pap. 14.95 (*1-59129-975-6*) PublishAmerica, Inc.

Roy, J. Soul Daddy. 1992. 224p. (YA). (gr. 7 up). 16.95 o.s.i (*0-15-277193-X*, Gulliver Bks.) Harcourt Children's Bks.

Rue, Nancy. The Ally. 1998. (Christian Heritage Ser.). 192p. (J). (gr. 3-7). pap. 5.99 (*1-56179-561-5*) Focus on the Family Publishing.

—The Misfit. 1998. (Christian Heritage Ser.). 192p. (J). (gr. 3-7). pap. 5.99 (*1-56179-560-7*) Focus on the Family Publishing.

—The Stunt. 1999. (Christian Heritage Ser.). 208p. (J). (gr. 3-7). pap. 5.99 (*1-56179-833-9*) Bethany Hse. Pubs.

Rust, Ann O'Connell. Torry Island. Rust, Allen F., ed. 2002. (Nonie of the Everglades Ser.: Vol. II). 94p. (J). (gr. 4-7). pap. 7.95 (*1-883203-06-6*) Amaro Bks.

Rutberg, Donald Paul. Running Through Kenya. 1999. (Illus.). 40p. (J). (gr. 3-8). pap. text 8.95 (*1-58521-011-0*) Books for Black Children, Inc.

Samton, Sheila. Amazing Aunt Agatha. 1990. (Ready-Set-Read Ser.). (Illus.). 24p. (J). (ps-3). lib. bdg. 21.40 o.p. (*0-8172-3575-2*); pap. 4.95 (*0-8114-6737-6*) Raintree Pubs.

Samton, Sheila White. Jenny's Journey. 1993. (Illus.). 32p. (J). (ps-3). pap. 4.99 o.s.i (*0-14-054308-2*, Puffin Bks.) Penguin Putnam Bks. for Young Readers.

Samuels, Alison. Christmas Soul: African-American Holiday Stories. 2001. (Illus.). 48p. (J). 17.99 (*0-7868-0521-8*, Jump at the Sun) Hyperion Bks. for Children.

Sanders, Scott Russel. A Place Called Freedom. 1997. (Illus.). 32p. (J). (gr. k-3). 16.00 (*0-689-80470-9*, Atheneum) Simon & Schuster Children's Publishing.

Ethnic Groups

Sanders, Scott Russell. A Place Called Freedom. 2001. (J). 12.14 (0-606-20854-2) Turtleback Bks.

Sapphire. Push. 1996. 192p. 20.00 o.s.i (0-679-44626-5) Random Hse., Inc.

Sargent, Dave & Sargent, Pat. Nubbin (Linebacked Apricot Dun: Freedom. 2003. (Saddle Up Ser.: Vol. 43). 42p. (J). mass mkt. 6.95 (1-56763-704-3) Ozark Publishing.

—Nubbin (Linebacked Apricot Dun) Freedom. 2003. (Saddle Up Ser.: Vol. 43). 42p. (J). lib. bdg. 22.60 (1-56763-703-5) Ozark Publishing.

Sawyer, Kem Knapp. Freedom Calls: Journey of a Slave Girl. 2001. v, 181p. (J). (gr. 3-6). lib. bdg. 17.95 (1-57249-206-6, WM Kids) White Mane Publishing Co., Inc.

Schertle, Alice. Down the Road. (Illus.). 40p. (J). (gr. k-3). 2000. pap. 6.00 (0-15-202471-9, Harcourt Paperbacks); 1995. 16.00 (0-15-276622-7) Harcourt Children's Bks.

—Down the Road. 2000. 12.15 (0-606-20324-9) Turtleback Bks.

Schlabach, Janet. Riverboat Runaways. 1999. (Illus.). 138p. (J). (gr. 4-8). pap. 15.95 (0-936389-75-3) Tudor Pubs., Inc.

Schoberle, Cecile & Stevenson, Harvey. Morning Sounds, Evening Sounds. 1994. (J). (gr. 4 up). pap. 14.00 o.p. (0-671-87437-3, Simon & Schuster Children's Publishing) Simon & Schuster Children's Publishing.

Schorsch, Laurence. Grandma's Visit. 1990. (Real Mother Goose Library). (Illus.). 32p. (J). (ps-3). 4.95 (1-56288-049-7) Checkerboard Pr., Inc.

Schotter, Roni. Efan the Great. 1986. (Illus.). 32p. (J). (gr. 2-5). 12.95 o.p. (0-688-04986-9); lib. bdg. 12.88 o.p. (0-688-04987-7) HarperCollins Children's Bk. Group.

—F Is for Freedom. 2000. (Illus.). 112p. (J). (gr. 2-5). pap. 15.99 (0-7894-2641-2, D K Ink) Dorling Kindersley Publishing, Inc.

Schraff, Anne. Freedom Knows No Color. 2000. 118p. (J). (0-7807-9270-X); pap. (0-7891-5136-7) Perfection Learning Corp.

Schroeder, Alan. Carolina Shout! 1995. (Illus.). 32p. (J). 14.89 o.s.i (0-8037-1678-8); 14.99 o.s.i (0-8037-1676-1) Penguin Putnam Bks. for Young Readers. (Dial Bks. for Young Readers).

—Ragtime Tumpie. (J). (ps-3). 1993. 32p. pap. 6.99 (0-316-77504-5); 1989. (Illus.). 16.95 o.p. (0-316-77497-9, Joy Street Bks.) Little Brown & Co.

—Satchmo's Blues. 1996. (Illus.). 32p. (J). (gr. k-3). 15.95 o.s.i (0-385-32046-9) Doubleday Publishing.

Schuett, Stacey, illus. Too Tight Shoes. 1997. (J). (0-7802-8023-7) Wright Group, The.

Schunk, Laurel. Black & Secret Midnight. 1998. 239p. (YA). (gr. 6-8). 24.99 (0-9661879-0-3, SKP98-41) St Kitts Pr.

Scott, Ann Herbert. Sam. 1967. (Illus.). (J). (ps-3). text 14.95 o.p. (0-07-055803-5) McGraw-Hill Cos., The.

—Sam. (Illus.). 40p. (J). (ps-3). 1996. pap. 5.95 o.s.i (0-698-11387-X, PaperStar); 1992. 14.95 o.s.i (0-399-22104-2, Philomel) Penguin Putnam Bks. for Young Readers.

—Sam. 1996. (J). 11.15 o.p. (0-606-09817-8) Turtleback Bks.

Scott, Stefanie. Everybody Say Moesha! 1997. (Moesha Ser.). 160p. (YA). (gr. 7 up). per. 3.99 (0-671-01147-2, Simon Pulse) Simon & Schuster Children's Publishing.

—Keeping It Real. 1997. (Moesha Ser.). 160p. (YA). (gr. 7 up). per. 3.99 (0-671-01148-0, Simon Pulse) Simon & Schuster Children's Publishing.

—Trippin' Out. 1997. (Moesha Ser.). 160p. (YA). (gr. 7 up). pap. 3.99 (0-671-01149-9, Simon Pulse) Simon & Schuster Children's Publishing.

Screen, Robert M. With My Face to the Rising Sun. 1977. (Illus.). 106p. (J). (gr. 5-9). 6.95 o.p. (0-15-298780-0) Harcourt Children's Bks.

Scruggs, Afi. Jump Rope Magic. 2000. (Illus.). 40p. (J). (ps-4). pap. 16.95 (0-590-69327-1, Blue Sky Pr., The) Scholastic, Inc.

Seabrooke, Brenda. The Bridges of Summer. 1992. 160p. (J). (gr. 5 up). 14.99 o.p. (0-525-65094-6, Dutton Children's Bks.) Penguin Putnam Bks. for Young Readers.

Sebestyen, Ouida. Words by Heart. 1979. 162p. (YA). (gr. 5 up). 15.95 (0-316-77931-8, Joy Street Bks.) Little Brown & Co.

—Words by Heart. 1997. 176p. (gr. 5 up). pap. text 5.50 (0-440-41346-X, Yearling); 1996. 144p. (YA). (gr. 4-7). mass mkt. 4.99 (0-440-22688-0, Dell Books for Young Readers); 1996. (YA). mass mkt. 5.99 (0-553-54250-8, Dell Books for Young Readers); 1992. (YA). mass mkt. o.s.i (0-553-54091-2, Dell Books for Young Readers); 1983. 144p. (J). (gr. 4-8). mass mkt. 4.50 o.s.i (0-553-27179-2, Starfire) Random Hse. Children's Bks.

—Words by Heart. 1996. (YA). 11.04 (0-606-02408-5) Turtleback Bks.

Shaik, Fatima. The Jazz of Our Street. (Illus.). 32p. (J). 2002. pap. 4.99 (0-14-056086-6, Puffin Bks.); 1998. 15.99 o.s.i (0-8037-1885-3, Dial Bks. for Young Readers); 1998. 15.89 o.s.i (0-8037-1886-1, Dial Bks. for Young Readers) Penguin Putnam Bks. for Young Readers.

—Melitte. 160p. (J). (gr. 5-9). 1999. (Illus.). pap. 4.99 o.s.i (0-14-130420-0, Puffin Bks.); 1997. 15.99 o.s.i (0-8037-2106-4, Dial Bks. for Young Readers) Penguin Putnam Bks. for Young Readers.

—Melitte. 2000. 11.04 (0-606-18432-5) Turtleback Bks.

Shange, Ntozake. Whitewash. 1997. (Illus.). 32p. (J). (gr. 2-5). 15.95 (0-8027-8490-9); lib. bdg. 16.85 (0-8027-8491-7) Walker & Co.

Sharpe, Stella G. Tobe: A Six-Year-Old Farmer. 1995. 162p. (J). pap. 9.95 o.p. (0-931761-21-2) Beckham Pubns. Group, Inc.

Shavers Gayle, Sharon. Family Picnic. 1997. (Stickers 'n' Shapes Ser.). (Illus.). 24p. (J). (gr. k-3). mass mkt. 3.99 (0-689-81318-X, Simon Spotlight/Nickelodeon) Simon & Schuster Children's Publishing.

Shelby, Anne. We Keep a Store. 1990. (Illus.). 32p. (J). (ps-2). 15.95 o.p. (0-531-05856-5); mass mkt. 16.99 o.p. (0-531-08456-6) Scholastic, Inc. (Orchard Bks.).

Shepard, Mary L. & Gaines, Edith M. Forty Acres; Little Jess & the Circus; Jubilee Day. McCluskey, John A., ed. 2nd ed. 1993. (Stories from Black History Series II: Vol. 2). (Illus.). (J). (gr. 4-7). pap. 2.00 (0-913678-26-0) New Day Pr.

Shotwell, Louisa R. Roosevelt Grady. 1963. (Illus.). 152p. (J). (gr. 4-6). 5.99 o.p. (0-529-03781-5) Penguin Putnam Bks. for Young Readers.

Siegelson, Kim L. Dancing the Ring Shout. 2000. (Illus.). 32p. (J). lib. bdg. 16.49 (0-7868-2396-8) Disney Pr.

—Dancing the Ring Shout. 2000. (Illus.). 32p. (J). 15.99 (0-7868-0453-X, Jump at the Sun) Hyperion Bks. for Children.

—Dancing the Ring Shout. 2000. (J). 16.00 (0-689-81699-5, Simon & Schuster Children's Publishing) Simon & Schuster Children's Publishing.

—Escape South. 2000. (Road to Reading Ser.). (Illus.). (J). (gr. 2-5). 78p. pap. 3.99 (0-307-26504-8); 80p. lib. bdg. 11.99 o.s.i (0-307-46504-7) Random Hse. Children's Bks. (Golden Bks.).

—Escape South. 2000. (J). 10.14 (0-606-18931-9) Turtleback Bks.

—In the Time of the Drums. 1999. (Jump at the Sun Bks.). (Illus.). 32p. (J). (gr. 1-4). 15.99 (0-7868-0436-X) Hyperion Bks. for Children.

—In the Time of the Drums. 1999. (J). 17.00 (0-689-80570-5); 17.00 (0-689-81084-9) Simon & Schuster Children's Publishing. (Simon & Schuster Children's Publishing).

Simmons, Clara A. Sauncey & Mr. King's Gallery. 1997. (Illus.). 30p. (J). (gr. 1-4). 10.95 (0-87033-498-0, Tidewater Pubs.) Cornell Maritime Pr., Inc.

Simon, Charnan. I Like to Win! 1999. (Real Kids Readers Ser.). (Illus.). 32p. (ps-1). (J). pap. 4.99 (0-7613-2087-3); lib. bdg. 18.90 (0-7613-2062-8) Millbrook Pr., Inc.

Skulicz, Matthew. Right on, Shane! 1972. (J). (gr. 7-11). 5.95 o.p. (0-399-20198-X) Putnam Publishing Group, The.

Sloan, Phyllis J. Postcard from Heaven. 1990. (Illus.). (J). 3.00 (0-940248-81-6) Guild Pr.

Slote, Alfred. Finding Buck McHenry. (Trophy Bk.). 256p. (J). 1993. (gr. 3-7). pap. 5.99 (0-06-440469-2, Harper Trophy); 1991. (gr. 3-7). 14.95 o.p. (0-06-021652-2); 1991. (gr. 4 up). lib. bdg. 15.89 (0-06-021653-0) HarperCollins Children's Bk. Group.

—Finding Buck McHenry. 1993. (J). 11.00 (0-606-02639-8) Turtleback Bks.

Smalls, Irene. Because You're Lucky. 1997. (Illus.). 32p. (J). (ps-3). 15.95 (0-316-79867-3) Little Brown & Co.

—Because You're Lucky. 2003. (Illus.). 32p. (J). (ps-1). pap. 5.99 (0-316-76425-6) Little Brown Children's Bks.

—Dawn & the Round-to-It. 1994. (Illus.). 40p. (J). (ps-3). pap. 15.00 (0-671-87166-8, Simon & Schuster Children's Publishing) Simon & Schuster Children's Publishing.

—Father's Day Blues: What Do You Do about Father's Day When All You Have Are Mothers? 1995. (Illus.). 32p. (J). 10.95 o.p. (0-681-00543-2) Borders Pr.

—Irene & the Big, Fine Nickel. (J). (ps-3). 1996. (Illus.). 32p. pap. 5.95 o.p. (0-316-79898-3); 1994. pap. (0-316-79879-7); 2nd ed. 2003. (Illus.). 32p. pap. 5.99 (0-316-69832-6); Vol. 1. 1991. (Illus.). 15.95 o.p. (0-316-79871-1) Little Brown & Co.

—Irene & the Big, Fine Nickel. 1991. (J). 11.15 o.p. (0-606-08783-4) Turtleback Bks.

—Irene Jennie & the Christmas Masquerade: The Johnkankus. 1996. (Illus.). 32p. (J). (ps-3). 15.95 o.p. (0-316-79878-9) Little Brown & Co.

—Jenny Reen & the Jack Muh Lantern on Halloween. 1996. (Illus.). 32p. (J). (gr. 1-5). 16.00 (0-689-31875-8, Atheneum) Simon & Schuster Children's Publishing.

—Jonathan & His Mommy. (Illus.). 32p. (J). (ps-3). 1994. pap. 5.95 (0-316-79880-0); 1992. 15.95 o.p. (0-316-79870-3) Little Brown & Co.

—Jonathan & His Mommy. 1992. 11.10 (0-606-06509-1) Turtleback Bks.

—Louise's Gift. 1996. (Illus.). 36p. (J). (ps-3). 15.95 o.p. (0-316-79877-0) Little Brown & Co.

—My Nana & Me. 2004. (Illus.). (J). 15.95 (0-316-16821-1) Little Brown & Co.

—A Strawbeater's Thanksgiving. 1998. (Illus.). 32p. (J). (gr. 2-5). 15.95 o.p. (0-316-79866-5) Little Brown & Co.

Smith, Charles, Jr., photos by. My Girl. 2001. (Motown Baby Love Ser.: Bk. 1). (Illus.). 12p. (J). (ps-k). bds. 6.99 (0-7868-0782-2) Hyperion Bks. for Children.

Smith, Charles R., Jr. Brown Sugar Babies. 2000. (Illus.). 32p. (J). (ps-k). 14.99 (0-7868-0622-2, Jump at the Sun) Hyperion Bks. for Children.

—Loki & Alex: The Adventures of a Dog & His Best Friend. 2001. (Illus.). 32p. (J). (ps-2). 14.99 (0-525-46700-9, Dutton Children's Bks.) Penguin Putnam Bks. for Young Readers.

Smith, Eddie. A Lullaby for Daddy. 1994. (Illus.). 32p. (J). (gr. 4-7). pap. 8.95 (0-86543-404-2); (ps). 16.95 (0-86543-403-4) Africa World Pr.

Smith, Kay Jordan. Skeeter. 1992. 216p. (YA). (gr. 7-7). pap. 6.95 (0-395-61621-2) Houghton Mifflin Co.

Smith, Kay Jordan, ed. Skeeter. 1989. (J). (gr. 6 up). 14.95 o.p. (0-395-49603-9) Houghton Mifflin Co.

—Skeeter. 1989. (J). 12.00 (0-606-01441-1) Turtleback Bks.

Smith, Patricia. Janna & the Kings. 2003. (Illus.). (J). 16.95 (1-58430-088-4) Lee & Low Bks., Inc.

Smith, Peaches. Marcy's Granny. 1996. (Illus.). 62p. (J). 17.25 (1-56763-184-3); pap. 2.95 (1-56763-185-1) Ozark Publishing.

Smothers, Ethel. The Hard Times Jar, RS. 2003. (Illus.). 32p. (J). 16.00 (0-374-32852-8, Farrar, Straus & Giroux (BYR)) Farrar, Straus & Giroux.

Smothers, Ethel Footman. Down in the Piney Woods. 2003. 128p. (J). 6.00 (0-8028-5248-3, Eerdmans Bks For Young Readers) Eerdmans, William B. Publishing Co.

—Down in the Piney Woods. (J). 1994. 156p. (gr. 3-7). pap. 4.99 o.s.i (0-679-84714-6, Random Hse. Bks. for Young Readers); 1992. 144p. (gr. 5-9). 14.00 o.s.i (0-679-80360-2, Knopf Bks. for Young Readers); 1992. 144p. (gr. 5-9). 14.99 o.s.i (0-679-90360-7, Knopf Bks. for Young Readers) Random Hse. Children's Bks.

—Down in the Piney Woods. 1992. (J). 9.09 (0-606-05813-3) Turtleback Bks.

—Moriah's Pond. 2003. 96p. (J). 7.00 (0-8028-5249-1, Eerdmans Bks For Young Readers) Eerdmans, William B. Publishing Co.

—Moriah's Pond. 1994. (J). lib. bdg. o.p. (0-679-94504-0) Knopf, Alfred A. Inc.

—Moriah's Pond. 1994. (Illus.). 128p. (J). 16.00 o.s.i (0-679-84504-6, Knopf Bks. for Young Readers) Random Hse. Children's Bks.

Snelling, Lauraine. Setting the Pace. 1996. (High Hurdles Ser.: No. 3). 176p. (Orig.). (YA). (gr. 6-9). pap. 5.99 (1-55661-507-8, Bethany Backyard) Bethany Hse. Pubs.

Snider, Catherine. Mommy Loves Jesus. 1993. (Illus.). 24p. (Orig.). (J). (ps-6). pap. 3.95 (0-8198-4731-3) Pauline Bks. & Media.

Sokoloff, Myka-Lynne. Little Book: Too Small Jill. 1997. (Sadlier Phonics Reading Program). (Illus.). 16p. (J). (0-8215-0961-6, Sadlier-Oxford) Sadlier, William H. Inc.

Sorenson, Margo. Shatter with Words: Langston Hughes. 1998. (Cover-to-Cover Biographical Novel Ser.). 103 p. (J). 5.95 (0-7891-2152-2) Perfection Learning Corp.

Sorenson, Margo, contrib. by. Shatter with Words: Langston Hughes. 1998. (Cover-to-Cover Biographical Novel Ser.). (Illus.). (J). (0-7807-6786-1) Perfection Learning Corp.

Southgate, Martha. Another Way to Dance. 1996. 192p. (YA). (gr. 7-12). 15.95 o.s.i (0-385-32191-0, Delacorte Pr.) Dell Publishing.

—Another Way to Dance. 1998. 208p. (YA). (gr. 7-12). reprint ed. mass mkt. 4.99 o.s.i (0-440-21968-X, Laurel Leaf) Random Hse. Children's Bks.

—Another Way to Dance. 1998. 10.55 (0-606-12878-6) Turtleback Bks.

Spinner, Stephanie. Bird Is the Word, 5. 1997. (Weebie Zone Ser.). (J). 9.15 o.p. (0-606-12058-0) Turtleback Bks.

Spinner, Stephanie & Weiss, Ellen. Bird Is the Word. 1997. (Weebie Zone Ser.: No. 5). (Illus.). 80p. (J). (gr. 2-4). lib. bdg. 13.89 (0-06-027590-1) HarperCollins Children's Bk. Group.

St. James, Synthia. Sunday. 1996. (Illus.). 32p. (J). (ps-3). lib. bdg. 15.95 o.p. (0-8075-7658-1) Whitman, Albert & Co.

Staples, Suzanne Fisher. Dangerous Skies, RS. 1996. 40p. (YA). (gr. 5 up). 16.00 (0-374-31694-5, Farrar, Straus & Giroux (BYR)) Farrar, Straus & Giroux.

—Dangerous Skies. 1998. 240p. (J). (gr. 5 up). pap. 5.99 (0-06-440683-0, Harper Trophy) HarperCollins Children's Bk. Group.

—Dangerous Skies. 1998. 12.00 (0-606-13312-7) Turtleback Bks.

Starkman, Neal. The Riddle. 1989. (Illus.). 50p. (Orig.). (J). (gr. 2-4). pap. 10.00 (0-935529-13-6) Comprehensive Health Education Foundation.

Starks, Virginia L. The Spirit of Ancient Africa. 1997. (Illus.). 40p. (J). (gr. 1-5). 16.95 (0-9656859-1-8) Black Pyramid Pr.

Steptoe, Javaka. The Jones Family Express. 2003. (Illus.). 40p. (J). (ps-4). 17.95 (1-58430-047-7) Lee & Low Bks., Inc.

Steptoe, John. Creativity. 2003. (Illus.). 32p. (J). (ps-3). pap. 5.95 (0-618-31677-9, Clarion Bks.) Houghton Mifflin Co. Trade & Reference Div.

Steptoe, John L. Baby Says. 1988. (Illus.). 32p. (J). (ps). 15.00 o.p. (0-688-07423-5); lib. bdg. 16.89 (0-688-07424-3) HarperCollins Children's Bk. Group.

—Baby Says. ALC Staff, ed. 1992. (Illus.). 28p. (J). (ps up). pap. 3.95 o.p. (0-688-11855-0, Morrow, William & Co.) Morrow/Avon.

—Creativity. 1997. (Illus.). 32p. (J). (ps-3). lib. bdg., tchr. ed. 17.00 (0-395-68706-3) Houghton Mifflin Co.

—Marcia. 1991. (Illus.). 8p. (YA). (gr. 7 up). pap. 3.99 o.s.i (0-14-034669-4, Puffin Bks.) Penguin Putnam Bks. for Young Readers.

—Marcia. 1976. (Illus.). 96p. (J). (gr. 7-11). 7.95 o.p. (0-670-45532-6) Viking Penguin.

Stern, Judith, et al. You Can Call Me Willy: A Story for Children about AIDS. 1996. (Illus.). 80p. (J). (ps-3). pap. 16.95 o.p. (0-945354-61-4) American Psychological Assn.

Stock, Catherine. Halloween Monster. (Festive Year Ser.). (Illus.). 32p. (J). (ps-1). 1990. mass mkt. 13.00 (0-02-788404-X, Atheneum); 1993. reprint ed. pap. 3.95 (0-689-71727-X, Aladdin) Simon & Schuster Children's Publishing.

—Halloween Monster. 1993. (J). 9.15 o.p. (0-606-05326-3) Turtleback Bks.

Stolz, Mary. Cezanne Pinto: A Memoir. 1997. 288p. (J). (gr. 5-9). pap. 4.99 (0-679-88933-7); 1994. 256p. (YA). (gr. 6 up). pap. o.p. (0-679-94917-8); 1994. 256p. (YA). (gr. 6 up). 16.00 o.s.i (0-679-84917-3) Random Hse. Children's Bks. (Knopf Bks. for Young Readers).

—Cezanne Pinto: A Memoir. 1997. (YA). (gr. 6 up). 11.04 (0-606-12904-9) Turtleback Bks.

—Coco Grimes. (Trophy Bk.). (J). 1995. 96p. (gr. 4-7). pap. 4.50 o.p. (0-06-440512-5, Harper Trophy); 1994. 128p. (gr. 3-6). lib. bdg. 13.89 o.p. (0-06-024233-7); 1994. 128p. (gr. 3-6). 14.00 o.p. (0-06-024232-9) HarperCollins Children's Bk. Group.

—Coco Grimes. 1996. (J). 9.70 o.p. (0-606-08507-6) Turtleback Bks.

—Go Fish. (Trophy Chapter Bks.). (Illus.). 80p. (J). 1993. (gr. 4-7). pap. 4.50 (0-06-440466-8, Harper Trophy); 1991. (gr. 2-6). 13.95 o.p. (0-06-025820-9); 1991. (gr. 2-6). lib. bdg. 14.89 (0-06-025822-5) HarperCollins Children's Bk. Group.

—Go Fish. 1993. (Trophy Chapter Bks.). (J). 10.65 (0-606-02653-3) Turtleback Bks.

—Stealing Home. 160p. (J). (gr. 3-6). 1994. (Illus.). pap. 5.99 (0-06-440528-1, Harper Trophy); 1992. lib. bdg. 14.89 o.p. (0-06-021157-1); 1992. 15.95 (0-06-021154-7) HarperCollins Children's Bk. Group.

—Stealing Home. 1994. 11.00 (0-606-06767-1) Turtleback Bks.

—Storm in the Night. (Trophy Picture Bk.). (Illus.). 32p. (J). (gr. k-3). 1990. pap. 5.99 (0-06-443256-4, Harper Trophy); 1988. 15.00 o.p. (0-06-025912-4); 1988. lib. bdg. 16.89 (0-06-025913-2) HarperCollins Children's Bk. Group.

—Storm in the Night. 1990. 12.10 (0-606-04814-6) Turtleback Bks.

Stowe, Harriet Beecher. Uncle Tom's Cabin. 1852. (YA). reprint ed. pap. text 28.00 (1-4047-8957-X) Classic Textbooks.

—Uncle Tom's Cabin. 1981. (Penguin American Library). (J). 14.05 o.p. (0-606-01538-8) Turtleback Bks.

Straight, Susan. Bear E. Bear. l.t. ed. 1995. (Illus.). 32p. (J). (ps-2). 14.95 o.p. (1-56282-526-7); lib. bdg. 15.49 o.p. (1-56282-527-5) Hyperion Bks. for Children.

Strickland, Brad. The Wrath of the Grinning Ghost. 2001. (Illus.). (J). 12.04 (0-606-21537-9) Turtleback Bks.

Strickland, Michael R. Haircuts at Sleepy Sam's. 2003. (Illus.). 32p. (J). (ps-3). 15.95 (1-56397-562-9) Boyds Mills Pr.

Stroud, Bettye. Down Home at Miss Dessa's. 1996. (Illus.). 32p. (J). (ps up). 14.95 (1-880000-39-3) Lee & Low Bks., Inc.

Stroud, Bettye & Lucas, Cedric, illus. The Leaving. 2001. 32p. (J). (gr. 1-4). 15.95 (*0-7614-5067-X*, Cavendish Children's Bks.) Cavendish, Marshall Corp.

Suen, Anastasia. Loose Tooth. 2002. (Viking Easy-To-Read Ser.). (Illus.). 32p. (J). (gr. k-3). 13.99 (*0-670-03536-X*) Penguin Putnam Bks. for Young Readers.

—The Loose Tooth. 2003. (Easy-to-Read Ser.). (Illus.). 32p. pap. 3.99 (*0-14-250064-X*, Puffin Bks.) Penguin Putnam Bks. for Young Readers.

Suranna, Keith. Simeon's Sandbox. 1997. (Gullah Gullah Island Ser.). (Illus.). 10p. (J). (ps-k). bds. 4.99 o.s.i (*0-689-81312-0*, Simon Spotlight/ Nickelodeon) Simon & Schuster Children's Publishing.

Swanson-Natsues, Lyn. Days of Adventure. 1996. (Illus.). 24p. (J). (ps-2). pap. 4.95 (*1-57255-117-8*) Mondo Publishing.

Switzer-Clarke, Eileen. Blossom: A Girl's Adventures in Revolutionary Rockland. 1998. (Illus.). 108p. (J). (gr. 3-6). pap. 8.00 (*0-911183-44-2*) Historical Society of Rockland County, The.

Tarpley, Natasha. Bippity Bop Barbershop. 2002. (Illus.). 32p. (J). (gr. k-3). 15.95 (*0-316-52284-8*) Little Brown Children's Bks.

—Destiny's Gift. Burrowes, Adjoa J., tr. & illus. by. 2004. (J). (*1-58430-156-2*) Lee & Low Bks., Inc.

—I Love My Hair! (Illus.). (J). 2003. 11p. bds. 6.99 (*0-316-52558-8*); 1998. 32p. 15.95 (*0-316-52275-9*) Little Brown & Co.

—I Love My Hair! 2001. (Illus.). 32p. (J). (gr. k-3). pap. 5.95 (*0-316-52375-5*) Little Brown Children's Bks.

Tate, Eleanora E. A Blessing in Disguise. 1995. 192p. (J). 14.95 o.s.i (*0-385-32103-1*, Delacorte Pr.) Dell Publishing.

—A Blessing in Disguise. 1996. 192p. (gr. 3-7). pap. text 3.99 o.s.i (*0-440-41209-9*, Yearling) Random Hse. Children's Bks.

—A Blessing in Disguise. 1996. (J). 9.09 o.p. (*0-606-09086-X*) Turtleback Bks.

—Blessing in Disguise. 1996. (J). 18.95 (*0-385-30997-X*, Dell Books for Young Readers) Random Hse. Children's Bks.

—Front Porch Stories at the One-Room School. 1992. 112p. (YA). 15.00 o.s.i (*0-553-08384-8*) Bantam Bks.

—Front Porch Stories at the One-Room School. 1993. (Illus.). 112p. (gr. 4-7). pap. text 4.99 (*0-440-40901-2*) Dell Publishing.

—Front Porch Stories at the One-Room School. 1993. (J). pap. o.p. (*0-440-90061-1*, Dell Books for Young Readers) Random Hse. Children's Bks.

—Front Porch Stories at the One-Room School. 1992. (J). 11.04 (*0-606-05838-9*) Turtleback Bks.

—Just an Overnight Guest. 1996. 250p. (J). (gr. 4-7). pap. 8.00 (*0-940975-65-3*); 15.00 o.p. (*0-940975-64-5*) Just Us Bks., Inc.

—The Minstrel's Melody. 2001. (American Girl Collection: Bk. 11). (Illus.). 160p. (J). (gr. 5-9). 9.95 (*1-58485-311-5*); pap. 5.95 (*1-58485-310-7*) Pleasant Co. Pubns. (American Girl).

—The Minstrel's Melody. 2001. (American Girl Collection). (Illus.). (J). 12.00 (*0-606-21331-7*) Turtleback Bks.

—The Secret of Gumbo Grove. 1996. 208p. (J). pap. 3.99 o.s.i (*0-440-41273-0*) Dell Publishing.

—The Secret of Gumbo Grove. 1988. 208p. (YA). mass mkt. 5.50 (*0-440-22716-X*, Dell Books for Young Readers); (gr. 7 up). mass mkt. 4.50 o.s.i (*0-553-27226-8*, Starfire) Random Hse. Children's Bks.

—The Secret of Gumbo Grove. 1987. (Illus.). 256p. (YA). (gr. 7-12). 12.95 o.p. (*0-531-15051-8*); lib. bdg. 12.90 o.p. (*0-531-10298-X*) Scholastic Library Publishing. (Watts, Franklin).

—The Secret of Gumbo Grove. 1998. (J). (gr. 4-7). 18.25 o.p. (*0-8446-6977-6*) Smith, Peter Pub., Inc.

—The Secret of Gumbo Grove. (J). 1997. 11.04 (*0-606-04041-2*); 1996. 9.09 o.p. (*0-606-10926-9*) Turtleback Bks.

—Thank You, Dr. Martin Luther King, Jr. 1991. 240p. (J). (gr. 4-7). pap. 4.50 o.s.i (*0-553-15886-4*) Bantam Bks.

—Thank You, Dr. Martin Luther King, Jr. 1997. 240p. (gr. 4-7). pap. text 4.99 (*0-440-41407-5*, Dell Books for Young Readers) Random Hse. Children's Bks.

—Thank You, Dr. Martin Luther King, Jr. 1990. (J). 13.95 o.p. (*0-531-15151-4*); lib. bdg. 14.90 o.p. (*0-531-10904-6*) Scholastic Library Publishing. (Watts, Franklin).

Taulbert, Clifton L. Little Cliff & the Porch People. Kane, Cindy, ed. 1999. (Illus.). 32p. (J). (ps-3). 16.99 (*0-8037-2174-9*); 15.89 o.p. (*0-8037-2175-7*) Penguin Putnam Bks. for Young Readers. (Dial Bks. for Young Readers).

Taylor, Ann & HarperCollins Staff. Baby Dance. 1999. (Growing Tree Ser.). (Illus.). 16p. (J). (ps up). 5.99 (*0-694-01206-8*, Harper Festival) HarperCollins Children's Bk. Group.

Taylor, Debbie. A Special Day in Harlem. Morrison, Frank, tr. & illus. by. 2004. (J). (*1-58430-165-1*) Lee & Low Bks., Inc.

Taylor, Mildred D. Elements of Literature: Roll of Thunder, Hear My Cry. 1989. pap. text, stu. ed. 15.33 (*0-03-023434-4*) Holt, Rinehart & Winston.

—The Friendship. (Illus.). 56p. 1998. (gr. 2-6). pap. 4.99 (*0-14-038964-4*, Puffin Bks.); 1987. (J). (gr. 2-6). 13.89 o.p. (*0-8037-0418-6*, Dial Bks. for Young Readers); 1987. (J). (gr. 4-7). 16.99 (*0-8037-0417-8*, Dial Bks. for Young Readers) Penguin Putnam Bks. for Young Readers.

—The Friendship. 1998. 10.14 (*0-606-12938-3*) Turtleback Bks.

—The Friendship & the Gold Cadillac. 1996. 96p. pap. text 3.99 o.p. (*0-440-41307-9*, Dell Books for Young Readers) Random Hse. Children's Bks.

—Friendship & the Gold Cadillac. 1989. 96p. (J). (gr. 2-6). pap. 3.99 o.s.i (*0-553-15765-5*, Skylark) Random Hse. Children's Bks.

—The Gold Cadillac. (Illus.). (J). 1998. 48p. (gr. 2-6). pap. 4.99 (*0-14-038963-6*); 1987. 4p. (gr. 2-6). 12.89 o.p. (*0-8037-0343-0*, Dial Bks. for Young Readers); 1987. 4p. (gr. 4-7). 16.99 (*0-8037-0342-2*, Dial Bks. for Young Readers) Penguin Putnam Bks. for Young Readers.

—The Gold Cadillac. 1998. 11.14 (*0-606-13433-6*) Turtleback Bks.

—The Land. 2001. 392p. (J). (gr. 7 up). 17.99 (*0-8037-1950-7*, Dial Bks. for Young Readers) Penguin Putnam Bks. for Young Readers.

—Land. 2003. 384p. (YA). pap. 6.99 (*0-14-250146-8*, Puffin Bks.) Penguin Putnam Bks. for Young Readers.

—Let the Circle Be Unbroken. 400p. (YA). 1991. (gr. 5-12). pap. 6.99 (*0-14-034892-1*, Puffin Bks.); 1981. (gr. 7 up). 17.99 (*0-8037-4748-9*, Dial Bks. for Young Readers) Penguin Putnam Bks. for Young Readers.

—Let the Circle Be Unbroken. 1991. 11.04 (*0-606-00558-7*) Turtleback Bks.

—Mississippi Bridge. 2002. (J). 12.87 (*0-7587-9586-6*) Book Wholesalers, Inc.

—Mississippi Bridge. (Illus.). 2000. 64p. (YA). (gr. 4-7). pap. 4.99 (*0-14-130817-6*, Puffin Bks.); 1990. 64p. (J). 15.99 o.s.i (*0-8037-0426-7*, Dial Bks. for Young Readers); 1990. 6p. (J). 13.89 o.p. (*0-8037-0427-5*, Dial Bks. for Young Readers) Penguin Putnam Bks. for Young Readers.

—Mississippi Bridge. 1992. (Illus.). 64p. (gr. 2-6). pap. text 4.50 (*0-553-15992-5*, Skylark); (J). pap. o.s.i (*0-553-54058-0*, Dell Books for Young Readers) Random Hse. Children's Bks.

—Mississippi Bridge. 2002. (J). (gr. 2-6). 19.75 (*0-8446-7213-0*) Smith, Peter Pub., Inc.

—Mississippi Bridge. 2000. 11.14 (*0-606-18434-1*); 1992. 9.19 o.p. (*0-606-00528-5*) Turtleback Bks.

—The Road to Memphis. 1992. 304p. (YA). (gr. 7-12). pap. 6.99 (*0-14-036077-8*, Puffin Bks.) Penguin Putnam Bks. for Young Readers.

—The Road to Memphis. Fogelman, Phyllis J., ed. 1990. (Illus.). 30p. (YA). (gr. 7 up). 16.99 (*0-8037-0340-6*, Dial Bks. for Young Readers) Penguin Putnam Bks. for Young Readers.

—Roll of Thunder, Hear My Cry. 1984. 224p. (YA). (gr. 8-12). mass mkt. 3.50 o.s.i (*0-553-25450-2*) Bantam Bks.

—Roll of Thunder, Hear My Cry. 2002. (Illus.). (J). 14.04 (*0-7587-0209-4*) Book Wholesalers, Inc.

—Roll of Thunder, Hear My Cry. 1993. (Golden Leaf Classics). 48p. (YA). (gr. 5 up). stu. ed. 9.95 (*1-56872-003-3*) Incentives For Learning.

—Roll of Thunder, Hear My Cry. l.t. ed. 2000. (LRS Large Print Cornerstone Ser.). 348p. (YA). (gr. 5-12). lib. bdg. 32.95 (*1-58118-057-8*, 23471) LRS.

—Roll of Thunder, Hear My Cry. l.t. ed. 1989. 304p. (YA). reprint ed. lib. bdg. 16.95 o.s.i (*1-55736-140-1*, Cornerstone Bks.) Pages, Inc.

—Roll of Thunder, Hear My Cry. 1999. (Masterpiece Series Access Editions). xvii, 205p. (J). pap. 10.95 (*0-8219-1985-7*, 35335) Paradigm Publishing, Inc.

—Roll of Thunder, Hear My Cry. (gr. 5-8). 1997. 288p. (YA). pap. 6.99 (*0-14-038451-0*, Puffin Bks.); 1991. 288p. (J). pap. 6.99 (*0-14-034893-X*); 1976. (Illus.). 290p. (YA). 16.99 o.s.i (*0-8037-7473-7*, Dial Bks. for Young Readers); 25th anniv. ed. 2001. (Illus.). 296p. (J). 17.99 (*0-8037-2647-3*, Fogelman, Phyllis Bks.) Penguin Putnam Bks. for Young Readers.

—Roll of Thunder, Hear My Cry. 1999. 60p. (gr. 6-8). stu. ed., ring bd. 12.99 (*1-58609-152-2*) Progeny Pr.

—Roll of Thunder, Hear My Cry. unabr. ed. 2001. (YA). audio 30.00 (*0-8072-0621-0*); audio 30.00 (*0-8072-0621-0*); 276p. (gr. 5 up). pap. 46.00 incl. audio (*0-8072-0678-4*); 276p. (gr. 5 up). pap. 46.00 incl. audio (*0-8072-0678-4*) Random Hse. Audio Publishing Group. (Listening Library).

—Roll of Thunder, Hear My Cry. 1998. (J). (gr. 5). pap. 3.95 (*0-439-04476-6*) Scholastic, Inc.

—Roll of Thunder, Hear My Cry. (YA). 1997. 12.04 (*0-606-11807-1*); 1991. 12.04 (*0-606-00720-2*) Turtleback Bks.

—Roll of Thunder, Hear My Cry: Let the Circle Be Unbroken, 3 vols., Set. 1996. (J). (gr. 4-7). 13.99 o.p. (*0-14-774347-8*, Puffin Bks.) Penguin Putnam Bks. for Young Readers.

—The Well: David's Story. 96p. (J). 1998. (gr. 4-7). pap. 5.99 (*0-14-038642-4*); 1995. (gr. 3-7). 15.99 (*0-8037-1802-0*, Dial Bks. for Young Readers); 1995. (gr. 4-7). 14.89 o.s.i (*0-8037-1803-9*, Dial Bks. for Young Readers) Penguin Putnam Bks. for Young Readers.

Teague, Mark. The Baby Tamer. 1997. (Illus.). 32p. (J). (ps-2). pap. 15.95 (*0-590-67712-8*) Scholastic, Inc.

Temple, Charles. On the Riverbank. 1992. (Illus.). 32p. (J). (ps-3). 14.95 o.p. (*0-395-61591-7*) Houghton Mifflin Co.

Temple, Frances. Tonight, by Sea. 1997. (Illus.). 160p. (J). (gr. 5 up). pap. 5.99 (*0-06-440670-9*, Harper Trophy) HarperCollins Children's Bk. Group.

—Tonight, by Sea. 1995. 160p. (gr. 7 up). (J). lib. bdg. 16.99 (*0-531-08749-2*); (YA). pap. 15.95 (*0-531-06899-4*) Scholastic, Inc. (Orchard Bks.).

Thigpen, Laura B. Bellfree's Leap to Better Grammar. 1996. (Illus.). 54p. (Orig.). (J). (gr. 4-9). pap. 8.00 (*0-9652368-0-3*) Wright Publishing, Inc.

Thomas, Jane Resh. Celebration! 1997. (Illus.). 32p. (J). (ps-3). lib. bdg. 15.49 (*0-7868-2160-4*); (Maggie Stories Ser.: Vol. 2). 14.95 (*0-7868-0189-1*) Hyperion Bks. for Children.

Thomas, Joyce Carol. Bright Shadow. 1983. (Avon Flare Book Ser.). 128p. (gr. 7 up). mass mkt. 4.99 (*0-380-84509-1*, Avon Bks.) Morrow/Avon.

—Bright Shadow. 1983. (Avon/Flare Bks.). 9.60 o.p. (*0-606-03029-8*) Turtleback Bks.

—The Golden Pasture. 144p. (YA). (gr. 7 up). 1987. pap. 2.50 o.p. (*0-590-33638-X*); 1986. 11.95 o.p. (*0-590-33681-9*) Scholastic, Inc.

—I Have Heard of a Land. (Trophy Picture Book Ser.). (Illus.). 32p. (J). 2000. (gr. k-3). pap. 5.99 (*0-06-443617-9*, Harper Trophy); 1998. (gr. 2-6). 15.95 (*0-06-023477-6*, Cotler, Joanna Bks.); 1998. (gr. 3 up). lib. bdg. 14.89 (*0-06-023478-4*, Cotler, Joanna Bks.) HarperCollins Children's Bk. Group.

—I Have Heard of a Land. 1998. 12.10 (*0-606-17563-6*) Turtleback Bks.

—Journey. 1990. (J). pap. 2.75 o.p. (*0-590-40628-0*); 1988. (YA). (gr. 7 up). pap. 12.95 o.p. (*0-590-40627-2*) Scholastic, Inc.

—Joy! 2001. 18p. (J). (ps-k). bds. 6.99 (*0-7868-0750-4*, Jump at the Sun) Hyperion Bks. for Children.

—Marked by Fire. 1982. (J). (gr. 7 up). pap. 4.50 o.s.i (*0-380-79327-X*, Avon Bks.) Morrow/Avon.

—When the Nightingale Sings. (Trophy Bk.). 160p. (YA). (gr. 7 up). 1994. (Illus.). pap. 3.95 (*0-06-440524-9*, Harper Trophy); 1992. 14.95 o.p. (*0-06-020294-7*); 1992. lib. bdg. 13.89 o.s.i (*0-06-020295-5*) HarperCollins Children's Bk. Group.

—You Are My Perfect Baby. 1999. (Joanna Cotler Bks.). (Illus.). 14p. (J). (ps up). 5.95 (*0-694-01096-0*, Harper Festival) HarperCollins Children's Bk. Group.

Thomas, Naturi. Uh-Oh! It's Mama's Birthday! 1997. (Illus.). 24p. (J). (gr. 1-4). lib. bdg. 13.95 (*0-8075-8268-9*) Whitman, Albert & Co.

Thomassie, Tynia. Mimi's Tutu. (Illus.). 32p. (J). (gr. k-2). 2002. mass mkt. 5.99 (*0-590-44021-7*, Scholastic Pr.); 1996. pap. 14.95 (*0-590-44020-9*) Scholastic, Inc.

—Mimi's Tutu. 2001. 12.14 (*0-606-22267-7*) Turtleback Bks.

Time-Life Books Editors. The Three Storytellers of Or: A Flexible-Thinking Book. Kagan, Neil & Ward, Elizabeth, eds. 1991. (Early Learning Program Ser.). (Illus.). 64p. (J). (ps-2). (*0-8094-9283-0*); lib. bdg. (*0-8094-9284-9*) Time-Life, Inc.

Tolan, Stephanie S. Flight of the Raven. 2001. 304p. (J). (gr. 5 up). 15.95 (*0-688-17419-1*); (Illus.). lib. bdg. 17.89 (*0-06-029620-8*, Harper Trophy) HarperCollins Children's Bk. Group.

Travis, L. Captured by a Spy. 1995. (Ben & Zack Ser.: Vol. 1). 144p. (J). (gr. 3-8). pap. 5.99 o.p. (*0-8010-8915-8*) Baker Bks.

—Union Army Black. 1995. (Ben & Zack Ser.: Bk. 4). 168p. (J). (gr. 3-8). pap. 5.99 o.p. (*0-8010-4037-X*) Baker Bks.

Turner, Glennette Tilley. Running for Our Lives. 1994. (Illus.). 208p. (J). (gr. 4-7). tchr. ed. 16.95 (*0-8234-1121-4*) Holiday Hse., Inc.

Tusa, Tricia. Maebelle's Suitcase. (Illus.). 32p. (J). (gr. k-3). 1987. lib. bdg. 15.00 o.s.i (*0-02-789250-6*, Simon & Schuster Children's Publishing); 1991. reprint ed. pap. 6.99 (*0-689-71444-0*, Aladdin) Simon & Schuster Children's Publishing.

—Maebelle's Suitcase. 1991. (Reading Rainbow Bks.). 12.14 (*0-606-12407-1*) Turtleback Bks.

Twain, Mark, et al. Pudd'nhead Wilson: Curriculum Unit. 2000. (Novel Ser.). 60p. (YA). (gr. 9-12). spiral bd. 18.95 (*1-56077-648-X*) Ctr. for Learning, The.

Udry, Janice May. What Mary Jo Shared. (Illus.). (J). (ps-3). 1991. 32p. mass mkt. 4.99 (*0-590-43757-7*); 1970. pap. 2.25 o.p. (*0-590-40731-7*) Scholastic, Inc.

—What Mary Jo Shared. 1966. (Illus.). 40p. (J). (ps-3). lib. bdg. 14.95 (*0-8075-8842-3*) Whitman, Albert & Co.

Van Raven, Pieter. Pickle & Price. 1990. 208p. (YA). (gr. 7 up). 14.95 o.s.i (*0-684-19162-8*, Atheneum) Simon & Schuster Children's Publishing.

Van Steenwyk, Elizabeth. My Name Is York. (Illus.). 32p. 2000. (ps-3). pap. 7.95 (*0-87358-758-8*); 1997. (J). (gr. 1-3). lib. bdg. 14.95 (*0-87358-650-6*) Northland Publishing. (Rising Moon Bks. for Young Readers).

Vander Zee, Ruth. Mississippi Morning. 2003. (J). (*0-8028-5211-4*, Eerdmans Bks For Young Readers) Eerdmans, William B. Publishing Co.

Vaughan, Marcia K. The Secret to Freedom. 2001. (Illus.). 32p. (J). (gr. 1-4). 16.95 (*1-58430-021-3*) Lee & Low Bks., Inc.

—Up the Learning Tree. 2003. (Illus.). (J). 16.96 (*1-58430-049-3*) Lee & Low Bks., Inc.

Velasquez, Gloria. Ankiza. 2001. (Roosevelt High School Ser.). 144p. (J). (gr. 2 up). pap. 9.95 (*1-55885-309-X*, Piñata Books) Arte Publico Pr.

—Ankiza's Rainbow. 2000. (Roosevelt High School Ser.). 160p. (J). (gr. 8-12). 16.95 (*1-55885-308-1*, Piñata Books) Arte Publico Pr.

Verniero, Joan C. You Can Call Me Willy: A Story for Children about AIDS. 1994. (Illus.). 32p. (J). (ps-3). pap. 8.95 (*0-945354-60-6*) American Psychological Assn.

Vertreace, Martha. Kelly in the Mirror. 1993. (Illus.). 32p. (J). (gr. 1-3). lib. bdg. 14.95 o.p. (*0-8075-4152-4*) Whitman, Albert & Co.

Viglucci, Pat C. Cassandra Robbins, Esq. 1987. 176p. (Orig.). (YA). (gr. 8-12). pap. 4.95 o.p. (*0-938961-01-2*, Stamp Out Sheep Pr.) Square 1 Pubs., Inc.

Vigna, Judith. Black Like Kyra, White Like Me. Tucker, Kathleen, ed. 1992. (Albert Whitman Concept Bks.). (Illus.). 32p. (J). (gr. 2-6). lib. bdg. 14.95 o.p. (*0-8075-0778-4*) Whitman, Albert & Co.

—Black Like Kyra, White Like Me. 1996. (Illus.). 32p. (J). (gr. 1-4). reprint ed. pap. 5.95 (*0-8075-0779-2*) Whitman, Albert & Co.

Voigt, Cynthia. Come a Stranger. 1987. 240p. (YA). (gr. 6 up). mass mkt. 3.95 o.s.i (*0-449-70246-4*, Fawcett) Ballantine Bks.

—Come a Stranger. 1995. 256p. (J). (gr. 7 up). mass mkt. 5.99 (*0-689-80444-X*, Simon Pulse); 1986. 208p. (YA). (gr. 6 up). 15.95 (*0-689-31289-X*, Atheneum) Simon & Schuster Children's Publishing.

—Come a Stranger. 1995. (J). 11.04 (*0-606-07384-1*) Turtleback Bks.

Wagner, Jane. J. T. 125p. (J). (gr. 3-5). pap. 3.00 (*0-8072-1403-5*, Listening Library) Random Hse. Audio Publishing Group.

—J. T. 1972. (Illus.). 128p. (gr. 3-8). pap. text 4.99 (*0-440-44275-3*, Yearling) Random Hse. Children's Bks.

—J. T. 1969. (J). 11.04 (*0-606-03662-8*) Turtleback Bks.

—J. T. 1987. (J). text o.p. (*0-442-29152-3*) Wiley, John & Sons, Inc.

Walker, Alice. Finding the Green Stone. 1991. (Illus.). 40p. (J). (gr. 2 up). 20.00 (*0-15-227538-X*) Harcourt Children's Bks.

—Finding the Green Stone. 1997. (J). pap. 6.00 (*0-15-201502-7*) Harcourt Trade Pubs.

—To Hell with Dying. 1993. (Illus.). 32p. (J). pap. 8.00 (*0-15-289074-2*) Harcourt Children's Bks.

—To Hell with Dying. 1988. (Illus.). 32p. (J). (ps up). 13.95 o.s.i (*0-15-289075-0*) Harcourt Trade Pubs.

Walker, Mary A. To Catch a Zombi. 1979. 204p. (J). (gr. 7-10). 8.95 o.s.i (*0-689-30725-X*, Atheneum) Simon & Schuster Children's Publishing.

Walker, Sylvia, illus. A Spicy-herby Day. 1997. (*0-7802-8025-3*) Wright Group, The.

Walter, Mildred Pitts. Because We Are. 1983. 192p. (J). (gr. 6 up). 11.95 o.p. (*0-688-02287-1*) HarperCollins Children's Bk. Group.

—Justin & the Best Biscuits in the World. 2002. (Illus.). (J). 13.40 (*0-7587-0371-6*) Book Wholesalers, Inc.

—Justin & the Best Biscuits in the World. 1986. (Illus.). 128p. (J). (gr. 4-7). 15.95 (*0-688-06645-3*) HarperCollins Children's Bk. Group.

—Justin & the Best Biscuits in the World. 1995. (Illus.). (J). (gr. 4). 9.00 (*0-395-73245-X*) Houghton Mifflin Co.

—Justin & the Best Biscuits in the World. 1999. (Illus.). 128p. (J). (gr. 3-5). pap. 4.99 (*0-679-89448-9*) Knopf, Alfred A. Inc.

—Justin & the Best Biscuits in the World. 1986. (J). 11.04 (*0-606-04714-X*) Turtleback Bks.

—Mariah Keeps Cool. 1990. 144p. (J). (gr. 3-7). lib. bdg. 15.00 (*0-02-792295-2*, Simon & Schuster Children's Publishing) Simon & Schuster Children's Publishing.

Ethnic Groups

—Mariah Loves Rock. 1988. 128p. (J). (gr. 3-7). lib. bdg. 13.95 o.p. (*0-02-792511-0*, Simon & Schuster Children's Publishing) Simon & Schuster Children's Publishing.

—Second Daughter: The Story of a Slave Girl. 1996. 176p. (YA). (gr. 7 up). pap. 15.95 (*0-590-48282-3*) Scholastic, Inc.

—Suitcase. 1999. (Illus.). 112p. (J). (gr. 3 up). 15.99 (*0-688-16547-8*) HarperCollins Children's Bk. Group.

—Trouble's Child. 1985. 128p. (J). (gr. 4 up). 11.95 o.p. (*0-688-04214-7*) HarperCollins Children's Bk. Group.

—Two & Too Much. 1990. (Illus.). 32p. (J). (ps-2). 13.95 o.p. (*0-02-792290-1*, Simon & Schuster Children's Publishing) Simon & Schuster Children's Publishing.

Walton, Darwin M. Dance, Kayla! 1998. 160p. (J). (gr. 4-6). lib. bdg. 14.95 o.p. (*0-8075-1453-5*) Whitman, Albert & Co.

Wampamba, Mazzi. The Kingdom of the South: The Long Journey. 1992. (Illus.). (J). (gr. 1-4). pap. 3.95 (*1-56411-045-1*) Conquering Bks.

Wangerin, Walter, Jr. Probity Jones & the Fear Not Angel. 1996. (Illus.). 32p. (J). (gr. 1-4). 16.99 (*0-8066-2992-4*, 9-2992, Augsburg Bks.) Augsburg Fortress, Pubs.

Warren, Cathy. Fred's First Day. 1984. (Illus.). 32p. (J). (gr. k up). 12.00 o.p. (*0-688-03813-1*); lib. bdg. 11.04 o.p. (*0-688-03814-X*) HarperCollins Children's Bk. Group.

Washington, Donna L. Double Dutch & the Voodoo Shoes: An Urban Folktale. 1991. (Adventures in Storytelling Ser.). (Illus.). 32p. (J). (ps-3). pap. 5.95 o.p. (*0-516-45133-2*); lib. bdg. 19.20 o.p. (*0-516-05133-4*) Scholastic Library Publishing. (Children's Pr.).

Washington, Vivian E. I Am Somebody, I Am Me: A Black Child's Credo. 1986. (Illus.). 35p. (Orig.). (J). (gr. 2-6). pap. 8.50 (*0-935132-07-4*) Fairfax, C.H. Co., Inc.

Waters, Linda. Slices of Chocolate Lives. 1993. 176p. (Orig.). (YA). pap. 4.95 (*0-9630887-0-X*) Ethnic Bks.

Watson, Jude. Tempestuous: Opal's Story. 1996. (Brides of Wildcat County Ser.). 192p. (J). (gr. 7 up). mass mkt. 5.99 (*0-689-81023-7*, Simon Pulse) Simon & Schuster Children's Publishing.

Watson, Kim. The Extra Thankful Thanksgiving. 2001. (Little Bill Ser.). (Illus.). 16p. (J). (gr. k-3). pap. 3.99 (*0-689-84190-6*, Simon Spotlight/ Nickelodeon) Simon & Schuster Children's Publishing.

—Just Like Dad. 2001. (Little Bill Ser.). (Illus.). 32p. (J). (gr. k-3). pap. 5.99 (*0-689-83999-5*, Simon Spotlight/Nickelodeon) Simon & Schuster Children's Publishing.

—Just Like Dad. 2001. (Little Bill Books for Beginning Readers Ser.). (Illus.). (J). 12.14 (*0-606-21276-0*) Turtleback Bks.

—A Trip to the Hospital. 2001. (Little Bill Books for Beginning Readers Ser.). (Illus.). (J). 9.65 (*0-606-21300-7*) Turtleback Bks.

Watson, Pat. Slam! Durst, Shirley J., ed. 2000. (YA). 9.95 (*1-58130-640-7*); 11.95 (*1-58130-641-5*) Novel Units, Inc.

Watts, Jeri H. Keepers. 2000. (Illus.). 32p. (gr. k up). (YA). 15.95 (*1-880000-58-X*); (J). pap. 6.95 (*1-58430-013-2*) Lee & Low Bks., Inc.

Wayne, Kyra P. Li'l Ol' Charlie. 1989. (Illus.). 88p. (Orig.). (J). pap. 8.95 o.p. (*0-931866-41-3*) Alpine Pubns., Inc.

Weatherford, Carole Boston. Freedom on the Menu: The Greensboro Sit-Ins. 2004. (J). (*0-8037-2860-3*, Dial Bks. for Young Readers) Penguin Putnam Bks. for Young Readers.

—Grandma & Me. 1996. (Illus.). 12p. (J). (ps-k). bds. 5.95 (*0-86316-252-5*) Writers & Readers Publishing, Inc.

—Juneteenth Jamboree. 1995. (Illus.). 24p. (J). (ps-3). 15.95 (*1-880000-18-0*) Lee & Low Bks., Inc.

—Me & My Family Tree. 1996. (Illus.). 12p. (J). (ps-k). bds. 5.95 (*0-86316-251-7*) Writers & Readers Publishing, Inc.

—Mighty Menfolk. 1996. (Illus.). 12p. (J). (ps-k). bds. 5.95 (*0-86316-253-3*) Writers & Readers Publishing, Inc.

Weik, Mary H. The Jazz Man. 2nd ed. 1993. (Illus.). 48p. (J). (gr. 3-7). reprint ed. pap. 4.99 (*0-689-71767-9*, Aladdin) Simon & Schuster Children's Publishing.

—The Jazz Man. 1996. 20.25 (*0-8446-6882-6*) Smith, Peter Pub., Inc.

Welber, Robert. The Train. 1972. (Illus.). (J). (gr. 1-4). lib. bdg. 5.99 o.p. (*0-394-92430-4*, Pantheon) Knopf Publishing Group.

Welty, Eudora. A Worn Path. 1993. (Creative Short Stories Ser.). 32p. (YA). (gr. 5-12). lib. bdg. 18.60 (*0-88682-471-0*, Creative Education) Creative Co., The.

Wenberg, Michael. Elizabeth's Song. 2003. (Illus.). 32p. (J). (gr. 3 up). lib. bdg. 23.93 (*0-8368-3572-7*) Stevens, Gareth Inc.

Wesley, Valerie Wilson. Freedom's Child. 1997. (Illus.). 32p. (J). (gr. 3-7). 16.00 (*0-689-80269-2*, Simon & Schuster Children's Publishing) Simon & Schuster Children's Publishing.

—Where Do I Go from Here? 144p. (J). (gr. 7-12). 1996. pap. 3.50 (*0-590-45607-5*); 1993. pap. 13.95 o.p. (*0-590-45606-7*) Scholastic, Inc.

—Where Do I Go from Here? 1993. 9.55 (*0-606-08660-9*) Turtleback Bks.

—Willimena. (J). Bk. 2. 2002. 12.99 (*0-7868-0466-1*); Bk. 3. Date not set. 12.99 (*0-7868-0523-4*); Bk. 4. Date not set. 12.99 (*0-7868-0524-2*) Hyperion Bks. for Children.

—Willimena Rules! Rule Book #2: How to Fish for Trouble. 2004. (Illus.). (J). (gr. 2-5). pap. 3.99 (*0-7868-1807-7*) Hyperion Bks. for Children.

Wezeman, Phyllis Vos. Benjamin Brody's Backyard Bag. 1991. (Illus.). 32p. (Orig.). (J). (gr. 1-5). pap. 11.95 (*0-87178-091-7*, 8917) Brethren Pr.

Whalin, W. Terry. Sojourner Truth: American Abolitionist. 1999. (Young Reader's Christian Library). (Illus.). 222p. (J). (gr. 8-12). pap. 1.39 (*1-57748-515-7*) Barbour Publishing, Inc.

Whitmore, Arvella. Trapped Between the Lash & the Gun. 2001. (YA). 12.04 (*0-606-21604-9*) Turtleback Bks.

—Trapped Between the Lash & the Gun: A Boy's Journey. Goyette, Cecile & Sherry, Toby, eds. 1999. 192p. (YA). (gr. 6-12). 16.99 (*0-8037-2384-9*, Dial Bks. for Young Readers) Penguin Putnam Bks. for Young Readers.

Whittle, Royce. 2U Black Children. 1996. (Illus.). 32p. (J). (gr. k-5). pap. 8.00 o.p. (*0-8059-3845-1*) Dorrance Publishing Co., Inc.

Wilkins, Verna A. Dave & the Tooth Fairy. 1996. (Illus.). 24p. (J). lib. bdg. 12.95 (*1-56674-120-3*) Forest Hse. Publishing Co., Inc.

Wilkins, Verna Allette. Dave & the Tooth Fairy. 1998. (Illus.). 24p. (J). (gr. 2 up). lib. bdg. 22.60 (*0-8368-2089-4*) Stevens, Gareth Inc.

—Toyin Fay. 1998. (Illus.). 24p. (J). (gr. 2 up). lib. bdg. 22.60 (*0-8368-2091-6*) Stevens, Gareth Inc.

Wilkinson, Brenda. Definitely Cool. 176p. (gr. 4-6). 1995. (J). mass mkt. 3.50 (*0-590-43842-5*); 1993. (Illus.). (YA). pap. 13.95 o.p. (*0-590-46186-9*) Scholastic, Inc.

—Definitely Cool. 1993. 8.60 o.p. (*0-606-07428-7*) Turtleback Bks.

—Ludell. 1985. 176p. mass mkt. 2.50 o.s.i (*0-553-26433-8*) Bantam Bks.

—Ludell. (Trophy Bk.). 176p. (J). 1992. (gr. 5 up). pap. 3.95 o.p. (*0-06-440419-6*, Harper Trophy); 1975. (gr. 7 up). lib. bdg. 14.89 o.p. (*0-06-026492-6*) HarperCollins Children's Bk. Group.

—Ludell & Willie. 1985. (Skylark Ser.). 144p. (J). (gr. 6 up). mass mkt. 2.25 o.s.i (*0-553-24995-9*) Bantam Bks.

—Ludell & Willie. 1977. (YA). (gr. 7 up). lib. bdg. 14.89 o.p. (*0-06-026488-8*) HarperCollins Children's Bk. Group.

—Ludell's New York Time. 1980. 192p. (YA). (gr. 7 up). 11.95 (*0-06-026497-7*); lib. bdg. 12.89 o.p. (*0-06-026498-5*) HarperCollins Children's Bk. Group.

—Not Separate, Not Equal. 1987. 192p. (J). (gr. 5 up). lib. bdg. 12.89 o.p. (*0-06-026482-9*) HarperCollins Children's Bk. Group.

Williams, Carol Lynch. Marciea's Melody. Utley, Jennifer, ed. 1996. (Latter-Day Daughters Ser.). (Illus.). 80p. (J). (gr. 3-9). pap. 4.95 (*1-56236-509-6*) Aspen Bks.

Williams-Garcia, Rita. Blue Tights. (YA). (gr. 7 up). 1996. 144p. pap. 5.99 (*0-14-038045-0*); 1988. 160p. 12.95 o.s.i (*0-525-67234-6*, Dutton Children's Bks.) Penguin Putnam Bks. for Young Readers.

—Catching the Wild Waiyuuzee. 2000. (Illus.). 32p. (J). (ps-3). 16.00 (*0-689-82601-X*, Simon & Schuster Children's Publishing) Simon & Schuster Children's Publishing.

—Fast Talk on a Slow Track. 1992. 192p. (YA). mass mkt. 3.99 o.p. (*0-553-29594-2*) Bantam Bks.

—Fast Talk on a Slow Track. (YA). (gr. 7-12). 1998. 190p. 5.99 (*0-14-130231-3*, Puffin Bks.); 1991. 176p. 15.00 o.s.i (*0-525-67334-2*, Dutton Children's Bks.) Penguin Putnam Bks. for Young Readers.

—Like Sisters on the Homefront. 176p. (gr. 7-12). 1998. pap. 5.99 (*0-14-038561-4*); 1995. (J). 15.99 (*0-525-67465-9*, Dutton Children's Bks.) Penguin Putnam Bks. for Young Readers.

—Like Sisters on the Homefront. 1998. (J). 12.04 (*0-606-12980-4*) Turtleback Bks.

—No Laughter Here. 2004. 144p. (J). 15.99 (*0-688-16247-9*); lib. bdg. 16.89 (*0-688-16248-7*) HarperCollins Pubs.

Williams, Karen L. When Africa Was Home. 1994. 13.10 (*0-606-12570-1*) Turtleback Bks.

Williams, Lori Aurelia. Shayla's Double Brown Baby Blues. 304p. 2003. (Illus.). (YA). pap. 7.99 (*0-689-85670-9*, Simon Pulse); 2001. (J). (gr. 7 up). 17.00 (*0-689-82469-6*, Simon & Schuster Children's Publishing) Simon & Schuster Children's Publishing.

—When Kambia Elaine Flew in from Neptune. unabr. ed. 2001. 256p. (YA). (gr. 7 up). pap. 50.00 incl. audio (*0-8072-8851-9*, Listening Library) Random Hse. Audio Publishing Group.

—When Kambia Elaine Flew in from Neptune. (Illus.). 256p. 2001. (J). pap. 10.00 (*0-689-84593-6*, Simon Pulse); 2000. (YA). (gr. 8 up). 17.00 (*0-689-82468-8*, Simon & Schuster Children's Publishing) Simon & Schuster Children's Publishing.

—When Kambia Elaine Flew in from Neptune. 2002. 16.05 (*0-606-22109-3*) Turtleback Bks.

Williams, Sherley Anne. Girls Together. 1999. (Illus.). 32p. (J). (ps-3). 16.00 (*0-15-230982-9*) Harcourt Children's Bks.

—Working Cotton. 2002. (Illus.). (J). 14.04 (*0-7587-0168-3*) Book Wholesalers, Inc.

—Working Cotton. (Illus.). 32p. (J). 1997. pap. 7.00 (*0-15-201482-9*, Harcourt Paperbacks); 1992. 17.00 (*0-15-299624-9*) Harcourt Children's Bks.

—Working Cotton. 1997. 13.15 (*0-606-12114-5*) Turtleback Bks.

Williamson, Mel & Ford, George. Walk On. 1972. (Illus.). 32p. (J). (gr. 3 up). 11.95 (*0-89388-042-6*) Okpaku Communications Corp.

Wilson, Beth P. Jenny. 1990. (Illus.). 32p. (J). (gr. k-3). lib. bdg. 13.95 (*0-02-793120-X*, Atheneum) Simon & Schuster Children's Publishing.

Wilson, Johnniece M. Oh, Brother. 128p. (J). (gr. 4-7). 1989. pap. 4.50 (*0-590-41001-6*, Scholastic Paperbacks); 1988. pap. 10.95 o.p. (*0-590-41363-5*) Scholastic, Inc.

—Oh, Brother. 1989. (J). 10.55 (*0-606-12457-8*) Turtleback Bks.

—Robin on His Own. (J). (gr. 4-6). 1992. 160p. mass mkt. 2.95 (*0-590-41809-2*, Scholastic Paperbacks); 1990. 12.95 o.p. (*0-590-41813-0*) Scholastic, Inc.

Winslow, Vicki. Follow the Leader. 1998. (Illus.). 224p. (gr. 2-6). pap. text 3.99 o.s.i (*0-440-41296-X*) Dell Publishing.

—Follow the Leader. 1998. 10.04 (*0-606-15531-7*) Turtleback Bks.

Wisehart, Randall. A Winding Road to Freedom. 1999. 184p. (J). (gr. 5-8). pap. 13.00 (*0-944350-47-X*) Friends United Pr.

Wisler, G. Clifton. The Raid. 128p. (J). (gr. 5 up). 1994. pap. 3.99 o.s.i (*0-14-036937-6*, Puffin Bks.); 1985. 11.95 o.p. (*0-525-67169-2*, Dutton Children's Bks.) Penguin Putnam Bks. for Young Readers.

Wojciechowska, Maia. Through the Broken Mirror with Alice. 1972. (J). (gr. 5 up). 5.95 o.p. (*0-15-286950-6*) Harcourt Children's Bks.

Woods, Brenda. The Red Rose Box. 2002. 160p. (J). (gr. 4-6). 16.99 (*0-399-23702-X*) Putnam Publishing Group, The.

Woodson, Jacqueline. Between Madison & Palmetto. 128p. (J). 1995. (gr. 5 up). pap. 3.50 o.s.i (*0-440-41062-2*); 1993. (gr. 1-6). 13.95 o.s.i (*0-385-30906-6*, Delacorte Pr.) Dell Publishing.

—Between Madison & Palmetto. 2002. 128p. (J). 16.99 (*0-399-23757-7*); (YA). pap. 5.99 (*0-698-11958-4*) Putnam Publishing Group, The.

—The Book Chase. 1994. (Ghostwriter Ser.). 112p. (J). (gr. 4-6). mass mkt. 3.50 o.s.i (*0-553-48190-8*) Bantam Bks.

—Dear One. 1991. (Laurel-Leaf Contemporary Fiction Ser.). 10.04 (*0-606-02589-8*) Turtleback Bks.

—The Dear One. 160p. 1992. (YA). mass mkt. 3.99 o.s.i (*0-440-21420-3*); 1991. (J). (gr. 4-7). 14.00 o.s.i (*0-385-30416-1*, Delacorte Pr.) Dell Publishing.

—The Dear One. 2004. 160p. pap. 6.99 (*0-14-250190-5*, Puffin Bks.) Penguin Putnam Bks. for Young Readers.

—The Dear One. 2004. 128p. (J). 17.99 (*0-399-23968-5*, Putnam & Grosset) Putnam Publishing Group, The.

—From the Notebooks of Melanin Sun. 160p. (gr. 7 up). 2003. (J). mass mkt. 5.99 (*0-590-45881-7*, Scholastic Paperbacks); 1995. (YA). pap. 14.95 o.p. (*0-590-45880-9*, Blue Sky Pr., The) Scholastic, Inc.

—From the Notebooks of Melanin Sun. 1997. (Point Signature Ser.). (J). 10.04 (*0-606-11357-6*) Turtleback Bks.

—The House You Pass on the Way. 2003. 128p. pap. 5.99 (*0-14-250191-3*, Puffin Bks.); 160p. (J). 16.99 (*0-399-23969-3*, G. P. Putnam's Sons) Penguin Putnam Bks. for Young Readers.

—The House You Pass on the Way. 1999. 128p. (YA). (gr. 7-12). mass mkt. 4.50 o.s.i (*0-440-22797-6*, Dell Books for Young Readers) Random Hse. Children's Bks.

—The House You Pass on the Way. 1999. 10.55 (*0-606-16085-X*) Turtleback Bks.

—Hush. 2002. 192p. (YA). (gr. 5-8). 15.99 (*0-399-23114-5*) Penguin Group (USA) Inc.

—Hush. 2003. 192p. pap. 5.99 (*0-14-250049-6*, Puffin Bks.) Penguin Putnam Bks. for Young Readers.

—I Hadn't Meant to Tell You This. 1994. 128p. (YA). (gr. 7 up). 15.95 o.s.i (*0-385-32031-0*, Delacorte Pr.) Dell Publishing.

—I Hadn't Meant to Tell You This. 1995. 128p. (YA). (gr. 7 up). mass mkt. 4.99 (*0-440-21960-4*, Dell Books for Young Readers) Random Hse. Children's Bks.

—I Hadn't Meant to Tell You This. 1995. (YA). (gr. 7 up). 10.55 (*0-606-08551-3*) Turtleback Bks.

—I Hadn't Meant To Tell You This. 1995. (YA). (gr. 7 up). mass mkt. 4.99 (*0-440-91087-0*, Dell Books for Young Readers) Random Hse. Children's Bks.

—If You Come Softly. 192p. (YA). (gr. 5 up). 2000. pap. 5.99 (*0-698-11862-6*); 1998. 15.99 (*0-399-23112-9*) Putnam Publishing Group, The.

—If You Come Softly. 2000. 11.04 (*0-606-17863-5*) Turtleback Bks.

—Last Summer with Maizon. 1991. 112p. (YA). pap. 3.99 o.s.i (*0-440-40555-6*) Dell Publishing.

—Last Summer with Maizon. 2002. 112p. (J). 16.99 (*0-399-23755-0*); (Illus.). 128p. (YA). (gr. 3-7). pap. 4.99 (*0-698-11929-0*) Putnam Publishing Group, The.

—Maizon at Blue Hill. 144p. 1993. (gr. 4-7). pap. text 3.99 o.s.i (*0-440-40899-7*); 1992. (J). (gr. 5-9). 14.00 o.s.i (*0-385-30796-9*, Delacorte Pr.) Dell Publishing.

—Maizon at Blue Hill. 2002. 144p. (J). 16.99 (*0-399-23756-9*); (YA). pap. 5.99 (*0-698-11957-6*) Putnam Publishing Group, The.

—Maizon at Blue Hill. 1992. (J). 10.04 (*0-606-05918-0*) Turtleback Bks.

—Our Gracie Aunt. 32p. 2002. (Illus.). (J). 15.99 (*0-7868-0620-6*, Jump at the Sun); 2001. lib. bdg. (*0-7868-2532-4*) Hyperion Bks. for Children.

—Sweet, Sweet Memory. 2000. (Illus.). 32p. (J). lib. bdg. 15.49 (*0-7868-2191-4*) Disney Pr.

—Sweet, Sweet Memory. 2000. (Illus.). 32p. (J). (gr. 1-4). 14.99 (*0-7868-0241-3*, Jump at the Sun) Hyperion Bks. for Children.

—Visiting Day. 2002. (Illus.). 32p. (J). (ps-3). pap. 15.95 (*0-590-40005-3*, Scholastic Pr.) Scholastic, Inc.

—A Way Out of No Way. 1997. 122p. (YA). (gr. 7-12). mass mkt. 4.50 o.s.i (*0-449-70460-2*, Fawcett) Ballantine Bks.

—We Had a Picnic This Sunday Past. 1998. (Illus.). 32p. (J). (ps-3). 14.99 (*0-7868-0242-1*); lib. bdg. 15.49 (*0-7868-2192-2*) Hyperion Bks. for Children.

Woodson, Jacqueline & Ransome, James. Visiting Day. 2001. (Illus.). (J). pap. (*0-590-55262-7*) Scholastic, Inc.

Woodtor, Dee P. Big Meeting. 1996. (Illus.). 40p. (J). (gr. k-3). 16.00 (*0-689-31933-9*, Atheneum) Simon & Schuster Children's Publishing.

Worth, Bonnie. The Lean, Green Urkel Machine. 1992. (Family Matters Ser.: No. 01). 96p. (J). (gr. 4-7). pap. 3.25 o.s.i (*0-440-40739-7*, Yearling) Random Hse. Children's Bks.

Wright, Courtni C. Journey to Freedom: A Story of the Underground Railroad. 1994. (Illus.). 32p. (J). (ps-3). tchr. ed. 16.95 (*0-8234-1096-X*); reprint ed. pap. 6.95 (*0-8234-1333-0*) Holiday Hse., Inc.

—Jumping the Broom. 1994. (Illus.). 32p. (J). (ps-3). tchr. ed. 15.95 (*0-8234-1042-0*) Holiday Hse., Inc.

Wright, Richard. Rite of Passage. 1994. 128p. (YA). lib. bdg. 13.89 o.p. (*0-06-023420-2*) HarperCollins Children's Bk. Group.

Wright, Richard A., ed. Black Boy: A Record of Childhood & Youth. 1989. (J). 18.05 (*0-606-00403-3*) Turtleback Bks.

Wyeth, Sharon Dennis. Always My Dad. (Illus.). (J). (gr. k-3). 1997. 32p. pap. 6.99 o.s.i (*0-679-88934-5*); 1994. 40p. 17.00 o.s.i (*0-679-83447-8*); 1994. 40p. 15.99 o.s.i (*0-679-93447-2*) Random Hse. Children's Bks. (Knopf Bks. for Young Readers).

—Always My Dad. 1997. 12.19 o.p. (*0-606-12873-5*) Turtleback Bks.

—Flying Free: Corey's Underground Railroad Diary, Bk. 2. 2002. (My America Ser.: Bk. 2). (Illus.). 112p. (J). (gr. 2-5). pap. 8.95 (*0-439-24443-9*); mass mkt. 4.99 (*0-439-36908-8*) Scholastic, Inc. (Scholastic Pr.).

—Freedom's Wings: Corey's Underground Railroad Diary, Bk. 1. (My America Ser.). (Illus.). 112p. (J). (gr. 4-7). 2002. mass mkt. 4.99 (*0-439-36907-X*); 2001. pap. 8.95 (*0-439-14100-1*) Scholastic, Inc. (Scholastic Pr.).

—Freedom's Wings: Corey's Underground Railroad Diary. 2001. (J). (gr. 4-7). 15.00 (*0-606-22804-7*) Turtleback Bks.

—Message in the Sky: Corey's Underground Railroad Diary, Bk. 3. 2003. (My America Ser.). 112p. (J). pap. 10.95 (*0-439-37057-4*); mass mkt. 4.99 (*0-439-37058-2*) Scholastic, Inc. (Scholastic Pr.).

—Once on This River. (J). (gr. 5-8). 1998. 160p. pap. 4.99 (*0-679-89446-2*, Random Hse. Bks. for Young Readers); 1997. 150p. 16.00 o.s.i (*0-679-88350-9*, Knopf Bks. for Young Readers) Random Hse. Children's Bks.

Asai, Carrie & Gray, Mitchel. The Book of the Wind. 2003. (Samurai Girl Ser.). (Illus.). 224p. (YA). pap. 6.99 (*0-689-86433-7*, Simon Pulse) Simon & Schuster Children's Publishing.

Chiu, Esther. The Lobster & the Sea. 1998. (Illus.). 32p. (J). (gr. 2-5). 14.95 (*1-879965-14-3*) Polychrome Publishing Corp.

Havill, Juanita. Jamaica & Brianna. 1993. (Illus.). 32p. (J). (ps-3). lib. bdg., tchr. ed. 16.00 (*0-395-64489-5*) Houghton Mifflin Co.

—Jamaica & Brianna. 1996. (Illus.). 32p. (J). (ps-3). pap. 5.95 (*0-395-77939-1*) Houghton Mifflin Co. Trade & Reference Div.

—Jamaica & Brianna. 1993. 11.15 o.p. (*0-606-08785-0*) Turtleback Bks.

Moss, Sally. Peter's Painting. 1995. (Illus.). 24p. (J). (ps-2). 13.95 (*1-57255-013-9*) Mondo Publishing.

Namioka, Lensey. Yang the Second & Her Secret Admirers. 2000. (Illus.). 144p. (gr. 4-7). pap. text 4.50 (*0-440-41641-8*, Yearling) Random Hse. Children's Bks.

—Yang the Second & Her Secret Admirers. 2000. 10.55 (*0-606-18794-4*) Turtleback Bks.

Say, Allen. Stranger in the Mirror. 1995. (Illus.). 32p. (J). (ps-3). 16.95 (*0-395-61590-9*) Houghton Mifflin Co.

—Stranger in the Mirror. 1995. 13.10 (*0-606-15724-7*) Turtleback Bks.

Suen, Anastasia. Toddler Two. (Illus.). (J). 2002. 20p. bds. 6.95 (*1-58430-052-3*); 2000. 22p. bds. 6.95 (*1-58430-015-9*) Lee & Low Bks., Inc.

—Toddler Two: Dos Anos. 2002. (ENG & SPA., Illus.). (J). bds. 5.95 (*1-58430-054-X*) Lee & Low Bks., Inc.

Wong, Shawn. American Knees. 240p. 1996. pap. 12.00 (*0-684-82275-X*); 1995. (J). 20.50 o.p. (*0-684-80304-6*) Simon & Schuster. (Simon & Schuster).

Yamanaka, Lois-Ann. Name Me Nobody. 2000. 229p. (J). (gr. 7-12). mass mkt. 5.99 (*0-7868-1466-7*) Disney Pr.

Yamate, Sandra S. The Best of Intentions. 1993. (Illus.). (J). (*1-879965-09-7*) Polychrome Publishing Corp.

B

BEDOUINS—FICTION

Abdel-Al, Mohamed. Weavers of Death. 1996. 158p. pap. 12.95 (*1-85756-285-2*) Janus Publishing Co. GBR. *Dist:* Paul & Co. Pubs. Consortium, Inc.

Ivey, Jean. Wadduda of the Desert: A Legend of the Arabian War Mare. 1998. (Illus.). 230p. (J). (gr. 4-12). pap. 9.95 (*0-9658891-3-0*) Elan Pr.

Temple, Frances. The Beduins' Gazelle. 1998. (Harper Trophy Bks.). (Illus.). 160p. (J). (gr. 7 up). pap. 5.99 (*0-06-440669-5*, Harper Trophy) HarperCollins Children's Bk. Group.

—The Beduins' Gazelle. 1996. 160p. (YA). (gr. 7 up). pap. 15.95 (*0-531-09519-3*); lib. bdg. 16.99 (*0-531-08869-3*) Scholastic, Inc. (Orchard Bks.).

BLACKS—FICTION

Ashley, Bernard. Little Soldier: A Novel. 240p. (J). 2003. mass mkt. 5.99 (*0-439-28502-X*); 2002. (Illus.). (gr. 9 up). pap. 16.95 (*0-439-22424-1*, Scholastic Pr.) Scholastic, Inc.

Bacon, Martha. Sophia Scrooby Preserved. 1972. (Illus.). 240p. (gr. 5-8). reprint ed. pap. 1.50 o.p. (*0-440-48153-8*) Dell Publishing.

Barnes, Joyce Annette. Amistad. 1997. (Illus.). 144p. (J). (gr. 5-9). pap. 4.99 o.s.i (*0-14-039063-4*, Puffin Bks.) Penguin Putnam Bks. for Young Readers.

Bell, Anthea, tr. Youpala, Queen of the Jungle. 1995. (Illus.). 32p. (J). (ps-3). tchr. ed. (*1-85697-625-4*) Kingfisher Publications, plc.

Bell, William. Zack. 1998. 176p. (YA). (gr. 5). pap. o.s.i (*0-385-25711-2*) Doubleday Canada, Ltd. CAN. *Dist:* Random Hse., Inc.

—Zack. l.t. ed. 2000. (LRS Large Print Cornerstone Ser.). 256p. (YA). (gr. 5-12). lib. bdg. 28.95 (*1-58118-072-1*, 23656) LRS.

—Zack. (Illus.). 192p. (YA). (gr. 7 up). 2000. mass mkt. 4.99 (*0-689-82529-3*, Simon Pulse); 1999. per. 16.95 (*0-689-82248-0*, Simon & Schuster Children's Publishing) Simon & Schuster Children's Publishing.

—Zack. 2000. (J). 11.04 (*0-606-20095-9*) Turtleback Bks.

Brady, Jennifer. Jambi & the Lions. Thatch, Nancy R., ed. 1992. (Books for Students by Students). (Illus.). 26p. (J). (gr. 4-7). lib. bdg. 15.95 (*0-933849-41-9*) Landmark Editions, Inc.

Cousins, Linda. Huggy Bean: A Desert Adventure. 1992. (Series 3). (Illus.). 28p. (J). pap. 5.95 o.p. (*0-936073-12-8*) Gumbs & Thomas Pubs., Inc.

—Huggy Bean: We Happened upon a Beautiful Place. 1992. (Series 2). (Illus.). 28p. (J). pap. 5.95 o.p. (*0-936073-13-6*) Gumbs & Thomas Pubs., Inc.

—Huggy Bean & the Origin of the Magic Kente Cloth. 1991. (Series 1). (Illus.). 28p. (J). pap. 5.95 o.p. (*0-936073-11-X*) Gumbs & Thomas Pubs., Inc.

Daly, Niki. Jamela's Dress, RS. (Illus.). (J). 2004. pap. 6.95 (*0-374-43720-3*); 1999. 32p. 16.00 (*0-374-33667-9*, Farrar, Straus & Giroux (BYR)) Farrar, Straus & Giroux.

—Jamela's Dress. 2001. (J). (ps-2). 26.95 incl. audio (*0-8045-6878-2*, 6878) Spoken Arts, Inc.

—Not So Fast, Songololo. 1998. (J). pap. 4.95 (*0-87628-975-8*) Ctr. for Applied Research in Education, The.

—Not So Fast, Songololo. 1987. 32p. (J). (ps-3). pap. 4.99 o.p. (*0-14-050715-9*, Puffin Bks.) Penguin Putnam Bks. for Young Readers.

—Not So Fast, Songololo. (Illus.). 32p. (J). (gr. k-3). 1996. pap. 6.99 (*0-689-80154-8*, Aladdin); 1986. 16.00 (*0-689-50367-9*, McElderry, Margaret K.) Simon & Schuster Children's Publishing.

—Not So Fast, Songololo. 1996. (J). 10.15 o.p. (*0-606-09700-7*) Turtleback Bks.

—Oh Jamela!, RS. 2001. (Illus.). 32p. (J). (ps-2). 16.00 (*0-374-35602-5*, Farrar, Straus & Giroux (BYR)) Farrar, Straus & Giroux.

Daly, Niki, illus. & text. Once upon a Time, RS. 2003. 40p. (J). (gr. k-3). 16.00 (*0-374-35633-5*, Farrar, Straus & Giroux (BYR)) Farrar, Straus & Giroux.

Deetlefs, Rene. The Song of Six Birds. 1999. (Illus.). 32p. (J). (ps-4). 15.99 o.s.i (*0-525-46314-3*, Dutton Children's Bks.) Penguin Putnam Bks. for Young Readers.

Dhondy, Farrukh. Black Swan. 1993. 208p. (YA). (gr. 6 up). 14.95 o.p. (*0-395-66076-9*) Houghton Mifflin Co.

Dickinson, Peter. AK. 1992. 240p. (YA). 15.00 o.s.i (*0-385-30608-3*) Dell Publishing.

Farmer, Nancy. Do You Know Me? 1994. (Illus.). 112p. (J). (gr. 3-7). pap. 5.99 (*0-14-036946-5*, Puffin Bks.) Penguin Putnam Bks. for Young Readers.

—Do You Know Me? 1993. (Illus.). 112p. (J). (gr. 3-5). pap. 15.95 (*0-531-05474-8*); (gr. 4-7). lib. bdg. 16.99 (*0-531-08624-0*) Scholastic, Inc. (Orchard Bks.).

—The Ear, the Eye & the Arm: A Novel. 1995. 320p. (YA). (gr. 4-7). pap. 5.99 (*0-14-037641-0*, Puffin Bks.) Penguin Putnam Bks. for Young Readers.

—The Ear, the Eye & the Arm: A Novel. 1994. 320p. (YA). (gr. 7 up). pap. 18.95 (*0-531-06829-3*); lib. bdg. 19.99 (*0-531-08679-8*) Scholastic, Inc. (Orchard Bks.).

—The Ear, the Eye & the Arm: A Novel. 1995. (YA). (gr. 7 up). 12.04 (*0-606-08279-4*) Turtleback Bks.

Foggo, Cheryl. One Thing That's True. unabr. ed. 2002. (Illus.). 120p. (YA). (gr. 5-9). pap. 5.95 (*1-55074-377-5*); 1998. 260p. (J). (gr. 4-7). (*1-55074-411-9*) Kids Can Pr., Ltd.

—Sam Finds a Monster. 2003. (Kids Can Read Ser.). (Illus.). 32p. (J). (gr. k-1). 14.95 (*1-55337-351-0*) Kids Can Pr., Ltd.

Gates, Susan. Bill's Baggy Pants. 2002. (Read-It! Readers Ser.). (Illus.). 32p. (J). (ps-3). lib. bdg. 18.60 (*1-4048-0050-6*) Picture Window Bks.

Gillard, Denise. Music from the Sky. 2001. (Illus.). 32p. (J). (gr. k-2). 15.95 (*0-88899-311-0*) Groundwood Bks. CAN. *Dist:* Publishers Group West.

Glasser, Margaret D. Kofi's Story. 1999. (Illus.). 28p. (J). (gr. k-3). pap. text 8.95 (*1-58521-003-X*) Books for Black Children, Inc.

Golden Books Staff. Blue's Quilt. 2003. (Blue's Clues Ser.). (Illus.). 32p. (J). (ps-2). pap. 4.99 (*0-307-10503-2*, Golden Bks.) Random Hse. Children's Bks.

Gray, Nigel. I'll Take You to Mrs. Cole. 1992. (Illus.). 32p. (J). (gr. k-5). 12.95 o.p. (*0-916291-39-1*) Kane/Miller Bk. Pubs.

Grifalconi, Ann. The Village That Vanished. 2002. (Illus.). 40p. (J). (gr. k up). 16.99 (*0-8037-2623-6*, Dial Bks. for Young Readers) Penguin Putnam Bks. for Young Readers.

Haarhoff, Dorian. Desert December. 1992. (Illus.). 32p. (J). (ps-3). 13.95 o.s.i (*0-395-61300-0*, Clarion Bks.) Houghton Mifflin Co. Trade & Reference Div.

Howard, Ellen. When Daylight Comes. 1985. 192p. (J). (gr. 5-9). lib. bdg. 14.95 o.p. (*0-689-31133-8*, Atheneum) Simon & Schuster Children's Publishing.

Isadora, Rachel. At the Crossroads. 1991. (Illus.). 32p. (J). (ps up). 16.00 o.s.i (*0-688-05270-3*); lib. bdg. 15.93 o.p. (*0-688-05271-1*) HarperCollins Children's Bk. Group. (Greenwillow Bks.).

—At the Crossroads. 1994. (Illus.). 32p. (J). (ps-3). reprint ed. pap. 5.95 (*0-688-13103-4*, Morrow, William & Co.) Morrow/Avon.

—At the Crossroads. 1994. 11.10 (*0-606-06192-4*) Turtleback Bks.

—Caribbean Dream. 2002. (Illus.). 32p. (J). pap. 6.99 (*0-698-11944-4*, PaperStar) Penguin Putnam Bks. for Young Readers.

—Over the Green Hills. 1992. 32p. (J). (ps up). lib. bdg. 13.93 o.p. (*0-688-10510-6*); (Illus.). 17.99 (*0-688-10509-2*) HarperCollins Children's Bk. Group. (Greenwillow Bks.).

James, Simon. Leon & Bob. 1997. (Illus.). 32p. (J). (gr. 1-4). 15.99 o.s.i (*1-56402-991-3*) Candlewick Pr.

Kroll, Virginia L. Africa Brothers & Sisters. (Illus.). 32p. (J). (ps-2). 1998. pap. 5.99 o.s.i (*0-689-81816-5*, Aladdin); 1993. lib. bdg. 15.00 (*0-02-751166-9*, Simon & Schuster Children's Publishing) Simon & Schuster Children's Publishing.

—Africa Brothers & Sisters. 1998. 12.14 (*0-606-12870-0*) Turtleback Bks.

Lewin, Hugh. Jafta & the Wedding. 1983. (Jafta Collection). (Illus.). 24p. (J). (gr. 1-3). pap. 4.95 o.s.i (*0-87614-497-0*); lib. bdg. 15.95 (*0-87614-210-2*) Lerner Publishing Group. (Carolrhoda Bks.).

Lisa, Nikola. Hallelujah! A Christmas Celebration. 2000. (Illus.). 32p. (J). (ps-3). 16.00 o.s.i (*0-689-81673-1*, Atheneum) Simon & Schuster Children's Publishing.

Maartens, Maretha. Paper Bird: A Novel of South Africa. 1991. 144p. (J). (gr. 4-9). 13.95 o.s.i (*0-395-56490-5*, Clarion Bks.) Houghton Mifflin Co. Trade & Reference Div.

Machado, Ana Maria. Nina Bonita. 1995. (SPA., Illus.). 24p. (J). (ps-3). pap. 6.99 (*980-257-165-2*, EK6355) Ekare, Ediciones VEN. *Dist:* AIMS International Bks., Inc., Kane/Miller Bk. Pubs., Lectorum Pubns., Inc.

—Nina Bonita. Iribarren, Elena, tr. from POR. (Illus.). 24p. (J). (ps-3). 1996. 9.95 o.p. (*0-916291-63-4*); 2001. reprint ed. pap. 6.95 (*1-929132-11-5*) Kane/Miller Bk. Pubs.

—Nina Bonita. 2001. (J). 13.10 (*0-606-20824-0*) Turtleback Bks.

Medearis, Angela Shelf. Seven Spools of Thread: A Kwanzaa Story. 2000. (Illus.). 40p. (J). (gr. 2-5). lib. bdg. 15.95 (*0-8075-7315-9*) Whitman, Albert & Co.

Mitchell, Rita Phillips. Hue Boy. 1999. (Illus.). 32p. (J). (gr. k-3). pap. 11.95 (*0-14-056354-7*) Penguin Bks., Ltd. GBR. *Dist:* Trafalgar Square.

—Hue Boy. (Picture Puffin Ser.). (J). (gr. k-3). 1997. 32p. pap. 4.99 o.s.i (*0-14-055995-7*); 1993. (Illus.). 320p. 13.99 o.s.i (*0-8037-1448-3*, Dial Bks. for Young Readers) Penguin Putnam Bks. for Young Readers.

—Hue Boy. 1997. (Picture Puffin Ser.). (J). 10.19 o.p. (*0-606-11487-4*) Turtleback Bks.

Moon, Nicola. Something Special. 1997. (Illus.). 32p. (J). (ps-1). 14.95 (*1-56145-137-1*) Peachtree Pubs., Ltd.

Murray, Millie. Cairo Hughes. 1997. (Livewire Ser.). 110p. (YA). (gr. 7-11). pap. 7.95 (*0-7043-4936-1*) Women's Pr., Ltd., The GBR. *Dist:* Trafalgar Square.

Naidoo, Beverley. Journey to Jo'burg: A South African Story. (Illus.). 96p. (J). (gr. 4-7). 1986. 14.95 o.p. (*0-397-32168-6*); 1986. lib. bdg. 16.89 (*0-397-32169-4*); 1988. reprint ed. pap. 4.99 (*0-06-440237-1*, Harper Trophy) HarperCollins Children's Bk. Group.

—Journey to Jo'burg: A South African Story. 1986. (J). 11.10 (*0-606-03834-5*) Turtleback Bks.

—No Turning Back: A Novel of South Africa. (J). (gr. 3-7). 1999. 208p. pap. 5.99 (*0-06-440749-7*); 1997. 208p. 15.89 (*0-06-027506-5*); 1996. 160p. 14.95 o.p. (*0-06-027505-7*) HarperCollins Children's Bk. Group. (Harper Trophy).

—No Turning Back: A Novel of South Africa. 1999. 12.00 (*0-606-15856-1*) Turtleback Bks.

Naidoo, Beverly. Journey to Jo'burg: A South African Story. 1995. (Longman Literature Ser.). pap. text 50.95 (*0-582-25402-7*) Addison-Wesley Longman, Ltd. GBR. *Dist:* Trans-Atlantic Pubns., Inc.

Northway, Jennifer. Get Lost, Laura! 1995. (Illus.). 32p. (J). (ps-2). pap. 10.95 o.s.i (*0-307-17520-0*, Golden Bks.) Random Hse. Children's Bks.

Perera, Hilda. Cuentos de Apolo. 3rd ed. 1975. (SPA., Illus.). 103p. (YA). (gr. 6 up). pap. 5.00 (*0-89729-438-6*) Ediciones Universal.

Picó, Fernando. The Red Comb. 1994. 11.10 (*0-606-08064-3*) Turtleback Bks.

Pirotta, Saviour. Follow That Cat! 1993. (Illus.). 32p. (J). (gr. k-3). 13.99 o.p. (*0-525-45125-0*, Dutton Children's Bks.) Penguin Putnam Bks. for Young Readers.

—Follow That Cat! (Illus.). 26p. (J). 4.98 o.p. (*0-8317-5016-2*) Smithmark Pubs., Inc.

Pullman, Philip. The Broken Bridge. (gr. 7 up). 1994. (Illus.). 224p. mass mkt. 5.50 (*0-679-84715-4*, Random Hse. Bks. for Young Readers); 1992. 256p. (YA). 15.99 o.s.i (*0-679-91972-4*, Knopf Bks. for Young Readers) Random Hse. Children's Bks.

—The Broken Bridge. 2002. (YA). 20.25 (*0-8446-7229-7*) Smith, Peter Pub., Inc.

—The Broken Bridge. 1994. 11.04 (*0-606-06945-3*) Turtleback Bks.

Rochman, Hazel, ed. Somehow Tenderness Survives: Stories of Southern Africa. (Charlotte Zolotow Bk.). (gr. 7 up). 1990. 208p. (J). mass mkt. 5.99 (*0-06-447063-6*, Harper Trophy); 1988. 160p. (YA). 12.95 (*0-06-025022-4*); 1988. 160p. (YA). lib. bdg. 14.89 o.p. (*0-06-025023-2*) HarperCollins Children's Bk. Group.

—Somehow Tenderness Survives: Stories of Southern Africa. 1990. 11.00 (*0-606-04802-2*) Turtleback Bks.

Romain, Trevor. The Other Side of the Invisible Fence. Willerman, Benne, ed. 1994. 96p. (J). (gr. 3-11). pap. 7.95 (*1-880092-17-4*) Bright Bks., Inc.

Sacks, Margaret. Themba. 1992. (Illus.). 48p. (J). (gr. 2-5). 12.00 o.p. (*0-525-67414-4*, Dutton Children's Bks.) Penguin Putnam Bks. for Young Readers.

Schrier, Jeffrey. On the Wings of Eagles. 1998. (Single Titles Ser.). (Illus.). 32p. (J). (ps up). 21.90 o.p. (*0-7613-0004-X*) Millbrook Pr., Inc.

Shahrokhimanesh, Doris J. Under the Veil. 1996. 282p. (Orig.). (YA). (gr. 10-12). pap. 19.95 (*0-9653158-0-0*) Under The Veil Pr.

Sisulu, Elinor B. The Day Gogo Went to Vote: South Africa, April 1994. (Illus.). 32p. (J). (ps-3). 1999. pap. 5.95 (*0-316-70271-4*); 1996. 15.95 o.p. (*0-316-70267-6*) Little Brown & Co.

Stewart, Dianne. The Dove. 1993. (Illus.). 32p. (J). (ps up). 14.00 o.p. (*0-688-11264-1*); lib. bdg. 13.93 o.p. (*0-688-11265-X*) HarperCollins Children's Bk. Group. (Greenwillow Bks.).

—El Regalo del Sol. 2001. (SPA., Illus.). 28p. (J). (ps-3). pap. 6.99 (*980-257-258-6*, EK(1977)) Ekare, Ediciones VEN. *Dist:* Kane/Miller Bk. Pubs., Lectorum Pubns., Inc.

—El Regalo del Sol, RS. 1996. (SPA., Illus.). 32p. (J). (gr. k up). 15.00 o.p. (*0-374-32425-5*, Farrar, Straus & Giroux (BYR)) Farrar, Straus & Giroux.

Stock, Catherine. Where Are You Going, Manyoni. 1993. (Illus.). 48p. (J). (ps-3). 16.99 (*0-688-10352-9*) HarperCollins Children's Bk. Group.

—Where Are You Going, Manyoni. 1993. (Illus.). 48p. (J). (ps-3). lib. bdg. 16.89 o.p. (*0-688-10353-7*, Morrow, William & Co.) Morrow/Avon.

Stuart, Morna. Marassa & Midnight. 1969. (gr. 5-8). pap. 1.25 o.p. (*0-440-45322-4*) Dell Publishing.

Taylor, Theodore. The Cay. l.t. ed. 1990. 154p. (J). (gr. k-6). reprint ed. lib. bdg. 15.95 o.p. (*1-55736-163-0*) Bantam Doubleday Dell Large Print Group, Inc.

—The Cay. (YA). (gr. 5 up). 1977. 416p. pap. 4.95 (*0-380-00142-X*); 1976. 512p. reprint ed. pap. 4.95 (*0-380-01003-8*) HarperCollins Children's Bk. Group. (Harper Trophy).

—The Cay. 2000. 171p. (J). 15.60 (*0-03-054604-4*) Holt, Rinehart & Winston.

—The Cay. 144p. 2003. (Illus.). (YA). (gr. 5). mass mkt. 5.50 (*0-440-22912-X*, Laurel Leaf); 2002. (gr. 4-7). pap. text 5.50 (*0-440-41663-9*, Yearling); 1987. (gr. 4-7). text 16.95 (*0-385-07906-0*, Delacorte Bks. for Young Readers) Random Hse. Children's Bks.

—The Cay. 1970. (J). 11.00 (*0-606-04889-8*); 1969. 11.04 (*0-606-02584-7*) Turtleback Bks.

Temple, Frances. Taste of Salt. 1994. (Trophy Bk.). 192p. (YA). (gr. 7 up). pap. 5.99 (*0-06-447136-5*, Harper Trophy) HarperCollins Children's Bk. Group.

—A Taste of Salt: A Story of Modern Haiti. 1992. 192p. (YA). (gr. 6-12). pap. 16.95 (*0-531-05459-4*); (gr. 7 up). lib. bdg. 17.99 (*0-531-08609-7*) Scholastic, Inc. (Orchard Bks.).

—A Taste of Salt: A Story of Modern Haiti. 1994. (J). 11.00 (*0-606-07117-2*) Turtleback Bks.

—Tonight, by Sea. 1997. 11.00 (*0-606-10955-2*) Turtleback Bks.

Williams, Michael. Crocodile Burning. 208p. (gr. 7 up). 1994. (J). pap. 3.99 o.s.i (*0-14-036793-4*, Puffin Bks.); 1992. (YA). 15.00 o.p. (*0-525-67401-2*, Dutton Children's Bks.) Penguin Putnam Bks. for Young Readers.

BUDDHISM—FICTION

Chaitanya, Krishna. Rohanta & Nandriya. 1979. (Nehru Library for Children). (Illus.). (J). (gr. 1-9). pap. 2.00 o.p. (*0-89744-179-6*) Auromere, Inc.

Demi, Hitz. Buddha Stories, ERS. 1997. (Illus.). 32p. (J). (gr. 1-4). 20.00 (*0-8050-4886-3*, Holt, Henry & Co. Bks. For Young Readers) Holt, Henry & Co.

Dharma Realm Buddhist University Staff. Human Roots: Buddhist Stories for Young Readers. 1984. (Illus.). 140p. (J). (gr. 3 up). pap. 5.00 (*0-88139-017-8*) Buddhist Text Translation Society.

Dharma Realm Buddhist University Staff, compiled by. Human Roots: Buddhist Stories for Young Readers. 1982. (Illus.). 89p. (J). (gr. 3 up). pap. 5.00 (*0-88139-500-5*) Buddhist Text Translation Society.

Dickinson, Peter. Tulku. 1979. (J). (gr. 7 up). 9.95 o.p. (*0-525-41571-8*, Dutton) Dutton/Plume.

Koja, Kathe. Buddha Boy, RS. 2003. 128p. (YA). (gr. 7 up). 16.00 o.s.i (*0-374-30998-1*, Farrar, Straus & Giroux (BYR)) Farrar, Straus & Giroux.

—Buddha Boy. l.t. ed. 2003. 113p. (J). 24.95 (*0-7862-6012-2*) Gale Group.

Thong, Roseanne. One Is a Drummer. (J). 14.95 (*0-8118-3772-6*) Chronicle Bks. LLC.
—Red Is a Dragon. 2001. (Illus.). 40p. (J). 14.95 (*0-8118-3177-9*) Chronicle Bks. LLC.
—Round is a Mooncake: A Book of Shapes. 2000. (Illus.). 40p. (J). (ps-k). 14.95 (*0-8118-2676-7*) Chronicle Bks. LLC.
Wong, Janet S. Apple Pie Fourth of July. 2002. (Illus.). 40p. (J). (ps-2). 16.00 (*0-15-202543-X*) Harcourt Children's Bks.
Yamada, Debbie Leung. Striking It Rich: Treasures from Gold Mountain. l.t. ed. 2001. (Illus.). 128p. (J). (gr. 4-8). 13.95 (*1-879965-21-6*) Polychrome Publishing Corp.
Yamate, Sandra S. Char Siu Bao Boy. 1991. (Illus.). 32p. (J). (gr. k-4). 12.95 o.p. (*1-879965-00-3*) Polychrome Publishing Corp.
Yamate, Sandra S. & Yao, Carolina, illus. Char Siu Bao Boy. 2000. 32p. (J). (ps-3). 15.95 (*1-879965-19-4*) Polychrome Publishing Corp.
Yang, Dori Jones. The Secret Voice of Gina Zhang. 2000. (American Girls Collection Ser.). 232p. (J). (gr. 4-6). 12.95 (*1-58485-204-6*); pap. 5.95 (*1-58485-203-8*) Pleasant Co. Pubns. (American Girl).
—The Secret Voice of Gina Zhang. 2000. 12.00 (*0-606-21790-8*) Turtleback Bks.
Yee, Lisa. Millicent Min, Girl Genius. 2003. 240p. (J). pap. 16.95 (*0-439-42519-0*, Levine, Arthur A. Bks.) Scholastic, Inc.
Yep, Laurence. Angelfish. 2001. 216p. (J). (gr. 5 up). 16.99 (*0-399-23041-6*, G. P. Putnam's Sons) Penguin Group (USA) Inc.
—Child of the Owl. 1990. (Golden Mountain Chronicles). 288p. (J). (gr. 7 up). pap. 6.99 (*0-06-440336-X*, Harper Trophy) HarperCollins Children's Bk. Group.
—Child of the Owl. 1977. (YA). (gr. 7-12). 16.12 (*0-06-026739-9*, 972926) HarperCollins Pubs.
—Child of the Owl. 1977. (J). 11.00 (*0-606-04634-8*) Turtleback Bks.
—Cockroach Cooties. 2001. 144p. (J). (gr. 3-7). pap. 5.99 (*0-7868-1338-5*) Hyperion Bks. for Children.
—The Cook's Family. 1998. (J). (*0-03-992907-8*) Holt, Rinehart & Winston.
—The Cook's Family. 1998. 186p. (J). (gr. 5-9). 15.99 o.p. (*0-399-22907-8*, G. P. Putnam's Sons) Penguin Group (USA) Inc.
—The Cook's Family. 1999. (Illus.). 192p. (J). (gr. 5-9). pap. 5.99 o.s.i (*0-698-11804-9*, PaperStar) Penguin Putnam Bks. for Young Readers.
—The Cook's Family. 1999. (J). 11.04 (*0-606-18932-7*) Turtleback Bks.
—The Cook's Family. 1999. (J). pap. 3.99 (*0-14-037472-8*, Viking) Viking Penguin.
—Dragonwings. 1993. (J). per. 6.50 (*0-8222-1326-5*) Dramatists Play Service, Inc.
—Dragonwings. 1975. (Golden Mountain Chronicles). 256p. (J). (gr. 5 up). lib. bdg. 16.89 (*0-06-026738-0*) HarperCollins Children's Bk. Group.
—Dragonwings. 1975. (YA). (gr. 7-12). 17.02 o.p. (*0-06-026737-2*, 972928) HarperCollins Pubs.
—Dragonwings. l.t. ed. 1990. 282p. (J). reprint ed. lib. bdg. 16.95 o.s.i (*1-55736-168-1*, Cornerstone Bks.) Pages, Inc.
—Dragonwings. 1975. (J). 12.00 (*0-606-00842-X*) Turtleback Bks.
—Dragonwings: Golden Mountain Chronicles: 1903. 25th ed. 1977. (Golden Mountain Chronicles). (Illus.). 336p. (J). (gr. 5 up). pap. 6.99 (*0-06-440085-9*, Harper Trophy) HarperCollins Children's Bk. Group.
—Dream Soul. (J). 2002. 256p. (gr. 3-7). pap. 6.99 (*0-06-440788-8*); 2000. (Illus.). 224p. (gr. 3-7). lib. bdg. 16.89 (*0-06-028390-4*); 2000. (Illus.). 256p. (gr. 7 up). 15.95 (*0-06-028389-0*) HarperCollins Children's Bk. Group.
—The Journal of Wong Ming-Chung: A Chinese Miner: California, 1852. 2000. (My Name Is America Ser.). (Illus.). 219p. (J). (gr. 4-8). pap. 10.95 (*0-590-38607-7*) Scholastic, Inc.
—The Magic Paintbrush. 2000. (Illus.). 96p. (J). (gr. 7 up). 14.95 (*0-06-028199-5*); lib. bdg. 13.89 (*0-06-028200-2*) HarperCollins Children's Bk. Group.
—The Magic Paintbrush. 2003. (Illus.). 96p. (J). (gr. 3-7). pap. 4.99 (*0-06-440852-3*) HarperCollins Pubs.
—Skunk Scout. 2003. (Illus.). 160p. (J). 15.99 (*0-7868-0670-2*) Hyperion Bks. for Children.
—Tiger's Apprentice. 2003. 192p. (J). (gr. 5 up). lib. bdg. 16.89 (*0-06-001014-2*) HarperCollins Children's Bk. Group.
—The Tiger's Apprentice. 2003. 192p. (J). (gr. 5 up). 15.99 (*0-06-001013-4*) HarperCollins Children's Bk. Group.
—The Tiger's Apprentice. l.t. ed. 2003. 221p. (J). 22.95 (*0-7862-5731-8*) Thorndike Pr.
—The Traitor. 2003. (Golden Mountain Chronicles Ser.). 320p. (J). 16.99 (*0-06-027522-7*); (Illus.). lib. bdg. 17.89 (*0-06-027523-5*) HarperCollins Children's Bk. Group.
—When the Circus Came to Town. 128p. (J). 2004. pap. 5.99 (*0-06-440965-1*, Harper Trophy); 2001. (Illus.). 14.95 (*0-06-029325-X*); 2001. (Illus.). lib. bdg. 14.89 (*0-06-029326-8*) HarperCollins Children's Bk. Group.
Yin. Coolies. (Illus.). 40p. 2003. pap. 7.99 (*0-14-250055-0*, Puffin Bks.); 2001. (J). 16.99 (*0-399-23227-3*, Philomel) Penguin Putnam Bks. for Young Readers.

COSSACKS—FICTION

Kimmel, Eric A. The Tartar's Sword. 1974. 288p. (J). (gr. 6 up). 6.95 o.p. (*0-698-20243-0*) Putnam Publishing Group, The.

CUBAN AMERICANS—FICTION

Acierno, Maria A. Children of Flight Pedro Pan. 1994. (Stories of the States Ser.). (Illus.). 80p. (J). (gr. 4-7). lib. bdg. 13.95 o.p. (*1-881889-52-1*) Silver Moon Pr.
Bernardo, Anilu. Loves Me, Loves Me Not. 1998. 169p. (gr. 6-12). (J). pap. 9.95 (*1-55885-259-X*); (YA). 16.95 o.p. (*1-55885-258-1*) Arte Publico Pr. (Piñata Books).
Brouwer, Sigmund. Hurricane Power: Track. 1999. (Sigmund Brouwer's Sports Mystery Ser.: Vol. 6). 128p. (J). (gr. 5-9). pap. 5.99 o.s.i (*0-8499-5818-0*) Nelson, Tommy.
Chapra, Mimi. Amelia's Kindergarten Fiesta. 2004. (Illus.). (J). 15.99 (*0-06-050255-X*); lib. bdg. 16.89 (*0-06-050256-8*) HarperCollins Pubs.
Dole, Mayra L. Drum, Chavi, Drum ! / Toca, Chavi, Toca! 2003. Tr. of Toca, Chavi, Toca!. (ENG & SPA., Illus.). 32p. (J). 16.95 (*0-89239-186-3*) Children's Bk. Pr.
Heller, Marion. Paco's Perro. 2001. 163p. (J). (gr. 5-9). pap. 12.95 (*1-56825-080-0*, 080.0) Rainbow Bks., Inc.
Mills, Claudia. Luisa's American Dream. 1984. 160p. (J). (gr. 7 up). pap. 11.95 o.p. (*0-02-767040-6*, Simon & Schuster Children's Publishing) Simon & Schuster Children's Publishing.
Osa, Nancy. Cuba 15. 2003. 288p. (YA). (gr. 7). lib. bdg. 17.99 (*0-385-90086-4*); (Illus.). 15.95 (*0-385-73021-7*) Random Hse. Children's Bks. (Delacorte Bks. for Young Readers).
Veciana-Suarez, Ana. The Flight to Freedom. 2002. (First Person Fiction Ser.). 208p. (J). (gr. 6-9). pap. 16.95 (*0-439-38199-1*, Orchard Bks.) Scholastic, Inc.

CUBANS—UNITED STATES—FICTION

Bernardo, Anilu. Fitting In. 1996. (J). 14.95 o.p. (*1-55885-176-3*); 200p. (gr. 7 up). pap. 9.95 (*1-55885-173-9*) Arte Publico Pr. (Piñata Books).
—Jumping off to Freedom. 1996. 198p. (YA). (gr. 4-7). pap. 9.95 (*1-55885-088-0*); (gr. 6-12). 14.95 o.p. (*1-55885-087-2*) Arte Publico Pr. (Piñata Books).
—Jumping off to Freedom. 1996. 16.00 (*0-606-13547-2*) Turtleback Bks.

CZECHS—UNITED STATES—FICTION

Gonzalez, Catherine G. Cherub in Stone. 1995. (Chaparral Book for Young Readers Ser.). 116p. (J). (gr. 7 up). pap. 12.95 (*0-87565-139-9*) Texas Christian Univ. Pr.

D

DRUIDS AND DRUIDISM—FICTION

Boyes, Vivien. The Druid's Head. 1998. (J). (gr. 4-8). pap. 13.95 (*0-8464-4596-4*) Beekman Pubs., Inc.
—The Druid's Head. 1997. (J). pap. 22.00 (*1-85902-459-9*) Gomer Pr. GBR. *Dist:* State Mutual Bk. & Periodical Service, Ltd.
Freeman, Martha. The Spy Wore Shades. 2001. (Illus.). 240p. (J). (gr. 3 up). 15.95 (*0-06-029269-5*); lib. bdg. 15.89 (*0-06-029270-9*) HarperCollins Children's Bk. Group.
—The Spy Wore Shades. Date not set. 160p. (YA). (gr. 3 up). pap. 4.99 (*0-06-440957-0*) HarperCollins Pubs.
Melling, O. R. The Druid's Tune. 1985. 240p. (J). (gr. 7 up). pap. 2.95 o.p. (*0-14-031778-3*, Penguin Bks.) Viking Penguin.
Pevsner, Stella. Jon, Flora, & the Odd-Eyed Cat. 1994. (Illus.). 160p. (J). 13.95 o.s.i (*0-395-67021-7*) Houghton Mifflin Co.
Pope, Elizabeth M. The Perilous Gard. 1992. (Puffin Newbery Library). (Illus.). 288p. (J). (gr. 4-7). pap. 6.99 o.s.i (*0-14-034912-X*, Puffin Bks.) Penguin Putnam Bks. for Young Readers.

DUTCH—UNITED STATES—FICTION

Joosse, Barbara M. The Morning Chair. 1995. (Illus.). 32p. (J). (ps-3). tchr. ed. 14.95 o.p. (*0-395-62337-5*, Clarion Bks.) Houghton Mifflin Co. Trade & Reference Div.
St. George, Judith S. The Shad Are Running. 1977. (Illus.). (J). (gr. 3-6). 5.29 o.p. (*0-399-61045-6*) Putnam Publishing Group, The.

E

ESKIMOS—FICTION

Andrew, Alice & Oscar, Ina. Tulukaruk Tunutellek-llu. l.t. ed. 1998. (ESK., Illus.). 8p. (J). (gr. k-3). pap. text 6.00 (*1-58084-017-5*) Lower Kuskokwim Schl. District.
Andrews, Jan. Very Last First Time. 2002. 32p. (J). 16.95 (*0-88899-043-X*) Groundwood Bks. CAN. *Dist:* Publishers Group West.
—Very Last First Time. 1986. (Illus.). 32p. (J). (gr. k-4). 17.00 o.p. (*0-689-50388-1*, McElderry, Margaret K.) Simon & Schuster Children's Publishing.
—Very Last First Time: An Inuit Tale. 1998. (Illus.). 32p. (J). (gr. k-3). per. 5.99 o.p. (*0-689-81960-9*, Aladdin) Simon & Schuster Children's Publishing.
Aspen, Jean. Arctic Son: Fulfilling the Dream. 1995. (Illus.). 250p. (J). 19.95 o.p. (*0-89732-173-1*) Menasha Ridge Pr., Inc.
Beim, Lorraine & Beim, Jerrold. Little Igloo. 1941. (Illus.). (J). (ps-3). 5.95 o.p. (*0-15-246145-0*) Harcourt Children's Bks.
Berlin, James, Sr. Cup'igtat Laanguarrutenka. l.t. ed. 1999. Tr. of My Yup'ik Eskimo Toys. (ESK., Illus.). 12p. (J). (gr. k-3). pap. text 17.00 (*1-58084-112-0*) Lower Kuskokwim Schl. District.
—My Yupik Eskimo Toys. l.t. ed. 1999. (Illus.). 12p. (J). (gr. k-3). pap. text 17.00 (*1-58084-074-4*) Lower Kuskokwim Schl. District.
—Yugtaat Naanguat. l.t. ed. 1999. Tr. of My Yup'ik Eskimo Toys. (ESK., Illus.). 12p. (J). (gr. k-3). pap. text 17.00 (*1-58084-075-2*) Lower Kuskokwim Schl. District.
Biggar, Joan R. Danger at Half-Moon Lake. 1991. (Adventure Quest Ser.). (Illus.). 143p. (J). (gr. 5-8). pap. 4.99 o.s.i (*0-570-04194-5*, 56-1653) Concordia Publishing Hse.
Brown, Kerry Hannula. Tupaq the Dreamer. 2001. (Illus.). 32p. (J). (ps-3). 15.95 (*0-7614-5076-9*, Cavendish Children's Bks.) Cavendish, Marshall Corp.
Carl, Elsie & Mann, Mary J. Eren'am Erenra. l.t. ed. 1998. (ESK., Illus.). 12p. (J). (gr. k-3). pap. text 6.00 (*1-58084-021-3*) Lower Kuskokwim Schl. District.
—Inaqam Ikamrcuallra. l.t. ed. 1997. (ESK., Illus.). 12p. (J). (gr. k-3). pap. text 6.00 (*1-58084-005-1*) Lower Kuskokwim Schl. District.
Cawston, Vee. Matuk, the Eskimo Boy. 1965. (Illus.). (J). (gr. 1-2). lib. bdg. 6.19 o.p. (*0-8313-0014-0*) Lantern Pr., Inc., Pubs.
Chadwick, Roxane. Don't Shoot. 1979. (Young Adult Fiction Ser.). (Illus.). 40p. (J). (gr. 2-9). lib. bdg. 7.95 o.p. (*0-8225-0706-4*, Lerner Pubns.) Lerner Publishing Group.
Conway, Diana Cohen. Northern Lights: A Hanukkah Story. 1994. (Illus.). 32p. (J). (ps-3). pap. 6.95 (*0-929371-80-1*) Kar-Ben Publishing.
Crawford, Kenneth C. Yuki. 1998. 96p. (J). (ps up). pap. 7.99 o.p. (*0-8280-1051-X*) Review & Herald Publishing Assn.
Dewey, Jennifer Owings. Minik's Story. 2003. (J). 15.95 (*0-7614-5134-X*) Cavendish, Marshall Corp.
Distribution Media Staff & Paulsen, Gary. Dogsong. 1986. (J). 21.33 incl. audio (*0-676-31628-X*) Ballantine Bks.
Edwardson, Debby Dahl. Whale Snow. 2003. (Illus.). 32p. (J). (gr. k-4). 15.95 (*1-57091-393-5*, Talewinds) Charlesbridge Publishing, Inc.
Fitka, Alice & Samuelson, Christine. Evekaq 'Viuq. l.t. ed. 1998. (ESK., Illus.). 12p. (J). (gr. k-3). pap. text 6.00 (*1-58084-018-3*) Lower Kuskokwim Schl. District.
George, Jean Craighead. Arctic Son. (Illus.). 32p. (J). (gr. k-4). 1999. pap. 5.99 (*0-7868-1179-X*); 1997. 14.95 (*0-7868-0315-0*); 1997. lib. bdg. 15.49 (*0-7868-2255-4*) Hyperion Bks. for Children.
—Arctic Son. 1999. (J). 12.14 (*0-606-17381-1*) Turtleback Bks.
—Julie. (Trophy Bk.). (Illus.). 240p. (gr. 5 up). 1996. (J). pap. 5.99 (*0-06-440573-7*, Harper Trophy); 1994. (J). 16.95 (*0-06-023528-4*); 1994. (YA). lib. bdg. 14.89 o.p. (*0-06-023529-2*) HarperCollins Children's Bk. Group.
—Julie. 1996. (YA). (gr. 5 up). 11.00 (*0-606-08788-5*) Turtleback Bks.
—Julie of the Wolves. l.t. ed. 1987. (Illus.). 260p. (J). (gr. 3-7). lib. bdg. 14.95 o.p. (*1-55736-053-7*) Bantam Doubleday Dell Large Print Group, Inc.
—Julie of the Wolves. 1986. (J). pap. 1.50 o.s.i (*0-440-84444-4*) Dell Publishing.
—Julie of the Wolves. l.t. ed. 1973. (Illus.). (J). lib. bdg. 6.95 o.p. (*0-8161-6102-X*, Macmillan Reference USA) Gale Group.
—Julie of the Wolves. (Julie of the Wolves Ser.). (Illus.). 2003. 176p. (J). pap. 5.99 (*0-06-054095-8*, Harper Trophy); 1996. 180p. (YA). (gr. 7 up). pap. 2.25 o.p. (*0-06-447146-2*, Harper Trophy); 1972. 192p. (J). (gr. 7 up). 15.99 (*0-06-021943-2*); 1972. 176p. (J). (gr. 7 up). pap. 5.99 (*0-06-440058-1*, Harper Trophy); 1972. 192p. (J). (gr. 7 up). lib. bdg. 16.89 (*0-06-021944-0*) HarperCollins Children's Bk. Group.
—Julie of the Wolves. 1974. (J). 12.00 (*0-606-03699-7*) Turtleback Bks.
—Julie y los Lobos. 1995. (SPA., Illus.). 184p. (YA). (gr. 5-8). 12.95 (*84-204-3206-7*) Alfaguara, Ediciones, S.A.- Grupo Santillana ESP. *Dist:* Santillana USA Publishing Co., Inc.
—Julie's Wolf Pack. (Julie of the Wolves Ser.). (Illus.). 208p. (J). (gr. 5 up). 1999. pap. 5.99 (*0-06-440721-7*, Harper Trophy); 1997. 16.95 (*0-06-027406-9*); 1997. lib. bdg. 17.89 (*0-06-027407-7*) HarperCollins Children's Bk. Group.
—Nutik & Amaroq Play Ball. (J). (gr. k-3). 2001. (Illus.). 40p. 15.95 (*0-06-028166-9*); 2000. 32p. pap. 5.95 (*0-06-443523-7*) HarperCollins Children's Bk. Group.
—Snow Bear. 1999. (Illus.). 32p. (J). (ps-3). lib. bdg. 16.49 (*0-7868-2398-4*) Disney Pr.
—Snow Bear. 2003. (Illus.). 32p. (J). (ps-3). pap. 5.99 (*0-7868-1733-X*) Hyperion Bks. for Children.
—Water Sky. 1989. (Trophy Bk.). (Illus.). 224p. (J). (gr. 6 up). pap. 5.99 (*0-06-440202-9*, Harper Trophy) HarperCollins Children's Bk. Group.
—The Wolf Pup Named Nutik. (J). (gr. k-3). 2001. (Illus.). 40p. 15.99 (*0-06-028164-2*); 2001. (Illus.). 40p. lib. bdg. 16.89 (*0-06-028165-0*); 2000. 32p. pap. 5.95 (*0-06-443522-9*) HarperCollins Children's Bk. Group.
George, Jean Craighead, et al. Snow Bear. 1999. (Illus.). 32p. (J). (ps-3). 15.99 (*0-7868-0456-4*) Disney Pr.
Gerber, Carole. Arctic Dreams. 1999. (Illus.). (J). (ps-2). 15.95 (*1-58089-021-0*, Whispering Coyote) Charlesbridge Publishing, Inc.
Griese, Arnold A. The Way of Our People. 1975. (Illus.). 90p. (J). (gr. 4-7). lib. bdg. 12.89 o.p. (*0-690-00707-8*) HarperCollins Children's Bk. Group.
Harper, Kenn. Give Me My Father's Body: The Life of Minik, the New York Eskimo. abr. ed. 2001. (Illus.). 256p. (YA). (gr. 7-12). pap. 5.99 (*0-7434-1257-5*, Simon Pulse) Simon & Schuster Children's Publishing.
Hill, Kirkpatrick. Minuk: Ashes in the Pathway. 2002. (Girls of Many Lands Ser.). (Illus.). 196p. (J). (gr. 4-7). 12.95 (*1-58485-596-7*); pap. 7.95 (*1-58485-520-7*) Pleasant Co. Pubns. (American Girl).
—Winter Camp. 1993. (Illus.). 192p. (J). (gr. 3-7). mass mkt. 15.00 o.s.i (*0-689-50588-4*, McElderry, Margaret K.) Simon & Schuster Children's Publishing.
Hoshino, Michio. Nanook's Gift. 1996. 36p. (ps-3). 15.95 (*1-56931-147-1*, Cadence Bks.) Viz Communications, Inc.
Houston, James. Drifting Snow: An Arctic Search. 1992. (Illus.). 160p. (YA). (gr. 5 up). lib. bdg. 13.95 o.s.i (*0-689-50563-9*, McElderry, Margaret K.) Simon & Schuster Children's Publishing.
—The Falcon Bow: An Arctic Legend. 1986. 96p. (J). (gr. 3-7). lib. bdg. 13.95 o.s.i (*0-689-50411-X*, McElderry, Margaret K.) Simon & Schuster Children's Publishing.
—Long Claws: An Arctic Adventure. 1995. (Illus.). (J). (gr. 6). 9.28 (*0-395-73262-X*) Houghton Mifflin Co.
—Wolf Run: A Caribou Eskimo Tale. 1971. (Illus.). (J). (gr. 2-5). 5.75 o.p. (*0-15-299104-2*) Harcourt Children's Bks.
Houston, James R. Akavak: An Inuit-Eskimo Legend. 1990. (Illus.). 80p. (YA). (gr. 4-7). pap. 9.00 o.s.i (*0-15-201731-3*, Harcourt Paperbacks) Harcourt Children's Bks.
—Long Claws: An Arctic Adventure. 97th ed. 1992. (Picture Puffin Ser.). (Illus.). 320p. (J). (ps-3). pap. 4.99 o.p. (*0-14-054522-0*, Puffin Bks.) Penguin Putnam Bks. for Young Readers.
Ilutsik, Paul, et al. Kuvyastek. l.t. ed. 1999. Tr. of Two Fishermen. (ESK.). 20p. (J). (gr. 3-5). pap. text 6.00 (*1-58084-172-4*) Lower Kuskokwim Schl. District.
Jenness, Aylette & Rivers, Alice. In Two Worlds: A Yup'ik Eskimo Family. 1989. (Illus.). (J). (gr. 6 up). 13.95 o.s.i (*0-395-42797-5*) Houghton Mifflin Co.
Jones, Loddie & Nicolai, Marie. Mayuralria. l.t. ed. 1997. (ESK., Illus.). 12p. (J). (gr. k-3). pap. text 6.00 (*1-58084-008-6*) Lower Kuskokwim Schl. District.
Joshua, Mary. Cayunqegtua. 1998. Tr. of I Like To. (ESK., Illus.). 8p. (J). (gr. k-3). pap. text 6.00 (*1-58084-026-4*) Lower Kuskokwim Schl. District.
Kairaiuak, Agnes & Shield, Sophie. Qucillgaq. l.t. ed. 1997. (ESK., Illus.). 16p. (J). (gr. k-3). pap. text 6.00 (*1-58084-011-6*) Lower Kuskokwim Schl. District.

Kittredge, Frances. Neeluk: An Eskimo Boy in the Days of the Whaling Ships. 2001. (Illus.). 88p. (J). (gr. 3-7). 18.95 (*0-88240-545-4*); pap. 11.95 (*0-88240-546-2*) Graphic Arts Ctr. Publishing Co. (Alaska Northwest Bks.).

Kortum, Jeanie. Ghost Vision. 1983. (Sierra Club Bks.). (Illus.). 160p. (J). (gr. 5-9). 10.95 o.p. (*0-394-86190-6*); lib. bdg. 10.99 o.p. (*0-394-96190-0*) Knopf Publishing Group. (Pantheon).

Kroll, Virginia L. The Seasons & Someone. 1994. (Illus.). 32p. (J). (ps-3). 15.00 (*0-15-271233-X*) Harcourt Trade Pubs.

Larson, Marie & Kern, Christina. Saaskaaq Suulutaalek. 1998. (ESK., Illus.). 12p. (J). (gr. k-3). pap. text 6.00 (*1-58084-016-7*) Lower Kuskokwim Schl. District.

Lehman-Wilzig, Tami. Keeping the Promise: A Torah's Journey. 2004. (J). pap. 6.95 (*1-58013-118-2*); (J). lib. bdg. (*1-58013-117-4*); (Illus.). 16.95 (*0-929371-79-8*) Kar-Ben Publishing.

Lincoln, Kelly J. Let's Go Storyknifing. l.t. ed. 1999. (Illus.). 12p. (J). (gr. k-3). pap. text 17.00 (*1-58084-066-3*) Lower Kuskokwim Schl. District.

—Yaaruiyarciqukug. l.t. ed. 1999. Tr. of Let's Go Story Knifing. (ESK., Illus.). 12p. (J). (gr. k-3). pap. text 17.00 (*1-58084-108-2*) Lower Kuskokwim Schl. District.

—Yaaruiyarluk. l.t. ed. 1999. Tr. of Let's Go Story Knifing. (ESK., Illus.). 12p. (J). (gr. k-3). pap. text 17.00 (*1-58084-067-1*) Lower Kuskokwim Schl. District.

Lincoln, Rosalie. Arnat Castun Pillerkat Assigeskuneng. l.t. ed. 1999. Tr. of What Girls Should Do When Eskimo Dancing. (ESK., Illus.). 16p. (J). (gr. k-3). pap. text 21.00 (*1-58084-111-2*) Lower Kuskokwim Schl. District.

—Nasaurluum Yurallra. l.t. ed. 1999. Tr. of What Girls Should Do When Eskimo Dancing. (ESK., Illus.). 16p. (J). (gr. k-3). pap. text 21.00 (*1-58084-065-5*) Lower Kuskokwim Schl. District.

—What Girls Should Do When Eskimo Dancing. l.t. ed. 1999. (Illus.). 16p. (J). (gr. k-3). pap. text 20.00 (*1-58084-064-7*) Lower Kuskokwim Schl. District.

Lipkind, William. Boy with a Harpoon. 1952. (Illus.). (J). (gr. 2-5). 4.50 o.p. (*0-15-210703-7*); lib. bdg. 3.56 o.p. (*0-15-210704-5*) Harcourt Children's Bks.

Luenn, Nancy. Nessa's Story - El Cuento de Nessa. Ada, Alma Flor, tr. 1994. (ENG & SPA., Illus.). 32p. (J). (gr. k-3). 14.95 (*0-689-31782-4*); 14.95 (*0-689-31919-3*) Simon & Schuster Children's Publishing. (Atheneum).

MacDiarmid, Jim. Neqem Ayuqucia Nallunritellruan-qaa... Nega! Collidge, Joseph, tr. l.t. ed. 1999. Tr. of Meet... a Fish!. (ESK., Illus.). 20p. (J). (gr. 3-5). pap. text 7.00 (*1-58084-176-7*) Lower Kuskokwim Schl. District.

Magdanz, James. Go Home, River. (Illus.). 32p. 2002. (YA). (ps up). pap. 8.95 (*0-88240-568-3*); 1996. (J). (gr. 4-7). 15.95 o.p. (*0-88240-476-8*) Graphic Arts Ctr. Publishing Co. (Alaska Northwest Bks.).

Marceau-Chenkie, Brittany. Naya, the Inuit Cinderella. l.t. ed. 1999. (Illus.). 24p. (J). (ps-3). pap. (*1-894303-05-9*) Raven Rock Publishing.

McDalton, Magdalena, et al. Kaviaq Kayangussulria. l.t. ed. 1997. (ESK., Illus.). 16p. (J). (gr. k-3). pap. text 6.00 (*1-58084-006-X*) Lower Kuskokwim Schl. District.

McDonald, Megan. Tundra Mouse: A Storyknife Tale. 1997. (Illus.). 32p. (J). (ps-2). pap. 15.95 (*0-531-30047-1*); lib. bdg. 16.99 (*0-531-33047-8*) Scholastic, Inc. (Orchard Bks.).

Mowat, Farley. The Snow Walker. 1976. (J). 10.95 o.p. (*0-316-58693-5*) Little Brown & Co.

Murphy, Claire Rudolf. Caribou Girl. 1955. (Illus.). 208p. (ps-3). pap. 16.95 (*1-57098-145-0*) Rinehart, Roberts Pubs.

Neeland, Barbara S. Coming of the Reindeer. 1966. (Illus.). (J). (gr. 1-4). lib. bdg. 6.19 o.p. (*0-8313-0080-9*) Lantern Pr., Inc., Pubs.

Newth, Mette. The Transformation, RS. Ingwersen, Faith, tr. from NOR. 2000. 208p. (J). (gr. 7-12). 16.00 (*0-374-37752-9*, Farrar, Straus & Giroux (BYR)) Farrar, Straus & Giroux.

Nicolai, Margaret. Kitaq Goes Ice Fishing. (Illus.). 32p. (gr. k up). 2002. (YA). pap. 8.95 (*0-88240-569-1*); 1998. (J). 15.95 o.p. (*0-88240-504-7*) Graphic Arts Ctr. Publishing Co. (Alaska Northwest Bks.).

O'Dell, Scott. Black Star, Bright Dawn. 1989. 112p. (gr. 7-12). mass mkt. 6.50 (*0-449-70340-1*, Fawcett) Ballantine Bks.

—Black Star, Bright Dawn. 1988. 144p. (YA). (gr. 7-7). tchr. ed. 17.00 (*0-395-47778-6*) Houghton Mifflin Co.

—Black Star, Bright Dawn. 1990. 10.55 (*0-606-01201-X*) Turtleback Bks.

Olick, Hilda. Kaviam Iqvaryallra. l.t. ed. 1999. (ESK., Illus.). 8p. (J). (gr. k-3). pap. text 14.50 (*1-58084-057-4*) Lower Kuskokwim Schl. District.

Olick, Hilda & Nicori, Helen. Nasaurluq Nunalinqig-telleq. l.t. ed. 1997. (ESK., Illus.). 8p. (J). (gr. k-3). pap. text 6.00 (*1-58084-009-4*) Lower Kuskokwim Schl. District.

—Wavigcuk Watqapik-llu. l.t. ed. 1998. (ESK., Illus.). 8p. (J). (gr. k-3). pap. text 6.00 (*1-58084-019-1*) Lower Kuskokwim Schl. District.

Orenstein, Denise G. Unseen Companions. 2003. 368p. (J). 15.99 (*0-06-052056-6*); lib. bdg. 16.89 (*0-06-052057-4*) HarperCollins Children's Bk. Group. (Tegen, Katherine Bks.).

Parish, Peggy. Ootah's Lucky Day. 1970. (I Can Read Bks.). (Illus.). 64p. (J). (ps-3). lib. bdg. 11.89 o.p. (*0-06-024645-6*) HarperCollins Children's Bk. Group.

Paulsen, Gary. Dogsong. 1999. (YA). 9.95 (*1-56137-342-7*) Novel Units, Inc.

—Dogsong. 1987. 192p. (J). (gr. 5-9). pap. 4.99 o.p. (*0-14-032235-3*, Puffin Bks.) Penguin Putnam Bks. for Young Readers.

—Dogsong. (Two Thousand Kids Picks Ser.). 2000. 192p. (J). (gr. 4-6). mass mkt. 2.99 (*0-689-83869-7*, Aladdin); 2000. 192p. (YA). (gr. 7 up). 16.00 (*0-689-83960-X*, Atheneum/Richard Jackson Bks.); 1999. 176p. (YA). (gr. 7 up). pap. 4.99 (*0-689-82700-8*, 076714004993, Simon Pulse); 1998. (J). (gr. 4-6). pap. 2.65 (*0-689-82165-4*, Aladdin); 1995. 192p. (YA). (gr. 7 up). mass mkt. 5.50 (*0-689-80409-1*, Simon Pulse); 1985. 192p. (YA). (gr. 7 up). lib. bdg. 16.00 (*0-02-770180-8*, Atheneum/Richard Jackson Bks.) Simon & Schuster Children's Publishing.

—Dogsong. l.t. ed. 2000. (Young Adult Ser.). (Illus.). 184p. (J). (gr. 8-12). 21.95 (*0-7862-2845-8*) Thorndike Pr.

—Dogsong. 1999. 11.04 (*0-606-16328-X*); 1995. (YA). 11.55 (*0-606-07437-6*) Turtleback Bks.

Petersen, Palle. Inunguak: The Little Greenlander. 1993. (Illus.). 32p. (J). (gr. 4-7). 14.00 o.p. (*0-688-09876-2*); (ps-3). lib. bdg. 13.93 o.p. (*0-688-09877-0*) HarperCollins Children's Bk. Group.

Rau, Dana Meachen. Arctic Adventure: Inuit Life in the 1800s. 1997. (Smithsonian Odyssey Ser.). (Illus.). (J). 32p. (gr. 1-4). pap. 5.95 (*1-56899-417-6*); 32p. (gr. 2-5). 14.95 (*1-56899-416-8*); 32p. (gr. 2-5). 19.95 incl. audio (*1-56899-423-0*, BC6005);Incl. toy. (gr. 2-5). 29.95 (*1-56899-418-4*);Incl. toy. 32p. (gr. 2-5). 35.95 incl. audio (*1-56899-421-4*);Incl. toy. 32p. (gr. 2-5). pap. 25.95 incl. audio (*1-56899-420-6*);Incl. toy. 32p. (gr. 2-5). pap. 25.95 incl. audio (*1-56899-420-6*);Incl. toy. 32p. (gr. 2-5). pap. 17.95 (*1-56899-419-2*) Soundprints.

Repp, Gloria. Charlie. 2002. (Illus.). 147p. (J). (*1-57924-817-9*) Jones, Bob Univ. Pr.

Rogers, Jean. Goodbye, My Island. 2001. (Illus.). 96p. (YA). (gr. 2 up). pap. 9.95 (*0-88240-538-1*, Alaska Northwest Bks.) Graphic Arts Ctr. Publishing Co.

—Goodbye, My Island. 1983. (Illus.). 96p. (J). (gr. 5-7). 15.00 o.p. (*0-688-01964-1*); lib. bdg. 14.93 o.p. (*0-688-01965-X*) HarperCollins Children's Bk. Group. (Greenwillow Bks.).

—King Island Christmas. (Illus.). 32p. (J). (ps-3). 1998. pap. 5.95 (*06881-6449-8*, Harper Trophy); 1985. 16.00 o.p. (*0-688-04236-8*, Greenwillow Bks.); 1985. lib. bdg. 15.93 o.p. (*0-688-04237-6*, Greenwillow Bks.) HarperCollins Children's Bk. Group.

—King Island Christmas. 1998. (J). 11.10 (*0-606-19040-6*) Turtleback Bks.

—Runaway Mittens. 1988. (Illus.). 24p. (J). (ps-3). 16.00 o.p. (*0-688-07053-1*); lib. bdg. 15.93 o.p. (*0-688-07054-X*) HarperCollins Children's Bk. Group. (Greenwillow Bks.).

—Runaway Mittens. 1988. (Illus.). 24p. (J). pap. 10.00 (*1-57833-108-0*) Todd Communications.

Samuelson, Christine & Fitka, Alice. Cingsiigek. l.t. ed. 1997. (ESK., Illus.). 12p. (J). (gr. k-3). pap. text 6.00 (*1-58084-004-3*) Lower Kuskokwim Schl. District.

Scott, Ann Herbert. On Mother's Lap. 2002. (Illus.). (J). 14.74 (*0-7587-3318-6*) Book Wholesalers, Inc.

—On Mother's Lap. 1994. 1p. (J). (-ps). pap. 9.95 incl. audio (*0-395-69173-7*, 111692); pap. 9.95 incl. audio (*0-395-69173-7*, 111692) Houghton Mifflin Co.

—On Mother's Lap. (Illus.). 32p. (J). (ps-ps). 2000. bds. 4.95 (*0-618-05159-7*); 1992. pap. 6.95 (*0-395-62976-4*); 1992. lib. bdg., tchr. ed. 16.00 (*0-395-58920-7*) Houghton Mifflin Co. Trade & Reference Div. (Clarion Bks.).

—On Mother's Lap. 1972. (Illus.). 39p. (J). (ps). pap. 6.95 o.p. (*0-07-055896-5*); text 12.95 o.p. (*0-07-055897-3*) McGraw-Hill Cos., The.

—On Mother's Lap. 1992. 13.10 (*0-606-06633-0*) Turtleback Bks.

—On Mothers Lap. 2001. (Early Readers Ser.: Vol. 3). (J). lib. bdg. (*1-59054-346-7*) Fitzgerald Bks.

Shaw-MacKinnon, Margaret. Tiktala. 1996. (Illus.). 32p. (J). (ps-3). 15.95 (*0-8234-1221-0*) Holiday Hse., Inc.

Shaw-MacKinnon, Margaret & Gal, Laszlo. Tiktala. (Illus.). 32p. 13.95 (*0-7737-2920-8*) Stoddart Kids CAN. *Dist:* Fitzhenry & Whiteside, Ltd.

Shield, Sophie. Can'giiq. l.t. ed. 1999. Tr. of Blackfish. (ESK., Illus.). 12p. (J). (gr. 3-5). pap. text 6.00 (*1-58084-175-9*) Lower Kuskokwim Schl. District.

Shield, Sophie & Kairaiuak, Agnes. Lak'aq. l.t. ed. 1997. (ESK., Illus.). 12p. (J). (gr. k-3). pap. text 6.00 (*1-58084-007-8*) Lower Kuskokwim Schl. District.

Sis, Peter. A Small Tall Tale from Far Far North, RS. 2001. (Illus.). 40p. (J). (gr. 1-4). pap. 6.95 (*0-374-46725-0*, Sunburst) Farrar, Straus & Giroux.

—A Small, Tall Tale from the Far, Far North. 1993. (Illus.). 40p. (J). (gr. k-5). 15.99 o.s.i (*0-679-94345-5*, Knopf Bks. for Young Readers) Random Hse. Children's Bks.

—A Small Tall Tale from the Far Far North, RS. 2001. (Illus.). 40p. (J). (gr. 1-4). 17.00 (*0-374-37075-3*, Farrar, Straus & Giroux (BYR)) Farrar, Straus & Giroux.

—A Small Tall Tale from the Far Far North. 1993. (Illus.). 40p. (J). (gr. k-5). 15.00 o.s.i (*0-679-84345-0*, Knopf Bks. for Young Readers) Random Hse. Children's Bks.

Sloat, Teri. Eye of the Needle. 1993. (Picture Puffin Ser.). (Illus.). (J). 10.19 o.p. (*0-606-05828-1*) Turtleback Bks.

Stafford, Liliana. Snow Bear. 2001. (Illus.). 32p. (J). (gr. 1-3). 15.95 (*0-439-26977-6*) Scholastic, Inc.

Stafford, Liliana & Davis, Lambert. Snow Bear. (Illus.). 32p. (J). (*0-88899-441-9*) Groundwood Bks.

Sullivan, Paul. Maata's Journal: A Novel. 2003. 240p. (J). 16.95 (*0-689-83463-2*, Atheneum) Simon & Schuster Children's Publishing.

Tunuchuk, Mary & Augustine, Abby. Panruum Pilugungella. l.t. ed. 1997. (ESK., Illus.). 8p. (J). (gr. k-3). pap. text 6.00 (*1-58084-010-8*) Lower Kuskokwim Schl. District.

Vanasse, Debra. Distant Enemy. 1997. 192p. (J). (gr. 5-9). 16.99 o.p. (*0-525-67549-3*) NAL.

Wassillie, Irene & Larson, Helen C. Ulap'ag Uliir. l.t. ed. 1997. (ESK., Illus.). 12p. (J). (gr. k-3). pap. text 6.00 (*1-58084-012-4*) Lower Kuskokwim Schl. District.

Whitman, Theresa M. & Lincoln, Kelly J. Yuralqinkuk Yaarcaq-llu. l.t. ed. 1998. (ESK., Illus.). 12p. (J). (gr. k-3). pap. text 6.00 (*1-58084-020-5*) Lower Kuskokwim Schl. District.

Winslow, Barbara. Dance on a Sealskin. (Illus.). 32p. (J). 2001. (ps-3). pap. 8.95 (*0-88240-559-4*); 1995. (gr. 4-7). 15.95 o.p. (*0-88240-443-1*) Graphic Arts Ctr. Publishing Co. (Alaska Northwest Bks.).

F

FINNS—UNITED STATES—FICTION

Clark, Ann Nolan. All This Wild Land. 1976. (J). (gr. 7-12). 7.95 o.p. (*0-670-11444-8*) Viking Penguin.

Durbin, William. The Journal of Otto Peltonen: A Finnish Immigrant: Hibbing, Minnesota, 1905. 2000. (My Name Is America Ser.). (Illus.). 163p. (J). (gr. 4-8). pap. 10.95 (*0-439-09254-X*) Scholastic, Inc.

Kingman, Lee. The Best Christmas. 1993. (Illus.). 96p. (J). (gr. 5 up). pap. 4.95 o.p. (*0-688-11838-0*, Morrow, William & Co.) Morrow/Avon.

Marvin, Isabel R. A Bride for Anna's Papa. 1994. (Illus.). 144p. (J). 14.95 o.p. (*0-915943-89-1*); (gr. 3-8). pap. 6.95 (*0-915943-93-X*) Milkweed Editions.

FRENCH—UNITED STATES—FICTION

Klein, Norma. Bizou. 1983. 168p. (J). (gr. 5-9). 11.50 o.p. (*0-670-17053-4*, Viking Children's Bks.) Penguin Putnam Bks. for Young Readers.

FRENCH-CANADIANS—FICTION

London, Jonathan. The Sugaring-Off Party. 1999. (J). pap. 5.99 (*0-14-056360-1*) Viking Penguin.

FRENCH-CANADIANS—UNITED STATES—FICTION

London, Jonathan. The Sugaring-Off Party. 1995. (Illus.). 32p. (J). 15.99 o.s.i (*0-525-45187-0*, Dutton Children's Bks.) Penguin Putnam Bks. for Young Readers.

G

GERMANS—UNITED STATES—FICTION

Benary-Isbert, Margot. Long Way Home. 1959. (J). (gr. 7 up). 5.95 o.p. (*0-15-248830-8*) Harcourt Children's Bks.

Bender, Esther. Virginia & the Tiny One. 1998. (Lemon Tree Ser.: Vol. 2). (Illus.). 104p. (J). (gr. 3-7). pap. 6.99 (*0-8361-9090-4*) Herald Pr.

Bodkin, Odds. The Christmas Cobwebs. 2001. (Illus.). 32p. (J). (gr. k-2). 16.00 (*0-15-201459-4*, Gulliver Bks.) Harcourt Children's Bks.

Hallman, Ruth. Secrets of a Silent Stranger. 1976. (Hiway Book). (J). 6.95 o.p. (*0-664-32598-X*) Westminster John Knox Pr.

Hoehne, Marcia. Emilie's Odyssey. (Immigrants Chronicles Ser.). 132p. (J). (gr. 3-7). pap. 5.99 (*0-7814-3081-X*) Cook Communications Ministries.

Hoff, Carol. Johnny Texas. 1992. (Illus.). (J). reprint ed. 160p. (gr. 3 up). pap. 13.95 (*0-937460-81-8*); 150p. (gr. 4 up). lib. bdg. 15.95 o.p. (*0-937460-80-X*) Hendrick-Long Publishing Co.

Hubbard, Coleen. Christmas in Silver Lake, l.t. ed. 1999. (Treasured Horses Collection). (Illus.). 128p. (J). (gr. 4 up). lib. bdg. 22.60 (*0-8368-2400-8*) Stevens, Gareth Inc.

Levitin, Sonia. Silver Days. 1992. 192p. (J). (gr. 4-7). reprint ed. pap. 4.99 (*0-689-71570-6*, Aladdin) Simon & Schuster Children's Publishing.

—Silver Days. 1992. 10.55 (*0-606-01597-3*) Turtleback Bks.

Liebig, Nelda J. Carrie & the Crazy Quilt. 1997. 88p. (Orig.). (J). (gr. 3-7). pap. 7.50 (*1-883953-19-7*) Midwest Traditions, Inc.

—Carrie & the Crazy Quilt. 1996. 96p. (Orig.). (J). pap. 7.50 (*1-883893-40-2*) WinePress Publishing.

Lindsay, Mela M. The Story of Johann: The Boy Who Longed to Come to America. 1991. (Illus.). 190p. (YA). 15.00 (*0-914222-18-X*) American Historical Society of Germans from Russia.

Rinaldi, Ann. Keep Smiling Through. 1996. 208p. (YA). (gr. 3-7). 13.00 o.s.i (*0-15-200768-7*) Harcourt Children's Bks.

GREEKS—FICTION

McLaren, Clemence. Inside the Walls of Troy. 1996. 208p. (YA). (gr. 7-12). 17.00 (*0-689-31820-0*, Atheneum) Simon & Schuster Children's Publishing.

—Inside the Walls of Troy: A Novel of the Women Who Lived the Trojan War. 1998. 208p. (YA). (gr. 7 up). reprint ed. mass mkt. 5.50 (*0-440-22749-6*, Laurel Leaf) Random Hse. Children's Bks.

—Inside the Walls of Troy: A Novel of the Women Who Lived the Trojan War. 1998. (J). 11.04 (*0-606-13519-7*) Turtleback Bks.

Napoli, Donna Jo. The Great God Pan. 2003. 160p. (J). lib. bdg. 17.99 (*0-385-90120-8*); (gr. 5). 15.95 (*0-385-32777-3*) Dell Publishing. (Delacorte Pr.).

Schreengost, Maity. Tasso of Tarpon Springs. 1998. (Illus.). 118p. (J). (gr. 3-6). pap. 5.95 (*0-929895-24-X*, Hoot Owl Bks.) Maupin Hse. Publishing.

GYPSIES—FICTION

Alexander, Lloyd. Gypsy Rizka. (gr. 3-7). 2000. (Illus.). 208p. (YA). pap. 5.99 (*0-14-130980-6*, Puffin Bks.); 1999. 144p. (J). 16.99 o.p. (*0-525-46121-3*, Dutton Children's Bks.) Penguin Putnam Bks. for Young Readers.

—Gypsy Rizka. unabr. ed. 2000. (YA). pap. 58.99 incl. audio (*0-7887-3954-9*, 41059X4) Recorded Bks., LLC.

Bemelmans, Ludwig. Madeline & the Gypsies. (Madeline Ser.). (Illus.). (J). (ps-3). 1977. 64p. pap. 5.99 o.s.i (*0-14-050261-0*, Puffin Bks.); 1959. 56p. 16.99 (*0-670-44682-3*, Viking Children's Bks.) Penguin Putnam Bks. for Young Readers.

—Madeline & the Gypsies. (Madeline Ser.). (J). (ps-3). 2000. (Illus.). 13.14 (*0-606-18428-7*); 1959. 10.19 o.p. (*0-606-01010-6*) Turtleback Bks.

Bradley, Kimberly Brubaker. One-of-a-Kind Mallie. 1999. 160p. (gr. 2-7). text 15.95 o.s.i (*0-385-32694-7*, Dell Books for Young Readers) Random Hse. Children's Bks.

Carlson, Natalie S. Family under the Bridge. 1958. (Illus.). 112p. (J). (gr. k-3). lib. bdg. 16.89 (*0-06-020991-7*) HarperCollins Children's Bk. Group.

—Family under the Bridge. 1989. (J). 12.00 (*0-606-04031-5*) Turtleback Bks.

Ficowski, Jerzy. Sister of the Birds & Other Gypsy Tales. Borski, Lucia, tr. 1976. (ENG & POL., Illus.). 80p. (J). (gr. 3-7). lib. bdg. 5.95 o.p. (*0-687-38596-2*) Abingdon Pr.

Gilman, Phoebe. The Gypsy Princess. ed. 1997. (J). (gr. 2). spiral bd. (*0-616-01652-2*) Canadian National Institute for the Blind/Institut National Canadien pour les Aveugles.

—The Gypsy Princess. 1997. (Illus.). 32p. (J). (ps-2). 15.95 (*0-590-86543-9*) Scholastic, Inc.

Greene, Bette. Them That Glitter & Them That Don't. 1984. (J). mass mkt. 2.25 o.p. (*0-449-70077-1*, Fawcett) Ballantine Bks.

Griffith, Connie. Surprise at Logan School. 1993. (Tootie McCarthy Ser.: Bk. 2). 128p. (Orig.). (J). (gr. 5-8). pap. 6.99 o.p. (*0-8010-3856-1*) Baker Bks.

—Surprise at Logan School. 1993. (Tootie McCarthy Ser.: Bk. 2). (Orig.). (J). (gr. 4-7). pap. 4.99 o.s.i (*0-8007-5464-6*) Revell, Fleming H. Co.

Jablonski, Carla. The Gypsy Enchantment. 2001. (Charmed Ser.). 192p. (YA). (gr. 7 up). reprint ed. E-Book 5.99 (*0-7434-2954-0*, Simon Pulse) Simon & Schuster Children's Publishing.

Lynch, Chris. Gypsy Davey. 1998. (Illus.). 192p. (J). (gr. 7-k). pap. 11.00 (*0-06-440730-6*) HarperCollins Pubs.

—Gypsy Davey. 1998. 17.05 (*0-606-15562-7*) Turtleback Bks.

Nussbaum, Al. Gypsy. 1978. (Pacesetters Ser.). (Illus.). 64p. (J). (gr. 4 up). lib. bdg. 9.25 o.p. (*0-516-02170-2*, Children's Pr.) Scholastic Library Publishing.

Patterson, Geoffrey. The Lion & the Gyspy. 1991. 32p. (J). (ps-3). 15.99 o.s.i (*0-385-41536-2*) Doubleday Publishing.

Pochocki, Ethel. The Gypsies' Tale. 1994. (Illus.). (J). (gr. 4 up). 15.00 o.p. (*0-671-79934-7*, Simon & Schuster Children's Publishing) Simon & Schuster Children's Publishing.

Roos, Stephen. The Gypsies Never Came. 2001. (Illus.). 128p. (J). (gr. 3-7). 15.00 (*0-689-83147-1*, Simon & Schuster Children's Publishing) Simon & Schuster Children's Publishing.

Roth, Susan L. Gypsy Bird Song, RS. 1991. (Illus.). 32p. (J). (gr. 1 up). 15.95 o.p. (*0-374-32825-0*, Farrar, Straus & Giroux (BYR)) Farrar, Straus & Giroux.

Snyder, Zilpha Keatley. The Gypsy Game. 1998. 240p. (J). (gr. 3-7). pap. text 5.50 (*0-440-41258-7*) Dell Publishing.

—The Gypsy Game. 1997. 224p. (gr. 3-7). text 15.95 o.s.i (*0-385-32266-6*, Dell Books for Young Readers) Random Hse. Children's Bks.

—The Gypsy Game. 1998. (J). 11.55 (*0-606-13104-3*) Turtleback Bks.

Springer, Nancy. The Boy on a Black Horse. 1994. 176p. (J). (gr. 5-9). 14.95 (*0-689-31840-5*, Atheneum) Simon & Schuster Children's Publishing.

Van Stockum, Hilda. Penengro, RS. 1972. (Illus.). 224p. (J). (gr. 4 up). 4.95 o.p. (*0-374-35787-0*, Farrar, Straus & Giroux (BYR)) Farrar, Straus & Giroux.

Vande Velde, Vivian. A Coming Evil. 1998. 212p. (J). (gr. 5-9). tchr. ed. 17.00 (*0-395-90012-3*) Houghton Mifflin Co.

Worth, Valerie. Gypsy Gold, RS. 176p. (gr. 12 up). 1986. (YA). pap. 3.45 o.p. (*0-374-42820-4*, Sunburst); 1983. (J). 10.95 o.p. (*0-374-32828-5*, Farrar, Straus & Giroux (BYR)) Farrar, Straus & Giroux.

Zach, Cheryl. The Gypsy's Warning. 1997. (Mind over Matter Ser.: No. 4). (J). (gr. 4-8). pap. 3.99 o.p. (*0-380-79168-4*, Avon Bks.) Morrow/Avon.

—The Gypsy's Warning. 1997. (Mind over Matter Ser.: No. 4). 128p. (J). (gr. 4-8). 9.09 o.p. (*0-606-12769-0*) Turtleback Bks.

H

HASIDISM—FICTION

Gravelle, Karen. Growing up in a Joyous Life; A Hasidic Childhood. 1999. (Growing Up in America Ser.). 24.00 o.p. (*0-531-11536-4*, Watts, Franklin) Scholastic Library Publishing.

HISPANIC AMERICANS—FICTION

Alvarez, Julia. Antes de Ser Libre. 2004. (SPA.). 176p. (YA). (gr. 7). lib. bdg. 17.99 (*0-375-91545-1*, Knopf Bks. for Young Readers) Random Hse. Children's Bks.

Bang, Molly. Tiger's Fall. 2003. 112p. (YA). (gr. 4-7). pap. 4.99 (*0-440-41876-3*, Yearling) Random Hse. Children's Bks.

Baylor, Byrd. Amigo. 2nd ed. 1989. (Illus.). 48p. (J). (gr. 1-7). reprint ed. pap. 5.99 (*0-689-71299-5*, Aladdin) Simon & Schuster Children's Publishing.

Castilla, Julia Mercedes. Emilio. 1999. 105p. (J). (gr. 4-7). pap. 9.95 (*1-55885-271-9*, Piñata Books) Arte Publico Pr.

Cisneros, Sandra. Hairs. 1997. Orig. Title: Pelitos. (J). 13.14 (*0-606-12960-X*) Turtleback Bks.

Cisneros, Sandra & Ybanez, Terry. Hairs. 1994. Orig. Title: Pelitos. (ENG & SPA., Illus.). 32p. (J). (ps-3). 15.00 o.s.i (*0-679-86171-8*, Knopf Bks. for Young Readers) Random Hse. Children's Bks.

Colato Lainez, Rene. Waiting for Papa: Esperando a Papa. Accardo, Anthony, tr. & illus. by. 2003. (ENG & SPA.). (J). (*1-55885-403-7*, Piñata Books) Arte Publico Pr.

De Anda, Diane. Dancing Miranda. Castilla, Julia Mercedes, tr. from ENG. 2001. Tr. of Baila, Miranda, Baila. (ENG & SPA., Illus.). 32p. (J). (ps-3). 14.95 (*1-55885-323-5*, Piñata Books) Arte Publico Pr.

de Paola, Tomie. Marcus Counts One, Two, Three. 2003. (Illus.). 14p. bds. 5.99 (*0-399-24011-X*) Penguin Group (USA) Inc.

—A New Barker in the House. 2002. (Illus.). 32p. (J). (ps-3). 13.99 (*0-399-23865-4*) Putnam Publishing Group, The.

del Castillo, Richard Griswold. Cesar Chavez: a Struggle for Justice / Cesar Chavez: La Lucha Por la Justicia. Colin, Jose Juan, tr. from ENG. 2002. (Hispanic Civil Rights Ser.). (ENG & SPA., Illus.). 32p. (J). (ps-3). 14.95 (*1-55885-324-3*, Piñata Books) Arte Publico Pr.

DeRubertis, Barbara. Count on Pablo. 1999. (Math Matters Ser.). (Illus.). 32p. (J). (gr. k-2). pap. 4.95 (*1-57565-090-8*) Kane Pr., The.

—Count on Pablo. 1999. (Math Matters Ser.). (Illus.). (J). 11.10 (*0-606-18217-9*) Turtleback Bks.

Dominguez, Kelli Kyle. The Perfect Pinata: La Pinata Perfecta. Mlawer, Teresa, tr. 2002. (ENG & SPA., Illus.). 32p. (J). (gr. k-3). lib. bdg. 14.95 (*0-8075-6495-8*) Whitman, Albert & Co.

Dorros, Arthur. Abuela. 2002. (Illus.). (J). 14.04 (*0-7587-1901-9*) Book Wholesalers, Inc.

—Abuela. (Picture Puffin Bks.). (J). (ps-1). 1997. (SPA.). 40p. pap. 6.99 (*0-14-056226-5*); 1997. (Illus.). 40p. pap. 6.99 (*0-14-056225-7*, Puffin Bks.); 1995. (SPA., Illus.). 48p. 15.99 (*0-525-45438-1*, Dutton Children's Bks.); 1991. (Illus.). 40p. 16.99 (*0-525-44750-4*, Dutton Children's Bks.) Penguin Putnam Bks. for Young Readers.

—Abuela. 1997. (Picture Puffin Ser.). 13.14 (*0-606-11019-4*); (J). 13.14 (*0-606-11018-6*) Turtleback Bks.

Draper, Sharon M. Romiette & Julio. (YA). (gr. 7-12). 2001. 336p. mass mkt. 4.99 (*0-689-84209-0*, Simon Pulse); 1999. (Illus.). 240p. 16.00 (*0-689-82180-8*, Atheneum) Simon & Schuster Children's Publishing.

Encinas, Carlos. The New Engine: La Maquina Nueva. 2001. (Illus.). (J). 15.95 (*1-885772-24-6*) Kiva Publishing, Inc.

English, Karen. Speak English for Us, Marisol! 2000. (Concept Book Ser.). (Illus.). 32p. (J). (gr. 1-4). lib. bdg. 14.95 (*0-8075-7554-2*) Whitman, Albert & Co.

Ewing, Lynne. Party Girl. 1998. (gr. 9-12). 144p. (J). 17.99 o.s.i (*0-679-99285-5*); 128p. (YA). 16.00 o.s.i (*0-679-89285-0*) Random Hse. Children's Bks. (Random Hse. Bks. for Young Readers).

—Party Girl. 1999. 128p. (gr. 9-11). mass mkt. 4.99 (*0-375-80210-X*) Random Hse., Inc.

—Party Girl. 1999. 11.04 (*0-606-17373-0*) Turtleback Bks.

Gershator, David. Bread Is for Eating, ERS. 1995. (J). 14.95 o.p. (*0-8050-3995-3*, Holt, Henry & Co. Bks. For Young Readers) Holt, Henry & Co.

—Bread Is for Eating. 1998. 13.10 (*0-606-13225-2*) Turtleback Bks.

Griffin, Peni R. The Music Thief, ERS. 2002. 160p. (YA). (gr. 5-8). 16.95 (*0-8050-7055-9*, Holt, Henry & Co. Bks. For Young Readers) Holt, Henry & Co.

—The Music Thief. l.t. ed. 2003. 190p. (J). 21.95 (*0-7862-5606-0*) Thorndike Pr.

Haugaard, Kay. No Place. 1999. (Illus.). 208p. (J). (gr. 3-8). 15.95 (*1-57131-616-7*); pap. 6.95 (*1-57131-617-5*) Milkweed Editions.

—No Place. 1999. (J). 13.00 (*0-606-19034-1*) Turtleback Bks.

Hollenbeck, K., retold by. Hispanic American: How the Corn Seeds Were Saved. 1994. (Graphic Learning Multicultural Literature Program Ser.). (ENG & SPA., Illus.). (J). (gr. k-5). 45.00 (*0-87746-434-0*) Graphic Learning.

Ibarra, Rosa, illus. Soledad Sigh-Sighs / Soledad Suspiros. 2003. Tr. of Soledad Suspiros. (ENG & SPA.). 32p. (J). 16.95 (*0-89239-180-4*) Children's Bk. Pr.

Jiménez, Francisco. Breaking Through. 2002. 208p. (J). (gr. 7). pap. 6.95 (*0-618-34248-6*) Houghton Mifflin Co.

Martin, Ann M. Amalia: Diary Three. 2000. (California Diaries). (Illus.). 144p. (YA). (gr. 6-8). mass mkt. 4.99 (*0-439-09548-4*) Scholastic, Inc.

—Amalia: Diary Three. 1999. (California Diaries). (Illus.). (YA). (gr. 6-8). 11.04 (*0-606-18525-9*) Turtleback Bks.

McConnie Zapater, Beatriz. Fiesta. 2004. (Multicultural Celebrations Ser.). (Illus.). 32p. (J). 4.95 (*1-59373-009-8*) Bunker Hill Publishing, Inc.

Mikaelsen, Ben. Sparrow Hawk Red. 1993. 224p. (J). (gr. 4-7). lib. bdg. 15.49 o.s.i (*1-56282-388-4*); (gr. 5-9). 15.99 (*1-56282-387-6*) Hyperion Bks. for Children.

—Sparrow Hawk Red. (J). 1995. o.s.i (*0-7868-1105-6*); 1994. 192p. (gr. 5-9). pap. 5.99 (*0-7868-1002-5*) Hyperion Pr.

—Sparrow Hawk Red. 1994. (J). 12.04 (*0-606-06758-2*) Turtleback Bks.

Montes, Marisa. A Crazy Mixed-Up Spanglish Day. 2003. (Get Ready for Gabi Ser.). (Illus.). 96p. (J). pap. 12.95 (*0-439-51710-9*, Scholastic Paperbacks); mass mkt. 3.99 (*0-439-47519-8*) Scholastic, Inc.

Montes, Marisa & Cepeda, Joe. Who's That Girl. 2003. (Get Ready for Gabi Ser.). 96-112p. (J). pap. 12.95 (*0-439-51711-7*, Scholastic Pr.) Scholastic, Inc.

Ozeta, Valerie. Legend of the Red Wolf. 2nd ed. 1999. (Illus.). 34p. (J). (gr. 3-7). pap. 5.95 (*0-9661687-1-2*) Red Wolf Publishing.

Rice, David. Crazy Loco. 2003. (Illus.). 144p. pap. 5.99 (*0-14-250056-9*, Puffin Bks.) Penguin Putnam Bks. for Young Readers.

Rodriguez, Luis J. It Doesn't Have to Be This Way (No Tiene Que Ser Asi) A Barrio Story (Una Historia del Barrio) 1999. (ENG & SPA., Illus.). 32p. (J). (gr. 1 up). 15.95 (*0-89239-161-8*) Children's Bk. Pr.

Rosa-Casanova, Sylvia. Mama Provi & the Pot of Rice. 1997. (Illus.). 32p. (J). (gr. k-3). 16.00 o.s.i (*0-689-31932-0*, Atheneum) Simon & Schuster Children's Publishing.

Starr, Meg. Alicia's Happy Day. (Illus.). (J). Date not set. 36p. pap. 5.95 (*1-932065-06-7*); 2003. 32p. 15.95 (*1-887734-85-6*) Star Bright Bks., Inc.

Torres, Leyla. El Festival de Cometas, RS. 2004. (SPA.). 16.00 (*0-374-32299-6*) Farrar, Straus & Giroux.

—The Kite Festival, RS. 2004. (J). 16.00 (*0-374-38054-6*, Farrar, Straus & Giroux (BYR)) Farrar, Straus & Giroux.

Valdes, Leslie. Dora's Christmas Parade. 2003. (Dora the Explorer Ser.). (Illus.). 32p. (J). pap. 5.99 (*0-689-85843-4*, Simon Spotlight/Nickelodeon) Simon & Schuster Children's Publishing.

—Happy Mother's Day, Mami! 2003. (Dora the Explorer Ser.). (Illus.). 24p. (J). pap. 3.99 (*0-689-85233-9*, Simon Spotlight/Nickelodeon) Simon & Schuster Children's Publishing.

Willson, Sarah. Dora's Halloween Adventure. 2003. (Dora the Explorer Ser.). (Illus.). 14p. (J). bds. 5.99 (*0-689-85844-2*, Simon Spotlight/Nickelodeon) Simon & Schuster Children's Publishing.

HOLOCAUST SURVIVORS—FICTION

Atlan, Liliane. The Passerby, ERS. Owens, Rochelle, tr. 1993. (Illus.). 96p. (YA). (gr. 7 up). 13.95 o.p. (*0-8050-3054-9*, Holt, Henry & Co. Bks. For Young Readers) Holt, Henry & Co.

Bat-Ami, Miriam. Two Suns in the Sky. 1999. 208p. (YA). (gr. 7-12). 17.95 (*0-8126-2900-0*) Cricket Bks.

—Two Suns in the Sky. 2001. 208p. (YA). pap. 6.99 (*0-14-230036-5*, Puffin Bks.) Penguin Putnam Bks. for Young Readers.

Bergman, Tamar. The Boy from over There. Halkin, Hillel, tr. from HEB. 1988. 192p. (J). (gr. 3-7). 13.95 o.p. (*0-395-43077-1*) Houghton Mifflin Co.

—Boy from over There. 1992. (J). (gr. 4-7). pap. 4.95 o.p. (*0-395-64370-8*) Houghton Mifflin Co.

Lakin, Patricia. Don't Forget. (Illus.). 32p. (gr. k-3). 2000. (YA). pap. 5.95 (*0-688-17522-8*); 1994. (J). 14.00 o.p. (*0-688-12075-X*); 1994. (J). lib. bdg. 13.93 (*0-688-12076-8*) Morrow/Avon. (Morrow, William & Co.).

Mamet, David. Bar Mitzvah. 1999. (Illus.). 45p. (YA). reprint ed. 27.00 (*0-7567-6490-4*) DIANE Publishing Co.

—Bar Mitzvah. 1999. (Illus.). 48p. (gr. 8). 26.95 o.p. (*0-8212-2546-4*) Little Brown & Co.

Mazer, Norma Fox. Good Night, Maman. 1999. (Illus.). 192p. (YA). (gr. 5-9). 16.00 (*0-15-201468-3*) Harcourt Children's Bks.

—Good Night, Maman. 2001. (Harper Trophy Bks.). 192p. (J). (gr. 5 up). pap. 5.99 (*0-06-440923-6*, Harper Trophy) HarperCollins Children's Bk. Group.

Orlev, Uri. The Island on Bird Street. Halkin, Hillel, tr. from HEB. 176p. (J). (gr. 4-6). 1992. pap. 6.95 (*0-395-61623-9*); 1984. tchr. ed. 16.00 (*0-395-33887-5*, 5-92515) Houghton Mifflin Co.

—The Island on Bird Street. Halkin, Hillel, tr. from HEB. 1984. (J). 12.00 (*0-606-00521-8*) Turtleback Bks.

—The Lady with the Hat. Halkin, Hillel, tr. 1995. 192p. (YA). (gr. 7 up). tchr. ed. 16.00 (*0-395-69957-6*) Houghton Mifflin Co.

—The Lady with the Hat. Halkin, Hillel, tr. from HEB. 1997. (Illus.). 192p. (J). (gr. 5-9). pap. 4.99 o.s.i (*0-14-038571-1*) Penguin Putnam Bks. for Young Readers.

—The Lady with the Hat. 1997. 10.09 o.p. (*0-606-13562-6*) Turtleback Bks.

Watts, Irene N. Goodbye Marianne. 1997. 48p. (YA). pap. 6.50 (*0-87602-350-2*) Anchorage Pr.

—Goodbye Marianne. 1998. 48p. (J). pap. (*1-896239-03-X*) Shillingford, J. Gordon Publishing.

HUNGARIANS—UNITED STATES—FICTION

Couric, Katherine. The Brand New Kid. 2000. (Illus.). 32p. (J). (gr. 2-3). 15.95 (*0-385-50030-0*) Doubleday Publishing.

Konigsburg, E. L. The Outcasts of 19 Schuyler Place. 2004. (Illus.). 304p. (J). 16.95 (*0-689-86636-4*, Atheneum) Simon & Schuster Children's Publishing.

I

INDIANS, TREATMENT OF—FICTION

Thomas, Estelle W. Gift of Laughter. 1967. (J). (gr. 7 up). 4.50 o.p. (*0-664-32395-2*) Westminster John Knox Pr.

INDIANS OF CENTRAL AMERICA—FICTION

Cameron, Ann. Colibri, RS. 2003. 240p. (J). 17.00 (*0-374-31519-1*, 53501559, Farrar, Straus & Giroux (BYR)) Farrar, Straus & Giroux.

Eboch, Chris. The Well of Sacrifice. 1999. (Illus.). 224p. (J). (gr. 5-9). tchr. ed. 16.00 (*0-395-90374-2*, Clarion Bks.) Houghton Mifflin Co. Trade & Reference Div.

González, Gaspar P. A Mayan Life. Elliott, Elaine, tr. from ENG. 1995. 230p. (Orig.). pap. 9.95 (*1-886502-01-3*) Yax Te' Foundation.

London, Jonathan. The Village Basket Weaver. 1996. (Illus.). 32p. (J). (ps-3). 14.99 o.p. (*0-525-45314-8*, Dutton Children's Bks.) Penguin Putnam Bks. for Young Readers.

Surany, Anico. The Golden Frog. 1963. (Illus.). (J). (gr. 3-5). 3.97 o.p. (*0-399-60199-6*) Putnam Publishing Group, The.

Wahl, Jan. Once When the World Was Green. 1996. (Illus.). 32p. (YA). (gr. 2 up). 14.95 o.p. (*1-883672-12-0*) Tricycle Pr.

Wisniewski, David. Rain Player. 1991. (Illus.). 32p. (J). (gr. 4-6). lib. bdg., tchr. ed. 17.00 (*0-395-55112-9*, Clarion Bks.) Houghton Mifflin Co. Trade & Reference Div.

INDIANS OF MEXICO—AZTECS—FICTION

Gaudiano, Andrea. Azteca: The Story of a Jaguar Warrior. 1992. (Illus.). 80p. (J). (gr. 7 up). pap. 7.95 o.p. (*1-879373-32-7*) Rinehart, Roberts Pubs.

Lattimore, Deborah Nourse. The Flame of Peace: A Tale of the Aztecs. 1991. (Trophy Picture Bk.). (Illus.). 48p. (J). (ps-3). pap. 7.95 (*0-06-443272-6*, Harper Trophy) HarperCollins Children's Bk. Group.

Malam, John. Indiana Jones Explores the Aztecs. 1996. (Illus.). 47p. (J). (gr. 5-8). 19.95 o.p. (*0-237-51219-X*) Evans Brothers, Ltd. GBR. *Dist:* Trafalgar Square.

McDaniel, Suellen R. Serpent Treasure. 1978. (gr. 4 up). 2.98 o.p. (*0-89587-007-X*) Blair, John F. Pub.

O'Dell, Scott. The Feathered Serpent, 001. 1981. 224p. (J). (gr. 7 up). 16.95 o.p. (*0-395-30851-8*) Houghton Mifflin Co.

INDIANS OF MEXICO—FICTION

Baker, Betty. Walk the World's Rim. 1965. 80p. (J). (gr. 5 up). lib. bdg. 14.89 o.p. (*0-06-020381-1*) HarperCollins Children's Bk. Group.

Bernard, Leonard. Itza: The Boy Who Rode a Jaguar. 1998. (Illus.). (J). (ps-3). 16.95 (*0-9634661-1-9*) Bernard Bks.

Bernard, Virginia. Eliza & the Sacred Mountain. 2000. (Going to Ser.). (Illus.). 128p. (J). (gr. 4-8). pap. 5.99 (*1-893577-05-8*) Four Corners Publishing Co., Inc.

Blevins, Wade. Se-lu's Song. 1996. (Cherokee Indian Legend Ser.: Vol. 7). (Illus.). 53p. (J). lib. bdg. 17.25 (*1-56763-133-9*) Ozark Publishing.

Brenner, Anita. A Hero by Mistake. 1953. (J). (gr. 1-5). lib. bdg. 4.95 o.p. (*0-201-09223-9*) Addison-Wesley Longman, Inc.

Harper, Jo. Delfino's Journey. 2000. viii, 184p. (J). (gr. 8-12). 15.95 (*0-89672-437-9*) Texas Tech Univ. Pr.

—Delfino's Journey, Grades 8-12. 2000. (Illus.). viii, 184p. (J). tchr. ed. 5.95 (*0-89672-442-5*) Texas Tech Univ. Pr.

Hays, Jim, illus. Marigolds for Dona Remedios. 1997. (*0-7802-8302-3*) Wright Group, The.

Kline, Trish. I Am Called Calpulli. 2001. (Illus.). 112p. (J). (gr. 4-7). 15.95 (*0-8234-1570-8*) Holiday Hse., Inc.

McGee, Charmayne. So Sings the Blue Deer. 1994. 160p. (J). (gr. 3-7). 14.95 (*0-689-31888-X*, Atheneum) Simon & Schuster Children's Publishing.

O'Dell, Scott. The Feathered Serpent, 001. 1981. 224p. (J). (gr. 7 up). 16.95 o.p. (*0-395-30851-8*) Houghton Mifflin Co.

Roy, Cal. The Painter of Miracles. 1974. 144p. (J). (gr. 7 up). 4.95 o.p. (*0-374-35728-5*) Farrar, Straus & Giroux.

Scieszka, Jon. Me Oh Maya. 2003. (Time Warp Trio Ser.). (Illus.). 80p. (J). 14.99 (*0-670-03629-3*, Viking) Viking Penguin.

Strock, Glen T., illus. The Butterfly Pyramid. 1997. (*0-7802-8321-X*) Wright Group, The.

Van Laan, Nancy. La Boda: A Mexican Wedding Celebration. 1996. (ENG & SPA., Illus.). 32p. (J). (ps-3). 15.95 o.p. (*0-316-89626-8*) Little Brown & Co.

Wisniewski, David. Rain Player. 1991. (Illus.). 32p. (J). (gr. 4-6). lib. bdg., tchr. ed. 17.00 (*0-395-55112-9*, Clarion Bks.) Houghton Mifflin Co. Trade & Reference Div.

Ethnic Groups

Witton, Dorothy. Crossroads for Chela. 1967. (J). (gr. 7-9). pap. (*0-671-29002-9*, Simon Pulse) Simon & Schuster Children's Publishing.

INDIANS OF MEXICO—MAYAS—FICTION

Brouwer, Sigmund. Sunrise at the Mayan Temple. (Accidental Detective Ser.: Vol. 10). (J). (gr. 3-7). 1995. 132p. pap. 5.99 o.p. (*1-56476-379-X*, 6-3379); 1992. pap. 4.99 (*0-89693-057-2*) Cook Communications Ministries.

Buja, John E. & Morrison, Melody. Ballcourt of Death: Novel. 2000. (Illus.). 128p. (gr. 7-12). pap. (*1-894303-23-7*) Raven Rock Publishing.

Eboch, Chris. The Well of Sacrifice. 1999. (Illus.). 224p. (J). (gr. 5-9). tchr. ed. 16.00 (*0-395-90374-2*, Clarion Bks.) Houghton Mifflin Co. Trade & Reference Div.

Harper, Piers. Turtle Quest. 1997. (Illus.). 32p. (J). (gr. 3-6). 14.99 o.p. (*1-56402-959-X*) Candlewick Pr.

Hunter, Evan. Find the Feathered Serpent. 1979. (J). lib. bdg. 9.95 o.p. (*0-8398-2519-6*, Macmillan Reference USA) Gale Group.

Mayan Pyramid Mystery. 2001. (Illus.). 10p. (J). 12.99 (*0-307-10617-9*, 10617, Golden Bks.) Random Hse. Children's Bks.

McCunney, Michelle. Mario's Mayan Journey. 1996. (Illus.). 32p. (J). (gr. 2-6). pap. 4.95 (*1-57255-203-4*) Mondo Publishing.

O'Dell, Scott. The Feathered Serpent, 001. 1981. 224p. (J). (gr. 7 up). 16.95 o.p. (*0-395-30851-8*) Houghton Mifflin Co.

Rhoads, Dorothy. The Corn Grows Ripe. 1993. (Puffin Newbery Library). (Illus.). 96p. (YA). (gr. 3-7). pap. 4.99 (*0-14-036313-0*, Puffin Bks.) Penguin Putnam Bks. for Young Readers.

—The Corn Grows Ripe. 1994. (J). 19.75 (*0-8446-6756-0*) Smith, Peter Pub., Inc.

—The Corn Grows Ripe. 1993. (J). 11.14 (*0-606-05215-1*) Turtleback Bks.

Talbert, Marc. Heart of a Jaguar. 1995. (J). 15.00 (*0-689-89018-4*) Simon & Schuster Bks. For Young Readers.

—Heart of a Jaguar. (gr. 7 up). 1997. 224p. (J). per. 4.99 (*0-689-81332-5*, Simon Pulse); 1995. 208p. (YA). 16.00 o.s.i (*0-689-80282-X*, Simon & Schuster Children's Publishing) Simon & Schuster Children's Publishing.

Wahl, Jan. Once When the World Was Green. 1996. (Illus.). 32p. (YA). (gr. 2 up). 14.95 o.p. (*1-883672-12-0*) Tricycle Pr.

INDIANS OF NORTH AMERICA—ABNAKI INDIANS—FICTION

Bruchac, Joseph. Dog People: Native Dog Stories. 1995. (Kids Ser.). (Illus.). 64p. (J). (gr. 4-7). 14.95 (*1-55591-228-1*) Fulcrum Publishing.

—The Winter People. 2002. (Illus.). 176p. (J). 16.99 (*0-8037-2694-5*, Dial Bks. for Young Readers) Penguin Putnam Bks. for Young Readers.

Dubois, Muriel L. Abenaki Captive. 16.00 (*0-9723410-0-5*) Apprentice Shop Bks., LLC.

—Abenaki Captive. 1994. (J). (gr. 4-7). lib. bdg. 15.95 o.s.i (*0-87614-753-8*, Carolrhoda Bks.) Lerner Publishing Group.

Epstein, Anne M. Good Stones, 001. 1977. (Illus.). 274p. (J). (gr. 5-9). 6.95 o.p. (*0-395-25154-0*) Houghton Mifflin Co.

Philbrook, Clem. Captured by the Abnakis. 1966. (Illus.). (J). (gr. 4-6). 6.95 o.p. (*0-8038-1080-6*) Hastings Hse. Daytrips Pubs.

INDIANS OF NORTH AMERICA—ACOMA INDIANS—FICTION

Thomasma, Kenneth. Naya Nuki: Shoshone Girl Who Ran. 1983. (J). pap. 7.99 (*1-880114-00-3*) Grandview Publishing Co.

INDIANS OF NORTH AMERICA—ALGONQUIAN INDIANS—FICTION

Cheatham, K. Follis. Spotted Flower & the Ponokomita. 1977. (Illus.). 92p. (J). (gr. 5-8). 7.95 o.p. (*0-664-32617-X*) Westminster John Knox Pr.

Dorris, Michael. Guests. 1994. 128p. (J). 13.95 (*0-7868-0047-X*); (gr. 3-7). lib. bdg. 14.49 o.s.i (*0-7868-2036-5*) Hyperion Bks. for Children.

—Guests. 1996. 128p. (J). (gr. 3-7). pap. 4.50 (*0-7868-1108-0*) Hyperion Paperbacks for Children.

—Guests. 1999. 128p. (J). (gr. 4 up). pap. 4.99 (*0-7868-1356-3*) Hyperion Pr.

—Guests. 1996. (J). 11.04 (*0-606-08759-1*) Turtleback Bks.

Hassinger, Peter. The Book of Alfar: Pyngyp. 2002. (Illus.). 272p. (J). (gr. 4 up). 15.95 (*0-06-028469-2*); lib. bdg. 15.89 (*0-06-028470-6*) HarperCollins Children's Bk. Group. (Geringer, Laura Bk.).

Lemieux, Margo. Full Worm Moon. 1994. (Illus.). 32p. (J). 15.00 o.p. (*0-688-12105-5*); lib. bdg. 14.93 o.p. (*0-688-12106-3*) Morrow/Avon. (Morrow, William & Co.).

INDIANS OF NORTH AMERICA—APACHE INDIANS—FICTION

Baker, Betty. Three Fools & a Horse. 1987. (Ready-to-Read Ser.). (Illus.). 64p. (J). (gr. 1-4). reprint ed. pap. 3.95 o.s.i (*0-689-71123-9*) Aladdin Paperbacks.

Burks, Brian. Runs with Horses. 1995. 128p. (YA). (gr. 7 up). 12.00 (*0-15-200264-2*); pap. 6.00 (*0-15-200994-9*, Harcourt Paperbacks) Harcourt Children's Bks.

—Runs with Horses. 1995. 11.05 (*0-606-09802-X*) Turtleback Bks.

—Walks Alone. 1998. 128p. (YA). (gr. 6-12). 16.00 (*0-15-201612-0*) Harcourt Children's Bks.

Dearen, Patrick. The Hidden Treasure of the Chisos. 2001. (Lone Star Heroes Ser.). 128p. (J). pap. 8.95 (*1-55622-829-5*, Republic of Texas Pr.) Wordware Publishing, Inc.

Ellison, Suzanne P. The Last Warrior. 1997. (J). (gr. 7-10). 140p. pap. 6.95 (*0-87358-679-4*); 240p. lib. bdg. 12.95 o.p. (*0-87358-678-6*) Northland Publishing. (Rising Moon Bks. for Young Readers).

Hamilton, Madelen C. Where the Thunderbirds Dwell. 1977. (Moody Pre-Teen Bks.). pap. 1.50 o.p. (*0-8024-3978-0*) Moody Pr.

Holmas, Stig. Apache Pass. Born, Anne, tr. (Illus.). 1996. 48p. (YA). (gr. 6-12). pap., tchr. ed. 9.95 o.p. (*1-57140-018-4*); 1996. 128p. (YA). (gr. 7 up). 15.95 (*1-57140-010-9*); 1955. 48p. (gr. 7 up). pap. 9.95 (*1-57140-011-7*) Rinehart, Roberts Pubs.

—Fire Wagons. Born, Anne, tr. from NOR. 1996. (Chiricahua Apache Ser.). (Illus.). (YA). (gr. 7 up). 128p. 15.95 o.p. (*1-57140-016-8*); 128p. pap. 9.95 o.p. (*1-57140-017-6*); 48p. pap., tchr. ed. 9.95 o.p. (*1-57140-019-2*) Rinehart, Roberts Pubs.

—Son-of-Thunder. Born, Anne, tr. from NOR. (Illus.). (gr. 7 up). 1999. (Chiricahua Apache Series / Stig Holmas Ser.: Vol. 1). 32p. pap. 16.95 (*0-943173-88-4*); 1993. 48p. (YA). pap., tchr. ed. 9.95 o.p. (*1-57140-020-6*) Rinehart, Roberts Pubs.

Kjelgaard, Jim. Wolf Brother. 1957. 189p. (J). (gr. 7 up). 6.95 o.p. (*0-8234-0152-9*) Holiday Hse., Inc.

Lacapa, Michael. Antelope Woman: An Apache Folktale. 1995. (Illus.). 48p. (J). (gr. 2-3). reprint ed. pap. 7.95 o.p. (*0-87358-647-6*, Rising Moon Bks. for Young Readers) Northland Publishing.

—The Flute Player: An Apache Folktale. 1995. (Illus.). 48p. (J). (gr. 1-3). reprint ed. pap. 7.95 o.p. (*0-87358-627-1*, Rising Moon Bks. for Young Readers) Northland Publishing.

Martinello, Marian, et al. Hopes, Prayers & Promises. 1986. (Texas Ser.: Vol. 2). (Illus.). 48p. (J). (gr. k-8). 12.95 (*0-935857-05-2*); pap. (*0-935857-06-0*) TexArt Services, Inc.

McKissack, Patricia C. Run Away Home. 1997. 128p. (J). (gr. 3-7). pap. 14.95 (*0-590-46751-4*) Scholastic, Inc.

Munch, Theodore W. & Winthrop, Robert D. Thunder on Forbidden Mountain. 1976. (J). (gr. 5-9). 6.95 o.p. (*0-664-32588-2*) Westminster John Knox Pr.

Paulsen, Gary. Canyons. 192p. 1991. (J). (gr. 4-7). mass mkt. 5.99 (*0-440-21023-2*); 1990. (YA). 15.95 o.s.i (*0-385-30153-7*, Delacorte Pr.) Dell Publishing.

—Canyons. 1991. (J). mass mkt. o.s.i (*0-440-80233-4*); 1990. (YA). o.s.i (*0-385-30201-0*) Random Hse. Children's Bks. (Dell Books for Young Readers).

—Canyons. 1992. (J). (gr. 4-8). 17.75 o.p. (*0-8446-6590-8*) Smith, Peter Pub., Inc.

Shope, Kimberly A. The Apache Blessing: A Modern Tale of Texas Indians. 1992. 24p. (J). (gr. 3-8). pap. 5.00 (*1-886210-03-9*) Tyketoon Young Author Publishing Co.

INDIANS OF NORTH AMERICA—ARAPAHOE INDIANS—FICTION

Eagle Walking Turtle. Full Moon Stories. 1997. (Illus.). 47p. (J). (gr. 3-7). lib. bdg. 16.49 (*0-7868-2175-2*) Hyperion Bks. for Children.

Full Moon Stories. 1997. (Illus.). 48p. (J). (gr. 3-7). 15.95 (*0-7868-0225-1*) Hyperion Bks. for Children.

Henty, G. A. In the Heart of the Rockies: A Story of Adventure in Colorado. E-Book 3.95 (*0-594-01719-X*) 1873 Pr.

—In the Heart of the Rockies: A Story of Adventure in Colorado. 2002. 370p. 29.95 (*1-59087-073-5*, GAH073); per. 19.95 (*1-59087-072-7*, GAH072) Althouse Pr.

—In the Heart of the Rockies: A Story of Adventure in Colorado. 1998. (Illus.). 385p. (YA). (gr. 4 up). reprint ed. pap. 16.95 (*1-890623-08-3*) Lost Classics Bk. Co.

—In the Heart of the Rockies: A Story of Adventure in Colorado. collector's ed. 2002. (Illus.). im. lthr. 38.85 (*1-4115-1341-X*); pap. 19.95 (*1-4115-0577-8*); 25.95 (*1-4115-0949-8*); pap. 17.95 (*1-4115-0174-8*) Polyglot Pr., Inc.

Korman, Susan. Horse Raid: An Arapaho Camp in the 1800s. 1998. (Smithsonian Odyssey Ser.: Vol. 10). (Illus.). 32p. (J). (gr. 2-5). 14.95 (*1-56899-613-6*); 19.95 incl. audio (*1-56899-615-2*, C6011); pap. 10.95 incl. audio (*1-56899-616-0*); pap. 5.95 (*1-56899-614-4*) Soundprints.

—Horse Raid: An Arapaho Camp in the 1800s. 1998. 12.10 (*0-606-16856-7*) Turtleback Bks.

—Horse Raid: An Arapaho Camp in the 1800's, Incl. toy. 1998. (Smithsonian Odyssey Ser.: Vol. 10). (Illus.). 32p. (J). (gr. 2-5). 19.95 o.p. incl. audio (*1-56899-619-5*); pap. o.p. incl. audio (*1-56899-620-9*); pap. 17.95 o.p. (*1-56899-618-7*); pap. o.p. incl. audio (*1-56899-620-9*) Soundprints.

—Horse Raid: An Arapaho Camp in the 1800s, Incl. toy. 1998. (Smithsonian Odyssey Ser.: Vol. 10). (Illus.). 32p. (J). (gr. 2-5). 29.95 o.p. (*1-56899-617-9*) Soundprints.

Ryan, Marla Felkins & Schmittroth, Linda, eds. Arapaho. 2004. (Tribes of Native America Ser.). (J). 26.20 (*1-56711-587-X*, Blackbirch Pr., Inc.) Gale Group.

Taylor, C. J. Guerrier Solitaire et le Fantome: An Arapaho Legend, Vol. 2. 1993. (Native Legends Ser.). (FRE., Illus.). 24p. (YA). (gr. 3 up). pap. 6.95 (*0-88776-309-X*) Tundra Bks. of Northern New York.

INDIANS OF NORTH AMERICA—BANNOCK INDIANS—FICTION

Thomasma, Kenneth. Doe Sia: Bannock Girl & the Handcart Pioneer. 1999. (Amazing Indian Children: 8). (J). (gr. 3-8). pap. 7.99 (*1-880114-20-8*) Grandview Publishing Co.

INDIANS OF NORTH AMERICA—CANADA—FICTION

Barber-Starkey, Joe. Jason & the Sea Otter. 1997. (Illus.). 32p. (J). reprint ed. pap. (*1-55017-162-3*) Harbour Publishing Co., Ltd.

Buchholz, Kate. How the Pinto Got Her Colour. ed. 1998. (J). (gr. 2). spiral bd. (*0-616-01606-9*) Canadian National Institute for the Blind/Institut National Canadien pour les Aveugles.

Buckey, Sarah Masters. Enemy in the Fort. (American Girl Collection: Bk. 13). (Illus.). 176p. (J). (gr. 4-7). 2001. 9.95 o.p. (*1-58485-307-7*); 2000. pap. 5.95 (*1-58485-306-9*) Pleasant Co. Pubns. (American Girl).

Bushey, Jeanne. A Sled Dog for Moshi. l.t. ed. 1994. (Illus.). 40p. (J). (ps-3). (*0-920534-85-6*) Hyperion Pr., Ltd.

Byron Through the Seasons: A Dene-English Story Book. 1994. (J). pap. 7.95 (*1-895618-33-9*) Fifth Hse. Pubs. CAN. *Dist:* Fitzhenry & Whiteside, Ltd.

Craven, Margaret. I Heard the Owl Call My Name. 1991. 250p. (J). (ps up). reprint ed. lib. bdg. 25.95 (*0-89966-854-2*) Buccaneer Bks., Inc.

—I Heard the Owl Call My Name. 1980. 160p. (gr. 7-12). mass mkt. 6.99 (*0-440-34369-0*, Laurel) Dell Publishing.

—I Heard the Owl Call My Name. 1973. (Illus.). 144p. 11.95 o.p. (*0-385-02586-6*) Doubleday Publishing.

—I Heard the Owl Call My Name. 1978. (Inspirational Ser.). 225p. reprint ed. lib. bdg. 9.95 o.p. (*0-8161-6203-4*, Macmillan Reference USA) Gale Group.

—I Heard the Owl Call My Name. 1973. 12.55 (*0-606-03572-9*) Turtleback Bks.

Dorion, Betty F. Melanie Bluelake's Dream. 1995. 156p. (J). (gr. 4-7). pap. 4.95 (*1-55050-081-3*) Coteau Bks. CAN. *Dist:* General Distribution Services, Inc.

Dubois, Muriel L. Abenaki Captive. 16.00 (*0-9723410-0-5*) Apprentice Shop Bks., LLC.

—Abenaki Captive. 1994. (J). (gr. 4-7). lib. bdg. 15.95 o.s.i (*0-87614-753-8*, Carolrhoda Bks.) Lerner Publishing Group.

Eckert, Allan W. Return to Hawk's Hill. (J). 2000. 208p. (gr. 7 up). pap. 6.99 (*0-316-00689-0*); 1999. 192p. pap. 4.99 (*0-316-20341-6*); 1998. (Illus.). 160p. (gr. 7-12). 15.95 o.p. (*0-316-21593-7*) Little Brown & Co.

—Return to Hawk's Hill. 2000. 12.00 (*0-606-17850-3*) Turtleback Bks.

Edmonds, Yvette. Yuit. 1996. 128p. (J). pap. 5.95 (*0-929141-20-2*, Napoleon Publishing) Napoleon Publishing/Rendezvous Pr. CAN. *Dist:* Words Distributing Co.

Houston, James. Ghost Paddle: A Northwest Coast Indian Tale. 1972. (Illus.). 64p. (J). (gr. 2-6). 5.50 o.p. (*0-15-230760-5*) Harcourt Children's Bks.

Houston, James R. River Runners: A Tale of Hardship & Bravery. 1992. 160p. (J). (gr. 5 up). pap. 4.50 o.s.i (*0-14-036093-X*, Puffin Bks.) Penguin Putnam Bks. for Young Readers.

Robinson, Margaret A. A Woman of Her Tribe. 1990. 144p. (YA). (gr. 7 up). mass mkt. 13.95 (*0-684-19223-3*, Atheneum) Simon & Schuster Children's Publishing.

Schwartz, Virginia Frances. Initiation. Morin, Paul, tr. 2003. 268p. (YA). (*1-55005-053-2*) Fitzhenry & Whiteside, Ltd.

Walters, Eric. War of the Eagles. 1998. 160p. (YA). (gr. 7-11). pap. 7.95 (*1-55143-099-1*); 14.00 (*1-55143-118-1*) Orca Bk. Pubs.

—War of the Eagles. 1998. 14.00 (*0-606-16742-0*) Turtleback Bks.

INDIANS OF NORTH AMERICA—CAPTIVITIES—FICTION

Buckey, Sarah Masters. Enemy in the Fort. (American Girl Collection: Bk. 13). (Illus.). 176p. (J). (gr. 4-7). 2001. 9.95 o.p. (*1-58485-307-7*); 2000. pap. 5.95 (*1-58485-306-9*) Pleasant Co. Pubns. (American Girl).

—Enemy in the Fort. 2001. (American Girl Collection). (Illus.). (J). 12.00 (*0-606-21180-2*) Turtleback Bks.

Keehn, Sally M. I Am Regina. 1993. (gr. 4-7). (J). pap. o.p. (*0-440-90037-9*); 240p. pap. text 4.99 o.s.i (*0-440-40754-0*) Dell Publishing.

—I Am Regina. 1991. 240p. (YA). (gr. 4-7). 17.99 (*0-399-21797-5*, Philomel) Penguin Putnam Bks. for Young Readers.

—I Am Regina. 1991. (J). 11.04 (*0-606-02681-9*) Turtleback Bks.

Keith, Harold. Komantcia. 1965. (J). (gr. 7 up). 9.95 o.p. (*0-690-47744-9*) HarperCollins Children's Bk. Group.

Lenski, Lois. Indian Captive: The Story of Mary Jemison. (Illus.). 272p. (J). 1994. (gr. 5 up). lib. bdg. 17.89 (*0-397-30076-X*); 1990. (gr. 7-9). 16.00 o.p. (*0-397-30072-7*) HarperCollins Children's Bk. Group.

—Indian Captive: The Story of Mary Jemison. 1995. 12.00 (*0-606-07706-5*) Turtleback Bks.

Lenski, Lois, illus. Indian Captive: The Story of Mary Jemison. 97th ed. 1995. 320p. (J). (gr. 5 up). pap. 6.99 (*0-06-446162-9*, Harper Trophy) HarperCollins Children's Bk. Group.

Mayne, William. Drift. 1986. 168p. (J). (gr. 4-6). 14.95 o.p. (*0-385-29446-8*, Delacorte Pr.) Dell Publishing.

Panagopoulos, Janie Lynn. Little Ship under Full Sail. 1997. 146p. (J). 15.95 (*0-938682-46-6*) River Road Pubns., Inc.

Philbrook, Clem. Captured by the Abnakis. 1966. (Illus.). (J). (gr. 4-6). 6.95 o.p. (*0-8038-1080-6*) Hastings Hse. Daytrips Pubs.

Schmidt, William & Monsma, Hester. Star Eye. 1979. (Voyager Ser.). (J). (gr. 5 up). pap. 2.50 o.p. (*0-8010-8166-1*) Baker Bks.

Smith, Mary P. Boy Captive of Old Deerfield. (Illus.). (J). (gr. 5-6). reprint ed. lib. bdg. 22.95 (*0-89190-961-3*, Rivercity Pr.) Amereon, Ltd.

Speare, Elizabeth George. Calico Captive. 1957. (Illus.). 288p. (J). (gr. 7 up). 17.00 o.p. (*0-395-07112-7*) Houghton Mifflin Co.

—Calico Captive. 1973. 288p. (gr. 4-7). pap. text 4.99 o.s.i (*0-440-41156-4*, Yearling) Random Hse. Children's Bks.

—Calico Captive. 1957. (J). 11.04 (*0-606-04179-6*) Turtleback Bks.

Steele, William O. Tomahawks & Trouble. 1955. (Illus.). (J). (gr. 3-6). 5.50 o.p. (*0-15-289084-X*) Harcourt Children's Bks.

Wheeler, Arville. White Squaw: The True Story of Jennie Wiley. 2000. (Illus.). 163p. (J). 14.95 (*0-945084-82-X*) Stuart, Jesse Foundation, The.

Wisler, G. Clifton. The Raid. 128p. (J). (gr. 5 up). 1994. pap. 3.99 o.s.i (*0-14-036937-6*, Puffin Bks.); 1985. 11.95 o.p. (*0-525-67169-2*, Dutton Children's Bks.) Penguin Putnam Bks. for Young Readers.

INDIANS OF NORTH AMERICA—CHEROKEE INDIANS—FICTION

Bannon, Kay Thorpe. Curious One: A Cherokee Story. 2001. (Illus.). 38p. (J). (ps-5). pap. 12.95 (*0-9669946-3-9*) Lobster Cove Publishing Co.

Bird, Traveller. The Path to Snowbird Mountain, RS. 1972. (Illus.). 96p. (J). (gr. 4 up). 3.95 o.p. (*0-374-35757-9*, Farrar, Straus & Giroux (BYR)) Farrar, Straus & Giroux.

Blevins, Wade. And Then the Feather Fell. 1996. (Cherokee Indian Legend Ser.: No. 1). (Illus.). 35p. (J). pap. 2.95 o.p. (*1-56763-097-9*); 17.25 (*1-56763-096-0*) Ozark Publishing.

—Atagahi's Gift. 51p. (J). (gr. 4-7). 1996. (Cherokee Indian Legend Ser.: Vol. 6). (Illus.). lib. bdg. 17.25 (*1-56763-135-5*); 1995. pap. text 2.95 o.p. (*1-56763-136-3*) Ozark Publishing.

—Se-lu's Song. 1996. (Cherokee Indian Legend Ser.: Vol. 7). (Illus.). 53p. (J). lib. bdg. 17.25 (*1-56763-133-9*) Ozark Publishing.

—The Wisdom Circle. 1993. (Cherokee Indian Legend Ser.: Vol. 5). (Illus.). 45p. (J). (gr. k-8). lib. bdg. 17.25 (*1-56763-075-8*); pap. 6.00 o.p. (*1-56763-076-6*) Ozark Publishing.

Bruchac, Joseph. The Journal of Jesse Smoke: A Cherokee Boy: Trail of Tears, 1838. 2001. (My Name Is America Ser.). (Illus.). 176p. (J). (gr. 4-8). pap. 10.95 (*0-439-12197-3*) Scholastic, Inc.

Bruchac, Joseph & Ross, Gayle. The Story of the Milky Way: A Cherokee Tale. 1995. (Illus.). 32p. (J). (ps-3). 15.99 o.p. (*0-8037-1737-7*, Dial Bks. for Young Readers) Penguin Putnam Bks. for Young Readers.

Haines, J. D. Flight of the Eagle. 2002. (Illus.). viii, 64p. (J). 14.95 (*1-57168-744-0*, Eakin Pr.) Eakin Pr.

Halverson, Lydia, illus. The Animals' Ballgame. 1992. (Adventures in Storytelling Ser.). 32p. (J). (ps-3). pap. 5.95 o.p. (*0-516-45139-1*); lib. bdg. 19.20 o.p. (*0-516-05139-3*) Scholastic Library Publishing. (Children's Pr.).

—The Animals' Ballgame (A Cherokee Story) 1995. (Adventures in Storytelling Ser.). 32p. (J). pap. 12.95 o.p. incl. audio (*0-516-07106-8*, Children's Pr.) Scholastic Library Publishing.

Johnston, Tony. Trail of Tears. 1998. (Illus.). (J). (*0-590-48519-9*, Blue Sky Pr., The) Scholastic, Inc.

L'Amour, Louis. The Cherokee Trail. 1996. 208p. mass mkt. 4.50 (*0-553-27047-8*); 1982. mass mkt. 2.95 o.s.i (*0-553-20846-2*) Bantam Bks.

—The Cherokee Trail. 1983. (General Ser.). lib. bdg. 12.95 o.p. (*0-8161-3464-2*, Macmillan Reference USA) Gale Group.

—The Cherokee Trail. 1982. (J). 10.55 (*0-606-01540-X*) Turtleback Bks.

Leppard, Lois Gladys. Mandie & the Cherokee Legend. 1983. (Mandie Bks.: No. 2). 144p. (J). (gr. 4-7). pap. 4.99 (*0-87123-321-5*) Bethany Hse. Pubs.

—Mandie & the Cherokee Legend. 1983. (Mandie Bks.: No. 2). (J). (gr. 4-7). 11.04 (*0-606-06126-6*) Turtleback Bks.

—Mandie & the Medicine Man. 1986. (Mandie Bks.: No. 6). 128p. (J). (gr. 4-7). pap. 4.99 (*0-87123-891-8*) Bethany Hse. Pubs.

—Mandie & the Medicine Man. 1986. (Mandie Bks.: No. 6). (J). (gr. 4-7). 11.04 (*0-606-06134-7*) Turtleback Bks.

—Mandie & the Midnight Journey. 1989. (Mandie Bks.: No. 13). 160p. (J). (gr. 4-7). pap. 4.99 (*1-55661-084-X*) Bethany Hse. Pubs.

—Mandie & the Midnight Journey. 1989. (Mandie Bks.: No. 13). (J). (gr. 4-7). 11.04 (*0-606-06135-5*) Turtleback Bks.

Moore, Lonnie W. & Moore, Iola. A Cherokee Spirit: The Saga of Oroville Annie & White Wolf. 1999. (Illus.). 45p. pap. 15.95 (*0-9661244-2-1*) I & L Publishing.

Pennington, Daniel. Itse Selu: Cherokee Harvest Festival. 1994. (Illus.). 32p. (J). (ps-3). 15.95 (*0-88106-851-9*, Talewinds); pap. 6.95 (*0-88106-850-0*, Talewinds); lib. bdg. 15.00 o.p. (*0-88106-852-7*) Charlesbridge Publishing, Inc.

—Itse Selu: Cherokee Harvest Festival. 1994. 13.10 (*0-606-06501-6*) Turtleback Bks.

Rockwood, Joyce. Groundhog's Horse, ERS. 1978. (J). 9.95 o.s.i (*0-03-021526-9*); (Illus.). 128p. (gr. 2-4). 12.95 o.p. (*0-8050-1173-0*) Holt, Henry & Co. (Holt, Henry & Co. Bks. For Young Readers).

—To Spoil the Sun, ERS. 1976. (J). (gr. k-3). o.p. (*0-03-018066-X*); 12.95 o.p. (*0-8050-0293-6*) Holt, Henry & Co. (Holt, Henry & Co. Bks. For Young Readers).

Roop, Peter & Roop, Connie. Ahyoka & the Talking Leaves. 1992. (Illus.). 48p. (J). (gr. 1 up). 15.00 o.p. (*0-688-10697-8*) HarperCollins Children's Bk. Group.

Roth, Susan L. Kanahena: A Cherokee Folktale. 1996. (Illus.). 32p. (J). (ps-3). pap. 5.99 o.s.i (*0-440-40826-1*, Yearling) Random Hse. Children's Bks.

—Kanahena: A Cherokee Story. 1988. (Illus.). 32p. (J). (gr. 1 up). 9.95 o.p. (*0-312-01722-7*) St. Martin's Pr.

—Kanahena: A Cherokee Story. 1996. 11.19 o.p. (*0-606-09508-X*) Turtleback Bks.

Smith, Florence B. Painted Eagle's Dream. 2001. 220p. pap. 8.00 (*1-893463-41-9*) Prickly Pr.

Steele, William O. The Cherokee Crown of Tannassy. 1977. 7.95 o.p. (*0-910244-99-5*) Blair, John F. Pub.

—The Man with the Silver Eyes. 1976. (J). (gr. 5 up). 5.95 o.p. (*0-15-251720-0*) Harcourt Children's Bks.

Stewart, Elizabeth J. On the Long Trail Home. 1994. (Illus.). 112p. (J). (gr. 4-6). tchr. ed. 15.00 (*0-395-68361-0*, Clarion Bks.) Houghton Mifflin Co. Trade & Reference Div.

Stroud, Virginia A. A Walk to the Great Mystery. 1995. (Illus.). 32p. (J). 14.99 o.s.i (*0-8037-1636-2*); 14.89 o.s.i (*0-8037-1637-0*) Penguin Putnam Bks. for Young Readers. (Dial Bks. for Young Readers).

Turnage, Sylvia D. Choestoe Songs. 1993. (Illus.). 24p. (Orig.). (J). pap. text 5.95 (*1-880726-01-7*) Turnage Publishing Co., Inc.

—The Choestoe Story. 1995. (Illus.). 28p. (Orig.). (J). (gr. k-5). pap. text 5.95 (*1-880726-00-9*) Turnage Publishing Co., Inc.

Vojtech, Anna, illus. The First Strawberries: A Cherokee Story. 1993. 32p. (J). (ps-3). 16.99 (*0-8037-1331-2*, Dial Bks. for Young Readers) Penguin Putnam Bks. for Young Readers.

INDIANS OF NORTH AMERICA—CHEYENNE INDIANS—FICTION

Benchley, Nathaniel. Only Earth & Sky Last Forever. 1974. (Trophy Bk.). 204p. (YA). (gr. 7 up). pap. 4.95 o.s.i (*0-06-440049-2*, Harper Trophy) HarperCollins Children's Bk. Group.

—Only Earth & Sky Last Forever. 1972. 196p. (J). (gr. 7 up). 10.95 o.p. (*0-06-020493-1*); lib. bdg. 8.79 o.p. (*0-06-020494-X*) HarperCollins Pubs.

—Only Earth & Sky Last Forever. 1992. (YA). (gr. 7 up). 17.25 o.p. (*0-8446-6583-5*) Smith, Peter Pub., Inc.

—Only Earth & Sky Last Forever. 1972. (J). 10.05 o.p. (*0-606-02346-1*) Turtleback Bks.

Bunting, Eve. Cheyenne Again. (Illus.). 32p. (J). (ps-3). 2002. pap. 5.95 (*0-618-19465-7*); 1995. 16.00 (*0-395-70364-6*) Houghton Mifflin Co. Trade & Reference Div. (Clarion Bks.).

Cohlene, Terri. Quillworker: A Cheyenne Legend. 1990. (Native American Legends Ser.). (Illus.). 48p. (J). (gr. 4-8). lib. bdg. 27.93 (*0-86593-004-X*) Rourke Publishing, LLC.

—Quillworker: A Cheyenne Legend. 1990. (Native American Legends Ser.). 11.10 (*0-606-05004-3*) Turtleback Bks.

Finley, Mary Pearce. Little Fox's Secret: The Mystery of Bent's Fort. 1999. (Illus.). 68p. (J). (gr. 3-4). lib. bdg. 15.95 (*0-86541-049-6*) Filter Pr., LLC.

—Soaring Eagle. 1998. 176p. (J). (gr. 5-7). pap. 8.95 (*1-57168-281-3*) Eakin Pr.

—Soaring Eagle. 1993. (YA). (gr. 6 up). pap. 16.00 (*0-671-75598-6*, Simon & Schuster Children's Publishing) Simon & Schuster Children's Publishing.

Gilliland, Hap. Alone in the Wilderness. 2001. (Illus.). 158p. (YA). (gr. 6-10). pap. 14.95 (*0-87961-257-6*) Naturegraph Pubs., Inc.

Goble, Paul. Death of the Iron Horse. (Illus.). 32p. (J). (gr. k-3). 1987. lib. bdg. 14.95 o.s.i (*0-02-737830-6*, Atheneum/Richard Jackson Bks.); 1993. reprint ed. pap. 5.99 (*0-689-71686-9*, Aladdin) Simon & Schuster Children's Publishing.

—Death of the Iron Horse. 1993. (J). 12.14 (*0-606-02590-1*) Turtleback Bks.

—Her Seven Brothers. (Illus.). 32p. (J). 1988. text 14.95 (*0-02-737960-4*, Simon & Schuster Children's Publishing); 1993. reprint ed. pap. 6.99 (*0-689-71730-X*, Aladdin) Simon & Schuster Children's Publishing.

—Her Seven Brothers. 1993. (J). 12.14 (*0-606-05873-7*) Turtleback Bks.

High, Linda Oatman. Winter Shoes for Shadow Horse. 2003. (Illus.). 32p. (J). (gr. k-3). 15.95 (*1-56397-472-X*) Boyds Mills Pr.

Holmes, Mary Z. Thunder Foot. 1992. (History's Children Ser.). (Illus.). 48p. (J). (gr. 4-5). lib. bdg. 21.36 o.p. (*0-8114-3500-8*) Raintree Pubs.

Irwin, Hadley. Jim Dandy. 1994. 144p. (J). (gr. 5-9). 15.00 (*0-689-50594-9*, McElderry, Margaret K.) Simon & Schuster Children's Publishing.

Penney, Grace Jackson. Moki. 1997. 160p. (gr. 3-7). pap. 4.99 o.s.i (*0-14-038430-8*) Penguin Putnam Bks. for Young Readers.

Sandoz, Mari. Horsecatcher. 1957. (J). 14.00 (*0-606-04402-7*) Turtleback Bks.

—Horsecatcher. 1957. 192p. (J). (gr. 8 up). 6.95 o.p. (*0-664-30063-4*) Westminster John Knox Pr.

—The Horsecatcher. 1986. 192p. (J). (gr. 5-8). 17.95 o.p. (*0-8032-4166-6*); (gr. 7 up). pap. 9.95 (*0-8032-9160-4*, Bison Bks.) Univ. of Nebraska Pr.

Sneve, Virginia Driving Hawk. The Cheyennes. 1996. (First Americans Book Ser.). (Illus.). 32p. (J). (gr. 4-7). tchr. ed. 16.95 (*0-8234-1250-4*) Holiday Hse., Inc.

Strigenz, Geri K., illus. Thunder Foot. 1992. (History's Children Ser.). 48p. (J). (gr. 4-5). pap. o.p. (*0-8114-6425-3*) Raintree Pubs.

Williams, Laura E. Cheyenne Rose. Korman, Susan, ed. 1997. (Magic Attic Club Ser.). (Illus.). 80p. (J). (gr. 2-6). 13.95 o.s.i (*1-57513-104-8*); pap. 5.95 (*1-57513-103-X*) Millbrook Pr., Inc. (Magic Attic Pr.).

—Cheyenne Rose. 1997. (Magic Attic Club Ser.). (J). (gr. 2-6). 12.10 (*0-606-19135-6*) Turtleback Bks.

Williams, Laura E. & Dodge, Bill. Cheyenne Rose. 1997. (Magic Attic Club Ser.). (Illus.). 80p. (J). (gr. 2-6). 18.90 (*1-57513-188-9*, Magic Attic Pr.) Millbrook Pr., Inc.

INDIANS OF NORTH AMERICA—CHIPPEWA INDIANS—FICTION

Barnouw, Victor. Dream of the Blue Heron. 1966. (Illus.). (J). (gr. 4-6). 4.50 o.p. (*0-440-02150-2*, Delacorte Pr.) Dell Publishing.

Reed, Nat. Thunderbird Gold. 1997. 154p. (J). (gr. 4-7). pap. 6.49 (*0-89084-919-6*, 103325) Jones, Bob Univ. Pr.

Wosmek, Frances. A Brown Bird Singing. 1986. (Illus.). 160p. (YA). (gr. 5-10). 11.95 o.p. (*0-688-06251-2*) HarperCollins Children's Bk. Group.

INDIANS OF NORTH AMERICA—CHUMASHAN INDIANS—FICTION

Dengler, Marianna. The Worry Stone. 1996. (Illus.). 40p. (J). (gr. 1-3). lib. bdg. 14.95 (*0-87358-642-5*, Rising Moon Bks. for Young Readers) Northland Publishing.

Spinka, Penina K. Mother's Blessing. 1993. 176p. mass mkt. 3.99 o.s.i (*0-449-70431-9*, Fawcett) Ballantine Bks.

—Mother's Blessing. 1992. 224p. (J). (gr. 5-9). lib. bdg. 14.95 o.s.i (*0-689-31758-1*, Atheneum) Simon & Schuster Children's Publishing.

INDIANS OF NORTH AMERICA—COMANCHE INDIANS—FICTION

Arbuckle, Scott. Zeb, the Cow's on the Roof Again! And Other Tales of Early Texas Dwellings. 1996. (Illus.). 120p. (J). (gr. 4-8). 15.95 (*1-57168-102-7*) Eakin Pr.

Beatty, Patricia. Wait for Me, Watch for Me, Eula Bee. 1978. (J). (gr. 7-9). 12.50 o.p. (*0-688-22151-3*); lib. bdg. 12.88 o.p. (*0-688-32151-8*) Morrow/Avon. (Morrow, William & Co.).

Benner, J. A. Uncle Comanche. 1996. (Chaparral Book for Young Readers Ser.). 174p. (Orig.). (J). (gr. 7 up). pap. 12.95 (*0-87565-152-6*) Texas Christian Univ. Pr.

Dearen, Patrick. Comanche Peace Pipe. 2001. (Lone Star Heroes Ser.). 300p. (J). (ps-3). pap. 8.95 (*1-55622-831-7*, Republic of Texas Pr.) Wordware Publishing, Inc.

Keith, Harold. Komantcia. 1965. (J). (gr. 7 up). 9.95 o.p. (*0-690-47744-9*) HarperCollins Children's Bk. Group.

—The Sound of Strings: Sequel to Komantcia. 1992. 175p. (Orig.). (J). (gr. 5 up). 17.00 (*0-927562-10-3*); pap. 10.00 o.p. (*0-927562-11-1*) Levite of Apache Publishing.

Lewis, Preston. Blanca Is My Name: Or, How I Saved the Buffalo on the Texas Plains. 2002. (Animal Legends Ser.: Vol. 2). (Illus.). x, 174p. (J). (*1-57168-699-1*); pap. (*1-57168-700-9*) Eakin Pr. (Eakin Pr.).

Meyer, Carolyn. Where the Broken Heart Still Beats: The Story of Cynthia Ann Parker. 1992. (Great Episodes Ser.). 192p. (J). (gr. 4-7). 16.95 o.s.i (*0-15-200639-7*, Gulliver Bks.) Harcourt Children's Bks.

Shefelman, Janice J., et al. Comanche Song. 2000. (Illus.). 255p. (J). (gr. 4-7). 17.95 (*1-57168-397-6*) Eakin Pr.

Werkley, Vicki. Girl-on-Fire. Laidig, Jean & HighPine, Gayle, eds. 1999. 230p. (YA). 14.95 (*1-58436-400-9*) Haven Bks.

Wisler, G. Clifton. Buffalo Moon. 1984. 144p. (J). (gr. 5-9). 10.95 o.p. (*0-525-67146-3*, 01063-320, Dutton Children's Bks.) Penguin Putnam Bks. for Young Readers.

INDIANS OF NORTH AMERICA—CREE INDIANS—FICTION

Mowat, Farley. Lost in the Barrens. 1956. (Illus.). (J). (gr. 7 up). 15.95 o.p. (*0-316-58638-2*, Joy Street Bks.) Little Brown & Co.

—Lost in the Barrens. 1985. 208p. (YA). (gr. 4-7). mass mkt. 5.50 (*0-553-27525-9*, Starfire) Random Hse. Children's Bks.

Oliviero, Jamie. The Fish Skin. 1993. (Illus.). 40p. (J). (ps-2). 14.95 o.s.i (*1-56282-401-5*); lib. bdg. 14.89 o.s.i (*1-56282-402-3*) Hyperion Bks. for Children.

Valgardson, W. D. Sarah & the People of Sand River. 1996. (Illus.). 44p. (J). (ps-3). 16.95 (*0-88899-255-6*) Groundwood Bks. CAN. *Dist:* Publishers Group West.

INDIANS OF NORTH AMERICA—CROW INDIANS—FICTION

Duey, Kathleen. Celou Sudden Shout: Idaho, 1826. 1998. (American Diaries Ser.: No. 9). 144p. (J). (gr. 3-7). pap. 4.50 o.s.i (*0-689-81622-7*, Aladdin) Simon & Schuster Children's Publishing.

—Celou Sudden Shout: Idaho, 1826. 1998. (American Diaries Ser.: No. 9). (J). (gr. 3-7). 10.55 (*0-606-13121-3*) Turtleback Bks.

Goble, Paul. Crow Chief: A Plains Indian Story. 1995. 11.15 o.p. (*0-606-09173-4*) Turtleback Bks.

Matcheck, Diane. The Sacrifice, RS. 1998. 208p. (J). (gr. 7-12). 16.00 o.p. (*0-374-36378-1*, Farrar, Straus & Giroux (BYR)) Farrar, Straus & Giroux.

—The Sacrifice. 1999. 224p. (J). (gr. 7-12). pap. 5.99 o.s.i (*0-14-130640-8*, Puffin Bks.) Penguin Putnam Bks. for Young Readers.

—The Sacrifice. 1999. 11.04 (*0-606-17598-9*) Turtleback Bks.

McGraw, Eloise Jarvis. The Moccasin Trail. 1986. (Puffin Newbery Library). 256p. (J). (gr. 4-7). pap. 5.99 (*0-14-032170-5*, Puffin Bks.) Penguin Putnam Bks. for Young Readers.

—The Moccasin Trail. 1952. (Illus.). (J). (gr. 5-8). 8.50 o.p. (*0-698-20092-6*, Coward-McCann) Putnam Publishing Group, The.

Ryniker, Alice D. Eagle Feather for a Crow. 1980. (Illus.). 80p. (J). (gr. 1-6). 9.95 o.p. (*0-932154-07-7*) Lowell Pr., The, Gallion Communications.

Sobol, Rose. Woman Chief. 1979. 112p. (YA). (gr. 5-9). pap. 1.25 o.s.i (*0-440-99657-0*, Laurel Leaf) Random Hse. Children's Bks.

INDIANS OF NORTH AMERICA—DAKOTA INDIANS—FICTION

Bennett, James. Dakota Dream. 1994. 144p. (YA). (gr. 7-9). pap. 14.95 o.p. (*0-590-46680-1*) Scholastic, Inc.

Calvert, Patricia. Betrayed! 224p. (J). 2004. (Illus.). pap. 4.99 (*0-689-86693-3*, Aladdin); 2002. (gr. 7 up). 16.00 (*0-689-83472-1*, Atheneum) Simon & Schuster Children's Publishing.

Distad, Audree. Dakota Sons. 1972. (Illus.). (J). (gr. 3-7). 144p. lib. bdg. 6.89 o.p. (*0-06-024778-9*); pap. 1.25 o.p. (*0-06-440050-6*) HarperCollins Pubs.

Howe, James, adapted by. Dances with Wolves: The Children's Picture Book. 2004. (Illus.). 64p. (YA). (gr. 2 up). 14.95 (*1-55704-104-0*) Newmarket Pr.

Kroll, Francis L. Young Sioux Warrior. 1980. (Illus.). (J). (gr. 4-7). lib. bdg. 6.19 o.p. (*0-8313-0074-4*) Lantern Pr., Inc., Pubs.

Martini, Teri. The Lucky Ghost Shirt. 1971. (Illus.). 112p. (J). (gr. 3-6). 4.50 o.p. (*0-664-32484-3*) Westminster John Knox Pr.

Matthaei, Gay & Grutman, Jewel. The Sketchbook of Thomas Blue Eagle. 2001. (Illus.). 72p. (J). (gr. 5 up). 16.95 o.p. (*0-8118-2908-1*) Chronicle Bks. LLC.

—The Sketchbook of Thomas Blue Eagle. 2001. (Illus.). 60p. (YA). (gr. 5-8). reprint ed. 17.00 (*0-7567-6295-2*) DIANE Publishing Co.

Osborne, Mary Pope. Buffalo Before Breakfast. 1999. (Magic Tree House Ser.: No. 18). (Illus.). (J). (gr. k-3). 20.00 (*0-375-80041-7*, Random Hse. Bks. for Young Readers) Random Hse. Children's Bks.

—Buffalo Before Breakfast. 1999. (Magic Tree House Ser.: No. 18). (Illus.). 96p. (gr. k-3). (J). pap. 3.99 (*0-679-89064-5*); lib. bdg. 11.99 (*0-679-99064-X*) Random Hse., Inc.

—Buffalo Before Breakfast. 1999. (Magic Tree House Ser.: No. 18). (J). (gr. k-3). lib. bdg. 10.14 (*0-606-16841-9*) Turtleback Bks.

Sandoz, Mari. The Story Catcher. 1986. (Illus.). 175p. (YA). (gr. 7 up). pap. 8.95 (*0-8032-9163-9*, Bison Bks.) Univ. of Nebraska Pr.

Sneve, Virginia Driving Hawk. The Chichi Hoohoo Bogeyman. 1993. (Illus.). 63p. (J). (gr. 4-7). pap. 6.95 o.p. (*0-8032-9219-8*, Bison Bks.) Univ. of Nebraska Pr.

—The Trickster & the Troll. 1997. (Illus.). 110p. (J). (gr. 4-8). text 25.00 (*0-8032-4261-1*, Bison Bks.) Univ. of Nebraska Pr.

—When Thunders Spoke. 1993. (Illus.). 95p. (J). (gr. 4-7). pap. 9.95 (*0-8032-9220-1*, Bison Bks.) Univ. of Nebraska Pr.

Turner, Ann Warren. The Girl Who Chased Away Sorrow: The Diary of Sarah Nita, a Navajo Girl, New Mexico, 1863. 1999. (Dear America Ser.). (Illus.). 200p. (J). (gr. 4-9). pap. 10.95 (*0-590-97216-2*, Scholastic Pr.) Scholastic, Inc.

Wangerin, Walter, Jr. The Crying for a Vision: A Novel. 2003. 346p. (J). 29.95 (*1-55725-342-0*) Paraclete Pr., Inc.

—The Crying for a Vision: A Novel. 1994. 288p. (J). (gr. 7 up). 16.00 o.p. (*0-671-79911-8*, Simon & Schuster Children's Publishing) Simon & Schuster Children's Publishing.

Warren, Mary P. Walk in My Moccasins. Lt. ed. 1966. (Illus.). (J). (gr. 4-6). 4.75 o.p. (*0-664-32373-1*) Westminster John Knox Pr.

Whelan, Gloria. Miranda's Last Stand. 144p. (J). (gr. 3-7). 2000. pap. 4.95 (*0-06-442097-3*, Harper Trophy); 1999. (Illus.). 14.95 (*0-06-028251-7*); 1999. (Illus.). lib. bdg. 14.89 (*0-06-028252-5*) HarperCollins Children's Bk. Group.

—Miranda's Last Stand. 2000. 11.00 (*0-606-19267-0*); 11.00 (*0-606-19988-8*) Turtleback Bks.

INDIANS OF NORTH AMERICA—DELAWARE INDIANS—FICTION

Curry, Jane Louise. Dark Shade. 1998. 168p. (YA). (gr. 7-12). 16.00 (*0-689-81812-2*, 870382, McElderry, Margaret K.) Simon & Schuster Children's Publishing.

Harrington, M. R. The Indians of New Jersey: Dickon Among the Lenapes. 1963. (Illus.). (J). (gr. 4-7). pap. 14.00 (*0-8135-0425-2*) Rutgers Univ. Pr.

Johnston, Norma. Feather in the Wind. 2001. (Illus.). 172p. (J). (gr. 5-9). 14.95 (*0-7614-5063-7*, Cavendish Children's Bks.) Cavendish, Marshall Corp.

Keehn, Sally M. Moon of Two Dark Horses. 1995. 224p. (J). (gr. 4-7). 16.95 o.p. (*0-399-22783-0*, Philomel) Penguin Putnam Bks. for Young Readers.

Osborne, Mary Pope. Standing in the Light: The Captive Diary of Catherine Carey Logan, Delaware Valley, Pennsylvania, 1763. 1998. (Dear America Ser.). (Illus.). 184p. (YA). (gr. 4-9). pap. 10.95 (*0-590-13462-0*, Scholastic Pr.) Scholastic, Inc.

Richter, Conrad. Elements of Literature: The Light in the Forest. 1989. pap., stu. ed. 15.33 (*0-03-023439-5*) Holt, Rinehart & Winston.

—The Light in the Forest. (YA). (gr. 7 up). 21.95 (*0-89190-333-X*) Amereon, Ltd.

—The Light in the Forest. 1994. 128p. (gr. 7-12). mass mkt. 6.50 (*0-449-70437-8*, Fawcett) Ballantine Bks.

—The Light in the Forest. 1990. 128p. (J). (gr. 5-12). mass mkt. 3.99 o.s.i (*0-553-26878-3*); 1986. mass mkt. o.s.i (*0-553-16642-5*) Bantam Bks.

—The Light in the Forest. 1991. (YA). (gr. 7 up). lib. bdg. 21.95 (*1-56849-064-X*) Buccaneer Bks., Inc.

—The Light in the Forest. 1953. (Illus.). (J). 23.00 o.s.i (*0-394-43314-9*); (YA). (gr. 7 up). lib. bdg. 5.99 o.p. (*0-394-91404-X*) Knopf, Alfred A. Inc.

—The Light in the Forest. 1986. (J). mass mkt. o.s.i (*0-553-16679-4*, Dell Books for Young Readers) Random Hse. Children's Bks.

—The Light in the Forest. 9999. pap. 1.95 o.p. (*0-590-02336-5*) Scholastic, Inc.

—The Light in the Forest. 1994. (YA). (gr. 7 up). 12.04 (*0-606-06903-8*) Turtleback Bks.

INDIANS OF NORTH AMERICA—EDUCATION—FICTION

Armstrong, Jeannette. Enwhisteetkwa: Walk in Water. 1986. (Illus.). 44p. (J). pap. text (*0-919441-12-2*) Theytus Bks., Ltd. CAN. *Dist:* Orca Bk. Pubs.

Chanin, Michael. Grandfather Four Winds & Rising Moon. 1994. (Illus.). 32p. (J). (ps-4). 14.95 (*0-915811-47-2*, Starseed Pr.) Kramer, H.J. Inc.

Darby, Maribeth. The Land of the Magic Sand: Salt, Yesterday & Today. 1994. 120p. (J). (gr. 5-6). 12.95 o.p. (*0-89015-973-4*) Eakin Pr.

Gould, Carol. The Drummers. Kaeden Corp. Staff, ed. 1995. (Illus.). 12p. (J). (gr. k-2). pap. text 4.95 (*1-879835-73-8*) Kaeden Corp.

Harrington, Michael O. The Ballad of Sara Doom: Myths, Messages, & Markers from the Culture Zone. 1995. (Illus.). 136p. (J). (gr. 7 up). pap. 14.85 (*1-880292-13-0*) LangMarc Publishing.

Hobbs, William. Far North. (J). 2004. (Illus.). 304p. pap. 5.99 (*0-06-054096-6*, Harper Trophy); 1997. 224p. (gr. 5 up). pap. 5.99 (*0-380-72536-3*); 1996. 240p. (gr. 5 up). 15.95 (*0-688-14192-7*) Harper-Collins Children's Bk. Group.

—Far North. 1997. (J). 11.04 (*0-606-11314-2*) Turtleback Bks.

Rodolph, Stormy. Quest for Courage, Vol. 4. 2nd ed. 1993. (Council for Indian Education Ser.). (Illus.). 112p. (J). (gr. 4-7). pap. 8.95 o.p. (*1-879373-57-2*) Rinehart, Roberts Pubs.

Sheldon, Dyan. Under the Moon. 1994. (Illus.). 32p. (J). (ps-3). 15.99 o.s.i (*0-8037-1670-2*, Dial Bks. for Young Readers) Penguin Putnam Bks. for Young Readers.

Thomas, Estelle W. Gift of Laughter. 1967. (J). (gr. 7 up). 4.50 o.p. (*0-664-32395-2*) Westminster John Knox Pr.

INDIANS OF NORTH AMERICA—FICTION

Aardema, Verna. Bringing the Rain to Kapiti Plain: A Nandi Tale. 2002. (Illus.). (J). 14.04 (*0-7587-2153-6*) Book Wholesalers, Inc.

—Bringing the Rain to Kapiti Plain: A Nandi Tale. 1981. (Reading Rainbow Bks.). 12.14 (*0-606-01606-6*) Turtleback Bks.

Adams, Patricia. Pocahontas, Indian Princess. 1987. 96p. (gr. 2-6). pap. text 3.25 o.s.i (*0-440-47067-6*, Yearling) Random Hse. Children's Bks.

Albers, Everett C. Lewis & Clark Meet the American Indians: As Told by Seaman the Dog. 1999. (Illus.). 32p. (J). (ps-11). pap. 3.95 (*0-9674002-0-1*) United Printing.

Alder, Elizabeth. Crossing the Panther's Path, RS. 2002. (Illus.). 240p. (J). 18.00 (*0-374-31662-7*, Farrar, Straus & Giroux (BYR)) Farrar, Straus & Giroux.

—Crossing the Panther's Path. 2003. (Young Adult Ser.). (YA). 24.95 (*0-7862-5013-5*) Thorndike Pr.

Alton, Jay. Thunder Hawk. 1997. (Illus.). 218p. (J). (ps-12). pap. 13.95 (*0-912382-34-1*) Black Letter Pr.

Annixter, Jane & Annixter, Paul. Horns of Plenty. 1960. 203p. (J). (gr. 7-11). 4.95 o.p. (*0-8234-0048-4*) Holiday Hse., Inc.

Applegate, Stanley. The Devil's Highway. 1998. (Illus.). 224p. (YA). (gr. 3-7). pap. 8.95 (*1-56145-184-3*, Peachtree Junior) Peachtree Pubs., Ltd.

—The Devil's Highway. 1998. (J). 15.00 (*0-606-19042-2*) Turtleback Bks.

Armstrong, Nancy. Navajo Long Walk. 1983. 88p. (J). (gr. 4-9). pap. 5.95 (*0-89992-083-7*) Council for Indian Education.

Asch, Connie. Tohono O'Odham (Papago) Indian Coloring Book. rev. ed. 1983. (Illus.). 32p. (Orig.). (J). (gr. 1-6). reprint ed. pap. 3.50 (*0-918080-60-6*) Treasure Chest Bks.

Back, Peg. Crickets & Corn. 1985. 3.50 (*0-377-00152-X*) Friendship Pr.

Baker, Betty. Shaman's Last Raid. 1963. (Illus.). (J). (gr. 3-6). lib. bdg. 10.89 o.p. (*0-06-020351-X*) HarperCollins Pubs.

Baker, Olaf. Where the Buffaloes Begin. 1985. (Picture Puffins Ser.). (Illus.). 48p. (J). (ps-3). pap. 6.99 (*0-14-050560-1*, Viking Children's Bks.) Penguin Putnam Bks. for Young Readers.

Banks, Lynne Reid. Behind the Scenes of The Indian in the Cupboard. 1995. 32p. (J). (gr. 4-7). mass mkt. 3.95 (*0-590-50984-5*) Scholastic, Inc.

—The Indian in the Cupboard. 1993. (Indian in the Cupboard Ser.: No. 1). (J). (gr. 4-7). 16.95 o.p. (*0-7451-5888-9*, Galaxy Children's Large Print) BBC Audiobooks America.

—The Indian in the Cupboard. (Indian in the Cupboard Ser.: No. 1). (Illus.). (gr. 4-7). 1985. 192p. text 16.95 (*0-385-17051-3*); 1980. (J). 15.95 (*0-385-17060-2*, 088464) Doubleday Publishing.

—The Indian in the Cupboard. (Indian in the Cupboard Ser.: No. 1). (J). (gr. 4-7). 1999. (Illus.). 192p. pap. 5.99 (*0-380-60012-9*); 1999. pap. 4.95 (*5-553-81211-9*); 1995. pap. 18.00 (*0-380-72643-2*); 1995. (Illus.). 208p. reprint ed. pap. 5.99 (*0-380-72558-4*) Morrow/Avon. (Avon Bks.).

—The Indian in the Cupboard. (Indian in the Cupboard Ser.: No. 1). 44p. (J). (gr. 4-7). 1999. 9.95 (*1-56137-225-0*); 1998. 11.95 (*1-56137-693-0*, NU6930SP) Novel Units, Inc.

—The Indian in the Cupboard. l.t. ed. 1988. (Indian in the Cupboard Ser.: No. 1). (J). (gr. 4-7). reprint ed. lib. bdg. 16.95 o.s.i (*1-55736-034-0*, Cornerstone Bks.) Pages, Inc.

—The Indian in the Cupboard. (J). (gr. 4-7). (Indian in the Cupboard Ser.: No. 1). 181p. pap. 4.99 (*0-8072-1433-7*); 181p. pap. 35.00 incl. audio (*0-8072-7308-2*, YA809SP); 2000. (Indian in the Cupboard Ser.: No. 1). audio 22.00 (*0-8072-7397-X*, 496005) Random Hse. Audio Publishing Group. (Listening Library).

—The Indian in the Cupboard. 1982. (Indian in the Cupboard Ser.: No. 1). (J). (gr. 4-7). 11.00 (*0-606-02215-5*) Turtleback Bks.

—The Indian in the Cupboard Study Guide. 1997. 16p. (J). mass mkt. 3.95 (*0-590-37364-1*) Scholastic, Inc.

—The Key to the Indian. 1998. (Indian in the Cupboard Ser.: No. 5). 240p. (J). (gr. 4-7). 16.00 (*0-380-97717-6*) HarperCollins Children's Bk. Group.

—The Key to the Indian. 1999. (Indian in the Cupboard Ser.: No. 5). (Illus.). 240p. (J). (gr. 4-7). mass mkt. 4.99 (*0-380-80373-9*, Avon Bks.) Morrow/Avon.

—The Key to the Indian. (Indian in the Cupboard Ser.: No. 5). 240p. (J). (gr. 4-7). pap. 4.99 (*0-8072-1551-1*, Listening Library) Random Hse. Audio Publishing Group.

—The Return of the Indian. l.t. ed. 1989. (Indian in the Cupboard Ser.: No. 2). (Illus.). 227p. (J). (gr. 4-7). lib. bdg. 15.95 o.p. (*1-55736-104-5*) Bantam Doubleday Dell Large Print Group, Inc.

—The Return of the Indian. 1986. (Indian in the Cupboard Ser.: No. 2). (Illus.). 192p. (gr. 4-7). text 16.95 (*0-385-23497-X*) Doubleday Publishing.

—The Return of the Indian. l.t. unabr. ed. 1989. (Indian in the Cupboard Ser.: No. 2). (J). (gr. 4-7). 22.95 incl. audio (*0-8161-9284-7*, Macmillan Reference USA) Gale Group.

—The Return of the Indian. (Indian in the Cupboard Ser.: No. 2). (J). (gr. 4-7). 1987. (Illus.). 208p. pap. 5.99 (*0-380-70284-3*); 1995. 192p. reprint ed. mass mkt. 4.50 (*0-380-72593-2*) Morrow/Avon. (Avon Bks.).

—The Return of the Indian. 1999. (Indian in the Cupboard Ser.: No. 2). (J). (gr. 4-7). 9.95 (*1-56137-232-3*) Novel Units, Inc.

—The Return of the Indian. (Indian in the Cupboard Ser.: No. 2). (J). (gr. 4-7). 189p. pap. 4.99 (*0-8072-1434-5*); 2000. audio 22.00 (*0-8072-7428-3*, YA 810 CXR); 2000. audio 22.00 (*0-8072-7428-3*, YA 810 CXR); 1990. pap. 35.00 incl. audio (*0-8072-7309-0*, YA810SP) Random Hse. Audio Publishing Group. (Listening Library).

—The Return of the Indian. 1986. (Indian in the Cupboard Ser.: No. 2). (J). (gr. 4-7). 11.04 (*0-606-03644-X*) Turtleback Bks.

—The Return of the Indian, The Secret of the Indian, The Mystery of the Cupboard. 1994. (Indian in the Cupboard Ser.: No. 1). (J). (gr. 4-7). pap. 19.95 (*0-380-72404-9*, Avon Bks.) Morrow/Avon.

—The Secret of the Indian. 1989. (Indian in the Cupboard Ser.: No. 3). 160p. (gr. 4-7). text 15.95 (*0-385-26292-2*) Doubleday Publishing.

—The Secret of the Indian. (Indian in the Cupboard Ser.: No. 3). (J). (gr. 4-7). 1990. (Illus.). 160p. pap. 5.99 (*0-380-71040-4*); 1995. 176p. reprint ed. mass mkt. 4.50 (*0-380-72594-0*) Morrow/Avon. (Avon Bks.).

Banks, Sarah Harrell. Remember My Name, No. 2. 1993. (Council for Indian Education Ser.). (Illus.). 120p. (J). (gr. 4-8). pap. 8.95 o.p. (*1-879373-38-6*) Rinehart, Roberts Pubs.

Batdorf, Carol. Seawolf: Building a Canoe. 1990. (Illus.). 24p. (Orig.). (J). (gr. 1-6). pap. 4.95 o.s.i (*0-88839-247-8*) Hancock Hse. Pubs.

—Tinka: A Day in a Little Girl's Life. 1990. (Illus.). 32p. (Orig.). (J). (gr. 1-6). pap. 5.95 (*0-88839-249-4*) Hancock Hse. Pubs.

Behrens, June. Snake... And Amy-Tsosie: A Navajo Sandpainting Story. Brower, Pauline, ed. 1996. (All Americans Series: Vol. 1). (Illus.). 32p. (J). (gr. 2-5). pap. text 6.95 (*1-889121-04-5*) York Hse., Pubs., Inc.

Benchley, Nathaniel. Red Fox & His Canoe. 2001. (Early Readers Ser.: Vol. 2). (J). lib. bdg. (*1-59054-085-9*) Fitzgerald Bks.

—Red Fox & His Canoe. (I Can Read Bks.). (Illus.). 64p. (J). (ps-1). 1964. lib. bdg. 15.89 o.p. (*0-06-020476-1*); 1985. reprint ed. pap. 3.99 (*0-06-444075-3*, Harper Trophy) HarperCollins Children's Bk. Group.

—Red Fox & His Canoe. 1985. (I Can Read Bks.). (J). (ps-1). 10.10 (*0-606-12497-7*) Turtleback Bks.

—Running Owl the Hunter. 1979. (I Can Read Bks.). (Illus.). 64p. (J). (ps-2). lib. bdg. 11.89 o.p. (*0-06-020454-0*) HarperCollins Children's Bk. Group.

—Small Wolf. (I Can Read Bks.). (Illus.). 64p. (J). 1994. (ps-3). pap. 3.99 (*0-06-444180-6*, Harper Trophy); 1986. (gr. 2-4). 14.95 o.p. (*0-06-020491-5*); 1972. (gr. 2-4). lib. bdg. 14.89 o.p. (*0-06-020492-3*) HarperCollins Children's Bk. Group.

—Small Wolf. 1994. (I Can Read Bks.). (Illus.). (J). (gr. 2-4). 10.10 (*0-606-06744-2*) Turtleback Bks.

Bennett, James. Dakota Dream. 1995. 144p. (YA). (gr. 7 up). mass mkt. 4.99 (*0-590-46681-X*, Scholastic Paperbacks) Scholastic, Inc.

Berkebile, Fred D. Captured! 1975. (Illus.). 176p. (gr. 4-9). pap. 1.50 o.p. (*0-912692-59-6*) Cook, David C. Publishing Co.

Berry, Gail. Little Fox & the Golden Hawk. 1991. (Illus.). 32p. (J). (gr. 1-9). 9.50 (*0-912411-36-8*) Open Horizons Publishing Co.

Bird, E. J. The Rainmakers. 1993. (Illus.). (J). (gr. 4-7). lib. bdg. 15.95 (*0-87614-748-1*, Carolrhoda Bks.) Lerner Publishing Group.

Blake, Robert J. Yudonsi: A Tale from the Canyons. 1999. (Illus.). 32p. (J). (ps-3). 15.99 o.p. (*0-399-23320-2*, Philomel) Penguin Putnam Bks. for Young Readers.

Blevins, Wade. And Then the Feather Fell. 1993. (Cherokee Indian Legend Ser.). (Illus.). 48p. (J). (gr. k-8). text 11.95 (*1-56763-060-X*) Ozark Publishing.

—Ganseti & the Legend of the Little People. 1993. (Cherokee Indian Legend Ser.: Vol. No. 4). (Illus.). 43p. (J). (gr. 2 up). pap. 6.00 o.p. (*1-56763-066-9*); lib. bdg. 17.25 (*1-56763-065-0*) Ozark Publishing.

—Legend of Little Deer. 1993. (Cherokee Indian Legend Ser.: Vol. No. 3). (Illus.). 49p. (J). (gr. 2 up). pap. 6.00 o.p. (*1-56763-074-X*) Ozark Publishing.

—Path of Destiny. 1993. (Cherokee Indian Legends Ser.: Vol. No. 2). (Illus.). 49p. (J). (gr. 2 up). pap. 6.00 o.p. (*1-56763-072-3*); lib. bdg. 17.25 (*1-56763-071-5*) Ozark Publishing.

Blevins, Winfred. Stone Song, a Novel of the Life of Crazy Horse. 1996. (J). 13.04 (*0-606-13818-8*) Turtleback Bks.

Blood, Charles L. & Link, Martin. The Goat in the Rug. 1984. (Illus.). 40p. (J). (ps-3). reprint ed. lib. bdg. 14.95 o.s.i (*0-02-710920-8*, Simon & Schuster Children's Publishing) Simon & Schuster Children's Publishing.

Blos, Joan W. Brothers of the Heart: A Story of the Old Northwest, 1837-1838. 2nd ed. 1993. 176p. (J). (gr. 3-7). reprint ed. pap. 4.99 (*0-689-71724-5*, Aladdin) Simon & Schuster Children's Publishing.

—Brothers of the Heart: A Story of the Old Northwest, 1837-1838. 1993. (J). 11.04 (*0-606-12203-6*) Turtleback Bks.

Blue, Rose. First Americans Story. 1955. 7.95 (*0-448-11101-2*) Penguin Putnam Bks. for Young Readers.

BlueWolf, James Don. Speaking for Fire. 2003. (Illus.). 44p. (J). (gr. 2-7). 14.95 (*1-887400-31-1*) Earthen Vessel Production, Inc.

Bly, Stephen A. The Buffalo's Last Stand. 2002. (Retta Barre's Oregon Trail Ser.: 2). 111p. (J). pap. 5.99 (*1-58134-392-2*) Crossway Bks.

—The Lost Wagon Train. 2002. (Retta Barre's Oregon Trail Ser.: Vol. 1). 110p. (J). pap. 5.99 (*1-58134-391-4*) Crossway Bks.

—The Plain Prairie Princess. 2002. (Retta Barre's Oregon Trail Ser.: 3). 108p. (J). pap. 5.99 (*1-58134-393-0*) Crossway Bks.

Boegehold, Betty D. A Horse Called Starfire. 1998. (Bank Street Reader Collection). (Illus.). 48p. (J). (gr. 2-4). lib. bdg. 21.26 (*0-8368-1763-X*) Stevens, Gareth Inc.

Bolognese, Don. Little Hawk's New Name. 1995. (Hello Reader! Ser.). (Illus.). 48p. (J). (ps-3). mass mkt. 3.99 (*0-590-48292-0*, Cartwheel Bks.) Scholastic, Inc.

—Little Hawk's New Name. 1995. (Hello Reader! Ser.). (J). 9.19 o.p. (*0-606-07795-2*) Turtleback Bks.

Borland, Hal. When the Legends Die. 1984. 304p. (YA). (gr. 8-12). mass mkt. 6.50 (*0-553-25738-2*) Bantam Bks.

—When the Legends Die. 9999. (J). pap. 1.95 o.s.i (*0-590-03172-4*) Scholastic, Inc.

—When the Legends Die. 1964. (YA). (gr. 6-12). 12.04 (*0-606-01571-X*) Turtleback Bks.

Bouchard, David. Qu'Appelle. 2002. (Illus.). 32p. (J). (gr. 3-6). 15.95 (*1-55192-475-7*) Raincoast Bk. Distribution CAN. *Dist:* Advanced Global Distribution Services.

Boutwell, Florence. Teresa & the Coeur d'Alene Indians: An Historical Adventure Story for Young & Old. 1998. (Illus.). 175 p. (J). (*0-87062-288-9*) Clark, Arthur H. Co.

Bowman, Eddie. The Dust of Butterfly Wings. 1997. (Illus.). (J). 17.25 (*1-56763-328-5*); pap. (*1-56763-329-3*) Ozark Publishing.

Bowman, Eva Jean. Chief Ninham: Forgotten Hero. 1999. (Illus.). 43p. (YA). (gr. 2 up). pap. 14.00 (*0-935790-04-7*) Muh-He-Con-Neew Pr.

Boyden, Linda. The Blue Roses. 2002. (Illus.). 32p. (J). (gr. 1-5). 16.95 (*1-58430-037-X*) Lee & Low Bks., Inc.

Bragg, Lynn E. A River Lost. 1995. (Illus.). 32p. (Orig.). (J). (gr. 2-8). pap. 12.95 (*0-88839-383-0*) Hancock Hse. Pubs.

Brittain, Bill. Shape-Changer. 1995. (Trophy Bk.). 112p. (J). (gr. 7 up). pap. 5.95 (*0-06-440514-1*, Harper Trophy) HarperCollins Children's Bk. Group.

—Shape-Changer. 1995. (J). 11.00 (*0-606-08453-3*) Turtleback Bks.

Brooks, Martha. Bone Dance. Date not set. 192p. (YA). (gr. 7 up). pap. (*0-88899-336-6*) Groundwood-Douglas & McIntyre CAN. *Dist:* Publishers Group West.

—Bone Dance. 1999. 192p. (YA). (gr. 7-12). mass mkt. 4.50 o.s.i (*0-440-22791-7*, Dell Books for Young Readers) Random Hse. Children's Bks.

—Bone Dance. 1997. (Illus.). 192p. (YA). (gr. 7-12). 16.95 (*0-531-30021-8*); lib. bdg. 17.99 (*0-531-33021-4*) Scholastic, Inc. (Orchard Bks.).

Brouwer, Sigmund. The Mystery Tribe of Camp Blackeagle. 2003. (Accidental Detectives Ser.). 144p. (J). pap. 5.99 (*0-7642-2570-7*) Bethany Hse. Pubs.

—The Mystery Tribe of Camp Blackeagle. (Accidental Detective Ser.: Vol. 2). 132p. 1997. pap. 4.99 o.p. (*0-89693-535-3*); 1994. (J). (gr. 4-7). pap. 4.99 o.p. (*1-56476-371-4*, 6-3371) Cook Communications Ministries.

Brown, Margaret Wise. David's Little Indian. 1992. 48p. (J). (ps-3). pap. 3.25 o.s.i (*0-440-40587-4*) Dell Publishing.

—David's Little Indian. 1992. (Illus.). 48p. (J). (gr. k-4). reprint ed. 11.95 o.s.i (*1-56282-209-8*) Hyperion Bks. for Children.

Brown, Towana J. Raglagger. 1989. (Illus.). 168p. (Orig.). (J). (gr. 5-7). pap. 3.50 (*0-9622060-2-4*) Brown, Towana J.

Brown, Vinson. Return of the Indian Spirit. Johnson, Phyllis, ed. 1995. (Illus.). 64p. (J). (gr. 3-7). text 6.95 o.p. (*0-89087-401-8*) Celestial Arts Publishing Co.

Brown, Virginia P. Cochula's Journey. 1996. 160p. (J). (gr. 5-8). 18.00 (*1-881320-40-5*, Black Belt Pr.) River City Publishing.

—The Gold Disc of Coosa. 7.95 o.p. (*0-87397-085-3*, Strode Pubs.) Circle Bk. Service, Inc.

Bruchac, James & Bruchac, Joseph. When the Chenoo Howls: Native American Tales of Terror. 1999. (Illus.). 136p. (J). (gr. 3-7). 16.95 (*0-8027-8638-3*); pap. 8.95 (*0-8027-7576-4*) Walker & Co.

Bruchac, Joseph. The Arrow over the Door. (Illus.). 96p. (J). 2002. pap. 4.99 (*0-14-130571-1*, Puffin Bks.); 1998. (gr. 2-4). 15.99 (*0-8037-2078-5*, Dial Bks. for Young Readers) Penguin Putnam Bks. for Young Readers.

—Crazy Horse's Vision. ed. 2001. (J). (gr. 1). spiral bd. (*0-616-07251-1*) Canadian National Institute for the Blind/Institut National Canadien pour les Aveugles.

—Eagle Song. 1997. (Illus.). 80p. (J). (gr. 2-4). 14.89 o.s.i (*0-8037-1919-1*); 14.99 o.p. (*0-8037-1918-3*) Penguin Putnam Bks. for Young Readers. (Dial Bks. for Young Readers).

—First Strawberries: A Cherokee Story. 1998. (Picture Bks.). (Illus.). 32p. (J). (ps-3). pap. 6.99 (*0-14-056409-8*, Puffin Bks.) Penguin Putnam Bks. for Young Readers.

—First Strawberries: A Cherokee Story. 1998. (Picture Puffin Ser.). 13.14 (*0-606-13388-7*) Turtleback Bks.

—Fox Song. 1993. (Illus.). 32p. (J). (ps). 14.95 o.p. (*0-399-22346-0*, Philomel) Penguin Putnam Bks. for Young Readers.

—The Heart of a Chief. 1998. 160p. (J). (gr. 4-7). 16.99 o.p. (*0-8037-2276-1*, Dial Bks. for Young Readers) Penguin Putnam Bks. for Young Readers.

—The Heart of a Chief. l.t. ed. 2002. 175p. (J). 21.95 (*0-7862-4453-4*) Thorndike Pr.

—The Heart of a Chief. 2001. (J). 12.04 (*0-606-21230-2*) Turtleback Bks.

—Sacajawea. 2001. 208p. (YA). (gr. 7 up). pap. 4.99 (*0-439-28068-0*) Scholastic, Inc.

—Squanto's Journey: The Story of the First Thanksgiving. 2000. (Illus.). 32p. (J). (gr. 2-5). 16.00 (0-15-201817-4, Silver Whistle) Harcourt Children's Bks.

—Squanto's Journey: The Story of the First Thanksgiving. 2000. (Illus.). 32p. (gr. 1-4). 19.98 (0-7398-3072-4) Raintree Pubs.

—The Warriors. 2003. 120p. (J). 15.95 (1-58196-002-6) Darby Creek Publishing.

—13 Moons on Turtle's Back: A Native American Year of Moons. 1997. 12.14 (0-606-12824-7) Turtleback Bks.

Buff, Mary & Buff, Conrad. Hah-Nee, 001. 1965. (J). (gr. 4-6). 5.95 o.p. (0-395-15081-7) Houghton Mifflin Co.

Bulla, Clyde Robert. Eagle Feather. 1994. (Illus.). 96p. (J). (gr. 3-7). pap. 4.99 (0-14-036730-6, Puffin Bks.) Penguin Putnam Bks. for Young Readers.

—Eagle Feather. 1994. 10.04 (0-606-06343-9) Turtleback Bks.

—Pocahontas & the Strangers. 1987. (Illus.). 176p. (J). (ps-3). mass mkt. 4.50 (0-590-43481-0) Scholastic, Inc.

Bulla, Clyde Robert & Syson, Michael. Conquista! 1978. (Illus.). (J). (gr. 2-5). lib. bdg. 12.89 (0-690-03871-2) HarperCollins Children's Bk. Group.

Burke, Wallace E. Night Hawk. 1994. (Anasazi Ser.: Bk. II). (Illus.). 225p. (Orig.). (YA). pap. 10.95 (0-9639014-1-9) WEB Publishing Co.

Butler, Amy. Virginia Bound. 2003. 192p. (J). (gr. 5-9). tchr. ed. 15.00 (0-618-24752-1, Clarion Bks.) Houghton Mifflin Co. Trade & Reference Div.

Byrd, Sandra. Indian Summer. 12th ed. 2000. (Secret Sisters Ser.: Vol. 12). 112p. (J). (gr. 3-7). pap. 4.95 (1-57856-270-8) WaterBrook Pr.

Calvert, Patricia. Betrayed! 224p. (J). 2004. (Illus.). pap. 4.99 (0-689-86693-3, Aladdin); 2002. (gr. 7 up). 16.00 (0-689-83472-1, Atheneum) Simon & Schuster Children's Publishing.

Cameron, Anne. Dreamspeaker. 2000. 128p. (YA). (gr. 7-9). mass mkt. 5.95 (0-7736-7482-9) Stoddart Kids CAN. Dist: Fitzhenry & Whiteside, Ltd.

Campbell Hale, Janet. Owl's Song. 1998. 153p. (J). pap. 12.95 (0-8263-1861-4) Univ. of New Mexico Pr.

Campbell, Karel. Blue Jay & the Monster. 1967. (Illus.). (J). (gr. k-5). lib. bdg. 3.95 o.p. (0-8225-0258-5) Lerner Publishing Group.

Cannon, A. E. Shadow Brothers. 1992. mass mkt. 3.99 (0-440-80328-4) Bantam Bks.

—Shadow Brothers. 1990. 9.09 (0-606-00748-2) Turtleback Bks.

—The Shadow Brothers. 1992. 192p. (YA). (gr. 7 up). mass mkt. 3.99 o.s.i (0-440-21167-0) Dell Publishing.

Castler, Leigh. The Boy Who Dreamed of an Acorn. 1994. (Illus.). 32p. (J). (ps up). 15.95 o.s.i (0-399-22547-1, Philomel) Penguin Putnam Bks. for Young Readers.

Cavanagh, Helen. Panther Glade. 1993. 160p. (J). (gr. 5-9). mass mkt. 16.00 (0-671-75617-6, Simon & Schuster Children's Publishing) Simon & Schuster Children's Publishing.

Chacon, Michelle N. & Strete, Craig K. How the Indians Bought the Farm. 1996. (Illus.). 32p. (J). (gr. k up). 15.00 o.p. (0-688-14130-7, Greenwillow Bks.) HarperCollins Children's Bk. Group.

Chandler, Edna W. Charley Brave. 1962. (Illus.). (gr. 3-5). 5.50 o.p. (0-8075-1129-3) Whitman, Albert & Co.

Chandonnet, Ann. Chief Stephen's Parky. 2nd ed. 1993. (Council for Indian Education Ser.). (Illus.). 80p. (J). (gr. 4-7). reprint ed. pap. 7.95 o.p. (1-879373-39-4) Rinehart, Roberts Pubs.

Chanin, Michael. The Chief's Blanket. 1998. (Illus.). 32p. (J). (ps-5). 14.95 (0-915811-78-2, Starseed Pr.) Kramer, H.J. Inc.

Cherokee Windsong. 1996. (Orig.). (YA). (gr. 10 up). lib. bdg. 15.00 o.p. (0-88092-301-6) Royal Fireworks Publishing Co.

Christian Family Classics. 1974. 128p. (gr. 5-8). pap. 1.25 o.p. (0-912692-47-2) Cook, David C. Publishing Co.

Clark, Ann Nolan. Bringer of the Mystery Dog. 2000. (Illus.). 48p. (J). (gr. k-5). pap. 6.95 (1-885772-20-3) Kiva Publishing, Inc.

Clark, Della R. Quiet One. 1992. (Illus.). 64p. (J). (ps-5). 15.00 (0-9631252-0-6) Desert Rose Publishing.

Clark, N. Laurie. It's Wesley! The Adirondack Guide. 1998. (Illus.). 32p. (J). (gr. k up). per. 14.95 (0-9641197-1-4) Clark Pubs.

Clifford, Eth. The Year of the Three-Legged Deer. Cuffari, Richard, tr. & illus. by. 2003. (Library of Indiana Classics). xix, 164p. (YA). 32.95 (0-253-34251-1); pap. 14.95 (0-253-21604-4) Indiana Univ. Pr.

Clifford, Mary L. When the Great Canoes Came. 1993. (Illus.). 144p. (J). 12.95 o.s.i (0-88289-926-0); (gr. 4-7). pap. 12.95 (1-56554-646-6) Pelican Publishing Co., Inc.

Coates, Belle. Mak, 001. 1981. (J). (gr. 5 up). 8.95 o.p. (0-395-31603-0) Houghton Mifflin Co.

Cochran, Sallie B. Brave Star & the Necklace. 1991. (Illus.). 23p. (Orig.). (J). (gr. 4-7). pap. 10.95 (0-9629612-0-5) Isabel's.

Coerr, Eleanor. The Bell Ringer & the Pirates. 1983. (I Can Read Bks.). (Illus.). 64p. (J). (ps-3). 9.95 (0-06-021354-X); lib. bdg. 10.89 o.p. (0-06-021355-8) HarperCollins Children's Bk. Group.

Cone, Molly. Number Four, 001. 1972. (Illus.). 160p. (J). (gr. 5-9). 6.95 o.p. (0-395-13889-2) Houghton Mifflin Co.

Connolly, Thomas E. A Coeur D'Alene Indian Story. 1990. 85p. (J). pap. 4.50 o.s.i (0-87770-483-X) Ye Galleon Pr.

Cooney, Caroline B. The Ransom of Mercy Carter. 2001. (Illus.). 256p. (YA). (gr. 7 up). 15.95 (0-385-32615-7, Delacorte Bks. for Young Readers) Random Hse. Children's Bks.

—The Ransom of Mercy Carter. 2002. 256p. (YA). (gr. 7 up). mass mkt. 5.50 (0-440-22775-5) Random Hse., Inc.

Cooper, James Fenimore. The Last of the Mohicans. 2002. (Great Illustrated Classics). (Illus.). 240p. (J). (gr. 3-8). lib. bdg. 21.35 (1-57765-692-X, ABDO & Daughters) ABDO Publishing Co.

—The Last of the Mohicans. 1964. (Airmont Classics Ser.). (J). (gr. 6 up). pap. 3.50 o.p. (0-8049-0005-1, CL-5) Airmont Publishing Co., Inc.

—The Last of the Mohicans. 1989. (Illus.). (J). (ps up). 26.95 (0-89968-254-5) Buccaneer Bks., Inc.

—The Last of the Mohicans. Wright, Robin S., ed. & abr. by. 1976. (Illus.). (J). (gr. 7 up). 7.95 o.p. (0-679-20372-9) McKay, David Co., Inc.

—The Last of the Mohicans. 1962. 432p. (J). (gr. 7). mass mkt. 2.95 o.p. (0-451-52329-6); (Illus.). mass mkt. 4.95 o.s.i (0-451-52503-5) NAL. (Signet Classics).

—The Last of the Mohicans. Farr, Naunerle C., ed. abr. ed. 1977. (Now Age Illustrated III Ser.). (Illus.). (J). (gr. 4-12). text 7.50 o.p. (0-88301-279-0); pap. text 2.95 (0-88301-267-7) Pendulum Pr., Inc.

—The Last of the Mohicans. 9999. (Children's Classics Ser.: No. 740-14). (Illus.). (J). (gr. 3-5). text 3.50 o.p. (0-7214-0789-7, Ladybird Bks.) Penguin Group (USA) Inc.

—The Last of the Mohicans. Vogel, Malvina, ed. 1992. (Great Illustrated Classics Ser.: Vol. 24). (Illus.). 240p. (J). (gr. 3-6). 9.95 (0-86611-975-2) Playmore, Inc., Pubs.

—The Last of the Mohicans. 1987. (Regents Illustrated Classics Ser.). (J). (gr. 7-12). pap. text 3.75 o.p. (0-13-523952-4, 20569) Prentice Hall, ESL Dept.

—The Last of the Mohicans. 1993. (Step into Classics Ser.). (Illus.). 112p. (J). (gr. 3-5). pap. 3.99 (0-679-84706-5, Random Hse. Bks. for Young Readers) Random Hse. Children's Bks.

—The Last of the Mohicans. 1986. (Illus.). 376p. (J). 75.00 o.s.i (0-684-18716-7); (YA). (gr. 4-7). 28.00 (0-684-18711-6) Simon & Schuster Children's Publishing. (Atheneum).

—The Last of the Mohicans. (Saddleback Classics). (J). 2001. (Illus.). 13.10 (0-606-21559-X); 1993. 10.04 (0-606-02705-X) Turtleback Bks.

—The Last of the Mohicans. abr. ed. 2002. (Scribner Storybook Classic Ser.). (Illus.). 64p. (J). (gr. 3-6). 18.95 (0-689-84068-3, Atheneum) Simon & Schuster Children's Publishing.

—The Last of the Mohicans. adapted ed. 1997. (Living Classics Ser.). (Illus.). 32p. (J). (gr. 3-7). 14.95 o.p. (0-7641-7048-1) Barron's Educational Series, Inc.

—The Last of the Mohicans. 1826. 423p. (YA). reprint ed. pap. text 28.00 (1-4047-2374-9) Classic Textbooks.

—The Last of the Mohicans. 2nd ed. 1998. (Illustrated Classic Book Ser.). (Illus.). 61p. (J). (gr. 3 up). reprint ed. pap. text 4.95 (1-56767-249-3) Educational Insights, Inc.

—Prairie. 1964. (Airmont Classics Ser.). (J). (gr. 8 up). mass mkt. 1.95 o.p. (0-8049-0041-8, CL-41) Airmont Publishing Co., Inc.

—Prairie. 1964. 416p. (YA). (gr. 10). mass mkt. 4.95 o.p. (0-451-52516-7, CE1780); mass mkt. 4.50 o.p. (0-451-52235-4) NAL. (Signet Classics).

Coren, Alan. Arthur's Last Stand. 1979. (Illus.). (J). (gr. 4-6). o.p. (0-316-15742-2) Little Brown & Co.

Cornelissen, Cornelia. Soft Rain: A Story of the Cherokee Trail of Tears. 1999. (Illus.). 128p. (gr. 3-7). pap. text 4.50 (0-440-41242-0) Bantam Bks.

—Soft Rain: A Story of the Cherokee Trail of Tears. 1999. (J). 10.55 (0-606-18968-8) Turtleback Bks.

Cossi, Olga. Fire Mate. rev. ed. 1991. (Council for Indian Education Ser.). 350p. (gr. 4-8). pap. 7.95 (1-879373-87-4) Rinehart, Roberts Pubs.

Creech, Sharon. Absolutely Normal Chaos; Walk Two Moons; Chasing Redbird. 2001. (J). (gr. 3-7). pap. 17.85 (0-06-441008-0, Harper Trophy) HarperCollins Children's Bk. Group.

—Chasing Redbird. 1998. (J). 11.00 (0-606-13265-1) Turtleback Bks.

Creel, Ann H. Water at the Blue Earth. 1998. (Illus.). 112p. (gr. 5-9). pap. 8.95 (1-57098-224-4) Rinehart, Roberts Pubs.

Crew, Linda. Nekomah Creek. (Illus.). 192p. (gr. 4-7). 1993. pap. text 3.99 o.s.i (0-440-40788-5); 1991. (J). 14.00 o.s.i (0-385-30442-0, Delacorte Pr.) Dell Publishing.

—Nekomah Creek. 2001. (Illus.). 192p. (gr. 4-7). pap. text 12.00 (0-375-89506-X, Random Hse. Bks. for Young Readers); 1991. (J). o.s.i (0-385-30379-3, Dell Books for Young Readers) Random Hse. Children's Bks.

—Nekomah Creek. 1991. 9.09 (0-606-05506-1) Turtleback Bks.

Crook, Connie Brummel. Maple Moon. unabr. ed. 1998. (Illus.). 32p. (YA). (ps-2). (0-7737-3017-6) Stoddart Kids.

—Maple Moon. 2000. (Illus.). 32p. (J). (ps-3). pap. 6.95 (0-7737-6098-9) Stoddart Kids CAN. Dist: Fitzhenry & Whiteside, Ltd.

Crum, Sally. Race to the Moonrise: An Ancient Journey. 1998. (Illus.). 99p. (J). pap. 9.95 (1-890437-21-2) Western Reflections Publishing Co.

Cunningham, Chet. Fort Blood. l.t. ed. 2002. (Thorndike Western Ser.). 224p. 25.95 (0-7862-3810-0) Gale Group.

Curry, Jane Louise. Back in the Beforetime: Tales of the California Indians. 1987. (Illus.). 144p. (J). (gr. 3-7). 17.95 (0-689-50410-1, McElderry, Margaret K.) Simon & Schuster Children's Publishing.

Cutler, Ebbitt. I Once Knew an Indian Woman. 1985. (Illus.). 72p. (J). (gr. 5 up). 7.95 o.p. (0-395-16044-8) Houghton Mifflin Co.

—I Once Knew an Indian Woman. (Illus.). E-Book 4.95 (0-88776-531-9) McClelland & Stewart/ Tundra Bks.

—I Once Knew an Indian Woman. 1975. (Illus.). 80p. (YA). (gr. 7 up). pap. 6.95 (0-88776-068-6) Tundra Bks. of Northern New York.

Dadey, Debbie. Cherokee Sister. 128p. (gr. 3-7). 2001. pap. text 4.50 o.s.i (0-440-41568-3, Yearling); 2000. text 14.95 o.s.i (0-385-32703-X, Delacorte Bks. for Young Readers) Random Hse. Children's Bks.

Dalgliesh, Alice. The Courage of Sarah Noble. 2002. (Illus.). (J). 13.40 (0-7587-0249-3) Book Wholesalers, Inc.

—The Courage of Sarah Noble. unabr. ed. 1954. (J). 24.20 incl. audio (0-7887-2658-7, 40818) Recorded Bks., LLC.

—The Courage of Sarah Noble. 9999. (J). pap. 1.95 o.s.i (0-590-30049-0) Scholastic, Inc.

—The Courage of Sarah Noble. (Illus.). 64p. (J). (gr. 2-6). reprint ed. 1987. 16.99 (0-684-18830-9, Atheneum); 2nd ed. 1991. pap. 4.99 (0-689-71540-4, Aladdin) Simon & Schuster Children's Publishing.

—The Courage of Sarah Noble. 2nd ed. 1991. (J). 11.14 (0-606-02070-5) Turtleback Bks.

Darwin, Beatrice, illus. If You Lived with the Sioux Indians. 1992. 80p. (J). (ps-3). pap. 5.99 o.s.i (0-590-45162-6) Scholastic, Inc.

Davis, R. Dell. Ashes & Sparks, Set. 1989. (Illus.). 172p. text 24.95 incl. audio (0-9616736-1-3) Franklin, J. Pub.

Davis, Russell B. & Ashabranner, Brent K. The Choctaw Code. 1994. (Illus.). 152p. (J). (gr. 4-8). reprint ed. lib. bdg. 19.50 (0-208-02377-1, Linnet Bks.) Shoe String Pr., Inc.

De Angulo, Jaime. Indian Tales. 1984. (Illus.). 256p. (YA). (gr. 5 up). pap. 7.95 o.p. (0-8090-0049-0, Hill & Wang) Farrar, Straus & Giroux.

De Coteau Orie, Sandra. Did You Hear Wind Sing Your Name? 1995. (Illus.). 32p. (J). (ps-3). 14.95 (0-8027-8350-3); lib. bdg. 15.85 (0-8027-8351-1) Walker & Co.

de Paola, Tomie, ed. & illus. The Legend of the Indian Paintbrush. 1988. 40p. (J). (ps-3). 16.99 (0-399-21534-4, G. P. Putnam's Sons) Penguin Group (USA) Inc.

Deans, Sis B. Blazing Bear. 1992. (Illus.). 40p. (J). (gr. 1-6). pap. 7.95 (0-932433-94-4) Windswept Hse. Pubs.

Dell, Pamela. Giles & Metacom: A Story about Plimouth Colony & the Wampanoag. 2002. (Illus.). 48p. (J). (gr. 3-8). lib. bdg. 27.07 (1-59187-012-7) Child's World, Inc.

Desai, Anita. The Village by the Sea. l.t. ed. 1988. 320p. (J). (gr. 5 up). 16.95 o.p. (0-7451-0655-2, Galaxy Children's Large Print) BBC Audiobooks America.

Deschaine, Scott. Screaming Eagle. 1999. (Illus.). 296p. (J). 19.95 (1-878181-04-1) Discovery Comics.

Destiny Calls - Pocahontas. 1995. (Picture Window Ser.). (Illus.). 30p. (J). (ps-4). 9.98 o.p. (1-57082-241-7) Mouse Works.

Deur, Lynne. Nishnawbe: A Story of Indians in Michigan. 1996. (J). 8.95 o.p. (0-938682-00-8) River Road Pubns., Inc.

Dhondy, Farrukh. Poona Company. 1985. 160p. (J). (gr. 6-8). 16.95 o.p. (0-575-03555-2) Gollancz, Victor GBR. Dist: Trafalgar Square.

Disney Staff. Pocahontas: An Unlikely Pair. 1997. (Disney's "Storytime Treasures" Library: Vol. 10). (Illus.). 44p. (J). (gr. 1-6). 3.49 o.p. (1-57973-006-X) Advance Pubs. LLC.

Dorris, Michael. Sees Behind Trees. l.t. ed. (J). 1997. pap. 4.95 o.s.i (0-7868-1290-7); 1997. 112p. (gr. 3-7). reprint ed. pap. 4.95 o.s.i (0-7868-1252-4); 1999. 128p. (gr. 4 up). mass mkt. 4.99 (0-7868-1357-1) Disney Pr.

—Sees Behind Trees. 1996. (Illus.). 128p. (J). (gr. 3 up). 14.95 o.p. (0-7868-0224-3); (YA). (gr. 4-7). lib. bdg. 15.49 (0-7868-2215-5) Hyperion Bks. for Children.

—Sees Behind Trees. 104p. (J). (gr. 4-6). pap. 4.95 (0-8072-1516-3); 1998. pap. 28.00 incl. audio (0-8072-7957-9, YA949SP) Random Hse. Audio Publishing Group. (Listening Library).

—Sees Behind Trees. 1997. (J). 11.04 (0-606-12807-7) Turtleback Bks.

—The Window. 1997. (Illus.). 112p. (J). (gr. 4 up). 16.95 (0-7868-0301-0) Hyperion Bks. for Children.

Doughty, Wayne D. Crimson Mocassins. 1972. (Trophy Bk.). 224p. (YA). (gr. 7 up). pap. 2.95 (0-06-440015-8, Harper Trophy) HarperCollins Children's Bk. Group.

Downie, Mary Alice. Scared Sarah. 2002. (Illus.). 65p. pap. (1-55041-714-2); 57p. (J). (gr. 3-6). (1-55041-712-6) Fitzhenry & Whiteside, Ltd.

Downing, Sybil & Barker, Jane Valentine. Mesas to Mountains. (Colorado Heritage Ser.). (Illus.). 47p. (J). (ps-8). reprint ed. pap. 7.95 (1-878611-04-6) Silver Rim Pr.

Duey, Kathleen. Celou Sudden Shout: Idaho, 1826. 1998. (American Diaries Ser.: No. 9). 144p. (J). (gr. 3-7). pap. 4.50 o.s.i (0-689-81622-7, Aladdin) Simon & Schuster Children's Publishing.

Duncklee, John. Quest for the Eagle Feather. Max, Jill, ed. 1997. (Illus.). (J). (gr. 3-6). 112p. pap. 6.95 o.p. (0-87358-657-3); 104p. lib. bdg. 12.95 o.p. (0-87358-668-9) Northland Publishing. (Rising Moon Bks. for Young Readers).

—Quest for the Eagle Feather. 1997. 13.10 (0-606-17149-5) Turtleback Bks.

Durrant, Lynda. Echohawk. 1998. 192p. (gr. 5-9). pap. text 4.50 o.s.i (0-440-41438-5, Dell Books for Young Readers) Random Hse. Children's Bks.

—Echohawk. 1998. 10.55 (0-606-15514-7) Turtleback Bks.

—Turtle Clan Journey. 1999. 176p. (J). (gr. 5-9). tchr. ed. 15.00 (0-395-90369-6, Clarion Bks.) Houghton Mifflin Co. Trade & Reference Div.

Durrant, Lynda, illus. Echohawk. 1996. 192p. (J). (gr. 4-6). tchr. ed. 16.00 (0-395-74430-X, Clarion Bks.) Houghton Mifflin Co. Trade & Reference Div.

Dyer, T. A. The Whipman Is Watching, 001. 1979. (J). (gr. 5-9). 7.95 o.p. (0-395-28581-X) Houghton Mifflin Co.

Dygert, Janice. Red Horse & the Buffalo Robe Man. Gilliland, Hap, ed. 1978. (Indian Culture Ser.). (Illus.). 36p. (J). (gr. 4-8). pap. 4.95 (0-89992-074-8) Council for Indian Education.

Edmiston, Jim. Little Eagle Lots of Owls. 1993. (Illus.). 32p. (J). (gr. k-3). 13.95 o.p. (0-395-65564-1) Houghton Mifflin Co.

Eldridge, Melinda. Salcott, the Indian Boy. (Publish-a-Book Ser.). (Illus.). 32p. (J). 1990. lib. bdg. 21.40 o.p. (0-8172-2778-4); 1989. lib. bdg. 21.40 o.p. (0-8172-2462-9) Raintree Pubs.

Erdrich, Lise. Bears Make Rock Soup: And Other Stories. 2002. (Illus.). 32p. (J). (gr. 1 up). 16.95 (0-89239-172-3) Children's Bk. Pr.

Esbensen, Barbara Juster. The Star Maiden: An Ojibway Tale. 1988. (J). 12.10 (0-606-00771-7) Turtleback Bks.

Faber, Gail & Lasagna, Michele. Clara Rides the Rancho. (Whispers Ser.). (Illus.). (J). (gr. 3-7). 2002. 52p. pap., tchr.'s training gde. ed. 10.95 (0-936480-17-3); 2001. 185p. 12.95 (0-936480-16-5); 2001. 185p. pap. 9.95 (0-936480-15-7) Magpie Pubns.

Feder, Harriet K. Death on Sacred Ground. 2001. (Young Adult Fiction Ser.). (Illus.). 192p. (J). (gr. 7-12). lib. bdg. 14.95 (0-8225-0741-2, Lerner Pubns.) Lerner Publishing Group.

Fleischman, Paul. Saturnalia. 1990. (Charlotte Zolotow Bk.). 128p. (YA). (gr. 7 up). 14.95 o.s.i (0-06-021912-2); lib. bdg. 14.89 o.s.i (0-06-021913-0) HarperCollins Children's Bk. Group.

Frame, Laurence A. The New Window (La Ventana Nueva), Vol. 1. 1994. (Native American - Mission Ser.). (ENG & SPA., Illus.). 30p. (J). (gr. 2-8). pap. 10.00 (1-884480-54-3) Sports Curriculum.

Francis, Lee & Bruchac, James, eds. Reclaiming the Vision: Past, Present, & Future: Native Voices for the Eighth Generation. 1996. (Illus.). 120p. (Orig.). (YA). (gr. 9-12). pap. 15.95 (0-87886-140-8) Ithaca Hse.

Francisco, Nia. Blue Horses for Navajo Women. 1988. (Illus.). 80p. (J). pap. 9.95 (0-912678-72-0, Greenfield Review Pr.) Greenfield Review Literary Ctr., Inc.

Freeman, Bill. Sioux Winter. 1999. (Illus.). 141p. (J). (gr. 3-7). pap. 6.95 (*1-55028-652-8*) Lorimer, James & Co. CAN. *Dist:* Orca Bk. Pubs.

Fregosi, Claudia. A Gift. 1976. (Illus.). (J). (gr. k-3). o.p. (*0-13-356220-4*) Prentice-Hall.

Friskey, Margaret. Indian Two Feet & His Eagle Feather. 1967. (Indian Two Feet Ser.). (Illus.). 64p. (J). (gr. k-3). lib. bdg. 15.93 o.p. (*0-516-03503-7*, Children's Pr.) Scholastic Library Publishing.

—Indian Two Feet & His Horse. 1959. (Illus.). 64p. (J). (gr. k-3). 15.93 o.p. (*0-516-03501-0*, Children's Pr.) Scholastic Library Publishing.

—Indian Two Feet & His Horse. 9999. (J). pap. 1.50 o.p. (*0-590-08056-3*) Scholastic, Inc.

—Indian Two Feet & the ABC Moose Hunt. 1977. (Indian Two Feet Ser.). (Illus.). 32p. (J). (gr. k-2). lib. bdg. 15.00 o.p. (*0-516-03500-2*, Children's Pr.) Scholastic Library Publishing.

—Indian Two Feet & the Wolf Cubs. 1971. (Illus.). 64p. (J). (gr. k-3). lib. bdg. 15.93 o.p. (*0-516-03506-1*, Children's Pr.) Scholastic Library Publishing.

—Indian Two Feet Rides Alone. 1980. (Indian Two Feet Ser.). (Illus.). 32p. (J). (gr. k-3). pap. 2.95 o.p. (*0-516-43523-X*); lib. bdg. 15.00 o.p. (*0-516-03523-1*) Scholastic Library Publishing. (Children's Pr.).

Fritz, Jean. The Good Giants & the Bad Pukwudgies. (Illus.). 40p. (J). (gr. 3-7). 1989. 5.95 o.s.i (*0-399-21732-0*); 1982. 10.95 o.p. (*0-399-20870-4*) Putnam Publishing Group, The. (Sandcastle Bks.).

Frye, Mary M. The Boy Who Almost Lost His Name, 5 vols., Vol .2. Willis, Henry J., tr. from CHO. 2001. (Illus.). 40p. (J). 20.00 (*0-9710250-1-0*) Choctaw Crafts & Bks.

Gage, Wilson. Secret of Indian Mound. 1974. (J). (gr. 4-6). pap. (*0-671-29718-X*, Simon Pulse) Simon & Schuster Children's Publishing.

Gallagher, Diana G. Poison in Paradise! 1996. (Secret World of Alex Mack Ser.: No. 9). 144p. (J). (gr. 4-7). pap. 3.99 (*0-671-00083-7*, Aladdin) Simon & Schuster Children's Publishing.

Garaway, Margaret K. Dezbah & the Dancing Tumbleweeds. 1990. (Illus.). 175p. (J). (gr. 3-5). pap. 7.95 o.p. (*0-918080-50-9*) Treasure Chest Bks.

Gardner, Sonia. Eagle Feather. 1997. (Illus.). 40p. (J). (gr. 3-6). 19.95 (*1-885101-17-1*) Writers Pr., Inc.

Garland, Sherry. The Last Rainmaker. 1997. 336p. (YA). (gr. 5-11). 12.00 (*0-15-200649-4*) Harcourt Children's Bks.

—The Last Rainmaker. 1997. (J). 12.05 (*0-606-11550-1*) Turtleback Bks.

—Rainmaker's Dream. 1997. 336p. (J). (gr. 8 up). pap. 6.00 o.s.i (*0-15-200652-4*, Harcourt Paperbacks) Harcourt Children's Bks.

George, Jean Craighead. Julie. (Trophy Bk.). (Illus.). 240p. (gr. 5 up). 1996. (J). pap. 5.99 (*0-06-440573-7*, Harper Trophy); 1994. (J). 16.95 (*0-06-023528-4*); 1994. (YA). lib. bdg. 14.89 o.p. (*0-06-023529-2*) HarperCollins Children's Bk. Group.

—Julie. 1996. (YA). (gr. 5 up). 11.00 (*0-606-08788-5*) Turtleback Bks.

—Julie of the Wolves. l.t. ed. 1987. (Illus.). 260p. (J). (gr. 3-7). lib. bdg. 14.95 o.p. (*1-55736-053-7*) Bantam Doubleday Dell Large Print Group, Inc.

—Julie of the Wolves. 1986. (J). pap. 1.50 o.s.i (*0-440-84444-4*) Dell Publishing.

—Julie of the Wolves. l.t. ed. 1973. (Illus.). (J). lib. bdg. 6.95 o.p. (*0-8161-6102-X*, Macmillan Reference USA) Gale Group.

—Julie of the Wolves. (Julie of the Wolves Ser.). (Illus.). 2003. 176p. (J). pap. 5.99 (*0-06-054095-8*, Harper Trophy); 1996. 180p. (YA). (gr. 7 up). pap. 2.25 o.p. (*0-06-447146-2*, Harper Trophy); 1972. 192p. (J). (gr. 7 up). 15.99 (*0-06-021943-2*); 1972. 176p. (J). (gr. 7 up). pap. 5.99 (*0-06-440058-1*, Harper Trophy); 1972. 192p. (J). (gr. 7 up). lib. bdg. 16.89 (*0-06-021944-0*) HarperCollins Children's Bk. Group.

—Julie of the Wolves. 1974. (J). 12.00 (*0-606-03699-7*) Turtleback Bks.

—Julie's Wolf Pack. (Julie of the Wolves Ser.). (Illus.). 208p. (J). (gr. 5 up). 1999. pap. 5.99 (*0-06-440721-7*, Harper Trophy); 1997. 16.95 (*0-06-027406-9*); 1997. lib. bdg. 17.89 (*0-06-027407-7*) HarperCollins Children's Bk. Group.

—The Talking Earth. (Trophy Bk.). 160p. (gr. 6 up). 1987. (J). pap. 5.99 (*0-06-440212-6*, Harper Trophy); 1983. (J). lib. bdg. 16.89 (*0-06-021976-9*); 1983. (YA). 14.00 (*0-06-021975-0*) HarperCollins Children's Bk. Group.

Gessner. Brother to the Navajo. 1979. (J). 8.95 o.p. (*0-525-66659-1*) NAL.

—To See a Witch. 1978. (J). 6.95 o.p. (*0-525-66589-7*) NAL.

Gilliland, Hap. Coyote's Pow-Wow. 1972. (Indian Culture Ser.). (Illus.). 31p. (J). (gr. k-4). pap. 4.95 (*0-89992-105-1*) Council for Indian Education.

—Flint's Rock. 2000. (Council for Indian Education Ser.). (Illus.). 80p. (gr. 4 up). pap. 8.95 (*1-879373-82-3*) Rinehart, Roberts Pubs.

Girion, Barbara. Indian Summer. 1990. (J). pap. 11.95 o.p. (*0-590-42636-2*) Scholastic, Inc.

Goble, Paul. Beyond the Ridge. (Illus.). 32p. (J). (ps-3). 1989. lib. bdg. 14.95 o.s.i (*0-02-736581-6*, Simon & Schuster Children's Publishing); 1993. reprint ed. pap. 5.99 (*0-689-71731-8*, Aladdin) Simon & Schuster Children's Publishing.

—Beyond the Ridge. 1993. 12.14 (*0-606-05159-7*) Turtleback Bks.

—Crow Chief: A Plains Indian Story. (Illus.). 32p. (J). (ps-3). 1996. mass mkt. 5.95 (*0-531-07064-6*); 1992. pap. 16.95 (*0-531-05947-2*) Scholastic, Inc. (Orchard Bks.).

—Gift of the Sacred Dog. 1980. (Reading Rainbow Bks.). (J). 12.14 (*0-606-02555-3*) Turtleback Bks.

—The Girl Who Loved Wild Horses. (Illus.). 32p. (J). (gr. k-3). 1986. reprint ed. pap. 3.95 o.s.i (*0-689-71082-8*, Aladdin); rev. ed. 1982. lib. bdg. 17.00 (*0-02-736570-0*, Atheneum/Richard Jackson Bks.); 2nd ed. 1993. reprint ed. pap. 6.99 (*0-689-71696-6*, Aladdin) Simon & Schuster Children's Publishing.

—The Girl Who Loved Wild Horses. 1986. (J). 12.14 (*0-606-03219-3*) Turtleback Bks.

—Love Flute. 1997. (Illus.). 32p. (J). (gr. k-3). pap. 6.99 (*0-689-81683-9*, Aladdin) Simon & Schuster Children's Publishing.

Godden, Rumer. The Valiant Chatti-Maker. 1983. (Illus.). 64p. (J). (gr. 3-7). 9.95 o.p. (*0-670-74236-8*, Viking Children's Bks.) Penguin Putnam Bks. for Young Readers.

Golden Gate Junior Books Staff. Little Too-Tall. 1988. (Magic Castle Readers Ser.). (Illus.). (J). pap. 3.50 o.p. (*0-516-45721-7*, Children's Pr.) Scholastic Library Publishing.

Golio, Janet & Golio, Mike. A Present from the Past. Anderson, David & Tronslin, Andrea, eds. 1995. (Environmental Adventure Ser.). 159p. (J). (gr. 4-6). pap. 8.95 (*0-9641330-5-9*) Portunus Publishing Co.

Golio, Janet, et al. A Present from the Past: Multimedia Edition. 2000. (Illus.). III, 157p. (J). (gr. 4-7). cd-rom 14.95 (*0-9704202-0-X*) GAGA.

Gould, Carol. My Native American School. l.t. ed. 1996. (Illus.). 16p. (J). (gr. k-2). pap. 4.95 (*1-879835-77-0*) Kaeden Corp.

Green, Timothy. Mystery of Coyote Canyon. 1994. (Illus.). 150p. (YA). (gr. 8-12). pap. 12.95 (*0-941270-83-1*) Ancient City Pr., Inc.

Gregory, Kristiana. Jenny of the Tetons. (Great Episodes Ser.). 2002. 192p. (YA). pap. 6.00 (*0-15-216770-6*); 1991. 160p. (YA). (gr. 3-7). pap. 6.00 o.p. (*0-15-200481-5*); 1989. 144p. (J). (gr. 4-7). 13.95 o.s.i (*0-15-200480-7*) Harcourt Children's Bks. (Gulliver Bks.).

—The Legend of Jimmy Spoon. (Great Episodes Ser.). 2002. 224p. (YA). pap. 6.00 (*0-15-216776-5*, Gulliver Bks.); 1991. 208p. (YA). (gr. 3-7). pap. 6.00 o.p. (*0-15-243812-2*, Gulliver Bks.); 1990. 165p. (J). (gr. 3-7). 15.95 (*0-15-200506-4*) Harcourt Children's Bks.

—The Legend of Jimmy Spoon. 1991. (J). (gr. 4-7). 12.05 (*0-606-12391-1*) Turtleback Bks.

Griese, Arnold A. Anna's Athabaskan Summer. 2003. (Illus.). 32p. (J). pap. 8.95 (*1-56397-650-1*) Boyds Mills Pr.

Grokett, Jan. Songs of the Orcas. l.t. ed. 2002. 48p. (J). per. 9.99 (*1-893108-72-4*) Neighborhood Pr. Publishing.

Grutman, Jewel & Matthaei, Gaye. The Ledgerbook of Thomas Blue Eagle. 1994. (Illus.). 72p. (J). (gr. 4-7). 17.95 (*1-56566-063-3*) LegacyWords Publishing.

Guest, Jacqueline. Lightning Rider. 2001. (YA). (gr. 6-9). 144p. bds. 4.99 (*1-55028-721-4*); 177p. pap. 4.99 (*1-55028-720-6*) Lorimer, James & Co. CAN. *Dist:* Orca Bk. Pubs.

Hahn, Elizabeth. The Creek. 1992. (Native American People Ser.: Set III). (Illus.). 32p. (J). (gr. 3-6). lib. bdg. 27.93 (*0-86625-393-9*) Rourke Publishing, LLC.

Hale, Janet C. The Owl's Song. 1974. 168p. (J). (gr. 7-11). 4.95 o.p. (*0-385-05020-8*) Doubleday Publishing.

—The Owl's Song. 1976. 144p. (YA). (gr. 7 up). pap. 2.50 (*0-380-00605-7*, 60212-1, Avon Bks.) Morrow/Avon.

Hamilton, Elizabeth L. Secret of Cachuma Lake: Travel Adventure for Young Adults #1. 2001. (Illus.). 144p. (YA). per. 9.95 (*0-9713749-7-X*) Quiet Impact, Inc.

Hamilton, Virginia. Arilla Sun Down. 1997. mass mkt. 4.99 (*0-590-05380-9*); 1995. 272p. (YA). (gr. 7 up). pap. 4.99 (*0-590-22223-6*, Scholastic Paperbacks) Scholastic, Inc.

—Arilla Sun Down. 1995. 11.04 (*0-606-07207-1*) Turtleback Bks.

Hamm, Diane J. Daughter of Suqua. 1997. 160p. (J). (gr. 5-7). lib. bdg. 14.95 o.p. (*0-8075-1477-2*) Whitman, Albert & Co.

Harrell, Beatrice O. Longwalker's Journey: A Novel of the Choctaw Trail of Tears. Kane, Cindy, ed. 1999. (Illus.). 144p. (J). (gr. 3-6). 15.99 o.p. (*0-8037-2380-6*); 15.89 (*0-8037-2383-0*) Penguin Putnam Bks. for Young Readers. (Dial Bks. for Young Readers).

Harrison, Sue. Sisu. 1997. (Illus.). 198p. (YA). (gr. 7-12). 16.95 (*1-882376-40-4*); pap. 11.95 (*1-882376-39-0*) Thunder Bay Pr.

Hart, Alison. Danger at the Wild West Show. 2003. (History Mysteries Ser.: Vol. 19). (Illus.). 163p. (J). 10.95 (*1-58485-718-8*); pap. 6.95 (*1-58485-717-X*) Pleasant Co. Pubns. (American Girl).

Hausman, Gerald. The Coyote Bead. 2000. E-Book 10.00 (*1-57174-992-6*) Hampton Roads Publishing Co., Inc.

—The Coyote Bead. 1999. E-Book 11.95 (*0-585-36563-6*) netLibrary, Inc.

—Ghost Walk: Native American Tales of the Spirit. 1991. (Illus.). 128p. (YA). pap. 11.95 (*0-933553-07-2*) Mariposa Printing & Publishing, Inc.

Hemmeter, Karla. Handmade Necklace. l.t. ed. 2004. (Illus.). 16p. (J). (ps-6). pap. 5.00 (*1-891452-11-8*, 1) Heart Arbor Bks.

Hewitt, William. Across the Wide River. 2003. 104p. (J). 11.95 (*0-8263-2978-0*) Univ. of New Mexico Pr.

Hide & Squeak, Meeko. 1995. (Squeeze Me Bks.). (Illus.). 10p. (J). (ps-1). 6.98 o.p. (*1-57082-100-3*) Mouse Works.

Highwater, Jamake. ANPANO: An American Indian Odyssey. (Illus.). 256p. 1993. (YA). (gr. 7 up). lib. bdg. 14.89 o.p. (*0-06-022878-4*); 1992. (J). (gr. 7 up). pap. 7.95 (*0-06-440437-4*, Harper Trophy); 1977. (J). (gr. 5-9). 14.00 (*0-397-31750-6*) HarperCollins Children's Bk. Group.

—The Ceremony of Innocence. 1985. (Charlotte Zolotow Bk.). 192p. (YA). (gr. 7 up). 12.95 (*0-06-022301-4*); lib. bdg. 12.89 o.p. (*0-06-022302-2*) HarperCollins Children's Bk. Group.

—The Ghost Horse Cycle: Trilogy: Legend Days, the Ceremony of Innocence & I Wear the Morning Star. 1997. 515p. (J). reprint ed. lib. bdg. 36.95 (*0-7351-0002-0*) Replica Bks.

—I Wear the Morning Star. 1986. (Charlotte Zolotow Bk.). 160p. (YA). (gr. 7 up). 12.95 (*0-06-022355-3*); lib. bdg. 12.89 o.p. (*0-06-022356-1*) HarperCollins Children's Bk. Group.

Hill, Gerald N. The Year of the Indians. 1985. (Illus.). 54p. (Orig.). (J). (gr. 4-7). pap. 4.95 (*0-912133-06-6*) Hilltop Publishing Co.

Hill, Kirkpatrick. Winter Camp. 1995. 192p. (J). (gr. 4-7). pap. 5.99 (*0-14-037076-5*, Puffin Bks.) Penguin Putnam Bks. for Young Readers.

—Winter Camp. 1993. (Illus.). 192p. (J). (gr. 3-7). mass mkt. 15.00 o.s.i (*0-689-50588-4*, McElderry, Margaret K.) Simon & Schuster Children's Publishing.

—Winter Camp. 1995. (J). 11.04 (*0-606-08391-X*) Turtleback Bks.

—The Year of Miss Agnes. 128p. (J). (gr. 3-7). 2002. pap. 4.99 (*0-689-85124-3*, Aladdin); 2000. 16.00 (*0-689-82933-7*, McElderry, Margaret K.) Simon & Schuster Children's Publishing.

Hirschi, Ron. Seya's Song. 1993. (Illus.). 32p. (J). (gr. 1 up). reprint ed. pap. 7.95 o.s.i (*0-912365-91-9*) Sasquatch Bks.

Hobbs, William. Beardream. 1997. (Illus.). 32p. (J). (gr. 1-3). 17.00 (*0-689-31973-8*, Atheneum) Simon & Schuster Children's Publishing.

—Bearstone. Harcourt Brace Staff, ed. 93rd ed. 1993. (J). pap. text 17.60 (*0-15-300368-5*) Harcourt Children's Bks.

—Bearstone. 1991. 160p. (J). (gr. 4-7). reprint ed. pap. 5.99 (*0-380-71249-0*, Avon Bks.) Morrow/Avon.

—Bearstone. 1989. 144p. (YA). (gr. 7 up). 17.00 (*0-689-31496-5*, Atheneum) Simon & Schuster Children's Publishing.

—Bearstone. 1989. 10.55 (*0-606-05058-2*) Turtleback Bks.

—The Big Wander. 1994. 192p. (J). (gr. 4-7). reprint ed. pap. 5.95 (*0-380-72140-6*, Avon Bks.) Morrow/Avon.

—The Big Wander. unabr. ed. 1997. (J). Class Set. (gr. 5). pap. 100.80 incl. audio (*0-7887-3498-9*, 46110); Homework Set. 47.75 incl. audio (*0-7887-1848-7*, 40628) Recorded Bks., LLC.

—The Big Wander. 1992. 160p. (J). (gr. 4-7). 17.00 (*0-689-31767-0*, Atheneum) Simon & Schuster Children's Publishing.

—The Big Wander. 1992. 11.00 (*0-606-06231-9*) Turtleback Bks.

—Far North. (J). 2004. (Illus.). 304p. pap. 5.99 (*0-06-054096-6*, Harper Trophy); 1997. 224p. (gr. 5 up). pap. 5.99 (*0-380-72536-3*); 1996. 240p. (gr. 5 up). 15.95 (*0-688-14192-7*) HarperCollins Children's Bk. Group.

—Far North. 1997. (J). 11.04 (*0-606-11314-2*) Turtleback Bks.

—Ghost Canoe. 1997. (Illus.). 208p. (J). (gr. 5-9). 15.95 (*0-688-14193-5*) HarperCollins Children's Bk. Group.

—Ghost Canoe. 1998. (Avon Camelot Bks.). 208p. (J). (gr. 5-9). pap. 5.99 (*0-380-72537-1*, Avon Bks.) Morrow/Avon.

—Ghost Canoe. 1998. (J). 11.00 (*0-606-13420-4*) Turtleback Bks.

—Kokopelli's Flute. 1997. 176p. (J). (gr. 5 up). pap. 5.99 (*0-380-72818-4*, Harper Trophy) HarperCollins Children's Bk. Group.

—Kokopelli's Flute. 1995. 160p. (J). (gr. 4-9). 16.00 (*0-689-31974-6*, Atheneum) Simon & Schuster Children's Publishing.

—Kokopelli's Flute. 1997. (J). 11.00 (*0-606-11541-2*) Turtleback Bks.

Hoff, Syd. Little Chief. 1961. (I Can Read Bks.). (Illus.). 64p. (J). (ps-3). lib. bdg. 13.89 o.p. (*0-06-022501-7*) HarperCollins Children's Bk. Group.

Hollenbeck, K., retold by. Native American: How the Hopi Stopped the Wind. 1994. (Graphic Learning Multicultural Literature Program Ser.). (ENG & SPA., Illus.). (J). (gr. k-5). tchr. ed. 45.00 (*0-87746-446-4*) Graphic Learning.

Holm, Jennifer L. Boston Jane: An Adventure. 2001. (Boston Jane Ser.). 288p. (J). (gr. 5 up). 16.95 (*0-06-028738-1*); (Illus.). lib. bdg. 17.89 (*0-06-028739-X*) HarperCollins Children's Bk. Group.

—Boston Jane: Wilderness Days. (Boston Jane Ser.). 256p. (J). 2004. pap. 5.99 (*0-06-440881-7*, Harper Trophy); 2002. (gr. 5 up). 16.99 (*0-06-029043-9*); 2002. (gr. 5 up). lib. bdg. 18.89 (*0-06-029044-7*) HarperCollins Children's Bk. Group.

Holman, Felice. Real. 1997. 160p. (J). (gr. 4-9). 16.00 (*0-689-80772-4*, Atheneum) Simon & Schuster Children's Publishing.

Holmes, Mary Z. Cross of Gold. 1992. (History's Children Ser.). (Illus.). 48p. (J). (gr. 4-5). pap. o.p. (*0-8114-6432-6*); lib. bdg. 21.36 o.p. (*0-8114-3507-5*) Raintree Pubs.

Hopkins, Suzette. Little Wolf's Christmas. 2003. (Illus.). 21p. (J). bds. 7.95 (*1-932133-72-0*) Writers' Collective, The.

Houghton Mifflin Company Staff. High Elk's Treasure. 1992. (Literature Experience 1993 Ser.). (J). (gr. 7). pap. 11.04 (*0-395-61839-8*) Houghton Mifflin Co.

Houston, James. Drifting Snow: An Arctic Search. 1992. (Illus.). 160p. (YA). (gr. 5 up). lib. bdg. 13.95 o.s.i (*0-689-50563-9*, McElderry, Margaret K.) Simon & Schuster Children's Publishing.

—Eagle Mask: A West Coast Indian Tale. 1966. (Illus.). (J). (gr. 2-6). 5.50 o.p. (*0-15-224444-1*) Harcourt Children's Bks.

—The Falcon Bow: An Arctic Legend. 1986. 96p. (J). (gr. 3-7). lib. bdg. 13.95 o.s.i (*0-689-50411-X*, McElderry, Margaret K.) Simon & Schuster Children's Publishing.

Houston, James R. Long Claws: An Arctic Adventure. 97th ed. 1992. (Picture Puffin Ser.). (Illus.). 320p. (J). (ps-3). pap. 4.99 o.p. (*0-14-054522-0*, Puffin Bks.) Penguin Putnam Bks. for Young Readers.

Hudson, Jan. Dawn Rider. 2000. 176p. (J). (gr. 5-9). pap. 4.99 o.s.i (*0-698-11859-6*, PaperStar); 1990. 192p. (YA). (gr. 6 up). 14.95 o.p. (*0-399-22178-6*, Philomel) Penguin Putnam Bks. for Young Readers.

—Dawn Rider. 1992. 176p. (YA). pap. 3.25 o.p. (*0-590-44987-7*, Scholastic Paperbacks) Scholastic, Inc.

—Dawn Rider. 2000. (Illus.). (J). 11.04 (*0-606-18399-X*) Turtleback Bks.

Huff, Gary. Indian Tales That Teach. 1988. 80p. (J). (gr. k-4). pap. text 10.00 (*0-87322-129-X*, 4919, YMCA of the U.S.A.) Human Kinetics Pubs.

Hull, Robert. Indian Stories. 1994. (Tales from Around the World Ser.). (Illus.). 48p. (J). (gr. 4-6). ring bd. 24.26 (*1-56847-189-0*, AS189-0) Raintree Pubs.

Hutchen, Paul. The Indian Cemetery. rev. ed. 1998. (Sugar Creek Gang Ser.: Vol. 13). 128p. (J). (gr. 4-7). mass mkt. 4.99 (*0-8024-7017-3*) Moody Pr.

Indian Woodcarver. 1978. (Sharazad Stories Ser.). (ARA., Illus.). (J). (gr. 5-8). pap. 3.50 o.p. (*0-86685-257-3*) International Bk. Ctr., Inc.

Ingoglia, Gina. Pocahontas. 1997. (Wonderful World of Disney Ser.). (Illus.). 80p. (J). (gr. 3-7). pap. 3.25 (*0-7868-4216-4*) Disney Pr.

Irbinskas, Heather. How Jackrabbit Got His Very Long Ears. 1994. (Illus.). 32p. (J). (gr. k up). lib. bdg. 15.95 (*0-87358-566-6*, Rising Moon Bks. for Young Readers) Northland Publishing.

Irwin, Hadley. We Are Mesquakie, We Are One. 1980. 128p. (YA). (gr. 5 up). 10.95 o.s.i (*0-912670-85-1*) Feminist Pr. at The City Univ. of New York.

Jackson, Bill, illus. The Rattlesnake Necklace. 1998. (Cover-to-Cover Bks.). (J). (*0-7807-6789-6*) Perfection Learning Corp.

Jackson, Dave & Jackson, Meta. The Warrior's Challenge: David Zeisberger. 1996. (Trailblazer Bks.: Vol. 20). (Illus.). 144p. (J). (gr. 3-7). pap. 5.99 (*1-55661-473-X*) Bethany Hse. Pubs.

Jackson, Helen H. Ramona: Wyeth Edition. 1939. (Illus.). (YA). (gr. 6 up). reprint ed. 17.95 o.s.i (*0-316-45467-2*) Little Brown & Co.

Jacobs, Paul S. James Printer: A Novel of King Philip's War. (J). (gr. 4-7). 2000. 224p. 4.50 (*0-590-97541-2*); 1997. 208p. pap. 15.95 (*0-590-16381-7*) Scholastic, Inc.

Jacobs, Shannon K. Boy Who Loved Morning. 1993. (J). (ps-3). 15.95 o.p. (*0-316-45556-3*) Little Brown & Co.

James, Betsy. The Mud Family. 1998. (Illus.). 32p. (J). pap. 10.95 (*0-19-512479-0*) Oxford Univ. Pr., Inc.

—The Mud Family. 1994. (Illus.). 32p. (J). (ps-3). 15.95 o.p. (*0-399-22549-8*, G. P. Putnam's Sons) Penguin Group (USA) Inc.

James, J. Alison. Sing for a Gentle Rain. 1990. 224p. (YA). (gr. 7 up). lib. bdg. 14.95 o.p. (*0-689-31561-9*, Atheneum) Simon & Schuster Children's Publishing.

Jeffers, Susan. Brother Eagle, Sister Sky: A Message from Chief Seattle. 1993. (Illus.). (J). pap. o.p. (*0-14-054514-X*) NAL.

Jeffers, Susan, illus. Brother Eagle, Sister Sky: A Message from Chief Seattle. 2002. 20p. (J). (gr. 3-5). reprint ed. 16.00 (*0-7567-5580-8*) DIANE Publishing Co.

Jelinek, Donald A. Survivor of the Alamo: The Saga of Moses Rose, Who Fought for France with Napoleon Bonaparta - & Then for Texas with Jim Bowle, Davy Crockett & William Barret Travis at the Alamo. 1999. (Illus.). 253p. pap. (*0-9704607-0-8*) Jelinck, Donald A.

Johnson, Rodney. The Curse of the Royal Ruby: A Rinnah Two Feathers Mystery. 2002. (J). 10.95 (*0-9663473-9-0*) UglyTown.

—The Secret of Dead Man's Mine: A Rinnah Two Feathers Mystery. 2001. (Illus.). 241p. (J). (gr. 4-7). pap. 12.00 (*0-9663473-3-1*) UglyTown.

Jones, Jennifer. Heetunka's Harvest: A Tale of the Plains Indians. 1994. (Council for Indian Education Ser.). (Illus.). 32p. (J). (gr. 1-5). 15.95 (*1-879373-17-3*) Rinehart, Roberts Pubs.

Jones, Jennifer Berry. Heetunka's Harvest: A Tale of the Plains Indians. 1998. (Council for Indian Education Ser.). (Illus.). 256p. (gr. k-7). 8.95 (*1-57098-235-X*, Rinehart, Roberts International) Rinehart, Roberts Pubs.

Kabel, Larassa, illus. The Buffalo Robe. 1998. (Cover-to-Cover Bks.). (J). (*0-7807-6778-0*) Perfection Learning Corp.

Kachel, Limana. Homer Littlebird's Rabbit: Cheyenne Indian Story for Children. 1983. 32p. (J). (ps-2). pap. 2.45 (*0-89992-084-5*) Council for Indian Education.

Kalman, Bobbie. Celebrating the Pow Wow. 1997. (Crabapples Ser.). (J). 12.10 (*0-606-12650-3*) Turtleback Bks.

Katschke, Judy. The Case of the Wild Wolf River. 1998. (New Adventures of Mary-Kate & Ashley Ser.). 87p. (J). (gr. 2-7). mass mkt. 3.99 (*0-590-29401-6*) Scholastic, Inc.

Katz, Welwyn W. False Face. 1988. 208p. (J). (gr. 5-9). lib. bdg. 14.95 o.s.i (*0-689-50456-X*, McElderry, Margaret K.) Simon & Schuster Children's Publishing.

Keehn, Sally M. Moon of the Two Dark Horses. 1997. 224p. (gr. 5-12). pap. text 3.99 o.s.i (*0-440-41287-0*) Dell Publishing.

Keith, Harold. Komantcia. 2nd ed. 1991. 299p. (YA). (gr. 5 up). reprint ed. 17.00 o.p. (*0-927562-03-0*); pap. 10.00 o.p. (*0-927562-02-2*) Levite of Apache Publishing.

Kerr, Rita. Grey Eagle: The Story of a Creek Indian Boy. 1997. (J). 13.95 (*1-57168-200-7*) Eakin Pr.

Killingsworth, Monte. Circle Within a Circle. 1994. 176p. (YA). (gr. 7 up). pap. 14.95 (*0-689-50598-1*, McElderry, Margaret K.) Simon & Schuster Children's Publishing.

Kirkpatrick, Katherine. Trouble's Daughter: The Story of Susanna Hutchinson, Indian Captive. 2000. 256p. (YA). (gr. 5-9). pap. 4.99 o.s.i (*0-440-41579-9*) Dell Publishing.

—Trouble's Daughter: The Story of Susanna Hutchinson, Indian Captive. 1998. 256p. (YA). (gr. 5-9). 14.95 o.s.i (*0-385-32600-9*) Doubleday Publishing.

—Trouble's Daughter: The Story of Susanna Hutchinson, Indian Captive. 2000. 11.04 (*0-606-17896-1*) Turtleback Bks.

Kissinger, Rosemary. Quanah Parker: Comanche Chief. 1991. (Illus.). 136p. (J). (ps-8). 19.95 (*0-88289-785-3*) Pelican Publishing Co., Inc.

Kittleman, Laurence R. Canyons Beyond the Sky. 1985. 228p. (J). (gr. 5-8). 13.95 o.s.i (*0-689-31138-9*, Atheneum) Simon & Schuster Children's Publishing.

Koller, Jackie French. The Primrose Way. (Great Episodes Ser.). 352p. (YA). (gr. 7-12). 1995. pap. 6.00 (*0-15-200372-X*); 1992. 15.95 o.s.i (*0-15-256745-3*) Harcourt Children's Bks. (Gulliver Bks.).

Kotzwinkle, William. The Return of Crazy Horse. 2001. (Illus.). 32p. (J). (ps-3). 16.95 (*1-58394-047-2*) Frog, Ltd.

Kroeber, Theodora. Ishi, Last of His Tribe, 001. 1964. (Illus.). 208p. (J). 14.95 o.s.i (*0-395-27644-6*) Houghton Mifflin Co.

—Ishi, Last of His Tribe. 1992. (J). mass mkt. o.s.i (*0-553-54066-1*, Dell Books for Young Readers) Random Hse. Children's Bks.

Kroll, Steven. John Quincy Adams: Letters from a Southern Planter's Son. 2001. (Dear Mr. President Ser.). (Illus.). 128p. (J). (gr. 4-6). 9.95 (*1-890817-93-7*) Winslow Pr.

Kusugak, Michael Arvaarluk. Arctic Stories. 1998. (Illus.). 40p. (J). (gr. k-6). pap. 6.95 (*1-55037-452-4*); lib. bdg. 18.95 (*1-55037-453-2*) Firefly Bks., Ltd.

—Arctic Stories. 1999. 13.10 (*0-606-16482-0*) Turtleback Bks.

Lacapa, Kathleen & Lacapa, Michael. Less Than Half, More Than Whole. 1994. (Illus.). 40p. (J). (gr. 1-3). lib. bdg. 14.95 o.p. (*0-87358-592-5*, Rising Moon Bks. for Young Readers) Northland Publishing.

Lampman, Evelyn S. Rattlesnake Cave. 1974. (Illus.). (J). (gr. 4-7). 7.95 o.p. (*0-689-30429-3*, McElderry, Margaret K.) Simon & Schuster Children's Publishing.

—Treasure Mountain. 2nd ed. 2000. (Eager Beaver Bks.). (Illus.). 220p. (J). (gr. 4). reprint ed. pap. 5.95 o.p. (*0-87595-231-3*) Oregon Historical Society Pr.

—Year of Small Shadow. 1971. 190p. (J). (gr. 5-7). 5.95 o.p. (*0-15-299815-2*) Harcourt Children's Bks.

Landrey, Wanda A. The Ghost of Spindletop Hill. 2000. (Illus.). xiii, 140p. (J). 15.95 (*1-57168-449-2*) Eakin Pr.

Larrabee, Lisa. Grandmother Five Baskets. (Illus.). (gr. 3-7). 2000. 128p. pap. 9.95 (*0-943173-90-6*); 1993. 64p. (J). 14.95 o.p. (*0-943173-86-8*) Rinehart, Roberts Pubs.

Lasky, Kathryn. Cloud Eyes. abr. ed. 1994. (Illus.). 32p. (J). (ps-3). 14.95 (*0-15-219168-2*) Harcourt Children's Bks.

The Last of the Mohicans. 2003. (Illus.). pap. 5.95 (*0-19-424403-2*) Oxford Univ. Pr., Inc.

Lawlor, Laurie. Wind on the River: A Story of the Civil War. (American Portraits Ser.). (Illus.). iv, 156p. (YA). (gr. 5-8). 2001. 12.64 (*0-8092-0582-3*); 2000. pap. 5.95 (*0-8092-0624-2*, 06242E) Jamestown.

Le Sueur, Meridel. Sparrow Hawk. 2000. (Wilderness Bks.). (Illus.). 176p. (YA). (gr. 7-12). reprint ed. pap. 10.95 (*0-930100-86-7*) Holy Cow! Pr.

Lee, Valerie. The Tales of Tuffy: Adventures of a Native American Boy. (J). E-Book 7.95 (*1-58820-515-0*); 2000. 100p. (gr. 4-7). pap. 10.85 (*1-58721-042-8*) 1stBooks Library.

Leech, Jay & Spencer, Zane. Bright Fawn & Me. 1979. (Illus.). (J). (ps-3). 12.95 o.p. (*0-690-03937-9*) HarperCollins Children's Bk. Group.

Lentz, Alice B. Tweetsie Adventure. 1995. (Illus.). 32p. (J). (ps-3). 9.95 (*1-57072-025-8*) Overmountain Pr.

Levin, Betty. Brother Moose. 1990. (J). (gr. 5 up). 12.95 o.p. (*0-688-09266-7*, Greenwillow Bks.) HarperCollins Children's Bk. Group.

Lewis, Paul Owen. Frog Girl. 1997. (Illus.). 32p. (J). (ps-5). 14.95 o.p. (*1-885223-57-9*) Beyond Words Publishing, Inc.

—Frog Girl. 1999. (Illus.). 32p. (J). (gr. 2 up). lib. bdg. 22.60 (*0-8368-2228-5*) Stevens, Gareth Inc.

—Frog Girl. 2003. 38p. tchr.'s planning gde. ed. 2.95 (*1-58246-009-4*) Tricycle Pr.

—Storm Boy. 1995. (Illus.). 32p. (J). (gr. k-3). 14.95 o.p. (*1-885223-12-9*) Beyond Words Publishing, Inc.

—Storm Boy. 1999. (Illus.). 32p. (J). (gr. 2 up). lib. bdg. 22.60 (*0-8368-2229-3*) Stevens, Gareth Inc.

—Storm Boy. 2003. (Illus.). 32p. (J). (gr. k-5). pap. 6.95 (*1-58246-057-4*); (gr. 1-4). 14.95 (*1-883672-96-1*) Tricycle Pr.

Lipsyte, Robert. The Brave. (Charlotte Zolotow Bk.). (gr. 7 up). 1993. 240p. (J). pap. 5.99 (*0-06-447079-2*, Harper Trophy); 1991. 208p. (YA). 15.00 o.p. (*0-06-023915-8*); 1991. 208p. (YA). lib. bdg. 14.89 o.p. (*0-06-023916-6*) HarperCollins Children's Bk. Group.

—Brave. 1993. (J). 11.00 (*0-606-02539-1*) Turtleback Bks.

—The Chief. 1993. 240p. (YA). (gr. 7 up). 15.00 o.p. (*0-06-021064-8*); lib. bdg. 14.89 o.p. (*0-06-021068-0*) HarperCollins Children's Bk. Group.

Lisle, Janet Taylor. The Crying Rocks. 2003. (Illus.). 208p. (YA). 16.95 (*0-689-85319-X*, Atheneum/Richard Jackson Bks.) Simon & Schuster Children's Publishing.

Little, Kimberley Griffiths. Enchanted Runner. 1999. (Avon Camelot Bks.). 149p. (J). (gr. 5-7). 15.00 (*0-380-97623-4*, Avon Bks.) Morrow/Avon.

—The Last Snake Runner. 2002. 208p. (J). (gr. 6-9). 15.95 (*0-375-81539-2*); lib. bdg. 17.99 (*0-375-91539-7*) Random Hse., Inc.

Littlesugar, Amy. A Portrait of Spotted Deer's Grandfather. 1997. (Illus.). 32p. (J). (gr. 2-6). lib. bdg. 15.95 (*0-8075-6622-5*) Whitman, Albert & Co.

Locker, Thomas. The Land of Gray Wolf. (Illus.). (J). (ps-3). 1996. 32p. pap. 6.99 o.s.i (*0-14-055741-5*, Puffin Bks.); 1991. 32p. 18.99 o.s.i (*0-8037-0936-6*, Dial Bks. for Young Readers); 1991. 320p. 15.89 o.p. (*0-8037-0937-4*, Dial Bks. for Young Readers) Penguin Putnam Bks. for Young Readers.

—The Land of Gray Wolf. 1996. (J). 13.14 (*0-606-09525-X*) Turtleback Bks.

Lockett, Sharon. No Moccasins Today. 1970. (J). (gr. 5-8). lib. bdg. 6.95 o.p. (*0-8407-6059-0*, Dutton Children's Bks.) Penguin Putnam Bks. for Young Readers.

Lodge, Sally. The Comanche. 1992. (Native American People Ser.: Set III). (Illus.). 32p. (J). (gr. 3-6). lib. bdg. 27.93 (*0-86625-390-4*) Rourke Publishing, LLC.

Loewen, Iris. My Kokum Called Today. ed. 1994. (J). (gr. 2). spiral bd. (*0-616-01704-9*) Canadian National Institute for the Blind/Institut National Canadien pour les Aveugles.

London, Jonathan. Giving Thanks. 2003. (Illus.). 32p. (J). 16.99 (*0-7636-1680-X*) Candlewick Pr.

Long, Devata. Seeing Is Sometimes Believing. Garza, Amy Ammons, ed. l.t. ed. 2001. (Illus.). 32p. (J). (gr. k-3). pap. 6.95 (*0-9651232-8-6*, AC505, Catch the Spirit of Appalachia) Ammons Communications, Ltd.

Long, Olivia. Thunderbirds & Thunderbeings. Date not set. (Our Precious Planet Ser.). (Illus.). 32p. (J). (ps-4). (*1-880042-10-X*) Shelf-Life Bks.

Lough, Loree. Dream Seekers: Roger William's Stand for Freedom. 3rd ed. 1998. (American Adventure Ser.: No. 3). (Illus.). (J). (gr. 3-7). pap. 3.97 (*1-57748-073-2*) Barbour Publishing, Inc.

—Dream Seekers: Roger William's Stand for Freedom. 1999. (American Adventure Ser.: No. 3). (Illus.). 144p. (J). (gr. 3-7). lib. bdg. 15.95 (*0-7910-5043-2*) Chelsea Hse. Pubs.

Luger, Harriett M. The Last Stronghold: A Story of the Modoc Indian, War, 1872-1873. 1995. (Illus.). x, 224p. (YA). (gr. 4-9). pap. text 17.50 (*0-208-02403-4*, Linnet Bks.) Shoe String Pr., Inc.

Luhrmann, Winifred B. Only Brave Tomorrows. 1989. (YA). (gr. 5-9). 13.95 o.p. (*0-395-47983-5*) Houghton Mifflin Co.

Lyons, Beth, retold by. Native American: When Coyote Stole Fire. 1994. (Graphic Learning Multicultural Literature Program Ser.). (ENG & SPA., Illus.). (J). (gr. k-5). tchr. ed. 45.00 (*0-87746-440-5*) Graphic Learning.

MacGregor, Miles. The Sunflower. Thatch, Nancy R., ed. 1994. (Books for Students by Students). (Illus.). 29p. (J). (gr. 3-6). lib. bdg. 15.95 (*0-933849-52-4*) Landmark Editions, Inc.

Maclay, Elise. The Earth Is My Mother. 2000. (Illus.). 175p. (J). (gr. 4-7). tchr. ed. 17.95 (*0-86713-044-X*, 85163) Greenwich Workshop Pr.

Magnuson, Diana, illus. Eagle Feathers. 1997. (*0-7802-8323-6*) Wright Group, The.

—The Gift. 1997. (*0-7802-8301-5*) Wright Group, The.

Mark of the Stone. 2000. 45p. (J). (gr. 3-6). per. 9.99 (*0-9707770-0-0*) Blue Horse Mukwa Publishing.

Markle, Sandra. Fledglings. 2003. 144p. (J). (gr. 5 up). pap. 9.95 (*1-56397-696-X*) Boyds Mills Pr.

—Fledglings. 2001. (J). 16.00 (*0-606-22053-4*) Turtleback Bks.

Marks, Dea, illus. Tall Shadow, a Navajo Boy. 1998. (Cover-to-Cover Bks.). (J). (*0-7807-7040-4*) Perfection Learning Corp.

Marsh, Carole. Pocahontas. 2002. (One Thousand Readers Ser.). (Illus.). 12p. (J). (gr. 2-6). pap. 2.95 (*0-635-01506-4*, 15064) Gallopade International.

—Pocahontas. 1995. (Classics Ser.). (Illus.). (ps-4). 96p. (J). 7.98 o.p. (*1-57082-114-3*); (SPA., 96p. (J). 7.98 o.p. (*1-57082-116-X*); 40p. (YA). 5.98 o.p. (*1-57082-115-1*) Mouse Works.

—Pocahontas. (Biographical Stories Ser.). (J). (gr. 1-5). pap. 5.72 o.p. (*0-8114-8304-5*); audio 8.49 o.p. (*0-8114-8339-8*) Raintree Pubs.

—Pocahontas. (Read-Along Ser.). (J). 7.99 incl. audio (*1-55723-739-5*); 7.99 incl. audio (*1-55723-739-5*); audio 11.99 (*1-55723-741-7*); audio compact disk 19.99 (*1-55723-743-3*); 1995. 11.99 incl. audio (*1-55723-745-X*); 1995. audio 11.99 (*1-55723-740-9*); 1995. audio compact disk 19.99 (*1-55723-742-5*) Walt Disney Records.

—Those Whose Names Were Terrible. 1994. (Lost Colony Collection). (Illus.). (Orig.). (J). (gr. 4-8). pap. 19.95 (*0-935326-48-0*) Gallopade International.

Martin, Bill, Jr. Knots on a Counting Rope. ed. 1989. (gr. 2). spiral bd. (*0-616-01713-8*) Canadian National Institute for the Blind/Institut National Canadien pour les Aveugles.

—Knots on a Counting Rope, ERS. 1993. (Illus.). 32p. (J). (ps-3). pap. 19.95 (*0-8050-2955-9*, Holt, Henry & Co. Bks. For Young Readers) Holt, Henry & Co.

—Knots on a Counting Rope. 1997. 13.10 (*0-606-12386-5*) Turtleback Bks.

Martin, Bill, Jr. & Archambault, John. Knots on a Counting Rope, ERS. 1987. (Illus.). 32p. (J). (ps-3). 16.95 (*0-8050-0571-4*, Holt, Henry & Co. Bks. For Young Readers) Holt, Henry & Co.

—Knots on a Counting Rope. unabr. ed. 1992. (J). (gr. k-5). pap. 17.90 incl. audio (*0-8045-6559-7*, 6559) Spoken Arts, Inc.

Martin, Bill, Jr., et al. Knots on a Counting Rope, ERS. 1997. (Illus.). 32p. (J). (ps-2). reprint ed. pap. 6.95 (*0-8050-5479-0*, Holt, Henry & Co. Bks. For Young Readers) Holt, Henry & Co.

Martin, Nora. The Eagle's Shadow. 1997. 176p. (YA). (gr. 5-9). pap. 15.95 (*0-590-36087-6*) Scholastic, Inc.

Mason, Tom. Red Wolf's Daughter. 2003. 128p. (gr. 5). pap. text 4.99 (*0-553-48761-2*, Random Hse. Bks. for Young Readers); lib. bdg. 12.99 (*0-553-13022-6*, Delacorte Bks. for Young Readers) Random Hse. Children's Bks.

Massey, Craig. Brown Shadow. Moore, Tracy, ed. & illus. by. rev. ed. 1996. 136p. (J). (gr. 5-9). reprint ed. mass mkt. 6.99 (*1-891635-02-6*) Moore Bks.

Matthaei, Gay & Grutman, Jewel. The Sketchbook of Thomas Blue Eagle. 2001. (Illus.). 72p. (J). (gr. 5 up). 16.95 o.p. (*0-8118-2908-1*) Chronicle Bks. LLC.

—The Sketchbook of Thomas Blue Eagle. 2001. (Illus.). 60p. (YA). (gr. 5-8). reprint ed. 17.00 (*0-7567-6295-2*) DIANE Publishing Co.

Matthaei, Gay & Grutman, Jewel H. The Journal Julia Singing Bear. 1996. (Illus.). 80p. (J). 19.95 o.p. (*1-56566-095-1*) Lickle Publishing, Inc.

Matthews, Kay. An Anasazi Welcome. 2004. (Illus.). 40p. (J). (gr. 4-7). pap. 6.95 (*1-878610-27-9*) Red Crane Bks., Inc.

Maxson, H. A. & Young, Claudia H. Lenapehoking: Land of the Delawares. 2001. 64p. (J). per. 8.95 (*0-9704692-1-7*) Bay Oak Pubs., Ltd.

Mayo, Gretchen W. North American Indian Stories, 4 vols., Set. 1990. (Illus.). 256p. (J). (gr. 5 up). pap. 23.80 (*0-8027-7341-9*) Walker & Co.

McCabe, Lianne & Brook, Jasmine. The Dreamcatcher: Keeping Hold of Your Dreams. 1999. (Illus.). 32p. (J). (gr. 4-7). 7.98 (*0-7651-0949-2*) Smithmark Pubs., Inc.

McDermott, Gerald. Flecha al Sol. unabr. ed. 1997. (SPA.). (J). (gr. 3-5). pap. 15.95 incl. audio (*0-87499-411-X*, LK7305) Live Oak Media.

—Flecha al Sol. (SPA.). (J). pap. 15.95 incl. audio Weston Woods Studios, Inc.

—Flecha al Sol (Arrow to the Sun) unabr. ed. 1997. (ENG & SPA.). (J). (gr. k-3). 22.95 incl. audio (*0-87499-412-8*) Live Oak Media.

—Flecha al Sol, Grades K-3. 1997. Tr. of Arrow to the Sun. (SPA., Illus.). pap., tchr. ed. 33.95 incl. audio (*0-87499-413-6*) Live Oak Media.

McElrath, William N. Indian Treasure on Rockhouse Creek. 1984. (J). (gr. 5-8). pap. 5.95 o.p. (*0-8054-4517-X*, 4245-17) Broadman & Holman Pubs.

McFarlane, Sheryl. Eagle Dreams. ed. 1997. (J). (gr. 1). spiral bd. (*0-616-01718-9*); (gr. 2). spiral bd. (*0-616-01719-7*) Canadian National Institute for the Blind/Institut National Canadien pour les Aveugles.

—Eagle Dreams. 1998. (Illus.). 32p. (J). (gr. k-3). pap. 6.95 (*1-55143-125-4*) Orca Bk. Pubs.

McFarlane, Sheryl & Lightburn, Ron. Eagle Dreams. 1994. (Illus.). 32p. (J). 9.95 o.p. (*1-55143-016-9*) Orca Bk. Pubs.

McGraw, Eloise Jarvis. Moccasin Trail. 1986. (Puffin Newbery Library). (J). 11.04 (*0-606-01321-0*) Turtleback Bks.

McKinley, Maura E. The Secret of the Eagle Feathers. 1997. (Publish-a-Book Ser.). (Illus.). 32p. (J). (gr. 1-6). lib. bdg. 22.83 (*0-8172-4436-0*) Raintree Pubs.

McLeod, Elaine. Lessons from Mother Earth. 2002. (Illus.). 24p. (J). (ps-1). 15.95 (*0-88899-312-9*) Groundwood Bks. CAN. *Dist:* Publishers Group West.

McLerran, Alice. The Ghost Dance. 2001. (Illus.). 32p. (J). (ps-3). pap. 6.95 (*0-618-11143-3*, Clarion Bks.) Houghton Mifflin Co. Trade & Reference Div.

McMurtry, Robby, tr. Song of Moon Pony. 2003. (J). 17.95 (*1-57168-740-8*, Eakin Pr.) Eakin Pr.

McNickle, D'Arcy. Runner in the Sun. 1987. (Zia Book Ser.). (Illus.). 249p. (J). (gr. 2 up). reprint ed. pap. 15.95 (*0-8263-0974-7*) Univ. of New Mexico Pr.

McNutt, Nan. The Bentwood Box. 5th ed. 1994. (Northwest Coast Indian Art Ser.). (Illus.). 36p. (Orig.). (J). (gr. 3-8). pap. text 9.95 (*0-9614534-7-8*) McNutt, Nan & Assocs.

Means, Florence C. Our Cup Is Broken, 001. 1969. (Illus.). (J). (gr. 7 up). 6.95 o.p. (*0-395-06937-8*) Houghton Mifflin Co.

Medearis, Angela Shelf. Dancing with the Indians. 1991. (Illus.). (J). (ps-3). 32p. tchr. ed. 16.95 (*0-8234-0893-0*); reprint ed. pap. 6.95 (*0-8234-1023-4*) Holiday Hse., Inc.

—Dancing with the Indians. 2000. (Illus.). (J). (gr. 1-6). 24.95 incl. audio (*0-87499-333-4*); pap. 15.95 incl. audio (*0-87499-332-6*); pap. 15.95 incl. audio (*0-87499-332-6*) Live Oak Media.

—Dancing with the Indians, Grades 1-6. 2000. (Illus.). (J). pap., tchr. ed. 37.95 incl. audio (*0-87499-334-2*) Live Oak Media.

Mikaelsen, Ben. Touching Spirit Bear. 2001. 256p. (J). (gr. 5 up). 15.99 (0-380-97744-3); 15.99 (0-380-97744-3); lib. bdg. 16.89 (0-06-029149-4) HarperCollins Children's Bk. Group.

Mills, Jackie. Sirena of Salado. 1991. (Illus.). 32p. (J). (gr. 2-7). 10.95 (0-9629284-0-2) Indian Trail Pr.

Mitchell, Barbara. Red Bird. 1996. (Illus.). (J). (gr. k-4). 32p. 16.00 (0-688-10859-8); lib. bdg. 15.93 o.p. (0-688-10860-1) HarperCollins Children's Bk. Group.

Momaday, N. Scott. Circle of Wonder: A Native American Christmas Story. 2001. (Illus.). 44p. 24.95 incl. audio (0-8263-2796-6) Univ. of New Mexico Pr.

Monjo, F. N. Indian Summer. 1968. (I Can Read Bks.). (Illus.). 192p. (J). (ps-3). lib. bdg. 13.89 o.p. (0-06-024328-7) HarperCollins Children's Bk. Group.

Montgomery, Rutherford G. Broken Fang. 2001. (Classic Ser.). (Illus.). 312p. (J). (gr. 4-7). pap. 15.95 (0-87004-416-8) Caxton Pr.

Monture, Joel. Cloudwalker: Contemporary Native American Stories. 1996. (Fulcrum Kids Ser.). (Illus.). 64p. (J). (gr. 4-7). 15.95 (1-55591-225-7) Fulcrum Publishing.

Moore, Ruth N. Peace Treaty. 1977. (Christian Peace Shelf Ser.). (Illus.). 154p. (J). (gr. 3-10). pap. 3.95 o.p. (0-8361-1805-7); text 4.95 o.p. (0-8361-1804-9) Herald Pr.

Morgan, Jill. Blood Brothers. 1996. (Illus.). 128p. (J). (gr. 3-7). pap. 4.50 o.s.i (0-06-440562-1, Harper Trophy) HarperCollins Children's Bk. Group.

—Blood Brothers. 1996. 9.60 o.p. (0-606-09087-8) Turtleback Bks.

Morris, Gilbert. The Rustlers of Panther Gap. 1994. (Ozark Adventures Ser.: Vol. 2). 144p. (J). (gr. 3-7). pap. 3.99 o.p. (0-8423-4393-8) Tyndale Hse. Pubs.

Morris, Oradel N. I Hear the Song of the Houmas: J'Entends la Chanson des Houmas. 1992. (Gens de la Louisiane - Peoples of Louisiana Ser.: Bk. 2). (Illus.). 160p. (J). 29.95 (0-944064-04-3) Paupieres Publishing Co.

Mouse Works Staff. Friends Forever: Friends Forever. 1995. (Illus.). (J). bds. 5.98 o.p. (1-57082-275-1) Mouse Works.

—Pocahontas: Meet the Characters. 1995. (Illus.). 20p. (J). 5.98 o.p. (1-57082-277-8) Mouse Works.

—Sharing Peace: Sharing Peace. 1995. (Illus.). (J). 7.98 o.p. (1-57082-281-6) Mouse Works.

—Where's Percy. 1995. (Illus.). (J). 7.98 o.p. (1-57082-270-0) Mouse Works.

Mowat, Farley. Lost in the Barrens. 1987. 256p. mass mkt. 6.99 (0-7710-6681-3) McClelland & Stewart/Tundra Bks.

—Lost in the Barrens. 1956. 11.55 (0-606-00513-7) Turtleback Bks.

Mulcahy, Lucille. Dark Arrow. 1995. (Illus.). 209p. (J). (gr. 7 up). pap. text 7.95 (0-8032-8220-6, Bison Bks.) Univ. of Nebraska Pr.

Murphy, Barbara B. Eagles in Their Flight. 1994. 192p. (J). (gr. 6 up). 14.95 o.s.i (0-385-32035-3, Delacorte Pr.) Dell Publishing.

Murphy, Elspeth Campbell. The Mystery of the Eagle Feather. 1995. (Three Cousins Detective Club Ser.: No. 9). (Illus.). 64p. (Orig.). (J). (gr. 2-5). pap. 3.99 (1-55661-413-6) Bethany Hse. Pubs.

Nelson, S. D. The Star People. 2003. (Illus.). 40p. (J). (gr. k-3). 14.95 (0-8109-4584-3) Abrams, Harry N., Inc.

Nez, Redwing T. Forbidden Talent. 1995. (Illus.). 32p. (J). (ps-3). lib. bdg. 14.95 o.p. (0-87358-605-0, Rising Moon Bks. for Young Readers) Northland Publishing.

O'Dell, Scott. Island of the Blue Dolphins. 1999. 208p. mass mkt. 2.99 o.s.i (0-440-22898-0) Bantam Bks.

—Island of the Blue Dolphins. 2002. (Illus.). (J). 15.00 (0-7587-0194-2) Book Wholesalers, Inc.

—Island of the Blue Dolphins. (J). 1997. mass mkt. 2.69 o.p. (0-440-22718-6); 1996. 192p. mass mkt. 2.49 o.s.i (0-440-22021-1); 1995. 192p. mass mkt. 4.50 (0-440-80102-8) Dell Publishing.

—Island of the Blue Dolphins. l.t. ed. 1974. (J). lib. bdg. 7.95 o.p. (0-8161-6170-4, Macmillan Reference USA) Gale Group.

—Island of the Blue Dolphins. 192p. (gr. 4-6). 1990. (Illus.). (J). tchr. ed. 22.00 (0-395-53680-4); 1960. (YA). tchr. ed. 16.00 (0-395-06962-9) Houghton Mifflin Co.

—Island of the Blue Dolphins. 184p. (J). (gr. 3-5). pap. 5.99 (0-8072-8327-4); 2000. pap. 35.00 incl. audio (0-8072-8326-6, YA163SP) Random Hse. Audio Publishing Group. (Listening Library).

—Island of the Blue Dolphins. 1996. 192p. (YA). mass mkt. 5.50 o.s.i (0-440-75312-0, Dell Books for Young Readers); 1995. (J). pap. 5.99 (0-440-91043-9, Dell Books for Young Readers); 1978. 208p. (YA). (gr. 5-9). mass mkt. 6.50 (0-440-94000-1, Laurel Leaf); 1971. 192p. (gr. 5-8). pap. text 6.50 (0-440-43988-4, Yearling) Random Hse. Children's Bks.

—Island of the Blue Dolphins. 9999. (J). pap. 1.50 o.s.i (0-590-02366-7) Scholastic, Inc.

—Island of the Blue Dolphins. 1960. (J). 12.04 (0-606-00877-2) Turtleback Bks.

—The Serpent Never Sleeps: A Novel of Jamestown & Pocahontas. 1987. (Illus.). 240p. (YA). (gr. 7 up). 17.00 o.s.i (0-395-44242-7) Houghton Mifflin Co.

—Sing down the Moon. (J). 1997. mass mkt. 2.69 o.p. (0-440-22736-4); 1991. mass mkt. 4.99 (0-440-80271-7) Dell Publishing.

—Sing down the Moon, 001. 1970. 144p. (YA). (gr. 7-7). tchr. ed. 18.00 (0-395-10919-1) Houghton Mifflin Co.

—Sing down the Moon. 1992. (Yearling Newbery Ser.). 144p. (gr. 5-9). pap. text 5.99 (0-440-40673-0, Yearling) Random Hse. Children's Bks.

—Sing down the Moon. 1970. (Laurel-Leaf Historical Fiction Ser.). (J). 11.55 (0-606-03442-0); 12.04 (0-606-00856-X) Turtleback Bks.

—Streams to the River, River to the Sea: A Novel of Sacagawea. 1987. 176p. (gr. 7-12). mass mkt. 5.99 (0-449-70244-8, Fawcett) Ballantine Bks.

—Streams to the River, River to the Sea: A Novel of Sacagawea. l.t. ed. 1989. 312p. (YA). (gr. 7 up). lib. bdg. 14.95 (0-8161-4811-2, Macmillan Reference USA) Gale Group.

—Streams to the River, River to the Sea: A Novel of Sacagawea. 1986. 208p. (YA). (gr. 7 up). tchr. ed. 16.00 (0-395-40430-4) Houghton Mifflin Co.

—Streams to the River, River to the Sea: A Novel of Sacagawea. 1986. (J). 12.04 (0-606-03695-4) Turtleback Bks.

—Zia. 1995. 192p. (gr. 4-7). (YA). mass mkt. 5.50 (0-440-21956-6); (J). pap. 5.50 (0-440-41001-0) Dell Publishing.

—Zia, 001. 1976. (Illus.). 192p. (YA). (gr. 7-7). tchr. ed. 18.00 (0-395-24393-9) Houghton Mifflin Co.

—Zia. 1978. 144p. (J). (gr. 4 up). mass mkt. 1.50 o.s.i (0-440-99904-9, Laurel Leaf) Random Hse. Children's Bks.

O'Dell, Scott, et al. Sing down the Moon. 1997. (Laurel-Leaf Historical Fiction Ser.). 128p. (YA). (gr. 4-7). mass mkt. 5.99 (0-440-97975-7, Laurel Leaf) Random Hse. Children's Bks.

Ogden, David. Dreambirds. 1997. (Illus.). 32p. (YA). (ps up). 16.95 (0-935699-09-0) Illumination Arts Publishing Co., Inc.

Oliphant, Pat, illus. Peter Becomes a Trail Man: The Story of a Boy's Journey on the Santa Fe Trail. 2002. 191p. (J). 12.95 (0-8263-2895-4) Univ. of New Mexico Pr.

Olsen, Sylvia. No Time to Say Goodbye. 2002. (Illus.). 194p. 6.95 (1-55039-121-6) Sono Nis Pr. CAN. *Dist:* Orca Bk. Pubs.

O'Meara, Walter. Sioux Are Coming, 001. 1971. (Illus.). (J). (gr. 3-7). 6.95 o.p. (0-395-12759-9) Houghton Mifflin Co.

Osborne, Mary Pope. Adaline Falling Star. unabr. ed. 2001. (YA). (gr. 5-9). audio 18.00 (0-8072-0430-7, Listening Library) Random Hse. Audio Publishing Group.

—Adaline Falling Star. 2000. (Illus.). vi, 170p. (J). (gr. 7-12). pap. 16.95 (0-439-05947-X, Scholastic Reference) Scholastic, Inc.

Osofsky, Audrey. Dreamcatcher. (Illus.). 32p. (J). (ps-2). 1999. mass mkt. 5.95 (0-531-07113-8); 1992. pap. 14.95 (0-531-05988-X); 1992. lib. bdg. 16.99 (0-531-08588-0) Scholastic, Inc. (Orchard Bks.).

—Dreamcatcher. 1999. lib. bdg. 12.10 (0-606-16921-0) Turtleback Bks.

Oughton, Jerrie. Music from a Place Called Half Moon. 1995. 176p. (YA). (gr. 7-7). 16.00 (0-395-70737-4) Houghton Mifflin Co.

—Music from a Place Called Half Moon. 1997. 176p. (YA). (gr. 5-9). mass mkt. 3.99 o.s.i (0-440-21999-X, Yearling) Random Hse. Children's Bks.

—Music from a Place Called Half Moon. 1997. 10.04 (0-606-11003-8) Turtleback Bks.

Palmer, Bernard. Silent Thunder. 1975. 96p. (J). (gr. 6-10). pap. 1.95 o.p. (0-87123-531-5, 200531) Bethany Hse. Pubs.

Parish, Peggy. Good Hunting, Blue Sky. (I Can Read Bks.). (Illus.). (J). 1991. 64p. (gr. k-3). pap. 3.99 (0-06-444148-2, Harper Trophy); 1988. 32p. (gr. k-3). lib. bdg. 15.89 (0-06-024662-6); 1988. 64p. (gr. 1-3). 14.00 (0-06-024661-8) HarperCollins Children's Bk. Group.

—Little Indian. 1968. (Illus.). (J). (ps-3). lib. bdg. 3.79 o.p. (0-671-65025-4, Simon & Schuster Children's Publishing) Simon & Schuster Children's Publishing.

Passey, Helen K. Speak to the Rain. 1989. 160p. (YA). (gr. 7 up). lib. bdg. 13.95 o.s.i (0-689-31489-2, Atheneum) Simon & Schuster Children's Publishing.

Paulsen, Gary. The Legend of Red Horse Cavern. 1994. (Gary Paulsen's World of Adventure Ser.). 80p. (gr. 4-7). pap. text 3.99 o.s.i (0-440-41023-1) Dell Publishing.

—The Legend of Red Horse Cavern. 1994. (J). pap. o.s.i (0-440-90109-X, Dell Books for Young Readers) Random Hse. Children's Bks.

—The Legend of Red Horse Cavern. 1994. (Gary Paulsen's World of Adventure Ser.). 10.14 (0-606-07141-5) Turtleback Bks.

Peck, Harriet Taylor. Secrets of the Stone, RS. 2000. (Illus.). 32p. (J). (ps-3). 16.00 (0-374-36648-9, Farrar, Straus & Giroux (BYR)) Farrar, Straus & Giroux.

Peck, Robert. Jo Silver. 1985. 144p. (J). (gr. 8-12). 9.95 o.p. (0-910923-20-5) Pineapple Pr., Inc.

Penn, Audrey. The Whistling Tree. 2003. 32p. (J). 16.95 (0-87868-852-8, Child & Family Pr.) Child Welfare League of America, Inc.

Penney, Grace Jackson. Moki, a Classic Story of a Young Cheyenne Girl. 1997. (J). 11.04 (0-606-11631-1) Turtleback Bks.

Perkins, Elavina & Johnson, Jerrold T., eds. Ashkii's Journey. 2001. (ENG & NAV., Illus.). (J). (1-893354-31-8) Salina Bookshelf.

Perkins, Stanley C. Arvilla & the Tattler Tree: The Fur Trader. 1994. (Illus.). 702p. (J). pap. 25.00 (0-9620249-4-5) Broadblade Pr.

Peyton, John L. Voices from the Ice. 1990. (Illus.). 56p. (J). (gr. 5-7). pap. 9.95 (0-939923-15-7) McDonald & Woodward Publishing Co., The.

Phillips, JoAnn. The Run According to Hawkeye. 1993. (Illus.). 24p. (Orig.). (J). pap. 9.95 (0-9638403-0-4) Cherokee Strip Centennial Foundation.

Pirone, James & Sweeney, Paula. Jake Montana: A Matter of Destiny. 1993. 124p. (YA). pap. 9.99 (0-88092-072-6); lib. bdg. 15.00 o.p. (0-88092-073-4) Royal Fireworks Publishing Co.

Polacco, Patricia. Boatride with Lillian Two-Blossom. 1989. (Illus.). 32p. (J). (ps-3). 16.99 (0-399-21470-4, Philomel) Penguin Putnam Bks. for Young Readers.

—Tikvah Means Hope. 1996. (Illus.). 48p. (J). (ps-3). pap. 5.99 o.s.i (0-440-41229-3, Yearling) Random Hse. Children's Bks.

Pomerantz, Charlotte. Timothy Tall Feather. 1986. (Illus.). 32p. (J). (gr. k-3). 12.95 o.p. (0-688-04246-5); lib. bdg. 12.93 o.p. (0-688-04247-3) HarperCollins Children's Bk. Group. (Greenwillow Bks.).

Porter, Donald. Medicine Shield. 1996. (White Indian Ser.: No. 28). 368p. (J). mass mkt. 5.50 o.s.i (0-553-56144-8) Bantam Bks.

Powell, Neva. The Long Crossing. 1998. (Illus.). 124p. (YA). (gr. 4-7). pap. 12.95 (0-9661072-2-5) Avocet Pr., Inc.

Praying, Jewell, et al. Chief Seattle & the Indian in the Moon: The Legend of Star Child & Mud Child. 1996. (Illus.). (J). (gr. 3 up). lib. bdg. o.p. (0-8037-1614-1, Dial Bks. for Young Readers) Penguin Putnam Bks. for Young Readers.

Preble, Donna. Yamino-Kwiti: A Story of Indian Life in the Los Angeles Area. 1983. (Illus.). 254p. (J). (gr. 4-10). reprint ed. pap. 6.95 o.p. (0-930588-09-6) Heyday Bks.

Price, Joan. Truth Is a Bright Star: A Hopi Adventure. 1995. 156p. (J). (gr. 3-7). pap. 9.95 o.p. (0-89087-333-X) Celestial Arts Publishing Co.

—Truth Is a Bright Star: A Hopi Adventure. 1997. 156p. (J). (gr. 3-7). pap. 9.95 o.p. (1-883672-62-7) Tricycle Pr.

Price, Joan & Meier, Scott T. Medicine Man. 2000. 124p. pap. 9.99 (0-88092-069-6) Royal Fireworks Publishing Co.

Priest, George E. The Great Winged Monster of the Piasa Valley: The Legend of the Piasa. 1998. (Illus.). 123p. (YA). (gr. 4-12). 17.00 (0-9678461-0-2); pap. 15.00 (0-9678461-1-0) Alton Museum of History & Art, Inc.

Purdy, Carol. Nesuya's Basket. 2000. (Council of Indian Education Ser.). (Illus.). 32p. (gr. 3-7). pap. 8.95 (1-57098-087-X) Rinehart, Roberts Pubs.

Qualey, Marsha. Revolutions of the Heart. 1993. 192p. (YA). (gr. 7 up). 16.00 (0-395-64168-3) Houghton Mifflin Co.

Quimby, Myrtle. Cougar. 1968. (Illus.). (J). (gr. 5-9). lib. bdg. o.p. (0-200-71993-9, 315770) Criterion Bks., Inc.

Raczek, Linda Theresa. Rainy's Powwow. 1999. (Illus.). 32p. (J). (gr. k-3). 15.95 (0-87358-686-7, Rising Moon Bks. for Young Readers) Northland Publishing.

Raphael, Taffy E. The Talking Earth. 2001. (Book Club Novel Guide Ser.). 56p. E-Book 9.95 (0-9656211-9-7) Small Planet Communications, Inc.

Razzell, Mary. Haida Quest. 2002. 160p. (YA). pap. (1-55017-249-2) Harbour Publishing Co., Ltd.

Reaver, Chap. A Little Bit Dead. 1992. 240p. (YA). (gr. 6 up). 15.00 (0-385-30801-9, Delacorte Pr.) Dell Publishing.

—A Little Bit Dead. 1992. 10.04 (0-606-06534-2) Turtleback Bks.

Reaver, Chap & Reaver, Herbert. A Little Bit Dead. 1994. 240p. (YA). (gr. 7 up). mass mkt. 3.99 o.s.i (0-440-21910-8) Dell Publishing.

Rees, Celia. Sorceress. 2003. 352p. (YA). bds. 8.99 (0-7636-2183-8); 2002. 336p. (J). (gr. 7-11). 15.99 (0-7636-1847-0) Candlewick Pr.

Rendon, Marcie R. Powwow Summer: A Family Celebrates the Circle of Life. 1996. (Illus.). (J). (gr. 1-5). lib. bdg. 22.60 o.s.i (0-87614-986-7); (gr. k-3). pap. 7.95 (1-57505-011-0) Lerner Publishing Group. (Carolrhoda Bks.).

RH Disney Staff. Bear with Me. 2003. (Illus.). (J). pap. 3.99 (0-7364-2174-2, RH/Disney) Random Hse. Children's Bks.

—Bears. 2003. (Illus.). 32p. (J). lib. bdg. 11.99 (0-7364-8026-9, RH/Disney) Random Hse. Children's Bks.

—Brother Bear. 2003. (Illus.). 24p. (J). 2.99 (0-7364-2176-9, RH/Disney) Random Hse. Children's Bks.

Rice, Bebe Faas. The Place at the Edge of the Earth. 2002. 192p. (J). (gr. 5-9). tchr. ed. 15.00 (0-618-15978-9) Houghton Mifflin Co.

Riddell, Chris. The Bear Dance. 1993. (Illus.). 32p. (J). (ps-4). pap. 7.95 o.s.i (0-671-79852-9, Simon & Schuster Children's Publishing) Simon & Schuster Children's Publishing.

Robinson, Marileta. Mr. Goat's Bad Good Idea: Three Stories. 1979. (J). (gr. 1-4). 11.50 (0-690-03862-3) HarperCollins Children's Bk. Group.

Rodolph, Stormy. Quest for Courage. 1984. (Indian Culture Ser.). (Illus.). 102p. (J). (gr. 4-12). pap. 6.95 (0-89992-092-6); (gr. 5-12). lib. bdg. 14.95 o.p. (0-89992-392-5) Council for Indian Education.

—Quest for Courage, Vol. 4. 2nd ed. 1993. (Council for Indian Education Ser.). (Illus.). 112p. (J). (gr. 4-7). pap. 8.95 o.p. (1-879373-57-2) Rinehart, Roberts Pubs.

Roop, Peter. Natosi: Strong Medicine. 1984. 32p. (J). (gr. 3-8). 8.45 o.p. (0-89992-390-9); pap. 4.95 (0-89992-090-X) Council for Indian Education.

—Sik-Ki-Mi. 1984. (Indian Culture Ser.). 32p. (J). (gr. 3-6). 7.96 o.s.i (0-89992-391-7); pap. 4.95 (0-89992-091-8) Council for Indian Education.

Roop, Peter & Roop, Connie. Girl of the Shining Mountains: Sacagawea's Story. 1999. 178p. (J). (gr. 3-7). 14.99 (0-7868-0492-0) Hyperion Bks. for Children.

—Sacagawea. 1999. (Illus.). 144p. (J). (gr. 3-7). lib. bdg. 15.49 (0-7868-2422-0) Hyperion Pr.

—Sacagawea: Girl of the Shining Mountains. 2003. (Illus.). 208p. (J). (gr. 3-7). pap. 5.99 (0-7868-1323-7) Hyperion Bks. for Children.

Root, Phyllis. The Listening Silence. 1992. (Illus.). 128p. (J). (gr. 3-7). 14.00 o.p. (0-06-025092-5); lib. bdg. 13.89 o.s.i (0-06-025093-3) HarperCollins Children's Bk. Group.

Rose, Wendy. What Happened When the Hopi Hit New York? 1982. (Chapbook Ser.). (Illus.). 56p. (Orig.). (J). pap. 3.50 (0-936556-08-0) Contact/II Pubns.

Rostkowski, Margaret I. Moon Dancer. 1995. (YA). (gr. 7 up). 224p. 11.00 o.s.i (0-15-276638-3); 192p. pap. 6.00 (0-15-200194-8) Harcourt Children's Bks.

—Moon Dancer. 1995. (J). 11.05 (0-606-09627-2) Turtleback Bks.

Rowland, Della. Story of Sacajawea. 1989. (J). pap. o.s.i (0-440-80124-9, Dell Books for Young Readers) Random Hse. Children's Bks.

Rue, Nancy. The Discovery. 2001. (Christian Heritage Ser.). (Illus.). 192p. (J). (gr. 3-7). pap. 5.99 (1-56179-862-2) Focus on the Family Publishing.

Ruemmler, John D. Smoke on the Water: A Novel of Jamestown & the Powhatans. 1992. (Illus.). 176p. (YA). (gr. 7 up). pap. 6.95 o.p. (1-55870-239-3, Betterway Bks.) F&W Pubns., Inc.

Rumbaut, Hendle. Dove Dream. 1994. (J). 13.95 o.p. (0-395-68393-9) Houghton Mifflin Co.

Russell, Sharman. Humpedback Fluteplayer. 1995. (J). o.p. (0-679-92408-6) Random Hse., Inc.

Rylant, Cynthia. Long Night Moon. 2003. (J). 15.95 (0-689-85426-9, Simon & Schuster Children's Publishing) Simon & Schuster Children's Publishing.

Sage, Doris E. The Littlest Chief. 1986. 155p. (J). (gr. 3-5). 9.95 o.p. (0-533-06696-4) Vantage Pr., Inc.

San Souci, Robert D. The Legend of Scarface. 1987. (Illus.). 40p. (J). (gr. k-3). pap. 7.00 o.s.i (0-385-15874-2) Doubleday Publishing.

—Sootface: An Ojibwa Cinderella Story. 1997. 13.14 (0-606-11863-2) Turtleback Bks.

—Sootface: Ojibwa Cin. 1994. (J). o.s.i (0-385-44612-8, Dell Books for Young Readers) Random Hse. Children's Bks.

Sanders, Evelin. Cherokee Windsong. 1996. 253p. (YA). (gr. 10 up). pap. 9.99 (0-88092-300-8, 3008) Royal Fireworks Publishing Co.

Sandoz, Mari. The Story Catcher. 1986. (Illus.). 175p. (YA). (gr. 7 up). pap. 8.95 (0-8032-9163-9, Bison Bks.) Univ. of Nebraska Pr.

Santiago, Chiori. Home to Medicine Mountain. 1998. (Illus.). 32p. (J). (gr. 1 up). 15.95 o.p. (0-89239-155-3) Children's Bk. Pr.

Sargent, Dave & Sargent, Pat. Charlie (Appaloosa) Be Brave #14. 2001. (Saddle Up Ser.). 36p. (J). pap. (1-56763-608-X); lib. bdg. 22.60 (1-56763-607-1) Ozark Publishing.

—Hoot: Be Creative. 2003. (Saddle Up Ser.: Vol. 35). (Illus.). 42p. (J). mass mkt. 6.95 (1-56763-696-9) Ozark Publishing.

—Hoot (Grullo) Be Creative. 2003. (Saddle Up Ser.: Vol. 35). (Illus.). 42p. (J). lib. bdg. 22.60 (*1-56763-695-0*) Ozark Publishing.

—Kiowa (paint) Be Thrustworthy #37. 2001. (Saddle Up Ser.). 36p. (J). pap. 6.95 (*1-56763-618-7*) Ozark Publishing.

—Kiowa (paint) Be Trustworthy #37. 2001. (Saddle Up Ser.). 36p. (J). lib. bdg. 22.60 (*1-56763-617-9*) Ozark Publishing.

—Mack (Medicine Hat Paint) Be a Leader. 2003. (Saddle Up Ser.: Vol. 39). 42p. (J). lib. bdg. 22.60 (*1-56763-699-3*); mass mkt. 6.95 (*1-56763-700-0*) Ozark Publishing.

—Whiskers (Roan) Pride & Peace. (Saddle Up Ser.: Vol. 59). (Illus.). 42p. (J). 2003. mass mkt. 6.95 (*1-56763-806-6*); 2002. lib. bdg. 22.60 (*1-56763-805-8*) Ozark Publishing.

Say, Allen. Home of the Brave. 2002. (Illus.). 32p. (J). lib. bdg. 17.00 (*0-618-21223-X*) Houghton Mifflin Co.

Schultz, James W. The Loud Mouthed Gun. 1984. (Indian Culture Ser.). 27p. (J). (gr. 4-8). pap. 4.95 (*0-89992-095-0*) Council for Indian Education.

—Story of Running Eagle. 1984. (Indian Culture Ser.). (J). (gr. 2-10). pap. 3.95 o.p. (*0-89992-093-4*) Council for Indian Education.

Schwartz, Ellen. Starshine at Camp Crescent Moon. 1995. 160p. (Orig.). (J). (gr. 3-7). pap. 6.95 (*0-919591-02-7*, Polestar Book Pubs.) Raincoast Bk. Distribution CAN. *Dist:* Publishers Group West.

Scieszka, Jon. The Good, the Bad & the Goofy. 1992. (Time Warp Trio Ser.). (Illus.). 80p. (J). (gr. 4-7). 14.99 (*0-670-84380-6*, Viking Children's Bks.) Penguin Putnam Bks. for Young Readers.

—The Good, the Bad & the Goofy. 1993. (Time Warp Trio Ser.). (J). 10.14 (*0-606-05847-8*) Turtleback Bks.

—The Good, the Bad, & the Goofy. 2004. (Time Warp Trio Ser.). (Illus.). 80p. pap. 4.99 (*0-14-240046-7*, Puffin Bks.) Penguin Putnam Bks. for Young Readers.

—The Good, the Bad & the Goofy. 1993. (Time Warp Trio Ser.). (Illus.). 80p. (J). (gr. 4-7). reprint ed. pap. 4.99 (*0-14-036170-7*) Penguin Putnam Bks. for Young Readers.

—Good, the Bad, & the Goofy Twt Promo. 2003. (Time Warp Trio Ser.). (Illus.). 76p. pap. 2.66 (*0-14-250132-8*, Puffin Bks.) Penguin Putnam Bks. for Young Readers.

Scott, Ann Herbert. Brave As a Mountain Lion. 1996. (Illus.). 32p. (J). (ps-3). lib. bdg., tchr. ed. 16.00 (*0-395-66760-7*, Clarion Bks.) Houghton Mifflin Co. Trade & Reference Div.

—On Mother's Lap. 2002. (Illus.). (J). 14.74 (*0-7587-3318-6*) Book Wholesalers, Inc.

—On Mother's Lap. 1994. 1p. (J). (-ps). pap. 9.95 incl. audio (*0-395-69173-7*, 111692); pap. 9.95 incl. audio (*0-395-69173-7*, 111692) Houghton Mifflin Co.

—On Mother's Lap. (Illus.). 32p. (J). (ps-ps). 2000. bds. 4.95 (*0-618-05159-7*); 1992. pap. 6.95 (*0-395-62976-4*); 1992. lib. bdg., tchr. ed. 16.00 (*0-395-58920-7*) Houghton Mifflin Co. Trade & Reference Div. (Clarion Bks.).

—On Mother's Lap. 1972. (Illus.). 39p. (J). (ps). pap. 6.95 o.p. (*0-07-055896-5*); text 12.95 o.p. (*0-07-055897-3*) McGraw-Hill Cos., The.

—On Mother's Lap. 1992. 13.10 (*0-606-06633-0*) Turtleback Bks.

—On Mothers Lap. 2001. (Early Readers Ser.: Vol. 3). (J). lib. bdg. (*1-59054-346-7*) Fitzgerald Bks.

Searcy, Margaret Z. The Charm of the Bear Claw Necklace. 1990. (Illus.). 80p. (J). reprint ed. (gr. 3-7). 13.95 (*0-88289-821-3*); (gr. 5-7). pap. 7.95 o.s.i (*0-88289-777-2*) Pelican Publishing Co., Inc.

—The Charm of the Bear Claw Necklace: A Story of Stone Age Southeastern Indians. 1981. (Illus.). 80p. (J). (gr. 4-5). 9.95 o.s.i (*0-8173-0060-0*) Univ. of Alabama Pr.

—Ikwa of the Mound-Builder Indians. 1989. (Illus.). 80p. (J). reprint ed. (gr. 3-7). 13.95 o.p. (*0-88289-762-4*); (gr. 4-7). pap. 7.95 (*0-88289-742-X*) Pelican Publishing Co., Inc.

—Wolf Dog of the Woodland Indians. 1991. (Illus.). 112p. (J). (gr. 4-7). pap. 8.95 (*0-88289-778-0*) Pelican Publishing Co., Inc.

—Wolf Dog of the Woodland Indians. 1982. (Illus.). 100p. (J). (gr. 4-8). 9.95 o.p. (*0-8173-0091-0*) Univ. of Alabama Pr.

Seton, Ernest Thompson. The Book of Woodcraft & Indian Lore. 1994. (Illus.). 590p. (YA). pap. 29.95 (*1-885529-11-2*) Stevens Publishing.

—Rolf in the Woods. E-Book 2.49 (*0-7574-0308-5*) Electric Umbrella Publishing.

—Rolf in the Woods: The Adventures of a Boy Scout with Indian Quonab & Little Dog Skookum. 1994. (Illus.). 436p. (YA). pap. 24.95 (*1-885529-09-0*) Stevens Publishing.

—Woodland Tales. 1994. (Illus.). 235p. (YA). pap. 14.95 (*1-885529-10-4*) Stevens Publishing.

Sewall, Marcia. People of the Breaking Day. 1997. (Aladdin Picture Bks.). 12.14 (*0-606-12789-5*) Turtleback Bks.

Sharpe, Susan. Spirit Quest. 1993. 128p. (J). (gr. 4-7). pap. 4.99 o.s.i (*0-14-036282-7*, Puffin Bks.) Penguin Putnam Bks. for Young Readers.

—Spirit Quest. 1991. (Illus.). 128p. (J). (gr. 4-6). lib. bdg. 13.95 (*0-02-782355-5*, Simon & Schuster Children's Publishing) Simon & Schuster Children's Publishing.

—Spirit Quest. 1993. 11.04 (*0-606-02904-4*) Turtleback Bks.

Shaw, Janet Beeler. Kirsten Learns a Lesson: A School Story. Thieme, Jeanne, ed. 1986. (American Girls Collection: Bk. 2). (Illus.). 80p. (J). (gr. 2 up). lib. bdg. 12.95 (*0-937295-82-5*, American Girl) Pleasant Co. Pubns.

—Kirsten Learns a Lesson: A School Story. 1986. (American Girls Collection: Bk. 2). (Illus.). (YA). (gr. 2 up). 12.10 (*0-606-02289-9*) Turtleback Bks.

—Kirsten on the Trail. 1999. (American Girls Short Stories Ser.). (Illus.). 56p. (YA). (gr. 2 up). 3.95 (*1-56247-764-1*, American Girl) Pleasant Co. Pubns.

Sheely, Robert. In the Hands of the Enemy. Killcoyne, Hope L., ed. 2003. (Adventures in America Ser.: Vol. 8). (J). 14.95 (*1-893110-31-1*) Silver Moon Pr.

Shefelman, Janice J. A Mare for Young Wolf. (Step into Reading Step 3 Bks.). (Illus.). 48p. 2004. (J). (gr. 2-4). lib. bdg. 11.99 (*0-679-93445-6*); 1993. (gr. 1-3). pap. 3.99 (*0-679-83445-1*) Random Hse. Children's Bks. (Random Hse. Bks. for Young Readers).

—Spirit of Iron. Eakin, Edwin M., ed. 1987. (Mina Jordan Ser.: No. 3). (Illus.). 136p. (J). (gr. 4-7). pap. 5.95 o.p. (*0-89015-624-7*); 13.95 (*0-89015-636-0*) Eakin Pr.

—Young Wolf & Spirit Horse. 1997. (Step into Reading Step 3 Bks.). (Illus.). 48p. (gr. 2-3). pap. 3.99 o.s.i (*0-679-88207-3*, Random Hse. Bks. for Young Readers) Random Hse. Children's Bks.

—Young Wolf & Spirit Horse. 1997. (Step into Reading Step 3 Bks.). (J). (gr. 2-3). 10.14 (*0-606-12126-9*) Turtleback Bks.

Siberell, Anne. Whale in the Sky. (Unicorn Paperbacks Ser.). (Illus.). 32p. (J). (ps-3). 1985. pap. 3.95 o.p. (*0-525-44197-2*); 1982. 13.95 o.s.i (*0-525-44021-6*) Penguin Putnam Bks. for Young Readers. (Dutton Children's Bks.).

Siegelson, Kim L. Escape South. 2000. (Road to Reading Ser.). (Illus.). (J). (gr. 2-5). 78p. pap. 3.99 (*0-307-26504-8*); 80p. lib. bdg. 11.99 o.s.i (*0-307-46504-7*) Random Hse. Children's Bks. (Golden Bks.).

—Escape South. 2000. (J). 10.14 (*0-606-18931-9*) Turtleback Bks.

Simmons, Marc. Millie Cooper's Ride: A True Story from History. 2002. (Illus.). 56p. (J). 16.95 (*0-8263-2925-X*) Univ. of New Mexico Pr.

Skurzynski, Gloria & Ferguson, Alane. Ghost Horses. 2000. (National Parks Mysteries Ser.: Vol. 6). (Illus.). 145p. (J). (gr. 4-7). 15.95 (*0-7922-7055-X*) National Geographic Society.

Smith, A. G. Plains Indians Punch-Out Panorama. 1994. (Illus.). (J). (gr. 4-7). pap. 4.95 (*0-486-27741-0*) Dover Pubns., Inc.

Smith, Cynthia. Indian Shoes. 2002. (Illus.). 80p. (J). (gr. 2-5). 15.95 (*0-06-029531-7*); lib. bdg. 15.89 (*0-06-029532-5*) HarperCollins Children's Bk. Group.

Smith, Cynthia Leitich. Rain Is Not My Indian Name. 2001. (Illus.). 144p. (J). (gr. 5-9). lib. bdg. 15.89 (*0-06-029504-X*) HarperCollins Children's Bk. Group.

—Rain Is Not My Indian Name. 2001. 144p. (J). (gr. 5-9). 15.95 (*0-688-17397-7*, Morrow, William & Co.) Morrow/Avon.

Smith, Debra. Hattie Marshall & the Mysterious Strangers. 1996. (Hattie Marshall Frontier Adventure Ser.: Vol. 3). 128p. (J). (gr. 7 up). pap. 4.99 o.p. (*0-89107-878-9*) Crossway Bks.

Smith, Patricia Clark. Weetamoo Heart of the Pocassets: Chief of the Pocassets, Massachusetts, 1653. 2003. (Royal Diaries Ser.). (Illus.). 208p. (J). 10.95 (*0-439-12910-9*) Scholastic, Inc.

Smith, Roland. The Last Lobo. 2001. (J). 12.04 (*0-606-21289-2*) Turtleback Bks.

Sneve, Virginia Driving Hawk. Jimmy Yellow Hawk. 1972. (Illus.). 80p. (J). (gr. 4-6). 10.95 o.p. (*0-8234-0197-9*) Holiday Hse., Inc.

Spalding-Stacy, Joanne. Black Eagle of the Nimapu. 1994. (J). pap. 9.95 o.p. (*0-87770-540-2*) Ye Galleon Pr.

Speare, Elizabeth George. The Sign of the Beaver. 1999. 160p. mass mkt. 2.99 o.s.i (*0-440-22830-1*) Bantam Bks.

—The Sign of the Beaver. 1997. mass mkt. 2.69 o.p. (*0-440-22730-5*); 1993. 144p. (J). (gr. 4-7). pap. 1.99 o.s.i (*0-440-21623-0*) Dell Publishing.

—The Sign of the Beaver. l.t. ed. 1988. 285p. (J). reprint ed. lib. bdg. 16.95 o.s.i (*1-55736-037-5*, Cornerstone Bks.) Pages, Inc.

—The Sign of the Beaver. 1984. 144p. (gr. 4-7). pap. text 5.99 (*0-440-47900-2*); 1994. 172p. (J). vinyl bd. 13.76 (*1-56956-563-5*, BR9513) Random Hse. Children's Bks. (Yearling).

—The Sign of the Beaver. 1983. 11.55 (*0-606-03391-2*) Turtleback Bks.

Spence, Peggy D. The Day of the Ogre Kachinas. 1993. (Illus.). 32p. (Orig.). (J). (gr. 3-9). pap. 4.95 o.p. (*0-89992-134-5*) Council for Indian Education.

Spinka, Penina Keen, ed. White Hare's Horses. 1991. 160p. (J). (gr. 5-9). lib. bdg. 13.95 o.s.i (*0-689-31654-2*, Atheneum) Simon & Schuster Children's Publishing.

Stainer, M. L. The Lyon's Cub. unabr. ed. 1998. (Book 2 of the Lyon Saga Ser.: Bk. 2). (Illus.). 162p. (YA). (gr. 5-10). pap. 6.95 (*0-9646904-6-2*); lib. bdg. 9.95 (*0-9646904-5-4*) Chicken Soup Pr., Inc.

—The Lyon's Throne. 1999. (Lyon Saga Ser.: Bk. 4). (Illus.). 153p. (YA). (gr. 5-9). pap. 6.95 (*1-893337-02-2*) Chicken Soup Pr., Inc.

Steele, Alexander. The Last of the Breed. Ryan, Kevin, ed. 1999. (Adventures of Wishbone Ser.: No. 16). (Illus.). 163p. (J). (gr. 2-5). pap. 3.99 o.p. (*1-57064-273-7*, Big Red Chair Bks.) Lyrick Publishing.

—The Last of the Breed. l.t. ed. 1999. (Adventures of Wishbone Ser.: No. 16). (Illus.). 163p. (J). (gr. 4 up). lib. bdg. 22.60 (*0-8368-2594-2*) Stevens, Gareth Inc.

Steele, D. Kelley. Fire in Her Hair: A Story of Friendship. l.t. ed. 2002. (Illus.). 40p. (J). (gr. 1-6). 18.95 (*0-9711534-0-X*) Hidden Path Pubn., Inc.

Steele, Mary Q. The True Men. 1976. 144p. (J). (gr. 5-9). 12.95 o.p. (*0-688-80052-1*); lib. bdg. 12.88 o.p. (*0-688-84052-3*) HarperCollins Children's Bk. Group. (Greenwillow Bks.).

Steele, William O. The War Party. 1978. (J). (gr. k-3). 4.95 o.p. (*0-15-294789-2*); (Illus.). pap. 1.95 o.p. (*0-15-694697-1*, Voyager Bks./Libros Viajeros) Harcourt Children's Bks.

—Year of the Bloody Sevens. 1963. (Illus.). (J). (gr. 4-6). 6.75 o.p. (*0-15-299800-4*) Harcourt Children's Bks.

Stenhouse, Ted. A Dirty Deed. 2003. 192p. (YA). (gr. 5-9). 16.95 (*1-55337-360-X*) Kids Can Pr., Ltd.

Stites, Clara. Katya of Fort Ross. 2001. (Illus.). 80p. (J). pap. 8.95 (*1-56474-379-9*) Fithian Pr.

Strelkoff, Tatiana. The Changer. 1995. (Illus.). 64p. (J). (gr. 4-6). pap. 12.95 (*0-945522-03-7*) Rebecca Hse.

Strete, Craig K. The Boy Who Became a Rattlesnake. 2004. (Illus.). 32p. (J). 15.99 (*0-399-23572-8*, Putnam & Grosset) Putnam Publishing Group, The.

—The World in Grandfather's Hands. 1995. 128p. (J). (gr. 4-7). 13.95 o.p. (*0-395-72102-4*, Clarion Bks.) Houghton Mifflin Co. Trade & Reference Div.

Strete, Craig K. & Chacon, Michelle N. How the Indians Bought the Farm. 1924. (Illus.). 32p. (J). lib. bdg. o.s.i (*0-688-14131-5*, Greenwillow Bks.) HarperCollins Children's Bk. Group.

Stroud, Virginia A. Doesn't Fall off His Horse. 1994. (Illus.). 32p. (J). 14.89 o.p. (*0-8037-1635-4*); (gr. 1-4). 15.99 o.p. (*0-8037-1634-6*) Penguin Putnam Bks. for Young Readers. (Dial Bks. for Young Readers).

Tanaka, Beatrice. The Chase: A Kutenai Indian Tale. 1991. (Illus.). 32p. (J). (ps-2). 14.99 o.s.i (*0-517-58624-X*, Random Hse. Bks. for Young Readers) Random Hse. Children's Bks.

Taylor, Bonnie Highsmith. Kodi's Mare. 2000. (Cover-to-Cover Novel Ser.). (Illus.). 82p. (J). (*0-7807-8962-8*); pap. (*0-7891-2929-9*) Perfection Learning Corp.

Taylor, C. J. Des Os dans un Panier. 1994. (Native Legends Ser.).Tr. of Native Stories of the Origin of People. (FRE., Illus.). 32p. (YA). (gr. 3 up). 17.95 o.p. (*0-88776-344-8*) Tundra Bks. of Northern New York.

—Deux Plumes et la Solitude Disparue. 1990. (Illus.). 24p. (J). (gr. 1-5). 13.95 o.p. (*0-88776-255-7*) Tundra Bks. of Northern New York.

—Deux-Plumes et la Solitude Disparue: An Abenaki Legend. 1993. (Native Legends Ser.). (FRE., Illus.). 24p. (YA). (gr. 3 up). pap. 6.99 (*0-88776-314-6*) Tundra Bks. of Northern New York.

—How Two-Feather Was Saved from Loneliness: An Abenaki Legend. (Native Legends Ser.). (Illus.). 24p. (J). (gr. 3-6). 1993. pap. 7.95 (*0-88776-282-4*); 1990. 13.95 o.p. (*0-88776-254-9*) Tundra Bks. of Northern New York.

—The Secret of the White Buffalo: An Oglala Sioux Legend. 1997. (Native Legends Ser.). (Illus.). 24p. (J). (gr. 3-7). pap. 6.95 (*0-88776-399-5*) Tundra Bks. of Northern New York.

Taylor, C. J., illus. & retold by. The Monster from the Swamp: Native Legends of Monsters, Demons & Other Creatures. 1995. (Native Legends Ser.). 32p. (J). (gr. 3-6). 17.99 (*0-88776-361-8*) Tundra Bks. of Northern New York.

Taylor, Drew Hayden. The Boy in the Treehouse/The Girl Who Loved Her Horses. 2001. 218p. (J). pap. 12.95 (*0-88922-441-2*) Talonbooks, Ltd. CAN. *Dist:* General Distribution Services, Inc.

Taylor, Morris. Top of the Hill. 1988. 64p. (J). (gr. 4-7). pap. 4.95 (*0-87961-183-9*) Naturegraph Pubs., Inc.

Thomas, Lowell P. The Panther & the Windigo. 2002. (Illus.). 264p. (YA). (gr. 5-9). per. 10.99 (*0-9668559-3-0*) East of the Sun Publishing.

Thomasma, Kenneth. Amee-nah: Zuni Boy Runs the Race of His Life. 1995. (Amazing Indian Children Ser.). (Illus.). 160p. (J). (gr. 6-9). pap. 5.99 o.p. (*0-8010-4054-X*) Baker Bks.

—Amee-nah: Zuni Boy Runs the Race of His Life. 1995. (Amazing Indian Children Ser.). (J). 12.05 o.p. (*0-606-10121-7*) Turtleback Bks.

—Amee-Nah: Zuni Boy Runs the Race of His Life. 1995. (Amazing Indian Children Ser.). (Illus.). 160p. (J). (gr. 6-9). 9.99 o.p. (*0-8010-4068-X*) Baker Bks.

—Doe Sia: Bannock Girl & the Handcart Pioneer. 1999. (Amazing Indian Children: Vol. 8). (J). (gr. 3-8). 12.99 (*1-880114-21-6*) Grandview Publishing Co.

—Doe Sia: Bannock Girl & the Handcart Pioneers. 1999. (Amazing Indian Children Ser.). (Illus.). 208p. (J). (gr. 6-9). pap. 5.99 o.p. (*0-8010-4438-3*) Baker Bks.

—Kunu: Winnebago Boy Escapes. 1989. (Amazing Indian Children Ser.: Bk. 4). (Illus.). 192p. (J). (gr. 6-9). reprint ed. 9.99 o.p. (*0-8010-8891-7*); pap. 5.99 (*0-8010-8892-5*) Baker Bks.

—Kunu: Winnebago Boy Escapes. 1989. (J). 12.99 (*1-880114-04-6*); pap. 7.99 (*1-880114-03-8*) Grandview Publishing Co.

—Kunu: Winnebago Boy Escapes. 1989. (Amazing Indian Children Ser.). 14.04 (*0-606-10243-4*) Turtleback Bks.

—Moho Wat: A Sheepeater Indian Boy Attempts a Rescue. 1994. (Amazing Indian Children Ser.). (Illus.). 192p. (J). (gr. 6-9). 9.99 o.p. (*0-8010-8918-2*); pap. 5.99 o.p. (*0-8010-8919-0*) Baker Bks.

—Moho Wat: Sheepeater Boy Attempts a Rescue. 1994. (Amazing Indian Children). (Illus.). 184p. (J). (gr. 3). 12.99 (*1-880114-14-3*); pap. 7.99 (*1-880114-13-5*) Grandview Publishing Co.

—Moho Wat: Sheepeater Boy Attempts a Rescue. 1994. (Amazing Indian Children Ser.). 12.05 o.p. (*0-606-10262-0*); (Illus.). (J). 14.04 (*0-606-21698-7*) Turtleback Bks.

—Naya Nuki: Shoshoni Girl Who Ran. 1983. (Amazing Indian Children Ser.). (Illus.). 176p. (J). (gr. 6-9). 9.99 o.p. (*0-8010-8869-0*); pap. 6.99 (*0-8010-8868-2*) Baker Bks.

—Naya Nuki: Shoshoni Girl Who Ran. 1991. (Amazing Indian Children Ser.). (J). 14.04 (*0-606-10268-X*) Turtleback Bks.

—Om-Kas-Toe: Blackfeet Twin Captures an Elkdog. (Amazing Indian Children Ser.). (Illus.). (J). (gr. 6-9). 1992. 216p. 9.99 o.p. (*0-8010-8883-6*); 1989. 224p. pap. 5.99 o.p. (*0-8010-8884-4*) Baker Bks.

—Om-Kas-Toe: Blackfeet Twin Captures an Elkdog. 1986. (Amazing Indian Children Ser.). 13.00 (*0-606-10272-8*) Turtleback Bks.

—Om-Kas-Toe: Blackfoot Twin Captures Elkdog. 1986. (J). pap. 7.99 (*1-880114-05-4*) Grandview Publishing Co.

—Pathki Nana: Kootenai Girl Solves a Mystery. 1991. (Amazing Indian Children Ser.). (Illus.). 168p. (J). (gr. 6-9). 9.99 o.p. (*0-8010-8901-8*); pap. 5.99 o.p. (*0-8010-8902-6*) Baker Bks.

—Pathki Nana: Kootenai Girl Solves a Mystery. 1991. (J). (gr. 3-8). pap. 7.99 o.p. (*1-880114-09-7*) Baker Bks.

—Pathki Nana: Kootenai Girl Solves a Mystery. 1991. (J). (gr. 3-8). 12.99 (*1-880114-10-0*) Grandview Publishing Co.

—Pathki Nana: Kootenai Girl Solves a Mystery. 1991. (Amazing Indian Children Ser.). 14.04 (*0-606-10281-7*) Turtleback Bks.

—Soun Tetoken: Nez Perce Boy Tames a Stallion. 1984. (Amazing Indian Children Ser.). 13.00 (*0-606-10303-1*) Turtleback Bks.

Trafzer, Clifford E. & Smith-Trafzer, Lee A. Creation of a California Tribe: Grandfather's Maidu Indian Tale. 1988. (Illus.). 45p. (Orig.). (J). (gr. 4-7). pap. 6.95 (*0-940113-18-X*) Sierra Oaks Publishing Co.

Travis, L. The Redheaded Orphan. 1995. (Ben & Zack Ser.: Vol. 3). 154p. (J). (gr. 3-8). pap. 5.99 o.p. (*0-8010-4023-X*) Baker Bks.

Turner, Ann Warren. Red Flower Goes West. 1999. (Illus.). 32p. (J). (gr. k-4). 14.99 (*0-7868-0313-4*) Hyperion Bks. for Children.

Turner, Ann Warren, et al. The Seasons of Bravery Collection: The Girl Who Chased Away Sorrow; A Time for Courage; I Thought My Soul Would Rise & Fly; The Journal of Biddy Owens, 4 vols. 2002. (Dear America Ser.). (J). pap. 19.96 (*0-439-12942-7*) Scholastic, Inc.

Urban, Betsy. Waiting for Deliverance. 2000. (Illus.). iv, 186p. (J). (gr. 7-12). pap. 17.95 (*0-531-30310-1*); lib. bdg. 18.99 (*0-531-33310-8*) Scholastic, Inc. (Orchard Bks.).

Van Camp, Richard. A Man Called Raven. 1997. (Illus.). 32p. (J). (gr. 1 up). 15.95 (*0-89239-144-8*) Children's Bk. Pr.

—A Man Called Raven. 1997. (Illus.). (J). lib. bdg. 21.20 o.p. (*0-516-20546-3*, Children's Pr.) Scholastic Library Publishing.

—What's the Most Beautiful Thing You Know about Horses? (Illus.). (J). 2003. pap. 7.95 (*0-89239-185-5*); 1998. 32p. (gr. 1 up). 15.95 (*0-89239-154-5*) Children's Bk. Pr.

—What's the Most Beautiful Thing You Know about Horses? 1998. (J). mass mkt. 21.27 o.p. (*0-516-21648-1*, Children's Pr.) Scholastic Library Publishing.

Van der Veer, Judy. Higher Than the Arrow. 1975. (J). (gr. 4-6). pap. 1.50 o.p. (*0-380-00194-2*, 44859-9, Avon Bks.) Morrow/Avon.

Van Leeuwen, Jean. When the White Man Came to Our Shores. 2004. (Illus.). 32p. (J). 16.99 (*0-8037-2544-2*, Dial Bks. for Young Readers) Penguin Putnam Bks. for Young Readers.

Vaughan, Marcia K. Night Dancer: Mythical Piper of the Native American Southwest. 2002. (Illus.). 32p. (J). (ps-2). pap. 16.95 (*0-439-35248-7*, Orchard Bks.) Scholastic, Inc.

Velasco, Vivian A. The Glass Teepee. 1997. (J). 8.95 o.p. (*0-533-12375-5*) Vantage Pr., Inc.

Vick, Helen H. Shadow. (Courage of the Stone Ser.). (gr. 4-9). 2000. 40p. pap. 15.95 (*1-57098-218-X*); 1955. 176p. pap. 9.95 (*1-57098-195-7*) Rinehart, Roberts Pubs.

Vincent, Bonnie J. The Little Big Foot & Family. (J). 4.95 o.p. (*0-533-06733-2*) Vantage Pr., Inc.

Von Ahnen, Katherine. Charlie Young Bear. 1994. (J). E-Book 4.95 (*1-57098-334-8*) Rinehart, Roberts Pubs.

Von Ahnen, Katherine & Young Bear, Joan A. Charlie Young Bear. Gilliland, Hap, ed. (Illus.). 32p. (J). (gr. 3-9). 1991. pap. 3.95 (*0-89992-128-0*); 1990. lib. bdg. 10.95 o.p. (*0-89992-428-X*) Council for Indian Education.

—Charlie Young Bear. 2000. (Council for Indian Education Ser.). (Illus.). 48p. (gr. 2-4). pap. 4.95 (*1-57098-001-2*) Rinehart, Roberts Pubs.

Waboose, Jan Bourdeau. Firedancers. 2000. (Illus.). 32p. (J). (ps-3). 14.95 (*0-7737-3138-5*) Stoddart Kids CAN. *Dist:* Fitzhenry & Whiteside, Ltd.

—Morning on the Lake. (J). (gr. k-4). 2002. 32p. pap. 5.95 (*1-55074-588-3*); 1998. (Illus.). 400p. (*1-55074-373-2*) Kids Can Pr., Ltd.

—Sky Sisters. 2000. (Illus.). 32p. (J). (ps-2). text 15.95 (*1-55074-697-9*) Kids Can Pr., Ltd.

—Skysisters. 2002. (Illus.). 32p. (J). (gr. k-3). pap. 5.95 (*1-55074-699-5*) Kids Can Pr., Ltd.

Wallace, Bill. The Final Freedom. 1997. 176p. (J). (gr. 3-7). per. 3.99 (*0-671-53000-3*, Aladdin) Simon & Schuster Children's Publishing.

Wargin, Kathy-Jo. The Legend of the Lady's Slipper. (Illus.). 48p. (J). (gr. k-5). 2003. pap. 7.95 (*1-58536-168-2*); 2001. 17.95 (*1-886947-74-0*) Sleeping Bear Pr.

Waterton, Betty. A Salmon for Simon. rev. ed. (Illus.). (J). (ps-1). 1998. 32p. pap. 4.95 (*0-88899-276-9*); 1996. 14.95 (*0-88899-265-3*) Groundwood Bks. CAN. *Dist:* Publishers Group West.

Webb, Denise. The Same Sun Was in the Sky. 1995. (Illus.). 32p. (J). (gr. k-3). lib. bdg. 14.95 o.p. (*0-87358-602-6*, Rising Moon Bks. for Young Readers) Northland Publishing.

Weechees. Sun Boy: Cou-Yan-Nai: Comanche Indian Story for Children. 1983. 32p. (J). (gr. 4-9). pap. 4.95 (*0-89992-082-9*) Council for Indian Education.

—Sun Boy & His Hunter's Bow. 1988. (Sun Boy Ser.). 32p. (J). (gr. 4-8). pap. 4.95 (*0-89992-115-9*) Council for Indian Education.

—Sun Boy & the Angry Panther. 1988. (Sun Boy Ser.). 32p. (J). (gr. 4-8). pap. 4.95 (*0-89992-114-0*) Council for Indian Education.

—Sun Boy & the Monster of To-Oh-Pah. 1988. (Sun Boy Ser.). 32p. (J). (gr. 4-8). pap. 4.95 (*0-89992-113-2*) Council for Indian Education.

Weir, Joan. Maybe Tomorrow. 2001. 256p. (YA). (gr. 5-9). pap. 5.95 (*0-7736-7486-1*) Stoddart Kids CAN. *Dist:* Fitzhenry & Whiteside, Ltd.

Welsch, Roger. Uncle Smoke Stories: Four Fires in the Big Belly Lodge of the Nehawka. 1994. (Illus.). 96p. (J). (gr. 3-7). lib. bdg. o.p. (*0-679-95450-3*) Knopf, Alfred A. Inc.

Wesche, Alice M. Runs Far, Son of the Chichimecs. 1982. (J). (gr. 3-7). pap. 9.95 o.p. (*0-89013-133-3*) Museum of New Mexico Pr.

Whelan, Gloria. Miranda's Last Stand. 144p. (J). (gr. 3-7). 2000. pap. 4.95 (*0-06-442097-3*, Harper Trophy); 1999. (Illus.). lib. bdg. 14.89 (*0-06-028252-5*) HarperCollins Children's Bk. Group.

—Miranda's Last Stand. 2000. 11.00 (*0-606-19267-0*); 11.00 (*0-606-19988-8*) Turtleback Bks.

—Night of the Full Moon. 1993. (Illus.). 64p. (J). (gr. 2-4). 15.00 o.s.i (*0-679-84464-3*); (gr. 4-7). 15.99 o.s.i (*0-679-94464-8*) Random Hse. Children's Bks. (Knopf Bks. for Young Readers).

—Night of the Full Moon. 1996. (Illus.). 64p. (J). (gr. 2-4). pap. 3.99 (*0-679-87276-0*) Random Hse., Inc.

—Return to the Island. 2000. 192p. (J). (gr. 4). lib. bdg. 15.89 (*0-06-028254-1*); 14.95 (*0-06-028253-3*) HarperCollins Children's Bk. Group.

—Return to the Island. 2002. 192p. (J). (gr. 4-7). pap. 5.95 (*0-06-440761-6*) HarperCollins Pubs.

White Deer of Autumn Staff. Ceremony-In the Circle of Life. 1983. (Heritage Bks.). (Illus.). 32p. (J). (gr. 3-6). reprint ed. lib. bdg. 14.65 o.p. (*0-940742-24-1*) Raintree Pubs.

—Ceremony in the Circle of Life. 1991. (Illus.). 32p. (J). (gr. 4-7). reprint ed. pap. 9.95 (*0-941831-68-X*) Beyond Words Publishing, Inc.

—The Great Change. 1992. (Illus.). 36p. (J). (gr. 4-7). pap. 14.95 (*0-941831-79-5*) Beyond Words Publishing, Inc.

—Native American Book of Knowledge. Roehm, Michelle, ed. 1992. (Native People, Native Ways Ser.: Vol. I). (Illus.). 88p. (J). (ps up). pap. 5.95 (*0-941831-42-6*) Beyond Words Publishing, Inc.

—The Native American Book of Life. Roehm, Michelle & Begay, Shonto W., eds. 1992. (Native People, Native Ways Ser.: Vol. II). (Illus.). 88p. (J). (gr. 2 up). pap. 5.95 (*0-941831-43-4*) Beyond Words Publishing, Inc.

Whitford-Garner, Donna. My Very First Pow Wow. 1997. (Illus.). 24p. (J). (gr. k-5). pap. 7.00 (*0-8059-4133-9*) Dorrance Publishing Co., Inc.

Wisniewski, David. The Wave of the Sea-Wolf. 1994. (Illus.). 32p. (J). (gr. 4-6). lib. bdg., tchr. ed. 17.00 (*0-395-66478-0*) Houghton Mifflin Co.

Wood, Nancy. The Girl Who Loved Coyotes: Stories of the Southwest. 1995. (Illus.). 48p. (J). (gr. k up). 16.00 (*0-688-13981-7*); lib. bdg. 15.93 o.p. (*0-688-13982-5*) Morrow/Avon. (Morrow, William & Co.).

Wooldridge, Jack. Jomin Lightfoot: A Potawatomi Fable. 1995. (Potawatomi Fables Ser.). 32p. (J). (gr. 1). pap. 7.00 (*1-887963-01-4*) Pota Pr.

—Mko Valley: A Potawatomi Fable. 1997. (Potawatomi Fables Ser.). (Illus.). 29p. (J). pap. 7.00 (*1-887963-11-1*) Pota Pr.

—Nisho: A Potawatomi Fable. 1997. (Potawatomi Fables Ser.). (Illus.). 29p. (J). pap. 7.00 (*1-887963-10-3*) Pota Pr.

—Potawatomi Pony: A Potawatomi Fable. 1995. (Potawatomi Fables Ser.). 32p. (J). (gr. 1). pap. 7.00 (*1-887963-02-2*) Pota Pr.

—Winnie Two-Shadows: A Potawatomi Fable. 1995. (Potawatomi Fables Ser.). 24p. (J). (gr. 1). pap. 7.00 (*1-887963-00-6*) Pota Pr.

Worcester, Donald E. Lone Hunter's Gray Pony. 1985. (Chaparral Bks.). (Illus.). 70p. (J). (gr. 4 up). 10.95 (*0-87565-001-5*) Texas Christian Univ. Pr.

—Lone Hunter's Gray Pony & Lone Hunter & the Cheyennes & War Pony, Set. 1992. (YA). (gr. 7 up). 29.95 o.p. (*0-87565-109-7*) Texas Christian Univ. Pr.

—War Pony. 1984. (Chaparral Bks.). (Illus.). 96p. (J). (gr. 4 up). reprint ed. 10.95 (*0-912646-85-3*) Texas Christian Univ. Pr.

Yerxa, Leo. Last Leaf First Snowflake to Fall. 1994. (Illus.). 32p. (J). (ps-3). pap. 16.95 o.p. (*0-531-06824-2*); lib. bdg. 17.99 (*0-531-08674-7*) Scholastic, Inc. (Orchard Bks.).

Youmans, Marly. The Curse of the Raven Mocker, RS. 2003. 288p. 18.00 (*0-374-31667-8*, Farrar, Straus & Giroux (BYR)) Farrar, Straus & Giroux.

INDIANS OF NORTH AMERICA—HISTORY—FICTION

Balch, Glenn. Horse of Two Colors. 1969. (Illus.). (J). (gr. 3-9). 7.95 o.p. (*0-690-40360-7*) HarperCollins Children's Bk. Group.

Cultures of the World, 6 bks., Set, Group 1. Incl. Burma. Saw Myat Yin. lib. bdg. 35.64 (*1-85435-299-7*); India. Srinivasan, Rodbika. lib. bdg. 35.64 (*1-85435-298-9*); Indonesia. Mirpuri, Gouri. lib. bdg. 35.64 (*1-85435-294-6*); Japan. Shelley, Rex. lib. bdg. 35.64 (*1-85435-297-0*); Malaysia. Munan, Heidi. lib. bdg. 35.64 (*1-85435-296-2*); Singapore. 2nd ed. Layton, Lesley. lib. bdg. 35.64 (*1-85435-295-4*); 128p. (J). (gr. 5-12). (Illus.). 1991. Set lib. bdg. 213.86 (*1-85435-293-8*, Benchmark Bks.) Cavendish, Marshall Corp.

Goble, Paul. Death of the Iron Horse. 1993. (Illus.). 32p. (J). (ps-3). reprint ed. pap. 5.99 (*0-689-71686-9*, Aladdin) Simon & Schuster Children's Publishing.

Jermyn, L. Cultures of the World - Group 2, 6 bks., Set 2nd ed. Incl. Brazil. Richard, Christopher. lib. bdg. 35.64 (*0-7614-1359-6*); Colombia. DuBois, Jill. lib. bdg. 35.64 (*0-7614-1361-8*, Benchmark Bks.); 144p. (J). (gr. 5 up). (Illus.). 2001. Set lib. bdg. 213.86 (*0-7614-1357-X*, Benchmark Bks.) Cavendish, Marshall Corp.

Sewall, Marcia. Thunder from a Clear Sky. 1995. (Illus.). 64p. (J). (ps-3). 17.00 (*0-689-31775-1*, Atheneum) Simon & Schuster Children's Publishing.

Shaffer, Elizabeth N. Hannah & the Indian King, Vol. 2. Pratt, Fran, ed. 2002. (Historical Novel Ser.). pap. 9.95 (*0-936369-35-3*) Son-Rise Pubns. & Distribution Co.

Thompson, Eileen. White Falcon. 1977. (gr. 9 up). lib. bdg. o.p. (*0-385-08651-2*) Doubleday Publishing.

INDIANS OF NORTH AMERICA—HOPI INDIANS—FICTION

Courlander, Harold. People of the Short Blue Corn: Tales & Legends of the Hopi Indians. 1970. (Illus.). (J). (gr. 4-6). 6.95 o.p. (*0-15-260525-8*) Harcourt Children's Bks.

Landau, Elaine. The Hopi. 1994. (First Bks.). 64p. (J). (gr. 4-6). lib. bdg. 21.00 o.p. (*0-531-20098-1*); (Illus.). pap. 6.95 o.p. (*0-531-15684-2*) Scholastic Library Publishing. (Watts, Franklin).

Latterman, Terry. Little Joe, a Hopi Indian Boy, Learns a Hopi Indian Secret. Hawkins, Mary E., ed. 1985. (Illus.). 32p. (J). (gr. 4-12). 12.95 (*0-934739-01-3*) Pussywillow Publishing Hse.

MacGregor, Rob. Prophecy Rock. 1995. 208p. (YA). (gr. 7-12). mass mkt. 16.00 o.s.i (*0-689-80056-8*, Simon & Schuster Children's Publishing) Simon & Schuster Children's Publishing.

Malotki, Ekkehart, tr. The Magic Hummingbird: A Hopi Folktale. 1996. (Illus.). 40p. (J). (ps-3). 15.95 (*1-885772-04-1*) Kiva Publishing, Inc.

Means, Florence C. Our Cup Is Broken, 001. 1969. (Illus.). (J). (gr. 7 up). 6.95 o.p. (*0-395-06937-8*) Houghton Mifflin Co.

Price, Joan. Truth Is a Bright Star. 2003. 156p. (J). (gr. 3-7). pap. 8.95 (*1-58246-055-8*) Tricycle Pr.

INDIANS OF NORTH AMERICA—HUPA INDIANS—FICTION

Oakley, Don. The Adventure of Christian Fast. 1989. (Illus.). 279p. (Orig.). (YA). (gr. 9 up). 12.95 (*0-9619465-1-2*); pap. 8.95 (*0-9619465-2-0*) Eyrie Pr.

INDIANS OF NORTH AMERICA—IROQUOIS INDIANS—FICTION

Baker, Betty. Little Runner of the Longhouse. (I Can Read Bks.). (Illus.). 64p. (J). (gr. k-3). 1989. pap. 3.99 (*0-06-444122-9*, Harper Trophy); 1962. lib. bdg. 15.89 (*0-06-020341-2*) HarperCollins Children's Bk. Group.

Bruchac, Joseph. Eagle Song. (Illus.). 80p. (J). (gr. 2-5). 1999. pap. 4.99 (*0-14-130169-4*, Puffin Bks.); 1997. 14.99 o.p. (*0-8037-1918-3*, Dial Bks. for Young Readers) Penguin Putnam Bks. for Young Readers.

—Eagle Song. 1999. (Puffin Chapters Ser.). 10.14 (*0-606-16833-8*) Turtleback Bks.

—Iroquois Stories: Heroes & Heroines, Monsters & Magic. (Illus.). (J). (gr. 3-7). 1995. 198p. 20.95 (*0-89594-234-8*); 1985. 200p. pap. 12.95 o.p. (*0-89594-167-8*) Crossing Pr., Inc., The.

Kelsey, Avonelle. Iroquois Medicine Woman. (Illus.). 300p. (Orig.). (YA). (*0-9640610-5-8*) Cheval International.

Pryor, Bonnie. American Adventures: Thomas in Danger, 1779. 2nd ed. 1999. (American Adventures Ser.). (Illus.). 176p. (J). (gr. 3-7). 15.99 (*0-688-16518-4*, Morrow, William & Co.) Morrow/Avon.

—Thomas in Danger, 1779. 2000. (American Adventures Ser.). 176p. (J). (gr. 3-7). pap. 4.95 (*0-380-73212-2*) Morrow/Avon.

INDIANS OF NORTH AMERICA—KIOWA INDIANS—FICTION

Hurmence, Belinda. Dixie in the Big Pasture. 1994. (J). (gr. 4 up). 13.95 o.s.i (*0-395-52002-9*) Clarion IND. *Dist:* Houghton Mifflin Co.

Stroud, Virginia A. Doesn't Fall off His Horse. 1994. (Illus.). 32p. (J). 14.89 o.p. (*0-8037-1635-4*); (gr. 1-4). 15.99 o.p. (*0-8037-1634-6*) Penguin Putnam Bks. for Young Readers. (Dial Bks. for Young Readers).

INDIANS OF NORTH AMERICA—MANDAN INDIANS—FICTION

Loveday, John. Goodbye, Buffalo Sky. 1997. 176p. (J). (gr. 7 up). 16.00 (*0-689-81370-8*, McElderry, Margaret K.) Simon & Schuster Children's Publishing.

INDIANS OF NORTH AMERICA—MOHAWK INDIANS—FICTION

Bennett, Jay. Deadly Gift. 1969. (J). (gr. 7 up). 4.50 o.p. (*0-8015-1968-3*, Dutton) Dutton/Plume.

Bruchac, Joseph. Children of the Longhouse. 1996. (Illus.). 160p. (J). (gr. 3-6). 14.89 o.s.i (*0-8037-1794-6*); 14.99 o.p. (*0-8037-1793-8*) Penguin Putnam Bks. for Young Readers. (Dial Bks. for Young Readers).

Carvell, Marlene. Who Will Tell My Brother? 2002. 160p. (J). 15.99 (*0-7868-0827-6*); 150p. (YA). pap. (*0-7868-1657-0*) Hyperion Bks. for Children.

Green, Richard G. Sing, Like a Hermit Thrush. Longboat, Dianne, ed. 1995. (Illus.). 132p. (Orig.). (J). (gr. 8-12). pap. 12.95 (*0-911737-01-4*) Ricara Features.

Peck, Robert Newton. Fawn. 1975. (J). (gr. 7 up). 14.95 o.s.i (*0-316-69652-8*) Little Brown & Co.

Wax, Wendy. Empire Dreams. 2000. (Adventures in America Ser.). (Illus.). 96p. (J). (gr. 4-7). lib. bdg. 14.95 (*1-893110-19-2*) Silver Moon Pr.

INDIANS OF NORTH AMERICA—NAVAHO INDIANS—FICTION

Armer, Laura A. Waterless Mountain. 1993. (Illus.). 240p. (J). (gr. 3-5). 16.00 o.s.i (*0-679-84502-X*, Knopf Bks. for Young Readers) Random Hse. Children's Bks.

Armstrong, Nancy. Navajo Long Walk. 2nd ed. 1999. (Council for Indian Education Ser.). (Illus.). 40p. (gr. 4-7). 8.95 (*1-879373-56-4*) Rinehart, Roberts Pubs.

Blood, Charles L. & Link, Martin. The Goat in the Rug. 1990. (Illus.). 40p. (J). (gr. k-3). reprint ed. pap. 5.99 (*0-689-71418-1*, Aladdin) Simon & Schuster Children's Publishing.

Browne, Vee. Monster Slayer: A Navajo Folktale. 1992. (Illus.). 32p. (J). (gr. 2-3). reprint ed. pap. 7.95 o.p. (*0-87358-626-3*) Northland Publishing.

Bulla, Clyde Robert. Indian Hill. 1963. (Illus.). (J). (gr. 2-5). 9.95 o.p. (*0-690-43626-2*) HarperCollins Children's Bk. Group.

Chanin, Michael. The Chief's Blanket. 1998. (Illus.). 32p. (J). (ps-5). 14.95 (*0-915811-78-2*, Starseed Pr.) Kramer, H.J. Inc.

Clark, Ann Nolan. Little Herder in Autumn. Harrington, John P., ed. Young, Robert W., tr. 1988. (ENG & NAV., Illus.). 96p. (J). reprint ed. (gr. 3 up). 19.95 o.p. (*0-941270-47-5*); (gr. 4-7). pap. 9.95 (*0-941270-46-7*) Ancient City Pr., Inc.

Crowder, Jack L., et al. Stephanie & the Coyote. Morgan, William, tr. 3rd rev. ed. (ENG & NAV., Illus.). 32p. (J). (gr. 3 up). reprint ed. pap. 4.95 (*0-9616589-0-8*) Crowder, Jack L.

Dewey, Jennifer Owings. Navajo Summer. (Illus.). 136p. (gr. 5-8). 2003. (YA). 9.95 (*1-56397-855-5*); 1998. (J). pap. 14.95 o.s.i (*1-56397-248-4*) Boyds Mills Pr.

Francisco, Nia. Blue Horses for Navajo Women. 1988. (Illus.). 80p. (J). pap. 9.95 (*0-912678-72-0*, Greenfield Review Pr.) Greenfield Review Literary Ctr., Inc.

Garaway, Margaret K. Ashkii & His Grandfather - Ashkii y el Abuelo. Cartes, Marie R., tr. (ENG & SPA., Illus.). 32p. (Orig.). (J). (gr. 2-10). 1996. pap. 8.95 (*0-9638851-6-2*); 1995. pap. 14.95 (*0-9638851-7-0*) Old Hogan Publishing Co.

—The Old Hogan. rev. ed. 1995. (Illus.). 32p. (Orig.). (J). (gr. k-6). pap. 4.95 (*0-9638851-0-3*) Old Hogan Publishing Co.

Garaway, Margaret Kahn. Ashkii & His Grandfather. 1989. (Illus.). 33p. (J). (gr. k-6). 5.95 o.p. (*0-918080-41-X*, 20974) Treasure Chest Bks.

Gessner. Brother to the Navajo. 1979. (J). 8.95 o.p. (*0-525-66659-1*) NAL.

Gessner, Lynne. Malcolm Yucca Seed. rev. ed. 1995. (Illus.). 63p. (J). (gr. 3-8). reprint ed. pap. 5.95 o.p. (*0-918080-63-0*) Treasure Chest Bks.

Grammer, Maurine. The Navajo Brothers & the Stolen Herd. 2004. (Illus.). 120p. (J). (gr. 4-7). pap. 9.95 (*1-878610-23-6*) Red Crane Bks., Inc.

Gray, Genevieve. The Magic Bears. 1975. (Blessingway Tales of a Navajo Family). (Illus.). 40p. (J). (gr. 4-9). pap. 3.95 o.p. (*0-88436-224-8*, ELA 129055) Paradigm Publishing, Inc.

—The Secret of the Mask. 1975. (Blessingway Tales of a Navajo Family). (Illus.). 40p. (J). (gr. 4-9). pap. 3.95 o.p. (*0-88436-222-1*) Paradigm Publishing, Inc.

—The Spiderweb Stone. 1975. (Blessingway Tales of a Navajo Family). (Illus.). 40p. (J). (gr. 4-9). pap. 3.95 o.p. (*0-88436-220-5*, ELA 129053) Paradigm Publishing, Inc.

—The Tall Singer. 1975. (Blessingway Tales of a Navajo Family). (Illus.). 40p. (J). (gr. 4-9). pap. 3.95 o.p. (*0-88436-218-3*, ELA 129052) Paradigm Publishing, Inc.

Green, Timothy. Mystery of Navajo Moon. (Illus.). 48p. (J). (ps-3). 1991. lib. bdg. 14.95 o.p. (*0-87358-523-2*); 1993. reprint ed. pap. 7.95 o.p. (*0-87358-577-1*) Northland Publishing.

—Twilight Boy. 1998. 127p. (J). (gr. 7 up). pap. 6.95 o.p. (*0-87358-640-9*); lib. bdg. 12.95 o.p. (*0-87358-670-0*) Northland Publishing. (Rising Moon Bks. for Young Readers).

—Twilight Boy. 1998. 13.00 (*0-606-16641-6*) Turtleback Bks.

Hausman, Gerald. The Coyote Bead. 1999. (Young Spirit Books Ser.). 144p. (J). (gr. 5-10). pap. 11.95 (*1-57174-145-3*) Hampton Roads Publishing Co., Inc.

Kent, Renee Holmes. J. J. Navajo Princess. 2000. (Adventures in Misty Falls Ser.: Vol. 3). (Illus.). vi, 114p. (J). (gr. 4-7). pap. 4.99 (*1-56309-763-X*, New Hope) Woman's Missionary Union.

Krantz, Hazel. Walks in Beauty. 1997. 192p. (YA). pap. 6.95 (*0-87358-671-9*); (J). (gr. 7 up). lib. bdg. 12.95 (*0-87358-667-0*) Northland Publishing. (Rising Moon Bks. for Young Readers).

Lauritzen, Jonreed. The Ordeal of the Young Hunter. 1954. (Illus.). (J). (gr. 5 up). 4.95 o.p. (*0-316-51640-6*) Little Brown & Co.

Maher, Ramona. Alice Yazzie's Year. 1977. (Illus.). (J). (gr. 3-6). 7.95 o.p. (*0-698-20432-8*) Putnam Publishing Group, The.

—Alice Yazzie's Year. 2003. (Illus.). 40p. (J). 15.95 (*1-58246-080-9*) Tricycle Pr.

Marks, Dea, illus. Tall Shadow, a Navajo Boy. 1998. (Cover-to-Cover Bks.). (J). (*0-7807-7040-4*) Perfection Learning Corp.

Momaday, N. Scott. Owl in the Cedar Tree. 1992. (Illus.). 116p. (J). (gr. 4-7). reprint ed. pap. 9.95 (*0-8032-8184-6*) Univ. of Nebraska Pr.

Moon, Sheila. Deepest Roots. 1986. (Illus.). 240p. (J). (gr. 8-12). pap. 8.95 (*0-917479-10-6*) Guild for Psychological Studies Publishing Hse.

—Knee-Deep in Thunder. 1986. (Illus.). 307p. (J). (gr. 8-12). reprint ed. pap. 11.95 (*0-917479-08-4*) Guild for Psychological Studies Publishing Hse.

O'Dell, Scott. Sing down the Moon. 1973. 138p. (J). (gr. 5 up). pap. 1.50 o.p. (*0-440-47975-4*) Dell Publishing.

Perrine, Mary. Salt Boy, 001. 1973. (Illus.). 32p. (J). (gr. k-3). reprint ed. pap. 0.95 o.p. (*0-395-17450-3*) Houghton Mifflin Co. Trade & Reference Div.

Pitts, Paul. Racing the Sun. 1988. 160p. (J). (gr. 4-7). pap. 5.99 (*0-380-75496-7*, Harper Trophy) HarperCollins Children's Bk. Group.

—Racing the Sun. 1988. 11.00 (*0-606-03897-3*) Turtleback Bks.

Richardson, Jean. The Courage Seed. 1993. (Illus.). 76p. (J). (gr. 4-5). 14.95 (*0-89015-902-5*) Eakin Pr.

Robinson, Marileta. Mr. Goat's Bad Good Idea: Three Stories. 1979. (J). (gr. 1-4). 11.50 (*0-690-03862-3*) HarperCollins Children's Bk. Group.

Roessel, Monty. Kinaalda: A Navajo Girl Grows Up. 1993. (We Are Still Here Ser.). (Illus.). 48p. (J). (gr. 4-6). pap. 6.95 (*0-8225-9641-5*, Lerner Pubns.) Lerner Publishing Group.

Schick, Eleanor. My Navajo Sister. 1996. (Illus.). 32p. (J). (ps-3). 16.00 (*0-689-80529-2*, Simon & Schuster Children's Publishing) Simon & Schuster Children's Publishing.

—Navajo Wedding Day: A Dine Marriage Ceremony. 1999. (Accelerated Reader Bks.). (Illus.). 40p. (J). (gr. k-3). 15.95 (*0-7614-5031-9*, Cavendish Children's Bks.) Cavendish, Marshall Corp.

Smiley, Virginia Kester. Swirling Sands. 2001. cd-rom 14.95 (*1-930430-18-3*) Waltsan Publishing, LLC.

Tapahonso, Luci. Songs of Shiprock Fair. 1999. (Illus.). 32p. (J). (ps-3). 15.95 (*1-885772-11-4*) Kiva Publishing, Inc.

Thomas, Marjorie W. Bidii. 2000. 32p. (J). pap. 9.95 (*1-893354-16-4*) Salina Bookshelf.

—White Nose the Sheep Dog: Chiilgai, Na'nilkaadii. 2000. 40p. pap. 9.00 (*1-893354-17-2*) Salina Bookshelf.

Whitethorne, Baje, Sr. Father's Boots: Azhe'e bikenidoots'osii. Marvin, Yellowhair & Jerrold, Johnson, eds. Darlene, Redhair, tr. 2001. (ENG & NAV., Illus.). 42p. (J). (gr. 1-6). text 17.95 (*1-893354-29-6*) Salina Bookshelf.

Whitethorne, Baje, Sr., illus. Sunpainters: Eclipse of the Navajo Sun. 2002. (J). (*1-893354-33-4*) Salina Bookshelf.

Wilson, Bennett. The Magic Feather: An Adventure in Navajo Land. 1989. (Illus.). 42p. (Orig.). (J). (gr. 1-6). pap. 5.00 o.p. (*0-918080-48-7*) Treasure Chest Bks.

Wunderli, Stephen. The Blue Between the Clouds, ERS. 1996. (J). (gr. 4-7). pap. 5.95 o.p. (*0-8050-4819-7*); 1992. 80p. (YA). (gr. 5 up). 13.95 o.p. (*0-8050-1772-0*) Holt, Henry & Co. (Holt, Henry & Co. Bks. For Young Readers).

INDIANS OF NORTH AMERICA—NEZ PERCE INDIANS—FICTION

Forman, James D. People of the Dream. 1974. 208p. (J). pap. 0.95 o.p. (*0-440-97337-6*, Laurel Leaf) Random Hse. Children's Bks.

Krupinski, Loretta. Best Friends. 1998. (Illus.). 32p. (J). (gr. k-4). 14.95 (*0-7868-0332-0*); lib. bdg. 15.49 (*0-7868-2356-9*) Hyperion Bks. for Children.

O'Dell, Scott & Hall, Elizabeth. Thunder Rolling in the Mountains. 1992. (Illus.). 144p. (YA). (gr. 7-7). 17.00 (*0-395-59966-0*) Houghton Mifflin Co.

Rushford, Patricia H. Betrayed. 1996. (Jennie McGrady Mysteries Ser.: No. 7). 192p. (Orig.). (J). (gr. 4-7). pap. 4.99 (*1-55661-560-4*, Bethany Backyard) Bethany Hse. Pubs.

Sanderson, William E. Nez Perce Buffalo Horse. 1972. (Illus.). (YA). (gr. 8-10). 4.95 o.p. (*0-87004-212-2*) Caxton Pr.

Shaw, Janet Beeler. Changes for Kaya: A Winter Story. 2002. (American Girls Collection: Bk. 6). (Illus.). 80p. (J). (gr. 2-7). 12.95 (*1-58485-434-0*); pap. 5.95 (*1-58485-433-2*) Pleasant Co. Pubns. (American Girl).

—Kaya: An American Girl. 2002. (American Girls Collection). (Illus.). (J). 74.95 o.p. (*1-56247-512-6*); (YA). (gr. 2). pap. 34.95 (*1-58485-511-8*, American Girl) Pleasant Co. Pubns.

—Kaya & Lone Dog: A Friendship Story. 2002. (American Girls Collection: Bk. 4). (Illus.). 96p. (J). (gr. 2-7). 12.95 (*1-58485-430-8*); pap. 5.95 (*1-58485-429-4*) Pleasant Co. Pubns. (American Girl).

—Kaya & the River Girl. 2003. (American Girls Collection). (Illus.). 38p. (J). pap. 4.95 (*1-58485-792-7*, American Girl) Pleasant Co. Pubns.

—Kaya Shows the Way: A Sister Story. 2002. (American Girls Collection: Bk. 5). (Illus.). 88p. (J). (gr. 2-7). 12.95 (*1-58485-432-4*); pap. 5.95 (*1-58485-431-6*) Pleasant Co. Pubns. (American Girl).

—Kaya's Escape! A Survival Story. 2002. (American Girls Collection: Bk. 2). (Illus.). 88p. (J). (gr. 2-7). 12.95 (*1-58485-426-X*); pap. 5.95 (*1-58485-425-1*) Pleasant Co. Pubns. (American Girl).

—Kaya's Hero: A Story of Giving. 2002. (American Girls Collection: Bk. 3). (Illus.). 88p. (J). (gr. 2-7). 12.95 (*1-58485-428-6*); pap. 5.95 (*1-58485-427-8*) Pleasant Co. Pubns. (American Girl).

—Meet Kaya: An American Girl. 2002. (American Girls Collection: Bk. 1). (Illus.). 80p. (J). (gr. 2-7). 12.95 (*1-58485-424-3*); pap. 5.95 (*1-58485-423-5*) Pleasant Co. Pubns. (American Girl).

Spalding-Stacy, Joanne. Black Eagle of the Nimapu. 1994. (J). pap. 9.95 o.p. (*0-87770-540-2*) Ye Galleon Pr.

Thomasma, Kenneth. Soun Tetoken: Nez Perce Boy Tames a Stallion. 1984. (J). pap. 7.99 (*1-880114-07-0*) Grandview Publishing Co.

INDIANS OF NORTH AMERICA—OGLALA INDIANS—FICTION

Bruchac, Joseph. Crazy Horse's Vision. 2000. (Illus.). 40p. (YA). (gr. 1 up). 16.95 (*1-880000-94-6*) Lee & Low Bks., Inc.

Johnson, Dorothy M. All the Buffalo Returning. 1996. 248p. (J). pap. 11.00 (*0-8032-7590-0*, Bison Bks.) Univ. of Nebraska Pr.

Kath, Sharon. Teepees on the Moon. 2001. 186p. (J). (gr. 8-12). 15.95 (*0-936389-85-0*) Tudor Pubs., Inc.

INDIANS OF NORTH AMERICA—OJIBWAY INDIANS—FICTION

Carter, Alden R. Crescent Moon. 1999. 153p. (J). (gr. 5-9). tchr. ed. 16.95 (*0-8234-1521-X*) Holiday Hse., Inc.

—Crescent Moon. 1999. (J). 15.95 (*0-590-29882-8*) Scholastic, Inc.

—Dogwolf. 1994. 272p. (J). (gr. 7-9). pap. 13.95 (*0-590-46741-7*) Scholastic, Inc.

Densmore, Frances. Dakota & Ojibwe People in Minnesota. 1977. (Illus.). 55p. (J). (gr. 5-8). pap. 3.50 o.p. (*0-87351-111-5*) Minnesota Historical Society Pr.

Durbin, William. Wintering. 208p. (YA). (gr. 5-7). 2000. (Illus.). pap. 4.50 (*0-440-22759-3*, Yearling); 1999. 14.95 (*0-385-32598-3*, Dell Books for Young Readers) Random Hse. Children's Bks.

Erdrich, Louise. The Birchbark House. 1999. (Illus.). 256p. (J). (gr. 4 up). 17.99 (*0-7868-0300-2*) Hyperion Bks. for Children.

—The Birchbark House. 2002. (Illus.). 256p. (J). (gr. 4 up). pap. 6.99 (*0-7868-1454-3*) Hyperion Paperbacks for Children.

—The Birchbark House. 1999. 192p. (YA). (gr. 4 up). lib. bdg. 15.49 (*0-7868-2241-4*) Hyperion Pr.

—The Birchbark House. l.t. ed. 2000. (Young Adult Ser.). 272p. (YA). (gr. 7-12). 20.95 (*0-7862-2178-X*) Thorndike Pr.

Ernst, Kathleen. Trouble at Fort la Pointe. 2000. (American Girl Collection: Bk. 7). (Illus.). 176p. (J). (gr. 5-9). pap. 5.95 (*1-58485-086-8*); 9.95 (*1-58485-087-6*) Pleasant Co. Pubns. (American Girl).

—Trouble at Fort la Pointe. 2000. (American Girl Collection). (Illus.). (J). 12.00 (*0-606-20956-5*) Turtleback Bks.

Gerber, Carole. Firefly Night. 2000. (Illus.). 32p. (J). (ps-1). 16.95 (*1-58089-051-2*); pap. 6.95 (*1-58089-066-0*) Charlesbridge Publishing, Inc. (Whispering Coyote).

—Firefly Night. 2000. 13.10 (*0-606-19687-0*) Turtleback Bks.

McCain, Becky R. Grandmother's Dreamcatcher. (Illus.). 32p. (J). (gr. k-3). 2001. pap. 6.95 (*0-8075-3032-8*); 1998. 15.95 (*0-8075-3031-X*) Whitman, Albert & Co.

Shaw, Janet Beeler. Kirsten & the Chippewa. 2002. (American Girls Short Stories Ser.). (Illus.). 56p. (J). 4.95 (*1-58485-479-0*, American Girl) Pleasant Co. Pubns.

Slipperjack, Ruby. Little Voice. 2001. (In the Same Boat Ser.: No. 4). (Illus.). 250p. (J). (gr. 4-6). pap. text 8.95 (*1-55050-182-8*) Coteau Bks. CAN. *Dist:* General Distribution Services, Inc.

Van Laan, Nancy. Shingebiss: An Ojibwe Legend. (Illus.). 32p. (J). (ps-3). 2002. pap. 6.95 (*0-618-21616-2*); 1997. lib. bdg., tchr. ed. 16.00 (*0-395-82745-0*) Houghton Mifflin Co.

Wood, Douglas. The Windigo's Return: A North Woods Story. 1996. (Illus.). 32p. (J). (ps-3). 16.00 (*0-689-80065-7*, Simon & Schuster Children's Publishing) Simon & Schuster Children's Publishing.

Wosmek, Frances. A Brown Bird Singing. 1993. (Illus.). 128p. (J). (gr. 5 up). pap. 4.95 o.p. (*0-688-04596-0*, Morrow, William & Co.) Morrow/Avon.

INDIANS OF NORTH AMERICA—PAIUTE INDIANS—FICTION

Austin, Mary H. Basket Woman: A Book of Indian Tales for Children. 1904. (J). 10.00 o.p. (*0-403-00001-7*) Scholarly Pr., Inc.

Fuchs, Bernie. Fastest Ride. 2004. 32p. (J). pap. 16.95 (*0-439-26645-9*, Blue Sky Pr., The) Scholastic, Inc.

Morrow, Mary F. Sarah Winnemucca: Paiute Native American Indian Stories. 1996. (Raintree-Rivilo American Indian Stories Ser.). 10.15 o.p. (*0-606-12504-3*) Turtleback Bks.

INDIANS OF NORTH AMERICA—PAPAGO INDIANS—FICTION

Cowley, Joy. Big Moon Tortilla. 2003. (Illus.). 32p. (J). pap. 7.95 (*1-59078-037-X*); (gr. 1-4). 14.95 (*1-56397-601-3*) Boyds Mills Pr.

INDIANS OF NORTH AMERICA—PAWNEE INDIANS—FICTION

Begay, Shonto W., illus. The Mud Pony. 1988. 32p. (J). (gr. k-4). 15.95 (*0-590-41525-5*) Scholastic, Inc.

Cohen, Caron Lee. The Mud Pony. 1992. 32p. (J). (ps-3). mass mkt. 4.99 o.s.i (*0-590-41526-3*) Scholastic, Inc.

Fradin, Dennis Brindell. The Pawnee. rev. ed. 1992. (New True Books Ser.). (Illus.). 48p. (J). (gr. 2-4). pap. 5.50 o.p. (*0-516-41155-1*); (ps-3). mass mkt. 21.00 o.p. (*0-516-01155-3*) Scholastic Library Publishing. (Children's Pr.).

Howell, War Cry. Gramma Curlychief's Pawnee Indian Stories. 3rd ed. 1991. (Comic Tale Easy Reader Ser.). (Illus.). 88p. (Orig.). (J). (gr. 5-12). 18.75 o.p. (*0-943864-20-8*) Davenport, May Pubs.

—Gramma Curlychief's Pawnee Indian Stories: Comic Tale Easy Reader. 3rd ed. 1991. (Comic Tale Easy Reader Ser.). (Illus.). 88p. (Orig.). (J). (gr. 5-12). pap. 4.95 (*0-943864-22-4*) Davenport, May Pubs.

Paulsen, Gary. Mr. Tucket. 1994. 176p. text 15.95 (*0-385-31169-9*, Delacorte Pr.) Dell Publishing.

—Mr. Tucket. 2000. (Illus.). 192p. (gr. 5-7). mass mkt. 2.99 o.s.i (*0-375-80680-6*, Random Hse. Bks. for Young Readers); 1996. (J). pap. 5.99 (*0-440-91097-8*, Dell Books for Young Readers); 1995. (Tucket Adventures Ser.: Vol. 1). 192p. (gr. 5 up). pap. text 4.99 (*0-440-41133-5*, Yearling); 1995. (J). pap. 5.99 (*0-440-91053-6*, Dell Books for Young Readers) Random Hse. Children's Bks.

—Mr. Tucket, unabr. ed. 1994. (J). (gr. 6). audio 27.00 (*0-7887-0010-3*, 94209E7) Recorded Bks., LLC.

—Mr. Tucket. 1995. 10.55 (*0-606-07895-9*) Turtleback Bks.

Remington, Gwen. The Pawnee. 2001. (Indigenous Peoples of North America Ser.). (Illus.). 96p. (YA). (gr. 4-12). lib. bdg. 27.45 (*1-56006-825-6*, LML00902-178157, Lucent Bks.) Gale Group.

INDIANS OF NORTH AMERICA—PUEBLO INDIANS—FICTION

Bryant, Kathleen. Kokopelli's Gift. 2002. (Illus.). 32p. (J). 15.95 (*1-885772-29-7*) Kiva Publishing, Inc.

Garland, Sherry. Indio. 1995. (Great Episodes Ser.). 304p. (YA). (gr. 7 up). 11.00 o.s.i (*0-15-238631-9*); pap. 6.00 (*0-15-200021-6*) Harcourt Children's Bks. (Gulliver Bks.).

—Indio. 1995. (Illus.). 10.10 o.p. (*0-606-09466-0*) Turtleback Bks.

Harcourt Brace Staff, ed. Pueblo Storyteller. 93rd ed. 1993. pap. text 14.00 (*0-15-300343-X*) Harcourt Children's Bks.

Keegan, Marcia. Pueblo Boy. 1997. 48p. (J). pap. 5.99 o.s.i (*0-14-036945-7*, Viking) Penguin Putnam Bks. for Young Readers.

Kita, Suzanne. The Mystery of the Anasazi at Frijoles Canyon. 2002. (Illus.). 96p. (J). 14.95 (*1-885772-26-2*) Kiva Publishing, Inc.

Lehr, Norma. Dance of the Crystal Skull. 1999. (Illus.). (J). (gr. 3-7). 115p. pap. 6.95 o.p. (*0-87358-725-1*); 238p. lib. bdg. 15.95 o.p. (*0-87358-724-3*) Northland Publishing. (Rising Moon Bks. for Young Readers).

—Dance of the Crystal Skull. 1999. (Illus.). (J). 13.00 (*0-606-18310-8*) Turtleback Bks.

Lyon, George Ella. Dreamplace. 1993. (Illus.). 32p. (J). (ps-2). mass mkt. 16.99 o.p. (*0-531-08616-X*); pap. 15.95 (*0-531-05466-7*) Scholastic, Inc. (Orchard Bks.).

—Dreamplace. 1998. (J). 13.10 (*0-606-13348-8*) Turtleback Bks.

McDermott, Gerald. Arrow to the Sun: A Pueblo Indian Tale. 2002. 48p. 15.95 (*957-632-204-9*) Formosan Magazine Pr., Ltd. CHN. *Dist:* Shen's Bks.

—Arrow to the Sun: A Pueblo Indian Tale. 1977. (Picture Puffin Ser.). 13.14 (*0-606-01088-2*) Turtleback Bks.

Mendel, Kathleen Lee. Whispering Clay. Valentine, Candy K., ed. 1992. (Illus.). 30p. (J). spiral bd. 11.00 (*1-878142-29-1*) Telstar.

Stine, Megan & Stine, H. William. Young Indiana Jones & the Lost Gold of Durango. 1993. (Young Indiana Jones Ser.: No. 10). 132p. (Orig.). (J). (gr. 4-6). pap. 3.50 o.s.i (*0-679-84926-2*, Random Hse. Bks. for Young Readers) Random Hse. Children's Bks.

Strete, Craig K. Big Thunder Magic. 1990. (Illus.). 32p. (J). (ps up). 12.95 o.p. (*0-688-08853-8*); lib. bdg. 12.88 o.p. (*0-688-08854-6*) HarperCollins Children's Bk. Group. (Greenwillow Bks.).

Thompson, Eileen. The Golden Coyote. 1981. (Illus.). 128p. (J). (gr. 3-7). 4.95 o.p. (*0-671-65193-5*, Simon & Schuster Children's Publishing) Simon & Schuster Children's Publishing.

Vallo, Lawrence. Tales of a Pueblo Boy: A Memoir. 2nd ed. 1987. (Illus.). 48p. (J). (gr. 6-9). pap. 5.95 (*0-86534-089-7*) Sunstone Pr.

Vick, Helen H. Shadow. (Courage of the Stone Ser.). (gr. 4-9). 2000. 40p. pap. 15.95 (*1-57098-218-X*); 1955. 176p. pap. 9.95 (*1-57098-195-7*) Rinehart, Roberts Pubs.

Weisman, Joan. The Storyteller. 1993. (Illus.). 32p. (J). 15.95 o.p. (*0-8478-1742-3*) Rizzoli International Pubns., Inc.

INDIANS OF NORTH AMERICA—SALISH INDIANS—FICTION

Harris, Christie. Secret in the Stlalakum Wild. 1972. (Illus.). (J). (gr. 4-6). 1.29 o.s.i (*0-689-30027-1*, Atheneum) Simon & Schuster Children's Publishing.

INDIANS OF NORTH AMERICA—SAUK INDIANS—FICTION

Anderson, Leone C. Sean's War. 1998. (Illus.). 192p. (J). (gr. 3-9). 16.95 (*0-9638819-4-9*) ShadowPlay Pr.

Jackson, Dave & Jackson, Neta. Abandoned on the Wild Frontier: Peter Cartwright. 1995. (Trailblazer Bks.: Vol. 15). (Illus.). 144p. (J). (gr. 3-7). pap. 5.99 (*1-55661-468-3*) Bethany Hse. Pubs.

Le Sueur, Meridel. Sparrow Hawk. 1966. (Illus.). (J). (gr. 5 up). lib. bdg. 5.19 o.s.i (*0-394-91658-1*, Knopf Bks. for Young Readers) Random Hse. Children's Bks.

INDIANS OF NORTH AMERICA—SEMINOLE INDIANS—FICTION

Ball, Zachary. Salvage Diver. 1961. 220p. (J). (gr. 7 up). 4.95 o.p. (*0-8234-0100-6*) Holiday Hse., Inc.

Kudlinski, Kathleen V. Night Bird: A Story of the Seminole Indians. (Once upon America Ser.). (Illus.). 64p. (J). (gr. 2-6). 1995. pap. 3.99 o.s.i (*0-14-034353-9*, Puffin Bks.); 1993. 12.99 o.s.i (*0-670-83157-3*, Viking Children's Bks.) Penguin Putnam Bks. for Young Readers.

McKissack, Patricia C. Run Away Home. 1997. 128p. (J). (gr. 3-7). pap. 14.95 (*0-590-46751-4*) Scholastic, Inc.

Moeller, Kathleen H. Hoketichee & the Manatee. 1998. (Books for Young Learners). (Illus.). 16p. (J). (gr. k-2). pap. text 5.00 (*1-57274-117-1*, A2745) Owen, Richard C. Pubs., Inc.

INDIANS OF NORTH AMERICA—SENECA INDIANS—FICTION

Harrington, M. R. The Iroquois Trail: Dickon among the Onondagas & Senecas. 1991. (Illus.). 215p. (YA). reprint ed. pap. text 9.95 (*0-8135-0480-5*) Rutgers Univ. Pr.

Lenski, Lois. Indian Captive: The Story of Mary Jemison. (Illus.). 272p. (J). 1994. (gr. 5 up). lib. bdg. 17.89 (*0-397-30076-X*); 1990. (gr. 7-9). 16.00 o.p. (*0-397-30072-7*) HarperCollins Children's Bk. Group.

—Indian Captive: The Story of Mary Jemison. 1995. 12.00 (*0-606-07706-5*) Turtleback Bks.

Lenski, Lois, illus. Indian Captive: The Story of Mary Jemison. 97th ed. 1995. 320p. (J). (gr. 5 up). pap. 6.99 (*0-06-446162-9*, Harper Trophy) HarperCollins Children's Bk. Group.

Panagopoulos, Janie Lynn. Little Ship under Full Sail. 1997. 146p. (J). 15.95 (*0-938682-46-6*) River Road Pubns., Inc.

Parker, Arthur C. Skunny Wundy Seneca Indian Tales. 1970. (Albert Whitman Folklore Ser.). (Illus.). (gr. 3 up). 5.95 o.p. (*0-8075-7405-8*) Whitman, Albert & Co.

INDIANS OF NORTH AMERICA—SHAWNEE INDIANS—FICTION

Allen, LeRoy. Shawnee Lance. 1970. (J). (gr. 3-7). lib. bdg. 4.58 o.p. (*0-440-07842-3*, Delacorte Pr.) Dell Publishing.

Bierhorst, John, ed. Ring in the Prairie. 1970. (Illus.). (J). (gr. 1-4). 7.95 o.p. (*0-8037-7462-1*); 7.45 o.p. (*0-8037-7461-3*) Penguin Putnam Bks. for Young Readers. (Dial Bks. for Young Readers).

Rinaldi, Ann. The Second Bend in the River. (J). 1999. 288p. (gr. 5-9). mass mkt. 4.99 (*0-590-74259-0*); 1997. pap. 15.95 (*0-590-74258-2*) Scholastic, Inc.

—The Second Bend in the River. 1999. 11.04 (*0-606-16581-9*) Turtleback Bks.

Watkins, Sherrin. Green Snake Ceremony. 1995. (Greyfeather Ser.). (Illus.). 408p. (J). (ps-5). 17.95 *(0-933031-89-0)* Council Oak Bks.

—White Bead Ceremony. (Greyfeather Ser.). (Illus.). (J). (gr. 1-5). 1995. 512p. 16.95 *(0-933031-92-0)*; 1994. 40p. o.p. *(0-933031-26-2)* Council Oak Bks.

INDIANS OF NORTH AMERICA—SIKSIKA INDIANS—FICTION

Ackerman, Ned. The Spirit Horse. 1998. 167p. (J). (gr. 5-9). pap. 15.95 *(0-590-39650-1)* Scholastic, Inc.

—Spirit Horse. 2002. 176p. (YA). mass mkt. 4.99 *(0-590-39720-6)* Scholastic, Inc.

Hudson, Jan. Sweetgrass. 1991. 160p. (YA). (gr. 7-9). pap. 3.99 *(0-590-43486-1)* Scholastic, Inc.

—Sweetgrass. 1984. 9.09 o.p. *(0-606-04820-0)* Turtleback Bks.

Oke, Janette. Drums of Change. 2003. (Classics for Girls Ser.). (Illus.). 176 p. (J). 9.99 *(0-7642-2714-9)* Bethany Hse. Pubs.

Roop, Peter. The Buffalo Jump. 1996. (Illus.). 32p. (J). (gr. 1-3). lib. bdg. 14.95 *(0-87358-616-6*, Rising Moon Bks. for Young Readers) Northland Publishing.

Yolen, Jane. Sky Dogs. 1990. (Illus.). 32p. (J). (ps-3). 15.95 o.s.i *(0-15-275480-6)*; 100.00 o.p. *(0-15-275481-4)* Harcourt Trade Pubs.

INDIANS OF NORTH AMERICA—SIOUX INDIANS—FICTION

Bunting, Eve. Moonstick: The Seasons of the Sioux. (Trophy Picture Book Ser.). (Illus.). 32p. (J). (gr. k-4). 2000. pap. 6.99 *(0-06-443619-5*, Harper Trophy); 1997. 15.95 *(0-06-024804-1*, Cotler, Joanna Bks.) HarperCollins Children's Bk. Group.

—Moonstick: The Seasons of the Sioux. unabr. ed. (J). 1998. audio 10.00 *(0-7887-1791-X*, 95263E7); 1997. 31.70 incl. audio *(0-7887-1832-0*, 40612); 1997. 167.80 incl. audio *(0-7887-3927-1*, 46348) Recorded Bks., LLC.

—Moonstick: The Seasons of the Sioux. 2000. 12.10 *(0-606-18706-5)* Turtleback Bks.

Dixon, Franklin W. Dead Man in Deadwood. Greenberg, Anne, ed. 1994. (Hardy Boys Casefiles Ser.: No. 87). 160p. (YA). (gr. 6 up). pap. 3.99 *(0-671-79471-X*, Simon Pulse) Simon & Schuster Children's Publishing.

Kretzer-Malvehy, Terry. Passage to Little Bighorn. 1999. 210p. (YA). (gr. 7 up). pap. 6.95 o.p. *(0-87358-713-8*, Rising Moon Bks. for Young Readers) Northland Publishing.

—Passage to Little Bighorn. 1999. 13.00 *(0-606-18313-2)* Turtleback Bks.

Paige, Harry W. Johnny Stands. 1982. 160p. (J). (gr. 5-9). 8.95 o.p. *(0-7232-6213-6*, Warne, Frederick) Penguin Putnam Bks. for Young Readers.

Pirone, James & Sweeney, Paula. Mystery at Deep Ravine. Kemnitz, Myrna, ed. 1996. (Jake Montana Ser.: Bk. 2). (YA). (gr. 7 up). pap. 9.99 *(0-88092-295-8)*; pap. 15.00 o.p. *(0-88092-296-6)* Royal Fireworks Publishing Co.

Robe, Rosebud Y. Tonweya & the Eagles. 1992. (Illus.). 118p. (J). (gr. 2-6). 13.89 o.s.i *(0-8037-8974-2*, Dial Bks. for Young Readers) Penguin Putnam Bks. for Young Readers.

Shubert, J. Lansing. The Legacy of George Partridgeberry. Steele, Robert, ed. 1990. (Illus.). 381p. (Orig.). (YA). (gr. 9-12). pap. 12.95 *(0-9627015-0-5)* Shubert, Joseph L.

Ulyatt, Kenneth. North Against the Sioux. 1978. (Illus.). (J). (gr. 3-5). pap. 1.50 o.p. *(0-14-030406-1*, Penguin Bks.) Viking Penguin.

Viola, Herman J. Sitting Bull: Sioux Native American Indian Stories. 1996. (Raintree-Rivilo American Indian Stories Ser.). 11.10 *(0-606-12519-1)* Turtleback Bks.

INDIANS OF NORTH AMERICA—UTE INDIANS—FICTION

Baltz, Terry & Baltz, Wayne. Night of the Falling Stars. 1995. 181p. (Orig.). (YA). (gr. 5 up). pap. 6.95 *(1-884610-51-X)* Prairie Divide Productions.

Creel, Ann H. Water at the Blue Earth. 1998. (Illus.). (gr. 5-9). 148p. (YA). 14.95 o.p. *(1-57098-209-0*, Rinehart, Roberts International); 112p. pap. 8.95 *(1-57098-224-4)* Rinehart, Roberts Pubs.

Hobbs, William. Beardance. 1993. 192p. (YA). (gr. 5-9). 17.00 *(0-689-31867-7*, Atheneum) Simon & Schuster Children's Publishing.

Raczek, Linda T. The Night the Grandfathers Danced. 1995. (Illus.). 32p. (J). (gr. k-3). lib. bdg. 14.95 o.p. *(0-87358-610-7)* Northland Publishing.

INDIANS OF NORTH AMERICA—WAMPANOAG INDIANS—FICTION

Sewall, Marcia. Thunder from a Clear Sky. 1995. (Illus.). 64p. (J). (ps-3). 17.00 *(0-689-31775-1*, Atheneum) Simon & Schuster Children's Publishing.

INDIANS OF NORTH AMERICA—ZUNI INDIANS—FICTION

Hillerman, Tony. The Boy Who Made Dragonfly: A Zuni Myth. abr. ed. 1995. 10.95 incl. audio *(0-944993-44-3)* Audio Literature.

—The Boy Who Made Dragonfly: A Zuni Myth. 1972. (Illus.). 144p. (J). (gr. 5 up). lib. bdg. 9.89 o.p. *(0-06-022312-X)* HarperCollins Pubs.

—The Boy Who Made Dragonfly: A Zuni Myth. 1986. (Illus.). 85p. (J). (gr. k-3). reprint ed. pap. 8.95 *(0-8263-0910-0)* Univ. of New Mexico Pr.

Thomasma, Kenneth. Amee-nah: Zuni Boy Runs the Race of His Life. 1995. (Amazing Indian Children Ser.). (Illus.). 160p. (J). (gr. 6-9). pap. 5.99 o.p. *(0-8010-4054-X)* Baker Bks.

—Amee-nah: Zuni Boy Runs the Race of His Life. 1995. (Amazing Indian Children Ser.). (Illus.). 176p. (J). (gr. 3-8). 12.99 *(1-880114-17-8)*; pap. 7.99 *(1-880114-15-1)* Grandview Publishing Co.

INDIANS OF SOUTH AMERICA—FICTION

Allende, Isabel. City of the Beasts. Peden, Margaret Sayers, tr. from SPA. 2002. Tr. of Ciudad de las Bestias. 416p. (J). (gr. 5 up). 19.99 *(0-06-050918-X)*; lib. bdg. 21.89 *(0-06-050917-1)* HarperCollins Children's Bk. Group.

—City of the Beasts. l.t. ed. 2002. Tr. of Ciudad de las Bestias. 400p. (J). (gr. 5). pap. 19.99 *(0-06-051195-8)* HarperCollins Pubs.

—City of the Beasts. 2004. Tr. of Ciudad de las Bestias. 432p. (J). pap. 7.99 *(0-06-053503-2*, Rayo) HarperTrade.

Andrews, Jan. Very Last First Time: An Inuit Tale. 1998. 12.14 *(0-606-13885-4)* Turtleback Bks.

Blair, David N. Fear the Condor. 1992. 144p. (YA). (gr. 7 up). 15.00 o.p. *(0-525-67381-4*, Dutton Children's Bks.) Penguin Putnam Bks. for Young Readers.

Garland, Sherry. Cabin 102. 1995. (Illus.). 252p. (J). (gr. 4-7). 11.00 *(0-15-200663-X)*; pap. 6.00 o.s.i *(0-15-200662-1*, Harcourt Paperbacks) Harcourt Children's Bks.

—Cabin 102. 1995. 12.05 *(0-606-09122-X)* Turtleback Bks.

Jackson, Dave & Jackson, Neta. Blinded by the Shining Path: Romulo Sauane. 2002. (Trailblazers Ser.). (Illus.). 144p. (J). (gr. 3-7). pap. 5.99 *(0-7642-2233-3)* Bethany Hse. Pubs.

Kendall, Sarita H. Ransom for a River Dolphin. 1993. 128p. (J). (gr. 3-6). lib. bdg. 19.95 o.p. *(0-8225-0735-8*, Lerner Pubns.) Lerner Publishing Group.

Krulik, Nancy E. Jungle to Jungle. 1997. 96p. (J). (gr. 3-7). pap. 4.95 o.p. *(0-7868-4119-2)* Disney Pr.

Newman, Shirlee Petkin. Isabella: A Wish for Miguel, Peru, 1820. 1997. (Girlhood Journeys Ser.: No. 1). (Illus.). 72p. (J). (gr. 2-6). pap. 5.99 *(0-689-81572-7*, Aladdin) Simon & Schuster Children's Publishing.

O'Dell, Scott. The Amethyst Ring, 001. 1983. 224p. (J). (gr. 7 up). 14.95 o.p. *(0-395-33886-7)* Houghton Mifflin Co.

Talbott, Hudson & Greenberg, Mark. Amazon Diary: The Jungle Adventures of Alex Winters. 1996. (Illus.). 48p. (J). (gr. 4-7). 15.95 o.s.i *(0-399-22916-7*, G. P. Putnam's Sons) Penguin Group (USA) Inc.

—Amazon Diary: The Jungle Adventures of Alex Winters. 1998. (Illus.). 48p. (J). (gr. k up). reprint ed. pap. 6.99 o.s.i *(0-698-11699-2*, PaperStar) Penguin Putnam Bks. for Young Readers.

Thomas, Rob. Green Thumb. unabr. ed. 2000. (YA). pap. 59.00 incl. audio *(0-7887-3641-8*, 41007) Recorded Bks., LLC.

—Green Thumb. (gr. 5-9). 2000. 192p. pap. 4.99 *(0-689-82886-1*, Aladdin); 1999. (Illus.). 186p. (YA). 16.00 o.s.i *(0-689-81780-0*, Simon & Schuster Children's Publishing) Simon & Schuster Children's Publishing.

—Green Thumb. 2000. 11.04 *(0-606-20048-7)* Turtleback Bks.

Topooco, Eusebio. Waira's First Journey. (J). (gr. 4 up). 1993. 15.00 o.p. *(0-688-12054-7)*; 1924. lib. bdg. o.p. *(0-688-12055-5)* HarperCollins Children's Bk. Group.

Upton, Peter. Green Hill Far Away. 1977. 10.95 o.s.i *(0-671-22344-5*, Simon & Schuster) Simon & Schuster.

Villoldo, Alberto. The First Story Ever Told. 1996. (Illus.). (J). (ps-3). 40p. 16.00 *(0-689-80515-2)*; 16.00 *(0-671-89729-2)* Simon & Schuster Children's Publishing. (Simon & Schuster Children's Publishing).

Yolen, Jane. Encuentro. Ada, Alma Flor, tr. 1996. (SPA., Illus.). 32p. (J). (gr. 4-7). pap. 6.00 *(0-15-201342-3*, HB2056, Voyager Bks./Libros Viajeros) Harcourt Children's Bks.

INUIT—FICTION

Bell, Hilari. Songs of Power. 2000. 219p. (J). (gr. 3-7). lib. bdg. 16.49 *(0-7868-2487-5)* Disney Pr.

—Songs of Power. 2000. 224p. (J). (gr. 3-7). 15.99 *(0-7868-0561-7)* Little Brown & Co.

Damjan, Mischa. Atuk. 2002. (Illus.). 32p. (J). (gr. k-3). 15.95 *(0-7358-1795-2)*; pap. 6.95 *(0-7358-1796-0)* North-South Bks., Inc.

—Atuk: A Story. (Illus.). 32p. (J). (gr. k-3). 1996. pap. 6.95 o.p. *(1-55858-590-7)*; 1990. 13.95 o.p. *(1-55858-091-3)* North-South Bks., Inc.

Devine, Monica. Carry Me, Mama. 2002. (Illus.). 24p. (J). (ps-3). 15.95 *(0-7737-3317-5)* Stoddart Kids CAN. *Dist:* Fitzhenry & Whiteside, Ltd.

Dewey, Jennifer Owings. Minik's Story. 2003. (J). 15.95 *(0-7614-5134-X)* Cavendish, Marshall Corp.

Easley, Mary Ann. I Am the Ice Worm. 2003. 128p. (J). (gr. 4-7). 16.95 *(1-56397-412-6)* Boyds Mills Pr.

—I Am the Ice Worm. 1998. 10.04 *(0-606-13500-6)* Turtleback Bks.

—I am the Ice Worm. 1998. 128p. (gr. 4-7). reprint ed. pap. text 3.99 o.s.i *(0-440-41444-X*, Yearling) Random Hse. Children's Bks.

Edwardson, Debby Dahl. Whale Snow. 2003. (Illus.). 32p. (J). (gr. k-4). 15.95 *(1-57091-393-5*, Talewinds) Charlesbridge Publishing, Inc.

George, Jean Craighead. Arctic Son. (Illus.). 32p. (J). (gr. k-4). 1999. pap. 5.99 *(0-7868-1179-X)*; 1997. 14.95 *(0-7868-0315-0)*; 1997. lib. bdg. 15.49 *(0-7868-2255-4)* Hyperion Bks. for Children.

—Arctic Son. 1999. (J). 12.14 *(0-606-17381-1)* Turtleback Bks.

Heinz, Brian J. Kayuktuk: An Arctic Quest. 1996. (Illus.). 40p. (J). (ps-3). 14.95 o.p. *(0-8118-0411-9)* Chronicle Bks. LLC.

—Nanuk: Lord of the Ice. 1998. (Illus.). 32p. (J). (gr. k-4). 15.89 o.s.i *(0-8037-2195-1*, Dial Bks. for Young Readers) Penguin Putnam Bks. for Young Readers.

Lavallee, Barbara, illus. Mama, Do You Love Me? Doll & Book Set. 1993. (J). 14.95 o.s.i *(0-8118-0521-2)* Chronicle Bks. LLC.

London, Jonathan. Ice Bear & Little Fox. 1998. (Illus.). 40p. (J). (ps-2). 15.99 *(0-525-45907-3*, Dutton Children's Bks.) Penguin Putnam Bks. for Young Readers.

Newth, Mette. The Transformation, RS. Ingwersen, Faith, tr. from NOR. 2000. 208p. (J). (gr. 7-12). 16.00 *(0-374-37752-9*, Farrar, Straus & Giroux (BYR)) Farrar, Straus & Giroux.

Rau, Dana Meachen. Arctic Adventure: Inuit Life in the 1800s. 1997. (Smithsonian Odyssey Ser.). (Illus.). (J). 32p. (gr. 1-4). pap. 5.95 *(1-56899-417-6)*; 32p. (gr. 2-5). 14.95 *(1-56899-416-8)*; 32p. (gr. 2-5). 19.95 incl. audio *(1-56899-423-0*, BC6005);Incl. toy. (gr. 2-5). 29.95 *(1-56899-418-4)*;Incl. toy. 32p. (gr. 2-5). 35.95 incl. audio *(1-56899-421-4)*;Incl. toy. 32p. (gr. 2-5). pap. 25.95 incl. audio *(1-56899-420-6)*;Incl. toy. 32p. (gr. 2-5). pap. 17.95 *(1-56899-419-2)*;Incl. toy. 32p. (gr. 2-5). pap. 25.95 incl. audio *(1-56899-420-6)* Soundprints.

Sage, James. Where the Great Bear Watches. 1993. (Illus.). 32p. (J). (ps-3). 13.99 o.p. *(0-670-84933-2*, Viking Children's Bks.) Penguin Putnam Bks. for Young Readers.

Stafford, Liliana. Snow Bear. 2001. (Illus.). 32p. (J). (gr. 1-3). 15.95 *(0-439-26977-6)* Scholastic, Inc.

Stafford, Liliana & Davis, Lambert. Snow Bear. (Illus.). 32p. (J). *(0-88899-441-9)* Groundwood Bks.

Sullivan, Paul. Maata's Journal: A Novel. 2003. 240p. (J). 16.95 *(0-689-83463-2*, Atheneum) Simon & Schuster Children's Publishing.

Wood, Ellen. Hundreds of Fish. 2000. (Notebooks Ser.). (Illus.). 40p. (YA). (gr. 4 up). 17.95 *(1-56846-162-3*, Creative Editions) Creative Co., The.

IRISH AMERICANS—FICTION

Armstrong, Jennifer. Patrick Doyle Is Full of Blarney. 1996. (First Stepping Stone Bks.). (Illus.). (J). (gr. 2-4). 80p. 16.00 o.s.i *(0-679-87285-X)*; 69p. 17.99 o.s.i *(0-679-97285-4)* Random Hse. Children's Bks. (Random Hse. Bks. for Young Readers).

—Patrick Doyle Is Full of Blarney. 1997. (Stepping Stone Book). (Illus.). 69p. (J). (gr. 2-4). pap. 3.99 o.s.i *(0-679-87787-8)* Random Hse., Inc.

—Patrick Doyle Is Full of Blarney. 1997. (Stepping Stone Bks.). (J). 9.19 o.p. *(0-606-11725-3)* Turtleback Bks.

Auch, Mary Jane. Ashes of Roses, ERS. 2002. 256p. (YA). (gr. 7-10). 16.95 *(0-8050-6686-1*, Holt, Henry & Co. Bks. For Young Readers) Holt, Henry & Co.

—Ashes of Roses. 2004. 256p. (YA). (gr. 7). mass mkt. 5.99 *(0-440-23851-X*, Laurel Leaf) Random Hse. Children's Bks.

Campbell Bartoletti, Susan, et al. The Journal of Finn Reardon, a Newsie. 2003. (My Name Is America Ser.). (Illus.). 192p. (J). pap. 10.95 *(0-439-18894-6*, Scholastic Pr.) Scholastic, Inc.

Conlon-McKenna, Marita. Wildflower Girl. 1992. (Illus.). 176p. (J). (gr. 4-7). 14.95 o.p. *(0-8234-0988-0)* Holiday Hse., Inc.

—Wildflower Girl. 1994. 176p. (J). (gr. 5 up). pap. 4.99 o.s.i *(0-14-036292-4*, Puffin Bks.) Penguin Putnam Bks. for Young Readers.

Dillon, Jana. Lucky O'Leprechaun Comes to America. 2001. (Illus.). 32p. (J). (ps-1). 14.95 *(1-56554-816-7)* Pelican Publishing Co., Inc.

Fenton, Edward. Duffy's Rocks. l.t. ed. 1999. (Golden Triangle Bks.). 240p. (YA). (gr. 8-12). pap. 9.95 *(0-8229-5706-X)* Univ. of Pittsburgh Pr.

Giff, Patricia Reilly. The Gift of the Pirate Queen. (Illus.). (gr. 4-6). 1982. 160p. (J). 11.95 o.s.i *(0-385-28338-5*, Delacorte Pr.); 1982. 160p. (J). lib. bdg. 11.95 o.s.i *(0-385-28339-3*, Delacorte Pr.); 1982. 160p. (J). 9.95 o.s.i *(0-440-02970-8*, Delacorte Pr.); 1982. 160p. (J). lib. bdg. 9.89 o.s.i *(0-440-02972-4*, Delacorte Pr.); 1983. 192p. reprint ed. pap. text 4.99 *(0-440-43046-1)* Dell Publishing.

Griffith, Connie. Mysterious Rescuer. 1994. (Tootie McCarthy Ser.: Bk. 4). 128p. (Orig.). (J). (gr. 6-9). pap. 6.99 o.p. *(0-8010-3865-0)* Baker Bks.

—Secret Behind Locked Doors. 1994. (Tootie McCarthy Ser.: Bk. 3). 128p. (J). (gr. 6-9). pap. 6.99 o.p. *(0-8010-3864-2)* Baker Bks.

—Surprise at Logan School. 1993. (Tootie McCarthy Ser.: Bk. 2). 128p. (Orig.). (J). (gr. 5-8). pap. 6.99 o.p. *(0-8010-3856-1)* Baker Bks.

—The Unexpected Weapon. 1993. (Tootie McCarthy Ser.: Bk. 1). 128p. (Orig.). (J). (gr. 5-8). pap. 6.99 o.p. *(0-8010-3858-8)* Baker Bks.

—The Unexpected Weapon. 1993. (Orig.). (J). (gr. 4-7). pap. 4.99 o.s.i *(0-8007-5463-8)* Revell, Fleming H. Co.

Holland, Isabelle. Paperboy. 1999. 144p. (J). (gr. 3-7). tchr. ed. 15.95 *(0-8234-1422-1)* Holiday Hse., Inc.

Kroll, Steven. Mary McLean & the St. Patrick's Day Parade. 32p. (J). 1991. (Illus.). (ps-3). pap. 15.95 *(0-590-43701-1)*; 1990. (gr. 4-7). mass mkt. 4.99 o.p. *(0-590-43702-X)* Scholastic, Inc.

—Mary McLean & the St. Patrick's Day Parade. 1991. (J). 9.15 o.p. *(0-606-05454-5)* Turtleback Bks.

Leppard, Lois Gladys. Mandie & Mollie: The Angel's Visit. 1998. (Mandie Bks.). 128p. (J). (gr. 3-9). text 9.99 o.s.i *(0-7642-2063-2)* Bethany Hse. Pubs.

Lynch, Chris. Blood Relations. 1996. (Blue Eyed Son Ser.: No. 2). (Illus.). (YA). 224p. (gr. 12 up). lib. bdg. 13.89 o.s.i *(0-06-025399-1)*; 192p. (gr. 7 up). pap. 4.50 o.s.i *(0-06-447122-5)* HarperCollins Children's Bk. Group. (Harper Trophy).

—Blood Relations. 1996. (Blue-Eyed Son Ser.: 2). (J). 9.60 o.p. *(0-606-09090-8)* Turtleback Bks.

—Dog Eat Dog. 1996. (Blue-Eyed Son Ser.: Vol. 3). (Illus.). 144p. (YA). (gr. 12 up). pap. 4.50 o.s.i *(0-06-447123-3)*; lib. bdg. 13.89 o.p. *(0-06-027210-4)* HarperCollins Children's Bk. Group. (Harper Trophy).

—Dog Eat Dog. 1996. (Blue-Eyed Son Ser.). (J). 9.60 o.p. *(0-606-09091-6)* Turtleback Bks.

—Mick. 1996. (Blue-Eyed Son Ser.: Bk. 1). (Illus.). 160p. (YA). (gr. 12 up). lib. bdg. 13.89 o.p. *(0-06-025397-5)*; mass mkt. 4.50 o.s.i *(0-06-447121-7*, Harper Trophy) HarperCollins Children's Bk. Group.

—Mick. 1996. (Blue-Eyed Son Ser.). (YA). 9.60 o.p. *(0-606-09089-4)* Turtleback Bks.

McCormack, Colette. After the Famine. 1996. 126p. (J). pap. 7.95 *(1-85594-142-2)* Attic Pr. IRL. *Dist:* International Specialized Bk. Services.

Nixon, Joan Lowery. Land of Promise. 1994. 176p. (YA). (gr. 5). mass mkt. 3.99 o.s.i *(0-440-21904-3)* Dell Publishing.

—Land of Promise. l.t. ed. 2001. (Ellis Island Stories Ser.). 169p. (J). (gr. 4 up). lib. bdg. 22.60 *(0-8368-2812-7)* Stevens, Gareth Inc.

Nolan, Janet. The St. Patrick's Day Shillelagh. 2002. (Illus.). 32p. (J). (gr. 2-4). lib. bdg. 15.95 *(0-8075-7344-2)* Whitman, Albert & Co.

Schneider, Mical. Annie Quinn in America. 2001. (J). 6.95 *(1-57505-535-X)* Carolrhoda Bks.

—Annie Quinn in America. 2001. (Adventures in Time Ser.). (Illus.). 252p. (J). (gr. 4-7). lib. bdg. 15.95 *(1-57505-510-4*, Carolrhoda Bks.) Lerner Publishing Group.

Shura, Mary Francis. Shoefull of Shamrock. 1991. 96p. (J). pap. 2.95 *(0-380-76169-6*, Avon Bks.) Morrow/Avon.

Watts, James F. The Irish Americans. 1995. (Immigrant Experience Ser.). (Illus.). 120p. (J). (gr. 7 up). pap. 9.95 *(0-7910-3388-0)* Chelsea Hse. Pubs.

Whitney, Kim Ablon. See You down the Road: A Novel. 2004. (J). (gr. 7). 192p. 15.95 *(0-375-82467-7)*; 176p. lib. bdg. 17.99 *(0-375-92467-1)* Random Hse. Children's Bks. (Knopf Bks. for Young Readers).

IRISH—UNITED STATES—FICTION

Armstrong, Jennifer. The Dreams of Mairhe Mehan. 1996. 119p. (J). (gr. 7-12). 18.00 o.s.i *(0-679-88152-2)* McKay, David Co., Inc.

—Patrick Doyle Is Full of Blarney. 1996. (First Stepping Stone Bks.). (Illus.). (J). (gr. 2-4). 80p. 16.00 o.s.i *(0-679-87285-X)*; 69p. 17.99 o.s.i *(0-679-97285-4)* Random Hse. Children's Bks. (Random Hse. Bks. for Young Readers).

Bolton, Carole. Search of Mary Katherine Mulloy. 1974. 192p. (J). 7.95 o.p. *(0-525-66392-4*, Dutton Children's Bks.) Penguin Putnam Bks. for Young Readers.

Conlon-McKenna, Marita. Wildflower Girl. 1992. (Illus.). 176p. (J). (gr. 4-7). 14.95 o.p. *(0-8234-0988-0)* Holiday Hse., Inc.

—Wildflower Girl. 1994. 176p. (J). (gr. 5 up). pap. 4.99 o.s.i *(0-14-036292-4*, Puffin Bks.) Penguin Putnam Bks. for Young Readers.

Denenberg, Barry. So Far from Home: The Diary of Mary Driscoll, an Irish Mill Girl, Lowell, Massachusetts, 1847. 1997. (Dear America Ser.). 166p. (J). (gr. 4-9). pap. 10.95 o.s.i (*0-590-92667-5*) Scholastic, Inc.

Dolman, Bob & Howard, Ron. Far & Away: A Newmarket Medallion Edition. 1993. (Illus.). (J). (gr. 3 up). pap. o.p. (*1-55704-145-8*) Newmarket Pr.

Giff, Patricia Reilly. The Gift of the Pirate Queen. 1982. (Illus.). 160p. (J). (gr. 4-6). 11.95 o.s.i (*0-385-28338-5*); lib. bdg. 11.95 o.s.i (*0-385-28339-3*) Dell Publishing. (Delacorte Pr.).

Griffith, Connie. The Shocking Discovery. 1994. (Tootie McCarthy Ser.: Bk. 5). 112p. (J). (gr. 5-8). pap. 6.99 o.p. (*0-8010-3866-9*) Baker Bks.

Kudlinski, Kathleen V. Shannon: A Chinatown Adventure, San Francisco, 1880. unabr. ed. 1996. (Girlhood Journeys Ser.). (Illus.). 71p. (J). (gr. 6-8). pap. 32.99 (*1-887327-06-1*) Aladdin Paperbacks.

—Shannon: A Chinatown Adventure, San Francisco, 1880. (Girlhood Journeys Ser.: Bk. 2). (J). 1997. 12.95 (*0-689-81204-3*, Simon & Schuster Children's Publishing); 1996. (Illus.). 72p. mass mkt. 5.99 (*0-689-80984-0*, Aladdin) Simon & Schuster Children's Publishing.

—Shannon: A Chinatown Adventure, San Francisco, 1880. 1996. (Girlhood Journeys Ser.: 2). (J). 11.19 o.p. (*0-606-10824-6*) Turtleback Bks.

—Shannon: Lost & Found, San Francisco, 1880. 1997. (Girlhood Journeys Ser.: Bk. 2). (Illus.). 72p. (J). (gr. 2-6). per. 5.99 (*0-689-80988-3*, Simon Pulse) Simon & Schuster Children's Publishing.

—Shannon: The Schoolmarm Mysteries, San Francisco, 1880. 1997. (Girlhood Journeys Ser.: No. 3). (Illus.). 72p. (J). (gr. 2-6). mass mkt. 5.99 (*0-689-81561-1*, Simon Pulse) Simon & Schuster Children's Publishing.

Kudlinski, Kathleen V. & Farnsworth, Bill. Shannon: A Chinatown Adventure, San Francisco, 1880. 1996. (Girlhood Journeys Ser.: 2). (Illus.). 72p. (J). (gr. 4-7). 13.00 o.s.i (*0-689-81138-1*, Simon & Schuster Children's Publishing) Simon & Schuster Children's Publishing.

Lasky, Kathryn. Prank. 1986. (J). (gr. 6 up). mass mkt. 2.75 o.s.i (*0-440-97144-6*, Laurel Leaf) Random Hse. Children's Bks.

Lawson, Robert. The Great Wheel. 1993. (Newbery Honor Roll Ser.). (Illus.). 180p. (J). (gr. 4-7). pap. 7.95 (*0-8027-7392-3*) Walker & Co.

—Great Wheel. 1999. (gr. 4-7). pap. 15.80 (*0-7857-0209-1*) Econo-Clad Bks.

—Great Wheel. 1993. (Newbery Honor Roll Ser.). (J). 13.05 o.p. (*0-606-02657-6*) Turtleback Bks.

Leppard, Lois Gladys. Mandie & Mollie: The Angel's Visit. 1998. (Mandie Bks.). 128p. (J). (gr. 3-9). text 9.99 o.s.i (*0-7642-2063-2*) Bethany Hse. Pubs.

Pastore, Clare. Journey to America, Vol. 1. 2002. 192p. mass mkt. 5.99 (*0-425-18735-7*) Berkley Publishing Group.

Rubel, Nicole. A Cowboy Named Ernestine. 2001. (Illus.). 32p. (J). (ps-3). 15.99 (*0-8037-2152-8*, Dial Bks. for Young Readers) Penguin Putnam Bks. for Young Readers.

Ward Weller, Frances. The Angel of Mill Street. 1998. (Illus.). 32p. (J). (ps-3). 15.99 o.p. (*0-399-23133-1*, G. P. Putnam's Sons) Penguin Putnam Bks. for Young Readers.

Wilkinson, Pamela F. Ridin' the Rainbow. 1983. (Illus.). 40p. (J). 10.95 o.p. (*0-931722-10-1*); pap. 5.95 o.p. (*0-931722-09-8*); lib. bdg. 10.95 o.p. (*0-931722-11-X*) Corona Publishing, Co.

ITALIAN AMERICANS—FICTION

Ayres, Katherine. Under Copp's Hill. 2000. (American Girl Collection: Bk. 8). (Illus.). 176p. (gr. 5 up). (J). 9.95 (*1-58485-089-2*); (YA). pap. 5.95 (*1-58485-088-4*) Pleasant Co. Pubns. (American Girl).

—Under Copp's Hill. 2000. (American Girl Collection). (Illus.). (J). 12.00 (*0-606-20963-8*) Turtleback Bks.

Bartone, Elisa. American Too. 1996. (Illus.). 40p. (J). (ps-3). 16.00 o.p. (*0-688-13278-2*); lib. bdg. 15.93 (*0-688-13279-0*) HarperCollins Children's Bk. Group.

Benson, Rita. Rosa's Diary. 1994. (Voyages Ser.). (Illus.). (J). 4.25 (*0-383-03772-7*) SRA/McGraw-Hill.

Creech, Sharon. Granny Torelli. 2003. (Illus.). 160p. (J). (gr. 4-7). lib. bdg. 16.89 (*0-06-029291-1*, Cotler, Joanna Bks.) HarperCollins Children's Bk. Group.

—Granny Torrelli Makes Soup. 2003. (Illus.). 160p. (J). (gr. 3-6). 15.99 (*0-06-029290-3*, HarperChildren's Audio) HarperCollins Children's Bk. Group.

Hoobler, Dorothy & Hoobler, Thomas. The Second Decade: Voyages. 2000. E-Book 21.90 (*0-585-35349-2*) netLibrary, Inc.

—The 1910s: Voyages. 2000. (Century Kids Ser.). (Illus.). 160p. (YA). (gr. 5-8). 22.90 (*0-7613-1601-9*) Millbrook Pr., Inc.

—The 1970s: Arguments. 2002. (Century Kids Ser.). (Illus.). 160p. (YA). (gr. 5-8). 22.90 (*0-7613-1607-8*) Millbrook Pr., Inc.

Lasky, Kathryn. Home at Last. 2003. (My America Ser.). 112p. (J). mass mkt. 4.99 (*0-439-20644-8*) Scholastic, Inc.

—Home at Last: Sofia's Immigrant Diary, Bk. 2. 2003. (My America Ser.). 112p. (J). pap. 12.95 (*0-439-44963-4*) Scholastic, Inc.

—Hope in My Heart: Sofia's Immigrant Diary, Bk. 1. 2003. (My America Ser.). 112p. (J). pap. 12.95 (*0-439-18875-X*) Scholastic, Inc.

Murphy, Jim. West to a Land of Plenty: The Diary of Teresa Angelino Viscardi, New York to Idaho Territory, 1883. 1998. (Dear America Ser.). (Illus.). 204p. (YA). (gr. 4-9). pap. 10.95 (*0-590-73888-7*) Scholastic, Inc.

Nobisso, Josephine. En Ingles, Por Supuesto. Orig. Title: In English, of Course. (SPA., Illus.). 32p. (J). 2004. 16.95 (*0-940112-14-0*); 2003. pap. 8.95 (*0-940112-16-7*) Gingerbread Hse.

Shulman, Irving. West Side Story. (Orig.). 1990. 160p. mass mkt. 5.99 (*0-671-72566-1*); 1983. (J). (gr. 8 up). mass mkt. 2.95 (*0-671-50448-7*); 1981. pap. 2.50 o.s.i (*0-671-44142-6*) Simon & Schuster. (Pocket).

Sirof, Harriet. Because She's My Friend. 1993. 192p. (J). (gr. 5-9). 16.00 (*0-689-31844-8*, Atheneum) Simon & Schuster Children's Publishing.

—Because She's My Friend. 2000. 196p. (gr. 4-7). pap. 13.95 (*0-595-09241-1*, Backinprint.com) iUniverse, Inc.

Winthrop, Elizabeth. Franklin Delano Roosevelt: Letters from a Mill Town Girl. 2001. (Dear Mr. President Ser.). (Illus.). 128p. (J). (gr. 4-6). 9.95 (*1-890817-61-9*) Winslow Pr.

J

JAMAICAN AMERICANS—FICTION

Pedlar, Elaine, tr. & illus. A Shelter in Our Car. 2004. 32p. 16.95 (*0-89239-189-8*) Children's Bk. Pr.

JAPANESE—UNITED STATES—FICTION

Blackburn, Joyce K. Suki & the Invisible Peacock. rev. ed. 1996. (Suki Ser.). (Illus.). 64p. (J). (ps-3). 14.95 (*1-881576-69-8*) Providence Hse. Pubs.

—Suki & the Old Umbrella. rev. ed. 1996. (Suki Ser.). (Illus.). 64p. (J). (ps-3). 14.95 (*1-881576-71-X*) Providence Hse. Pubs.

—Suki & the Wonder Star. rev. ed. 1996. (Suki Ser.). (Illus.). 64p. (J). (ps-3). 14.95 (*1-881576-72-8*) Providence Hse. Pubs.

Bonham, Frank. Burma Rifles: A Story of Merrill's Marauders. 1960. (J). (gr. 5 up). 7.95 o.p. (*0-690-16147-6*) HarperCollins Children's Bk. Group.

Brown, Janet Mitsui. Thanksgiving at Obaachan's. 1994. (Illus.). 36p. (J). (ps-3). 15.95 (*1-879965-07-0*) Polychrome Publishing Corp.

Bunting, Eve. So Far from the Sea. 1998. (Illus.). 32p. (J). (gr. 4-6). lib. bdg., tchr. ed. 16.00 (*0-395-72095-8*, Clarion Bks.) Houghton Mifflin Co. Trade & Reference Div.

Hosozawa-Nagano, Elaine. Chopsticks from America. 1994. (Illus.). 64p. (YA). (gr. 5 up). 16.95 (*1-879965-11-9*) Polychrome Publishing Corp.

Hutchinson, William M. Promised Year. 1959. (Illus.). (J). (gr. 4-6). 6.50 o.p. (*0-15-263866-0*) Harcourt Children's Bks.

Igus, Toyomi. Two Mrs. Gibsons. 1996. (Illus.). 32p. (YA). (gr. 4-7). 14.95 (*0-89239-135-9*) Children's Bk. Pr.

—Two Mrs. Gibsons. 1996. (Illus.). 32p. (J). (gr. 2-4). lib. bdg. 19.90 (*0-516-20001-1*, Children's Pr.) Scholastic Library Publishing.

Irwin, Hadley. Kim-Kimi. 1988. 208p. (J). (gr. 4-7). pap. 5.99 (*0-14-032593-X*, Puffin Bks.) Penguin Putnam Bks. for Young Readers.

—Kim-Kimi. 1987. 208p. (YA). (gr. 7 up). 16.00 (*0-689-50428-4*, McElderry, Margaret K.) Simon & Schuster Children's Publishing.

—Kim-Kimi. 1988. (J). 12.04 (*0-606-03839-6*) Turtleback Bks.

Johnston, Tony. Fishing Sunday. (Illus.). (J). (gr. k-3). 1996. 32p. 16.00 (*0-688-13458-0*); 1924. lib. bdg. o.p. (*0-688-13538-2*) Morrow/Avon. (Morrow, William & Co.).

—Fishing Sunday. 2001. (Illus.). (J). E-Book (*1-58824-234-X*); E-Book (*1-59019-213-3*) ipicturebooks, LLC.

Kroll, Virginia L. Pink Paper Swans. 1994. (Illus.). 32p. (J). (gr. k-5). 15.00 (*0-8028-5081-2*, Eerdmans Bks For Young Readers) Eerdmans, William B. Publishing Co.

Kudlinski, Kathleen V. Pearl Harbor Is Burning! A Story of World War II. 1993. (Once upon America Ser.). (Illus.). 64p. (J). (gr. 2-6). pap. 4.99 (*0-14-034509-4*, Puffin Bks.) Penguin Putnam Bks. for Young Readers.

Lancaster, Clay. Michiko: Or Mrs. Belmont's Brownstone on Brooklyn Heights. 1966. (Illus.). (J). (gr. k-4). 3.85 o.p. (*0-8048-0402-8*) Tuttle Publishing.

McCoy, Karen Kawamoto. Bon Odori Dancer. 1998. (Illus.). 32p. (J). (gr. 1-4). 14.95 (*1-879965-16-X*) Polychrome Publishing Corp.

Means, Florence C. The Moved-Outers. 1945. (J). (gr. 7-9). 5.95 o.p. (*0-395-06933-5*) Houghton Mifflin Co.

—The Moved-Outers. 1993. 156p. (J). pap. 7.95 (*0-8027-7386-9*) Walker & Co.

Meyer, Kathleen A. I Have a New Friend. 1995. (Illus.). 32p. (J). (gr. 3-7). 10.95 o.p. (*0-8120-6532-8*); (ps-2). pap. 4.95 (*0-8120-9408-5*) Barron's Educational Series, Inc.

Mochizuki, Ken. Heroes. 1995. (Illus.). 32p. (J). (ps-3). 15.95 (*1-880000-16-4*) Lee & Low Bks., Inc.

Okimoto, Jean Davies. Talent Night. 1995. 176p. (YA). (gr. 7-9). pap. 14.95 (*0-590-47809-5*) Scholastic, Inc.

Poynter, Margaret. A Time Too Swift. 1990. 224p. (J). (gr. 5 up). lib. bdg. 14.95 o.p. (*0-689-31146-X*, Atheneum) Simon & Schuster Children's Publishing.

Salisbury, Graham. Under the Blood Red Sun. 1994. 256p. (gr. 6-8). text 15.95 o.s.i (*0-385-32099-X*, Delacorte Pr.) Dell Publishing.

—Under the Blood Red Sun. 1995. 256p. (gr. 5-8). pap. text 5.50 (*0-440-41139-4*, Yearling) Random Hse. Children's Bks.

—Under the Blood Red Sun. 1995. (J). 11.04 (*0-606-08654-4*) Turtleback Bks.

Savin, Marcia. The Moon Bridge. 1992. 176p. (J). (gr. 4-6). pap. 13.95 o.p. (*0-590-45873-6*) Scholastic, Inc.

Say, Allen. Grandfather's Journey. 1993. (Illus.). 32p. (J). (ps-3). lib. bdg., tchr. ed. 16.95 (*0-395-57035-2*) Houghton Mifflin Co.

Shigekawa, Marlene. Blue Jay in the Desert. 1993. (Illus.). 36p. (J). (gr. 1-5). 14.95 (*1-879965-04-6*) Polychrome Publishing Corp.

Tung, Angela. Song of the Stranger. Artenstein, Michael, ed. 1999. (Roxbury Park Bks.). (J). 192p. (gr. 3-7). pap. 4.95 (*1-56565-948-1*, 09481W); 96p. (gr. 5-8). 12.95 (*1-56565-774-8*, 07748W) Lowell Hse. (Roxbury Park).

Uchida, Yoshiko. The Best Bad Thing. 1986. 136p. (J). (gr. 4-7). reprint ed. pap. 4.95 o.s.i (*0-689-71069-0*, Aladdin) Simon & Schuster Children's Publishing.

—A Jar of Dreams. 1998. (J). pap. 3.95 (*0-87628-469-1*) Ctr. for Applied Research in Education, The.

—A Jar of Dreams. 1995. (J). (gr. 6). 9.28 (*0-395-73263-8*) Houghton Mifflin Co.

—A Jar of Dreams. (gr. 5-9). 1985. 131p. (J). pap. 3.95 o.s.i (*0-689-71041-0*, Aladdin); 1981. 144p. (YA). 16.00 (*0-689-50210-9*, McElderry, Margaret K.); 2nd ed. 1993. 144p. (YA). reprint ed. pap. 4.99 (*0-689-71672-9*, Aladdin) Simon & Schuster Children's Publishing.

—A Jar of Dreams. 1981. (J). 11.04 (*0-606-03337-8*) Turtleback Bks.

—Journey Home. (Illus.). 144p. (J). 1978. (gr. 5-9). 16.00 (*0-689-50126-9*, McElderry, Margaret K.); 2nd ed. 1992. (gr. 4-7). reprint ed. pap. 4.99 (*0-689-71641-9*, Aladdin) Simon & Schuster Children's Publishing.

—Journey to Topaz: A Story of the Japanese-American Evacuation. 1985. 16.00 (*0-606-04381-0*) Turtleback Bks.

Yamamoto, Hosaye & Cheung, King-Kok, eds. Seventeen Syllables. 1994. (Woman Writers: Text & Contexts Ser.). 230p. (C). text 35.00 (*0-8135-2052-5*) Rutgers Univ. Pr.

Yamate, Sandra S. Day of Remembrance. Date not set. (J). 12.95 (*1-879965-12-7*) Polychrome Publishing Corp.

Yashima, Taro. Umbrella. 1970. pap. 1.25 o.p. (*0-670-05031-8*, Dutton Children's Bks.) Penguin Putnam Bks. for Young Readers.

—Umbrella. 1985. (Viking Seafarer Bks.). 12.14 (*0-606-05078-7*) Turtleback Bks.

—Umbrella. 1958. 3.37 o.p. (*0-670-73859-X*, Viking) Viking Penguin.

JAPANESE AMERICANS—FICTION

Banks, Jacqueline Turner. A Day for Vincent Chin & Me. 2001. (Illus.). 112p. (J). (gr. 5-9). 15.00 (*0-618-13199-X*) Houghton Mifflin Co.

Blackburn, Joyce K. Suki & the Magic Sand Dollar. rev. ed. 1996. (Suki Ser.). (Illus.). 64p. (J). (ps-3). 14.95 (*1-881576-70-1*) Providence Hse. Pubs.

Crilley, Mark. Akiko & the Alpha Centauri 5000. 2003. (Illus.). 160p. (J). 9.95 (*0-385-72969-3*, Delacorte Pr.) Dell Publishing.

—Akiko & the Great Wall of Trudd. 2001. E-Book 3.99 (*1-59061-579-4*) Adobe Systems, Inc.

—Akiko & the Great Wall of Trudd. 2001. (Illus.). 176p. (J). (ps-3). 9.95 (*0-385-32727-7*, Delacorte Bks. for Young Readers) Random Hse. Children's Bks.

—Akiko & the Journey to Toog. 2003. (Illus.). 176p. (gr. 3). text 9.95 (*0-385-73042-X*, Delacorte Bks. for Young Readers) Random Hse. Children's Bks.

—Akiko in the Castle of Alia Rellapor. 2001. (Akiko Ser.). (J). E-Book 3.99 (*1-59061-395-3*) Adobe Systems, Inc.

—Akiko in the Castle of Alia Rellapor. 2001. (Illus.). 176p. (J). (gr. 3-5). 9.95 (*0-385-32728-5*, Dell Books for Young Readers) Random Hse. Children's Bks.

—Akiko in the Sprubly Islands. 2001. (Akiko Ser.). (J). E-Book 3.99 (*1-59061-396-1*) Adobe Systems, Inc.

—Akiko in the Sprubly Islands. 2001. (Akiko Ser.: Vol. 2). (Illus.). 176p. (gr. 3-3). pap. text 4.99 (*0-440-41651-5*, Yearling) Random Hse. Children's Bks.

—Akiko in the Sprubly Islands. Simpson, Fiona, ed. 2000. (Akiko Ser.: Vol. 2). (Illus.). 176p. (J). (gr. 4-7). 9.95 (*0-385-32726-9*, Delacorte Bks. for Young Readers) Random Hse. Children's Bks.

—Akiko on the Planet Smoo. 2001. (Akiko Ser.). (J). E-Book 3.99 (*1-59061-397-X*) Adobe Systems, Inc.

—Akiko on the Planet Smoo. 2000. (Illus.). 176p. (gr. 3-7). text 9.95 (*0-385-32724-2*, Delacorte Pr.) Dell Publishing.

—Akiko on the Planet Smoo: Akiko in the Sprubly Islands. 2001. (Akiko Ser.: Vol. 1). (Illus.). 176p. (gr. 3-3). pap. text 4.99 (*0-440-41648-5*, Dell Books for Young Readers) Random Hse. Children's Bks.

Denenberg, Barry. The Journal of Ben Uchida: Citizen 13559, Mirror Lake Internment Camp: California, 1942. 1999. (My Name Is America Ser.). (Illus.). 156p. (J). (gr. 4-8). pap. 10.95 (*0-590-48531-8*, Scholastic Pr.) Scholastic, Inc.

Dunbar, Jake. Crashers. 1999. (Roxbury Park Bks.). 160p. (J). (gr. 4-7). o.p. (*0-7373-0300-X*, 0300XW) Lowell Hse.

Falwell, Cathryn. Butterflies for Kiri. 2003. (Illus.). (J). (*1-58430-100-7*) Lee & Low Bks., Inc.

Hawes, Louise. Rosey in the Present Tense. l.t. ed. 2002. (Young Adult Ser.). 186p. (J). 22.95 (*0-7862-4418-6*) Thorndike Pr.

—Rosey in the Present Tense. 1999. (Illus.). (J). 14.00 (*0-606-20488-1*) Turtleback Bks.

—Rosey in the Present Tense. 2000. (Illus.). 192p. (gr. 8-12). pap. 7.95 (*0-8027-7603-5*); 1999. 176p. (YA). (gr. 7). 15.95 (*0-8027-8685-5*) Walker & Co.

Hennelly, Nilsson. Keeper of the River. 1999. (Rafters Ser.: Vol. 2). 144p. (J). (gr. 3-7). 12.95 (*0-7373-0317-4*, 03174W); pap. 4.95 (*0-7373-0299-2*, 02992W) Lowell Hse. (Roxbury Park).

Icenoggle, Jodi. America's Betrayal. 2001. 208p. (J). (gr. 7 up). 7.95 (*1-57249-252-X*, WM Kids) White Mane Publishing Co., Inc.

Kadohata, Cynthia. Kirakira. 2004. (Illus.). 256p. (J). 15.95 (*0-689-85639-3*, Atheneum) Simon & Schuster Children's Publishing.

Mochizuki, Ken. Beacon Hill Boys. 2002. 201p. (YA). pap. 4.95 (*0-439-24906-6*); 208p. (J). (gr. 9 up). pap. 16.95 (*0-439-26749-8*, Scholastic Pr.) Scholastic, Inc.

Noguchi, Rick & Jenks, Deneen. Flowers from Mariko. 2001. (Illus.). 32p. (J). (gr. 1 up). 16.95 (*1-58430-032-9*) Lee & Low Bks., Inc.

Okimoto, Jean Davies. Talent Night. 2000. 180p. (gr. 7-12). pap. 12.95 (*0-595-00795-3*, Backinprint.com) iUniverse, Inc.

Rue, Nancy N. The Stand. 2001. (Christian Heritage Ser.). 192p. (J). (gr. 3-8). pap. 5.99 (*1-56179-893-2*) Focus on the Family Publishing.

Sakai, Kimiko. Sachiko Means Happiness. (ENG & KOR., Illus.). 24p. (J). (gr. 1 up). 1994. pap. 6.95 (*0-89239-122-7*); 1990. 14.95 o.p. (*0-89239-065-4*) Children's Bk. Pr.

—Sachiko Means Happiness. 1990. 13.10 (*0-606-06707-8*) Turtleback Bks.

Say, Allen. Home of the Brave. 2002. (Illus.). 32p. (J). lib. bdg. 17.00 (*0-618-21223-X*) Houghton Mifflin Co.

—Tea with Milk. 2002. (Illus.). (J). 24.36 (*0-7587-3768-8*) Book Wholesalers, Inc.

—Tea with Milk. 1999. (Illus.). 32p. (J). (ps-3). lib. bdg., tchr. ed. 17.00 (*0-395-90495-1*) Houghton Mifflin Co.

Smith, Greg Leitich. Ninjas, Piranhas, & Galileo. 2003. 192p. (J). (gr. 3-6). 15.95 (*0-316-77854-0*) Little Brown & Co.

Terasaki, Stanley Todd. Ghosts for Breakfast. 2002. (Illus.). 32p. (J). (gr. k-4). 16.95 (*1-58430-046-9*) Lee & Low Bks., Inc.

Trottier, Maxine & Morin, Paul. Flags. l.t. ed. 1999. (Illus.). 32p. (J). (ps-3). 16.95 (*0-7737-3136-9*) Stoddart Kids CAN. *Dist:* Fitzhenry & Whiteside, Ltd.

Wahl, Jan. Candy Shop. 2004. (J). (*1-57091-508-3*) Charlesbridge Publishing, Inc.

Walters, Eric. Caged Eagles. 2001. 244p. (gr. 7-11). (J). pap. 7.95 (*1-55143-139-4*); (YA). 15.95 (*1-55143-182-3*) Orca Bk. Pubs.

Wells, Rosemary. Practice Makes Perfect. 2002. (Yoko & Friends School Days Ser.: No. 10). (Illus.). 32p. (J). (gr. k-2). 9.99 (*0-7868-0725-3*) Disney Pr.

—Read Me a Story. 2002. (Yoko & Friends School Days Ser.: No. 8). 32p. (J). 9.99 (*0-7868-0727-X*); pap. 4.99 (*0-7868-1533-7*, Volo) Hyperion Bks. for Children.
—When I Grow Up. 2003. (Yoko & Friends School Days Ser.). (Illus.). 32p. (J). 9.95 (*0-7868-0731-8*); pap. 9.99 (*0-7868-1537-X*) Hyperion Bks. for Children. (Volo).
—Yoko's Paper Cranes. 2001. (Illus.). 32p. (J). (ps-2). 15.99 (*0-7868-0737-7*); lib. bdg. 16.49 (*0-7868-2602-9*) Hyperion Bks. for Children.

JEWISH-ARAB RELATIONS—FICTION

Banks, Lynne Reid. Broken Bridge. 1996. 336p. (J). (gr. 7 up). pap. 6.99 (*0-380-72384-0*, Harper Trophy) HarperCollins Children's Bk. Group.
—Broken Bridge. 1995. (Illus.). 336p. (YA). (gr. 5 up). 16.00 (*0-688-13595-1*, Morrow, William & Co.) Morrow/Avon.
—Broken Bridge. 1996. 10.55 (*0-606-09105-X*) Turtleback Bks.
Clinton, Cathryn. A Stone in My Hand. 2002. 208p. (J). (gr. 5-12). 15.99 (*0-7636-1388-6*) Candlewick Pr.
Levine, Anna. Running on Eggs. 1999. 128p. (YA). (gr. 5-9). 15.95 (*0-8126-2875-6*) Cricket Bks.
Ofek, Uriel. Smoke over Golan: A Novel of the 1973 Yom Kippur War in Israel. Taslitt, Israel I., tr. from HEB. 1979. (Illus.). 192p. (J). (gr. 4-7). lib. bdg. 12.89 o.p. (*0-06-024614-6*) HarperCollins Children's Bk. Group.

JEWS—CZECHOSLOVAKIA—FICTION

Kanefield, Teri. Rivka's Way. 2001. (Illus.). 137p. (J). (gr. 5-9). 15.95 (*0-8126-2870-5*) Cricket Bks.

JEWS—FICTION

Abraham, Michelle Shapiro. Good Morning, Boker Tov. 2002. (Illus.). (J). pap. 6.00 (*0-8074-0783-6*) UAHC Pr.
—Good Night, Lilah Tov. 2002. (Illus.). (J). pap. 6.00 (*0-8074-0784-4*) UAHC Pr.
Abrahamson, Ruth. The Kingston Castle. 1991. (Illus.). 102p. (J). (gr. 3-8). 10.95 o.p. (*0-922613-42-7*); pap. 8.95 o.p. (*0-922613-43-5*) Hachai Publishing.
Abramson, Ruth. The Cresta Adventure. 1989. (J). (gr. 4-7). 8.95 o.p. (*0-87306-493-3*) Feldheim, Philipp Inc.
Adelson, Leone. The Mystery Bear: A Purim Story. Howland, Naomi, tr. & illus. by. 2004. (J). (*0-618-33727-X*, Clarion Bks.) Houghton Mifflin Co. Trade & Reference Div.
Adler, David A. A Children's Treasure of Chassidic Tales. 1981. (ArtScroll Youth Ser.). (Illus.). 64p. (YA). (gr. 4-12). 8.95 o.p. (*0-89906-785-9*); pap. 5.95 o.p. (*0-89906-786-7*) Mesorah Pubns., Ltd.
—The Number on My Grandfather's Arm. 1987. (Illus.). 28p. (J). (ps-3). 10.95 (*0-8074-0328-8*, 103641) UAHC Pr.
—One Yellow Daffodil: A Hanukkah Story. (Illus.). 32p. (J). (gr. 1-5). 1999. pap. 6.00 (*0-15-202094-2*, Harcourt Paperbacks); 1995. 16.00 o.s.i (*0-15-200537-4*, Gulliver Bks.) Harcourt Children's Bks.
Adler, E. Donny & Deeny K'Teemy Help the King. 1990. (Middos Ser.). (J). 7.99 (*0-89906-505-8*) Mesorah Pubns., Ltd.
Aleichem, Sholem. Tevye the Dairyman. Simons, Joseph, ed. Katz, Miriam, tr. 1994. (YID., Illus.). 160p. (YA). (gr. 10-12). pap. 12.95 o.p. (*0-934710-31-7*) Simon, Rachelle.
Aleichem, Sholem, et al. A Treasury of Sholom Aleichem Children's Stories. Shevrin, Aliza, tr. from YID. & selected by by. 1996. (Illus.). 368p. (J). (ps up). 30.00 (*1-56821-926-1*) Aronson, Jason Pubs.
Allen, Norman. Lies My Father Told Me. 1975. (J). (gr. 7). mass mkt. 1.95 o.p. (*0-451-09830-7*, J9830, Signet Bks.) NAL.
Appleman, Harlene & Shapiro, Jane. A Seder for Tu B'Shevat. 1984. (Illus.). 32p. (J). (ps up). pap. 3.95 (*0-930494-39-3*) Kar-Ben Publishing.
Aroner, Miriam & Haas, Shelly O. The Kingdom of Singing Birds. 1993. (Illus.). 32p. (J). (gr. 1-5). 13.95 (*0-929371-43-7*); (ps-3). pap. 5.95 (*0-929371-44-5*) Kar-Ben Publishing.
Atlan, Liliane. The Passerby, ERS. Owens, Rochelle, tr. 1993. (Illus.). 96p. (YA). (gr. 7 up). 13.95 o.p. (*0-8050-3054-9*, Holt, Henry & Co. Bks. For Young Readers) Holt, Henry & Co.
Baer, Edith. A Frost in the Night: A Childhood on the Eve of the Third Reich. 1980. 224p. 8.95 o.p. (*0-394-84364-9*, Pantheon) Knopf Publishing Group.
—Walk the Dark Streets, RS. 1998. 272p. (YA). (gr. 4-7). 18.00 o.p. (*0-374-38229-8*, Farrar, Straus & Giroux (BYR)) Farrar, Straus & Giroux.
—Walk the Dark Streets. 1996. lib. bdg. 10.00 o.p. (*0-394-90596-2*, Random Hse. Bks. for Young Readers) Random Hse. Children's Bks.
Bandes, Hanna. Reb Aharon's Treasure. 1993. (Illus.). 104p. (J). (gr. 2-5). 8.95 o.p. (*1-56871-034-8*) Targum Pr., Inc.
Banks, Lynne Reid. Broken Bridge. 1996. 336p. (J). (gr. 7 up). pap. 6.99 (*0-380-72384-0*, Harper Trophy) HarperCollins Children's Bk. Group.
—Broken Bridge. 1995. (Illus.). 336p. (YA). (gr. 5 up). 16.00 (*0-688-13595-1*, Morrow, William & Co.) Morrow/Avon.
—Broken Bridge. 1996. 10.55 (*0-606-09105-X*) Turtleback Bks.
—One More River. 1996. (YA). (gr. 7 up). pap. 4.50 (*0-380-72755-2*, Avon Bks.); 1993. 256p. (J). (gr. 4-7). pap. 5.99 (*0-380-71563-5*, Avon Bks.); 1992. 256p. (YA). (gr. 5 up). 14.00 (*0-688-10893-8*, Morrow, William & Co.) Morrow/Avon.
—One More River. 1992. 11.04 (*0-606-05525-8*) Turtleback Bks.
Barrie, Barbara. Lone Star. (J). 1992. 192p. (gr. 4-7). pap. 3.50 o.s.i (*0-440-40718-4*, Yearling); 1990. o.s.i (*0-385-30192-8*, Dell Books for Young Readers) Random Hse. Children's Bks.
Bat-Ami, Miriam. Two Suns in the Sky. 1999. 208p. (YA). (gr. 7-12). 17.95 (*0-8126-2900-0*) Cricket Bks.
—Two Suns in the Sky. 2001. 208p. (YA). pap. 6.99 (*0-14-230036-5*, Puffin Bks.) Penguin Putnam Bks. for Young Readers.
Baylis-White, Mary. Sheltering Rebecca. 112p. (J). 1993. (gr. 5-9). pap. 3.99 o.p. (*0-14-036448-X*, Puffin Bks.); 1991. (gr. 3-7). 14.95 o.p. (*0-525-67349-0*, Dutton Children's Bks.) Penguin Putnam Bks. for Young Readers.
Beim, Lorraine. Carol's Side of the Street. 1951. (Illus.). (J). (gr. 3-6). 4.95 o.p. (*0-15-214641-5*) Harcourt Children's Bks.
Bell, Mary Reeves. Checkmate in the Carpathians. 2000. (Passport to Danger Ser.: Vol. 4). (Illus.). 208p. (J). (gr. 7-12). pap. 5.99 o.p. (*1-55661-551-5*) Bethany Hse. Pubs.
—Secret of Mezuzah. 1999. (Passport to Danger Ser.: Vol. 1). 208p. (J). (gr. 7-12). pap. 5.99 o.p. (*1-55661-549-3*) Bethany Hse. Pubs.
—Secret of Mezuzah. 1999. (J). 12.04 (*0-606-18974-2*) Turtleback Bks.
Bellafiore, Sharyn. Amos & Abraham. 1994. (Illus.). 32p. (J). (gr. k-5). lib. bdg. 14.95 (*1-56148-139-4*) Good Bks.
Benenfeld, Rikki. I Go to School. 1998. (Illus.). 32p. (J). (ps-k). 9.95 (*0-922613-82-6*) Hachai Publishing.
—Let's Go to Shul. 2002. (Illus.). 24p. (J). (ps-1). 9.95 (*1-929628-08-0*) Hachai Publishing.
Bennett, Cherie. Anne Frank & Me. 2002. 352p. (J). pap. 6.99 (*0-698-11973-8*, PaperStar) Penguin Putnam Bks. for Young Readers.
Bennett, Cherie & Gottesfeld, Jeff. Anne Frank & Me. 2001. 291p. (J). (gr. 7 up). 18.99 (*0-399-23329-6*, G. P. Putnam's Sons) Penguin Group (USA) Inc.
Bernays, Anne. Growing Up Rich. 1975. 352p. 7.95 o.p. (*0-316-09185-5*) Little Brown & Co.
Biers-Ariel, Matt. The Seven Species. 2003. (Illus.). 19.95 (*0-8074-0852-2*) UAHC Pr.
—Solomon & the Trees. 2000. (Illus.). (J). 12.95 (*0-8074-0749-6*) UAHC Pr.
Birnhack, Sarah. Happy Is the Heart: A Year in the Life of a Jewish Girl. 1976. (Illus.). (J). (gr. 5-8). 7.95 o.p. (*0-87306-131-4*) Feldheim, Philipp Inc.
Blanc, Esther Silverstein & Eagle, Godeane. Long Johns for a Small Chicken. 2003. (J). 16.95 (*1-884244-23-8*) Volcano Pr.
Blatt, Evelyn. More Precious Than Gold: A Story of Inquisition Spain in the 1490's. Gardner, Eve-Lynn J., ed. 2002. (Illus.). 200p. (J). (gr. 2-5). pap. 8.95 (*1-929628-10-2*) Hachai Publishing.
Blumberg, Sherry H. Rooftop Secrets, Grades 7-9: And Other Stories of Anti-Semitism. 1987. (Illus.). 144p. pap., tchr. ed. 5.00 (*0-8074-0326-1*, 201441) UAHC Pr.
Bogot, Howard I. Becky & Benny Thank God. 1996. (Illus.). 20p. (J). (ps-1). 9.95 (*0-88123-065-0*) Central Conference of American Rabbis/ CCAR Press.
Bogot, Howard I. & Bogot, Mary K. Seder with the Animals. 1996. 32p. (J). (ps up). pap. 10.95 (*0-88123-067-7*) Central Conference of American Rabbis/ CCAR Press.
Brodie, Deborah, ed. Stories My Grandfather Should Have Told Me. 1976. (Illus.). (J). (gr. 2-6). 6.95 o.p. (*0-88482-752-6*) Hebrew Publishing Co.
Brooks, Jerome. Make Me a Hero. 1980. 176p. (J). (gr. 5-9). 9.95 o.p. (*0-525-34475-6*, 0966-290, Dutton) Dutton/Plume.
Buckvar, Felice. Dangerous Dream. Kemnitz, Myrna, ed. 1998. 123p. (J). pap. 9.99 (*0-88092-277-X*, 277X) Royal Fireworks Publishing Co.
Bush, Lawrence. Emma Ansky-Levine & Her Mitzvah Machine. 1991. (Do-It-Yourself Jewish Adventure Ser.). (Illus.). 128p. (J). (gr. 4-7). pap. 7.95 (*0-8074-0458-6*, 123933) UAHC Pr.
—Rooftop Secrets: And Other Stories of Anti-Semitism. 1986. (Illus.). 144p. (J). (gr. 4-7). pap. 9.95 (*0-8074-0314-8*, 121720) UAHC Pr.
Carney, Karen L. What Is the Meaning of Shiva. rev. ed. 2001. (Barklay & Eve Ser.: Bk. 3). Orig. Title: Barklay & Eve. (Illus.). (J). pap. 6.95 (*0-9667820-2-X*) Dragonfly Publishing.
Carter, Peter. The Hunted, RS. 1994. 320p. (J). 17.00 o.p. (*0-374-33520-6*, Farrar, Straus & Giroux (BYR)) Farrar, Straus & Giroux.
Chaikin, Miriam. Aviva's Piano. 1986. (Illus.). 48p. (J). (gr. 2-4). 12.20 o.p. (*0-89919-367-6*, Clarion Bks.) Houghton Mifflin Co. Trade & Reference Div.
—Feathers in the Wind. 1989. (Charlotte Zolotow Bk.). (Illus.). 64p. (J). (gr. 3-5). 10.95 (*0-06-021162-8*); lib. bdg. 10.89 o.p. (*0-06-021163-6*) HarperCollins Children's Bk. Group.
—How Yossi Beat the Evil Urge. 1983. (Charlotte Zolotow Bk.). (Illus.). 64p. (J). (gr. 3-5). o.p. (*0-06-021184-9*); lib. bdg. 11.89 o.p. (*0-06-021185-7*) HarperCollins Children's Bk. Group.
—Yossi Tries to Help God. 1987. (Charlotte Zolotow Bk.). (Illus.). 80p. (J). (gr. 3-5). 11.95 (*0-06-021197-0*); lib. bdg. 11.89 o.p. (*0-06-021198-9*) HarperCollins Children's Bk. Group.
Chapman, Carol. The Tale of Meshka the Kvetch. 1980. (Illus.). 32p. (J). (gr. k-3). 13.95 o.p. (*0-525-40745-6*, Dutton Children's Bks.) Penguin Putnam Bks. for Young Readers.
Charles, Freda. The Mystery of Missing Challah. 1981. (Illus.). 40p. (J). (ps). pap. 5.95 o.p. (*0-8246-0264-1*) Jonathan David Pubs., Inc.
Cohen, Barbara. The Carp in the Bathtub. 1972. (Illus.). 48p. (J). (gr. 1-5). 13.95 o.p. (*0-688-41627-6*); lib. bdg. 15.93 o.p. (*0-688-51627-0*) HarperCollins Children's Bk. Group.
—The Carp in the Bathtub. (J). (gr. 2-4). 48p. pap. 5.95 (*0-8072-1332-2*); 1982. pap. 17.00 incl. audio (*0-8072-0022-0*, FTR66 SP) Random Hse. Audio Publishing Group. (Listening Library).
—The Carp in the Bathtub. 1972. (J). 12.10 (*0-606-03993-7*) Turtleback Bks.
—Here Come the Purim Players! 1984. (Illus.). 32p. (J). (gr. 1-4). lib. bdg. 12.88 o.p. (*0-688-02108-5*) HarperCollins Children's Bk. Group.
—The Secret Grove. 1985. (Illus.). 32p. (J). (gr. 4-6). 8.95 (*0-8074-0301-6*, 101065) UAHC Pr.
Cohen, Sholom. The Lopsided Yarmulke. 1995. (Yitz Berg from Pittsburgh Ser.). (J). (gr. 3 up). pap. 6.95 o.p. (*0-922613-51-6*) Hachai Publishing.
Cohen, Susan J., illus. The Donkey's Story. 1988. 32p. (J). (gr. k-5). 12.95 o.p. (*0-688-04104-3*); lib. bdg. 12.88 o.p. (*0-688-04105-1*) HarperCollins Children's Bk. Group.
Colish, Chana. The Great Mitzvah Fair. 1982. (Illus.). 13p. (J). reprint ed. spiral bd. 11.00 (*0-8266-0356-4*, Merkos L'Inyonei Chinuch) Kehot Pubn. Society.
Collins, Alan. Joshua. 1995. 130p. (YA). pap. 14.95 (*0-7022-2809-5*) Univ. of Queensland Pr. AUS. *Dist:* International Specialized Bk. Services.
Cook Waldron, Kathleen. Wilderness Passover. 1994. (Northern Lights Books for Children Ser.). (Illus.). 32p. (J). (gr. 4-7). 13.95 o.p. (*0-88995-112-8*) Red Deer Pr. CAN. *Dist:* General Distribution Services, Inc.
Cope, Jane, illus. A Treasury of Jewish Stories. 1996. 160p. (J). (gr. k-4). pap. o.s.i (*0-7534-5028-3*) Kingfisher Publications, plc.
Crosby, Ruthann. Miracle in the Glass. Godfrey, Ellen F. et al, eds. 1996. (Illus.). 32p. (Orig.). pap. 19.95 incl. audio (*0-9649962-0-0*) Gabriel's Gatherings, Inc.
Cushnir, Howard. The Secret Spinner: Tales of Rav Gedalia. 1985. (Illus.). 48p. (J). (gr. 2-5). pap. 5.95 o.p. (*0-930494-47-4*) Kar-Ben Publishing.
Dell, Pamela. The Gold Coin: A Story about New York City's Lower East Side. 2002. (Illus.). 48p. (J). (gr. 3-8). lib. bdg. 27.07 (*1-59187-017-8*) Child's World, Inc.
Douglas, Kirk. The Broken Mirror. 1997. (Illus.). 96p. (J). per. 13.00 (*0-689-81493-3*, Simon & Schuster Children's Publishing) Simon & Schuster Children's Publishing.
Dreams in the Golden Country: The Diary of Zipporah Feldman, a Jewish Immigrant Girl. 2003. (J). lib. bdg. 12.95 (*0-439-55502-7*) Scholastic, Inc.
Drucker, Malka. Grandma's Latkes. (Illus.). 32p. (J). 1996. pap. 6.00 o.s.i (*0-15-201388-1*, Voyager Bks./Libros Viajeros); 1992. 13.95 o.s.i (*0-15-200468-8*, Gulliver Bks.) Harcourt Children's Bks.
—Grandma's Latkes. 1996. 12.15 (*0-606-10201-9*) Turtleback Bks.
—Jacob's Rescue: A Holocaust Story. 1993. 128p. (J). 15.95 o.s.i (*0-385-32519-3*, Dell Books for Young Readers) Random Hse. Children's Bks.
—Jacob's Rescue: A Holocaust Story. 1993. 10.55 (*0-606-06504-0*) Turtleback Bks.
Drucker, Malka & Halperin. Jacob's Rescue: A Holocaust Story. 1994. (J). pap. o.p. (*0-440-90106-5*) Dell Publishing.
Drucker, Malka & Halperin, Michael. Jacob's Rescue: A Holocaust Story. 1993. 128p. (J). (gr. 4-7). 15.95 o.s.i (*0-553-08976-5*, Skylark) Random Hse. Children's Bks.
Drucker, Malka, et al. Jacob's Rescue: A Holocaust Story. 1994. 128p. (gr. 2-6). pap. text 4.99 (*0-440-40965-9*) Dell Publishing.
Edwards, Michelle. A Baker's Portrait. 1991. (Illus.). 32p. (J). (gr. k up). lib. bdg. 13.88 o.p. (*0-688-09713-8*) HarperCollins Children's Bk. Group.
—Chicken Man. 1994. (Illus.). 32p. (J). (ps up). reprint ed. pap. 4.95 o.p. (*0-688-13106-9*, Morrow, William & Co.) Morrow/Avon.
Elias, Miriam L. Families, Etc. 1991. (J). 12.95 o.p. (*0-87306-576-X*) Feldheim, Philipp Inc.
—Shimmy the Youngest. 1994. (Illus.). 32p. (J). pap. text 6.95 (*0-922613-72-9*) Hachai Publishing.
—Thanks to You! 1994. (J). 12.95 (*0-87306-663-4*); pap. 9.95 (*0-87306-664-2*) Feldheim, Philipp Inc.
Elmer, Robert. Follow the Star. 1997. (Young Underground Ser.: Vol. 7). 176p. (J). (gr. 3-8). pap. 5.99 (*1-55661-660-0*) Bethany Hse. Pubs.
—Peace Rebel. 2000. (Promise of Zion Ser.: Vol. 2). 160p. (J). (gr. 3-7). pap. 5.99 (*0-7642-2297-X*) Bethany Hse. Pubs.
—Promise Breaker. 2000. (Promise of Zion Ser.: Vol. 1). 176p. (J). (gr. 3-7). pap. 5.99 (*0-7642-2296-1*) Bethany Hse. Pubs.
Elsant, Martin. Bar Mitzvah Lessons. 1993. 96p. (YA). (gr. 7 up). 5.95 (*1-881283-01-1*) Alef Design Group.
Emerman, Ellen. Just Right: The Story of a Jewish Home. Rosenfeld, Dina, ed. 1999. (Illus.). 32p. (J). (ps-1). 9.95 (*0-922613-91-5*) Hachai Publishing.
Estrin, Leibel. The Man Who Rode with Eliyahu Hanavi. 1990. (Illus.). 32p. (J). (ps-3). 9.95 o.p. (*0-922613-23-0*); pap. 7.95 o.p. (*0-922613-24-9*) Hachai Publishing.
—The Story of Danny Three Times. 1989. (Illus.). 32p. (J). (ps-1). 9.95 (*0-922613-10-9*); pap. 6.95 (*0-922613-11-7*) Hachai Publishing.
Feder, Harriet K. Death on Sacred Ground. 2001. (Young Adult Fiction Ser.). (Illus.). 192p. (J). (gr. 7-12). lib. bdg. 14.95 (*0-8225-0741-2*, Lerner Pubns.) Lerner Publishing Group.
—It Happened in Shushan: A Purim Story. 1988. (Illus.). (J). (ps-3). pap. 3.95 (*0-930494-75-X*) Kar-Ben Publishing.
—Mystery in Miami Beach: A Vivi Hartman Adventure. 1992. (Lerner Mysteries Ser.). 176p. (YA). (gr. 5-8). lib. bdg. 14.95 (*0-8225-0733-1*, Lerner Pubns.) Lerner Publishing Group.
—Mystery of the Kaifeng Scroll: A Vivi Hartman Adventure. 1995. (Lerner Mysteries Ser.). 144p. (YA). (gr. 5-8). lib. bdg. 14.95 (*0-8225-0739-0*, Lerner Pubns.) Lerner Publishing Group.
Feder, Paula K. The Feather-Bed Journey. 1995. (Illus.). (J). (ps-3). lib. bdg. 15.95 (*0-8075-2330-5*) Whitman, Albert & Co.
Feldman, Eve B. Seymour, the Formerly Fearful. 2000. 164p. (gr. 4-7). pap. 11.95 (*0-595-00391-5*, Backinprint.com) iUniverse, Inc.
Fenton, Anne. Tikun Olam: Fixing the World. 1997. (Illus.). 32p. (J). (gr. 1-4). 15.95 (*1-57129-049-4*, Lumen Editions) Brookline Bks., Inc.
Finkelstein, Ruth. Big Like Me. 2001. (Illus.). 32p. (J). 9.95 (*1-929628-04-8*) Hachai Publishing.
Firer, Benzion. Saadiah Weissman. 1982. 140p. (J). (gr. 5-12). 10.95 o.p. (*0-87306-294-9*) Feldheim, Philipp Inc.
—The Twins. Scae, Bracha, tr. from HEB. 1983. 230p. (J). (gr. 4-8). 10.95 (*0-87306-279-5*); pap. 7.95 (*0-87306-340-6*) Feldheim, Philipp Inc.
Flam, Chanie. Erev Shabbos. (Goldie Gold Board Book Ser.: Vol. 2). (Illus.). (J). (ps-1). bds. 4.95 (*1-58330-026-0*) Feldheim, Philipp Inc.
Forman, James. My Enemy, My Brother. 1981. (Illus.). 256p. (J). 9.95 o.p. (*0-525-66735-0*, Dutton Children's Bks.) Penguin Putnam Bks. for Young Readers.
—The Survivor, RS. 1976. 288p. (J). (gr. 7 up). 11.95 o.p. (*0-374-37312-4*, Farrar, Straus & Giroux (BYR)) Farrar, Straus & Giroux.
Frankel, Ellen & Levine, Sarah. Tell It Like It Is: Tough Choices for Today's Teens. 1995. (YA). 16.95 o.p. (*0-88125-522-X*) Ktav Publishing Hse., Inc.
Freund, Chavie. Read Me Beraishis. 1990. (Illus.). 44p. (J). (gr. k-2). 14.95 (*1-56062-042-0*, CRM102H) CIS Communications, Inc.
Fruchter, Yaakov. The Best of Olmeinu - Book Three: Chanukah & Other Stories, Bk. 3. Scherman, Nosson, ed. 1982. (ArtScroll Youth Ser.). (Illus.). 160p. (YA). (gr. 5-12). 10.95 o.p. (*0-89906-754-9*); pap. 7.95 o.p. (*0-89906-755-7*) Mesorah Pubns., Ltd.
—The Best of Olomeinu: Pesach & Other Stories, Bk. 5. Scherman, Nosson, ed. 1984. (ArtScroll Youth Ser.). (Illus.). 160p. (YA). (gr. 5-12). 10.95 o.p. (*0-89906-758-1*) Mesorah Pubns., Ltd.
—The Best of Olomeinu: Shabos & Other Stories, Bk. 2. Scherman, Nosson, ed. 1982. (ArtScroll Youth Ser.). (Illus.). 160p. (gr. 5-12). (J). pap. 9.99 o.p. (*0-89906-753-0*); (YA). 10.95 o.p. (*0-89906-752-2*) Mesorah Pubns., Ltd.
—The Best of Olomeinu: Stories for All Year Round, Bk. 1. Scherman, Nosson, ed. 1981. (ArtScroll Youth Ser.). (Illus.). 160p. (YA). (gr. 5-12). 10.95 o.p. (*0-89906-750-6*); pap. 7.95 o.p. (*0-89906-751-4*) Mesorah Pubns., Ltd.

—The Best of Olomeinu: Succos & Other Stories, Bk. 6. Scherman, Nosson, ed. 1984. (ArtScroll Youth Ser.). (Illus.). 160p. (J). (gr. 5-12). 12.99 o.p. (*0-89906-760-3*); pap. 9.99 o.p. (*0-89906-761-1*) Mesorah Pubns., Ltd.

Fructer, Yaakov. The Best of Olomeinu: Purim & Other Stories, Bk. 7. Scherman, Nosson, ed. 1986. (ArtScroll Youth Ser.). (Illus.). 160p. (YA). (gr. 5-12). 10.95 o.p. (*0-89906-762-X*); pap. 7.95 o.p. (*0-89906-763-8*) Mesorah Pubns., Ltd.

Fuchs, Yitzchak Y. Halichos Bas Yisroel, 2 vols. Dombey, Moshe, tr. 1987. 41.95 (*1-58330-035-X*);Vol. 1. (J). (gr. 7-12). 19.95 (*0-87306-397-X*) Feldheim, Philipp Inc.

Gaberman, Judith. One-Way to Ansonia. 2000. 196p. pap. 12.95 (*0-595-15830-7*, Backinprint.com) iUniverse, Inc.

Gantz, David. Davey's Hanukkah Golem. 1991. (Illus.). 32p. (J). (gr. k-3). 14.95 o.p. (*0-8276-0380-0*) Jewish Pubn. Society.

Ganz, Yaffa. Hello Heddy Levi. 1989. (J). (gr. 4-7). 11.95 (*0-87306-480-1*) Feldheim, Philipp Inc.

—Savta Simcha & the Roundabout Journey to Jerusalem. 2000. (Illus.). (J). 15.95 (*1-58330-452-5*) Feldheim, Philipp Inc.

—Savta Simcha, Uncle Nechemya & the Very Strange Stone in the Garden. 1992. (Illus.). (J). 14.95 (*0-87306-618-9*) Feldheim, Philipp Inc.

—Shuki's Upside-Down Dream. 1986. (Illus.). (J). (gr. k-3). 9.95 (*0-87306-384-8*) Feldheim, Philipp Inc.

Garfunkel, Debby. Baker's Dozen No. 9: Through Thick & Thin. 1993. 144p. (Orig.). (J). (gr. 4-9). pap. 8.95 o.p. (*1-56871-024-0*) Targum Pr., Inc.

Garren, Devorah-Leah. Shabbos Is Coming! We're Lost in the Zoo! 1999. (Illus.). 32p. (J). (ps-3). 12.95 (*1-880582-32-5*) Judaica Pr., Inc., The.

Garrett, Sandra G. & Williams, Philip C. The Smugglers' Secret. 1994. (Screech Owl Mysteries Ser.). 32p. (J). (gr. k-5). lib. bdg. 19.93 (*0-86625-501-X*) Rourke Publishing, LLC.

Geller, Beverly. The Shalom Zachar. 1991. (Illus.). 47p. (J). (ps-1). 12.95 (*0-935063-69-2*, CCB106H) CIS Communications, Inc.

Geller, Beverly Mach. The Mitzvah Girl. 2000. (Illus.). 24p. (J). (ps-3). 12.95 (*965-229-203-6*) Gefen Publishing Hse., Ltd ISR. *Dist:* Gefen Bks.

Gellman, Ellie. Justin's Hebrew Name. 1988. (Illus.). 32p. (J). (gr. k-3). 10.95 o.p. (*0-930494-83-0*); pap. 4.95 o.p. (*0-930494-78-4*) Kar-Ben Publishing.

Geras, Adele. Golden Windows: And Other Stories of Jerusalem. 1993. (Willa Perlman Bks.). 160p. (J). (gr. 3-7). 14.95 o.p. (*0-06-022941-1*); lib. bdg. 13.89 o.p. (*0-06-022942-X*) HarperCollins Children's Bk. Group.

Getting Started. 1992. (Brookville Chese Committee Ser. - Tamar Bks.: Vol. I). (J). pap. 7.99 (*0-89906-136-2*) Mesorah Pubns., Ltd.

Gettinger, Shifrah. A Very Special Gift. 1993. (Illus.). 32p. (J). (ps-3). 9.95 (*0-922613-52-4*); pap. text 6.95 (*0-922613-53-2*) Hachai Publishing.

Gikow, Louise. The Shalom Sesame Players Present: The Story of Passover. 1994. (Sharing Passover Ser.). (Illus.). 36p. (J). 12.95 (*1-56086-201-7*); 14.95 incl. audio (*1-56086-200-9*) Sisu Home Entertainment, Inc.

Goetz, Bracha D. Nicanor Knew the Secret. Zakutinsky, Ruth, ed. 1992. (E Z Reader Ser.). (Illus.). 32p. (J). (gr. 3). lib. bdg. 6.95 o.p. (*0-911643-14-1*) Aura Printing, Inc.

Gold, Auner. The Purple Ring. 1986. (Ruach Ami Ser.). (Illus.). 191p. (YA). (gr. 9-12). pap. 11.95 (*0-935063-15-3*) CIS Communications, Inc.

Gold, Avner. The Purple Ring. 1986. (Ruach Ami Ser.). (Illus.). 191p. (YA). (gr. 9-12). 15.95 (*0-935063-16-1*, CRA106H) CIS Communications, Inc.

Goldin, Barbara Diamond. The Magician's Visit: A Passover Tale. (Illus.). 32p. (J). 1995. pap. 4.99 o.s.i (*0-14-054455-0*, Puffin Bks.); 1993. 13.99 o.p. (*0-670-84905-7*, Viking Children's Bks.); 1993. 14.99 o.s.i (*0-670-84840-9*, Viking Children's Bks.) Penguin Putnam Bks. for Young Readers.

—While the Candles Burn: Eight Stories for Hanukkah. 1996. (Illus.). 64p. (J). 16.99 o.s.i (*0-670-85875-7*, Viking) Penguin Putnam Bks. for Young Readers.

—While the Candles Burn: Eight Stories for Hanukkah. 1999. 13.14 (*0-606-17434-6*) Turtleback Bks.

Goldstein, Andrew. My Jewish Home. 2000. (Illus.). 12p. (J). bds. 4.95 (*1-58013-070-4*) Kar-Ben Publishing.

Goodman, David R. The Mitzvah Mouse: Children Do Good Deeds. 1992. 24p. (J). 8.95 (*965-229-069-6*) Gefen Publishing Hse., Ltd ISR. *Dist:* Gefen Bks.

Goodman, Ruth F. Pen Pals: What It Means to Be Jewish in Israel & America. 1996. 96p. (YA). (gr. 7 up). 14.95 (*1-56474-159-1*) Fithian Pr.

Goodman, Sarah. Shani Plus Three. 1993. (B. Y. High Ser.: No. 7). 176p. (J). (gr. 6-9). 9.95 o.p. (*1-56871-028-3*) Targum Pr., Inc.

Gorbaty, Norman, illus. Seder with the Animals. 1996. 32p. (J). (ps-3). 16.95 (*0-88123-066-9*) Central Conference of American Rabbis/ CCAR Press.

Gottesman, Meir U. Chaimkel the Dreamer. 1987. (Illus.). 157p. (J). (gr. 3-5). 11.95 (*0-935063-26-9*, CJR101H); pap. 8.95 (*0-935063-27-7*, CJR101S) CIS Communications, Inc.

Gottlieb, Yaffa L. My Upsheren Book. 1991. (Illus.). 32p. (J). (ps-1). 9.95 (*0-922613-37-0*); pap. 6.95 (*0-922613-38-9*) Hachai Publishing.

Gray, Elmer L. Furious & Free. 1984. (J). (gr. 10 up). 7.95 o.p. (*0-8054-7320-3*) Broadman & Holman Pubs.

Greenberg, Joanne. I Never Promised You a Rose Garden. 2004. 288p. pap. 13.95 (*0-451-21120-0*); 1989. (Illus.). 256p. (YA). (gr. 5-12). mass mkt. 6.99 (*0-451-16031-2*, AE3136, Signet Bks.); 1977. mass mkt. 1.75 o.p. (*0-451-07722-9*, Signet Bks.); 1969. mass mkt. 0.75 o.p. (*0-451-02592-X*, Signet Bks.); 1969. mass mkt. 0.95 o.p. (*0-451-03853-3*, Signet Bks.); 1965. mass mkt. 1.50 o.p. (*0-451-07473-4*, Signet Bks.); 1965. mass mkt. 1.25 o.p. (*0-451-04835-0*, Signet Bks.); 1965. mass mkt. 1.95 o.p. (*0-451-08737-2*, Signet Bks.); 1965. mass mkt. 3.50 o.p. (*0-451-15305-7*, Signet Bks.); 1965. mass mkt. 2.95 o.p. (*0-451-13747-7*, Signet Bks.); 1965. mass mkt. 2.50 o.p. (*0-451-13136-3*, Signet Bks.); 1965. mass mkt. 2.25 o.p. (*0-451-09700-9*, Signet Bks.) NAL.

—I Never Promised You a Rose Garden. 256p. (YA). (gr. 7 up). pap. 5.99 (*0-8072-1362-4*, Listening Library) Random Hse. Audio Publishing Group.

—I Never Promised You a Rose Garden. 1964. 12.04 (*0-606-00838-1*) Turtleback Bks.

Greenburg, Dan. My Grandma, Major League Slugger, Vol. 24. 2001. (Zack Files Ser.: No. 24). (Illus.). 64p. (J). (gr. 2-5). mass mkt. 4.99 (*0-448-42550-5*, Grosset & Dunlap) Penguin Putnam Bks. for Young Readers.

Greene, Bette. Morning Is a Long Time Coming. 1993. 272p. (YA). (gr. 7-12). mass mkt. 4.99 o.s.i (*0-440-21893-4*) Dell Publishing.

—Morning Is a Long Time Coming. 1978. (J). (gr. 9 up). 10.95 o.p. (*0-8037-5496-5*, Dial Bks. for Young Readers) Penguin Putnam Bks. for Young Readers.

—Morning Is a Long Time Coming. 1988. (YA). mass mkt. 2.95 o.s.i (*0-553-27354-X*, Starfire) Random Hse. Children's Bks.

—Morning Is a Long Time Coming. (gr. 7-9). 1983. (Illus.). pap. (*0-671-47618-1*); 1980. (J). pap. (*0-671-42456-4*) Simon & Schuster Children's Publishing. (Simon Pulse).

—Morning Is a Long Time Coming. 1978. 9.60 o.p. (*0-606-05928-8*) Turtleback Bks.

—Summer of My German Soldier. 2003. (Illus.). 256p. (J). 16.99 (*0-8037-2869-7*, Dial Bks. for Young Readers) Penguin Putnam Bks. for Young Readers.

—Summer of My German Soldier. 2000. (YA). (gr. 6 up). 20.50 (*0-8446-7144-4*) Smith, Peter Pub., Inc.

—Summer of My German Soldier. 1999. 11.04 (*0-606-17432-X*) Turtleback Bks.

Greene, Jacqueline D. Butchers & Bakers Rabbis & Kings. 1984. (Illus.). 32p. (J). (gr. 1-6). 10.95 o.p. (*0-930494-27-X*); pap. 4.95 o.p. (*0-930494-28-8*) Kar-Ben Publishing.

Greene, Jacqueline Dembar. One Foot Ashore. (J). 2000. 208p. (gr. 3-6). pap. 8.95 (*0-8027-7601-9*); 1994. 144p. (gr. 4-6). 16.95 (*0-8027-8281-7*) Walker & Co.

Greene, Patricia B. The Sabbath Garden. 1993. (Illus.). 224p. (YA). (gr. 7 up). 15.99 o.p. (*0-525-67430-6*, Dutton Children's Bks.) Penguin Putnam Bks. for Young Readers.

Grishaver, Joel Lurie. Tanta Teva & the Magic Booth. 1993. (Illus.). 80p. (J). (gr. 4-7). pap. 5.95 (*1-881283-00-3*) Alef Design Group.

Grode, Phyllis A. Sophie's Name. 1990. (Illus.). 32p. (J). (gr. k-3). 12.95 (*0-929371-18-6*); pap. 4.95 (*0-929371-19-4*) Kar-Ben Publishing.

Groner, Judye & Wikler, Madeline. Where Is the Afikomen? 1985. (Illus.). 12p. (J). (ps). bds. 4.95 o.p. (*0-930494-52-0*) Kar-Ben Publishing.

Gunsher, Cheryl. Lev the Lucky Lulav. 1993. (Illus.). 24p. (J). (ps). 10.00 (*1-881602-01-X*) Prism Pr.

Hall, Robert F. Blind Bartimaeus: Little Blind Shepard Boy - A Jewish Christmas Story, Vol. 1. 1996. (Illus.). 32p. (YA). (gr. 7-12). 11.90 (*0-9651296-0-8*) Hall, Robert F.

Halpern, Chaiky. The Dink That Stopped the Clock. 1985. (Sifrei Rimon Ser.). 24p. (Orig.). (J). (ps-3). pap. 2.95 (*0-87306-379-1*) Feldheim, Philipp Inc.

Halpern, Chaiky, illus. The Dangerous Dreidle Ride. 1981. (J). (ps-3). pap. 2.95 (*0-87306-249-3*) Feldheim, Philipp Inc.

Hannigan, Lynne. Sam's Passover. (J). pap. 5.95 (*0-7136-4084-7*, 93342) A & C Black GBR. *Dist:* Lubrecht & Cramer, Ltd.

Harber, Frances. The Brothers' Promise. 1998. (Illus.). 32p. (J). (gr. 1-5). lib. bdg. 15.95 o.p. (*0-8075-0900-0*) Whitman, Albert & Co.

Hart, Jan S. Hanna, the Immigrant. Roberts, Melissa, ed. 1991. (Illus.). 114p. (J). (gr. 6-8). 12.95 o.p. (*0-89015-805-3*) Eakin Pr.

—Hanna, the Immigrant. rev. ed. 1997. (Illus.). 114p. (J). (gr. 3-6). 12.95 (*0-9644559-1-9*) Hart Publishing.

—The Many Adventures of Minnie. 1992. (Illus.). 96p. (J). (gr. 4-7). 12.95 o.p. (*0-89015-859-2*) Eakin Pr.

—The Many Adventures of Minnie. 1997. (Illus.). 111p. (J). (gr. 3-6). reprint ed. 12.95 (*0-9644559-2-7*) Hart Publishing.

Hausman, Gerald. Night Flight. 1996. 144p. (J). (gr. 5-9). 15.95 o.s.i (*0-399-22758-X*, Philomel) Penguin Putnam Bks. for Young Readers.

Hautzig, Esther. Riches. 1992. (Charlotte Zolotow Bk.). (Illus.). 32p. (J). (gr. 3 up). 14.00 (*0-06-022259-X*); lib. bdg. 13.89 o.p. (*0-06-022260-3*) HarperCollins Children's Bk. Group.

Hautzig, Esther Rudomin. A Picture of Grandmother, RS. 2002. (Illus.). 80p. (J). (gr. 2-5). 15.00 (*0-374-35920-2*, Farrar, Straus & Giroux (BYR)) Farrar, Straus & Giroux.

Heller, Linda. The Castle on Hester Street. (Illus.). 32p. (J). 1990. (gr. k-3). pap. 4.95 (*0-8276-0323-1*); 1982. (gr. 1-3). 9.95 o.s.i (*0-8276-0206-5*, 496) Jewish Pubn. Society.

Herman, Charlotte. How Yussel Caught the Gefilte Fish: A Shabbos Story. 1999. (Illus.). 32p. (J). (gr. k-3). 16.99 o.p. (*0-525-45449-7*, Dutton Children's Bks.) Penguin Putnam Bks. for Young Readers.

Hershenhorn, Esther. Chicken Soup by Heart. 2001. (Illus.). (J). (gr. k-3). 16.95 (*0-689-82665-6*, Simon & Schuster Children's Publishing) Simon & Schuster Children's Publishing.

Hesse, Karen. Letters from Rifka. ERS. 1992. 160p. (YA). (gr. 4-7). 16.95 (*0-8050-1964-2*, Holt, Henry & Co. Bks. For Young Readers) Holt, Henry & Co.

—Letters from Rifka. 1993. 160p. (J). (gr. 3-7). reprint ed. pap. 5.99 (*0-14-036391-2*, Puffin Bks.) Penguin Putnam Bks. for Young Readers.

—Letters from Rifka. 1993. (J). 11.04 (*0-606-05905-9*) Turtleback Bks.

Hest, Amy. The Friday Nights of Nana. 2001. (Illus.). 32p. (J). (ps-2). 15.99 (*0-7636-0658-8*) Candlewick Pr.

—Love You, Soldier. 1993. 4p. (J). (gr. 4-7). pap. 4.99 o.p. (*0-14-036174-X*, Puffin Bks.) Penguin Putnam Bks. for Young Readers.

—Love You, Soldier. 1991. 48p. (J). (gr. 2-5). text 13.95 o.p. (*0-02-743635-7*, Simon & Schuster Children's Publishing) Simon & Schuster Children's Publishing.

—Love You, Soldier. 1993. 11.14 (*0-606-02730-0*) Turtleback Bks.

—The Private Notebook of Katie Roberts, Age 11. 1995. (Illus.). 80p. (J). (gr. 3-6). 14.99 o.s.i (*1-56402-474-1*) Candlewick Pr.

—The Private Notebook of Katie Roberts, Age 11. 1996. 10.14 (*0-606-09768-6*) Turtleback Bks.

Hest, Amy & Lamut, Sonja. Love You, Soldier. 2000. (Illus.). 80p. (J). (gr. 3-7). 14.99 o.s.i (*0-7636-0943-9*) Candlewick Pr.

Hirsh, Marilyn. I Love Hanukkah. 1984. (Illus.). 32p. (J). (ps-3). pap. 5.95 o.p. (*0-8234-0622-9*); lib. bdg. 13.95 o.p. (*0-8234-0525-7*) Holiday Hse., Inc.

—Where Is Yonkele? 1988. 32p. (J). (ps-1). pap. 6.95 o.p. (*0-8276-0294-4*) Jewish Pubn. Society.

Hodes, Loren. Too Big, Too Little. . . Just Right! 2002. (Illus.). (J). 9.95 (*1-880582-72-4*, TTTH) Judaica Pr., Inc., The.

Hoestlandt, Jo. Star of Fear, Star of Hope. Polizzotti, Mark, tr. from FRE. Tr. of Grande Peur sous les Etoiles. (Illus.). 32p. (J). (gr. 2-5). 1995. lib. bdg. 16.85 (*0-8027-8374-0*); 2000. reprint ed. 16.95 (*0-8027-8373-2*); 2000. reprint ed. pap. 8.95 (*0-8027-7588-8*) Walker & Co.

Hoffman, Allen. Big League Dreams. 1999. (Small Worlds Ser.). 296p. pap. 12.95 (*0-7892-0583-1*) Abbeville Pr., Inc.

Holland, Cheri. Maccabee Jamboree: A Hanukkah Countdown. 1998. (Illus.). 24p. (J). (ps-3). pap. 4.95 (*1-58013-019-4*) Kar-Ben Publishing.

Howe, Irving. Favorite Yiddish Stories. Greenberg, Eliezer, ed. 1992. 128p. (J). reprint ed. 5.99 o.s.i (*0-517-06656-4*) Random Hse. Value Publishing.

Hubner, Carol K. Silent Shofar. (Illus.). (J). (gr. 3 up). 6.95 o.p. (*0-910818-53-3*); 1983. pap. 6.95 o.p. (*0-910818-54-1*) Judaica Pr., Inc., The.

—The Tattered Tallis. 1979. (Judaica Youth Ser.). (Illus.). 128p. (J). (gr. 3-8). 5.95 o.p. (*0-910818-19-3*) Judaica Pr., Inc., The.

Hughes, Shirley. The Lion & the Unicorn. 1999. (Illus.). 64p. (J). (gr. 2-6). pap. 17.95 o.p. (*0-7894-2555-6*, D K Ink) Dorling Kindersley Publishing, Inc.

Hunt, Angela Elwell. The Deadly Chase. 1996. (Colonial Captives Ser.: Bk. 2). 240p. (J). (gr. 3-7). pap. 8.99 o.p. (*0-8423-0330-8*) Tyndale Hse. Pubs.

—The Deadly Chase. 2000. (Colonial Captives Ser.: Vol. 2). 192p. (gr. 4-7). pap. 12.95 (*0-595-08997-6*, Backinprint.com) iUniverse, Inc.

Hurwitz, Johanna. Dear Emma. 2002. (Illus.). 160p. (J). 15.99 (*0-06-029840-5*); lib. bdg. 17.89 (*0-06-029841-3*) HarperCollins Children's Bk. Group.

—The Rabbi's Girls. 2002. Orig. Title: The Diddakoi. (Illus.). 144p. (J). pap. 5.95 (*0-06-447370-8*, Harper Trophy) HarperCollins Children's Bk. Group.

—The Rabbi's Girls. 1989. Orig. Title: The Diddakoi. (Illus.). 160p. (J). (gr. 3-7). pap. 4.99 o.p. (*0-14-032951-X*, Puffin Bks.) Penguin Putnam Bks. for Young Readers.

Isaacs, Anne. Torn Thread. 2002. 192p. (YA). mass mkt. 4.99 (*0-590-60364-7*, Scholastic Paperbacks); 2000. (Illus.). 188p. (J). (gr. 5-9). pap. 15.95 o.p. (*0-590-60363-9*, Scholastic Reference) Scholastic, Inc.

Jessup, Jack. A Donkey Named Rico. 2001. 497p. lib. bdg. (*0-7541-1539-9*) Minerva Pr.

Johnson, Lissa Halls. The Worst Wish. 2000. (Kidwitness Tales Ser.). (Illus.). 128p. (J). (gr. 3-7). pap. 5.99 (*1-56179-882-7*) Bethany Hse. Pubs.

Johnston, Tony. The Harmonica. 2004. (J). (*1-57091-547-4*) Charlesbridge Publishing, Inc.

Jules, Jacqueline. The Hardest Word: A Yom Kippur Story. 2001. 32p. (J). 17.95 (*1-58013-030-5*); (Illus.). pap. 6.95 (*1-58013-028-3*) Kar-Ben Publishing.

Kacer, Kathy. Clara's War. 2001. (Holocaust Remembrance Ser.). (Illus.). 128p. (YA). (gr. 5 up). pap. 5.95 (*1-896764-42-8*) Second Story Pr. CAN. *Dist:* Univ. of Toronto Pr.

Kalechofsky, Roberta. A Boy, a Chicken & the Lion of Judah: How Ari Became a Vegetarian. 1995. (Illus.). 45p. (J). (gr. 2-5). pap. 8.00 (*0-916288-39-0*) Micah Pubns.

Kamins, Tamar. Rivky's Great Idea. (B. Y. Times Kid Sisters Ser.: No. 3). 107p. (J). (gr. 4-7). pap. 7.95 o.p. (*1-56871-004-6*) Feldheim, Philipp Inc.

Karkowsky, Nancy. Grandma's Soup. 1989. (Illus.). 32p. (J). (gr. k-5). 8.95 o.p. (*0-930494-98-9*); pap. 5.95 (*0-930494-99-7*) Kar-Ben Publishing.

Kaye, Marilyn. The Atonement of Mindy Wise. VanDoren, Liz, ed. 1991. 160p. (YA). (gr. 7 up). 15.95 (*0-15-200402-5*, Gulliver Bks.) Harcourt Children's Bks.

Kendall, Jonathan P. My Name Is Rachamim. 1987. (Illus.). (J). (ps-3). 7.95 (*0-8074-0321-0*, 123925) UAHC Pr.

Kerr, Judith. The Other Way Round. 1975. 256p. (J). (gr. 6 up). 8.95 o.p. (*0-698-20335-6*) Putnam Publishing Group, The.

—When Hitler Stole Pink Rabbit. 1997. Tr. of Cuando Hitler Robo el Conejo Rosa. (Illus.). 192p. (J). (gr. 3-7). pap. 5.99 (*0-698-11589-9*, PaperStar) Penguin Putnam Bks. for Young Readers.

—When Hitler Stole Pink Rabbit. 1972. Tr. of Cuando Hitler Robo el Conejo Rosa. (Illus.). (YA). (gr. 6 up). 14.95 o.p. (*0-698-20182-5*, Coward-McCann) Putnam Publishing Group, The.

—When Hitler Stole Pink Rabbit. 1987. Tr. of Cuando Hitler Robo el Conejo Rosa. 192p. (J). (gr. 3 up). pap. 3.99 o.p. (*0-440-49017-0*, Yearling) Random Hse. Children's Bks.

—When Hitler Stole Pink Rabbit. 1997. Tr. of Cuando Hitler Robo el Conejo Rosa. (J). 11.04 (*0-606-12845-X*) Turtleback Bks.

Kimmel, Eric A. Asher & the Capmakers: A Hanukkah Story. 1993. (Illus.). 32p. (J). (ps-3). tchr. ed. 15.95 (*0-8234-1031-5*) Holiday Hse., Inc.

—The Chanukkah Tree. 1988. (Illus.). 32p. (J). (ps-3). tchr. ed. 16.95 (*0-8234-0705-5*) Holiday Hse., Inc.

—A Cloak for the Moon: A Tale of Rabbi Nachman of Bratslav. 2001. (Illus.). 32p. (J). (ps-3). tchr. ed. 16.95 (*0-8234-1493-0*) Holiday Hse., Inc.

—Hershel of Ostropol. 1981. (Illus.). 40p. (J). (gr. 1 up). 7.95 o.p. (*0-8276-0192-1*, 479) Jewish Pubn. Society.

—Nicanor's Gate. 1979. (Illus.). 32p. (J). (gr. k-4). 5.95 o.p. (*0-8276-0168-9*, 442) Jewish Pubn. Society.

—When Mindy Saved Hanukkah. 1998. (Illus.). 32p. (J). (ps-2). pap. 15.95 (*0-590-37136-3*) Scholastic, Inc.

—Zigazak! A Magical Hanukkah Night. 2001. (Illus.). 32p. (J). (ps-3). 15.95 (*0-385-32652-1*, Doubleday Bks. for Young Readers); lib. bdg. 17.99 (*0-385-90004-X*, Dell Books for Young Readers) Random Hse. Children's Bks.

Kimmel, Eric A. & Weihs, Erika. Days of Awe: Stories for Rosh Hashanah & Yom Kippur. 1991. 48p. (J). (gr. 4-7). 14.50 o.p. (*0-670-82772-X*, Viking Children's Bks.) Penguin Putnam Bks. for Young Readers.

Kimmelman, Leslie. The Runaway Latkes. 2000. (Illus.). 32p. (J). (ps-2). lib. bdg. 15.95 (*0-8075-7176-8*) Whitman, Albert & Co.

—Sound the Shofar! A Story for Rosh Hashanah & Yom Kippur. 1998. (Illus.). 32p. (J). (ps-1). 15.99 (*0-06-027501-4*) HarperCollins Children's Bk. Group.

Kirsh, Sharon. Fitting in. 1995. 144p. (YA). (gr. 5-9). pap. 4.95 (*0-929005-74-0*) Second Story Pr. CAN. *Dist:* Orca Bk. Pubs.

Klein-Ehlich, Tzvia. A Children's Treasure of Sephardic Tales. 1985. (ArtScroll Youth Ser.). (Illus.). 64p. (YA). (gr. 4-10). 12.99 (*0-89906-787-5*); pap. 9.99 (*0-89906-788-3*) Mesorah Pubns., Ltd.

Klein, Leah. Dollars & Sense. 1993. (B. Y. Times: No. 11). 144p. (J). pap. 8.95 o.p. (*1-56871-005-4*) Targum Pr., Inc.

—Nechama on Strike. 1993. (B. Y. Times Ser.: No. 14). 132p. (Orig.). (J). (gr. 4-9). pap. 8.95 o.p. (*1-56871-029-1*) Targum Pr., Inc.

—Sarah's Room. (B. Y. Times Kid Sisters Ser.: No. 4). 106p. (J). pap. 7.95 o.p. (*1-56871-008-9*) Targum Pr., Inc.

—Talking It Over. 1993. (B. Y. Times: No. 12). 149p. (J). pap. 8.95 o.p. (*1-56871-010-0*) Targum Pr., Inc.

Klein, Norma. Snapshots. 1986. 128p. (J). mass mkt. 2.50 o.s.i (*0-449-70157-3*, Fawcett) Ballantine Bks.

—Snapshots. 1984. (J). (gr. 7 up). 12.95 o.p. (*0-8037-0129-2*, 01258-370, Dial Bks. for Young Readers) Penguin Putnam Bks. for Young Readers.

Klein, Rachel. The Moth Diaries: A Novel. 2002. 256p. (YA). text 24.00 (*1-58243-205-8*, Counterpoint Pr.) Basic Bks.

Kogan, Mark. Archivist, Vol. 1. Khotianovsky, Olga, ed. 1990. (RUS., Illus.). 300p. (Orig.). (YA). (gr. 9-12). pap. text (*0-9624922-0-5*) HAZAR.

Konigsburg, E. L. About the B'nai Bagels. 1985. (Illus.). 176p. (gr. 4-7). pap. text 4.50 (*0-440-40034-1*, Yearling) Random Hse. Children's Bks.

—About the B'nai Bagels. 1971. (Illus.). 176p. (J). (gr. 4-6). text 14.95 o.s.i (*0-689-20631-3*, Atheneum) Simon & Schuster Children's Publishing.

—About the B'nai Bagels. 1985. 10.55 (*0-606-00897-7*) Turtleback Bks.

Krantz, Hazel. Look to the Hills. 1995. 224p. (J). 14.95 (*0-8276-0552-8*); (gr. 4-7). pap. 9.95 (*0-8276-0571-4*) Jewish Pubn. Society.

Kranzler, Gershon. At B. A. T. T. 1978. 156p. reprint ed. 11.00 (*0-8266-0368-8*, Merkos L'Inyonei Chinuch) Kehot Pubn. Society.

—The Broken Bracelet. 1967. 218p. (YA). reprint ed. 12.00 (*0-8266-0367-X*, Merkos L'Inyonei Chinuch) Kehot Pubn. Society.

—The Coachman & Other Stories. (Illus.). 174p. (YA). reprint ed. 12.00 (*0-8266-0328-9*, Merkos L'Inyonei Chinuch) Kehot Pubn. Society.

—The Glass Blower of Venice & Other Stories. Waldman, Bryna, tr. (Illus.). 96p. (YA). reprint ed. 11.00 (*0-8266-0348-3*, Merkos L'Inyonei Chinuch) Kehot Pubn. Society.

—The Precious Little Spice Box & Other Stories. 1988. (Illus.). 110p. (YA). 11.00 (*0-8266-0347-5*, Merkos L'Inyonei Chinuch) Kehot Pubn. Society.

—The Reunion & Other Stories. (Illus.). 156p. (YA). reprint ed. 12.00 (*0-8266-0327-0*, Merkos L'Inyonei Chinuch) Kehot Pubn. Society.

—The Secret Code & Other Stories. (Illus.). 108p. (YA). reprint ed. 11.00 (*0-8266-0344-0*, Merkos L'Inyonei Chinuch) Kehot Pubn. Society.

—Seder in Herlin & Other Stories. 2003. (Illus.). 108p. (YA). (gr. 5-9). reprint ed. 14.00 (*0-8266-0343-2*, Merkos L'Inyonei Chinuch) Kehot Pubn. Society.

—The Silver Rings & Other Stories. (Illus.). 162p. (YA). reprint ed. 12.00 (*0-8266-0329-7*, Merkos L'Inyonei Chinuch) Kehot Pubn. Society.

—Yoshko the Dumbbell. (J). (gr. 4-9). pap. 6.95 o.p. (*0-87306-246-9*) Feldheim, Philipp Inc.

Kranzler, Gershon & Waldman, Bryna, illus. Chanan & His Violin & Other Stories. 1999. 132p. (J). (gr. 4-8). 12.00 (*0-8266-0349-1*) Kehot Pubn. Society.

Krasnopolsky, Fara L. I Remember. 1995. (Illus.). 176p. (J). 15.95 o.p. (*0-395-67401-8*, Clarion Bks.) Houghton Mifflin Co. Trade & Reference Div.

Kravetz, Nathan. Moscow, Farewell! A Russian Boys Adventure in Times Past. 2000. 164p. (gr. 7-12). pap. 20.99 (*0-7388-2854-8*) Xlibris Corp.

Kushner, Donn. Uncle Jacob's Ghost Story, ERS. 1986. 144p. (J). (gr. 4-9). o.p. (*0-03-006502-X*, Holt, Henry & Co. Bks. For Young Readers) Holt, Henry & Co.

Laird, Christa. But Can the Phoenix Sing? 1995. 224p. (YA). (gr. 7 up). 16.00 o.s.i (*0-688-13612-5*, Greenwillow Bks.) HarperCollins Children's Bk. Group.

—Shadow of the Wall. 1990. 144p. (YA). (gr. 7 up). 12.95 o.p. (*0-688-09336-1*, Greenwillow Bks.) HarperCollins Children's Bk. Group.

—Shadow of the Wall. 1997. 144p. (gr. 6-12). mass mkt. 4.95 (*0-688-15291-0*, Morrow, William & Co.) Morrow/Avon.

—Shadow of the Wall. 1997. 11.00 (*0-606-11832-2*) Turtleback Bks.

Lakin, Patricia. Don't Forget. 2000. (Illus.). 32p. (YA). (gr. k-3). pap. 5.95 (*0-688-17522-8*, Morrow, William & Co.) Morrow/Avon.

Lanton, Sandy. Daddy's Chair. 1991. (Illus.). 32p. (J). (gr. k-4). 12.95 o.p. (*0-929371-51-8*) Kar-Ben Publishing.

—Daddy's Chair. 2000. (Illus.). 32p. (J). (gr. k-2). 14.95 (*0-9702482-0-2*); pap. 6.95 (*0-9702482-1-0*) Lanton Haas Pr.

—Lots of Latkes: A Hanukkah Story. 2003. (Illus.). (J). lib. bdg. 14.95 (*1-58013-091-7*) Kar-Ben Publishing.

Lasky, Kathryn. Marven of the Great North Woods. (Illus.). 48p. (J). (gr. 1-4). 2002. pap. 7.00 (*0-15-216826-5*, Voyager Bks./Libros Viajeros); 1997. 16.00 (*0-15-200104-2*) Harcourt Children's Bks.

—The Night Journey. 1986. (J). 12.95 o.p. (*0-670-80935-7*, Viking Children's Bks.); (Illus.). 160p. (gr. 4-7). pap. 5.99 (*0-14-032048-2*, Puffin Bks.) Penguin Putnam Bks. for Young Readers.

—The Night Journey. 2002. (YA). (gr. 6 up). 20.25 (*0-8446-7210-6*) Smith, Peter Pub., Inc.

Lazewnik, Libby. Absolutely Shira. 1993. 190p. (J). (gr. 6-9). 12.95 o.p. (*1-56871-032-1*) Targum Pr., Inc.

Leader, R. L. Faithful Soldiers. 1989. (J). (gr. 7 up). 12.95 o.p. (*0-944070-12-4*) Targum Pr., Inc.

Leah, Devora, ed. Lost Erev Shabbos in the Zoo. rev. ed. 1986. (Illus.). 32p. (J). (gr. k-3). 9.95 o.p. (*0-910818-56-8*) Judaica Pr., Inc., The.

Leah, Devorah. Lost Erev Shabbos in the Zoo. rev. ed. 1986. (Illus.). 32p. (J). (gr. k-3). pap. 7.95 o.p. (*0-910818-57-6*) Judaica Pr., Inc., The.

Lebovics, Aydel. The Teeny Tiny Yarmulka. 1982. (Illus.). 32p. (J). reprint ed. 11.00 (*0-8266-0360-2*, Merkos L'Inyonei Chinuch) Kehot Pubn. Society.

—The Wind & the Sukkah. 1982. (Illus.). 32p. (J). reprint ed. 11.00 (*0-8266-0361-0*, Merkos L'Inyonei Chinuch) Kehot Pubn. Society.

—Zaydie's Special Esrogim. 1991. (Illus.). 28p. (J). reprint ed. 12.00 (*0-8266-0357-2*, Merkos L'Inyonei Chinuch) Kehot Pubn. Society.

Lehman, Marcus. The Adopted Princess. Mindel, Nissan, tr. from GER. (Illus.). 74p. (YA). reprint ed. 11.00 (*0-8266-0334-3*, Merkos L'Inyonei Chinuch) Kehot Pubn. Society.

—Bustenai. 1982. (Illus.). 144p. (YA). reprint ed. 12.00 (*0-8266-0340-8*, Merkos L'Inyonei Chinuch) Kehot Pubn. Society.

—Meor Hagolah: Rabbenu Gershom. Hartheimer, Eva J., tr. from GER. (Illus.). 174p. (YA). reprint ed. 12.00 (*0-8266-0342-4*, Merkos L'Inyonei Chinuch) Kehot Pubn. Society.

—Out of the Depths. Mindel, Nissan, tr. from GER. (Illus.). 108p. (YA). reprint ed. 11.00 (*0-8266-0336-X*, Merkos L'Inyonei Chinuch) Kehot Pubn. Society.

—Unpaid Ransom. Mindel, Nissan, tr. from GER. (Illus.). 74p. (YA). reprint ed. 11.00 (*0-8266-0338-6*, Merkos L'Inyonei Chinuch) Kehot Pubn. Society.

Lehmann, Marcus. Family y Aguilar. (J). (gr. 7 up). 9.95 o.p. (*0-87306-122-5*) Feldheim, Philipp Inc.

Leiberman, Sara. A Trip to Mezuza Land. Colish, Chanah, ed. 1988. (Illus.). 48p. (J). reprint ed. 13.00 (*0-8266-0364-5*, Merkos L'Inyonei Chinuch) Kehot Pubn. Society.

Lepon, Shoshana. Hillel Builds a House. 1993. (Illus.). 32p. (J). (ps-3). pap. 5.95 (*0-929371-42-9*) Kar-Ben Publishing.

Lester, Julius. Pharaoh's Daughter: A Novel of Ancient Egypt. 2000. (Illus.). 192p. (YA). (gr. 7-12). 17.00 (*0-15-201826-3*, Silver Whistle) Harcourt Children's Bks.

—Pharaoh's Daughter: A Novel of Ancient Egypt. 2002. 192p. (J). (gr. 5 up). pap. 5.99 (*0-06-440969-4*, Harper Trophy) HarperCollins Children's Bk. Group.

Levine, Gail Carson. Dave at Night. 2001. 12.00 (*0-606-21137-3*) Turtleback Bks.

Levitin, Sonia. The Cure. 1999. 192p. (YA). (gr. 5 up). 16.00 (*0-15-201827-1*, Silver Whistle) Harcourt Children's Bks.

—The Cure. 2000. 256p. (J). (gr. 7 up). pap. 5.99 (*0-380-73298-X*, Harper Trophy) HarperCollins Children's Bk. Group.

—The Golem & the Dragon Girl. 1994. 176p. (YA). mass mkt. 3.99 o.s.i (*0-449-70441-6*, Fawcett) Ballantine Bks.

—The Golem & the Dragon Girl. 1993. 192p. (J). (gr. 3-7). 14.89 o.p. (*0-8037-1281-2*); 14.99 o.p. (*0-8037-1280-4*) Penguin Putnam Bks. for Young Readers. (Dial Bks. for Young Readers).

—Journey to America. 2nd ed. (Illus.). 160p. (J). (gr. 4-7). 1993. 16.00 (*0-689-31829-4*, Atheneum); 1987. reprint ed. pap. 4.99 (*0-689-71130-1*, Aladdin) Simon & Schuster Children's Publishing.

—Journey to America. 2nd ed. 1987. 11.04 (*0-606-00503-X*) Turtleback Bks.

—The Return. 1988. 192p. (gr. 7 up). mass mkt. 5.99 (*0-449-70280-4*, Fawcett) Ballantine Bks.

—The Return. 1987. 224p. (YA). (gr. 5 up). 16.00 (*0-689-31309-8*, Atheneum) Simon & Schuster Children's Publishing.

—The Singing Mountain. (YA). (gr. 7-12). 1998. 272p. 17.00 (*0-689-80809-7*, Simon & Schuster Children's Publishing); 2000. 304p. reprint ed. mass mkt. 4.99 (*0-689-83523-X*, Simon Pulse) Simon & Schuster Children's Publishing.

Lewin, Waldtraut. Freedom Beyond the Sea. Crawford, Elizabeth D., tr. 2001. 272p. (YA). (gr. 9 up). 15.95 (*0-385-32705-6*, Delacorte Pr.) Dell Publishing.

—Freedom Beyond the Sea. 2003. 272p. (YA). (gr. 9-12). mass mkt. 5.50 (*0-440-22868-9*, Laurel Leaf) Random Hse. Children's Bks.

Lewis, Shari. One-Minute Jewish Stories. 1993. (Illus.). 48p. (J). pap. 5.99 o.s.i (*0-440-40878-4*) Dell Publishing.

Lieberman, Syd. The Wise Shoemaker of Studena. (J). (gr. 5-8). audio 24.95 o.p. (*0-8276-0536-6*); 1994. (Illus.). 32p. 15.95 (*0-8276-0509-9*) Jewish Pubn. Society.

Littlefield, Holly. Fire at the Triangle Factory. 1996. (On My Own History Ser.). (Illus.). 48p. (J). (gr. 1-3). pap. 6.95 (*0-87614-970-0*); lib. bdg. 21.27 (*0-87614-868-2*) Lerner Publishing Group. (Carolrhoda Bks.).

Lowry, Lois. Number the Stars. (J). 1996. 144p. mass mkt. 2.49 o.s.i (*0-440-22033-5*); 1994. 144p. pap. 3.99 (*0-440-91002-1*); 1992. 144p. (gr. 4-7). mass mkt. 1.99 o.s.i (*0-440-21372-X*); 1990. 144p. pap. 3.50 o.s.i (*0-440-70031-0*); 1990. pap. o.p. (*0-440-80164-8*) Dell Publishing.

—Number the Stars. 1996. (J). pap. 5.60 (*0-87129-711-6*, N45) Dramatic Publishing Co.

—Number the Stars. (J). 1995. (gr. 6). 9.28 (*0-395-73270-0*); 1992. (gr. 6). pap. 11.04 (*0-395-61834-7*); 1989. 144p. (gr. 4-6). tchr. ed. 16.00 (*0-395-51060-0*) Houghton Mifflin Co.

—Number the Stars. 1992. (J). pap. 3.50 (*0-440-80291-1*, Dell Books for Young Readers); 1990. 144p. (gr. 5-9). pap. text 5.99 (*0-440-40327-8*, Yearling); 1998. 144p. (YA). (gr. 4-7). reprint ed. mass mkt. 5.99 (*0-440-22753-4*, Laurel Leaf) Random Hse. Children's Bks.

—Number the Stars. (J). 1998. 12.04 (*0-606-13670-3*); 1989. 12.04 (*0-606-04493-0*) Turtleback Bks.

—Number the Stars - Musical. 1998. 33p. pap. 5.95 (*0-87129-834-1*, N03) Dramatic Publishing Co.

—Quien Cuenta las Estrellas. 5th ed. 1998. (SPA., Illus.). 152p. (J). 8.95 (*84-239-8867-8*) Espasa Calpe, S.A. ESP. *Dist:* Continental Bk. Co., Inc.

Mack, Tracy. Birdland. 2003. 224p. (J). pap. 16.95 (*0-439-53590-5*) Scholastic, Inc.

Mackall, Dandi Daley. Who'll Light the Chanukah Candles? 2003. (Illus.). 16p. (J). pap. 4.99 (*0-689-85025-5*, Little Simon) Simon & Schuster Children's Publishing.

Mamet, David. Bar Mitzvah. 1999. (Illus.). 45p. (YA). reprint ed. 27.00 (*0-7567-6490-4*) DIANE Publishing Co.

—Bar Mitzvah. 1999. (Illus.). 48p. (gr. 8). 26.95 o.p. (*0-8212-2546-4*) Little Brown & Co.

Marcus, Audrey Friedman & Zwerin, Raymond A. Like a Maccabee. 1991. (Illus.). 32p. (J). (ps-3). 11.95 (*0-8074-0445-4*, 102564) UAHC Pr.

Matas, Carol. After the War: The Story Behind Exodus. 1996. 144p. (YA). (gr. 5-10). pap. 16.99 o.p. (*0-590-24758-1*) Scholastic, Inc.

—After the War: The Story Behind Exodus. 128p. (gr. 7-11). 1997. (YA). mass mkt. 4.99 (*0-689-80722-8*, Simon Pulse); 1996. (J). lib. bdg. 16.00 (*0-689-80350-8*, Simon & Schuster Children's Publishing) Simon & Schuster Children's Publishing.

—After the War: The Story Behind Exodus. 1997. (J). 10.55 (*0-606-13077-2*) Turtleback Bks.

—The Garden. 1998. 144p. (gr. 7-12). per. 4.99 (*0-689-80723-6*, Simon Pulse) Simon & Schuster Children's Publishing.

—The Garden. 1998. 11.04 (*0-606-15542-2*) Turtleback Bks.

—Greater Than Angels. 1998. Orig. Title: Contagion of Good. 160p. (J). (gr. 7-12). pap. 16.00 (*0-689-81353-8*, Simon & Schuster Children's Publishing) Simon & Schuster Children's Publishing.

—In My Enemy's House. 176p. (gr. 7-12). 2000. (YA). pap. 4.99 (*0-689-82400-9*, Simon Pulse); 1999. (J). per. 16.00 (*0-689-81354-6*, Simon & Schuster Children's Publishing) Simon & Schuster Children's Publishing.

—Lisa's War. 1991. 128p. (J). (gr. 7-9). pap. 2.99 o.p. (*0-590-43517-5*) Scholastic, Inc.

—Lisa's War. 1989. 128p. (YA). (gr. 7 up). text 15.00 o.s.i (*0-684-19010-9*, Atheneum) Simon & Schuster Children's Publishing.

—The Primrose Path. 1995. 14.00 (*0-606-17171-1*) Turtleback Bks.

—Rebecca. 2000. (Illus.). 160p. (J). mass mkt. (*0-439-98718-0*) Scholastic, Inc.

—Sparks Fly Upward. 2002. 192p. (YA). (gr. 5-9). 15.00 (*0-618-15964-9*, Clarion Bks.) Houghton Mifflin Co. Trade & Reference Div.

Mazer, Harry. The Last Mission. (Laurel-Leaf Historical Fiction Ser.). (gr. 7 up). 1981. 192p. (YA). mass mkt. 5.50 (*0-440-94797-9*, Laurel); 1979. (J). 7.95 o.s.i (*0-440-05774-4*, Delacorte Pr.) Dell Publishing.

—The Last Mission. 192p. (YA). (gr. 7 up). pap. 4.99 (*0-8072-1366-7*, Listening Library) Random Hse. Audio Publishing Group.

—Last Mission. 1979. (Laurel-Leaf Historical Fiction Ser.). 11.04 (*0-606-02154-X*) Turtleback Bks.

Mazer, Norma Fox. Good Night, Maman. 2001. (Illus.). (J). 11.00 (*0-606-21217-5*) Turtleback Bks.

Medoff, Francine. The Mouse in the Matzah Factory. (Illus.). (J). (ps-3). 2003. pap. 6.95 (*1-58013-048-8*); 1983. 40p. o.p. (*0-930494-18-0*); 1983. 40p. pap. 5.95 o.p. (*0-930494-19-9*) Kar-Ben Publishing.

Meiseles, Shayna. The Bat Mitzvah Club: Debbie's Story. 2001. (Illus.). 243p. (J). (gr. 5-7). 14.00 (*0-8266-0029-8*) Kehot Pubn. Society.

Melmed, Laura Krauss. Moishe's Miracle: A Hanukkah Story. 2000. (Illus.). 32p. (J). (ps up). 15.95 (*0-688-14682-1*); 15.95 (*0-688-14682-1*); lib. bdg. 15.89 (*0-688-14683-X*) HarperCollins Children's Bk. Group.

Melnikoff, Pamela. Plots & Players. 1996. (Illus.). 160p. (YA). (gr. 8 up). pap. 9.95 (*0-8276-0576-5*) Jewish Pubn. Society.

—Plots & Players. 1989. 160p. (J). 9.95 o.p. (*0-87226-406-8*, Bedrick, Peter Bks.) McGraw-Hill Children's Publishing.

—The Star & the Sword. 1994. (Illus.). 140p. (J). (gr. 5-7). pap. 8.95 (*0-8276-0528-5*) Jewish Pubn. Society.

Merling, Beryl & Dershowitz, Yosef. Olomeinu Gems: Stories for All Year Round. 1987. (ArtScroll Youth Ser.). (Illus.). 128p. (J). (gr. 5-12). 12.99 o.p. (*0-89906-764-6*); pap. 9.99 o.p. (*0-89906-765-4*) Mesorah Pubns., Ltd.

Meyer, Carolyn. Gideon's People. 1996. (Gulliver Bks.). 304p. (J). (gr. 4-7). 12.00 (*0-15-200303-7*); pap. 6.00 (*0-15-200304-5*) Harcourt Children's Bks. (Gulliver Bks.).

—Gideon's People. 1996. 12.05 (*0-606-15548-1*) Turtleback Bks.

Miklowitz, Gloria D. The Enemy Has a Face. (YA). 2004. 143p. pap. 8.00 (*0-8028-5261-0*); 2003. 148p. 16.00 (*0-8028-5243-2*) Eerdmans, William B. Publishing Co. (Eerdmans Bks For Young Readers).

Miller, Deborah. Fins & Scales: A Kosher Tale. 1992. (Illus.). 32p. (J). (gr. 1-4). pap. 6.95 (*0-929371-26-7*) Kar-Ben Publishing.

Miller, Deborah & Ostrove, Karen. Fins & Scales: A Kosher Tale. 2004. (Israel Ser.). (Illus.). 32p. (J). (gr. 1-3). pap. 4.95 (*0-929371-25-9*) Kar-Ben Publishing.

Miller, Deborah U. Poppy Seeds, Too: A Twisted Tale for Shabbat. 1982. (Illus.). 48p. (J). (ps-3). pap. 4.95 o.p. (*0-930494-17-2*) Kar-Ben Publishing.

Mills, Steven L. Rafi's Search for the Torah Munching Monster. 2001. (Illus.). (J). (*1-881283-31-3*) Alef Design Group.

Milstein, Linda B. Miami-Nanny Stories. 1994. (Illus.). (J). 16.00 o.p. (*0-688-11151-3*); lib. bdg. 15.93 o.p. (*0-688-11152-1*) Morrow/Avon. (Morrow, William & Co.).

Mindel, Nissan. The Call of the Shofar. 1971. (Illus.). 64p. (YA). reprint ed. 11.00 (*0-8266-0345-9*, Merkos L'Inyonei Chinuch) Kehot Pubn. Society.

—Dertzeil Mir A Ma'aseh. (YID., Illus.). (YA). (gr. 4-9). reprint ed. Vol. 1. 1988. 274p. 12.00 (*0-8266-0386-6*); Vol. 2. 1994. 265p. 12.00 (*0-8266-0387-4*) Kehot Pubn. Society. (Merkos L'Inyonei Chinuch).

Mindel, Nissan, ed. The Secret of Success & Other Stories. 1973. (Illus.). 64p. (YA). reprint ed. 11.00 (*0-8266-0346-7*, Merkos L'Inyonei Chinuch) Kehot Pubn. Society.

Morpurgo, Michael. Waiting for Anya. l.t. ed. 1992. 240p. (J). 13.95 o.p. (*0-7451-1527-6*, Galaxy Children's Large Print) BBC Audiobooks America.

—Waiting for Anya. 1997. 176p. (gr. 5-9). pap. 5.99 (*0-14-038431-6*); 1991. 174p. (J). 14.99 o.s.i (*0-670-83735-0*, Viking Children's Bks.) Penguin Putnam Bks. for Young Readers.

—Waiting for Anya. 1997. (J). 11.04 (*0-606-12044-0*) Turtleback Bks.

Muchnik, Michael. David Comes Home. 1984. (Illus.). 48p. (J). reprint ed. 7.00 (*0-8266-0350-5*, Merkos L'Inyonei Chinuch) Kehot Pubn. Society.

—The Double Decker Purple Shul Bus. 1984. (Illus.). 48p. (J). reprint ed. 7.00 (*0-8266-0352-1*, Merkos L'Inyonei Chinuch) Kehot Pubn. Society.

—Hershel's Houseboat. 1984. (Illus.). 48p. (J). reprint ed. 7.00 (*0-8266-0354-8*, Merkos L'Inyonei Chinuch) Kehot Pubn. Society.

—Leah & Leibel's Lighthouse. 1984. (Illus.). 48p. (J). reprint ed. 7.00 (*0-8266-0355-6*, Merkos L'Inyonei Chinuch) Kehot Pubn. Society.

—The Scribe Who Lived in a Tree. 1984. (Illus.). 48p. (J). reprint ed. 7.00 (*0-8266-0351-3*, Merkos L'Inyonei Chinuch) Kehot Pubn. Society.

—Tuvia's Train That Had No End. 1984. (Illus.). 48p. (J). reprint ed. 7.00 (*0-8266-0353-X*, Merkos L'Inyonei Chinuch) Kehot Pubn. Society.

Nerlove, Miriam. Flowers on the Wall. 1996. (Illus.). 32p. (J). (gr. k-3). 16.00 (*0-689-50614-7*, McElderry, Margaret K.) Simon & Schuster Children's Publishing.

Ethnic Groups

Nestlebaum, Chana. The Mookster's Mitzvah Mishaps. 1991. (Illus.). 32p. (J). (gr. k-4). 12.95 (*0-910818-26-6*); pap. 9.95 (*0-910818-27-4*) Judaica Pr., Inc., The.

Netzarel, Orly. Yellow, Yellow-Brown, Yellow-Brown & Black. 2001. 160p. pap. 11.95 (*0-595-18742-0*, Writers Club Pr.) iUniverse, Inc.

Neville, Emily C. Berries Goodman. 1975. (Trophy Bk.). (J). (gr. 5-9). pap. 3.95 o.p. (*0-06-440072-7*, Harper Trophy) HarperCollins Children's Bk. Group.

Nivola, Claire A. Elisabeth, RS. 1996. (Illus.). 32p. (J). (ps-3). 16.00 o.p. (*0-374-32085-3*, Farrar, Straus & Giroux (BYR)) Farrar, Straus & Giroux.

Nolan, Han. If I Should Die Before I Wake. (YA). (gr. 7-12). 1996. 304p. pap. 6.00 o.s.i (*0-15-238041-8*, Harcourt Paperbacks); 1994. 240p. 18.00 (*0-15-238040-X*) Harcourt Children's Bks.

Now I Am Thee. (Yoni Gold Board Book Ser.). bds. 4.95 (*1-58330-153-4*) Feldheim, Philipp Inc.

Nurenberg, Thelma. The Time of Anger. 1975. (J). (gr. 5 up). o.p. (*0-200-00153-1*) Criterion Bks., Inc.

Oberman, Sheldon. Always Prayer Shawl. 1997. (Picture Puffin Ser.). (Illus.). 40p. (J). (ps-3). pap. 6.99 (*0-14-056157-9*) Penguin Putnam Bks. for Young Readers.

—Always Prayer Shawl. 1997. (Picture Puffin Ser.). (J). 13.14 (*0-606-11034-8*) Turtleback Bks.

—Always Prayer Shawl. 1999. 40p. (J). pap. 5.99 (*0-14-038214-3*) Viking Penguin.

—By the Hanukkah Light. 1997. (Illus.). 32p. (J). (gr. 1-4). 15.95 (*1-56397-658-7*) Boyds Mills Pr.

Olidort, Baila. Quarters & Dimes & Nickels & Pennies. 1993. (Illus.). 24p. (J). reprint ed. 12.00 (*0-8266-0358-0*, Merkos L'Inyonei Chinuch) Kehot Pubn. Society.

Oppenheim, Shulamith L. Appleblossom. (Illus.). 30p. (J). 3.98 o.p. (*0-8317-0006-8*) Smithmark Pubs., Inc.

Oppenheim, Shulamith Levey. Appleblossom. Yolen, Jane, ed. 1991. (Illus.). 40p. (J). (gr. 1-7). 14.95 (*0-15-203750-0*) Harcourt Children's Bks.

Orlev, Uri. The Lady with the Hat. Halkin, Hillel, tr. 1995. 192p. (YA). (gr. 7 up). tchr. ed. 16.00 (*0-395-69957-6*) Houghton Mifflin Co.

—The Lady with the Hat. Halkin, Hillel, tr. from HEB. 1997. (Illus.). 192p. (J). (gr. 5-9). pap. 4.99 o.s.i (*0-14-038571-1*) Penguin Putnam Bks. for Young Readers.

—The Lady with the Hat. 1997. 10.09 o.p. (*0-606-13562-6*) Turtleback Bks.

—Lydia: Queen of Palestine. Halkin, Hillel, tr. from HEB. 1993. Tr. of Lidyah: Malkat Erest Yisrael. 176p. (J). 13.95 o.p. (*0-395-65660-5*) Houghton Mifflin Co.

—Lydia, Queen of Palestine. Halkin, Hillel, tr. 1995. (Illus.). 176p. (J). (gr. 5-9). pap. 4.99 o.s.i (*0-14-037089-7*, Puffin Bks.) Penguin Putnam Bks. for Young Readers.

—Lydia, Queen of Palestine. 1995. 9.09 o.p. (*0-606-07817-7*) Turtleback Bks.

Oxley, A. T. Nathan the Littlest Disciple. 2000. (Illus.). pap. 12.00 o.p. (*0-8059-5044-3*) Dorrance Publishing Co., Inc.

Panas, Peter. The Shalom Sesame Players Present: The Story of Passover. 1994. (Sharing Passover Ser.). (Illus.). 32p. (J). pap. 17.95 incl. VHS (*1-56086-211-4*) Sisu Home Entertainment, Inc.

Panas, Peter, illus. The Shalom Sesame Players Present: The Story of Passover. 1994. (Sharing Passover Ser.). 32p. (J). pap. 5.95 (*1-56086-202-5*) Sisu Home Entertainment, Inc.

Pape, David S., ed. The Story Hour: A Collection for Young Readers, Vol. 2. 1995. (Illus.). 160p. (J). (gr. 3-9). 11.95 (*0-922613-65-6*) Hachai Publishing.

—The Story Hour Vol. 1: A Collection for Young Readers. 1994. (Illus.). 166p. (J). (gr. 3 up). 11.95 o.s.i (*0-922613-64-8*) Hachai Publishing.

Parrish, Shelley Berlin. Sharing Grandma's Gift. 2000. (Illus.). 40p. (J). 18.00 (*0-89716-936-0*) Peanut Butter Publishing.

Pausewang, Gudrun. Final Journey. Crampton, Patricia, tr. 1998. 160p. (YA). (gr. 7-12). pap. 5.99 (*0-14-130104-X*, Puffin Bks.) Penguin Putnam Bks. for Young Readers.

—Final Journey. 1996. 160p. (J). (gr. 7-12). 15.99 o.p. (*0-670-86456-0*) Penguin Putnam Bks. for Young Readers.

Pearl, Sydelle. Elijah's Tears: Stories for the Jewish Holidays, ERS. 1996. (Illus.). 64p. (J). (ps-3). 14.95 o.p. (*0-8050-4627-5*, Holt, Henry & Co. Bks. For Young Readers) Holt, Henry & Co.

—Elijah's Tears: Stories for the Jewish Holidays. 2004. 80p. (J). 14.95 (*1-58980-178-4*) Pelican Publishing Co., Inc.

Penn, Malka. The Hanukkah Ghosts. 1995. 80p. (J). (gr. 3-7). 14.95 (*0-8234-1145-1*) Holiday Hse., Inc.

Perrin, Randy, et al. Time Like a River. 1999. 144p. (YA). (gr. 5 up). 14.95 (*1-57143-061-X*) RDR Bks.

Pfitsch, Patricia C. The Deeper Song. 1998. 160p. (YA). (gr. 7-12). 16.00 o.s.i (*0-689-81183-7*, Simon & Schuster Children's Publishing) Simon & Schuster Children's Publishing.

Polacco, Patricia. The Butterfly. 2000. (Illus.). 48p. (J). (ps-3). 16.99 (*0-399-23170-6*, Philomel) Penguin Putnam Bks. for Young Readers.

—A Christmas Tapestry. 2002. (Illus.). 48p. (J). (gr. k-3). 16.99 (*0-399-23955-3*, G. P. Putnam's Sons) Penguin Putnam Bks. for Young Readers.

—The Keeping Quilt. 2002. (Illus.). (J). 26.17 (*0-7587-2927-8*) Book Wholesalers, Inc.

—The Keeping Quilt. (Illus.). (J). (ps-3). 2001. 32p. pap. 6.99 (*0-689-84447-6*, Aladdin); 10th anniv. ed. 1998. 48p. 17.95 (*0-689-82090-9*, Simon & Schuster Children's Publishing) Simon & Schuster Children's Publishing.

—The Keeping Quilt. 2001. (J). (gr. k-3). 26.95 incl. audio (*0-8045-6842-1*, 6842); 26.95 incl. audio (*0-8045-6842-1*, 6842) Spoken Arts, Inc.

—The Keeping Quilt. 2001. (J). 13.14 (*0-606-20749-X*) Turtleback Bks.

—Mrs. Katz & Tush. 1993. pap. 19.95 o.s.i incl. audio (*0-553-45913-9*) Bantam Bks.

—Mrs. Katz & Tush. 2002. (Illus.). (J). 14.79 (*0-7587-3191-4*) Book Wholesalers, Inc.

—Mrs. Katz & Tush. ed. 1994. (J). (gr. 2). spiral bd. (*0-616-01760-X*) Canadian National Institute for the Blind/Institut National Canadien pour les Aveugles.

—Mrs. Katz & Tush. 1994. (Picture Yearling Ser.). (Illus.). 32p. (ps-3). pap. text 6.99 (*0-440-40936-5*) Dell Publishing.

—Mrs. Katz & Tush. (J). 1993. mass mkt. o.p. (*0-440-90065-4*); 1992. (Illus.). 15.00 (*0-553-08122-5*); 1991. mass mkt. o.s.i (*0-553-53092-5*) Random Hse. Children's Bks. (Dell Books for Young Readers).

—Mrs. Katz & Tush. 1994. 13.14 (*0-606-05930-X*) Turtleback Bks.

Pomeranc, Marion H. The Hand-Me-down Horse. 1996. (Illus.). 32p. (J). (ps-3). lib. bdg. 15.95 o.p. (*0-8075-3141-3*) Whitman, Albert & Co.

Pressler, Mirjam. Malka. Murdoch, Brian, tr. from GER. 2003. 286p. (YA). (gr. 9-12). 18.99 (*0-399-23984-7*, Philomel) Penguin Putnam Bks. for Young Readers.

—Shylock's Daughter. Murdoch, Brian, tr. from GER. 2001. (Illus.). 272p. (J). (gr. 9 up). 17.99 (*0-8037-2667-8*, Dial Bks. for Young Readers) Penguin Putnam Bks. for Young Readers.

Propp, Vera W. When the Soldiers Were Gone. 1999. 112p. (YA). (gr. 5-9). 14.99 (*0-399-23325-3*) Penguin Group (USA) Inc.

—When the Soldiers Were Gone. 2001. (Illus.). (J). 11.04 (*0-606-20989-1*) Turtleback Bks.

Pullman, Philip. The Tiger in the Well. 1996. (YA). 11.04 (*0-606-09969-7*) Turtleback Bks.

Pushker, Gloria T. Toby Belfer & the High Holy Days. 2001. (Illus.). 32p. (J). 14.95 (*1-56554-765-9*) Pelican Publishing Co., Inc.

—Toby Belfer Never Had a Christmas Tree. 1991. (Illus.). 32p. (J). (gr. k-3). reprint ed. 14.95 (*0-88289-855-8*) Pelican Publishing Co., Inc.

Radin, Ruth Y. Escape to the Forest: Based on a True Story of the Holocaust. (Illus.). 96p. (J). (gr. 4 up). 2001. pap. 4.25 (*0-06-440822-1*); 2000. 14.99 (*0-06-028520-6*); 2000. lib. bdg. 13.89 (*0-06-028521-4*) HarperCollins Children's Bk. Group.

Rael, Elsa Okon. When Zaydeh Danced on Eldridge Street. 1997. (Illus.). 40p. (J). (gr. k-4). 16.00 o.s.i (*0-689-80451-2*, Simon & Schuster Children's Publishing) Simon & Schuster Children's Publishing.

Ray, Karen. To Cross a Line. 1994. 160p. (YA). (gr. 7 up). pap. 15.95 (*0-531-06831-5*); lib. bdg. 16.99 (*0-531-08681-X*) Scholastic, Inc. (Orchard Bks.).

Reudor Staff. Are Pigeons Kosher? 1998. (Reudor's the Doodle Family Ser.). (Illus.). 96p. (J). (gr. 3-12). pap. 5.95 (*1-886611-05-X*) Atara Publishing.

—My Dog Is Jewish: Reudor's the Doodle Family. 1998. (Rhyme Time Doodles Ser.). (Illus.). 24p. (J). (gr. 1-12). 7.95 (*1-886611-03-3*) Atara Publishing.

—My Shabbat Palace: Reudor's the Doodle Family. (Rhyme Time Doodles Ser.). (Illus.). 24p. (J). (gr. 1-12). 7.95 o.p. (*1-886611-04-1*) Atara Publishing.

Richter, Hans P. Friedrich. 1987. (Novels Ser.). 160p. (J). (gr. 7-12). pap. 4.99 (*0-14-032205-1*, Puffin Bks.) Penguin Putnam Bks. for Young Readers.

—Friedrich. 1992. (J). (gr. 6 up). 20.25 (*0-8446-6573-8*) Smith, Peter Pub., Inc.

Ringgold, Faith. Bonjour, Lonnie. 1996. (Illus.). 32p. (J). (gr. k-4). 15.95 (*0-7868-0076-3*); (gr. 4-7). lib. bdg. 16.49 (*0-7868-2062-4*) Hyperion Bks. for Children.

Rocklin, Joanne. Strudel Stories. 1999. 144p. (gr. 3-7). text 14.95 (*0-385-32602-5*, Delacorte Pr.) Dell Publishing.

—Strudel Stories. 2000. (Illus.). 144p. (gr. 3-7). pap. text 4.50 o.s.i (*0-440-41509-8*, Yearling) Random Hse. Children's Bks.

—Strudel Stories. l.t. ed. 2000. (Illus.). 102p. (J). (gr. 4-7). 21.95 (*0-7862-2770-2*) Thorndike Pr.

Roddy, Lee. Galen & Goliath. 2001. (Kidwitness Tales Ser.: Vol. 5). (Illus.). 128p. (J). (gr. 4-7). pap. 5.99 o.p. (*1-56179-955-6*) Focus on the Family Publishing.

Rogasky, Barbara. Gilgul. 2002. (Illus.). (J). (*0-8234-1619-4*) Holiday Hse., Inc.

Rogers, Kirby. Operation Dewey. 2002. (Illus.). ix, 100p. (J). pap. (*1-877633-65-8*) Luthers.

Romm, J. Leonard. The Swastika on the Synagogue Door. 1984. (Lazarus Family Mystery Ser.). 180p. (Orig.). (J). (gr. 3-10). pap. 6.95 o.p. (*0-940646-53-6*) Rossel Bks.

Roseman, Kenneth D. The Melting Pot: An Adventure in New York. 1984. (Do-It-Yourself Jewish Adventure Ser.). (Illus.). 144p. (J). (gr. 4-7). pap. 8.95 (*0-8074-0269-9*, 146065) UAHC Pr.

Rosen, Michael J. The Blessing of the Animals, RS. 2000. (Illus.). 96p. (J). (gr. 3-7). 15.00 (*0-374-30838-1*, Farrar, Straus & Giroux (BYR)) Farrar, Straus & Giroux.

Rosen, Sybil. Speed of Light. 2001. 176p. (J). (gr. 4-7). pap. 4.99 (*0-689-84151-5*, Aladdin) Simon & Schuster Children's Publishing.

—Speed of Light. 2001. (J). 11.04 (*0-606-20923-9*) Turtleback Bks.

Rosenberg, Liz. Heart & Soul. 1996. 224p. (YA). (gr. 7 up). pap. 5.00 o.s.i (*0-15-201270-2*, Harcourt Paperbacks) Harcourt Children's Bks.

—Heart & Soul. 1996. 224p. (YA). (gr. 7 up). 11.00 (*0-15-200942-6*) Harcourt Trade Pubs.

Rosenfeld, Dina. All about Us. 1989. (Illus.). 32p. (J). (ps-k). 9.95 (*0-922613-02-8*); pap. 6.95 o.p. (*0-922613-03-6*) Hachai Publishing.

—Five Alive: My Yom Tov Five Senses. 2002. (Illus.). 32p. (J). (ps-k). 9.95 (*1-929628-09-9*) Hachai Publishing.

—Labels for Laibel. 1990. (Illus.). 32p. (J). (ps-1). pap. 6.95 o.p. (*0-922613-36-2*) Hachai Publishing.

—A Little Boy Named Avram. 1989. (Little Greats Ser.). (Illus.). 32p. (J). (ps up). 9.95 (*0-922613-08-7*); pap. 6.95 (*0-922613-09-5*) Hachai Publishing.

—Yossi & Laibel Hot on the Trail. 1991. (Illus.). 32p. (J). (ps-1). 9.95 (*0-922613-47-8*); pap. 6.95 (*0-922613-48-6*) Hachai Publishing.

Rosenfeld, Dina H. Tiny Treasures: The Wonderful World of a Jewish Child. 1988. (Illus.). 26p. (J). reprint ed. 12.00 (*0-8266-0365-3*, Merkos L'Inyonei Chinuch) Kehot Pubn. Society.

—A Tree Full of Mitzvos. 1985. (Illus.). 48p. (J). reprint ed. 12.00 (*0-8266-0363-7*, Merkos L'Inyonei Chinuch) Kehot Pubn. Society.

Rosoff, David. Growing up: A Bar Mitzvah Story. 1984. (J). (gr. 6-8). 13.00 o.p. (*0-87306-370-8*) Feldheim, Philipp Inc.

Ross, Lillian Hammer. Buba Leah & Her Paper Children. 1991. (Illus.). 32p. (J). (gr. k-3). 17.95 (*0-8276-0375-4*) Jewish Pubn. Society.

Rossoff, Donald. The Perfect Prayer. 2003. (Illus.). (J). 13.95 (*0-8074-0853-0*) UAHC Pr.

Roth-Hano, Renee. Safe Harbors. 1993. 224p. (YA). (gr. 12 up). 16.95 o.p. (*0-02-777795-2*, Simon & Schuster Children's Publishing) Simon & Schuster Children's Publishing.

—Touch Wood: A Girlhood in Occupied France. 1989. (ALA Notable Bk.). 304p. (J). (gr. 5 up). pap. 5.99 o.p. (*0-14-034085-8*, Puffin Bks.) Penguin Putnam Bks. for Young Readers.

—Touch Wood: A Girlhood in Occupied France. 1988. 304p. (J). (gr. 5-9). 16.95 o.p. (*0-02-777340-X*, Simon & Schuster Children's Publishing) Simon & Schuster Children's Publishing.

Roth, Philip. The Conversion of the Jews. 1993. (Short Stories Ser.). 32p. (YA). (gr. 5 up). lib. bdg. 18.60 (*0-88682-506-7*, Creative Education) Creative Co., The.

Rothenberg, Joan. Inside-Out Grandma: A Hanukkah Story. 1997. (Illus.). 32p. (J). (ps-3). reprint ed. pap. 5.95 (*0-7868-1200-1*) Disney Pr.

—Inside-Out Grandma: A Hanukkah Story. 1995. (Illus.). 32p. (J). (ps-3). 14.95 (*0-7868-0107-7*); lib. bdg. 15.49 (*0-7868-2092-6*) Hyperion Bks. for Children.

—Inside-Out Grandma: A Hanukkah Story. 1997. (J). 12.10 (*0-606-13520-0*) Turtleback Bks.

Rothstein, Chaya L. The Mentchkins Make Shabbos. 1986. (Sifrei Rimon Ser.). (Illus.). (J). (ps-2). pap. 2.95 (*0-87306-401-1*) Feldheim, Philipp Inc.

Rouss, Sylvia. The Littlest Candlesticks. 2002. (Littlest Ser.). (Illus.). 32p. (J). 14.95 (*1-930143-48-6*) Pitspopany Pr.

—Sammy Spider's First Passover. 1995. (Illus.). 32p. (J). (ps-2). 14.95 o.p. (*0-929371-81-X*) Kar-Ben Publishing.

—Sammy Spider's First Rosh Hashanah. 1996. (Illus.). 32p. (J). (ps-2). 14.95 o.p. (*0-929371-98-4*) Kar-Ben Publishing.

—Sammy Spider's First Shabbat. 1997. (Illus.). 32p. (J). (ps-3). 14.95 (*1-58013-007-0*) Kar-Ben Publishing.

Rouss, Sylvia A. Aaron's Bar Mitzvah. Dubois, Liz Goulet, tr. & illus. by. 2003. (J). 14.95 (*0-8246-0447-4*) Jonathan David Pubs., Inc.

—My Baby Brother: What a Miracle! 2002. (J). 14.95 (*0-8246-0445-8*) Jonathan David Pubs., Inc.

—Sammy Spider's First Hanukkah. 1993. (Illus.). (J). 13.95 o.p. (*0-929371-45-3*); 32p. pap. 7.95 (*0-929371-46-1*) Kar-Ben Publishing.

—Sammy Spider's First Purim. 2000. (Illus.). (J). (ps-2). 32p. pap. 6.95 (*1-58013-062-3*); 6.95 (*1-58013-061-5*) Kar-Ben Publishing.

—Sammy Spider's First Rosh Hashanah. 1996. (Illus.). 32p. (J). (ps-2). pap. 6.95 (*0-929371-99-2*) Kar-Ben Publishing.

—Sammy Spider's First Shabbat. 1997. (Illus.). 32p. (J). (ps-3). pap. 6.95 (*1-58013-006-2*) Kar-Ben Publishing.

Rubin, Chana S. A Time to Heal. 1991. 235p. (C). 17.95 (*1-56062-067-6*, CFR111H) CIS Communications, Inc.

Rubinstein, Reva. We Are One Family. Zakutinsky, Ruth, ed. 1992. (Illus.). 24p. (J). (gr. 1-3). lib. bdg. 9.95 o.p. (*0-911643-15-X*) Aura Printing, Inc.

Rudolph, Lieba. The Best Call of All. 1998. (Illus.). (J). 12.00 (*0-8266-0025-5*, Merkos L'Inyonei Chinuch) Kehot Pubn. Society.

Sachs, Marilyn. Another Day. 1997. 176p. (J). (gr. 5-9). 15.99 o.p. (*0-525-45787-9*) Penguin Putnam Bks. for Young Readers.

—Call Me Ruth. 1995. 11.00 (*0-606-07333-7*) Turtleback Bks.

—A Pocket Full of Seeds. 1994. (Illus.). 144p. (YA). (gr. 5-9). pap. 5.99 o.s.i (*0-14-036593-1*, Puffin Bks.) Penguin Putnam Bks. for Young Readers.

—A Pocket Full of Seeds. 1995. 19.75 (*0-8446-6796-X*) Smith, Peter Pub., Inc.

—A Pocket Full of Seeds. 1994. 11.04 (*0-606-05978-4*) Turtleback Bks.

Safran, Faigy. Uncle Moishy Visits Torah Island. (Illus.). (J). pap. 5.99 (*0-89906-806-5*, UM1P); 1987. 32p. (gr. 2-8). pap. 5.95 o.p. (*0-89906-807-3*) Mesorah Pubns., Ltd.

Salop, Byrd. The Kiddush Cup Who Hated Wine. 1981. (Illus.). 32p. (J). (gr. 1 up). pap. 5.95 o.p. (*0-8246-0265-X*) Jonathan David Pubs., Inc.

Sandman, Rochel. As Big As an Egg: A Story about Giving. Rosenfeld, Dina, ed. 1995. (Illus.). 32p. (J). (gr. 2 up). 9.95 (*0-922613-77-X*) Hachai Publishing.

Saypol, Judyth R. & Wikler, Madeline. My Very Own Shavuot Book. 1982. (Illus.). 28p. (J). (gr. k-6). pap. 3.95 o.p. (*0-930494-15-6*) Kar-Ben Publishing.

Schachnowitz, Selig. Light from the West. Leftwich, Joseph, tr. (J). (gr. 7 up). 8.95 o.p. (*0-87306-124-1*) Feldheim, Philipp Inc.

Schanzer, Rosalyn, illus. In the Synagogue. 1991. 12p. (J). (ps). bds. 4.95 (*0-929371-60-7*) Kar-Ben Publishing.

Scherman, Nosson. Tales From the Rebbe's Table. 1986. (ArtScroll Youth Ser.). (Illus.). 32p. (J). 10.99 o.p. (*0-89906-789-1*); pap. 7.99 o.p. (*0-89906-790-5*) Mesorah Pubns., Ltd.

—Tales from the Yeshiva World. 1986. (ArtScroll Youth Ser.). (Illus.). 32p. (J). 11.99 o.p. (*0-89906-791-3*); pap. 8.99 o.p. (*0-89906-792-1*) Mesorah Pubns., Ltd.

Schleimer, Sarah M. Far from the Place We Called Home. 1994. (J). 16.95 (*0-87306-667-7*) Feldheim, Philipp Inc.

Schmidt, Gary D. Mara's Stories: Glimmers in the Darkness, ERS. 2001. 128p. (J). (gr. 5 up). 16.95 (*0-8050-6794-9*, Holt, Henry & Co. Bks. For Young Readers) Holt, Henry & Co.

Schnur, Steven. The Koufax Dilemma. 1997. (Illus.). 186p. (J). (gr. 5 up). 15.00 (*0-688-14221-4*, Morrow, William & Co.) Morrow/Avon.

—The Koufax Dilemma. 2001. 196p. pap. 14.95 (*0-595-19998-4*, Backinprint.com) iUniverse, Inc.

—The Narrowest Bar Mitzvah. 1986. (Illus.). 48p. (Orig.). (J). (gr. 4-6). pap. text 6.95 o.p. (*0-8074-0316-4*, 123923) UAHC Pr.

—The Return of Morris Schumsky. 1987. (Illus.). 48p. (J). (gr. 4-7). pap. 6.95 (*0-8074-0358-X*, 123927) UAHC Pr.

—The Tie Man's Miracle: A Chanukah Tale. 1995. (Illus.). 32p. (J). (ps-3). 16.00 (*0-688-13463-7*, Morrow, William & Co.) Morrow/Avon.

Schotter, Roni. Northern Fried Chicken. 1983. (J). (gr. 6-9). 10.95 o.p. (*0-399-20920-4*, Philomel) Penguin Putnam Bks. for Young Readers.

—Passover Magic. (Illus.). 32p. (J). 1998. (ps-3). pap. 6.95 (*0-316-77928-8*); 1995. (gr. 1-8). 15.95 o.p. (*0-316-77468-5*) Little Brown & Co.

—Passover Magic. 1998. (J). 12.10 (*0-606-13696-7*) Turtleback Bks.

—Purim Play. 1998. (Illus.). 32p. (J). (ps-3). 15.95 o.p. (*0-316-77518-5*) Little Brown & Co.

Schraff, Anne. Darkness. 2000. 119p. (J). (*0-7807-9367-6*); pap. (*0-7891-5183-9*) Perfection Learning Corp.

Schrier, Jeffrey. On the Wings of Eagles. 1998. (Single Titles Ser.). (Illus.). 32p. (J). (ps up). 21.90 o.p. (0-7613-0004-X) Millbrook Pr., Inc.

Schuman, Burt E. Chanukah on the Prairie. 2002. (J). 12.95 (0-8074-0814-X) UAHC Pr.

Schur, Maxine R. The Circlemaker. 192p. (YA). (gr. 5 up). 1996. pap. 5.99 (0-14-037997-5, Puffin Bks.); 1994. 14.99 o.s.i (0-8037-1354-1, Dial Bks. for Young Readers) Penguin Putnam Bks. for Young Readers.

—The Circlemaker. 1996. (YA). (gr. 5 up). 11.04 (0-606-09149-1) Turtleback Bks.

—Day of Delight: A Jewish Sabbath in Ethiopia. 1994. (Illus.). 40p. (J). (gr. k-4). 15.99 o.s.i (0-8037-1413-0); 15.89 o.p. (0-8037-1414-9) Penguin Putnam Bks. for Young Readers. (Dial Bks. for Young Readers).

—Sacred Shadows. (J). (gr. 6-9). 1999. 14.99 (0-8037-1800-4); 1997. 224p. 15.99 o.p. (0-8037-2295-8) Penguin Putnam Bks. for Young Readers. (Dial Bks. for Young Readers).

—When I Left My Village. 1996. (Illus.). 64p. (J). (gr. 1-5). 14.99 o.s.i (0-8037-1561-7); 14.89 o.s.i (0-8037-1562-5) Penguin Putnam Bks. for Young Readers. (Dial Bks. for Young Readers).

Schwartz, Amy. Mrs. Moskowitz & the Sabbath Candlesticks. 1983. (Illus.). 32p. (J). (gr. k-5). pap. 4.95 (0-8276-0231-6); (gr. 4-7). pap. 7.95 (0-8276-0372-X) Jewish Pubn. Society.

Schwartz, Howard. The Day the Rabbi Disappeared: Jewish Holiday Tales of Magic. 2000. (Illus.). 224p. (J). (ps-3). 15.99 o.s.i (0-670-88733-1, Viking Children's Bks.) Penguin Putnam Bks. for Young Readers.

—A Journey to Paradise: And Other Jewish Tales. 2000. (Jewish Storyteller Ser.). (Illus.). 48p. (J). (ps-4). pap. 9.95 (0-943706-16-5) Pitspopany Pr.

Schweiger-Dmi'el, Itzhak. Hanna's Sabbath Dress. 1994. (Illus.). (J). 16.00 (0-671-51008-8, Simon & Schuster Children's Publishing) Simon & Schuster Children's Publishing.

Scott, Walter, Sr. Ivanhoe. 2002. (Great Illustrated Classics). (Illus.). 240p. (J). (gr. 3-8). lib. bdg. 21.35 (1-57765-811-6, ABDO & Daughters) ABDO Publishing Co.

—Ivanhoe. (SPA., Illus.). 176p. (YA). 14.95 (84-7281-096-8, AF1096) Auriga, Ediciones S.A. ESP. *Dist:* Continental Bk. Co., Inc.

—Ivanhoe. 1991. (Wishbone Classics Ser.: No. 12). (J). (gr. 3-7). 13.00 (0-606-17587-3) Turtleback Bks.

Segal, Jerry. The Place Where Nobody Stopped. 1991. (Illus.). 160p. (J). (gr. 6-8). 15.95 o.p. (0-531-05897-2); mass mkt. 16.99 o.p. (0-531-08497-3) Scholastic, Inc. (Orchard Bks.).

Segal, Yocheved. Golden Shoes: And Other Stories. Falk, Esther, tr. from HEB. 1982. (Jewish Youth Classics Ser.: Vol. 2). (Illus.). 192p. (J). (gr. 4-9). text 8.95 o.p. (0-87306-123-3) Feldheim, Philipp Inc.

Semel, Nava. Flying Lessons. Halkin, Hillel, tr. 1995. Orig. Title: Moris Havivel Melamid La-uf. (Illus.). 112p. (YA). (gr. 5 up). 14.00 o.p. (0-689-80161-0, Simon & Schuster Children's Publishing) Simon & Schuster Children's Publishing.

Sevela, Ephraim. We Were Not Like Other People. Bouis, Antonina W., tr. from RUS. 1989. 224p. (YA). (gr. 7 up). 13.95 (0-06-025507-2); lib. bdg. 14.89 o.p. (0-06-025508-0) HarperCollins Children's Bk. Group.

—Why There Is No Heaven on Earth. Lourie, Richard, tr. 1982. (RUS.). 224p. (YA). (gr. 7 up). o.p. (0-06-025502-1); lib. bdg. 10.89 o.p. (0-06-025503-X) HarperCollins Children's Bk. Group.

Shalev, Meir. My Father Always Embarrasses Me. Klein, Zanvel, ed. Herrmann, Dagmar, tr. from HEB. 1990. (Illus.). 30p. (J). (gr. k-3). 12.95 (0-922984-02-6) Wellington Publishing, Inc.

Sharon, Lynn. Angelicum: Jewish Sci-Fi. 1999. pap. text 9.95 (0-943706-63-7) Pitspopany Pr.

Shemtov, Ester G. Mindy Gets Her Reward & Other Stories for Children. (Illus.). 62p. (Orig.). (YA). reprint ed. pap. 7.00 (0-8266-0366-1, Merkos L'Inyonei Chinuch) Kehot Pubn. Society.

Sherman, Eileen B. Independence Avenue. 1990. 154p. (J). (gr. 5-8). 14.95 (0-8276-0367-3) Jewish Pubn. Society.

—Monday in Odessa. 1986. (YA). (gr. 5-9). 12.95 o.p. (0-8276-0262-6) Jewish Pubn. Society.

Shiefman, Vicky. Good-Bye to the Trees. 1993. 160p. (J). (gr. 4-8). 14.95 o.p. (0-689-31806-5, Atheneum) Simon & Schuster Children's Publishing.

Sholem Aleichem. Holiday Tales. Shevrin, Aliza, tr. from YID. 2003. 128p. (J). pap. 6.95 (0-486-42864-8) Dover Pubns., Inc.

Sidi, Smadar S. Little Daniel & the Jewish Delicacies. 1988. (Illus.). (J). (ps-5). 9.95 (1-55774-028-3) Lambda Pubs., Inc.

Sigal, Maxine Handelman. Shabbat Angels. 2002. (J). pap. 13.95 (0-8074-0865-4) UAHC Pr.

Silberman, Shoshana. A Family Haggadah II. (Illus.). 64p. 1997. (gr. 5). pap. 4.95 (0-929371-96-8); 2003. (J). pap. 9.95 (1-58013-014-3) Kar-Ben Publishing.

Silton, Faye. Of Heroes, Hooks & Heirlooms. 1997. 100p. (YA). pap. 9.95 (0-8276-0649-4); 1996. 120p. (J). (gr. 4 up). 14.95 o.p. (0-8276-0582-X) Jewish Pubn. Society.

Silver, Norman. An Eye for Color. 1993. 192p. (YA). (gr. 8 up). 14.99 o.p. (0-525-44859-4, Dutton Children's Bks.) Penguin Putnam Bks. for Young Readers.

—Python Dance. 1993. 240p. (YA). 14.99 o.p. (0-525-45161-7) Penguin Putnam Bks. for Young Readers.

Silverman, Erica & Sholem Aleichem. When the Chickens Went on Strike. 2003. (Illus.). 32p. (J). 15.99 (0-525-46862-5, Dutton Children's Bks.) Penguin Putnam Bks. for Young Readers.

Silverman, Maida. The Glass Menorah & Other Stories for Jewish Holidays. 1992. (Illus.). 64p. (J). (gr. 1-4). 14.95 o.p. (0-02-782682-1, Simon & Schuster Children's Publishing) Simon & Schuster Children's Publishing.

Silverman, Manuel S. Rosie & the Mole: The Story of a Bris. 1999. (Illus.). 48p. (J). (gr. 1-4). 16.95 (0-943706-22-X); pap. 9.95 (0-943706-20-3) Pitspopany Pr.

Simpson, Lesley. The Purim Surprise. 2004. (Purim Ser.). (J). pap. 6.95 (1-58013-090-9) Lerner Publishing Group.

—The Shabbat Box. 2001. (Illus.). 32p. (J). pap. 6.95 (1-58013-027-5) Kar-Ben Publishing.

Singer, Isaac Bashevis. Joseph & Koza, or, The Sacrifice to the Vistula, RS. Singer, Isaac Bashevis & Shub, Elizabeth, trs. 1970. (Illus.). (J). (ps-3). 4.95 o.p. (0-374-33795-0, Farrar, Straus & Giroux (BYR)) Farrar, Straus & Giroux.

—Naftali the Storyteller & His Horse, Sus: And Other Stories, RS. 1976. (Illus.). 144p. (J). (gr. 4 up). 16.00 o.p. (0-374-35490-1, Farrar, Straus & Giroux (BYR)) Farrar, Straus & Giroux.

—A Tale of Three Wishes, RS. 1976. (Illus.). 32p. (J). (ps-3). 14.00 o.s.i (0-374-37370-1, Farrar, Straus & Giroux (BYR)) Farrar, Straus & Giroux.

—Zlateh the Goat & Other Stories. 2001. (Sendak Reissues Ser.). (Illus.). 104p. (J). (gr. 4-7). 15.95 (0-06-028477-3); (ps-1). reprint ed. lib. bdg. 15.89 (0-06-028478-1) HarperCollins Children's Bk. Group.

—Zlateh the Goat & Other Stories. 1966. (J). lib. bdg. 15.89 o.s.i (0-06-025699-0) HarperCollins Pubs.

—Zlateh the Goat & Other Stories. 1984. (J). 13.00 (0-606-02374-7) Turtleback Bks.

Singer, Isaac Bashevis, et al. The Safe Deposit & Other Stories about Grandparents, Old Lovers & Crazy Old Men. 1989. (Masterworks of Modern Jewish Writings Ser.). 360p. (J). 19.95 (1-55876-013-X) Wiener, Markus Pubs., Inc.

Siskind, Leda. The Hopscotch Tree. 1992. 128p. (J). (gr. 4-7). 15.00 o.s.i (0-553-08715-0) Bantam Bks.

—The Hopscotch Tree. 1995. 128p. (J). (gr. 3-7). pap. 3.50 o.s.i (0-440-40959-4, Yearling) Random Hse. Children's Bks.

—The Hopscotch Tree. 1995. 8.60 o.p. (0-606-07661-1) Turtleback Bks.

Smith, Annette. Terror in Cairo. 1979. (Illus.). (J). (gr. 4-7). 2.95 o.p. (0-15-284812-6) Harcourt Children's Bks.

Snyder, Carol. God Must Like Cookies, Too. 1993. (Illus.). 32p. (J). (ps-3). 16.95 (0-8276-0423-8) Jewish Pubn. Society.

Sonderling, Eric. A Knock at the Door. 1997. (Publish-a-Book Ser.). (Illus.). (J). (ps-3). 32p. lib. bdg. 22.83 (0-8172-4434-4); 28p. pap. 5.95 (0-8172-7211-9) Raintree Pubs.

Spinelli, Jerry. Milkweed. unabr. ed. 2003. (J). audio 25.00 (0-8072-1858-8, Listening Library) Random Hse. Audio Publishing Group.

—Milkweed. 2003. (Illus.). 224p. (J). (gr. 5). 15.95 (0-375-81374-8); lib. bdg. 17.99 (0-375-91374-2) Random Hse. Children's Bks.

Starting First Grade. (Tami & Moishy Ser.: Vol. 4). bds. 6.95 (1-58330-968-3) Feldheim, Philipp Inc.

Steiner, Connie C. On Eagles Wings & Other Things. 1987. 32p. (J). (gr. k-4). 16.95 o.p. (0-8276-0274-X) Jewish Pubn. Society.

Steiner, Lili. My Bubbe - My Grandmother. 1998. (Illus.). 24p. (J). pap. 14.95 (1-891397-02-8) Steiner, Lili Pubns.

—My Zaidah - My Grandfather. 1998. (My Jewish Family Series with a Bissel Yiddish). (Illus.). 24p. (J). pap. 14.95 (1-891397-01-X) Steiner, Lili Pubns.

—My Zeesa Jessica My Sweet Jessica. 1997. (My Jewish Family Series with a Bissel Yiddish). (Illus.). 24p. pap. 14.95 (1-891397-00-1) Steiner, Lili Pubns.

Stillerman, Marci. Nine Spoons: A Chanukah Story. Rosenfeld, D. L., ed. 1998. (Illus.). 32p. (J). (gr. k-3). 11.95 (0-922613-84-2) Hachai Publishing.

Stuchner, Joan Betty. The Kugel Valley Klezmer Band. 2001. (Illus.). 32p. (J). (ps-3). 15.95 (1-56656-430-1, Crocodile Bks.) Interlink Publishing Group, Inc.

Suhl, Yuri. On the Other Side of the Gate. 1975. 160p. (gr. 7 up). lib. bdg. 5.90 o.p. (0-531-02792-9, Watts, Franklin) Scholastic Library Publishing.

Taniuchi, Yutaka. The Miracle Visas. 2001. 176p. (J). (gr. 4-7). 16.95 (965-229-256-7) Gefen Publishing Hse., Ltd ISR. *Dist:* Gefen Bks.

Tarbescu, Edith. Annushka's Voyage. 1998. (Illus.). 32p. (J). (ps-3). tchr. ed. 15.00 (0-395-64366-X) Houghton Mifflin Co.

Taylor, Marilyn. Faraway Home. 2000. 224p. (J). (gr. 5 up). pap. 7.95 (0-86278-643-6) O'Brien Pr., Ltd., The IRL. *Dist:* Independent Pubs. Group.

Tene, Enjamin. In the Shade of the Chestnut Tree. Ben-Joseph, Reuben, tr. 1981. (Illus.). 144p. (J). (gr. 5 up). 8.95 o.p. (0-8276-0186-7, 470) Jewish Pubn. Society.

The Three Messengers. 2000. (J). 7.00 (0-930213-62-9) Breslov Research Institute.

Tobias, Tobi. Pot Luck. 1993. (Illus.). 32p. (J). 15.00 o.p. (0-688-09824-X) HarperCollins Children's Bk. Group.

Topek, Susan R. A Holiday for Noah. 1990. (Illus.). 24p. (J). (ps). pap. 4.95 o.p. (0-929371-08-9); pap. 5.95 (0-929371-07-0) Kar-Ben Publishing.

Travis, Lucille. Tirzah. Garber, S. David, ed. 1991. 160p. (Orig.). (J). (gr. 4-7). pap. 5.99 (0-8361-3546-6) Herald Pr.

Treseder, Terry W. Hear O Israel: A Story of the Warsaw Ghetto. 1990. (Illus.). 48p. (J). (gr. 3 up). text 13.95 o.s.i (0-689-31456-6, Atheneum) Simon & Schuster Children's Publishing.

Tunis, John R. Keystone Kids. (J). 1990. (Baseball Diamonds Ser.: Vol. 3). 256p. (gr. 4-7). pap. 6.00 (0-15-242388-5, Odyssey Classics); 1987. 239p. (gr. 3-7). reprint ed. pap. 4.95 o.p. (0-15-200495-5, Gulliver Bks.) Harcourt Children's Bks.

—Keystone Kids. 1990. 256p. (J). (gr. 3-7). 14.95 (0-15-242389-3) Harcourt Trade Pubs.

—Keystone Kids. 1987. (Baseball Diamonds Ser.). (J). 10.00 (0-606-04460-4) Turtleback Bks.

Tyberg, Sarah. Shaindy Strikes Again. 1993. (Illus.). 167p. (J). (gr. 6-8). 10.95 o.p. (1-56871-030-5) Targum Pr., Inc.

Van Hansel, E. Benjy's Room. (Middos Ser.). (J). 7.99 (0-89906-991-6) Mesorah Pubns., Ltd.

Vande Velde, Vivian. A Coming Evil. 1998. 212p. (J). (gr. 5-9). tchr. ed. 17.00 (0-395-90012-3) Houghton Mifflin Co.

Vineberg, Ethel. Grandmother Came from Dworitz: A Jewish Love Story. 1987. (Illus.). 44p. (J). (gr. 4 up). reprint ed. pap. 3.95 o.p. (0-88776-195-X) Tundra Bks. of Northern New York.

Vogiel, Eva. Facing the Music. 2003. 284p. 19.95 (1-880582-94-5) Judaica Pr., Inc., The.

Voigt, Cynthia. David & Jonathan. 256p. (J). (gr. 7-9). 1994. mass mkt. 3.95 (0-590-45166-9); 1992. pap. 14.95 (0-590-45165-0) Scholastic, Inc.

—David & Jonathan. 1992. (Point Ser.). 9.05 o.p. (0-606-06310-2) Turtleback Bks.

Vorst, Rochel Groner. The Sukkah That I Built. 2002. (Illus.). 26p. (J). (ps-k). 9.95 (1-929628-07-2) Hachai Publishing.

Vos, Ida. Anna Is Still Here. Edelstein, Terese & Smidt, Inez, trs. from DUT. 1993. 144p. (J). (gr. 4-6). tchr. ed. 15.00 o.s.i (0-395-65368-1) Houghton Mifflin Co.

—Anna Is Still Here. Edelstein, Terese & Smidt, Inez, trs. 1995. 144p. (J). (gr. 4-7). pap. 5.99 (0-14-036909-0, Puffin Bks.) Penguin Putnam Bks. for Young Readers.

—Anna is Still Here. 1995. 11.04 (0-606-07199-7) Turtleback Bks.

—Dancing on the Bridge of Avignon. Edelstein, Terese & Smidt, Inez, trs. from DUT. 1995. Tr. of Dansen ob de Brug van Avignon. 192p. (YA). (gr. 7-7). 14.95 (0-395-72039-7) Houghton Mifflin Co.

—Hide & Seek. Edelstein, Terese & Smidt, Inez, trs. 1991. Orig. Title: Wie Niet Weg Is Word Gezien. 144p. (J). (gr. 4-6). tchr. ed. 16.00 (0-395-56470-0) Houghton Mifflin Co.

—Hide & Seek. Edelstein, Terese & Smidt, Inez, trs. from DUT. 1995. Orig. Title: Wie Niet Weg Is Word Gezien. 144p. (J). (gr. 4-7). pap. 4.99 (0-14-036908-2, Puffin Bks.) Penguin Putnam Bks. for Young Readers.

—Hide & Seek. 1995. Orig. Title: Wie Niet Weg Is Word Gezien. 11.04 (0-606-07644-1) Turtleback Bks.

Waldman, Neil. The Never-Ending Greenness. 1997. (Illus.). 40p. (J). 16.00 (0-688-14479-9); lib. bdg. 15.93 o.p. (0-688-14480-2) Morrow/Avon. (Morrow, William & Co.).

Wasserman, Mira. Too Much of a Good Thing. 2003. (Illus.). (J). 6.95 (1-58013-066-6); lib. bdg. 14.95 (1-58013-082-8) Kar-Ben Publishing.

Watts, Irene N. Finding Sophie. 2002. 144p. (YA). (gr. 5). pap. 6.95 (0-88776-613-7) Tundra Bks. of Northern New York.

—Goodbye Marianne. 1997. 48p. (YA). pap. 6.50 (0-87602-350-2) Anchorage Pr.

—Goodbye Marianne. 1998. 48p. (J). pap. (1-896239-03-X) Shillingford, J. Gordon Publishing.

—Remember Me: A Search for Refuge in Wartime Britain. 2000. 192p. (YA). (gr. 5 up). pap. 7.95 (0-88776-519-X) Tundra Bks. of Northern New York.

Waysman, Dvora. Back of Beyond: A Bar Mitzvah Journey. Mayerson, Chaim, ed. 1996. (Illus.). 144p. (J). (gr. 6-9). pap. 4.95 (0-943706-54-8) Pitspopany Pr.

Weber, Ilse. Mendel Rosenbusch: Tales for Jewish Children. Fisher, Hans & Fisher, Ruth, trs. from CZE. 2001. Orig. Title: Mendel Rosenbusch: Geschichen Fur Jud Kinder. 232p. (J). (gr. 3-7). 14.00 (1-928746-19-5) Herodias.

Weil, Judith. School for One. 1992. (J). (gr. 4 up). 11.95 o.p. (0-87306-620-0); pap. 9.95 (0-87306-621-9) Feldheim, Philipp Inc.

Weilerstein, Sadie R. Best of K'tonton. 1980. (Illus.). 96p. (J). (gr. 1 up). 9.95 o.p. (0-8276-0184-0) Jewish Pubn. Society.

—K'tonton in the Circus: A Hanukkah Adventure. (Illus.). 96p. (J). (gr. 2 up). pap. 9.95 o.p. (0-8276-0303-7) Jewish Pubn. Society.

Weilerstein, Sadie Rose. Best of K'tonton. (Illus.). 94p. (J). (gr. 1 up). pap. 9.95 (0-8276-0187-5) Jewish Pubn. Society.

—K'tonton's Sukkot Adventure. 1993. (Illus.). 36p. (J). (ps-3). 9.95 (0-8276-0502-1) Jewish Pubn. Society.

Weinbach, Shaindel. The Three Merchants: And Other Stories. 1983. (ArtScroll Youth Ser.). (Illus.). 160p. (YA). (gr. 6-12). 14.99 (0-89906-768-9); pap. 11.99 o.p. (0-89906-769-7) Mesorah Pubns., Ltd.

Weinbach, Sheindel. Avi Names His Price. 1976. (Illus.). (J). (gr. 2-5). 6.95 o.p. (0-87306-119-5) Feldheim, Philipp Inc.

Weiss, Nicki. Stone Men. 1993. (Illus.). 32p. (J). (ps up). lib. bdg. 13.93 o.p. (0-688-11016-9, Greenwillow Bks.) HarperCollins Children's Bk. Group.

Weissenberg, Fran. The Streets Are Paved with Gold. 1990. (Illus.). 160p. (Orig.). (YA). (ps up). pap. 6.95 (0-943173-51-5) Rinehart, Roberts Pubs.

Werlin, Nancy. Are You Alone on Purpose? 1994. 208p. (YA). (gr. 7-7). tchr. ed. 16.00 (0-395-67350-X) Houghton Mifflin Co.

Wild, Margaret. Let the Celebrations Begin! (Illus.). 32p. (J). (ps-3). 1996. mass mkt. 6.95 (0-531-07076-X); 1991. 15.95 o.p. (0-531-05937-5); 1991. lib. bdg. 16.99 (0-531-08537-6) Scholastic, Inc. (Orchard Bks.).

—Let the Celebrations Begin! 1996. (J). 13.10 (0-606-09541-1) Turtleback Bks.

Willett, Fangette H. The Boy Who Found Hashem. 1998. (Illus.). ii, 14p. (J). (gr. 1-5). pap. 4.95 (0-9642613-1-6) KinderWord.

Williams, Laura E. Behind the Bedroom Wall. 1996. (Illus.). (J). 184p. (gr. 4-7). pap. 6.95 (1-57131-606-X); 200p. (gr. 7 up). 15.95 (1-57131-607-8) Milkweed Editions.

—Behind the Bedroom Wall. 1996. (J). 13.00 (0-606-13079-9) Turtleback Bks.

Willson, Sarah. The Rugrats Book of Chanukah. 1997. (Rugrats Ser.). (Illus.). 32p. (J). (ps-2). pap. 5.99 (0-689-81676-6, Simon Spotlight/Nickelodeon) Simon & Schuster Children's Publishing.

Wing, Natasha. Jalapeno Bagels. 1995. (Illus.). (J). (gr. k-3). 16.00 (0-02-793077-7, Simon & Schuster Children's Publishing) Simon & Schuster Children's Publishing.

Wing, Natasha & Casilla, Robert. Jalapeno Bagels. 1996. (Illus.). 32p. (J). (gr. k-3). 16.95 (0-689-80530-6, Atheneum) Simon & Schuster Children's Publishing.

Winkler, Gershon. The Hostage Torah. 1981. (Judaica Youth Ser.). (Illus.). (J). (gr. 7 up). 6.95 o.p. (0-910818-33-9); pap. 7.95 (0-910818-34-7) Judaica Pr., Inc., The.

—They Called Her Rebbe, the Maiden of Ludmir. Greenspan, Marlene & Goldman, Reva S., eds. 1990. (Illus.). 200p. (Orig.). (YA). (gr. 9 up). 16.95 (0-910818-83-5); pap. 12.95 (0-910818-90-8) Judaica Pr., Inc., The.

Winter, Kathryn. Katarina. 1998. 272p. (J). (gr. 5-9). 17.00 o.p. (0-374-33984-8, Farrar, Straus & Giroux (BYR)) Farrar, Straus & Giroux.

—Katarina: A Novel. 1999. 257p. (gr. 6-8). mass mkt. 4.99 (0-439-09904-8) Scholastic, Inc.

Wiseman, Eva. My Canary Yellow Star. 2001. (Illus.). 240p. (J). (gr. 3-7). pap. 6.95 (0-88776-533-5) Tundra Bks. of Northern New York.

Wohl, Lauren L. Matzoh Mouse. (Charlotte Zolotow Bk.). (Illus.). 32p. (J). (gr. k-3). 1993. pap. 4.95 (0-06-443323-4, Harper Trophy); 1991. 14.95 o.p. (0-06-026580-9); 1991. lib. bdg. 13.89 o.p. (0-06-026581-7) HarperCollins Children's Bk. Group.

Woodruff, Elvira. The Memory Coat. 1999. (Illus.). 32p. (J). (gr. 2-5). pap. 15.95 (0-590-67717-9) Scholastic, Inc.

Yaffe, Rochel. Rambam: The Story of Rabbi Moshe Ben Maimon. 1992. (Illus.). 220p. (YA). (gr. 8 up). 12.95 (*0-922613-14-1*); pap. 10.95 (*0-922613-15-X*) Hachai Publishing.

Yolen, Jane. And Twelve Chinese Acrobats. 1995. (Illus.). 50p. (J). 15.95 o.p. (*0-399-22691-5*, Philomel) Penguin Putnam Bks. for Young Readers.

—The Devil's Arithmetic. 2002. (J). 13.19 (*0-7587-9594-7*) Book Wholesalers, Inc.

—The Devil's Arithmetic. 176p. 2004. (Illus.). pap. 5.99 (*0-14-240109-9*, Puffin Bks.); 1990. (YA). (gr. 5-9). pap. 5.99 (*0-14-034535-3*, Puffin Bks.); 1988. (YA). 15.99 (*0-670-81027-4*, Viking Children's Bks.) Penguin Putnam Bks. for Young Readers.

—The Devil's Arithmetic. 1990. (YA). 11.04 (*0-606-04653-4*) Turtleback Bks.

Yorinks, Arthur. The Flying Latke. ed. 2000. (J). (gr. 2). spiral bd. (*0-616-03066-5*) Canadian National Institute for the Blind/Institut National Canadien pour les Aveugles.

—The Flying Latke. 1999. (Illus.). 32p. (J). (gr. k-3). 16.95 (*0-689-82597-8*, Simon & Schuster Children's Publishing) Simon & Schuster Children's Publishing.

Zakon, Miriam S. The Egyptian Star. 1983. (Judaica Youth Ser.). (Illus.). (J). (gr. 3-9). 114p. 6.95 o.p. (*0-910818-47-9*); 128p. pap. 6.95 (*0-910818-48-7*) Judaica Pr., Inc., The.

Zakutinsky, Ruth. The Wonder Worm. 1992. (E Z Reader Ser.). (Illus.). 24p. (J). (gr. k-3). lib. bdg. 6.95 o.p. (*0-911643-17-6*) Aura Printing, Inc.

Zalben, Jane Breskin. Beni's First Wedding, ERS. 1998. (Illus.). 32p. (J). (ps-2). 14.95 (*0-8050-4846-4*, Holt, Henry & Co. Bks. For Young Readers) Holt, Henry & Co.

—The Fortuneteller in 5B, ERS. 1991. (Illus.). 144p. (J). (gr. 4-7). 14.95 o.p. (*0-8050-1537-X*, Holt, Henry & Co. Bks. For Young Readers) Holt, Henry & Co.

—The Fortuneteller in 5B. 1993. 160p. (J). (gr. 4-6). pap. 2.95 o.p. (*0-590-46041-2*) Scholastic, Inc.

—The Fortuneteller in 5B. 2000. 160p. (gr. 4-7). pap. 15.95 (*0-595-14657-0*, Backinprint.com) iUniverse, Inc.

—Happy New Year, Beni, ERS. 1993. (Illus.). 32p. (J). (ps-3). 13.95 (*0-8050-1961-8*, Holt, Henry & Co. Bks. For Young Readers) Holt, Henry & Co.

Zemach, Margot. Siempre Puede Ser Peor, RS. Marcuse, Aida E., tr. 1992. (SPA., Illus.). 32p. (J). (ps-3). 17.00 o.p. (*0-374-36907-0*, Mirasol/Libros Juveniles) Farrar, Straus & Giroux.

Ziefert, Harriet. What Is Passover? 1994. (Lift-the-Flap Story Ser.). (Illus.). 16p. (J). (ps-2). 6.95 (*0-694-00482-0*, Harper Festival) HarperCollins Children's Bk. Group.

Zucker, Jonny. Four Special Questions: A Passover Story. 2003. (Festival Time! Ser.). (Illus.). 24p. (J). (ps-2). pap. 6.95 (*0-7641-2267-3*) Barron's Educational Series, Inc.

—It's Party Time! A Purim Story. 2003. (Festival Time! Ser.). (Illus.). 24p. (J). (ps-2). pap. 6.95 (*0-7641-2268-1*) Barron's Educational Series, Inc.

Zusman, Evelyn. The Passover Parrot. 1984. (Illus.). 40p. (J). (ps-3). 10.95 o.p. (*0-930494-29-6*); pap. 4.95 o.p. (*0-930494-30-X*) Kar-Ben Publishing.

Zyskind, Sara. Struggle. 1989. 288p. (J). lib. bdg. 22.95 o.p. (*0-8225-0772-2*, Lerner Pubns.) Lerner Publishing Group.

Zytman, Leah. The Bravest Fireman. 1998. (Illus.). 32p. (J). (ps-1). 9.95 (*0-922613-88-5*) Hachai Publishing.

JEWS—HISTORY—FICTION

Benderly, Beryl Lieff. Jason's Miracle: A Hanukkah Story. 2000. (Illus.). 114p. (J). (gr. 4-8). lib. bdg. 14.95 (*0-8075-3781-0*) Whitman, Albert & Co.

Cheng, Andrea. Marika. 2002. 168p. (J). (gr. 5 up). 16.95 (*1-886910-78-2*, Front Street) Front Street, Inc.

Cohen, Barbara. Yussel's Prayer: A Yom Kippur Story. 1981. (Illus.). 32p. (J). (gr. k-4). 12.95 o.p. (*0-688-00460-1*); lib. bdg. 14.93 o.p. (*0-688-00461-X*) HarperCollins Children's Bk. Group.

Cohen, Sholem. Yitzy & the G. O. L. E. M. 1992. (Yitz Berg from Pittsburgh Ser.). 128p. (J). (gr. 4-8). pap. text 6.95 o.p. (*0-922613-50-8*) Hachai Publishing.

Crowley, Bridget. Feast of Fools. 2003. 272p. (J). (gr. 5-9). 15.95 (*0-689-86512-0*, McElderry, Margaret K.) Simon & Schuster Children's Publishing.

Dennis, Jeanne Gowen & Seifert, Sheila. Attack! Hohn, David, tr. & illus. by. 2003. (Strive to Thrive Ser.). (J). pap. 4.99 (*0-7814-3894-2*) Cook Communications Ministries.

—Deadly Expedition! Hohn, David, tr. & illus. by. 2003. (J). pap. 4.99 (*0-7814-3897-7*) Cook Communications Ministries.

—Trapped! Hohn, David, tr. & illus. by. 2003. (J). pap. 4.99 (*0-7814-3898-5*) Cook Communications Ministries.

Eisenberg, Ronald L. The Iguana Corps of the Haganah. 1977. (J). (gr. 6-9). 5.95 o.p. (*0-8197-0456-3*) Bloch Publishing Co.

Gold, Avner. Envoy from Vienna. 1986. (Ruach Ami Ser.). 185p. (YA). (gr. 9-12). 15.95 (*0-935063-22-6*, CRA107H); pap. 12.95 (*0-935063-21-8*, CRA107S) CIS Communications, Inc.

Hernandez, David. Land of the Pharaohs. 2003. (Adventures of Toby Digz Ser.). (Illus.). 96p. (J). 5.99 (*1-4003-0195-5*) Nelson, Tommy.

Kelly, Clint & Ware, Jim. Escape Underground & the Prophet's Kid. 2001. (KidWitness Tales Ser.). 128p. (J). (gr. 3-8). pap. 5.99 (*1-56179-965-3*) Bethany Hse. Pubs.

Kerr, Judith. When Hitler Stole Pink Rabbit.Tr. of Cuando Hitler Robo el Conejo Rosa. (SPA.). 172p. 11.95 (*84-204-3201-6*) Santillana USA Publishing Co., Inc.

Levitin, Sonia. Escape from Egypt. 1996. 272p. (YA). (gr. 7 up). pap. 5.99 o.p. (*0-14-037537-6*, Puffin Bks.) Penguin Putnam Bks. for Young Readers.

—Escape from Egypt: A Novel. 1994. (YA). (gr. 7 up). 16.95 o.p. (*0-316-52273-2*) Little Brown & Co.

—Escape from Egypt: A Novel. 1996. 12.04 (*0-606-08678-1*) Turtleback Bks.

Maltz, Fran. Keeping Faith in the Dust. 1999. (Illus.). 72p. (J). (gr. 4-7). pap. 7.95 (*1-881283-25-9*) Alef Design Group.

Margolin, Miriam. Little Stories for Little Children. 1986. (Illus.). 32p. (J). (gr. k-3). reprint ed. 11.95 o.p. (*0-918825-53-9*) Moyer Bell.

Matas, Carol. Rosie in New York City: Gotcha! 2003. (Illus.). 128p. (J). (gr. 3-6). pap. 4.99 (*0-689-85714-4*, Aladdin) Simon & Schuster Children's Publishing.

Miklowitz, Gloria D. Masada: The Last Fortress. 1999. 198p. (J). (gr. 4-7). 16.00 (*0-8028-5165-7*, Eerdmans Bks For Young Readers) Eerdmans, William B. Publishing Co.

—Secrets in the House of Delgado. (gr. 4 up). 2002. 192p. (YA). pap. 8.00 (*0-8028-5210-6*); 2001. (Illus.). x, 182p. (J). 16.00 (*0-8028-5206-8*) Eerdmans, William B. Publishing Co. (Eerdmans Bks For Young Readers).

Napoli, Donna Jo. Daughter of Venice. 2003. 288p. (YA). (gr. 7). mass mkt. 5.50 (*0-440-22928-6*, Dell Books for Young Readers) Random Hse. Children's Bks.

Narell, Irena. Joshua: Fighter for Bar Kochba. (J). (gr. 6-12). 1979. 8.95 o.p. (*0-934764-02-6*); 1978. pap. 5.95 (*0-934764-01-8*) Akiba Pr.

Orgel, Doris. A Certain Magic. 1976. 192p. (J). (gr. 5 up). 7.95 o.p. (*0-8037-5405-1*, Dial Bks. for Young Readers) Penguin Putnam Bks. for Young Readers.

Orlev, Uri. The Island on Bird Street. Halkin, Hillel, tr. from HEB. 176p. (J). (gr. 4-6). 1992. pap. 6.95 (*0-395-61623-9*); 1984. tchr. ed. 16.00 (*0-395-33887-5*, 5-92515) Houghton Mifflin Co.

—The Island on Bird Street. Halkin, Hillel, tr. from HEB. 1984. (J). 12.00 (*0-606-00521-8*) Turtleback Bks.

—The Man from the Other Side. Halkin, Hillel, tr. from HEB. 1991. 192p. (YA). (gr. 7-7). tchr. ed. 16.00 (*0-395-53808-4*) Houghton Mifflin Co.

—The Man from the Other Side. Halkin, Hillel, tr. from HEB. 1995. (Illus.). 192p. (J). (gr. 5-9). pap. 5.99 (*0-14-037088-9*, Puffin Bks.) Penguin Putnam Bks. for Young Readers.

—The Man from the Other Side. Halkin, Hillel, tr. from HEB. 1995. 11.04 (*0-606-07834-7*) Turtleback Bks.

Ray, Karen. To Cross a Line. 1995. 160p. (YA). (gr. 7 up). pap. 5.99 o.p. (*0-14-037587-2*, Puffin Bks.) Penguin Putnam Bks. for Young Readers.

—To Cross a Line. 1995. 10.04 (*0-606-08679-X*) Turtleback Bks.

Ray, Mary. Beyond the Desert Gate. 2001. (Young Adult Bookshelf Ser.). (Illus.). 190p. (YA). (gr. 3-9). 11.95 (*1-883937-54-X*, 54-X) Bethlehem Bks.

—Beyond the Desert Gate. 1977. (Illus.). 160p. (J). o.p. (*0-571-10988-8*) Faber & Faber Ltd.

Roseman, Kenneth D. Escape from the Holocaust. 1985. (Do-It-Yourself Jewish Adventure Ser.). (Illus.). 192p. (J). (gr. 4-7). pap. 8.95 (*0-8074-0307-5*, 140070) UAHC Pr.

Schachnowitz, Selig. Avrohom ben Avrohom: The Famous Historical Novel About the Ger Tzedek of Vilna. (YA). (gr. 7 up). 12.95 o.p. (*0-87306-134-9*) Feldheim, Philipp Inc.

Sender, Ruth Minsky. To Life. 1988. 192p. (YA). (gr. 7 up). lib. bdg. 14.95 (*0-02-781831-4*, Simon & Schuster Children's Publishing) Simon & Schuster Children's Publishing.

Siegel, Bruce H. Champion & Jewboy. 1995. (Illus.). 144p. (J). (gr. 8 up). 6.95 (*1-881283-11-9*) Alef Design Group.

Stadtler, Bea. Story of Dona Gracia Mendes. 1969. (Illus.). (J). (gr. 6-9). 4.50 (*0-8381-0734-6*) United Synagogue of America Bk. Service.

JEWS—NEW YORK (N.Y.)—FICTION

Hest, Amy. When Jessie Came Across the Sea. (Illus.). 40p. 2003. bds. 6.99 (*0-7636-1274-X*); 1997. (J). (gr. 1-7). 16.99 (*0-7636-0094-6*) Candlewick Pr.

Karp, Naomi J. The Turning Point. 1976. (J). (gr. 5). 6.95 o.p. (*0-15-291238-X*) Harcourt Children's Bks.

Lasky, Kathryn. Dreams in the Golden Country: The Diary of Zipporah Feldman, a Jewish Immigrant Girl, New York City, 1903. (Dear America Ser.). (YA). 2002. E-Book 9.95 (*0-439-42539-5*); 1998. (Illus.). 188p. (gr. 4-9). pap. 10.95 (*0-590-02973-8*) Scholastic, Inc.

Levine, Gail Carson. Dave at Night. 288p. (J). 2001. (gr. 3-7). pap. 5.99 (*0-06-440747-0*, Harper Trophy); 1999. (Illus.). (gr. k-3). lib. bdg. 16.89 (*0-06-028154-5*); 1999. (gr. k-4). 16.99 (*0-06-028153-7*) HarperCollins Children's Bk. Group.

—Dave at Night. unabr. ed. 2001. 278p. (J). (gr. 4-6). pap. 37.00 incl. audio (*0-8072-8379-7*, YA174SP, Listening Library) Random Hse. Audio Publishing Group.

—Dave at Night. 1999. (YA). pap., stu. ed. 69.95 incl. audio (*0-7887-3794-5*, 41038); pap., stu. ed. 69.95 incl. audio (*0-7887-3794-5*, 41038) Recorded Bks., LLC.

—Dave at Night. l.t. ed. 2001. (Illus.). 295p. (J). (gr. 4-7). 22.95 (*0-7862-2972-1*) Thorndike Pr.

Rael, Elsa Okon. When Zaydeh Danced on Eldridge Street. 1997. (Illus.). 40p. (J). (gr. k-4). 16.00 o.s.i (*0-689-80451-2*, Simon & Schuster Children's Publishing) Simon & Schuster Children's Publishing.

JEWS—SOVIET UNION—FICTION

Burstein, Chaya M. Rifka Bangs the Teakettle. 1970. (Illus.). (J). (gr. 4-6). 4.95 o.p. (*0-15-266944-2*) Harcourt Children's Bks.

Heyman, Anita. Exit from Home. 1977. (Illus.). (J). (gr. 7 up). 7.50 o.p. (*0-517-52903-3*, Crown) Crown Publishing Group.

Howland, Naomi. Latkes, Latkes, Good to Eat: A Chanukah Story. 1999. (Illus.). 32p. (J). (ps-3). lib. bdg., tchr. ed. 16.00 (*0-395-89903-6*, Clarion Bks.) Houghton Mifflin Co. Trade & Reference Div.

Lasky, Kathryn. The Night Journey. 1986. (J). 12.95 o.p. (*0-670-80935-7*, Viking Children's Bks.) Penguin Putnam Bks. for Young Readers.

Lisowski, Gabriel, adapted by. How Tevye Became a Milkman, ERS. 1976. (Illus.). 32p. (J). (gr. 1-3). o.p. (*0-03-016636-5*, Holt, Henry & Co. Bks. For Young Readers) Holt, Henry & Co.

Margolin, Miriam. Little Stories for Little Children. 1986. (Illus.). 32p. (J). (gr. k-3). reprint ed. 11.75 o.p. (*0-918825-55-5*) Moyer Bell.

Matas, Carol. Sworn Enemies. 1994. 144p. (YA). mass mkt. 3.99 o.s.i (*0-440-21900-0*) Dell Publishing.

—Sworn Enemies. 1993. (J). mass mkt. o.p. (*0-440-90069-7*, Dell Books for Young Readers) Random Hse. Children's Bks.

—Sworn Enemies. 1993. 9.09 o.p. (*0-606-06043-X*) Turtleback Bks.

Sandman, Rochel. Perfect Porridge: A Story about Kindness. 2000. (Illus.). 32p. (J). (ps-2). 9.95 (*0-922613-92-3*) Hachai Publishing.

Schur, Maxine R. The Circlemaker. 1996. 192p. (YA). (gr. 5 up). 1996. pap. 5.99 (*0-14-037997-5*, Puffin Bks.); 1994. 14.99 o.s.i (*0-8037-1354-1*, Dial Bks. for Young Readers) Penguin Putnam Bks. for Young Readers.

—The Circlemaker. 1996. (YA). (gr. 5 up). 11.04 (*0-606-09149-1*) Turtleback Bks.

Segal, Jerry. The Place Where Nobody Stopped. Cohn, Amy, ed. 1994. (Illus.). 160p. (J). (gr. 5 up). reprint ed. pap. 4.95 o.p. (*0-688-12567-0*, Morrow, William & Co.) Morrow/Avon.

Steinberg, Fannie. Birthday in Kishinev. 1979. (Illus.). (J). (gr. 4-9). 6.95 o.p. (*0-8276-0111-5*, 434) Jewish Pubn. Society.

JEWS—UNITED STATES—FICTION

Abelove, Joan. Saying It Out Loud. 2001. 144p. (J). (gr. 7 up). pap. 5.99 (*0-14-131227-0*, Puffin Bks.) Penguin Putnam Bks. for Young Readers.

Adler, David A. One Yellow Daffodil: A Hanukkah Story. (Illus.). 32p. (J). (gr. 1-5). 1999. pap. 6.00 (*0-15-202094-2*, Harcourt Paperbacks); 1995. 16.00 o.s.i (*0-15-200537-4*, Gulliver Bks.) Harcourt Children's Bks.

Altman, Linda Jacobs. The Legend of Freedom Hill. (Illus.). (J). 2003. pap. (*1-58430-169-4*); 2000. 32p. 15.95 (*1-58430-003-5*) Lee & Low Bks., Inc.

Atlas, Susan. Passover Passage. 1991. 96p. (YA). (gr. 4-7). pap. 5.95 (*0-933873-46-8*) Torah Aura Productions.

Baer, Julie, illus. & text. I Only Like What I Like. 2003. 32p. (J). 15.99 (*1-932188-00-2*) Bollix Bks.

Bat-Ami, Miriam. Dear Elijah: A Passover Story, RS. 1995. 96p. (J). (gr. 4-7). 14.00 o.p. (*0-374-31755-0*, Farrar, Straus & Giroux (BYR)) Farrar, Straus & Giroux.

—Dear Elijah: A Passover Story. 1997. 106p. (J). pap. 9.95 (*0-8276-0592-7*) Jewish Pubn. Society.

Blos, Joan W. Brooklyn Doesn't Rhyme. (Illus.). 96p. (gr. 3-7). 2000. pap. 4.50 (*0-689-83557-4*, Aladdin); 1994. (J). 16.00 o.s.i (*0-684-19694-8*, Atheneum) Simon & Schuster Children's Publishing.

Blume, Judy. Starring Sally J. Freedman As Herself. 1982. 296p. (J). (gr. 4-7). 17.00 (*0-02-711070-2*, Atheneum/Richard Jackson Bks.) Simon & Schuster Children's Publishing.

Chaikin, Miriam. Finders Weepers. 2001. 136p. pap. 11.95 (*0-595-19878-3*, Backinprint.com) iUniverse, Inc.

—I Should Worry, I Should Care. 1979. (Illus.). (J). (gr. 3-6). 12.89 o.p. (*0-06-021174-1*); lib. bdg. 11.89 o.p. (*0-06-021175-X*) HarperCollins Children's Bk. Group.

—I Should Worry, I Should Care. 2000. (Illus.). 116p. (gr. 4-7). pap. 9.95 (*0-595-09011-7*, Backinprint.com) iUniverse, Inc.

Chapman, Carol. The Tale of Meshka the Kvetch. 1993. 32p. (J). (ps-3). pap. 4.99 o.s.i (*0-14-054787-8*, Puffin Bks.) Penguin Putnam Bks. for Young Readers.

Cohen, Barbara. Make a Wish, Molly. 1995. 48p. (gr. 4-7). pap. text 3.99 (*0-440-41058-4*); 1994. (Illus.). 40p. (J). 14.95 o.s.i (*0-385-31079-X*, Delacorte Pr.) Dell Publishing.

—Make a Wish, Molly. 1993. (J). o.s.i (*0-385-44599-7*) Doubleday Publishing.

—Make a Wish, Molly. 1994. (J). pap. 4.50 (*0-440-91018-8*, Dell Books for Young Readers) Random Hse. Children's Bks.

—Make a Wish, Molly. 1995. (J). 10.14 (*0-606-07831-2*) Turtleback Bks.

—Make a Wish Molly. 1995. (Illus.). (J). 10.55 (*0-7857-5404-0*) Econo-Clad Bks.

—Molly's Pilgrim. 1990. (First Skylark Ser.). (Illus.). 48p. (J). (gr. k-3). pap. 3.50 o.s.i (*0-553-15833-3*) Bantam Bks.

—Molly's Pilgrim. 1990. (Yearling Ser.). (Illus.). 48p. (J). (gr. k-3). pap. text 3.50 o.s.i (*0-440-41057-6*) Dell Publishing.

—Molly's Pilgrim. (Illus.). 32p. (J). 1983. (gr. 2-5). 16.00 o.p. (*0-688-02103-4*); 1983. (gr. 2-5). lib. bdg. 15.93 o.p. (*0-688-02104-2*); 1998. (ps-3). 15.99 (*0-688-16279-7*) HarperCollins Children's Bk. Group.

—Molly's Pilgrim. rev. ed. 1998. (Illus.). 32p. (J). (gr. 1-4). pap. 3.99 (*0-688-16280-0*); pap. 3.99 (*0-688-16280-0*) Morrow/Avon. (Morrow, William & Co.).

—Molly's Pilgrim. 1991. (J). pap. o.s.i (*0-553-54012-2*, Dell Books for Young Readers) Random Hse. Children's Bks.

—Molly's Pilgrim. 1990. (Bantam First Skylark Bks.). (J). 8.70 o.p. (*0-606-04748-4*) Turtleback Bks.

Cone, Molly. Promise Is a Promise, 001. 1964. (Illus.). (J). (gr. 7-9). 8.95 o.p. (*0-395-06703-0*) Houghton Mifflin Co.

Feldman, Eve B. Seymour, the Formerly Fearful. 1990. 160p. (J). (gr. 3-6). 13.95 o.p. (*0-02-734371-5*, Simon & Schuster Children's Publishing) Simon & Schuster Children's Publishing.

Fuchs, Menucha. Hand in Hand: Stories about You & Me. Goldfield, Zelda, tr. from HEB. 1999. (Children's Learning Ser.: Vol. 2). (Illus.). 48p. (J). (gr. 1-4). pap. 4.95 (*1-880582-43-0*) Judaica Pr., Inc., The.

Goldin, Barbara Diamond. Night Lights: A Sukkot Story. 1995. (Illus.). 32p. (J). (ps-3). 15.00 o.s.i (*0-15-200536-6*, Gulliver Bks.) Harcourt Children's Bks.

—Night Lights: A Sukkot Story. 2002. (Illus.). (J). (ps-3). 2.00 (*0-8074-0803-4*) UAHC Pr.

Goodman, Henry. The New Country: Stories from the Yiddish about Life in America. abr. ed. 2000. (Judaic Traditions in Literature, Music & Art Ser.). (Illus.). xxix, 243p. 26.95 (*0-8156-0669-9*) Syracuse Univ. Pr.

Greene, Bette. Summer of My German Soldier. 1984. 208p. (YA). (gr. 7-12). mass mkt. 2.95 o.s.i (*0-553-27247-0*) Bantam Bks.

—Summer of My German Soldier. 1993. 208p. (YA). mass mkt. 5.50 o.s.i (*0-440-21892-6*) Dell Publishing.

—Summer of My German Soldier. l.t. ed. 2000. (LRS Large Print Cornerstone Ser.). 305p. (YA). (gr. 6-12). lib. bdg. 29.95 (*1-58118-059-4*, 23473) LRS.

—Summer of My German Soldier. l.t. ed. 1989. 272p. (YA). reprint ed. lib. bdg. 16.95 o.s.i (*1-55736-134-7*, Cornerstone Bks.) Pages, Inc.

—Summer of My German Soldier. 2003. (Illus.). 256p. (J). 16.99 (*0-8037-2869-7*, Dial Bks. for Young Readers); 1999. (Illus.). 208p. (J). (gr. 5-9). pap. 6.99 (*0-14-130636-X*, Puffin Bks.); 1973. 240p. (YA). (gr. 7 up). 14.99 o.s.i (*0-8037-8321-3*, Dial Bks. for Young Readers) Penguin Putnam Bks. for Young Readers.

—Summer of My German Soldier. 1993. (YA). mass mkt. o.p. (*0-440-90056-5*, Dell Books for Young Readers) Random Hse. Children's Bks.

—Summer of My German Soldier. 2000. (YA). (gr. 6 up). 20.50 (*0-8446-7144-4*) Smith, Peter Pub., Inc.

—Summer of My German Soldier. 1999. 11.04 (*0-606-17432-X*); 1975. (YA). 10.09 o.p. (*0-606-05063-9*) Turtleback Bks.

Ethnic Groups

Herman, Charlotte. What Happened to Heather Hopkowitz? 1994. 186p. (J). (gr. 4 up). pap. 9.95 *(0-8276-0520-X)* Jewish Pubn. Society.

Hesse, Karen. A Time of Angels. 1997. (Illus.). 256p. (J). (gr. 5-9). reprint ed. pap. 5.95 *(0-7868-1209-5)* Disney Pr.

—A Time of Angels. 256p. 1997. pap. 5.95 o.s.i *(0-7868-1303-2)*; 1995. (J). (gr. 5-9). 15.95 *(0-7868-0087-9)*; 1995. (J). (gr. 5-9). lib. bdg. 16.49 *(0-7868-2072-1)* Hyperion Bks. for Children.

—A Time of Angels. 1997. 12.00 *(0-606-13088-8)* Turtleback Bks.

Hesse, Karen & Hesse, Hermann. Time of Angels. rev. ed. 2000. (J). 240p. (gr. 4-7). lib. bdg. 17.49 *(0-7868-2534-0)*; 277p. (gr. 5-9). 16.99 *(0-7868-0621-4)* Hyperion Pr.

Holmes, Mary Z. Dear Dad. 1992. (History's Children Ser.). (Illus.). 48p. (J). (gr. 4-5). pap. o.p. *(0-8114-6428-8)*; lib. bdg. 21.36 o.p. *(0-8114-3503-2)* Raintree Pubs.

Hurwitz, Johanna. Once I Was a Plum Tree. 1980. (Illus.). 160p. (J). (gr. 4-6). lib. bdg. 12.93 o.p. *(0-688-32223-9*, Morrow, William & Co.) Morrow/Avon.

Irwin, Hadley. Sarah with an "H" 1996. 144p. (J). (gr. 7 up). 16.00 *(0-689-80949-2*, McElderry, Margaret K.) Simon & Schuster Children's Publishing.

Kilpatrick, Susan. Molly's Pilgrim. 1995. (Literature Unit Ser.). (Illus.). 48p. pap., tchr. ed. 7.99 *(1-55734-535-X*, TCA0535) Teacher Created Materials, Inc.

Kornblatt, Marc. Understanding Buddy. l.t. ed. 2002. 100p. (J). 21.95 *(0-7862-3712-0)* Gale Group.

—Understanding Buddy. 2001. (Illus.). 128p. (J). (gr. 4-6). 16.00 *(0-689-83215-X*, McElderry, Margaret K.) Simon & Schuster Children's Publishing.

Koss, Amy Goldman. How I Saved Hanukkah. 1998. (Illus.). 96p. (J). (gr. 2-5). 15.99 *(0-8037-2241-9*, Dial Bks. for Young Readers) Penguin Putnam Bks. for Young Readers.

Krulik, Nancy E. Penny & the Four Questions. 1993. (Read with Me Ser.). (Illus.). 32p. (J). (ps-3). mass mkt. 3.25 *(0-590-46339-X)* Scholastic, Inc.

Lakin, Patricia. Don't Forget. (Illus.). 32p. (gr. k-3). 2000. (YA). pap. 5.95 *(0-688-17522-8)*; 1994. (J). 14.00 o.p. *(0-688-12075-X)*; 1994. (J). lib. bdg. 13.93 *(0-688-12076-8)* Morrow/Avon. (Morrow, William & Co.).

Lasky, Kathryn. Pageant. 1986. 240p. (YA). (gr. 7 up). lib. bdg. 14.95 o.p. *(0-02-751720-9*, Simon & Schuster Children's Publishing) Simon & Schuster Children's Publishing.

Lehrman, Robert. The Store That Mama Built. 1992. 128p. (J). (gr. 3-7). lib. bdg. 13.95 *(0-02-754632-2*, Simon & Schuster Children's Publishing) Simon & Schuster Children's Publishing.

Levinson, Riki. Soon, Annala. 1993. (Illus.). 32p. (J). (ps-2). mass mkt. 15.95 o.p. *(0-531-05494-2)*; mass mkt. 16.99 o.p. *(0-531-08644-5)* Scholastic, Inc. (Orchard Bks.).

Levitin, Sonia. Silver Days. 1992. 192p. (J). (gr. 4-7). reprint ed. pap. 4.99 *(0-689-71570-6*, Aladdin) Simon & Schuster Children's Publishing.

—Silver Days. 1992. 10.55 *(0-606-01597-3)* Turtleback Bks.

Little, Jean. Kate. (Trophy Bk.). 174p. (J). (gr. 5-8). 1973. pap. 3.95 o.s.i *(0-06-440037-9*, Harper Trophy); 1971. (Illus.). lib. bdg. 12.89 o.p. *(0-06-023914-X)* HarperCollins Children's Bk. Group.

Littman, Jennifer. Matzo Ball Soup: The Balls That Bobbed in the Broth That Bubbe Brewed. 1997. (Illus.). 32p. (Orig.). (J). (ps-2). pap. 7.95 *(0-9656431-0-7)* Brickford Lane Pubs.

Lutz, Norma Jean. Battling the Klan. 39th ed. 1998. (American Adventure Ser.: No. 39). (Illus.). (J). (gr. 3-7). pap. 3.97 *(1-57748-453-3)* Barbour Publishing, Inc.

Machlin, Mikki. My Name Is Not Gussie. 1999. (Illus.). 32p. (J). (ps-3). lib. bdg., tchr. ed. 16.00 *(0-395-95646-3)* Houghton Mifflin Co.

Manushkin, Fran. Hooray for Hanukkah! 2001. (Illus.). 40p. (J). (gr. k-3). 9.99 *(0-375-81043-9)*; lib. bdg. 11.99 *(0-375-91043-3)* Random Hse. Children's Bks. (Random Hse. Bks. for Young Readers).

—Sophie & the Shofar. 2001. (Illus.). (J). 12.95 *(0-8074-0751-8)* UAHC Pr.

Matas, Carol. The War Within: A Novel of the Civil War. 2001. (Illus.). 160p. (J). (gr. 5-8). 16.00 *(0-689-82935-3*, Simon & Schuster Children's Publishing) Simon & Schuster Children's Publishing.

—The War Within: A Novel of the Civil War. 2003. (J). 22.95 *(0-7862-5499-8)* Thorndike Pr.

Mazer, Norma Fox. Good Night, Maman. 1999. (Illus.). 192p. (YA). (gr. 5-9). 16.00 *(0-15-201468-3)* Harcourt Children's Bks.

—Good Night, Maman. 2001. (Harper Trophy Bks.). 192p. (J). (gr. 5 up). pap. 5.99 *(0-06-440923-6*, Harper Trophy) HarperCollins Children's Bk. Group.

Meyer, Carolyn. Drummers of Jericho. 1995. 320p. (YA). (gr. 5-9). 11.00 *(0-15-200441-6)*; pap. 6.00 *(0-15-200190-5)* Harcourt Children's Bks. (Gulliver Bks.).

—Drummers of Jericho. 1995. 11.05 *(0-606-10997-8)* Turtleback Bks.

Michelson, Richard. Grandpa's Gamble. 1999. (Accelerated Reader Bks.). (Illus.). 32p. (J). (ps up). 15.95 *(0-7614-5034-3*, Cavendish Children's Bks.) Cavendish, Marshall Corp.

—Too Young for Yiddish. 2002. (Illus.). 32p. (J). (gr. k-4). 15.95 *(0-88106-118-2)* Charlesbridge Publishing, Inc.

Millman, M. C. Cheery Bim Band No. 5: In the Spotlight! 1994. 141p. (J). (gr. 5-8). 12.95 *(1-56062-265-2*, CJR144H) CIS Communications, Inc.

—Cheery Bim Band No. 6: Trumpet Trouble. 1994. 176p. (J). (gr. 5-8). 13.95 *(1-56062-271-7*, CJR146H) CIS Communications, Inc.

Moss, Marissa. Hannah's Journal: The Story of an Immigrant Girl. (Young American Voices Ser.). (Illus.). 56p. (J). (gr. 3-7). 2002. pap. 7.00 *(0-15-216329-8)*; 2000. 15.00 *(0-15-202155-8)* Harcourt Children's Bks. (Silver Whistle).

—In America. 1994. (Illus.). 32p. (J). 14.99 o.s.i *(0-525-45152-8*, Dutton Children's Bks.) Penguin Putnam Bks. for Young Readers.

Newman, Leslea. Fat Chance. 1994. 224p. (J). (gr. 3-7). 15.95 o.p. *(0-399-22760-1*, G. P. Putnam's Sons) Penguin Group (USA) Inc.

—Fat Chance. 1996. 224p. (YA). (gr. 7 up). pap. 5.99 *(0-698-11406-X*, PaperStar) Penguin Putnam Bks. for Young Readers.

—Fat Chance. 1996. 11.04 *(0-606-10806-8)* Turtleback Bks.

Nixon, Joan Lowery. Land of Hope. 1993. (Ellis Island Ser.: No. 1). 176p. (YA). (gr. 7 up). mass mkt. 4.99 *(0-440-21597-8)* Dell Publishing.

—Land of Hope. 1992. (Ellis Island Ser.). (J). 10.55 *(0-606-05265-8)* Turtleback Bks.

—The Land of Hope. 1992. (Ellis Island Novels Ser.: Bk. 1). 176p. (YA). 16.00 o.s.i *(0-553-08110-1)* Bantam Bks.

—Land of Hope. l.t. ed. 2001. (Ellis Island Stories Ser.). 171p. (J). (gr. 4 up). lib. bdg. 22.60 *(0-8368-2811-9)* Stevens, Gareth Inc.

Polacco, Patricia. The Trees of the Dancing Goats. 2002. (Illus.). (J). 25.11 *(0-7587-3858-7)* Book Wholesalers, Inc.

—The Trees of the Dancing Goats. 32p. (J). 2000. (Illus.). (gr. k-3). pap. 6.99 *(0-689-83857-3*, Aladdin); 1997. (gr. k-5). pap. 22.00 incl. audio compact disk *(0-689-81193-4*, Simon & Schuster Children's Publishing); 1997. (gr. k-5). pap. 22.00 incl. audio compact disk *(0-689-81193-4*, Simon & Schuster Children's Publishing); 1996. (Illus.). (gr. 4-7). 16.00 *(0-689-80862-3*, Simon & Schuster Children's Publishing) Simon & Schuster Children's Publishing.

—The Trees of the Dancing Goats. 2000. 13.14 *(0-606-20094-0)* Turtleback Bks.

Portnoy, Mindy A. Matzah Ball. 1994. (Illus.). (J). 13.95 o.p. *(0-929371-68-2)*; 32p. (gr. 1-5). pap. 6.95 *(0-929371-69-0)* Kar-Ben Publishing.

Pushker, Gloria T. A Belfer Bar Mitzvah. 1995. (Illus.). 32p. (J). (gr. 4-7). 14.95 *(1-56554-095-6)* Pelican Publishing Co., Inc.

Pushker, Gloria Teles. Toby Belfer Visits Ellis Island. 2003. (Illus.). 32p. (J). 14.95 *(1-58980-117-2)* Pelican Publishing Co., Inc.

Rael, Elsa Okon. Rivka's First Thanksgiving. 2001. (Illus.). 32p. (J). (gr. k-3). 16.00 *(0-689-83901-4*, McElderry, Margaret K.) Simon & Schuster Children's Publishing.

—What Zeesie Saw on Delancey Street. (Illus.). 40p. (J). (ps-3). 2000. pap. 6.99 *(0-689-83535-3*, Aladdin); 1996. 16.00 *(0-689-80549-7*, Simon & Schuster Children's Publishing) Simon & Schuster Children's Publishing.

—What Zeesie Saw on Delancey Street. 2000. 12.14 *(0-606-17943-7)* Turtleback Bks.

Rappaport, Doreen. Menorah. 2000. 32p. (J). 15.99 *(0-7868-0400-9)*; lib. bdg. 16.49 *(0-7868-2352-6)* Hyperion Bks. for Children.

Rinn, Miriam. The Saturday Secret. 1999. (Illus.). 144p. (J). (gr. 4-7). pap. 7.95 *(1-881283-26-7)* Alef Design Group.

Roseman, Kenneth D. The Other Side of the Hudson: A Jewish Immigrant Adventure. 1993. (Do-It-Yourself Jewish Adventure Ser.). (Illus.). 140p. (J). (gr. 4-7). pap. 8.95 *(0-8074-0506-X*, 140061) UAHC Pr.

Rosen, Michael J. The Blessing of the Animals, RS. 2000. (Illus.). 96p. (J). (gr. 3-7). 15.00 *(0-374-30838-1*, Farrar, Straus & Giroux (BYR)) Farrar, Straus & Giroux.

—Chanukah Lights Everywhere. 2001. (Illus.). 32p. (J). (ps-2). 16.00 *(0-15-202447-6*, Gulliver Bks.) Harcourt Children's Bks.

—Chanukah Lights Everywhere. 2000. (Illus.). (J). *(0-15-201810-7)* Harcourt Trade Pubs.

Rosen, Sybil & Nielsen, Cliff. Speed of Light. 1999. 169p. (J). (gr. 5-9). 16.00 *(0-689-82437-8*, Atheneum/Anne Schwartz Bks.) Simon & Schuster Children's Publishing.

Rothenberg, Joan. Matzah Ball Soup: A Passover Story. 1999. 32p. (J). 14.99 *(0-7868-0574-9)* Disney Pr.

—Matzah Ball Soup: A Passover Story. 1999. (Illus.). 32p. (J). (ps-3). 14.99 *(0-7868-0202-2)*; lib. bdg. 15.49 *(0-7868-2170-1)* Hyperion Bks. for Children.

Ruby, Lois. Swindletop. 2000. (Illus.). 127p. (J). 15.95 *(1-57168-393-3)* Eakin Pr.

—Swindletop. 2000. E-Book 15.95 *(0-585-27649-8)* netLibrary, Inc.

Sachs, Marilyn. Call Me Ruth. 1995. 224p. (J). (gr. 4-7). pap. 4.95 *(0-688-13737-7*, Harper Trophy) HarperCollins Children's Bk. Group.

—Call Me Ruth. 1996. (J). (gr. 3 up). 18.75 o.p. *(0-8446-6905-9)* Smith, Peter Pub., Inc.

—Peter & Veronica. 1995. 160p. (J). (gr. 4-7). pap. 5.99 *(0-14-037082-X*, Puffin Bks.) Penguin Putnam Bks. for Young Readers.

Satten, Sandra C. In the Thirteenth Year. 1999. (Illus.). 72p. (YA). (ps up). pap. 7.95 *(1-881283-24-0)* Alef Design Group.

Shecter, Ben. Someplace Else. 1971. (Illus.). (J). (gr. 3-7). lib. bdg. 8.89 o.p. *(0-06-025577-3)* Harper-Collins Pubs.

Siegel, Bruce H. Sing Time. 1997. (Illus.). 64p. (J). (gr. 3-6). 5.95 *(1-881283-14-3)* Alef Design Group.

Snyder, Carol. Ike & Mama & the Block Wedding. 1979. (Illus.). (J). (gr. 2-6). 7.95 o.s.i *(0-698-20461-1*, Coward-McCann) Putnam Publishing Group, The.

Summer of My German Soldier. 1999. (YA). 9.95 *(1-56137-113-0)* Novel Units, Inc.

Talbert, Marc. Star of Luis. 1999. 192p. (J). (gr. 5-9). tchr. ed. 15.00 *(0-395-91423-X*, Clarion Bks.) Houghton Mifflin Co. Trade & Reference Div.

Tobias, Tobi. Pot Luck. 1993. (Illus.). (J). (ps-3). lib. bdg. 14.93 o.p. *(0-688-09825-8)* HarperCollins Children's Bk. Group.

Topek, Susan R. A Taste for Noah. 1993. (Illus.). 24p. (J). (gr. k-1). 12.95 *(0-929371-39-9)*; pap. 5.95 *(0-929371-40-2)* Kar-Ben Publishing.

Yorinks, Arthur. The Flying Latke. 2002. 32p. pap. 6.99 *(0-689-85348-3*, Aladdin) Simon & Schuster Children's Publishing.

Zalben, Jane Breskin. Pearl's Passover: A Family Celebration Through Stories, Recipes, Crafts & Songs. 2002. (Illus.). 48p. (J). (gr. k-3). 16.00 *(0-689-81487-9*, Simon & Schuster Children's Publishing) Simon & Schuster Children's Publishing.

—Unfinished Dreams: A Poignant Coming-of-Age Novel about Dreams Cut Short by AIDS. 1996. 176p. (J). (gr. 4-7). 16.00 o.s.i *(0-689-80033-9*, Simon & Schuster Children's Publishing) Simon & Schuster Children's Publishing.

K

KIBBUTZIM—FICTION

Banks, Lynne Reid. One More River. 1996. (YA). (gr. 7 up). pap. 4.50 *(0-380-72755-2*, Avon Bks.); 1993. 256p. (J). (gr. 4-7). pap. 5.99 *(0-380-71563-5*, Avon Bks.); 1992. 256p. (YA). (gr. 5 up). 14.00 *(0-688-10893-8*, Morrow, William & Co.) Morrow/Avon.

—One More River. 1992. 11.04 *(0-606-05525-8)* Turtleback Bks.

Bergman, Tamar. The Boy from over There. Halkin, Hillel, tr. from HEB. 1988. 192p. (J). (gr. 3-7). 13.95 o.p. *(0-395-43077-1)* Houghton Mifflin Co.

—Boy from over There. 1992. (J). (gr. 4-7). pap. 4.95 o.p. *(0-395-64370-8)* Houghton Mifflin Co.

Chaikin, Miriam. Aviva's Piano. 1986. (Illus.). 48p. (J). (gr. 2-4). 12.20 o.p. *(0-89919-367-6*, Clarion Bks.) Houghton Mifflin Co. Trade & Reference Div.

Edwards, Michelle. Chicken Man. 1991. (J). (ps-3). lib. bdg. 13.88 o.p. *(0-688-09709-X)*; (Illus.). 32p. 13.95 *(0-688-09708-1)* HarperCollins Children's Bk. Group.

—Chicken Man. 1994. (Illus.). 32p. (J). (ps up). reprint ed. pap. 4.95 o.p. *(0-688-13106-9*, Morrow, William & Co.) Morrow/Avon.

Orlev, Uri. The Lady with the Hat. Halkin, Hillel, tr. 1995. 192p. (YA). (gr. 7 up). tchr. ed. 16.00 *(0-395-69957-6)* Houghton Mifflin Co.

—The Lady with the Hat. Halkin, Hillel, tr. from HEB. 1997. (Illus.). 192p. (J). (gr. 5-9). pap. 4.99 o.s.i *(0-14-038571-1)* Penguin Putnam Bks. for Young Readers.

—The Lady with the Hat. 1997. 10.09 o.p. *(0-606-13562-6)* Turtleback Bks.

—Lydia: Queen of Palestine. Halkin, Hillel, tr. from HEB. 1993. Tr. of Lidyah: Malkat Erest Yisrael. 176p. (J). 13.95 o.p. *(0-395-65660-5)* Houghton Mifflin Co.

Shamir, Moshe. The Fifth Wheel. Hodes, Aubrey, tr. from HEB. rev. ed. 1986. (Illus.). 115p. (YA). (gr. 8 up). reprint ed. pap. 8.95 o.p. *(0-917883-02-0)* Benmir Bks.

KOREAN AMERICANS—FICTION

Bercaw, Edna C. Halmoni's Day. 2000. (Illus.). 32p. (J). (gr. k-3). 16.99 *(0-8037-2444-6*, Dial Bks. for Young Readers) Penguin Putnam Bks. for Young Readers.

Cogan, Kim & Paek, Min, trs. Cooper's Lesson. 2004. (ENG & KOR., Illus.). 32p. 16.95 *(0-89239-193-6)* Children's Bk. Pr.

Czech, Jan M. An American Face. 2000. (Illus.). (J). (ps-3). 8.95 *(0-87868-718-1*, Child & Family Pr.) Child Welfare League of America, Inc.

—The Coffee Can Kid. 2002. (Illus.). (J). per. 8.95 *(0-87868-821-8*, Child & Family Pr.) Child Welfare League of America, Inc.

Kline, Suzy. Horrible Harry & the Dragon War. 2002. (Illus.). 64p. (J). (gr. 1-3). text 13.99 *(0-670-03559-9)* Penguin Putnam Bks. for Young Readers.

—Horrible Harry & the Drop of Doom. (Horrible Harry Ser.: No. 9). (Illus.). 64p. (J). (gr. 2-4). 2000. pap. 3.99 *(0-14-037256-3*, Puffin Bks.); 1998. 13.99 *(0-670-85849-8)* Penguin Putnam Bks. for Young Readers.

Kline, Suzy & Remkiewicz, Frank. Horrible Harry & the Dragon War. 2003. (Illus.). 64p. pap. 3.99 *(0-14-250166-2*, Puffin Bks.) Penguin Putnam Bks. for Young Readers.

Lee, Marie G. F Is for Fabuloso. 1999. 192p. (J). (gr. 5-9). 15.95 *(0-380-97648-X)* HarperCollins Children's Bk. Group.

—Finding My Voice. 1994. 176p. (J). mass mkt. 3.99 o.s.i *(0-440-21896-9)* Dell Publishing.

—Finding My Voice. 2001. 224p. (J). (gr. 7 up). pap. 5.99 *(0-06-447245-0*, Harper Trophy) HarperCollins Children's Bk. Group.

—Finding My Voice. 1992. 176p. (YA). (gr. 6 up). 13.95 o.p. *(0-395-62134-8)* Houghton Mifflin Co.

—Finding My Voice. 1994. 9.09 o.p. *(0-606-06979-8)* Turtleback Bks.

—If It Hadn't Been for Yoon Jun. 1993. 144p. (J). (gr. 3-7). 13.95 o.p. *(0-395-62941-1)* Houghton Mifflin Co.

—If It Hadn't Been for Yoon Jun. 1995. 144p. (J). (gr. 4-7). pap. 3.99 *(0-380-72347-6*, Avon Bks.) Morrow/Avon.

—If It Hadn't Been for Yoon Jun. 1995. 10.04 *(0-606-07695-6)* Turtleback Bks.

—Necessary Roughness. 1996. (YA). (gr. 7 up). 176p. lib. bdg. 14.89 *(0-06-025130-1)*; (Illus.). 240p. 15.95 *(0-06-025124-7)* HarperCollins Children's Bk. Group.

—Night of the Chupacabras. 1999. 128p. (gr. 3-7). pap. 3.99 *(0-380-79773-9*, Avon Bks.) Morrow/Avon.

—Night of the Chupacabras. 1999. 10.04 *(0-606-17336-6)* Turtleback Bks.

Lewis, Beverly. Better Than Best. 2000. (Girls Only (Go!) Ser.: Vol. 6). (Illus.). 128p. (J). (gr. 3-8). pap. 5.99 *(1-55661-641-4)* Bethany Hse. Pubs.

—The Chicken Pox Panic. 1995. (Cul-de-Sac Kids Ser.: Vol. 2). 80p. (J). (gr. 2-5). pap. 3.99 *(1-55661-626-0)* Bethany Hse. Pubs.

Littleton, Mark. Sarah's Secret. 2001. (Ally OConnor Adventures Ser.: Vol. 2). 112p. (J). (gr. 4-7). pap. 5.99 *(0-8010-4489-8)* Baker Bks.

Na, An. A Step from Heaven. 2001. 176p. (J). (gr. 7 up). 15.95 *(1-886910-58-8*, Front Street) Front Street, Inc.

—A Step from Heaven. l.t. ed. 2002. 193p. (J). 22.95 *(0-7862-4126-8)* Gale Group.

—A Step from Heaven. 2003. (Illus.). 160p. (YA). pap. 7.99 *(0-14-250027-5*, Puffin Bks.) Penguin Putnam Bks. for Young Readers.

—A Step from Heaven. unabr. ed. 2002. (YA). (gr. 3 up). audio 25.00 *(0-8072-0721-7*, Listening Library) Random Hse. Audio Publishing Group.

Pak, Soyung. Dear Juno. 1999. (Illus.). 32p. (J). (ps-2). 15.99 *(0-670-88252-6)* Penguin Putnam Bks. for Young Readers.

—Sumi's First Day of School Ever. 2003. (Illus.). 32p. (J). (ps-2). text 15.99 *(0-670-03522-X*, Viking) Viking Penguin.

Recorvits, Helen. My Name Is Yoon, RS. 2003. (Illus.). 32p. (J). (gr. k-3). 16.00 *(0-374-35114-7*, Farrar, Straus & Giroux (BYR)) Farrar, Straus & Giroux.

Son, John. Finding My Hat. 2003. (First Person Fiction Ser.). 192p. (J). pap. 16.95 *(0-439-43538-2*, Orchard Bks.) Scholastic, Inc.

KOREANS—UNITED STATES—FICTION

Balgassi, Haemi. Tae's Sonata. 1997. (Illus.). 128p. (J). (gr. 4-6). tchr. ed. 15.00 *(0-395-84314-6*, Clarion Bks.) Houghton Mifflin Co. Trade & Reference Div.

Choi, Sook-Nyul. The Best Older Sister. 1997. (First Choice Chapter Book Ser.). (Illus.). 48p. (J). (gr. k-3). 13.95 o.s.i *(0-385-32208-9)*; pap. 3.99 o.s.i *(0-440-41149-1)* Random Hse. Children's Bks. (Dell Books for Young Readers).

—Gathering of Pearls. 1994. 176p. (YA). (gr. 7 up). tchr. ed. 16.00 (*0-395-67437-9*) Houghton Mifflin Co.

—Halmoni & the Picnic. 1993. (Illus.). 32p. (J). (ps-3). lib. bdg., tchr. ed. 16.00 (*0-395-61626-3*) Houghton Mifflin Co.

—Yummi & Halmoni's Trip. 1997. (Illus.). 32p. (J). (ps-3). tchr. ed. 15.00 o.s.i (*0-395-81180-5*) Houghton Mifflin Co.

Choi, Yangsook. New Cat, RS. 1999. (Illus.). 32p. (J). (ps-3). 16.00 (*0-374-35512-6*, Farrar, Straus & Giroux (BYR)) Farrar, Straus & Giroux.

—New Cat. 1999. E-Book (*1-59019-453-5*); (J). E-Book 12.99 (*1-59019-463-2*) ipicturebooks, LLC.

Griffiths, Ann H. Korean Americans. 1991. (New Americans Ser.). (Illus.). 128p. (YA). (gr. 6-10). lib. bdg. 17.95 o.p. (*0-8160-2300-X*) Facts on File Inc.

Heo, Yumi. Father's Rubber Shoes. 1996. (Illus.). 32p. (J). (ps-3). pap. 15.95 (*0-531-06873-0*); lib. bdg. 16.99 (*0-531-08723-9*) Scholastic, Inc. (Orchard Bks.).

Kline, Suzy. Song Lee & the Hamster Hunt. (Song Lee Ser.). 64p. (J). 2000. (Illus.). (gr. 2-5). pap. 3.99 o.s.i (*0-14-130707-2*, Puffin Bks.); 1996. (gr. 4-7). pap. 3.99 o.s.i (*0-14-036317-3*, Puffin Bks.); 1994. (Illus.). (gr. 2-6). 12.99 o.s.i (*0-670-84773-9*, Viking Children's Bks.) Penguin Putnam Bks. for Young Readers.

—Song Lee & the Hamster Hunt. 1996. (J). 10.14 (*0-606-09874-7*) Turtleback Bks.

—Song Lee & the "I Hate You" Notes. 1999. (Song Lee Ser.). (Illus.). 64p. (J). (gr. 2-5). 13.99 (*0-670-87887-1*) Penguin Putnam Bks. for Young Readers.

—Song Lee & the Leech Man. 1997. (Puffin Chapters Ser.). (J). 10.14 (*0-606-11862-4*) Turtleback Bks.

—Song Lee in Room 2B. (Song Lee Ser.). 64p. (J). (gr. 2-5). 1999. pap. 3.99 (*0-14-130408-1*, Puffin Bks.); 1993. (Illus.). 13.99 o.s.i (*0-670-84772-0*, Viking Children's Bks.) Penguin Putnam Bks. for Young Readers.

Lee, Lauren. Stella: On the Edge of Popularity. 1994. 184p. (J). (gr. 4-8). 10.95 (*1-879965-08-9*) Polychrome Publishing Corp.

Lee, Marie G. Necessary Roughness. 1996. (YA). (gr. 7 up). 176p. lib. bdg. 14.89 (*0-06-025130-1*); (Illus.). 240p. 15.95 (*0-06-025124-7*) HarperCollins Children's Bk. Group.

—Night of the Chupacabras. 1998. (Avon Camelot Bks.). 144p. (J). (gr. 3-7). 14.00 o.p. (*0-380-97706-0*, Avon Bks.) Morrow/Avon.

—Saying Goodbye. 1994. 240p. (YA). (gr. 7 up). tchr. ed. 16.00 (*0-395-67066-7*) Houghton Mifflin Co.

Lewis, Beverly. Fiddlesticks. 1997. (Cul-de-Sac Kids Ser.: Vol. 11). 80p. (J). (gr. 2-5). pap. 3.99 (*1-55661-911-1*) Bethany Hse. Pubs.

Myers, Anna. Rosie's Tiger. 1994. 128p. (J). (gr. 4-7). 14.95 (*0-8027-8305-8*) Walker & Co.

Paek, Min. Aekyung's Dream. 1979. (Fifth World Tales Ser.). (Illus.). 24p. (J). (gr. 2-9). pap. 5.95 o.p. (*0-89239-018-2*) Children's Bk. Pr.

Park, Frances & Park, Ginger. Goodbye, 382 Shin Dang Dong. 2002. (Illus.). 32p. (J). (gr. k-3). 16.95 (*0-7922-7985-9*) National Geographic Society.

Rhie, Schi-Zhin. Soon-Hee in America. 1977. (Illus.). 36p. (J). (gr. k-3). 8.50 (*0-930878-00-0*) Hollym International Corp.

Sinykin, Sheri Cooper. The Buddy Trap. 1991. 144p. (J). (gr. 3-7). lib. bdg. 13.95 o.p. (*0-689-31674-7*, Atheneum) Simon & Schuster Children's Publishing.

Soto, Gary. Canto Familiar. 1995. (Illus.). 88p. (J). (ps-3). 18.00 (*0-15-200067-4*) Harcourt Children's Bks.

Wong, Janet S. The Trip Back Home. 2000. (Illus.). 32p. (J). (ps-2). 16.00 (*0-15-200784-9*) Harcourt Children's Bks.

KWANZAA—FICTION

Ball, Lynda Anne. Kwanzaa Teddy, The Curious Bear. 2001. (Adventures of KT). (Illus.). 32p. (J). (ps-2). per. 6.95 (*1-889383-11-2*) Angel Pubns.

Ballard, Bobbie. My Kwanzaa Story. 1993. (Illus.). 48p. (J). (gr. k-6). 6.95 (*0-9639349-0-2*) Ujamaa Enterprises, Inc.

Burden-Patmon, Denise. Imani's Gift at Kwanzaa. 48.95 (*0-8136-2248-4*) Modern Curriculum Pr.

—Imani's Gift at Kwanzaa. 1993. (Illus.). 32p. (J). (ps-3). pap. 4.95 (*0-671-79841-3*, Aladdin) Simon & Schuster Children's Publishing.

—Imani's Gift at Kwanzaa. 1993. (J). 11.10 (*0-606-05372-7*) Turtleback Bks.

Chocolate, Deborah M. Newton. A Very Special Kwanzaa. 1996. (J). (gr. 5-7). pap. 3.99 (*0-590-84862-3*) Scholastic, Inc.

—A Very Special Kwanzaa. 1996. 10.04 (*0-606-10353-8*) Turtleback Bks.

Cole, Harriette. Kwanzaa. 2003. (J). lib. bdg. 20.49 (*0-7868-2606-1*) Disney Pr.

Gayle, Sharon Shavers. A Kwanzaa Miracle. 1996. 8.15 o.p. (*0-606-10246-9*) Turtleback Bks.

Goggins, Alfonza R. & Lamar, Angela M. Father Kwanzaa Vol. I: The Spirit of Kwanzaa. Spenser, Delores, ed. 1997. (Illus.). (J). (gr. 4 up). pap. 9.95 (*0-9654203-0-2*) Spiritual Moon Publishing, Ltd.

—Father Kwanzaa Vol. II: The Intent of Kwanzaa. Spenser, Delores, ed. 1997. (Illus.). (YA). pap. 9.95 (*0-9654203-1-0*) Spiritual Moon Publishing, Ltd.

—Father Kwanzaa Vol. III: The Faith of Kwanzaa. Spenser, Delores, ed. 1997. (Illus.). (YA). pap. 9.95 (*0-9654203-2-9*) Spiritual Moon Publishing, Ltd.

Greene, Stephanie. The Rugrats First Kwanzaa. 2001. (Rugrats Ser.). (Illus.). 32p. (J). (ps-2). pap. 5.99 (*0-689-84191-4*, Simon Spotlight/Nickelodeon) Simon & Schuster Children's Publishing.

Holub, Joan. Kwanzaa Kids. 2002. (Lift-the-Flap Book Ser.). (Illus.). 16p. (J). pap. 6.99 (*0-14-230199-X*, Puffin Bks.) Penguin Putnam Bks. for Young Readers.

Hoyt-Goldsmith, Diane. Mark's Kwanzaa Celebration. Evento, Susan, ed. 1996. (Big America Ser.). (Illus.). 16p. (Orig.). (J). (gr. 1-3). pap. 3.95 (*1-56784-199-6*); pap. 17.95 (*1-56784-198-8*) Newbridge Educational Publishing.

Katz, Karen. My First Kwanzaa, ERS. 2003. (Illus.). 32p. (J). 14.95 (*0-8050-7077-X*, Holt, Henry & Co. Bks. For Young Readers) Holt, Henry & Co.

Mathis, Sharon Bell. Listen for the Fig Tree. 1990. 176p. (J). (gr. 7 up). pap. 4.99 o.s.i (*0-14-034364-4*, Puffin Bks.) Penguin Putnam Bks. for Young Readers.

—Listen for the Fig Tree. 1974. 176p. (J). (gr. 7 up). 9.95 o.p. (*0-670-43016-1*) Viking Penguin.

McKissack, Patricia C. & McKissack, Fredrick L. Messy Bessey's Holidays. 1999. (Rookie Readers Ser.). (Illus.). 32p. (J). (gr. 1-2). lib. bdg. 19.00 (*0-516-20829-2*, Children's Pr.) Scholastic Library Publishing.

Medearis, Angela Shelf. Seven Spools of Thread: A Kwanzaa Story. 2000. (Illus.). 40p. (J). (gr. 2-5). lib. bdg. 15.95 (*0-8075-7315-9*) Whitman, Albert & Co.

Metzger, Steve. Dinofours, Our Holiday Show! 2002. (J). 3.50 (*0-439-38218-1*) Scholastic, Inc.

Moore, Miriam. The Kwanzaa Contest. 1996. (Hyperion Chapters Ser.). (Illus.). 64p. (J). (gr. 4-7). pap. 3.95 (*0-7868-1122-6*) Disney Pr.

—The Kwanzaa Contest. 1996. 10.10 (*0-606-10245-0*) Turtleback Bks.

Moore, Miriam & Taylor, Penny. The Kwanzaa Contest. 1997. (Illus.). 64p. (J). lib. bdg. 14.49 (*0-7868-2336-4*) Disney Pr.

—The Kwanzaa Contest. 1996. (Illus.). 64p. (J). (gr. 3-4). 13.95 (*0-7868-0261-8*) Hyperion Bks. for Children.

St. James, Synthia. It's Kwanzaa Time: A Lift the Flap Story. 2001. (Lift-the-Flap Bks.). (Illus.). 16p. (J). pap. 5.99 (*0-689-84163-9*, Little Simon) Simon & Schuster Children's Publishing.

Walter, Mildred Pitts. Have a Happy... A Novel about Kwanzaa. 1989. (Illus.). 144p. (J). (gr. 3-6). 16.00 o.p. (*0-688-06923-1*) HarperCollins Children's Bk. Group.

—Have a Happy... A Novel about Kwanzaa. 1990. 96p. (J). (gr. 4-7). reprint ed. pap. 3.99 (*0-380-71314-4*, Avon Bks.) Morrow/Avon.

—Have a Happy... A Novel about Kwanzaa. 1990. (J). 10.14 (*0-606-04691-7*) Turtleback Bks.

L

LATIN AMERICANS—FICTION

Hughes, Monica. A Handful of Seeds. 1996. (Illus.). 32p. (J). (ps-3). pap. 15.95 (*0-531-09498-7*, Orchard Bks.) Scholastic, Inc.

Joseph, Lynn. The Color of My Words. 2000. (Illus.). 144p. (J). (gr. 3-7). 14.99 (*0-06-028232-0*, Cotler, Joanna Bks.) HarperCollins Children's Bk. Group.

Madrigal, Antonio Hernandez. Erandi's Braids. 2001. (Illus.). (J). 13.14 (*0-606-21181-0*) Turtleback Bks.

LITHUANIANS—UNITED STATES—FICTION

Ruby, Lois. Swindletop. 2000. (Illus.). 127p. (J). 15.95 (*1-57168-393-3*) Eakin Pr.

—Swindletop. 2000. E-Book 15.95 (*0-585-27649-8*) netLibrary, Inc.

M

MAORI (NEW ZEALAND PEOPLE)—FICTION

Anderson, Margaret J. Light in the Mountain. 1982. (Illus.). 192p. (J). (gr. 5-9). 9.99 o.s.i (*0-394-94791-6*); 9.95 o.s.i (*0-394-84791-1*) Random Hse. Children's Bks. (Knopf Bks. for Young Readers).

Bacon, Ron. Fish of Our Fathers. 1989. (Illus.). 36p. (J). (ps-3). 11.99 (*0-85953-301-8*) Child's Play of England GBR. *Dist:* Child's Play-International.

Ihimaera, Witi. The Whale Rider. 2003. 152p. (YA). (gr. 3-6). 17.00 (*0-15-205017-5*) Harcourt Children's Bks.

Lattimore, Deborah Nourse. Punga: The Goddess of Ugly. 1993. (Illus.). 32p. (J). (ps-3). 14.95 o.s.i (*0-15-292862-6*) Harcourt Trade Pubs.

Savage, Deborah. A Stranger Calls Me Home. 1992. 240p. (J). (gr. 4-7). 14.95 (*0-395-59424-3*) Houghton Mifflin Co.

MASAI (AFRICAN PEOPLE)—FICTION

Bothwell, Jean. African Herdboy: A Story of the Masai. 1970. (Illus.). (J). (gr. 4-6). 5.25 o.p. (*0-15-201630-9*) Harcourt Children's Bks.

Kroll, Virginia L. Masai & I. 32p. (J). (ps-2). 1997. pap. 5.99 (*0-689-80454-7*, Aladdin); 1992. (Illus.). lib. bdg. 16.00 (*0-02-751165-0*, Simon & Schuster Children's Publishing) Simon & Schuster Children's Publishing.

—Masai & I. 1997. 12.14 (*0-606-11601-X*) Turtleback Bks.

MacDonald, Susan. Nanta's Lion. 1924. (J). lib. bdg. o.s.i (*0-688-13999-X*, Morrow, William & Co.) Morrow/Avon.

—Nanta's Lion: A Search - & - Find Adventure. 1995. (Illus.). 24p. (J). (ps-3). 15.00 (*0-688-13125-5*, Morrow, William & Co.) Morrow/Avon.

Morris, Gilbert. Painted Warriors & Wild Lions - Travels in Africa. 2001. (Adventures of the Kerrigan Kids Ser.). (Illus.). 128p. (J). (gr. 3-7). pap. 5.99 (*0-8024-1578-4*) Moody Pr.

Quintana, Anton. The Baboon King. Nieuwenhuizen, John, tr. 1999. (DUT.). 192p. (YA). (gr. 7-12). 16.95 (*0-8027-8711-8*) Walker & Co.

Smith, Roland. Thunder Cave. 1997. 256p. (J). (gr. 5-9). pap. 5.95 (*0-7868-1159-5*) Disney Pr.

—Thunder Cave. (YA). (gr. 5 up). 1997. (Illus.). 272p. lib. bdg. 17.49 (*0-7868-2055-1*); 1995. 277p. 16.95 o.s.i (*0-7868-0068-2*) Hyperion Bks. for Children.

—Thunder Cave. 1997. (J). 12.00 (*0-606-11987-6*) Turtleback Bks.

MENNONITES—FICTION

Bender, Lucy E. Outside World. 1969. (Illus.). 112p. (J). (gr. 10 up). 4.95 o.p. (*0-8361-1585-6*) Herald Pr.

High, Linda Oatman. A Stone's Throw from Paradise. 1997. 143p. (YA). (gr. 5-9). pap. 5.00 (*0-8028-5142-8*, Eerdmans Bks For Young Readers) Eerdmans, William B. Publishing Co.

Hostetter, Joyce M. Best Friends Forever. 1995. (Illus.). 96p. (J). (gr. 3-5). pap. 5.95 (*0-377-00297-6*) Friendship Pr.

Jackson, Dave & Jackson, Neta. The Betrayer's Fortune: Menno Simons. 1994. (Trailblazer Bks.: Vol. 14). 144p. (J). (gr. 3-7). pap. 5.99 (*1-55661-467-5*) Bethany Hse. Pubs.

Kauffmann, Joel. The Weight. 1980. 176p. (J). pap. 5.95 o.p. (*0-8361-3335-8*) Herald Pr.

Smucker, Barbara. Selina & the Bear Paw Quilt. 1996. (Illus.). 32p. (J). (gr. 1-5). 16.00 o.s.i (*0-517-70904-X*, Crown) Crown Publishing Group.

—Selina & the Shoo-Fly Pie. 1999. (Illus.). 32p. (J). (ps-3). 15.95 (*0-7737-3018-4*) Stoddart Kids CAN. *Dist:* Fitzhenry & Whiteside, Ltd.

Sorensen, Virginia. Plain Girl. 1955. (Illus.). (J). (gr. 4-6). 6.50 o.p. (*0-15-262434-1*) Harcourt Children's Bks.

Stark, Lynette. Escape from Heart. 2000. 224p. (YA). (gr. 7-10). 17.00 o.s.i (*0-15-202385-2*) Harcourt Children's Bks.

Towell, Anne. The Hollow Locust Tree. 1998. 100p. (YA). (gr. 5-10). 16.95 o.p. (*0-88753-307-8*) Black Moss Pr. CAN. *Dist:* Firefly Bks., Ltd.

Vernon, Louise A. Beggars Bible: An Illustrated Historical Fiction of John Wycliffe. 1971. (Illus.). 128p. (J). (gr. 4-7). 7.99 (*0-8361-1732-8*) Herald Pr.

—Secret Church. 1967. (Illus.). 128p. (J). (gr. 4-7). pap. 7.99 (*0-8361-1783-2*) Herald Pr.

Vogt, Esther Loewen. A Race for Land. 1992. 112p. (J). (gr. 4-7). pap. 5.99 o.p. (*0-8361-3575-X*) Herald Pr.

Yoder, Wanda M. Ricky & the Hammond Cousins. 1996. 170p. (Orig.). (YA). (gr. 5 up). pap. 5.95 (*0-87813-562-6*) Christian Light Pubns., Inc.

MEXICAN AMERICANS—FICTION

Ada, Alma Flor. I Love Saturdays y Domingos. (gr. k-3). 2002. (Illus.). 32p. (J). 16.95 (*0-689-31819-7*, Atheneum); 1999. (SPA.). pap. 4.95 (*0-689-80591-8*, Aladdin) Simon & Schuster Children's Publishing.

Alexander Greene, Alesia. A Mural for Mamita. Lara, Susana, tr. 2001. Tr. of Mural Para Mamita. (ENG & SPA., Illus.). (J). 8.95 (*1-56123-154-1*, MFMC) Centering Corp.

Alexander, Liza. My Name Is Rosita. 1999. (Golden's Sesame Street Ser.). (Illus.). 24p. (J). (ps-k). pap. 1.79 o.s.i (*0-307-91613-8*, Golden Bks.) Random Hse. Children's Bks.

Anaya, Rudolfo A. Farolitos for Abuelo. 1999. (Illus.). 32p. (J). (gr. k-4). pap. 15.99 (*0-7868-0237-5*); lib. bdg. 16.49 (*0-7868-2186-8*) Hyperion Bks. for Children.

—The Farolitos of Christmas. 1995. (Illus.). 32p. (J). (gr. k-4). lib. bdg. 16.49 (*0-7868-2047-0*); 16.95 (*0-7868-0060-7*) Hyperion Bks. for Children.

Anzaldua, Gloria. Prietita & the Ghost Woman (Prietita y la Llorona) 1996. (ENG & SPA., Illus.). 32p. (J). (gr. 1 up). 17.50 (*0-89239-136-7*, CBP367) Children's Bk. Pr.

—Prietita & the Ghost Woman (Prietita y la Llorona) 1996. (Illus.). 32p. (J). (gr. 2-4). 19.90 (*0-516-20000-3*, Children's Pr.) Scholastic Library Publishing.

Armas, Teresa. Remembering Grandma / Recordando a Abuela. Baeza Ventura, Gabriela, tr. from ENG. 2003. (ENG & SPA., Illus.). 32p. (J). 14.95 (*1-55885-344-8*, Piñata Books) Arte Publico Pr.

Baca, Ana. Benito's Bizcochitos. Castilla, Julia Mercedes, tr. 1999. Tr. of Bizcochitos de Benito. (Illus.). (J). pap. 7.95 o.s.i (*1-55885-265-4*); 32p. 14.95 (*1-55885-264-6*, Piñata Books) Arte Publico Pr.

—Chiles for Benito/Chiles para Benito. Colin, Jose Juan, tr. 2003. (ENG & SPA., Illus.). 32p. (J). 14.95 (*1-55885-389-8*, Piñata Books) Arte Publico Pr.

Balmes, Kathy. Thunder on the Sierra. 2001. (Adventures in America Ser.). (Illus.). 96p. (J). (gr. 3-7). lib. bdg. 14.95 (*1-893110-10-9*) Silver Moon Pr.

Barron, Marietta. Two Worlds. (J). 1999. 94p. pap. 9.99 (*0-88092-120-X*, 120-X); 1994. 93p. (gr. 4-6). lib. bdg. 15.00 o.p. (*0-88092-121-8*) Royal Fireworks Publishing Co.

Bertrand, Diane Gonzales. Alicia's Treasure. 1996. 125p. (J). (gr. 3-7). 14.95 o.p. (*1-55885-085-6*); (gr. 4-7). pap. 7.95 (*1-55885-086-4*) Arte Publico Pr. (Piñata Books).

—Close to the Heart. 1991. 192p. 13.95 o.p. (*0-8034-8890-4*) Bouregy, Thomas & Co., Inc.

—The Empanadas That Abuela Made/Las Empandas Que Hacia la Abuela. Ventura, Gabriela Baeza, tr. 2003. (ENG & SPA., Illus.). 32p. (J). 14.95 (*1-55885-388-X*, Piñata Books) Arte Publico Pr.

—Family, Familia. Castilla, Julia Mercedes, tr. 1999. (Illus.). (J). (ps-3). pap. 7.95 o.s.i (*1-55885-270-0*, Piñata Books) Arte Publico Pr.

—The Last Doll (La Ultima Muneca) Balestra, Alejandra, tr. 2001. (ENG & SPA., Illus.). 32p. (J). (ps-2). 14.95 (*1-55885-290-5*) Arte Publico Pr.

—Sweet Fifteen. 1996. 296p. (YA). (gr. 6-12). pap. text 7.95 o.p. (*1-55885-184-4*) Arte Publico Pr.

—Trino's Choice. 1999. 124p. (J). (gr. 4-7). 16.95 (*1-55885-279-4*); (Illus.). (gr. 5-11). pap. 9.95 (*1-55885-268-9*) Arte Publico Pr. (Piñata Books).

—Trino's Choice. 1999. 16.00 (*0-606-17956-9*) Turtleback Bks.

—Trino's Time. 2001. (Illus.). 128p. (J). (gr. 6 up). 14.95 (*1-55885-316-2*); (gr. 7 up). pap. 9.95 (*1-55885-317-0*) Arte Publico Pr.

—Uncle Chente's Picnic. Castilla, Julia Mercedes, tr. 2001. Tr. of Picnic de Tio Chente. (ENG & SPA., Illus.). 32p. (J). (ps-3). 14.95 (*1-55885-337-5*, Piñata Books) Arte Publico Pr.

Bledsoe, Lucy Jane. Cougar Canyon. 2001. 130p. (J). (gr. 3-6). tchr. ed. 16.95 (*0-8234-1599-6*) Holiday Hse., Inc.

Brammer, Ethriam Cash. Alla en el Rancho Grande: The Rowdy, Rowdy Ranch. Cruz, D. Nina, tr. & illus. by. 2003. (ENG & SPA.). (J). (*1-55885-409-6*, Piñata Books) Arte Publico Pr.

—My Tata's Guitar / la Guitarra de Mi Tata. 2003. (ENG & SPA., Illus.). 32p. (J). 14.95 (*1-55885-369-3*, Piñata Books) Arte Publico Pr.

Bray, Marian. The Bounty Hunter. 1992. (Reba Novel Ser.: Vol. 1). 144p. (YA). pap. 5.99 o.p. (*0-310-54351-7*) Zondervan.

Bulla, Clyde Robert. The Paint Brush Kid. (Stepping Stone Bks.). (Illus.). 80p. (J). 1999. (gr. 2-4). lib. bdg. 11.99 (*0-679-99282-0*); 1998. (gr. 4-7). pap. 3.99 (*0-679-89282-6*) Random Hse. Children's Bks. (Random Hse. Bks. for Young Readers).

Bunting, Eve. A Day's Work. 2002. (Illus.). (J). 13.79 (*0-7587-2361-X*) Book Wholesalers, Inc.

—A Day's Work. 1994. (Illus.). 32p. (J). (gr. k-3). lib. bdg., tchr. ed. 16.00 (*0-395-67321-6*) Houghton Mifflin Co.

—A Day's Work. 1997. (Illus.). 32p. (J). (gr. k-3). pap. 5.95 (*0-395-84518-1*, Clarion Bks.) Houghton Mifflin Co. Trade & Reference Div.

—A Day's Work. 1997. (J). 12.10 (*0-606-11243-X*) Turtleback Bks.

—Going Home. 1998. (Trophy Picture Book Ser.). (Illus.). 32p. (J). (ps-3). pap. 6.99 (*0-06-443509-1*, Harper Trophy) HarperCollins Children's Bk. Group.

—Going Home. 1998. 13.10 (*0-606-15551-1*) Turtleback Bks.

Calhoun, Mary. Tonio's Cat. 1996. (Illus.). 32p. (YA). (gr. k up). lib. bdg. 15.93 (*0-688-13315-0*); 16.00 (*0-688-13314-2*) Morrow/Avon. (Morrow, William & Co.).

Campos, Tito. Muffler Man. Vigil-Pion, Evangelina, tr. 2001. Tr. of Hombre Mofle. (ENG & SPA., Illus.). 32p. (J). (ps-3). 14.95 (*1-55885-318-9*, Piñata Books) Arte Publico Pr.

Canales, Viola. Orange Candy Slices & Other Secret Tales. 2001. 176p. (J). pap. 9.95 (*1-55885-332-4*, Piñata Books) Arte Publico Pr.

Cano, Robin B. Lucita Regresa a Oaxaca (Lucita Comes Home to Oaxaca) Ricardez, Rafael E., tr. 1998. (ENG & SPA., Illus.). 32p. (J). (gr. 3-6). 16.95 (*1-56492-111-5*) Laredo Publishing Co., Inc.

Cano, Robin B., et al. Ramona Viaja Al Norte (North with Ramona) 1998. (Tales in Two Languages, LS Ser.). (ENG & SPA.). (J). (gr. 3-6). 16.95 (*1-56492-254-5*) Laredo Publishing Co., Inc.

Caraballo, Samuel. Estrellita Se Despide de Su Isla. Caraballo, Samuel, tr. 2002. Tr. of Estrellita Says Good-Bye to Her Island. (ENG & SPA., Illus.). 32p. (J). 14.95 (*1-55885-338-3*, Piñata Books) Arte Publico Pr.

Cazet, Denys. Born in the Gravy. 1993. (Illus.). 32p. (J). (ps-1). mass mkt. 15.99 o.p. (*0-531-08638-0*); pap. 15.95 (*0-531-05488-8*) Scholastic, Inc. (Orchard Bks.).

Ciavonne, Jean. Carlos, Light the Farolito. 1995. (Illus.). 32p. (J). (ps-3). 15.00 o.p. (*0-395-66759-3*, Clarion Bks.) Houghton Mifflin Co. Trade & Reference Div.

Colman, Hila. That's the Way It Is, Amigo. 1975. (Illus.). 96p. (J). (gr. 6 up). 11.95 (*0-690-00750-7*) HarperCollins Children's Bk. Group.

Cook, Jean Thor. Los Amiguitos' Fiesta. Wilson, Lincoln, ed. l.t. ed. 2001. Tr. of Little Friends' Fiesta. (SPA., Illus.). 28p. (J). (ps-3). 17.00 (*0-9708940-0-7*) Gently Worded Bks., LLC.

Covault, Ruth M. Pablo & Pimienta (Pablo y Pimienta) 1994. (ENG & SPA., Illus.). 32p. (J). (gr. 1-3). lib. bdg. 14.95 o.p. (*0-87358-588-7*, NP887, Rising Moon Bks. for Young Readers) Northland Publishing.

Cuyler, Margery. From Here to There, ERS. 1999. (Illus.). 32p. (J). (ps-2). 16.95 (*0-8050-3191-X*, Holt, Henry & Co. Bks. For Young Readers) Holt, Henry & Co.

—From Here to There. 1999. (Illus.). E-Book (*1-58824-612-4*); E-Book (*1-58824-598-5*); E-Book (*1-58824-572-1*) ipicturebooks, LLC.

De Anda, Diane. Kikiriki. Ventura, Gabriela Baeza, tr. 2002. (ENG & SPA.). (J). (*1-55885-382-0*, Piñata Books) Arte Publico Pr.

De la Garza, Beatriz. Pillars of Gold & Silver. 1997. 260p. (YA). (gr. 6-12). pap. 9.95 (*1-55885-206-9*, Piñata Books) Arte Publico Pr.

—Pillars of Gold & Silver. 1997. 16.00 (*0-606-16042-6*) Turtleback Bks.

Dorros, Arthur. Isla. Orig. Title: The Island. (Illus.). (ps-1). 1999. 40p. pap. 5.99 (*0-14-056505-1*, Puffin Bks.); 1995. (SPA., 48p. (J). 16.99 (*0-525-45149-8*, Dutton Children's Bks.) Penguin Putnam Bks. for Young Readers.

—Isla. 1999. Orig. Title: The Island. 13.14 (*0-606-16811-7*); 12.14 (*0-606-16810-9*) Turtleback Bks.

—La Isla. 1999. (Picture Puffins Ser.). (SPA., Illus.). 32p. (J). (gr. k-3). pap. 6.99 (*0-14-056541-8*, DT8806, Puffin Bks.) Penguin Putnam Bks. for Young Readers.

—Radio Man: Don Radio: A Story in English & Spanish. Dorros, Sandra M., tr. 1993. (ENG & SPA., Illus.). 40p. (J). (gr. 1-5). lib. bdg. 15.89 o.p. (*0-06-021548-8*) HarperCollins Children's Bk. Group.

—Radio Man: Don Radio: A Story in English & Spanish. Dorros, Sandra, tr. 1995. (ENG & SPA.). (J). (gr. 4). 9.00 (*0-395-73244-1*) Houghton Mifflin Co.

—Radio Man: Don Radio: A Story in English & Spanish. 1997. (Trophy Picture Bks.). 13.10 (*0-606-11777-6*) Turtleback Bks.

—Radio Man (Don Radio) A Story in English & Spanish. 1997. (Harper Arco Iris Ser.). (SPA., Illus.). 40p. (J). (gr. 1-5). reprint ed. pap. 6.99 (*0-06-443482-6*, Rayo) HarperTrade.

—Radio Man/Don Radio: A Story. Dorros, Sandra M., tr. 1993. (ENG & SPA., Illus.). 40p. (J). (gr. 1-5). 16.00 o.p. (*0-06-021547-X*, L-38181-00) HarperCollins Children's Bk. Group.

—When the Pigs Took Over. 2002. (Illus.). 32p. (J). (ps-2). 15.99 (*0-525-42030-4*, Dutton Children's Bks.) Penguin Putnam Bks. for Young Readers.

Dumas Lachtman, Ofelia. Call Me Consuelo. 1997. 152p. (YA). (gr. 3-7). 14.95 o.p. (*1-55885-188-7*); (Illus.). pap. 9.95 (*1-55885-187-9*) Arte Publico Pr. (Piñata Books).

Dunnahoo, Terry. This Is Espie Sanchez. 1976. (J). (gr. 4-7). 7.95 o.p. (*0-525-41130-5*, Dutton) Dutton/Plume.

—Who Needs Espie Sanchez? 1977. (J). (gr. 4-7). 7.95 o.p. (*0-525-42704-X*, Dutton) Dutton/Plume.

Elya, Susan Middleton. Home at Last. 2001. (Illus.). (J). 16.95 (*1-58430-020-5*) Lee & Low Bks., Inc.

Flores, Bettina R. Chiquita's Diary: A Hispanic Girl's Inspiring & Heroic Quest for a Better Life. Allison, Marian & Letner, Ruth, eds. 1996. (Escape Ser.: Bk. 1). (Illus.). 186p. (Orig.). (YA). (gr. 7-12). pap., tchr. ed. 13.50 (*0-9625777-7-4*) Pepper Vine Pr.

Freschet, Gina. Beto Goes Bump in the Night, RS. 2001. (Illus.). 32p. (J). (gr. k-3). 16.00 (*0-374-31720-8*, Farrar, Straus & Giroux (BYR)) Farrar, Straus & Giroux.

Galindo, Mary Sue & Howard, Pauline Rodriguez. Icy Watermelon. 2000. Tr. of Sandia Fria. (ENG & SPA., Illus.). 32p. (J). (ps-2). 14.95 (*1-55885-306-5*, Piñata Books) Arte Publico Pr.

Gonzales Bertrand, Diane. Family, Familia. Castilla, Julia Mercedes, tr. 1999. (SPA., Illus.). 32p. (J). (ps-3). 14.95 (*1-55885-269-7*, Piñata Books) Arte Publico Pr.

—Sip, Slurp, Soup, Soup. 1997. (SPA., Illus.). 32p. (J). (ps-2). 14.95 (*1-55885-183-6*, Piñata Books) Arte Publico Pr.

Gonzales Bertrand, Diane, et al. Close to the Heart. 2001. (Illus.). 144p. (J). pap. 9.95 (*1-55885-319-7*, Piñata Books) Arte Publico Pr.

Gonzalez, Catherine T. Chacho & Ellie Sanchez, Citizens. 1998. 96p. (J). (gr. 4). 13.95 (*1-57168-114-0*) Eakin Pr.

Gonzalez Jensen, Margarita. And Then It Was Sugar. 1997. (Illus.). (*0-7802-8318-X*) Wright Group, The.

Gonzalez, Maya Christina, tr. & illus. Nana's Chicken Coop Surprise: Nana, Que Sorpresa! 2004. (ENG & SPA.). (J). (*0-89239-190-1*) Children's Bk. Pr.

Grattan-Dominguez, Alejandro. Breaking Even. 1997. 250p. (YA). (gr. 9 up). pap. 11.95 (*1-55885-213-1*) Arte Publico Pr.

Harper, Jo. Delfino's Journey. 2000. viii, 184p. (J). (gr. 8-12). 15.95 (*0-89672-437-9*) Texas Tech Univ. Pr.

—Delfino's Journey, Grades 8-12. 2000. (Illus.). viii, 184p. (J). tchr. ed. 5.95 (*0-89672-442-5*) Texas Tech Univ. Pr.

Haslam, Gerald W. & Haslam, Janice E. Manuel & the Madman. 2000. viii, 206p. (J). pap. 9.95 (*0-915685-11-6*) Devil Mountain Bks.

Havill, Juanita. Treasure Map. 1992. (Illus.). 32p. (J). (ps-3). lib. bdg., tchr. ed. 16.00 (*0-395-57817-5*) Houghton Mifflin Co.

Head, Judith. Mud Soup. 2003. (Illus.). 48p. (J). (gr. 1-3). pap. 3.99 (*0-375-81087-0*); lib. bdg. 11.99 (*0-375-91087-5*) Random Hse. Children's Bks. (Random Hse. Bks. for Young Readers).

Hernandez, Irene B. The Secret of Two Brothers. 1995. 182p. (YA). (gr. 7-12). pap. 9.95 (*1-55885-142-9*, Piñata Books) Arte Publico Pr.

—The Secret of Two Brothers. 1995. 16.00 (*0-606-16039-6*) Turtleback Bks.

Hernandez, Jo Ann Y. White Bread Competition. 1997. 208p. (YA). (gr. 6-12). pap. 9.95 (*1-55885-210-7*, Piñata Books) Arte Publico Pr.

Herrera, Juan F. Crashboomlove: A Novel in Verse. 1999. 176p. 18.95 (*0-8263-2113-5*); (gr. 8-12). pap. 11.95 (*0-8263-2114-3*) Univ. of New Mexico Pr.

Herrera, Juan Felipe. Crashboomlove: A Novel in Verse. 2000. 17.00 (*0-606-19432-0*) Turtleback Bks.

—Grandma & Me at the Flea / Los Meros Meros Remateros. Rohmer, Harriet & Cumpiano, Ina, eds. 2002. Tr. of Los Meros Meros Remateros. (ENG & SPA., Illus.). 32p. (J). (gr. 1 up). 15.95 (*0-89239-171-5*) Children's Bk. Pr.

—Super Cilantro Girl / la Supernina Del Cilantro. 2003. Tr. of Supernina Del Cilantro. (ENG & SPA., Illus.). 32p. (J). 16.95 (*0-89239-187-1*) Children's Bk. Pr.

Jimenez, Francisco. Cajas de Carton: The Circuit Spanish Edition. 2002. (SPA., Illus.). 208p. (J). (gr. 5 up). pap. 6.95 (*0-618-22616-8*) Houghton Mifflin Co.

—Senderos Fronterizos: Breaking Through Spanish Edition. 2002. (SPA., Illus.). 208p. (J). tchr. ed. 15.00 (*0-618-22617-6*); (gr. 5 up). pap. 6.95 (*0-618-22618-4*) Houghton Mifflin Co.

Jimenez, Francisco, ed. Cajas de Carton: The Circuit Spanish Edition. 2002. (SPA., Illus.). 208p. (J). (gr. 5). tchr. ed. 15.00 (*0-618-22615-X*) Houghton Mifflin Co.

Jiménez, Francisco. Breaking Through: A Migrant Child's Journey from the Fields. 2001. (Illus.). 208p. (YA). (gr. 7 up). tchr. ed. 15.00 (*0-618-01173-0*) Houghton Mifflin Co.

—The Christmas Gift. 2000. Tr. of Regalo de Navidad. (ENG & SPA., Illus.). 32p. (J). (ps-3). lib. bdg., tchr. ed. 15.00 (*0-395-92869-9*) Houghton Mifflin Co. Trade & Reference Div.

—La Mariposa. (SPA., Illus.). 40p. (J). 2000. (gr. 3-5). pap. 5.95 (*0-618-07036-2*, HM3550); 1998. (ps-3). lib. bdg., tchr. ed. 16.00 (*0-395-81663-7*) Houghton Mifflin Co.

—La Mariposa. 2000. (SPA., Illus.). 40p. (J). (ps-3). pap. 5.95 (*0-618-07317-5*) Houghton Mifflin Co. Trade & Reference Div.

Johnson, Dorothy T. One Day, Mother/Un Dia, Madre. 1996. (ENG & SPA.). (Orig.). (J). (gr. 1-6). pap. 6.95 o.p. (*0-533-11716-X*) Vantage Pr., Inc.

Johnston, Tony. Angel City. 2002. (Illus.). (J). (*0-399-23405-5*, Philomel) Penguin Putnam Bks. for Young Readers.

—Any Small Goodness: A Novel of the Barrio. 128p. (J). 2003. mass mkt. 4.99 (*0-439-23384-4*, Scholastic Paperbacks); 2001. (Illus.). (gr. 4 up). pap. 15.95 (*0-439-18936-5*, Blue Sky Pr., The) Scholastic, Inc.

—Uncle Rain Cloud. 2001. (Illus.). 32p. (J). (gr. k-4). 15.95 (*0-88106-371-1*) Charlesbridge Publishing, Inc.

Johnston, Tony & Vanden Broeck, Fabrizio. Uncle Rain Cloud. 2003. pap. 6.95 (*0-88106-372-X*) Charlesbridge Publishing, Inc.

Krumgold, Joseph. And Now Miguel. 1990. (Literature Experience 1991 Ser.). (J). (gr. 6). pap. 11.04 (*0-395-55172-2*) Houghton Mifflin Co.

Lachtman, Ofelia Dumas. Big Enough (Bastante Grande) Canetti, Yanitzia, tr. 1998. (ENG & SPA., Illus.). 32p. (J). (ps-2). 14.95 (*1-55885-221-2*, Piñata Books) Arte Publico Pr.

—Pepita Thinks Pink (Pepita y el Color Rosado) 1998. (ENG & SPA., Illus.). 32p. (J). (ps-2). 14.95 (*1-55885-222-0*, Piñata Books) Arte Publico Pr.

Lachtman, Ofellia Dumas. The Summer of El Pintor. 2001. (Illus.). 234p. (J). (gr. 11 up). pap. 9.95 (*1-55885-327-8*) Arte Publico Pr.

Lee, Marie G. Night of the Chupacabras. (gr. 3-7). 1999. 128p. pap. 3.99 (*0-380-79773-9*); 1998. 144p. (J). 14.00 o.p. (*0-380-97706-0*) Morrow/Avon. (Avon Bks.).

—Night of the Chupacabras. 1999. 10.04 (*0-606-17336-6*) Turtleback Bks.

Levene, Nancy S. Hero for a Season. Reck, Sue, ed. 1994. (T. J. Book Ser.: Vol. 4). (Illus.). 96p. (J). (gr. 2-5). pap. 4.99 (*0-7814-0702-8*) Cook Communications Ministries.

Levy, Janice. Abuelito Eats with His Fingers. 1998. (Illus.). 32p. (J). 14.95 (*1-57168-177-9*) Eakin Pr.

Lopez, Loretta. The Birthday Swap. (Illus.). 32p. (J). (gr. k-3). 1999. pap. 6.95 (*1-880000-89-X*); 1997. 15.95 (*1-880000-47-4*) Lee & Low Bks., Inc.

—The Birthday Swap. 1997. 13.10 (*0-606-17378-1*) Turtleback Bks.

—Que Sorpresa de Cumpleanos. 1997. Tr. of Birthday Swap. 13.10 (*0-606-12795-X*) Turtleback Bks.

—Que Sorpresa de Cumpleanos! 1997. (SPA., Illus.). 32p. (J). (ps-3). 15.95 (*1-880000-55-5*, LW6614) Lee & Low Bks., Inc.

Lopez, Loretta & Lee, Hector Viveros. Que Sorpresa de Cumpleanos! 1997. (SPA., Illus.). 32p. (J). (ps-3). pap. 6.95 (*1-880000-56-3*, LW6611) Lee & Low Bks., Inc.

Luenn, Nancy. A Gift for Abuelita: Celebrating the Day of the Dead. 1998. Tr. of Un Regalo para Abuelita: En Celebration del Dia de los Muertos. (ENG & SPA., Illus.). 32p. (J). (gr. k-3). 15.95 (*0-87358-688-3*, Rising Moon Bks. for Young Readers) Northland Publishing.

Madison, Winifred. Maria Luisa. 1971. 192p. (J). (gr. 4-9). lib. bdg. 9.89 o.p. (*0-397-31280-6*) HarperCollins Children's Bk. Group.

Makris, Kathryn. The Wrong Love. 1986. 176p. (Orig.). (J). (gr. 7 up). pap. 2.25 o.p. (*0-590-33931-1*) Scholastic, Inc.

Marquez, Pablo. Benito's Treasure Hunt. 2000. (J). pap. 7.00 (*0-533-13567-2*) Vantage Pr., Inc.

Marsden, Carolyn. Mama Had to Work on Christmas. 2003. (Illus.). 80p. (J). (gr. 2-5). 14.99 (*0-670-03635-8*, Viking) Viking Penguin.

Martin, Patricia. The Bellringer of San Agustin. Armas, Linda M., ed. 1980. (Illus.). 20p. (J). (gr. k-6). pap. 3.50 o.p. (*0-918358-12-4*) Pajarito Pubns.

Martinez, Victor. Parrot in the Oven. 1998. 224p. (gr. 7 up). (Illus.). (J). pap. 5.99 (*0-06-447186-1*, Harper Trophy); audio 16.95 (*0-694-70093-2*) HarperCollins Children's Bk. Group.

—Parrot in the Oven: Mi Vida: A Novel. 1996. (Joanna Cotler Bks.). (Illus.). 224p. (J). (gr. 7 up). 16.99 (*0-06-026704-6*); lib. bdg. 16.89 (*0-06-026706-2*) HarperCollins Children's Bk. Group. (Cotler, Joanna Bks.).

—Parrot in the Oven: Mi Vida: A Novel. 1998. 12.00 (*0-606-13695-9*) Turtleback Bks.

Martini, Teri. Feliz Navidad, Pablo. 1990. (Illus.). (J). (gr. 4 up). pap. 2.95 o.p. (*0-8091-6597-X*) Paulist Pr.

Marvin, Isabel R. Josefina & the Hanging Tree. 1992. (Chaparral Book Ser.). 128p. (YA). (gr. 7 up). pap. 9.95 (*0-87565-103-8*) Texas Christian Univ. Pr.

McGinley, Jerry. Joaquin Strikes Back. 1998. 158p. (YA). (gr. 5-10). 18.95 (*0-936389-58-3*) Tudor Pubs., Inc.

Medina, Jane. My Name Is Jorge: On Both Sides of the River. 2003. (ENG & SPA., Illus.). 48p. (J). (gr. 2-5). 15.95 (*1-56397-811-3*) Boyds Mills Pr.

Mora, Pat. The Bakery Lady. Mora, Pat & Ventura, Gabriela Baeza, trs. 2001. Tr. of Se?Ora de la Panaderia. (ENG & SPA., Illus.). 32p. (J). (ps-3). 14.95 (*1-55885-343-X*, Piñata Books) Arte Publico Pr.

—A Birthday Basket for Tia. 1998. (J). pap. 4.99 (*0-87628-395-4*) Ctr. for Applied Research in Education, The.

—A Birthday Basket for Tia. (Aladdin Picture Bks.). (Illus.). 32p. (J). (ps-1). 1997. pap. 5.99 (*0-689-81328-7*, Aladdin); 1997. (SPA., mass mkt. 5.99 (*0-689-81325-2*, Aladdin); 1992. 16.00 (*0-02-767400-2*, Simon & Schuster Children's Publishing) Simon & Schuster Children's Publishing.

—A Birthday Basket for Tia. 1997. (Aladdin Picture Bks.). 12.14 (*0-606-11133-6*) Turtleback Bks.

—Maria Paints the Hills. 2002. (J). 19.95 o.p. (*0-89013-401-4*); pap. 9.95 (*0-89013-410-3*) Museum of New Mexico Pr.

—The Rainbow Tulip. (Illus.). 32p. (J). 2003. pap. 6.99 (*0-14-250009-7*, Puffin Bks.); 1999. 16.99 (*0-670-87291-1*) Penguin Putnam Bks. for Young Readers.

—Tomas & the Library Lady. 2000. (Illus.). 32p. (gr. k-3). pap. 6.99 (*0-375-80349-1*) Knopf, Alfred A. Inc.

—Tomas & the Library Lady. 1997. (Illus.). 40p. (ps-3). (J). 17.00 (*0-679-80401-3*); lib. bdg. 18.99 (*0-679-90401-8*) Random Hse., Inc.

—Tomas & the Library Lady. 2000. 13.14 (*0-606-18093-1*) Turtleback Bks.

—Tomas y la Senora de la Biblioteca. ed. 2000. (J). (gr. 1). spiral bd. (*0-616-03092-4*) Canadian National Institute for the Blind/Institut National Canadien pour les Aveugles.

—Tomas y la Senora de la Biblioteca. 1997. (SPA., Illus.). 40p. (J). (gr. 1-3). pap. 7.99 (*0-679-84173-3*); (ps-3). 18.99 o.s.i (*0-679-94173-8*) Random Hse. Children's Bks. (Knopf Bks. for Young Readers).

—Tomas y la Senora de la Biblioteca/Tomas & the Library Lady. 1997. (J). 14.14 (*0-606-11996-5*) Turtleback Bks.

Myers, Anna. Stolen by the Sea. 2001. 160p. (J). (gr. 3-7). 16.95 (*0-8027-8787-8*) Walker & Co.

Ogan, Margaret & Ogan, George. Tennis Bum. 1976. (Hiway Book). (J). 6.95 o.p. (*0-664-32593-9*) Westminster John Knox Pr.

Ortega, Cristina. Los Ojos del Tejedor: Through the Eyes of the Weaver. 1997. (Illus.). 64p. (YA). (gr. 4-7). pap. 14.95 (*0-940666-81-2*) Clear Light Pubs.

Paley, Nina, illus. Inside-Out Feelings. 1993. (Contemporary Health Ser.). (J). 3.00 (*1-56071-315-1*) ETR Assocs.

Perez, Amada Irma. My Diary from Here to There / Mi Diario de Aqui Hasta Alla. 2002. Tr. of Mi Diario de Aqui Hasta Alla. (ENG & SPA., Illus.). 32p. (J). (gr. 2-5). 16.95 (*0-89239-175-8*) Children's Bk. Pr.

—My Very Own Room (Mi Propio Cuartito) 2000. (ENG & SPA., Illus.). 32p. (J). (gr. 1 up). 15.95 (*0-89239-164-2*) Children's Bk. Pr.

Perez, L. King. First Day in Grapes. 2002. (Illus.). 32p. (J). (gr. 1-3). 16.95 (*1-58430-045-0*) Lee & Low Bks., Inc.

—Ghoststalking. 1994. (Middle Grade Fiction Ser.). (Illus.). 48p. (J). (ps-3). lib. bdg. 19.93 (*0-87614-821-6*, Carolrhoda Bks.) Lerner Publishing Group.

Podoshen, Lois. Paco's Garden. 1999. (Books for Young Learners). (Illus.). 12p. (J). (gr. k-2). pap. text 5.00 (*1-57274-235-6*) Owen, Richard C. Pubs., Inc.

Politi, Leo. Three Stalks of Corn. 1994. (Illus.). 32p. (J). (gr. k-3). reprint ed. pap. 4.95 o.s.i (*0-689-71782-2*, Aladdin) Simon & Schuster Children's Publishing.

Rice, David L. Crazy Loco: Stories about Growing up Chicano in Southern Texas. 2001. (Illus.). 160p. (J). (gr. 7 up). 16.99 (*0-8037-2598-1*, Dial Bks. for Young Readers) Penguin Putnam Bks. for Young Readers.

Rodriguez, Luis J. America Is Her Name. 2004. (Illus.). 32p. (J). (gr. 4-7). 15.95 (*1-880684-40-3*) Curbstone Pr.

—La Llaman America. Villanueva, Tino, tr. 2004. (SPA., Illus.). 32p. (J). (gr. 4-7). 15.95 (*1-880684-41-1*) Curbstone Pr.

Romeyn, Debra. Juan & Mariano #1: Passage to Monterey. May, Dan, tr. & illus. by. 2003. 39p. (J). pap. 9.95 (*0-9729016-0-4*) Gossamer Bks.

Rosa-Casanova, Sylvia. Mama Provi & the Pot of Rice. 2001. (Illus.). 32p. (ps-3). pap. 5.99 (*0-689-84249-X*, Aladdin) Simon & Schuster Children's Publishing.

Ryan, Pam Muñoz. Esperanza Renace. 2002. (SPA., Illus.). 272p. (YA). (gr. 4-9). pap. 4.99 (*0-439-39885-1*, Scholastic en Espanola) Scholastic, Inc.

—Esperanza Rising. (Illus.). (gr. 4-9). 2002. 272p. (YA). mass mkt. 4.99 (*0-439-12042-X*); 2000. 262p. (J). pap. 15.95 (*0-439-12041-1*, Scholastic Pr.) Scholastic, Inc.

Sachs, Marilyn. Ghosts in the Family. 1995. 176p. (J). (gr. 3-6). 15.99 o.s.i (*0-525-45421-7*, Dutton Children's Bks.) Penguin Putnam Bks. for Young Readers.

Saenz, Benjamin Alire. A Gift from Papa Diego (Un Regalo de Papa Diego) 2004. (ENG & SPA., Illus.). 40p. (J). (gr. k-7). pap. 10.95 (*0-938317-33-4*) Cinco Puntos Pr.

Ethnic Groups

Sagel, Jim. Always the Heart. 1998. (Red Crane Literature Ser.).Tr. of Siempre el Corazon. (ENG & SPA., Illus.). 168p. (YA). (gr. 8-12). pap. 12.95 (*1-878610-68-6*) Red Crane Bks., Inc.

—Garden of Stories: Jardin de Cuentos. 1996. (Bilingual Ser.).Tr. of Jardin de Cuentos. (SPA., Illus.). 112p. (YA). (gr. 7 up). pap. 12.95 (*1-878610-55-4*) Red Crane Bks., Inc.

Saldana, Rene, Jr. Finding Our Way. 2003. 128p. (J). (gr. 7). 15.95 (*0-385-73051-9*, Delacorte Pr.) Dell Publishing.

—Finding Our Way. 2003. 128p. (YA). (gr. 7-12). lib. bdg. 17.99 (*0-385-90077-5*, Lamb, Wendy) Random Hse. Children's Bks.

—The Jumping Tree. 2002. (Illus.). 192p. (YA). (gr. 5). mass mkt. 5.50 (*0-440-22881-6*, Laurel Leaf) Random Hse. Children's Bks.

—The Jumping Tree: A Novel. 2001. (Illus.). 192p. (YA). (gr. 5-9). 14.95 (*0-385-32725-0*, Delacorte Bks. for Young Readers) Random Hse. Children's Bks.

Sandin, Joan. Coyote School News, ERS. 2003. (Illus.). 48p. (J). 17.95 (*0-8050-6558-X*, Holt, Henry & Co. Bks. For Young Readers) Holt, Henry & Co.

Sandoval, Victor. Roll over, Big Toben. 2003. 160p. (J). pap. 9.95 (*1-55885-401-0*, Piñata Books) Arte Publico Pr.

Santana, Patricia. Motorcycle Ride on the Sea of Tranquillity. 2002. 276p. (YA). 19.95 (*0-8263-2435-5*) Univ. of New Mexico Pr.

Schraff, Anne. Under My Sombrero. 1999. (Books for Young Learners). (Illus.). 12p. (J). (gr. k-2). pap. 5.00 o.s.i (*1-57274-152-X*, 2827) Owen, Richard C. Pubs., Inc.

Schreck, Karen Halvorsen. Lucy's Family Tree. 2001. (Illus.). 40p. (J). (gr. 1-5). text 16.95 (*0-88448-225-1*, Harpswell Pr.) Tilbury Hse. Pubs.

Sito, Gary. Big Bushy Mustache. 1998. (Illus.). 32p. (J). (gr. k-3). 18.99 o.s.i (*0-679-98030-X*) Random Hse., Inc.

Soto, Gary. The Afterlife: A Novel. 2003. 176p. (J). (gr. 6 up). 16.00 (*0-15-204774-3*, 53597422) Harcourt Children's Bks.

—Baseball in April & Other Stories. 1998. (SPA., Illus.). 149p. (ps up). 14.30 (*968-16-4838-2*) Fondo de Cultura Economica USA.

—Baseball in April & Other Stories. (YA). 1991. (SPA.). 125p. (gr. 5 up). pap. 6.00 o.p. (*0-15-205721-8*, Odyssey Classics); 1990. 128p. (gr. 5 up). 16.00 o.s.i (*0-15-205720-X*); 10th anniv. ed. 2000. (SPA.). 128p. (gr. 3-7). 16.00 (*0-15-202573-1*); 10th anniv. ed. 2000. (Illus.). 128p. (gr. 3-7). pap. 6.00 (*0-15-202567-7*, Harcourt Paperbacks) Harcourt Children's Bks.

—Baseball in April & Other Stories. 1990. (J). 12.05 (*0-606-00300-2*) Turtleback Bks.

—Big Bushy Mustache. 1998. (Illus.). 32p. (J). (gr. k-3). 17.00 o.s.i (*0-679-88030-5*) Random Hse., Inc.

—Boys at Work. 1996. (Illus.). 144p. (gr. 3-7). pap. text 3.99 o.s.i (*0-440-41221-8*, Yearling); 1995. (J). 19.95 (*0-385-44634-9*, Dell Books for Young Readers) Random Hse. Children's Bks.

—Boys at Work. 1996. (J). 9.09 o.p. (*0-606-09102-5*) Turtleback Bks.

—Buried Onions. 1997. 160p. (YA). (gr. 7-12). 17.00 (*0-15-201333-4*) Harcourt Children's Bks.

—Buried Onions. 10th ed. 1999. (Ageless Bks.). 160p. (J). (gr. 7-10). pap. 11.00 (*0-06-440771-3*, Harper Trophy) HarperCollins Children's Bk. Group.

—The Cat's Meow. 1995. (Illus.). 80p. (J). (gr. 4-7). pap. 13.95 (*0-590-47001-9*) Scholastic, Inc.

—Chato & the Party Animals. 2000. (Illus.). 32p. (J). (ps-3). 15.99 (*0-399-23159-5*, G. P. Putnam's Sons) Penguin Group (USA) Inc.

—Chato & the Party Animals. 2004. (Illus.). 32p. (J). 6.99 (*0-14-240032-7*, Puffin Bks.) Penguin Putnam Bks. for Young Readers.

—Chato y Su Cena. Ada, Alma Flor, tr. 1998. (SPA., Illus.). (gr. k-3). pap., tchr. ed. 37.95 incl. audio (*0-87499-439-X*); (J). pap. 15.95 incl. audio (*0-87499-437-3*) Live Oak Media.

—If the Shoe Fits. 2002. (Illus.). 32p. (J). (gr. 4-8). 15.99 (*0-399-23420-9*) Penguin Group (USA) Inc.

—Jesse. 1994. 176p. (YA). (gr. 7 up). 17.00 (*0-15-240239-X*) Harcourt Children's Bks.

—Jesse, unabr. ed. 2000. (YA). pap. 42.24 incl. audio (*0-7887-3188-2*, 40923X4) Recorded Bks., LLC.

—Jesse. 1996. 160p. (YA). (gr. 7 up). pap. 4.99 (*0-590-52837-8*) Scholastic, Inc.

—Jesse. 1996. 11.04 (*0-606-09489-X*) Turtleback Bks.

—Local News. 1993. 144p. (J). (gr. 7-12). 14.00 (*0-15-248117-6*) Harcourt Trade Pubs.

—Local News. 1994. (Point Signature Ser.). 160p. (YA). (gr. 7 up). mass mkt. 4.99 (*0-590-48446-X*) Scholastic, Inc.

—Local News: A Collection of Stories. 1993. (Point Signature Ser.). 11.04 (*0-606-06545-8*) Turtleback Bks.

—The Mustache. 1995. (Illus.). (J). 14.95 (*0-399-22617-6*, G. P. Putnam's Sons) Penguin Group (USA) Inc.

—My Little Car. 2015. Tr. of Mi Carrito. (J). 15.95 (*0-399-23220-6*) Penguin Group (USA) Inc.

—Off & Running. 1996. (Illus.). 144p. (gr. 4-7). text 15.95 o.s.i (*0-385-32181-3*, Delacorte Pr.) Dell Publishing.

—Off & Running. 1997. (Illus.). 144p. (gr. 3-7). pap. text 4.50 o.s.i (*0-440-41432-6*, Dell Books for Young Readers) Random Hse. Children's Bks.

—Off & Running. 1997. 9.60 (*0-606-13673-8*) Turtleback Bks.

—Pacific Crossing. 1992. 144p. (YA). (gr. 4-7). 17.00 (*0-15-259187-7*) Harcourt Children's Bks.

—The Pool Party. 1993. (Illus.). 112p. (J). 13.95 (*0-385-30890-6*, Delacorte Pr.) Dell Publishing.

—Que Monton de Tamales! 1996. (SPA., Illus.). 32p. (J). (ps-3). pap. 6.99 (*0-698-11413-2*, PaperStar) Penguin Putnam Bks. for Young Readers.

—The Skirt. 1996. (J). pap. 4.50 (*0-440-91096-X*, Dell Books for Young Readers) Random Hse. Children's Bks.

—Snapshots from the Wedding. 1997. (Illus.). 32p. (J). (ps-3). 15.99 o.p. (*0-399-22808-X*) Penguin Group (USA) Inc.

—Snapshots from the Wedding. 1998. (Illus.). 32p. (J). (ps-3). pap. 5.99 (*0-698-11752-2*, PaperStar) Penguin Putnam Bks. for Young Readers.

—Snapshots from the Wedding. 1998. 12.14 (*0-606-15961-4*) Turtleback Bks.

—Summer on Wheels. 1995. 176p. (J). (gr. 4-6). pap. 13.95 (*0-590-48365-X*) Scholastic, Inc.

—Taking Sides. 2000. (YA). pap., stu. ed. 45.25 incl. audio (*0-7887-3656-6*, 41022X4) Recorded Bks., LLC.

—Too Many Tamales. 1993. (Illus.). 32p. (J). (ps-3). 16.99 (*0-399-22146-8*, G. P. Putnam's Sons) Penguin Putnam Bks. for Young Readers.

Spurr, Elizabeth. Lupe & Me. 1995. (Illus.). 40p. (J). (gr. 4-7). 13.00 (*0-15-200522-6*, Red Wagon Bks.) Harcourt Children's Bks.

—Mama's Birthday Surprise. 1996. (Hyperion Chapters Ser.). (Illus.). 64p. (J). (gr. 1-4). pap. 3.95 (*0-7868-1124-2*) Disney Pr.

—Mama's Birthday Surprise. 1996. (Hyperion Chapters Ser.). (Illus.). 64p. (J). (gr. 4-7). 13.95 o.s.i (*0-7868-0265-0*) Hyperion Bks. for Children.

Stanley, Diane. Elena. 1996. 64p. (J). (gr. 3-7). 13.95 (*0-7868-0256-1*); lib. bdg. 14.49 (*0-7868-2211-2*) Hyperion Bks. for Children.

Stites, Clara. Rosalba of Santa Juanita: A California Story. 2002. (Illus.). 80p. (J). pap. 8.95 (*1-56474-394-2*) Fithian Pr.

Summers, James L. You Can't Make It by Bus. 1969. (J). (gr. 7 up). 3.95 o.p. (*0-664-32450-9*) Westminster John Knox Pr.

Talbert, Marc. Star of Luis. 1999. 192p. (J). (gr. 5-9). tchr. ed. 15.00 (*0-395-91423-X*, Clarion Bks.) Houghton Mifflin Co. Trade & Reference Div.

—A Sunburned Prayer. 112p. (J). 1997. (gr. 5-9). pap. 4.50 (*0-689-81326-0*, Aladdin); 1995. (gr. 4-7). mass mkt. 14.00 o.s.i (*0-689-80125-4*, Simon & Schuster Children's Publishing) Simon & Schuster Children's Publishing.

—A Sunburned Prayer. 1997. 10.55 (*0-606-11938-8*) Turtleback Bks.

Taylor, Theodore. Maria. 1993. 80p. (J). (gr. 4-7). pap. 3.99 o.s.i (*0-380-72120-1*, Avon Bks.) Morrow/Avon.

—Maria: A Christmas Story. abr. ed. 1992. (Illus.). 96p. (J). (gr. 4-7). 15.00 o.s.i (*0-15-217763-9*) Harcourt Children's Bks.

—Maria: A Christmas Story. 1993. (J). 10.14 (*0-606-05452-9*) Turtleback Bks.

Thomas, Jane Resh. Lights on the River. 1994. (Illus.). 32p. (J). (ps-3). 15.95 (*0-7868-0004-6*); lib. bdg. 16.49 (*0-7868-2003-9*) Hyperion Bks. for Children.

—Lights on the River. 1996. (Illus.). 32p. (J). (ps-3). pap. 4.95 o.p. (*0-7868-1132-3*) Hyperion Paperbacks for Children.

Tripp, Valerie. Again, Josefina! 2000. (American Girls Short Stories Ser.). (Illus.). 56p. (YA). (gr. 2 up). 3.95 (*1-58485-032-9*, American Girl) Pleasant Co. Pubns.

—Asi es Josefina: Una Nina Americana. 1998. (American Girls Collection: Bk. 1). (SPA.). 432p. (J). (gr. 2 up). pap. 34.95 (*1-56247-706-4*) Pleasant Co. Pubns.

—Asi es Josefina: Una Nina Americana. Moreno, Jose, tr. 1997. (American Girls Collection: Bk. 1). (SPA., Illus.). 96p. (J). (gr. 2 up). pap. 5.95 (*1-56247-496-0*, PE6901, American Girl) Pleasant Co. Pubns.

—Asi es Josefina: Una Nina Americana. 1997. (American Girls Collection: Bk. 1). (SPA., Illus.). (YA). (gr. 2 up). 12.10 (*0-606-11060-7*) Turtleback Bks.

—Cambios para Josefina: Un Cuento de Invierno. 1998. (American Girls Collection: Bk. 6). (SPA., Illus.). 80p. (J). (gr. 2 up). pap. 5.95 (*1-56247-595-9*, BT5959, American Girl) Pleasant Co. Pubns.

—Changes for Josefina: A Winter Story. 1998. (American Girls Collection: Bk. 6). (Illus.). 80p. (J). (gr. 2 up). 12.95 (*1-56247-592-4*); pap. 5.95 (*1-56247-591-6*) Pleasant Co. Pubns. (American Girl).

—Changes for Josefina: A Winter Story. 1998. (American Girls Collection: Bk. 6). (Illus.). (YA). (gr. 2 up). 12.10 (*0-606-13264-3*) Turtleback Bks.

—Feliz Cumpleanos, Josefina! Un Cuento de Primavera. 1998. (American Girls Collection: Bk. 4). (SPA., Illus.). 80p. (J). (gr. 2 up). pap. 5.95 (*1-56247-593-2*, BT5932, American Girl) Pleasant Co. Pubns.

—Happy Birthday, Josefina! A Springtime Story. 1998. (American Girls Collection: Bk. 4). (Illus.). 80p. (J). (gr. 2 up). 12.95 (*1-56247-588-6*); pap. 5.95 (*1-56247-587-8*) Pleasant Co. Pubns. (American Girl).

—Happy Birthday, Josefina! A Springtime Story. 1998. (American Girls Collection: Bk. 4). (Illus.). (YA). (gr. 2 up). 12.10 (*0-606-13381-X*); 12.10 (*0-606-13456-5*) Turtleback Bks.

—Josefina Aprende une Leccion: Un Cuento de la Escuela. Moreno, Jose, tr. 1997. (American Girls Collection: Bk. 2). (SPA., Illus.). 80p. (J). (gr. 2 up). pap. 5.95 (*1-56247-497-9*, BT4979, American Girl) Pleasant Co. Pubns.

—Josefina Entra en Accion: Un Cuento de Verano. Morano, Jose, tr. 1998. (American Girls Collection: Bk. 5). (SPA., Illus.). 80p. (J). (gr. 2 up). pap. 5.95 (*1-56247-594-0*, BT5940, American Girl) Pleasant Co. Pubns.

—Josefina Entra en Accion: Un Cuento de Verano. 1998. (American Girls Collection: Bk. 5). (SPA., Illus.). (YA). (gr. 2 up). 12.10 (*0-606-13540-5*) Turtleback Bks.

—Josefina Learns a Lesson: A School Story. 1997. (American Girls Collection: Bk. 2). (Illus.). 80p. (J). (gr. 2 up). pap. 5.95 (*1-56247-517-7*); lib. bdg. 12.95 (*1-56247-518-5*) Pleasant Co. Pubns. (American Girl).

—Josefina Learns a Lesson: A School Story. 1997. (American Girls Collection: Bk. 2). (Illus.). (YA). (gr. 2 up). 12.10 (*0-606-11524-2*) Turtleback Bks.

—Josefina Saves the Day: A Summer Story. 1998. (American Girls Collection: Bk. 5). (Illus.). 80p. (J). (gr. 2 up). 12.95 (*1-56247-590-8*); pap. 5.95 (*1-56247-589-4*) Pleasant Co. Pubns. (American Girl).

—Josefina Saves the Day: A Summer Story. 1998. (American Girls Collection: Bk. 5). (Illus.). (YA). (gr. 2 up). 12.10 (*0-606-13541-3*) Turtleback Bks.

—Josefina's Short Story Set: A Reward for Josefina; Again, Josefina!; Just Josefina, 3 vols. 2002. (American Girls Short Stories Ser.). (Illus.). (YA). (gr. 2). 11.95 (*1-58485-495-2*, American Girl) Pleasant Co. Pubns.

—Josefina's Song. 2001. (American Girls Short Stories Ser.). (Illus.). 56p. (YA). (gr. 2 up). 3.95 (*1-58485-272-0*, American Girl) Pleasant Co. Pubns.

—Josefina's Story Collection. 2001. (American Girls Collection). (Illus.). 406p. (J). (gr. 2 up). 29.95 (*1-58485-442-1*, American Girl) Pleasant Co. Pubns.

—Josefina's Surprise: A Christmas Story. 1997. (American Girls Collection: Bk. 3). (Illus.). 80p. (J). (gr. 2 up). pap. 5.95 (*1-56247-519-3*); lib. bdg. 12.95 (*1-56247-520-7*) Pleasant Co. Pubns. (American Girl).

—Josefina's Surprise: A Christmas Story. 1997. (American Girls Collection: Bk. 3). (Illus.). (YA). (gr. 2 up). 12.10 (*0-606-11525-0*) Turtleback Bks.

—Just Josefina. 2002. (American Girls Short Stories Ser.). (Illus.). 64p. (J). 4.95 (*1-58485-478-2*, American Girl) Pleasant Co. Pubns.

—Meet Josefina: An American Girl. 1997. (American Girls Collection: Bk. 1). (Illus.). 96p. (J). (gr. 2 up). pap. 5.95 (*1-56247-515-0*); lib. bdg. 12.95 (*1-56247-516-9*) Pleasant Co. Pubns. (American Girl).

—Meet Josefina: An American Girl. 1997. (American Girls Collection: Bk. 1). (Illus.). (YA). (gr. 2 up). 12.10 (*0-606-11614-1*) Turtleback Bks.

—A Reward for Josefina. 1999. (American Girls Short Stories Ser.). (Illus.). 56p. (YA). (gr. 2 up). 3.95 (*1-56247-763-3*, American Girl) Pleasant Co. Pubns.

—Una Sorpresa para Josefina: Un Cuento de Navidad. Moreno, Jose, tr. 1997. (American Girls Collection: Bk. 3). (SPA., Illus.). 80p. (J). (gr. 2 up). pap. 5.95 (*1-56247-498-7*, BT4987, American Girl) Pleasant Co. Pubns.

—Una Sorpresa para Josefina: Un Cuento de Navidad. 1997. (American Girls Collection: Bk. 3). (SPA.). (YA). (gr. 2 up). 12.10 (*0-606-12025-4*) Turtleback Bks.

—Thanks to Josefina. 2003. (American Girls Collection). (Illus.). 39p. (J). pap. 4.95 (*1-58485-698-X*, American Girl) Pleasant Co. Pubns.

Velasquez, Gloria. Maya's Divided World. 1995. (Roosevelt High School Series Bks.). 125p. (YA). (gr. 4-7). 12.95 (*1-55885-126-7*); pap. 9.95 (*1-55885-131-3*) Arte Publico Pr. (Piñata Books).

—Tommy Stands Alone. 1995. (Roosevelt High School Series Bks.). 135p. (YA). (gr. 7 up). pap. 9.95 (*1-55885-147-X*); 14.95 (*1-55885-146-1*) Arte Publico Pr. (Piñata Books).

—Tommy Stands Alone. 1995. (Roosevelt High School Ser.). 16.00 (*0-606-16337-9*) Turtleback Bks.

Whitney, Phyllis A. A Long Time Coming. 1.t. ed. 2002. (YA). lib. bdg. 27.95 (*1-58547-184-4*, Premier) Ctr. Point Large Print.

—A Long Time Coming. 1980. 245p. mass mkt. 1.50 o.p. (*0-451-09310-0*, W9310, Signet Bks.) NAL.

Wing, Natasha. Jalapeno Bagels. 1995. (Illus.). (J). (gr. k-3). 16.00 (*0-02-793077-7*, Simon & Schuster Children's Publishing) Simon & Schuster Children's Publishing.

Wing, Natasha & Casilla, Robert. Jalapeno Bagels. 1996. (Illus.). 32p. (J). (gr. k-3). 16.95 (*0-689-80530-6*, Atheneum) Simon & Schuster Children's Publishing.

MONGO (AFRICAN PEOPLE)—FICTION

Moore, Miriam & Taylor, Penny. Koi's Python. 1998. (Hyperion Chapters Ser.). (Illus.). 64p. (J). (gr. 3-4). pap. 3.95 (*0-7868-1227-3*) Hyperion Bks. for Children.

—Koi's Python. 1998. (Hyperion Chapters Ser.). (Illus.). 64p. (J). (gr. 3-4). lib. bdg. 14.49 (*0-7868-2285-6*) Hyperion Pr.

MONGOLS—FICTION

McCaughrean, Geraldine. The Kite Rider. (J). (gr. 7 up). 2003. (Illus.). 320p. pap. 6.99 (*0-06-441091-9*); 2002. 288p. lib. bdg. 16.89 (*0-06-623875-7*) HarperCollins Children's Bk. Group.

—The Kite Rider. 2002. (Illus.). 288p. (J). (gr. 7 up). 15.95 (*0-06-623874-9*) HarperCollins Pubs.

MORMONS AND MORMONISM—FICTION

Andersen, C. B. The Book of Mormon Sleuth Vol. 3: The Hidden Path. 2003. ix, 214p. (J). pap. (*1-57008-988-4*) Deseret Bk. Co.

Anderson, Launi K. Clarissa's Crossing. 1995. (Latter-Day Daughters Ser.: Vol. 2). 80p. (J). (gr. 2 up). pap. 4.95 (*1-56236-500-2*) Aspen Bks.

—Clarissa's Heart. 1998. (Latter-Day Daughters Ser.). 5.95 (*1-57345-416-8*) Deseret Bk. Co.

—Ellie's Gold. 1995. (Latter-Day Daughters Ser.). (J). pap. 4.95 (*1-56236-505-3*) Aspen Bks.

—Janey's Own. 1997. (Latter-Day Daughters Ser.). (J). pap. o.p. (*1-57345-319-6*, Cinnamon Tree) Deseret Bk. Co.

—Maren's Hope. 1995. (Latter-Day Daughters Ser.). (Illus.). 80p. (J). pap. 4.95 (*1-56236-503-7*) Aspen Bks.

—Sadie's Trade. 1998. (Latter-Day Daughters Ser.). (J). o.p. (*1-57345-415-X*) Deseret Bk. Co.

—Violet's Garden. 1996. (Latter-Day Daughters Ser.). (Illus.). 80p. (J). (gr. 3-9). pap. 4.95 (*1-56236-506-1*) Aspen Bks.

Bergera, Janet. Vital Signs: A Mission of the Heart. 1995. (J). pap. 9.95 (*1-55503-773-9*, 01111817) Covenant Communications, Inc.

Blum, Vicki. The Trouble with Spitt. 1996. 108p. (Orig.). (J). (gr. 4-8). pap. o.p. (*1-57345-147-9*) Deseret Bk. Co.

Bowen, Annette P. Get a Life, Jennifer Parker. 1993. vi, 201p. (Orig.). (YA). (gr. 8-12). pap. 8.95 (*0-87579-756-3*) Deseret Bk. Co.

—Live & Learn, Jennifer Parker. 1995. 180p. (Orig.). (YA). (gr. 9-12). pap. 9.95 (*0-87579-879-9*) Deseret Bk. Co.

Brigham Young & the Robin Soup. 1988. (Keepsake Bookcards Ser.). 12p. (J). pap. text 1.95 o.p. (*0-929985-01-X*) Jackman Publishing.

Call, Brian D., tr. & illus. Sarah's Cloud. 2003. (J). (*1-57008-955-8*) Deseret Bk. Co.

Cantwell, Lee G. Finders Keepers. 1996. pap. o.p. (*1-57008-224-3*, Bookcraft, Inc.) Deseret Bk. Co.

Carter, Ron. The Case of the Golden Spike Kidnappers. 1996. (Brigham's Ghost Brigade Ser.). (J). pap. (*0-9643672-6-2*) Harbour Bks.

Crane, Cheri J. Forever Kate. 1997. (J). pap. 12.95 (*1-57734-127-9*, 01112902) Covenant Communications, Inc.

—Kate's Return. 1996. (J). pap. 13.95 (*1-55503-982-0*, 01112457) Covenant Communications, Inc.

—Kate's Turn: A Novel. 1994. (J). pap. 11.95 (*1-55503-715-1*, 019404) Covenant Communications, Inc.

Crowther, Jean D. Growing up a Mormon. rev. ed. 1993. (J). reprint ed. 10.98 (*0-88290-485-X*, 1300) Horizon Pubs. & Distributors, Inc.

—Growing up in the Church: Gospel Principles & Practices for Children. rev. ed. 1973. (Illus.). 84p. (J). (gr. 2-6). reprint ed. 9.98 (*0-88290-024-2*) Horizon Pubs. & Distributors, Inc.

Embry-Litchman, Kristin. All Is Well. 1998. (Illus.). 128p. (gr. 4-7). text 14.95 o.s.i (*0-385-32592-4*, Delacorte Pr.) Dell Publishing.

—All Is Well. 1999. 128p. (gr. 4-7). pap. text 3.99 o.s.i (*0-440-41488-1*, Dell Books for Young Readers) Random Hse. Children's Bks.

—All Is Well. 1999. 10.04 (*0-606-16714-5*) Turtleback Bks.

Gallacher, Marcie. Amaryllis Lilies. 1996. (Values for Young Women Ser.). pap. 7.95 o.p. (*0-15-623645-1*) Aspen Bks.

Gostick, Adrian R. Jessica's Search: The Secret of Ballycater Cove. 1998. (J). 1.99 (*1-57345-436-2*) Deseret Bk. Co.

Heimerdinger, Chris. Tennis Shoes & the Seven Churches. 1997. (J). pap. 6.95 (*1-57734-217-8*, 01113275) Covenant Communications, Inc.

—Tower of Thunder: A Novel. 2003. 406p. (YA). 14.95 (*1-59156-177-9*) Covenant Communications.

Hughes, Dean. Cornbread & Prayer. 1988. 143p. (YA). (gr. 7-12). 8.95 o.p. (*0-87579-135-2*) Deseret Bk. Co.

—Facing the Enemy. 143p. (J). 1982. (gr. 6-12). 6.95 o.p. (*0-87747-928-3*); 1991. (gr. 3-9). reprint ed. pap. 4.95 o.p. (*0-87579-498-X*) Deseret Bk. Co.

—Lucky Comes Home. 1994. (Lucky Ladd Ser.: Bk. 10). 138p. (Orig.). (J). (gr. 4-6). pap. o.p. (*0-87579-941-8*, Cinnamon Tree) Deseret Bk. Co.

—Lucky Fights Back. 1991. (Lucky Ladd Ser.: Bk. 4). 150p. (Orig.). (J). (gr. 3-6). pap. text 4.95 (*0-87579-559-5*, Cinnamon Tree) Deseret Bk. Co.

—Lucky in Love. 1993. (Lucky Ladd Ser.: No. 9). 161p. (Orig.). (J). (gr. 3-7). pap. 4.95 (*0-87579-805-5*, Cinnamon Tree) Deseret Bk. Co.

—Lucky's Cool Club. 1993. (Lucky Ladd Ser.: No. 8). 141p. (Orig.). (J). (gr. 3-7). pap. 4.95 o.p. (*0-87579-786-5*, Cinnamon Tree) Deseret Bk. Co.

—Lucky's Gold Mine. 1990. (Lucky Ladd Ser.: Bk. 3). 132p. (Orig.). (J). (gr. 3-6). pap. 4.95 (*0-87579-350-9*, Cinnamon Tree) Deseret Bk. Co.

—Under the Same Stars. 1979. (J). (gr. 7-12). 6.95 o.p. (*0-87747-750-7*) Trafalgar Square.

Hulme, Joy N. Through the Open Door. 2000. 176p. (J). (gr. 4-6). 14.95 (*0-380-97870-9*) HarperCollins Children's Bk. Group.

Johnson-Choong, Shelly. A Light to Come Home By. 1996. (YA). pap. 9.95 o.p. (*1-55503-816-6*, 01112120) Covenant Communications, Inc.

Johnson, Marjorie. Book of Mormon Stories for Little Children. 1976. (Books for LDS Children). (Illus.). 96p. (Orig.). (J). (ps-7). pap. 8.98 (*0-88290-063-3*) Horizon Pubs. & Distributors, Inc.

Johnson, Sherrie. The Broken Bow. 1994. (J). pap. 4.95 o.p. (*0-87579-253-7*) Deseret Bk. Co.

—A House with Wings. 1995. (J). pap. 7.95 (*1-56236-309-3*) Aspen Bks.

Levitin, Sonia. Clem's Chances. 2001. (Illus.). 208p. (J). (gr. 2-7). pap. 17.95 (*0-439-29314-6*, Orchard Bks.) Scholastic, Inc.

Littke, Lael. Searching for Selene. 2003. 203p. (J). pap. 13.95 (*1-59038-179-3*) Deseret Bk. Co.

Littke, Lael J. The Bridesmaids' Dress Disaster. 1994. (Bee There Ser.: Bk. 5). viii, 155p. (Orig.). (J). (gr. 3-7). pap. 4.95 (*0-87579-940-X*, Cinnamon Tree) Deseret Bk. Co.

—The Phantom Fair. 1996. (Bee There Ser.: Bk. 7). 156p. (J). (gr. 3-7). pap. 6.95 (*1-57345-200-9*, Cinnamon Tree) Deseret Bk. Co.

—Star of the Show. 1993. (Bee There Ser.: Bk. 3). 162p. (Orig.). (J). (gr. 3-7). pap. o.p. (*0-87579-785-7*, Cinnamon Tree) Deseret Bk. Co.

—There's a Snake at Girls' Camp. 1994. (Bee There Ser.: No. 4). (Orig.). (J). (gr. 3-7). pap. 4.95 (*0-87579-845-4*, Cinnamon Tree) Deseret Bk. Co.

Lundberg, Joy S. Book of Mormon Summer. 1991. (J). (gr. 5-8). 6.95 o.p. (*0-915029-00-6*) Riverpark Publishing Co.

McCloud, Susan Evans. Mormon Girls Bk. 4: New Friends. 1996. pap. 5.95 (*1-57008-282-0*, Bookcraft, Inc.) Deseret Bk. Co.

—Mormon Girls Bk. 5: A Lesson Learned. 1996. pap. 5.95 (*1-57008-283-9*, Bookcraft, Inc.) Deseret Bk. Co.

—Mormon Girls Bk. 6: The Little Stranger. 1996. pap. 5.95 (*1-57008-284-7*, Bookcraft, Inc.) Deseret Bk. Co.

Norton, Tamra. Molly Mormon? Myth or Me? 2002. (Illus.). 170p. (J). pap. 12.95 (*1-55517-606-2*, Bonneville Bks.) Cedar Fort, Inc./CFI Distribution.

Palmer, Katheryn Ann. Butterfly Dust. 1996. (Values for Young Women Ser.). 185p. (YA). pap. 7.95 (*1-56236-452-9*) Aspen Bks.

Petersen, Emma M. Book of Mormon Stories for Young LDS. 1996. pap. o.p. (*1-57008-257-X*, Bookcraft, Inc.) Deseret Bk. Co.

Rada, James R., Jr. Logan's Fire. 1996. (YA). o.p. (*1-55503-841-7*) Covenant Communications, Inc.

Rallison, Janette. Deep Blue Eyes & Other Lies. 1996. 272p. (Orig.). (J). (gr. 7-12). mass mkt. o.p. (*1-57345-191-6*) Deseret Bk. Co.

Richardson, Boyd C. Danger Trail: Knife Thrower's Journey West. 1995. (J). pap. 9.95 o.p. (*1-55503-777-1*, 01111795) Covenant Communications, Inc.

Robinson, Bonnie. Through the Mists of Darkness. 1996. (YA). pap. 8.95 o.p. (*1-55503-693-7*, 01111728) Covenant Communications, Inc.

Robison, Pamela L. Alma. 1985. 90p. (J). (gr. 5-10). pap. 6.25 o.p. (*0-8309-0409-3*) Herald Publishing Hse.

Rostrom, Laura Lee. My Book of Mormon Storybook: 90 Favorite Stories. 1999. (Illus.). (J). (ps-6). 19.95 (*1-55517-352-7*) Cedar Fort, Inc./CFI Distribution.

Rowley, Brent. My Body Fell Off! A Novel. 1997. (J). 9.95 o.p. (*1-57734-130-9*) Covenant Communications, Inc.

—Out for Revenge. 1998. (J). 11.95 o.p. (*1-57734-312-3*) Covenant Communications, Inc.

Sealy, Shirley. I, Jason. (YA). pap. 6.95 o.p. (*1-55503-247-8*, 29004721) Covenant Communications, Inc.

Searle, Don L. Light in the Harbor. 1991. viii, 245p. (Orig.). (J). pap. 8.95 o.p. (*0-87579-528-5*) Deseret Bk. Co.

Stansfield, Anita. A Promise of Forever: A Novel. 1997. pap. 11.95 (*1-57734-060-4*, 01112716) Covenant Communications, Inc.

Thomasma, Kenneth. Doe Sia: Bannock Girl & the Handcart Pioneer. 1999. (Amazing Indian Children: 8). (J). (gr. 3-8). pap. 7.99 (*1-880114-20-8*); 12.99 (*1-880114-21-6*) Grandview Publishing Co.

—Doe Sia: Bannock Girl & the Handcart Pioneers. 1999. (Amazing Indian Children Ser.). (Illus.). 208p. (J). (gr. 6-9). 9.99 o.p. (*0-8010-4428-6*); pap. 5.99 o.p. (*0-8010-4438-3*) Baker Bks.

—Doe Sia: Bannock Girl & the Handcart Pioneers. 1999. (Illus.). (J). 14.04 (*0-606-21884-X*) Turtleback Bks.

Tolman, Louise L. Jake & the Pigs. 1985. 140p. (gr. 7-12). 6.95 o.p. (*0-87747-952-6*) Deseret Bk. Co.

Wells, Marian. The Wedding Dress. 1982. 272p. (J). pap. 7.99 o.p. (*0-87123-610-9*) Bethany Hse. Pubs.

Weyland, Jack. Brittany. 1997. v, 234p. (J). 15.95 (*1-57345-303-X*) Deseret Bk. Co.

—Charly. 1992. 98p. (YA). (gr. 9-12). reprint ed. pap. 4.95 o.p. (*0-87579-619-2*) Deseret Bk. Co.

—If Talent Were Pizza. 1993. 118p. (YA). (gr. 8-12). pap. 6.95 (*0-87579-696-6*) Deseret Bk. Co.

—Jake. 1998. 171 p. (J). o.p. (*1-57345-447-8*) Deseret Bk. Co.

—Lean on Me. 1996. vii, 279p. (J). 14.95 (*1-57345-214-9*) Deseret Bk. Co.

—Michelle & Debra. 137p. (YA). (gr. 7-12). 1995. pap. 5.95 (*0-87579-959-0*); 1990. o.p. (*0-87579-369-X*) Deseret Bk. Co.

—Night on Lone Wolf Mountain & Other Short Stories. 1996. vii, 210p. (YA). (gr. 8-12). 14.95 (*1-57345-113-4*) Deseret Bk. Co.

—On the Run. 1995. 188p. (YA). (gr. 9-12). 13.95 (*0-87579-891-8*) Deseret Bk. Co.

Williams, Carol Lynch. Anna's Gift. 1995. (Latter-Day Daughters Ser.: Vol. 1). 80p. (J). (gr. 2 up). pap. 4.95 (*1-56236-501-0*) Aspen Bks.

—Catherine's Remembrance. 1997. (Latter-Day Daughters Ser.). (J). pap. 4.95 (*1-57345-296-3*, Cinnamon Tree) Deseret Bk. Co.

—Esther's Celebration. 1996. (Latter-Day Daughters Ser.). (Illus.). 80p. (J). (gr. 3-9). pap. 4.95 (*1-56236-507-X*) Aspen Bks.

—Laurel's Flight. 1995. (Latter-Day Daughters Ser.). (Illus.). 80p. (J). pap. 4.95 (*1-56236-502-9*) Aspen Bks.

—Marciea's Melody. Utley, Jennifer, ed. 1996. (Latter-Day Daughters Ser.). (Illus.). 80p. (J). (gr. 3-9). pap. 4.95 (*1-56236-509-6*) Aspen Bks.

—Sarah's Quest. 1995. (Latter-Day Daughters Ser.). (J). pap. 4.95 (*1-56236-504-5*) Aspen Bks.

—Victoria's Courage. 1998. (Latter-Day Daughters Ser.). (J). 5.95 (*1-57345-434-6*) Deseret Bk. Co.

Yates, Alma J. Ghosts in the Baker Mine. 1992. 197p. (Orig.). (J). (gr. 3-7). pap. 4.95 (*0-87579-581-1*) Deseret Bk. Co.

Yates, Dan. An Angel in the Family: A Novel. 1999. (Illus.). 188 p. pap. 12.95 (*1-57734-282-8*, 01113461) Covenant Communications, Inc.

MUSLIMS—FICTION

Clinton, Cathryn. A Stone in My Hand. 2002. 208p. (J). (gr. 5-12). 15.99 (*0-7636-1388-6*) Candlewick Pr.

Clyde, Ahmad. Cheng Ho's Voyage. 1981. (Illus.). 32p. (Orig.). (J). (gr. 3-7). pap. 2.50 (*0-89259-021-1*) American Trust Pubns.

Fama, Elizabeth. Overboard. 2002. (Illus.). 192p. (YA). (gr. 6-9). 15.95 (*0-8126-2652-4*) Cricket Bks.

Ghazi, A., ed. The First Ones: The Makkan Sahabah. Siddiqui, A. Sayeed, tr. 1999. (Stories of the Sahabah Ser.: Vol. II). (Illus.). 145p. (YA). (gr. 7-10). pap. 10.00 (*1-56316-451-5*) IQRA International Educational Foundation.

—Those Promised Paradise. Siddiqui, M. Sayeed, tr. & illus. by. 1999. (Stories of the Sahabah Ser.: Vol. I). 256p. (YA). (gr. 7-10). pap. 10.00 (*1-56316-374-8*) IQRA International Educational Foundation.

Ismail, Suzy. The BFF Sisters: Jennah's New Friends. 2001. 64p. (J). (*1-59008-005-X*) amana-pubns.

Jackson, Dave & Jackson, Neta. Risking the Forbidden Game: Maude Cary. 2002. (Trailblazers Ser.). (Illus.). 160p. (J). (gr. 3-7). pap. 5.99 (*0-7642-2234-1*) Bethany Hse. Pubs.

Klaus, Sandra. Mustafas Geheimnis: Ein Moslemischer Junge auf der Suche nach Gott. Date not set. Tr. of Mustapha's Secret - A Muslim Boy's Search to Know God. (GER., Illus.). (J). (gr. 2-7). pap. (*0-9617490-6-7*) Gospel Missionary Union.

—Mustapha's Secret: A Muslim Boy's Search to Know God. 2nd ed. 1997. (Illus.). 42p. (J). (gr. 2-7). spiral bd. 11.95 (*1-890940-00-3*) Gospel Missionary Union.

—Tainata na Mustapha. Date not set. Tr. of Mustapha's Secret. (BUL.). (J). (gr. 2-7). pap. (*1-890940-04-6*) Gospel Missionary Union.

Oppenheim, Shulamith Levey. Ali & the Magic Stew. 2003. (Illus.). 32p. (YA). (gr. k up). 15.95 (*1-56397-869-5*) Boyds Mills Pr.

Shofi, Saima. The Mansurs Find a Home. 1996. 30p. (J). pap. (*0-9642101-5-0*) Al-Huda Pubs.

Williams, Tad & Crosby, Rodney. Child of an Ancient City. Hoffman, Nina Kiriki, ed. 1999. 288p. pap. text 6.99 (*0-8125-7211-4*, Tor Bks.) Doherty, Tom Assocs., LLC.

Williams, Tad & Hoffman, Nina K. Child of an Ancient City. 1994. 288p. reprint ed. mass mkt. 6.99 o.p. (*0-8125-3391-7*, Tor Bks.) Doherty, Tom Assocs., LLC.

—Child of an Ancient City. 1992. (Dragonflight Ser.). (Illus.). 144p. lib. bdg. 16.00 o.s.i (*0-689-31577-5*, Atheneum) Simon & Schuster Children's Publishing.

Williams, Tad & Hoffman, Nina Kiriki. Child of an Ancient City. 1992. E-Book (*1-58824-903-4*) ipicturebooks, LLC.

N

NORMANS—FICTION

McCaughren, Tom. Ride a Pale Horse. 1998. 144p. (YA). (gr. 4 up). 13.95 (*1-901737-08-X*) Anvil Bks., Ltd. IRL. *Dist:* Irish Bks. & Media, Inc.

NORTHMEN—FICTION

Abraham, Norma J. Erik of the Dragon Ships. 1983. (Illus.). 163p. (Orig.). (J). (gr. 8-11). pap. 3.95 (*0-912661-00-3*) Woodsong Graphics, Inc.

Arthur, Ruth M. On the Wasteland. 1975. (Illus.). 176p. (J). (gr. 4-8). 5.95 o.p. (*0-689-30473-0*, Atheneum) Simon & Schuster Children's Publishing.

Benchley, Nathaniel. Beyond the Mists. 1975. 160p. (YA). (gr. 7 up). 13.95 (*0-06-020459-1*); lib. bdg. 10.89 o.p. (*0-06-020460-5*) HarperCollins Children's Bk. Group.

—Snorri & the Strangers. 1976. (I Can Read Bks.). (Illus.). (J). (ps-3). 11.95 (*0-06-020457-5*) HarperCollins Children's Bk. Group.

Boucher, Alan. The Land Seekers, RS. 1968. (J). (gr. 7 up). 3.50 o.p. (*0-374-34323-3*, Farrar, Straus & Giroux (BYR)) Farrar, Straus & Giroux.

Bulla, Clyde Robert. Viking Adventure. 1963. (Illus.). (J). (gr. 3-6). lib. bdg. 7.89 o.p. (*0-690-86015-3*) HarperCollins Children's Bk. Group.

Campbell, Civardi. Viking Raiders. 1977. (Time Travelers Bks.). (J). (gr. 4-9). 7.95 o.p. (*0-86020-086-8*); pap. 6.95 (*0-86020-085-X*); lib. bdg. 14.95 (*0-88110-102-8*) EDC Publishing. (Usborne).

Carter, Avis M. One Day with the Vikings. 1974. (Day Book Ser.). 48p. (J). (gr. 3 up). 6.95 o.p. (*0-200-00137-X*) Criterion Bks., Inc.

Coatsworth, Elizabeth. Jock's Island. 1969. (Seafarer Ser.). (Illus.). (J). (gr. 7 up). 0.65 o.p. (*0-670-05026-1*, Penguin Bks.) Viking Penguin.

Crossley-Holland, Kevin, ed. The Faber Book of Northern Legends. 1983. (Illus.). 156p. (J). (gr. 3 up). o.p. (*0-571-10912-8*); pap. o.p. (*0-571-13165-4*) Faber & Faber Ltd.

Deary, Terry. Vicious Vikings. 1998. (Horrible Histories Ser.). (J). (gr. 7-12). mass mkt. 4.50 (*0-590-49849-5*) Scholastic, Inc.

Dixon, Franklin W. The Viking's Revenge, 1997. (Hardy Boys Casefiles Ser.: No. 124). 160p. (YA). (gr. 6 up). pap. 3.99 (*0-671-56124-3*, Simon Pulse) Simon & Schuster Children's Publishing.

Goscinny, René. Le Bouclier Arverne. 1990. (FRE.). (J). (gr. 7-9). 24.95 (*0-8288-5120-4*, FC883) French & European Pubns., Inc.

—Le Combat des Chefs. 1990. (FRE.). (J). (gr. 7-9). 24.95 (*0-8288-5121-2*, FC879) French & European Pubns., Inc.

Goscinny, René & Uderzo, M. Asterix & the Goths. 1990. (Illus.). (J). (gr. 7-10). 24.95 (*0-8288-4919-6*) French & European Pubns., Inc.

—Asterix Gladiator. 1990. (LAT., Illus.). (J). 24.95 (*0-8288-4943-9*) French & European Pubns., Inc.

—Asterix in Britain. 1990. (Illus.). (J). 24.95 (*0-8288-4944-7*) French & European Pubns., Inc.

—Le Domaine des Dieux. 1990. (FRE., Illus.). (J). (gr. 7-9). 24.95 (*0-8288-5123-9*, FC886) French & European Pubns., Inc.

—The Great Crossing. 1990. (Illus.). (J). 24.95 (*0-8288-4971-4*) French & European Pubns., Inc.

Haugaard, Erik Christian. Hakon of Rogen's Saga, 001. 1963. (Illus.). (J). (gr. 7 up). 6.95 o.p. (*0-395-06803-7*) Houghton Mifflin Co.

—Leif the Unlucky, 001. 1982. (J). (gr. 7 up). 9.95 o.p. (*0-395-32156-5*) Houghton Mifflin Co.

—Slave's Tale, 001. 1965. (Illus.). (J). (gr. 7 up). 7.95 o.p. (*0-395-06804-5*) Houghton Mifflin Co.

Janeway, Elizabeth. The Vikings. 1981. (Landmark Bks.: No. 7). (Illus.). 160p. (gr. 5-8). pap. text 5.99 o.s.i (*0-394-84885-3*, Random Hse. Bks. for Young Readers) Random Hse. Children's Bks.

Jones, Terry. The Saga of Erik the Viking. l.t. ed. 1990. 248p. (J). (gr. 3 up). 16.95 (*0-7451-1152-1*, Macmillan Reference USA) Gale Group.

—The Saga of Erik the Viking. 1987. (Illus.). 144p. (J). (gr. 4 up). 15.95 o.p. (*0-8052-3876-X*, Schocken) Knopf Publishing Group.

—The Saga of Erik the Viking. 1998. (Illus.). 144p. (J). 19.95 (*1-86205-225-5*) Pavilion Bks., Ltd. GBR. *Dist:* Trafalgar Square.

—The Saga of Erik the Viking. (Illus.). (J). 1993. 192p. (gr. 3-7). pap. 3.99 o.s.i (*0-14-032261-2*); 1986. 144p. (ps up). pap. 9.99 o.p. (*0-14-031713-9*) Penguin Putnam Bks. for Young Readers. (Puffin Bks.).

Katz, Welwyn W. Out of the Dark. 1996. 192p. (YA). (gr. 4). pap. 5.95 (*0-88899-262-9*) Groundwood Bks. CAN. *Dist:* Publishers Group West.

—Out of the Dark. 1996. 192p. (J). (gr. 6-9). 16.00 (*0-689-80947-6*, McElderry, Margaret K.) Simon & Schuster Children's Publishing.

Leighton, Margaret. Voyage to Coromandel, RS. 1965. (J). (gr. 7 up). 3.25 o.p. (*0-374-38217-4*, Farrar, Straus & Giroux (BYR)) Farrar, Straus & Giroux.

Malam, John. Indiana Jones Explores the Vikings. 1996. (Illus.). 47p. (J). (gr. 5-8). 22.95 (*0-237-51222-X*) Evans Brothers, Ltd. GBR. *Dist:* Trafalgar Square.

Molan, Christine, as told by. The Viking Saga. 1985. (Legends & Folktales Ser.). (Illus.). 32p. (J). (gr. k-5). pap. 9.27 o.p. (*0-8172-2511-0*); lib. bdg. 19.97 o.p. (*0-8172-2503-X*) Raintree Pubs.

Mullen, Michael. Sea Wolves from the North. 1994. (Illus.). 96p. (YA). reprint ed. pap. (*0-920911-03-X*) Breakwater Bks., Ltd.

Newman, Roger C. Murtagh the Warrior. 1997. 144p. pap. 8.95 (*0-947962-98-0*) Dufour Editions, Inc.

Packard, Edward. Viking Raiders. 1992. (Choose Your Own Adventure Ser.: No. 128). 128p. (J). (gr. 4-8). pap. 3.25 o.s.i (*0-553-29302-8*) Bantam Bks.

Stone, Rosetta. Because a Little Bug Went Ka-Choo! 1975. (Illus.). 48p. (ps-3). 8.99 (*0-394-83130-6*) Beginner Bks.

Stroud, Jonathan. The Viking Saga of Harri Bristlebeard. 1997. (Illus.). 32p. (J). (gr. 3-7). 14.99 o.p. (*0-7636-0270-1*) Candlewick Pr.

Sutcliff, Rosemary. Blood Feud. 1977. (J). (gr. 4 up). 7.50 o.p. (*0-525-26730-1*, Dutton) Dutton/Plume.

Treece, Henry. Road to Miklagard. 1957. (Illus.). (J). (gr. 6-10). 26.95 (*0-87599-118-1*) Phillips, S.G. Inc.

—Viking's Dawn. 1956. (Illus.). (J). (gr. 7-9). 22.95 o.p. (*0-87599-117-3*) Phillips, S.G. Inc.

—Westward to Vinland. 1967. (Illus.). (J). (gr. 8 up). 22.95 o.p. (*0-87599-136-X*) Phillips, S.G. Inc.

NORWEGIANS—UNITED STATES—FICTION

Archer, Marion F. There Is a Happy Land. 1963. (Illus.). (gr. 5-7). 5.95 o.p. (*0-8075-7861-4*) Whitman, Albert & Co.

Forbes, Kathryn. Mama's Bank Account. 1968. 154p. reprint ed. pap. 10.00 (*0-15-656377-0*, Harvest Bks.) Harcourt Trade Pubs.

Lurie, April. Dancing in the Streets of Brooklyn. 2002. 208p. lib. bdg. 17.99 (*0-385-90066-X*); (gr. 3-7). text 15.95 (*0-385-72942-1*) Random Hse., Inc.

P

PANAMANIANS IN NEW YORK (CITY)—FICTION

Chambers, Veronica. Marisol & Magdalena: The Sound of Our Sisterhood. 2001. 176p. (J). (gr. 3-7). pap. 5.99 (*0-7868-1304-0*) Hyperion Bks. for Children.

—Marisol & Magdalena: The Sound of Our Sisterhood. 1998. 141p. (gr. 3-7). (J). 14.95 (*0-7868-0437-8*); (YA). lib. bdg. 15.49 (*0-7868-2385-2*) Hyperion Pr.

PASSOVER—FICTION

Atlas, Susan. Passover Passage. 1991. 96p. (YA). (gr. 4-7). pap. 5.95 (*0-933873-46-8*) Torah Aura Productions.

Bat-Ami, Miriam. Dear Elijah: A Passover Story, RS. 1995. 96p. (J). (gr. 4-7). 14.00 o.p. (*0-374-31755-0*, Farrar, Straus & Giroux (BYR)) Farrar, Straus & Giroux.

—Dear Elijah: A Passover Story. 1997. 106p. (J). pap. 9.95 (*0-8276-0592-7*) Jewish Pubn. Society.

Feder, Harriet K. Not Yet, Elijah! 1989. (Illus.). 32p. (J). (gr. k-3). 10.95 o.p. (*0-930494-94-6*); pap. 4.95 o.p. (*0-930494-95-4*) Kar-Ben Publishing.

Gikow, Louise. The Shalom Sesame Players Present: The Story of Passover. 1994. (Sharing Passover Ser.). (Illus.). 36p. (J). 12.95 (*1-56086-201-7*); 14.95 incl. audio (*1-56086-200-9*) Sisu Home Entertainment, Inc.

Goldin, Barbara Diamond. The Magician's Visit: A Passover Tale. (Illus.). 32p. (J). 1995. pap. 4.99 o.s.i (*0-14-054455-0*, Puffin Bks.); 1993. 13.99 o.p. (*0-670-84905-7*, Viking Children's Bks.); 1993. 14.99 o.s.i (*0-670-84840-9*, Viking Children's Bks.) Penguin Putnam Bks. for Young Readers.

—The Magician's Visit: A Passover Tale. 1995. 10.19 o.p. (*0-606-07827-4*) Turtleback Bks.

Groner, Judye & Wikler, Madeline. Where Is the Afikomen? 1985. (Illus.). 12p. (J). (ps). bds. 4.95 o.p. (*0-930494-52-0*) Kar-Ben Publishing.

Hannigan, Lynne. Sam's Passover. (J). pap. 5.95 (*0-7136-4084-7*, 93342) A & C Black GBR. *Dist:* Lubrecht & Cramer, Ltd.

Herold, Ann B. The Mysterious Passover Visitors. 1989. (Illus.). 112p. (Orig.). (J). (gr. 4-7). pap. 5.99 (*0-8361-3494-X*) Herald Pr.

Heymsfeld, Carla. The Matzah Ball Fairy. 1996. (Illus.). 32p. (J). (ps-3). 12.95 (*0-8074-0600-7*, 101070) UAHC Pr.

Howland, Naomi. The Matzah Man: A Passover Story. 2002. (Illus.). 32p. (J). (ps-3). lib. bdg. 15.00 (*0-618-11750-4*, Clarion Bks.) Houghton Mifflin Co. Trade & Reference Div.

Krulik, Nancy E. No Matzoh for Me. 2003. (Reading Railroad Bks.). (Illus.). 32p. (J). mass mkt. 3.49 (*0-448-43119-X*, Grosset & Dunlap) Penguin Putnam Bks. for Young Readers.

—Penny & the Four Questions. 1993. (Read with Me Ser.). (Illus.). 32p. (J). (ps-3). mass mkt. 3.25 (*0-590-46339-X*) Scholastic, Inc.

Manushkin, Fran. The Matzah That Papa Brought Home. 1995. (Illus.). 32p. (J). (ps-2). pap. 14.95 (*0-590-47146-5*) Scholastic, Inc.

Miller, Deborah U. Only Nine Chairs-A Tall Tale for Passover. 1982. (Illus.). 40p. (J). (ps-3). 9.95 o.p. (*0-930494-12-1*) Kar-Ben Publishing.

Miller, Deborah U. & Ostrove, Karen. Only Nine Chairs - A Tall Tale for Passover. 1982. (Illus.). 40p. (J). (ps-3). pap. 5.95 (*0-930494-13-X*) Kar-Ben Publishing.

Newman, Leslea. Matzo Ball Moon. 1998. 15.00 (*0-395-71519-9*) Houghton Mifflin Co.

—Matzo Ball Moon. 1998. (Illus.). 32p. (J). (ps-3). lib. bdg., tchr. ed. 15.00 (*0-395-71530-X*, Clarion Bks.) Houghton Mifflin Co. Trade & Reference Div.

Oppenheim, Shulamith L. Appleblossom. (Illus.). 30p. (J). 3.98 o.p. (*0-8317-0006-8*) Smithmark Pubs., Inc.

Oppenheim, Shulamith Levey. Appleblossom. Yolen, Jane, ed. 1991. (Illus.). 40p. (J). (gr. 1-7). 14.95 (*0-15-203750-0*) Harcourt Children's Bks.

Panas, Peter. The Shalom Sesame Players Present: The Story of Passover. 1994. (Sharing Passover Ser.). (Illus.). 32p. (J). pap. 17.95 incl. VHS (*1-56086-211-4*) Sisu Home Entertainment, Inc.

Panas, Peter, illus. The Shalom Sesame Players Present: The Story of Passover. 1994. (Sharing Passover Ser.). 32p. (J). pap. 5.95 (*1-56086-202-5*) Sisu Home Entertainment, Inc.

Peretz, Yitskhok Leybush. The Magician. 1985. (Illus.). 32p. (J). (gr. k-6). lib. bdg. 12.95 o.s.i (*0-02-782770-4*, Simon & Schuster Children's Publishing) Simon & Schuster Children's Publishing.

Portnoy, Mindy A. Matzah Ball. 1994. (Illus.). (J). 13.95 o.p. (*0-929371-68-2*); 32p. (gr. 1-5). pap. 6.95 (*0-929371-69-0*) Kar-Ben Publishing.

Pushker, Gloria T. Toby Belfer's Seder: A Passover Story Retold. 1994. (Illus.). 32p. (J). (ps-3). 14.95 (*0-88289-987-2*) Pelican Publishing Co., Inc.

Rosten, Norman. The Wine Glass. 1978. (Illus.). (J). (gr. 3-7). 6.95 o.p. (*0-8027-6318-9*); lib. bdg. 6.85 o.p. (*0-8027-6319-7*) Walker & Co.

Rothenberg, Joan. Matzah Ball Soup: A Passover Story. 1999. 32p. (J). 14.99 (*0-7868-0574-9*) Disney Pr.

—Matzah Ball Soup: A Passover Story. 1999. (Illus.). 32p. (J). (ps-3). 14.99 (*0-7868-0202-2*); lib. bdg. 15.49 (*0-7868-2170-1*) Hyperion Bks. for Children.

Rouss, Sylvia. Sammy Spider's First Passover. 1995. (Illus.). 32p. (J). (ps-2). 14.95 o.p. (*0-929371-81-X*) Kar-Ben Publishing.

Rouss, Sylvia A. Sammy Spider's First Passover. 1995. (Illus.). 32p. (J). (ps-2). pap. 6.95 (*0-929371-82-8*) Kar-Ben Publishing.

Schilder, Rosalind. Dayenu, or How Uncle Murray Saved the Seder. 1988. (Illus.). 32p. (Orig.). (J). (ps-3). pap. 5.95 o.p. (*0-930494-76-8*) Kar-Ben Publishing.

Schotter, Roni. Passover Magic. (Illus.). 32p. (J). 1998. (ps-3). pap. 6.95 (*0-316-77928-8*); 1995. (gr. 1-8). 15.95 o.p. (*0-316-77468-5*) Little Brown & Co.

—Passover Magic. 1998. (J). 12.10 (*0-606-13696-7*) Turtleback Bks.

Swartz, Leslie. First Passover. 1994. (Illus.). 32p. (J). (ps-3). pap. 5.95 (*0-671-88025-X*, Aladdin) Simon & Schuster Children's Publishing.

Topek, Susan R. A Taste for Noah. 1993. (Illus.). 24p. (J). (gr. k-1). 12.95 (*0-929371-39-9*); pap. 5.95 (*0-929371-40-2*) Kar-Ben Publishing.

Wikler, Madeline & Groner, Judye. I Have Four Questions. 1989. (Illus.). 12p. (J). (ps). bds. 4.95 o.p. (*0-930494-90-3*) Kar-Ben Publishing.

Zalben, Jane Breskin. Pearl's Passover: A Family Celebration Through Stories, Recipes, Crafts & Songs. 2002. (Illus.). 48p. (J). (gr. k-3). 16.00 (*0-689-81487-9*, Simon & Schuster Children's Publishing) Simon & Schuster Children's Publishing.

Ziefert, Harriet. What Is Passover? 1994. (Lift-the-Flap Story Ser.). (Illus.). 16p. (J). (ps-2). 6.95 (*0-694-00482-0*, Harper Festival) HarperCollins Children's Bk. Group.

Zucker, Jonny. Four Special Questions: A Passover Story. 2003. (Festival Time! Ser.). (Illus.). 24p. (J). (ps-2). pap. 6.95 (*0-7641-2267-3*) Barron's Educational Series, Inc.

PENNSYLVANIA DUTCH—FICTION

Irion, Ruth H. The Christmas Cookie Tree. 1976. (Illus.). (J). 6.95 o.p. (*0-664-32586-6*) Westminster John Knox Pr.

Long, Lucile. Anna Elizabeth-Seventeen. 1978. (J). pap. 2.25 o.p. (*0-87178-041-0*) Brethren Pr.

Milhous, Katherine. Egg Tree. 1971. (Egg Tree Ser.: Vol. 1). (Illus.). 32p. (J). (gr. 1-4). 16.00 (*0-684-12716-4*, Atheneum) Simon & Schuster Children's Publishing.

—The Egg Tree. 2nd ed. 1992. (Illus.). 32p. (J). (gr. 1-4). pap. 5.99 (*0-689-71568-4*, Aladdin) Simon & Schuster Children's Publishing.

Monjo, F. N. Rudi & the Distelfink. 1972. 32p. (J). 5.95 o.p. (*0-525-61002-2*, Dutton) Dutton/Plume.

Sorensen, Virginia. Plain Girl. 1955. (Illus.). (J). (gr. 4-6). 6.50 o.p. (*0-15-262434-1*) Harcourt Children's Bks.

Stoltsfus, John R. The Day on the Farm with Samuel: The Life of an Amish Boy. 1995. (Illus.). 32p. (J). 16.95 (*0-9646590-0-X*) J&M Publishing.

POLES—UNITED STATES—FICTION

Bartoletti, Susan Campbell. Dancing with Dziadziu. 1997. (Illus.). 40p. (J). (ps-3). 15.00 (*0-15-200675-3*) Harcourt Children's Bks.

Blos, Joan W. Brooklyn Doesn't Rhyme. (Illus.). 96p. (gr. 3-7). 2000. pap. 4.50 (*0-689-83557-4*, Aladdin); 1994. (J). 16.00 o.s.i (*0-684-19694-8*, Atheneum) Simon & Schuster Children's Publishing.

Pastore, Clare. Journey to America: Aniela Kaminski's Story, Vol. 2. 2002. 192p. mass mkt. 5.99 (*0-425-18816-7*) Berkley Publishing Group.

Strigenz, Geri K., illus. For Bread. 1992. (History's Children Ser.). 48p. (J). (gr. 4-5). pap. o.p. (*0-8114-6426-1*); lib. bdg. 21.36 o.p. (*0-8114-3501-6*) Raintree Pubs.

POLISH AMERICANS—FICTION

Armstrong, Jennifer. Theodore Roosevelt: Letters from a Young Coal Miner. 2001. (Dear Mr. President Ser.: Vol. 1). (Illus.). 118p. (J). (gr. 4-7). 8.95 (*1-890817-27-9*) Winslow Pr.

Bartoletti, Susan Campbell. A Coal Miner's Bride: The Diary of Anetka Kaminski, Lattimer, Pennsylvania, 1896. 2000. (Dear America Ser.). (Illus.). 219p. (J). (gr. 4-9). pap. 10.95 (*0-439-05386-2*, Scholastic Pr.) Scholastic, Inc.

Cushman, Karen. Rodzina. 2003. 208p. (J). (gr. 5-9). tchr. ed. 16.00 (*0-618-13351-8*, Clarion Bks.) Houghton Mifflin Co. Trade & Reference Div.

—Rodzina. unabr. ed. 2003. (J). (gr. 7-7). audio 26.00 (*0-8072-1576-7*, Listening Library) Random Hse. Audio Publishing Group.

Estes, Eleanor. The Hundred Dresses. 2002. (Illus.). (J). 13.19 (*0-7587-0272-8*) Book Wholesalers, Inc.

—The Hundred Dresses. (Illus.). 88p. (J). 1944. (gr. 4-7). 16.00 (*0-15-237374-8*); 1974. (gr. 1-5). reprint ed. pap. 6.00 (*0-15-642350-2*, Voyager Bks./Libros Viajeros) Harcourt Children's Bks.

—The Hundred Dresses. 1971. (J). (gr. 4-7). 12.15 (*0-606-03310-6*) Turtleback Bks.

Raphael, Marie. Streets of Gold. rev. ed. 2001. (Illus.). 224p. (J). (gr. 5 up). pap. 9.95 (*0-89255-256-5*) Persea Bks., Inc.

—Streets of Gold: A Novel. Sena, Jerry, ed. 1998. (Illus.). 216p. (J). (gr. 6-9). per. 7.95 (*1-883088-05-4*) Source Productions, Inc.

PUERTO RICANS—NEW YORK (N. Y.)—FICTION

Belpré, Pura. Santiago: Spanish Language Edition. 1971. (SPA., Illus.). (J). (gr. k-3). 7.95 o.p. (*0-7232-6020-6*, Warne, Frederick) Penguin Putnam Bks. for Young Readers.

Fleischman, H. Samuel. Gang Girl. 1967. (gr. 7-8). 5.95 o.p. (*0-385-06290-7*) Doubleday Publishing.

Garcia, Richard, et al. My Aunt Otilia's Spirits: Los Espiritus de mi Tia Otilia. 1978. (Fifth World Tales Ser.). (Illus.). (J). (gr. k-6). pap. text 4.95 o.p. (*0-89239-016-6*) Children's Bk. Pr.

Gray, Genevieve. The Dark Side of Nowhere. 1977. (Time of Danger, Time for Courage Ser.). (Illus.). (J). (gr. 3-9). pap. 3.95 o.p. (*0-88436-391-0*, 35298) Paradigm Publishing, Inc.

Lewiton, Mina. That Bad Carlos. 1964. (Illus.). (J). (gr. 2-6). lib. bdg. 8.79 o.p. (*0-06-023846-1*) HarperCollins Pubs.

Martel, Cruz. Yagua Days. 1995. (Illus.). (J). (gr. 3). 8.60 (*0-395-73235-2*) Houghton Mifflin Co.

—Yagua Days. 1987. (Pied Piper Bks.). (Illus.). 40p. (J). (ps-3). 11.89 o.p. (*0-8037-9766-4*); pap. 4.95 o.p. (*0-8037-0457-7*) Penguin Putnam Bks. for Young Readers. (Dial Bks. for Young Readers).

Mohr, Nicholasa. El Bronx Remembered. 1994. (J). 20.75 (*0-8446-6779-X*) Smith, Peter Pub., Inc.

—El Bronx Remembered: A Novella & Stories. 1975. 256p. (YA). (gr. 7 up). lib. bdg. 13.89 o.p. (*0-06-024314-7*) HarperCollins Children's Bk. Group.

—In Nueva York. 2nd ed. 1988. 194p. (YA). (gr. 8-12). reprint ed. pap. 10.95 o.p. (*0-934770-78-6*) Arte Publico Pr.

—In Nueva York. 1977. (J). (gr. 7 up). 7.95 o.p. (*0-8037-4044-1*, Dial Bks. for Young Readers) Penguin Putnam Bks. for Young Readers.

—In Nueva York. 1988. 17.00 (*0-606-16041-8*) Turtleback Bks.

—Nilda. 2nd ed. 1986. 292p. (YA). (ps up). pap. 11.95 (*0-934770-61-1*) Arte Publico Pr.

—Nilda. 1973. (Illus.). 272p. (YA). (gr. 5 up). 8.96 o.p. (*0-06-024331-7*); lib. bdg. 13.89 o.p. (*0-06-024332-5*) HarperCollins Children's Bk. Group.

Scott, James. When I Was Puerto Rican: Reproducible Teaching Unit. 2001. 55p. (YA). (gr. 7-12). tchr. ed., ring bd. 29.50 (*1-58049-281-9*, TU167) Prestwick Hse., Inc.

Shulman, Irving. West Side Story. (Orig.). 1990. 160p. mass mkt. 5.99 (*0-671-72566-1*); 1983. (J). (gr. 8 up). mass mkt. 2.95 (*0-671-50448-7*); 1981. pap. 2.50 o.s.i (*0-671-44142-6*) Simon & Schuster. (Pocket).

Speevack, Yetta. The Spider Plant. 1974. (J). (gr. 4-6). pap. (*0-671-29638-8*, Simon Pulse) Simon & Schuster Children's Publishing.

PUERTO RICANS—UNITED STATES—FICTION

Aust, Patricia H. Benni & Victoria: Friends Through Time. 1996. (Illus.). 117p. (J). (ps-5). pap. 5.95 (*0-87868-629-0*, Child & Family Pr.) Child Welfare League of America, Inc.

Cofer, Judith Ortiz. An Island Like You. 1996. 128p. (J). (gr. 7 up). 5.99 (*0-14-038068-X*, Puffin Bks.) Penguin Putnam Bks. for Young Readers.

Cowley, Joy. Gracias, the Thanksgiving Turkey. 1996. (Illus.). 32p. (J). (ps-3). pap. 15.95 (*0-590-46976-2*) Scholastic, Inc.

Kesselman, Wendy Ann. Joey. 1972. (Illus.). 64p. (Orig.). (J). (gr. 3-6). 5.95 o.p. (*0-88208-005-9*); pap. 3.95 o.p. (*0-88208-031-8*) Chicago Review Pr., Inc. (Hill, Lawrence Bks.).

Lewiton, Mina. Candita's Choice. 1959. (Illus.). (J). (gr. 3-6). lib. bdg. 8.79 o.p. (*0-06-023821-6*) HarperCollins Pubs.

Mohr, Nicholasa. Felita. 1999. 11.04 (*0-606-17413-3*) Turtleback Bks.

—Going Home. 1986. (YA). (gr. 5-8). 20p. 14.95 o.s.i (*0-8037-0269-8*); 176p. 11.89 o.p. (*0-8037-0338-4*) Penguin Putnam Bks. for Young Readers. (Dial Bks. for Young Readers).

Montes, Marisa. Something Wicked's in Those Woods. 2000. 224p. (YA). (gr. 7-12). 17.00 (*0-15-202391-7*) Harcourt Children's Bks.

Ortiz Cofer, Judith. An Island Like You: Stories of the Barrio. 1995. 176p. (YA). (gr. 7 up). (SPA.). pap. 15.95 (*0-531-06897-8*); lib. bdg. 16.99 (*0-531-08747-6*) Scholastic, Inc. (Orchard Bks.).

Simon, Norma. What Do I Do. 1969. (Albert Whitman Concept Bks.). (Illus.). (J). (ps-2). 7.50 o.p. (*0-8075-8822-9*) Whitman, Albert & Co.

—What Do I Do? 1969. (Albert Whitman Concept Bks.). (SPA., Illus.). 40p. (J). (ps-3). lib. bdg. 14.95 o.p. (*0-8075-8823-7*) Whitman, Albert & Co.

Steptoe, John. Creativity. 2003. (Illus.). 32p. (J). (ps-3). pap. 5.95 (*0-618-31677-9*, Clarion Bks.) Houghton Mifflin Co. Trade & Reference Div.

Steptoe, John L. Creativity. 1997. (Illus.). 32p. (J). (ps-3). lib. bdg., tchr. ed. 17.00 (*0-395-68706-3*) Houghton Mifflin Co.

Tamar, Erika. Alphabet City Ballet. 1996. 176p. (J). (gr. 3-7). lib. bdg. 14.89 o.p. (*0-06-027329-1*); 14.95 o.p. (*0-06-027328-3*) HarperCollins Children's Bk. Group.

Velasquez, Eric. Grandma's Records. 2001. (Illus.). 32p. (J). (gr. k-3). 17.85 (*0-8027-8761-4*); 16.95 (*0-8027-8760-6*) Walker & Co.

Velasquez, Eric & de la Vega, Eida. Los Discos de Mi Abuela. 2002. (SPA., Illus.). (J). (gr. 1-3). 16.95 (*1-930332-21-1*, LC7246) Lectorum Pubns., Inc.

Velasquez, Gloria. Rina's Family Secret. 1998. 112p. (J). 16.95 o.p. (*1-55885-236-0*, Piñata Books) Arte Publico Pr.

PURIM—FICTION

Adelson, Leone. The Mystery Bear: A Purim Story. Howland, Naomi, tr. & illus. by. 2004. (J). (*0-618-33727-X*, Clarion Bks.) Houghton Mifflin Co. Trade & Reference Div.

Cohen, Barbara. Here Come the Purim Players! 1984. (Illus.). 32p. (J). (gr. 1-4). 12.00 o.p. (*0-688-02106-9*); lib. bdg. 12.88 o.p. (*0-688-02108-5*) HarperCollins Children's Bk. Group.

—Here Come the Purim Players! 1998. (Illus.). (J). (ps-3). 12.95 (*0-8074-0645-7*, 101251) UAHC Pr.

Geller, Beverly Mach. The Mitzvah Girl. 2000. (Illus.). 24p. (J). (ps-3). 12.95 (*965-229-203-6*) Gefen Publishing Hse., Ltd ISR. *Dist:* Gefen Bks.

Gettinger, Shifrah. A Very Special Gift. 1993. (Illus.). 32p. (J). (ps-3). 9.95 (*0-922613-52-4*); pap. text 6.95 (*0-922613-53-2*) Hachai Publishing.

Goldin, Barbara Diamond. Cakes & Miracles: A Purim Tale. 1993. (Illus.). 320p. (J). reprint ed. pap. 4.99 o.s.i (*0-14-054871-8*, Puffin Bks.) Penguin Putnam Bks. for Young Readers.

—Cakes & Miracles: A Purin Tale. 1991. (Illus.). (J). (ps-3). 15.00 o.p. (*0-670-83047-X*, Viking Children's Bks.) Penguin Putnam Bks. for Young Readers.

Rouss, Sylvia A. Sammy Spider's First Purim. 2000. (Illus.). (J). (ps-2). 32p. pap. 6.95 (*1-58013-062-3*); 6.95 (*1-58013-061-5*) Kar-Ben Publishing.

Sidon, Ephraim. The Animated Megillah. 1987. (Animated Holydays Ser.). 54p. (J). (gr. 1-5). 14.95 o.p. (*0-8246-0324-9*) Jonathan David Pubs., Inc.

Simpson, Lesley. The Purim Surprise. 2004. (Purim Ser.). (J). pap. 6.95 (*1-58013-090-9*) Lerner Publishing Group.

Topek, Susan R. A Costume for Noah: A Purim Story. (Illus.). 24p. (J). (ps-1). 1996. 13.95 (*0-929371-91-7*); 1995. pap. 5.95 (*0-929371-90-9*) Kar-Ben Publishing.

Zalben, Jane Breskin. Goldie's Purim, ERS. 1991. (Illus.). 32p. (J). (ps-2). 13.95 o.p. (*0-8050-1227-3*, Holt, Henry & Co. Bks. For Young Readers) Holt, Henry & Co.

Zwerin, Raymond A. & Marcus, Audrey F. A Purim Album. 1982. (Illus.). 32p. (J). (gr. k-3). 10.95 o.p. (*0-8074-0154-4*, 101250) UAHC Pr.

PURITANS—FICTION

Duey, Kathleen. Sarah Anne Hartford: Massachusetts, 1651. 1996. (American Diaries Ser.: No. 1). (Illus.). 144p. (J). (gr. 3-7). pap. 4.99 (*0-689-80384-2*, Simon Pulse) Simon & Schuster Children's Publishing.

—Sarah Anne Hartford: Massachusetts, 1651. 1996. (American Diaries Ser.: No. 1). (J). (gr. 3-7). 10.55 (*0-606-08985-3*) Turtleback Bks.

Gilson, Jamie. Stink Alley. 2002. 192p. (J). (gr. 3 up). 15.95 (*0-688-17864-2*); lib. bdg. 15.89 (*0-06-029217-2*) HarperCollins Children's Bk. Group.

Hawthorne, Nathaniel. The Scarlet Letter. 2nd ed. 1998. (Illustrated Classic Book Ser.). (Illus.). 61p. (J). (gr. 3 up). reprint ed. pap. text 4.95 (*1-56767-265-5*) Educational Insights, Inc.

Holberg, Ruth L. Kate & the Devil. 1968. (Illus.). (J). (gr. 4-6). 4.95 o.p. (*0-8038-3931-6*) Hastings Hse. Daytrips Pubs.

Jackson, Dave & Jackson, Neta. Traitor in the Tower: John Bunyan. 1997. (Trailblazer Bks.: Vol. 22). (Illus.). 144p. (J). (gr. 3-7). pap. 5.99 (*1-55661-741-0*) Bethany Hse. Pubs.

Kelley, Nancy J. The Whispering Rod: A Tale of Old Massachusetts. 2002. 160p. (J). lib. bdg. 17.95 (*1-57249-248-1*, WM Kids) White Mane Publishing Co., Inc.

Lawlor, Laurie. Saturn Coupes/Sedans Wagons 1630. 1998. (American Sisters Ser.: 03). 192p. (J). (gr. 3-7). 9.00 (*0-671-01552-4*, Aladdin) Simon & Schuster Children's Publishing.

—Voyage to a Free Land 1630. 2001. (American Sisters Ser.: Vol. 3). 192p. (J). (gr. 3-6). reprint ed. pap. 4.50 (*0-671-77562-6*, Aladdin) Simon & Schuster Children's Publishing.

Matchette, Katharine E. Libby's Choice. 1995. 157p. (YA). (gr. 6-12). pap. 8.75 (*0-9645045-0-2*) Deka Pr.

Monjo, F. N. & Quackenbush, Robert. The House on Stink Alley, ERS. 1977. (gr. k-4). o.p. (*0-03-016651-9*, Holt, Henry & Co. Bks. For Young Readers) Holt, Henry & Co.

Petry, Ann. Tituba of Salem Village. (Trophy Bk.). (YA). 1991. 272p. (gr. 5 up). pap. 5.99 (*0-06-440403-X*, Harper Trophy); 1964. (gr. 7-11). 14.95 (*0-690-82677-X*) HarperCollins Children's Bk. Group.

Phelps, Winston. Puritan Roots. 1987. (Illus.). xvii, 92p. (Orig.). (J). (gr. 7 up). pap. 7.00 o.p. (*1-55613-077-5*) Heritage Bks.

Rees, Celia. Witch Child. (gr. 7 up). 2002. 304p. (YA). bds. 8.99 (*0-7636-1829-2*); 2001. 272p. (J). 15.99 (*0-7636-1421-1*) Candlewick Pr.

—Witch Child. l.t. ed. 2002. (Young Adult Ser.). 284p. (J). 22.95 (*0-7862-3896-8*) Gale Group.

Rue, Nancy. The Accused. 1998. (Christian Heritage Ser.). 224p. (J). (gr. 3-7). pap. 5.99 (*1-56179-398-1*) Focus on the Family Publishing.
—The Secret. 1998. (Christian Heritage Ser.). 192p. (Orig.). (J). (gr. 3-7). pap. 5.99 (*1-56179-443-0*) Focus on the Family Publishing.
Speare, Elizabeth George. The Witch of Blackbird Pond. l.t. ed. 1989. 280p. (J). reprint ed. lib. bdg. 15.95 o.s.i (*1-55736-138-X*) Bantam Doubleday Dell Large Print Group, Inc.
—The Witch of Blackbird Pond. 2002. (Illus.). (J). 14.47 (*0-7587-0227-2*) Book Wholesalers, Inc.
—The Witch of Blackbird Pond. 1997. mass mkt. 2.69 o.p. (*0-440-22721-6*) Dell Publishing.
—The Witch of Blackbird Pond. (Illus.). 2001. 288p. (YA). (gr. 7-9). tchr. ed. 22.00 (*0-395-91367-5*); 1958. 256p. (J). (gr. 4-6). tchr. ed. 16.00 (*0-395-07114-3*) Houghton Mifflin Co.
—The Witch of Blackbird Pond. 2002. (J). (gr. 4-7). 32.00 incl. audio (*0-8072-0749-7*); (gr. 4-7). 32.00 incl. audio (*0-8072-0749-7*); (gr. 4-7). pap., tchr.'s planning gde. ed. 37.00 incl. audio (*0-8072-0862-0*); (gr. 4-7). pap., tchr.'s planning gde. ed. 37.00 incl. audio (*0-8072-0862-0*); (gr. 3-7). audio 26.00 (*0-8072-0748-9*) Random Hse. Audio Publishing Group. (Listening Library).
—The Witch of Blackbird Pond. 1987. (YA). (gr. 7 up). 12.04 (*0-606-00107-7*) Turtleback Bks.
Vernon, Louise A. Peter & the Pilgrims. 2nd ed. 2002. (Illus.). 119p. (J). (gr. 4-9). pap. 7.99 (*0-8361-9226-5*) Herald Pr.

R

RACIALLY MIXED PEOPLE—FICTION

Bell, William. Zack. 1998. 176p. (YA). (gr. 5). pap. o.s.i (*0-385-25711-2*) Doubleday Canada, Ltd. CAN. *Dist:* Random Hse., Inc.
—Zack. l.t. ed. 2000. (LRS Large Print Cornerstone Ser.). 256p. (YA). (gr. 5-12). lib. bdg. 28.95 (*1-58118-072-1*, 23656) LRS.
—Zack. (Illus.). 192p. (YA). (gr. 7 up). 2000. mass mkt. 4.99 (*0-689-82529-3*, Simon Pulse); 1999. per. 16.95 (*0-689-82248-0*, Simon & Schuster Children's Publishing) Simon & Schuster Children's Publishing.
—Zack. 2000. (J). 11.04 (*0-606-20095-9*) Turtleback Bks.
Binch, Caroline, illus. Silver Shoes. 2001. 32p. (J). pap. 15.95 (*0-7894-7905-2*, D K Ink) Dorling Kindersley Publishing, Inc.
Cheng, Andrea. Grandfather Counts. (Illus.). (J). 2003. pap. (*1-58430-158-9*); 2000. 32p. 15.95 (*1-58430-010-8*) Lee & Low Bks., Inc.
Cogan, Kim & Paek, Min, trs. Cooper's Lesson. 2004. (ENG & KOR., Illus.). 32p. 16.95 (*0-89239-193-6*) Children's Bk. Pr.
Crutcher, Chris. Whale Talk. 2001. 224p. (J). (gr. 7 up). 15.99 (*0-688-18019-1*); lib. bdg. 16.89 (*0-06-029369-1*) HarperCollins Children's Bk. Group. (Greenwillow Bks.).
—Whale Talk. unabr. ed. 2002. (gr. 5 up). audio 26.00 (*0-8072-0708-X*, Listening Library) Random Hse. Audio Publishing Group.
—Whale Talk. 2002. 224p. (YA). (gr. 7). mass mkt. 5.50 (*0-440-22938-3*, Laurel Leaf) Random Hse. Children's Bks.
Davol, Marguerite. Black, White, Just Right! 1993. (Albert Whitman Concept Bks.). (Illus.). 32p. (J). (gr. k-3). lib. bdg. 14.95 (*0-8075-0785-7*) Whitman, Albert & Co.
Dell, Pamela. Half-Breed: The Story of Two Boys During the Klondike Gold Rush. 2003. (J). (*1-59187-044-5*) Tradition Publishing Co.
Dorris, Michael. The Window. 1999. 112p. (J). (gr. 4 up). pap. 4.99 (*0-7868-1317-2*) Disney Pr.
—The Window. 1997. (Illus.). 112p. (J). (gr. 4 up). 16.95 (*0-7868-0301-0*); lib. bdg. 17.49 (*0-7868-2240-6*) Hyperion Bks. for Children.
—The Window. 1999. 112p. (J). (gr. 4 up). pap. 4.99 (*0-7868-1373-3*) Hyperion Pr.
Ernst, Kathleen. Trouble at Fort la Pointe. 2000. (American Girl Collection: Bk. 7). (Illus.). 176p. (J). (gr. 5-9). pap. 5.95 (*1-58485-086-8*); 9.95 (*1-58485-087-6*) Pleasant Co. Pubns. (American Girl).
—Trouble at Fort la Pointe. 2000. (American Girl Collection). (Illus.). (J). 12.00 (*0-606-20956-5*) Turtleback Bks.
Flood, Pansie Hart. It's Test Day, Tiger Turcotte. Wummer, Amy, tr. & illus. by. 2004. (Young Reader Fiction Ser.). (YA). pap. 6.95 (*1-57505-670-4*, Carolrhoda Bks.) Lerner Publishing Group.
—Tiger Turcotte & the Trouble with Tests. Wummer, Amy, tr. & illus. by. 2004. (Young Reader Fiction Ser.). (YA). lib. bdg. 14.95 (*1-57505-056-0*, Carolrhoda Bks.) Lerner Publishing Group.
Garland, Sherry. The Last Rainmaker. 1997. 336p. (YA). (gr. 5-11). 12.00 (*0-15-200649-4*) Harcourt Children's Bks.
—The Last Rainmaker. 1997. (J). 12.05 (*0-606-11550-1*) Turtleback Bks.
—Valley of the Moon: The Diary of Maria Rosalia de Milagros, Sonoma Valley, Alta California, 1846. 2001. (Dear America Ser.). (Illus.). 224p. (J). (gr. 4-9). pap. 10.95 (*0-439-08820-8*) Scholastic, Inc.
Hamilton, Virginia. Plain City. (Barco de Vapor). (SPA.). 176p. (YA). (gr. 5-8). 6.95 (*84-348-4686-1*, LEC6861) SM Ediciones ESP. *Dist:* Continental Bk. Co., Inc.
—Plain City. (J). 2003. 208p. (gr. 4-7). mass mkt. 5.99 (*0-590-47365-4*, Scholastic Paperbacks); 1993. 176p. (gr. 3-7). pap. 13.95 (*0-590-47364-6*) Scholastic, Inc.
—Plain City. 1993. (J). 11.04 (*0-606-08020-1*) Turtleback Bks.
Haslam, Gerald W. & Haslam, Janice E. Manuel & the Madman. 2000. viii, 206p. (J). pap. 9.95 (*0-915685-11-6*) Devil Mountain Bks.
Hesse, Karen. Aleutian Sparrow. unabr. ed. 2003. (J). (gr. 7). audio 12.99 (*0-8072-1966-5*, Listening Library) Random Hse. Audio Publishing Group.
—Aleutian Sparrow. 2003. (Illus.). 160p. (J). (gr. 5-9). 16.95 (*0-689-86189-3*, McElderry, Margaret K.) Simon & Schuster Children's Publishing.
Igus, Toyomi. Two Mrs. Gibsons. 1996. (Illus.). 32p. (YA). (gr. 4-7). 14.95 (*0-89239-135-9*) Children's Bk. Pr.
—Two Mrs. Gibsons. 1996. (Illus.). 32p. (J). (gr. 2-4). lib. bdg. 19.90 (*0-516-20001-1*, Children's Pr.) Scholastic Library Publishing.
Johnson, Angela. The Aunt in Our House. 1996. (Illus.). 32p. (J). (ps-3). pap. 15.95 (*0-531-09502-9*); lib. bdg. 16.99 (*0-531-08852-9*) Scholastic, Inc. (Orchard Bks.).
Kallok, Emma. Gem. 2003. (Illus.). 32p. (J). (gr. k-2). 14.95 (*1-58246-027-2*) Tricycle Pr.
Katz, Karen. The Colors of Us, ERS. (Illus.). 32p. (J). (ps-3). 2002. pap. 6.95 (*0-8050-7163-6*); 1999. 17.00 (*0-8050-5864-8*) Holt, Henry & Co. (Holt, Henry & Co. Bks. For Young Readers).
Kim, Kenneth H. Half & Half. Parker, Liz, ed. 1993. (Take Ten Bks.). (Illus.). 51p. (YA). (gr. 6-12). pap. text 3.95 o.p. (*1-56254-091-2*) Saddleback Publishing, Inc.
Little, Kimberley Griffiths. Enchanted Runner. 1999. (Avon Camelot Bks.). 149p. (J). (gr. 5-7). 15.00 (*0-380-97623-4*, Avon Bks.) Morrow/Avon.
—The Last Snake Runner. 2002. 208p. (J). (gr. 6-9). 15.95 (*0-375-81539-2*); lib. bdg. 17.99 (*0-375-91539-7*) Random Hse., Inc.
McCaffrey, Tony. Emmanuel McClue & The Mystery of the Shroud. 2002. 155p. (J). (gr. 5-9). pap. 11.95 (*1-929039-08-5*) Ambassador Bks., Inc.
Meyer, Carolyn. Jubilee Journey. 1997. 288p. (YA). (gr. 5-9). 13.00 (*0-15-201377-6*); pap. 6.00 (*0-15-201591-4*) Harcourt Children's Bks. (Gulliver Bks.).
—Jubilee Journey. 1997. 12.05 (*0-606-14244-4*) Turtleback Bks.
Monk, Isabell. Hope. 1998. (Picture Bks.). (Illus.). 32p. (J). (ps-3). lib. bdg. 15.95 (*1-57505-230-X*, Carolrhoda Bks.) Lerner Publishing Group.
Murphy, Rita. Black Angels. 2002. 176p. (gr. 4). pap. text 4.99 (*0-440-22934-0*) Random Hse., Inc.
Namioka, Lensey. Half & Half. 2003. 144p. lib. bdg. 17.99 (*0-385-90072-4*); (gr. 3-7). text 15.95 (*0-385-73038-1*) Random Hse. Children's Bks. (Delacorte Bks. for Young Readers).
Osborne, Mary Pope. Adaline Falling Star. unabr. ed. 2001. (YA). (gr. 5-9). audio 18.00 (*0-8072-0430-7*, Listening Library) Random Hse. Audio Publishing Group.
—Adaline Falling Star. 2000. (Illus.). vi, 170p. (J). (gr. 7-12). pap. 16.95 (*0-439-05947-X*, Scholastic Reference) Scholastic, Inc.
Peck, Richard. The River Between Us. 2003. 176p. (J). 16.99 (*0-8037-2735-6*, Dial Bks. for Young Readers) Penguin Putnam Bks. for Young Readers.
Platt, Randall. The Likes of Me. 2000. 256p. (YA). (gr. 9 up). 15.95 o.s.i (*0-385-32692-0*, Delacorte Pr.) Dell Publishing.
—The Likes of Me. 2001. 256p. (YA). (gr. 9 up). reprint ed. mass mkt. 5.50 o.s.i (*0-440-22880-8*, Laurel Leaf) Random Hse. Children's Bks.
Reynolds, Marilynn. If You Loved Me. 1999. (True-to-Life Series from Hamilton High: Vol. 7). 32p. pap., tchr. ed. 2.50 (*1-885356-59-5*); 224p. (YA). (gr. 7-12). pap. 8.95 (*1-885356-55-2*); (Illus.). 224p. (J). (gr. 7-12). 15.95 o.p. (*1-885356-54-4*) Morning Glory Pr., Inc.
Rinaldi, Ann. The Education of Mary: A Little Miss of Color, 1832. 2000. 256p. (J). (gr. 6-8). 15.99 (*0-7868-0532-3*, Jump at the Sun) Hyperion Bks. for Children.
—The Education of Mary: A Little Miss of Color, 1832. 2000. 254p. (J). pap. (*0-7868-1377-6*) Hyperion Pr.
—Rime of Mary Christian. 2004. 224p. (J). 15.99 (*0-06-029638-0*); lib. bdg. 16.89 (*0-06-029639-9*) HarperCollins Pubs.
Saksena, Kate. Hang on in There, Shelley. 2003. 219p. (J). 16.95 (*1-58234-822-7*, Bloomsbury Children) Bloomsbury Publishing.
Senisi, Ellen B. For My Family, Love, Allie. 1998. (Illus.). 32p. (J). (ps-3). lib. bdg. 14.95 o.p. (*0-8075-2539-1*) Whitman, Albert & Co.
Skurzynski, Gloria & Ferguson, Alane. Escape from Death, No. 9. 2002. (Mysteries in Our National Parks Ser.: Vol. 9). 160p. (J). pap. 5.95 (*0-7922-6782-6*) National Geographic Society.
—Escape from Fear. 2002. (Mysteries in Our National Parks Ser.: Vol. 9). 160p. (J). 15.95 (*0-7922-6780-X*) National Geographic Society.
Sweeney, Joyce. Waiting for June. 2003. 144p. (YA). 15.95 (*0-7614-5138-2*, Cavendish Children's Bks.) Cavendish, Marshall Corp.
Taylor, Mildred D. The Land. 2001. 392p. (J). (gr. 7 up). 17.99 (*0-8037-1950-7*); 1999. pap. 15.89 (*0-8037-1951-5*) Penguin Putnam Bks. for Young Readers. (Dial Bks. for Young Readers).
—Land. 2003. 384p. (YA). pap. 6.99 (*0-14-250146-8*, Puffin Bks.) Penguin Putnam Bks. for Young Readers.
Vigil-Pianon, Evangelina & Torrecilla, Pablo. Marina's Muumuu: El Muumuu de Marina. 2001. (ENG & SPA., Illus.). (J). pap. 9.95 (*1-55885-351-0*, Piñata Books) Arte Publico Pr.
Vigil-Pion, Evangelina. Marina's Muumuu. 2001. Tr. of Muumuu de Marina. (ENG & SPA., Illus.). 32p. (J). (ps-3). 14.95 (*1-55885-350-2*, Piñata Books) Arte Publico Pr.
Viglucci, Patricia C. Sun Dance at Turtle Rock. 1996. (Illus.). 128p. (Orig.). (J). (gr. 4-7). pap. 4.95 (*0-9645914-9-9*, Stone Pine Bks.) Patri Pubns.
Wilson, Barbara. A Clear Spring. 2004. (Girls First! Ser.: Vol. 1). 173p. (J). pap. 12.50 (*1-55861-277-7*) Feminist Pr. at The City Univ. of New York.
Woodson, Jacqueline. The House You Pass on the Way. 2003. 128p. pap. 5.99 (*0-14-250191-3*, Puffin Bks.); 160p. (J). 16.99 (*0-399-23969-3*, G. P. Putnam's Sons) Penguin Putnam Bks. for Young Readers.
—The House You Pass on the Way. 1999. 128p. (YA). (gr. 7-12). mass mkt. 4.50 o.s.i (*0-440-22797-6*, Dell Books for Young Readers) Random Hse. Children's Bks.
—The House You Pass on the Way. 1999. 10.55 (*0-606-16085-X*) Turtleback Bks.
—Miracle's Boys. 2000. 192p. (YA). (gr. 5 up). 15.99 (*0-399-23113-7*) Penguin Group (USA) Inc.
—Miracle's Boys. l.t. ed. 2001. 120p. (J). 24.95 (*0-7862-3476-8*) Thorndike Pr.
Wyeth, Sharon Dennis. Ginger Brown: Too Many Houses. 1996. (Illus.). 80p. (J). (ps-3). 11.99 o.s.i (*0-679-95437-6*); (gr. 1-4). pap. 3.99 o.s.i (*0-679-85437-1*) Random Hse. Children's Bks. (Random Hse. Bks. for Young Readers).
—Ginger Brown: Too Many Houses. 1996. 9.19 o.p. (*0-606-09327-3*) Turtleback Bks.
—The World of Daughter McGuire. (J). 1996. pap. 4.99 (*0-440-91105-2*, Dell Books for Young Readers); 1995. 176p. (gr. 3-7). pap. 3.99 o.s.i (*0-440-41114-9*, Yearling) Random Hse. Children's Bks.
—The World of Daughter McGuire. 2001. 176p. (gr. 3-7). pap. text 12.00 (*0-375-89502-7*) Random Hse., Inc.
—The World of Daughter McGuire. 1995. (J). 9.09 o.p. (*0-606-08664-1*) Turtleback Bks.
Yep, Laurence. Angelfish. 2001. 216p. (J). (gr. 5 up). 16.99 (*0-399-23041-6*, G. P. Putnam's Sons) Penguin Group (USA) Inc.
Young, Karen. Cobwebs from the Sky. Date not set. (J). 15.99 (*0-06-029761-1*, Greenwillow Bks.) HarperCollins Children's Bk. Group.

RUSSIAN AMERICANS—FICTION

Best, Cari. Three Cheers for Catherine the Great. 2001. (J). (gr. k-4). audio 6.95 (*1-55592-984-2*) Weston Woods Studios, Inc.
—Three Cheers for Catherine the Great! 1999. (Illus.). 32p. (J). (ps-3). pap. 16.99 (*0-7894-2622-6*, D K Ink) Dorling Kindersley Publishing, Inc.
—Three Cheers for Catherine the Great!, RS. 2003. (Illus.). 32p. (J). pap. 6.95 (*0-374-47551-2*, Sunburst) Farrar, Straus & Giroux.
—When Catherine the Great & I Were Eight, RS. 2003. (Illus.). 32p. (gr. k-3). 16.00 (*0-374-39954-9*, Farrar, Straus & Giroux (BYR)) Farrar, Straus & Giroux.
Cohen, Barbara. Make a Wish, Molly. 1995. 48p. (gr. 4-7). pap. text 3.99 (*0-440-41058-4*); 1994. (Illus.). 40p. (J). 14.95 o.s.i (*0-385-31079-X*, Delacorte Pr.) Dell Publishing.
—Make a Wish, Molly. 1993. (J). o.s.i (*0-385-44599-7*) Doubleday Publishing.
—Make a Wish, Molly. 1994. (J). pap. 4.50 (*0-440-91018-8*, Dell Books for Young Readers) Random Hse. Children's Bks.
—Make a Wish, Molly. 1995. (J). 10.14 (*0-606-07831-2*) Turtleback Bks.
—Make a Wish Molly. 1995. (Illus.). (J). 10.55 (*0-7857-5404-0*) Econo-Clad Bks.
—Molly's Pilgrim. 1990. (First Skylark Ser.). (Illus.). 48p. (J). (gr. k-3). pap. 3.50 o.s.i (*0-553-15833-3*) Bantam Bks.
—Molly's Pilgrim. 1990. (Yearling Ser.). (Illus.). 48p. (J). (gr. k-3). pap. text 3.50 o.s.i (*0-440-41057-6*) Dell Publishing.
—Molly's Pilgrim. (Illus.). 32p. (J). 1983. (gr. 2-5). 16.00 o.p. (*0-688-02103-4*); 1983. (gr. 2-5). lib. bdg. 15.93 o.p. (*0-688-02104-2*); 1998. (ps-3). 15.99 (*0-688-16279-7*) HarperCollins Children's Bk. Group.
—Molly's Pilgrim. rev. ed. 1998. (Illus.). 32p. (J). (gr. 1-4). pap. 3.99 (*0-688-16280-0*); pap. 3.99 (*0-688-16280-0*) Morrow/Avon. (Morrow, William & Co.).
—Molly's Pilgrim. 1991. (J). pap. o.s.i (*0-553-54012-2*, Dell Books for Young Readers) Random Hse. Children's Bks.
—Molly's Pilgrim. 1990. (Bantam First Skylark Bks.). (J). 8.70 o.p. (*0-606-04748-4*) Turtleback Bks.
Cohen, Miriam. Mimmy & Sophie, RS. 1999. (Illus.). 40p. (J). (gr. k up). 16.00 (*0-374-34988-6*, Farrar, Straus & Giroux (BYR)) Farrar, Straus & Giroux.
Gaberman, Judith. One-Way to Ansonia. 2000. 196p. pap. 12.95 (*0-595-15830-7*, Backinprint.com) iUniverse, Inc.
Hamilton, Morse. Yellow Blue Bus Means I Love You. (YA). (gr. 7 up). 2000. 192p. pap. 6.99 (*0-380-73301-3*); 1994. 14.00 o.p. (*0-688-12800-9*) HarperCollins Children's Bk. Group. (Greenwillow Bks.).
Kalman, Esther. Tchaikovsky Discovers America. (Illus.). (J). (gr. k-3). 2000. 48p. mass mkt. 6.95 (*0-531-07168-5*); 1995. 40p. pap. 14.98 (*0-531-06894-3*) Scholastic, Inc. (Orchard Bks.).
Kilpatrick, Susan. Molly's Pilgrim. 1995. (Literature Unit Ser.). (Illus.). 48p. pap., tchr. ed. 7.99 (*1-55734-535-X*, TCA0535) Teacher Created Materials, Inc.
Lehrman, Robert. The Store That Mama Built. 1992. 128p. (J). (gr. 3-7). lib. bdg. 13.95 (*0-02-754632-2*, Simon & Schuster Children's Publishing) Simon & Schuster Children's Publishing.
Levitin, Sonia. A Piece of Home. 1996. (Illus.). 32p. (J). (ps-3). 14.89 o.s.i (*0-8037-1626-5*); 14.99 o.s.i (*0-8037-1625-7*) Penguin Putnam Bks. for Young Readers. (Dial Bks. for Young Readers).
Machlin, Mikki. My Name Is Not Gussie. 1999. (Illus.). 32p. (J). (ps-3). lib. bdg., tchr. ed. 16.00 (*0-395-95646-3*) Houghton Mifflin Co.
Polacco, Patricia. The Trees of the Dancing Goats. 2002. (Illus.). (J). 25.11 (*0-7587-3858-7*) Book Wholesalers, Inc.
—The Trees of the Dancing Goats. 32p. (J). 2000. (Illus.). (gr. k-3). pap. 6.99 (*0-689-83857-3*, Aladdin); 1997. (gr. k-5). pap. 22.00 incl. audio compact disk (*0-689-81193-4*, Simon & Schuster Children's Publishing); 1997. (gr. k-5). pap. 22.00 incl. audio compact disk (*0-689-81193-4*, Simon & Schuster Children's Publishing); 1996. (Illus.). (gr. 4-7). 16.00 (*0-689-80862-3*, Simon & Schuster Children's Publishing) Simon & Schuster Children's Publishing.
—The Trees of the Dancing Goats. 2000. 13.14 (*0-606-20094-0*) Turtleback Bks.
Pryor, Bonnie. The Dream Jar. 1996. (Illus.). (J). (gr. k-3). 32p. 16.00 o.p. (*0-688-13061-5*); lib. bdg. 15.89 (*0-688-13062-3*) Morrow/Avon. (Morrow, William & Co.).
Rosenblum, Richard. Journey to the Golden Land. 1992. (Illus.). 32p. (J). (gr. k-4). 9.95 (*0-8276-0405-X*) Jewish Pubn. Society.
Sachs, Marilyn. Call Me Ruth. 1995. 224p. (J). (gr. 4-7). pap. 4.95 (*0-688-13737-7*, Harper Trophy) HarperCollins Children's Bk. Group.
—Call Me Ruth. 1996. (J). (gr. 3 up). 18.75 o.p. (*0-8446-6905-9*) Smith, Peter Pub., Inc.
Shiefman, Vicky. Good-Bye to the Trees. 1993. 160p. (J). (gr. 4-8). 14.95 o.p. (*0-689-31806-5*, Atheneum) Simon & Schuster Children's Publishing.
Tarbescu, Edith. Annushka's Voyage. 1998. (Illus.). 32p. (J). (ps-3). tchr. ed. 15.00 (*0-395-64366-X*) Houghton Mifflin Co.
Vogt, Esther Loewen. A Race for Land. 1992. 112p. (J). (gr. 4-7). pap. 5.99 o.p. (*0-8361-3575-X*) Herald Pr.

S

SCOTS—UNITED STATES—FICTION

Lunn, Janet. Shadow in Hawthorn Bay. 1988. 192p. (J). (gr. 5-9). pap. 3.95 o.p. (*0-14-032436-4*, Puffin Bks.) Penguin Putnam Bks. for Young Readers.
—Shadow in Hawthorn Bay. 1987. 192p. (YA). (gr. 7 up). 13.95 o.s.i (*0-684-18843-0*, Atheneum) Simon & Schuster Children's Publishing.

SHAVUOT—FICTION

Wengrov, Charles. The Story of Shavuot. 1965. (Shulsinger Holiday Ser.). (Illus.). (J). (gr. k-7). pap. 2.50 o.s.i (*0-914080-55-5*) Shulsinger Sales, Inc.

SOCIETY OF FRIENDS—FICTION

Avi. Night Journeys. 160p. (J). 2000. (Illus.). (gr. 3-7). pap. 5.99 (*0-380-73242-4*, Harper Trophy); 1994. (gr. 5 up). reprint ed. pap. 4.95 (*0-688-13628-1*) HarperCollins Children's Bk. Group.

—Night Journeys. 1994. 160p. (YA). (gr. 5 up). reprint ed. 15.00 o.p. (*0-688-05298-3*, Morrow, William & Co.) Morrow/Avon.

—Night Journeys, unabr. ed. 1997. (YA). 40.20 incl. audio (*0-7887-1838-X*, 40618); (J). (gr. 6). audio 27.00 (*0-7887-1795-2*, 95267E7) Recorded Bks., LLC.

—Night Journeys. 2000. 11.04 (*0-606-17978-X*); 1994. 10.05 o.p. (*0-606-06621-7*) Turtleback Bks.

Beatty, Patricia. Who Comes with Cannons? 1992. 192p. (J). (gr. 4-7). 15.99 (*0-688-11028-2*) HarperCollins Children's Bk. Group.

Bruchac, Joseph. The Arrow over the Door. (Illus.). 96p. (J). 2002. pap. 4.99 (*0-14-130571-1*, Puffin Bks.); 1998. (gr. 2-4). 15.99 (*0-8037-2078-5*, Dial Bks. for Young Readers) Penguin Putnam Bks. for Young Readers.

Clark, Marnie, et al, eds. Lighting Candles in the Dark: Stories of Courage & Love in Action. 1992. (Illus.). 215p. (Orig.). (YA). reprint ed. per. 13.00 (*0-9620912-3-5*) Quaker Press of Friends General Conference.

Cromer, Mary L. Stories for Jason. 1993. 110p. (J). pap. 9.00 (*0-944350-28-3*) Friends United Pr.

De Angeli, Marguerite. Thee, Hannah! 1970. (Illus.). 96p. (J). (gr. 2-5). 15.95 o.s.i (*0-385-07525-1*) Doubleday Publishing.

—Thee, Hannah! 2nd ed. 2000. (Illus.). 112p. (J). (gr. 3-7). pap. 15.99 (*0-8361-9106-4*) Herald Pr.

Hedstrom, Deborah. From Settlement to City with Benjamin Franklin. 1997. (My American Journey Ser.). (Illus.). 19.99 o.p. (*1-57673-164-2*) Multnomah Pubs., Inc.

Jackson, Dave & Jackson, Neta. Thieves of Tyburn Square: Elizabeth Fry. 1995. (Trailblazer Bks.: Vol. 17). (Illus.). 144p. (J). (gr. 3-7). pap. 5.99 (*1-55661-470-5*) Bethany Hse. Pubs.

Luttrell, Ida. The Bear Next Door. 1991. (I Can Read Bks.). (Illus.). 64p. (J). (gr. 1-3). lib. bdg. 15.89 o.p. (*0-06-024024-5*); 11.95 (*0-06-024023-7*) HarperCollins Children's Bk. Group.

Newman, Daisy. I Take Thee, Serenity, 001. 1975. 320p. (J). 8.95 o.p. (*0-395-20551-4*) Houghton Mifflin Co.

Rinaldi, Ann. Finishing Becca: A Story about Peggy Shippen & Benedict Arnold. (Great Episodes Ser.). 384p. (YA). 2004. pap. (*0-15-205079-5*); 1994. (gr. 7 up). 12.00 (*0-15-200880-2*); 1994. (gr. 7 up). pap. 6.00 o.s.i (*0-15-200879-9*) Harcourt Children's Bks. (Gulliver Bks.).

—Finishing Becca: A Story about Peggy Shippen & Benedict Arnold. 1994. 12.05 (*0-606-14207-X*) Turtleback Bks.

Ruby, Lois. Steal Away Home. 1997. pap. 1.95 o.p. (*0-590-03322-0*) Scholastic, Inc.

—Steal Away Home. 1999. 208p. (J). (gr. 3-7). pap. 4.99 (*0-689-82435-1*, Aladdin) Simon & Schuster Children's Publishing.

—Steal Away Home. 1999. 11.04 (*0-606-15921-5*) Turtleback Bks.

Smith, Susan. Sonya Begonia & the Eleventh Birthday Blues. 1990. (Best Friends Ser.). (Orig.). (J). (gr. 3-7). pap. 2.75 (*0-671-73033-9*, Aladdin) Simon & Schuster Children's Publishing.

Snedeker, Caroline Dale. Downright Dencey. 1927. (J). (gr. 3-7). 3.95 o.p. (*0-385-07284-8*) Doubleday Publishing.

Steele, William O. The Man with the Silver Eyes. 1976. (J). (gr. 5 up). 5.95 o.p. (*0-15-251720-0*) Harcourt Children's Bks.

Turkle, Brinton. Obadiah the Bold. (Illus.). (J). (gr. k-3). 1977. 4p. pap. 4.99 o.s.i (*0-14-050233-5*, Puffin Bks.); 1965. 13.95 o.p. (*0-670-52001-2*, Viking Children's Bks.) Penguin Putnam Bks. for Young Readers.

—Thy Friend, Obadiah. 1969. (Illus.). (J). (gr. k-3). 13.95 o.p. (*0-670-71229-9*, Viking Children's Bks.) Penguin Putnam Bks. for Young Readers.

SWEDES—UNITED STATES—FICTION

Ericson, Stig. Dan Henry in the Wild West. Teal, Thomas, tr. 1976. (J). (gr. 5-9). 5.95 o.p. (*0-440-01659-2*, Delacorte Pr.) Dell Publishing.

Lindquist, Jennie D. Crystal Tree. 1966. (Illus.). (J). (gr. 3-7). 6.79 o.p. (*0-06-023894-1*) HarperCollins Pubs.

—Golden Name Day. 1955. (Illus.). (J). (gr. 3-6). pap. 1.50 o.p. (*0-06-440024-7*); lib. bdg. 11.89 o.p. (*0-06-023881-X*) HarperCollins Pubs.

Munson, Sammye. Hej Texas, Goodbye Sweden. 1994. 128p. (J). (gr. 5-6). 13.95 (*0-89015-948-3*) Eakin Pr.

Rew, Lois J. God's Green Liniment. 1981. (Illus.). 204p. (Orig.). (J). (gr. 3-8). pap. 8.99 (*0-938462-02-4*) Green Leaf Pr.

SWISS—UNITED STATES—FICTION

Brummett, Nancy Parker. Journey of Elisa: From Switzerland to America. (Immigrants Chronicles Ser.). 132p. (J). (gr. 3-7). pap. 5.99 (*0-7814-3286-3*) Cook Communications Ministries.

T

TUAREGS—FICTION

Kaufmann, Herbert. Adventure in the Desert. 1961. (Illus.). (J). (gr. 7 up). 12.95 (*0-8392-3000-1*) Astor-Honor, Inc.

—Lost Sahara Trail. 1962. (J). (gr. 7 up). 12.95 (*0-8392-3022-2*) Astor-Honor, Inc.

V

VIETNAMESE AMERICANS—FICTION

Breckler, Rosemary K. Hoang Breaks the Lucky Teapot. 1992. (Illus.). 32p. (J). (gr. k-3). tchr. ed. 13.95 o.s.i (*0-395-57031-X*) Houghton Mifflin Co.

Garland, Sherry. My Father's Boat. 1998. (Illus.). 32p. (J). (gr. k-3). pap. 15.95 (*0-590-47867-2*) Scholastic, Inc.

—Shadow of the Dragon. 1994. (J). pap. 3.95 (*0-15-200295-2*); 1993. (Illus.). 368p. (YA). (gr. 7 up). 10.95 (*0-15-273530-5*); 1993. (Illus.). 320p. (YA). (gr. 7 up). pap. 6.00 (*0-15-273532-1*, Harcourt Paperbacks) Harcourt Children's Bks.

Good Morning, Vietnam, Good Afternoon, USA. 2000. (*0-9703585-0-4*) Hudson, Anna E.

Harman, Betty & Meador, Nancy. The Moon Rock Heist. 1988. 112p. (J). (gr. 6-7). 13.95 (*0-89015-667-0*) Eakin Pr.

Holmes, Mary Z. Dust of Life. 1992. (History's Children Ser.). (Illus.). 48p. (J). (gr. 4-5). pap. o.p. (*0-8114-6429-6*); lib. bdg. 21.36 o.p. (*0-8114-3504-0*) Raintree Pubs.

McKay, Lawrence, Jr. Journey Home. 2000. (Illus.). 32p. (J). (ps-5). 15.95 (*1-880000-65-2*); pap. 6.95 (*1-58430-005-1*) Lee & Low Bks., Inc.

—Journey Home. 1998. (Illus.). (J). 13.10 (*0-606-18247-0*) Turtleback Bks.

Mills, Charles. Voyager. 157p. (J). reprint ed. pap. 48.70 (*0-7837-6401-4*, 204611700010) Bks. on Demand.

—Voyager. Johnson, Jeannette, ed. 1989. 160p. (J). pap. 7.95 o.p. (*0-8280-0491-9*) Review & Herald Publishing Assn.

—Voyager, II. 1991. 192p. (Orig.). (J). (gr. 5-8). pap. 7.99 o.p. (*0-8280-0595-8*) Review & Herald Publishing Assn.

Mosher, Richard. Zazoo. 2001. 224p. (YA). (gr. 7 up). tchr. ed. 16.00 (*0-618-13534-0*, Clarion Bks.) Houghton Mifflin Co. Trade & Reference Div.

Pastore, Clare. Journey to America: Chantrea's Voyage, Vol. 3. 2002. 192p. mass mkt. 5.99 (*0-425-18857-4*) Berkley Publishing Group.

Paterson, Katherine. Park's Quest. 160p. (J). 1989. (gr. 4-7). pap. 5.99 (*0-14-034262-1*, Puffin Bks.); 1988. (gr. 5 up). 13.99 o.s.i (*0-525-67258-3*, Dutton Children's Bks.) Penguin Putnam Bks. for Young Readers.

—Park's Quest. 1988. 11.04 (*0-606-02743-2*) Turtleback Bks.

Pettit, Jayne. My Name Is San Ho. 1992. 192p. (J). 13.95 o.p. (*0-590-44172-8*) Scholastic, Inc.

Skurzynski, Gloria & Ferguson, Alane. Rage of Fire. 160p. (J). (gr. 3-7). 2001. (Mysteries in Our National Parks Ser.). pap. 5.95 (*0-7922-7653-1*); 1999. (National Parks Mysteries Ser.: No. 2). (Illus.). 15.95 (*0-7922-7035-5*) National Geographic Society.

Sommer, Karen. New Kids on the Block. 1987. (Satch Ser.). 132p. (J). (gr. 3-7). pap. 4.99 o.p. (*0-89191-746-2*) Cook Communications Ministries.

Tamar, Erika. The Truth about Kim O'Hara. 1992. 192p. (J). (gr. 6-9). 14.95 o.p. (*0-689-31789-1*, Atheneum) Simon & Schuster Children's Publishing.

Tran, Truong. Going Home, Coming Home / Ve Nha Tham Que Hu'O'Ng. 2003. Tr. of Ve Nha Tham Que Hu'O'Ng. (ENG & VIE., Illus.). 32p. (J). 16.95 (*0-89239-179-0*) Children's Bk. Pr.

Windle, Jeanette. Secret of the Dragon Mark. 2002. (Parker Twins Ser.: No. 5). 160p. (J). (gr. 3-8). 5.99 (*0-8254-4149-8*) Kregel Pubns.

—Secret of the Dragon Mark. 1996. (Twin Pursuits Ser.: No. 2). 128p. pap. 4.99 o.p. (*0-88070-905-7*, Multnomah Bks.) Multnomah Pubs., Inc.

Z

ZULU (AFRICAN PEOPLE)—FICTION

Ferreira, Anton. Zulu Dog, RS. 2002. (Illus.). 208p. (J). (gr. 5 up). 16.00 (*0-374-39223-4*, Farrar, Straus & Giroux (BYR)) Farrar, Straus & Giroux.

Welch, Ronald. Zulu Warrior. 1974. (gr. 3-8). o.p. (*0-7153-6555-X*) David & Charles Pubs.

HISTORICAL EVENTS

A

ABOLITIONISTS—FICTION

Burton, Hester. To Ravensrigg. 1977. (J). 10.78 (*0-690-01354-X*) HarperCollins Children's Bk. Group.

Kay, Alan N. On the Trail of John Brown's Body. 2001. (Young Heroes of History Ser.: Vol. 2). (Illus.). 175p. (J). (gr. 4-7). pap. 5.95 (*1-57249-239-2*, 1572492406, Burd Street Pr.) White Mane Publishing Co., Inc.

Krisher, Trudy B. Uncommon Faith. 2003. 263p. (J). tchr. ed. 17.95 (*0-8234-1791-3*) Holiday Hse., Inc.

Lasky, Kathryn. True North: A Novel of the Underground Railroad. 208p. 1998. (J). (gr. 5-9). mass mkt. 4.99 (*0-590-20524-2*); 1996. (YA). (gr. 7 up). pap. 15.95 (*0-590-20523-4*) Scholastic, Inc. (Blue Sky Pr., The).

—True North: A Novel of the Underground Railroad. 1998. (J). 11.04 (*0-606-13874-9*) Turtleback Bks.

Lyons, Mary E. & Branch, Muriel M. Dear Ellen Bee: A Civil War Scrapbook of Two Union Spies. 2000. (Illus.). 176p. (J). (gr. 4 up). 17.95 (*0-689-82379-7*, Atheneum) Simon & Schuster Children's Publishing.

Pryor, Bonnie. Joseph: 1861 - A Rumble of War. 2000. (Illus.). (J). 10.55 (*0-606-17975-5*) Turtleback Bks.

—Joseph: 1861 - a Rumble of War. 1999. (American Adventures Ser.). (Illus.). 176p. (J). (gr. 3-7). 14.95 (*0-688-15671-1*) HarperCollins Children's Bk. Group.

—Joseph: 1861—A Rumble of War. 2000. (American Adventures Ser.). (Illus.). 176p. (J). (gr. 3-7). pap. 4.50 (*0-380-73103-7*, Harper Trophy) HarperCollins Children's Bk. Group.

Rees, Douglas. Lightning Time. 1997. (Illus.). 172p. (J). (gr. 5-9). pap. 15.95 o.p. (*0-7894-2458-4*) Dorling Kindersley Publishing, Inc.

—Lightning Time. 1999. 176p. (J). (gr. 5-9). pap. 4.99 (*0-14-130317-4*, Puffin Bks.) Penguin Putnam Bks. for Young Readers.

—Lightning Time. 1999. 11.04 (*0-606-19069-4*) Turtleback Bks.

Rinaldi, Ann. Mine Eyes Have Seen. 1997. (Illus.). 288p. (J). (gr. 7-12). pap. 16.95 (*0-590-54318-0*) Scholastic, Inc.

—Mine Eyes Have Seen. 2002. 11.04 (*0-606-22271-5*) Turtleback Bks.

Rosen, Michael J. A School for Pompey Walker. 1995. (Illus.). 48p. (J). (gr. 4-7). 16.00 (*0-15-200114-X*) Harcourt Children's Bks.

Underwood, Betty. The Forge & the Forest, 001. 1975. (Illus.). 240p. (YA). (gr. 6 up). 6.95 o.p. (*0-395-20492-5*) Houghton Mifflin Co.

Weinberg, Larry. Ghost Hotel. 1994. 9.05 o.p. (*0-606-06409-5*) Turtleback Bks.

Williams, Jeanne. Freedom Trail. 1973. 160p. (YA). (gr. 6 up). 5.95 o.p. (*0-399-20336-2*) Putnam Publishing Group, The.

Yates, Elizabeth. Prudence Crandall: Woman of Courage. 1955. (Illus.). (J). (gr. 7 up). 8.50 o.p. (*0-525-37883-9*, Dutton) Dutton/Plume.

ALAMO (SAN ANTONIO, TEX.)—FICTION

Casad, Mary Brooke. Bluebonnet at the Alamo. 1995. (Illus.). 40p. (J). (ps-3). pap. 6.95 (*1-57168-027-6*) Eakin Pr.

Cousins, Margaret. The Boy in the Alamo. 1983. (Illus.). 180p. (J). (gr. 5-7). reprint ed. pap. 8.95 (*0-931722-26-8*) Corona Publishing, Co.

Garland, Sherry. In the Shadow of the Alamo. 2001. (Great Episodes Ser.). 288p. (YA). (gr. 5-8). 17.00 (*0-15-201744-5*, Gulliver Bks.) Harcourt Children's Bks.

Love, D. Anne. I Remember the Alamo. 1999. 156p. (J). (gr. 3-7). tchr. ed. 15.95 (*0-8234-1426-4*) Holiday Hse., Inc.

—I Remember the Alamo. 2001. 176p. (gr. 4-7). pap. text 4.50 (*0-440-41697-3*, Yearling) Random Hse. Children's Bks.

Rice, James. Texas Jack at the Alamo. 1989. (Illus.). 32p. (YA). (gr. 2 up). 14.95 (*0-88289-725-X*) Pelican Publishing Co., Inc.

—Victor Lopez at the Alamo. 2001. (Illus.). 128p. (J). (gr. 3-7). pap. 12.95 (*1-56554-866-3*) Pelican Publishing Co., Inc.

Richardson, Jean. When Grandpa Had Fangs. 1997. (Illus.). 32p. (J). (gr. 2-3). 14.95 (*1-57168-175-2*) Eakin Pr.

Rogers, Lisa Waller. Angel of the Alamo. 2000. (Illus.). 48p. (J). (gr. 3-8). 18.95 (*0-87443-125-5*, 125-5); pap. 8.95 (*0-87443-126-3*, 126-3) Benson, W. S. & Co., Inc.

—Remember the Alamo! The Runaway Scrape Diary of Belle Wood. 2003. (Lone Star Journals: Bk. 3). 176p. (J). 15.95 (*0-89672-497-2*) Texas Tech Univ. Pr.

Schaller, Bob. Treasure in Texas. 2001. (X-Country Adventures Ser.). 128p. (J). (gr. 3-6). pap. 5.99 o.p. (*0-8010-4492-8*) Baker Bks.

Stover, Jill. Alamo Across Texas. 1993. (Illus.). (J). (ps-3). lib. bdg. 12.93 o.p. (*0-688-11713-9*) HarperCollins Children's Bk. Group.

Warner, Gertrude Chandler, creator. The Mystery at the Alamo. 1997. (Boxcar Children Ser.: No. 58). (J). (gr. 2-5). 10.00 (*0-606-11161-1*) Turtleback Bks.

—The Mystery at the Alamo. 1997. (Boxcar Children Ser.: No. 58). (J). (gr. 2-5). lib. bdg. 13.95 (*0-8075-5436-7*); mass mkt. 3.95 (*0-8075-5437-5*) Whitman, Albert & Co.

Wheatly, Mark. Build the Alamo. Eakin, Ed, ed. 1989. (Illus.). 32p. (J). (gr. 4-5). 10.95 o.p. (*0-89015-721-9*) Eakin Pr.

AMERICA—DISCOVERY AND EXPLORATION—FICTION

Bresnick-Perry, Roslyn. Leaving for America. 1992. (Illus.). 32p. (YA). (ps-3). 14.95 (*0-89239-105-7*) Children's Bk. Pr.

Brown, Virginia P. Cochula's Journey. 1996. 160p. (J). (gr. 5-8). 18.00 (*1-881320-40-5*, Black Belt Pr.) River City Publishing.

Bulla, Clyde Robert & Syson, Michael. Conquista! 1978. (Illus.). (J). (gr. 2-5). lib. bdg. 12.89 (*0-690-03871-2*) HarperCollins Children's Bk. Group.

Campbell, Donna. Pale as the Moon. 1999. (Carolina Young People Ser.). (Illus.). 104p. (J). (gr. 4-8). pap. 10.95 (*1-928556-02-7*) Coastal Carolina Pr.

Clifford, Mary L. When the Great Canoes Came. 1993. (Illus.). 144p. (J). 12.95 o.s.i (*0-88289-926-0*); (gr. 4-7). pap. 12.95 (*1-56554-646-6*) Pelican Publishing Co., Inc.

Dorris, Michael. Guests. 1994. 128p. (J). 13.95 (*0-7868-0047-X*); (gr. 3-7). lib. bdg. 14.49 o.s.i (*0-7868-2036-5*) Hyperion Bks. for Children.

—Guests. 1996. 128p. (J). (gr. 3-7). pap. 4.50 (*0-7868-1108-0*) Hyperion Paperbacks for Children.

—Guests. 1999. 128p. (J). (gr. 4 up). pap. 4.99 (*0-7868-1356-3*) Hyperion Pr.

—Guests. 1996. (J). 11.04 (*0-606-08759-1*) Turtleback Bks.

—Morning Girl. 80p. 1994. (YA). (gr. 4-7). pap. 4.95 (*1-56282-661-1*); 1992. (J). 12.95 o.p. (*1-56282-284-5*); 1992. (YA). (gr. 3 up). lib. bdg. 13.49 o.s.i (*1-56282-285-3*) Hyperion Bks. for Children.

—Morning Girl. 1999. 80p. (J). (gr. 4 up). pap. text 4.99 (*0-7868-1372-5*); mass mkt. 4.99 (*0-7868-1358-X*) Hyperion Pr.

—Morning Girl. 1994. (J). 11.14 (*0-606-06583-0*) Turtleback Bks.

Fritz, Jean. Brendan the Navigator: A History Mystery about the Discovery of America. 1979. 31p. (gr. 1-6). 17.99 (*0-399-23326-1*) Penguin Group (USA) Inc.

—Brendan the Navigator: A History Mystery about the Discovery of America. 1999. (gr. 1-6). pap. 5.99 (*0-698-11759-X*) Penguin Putnam Bks. for Young Readers.

Garfield, Henry. The Lost Voyage of John Cabot. 2004. (YA). (*0-689-85173-1*, Atheneum/Richard Jackson Bks.) Simon & Schuster Children's Publishing.

Garland, Sherry. Indio. 1995. (Great Episodes Ser.). 304p. (YA). (gr. 7 up). 11.00 o.s.i (*0-15-238631-9*); pap. 6.00 (*0-15-200021-6*) Harcourt Children's Bks. (Gulliver Bks.).

—Indio. 1995. (Illus.). 10.10 o.p. (*0-606-09466-0*) Turtleback Bks.

Hays, Wilma P. Noko, Captive of Columbus. 1967. (Illus.). (J). (gr. 3-7). 4.49 o.p. (*0-698-30259-1*) Putnam Publishing Group, The.

Hewlett, Maurice. Gudrid the Fair. (J). E-Book 3.95 (*0-594-02441-2*) 1873 Pr.

Martin, Susan. I Sailed with Columbus: The Adventures of a Ship's Boy. 1991. (Illus.). 154p. (YA). (gr. 8-10). reprint ed. 18.00 (*0-7567-6043-7*) DIANE Publishing Co.

—I Sailed with Columbus: The Adventures of a Ship's Boy. 1991. (Illus.). 154p. (YA). (gr. 5 up). 17.95 o.p. (*0-87951-431-0*) Overlook Pr., The.

Merino, Jose M. The Gold of Dreams, RS. Lane, Helen, tr. 1992. 224p. (YA). (gr. 7 up). 15.00 o.p. (*0-374-32692-4*, Farrar, Straus & Giroux (BYR)) Farrar, Straus & Giroux.

Merino, Jose Maria. Beyond the Ancient Cities, RS. Lane, Helen, tr. from SPA. 1994. Tr. of Tierra del Tiempo Perdido. 208p. (J). 16.00 o.p. (*0-374-34307-1*, Farrar, Straus & Giroux (BYR)) Farrar, Straus & Giroux.

Nelson-Hernandez, Natalie. Mapmakers of the Western Trails: The Story of John Charles Fremont. 1997. (Illus.). 128p. (J). (gr. 3-8). pap. 9.95 o.p. (*0-9644386-2-3*) Santa Ines Pubns.

O'Dell, Scott. The King's Fifth. 2002. (Illus.). (J). 24.36 (*0-7587-0284-1*) Book Wholesalers, Inc.

O'Dell, Scott, et al. The King's Fifth. 1966. (Illus.). 272p. (YA). (gr. 7 up). tchr. ed. 17.00 (*0-395-06963-7*) Houghton Mifflin Co.

Parish, Helen R. Estebanico. 1974. 128p. (J). (gr. 7 up). 5.95 o.p. (*0-670-29814-X*) Viking Penguin.

Piercy, Patricia A. The Great Encounter: A Special Meeting Before Columbus. 1991. (Illus.). 41p. (J). (gr. 2-5). pap. 6.95 (*0-913543-26-8*) African American Images.

Stainer, M. L. The Lyon's Crown. 2000. (Lyon Saga Ser.: No. 5). (Illus.). 165p. (J). (gr. 5-9). lib. bdg. 9.95 (*1-893337-03-0*); pap. 6.95 (*1-893337-04-9*) Chicken Soup Pr., Inc.

—The Lyon's Throne. 1999. (Lyon Saga Ser.: Bk. 4). (Illus.). 153p. (YA). (gr. 5-9). pap. 6.95 (*1-893337-02-2*) Chicken Soup Pr., Inc.

Whittier, Mary Ann. Tales from 1492. (YA). (gr. 7 up). lib. bdg. 19.99 (*0-89824-981-3*) Royal Fireworks Publishing Co.

B

BACON'S REBELLION, 1676—FICTION

Harrah, Madge. My Brother, My Enemy. 1997. 144p. (YA). (gr. 5-9). 16.00 (*0-689-80968-9*, Simon & Schuster Children's Publishing) Simon & Schuster Children's Publishing.

BEAGLE EXPEDITION (1831-1836)—FICTION

Weaver, Anne H. The Voyage of the Beetle: A Journey Around the World with Charles Darwin & the Search for the Solution to the Mystery of Mysteries, As Narrated by Rosie, an Articulate Beetle. Lawrence, George, tr. & illus. by. 2004. 80p. lib. bdg. 26.90 (*0-7613-2923-4*) Millbrook Pr., Inc.

BERLIN WALL, BERLIN, GERMANY, 1961-1989—FICTION

Degens, T. Freya on the Wall. 1997. 288p. (J). 19.00 o.s.i (*0-15-200210-3*) Harcourt Trade Pubs.

Disch, Irene & Enzensberger, Hans Magnus. Esterhazy. 1994. (Illus.). 32p. 16.95 o.p. (*0-88682-731-0*, Creative Education) Creative Co., The.

Larson, Lloyd. He is Risen! SAB. (Illus.). pap. (*0-7390-1978-3*, 2008) Alfred Publishing Co., Inc.

Lutzeier, Elizabeth. The Wall. 1992. 160p. (J). (gr. 5-9). 14.95 o.p. (*0-8234-0987-2*) Holiday Hse., Inc.

Stapleton, Peter. New Directions for a Musical Church. 1975. 120p. pap. 5.25 o.p. (*0-8042-1765-3*) Westminster John Knox Pr.

BOSTON TEA PARTY, 1773—FICTION

Grote, JoAnn A. The American Revolution. 1999. (American Adventure Ser.: No. 11). (J). (gr. 3-7). (*0-7910-5591-4*) Chelsea Hse. Pubs.

Hemphill, Kris. A Secret Party in Boston Harbor. 1998. (Mysteries in Time Ser.: Vol. 6). (Illus.). 96p. (J). (gr. 4-7). text 14.95 (*1-881889-88-2*) Silver Moon Pr.

Seabrooke, Brenda. The Chester Town Tea Party. 1991. (Illus.). 30p. (J). (ps-3). 8.95 (*0-87033-422-0*, Tidewater Pubs.) Cornell Maritime Pr., Inc.

Stanley, Diane. Joining the Boston Tea Party. 2001. (Time-Traveling Twins Ser.: No. 2). (Illus.). 48p. (J). (gr. k-5). 15.99 (*0-06-027067-5*); lib. bdg. 15.89 (*0-06-027068-3*) HarperCollins Children's Bk. Group. (Cotler, Joanna Bks.).

Stein, R. Conrad. The Boston Tea Party. (Cornerstones of Freedom Ser.). (Illus.). 32p. (J). (gr. 4-6). 1998. pap. 5.95 (*0-516-26285-8*); 1996. lib. bdg. 21.00 (*0-516-20005-4*) Scholastic Library Publishing. (Children's Pr.).

BYZANTINE EMPIRE—FICTION

Barrett, Tracy. Anna of Byzantium. 224p. (YA). (gr. 7-12). 2000. mass mkt. 4.50 (*0-440-41536-5*, Laurel Leaf); 1999. (Illus.). 14.95 (*0-385-32626-2*, Dell Books for Young Readers) Random Hse. Children's Bks.

—Anna of Byzantium. 2000. 10.55 (*0-606-19742-7*) Turtleback Bks.

Paton Walsh, Jill. The Emperor's Winding Sheet, RS. 288p. (gr. 7 up). 1992. (YA). pap. 4.95 o.p. (*0-374-42121-8*, Sunburst); 1974. (J). 13.95 o.p. (*0-374-32160-4*, Farrar, Straus & Giroux (BYR)) Farrar, Straus & Giroux.

—The Emperor's Winding Sheet. 1993. (J). (gr. 4-9). 18.00 o.p. (*0-8446-6665-3*) Smith, Peter Pub., Inc.

C

CHILDREN'S CRUSADE, 1212—FICTION

Beckman, Thea. Crusade in Jeans. 2003. (J). 14.95 (*1-886910-96-0*, Front Street) Front Street, Inc.

Janasik, Steven M. A Journey of Innocents. 1999. (Illus.). 340p. 25.95 (*0-9659417-2-8*); pap. 16.95 (*0-9659417-3-6*) Century Pr.

Thompson, Brenda & Overbeck, Cynthia. The Children's Crusade. 1977. (First Fact Bks.). (Illus.). (J). (gr. k-3). lib. bdg. 4.95 o.p. (*0-8225-1353-6*, Lerner Pubns.) Lerner Publishing Group.

CONNECTICUT—HISTORY—FICTION

Evan, Frances Y. The Forgotten Flag: Revolutionary Struggle in Connecticut. 2003. 92p. (J). 5.95 (*1-57249-338-0*, WM Kids) White Mane Publishing Co., Inc.

Underwood, Betty. Tamarack Tree, 001. 1971. (Illus.). (J). (gr. 5-9). 5.95 o.p. (*0-395-12761-0*) Houghton Mifflin Co.

Van Leeuwen, Jean. Hannah's Helping Hands. Fogelman, Phyllis, ed. 1999. (Pioneer Daughters Ser.: No. 2). (Illus.). 96p. (J). (gr. 2-5). 13.99 o.p. (*0-8037-2447-0*, Dial Bks. for Young Readers) Penguin Putnam Bks. for Young Readers.

Yates, Elizabeth. Prudence Crandall: Woman of Courage. 1955. (Illus.). (J). (gr. 7 up). 8.50 o.p. (*0-525-37883-9*, Dutton) Dutton/Plume.

CRIMEAN WAR, 1853-1856—FICTION

Jackson, Dave & Jackson, Neta. The Drummer Boy's Battle: Florence Nightingale. 1997. (Trailblazer Bks.: Vol. 21). (Illus.). 144p. (J). (gr. 3-7). pap. 5.99 (*1-55661-740-2*) Bethany Hse. Pubs.

CRUSADES—FICTION

Bradford, Karleen. There Will Be Wolves. 1996. 208p. (YA). (gr. 7-12). 15.99 o.p. (*0-525-67539-6*, Dutton Children's Bks.) Penguin Putnam Bks. for Young Readers.

Celestri, John. The Christian Crusader: Web of Lies...Chains of Sin. 1993. (Illus.). 80p. (Orig.). (J). (gr. 3-6). pap. 4.99 (*0-9634183-2-7*) C C Publishing.

Henty, G. A. Winning His Spurs: A Tale of the Crusades. 2000. 252p. (J). E-Book 9.95 (*0-594-02413-7*) 1873 Pr.

Jocson, Antonio & Christian, J. E. The Children's Crusade. 1998. (Illus.). 84p. (J). (gr. 3 up). 22.00 (*1-890963-27-5*, LB Bks.) Liberty Bell Productions.

Patterson, James & Gross, Andrew. The Jester. 2004. 496p. mass mkt. 7.99 (*0-446-61384-3*, Warner Vision) Warner Bks., Inc.

Tullus & the Ransom Gold. 1974. (Illus.). 96p. (gr. 4-5). pap. 1.25 o.p. (*0-912692-33-2*) Cook, David C. Publishing Co.

Tullus in the Deadly Whirlpool. 1974. (Illus.). 96p. (gr. 4-5). pap. 1.25 o.p. (*0-912692-34-0*) Cook, David C. Publishing Co.

E

EGYPT—HISTORY—FICTION

Anderson, Scoular. A Puzzling Day in the Land of the Pharaohs. 1996. (Illus.). 32p. (J). (gr. 4-7). 14.99 o.p. (*1-56402-877-1*) Candlewick Pr.

Banks, Lynne Reid. Moses in Egypt: A Novel Inspired by The Prince of Egypt & The Book of Exodus. 1998. (Prince of Egypt Ser.). (Illus.). 128p. (J). (gr. 5-9). pap. text 4.99 (*0-8499-5898-9*) Nelson, Tommy.

Bunting, Eve. I Am the Mummy Heb-Nefert. (Illus.). 32p. (J). 2000. (ps-3). pap. 6.00 (*0-15-202464-6*, Harcourt Paperbacks); 1997. (gr. 2-7). 15.00 (*0-15-200479-3*) Harcourt Children's Bks.

Clements, Andrew. Temple Cat. 1996. (Illus.). 32p. (J). (gr. k-3). tchr. ed. 16.00 o.p. (*0-395-69842-1*, Clarion Bks.) Houghton Mifflin Co. Trade & Reference Div.

—Temple Cat. 1999. (J). 16.00 (*0-689-80248-X*, Simon & Schuster Children's Publishing) Simon & Schuster Children's Publishing.

Gregory, Kristiana. Cleopatra VII: Daughter of the Nile, Egypt, 57 B. C. 1999. (Royal Diaries Ser.). (Illus.). 221p. (J). (gr. 4-8). 10.95 (*0-590-81975-5*, Scholastic Pr.) Scholastic, Inc.

Henty, G. A. The Cat of Bubastes: A Tale of Ancient Egypt. 2000. 252p. (J). E-Book 3.95 (*0-594-02869-8*) 1873 Pr.

—The Cat of Bubastes: A Tale of Ancient Egypt. 2002. 288p. (J). pap. 6.95 (*0-486-42363-8*) Dover Pubns., Inc.

Hernandez, David. Land of the Pharaohs. 2003. (Adventures of Toby Digz Ser.). (Illus.). 96p. (J). 5.99 (*1-4003-0195-5*) Nelson, Tommy.

Howard, Annabelle. The Great Wonder: The Building of the Great Pyramid. 1996. (Smithsonian Odyssey Ser.). 32p. (J). (gr. 2-5). pap. 7.95 incl. audio (*1-56899-358-7*, C6002); (Illus.). (gr. 2-5). 14.95 (*1-56899-350-1*); (Illus.). (gr. 2-5). 19.95 incl. audio (*1-56899-355-2*, BC6002); (Illus.). (gr. 4-7). pap. 5.95 (*1-56899-351-X*);Incl. toy. (Illus.). (gr. 2-5). 29.95 (*1-56899-352-8*);Incl. toy. (Illus.). (gr. 2-5). pap. 17.95 (*1-56899-353-6*) Soundprints.

—The Great Wonder: The Building of the Great Pyramid. 1996. (Smithsonian Institution Odyssey Ser.). 11.15 o.p. (*0-606-10204-3*) Turtleback Bks.

Lester, Julius. Pharaoh's Daughter: A Novel of Ancient Egypt. 2000. (Illus.). 192p. (YA). (gr. 7-12). 17.00 (*0-15-201826-3*, Silver Whistle) Harcourt Children's Bks.

—Pharaoh's Daughter: A Novel of Ancient Egypt. 2002. 192p. (J). (gr. 5 up). pap. 5.99 (*0-06-440969-4*, Harper Trophy) HarperCollins Children's Bk. Group.

Meadowcroft, Enid L. Scarab for Luck. 1964. (Illus.). (J). (gr. 3-7). 7.95 o.p. (*0-690-72027-0*) HarperCollins Children's Bk. Group.

Scieszka, Jon. Tut Tut. (SPA.). (YA). (gr. 5-8). pap. 8.95 (*958-04-5046-3*, NR7010) Norma S.A. COL. *Dist:* Distribuidora Norma, Inc., Lectorum Pubns., Inc.

—Tut Tut. (Time Warp Trio Ser.). (Illus.). 80p. 2004. pap. 4.99 (*0-14-240047-5*, Puffin Bks.); 1998. (J). (gr. 2-6). pap. 4.99 (*0-14-036360-2*) Penguin Putnam Bks. for Young Readers.

—Tut,Tut. 1996. (Time Warp Trio Ser.). (Illus.). 80p. (J). (gr. 4-7). text 14.99 (*0-670-84832-8*, Viking Children's Bks.) Penguin Putnam Bks. for Young Readers.

—Tut,Tut. 1998. (Time Warp Trio Ser.). 11.14 (*0-606-13879-X*) Turtleback Bks.

Shakespeare, William. Antony & Cleopatra. Gill, Roma, ed. 2002. (Oxford School Shakespeare Ser.). (Illus.). 224p. pap. text 7.95 (*0-19-832057-4*) Oxford Univ. Pr., Inc.

—Antony & Cleopatra. 2002. (Shakespeare Collection). (Illus.). 46p. (J). 9.95 o.p. (*0-19-521793-4*) Oxford Univ. Pr., Inc.

Sturges, Philomen. Crocky Dilly. 1998. (Illus.). 32p. (J). (ps-3). 14.95 (*0-87846-458-1*) Museum of Fine Arts, Boston.

Terry Deary's Dreadful Day in Ancient Egypt. 2004. 48p. (J). pap. 14.99 (*0-7894-9264-4*) Dorling Kindersley Publishing, Inc.

EUROPE—HISTORY—FICTION

Comrie, Margaret S. The Heroes of Castle Bretten. 2003. (Illus.). 229p. (J). (*1-894666-65-8*) Inheritance Pubns.

Dickinson, Peter. The Tears of the Salamander. 2003. 208p. lib. bdg. 18.99 (*0-385-90125-9*); (Illus.). (gr. 5). text 16.95 (*0-385-73098-5*) Random Hse. Children's Bks. (Lamb, Wendy).

Henty, G. A. Won by the Sword: A Story of the Thirty Years' War. 2000. 252p. (J). E-Book 3.95 (*0-594-02425-0*) 1873 Pr.

McGuire, Leslie & Golden Books Staff. In the Dark of the Night, 12 vols., Set. 1997. (Disney Ser.). (Illus.). 32p. (J). (gr. k-2). pap. 2.99 o.s.i (*0-307-20011-6*, Golden Bks.) Random Hse. Children's Bks.

Petrie, Glen. Lucy & the Pirates. 2001. (Illus.). 32p. (J). (gr. k-5). pap. 6.95 (*1-896580-38-6*) Interlink Publishing Group, Inc.

—Lucy & the Pirates. 2000. (Illus.). 32p. (J). (gr. k-4). text 14.95 (*1-896580-02-5*) Tradewind Bks. CAN. *Dist:* Tricycle Pr.

Priestley, Chris. Death & the Arrow. 2004. 169p. (J). pap. (*0-440-86514-X*, Corgi) Bantam Bks.

—Death & the Arrow. 2003. (Illus.). 176p. (J). (gr. 7). lib. bdg. 17.99 (*0-375-92466-3*); 15.95 (*0-375-82466-9*) Random Hse. Children's Bks.

Steiner, Connie Colker. Shoes for Amelie. 2001. (Illus.). 48p. (J). (gr. 3-7). 12.95 (*1-894222-37-7*) Lobster Pr. CAN. *Dist:* Publishers Group West.

Treece, Henry. Men of the Hills. 1958. (Illus.). (J). (gr. 6-9). 26.95 (*0-87599-115-7*) Phillips, S.G. Inc.

—Ride into Danger. 1959. (Illus.). (J). (gr. 7-10). 26.95 (*0-87599-113-0*) Phillips, S.G. Inc.

Wilson, John. Lost in Spain. (Illus.). 174p. (YA). 2000. (gr. 8-12). (*1-55041-550-6*); 1999. (gr. 7-10). pap. (*1-55041-523-9*) Fitzhenry & Whiteside, Ltd.

F

FRANCE—HISTORY—FICTION

Alcock, Deborah. Done & Dared in Old France. 2002. (Huguenot Inheritance Ser.: Vol. 7). (Illus.). 286p. (J). (*1-894666-03-8*) Inheritance Pubns.

Bazaldua, Barbara, et al. Quasimodo the Hero. 1997. (Golden Book Ser.). (Illus.). 24p. (J). (ps-k). o.p. (*0-307-98797-3*, Golden Bks.) Random Hse. Children's Bks.

Bennett, Cherie. Anne Frank & Me. 2002. 352p. (J). pap. 6.99 (*0-698-11973-8*, PaperStar) Penguin Putnam Bks. for Young Readers.

Bennett, Cherie & Gottesfeld, Jeff. Anne Frank & Me. 2001. 291p. (J). (gr. 7 up). 18.99 (*0-399-23329-6*, G. P. Putnam's Sons) Penguin Group (USA) Inc.

Bollinger, Marilyn. The Hunchback of Notre Dame: Quasimodo Finds a Friend. 1996. (Magic Touch Talking Bks.). (Illus.). 22p. (J). (ps-2). 19.99 (*1-888208-16-3*) Hasbro, Inc.

Carr, Jan. The Hunchback of Notre Dame: Upside Down & Topsy-Turvy. 1996. (Illus.). 24p. (J). (gr. k-3). 12.89 o.p. (*0-7868-5040-X*); 12.95 o.p. (*0-7868-3090-5*) Disney Pr.

Casanova, Mary. Cecile: Gates of Gold. 2002. (Girls of Many Lands Ser.). (Illus.). 194p. (J). 12.95 (*1-58485-594-0*); pap. 7.95 (*1-58485-518-5*) Pleasant Co. Pubns. (American Girl).

—Curse of a Winter Moon. 2000. 137p. (J). 15.99 (*0-7868-0547-1*); 144p. (YA). lib. bdg. 16.49 (*0-7868-2475-1*) Hyperion Bks. for Children.

—Curse of a Winter Moon. 2002. (Illus.). 144p. (J). pap. 5.99 (*0-7868-1602-3*) Hyperion Paperbacks for Children.

Cuddy, Robbin, illus. The Hunchback of Notre Dame Illustrated Classic. 1996. 96p. (J). 14.95 (*0-7868-3089-1*) Disney Pr.

Davis, Kathryn. Versailles. l.t. ed. 2003. 25.95 (*1-58724-394-6*, Wheeler Publishing, Inc.) Gale Group.

—Versailles. 2003. 240p. pap. 13.95 (*0-316-73761-5*, Back Bay) Little Brown & Co.

Disney Staff. The Hunchback of Notre Dame: The Hidden Hero. 1997. (Disney's "Storytime Treasures" Library: Vol. 16). (Illus.). 44p. (J). (gr. 1-6). 3.49 o.p. (*1-57973-012-4*) Advance Pubs. LLC.

Distribooks Inc. Staff. Asterix Bind-Ups: Asterix & Friends. 1998. (Asterix Ser.). (Illus.). (J). 29.95 (*0-340-72755-1*) Hodder & Stoughton, Ltd. GBR. *Dist:* Distribooks, Inc., Lubrecht & Cramer, Ltd., Trafalgar Square.

Dumas, Alexandre. The Three Musketeers. 2002. (Great Illustrated Classics). (Illus.). 240p. (J). (gr. 3-8). lib. bdg. 21.35 (*1-57765-803-5*, ABDO & Daughters) ABDO Publishing Co..

Floyer, Edith S. The Young Huguenots. 1998. (Huguenots Inheritance Ser.). 9.95 (*0-921100-65-5*) Inheritance Pubns.

Fontes, Justine. The Hunchback of Notre Dame: Big Golden Book. 1996. (Illus.). 24p. (J). (ps-3). o.p. (*0-307-10378-1*, Golden Bks.) Random Hse. Children's Bks.

Forever Free. 1996. 10p. (J). 7.98 o.p. (*1-57082-322-7*) Mouse Works.

Friedman, Michael Jan. Hunchdog of Notre Dame. 1997. (Adventures of Wishbone Ser.: No. 5). (Illus.). 144p. (J). (gr. 2-5). mass mkt. 3.99 o.p. (*1-57064-270-2*, Big Red Chair Bks.) Lyrick Publishing.

—Hunchdog of Notre Dame. l.t. ed. 1999. (Adventures of Wishbone Ser.: No. 5). (Illus.). 139p. (J). (gr. 4 up). lib. bdg. 22.60 (*0-8368-2301-X*) Stevens, Gareth Inc.

Garden, Nancy. Dove & Sword. 1997. (J). mass mkt. 4.99 (*0-590-92949-6*) Scholastic, Inc.

—Dove & Sword: A Novel of Joan of Arc, RS. 1995. 304p. (YA). (gr. 7 up). 17.00 o.p. (*0-374-34476-0*, Farrar, Straus & Giroux (BYR)) Farrar, Straus & Giroux.

Girlhood Journeys, Inc., Staff. Marie: Summer in the Country, Paris, 1775. 1997. (Girlhood Journeys Ser.: 3). (Illus.). 69p. (J). (gr. 2-6). per. 5.99 (*0-689-81562-X*, Simon Pulse) Simon & Schuster Children's Publishing.

Golden Books Staff. Hide-And-Seek, Djali. 1997. (Golden Book Ser.). (Illus.). 24p. (J). o.p. (*0-307-10569-5*, Golden Bks.) Random Hse. Children's Bks.

—The Hunchback of Notre Dame. 1999. (Song Book & Tape Ser.). (J). (ps-3). pap. 6.98 o.p. incl. audio (*0-307-47720-7*, Golden Bks.) Random Hse. Children's Bks.

Goscinny, René. Absolutely Asterix. 1998. (Illus.). (J). text 29.95 (*0-340-72756-X*) Hodder & Stoughton, Ltd. GBR. *Dist:* Lubrecht & Cramer, Ltd., Trafalgar Square.

—Asterix: La Galere D'Obelix. 1996. (FRE.). 48p. (J). 24.95 (*0-7859-9352-5*) French & European Pubns., Inc.

—Asterix & Caesar's Gift. 1995. (Asterix Ser.). (Illus.). 44p. (J). (gr. 4-7). reprint ed. pap. 10.95 (*0-917201-68-X*) Dargaud Publishing Co. FRA. *Dist:* Distribooks, Inc.

—Asterix & Caesar's Gift, No. 19. (Illus.). 48p. (J). pap. text 9.95 (*0-340-23301-X*) International Language Centre.

—Asterix & Cleopatra. 1995. (Asterix Ser.). (Illus.). 44p. (J). (gr. 4-7). pap. 10.95 (*0-917201-75-2*) Dargaud Publishing Co. FRA. *Dist:* Distribooks, Inc.

—Asterix & Cleopatra, No. 4. 1976. (Asterix Ser.). (Illus.). (J). pap. text 9.95 (*0-340-17220-7*) International Language Centre.

—Asterix & Obelix All at Sea. 1996. 64p. (J). 24.95 (*0-7859-9452-1*) French & European Pubns., Inc.

—Asterix & the Banquet. 1995. (Asterix Ser.). (Illus.). 44p. (J). (gr. 4-7). reprint ed. pap. 10.95 (*0-917201-71-X*) Dargaud Publishing Co. FRA. *Dist:* Distribooks, Inc.

—Asterix & the Big Fight. 1995. (Asterix Ser.). (Illus.). 44p. (J). (gr. 4-7). reprint ed. pap. 10.95 (*0-917201-58-2*) Dargaud Publishing Co. FRA. *Dist:* Distribooks, Inc.

—Asterix & the Big Fight. 1976. (Asterix Ser.: No. 9). (Illus.). (J). pap. text 9.95 (*0-340-19167-8*) International Language Centre.

—Asterix & the Black Gold. 1984. (J). (gr. 4-7). pap. 10.95 (*0-340-32367-1*) Hodder & Stoughton, Ltd. GBR. *Dist:* Distribooks, Inc.

—Asterix & the Cauldron. 1995. (Asterix Ser.). (Illus.). 44p. (J). (gr. 4-7). reprint ed. pap. 10.95 (*0-917201-66-3*) Dargaud Publishing Co. FRA. *Dist:* Distribooks, Inc.

—Asterix & the Cauldron, No. 17. 1976. (Asterix Ser.). (Illus.). 48p. (J). pap. text 9.95 (*0-340-22711-7*) International Language Centre.

—Asterix & the Chieftain's Shield. 1995. (Asterix Ser.). (Illus.). 44p. (J). (gr. 4-7). reprint ed. pap. 10.95 (*0-917201-67-1*) Dargaud Publishing Co. FRA. *Dist:* Distribooks, Inc.

—Asterix & the Golden Sickle. 1995. (Asterix Ser.). (Illus.). 44p. (J). (gr. 4-7). reprint ed. pap. 10.95 (*0-917201-64-7*) Dargaud Publishing Co. FRA. *Dist:* Distribooks, Inc.

—Asterix & the Great Crossing. 1995. (Asterix Ser.). (Illus.). 44p. (J). (gr. 4-7). pap. 10.95 (*0-917201-65-5*) Dargaud Publishing Co. FRA. *Dist:* Distribooks, Inc.

—Asterix & the Great Divide. 1982. (Adventures of Asterix Ser.: No. 26). (J). pap. text 10.95 (*0-340-27627-4*) Hodder & Stoughton, Ltd. GBR. *Dist:* Distribooks, Inc.

—Asterix & the Laurel Wreath. 1995. (Asterix Ser.). (Illus.). 44p. (J). (gr. 4-7). reprint ed. pap. 10.95 (*0-917201-62-0*) Dargaud Publishing Co. FRA. *Dist:* Distribooks, Inc.

—Asterix & the Normans. 1995. (Asterix Ser.). (Illus.). 44p. (J). (gr. 4-7). reprint ed. pap. 10.95 (*0-917201-69-8*) Dargaud Publishing Co. FRA. *Dist:* Distribooks, Inc.

—Asterix & the Normans. (Illus.). (J). pap. 9.95 (*0-02-497290-8*) International Language Centre.

—Asterix & the Roman Agent. 1995. (Asterix Adventure Ser.). (Illus.). 44p. (J). reprint ed. pap. 10.95 (*0-917201-59-0*) Dargaud Publishing Co. FRA. *Dist:* Distribooks, Inc.

—Asterix & the Roman Agent, No. 10. 1976. (Asterix Ser.: No. 10). (Illus.). (J). pap. text 9.95 (*0-340-19168-6*) International Language Centre.

—Asterix & the Soothsayer. 1995. (Asterix Ser.). (Illus.). 44p. (J). (gr. 4-7). reprint ed. pap. 10.95 (*0-917201-63-9*) Dargaud Publishing Co. FRA. *Dist:* Distribooks, Inc.

—Asterix & the Soothsayer, No. 14. 1976. (Asterix Ser.). (Illus.). 48p. (J). pap. text 9.95 (*0-340-20697-7*) International Language Centre.

—Asterix at the Olympic Games. 1995. (Asterix Ser.). (Illus.). 44p. (J). (gr. 4-7). pap. 10.95 (*0-917201-61-2*) Dargaud Publishing Co. FRA. *Dist:* Distribooks, Inc.

—Asterix at the Olympic Games, No. 12. 1976. (Asterix Ser.: No. 12). (Illus.). (J). pap. text 9.95 (*0-340-19169-4*) International Language Centre.

—Asterix aux Jeux Olympiques. 1990. (FRE.). (J). (gr. 7-9). 24.95 (*0-8288-5109-3*, FC884) French & European Pubns., Inc.

—Asterix Chez les Bretons. 1990. (FRE.). (J). (gr. 7-9). 24.95 (*0-8288-5108-5*, FC880) French & European Pubns., Inc.

—Asterix Chez les Helvetes. 1990. (FRE., Illus.). (J). (gr. 7-9). 24.95 (*0-8288-5110-7*, FC889) French & European Pubns., Inc.

—Asterix Conquers America. 1997. (Asterix Ser.: Vol. 34). (J). pap. text 10.95 (*0-340-65347-7*) Hodder & Stoughton, Ltd. GBR. *Dist:* Distribooks, Inc., Lubrecht & Cramer, Ltd., Trafalgar Square.

—Asterix en Hispanie. 1990. (FRE., Illus.). (J). (gr. 7-9). 24.95 (*0-8288-5111-5*, FC887) French & European Pubns., Inc.

—Asterix et Cleopatre. 1990. (FRE.). (J). (gr. 7-9). 24.95 (*0-8288-5112-3*, FC878) French & European Pubns., Inc.

—Asterix et la Serpe d'or. 1990. (FRE., Illus.). (J). (gr. 3-8). 24.95 (*0-8288-4939-0*) French & European Pubns., Inc.

—Asterix et la Surprise de Cesar. 1993. (FRE.). 64p. (J). lib. bdg. 24.95 (*0-7859-3651-3*, 2865030044) French & European Pubns., Inc.

—Asterix et le Chaudron. 1990. (FRE., Illus.). (J). (gr. 7-9). 24.95 (*0-8288-5113-1*, FC885) French & European Pubns., Inc.

—Asterix et les Goths. 1990. (FRE.). (J). (gr. 7-9). 24.95 (*0-8288-5114-X*, FC875) French & European Pubns., Inc.

—Asterix et les Normands. 1990. (FRE.). (J). (gr. 7-9). 24.95 (*0-8288-5115-8*, FC881) French & European Pubns., Inc.

—Asterix Gladiateur. 1990. (FRE.). (J). (gr. 7-9). 24.95 (*0-8288-5116-6*, FC876) French & European Pubns., Inc.

—Asterix in Belgium. 1995. (Asterix Ser.). (Illus.). 44p. (J). (gr. 4-7). reprint ed. pap. 10.95 (*0-917201-73-6*) Dargaud Publishing Co. FRA. *Dist:* Distribooks, Inc.

—Asterix in Belgium, No. 25. (Illus.). (J). pap. text 9.95 (*0-340-27753-X*) International Language Centre.

—Asterix in Britain. 1995. (Asterix Ser.). (Illus.). 44p. (J). (gr. 4-7). pap. 10.95 (*0-917201-74-4*) Dargaud Publishing Co. FRA. *Dist:* Distribooks, Inc.

—Asterix in Britain, No. 3. 1976. (Asterix Ser.). (Illus.). (J). pap. text 9.95 (*0-340-17221-5*) International Language Centre.

—Asterix in Corsica. 1995. (Asterix Ser.). (Illus.). 44p. (J). (gr. 4-7). reprint ed. pap. 10.95 (*0-917201-72-8*) Dargaud Publishing Co. FRA. *Dist:* Distribooks, Inc.

—Asterix in Corsica, No. 24. (Illus.). 48p. (J). pap. text 9.95 (*0-340-27754-8*) International Language Centre.

—Asterix in Spain. 1995. (Asterix Ser.). (Illus.). 44p. (J). (gr. 4-7). reprint ed. pap. 10.95 (*0-917201-51-5*) Dargaud Publishing Co. FRA. *Dist:* Distribooks, Inc.

—Asterix in Spain, No. 2. 1976. (Asterix Ser.). (Illus.). (J). pap. text 9.95 (*0-340-18326-8*) International Language Centre.

—Asterix in Switzerland. 1995. (Asterix Ser.). (Illus.). 44p. (J). (gr. 4-7). reprint ed. pap. 10.95 (*0-917201-57-4*) Dargaud Publishing Co. FRA. *Dist:* Distribooks, Inc.

—Asterix in Switzerland. 1976. (Asterix Ser.: No. 8). (Illus.). (J). pap. text 9.95 (*0-340-19270-4*) International Language Centre.

—Asterix la Zizanie. 1990. (FRE., Illus.). (J). (gr. 7-9). 24.95 (*0-8288-5117-4*, FC888) French & European Pubns., Inc.

—Asterix le Gaulois. 1990. (FRE.). (J). (gr. 7-9). 24.95 (*0-8288-5118-2*, FC873) French & European Pubns., Inc.

—Asterix Legionnaire. 1990. (FRE.). (J). (gr. 7-9). 24.95 (*0-8288-5119-0*, FC882) French & European Pubns., Inc.

—Asterix the Gaul. (Illus.). (J). pap. text 9.95 (*0-340-17210-X*) International Language Centre.

—Asterix the Gladiator. 1995. (Asteric Comic Book Ser.). (Illus.). 44p. (J). (gr. 4-7). reprint ed. pap. 10.95 (*0-917201-55-8*) Dargaud Publishing Co. FRA. *Dist:* Distribooks, Inc.

—Asterix the Gladiator. 1976. (Asterix Ser.: No. 6). (Illus.). (J). pap. text 9.95 (*0-340-18320-9*) International Language Centre.

—Asterix the Legionary. 1995. (Asterix Ser.). (Illus.). 44p. (J). (gr. 4-7). pap. 10.95 (*0-917201-56-6*) Dargaud Publishing Co. FRA. *Dist:* Distribooks, Inc.

—Asterix the Legionary. 1976. (Asterix Ser.: No. 7). (Illus.). (J). pap. text 9.95 (*0-340-18321-7*) International Language Centre.

—Asterix vs. Caesar. 1997. (Adventures of Asterix Ser.: No. 29). (J). pap. text 10.95 (*0-340-39723-3*) Hodder & Stoughton, Ltd. GBR. *Dist:* Distribooks, Inc.

—The Banquet, No. 23. (Illus.). (J). pap. text 9.95 (*0-340-26429-2*) International Language Centre.

—The Chieftain's Shield, No. 18. 1977. (Asterix Ser.). (Illus.). 48p. (J). pap. text 9.95 (*0-340-22710-9*) International Language Centre.

—The Golden Sickle, No. 15. 1976. (Asterix Ser.). (Illus.). 48p. (J). pap. text 9.95 (*0-340-21209-8*) International Language Centre.

—The Great Crossing, No. 16. 1976. (Asterix Ser.). (Illus.). 48p. (J). pap. text 9.95 (*0-340-21589-5*) International Language Centre.

—How Obelix Fell into Magic Pot, Bk. 33. 1997. (J). text 9.95 (*0-340-65148-2*) Hodder Arnold GBR. *Dist:* Oxford Univ. Pr., Inc.

—The Laurel Wreath, No. 13. 1976. (Asterix Ser.). (Illus.). 48p. (J). pap. text 9.95 (*0-340-20699-3*) International Language Centre.

—The Mansion of the Gods. 1976. (Asterix Ser.: No. 11). (Illus.). (J). pap. text 9.95 (*0-340-19269-0*) International Language Centre.

—The Mansions of the Gods. 1995. (Asterix Ser.). (Illus.). 44p. (J). (gr. 4-7). reprint ed. pap. 10.95 (*0-917201-60-4*) Dargaud Publishing Co. FRA. *Dist:* Distribooks, Inc.

—Obelix & Company. 1995. (Asterix Ser.). (Illus.). 44p. (J). (gr. 4-7). reprint ed. pap. 10.95 (*0-917201-70-1*) Dargaud Publishing Co. FRA. *Dist:* Distribooks, Inc.

—Obelix & Company, No. 22. (Illus.). 48p. (J). pap. text 9.95 (*0-340-25307-X*) International Language Centre.

—The Twelve Tasks of Asterix, No. 21. (Illus.). 56p. (J). pap. text 9.95 (*0-340-27647-9*) International Language Centre.

Goscinny, René & Uderzo, Albert. Asterix Aetepekioe en Oayammie. 1992. (GRE.). (J). 24.95 (*0-7859-1040-9*, 9602202661) French & European Pubns., Inc.

—Asterix & Maestria. 1992. (GER.). (J). 24.95 (*0-7859-1025-5*, 3770400291) French & European Pubns., Inc.

—Asterix & Son. 1992. (J). 19.95 (*0-7859-1047-6*, 0-340-330082) French & European Pubns., Inc.

—Asterix & Son. 1983. (Asterix Ser.: No. 28). (J). pap. text 10.95 (*0-340-35331-7*) Hodder & Stoughton, Ltd. GBR. *Dist:* Distribooks, Inc.

—Asterix & the Banquet. 1992. (J). 19.95 (*0-7859-1042-5*, 0-340-231742) French & European Pubns., Inc.

—Asterix & the Black Gold. 1992. (J). 19.95 (*0-7859-1046-8*, 0-340-27476X) French & European Pubns., Inc.

—Asterix & the Great Divide. 1992. (J). 19.95 (*0-7859-1045-X*, 0-340-259884) French & European Pubns., Inc.

—Asterix & the Magic Carpet. 1992. (J). 19.95 (*0-7859-1048-4*, 0-340-409576) French & European Pubns., Inc.

—Asterix Apud Brittannos. 1992. (LAT.). (J). 24.95 (*0-7859-1029-8*, 3770400593) French & European Pubns., Inc.

—Asterix Atque Olla Cypria. 1992. (LAT.). (J). 24.95 (*0-7859-1033-6*, 3770400666) French & European Pubns., Inc.

—Asterix aux Jeux Olympiques. 1992. (FRE.). (J). 19.95 (*0-7859-0986-9*, 2205003208) French & European Pubns., Inc.

—Asterix Certamen Principum. 1992. (LAT.). (J). 24.95 (*0-7859-1027-1*, 3770400577) French & European Pubns., Inc.

—Asterix Chez les Bretons. 1992. (FRE.). (J). 19.95 (*0-7859-1075-1*, 220500185X) French & European Pubns., Inc.

—Asterix Chez les Helvetes. 1992. (FRE.). (J). 19.95 (*0-7859-0989-3*, 2205005162) French & European Pubns., Inc.

—Asterix Chez Rahazade. 1992. (FRE.). (J). 19.95 (*0-7859-1016-6*, 2864970201) French & European Pubns., Inc.

—Asterix Clipeus Arvernus. 1992. (LAT.). (J). 24.95 (*0-7859-1077-8*, 377040064X) French & European Pubns., Inc.

—Asterix en Corse. 1992. (FRE.). (J). 19.95 (*0-7859-0991-5*, 2205006940) French & European Pubns., Inc.

—Asterix en Hispania. 1992. (SPA.). (J). 24.95 (*0-7859-1039-5*, 8475100287) French & European Pubns., Inc.

—Asterix en Hispanie. 1992. (FRE.). (J). 24.95 (*0-7859-0988-5*, 2205003941) French & European Pubns., Inc.

—Asterix et Cleopatra. 1992. (LAT.). (J). 24.95 (*0-7859-1026-3*, 3770400569) French & European Pubns., Inc.

—Asterix et Cleopatre. 1992. (FRE.). (J). 19.95 (*0-7859-0981-8*, 2205001574) French & European Pubns., Inc.

—Asterix et la Surprise de Cesar. 1992. (FRE.). (J). 24.95 (*0-7859-0993-1*, 2205030044) French & European Pubns., Inc.

—Asterix et le Chaudron. 1992. (FRE.). (J). 19.95 (*0-7859-0987-7*, 2205003364) French & European Pubns., Inc.

—Asterix et les Normands. 1992. (FRE.). (J). 19.95 (*0-7859-0983-4*, 2205001906) French & European Pubns., Inc.

—Asterix et Normanni. 1992. (LAT.). (J). 24.95 (*0-7859-1031-X*, 3770400615) French & European Pubns., Inc.

—Asterix Gladiateur. 1992. (FRE.). (J). 19.95 (*0-7859-0980-X*, 2205001345) French & European Pubns., Inc.

—Asterix in Belgium. 1992. (J). 19.95 (*0-7859-1044-1*, 0-340-257350) French & European Pubns., Inc.

—Asterix in Corsica. 1992. (J). 19.95 (*0-7859-1043-3*, 240741) French & European Pubns., Inc.

—Asterix in Hispania. 1992. (LAT.). (J). 24.95 (*0-7859-1034-4*, 3770400674) French & European Pubns., Inc.

—Asterix la Rosa y la Espada. 1992. (SPA.). (J). 24.95 (*0-7859-1038-7*, 8474199123) French & European Pubns., Inc.

—Asterix la Rose et le Glaive. 1992. (FRE.). (J). 24.95 (*0-7859-1017-4*, 2864970538) French & European Pubns., Inc.

—Asterix le Gaulois. 1992. (FRE.). (J). 19.95 (*0-7859-0979-6*, 2205000969) French & European Pubns., Inc.

—Asterix Legionnaire. 1992. (FRE.). (J). 19.95 (*0-7859-0984-2*, 2205002309) French & European Pubns., Inc.

—Asterix Olympius. 1992. (LAT.). (J). 24.95 (*0-7859-0959-1*, 0-377-040658) French & European Pubns., Inc.

—Asterix Orientalis. 1992. (LAT.). (J). 24.95 (*0-7859-1035-2*, 3770400682) French & European Pubns., Inc.

—Comment Obelix est Tombe dans la Marmite. 1992. (FRE.). (J). 24.95 (*0-7859-1050-6*, 0-340-517727) French & European Pubns., Inc.

—Le Coup de Menhir. 1993. (FRE.). 64p. (J). lib. bdg. 19.95 (*0-7859-3652-1*, 2865030051) French & European Pubns., Inc.

—Filius Asterix. 1992. (LAT.). (J). 24.95 (*0-7859-1032-8*, 3770400623) French & European Pubns., Inc.

—How Obelix Fell into the Magic Potion When He Was a Little Boy. 1992. (J). 24.95 (*0-7859-1049-2*, 0-340-511273) French & European Pubns., Inc.

—Obelix & Co. 1992. (J). 24.95 (*0-7859-1041-7*, 0-340-227095) French & European Pubns., Inc.

—Obelix GMBH Co. 1992. (GER.). (J). 24.95 (*0-7859-1021-2*, 3770400232) French & European Pubns., Inc.

—Der Sohn des Asterix. 1992. (GER.). (J). 24.95 (*0-7859-1024-7*, 3770400275) French & European Pubns., Inc.

—Uderzo de Flamberge a Asterix. 1993. (FRE.). 64p. (J). 24.95 (*0-7859-3653-X*, 2865030077) French & European Pubns., Inc.

Goscinny, René & Uderzo, M. Asterix: Comment Obelix est Tombe dans la Marmite du Druide Quand Il Etait Petit. 1990. (FRE.). (J). 24.95 (*0-8288-8597-4*) French & European Pubns., Inc.

—Asterix: How Obelix Fell into the Magic Cauldron When He Was a Little Boy. 1990. (J). 24.95 (*0-8288-8594-X*) French & European Pubns., Inc.

—Asterix als Gladiator. 1992. (GER., Illus.). (J). (gr. 7-10). 24.95 (*0-8288-4923-4*) French & European Pubns., Inc.

—Asterix als Legionar. 1992. (GER., Illus.). (J). (gr. 7-10). 24.95 (*0-8288-4924-2*) French & European Pubns., Inc.

—Asterix & Caesar's Gift. 1990. (Illus.). (J). (gr. 7-10). 24.95 (*0-8288-4915-3*) French & European Pubns., Inc.

—Asterix & Cleopatra. 1990. (Illus.). (J). (gr. 7-10). 24.95 (*0-8288-4916-1*) French & European Pubns., Inc.

—Asterix & Operation Getafix. 1990. (J). 24.95 (*0-8288-8570-2*) French & European Pubns., Inc.

—Asterix & Son. 1990. (J). 24.95 (*0-8288-8568-0*) French & European Pubns., Inc.

—Asterix & the Banquet. 1990. (J). 24.95 (*0-8288-8590-7*) French & European Pubns., Inc.

—Asterix & the Big Fight. 1990. (Illus.). (J). (gr. 7-10). 24.95 (*0-8288-4917-X*) French & European Pubns., Inc.

—Asterix & the Black Gold. 1990. (J). 24.95 (*0-8288-8592-3*) French & European Pubns., Inc.

—Asterix & the Chieftain's Shield. 1990. (Illus.). (J). (gr. 7-10). 24.95 (*0-8288-4918-8*) French & European Pubns., Inc.

—Asterix & the Goths. 1990. (Illus.). (J). (gr. 7-10). 24.95 (*0-8288-4919-6*) French & European Pubns., Inc.

—Asterix & the Great Divide. 1990. (J). 24.95 (*0-8288-8567-2*) French & European Pubns., Inc.

—Asterix & the Laurel Wreath. 1990. (Illus.). (J). (gr. 7-10). 24.95 (*0-8288-4920-X*) French & European Pubns., Inc.

—Asterix & the Magic Carpet. 1990. (J). 24.95 (*0-8288-8569-9*) French & European Pubns., Inc.

—Asterix & the Normans. 1990. (Illus.). (J). (gr. 7-10). 24.95 (*0-8288-4921-8*) French & European Pubns., Inc.

—Asterix & the Roman Agent. 1990. (Illus.). (J). (gr. 7-10). 24.95 (*0-8288-4922-6*) French & European Pubns., Inc.

—Asterix apud Gothos. 1990. (LAT., Illus.). (J). (gr. 7-10). lib. bdg. 24.95 (*0-8288-4925-0*) French & European Pubns., Inc.

—Asterix at the Olympic Games. 1990. (Illus.). (J). (gr. 7-10). 24.95 (*0-8288-4926-9*) French & European Pubns., Inc.

—Asterix auf Korsika. 1990. (GER., Illus.). (J). (gr. 7-10). lib. bdg. 24.95 (*0-8288-4927-7*) French & European Pubns., Inc.

—Asterix bei den Briten. 1990. (GER., Illus.). (J). (gr. 7-10). lib. bdg. 24.95 (*0-8288-4928-5*) French & European Pubns., Inc.

—Asterix bei den Olympischen Spielen. 1990. (GER., Illus.). (J). (gr. 7-10). lib. bdg. 24.95 (*0-8288-4929-3*) French & European Pubns., Inc.

—Asterix bei den Schweizern. 1990. (GER., Illus.). (J). (gr. 7-10). lib. bdg. 24.95 (*0-8288-4930-7*) French & European Pubns., Inc.

—Asterix chez les Belges. 1990. (FRE., Illus.). (J). (gr. 7-10). 24.95 (*0-8288-4931-5*) French & European Pubns., Inc.

—Asterix Chez Rahazade. 1990. (FRE.). (J). 24.95 (*0-8288-8572-9*) French & European Pubns., Inc.

—Asterix der Gallier. 1990. (GER., Illus.). (J). (gr. 7-10). lib. bdg. 24.95 (*0-8288-4932-3*) French & European Pubns., Inc.

—Asterix el Galo. (SPA., Illus.). (J). (gr. 7-10). 24.95 (*0-8288-4933-1*) French & European Pubns., Inc.

Historical Events

—Asterix en Bretana. 1990. (SPA., Illus.). (J). (gr. 7-10). lib. bdg. 24.95 (*0-8288-4934-X*) French & European Pubns., Inc.

—Asterix en Corcega. 1990. (SPA., Illus.). (J). (gr. 7-10). lib. bdg. 24.95 (*0-8288-4935-8*) French & European Pubns., Inc.

—Asterix en Corse. 1990. (FRE., Illus.). (J). (gr. 7-10). 24.95 (*0-8288-4936-6*) French & European Pubns., Inc.

—Asterix en Helvecia. 1990. (SPA., Illus.). (J). (gr. 7-10). lib. bdg. 24.95 (*0-8288-4937-4*) French & European Pubns., Inc.

—Asterix en los Juegos Olimpicos. 1990. (SPA., Illus.). (J). (gr. 7-10). lib. bdg. 24.95 (*0-8288-4938-2*) French & European Pubns., Inc.

—Asterix et la Rose et le Glaive. 1990. (FRE.). (J). 24.95 (*0-8288-8573-7*) French & European Pubns., Inc.

—Asterix Gallus. 1990. (LAT., Illus.). (J). (gr. 7-10). lib. bdg. 24.95 (*0-8288-4941-2*) French & European Pubns., Inc.

—Asterix Gladiador. 1990. (SPA., Illus.). (J). (gr. 7-10). lib. bdg. 24.95 (*0-8288-4942-0*) French & European Pubns., Inc.

—Asterix Gladiator. 1990. (LAT., Illus.). (J). 24.95 (*0-8288-4943-9*) French & European Pubns., Inc.

—Asterix in Belgium. 1990. (J). 24.95 (*0-8288-8591-5*) French & European Pubns., Inc.

—Asterix in Britain. 1990. (Illus.). (J). 24.95 (*0-8288-4944-7*) French & European Pubns., Inc.

—Asterix in Corsica. 1990. (J). 24.95 (*0-8288-8566-4*) French & European Pubns., Inc.

—Asterix in Spain. 1990. (Illus.). (J). 24.95 (*0-8288-4945-5*) French & European Pubns., Inc.

—Asterix in Spanien. 1990. (GER., Illus.). (J). lib. bdg. 24.95 (*0-8288-4946-3*) French & European Pubns., Inc.

—Asterix in Switzerland. 1990. (Illus.). (J). lib. bdg. 24.95 (*0-8288-4947-1*) French & European Pubns., Inc.

—Asterix iter Gallicum. 1990. (LAT., Illus.). (J). lib. bdg. 24.95 (*0-8288-4948-X*) French & European Pubns., Inc.

—Asterix Legionario. 1990. (SPA., Illus.). (J). lib. bdg. 24.95 (*0-8288-4949-8*) French & European Pubns., Inc.

—Asterix, Obelix & Company. 1990. (J). 24.95 (*0-8288-8565-6*) French & European Pubns., Inc.

—Asterix the Gaul. 1990. (Illus.). (J). 24.95 (*0-8288-4950-1*) French & European Pubns., Inc.

—Asterix the Gladiator. 1990. (Illus.). (J). 24.95 (*0-8288-4951-X*) French & European Pubns., Inc.

—Asterix the Legionary. 1990. (Illus.). (J). 24.95 (*0-8288-4952-8*) French & European Pubns., Inc.

—Asterix und die Goten. 1990. (GER., Illus.). (J). lib. bdg. 24.95 (*0-8288-4953-6*) French & European Pubns., Inc.

—Asterix und Kleopatra. 1990. (GER., Illus.). (J). lib. bdg. 24.95 (*0-8288-4954-4*) French & European Pubns., Inc.

—Asterix Versus Caesar. 1990. (J). 24.95 (*0-8288-8593-1*) French & European Pubns., Inc.

—Asterix y Cleopatra. 1990. (SPA., Illus.). (J). lib. bdg. 24.95 (*0-8288-4955-2*) French & European Pubns., Inc.

—Asterix y el Caldero. 1990. (SPA., Illus.). (J). lib. bdg. 24.95 (*0-8288-4956-0*) French & European Pubns., Inc.

—Asterix y los Godos. 1990. (SPA., Illus.). (J). lib. bdg. 24.95 (*0-8288-4957-9*) French & European Pubns., Inc.

—Asterix y los Normandos. 1990. (SPA., Illus.). (J). lib. bdg. 24.95 (*0-8288-4958-7*) French & European Pubns., Inc.

—Obelix et Compagnie. 1990. (FRE., Illus.). (J). 24.95 (*0-8288-5479-3*) French & European Pubns., Inc.

—Streit um Asterix. (GER., Illus.). (J). 24.95 (*0-8288-4906-4*) French & European Pubns., Inc.

Goscinny, René, et al. Asterix & the Goths. 1995. (Asterix Ser.). (Illus.). 44p. (J). (gr. 4-7). reprint ed. pap. 10.95 (*0-917201-54-X*) Dargaud Publishing Co. FRA. *Dist:* Distribooks, Inc.

—Asterix the Gaul. 1995. (Asterix Ser.). (Illus.). 44p. (J). (gr. 4-7). reprint ed. pap. 10.95 (*0-917201-50-7*) Dargaud Publishing Co. FRA. *Dist:* Distribooks, Inc.

Gregory, Kristiana. Eleanor: Crown Jewel of Aquitaine. 2002. (Royal Diaries Ser.). 112p. (YA). (gr. 4-9). 10.95 (*0-439-16484-2*, Scholastic Pr.) Scholastic, Inc.

Harchy, Philippe, illus. The Hunchback of Notre Dame Pop-up Book. 1996. 12p. (J). (gr. k-3). 12.95 o.p. (*0-7868-3091-3*) Disney Pr.

Haseley, Dennis. Horses with Wings. 1993. (Laura Geringer Bks.). (Illus.). 32p. (J). (gr. k up). 16.00 (*0-06-022885-7*); lib. bdg. 15.89 (*0-06-022886-5*) HarperCollins Children's Bk. Group.

Henty, G. A. St. Bartholomew's Eve: A Tale of the Huguenot Wars. (J). E-Book 3.95 (*0-594-02403-X*) 1873 Pr.

Hugo, Victor. The Hunchback of Notre-Dame. 2000. (Giant Courage Classics Ser.). 704p. (YA). 9.00 o.p. (*0-7624-0563-5*, Courage Bks.) Running Pr. Bk. Pubs.

—The Hunchback of Notre Dame. 1968. (Airmont Classics Ser.). (YA). (gr. 11 up). mass mkt. 2.25 (*0-8049-0162-7*, CL-162) Airmont Publishing Co., Inc.

—The Hunchback of Notre Dame. 1998. (Illustrated Classic Book Ser.). (Illus.). 61p. (J). (gr. 3 up). pap. text 4.95 (*1-56767-247-7*) Educational Insights, Inc.

—The Hunchback of Notre Dame. (Young Collector's Illustrated Classics Ser.). (Illus.). 192p. (J). (gr. 3-7). 9.95 (*1-56156-458-3*) Kidsbooks, Inc.

—The Hunchback of Notre Dame. Hanft, Joshua, ed. 1994. (Great Illustrated Classics Ser.: Vol. 36). (Illus.). 240p. (J). (gr. 3-6). 9.95 (*0-86611-987-6*) Playmore, Inc., Pubs.

—The Hunchback of Notre Dame. 1987. (Regents Illustrated Classics Ser.). 62p. (YA). (gr. 7-12). pap. text 3.75 o.p. (*0-13-448085-6*, 20519) Prentice Hall, ESL Dept.

—The Hunchback of Notre Dame. (Short Classics Ser.). (Illus.). 48p. (J). (gr. 4 up). 1983. pap. 9.27 o.p. (*0-8172-2010-0*); 1981. lib. bdg. 24.26 o.p. (*0-8172-1671-5*) Raintree Pubs.

—The Hunchback of Notre Dame. 1995. (Illus.). 416p. (J). 12.99 o.s.i (*0-517-12375-4*) Random Hse. Value Publishing.

—The Hunchback of Notre Dame. 1995. (Step into Classics Ser.). 112p. (J). (gr. 3-5). pap. 3.99 (*0-679-87429-1*) Random Hse., Inc.

—The Hunchback of Notre Dame. (gr. k-3). 1997. (Illus.). 40p. (J). pap. 15.95 (*0-531-30055-2*, Orchard Bks.); 1996. (YA). mass mkt. 4.50 (*0-590-93808-8*, Scholastic Paperbacks) Scholastic, Inc.

—The Hunchback of Notre Dame. 1996. 112p. (J). (gr. 4-7). per. 4.50 (*0-689-81027-X*, Aladdin) Simon & Schuster Children's Publishing.

—Hunchback of Notre Dame. 2002. (Great Illustrated Classics). (Illus.). 240p. (J). (gr. 3-8). lib. bdg. 21.35 (*1-57765-813-2*, ABDO & Daughters) ABDO Publishing Co.

—The Hunchback of Notre Dame. unabr. ed. 1998. (Wordsworth Classics Ser.). (YA). (gr. 6-12). 5.27 (*0-89061-068-1*, R0681WW) Jamestown.

—The Hunchback of Notre Dame. abr. ed. 2001. (YA). (gr. 5-12). audio 16.95 (*1-56994-529-2*) Monterey Media, Inc.

—The Hunchback of Notre Dame. abr. ed. 1996. (J). 12.98 o.p. (*0-7871-1081-7*); (gr. 4-7). audio 6.95 o.p. (*0-7871-0992-4*, 628697) NewStar Media, Inc.

—The Hunchback of Notre Dame. abr. ed. 1997. (Puffin Classics Ser.). (Illus.). 320p. (YA). (gr. 5-9). pap. 4.99 (*0-14-038253-4*) Penguin Putnam Bks. for Young Readers.

—The Hunchback of Notre Dame. abr. ed. 1996. 288p. (YA). mass mkt. 4.50 o.s.i (*0-440-22675-9*, Dell Books for Young Readers) Random Hse. Children's Bks.

—The Hunchback of Notre Dame: With a Discussion of Compassion. Butterfield, Ned, tr. & illus. by. 2003. (Values in Action Illustrated Classics Ser.). (J). (*1-59203-049-1*) Learning Challenge, Inc.

—The Hunchback of Notre Dame Readalong. 1994. (Illustrated Classics Collection). 64p. pap. 14.95 incl. audio (*0-7854-0683-2*, 40399); pap. 13.50 o.p. incl. audio (*1-56103-487-8*) American Guidance Service, Inc.

Hugo, Victor, et al. The Hunchback of Notre Dame. 1997. (Eyewitness Classics Ser.). (Illus.). 64p. (J). (gr. 3-6). pap. 14.95 o.p. (*0-7894-1491-0*) Dorling Kindersley Publishing, Inc.

The Hunchback of Notre Dame. 1996. 96p. pap. 14.95 (*0-7935-6655-X*) Leonard, Hal Corp.

The Hunchback of Notre Dame. 1991. (Short Classics Ser.). 48p. (J). pap. 34.00 (*0-8114-6963-8*) Raintree Pubs.

The Hunchback of Notre Dame. (Read-Along Ser.). (J). 7.99 incl. audio (*1-55723-992-4*); 1996. audio 11.99 (*1-55723-987-8*) Walt Disney Records.

The Hunchback of Notre Dame Read-Along. 1996. (J). (*1-55723-993-2*) Walt Disney Records.

Ingoglia, Gina. The Hunchback of Notre Dame. 1996. (Illus.). 96p. (J). lib. bdg. 15.49 (*0-7868-5034-5*) Disney Pr.

—The Hunchback of Notre Dame Junior Novelization. 1996. 96p. (J). (gr. 2-6). pap. 3.95 o.p. (*0-7868-4062-5*) Disney Pr.

Jennings, Patrick. The Wolving Time. 2003. 208p. (J). 15.95 (*0-439-39555-0*) Scholastic, Inc.

Lasky, Kathryn. Marie Antoinette: Princess of Versailles, Austria-France, 1544. 2000. (Royal Diaries Ser.). (Illus.). 236p. (J). (gr. 4-8). 10.95 (*0-439-07666-8*) Scholastic, Inc.

—Mary, Queen of Scots: Queen Without a Country, France, 1553. 2002. (Royal Diaries Ser.). (Illus.). 208p. (J). (gr. 4-8). 10.95 (*0-439-19404-0*, Scholastic Pr.) Scholastic, Inc.

Litowinski, Olga. The Pawloined Paper. 1998. (Adventures of Wishbone Ser.: No. 11). (Illus.). 137p. (J). (gr. 2-5). pap. 3.99 o.p. (*1-57064-276-1*, Big Red Chair Bks.) Lyrick Publishing.

—The Pawloined Paper. l.t. ed. 1999. (Adventures of Wishbone Ser.: No. 11). (Illus.). (J). (gr. 4 up). lib. bdg. 22.60 (*0-8368-2589-6*) Stevens, Gareth Inc.

Morpurgo, Michael. Waiting for Anya. l.t. ed. 1992. 240p. (J). 13.95 o.p. (*0-7451-1527-6*, Galaxy Children's Large Print) BBC Audiobooks America.

—Waiting for Anya. 1997. 176p. (gr. 5-9). pap. 5.99 (*0-14-038431-6*); 1991. 174p. (J). 14.99 o.s.i (*0-670-83735-0*, Viking Children's Bks.) Penguin Putnam Bks. for Young Readers.

—Waiting for Anya. 1997. (J). 11.04 (*0-606-12044-0*) Turtleback Bks.

Mouse Works Staff. The Hunchback of Notre Dame. 1996. (J). 5.98 o.p. (*1-57082-279-4*); 8p. 5.98 o.p. (*1-57082-273-5*); 96p. 7.98 o.p. (*1-57082-173-9*) Mouse Works.

Orczy, Baroness Emmuska. The Scarlet Pimpernel. 1974. (Signet Classics). 256p. (J). (gr. 7). mass mkt. 4.95 o.s.i (*0-451-52315-6*, Signet Classics) NAL.

—The Scarlet Pimpernel. Farr, Naunerle C., ed. 1978. (Now Age Illustrated IV Ser.). (Illus.). (J). (gr. 4-12). stu. ed. 1.25 (*0-88301-345-2*); text 7.50 o.p. (*0-88301-333-9*); pap. text 2.95 (*0-88301-321-5*) Pendulum Pr., Inc.

—The Scarlet Pimpernel. 1989. (Classics for Young Readers Ser.). 256p. (J). (gr. 5 up). pap. 4.99 o.p. (*0-14-035056-X*, Puffin Bks.) Penguin Putnam Bks. for Young Readers.

—The Scarlet Pimpernel. 1989. (J). (gr. k-6). pap. 3.50 o.s.i (*0-440-40220-4*, Yearling) Random Hse. Children's Bks.

—The Scarlet Pimpernel, unabr. ed. 2000. (YA). audio 60.00 Recorded Bks., LLC.

—The Scarlet Pimpernel Readalong. 1994. (Illustrated Classics Collection). 64p. pap. 13.50 o.p. incl. audio (*1-56103-608-0*); pap. 14.95 incl. audio (*0-7854-0771-5*, 40520) American Guidance Service, Inc.

Orczy, Baroness Emmuska, et al. The Scarlet Pimpernel. 1997. (Puffin Classics Ser.). (Illus.). 336p. (YA). (gr. 5 up). pap. 5.99 (*0-14-037454-X*, Puffin Bks.) Penguin Putnam Bks. for Young Readers.

Rostand, Edmond. Cyrano de Bergerac. 8.97 (*0-673-58340-6*) Addison-Wesley Longman, Inc.

—Cyrano de Bergerac. 1999. 11.95 (*1-56137-622-1*) Novel Units, Inc.

Roth-Hano, Renee. Touch Wood: A Girlhood in Occupied France. 1989. (ALA Notable Bk.). 304p. (J). (gr. 5 up). pap. 5.99 o.p. (*0-14-034085-8*, Puffin Bks.) Penguin Putnam Bks. for Young Readers.

—Touch Wood: A Girlhood in Occupied France. 1988. 304p. (J). (gr. 5-9). 16.95 o.p. (*0-02-777340-X*, Simon & Schuster Children's Publishing) Simon & Schuster Children's Publishing.

Sauerwein, Leigh. A Song for Eloise. 2003. (YA). 15.95 (*1-886910-90-1*, Front Street) Front Street, Inc.

Skurzynski, Gloria. Spider's Voice. 1999. (Illus.). 144p. (YA). (gr. 7 up). 16.95 (*0-689-82149-2*, Atheneum) Simon & Schuster Children's Publishing.

Sohl, Marcia & Dackerman, Gerald. The Hunchback of Notre Dame: Student Activity Book. 1976. (Now Age Illustrated Ser.). (Illus.). (J). (gr. 4-10). stu. ed. 1.25 (*0-88301-189-1*) Pendulum Pr., Inc.

Timmermans, Gommaar. The Little White Hen & the Emperor of France. 1976. (ENG & GER., Illus.). 32p. (J). lib. bdg. 6.95 o.p. (*0-201-09332-4*) Addison-Wesley Longman, Inc.

Tucker, Charlotte Maria. Driven into Exile: A Story of the Huguenots. 2003. (Huguenot Inheritance Ser.: Vol. 5). 141p. (J). (*0-921100-66-3*) Inheritance Pubns.

Uderzo, Albert & Goscinny, René. The Complete Guide to Asterix. Bell, Anthea & Hockridge, Derek, trs. from FRE. 1997. (Adventures of Asterix Ser.). (Illus.). 105p. (J). reprint ed. 29.95 o.p. (*0-340-65346-9*) Distribooks, Inc.

Van der Jagt, A. The Secret Mission, No. 2. 2001. (Huguenots Inheritance Ser.: Vol. 2). (Illus.). 187p. (J). (*0-921100-18-3*) Inheritance Pubns.

Van Gool Studio Staff, illus. The Hunchback of Notre Dame. 1995. (Classic Ser.). 64p. (J). (ps-1). 4.98 o.p. (*0-8317-1653-3*) Smithmark Pubs., Inc.

Vogiel, Eva. Facing the Music. 2003. 284p. 19.95 (*1-880582-94-5*) Judaica Pr., Inc., The.

Watson, Pat. The Scarlet Pimpernel. Robbins, Dawn Michelle, ed. 2000. (YA). 9.95 (*1-58130-638-5*); 11.95 (*1-58130-639-3*) Novel Units, Inc.

Weingartner, Amy. The Hunchback of Notre Dame. 1996. (Illus.). 48p. pap. text 4.95 o.p. (*0-7851-0225-6*) Marvel Enterprises.

Woodruff, Elvira. Dear Napoleon, I Know You're Dead, But... 1996. (J). pap. 4.50 (*0-440-91110-9*, Dell Books for Young Readers) Random Hse. Children's Bks.

FRANCE—HISTORY—TO 1328—FICTION

Almedingen, E. M. A Candle at Dusk, RS. 1969. (J). (gr. 7 up). 3.75 o.p. (*0-374-31056-4*, Farrar, Straus & Giroux (BYR)) Farrar, Straus & Giroux.

Konigsburg, E. L. A Proud Taste for Scarlet & Miniver. 1973. (Proud Taste for Scarlet Minvr Nrf Ser.: Vol. 1). (Illus.). 208p. (J). (gr. 4-7). 18.95 (*0-689-30111-1*, Atheneum) Simon & Schuster Children's Publishing.

FRANCE—HISTORY—HOUSE OF VALOIS, 1328-1589—FICTION

Dana, Barbara. Young Joan. 1997. (Illus.). 352p. (J). (gr. 5 up). pap. 6.99 (*0-06-440661-X*, Harper Trophy); 1991. 384p. (YA). (gr. 7 up). 17.95 (*0-06-021422-8*); 1991. 384p. (YA). (gr. 7 up). lib. bdg. 17.89 o.p. (*0-06-021423-6*) HarperCollins Children's Bk. Group.

—Young Joan. 1997. 12.00 (*0-606-12125-0*) Turtleback Bks.

Scott, Walter, Sr. Quentin Durward. 1967. (Airmont Classics Ser.). (J). (gr. 9 up). mass mkt. 2.50 o.p. (*0-8049-0132-5*, CL-132) Airmont Publishing Co., Inc.

Twain, Mark, et al. Joan of Arc. 1996. (Wishbone Classics Ser.: No. 4). (Illus.). 128p. (gr. 3-7). mass mkt. 3.99 (*0-06-106418-1*, HarperEntertainment) Morrow/Avon.

FRANCE—HISTORY—BOURBONS, 1589-1789—FICTION

Matas, Carol. The Burning Time. 1996. 128p. (J). (gr. 7). mass mkt. 3.99 o.p. (*0-440-21978-7*) Dell Publishing.

Raymond, Grace. How They Kept the Faith: A Tale of the Huguenots of Languedoc. 1996. (Huguenots Inheritance Ser.). (J). 12.90 (*0-921100-64-7*) Inheritance Pubns.

FRANCE—HISTORY—REVOLUTION, 1789-1799—FICTION

Barkan, Joanne. A Tale of Two Sitters. 1998. (Adventures of Wishbone Ser.: No. 9). (Illus.). 144p. (J). (gr. 2-5). mass mkt. 3.99 o.p. (*1-57064-277-X*, Big Red Chair Bks.) Lyrick Publishing.

—A Tale of Two Sitters. l.t. ed. 1999. (Adventures of Wishbone Ser.: No. 9). (Illus.). 144p. (J). (gr. 4 up). lib. bdg. 22.60 (*0-8368-2305-2*) Stevens, Gareth Inc.

Bassett, Jennifer, ed. A Tale of Two Cities. 1995. (Illus.). 80p. (J). pap. text 5.95 o.p. (*0-19-422727-8*) Oxford Univ. Pr., Inc.

Dickens, Charles. A Tale of Two Cities. 2002. (Great Illustrated Classics). (Illus.). 240p. (J). (gr. 3-8). lib. bdg. 21.35 (*1-57765-802-7*, ABDO & Daughters) ABDO Publishing Co.

—A Tale of Two Cities. 1976. (Illus.). (gr. 7 up). 7.95 o.p. (*0-679-20374-5*) McKay, David Co., Inc.

—A Tale of Two Cities. 9999. (Children's Classics Ser.: No. 740-6). (Illus.). (J). (gr. 3-5). text 3.50 o.p. (*0-7214-0710-2*, Ladybird Bks.) Penguin Group (USA) Inc.

—A Tale of Two Cities. (Illus.). (J). (gr. 4-6). 1982. 5.95 o.p. (*0-448-11023-7*); 1948. 12.95 o.s.i (*0-448-06023-X*) Penguin Putnam Bks. for Young Readers. (Grosset & Dunlap).

—A Tale of Two Cities. Vogel, Malvina, ed. 1993. (Great Illustrated Classics Ser.: Vol. 26). (Illus.). 240p. (J). (gr. 3-6). 9.95 (*0-86611-977-9*) Playmore, Inc., Pubs.

—A Tale of Two Cities. 1983. (Short Classics Ser.). (Illus.). (J). (gr. 4 up). pap. 9.27 o.p. (*0-8172-2022-4*); lib. bdg. 24.26 o.p. (*0-8172-1658-8*) Raintree Pubs.

—A Tale of Two Cities. 1981. (Keith Jennison Large Type Bks.). (gr. 5 up). lib. bdg. 8.95 o.p. (*0-531-00288-8*, Watts, Franklin) Scholastic Library Publishing.

—A Tale of Two Cities. 1997. 11.00 (*0-606-00203-0*) Turtleback Bks.

Gerstein, Mordicai. Victor: A Novel Based on the Life of Victor, the Savage of Aveyron, RS. 1998. 224p. (YA). (gr. 4-7). 17.00 o.p. (*0-374-38142-9*, Farrar, Straus & Giroux (BYR)) Farrar, Straus & Giroux.

Hess, Donna L. In Search of Honor. 1991. 154p. (YA). (gr. 7 up). pap. 6.49 (*0-89084-595-6*, 055673) Jones, Bob Univ. Pr.

Hugo, Victor & Kulling, Monica. Les Miserables. 1995. (Step into Classics Ser.). (Illus.). 112p. (gr. 3-5). pap. text 3.99 (*0-679-86668-X*) Random Hse., Inc.

Orczy, Baroness Emmuska. The Scarlet Pimpernel. 1974. (Signet Classics). 256p. (J). (gr. 7). mass mkt. 4.95 o.s.i (*0-451-52315-6*, Signet Classics) NAL.

—The Scarlet Pimpernel. Farr, Naunerle C., ed. 1978. (Now Age Illustrated IV Ser.). (Illus.). (J). (gr. 4-12). stu. ed. 1.25 (*0-88301-345-2*); text 7.50 o.p. (*0-88301-333-9*); pap. text 2.95 (*0-88301-321-5*) Pendulum Pr., Inc.

—The Scarlet Pimpernel. 1989. (Classics for Young Readers Ser.). 256p. (J). (gr. 5 up). pap. 4.99 o.p. (*0-14-035056-X*, Puffin Bks.) Penguin Putnam Bks. for Young Readers.

Historical Events

—The Scarlet Pimpernel. 1989. (J). (gr. k-6). pap. 3.50 o.s.i (*0-440-40220-4*, Yearling) Random Hse. Children's Bks.

—The Scarlet Pimpernel, unabr. ed. 2000. (YA). audio 60.00 Recorded Bks., LLC.

—The Scarlet Pimpernel Readalong. 1994. (Illustrated Classics Collection). 64p. pap. 13.50 o.p. incl. audio (*1-56103-608-0*); pap. 14.95 incl. audio (*0-7854-0771-5*, 40520) American Guidance Service, Inc.

Orczy, Baroness Emmuska, et al. The Scarlet Pimpernel. 1997. (Puffin Classics Ser.). (Illus.). 336p. (YA). (gr. 5 up). pap. 5.99 (*0-14-037454-X*, Puffin Bks.) Penguin Putnam Bks. for Young Readers.

Prowense, Mary J. Pamela & the Revolution. Schatz, Molly, ed. 1993. (Illus.). 130p. (J). (gr. 7 up). 12.95 (*0-9635107-2-X*) Marc Anthony Publishing.

Watson, Pat. The Scarlet Pimpernel. Robbins, Dawn Michelle, ed. 2000. (YA). 9.95 (*1-58130-638-5*); 11.95 (*1-58130-639-3*) Novel Units, Inc.

FRANCE—HISTORY—1799-1914—FICTION

Dickens, Charles. A Tale of Two Cities. 2000. (Illus.). 96p. pap. text 5.95 (*0-19-423047-3*) Oxford Univ. Pr., Inc.

—A Tale of Two Cities. (Saddleback Classics). 1999. (Illus.). (J). 13.10 (*0-606-21570-0*); 1996. 12.04 (*0-606-13049-7*) Turtleback Bks.

Dumas, Alexandre. The Count of Monte Cristo. 2002. (Great Illustrated Classics). (Illus.). 240p. (J). (gr. 3-8). lib. bdg. 21.35 (*1-57765-684-9*, ABDO & Daughters) ABDO Publishing Co.

—The Count of Monte Cristo: Abridged & Illustrated. Vogel, Malvina, ed. 1993. (Great Illustrated Classics Ser.: Vol. 28). (Illus.). 240p. (J). (gr. 3-6). 9.95 (*0-86611-979-5*) Playmore, Inc., Pubs.

—The Count of Monte Cristo: Abridged for Children. abr. ed. 1996. (Classics for Young Readers Ser.). (Illus.). 400p. (YA). (gr. 4-7). pap. 4.99 (*0-14-037353-5*, Puffin Bks.) Penguin Putnam Bks. for Young Readers.

—The Count of Monte Cristo: Adapted & Illustrated. 1987. (Regents Illustrated Classics Ser.). (YA). (gr. 7-12). pap. text 4.50 o.p. (*0-13-183336-7*, 20557) Prentice Hall, ESL Dept.

Gerstein, Mordicai. Victor: A Novel Based on the Life of Victor, the Savage of Aveyron, RS. 1998. 224p. (YA). (gr. 4-7). 17.00 o.p. (*0-374-38142-9*, Farrar, Straus & Giroux (BYR)) Farrar, Straus & Giroux.

Selinko, Annemarie. Desiree. 1953. (J). 17.95 o.p. (*0-688-01448-8*, Morrow, William & Co.) Morrow/Avon.

FRANCE—HISTORY—CONSULATE AND EMPIRE, 1799-1815—FICTION

Robbins, Ruth. The Emperor & the Drummer Boy. 1962. (Illus.). (J). (gr. 2-6). 4.95 o.p. (*0-87466-043-2*); lib. bdg. 5.38 o.p. (*0-87466-011-4*) Houghton Mifflin Co.

Wheeler, Thomas G. Fanfare for the Stalwart. 1967. (J). (gr. 8 up). 26.95 (*0-87599-139-4*) Phillips, S.G. Inc.

FRANCE—HISTORY—GERMAN OCCUPATION, 1940-1945—FICTION

Bradley, Kimberly Brubaker. For Freedom: The Story of a French Spy. 2003. 192p. lib. bdg. 17.99 (*0-385-90087-2*); (gr. 5-9). text 15.95 (*0-385-72961-8*) Random Hse. Children's Bks.

Maguire, Gregory. The Good Liar. 1999. 144p. (J). (gr. 5-9). tchr. ed. 15.00 (*0-395-90697-0*, Clarion Bks.) Houghton Mifflin Co. Trade & Reference Div.

Matas, Carol. Greater Than Angels. 1998. Orig. Title: Contagion of Good. 160p. (J). (gr. 7-12). pap. 16.00 (*0-689-81353-8*, Simon & Schuster Children's Publishing) Simon & Schuster Children's Publishing.

Polacco, Patricia. The Butterfly. 2000. (Illus.). 48p. (J). (ps-3). 16.99 (*0-399-23170-6*, Philomel) Penguin Putnam Bks. for Young Readers.

Sachs, Marilyn. A Pocket Full of Seeds. 1994. (Illus.). 144p. (YA). (gr. 5-9). pap. 5.99 o.s.i (*0-14-036593-1*, Puffin Bks.) Penguin Putnam Bks. for Young Readers.

—A Pocket Full of Seeds. 1995. 19.75 (*0-8446-6796-X*) Smith, Peter Pub., Inc.

—A Pocket Full of Seeds. 1994. 11.04 (*0-606-05978-4*) Turtleback Bks.

Vande Velde, Vivian. A Coming Evil. 1998. 212p. (J). (gr. 5-9). tchr. ed. 17.00 (*0-395-90012-3*) Houghton Mifflin Co.

FRONTIER AND PIONEER LIFE—FICTION

Aaron, Chester. An American Ghost. 1973. (Illus.). 192p. (J). (gr. 5 up). 5.95 o.p. (*0-15-203050-6*) Harcourt Children's Bks.

Ackerman, Karen. Araminta's Paint Box. (Illus.). 32p. (J). (gr. 1-3). 1998. pap. 6.99 (*0-689-82091-7*, Aladdin); 1990. lib. bdg. 13.95 (*0-689-31462-0*, Atheneum) Simon & Schuster Children's Publishing.

—Araminta's Paint Box. 1998. 12.14 (*0-606-15439-6*) Turtleback Bks.

Aldrich, Bess S. A Lantern in Her Hand. 1997. 256p. (YA). (gr. 8 up). pap. 6.99 (*0-14-038428-6*) Penguin Putnam Bks. for Young Readers.

—A Lantern in Her Hand. l.t. ed. 1982. 433p. reprint ed. o.p. (*0-89621-330-7*) Thorndike Pr.

—A Lantern in Her Hand. 1997. (J). 12.04 (*0-606-11546-3*) Turtleback Bks.

Alef, Daniel. Centennial Stories: A Living History of San Francisco. 2nd ed. 2000. (Illus.). 227p. (J). pap. 15.95 (*0-9700174-2-1*) Maxit Publishing, Inc.

Alter, Judith M. Luke & the Van Zandt County War. 1984. (Chaparral Bks.). (Illus.). 132p. (J). (gr. 4 up). 14.95 (*0-912646-88-8*) Texas Christian Univ. Pr.

Alter, Judy. Sam Houston Is My Hero. 2003. (Chaparral Book for Young Readers Ser.). 140p. (J). pap. 15.95 (*0-87565-277-8*) Texas Christian Univ. Pr.

Altsheler, Joseph A. Kentucky Frontiersmen: The Adventures of Henry Ware, Hunter & Border Fighter. Kenton, Nathaniel, ed. rev. ed. 1988. (Kentucky Frontiersmen Ser.: Vol. 1). (Illus.). 256p. (J). (gr. 5-10). 16.95 (*0-929146-01-8*) Voyageur Publishing Co.

Anderson, Laurie K. Clarissa's Heart. 1998. (Latter-Day Daughters Ser.). 5.95 (*1-57345-416-8*) Deseret Bk. Co.

—Ellie's Gold. 1995. (Latter-Day Daughters Ser.). (J). pap. 4.95 (*1-56236-505-3*) Aspen Bks.

—Maren's Hope. 1995. (Latter-Day Daughters Ser.). (Illus.). 80p. (J). pap. 4.95 (*1-56236-503-7*) Aspen Bks.

—Sadie's Trade. 1998. (Latter-Day Daughters Ser.). (J). o.p. (*1-57345-415-X*) Deseret Bk. Co.

—Violet's Garden. 1996. (Latter-Day Daughters Ser.). (Illus.). 80p. (J). (gr. 3-9). pap. 4.95 (*1-56236-506-1*) Aspen Bks.

Anderson, Leone C. Sean's War. 1998. (Illus.). 192p. (J). (gr. 3-9). 16.95 (*0-9638819-4-9*); pap. 10.95 (*0-9638819-5-7*) ShadowPlay Pr.

Anderson, Rian B. A Christmas Prayer. 2001. (J). 2.95 (*1-57734-900-8*) Covenant Communications.

Antle, Nancy. Beautiful Land: A Story of the Oklahoma Land Rush. 1994. (Once upon America Ser.). (Illus.). 64p. (J). (gr. 2-6). 12.99 o.p. (*0-670-85304-6*, Viking Children's Bks.) Penguin Putnam Bks. for Young Readers.

Applegate, Stanley. The Devil's Highway. 1998. (Illus.). 224p. (YA). (gr. 3-7). pap. 8.95 (*1-56145-184-3*, Peachtree Junior) Peachtree Pubs., Ltd.

—The Devil's Highway. 1998. (J). 15.00 (*0-606-19042-2*) Turtleback Bks.

—Natchez under-the-Hill. 1999. (Illus.). 186p. (YA). (gr. 3-7). pap. 8.95 (*1-56145-191-6*, 51916) Peachtree Pubs., Ltd.

Arbuckle, Scott. Zeb, the Cow's on the Roof Again! And Other Tales of Early Texas Dwellings. 1996. (Illus.). 120p. (J). (gr. 4-8). 15.95 (*1-57168-102-7*) Eakin Pr.

Archer, Marion F. Sarah Jane. 1971. (Illus.). (gr. 5-8). 5.95 o.p. (*0-8075-7241-1*) Whitman, Albert & Co.

Armstrong, Jennifer. Black-Eyed Susan. 1995. (Illus.). 128p. (J). (gr. 4-7). 15.00 o.s.i (*0-517-70107-3*) Random Hse., Inc.

Arrington, Frances. Bluestem. 2000. (Illus.). 140p. (J). (gr. 5-9). 16.99 (*0-399-23564-7*, G. P. Putnam's Sons) Penguin Putnam Bks. for Young Readers.

—Bluestem. 2001. (J). 12.04 (*0-606-22050-X*) Turtleback Bks.

—Prairie Whispers. 2003. 176p. (YA). (gr. 5-9). 17.99 (*0-399-23975-8*, Philomel) Penguin Putnam Bks. for Young Readers.

Auch, Mary Jane. Journey to Nowhere, ERS. 1997. 128p. (J). (gr. 4-7). 16.95 (*0-8050-4922-3*, Holt, Henry & Co. Bks. For Young Readers) Holt, Henry & Co.

—The Road to Home, ERS. 2000. 224p. (YA). (gr. 5-8). 16.95 (*0-8050-4921-5*, Holt, Henry & Co. Bks. For Young Readers) Holt, Henry & Co.

—The Road to Home. 2002. 224p. (gr. 5). pap. text 4.99 (*0-440-41805-4*, Random Hse. Bks. for Young Readers) Random Hse. Children's Bks.

Ayres, Katherine. Silver Dollar Girl. 2002. (Illus.). 208p. (gr. 3-7). pap. text 4.99 (*0-440-41705-8*, Laurel Leaf) Random Hse. Children's Bks.

Bagdon, Paul. Scrapper John: Valley of the Spotted Horse. 1992. (J). (gr. 4-7). pap. 3.50 (*0-380-76416-4*, Avon Bks.) Morrow/Avon.

Baker, Betty. Little Runner of the Longhouse. 1989. (I Can Read Bks.). (J). (gr. 1-3). 10.10 (*0-606-12401-2*) Turtleback Bks.

Ball, Zachary. North to Abilene. 1960. (Illus.). 199p. (J). (gr. 7-9). 3.95 o.p. (*0-8234-0079-4*) Holiday Hse., Inc.

Balmes, Kathy. Thunder on the Sierra. 2001. (Adventures in America Ser.). (Illus.). 96p. (J). (gr. 3-7). lib. bdg. 14.95 (*1-893110-10-9*) Silver Moon Pr.

Baltazzi, Evan S. Dog Gone West: A Western for Dog Lovers. 1994. (Illus.). 115p. (Orig.). (YA). (gr. 7 up). pap. 3.95 (*0-918948-05-3*) Evanel Assocs.

Barsotti, Joan B. Grandmother's Bell & the Wagon Train, 1849. (Illus.). 32p. (J). (gr. 1-5). 1997. 14.95 (*0-9642112-4-6*); 1996. pap. 6.95 (*0-9642112-3-8*) Barsotti Bks.

Bartlow, Evelyn A. Emily & the Santa Fe Trail. unabr. ed. 1998. (Illus.). 64p. (J). (gr. 4-7). pap. 8.00 (*1-890826-04-9*) Rock Creek Pr., LLC.

Bauer, Marion Dane. Land of the Buffalo Bones: The Diary of Mary Elizabeth Rodgers, an English Girl in Minnesota. 2003. (Dear America Ser.). (Illus.). 240p. (J). pap. 12.95 (*0-439-22027-0*) Scholastic, Inc.

Benchley, Nathaniel. Gone & Back. 1972. (I Can Read Bks.). (J). (ps-3). pap. 1.95 (*0-06-440016-6*, Harper Trophy) HarperCollins Children's Bk. Group.

Bender, Esther. Elisabeth & the Windmill. 2003. (Lemon Tree Ser.). 112p. (J). (gr. 3-7). pap. 6.99 (*0-8361-9204-4*) Herald Pr.

—Virginia & the Tiny One. 1998. (Lemon Tree Ser.: Vol. 2). (Illus.). 104p. (J). (gr. 3-7). pap. 6.99 (*0-8361-9090-4*) Herald Pr.

Benton, Amanda. Silent Stranger. 1998. pap. 3.99 (*0-380-79222-2*, Avon Bks.) Morrow/Avon.

—Silent Stranger. 1998. 10.04 (*0-606-16165-1*) Turtleback Bks.

Blakeslee, Ann R. A Different Kind of Hero. 1997. (Accelerated Reader Bks.). (Illus.). 144p. (J). (gr. 5-9). 14.95 (*0-7614-5000-9*, Cavendish Children's Bks.) Cavendish, Marshall Corp.

Blanc, Esther Silverstein & Eagle, Godeane. Long Johns for a Small Chicken. 2003. (J). 16.95 (*1-884244-23-8*) Volcano Pr.

Blevins, Wade. Se-lu's Song. 1996. (Cherokee Indian Legend Ser.: Vol. 7). (Illus.). 53p. (J). lib. bdg. 17.25 (*1-56763-133-9*) Ozark Publishing.

Blos, Joan W. Brothers of the Heart: A Story of the Old Northwest, 1837-1838. 2nd ed. 1993. 176p. (J). (gr. 3-7). reprint ed. pap. 4.99 (*0-689-71724-5*, Aladdin) Simon & Schuster Children's Publishing.

—Brothers of the Heart: A Story of the Old Northwest, 1837-1838. 1993. (J). 11.04 (*0-606-12203-6*) Turtleback Bks.

Bly, Stephen. Dangerous Ride Across Humboldt Flats. 2003. 128p. (J). pap. 6.99 (*1-58134-472-4*) Crossway Bks.

—Daring Rescue at Sonora Pass. 2003. 144p. (J). pap. 6.99 (*1-58134-471-6*) Crossway Bks.

Bly, Stephen A. The Adventures of Nathan T. Riggins, 31 vols., Vol. 1. 2001. 384p. (J). (gr. 4-9). reprint ed. pap. 10.99 (*1-58134-235-7*) Crossway Bks.

—The Adventures of Nathan T. Riggins Bks. 4-6, 31 vols., Vol. 2. 2001. 384p. (J). (gr. 4-9). reprint ed. pap. 10.99 (*1-58134-234-9*) Crossway Bks.

—The Buffalo's Last Stand. 2002. (Retta Barre's Oregon Trail Ser.: 2). 111p. (J). pap. 5.99 (*1-58134-392-2*) Crossway Bks.

—Coyote True, No. 2. 1992. (Nathan T. Riggins Western Adventure Ser.: Bk. 2). 128p. (J). (gr. 4-7). pap. 4.99 o.p. (*0-89107-680-8*) Crossway Bks.

—The Dog Who Would Not Smile, No. 1. 1992. (Nathan T. Riggins Western Adventure Ser.: Vol. 1). 128p. (J). (gr. 4-7). pap. 4.99 o.p. (*0-89107-656-5*) Crossway Bks.

—The Lost Wagon Train. 2002. (Retta Barre's Oregon Trail Ser.: Vol. 1). 110p. (J). pap. 5.99 (*1-58134-391-4*) Crossway Bks.

—The Plain Prairie Princess. 2002. (Retta Barre's Oregon Trail Ser.: 3). 108p. (J). pap. 5.99 (*1-58134-393-0*) Crossway Bks.

—You Can Always Trust a Spotted Horse, No. 3. 1993. (Nathan T. Riggins Western Adventure Ser.: Vol. 3). 128p. (J). (gr. 4-7). pap. 4.99 o.p. (*0-89107-716-2*) Crossway Bks.

Boonstra, Jean Elizabeth. Miss Button & the Schoolboard: Sarah 1842-1844. 2002. 95p. (J). (*0-8163-1874-3*) Pacific Pr. Publishing Assn.

—Sarah's Disappointment: Sarah 1842-1844. 2002. 95p. (J). (*0-8163-1888-3*) Pacific Pr. Publishing Assn.

—Secret in the Family A: Sarah 1842-1844. 2002. 95p. (J). (*0-8163-1887-5*) Pacific Pr. Publishing Assn.

—Song for Grandfather A: Sarah 1842-1844. 2002. 95p. (J). (*0-8163-1873-5*) Pacific Pr. Publishing Assn.

Bouchard, Dave. The Journal of Etienne Mercier. 1998. (Illus.). 40p. (J). 22.95 o.p. incl. audio compact disk (*1-55143-126-2*) Orca Bk. Pubs.

Boutwell, Florence. Love According to Teresa. 2000. (Illus.). 190p. (J). (*0-87062-298-6*, Millwood Publishing) Clark, Arthur H. Co.

—Teresa & the Coeur d'Alene Indians: An Historical Adventure Story for Young & Old. 1998. (Illus.). 175 p. (J). (*0-87062-288-9*) Clark, Arthur H. Co.

—Teresa of Northwood Prairie: An Historical Adventure Story for Young & Old. 1998. (Illus.). 175p. (J). 17.95 (*0-87062-284-6*) Clark, Arthur H. Co.

Bradley, Kimberly Brubaker. Weaver's Daughter. l.t. ed. 2002. 173p. (J). 21.95 (*0-7862-3763-5*) Gale Group.

—Weaver's Daughter. 2000. (Illus.). 160p. (gr. 3-7). text 14.95 (*0-385-32769-2*, Delacorte Bks. for Young Readers) Random Hse. Children's Bks.

Brandis, Marianne. The Quarter-Pie Window. 1985. 204p. (YA). pap. (*0-88984-085-7*) Porcupine's Quill, Inc.

—The Quarter-Pie Window. 2003. (Illus.). 232p. (YA). (gr. 6-9). pap. 9.95 (*0-88776-624-2*) Tundra Bks. of Northern New York.

Brenner, Barbara. Wagon Wheels. (I Can Read Bks.). (Illus.). 64p. (J). (gr. k-3). 1978. 15.95 (*0-06-020668-3*); 1978. lib. bdg. 15.89 (*0-06-020669-1*); unabr. ed. 1995. pap. 8.99 incl. audio (*0-694-70001-0*); 97th ed. 1997. pap. 3.99 (*0-06-444052-4*, Harper Trophy) HarperCollins Children's Bk. Group.

—Wagon Wheels. 1978. (I Can Read Bks.). (J). (gr. 2-4). 10.10 (*0-606-02372-0*) Turtleback Bks.

Brink, Carol R. Caddie Woodlawn. l.t. ed. 1988. (YA). (gr. 5 up). reprint ed. lib. bdg. 16.95 o.s.i (*1-55736-043-X*, Cornerstone Bks.) Pages, Inc.

—Caddie Woodlawn. (J). 9999. pap. 2.50 o.s.i (*0-590-10121-8*); 1997. (Illus.). 16p. mass mkt. 3.95 (*0-590-37359-5*) Scholastic, Inc.

—Caddie Woodlawn. 1990. (Illus.). 288p. (J). (gr. 3-7). pap. 5.99 (*0-689-71370-3*, Aladdin); 1973. (Illus.). 288p. (J). (gr. 3-7). 17.00 (*0-02-713670-1*, Simon & Schuster Children's Publishing); 2nd ed. 1997. 288p. (YA). (gr. 3-7). mass mkt. 5.50 (*0-689-81521-2*, Simon Pulse); Vol. 1. 1999. pap. 2.99 (*0-689-82969-8*, Aladdin) Simon & Schuster Children's Publishing.

—Caddie Woodlawn. (J). 2001. (Illus.). 11.55 (*0-606-20588-8*); 1970. 11.04 (*0-606-02490-5*) Turtleback Bks.

—Magical Melons. 1990. (Illus.). 208p. (J). (gr. 4-7). reprint ed. pap. 4.99 (*0-689-71416-5*, Aladdin) Simon & Schuster Children's Publishing.

—Magical Melons. 1990. (J). 10.00 (*0-606-04473-6*) Turtleback Bks.

Brown, Cinita D. The Black Kettle Ride. 1997. (Illus.). (J). 25.25 (*1-56763-291-2*); pap. (*1-56763-292-0*) Ozark Publishing.

Brown, Irene Bennett. Skitterbrain. 1992. (Sunflower Editions Ser.). (Illus.). 128p. (J). (gr. 4 up). reprint ed. pap. 6.95 o.p. (*0-936085-21-5*) Blue Heron Publishing.

—Skitterbrain. l.t. ed. 2002. 158p. (J). 21.95 (*0-7862-4646-4*) Thorndike Pr.

Buchanan, William J. One Last Time. 1992. (Orig.). (YA). pap. 2.99 (*0-380-76152-1*, Avon Bks.) Morrow/Avon.

Buckey, Sarah Masters. Enemy in the Fort. (American Girl Collection: Bk. 13). (Illus.). 176p. (J). (gr. 4-7). 2001. 9.95 o.p. (*1-58485-307-7*); 2000. pap. 5.95 (*1-58485-306-9*) Pleasant Co. Pubns. (American Girl).

—Enemy in the Fort. 2001. (American Girl Collection). (Illus.). (J). 12.00 (*0-606-21180-2*) Turtleback Bks.

Bulla, Clyde Robert. Secret Valley. (Trophy Bk.). (Illus.). (J). (gr. 2-5). 1993. 112p. pap. 4.50 (*0-06-440456-0*, Harper Trophy); 1949. lib. bdg. 7.95 o.p. (*0-690-72383-0*) HarperCollins Children's Bk. Group.

—White Bird. 1966. (Illus.). (J). (gr. 2-5). 7.95 o.p. (*0-690-88499-0*) HarperCollins Children's Bk. Group.

Bunting, Eve. Dandelions. 1995. (Illus.). 48p. (J). (ps-3). 16.00 (*0-15-200050-X*) Harcourt Children's Bks.

Burks, Brian. Soldier Boy. 1997. 160p. (YA). (gr. 7 up). 12.00 (*0-15-201218-4*); pap. 6.00 (*0-15-201219-2*, Harcourt Paperbacks) Harcourt Children's Bks.

Byars, Betsy C. The Golly Sisters Go West: An I Can Read Book. (I Can Read Bks.). (Illus.). 64p. (J). 1989. (gr. k-3). pap. 3.99 (*0-06-444132-6*, Harper Trophy); 1986. (gr. k-3). lib. bdg. 16.89 (*0-06-020884-8*, Harper Trophy); 1986. (gr. 2-4). 11.95 (*0-06-020883-X*); 1995. (ps-3). 8.99 incl. audio (*0-694-70027-4*) HarperCollins Children's Bk. Group.

—The Golly Sisters Go West: An I Can Read Book. 2000. (YA). pap. 23.20 incl. audio (*0-7887-4335-X*, 41130) Recorded Bks., LLC.

—The Golly Sisters Go West: An I Can Read Book. 1985. (I Can Read Bks.). (J). (gr. 2-4). 10.10 (*0-606-04234-2*) Turtleback Bks.

—The Golly Sisters Ride Again: An I Can Read Book. 1994. (I Can Read Bks.). (Illus.). 64p. (J). (gr. k-3). lib. bdg. 15.89 (*0-06-021564-X*); 14.95 o.p. (*0-06-021563-1*) HarperCollins Children's Bk. Group.

—Hooray for the Golly Sisters! An I Can Read Book. 1990. (I Can Read Bks.). (Illus.). 64p. (J). (gr. k-3). lib. bdg. 15.89 (*0-06-020899-6*); (gr. 2-4). 15.95 o.p. (*0-06-020898-8*) HarperCollins Children's Bk. Group.

—Trouble River. (Illus.). (J). (gr. 3-7). 1989. 128p. pap. 4.99 (*0-14-034243-5*, Puffin Bks.); 1969. 160p. 14.99 o.s.i (*0-670-73257-5*, Viking Children's Bks.) Penguin Putnam Bks. for Young Readers.

—Trouble River. 1989. (J). 11.04 (*0-606-04396-9*) Turtleback Bks.

—Trouble River. 1972. (Seafarer Ser.). (Illus.). (J). (gr. 3-8). 0.95 o.p. (*0-670-05064-4*, Penguin Bks.) Viking Penguin.

Calvert, Patricia. Betrayed! 224p. (J). 2004. (Illus.). pap. 4.99 (*0-689-86693-3*, Aladdin); 2002. (gr. 7 up). 16.00 (*0-689-83472-1*, Atheneum) Simon & Schuster Children's Publishing.
—Bigger. 144p. (J). 2003. pap. 4.99 (*0-689-86003-X*, Aladdin); 1994. (gr. 4-6). 16.00 (*0-684-19685-9*, Atheneum) Simon & Schuster Children's Publishing.
—Bigger. 1994. 10.00 (*0-606-07287-X*) Turtleback Bks.
Canfield, Dorothy. The Bent Twig. 1981. 334p. (J). reprint ed. lib. bdg. 17.95 o.p. (*0-89966-343-5*) Buccaneer Bks., Inc.
Cannon, A. E. Charlotte's Rose. 2004. 256p. (gr. 3-7). pap. text 5.50 (*0-440-41840-2*, Yearling) Random Hse. Children's Bks.
—Charlotte's Rose. 2002. (Illus.). 256p. (gr. 3-7). text 15.95 (*0-385-72966-9*) Random Hse., Inc.
Carey, Mary. Two for Texas: The Extraordinary Story of Kian & Jane Long. 1999. (J). 14.95 (*1-57168-292-9*) Eakin Pr.
Carroll, Betty Casbeer. The Foothill Spirits! Frontier Life & the Shawnees. 2001. 137p. pap. 17.95 (*0-595-17708-5*, Writer's Showcase Pr.) iUniverse, Inc.
Carter, Peter. Borderlands, RS. 432p. 1993. (YA). pap. 4.95 o.p. (*0-374-40883-1*, Aerial); 1990. 17.00 o.p. (*0-374-30895-0*, Farrar, Straus & Giroux (BYR)) Farrar, Straus & Giroux.
—Borderlands. 1993. (Aerial Fiction Ser.). (J). 10.05 o.p. (*0-606-05764-1*) Turtleback Bks.
Castleberry, Stephen B. & Castleberry, Susie L. Our Homestead Story: The First Years. 1996. 210p. pap. 7.50 o.s.i (*1-891907-02-6*) Castleberry Farms Pr.
Chandler, Roy F. & Chandler, Katherine R. The Gun of Joseph Smith. 1987. 106p. (J). (gr. 4 up). 7.95 o.p. (*0-87579-086-0*) Deseret Bk. Co.
Childers, Bob, contrib. by. Home Beyond the Mountains. 1997. (*1-890795-00-3*) Revelation I Publishing.
Citra, Becky. Danger at the Landings. 2002. (Illus.). 96p. (J). (gr. 2-6). pap. 4.99 (*1-55143-232-3*) Orca Bk. Pubs.
—The Freezing Moon. 2001. (Young Reader Ser.). (Illus.). 96p. (J). (gr. 2-6). pap. 4.99 (*1-55143-181-5*) Orca Bk. Pubs.
Clark, Ann Nolan. All This Wild Land. 1976. (J). (gr. 7-12). 7.95 o.p. (*0-670-11444-8*) Viking Penguin.
Clifford, Eth. Search for the Crescent Moon, 001. 1974. (Illus.). 256p. (J). (gr. 7-12). 5.95 o.p. (*0-395-16035-9*) Houghton Mifflin Co.
—The Year of the Three-Legged Deer. Cuffari, Richard, tr. & illus. by. 2003. (Library of Indiana Classics). xix, 164p. (YA). 32.95 (*0-253-34251-1*); pap. 14.95 (*0-253-21604-4*) Indiana Univ. Pr.
Coerr, Eleanor. The Josefina Story Quilt. 1989. (I Can Read Bks.). (Illus.). 64p. (J). (gr. k-3). pap. 3.99 (*0-06-444129-6*, Harper Trophy) HarperCollins Children's Bk. Group.
Conrad, Pam. My Daniel. 1989. 144p. (gr. 5 up). (J). lib. bdg. 16.89 (*0-06-021314-0*); (YA). 13.95 (*0-06-021313-2*) HarperCollins Children's Bk. Group.
—Prairie Songs. (Trophy Book Ser.). (Illus.). 176p. (gr. 5 up). 1987. (YA). pap. 5.99 (*0-06-440206-1*, Harper Trophy); 1985. (J). lib. bdg. 15.89 (*0-06-021337-X*) HarperCollins Children's Bk. Group.
—Prairie Songs. 1985. (Illus.). (J). (gr. 4-7). 14.00 o.s.i (*0-06-021336-1*, 236070) HarperCollins Pubs.
—Prairie Songs. 1995. 19.50 (*0-8446-6812-5*) Smith, Peter Pub., Inc.
—Prairie Songs. 1987. (J). 11.00 (*0-606-03639-3*) Turtleback Bks.
Constant, Alberta W. Miss Charity Comes to Stay. 1959. (Illus.). (J). (gr. 5-9). 8.95 o.p. (*0-690-54490-1*) HarperCollins Children's Bk. Group.
Cook, David C. Publishing Staff. Ambush. 1977. (Illus.). (gr. 2-5). pap. 1.95 o.p. (*0-89191-076-X*, 08748) Cook, David C. Publishing Co.
Cooper, James Fenimore. The Leatherstocking Saga. (J). (gr. 5-6). 44.95 (*0-8488-0059-1*) Amereon, Ltd.
—The Pioneers. 1964. (Airmont Classics Ser.). (J). (gr. 8 up). mass mkt. 1.95 o.p. (*0-8049-0049-3*, CL-49) Airmont Publishing Co., Inc.
—The Pioneers. 1823. 477p. (YA). reprint ed. pap. text 28.00 (*1-4047-2371-4*) Classic Textbooks.
—The Pioneers. 1964. 448p. (YA). mass mkt. 6.95 (*0-451-52521-3*); mass mkt. 4.50 o.p. (*0-451-52339-3*) NAL. (Signet Classics).
Creel, Ann H. Water at the Blue Earth. 1998. (Illus.). (gr. 5-9). 148p. (YA). 14.95 o.p. (*1-57098-209-0*, Rinehart, Roberts International); 112p. pap. 8.95 (*1-57098-224-4*) Rinehart, Roberts Pubs.
Crompton, Anne E. Johnny's Trail. 1986. 112p. 6.95 (*0-87785-131-X*) Swedenborg Foundation, Inc.
Crook, Connie Brummel. The Perilous Year. 2003. 197p. (YA). (*1-55041-816-5*) Fitzhenry & Whiteside, Ltd.
Cullen, Lynn. Diary of Nelly Vandorn. 2002. (Nelly in the Wilderness Ser.). 192p. (J). (gr. 3-6). lib. bdg. 15.89 (*0-06-029134-6*); 15.95 (*0-06-029133-8*) HarperCollins Children's Bk. Group.
—Diary of Nelly Vandorn. Date not set. 128p. (gr. 3 up). mass mkt. 4.99 (*0-06-440926-0*) HarperCollins Pubs.
Curtis, Rebecca S. Charlotte Avery on Isle Royale. 1995. 192p. (J). 14.95 o.p. (*1-883953-09-X*) Midwest Traditions, Inc.
Cushman, Karen. The Ballad of Lucy Whipple. 1996. 208p. (YA). (gr. 7-9). tchr. ed. 15.00 (*0-395-72806-1*, Clarion Bks.) Houghton Mifflin Co. Trade & Reference Div.
Dalgliesh, Alice. The Courage of Sarah Noble. 2002. (Illus.). (J). 13.40 (*0-7587-0249-3*) Book Wholesalers, Inc.
—The Courage of Sarah Noble. unabr. ed. 1954. (J). 24.20 incl. audio (*0-7887-2658-7*, 40818) Recorded Bks., LLC.
—The Courage of Sarah Noble. 9999. (J). pap. 1.95 o.s.i (*0-590-30049-0*) Scholastic, Inc.
—The Courage of Sarah Noble. (Illus.). (J). reprint ed. 1987. 64p. (gr. 2-6). 16.99 (*0-684-18830-9*, Atheneum); 1986. 60p. (gr. 1-5). pap. 4.95 o.s.i (*0-689-71057-7*, Aladdin); 2nd ed. 1991. 64p. (gr. 2-5). pap. 4.99 (*0-689-71540-4*, Aladdin) Simon & Schuster Children's Publishing.
—The Courage of Sarah Noble. 2nd ed. 1991. (J). 11.14 (*0-606-02070-5*) Turtleback Bks.
Davis, Tim. More Tales from Dust River Gulch. 2002. (Tales from Dust River Gulch Ser.). (Illus.). 108p. (J). (gr. 4-6). 6.49 (*1-57924-855-1*) Jones, Bob Univ. Pr.
—Tales from Dust River Gulch. 1997. (Illus.). 102p. (J). (gr. 4-7). pap. 6.49 (*0-89084-896-3*, 102517) Jones, Bob Univ. Pr.
De Angeli, Marguerite. Copper-Toed Boots. 1938. (gr. k-4). 5.95 o.p. (*0-385-07264-3*) Doubleday Publishing.
Dearen, Patrick. Comanche Peace Pipe. 2001. (Lone Star Heroes Ser.). 300p. (J). (ps-3). pap. 8.95 (*1-55622-831-7*, Republic of Texas Pr.) Wordware Publishing, Inc.
Dengler, Sandy. Arizona Longhorn Adventure. 1980. (Pioneer Family Adventure Ser.). 128p. (J). (gr. 5-8). pap. 2.95 o.p. (*0-8024-0299-2*) Moody Pr.
—The Horse Who Loved Picnics. 1980. (Pioneer Family Adventure Ser.). 128p. (J). (gr. 4-8). pap. 2.95 o.p. (*0-8024-3589-0*) Moody Pr.
Domnick, Howard. Danny on the Pioneer Trail. 2001. (Illus.). 93p. (YA). pap. 10.00 (*0-9715419-3-0*) Domnick, Howard.
Donahue, Marilyn C. The Valley in Between. 1987. (J). 15.85 (*0-8027-6745-1*); (YA). (gr. 5 up). 14.95 (*0-8027-6731-1*); (YA). (gr. 5 up). lib. bdg. 15.85 (*0-8027-6733-8*) Walker & Co.
Downie, Mary Alice. Scared Sarah. 2002. (Illus.). 65p. pap. (*1-55041-714-2*) Fitzhenry & Whiteside, Ltd.
Duey, Kathleen. Celou Sudden Shout: Idaho, 1826. 1998. (American Diaries Ser.: No. 9). 144p. (J). (gr. 3-7). pap. 4.50 o.s.i (*0-689-81622-7*, Aladdin) Simon & Schuster Children's Publishing.
—Celou Sudden Shout: Idaho, 1826. 1998. (American Diaries Ser.: No. 9). (J). (gr. 3-7). 10.55 (*0-606-13121-3*) Turtleback Bks.
—Ellen Elizabeth Hawkins: Mobeetie, Texas, 1886. 1997. (American Diaries Ser.: No. 6). (Illus.). 144p. (J). (gr. 3-7). pap. 4.99 (*0-689-81409-7*, Aladdin) Simon & Schuster Children's Publishing.
—Ellen Elizabeth Hawkins: Mobeetie, Texas, 1886. 1997. (American Diaries Ser.: No. 6). (J). (gr. 3-7). 10.55 (*0-606-11037-2*) Turtleback Bks.
—Willow Chase: Kansas Territory, 1847. 1997. (American Diaries Ser.: No. 5). 144p. (J). (gr. 3-7). pap. 4.50 (*0-689-81355-4*, Aladdin) Simon & Schuster Children's Publishing.
—Willow Chase: Kansas Territory, 1847. 1997. (American Diaries Ser.: No. 5). (J). (gr. 3-7). 10.55 (*0-606-11036-4*) Turtleback Bks.
Durbin, William. Blackwater Ben. 2003. 208p. (gr. 5). text 15.95 (*0-385-72928-6*); lib. bdg. 17.99 (*0-385-90149-6*) Random Hse. Children's Bks. (Delacorte Bks. for Young Readers).
—Song of Sampo Lake. 2002. 224p. (gr. 4-7). lib. bdg. 17.99 (*0-385-90055-4*); (gr. 5 up). text 15.95 (*0-385-32731-5*) Dell Publishing. (Delacorte Pr.).
—Song of Sampo Lake. 2004. 224p. (gr. 5). pap. text 5.50 (*0-440-22899-9*, Yearling) Random Hse. Children's Bks.
Durrant, Lynda. The Sun, the Rain, & the Apple Seed: A Novel of Johnny Appleseed's Life. 2003. 208p. (J). (gr. 5-9). tchr. ed. 15.00 (*0-618-23487-X*, Clarion Bks.) Houghton Mifflin Co. Trade & Reference Div.
Easton. Blood & Money. 1998. 20.00 (*0-7862-1103-2*, Macmillan Reference USA) Gale Group.
Easton, Robert. Blood & Money. 1998. (Western Ser.). 372p. 19.95 (*0-7862-1154-7*, Five Star) Gale Group.
Ellis, Mel. An Eagle to the Wind, ERS. 1978. (J). o.p. (*0-03-022766-6*, Holt, Henry & Co. Bks. For Young Readers) Holt, Henry & Co.
Ellsworth, Loretta. The Shrouding Woman, ERS. 2002. 160p. (YA). (gr. 5-8). 16.95 (*0-8050-6651-9*, Holt, Henry & Co. Bks. For Young Readers) Holt, Henry & Co.
Embry-Litchman, Kristin. All Is Well. 1998. (Illus.). 128p. (gr. 4-7). text 14.95 o.s.i (*0-385-32592-4*, Delacorte Pr.) Dell Publishing.
—All Is Well. 1999. 128p. (gr. 4-7). pap. text 3.99 o.s.i (*0-440-41488-1*, Dell Books for Young Readers) Random Hse. Children's Bks.
—All Is Well. 1999. 10.04 (*0-606-16714-5*) Turtleback Bks.
Ericson, Stig. Dan Henry in the Wild West. Teal, Thomas, tr. 1976. (J). (gr. 5-9). 5.95 o.p. (*0-440-01659-2*, Delacorte Pr.) Dell Publishing.
Ernst, Kathleen. Whistler in the Dark. 2002. (American Girl Collection: Bk. 16). (Illus.). 176p. (J). 10.95 (*1-58485-486-3*); pap. 6.95 (*1-58485-485-5*) Pleasant Co. Pubns. (American Girl).
Eubanks, Toni. Journey Home: Passage to Womanhood. 1996. 158 p. (J). 11.99 (*1-56256-413-7*) Peoples Publishing Group, Inc., The.
Faber, Gail & Lasagna, Michele. Clara Rounds Cape Horn. 1997. (Whispers Ser.). (Illus.). 50p. pap., tchr. ed. 10.95 (*0-936480-14-9*); 113p. (J). (gr. 4-8). 12.95 (*0-936480-13-0*); 113p. (J). (gr. 4-8). pap. 9.95 (*0-936480-12-2*) Magpie Pubns.
Fahey, Effie. Patience of Dearing Bay. (Illus.). 151p. (J). pap. (*0-920576-57-5*) Caitlin Pr., Inc.
Field, Rachel. Calico Bush. 1990. (Yearling Newbery Ser.). (J). 10.09 o.p. (*0-606-12208-7*) Turtleback Bks.
Finley, Martha. Elsie at Nantucket. 1998. (Elsie Bks.: Vol. 10). (J). (gr. 7-12). pap. 6.99 (*1-888306-46-7*) Holly Hall Pubns., Inc.
—Elsie Dinsmore. 1976. 22.95 (*0-8488-1311-1*) Amereon, Ltd.
—Elsie Dinsmore. 1979. (Popular Culture in America Ser.). (Illus.). 342p. (YA). (gr. 7 up). reprint ed. 41.95 (*0-405-06372-5*) Ayer Co. Pubs., Inc.
—Elsie Dinsmore. 1987. 332p. (J). (gr. 7-12). reprint ed. lib. bdg. 27.95 (*0-89966-332-X*) Buccaneer Bks., Inc.
—Elsie Dinsmore. rev. ed. 1997. (Elsie Bks.: Vol. 1). 253p. (J). (gr. 7-12). pap. 6.99 (*1-888306-31-9*, Full Quart Pr.) Holly Hall Pubns., Inc.
—Elsie's Girlhood, 28. rev. ed. 1997. (Elsie Bks.: Vol. 3). 300p. (J). (gr. 7-12). pap. 6.99 (*1-888306-33-5*, Full Quart Pr.) Holly Hall Pubns., Inc.
—Elsie's Holidays at Roselands. 1997. (Elsie Books: Vol. 2). 274p. (J). mass mkt. 5.99 (*1-931343-06-3*) Hibbard Pubns., Inc.
—Elsie's Holidays at Roselands, 28. rev. ed. 1997. (Elsie Bks.: Vol. 2). 274p. (J). (gr. 7-12). pap. 6.99 (*1-888306-32-7*, Full Quart Pr.) Holly Hall Pubns., Inc.
—Elsie's Holidays at Roselands. 1993. (Elsie Dinsmore Ser.: Bk. 2). (Illus.). 360p. (gr. 4-7). 28.99 (*1-58960-264-1*) Sovereign Grace Pubs., Inc.
—Elsie's Kith & Kin. 2001. (Elsie Books: Vol. 12). 228p. (J). (gr. 4-7). mass mkt. 5.99 (*1-931343-03-9*) Hibbard Pubns., Inc.
—Elsie's Kith & Kin. 1998. (Elsie Bks.: Vol. 12). pap. 6.99 (*1-888306-48-3*) Holly Hall Pubns., Inc.
—Elsie's Kith & Kin. 1996. (Elsie Dinsmore Ser.: Bk. 12). (Illus.). 352p. (gr. 4-7). 28.99 (*1-58960-274-9*) Sovereign Grace Pubs., Inc.
—Elsie's New Relations. 1998. (Elsie Bks.: Vol. 9). (J). (gr. 7-12). pap. 6.99 (*1-888306-45-9*) Holly Hall Pubns., Inc.
—Elsie's Womanhood, 28. rev. ed. 1997. (Elsie Bks.: No. 4). 287p. (J). (gr. 7-12). pap. 6.99 (*1-888306-34-3*, Full Quart Pr.) Holly Hall Pubns., Inc.
—Millie Keith Boxed Set 1-4. 2002. 224p. 34.99 (*1-928749-65-8*) Mission City Pr., Inc.
—The Two Elsies. 1998. (Elsie Bks.: Vol. 11). (J). (gr. 7-12). pap. 6.99 (*1-888306-47-5*) Holly Hall Pubns., Inc.
Finley, Mary Peace. Meadow Lark. 2003. (YA). 15.95 (*0-86541-070-4*) Filter Pr., LLC.
Finley, Mary Peace. White Grizzly. 2000. (gr. 5-9). (Illus.). 215p. (J). 15.95 (*0-86541-053-4*); 216p. (YA). pap. 8.95 (*0-86541-058-5*) Filter Pr., LLC.
Fleischman, Paul. The Borning Room. 1991. (Charlotte Zolotow Bk.). 80p. (YA). (gr. 6 up). 14.95 o.s.i (*0-06-023762-7*); lib. bdg. 14.89 o.p. (*0-06-023785-6*) HarperCollins Children's Bk. Group.
Flory, Jane. The Golden Venture, 001. 1976. (Illus.). 224p. (J). (gr. 5-9). 7.95 o.p. (*0-395-24377-7*) Houghton Mifflin Co.
Fontes, Ron & Fontes, Justine. Calamity Jane at Fort Sanders. 1992. (Disney's American Frontier Ser.: Bk. 8). (Illus.). 80p. (J). (gr. 1-4). lib. bdg. 12.89 o.s.i (*1-56282-265-9*); (ps-3). pap. 3.50 (*1-56282-264-0*) Disney Pr.
—Davy Crockett & the Highwaymen. 1992. (Disney's American Frontier Ser.: Bk. 6). (Illus.). 80p. (J). (gr. 1-4). pap. 3.50 o.s.i (*1-56282-260-8*); lib. bdg. 12.89 o.s.i (*1-56282-261-6*) Disney Pr.
Frazier, Neta L. Stout-Hearted Seven. 1973. (J). (gr. 4-6). 5.95 o.p. (*0-15-281450-7*) Harcourt Children's Bks.
Freeman, Bill. Ambush in the Foothills. 2001. (Bains Ser.). (Illus.). 160p. (J). (gr. 3-7). mass mkt. 6.95 (*1-55028-716-8*) Lorimer, James & Co. CAN. *Dist:* Orca Bk. Pubs.
—First Spring on the Grand Banks. 1978. (Bains Ser.). (Illus.). 215p. (J). mass mkt. 9.95 (*0-88862-220-1*); bds. 16.95 (*0-88862-221-X*) Lorimer, James & Co. CAN. *Dist:* Formac Distributing, Ltd.
—First Spring on the Grand Banks, Grades 5-10. 1981. (Bains Ser.). (Illus.). 80p. tchr. ed., spiral bd. 6.95 (*0-88862-431-X*) Lorimer, James & Co. CAN. *Dist:* Formac Distributing, Ltd.
—Prairie Fire! 1998. 196p. (J). (gr. 3-7). pap. 6.95 (*1-55028-608-0*) Lorimer, James & Co. CAN. *Dist:* Orca Bk. Pubs.
Freeman, Marcia S. The Gift. 2001. (Illus.). 31p. (J). 14.95 (*0-929895-51-7*) Maupin Hse. Publishing.
Fritz, Jean. The Cabin Faced West. 1997. (Illus.). 128p. (J). (gr. 4-7). 15.99 (*0-399-23223-0*, G. P. Putnam's Sons) Penguin Group (USA) Inc.
—The Cabin Faced West. 1987. (Classics for Young Readers Ser.). (Illus.). 128p. (J). (gr. 3-7). pap. 5.99 o.s.i (*0-14-032256-6*, Puffin Bks.) Penguin Putnam Bks. for Young Readers.
—The Cabin Faced West. 1958. (Illus.). 128p. (J). (gr. 4-7). 14.95 o.s.i (*0-698-20016-0*, Coward-McCann) Putnam Publishing Group, The.
Fugate, Clara T. The Legend of Natural Tunnel: La Leyenda del Tunel Natural. Calvera, Elizabeth C., ed. Socarras-Roufagalas, Gilda, tr. 1986. (Tales of the Virginia Wilderness Ser.: No. 1). (ENG & SPA., Illus.). 78p. (Orig.). (YA). (gr. 6-12). pap. 5.95 (*0-936015-02-0*) Pocahontas Pr., Inc.
Gagliano, Eugene. The Secret of the Black Widow. 2002. 67p. (J). pap. 5.95 (*1-57249-286-4*, WM Kids) White Mane Publishing Co., Inc.
Garland, Sherry. A Line in the Sand: The Alamo Diary of Lucinda Lawrence, Gonzales, Texas, 1836. 1998. (Dear America Ser.). (Illus.). 201p. (YA). (gr. 4-9). pap. 10.95 (*0-590-39466-5*, Scholastic Pr.) Scholastic, Inc.
Gerrard, Roy. Rosie & the Rustlers, RS. 1991. (Illus.). 32p. (J). (ps-3). pap. 6.95 (*0-374-46339-5*, Sunburst) Farrar, Straus & Giroux.
—Wagons West!, RS. 32p. (J). (ps-3). 2000. (Illus.). pap. 5.95 (*0-374-48210-1*, Sunburst); 1996. 15.00 (*0-374-38249-2*, Farrar, Straus & Giroux (BYR)) Farrar, Straus & Giroux.
—Wagons West! 2000. (Illus.). (J). 12.10 (*0-606-20401-6*) Turtleback Bks.
Gilson, Jamie. Wagon Train 911. (gr. 3 up). 1996. 160p. (J). 15.00 o.p. (*0-688-14550-7*); 1924. (YA). lib. bdg. o.s.i (*0-688-14551-5*) HarperCollins Children's Bk. Group.
—Wagon Train 911. 1998. (J). 11.00 (*0-606-13090-X*) Turtleback Bks.
Glass, Andrew. Bewildered for Three Days: As to Why Daniel Boone Never Wore His Coonskin Cap. 2000. (Illus.). 32p. (J). (gr. 1-5). tchr. ed. 16.95 (*0-8234-1446-9*) Holiday Hse., Inc.
—Folks Call Me Appleseed John. 1995. (Illus.). 48p. (J). (gr. 1-5). 15.95 o.p. (*0-385-32045-0*) Doubleday Publishing.
—Folks Call Me Appleseed John. 1998. (Picture Yearling Book Ser.). (Illus.). 48p. (gr. 1-4). pap. text 6.99 o.s.i (*0-440-41466-0*, Dell Books for Young Readers) Random Hse. Children's Bks.
—Folks Call Me Appleseed John. unabr. ed. 1998. (J). Class Set. 102.70 incl. audio (*0-7887-2552-1*, 46722); Homework. 27.24 incl. audio (*0-7887-2247-6*, 40731) Recorded Bks., LLC.
—Folks Call Me Appleseed John. 1998. 13.14 (*0-606-13393-3*) Turtleback Bks.
—The Sweetwater Run: The Story of Buffalo Bill Cody & the Pony Express. 1998. (Picture Yearling Book Ser.). 48p. (gr. 1-5). pap. text 6.99 o.s.i (*0-440-41186-6*) Dell Publishing.
Glaze, Lynn. Seasons of the Trail. 2000. (Adventures in America Ser.). (Illus.). 96p. (J). (gr. 3-7). lib. bdg. 14.95 (*1-893110-20-6*) Silver Moon Pr.
Graef, Renee, illus. The Adventures of Laura & Jack. 1997. (Little House Ser.: No. 1). 80p. (J). (gr. 3-6). pap. 4.25 (*0-06-442045-0*, Harper Trophy); lib. bdg. 14.89 (*0-06-027130-2*) HarperCollins Children's Bk. Group.
—The Adventures of Laura & Jack. 1997. (Little House Chapter Bks.: No. 1). 80p. (J). (gr. 3-6). 10.40 (*0-606-10736-3*) Turtleback Bks.
—Animal Adventures. 1997. (Little House Ser.: No. 3). 80p. (J). (gr. 3-6). pap. 4.25 (*0-06-442050-7*, Harper Trophy); lib. bdg. 13.89 o.p. (*0-06-027148-5*) HarperCollins Children's Bk. Group.
—Animal Adventures. 1997. (Little House Chapter Bks.: No. 3). (J). (gr. 3-6). 10.40 (*0-606-11045-3*) Turtleback Bks.
—Hard Times on the Prairie. adapted ed. 1998. (Little House Ser.: No. 8). 80p. (J). (gr. 3-6). pap. 4.25 (*0-06-442077-9*, Harper Trophy); lib. bdg. 15.89 (*0-06-027792-0*) HarperCollins Children's Bk. Group.
—Laura & Mr. Edwards. 1999. (Little House Ser.: No. 13). 80p. (J). (gr. 3-6). pap. 4.25 (*0-06-442084-1*, Harper Trophy); lib. bdg. 14.89 (*0-06-027949-4*) HarperCollins Children's Bk. Group.

—Laura & Nellie. 2000. (Little House Ser.: No. 5). 80p. (J). (gr. 3-6). pap. 4.25 (*0-06-442060-4*, Harper Trophy) HarperCollins Children's Bk. Group.

—Laura & Nellie. 1998. (Little House Chapter Bks.: No. 5). 80p. (J). (gr. 3-6). lib. bdg. 14.89 o.p. (*0-06-027496-4*) HarperCollins Pubs.

—Laura & Nellie. 1998. (Little House Chapter Bks.: No. 5). (J). (gr. 3-6). 10.40 (*0-606-12979-0*) Turtleback Bks.

—Laura's Ma. 1999. (Little House Ser.: No. 11). 80p. (J). (gr. 3-6). pap. 4.25 (*0-06-442083-3*, Harper Trophy); lib. bdg. 14.89 (*0-06-027897-8*) HarperCollins Children's Bk. Group.

—Laura's Pa. 1999. (Little House Ser.: No. 12). 80p. (J). (gr. 3-6). lib. bdg. 14.89 (*0-06-027896-X*) HarperCollins Children's Bk. Group.

—Little House Farm Days. adapted ed. 1998. (Little House Ser.: No. 7). 80p. (J). (gr. 3-6). pap. 4.25 (*0-06-442078-7*); lib. bdg. 13.89 o.p. (*0-06-027793-9*) HarperCollins Children's Bk. Group. (Harper Trophy).

—Little House Friends. 1998. (Little House Ser.: No. 9). 80p. (J). (gr. 3-6). pap. 4.25 (*0-06-442080-9*, Harper Trophy) HarperCollins Children's Bk. Group.

—Little House Friends. 1998. (Little House Chapter Bks.: No. 9). 80p. (J). (gr. 3-6). lib. bdg. 14.89 (*0-06-027894-3*) HarperCollins Pubs.

—Little House Parties. 1999. (Little House Ser.: No. 14). 80p. (J). (gr. 3-6). pap. 4.25 (*0-06-442085-X*, Harper Trophy); lib. bdg. 14.89 (*0-06-027951-6*) HarperCollins Children's Bk. Group.

—Pioneer Sisters. 1997. (Little House Ser.: No. 2). 80p. (J). (gr. 3-6). pap. 4.25 (*0-06-442046-9*, Harper Trophy); (gr. 2-5). lib. bdg. 14.89 o.p. (*0-06-027132-9*) HarperCollins Children's Bk. Group.

—Pioneer Sisters. 1997. (Little House Chapter Bks.: No. 2). (J). (gr. 3-6). 10.40 (*0-606-10905-6*) Turtleback Bks.

—School Days. (Little House Ser.: No. 4). 80p. (J). 1997. (gr. 2-4). pap. 4.25 (*0-06-442049-3*, Harper Trophy); 1997. (gr. 3-6). lib. bdg. 13.89 o.p. (*0-06-027146-9*); 1998. (gr. 3-6). pap. 4.95 o.p. (*0-694-01175-4*) HarperCollins Children's Bk. Group.

—School Days. 1997. (Little House Chapter Bks.: No. 4). (J). (gr. 3-6). 10.40 (*0-606-11817-9*) Turtleback Bks.

Graham, Christine. When Pioneer Wagons Rumbled West. 1998. (Illus.). 32p. (J). (ps-3). 14.95 (*1-57345-272-6*, Shadow Mountain) Deseret Bk. Co.

Gray, Dianne E. Holding up the Earth. l.t. ed. 2002. (Young Adult Ser.). 198p. (J). 22.95 (*0-7862-3889-5*) Gale Group.

—Holding up the Earth. 2000. 224p. (J). (gr. 5-9). tchr. ed. 15.00 (*0-618-00703-2*) Houghton Mifflin Co. Trade & Reference Div.

Greenwood, Barbara. A Pioneer Story: The Daily Life of a Canadian Family in 1840. 1994. (Illus.). 520p. (J). pap. (*1-55074-128-4*) Kids Can Pr., Ltd.

Gregory, Kristiana. The Great Railroad Race: The Diary of Libby West, Utah Territory, 1868. 1999. (Dear America Ser.). (Illus.). 203p. (J). (gr. 4-9). mass mkt. 10.95 (*0-590-10991-X*) Scholastic, Inc.

—Jimmy Spoon & the Pony Express. 1994. 144p. (J). (gr. 4-7). pap. 3.99 (*0-590-46577-5*) Scholastic, Inc.

—A Journey of Faith. 2003. (Prairie River Ser.: No. 1). 224p. (J). (gr. 3-8). mass mkt. 4.99 (*0-439-43991-4*, Scholastic Paperbacks) Scholastic, Inc.

—Prairie River 2: A Grateful Harvest. 2003. (Prairie River Ser.: No. 2). 208p. (J). mass mkt. 4.99 (*0-439-43993-0*) Scholastic, Inc.

—Prairie River 3. 2004. (Prairie River Ser.: No. 3). (J). per. (*0-439-44001-7*) Scholastic, Inc.

—Prairie River 4. 2004. (Prairie River Ser.: No. 4). (J). per. (*0-439-44003-3*) Scholastic, Inc.

Gregory, Kristiana & Philbrick, Rodman. The Heading West Collection: Seeds of Hope; The Greatest Railroad Race; Across the Wide & Lonesome Prairie; The Journal of Douglas Deeds, 4 vols. 2002. (Dear America Ser.). (J). pap. 19.96 (*0-439-12941-9*) Scholastic, Inc.

Grossman, Bill. Cowboy Ed. 1993. (Laura Geringer Bks.). (Illus.). 32p. (J). (ps-2). 15.00 (*0-06-021570-4*); lib. bdg. 14.89 (*0-06-021571-2*) HarperCollins Children's Bk. Group.

Guy, Glen E. The Trail to Wrangell: The Adventures of Dusty Sourdough, Vol. 2. 1995. (Illus.). 105p. (Orig.). (J). pap. 7.95 (*0-9644491-3-7*) Old Alaska Today.

Hahn, Mary Downing. The Gentleman Outlaw & Me, Eli: A Story of the Old West. 1996. (Illus.). 224p. (YA). (gr. 7-7). tchr. ed. 15.00 (*0-395-73083-X*, Clarion Bks.) Houghton Mifflin Co. Trade & Reference Div.

Harrell, Beatrice O. Longwalker's Journey: A Novel of the Choctaw Trail of Tears. Kane, Cindy, ed. 1999. (Illus.). 144p. (J). (gr. 3-6). 15.99 o.p. (*0-8037-2380-6*); 15.89 (*0-8037-2383-0*) Penguin Putnam Bks. for Young Readers. (Dial Bks. for Young Readers).

Harrison, Nick. While Yet We Live. 1991. (Ann of the Prairie Ser.: Vol. 4). 224p. (YA). pap. 6.95 o.p. (*0-940652-08-0*) Sunrise Bks.

Harte, Bret. The Outcasts of Poker Flat. 1982. (Short Story Library). (Illus.). 48p. (YA). (gr. 4 up). lib. bdg. 13.95 o.p. (*0-87191-768-8*, Creative Education) Creative Co., The.

—The Outcasts of Poker Flat. 1968. 58p. (YA). (gr. 10 up). pap. 3.60 (*0-87129-547-4*, O27) Dramatic Publishing Co.

—The Outcasts of Poker Flat. 1995. (Jamestown Classics Ser.). (J). pap., stu. ed. 5.99 (*0-89061-052-5*) Jamestown.

Harvey, Amanda. The Iron Needle. 1994. (Illus.). (J). 15.00 o.p. (*0-688-13192-1*) HarperCollins Children's Bk. Group.

Harvey, Brett. My Prairie Year: Based on the Diary of Elenore Plaisted. 1986. (Illus.). 40p. (J). (gr. 1-4). tchr. ed. 15.95 o.p. (*0-8234-0604-0*) Holiday Hse., Inc.

Hay, John Williams. Rover & Coo Coo. 1995. (J). 12.95 o.p. (*0-671-75217-0*, Simon & Schuster Children's Publishing) Simon & Schuster Children's Publishing.

Henry, Marguerite. San Domingo: The Medicine Hat Stallion. 1986. (Illus.). 224p. (J). (gr. 2-9). 8.95 o.s.i (*0-528-82443-0*, Simon & Schuster Children's Publishing) Simon & Schuster Children's Publishing.

Henson, Heather. Christmas Stories: Adapted from the Little House Books by Laura Ingalls Wilder. 1998. (Little House Chapter Bks.: No. 9). (Illus.). 80p. (J). (gr. 3-6). lib. bdg. 14.89 (*0-06-027895-1*) HarperCollins Pubs.

Henty, G. A. In the Heart of the Rockies: A Story of Adventure in Colorado. E-Book 3.95 (*0-594-01719-X*) 1873 Pr.

—In the Heart of the Rockies: A Story of Adventure in Colorado. 2002. 370p. 29.95 (*1-59087-073-5*, GAH073); per. 19.95 (*1-59087-072-7*, GAH072) Althouse Pr.

—In the Heart of the Rockies: A Story of Adventure in Colorado. 1998. (Illus.). 385p. (YA). (gr. 4 up). reprint ed. pap. 16.95 (*1-890623-08-3*) Lost Classics Bk. Co.

—In the Heart of the Rockies: A Story of Adventure in Colorado. collector's ed. 2002. (Illus.). im. lthr. 38.85 (*1-4115-1341-X*); pap. 19.95 (*1-4115-0577-8*); 25.95 (*1-4115-0949-8*); pap. 17.95 (*1-4115-0174-8*) Polyglot Pr., Inc.

Hermes, Patricia. Calling Me Home. 1998. (Avon Camelot Bks.). 144p. (J). (gr. 4-7). 15.00 (*0-380-97451-7*, Eos) Morrow/Avon.

—Calling Me Home. 1999. (Illus.). (J). 10.04 (*0-606-17961-5*) Turtleback Bks.

—A Perfect Place: Joshua's Oregon Trail Diary, Bk. 2. 2002. (My America Ser.: Bk. 2). 128p. (J). (gr. 2-5). pap. 10.95 (*0-439-19999-9*); mass mkt. 4.99 (*0-439-38900-3*) Scholastic, Inc. (Scholastic Pr.).

—Westward to Home: Joshua's Oregon Trail Diary, Bk. 1. 2001. (My America Ser.). (Illus.). 112p. (J). (gr. 4-8). pap. 10.95 (*0-439-11209-5*) Scholastic, Inc.

—Westward to Home: The Oregon Trail 1848. 2002. (Joshua's Oregon Trail Diary Ser.: Bk. 1). 112p. (J). (gr. 2-5). mass mkt. 4.99 (*0-439-38899-6*, Scholastic Pr.) Scholastic, Inc.

Hite, Sid. Stick & Whittle. 2000. (Illus.). 208p. (J). (gr. 5 up). pap. 16.95 (*0-439-09828-9*) Scholastic, Inc.

Holeman, Linda. Promise Song. 1997. 264p. (YA). (gr. 6-9). pap. 6.95 (*0-88776-387-1*) Tundra Bks. of Northern New York.

Holland, Isabelle. The Promised Land. 1996. 176p. (J). (gr. 3-7). pap. 15.95 (*0-590-47176-7*) Scholastic, Inc.

Holm, Jennifer L. Boston Jane: An Adventure. 2001. (Boston Jane Ser.). 288p. (J). (gr. 5 up). 16.95 (*0-06-028738-1*); (Illus.). lib. bdg. 17.89 (*0-06-028739-X*) HarperCollins Children's Bk. Group.

—Boston Jane: An Adventure. 2002. (Boston Jane Ser.). 288p. (J). (gr. 5 up). pap. 6.99 (*0-06-440849-3*) HarperCollins Pubs.

—Boston Jane: Wilderness Days. (Boston Jane Ser.). 256p. (J). 2004. pap. 5.99 (*0-06-440881-7*, Harper Trophy); 2002. (gr. 5 up). 16.99 (*0-06-029043-9*); 2002. (gr. 5 up). lib. bdg. 18.89 (*0-06-029044-7*) HarperCollins Children's Bk. Group.

—Our Only May Amelia. (Harper Trophy Bks.). (Illus.). 272p. (gr. 4 up). 2001. (J). pap. 5.99 (*0-06-440856-6*, Harper Trophy); 1999. (J). 16.99 (*0-06-027822-6*); 1999. (YA). lib. bdg. 15.89 (*0-06-028354-8*) HarperCollins Children's Bk. Group.

—Our Only May Amelia. unabr. ed. 2001. 253p. (J). (gr. 4-6). pap. 35.00 incl. audio (*0-8072-8366-5*, YA191SP, Listening Library) Random Hse. Audio Publishing Group.

—Our Only May Amelia. l.t. ed. 2000. (Illus.). 261p. (J). (ps up). 21.95 (*0-7862-2742-7*) Thorndike Pr.

Hopkinson, Deborah. Packet of Seeds. 2004. 32p. (J). 15.99 (*0-06-009089-8*); lib. bdg. 16.89 (*0-06-009090-1*) HarperCollins Children's Bk. Group. (Greenwillow Bks.).

—Pioneer Summer. 2002. (Ready-for-Chapters Ser.). (Illus.). 80p. (J). (gr. 1-4). pap. 3.99 (*0-689-84349-6*, Aladdin) Simon & Schuster Children's Publishing.

—Prairie Skies: Cabin in the Snow. 2002. (Ready-for-Chapters Ser.). 80p. (J). pap. 3.99 (*0-689-84351-8*, Aladdin); lib. bdg. 11.89 (*0-689-84352-6*, Aladdin Library) Simon & Schuster Children's Publishing.

Howard, Ellen. The Chickenhouse House. 1991. (Illus.). 64p. (J). (gr. 2-5). lib. bdg. 13.00 (*0-689-31695-X*, Atheneum) Simon & Schuster Children's Publishing.

—The Log Cabin Christmas. 2000. (Illus.). 32p. (J). (ps-3). tchr. ed. 16.95 (*0-8234-1381-0*) Holiday Hse., Inc.

—The Log Cabin Church. 2002. (Illus.). (J). (gr. k-3). tchr. ed. 16.95 (*0-8234-1740-9*) Holiday Hse., Inc.

Hubbard, Louise G. Grandfather's Gold Watch. 1997. (Illus.). 32p. (J). (ps-3). 11.95 (*1-57345-242-4*, Shadow Mountain) Deseret Bk. Co.

Hudson, Jan. Sweetgrass. 1999. 168p. (YA). (gr. 5-9). pap. 5.99 (*0-698-11763-8*) Penguin Putnam Bks. for Young Readers.

—Sweetgrass. 2002. (YA). (gr. 5-10). 20.50 (*0-8446-7209-2*) Smith, Peter Pub., Inc.

—Sweetgrass. 1999. 12.04 (*0-606-16851-6*) Turtleback Bks.

Hulme, Joy N. Climbing the Rainbow. 2004. 224p. (J). 15.99 (*0-380-81572-9*); lib. bdg. 16.89 (*0-06-054304-3*) HarperCollins Pubs.

—Through the Open Door. 2000. 176p. (J). (gr. 4-6). 14.95 (*0-380-97870-9*) HarperCollins Children's Bk. Group.

Hurmence, Belinda. Dixie in the Big Pasture. 1994. (J). (gr. 4 up). 13.95 o.s.i (*0-395-52002-9*) Clarion IND. *Dist:* Houghton Mifflin Co.

Hurst, Carol Otis & Otis, Rebecca. A Killing in Plymouth Colony. 2003. 160p. (J). (gr. 5-9). tchr. ed. 15.00 (*0-618-27597-5*) Houghton Mifflin Co.

Ingoglia, Gina. Sacajawea & the Journey to the Pacific. 1992. (Disney's American Frontier Ser.: Bk. 7). (Illus.). 80p. (J). (gr. 1-4). pap. 3.50 (*1-56282-262-4*); lib. bdg. 12.89 o.s.i (*1-56282-263-2*) Disney Pr.

Ingold, Jeanette. The Big Burn. (YA). 2003. 320p. pap. 6.95 (*0-15-204924-X*, Harcourt Paperbacks); 2002. 304p. 17.00 (*0-15-216470-7*) Harcourt Children's Bks.

—Mountain Solo. 2003. 320p. (J). 17.00 (*0-15-202670-3*) Harcourt Children's Bks.

Irwin, Hadley. Jim Dandy. 1994. 144p. (J). (gr. 5-9). 15.00 (*0-689-50594-9*, McElderry, Margaret K.) Simon & Schuster Children's Publishing.

Isaacs, Anne. Swamp Angel. 2002. (Illus.). (J). 14.04 (*0-7587-0152-7*) Book Wholesalers, Inc.

—Swamp Angel. (Illus.). 48p. (J). (ps-3). 2000. pap. 6.99 (*0-14-055908-6*); 1994. 16.99 (*0-525-45271-0*, Dutton Children's Bks.) Penguin Putnam Bks. for Young Readers.

—Swamp Angel. 2000. 13.14 (*0-606-18453-8*) Turtleback Bks.

—Swamp Angel. 2001. (J). (gr. k-4). 6.95 (*1-55592-985-0*) Weston Woods Studios, Inc.

James, Will. Cowboy in the Making. 2001. (Illus.). 92p. (J). 15.00 (*0-87842-439-3*) Mountain Pr. Publishing Co., Inc.

Johnson, Annabel & Johnson, Edgar. Golden Touch. 1963. (J). (gr. 7 up). lib. bdg. 12.89 o.p. (*0-06-022856-3*) HarperCollins Pubs.

Johnson, Sherrie. A House with Wings. 1995. (J). pap. 7.95 (*1-56236-309-3*) Aspen Bks.

Johnston, Tony. The Sunsets of the West. 2002. (Illus.). 32p. (J). (gr. k up). 16.99 (*0-399-22659-1*) Putnam Publishing Group, The.

Jones, Veda Boyd. Adventure in the Wilderness: The Journey to Cincinnati's Frontier. 13th ed. 1998. (American Adventure Ser.: No. 13). (Illus.). (J). (gr. 3-7). pap. 3.97 (*1-57748-230-1*) Barbour Publishing, Inc.

—Adventure in the Wilderness: The Journey to Cincinnati's Frontier, 1999. (American Adventure Ser.: No. 13). (Illus.). 143p. (J). (gr. 3-7). lib. bdg. 19.75 (*0-7910-5587-6*) Chelsea Hse. Pubs.

Kabel, Larassa, illus. Rocky Mountain Summer. 1998. (Cover-to-Cover Bks.). (J). (*0-7807-6790-X*) Perfection Learning Corp.

Karim, Roberta. Kindle Me a Riddle: A Pioneer Story. 1999. (Illus.). 32p. (J). (gr. k-3). 16.00 (*0-688-16203-7*); lib. bdg. 16.89 (*0-688-16204-5*) HarperCollins Children's Bk. Group. (Greenwillow Bks.).

Karr, Kathleen. Go West, Young Women! 1997. (Petticoat Party Ser.). 9.60 o.p. (*0-606-11741-5*) Turtleback Bks.

—Oh, Those Harper Girls!, RS. 1992. 176p. (YA). (gr. 7 up). 16.00 o.p. (*0-374-35609-2*, Farrar, Straus & Giroux (BYR)) Farrar, Straus & Giroux.

Keith, Harold. The Obstinate Land. 1977. (J). (gr. 5 up). 11.49 o.p. (*0-690-01319-1*) HarperCollins Children's Bk. Group.

Kelley, Nancy J. The Whispering Rod: A Tale of Old Massachusetts. 2002. 160p. (J). lib. bdg. 17.95 (*1-57249-248-1*, WM Kids) White Mane Publishing Co., Inc.

Kent, Peter. Quest for the West in Search of Gold. 1997. 6. (Illus.). 32p. (J). (gr. 3-6). 22.40 (*0-7613-0302-2*) Millbrook Pr., Inc.

Kerr, Rita. The Ghost of Panna Maria. Eakin, Ed, ed. 1990. (Illus.). 96p. (J). (gr. 2-4). pap. 3.95 o.p. (*0-89015-803-7*); (gr. 3-4). 13.95 (*0-89015-791-X*) Eakin Pr.

—The Texas Cowboy. 1996. (Illus.). 96p. (J). (gr. 2-4). 13.95 (*1-57168-105-1*) Eakin Pr.

—Texas Marvel. Roberts, Melissa, ed. 1987. 64p. (J). (gr. 5-6). 13.95 (*0-89015-597-6*) Eakin Pr.

Ketteman, Helen. Shoeshine Whittaker. 1999. (Illus.). 32p. (J). (gr. k-3). 15.95 (*0-8027-8714-2*); lib. bdg. 16.85 (*0-8027-8715-0*) Walker & Co.

Kimmel, Cody. To the Frontier. 2004. (Adventures of Young Buffalo Bill Ser.). 192p. (J). pap. 5.99 (*0-06-440894-9*, Harper Trophy) HarperCollins Children's Bk. Group.

Kimmel, Cody E. In the Eye of the Storm. 2003. (Adventures of Young Buffalo Bill Ser.). (Illus.). 144p. (J). (gr. 3-7). 15.99 (*0-06-029115-X*); lib. bdg. 16.89 (*0-06-029116-8*) HarperCollins Children's Bk. Group.

Kimmel, Elizabeth Cody. One Sky above Us. 2002. (Adventures of Young Buffalo Bill Ser.). (Illus.). 192p. (J). (gr. 3-6). 15.99 (*0-06-029119-2*); lib. bdg. 17.89 (*0-06-029120-6*) HarperCollins Children's Bk. Group.

—To the Frontier. 2002. (Adventures of Young Buffalo Bill Ser.). (Illus.). 192p. (J). (gr. k-3). lib. bdg. 15.89 (*0-06-029118-4*); (gr. 4-7). 15.95 (*0-06-029117-6*) HarperCollins Children's Bk. Group.

Kingsley, Charles. Westward Ho! deluxe ltd. ed. 1992. (Scribners Illustrated Classics Ser.). (Illus.). 432p. (YA). (gr. 7 up). 75.00 o.s.i (*0-684-19443-0*); 26.95 (*0-684-19444-9*) Simon & Schuster Children's Publishing. (Atheneum).

Kinsey-Warnock, Natalie. Wilderness Cat. 1992. (Illus.). 32p. (J). (ps-3). 14.99 o.s.i (*0-525-65068-7*, Dutton Children's Bks.) Penguin Putnam Bks. for Young Readers.

Kirkpatrick, Katherine. The Voyage of the Continental. 2002. (Illus.). 297p. (J). (gr. 7 up). tchr. ed. 16.95 (*0-8234-1580-5*) Holiday Hse., Inc.

Kirsten Saves the Day: A Summer Story. 2001. (Frequently Requested Ser.). lib. bdg. (*1-59054-094-8*) Fitzgerald Bks.

Kjelgaard, Jim. Buckskin Brigade. 1947. (Illus.). 310p. (J). (gr. 7-11). 5.95 o.p. (*0-8234-0014-X*) Holiday Hse., Inc.

Koller, Jackie French. The Primrose Way. 1992. (Great Episodes Ser.). 352p. (YA). (gr. 7-12). 15.95 o.s.i (*0-15-256745-3*, Gulliver Bks.) Harcourt Children's Bks.

Kramer, Sydelle A. Wagon Train. 1997. (All Aboard Reading Ser.). 10.14 (*0-606-12841-7*) Turtleback Bks.

Krantz, Hazel. Look to the Hills. 1995. 224p. (J). 14.95 (*0-8276-0552-8*); (gr. 4-7). pap. 9.95 (*0-8276-0571-4*) Jewish Pubn. Society.

Krensky, Stephen. Striking It Rich: The Story of the California Gold Rush. 1996. (Ready-to-Read Ser.). (Illus.). 48p. (J). (ps-3). 15.00 (*0-689-80804-6*, Simon & Schuster Children's Publishing) Simon & Schuster Children's Publishing.

Kudlinski, Kathleen V. Facing West: A Story of the Oregon Trail. (Once upon America Ser.). (Illus.). 64p. (J). (gr. 2-6). 1996. pap. 5.99 (*0-14-036914-7*); 1994. 12.99 o.s.i (*0-670-85451-4*, Viking Children's Bks.) Penguin Putnam Bks. for Young Readers.

Kurtz, Jane. I'm Sorry, Almira Ann, ERS. 1999. (Illus.). 120p. (J). (gr. 4-7). 15.95 (*0-8050-6094-4*, Holt, Henry & Co. Bks. For Young Readers) Holt, Henry & Co.

LaFaye, A. Worth. 2004. (J). (*0-689-85730-6*, Simon & Schuster Children's Publishing) Simon & Schuster Children's Publishing.

Lane, Rose Wilder. Young Pioneers. 1976. (Little House Ser.). 17.95 (*0-8488-0557-7*) Amereon, Ltd.

—Young Pioneers. 1976. (Little House Ser.). 128p. (gr. 6-12). pap. 1.95 o.p. (*0-553-20173-5*, 20173-5) Bantam Bks.

—Young Pioneers. 1998. (Little House Ser.). (Illus.). 192p. (J). (gr. 3 up). pap. 5.99 (*0-06-440698-9*, Harper Trophy) HarperCollins Children's Bk. Group.

—Young Pioneers. 1976. (Little House Ser.). 10.95 o.p. (*0-07-036205-X*) McGraw-Hill Cos., The.

—Young Pioneers. 1998. (Little House Ser.). (YA). (gr. 3 up). 12.00 (*0-606-17778-7*) Turtleback Bks.

LaPietra, Mary. A Tomahawk for Christmas. 1976. (gr. 5 up). pap. 1.50 o.p. (*0-89191-052-2*) Cook, David C. Publishing Co.

Historical Events

—Carlota. 1977. (J). 10.55 (*0-606-04137-0*) Turtleback Bks.

Oke, Janette. A Bride for Donnigan. 1993. (Women of the West Ser.). 224p. pap. 11.99 (*1-55661-327-X*); 240p. pap. 12.99 o.p. (*1-55661-328-8*) Bethany Hse. Pubs.

Oliphant, Pat, illus. Peter Becomes a Trail Man: The Story of a Boy's Journey on the Santa Fe Trail. 2002. 191p. (J). 12.95 (*0-8263-2895-4*) Univ. of New Mexico Pr.

Orton, Helen F. Secret of the Rosewood Box. 1937. (Illus.). (J). (gr. 4-6). 8.95 o.p. (*0-397-31596-1*) HarperCollins Children's Bk. Group.

Osborne, Mary Pope. Ghost Town at Sundown. unabr. ed. 2001. (Magic Tree House Ser. : No. 10). 73p. (J). (gr. k-4). pap. 17.00 incl. audio (*0-8072-0535-4*, Listening Library) Random Hse. Audio Publishing Group.

—Ghost Town at Sundown. 1997. (Magic Tree House Ser.: No. 10). (Illus.). 96p. (gr. k-3). pap. 3.99 (*0-679-88339-8*);No. 10. lib. bdg. 11.99 (*0-679-98339-2*) Random Hse. Children's Bks. (Random Hse. Bks. for Young Readers).

—Ghost Town at Sundown. 1997. (Magic Tree House Ser.: No. 10). (Illus.). (J). (gr. k-3). 10.04 (*0-606-12709-7*) Turtleback Bks.

—Twister on Tuesday. 2001. (Magic Tree House Ser.: No. 23). (Illus.). 96p. (J). (gr. k-3). pap. 3.99 (*0-679-89069-6*); lib. bdg. 11.99 (*0-679-99069-0*) Random Hse. Children's Bks. (Random Hse. Bks. for Young Readers).

—Twister on Tuesday. 2001. (Magic Tree House Ser.). (Illus.). (J). 10.04 (*0-606-21498-4*) Turtleback Bks.

Pamplin, Laurel J. Masquerade on the Western Trail. Roberts, M., ed. 1991. (Illus.). 112p. (J). (gr. 6-7). 13.95 (*0-89015-755-3*) Eakin Pr.

Parish, Peggy. Granny & the Desperadoes. 1996. (Ready-to-Read Ser.: Level 2). (Illus.). 48p. (J). (ps-3). mass mkt. 3.99 (*0-689-80877-1*, Aladdin); mass mkt. 14.00 (*0-689-80878-X*, Simon & Schuster Children's Publishing) Simon & Schuster Children's Publishing.

—Granny & the Desperadoes. 1996. (Ready-to-Read Ser.). (J). 10.14 (*0-606-09351-6*) Turtleback Bks.

Patneaude, David. The Last Man's Reward. 1998. (J). 11.00 (*0-606-13564-2*) Turtleback Bks.

Paulsen, Gary. Call Me Francis Tucket. (Tucket Adventures Ser.: Vol. 2). 112p. (gr. 4-7). 1996. (J). pap. text 4.50 (*0-440-41270-6*); 1995. text 15.95 (*0-385-32116-3*, Delacorte Pr.) Dell Publishing.

—Call Me Francis Tucket. 1996. 10.55 (*0-606-10766-5*) Turtleback Bks.

—Mr. Tucket. 1994. 176p. text 15.95 (*0-385-31169-9*, Delacorte Pr.) Dell Publishing.

—Mr. Tucket. 2000. (Illus.). 192p. (gr. 5-7). mass mkt. 2.99 o.s.i (*0-375-80680-6*, Random Hse. Bks. for Young Readers); 1996. (J). pap. 5.99 (*0-440-91097-8*, Dell Books for Young Readers); 1995. (Tucket Adventures Ser.: Vol. 1). 192p. (gr. 5 up). pap. text 4.99 (*0-440-41133-5*, Yearling); 1995. (J). pap. 5.99 (*0-440-91053-6*, Dell Books for Young Readers) Random Hse. Children's Bks.

—Mr. Tucket. 1995. 10.55 (*0-606-07895-9*) Turtleback Bks.

—Tucket's Gold. 1999. (Tucket Adventures Ser.: Vol. 4). 112p. (gr. 4-7). text 15.95 (*0-385-32501-0*) Bantam Bks.

—Tucket's Gold. 2001. (Tucket Adventures Ser.). 112p. (gr. 4-7). pap. text 4.50 (*0-440-41376-1*, Dell Books for Young Readers) Random Hse. Children's Bks.

—Tucket's Gold. 2001. (J). 10.55 (*0-606-20958-1*) Turtleback Bks.

Pearce, Jonathan. The Far Side of the Moon: A California Story. 2nd ed. 2003. viii, 130p. (J). per. 15.95 (*1-59411-011-5*) Writers' Collective, The.

Pellowski, Anne. First Farm in the Valley: Anna's Story. 1982. (Illus.). 192p. (J). (gr. 3-6). 9.95 o.s.i (*0-399-20887-9*, Philomel) Penguin Putnam Bks. for Young Readers.

Penson, Mary. You're an Orphan, Mollie Brown. 1993. (Illus.). 122p. (J). pap. 9.95 o.p. (*0-87565-111-9*) Texas Christian Univ. Pr.

Pepper Bird Staff. Wild Frontier: Adventures of Jean Baptiste Du Sable. 1993. (Multicultural Historical Fiction Ser.). (Illus.). 48p. (Orig.). (J). (gr. 4-7). pap. 4.95 (*1-56817-003-3*) Pepper Bird Publishing.

Perkins, Stanley C. Arvilla & the Tattler Tree: The Fur Trader. 1994. (Illus.). 702p. (J). 30.00 (*0-9614640-9-7*); pap. 25.00 (*0-9620249-4-5*) Broadblade Pr.

Pfitsch, Patricia C. Riding the Flume. 2002. (Illus.). 240p. (J). (gr. 5-8). 16.95 (*0-689-83823-9*, Simon & Schuster Children's Publishing) Simon & Schuster Children's Publishing.

Plowhead, Ruth Gipson. Lucretia Ann on the Oregon Trail. 8th ed. 1997. (Classic Ser.). (Illus.). 250p. (J). (gr. 4-8). reprint ed. pap. 10.95 (*0-87004-360-9*, 036090) Caxton Pr.

Pryor, Bonnie. Luke: 1849 - On the Golden Trail. 1999. (American Adventures Ser.). (Illus.). 272p. (J). (gr. 3-7). 15.00 (*0-688-15670-3*) HarperCollins Children's Bk. Group.

—Luke: 1849—On the Golden Trail. 2000. (American Adventures Ser.). (Illus.). 176p. (J). (gr. 3-7). pap. 4.50 (*0-380-73102-9*, Harper Trophy) HarperCollins Children's Bk. Group.

—Luke: 1849-On the Golden Trail. 2000. (Illus.). (J). 10.55 (*0-606-17977-1*) Turtleback Bks.

—Thomas: Patriots on the Run. 1998. (American Adventures Ser.: No. 1). (Illus.). 160p. (J). (gr. 3-7). 15.95 (*0-688-15669-X*) HarperCollins Children's Bk. Group.

Rees, Celia. Witch Child. (gr. 7 up). 2002. 304p. (YA). bds. 8.99 (*0-7636-1829-2*); 2001. 272p. (J). 15.99 (*0-7636-1421-1*) Candlewick Pr.

—Witch Child. l.t. ed. 2002. (Young Adult Ser.). 284p. (J). 22.95 (*0-7862-3896-8*) Gale Group.

Rees, Shirley. Hannah Stands Tall. 2002. 130p. (J). pap. 10.95 (*1-55517-652-6*, 76526, Bonneville Bks.) Cedar Fort, Inc./CFI Distribution.

Reiss, Kathryn. Riddle of the Prairie Bride. 2001. (American Girl Collection: Bk. 12). (Illus.). 176p. (J). (gr. 3-6). pap. 5.95 (*1-58485-308-5*); 9.95 o.p. (*1-58485-309-3*) Pleasant Co. Pubns. (American Girl).

—Riddle of the Prairie Bride. 2001. (American Girl Collection). (Illus.). (J). 12.00 (*0-606-21400-3*) Turtleback Bks.

Reuther, Ruth E. Meet at the Falls: The Story of the Pioneers. McCall, Jody, ed. 1989. (Series 2). (Illus.). (J). pap. text (*0-9622632-1-4*) Wee-Chee-Taw Publishing.

Reynolds, Marilynn. The Prairie Fire. (Illus.). 32p. (J). (ps-3). 2001. pap. 7.95 (*1-55143-175-0*); 1999. pap. 14.95 o.s.i (*1-55143-137-8*) Orca Bk. Pubs.

Richardson, Arleta. Prairie Homestead. 1994. (Orphans' Journey Ser.: Vol. 3). 144p. (J). (gr. 4-7). pap. 4.99 (*0-7814-0091-0*) Cook Communications Ministries.

Richardson, Boyd C. Danger Trail: Knife Thrower's Journey West. 1995. (J). pap. 9.95 o.p. (*1-55503-777-1*, 01111795) Covenant Communications, Inc.

Richter, Conrad. Elements of Literature: The Light in the Forest. 1989. pap., stu. ed. 15.33 (*0-03-023439-5*) Holt, Rinehart & Winston.

—The Light in the Forest. (YA). (gr. 7 up). 21.95 (*0-89190-333-X*) Amereon, Ltd.

—The Light in the Forest. 1994. 128p. (gr. 7-12). mass mkt. 6.50 (*0-449-70437-8*, Fawcett) Ballantine Bks.

—The Light in the Forest. 1990. 128p. (J). (gr. 5-12). mass mkt. 3.99 o.s.i (*0-553-26878-3*); 1986. mass mkt. o.s.i (*0-553-16642-5*) Bantam Bks.

—The Light in the Forest. 1991. (YA). (gr. 7 up). lib. bdg. 21.95 (*1-56849-064-X*) Buccaneer Bks., Inc.

—The Light in the Forest. 1953. (Illus.). (J). 23.00 o.s.i (*0-394-43314-9*); (YA). (gr. 7 up). lib. bdg. 5.99 o.p. (*0-394-91404-X*) Knopf, Alfred A. Inc.

—The Light in the Forest. 1986. (J). mass mkt. o.s.i (*0-553-16679-4*, Dell Books for Young Readers) Random Hse. Children's Bks.

—The Light in the Forest. 9999. pap. 1.95 o.p. (*0-590-02336-5*) Scholastic, Inc.

—The Light in the Forest. 1994. (YA). (gr. 7 up). 12.04 (*0-606-06903-8*) Turtleback Bks.

Riefe, Barbara. Amelia Dale Archer Story. 1998. 304p. (YA). (gr. 8 up). 22.95 o.p. (*0-312-86077-3*, Forge Bks.) Doherty, Tom Assocs., LLC.

Rinaldi, Ann. Ride Into Morning: The Story of Tempe Wick. 1995. (Great Episodes Ser.). (J). 10.10 o.p. (*0-606-08074-0*) Turtleback Bks.

—The Second Bend in the River. (J). 1999. 288p. (gr. 5-9). mass mkt. 4.99 (*0-590-74259-0*); 1997. pap. 15.95 (*0-590-74258-2*) Scholastic, Inc.

—The Second Bend in the River. 1999. 11.04 (*0-606-16581-9*) Turtleback Bks.

—A Stitch in Time. (Quilt Trilogy Ser.: Vol. 1). 320p. (J). (gr. 7 up). 1995. mass mkt. 5.99 (*0-590-46056-0*); 1994. pap. 13.95 (*0-590-46055-2*) Scholastic, Inc.

—A Stitch in Time. 1994. (Quilt Trilogy Ser.). (J). 11.04 (*0-606-08206-9*) Turtleback Bks.

Ritthaler, Shelly. Heart of the Hills. 1996. (American Dreams Ser.). 9.09 o.p. (*0-606-10210-8*) Turtleback Bks.

Rizzo, Kay D. Wagon Train West. 2003. 96p. (J). (*0-8163-1986-3*) Pacific Pr. Publishing Assn.

Roberts, Sally A. The Legend of Crystal Lake. (Illus.). vi, 135p. (J). 2001. pap. (*1-57168-557-X*, Eakin Pr.); 2000. 16.95 (*1-57168-369-0*) Eakin Pr.

Rogers, Lisa Waller. Remember the Alamo! The Runaway Scrape Diary of Belle Wood. 2003. (Lone Star Journals: Bk. 3). 176p. (J). 15.95 (*0-89672-497-2*) Texas Tech Univ. Pr.

Ruckman, Ivy. In Care of Cassie Tucker. 1998. 176p. (gr. 5-8). text 14.95 o.s.i (*0-385-32514-2*, Dell Books for Young Readers) Random Hse. Children's Bks.

Rudolph, Marian. Lovina's Song: A Pioneer Girl's Journey with the Donner Party. 1998. (Illus.). 192p. (J). pap. 11.95 (*1-883965-43-8*) Rattle OK Pubns.

Rylant, Cynthia. Old Town in the Green Groves: Laura Ingalls Wilder's Lost Little House Years. 2002. (Little House Ser.). (Illus.). 176p. (J). (gr. 3-7). lib. bdg. 16.89 (*0-06-029562-7*); (ps-1). 15.99 (*0-06-029561-9*) HarperCollins Children's Bk. Group.

Saban, Vera. The Westering: Joanna. 1994. (This Is America Ser.). (J). 15.95 (*0-914565-43-5*) Capstan Pubns.

Sanders, Scott R. Aurora Means Dawn. 1998. 12.14 (*0-606-13155-8*) Turtleback Bks.

Sanders, Scott Russell. Aurora Means Dawn. (Illus.). 32p. (J). (gr. k-3). 1998. pap. 5.99 (*0-689-81907-2*, Aladdin); 1989. 16.00 (*0-02-778270-0*, Atheneum) Simon & Schuster Children's Publishing.

—The Floating House. 1995. (Illus.). 40p. (J). (ps-3). 17.00 (*0-02-778137-2*, Atheneum) Simon & Schuster Children's Publishing.

—Here Comes the Mystery Man. 1993. (Illus.). 32p. (J). (gr. k-5). text 15.95 (*0-02-778145-3*, Atheneum) Simon & Schuster Children's Publishing.

—A Place Called Freedom. 2001. (J). 12.14 (*0-606-20854-2*) Turtleback Bks.

—Warm As Wool. 1992. (Illus.). 32p. (J). (gr. k-5). mass mkt. 16.00 (*0-02-778139-9*, Atheneum) Simon & Schuster Children's Publishing.

—Warm As Wool. 1998. 12.14 (*0-606-15877-4*) Turtleback Bks.

Sandin, Joan. Pioneer Bear. 1995. (Step into Reading Step 2 Bks.). (J). (gr. 1-3). 10.14 (*0-606-08015-5*) Turtleback Bks.

Sargent, Dave & Sargent, Pat. Ben (Bay Sabino) Help Others #2. 2001. (Saddle Up Ser.). 36p. (J). pap. 6.95 (*1-56763-644-6*); lib. bdg. 22.60 (*1-56763-643-8*) Ozark Publishing.

—Pete: Be a Hero. 2003. (Saddle Up Ser.: Vol. 46). 42p. (J). lib. bdg. 22.60 (*1-56763-707-8*) Ozark Publishing.

—Pete (Pink-Skinned Palomino) Be a Hero. 2003. (Saddle Up Ser.: Vol. 46). 42p. (J). mass mkt. 6.95 (*1-56763-708-6*) Ozark Publishing.

—Stinky (sorrel) Don't Be Mischievous #56: Don't Be Mischievous #56. 2001. (Saddle Up Ser.). 36p. (J). pap. (*1-56763-666-7*); lib. bdg. 22.60 (*1-56763-665-9*) Ozark Publishing.

Sauerwein, Leigh. The Way Home, RS. 1994. 96p. (J). (gr. 7 up). 15.00 o.p. (*0-374-38247-6*, Farrar, Straus & Giroux (BYR)) Farrar, Straus & Giroux.

Schulman, Audrey. A House Named Brazil. 2001. 320p. pap. 13.95 (*0-380-80880-3*, Perennial) HarperTrade.

—A House Named Brazil. 2000. (Illus.). 301p. 23.00 (*0-380-97799-0*, Morrow, William & Co.) Morrow/Avon.

Schulte, Elaine L. Daniel Colton Kidnapped. 2002. (Colton Cousins Adventure Ser.: Bk. 4). (Illus.). 138p. (J). 6.49 (*1-57924-566-8*) Jones, Bob Univ. Pr.

—Daniel Colton Kidnapped. 1993. (Colton Cousins Adventure Ser.: Vol. 4). (Illus.). 144p. (J). (gr. 3-7). pap. 5.99 o.p. (*0-310-57261-4*) Zondervan.

—Daniel Colton under Fire. 2001. (Illus.). 137p. (J). pap. 6.49 (*1-57924-564-1*) Jones, Bob Univ. Pr.

—Daniel Colton under Fire. 1992. (Colton Cousins Adventure Ser.: Vol. 2). 144p. pap. 5.99 o.p. (*0-310-54821-7*) Zondervan.

—Suzannah & the Secret Coins. 2001. (Colton Cousins Adventure Ser.). (Illus.). 130p. (J). (gr. 4-7). 6.49 (*1-57924-563-3*) Jones, Bob Univ. Pr.

—Suzannah Strikes Gold. 2001. (Illus.). 144p. (J). pap. 6.49 (*1-57924-565-X*) Jones, Bob Univ. Pr.

—Suzannah Strikes Gold. 1992. (Colton Cousins Adventure Ser.: Vol. 3). 144p. (J). pap. 5.99 o.p. (*0-310-54611-7*) Zondervan.

Seely, Debra. Grasslands. 2002. (Illus.). 170p. (J). (gr. 5-9). tchr. ed. 16.95 (*0-8234-1731-X*) Holiday Hse., Inc.

Seymour, Peter. Frontier Town, ERS. 1982. (Illus.). (J). (gr. 1-4). o.p. (*0-03-062077-5*, Holt, Henry & Co. Bks. For Young Readers) Holt, Henry & Co.

Shannon, George. The Gang & Mrs. Higgins. 1981. (Greenwillow Read-Alone Bks.). (Illus.). 48p. (J). (gr. 1-3). 8.50 o.p. (*0-688-80303-2*); lib. bdg. 8.88 o.p. (*0-688-84303-4*) HarperCollins Children's Bk. Group. (Greenwillow Bks.).

Shaw, Janet Beeler. Changes for Kirsten: A Winter Story. 1988. (American Girls Collection: Bk. 6). (Illus.). 65p. (YA). (gr. 2 up). 12.95 o.p. (*0-937295-44-2*) Pleasant Co. Pubns.

—Changes for Kirsten: A Winter Story. Thieme, Jeanne, ed. 1988. (American Girls Collection: Bk. 6). (Illus.). 80p. (J). (gr. 2 up). pap. 5.95 (*0-937295-45-0*); lib. bdg. 12.95 (*0-937295-94-9*) Pleasant Co. Pubns. (American Girl).

—Changes for Kirsten: A Winter Story. 1988. (American Girls Collection: Bk. 6). (Illus.). (YA). (gr. 2 up). 12.10 (*0-606-03749-7*) Turtleback Bks.

—Happy Birthday, Kirsten! A Springtime Story. Thieme, Jeanne, ed. 1987. (American Girls Collection: Bk. 4). (Illus.). 72p. (gr. 2 up). (J). 12.95 (*0-937295-88-4*, American Girl); (J). pap. 5.95 (*0-937295-33-7*, American Girl); (YA). 12.95 o.p. (*0-937295-32-9*) Pleasant Co. Pubns.

—Happy Birthday, Kirsten! A Springtime Story. 1987. (American Girls Collection: Bk. 4). (Illus.). (YA). (gr. 2 up). 12.10 (*0-606-03798-5*) Turtleback Bks.

—Kirsten & the Chippewa. 2002. (American Girls Short Stories Ser.). (Illus.). 56p. (J). 4.95 (*1-58485-479-0*, American Girl) Pleasant Co. Pubns.

—Kirsten Keepsake Boxed Set: Meet Kirsten; Kirsten Learns a Lesson; Kirsten's Surprise; Happy Birthday, Kirsten!; Kirsten Saves the Day; Changes for Kirsten. 1988. (American Girls Collection). (Illus.). 432p. (YA). (gr. 2 up). 84.95 o.s.i (*0-937295-50-7*); pap. 44.95 o.s.i (*0-937295-51-5*) Pleasant Co. Pubns.

—Kirsten Learns a Lesson: A School Story. Thieme, Jeanne, ed. 1986. (American Girls Collection: Bk. 2). (Illus.). (gr. 2 up). 80p. (J). pap. 5.95 (*0-937295-10-8*, American Girl); 80p. (J). lib. bdg. 12.95 (*0-937295-82-5*, American Girl); 72p. (YA). 12.95 o.p. (*0-937295-09-4*) Pleasant Co. Pubns.

—Kirsten Learns a Lesson: A School Story. 1986. (American Girls Collection: Bk. 2). (Illus.). (YA). (gr. 2 up). 12.10 (*0-606-02289-9*) Turtleback Bks.

—Kirsten on the Trail. 1999. (American Girls Short Stories Ser.). (Illus.). 56p. (YA). (gr. 2 up). 3.95 (*1-56247-764-1*, American Girl) Pleasant Co. Pubns.

—Kirsten Saves the Day: A Summer Story. Thieme, Jeanne, ed. 1988. (American Girls Collection: Bk. 5). (Illus.). (gr. 2 up). 80p. (J). pap. 5.95 (*0-937295-39-6*, American Girl); 66p. (J). lib. bdg. 12.95 (*0-937295-91-4*, American Girl); 72p. (YA). 12.95 o.p. (*0-937295-38-8*) Pleasant Co. Pubns.

—Kirsten Saves the Day: A Summer Story. 1988. (American Girls Collection: Bk. 5). (Illus.). (YA). (gr. 2 up). 12.10 (*0-606-03840-X*) Turtleback Bks.

—Kirsten Snowbound! 2001. (American Girls Short Stories Ser.). (Illus.). 56p. (J). (gr. 2). 3.95 (*1-58485-273-9*, American Girl) Pleasant Co. Pubns.

—Kirsten's Boxed Set: Meet Kirsten; Kirsten Learns a Lesson; Kirsten's Surprise; Happy Birthday, Kirsten!; Kirsten Saves the Day; Changes for Kirsten. 1991. (American Girls Collection: Bks. 1-6). (Illus.). 400p. (YA). (gr. 2 up). 74.95 o.p. (*1-56247-012-4*) Pleasant Co. Pubns.

—Kirsten's Boxed Set: Meet Kirsten; Kirsten Learns a Lesson; Kirsten's Surprise; Happy Birthday, Kirsten!; Kirsten Saves the Day; Changes for Kirsten, 6 bks. Thieme, Jeanne, ed. 1990. (American Girls Collection: Bks. 1-6). (Illus.). (J). 388p. (gr. 2 up). 74.95 (*1-56247-049-3*); 400p. (gr. 3-7). pap. 34.95 (*0-937295-76-0*) Pleasant Co. Pubns. (American Girl).

—Kirsten's Promise. 2003. (American Girls Collection). (Illus.). 38p. (J). pap. 4.95 (*1-58485-696-3*, American Girl) Pleasant Co. Pubns.

—Kirsten's Short Story Set: Kirsten on the Trail; Kirsten & the New Girl; Kirsten & the Chippewa, 3 vols. 2002. (American Girls Short Stories Ser.). (Illus.). (YA). (gr. 2). 11.95 (*1-58485-496-0*, American Girl) Pleasant Co. Pubns.

—Kirsten's Story Collection. 2001. (American Girls Collection). (Illus.). 366p. (J). (gr. 2 up). 29.95 (*1-58485-443-X*, American Girl) Pleasant Co. Pubns.

—Kirsten's Surprise: A Christmas Story. Thieme, Jeanne, ed. 1986. (American Girls Collection: Bk. 3). (Illus.). 72p. (gr. 2 up). (J). pap. 5.95 (*0-937295-19-1*, American Girl); (J). lib. bdg. 12.95 (*0-937295-85-X*, American Girl); (YA). 12.95 o.p. (*0-937295-18-3*) Pleasant Co. Pubns.

—Kirsten's Surprise: A Christmas Story. 1986. (American Girls Collection: Bk. 3). (Illus.). (YA). (gr. 2 up). 12.10 (*0-606-02290-2*) Turtleback Bks.

—Meet Kirsten: An American Girl. Thieme, Jeanne, ed. 1986. (American Girls Collection: Bk. 1). (Illus.). 72p. (gr. 2 up). (J). lib. bdg. 12.95 (*0-937295-79-5*, American Girl); (YA). pap. 5.95 (*0-937295-01-9*, American Girl); (YA). 12.95 o.p. (*0-937295-00-0*) Pleasant Co. Pubns.

—Meet Kirsten: An American Girl. 1986. (American Girls Collection: Bk. 1). (Illus.). (YA). (gr. 2 up). 12.10 (*0-606-02754-8*) Turtleback Bks.

Shefelman, Janice J. A Paradise Called Texas. 1983. (Illus.). 128p. (J). (gr. 4-5). 13.95 (*0-89015-409-0*); pap. 6.95 (*0-89015-506-2*) Eakin Pr.

—Spirit of Iron. Eakin, Edwin M., ed. 1987. (Mina Jordan Ser.: No. 3). (Illus.). 136p. (J). (gr. 4-7). pap. 5.95 o.p. (*0-89015-624-7*); 13.95 (*0-89015-636-0*) Eakin Pr.

Smith, Debra. Hattie Marshall & the Mysterious Strangers. 1996. (Hattie Marshall Frontier Adventure Ser.: Vol. 3). 128p. (J). (gr. 7 up). pap. 4.99 o.p. (*0-89107-878-9*) Crossway Bks.

Smith, Janice Lee. Jess & the Stinky Cowboys. 2004. (Dial Easy-To-Read Ser.). (Illus.). 48p. (J). 14.99 (*0-8037-2641-4*, Dial Bks. for Young Readers) Penguin Putnam Bks. for Young Readers.

Sommer, Carl. Light Your Candle. 2000. (Another Sommer-Time Story Ser.). (Illus.). 48p. (J). (gr. 1-4). 9.95 (*1-57537-019-0*); (ps-4). lib. bdg. 16.95 (*1-57537-068-9*) Advance Publishing, Inc.

—Light Your Candle Read-along Cassette. 2003. (Another Sommer-Time Story Ser.). (Illus.). 48p. (J). 16.95 incl. audio (*1-57537-567-2*) Advance Publishing, Inc.
—Light Your Candle Read-along CD. 2003. (Another Sommer-Time Story Ser.). (Illus.). 48p. (J). 16.95 incl. audio compact disk (*1-57537-518-4*) Advance Publishing, Inc.
Sorensen, Henri. New Hope. 1998. 32p. (J). pap. 5.99 o.p. (*0-14-056359-8*, Puffin Bks.) Penguin Putnam Bks. for Young Readers.
Speare, Elizabeth George. The Sign of the Beaver. 1999. 160p. mass mkt. 2.99 o.s.i (*0-440-22830-1*) Bantam Bks.
—The Sign of the Beaver. 1997. mass mkt. 2.69 o.p. (*0-440-22730-5*); 1993. 144p. (J). (gr. 4-7). pap. 1.99 o.s.i (*0-440-21623-0*) Dell Publishing.
—The Sign of the Beaver. 1983. 144p. (J). (gr. 5-9). tchr. ed. 16.00 (*0-395-33890-5*) Houghton Mifflin Co.
—The Sign of the Beaver. l.t. ed. 1988. 285p. (J). reprint ed. lib. bdg. 16.95 o.s.i (*1-55736-037-5*, Cornerstone Bks.) Pages, Inc.
—The Sign of the Beaver. 1984. 144p. (gr. 4-7). pap. text 5.99 (*0-440-47900-2*); 1994. 172p. (J). vinyl bd. 13.76 (*1-56956-563-5*, BR9513) Random Hse. Children's Bks. (Yearling).
—The Sign of the Beaver. 1983. 11.55 (*0-606-03391-2*) Turtleback Bks.
Sperry, Armstrong. Wagons Westward: The Old Trail to Santa Fe. 2000. (Illus.). 208p. (YA). pap. 14.95 (*1-56792-128-0*) Godine, David R. Pub.
Spooner, Michael. Daniel's Walk. 2004. (J). pap. 6.95 (*0-8050-7543-7*); ERS. 2001. (Illus.). 224p. (YA). (gr. 7 up). 16.95 (*0-8050-6750-7*) Holt, Henry & Co. (Holt, Henry & Co. Bks. For Young Readers).
Stahl, Hilda. Kayla O'Brian & the Runaway Orphans. 1991. (Kayla O'Brian Adventure Ser.). 128p. (J). (gr. 4-7). pap. 4.99 o.p. (*0-89107-631-X*) Crossway Bks.
—Sadie Rose & the Champion Sharpshooter. 1991. (Sadie Rose Adventure Ser.: No. 7). 128p. (J). (gr. 4-7). pap. 4.99 o.p. (*0-89107-630-1*) Crossway Bks.
—Sadie Rose & the Mad Fortune Hunters. 1990. (Sadie Rose Adventure Ser.: No. 5). 128p. (J). (gr. 4-7). pap. 4.99 o.p. (*0-89107-578-X*) Crossway Bks.
—Sadie Rose & the Mysterious Stranger. 1993. (Sadie Rose Adventure Ser.: No. 11). 128p. (J). (gr. 4-7). pap. 4.99 o.p. (*0-89107-747-2*) Crossway Bks.
Stanley, Diane. Roughing It on the Oregon Trail. (Time-Traveling Twins Ser.: No. 1). (Illus.). 48p. (J). (gr. k-5). 2001. pap. 5.95 (*0-06-449006-8*, Harper Trophy); 2000. 15.95 (*0-06-027065-9*, Cotler, Joanna Bks.); 2000. lib. bdg. 15.89 (*0-06-027066-7*, Cotler, Joanna Bks.) HarperCollins Children's Bk. Group.
Steber, Rick. Loggers. 1989. (Tales of the Wild West Ser.: Vol. 7). (Illus.). 60p. pap. 4.95 (*0-945134-07-X*) Bonanza Publishing.
—Mountain Men. 1990. (Tales of the Wild West Ser.: Vol. 8). (Illus.). 60p. pap. 4.95 (*0-945134-08-8*); (J). lib. bdg. 14.95 (*0-945134-86-X*) Bonanza Publishing.
Steele, William O. Buffalo Knife. 1990. 192p. (J). (gr. 3-7). pap. 3.95 o.s.i (*0-15-213212-0*, Odyssey Classics) Harcourt Children's Bks.
—Buffalo Knife. 1990. (J). 9.05 o.p. (*0-606-03139-1*) Turtleback Bks.
—The Buffalo Knife. 1968. (Illus.). (J). (gr. 4-6). reprint ed. pap. 2.75 o.p. (*0-15-614750-5*, Voyager Bks./Libros Viajeros) Harcourt Children's Bks.
—Daniel Boone's Echo. 1957. (Illus.). (J). (gr. k-3). 5.95 o.p. (*0-15-221980-3*) Harcourt Children's Bks.
—Far Frontier. 1959. (Illus.). (J). (gr. 3-7). 5.50 o.p. (*0-15-227171-6*) Harcourt Children's Bks.
—Flaming Arrows. (J). (gr. 4-7). 1990. 192p. pap. 3.95 (*0-15-228427-3*, Odyssey Classics); 1957. (Illus.). 5.95 o.p. (*0-15-228424-9*); 1972. (Illus.). reprint ed. pap. 1.15 o.p. (*0-15-631550-5*, Voyager Bks./Libros Viajeros) Harcourt Children's Bks.
—Flaming Arrows. 1992. (J). 17.50 o.p. (*0-8446-6506-1*) Smith, Peter Pub., Inc.
—The Lone Hunt. 1976. (Illus.). 176p. (J). (gr. 4-6). reprint ed. pap. 1.75 o.p. (*0-15-652983-1*, Voyager Bks./Libros Viajeros) Harcourt Children's Bks.
—Tomahawks & Trouble. 1955. (Illus.). (J). (gr. 3-6). 5.50 o.p. (*0-15-289084-X*) Harcourt Children's Bks.
—Trail Through Danger. 1965. (Illus.). (J). (gr. 4-6). 4.95 o.p. (*0-15-289661-9*) Harcourt Children's Bks.
—Wilderness Journey. 1953. (Illus.). (J). (gr. 4-6). 6.75 o.p. (*0-15-297318-4*) Harcourt Children's Bks.
—Year of the Bloody Sevens. 1963. (Illus.). (J). (gr. 4-6). 6.75 o.p. (*0-15-299800-4*) Harcourt Children's Bks.
Steig, Jeanne. Tales from Gizzards Grill. 2004. (J). (*0-06-000959-4*); lib. bdg. (*0-06-000960-8*) HarperCollins Children's Bk. Group. (Cotler, Joanna Bks.).
Stevens, Carla. Trouble for Lucy, 001. 1979. (Illus.). (J). (gr. 2-6). 13.95 o.p. (*0-395-28971-8*, Clarion Bks.) Houghton Mifflin Co. Trade & Reference Div.
—Trouble for Lucy. 1987. (J). 12.10 (*0-606-03667-9*) Turtleback Bks.
Stewart, George R. The Pioneers Go West. 1987. (Landmark Bks.). 160p. (YA). (gr. 4-9). reprint ed. pap. 5.99 (*0-394-89180-5*, Random Hse. Bks. for Young Readers) Random Hse. Children's Bks.
Stites, Clara. Lixia of Gold Mountain: A Story of Early California. 2003. (Illus.). 64p. (J). pap. 8.95 (*1-56474-421-3*) Fithian Pr.
Stone, B. J. Girl on the Bluff. 1999. (Illus.). 124p. (J). (gr. 4-6). 14.95 (*1-57168-280-5*) Eakin Pr.
Story, Bettie W. River of Fire. 1978. pap. 1.95 o.p. (*0-89191-170-7*) Cook, David C. Publishing Co.
Strand, Keith. Grandfather's Christmas Tree. 1999. (Illus.). 32p. (J). (ps-3). 16.00 (*0-15-201821-2*, Silver Whistle) Harcourt Children's Bks.
—Grandfather's Christmas Tree. 2002. (Illus.). 32p. (J). (gr. k-3). pap. 6.00 (*0-15-216374-3*, Voyager Bks./Libros Viajeros) Harcourt Children's Bks.
Strigenz, Geri K. Year of the Sevens. 1992. (History's Children Ser.). (Illus.). 48p. (J). (gr. 4-5). pap. o.p. (*0-8114-6430-X*) Raintree Pubs.
Strigenz, Geri K., illus. Year of the Sevens. 1992. (History's Children Ser.). 48p. (J). (gr. 4-5). lib. bdg. 21.36 o.p. (*0-8114-3505-9*) Raintree Pubs.
Stutson, Caroline. Prairie Primer A to Z. (Illus.). 32p. (ps-1). 1999. pap. 5.99 o.s.i (*0-14-056551-5*); 1996. (J). 15.99 o.s.i (*0-525-45163-3*, Dutton Children's Bks.) Penguin Putnam Bks. for Young Readers.
—Prairie Primer A to Z. 1999. 12.14 (*0-606-16783-8*) Turtleback Bks.
Sullivan, Arlene R. The Journey of Hanna Heart: You Never Know Where the Wind Will Blow. 1998. (Illus.). 16p. (J). (gr. k-5). pap. 12.95 (*0-9665793-0-5*) Changing Images Art Foundation, Inc.
Susi, Geraldine Lee. My Father, My Companion: Life at the Hollow, Chief Justice John Marshall's Boyhood Home in Virginia. 2001. (Illus.). 96p. (J). (gr. 4-9). pap. 10.95 (*1-889324-22-1*) EPM Pubns., Inc.
Tedrow, T. L. Days of Laura Ingalls Wilder, Vol. 2: Children of Promise. 1992. (J). pap. 4.99 o.p. (*0-8407-3398-4*) Nelson, Thomas Inc.
—Days of Laura Ingalls Wilder, Vol. 3: Good Neighbors. 1992. (J). pap. 4.99 o.p. (*0-8407-3399-2*) Nelson, Thomas Inc.
—Days of Laura Ingalls Wilder, Vol. 4: Home to the Prairie. 1992. (J). pap. 4.99 o.p. (*0-8407-3401-8*) Nelson, Thomas Inc.
—Land of Promise. 1992. (Days of Laura Ingalls Wilder Ser.: Bk. 8). (J). 4.99 o.p. (*0-8407-7735-3*) Nelson, Thomas Inc.
—Land of Promise. 1992. (Days of Laura Ingalls Wilder Ser.). (J). 10.09 o.p. (*0-606-12388-1*) Turtleback Bks.
—Mountain Miracle. 1992. (Days of Laura Ingalls Wilder Ser.). (J). 10.09 o.p. (*0-606-12431-4*) Turtleback Bks.
Thoene, Brock & Thoene, Bodie. Gold Rush Prodigal. 1991. (Saga of the Sierras Ser.: Bk. 3). 224p. (J). (ps up). pap. 8.99 o.p. (*1-55661-162-5*) Bethany Hse. Pubs.
Thomas, Carroll. Riding by Starlight: A Matty Trescott Novel. 2002. (Illus.). ix, 173p. (J). 9.95 (*1-57525-315-1*) Smith & Kraus Pubs., Inc.
Thomas, Joyce Carol. I Have Heard of a Land. (Trophy Picture Book Ser.). (Illus.). 32p. (J). 2000. (gr. k-3). pap. 5.99 (*0-06-443617-9*, Harper Trophy); 1998. (gr. 2-6). 15.95 (*0-06-023477-6*, Cotler, Joanna Bks.); 1998. (gr. 3 up). lib. bdg. 14.89 (*0-06-023478-4*, Cotler, Joanna Bks.) HarperCollins Children's Bk. Group.
—I Have Heard of a Land. 1998. 12.10 (*0-606-17563-6*) Turtleback Bks.
Thomasma, Kenneth. Doe Sia: Bannock Girl & the Handcart Pioneer. 1999. (Amazing Indian Children: Vol. 8). (J). (gr. 3-8). 12.99 (*1-880114-21-6*) Grandview Publishing Co.
—Doe Sia: Bannock Girl & the Handcart Pioneers. 1999. (Amazing Indian Children Ser.). (Illus.). 208p. (J). (gr. 6-9). 9.99 o.p. (*0-8010-4428-6*) Baker Bks.
—Doe Sia: Bannock Girl & the Handcart Pioneers. 1999. (Illus.). (J). 14.04 (*0-606-21884-X*) Turtleback Bks.
Thompson, Gare. Our Journey West. 2003. (I Am American Ser.). (Illus.). 40p. (J). pap. 6.99 (*0-7922-5178-4*) National Geographic Society.
Travis, L. The Redheaded Orphan. 1995. (Ben & Zack Ser.: Vol. 3). 154p. (J). (gr. 3-8). pap. 5.99 o.p. (*0-8010-4023-X*) Baker Bks.
Turner, Ann Warren. Dakota Dugout. 1989. (Reading Rainbow Bks.). (Illus.). 32p. (J). (ps-3). reprint ed. pap. 7.60 (*0-689-71296-0*, Aladdin) Simon & Schuster Children's Publishing.
—Dakota Dugout. 1989. (Reading Rainbow Bks.). (J). 11.14 (*0-606-04191-5*) Turtleback Bks.
—Mississippi Mud: 3 Prairie Journals. 1997. (Illus.). 48p. (J). (gr. 2-5). 16.95 (*0-06-024432-1*); lib. bdg. 16.89 o.p. (*0-06-024433-X*) HarperCollins Children's Bk. Group.
Urban, Betsy. Waiting for Deliverance. 2000. (Illus.). iv, 186p. (J). (gr. 7-12). pap. 17.95 (*0-531-30310-1*); lib. bdg. 18.99 (*0-531-33310-8*) Scholastic, Inc. (Orchard Bks.).
Van Leeuwen, Jean. Going West. (Picture Puffin Bks.). (Illus.). (J). (gr. k-3). 1997. 48p. pap. 5.99 (*0-14-056096-3*); 1992. 48p. 17.99 o.s.i (*0-8037-1027-5*, Dial Bks. for Young Readers); 1992. 4p. 14.89 o.p. (*0-8037-1028-3*, Dial Bks. for Young Readers) Penguin Putnam Bks. for Young Readers.
—Going West. 1997. (Picture Puffin Ser.). 12.14 (*0-606-11398-3*) Turtleback Bks.
—Hannah of Fairfield. 2000. (Pioneer Daughters Ser.: No. 1). (Illus.). 96p. (J). (gr. 2-5). pap. 4.99 (*0-14-130499-5*, Puffin Bks.) Penguin Putnam Bks. for Young Readers.
—Hannah's Helping Hands. 2000. (Pioneer Daughters Ser.: No. 2). (Illus.). 96p. (J). (gr. 2-5). pap. 5.99 (*0-14-130500-2*, Puffin Bks.) Penguin Putnam Bks. for Young Readers.
—Nothing Here but Trees. 1998. (Illus.). 32p. (J). (ps-3). 15.89 o.p. (*0-8037-2180-3*); 15.99 o.p. (*0-8037-2178-1*) Penguin Putnam Bks. for Young Readers. (Dial Bks. for Young Readers).
Verla, Kay. Covered Wagons, Bumpy Trails. 2000. (Illus.). 32p. (J). (ps-3). 15.99 (*0-399-22928-0*, G. P. Putnam's Sons) Penguin Group (USA) Inc.
Vogt, Esther Loewen. A Race for Land. 1992. 112p. (J). (gr. 4-7). pap. 5.99 o.p. (*0-8361-3575-X*) Herald Pr.
—Turkey Red. 1975. (Illus.). 128p. (gr. 6-7). pap. 2.25 o.p. (*0-912692-68-5*) Cook, David C. Publishing Co.
—Turkey Red. 1987. (Junior-Teen Companion Ser.). 104p. (J). pap. 4.95 o.p. (*0-919797-62-8*) Kindred Productions.
Waddell, Martin. Little Obie & the Flood. (J). (gr. 3-6). 1996. bds. 4.99 o.p. (*1-56402-857-7*); 1992. (Illus.). 80p. 13.95 o.p. (*1-56402-106-8*) Candlewick Pr.
—Little Obie & the Flood. 1996. 10.19 o.p. (*0-606-09562-4*) Turtleback Bks.
—Little Obie & the Kidnap. 1994. (Illus.). 80p. (J). (gr. 3-6). 14.95 o.p. (*1-56402-352-4*) Candlewick Pr.
Wallace, Bill. Red Dog. 1987. 192p. (J). (gr. 4-7). tchr. ed. 16.95 (*0-8234-0650-4*) Holiday Hse., Inc.
—Red Dog. 2002. 192p. (J). pap. 4.99 (*0-689-85394-7*, Aladdin); 1989. 176p. (YA). (gr. 4 up). pap. 4.99 (*0-671-70141-X*, Simon Pulse) Simon & Schuster Children's Publishing.
—Red Dog. 1987. 11.04 (*0-606-03899-X*) Turtleback Bks.
Waters, Kate. Andrew McClure & the Headless Horseman: An Adventure in Prairietown, Indiana, 1836. 1984. (Illus.). 40p. (J). (gr. 1-4). pap. 15.95 (*0-590-45503-6*) Scholastic, Inc.
Watson, Jude. Audacious: Ivy's Story. 1995. (Brides of Wildcat County Ser.: No. 3). 192p. (YA). (gr. 7 up). per. 3.95 (*0-689-80328-1*, Simon Pulse) Simon & Schuster Children's Publishing.
—Brides of Independence, No. 4. 1996. (Brides of Wildcat County Ser.). 192p. (J). (gr. 7 up). pap. 3.95 (*0-689-80329-X*, Simon Pulse) Simon & Schuster Children's Publishing.
—Scandalous No. 2: Eden's Story. 1995. (Brides of Wildcat County Ser.). 192p. (J). (gr. 7 up). mass mkt. 3.95 (*0-689-80327-3*, Simon Pulse) Simon & Schuster Children's Publishing.
—Tempestuous: Opal's Story. 1996. (Brides of Wildcat County Ser.). 192p. (J). (gr. 7 up). mass mkt. 5.99 (*0-689-81023-7*, Simon Pulse) Simon & Schuster Children's Publishing.
Watts, Leander. Wild Ride to Heaven. 2003. 176p. (J). (gr. 5-9). tchr. ed. 16.00 (*0-618-26805-7*) Houghton Mifflin Co.
Weidt, Maryann N. Wild Bill Hickok. (Illus.). (J). 1992. 11.00 o.p. (*0-688-10089-9*); 1924. lib. bdg. o.s.i (*0-688-10090-2*) HarperCollins Children's Bk. Group.
Welch, Catherine A. Clouds of Terror. (On My Own History Ser.). (Illus.). (J). (gr. 1-3). 1994. 56p. pap. 6.95 (*0-87614-639-6*); 1993. 48p. lib. bdg. 21.27 (*0-87614-771-6*) Lerner Publishing Group. (Carolrhoda Bks.).
Whelan, Gloria. Night of the Full Moon. 1993. (Illus.). 64p. (J). (gr. 2-4). 15.00 o.s.i (*0-679-84464-3*); (gr. 4-7). 15.99 o.s.i (*0-679-94464-8*) Random Hse. Children's Bks. (Knopf Bks. for Young Readers).
—Night of the Full Moon. 1996. (Illus.). 64p. (J). (gr. 2-4). pap. 3.99 (*0-679-87276-0*) Random Hse., Inc.
—Return to the Island. 2000. 192p. (J). (gr. 4). lib. bdg. 15.89 (*0-06-028254-1*); 14.95 (*0-06-028253-3*) HarperCollins Children's Bk. Group.
—Return to the Island. 2002. 192p. (J). (gr. 4-7). pap. 5.95 (*0-06-440761-6*) HarperCollins Pubs.
—The Wanigan: A Life on the River. (Illus.). 144p. (gr. 3-7). 2003. (YA). pap. 4.99 (*0-440-41882-8*, Dell Books for Young Readers); 2002. (J). 14.95 (*0-375-81429-9*, Knopf Bks. for Young Readers); 2002. (J). lib. bdg. 16.99 (*0-375-91429-3*, Knopf Bks. for Young Readers) Random Hse. Children's Bks.
White, Jack N. The Canebrake Kids: The Trip to Texas. 1996. (Illus.). 120p. (J). (gr. 4-6). 12.95 o.p. (*1-57168-111-6*) Eakin Pr.
The Wild, Wild West: Search & Color. gif. ed. 1990. pap. o.s.i (*0-679-80380-7*, Random Hse. Bks. for Young Readers) Random Hse. Children's Bks.
Wilder, Laura Ingalls. Animal Adventures. 2000. (Little House Chapter Bks.: No. 3). (Illus.). 48p. (J). (gr. 3-6). pap. (*0-7666-0608-2*) Modern Publishing.
—Animal Adventures. 2000. (Little House Chapter Bks.). (Illus.). 80p. (J). (gr. 3-6). Teaching Resource Ctr.
—Bedtime for Laura. 1996. (My First Little House Bks.). (Illus.). 10p. (J). (ps). 3.95 o.s.i (*0-694-00779-X*, Harper Festival) HarperCollins Children's Bk. Group.
—By the Shores of Silver Lake. (Little House Ser.). (J). (gr. 3-6). lib. bdg. 23.95 (*0-8488-2117-3*) Amereon, Ltd.
—By the Shores of Silver Lake. (Little House Ser.). 304p. (J). 2003. pap. 5.99 (*0-06-052240-2*); 1953. (Illus.). (gr. 3-7). pap. 6.99 (*0-06-440005-0*, Harper Trophy); 1953. (Illus.). (gr. 3-6). 16.99 (*0-06-026416-0*); 1953. (Illus.). (gr. 3-7). lib. bdg. 17.89 (*0-06-026417-9*) HarperCollins Children's Bk. Group.
—By the Shores of Silver Lake. 2002. (LRS Large Print Cornerstone Ser.). (J). lib. bdg. 35.95 (*1-58118-098-5*) LRS.
—By the Shores of Silver Lake. l.t. ed. 1990. (Little House Ser.). (J). (gr. 3-6). reprint ed. lib. bdg. 16.95 o.p. (*1-55736-176-2*, Cornerstone Bks.) Pages, Inc.
—By the Shores of Silver Lake. 9999. (J). pap. 2.50 o.s.i (*0-590-01401-3*) Scholastic, Inc.
—By the Shores of Silver Lake. 1981. (Little House Ser.). (J). (gr. 3-6). 11.00 (*0-606-02488-3*) Turtleback Bks.
—La Casa de la Pradera. 1990. 14.55 (*0-606-10433-X*) Turtleback Bks.
—Christmas in the Big Woods. (My First Little House Bks.). (Illus.). (J). (ps-1). 1996. 80p. 3.25 o.p. (*0-694-00877-X*, Harper Festival); 1995. 40p. 14.99 (*0-06-024752-5*); 1995. 40p. lib. bdg. 12.89 o.p. (*0-06-024753-3*) HarperCollins Children's Bk. Group.
—Christmas in the Big Woods. 1995. (My First Little House Bks.). (Illus.). (J). (ps-1). 12.10 (*0-606-10772-X*) Turtleback Bks.
—County Fair. 1998. (My First Little House Bks.). (Illus.). 32p. (J). (ps-3). pap. 5.99 (*0-06-443493-1*, Harper Trophy) HarperCollins Children's Bk. Group.
—County Fair. 1998. (My First Little House Bks.). 11.10 (*0-606-15492-2*) Turtleback Bks.
—Dance at Grandpa's. (My First Little House Bks.). (Illus.). (J). (ps-1). 1996. 80p. 3.25 o.p. (*0-694-00885-0*, Harper Festival); 1994. 40p. lib. bdg. 11.89 o.p. (*0-06-023879-8*); 1994. 40p. 12.95 o.p. (*0-06-023878-X*) HarperCollins Children's Bk. Group.
—The Deer in the Wood. (My First Little House Bks.). (Illus.). (J). (ps-3). 1999. 32p. pap. 5.99 (*0-06-443498-2*, Harper Trophy); 1996. 32p. pap. 3.25 (*0-694-00879-6*, Harper Festival); 1995. 40p. 11.95 o.p. (*0-06-024881-5*); 1995. 40p. lib. bdg. 11.89 o.p. (*0-06-024882-3*) HarperCollins Children's Bk. Group.
—The Deer in the Wood. (My First Little House Bks.). 1999. 12.10 (*0-606-15841-3*); 1996. (Illus.). (J). 8.20 o.p. (*0-606-10780-0*) Turtleback Bks.
—The Early Years Collection: Little House in the Big Woods; Little House on the Prairie; On the Banks of Plum Creek; By the Shores of Silver Lake; The Long Winter, 5 vols. 1993. (Little House Ser.). (Illus.). (J). (gr. 4-7). pap. 34.95 (*0-06-440476-5*, Harper Trophy) HarperCollins Children's Bk. Group.
—The First Four Years. (Little House Ser.). (J). 2003. 144p. pap. 5.99 (*0-06-052243-7*); 1971. (Illus.). 160p. (gr. 3-7). lib. bdg. 17.89 (*0-06-026427-6*); 1971. (Illus.). 160p. (ps-2). 16.99 (*0-06-026426-8*); 1953. (Illus.). 160p. (gr. 5 up). pap. 6.99 (*0-06-440031-X*, Harper Trophy) HarperCollins Children's Bk. Group.
—The First Four Years. l.t. ed. 2002. (LRS Large Print Cornerstone Ser.). (Illus.). (J). lib. bdg. 27.95 (*1-58118-103-5*, 25535) LRS.
—The First Four Years. 1971. (Little House Ser.). (J). (gr. 3-6). 11.00 (*0-606-03250-9*) Turtleback Bks.
—Going to Town. (My First Little House Bks.). (Illus.). (J). (ps-1). 1997. 12p. 3.25 (*0-694-00955-5*, Harper Festival); 1996. 32p. pap. 5.95 (*0-06-443452-4*, Harper Trophy); 1995. 40p. 11.95 o.p. (*0-06-023012-6*); 1995. 40p. lib. bdg. 11.89 o.p. (*0-06-023013-4*) HarperCollins Children's Bk. Group.

—Going to Town. 1995. (My First Little House Bks.). (Illus.). (J). (ps-1). 12.10 (*0-606-09335-4*) Turtleback Bks.

—Going West. (My First Little House Bks.). (Illus.). (J). (ps-1). 1997. 32p. 3.25 (*0-694-00951-2*, Harper Festival); 1996. 40p. lib. bdg. 11.89 o.p. (*0-06-027168-X*); 1996. 40p. 12.95 o.p. (*0-06-027167-1*) HarperCollins Children's Bk. Group.

—Hello, Laura! 1996. (My First Little House Bks.). (Illus.). 10p. (J). (ps). 3.95 o.p. (*0-694-00776-5*, Harper Festival) HarperCollins Children's Bk. Group.

—Laura & Mr. Edwards. 1999. (Little House Chapter Bks.: No. 13). (J). (gr. 3-6). 10.40 (*0-606-16685-8*) Turtleback Bks.

—Laura's Garden. 1996. (My First Little House Bks.). (Illus.). 10p. (J). (ps). 3.95 o.p. (*0-694-00778-1*, Harper Festival) HarperCollins Children's Bk. Group.

—Laura's Ma. 1999. (Little House Chapter Bks.: No. 11). (J). (gr. 3-6). 10.40 (*0-606-15839-1*) Turtleback Bks.

—Laura's Pa. 1999. (Little House Ser.: No. 12). (Illus.). 80p. (J). (gr. 3-6). pap. 4.25 (*0-06-442082-5*, Harper Trophy) HarperCollins Children's Bk. Group.

—Laura's Pa. 1999. (Little House Chapter Bks.: No. 12). (J). (gr. 3-6). 10.40 (*0-606-15840-5*) Turtleback Bks.

—A Little House Birthday. 1997. (My First Little House Bks.). (Illus.). 40p. (J). (ps-3). 13.99 (*0-06-025928-0*) HarperCollins Children's Bk. Group.

—A Little House Birthday. 1997. (My First Little House Bks.). (Illus.). 40p. (J). (ps-1). lib. bdg. 12.89 o.p. (*0-06-025929-9*) HarperCollins Pubs.

—A Little House Christmas: Holiday Stories from the Little House Books. (Little House Ser.). (Illus.). (J). 1994. 96p. (gr. 3-6). lib. bdg. 18.89 o.p. (*0-06-024270-1*); 1994. 80p. (gr. 3-6). 18.95 o.p. (*0-06-024269-8*); No. 2. 1997. 112p. (gr. 3-6). lib. bdg. 19.89 (*0-06-027490-5*); Vol. 2. 2nd ed. 1997. 32p. (gr. k-3). 19.95 (*0-06-027489-1*) HarperCollins Children's Bk. Group.

—A Little House Christmas: Holiday Stories from the Little House Books. 1995. (Little House Ser.). (Illus.). (J). (gr. 3-6). 16.10 (*0-606-12983-9*) Turtleback Bks.

—The Little House Collection, 9 bks., Set. 2003. (YA). pap. 49.99 (*0-06-052996-2*, Avon Bks.) Morrow/Avon.

—Little House Friends. 1998. (Little House Chapter Bks.: No. 9). (J). (gr. 3-6). 10.40 (*0-606-17698-5*) Turtleback Bks.

—Little House "History Comes to Life" Event Kit. 2000. (J). (*0-06-028839-6*) HarperCollins Children's Bk. Group.

—Little House in the Big Woods. (Little House Ser.). (J). 2003. 176p. pap. 5.99 (*0-06-052236-4*); 1953. (Illus.). 256p. (gr. 3-6). pap. 6.99 (*0-06-440001-8*, Harper Trophy); 1953. (Illus.). 256p. (gr. 3-6). 16.99 (*0-06-026430-6*); 1953. (Illus.). 256p. (gr. 3-6). lib. bdg. 17.89 (*0-06-026431-4*) HarperCollins Children's Bk. Group.

—Little House in the Big Woods. l.t. ed. 1987. (Little House Ser.). 161p. (J). (gr. 3-6). reprint ed. lib. bdg. 14.95 o.p. (*1-85089-913-4*) ISIS Large Print Bks. GBR. *Dist:* Transaction Pubs.

—Little House in the Big Woods. l.t. ed. 2000. (Little House Ser.). (Illus.). 244p. (J). (gr. 3-6). lib. bdg. 28.95 (*1-58118-078-0*, 24070) LRS.

—Little House in the Big Woods. 2003. audio compact disk 25.95 (*0-06-054398-1*, HarperEntertainment); 1990. (J). (gr. 3-6). pap. 3.50 o.p. (*0-06-107005-X*, HarperTorch) Morrow/Avon.

—Little House in the Big Woods. 1971. (Little House). (J). (gr. 3-6). 12.00 (*0-606-03811-6*) Turtleback Bks.

—Little House in the Big Woods A Special Read Aloud Edition. 2001. (Little House Ser.). (Illus.). 256p. (J). (gr. k-4). 19.95 (*0-06-029647-X*) HarperCollins Children's Bk. Group.

—Little House in the Big Woods A Special Read Aloud Edition. 2001. (Little House Ser.). (Illus.). 256p. (J). (gr. 3-5). lib. bdg. 19.89 (*0-06-029648-8*) HarperCollins Pubs.

—Little House on the Prairie. 1991. (Little House Ser.). 250p. (J). (gr. 3-6). reprint ed. lib. bdg. 19.95 (*0-89966-868-2*) Buccaneer Bks., Inc.

—Little House on the Prairie. (Little House Ser.). (J). 2003. 272p. pap. 5.99 (*0-06-052237-2*); 1999. (Illus.). 320p. (gr. 3-6). 29.95 (*0-06-028244-4*); 1953. (Illus.). 352p. (gr. 3-6). pap. 6.99 (*0-06-440002-6*, Harper Trophy); 1997. (Illus.). 352p. (gr. 3-6). 24.95 o.s.i (*0-06-027723-8*); 1953. (Illus.). 320p. (gr. k-3). lib. bdg. 17.89 (*0-06-026446-2*); 1953. (Illus.). 352p. (ps-2). 16.99 (*0-06-026445-4*) HarperCollins Children's Bk. Group.

—Little House on the Prairie. 2003. audio compact disk 25.95 (*0-06-054399-X*, Access Pr.) HarperInformation.

—Little House on the Prairie. 1975. (Little House Ser.). (J). (gr. 3-6). pap. 5.50 o.p. (*0-06-080357-6*, P357, Perennial) HarperTrade.

—Little House on the Prairie. l.t. ed. 1999. (Little House Ser.). (Illus.). 420p. (J). (gr. 3-6). lib. bdg. 35.95 (*1-58118-051-9*, 22771) LRS.

—Little House on the Prairie. 1998. (Little House Ser.). (Illus.). 256p. (J). (gr. 3-6). 9.99 o.p. (*1-897954-27-1*) M Q Pubns. GBR. *Dist:* Independent Pubs. Group.

—Little House on the Prairie. 1990. (Little House Ser.). (J). (gr. 3-6). pap. 3.50 (*0-06-107006-8*, HarperTorch) Morrow/Avon.

—Little House on the Prairie. 1999. (Little House Ser.). (J). (gr. 3-6). 11.95 (*1-56137-834-8*) Novel Units, Inc.

—Little House on the Prairie. 9999. (Little House Ser.). (J). (gr. 3-6). pap. 2.50 o.s.i (*0-590-02111-7*) Scholastic, Inc.

—Little House on the Prairie. 1981. (Little House). (J). (gr. 3-6). 12.00 (*0-606-03812-4*) Turtleback Bks.

—Little House on the Prairie: Book & Charm. 2002. (Charming Classics Ser.). (Illus.). 352p. (J). pap. 6.99 (*0-06-000046-5*, Harper Festival) HarperCollins Children's Bk. Group.

—Little House Parties. 1999. (Little House Chapter Bks.: No. 14). (J). (gr. 3-6). 10.40 (*0-606-16686-6*) Turtleback Bks.

—Little House Sisters: Collected Stories from the Little House Books. 1997. (Little House Ser.). (Illus.). 96p. (J). (gr. 3-7). 19.95 (*0-06-027587-1*) HarperCollins Children's Bk. Group.

—A Little Prairie House. (My First Little House Bks.). (Illus.). (J). (ps-3). 1999. 32p. pap. 5.99 (*0-06-443526-1*, Harper Trophy); 1998. 40p. 14.99 (*0-06-025907-8*); 1998. 40p. lib. bdg. 13.89 (*0-06-025908-6*) HarperCollins Children's Bk. Group.

—A Little Prairie House. 1998. (My First Little House Bks.). 12.10 (*0-606-16687-4*) Turtleback Bks.

—Little Town on the Prairie. (Little House Ser.). (J). 2003. 320p. pap. 5.99 (*0-06-052242-9*); 2000. (gr. 3-6). pap. 9.90 (*0-06-449101-3*, Harper Trophy); 1953. (Illus.). 320p. (gr. 3-7). pap. 6.99 (*0-06-440007-7*, Harper Trophy); 1953. (Illus.). 320p. (gr. 3-7). 16.99 (*0-06-026450-0*); 1953. (Illus.). 320p. (gr. 3-7). lib. bdg. 17.89 (*0-06-026451-9*) HarperCollins Children's Bk. Group.

—Little Town on the Prairie. l.t. ed. 2002. (LRS Large Print Cornerstone Ser.). (Illus.). (J). lib. bdg. 35.95 (*1-58118-101-9*, 25533) LRS.

—Little Town on the Prairie. 1981. (Little House Ser.). (J). (gr. 3-6). 12.00 (*0-606-03820-5*) Turtleback Bks.

—The Long Winter. (Little House Ser.). (J). 2003. 368p. pap. 5.99 (*0-06-052241-0*); 1953. (Illus.). 352p. (gr. 3-7). pap. 6.99 (*0-06-440006-9*, Harper Trophy); 1953. (Illus.). 352p. (gr. k-3). lib. bdg. 17.89 (*0-06-026461-6*); 1953. (Illus.). 352p. (ps-2). 16.99 (*0-06-026460-8*) HarperCollins Children's Bk. Group.

—The Long Winter. l.t. ed. 2002. (LRS Large Print Cornerstone Ser.). (Illus.). (J). lib. bdg. 35.95 (*1-58118-100-0*) LRS.

—The Long Winter. 1995. (Little House Ser.). (J). (gr. 3-6). pap. 2.50 (*0-590-30094-6*) Scholastic, Inc.

—The Long Winter. 1981. (Little House Ser.). (J). (gr. 3-6). 12.00 (*0-606-03846-9*) Turtleback Bks.

—My Little House: Animal Adventures; School Days; Pioneer Sisters; The Adventures of Laura & Jack, 4 bks., Set. 1998. (Little House Ser.). (Illus.). (J). (gr. 2-5). pap. 16.95 o.p. (*0-06-449438-1*) HarperCollins Children's Bk. Group.

—My Little House ABC. 1997. (My First Little House Bks.). (Illus.). 24p. (J). (ps). 7.95 o.p. (*0-06-025984-1*); lib. bdg. 7.89 o.p. (*0-06-025985-X*) HarperCollins Children's Bk. Group.

—My Little House Birthday Book. 1996. (Illus.). 40p. (J). (gr. 3-7). 7.95 o.p. (*0-694-00875-3*, Harper Festival) HarperCollins Children's Bk. Group.

—My Little House Book of Animals. 1998. (My First Little House Bks.). (Illus.). (J). (ps). lib. bdg. (*0-06-025993-0*); 24p. 7.95 o.p. (*0-06-025992-2*) HarperCollins Children's Bk. Group.

—My Little House Book of Family. 1998. (My First Little House Bks.). (Illus.). (J). (ps). lib. bdg. (*0-06-025989-2*) HarperCollins Children's Bk. Group.

—My Little House 123. 1997. (My First Little House Bks.). (Illus.). 24p. (J). (ps). 7.95 o.p. (*0-06-025986-8*); lib. bdg. 7.89 o.p. (*0-06-025987-6*) HarperCollins Children's Bk. Group.

—On the Banks of Plum Creek. (Little House Ser.). (J). 2003. 304p. pap. 5.99 (*0-06-052239-9*); 1953. (Illus.). 352p. (gr. 3-7). pap. 6.99 (*0-06-440004-2*, Harper Trophy); rev. ed. 1953. (Illus.). 352p. (gr. 3-7). lib. bdg. 17.89 (*0-06-026471-3*); 32nd rev. ed. 1953. (Illus.). 352p. (gr. 3-7). 16.99 (*0-06-026470-5*) HarperCollins Children's Bk. Group.

—On the Banks of Plum Creek. 2003. 96p. audio compact disk 25.95 (*0-06-054400-7*, Access Pr.) HarperInformation.

—On the Banks of Plum Creek. l.t. ed. 2002. (LRS Large Print Cornerstone Ser.). (Illus.). (J). lib. bdg. 35.95 (*1-58118-099-3*, 25531) LRS.

—On the Banks of Plum Creek. 9999. (Little House Ser.). (J). (gr. 3-6). pap. 2.95 o.s.i (*0-590-11889-7*) Scholastic, Inc.

—On the Banks of Plum Creek. 1971. (Little House Ser.). (J). (gr. 3-6). 12.00 (*0-606-04233-4*) Turtleback Bks.

—On the Way Home: The Diary of a Trip from South Dakota to Mansfield, Missouri, in 1894. Lane, Rose W., ed. (Little House Ser.). 1976. (Illus.). 112p. (J). (gr. 7 up). pap. 5.99 (*0-06-440080-8*, Harper Trophy); 1962. 128p. (YA). (gr. 12 up). lib. bdg. 15.89 o.s.i (*0-06-026490-X*); 60th ed. 1962. 128p. (J). (gr. 7 up). 16.99 (*0-06-026489-6*) HarperCollins Children's Bk. Group.

—Prairie Day. (My First Little House Bks.). (Illus.). (J). (ps-1). 1997. 40p. lib. bdg. 11.89 o.p. (*0-06-025906-X*); 1997. 40p. 12.95 o.p. (*0-06-025905-1*); 1998. 32p. pap. 5.99 (*0-06-443504-0*, Harper Trophy) HarperCollins Children's Bk. Group.

—Prairie Day. 1998. (My First Little House Bks.). (Illus.). (J). (ps-1). 12.10 (*0-606-13719-X*) Turtleback Bks.

—Santa Comes to Little House. 2001. (Little House Picture Bks.). (Illus.). 32p. (J). (ps-3). 15.95 (*0-06-025938-8*); lib. bdg. 15.89 (*0-06-025939-6*) HarperCollins Children's Bk. Group.

—Summertime in the Big Woods. 1996. (My First Little House Bks.). (Illus.). (J). (ps-3). 40p. 14.99 (*0-06-025934-5*); 80p. lib. bdg. 11.89 o.p. (*0-06-025937-X*) HarperCollins Children's Bk. Group.

—These Happy Golden Years. (Little House Ser.). (J). 2003. 336p. pap. 5.99 (*0-06-052315-8*); 1953. (Illus.). 304p. (gr. 3-7). pap. 6.99 (*0-06-440008-5*, Harper Trophy); 1953. (Illus.). 304p. (gr. 3-7). 16.99 (*0-06-026480-2*); 1953. (Illus.). 304p. (gr. 3-7). lib. bdg. 17.89 (*0-06-026481-0*) HarperCollins Children's Bk. Group.

—These Happy Golden Years. l.t. ed. (J). (gr. 3-6). 35.95 (*1-58118-102-7*) LRS.

—These Happy Golden Years. 1971. (Little House Ser.). (J). (gr. 3-6). 11.00 (*0-606-05071-X*) Turtleback Bks.

—Winter Days in the Big Woods. (My First Little House Bks.). (Illus.). (J). (ps-1). 1996. 80p. 3.25 o.p. (*0-694-00876-1*, Harper Festival); 1994. 40p. lib. bdg. 11.89 o.p. (*0-06-023022-3*); 1994. 40p. 12.00 (*0-06-023014-2*) HarperCollins Children's Bk. Group.

—Winter on the Farm. 1997. (My First Little House Bks.). (Illus.). 32p. (J). (ps-1). 3.25 (*0-694-00950-4*, Harper Festival) HarperCollins Children's Bk. Group.

Wilder, Laura Ingalls & Graef, Renee. My Little House Book of Family. 1998. (My First Little House Bks.). (Illus.). 24p. (J). (ps). 7.95 o.p. (*0-06-025988-4*) HarperCollins Pubs.

—Summertime in the Big Woods. 2000. (My First Little House Bks.). (Illus.). 40p. (J). (ps-3). pap. 5.99 (*0-06-443497-4*, Harper Trophy) HarperCollins Children's Bk. Group.

Wiley, Melissa. Little House Chapter Book, No. 26. 2001. (J). pap. (*0-06-442112-0*, Harper Trophy) HarperCollins Children's Bk. Group.

Wilkes, Maria D. Brookfield Days. 1999. (Little House Chapter Bks.: No. 1). (Illus.). 80p. (J). (gr. 3-6). pap. 4.25 (*0-06-442086-8*, Harper Trophy) HarperCollins Children's Bk. Group.

—Brookfield Days. 1999. (Little House Chapter Bks.: No. 1). (Illus.). 80p. (J). (gr. 3-6). lib. bdg. 14.89 (*0-06-027952-4*) HarperCollins Pubs.

—Brookfield Days. 1999. (Little House Chapter Bks.: No.1). (Illus.). (J). (gr. 3-6). 10.40 (*0-606-18680-8*) Turtleback Bks.

—Brookfield Friends. 2000. (Little House Chapter Bks.: No. 4). (Illus.). 80p. (J). (gr. 3-6). pap. 4.25 (*0-06-442107-4*, Harper Trophy); lib. bdg. 14.89 (*0-06-028552-4*) HarperCollins Children's Bk. Group.

—Frontier Family. 2000. (Little House Chapter Bks.: No. 3). (Illus.). 80p. (J). (gr. 3-6). pap. 4.25 (*0-06-442094-9*, Harper Trophy) HarperCollins Children's Bk. Group.

—Little Clearing in the Woods. adapted ed. 1998. (Little House Ser.). (Illus.). 336p. (J). (gr. 3-7). lib. bdg. 15.89 (*0-06-026998-7*) HarperCollins Children's Bk. Group.

—Little Clearing in the Woods. 1998. (Little House Ser.). (Illus.). 336p. (J). (gr. 3-7). 15.95 (*0-06-026997-9*); pap. 5.99 (*0-06-440652-0*) HarperCollins Pubs.

—Little House in Brookfield. 1996. (Little House Ser.). (Illus.). 320p. (J). (gr. 3-7). 16.95 (*0-06-026459-4*); pap. 5.99 (*0-06-440610-5*, Harper Trophy); lib. bdg. 14.89 o.p. (*0-06-026462-4*) HarperCollins Children's Bk. Group.

—Little House in Brookfield. 1996. (Little House Ser.). (Illus.). (J). (gr. 3-6). 11.00 (*0-606-09559-4*) Turtleback Bks.

—Little Town at the Crossroads. 1997. (Little House Ser.). (Illus.). 368p. (J). (gr. 3-7). lib. bdg. 15.89 o.p. (*0-06-026996-0*); (gr. 4 up). 16.95 (*0-06-026995-2*) HarperCollins Children's Bk. Group.

—A New Little Cabin. 2001. (Little House Chapter Bks.: Vol. 5). (Illus.). 80p. (J). (gr. 2-5). pap. 4.25 (*0-06-442109-0*, Harper Trophy); lib. bdg. 14.89 (*0-06-028554-0*) HarperCollins Children's Bk. Group.

—A New Little Cabin. 2001. (Little House Chapter Bks.). (Illus.). (J). (gr. 2-5). 10.40 (*0-606-20592-6*) Turtleback Bks.

—On Top of Concord Hill. 2000. (Little House Ser.). (Illus.). 288p. (J). (gr. 3-7). 15.95 (*0-06-026999-5*); pap. 5.99 (*0-06-440689-X*, Harper Trophy); lib. bdg. 15.89 (*0-06-027003-9*) HarperCollins Children's Bk. Group.

Wilkes, Maria D., et al. The Little House Pioneer Girls, 3 vols. 1998. (J). (gr. 3-7). pap. 14.85 (*0-06-440709-8*, Harper Trophy) HarperCollins Children's Bk. Group.

Wilkins, Celia. Across the Rolling River. 2001. (Little House Ser.). (Illus.). 272p. (J). 16.95 (*0-06-027004-7*); lib. bdg. 16.89 (*0-06-027005-5*); (gr. 5 up). pap. 5.99 (*0-06-440734-9*, Harper Trophy) HarperCollins Children's Bk. Group.

Williams, Carol Lynch. Catherine's Remembrance. 1997. (Latter-Day Daughters Ser.). (J). pap. 4.95 (*1-57345-296-3*, Cinnamon Tree) Deseret Bk. Co.

—Laurel's Flight. 1995. (Latter-Day Daughters Ser.). (Illus.). 80p. (J). pap. 4.95 (*1-56236-502-9*) Aspen Bks.

Williams, David. Grandma Essie's Covered Wagon. 1993. (Illus.). 48p. (J). (ps-3). 16.00 o.s.i (*0-679-80253-3*, Knopf Bks. for Young Readers) Random Hse. Children's Bks.

Williams, Jeanne. Winter Wheat. 1975. 162p. (J). (gr. 6-8). 6.95 o.p. (*0-399-20445-8*) Putnam Publishing Group, The.

Wilson, Laura. How I Survived the Oregon Trail: The Journal of Jesse Adams. 1999. (Time Travellers Ser.). (Illus.). 38p. (J). (gr. 4-7). pap. 9.95 (*0-688-17276-8*) Morrow/Avon.

Wisler, G. Clifton. Jericho's Journey. 144p. (J). 1995. (gr. 4-7). pap. 5.99 (*0-14-037065-X*, Puffin Bks.); 1993. (gr. 5-9). 13.99 o.s.i (*0-525-67428-4*, Dutton Children's Bks.) Penguin Putnam Bks. for Young Readers.

—Jericho's Journey. 1995. 11.04 (*0-606-07737-5*) Turtleback Bks.

—The Raid. 128p. (J). (gr. 5 up). 1994. pap. 3.99 o.s.i (*0-14-036937-6*, Puffin Bks.); 1985. 11.95 o.p. (*0-525-67169-2*, Dutton Children's Bks.) Penguin Putnam Bks. for Young Readers.

Wittmann, Patricia. Buffalo Thunder. 1997. (Accelerated Reader Bks.). (Illus.). 32p. (J). (gr. k-3). 15.95 (*0-7614-5001-7*, Cavendish Children's Bks.) Cavendish, Marshall Corp.

Woodruff, Elvira. Dear Levi: Letters from the Overland Trail. 1994. (Illus.). (J). (gr. 3-7). 15.00 o.s.i (*0-679-84641-7*); 119p. (gr. 4-7). 16.99 o.s.i (*0-679-94641-1*) Random Hse. Children's Bks. (Knopf Bks. for Young Readers).

Wyman, Andrea. Red Sky at Morning. 1991. 240p. (J). (gr. 4-7). 15.95 o.p. (*0-8234-0903-1*) Holiday Hse., Inc.

—Red Sky at Morning. 1997. pap. 3.99 o.p. (*0-380-72877-X*, Avon Bks.) Morrow/Avon.

—Red Sky at Morning. 1997. 9.09 o.p. (*0-606-10908-0*) Turtleback Bks.

Yates, Elizabeth. Carolina's Courage. 1964. (Illus.). (J). (gr. 3-5). 7.50 o.p. (*0-525-27480-4*, Dutton) Dutton/Plume.

Yep, Laurence. When the Circus Came to Town. 128p. (J). 2004. pap. 5.99 (*0-06-440965-1*, Harper Trophy); 2001. (Illus.). 14.95 (*0-06-029325-X*); 2001. (Illus.). lib. bdg. 14.89 (*0-06-029326-8*) HarperCollins Children's Bk. Group.

G

GERMANY—HISTORY—FICTION

Baer, Frank. Max's Gang. 1983. 324p. (J). (gr. 7 up). o.p. (*0-316-07517-5*) Little Brown & Co.

Benary-Isbert, Margot. Under a Changing Moon. 1998. (Young Adult Bookshelf Ser.). 326p. (J). (gr. 9-12). reprint ed. pap. 14.95 (*1-883937-33-7*, 33-7) Bethlehem Bks.

Chetkowski, Emily. Gooseman. 2001. (J). 11.95 (*1-880158-32-9*) Townsend Pr.

Degens, T. The Visit. 1982. 168p. (J). (gr. 7 up). 11.95 o.p. (*0-670-74712-2*, Viking Children's Bks.) Penguin Putnam Bks. for Young Readers.

Disch, Irene & Enzensberger, Hans Magnus. Esterhazy. 1995. (Illus.). 32p. (J). (ps-5). 16.95 o.p. (*0-15-200921-3*) Harcourt Trade Pubs.

Forman, James. Traitors, RS. 1968. 256p. (J). (gr. 7 up). 3.95 o.p. (*0-374-37722-7*, Farrar, Straus & Giroux (BYR)) Farrar, Straus & Giroux.

GETTYSBURG, BATTLE OF, GETTYSBURG, PA., 1863—FICTION

GLACIAL EPOCH—FICTION

GREAT BRITAIN—HISTORY—FICTION

—The Light Beyond the Forest: The Quest for the Holy Grail. 1994. 11.04 (*0-606-07024-9*) Turtleback Bks.
—The Shining Company, RS. 1990. (Illus.). 304p. 14.95 o.p. (*0-374-36807-4*, Farrar, Straus & Giroux (BYR)) Farrar, Straus & Giroux.
Tolhurst, Marilyn. Knights Treasure Chest: The Age of Adventure, to Unlock & Discover. 2001. (Treasure Chest Ser.). (Illus.). 32p. (J). (gr. 4-7). pap. text 19.95 (*1-56138-545-X*) Running Pr. Bk. Pubs.
Tomlinson, Theresa. The Forest Wife. 1997. 176p. (gr. 5-9). pap. text 4.50 o.s.i (*0-440-41350-8*, Yearling) Random Hse. Children's Bks.
—The Forestwife. 1997. 176p. (J). pap. 3.99 (*0-440-91310-1*, Dell Books for Young Readers) Random Hse. Children's Bks.
—The Forestwife. 1993. (J). o.p. (*1-85681-193-X*) Random Hse. of Canada, Ltd. CAN. *Dist:* Random Hse., Inc.
—The Forestwife. 1995. 176p. (YA). (gr. 7 up). lib. bdg. 17.99 (*0-531-08750-6*, Orchard Bks.) Scholastic, Inc.
—The Forestwife. 1997. 10.55 (*0-606-11344-4*) Turtleback Bks.
Twain, Mark. The Prince & the Pauper. 2002. (Great Illustrated Classics). (Illus.). 240p. (J). (gr. 3-8). lib. bdg. 21.35 (*1-57765-698-9*, ABDO & Daughters) ABDO Publishing Co.
—The Prince & the Pauper. (Illus.). 72p. (YA). (gr. 4 up). pap. 7.95 (*1-55576-096-1*, EDN206B) AV Concepts Corp.
—The Prince & the Pauper. 1999. (YA). reprint ed. pap. text 28.00 (*1-4047-1120-1*) Classic Textbooks.
—The Prince & the Pauper. abr. ed. 1996. (Children's Classics Ser.). (Illus.). (J). 6.95 o.p. (*0-7871-0639-9*); 19.95 o.p. (*0-7871-0638-0*, 694016) NewStar Media, Inc.
—The Prince & the Pauper. 2003. (Modern Library Classics). (Illus.). 240p. pap. 8.95 (*0-375-76112-8*, Modern Library) Random House Adult Trade Publishing Group.
Vandersteen, Willy. The Circle of Power. 1998. (Greatest Adventures of Spike & Suzy Ser.: Vol. 2). (Illus.). 56p. (J). (gr. 2-9). 11.95 (*0-9533178-1-1*) Intes International (UK) Ltd. GBR. *Dist:* Diamond Book Distributors, Inc.
Willard, Barbara. If All the Swords in England. 2000. (Living History Library). (Illus.). x, 181p. (J). (gr. 8-12). reprint ed. pap. 12.95 (*1-883937-49-3*, 49-3) Bethlehem Bks.
Yolen, Jane. Sword of the Rightful King: A Novel of King Arthur. 2003. (Illus.). 368p. (J). 17.00 (*0-15-202527-8*) Harcourt Children's Bks.

GREAT BRITAIN—HISTORY, NAVAL—FICTION

Kent, Alexander. Richard Bolitho-Midshipman. 1976. 160p. (J). (gr. 6 up). 6.95 o.p. (*0-399-20514-4*) Putnam Publishing Group, The.
Pope, Dudley. Governor Ramage, R. N. A Novel. 1973. 340p. (J). o.s.i (*0-671-21582-5*, Simon & Schuster) Simon & Schuster.

GREAT BRITAIN—HISTORY—TO 1066—FICTION

Alder, Elizabeth. The King's Shadow. 1997. 272p. (YA). (gr. 7-12). mass mkt. 4.99 (*0-440-22011-4*) Dell Publishing.
—The King's Shadow, RS. 1995. 192p. (YA). (gr. 6 up). 17.00 o.p. (*0-374-34182-6*, Farrar, Straus & Giroux (BYR)) Farrar, Straus & Giroux.
—The King's Shadow. 1997. (J). 10.55 (*0-606-11000-3*) Turtleback Bks.
Bulla, Clyde Robert. The Beast of Lor. 1977. (Illus.). (J). (gr. 3-7). 12.95 (*0-690-01377-9*) HarperCollins Children's Bk. Group.
Clements, Bruce. Prison Window, Jerusalem Blue, RS. 1977. 256p. (J). (gr. 7 up). 12.95 o.p. (*0-374-36126-6*, Farrar, Straus & Giroux (BYR)) Farrar, Straus & Giroux.
Leighton, Margaret. Journey for a Princess, RS. 1960. 224p. (J). (gr. 7 up). 3.95 o.p. (*0-374-33828-0*, Farrar, Straus & Giroux (BYR)) Farrar, Straus & Giroux.
Malone, Patricia. The Legend of Lady Ilena. 2002. (Illus.). 240p. (YA). (gr. 7 up). 15.95 (*0-385-72915-4*); lib. bdg. 17.99 (*0-385-90030-9*) Dell Publishing. (Delacorte Pr.).
—The Legend of Lady Ilena. 2003. 240p. (YA). (gr. 7). mass mkt. 5.50 (*0-440-22909-X*, Laurel Leaf) Random Hse. Children's Bks.
McCaffrey, Anne. Black Horses for the King. 1998. 224p. mass mkt. 6.99 (*0-345-42257-0*, Del Rey) Ballantine Bks.
—Black Horses for the King. 1996. 240p. (YA). (gr. 7 up). 17.00 (*0-15-227322-0*) Harcourt Children's Bks.
—Black Horses for the King. 1997. 17.00 (*0-606-14166-9*) Turtleback Bks.
Ray, Mary. Spring Tide. 1979. (Illus.). 174p. (J). (gr. 5-9). pap. o.p. (*0-571-11331-1*) Faber & Faber Ltd.
Ross, Stewart. Down with the Romans! 1996. (Illus.). 62p. (J). pap. 8.95 (*0-237-51635-7*) Evans Brothers, Ltd. GBR. *Dist:* Trafalgar Square.
San Souci, Robert D. Young Lancelot. 1998. (J). 13.14 (*0-606-13937-0*) Turtleback Bks.
Sutcliff, Rosemary. The Eagle of the Ninth, RS. 1993. 264p. (J). (gr. 7 up). pap. 5.95 (*0-374-41930-2*, Sunburst) Farrar, Straus & Giroux.
—The Eagle of the Ninth. 1987. (Illus.). 264p. (J). 20.00 o.p. (*0-19-271037-0*) Oxford Univ. Pr., Inc.
—The Lantern Bearers, RS. 1994. 40p. (J). (gr. 7 up). pap. 6.95 (*0-374-44302-5*, Sunburst) Farrar, Straus & Giroux.
—The Lantern Bearers. 1979. (New Oxford Library Ser.). (Illus.). (J). (gr. 4 up). reprint ed. 4.95 o.p. (*0-19-277082-9*) Oxford Univ. Pr., Inc.
—The Lantern Bearers. 1995. (J). 20.00 (*0-8446-6837-0*) Smith, Peter Pub., Inc.
—The Lantern Bearers. 1994. 12.00 (*0-606-17793-0*) Turtleback Bks.
—Outcast, RS. 1995. (Illus.). 40p. (J). (gr. 7 up). pap. 7.95 (*0-374-45673-9*, Sunburst) Farrar, Straus & Giroux.
—Outcast. 1979. (Alpha Bks.). (J). pap. text 2.95 o.p. (*0-19-424210-2*) Oxford Univ. Pr., Inc.
—Outcast. 1995. (J). 11.05 o.p. (*0-606-09726-0*) Turtleback Bks.
—The Silver Branch, RS. 1993. 228p. (J). (gr. 7 up). pap. 6.95 (*0-374-46648-3*, Sunburst) Farrar, Straus & Giroux.
—The Silver Branch. 1994. (J). 20.25 (*0-8446-6780-3*) Smith, Peter Pub., Inc.
—Song for a Dark Queen. 1979. (J). (gr. 7 up). 11.95 o.p. (*0-690-03911-5*); lib. bdg. 8.79 o.p. (*0-690-03912-3*) HarperCollins Children's Bk. Group.
—Sword Song, RS. 1998. 288p. (J). (gr. 7-12). 18.00 (*0-374-37363-9*, Farrar, Straus & Giroux (BYR)) Farrar, Straus & Giroux.
Tingle, Rebecca. Far Traveler. 2003. (J). (*0-399-23890-5*, G. P. Putnam's Sons) Penguin Putnam Bks. for Young Readers.
Wein, Elizabeth. Winter Prince. 2003. (Firebird Ser.). (Illus.). 224p. (YA). pap. 6.99 (*0-14-250014-3*, Puffin Bks.) Penguin Putnam Bks. for Young Readers.

GREAT BRITAIN—HISTORY—NORMAN PERIOD, 1066-1154—FICTION

Chaucer, Geoffrey. The Canterbury Tales. Hieatt, A. Kent & Hieatt, Constance B., eds. 1982. (Bantam Classics Ser.). 448p. (gr. 9-12). mass mkt. 5.99 (*0-553-21082-3*, Bantam Classics) Bantam Bks.
—The Canterbury Tales. 1990. 496p. (J). (ps-8). reprint ed. lib. bdg. 29.95 o.p. (*0-89966-671-X*) Buccaneer Bks., Inc.
—The Canterbury Tales. 1985. (Illus.). (gr. 7 up). 10.95 o.p. (*0-385-00028-6*) Doubleday Publishing.
—The Canterbury Tales. adapted ed. (YA). (gr. 5-12). text 9.95 (*0-8359-0869-0*) Globe Fearon Educational Publishing.
—The Canterbury Tales. 1988. (Illus.). 104p. (J). (gr. 5 up). 21.99 (*0-688-06201-6*) HarperCollins Children's Bk. Group.
—The Canterbury Tales, ERS. 1988. (Illus.). 80p. (YA). (gr. 4 up). 17.95 o.p. (*0-8050-0904-3*, Holt, Henry & Co. Bks. For Young Readers) Holt, Henry & Co.
—The Canterbury Tales. 1997. (Puffin Classics Ser.). (Illus.). 128p. (YA). (gr. 4-7). pap. 3.99 (*0-14-038053-1*) Penguin Putnam Bks. for Young Readers.
—The Canterbury Tales. 1983. (Short Classics Ser.). (Illus.). 48p. (J). (gr. 4 up). lib. bdg. 24.26 o.p. (*0-8172-1666-9*) Raintree Pubs.
Goodman, Joan Elizabeth. The Winter Hare. 1996. (Illus.). 272p. (YA). (gr. 7-7). tchr. ed. 17.00 (*0-395-78569-3*) Houghton Mifflin Co.
La Fevers, Robin. The Falconmaster. 2003. 176p. (J). 16.99 (*0-525-46993-1*, Dutton Children's Bks.) Penguin Putnam Bks. for Young Readers.
McGraw, Eloise Jarvis. The Striped Ships. 1991. 240p. (YA). (gr. 7 up). 15.95 o.s.i (*0-689-50532-9*, McElderry, Margaret K.) Simon & Schuster Children's Publishing.
Peart, Hendry. Red Falcons of Tremoine. 1965. (Illus.). (J). (gr. 5-9). lib. bdg. 5.69 o.p. (*0-394-91537-2*, Knopf Bks. for Young Readers) Random Hse. Children's Bks.

GREAT BRITAIN—HISTORY—PLANTAGENETS, 1154-1399—FICTION

Cadnum, Michael. In a Dark Wood: A Novel. 1999. (Illus.). 256p. (J). (gr. 9-12). pap. 6.99 (*0-14-130638-6*, Puffin Bks.) Penguin Putnam Bks. for Young Readers.
—In a Dark Wood: A Novel. 1998. 246p. (YA). (gr. 7-12). pap. 17.95 (*0-531-30071-4*); lib. bdg. 18.99 (*0-531-33071-0*) Scholastic, Inc. (Orchard Bks.).
Gray, Elizabeth J. Adam of the Road. (Illus.). 320p. (J). (gr. 4-7). 1942. 18.99 (*0-670-10435-3*, Viking Children's Bks.); 1987. reprint ed. pap. 5.99 (*0-14-032464-X*, Puffin Bks.) Penguin Putnam Bks. for Young Readers.
—Adam of the Road. 1987. (J). 12.04 (*0-606-03539-7*) Turtleback Bks.
—Adam of the Road. 1942. (J). 4.53 o.p. (*0-670-10436-1*, Viking) Viking Penguin.
Ivanhoe. 1988. (Short Classics Ser.). (Illus.). 48p. (J). (gr. 4 up). pap. 9.27 o.p. (*0-8172-2769-5*) Raintree Pubs.
Lang, Andrew, ed. The Story of Robin Hood, & Other Tales of Adventure & Battle. 1968. (Illus.). (J). (gr. 5 up). 3.95 o.p. (*0-8052-3253-2*, Schocken) Knopf Publishing Group.
Lasky, Kathryn. Robin Hood: The Boy Who Became a Legend. 1999. (J). (*0-590-25933-4*, Blue Sky Pr., The) Scholastic, Inc.
Mayer, Marianna. Ivanhoe. 2003. (Illus.). 48p. (J). 16.95 (*1-58717-248-8*); lib. bdg. 17.50 (*1-58717-249-6*) SeaStar Bks.
Mooser, Stephen. Young Marian's Adventures in Sherwood Forest. 1997. 143p. (J). pap. 4.95 (*0-88166-277-1*) Meadowbrook Pr.
Scott, Walter, Sr. Ivanhoe. 1977. (McKay Illustrated Classics Ser.). (gr. 7 up). 7.95 o.p. (*0-679-20394-X*) McKay, David Co., Inc.
—Ivanhoe. 1978. (Illus.). (J). (gr. 4-12). text 7.50 o.p. (*0-88301-327-4*) Pendulum Pr., Inc.
—Ivanhoe. Farr, Naunerle C., ed. 1978. (Now Age Illustrated III Ser.). (Illus.). (J). (gr. 4-12). stu. ed. 1.25 (*0-88301-339-8*); pap. text 2.95 (*0-88301-315-0*) Pendulum Pr., Inc.
—Ivanhoe. Hanft, Josua, ed. 1994. (Great Illustrated Classics Ser.: Vol. 35). (Illus.). 240p. (J). (gr. 3-6). 9.95 (*0-86611-986-8*) Playmore, Inc., Pubs.
—Ivanhoe. 1988. (Short Classics Ser.). (Illus.). 48p. (J). (gr. 4 up). lib. bdg. 24.26 o.p. (*0-8172-2765-2*) Raintree Pubs.
—Ivanhoe. (J). 1997. (Wishbone Classics Ser.: No. 12). (gr. 2-5). 10.04 (*0-606-12105-6*); 1962. 12.00 (*0-606-02708-4*) Turtleback Bks.
—Ivanhoe Readalong. 1994. (Illustrated Classics Collection). 64p. pap. 14.95 incl. audio (*0-7854-0765-0*, 40502) American Guidance Service, Inc.
Scott, Walter, Sr. & Wright, Robin S. Ivanhoe. 1972. 128 P.p. (*0-8212-0471-8*) Little Brown & Co.
Scott, Walter, Sr., et al. Ivanhoe. (Classics Illustrated Ser.). (Illus.). 52p. (YA). pap. 4.95 (*1-57209-023-5*) Classics International Entertainment, Inc.
Shakespeare, William. Henry IV. 1967. (Airmont Shakespeare Ser.). (YA). (gr. 10 up). Pt. I. mass mkt. 0.60 o.p. (*0-8049-1018-9*, S18); Pt. 2. mass mkt. 1.25 o.p. (*0-8049-1019-7*, S19) Airmont Publishing Co., Inc.
—Richard II. 1966. (Airmont Shakespeare Ser.). (YA). (gr. 9 up). mass mkt. 0.60 o.p. (*0-8049-1014-6*, S14) Airmont Publishing Co., Inc.
Tomlinson, Theresa. Child of the May. 1998. (YA). (gr. 5 up). 120p. mass mkt. 16.99 o.p. (*0-531-33118-0*); (Illus.). 128p. pap. 15.95 (*0-531-30118-4*) Scholastic, Inc. (Orchard Bks.).
Trease, Geoffrey. The Barons' Hostage. 1975. (J). (gr. 5 up). 6.50 o.p. (*0-8407-6434-0*, Dutton Children's Bks.) Penguin Putnam Bks. for Young Readers.
Wheeler, Thomas G. All Men Tall. 1969. (J). (gr. 8 up). 26.95 (*0-87599-157-2*) Phillips, S.G. Inc.

GREAT BRITAIN—HISTORY—LANCASTER AND YORK, 1399-1485—FICTION

Alphin, Elaine Marie. Tournament of Time. 1994. 125p. (Orig.). (J). (gr. 4-6). pap. 3.95 (*0-9643683-0-7*) Bluegrass Bks.
Pyle, Howard. Men of Iron. 25.95 (*0-8488-1131-3*) Amereon, Ltd.

GREAT BRITAIN—HISTORY—WARS OF THE ROSES, 1455-1485—FICTION

Clayton, Elaine. The Yeoman's Daring Daughter & the Princes in the Tower. 1999. (Illus.). 40p. (J). (ps-3). 17.00 o.s.i (*0-517-70984-8*); 18.99 o.s.i (*0-517-70985-6*) Crown Publishing Group.
Harnett, Cynthia. The Writing on the Hearth. 1973. (Illus.). 320p. (J). (gr. 7 up). 9.95 o.p. (*0-670-79119-9*) Viking Penguin.
Stevenson, Robert Louis. The Black Arrow. 1964. (Airmont Classics Ser.). (J). (gr. 6 up). mass mkt. 2.95 o.p. (*0-8049-0020-5*, CL-20) Airmont Publishing Co., Inc.
—The Black Arrow. 1967. (Dent's Illustrated Children's Classics Ser.). (Illus.). (J). reprint ed. 9.00 o.p. (*0-460-05040-0*) Biblio Distribution.
—The Black Arrow. 1990. 288p. (J). (gr. 4 up). pap. 3.50 o.s.i (*0-440-40359-6*) Dell Publishing.
—The Black Arrow. 1998. 269p. (YA). (gr. 7 up). pap. text 3.99 (*0-8125-6562-2*, Tor Classics) Doherty, Tom Assocs., LLC.
—The Black Arrow. 2001. (Juvenile Classics). 272p. (J). pap. 3.00 (*0-486-41820-0*) Dover Pubns., Inc.
—The Black Arrow. 1997. (J). 8.05 o.p. (*0-606-12193-5*) Turtleback Bks.
—The Black Arrow. 2003. (Children's Classics). 304p. (J). (gr. 3-6). pap. 3.95 (*1-85326-161-0*) Wordsworth Editions, Ltd. GBR. *Dist:* Advanced Global Distribution Services.
—The Black Arrow: A Tale of the Two Roses. 1987. (Illustrated Classics Ser.). (Illus.). 336p. (J). (gr. 4-7). 28.00 (*0-684-18877-5*, Atheneum) Simon & Schuster Children's Publishing.

GREAT BRITAIN—HISTORY—TUDORS, 1485-1603—FICTION

Cadnum, Michael. Ship of Fire. 2003. 208p. (YA). 16.99 (*0-670-89907-0*, Viking) Viking Penguin.
Fecher, Constance. Heir to Pendarrow, RS. 1969. 192p. (J). (gr. 7 up). 3.75 o.p. (*0-374-32937-0*, Farrar, Straus & Giroux (BYR)) Farrar, Straus & Giroux.
Kingsley, Charles. Westward Ho. 1968. (Airmont Classics Ser.). (J). (gr. 8 up). mass mkt. 1.25 o.p. (*0-8049-0184-8*, CL-184) Airmont Publishing Co., Inc.
MacInnes, Colin. Three Years to Play. 1970. 354p. (J). 6.95 o.p. (*0-374-27681-1*) Farrar, Straus & Giroux.
Meyer, Carolyn. Doomed Queen Anne. 2002. (Young Royals Ser.). (Illus.). 240p. (YA). (gr. 7 up). 17.00 (*0-15-216523-1*, Gulliver Bks.) Harcourt Children's Bks.
Willard, Barbara. The Iron Lily. 1974. 176p. (J). (gr. 5-7). lib. bdg. 5.95 o.p. (*0-525-32592-1*, Dutton) Dutton/Plume.

GREAT BRITAIN—HISTORY—STUARTS, 1603-1714—FICTION

Bassett, Jennifer, ed. The Children of the New Forest. 1996. (Illus.). 48p. (J). pap. text 5.95 o.p. (*0-19-422748-0*) Oxford Univ. Pr., Inc.
Blackmore, Richard D. Lorna Doone. unabr. ed. 1964. (Classics Ser.). (YA). (gr. 8 up). mass mkt. 3.50 o.p. (*0-8049-0149-X*, CL-149) Airmont Publishing Co., Inc.
—Lorna Doone. 1974. (Dent's Illustrated Children's Classics Ser.). (Illus.). 505p. (J). reprint ed. 9.00 o.p. (*0-460-05022-2*) Biblio Distribution.
Burton, Hester. Beyond the Weir Bridge. 1970. (Illus.). (J). (gr. 6 up). 4.95 o.p. (*0-690-14052-5*) HarperCollins Children's Bk. Group.
—Kate Ryder. 1975. (Illus.). 160p. (J). (gr. 7 up). 10.95 (*0-690-00978-X*) HarperCollins Children's Bk. Group.
Daringer, Helen F. Pilgrim Kate. 1949. (Illus.). (J). (gr. 7 up). 4.95 o.p. (*0-15-261897-X*) Harcourt Children's Bks.
Fecher, Constance. The Link Boys. 1971. (Illus.). 192p. (J). (gr. 4 up). 4.50 o.p. (*0-374-34497-3*) Farrar, Straus & Giroux.
Forrester, Sandra. Wheel of the Moon. 2000. 176p. (J). (gr. 5 up). lib. bdg. 15.89 (*0-06-029203-2*); (Illus.). 15.95 (*0-688-17149-4*) HarperCollins Children's Bk. Group.
Marryat, Frederick. The Children of the New Forest. 1996. (Andre Deutsch Classics). 336p. (J). (gr. 5-8). 11.95 (*0-233-99077-1*) Andre Deutsch GBR. *Dist:* Trafalgar Square, Trans-Atlantic Pubns., Inc.
—The Children of the New Forest. 1977. (Dent's Illustrated Children's Classics Ser.). (Illus.). 325p. (J). reprint ed. 9.00 o.p. (*0-460-05032-X*) Biblio Distribution.
—The Children of the New Forest. 1990. (J). reprint ed. lib. bdg. 21.95 o.p. (*0-89966-700-7*) Buccaneer Bks., Inc.
—The Children of the New Forest. (Illus.). 307p. (J). mass mkt. 8.95 (*0-340-68983-8*) Hodder & Stoughton, Ltd. GBR. *Dist:* Lubrecht & Cramer, Ltd., Trafalgar Square.
—The Children of the New Forest. Butts, Dennis, ed. 1992. (Oxford World's Classics Ser.). 262p. (J). pap. 7.95 o.p. (*0-19-282725-1*) Oxford Univ. Pr., Inc.
—The Children of the New Forest. (Illus.). 304p. (J). pap. 7.95 o.p. (*0-14-130262-3*) Penguin Bks., Ltd. GBR. *Dist:* Trafalgar Square.
—The Children of the New Forest. 1984. (Classics for Young Readers Ser.). 304p. (J). (gr. 4-6). pap. 2.25 o.p. (*0-14-035019-5*, Puffin Bks.) Penguin Putnam Bks. for Young Readers.
Sutcliff, Rosemary. Simon. 1980. (Illus.). (J). (gr. 6 up). reprint ed. 17.95 o.p. (*0-19-271442-2*) Oxford Univ. Pr., Inc.
Vernon, Louise A. The King's Book. 2nd ed. 1980. (Illus.). 128p. (YA). (gr. 4). pap. 7.99 (*0-8361-1933-9*) Herald Pr.
Wallace, M. Imelda, Sr. Outlaws of Ravenhurst. (Illus.). 1950. (J). (gr. 6-10). 12.95 (*0-910334-25-0*); 1950. (J). (gr. 6-10). pap. 15.00 (*0-910334-26-9*); 1996. 232p. (YA). (gr. 5 up). reprint ed. 20.00 (*0-911845-32-1*) Neumann Pr., The.

GREAT BRITAIN—HISTORY—PURITAN REVOLUTION, 1642-1660—FICTION

Fecher, Constance. Venture for a Crown, RS. 1968. (J). (gr. 7 up). 3.50 o.p. (*0-374-38118-6*, Farrar, Straus & Giroux (BYR)) Farrar, Straus & Giroux.
Gordon, Shirley. Crystal Is My Friend. 1978. (Illus.). (J). pap. 7.95 o.p. (*0-06-022112-7*); lib. bdg. 10.89 o.p. (*0-06-022113-5*) HarperCollins Children's Bk. Group.
Haugaard, Erik Christian. Cromwell's Boy. (gr. 7-7). 1990. 192p. (YA). pap. 8.95 (*0-395-54975-2*); 1978. 224p. (J). 7.95 o.p. (*0-395-27203-3*) Houghton Mifflin Co.
—A Messenger for Parliament, 001. 1976. (Illus.). (J). 6.95 o.p. (*0-395-24392-0*) Houghton Mifflin Co.

Weir, Rosemary. Blood Royal, RS. 1973. (Illus.). 176p. (J). (gr. 7 up). 6.95 o.p. (*0-374-30845-4*, Farrar, Straus & Giroux (BYR)) Farrar, Straus & Giroux.

GREAT BRITAIN—HISTORY—18TH CENTURY—FICTION

Garfield, Leon. Footsteps, RS. 2001. 208p. (gr. 7 up). pap. 6.95 (*0-374-42441-1*, Sunburst) Farrar, Straus & Giroux.

—Footsteps. 1988. (J). (gr. k-6). pap. 3.25 o.s.i (*0-440-40102-X*, Yearling) Random Hse. Children's Bks.

—Smith. l.t. ed. 1991. (J). (gr. 1-8). 16.95 o.p. (*0-7451-0448-7*, Galaxy Children's Large Print) BBC Audiobooks America.

—Smith. 1987. (J). (gr. k-6). pap. 4.95 o.s.i (*0-440-48044-2*) Dell Publishing.

—Smith, RS. 2000. 216p. (YA). (gr. 7-12). 18.00 (*0-374-37082-6*, Farrar, Straus & Giroux (BYR)); pap. 7.95 (*0-374-46762-5*, Sunburst) Farrar, Straus & Giroux.

—Smith. 1967. (Illus.). (YA). (gr. 7 up). lib. bdg. 5.99 o.p. (*0-394-91641-7*, Pantheon) Knopf Publishing Group.

—Smith. 1991. (J). (gr. 6-10). 16.00 o.p. (*0-8446-6455-3*) Smith, Peter Pub., Inc.

—Smith. 2000. (J). 13.00 (*0-606-21674-X*) Turtleback Bks.

—The Sound of Coaches. 1974. 256p. (J). (gr. 7 up). 5.95 o.p. (*0-670-65834-0*) Viking Penguin.

Gavin, Jamila. Coram Boy, RS. 2001. (Illus.). 336p. (J). (gr. 7-9). 19.00 (*0-374-31544-2*, Farrar, Straus & Giroux (BYR)) Farrar, Straus & Giroux.

Hutchinson, Robert. Over the Sea to Skye. 1997. (Illus.). 96p. (J). (ps-12). 14.95 (*1-56313-907-3*) BrownTrout Pubs., Inc.

Snodin, David. A Mighty Ferment: Britain in the Age of Revolution, 1750-1850, 001. 1979. (Illus.). 128p. (J). (gr. 6 up). 8.95 o.p. (*0-395-28925-4*, Clarion Bks.) Houghton Mifflin Co. Trade & Reference Div.

GREAT BRITAIN—HISTORY—1714-1837—FICTION

Forester, C. S. Lieutenant Hornblower. 1984. 306p. pap. 14.95 o.p. (*0-316-28921-3*, Back Bay); 1952. (J). (gr. 7 up). 17.95 (*0-316-28907-8*) Little Brown & Co.

—Lord Hornblower. 1946. (J). (gr. 7 up). 17.95 o.p. (*0-316-28908-6*) Little Brown & Co.

Meyrick, Bette. Invasion! 1991. (Illus.). 70p. (YA). pap. 23.00 (*0-86383-773-5*) Gomer Pr. GBR. *Dist:* State Mutual Bk. & Periodical Service, Ltd.

GREAT BRITAIN—HISTORY—19TH CENTURY—FICTION

Avery, Gillian. The Echoing Green: Memories of Victorian Youth. 1974. (Illus.). 256p. (J). (gr. 7 up). 8.95 o.p. (*0-670-28837-3*) Viking Penguin.

Avery, Gillian, ed. Victorian Doll Stories. 1969. (Illus.). 140p. (J). (gr. 4 up). 4.50 o.p. (*0-8052-3275-3*); pap. 2.95 o.p. (*0-8052-0224-2*) Knopf Publishing Group. (Schocken).

Burgess, Melvin. The Copper Treasure. 2002. (Illus.). 112p. (J). (gr. 4-7). pap. 4.95 (*0-380-73325-0*, Harper Trophy) HarperCollins Children's Bk. Group.

—The Copper Treasure, ERS. 2000. (Illus.). 104p. (J). (gr. 4-7). 15.95 (*0-8050-6381-1*, Holt, Henry & Co. Bks. For Young Readers) Holt, Henry & Co.

Burnett, Frances Hodgson. Little Lord Fauntleroy. (J). 21.95 (*0-8488-0792-8*) Amereon, Ltd.

—Little Lord Fauntleroy. 1987. (Classics Ser.). 192p. mass mkt. 2.95 o.s.i (*0-553-21202-8*, Bantam Classics) Bantam Bks.

—Little Lord Fauntleroy. (J). 1977. 21.95 o.p. (*0-89967-002-4*); 1981. (Illus.). 252p. (gr. 5-7). reprint ed. lib. bdg. 21.95 (*0-89966-288-9*) Buccaneer Bks., Inc.

—Little Lord Fauntleroy. 1990. 224p. (J). (gr. k-6). pap. 3.50 o.s.i (*0-440-44764-X*) Dell Publishing.

—Little Lord Fauntleroy. 1976. (Classics of Children's Literature, 1621-1932: Vol. 53). (Illus.). (J). reprint ed. lib. bdg. 46.00 o.p. (*0-8240-2302-1*) Garland Publishing, Inc.

—Little Lord Fauntleroy. 1993. (Illus.). 160p. (YA). (gr. 5 up). 18.95 (*0-87923-958-1*) Godine, David R. Pub.

—Little Lord Fauntleroy. 1995. (Everyman's Library Children's Classics Ser.). (Illus.). (J). (gr. 4-7). 13.95 (*0-679-44474-2*, Everyman's Library) Knopf Publishing Group.

—Little Lord Fauntleroy. 1992. 224p. (YA). mass mkt. 2.95 o.s.i (*0-451-52559-0*, Signet Classics) NAL.

—Little Lord Fauntleroy. 1993. (Oxford World's Classics Ser.). 208p. (J). pap. 7.95 o.p. (*0-19-282961-0*) Oxford Univ. Pr., Inc.

—Little Lord Fauntleroy. (Puffin Classics Ser.). (YA). 1996. (Illus.). 238p. (gr. 5-9). 4.99 (*0-14-036753-5*); 1985. 176p. (gr. 7 up). pap. 3.50 o.p. (*0-14-035025-X*) Penguin Putnam Bks. for Young Readers. (Puffin Bks.).

—Little Lord Fauntleroy. (Illus.). (J). pap. 21.95 (*0-590-74607-3*) Scholastic, Inc.

—Little Lord Fauntleroy. 1994. (Puffin Classics). (J). 11.04 (*0-606-09560-8*) Turtleback Bks.

—Little Lord Fauntleroy. 1998. (Children's Library). (J). (gr. 4-7). pap. 3.95 (*1-85326-130-0*, 1300WW) Wordsworth Editions, Ltd. GBR. *Dist:* Combined Publishing.

Carter, Peter. The Black Lamp. 1975. 175p. (gr. 5 up). 6.95 o.p. (*0-8407-6468-5*, Dutton Children's Bks.) Penguin Putnam Bks. for Young Readers.

Dickens, Charles. Oliver Twist: With a Discussion of Honesty. 2003. (Values in Action Illustrated Classics Ser.). (J). (*1-59203-051-3*) Learning Challenge, Inc.

Dunkle, Clare B. The Hollow Kingdom, ERS. 2003. (Illus.). 240p. (YA). 16.95 (*0-8050-7390-6*, Holt, Henry & Co. Bks. For Young Readers) Holt, Henry & Co.

Goodall, John S. An Edwardian Summer. 1976. (Illus.). 72p. (J). (ps up). 6.95 o.p. (*0-689-50062-9*, McElderry, Margaret K.) Simon & Schuster Children's Publishing.

Greaves, Margaret. Cat's Magic. 1981. 192p. (J). (gr. 5 up). o.p. (*0-06-022122-4*); lib. bdg. 11.89 o.p. (*0-06-022123-2*) HarperCollins Children's Bk. Group.

MacDonald, George. At the Back of the North Wind. 1966. (Airmont Classics Ser.). (Illus.). (YA). (gr. 5 up). mass mkt. 1.50 o.p. (*0-8049-0100-7*, CL-100) Airmont Publishing Co., Inc.

—At the Back of the North Wind. (Young Reader's Christian Library). 1991. (Illus.). 224p. (J). (gr. 3-7). pap. 1.39 o.p. (*1-55748-188-1*); 1988. 384p. 8.97 o.p. (*1-55748-024-9*) Barbour Publishing, Inc.

—At the Back of the North Wind. 1987. (Illus.). (YA). (gr. 5 up). reprint ed. pap. 8.95 o.s.i (*0-8052-0595-0*, Schocken) Knopf Publishing Group.

—At the Back of the North Wind. 1985. (Classics for Young Readers Ser.). 336p. (J). (gr. 4-6). pap. 3.50 o.p. (*0-14-035030-6*, Puffin Bks.) Penguin Putnam Bks. for Young Readers.

—At the Back of the North Wind. 1990. 352p. (J). 12.99 o.s.i (*0-517-69120-5*) Random Hse. Value Publishing.

—At the Back of the North Wind. Watson, Jean, ed. 1981. (Illus.). 128p. (J). (gr. 3-7). reprint ed. 7.95 o.p. (*0-310-42340-6*, 9065P) Zondervan.

Macdonald, Shelagh. No End to Yesterday. 1979. (Illus.). (J). (gr. 7 up). 9.95 o.p. (*0-233-96865-2*) Andre Deutsch GBR. *Dist:* Trafalgar Square, Trans-Atlantic Pubns., Inc.

Pullman, Philip. The Ruby in the Smoke. 1987. 208p. (YA). (gr. 7 up). 11.95 o.s.i (*0-394-88826-X*); 1987. 208p. (YA). (gr. 7 up). 11.99 o.s.i (*0-394-98826-4*); 1988. 240p. (gr. 5-8). reprint ed. mass mkt. 5.50 (*0-394-89589-4*) Random Hse. Children's Bks. (Knopf Bks. for Young Readers).

—The Ruby in the Smoke. 2002. (YA). 20.50 (*0-8446-7230-0*) Smith, Peter Pub., Inc.

—The Ruby in the Smoke. 1985. (J). 11.04 (*0-606-04047-1*) Turtleback Bks.

—Shadow in the North. 1988. 320p. (YA). (gr. 7 up). 12.95 o.s.i (*0-394-89453-7*, Knopf Bks. for Young Readers) Random Hse. Children's Bks.

—Shadow in the North. 1988. (YA). 11.04 (*0-606-04320-9*) Turtleback Bks.

—The Tiger in the Well. 1996. (YA). 11.04 (*0-606-09969-7*) Turtleback Bks.

Stretton, Hesba. Lost Gip. 2003. (Golden Inheritance Ser.: Vol. 7). (Illus.). 121p. (J). (*0-921100-93-0*) Inheritance Pubns.

Wood, Colin. A Confusion of Time. 1977. (J). 6.95 o.p. (*0-525-66553-6*, Dutton Children's Bks.) Penguin Putnam Bks. for Young Readers.

H

HAWAII—HISTORY—FICTION

Gomes, Bernadette. Maile & the Marvelous One. 1984. (Treasury of Children's Hawaiian Stories Ser.). (Illus.). (J). (gr. 3-6). 6.95 o.p. (*0-916630-40-4*) Press Pacifica, Ltd.

McLane, Gretel B. Kailia & the King's Horse. 1982. (Illus.). 96p. (J). (gr. 4-6). 7.95 o.p. (*0-916630-28-5*) Press Pacifica, Ltd.

—Kalia & the King's Horse. 1994. (Illus.). 88p. (J). (gr. 3-7). pap. 8.95 (*0-916630-70-6*) Press Pacifica, Ltd.

Rumford, James. The Island-below-the-Star. 1998. (Illus.). 32p. (J). (ps-3). tchr. ed. 16.00 (*0-395-85159-9*) Houghton Mifflin Co.

—When Silver Needles Swam: The Story of Tutu's Quilt. 1998. (ENG & HAW., Illus.). 30p. (J). (gr. 1-6). 10.95 (*1-891839-00-4*) Manoa Pr.

Thompson, Vivian L. Hawaiian Tales of Heroes & Champions. 1971. (Illus.). 128p. (J). (gr. 3-6). lib. bdg. 7.95 o.p. (*0-8234-0192-8*) Holiday Hse., Inc.

Titcomb, Margaret. Voyage of the Flying Bird. 1970. (Illus.). (J). (gr. 7-9). 4.35 o.p. (*0-8048-0723-X*) Tuttle Publishing.

Yamashita, Susan. The Menehune & the Nene. 1984. (Treasury of Children's Hawaiian Stories Ser.). (Illus.). (J). (gr. 3-6). 9.95 (*0-916630-42-0*) Press Pacifica, Ltd.

HISTORY, ANCIENT—FICTION

Anderson, Paul L. For Freedom & for Gaul. 1931. (Illus.). (YA). (gr. 7-11). pap. 18.00 (*0-8196-0102-0*) Biblo & Tannen Booksellers & Pubs., Inc.

Banks, Lynne Reid. Moses in Egypt: A Novel Inspired by The Prince of Egypt & The Book of Exodus. 1998. (Prince of Egypt Ser.). 128p. (J). (gr. 5-9). pap. text 4.99 (*0-8499-5898-9*) Nelson, Tommy.

Crow, Donna Fletcher. Professor Q's Mysterious Machine. 1983. (Making Choices Ser.: No. 3). (J). (gr. 3-8). pap. 3.95 o.p. (*0-89191-562-1*) Cook Communications Ministries.

Dickinson, Peter. The Dancing Bear. 1973. (Illus.). 256p. (J). (gr. 7 up). 6.95 o.p. (*0-316-18426-8*) Little Brown & Co.

Gaines, Charles K. By the Will of Apollo: Being the Strange Adventures of Cylon, a Spearman of Athens, with Koria of Apollo's Temple, As Related by Himself. 1976. 448p. (YA). (gr. 6 up). 24.95 (*0-8265-1204-6*) Vanderbilt Univ. Pr.

—Gorgo: A Romance of Old Athens. 1976. 526p. (YA). (gr. 6 up). reprint ed. 24.95 (*0-8265-1203-8*) Vanderbilt Univ. Pr.

Golden. Flintstones. 1994. (Illus.). 12p. (J). (ps-3). pap. 1.79 o.s.i (*0-307-08452-3*, Golden Bks.) Random Hse. Children's Bks.

Lawrence, Carol. Twelve Tasks of Flavia Gemina. 2004. (Roman Mysteries Ser.). 192p. 15.95 (*0-7613-1587-X*); lib. bdg. 22.90 (*0-7613-2607-3*) Millbrook Pr., Inc. (Roaring Brook Pr.).

Seigelson, Kim. Trembling Earth. 2004. 17.99 (*0-399-24021-7*, Philomel) Penguin Putnam Bks. for Young Readers.

Smith, Robert Kimmel. The Squeaky Wheel. 1992. 192p. (J). (gr. 4-7). pap. 3.99 o.s.i (*0-440-40631-5*, Yearling) Random Hse. Children's Bks.

Sutcliff, Rosemary. Warrior Scarlet, RS. 1994. 40p. (J). (gr. 4-7). pap. 7.95 (*0-374-48244-6*, Sunburst) Farrar, Straus & Giroux.

What Water Taught the First People: A Story about Peacefulness. 1998. (Excellence in Character Series Storybks.). (Illus.). 30p. (J). (gr. k-8). pap. 6.00 (*1-58259-023-0*) Global Classroom, The.

Williamson, Joanne S. And Forever Free. 1966. (Illus.). (J). (gr. 7 up). lib. bdg. 5.39 o.p. (*0-394-91127-X*, Knopf Bks. for Young Readers) Random Hse. Children's Bks.

Zeman, Ludmila. Le Roi Gilgamesh. Boileau, Michele, tr. from ENG. 1993. (FRE., Illus.). 24p. (J). (gr. 3 up). 19.95 (*0-88776-288-3*) Tundra Bks. of Northern New York.

Zeman, Ludmila & Boileau, Michele. Le Roi Gilgamesh. 2000. (FRE., Illus.). 24p. (J). (gr. 3). pap. 9.95 (*0-88776-526-2*) Tundra Bks. of Northern New York.

HOLOCAUST, JEWISH (1939-1945)—FICTION

Adler, David A. Hiding from the Nazis. 2000. (Illus.). (J). pap. 6.95 (*0-8234-1666-6*) Holiday Hse., Inc.

—One Yellow Daffodil: A Hanukkah Story. (Illus.). 32p. (J). (gr. 1-5). 1999. pap. 6.00 (*0-15-202094-2*, Harcourt Paperbacks); 1995. 16.00 o.s.i (*0-15-200537-4*, Gulliver Bks.) Harcourt Children's Bks.

Almagor, Gila. Under the Domim Tree. Schenker, Hillel, tr. 1995. 176p. (J). (gr. 7 up). 15.00 (*0-671-89020-4*, Simon & Schuster Children's Publishing) Simon & Schuster Children's Publishing.

Baylis-White, Mary. Sheltering Rebecca. 112p. (J). 1993. (gr. 5-9). pap. 3.99 o.p. (*0-14-036448-X*, Puffin Bks.); 1991. (gr. 3-7). 14.95 o.p. (*0-525-67349-0*, Dutton Children's Bks.) Penguin Putnam Bks. for Young Readers.

Bennett, Cherie. Anne Frank & Me. 2002. 352p. (J). pap. 6.99 (*0-698-11973-8*, PaperStar) Penguin Putnam Bks. for Young Readers.

Bennett, Cherie & Gottesfeld, Jeff. Anne Frank & Me. 2001. 291p. (J). (gr. 7 up). 18.99 (*0-399-23329-6*, G. P. Putnam's Sons) Penguin Group (USA) Inc.

Cormier, Robert. Tunes for Bears to Dance To. 1992. 112p. (J). (gr. 5 up). 15.00 o.s.i (*0-385-30818-3*, Delacorte Pr.) Dell Publishing.

Crosby, Ruthann. Miracle in the Glass. Godfrey, Ellen F. et al, eds. 1996. (Illus.). 32p. (Orig.). pap. 19.95 incl. audio (*0-9649962-0-0*) Gabriel's Gatherings, Inc.

Deedy, Carmen Agra. The Yellow Star: The Legend of King Christian X of Denmark. 2000. (Illus.). 32p. (J). (gr. 3-7). 16.95 (*1-56145-208-4*) Peachtree Pubs., Ltd.

Denenberg, Barry. One Eye Laughing, the Other Weeping: The Diary of Julie Weiss, Vienna, Austria to New York, 1938. (Dear America Ser.). 2002. (YA). E-Book 4.50 (*0-439-42545-X*); 2000. (Illus.). 250p. (J). (gr. 4-9). pap. 12.95 (*0-439-09518-2*) Scholastic, Inc.

Douglas, Kirk. The Broken Mirror. 1997. (Illus.). 96p. (J). per. 13.00 (*0-689-81493-3*, Simon & Schuster Children's Publishing) Simon & Schuster Children's Publishing.

Drucker, Malka. Jacob's Rescue: A Holocaust Story. 1993. 128p. (J). 15.95 o.s.i (*0-385-32519-3*, Dell Books for Young Readers) Random Hse. Children's Bks.

—Jacob's Rescue: A Holocaust Story. 1993. 10.55 (*0-606-06504-0*) Turtleback Bks.

Drucker, Malka & Halperin. Jacob's Rescue: A Holocaust Story. 1994. (J). pap. o.p. (*0-440-90106-5*) Dell Publishing.

Drucker, Malka & Halperin, Michael. Jacob's Rescue: A Holocaust Story. 1993. 128p. (J). (gr. 4-7). 15.95 o.s.i (*0-553-08976-5*, Skylark) Random Hse. Children's Bks.

Drucker, Malka, et al. Jacob's Rescue: A Holocaust Story. 1994. 128p. (gr. 2-6). pap. text 4.99 (*0-440-40965-9*) Dell Publishing.

Feder, Paula K. The Feather-Bed Journey. 1995. (Illus.). (J). (ps-3). lib. bdg. 15.95 (*0-8075-2330-5*) Whitman, Albert & Co.

Goldman, Alex J. I Am a Holocaust Torah. 1999. (Illus.). (gr. 4-7). 14.95 (*965-229-154-4*) Gefen Publishing Hse., Ltd ISR. *Dist:* Gefen Bks.

Hoestlandt, Jo. Star of Fear, Star of Hope. Polizzotti, Mark, tr. from FRE. Tr. of Grande Peur sous les Etoiles. (Illus.). 32p. (J). (gr. 2-5). 1995. lib. bdg. 16.85 (*0-8027-8374-0*); 2000. reprint ed. 16.95 (*0-8027-8373-2*); 2000. reprint ed. pap. 8.95 (*0-8027-7588-8*) Walker & Co.

Isaacs, Anne. Torn Thread. 2002. 192p. (YA). mass mkt. 4.99 (*0-590-60364-7*, Scholastic Paperbacks); 2000. (Illus.). 188p. (J). (gr. 5-9). pap. 15.95 o.p. (*0-590-60363-9*, Scholastic Reference) Scholastic, Inc.

Johnston, Tony. The Harmonica. 2004. (J). (*1-57091-547-4*) Charlesbridge Publishing, Inc.

Jules, Jacqueline. The Grey Striped Shirt: How Grandma & Grandpa Survived the Holocaust. 1994. (Illus.). 64p. (J). (gr. 3-6). 13.95 o.p. (*1-881283-06-2*) Alef Design Group.

Kacer, Kathy. Clara's War. 2001. (Holocaust Remembrance Ser.). (Illus.). 128p. (YA). (gr. 5 up). pap. 5.95 (*1-896764-42-8*) Second Story Pr. CAN. *Dist:* Univ. of Toronto Pr.

Kerr, Judith. When Hitler Stole Pink Rabbit. 1997. Tr. of Cuando Hitler Robo el Conejo Rosa. (Illus.). 192p. (J). (gr. 3-7). pap. 5.99 (*0-698-11589-9*, PaperStar) Penguin Putnam Bks. for Young Readers.

—When Hitler Stole Pink Rabbit. 1972. Tr. of Cuando Hitler Robo el Conejo Rosa. (Illus.). (YA). (gr. 6 up). 14.95 o.p. (*0-698-20182-5*, Coward-McCann) Putnam Publishing Group, The.

—When Hitler Stole Pink Rabbit. 1987. Tr. of Cuando Hitler Robo el Conejo Rosa. 192p. (J). (gr. 3 up). pap. 3.99 o.p. (*0-440-49017-0*, Yearling) Random Hse. Children's Bks.

—When Hitler Stole Pink Rabbit.Tr. of Cuando Hitler Robo el Conejo Rosa. (SPA.). 172p. 11.95 (*84-204-3201-6*) Santillana USA Publishing Co., Inc.

—When Hitler Stole Pink Rabbit. 1997. Tr. of Cuando Hitler Robo el Conejo Rosa. (J). 11.04 (*0-606-12845-X*) Turtleback Bks.

Laird, Christa. Shadow of the Wall. 1990. 144p. (YA). (gr. 7 up). 12.95 o.p. (*0-688-09336-1*, Greenwillow Bks.) HarperCollins Children's Bk. Group.

—Shadow of the Wall. 1997. 144p. (gr. 6-12). mass mkt. 4.95 (*0-688-15291-0*, Morrow, William & Co.) Morrow/Avon.

—Shadow of the Wall. 1997. 11.00 (*0-606-11832-2*) Turtleback Bks.

Levitin, Sonia. Room in the Heart. 2003. 304p. (J). 16.99 (*0-525-46871-4*, Dutton Children's Bks.) Penguin Putnam Bks. for Young Readers.

Lustig, Arnost. Dita Saxova. 1994. 320p. (J). 64.00 (*0-8101-1131-4*) Northwestern Univ. Pr.

Matas, Carol. After the War: The Story Behind Exodus. 1996. 144p. (YA). (gr. 5-10). pap. 16.99 o.p. (*0-590-24758-1*) Scholastic, Inc.

—After the War: The Story Behind Exodus. 128p. (gr. 7-11). 1997. (YA). mass mkt. 4.99 (*0-689-80722-8*, Simon Pulse); 1996. (J). lib. bdg. 16.00 (*0-689-80350-8*, Simon & Schuster Children's Publishing) Simon & Schuster Children's Publishing.

—After the War: The Story Behind Exodus. 1997. (J). 10.55 (*0-606-13077-2*) Turtleback Bks.

—Daniel's Story. 1993. 144p. (J). (gr. 4-6). pap. 13.95 o.p. (*0-590-46920-7*); mass mkt. 4.99 (*0-590-46588-0*) Scholastic, Inc.

—Daniel's Story. 1993. 11.04 (*0-606-07412-0*) Turtleback Bks.

—The Garden. 1998. 144p. (gr. 7-12). per. 4.99 (*0-689-80723-6*, Simon Pulse) Simon & Schuster Children's Publishing.

—The Garden. 1998. 11.04 (*0-606-15542-2*) Turtleback Bks.

—Greater Than Angels. 1998. Orig. Title: Contagion of Good. 160p. (J). (gr. 7-12). pap. 16.00 (*0-689-81353-8*, Simon & Schuster Children's Publishing) Simon & Schuster Children's Publishing.

Mazer, Norma Fox. Good Night, Maman. 1999. (Illus.). 192p. (YA). (gr. 5-9). 16.00 (*0-15-201468-3*) Harcourt Children's Bks.

—Good Night, Maman. 2001. (Harper Trophy Bks.). 192p. (J). (gr. 5 up). pap. 5.99 (*0-06-440923-6*, Harper Trophy) HarperCollins Children's Bk. Group.

—Good Night, Maman. 2001. (Illus.). (J). 11.00 (*0-606-21217-5*) Turtleback Bks.

Melnikoff, Pamela. Prisoner in Time. 2001. 142p. (J). (gr. 5-8). pap. 9.95 (*0-8276-0735-0*) Jewish Pubn. Society.

Morpurgo, Michael. Waiting for Anya. Lt. ed. 1992. 240p. (J). 13.95 o.p. (*0-7451-1527-6*, Galaxy Children's Large Print) BBC Audiobooks America.

—Waiting for Anya. 1997. 176p. (gr. 5-9). pap. 5.99 (*0-14-038431-6*); 1991. 174p. (J). 14.99 o.s.i (*0-670-83735-0*, Viking Children's Bks.) Penguin Putnam Bks. for Young Readers.

—Waiting for Anya. 1997. (J). 11.04 (*0-606-12044-0*) Turtleback Bks.

Moskin, Marietta D. I Am Rosemarie. 1991. (J). mass mkt. o.p. (*0-440-80280-6*) Dell Publishing.

—I Am Rosemarie. 1999. 258p. pap. 12.95 (*0-7351-0226-0*); lib. bdg. 24.95 (*0-7351-0225-2*) Replica Bks.

—I Am Rosemarie. 2000. (J). pap. 1.95 (*0-590-04278-5*) Scholastic, Inc.

—I am Rosemarie. 1986. 256p. (J). (gr. k-12). mass mkt. 2.95 o.s.i (*0-440-94066-4*, Laurel Leaf) Random Hse. Children's Bks.

Nerlove, Miriam. Flowers on the Wall. 1996. (Illus.). 32p. (J). (gr. k-3). 16.00 (*0-689-50614-7*, McElderry, Margaret K.) Simon & Schuster Children's Publishing.

Newbery, Linda. Sisterland. 2004. 384p. (J). (gr. 7). 15.95 (*0-385-75026-9*); lib. bdg. 17.99 (*0-385-75035-8*) Random Hse. Children's Bks. (Fickling, David Bks.).

Nivola, Claire A. Elisabeth, RS. 1996. (Illus.). 32p. (J). (ps-3). 16.00 o.p. (*0-374-32085-3*, Farrar, Straus & Giroux (BYR)) Farrar, Straus & Giroux.

Nolan, Han. If I Should Die Before I Wake. (YA). (gr. 7-12). 1996. 304p. pap. 6.00 o.s.i (*0-15-238041-8*, Harcourt Paperbacks); 1994. 240p. 18.00 (*0-15-238040-X*) Harcourt Children's Bks.

—If I Should Die Before I Wake. 1998. (C). 18.00 o.s.i (*0-15-202010-1*) Harcourt Trade Pubs.

Norman, Hilary. The Pact. 1997. 432p. (YA). 24.95 o.p. (*0-525-94256-4*) Dutton/Plume.

Oppenheim, Shulamith Levey. The Lily Cupboard. 2nd ed. 1995. (Charlotte Zolotow Bk.). (Illus.). 32p. (J). (gr. k-3). pap. 6.99 (*0-06-443393-5*, Harper Trophy) HarperCollins Children's Bk. Group.

Orlev, Uri. The Lady with the Hat. Halkin, Hillel, tr. 1995. 192p. (YA). (gr. 7 up). tchr. ed. 16.00 (*0-395-69957-6*) Houghton Mifflin Co.

—The Lady with the Hat. Halkin, Hillel, tr. from HEB. 1997. (Illus.). 192p. (J). (gr. 5-9). pap. 4.99 o.s.i (*0-14-038571-1*) Penguin Putnam Bks. for Young Readers.

—The Lady with the Hat. 1997. 10.09 o.p. (*0-606-13562-6*) Turtleback Bks.

—The Man from the Other Side. Halkin, Hillel, tr. from HEB. 1991. 192p. (YA). (gr. 7-7). tchr. ed. 16.00 (*0-395-53808-4*) Houghton Mifflin Co.

—The Man from the Other Side. Halkin, Hillel, tr. from HEB. 1995. (Illus.). 192p. (J). (gr. 5-9). pap. 5.99 (*0-14-037088-9*, Puffin Bks.) Penguin Putnam Bks. for Young Readers.

—The Man from the Other Side. Halkin, Hillel, tr. from HEB. 1995. 11.04 (*0-606-07834-7*) Turtleback Bks.

—Run Boy, Run. Halkin, Hillel, tr. from HEB. 2003. 192p. (YA). (gr. 5 up). tchr. ed. 15.00 (*0-618-16465-0*, Lorraine, A. Walter) Houghton Mifflin Co. Trade & Reference Div.

Pausewang, Gudrun. Final Journey. Crampton, Patricia, tr. 1998. 160p. (YA). (gr. 7-12). pap. 5.99 (*0-14-130104-X*, Puffin Bks.) Penguin Putnam Bks. for Young Readers.

—Final Journey. 1996. 160p. (J). (gr. 7-12). 15.99 o.p. (*0-670-86456-0*) Penguin Putnam Bks. for Young Readers.

Pressler, Mirjam. Malka. Murdoch, Brian, tr. from GER. 2003. 286p. (YA). (gr. 9-12). 18.99 (*0-399-23984-7*, Philomel) Penguin Putnam Bks. for Young Readers.

Propp, Vera W. When the Soldiers Were Gone. 2001. (Illus.). (J). 11.04 (*0-606-20989-1*) Turtleback Bks.

Radin, Ruth Y. Escape to the Forest: Based on a True Story of the Holocaust. (Illus.). 96p. (J). (gr. 4 up). 2001. pap. 4.25 (*0-06-440822-1*); 2000. 14.99 (*0-06-028520-6*); 2000. lib. bdg. 13.89 (*0-06-028521-4*) HarperCollins Children's Bk. Group.

Ross, Stewart. The Star Houses: A Story from the Holocaust. 2002. (Survivors Ser.). 96p. (J). (gr. 5-8). pap. 4.95 (*0-7641-2204-5*) Barron's Educational Series, Inc.

Roth-Hano, Renee. Touch Wood: A Girlhood in Occupied France. 1989. (ALA Notable Bk.). 304p. (J). (gr. 5 up). pap. 5.99 o.p. (*0-14-034085-8*, Puffin Bks.) Penguin Putnam Bks. for Young Readers.

—Touch Wood: A Girlhood in Occupied France. 1988. 304p. (J). (gr. 5-9). 16.95 o.p. (*0-02-777340-X*, Simon & Schuster Children's Publishing) Simon & Schuster Children's Publishing.

Schleimer, Sarah M. Far from the Place We Called Home. 1994. (J). 16.95 (*0-87306-667-7*) Feldheim, Philipp Inc.

Schmidt, Gary D. Mara's Stories: Glimmers in the Darkness, ERS. 2001. 128p. (J). (gr. 5 up). 16.95 (*0-8050-6794-9*, Holt, Henry & Co. Bks. For Young Readers) Holt, Henry & Co.

Schnur, Steven. The Shadow Children. 1994. (Illus.). 96p. (J). (gr. 3 up). 16.99 (*0-688-13281-2*) HarperCollins Children's Bk. Group.

—The Shadow Children. 1994. (Illus.). 192p. (J). (gr. 4-7). 15.89 o.p. (*0-688-13831-4*, Morrow, William & Co.) Morrow/Avon.

Schwartz, Ellen. Jesse's Star. 2000. (Young Reader Ser.). (Illus.). 108p. (J). (gr. 4-7). pap. 4.99 (*1-55143-143-2*) Orca Bk. Pubs.

Sender, Ruth Minsky. The Cage. 1997. 256p. (YA). (gr. 7-12). mass mkt. 5.50 (*0-689-81321-X*, Simon Pulse) Simon & Schuster Children's Publishing.

Siegel, Bruce H. Champion & Jewboy. 1995. (Illus.). 144p. (J). (gr. 8 up). 6.95 (*1-881283-11-9*) Alef Design Group.

Silton, Faye. Of Heroes, Hooks & Heirlooms. 1997. 100p. (YA). pap. 9.95 (*0-8276-0649-4*); 1996. 120p. (J). (gr. 4 up). 14.95 o.p. (*0-8276-0582-X*) Jewish Pubn. Society.

Spinelli, Jerry. Milkweed. unabr. ed. 2003. (J). audio 25.00 (*0-8072-1858-8*, Listening Library) Random Hse. Audio Publishing Group.

—Milkweed. 2003. (Illus.). 224p. (J). (gr. 5). 15.95 (*0-375-81374-8*); lib. bdg. 17.99 (*0-375-91374-2*) Random Hse. Children's Bks.

Taylor, Marilyn. Faraway Home. 2000. 224p. (J). (gr. 5 up). pap. 7.95 (*0-86278-643-6*) O'Brien Pr., Ltd., The IRL. *Dist:* Independent Pubs. Group.

Treseder, Terry W. Hear O Israel: A Story of the Warsaw Ghetto. 1990. (Illus.). 48p. (J). (gr. 3 up). text 13.95 o.s.i (*0-689-31456-6*, Atheneum) Simon & Schuster Children's Publishing.

Voigt, Cynthia. David & Jonathan. 256p. (J). (gr. 7-9). 1994. mass mkt. 3.95 (*0-590-45166-9*); 1992. pap. 14.95 (*0-590-45165-0*) Scholastic, Inc.

—David & Jonathan. 1992. (Point Ser.). 9.05 o.p. (*0-606-06310-2*) Turtleback Bks.

Vos, Ida. Anna Is Still Here. Edelstein, Terese & Smidt, Inez, trs. from DUT. 1993. 144p. (J). (gr. 4-6). tchr. ed. 15.00 o.s.i (*0-395-65368-1*) Houghton Mifflin Co.

—Anna Is Still Here. Edelstein, Terese & Smidt, Inez, trs. 1995. 144p. (J). (gr. 4-7). pap. 5.99 (*0-14-036909-0*, Puffin Bks.) Penguin Putnam Bks. for Young Readers.

—Anna is Still Here. 1995. 11.04 (*0-606-07199-7*) Turtleback Bks.

Waldman, Neil. The Never-Ending Greenness. 1997. (Illus.). 40p. (J). 16.00 (*0-688-14479-9*); lib. bdg. 15.93 o.p. (*0-688-14480-2*) Morrow/Avon. (Morrow, William & Co.).

Wild, Margaret. Let the Celebrations Begin! (Illus.). 32p. (J). (ps-3). 1996. mass mkt. 6.95 (*0-531-07076-X*); 1991. 15.95 o.p. (*0-531-05937-5*); 1991. lib. bdg. 16.99 (*0-531-08537-6*) Scholastic, Inc. (Orchard Bks.).

—Let the Celebrations Begin! 1996. (J). 13.10 (*0-606-09541-1*) Turtleback Bks.

Williams, Laura E. Behind the Bedroom Wall. 1996. (Illus.). (J). 184p. (gr. 4-7). pap. 6.95 (*1-57131-606-X*); 200p. (gr. 7 up). 15.95 (*1-57131-607-8*) Milkweed Editions.

—Behind the Bedroom Wall. 1996. (J). 13.00 (*0-606-13079-9*) Turtleback Bks.

Wiseman, Eva. My Canary Yellow Star. 2001. (Illus.). 240p. (J). (gr. 3-7). pap. 6.95 (*0-88776-533-5*) Tundra Bks. of Northern New York.

Yolen, Jane. The Devil's Arithmetic. 2002. (J). 13.19 (*0-7587-9594-7*) Book Wholesalers, Inc.

—The Devil's Arithmetic. 176p. 2004. (Illus.). pap. 5.99 (*0-14-240109-9*, Puffin Bks.); 1990. (YA). (gr. 5-9). pap. 5.99 (*0-14-034535-3*, Puffin Bks.); 1988. (YA). 15.99 (*0-670-81027-4*, Viking Children's Bks.) Penguin Putnam Bks. for Young Readers.

—The Devil's Arithmetic. 1990. (YA). 11.04 (*0-606-04653-4*) Turtleback Bks.

Zyskind, Sara. Struggle. 1989. 288p. (J). lib. bdg. 22.95 o.p. (*0-8225-0772-2*, Lerner Pubns.) Lerner Publishing Group.

HUNDRED YEARS' WAR, 1339-1453—FICTION

Doyle, Arthur Conan. The White Company. 1988. (Books of Wonder). (Illus.). 362p. (J). (gr. 2 up). 24.99 (*0-688-07817-6*) HarperCollins Children's Bk. Group.

Wheeler, Thomas G. All Men Tall. 1969. (J). (gr. 8 up). 26.95 (*0-87599-157-2*) Phillips, S.G. Inc.

I

IRAQ-KUWAIT CRISIS, 1990-1991—FICTION

Alshalabi, Firyal M. Summer 1990. 1999. 138 p. pap. text 6.99 (*0-9669988-0-4*) Aunt Strawberry Bks.

Giff, Patricia Reilly. The War Began at Supper: Letters to Miss Loria. 1991. 80p. (J). (gr. 4-7). pap. 2.95 o.s.i (*0-440-40572-6*) Dell Publishing.

—The War Began at Supper: Letters to Miss Loria. 1991. 80p. (J). 11.00 o.s.i (*0-385-30530-3*) Doubleday Publishing.

Qualey, Marsha. Hometown. 1995. 192p. (YA). (gr. 7). tchr. ed. 14.95 o.p. (*0-395-72666-2*) Houghton Mifflin Co.

ISRAEL—HISTORY—FICTION

Kubie, Nora B. Jews of Israel: History & Sources. Silberman, Mark, ed. 1975. (Illus.). 128p. (J). (gr. 5-6). pap. text 3.95 o.p. (*0-87441-246-3*) Behrman Hse., Inc.

Weilerstein, Sadie R. K'tonton in Israel, 3 bks., Set. 1988. (Illus.). (J). (ps-6). pap. 6.95 o.p. (*0-944633-32-3*) Chernak, Judy Productions.

ISRAEL-ARAB WAR, 1967—FICTION

Banks, Lynne Reid. One More River. 1996. (YA). (gr. 7 up). pap. 4.50 (*0-380-72755-2*, Avon Bks.); 1993. 256p. (J). (gr. 4-7). pap. 5.99 (*0-380-71563-5*, Avon Bks.); 1992. 256p. (YA). (gr. 5 up). 14.00 (*0-688-10893-8*, Morrow, William & Co.) Morrow/Avon.

—One More River. 1992. 11.04 (*0-606-05525-8*) Turtleback Bks.

Elmer, Robert. True Betrayer: A Close Call or a Sinister Coincidence???? 2002. (Promise of Zion Ser.). 160p. (J). (gr. 3-8). pap. 5.99 (*0-7642-2314-3*) Bethany Hse. Pubs.

Reboul, Antoine. Thou Shall Not Kill. Craig, Stephanie, tr. 1969. Orig. Title: Tu Ne Tueras Point. (J). (gr. 5-8). 26.95 (*0-87599-161-0*) Phillips, S.G. Inc.

ITALY—HISTORY—FICTION

Alexander, Lloyd. The Rope Trick. 2002. 256p. (J). (gr. 3-6). 16.99 (*0-525-47020-4*) Penguin Putnam Bks. for Young Readers.

Bradford, Emma. Kat & the Missing Notebooks. 1999. (Stardust Classics: No. 4). (Illus.). 119p. (J). (gr. 2-5). 12.95 (*1-889514-27-6*); pap. 5.95 (*1-889514-28-4*) Dolls Corp.

Guarnieri, Paolo. A Boy Named Giotto, RS. Galassi, Jonathan, tr. from ITA. 1999. (Illus.). 32p. (J). (gr. k-4). 17.00 (*0-374-30931-0*, Farrar, Straus & Giroux (BYR)) Farrar, Straus & Giroux.

Konigsburg, E. L. The Second Mrs. Giaconda. 3rd ed. (J). pap. text 4.95 (*0-13-800061-1*) Prentice Hall (Schl. Div.).

—The Second Mrs. Giaconda. 160p. (J). (gr. 5-9). 1998. pap. 4.99 (*0-689-82121-2*); 1978. (Illus.). pap. 5.95 (*0-689-70450-X*) Simon & Schuster Children's Publishing. (Aladdin).

—The Second Mrs. Giaconda. 1998. 11.04 (*0-606-16213-5*) Turtleback Bks.

Napoli, Donna Jo. The Daughter of Venice. 2002. 288p. (YA). lib. bdg. 18.99 (*0-385-90036-8*); (gr. 7-7). 16.95 (*0-385-32780-3*) Dell Publishing. (Delacorte Pr.).

—Daughter of Venice. 2003. 288p. (YA). (gr. 7). mass mkt. 5.50 (*0-440-22928-6*, Dell Books for Young Readers) Random Hse. Children's Bks.

Pressler, Mirjam. Shylock's Daughter. Murdoch, Brian, tr. from GER. 2001. (Illus.). 272p. (J). (gr. 9 up). 17.99 (*0-8037-2667-8*, Dial Bks. for Young Readers) Penguin Putnam Bks. for Young Readers.

J

JAMESTOWN (VA.)—HISTORY—FICTION

Hermes, Patricia. Our Strange New Land: Elizabeth's Jamestown Colony Diary. 2000. (My America Ser.). (Illus.). 112p. (J). (gr. 2-5). pap. 8.95 (*0-439-11208-7*, Scholastic Pr.) Scholastic, Inc.

—Our Strange New Land Bk. 1: Elizabeth's Jamestown Colony Diary. 2002. (My America Ser.: Bk. 1). (Illus.). 112p. (J). (gr. 2-5). mass mkt. 4.99 (*0-439-36898-7*, Scholastic Pr.) Scholastic, Inc.

—Season of Promise: Elizabeth's Jamestown Colony Diary. 2002. (My America Ser.: Bk. 3). (Illus.). (J). (gr. 2-5). 128p. pap. 10.95 (*0-439-38898-8*); 144p. mass mkt. 4.99 (*0-439-27206-8*) Scholastic, Inc. (Scholastic Pr.).

Lees, Stuart. The Lucky Sovereign. 2002. (Illus.). (J). (gr. 3-5). 15.95 (*1-57091-488-5*, Talewinds) Charlesbridge Publishing, Inc.

Lees, Stuart, illus. The Lucky Sovereign. 2002. (J). pap. (*1-57091-489-3*, Talewinds) Charlesbridge Publishing, Inc.

Tunis, Edwin. Shaw's Fortune: The Picture Story of a Colonial Plantation. 1976. (Illus.). 64p. (J). (gr. 2-6). o.p. (*0-690-01066-4*) HarperCollins Children's Bk. Group.

K

KANSAS—HISTORY—FICTION

Kimmel, Cody E. In the Eye of the Storm. 2003. (Adventures of Young Buffalo Bill Ser.). (Illus.). 144p. (J). (gr. 3-7). 15.99 (*0-06-029115-X*); lib. bdg. 16.89 (*0-06-029116-8*) HarperCollins Children's Bk. Group.

Kimmel, Elizabeth Cody. One Sky above Us. 2002. (Adventures of Young Buffalo Bill Ser.). (Illus.). 192p. (J). (gr. 3-6). 15.99 (*0-06-029119-2*); lib. bdg. 17.89 (*0-06-029120-6*) HarperCollins Children's Bk. Group.

—To the Frontier. 2002. (Adventures of Young Buffalo Bill Ser.). (Illus.). 192p. (J). (gr. k-3). lib. bdg. 15.89 (*0-06-029118-4*); (gr. 4-7). 15.95 (*0-06-029117-6*) HarperCollins Children's Bk. Group.

McMullan, Kate. A Fine Start: Meg's Prairie Diary, Bk. 3. 2003. (My America Ser.). 112p. (J). pap. 12.95 (*0-439-37061-2*); mass mkt. 4.99 (*0-439-37062-0*) Scholastic, Inc.

Ruby, Lois. Soon Be Free. 2000. (Illus.). 320p. (J). (gr. 3-7). 17.00 (*0-689-83266-4*, Simon & Schuster Children's Publishing) Simon & Schuster Children's Publishing.

KING PHILIP'S WAR, 1675-1676—FICTION

Jacobs, Paul S. James Printer: A Novel of King Philip's War. (J). (gr. 4-7). 2000. 224p. 4.50 (*0-590-97541-2*); 1997. 208p. pap. 15.95 (*0-590-16381-7*) Scholastic, Inc.

Luhrmann, Winifred B. Only Brave Tomorrows. 1989. (YA). (gr. 5-9). 13.95 o.p. (*0-395-47983-5*) Houghton Mifflin Co.

Matchette, Katharine E. Libby's Choice. 1995. 157p. (YA). (gr. 6-12). pap. 8.75 (*0-9645045-0-2*) Deka Pr.

Sewall, Marcia. Thunder from a Clear Sky. 1995. (Illus.). 64p. (J). (ps-3). 17.00 (*0-689-31775-1*, Atheneum) Simon & Schuster Children's Publishing.

KOREAN WAR, 1950-1953—FICTION

Balgassi, Haemi. Peacebound Trains. (Illus.). 48p. (J). (gr. 4-6). 2000. pap. 6.95 (*0-618-04030-7*); 1996. tchr. ed. 15.00 (*0-395-72093-1*) Houghton Mifflin Co. Trade & Reference Div. (Clarion Bks.).

Barbeau, Clayton C. The Ikon. 2nd ed. 1995. 256p. 19.95 (*0-9633157-0-6*) Ikon Pr.

Choi, Sook-Nyul. Year of Impossible Goodbyes. 1991. 176p. (YA). (gr. 7-7). tchr. ed. 16.00 (*0-395-57419-6*) Houghton Mifflin Co. Trade & Reference Div.

Salter, James. The Hunters. 1997. 224p. 22.00 (*1-887178-36-8*, Counterpoint Pr.) Basic Bks.

L

LEWIS AND CLARK EXPEDITION (1804-1806)—FICTION

Albers, Everett C. Lewis & Clark Meet the American Indians: As Told by Seaman the Dog. 1999. (Illus.). 32p. (J). (ps-11). pap. 3.95 (*0-9674002-0-1*) United Printing.

Ambrose, Stephen E. This Vast Land: A Young Man's Journal of the Lewis & Clark Expedition. 2003. (Illus.). 304p. (YA). 17.95 (*0-689-86448-5*, Simon & Schuster Children's Publishing) Simon & Schuster Children's Publishing.

Barrett, Robert, illus. Seaman's Journal. 2002. 32p. (J). 15.95 (*0-8249-5442-4*) Ideals Pubns.

Bohner, Charles H. Bold Journey: West with Lewis & Clark. 2004. 192p. (J). (gr. 5-9). pap. 5.95 (*0-618-43718-5*); 1989. (Illus.). 192p. (YA). (gr. 7-7). pap. 6.95 (*0-395-54978-7*); 1985. (Illus.). 171p. (J). (gr. 5 up). 13.95 o.p. (*0-395-36691-7*) Houghton Mifflin Co.

—Bold Journey: West with Lewis & Clark. 1985. (J). 13.00 (*0-606-04618-6*) Turtleback Bks.

Carlson, Nolan. Lewis & Clark & Davey Hutchins. 1994. (Illus.). 158p. (Orig.). (J). (gr. 4-8). pap. 6.95 (*1-882420-08-X*, 1-882420-08-X) Hearth Publishing.

Hedstrom, Debbie. From East to West with Lewis & Clark. 1997. (My American Journey Ser.). (J). (gr. 4-7). 19.99 o.p. (*1-57673-066-2*) Questar, Inc.

Karwoski, Gail Langer. Seaman: The Dog Who Explored the West with Lewis & Clark. 2003. (Illus.). 192p. (J). (gr. 3-7). pap. 8.95 (*1-56145-190-8*, 51908) Peachtree Pubs., Ltd.

—Seaman: The Dog Who Explored the West with Lewis & Clark. 1999. 15.00 (*0-606-17742-6*) Turtleback Bks.

LITTLE BIGHORN, BATTLE OF THE, MONT., 1876—FICTION

LONDON (ENGLAND)—HISTORY—FICTION

M

MARATHON, BATTLE OF, 490 B.C.—FICTION

MASSACHUSETTS—HISTORY—FICTION

MAYFLOWER (SHIP)—FICTION

Shaffer, Elizabeth. Daughter of the Dawn: A Mayflower Romance. 1992. (American Heritage Ser.). (Illus.). (J). 9.95 (*0-936369-72-8*) Son-Rise Pubns. & Distribution Co.

Waters, Kate. On the Mayflower: The Voyage of the Ship's Apprentice & a Passenger Girl. 1996. (Illus.). 40p. (J). (gr. 1-4). pap. 16.95 (*0-590-67308-4*) Scholastic, Inc.

MEXICAN WAR, 1846-1848—FICTION

Dell, Pamela. Blood in the Water: A Story of Friendship During the Mexican War. 2003. (J). (*1-59187-042-9*) Tradition Publishing Co.

Neugeboren, Jay. Poli - A Mexican Boy in Early Texas. (Multicultural Texas Ser.). (Illus.). 120p. (YA). (gr. 7 up). 1992. pap. 7.95 (*0-931722-74-8*); 1989. 13.95 o.p. (*0-931722-72-1*) Corona Publishing, Co.

Shaara, Jeff. Gone for Soldiers: A Novel of the Mexican War. 2003. 512p. mass mkt. 7.99 (*0-345-42752-1*) Ballantine Bks.

MEXICO—HISTORY—CONQUEST, 1519-1540—FICTION

Coleman, Eleanor S. Cross & the Sword of Cortes. 1981. (Illus.). (J). (gr. 5 up). 3.95 o.p. (*0-671-65018-1*, Simon & Schuster Children's Publishing) Simon & Schuster Children's Publishing.

Henty, G. A. By Right of Conquest: Or with Cortez in Mexico. (J). E-Book 3.95 (*0-594-02375-0*) 1873 Pr.

Jacobs, William J. Cortes: Conquerer of Mexico. 1994. (Illus.). 64p. (J). (gr. 4-6). lib. bdg. 21.00 o.p. (*0-531-20138-4*, Watts, Franklin) Scholastic Library Publishing.

Mathews, Sally Schofer. The Sad Night: The Story of an Aztec Victory & a Spanish Loss. 1994. (Illus.). 40p. (J). (gr. 4-6). tchr. ed. 17.00 (*0-395-63035-5*, BS0355, Clarion Bks.) Houghton Mifflin Co. Trade & Reference Div.

MEXICO—HISTORY—SPANISH COLONY, 1540-1810—FICTION

de Trevino, Elizabeth Borton. Nacar, the White Deer, RS. 1963. (Illus.). 160p. (J). (gr. 4 up). 3.95 o.p. (*0-374-35478-2*, Farrar, Straus & Giroux (BYR)) Farrar, Straus & Giroux.

Gray, Genevieve. How Far, Felipe? 1978. (I Can Read Bks.). (Illus.). 64p. (J). (ps-3). lib. bdg. 11.89 o.p. (*0-06-022108-9*) HarperCollins Children's Bk. Group.

McCay, William. The Treasure of Don Diego. 1998. (Zorro Ser.: No. 1). 160p. (Orig.). (J). (gr. 3-6). pap. 4.50 (*0-671-51968-9*, Aladdin) Simon & Schuster Children's Publishing.

MEXICO—HISTORY—WARS OF INDEPENDENCE, 1810-1821—FICTION

Borton de Trevino, Elizabeth. Leona, a Love Story, RS. 1994. 176p. (J). 15.00 o.p. (*0-374-34382-9*, Farrar, Straus & Giroux (BYR)) Farrar, Straus & Giroux.

Kahl, Gunter. El Ejercito y la Formacion del Estado en los Comienzos de la Independencia de Mexico (The Army & the Creation of the State During the Mexican Independence) 1997. (SPA.). 276p. 16.99 (*968-16-4300-3*) Fondo de Cultura Economica USA.

MIDDLE AGES—FICTION

Anno, Mitsumasa. Anno's Medieval World. (Illus.). 56p. (J). (gr. 3 up). 1990. 16.95 o.p. (*0-399-20742-2*); 1980. 12.99 o.s.i (*0-399-61153-3*) Penguin Putnam Bks. for Young Readers. (Philomel).

Ashley, Mike, ed. The Chronicles of the Holy Grail. 1996. 448p. (YA). pap. 12.95 (*0-7867-0363-6*, Carroll & Graf Pubs.) Avalon Publishing Group.

Avi. Crispin: The Cross of Lead. 2002. 256p. (J). (gr. 6-9). lib. bdg. 16.49 (*0-7868-2647-9*) Disney Pr.

—Crispin: The Cross of Lead. 2002. (Illus.). 256p. (J). (gr. 3-7). 15.99 (*0-7868-0828-4*) Hyperion Bks. for Children.

—Crispin: The Cross of Lead. 2003. (Young Adult Ser.). 303p. (J). 25.95 (*0-7862-5501-3*) Thorndike Pr.

Barrett, Tracy. Anna of Byzantium. 224p. (YA). (gr. 7-12). 2000. mass mkt. 4.50 (*0-440-41536-5*, Laurel Leaf); 1999. (Illus.). 14.95 (*0-385-32626-2*, Dell Books for Young Readers) Random Hse. Children's Bks.

—Anna of Byzantium. 2000. 10.55 (*0-606-19742-7*) Turtleback Bks.

Bodger, Joan. The Forest Family. (Illus.). 112p. (J). (gr. 3-7). 2001. pap. 7.95 (*0-88776-579-3*); 1999. 16.95 (*0-88776-485-1*) Tundra Bks. of Northern New York.

Brittain, Bill. The Wizards & the Monster. 1994. (Illus.). (J). (gr. 2-5). 80p. lib. bdg. 11.89 o.p. (*0-06-024456-9*); 88p. 11.95 o.p. (*0-06-024454-2*) HarperCollins Children's Bk. Group.

Browne, Dik. Hagar the Horrible: My Feet Are Really Drunk. 1981. (Hagar the Horrible Ser.: No. 10). 128p. (J). (gr. 3 up). 1.75 o.s.i (*0-448-17009-4*) Ace Bks.

Bulla, Clyde Robert. The Sword in the Tree. 1956. (Illus.). (J). (gr. 2-5). 12.95 (*0-690-79908-X*) HarperCollins Children's Bk. Group.

Cadnum, Michael. Daughter of the Wind. 2003. 272p. (J). 17.95 (*0-439-35224-X*, Orchard Bks.) Scholastic, Inc.

—Forbidden Forest: The Story of Little John & the Robin Hood. 2002. 224p. (J). (gr. 7 up). pap. 17.95 (*0-439-31774-6*, Orchard Bks.) Scholastic, Inc.

—The Leopard Sword. 2002. 224p. (J). (gr. 7 up). 15.99 (*0-670-89908-9*, Viking) Viking Penguin.

Cohen, Barbara. Robin Hood & Little John. 1998. 12.14 (*0-606-13744-0*) Turtleback Bks.

Comrie, Margaret S. The Heroes of Castle Bretten. 2003. (Illus.). 229p. (J). (*1-894666-65-8*) Inheritance Pubns.

Crossley-Holland, Kevin. At the Crossing-Places. 2002. (Arthur Trilogy: Bk. 2). (J). 394p. pap. 5.99 (*0-439-26599-1*); 352p. (gr. 9 up). 17.95 (*0-439-26598-3*) Scholastic, Inc. (Levine, Arthur A. Bks.).

—The Seeing Stone. unabr. ed. 2001. (YA). audio 30.00 (*0-8072-0538-9*, Listening Library) Random Hse. Audio Publishing Group.

—The Seeing Stone. 2002. (Arthur Trilogy: Vol. 1). 352p. (YA). (gr. 5 up). pap. 6.99 (*0-439-43524-2*, Levine, Arthur A. Bks.) Scholastic, Inc.

Crowley, Bridget. Feast of Fools. 2003. 272p. (J). (gr. 5-9). 15.95 (*0-689-86512-0*, McElderry, Margaret K.) Simon & Schuster Children's Publishing.

Curley, Daniel. Billy Beg & the Bull. 1978. (Illus.). (J). (gr. 4-6). o.p. (*0-690-03808-9*); lib. bdg. 6.79 o.p. (*0-690-03831-3*) HarperCollins Children's Bk. Group.

Cushman, Karen. Catherine, Called Birdy. 2002. (Illus.). (J). 15.00 (*0-7587-0246-9*) Book Wholesalers, Inc.

—Catherine, Called Birdy. 1995. 224p. (J). (gr. 7 up). pap. 6.50 (*0-06-440584-2*, Harper Trophy) HarperCollins Children's Bk. Group.

—Catherine, Called Birdy. 1995. (YA). (gr. 6 up). pap. 3.95 o.p. (*0-06-449683-X*) HarperCollins Pubs.

—Catherine, Called Birdy. 1994. 176p. (YA). (gr. 7 up). tchr. ed. 16.00 (*0-395-68186-3*, Clarion Bks.) Houghton Mifflin Co. Trade & Reference Div.

—Catherine, Called Birdy. 1995. (YA). (gr. 6 up). 12.00 (*0-606-07355-8*) Turtleback Bks.

—Catherine, Called Birdy: And The Midwife's Apprentice. 1999. (YA). (gr. 3-7). pap. text 7.50 o.p. (*0-06-449365-2*) HarperCollins Pubs.

—Matilda Bone. 2002. 13.94 (*1-4046-1906-2*) Book Wholesalers, Inc.

—Matilda Bone. 2000. (Illus.). 167p. (YA). (gr. 5-9). tchr. ed. 15.00 (*0-395-88156-0*, Clarion Bks.) Houghton Mifflin Co. Trade & Reference Div.

—Matilda Bone. unabr. ed. 2000. (J). (gr. 4-8). audio 30.00 (*0-8072-8737-7*, YA252CX, Listening Library) Random Hse. Audio Publishing Group.

—Matilda Bone. 2002. 176p. (J). (gr. 5-7). reprint ed. pap. 5.50 (*0-440-41822-4*, Yearling) Random Hse. Children's Bks.

—Matilda Bone. Lt. ed. 2001. (Young Adult Ser.). 184p. (J). (gr. 8-12). 23.95 (*0-7862-3212-9*) Thorndike Pr.

—The Midwife's Apprentice. 2002. (Illus.). (J). 14.47 (*0-7587-0202-7*) Book Wholesalers, Inc.

—The Midwife's Apprentice. 1996. (Trophy Bk.). (Illus.). 128p. (J). (gr. 7 up). pap. 5.99 (*0-06-440630-X*, Harper Trophy) HarperCollins Children's Bk. Group.

—The Midwife's Apprentice. 1995. 128p. (YA). (gr. 7 up). tchr. ed. 12.00 (*0-395-69229-6*, Clarion Bks.) Houghton Mifflin Co. Trade & Reference Div.

—The Midwife's Apprentice. 1996. 12.00 (*0-606-09612-4*) Turtleback Bks.

Dayton, Dorothy. The Epic of Alexandra. 1979. (Illus.). (gr. 4 up). 4.98 o.p. (*0-89587-015-0*) Blair, John F. Pub.

De Angeli, Marguerite. The Door in the Wall. 1997. 128p. (J). mass mkt. 2.69 o.p. (*0-440-22740-2*) Dell Publishing.

—The Door in the Wall. 1996. (J). pap. 4.99 (*0-440-91164-8*, Dell Books for Young Readers); 1998. (Illus.). 128p. (YA). (gr. 5-9). reprint ed. mass mkt. 4.99 (*0-440-22779-8*, Laurel Leaf) Random Hse. Children's Bks.

—The Door in the Wall. 1984. (J). mass mkt. 2.50 o.p. (*0-590-40968-9*) Scholastic, Inc.

—The Door in the Wall. 1995. (J). (gr. 3-6). 20.25 (*0-8446-6834-6*) Smith, Peter Pub., Inc.

—The Door in the Wall. 1998. 11.04 (*0-606-13344-5*); 1977. (J). 11.04 (*0-606-03234-7*) Turtleback Bks.

—The Door in the Wall: Story of Medieval London. 1990. (Yearling Newbery Ser.). (Illus.). 128p. (J). (gr. 5-9). reprint ed. pap. text 5.50 (*0-440-40283-2*) Dell Publishing.

—The Door in the Wall: Story of Medieval London. 1989. (Illus.). 128p. (gr. 4-7). text 16.95 (*0-385-07283-X*) Doubleday Publishing.

Deary, Terry. Measly Middle Ages. 1998. (Horrible Histories Ser.). (J). (gr. 7-12). mass mkt. 4.50 (*0-590-49848-7*) Scholastic, Inc.

Denney, James D. Doorway to Doom. 2002. (Illus.). 144p. (J). (gr. 3-7). 5.99 (*1-4003-0040-1*) Nelson, Tommy.

Domanska, Janina. What Happens Next? 1983. (Illus.). 32p. (J). (gr. k-3). 11.50 o.p. (*0-688-01748-7*); lib. bdg. 12.88 o.p. (*0-688-01749-5*) HarperCollins Children's Bk. Group. (Greenwillow Bks.).

Doyle, Arthur Conan. The White Company. 1988. (Books of Wonder). (Illus.). 362p. (J). (gr. 2 up). 24.99 (*0-688-07817-6*) HarperCollins Children's Bk. Group.

Doyle, Debra. The Knight's Wyrd. 1997. (Magic Carpet Books Ser.). (J). 12.05 (*0-606-11539-0*) Turtleback Bks.

Doyle, Debra & MacDonald, James D. The Knight's Wyrd. 1992. 176p. (YA). (gr. 7 up). 16.95 o.s.i (*0-15-200764-4*) Harcourt Children's Bks.

Doyle, Debra & MacDonald, James D. The Knight's Wyrd. 1997. 320p. (YA). pap. 6.00 (*0-15-201520-5*, Magic Carpet Bks.) Harcourt Children's Bks.

Ellis, Anne L. The Dragon of Middlethorpe, ERS. 1991. (Illus.). 192p. (J). (gr. 4-7). 14.95 o.p. (*0-8050-1713-5*, Holt, Henry & Co. Bks. For Young Readers) Holt, Henry & Co.

French, Allen. The Red Keep: A Story of Burgundy in the Year 1165. 1997. (Adventure Library). (Illus.). 380p. (Orig.). (J). (gr. 5-12). pap. 14.95 (*1-883937-29-9*, 29-9) Bethlehem Bks.

Friend in Need. 1996. (J). 9.98 o.p. (*1-57082-341-3*) Mouse Works.

Gerrard, Roy. Sir Cedric, RS. 1984. (Illus.). 32p. (J). (gr. 2 up). 14.95 o.p. (*0-374-36959-3*, Farrar, Straus & Giroux (BYR)) Farrar, Straus & Giroux.

Goodman, Joan Elizabeth. The Winter Hare. 1996. (Illus.). 272p. (YA). (gr. 7-7). tchr. ed. 17.00 (*0-395-78569-3*) Houghton Mifflin Co.

Gray, Elizabeth J. Adam of the Road. (Illus.). 320p. (J). (gr. 4-7). 1942. 18.99 (*0-670-10435-3*, Viking Children's Bks.); 1987. reprint ed. pap. 5.99 (*0-14-032464-X*, Puffin Bks.) Penguin Putnam Bks. for Young Readers.

—Adam of the Road. 1987. (J). 12.04 (*0-606-03539-7*) Turtleback Bks.

—Adam of the Road. 1942. (J). 4.53 o.p. (*0-670-10436-1*, Viking) Viking Penguin.

Gripe, Maria. In the Time of the Bells. La Farge, Sheila & Gripe, Herald, trs. 1976. (Illus.). (J). (gr. 7 up). 6.95 o.s.i (*0-440-04012-4*); lib. bdg. 6.46 o.s.i (*0-440-04014-0*) Dell Publishing. (Delacorte Pr.).

Haahr, Berit I. The Minstrel's Tale. 2000. (Illus.). 256p. (YA). (gr. 7 up). 15.95 (*0-385-32713-7*, Dell Books for Young Readers) Random Hse. Children's Bks.

Hartman, Rachel. Amy Unbounded: Belondweg Blossoming. 2002. 208p. (J). pap. 16.95 (*0-9717900-0-0*) Pug House Pr.

Hildick, E. W. The Case of the Dragon in Distress. 1991. (McGurk Mystery Ser.). 160p. (J). (gr. 4-7). 13.95 o.p. (*0-02-743931-3*, Simon & Schuster Children's Publishing) Simon & Schuster Children's Publishing.

Jinks, Catherine. Pagan in Exile. 2004. 336p. (J). 15.99 (*0-7636-2020-3*) Candlewick Pr.

Jordan, Sherryl. The Hunting of the Last Dragon. (J). (gr. 7 up). 2003. 256p. pap. 5.99 (*0-06-447231-0*); 2002. 192p. 15.95 (*0-06-028902-3*); 2002. 192p. lib. bdg. 15.89 (*0-06-028903-1*) HarperCollins Children's Bk. Group.

Kelly, Eric P. The Trumpeter of Krakow. 224p. 1992. (Illus.). (YA). (gr. 7 up). reprint ed. mass mkt. 4.99 (*0-689-71571-4*, Simon Pulse); 1968. (Illus.). (YA). (gr. 7 up). reprint ed. 17.95 (*0-02-750140-X*, Simon & Schuster Children's Publishing); Vol. 1. 1999. (J). (gr. 4-7). mass mkt. 2.99 o.s.i (*0-689-82992-2*, Aladdin) Simon & Schuster Children's Publishing.

—The Trumpeter of Krakow. 1973. (J). 11.04 (*0-606-05074-4*) Turtleback Bks.

Kemp, Gene. Jason Bodger & the Priory Ghost. 1985. (Illus.). 144p. (J). (gr. 5-8). 12.95 o.p. (*0-571-13645-1*) Faber & Faber, Inc.

Kirwan, Anna. Juliet: A Dream Takes Flight, England, 1339. 1997. (Girlhood Journeys Ser.: Bk. 2). (Orig.). (J). 12.95 (*0-689-81203-5*, Simon & Schuster Children's Publishing) Simon & Schuster Children's Publishing.

—Juliet: A Secret Takes Flight, England, 1339. 1996. (Girlhood Journeys Ser.). (Illus.). 72p. (J). mass mkt. 5.99 (*0-689-80983-2*, Aladdin) Simon & Schuster Children's Publishing.

—Juliet: Midsummer at Greenchapel, Bk. 3. 1997. (Girlhood Journeys Ser.: No. 3). (Illus.). 72p. (J). (gr. 2-6). pap. 5.99 (*0-689-81560-3*, Simon Pulse) Simon & Schuster Children's Publishing.

—Juliet: Rescue at Marlehead Manor, England. 1997. (Girlhood Journeys Ser.: Bks. 2). (Illus.). 72p. (J). (gr. 2-6). per. 5.99 (*0-689-80987-5*, Aladdin) Simon & Schuster Children's Publishing.

Klein-Gousseff, Catherine. The Perfect Knight. Negrin, Fabian, tr. from FRE. & illus. by. 2004. (J). (*0-89236-739-3*) Getty Pubns.

Krensky, Stephen. We Just Moved! 1998. (Hello Reader! Ser.). (Illus.). (J). mass mkt. 3.99 (*0-590-33127-2*) Scholastic, Inc.

Ladd, Louise. The Anywhere Ring No.. 2: Castle in Time. 1995. (Illus.). 160p. (J). mass mkt. 4.50 o.s.i (*0-425-15048-8*) Berkley Publishing Group.

Lasker, Joe. Merry Ever After: The Story of Two Medieval Weddings. 1976. (Illus.). (J). (gr. k-3). 9.95 o.p. (*0-670-47257-3*) Viking Penguin.

Lasky, Kathryn. Grace the Pirate. 1997. (Hyperion Chapters Ser.). (Illus.). 64p. (J). (gr. 3-4). pap. 3.95 (*0-7868-1147-1*) Disney Pr.

—Grace the Pirate. 1997. (Chapters Ser.). (Illus.). 64p. (J). (gr. 3-4). lib. bdg. 14.49 (*0-7868-2236-8*) Hyperion Paperbacks for Children.

Levitin, Sonia. The Cure. 1999. 192p. (YA). (gr. 5 up). 16.00 (*0-15-201827-1*, Silver Whistle) Harcourt Children's Bks.

—The Cure. 2000. 256p. (J). (gr. 7 up). pap. 5.99 (*0-380-73298-X*, Harper Trophy) HarperCollins Children's Bk. Group.

Llywelyn, Morgan. Brian Boru: Emperor of the Irish. 1995. (Illus.). 160p. (J). (gr. 5-10). 14.95 o.p. (*0-312-85623-7*, Tor Bks.) Doherty, Tom Assocs., LLC.

Love, D. Anne. The Puppeteer's Apprentice. 2003. 192p. (J). 16.95 (*0-689-84424-7*, McElderry, Margaret K.) Simon & Schuster Children's Publishing.

MacDonald, Fiona. Castle Seige. 1997. (Microstickers Ser.). (Illus.). 24p. (J). (gr. 4-6). pap. 9.99 o.p. (*1-57584-030-8*) Reader's Digest Children's Publishing, Inc.

Malone, Patricia. The Legend of Lady Ilena. 2002. (Illus.). 240p. (YA). (gr. 7 up). 15.95 (*0-385-72915-4*); lib. bdg. 17.99 (*0-385-90030-9*) Dell Publishing. (Delacorte Pr.).

—The Legend of Lady Ilena. 2003. 240p. (YA). (gr. 7). mass mkt. 5.50 (*0-440-22909-X*, Laurel Leaf) Random Hse. Children's Bks.

Marcuse, Katherine. The Devil's Workshop. 1979. (Illus.). (J). (gr. 3-7). 6.50 o.p. (*0-687-10506-4*) Abingdon Pr.

McMullan, Kate. Countdown to the Year 1000. 2003. (Dragon Slayer's Academy Ser.). (Illus.). 112p. mass mkt. 4.99 (*0-448-43508-X*, Grosset & Dunlap) Penguin Putnam Bks. for Young Readers.

Morressy, John. The Juggler. 1998. 112p. (YA). (gr. 12 up). pap. 5.95 (*0-06-447174-8*, Harper Trophy) HarperCollins Children's Bk. Group.

—The Juggler, ERS. 1996. 272p. (YA). (gr. 6-12). 16.95 o.s.i (*0-8050-4217-2*, Holt, Henry & Co. Bks. For Young Readers) Holt, Henry & Co.

Myers, Anna. Graveyard Girl. 128p. (J). (gr. 3-7). 2001. pap. 7.95 (*0-8027-7607-8*); 1995. 14.95 (*0-8027-8260-4*) Walker & Co.

Napoli, Donna Jo. Breath. 2003. (Illus.). 272p. (YA). 16.95 (*0-689-86174-5*, Atheneum) Simon & Schuster Children's Publishing.

Osborne, Mary Pope. The Knight at Dawn. unabr. ed. 2001. (Magic Tree House Ser. : No. 2). 66p. (J). (gr. k-4). pap. 17.00 incl. audio (*0-8072-0331-9*, Listening Library) Random Hse. Audio Publishing Group.

—The Knight at Dawn. 1993. (Magic Tree House Ser.: No. 2). (Illus.). 80p. (gr. k-3). lib. bdg. 11.99 (*0-679-92412-4*); (J). pap. 3.99 (*0-679-82412-X*) Random Hse. Children's Bks. (Random Hse. Bks. for Young Readers).

—The Knight at Dawn. 1993. (Magic Tree House Ser.: No. 2). (Illus.). (J). (gr. k-3). 10.14 (*0-606-09518-7*) Turtleback Bks.

Pernoud, R. Egine & Clift, Dominique. A Troubadour. 1997. (Day with Ser.). (Illus.). 48p. (J). (gr. 5-7). lib. bdg. 22.60 (*0-8225-1915-1*, Runestone Pr.) Lerner Publishing Group.

Platt, Richard. Castle Diary: The Journal of Tobias Burgess. 2003. (Illus.). 128p. pap. 6.99 (*0-7636-2164-1*) Candlewick Pr.

—Castle Diary: The Journal of Tobias Burgess, Page. 2001. (J). 14.14 (*0-606-22543-9*) Turtleback Bks.

Platt, Rickard. Castle Diary: The Journal of Tobias Burgess, Page. 1999. (Illus.). 64p. (J). (gr. 4-8). 21.99 (*0-7636-0489-5*) Candlewick Pr.

Rosen, Sidney & Rosen, Dorothy. The Magician's Apprentice. 1993. (J). (gr. 4-7). lib. bdg. 19.95 (*0-87614-809-7*, Carolrhoda Bks.) Lerner Publishing Group.

Sauerwein, Leigh. A Song for Eloise. 2003. (YA). 15.95 (*1-886910-90-1*, Front Street) Front Street, Inc.

Scarry, Huck. Looking into the Middle Ages. 1985. (Illus.). 12p. (J). (gr. 2 up). 12.50 (*0-06-025224-3*) HarperCollins Children's Bk. Group.

Scott, Deborah. The Kid Who Got Zapped Through Time. (J). (gr. 3-7). 1998. pap. 3.99 o.p. (*0-380-72850-8*); 1997. 160p. 14.00 (*0-380-97356-1*) Morrow/Avon. (Avon Bks.).

Sherman, Josepha. Windleaf. 1993. 128p. (YA). (gr. 7 up). 14.95 (*0-8027-8259-0*) Walker & Co.

Skurzynski, Gloria. Spider's Voice. 1999. (Illus.). 144p. (YA). (gr. 7 up). 16.95 (*0-689-82149-2*, Atheneum) Simon & Schuster Children's Publishing.

Springer, Nancy. Lionclaw: A Tale of Rowan Hood. 2002. 160p. (J). (gr. 4-7). 16.99 (*0-399-23716-X*, G. P. Putnam's Sons) Penguin Putnam Bks. for Young Readers.

—Rowan Hood. 2002. 176p. (J). pap. 5.99 (*0-698-11972-X*, PaperStar) Penguin Putnam Bks. for Young Readers.

—Rowan Hood, Outlaw Girl of Sherwood Forest. 2001. (Illus.). 170p. (J). (gr. 5-10). 16.99 (*0-399-23368-7*, G. P. Putnam's Sons) Penguin Putnam Bks. for Young Readers.

Strauss, Victoria. The Lady of Rhuddesmere. 1982. 240p. (J). (gr. 7 up). 8.95 o.p. (*0-7232-6210-1*, Warne, Frederick) Penguin Putnam Bks. for Young Readers.

Temple, Frances. The Ramsay Scallop. 1994. 320p. (J). (gr. 7 up). pap. 18.95 (*0-531-06836-6*); lib. bdg. 19.99 (*0-531-08686-0*) Scholastic, Inc. (Orchard Bks.).

Tomlinson, Theresa. Child of the May. 1998. (YA). (gr. 5 up). 120p. mass mkt. 16.99 o.p. (*0-531-33118-0*); (Illus.). 128p. pap. 15.95 (*0-531-30118-4*) Scholastic, Inc. (Orchard Bks.).

Waite, Michael P. Sylvester the Jester. 1992. 32p. (J). (ps-3). pap. 9.99 (*0-7814-0033-3*) Cook Communications Ministries.

Warkentin, Karla. Mystery in Medieval Castle. 2004. (J). pap. 7.99 (*0-7814-4025-4*) Cook Communications Ministries.

Williams, Laura. The Executioner's Daughter, ERS. 2000. 134p. (YA). (gr. 5-8). 16.95 (*0-8050-6234-3*, Holt, Henry & Co. Bks. For Young Readers) Holt, Henry & Co.

Yolen, Jane. Sword of the Rightful King: A Novel of King Arthur. 2003. (Illus.). 368p. (J). 17.00 (*0-15-202527-8*) Harcourt Children's Bks.

MOGUL EMPIRE—FICTION

Lasky, Kathryn. Jahanara: Princess of Princesses. 2002. (Royal Diaries Ser.). 192p. (J). (gr. 4-8). 10.95 (*0-439-22350-4*, Scholastic Pr.) Scholastic, Inc.

N

NEBRASKA—HISTORY—FICTION

Blanc, Esther Silverstein & Eagle, Godeane. Long Johns for a Small Chicken. 2003. (J). 16.95 (*1-884244-23-8*) Volcano Pr.

Figley, Marty Rhodes. The Schoolchildren's Blizzard. 2004. (On My Own History Ser.). (J). pap. 5.95 (*1-57505-619-4*, Carolrhoda Bks.) Lerner Publishing Group.

Gray, Dianne E. Together Apart. 2002. 208p. (J). (gr. 5-9). tchr. ed. 16.00 (*0-618-18721-9*) Houghton Mifflin Co.

Hoffman, Emily Allen. A Friend of the Enemy. 2003. 108p. (J). pap. 7.95 (*1-57249-312-7*, WM Kids) White Mane Publishing Co., Inc.

Hopkinson, Deborah. Pioneer Summer. 2002. (Prairie Skies Trilogy: No. 1). (Illus.). 80p. (J). (gr. 1-3). lib. bdg. 11.89 (*0-689-84350-X*, Aladdin Library) Simon & Schuster Children's Publishing.

LaFaye, A. Worth. 2004. (J). (*0-689-85730-6*, Simon & Schuster Children's Publishing) Simon & Schuster Children's Publishing.

Levinson, Nancy. Prairie Friends. 2003. (I Can Read Book Ser.). (Illus.). 64p. (J). (gr. 2-4). 15.99 (*0-06-028001-8*) HarperCollins Pubs.

NEW ORLEANS (LA.), BATTLE OF, 1815—FICTION

Robinet, Harriette Gillem. The Twins, the Pirates & the Battle of New Orleans. 1997. 144p. (J). (gr. 3-7). 15.00 o.s.i (*0-689-81208-6*, Atheneum) Simon & Schuster Children's Publishing.

Sargent, Dave & Sargent, Pat. Snow (white) Be Truthful #53. 2001. (Saddle Up Ser.). 36p. (J). pap. 6.95 (*1-56763-624-1*); lib. bdg. 22.60 (*1-56763-623-3*) Ozark Publishing.

NEW YORK (N.Y.)—HISTORY—FICTION

Avi. The Mayor of Central Park. 2003. (Illus.). 208p. (J). (gr. 3-6). 15.99 (*0-06-000682-X*); lib. bdg. 16.89 (*0-06-051556-2*) HarperCollins Pubs.

Collier, James Lincoln. Chipper. 2001. (Illus.). 144p. (J). (gr. 5-9). 14.95 (*0-7614-5084-X*, Cavendish Children's Bks.) Cavendish, Marshall Corp.

Constiner, Merle. Sumatra Alley. 1971. (J). (gr. 6 up). 6.95 o.p. (*0-525-66126-3*, Dutton Children's Bks.) Penguin Putnam Bks. for Young Readers.

Holland, Isabelle. Behind the Lines. (Point Ser.). (gr. 7 up). 1997. 208p. (J). mass mkt. 4.50 (*0-590-45114-6*); 1994. (Illus.). 240p. (YA). pap. 13.95 (*0-590-45113-8*) Scholastic, Inc.

—Behind the Lines. 1997. (Point Ser.). 10.55 (*0-606-11104-2*) Turtleback Bks.

Hurwitz, Johanna. Dear Emma. 2002. (Illus.). 160p. (J). 15.99 (*0-06-029840-5*) HarperCollins Children's Bk. Group.

Killcoyne, Hope L. The Lost Village of Central Park. 1999. (Mysteries in Time Ser.: Vol. 9). (Illus.). 89p. (J). (gr. 3-7). lib. bdg. 14.95 (*1-893110-02-8*) Silver Moon Pr.

Lasky, Kathryn. Hope in My Heart: Sofia's Immigrant Diary, Bk. 1. 2003. (My America Ser.). 112p. (J). pap. 12.95 (*0-439-18875-X*) Scholastic, Inc.

Levine, Beth Seidel. When Christmas Comes Again: The World War I Diary of Simone Spencer. 2002. (Dear America Ser.). (Illus.). 112p. (J). (gr. 4-9). pap. 10.95 (*0-439-43982-5*, Scholastic Pr.) Scholastic, Inc.

Moskin, Marietta. Adam & the Wishing Charm. 1977. (Illus.). (J). (gr. 3-5). 5.95 o.p. (*0-698-20404-2*) Putnam Publishing Group, The.

—Day of the Blizzard. 1978. (Illus.). (J). (gr. 3-7). 7.95 o.p. (*0-698-20468-9*) Putnam Publishing Group, The.

Nixon, Joan Lowery. Land of Hope. l.t. ed. 2001. (Ellis Island Stories Ser.). 171p. (J). (gr. 4 up). lib. bdg. 22.60 (*0-8368-2811-9*) Stevens, Gareth Inc.

Osborne, Mary Pope, et al. A Time to Dance: Virginia's Civil War Diary, Bk. 3. 2003. (My America Ser.). 112p. (J). pap. 12.95 (*0-439-44341-5*); mass mkt. 4.99 (*0-439-44343-1*) Scholastic, Inc.

Pfeffer, Susan Beth & Alcott, Louisa May. Beth's Story. 1997. (Portraits of Little Women Ser.). 112p. (gr. 3-7). text 9.95 o.s.i (*0-385-32526-6*, Delacorte Pr.) Dell Publishing.

Stevens, Carla. Anna, Grandpa & the Big Storm. 1982. (Illus.). 48p. (J). (gr. 6-9). 13.95 o.p. (*0-89919-066-9*, Clarion Bks.) Houghton Mifflin Co. Trade & Reference Div.

—Anna, Grandpa & the Big Storm. 1982. (Young Puffin Read Alone Ser). (J). 9.19 o.p. (*0-606-02802-1*) Turtleback Bks.

—Anna, Grandpa, & the Big Storm. 1998. (Puffin Chapters for Readers on the Move Ser.). (Illus.). 64p. (J). (gr. 2-5). pap. 4.99 (*0-14-130083-3*, Puffin Bks.) Penguin Putnam Bks. for Young Readers.

—Anna, Grandpa, & the Big Storm. 1998. (Illus.). (J). 11.14 (*0-606-21777-0*) Turtleback Bks.

Travis, L. Thief from Five Points. 1995. (Ben & Zack Ser.: Bk. 2). 168p. (J). (gr. 3-8). pap. 5.99 o.p. (*0-8010-8916-6*) Baker Bks.

NEW YORK (STATE)—HISTORY—FICTION

Cohen, Nancy Lipson. Exploring Orange: Adventures in Orange County, New York. 2000. (Illus.). 62p. (J). (gr. 3-6). pap. 9.99 (*0-88092-556-6*) Royal Fireworks Publishing Co.

Donnelly, Jennifer. A Northern Light. 2003. (Illus.). 400p. (YA). (gr. 7-12). 17.00 (*0-15-216705-6*) Harcourt Children's Bks.

—A Northern Light. unabr. ed. 2003. (J). (gr. 7). audio 30.00 (*0-8072-0895-7*, Listening Library) Random Hse. Audio Publishing Group.

Giff, Patricia Reilly. Columbus Circle. 1988. (Orig.). (J). (gr. k-6). pap. 2.75 o.s.i (*0-440-40036-8*, Yearling) Random Hse. Children's Bks.

Goodman, Joan Elizabeth. Hope's Crossing. 1998. (Illus.). 224p. (J). (gr. 4-6). tchr. ed. 16.00 (*0-395-86195-0*) Houghton Mifflin Co.

—Hope's Crossing. 1999. (Illus.). 160p. (J). (gr. 3-7). pap. 5.99 (*0-698-11807-3*, Puffin Bks.) Penguin Putnam Bks. for Young Readers.

—Hope's Crossing. 1999. 12.04 (*0-606-19068-6*) Turtleback Bks.

Kirkpatrick, Katherine. Redcoats & Petticoats. 1999. (Illus.). 32p. (J). (gr. 1-5). tchr. ed. 15.95 (*0-8234-1416-7*) Holiday Hse., Inc.

Kohl, Susan. The Ghost of Gracie Mansion. 1999. (Mysteries in Time Ser.: Vol. 8). (Illus.). 96p. (J). (gr. 3-7). lib. bdg. 14.95 (*1-893110-04-4*) Silver Moon Pr.

Lonergan, Carroll V. Brave Boys of Old Fort Ticonderoga. 1987. (YA). (gr. 6 up). 192p. o.p. (*0-932334-57-1*); 144p. pap. 7.95 (*1-55787-018-7*, NY16028) Heart of the Lakes Publishing. (Empire State Bks.).

Quackenbush, Robert M. Daughter of Liberty: A True Story of the American Revolution. 1999. 64p. (J). (gr. 2-4). lib. bdg. 15.49 (*0-7868-2355-0*) Hyperion Pr.

Rizzo, Kay D. & Ferree, Dennis. The Not-So-Secret Mission. 2003. 96p. (J). (*0-8163-1966-9*) Pacific Pr. Publishing Assn.

Sterman, Betsy. Saratoga Secret. 1998. 176p. (YA). (gr. 5-9). 16.99 (*0-8037-2332-6*, Dial Bks. for Young Readers) Penguin Putnam Bks. for Young Readers.

Watts, Leander. Stonecutter. 2002. (Illus.). 224p. (J). (gr. 5-9). tchr. ed. 15.00 (*0-618-16474-X*) Houghton Mifflin Co.

NORWAY—HISTORY—FICTION

Bernhardsen, Christian. Fight in the Mountains. Sinding, Franey, tr. 1968. (J). (gr. 7 up). 4.50 o.p. (*0-15-227523-1*) Harcourt Children's Bks.

Emberley, Michael. Welcome Back, Sun. 1993. (J). (gr. 4 up). 14.95 o.p. (*0-316-23647-0*) Little Brown & Co.

Haugaard, Erik Christian. Hakon of Rogen's Saga, 001. 1963. (Illus.). (J). (gr. 7 up). 6.95 o.p. (*0-395-06803-7*) Houghton Mifflin Co.

Hopkins, Andrea. Harald the Ruthless: The Saga of the Last Viking, ERS. 1996. (Illus.). 64p. (YA). (gr. 7 up). 16.95 o.p. (*0-8050-3176-6*, Holt, Henry & Co. Bks. For Young Readers) Holt, Henry & Co.

Senje, Sigurd. Escape! Ramsden, Evelyn, tr. 1966. (YA). (gr. 7 up). pap. 1.25 o.p. (*0-15-629041-3*, Voyager Bks./Libros Viajeros) Harcourt Children's Bks.

Vestly, Anne-Catherine. Hello, Aurora. Amos, Eileen, tr. from NOR. 1974. (Illus.). 96p. (J). (gr. 3-6). 7.95 (*0-690-00513-X*) HarperCollins Children's Bk. Group.

O

OHIO—HISTORY—FICTION

Fradin, Dennis Brindell. Ohio: In Words & Pictures. 1977. (Young People's Stories of Our States Ser.). (Illus.). 48p. (J). (gr. 2-5). pap. 4.95 o.p. (*0-516-43935-9*); mass mkt. 17.27 o.p. (*0-516-03935-0*) Scholastic Library Publishing. (Children's Pr.).

Kallevig, Christine P. Carry Me Home Cuyahoga: A Historical Novel. 1996. (Illus.). 112p. (J). (gr. 4-6). 16.95 (*0-9628769-8-4*); pap. 9.95 (*0-9628769-7-6*) Storytime Ink International.

Marsh, Carole. Ohio Government! The Cornerstone of Everyday Life in Our State! 1996. (Carole Marsh Ohio Bks.). (Illus.). (J). (gr. 3-12). pap. 19.95 (*0-7933-6287-3*); cd-rom 29.95 (*0-7933-6288-1*) Gallopade International.

Sanders, Scott Russell. Aurora Means Dawn. (Illus.). 32p. (J). (gr. k-3). 1998. pap. 5.99 (*0-689-81907-2*, Aladdin); 1989. 16.00 (*0-02-778270-0*, Atheneum) Simon & Schuster Children's Publishing.

OKLAHOMA—HISTORY—FICTION

Antle, Nancy. Beautiful Land: A Story of the Oklahoma Land Rush. 1994. (Once upon America Ser.). (Illus.). 64p. (J). (gr. 2-6). 12.99 o.p. (*0-670-85304-6*, Viking Children's Bks.) Penguin Putnam Bks. for Young Readers.

Griffis, Molly Levite. The Feester Filibuster. 2002. (Illus.). vi, 236p. (J). 18.95 (*1-57168-693-2*, Eakin Pr.) Eakin Pr.

Keith, Harold. The Obstinate Land: Cherokee Strip Run of 1893. 2nd ed. 1993. 214p. (J). (gr. 4 up). reprint ed. pap. 12.95 o.p. (*0-927562-15-4*) Levite of Apache Publishing.

Kirschstein, Carolyn V. Hooray for Oklahoma Eighteen Eighty-Nine. 1989. (Illus.). 72p. (J). (gr. k-4). 9.95 (*0-926521-00-4*) B.C. Publishing, Inc.

McCaughrean, Geraldine. Stop the Train. 2003. 304p. (J). (gr. 5 up). 16.99 (*0-06-050749-7*); lib. bdg. 17.89 (*0-06-050750-0*) HarperCollins Pubs.

Myers, Anna. Tulsa Burning. 2002. (Illus.). 184p. (J). (gr. 3-7). 16.95 (*0-8027-8829-7*) Walker & Co.

Thomas, Joyce Carol. I Have Heard of a Land. (Trophy Picture Book Ser.). (Illus.). 32p. (J). 2000. (gr. k-3). pap. 5.99 (*0-06-443617-9*, Harper Trophy); 1998. (gr. 2-6). 15.95 (*0-06-023477-6*, Cotler, Joanna Bks.); 1998. (gr. 3 up). lib. bdg. 14.89 (*0-06-023478-4*, Cotler, Joanna Bks.) HarperCollins Children's Bk. Group.

—I Have Heard of a Land. 1998. 12.10 (*0-606-17563-6*) Turtleback Bks.

Vogt, Esther Loewen. A Race for Land. 1992. 112p. (J). (gr. 4-7). pap. 5.99 o.p. (*0-8361-3575-X*) Herald Pr.

OREGON NATIONAL HISTORIC TRAIL—FICTION

Arntson, Herbert E. Caravan to Oregon. 1957. (Illus.). (J). (gr. 7-11). 8.95 o.p. (*0-8323-0164-7*) Binford & Mort Publishing.

Bly, Stephen A. The Buffalo's Last Stand. 2002. (Retta Barre's Oregon Trail Ser.: 2). 111p. (J). pap. 5.99 (*1-58134-392-2*) Crossway Bks.

—The Lost Wagon Train. 2002. (Retta Barre's Oregon Trail Ser.: Vol. 1). 110p. (J). pap. 5.99 (*1-58134-391-4*) Crossway Bks.

—The Plain Prairie Princess. 2002. (Retta Barre's Oregon Trail Ser.: 3). 108p. (J). pap. 5.99 (*1-58134-393-0*) Crossway Bks.

Carr, Mary J. Children of the Covered Wagon. rev. ed. 1957. (Illus.). (J). (gr. 3-7). o.p. (*0-690-18987-7*) HarperCollins Children's Bk. Group.

Gregory, Kristiana. Across the Wide & Lonesome Prairie: The Oregon Trail Diary of Hattie Campbell, 1847. 1997. (Dear America Ser.). Orig. Title: Prairie Dust. (Illus.). 128p. (YA). (gr. 4-9). pap. 10.95 (*0-590-22651-7*, 22651) Scholastic, Inc.

Kudlinski, Kathleen V. Facing West: A Story of the Oregon Trail. (Once upon America Ser.). (Illus.). 64p. (J). (gr. 2-6). 1996. pap. 5.99 (*0-14-036914-7*); 1994. 12.99 o.s.i (*0-670-85451-4*, Viking Children's Bks.) Penguin Putnam Bks. for Young Readers.

Kurtz, Jane. I'm Sorry, Almira Ann, ERS. 1999. (Illus.). 120p. (J). (gr. 4-7). 15.95 (*0-8050-6094-4*, Holt, Henry & Co. Bks. For Young Readers) Holt, Henry & Co.

Levine, Ellen. The Journal of Jedediah Barstow, an Emigrant on the Oregon Trail: Overland, 1845. 2002. (My Name Is America Ser.). (Illus.). 192p. (J). (gr. 4-9). 10.95 (*0-439-06310-8*, Scholastic Pr.) Scholastic, Inc.

Meader, Stephen W. Keep 'em Rolling. 1967. (Illus.). (J). (gr. 7 up). 4.95 o.p. (*0-15-242195-5*) Harcourt Children's Bks.

Mercati, Cynthia. Wagons Ho! A Diary of the Oregon Trail. 2000. (Cover-to-Cover Bks.). (Illus.). 56p. (J). 15.95 (*0-7807-9011-1*); pap. (*0-7891-5039-5*) Perfection Learning Corp.

Morrow, Honore. On to Oregon! 1991. (Illus.). 240p. (J). (gr. 5-9). reprint ed. pap. 6.99 (*0-688-10494-0*, Harper Trophy) HarperCollins Children's Bk. Group.

—On to Oregon! 1946. (Illus.). (J). (gr. 4-7). reprint ed. 16.00 o.p. (*0-688-21639-0*, Morrow, William & Co.) Morrow/Avon.

Plowhead, Ruth G. Lucretia Ann on the Oregon Trail. 1969. (Illus.). (J). (gr. 4-7). 4.50 o.p. (*0-87004-136-3*) Caxton Pr.

Plowhead, Ruth Gipson. Lucretia Ann on the Oregon Trail. 8th ed. 1997. (Classic Ser.). (Illus.). 250p. (J). (gr. 4-8). reprint ed. pap. 10.95 (*0-87004-360-9*, 036090) Caxton Pr.

—Lucretia Ann on the Sagebrush Plains. 2001. (Classic Ser.). (Illus.). 358p. (J). (gr. 4-7). pap. 18.95 (*0-87004-408-7*) Caxton Pr.

Schulte, Elaine L. Daniel Colton under Fire. 2001. (Illus.). 137p. (J). pap. 6.49 (*1-57924-564-1*) Jones, Bob Univ. Pr.

—Daniel Colton under Fire. 1992. (Colton Cousins Adventure Ser.: Vol. 2). 144p. pap. 5.99 o.p. (*0-310-54821-7*) Zondervan.

Spooner, Michael. Daniel's Walk. 2004. (J). pap. 6.95 (*0-8050-7543-7*); ERS. 2001. (Illus.). 224p. (YA). (gr. 7 up). 16.95 (*0-8050-6750-7*) Holt, Henry & Co. (Holt, Henry & Co. Bks. For Young Readers).

Stanley, Diane. Roughing It on the Oregon Trail. (Time-Traveling Twins Ser.: No. 1). (Illus.). 48p. (J). (gr. k-5). 2001. pap. 5.95 (*0-06-449006-8*, Harper Trophy); 2000. 15.95 (*0-06-027065-9*, Cotler, Joanna Bks.); 2000. lib. bdg. 15.89 (*0-06-027066-7*, Cotler, Joanna Bks.) HarperCollins Children's Bk. Group.

Stevens, Carla. Trouble for Lucy, 001. 1979. (Illus.). (J). (gr. 2-6). 13.95 o.p. (*0-395-28971-8*, Clarion Bks.) Houghton Mifflin Co. Trade & Reference Div.

—Trouble for Lucy. 1987. (J). 12.10 (*0-606-03667-9*) Turtleback Bks.

Van Leeuwen, Jean. Bound for Oregon. 1994. 176p. (YA). (gr. 4-7). 15.89 o.s.i (*0-8037-1527-7*); (Illus.). 14.99 o.s.i (*0-8037-1526-9*) Penguin Putnam Bks. for Young Readers. (Dial Bks. for Young Readers).

Wilson, Laura. How I Survived the Oregon Trail: The Journal of Jesse Adams. 1999. (Time Travellers Ser.). (Illus.). 38p. (J). (gr. 4-7). pap. 9.95 (*0-688-17276-8*) Morrow/Avon.

OVERLAND JOURNEYS TO THE PACIFIC—FICTION

Ackerman, Karen. Araminta's Paint Box. 1998. (Illus.). 32p. (J). (gr. 1-3). pap. 6.99 (*0-689-82091-7*, Aladdin) Simon & Schuster Children's Publishing.

—Araminta's Paint Box. 1998. 12.14 (*0-606-15439-6*) Turtleback Bks.

Baird, Janet H. Journey to the Edge of Nowhere. 132p. (J). (gr. 3-7). 2000. (Illus.). pap. 6.95 (*1-889658-15-4*); 1999. 11.95 (*1-889658-19-7*) New Canaan Publishing Co., Inc.

Bly, Stephen A. The Lost Wagon Train. 2002. (Retta Barre's Oregon Trail Ser.: Vol. 1). 110p. (J). pap. 5.99 (*1-58134-391-4*) Crossway Bks.

—The Plain Prairie Princess. 2002. (Retta Barre's Oregon Trail Ser.: 3). 108p. (J). pap. 5.99 (*1-58134-393-0*) Crossway Bks.

Carr, Mary J. Children of the Covered Wagon. rev. ed. 1957. (Illus.). (J). (gr. 3-7). o.p. (*0-690-18987-7*) HarperCollins Children's Bk. Group.

Coerr, Eleanor. The Josefina Story Quilt. 1986. (I Can Read Bks.). (Illus.). 64p. (J). (gr. k-3). 15.99 (*0-06-021348-5*); lib. bdg. 16.89 (*0-06-021349-3*) HarperCollins Children's Bk. Group.

Duey, Kathleen. Willow Chase: Kansas Territory, 1847. 1997. (American Diaries Ser.: No. 5). 144p. (J). (gr. 3-7). pap. 4.50 (*0-689-81355-4*, Aladdin) Simon & Schuster Children's Publishing.

—Willow Chase: Kansas Territory, 1847. 1997. (American Diaries Ser.: No. 5). (J). (gr. 3-7). 10.55 (*0-606-11036-4*) Turtleback Bks.

Fleischman, Sid. Mr. Mysterious & Company. 1972. (gr. 3-6). pap. 1.25 o.p. (*0-440-45883-8*) Dell Publishing.

—Mr. Mysterious & Company. 1997. (Illus.). 160p. (J). (gr. 3 up). 15.00 (*0-688-14921-9*); 15.00 (*0-688-14921-9*) HarperCollins Children's Bk. Group. (Greenwillow Bks.).

—Mr. Mysterious & Company. 1962. (Illus.). (J). (gr. 4-6). 14.95 o.s.i (*0-316-28578-1*, Joy Street Bks.) Little Brown & Co.

Frazier, Neta L. Stout-Hearted Seven. 1973. (J). (gr. 4-6). 5.95 o.p. (0-15-281450-7) Harcourt Children's Bks.

Gerrard, Roy. Wagons West!, RS. 32p. (J). (ps-3). 2000. (Illus.). pap. 5.95 (0-374-48210-1, Sunburst); 1996. 15.00 (0-374-38249-2, Farrar, Straus & Giroux (BYR)) Farrar, Straus & Giroux.

—Wagons West! 2000. (Illus.). (J). 12.10 (0-606-20401-6) Turtleback Bks.

Gilson, Jamie. Wagon Train 911. 1996. 160p. (J). (gr. 3 up). 15.00 o.p. (0-688-14550-7) HarperCollins Children's Bk. Group.

Graham, Christine. When Pioneer Wagons Rumbled West. 1998. (Illus.). 32p. (J). (ps-3). 14.95 (1-57345-272-6, Shadow Mountain) Deseret Bk. Co.

Gregory, Kristiana. Across the Wide & Lonesome Prairie: The Oregon Trail Diary of Hattie Campbell, 1847. 1997. (Dear America Ser.). Orig. Title: Prairie Dust. (Illus.). 128p. (YA). (gr. 4-9). pap. 10.95 (0-590-22651-7, 22651) Scholastic, Inc.

Hays, Wilma P. For Ma & Pa: On the Oregon Trail 1844. 1972. (Illus.). 64p. (J). (gr. 3-6). 4.49 o.p. (0-698-30425-X) Putnam Publishing Group, The.

Hermes, Patricia. Westward to Home: Joshua's Oregon Trail Diary, Bk. 1. 2001. (My America Ser.). (Illus.). 112p. (J). (gr. 4-8). pap. 10.95 (0-439-11209-5) Scholastic, Inc.

Karr, Kathleen. Go West, Young Women!, No. 1. 1996. (Petticoat Party Ser.: Vol. 1). 208p. (gr. 5 up). (J). lib. bdg. 14.89 o.p. (0-06-027152-3); (YA). 14.95 o.p. (0-06-027151-5) HarperCollins Children's Bk. Group.

Kimmel, Elizabeth Cody. West on the Wagon Train. 2003. (Adventures of Young Buffalo Bill Ser.). (Illus.). 160p. (J). 15.99 (0-06-029113-3); lib. bdg. 16.89 (0-06-029114-1) HarperCollins Pubs.

Kudlinski, Kathleen V. Facing West: A Story of the Oregon Trail. (Once upon America Ser.). (Illus.). 64p. (J). (gr. 2-6). 1996. pap. 5.99 (0-14-036914-7); 1994. 12.99 o.s.i (0-670-85451-4, Viking Children's Bks.) Penguin Putnam Bks. for Young Readers.

Kurtz, Jane. I'm Sorry, Almira Ann, ERS. 1999. (Illus.). 120p. (J). (gr. 4-7). 15.95 (0-8050-6094-4, Holt, Henry & Co. Bks. For Young Readers) Holt, Henry & Co.

Levine, Ellen. The Journal of Jedediah Barstow, an Emigrant on the Oregon Trail: Overland, 1845. 2002. (My Name Is America Ser.). (Illus.). 192p. (J). (gr. 4-9). 10.95 (0-439-06310-8, Scholastic Pr.) Scholastic, Inc.

Levitin, Sonia. Clem's Chances. 2001. (Illus.). 208p. (J). (gr. 2-7). pap. 17.95 (0-439-29314-6, Orchard Bks.) Scholastic, Inc.

McDonald, Megan, et al. All the Stars in the Sky: The Santa Fe Trail Diary of Florrie Ryder. 2003. (Dear America Ser.). 192p. (J). pap. 10.95 (0-439-16963-1) Scholastic, Inc.

Meader, Stephen W. Keep 'em Rolling. 1967. (Illus.). (J). (gr. 7 up). 4.95 o.p. (0-15-242195-5) Harcourt Children's Bks.

Mercati, Cynthia. Wagons Ho! A Diary of the Oregon Trail. 2000. (Cover-to-Cover Bks.). (Illus.). 56p. (J). 15.95 (0-7807-9011-1); pap. (0-7891-5039-5) Perfection Learning Corp.

Morris, Neil. Wagon Wheels Roll West. 1989. (Tales of the Old West Ser.). (Illus.). 32p. (J). (gr. 3-8). lib. bdg. 9.95 o.p. (1-85435-167-2) Cavendish, Marshall Corp.

Paulsen, Gary. Mr. Tucket. 1994. 176p. text 15.95 (0-385-31169-9, Delacorte Pr.) Dell Publishing.

—Mr. Tucket. 2000. (Illus.). 192p. (gr. 5-7). mass mkt. 2.99 o.s.i (0-375-80680-6, Random Hse. Bks. for Young Readers); 1996. (J). pap. 5.99 (0-440-91097-8, Dell Books for Young Readers); 1995. (Tucket Adventures Ser.: Vol. 1). 192p. (gr. 5 up). pap. text 4.99 (0-440-41133-5, Yearling); 1995. (J). pap. 5.99 (0-440-91053-6, Dell Books for Young Readers) Random Hse. Children's Bks.

—Mr. Tucket, unabr. ed. 1994. (J). (gr. 6). audio 27.00 (0-7887-0010-3, 94209E7) Recorded Bks., LLC.

—Mr. Tucket. 1995. 10.55 (0-606-07895-9) Turtleback Bks.

Philbrick, Rodman. The Journal of Douglas Allen Deeds: The Donner Party Expedition, 1846. 2001. (My Name Is America Ser.). (Illus.). 224p. (J). (gr. 4-9). pap. 10.95 (0-439-21600-1) Scholastic, Inc.

Ray, Mary Lyn. Alvah & Arvilla. 1994. (Illus.). 32p. (J). (ps-3). 14.95 (0-15-202655-X) Harcourt Children's Bks.

Rizzo, Kay D. Wagon Train West. 2003. 96p. (J). (0-8163-1986-3) Pacific Pr. Publishing Assn.

Sargent, Dave & Sargent, Pat. Dizzy (claybank) Have Courage #22. 2001. 36p. (J). pap. 6.95 (1-56763-680-2); lib. bdg. 22.60 (1-56763-679-9) Ozark Publishing.

Schulte, Elaine L. Daniel Colton under Fire. 2001. (Illus.). 137p. (J). pap. 6.49 (1-57924-564-1) Jones, Bob Univ. Pr.

—Daniel Colton under Fire. 1992. (Colton Cousins Adventure Ser.: Vol. 2). 144p. pap. 5.99 o.p. (0-310-54821-7) Zondervan.

—Suzannah Strikes Gold. 2001. (Illus.). 144p. (J). pap. 6.49 (1-57924-565-X) Jones, Bob Univ. Pr.

—Suzannah Strikes Gold. 1992. (Colton Cousins Adventure Ser.: Vol. 3). 144p. (J). pap. 5.99 o.p. (0-310-54611-7) Zondervan.

Spooner, Michael. Daniel's Walk. 2004. (J). pap. 6.95 (0-8050-7543-7); ERS. 2001. (Illus.). 224p. (YA). (gr. 7 up). 16.95 (0-8050-6750-7) Holt, Henry & Co. (Holt, Henry & Co. Bks. For Young Readers).

Stanley, Diane. Roughing It on the Oregon Trail. (Time-Traveling Twins Ser.: No. 1). (Illus.). 48p. (J). (gr. k-5). 2001. pap. 5.95 (0-06-449006-8, Harper Trophy); 2000. 15.95 (0-06-027065-9, Cotler, Joanna Bks.); 2000. lib. bdg. 15.89 (0-06-027066-7, Cotler, Joanna Bks.) HarperCollins Children's Bk. Group.

Taylor, Theodore. Walking up a Rainbow: Being the True Version of the Long & Hazardous Journey of Susan D. Carlisle, Mrs. Myrtle Dessery, Drover Bert Pettit & Cowboy Clay Carmer & Others. abr. ed. 1994. 276p. (YA). (gr. 7 up). 14.95 o.s.i (0-15-294512-1) Harcourt Trade Pubs.

Thompson, Gare. Our Journey West. 2003. (I Am American Ser.). (Illus.). 40p. (J). pap. 6.99 (0-7922-5178-4) National Geographic Society.

Turner, Ann Warren. Mississippi Mud: 3 Prairie Journals. 1997. (Illus.). 48p. (J). (gr. 2-5). 16.95 (0-06-024432-1); lib. bdg. 16.89 o.p. (0-06-024433-X) HarperCollins Children's Bk. Group.

—Red Flower Goes West. 1999. (Illus.). 32p. (J). (gr. k-4). lib. bdg. 15.49 (0-7868-2253-8) Disney Pr.

—Red Flower Goes West. Date not set. (Illus.). 32p. (J). pap. 15.49 (0-7868-1177-3) Hyperion Bks. for Children.

—Red Flower Goes West: Book Club Edition. 1999. 32p. (J). pap. 14.99 (0-7868-0575-7) Disney Pr.

Van Leeuwen, Jean. Bound for Oregon. 1994. 176p. (YA). (gr. 4-7). 15.89 o.s.i (0-8037-1527-7); (Illus.). 14.99 o.s.i (0-8037-1526-9) Penguin Putnam Bks. for Young Readers. (Dial Bks. for Young Readers).

—Going West. 1997. (Picture Puffin Bks.). (Illus.). 48p. (J). (gr. k-3). pap. 5.99 (0-14-056096-3) Penguin Putnam Bks. for Young Readers.

Verla, Kay. Covered Wagons, Bumpy Trails. 2000. (Illus.). 32p. (J). (ps-3). 15.99 (0-399-22928-0, G. P. Putnam's Sons) Penguin Group (USA) Inc.

Wilson, Laura. How I Survived the Oregon Trail: The Journal of Jesse Adams. 1999. (Time Travellers Ser.). (Illus.). 38p. (J). (gr. 4-7). pap. 9.95 (0-688-17276-8) Morrow/Avon.

Woodruff, Elvira. Dear Levi: Letters from the Overland Trail. 1994. (Illus.). (J). (gr. 3-7). 15.00 o.s.i (0-679-84641-7); 119p. (gr. 4-7). 16.99 o.s.i (0-679-94641-1) Random Hse. Children's Bks. (Knopf Bks. for Young Readers).

P

PARIS (FRANCE)—HISTORY—FICTION

Bollinger, Marilyn. The Hunchback of Notre Dame: Quasimodo Finds a Friend. 1996. (Magic Touch Talking Bks.). (Illus.). 22p. (J). (ps-2). 19.99 (1-888208-16-3) Hasbro, Inc.

Carr, Jan. The Hunchback of Notre Dame: Upside Down & Topsy-Turvy. 1996. (Illus.). 24p. (J). (gr. k-3). 12.89 o.p. (0-7868-5040-X); 12.95 o.p. (0-7868-3090-5) Disney Pr.

Cuddy, Robbin, illus. The Hunchback of Notre Dame Illustrated Classic. 1996. 96p. (J). 14.95 (0-7868-3089-1) Disney Pr.

Dickens, Charles. A Tale of Two Cities. 1995. (Longman Classics Ser.). (Illus.). (J). pap. text 7.87 o.p. (0-582-03047-1, TG7550) Addison-Wesley Longman, Inc.

Disney Staff. The Hunchback of Notre Dame: The Hidden Hero. 1997. (Disney's "Storytime Treasures" Library: Vol. 16). (Illus.). 44p. (J). (gr. 1-6). 3.49 o.p. (1-57973-012-4) Advance Pubs. LLC.

Fontes, Justine. The Hunchback of Notre Dame: Big Golden Book. 1996. (Illus.). 24p. (J). (ps-3). o.p. (0-307-10378-1, Golden Bks.) Random Hse. Children's Bks.

Friedman, Michael Jan. Hunchdog of Notre Dame. 1997. (Adventures of Wishbone Ser.: No. 5). (Illus.). 144p. (J). (gr. 2-5). mass mkt. 3.99 o.p. (1-57064-270-2, Big Red Chair Bks.) Lyrick Publishing.

Golden Books Staff. The Hunchback of Notre Dame. 1999. (Song Book & Tape Ser.). (J). (ps-3). pap. 6.98 o.p. incl. audio (0-307-47720-7, Golden Bks.) Random Hse. Children's Bks.

Harchy, Philippe, illus. The Hunchback of Notre Dame Pop-up Book. 1996. 12p. (J). (gr. k-3). 12.95 o.p. (0-7868-3091-3) Disney Pr.

Hugo, Victor. The Hunchback of Notre-Dame. 2000. (Giant Courage Classics Ser.). 704p. (YA). 9.00 o.p. (0-7624-0563-5, Courage Bks.) Running Pr. Bk. Pubs.

—The Hunchback of Notre Dame. 1968. (Airmont Classics Ser.). (YA). (gr. 11 up). mass mkt. 2.25 (0-8049-0162-7, CL-162) Airmont Publishing Co., Inc.

—The Hunchback of Notre Dame. 1998. (Illustrated Classic Book Ser.). (Illus.). 61p. (J). (gr. 3 up). pap. text 4.95 (1-56767-247-7) Educational Insights, Inc.

—The Hunchback of Notre Dame. (Young Collector's Illustrated Classics Ser.). (Illus.). 192p. (J). (gr. 3-7). 9.95 (1-56156-458-3) Kidsbooks, Inc.

—The Hunchback of Notre Dame. Hanft, Joshua, ed. 1994. (Great Illustrated Classics Ser.: Vol. 36). (Illus.). 240p. (J). (gr. 3-6). 9.95 (0-86611-987-6) Playmore, Inc., Pubs.

—The Hunchback of Notre Dame. 1987. (Regents Illustrated Classics Ser.). 62p. (YA). (gr. 7-12). pap. text 3.75 o.p. (0-13-448085-6, 20519) Prentice Hall, ESL Dept.

—The Hunchback of Notre Dame. (Short Classics Ser.). (Illus.). 48p. (J). (gr. 4 up). 1983. pap. 9.27 o.p. (0-8172-2010-0); 1981. lib. bdg. 24.26 o.p. (0-8172-1671-5) Raintree Pubs.

—The Hunchback of Notre Dame. 1995. (Illus.). 416p. (J). 12.99 o.s.i (0-517-12375-4) Random Hse. Value Publishing.

—The Hunchback of Notre Dame. 1995. (Step into Classics Ser.). 112p. (J). (gr. 3-5). pap. 3.99 (0-679-87429-1) Random Hse., Inc.

—The Hunchback of Notre Dame. (gr. k-3). 1997. (Illus.). 40p. (J). pap. 15.95 (0-531-30055-2, Orchard Bks.); 1996. (YA). mass mkt. 4.50 (0-590-93808-8, Scholastic Paperbacks) Scholastic, Inc.

—The Hunchback of Notre Dame. 1996. 112p. (J). (gr. 4-7). per. 4.50 (0-689-81027-X, Aladdin) Simon & Schuster Children's Publishing.

—Hunchback of Notre Dame. 2002. (Great Illustrated Classics). (Illus.). 240p. (J). (gr. 3-8). lib. bdg. 21.35 (1-57765-813-2, ABDO & Daughters) ABDO Publishing Co.

—The Hunchback of Notre Dame. unabr. ed. 1998. (Wordsworth Classics Ser.). (YA). (gr. 6-12). 5.27 (0-89061-068-1, R0681WW) Jamestown.

—The Hunchback of Notre Dame. abr. ed. 2001. (YA). (gr. 5-12). audio 16.95 (1-56994-529-2) Monterey Media, Inc.

—The Hunchback of Notre Dame. abr. ed. 1996. (J). 12.98 o.p. (0-7871-1081-7); (gr. 4-7). audio 6.95 o.p. (0-7871-0992-4, 628697) NewStar Media, Inc.

—The Hunchback of Notre Dame. abr. ed. 1997. (Puffin Classics Ser.). (Illus.). 320p. (YA). (gr. 5-9). pap. 4.99 (0-14-038253-4) Penguin Putnam Bks. for Young Readers.

—The Hunchback of Notre Dame. abr. ed. 1996. 288p. (YA). mass mkt. 4.50 o.s.i (0-440-22675-9, Dell Books for Young Readers) Random Hse. Children's Bks.

—The Hunchback of Notre Dame Readalong. 1994. (Illustrated Classics Collection). 64p. pap. 14.95 incl. audio (0-7854-0683-2, 40399); pap. 13.50 o.p. incl. audio (1-56103-487-8) American Guidance Service, Inc.

Hugo, Victor, et al. The Hunchback of Notre Dame. 1997. (Eyewitness Classics Ser.). (Illus.). 64p. (J). (gr. 3-6). pap. 14.95 o.p. (0-7894-1491-0) Dorling Kindersley Publishing, Inc.

The Hunchback of Notre Dame. 1996. 96p. pap. 14.95 (0-7935-6655-X) Leonard, Hal Corp.

The Hunchback of Notre Dame. 1991. (Short Classics Ser.). 48p. (J). pap. 34.00 (0-8114-6963-8) Raintree Pubs.

The Hunchback of Notre Dame. (Read-Along Ser.). (J). 7.99 incl. audio (1-55723-992-4); 7.99 incl. audio (1-55723-992-4); 1996. audio 11.99 (1-55723-987-8) Walt Disney Records.

The Hunchback of Notre Dame Read-Along. 1996. (J). (1-55723-993-2) Walt Disney Records.

Ingoglia, Gina. The Hunchback of Notre Dame. 1996. (Illus.). 96p. (J). lib. bdg. 15.49 (0-7868-5034-5) Disney Pr.

—The Hunchback of Notre Dame Junior Novelization. 1996. 96p. (J). (gr. 2-6). pap. 3.95 o.p. (0-7868-4062-5) Disney Pr.

Knight, Joan. Charlotte Goes to Paris. 2003. (Illus.). 52p. (J). 16.95 (0-8118-3766-1) Chronicle Bks. LLC.

Lamensdorf, Len. The Raging Dragon. 2000. (Will to Conquer Ser.: Vol. 2). 350p. (YA). (gr. 5-12). 22.95 (0-9669741-7-4) SeaScape Pr., Ltd.

McAlpine, Gordon. Mystery Box. 2003. 194p. (YA). 16.95 (0-8126-2680-X) Cricket Bks.

Mouse Works Staff. The Hunchback of Notre Dame. 1996. (J). 5.98 o.p. (1-57082-279-4); 8p. 5.98 o.p. (1-57082-273-5) Mouse Works.

Robertson, Barbara. Rosemary in Paris: Back to 1889. 2001. (Hourglass Adventures Ser.: Bk. 2). (Illus.). 121p. (J). (gr. 4-7). pap. 4.95 (1-890817-56-2) Winslow Pr.

Sohl, Marcia & Dackerman, Gerald. The Hunchback of Notre Dame: Student Activity Book. 1976. (Now Age Illustrated Ser.). (Illus.). (J). (gr. 4-10). stu. ed. 1.25 (0-88301-189-1) Pendulum Pr., Inc.

Van Gool Studio Staff, illus. The Hunchback of Notre Dame. 1995. (Classic Ser.). 64p. (J). (ps-1). 4.98 o.p. (0-8317-1653-3) Smithmark Pubs., Inc.

Weingartner, Amy. The Hunchback of Notre Dame. 1996. (Illus.). 48p. pap. text 4.95 o.p. (0-7851-0225-6) Marvel Enterprises.

PEARL HARBOR (HAWAII), ATTACK ON, 1941—FICTION

Denenberg, Barry. Early Sunday Morning: The Pearl Harbor Diary of Amber Billows, Hawaii, 1941. 2001. (Dear America Ser.). (Illus.). 192p. (J). (gr. 4-9). pap. 10.95 (0-439-32874-8) Scholastic, Inc.

Duey, Kathleen. Janey G. Blue: Pearl Harbor 1941. 2001. (American Diaries Ser.: No. 18). (Illus.). 144p. (J). (gr. 3-7). pap. 4.99 (0-689-84404-2, Aladdin) Simon & Schuster Children's Publishing.

Early Sunday Morning: The Pearl Harbor Diary of Amber Billows. 2003. (J). lib. bdg. 12.95 (0-439-55513-2) Scholastic, Inc.

Holder, Nancy. Pearl Harbor 1941. 2001. (Illus.). 208p. (YA). (gr. 9-12). pap. 4.99 (0-671-03927-X, Simon Pulse) Simon & Schuster Children's Publishing.

Kudlinski, Kathleen V. Pearl Harbor Is Burning! A Story of World War II. (Once upon America Ser.). 64p. (J). (gr. 2-6). 1993. (Illus.). pap. 4.99 (0-14-034509-4, Puffin Bks.); 1991. 11.95 o.p. (0-670-83475-0, Viking Children's Bks.) Penguin Putnam Bks. for Young Readers.

LeSourd, Nancy. The Personal Correspondence of Catherine Clark & Meredith Lyons. 2004. 224p. 9.99 (0-310-70353-0) Zondervan.

Mazer, Harry. A Boy at War: A Novel of Pearl Harbor. 112p. (J). (gr. 5-9). 2002. pap. 4.99 (0-689-84160-4, Aladdin); 2001. (Illus.). 15.00 (0-689-84161-2, Simon & Schuster Children's Publishing) Simon & Schuster Children's Publishing.

Salisbury, Graham. Under the Blood Red Sun. 1994. 256p. (gr. 6-8). text 15.95 o.s.i (0-385-32099-X, Delacorte Pr.) Dell Publishing.

—Under the Blood Red Sun. 1995. 256p. (gr. 5-8). pap. text 5.50 (0-440-41139-4, Yearling) Random Hse. Children's Bks.

—Under the Blood Red Sun. 1995. (J). 11.04 (0-606-08654-4) Turtleback Bks.

PILGRIMS (NEW PLYMOUTH COLONY)—FICTION

Bulla, Clyde Robert. John Billington, Friend of Squanto. 1956. (Illus.). (J). (gr. 2-5). 11.49 o.p. (0-690-46253-0) HarperCollins Children's Bk. Group.

Cauper, Eunice. The Story of the Pilgrims & Their Indian Friends: A Thanksgiving Story for Children. 5th ed. 1990. (Illus.). 15p. (J). pap. 4.95 (0-9617551-1-3) Cauper, Eunice.

Clapp, Patricia C. Constance. 1991. 256p. (J). (gr. 7 up). reprint ed. pap. 6.99 (0-688-10976-4, Harper Trophy) HarperCollins Children's Bk. Group.

—Constance: A Story of Early Plymouth. 1993. (J). (gr. 5-9). 20.25 (0-8446-6647-5) Smith, Peter Pub., Inc.

Cohen, Barbara. Molly y los Peregrinos. Fiol, Maria A., tr. 1997. (SPA., Illus.). 32p. (J). (gr. 2-4). pap. 6.95 (1-880507-34-X, LC7322) Lectorum Pubns., Inc.

Daringer, Helen F. Pilgrim Kate. 1949. (Illus.). (J). (gr. 7 up). 4.95 o.p. (0-15-261897-X) Harcourt Children's Bks.

Daugherty, James. The Landing of the Pilgrims. (Landmark Bks.). (Illus.). 160p. (J). (gr. 5-7). reprint ed. 1981. pap. 5.99 (0-394-84697-4); 1963. 8.99 o.p. (0-394-90302-1) Random Hse. Children's Bks. (Random Hse. Bks. for Young Readers).

—The Landing of the Pilgrims. 1978. (Landmark Bks.). (J). 12.04 (0-606-02153-1) Turtleback Bks.

Dillon, Ellis. The Seekers. 1987. (J). pap. 3.95 o.p. (0-14-032320-1, Puffin Bks.) Penguin Putnam Bks. for Young Readers.

Gay, David. Voyage to Freedom: Story of the Pilgrim Fathers. 1984. (Illus.). 160p. (J). (gr. 4-7). pap. 8.99 (0-85151-384-0) Banner of Truth, The.

Grote, JoAnn A. Danger in the Harbor: Grain Riots Threaten Boston. 6th ed. 1998. (American Adventure Ser.: No. 6). (Illus.). (J). (gr. 3-7). pap. 3.97 (1-57748-147-X) Barbour Publishing, Inc.

Hall, Elvajean. Margaret Pumphrey's Pilgrim Stories. 1991. 128p. (J). pap. 2.95 o.p. (0-590-45202-9, Scholastic Paperbacks) Scholastic, Inc.

Harness, Cheryl. Three Young Pilgrims. (Illus.). 40p. (J). (gr. k-5). 1995. pap. 5.95 (0-689-80208-0, Aladdin); 1992. 16.00 (0-02-742643-2, Simon & Schuster Children's Publishing) Simon & Schuster Children's Publishing.

—Three Young Pilgrims. 1995. (J). 12.10 (0-606-08301-4) Turtleback Bks.

Hays, Wilma P. Naughty Little Pilgrim. 1969. (Illus.). (J). (gr. 1-3). 4.95 o.p. (0-679-24057-8, 240967) McKay, David Co., Inc.

—Pilgrim Thanksgiving. 1955. (Illus.). (J). (gr. 2-4). 4.99 o.p. (0-698-30281-8) Putnam Publishing Group, The.

Hennessy, G. B. One Little, Two Little, Three Little Pilgrims. 2001. 32p. pap. 6.99 (*0-14-230006-3*, Puffin Bks.) Penguin Putnam Bks. for Young Readers.

Jackson, Dave & Jackson, Neta. The Mayflower Secret: Governor William Bradford. 1998. (Trailblazer Bks.: Vol. 26). (Illus.). 160p. (J). (gr. 3-7). pap. 5.99 (*0-7642-2010-1*) Bethany Hse. Pubs.

Lasky, Kathryn & Gregory, Kristiana. A Journey to the New World: The Diary of Remember Patience Whipple, Mayflower, 1620. 1996. (Dear America Ser.). (Illus.). 176p. (YA). (gr. 4-9). 10.95 Scholastic, Inc.

Lawton, Wendy. Almost Home: A Story Based on the Life of the Mayflower's Mary Chilton. 2003. (Daughters of the Faith Ser.). 143p. (J). 5.99 (*0-8024-3637-4*) Moody Pr.

Lough, Loree. Dream Seekers: Roger William's Stand for Freedom. 3rd ed. 1998. (American Adventure Ser.: No. 3). (Illus.). (J). (gr. 3-7). pap. 3.97 (*1-57748-073-2*) Barbour Publishing, Inc.

—Dream Seekers: Roger William's Stand for Freedom. 1999. (American Adventure Ser.: No. 3). (Illus.). 144p. (J). (gr. 3-7). lib. bdg. 15.95 (*0-7910-5043-2*) Chelsea Hse. Pubs.

—Fire by Night: The Great Fire Devastates Boston. 4th ed. 1998. (American Adventure Ser.: No. 4). (Illus.). (J). (gr. 3-7). pap. 3.97 (*1-57748-074-0*) Barbour Publishing, Inc.

Lowitz, Sadyebeth & Lowitz, Anson. The Pilgrims' Party. 1977. (gr. k-3). pap. 0.95 o.p. (*0-440-47153-2*) Dell Publishing.

—The Pilgrims' Party. 1967. (Really Truly Stories Ser.). 76p. (J). (gr. 2 up). lib. bdg. 3.95 o.p. (*0-8225-0133-3*) Lerner Publishing Group.

Lutz, Norma Jean. Maggie's Choice: Jonathan Edwards & the Great Awakening. 8th ed. 1998. (American Adventure Ser.: No. 8). (Illus.). (J). (gr. 3-7). pap. 3.97 (*1-57748-145-3*) Barbour Publishing, Inc.

Meadowcroft, Enid L. First Year. 1946. (Illus.). (J). (gr. 5 up). 10.95 o.p. (*0-690-30349-1*) HarperCollins Children's Bk. Group.

Moger, Susan. Pilgrims. 1995. (J). 9.95 (*0-590-49787-1*) Scholastic, Inc.

Molloy, Anne. Years before the Mayflower: The Pilgrims in Holland. 1972. 160p. (J). (gr. 5-10). 5.95 o.p. (*0-8038-0734-1*) Hastings Hse. Daytrips Pubs.

Morris, Gilbert. The Dangerous Voyage. 1995. (Time Navigators Ser.: Vol. 1). 160p. (J). (gr. 6-9). pap. 5.99 o.p. (*1-55661-395-4*) Bethany Hse. Pubs.

Osborne, Mary Pope. Thanksgiving on Thursday. 2002. (Magic Tree House Ser.). (Illus.). 96p. (gr. 1-4). lib. bdg. 11.99 (*0-375-90615-0*); pap. 3.99 (*0-375-80615-6*) Random Hse., Inc.

Peach. Pilgrim Fathers. 1972. (Ladybird Ser.). (J). (gr. 2-7). 2.50 o.p. (*0-87508-855-4*) Christian Literature Crusade, Inc.

Pumphrey, Margaret. Pilgrim Stories. 9999. 144p. (J). (gr. 2-5). pap. 1.95 o.p. (*0-590-01352-1*) Scholastic, Inc.

Pumphrey, Margaret B. Stories of the Pilgrims. McHugh, Michael J., ed. 1991. (Illus.). 240p. (J). (gr. 3-5). pap. text 6.00 (*1-930092-36-9*, CLP29545) Christian Liberty Pr.

Reece, Colleen L. The Mayflower Adventure. 1998. (American Adventure Ser.: No. 1). (Illus.). (J). (gr. 3-7). 3.97 (*1-57748-059-7*) Barbour Publishing, Inc.

—The Mayflower Adventure. 1999. (American Adventure Ser.: No. 1). 144p. (J). (gr. 3-7). lib. bdg. 15.95 (*0-7910-5041-6*) Chelsea Hse. Pubs.

—Plymouth Pioneers. 2nd ed. 1998. (American Adventure Ser.: No. 2). (Illus.). (J). (gr. 3-7). pap. 3.97 (*1-57748-060-0*) Barbour Publishing, Inc.

—Plymouth Pioneers. 1998. (American Adventure Ser.: No. 2). (Illus.). 142p. (J). (gr. 3-7). lib. bdg. 15.95 (*0-7910-5042-4*) Chelsea Hse. Pubs.

Rinaldi, Ann. The Journal of Jasper Jonathan Pierce: A Pilgrim Boy: Plymouth Plantation, 1620. 2000. (My Name Is America Ser.). (Illus.). 155p. (J). (gr. 4-8). pap. 10.95 (*0-590-51078-9*) Scholastic, Inc.

Roop, Connie & Roop, Peter, eds. Pilgrim Voices: Our First Year in the New World. 1997. (Illus.). 48p. (J). (gr. 3-7). pap. 8.95 (*0-8027-7530-6*) Walker & Co.

Sewall, Marcia. The Pilgrims of Plimoth. 1996. 48p. (J). (ps-3). pap. 6.99 (*0-689-80861-5*, Aladdin) Simon & Schuster Children's Publishing.

Stanley, Diane. Being Thankful at Plymouth Plantation. 2003. (Illus.). (J). 15.99 (*0-06-027069-1*); lib. bdg. 16.89 (*0-06-027076-4*) HarperCollins Children's Bk. Group. (Cotler, Joanna Bks.).

Taylor, Helen L. Little Pilgrim's Progress. 1982. (J). (gr. 4-7). pap. 7.99 (*0-8024-4926-3*, 551) Moody Pr.

Vernon, Louise A. Peter & the Pilgrims. 2nd ed. 2002. (Illus.). 119p. (J). (gr. 4-9). pap. 7.99 (*0-8361-9226-5*) Herald Pr.

Waters, Kate. On the Mayflower: The Voyage of the Ship's Apprentice & a Passenger Girl. 1996. (Illus.). 40p. (J). (gr. 1-4). pap. 16.95 (*0-590-67308-4*) Scholastic, Inc.

—Samuel Eaton's Day: A Day in the Life of a Pilgrim Boy. 1993. 12.14 (*0-606-10298-1*) Turtleback Bks.

—Sarah Morton's Day: A Day in the Life of a Pilgrim Girl. 1993. 32p. (J). (ps-3). pap. 5.99 (*0-590-47400-6*) Scholastic, Inc.

PONY EXPRESS—FICTION

Bailer, Darice. The Pony Express. 2003. (J). pap. 3.95 (*1-59249-019-0*) Soundprints.

—Wanted - A Few Bold Riders: A Story of the Pony Express. 1997. (Smithsonian Odyssey Ser.). (Illus.). 32p. (J). (gr. 2-5). 14.95 (*1-56899-464-8*); pap. 5.95 (*1-56899-465-6*) Soundprints.

Champlin, Tim. Swift Thunder. 1998. (Western Ser.). 230p. 19.95 (*0-7862-1160-1*, Five Star) Gale Group.

Coerr, Eleanor. Buffalo Bill & the Pony Express. (I Can Read Bks.). (Illus.). 64p. (J). (gr. k-3). 1995. lib. bdg. 15.89 (*0-06-023373-7*); 1994. 15.95 o.p. (*0-06-023372-9*) HarperCollins Children's Bk. Group.

—Buffalo Bill & the Pony Express. 1996. (I Can Read Bks.). (J). (gr. 2-4). 10.10 (*0-606-09115-7*) Turtleback Bks.

Fontes, Ron & Fontes, Justine. Wild Bill Hickok & the Rebel Raiders. 1993. (Disney's American Frontier Ser.: Bk. 10). (Illus.). 80p. (J). (gr. 1-4). lib. bdg. 12.89 o.s.i (*1-56282-494-5*); pap. 3.50 o.p. (*1-56282-493-7*) Disney Pr.

Fuchs, Bernie. Fastest Ride. 2004. 32p. (J). pap. 16.95 (*0-439-26645-9*, Blue Sky Pr., The) Scholastic, Inc.

Glass, Andrew. The Sweetwater Run: The Story of Buffalo Bill Cody & the Pony Express. 1998. (Picture Yearling Book Ser.). 48p. (gr. 1-5). pap. text 6.99 o.s.i (*0-440-41186-6*) Dell Publishing.

Gould, Arlen. Pony Express. 1997. (J). (*0-517-59825-6*); lib. bdg. (*0-517-59826-4*) Random Hse. Children's Bks. (Random Hse. Bks. for Young Readers).

Gregory, Kristiana. Jimmy Spoon & the Pony Express. 1994. 144p. (J). (gr. 4-7). pap. 3.99 (*0-590-46577-5*) Scholastic, Inc.

—Jimmy Spoon & the Pony Express. 1997. (J). 10.55 (*0-606-11520-X*) Turtleback Bks.

Knowlton, Laurie Lazzaro. Why Cowboys Need a Pardner. 200th ed. 1998. (Illus.). 32p. (J). (gr. k-3). 14.95 (*1-56554-336-X*) Pelican Publishing Co., Inc.

McDonald, Brix. Riding on the Wind. 1998. 243p. (YA). (gr. 5-10). pap. 5.95 (*0-9661306-0-X*) Avenue Publishing.

Sargent, Dave & Sargent, Pat. Jet (Jet Black) Good Attitude. 2001. (Saddle Up Ser.). 36p. (J). pap. 6.95 (*1-56763-616-0*) Ozark Publishing.

—Jet (Jet Black) Good Attitude #36. 2001. (Saddle Up Ser.). 36p. (J). lib. bdg. 22.60 (*1-56763-615-2*) Ozark Publishing.

Schnetzler, Pattie L. Fast 'n Snappy. Manning, Jane K., tr. & illus. by. 2004. (Carolrhoda Picture Books Ser.). (J). lib. bdg. 15.95 (*1-57505-539-2*, Carolrhoda Bks.) Lerner Publishing Group.

Tate, Nikki. Jo's Triumph. 2002. (Illus.). 160p. (J). (gr. 2-6). pap. 4.99 (*1-55143-199-8*) Orca Bk. Pubs.

Thomas, Carroll. Riding by Starlight: A Matty Trescott Novel. 2002. (Illus.). ix, 173p. (J). 9.95 (*1-57525-315-1*) Smith & Kraus Pubs., Inc.

Watson, Jude. Brides of Independence, No. 4. 1996. (Brides of Wildcat County Ser.). 192p. (J). (gr. 7 up). pap. 3.95 (*0-689-80329-X*, Simon Pulse) Simon & Schuster Children's Publishing.

PREHISTORIC PEOPLES—FICTION

Barringer, D. Moreau. And the Waters Prevailed. 1956. (J). (gr. 4-9). 6.95 o.p. (*0-525-25598-2*, Dutton) Dutton/Plume.

Bato, Joseph. The Sorcerer. 1976. (gr. 7 up). 6.95 o.p. (*0-679-20363-X*) McKay, David Co., Inc.

Baylor, Byrd. One Small Blue Bead. 2nd ed. 1992. (Illus.). 32p. (J). (ps-3). 17.00 (*0-684-19334-5*, Atheneum) Simon & Schuster Children's Publishing.

Brennan, J. H. Shiva: An Adventure of the Ice Age. (Trophy Bk.). (gr. 5 up). 1992. 208p. (YA). pap. 3.95 o.p. (*0-06-440392-0*, Harper Trophy); 1990. 192p. (J). 13.95 (*0-397-32453-7*); 1990. 192p. (J). lib. bdg. 13.89 o.p. (*0-397-32454-5*) HarperCollins Children's Bk. Group.

—Shiva Accused: An Adventure of the Ice Age. 1991. 288p. (gr. 5 up). (J). lib. bdg. 16.89 (*0-06-020742-6*); (YA). 16.95 o.p. (*0-06-020741-8*) HarperCollins Children's Bk. Group.

—Shiva's Challenge: An Adventure of the Ice Age. (Trophy Bk.). 224p. (gr. 5 up). 1993. (J). pap. 4.95 (*0-06-440460-9*, Harper Trophy); 1992. (J). 17.00 (*0-06-020825-2*); 1992. (YA). lib. bdg. 16.89 (*0-06-020826-0*) HarperCollins Children's Bk. Group.

Briggs, Raymond. Ug: Boy Genius of the Stone Age & His Search for Soft Trousers. 2002. (Illus.). 32p. (J). (gr. 3-6). 15.95 (*0-375-81611-9*); lib. bdg. 17.99 (*0-375-91611-3*) Random Hse. Children's Bks. (Knopf Bks. for Young Readers).

Brooke, William J. A Is for AARRGH! 256p. (J). (gr. 5 up). 2000. pap. 5.95 (*0-06-440889-2*, Harper Trophy); 1999. lib. bdg. 14.89 (*0-06-023394-X*) HarperCollins Children's Bk. Group.

Chapman, Carol. Ig Lives in a Cave. 1979. (Smart Cat Bks.). (Illus.). (J). (ps-3). 7.95 o.p. (*0-525-32534-4*, Dutton) Dutton/Plume.

Cowley, Marjorie. Dar & the Spear Thrower. 1994. 128p. (J). (gr. 4-6). tchr. ed. 15.00 (*0-395-68132-4*, Clarion Bks.) Houghton Mifflin Co. Trade & Reference Div.

Craig, Ruth. Malu's Wolf. 1995. 192p. (J). (gr. 3-7). pap. 15.95 (*0-531-09484-7*); lib. bdg. 16.99 (*0-531-08784-0*) Scholastic, Inc. (Orchard Bks.).

Crowell, Pers. King Moo, the Wordmaker. 1976. (Illus.). (J). (gr. 1-3). 5.95 o.p. (*0-87004-253-X*) Caxton Pr.

Crum, Sally. Race to the Moonrise: An Ancient Journey. 1998. (Illus.). 99p. (J). pap. 9.95 (*1-890437-21-2*) Western Reflections Publishing Co.

Denzel, Justin F. Hunt for the Last Cat. 1991. (YA). (gr. 5 up). 14.95 o.s.i (*0-399-22101-8*, Philomel) Penguin Putnam Bks. for Young Readers.

—Return to the Painted Cave. 1997. 208p. (J). (gr. 5-8). 16.95 o.p. (*0-399-23117-X*, Philomel) Penguin Putnam Bks. for Young Readers.

Dickinson, Peter. A Bone from a Dry Sea. 1993. 208p. (J). 16.00 o.s.i (*0-385-30821-3*, Delacorte Pr.) Dell Publishing.

—The Kin: Noli's Story. 1998. (Library Ser.). 211p. (J). (gr. 4-8). 14.99 o.s.i (*0-399-23328-8*); (gr. 5-9). 3.99 o.p. (*0-448-41710-3*) Penguin Putnam Bks. for Young Readers. (Grosset & Dunlap).

Dubowski, Cathy. Cave Boy. 1988. (Step into Reading Step 1 Bks.). (J). (ps-1). 10.14 (*0-606-12216-8*) Turtleback Bks.

Evarts, Hal. Jay Jay & the Peking Monster. 1984. (J). (gr. 5-9). 15.75 (*0-8446-6166-X*) Smith, Peter Pub., Inc.

Ferris, Jean. Signs of Life, RS. 1995. 160p. (J). (gr. 7 up). 14.00 o.p. (*0-374-36909-7*, Farrar, Straus & Giroux (BYR)) Farrar, Straus & Giroux.

Geren, Carl. Shell Hunter. 1977. (Illus.). (J). (gr. 2-5). lib. bdg. 7.95 o.p. (*0-516-03611-4*, Children's Pr.) Scholastic Library Publishing.

Harnishfeger, Lloyd C. Hunters of the Black Swamp. 1971. (Real Life Bks.). (Illus.). (J). (gr. 5-11). lib. bdg. 5.95 o.p. (*0-8225-0701-3*, Lerner Pubns.) Lerner Publishing Group.

Hoff, Syd. Stanley. (I Can Read Bks.). (Illus.). 64p. (J). (gr. k-3). 1978. pap. 3.95 (*0-06-444010-9*, Harper Trophy); 1962. lib. bdg. 15.89 (*0-06-022536-X*); 1962. 13.00 (*0-06-022535-1*) HarperCollins Children's Bk. Group.

Kjelgaard, Jim. Fire-Hunter. 1993. reprint ed. lib. bdg. 21.95 (*1-56849-112-3*) Buccaneer Bks., Inc.

Lasky, Kathryn. The First Painter. 2000. (Illus.). 40p. (J). (gr. 2-12). pap. 16.95 o.p. (*0-7894-2578-5*, D K Ink) Dorling Kindersley Publishing, Inc.

May, Scott. The Yuggs: A Bird in the Hat. 2000. (Illus.). 24p. (J). (gr. 1-3). pap. (*0-9701450-3-9*) Long Hill Productions, Inc.

Osborne, Chester G. The Memory String. 1984. 168p. (J). (gr. 4-8). 11.95 o.s.i (*0-689-31020-X*, Atheneum) Simon & Schuster Children's Publishing.

Osborne, Mary Pope. Sunset of the Sabertooth. 1996. (Magic Tree House Ser.: No. 7). (Illus.). 80p. (gr. k-3). (J). lib. bdg. 11.99 (*0-679-96373-1*); pap. 3.99 (*0-679-86373-7*) Random Hse. Children's Bks. (Random Hse. Bks. for Young Readers).

—Sunset of the Sabertooth. 1996. (Magic Tree House Ser.: No. 7). (Illus.). 158p. (J). (gr. k-3). 10.14 (*0-606-09913-1*) Turtleback Bks.

Scieszka, Jon. Your Mother Was a Neanderthal. (Time Warp Trio Ser.). (Illus.). 80p. 2004. pap. 4.99 (*0-14-240048-3*, Puffin Bks.); 1995. (J). (gr. 2-6). pap. 4.99 (*0-14-036372-6*, Puffin Bks.); 1993. (J). (gr. 2-6). 14.99 (*0-670-84481-0*, Viking Children's Bks.) Penguin Putnam Bks. for Young Readers.

—Your Mother Was a Neanderthal. 1995. (Time Warp Trio Ser.). (J). 11.14 (*0-606-08411-8*) Turtleback Bks.

—Your Mother Was a Neanderthal Twt Promo. 2003. (Time Warp Trio Ser.). (Illus.). 76p. pap. 2.66 (*0-14-250134-4*, Puffin Bks.) Penguin Putnam Bks. for Young Readers.

Sharratt, Nick. Caveman Dave. 1996. (Illus.). (J). (ps up). bds. 2.99 o.p. (*1-56402-476-8*) Candlewick Pr.

Shykoff, Henry. Just a Little Later with Eevo & Sim. 2001. (Illus.). 132p. (J). pap. (*1-896219-73-X*) Natural Heritage/Natural History, Inc.

Stanley, Diane. A Time Apart. (J). (gr. 5 up). 2001. 272p. pap. 5.99 (*0-380-81030-1*, Harper Trophy); 1999. (Illus.). 256p. 15.95 (*0-688-16997-X*) HarperCollins Children's Bk. Group.

Stanley, George Edward. Bugs for Breakfast. 1996. (Scaredy Cats Ser.: No. 2). (Illus.). 80p. (J). (gr. 1-4). per. 3.99 (*0-689-80857-7*, Aladdin) Simon & Schuster Children's Publishing.

—Bugs for Breakfast. 1996. (Scaredy Cats Ser.: No. 2). (Illus.). (J). (gr. 1-4). 9.19 o.p. (*0-606-10921-8*) Turtleback Bks.

Steele, William O. The Magic Amulet. 1979. (J). (gr. 5 up). 6.95 o.p. (*0-15-250427-3*) Harcourt Children's Bks.

Tannen, Mary. Huntley Nutley & the Missing Link. 1983. (Illus.). 128p. (J). (gr. 3-5). 9.95 o.p. (*0-394-85759-3*); lib. bdg. 9.99 o.p. (*0-394-95759-8*) Random Hse. Children's Bks. (Knopf Bks. for Young Readers).

Turnbull, Ann. Maroo of the Winter Caves. 144p. 1990. (Illus.). (J). (gr. 4-6). pap. 6.95 (*0-395-54795-4*); 1984. (J). (gr. 4-7). 14.95 o.p. (*0-89919-304-8*); 20th ed. 2004. (J). 15.00 (*0-618-43408-9*); 20th ed. 2004. (YA). pap. 6.95 (*0-618-44299-5*) Houghton Mifflin Co. Trade & Reference Div. (Clarion Bks.).

—Maroo of the Winter Caves. 1984. (J). 13.00 (*0-606-04740-9*) Turtleback Bks.

Turner, Ann Warren. Time of the Bison. 1987. (Illus.). 64p. (J). (gr. 2-6). 13.95 o.p. (*0-02-789300-6*, Simon & Schuster Children's Publishing) Simon & Schuster Children's Publishing.

Wibberley, Leonard. Attar of the Ice Valley, RS. 1968. 176p. (J). (gr. 6 up). 11.95 o.p. (*0-374-30451-3*, Farrar, Straus & Giroux (BYR)) Farrar, Straus & Giroux.

Wood, Audrey. The Tickleoctopus. 1994. (Illus.). 48p. (J). (ps-3). 17.00 (*0-15-287000-8*) Harcourt Children's Bks.

R

RECONSTRUCTION—FICTION

Hansen, Joyce. The Heart Calls Home. 2002. 256p. (J). (gr. 7 up). pap. 5.95 (*0-380-73294-7*, Harper Trophy) HarperCollins Children's Bk. Group.

—The Heart Calls Home. 1999. viii, 175p. (J). (gr. 7-12). 16.95 (*0-8027-8636-7*) Walker & Co.

—I Thought My Soul Would Rise & Fly: The Diary of Patsy, a Freed Girl, Mars Bluff, South Carolina, 1865. 1997. (Dear America Ser.). (Illus.). 202p. (J). (gr. 4-9). pap. 10.95 (*0-590-84913-1*) Scholastic, Inc.

Osborne, Mary Pope, et al. A Time to Dance: Virginia's Civil War Diary, Bk. 3. 2003. (My America Ser.). 112p. (J). pap. 12.95 (*0-439-44341-5*); mass mkt. 4.99 (*0-439-44343-1*) Scholastic, Inc.

Robinet, Harriette Gillem. Forty Acres & Maybe a Mule. 2000. (YA). (gr. 3 up). pap. 52.00 incl. audio (*0-7887-4332-5*, 41127) Recorded Bks., LLC.

—Forty Acres & Maybe a Mule. (Jean Karl Bks.). 144p. (J). (gr. 3-7). 1998. (Illus.). 16.95 (*0-689-82078-X*, Atheneum); 2000. reprint ed. pap. 4.99 (*0-689-83317-2*, Aladdin) Simon & Schuster Children's Publishing.

—Forty Acres & Maybe a Mule. l.t. ed. 2001. (Illus.). 184p. (J). (gr. 4-7). 21.95 (*0-7862-2704-4*) Thorndike Pr.

—Forty Acres & Maybe a Mule. 2000. 11.04 (*0-606-17824-4*) Turtleback Bks.

Trelease, Allen W. Reconstruction: The Great Experiment. 1970. (Illus.). (J). (gr. 7 up). lib. bdg. 9.79 o.p. (*0-06-026123-4*) HarperCollins Pubs.

REFORMATION—FICTION

Prins, Piet. When the Morning Came. Deboer, Gertrude, tr. from DUT. 1989. (Struggle for Freedom Ser.: No. 1). (Illus.). 158p. (Orig.). (J). pap. 8.90 (*0-921100-12-4*) Inheritance Pubns.

Van Heerde, Gerrit. The Man with the Red Beard. 2002. (J). (*0-9579517-0-1*) Inheritance Pubns.

Vernon, Louise A. The King's Book. 2nd ed. 1980. (Illus.). 128p. (YA). (gr. 4). pap. 7.99 (*0-8361-1933-9*) Herald Pr.

RENAISSANCE—FICTION

Avi. Midnight Magic. 2001. 11.04 (*0-606-22158-1*) Turtleback Bks.

Bradford, Emma. Kat & the Missing Notebooks. 1999. (Stardust Classics: No. 4). (Illus.). 119p. (J). (gr. 2-5). 12.95 (*1-889514-27-6*); pap. 5.95 (*1-889514-28-4*) Dolls Corp.

Caselli, Giovanni. The Everyday Life of a Cathedral Builder. 1992. (Everyday Life of Ser.). (Illus.). 32p. (J). (gr. 3-6). lib. bdg. 12.95 o.s.i (*0-87226-115-8*, Bedrick, Peter Bks.) McGraw-Hill Children's Publishing.

Juster, Norton. Alberic the Wise. 1992. (Illus.). 28p. (J). (gr. 1 up). 16.95 (*0-88708-243-2*, Simon & Schuster Children's Publishing) Simon & Schuster Children's Publishing.

Reilly, Robert T. Red Hugh, Prince of Donegal. 1997. (Living History Library). (Illus.). 155p. (J). (gr. 5-7). pap. 12.95 (*1-883937-22-1*, 22-1) Bethlehem Bks.

Historical Events

Vergés, GlÓria & Vergés, Oiol. El Renacimiento (The Renaissance) 1988. (Journey Through History Ser.). (ENG & SPA., Illus.). 32p. (J). (gr. 1-4). pap. 7.95 (*0-8120-3397-3*, BA3397) Barron's Educational Series, Inc.

—The Renaissance. 1988. (Journey Through History Ser.). (Illus.). 32p. (J). (gr. 2-4). pap. 6.95 o.p. (*0-8120-3396-5*) Barron's Educational Series, Inc.

RIEL REBELLION, 1885—FICTION

Bayle, B. J. Battle Cry at Batoche. 2001. (Illus.). 144p. pap. 5.95 (*0-88878-414-7*) Beach Holme Pubs., Ltd. CAN. *Dist:* Strauss Consultants.

ROANOKE ISLAND—HISTORY—FICTION

Forrester, Sandra. Sound the Jubilee. 1995. 192p. (YA). (gr. 5-9). 15.99 o.s.i (*0-525-67486-1*, Dutton Children's Bks.) Penguin Putnam Bks. for Young Readers.

Levitin, Sonia. Roanoke: A Novel of the Lost Colony. 2000. 288p. (YA). (gr. 7-12). mass mkt. 4.99 (*0-689-83785-2*, Simon Pulse) Simon & Schuster Children's Publishing.

Maden, Mary. In Search of the Lost Colony. 1996. (Outer Banks Animals Adventure Ser.: No. 3). (Illus.). 20p. (Orig.). (J). (gr. 2-5). pap. 5.95 (*0-9646970-2-5*) Dog & Pony Publishing.

Stainer, M. L. The Lyon's Cub. unabr. ed. 1998. (Book 2 of the Lyon Saga Ser.: Bk. 2). (Illus.). 162p. (YA). (gr. 5-10). pap. 6.95 (*0-9646904-6-2*); lib. bdg. 9.95 (*0-9646904-5-4*) Chicken Soup Pr., Inc.

—The Lyon's Throne. 1999. (Lyon Saga Ser.: Bk. 4). (Illus.). 153p. (YA). (gr. 5-9). pap. 6.95 (*1-893337-02-2*) Chicken Soup Pr., Inc.

ROME—HISTORY—FICTION

Anderson, Paul L. Pugnax the Gladiator. 1939. (Illus.). (J). (gr. 7-11). pap. 18.00 (*0-8196-0104-7*) Biblo & Tannen Booksellers & Pubs., Inc.

—With the Eagles. 1929. (Illus.). (J). (gr. 7-11). pap. 21.00 (*0-8196-0100-4*) Biblo & Tannen Booksellers & Pubs., Inc.

Brown, Brian & Melrose, Andrew. Breakout! 1996. (Storykeepers Ser.: Vol. 1). (Illus.). 24p. (J). (ps-3). pap. 3.99 (*0-310-20213-2*) Zondervan.

—Raging Waters. 1996. (Storykeepers Ser.: Vol. 2). (Illus.). 64p. (J). (ps-3). pap. 3.99 (*0-310-20329-5*) Zondervan.

Chariots of Fire. Date not set. (Nelson Readers Ser.: 2). (J). pap. text (*0-17-557036-1*) Addison-Wesley Longman, Inc.

Church, Alfred J. Lucius, Adventures of a Roman Boy. 1969. (YA). (gr. 7-11). 22.00 (*0-8196-0108-X*) Biblo & Tannen Booksellers & Pubs., Inc.

Deary, Terry. Rotten Romans. 1997. (J). mass mkt. 3.99 (*0-590-73893-3*) Scholastic, Inc.

Dunster, Mark. Andronicus. 1996. 19p. (Orig.). (YA). (gr. 9-12). pap. 5.00 (*0-89642-297-6*) Linden Pubs.

Lawrence, Carol. The Dolphins of Laurentium. 2003. (Roman Mysteries Ser.: Bk. 5). 176p. (gr. 6-9). 15.95 (*0-7613-2349-X*); lib. bdg. 22.90 (*0-7613-2606-5*) Millbrook Pr., Inc. (Roaring Brook Pr.).

Lawrence, Caroline. The Pirates of Pompeii. 2003. (Roman Mysteries Ser.: Bk. III). 160p. (gr. 6-9). lib. bdg. 22.90 (*0-7613-2604-9*); (YA). 15.95 (*0-7613-1584-5*) Millbrook Pr., Inc. (Roaring Brook Pr.).

—The Thieves of Ostia. 2002. (Roman Mysteries Ser.). (Illus.). 160p. (gr. 6-9). lib. bdg. 22.90 (*0-7613-2602-2*, Roaring Brook Pr.) Millbrook Pr., Inc.

—The Thieves of Ostia: A Roman Mystery. 2002. 9. (Illus.). 160p. (gr. 4-9). 15.95 (*0-7613-1582-9*, Roaring Brook Pr.) Millbrook Pr., Inc.

Morris, Neil & Morris, Ting. Battle of the Gladiators. 1991. (Tales of the Ancient Romans Ser.). (Illus.). 24p. (J). (gr. 3-5). 13.95 o.s.i (*0-237-51021-9*) Evans Brothers, Ltd. GBR. *Dist:* Trafalgar Square.

—In the Slave Market. 1991. (Tales of the Ancient Romans Ser.). (Illus.). 24p. (J). (gr. 3-5). 13.95 o.s.i (*0-237-51019-7*) Evans Brothers, Ltd. GBR. *Dist:* Trafalgar Square.

Moss, Marissa. Galen: My Life in Imperial Rome. 2002. (Ancient World Journals). (Illus.). 48p. (J). (gr. 3-7). 15.00 (*0-15-216535-5*, Silver Whistle) Harcourt Children's Bks.

Ray, Mary. Beyond the Desert Gate. 2001. (Young Adult Bookshelf Ser.). (Illus.). 190p. (YA). (gr. 3-9). 11.95 (*1-883937-54-X*, 54-X) Bethlehem Bks.

—Beyond the Desert Gate. 1977. (Illus.). 160p. (J). o.p. (*0-571-10988-8*) Faber & Faber Ltd.

—The Ides of April, RS. 1975. 160p. (J). (gr. 7 up). 6.95 o.p. (*0-374-33626-1*, Farrar, Straus & Giroux (BYR)) Farrar, Straus & Giroux.

Rubalcaba, Jill. The Wadjet Eye. 2000. (Illus.). 160p. (J). (gr. 4-6). tchr. ed. 15.00 (*0-395-68942-2*, Clarion Bks.) Houghton Mifflin Co. Trade & Reference Div.

Wallace, Lew. Ben-Hur. (SPA., Illus.). (YA). 11.95 (*84-7281-099-2*, AF1099) Auriga, Ediciones S.A. ESP. *Dist:* Continental Bk. Co., Inc.

—Ben-Hur. 1977. (McKay Illustrated Classics Ser.). (gr. 7 up). 7.95 o.p. (*0-679-20392-3*) McKay, David Co., Inc.

—Ben Hur. 1981. 450p. (YA). (ps up). reprint ed. lib. bdg. 35.95 (*0-89966-289-7*) Buccaneer Bks., Inc.

Wells, Reuben F. With Caesar's Legions. 1951. (Illus.). (J). (gr. 7-11). pap. 20.00 (*0-8196-0110-1*) Biblo & Tannen Booksellers & Pubs., Inc.

ROME (ITALY)—FICTION

Doyle, Peter R. Kidnapped in Rome. 1996. (Daring Adventure Ser.: Vol. 9). (J). (gr. 4). pap. 5.99 o.p. (*1-56179-480-5*) Focus on the Family Publishing.

Klass, David. Danger Zone. (Point Signature Ser.). 240p. (YA). (gr. 7-12). 1998. mass mkt. 4.99 (*0-590-48591-1*); 1996. pap. 16.95 (*0-590-48590-3*) Scholastic, Inc.

—Danger Zone. 1998. (J). 11.04 (*0-606-13080-2*) Turtleback Bks.

S

SCOTLAND—HISTORY—FICTION

Banks, Lynne Reid. The Dungeon. 2002. 288p. (J). (gr. 7 up). lib. bdg. 17.89 (*0-06-623783-1*) HarperCollins Children's Bk. Group.

—The Dungeon. 2002. 288p. (J). (gr. 7 up). 16.99 (*0-06-623782-3*) HarperCollins Pubs.

Bond, Douglas. King's Arrow. 2003. (Crown & Covenant Ser.). (Illus.). 208p. (J). per. 9.99 (*0-87552-743-4*) P&R Publishing.

Breslin, Theresa. Remembrance. 304p. (YA). 2004. (gr. 7). mass mkt. 6.50 (*0-440-23778-5*, Laurel Leaf); 2002. lib. bdg. 18.99 (*0-385-90067-8*, Delacorte Bks. for Young Readers); 2002. (gr. 7 up). 16.95 (*0-385-73015-2*, Delacorte Bks. for Young Readers) Random Hse. Children's Bks.

Douglas, Bond. Duncan's War. 2002. (Crown & Covenant Ser.). (Illus.). viii, 277p. (J). per. 9.99 (*0-87552-742-6*) P&R Publishing.

Forman, James D. Prince Charlie's Year. 1991. 144p. (YA). (gr. 7 up). lib. bdg. 13.95 o.p. (*0-684-19242-X*, Atheneum) Simon & Schuster Children's Publishing.

Henty, G. A. In Freedom's Cause: A Story of Wallace & Bruce. 2000. 252p. (J). E-Book 3.95 (*0-594-02391-2*) 1873 Pr.

—In Freedom's Cause: A Story of Wallace & Bruce. McHugh, Michael J., ed. 1998. (Illus.). 258p. (YA). (gr. 8 up). pap. text 9.00 (*1-930092-20-2*, CLP29680) Christian Liberty Pr.

—In Freedom's Cause: A Story of Wallace & Bruce. 2002. 320p. (J). pap. 6.95 (*0-486-42362-X*) Dover Pubns., Inc.

—In Freedom's Cause: A Story of Wallace & Bruce. (Illus.). 2000. 337p. (J). pap. 14.99 (*1-887159-35-5*); 1996. 351p. (YA). 20.99 (*1-887159-03-7*) Preston-Speed Pubns.

Hunter, Mollie. The King's Swift Rider: A Novel on Robert the Bruce. 2000. (Illus.). 336p. (J). (gr. 7 up). pap. 5.95 (*0-06-447216-7*, Harper Trophy) HarperCollins Children's Bk. Group.

—The King's Swift Rider: A Novel on Robert the Bruce. 1998. 256p. (J). (gr. 7 up). 16.95 (*0-06-027186-8*) HarperCollins Pubs.

—The King's Swift Rider: A Novel on Robert the Bruce. 2000. (Illus.). (J). 12.00 (*0-606-18701-4*) Turtleback Bks.

—The Stronghold. 1974. 256p. (YA). (gr. 8 up). o.p. (*0-06-022653-6*); lib. bdg. 10.89 o.p. (*0-06-022654-4*) HarperCollins Pubs.

—The Thirteenth Member. 2002. (Kelpies Ser.). (Illus.). 192p. (J). pap. (*0-86315-405-0*) Floris Bks. GBR. *Dist:* SteinerBooks, Inc.

Hutchinson, Robert. Over the Sea to Skye. 1997. (Illus.). 96p. (J). (ps-12). 14.95 (*1-56313-907-3*) BrownTrout Pubs., Inc.

McGoldrick, May. Tess & the Highlander. 2002. (Avon True Romance Ser.). 272p. (J). pap. 4.99 (*0-06-000486-X*, Avon) HarperCollins Children's Bk. Group.

Porter, Jane. The Scottish Chiefs. Smith, Nora A. & Wiggin, Kate Douglas, eds. & trs. by. from SCO. 1991. (Scribner Illustrated Classics Ser.). (Illus.). 520p. (YA). (gr. 7 up). 29.00 (*0-684-19340-X*, Atheneum) Simon & Schuster Children's Publishing.

—The Scottish Chiefs. deluxe ltd. ed. 1991. (Scribners Illustrated Classics Ser.). (Illus.). 528p. (J). 75.00 o.s.i (*0-684-19339-6*, Atheneum) Simon & Schuster Children's Publishing.

Smith, Kathryn. Emily & the Scot. 2002. (Avon True Romance Ser.). 288p. (J). pap. 4.99 (*0-06-000619-6*, Avon) HarperCollins Children's Bk. Group.

Stevenson, Robert Louis. Kidnapped. 2002. (Great Illustrated Classics). (Illus.). 240p. (J). (gr. 3-8). lib. bdg. 21.35 (*1-57765-690-3*, ABDO & Daughters) ABDO Publishing Co.

—Kidnapped. 1988. mass mkt. 2.25 (*0-938819-68-2*, Aerie) Doherty, Tom Assocs., LLC.

—The Master of Ballantrae. 2003. 160p. pap. 2.00 (*0-486-42685-8*) Dover Pubns., Inc.

—The Works of Robert Louis Stevenson: Treasure Island, Kidnapped, The Strange Case of Dr. Jekyll & Mr. Hyde. 1995. (Classic Bonded Leather Ser.). 800p. (YA). 24.95 o.p. (*0-681-10373-6*) Borders Pr.

Sutcliff, Rosemary. Bonnie Dundee. 1984. (J). (gr. 7). 12.50 o.p. (*0-525-44094-1*, Dutton) Dutton/Plume.

Wiley, Melissa. Down to the Bonny Glen: Martha Years. 2001. (Little House Ser.). (Illus.). 336p. (J). (gr. 3-7). 16.95 (*0-06-027985-0*); pap. 5.99 (*0-06-440714-4*, Harper Trophy); lib. bdg. 16.89 (*0-06-028204-5*) HarperCollins Children's Bk. Group.

Yolen, Jane & Harris, Robert J. The Queen's Own Fool. 2000. (Illus.). viii, 390p. (J). (gr. 5-9). 19.99 (*0-399-23380-6*, Philomel) Penguin Putnam Bks. for Young Readers.

SOVIET UNION—HISTORY—FICTION

Almedingen, E. M. The Crimson Oak. 1983. 112p. (J). (gr. 6-9). 9.95 o.p. (*0-698-20569-3*, Coward-McCann) Putnam Publishing Group, The.

Asmar, Ramsey. The Birth of a New Tradition. 1992. (Publish-a-Book Ser.). (Illus.). 32p. (J). (gr. 3-4). lib. bdg. 22.83 (*0-8114-3583-0*) Raintree Pubs.

Cusack, Isabel L. Ivan the Great. 1978. (Illus.). (J). (gr. 1-4). o.p. (*0-690-03860-7*); lib. bdg. 5.79 o.p. (*0-690-03861-5*) HarperCollins Children's Bk. Group.

Franklin, Kristine L. The Wolfhound. 1996. (Illus.). 32p. (J). lib. bdg. 15.93 o.p. (*0-688-13675-3*); 16.00 (*0-688-13674-5*) HarperCollins Children's Bk. Group.

Heyman, Anita. Exit from Home. 1977. (Illus.). (J). (gr. 7 up). 7.50 o.p. (*0-517-52903-3*, Crown) Crown Publishing Group.

Meyer, Carolyn. Anastasia: Last Grand Duchess, Russia, 1914. 2000. (Royal Diaries Ser.). (Illus.). 220p. (J). (gr. 4-8). 10.95 (*0-439-12908-7*) Scholastic, Inc.

Plowman, Stephanie. Three Lives for the Czar. 1970. (J). (gr. 9-12). 4.95 o.p. (*0-395-07032-5*) Houghton Mifflin Co.

Ter Haar, Jaap. Boris. Mearns, Martha, tr. 1970. (Illus.). (J). (gr. 4-6). 4.50 o.p. (*0-440-00747-X*, Delacorte Pr.) Dell Publishing.

Verne, Jules. Michael Strogoff. 1997. (Scribner Illustrated Classics Ser.). (Illus.). 416p. (J). (gr. 4-7). 25.00 (*0-689-81096-2*, Atheneum) Simon & Schuster Children's Publishing.

—Miguel Strogoff. 2002. (SPA.). 14.95 (*84-392-0915-0*, EV30597); 2001. (*84-305-2204-2*); 2001. (SPA.). (*84-305-7143-4*); 1985. (SPA.). 96p. (*84-305-1437-6*) Lectorum Pubns., Inc.

Wulffson, Don. Soldier X. 2003. 240p. (YA). pap. 6.99 (*0-14-250073-9*, Puffin Bks.) Penguin Putnam Bks. for Young Readers.

Wulffson, Don L. Soldier X. 2001. 244p. (J). (gr. 5-9). 16.99 (*0-670-88863-X*, Viking Children's Bks.) Penguin Putnam Bks. for Young Readers.

Zei, Alki. The Sound of the Dragon's Feet. Fenton, Edward, tr. 1979. (J). (gr. 5-7). 8.50 o.p. (*0-525-39712-4*, Dutton) Dutton/Plume.

SPAIN—HISTORY—FICTION

Blatt, Evelyn. More Precious Than Gold: A Story of Inquisition Spain in the 1490's. Gardner, Eve-Lynn J., ed. 2002. (Illus.). 200p. (J). (gr. 2-5). pap. 8.95 (*1-929628-10-2*) Hachai Publishing.

Lehmann, Marcus. Family y Aguilar. (J). (gr. 7 up). 9.95 o.p. (*0-87306-122-5*) Feldheim, Philipp Inc.

Meyer, Carolyn, contrib. by. Isabel: Jewel of Castilla, Spain, 1466. 2000. (Royal Diaries Ser.). (Illus.). 204p. (J). (gr. 4-8). 10.95 (*0-439-07805-9*) Scholastic, Inc.

Miklowitz, Gloria D. Secrets in the House of Delgado. (gr. 4 up). 2002. 192p. (YA). pap. 8.00 (*0-8028-5210-6*); 2001. (Illus.). x, 182p. (J). 16.00 (*0-8028-5206-8*) Eerdmans, William B. Publishing Co. (Eerdmans Bks For Young Readers).

Myers, Walter Dean. Three Swords for Granada. 2002. (Illus.). 80p. (J). (gr. 2-5). tchr. ed. 15.95 (*0-8234-1676-3*) Holiday Hse., Inc.

Wilson, John. Lost in Spain. (Illus.). 174p. (YA). 2000. (gr. 8-12). (*1-55041-550-6*); 1999. (gr. 7-10). pap. (*1-55041-523-9*) Fitzhenry & Whiteside, Ltd.

STONE AGE—FICTION

Beall, Pamela Conn. Pebbles & Bamm-Bamm Find Things to Do. 1984. (J). (gr. k-3). 9.95 o.s.i (*0-8431-4127-1*, Grosset & Dunlap) Penguin Putnam Bks. for Young Readers.

Clement, Claude. Musician from the Darkness. 1990. (Illus.). 32p. (J). 14.95 o.s.i (*0-316-14740-0*) Little Brown & Co.

Craig, Ruth. Malu's Wolf. 1997. 192p. (J). pap. 4.99 o.s.i (*0-14-038604-1*, Puffin Bks.) Penguin Putnam Bks. for Young Readers.

—Malu's Wolf. 1995. 192p. (J). (gr. 3-7). pap. 15.95 (*0-531-09484-7*); lib. bdg. 16.99 (*0-531-08784-0*) Scholastic, Inc. (Orchard Bks.).

Flintstones Standee. 9999. (J). o.p. (*0-448-40993-3*) Penguin Putnam Bks. for Young Readers.

Fradin, Dennis Brindell. Early Man: The New Spear. 1979. (Prehistoric Tales). (Illus.). 48p. (J). (gr. 2-5). lib. bdg. 8.65 o.p. (*0-516-03854-0*, Children's Pr.) Scholastic Library Publishing.

Golden Western Staff. Flintstones. 9999. (Illus.). (J). (ps-3). pap. o.p. (*0-307-74042-0*, Golden Bks.) Random Hse. Children's Bks.

Hardy, Linda. Come into My Cave: A Prehistoric Novel. 1998. 104p. (J). (gr. 4-9). pap. 12.95 (*0-9656945-2-6*) LHA Bks.

Kipling, Rudyard. How the Alphabet Was Made. 1972. audio 11.00 o.s.i (*0-694-50882-9*, CDL 5, Caedmon) HarperTrade.

—How the First Letter Was Written. 1987. (Just So Stories Ser.). (Illus.). 32p. (J). (gr. 1-5). lib. bdg. 10.95 o.p. (*0-87226-138-7*, Bedrick, Peter Bks.) McGraw-Hill Children's Publishing.

Kotzwinkle, William. The Elephant Boy, RS. 1970. (J). (ps-3). 3.95 o.p. (*0-374-32013-6*, Farrar, Straus & Giroux (BYR)) Farrar, Straus & Giroux.

Linevski, A. An Old Tale Carved Out of Stone. Polushkin, Maria, tr. 1973. (ENG & RUS.). 256p. (J). (gr. 7 up). 1.49 o.p. (*0-517-50263-1*, Crown) Crown Publishing Group.

Little Golden Books Staff. Flintstones. 1994. 56p. (J). (ps up). pap. 1.69 o.s.i (*0-307-08577-5*, Golden Bks.) Random Hse. Children's Bks.

Paton Walsh, Jill. Toolmaker. 1974. (Illus.). (J). (gr. 3-6). 4.95 o.p. (*0-8164-3109-4*) Houghton Mifflin Co.

Scieszka, Jon. Your Mother Was a Neanderthal. (Time Warp Trio Ser.). (Illus.). 80p. 2004. pap. 4.99 (*0-14-240048-3*, Puffin Bks.); 1995. (J). (gr. 2-6). pap. 4.99 (*0-14-036372-6*, Puffin Bks.); 1993. (J). (gr. 2-6). 14.99 (*0-670-84481-0*, Viking Children's Bks.) Penguin Putnam Bks. for Young Readers.

—Your Mother Was a Neanderthal. 1995. (Time Warp Trio Ser.). (J). 11.14 (*0-606-08411-8*) Turtleback Bks.

Searcy, Margaret Z. Wolf Dog of the Woodland Indians. 1982. (Illus.). 100p. (J). (gr. 4-8). 9.95 o.p. (*0-8173-0091-0*) Univ. of Alabama Pr.

Unknown. Fred Flintstone's Surprising Corn. 1984. (J). (gr. k-3). 90.00 o.s.i (*0-8431-4161-1*, Price Stern Sloan) Penguin Putnam Bks. for Young Readers.

Various. Fred's Big Cleaning Day. (J). (gr. k-3). 20.00 o.p. (*0-8431-4160-3*, Price Stern Sloan) Penguin Putnam Bks. for Young Readers.

T

TITANIC (STEAMSHIP)—FICTION

Bunting, Eve. SOS Titanic. 1996. 256p. (YA). (gr. 7 up). pap. 6.00 (*0-15-201305-9*, Harcourt Paperbacks); (Illus.). 13.00 (*0-15-200271-5*) Harcourt Children's Bks.

—SOS Titanic. 1996. (J). 12.05 (*0-606-09878-X*) Turtleback Bks.

Crew, Gary. Pig on the Titanic: A True Story. 2005. (J). (*0-06-052305-0*); lib. bdg. (*0-06-052306-9*) HarperCollins Pubs.

Duey, Kathleen & Bale, Karen. Titanic, April 14, 1912. 1998. (Survival! Ser.: No. 1). (J). (gr. 4-7). 10.04 (*0-606-17580-6*) Turtleback Bks.

Duey, Kathleen & Bale, Karen A. Titanic, April 14, 1912. 1998. (Survival! Ser.: No. 1). (J). (gr. 3-7). 10.04 (*0-606-13047-0*) Turtleback Bks.

Duey, Kathleen, et al. Titanic, April 14, 1912. 1998. (Survival! Ser.: No. 1). 176p. (J). (gr. 4-7). pap. 4.99 (*0-689-81311-2*, Aladdin) Simon & Schuster Children's Publishing.

Henkel, Virginia. Letters from the Past. 1990. (Highgate Collection). (Illus.). 24p. (J). (gr. k-4). lib. bdg. 15.96 o.p. (*0-8114-2698-X*) Raintree Pubs.

Jenner, Caryn. Survivors: The Night the Titanic Sank. 2001. (Readers Ser.). (Illus.). 32p. (J). (ps-3). pap. 12.95 (*0-7894-7374-7*); pap. 3.95 (*0-7894-7373-9*) Dorling Kindersley Publishing, Inc. (D K Ink).

Lawlor, Laurie. A Titanic Journey Across the Sea 1912. (American Sisters Ser.: Vol. 2). (J). 1998. 208p. (gr. 4-7). 9.00 (*0-671-02718-2*); 2000. (Illus.). 224p. (gr. 3-6). pap. 4.50 (*0-671-77559-6*) Simon & Schuster Children's Publishing. (Aladdin).

Martin, Les. Young Indiana Jones & the Titanic Adventure. 1993. (Young Indiana Jones Ser.: No. 9). 132p. (Orig.). (J). (gr. 4-6). pap. 3.50 o.s.i (*0-679-84925-4*, Random Hse. Bks. for Young Readers) Random Hse. Children's Bks.

McKeown, Arthur. Titanic: Read to Read Level 2. 1998. (Ready-to-Read Ser.). (Illus.). 48p. (J). (gr. 1-4). pap. 3.99 (*0-689-82476-9*, Aladdin) Simon & Schuster Children's Publishing.

McKeown, Arthur & Hogan, Peter. Titanic: Read to Read Level 2. 1996. (Illus.). 48p. pap. 7.95 (*1-85371-516-6*) Poolbeg Pr. IRL. *Dist:* Dufour Editions, Inc.

Osborne, Mary Pope. Tonight on the Titanic. 1999. (Magic Tree House Ser.: No. 17). (Illus.). 96p. (J). (gr. k-3). lib. bdg. 11.99 (*0-679-99063-1*); pap. 3.99 (*0-679-89063-7*) Random Hse., Inc.

—Tonight on the Titanic. 1999. (Magic Tree House Ser.: No. 17). (J). (gr. k-3). 10.14 (*0-606-16894-X*) Turtleback Bks.

Peck, Richard. Amanda/Miranda. 1981. 544p. (YA). (gr. 7 up). pap. 2.95 o.p. (*0-380-53850-4*, 53850-5, Avon Bks.) Morrow/Avon.

—Amanda/Miranda. Kane, Cindy, ed. abr. ed. 1999. (Illus.). 176p. (YA). (gr. 7-12). 16.99 (*0-8037-2489-6*, Dial Bks. for Young Readers) Penguin Putnam Bks. for Young Readers.

—Amanda/Miranda. 1980. 12.95 o.p. (*0-670-11530-4*) Viking Penguin.

Spedden, Daisy C. S. Polar the Titanic Bear. 1998. 17.95 (*0-316-80924-1*); 1994. (Illus.). 64p. (J). (gr. 3-7). 17.95 (*0-316-80625-0*) Little Brown & Co.

Tanaka, Shelley. I Was There: On Board the Titanic - What It Was Like When the Great Liner Sank. 1996. (I Was There Ser.). (Illus.). 48p. (J). (gr. 4-7). 16.95 (*0-7868-0283-9*) Hyperion Bks. for Children.

—On Board the Titanic. 1997. (Illus.). 16.45 (*0-7868-1269-9*) Hyperion Pr.

—On Board the Titanic: What It Was Like When the Great Liner Sank. 1998. (I Was There Ser.). (Illus.). 48p. (J). (gr. 4-6). pap. 7.99 (*0-7868-1318-0*) Hyperion Pr.

—On Board the Titanic: What It Was Like When the Great Liner Sank. 1999. (Illus.). (J). 13.10 (*0-606-15659-3*) Turtleback Bks.

White, Ellen Emerson. Voyage on the Great Titanic: The Diary of Margaret Ann Brady, R. M. S. Titanic, 1912. 1998. (Illus.). 197p. (YA). (gr. 4-9). pap. 10.95 (*0-590-96273-6*, Scholastic Pr.) Scholastic, Inc.

Williams, Barbara. Making Waves. 2000. (Illus.). 215p. (J). (gr. 4-8). 17.99 o.s.i (*0-8037-2515-9*, Dial Bks. for Young Readers) Penguin Putnam Bks. for Young Readers.

—Titanic Crossing. 1995. 176p. (J). (gr. 4-7). 15.99 o.s.i (*0-8037-1790-3*); 15.89 o.p. (*0-8037-1791-1*) Penguin Putnam Bks. for Young Readers. (Dial Bks. for Young Readers).

—Titanic Crossing. 1997. 167p. (J). (gr. 3-7). mass mkt. 4.50 (*0-590-94464-9*) Scholastic, Inc.

—Titanic Crossing. 1997. 10.55 (*0-606-12829-8*) Turtleback Bks.

Wilson, Lynda. The Virtual Zone: Titanic's Race to Disaster. 2001. (On Time's Wing Ser.). (Illus.). 104p. (J). (gr. 3-7). pap. 6.95 (*1-896184-96-0*) Roussan Pubs., Inc./Roussan Editeur, Inc. CAN. *Dist:* Orca Bk. Pubs.

U

UNDERGROUND RAILROAD—FICTION

Armstrong, Jennifer. Steal Away. 224p. 1993. (J). (gr. 3-7). pap. 4.50 (*0-590-46921-5*, Scholastic Paperbacks); 1992. (YA). (gr. 6 up). mass mkt. 16.99 o.p. (*0-531-08583-X*, Orchard Bks.); 1992. (YA). (gr. 6 up). 15.95 o.p. (*0-531-05983-9*, Orchard Bks.) Scholastic, Inc.

—Steal Away. 1992. (J). 10.55 (*0-606-05623-8*) Turtleback Bks.

Ayres, Katherine. North by Night: A Story of the Underground Railroad. 1998. 192p. (gr. 5-9). text 15.95 o.s.i (*0-385-32564-9*, Delacorte Pr.) Dell Publishing.

—Stealing South: A Story of the Underground Railroad. 208p. (gr. 5-9). 2002. pap. text 4.99 (*0-440-41801-1*, Yearling); 2001. (Illus.). text 14.95 o.s.i (*0-385-72912-X*, Delacorte Bks. for Young Readers) Random Hse. Children's Bks.

—Stealing South: A Story of the Underground Railroad. Lt. ed. 2002. (Young Adult Ser.). 231p. (J). 22.95 (*0-7862-4422-4*) Thorndike Pr.

Beatty, Patricia. Jayhawker. 1995. (Illus.). 224p. (J). (gr. 7 up). pap. 6.99 (*0-688-14422-5*) HarperCollins Children's Bk. Group.

—Jayhawker. 1991. 224p. (YA). (gr. 5 up). 16.00 o.p. (*0-688-09850-9*); 1924. (J). lib. bdg. o.s.i (*0-688-09851-7*) Morrow/Avon. (Morrow, William & Co.).

—Jayhawker. 1995. 12.00 (*0-606-07734-0*) Turtleback Bks.

—Who Comes with Cannons? 1992. 192p. (J). (gr. 4-7). 15.99 (*0-688-11028-2*) HarperCollins Children's Bk. Group.

Brenaman, Miriam. Evvy's Civil War. 2002. 224p. (J). (gr. 7-10). 18.99 (*0-399-23713-5*) Penguin Group (USA) Inc.

—Evvy's Civil War. 2004. (Illus.). 224p. pap. 6.99 (*0-14-240039-4*, Puffin Bks.) Penguin Putnam Bks. for Young Readers.

Bryant, Louella. The Black Bonnet. 1996. (YA). (gr. 5 up). pap. 12.95 (*1-881535-22-3*) New England Pr., Inc., The.

Carbone, Elisa. Stealing Freedom. 272p. (gr. 5-8). 2001. (Illus.). (YA). pap. 5.50 (*0-440-41707-4*, Dell Books for Young Readers); 1998. lib. bdg. 18.99 o.s.i (*0-679-99307-X*, Random Hse. Bks. for Young Readers); 1998. (Illus.). (YA). 17.00 o.s.i (*0-679-89307-5*, Random Hse. Bks. for Young Readers) Random Hse. Children's Bks.

Carbone, Elisa Lynn. Stealing Freedom. 2002. (EMC Masterpiece Series Access Editions). (Illus.). xix, 284p. (J). 14.60 (*0-8219-2507-5*) EMC/Paradigm Publishing.

Charbonneau, Eileen. Honor to the Hills. (J). 1997. (Woods Family Saga: Vol. 3). (FRE.). 238p. (gr. 8-12). mass mkt. 3.99 (*0-8125-5187-7*); 1996. 192p. (gr. 7-12). 18.95 (*0-312-86094-3*) Doherty, Tom Assocs., LLC. (Tor Bks.).

—Honor to the Hills, 3. 1997. (Woods Family Saga). 10.04 (*0-606-11477-7*) Turtleback Bks.

Connelly, Bernardine. Follow the Drinking Gourd. 1993. (Illus.). (J). 14.95 (*0-88708-336-6*); 19.95 incl. audio (*0-88708-335-8*) Simon & Schuster Children's Publishing. (Simon & Schuster Children's Publishing).

Cromer, Mary L. Stories for Jason. 1993. 110p. (J). pap. 9.00 (*0-944350-28-3*) Friends United Pr.

Dahlberg, Maurine F. The Spirit & Gilly Bucket, RS. 2002. 240p. (J). (gr. 3-7). 18.00 (*0-374-31677-5*, Farrar, Straus & Giroux (BYR)) Farrar, Straus & Giroux.

Dell, Pamela. Aquila's Drinking Gourd: A Story of the Underground Railroad. 2002. (Illus.). 48p. (J). lib. bdg. 27.07 (*1-59187-013-5*) Child's World, Inc.

Draper, Sharon M. Ziggy & the Black Dinosaurs: Lost in the Tunnel of Time. (Ziggy & the Black Dinosaurs Ser.: No. 2). (Illus.). 96p. (J). (gr. 3-7). 1996. pap. 6.00 (*0-940975-63-7*); 1994. 14.00 o.p. (*0-940975-47-5*) Just Us Bks., Inc.

Edwards, Pamela Duncan. Barefoot: Escape on the Underground Railroad. 1997. (Illus.). 32p. (J). (gr. k-4). 15.99 (*0-06-027137-X*); lib. bdg. 15.89 (*0-06-027138-8*) HarperCollins Children's Bk. Group.

—Barefoot: Escape on the Underground Railroad. 1998. 12.10 (*0-606-15847-2*) Turtleback Bks.

Fritz, Jean. Brady. 1987. (Illus.). 224p. (J). (gr. 7 up). reprint ed. pap. 5.99 o.s.i (*0-14-032258-2*, Puffin Bks.) Penguin Putnam Bks. for Young Readers.

—Brady. 1960. (J). (gr. 4-8). 9.95 o.p. (*0-698-20014-4*, Coward-McCann) Putnam Publishing Group, The.

—Brady. 1993. (J). (gr. 5-9). 20.75 (*0-8446-6644-0*) Smith, Peter Pub., Inc.

—Brady. 1987. (J). 10.09 o.p. (*0-606-03555-9*) Turtleback Bks.

Gayle, Sharon Shavers. Emma's Escape: A Story of America's Underground Railroad. 2003. (J). pap. 3.95 (*1-59249-021-2*) Soundprints.

Guccione, Leslie Davis. Come Morning. (Adventures in Time Ser.). 120p. (J). (gr. 4-7). 1995. lib. bdg. 15.95 (*0-87614-892-5*); 1997. (Illus.). reprint ed. pap. 6.95 (*1-57505-228-8*) Lerner Publishing Group. (Carolrhoda Bks.).

Hamilton, Virginia. The House of Dies Drear. Lt. ed. 2001. 305p. lib. bdg. 29.95 (*1-58118-087-X*) LRS.

—The House of Dies Drear. 1998. 32p. 9.95 (*1-56137-516-0*, NU5168) Novel Units, Inc.

—The House of Dies Drear. 2001. (Assessment Packs Ser.). 15p. pap. text 15.95 (*1-58303-122-7*) Pathways Publishing.

—The House of Dies Drear. 8.97 (*0-13-437491-6*) Prentice Hall PTR.

—The House of Dies Drear. (Illus.). 256p. (YA). 1984. (gr. 7 up). mass mkt. 5.99 (*0-02-043520-7*, Simon Pulse); 1968. (gr. 4-7). 18.95 (*0-02-742500-2*, Simon & Schuster Children's Publishing) Simon & Schuster Children's Publishing.

—The House of Dies Drear. 1984. (Dies Drear Chronicle Ser.). (J). 11.04 (*0-606-03314-9*) Turtleback Bks.

Hedstrom, Deborah. From Settlement to City with Benjamin Franklin. 1997. (My American Journey Ser.). (Illus.). 19.99 o.p. (*1-57673-164-2*) Multnomah Pubs., Inc.

Holub, Joan. Glory's Freedom: A Story of the Underground Railroad. 2003. (Doll Hospital Ser.: No. 3). (Illus.). 118p. (J). (gr. 2-6). mass mkt. 3.99 (*0-439-40180-1*, Scholastic Paperbacks) Scholastic, Inc.

Hopkinson, Deborah. Under the Quilt of Night. 2002. (Illus.). 40p. (J). 16.00 (*0-689-82227-8*, Atheneum/Anne Schwartz Bks.) Simon & Schuster Children's Publishing.

Houston, Gloria M. Bright Freedom's Song: A Story of the Underground Railroad. 1998. (Illus.). 160p. (YA). (gr. 5 up). 16.00 (*0-15-201812-3*, Silver Whistle) Harcourt Children's Bks.

Johnson, P. Mysterious Signal. 1998. (Riverboat Adventures Ser.: Vol. 5). 176p. (J). (gr. 3-8). pap. 5.99 o.p. (*1-55661-355-5*) Bethany Hse. Pubs.

Kay, Alan N. Send 'Em South. 2001. (Young Heroes of History Ser.: Vol. 1). (Illus.). 145p. (J). (gr. 3-6). pap. 5.95 (*1-57249-208-2*, WM Kids) White Mane Publishing Co., Inc.

Lasky, Kathryn. True North: A Novel of the Underground Railroad. 208p. 1998. (J). (gr. 5-9). mass mkt. 4.99 (*0-590-20524-2*); 1996. (YA). (gr. 7 up). pap. 15.95 (*0-590-20523-4*) Scholastic, Inc. (Blue Sky Pr., The).

—True North: A Novel of the Underground Railroad. 1998. (J). 11.04 (*0-606-13874-9*) Turtleback Bks.

Lawrence. Harriet & the Promise Land. 1998. (J). pap. 5.99 (*0-87628-392-X*) Ctr. for Applied Research in Education, The.

Mathews, Marcia M. The Freedom Star. 1971. (Illus.). (J). (gr. 3-6). 4.39 o.p. (*0-698-30094-7*, Coward-McCann) Putnam Publishing Group, The.

McCusker, Paul. The Dark Passage. 1996. (Adventures in Odyssey Ser.: Vol. 9). 112p. (J). (gr. 3-7). 4.99 (*1-56179-474-0*) Focus on the Family Publishing.

—Freedom Run. 1996. (Adventures in Odyssey Ser.: Bk. 10). 107p. (J). (gr. 3-7). 4.99 (*1-56179-475-9*) Focus on the Family Publishing.

McKissack, Patricia C. A Picture of Freedom: The Diary of Clotee, a Slave Girl, Belmont Plantation, Virginia, 1859. 1997. (Dear America Ser.). (Illus.). 195p. (YA). (gr. 4-9). pap. 10.95 (*0-590-25988-1*) Scholastic, Inc.

Meltzer, Milton. Underground Man. 1990. (Great Episodes Ser.). (J). 224p. (gr. 3-7). 14.95 (*0-15-200617-6*, Gulliver Bks.); 288p. (gr. 4-7). pap. 7.00 (*0-15-292846-4*, Odyssey Classics) Harcourt Children's Bks.

—Underground Man. 1972. 224p. (J). (gr. 6 up). 6.95 o.s.i (*0-87888-051-8*, Simon & Schuster Children's Publishing) Simon & Schuster Children's Publishing.

—Underground Man. 1990. 10.05 o.p. (*0-606-04836-7*) Turtleback Bks.

Monjo, F. N. The Drinking Gourd: A Story of the Underground Railroad. 2002. (Illus.). (J). 12.34 (*0-7587-5177-X*) Book Wholesalers, Inc.

—The Drinking Gourd: A Story of the Underground Railroad. 1970. (I Can Read Bks.). (Illus.). 64p. (J). (gr. k-3). 15.95 (*0-06-024329-5*); lib. bdg. 15.89 (*0-06-024330-9*) HarperCollins Children's Bk. Group.

—The Drinking Gourd: A Story of the Underground Railroad. unabr. ed. 1991. (I Can Read Bks.). (Illus.). 64p. (J). (gr. k-3). 8.99 incl. audio (*1-55994-355-6*, TBC 3556, HarperAudio) HarperTrade.

—La Osa Menor: Una Historia del Ferrocarril Subterraneo. Mlawer, Teresa, tr. 1997. (Ya Se Leer Ser.). (SPA., Illus.). 64p. (J). (gr. k-3). pap. 4.95 o.p. (*0-06-444217-9*) HarperCollins Children's Bk. Group.

—La Osa Menor: Una Historia del Ferrocarril Subterraneo. Mlawer, Teresa, tr. 2001. (SPA., Illus.). (J). (gr. 3-10). pap. 6.95 (*1-880507-90-0*, LC7973); ring bd. 15.95 (*1-880507-91-9*, LC7976) Lectorum Pubns., Inc.

—La Osa Menor: Una Historia del Ferrocarril Subterraneo. 2001. 12.10 (*0-606-21286-8*); 1997. 10.15 o.p. (*0-606-10860-2*) Turtleback Bks.

Morrow, Barbara Olenyik. A Good Night for Freedom. 2003. (Illus.). (J). (gr. k-3). tchr. ed. 16.95 (*0-8234-1709-3*) Holiday Hse., Inc.

Nelson, Vaunda Micheaux. Almost to Freedom. 2003. (Carolrhoda Picture Books Ser.). (Illus.). 40p. (J). (gr. 1-5). 15.95 (*1-57505-342-X*, Carolrhoda Bks.) Lerner Publishing Group.

Nordan, Robert. The Secret Road. 2001. (Illus.). 144p. (J). (gr. 4-6). tchr. ed. 16.95 (*0-8234-1543-0*) Holiday Hse., Inc.

Pearsall, Shelley. Trouble Don't Last. 256p. 2003. (gr. 3-7). pap. text 5.50 (*0-440-41811-9*, Dell Books for Young Readers); 2002. (Illus.). (gr. 4-8). text 14.95 (*0-375-81490-6*, Random Hse. Bks. for Young Readers); 2002. (Illus.). (gr. 4-8). lib. bdg. 16.99 (*0-375-91490-0*, Random Hse. Bks. for Young Readers) Random Hse. Children's Bks.

Pinkney, Andrea Davis. Silent Thunder: A Civil War Story. (J). 2001. 224p. (gr. 3-7). pap. 5.99 (*0-7868-1569-8*, Jump at the Sun); 1999. (Illus.). 208p. (gr. 4-7). 15.99 (*0-7868-0439-4*) Hyperion Bks. for Children.

—Silent Thunder: A Civil War Story. 2001. (J). 12.04 (*0-606-21434-8*) Turtleback Bks.

Ransom, Candice F. Liberty Street. 2003. (J). lib. bdg. 17.85 (*0-8027-8871-8*); (Illus.). 16.95 (*0-8027-8869-6*) Walker & Co.

Riggio, Anita. Secret Signs: Along the Underground Railroad. 2003. (Illus.). 32p. (J). (gr. k-3). 15.95 (*1-56397-555-6*) Boyds Mills Pr.

—Secret Signs: An Escape through the Underground Railroad. 2003. (Illus.). 32p. (J). (gr. k-3). pap. 8.95 (*1-59078-072-8*) Boyds Mills Pr.

Ringgold, Faith. Aunt Harriet's Underground Railroad in the Sky. 1995. (Illus.). 32p. (ps-3). pap. 6.99 (*0-517-88543-3*) Crown Publishing Group.

—Aunt Harriet's Underground Railroad in the Sky. 1992. (Illus.). 32p. (J). (ps-3). lib. bdg. 17.99 o.s.i (*0-517-58768-8*); 16.00 o.s.i (*0-517-58767-X*) Random Hse. Children's Bks. (Random Hse. Bks. for Young Readers).

—Aunt Harriet's Underground Railroad in the Sky. 1995. (J). 13.14 (*0-606-08478-9*) Turtleback Bks.

Rosen, Michael J. A School for Pompey Walker. 1995. (Illus.). 48p. (J). (gr. 4-7). 16.00 (*0-15-200114-X*) Harcourt Children's Bks.

Ruby, Lois. Soon Be Free. 2000. (Illus.). 320p. (J). (gr. 3-7). 17.00 (*0-689-83266-4*, Simon & Schuster Children's Publishing) Simon & Schuster Children's Publishing.

—Steal Away Home. 1997. pap. 1.95 o.p. (*0-590-03322-0*) Scholastic, Inc.

—Steal Away Home. 1999. 208p. (J). (gr. 3-7). pap. 4.99 (*0-689-82435-1*, Aladdin) Simon & Schuster Children's Publishing.

—Steal Away Home. 1999. 11.04 (*0-606-15921-5*) Turtleback Bks.

Sargent, Dave & Sargent, Pat. Nubbin (Linebacked Apricot Dun): Freedom. 2003. (Saddle Up Ser.: Vol. 43). 42p. (J). mass mkt. 6.95 (*1-56763-704-3*) Ozark Publishing.

—Nubbin (Linebacked Apricot Dun) Freedom. 2003. (Saddle Up Ser.: Vol. 43). 42p. (J). lib. bdg. 22.60 (*1-56763-703-5*) Ozark Publishing.

Schlabach, Janet. Riverboat Runaways. 1999. (Illus.). 138p. (J). (gr. 4-8). pap. 15.95 (*0-936389-75-3*) Tudor Pubs., Inc.

Schotter, Roni. F Is for Freedom. 2000. (Illus.). 112p. (J). (gr. 2-5). pap. 15.99 (*0-7894-2641-2*, D K Ink) Dorling Kindersley Publishing, Inc.

Schwartz, Virginia Frances. If I Just Had Two Wings. (Illus.). (J). 220p. pap. 9.95 (*0-7737-6192-6*); 2001. 221p. (gr. 5 up). 15.95 (*0-7737-3302-7*) Stoddart Kids CAN. *Dist:* Fitzhenry & Whiteside, Ltd.

Stengel, Joyce A. Mystery at Kittiwake Bay. 2001. 176p. (J). pap. 4.99 (*0-689-84595-2*, Aladdin) Simon & Schuster Children's Publishing.

Stolz, Mary. Cezanne Pinto: A Memoir. 1997. 288p. (J). (gr. 5-9). pap. 4.99 (*0-679-88933-7*); 1994. 256p. (YA). (gr. 6 up). pap. o.p. (*0-679-94917-8*); 1994. 256p. (YA). (gr. 6 up). 16.00 o.s.i (*0-679-84917-3*) Random Hse. Children's Bks. (Knopf Bks. for Young Readers).

—Cezanne Pinto: A Memoir. 1997. (YA). (gr. 6 up). 11.04 (*0-606-12904-9*) Turtleback Bks.

Turner, Glennette Tilley. Running for Our Lives. 1994. (Illus.). 208p. (J). (gr. 4-7). tchr. ed. 16.95 (*0-8234-1121-4*) Holiday Hse., Inc.

Vande Velde, Vivian. There's a Dead Person Following My Sister Around. 2001. 160p. (J). pap. 4.99 (*0-14-131281-5*, Puffin Bks.) Penguin Putnam Bks. for Young Readers.

Vaughan, Marcia K. The Secret to Freedom. 2001. (Illus.). 32p. (J). (gr. 1-4). 16.95 (*1-58430-021-3*) Lee & Low Bks., Inc.

Warburton, Carol. Edge of Night: A Novel. 2002. (Illus.). 278p. (YA). (*1-59156-013-6*) Covenant Communications.

Weinberg, Larry. Ghost Hotel. 1994. 9.05 o.p. (*0-606-06409-5*) Turtleback Bks.

—Return to Ghost Hotel. 1996. 9.05 o.p. (*0-606-09785-6*) Turtleback Bks.

Williams, Jeanne. Freedom Trail. 1973. 160p. (YA). (gr. 6 up). 5.95 o.p. (*0-399-20336-2*) Putnam Publishing Group, The.

Williamson, Denise. When Stars Begin to Fall. 2000. (Roots of Faith Ser.: Vol. 2). 448p. pap. 12.99 (*1-55661-883-2*) Bethany Hse. Pubs.

Winter, Jeanette. Follow the Drinking Gourd. 2002. (Illus.). (J). 15.74 (*0-7587-2527-2*) Book Wholesalers, Inc.

—Follow the Drinking Gourd. 48p. (J). (gr. 1-4). 1989. 17.99 o.s.i (*0-394-99694-1*); 1988. (Illus.). 17.00 o.s.i (*0-394-89694-7*) Random Hse. Children's Bks. (Knopf Bks. for Young Readers).

—Follow the Drinking Gourd. 1992. (J). 14.14 (*0-606-01542-6*) Turtleback Bks.

Wisehart, Randall. A Winding Road to Freedom. 1999. 184p. (J). (gr. 5-8). pap. 13.00 (*0-944350-47-X*) Friends United Pr.

Woodruff, Elvira. Dear Austin: Letters from the Underground Railroad. 1998. (Illus.). 144p. (YA). (gr. 5-8). 16.00 o.s.i (*0-679-88594-3*, Knopf Bks. for Young Readers) Random Hse. Children's Bks.

—Dear Austin: Letters from the Underground Railroad. 2000. (Illus.). (J). 11.04 (*0-606-18811-8*) Turtleback Bks.

Wright, Courtni C. Journey to Freedom: A Story of the Underground Railroad. 1994. (Illus.). 32p. (J). (ps-3). tchr. ed. 16.95 (*0-8234-1096-X*); reprint ed. pap. 6.95 (*0-8234-1333-0*) Holiday Hse., Inc.

Wyeth, Sharon Dennis. Freedom's Wings: Corey's Underground Railroad Diary, Bk. 1. (My America Ser.). (Illus.). 112p. (J). (gr. 4-7). 2002. mass mkt. 4.99 (*0-439-36907-X*); 2001. pap. 8.95 (*0-439-14100-1*) Scholastic, Inc. (Scholastic Pr.).

—Freedom's Wings: Corey's Underground Railroad Diary. 2001. (J). (gr. 4-7). 15.00 (*0-606-22804-7*) Turtleback Bks.

—Message in the Sky: Corey's Underground Railroad Diary, Bk. 3. 2003. (My America Ser.). 112p. (J). pap. 10.95 (*0-439-37057-4*); mass mkt. 4.99 (*0-439-37058-2*) Scholastic, Inc. (Scholastic Pr.).

UNITED STATES—HISTORY—FICTION

Across the Wide & Lonesome Prairie: The Oregon Trail Diary of Hattie Campbell. 2003. (J). lib. bdg. 12.95 (*0-439-55508-6*) Scholastic, Inc.

Adler, David A. Mama Played Baseball. 2003. (Illus.). 32p. (J). 16.00 (*0-15-202196-5*) Harcourt Children's Bks.

Alter, Judy. Sam Houston Is My Hero. 2003. (Chaparral Book for Young Readers Ser.). 140p. (J). pap. 15.95 (*0-87565-277-8*) Texas Christian Univ. Pr.

Antle, Nancy. Sam's Wild West Show: Level 3. 1998. (Puffin Easy-to-Read Program Ser.). (Illus.). 48p. (J). (gr. 1-4). pap. 3.99 o.s.i (*0-14-130133-3*, Puffin Bks.) Penguin Putnam Bks. for Young Readers.

Archer, Myrtle. In the Wilderness. rev. ed. 1986. 220p. (J). reprint ed. pap. 6.95 (*0-9615263-0-0*) Ames Publishing Co.

Armistead, John. The Return of Gabriel. 2002. (Illus.). 240p. (J). (gr. 3-8). 17.95 (*1-57131-637-X*); pap. 6.95 (*1-57131-638-8*) Milkweed Editions.

Armstrong, Jennifer. Becoming Mary Mehan. 2002. (Illus.). 320p. (YA). (gr. 7). mass mkt. 6.99 (*0-440-22961-8*, Laurel Leaf) Random Hse. Children's Bks.

Arntson, Herbert E. Caravan to Oregon. 1957. (Illus.). (J). (gr. 7-11). 8.95 o.p. (*0-8323-0164-7*) Binford & Mort Publishing.

Atwell, Debby. Pearl. 2001. (Illus.). 32p. (J). (ps-3). tchr. ed. 16.00 (*0-395-88416-0*) Houghton Mifflin Co.

Avi. The Escape from Home. 1997. (Beyond the Western Sea Ser.: Bk. 1). 336p. (J). (gr. 5-9). pap. 6.99 (*0-380-72875-3*, Harper Trophy) HarperCollins Children's Bk. Group.

—Lord Kirkle's Money. 1998. (Beyond the Western Sea Ser.: Vol. 2). 432p. (J). (gr. 5-9). reprint ed. pap. 6.99 (*0-380-72876-1*, Harper Trophy) HarperCollins Children's Bk. Group.

Aylesworth, Jim. Mr. McGill Goes to Town, ERS. 1992. (Illus.). 32p. (J). (gr. k-2). pap. 4.95 o.p. (*0-8050-2096-9*, Holt, Henry & Co. Bks. For Young Readers) Holt, Henry & Co.

Brooks, Nigel & Horner, Abigail. Town Mouse House: How We Lived One Hundred Years Ago. 2000. (Illus.). 32p. (J). (gr. k-3). 15.95 (*0-8027-8732-0*) Walker & Co.

Bruchac, Joseph. Bowman's Store: A Journey to Myself. 2001. (Illus.). 328p. (YA). (gr. 7 up). pap. 6.95 (*1-58430-027-2*) Lee & Low Bks., Inc.

—Bowman's Store: A Journey to Myself. 1997. (Illus.). 320p. (YA). (gr. 7 up). 17.99 o.s.i (*0-8037-1997-3*, Dial Bks. for Young Readers) Penguin Putnam Bks. for Young Readers.

—Children of the Longhouse. 1996. (Illus.). 160p. (J). (gr. 3-7). 14.99 o.p. (*0-8037-1793-8*, Dial Bks. for Young Readers) Penguin Putnam Bks. for Young Readers.

—Eagle Song. 1997. (Illus.). 80p. (J). (gr. 2-5). 14.99 o.p. (*0-8037-1918-3*, Dial Bks. for Young Readers) Penguin Putnam Bks. for Young Readers.

Call me. 2003. (J). mass mkt. 2.25 (*0-590-33766-1*) Scholastic, Inc.

Carbone, Elisa. Storm Warriors. 2002. 176p. (gr. 3-7). pap. text 5.50 (*0-440-41879-8*) Random Hse., Inc.

Carter, Russell G. A Patriot Lad of Old Cape Cod. 1975. (Illus.). 224p. (J). (gr. 6-8). reprint ed. 4.95 o.p. (*0-88492-007-0*); pap. 1.95 o.p. (*0-88492-008-9*) Sullwold, William S. Publishing.

Chambers, Veronica. Amistad Rising: A Story of Freedom. Bowen, Shelly & Johnston, Allyn M., eds. 1998. (Illus.). 40p. (J). (gr. 3-7). 16.00 o.s.i (*0-15-201803-4*) Harcourt Children's Bks.

—Amistad Rising: A Story of Freedom. 1998. (Illus.). 40p. (J). (gr. 4-7). lib. bdg. 16.98 (*0-8172-5510-9*) Raintree Pubs.

A Coal Miner's Bride: The Diary of Anetka Kaminska. 2003. (J). lib. bdg. 12.95 (*0-439-55510-8*) Scholastic, Inc.

Cochrane, Patricia A. Purely Rosie Pearl. 1997. 144p. (gr. 4-7). pap. text 3.99 o.s.i (*0-440-41344-3*) Dell Publishing.

Coleman, Wim & Perrin, Pat. Sister Anna: A Story of Shaker Life. 2000. 232p. (J). (gr. 5-12). pap. 10.95 (*1-57960-059-X*) Discovery Enterprises, Ltd.

Collier, James & Collier, Christopher. Who Is Carrie? 2001. 176p. (gr. 5-7). pap. text 12.00 (*0-375-89503-5*) Random Hse., Inc.

Conlon-McKenna, Marita. Fields of Home. 1997. (Illus.). 192p. (J). (gr. 3-7). pap. 15.95 (*0-8234-1295-4*) Holiday Hse., Inc.

Cooney, Caroline B. The Ransom of Mercy Carter. 2001. (Illus.). 256p. (YA). (gr. 7 up). 15.95 (*0-385-32615-7*, Delacorte Bks. for Young Readers) Random Hse. Children's Bks.

—The Ransom of Mercy Carter. 2002. 256p. (YA). (gr. 7 up). mass mkt. 5.50 (*0-440-22775-5*) Random Hse., Inc.

Curley, Daniel. Hilarion, 001. 1979. (J). (gr. 5-9). 6.95 o.p. (*0-395-28268-3*) Houghton Mifflin Co.

Curtis, Alice Turner. A Little Maid of New England, 2 vols. in 1. 1991. (J). 7.99 o.s.i (*0-517-06494-4*) Random Hse. Value Publishing.

Davis, Ossie. Just Like Martin. 2001. (J). pap. (*0-7868-1642-2*); 176p. lib. bdg. 16.49 (*0-7868-2632-0*) Hyperion Bks. for Children. (Jump at the Sun).

—Just Like Martin. 1995. 224p. (YA). (gr. 5-9). pap. 5.99 (*0-14-037095-1*, Puffin Bks.) Penguin Putnam Bks. for Young Readers.

—Just Like Martin. 1992. 208p. (YA). (gr. 5-9). pap. 15.00 (*0-671-73202-1*, Simon & Schuster Children's Publishing) Simon & Schuster Children's Publishing.

—Just Like Martin. 1996. (J). (gr. 5-9). 19.50 o.p. (*0-8446-6897-4*) Smith, Peter Pub., Inc.

—Just Like Martin. 1995. (YA). 12.04 (*0-606-07756-1*) Turtleback Bks.

Denenberg, Barry. Mirror, Mirror on the Wall: The Diary of Bess Brennan. 2002. (Dear America Ser.). (Illus.). 144p. (J). (gr. 4-9). pap. 10.95 (*0-439-19446-6*, Scholastic Pr.) Scholastic, Inc.

Donahue, John. An Island Far from Home. 1995. (Adventures in Time Ser.). 180p. (J). (gr. 4-7). lib. bdg. 15.95 (*0-87614-859-3*, Carolrhoda Bks.) Lerner Publishing Group.

Drexler, Sam & Shelby, Fay. Lost in Spillville. 2000. (Erika & Oz Adventures in American History Ser.: Vol. 1). (Illus.). 150p. (J). (gr. 5-9). pap. 6.99 (*0-9669988-1-2*) Aunt Strawberry Bks.

Duey, Kathleen. Nell Dunne: New York City 1899. 2000. (American Diaries Ser.: No. 16). (Illus.). 144p. (J). (gr. 3-7). pap. 4.99 (*0-689-83555-8*, Aladdin) Simon & Schuster Children's Publishing.

—Nell Dunne: New York City 1899. 2000. (American Diaries Ser.: No. 16). (J). (gr. 3-7). 10.55 (*0-606-17903-8*) Turtleback Bks.

—Rosa Moreno: Hollywood, California, 1934. 1999. (American Diaries Ser.: No. 14). 140p. (J). (gr. 3-7). per. 4.50 (*0-689-83126-9*, Aladdin) Simon & Schuster Children's Publishing.

—Rosa Moreno: Hollywood, California, 1934. 1999. (American Diaries Ser.: No. 14). (J). (gr. 3-7). 10.55 (*0-606-17200-9*) Turtleback Bks.

Duey, Kathleen & Bale, Karen A. Blizzard, Estes Park, Colorado, 1886. 1998. (Survival! Ser.: No. 3). (Illus.). 160p. (J). (gr. 4-7). pap. 4.99 (*0-689-81309-0*, Aladdin) Simon & Schuster Children's Publishing.

Durrant, Lynda. Betsy Zane: The Rose of Fort Henry. 2002. 208p. (gr. 5). pap. text 4.99 (*0-440-41834-8*, Yearling) Random Hse. Children's Bks.

Ernst, Kathleen. The Bravest Girl in Sharpsburg. 1998. (White Mane Kids Ser.: Vol. 5). (Illus.). 238p. (YA). (gr. 3-7). pap. 8.95 (*1-57249-083-7*, WM Kids) White Mane Publishing Co., Inc.

Farhi, Roslyn. Molly's Century. 1999. (Illus.). 32p. (J). (gr. k-4). pap. 9.95 (*0-9660599-1-3*) Nostalgia Pubns.

Fennessey, Sharon. The Loom & the Lash. 1998. (J). (gr. 5-9). pap. 12.00 (*1-57960-042-5*) Discovery Enterprises, Ltd.

Fiore, Peter A., illus. Hand in Hand: An American History Through Poetry. 1994. 144p. (J). (gr. 3-7). 21.95 (*0-671-73315-X*, Simon & Schuster Children's Publishing) Simon & Schuster Children's Publishing.

Fryer, Jane Eayre. The Mary Frances Housekeeper: Adventures among the Doll People. 1998. (Mary Frances Ser.: Vol. 3). (Illus.). 254p. (J). (gr. 3-8). pap. 28.00 (*0-916896-92-7*) Lacis Pubns.

Gauch, Patricia. Thunder in Gettysburg. 1996. (J). pap. 4.50 (*0-440-91190-7*, Dell Books for Young Readers) Random Hse. Children's Bks.

Giff, Patricia Reilly. Lily's Crossing. 2002. (Illus.). (J). 13.94 (*0-7587-0287-6*) Book Wholesalers, Inc.

—Lily's Crossing. 1997. 192p. (gr. 3-7). text 15.95 (*0-385-32142-2*, Delacorte Pr.) Dell Publishing.

—Lily's Crossing. 1999. (Yearling Newbery Ser.). 208p. (gr. 3-7). pap. text 5.50 (*0-440-41453-9*, Dell Books for Young Readers) Random Hse. Children's Bks.

—Lily's Crossing. l.t. ed. 2000. (Illus.). 200p. (J). (ps up). 22.95 (*0-7862-2771-0*) Thorndike Pr.

—Lily's Crossing. 1999. (Yearling Newbery Ser.). (Illus.). (J). 11.55 (*0-606-14423-4*) Turtleback Bks.

The Girl Who Chased Away Sorrow: The Diary of Sarah Nita, a Navajo Girl. 2003. (J). lib. bdg. 12.95 (*0-439-55539-6*) Scholastic, Inc.

Greenfield, Eloise. Easter Parade. 1998. (Illus.). 64p. (J). (gr. 1-5). 13.95 (*0-7868-0326-6*); lib. bdg. 14.49 (*0-7868-2271-6*) Hyperion Bks. for Children.

Grote, JoAnn A. The Flu Epidemic. 37th ed. 1998. (American Adventure Ser.: No. 37). (Illus.). (J). (gr. 3-7). pap. 3.97 (*1-57748-451-7*) Barbour Publishing, Inc.

—Queen Anne's War. 5th ed. 1998. (American Adventure Ser.: No. 5). (Illus.). (J). (gr. 3-7). pap. 3.97 (*1-57748-146-1*) Barbour Publishing, Inc.

Harrah, Madge. My Brother, My Enemy. 1997. 144p. (YA). (gr. 5-9). 16.00 (*0-689-80968-9*, Simon & Schuster Children's Publishing) Simon & Schuster Children's Publishing.

Hedstrom, Deborah. From Log Cabin to White House with Abraham Lincoln, No. 7. 1998. (My American Journey Ser.: Vol. 7). (YA). (ps-3). 19.99 o.p. (*1-57673-300-9*) Multnomah Pubs., Inc.

—From Mississippi Mud to California Gold with Mark Twain. 1998. (My American Journey Ser.: No. 8). 19.99 o.p. (*1-57673-301-7*) Multnomah Pubs., Inc.

Hinman, Bonnie. Earthquake in Cincinnati: Disaster Changes Life Forever. 14th ed. 1998. (American Adventure Ser.: No. 14). (Illus.). (J). (gr. 3-7). pap. 3.97 (*1-57748-231-X*) Barbour Publishing, Inc.

Hinson, Robert. Of Fairfield Plantation. 1997. 64p. (YA). (gr. 7-12). pap. 5.95 (*1-890424-00-5*) D-N Publishing.

Hobbs, Valerie. Sonny's War, RS. 2002. 224p. (YA). (gr. 7 up). 16.00 (*0-374-37136-9*, Farrar, Straus & Giroux (BYR)) Farrar, Straus & Giroux.

Hoobler, Dorothy & Hoobler, Thomas. The 1960s: Rebels, 2001. (Century Kids Ser.). (Illus.). 160p. (J). (gr. 5-8). 22.90 (*0-7613-1606-X*) Millbrook Pr., Inc.

Hopkinson, Deborah. Our Kansas Home. 2003. (Prairie Skies Ser.: Bk. 3). 80p. (J). pap. 3.99 (*0-689-84353-4*, Aladdin) Simon & Schuster Children's Publishing.

—Prairie Skies: Our Kansas Home. 2003. (Prairie Skies Ser.). 80p. (J). lib. bdg. 11.89 (*0-689-84354-2*, Aladdin Library) Simon & Schuster Children's Publishing.

Hughes, Barbara. Then & Now. (Livewire Ser.). (YA). (gr. 6-9). pap. 8.95 (*0-7043-4930-2*) Women's Pr., Ltd., The GBR. *Dist:* Trafalgar Square.

I Thought My Soul Would Rise & Fly: The Diary of Patsy, a Freed Girl. 2003. (J). lib. bdg. 12.95 (*0-439-55505-1*) Scholastic, Inc.

Irwin, Ann & Reida, Bernice. Until We Reach the Valley. 1979. (Illus.). 173p. (J). (gr. 4-7). pap. 1.50 o.p. (*0-380-43398-2*, 43398-2, Avon Bks.) Morrow/Avon.

Irwin, Hadley. Be Somebody. 1988. 160p. mass mkt. 2.50 o.p. (*0-451-15303-0*, Signet Bks.) NAL.

—Be Somebody. 1984. 180p. (J). (gr. 4-7). 13.95 o.s.i (*0-689-50308-3*, McElderry, Margaret K.) Simon & Schuster Children's Publishing.

Johnson, Dolores. Now Let Me Fly: The Story of a Slave Family. 1998. pap. 5.99 (*0-87628-977-4*) Ctr. for Applied Research in Education, The.

—Now Let Me Fly: The Story of a Slave Family. 32p. (ps-3). 1997. pap. 6.99 (*0-689-80966-2*, Aladdin); 1993. (Illus.). (J). lib. bdg. 15.00 (*0-02-747699-5*, Atheneum) Simon & Schuster Children's Publishing.

—Now Let Me Fly: The Story of a Slave Family. 1997. 12.14 (*0-606-11692-3*) Turtleback Bks.

Johnson, Mabel. Escape from Scrooby. 1975. (J). (gr. 7 up). pap. 4.50 (*0-9600838-2-0*) Johnson, Mabel Quality Paperbacks.

Johnston, Norma. Lotta's Progress. 1997. 160p. (J). (gr. 3-7). mass mkt. 14.00 o.p. (*0-380-97367-7*, Avon Bks.) Morrow/Avon.

Jones, Veda Boyd. Cincinnati Epidemic. 17th ed. 1998. (American Adventure Ser.: No. 17). (Illus.). (J). (gr. 3-7). pap. 3.97 (*1-57748-255-7*) Barbour Publishing, Inc.

The Journal of Ben Uchida: Citizen 13559. 2003. (J). lib. bdg. 12.95 (*0-439-55530-2*) Scholastic, Inc.

The Journal of Douglas Allen Deeds: The Donner Party Expedition. 2003. (J). lib. bdg. 12.95 (*0-439-55519-1*) Scholastic, Inc.

The Journal of James Edmond Pease: A Civil War Union Soldier. 2003. (J). lib. bdg. 12.95 (*0-439-55537-X*) Scholastic, Inc.

The Journal of Jasper Jonathan Pierce: A Pilgrim Boy: Plymouth Plantation, 1620. 2003. (J). lib. bdg. 12.95 (*0-439-55511-6*) Scholastic, Inc.

The Journal of Otto Peltonen: A Finnish Immigrant. 2003. (J). lib. bdg. 12.95 (*0-439-55500-0*) Scholastic, Inc.

Karr, Kathleen. Dwight D. Eisenhower: Letters from a New Jersey Schoolgirl. 2002. (Dear Mr. President Ser.). (Illus.). 128p. (YA). 9.95 (*1-58837-007-0*) Winslow Pr.

—Spy in the Sky. 1997. (Hyperion Chapters Ser.). (Illus.). 64p. (J). (gr. 3-4). pap. 3.95 (*0-7868-1165-X*) Disney Pr.

—Spy in the Sky. 1997. (Illus.). (J). 10.10 (*0-606-20493-8*) Turtleback Bks.

Keehn, Sally M. Moon of the Two Dark Horses. 1997. 224p. (gr. 5-12). pap. text 3.99 o.s.i (*0-440-41287-0*) Dell Publishing.

Kinsey-Warnock, Natalie. Gifts from the Sea. 2003. (Illus.). 128p. (J). (gr. 5). 14.95 (*0-375-82257-7*); lib. bdg. 16.99 (*0-375-92257-1*) Random Hse. Children's Bks. (Knopf Bks. for Young Readers).

Langton, Jane. The Fragile Flag. 2002. (Hall Family Chronicles). 272p. (J). (gr. 5 up). pap. 5.95 (*0-06-440311-4*, Harper Trophy) HarperCollins Children's Bk. Group.

Langton, Jane & Blegvad, Erik. The Fragile Flag. 1984. (Illus.). 224p. (J). (gr. 3-7). 13.00 (*0-06-023698-1*); lib. bdg. 14.89 o.p. (*0-06-023699-X*) HarperCollins Children's Bk. Group.

Lasky, Kathryn. A Time for Courage: The Suffragette Diary of Kathleen Bowen, Washington D. C., 1917. 2002. (Dear America Ser.). (Illus.). 176p. (J). (gr. 4-9). pap. 10.95 (*0-590-51141-6*, Scholastic Pr.) Scholastic, Inc.

Lawlor, Laurie. Horseback on the Old Post Road from Boston to New York 1704. 2000. (American Sisters Ser.: Vol. 7). (Illus.). 192p. (J). (gr. 7-12). 9.00 (*0-671-03923-7*, Aladdin) Simon & Schuster Children's Publishing.

Levero, Diane. What So Proudly We Hail'd. Kemnitz, Myrna, ed. 1999. (Illus.). 302p. (YA). pap. 7.99 (*0-88092-054-8*, 0548) Royal Fireworks Publishing Co.

A Light in the Storm: The Civil War Diary of Amelia Martin. 2003. (J). lib. bdg. 12.95 (*0-439-55535-3*) Scholastic, Inc.

Light, Steve. Uncle Sam: A Press Out & Play Book. 2002. (Illus.). 8p. (J). (gr. k-1). bds. 7.95 (*0-8109-3498-1*) Abrams, Harry N., Inc.

Liles, Maurine W. Dona Maria, la Ranchera. 2000. (Illus.). viii, 152p. (J). 15.95 (*1-57168-381-X*) Eakin Pr.

Loesch, Joe. The Pony Express: With Buffalo Biff & Farley's Raiders, 7 vols., Vol. 7. abr. ed. 2001. (Backyard Adventure Ser.: Vol. 7). 56p. (J). pap. 14.95 incl. audio (*1-887729-79-8*); pap. 16.95 incl. audio compact disk (*1-887729-80-1*) Toy Box Productions.

Longmeyer, Carole M. The Lost Colony Storybook. 1994. (Lost Colony Collection). (Illus.). (J). (gr. 4 up). pap. 19.95 (*0-935326-38-3*) Gallopade International.

Lunn, Janet. Charlotte. 1998. (Illus.). 32p. (J). (gr. 2-4). 15.95 (*0-88776-383-9*) Tundra Bks. of Northern New York.

Lyons, Mary E. & Branch, Muriel M. Dear Ellen Bee: A Civil War Scrapbook of Two Union Spies. 2000. (Illus.). 176p. (J). (gr. 4 up). 17.95 (*0-689-82379-7*, Atheneum) Simon & Schuster Children's Publishing.

MacBride, Roger Lea. Rose at Rocky Ridge. 2000. (Little House Chapter Bks.: No. 2). (Illus.). 80p. (J). (gr. 2-5). pap. 4.25 (*0-06-442093-0*, Harper Trophy); lib. bdg. 14.89 (*0-06-028156-1*) HarperCollins Children's Bk. Group.

—Rose at Rocky Ridge. 2000. (Little House Chapter Bks.: No. 2). (Illus.). (J). (gr. 3-6). 10.40 (*0-606-20478-4*) Turtleback Bks.

Massie, Elizabeth. Barbara's Escape. 1997. (Daughters of Liberty Ser.). 10.04 (*0-606-12672-4*) Turtleback Bks.

—Patsy & the Declaration. 1997. (Daughters of Liberty Ser.). 10.04 (*0-606-12671-6*) Turtleback Bks.

—Patsy's Discovery. 1997. (Daughters of Liberty Ser.). 10.04 (*0-606-11239-1*) Turtleback Bks.

McWilliams, K. J. The Journal of Darien Dexter Duff, An Emancipated Slave. 2002. (Illus.). 182p. (YA). (gr. 4-9). 21.45 (*1-4033-5675-0*); pap. 14.50 (*1-4033-5674-2*) 1stBooks Library.

Miller, Susan Martins. The Streetcar Riots. 29th ed. 1998. (American Adventure Ser.: No. 28). (Illus.). (J). (gr. 3-7). pap. 3.97 (*1-57748-290-5*) Barbour Publishing, Inc.

—Time For Battle. 1998. (American Adventure Ser.: No. 22). (Illus.). (J). (gr. 3-7). 3.97 (*1-57748-260-3*) Barbour Publishing, Inc.

Mills, Judith Christine, et al. The Stonehook Schooner. 1997. (Illus.). 32p. (J). (gr. k-2). 14.95 (*1-55013-653-4*) Firefly Bks., Ltd.

—The Stonehook Schooner. 1997. (Illus.). 32p. (J). (gr. k-2). pap. 4.95 (*1-55013-719-0*) Key Porter Bks. CAN. *Dist:* Firefly Bks., Ltd.

Mitchell, Barbara. Cornstalks & Cannonballs. 1992. (J). pap. o.p. (*0-440-80331-4*) Dell Publishing.

My Secret War: The World War II Diary of Madeline Beck. 2003. (J). lib. bdg. 12.95 (*0-439-55512-4*) Scholastic, Inc.

Nixon, Joan Lowery. David's Search. 2000. (Orphan Train Children Ser.: Vol. 4). (Illus.). 144p. (gr. 2-6). pap. text 4.50 (*0-440-41315-X*, Yearling) Random Hse. Children's Bks.

—David's Search. 2000. 10.55 (*0-606-17831-7*) Turtleback Bks.

—Lucy's Wish. 1998. (Orphan Train Ser.: No. 1). (Illus.). 128p. (gr. 4-6). text 9.95 o.s.i (*0-385-32293-3*, Dell Books for Young Readers) Random Hse. Children's Bks.

Ormondroyd, Edward. Castaways on Long Ago. 1985. (J). pap. 2.25 o.s.i (*0-553-15457-5*) Bantam Bks.

Owens, Tom. Free to Learn. 2000. (Cover-to-Cover Bks.). (Illus.). 55p. (J). 15.95 (*0-7807-9314-5*); pap. (*0-7891-5164-2*) Perfection Learning Corp.

Pagnucci, Franco & Pagnucci, Susan. Paul Revere & Other Story Hours. 1988. (Illus.). 72p. (Orig.). (J). (gr. k-6). pap. 8.99 (*0-929326-00-8*) Bur Oak Pr., Inc.

Pascal, Francine, creator. The Patmans of Sweet Valley. 1996. (Sweet Valley Saga Ser.). 352p. (gr. 7 up). mass mkt. 4.50 o.s.i (*0-553-57023-4*) Bantam Bks.

Pickford, Susan B. The Drama of la Amistad. 1998. (J). (gr. 5-9). pap. 12.00 (*1-57960-034-4*) Discovery Enterprises, Ltd.

A Picture of Freedom: The Diary of Clotee, a Slave Girl. 2003. (J). lib. bdg. 12.95 (*0-439-55501-9*) Scholastic, Inc.

Pleasant Company Staff, ed. Addy's Pastimes: Activities from the Past for Girls of Today, 4 bks., Set. 1995. (American Girls Collection). (Illus.). 160p. (YA). (gr. 2 up). pap. 22.95 (*1-56247-261-5*) Pleasant Co. Pubns.

—Felicity's Pastimes: Activities from the Past for Girls of Today, 4 bks., Set. 1995. (American Girls Collection). (Illus.). 160p. (YA). (gr. 2 up). pap. 22.95 (*1-56247-259-3*) Pleasant Co. Pubns.

—Kirsten's Pastimes: Activities from the Past for Girls of Today, 4 bks., Set. 1995. (American Girls Collection). (Illus.). 168p. (YA). (gr. 2 up). pap. 22.95 (*1-56247-260-7*) Pleasant Co. Pubns.

—Molly's Pastimes: Activities from the Past for Girls of Today, 4 bks., Set. 1995. (American Girls Collection). (Illus.). 160p. (YA). (gr. 2 up). text 22.95 (*1-56247-263-1*) Pleasant Co. Pubns.

—Samantha's Pastimes: Activities from the Past of Girls of Today, 4 bks., Set. 1995. (American Girls Collection). (Illus.). 160p. (YA). (gr. 2 up). pap. text 22.95 (*1-56247-262-3*) Pleasant Co. Pubns.

Pleasant Company Staff, et al. Meet the American Girls, 5 bks., Set. 1993. (American Girls Collection Ser.). (Illus.). (YA). (gr. 2 up). pap. 28.95 o.p. (*1-56247-096-5*) Pleasant Co. Pubns.

Recorvits, Helen. Where Heroes Hide, RS. 2002. (Illus.). 144p. (J). (gr. 4-6). 16.00 (*0-374-33057-3*, Farrar, Straus & Giroux (BYR)) Farrar, Straus & Giroux.

Reece, Colleen L. Plymouth Pioneers. 1998. (American Adventure Ser.: No. 2). (Illus.). 142p. (J). (gr. 3-7). lib. bdg. 15.95 (*0-7910-5042-4*) Chelsea Hse. Pubs.

Reeder, Carolyn. Captain Kate. 2002. 210p. (J). (gr. 4-7). reprint ed. pap. 6.50 (*1-890920-14-2*) Children's Literature.

—Captain Kate. 2000. 224p. (J). (gr. 3-7). pap. 4.99 (*0-380-79668-6*) Morrow/Avon.

—Captain Kate. 1999. (Illus.). (J). 11.04 (*0-606-17963-1*) Turtleback Bks.

Ritthaler, Shelly. With Love, Amanda. 1997. (YA). pap. 3.99 (*0-380-78375-4*, Avon Bks.) Morrow/Avon.

—With Love, Amanda. 1997. (American Dreams Ser.). (YA). 9.09 o.p. (*0-606-10976-5*) Turtleback Bks.

Sanders, Scott Russel. A Place Called Freedom. 1997. (Illus.). 32p. (J). (gr. k-3). 16.00 (*0-689-80470-9*, Atheneum) Simon & Schuster Children's Publishing.

Sargent, Dave & Sargent, Pat. Freckles: Be Proud of Old Glory. 2003. (Saddle Up Ser.: Vol. 26). (Illus.). 42p. (J). mass mkt. 6.95 (*1-56763-810-4*) Ozark Publishing.

—Freckles (Flea-Bitten Grey) Be Proud of Old Glory. 2003. (Saddle Up Ser.: Vol. 26). (Illus.). 42p. (J). lib. bdg. 22.60 (*1-56763-809-0*) Ozark Publishing.

—Popcorn (Blue Corn) Work Hard #47. 2001. (Saddle Up Ser.). 36p. (J). pap. 6.95 (*1-56763-660-8*); lib. bdg. 22.60 (*1-56763-659-4*) Ozark Publishing.

Schulte, Elaine. My American Heros. 1999. 24.99 o.p. (*1-57673-241-X*) Multnomah Pubs., Inc.

Schulz, Charles M. Here's to You, America! 2002. (Peanuts Ser.). (Illus.). 32p. (J). (ps-3). pap. 5.99 (*0-689-85163-4*, Little Simon) Simon & Schuster Children's Publishing.

Seeds of Hope: The Gold Rush Diary of Susanna Fairchild. 2003. (J). lib. bdg. 12.95 (*0-439-55509-4*) Scholastic, Inc.

Shaw, Valerie Trip & Adler, Porter. Meet the American Girls, 7 vols., Set. 2000. (Illus.). (J). (gr. 4-7). 39.95 (*1-58485-236-4*) Pleasant Co. Pubns.

Skolsky, Mindy Warshaw. Love from Your Friend, Hannah. 1998. (Illus.). 256p. (J). (gr. 3-7). pap. 17.95 o.p. (*0-7894-2492-4*) Dorling Kindersley Publishing, Inc.

So Far from Home: The Diary of Mary Driscoll, an Irish Mill Girl. 2003. (J). lib. bdg. 12.95 (*0-439-55506-X*) Scholastic, Inc.

Spicer-Zerner, Jessie & Brooks, Andrea, illus. One Hundred Years Ago. 1983. 96p. (J). 7.95 o.p. (*0-448-81691-1*, Grosset & Dunlap) Penguin Putnam Bks. for Young Readers.

Standing in the Light: The Captive Diary of Catharine Carey Logan. 2003. (J). lib. bdg. 12.95 (*0-439-55515-9*) Scholastic, Inc.

Stephens, Amanda. Freedom at Any Price. 2003. (Liberty's Kids Ser.). (Illus.). 112p. (J). (gr. 3-7). 6.99 (*0-448-43247-1*, Grosset & Dunlap) Penguin Putnam Bks. for Young Readers.

Stevenson, Augusta. George Washington & Abraham Lincoln. 2003. (Childhood of Famous Americans Ser.). (Illus.). 384p. (J). pap. 6.99 (*0-689-85624-5*, Aladdin) Simon & Schuster Children's Publishing.

Susi, Geraldine Lee. My Father, My Companion: Life at the Hollow, Chief Justice John Marshall's Boyhood Home in Virginia. 2001. (Illus.). 96p. (J). (gr. 4-9). pap. 10.95 (*1-889324-22-1*) EPM Pubns., Inc.

Thomas, Carroll. Blue Creek Farm: A Matty Trescott Novel. 2000. (Illus.). 185p. (J). pap. 9.95 (*1-57525-243-0*) Smith & Kraus Pubs., Inc.

A Time for Courage: The Suffragette Diary of Kathleen Bowen. 2003. (J). lib. bdg. 12.95 (*0-439-55542-6*) Scholastic, Inc.

Trent, J. P. Freedom's Fire. 2000. (Illus.). 160p. (J). (gr. 4-7). pap. 4.50 (*0-439-18926-8*) Scholastic, Inc.

—Freedom's Fire. 2000. (Illus.). (J). 10.55 (*0-606-18874-6*) Turtleback Bks.

Tripp, Valerie. Josefina: Meet Josefina; Josefina Learns a Lesson; Josefina's Surprise; Happy Birthday, Josefina; Josefina Saves the Day; Changes for Josefina, Set. 1997. (American Girls Collection: Bks. 1-3). (Illus.). (J). (gr. 2-7). pap. 16.95 o.p. (*1-56247-535-5*) Pleasant Co. Pubns.

—Molly's Boxed Set: Meet Molly; Molly Learns a Lesson; Molly's Surprise; Happy Birthday, Molly!; Molly Saves the Day; Changes for Molly, 6 bks. Thieme, Jeanne, ed. 1992. (American Girls Collection: Bks. 1-6). (Illus.). 398p. (YA). (gr. 2 up). 74.95 (*1-56247-051-5*, American Girl) Pleasant Co. Pubns.

—Molly's Boxed Set: Meet Molly; Molly Learns a Lesson; Molly's Surprise; Happy Birthday, Molly!; Molly Saves the Day; Changes for Molly. 1991. (American Girls Collection: Bks. 1-6). (Illus.). 432p. (YA). (gr. 2 up). 74.95 o.p. (*1-56247-014-0*) Pleasant Co. Pubns.

—Molly's Boxed Set: Meet Molly; Molly Learns a Lesson; Molly's Surprise; Happy Birthday, Molly!; Molly Saves the Day; Changes for Molly, 6 bks. Thieme, Jeanne, ed. 1991. (American Girls Collection: Bks. 1-6). (Illus.). 398p. (YA). pap. 34.95 (*0-937295-78-7*, American Girl) Pleasant Co. Pubns.

Van Leeuwen, Jean. Hannah's Helping Hands. Fogelman, Phyllis, ed. 1999. (Pioneer Daughters Ser.: No. 2). (Illus.). 96p. (J). (gr. 2-5). 13.99 o.p. (*0-8037-2447-0*, Dial Bks. for Young Readers) Penguin Putnam Bks. for Young Readers.

Weiss, Ellen. Voting Rights Days. 2002. (Hitty's Travels Ser.: Vol. 3). (Illus.). 64p. (J). lib. bdg. 11.89 (*0-689-85059-X*, Aladdin Library) Simon & Schuster Children's Publishing.

When Will This Cruel War Be Over? The Civil War Diary of Emma Simpson. 2003. (J). lib. bdg. 12.95 (*0-439-55517-5*) Scholastic, Inc.

White, Ellen Emerson. Where Have All the Flowers Gone? The Diary of Molly Mackenzie Flaherty, Boston, Massachusetts, 1968. 2002. (Dear America Ser.). (Illus.). 176p. (J). (gr. 4-9). pap. 10.95 (*0-439-14889-8*, Scholastic Pr.) Scholastic, Inc.

The Winter of Red Snow: The Revolutionary War Diary of Abigail Jane Stewart, Valley Forge, Pennsylvania, 1777. 2003. (J). lib. bdg. 12.95 (*0-439-55507-8*) Scholastic, Inc.

Yarbough, Camille. The Little Tree Growing in the Shade. 1996. (Illus.). 64p. (J). (gr. 2-5). 18.95 o.s.i (*0-399-21204-3*, G. P. Putnam's Sons) Penguin Group (USA) Inc.

Young, Karen Romano. Outside In. 2002. 192p. (J). (gr. 5 up). lib. bdg. 16.89 (*0-06-029368-3*); (Illus.). 16.95 (*0-688-17363-2*) HarperCollins Children's Bk. Group. (Greenwillow Bks.).

UNITED STATES—HISTORY—COLONIAL PERIOD, CA. 1600-1775—FICTION

Albrecht, Lillie V. Spinning Wheel Secret. 1965. (Illus.). (J). (gr. 4-6). lib. bdg. 3.99 o.p. (*0-8038-6668-2*) Hastings Hse. Daytrips Pubs.

Avi. Night Journeys. 160p. (J). 2000. (Illus.). (gr. 3-7). pap. 5.99 (*0-380-73242-4*, Harper Trophy); 1994. (gr. 5 up). reprint ed. pap. 4.95 (*0-688-13628-1*) HarperCollins Children's Bk. Group.

—Night Journeys, unabr. ed. 1997. (YA). 40.20 incl. audio (*0-7887-1838-X*, 40618); (J). (gr. 6). audio 27.00 (*0-7887-1795-2*, 95267E7) Recorded Bks., LLC.

—Night Journeys. 2000. 11.04 (*0-606-17978-X*); 1994. 10.05 o.p. (*0-606-06621-7*) Turtleback Bks.

Bangs, Edward. Steven Kellogg's Yankee Doodle. 1996. (J). 12.14 (*0-606-10097-0*) Turtleback Bks.

Berkey, Ben B. Liberty Hill. 1983. (Upper Grade Bk.). (Illus.). (gr. 4-6). lib. bdg. 2.00 o.p. (*0-513-00361-4*) Denison, T. S. & Co., Inc.

Blackburn, Joyce K. The Bloody Summer of Seventeen Forty-Two: A Colonial Boy's Journal. 1985. (Illus.). 64p. (J). (gr. 5-8). pap. 7.95 (*0-930803-00-0*) Fort Frederica Assn., Inc.

Bolin, J. J. Yankee Doodle & the Secret Society. 1997. (Cover-to-Cover Bks.). (Illus.). 54p. (J). (*0-7807-6715-2*, Covercraft) Perfection Learning Corp.

Borden, Louise. Sleds on Boston Common: A Story from the American Revolution. 2000. (Illus.). 40p. (J). (gr. 3-7). 17.00 (*0-689-82812-8*, McElderry, Margaret K.) Simon & Schuster Children's Publishing.

Bulla, Clyde Robert. Charlie's House. 1993. (Illus.). 96p. (J). (gr. 3-6). 14.00 o.s.i (*0-679-83841-4*, Knopf Bks. for Young Readers) Random Hse. Children's Bks.

—A Lion to Guard Us. (Trophy Bk.). (Illus.). (J). 1989. 128p. (gr. 3 up). pap. 4.99 (*0-06-440333-5*, Harper Trophy); 1981. (gr. 2-5). 14.00 o.p. (*0-690-04096-2*); 1981. 128p. (gr. 7 up). lib. bdg. 16.89 (*0-690-04097-0*) HarperCollins Children's Bk. Group.

—A Lion to Guard Us. 1983. (Illus.). 128p. (J). reprint ed. pap. 2.25 o.p. (*0-590-33788-2*) Scholastic, Inc.

—A Lion to Guard Us. 1989. (J). 11.00 (*0-606-04267-9*) Turtleback Bks.

Burt, Barbara. The Eve of Revolution: The Colonial Adventures of Benjamin Wilcox. 2003. (I Am American Ser.). (J). pap. 6.99 (*0-7922-5211-X*) National Geographic Society.

Butters, Dorothy G. The Bells of Freedom. 1984. (Illus.). (J). (gr. 4-8). 16.00 (*0-8446-6162-7*) Smith, Peter Pub., Inc.

Coombs, Karen M. Sarah on Her Own. 1996. (American Dreams Ser.). 9.09 o.p. (*0-606-09818-6*) Turtleback Bks.

Coombs, Karen Mueller. Sarah on Her Own. 1996. (American Dreams Ser.). 240p. (YA). (gr. 7 up). mass mkt. 3.99 (*0-380-78275-8*, Avon Bks.) Morrow/Avon.

Crandell, Myra C. Molly & the Regicides. 1968. (Illus.). (J). (gr. 6 up). lib. bdg. 3.79 o.p. (*0-671-65015-7*, Simon & Schuster Children's Publishing) Simon & Schuster Children's Publishing.

Dillon, Eilis. The Seekers. 1986. 144p. (J). (gr. 5-9). 12.95 o.p. (*0-684-18595-4*, Atheneum) Simon & Schuster Children's Publishing.

Duey, Kathleen. Sarah Anne Hartford: Massachusetts, 1651. 1996. (American Diaries Ser.: No. 1). (Illus.). 144p. (J). (gr. 3-7). pap. 4.99 (*0-689-80384-2*, Simon Pulse) Simon & Schuster Children's Publishing.

—Sarah Anne Hartford: Massachusetts, 1651. 1996. (American Diaries Ser.: No. 1). (J). (gr. 3-7). 10.55 (*0-606-08985-3*) Turtleback Bks.

—Summer MacCleary: Virginia, 1749. 1998. (American Diaries Ser.: Vol. 10). (J). (gr. 3-7). 10.04 (*0-606-13120-5*) Turtleback Bks.

—Summer McCleary: Virginia, 1749. 1998. (American Diaries Ser.: No. 10). 144p. (J). (gr. 3-7). pap. 4.50 o.s.i (*0-689-81623-5*, Aladdin) Simon & Schuster Children's Publishing.

Edmonds, Walter D. The Matchlock Gun. 1989. (Illus.). 64p. (J). (ps-3). 16.99 (*0-399-21911-0*, G. P. Putnam's Sons) Penguin Group (USA) Inc.

—The Matchlock Gun. 1998. (Illus.). 64p. (J). (gr. 3-7). pap. 5.99 (*0-698-11680-1*, PaperStar) Penguin Putnam Bks. for Young Readers.

Fann, Marcia M. American Made: The Colonial Child of 1740. rev. ed. 1997. (Illus.). 48p. (J). (gr. k-6). pap. 2.50 (*0-9619421-3-4*) Great American Coloring Bk., Inc.

Fleming, Candace. The Hatmaker's Sign. 2000. (Illus.). 40p. (J). (gr. k-4). mass mkt. 6.95 o.s.i (*0-531-07174-X*, Orchard Bks.) Scholastic, Inc.

Forest, Heather. Baker's Dozen: A Colonial American Tale. 1988. (Voyager Bks.). (J). 12.15 (*0-606-05748-X*) Turtleback Bks.

Forrester, Sandra. Wheel of the Moon. 2000. 176p. (J). (gr. 5 up). lib. bdg. 15.89 (*0-06-029203-2*); (Illus.). 15.95 (*0-688-17149-4*) HarperCollins Children's Bk. Group.

Grand, Gordon. Col. Weatherford & His Friends. 1991. (Fifty Greatest Bks.). (Illus.). 242p. (YA). (gr. 10 up). reprint ed. lthr. 40.00 o.p. (*1-56416-026-2*) Derrydale Pr., The.

—Colonel Weatherford's Young Entry: Being an Account of the South Dorchester Ratters & Other Genteel Diversions Suitable for Children. 1991. (Illus.). 214p. (YA). (gr. 10 up). reprint ed. lthr. 40.00 o.p. (*1-56416-028-9*) Derrydale Pr., The.

—Old Man: And Other Colonel Weatherford Stories. 1991. (Fifty Greatest Bks.). (Illus.). 239p. (YA). (gr. 10 up). reprint ed. lthr. 40.00 o.p. (*1-56416-027-0*) Derrydale Pr., The.

Grote, JoAnn A. Danger in the Harbor: Grain Riots Threaten Boston. 1999. (American Adventure Ser.: No. 6). (Illus.). 144p. (J). (gr. 3-7). lib. bdg. 15.95 (*0-7910-5046-7*) Chelsea Hse. Pubs.

—Queen Anne's War. 1999. (American Adventure Ser.: No. 5). 144p. (J). (gr. 3-7). lib. bdg. 15.95 (*0-7910-5045-9*) Chelsea Hse. Pubs.

Haley, Gail E. Jack Jouett's Ride. 1973. (Illus.). 32p. (J). (gr. k-3). 5.95 o.p. (*0-670-40466-7*) Viking Penguin.

Hamilton, Elizabeth L. Passport to Courage. 2002. (Character-in-Action Ser.: Bk. 1). 384p. (YA). per. 19.95 (*0-9713749-3-7*) Quiet Impact, Inc.

Harmon, Lyn. Flight to Jewell Island. 2001. (Illus.). 148p. (gr. 4-7). pap. 10.95 (*0-595-16337-8*, Backinprint.com) iUniverse, Inc.

Hays, Wilma P. Naughty Little Pilgrim. 1969. (Illus.). (J). (gr. 1-3). 4.95 o.p. (*0-679-24057-8*, 240967) McKay, David Co., Inc.

—Siege: The Story of St. Augustine in 1702. 1976. (Illus.). 96p. (J). (gr. 3-6). 6.95 o.p. (*0-698-20357-7*) Putnam Publishing Group, The.

Hemphill, Kris. A Secret Party in Boston Harbor. 1998. (Mysteries in Time Ser.: Vol. 6). (Illus.). 96p. (J). (gr. 4-7). text 14.95 (*1-881889-88-2*) Silver Moon Pr.

Hermes, Patricia. Our Strange New Land: Elizabeth's Jamestown Colony Diary. 2000. (My America Ser.). (Illus.). 112p. (J). (gr. 2-5). pap. 8.95 (*0-439-11208-7*, Scholastic Pr.) Scholastic, Inc.

—Season of Promise: Elizabeth's Jamestown Colony Diary. 2002. (My America Ser.: Bk. 3). (Illus.). (J). (gr. 2-5). 128p. pap. 10.95 (*0-439-38898-8*); 144p. mass mkt. 4.99 (*0-439-27206-8*) Scholastic, Inc. (Scholastic Pr.).

—The Starving Time Bk. 2: Elizabeth's Jamestown Colony Diary. (My America Ser.: Bk. 2). (Illus.). 112p. (J). (gr. 2-5). 2002. mass mkt. 4.99 (*0-439-36902-9*); 2001. pap. 8.95 (*0-439-19998-0*) Scholastic, Inc. (Scholastic Pr.).

Hilton, Suzanne. We the People: The Way We Were, 1783-1793. 1981. (Junior Literary Guild Selection Ser.). (Illus.). 206p. (J). (gr. 6-9). 12.95 o.p. (*0-664-32685-4*) Westminster John Knox Pr.

Holberg, Ruth L. Kate & the Devil. 1968. (Illus.). (J). (gr. 4-6). 4.95 o.p. (*0-8038-3931-6*) Hastings Hse. Daytrips Pubs.

Howard, Ginger. William's House. 2001. (Illus.). 32p. (J). (gr. k-3). 22.90 (*0-7613-1674-4*) Millbrook Pr., Inc.

Jones, Elizabeth McDavid. Mystery on Skull Island. 2001. (American Girl Collection: Bk. 15). (Illus.). 192p. (J). 9.95 (*1-58485-342-5*); pap. 5.95 (*1-58485-341-7*) Pleasant Co. Pubns. (American Girl).

Karr, Kathleen. Phoebe's Folly. 1996. (Petticoat Party Ser.: Vol. 2). (gr. 5 up). 208p. (J). pap. 14.89 o.p. (*0-06-027154-X*); 80p. (YA). 14.95 o.p. (*0-06-027153-1*) HarperCollins Children's Bk. Group.

Kay, Verla. Tattered Sails. 2001. (Illus.). 32p. (J). 15.99 (*0-399-23345-8*, Ace/Putnam) Penguin Group (USA) Inc.

Konz, Helen S. Builders of the Nation. 1999. 212p. reprint ed. o.p. (*0-9658183-2-2*) Heloukon Publishing.

Laird, Marnie. Water Rat. 1998. (Illus.). 196p. (J). (gr. 4-7). 15.95 (*1-890817-08-2*) Winslow Pr.

Lawlor, Laurie. Horseback on the Boston Post Road 1704. 2002. (American Sisters Ser.: Vol. 7). 208p. (YA). pap. 4.99 (*0-7434-3626-1*, Aladdin) Simon & Schuster Children's Publishing.

Lawson, Robert. Mr. Revere & I. (Illus.). (J). 1988. 152p. (gr. 4-7). pap. 6.99 (*0-316-51729-1*); 1953. (gr. 7-10). 16.95 o.p. (*0-316-51739-9*) Little Brown & Co.

—Mr. Revere & I. 1973. (J). (gr. 3-6). pap. 2.95 o.s.i (*0-440-45897-8*, Yearling) Random Hse. Children's Bks.

Lutz, Norma Jean. Smallpox Strikes! Cotton Mather's Bold Experiment. 7th ed. 1998. (American Adventure Ser.: No. 7). (Illus.). (J). (gr. 3-7). pap. 3.97 (*1-57748-144-5*) Barbour Publishing, Inc.

—Smallpox Strikes! Cotton Mather's Bold Experiment. 1999. (American Adventure Ser.: No. 7). (Illus.). 144p. (J). (gr. 3-7). lib. bdg. 15.95 (*0-7910-5047-5*) Chelsea Hse. Pubs.

Massie, Elizabeth. Barbara's Escape. 1997. (Daughters of Liberty Ser.: Vol. 3). 144p. (J). (gr. 3-6). pap. 3.99 (*0-671-00134-5*, Aladdin) Simon & Schuster Children's Publishing.

McDonald, Megan. Shadows in the Glasshouse. 2000. (American Girl Collection: Bk. 10). (Illus.). 160p. (J). (gr. 4-6). 9.95 (*1-58485-093-0*); pap. 5.95 (*1-58485-092-2*) Pleasant Co. Pubns. (American Girl).

—Shadows in the Glasshouse. 2000. (American Girl Collection). (Illus.). (J). 12.00 (*0-606-20906-9*) Turtleback Bks.

McGovern, Ann. If You Lived in Colonial Times. 1992. (Illus.). 80p. (J). (gr. 2-5). pap. 5.99 o.s.i (*0-590-45160-X*) Scholastic, Inc.

Meadowcroft, Enid L. First Year. 1946. (Illus.). (J). (gr. 5 up). 10.95 o.p. (*0-690-30349-1*) HarperCollins Children's Bk. Group.

Nixon, Joan Lowery. Ann's Story, 1747. 2001. (Young Americans Ser.). 160p. (gr. 3-7). pap. text 4.50 (*0-440-41629-9*, Dell Books for Young Readers) Random Hse. Children's Bks.

—Caesar's Story, 1759. 2002. (Young Americans). 176p. (gr. 3-7). pap. text 4.50 (*0-440-41632-9*, Delacorte Bks. for Young Readers) Random Hse. Children's Bks.

—John's Story 1775: Colonial Williamsburg. 2001. (Young Americans Ser.). (Illus.). 176p. (gr. 3-7). text 9.95 (*0-385-32688-2*, Dell Books for Young Readers) Random Hse. Children's Bks.

—Will's Story 1771. 2001. (Young Americans). (Illus.). 176p. (gr. 2-6). text 9.95 o.s.i (*0-385-32682-3*, Delacorte Bks. for Young Readers) Random Hse. Children's Bks.

Paul Revere Play Set & Booklet: 15 Pieces Include 5" Figures, Horse, Steeple, Lanterns. 1999. (Illus.). 32p. (J). (gr. k-7). 28.00 (*0-9677511-1-X*) Child Light.

Peck, Robert Newton. Hang for Treason. 1976. 6.95 o.p. (*0-385-07337-2*) Doubleday Publishing.

Pfeffer, Susan Beth. Meg's Story. 2001. (Portraits of Little Women Ser.). (Illus.). (J). 10.55 (*0-606-21327-9*) Turtleback Bks.

Richter, Conrad. Elements of Literature: The Light in the Forest. 1989. pap., stu. ed. 15.33 (*0-03-023439-5*) Holt, Rinehart & Winston.

—The Light in the Forest. (YA). (gr. 7 up). 21.95 (*0-89190-333-X*) Amereon, Ltd.
—The Light in the Forest. 1994. 128p. (gr. 7-12). mass mkt. 6.50 (*0-449-70437-8*, Fawcett) Ballantine Bks.
—The Light in the Forest. 1990. 128p. (J). (gr. 5-12). mass mkt. 3.99 o.s.i (*0-553-26878-3*); 1986. mass mkt. o.s.i (*0-553-16642-5*) Bantam Bks.
—The Light in the Forest. 1991. (YA). (gr. 7 up). lib. bdg. 21.95 (*1-56849-064-X*) Buccaneer Bks., Inc.
—The Light in the Forest. 1953. (Illus.). (J). 23.00 o.s.i (*0-394-43314-9*); (YA). (gr. 7 up). lib. bdg. 5.99 o.p. (*0-394-91404-X*) Knopf, Alfred A. Inc.
—The Light in the Forest. 1986. (J). mass mkt. o.s.i (*0-553-16679-4*, Dell Books for Young Readers) Random Hse. Children's Bks.
—The Light in the Forest. 9999. pap. 1.95 o.p. (*0-590-02336-5*) Scholastic, Inc.
—The Light in the Forest. 1994. (YA). (gr. 7 up). 12.04 (*0-606-06903-8*) Turtleback Bks.
Rinaldi, Ann. The Fifth of March: A Story of the Boston Massacre. (Great Episodes Ser.). 352p. (YA). 2004. pap. (*0-15-205078-7*); 1993. (Illus.). (gr. 5 up). 13.00 (*0-15-200343-6*) Harcourt Children's Bks. (Gulliver Bks.).
—The Journal of Jasper Jonathan Pierce: A Pilgrim Boy: Plymouth Plantation, 1620. 2000. (My Name Is America Ser.). (Illus.). 155p. (J). (gr. 4-8). pap. 10.95 (*0-590-51078-9*) Scholastic, Inc.
—Time Enough for Drums. 2000. 256p. (YA). (gr. 7 up). mass mkt. 5.50 (*0-440-22850-6*, Dell Books for Young Readers) Random Hse. Children's Bks.
—Time Enough for Drums. 2000. 10.55 (*0-606-18002-8*) Turtleback Bks.
Schneider, Rex, illus. Yankee Doodle & the Secret Society. 1997. (Cover-to-Cover Bks.). (J). (*0-7891-2006-2*) Perfection Learning Corp.
Traylor, Sarah M. The Red Wind. 1977. (Illus.). (J). (gr. 5 up). 5.95 o.p. (*0-687-35881-7*) Abingdon Pr.
Tripp, Valerie. Felicity Takes a Dare. 2001. (American Girls Short Stories Ser.). (Illus.). 56p. (J). (gr. 2-7). 3.95 (*1-58485-271-2*, American Girl) Pleasant Co. Pubns.
—Felicity's Boxed Set: Meet Felicity; Felicity Learns a Lesson; Felicity's Surprise; Happy Birthday, Felicity!; Felicity Saves the Day; Changes for Felicity, 6 bks. 1992. (American Girls Collection: Bks. 1-6). (Illus.). 412p. (J). (gr. 2 up). 74.95 (*1-56247-045-0*, American Girl) Pleasant Co. Pubns.
—Felicity's Short Story Set: Felicity's New Sister; Felicity's Dancing Shoes; Felicity Discovers a Secret, 3 vols. 2002. (American Girls Short Stories Ser.). (Illus.). (YA). (gr. 2). 11.95 (*1-58485-494-4*, American Girl) Pleasant Co. Pubns.
—Felicity's Story Collection. 2001. (American Girls Collection). (Illus.). 390p. (J). (gr. 2 up). 29.95 (*1-58485-441-3*, American Girl) Pleasant Co. Pubns.
Trottier, Maxine. By the Standing Stone. 2001. (Circle of Silver Chronicles Ser.). (Illus.). 246p. (YA). (gr. 7-12). pap. 7.95 (*0-7737-6138-1*) Stoddart Kids CAN. *Dist:* Fitzhenry & Whiteside, Ltd.
Turner, Ann Warren. Love Thy Neighbor: The Tory Diary of Prudence Emerson. 2003. (Dear America Ser.). (Illus.). 192p. (J). pap. 10.95 (*0-439-15308-5*) Scholastic, Inc.
Van Leeuwen, Jean. Hannah's Helping Hands. Fogelman, Phyllis, ed. 1999. (Pioneer Daughters Ser.: No. 2). (Illus.). 96p. (J). (gr. 2-5). 13.99 o.p. (*0-8037-2447-0*, Dial Bks. for Young Readers) Penguin Putnam Bks. for Young Readers.
Witt, Betty. The Adventures of Truncus. 1998. (Illus.). 72p. (J). (gr. 4-5). pap. 8.00 o.p. (*0-8059-4335-8*) Dorrance Publishing Co., Inc.

UNITED STATES—HISTORY—FRENCH AND INDIAN WAR, 1755-1763—FICTION

Cooper, James Fenimore. The Last of the Mohicans. 2002. (Great Illustrated Classics). (Illus.). 240p. (J). (gr. 3-8). lib. bdg. 21.35 (*1-57765-692-X*, ABDO & Daughters) ABDO Publishing Co.
—The Last of the Mohicans. 1964. (Airmont Classics Ser.). (J). (gr. 6 up). pap. 3.50 o.p. (*0-8049-0005-1*, CL-5) Airmont Publishing Co., Inc.
—The Last of the Mohicans. 1989. (Illus.). (J). (ps up). 26.95 (*0-89968-254-5*) Buccaneer Bks., Inc.
—The Last of the Mohicans. 1989. (gr. 4-6). audio 11.00 o.p. (*1-55994-075-1*, CPN 1239, Caedmon) HarperTrade.
—The Last of the Mohicans. Wright, Robin S., ed. & abr. by. 1976. (Illus.). (J). (gr. 7 up). 7.95 o.p. (*0-679-20372-9*) McKay, David Co., Inc.
—The Last of the Mohicans. 1962. 432p. (J). (gr. 7). mass mkt. 2.95 o.p. (*0-451-52329-6*); (Illus.). mass mkt. 4.95 o.s.i (*0-451-52503-5*) NAL. (Signet Classics).
—The Last of the Mohicans. Farr, Naunerle C., ed. abr. ed. 1977. (Now Age Illustrated III Ser.). (Illus.). (J). (gr. 4-12). text 7.50 o.p. (*0-88301-279-0*); pap. text 2.95 (*0-88301-267-7*) Pendulum Pr., Inc.
—The Last of the Mohicans. 9999. (Children's Classics Ser.: No. 740-14). (Illus.). (J). (gr. 3-5). text 3.50 o.p. (*0-7214-0789-7*, Ladybird Bks.) Penguin Group (USA) Inc.
—The Last of the Mohicans. Vogel, Malvina, ed. 1992. (Great Illustrated Classics Ser.: Vol. 24). (Illus.). 240p. (J). (gr. 3-6). 9.95 (*0-86611-975-2*) Playmore, Inc., Pubs.
—The Last of the Mohicans. 1987. (Regents Illustrated Classics Ser.). (J). (gr. 7-12). pap. text 3.75 o.p. (*0-13-523952-4*, 20569) Prentice Hall, ESL Dept.
—The Last of the Mohicans. 1993. (Step into Classics Ser.). (Illus.). 112p. (J). (gr. 3-5). pap. 3.99 (*0-679-84706-5*, Random Hse. Bks. for Young Readers) Random Hse. Children's Bks.
—The Last of the Mohicans. 1986. (Illus.). 376p. (J). 75.00 o.s.i (*0-684-18716-7*); (YA). (gr. 4-7). 28.00 (*0-684-18711-6*) Simon & Schuster Children's Publishing. (Atheneum).
—The Last of the Mohicans. (Saddleback Classics). (J). 2001. (Illus.). 13.10 (*0-606-21559-X*); 1993. 10.04 (*0-606-02705-X*) Turtleback Bks.
—The Last of the Mohicans. abr. ed. 2002. (Scribner Storybook Classic Ser.). (Illus.). 64p. (J). (gr. 3-6). 18.95 (*0-689-84068-3*, Atheneum) Simon & Schuster Children's Publishing.
—The Last of the Mohicans. adapted ed. 1997. (Living Classics Ser.). (Illus.). 32p. (J). (gr. 3-7). 14.95 o.p. (*0-7641-7048-1*) Barron's Educational Series, Inc.
—The Last of the Mohicans. 1826. 423p. (YA). reprint ed. pap. text 28.00 (*1-4047-2374-9*) Classic Textbooks.
—The Last of the Mohicans. 2nd ed. 1998. (Illustrated Classic Book Ser.). (Illus.). 61p. (J). (gr. 3 up). reprint ed. pap. text 4.95 (*1-56767-249-3*) Educational Insights, Inc.
De Varona, Frank. Bernardo de Galvez. 1990. (Hispanic Stories Ser.). (ENG & SPA., Illus.). 32p. (J). lib. bdg. 5.00 o.p. (*0-8172-3379-2*) Raintree Pubs.
Henty, G. A. With Wolfe in Canada: The Winning of a Continent. 2001. (Illus.). 353p. (J). pap. 13.99 (*0-921100-87-6*); text 19.99 (*0-921100-86-8*) Inheritance Pubns.
—With Wolfe in Canada: The Winning of a Continent. (Illus.). 353p. 2000. (gr. 8-12). pap. 14.99 (*1-887159-30-4*); 1998. (J). lib. bdg. 20.99 (*1-887159-18-5*) Preston-Speed Pubns.
Keehn, Sally M. I Am Regina. 1993. (gr. 4-7). (J). pap. o.p. (*0-440-90037-9*); 240p. pap. text 4.99 o.s.i (*0-440-40754-0*) Dell Publishing.
—I Am Regina. 1991. 240p. (YA). (gr. 4-7). 17.99 (*0-399-21797-5*, Philomel) Penguin Putnam Bks. for Young Readers.
—I Am Regina. 1991. (J). 11.04 (*0-606-02681-9*) Turtleback Bks.
McKissack, Pat, tr. Look to the Hills: The Diary of Lozette Moreau, a French Slave Girl. 2004. (Dear America Ser.). 192p. (J). pap. 10.95 (*0-439-21038-0*) Scholastic, Inc.
Moore, Ruth N. Peace Treaty. 1977. (Christian Peace Shelf Ser.). (Illus.). 154p. (J). (gr. 3-10). pap. 3.95 o.p. (*0-8361-1805-7*); text 4.95 o.p. (*0-8361-1804-9*) Herald Pr.
Mott, Michael. Master Entrick. 1986. (J). (gr. 3-6). reprint ed. pap. 2.95 o.s.i (*0-440-45818-8*, Yearling) Random Hse. Children's Bks.
Speare, Elizabeth George. Calico Captive. 1957. (Illus.). 288p. (J). (gr. 7 up). 17.00 o.p. (*0-395-07112-7*) Houghton Mifflin Co.
—Calico Captive. 1973. 288p. (gr. 4-7). pap. text 4.99 o.s.i (*0-440-41156-4*, Yearling) Random Hse. Children's Bks.
—Calico Captive. 1957. (J). 11.04 (*0-606-04179-6*) Turtleback Bks.

UNITED STATES—HISTORY—REVOLUTION, 1775-1783—FICTION

Armstrong, Tom, illus. Brave Journey: Launching of the United States. 1975. 208p. (J). (gr. 3-7). lib. bdg. 7.95 o.p. (*0-687-03965-7*) Abingdon Pr.
Arnow, Harriette Louisa Simpson. Kentucky Trace: A Novel of the American Revolution. 1974. 10.00 o.p. (*0-394-48990-X*, Knopf Bks. for Young Readers) Random Hse. Children's Bks.
Avi. The Fighting Ground. 160p. 1984. (Illus.). (J). (gr. 4 up). lib. bdg. 16.89 (*0-397-32074-4*); 1984. (Illus.). (YA). (gr. 5 up). 12.95 (*0-397-32073-6*); 1987. (J). (gr. 3-7). reprint ed. pap. 5.99 (*0-06-440185-5*, Harper Trophy) HarperCollins Children's Bk. Group.
—The Fighting Ground. 1987. (J). 11.00 (*0-606-01662-7*) Turtleback Bks.
Benchley, Nathaniel. George the Drummer Boy. 1977. (I Can Read Bks.). (Illus.). 64p. (J). (gr. k-3). lib. bdg. 16.89 (*0-06-020501-6*); (gr. 2-4). 14.00 (*0-06-020500-8*) HarperCollins Children's Bk. Group.
—Sam the Minuteman. (I Can Read Bks.). (Illus.). 64p. (J). 1987. (gr. k-3). pap. 3.99 (*0-06-444107-5*, Harper Trophy); 1969. (gr. k-3). lib. bdg. 16.89 (*0-06-020480-X*); 1969. (gr. 2-4). 11.95 (*0-06-020479-6*) HarperCollins Children's Bk. Group.
—Sam the Minuteman. abr. ed. 1991. (I Can Read Bks.). (Illus.). 64p. (J). (gr. k-3). 8.99 incl. audio (*1-55994-354-8*, TBC 3548, HarperAudio) HarperTrade.
—Sam the Minuteman. 1987. (I Can Read Bks.). (Illus.). (J). (gr. 2-4). 10.10 (*0-606-03264-9*) Turtleback Bks.
Beyer, Audrey W. Katharine Leslie. 1963. (Illus.). (J). (gr. 7 up). lib. bdg. 4.99 o.p. (*0-394-91298-5*, Knopf Bks. for Young Readers) Random Hse. Children's Bks.
Bjerregaard, Marcia. First Heroes for Freedom. 2000. (Adventures in America Ser.). (Illus.). 92p. (J). (gr. 3-7). lib. bdg. 14.95 (*1-893110-17-6*) Silver Moon Pr.
Blackburn, Joyce K. Phoebe's Secret Diary: Daily Life & First Romance of a Colonial Girl, 1742. 1993. (Illus.). 56p. (Orig.). (J). (gr. 5-8). pap. 7.95 (*0-930803-01-9*) Fort Frederica Assn., Inc.
Blackwood, Gary. The Year of the Hangman. 2004. 272p. pap. 5.99 (*0-14-240078-5*, Puffin Bks.) Penguin Putnam Bks. for Young Readers.
Blackwood, Gary L. The Year of the Hangman. 2002. 196p. (YA). (gr. 9 up). 16.99 (*0-525-46921-4*, Dutton Children's Bks.) Penguin Putnam Bks. for Young Readers.
Boyd, James. Drums. 1995. (Scribner Illustrated Classics Ser.). (Illus.). 432p. (YA). (gr. 4-7). 25.00 (*0-689-80176-9*, Atheneum); (gr. 7 up). 75.00 o.s.i (*0-689-80177-7*, Simon & Schuster Children's Publishing) Simon & Schuster Children's Publishing.
Brady, Esther W. Toliver's Secret. 1988. (Illus.). (J). (gr. 3-5). 6.95 o.s.i (*0-517-52621-2*, Crown) Crown Publishing Group.
—Toliver's Secret. 1986. (Illus.). (J). (gr. 3-5). pap. 1.50 o.p. (*0-380-45914-0*, 45914-0, Avon Bks.) Morrow/Avon.
Brown, Drollene P. Sybil Rides for Independence. Levine, Abby, ed. 1985. (Illus.). 48p. (J). (gr. 2-5). 12.95 o.p. (*0-8075-7684-0*) Whitman, Albert & Co.
Bruchac, Joseph. The Arrow over the Door. (Illus.). 96p. (J). 2002. pap. 4.99 (*0-14-130571-1*, Puffin Bks.); 1998. (gr. 2-4). 15.99 (*0-8037-2078-5*, Dial Bks. for Young Readers) Penguin Putnam Bks. for Young Readers.
Burt, Barbara. The Eve of Revolution: The Colonial Adventures of Benjamin Wilcox. 2003. (I Am American Ser.). (J). pap. 6.99 (*0-7922-5211-X*) National Geographic Society.
Campbell, Donna. An Independent Spirit: The Tale of Betsy Dowdy & Black Bess. 2002. (Legends of the Carolinas Ser.). 200p. (J). 8.95 (*1-928556-35-3*) Coastal Carolina Pr.
Cavanna, Betty. Ruffles & Drums. 1975. (Illus.). (J). (gr. 7-9). 12.95 o.p. (*0-688-22035-5*); lib. bdg. 9.12 o.p. (*0-688-32035-X*) Morrow/Avon. (Morrow, William & Co.).
Cavanna, Betty A. Touch of Magic. 1961. (Illus.). (J). (gr. 6-9). 5.75 o.p. (*0-664-32253-0*) Westminster John Knox Pr.
Chalk, Gary. Yankee Doodle. 1993. (Illus.). 32p. (J). (ps-3). pap. 14.95 o.p. (*1-56458-202-7*) Dorling Kindersley Publishing, Inc.
Clyne, Patricia E. The Corduroy Road. 1984. (Illus.). (J). (gr. 5-9). 15.75 (*0-8446-6163-5*) Smith, Peter Pub., Inc.
Collier, James Lincoln. War Comes to Willy Freeman. 1983. (J). 12.95 (*0-440-09642-1*) Dell Publishing.
—War Comes to Willy Freeman. 1987. (Arabus Family Saga Ser.). (J). 11.55 (*0-606-03076-X*) Turtleback Bks.
Collier, James Lincoln & Collier, Christopher. The Bloody Country. 1985. (Point Ser.). 192p. (YA). (gr. 4-7). pap. 4.50 (*0-590-43126-9*) Scholastic, Inc.
—The Bloody Country. 1984. 192p. (YA). (gr. 7 up). 13.95 o.s.i (*0-02-722960-2*, Simon & Schuster Children's Publishing) Simon & Schuster Children's Publishing.
—My Brother Sam Is Dead. 1977. 182p. (J). (gr. 7 up). 1.25 o.p. (*0-590-40666-3*); 1977. 182p. (J). (gr. 7 up). pap. 2.50 o.p. (*0-590-40737-6*); 2003. (Illus.). 224p. (YA). (gr. 5-9). mass mkt. 5.99 (*0-590-42792-X*) Scholastic, Inc. (Scholastic Paperbacks).
—My Brother Sam Is Dead. 1984. 224p. (YA). (gr. 7 up). 17.95 (*0-02-722980-7*, Simon & Schuster Children's Publishing) Simon & Schuster Children's Publishing.
—War Comes to Willy Freeman. 1987. (Arabus Family Saga Ser.: Vol. 1). 192p. (gr. 4-7). pap. text 5.50 (*0-440-49504-0*, Yearling) Random Hse. Children's Bks.
—War Comes to Willy Freeman. 1992. (J). (gr. 4-6). 17.25 o.p. (*0-8446-6596-7*) Smith, Peter Pub., Inc.
Cover, Arthur B. American Revolutionary. 1985. (Time Machine Ser.: No. 10). (Illus.). 144p. (J). (gr. 7-12). mass mkt. 2.50 o.s.i (*0-553-26773-6*) Bantam Bks.
—American Revolutionary. (Time Machine Ser.: Vol. 10). E-Book (*1-58824-440-7*) ipicturebooks, LLC.
Curtis, Alice Turner. A Little Maid of Massachusetts Bay Colony. 2004. (Little Maid Ser.). (Illus.). 192p. (J). (gr. 4-7). reprint ed. pap. 9.95 (*1-55709-329-6*) Applewood Bks.
—A Little Maid of Narragansett Bay. 2004. (Little Maid Ser.). (Illus.). 210p. (J). (gr. 1-6). reprint ed. pap. 9.95 (*1-55709-334-2*) Applewood Bks.
—A Little Maid of Old Connecticut. 2004. (Little Maid Ser.). (Illus.). 192p. (J). (gr. 4-7). reprint ed. pap. 9.95 (*1-55709-328-8*) Applewood Bks.
—A Little Maid of Ticonderoga. 2004. (Little Maid Ser.). (Illus.). 192p. (J). (gr. 4-7). reprint ed. pap. 9.95 (*1-55709-330-X*) Applewood Bks.
—A Little Maid of Virginia. 2004. (Little Maid Ser.). (Illus.). 192p. (J). (gr. 1-3). reprint ed. pap. 9.95 (*1-55709-333-4*) Applewood Bks.
Cuyler, Margery. The Battlefield Ghost. (Illus.). (J). 2002. 112p. mass mkt. 3.99 (*0-590-10849-2*, Scholastic Paperbacks); 1999. 103p. (gr. 2-4). pap. 15.95 (*0-590-10848-4*) Scholastic, Inc.
Dell, Pamela. Freedom's Light: A Story about Paul Revere's Midnight Ride. 2002. (Illus.). 48p. (J). lib. bdg. 27.07 (*1-59187-016-X*) Child's World, Inc.
Denenberg, Barry. The Journal of William Thomas Emerson: A Revolutionary War Patriot: Boston, Massachusetts, 1774. 1998. (My Name Is America Ser.). (Illus.). 156p. (J). (gr. 4-8). pap. 10.95 o.s.i (*0-590-31350-9*, Scholastic Pr.) Scholastic, Inc.
Doughty, Wayne D. Crimson Mocassins. 1972. (Trophy Bk.). 224p. (YA). (gr. 7 up). pap. 2.95 (*0-06-440015-8*, Harper Trophy) HarperCollins Children's Bk. Group.
Downie, Mary Alice. Honor Bound. Date not set. (Illus.). 216p. (YA). 12.95 (*1-55082-026-5*); pap. 7.95 (*1-55082-027-3*) Quarry Pr. CAN. *Dist:* LPC/InBook.
Doyle, Peter R. Independence. 1997. (Drums of War Ser.: Vol. 1). 170p. (Orig.). (J). (gr. 4-12). pap. 7.95 (*1-887456-06-6*) Providence Foundation.
Duey, Kathleen. Mary Alice Peale: Philadelphia, 1777. 1996. (American Diaries Ser.: No. 4). 144p. (J). (gr. 3-7). pap. 4.99 (*0-689-80387-7*, Simon Pulse) Simon & Schuster Children's Publishing.
—Mary Alice Peale: Philadelphia, 1777. 1996. (American Diaries Ser.: No. 4). (J). (gr. 3-7). 10.55 (*0-606-10739-8*) Turtleback Bks.
Duncombe, Frances. Summer of the Burning. 1976. (Illus.). 180p. (J). (gr. 5-9). 7.95 o.p. (*0-399-20513-6*) Putnam Publishing Group, The.
Durrant, Linda. Betsy Zane, the Rose of Fort Henry. 2000. 176p. (J). (gr. 5-9). tchr. ed. 15.00 (*0-395-97899-8*, Clarion Bks.) Houghton Mifflin Co. Trade & Reference Div.
Evan, Frances Y. The Forgotten Flag: Revolutionary Struggle in Connecticut. 2003. 92p. (J). 5.95 (*1-57249-338-0*, WM Kids) White Mane Publishing Co., Inc.
Fast, Howard. April Morning. 1983. 208p. (gr. 6 up). mass mkt. 6.99 (*0-553-27322-1*) Bantam Bks.
—April Morning. 9999. (J). pap. 2.25 o.p. (*0-590-02283-0*) Scholastic, Inc.
—The Crossing. 1984. (Illus.). 213p. (J). reprint ed. pap. 12.95 (*0-911020-10-1*) New Jersey Historical Society.
Favole, Robert J. Through the Wormhole. 2001. (Illus.). 192p. (J). (gr. 5-10). 17.95 (*1-930826-00-1*) Flywheel Publishing Co.
Finlayson, Ann. Rebecca's War. 1972. (Illus.). 280p. (J). (gr. 6 up). 5.95 o.p. (*0-7232-6090-7*, Warne, Frederick) Penguin Putnam Bks. for Young Readers.
—Redcoat in Boston. 1971. (J). (gr. 7-12). 5.95 o.p. (*0-7232-6089-3*, Warne, Frederick) Penguin Putnam Bks. for Young Readers.
Forbes, Esther. Johnny Tremain. 1999. 272p. (gr. 5-9). mass mkt. 2.99 o.s.i (*0-440-22827-1*) Bantam Bks.
—Johnny Tremain. 1986. (J). pap. 3.50 o.s.i (*0-440-80053-6*) Dell Publishing.
—Johnny Tremain. 1998. (Illus.). 288p. (YA). (gr. 5-9). tchr. ed. 20.00 (*0-395-90011-5*) Houghton Mifflin Co.
—Johnny Tremain. 2002. (Illus.). (J). 15.00 (*0-7587-0196-9*) Book Wholesalers, Inc.
—Johnny Tremain. 2002. (EMC Masterpiece Series Access Editions). (Illus.). xvi, 308p. (J). 10.95 (*0-8219-2408-7*) EMC/Paradigm Publishing.
—Johnny Tremain: A Novel for Old & Young. 1987. 12.04 (*0-606-00901-9*) Turtleback Bks.
Forbes, Esther Hoskins. Johnny Tremain. 1943. (Illus.). 288p. (YA). (gr. 7-7). tchr. ed. 16.00 (*0-395-06766-9*) Houghton Mifflin Co.
—Johnny Tremain: Illustrated American Classics. Date not set. (J). lib. bdg. 22.95 (*0-8488-1318-9*) Amereon, Ltd.
—Johnny Tremain: Illustrated American Classics. l.t. ed. 1987. 354p. (J). (gr. 3-7). lib. bdg. 14.95 o.s.i (*1-55736-023-5*) Bantam Doubleday Dell Large Print Group, Inc.
—Johnny Tremain: Illustrated American Classics. 1981. 305p. (J). reprint ed. lib. bdg. 27.95 (*0-89966-306-0*) Buccaneer Bks., Inc.
—Johnny Tremain: Illustrated American Classics. 1996. 288p. (J). mass mkt. 2.49 o.s.i (*0-440-22024-6*); 1988. (J). mass mkt. o.p. (*0-440-80073-0*); 1987. (Illus.). 288p. (J). (gr. 4-7). pap. text 6.50 (*0-440-44250-8*) Dell Publishing.

—Johnny Tremain: Illustrated American Classics, 2 vols., Set. 1.t. ed. reprint ed. (*0-89064-029-7*) National Assn. for Visually Handicapped.

—Johnny Tremain: Illustrated American Classics. 1996. (J). mass mkt. 6.99 (*0-440-91100-1*, Dell Books for Young Readers); 1987. (Illus.). 272p. (YA). (gr. 4-7). mass mkt. 6.50 (*0-440-94250-0*, Yearling) Random Hse. Children's Bks.

—Johnny Tremain: Illustrated American Classics. 1987. (J). (gr. 4-8). pap. 19.75 o.p. (*0-8446-6600-9*) Smith, Peter Pub., Inc.

Ford, Paul L. Janice Meredith. 1967. (Airmont Classics Ser.). (J). (gr. 11 up). mass mkt. 0.95 o.p. (*0-8049-0148-1*, CL-148) Airmont Publishing Co., Inc.

Forman, James. Cow Neck Rebels, RS. 1969. 256p. (J). (gr. 7 up). 3.95 o.p. (*0-374-31617-1*, Farrar, Straus & Giroux (BYR)) Farrar, Straus & Giroux.

Fritz, Jean. And Then What Happened, Paul Revere? 1996. (Illus.). 48p. (J). (gr. 4-7). pap. 6.99 (*0-698-11351-9*, PaperStar) Penguin Putnam Bks. for Young Readers.

—Early Thunder. 1967. (Illus.). (J). (gr. 7-11). 15.95 o.s.i (*0-698-20036-5*, Coward-McCann) Penguin Group (USA) Inc.

Garvie, Maureen McCallum & Beaty, Mary. George Johnson's War. (Illus.). (YA). (gr. 7 up). 2003. 248p. pap. 8.95 (*0-88899-468-0*); 2002. 224p. 15.95 (*0-88899-465-6*) Groundwood Bks. CAN. *Dist:* Publishers Group West.

Gauch, Patricia L. Aaron & the Green Mountain Boys. 1972. (Break-of-Day Bks.). (Illus.). (J). (gr. 1-4). 6.99 o.p. (*0-698-30423-3*) Putnam Publishing Group, The.

—Aaron & the Green Mountain Boys. 1988. (Illus.). 64p. (J). (gr. 1-4). 10.95 o.p. (*0-936915-05-6*); pap. 5.95 o.p. (*1-55870-220-2*) Shoe Tree Pr.

—This Time, Tempe Wick? 1992. (Illus.). 48p. (J). (ps-3). 15.99 o.p. (*0-399-21880-7*, G. P. Putnam's Sons) Penguin Group (USA) Inc.

—This Time, Tempe Wick? 1974. (Illus.). 48p. (J). (gr. 2-6). 6.95 o.p. (*0-698-20300-3*, Coward-McCann) Putnam Publishing Group, The.

Gerrard, Roy. Sir Cedric Rides Again, RS. 1988. (Illus.). 32p. (J). (ps-3). pap. 5.95 (*0-374-46662-9*, Sunburst) Farrar, Straus & Giroux.

Gillett, Mary C. Bugles at the Border. 1968. (Illus.). 220p. (YA). (gr. 6 up). lib. bdg. 3.98 o.p. (*0-910244-50-2*) Blair, John F. Pub.

Goll, Reinhold W. Valley Forge Rebel. 1974. 211p. (J). (gr. 5-10). 6.95 o.p. (*0-8059-1994-5*) Dorrance Publishing Co., Inc.

Goodman, Joan Elizabeth. Hope's Crossing. 1998. (Illus.). 224p. (J). (gr. 4-6). tchr. ed. 16.00 (*0-395-86195-0*) Houghton Mifflin Co.

—Hope's Crossing. 1999. (Illus.). 160p. (J). (gr. 3-7). pap. 5.99 (*0-698-11807-3*, Puffin Bks.) Penguin Putnam Bks. for Young Readers.

—Hope's Crossing. 1999. 12.04 (*0-606-19068-6*) Turtleback Bks.

Gregory, Kristiana. Five Smooth Stones: Hope's Revolutionary War Diary. 2001. (My America Ser.). (Illus.). 112p. (J). (gr. 4-7). pap. 8.95 (*0-439-14827-8*, Scholastic Pr.) Scholastic, Inc.

—Five Smooth Stones Bk. 1: Hope's Revolutionary War Diary. 2002. (My America Ser.). (Illus.). 112p. (J). (gr. 2-5). mass mkt. 4.99 (*0-439-36905-3*, Scholastic Pr.) Scholastic, Inc.

—My America Hope's Revolutionary War. 2004. (My America Ser.). (J). pap. 12.95 (*0-439-37053-1*) Scholastic, Inc.

—We Are Patriots Bk. 2: Hope's Revolutionary War Diary, Philadelphia, 1777. 2002. (My America Ser.). (Illus.). 112p. (J). (gr. 2-5). pap. 8.95 (*0-439-21039-9*); mass mkt. 4.99 (*0-439-36906-1*) Scholastic, Inc. (Scholastic Pr.).

—The Winter of Red Snow: The Revolutionary War Diary of Abigail Jane Stewart, Valley Forge, Pennsylvania, 1777. 1996. (Dear America Ser.). (Illus.). 176p. (YA). (gr. 4-9). pap. 10.95 (*0-590-22653-3*) Scholastic, Inc.

Gregory, Kristiana, et al. The Birth of Our Nation Collection: Winter of Red Snow; Standing in the Light; Journey to the New World; Journal of Jasper J. Pierce, 4 vols. 2002. (Dear America Ser.). (J). pap. 19.96 (*0-439-12938-9*) Scholastic, Inc.

Griffin, A. J. Asa's Choice. 2002. 156p. (YA). pap. 9.99 (*0-88092-566-3*, 566-3) Royal Fireworks Publishing Co.

Griffin, Judith Berry. Phoebe, the Spy. 2002. (Illus.). 48p. (J). pap. 6.99 (*0-698-11956-8*, PaperStar) Penguin Putnam Bks. for Young Readers.

Grote, JoAnn A. The American Revolution. 1998. (American Adventure Ser.: No. 11). (Illus.). (J). (gr. 3-7). pap. 3.97 (*1-57748-158-5*) Barbour Publishing, Inc.

—The American Victory: A New Nation Is Born. 12th ed. 1998. (American Adventure Ser.: No. 12). (Illus.). (J). (gr. 3-7). pap. 3.97 (*1-57748-159-3*) Barbour Publishing, Inc.

Gutman, Dan. Qwerty Stevens, Stuck in Time with Benjamin Franklin. 2002. (Illus.). 192p. (J). (gr. 5-8). 16.95 (*0-689-84553-7*, Simon & Schuster Children's Publishing) Simon & Schuster Children's Publishing.

Guzman, Lila & Guzman, Rick. Lorenzo's Secret Mission. 2001. 144p. (J). pap. 9.95 (*1-55885-341-3*, Piñata Books) Arte Publico Pr.

Hall, Marjory. The Other Girl. 1974. 184p. (J). (gr. 5-8). 5.25 o.p. (*0-664-32542-4*) Westminster John Knox Pr.

Hedstrom, Deborah. From Colonies to Country with George Washington. 1997. (My American Journey Ser.). 45p. (J). (gr. 4-7). 19.99 (*1-57673-155-3*) Questar, Inc.

Hilbtecht, Sharron. The Drummer Boy. 2004. 85p. (J). pap. 6.95 (*1-889658-35-9*) New Canaan Publishing Co., Inc.

Holt, Rinehart and Winston Staff. The Fifth of March: A Story of the Boston Massacre. 2nd ed. 2002. (J). text 4.80 (*0-03-073524-6*) Holt, Rinehart & Winston.

Hominick, Judy & Spreier, Jeanne. Ride for Freedom: The Story of Sybil Ludington. 2001. (Heroes to Remember Ser.). (Illus.). 52p. (J). 14.95 (*1-893110-24-9*) Silver Moon Pr.

Houghton Mifflin Company Staff, ed. Johnny Tremain. 1990. (Literature Experience 1991 Ser.). (J). (gr. 8). pap. 11.04 (*0-395-55185-4*) Houghton Mifflin Co.

Huntington, Lee P. Brothers in Arms. 1976. (Illus.). 64p. (J). (gr. 7-10). 5.95 o.p. (*0-914378-18-X*); pap. 3.95 o.p. (*0-914378-24-4*) Countryman Pr.

Jensen, Dorothea. The Riddle of Penncroft Farm. (Odyssey/Great Episodes Book Ser.). (J). (gr. 4-7). 1991. 192p. pap. 6.00 (*0-15-266908-6*); 1989. 272p. 16.00 (*0-15-200574-9*) Harcourt Children's Bks. (Gulliver Bks.).

Johnston, Mary. To Have & to Hold. 1968. (Airmont Classics Ser.). (YA). (gr. 8 up). mass mkt. 1.95 o.p. (*0-8049-0160-0*, CL-160) Airmont Publishing Co., Inc.

Jones, Peter. Rebel in the Night. 1971. (J). (gr. 7 up). 5.95 o.p. (*0-8037-7282-3*, Dial Bks. for Young Readers) Penguin Putnam Bks. for Young Readers.

Keehn, Sally M. Moon of Two Dark Horses. 1995. 224p. (J). (gr. 4-7). 16.95 o.p. (*0-399-22783-0*, Philomel) Penguin Putnam Bks. for Young Readers.

Kirkpatrick, Katherine. Redcoats & Petticoats. 1999. (Illus.). 32p. (J). (gr. 1-5). tchr. ed. 15.95 (*0-8234-1416-7*) Holiday Hse., Inc.

Koger, Earl. Jocko: A Legend of the American Revolution. 1976. (Illus.). (J). (gr. 2 up). lib. bdg. o.p. (*0-13-510040-2*) Prentice-Hall.

Krensky, Stephen. Dangerous Crossing: The Revolutionary Voyage of John & John Quincy Adams. Harlin, Greg, tr. & illus. by. 2005. 32p. (J). 16.99 (*0-525-46966-4*, Dutton Children's Bks.) Penguin Putnam Bks. for Young Readers.

Lavender, William. Just Jane: A Daughter of England Caught in the Struggle of the American Revolution. 2002. (Great Episodes Ser.). 288p. (YA). 17.00 (*0-15-202587-1*, Gulliver Bks.) Harcourt Children's Bks.

Lawrence, Mildred. Touchmark. 1975. (Illus.). 192p. (J). (gr. 4-7). 7.50 o.p. (*0-15-289603-1*) Harcourt Children's Bks.

Lee, Beverly. The Secret of Van Rink's Cellar. 1979. (Books for Adults & Young Adults). 180p. (J). (gr. 4 up). 17.50 o.p. (*0-8225-0763-3*, Lerner Pubns.) Lerner Publishing Group.

Lowrey, Janette S. Six Silver Spoons. 1971. (I Can Read Bks.). (Illus.). 64p. (J). (ps-3). lib. bdg. 10.89 o.p. (*0-06-024037-7*) HarperCollins Children's Bk. Group.

Lunn, Janet. Hollow Tree. 2000. (Illus.). 208p. (J). (gr. 5-9). 15.99 (*0-670-88949-0*, Viking) Penguin Putnam Bks. for Young Readers.

Luttrell, Wanda. Stranger in Williamsburg. 196p. 2010. (Sarah's Journey Ser.: Vol. 2). (J). (gr. 4-7). pap. 6.99 (*0-7814-0902-0*); 1995. (YA). 12.99 (*0-7814-0235-2*) Cook Communications Ministries.

Lutz, Norma Jean. Enemy or Friend? 20th ed. 1998. (American Adventure Ser.: No. 20). (Illus.). (J). (gr. 3-7). pap. 3.97 (*1-57748-258-1*) Barbour Publishing, Inc.

—Fight for Freedom. 19th ed. 1998. (American Adventure Ser.: No. 19). (Illus.). (J). (gr. 3-7). pap. 3.97 (*1-57748-257-3*) Barbour Publishing, Inc.

Maddox, Hugh. Billy Boll Weevil. 1976. 2.50 o.p. (*0-87397-097-7*, Strode Pubs.) Circle Bk. Service, Inc.

Marko, Katherine M. Away to Fundy Bay. 1985. (Walker's American History Series for Young People). (Illus.). 128p. (J). (gr. 4 up). 11.95 o.s.i (*0-8027-6576-9*); lib. bdg. 12.85 o.s.i (*0-8027-6594-7*) Walker & Co.

Massey, Craig. Indian Drums & Broken Arrows. rev. ed. 1996. (Illus.). 136p. (J). (gr. 5-9). reprint ed. mass mkt. 6.99 (*1-891635-01-8*) Moore Bks.

Massie, Elizabeth. Patsy's Discovery. 1997. (Daughters of Liberty Ser.: No. 1). 144p. (J). (gr. 3 up). pap. 3.99 (*0-671-00132-9*, Aladdin) Simon & Schuster Children's Publishing.

McGahan, Mary. Raid at Red Mill. 2001. (Adventures in America Ser.). (Illus.). 96p. (J). (gr. 3-7). lib. bdg. 14.95 (*1-893110-11-7*) Silver Moon Pr.

Meadowcroft, Enid L. Silver for General Washington: A Story of Valley Forge. rev. ed. 1967. (Illus.). (J). (gr. 3-7). o.p. (*0-690-73731-9*) HarperCollins Children's Bk. Group.

Miller, Susan Martins. The Boston Massacre. 10th ed. 1998. (American Adventure Ser.: No. 10). (Illus.). (J). (gr. 3-7). pap. 3.97 (*1-57748-157-7*) Barbour Publishing, Inc.

—The Boston Massacre. 1999. (American Adventure Ser.: No. 10). 144p. (J). (gr. 3-7). lib. bdg. 15.95 (*0-7910-5584-1*) Chelsea Hse. Pubs.

—Boston Revolts! 9th ed. 1998. (American Adventure Ser.: No. 9). (Illus.). (J). (gr. 3-7). 3.97 (*1-57748-156-9*) Barbour Publishing, Inc.

—Boston Revolts! 1999. (American Adventure Ser.: No. 9). (Illus.). 144p. (J). (gr. 3-7). lib. bdg. 15.95 (*0-7910-5583-3*) Chelsea Hse. Pubs.

Monjo, F. N. King George's Head Was Made of Lead. 1974. (Illus.). 48p. (J). (gr. 1-3). 5.95 o.p. (*0-698-20298-8*) Putnam Publishing Group, The.

—Zenas & the Shaving Mill. 1976. (Illus.). 48p. (J). (gr. 3-6). 5.95 o.p. (*0-698-20326-7*) Putnam Publishing Group, The.

Moore, Ruth N. Distant Thunder: A Sequel to the Christmas Surprise. 1991. (Illus.). 160p. (Orig.). (J). (gr. 4-7). pap. 6.99 (*0-8361-3557-1*) Herald Pr.

—Hiding the Bell. 1968. (Illus.). (J). (gr. 4-6). 5.25 o.p. (*0-664-32412-6*) Westminster John Knox Pr.

Moss, Marissa. Emma's Journal: The Story of a Colonial Girl. (Young American Voices Ser.: Bk. 2). (Illus.). 56p. (J). (gr. 3-7). 2001. pap. 7.00 (*0-15-216325-5*); 1999. 15.00 (*0-15-202025-X*) Harcourt Children's Bks. (Silver Whistle).

Murphy, Jim. A Young Patriot: The American Revolution As Experienced by One Boy. 1998. (J). 13.00 (*0-606-13941-9*) Turtleback Bks.

Myers, Anna. The Keeping Room. 1999. (Illus.). 128p. (J). (gr. 3-7). pap. 5.99 (*0-14-130468-5*) Penguin Putnam Bks. for Young Readers.

—The Keeping Room. 1999. 11.04 (*0-606-16786-2*) Turtleback Bks.

—The Keeping Room. 1997. 144p. (J). (gr. 3-7). 16.95 (*0-8027-8641-3*) Walker & Co.

O'Dell, Scott. Sara Bishop. 1988. (YA). (gr. 7 up). mass mkt. 2.95 o.p. (*0-590-44363-1*) Scholastic, Inc.

—Sarah Bishop, 001. 1980. 192p. (YA). (gr. 7 up). tchr. ed. 16.00 (*0-395-29185-2*) Houghton Mifflin Co.

Olasky, Susan. Annie Henry: Adventures in the American Revolution. 2003. (Illus.). 528p. (J). pap. 16.99 (*1-58134-521-6*) Crossway Bks.

—Annie Henry & the Birth of Liberty. 1995. (Adventures of the American Revolution Ser.: Vol. 2). 128p. (J). (gr. 3-7). pap. 5.99 (*0-89107-842-8*) Crossway Bks.

—Annie Henry & the Redcoats: Adventures of the American Revolution. 1996. (Adventures of the American Revolution Ser.: Vol. 4). 128p. (J). (gr. 3-7). pap. 5.99 (*0-89107-908-4*) Crossway Bks.

Osborne, Mary Pope. Revolutionary War on Wednesday. Loehr, Mallory, ed. 2000. (Magic Tree House Ser.: No. 22). (Illus.). 96p. (J). (gr. k-3). lib. bdg. 11.99 (*0-679-99068-2*); pap. 3.99 (*0-679-89068-8*) Random Hse. Children's Bks. (Random Hse. Bks. for Young Readers).

—Revolutionary War on Wednesday. 2000. (Magic Tree House Ser.: No. 22). (J). (gr. k-3). 10.04 (*0-606-19907-1*) Turtleback Bks.

Owens, Tom. The Bravest Blacksmith. 2000. (Cover-to-Cover Bks.). (Illus.). 56p. (J). (*0-7807-9266-1*) Perfection Learning Corp.

—Flames of Freedom. 2001. (Cover-to-Cover Bks.). (Illus.). 54p. (J). (*0-7807-9040-5*) Perfection Learning Corp.

Paulsen, Gary. The Rifle. 1995. 112p. (YA). (gr. 7 up). 17.00 (*0-15-292880-4*) Harcourt Children's Bks.

—The Rifle. 1997. 112p. (YA). (gr. 7-12). mass mkt. 4.99 (*0-440-21920-5*, Laurel Leaf) Random Hse. Children's Bks.

—The Rifle. 1997. 11.04 (*0-606-11800-4*) Turtleback Bks.

Peck, Robert Newton. Rabbits & Redcoats. 1976. (Illus.). 64p. (J). (gr. 3-6). 6.95 o.s.i (*0-8027-6241-7*); lib. bdg. 6.85 o.s.i (*0-8027-6242-5*) Walker & Co.

Pope, Elizabeth M. The Sherwood Ring, 001. 1958. (Illus.). (J). (gr. 7 up). 7.95 o.p. (*0-395-07033-3*) Houghton Mifflin Co.

Pryor, Bonnie. American Adventures: Thomas in Danger, 1779. 2nd ed. 1999. (American Adventures Ser.). (Illus.). 176p. (J). (gr. 3-7). 15.99 (*0-688-16518-4*, Morrow, William & Co.) Morrow/Avon.

—Thomas: Patriots on the Run. 1998. (American Adventures Ser.: No. 1). (Illus.). 160p. (J). (gr. 3-7). 15.95 (*0-688-15669-X*) HarperCollins Children's Bk. Group.

—Thomas: 1778—Patriots on the Run. 2000. (American Adventures Ser.). (Illus.). 160p. (J). (gr. 3-7). pap. 5.99 (*0-380-73088-X*, Avon Bks.) Morrow/Avon.

—Thomas in Danger, 1779. 2000. (American Adventures Ser.). 176p. (J). (gr. 3-7). pap. 4.95 (*0-380-73212-2*) Morrow/Avon.

Quackenbush, Robert M. Daughter of Liberty: A True Story of the American Revolution. 1999. 64p. (J). (gr. 2-4). pap. 4.99 (*0-7868-1286-9*); lib. bdg. 15.49 (*0-7868-2355-0*) Hyperion Pr.

Reit, Seymour V. Guns for General Washington. 1990. (Great Episodes Ser.). (Illus.). 144p. (C). (gr. 3-7). 15.95 o.s.i (*0-15-200466-1*, Gulliver Bks.) Harcourt Children's Bks.

—Guns for General Washington: A Story of the American Revolution. 2001. (Great Episodes Ser.). 160p. (YA). (gr. 5-9). pap. 6.00 (*0-15-216435-9*, Gulliver Bks.) Harcourt Children's Bks.

Richards, Kitty. Star-Spangled Babies. 1999. (Rugrats Chapter Bks.: No. 3). (Illus.). 64p. (J). (gr. 1-4). pap. 3.99 (*0-689-82891-8*, Simon Spotlight) Simon & Schuster Children's Publishing.

Rinaldi, Ann. The Fifth of March: A Story of the Boston Massacre. 1993. (Great Episodes Ser.). (Illus.). 352p. (YA). (gr. 7 up). pap. 6.00 (*0-15-227517-7*, Gulliver Bks.) Harcourt Children's Bks.

—Finishing Becca: A Story about Peggy Shippen & Benedict Arnold. (Great Episodes Ser.). 384p. (YA). 2004. pap. (*0-15-205079-5*); 1994. (gr. 7 up). 12.00 (*0-15-200880-2*); 1994. (gr. 7 up). pap. 6.00 o.s.i (*0-15-200879-9*) Harcourt Children's Bks. (Gulliver Bks.).

—Finishing Becca: A Story about Peggy Shippen & Benedict Arnold. 1994. 12.05 (*0-606-14207-X*) Turtleback Bks.

—Or Give Me Death: A Novel of Patrick Henry's Family. 2003. (Great Episodes Ser.). 240p. (J). 17.00 (*0-15-216687-4*) Harcourt Children's Bks.

—A Ride into Morning: The Story of Tempe Wick. Grove, Karen, ed. 1991. (Great Episodes Ser.). 368p. (YA). (gr. 7 up). 15.95 (*0-15-200573-0*, Gulliver Bks.) Harcourt Children's Bks.

—The Secret of Sarah Revere. (Great Episodes Ser.). 336p. (YA). 2003. pap. 6.95 (*0-15-204684-4*); 1995. (gr. 7 up). 13.00 (*0-15-200393-2*, Gulliver Bks.); 1995. (gr. 7 up). pap. 6.00 o.s.i (*0-15-200392-4*, Gulliver Bks.) Harcourt Children's Bks.

Roop, Peter & Roop, Connie. An Eye for an Eye: A Story of the American Revolution. 2001. (Jamestown Classics Ser.). (Illus.). 168p. (YA). (gr. 5-8). 12.64 (*0-8092-0587-4*) Jamestown.

Rosenburg, John M. First in War: George Washington in the American Revolution. 1998. (Single Titles Ser.: up). (Illus.). 256p. (gr. 7-12). 25.90 (*0-7613-0311-1*) Millbrook Pr., Inc.

Rue, Nancy. The Burden. 1998. (Christian Heritage Ser.). 192p. (J). (gr. 3-7). pap. 5.99 (*1-56179-517-8*) Focus on the Family Publishing.

—The Invasion. 1998. (Christian Heritage Ser.). 192p. (J). (gr. 3-7). pap. 5.99 (*1-56179-541-0*) Focus on the Family Publishing.

—The Prisoner. 1998. (Christian Heritage Ser.). 192p. (J). (gr. 3-7). pap. 5.99 (*1-56179-518-6*) Focus on the Family Publishing.

—The Rebel. 1998. (Christian Heritage Ser.). 192p. (J). (gr. 3-7). pap. 5.99 (*1-56179-478-3*) Focus on the Family Publishing.

—The Thief. 1998. (Christian Heritage Ser.). 192p. (J). (gr. 3-7). pap. 5.99 (*1-56179-479-1*) Focus on the Family Publishing.

Sargent, Dave & Sargent, Pat. Dan (Dappled Mahogany Bay) Determination #21. 2001. (Saddle Up Ser.). 36p. (J). pap. 6.95 (*1-56763-652-7*); lib. bdg. 22.60 (*1-56763-651-9*) Ozark Publishing.

Schick, Alice & Allen, Marjorie N. The Remarkable Ride of Israel Bissell As Related by Molly the Crow. 1976. (Illus.). (J). (gr. k-3). 5.95 o.p. (*0-397-31676-3*) HarperCollins Children's Bk. Group.

Schurfranz, Vivian. A Message for General Washington. 1998. (Stories of the States Ser.: Vol. 10). 92p. (J). (gr. 4-7). lib. bdg. 14.95 (*1-881889-89-0*) Silver Moon Pr.

Smith, Mary P. Boys & Girls of Seventy-Seven. Silvester, Susan B., ed. 2nd ed. 1987. (Old Deerfield Ser.). (Illus.). 333p. (YA). (gr. 5 up). reprint ed. 17.00 o.p. (*0-913993-08-5*) Paideia Pubs.

Smyth, Donna. Loyalist Runaway. 1995. 136p. (YA). (gr. 5 up). (*0-88780-087-4*); pap. (*0-88780-086-6*) Formac Distributing, Ltd.

Snow, Richard F. Freelon Starbird, 001. 1976. (Illus.). 240p. (J). (gr. 7 up). 7.95 o.p. (*0-395-24275-4*) Houghton Mifflin Co.

Stephens, Amanda. Fire in Their Hearts. 2003. (Illus.). 128p. (J). bds. 6.99 (*0-448-43269-2*, Grosset & Dunlap) Penguin Putnam Bks. for Young Readers.

—New Kind of Hero. 2003. (Illus.). 128p. bds. 6.99 (*0-448-43268-4*, Grosset & Dunlap) Penguin Putnam Bks. for Young Readers.

Sterman, Betsy. Saratoga Secret. 1998. 176p. (YA). (gr. 5-9). 16.99 (*0-8037-2332-6*, Dial Bks. for Young Readers) Penguin Putnam Bks. for Young Readers.

Stratemeyer, Edward. The Minute Boys of Bunker Hill. (Illus.). (J). (gr. 4-8). 1996. 304p. reprint ed. pap. 17.95 o.p. (*0-9652735-0-4*); 1998. 316p. pap. 14.95 (*1-890623-05-9*) Lost Classics Bk. Co.

Strigenz, Geri K. Year of the Sevens. 1992. (History's Children Ser.). (Illus.). 48p. (J). (gr. 4-5). pap. o.p. (*0-8114-6430-X*) Raintree Pubs.

Strigenz, Geri K., illus. Year of the Sevens. 1992. (History's Children Ser.). (Illus.). 48p. (J). (gr. 4-5). lib. bdg. 21.36 o.p. (*0-8114-3505-9*) Raintree Pubs.

Sweetzer, Anna Leah, et al. Treason Stops at Oyster Bay. 1999. (Mysteries in Time Ser.: Vol. 7). (Illus.). 90p. (J). (gr. 3-7). lib. bdg. 14.95 (*1-893110-03-6*) Silver Moon Pr.

Switzer-Clarke, Eileen. Blossom: A Girl's Adventures in Revolutionary Rockland. 1998. (Illus.). 108p. (J). (gr. 3-6). pap. 8.00 (*0-911183-44-2*) Historical Society of Rockland County, The.

Turner, Ann Warren. Katie's Trunk. (Illus.). 32p. (J). (gr. k-3). 1997. pap. 6.99 (*0-689-81054-7*, Aladdin); 1992. lib. bdg. 15.00 (*0-02-789512-2*, Simon & Schuster Children's Publishing) Simon & Schuster Children's Publishing.

—Love Thy Neighbor: The Tory Diary of Prudence Emerson. 2003. (Dear America Ser.). (Illus.). 192p. (J). pap. 10.95 (*0-439-15308-5*) Scholastic, Inc.

—What Did I Know of Freedom? 2004. 32p. (J). (ps-3). 15.99 (*0-06-027579-0*); lib. bdg. 16.89 (*0-06-027580-4*) HarperCollins Children's Bk. Group.

Turner Curtis, Alice. Little Maid of Mohawk Valley. 2004. (Little Maid Ser.). 189p. (J). (gr. 1-3). pap. text 9.95 (*1-55709-337-7*) Applewood Bks.

Van Leeuwen, Jean. Hannah of Fairfield. Fogelman, Phyllis J., ed. 1999. (Pioneer Daughters Ser.: No. 1). (Illus.). 96p. (J). (gr. 2-5). 15.99 (*0-8037-2335-0*, Dial Bks. for Young Readers) Penguin Putnam Bks. for Young Readers.

—Hannah of Fairfield. Fogelman, Phyllis, ed. 1999. (Pioneer Daughters Ser.: No. 1). (Illus.). 96p. (J). (gr. 2-5). 14.89 (*0-8037-2336-9*, Dial Bks. for Young Readers) Penguin Putnam Bks. for Young Readers.

—Hannah's Winter of Hope. 2000. (Pioneer Daughters Ser.). (Illus.). 96p. (J). (gr. 2-5). 14.99 (*0-8037-2492-6*, Dial Bks. for Young Readers) Penguin Putnam Bks. for Young Readers.

Walker, Sally M. The 18 Penny Goose. 1998. (I Can Read Bks.). (Illus.). 64p. (J). (gr. k-3). lib. bdg. 15.89 (*0-06-027557-X*) HarperCollins Children's Bk. Group.

—The 18 Penny Goose. 1998. (I Can Read Bks.). (Illus.). 64p. (J). (ps-4). 14.95 o.p. (*0-06-027556-1*) HarperCollins Pubs.

Waters, Kate. Mary Geddy's Day: A Colonial Girl in Williamsburg. (Illus.). 40p. (J). 2002. pap. 5.99 (*0-590-92928-3*, Scholastic Paperbacks); 1999. (gr. 1-4). pap. 16.95 (*0-590-92925-9*) Scholastic, Inc.

Wibberley, Leonard. John Treegate's Musket, RS. 1986. 224p. (J). (gr. 7 up). pap. 3.95 o.p. (*0-374-43788-2*, Sunburst) Farrar, Straus & Giroux.

—John Treegate's Musket. 1993. (J). (gr. 5 up). 16.80 o.p. (*0-8446-6655-6*) Smith, Peter Pub., Inc.

Wisler, G. Clifton. The King's Mountain. 2002. 160p. (J). (gr. 5 up). lib. bdg. 15.89 (*0-06-623793-9*) HarperCollins Children's Bk. Group.

Woodruff, Elvira. In George Washington's Socks. 1991. 176p. (J). 13.95 o.p. (*0-590-44035-7*) Scholastic, Inc.

UNITED STATES—HISTORY—1783-1809—FICTION

Bourne, Miriam A. Patsy Jefferson's Diary. 1976. (Illus.). 96p. (J). (gr. 5-11). 5.95 o.p. (*0-698-20352-6*) Putnam Publishing Group, The.

Collier, James Lincoln. Jump Ship to Freedom. 1996. (J). pap. 5.99 (*0-440-91158-3*, Dell Books for Young Readers) Random Hse. Children's Bks.

—Jump Ship to Freedom. 1987. (Arabus Family Saga Ser.). (J). 11.55 (*0-606-02265-1*) Turtleback Bks.

Collier, James Lincoln & Collier, Christopher. Jump Ship to Freedom. 1987. (Arabus Family Saga Ser.: Vol. 2). 208p. (gr. 4-7). pap. text 5.50 (*0-440-44323-7*, Yearling) Random Hse. Children's Bks.

—Who Is Carrie? 1984. 192p. (J). (gr. 4-6). 14.95 o.s.i (*0-385-29295-3*, Delacorte Pr.) Dell Publishing.

—Who Is Carrie? 1987. (Arabus Family Saga Ser.: Vol. 3). 176p. (gr. 5-7). pap. text 4.99 o.s.i (*0-440-49536-9*, Yearling) Random Hse. Children's Bks.

—Who Is Carrie? 1987. (Arabus Family Saga Ser.). (J). 11.04 (*0-606-03505-2*) Turtleback Bks.

—The Winter Hero. 1985. (YA). 132p. (gr. 9 up). pap. 3.50 (*0-590-42604-4*); 208p. (gr. 7 up). reprint ed. 1.25 o.p. (*0-590-40680-9*, Scholastic Paperbacks); 208p. (gr. 7 up). reprint ed. pap. 2.25 o.p. (*0-590-33696-7*, Scholastic Paperbacks) Scholastic, Inc.

—The Winter Hero. 1984. 160p. (YA). (gr. 7 up). 11.95 o.p. (*0-02-722990-4*, Simon & Schuster Children's Publishing) Simon & Schuster Children's Publishing.

Lomask, Milton. The Spirit of 1787: The Making of Our Constitution, RS. 1980. 224p. (J). (gr. 7 up). 10.95 o.p. (*0-374-37149-0*, Farrar, Straus & Giroux (BYR)) Farrar, Straus & Giroux.

Wood, Frances M. Becoming Rosemary. 1998. 256p. (gr. 7-12). pap. text 3.99 o.s.i (*0-440-41238-2*) Dell Publishing.

—Becoming Rosemary. 1998. (J). 10.04 (*0-606-13186-8*) Turtleback Bks.

UNITED STATES—HISTORY—1783-1865—FICTION

Armstrong, Jennifer. Thomas Jefferson: Letters from a Philadelphia Bookworm. 2001. (Dear Mr. President Ser.: Vol. 2). (Illus.). 117p. (J). (gr. 5-7). 8.95 (*1-890817-30-9*) Winslow Pr.

Brown, Jane C., illus. George Washington's Ghost. 1994. 96p. (J). 13.95 o.p. (*0-395-69452-3*) Houghton Mifflin Co.

Collier, James Lincoln & Collier, Christopher. Jump Ship to Freedom. 1981. 192p. (J). (gr. 4-6). pap. 13.95 o.s.i (*0-385-28484-5*, Delacorte Pr.) Dell Publishing.

De Angeli, Marguerite. Whistle for the Crossing. 1977. (gr. 2-5). 5.95 o.p. (*0-385-11552-0*); lib. bdg. 5.95 o.p. (*0-385-11553-9*) Doubleday Publishing.

Fradin, Dennis Brindell. The Connecticut Colony. 1990. (Thirteen Colonies Ser.). (Illus.). 160p. (YA). (gr. 4-12). lib. bdg. 33.50 (*0-516-00393-3*, Children's Pr.) Scholastic Library Publishing.

Hopkinson, Deborah. Under the Quilt of Night. 2002. (Illus.). 40p. (J). 16.00 (*0-689-82227-8*, Atheneum/Anne Schwartz Bks.) Simon & Schuster Children's Publishing.

Marriott, Donna. What Are the Other Kids Doing While You Teach Small Groups?, Grades 1-3. Kupperstein, Joel, ed. 1997. (Illus.). 160p. pap., tchr. ed. 16.99 (*1-57471-293-4*, 3345) Creative Teaching Pr., Inc.

Rees, Douglas. Lightning Time. 1997. (Illus.). 172p. (J). (gr. 5-9). pap. 15.95 o.p. (*0-7894-2458-4*) Dorling Kindersley Publishing, Inc.

—Lightning Time. 1999. 176p. (J). (gr. 5-9). pap. 4.99 (*0-14-130317-4*, Puffin Bks.) Penguin Putnam Bks. for Young Readers.

—Lightning Time. 1999. 11.04 (*0-606-19069-4*) Turtleback Bks.

Stone, Irving. The President's Lady: A Novel about Rachel & Andrew Jackson. 1951. 360p. (J). 24.95 o.s.i (*0-385-04362-7*) Doubleday Publishing.

Tibbitts, Casey. Place of Honor. 2000. 424p. pap. 22.95 (*0-595-16628-8*, Writers Club Pr.) iUniverse, Inc.

Wanttaja, Ronald. The Price of Command: Nate Lawton's War of 1812. Kemnitz, Myrna, ed. 1998. (Illus.). 330p. (J). pap. 9.99 (*0-88092-286-9*, 2869) Royal Fireworks Publishing Co.

Yep, Laurence. The Journal of Wong Ming-Chung: A Chinese Miner: California, 1852. 2000. (My Name Is America Ser.). (Illus.). 219p. (J). (gr. 4-8). pap. 10.95 (*0-590-38607-7*) Scholastic, Inc.

UNITED STATES—HISTORY—19TH CENTURY—FICTION

Ambrose, Stephen E. This Vast Land: A Young Man's Journal of the Lewis & Clark Expedition. 2003. (Illus.). 304p. (YA). 17.95 (*0-689-86448-5*, Simon & Schuster Children's Publishing) Simon & Schuster Children's Publishing.

Fletcher, Susan. Walk Across the Sea. 2003. (Illus.). 224p. (J). pap. 4.99 (*0-689-85707-1*, Aladdin) Simon & Schuster Children's Publishing.

The Great Railroad Race: The Diary of Libby West. 2003. (J). lib. bdg. 12.95 (*0-439-55533-7*) Scholastic, Inc.

Hart, Alison. Fires of Jubilee. 2003. (Illus.). 192p. (J). pap. 4.99 (*0-689-85528-1*, Aladdin) Simon & Schuster Children's Publishing.

Kimmel, Cody. One Sky Above Us. 2004. (Adventures of Young Buffalo Bill Ser.). 192p. (J). pap. 5.99 (*0-06-440895-7*, Harper Trophy) HarperCollins Children's Bk. Group.

Rees, Shirley. Hannah Stands Tall. 2002. 130p. (J). pap. 10.95 (*1-55517-652-6*, 76526, Bonneville Bks.) Cedar Fort, Inc./CFI Distribution.

Tripp, Valerie. Josefina's Boxed Set: Meet Josefina; Josefina Learns a Lesson; Josefina's Surprise; Happy Birthday, Josefina; Josefina Saves the Day; Changes for Josefina, 6 bks. 1998. (American Girls Collection: Bks. 1-6). (Illus.). 432p. (J). (gr. 2-7). 74.95 (*1-56247-676-9*, American Girl) Pleasant Co. Pubns.

Whelan, Gloria. Fruitlands. 2004. 128p. (J). pap. 5.99 (*0-06-441084-6*, Harper Trophy) HarperCollins Children's Bk. Group.

—The Wanigan: A Life on the River. 2003. (Illus.). 144p. (YA). (gr. 3-7). pap. 4.99 (*0-440-41882-8*, Dell Books for Young Readers) Random Hse. Children's Bks.

UNITED STATES—HISTORY—WAR OF 1812—FICTION

Alder, Elizabeth. Crossing the Panther's Path, RS. 2002. (Illus.). 240p. (J). 18.00 (*0-374-31662-7*, Farrar, Straus & Giroux (BYR)) Farrar, Straus & Giroux.

—Crossing the Panther's Path. 2003. (Young Adult Ser.). (YA). 24.95 (*0-7862-5013-5*) Thorndike Pr.

Benton, Amanda. Silent Stranger. 1998. pap. 3.99 (*0-380-79222-2*, Avon Bks.) Morrow/Avon.

—Silent Stranger. 1998. 10.04 (*0-606-16165-1*) Turtleback Bks.

Brown, Duncan. The Monkey's Constitution. 1997. (Illus.). 88p. (J). (gr. 4-8). pap. 9.95 (*1-57960-030-1*) Discovery Enterprises, Ltd.

Crook, Connie Brummel. Laura Secord's Brave Walk. 2001. (Illus.). 24p. (J). (gr. 1-4). 14.95 (*1-896764-34-7*) Second Story Pr. CAN. *Dist:* Orca Bk. Pubs.

Greeson, Janet. An American Army of Two. 1999. (On My Own Biography Ser.). (Illus.). (J). 12.00 (*0-606-21902-1*) Turtleback Bks.

Hall, Marjory. The Gold-Lined Box. 2003. 224p. (YA). 11.95 (*0-9714612-6-0*) Green Mansion Pr. LLC.

—The Gold-Lined Box. 1968. 198p. (J). (gr. 5-9). 4.25 o.p. (*0-664-32420-7*) Westminster John Knox Pr.

Kimball, K. M. The Star Spangled Secret. 2001. (Mystery Ser.). 240p. (J). (gr. 5-7). pap. 4.99 (*0-689-84550-2*, Aladdin) Simon & Schuster Children's Publishing.

Mandrell, Louise & Collins, Ace. Sunrise over the Harbor: A Story about the Meaning of Independence Day. 1993. (Children's Holiday Adventure Ser.: Vol. 16). (Illus.). 32p. (J). (ps-3). 12.95 o.p. (*1-56530-040-8*) Summit Publishing Group - Legacy Bks.

McCully, Emily Arnold. The Battle for St. Michaels. 2002. (I Can Read Chapter Bks.). (Illus.). 64p. (J). (gr. 3 up). 15.99 (*0-06-028728-4*); lib. bdg. 17.89 (*0-06-028729-2*) HarperCollins Children's Bk. Group.

—The Battle for St. Michaels. 2004. (I Can Read Book 4 Ser.). 64p. (J). (gr. k-3). pap. 3.99 (*0-06-444278-0*) HarperCollins Pubs.

Meader, Stephen W. Clear for Action. 1940. (Illus.). (J). (gr. 7 up). 4.95 o.p. (*0-15-218937-8*) Harcourt Children's Bks.

Midgley, Amy. Silent Stranger. 1997. 160p. (J). (gr. 5-7). mass mkt. 14.00 o.p. (*0-380-97486-X*, Avon Bks.) Morrow/Avon.

Minahan, John A. Abigail's Drum. 1995. (Illus.). 64p. (J). (gr. 3-5). text 15.95 (*0-945912-25-0*) Pippin Pr.

Mitchell, Barbara. Cornstalks & Cannonballs. 1980. (Carolrhoda On My Own Bks.). (Illus.). (J). (gr. k-4). lib. bdg. 9.95 o.p. (*0-87614-121-1*, Carolrhoda Bks.) Lerner Publishing Group.

Perkins, Lucy F. American Twins of 1812. (J). (gr. 2-5). 20.95 (*0-89190-473-5*) Amereon, Ltd.

—American Twins of 1812. 1969. (Walker's Twins Ser.). (Illus.). (J). (gr. 2-5). lib. bdg. 4.85 o.s.i (*0-8027-6007-4*) Walker & Co.

Perkins, Stanley C. Arvilla & the Tattler Tree: The Fur Trader. 1994. (Illus.). 702p. (J). 30.00 (*0-9614640-9-7*); pap. 25.00 (*0-9620249-4-5*) Broadblade Pr.

Rinaldi, Ann. Broken Days. (Quilt Trilogy Ser.: Vol. 2). 288p. 1997. (J). mass mkt. 5.99 o.s.i (*0-590-46054-4*, Scholastic Paperbacks); 1995. (YA). (gr. 7 up). pap. 14.95 (*0-590-46053-6*) Scholastic, Inc.

—Broken Days. 1997. (Quilt Trilogy Ser.). 11.04 (*0-606-11167-0*) Turtleback Bks.

Roberts, Kenneth Lewis. Captain Caution. Date not set. 224p. 21.95 (*0-8488-2382-6*) Amereon, Ltd.

Robinet, Harriette Gillem. Washington City Is Burning. 1996. 160p. (J). (gr. 3-7). 16.95 (*0-689-80773-2*, Atheneum) Simon & Schuster Children's Publishing.

Sargent, Dave & Sargent, Pat. Snow (white) Be Truthful #53. 2001. (Saddle Up Ser.). 36p. (J). pap. 6.95 (*1-56763-624-1*); lib. bdg. 22.60 (*1-56763-623-3*) Ozark Publishing.

Simmons, Marc. Millie Cooper's Ride: A True Story from History. 2002. (Illus.). 56p. (J). 16.95 (*0-8263-2925-X*) Univ. of New Mexico Pr.

Sutherland, Robert. A River Apart. 2002. 178p. pap. (*1-55041-646-4*) Fitzhenry & Whiteside, Ltd.

Whelan, Gloria. Once on This Island. (Trophy Bk.). 192p. (J). 1996. (gr. 3-7). pap. 5.99 (*0-06-440619-9*, Harper Trophy); 1995. (gr. k-3). 16.99 (*0-06-026248-6*); 1995. (gr. 3-7). lib. bdg. 14.89 (*0-06-026249-4*) HarperCollins Children's Bk. Group.

—Once on This Island. 1996. (J). 11.00 (*0-606-09709-0*) Turtleback Bks.

Wibberley, Leonard. The Last Battle, RS. 1976. 208p. (J). (gr. 4-8). 7.95 o.p. (*0-374-34349-7*, Farrar, Straus & Giroux (BYR)) Farrar, Straus & Giroux.

—Red Pawns, RS. 1973. 192p. (J). (gr. 7 up). 5.95 o.p. (*0-374-36240-8*, Farrar, Straus & Giroux (BYR)) Farrar, Straus & Giroux.

Wiley, Melissa. Little House by Boston Bay. 1999. (Little House Ser.). (Illus.). 208p. (J). (gr. 3-7). 15.95 (*0-06-027011-X*); (gr. 3-7). pap. 5.99 (*0-06-440737-3*, Harper Trophy); (ps-3). lib. bdg. 16.89 (*0-06-028201-0*) HarperCollins Children's Bk. Group.

—On Tide Mill Lane, No. 2. 2001. (Little House Ser.). (Illus.). 272p. (J). (gr. k-4). 16.95 (*0-06-027013-6*); (gr. 3-7). lib. bdg. 16.89 (*0-06-027014-4*) HarperCollins Children's Bk. Group.

Winstead, Amy. The Star-Spangled Banner. Dacey, Bob & Bandelin, Debra, trs. 2003. (Illus.). 32p. (J). 16.95 (*0-8249-5462-9*, Ideals Pr.) Ideals Pubns.

UNITED STATES—HISTORY—1815-1861—FICTION

Hill, Elizabeth S. The Banjo Player. 1993. 208p. (J). (gr. 5-9). 14.99 o.p. (*0-670-84967-7*, Viking Children's Bks.) Penguin Putnam Bks. for Young Readers.

—The Banjo Player. 1999. pap. 4.99 (*0-14-036422-6*) Viking Penguin.

Hough, Emerson. 54-40 or Fight. 2000. 252p. (J). E-Book 3.95 (*0-594-02461-7*) 1873 Pr.

Kroll, Steven. John Quincy Adams: Letters from a Southern Planter's Son. 2001. (Dear Mr. President Ser.). (Illus.). 128p. (J). (gr. 4-6). 9.95 (*1-890817-93-7*) Winslow Pr.

Kudlinski, Kathleen V. Lone Star: A Story of the Texas Rangers. (Once upon America Ser.). (Illus.). 64p. (J). (gr. 2-6). 1996. pap. 3.99 o.s.i (*0-14-036645-8*, Puffin Bks.); 1994. 12.99 o.p. (*0-670-85179-5*, Viking Children's Bks.) Penguin Putnam Bks. for Young Readers.

—Lone Star: A Story of the Texas Rangers. 1996. (Once upon America Ser.). (J). (gr. 2-6). 9.19 o.p. (*0-606-09571-3*) Turtleback Bks.

Luttrell, Wanda. Hannah's Sojourn. 2000. (Immigrants Chronicles Ser.). 132p. (J). (gr. 3-7). pap. 5.99 (*0-7814-3082-8*) Cook Communications Ministries.

Nixon, Joan Lowery. A Place to Belong. 1990. (Orphan Train Quartet Ser.: No. 4). 160p. (J). mass mkt. 4.50 o.s.i (*0-553-28485-1*) Bantam Bks.

—A Place to Belong. 160p. 1996. (Orphan Train Adventures Ser.: No. 4). (gr. 4-7). mass mkt. 4.50 (*0-440-22696-1*, Dell Books for Young Readers); 1989. (Orphan Train Quartet Ser.: Bk. 4). (YA). 14.95 o.s.i (*0-553-05803-7*, Starfire) Random Hse. Children's Bks.

—A Place to Belong. 1996. (Orphan Train Quartet Ser.). (J). 10.55 (*0-606-04516-3*) Turtleback Bks.

—Place to Belong. 1990. (J). mass mkt. o.s.i (*0-553-16965-3*, Dell Books for Young Readers) Random Hse. Children's Bks.

Norton, Andre. Stand to Horse. 1968. (J). (gr. 7 up). reprint ed. pap. 0.75 o.p. (*0-15-684890-2*, Voyager Bks./Libros Viajeros) Harcourt Children's Bks.

Paterson, Katherine. Jip, His Story. (Puffin Novel Ser.). 192p. (gr. 5-9). 1998. (YA). pap. 5.99 (*0-14-038674-2*); 1996. (J). 15.99 o.s.i (*0-525-67543-4*, Dutton Children's Bks.) Penguin Putnam Bks. for Young Readers.

—Jip, His Story, Set. unabr. ed. 1997. (J). (gr. 2). 57.99 incl. audio (*0-7887-1711-1*, 40579) Recorded Bks., LLC.

—Jip, His Story. 1998. 12.04 (*0-606-15596-1*) Turtleback Bks.

UNITED STATES—HISTORY—CIVIL WAR, 1861-1865—FICTION

Alphin, Elaine Marie. The Ghost Cadet, ERS. 1991. 88p. (J). (gr. 4-6). 14.95 o.p. (*0-8050-1614-7*, Holt, Henry & Co. Bks. For Young Readers) Holt, Henry & Co.

Alter, Robert E. High Spy. 1973. (Illus.). (J). (gr. 5 up). 5.29 o.p. (*0-399-60260-7*) Putnam Publishing Group, The.

Archer, Myrtle. In the Wilderness. rev. ed. 1986. 220p. (J). reprint ed. pap. 6.95 (*0-9615263-0-0*) Ames Publishing Co.

Armstrong, Jennifer. The Dreams of Mairhe Mehan. 1996. 119p. (J). (gr. 7-12). 18.00 o.s.i (*0-679-88152-2*) McKay, David Co., Inc.

Avi. Punch with Judy. 1997. (Illus.). 160p. (J). (gr. 5 up). pap. 4.50 (*0-380-72980-6*, Harper Trophy) HarperCollins Children's Bk. Group.

—Punch with Judy. 1994. 176p. (YA). (gr. 6 up). mass mkt. 3.99 o.p. (*0-380-72253-4*, Avon Bks.) Morrow/Avon.

—Punch with Judy. 1997. 10.55 (*0-606-11771-7*); 1993. 9.09 o.p. (*0-606-06684-5*) Turtleback Bks.

Banks, Sarah Harrell. Abraham's Battle: A Novel of Gettysburg. 96p. (gr. 4-7). 2001. pap. 4.50 (*0-689-84046-2*, Aladdin); 1999. (J). 15.95 (*0-689-81779-7*, Atheneum/Anne Schwartz Bks.) Simon & Schuster Children's Publishing.

Bartoletti, Susan Campbell. No Man's Land. 1999. 176p. (J). (gr. 5-9). pap. 15.95 (*0-590-38371-X*, Blue Sky Pr., The) Scholastic, Inc.

Beachy, J. Wayne. A Bird of Peace Is Born in Petersburg. 1981. (Illus.). (Orig.). (J). (gr. 5). pap. 2.50 (*0-9608084-0-X*) Hawkins, Beverly Studio & Gallery.

Historical Events

Bearden, Romare. Li'l Dan the Drummer Boy: A Civil War Story. 2003. (Illus.). 40p. (J). 18.95 incl. audio compact disk (*0-689-86237-7*, Simon & Schuster Children's Publishing) Simon & Schuster Children's Publishing.

Beatty, Patricia. Be Ever Hopeful, Hannalee. 1988. 208p. (J). (gr. 5-9). 16.00 o.p. (*0-688-07502-9*, Morrow, William & Co.) Morrow/Avon.

—Charley Skedaddle. 1987. 192p. (YA). (gr. 5-9). 16.00 o.p. (*0-688-06687-9*, Morrow, William & Co.) Morrow/Avon.

—Charley Skedaddle. 1997. (Literature Units Ser.). (Illus.). 48p. (gr. 5-8). pap., tchr. ed. 7.99 (*1-55734-565-1*, TCA0565) Teacher Created Materials, Inc.

—Charley Skedaddle. 1987. (J). 11.00 (*0-606-04029-3*) Turtleback Bks.

—Jayhawker. 1995. (Illus.). 224p. (J). (gr. 7 up). pap. 6.99 (*0-688-14422-5*) HarperCollins Children's Bk. Group.

—Jayhawker. 1991. 224p. (YA). (gr. 5 up). 16.00 o.p. (*0-688-09850-9*); 1924. (J). lib. bdg. o.s.i (*0-688-09851-7*) Morrow/Avon. (Morrow, William & Co.).

—Jayhawker. 1995. 12.00 (*0-606-07734-0*) Turtleback Bks.

—Who Comes with Cannons? 1992. 192p. (J). (gr. 4-7). 15.99 (*0-688-11028-2*) HarperCollins Children's Bk. Group.

Bellerophon Books Staff. Johnny Reb. 1993. (J). (gr. 4-7). pap. 4.95 (*0-88388-180-2*) Bellerophon Bks.

Benner, Judith A. Lone Star Rebel. 1971. (Illus.). (gr. 6 up). lib. bdg. 7.95 o.p. (*0-910244-62-6*) Blair, John F. Pub.

Bierce, Ambrose. Chickamauga. 1988. (Classic Short Stories on Tape Ser.). (YA). (gr. 9-12). ring bd. 38.00 (*1-878298-23-2*) Balance Publishing Co.

—A Horseman in the Sky. rev. ed. 1985. (Read-along Radio Dramas Ser.). (YA). (gr. 7-12). ring bd. 38.00 (*1-878298-17-8*) Balance Publishing Co.

Biros, Florence K. Dog Jack. Libb, Melva, ed. 1988. (American Heritage Ser.). (Illus.). 192p. (Orig.). (J). pap. 6.95 o.p. (*0-936369-22-1*) Son-Rise Pubns. & Distribution Co.

Biros, Florence W. Dog Jack: Heart-Warming Story of a Slave Boy & His Best Friend. 2nd rev. ed. 2001. (Illus.). (YA). (gr. 5 up). pap. 9.95 (*0-936369-47-7*) Son-Rise Pubns. & Distribution Co.

Blair, Margaret W. Brothers at War. 1996. (White Mane Kids Ser.: Vol. No. 4). 154p. (YA). (gr. 5-9). pap. 7.95 (*1-57249-049-7*, WM Kids) White Mane Publishing Co., Inc.

—House of Spies: Danger in the Civil War. 1999. (White Mane Kids Ser.: Vol. 7). (Illus.). 169p. (YA). (ps up). pap. 8.95 (*1-57249-161-2*, WM Kids) White Mane Publishing Co., Inc.

Brenaman, Miriam. Evvy's Civil War. 2002. 224p. (J). (gr. 7-10). 18.99 (*0-399-23713-5*) Penguin Group (USA) Inc.

—Evvy's Civil War. 2004. (Illus.). 224p. pap. 6.99 (*0-14-240039-4*, Puffin Bks.) Penguin Putnam Bks. for Young Readers.

Brill, Marlene Targ. Diary of a Drummer Boy. 1998. (Illus.). 48p. (J). (gr. 4-6). 23.90 (*0-7613-0118-6*) Millbrook Pr., Inc.

—The Diary of a Drummer Boy. 2000. (I Know America Ser.: 6). (Illus.). 48p. (J). (gr. 4-6). pap. 8.95 (*0-7613-1388-5*, Copper Beech Bks.) Millbrook Pr., Inc.

Bunting, Eve. The Blue & the Gray. (Illus.). 32p. (gr. k-2). 2001. pap. 5.99 (*0-590-60200-4*); 1996. (J). pap. 14.95 (*0-590-60197-0*) Scholastic, Inc.

Burchard, Peter. Bimby. 1968. (Illus.). (J). (gr. 3-7). 6.95 o.p. (*0-698-20012-8*) Putnam Publishing Group, The.

Burrows, D. R. Sound of the Bugle. 1973. 224p. (J). (gr. 6-9). pap. 3.50 o.p. (*0-570-03145-1*, 12-2529) Concordia Publishing Hse.

Chass, Vikentia. The Visiting Angels. 1999. 16p. (J). (gr. k-6). pap. 8.00 (*0-8059-4713-2*) Dorrance Publishing Co., Inc.

Clapp, Patricia C. The Tamarack Tree. 1988. 256p. (J). (gr. 5-9). pap. 3.95 o.p. (*0-14-032406-2*, Puffin Bks.) Penguin Putnam Bks. for Young Readers.

Clary, Margie Willis. Make It Three: The Story of the CSS H. L. Hunley, Civil War Submarine. 2001. (Illus.). 110p. (J). 9.95 (*0-87844-158-1*) Sandlapper Publishing Co., Inc.

Climo, Shirley. A Month of 7 Days. 1987. 192p. (YA). (gr. 5 up). 12.95 o.p. (*0-690-04658-8*); lib. bdg. 13.89 o.p. (*0-690-04656-1*) HarperCollins Children's Bk. Group.

Collier, James Lincoln & Collier, Christopher. With Every Drop of Blood. 256p. 1996. (Illus.). (YA). (gr. 4-7). mass mkt. 5.99 (*0-440-21983-3*); 1994. (J). 16.95 o.s.i (*0-385-32028-0*, Delacorte Pr.) Dell Publishing.

Connell, Kate. Yankee Blue or Rebel Grey: The Civil War Adventures of Sam Shaw. 2003. (I Am American Ser.). (Illus.). 40p. (J). pap. 6.99 (*0-7922-5179-2*) National Geographic Society.

Crane, Stephen. The Red Badge of Courage. 2002. (Great Illustrated Classics). (Illus.). 240p. (J). (gr. 3-8). lib. bdg. 21.35 (*1-57765-699-7*, ABDO & Daughters) ABDO Publishing Co.

—The Red Badge of Courage. (Illus.). 72p. (YA). (gr. 4 up). pap. 7.95 (*0-931334-42-X*, EDN302B) AV Concepts Corp.

—The Red Badge of Courage. (Modern Library Ser.). (J). E-Book 4.95 (*1-931208-32-8*) Adobe Systems, Inc.

—The Red Badge of Courage. 1994. (Illustrated Classics Collection). 64p. (J). pap. 3.60 o.p. (*1-56103-435-5*) American Guidance Service, Inc.

—The Red Badge of Courage. 1981. (Bantam Classics Ser.). 160p. (gr. 7-12). mass mkt. 3.95 (*0-553-21011-4*, Bantam Classics) Bantam Bks.

—The Red Badge of Courage. 1971. (Dent's Illustrated Children's Classics Ser.). (Illus.). (J). 9.00 o.p. (*0-460-05090-7*) Biblio Distribution.

—The Red Badge of Courage. 1990. 162p. (YA). mass mkt. 3.99 (*0-8125-0479-8*, Tor Classics); 1987. mass mkt. 1.95 (*0-938819-08-9*, Aerie) Doherty, Tom Assocs., LLC.

—The Red Badge of Courage. (J). 2004. 128p. pap. 2.50 (*0-486-43422-2*); 1991. (Illus.). 112p. pap. 1.50 (*0-486-26465-3*) Dover Pubns., Inc.

—The Red Badge of Courage. (YA). (gr. 6-12). pap. text 10.50 (*0-8359-0462-8*) Globe Fearon Educational Publishing.

—The Red Badge of Courage. Pacemaker Staff, ed. 1991. (YA). (gr. 5-12). pap. 9.95 (*0-8224-9356-X*) Globe Fearon Educational Publishing.

—The Red Badge of Courage. 1977. (American Classics). (gr. 9-12). tchr. ed. 3.85 o.p. (*0-88343-418-0*); pap. text 4.62 o.p. (*0-88343-417-2*); (YA). tchr. ed. 57.00 o.p. (*0-88343-428-8*) McDougal Littell Inc.

—The Red Badge of Courage. 1996. (Wishbone Classics Ser.: No. 10). 128p. (gr. 3-7). mass mkt. 4.25 (*0-06-106497-1*, HarperEntertainment) Morrow/Avon.

—The Red Badge of Courage. 1988. (Short Classics Learning Files Ser.). (J). (gr. 4 up). 22.00 o.p. (*0-8172-2189-1*, HarperTorch) Morrow/Avon.

—The Red Badge of Courage. 1999. (Masterpiece Series Access Editions). (J). 10.95 (*0-8219-1981-4*) Paradigm Publishing, Inc.

—The Red Badge of Courage. Shapiro, Irwin, ed. 1973. (Now Age Illustrated Ser.). (Illus.). 64p. (J). (gr. 5-10). 7.50 o.p. (*0-88301-214-6*); pap. 2.95 (*0-88301-101-8*) Pendulum Pr., Inc.

—The Red Badge of Courage. (Illus.). 224p. 2003. (J). pap. 3.99 (*0-14-250094-1*); 1995. (YA). (gr. 4-7). pap. 4.99 (*0-14-036710-1*) Penguin Putnam Bks. for Young Readers. (Puffin Bks.).

—The Red Badge of Courage. Hanft, Joshua, ed. 1993. (Great Illustrated Classics Ser.: Vol. 27). (Illus.). 240p. (J). (gr. 3-6). 9.95 (*0-86611-978-7*) Playmore, Inc., Pubs.

—The Red Badge of Courage. (J). (gr. 4-7). 1993. 32p. pap. 4.95 (*0-8114-6837-2*); 1983. (Illus.). 48p. pap. 9.27 o.p. (*0-8172-2019-4*); 1983. (Illus.). 48p. lib. bdg. 24.26 o.p. (*0-8172-1670-7*) Raintree Pubs.

—The Red Badge of Courage. 1988. (Portland House Illustrated Classics Ser.). (Illus.). 224p. (YA). 9.99 o.s.i (*0-517-66844-0*) Random Hse. Value Publishing.

—The Red Badge of Courage. 1984. (Keith Jennison Large Type Bks.). (gr. 6 up). lib. bdg. 7.95 o.p. (*0-531-00270-5*, Watts, Franklin) Scholastic Library Publishing.

—The Red Badge of Courage. 2002. (Scribner Classic Ser.). (J). 25.00 (*0-689-82000-3*, Atheneum) Simon & Schuster Children's Publishing.

—The Red Badge of Courage. (J). 1999. (Saddleback Classics). (Illus.). 13.10 (*0-606-21565-4*); 1996. (Wishbone Classics Ser.: No. 10). (gr. 3-7). 10.04 (*0-606-10974-9*) Turtleback Bks.

—The Red Badge of Courage. Hegarty, Carol, ed. 1998. (Classics Ser.: Set I). (Illus.). 79p. (YA). (gr. 5-12). pap. 6.95 (*1-56254-270-2*, SP2702) Saddleback Publishing, Inc.

—The Red Badge of Courage. unabr. ed. 1962. (Classics Ser.). (YA). (gr. 7 up). mass mkt. 2.50 (*0-8049-0003-5*, CL-3) Airmont Publishing Co., Inc.

—The Red Badge of Courage. 1895. 209p. (YA). reprint ed. pap. text 28.00 (*1-4047-2426-5*) Classic Textbooks.

—The Red Badge of Courage. unabr. ed. 1998. (Wordsworth Classics Ser.). (YA). (gr. 6-12). 5.27 o.p. (*0-89061-567-5*, R5675WW) Jamestown.

—The Red Badge of Courage. Dixson, Robert James, ed. rev. ed. 1987. (American Classics: Bk. 10). (J). (gr. 9 up). pap. text 5.75 o.p. (*0-13-024605-0*, 18129) Prentice Hall, ESL Dept.

—The Red Badge of Courage. abr. ed. 1986. (Random House-Reader's Digest Best Loved Audiobks.). (J). pap. 16.00 o.s.i incl. audio (*0-394-55729-8*) Random Hse., Inc.

—The Red Badge of Courage. 1972. 180p. (YA). (gr. 7-12). reprint ed. 1.25 o.p. (*0-590-40678-7*); pap. 2.25 (*0-590-02117-6*) Scholastic, Inc.

—The Red Badge of Courage. unabr. ed. 2002. (YA). pap. incl. audio compact disk (*1-58472-313-0*, In Audio) Sound Room Pubs., Inc.

—The Red Badge of Courage: With a Discussion of Self-Esteem. 2003. (Values in Action Illustrated Classics Ser.). (Illus.). 190p. (J). (*1-59203-034-3*) Learning Challenge, Inc.

—The Red Badge of Courage & Other Stories. unabr. ed. 1999. (J). (gr. 1-8). audio 40.00 BBC Audiobooks America.

—The Red Badge of Courage & Other Writings. Chase, Richard, ed. 1972. (YA). (gr. 9 up). pap. 16.36 (*0-395-05143-6*, Riverside Editions) Houghton Mifflin Co.

—La Roja Insignia del Valor. 2002. (Clover Ser.). (SPA., Illus.). 224p. (YA). 11.50 (*84-392-8013-0*, EV4334) Lectorum Pubns., Inc.

Crisp, Marty. Private Captain: A Story of Gettysburg. 2001. (Illus.). 293p. (J). (gr. 7-12). 18.99 (*0-399-23577-9*, Philomel) Penguin Putnam Bks. for Young Readers.

Crist-Evans, Craig. Moon over Tennessee: A Boy's Civil War Journal. (Illus.). (J). 2003. 64p. pap. 6.95 (*0-618-31107-6*); 1999. 62p. (gr. 4-6). tchr. ed. 15.00 (*0-395-91208-3*) Houghton Mifflin Co.

Curtis, Alice Turner. Yankee Girl at Fort Sumter. 2004. (Yankee Girl Ser.). 190p. (J). (gr. 4-7). pap. text 9.95 (*1-55709-525-6*) Applewood Bks.

Daringer, Helen F. Mary Montgomery, Rebel. 1948. (Illus.). (J). (gr. 7 up). 4.95 o.p. (*0-15-252231-X*) Harcourt Children's Bks.

Davis, Burke. Appomattox: Closing Struggle of the Civil War. 1963. (Breakthrough Bks.). (Illus.). (J). (gr. 5 up). 9.89 o.p. (*0-06-021401-5*) HarperCollins Pubs.

Denenberg, Barry. When Will This Cruel War Be Over? The Civil War Diary of Emma Simpson, Gordonsville, Virginia, 1864. 1996. (Dear America Ser.). (Illus.). 156p. (YA). (gr. 4-9). pap. 10.95 (*0-590-22862-5*) Scholastic, Inc.

Denslow, Sharon Phillips. All Their Names Were Courage. 2003. 144p. (J). 15.99 (*0-06-623810-2*); pap. 16.89 (*0-06-623809-9*) HarperCollins Children's Bk. Group. (Greenwillow Bks.).

Dionne, Wanda. A Yank among Us. 1997. 176p. (J). (gr. 6). pap. 12.95 (*1-57168-108-6*) Eakin Pr.

Doyle, Arthur Conan. Las Aventuras de Sherlock Holmes. 2002. (Clover Ser.). (SPA., Illus.). 369p. (YA). (*84-392-8023-8*, EV5544) Gaviota Ediciones ESP. *Dist:* Lectorum Pubns., Inc.

Duey, Kathleen. Amelina Carrett: Bayou Grand Coeur, Louisiana 1863. 1999. (American Diaries Ser.: No. 12). 144p. (J). (gr. 3-7). pap. 3.99 (*0-689-82402-5*, Aladdin) Simon & Schuster Children's Publishing.

—Amelina Carrett: Thibodeau, Louisiana 1870. 1999. (American Diaries Ser.: No. 12). (J). (gr. 3-7). 10.04 (*0-606-16281-X*) Turtleback Bks.

—Emma Eileen Grove: Mississippi, 1865. 1996. (American Diaries Ser.: No. 2). (Illus.). 144p. (J). (gr. 3-7). pap. 4.99 (*0-689-80385-0*, Aladdin) Simon & Schuster Children's Publishing.

—Emma Eileen Grove: Mississippi, 1865. 1996. (American Diaries Ser.: No. 2). (J). (gr. 3-7). 10.55 (*0-606-08986-1*) Turtleback Bks.

—Maddie Retta Lauren: Sandersville, Georgia, 1864. 2000. (American Diaries Ser.: No. 15). (Illus.). 141p. (J). (gr. 3-7). pap. 4.50 (*0-689-83377-6*, Aladdin) Simon & Schuster Children's Publishing.

—Maddie Retta Lauren: Sandersville, Georgia, 1864. 2000. (American Diaries Ser.: No. 15). (J). (gr. 3-7). 10.55 (*0-606-17902-X*) Turtleback Bks.

Easton. Blood & Money. 1998. 20.00 (*0-7862-1103-2*, Macmillan Reference USA) Gale Group.

Easton, Robert. Blood & Money. 1998. (Western Ser.). 372p. 19.95 (*0-7862-1154-7*, Five Star) Gale Group.

Ekberg, Nancy. What Kind of War Was It, Anyhow? Reynolds, Rhonda, tr. & illus. by. 2003. 45p. (J). pap. 8.95 (*1-58838-085-8*, Junebug Bks.) NewSouth, Inc.

Ernst, Kathleen. Ghosts of Vicksburg. 2003. (White Main Kids Ser.: 13). (Illus.). 180p. (J). pap. 8.95 (*1-57249-322-4*, WM Kids) White Mane Publishing Co., Inc.

—Night Riders of Harper's Ferry. 1996. (Kids Ser.: No. 2). (Illus.). 152p. (YA). (gr. 5 up). pap. 7.95 (*1-57249-013-6*, WM Kids) White Mane Publishing Co., Inc.

Fedor, Janis M. Girl Lieutenant in Blue, Vol. 2. 2002. 166p. (YA). (gr. 5-6). pap. 9.95 (*0-936369-38-8*) Son-Rise Pubns. & Distribution Co.

Filegar, James. Fathers, Sons, & Brothers: Book One. 2003. 191p. (J). pap. 19.95 (*1-59129-908-X*) PublishAmerica, Inc.

Fleischman, Paul. Bull Run. (gr. 5 up). 1995. (Illus.). 128p. (J). pap. 4.99 (*0-06-440588-5*, Harper Trophy); 1993. 112p. (YA). 14.95 (*0-06-021446-5*); 1993. (Illus.). 112p. (YA). lib. bdg. 16.89 (*0-06-021447-3*, Geringer, Laura Bk.) HarperCollins Children's Bk. Group.

—Bull Run. 1995. (J). 11.00 (*0-606-07326-4*) Turtleback Bks.

Forman, James. Song of Jubilee, RS. 1971. 192p. (J). (gr. 7 up). 10.95 o.p. (*0-374-37142-3*, Farrar, Straus & Giroux (BYR)) Farrar, Straus & Giroux.

Forman, James D. Becca's Story. 1992. 192p. (YA). (gr. 7 up). lib. bdg. 15.00 (*0-684-19332-9*, Atheneum) Simon & Schuster Children's Publishing.

Forrester, Sandra. Sound the Jubilee. 1995. 192p. (YA). (gr. 5-9). 15.99 o.s.i (*0-525-67486-1*, Dutton Children's Bks.) Penguin Putnam Bks. for Young Readers.

Fritz, Jean. Stonewall. 1997. (J). 12.04 (*0-606-11916-7*) Turtleback Bks.

Gauch, Patricia L. Thunder at Gettysburg. 1990. (Yearling Book Ser.). 64p. (ps-3). pap. text 3.99 o.s.i (*0-440-41075-4*) Dell Publishing.

—Thunder at Gettysburg. 1990. (Illus.). 48p. (J). (ps-3). 18.99 o.p. (*0-399-22201-4*, G. P. Putnam's Sons) Penguin Putnam Bks. for Young Readers.

Gibboney, Douglas Lee. Stonewall Jackson at Gettysburg. 2002. (Illus.). 132p. (YA). pap. 12.95 (*1-57249-317-8*, Burd Street Pr.) White Mane Publishing Co., Inc.

Gurasich, Marjorie A. A House Divided. 1994. (Chaparral Book Ser.). 170p. (J). (gr. 7 up). pap. 9.95 (*0-87565-122-4*) Texas Christian Univ. Pr.

Hahn, Mary Downing. Hear the Wind Blow. 2003. (Illus.). 224p. (J). (gr. 5-9). tchr. ed. 15.00 (*0-618-18190-3*, Clarion Bks.) Houghton Mifflin Co. Trade & Reference Div.

—Promises to the Dead. 2002. 208p. (J). (gr. 3 up). pap. 5.95 (*0-06-440982-1*, Harper Trophy) HarperCollins Children's Bk. Group.

—Promises to the Dead. 2000. 208p. (J). (gr. 5-9). tchr. ed. 15.00 (*0-395-96394-X*, Clarion Bks.) Houghton Mifflin Co. Trade & Reference Div.

Hahn, Stephen. Pike McCallister. 1998. 253p. (YA). (gr. 6 up). per. 14.95 (*1-888125-29-2*) Publication Consultants.

Haislip, Phyllis Hall. Lottie's Courage: A Contraband Slave's Story. 2003. (Illus.). 120p. (J). pap. 7.95 (*1-57249-311-9*, WM Kids) White Mane Publishing Co., Inc.

Hall, Beverly B. The Secret of the Lion's Head. 1995. (Illus.). 164p. (J). (gr. 5 up). pap. 7.95 (*0-942597-92-3*, WM Kids) White Mane Publishing Co., Inc.

Hall, Marjory. The Carved Wooden Ring. 1972. 176p. (J). (gr. 6 up). 4.75 o.s.i (*0-664-32506-8*) Westminster John Knox Pr.

Hansen, Joyce. Out from This Place. 1988. 10.55 (*0-606-00682-6*) Turtleback Bks.

—Out from This Place. 1988. 13.95 (*0-8027-6816-4*) Walker & Co.

—Out from this Place. 1992. 144p. (J). (gr. 4-7). pap. 5.99 (*0-380-71409-4*, Avon Bks.) Morrow/Avon.

—Which Way Freedom. 1992. 128p. (J). (gr. 4-7). pap. 4.99 (*0-380-71408-6*, Avon Bks.) Morrow/Avon.

—Which Way to Freedom? 1991. 13.85 o.p. (*0-8027-6623-4*) Walker & Co.

Harness, Cheryl. Ghosts of the Civil War. 2002. (Illus.). 48p. (J). 17.00 (*0-689-83135-8*, Simon & Schuster Children's Publishing) Simon & Schuster Children's Publishing.

Hemingway, Edith M. & Shields, Jacqueline C. Broken Drum. 1996. (Kids Ser.: Vol. No. 3). 172p. (YA). (gr. 5-7). pap. 8.95 (*1-57249-027-6*, WM Kids) White Mane Publishing Co., Inc.

—Rebel Hart. 2000. (White Mane Kids Ser.: Vol. 8). (Illus.). xi, 173p. (J). (gr. 3-12). pap. 8.95 (*1-57249-186-8*, WM Kids) White Mane Publishing Co., Inc.

Henty, G. A. With Lee in Virginia: A Story of the American Civil War. 2000. 252p. (J). E-Book 3.95 (*0-594-02419-6*) 1873 Pr.

Hesse, Karen. A Light in the Storm: The Civil War Diary of Amelia Martin, Fenwick Island, Delaware, 1861. (Dear America Ser.). 2002. (YA). E-Book 9.95 (*0-439-42541-7*); 1999. (Illus.). 169p. (J). (gr. 4-9). pap. 10.95 (*0-590-56733-0*, Scholastic Pr.) Scholastic, Inc.

Hesse, Karen, et al. The Nation at War: Civil War Collection: A Light in the Storm; When Will This Cruel War Be Over?; A Picture of Freedom; The Journal of James Edmond Pease, 4 vols. 2002. (Dear America Ser.). (J). pap. 19.96 (*0-439-12939-7*) Scholastic, Inc.

Hill, Pamela Smith. A Voice from the Border. 1998. 320p. (YA). (gr. 7-12). tchr. ed. 16.95 (*0-8234-1356-X*) Holiday Hse., Inc.

Hite, Sid. The Journal of Rufus Rowe: A Witness to the Battle of Fredricksburg. 2003. (My Name Is America Ser.). 144p. (J). pap. 10.95 (*0-439-35364-5*) Scholastic, Inc.

—Stick & Whittle. 2001. 208p. (YA). (gr. 5 up). mass mkt. 4.99 (*0-439-09829-7*) Scholastic, Inc.

Hopkinson, Deborah. A Band of Angels: A Story Inspired by the Jubilee Singers. 1999. (Anne Schwartz Bks.). (Illus.). 40p. (J). (gr. 1-4). 16.00 (*0-689-81062-8*, Atheneum/Anne Schwartz Bks.) Simon & Schuster Children's Publishing.

—Billy & the Rebel. 2001. (Ready-to-Read Ser.). (Illus.). (J). lib. bdg. 15.00 (*0-689-83964-2*, Atheneum) Simon & Schuster Children's Publishing.

Houston, Gloria M. Mountain Valor. 1994. (Illus.). 240p. (YA). (gr. 8 up). 15.95 o.s.i (*0-399-22519-6*, Philomel) Penguin Putnam Bks. for Young Readers.

Hubalek, Linda K. Stitch of Courage: A Woman's Fight for Freedom. 1996. (Trail of Thread Ser.: Bk. 3). (Illus.). 120p. (Orig.). pap. 9.95 (*1-886652-08-2*) Butterfield Bks., Inc.

Hughes, Pat. Guerilla Season, RS. 2003. 336p. (J). 18.00 (*0-374-32811-0*, Farrar, Straus & Giroux (BYR)) Farrar, Straus & Giroux.

Hunt, Irene. Across Five Aprils. (J). 1985. 2.50 o.s.i (*0-441-00318-4*); 1984. 2.25 o.s.i (*0-441-00317-6*); 1983. 2.25 o.s.i (*0-441-00316-8*) Ace Bks.

—Across Five Aprils. 2002. 224p. (J). mass mkt. 4.99 (*0-425-18278-9*); 1986. 192p. (gr. 4-7). mass mkt. 4.99 (*0-425-10241-6*) Berkley Publishing Group.

—Across Five Aprils. 1999. (J). pap. 1.95 (*0-590-05178-4*) Scholastic, Inc.

—Across Five Aprils. 1986. 11.04 (*0-606-00289-8*) Turtleback Bks.

Hurmence, Belinda. Tancy. 1984. 224p. (J). (gr. 6 up). 12.95 o.p. (*0-89919-228-9*, Clarion Bks.) Houghton Mifflin Co. Trade & Reference Div.

Johnson, Nancy. My Brother's Keeper: A Civil War Story. (gr. 4-7). 2001. pap. 9.95 (*0-89272-433-1*); 1997. 152p. (J). 14.95 (*0-89272-414-5*) Down East Bks.

Johnston, Annie F. The Little Colonel. 2004. (Little Colonel Ser.). (Illus.). 192p. (J). (gr. 4-7). reprint ed. pap. 9.95 (*1-55709-315-6*) Applewood Bks.

—The Little Colonel. 1974. (Illus.). (J). 145p. (gr. 5-9). 8.95 o.p. (*0-88289-050-6*); 168p. (gr. 4-7). pap. 16.95 (*1-56554-542-7*) Pelican Publishing Co., Inc.

Johnston, Tony. The Wagon. (Illus.). 40p. (J). (ps-3). 1999. mass mkt. 5.95 (*0-688-16694-6*, Morrow, William & Co.); 1996. lib. bdg. 15.89 o.s.i (*0-688-13537-4*); 1996. 17.00 (*0-688-13457-2*, Morrow, William & Co.) Morrow/Avon.

Joinson, Carla. March of Glory. 1994. 125p. (YA). (gr. 9-12). pap. 9.99 o.p. (*0-88092-083-1*); lib. bdg. 9.99 (*0-88092-082-3*) Royal Fireworks Publishing Co.

Jones, Elizabeth McDavid. Watcher in the Piney Woods. 2000. (American Girl Collection: Bk. 9). (Illus.). 160p. (gr. 5-7). (J). pap. 5.95 (*1-58485-090-6*); (YA). 9.95 (*1-58485-091-4*) Pleasant Co. Pubns. (American Girl).

—Watcher in the Piney Woods. 2000. (American Girl Collection). (Illus.). (J). 12.00 (*0-606-20981-6*) Turtleback Bks.

Joslyn, Mauriel. Shenandoah Autumn: Courage under Fire. 1999. (WM Kids Ser.). 164p. (YA). (gr. 4-7). pap. 8.95 (*1-57249-137-X*, WM Kids) White Mane Publishing Co., Inc.

Karr, Kathleen. Spy in the Sky. 1997. (Hyperion Chapters Ser.). (Illus.). 64p. (YA). (gr. 3-4). lib. bdg. 14.49 (*0-7868-2239-2*) Hyperion Bks. for Children.

Kassem, Lou. Listen for Rachel. 1992. 176p. (J). (gr. 5). mass mkt. 3.99 (*0-380-71231-8*, Avon Bks.) Morrow/Avon.

Kay, Alan N. No Girls Allowed. 2003. (Young Heroes of History: Vol. 5). (Illus.). 140p. (J). pap. 6.95 (*1-57249-324-0*, WM Kids) White Mane Publishing Co., Inc.

—Nowhere to Turn. 2002. (Young Heroes of History: 4). (Illus.). 164p. (J). pap. 6.95 (*1-57249-297-X*, WM Kids) White Mane Publishing Co., Inc.

Keehn, Sally M. Anna Sunday. 272p. 2004. (Illus.). pap. 6.99 (*0-14-240026-2*, Puffin Bks.); 2002. (J). (gr. 5-9). 18.99 (*0-399-23875-1*, Philomel) Penguin Putnam Bks. for Young Readers.

Keith, Harold. Rifles for Watie. (gr. 7 up). 1991. 352p. (J). lib. bdg. 16.89 (*0-690-04907-2*); 1987. 352p. (J). mass mkt. 5.99 (*0-06-447030-X*, Harper Trophy); 1957. 322p. (YA). 14.95 o.p. (*0-690-70181-0*) HarperCollins Children's Bk. Group.

—Rifles for Watie. 1987. (J). 12.00 (*0-606-03520-6*) Turtleback Bks.

Kidd, Ronald. Family under Fire: A Story of the Civil War. 1995. (River Country Classics Ser.). 80p. (J). (gr. 2-8). 14.95 (*0-9648140-0-5*) Chattanooga Regional History Museum.

Kirkland, Joseph. The Captain of Company K. (Americans in Fiction Ser.). (Illus.). (J). reprint ed. pap. text 12.95 (*0-89197-690-6*); lib. bdg. 27.00 (*0-8398-1057-1*) Irvington Pubs.

—The Captain of Company K. 1988. (Collected Works of Joseph Kirkland). (J). reprint ed. lib. bdg. 79.00 (*0-7812-1319-3*) Reprint Services Corp.

Lawlor, Laurie. Wind on the River: A Story of the Civil War. (American Portraits Ser.). (Illus.). iv, 156p. (YA). (gr. 5-8). 2001. 12.64 (*0-8092-0582-3*); 2000. pap. 5.95 (*0-8092-0624-2*, 06242E) Jamestown.

LeSourd, Nancy. The Personal Correspondence of Emma Edmunds & Mollie Turner. 2004. 224p. 9.99 (*0-310-70352-2*) Zondervan.

Love, D. Anne. Three Against the Tide. 1998. 162p. (J). (gr. 4-7). tchr. ed. 15.95 (*0-8234-1400-0*) Holiday Hse., Inc.

—Three Against the Tide. 2000. (Illus.). 192p. (gr. 4-7). pap. text 4.50 (*0-440-41634-5*, Yearling) Random Hse. Children's Bks.

—Three Against the Tide. 2000. 10.55 (*0-606-18909-2*) Turtleback Bks.

Lutz, Norma Jean. The Rebel Spy. 23rd ed. 1998. (American Adventure Ser.: No. 23). (Illus.). (J). (gr. 3-7). pap. 3.97 (*1-57748-267-0*) Barbour Publishing, Inc.

—War's End. 24th ed. 1998. (American Adventure Ser.: No. 24). (Illus.). (J). (gr. 3-7). pap. 3.97 (*1-57748-268-9*) Barbour Publishing, Inc.

Lynch, Marcia. United in Freedom. 2000. (Cover-to-Cover Bks.). (Illus.). 92p. (J). (*0-7807-9068-5*); pap. (*0-7891-5102-2*) Perfection Learning Corp.

Lyon, George Ella. Cecil's Story. 1995. (Illus.). 32p. (J). (ps-3). mass mkt. 5.95 (*0-531-07063-8*, Orchard Bks.) Scholastic, Inc.

—Cecil's Story. 1995. 12.10 (*0-606-08712-5*) Turtleback Bks.

—Here & Then. 1994. 128p. (J). (gr. 4-7). pap. 15.95 (*0-531-06866-8*); (gr. 5-7). mass mkt. 16.99 o.p. (*0-531-08716-6*) Scholastic, Inc. (Orchard Bks.).

Marius, Richard. After the War. 1994. 640p. (J). reprint ed. pap. 16.95 o.s.i (*1-55853-273-0*) Rutledge Hill Pr.

Marten, James. The Boy of Chancellorville & Other Civil War Stories. 2002. (Illus.). 128p. (J). (gr. 4 up). 20.00 (*0-19-514163-6*) Oxford Univ. Pr., Inc.

Masi, Doris H. Pride O' the Hilltop. 1992. 140p. (J). per. 12.00 (*0-9628208-6-5*) Canal Side Pubs.

Masters, Susan Rowan. Night Journey to Vicksburg. Killcoyne, Hope L., ed. 2003. (J). 14.95 (*1-893110-30-3*) Silver Moon Pr.

Matas, Carol. The War Within: A Novel of the Civil War. 2001. (Illus.). 160p. (J). (gr. 5-8). 16.00 (*0-689-82935-3*, Simon & Schuster Children's Publishing) Simon & Schuster Children's Publishing.

—The War Within: A Novel of the Civil War. 2003. (J). 22.95 (*0-7862-5499-8*) Thorndike Pr.

McKissack, Patricia C. A Picture of Freedom: The Diary of Clotee, a Slave Girl, Belmont Plantation, Virginia, 1859. 1997. (Dear America Ser.). (Illus.). 195p. (YA). (gr. 4-9). pap. 10.95 (*0-590-25988-1*) Scholastic, Inc.

McPherson, Betty. A Picnic at Bull Run. 1991. (Pocket Tales Ser.: Bk. 3). (Illus.). 40p. (J). (ps-1). 6.00 (*0-918823-05-6*) Boyce Pubns.

McPherson, James M. Fields of Fury: The American Civil War. 2002. (Illus.). 96p. (J). (gr. 5-8). 22.95 (*0-689-84833-1*, Atheneum) Simon & Schuster Children's Publishing.

Meader, Stephen W. Muddy Road to Glory. 1963. (Illus.). (J). (gr. 7 up). 4.95 o.p. (*0-15-256260-5*) Harcourt Children's Bks.

Mildred's Boys & Girls. 2001. (Mildred Classics Ser.: Vol. 6). 288p. pap. 5.95 (*1-58182-232-4*) Cumberland Hse. Publishing.

Miner, Jane C. Corey, No. 22. 1987. 192p. (Orig.). (J). (gr. 5-10). pap. 2.50 o.p. (*0-590-40395-8*) Scholastic, Inc.

Monjo, F. N. La Osa Menor: Una Historia del Ferrocarril Subterraneo. Mlawer, Teresa, tr. 1997. (Ya Se Leer Ser.). (SPA., Illus.). 64p. (J). (gr. k-3). pap. 4.95 o.p. (*0-06-444217-9*) HarperCollins Children's Bk. Group.

—La Osa Menor: Una Historia del Ferrocarril Subterraneo. Mlawer, Teresa, tr. 2001. (SPA., Illus.). (J). (gr. 3-10). pap. 6.95 (*1-880507-90-0*, LC7973); ring bd. 15.95 (*1-880507-91-9*, LC7976) Lectorum Pubns., Inc.

—La Osa Menor: Una Historia del Ferrocarril Subterraneo. 2001. 12.10 (*0-606-21286-8*); 1997. 10.15 o.p. (*0-606-10860-2*) Turtleback Bks.

Monte, Emily C. The Lost Sword of the Confederate Ghost: A Mystery in Two Centuries. 1999. 116p. (J). (gr. 4-7). 5.99 (*1-57249-132-9*) White Mane Publishing Co., Inc.

Morris, Gilbert. The Battle of Lookout Mountain. 1996. (Bonnets & Bugles Ser.: No. 7). (J). (gr. 8 up). pap. 5.99 (*0-8024-0917-2*, 564) Moody Pr.

—Blockade Runner. 1996. (Bonnets & Bugles Ser.: No. 5). 151p. (J). (gr. 7 up). pap. 5.99 (*0-8024-0915-6*, 565) Moody Pr.

—Bring the Boys Home. 1997. (Bonnets & Bugles Ser.: No. 10). 128p. (J). (gr. 5-9). pap. 5.99 (*0-8024-0920-2*, 3) Moody Pr.

—Drummer Boy at Bull Run. 1995. (Bonnets & Bugles Ser.: No. 1). (J). (gr. 5-9). pap. 5.99 (*0-8024-0911-3*, 566) Moody Pr.

—Encounter at Cold Harbor. 1997. (Bonnets & Bugles Ser.: No. 8). 160p. (J). (gr. 5-9). pap. 5.99 (*0-8024-0918-0*, 567) Moody Pr.

—Fire over Atlanta. 1997. (Bonnets & Bugles Ser.: No. 9). 168p. (J). (gr. 5-9). pap. 5.99 (*0-8024-0919-9*, 568) Moody Pr.

—The Gallant Boys of Gettysburg. 1996. (Bonnets & Bugles Ser.: No. 6). (J). (gr. 7 up). pap. 5.99 (*0-8024-0916-4*, 569) Moody Pr.

—Secret of Richmond Manor. 1995. (Bonnets & Bugles Ser.: No. 3). (J). (gr. 7 up). pap. 5.99 (*0-8024-0913-X*, 570) Moody Pr.

—The Soldier Boy's Discovery. 1996. (Bonnets & Bugles Ser.: No. 4). (J). (gr. 7 up). pap. 5.99 (*0-8024-0914-8*, 571) Moody Pr.

—Yankee Belles in Dixie. 1995. (Bonnets & Bugles Ser.: No. 2). 164p. (J). (gr. 7-12). pap. 5.99 (*0-8024-0912-1*, 572) Moody Pr.

Murphy, Jim. The Journal of James Edmond Pease: A Civil War Union Soldier: Virginia, 1863. 1998. (My Name Is America Ser.). (Illus.). 173p. (J). (gr. 4-8). pap. 10.95 (*0-590-43814-X*, Scholastic Pr.) Scholastic, Inc.

Nixon, Joan Lowery. A Dangerous Promise. 1995. (Orphan Train Adventures Ser.: Vol. 5). 160p. (YA). (gr. 4-7). mass mkt. 4.99 (*0-440-21965-5*, Laurel Leaf) Random Hse. Children's Bks.

—Keeping Secrets. 1995. (Orphan Train Adventures Ser.). 176p. (J). 15.95 o.s.i (*0-385-32139-2*, Delacorte Pr.) Dell Publishing.

O'Dell, Scott. The Two Hundred Ninety, 001. 1976. (J). (gr. 5-9). 16.95 o.p. (*0-395-24737-3*) Houghton Mifflin Co.

Optic, Oliver. On the Blockade. 1999. (Blue & the Gray Ser.). (Illus.). 358p. (J). (gr. 4 up). reprint ed. pap. 14.95 (*1-890623-10-5*) Lost Classics Bk. Co.

—Within the Enemy's Lines. 1998. (Blue & the Gray Ser.). (Illus.). 350p. (YA). (gr. 4 up). reprint ed. pap. 14.95 (*1-890623-09-1*) Lost Classics Bk. Co.

Osborne, Mary Pope. After the Rain: Virginia's Civil War Diary, Bk. 2. 2002. (My America Ser.). 112p. (J). (gr. 2-5). pap. 8.95 o.s.i (*0-439-20138-1*); (Illus.). mass mkt. 4.99 (*0-439-36904-5*) Scholastic, Inc. (Scholastic Pr.).

—Civil War on Sunday. 2000. (Magic Tree House Ser.: No. 21). (Illus.). 96p. (J). (gr. k-3). lib. bdg. 11.99 (*0-679-99067-4*); pap. 3.99 (*0-679-89067-X*) Random Hse. Children's Bks. (Random Hse. Bks. for Young Readers).

—Civil War on Sunday. 2000. (Magic Tree House Ser.: No. 21). (Illus.). (J). (gr. k-3). 10.04 (*0-606-18852-5*) Turtleback Bks.

—My Brother's Keeper: Virginia's Civil War Diary, Bk. 1. 2000. (My America Ser.). (Illus.). 112p. (J). (gr. 4-7). pap. 8.95 (*0-439-15307-7*, Scholastic Pr.) Scholastic, Inc.

Oughton, Jerrie. The War in Georgia. 1999. 192p. (YA). (gr. 7 up). mass mkt. 4.50 o.s.i (*0-440-22752-6*, Dell Books for Young Readers) Random Hse. Children's Bks.

—The War in Georgia. 1999. 10.55 (*0-606-16444-8*) Turtleback Bks.

Page, Thomas Nelson. Among the Camps. 1891. (YA). reprint ed. pap. text 28.00 (*1-4047-4690-0*) Classic Textbooks.

—Among the Camps. 1996. (J). 17.99 (*0-87377-173-7*) GAM Pubns.

—Two Little Confederates. 1996. (J). 17.99 (*0-87377-174-5*) GAM Pubns.

Paulsen, Gary. A Soldier's Heart: Being the Story of the Enlistment & Due Service of the Boy Charley Goddard in the First Minnesota Volunteers. 1998. 128p. (YA). (gr. 7-12). 15.95 (*0-385-32498-7*) Doubleday Publishing.

Peck, Richard. The River Between Us. 2003. 176p. (J). 16.99 (*0-8037-2735-6*, Dial Bks. for Young Readers) Penguin Putnam Bks. for Young Readers.

Pfeffer, Susan Beth. Devil's Den. 1998. 115p. (J). (gr. 3-7). 15.95 (*0-8027-8650-2*) Walker & Co.

Phillips, Michael. Land of the Brave & the Free. 1993. (Journals of Corrie Belle Hollister: Vol. 7). 320p. (J). (gr. 4-7). pap. 10.99 o.p. (*1-55661-308-3*) Bethany Hse. Pubs.

Pinkney, Andrea Davis. Silent Thunder: A Civil War Story. 2001. 224p. (J). (gr. 3-7). pap. 5.99 (*0-7868-1569-8*, Jump at the Sun); 1999. (Illus.). 208p. (J). (gr. 4-7). 15.99 (*0-7868-0439-4*); 1999. (Illus.). 208p. (YA). (gr. 4-7). lib. bdg. 16.49 (*0-7868-2388-7*) Hyperion Bks. for Children.

—Silent Thunder: A Civil War Story. 2001. (J). 12.04 (*0-606-21434-8*) Turtleback Bks.

Plunkett, N. Geraldine. Nathan's Secret. 2000. (Illus.). 87p. (J). pap. 7.95 (*0-87178-029-1*) Brethren Pr.

Polacco, Patricia. Pink & Say. 2002. (Illus.). (J). 23.64 (*0-7587-3418-2*) Book Wholesalers, Inc.

—Pink & Say. 1994. (Illus.). 48p. (J). (ps-5). 16.99 (*0-399-22671-0*, Philomel) Penguin Putnam Bks. for Young Readers.

—Pink & Say. 2001. (J). 27.95 incl. audio (*0-8045-6835-9*, 6835); 27.95 incl. audio (*0-8045-6835-9*, 6835) Spoken Arts, Inc.

Porter. Addy's Short Story Set: High Hopes for Addy; Addy's Little Brother; Addy Studies Freedom, 3 vols. 2002. (American Girls Short Stories Ser.). (Illus.). (YA). (gr. 2). 11.95 (*1-58485-497-9*, American Girl) Pleasant Co. Pubns.

Porter, Connie Rose. Addy Learns a Lesson: A School Story. Johnson, Roberta, ed. 1993. (American Girls Collection: Bk. 2). (Illus.). 80p. (J). (gr. 2 up). 12.95 (*1-56247-078-7*); pap. 5.95 (*1-56247-077-9*) Pleasant Co. Pubns. (American Girl).

—Addy Learns a Lesson: A School Story. 1993. (American Girls Collection: Bk. 2). (Illus.). (YA). (gr. 2 up). 12.10 (*0-606-05103-1*) Turtleback Bks.

—Addy Saves the Day: A Summer Story. Johnson, Roberta, ed. 1993. (American Girls Collection: Bk. 5). (Illus.). 80p. (YA). (gr. 2 up). 12.95 (*1-56247-084-1*); pap. 5.95 (*1-56247-083-3*) Pleasant Co. Pubns. (American Girl).

—Addy Saves the Day: A Summer Story. Johnson, Roberta, ed. 1993. (American Girls Collection: Bk. 5). (Illus.). (YA). (gr. 2 up). 12.10 (*0-606-06160-6*) Turtleback Bks.

—Addy's Boxed Set: Meet Addy; Addy Learns a Lesson; Addy's Surprise; Happy Birthday; Addy!; Addy Saves the Day; Changes for Addy, 6 bks. Johnson, Roberta, ed. 1994. (American Girls Collection: Bks. 1-6). (Illus.). 392p. (YA). pap. 34.95 (*1-56247-087-6*); (gr. 2 up). 74.95 (*1-56247-088-4*) Pleasant Co. Pubns. (American Girl).

—Addy's Story Collection. 2001. (American Girls Collection). (Illus.). 370p. (J). (gr. 2 up). 29.95 (*1-58485-444-8*, American Girl) Pleasant Co. Pubns.

—Addy's Surprise: A Christmas Story. Johnson, Roberta, ed. 1993. (American Girls Collection: Bk. 3). (Illus.). 80p. (J). (gr. 2 up). 12.95 (*1-56247-080-9*); pap. 5.95 (*1-56247-079-5*) Pleasant Co. Pubns. (American Girl).

—Addy's Surprise: A Christmas Story. 1993. (American Girls Collection: Bk. 3). (Illus.). (YA). (gr. 2 up). 12.10 (*0-606-05104-X*) Turtleback Bks.

—Changes for Addy: A Winter Story. Johnson, Roberta, ed. 1994. (American Girls Collection: Bk. 6). (Illus.). 72p. (YA). (gr. 2 up). 12.95 (*1-56247-086-8*); pap. 5.95 (*1-56247-085-X*) Pleasant Co. Pubns. (American Girl).

—Changes for Addy: A Winter Story. 1994. (American Girls Collection: Bk. 6). (Illus.). (YA). (gr. 2 up). 12.10 (*0-606-06272-6*) Turtleback Bks.

—Happy Birthday, Addy! A Springtime Story. 1993. (American Girls Collection: Bk. 4). (Illus.). 72p. (YA). (gr. 2 up). 12.95 (*1-56247-082-5*, American Girl) Pleasant Co. Pubns.

—Happy Birthday, Addy! A Springtime Story. Johnson, Roberta, ed. 1993. (American Girls Collection: Bk. 4). (Illus.). 72p. (YA). (gr. 2 up). pap. 5.95 (*1-56247-081-7*, American Girl) Pleasant Co. Pubns.

—Happy Birthday, Addy! A Springtime Story. 1994. (American Girls Collection: Bk. 4). (Illus.). (YA). (gr. 2 up). 12.10 (*0-606-06439-7*) Turtleback Bks.

—Meet Addy: An American Girl. Johnson, Roberta, ed. 1993. (American Girls Collection: Bk. 1). (Illus.). 80p. (J). (gr. 2 up). pap. 5.95 (*1-56247-075-2*); lib. bdg. 12.95 (*1-56247-076-0*) Pleasant Co. Pubns. (American Girl).

—Meet Addy: An American Girl. 1993. (American Girls Collection: Bk. 1). (Illus.). (YA). (gr. 2 up). 12.10 (*0-606-05459-6*) Turtleback Bks.

Pryor, Bonnie. Joseph: 1861 - A Rumble of War. 2000. (Illus.). (J). 10.55 (*0-606-17975-5*) Turtleback Bks.

—Joseph: 1861 - a Rumble of War. 1999. (American Adventures Ser.). (Illus.). 176p. (J). (gr. 3-7). 14.95 (*0-688-15671-1*) HarperCollins Children's Bk. Group.

—Joseph: 1861—A Rumble of War. 2000. (American Adventures Ser.). (Illus.). 176p. (J). (gr. 3-7). pap. 4.50 (*0-380-73103-7*, Harper Trophy) HarperCollins Children's Bk. Group.

—Joseph's Choice, 1861. 2000. (American Adventures Ser.). (Illus.). 176p. (J). (gr. 3 up). 15.99 (*0-688-17633-X*); 14.89 (*0-06-029226-1*) HarperCollins Children's Bk. Group.

Putnam. The Spy Doll. 1979. (J). 6.95 o.p. (*0-525-66667-2*) NAL.

Reasoner, James. Savannah. 2003. (Civil War Battle Ser.: Vol. 9). 432p. 22.95 (*1-58182-328-2*) Cumberland Hse. Publishing.

Reeder, Carolyn. Across the Lines. 1998. 224p. (J). (gr. 4-7). pap. 5.99 (*0-380-73073-1*, Harper Trophy) HarperCollins Children's Bk. Group.

—Across the Lines. 1997. 224p. (J). (gr. 3-7). 17.00 (*0-689-81133-0*, Atheneum) Simon & Schuster Children's Publishing.

—Across the Lines. 1998. 11.00 (*0-606-15426-4*) Turtleback Bks.

—Before the Creeks Ran Red. 2003. 384p. (J). (gr. 5 up). 16.99 (*0-06-623615-0*); lib. bdg. 17.89 (*0-06-623616-9*) HarperCollins Pubs.

—Captain Kate. 1999. (Avon Camelot Bks.). 224p. (J). (gr. 4-7). 15.00 (*0-380-97628-5*, Avon Bks.) Morrow/Avon.

—Shades of Gray. 1991. 160p. (YA). (gr. 4-9). pap. 4.99 o.p. (*0-380-71232-6*, Avon Bks.) Morrow/Avon.

—Shades of Gray. 3rd ed. 1994. pap. text 3.50 (*0-13-800046-8*) Prentice Hall (Schl. Div.).

—Shades of Gray. 1999. 160p. (J). (gr. 3-7). pap. 4.99 (*0-689-82696-6*, 076714004993, Aladdin); 1989. 176p. (YA). (gr. 7 up). lib. bdg. 16.00 (*0-02-775810-9*, Simon & Schuster Children's Publishing) Simon & Schuster Children's Publishing.

—Shades of Gray. 1991. 9.60 o.p. (*0-606-04873-1*) Turtleback Bks.

Reisberg, Joanne A. Save the Colors: A Civil War Battle Cry. 2001. (Young Americans Ser.: Vol. 5). (Illus.). 92p. (J). 5.95 (*1-57249-247-3*, WM Kids) White Mane Publishing Co., Inc.

Richards, R. W. A Southern Yarn. Bogart, Jeffrey, ed. 1990. (Illus.). (Orig.). (YA). pap. 12.95 (*0-9625502-0-5*) RoKarn Pubns.

Rifles for Watie. 1999. (YA). 9.95 (*1-56137-598-5*) Novel Units, Inc.

Rinaldi, Ann. An Acquaintance with Darkness. (Great Episodes Ser.). 304p. (YA). (gr. 7 up). 1999. pap. 6.00 (*0-15-202197-3*, Harcourt Paperbacks); 1997. 16.00 (*0-15-201294-X*, Gulliver Bks.) Harcourt Children's Bks.

—An Acquaintance with Darkness. 1999. 12.05 (*0-606-16525-8*) Turtleback Bks.

—Amelia's War. 1999. 265p. (J). (gr. 6-8). pap. 15.95 (*0-590-11744-0*) Scholastic, Inc.

—Girl in Blue. 2001. (Illus.). 272p. (J). (gr. 4-9). pap. 15.95 (*0-439-07336-7*) Scholastic, Inc.

—In My Father's House. (Point Ser.). 336p. (YA). 1994. (gr. 8-12). mass mkt. 4.99 (*0-590-44731-9*); 1993. (Illus.). (gr. 7-9). pap. 14.95 (*0-590-44730-0*) Scholastic, Inc.

—In My Father's House. 1993. 11.04 (*0-606-07012-5*) Turtleback Bks.

—The Last Silk Dress. 1990. 352p. (YA). mass mkt. 4.99 o.s.i (*0-553-28315-4*) Bantam Bks.

—The Last Silk Dress. 1999. 352p. (YA). (gr. 7). mass mkt. 5.99 (*0-440-22861-1*) Bantam Dell Publishing Group.

—The Last Silk Dress. 1988. 368p. (YA). (gr. 5 up). 15.95 o.p. (*0-8234-0690-3*) Holiday Hse., Inc.

—The Last Silk Dress. 1988. (J). 11.55 (*0-606-04464-7*) Turtleback Bks.

Robertson, William P. & Rimer, David. The Bucktails' Shenandoah March. 2002. (WM Kids Ser.: Vol. 12). (Illus.). 170p. (J). pap. 7.95 (*1-57249-293-7*, WM Kids) White Mane Publishing Co., Inc.

—Hayfoot, Strawfoot: The Bucktail Recruits. 2001. (Illus.). 170p. (J). pap. 7.95 (*1-57249-250-3*, WM Kids) White Mane Publishing Co., Inc.

Roddy, Lee. Cry of Courage. l.t. ed. 1999. (Paperback Ser.). 213p. (gr. 6-9). pap. 22.95 (*0-7838-8611-X*) Thorndike Pr.

—Risking the Dream. 2000. (Between Two Flags Ser.: Vol. 6). (Illus.). 176p. (J). (gr. 6-9). pap. 5.99 o.p. (*0-7642-2030-6*) Bethany Hse. Pubs.

—Uprising at Dawn. 2000. (Between Two Flags Ser.: Vol. 5). (Illus.). 160p. (J). (gr. 6-9). pap. 5.99 o.p. (*0-7642-2029-2*) Bethany Hse. Pubs.

Rosholt, Malcolm & Rosholt, Margaret. The Story of Old Abe Wisconsin's Civil War Hero. 1987. (Illus.). 110p. (J). (gr. 4-12). 14.95 o.p. (*0-910417-09-1*) Rosholt Hse.

Sappey, Maureen S. Dreams of Ships, Dreams of Julia: At Sea with the Monitor & the Merrimack-Virginia, 1862. 1998. (Young American Ser.: Vol. 2). (Illus.). 140p. (YA). (gr. 4-7). 5.99 (*1-57249-134-5*) White Mane Publishing Co., Inc.

—A Rose at Bull Run: Romance & Realities at First Bull Run. 1999. (Young American Ser.: Vol. 1). (Illus.). 100p. (YA). (gr. 4-7). 5.99 (*1-57249-133-7*) White Mane Publishing Co., Inc.

—Yankee Spy. 1999. (Young American Ser.: Vol. 3). (Illus.). 140p. (J). (gr. 4-7). 5.99 (*1-57249-135-3*) White Mane Publishing Co., Inc.

Sescoe, Vincent E. Double Time. 2001. (Illus.). (gr. 6-12). 191p. (J). 17.95 (*1-930093-00-4*); 192p. (YA). pap. 6.95 (*1-930093-06-3*) Brookfield Reader, Inc., The.

Severance, John B. Braving the Fire. 2002. (Illus.). 160p. (YA). (gr. 5-9). tchr. ed. 15.00 (*0-618-22999-X*, Clarion Bks.) Houghton Mifflin Co. Trade & Reference Div.

Severs, Vesta N. Lucinda. 1983. (Midwestern Memories Ser.). (Illus.). (J). (gr. 5-9). 4.95 o.p. (*0-570-07805-9*, 39-1000); pap. 3.50 o.p. (*0-570-07800-8*, 39-1010) Concordia Publishing Hse.

Seymour, Tres. We Played Marbles. 1998. (Illus.). 32p. (J). (gr. k-4). pap. 15.95 (*0-531-30074-9*); lib. bdg. 16.99 (*0-531-33074-5*) Scholastic, Inc. (Orchard Bks.).

Shaffer, Elizabeth N. Hannah & the Indian King, Vol. 2. Pratt, Fran, ed. 2002. (Historical Novel Ser.). pap. 9.95 (*0-936369-35-3*) Son-Rise Pubns. & Distribution Co.

Simpson, Kathleen. Shiloh. 2002. (Literature Circle Guides Ser.). 32p. mass mkt. 5.95 (*0-439-35539-7*) Scholastic, Inc.

Smith, Debra West. Yankees on the Doorstep: The Story of Sarah Morgan. 2001. (Illus.). 176p. (J). (gr. 3-7). pap. 10.95 (*1-56554-872-8*) Pelican Publishing Co., Inc.

Sohl, Marcia & Dackerman, Gerald. The Red Badge of Courage: Student Activity Book. 1976. (Now Age Illustrated Ser.). (Illus.). 16p. (J). (gr. 4-10). pap. 1.25 (*0-88301-184-0*) Pendulum Pr., Inc.

Spier, Peter. The Star-Spangled Banner. 1973. (Illus.). 48p. (J). (gr. 1 up). 11.95 o.s.i (*0-385-07746-7*); 15.00 o.s.i (*0-385-09458-2*) Doubleday Publishing.

—The Star-Spangled Banner. 1992. (Reading Rainbow Bks.). (Illus.). 56p. (ps-3). pap. text 10.95 (*0-440-40697-8*, Yearling) Random Hse. Children's Bks.

—The Star-Spangled Banner. 2002. (J). (ps-6). 24.95 incl. audio (*1-55592-160-4*); 24.95 incl. audio (*1-55592-160-4*); pap. 18.95 incl. audio compact disk (*1-55592-143-4*); pap. 18.95 incl. audio compact disk (*1-55592-143-4*); pap. 12.95 incl. audio (*1-55592-144-2*); pap. 18.95 incl. audio compact disk (*1-55592-161-2*); pap. 12.95 incl. audio (*1-55592-144-2*) Weston Woods Studios, Inc.

Steele, William O. The Perilous Road. (J). (gr. 3-7). 1990. 176p. pap. 6.00 (*0-15-260647-5*, Odyssey Classics); 1965. (Illus.). pap. 3.95 o.p. (*0-15-671696-8*, Voyager Bks./Libros Viajeros); 1958. (Illus.). 9.95 o.p. (*0-15-260644-0*) Harcourt Children's Bks.

Stevens, C. A. The Jonah. Palmer, Mary, ed. 1995. (Illus.). 48p. (J). (gr. 1-6). pap. 8.95 (*1-883650-26-7*) Windswept Hse. Pubs.

Stites, Clara. Naming the Stones. 2002. (Illus.). 46p. (J). (*0-932027-72-5*) Spinner Pubns., Inc.

Stolz, Mary. A Ballad of the Civil War. 1997. (Illus.). (J). 64p. (gr. 3-5). 14.95 (*0-06-027362-3*); 80p. (gr. 2-6). lib. bdg. 13.89 (*0-06-027363-1*) HarperCollins Children's Bk. Group.

—A Ballad of the Civil War. 1998. (Trophy Chapter Bks.). (Illus.). 64p. (J). (gr. 2-5). pap. 4.25 (*0-06-442088-4*) HarperCollins Pubs.

—A Ballad of the Civil War. 1998. 10.40 (*0-606-15450-7*) Turtleback Bks.

Strait, Mel. Strange Tales of the Civil War. 2002. cd-rom 14.95 (*1-930430-20-5*) Waltsan Publishing, LLC.

Susi, Geraldine Lee. Looking Back: A Boy's Civil War Memories. 2001. (Illus.). 128p. (J). (gr. 3-7). pap. 11.95 (*1-880664-34-8*) E. M. Productions.

—Looking for Pa: A Civil War Journey from Catlett to Manassas, 1861. 2nd ed. 2001. (Illus.). 127p. (J). (gr. 4-7). pap. 10.95 (*1-880664-33-X*) E. M. Productions.

—Looking for Pa: A Civil War Journey from Catlett to Manassas, 1861. 1995. (Illus.). 128p. (J). (gr. 5-7). pap. 9.95 (*0-939009-87-0*, EPM Pubns.) Howell Pr.

Sykes, Shelley & Szymanski, Lois. A Whisper of War. 2003. (J). (*1-57249-327-5*, WM Kids) White Mane Publishing Co., Inc.

Tallent, Mary. The Secret at Robert's Roost. 1988. 161p. (J). (gr. 4-7). pap. 3.95 o.p. (*0-941711-05-6*) Wyrick & Co.

Tate, Suzanne. Burnside & Sideburns: A Tale of Civil War Days. 2000. (Suzanne Tate's History Ser.). (Illus.). 32p. (J). (gr. k-4). pap. 4.95 (*1-878405-28-4*) Nags Head Art, Inc.

Thomas, Carroll. Matty's War. 1999. (J). (Illus.). 164p. (gr. 4-7). pap. 9.95 (*1-57525-206-6*); (*1-57525-205-8*) Smith & Kraus Pubs., Inc.

Tolliver, Ruby C. Muddy Banks. 1987. (Chaparral Book for Young Readers Ser.). (Illus.). 154p. (J). (gr. 4). pap. 11.95 (*0-87565-049-X*); 14.95 o.p. (*0-87565-062-7*) Texas Christian Univ. Pr.

Townsend, Tom. The Battle of Galveston. Eakin, Edwin M., ed. 1989. (Illus.). 80p. (J). (gr. 6-7). pap. 7.95 o.p. (*0-89015-713-8*); (YA). (gr. 9-11). 10.95 o.p. (*0-89015-685-9*) Eakin Pr.

Travis, L. Captured by a Spy. 1995. (Ben & Zack Ser.: Vol. 1). 144p. (J). (gr. 3-8). pap. 5.99 o.p. (*0-8010-8915-8*) Baker Bks.

—Union Army Black. 1995. (Ben & Zack Ser.: Bk. 4). 168p. (J). (gr. 3-8). pap. 5.99 o.p. (*0-8010-4037-X*) Baker Bks.

Turner, Ann Warren. Drummer Boy: Marching to the Civil War. 1998. (Illus.). 32p. (J). (ps-3). 16.95 (*0-06-027696-7*); lib. bdg. 16.89 (*0-06-027697-5*) HarperCollins Children's Bk. Group.

Venner, Thomas. Young Heroes of Gettysburg. 2000. (White Mane Kids Ser.: Vol. 10). (Illus.). vi, 172p. (J). (gr. 4-7). pap. 8.95 (*1-57249-200-7*, WM Kids) White Mane Publishing Co., Inc.

Webber, Earlynne. The Secret of the Big Thicket. 1994. (J). pap. 7.95 o.p. (*0-89015-958-0*) Eakin Pr.

Weik, Mary H. A House on Liberty Street. 1973. (Illus.). 80p. (J). (gr. 5 up). 4.50 o.p. (*0-689-30098-0*, Atheneum) Simon & Schuster Children's Publishing.

Weiss, Ellen. Civil War Days. 2001. (Hitty's Travels Ser.: No. 1). (Illus.). 80p. (J). pap. 3.99 (*0-689-84671-1*, Aladdin) Simon & Schuster Children's Publishing.

Whitney, Phyllis A. Step to the Music. 1953. (J). (gr. 7 up). 11.20 (*0-690-77352-8*) HarperCollins Children's Bk. Group.

Wilhelm, Doug. Gunfire at Gettysburg. 1994. (Choose Your Own Adventure Ser.: No. 151). 128p. (J). (gr. 4-8). pap. 3.50 o.s.i (*0-553-56393-9*) Bantam Bks.

—Gunfire at Gettysburg. 1994. (Choose Your Own Adventure Ser.: No. 151). (J). (gr. 4-8). 8.60 o.p. (*0-606-06997-6*) Turtleback Bks.

Williams, George F. Bullet & Shell: The Civil War As the Soldier Saw It. 1992. (Illus.). 480p. 9.98 o.p. (*0-681-41497-9*) Borders Pr.

Wisler, G. Clifton. The Drummer Boy of Vicksburg. 1997. 144p. (YA). (gr. 5-9). 15.99 (*0-525-67537-X*, Dutton Children's Bks.) Penguin Putnam Bks. for Young Readers.

—Drummer Boy of Vicksburg. 1999. (Illus.). 144p. (YA). (gr. 4-7). pap. 5.99 (*0-14-038673-4*, Puffin Bks.) Penguin Putnam Bks. for Young Readers.

—Mr. Lincoln's Drummer. 144p. (YA). (gr. 5-9). 1997. pap. 5.99 (*0-14-038542-8*); 1995. 15.99 o.s.i (*0-525-67463-2*, Dutton Children's Bks.) Penguin Putnam Bks. for Young Readers.

—Mr. Lincoln's Drummer. 1997. (YA). 11.04 (*0-606-10986-2*) Turtleback Bks.

—Mustang Flats. 1997. 128p. (YA). (gr. 5-9). 14.99 o.s.i (*0-525-67544-2*, Dutton Children's Bks.) Penguin Putnam Bks. for Young Readers.

—Red Cap. 176p. (gr. 5 up). 1994. (YA). pap. 5.99 (*0-14-036936-8*, Puffin Bks.); 1991. (J). 15.99 o.p. (*0-525-67337-7*, Dutton Children's Bks.) Penguin Putnam Bks. for Young Readers.

—Red Cap, 2000. (YA). pap., stu. ed. 41.24 incl. audio (*0-7887-3629-9*, 41018X4); pap., stu. ed. 41.24 incl. audio (*0-7887-3629-9*, 41018X4) Recorded Bks., LLC.

—Red Cap. 2001. (YA). 20.25 (*0-8446-7196-7*) Smith, Peter Pub., Inc.

—Red Cap. 1994. 11.04 (*0-606-06691-8*) Turtleback Bks.

—Run the Blockade. 2000. (Illus.). 128p. (J). (gr. 5 up). lib. bdg. 15.89 (*0-06-029208-3*) HarperCollins Children's Bk. Group.

—Run the Blockade. 2000. (Illus.). 122p. (J). (gr. 5-9). 15.95 (*0-688-16538-9*, Morrow, William & Co.) Morrow/Avon.

UNITED STATES—HISTORY—1865-1898—FICTION

Dionne, Wanda. The Couturiere of Galvez. 1993. (Illus.). (J). (gr. 6-7). 176p. 15.95 o.p. (*0-89015-860-6*); pap. 9.95 (*1-57168-161-2*) Eakin Pr.

—The Couturiere of Galvez. 1993. E-Book 9.95 (*0-585-23700-X*) netLibrary, Inc.

Grote, JoAnn A. Centennial Celebration. 25th ed. 1998. (American Adventure Ser.: No. 25). (Illus.). (J). (gr. 3-7). pap. 3.97 (*1-57748-287-5*) Barbour Publishing, Inc.

Hansen, Joyce. The Heart Calls Home. 2002. 256p. (J). (gr. 7 up). pap. 5.95 (*0-380-73294-7*, Harper Trophy) HarperCollins Children's Bk. Group.

—The Heart Calls Home. 1999. viii, 175p. (J). (gr. 7-12). 16.95 (*0-8027-8636-7*) Walker & Co.

—I Thought My Soul Would Rise & Fly: The Diary of Patsy, a Freed Girl, Mars Bluff, South Carolina, 1865. 1997. (Dear America Ser.). (Illus.). 202p. (J). (gr. 4-9). pap. 10.95 (*0-590-84913-1*) Scholastic, Inc.

—Which Way Freedom? 1987. (Walker's American History Series for Young People). (J). lib. bdg. 13.85 (*0-8027-6636-6*) Walker & Co.

LaFaye, A. Edith Shay. 1998. 160p. (YA). (gr. 6-12). 15.99 o.s.i (*0-670-87598-8*) Penguin Putnam Bks. for Young Readers.

—Edith Shay. 2001. 192p. (YA). (gr. 7 up). pap. 4.99 (*0-689-84228-7*, Simon Pulse) Simon & Schuster Children's Publishing.

Lawlor, Laurie. Old Crump: The True Story of a Trip West. 2002. (Illus.). 32p. (J). (gr. 2-4). tchr. ed. 16.95 (*0-8234-1608-9*) Holiday Hse., Inc.

L'Engle, Madeleine. The Other Side of the Sun. 1971. 344p. (J). 6.95 o.s.i (*0-374-22805-1*) Farrar, Straus & Giroux.

MacBride, Roger Lea. Bachelor Girl. 1999. (Little House Ser.). (Illus.). 256p. (J). (gr. 3-6). 15.95 (*0-06-027755-6*); (gr. 3-6). lib. bdg. 15.89 (*0-06-028434-X*); (gr. 5 up). pap. 5.99 (*0-06-440691-1*, Harper Trophy) HarperCollins Children's Bk. Group.

—Bachelor Girl. 1999. (Little House Ser.). (Illus.). (J). (gr. 3-6). 11.00 (*0-606-18676-X*) Turtleback Bks.

Robinet, Harriette Gillem. Forty Acres & Maybe a Mule. 2000. (YA). (gr. 3 up). pap. 52.00 incl. audio (*0-7887-4332-5*, 41127); pap. 52.00 incl. audio (*0-7887-4332-5*, 41127) Recorded Bks., LLC.

—Forty Acres & Maybe a Mule. (Jean Karl Bks.). 144p. (J). (gr. 3-7). 1998. (Illus.). 16.95 (*0-689-82078-X*, Atheneum); 2000. reprint ed. pap. 4.99 (*0-689-83317-2*, Aladdin) Simon & Schuster Children's Publishing.

—Forty Acres & Maybe a Mule. l.t. ed. 2001. (Illus.). 184p. (J). (gr. 4-7). 21.95 (*0-7862-2704-4*) Thorndike Pr.

—Forty Acres & Maybe a Mule. 2000. 11.04 (*0-606-17824-4*) Turtleback Bks.

Travis, L. The Redheaded Orphan. 1995. (Ben & Zack Ser.: Vol. 3). 154p. (J). (gr. 3-8). pap. 5.99 o.p. (*0-8010-4023-X*) Baker Bks.

Zach, Cheryl. Hearts Divided. 1995. (Southern Angels Ser.: No. 1). 256p. (YA). (gr. 7 up). mass mkt. 3.99 o.s.i (*0-553-56217-7*) Bantam Bks.

—Hearts Divided. 1995. (Southern Angels Ser.). 9.09 o.p. (*0-606-08184-4*) Turtleback Bks.

UNITED STATES—HISTORY—WAR OF 1898—FICTION

Howard, Elizabeth Fitzgerald. Papa Tells Chita a Story. (Illus.). 32p. (J). (ps-2). 1998. pap. 5.99 (*0-689-82220-0*, Aladdin); 1995. 15.00 (*0-02-744623-9*, Simon & Schuster Children's Publishing) Simon & Schuster Children's Publishing.

—Papa Tells Chita a Story. 1998. 12.14 (*0-606-15670-4*) Turtleback Bks.

Sargent, Dave & Sargent, Pat. Buckshot (Blue Eyed Chestnet) Mind Your Manners #8. 2001. (Saddle Up Ser.). 36p. (J). pap. (*1-56763-674-8*) Ozark Publishing.

—Buckshot (Blue Eyed Chestnut) Mind Your Manners #8. 2001. (Saddle Up Ser.). 36p. (J). lib. bdg. 22.60 (*1-56763-673-X*) Ozark Publishing.

UNITED STATES—HISTORY—20TH CENTURY—FICTION

Boling, Katharine. January 1905. 2004. 160p. (J). 16.00 (*0-15-205119-8*) Harcourt Children's Bks.

Matas, Carol. Rosie in Chicago: Play Ball! 2003. (Illus.). 128p. (J). pap. 4.99 (*0-689-85715-2*, Aladdin) Simon & Schuster Children's Publishing.

V

VIETNAMESE CONFLICT, 1961-1975—FICTION

Antle, Nancy. Lost in the War. 1998. 144p. (YA). (gr. 6-12). 15.99 o.s.i (*0-8037-2299-0*, Dial Bks. for Young Readers) Penguin Putnam Bks. for Young Readers.

—Touch Choices: A Story of the Vietnam War. 1993. (Once upon America Ser.). (Illus.). 64p. (J). (gr. 2-6). 12.99 o.p. (*0-670-84879-4*, Viking Children's Bks.) Penguin Putnam Bks. for Young Readers.

Ashabranner, Brent K. Always to Remember: The Story of the Vietnam Veterans Memorial. 1988. (Illus.). 40p. (J). (gr. 6 up). 14.95 o.p. (*0-399-22031-3*, G. P. Putnam's Sons) Penguin Group (USA) Inc.

Boyd, Candy Dawson. Charlie Pippin. 1988. 192p. (J). (gr. 4-7). pap. 5.99 (*0-14-032587-5*, Puffin Bks.) Penguin Putnam Bks. for Young Readers.

—Charlie Pippin. 1987. 192p. (J). (gr. 3-7). lib. bdg. 14.95 o.s.i (*0-02-726350-9*, Simon & Schuster Children's Publishing) Simon & Schuster Children's Publishing.

—Charlie Pippin. 1987. (J). 11.04 (*0-606-03752-7*) Turtleback Bks.

Breckler, Rosemary. Sweet Dried Apples: A Vietnamese Wartime Childhood. 1996. (Illus.). 32p. (J). (gr. 1-4). tchr. ed. 15.95 o.p. (*0-395-73570-X*) Houghton Mifflin Co.

Brown, Larry. Dirty Work. 1989. 252p. 16.95 (*0-945575-20-3*) Algonquin Bks. of Chapel Hill.

—Dirty Work. 1990. (Vintage Contemporaries Ser.). 256p. pap. 13.00 (*0-679-73049-4*, Vintage) Knopf Publishing Group.

Cam, John B. Vietnam Blues: Every American Who Fought in Vietnam is a Nero. 1988. 272p. (J). mass mkt. 3.25 (*0-87067-730-6*) Holloway Hse. Publishing Co.

Crist-Evans, Craig. Amaryllis. 2003. 208p. (YA). 15.99 (*0-7636-1863-2*) Candlewick Pr.

Easton, Kelly. The Life History of a Star. 208p. (YA). 2002. pap. 6.99 (*0-689-85270-3*, Simon Pulse); 2001. (Illus.). (gr. 7 up). 16.00 (*0-689-83134-X*, McElderry, Margaret K.) Simon & Schuster Children's Publishing.

—The Life History of a Star. l.t. ed. 2002. (Young Adult Ser.). 200p. 22.95 (*0-7862-4786-X*) Thorndike Pr.

Emerson, Zack. Hill Five Hundred Sixty-Eight. 1991. (Echo Company Ser.: No. 2). (YA). mass mkt. 2.95 o.p. (*0-590-44592-8*) Scholastic, Inc.

—Stand Down. 1992. (Echo Company Ser.: No. 4). 128p. (J). pap. 2.95 o.p. (*0-590-44594-4*, Scholastic Paperbacks) Scholastic, Inc.

—'Tis the Season. 1991. (Echo Company Ser.: No. 3). 256p. (J). mass mkt. 2.95 o.p. (*0-590-44593-6*) Scholastic, Inc.

—Welcome to Vietnam. 1991. (Echo Company Ser.: No. 1). (YA). pap. 2.95 o.p. (*0-590-44591-X*) Scholastic, Inc.

Franklin, Kristine L. Dove Song. 1999. (Illus.). 192p. (J). (gr. 5-9). 16.99 (*0-7636-0409-7*) Candlewick Pr.

Gifford, Clive. The Water Puppets: A Story from the War in Vietnam. 2002. (Survivors Ser.). 96p. (J). (gr. 5-8). pap. 4.95 (*0-7641-2206-1*); (Illus.). 12.95 (*0-7641-5531-8*) Barron's Educational Series, Inc.

Graham, Gail. Cross-Fire: A Vietnam Novel. 1972. (YA). (gr. 7 up). lib. bdg. 5.99 o.p. (*0-394-92380-4*, Pantheon) Knopf Publishing Group.

Hahn, Mary Downing. December Stillness. 1988. 192p. (YA). (gr. 5-9). 14.95 o.p. (*0-89919-758-2*, Clarion Bks.) Houghton Mifflin Co. Trade & Reference Div.

—December Stillness. 1990. 192p. (J). (gr. 7 up). pap. 5.99 (*0-380-70764-0*, Avon Bks.) Morrow/Avon.
—December Stillness. 1990. (J). 11.04 (*0-606-04652-6*) Turtleback Bks.
Hobbs, Valerie. Sonny's War, RS. 2002. 224p. (YA). (gr. 7 up). 16.00 (*0-374-37136-9*, Farrar, Straus & Giroux (BYR)) Farrar, Straus & Giroux.
Hoobler, Dorothy & Hoobler, Thomas. The 1970s: Arguments. 2002. (Century Kids Ser.). (Illus.). 160p. (YA). (gr. 5-8). 22.90 (*0-7613-1607-8*) Millbrook Pr., Inc.
Jensen, Kathryn. Pocket Change. 1991. 192p. (YA). (gr. 7 up). pap. 2.95 o.p. (*0-590-43419-5*, Scholastic Paperbacks) Scholastic, Inc.
—Pocket Change. 1989. 176p. (YA). (gr. 7 up). text 14.95 o.s.i (*0-02-747731-2*, Simon & Schuster Children's Publishing) Simon & Schuster Children's Publishing.
Jones, Adrienne. Long Time Passing. 1990. (Charlotte Zolotow Bk.). 256p. (YA). (gr. 7 up). 14.95 (*0-06-023055-X*); lib. bdg. 14.89 o.p. (*0-06-023056-8*) HarperCollins Children's Bk. Group.
Myers, Walter Dean. Fallen Angels. 2002. (Illus.). (J). 13.19 (*0-7587-0353-8*) Book Wholesalers, Inc.
—Fallen Angels. 320p. (gr. 7-12). 2003. (J). mass mkt. 5.95 (*0-590-40943-3*, Scholastic Paperbacks); 1988. (YA). pap. 16.95 (*0-590-40942-5*) Scholastic, Inc.
—Fallen Angels. 1988. (J). 11.04 (*0-606-04220-2*) Turtleback Bks.
Nelson, Theresa. And One for All. 1989. 192p. (J). (gr. 6-8). mass mkt. 15.99 o.p. (*0-531-08404-3*); (YA). (gr. 4-7). pap. 16.95 (*0-531-05804-2*) Scholastic, Inc. (Orchard Bks.).
—And One for All. 1991. 10.55 (*0-606-04866-9*) Turtleback Bks.
Okimoto, Jean Davies. Jason's Women. 2000. 220p. (gr. 4-7). pap. 12.95 (*0-595-00797-X*, Backinprint-.com) iUniverse, Inc.
Paulsen, Gary. The Car. 1994. 192p. (YA). (gr. 7 up). 17.00 (*0-15-292878-2*) Harcourt Children's Bks.
Pettit, Jayne. My Name Is San Ho. 1992. 192p. (J). 13.95 o.p. (*0-590-44172-8*) Scholastic, Inc.
Pevsner, Stella & Tang, Fay. Sing for Your Father, Su Phan. 1997. (Illus.). 112p. (J). (gr. 4-6). 14.00 o.s.i (*0-395-82267-X*, Clarion Bks.) Houghton Mifflin Co. Trade & Reference Div.
—Sing for Your Father, Su Phan. 1999. 10.55 (*0-606-16709-9*) Turtleback Bks.
Qualey, Marsha. Come in from the Cold. 1994. 224p. (YA). (gr. 7 up). tchr. ed. 16.00 (*0-395-68986-4*) Houghton Mifflin Co.
Ritter, John H. Over the Wall. 2000. (Illus.). 312p. (YA). (gr. 5 up). 17.99 (*0-399-23489-6*, Philomel) Penguin Putnam Bks. for Young Readers.
Rostkowski, Margaret I. The Best of Friends. 1989. 192p. (YA). (gr. 7 up). 12.95 (*0-06-025104-2*); lib. bdg. 12.89 o.p. (*0-06-025105-0*) HarperCollins Children's Bk. Group.
Santana, Patricia. Motorcycle Ride on the Sea of Tranquillity. 2002. 276p. (YA). 19.95 (*0-8263-2435-5*) Univ. of New Mexico Pr.
Schraff, Anne. The Greatest Heroes. 2000. 143p. (J). (*0-7807-9271-8*); pap. (*0-7891-5133-2*) Perfection Learning Corp.
Shoup, Barbara. Stranded in Harmony. 2001. 194p. (YA). pap. 15.95 (*1-57860-094-4*) Emmis Bks.
—Stranded in Harmony. 1997. 192p. (YA). (gr. 7 up). 17.95 (*0-7868-0287-1*); lib. bdg. 18.49 (*0-7868-2284-8*) Hyperion Bks. for Children.
Talbert, Marc. The Purple Heart. 1992. (Willa Perlman Bks.). 144p. (J). (gr. 4-8). lib. bdg. 14.89 o.p. (*0-06-020429-X*); 14.95 (*0-06-020428-1*) HarperCollins Children's Bk. Group.
Testa, Maria. Almost Forever. 2003. 80p. (J). 14.99 (*0-7636-1996-5*) Candlewick Pr.
Warren, Andrea. Escape from Saigon: Vietnamese War Orphan Became an American, RS. 2004. (J). (*0-374-32224-4*) Farrar, Straus & Giroux.
White, Ellen E. The Road Home. (YA). (gr. 7 up). 1997. 480p. mass mkt. 4.99 (*0-590-46738-7*); 1995. 464p. pap. 15.95 (*0-590-46737-9*) Scholastic, Inc.
—The Road Home. 1997. (J). 11.04 (*0-606-12800-X*) Turtleback Bks.
White, Ellen Emerson. Where Have All the Flowers Gone? The Diary of Molly Mackenzie Flaherty, Boston, Massachusetts, 1968. 2002. (Dear America Ser.). (Illus.). 176p. (J). (gr. 4-9). pap. 10.95 (*0-439-14889-8*, Scholastic Pr.) Scholastic, Inc.
Wolitzer, Meg. Caribou. 1986. (Starfire Ser.). 176p. (YA). (gr. 7-12). mass mkt. 2.50 o.s.i (*0-553-25560-6*) Bantam Bks.

VIKINGS—FICTION

Bailey, Linda. Adventures with the Vikings. 2001. (Good Times Travel Agency Ser.). (Illus.). 48p. (J). (gr. 3-7). pap. 7.95 (*1-55074-544-1*);No. 3. 14.95 (*1-55074-542-5*) Kids Can Pr., Ltd.
Cadnum, Michael. Daughter of the Wind. 2003. 272p. (J). 17.95 (*0-439-35224-X*, Orchard Bks.) Scholastic, Inc.
—Raven of the Waves. 2001. 200p. (YA). (gr. 9 up). pap. 17.95 (*0-531-30334-9*, Orchard Bks.) Scholastic, Inc.
Cowell, Cressida. Hiccup the Seasick Viking. 2000. (Illus.). 40p. (J). (gr. k-3). pap. 15.95 (*0-531-30278-4*, Orchard Bks.) Scholastic, Inc.
Cowell, Cressida, tr. How to Train Your Dragon. 2004. 224p. (J). 10.95 (*0-316-73737-2*) Little Brown & Co.
Foster, Scarlett R. Secret of the Viking Dagger. Qualben, James D., ed. 1997. 144p. (J). (gr. 4-7). pap. 7.95 (*1-880292-55-6*); lib. bdg. 15.95 (*1-880292-56-4*) LangMarc Publishing. (North Sea Pr.).
Gafford, Deborah. Swept Away Stories: Visit with a Viking. (J). E-Book 5.95 (*1-930756-48-8*, Bookmice) McGraw Publishing, Inc.
—Swept Away Stories - Visit with a Viking. 1999. (J). E-Book 4.50 (*1-930364-21-0*, Bookmice) McGraw Publishing, Inc.
Harrison, Cora. The Viking at Drumshee. 2001. 128p. pap. 7.95 (*0-86327-788-8*) Interlink Publishing Group, Inc.
Hauger, Torill Thorstad. Escape from the Vikings. Hamnes, Lisa, ed. Born, Anne, tr. from NOR. 2000. Orig. Title: Flukten Fra Vikingene. (Illus.). 175p. (J). (gr. 4-12). pap. (*1-57534-013-5*) Skandisk, Inc.
Henighan, Tom. Viking Quest. 2001. 120p. pap. 5.95 (*0-88878-421-X*, Sandcastle Bks.) Beach Holme Pubs., Ltd. CAN. *Dist:* Strauss Consultants.
Osborne, Mary Pope. Viking Ships at Sunrise. unabr. ed. 2002. (Magic Tree House Ser. : Vol. 15). 71p. (J). (gr. k-4). pap. 17.00 incl. audio (*0-8072-0784-5*, LFTR 243 SP, Listening Library) Random Hse. Audio Publishing Group.
—Viking Ships at Sunrise. 1998. (Magic Tree House Ser.: No. 15). (Illus.). 96p. (J). (gr. k-3). pap. 3.99 (*0-679-89061-0*); lib. bdg. 11.99 (*0-679-99061-5*) Random Hse., Inc.
—Viking Ships at Sunrise. 1998. (Magic Tree House Ser.: No. 15). (J). (gr. k-3). 10.14 (*0-606-15755-7*) Turtleback Bks.
Schachner, Judith Byron. Yo, Vikings! 2002. (Illus.). 32p. (J). (gr. k-4). 16.99 (*0-525-46889-7*, Dutton Children's Bks.) Penguin Putnam Bks. for Young Readers.
Scieszka, Jon. Viking It & Liking It. (Time Warp Trio Ser.). (Illus.). 2004. pap. 4.99 (*0-14-240002-5*, Puffin Bks.); 2002. 80p. (J). 14.99 (*0-670-89918-6*, Viking Children's Bks.) Penguin Putnam Bks. for Young Readers.
Strong, Jeremy. Viking at School. l.t. ed. (J). 2000. (Illus.). pap. (*0-7540-6093-4*); 2003. 104p. pap. 24.95 incl. audio (*0-7540-6230-9*, RA031, Galaxy Children's Large Print) BBC Audiobooks America.
Sutcliff, Rosemary. Sword Song, RS. 1998. 288p. (J). (gr. 7-12). 18.00 (*0-374-37363-9*, Farrar, Straus & Giroux (BYR)) Farrar, Straus & Giroux.
Tebbetts, Christopher. The Land of the Dead: Viking Saga, Vol. 3. 2003. (Viking Ser.: Vol. 3). 192p. (J). pap. 5.99 (*0-14-250031-3*, Puffin Bks.) Penguin Putnam Bks. for Young Readers.
—The Quest for Faith. 2003. (Viking Ser.). 192p. (J). pap. 5.99 (*0-14-250030-5*, Puffin Bks.) Penguin Putnam Bks. for Young Readers.
—Viking Pride, Vol. 1. 2003. (Viking Ser.). 192p. (J). pap. 5.99 (*0-14-250029-1*, Puffin Bks.) Penguin Putnam Bks. for Young Readers.
Tingle, Rebecca. The Edge on the Sword. 2003. (Sailing Mystery Ser.). 288p. (J). pap. 6.99 (*0-14-250058-5*, Puffin Bks.) Penguin Putnam Bks. for Young Readers.

W

WORLD WAR, 1914-1918—FICTION

Anderson, Launi K. Gracie's Angel. Utley, Jennifer, ed. 1996. (Latter-Day Daughters Ser.). (Illus.). 80p. (J). (gr. 3-9). pap. 4.95 (*1-56236-508-8*) Aspen Bks.
Bawden, Nina. The Real Plato Jones. 1996. 176p. (J). (gr. 5-9). pap. 4.99 o.s.i (*0-14-037947-9*, Puffin Bks.) Penguin Putnam Bks. for Young Readers.
Breslin, Theresa. Remembrance. 304p. (YA). 2004. (gr. 7). mass mkt. 6.50 (*0-440-23778-5*, Laurel Leaf); 2002. lib. bdg. 18.99 (*0-385-90067-8*, Delacorte Bks. for Young Readers); 2002. (gr. 7 up). 16.95 (*0-385-73015-2*, Delacorte Bks. for Young Readers) Random Hse. Children's Bks.
Dank, Milton. Khaki Wings. 1980. 160p. (J). (gr. 8-12). pap. 8.95 o.s.i (*0-385-28523-X*, Delacorte Pr.) Dell Publishing.
—Red Flight Two. 1981. 224p. (J). (gr. 7 up). 12.95 o.p. (*0-385-28840-9*, Delacorte Pr.) Dell Publishing.
Debon, Nicolas. A Brave Soldier. 2002. (Illus.). 32p. (YA). (gr. 1 up). 15.95 (*0-88899-481-8*) Groundwood Bks. CAN. *Dist:* Publishers Group West.
Dubois, William P. The Forbidden Forest. 1978. (Ursula Nordstrom Bks.). (J). (gr. 2 up). 7.95 o.p. (*0-06-024699-5*); lib. bdg. 7.89 o.p. (*0-06-024700-2*) HarperCollins Pubs.
Gee, Maurice. The Champion. 1993. (Illus.). 176p. (J). (gr. 5-9). pap. 16.00 (*0-671-86561-7*, Simon & Schuster Children's Publishing) Simon & Schuster Children's Publishing.
Hamisch, Siegfried R. The Bunker... on Edelweiss Mountain. 2001. 107p. 16.95 (*1-57197-282-X*) Pentland Pr., Inc.
Harrar, George. The Trouble with Jeremy Change. 2003. (Illus.). 176p. (YA). pap. 6.95 (*1-57131-646-9*); (J). 16.95 (*1-57131-647-7*) Milkweed Editions.
Harris, Ruth Elwin. Julia's Story. 2002. 304p. (YA). (gr. 7 up). bds. 5.99 (*0-7636-1706-7*) Candlewick Pr.
Harrison, Charles Yale. Generals Die in Bed: A Story from the Trenches. 2002. (Illus.). 180p. (YA). (gr. 9). 18.95 (*1-55037-731-0*); per. 7.95 (*1-55037-730-2*) Annick Pr., Ltd. CAN. *Dist:* Firefly Bks., Ltd.
Howard-Douglas, Daisy. Jad & Old Ananias. 1999. (Illus.). (J). (gr. 3-6). 12.95 o.p. (*0-533-13028-X*) Vantage Pr., Inc.
Jones, Elizabeth McDavid. The Night Flyers. 1999. (American Girl Collection: Bk. 3). (Illus.). 160p. (J). (gr. 5-9). 9.95 (*1-56247-815-X*); pap. 5.95 (*1-56247-759-5*) Pleasant Co. Pubns. (American Girl).
—The Night Flyers. 1999. 12.00 (*0-606-17518-0*) Turtleback Bks.
Kacer, Kathy. The Night Spies. 2003. (Illus.). 148p. (J). pap. 5.95 (*1-896764-70-3*) Orca Bk. Pubs.
Karr, Kathleen. In the Kaiser's Clutch, RS. 1995. 182p. (J). (gr. 4-7). 16.00 o.p. (*0-374-33638-5*, Farrar, Straus & Giroux (BYR)) Farrar, Straus & Giroux.
Kinsey-Warnock, Natalie. The Night the Bells Rang. 1991. (Illus.). 80p. (J). (gr. 4 up). 13.99 o.s.i (*0-525-65074-1*, Dutton Children's Bks.) Penguin Putnam Bks. for Young Readers.
—The Night the Bells Rang. 2001. (J). (gr. 1-5). 19.75 (*0-8446-7180-0*) Smith, Peter Pub., Inc.
—The Night the Bells Rang. 2000. 11.04 (*0-606-20367-2*) Turtleback Bks.
Kudlinski, Kathleen V. Hero over Here: A Story of World War I. (Once upon America Ser.). (Illus.). 64p. (J). (gr. 2-6). 1992. pap. 3.99 o.s.i (*0-14-034286-9*, Puffin Bks.); 1990. 13.00 o.p. (*0-670-83050-X*, Viking Children's Bks.) Penguin Putnam Bks. for Young Readers.
Lasky, Kathryn. A Time for Courage: The Suffragette Diary of Kathleen Bowen, Washington D. C., 1917. 2002. (Dear America Ser.). (Illus.). 176p. (J). (gr. 4-9). pap. 10.95 (*0-590-51141-6*, Scholastic Pr.) Scholastic, Inc.
Lawrence, Iain. Lord of the Nutcracker Men. 2001. 224p. (gr. 5 up). text 15.95 (*0-385-72924-3*, Delacorte Pr.) Dell Publishing.
—Lord of the Nutcracker Men. l.t. ed. 2002. 280p. (J). 24.95 (*0-7862-4155-1*) Gale Group.
—Lord of the Nutcracker Men. (gr. 5). 2003. 240p. pap. 5.99 (*0-440-41812-7*, Laurel Leaf); 2001. 224p. lib. bdg. 17.99 (*0-385-90024-4*, Delacorte Bks. for Young Readers) Random Hse. Children's Bks.
Levine, Beth Seidel. When Christmas Comes Again: The World War I Diary of Simone Spencer. 2002. (Dear America Ser.). (Illus.). 112p. (J). (gr. 4-9). pap. 10.95 (*0-439-43982-5*, Scholastic Pr.) Scholastic, Inc.
Lindquist, Susan H. Summer Soldiers. 1999. (Illus.). 192p. (gr. 5-9). text 14.95 o.s.i (*0-385-32641-6*, Dell Books for Young Readers) Random Hse. Children's Bks.
Lindquist, Susan Hart. Summer Soldiers. 2000. 192p. (gr. 5-9). pap. text 4.50 o.s.i (*0-440-41537-3*, Yearling) Random Hse. Children's Bks.
—Summer Soldiers. 2000. 10.55 (*0-606-19132-1*) Turtleback Bks.
Lutz, Norma Jean. The Great War. 36th ed. 1998. (American Adventure Ser.: No. 36). (Illus.). (J). (gr. 3-7). pap. 3.97 (*1-57748-411-8*) Barbour Publishing, Inc.
Martin, Les, adapted by. Prisoner of War. 1993. (Young Indiana Jones Chronicles: No. 8). (Illus.). 136p. (Orig.). (J). (gr. 4-6). pap. 3.50 o.s.i (*0-679-84389-2*, Random Hse. Bks. for Young Readers) Random Hse. Children's Bks.
McCutcheon, Elsie. Summer of the Zeppelin, RS. 1985. 168p. (J). (gr. 5 up). 11.95 o.p. (*0-374-37294-2*, Farrar, Straus & Giroux (BYR)) Farrar, Straus & Giroux.
Miller, Calvin. Snow. 1998. 160p. (YA). (gr. 8 up). 12.99 (*0-7642-2152-3*) Bethany Hse. Pubs.
Montgomery, L. M. Rilla of Ingleside. 1976. (Avonlea Ser.: No. 8). 286p. (YA). (gr. 5-8). 23.95 (*0-8488-0592-5*) Amereon, Ltd.
—Rilla of Ingleside. (Avonlea Ser.: No. 8). (YA). (gr. 5-8). 1987. 288p. mass mkt. 3.99 (*0-7704-2185-7*); 1985. 304p. mass mkt. 4.50 (*0-553-26922-4*) Bantam Bks.
—Rilla of Ingleside. unabr. ed. 1998. (Avonlea Ser.: No. 8). (YA). (gr. 5-8). audio 56.95 (*0-7861-1275-1*, 2172) Blackstone Audio Bks., Inc.
—Rilla of Ingleside. 1985. (Avonlea Ser.: No. 8). 288p. (YA). (gr. 5-8). mass mkt. 2.95 o.s.i (*0-553-25241-0*, Starfire) Random Hse. Children's Bks.
—Rilla of Ingleside. 1997. (Avonlea Ser.: No. 8). (Illus.). (YA). (gr. 5-8). 7.99 (*0-517-18083-9*) Random Hse. Value Publishing.
—Rilla of Ingleside. 1985. (Avonlea Ser.: No. 8). (YA). (gr. 5-8). 10.04 (*0-606-00747-4*) Turtleback Bks.
Morpurgo, Michael. Farm Boy. 1999. (Illus.). 74p. (YA). pap. 16.95 (*1-86205-192-5*) Pavilion Bks., Ltd. GBR. *Dist:* Trafalgar Square.
Myers, Anna. The Fire in the Hills. 1998. (Puffin Novel Ser.). 176p. (J). (gr. 7-12). pap. 5.99 o.s.i (*0-14-130074-4*, Puffin Bks.) Penguin Putnam Bks. for Young Readers.
Newbery, Linda. The Shell House. 2002. 352p. (J). (gr. 7-11). 15.95 (*0-385-75011-0*) Doubleday Publishing.
—The Shell House. 2004. 352p. (YA). (gr. 7-11). mass mkt. 6.50 (*0-440-23786-6*, Laurel Leaf) Random Hse. Children's Bks.
Olesky, Walter. The Golden Goat. 1981. (Voyager Ser.). (gr. 5-8). pap. 2.95 o.p. (*0-8010-6700-6*) Baker Bks.
Oneal, Zibby. A Long Way to Go: A Story of Women's Right to Vote. (Once upon America Ser.). (Illus.). 64p. (J). (gr. 2-6). 1992. pap. 4.99 (*0-14-032950-1*, Puffin Bks.); 1990. 11.95 o.p. (*0-670-82532-8*, Viking Children's Bks.) Penguin Putnam Bks. for Young Readers.
—A Long Way to Go: A Story of Women's Right to Vote. 1992. (Once upon America Ser.). (J). (gr. 2-6). 11.14 (*0-606-01718-6*) Turtleback Bks.
Rabin, Staton. Casey over There. 1994. (Illus.). 32p. (J). (ps-3). 14.95 (*0-15-253186-6*) Harcourt Trade Pubs.
Remarque, Erich Maria. All Quiet on the Western Front: With Related Readings. Wheen, A. W., tr. from GER. 2002. (EMC Masterpiece Series Access Editions). (Illus.). xxv, 249p. (YA). 14.60 (*0-8219-2420-6*) EMC/Paradigm Publishing.
Skurzynski, Gloria. Good-Bye, Billy Radish. 1992. (Illus.). 160p. (YA). (gr. 5 up). lib. bdg. 15.00 (*0-02-782921-9*, Simon & Schuster Children's Publishing) Simon & Schuster Children's Publishing.
Sonderling, Eric. A Knock at the Door. 1997. (Publish-a-Book Ser.). (Illus.). (J). (ps-3). 32p. lib. bdg. 22.83 (*0-8172-4434-4*); 28p. pap. 5.95 (*0-8172-7211-9*) Raintree Pubs.
Voigt, Cynthia. Tree by Leaf. 1989. 176p. (J). (gr. 7 up). mass mkt. 4.50 o.s.i (*0-449-70334-7*, Fawcett) Ballantine Bks.
—Tree by Leaf. (J). (gr. 4-7). 2000. 240p. pap. 4.99 (*0-689-83527-2*, Aladdin); 1988. 208p. 15.95 (*0-689-31403-5*, Atheneum) Simon & Schuster Children's Publishing.
—Tree by Leaf. 1989. (J). 9.60 o.p. (*0-606-01223-0*) Turtleback Bks.
Welch, Ronald. Tank Commander. 1974. 192p. (J). (gr. 6-10). 6.95 o.p. (*0-8407-6388-3*, Dutton Children's Bks.) Penguin Putnam Bks. for Young Readers.
Wells, Rosemary. The Language of Doves. 1996. (Illus.). 32p. (J). (ps-3). 14.99 o.p. (*0-8037-1471-8*); 14.89 o.p. (*0-8037-1472-6*) Penguin Putnam Bks. for Young Readers. (Dial Bks. for Young Readers).
—Waiting for the Evening Star. 1993. (Illus.). (J). (gr. k-3). 400p. 15.00 o.s.i (*0-8037-1398-3*); 32p. 14.89 o.p. (*0-8037-1399-1*) Penguin Putnam Bks. for Young Readers. (Dial Bks. for Young Readers).

WORLD WAR, 1939-1945—FICTION

Ackerman, Karen. When Mama Retires. 1992. (Illus.). 40p. (J). (ps-3). 15.00 o.s.i (*0-679-80289-4*); 15.99 o.s.i (*0-679-90289-9*) Random Hse. Children's Bks. (Knopf Bks. for Young Readers).
Anderson, Margaret J. Searching for Shona. 1978. (J). (gr. 5-8). 6.95 o.p. (*0-394-83724-X*); lib. bdg. 6.99 o.p. (*0-394-93724-4*) Random Hse. Children's Bks. (Knopf Bks. for Young Readers).
Anderson, Rachel. Paper Faces. l.t. ed. 1993. 216p. (J). 13.95 o.p. (*0-7451-1683-3*, Galaxy Children's Large Print) BBC Audiobooks America.
—Paper Faces, ERS. 1993. 88p. (J). (gr. 4-7). 14.95 o.p. (*0-8050-2527-8*, Holt, Henry & Co. Bks. For Young Readers) Holt, Henry & Co.
Arnothy, Christine. I Am Fifteen—& I Don't Want to Die. 1986. 128p. (J). (gr. 7 up). reprint ed. pap. 2.50 o.p. (*0-590-40322-2*, Scholastic Paperbacks) Scholastic, Inc.
Attema, Martha. Daughter of Light. 2001. (Young Reader Ser.). (Illus.). 144p. (J). (gr. 3-6). pap. 4.99 (*1-55143-179-3*) Orca Bk. Pubs.
—Daughter of Light. 2001. (J). 11.04 (*0-606-22770-9*) Turtleback Bks.
Avi. Don't You Know There's a War On? 208p. (J). 2003. pap. 5.99 (*0-380-81544-3*, Harper Trophy); 2001. (gr. 3 up). lib. bdg. 16.89 (*0-06-029214-8*) HarperCollins Children's Bk. Group.

Historical Events

Haugaard, Erik Christian. The Little Fishes. 1967. (Illus.). (J). (gr. 6-8). 6.95 o.p. *(0-395-06802-9)* Houghton Mifflin Co.

Heneghan, James. Wish Me Luck, RS. 1997. 195p. (J). (gr. 7-12). 16.00 o.p. *(0-374-38453-3,* Farrar, Straus & Giroux (BYR)) Farrar, Straus & Giroux.

Hermes, Patricia. In God's Novel. 2000. (Illus.). (J). 15.95 *(0-7614-5074-2)* Cavendish, Marshall Corp.

—Sweet by & By. 2002. 208p. (J). (gr. 3-6). 15.99 *(0-380-97452-5)* HarperCollins Pubs.

Hertenstein, Jane. Beyond Paradise. 1999. (Illus.). 168p. (YA). (gr. 7 up). 16.00 *(0-688-16381-5,* Morrow, William & Co.) Morrow/Avon.

Hesse, Karen. Aleutian Sparrow. unabr. ed. 2003. (J). (gr. 7). audio 12.99 *(0-8072-1966-5,* Listening Library) Random Hse. Audio Publishing Group.

—Aleutian Sparrow. 2003. (Illus.). 160p. (J). (gr. 5-9). 16.95 *(0-689-86189-3,* McElderry, Margaret K.) Simon & Schuster Children's Publishing.

Hest, Amy. Love You, Soldier. 1993. 4p. (J). (gr. 4-7). pap. 4.99 o.p. *(0-14-036174-X,* Puffin Bks.) Penguin Putnam Bks. for Young Readers.

—Love You, Soldier. 1991. 48p. (J). (gr. 2-5). text 13.95 o.p. *(0-02-743635-7,* Simon & Schuster Children's Publishing) Simon & Schuster Children's Publishing.

—Love You, Soldier. 1993. 11.14 *(0-606-02730-0)* Turtleback Bks.

Hest, Amy & Lamut, Sonja. Love You, Soldier. 2000. (Illus.). 80p. (J). (gr. 3-7). 14.99 o.s.i *(0-7636-0943-9)* Candlewick Pr.

Higa, Tomiko. The Girl with the White Flag. Britton, Dorothy, tr. 1992. (Illus.). 144p. (J). (gr. 5 up). pap. 3.50 o.s.i *(0-440-40720-6,* Yearling) Random Hse. Children's Bks.

Hoffman, Emily Allen. A Friend of the Enemy. 2003. 108p. (J). pap. 7.95 *(1-57249-312-7,* WM Kids) White Mane Publishing Co., Inc.

Holder, Nancy. Pearl Harbor 1941. 2001. (Illus.). 208p. (YA). (gr. 9-12). pap. 4.99 *(0-671-03927-X,* Simon Pulse) Simon & Schuster Children's Publishing.

Holm, Anne S. North to Freedom. 1999. (Illus.). (J). (gr. 4-7). pap. 13.40 *(0-8335-1289-7)* Econo-Clad Bks.

—North to Freedom. 1990. 256p. (YA). (gr. 4-7). pap. 6.00 *(0-15-257553-7,* Odyssey Classics) Harcourt Children's Bks.

—North to Freedom. Kingsland, L. W., tr. (YA). (gr. 7 up). 1965. 5.95 o.p. *(0-15-257550-2)*; 1974. 190p. reprint ed. pap. 5.95 o.p. *(0-15-666100-4,* Voyager Bks./Libros Viajeros) Harcourt Children's Bks.

—North to Freedom. 1984. (J). (gr. 5-9). 17.55 o.p. *(0-8446-6156-2)* Smith, Peter Pub., Inc.

—North to Freedom. 1965. (J). 12.05 *(0-606-02214-7)* Turtleback Bks.

Holmes, Mary Z. Dear Dad. 1992. (History's Children Ser.). (Illus.). 48p. (J). (gr. 4-5). pap. o.p. *(0-8114-6428-8)*; lib. bdg. 21.36 o.p. *(0-8114-3503-2)* Raintree Pubs.

Holt, Gerald. Tails of Flame. unabr. ed. 1996. 242p. (J). (gr. 3-6). mass mkt. 4.95 *(0-7736-7431-4)* Stoddart Kids CAN. *Dist:* Fitzhenry & Whiteside, Ltd.

Hoobler, Dorothy & Hoobler, Thomas. The 1940s: Secrets. 2001. (Century Kids Ser.). (Illus.). 160p. (YA). (gr. 5-8). 22.90 *(0-7613-1604-3)* Millbrook Pr., Inc.

Houston, Gloria M. But No Candy. 1992. (Illus.). 32p. (J). (ps-3). 14.95 o.p. *(0-399-22142-5,* Philomel) Penguin Putnam Bks. for Young Readers.

Hughes, Dean. Soldier Boys. (YA). 2003. (Illus.). 240p. mass mkt. 4.99 *(0-689-86021-8,* Simon Pulse); 2001. 176p. (gr. 4-6). 16.95 *(0-689-81748-7,* Atheneum) Simon & Schuster Children's Publishing.

Hughes, Monica. Blaine's Way. 1.t. ed. 1989. 334p. lib. bdg. 11.95 o.p. *(1-85057-581-9,* Macmillan Reference USA) Gale Group.

—Blaine's Way. 1996. 224p. (YA). (gr. 7 up). mass mkt. 4.95 *(0-7736-7445-4)* Stoddart Kids CAN. *Dist:* Fitzhenry & Whiteside, Ltd.

Hughes, Shirley. The Lion & the Unicorn. 1999. (Illus.). 64p. (J). (gr. 2-6). pap. 17.95 o.p. *(0-7894-2555-6,* D K Ink) Dorling Kindersley Publishing, Inc.

Hyman, John H. The Relationship. 1995. (Illus.). 251p. (YA). (gr. 7 up). 16.95 *(1-880664-14-3)* E. M. Productions.

Icenoggle, Jodi. America's Betrayal. 2001. 208p. (J). (gr. 7 up). 7.95 *(1-57249-252-X,* WM Kids) White Mane Publishing Co., Inc.

Innocenti, Roberto. Rose Blanche. 32p. 17.00 *(1-56846-189-5)* Creative Co., The.

—Rose Blanche. 1996. (J). 17.00 o.s.i *(0-15-201607-4)* Harcourt Children's Bks.

—Rose Blanche. Gallaz, Christophe, ed. 1996. (Illus.). 32p. (J). pap. 8.00 o.p. *(0-15-200917-5)*; 17.00 o.p. *(0-15-200918-3)* Harcourt Trade Pubs.

—Rose Blanche. 1991. (Illus.). 32p. (YA). (gr. 2 up). 15.95 o.p. *(1-55670-207-8)* Stewart, Tabori & Chang.

—Rose Blanche. 1996. 13.20 o.p. *(0-606-10913-7)* Turtleback Bks.

Innocenti, Roberto & Gallaz, Christophe. Rose Blanche: Based on the Original Idea of Roberto Innocenti. Coventry, Martha, tr. from FRE. 1995. (Illus.). 32p. (YA). (gr. 6 up). lib. bdg. 22.60 o.p. *(0-87191-994-X,* Creative Education) Creative Co., The.

Isaacs, Anne. Tom Thread. 2002. 192p. (YA). mass mkt. 4.99 *(0-590-60364-7,* Scholastic Paperbacks); 2000. (Illus.). 188p. (J). (gr. 5-9). pap. 15.95 o.p. *(0-590-60363-9,* Scholastic Reference) Scholastic, Inc.

Johnston, Tony. The Harmonica. 2004. (J). *(1-57091-547-4)* Charlesbridge Publishing, Inc.

Keefer, Janice Kulyk. Anna's Goat. 2001. (Illus.). 32p. (J). (ps-3). 15.95 *(1-55143-153-X)* Orca Bk. Pubs.

Keneally, Thomas. Schindler's List. 1994. 528p. pap. 6.50 o.s.i *(0-671-51171-8,* Touchstone) Simon & Schuster.

Kerr, Judith. When Hitler Stole Pink Rabbit. 1997. Tr. of Cuando Hitler Robo el Conejo Rosa. (Illus.). 192p. (J). (gr. 3-7). pap. 5.99 *(0-698-11589-9,* PaperStar) Penguin Putnam Bks. for Young Readers.

—When Hitler Stole Pink Rabbit. 1972. Tr. of Cuando Hitler Robo el Conejo Rosa. (Illus.). (YA). (gr. 6 up). 14.95 o.p. *(0-698-20182-5,* Coward-McCann) Putnam Publishing Group, The.

—When Hitler Stole Pink Rabbit. 1987. Tr. of Cuando Hitler Robo el Conejo Rosa. 192p. (J). (gr. 3 up). pap. 3.99 o.p. *(0-440-49017-0,* Yearling) Random Hse. Children's Bks.

—When Hitler Stole Pink Rabbit. 1997. Tr. of Cuando Hitler Robo el Conejo Rosa. (J). 11.04 *(0-606-12845-X)* Turtleback Bks.

Kerr, M. E. Slap Your Sides. 208p. (J). (gr. 7 up). 2003. pap. 5.99 *(0-06-447274-4)*; 2001. 15.95 *(0-06-029481-7)*; 2001. lib. bdg. 16.89 *(0-06-029482-5)* HarperCollins Children's Bk. Group.

King-Smith, Dick. The Crowstarver. 1.t. ed. 2000. (J). (Illus.). pap. *(0-7540-6095-0)*; 216p. pap. incl. audio *(0-7540-6228-7,* RA029, Chivers Children's Audio Bks.) BBC Audiobooks America.

—Spider Sparrow. unabr. ed. 2000. (J). (gr. 4-6). 176p. 35.00 incl. audio *(0-8072-8407-6)*; audio 30.00 *(0-8072-8406-8)* Random Hse. Audio Publishing Group. (Listening Library).

—Spider Sparrow. 2001. 176p. (gr. 5 up). pap. text 4.99 *(0-440-41664-7,* Yearling) Random Hse. Children's Bks.

—Spider Sparrow. 2002. (YA). (gr. 5-9). 20.50 *(0-8446-7221-1)* Smith, Peter Pub., Inc.

—Spider Sparrow. 2001. (Illus.). (J). 11.04 *(0-606-21445-3)* Turtleback Bks.

Klar, Elizabeth. Lily's Crossing. Robbins, Dawn Michelle, ed. 2000. (J). 9.95 *(1-58130-644-X)*; 11.95 *(1-58130-645-8)* Novel Units, Inc.

Kochenderfer, Lee. The Victory Garden. Date not set. 176p. (J). pap. text 4.99 *(0-440-41703-1,* Yearling) Dell Bks. for Young Readers CAN. *Dist:* Random Hse. of Canada, Ltd.

—The Victory Garden. 2002. (Illus.). 176p. (gr. 3-7). text 14.95 *(0-385-32788-9,* Delacorte Pr.) Dell Publishing.

Kudlinski, Kathleen V. Pearl Harbor Is Burning! A Story of World War II. 1993. (Once upon America Ser.). (Illus.). 64p. (J). (gr. 2-6). pap. 4.99 *(0-14-034509-4,* Puffin Bks.) Penguin Putnam Bks. for Young Readers.

Laird, Christa. But Can the Phoenix Sing? 1995. 224p. (YA). (gr. 7 up). 16.00 o.s.i *(0-688-13612-5,* Greenwillow Bks.) HarperCollins Children's Bk. Group.

—Shadow of the Wall. 1990. 144p. (YA). (gr. 7 up). 12.95 o.p. *(0-688-09336-1,* Greenwillow Bks.) HarperCollins Children's Bk. Group.

—Shadow of the Wall. 1997. 144p. (gr. 6-12). mass mkt. 4.95 *(0-688-15291-0,* Morrow, William & Co.) Morrow/Avon.

—Shadow of the Wall. 1997. 11.00 *(0-606-11832-2)* Turtleback Bks.

Lee, Milly. Nim & the War Effort. (Illus.). (J). 1997. o.p. *(0-374-22262-2)*; RS. 2002. 40p. pap. 5.95 *(0-374-45506-6,* Sunburst); RS. 1997. 40p. (gr. 1 up). 16.00 *(0-374-35523-1,* Farrar, Straus & Giroux (BYR)) Farrar, Straus & Giroux.

LeSourd, Nancy. The Personal Correspondence of Catherine Clark & Meredith Lyons. 2004. 224p. 9.99 *(0-310-70353-0)* Zondervan.

Levin, Jane W. Star of Danger. 1966. (Illus.). (J). (gr. 7 up). 5.50 o.p. *(0-15-279380-1)* Harcourt Children's Bks.

Levitin, Sonia. Room in the Heart. 2003. 304p. (J). 16.99 *(0-525-46871-4,* Dutton Children's Bks.) Penguin Putnam Bks. for Young Readers.

Lingard, Joan. Tug of War. 1992. 208p. (J). (gr. 5 up). pap. 4.50 o.p. *(0-14-036072-7,* Puffin Bks.); 1990. 20p. (YA). (gr. 7 up). 15.00 o.p. *(0-525-67306-7,* Dutton Children's Bks.) Penguin Putnam Bks. for Young Readers.

Lisle, Janet Taylor. The Art of Keeping Cool. (Illus.). (J). (gr. 5-9). 2002. 256p. pap. 4.99 *(0-689-83788-7,* Aladdin); 2000. 216p. 17.00 *(0-689-83787-9,* Atheneum/Richard Jackson Bks.) Simon & Schuster Children's Publishing.

—The Art of Keeping Cool. 1.t. ed. 2001. 207p. (J). 21.95 *(0-7862-3427-X)* Thorndike Pr.

—Sirens & Spies. 2002. (Illus.). 224p. (YA). (gr. 5 up). pap. 4.99 *(0-689-84457-3,* Aladdin); 1985. 192p. (J). (gr. 7 up). lib. bdg. 14.95 o.p. *(0-02-759150-6,* Simon & Schuster Children's Publishing) Simon & Schuster Children's Publishing.

—Sirens & Spies. 1.t. ed. 2003. (Young Adult Ser.). 22.95 *(0-7862-5378-9)* Thorndike Pr.

Little, Jean. Listen for the Singing. 1977. (J). (gr. 5-7). 9.95 o.p. *(0-525-33705-9,* Dutton) Dutton/Plume.

Littlesugar, Amy. Lisette's Angel. 2002. (Illus.). 32p. (J). (gr. 2-4). 15.99 *(0-8037-2435-7,* Dial Bks. for Young Readers) Penguin Putnam Bks. for Young Readers.

Lowry, Lois. Autumn Street, 001. 1980. 192p. (J). (gr. 4-6). tchr. ed. 16.00 *(0-395-27812-0)* Houghton Mifflin Co.

—Autumn Street. 1980. 10.55 *(0-606-02576-6)* Turtleback Bks.

—Number the Stars. (J). 1996. 144p. mass mkt. 2.49 o.s.i *(0-440-22033-5)*; 1994. 144p. pap. 3.99 *(0-440-91002-1)*; 1992. 144p. (gr. 4-7). mass mkt. 1.99 o.s.i *(0-440-21372-X)*; 1990. 144p. pap. 3.50 o.s.i *(0-440-70031-0)*; 1990. pap. o.p. *(0-440-80164-8)* Dell Publishing.

—Number the Stars. (J). 1995. (gr. 6). 9.28 *(0-395-73270-0)*; 1992. (gr. 6). pap. 11.04 *(0-395-61834-7)*; 1989. 144p. (gr. 4-6). tchr. ed. 16.00 *(0-395-51060-0)* Houghton Mifflin Co.

—Number the Stars. 1992. (J). pap. 3.50 *(0-440-80291-1,* Dell Books for Young Readers); 1990. 144p. (gr. 5-9). pap. text 5.99 *(0-440-40327-8,* Yearling); 1998. 144p. (YA). (gr. 4-7). reprint ed. mass mkt. 5.99 *(0-440-22753-4,* Laurel Leaf) Random Hse. Children's Bks.

—Number the Stars. (J). 1998. 12.04 *(0-606-13670-3)*; 1989. 12.04 *(0-606-04493-0)* Turtleback Bks.

—Number the Stars - Musical. 1998. 33p. pap. 5.95 *(0-87129-834-1,* N03) Dramatic Publishing Co.

—Quien Cuenta las Estrellas. 5th ed. 1998. (SPA., Illus.). 152p. (J). 8.95 *(84-239-8867-8)* Espasa Calpe, S.A. ESP. *Dist:* Continental Bk. Co., Inc.

Lurie, April. Dancing in the Streets of Brooklyn. 2002. 208p. lib. bdg. 17.99 *(0-385-90066-X)*; (gr. 3-7). text 15.95 *(0-385-72942-1)* Random Hse., Inc.

Maguire, Gregory. The Good Liar. 1999. 144p. (J). (gr. 5-9). tchr. ed. 15.00 *(0-395-90697-0,* Clarion Bks.) Houghton Mifflin Co. Trade & Reference Div.

Manley, Joan B. She Flew No Flags. 1995. 272p. (YA). (gr. 7-7). tchr. ed. 16.00 *(0-395-71130-4)* Houghton Mifflin Co.

Marko, Katherine M. Hang Out the Flag. 1992. 160p. (J). (gr. 3-7). text 13.95 o.p. *(0-02-762320-3,* Simon & Schuster Children's Publishing) Simon & Schuster Children's Publishing.

Marx, Trish. Hanna's Cold Winter. 1993. (Illus.). 32p. (J). (ps-3). lib. bdg. 15.95 o.s.i *(0-87614-772-4,* Carolrhoda Bks.) Lerner Publishing Group.

Matas, Carol. Greater Than Angels. 1998. Orig. Title: Contagion of Good. 160p. (J). (gr. 7-12). pap. 16.00 *(0-689-81353-8,* Simon & Schuster Children's Publishing) Simon & Schuster Children's Publishing.

—In My Enemy's House. 176p. (gr. 7-12). 2000. (YA). pap. 4.99 *(0-689-82400-9,* Simon Pulse); 1999. (J). per. 16.00 *(0-689-81354-6,* Simon & Schuster Children's Publishing) Simon & Schuster Children's Publishing.

Matus, Joel. Leroy & the Caveman. 1993. 144p. (J). (gr. 3-7). 13.95 o.s.i *(0-689-31812-X,* Atheneum) Simon & Schuster Children's Publishing.

Mazer, Harry. The Last Mission. (Laurel-Leaf Historical Fiction Ser.). (gr. 7 up). 1981. 192p. (YA). mass mkt. 5.50 *(0-440-94797-9,* Laurel); 1979. (J). 7.95 o.s.i *(0-440-05774-4,* Delacorte Pr.) Dell Publishing.

—The Last Mission. 192p. (YA). (gr. 7 up). pap. 4.99 *(0-8072-1366-7,* Listening Library) Random Hse. Audio Publishing Group.

—Last Mission. 1979. (Laurel-Leaf Historical Fiction Ser.). 11.04 *(0-606-02154-X)* Turtleback Bks.

McNaughton, Janet. Make or Break Spring. 1999. 192p. (YA). (gr. 7 up). pap. *(1-895387-93-0)* Creative Bk. Publishing.

McSwigan, Marie. Snow Treasure. 1967. (Illus.). (J). (gr. 3-7). 9.95 o.p. *(0-525-39556-3,* Dutton) Dutton/Plume.

—Snow Treasure. 9999. (Illus.). (J). (gr. 6-9). pap. 2.50 o.p. *(0-590-41148-9)* Scholastic, Inc.

Means, Florence C. The Moved-Outers. 1993. 156p. (J). pap. 7.95 *(0-8027-7386-9)* Walker & Co.

Michener, James A. South Pacific. 1992. (Performing Arts Ser.). (Illus.). 40p. (J). 16.95 o.s.i *(0-15-200618-4,* Gulliver Bks.) Harcourt Children's Bks.

Mochizuki, Ken. Baseball Saved Us. (Illus.). 32p. (J). 1997. (gr. 2 up). pap. 11.40 *(1-880000-19-9)*; 1993. (ps up). 15.95 *(1-880000-01-6)* Lee & Low Bks., Inc.

—Baseball Saved Us. 1993. 13.10 *(0-606-08914-4)* Turtleback Bks.

Morpurgo, Michael. Billy the Kid. 2000. (Illus.). 80p. (J). 22.95 *(1-86205-361-8)* Pavilion Bks., Ltd. GBR. *Dist:* Trafalgar Square.

Mullally, Frederic. Hitler Has Won. 1975. ix, 293p. (YA). 2.75 *(0-333-18428-9)* Macmillan U.K. GBR. *Dist:* Trans-Atlantic Pubns., Inc.

—Hitler Has Won: A Novel. 1975. 318p. (J). o.p. *(0-671-22074-8,* Simon & Schuster) Simon & Schuster.

Murphy, Claire Rudolf. Gold Star Sister. 176p. (J). (gr. 5-9). 1996. pap. 4.99 o.s.i *(0-14-037744-1,* Puffin Bks.); 1994. 14.99 o.p. *(0-525-67492-6,* Dutton Children's Bks.) Penguin Putnam Bks. for Young Readers.

Myers, Anna. Captain's Command. 2001. 144p. (gr. 4-7). pap. text 4.50 *(0-440-41699-X,* Yearling) Random Hse. Children's Bks.

—Captain's Command. 1999. 144p. (YA). (gr. 5-9). 15.95 *(0-8027-8706-1)* Walker & Co.

—Fire in the Hills. 1996. 192p. (YA). (gr. 7 up). 15.95 *(0-8027-8421-6)* Walker & Co.

Myers, Walter Dean. The Journal of Scott Pendleton Collins: A World War II Soldier: Normandy, France 1944. 1999. (My Name Is America Ser.). (Illus.). 140p. (J). (gr. 4-8). pap. 10.95 *(0-439-05013-8)* Scholastic, Inc.

Nanus, Susan & Kornblatt, Marc. Mission to World War Two. 1986. (Time Machine Ser.: No. 11). 144p. (Orig.). (J). (gr. 4 up). mass mkt. 2.25 o.s.i *(0-553-25431-6)* Bantam Bks.

Napoli, Donna Jo. Stones in Water. 224p. (YA). (gr. 5-9). 1997. 16.99 o.s.i *(0-525-45842-5,* Dutton Children's Bks.); 1999. (Illus.). reprint ed. pap. 5.99 *(0-14-130600-9,* Puffin Bks.) Penguin Putnam Bks. for Young Readers.

—Stones in Water. 1999. 11.04 *(0-606-17262-9)* Turtleback Bks.

Nolan, Peggy. The Spy Who Came in from the Sea. 2000. 129p. (J). (gr. 5-9). 14.95 *(1-56164-186-3)* Pineapple Pr., Inc.

Oberman, Sheldon. By the Hanukkah Light. 1997. (Illus.). 32p. (J). (gr. 1-4). 15.95 *(1-56397-658-7)* Boyds Mills Pr.

Olson, Gene. Drop into Hell. 1969. (YA). (gr. 8 up). 3.75 o.p. *(0-664-32436-3)* Westminster John Knox Pr.

Oppenheim, Shulamith L. The Lily Cupboard. 1992. (Charlotte Zolotow Bk.). (Illus.). 32p. (J). (gr. 1-3). 15.00 o.p. *(0-06-024669-3)*; lib. bdg. 14.89 o.p. *(0-06-024670-7)* HarperCollins Children's Bk. Group.

Orlev, Uri. The Island on Bird Street. Halkin, Hillel, tr. from HEB. 176p. (J). (gr. 4-6). 1992. pap. 6.95 *(0-395-61623-9)*; 1984. tchr. ed. 16.00 *(0-395-33887-5,* 5-92515) Houghton Mifflin Co.

—The Island on Bird Street. Halkin, Hillel, tr. from HEB. 1984. (J). 12.00 *(0-606-00521-8)* Turtleback Bks.

—Lydia: Queen of Palestine. Halkin, Hillel, tr. from HEB. 1993. Tr. of Lidyah: Malkat Erest Yisrael. 176p. (J). 13.95 o.p. *(0-395-65660-5)* Houghton Mifflin Co.

—Lydia, Queen of Palestine. Halkin, Hillel, tr. 1995. (Illus.). 176p. (J). (gr. 5-9). pap. 4.99 o.s.i *(0-14-037089-7,* Puffin Bks.) Penguin Putnam Bks. for Young Readers.

—Lydia, Queen of Palestine. 1995. 9.09 o.p. *(0-606-07817-7)* Turtleback Bks.

—The Man from the Other Side. Halkin, Hillel, tr. from HEB. 1991. 192p. (YA). (gr. 7-7). tchr. ed. 16.00 *(0-395-53808-4)* Houghton Mifflin Co.

—The Man from the Other Side. Halkin, Hillel, tr. from HEB. 1995. (Illus.). 192p. (J). (gr. 5-9). pap. 5.99 *(0-14-037088-9,* Puffin Bks.) Penguin Putnam Bks. for Young Readers.

—The Man from the Other Side. Halkin, Hillel, tr. from HEB. 1995. 11.04 *(0-606-07834-7)* Turtleback Bks.

Osborne, Mary Pope. My Secret War: The World War II Diary of Madeline Beck, Long Island, New York 1941. (Dear America Ser.). 2002. E-Book 9.95 *(0-439-42543-3)*; 2000. (Illus.). 185p. (J). (gr. 4-9). pap. 10.95 *(0-590-68715-8)* Scholastic, Inc.

Osborne, Mary Pope, et al. The Nation at War: World War II Collection: My Secret War, Early Sunday Morning; Journal of Ben Uchida; Journal of Scott Pendleton Collins, 4 vols. 2002. (Dear America Ser.). (J). pap. 19.96 *(0-439-12943-5)* Scholastic, Inc.

Oughton, Jerrie. The War in Georgia. 1997. 192p. (J). (gr. 7-10). tchr. ed. 14.95 o.p. *(0-395-81568-1)* Houghton Mifflin Co.

—The War in Georgia. 1999. 192p. (YA). (gr. 7 up). mass mkt. 4.50 o.s.i *(0-440-22752-6,* Dell Books for Young Readers) Random Hse. Children's Bks.

—The War in Georgia. 1999. 10.55 *(0-606-16444-8)* Turtleback Bks.

Park, Linda Sue. When My Name Was Keoko. 2002. 208p. (YA). (gr. 5-9). 16.00 (0-618-13335-6, Clarion Bks.) Houghton Mifflin Co. Trade & Reference Div.

—When My Name Was Keoko. 2004. (Illus.). 208p. (gr. 5). pap. 5.50 (0-440-41944-1, Yearling) Random Hse. Children's Bks.

Pastore, Clare. Aniela Kaminski's Story: A Voyage from Poland During World War II, No. 2. 2001. 192p. (J). (gr. 4-7). bds. 9.95 o.s.i (0-425-17784-X) Berkley Publishing Group.

—Journey to America: Aniela Kaminski's Story, Vol. 2. 2002. 192p. mass mkt. 5.99 (0-425-18816-7) Berkley Publishing Group.

Paterson, John & Kath. Blueberries for the Queen. 2004. (Illus.). (J). lib. bdg. (0-06-623943-5) HarperCollins Pubs.

Paterson, John & Paterson, Katherine. Blueberries for the Queen. Jeffers, Susan, tr. & illus. by. 2004. (J). (0-06-623942-7) HarperCollins Pubs.

Paterson, Katherine. Ame a Jacob: Jacob Have I Loved. 1995. (SPA.). 216p. (J). 11.50 o.p. (84-204-3649-6) Santillana USA Publishing Co., Inc.

Paton Walsh, Jill. Fireweed, RS. 1970. 144p. (J). (gr. 6 up). 14.95 o.p. (0-374-32310-0, Farrar, Straus & Giroux (BYR)) Farrar, Straus & Giroux.

Patterson, Don. Fighter Escort. Parenteau, Mary, ed. 1999. (Tales of the R. A. F. Ser.). (Illus.). 92p. (J). (gr. 3-8). per. 7.95 (1-929031-09-2) Hindsight, Ltd.

Paulsen, Gary. The Cookcamp. 1992. 128p. (gr. 5-6). pap. text 4.50 o.s.i (0-440-40704-4, Yearling); (J). pap. o.s.i (0-440-80301-2, Dell Books for Young Readers) Random Hse. Children's Bks.

—The Cookcamp. 128p. (J). 2003. pap. 4.99 (0-439-52357-5, Scholastic Paperbacks); 1991. (gr. 2-6). pap. 15.95 (0-531-05927-8, Orchard Bks.); 1991. (gr. 5-7). mass mkt. 16.99 o.p. (0-531-08527-9, Orchard Bks.) Scholastic, Inc.

—The Quilt. 2004. 96p. (YA). (gr. 3-7). 15.95 (0-385-72950-2); lib. bdg. 17.99 (0-385-90886-5) Random Hse. Children's Bks. (Lamb, Wendy).

Pausewang, Gudrun. Final Journey. Crampton, Patricia, tr. 1998. 160p. (YA). (gr. 7-12). pap. 5.99 (0-14-130104-X, Puffin Bks.) Penguin Putnam Bks. for Young Readers.

—Final Journey. 1996. 160p. (J). (gr. 7-12). 15.99 o.p. (0-670-86456-0) Penguin Putnam Bks. for Young Readers.

Pelgrom, Els. The Winter When Time Was Frozen. Rudnik, Maryka & Rudnik, Raphael, trs. from DUT. 1980. Tr. of De Kinderen Van Het Achtste Woud. 256p. (J). (gr. 4-6). 13.00 o.p. (0-688-22247-1); lib. bdg. 12.88 o.p. (0-688-32247-6) Morrow/Avon. (Morrow, William & Co.).

Pfeffer, Wendy. The Gooney War. 1990. (Illus.). 48p. (Orig.). (J). (gr. 2-6). pap. 5.95 o.p. (1-55870-155-9) Shoe Tree Pr.

Platt, Randall Beth. Honor Bright. 240p. (YA). (gr. 7-12). 1998. mass mkt. 4.50 o.s.i (0-440-21987-6, Laurel Leaf); 1997. 14.95 o.s.i (0-385-32216-X, Dell Books for Young Readers) Random Hse. Children's Bks.

—Honor Bright. 1998. 10.55 (0-606-13486-7) Turtleback Bks.

Polacco, Patricia. The Butterfly. 2000. (Illus.). 48p. (J). (ps-3). 16.99 (0-399-23170-6, Philomel) Penguin Putnam Bks. for Young Readers.

Poynter, Margaret. A Time Too Swift. 1990. 224p. (J). (gr. 5 up). lib. bdg. 14.95 o.p. (0-689-31146-X, Atheneum) Simon & Schuster Children's Publishing.

Propp, Vera W. When the Soldiers Were Gone. 1999. 112p. (YA). (gr. 5-9). 14.99 (0-399-23325-3) Penguin Group (USA) Inc.

Radin, Ruth Y. Escape to the Forest: Based on a True Story of the Holocaust. (Illus.). 96p. (J). (gr. 4 up). 2001. pap. 4.25 (0-06-440822-1); 2000. 14.99 (0-06-028520-6); 2000. lib. bdg. 13.89 (0-06-028521-4) HarperCollins Children's Bk. Group.

Redmond, Shirley-Raye. Pigeon Hero! 2003. (Ready-to-Reads Ser.). (Illus.). 32p. (J). pap. 3.99 (0-689-85486-2, Aladdin); lib. bdg. 11.89 (0-689-85487-0, Aladdin Library) Simon & Schuster Children's Publishing.

Reed, Nancy Amis. The Orphans of Normandy: A True Story of World War II Told Through Drawings by Children. 2003. (Illus.). 48p. (J). 17.95 (0-689-84143-4, Atheneum) Simon & Schuster Children's Publishing.

Reeder, Carolyn. Foster's War. 2000. 272p. (J). (gr. 4-7). pap. 4.50 (0-590-09856-X); 1998. 224p. (YA). (gr. 5-9). pap. 16.95 o.p. (0-590-09846-2) Scholastic, Inc.

Rees, David. The Exeter Blitz. 1980. (J). 7.95 o.p. (0-525-66683-4, Dutton Children's Bks.) Penguin Putnam Bks. for Young Readers.

Reid, Charles. Hurricanes over London. 2001. (Illus.). 152p. (J). (gr. 3-9). pap. 8.95 (0-921870-82-5) Ronsdale Pr. CAN. *Dist:* General Distribution Services, Inc.

Reiss, Johanna. The Journey Back. 1987. (Trophy Keypoint Bks.). 224p. (J). (gr. 5 up). pap. 5.99 (0-06-447042-3, Harper Trophy) HarperCollins Children's Bk. Group.

—The Upstairs Room. 1984. (J). mass mkt. 2.50 o.s.i (0-553-24784-0) Bantam Bks.

—The Upstairs Room. (gr. 7 up). 1990. 208p. (J). pap. 5.99 (0-06-440370-X, Harper Trophy); 1987. 196p. (YA). lib. bdg. 14.89 o.p. (0-690-04702-9); 1972. 208p. (J). 16.99 (0-690-85127-8) HarperCollins Children's Bk. Group.

—The Upstairs Room. 2000. (YA). pap., stu. ed. 49.20 incl. audio (0-7887-3659-0, 41025X4) Recorded Bks., LLC.

—The Upstairs Room. 1972. (J). 12.00 (0-606-04132-X) Turtleback Bks.

—Upstairs Room. 1987. (Trophy Keypoint Bks.). 192p. (J). (gr. 7 up). reprint ed. pap. 5.99 (0-06-447043-1, Harper Trophy) HarperCollins Children's Bk. Group.

Reuter, Bjarne. The Boys from St. Petri. 1994. 224p. (YA). (gr. 6 up). 15.99 o.s.i (0-525-45121-8, Dutton Children's Bks.) Penguin Putnam Bks. for Young Readers.

—Boys from St. Petri. 1996. 11.04 (0-606-08704-4) Turtleback Bks.

Rice, Mel. Secrets in the Sky. 2001. (Lone Star Heroine Ser.). (Illus.). 106p. (J). (gr. 4-7). pap. 8.95 (1-55622-787-6, Republic of Texas Pr.) Wordware Publishing, Inc.

Rinaldi, Ann. Keep Smiling Through. 1996. 208p. (YA). (gr. 3-7). 13.00 o.s.i (0-15-200768-7); (J). (gr. 4-7). pap. 6.00 (0-15-201072-6, Harcourt Paperbacks) Harcourt Children's Bks.

Riordan, James. The Enemy: A Story from World War II. 2002. (Survivors Ser.). 96p. (J). (gr. 5-8). pap. 4.95 (0-7641-2203-7); (Illus.). 12.95 (0-7641-5526-1) Barron's Educational Series, Inc.

Rogers, Kirby. Operation Dewey. 2002. (Illus.). ix, 100p. (J). pap. (1-877633-65-8) Luthers.

Roseman, Kenneth D. Escape from the Holocaust. 1985. (Do-It-Yourself Jewish Adventure Ser.). (Illus.). 192p. (J). (gr. 4-7). pap. 8.95 (0-8074-0307-5, 140070) UAHC Pr.

Rue, Nancy. The Discovery. 2001. (Christian Heritage Ser.). (Illus.). 192p. (J). (gr. 3-7). pap. 5.99 (1-56179-862-2) Focus on the Family Publishing.

Rue, Nancy N. The Mission. 2001. (Christian Heritage Ser.). 192p. (J). (gr. 3-8). pap. 5.99 o.s.i (1-56179-894-0) Focus on the Family Publishing.

—The Struggle. 2002. (Christian Heritage Ser.). 192p. (J). pap. 5.99 (1-56179-895-9) Bethany Hse. Pubs.

Rydberg, Ernie & Rydberg, Lou. The Shadow Army. 1976. 160p. (J). 7.95 o.p. (0-525-66493-9, Dutton Children's Bks.) Penguin Putnam Bks. for Young Readers.

Rylant, Cynthia. I Had Seen Castles. 1995. 112p. (YA). (gr. 7 up). pap. 5.00 (0-15-200374-6, Harcourt Paperbacks) Harcourt Children's Bks.

—I Had Seen Castles. 1993. 112p. (YA). (gr. 7 up). 10.95 o.s.i (0-15-238003-5) Harcourt Trade Pubs.

—I Had Seen Castles. 1995. 11.05 (0-606-07683-2) Turtleback Bks.

Salisbury, Graham. Under the Blood Red Sun. 1994. 256p. (gr. 6-8). text 15.95 o.s.i (0-385-32099-X, Delacorte Pr.) Dell Publishing.

—Under the Blood Red Sun. 1995. 256p. (gr. 5-8). pap. text 5.50 (0-440-41139-4, Yearling) Random Hse. Children's Bks.

—Under the Blood Red Sun. 1995. (J). 11.04 (0-606-08654-4) Turtleback Bks.

Savery, Constance. Enemy Brothers. 2001. (Living History Library). 304p. (J). (gr. 5-12). reprint ed. pap. 13.95 (1-883937-50-7, 50-7) Bethlehem Bks.

Savin, Marcia. The Moon Bridge. 1992. 176p. (J). (gr. 4-6). pap. 13.95 o.p. (0-590-45873-6) Scholastic, Inc.

Say, Allen. Home of the Brave. 2002. (Illus.). 32p. (J). lib. bdg. 17.00 (0-618-21223-X) Houghton Mifflin Co.

Schleimer, Sarah M. Far from the Place We Called Home. 1994. (J). 16.95 (0-87306-667-7) Feldheim, Philipp Inc.

Seabrooke, Brenda. Haunting at Stratton Falls. 2000. (Illus.). 160p. (J). (gr. 5-7). 15.99 (0-525-46389-5, Dutton Children's Bks.) Penguin Putnam Bks. for Young Readers.

Senje, Sigurd. Escape! Ramsden, Evelyn, tr. 1966. (YA). (gr. 7 up). pap. 1.25 o.p. (0-15-629041-3, Voyager Bks./Libros Viajeros) Harcourt Children's Bks.

Serraillier, Ian. Escape from Warsaw. 218p. (gr. 7-12). 1990. (Illus.). (YA). pap. 4.99 (0-590-43715-1); 1972. (J). reprint ed. pap. 2.50 o.p. (0-590-41176-4) Scholastic, Inc.

—Escape from Warsaw. 1972. 11.04 (0-606-03096-4) Turtleback Bks.

—The Silver Sword. 1959. (Illus.). (J). (gr. 7-9). 32.95 (0-87599-104-1) Phillips, S.G. Inc.

Sevela, Ephraim. Why There Is No Heaven on Earth. Lourie, Richard, tr. 1982. (RUS.). 224p. (YA). (gr. 7 up). (0-06-025502-1); lib. bdg. 10.89 o.p. (0-06-025503-X) HarperCollins Children's Bk. Group.

Shemin, Margaretha. The Little Riders. 1993. (Illus.). 80p. (J). (gr. 4 up). reprint ed. pap. 4.95 (0-688-12499-2) HarperCollins Children's Bk. Group.

Shirreffs, Gordon D. Torpedoes Away. 1967. (J). (gr. 6-8). 3.75 o.p. (0-664-32407-X) Westminster John Knox Pr.

Slasienski, Bruce E. Deep in My Polish Heart. 2000. 510p. E-Book 10.95 (1-929072-50-3) Booklocker-.com, Inc.

—Deep in My Polish Heart. 2000. 560p. pap. 26.99 (0-7388-2389-9); E-Book 8.00 (0-7388-8673-4) Xlibris Corp.

Slate, Joseph. Crossing the Trestle. 1999. (Accelerated Reader Bks.). 144p. (J). (gr. 3-7). 14.95 (0-7614-5053-X, Cavendish Children's Bks.) Cavendish, Marshall Corp.

Spinelli, Jerry. Milkweed. unabr. ed. 2003. (J). audio 25.00 (0-8072-1858-8, Listening Library) Random Hse. Audio Publishing Group.

—Milkweed. 2003. (Illus.). 224p. (J). (gr. 5). 15.95 (0-375-81374-8); lib. bdg. 17.99 (0-375-91374-2) Random Hse. Children's Bks.

Stevenson, James. Don't You Know There's a War On? 1992. (Illus.). 32p. (J). (gr. k-8). 14.00 o.p. (0-688-11383-4, Greenwillow Bks.) HarperCollins Children's Bk. Group.

—Don't You Know There's a War On. 1992. (Illus.). 32p. (J). (ps-3). lib. bdg. 15.89 (0-688-11384-2, Greenwillow Bks.) HarperCollins Children's Bk. Group.

Streatfeild, Noel. When the Sirens Wailed. 1976. (Illus.). (J). (gr. 4-6). 5.95 o.p. (0-394-83147-0); lib. bdg. 6.99 o.p. (0-394-93147-5) Random Hse. Children's Bks. (Random Hse. Bks. for Young Readers).

Summer of My German Soldier. 1999. (YA). 9.95 (1-56137-113-0) Novel Units, Inc.

Swindells, Robert. Blitzed. 2003. 176p. (J). pap. 8.95 (0-440-86397-X) Transworld Publishers Ltd. GBR. *Dist:* Trafalgar Square.

Taylor, Theodore. The Bomb. abr. ed. 1995. 208p. (YA). (gr. 7 up). 15.00 (0-15-200867-5) Harcourt Children's Bks.

—The Bomb. 1997. 176p. (J). (gr. 7 up). pap. 5.99 (0-380-72723-4, Harper Trophy) HarperCollins Children's Bk. Group.

—The Bomb. 1997. 11.04 (0-606-11146-8) Turtleback Bks.

Terlouw, Jan. Winter in Wartime. 1976. 144p. (J). (gr. 7-12). lib. bdg. 7.95 o.p. (0-07-063504-8) McGraw-Hill Cos., The.

Thesman, Jean. Molly Donnelly. 1993. 192p. (YA). (gr. 7-9). tchr. ed. 16.00 (0-395-64348-1) Houghton Mifflin Co.

—Molly Donnelly. 1994. 192p. (YA). mass mkt. 4.50 (0-380-72252-6, Avon Bks.) Morrow/Avon.

—Molly Donnelly. 1993. 9.60 o.p. (0-606-06574-1) Turtleback Bks.

Todd, Leonard. The Best Kept Secret of the War. 1984. 176p. (J). (gr. 4-7). 9.95 o.p. (0-394-86569-3, Knopf Bks. for Young Readers) Random Hse. Children's Bks.

Townsend, Tom. Nadia of the Night Witches. Kemnitz, Myrna, ed. 1998. 153p. (J). pap. 9.99 (0-88092-273-7, 2737) Royal Fireworks Publishing Co.

Treseder, Terry W. Hear O Israel: A Story of the Warsaw Ghetto. 1990. (Illus.). 48p. (J). (gr. 3 up). text 13.95 o.s.i (0-689-31456-6, Atheneum) Simon & Schuster Children's Publishing.

Trevor, William. Nights at the Alexandra. 1988. (Harper Short Novel Ser.). (Illus.). 80p. reprint ed. pap. 5.95 o.p. (0-06-091513-7, PL 1513, Perennial) HarperTrade.

Tripp, Valerie. Happy Birthday, Molly! A Springtime Story. Thieme, Jeanne, ed. 1987. (American Girls Collection: Bk. 4). (Illus.). 72p. (YA). (gr. 2 up). 12.95 o.p. (0-937295-36-1) Pleasant Co. Pubns.

—Meet Molly: An American Girl. Thieme, Jeanne, ed. 1986. (American Girls Collection: Bk. 1). (Illus.). 72p. (gr. 2 up). (J). lib. bdg. 12.95 (0-937295-81-7, American Girl); (YA). pap. 5.95 (0-937295-07-8, American Girl); (YA). 12.95 o.p. (0-937295-06-X) Pleasant Co. Pubns.

—Meet Molly: An American Girl. 1986. (American Girls Collection: Bk. 1). (Illus.). (YA). (gr. 2 up). 12.10 (0-606-02769-6) Turtleback Bks.

—Molly & the Movie Star. 2000. (American Girls Short Stories Ser.). (Illus.). 56p. (YA). (gr. 2 up). 3.95 (1-58485-036-1, American Girl) Pleasant Co. Pubns.

—Molly Learns a Lesson: A School Story. 1986. (American Girls Collection: Bk. 2). (Illus.). 80p. (YA). (gr. 2 up). pap. 5.95 (0-937295-16-7, American Girl) Pleasant Co. Pubns.

—Molly Learns a Lesson: A School Story. Thieme, Jeanne, ed. 1986. (American Girls Collection: Bk. 2). (Illus.). (gr. 2 up). 80p. (J). lib. bdg. 12.95 (0-937295-84-1, American Girl); 72p. (YA). 12.95 o.p. (0-937295-15-9) Pleasant Co. Pubns.

—Molly Learns a Lesson: A School Story. 1986. (American Girls Collection: Bk. 2). (Illus.). (YA). (gr. 2 up). 12.10 (0-606-02824-2) Turtleback Bks.

—Molly Saves the Day: A Summer Story. Thieme, Jeanne, ed. 2001. (Frequently Requested Ser.). lib. bdg. (1-59054-095-6) Fitzgerald Bks.

—Molly Takes Flight. 1999. (American Girls Short Stories Ser.). (Illus.). 56p. (YA). (gr. 2 up). 3.95 (1-56247-767-6, American Girl) Pleasant Co. Pubns.

—Molly's Short Story Set: Molly Takes Flight; Molly & the Movie Star; Molly's A+ Partner, 3 vols. 2002. (American Girls Short Stories Ser.). (Illus.). (YA). (gr. 2). 11.95 (1-58485-499-5, American Girl) Pleasant Co. Pubns.

—Molly's Story Collection. 2001. (American Girls Collection). (Illus.). 374p. (J). (gr. 2 up). 29.95 (1-58485-447-2, American Girl) Pleasant Co. Pubns.

—Molly's Surprise: A Christmas Story. Thieme, Jeanne, ed. 1986. (American Girls Collection: Bk. 3). (Illus.). (gr. 2 up). 80p. (J). lib. bdg. 12.95 (0-937295-87-6, American Girl); 80p. (YA). pap. 5.95 (0-937295-25-6, American Girl); 72p. (YA). 12.95 o.p. (0-937295-24-8) Pleasant Co. Pubns.

—Molly's Surprise: A Christmas Story. 1986. (American Girls Collection: Bk. 3). (Illus.). (YA). (gr. 2 up). 12.10 (0-606-02827-7) Turtleback Bks.

Tunnell, Michael O. Brothers in Valor: Story of Resistance. 2001. 260p. (J). (gr. 6-10). tchr. ed. 16.95 (0-8234-1541-4) Holiday Hse., Inc.

Turnbull, Ann. Room for a Stranger. 1996. 128p. (J). (gr. 5-9). 15.99 o.p. (1-56402-868-2) Candlewick Pr.

Uchida, Yoshiko. The Bracelet. 1993. (Illus.). 32p. (J). (ps-3). 16.99 (0-399-22503-X, Philomel) Penguin Putnam Bks. for Young Readers.

Van Steenwyk, Elizabeth. A Traitor among Us. 143p. (J). (gr. 4-7). 1999. pap. 6.00 (0-8028-5157-6); 1998. 15.00 (0-8028-5150-9) Eerdmans, William B. Publishing Co. (Eerdmans Bks For Young Readers).

—A Traitor among Us. 1999. 12.05 (0-606-17601-2) Turtleback Bks.

Van Stockum, Hilda. The Mitchells: Five for Victory. 1995. (Mitchells Ser.: Vol. 1). (Illus.). 250p. (J). (gr. 4-7). reprint ed. pap. 12.95 (1-883937-05-1, 05-1) Bethlehem Bks.

—The Winged Watchman. 1995. (Living History Library). (Illus.). 204p. (J). (gr. 4-7). reprint ed. pap. 12.95 (1-883937-07-8, 07-8) Bethlehem Bks.

—Winged Watchman, RS. (Illus.). 228p. (J). (gr. 4 up). 1985. pap. 3.45 o.p. (0-374-48405-8, Sunburst); 1963. 6.95 o.p. (0-374-38448-7, Farrar, Straus & Giroux (BYR)) Farrar, Straus & Giroux.

Vande Velde, Vivian. A Coming Evil. 1998. 212p. (J). (gr. 5-9). tchr. ed. 17.00 (0-395-90012-3) Houghton Mifflin Co.

Vander Els, Betty. The Bombers' Moon, RS. 1992. 168p. (J). (gr. 5 up). pap. 4.50 o.p. (0-374-40877-7, Sunburst) Farrar, Straus & Giroux.

Vos, Ida. Dancing on the Bridge of Avignon. Edelstein, Terese & Smidt, Inez, trs. from DUT. 1995. Tr. of Dansen ob de Brug van Avignon. 192p. (YA). (gr. 7-7). 14.95 (0-395-72039-7) Houghton Mifflin Co.

—Hide & Seek. Edelstein, Terese & Smidt, Inez, trs. 1991. Orig. Title: Wie Niet Weg Is Word Gezien. 144p. (J). (gr. 4-6). tchr. ed. 16.00 (0-395-56470-0) Houghton Mifflin Co.

—Hide & Seek. Edelstein, Terese & Smidt, Inez, trs. from DUT. 1995. Orig. Title: Wie Niet Weg Is Word Gezien. 144p. (J). (gr. 4-7). pap. 4.99 (0-14-036908-2, Puffin Bks.) Penguin Putnam Bks. for Young Readers.

—Hide & Seek. 1995. Orig. Title: Wie Niet Weg Is Word Gezien. 11.04 (0-606-07644-1) Turtleback Bks.

Walters, Eric. Caged Eagles. 2001. 244p. (gr. 7-11). (J). pap. 7.95 (1-55143-139-4); (YA). 15.95 (1-55143-182-3) Orca Bk. Pubs.

—War of the Eagles. 1998. 160p. (YA). (gr. 7-11). pap. 7.95 (1-55143-099-1); 14.00 (1-55143-118-1) Orca Bk. Pubs.

—War of the Eagles. 1998. 14.00 (0-606-16742-0) Turtleback Bks.

Watkins, Yoko Kawashima. So Far from the Bamboo Grove. 192p. (J). (gr. 3-6). 1986. 16.00 o.p. (0-688-06110-9); 1994. (Illus.). reprint ed. pap. 5.99 (0-688-13115-8, HarperTempest) HarperCollins Children's Bk. Group.

Watts, Irene N. Finding Sophie. 2002. 144p. (YA). (gr. 5). pap. 6.95 (0-88776-613-7) Tundra Bks. of Northern New York.

—Good-Bye, Marianne: A Story of Growing up in Nazi Germany. 1998. 112p. (J). (gr. 3-7). pap. 7.95 (0-88776-445-2) Tundra Bks. of Northern New York.

—Remember Me: A Search for Refuge in Wartime Britain. 2000. 192p. (YA). (gr. 5 up). pap. 7.95 (*0-88776-519-X*) Tundra Bks. of Northern New York.

Westall, Robert. Fathom Five. 1990. (YA). 17.25 o.p. (*0-8446-6664-5*) Smith, Peter Pub., Inc.

—The Kingdom by the Sea, RS. 1991. 176p. (J). (gr. 4-7). 15.00 o.p. (*0-374-34205-9*, Farrar, Straus & Giroux (BYR)) Farrar, Straus & Giroux.

—The Machine-Gunners. (J). 1997. (Illus.). 192p. (gr. 7 up). pap. 5.95 (*0-688-15498-0*, Harper Trophy); 1977. 186p. (gr. 5-9). lib. bdg. 13.93 o.p. (*0-688-84055-8*, Greenwillow Bks.); 1976. 186p. (gr. 5-9). 8.25 o.p. (*0-688-80055-6*, Greenwillow Bks.) HarperCollins Children's Bk. Group.

—Time of Fire. 1997. 176p. (J). (gr. 5-9). 15.95 (*0-590-47746-3*) Scholastic, Inc.

Wickham, Martha. A Golden Age: The Golden Age of Radio. 1996. (Smithsonian Odyssey Ser.). (Illus.). 32p. (J). (gr. 2-5). 19.95 incl. audio (*1-56899-373-0*, BC6004); (gr. 4-7). 14.95 (*1-56899-371-4*); (gr. 4-7). pap. 5.95 (*1-56899-372-2*);Incl. toy. (gr. 2-5). 29.95 (*1-56899-375-7*);Incl. toy. (gr. 2-5). pap. 17.95 (*1-56899-376-5*) Soundprints.

Wilhelm, Doug. Shadow of the Swastika. 1995. (Choose Your Own Adventure Ser.: No. 163). (J). (gr. 4-8). 8.60 o.p. (*0-606-08148-8*) Turtleback Bks.

Winter, Kathryn. Katarina. 1998. 272p. (J). (gr. 5-9). 17.00 o.p. (*0-374-33984-8*, Farrar, Straus & Giroux (BYR)) Farrar, Straus & Giroux.

—Katarina: A Novel. 1999. 257p. (gr. 6-8). mass mkt. 4.99 (*0-439-09904-8*) Scholastic, Inc.

Wolff, Virginia Euwer. Bat 6. 256p. (J). (gr. 4-6). pap. 4.99 (*0-8072-8223-5*); 2000. pap. 35.00 incl. audio (*0-8072-8222-7*, YYA144SP) Random Hse. Audio Publishing Group. (Listening Library).

—Bat 6. 240p. (YA). (gr. 5-9). 2000. (Illus.). mass mkt. 4.99 o.s.i (*0-590-89800-0*, Scholastic Reference); 1998. pap. 16.95 (*0-590-89799-3*) Scholastic, Inc.

—Bat 6. 2000. (Illus.). (J). 11.04 (*0-606-18516-X*) Turtleback Bks.

Woodford, Peggy. Backwater War, RS. 1975. 192p. (J). (gr. 7 up). 6.95 o.p. (*0-374-30477-7*, Farrar, Straus & Giroux (BYR)) Farrar, Straus & Giroux.

Wulffson, Don. Soldier X. 2003. 240p. (YA). pap. 6.99 (*0-14-250073-9*, Puffin Bks.) Penguin Putnam Bks. for Young Readers.

Wulffson, Don L. Soldier X. 2001. 244p. (J). (gr. 5-9). 16.99 (*0-670-88863-X*, Viking Children's Bks.) Penguin Putnam Bks. for Young Readers.

Yates, Elizabeth. American Haven. 2002. (Illus.). 112p. (J). (*1-57924-896-9*) Jones, Bob Univ. Pr.

Yep, Laurence. Hiroshima. 64p. (J). (gr. 4-7). 1996. mass mkt. 2.99 (*0-590-20833-0*); 1995. pap. 9.95 (*0-590-20832-2*) Scholastic, Inc.

—Hiroshima: A Novella. 1996. (J). 10.65 (*0-606-09414-8*) Turtleback Bks.

Ylvisaker, Anne. Dear Papa. 2002. 192p. (J). (gr. 5-8). 15.99 (*0-7636-1618-4*) Candlewick Pr.

Zindel, Paul. The Gadget. 2001. 192p. (J). (gr. 6 up). lib. bdg. 16.89 (*0-06-028255-X*) HarperCollins Children's Bk. Group.

—The Gadget. 2003. (Illus.). 192p. (YA). (gr. 7). mass mkt. 5.50 (*0-440-22951-0*, Laurel Leaf) Random Hse. Children's Bks.

MISCELLANEOUS

D

DRAGONS—FICTION

Adrian, Raeside. Dennis the Dragon. 1994. 32p. pap. 5.95 o.p. (*0-385-25431-8*) Doubleday Publishing.

Albee, Sarah. The Dragon's Scales. 1998. (Step into Reading & Math Step 2 Bks.). 48p. (J). (gr. k-3). lib. bdg. 11.99 (*0-679-98381-3*, Random Hse. Bks. for Young Readers) Random Hse. Children's Bks.

—The Dragon's Scales. 1998. (Step Into Reading & Math Bks.). (Illus.). 48p. (J). (gr. k-3). pap. 3.99 (*0-679-88381-9*) Random Hse., Inc.

—The Dragon's Scales. 1998. (Step into Reading & Math Step 2 Bks.). (J). (gr. 1-3). 10.14 (*0-606-13960-5*) Turtleback Bks.

Anderson, Bendix. Quetzal & the Cool School. 2000. (Dragon Tales Ser.). (Illus.). 24p. (J). (ps-k). pap. 3.25 o.p. (*0-375-80634-2*, Random Hse. Bks. for Young Readers) Random Hse. Children's Bks.

Awdry, Wilbert V. Thomas, Percy, & the Dragon. 1994. (Thomas the Tank Engine Photographic Board Bks.). (Illus.). 16p. (J). (ps). 3.99 o.s.i (*0-679-86183-1*, Random Hse. Bks. for Young Readers) Random Hse. Children's Bks.

Base, Graeme. The Discovery of Dragons. 1996. (Illus.). 36p. (gr. 5-7). 16.95 (*0-8109-3237-7*) Abrams, Harry N. , Inc.

Bass, Jules. Herb, the Vegetarian Dragon. 2000. (Illus.). 32p. (J). (gr. 1-5). reprint ed. pap. 5.99 (*1-84148-127-0*) Barefoot Bks., Inc.

—Herb, the Vegetarian Dragon. 2001. (J). 12.14 (*0-606-19750-8*) Turtleback Bks.

Baumgart, Klaus. Anna & the Little Green Dragon. 1992. (Little Green Dragon Ser.). (Illus.). 32p. (J). (ps-3). 12.95 o.s.i (*1-56282-166-0*); lib. bdg. 13.49 o.s.i (*1-56282-167-9*) Hyperion Bks. for Children.

—Anna & the Little Green Dragon. 1995. (Little Green Dragon Ser.). (Illus.). 32p. (J). (ps-3). pap. 4.95 o.s.i (*0-7868-1050-5*) Hyperion Paperbacks for Children.

—Anna & the Little Green Dragon. 1992. 10.15 o.p. (*0-606-07198-9*) Turtleback Bks.

—The Little Green Dragon Steps Out. 1992. (Little Green Dragon Ser.). (Illus.). 32p. (J). (ps-3). 12.95 (*1-56282-254-3*); lib. bdg. 13.49 o.s.i (*1-56282-255-1*) Hyperion Bks. for Children.

—The Little Green Dragon Steps Out. 1994. (Little Green Dragon Ser.). (Illus.). 32p. (J). (ps-3). pap. 4.95 o.s.i (*0-7868-1006-8*) Hyperion Paperbacks for Children.

Befelar, Roger. Too Many Dragons: Great Adventures. 1997. (Great Adventures Ser.). (Illus.). 24p. (Orig.). (J). (ps up). pap. 2.99 o.p. (*0-88743-451-7*, 06781) School Zone Publishing Co.

Bergsma, Jody Lynn. The Little Wizard. l.t. ed. 2000. (Illus.). 32p. (J). (ps-7). 15.95 (*0-935699-19-8*) Illumination Arts Publishing Co., Inc.

Bergsma, Jody Lynn, et al. Dragon. 1999. (Illus.). 32p. (J). (ps-7). 15.95 (*0-935699-17-1*) Illumination Arts Publishing Co., Inc.

Blake-Brekke, Carri. Panuk, Princess & Prince. 2002. (J). pap. (*0-9720549-1-X*) Mom's Pride Enterprises.

Bremer, Michael. Ronald Dragon: An Electronic Storybook. 2000. (Illus.). 32p. (J). (ps up). cd-rom 9.95 (*0-9669949-7-3*) UnTechnical Pr.

Broger, Achim. Historia de Dragolina (Story of Little Dragon) 4th ed. (SPA., Illus.). 32p. 14.95 (*84-261-1924-7*) Juventud, Editorial ESP. *Dist:* AIMS International Bks., Inc.

Brouillet, Chrystine. Mon Frere, le Dragon. 2001. (Premier Roman Ser.: 115). (FRE., Illus.). 64p. (J). pap. 8.95 (*2-89021-543-1*) La Courte Echelle CAN. *Dist:* Firefly Bks., Ltd.

Brouillet, Chrystine & Dion, Nathalie. Mon Frere, le Dragon. 2001. (FRE., Illus.). 64p. (J). pap. 8.95 (*2-89021-531-8*) La Courte Echelle CAN. *Dist:* Firefly Bks., Ltd.

Brovelli, Tito Alberto. Kiko, el Dragon Desobediente: Cuentos Bilingues. Anderson, Kirk, tr. 2000. Tr. of Kiko, the Disobedient Dragon: Bilingual Stories. (ENG & SPA., Illus.). 24p. (YA). (gr. k up). 14.95 (*0-9673032-2-2*) Sweet Dreams Bilingual Pubs.

Camp, Martin. Why Alligators Don't Have Wings. 1994. (Illus.). 32p. (J). (ps-5). 13.95 (*1-880092-06-9*) Bright Bks., Inc.

Carter, Angela. Sea-Cat & Dragon King. 2002. (Illus.). 93p. (J). (gr. 2-4). 12.95 (*1-58234-768-9*, Bloomsbury Children) Bloomsbury Publishing.

Carus, Marianne, ed. Fire & Wings: Dragon Tales from East & West. 2002. (Illus.). ix, 146p. (J). (gr. 4-7). 17.95 (*0-8126-2664-8*) Cricket Bks.

Cason, Sue. Dragon Trouble. 1999. (Supa Doopers Ser.). (Illus.). 64p. (J). (*0-7608-3289-7*) Sundance Publishing.

Cave, Kathryn. You've Got Dragons. 2003. (Illus.). (J). (gr. 1-5). 16.95 (*1-56145-284-X*) Peachtree Pubs., Ltd.

Charlotte Latin School Staff. Ann & the Dragon. 2001. 32p. (J). per. 4.95 (*0-9707920-0-X*) Charlotte's Storybooks.

Cherry, Lynne. The Dragon & the Unicorn. 1995. (Gulliver Green Book Ser.). (Illus.). 40p. (J). (gr. 1-5). 16.00 (*0-15-224193-0*, Gulliver Bks.) Harcourt Children's Bks.

—The Dragon & the Unicorn. 2001. (J). (gr. 1-5). pap. 17.95 incl. audio Spoken Arts, Inc.

—The Dragon & the Unicorn. 1998. 13.15 (*0-606-13347-X*) Turtleback Bks.

Christian, Peggy. The Bookstore Mouse. (Illus.). 144p. 2002. (YA). (gr. 3-7). pap. 5.95 (*0-15-204564-3*, Harcourt Paperbacks); 1995. (J). (gr. 4-7). 17.00 (*0-15-200203-0*) Harcourt Children's Bks.

Clark, John T. & Clark, Nicole K. Adventures in Dreamtime. l.t. ed. 1998. (Illus.). 32p. (J). (gr. k-2). 15.95 (*1-892176-12-2*) PremaNations Publishing.

Clark, Margaret. A Treasury of Dragon Stories. 2002. (Kingfisher Treasury of Stories Ser.: Vol. 13). (Illus.). 160p. (J). pap. 5.95 (*0-7534-5568-4*, Kingfisher) Houghton Mifflin Co. Trade & Reference Div.

—A Treasury of Dragon Stories. 1997. 13.00 (*0-606-16562-2*) Turtleback Bks.

Coleman, Sheila. Dinky, the Pint-Size Dragon. 1986. (Appleseed Ser.). 24p. (J). pap. 2.95 o.p. (*0-8407-6693-9*) Nelson, Thomas Inc.

Cooper, Susan. Matthew's Dragon. (Illus.). 32p. (J). (ps-3). 1991. 14.95 (*0-689-50512-4*, McElderry, Margaret K.); 1994. reprint ed. pap. 6.99 (*0-689-71794-6*, Aladdin) Simon & Schuster Children's Publishing.

—Matthew's Dragon. 1994. (J). 12.14 (*0-606-05921-0*) Turtleback Bks.

Cosgrove, Stephen. The Muffin Dragon. 2001. (Serendipity Bks.). (Illus.). 32p. (J). 4.99 (*0-8431-7687-3*, Price Stern Sloan) Penguin Putnam Bks. for Young Readers.

Coville, Bruce. The Dragonslayers. unabr. ed. 1998. 119p. (J). (gr. 3-5). pap. 23.00 incl. audio (*0-8072-7988-9*, YA958SP, Listening Library) Random Hse. Audio Publishing Group.

—The Dragonslayers. MacDonald, Patricia, ed. 1994. (Illus.). 128p. (J). (gr. 3-6). 14.00 (*0-671-89036-0*, Simon & Schuster Children's Publishing); (gr. 4-7). pap. 4.99 (*0-671-79832-4*, Aladdin) Simon & Schuster Children's Publishing.

—The Dragonslayers. 1994. (J). 10.04 (*0-606-06337-4*) Turtleback Bks.

—Jeremy Thatcher, Dragon Hatcher. 2002. (Magic Shop Bks.). (Illus.). 168p. (YA). (gr. 3-7). 17.00 (*0-15-204614-3*) Harcourt Children's Bks.

—Jeremy Thatcher, Dragon Hatcher. (J). 148p. (gr. 4-6). pap. 4.50 (*0-8072-1471-X*); 2000. (gr. 4-7). audio 18.00 (*0-8072-7559-X*); 1995. 148p. (gr. 3-6). pap. 28.00 incl. audio (*0-8072-7532-8*, YA873SP) Random Hse. Audio Publishing Group. (Listening Library).

—Jeremy Thatcher, Dragon Hatcher. 2001. 160p. (YA). mass mkt. 4.99 (*0-7434-3465-X*, Aladdin) Simon & Schuster Children's Publishing.

Cowell, Cressida, tr. How to Train Your Dragon. 2004. 224p. (J). 10.95 (*0-316-73737-2*) Little Brown & Co.

Deedy, Carmen Agra. The Library Dragon. 1994. (Illus.). 32p. (J). (gr. 4-7). 16.95 (*1-56145-091-X*) Peachtree Pubs., Ltd.

Demi, Hitz. Demi's Dragons & Fantastic Creatures, ERS. 1993. (Illus.). 88p. (J). (ps-2). 19.95 o.p. (*0-8050-2564-2*, Holt, Henry & Co. Bks. For Young Readers) Holt, Henry & Co.

Dennis, Anne. Taming the Diabetes Dragon. Mitchell, Barb, ed. 1998. (Illus.). 24p. (J). (gr. 3-7). pap. 14.95 (*1-891383-03-5*) JayJo Bks., LLC.

Dennis the Dragon. 1984. (Ladybird Bks.). (ARA., Illus.). 52p. (J). 4.95 (*0-86685-197-6*, LDL174) International Bk. Ctr., Inc.

Dennis the Dragon. 1990. (Ladybird Bks.). (ARA., Illus.). 14.95 incl. audio (*0-86685-198-4*, LDL119C) Librairie du Liban Pubns. FRA. *Dist:* International Bk. Ctr., Inc.

Dennis the Dragon. 9999. (Rhyming Stories Ser.: No. 401-16). (Illus.). (J). (ps). pap. 3.50 o.p. (*0-7214-0611-4*, Ladybird Bks.) Penguin Group (USA) Inc.

Dennis the Dragon Finds a New Job. 9999. (Rhyming Stories Ser.: No. 401-17). (Illus.). (J). (ps). pap. 3.50 o.p. (*0-7214-0753-6*, Ladybird Bks.) Penguin Group (USA) Inc.

Dixon, Andy, ed. En Busca del Dragon. 1998. (Fantasy Adventures Ser.).Tr. of Dragon Quest. (SPA., Illus.). (YA). 32p. (gr. 4-7). pap. 8.95 (*0-7460-3433-4*); 68p. (gr. 3 up). lib. bdg. 16.95 (*1-58086-207-1*) EDC Publishing. (Usborne).

Donaldson, Julia. Room on the Broom. (Illus.). 32p. (J). (gr. k-2). 2003. pap. 6.99 (*0-14-250112-3*, Puffin Bks.); 2001. 15.99 (*0-8037-2657-0*, Dial Bks. for Young Readers) Penguin Putnam Bks. for Young Readers.

Downer, Ann. Hatching Magic. 2003. 256p. (J). 16.95 (*0-689-02932-2*, Simon & Schuster Children's Publishing); (Illus.). (gr. 7). 16.95 (*0-689-83400-4*, Atheneum) Simon & Schuster Children's Publishing.

Dragon: Including Toy. 2001. (Jigsaw Ser.). 20p. (J). 7.95 (*968-5308-21-7*) Silver Dolphin Spanish Editions MEX. *Dist:* Publishers Group West.

Drake, Ernest, et al. Dragonology: The Complete Book of Dragons. 2003. (Illus.). 32p. (J). 18.99 (*0-7636-2329-6*) Candlewick Pr.

Ellis, Anne L. The Dragon of Middlethorpe, ERS. 1991. (Illus.). 192p. (J). (gr. 4-7). 14.95 o.p. (*0-8050-1713-5*, Holt, Henry & Co. Bks. For Young Readers) Holt, Henry & Co.

Escrivá, Vivi. Olmo & the Dragon. unabr. ed. 1997. (SPA., Illus.). 24p. (Orig.). (J). (gr. 3-10). pap. 9.95 (*1-56492-219-7*) Laredo Publishing Co., Inc.

Evslin, Bernard. The Dragon of Boeotia. 1987. (Monsters of Mythology Ser.). (Illus.). 104p. (J). (gr. 4-7). lib. bdg. 19.95 (*1-55546-246-4*) Chelsea Hse. Pubs.

Ferrone, John M. Gus & the Golden Dragon. Date not set. (Illus.). 36p. (ps-5). pap. 16.95 (*1-928811-02-7*) Story Stuff, Inc.

Fienberg, Anna & Fienberg, Barbara. The Big Big Big Book of Tashi. 2002. (Illus.). 448p. (J). (gr. 1-5). pap. 11.95 (*1-86508-563-4*) Allen & Unwin Pty., Ltd. AUS. *Dist:* Independent Pubs. Group.

Fletcher, Susan. Flight of the Dragon Kyn. 224p. (gr. 5-9). 1997. (J). pap. 4.99 (*0-689-81515-8*, Aladdin); 1993. (YA). 17.00 (*0-689-31880-4*, Atheneum) Simon & Schuster Children's Publishing.

—Flight of the Dragon Kyn. 1997. 11.04 (*0-606-12701-1*) Turtleback Bks.

Fontes, Ron. To Fly with Dragons. Kleinberg, Naomi, ed. 2000. (Sparkle Storybook Ser.). (Illus.). 32p. (J). (ps-3). 8.99 (*0-375-80661-X*, Random Hse. Bks. for Young Readers) Random Hse. Children's Bks.

Friedman, Jim. The Mysterious Misadventures of Foy Rin Jin: A Decidedly Dysfunctional Dragon. 1999. (Illus.). 32p. (J). (ps-3). lib. bdg. 15.89 (*0-06-028551-6*) HarperCollins Children's Bk. Group.

—The Mysterious Misadventures of Foy Rin Jin: A Decidedly Dysfunctional Dragon. 1999. (Illus.). 32p. (J). (ps-3). 15.95 (*0-06-028000-X*, Perennial) HarperTrade.

Galchutt, David. There Was Magic Inside. 1993. (Illus.). 40p. (J). (ps-2). pap. 14.00 (*0-671-75978-7*, Simon & Schuster Children's Publishing) Simon & Schuster Children's Publishing.

Gannett, Ruth Stiles. Elmer & the Dragon. 2002. (Illus.). (J). 14.47 (*0-7587-9151-8*) Book Wholesalers, Inc.

—Elmer & the Dragon. 2004. 32p. (J). (gr. 3-6). pap. 6.99 (*0-440-41761-9*) Dell Publishing.

—Elmer & the Dragon. (Tales of My Father's Dragon Ser.: Bk. 2). 87p. (J). (gr. 3-6). pap. 4.99 incl. audio (*0-8072-1288-1*); pap. 4.99 incl. audio (*0-8072-1288-1*); 1997. pap. 17.00 incl. audio (*0-8072-0244-4*, FTR178SP) Random Hse. Audio Publishing Group. (Listening Library).

—Elmer & the Dragon. (Illus.). (J). 1987. (Tales of My Father's Dragon Ser.: Bk. 2). 96p. (gr. 5-8). pap. 5.99 (*0-394-89049-3*, Knopf Bks. for Young Readers); 1964. (gr. 4-6). 9.99 o.s.i (*0-394-91120-2*, Random Hse. Bks. for Young Readers) Random Hse. Children's Bks.

—Elmer & the Dragon. 1950. (J). (gr. 3-6). 2.95 o.p. (*0-394-81120-8*) Random Hse., Inc.

—Elmer & the Dragon. 1987. (Tales of My Father's Dragon Ser.: Bk. 2). (J). (gr. 3-6). 11.04 (*0-606-01539-6*) Turtleback Bks.

—My Father's Dragon. 2002. (Illus.). (J). 14.47 (*0-7587-0296-5*) Book Wholesalers, Inc.

—My Father's Dragon. 1990. 88p. (J). (gr. 3-6). reprint ed. lib. bdg. 29.95 (*0-89966-701-5*) Buccaneer Bks., Inc.

—My Father's Dragon. 1980. (J). (gr. 3-6). pap. 1.25 o.p. (*0-440-45628-2*) Dell Publishing.

—My Father's Dragon. (Tales of My Father's Dragon Ser.: Bk. 1). 87p. (J). (gr. 3-6). pap. 4.99 o.p. incl. audio (*0-8072-1286-5*, Listening Library) Random Hse. Audio Publishing Group.

—My Father's Dragon. (Illus.). 1987. (Tales of My Father's Dragon Ser.: Bk. 1). 96p. (gr. 5-8). pap. text 5.99 (*0-394-89048-5*, Knopf Bks. for Young Readers); 1986. (Tales of My Father's Dragon Ser.: Bk. 1). 88p. (J). (gr. 3-6). 14.95 o.s.i (*0-394-88460-4*, Random Hse. Bks. for Young Readers); 1948. 88p. (J). (gr. 3-6). 14.99 o.s.i (*0-394-91438-4*, Random Hse. Bks. for Young Readers) Random Hse. Children's Bks.

—My Father's Dragon. 1987. (Tales of My Father's Dragon Ser.: Bk. 1). (J). (gr. 3-6). 11.04 (*0-606-02929-X*) Turtleback Bks.

—Three Tales of My Father's Dragon. (Illus.). 1997. 256p. (gr. 3-6). 16.95 (*0-679-88911-6*, Random Hse. Bks. for Young Readers); 1987. 96p. (J). (gr. 2-5). 12.00 o.s.i (*0-394-89136-8*, Knopf Bks. for Young Readers); 50th anniv. ed. 1997. 256p. (J). (gr. 3-6). 17.99 (*0-679-98911-0*, Random Hse. Bks. for Young Readers) Random Hse. Children's Bks.

Glaze, Sandra. Willobe of Wuzz. 1997. (Illus.). 84p. (J). (gr. 1-5). pap. 8.95 (*0-921870-48-5*) Ronsdale Pr. CAN. *Dist:* General Distribution Services, Inc.

Goodhart, Pippa. Arthur's Tractor. 2003. (Illus.). 32p. (J). (ps-3). 15.95 (*1-58234-847-2*, Bloomsbury Children) Bloomsbury Publishing.

Grahame, Kenneth. The Reluctant Dragon. 2003. (J). 15.99 (*0-7636-2199-4*) Candlewick Pr.

—Reluctant Dragon. 2004. 40p. (J). 16.95 (*0-439-45581-2*) Scholastic, Inc.

Gray, Luli. Falcon & the Charles Street Witch. 2002. 144p. (J). (gr. 5-9). 15.00 (*0-618-16410-3*) Houghton Mifflin Co.

—Falcon's Egg. 1997. 144p. (J). (gr. 3-6). pap. text 4.50 o.s.i (*0-440-41247-1*) Dell Publishing.

—Falcon's Egg. 1995. 144p. (J). (gr. 4-6). tchr. ed. 16.00 (*0-395-71128-2*) Houghton Mifflin Co.

—Falcon's Egg. 1997. 10.55 (*0-606-11311-8*) Turtleback Bks.

Hall, Willis. Dragon Days. l.t. ed. 1991. (Lythway Ser.). 200p. (J). (gr. 3-7). 16.95 o.p. (*0-7451-1294-3*, Galaxy Children's Large Print) BBC Audiobooks America.

Hicks, Bob. Cornelius, the Little Dragon Book. 2004. (J). ring bd. incl. audio compact disk (*0-9722036-5-6*) T. E. Publishing, Inc.

Hillert, Margaret. Come to School, Dear Dragon. 2002. (Illus.). (J). 15.00 (0-7587-9456-8) Book Wholesalers, Inc.

—Come to School, Dear Dragon. (J). (ps-k). 1985. (Illus.). pap. 5.10 (0-8136-5633-8); 1985. (Illus.). lib. bdg. 7.95 (0-8136-5133-6, TK2966); 1984. (0-87895-878-9) Modern Curriculum Pr.

—Come to School, Dear Dragon. 1985. 12.20 (0-606-14018-2) Turtleback Bks.

—A Friend for Dear Dragon. 1985. (Illus.). (J). (ps-k). pap. 5.10 (0-8136-5636-2, TK2973); lib. bdg. 7.95 (0-8136-5136-0, TK2972) Modern Curriculum Pr.

—A Friend for Dear Dragon. 1985. 12.20 (0-606-14021-2) Turtleback Bks.

—Go to Sleep Dear Dragon. (J). (ps-k). 1985. (Illus.). pap. 5.10 (0-8136-5635-4, TK2971); 1985. (Illus.). lib. bdg. 7.95 (0-8136-5135-2, TK2970); 1984. (0-87895-880-0) Modern Curriculum Pr.

—Go to Sleep Dear Dragon. 1985. 12.20 (0-606-14024-7) Turtleback Bks.

—Happy Birthday, Dear Dragon. 2002. (Illus.). (J). 15.00 (0-7587-9477-0) Book Wholesalers, Inc.

—Happy Birthday, Dear Dragon. 1977. (Illus.). (J). (ps-k). pap. 5.10 (0-8136-5521-8, TK2309); lib. bdg. 7.95 (0-8136-5021-6, TK2308) Modern Curriculum Pr.

—Happy Birthday, Dear Dragon. 1977. 12.20 (0-606-14026-3) Turtleback Bks.

—Happy Easter, Dear Dragon. 1981. (Illus.). (J). (ps). pap. 5.10 (0-8136-5522-6, TK2311); lib. bdg. 7.95 (0-8136-5022-4, TK2310) Modern Curriculum Pr.

—Happy Easter, Dear Dragon. 1981. 12.20 (0-606-14027-1) Turtleback Bks.

—Help for Dear Dragon. (J). 1984. (0-87895-876-2); 1981. (Illus.). pap. 5.10 (0-8136-5631-1, TK2963); 1981. (Illus.). lib. bdg. 7.95 (0-8136-5131-X, TK2962) Modern Curriculum Pr.

—Help for Dear Dragon. 1985. 12.20 (0-606-14028-X) Turtleback Bks.

—I Love You, Dear Dragon. 1981. (Illus.). (J). (ps). pap. 5.10 (0-8136-5523-4); lib. bdg. 7.95 (0-8136-5023-2) Modern Curriculum Pr.

—I Love You, Dear Dragon. 1981. 12.20 (0-606-14031-X) Turtleback Bks.

—I Need You, Dear Dragon. (J). (ps) 1985. (Illus.). pap. 5.10 (0-8136-5634-6, TK2969); 1985. (Illus.). lib. bdg. 7.95 (0-8136-5134-4, TK2968); 1984. (0-87895-879-7) Modern Curriculum Pr.

—I Need You, Dear Dragon. 1985. 12.20 (0-606-14032-8) Turtleback Bks.

—It's Circus Time, Dear Dragon. (ps). 1985. (Illus.). (J). pap. 5.10 (0-8136-5632-X, TK2965); 1985. (Illus.). (J). lib. bdg. 7.95 (0-8136-5132-8, TK2964); 1984. (0-87895-877-0) Modern Curriculum Pr.

—It's Circus Time, Dear Dragon. 1985. 12.20 (0-606-14033-6) Turtleback Bks.

—It's Halloween Time, Dear Dragon. 1981. (Illus.). (J). (ps). pap. 5.10 (0-8136-5524-2, TK2319); lib. bdg. 7.95 (0-8136-5024-0, TK2318) Modern Curriculum Pr.

—Let's Go Dear Dragon. 1981. (Illus.). (J). (ps). pap. 5.10 (0-8136-5525-0, TK2323); lib. bdg. 7.95 (0-8136-5025-9, TK2322) Modern Curriculum Pr.

—Merry Christmas, Dear Dragon. 1981. (Illus.). (J). (ps). pap. 5.10 (0-8136-5526-9, TK2345); lib. bdg. 7.95 (0-8136-5026-7, TK2344) Modern Curriculum Pr.

—Merry Christmas, Dear Dragon. 1981. 12.20 (0-606-14045-X) Turtleback Bks.

Hillman, Elizabeth. Min-Yo & the Moon Dragon. (Illus.). 32p. (J). (ps-3). 1992. 14.95 o.s.i (0-15-254230-2); 1996. pap. 5.00 (0-15-200985-X) Harcourt Children's Bks.

—Min-Yo & the Moon Dragon. 1996. 10.20 o.p. (0-606-09617-5) Turtleback Bks.

Hodges, Margaret. Saint George & the Dragon. 2002. (Illus.). (J). 13.79 (0-7587-0070-9) Book Wholesalers, Inc.

—Saint George & the Dragon. braille ed. 2000. (J). (gr. 2). spiral bd. (0-616-01675-1) Canadian National Institute for the Blind/Institut National Canadien pour les Aveugles.

Howard, Arthur. Serious Trouble. 2003. (Illus.). 32p. (J). 16.00 (0-15-202664-9) Harcourt Children's Bks.

Hunter, Jana Novotny. Little Ones Do. 2001. (Illus.). 32p. (J). (ps-k). 14.99 o.s.i (0-525-46690-8, Dutton Children's Bks.) Penguin Putnam Bks. for Young Readers.

Inches, Alison. In the Mushroom Meadow. 2002. (Illus.). 24p. (J). (gr. k-3). pap. 3.25 (0-375-81479-5) Random Hse., Inc.

—Picture Perfect. 2002. (Illus.). 24p. (J). pap. 3.25 (0-375-81607-0) Random Hse., Inc.

Johnson, Sandi. Dorp (Lost) Moon-Star Records, 2 vols. l.t. ed. 2003. (Illus.). 10p. (J). (gr. k-5). spiral bd. 5.99 (1-929063-33-4, 330) Moons & Stars Publishing For Children.

—Dorp the Scottish Dragon: Conquest City. Johnson, Britt, ed. 1999. (Conquest City Ser.: Vol. 7). (Illus.). 35p. (J). (ps-6). 10.99 (1-929063-06-7, 142) Moons & Stars Publishing For Children.

—Dorp the Scottish Dragon: Scotland, 7 vols. Johnson, Britt, ed. 2nd rev. ed. 1986. (Lost from Loch Lomond Ser.: Bk. 1). (Illus.). 58p. (J). (ps-6). 9.99 (1-929063-00-8, 101) Moons & Stars Publishing For Children.

—Dorp the Scottish Dragon Bk. 1: Lost, 7 vols. Johnson, Britt, ed. 3rd rev. ed. 1999. (Little Choo-Choo Bks.). (Illus.). 35p. (J). (ps-6). 10.99 (1-929063-10-5, 110) Moons & Stars Publishing For Children.

—Dorp the Scottish Dragon Bk. 2: Dragon Love. Johnson, Britt, ed. 1987. (Little Choo-Choo Bks.). 35p. (J). (ps-6). 4.99 (1-929063-01-6, 102) Moons & Stars Publishing For Children.

—Dorp the Scottish Dragon Bk. 3: Hollywood, 7 vols. Johnson, Britt, ed. 1987. (Little Choo-Choo Bks.). 31p. (J). (ps-6). 4.99 (1-929063-02-4, 103) Moons & Stars Publishing For Children.

—Dorp the Scottish Dragon Bk. 4: New York Christmas: Moon-Star Storys. Johnson, Britt, ed. 1987. (Little Choo-Choo Bks.). (Illus.). 24p. (J). (ps-6). spiral bd. 9.99 (1-929063-03-2, 104) Moons & Stars Publishing For Children.

—Dorp the Scottish Dragon Bk. 5: Sun-n-Fun in Florida. Johnson, Britt, ed. 1987. (Little Choo-Choo Bks.). 35p. (J). (ps-6). 4.99 (1-929063-04-0, 105) Moons & Stars Publishing For Children.

—Dorp the Scottish Dragon Bk. 6: A Lone Star Story. Johnson, Britt, ed. 1987. (Little Choo-Choo Bks.). (Illus.). 40p. (J). (ps-6). 10.99 (1-929063-05-9, 106) Moons & Stars Publishing For Children.

Jones, Shelagh. Derrynaluscha Dragon. 1991. 126p. (J). pap. 8.95 (0-947962-57-3) Dufour Editions, Inc.

Jordan, Apple. Simon Says: A Spanish-English Word Book. 2002. (ENG & SPA., Illus.). 24p. (J). (gr. k-3). pap. 3.25 (0-375-81527-9, Random Hse. Bks. for Young Readers) Random Hse. Children's Bks.

Jordan, Sherryl. The Hunting of the Last Dragon. (J). (gr. 7 up). 2003. 256p. pap. 5.99 (0-06-447231-0); 2002. 192p. 15.95 (0-06-028902-3); 2002. 192p. lib. bdg. 15.89 (0-06-028903-1) HarperCollins Children's Bk. Group.

Kent, Jack, illus. There's No Such Thing As a Dragon. (J). (ps-1). 2001. 40p. 9.95 o.s.i (0-307-10214-9); 1975. 24p. pap. o.p. (0-307-11841-X) Random Hse. Children's Bks. (Golden Bks.).

Koller, Jackie French. A Dragon in the Family. 1993. (Springboard Bks.). (Illus.). (J). 12.95 o.p. (0-316-50151-4) Little Brown & Co.

—A Dragon in the Family. 1996. (Illus.). 64p. (J). (gr. 2-5). reprint ed. per. 3.99 (0-671-89786-1, Aladdin) Simon & Schuster Children's Publishing.

—A Dragon in the Family. 1996. 9.19 o.p. (0-606-09207-2) Turtleback Bks.

—Dragon Quest. 1990. (J). (ps-4). 10.95 o.s.i (0-316-50148-4) Little Brown & Co.

—Dragon Quest. 1997. (Dragonling Ser.: Vol. 3). (Illus.). 96p. (YA). (gr. 2-5). per. 3.50 (0-671-00193-0, Aladdin) Simon & Schuster Children's Publishing.

—Dragon Quest. 1997. 8.60 o.p. (0-606-11278-2) Turtleback Bks.

—Dragon Trouble. 1997. (Dragonling Ser.: No. 5). (Illus.). 96p. (J). (gr. 2-5). per. 3.50 (0-671-01399-8, Aladdin) Simon & Schuster Children's Publishing.

—Dragon Trouble. 1997. (Dragonling Ser.). 9.55 (0-606-12922-7) Turtleback Bks.

—Dragonling. 1995. (Dragonling Ser.: 1). (J). 9.19 (0-606-09211-0) Turtleback Bks.

—The Dragonling. 1995. (Dragonling Ser.). 64p. (J). (gr. 2-5). pap. 3.99 (0-671-86790-3, Aladdin) Simon & Schuster Children's Publishing.

—The Dragonling Collector's Edition. (Dragonling Ser.: Vol. 2). (J). (gr. 2-5). 2001. (Illus.). 272p. reprint ed. pap. 5.99 (0-7434-1020-3); Set. 2000. 224p. pap. 5.99 (0-7434-1019-X) Simon & Schuster Children's Publishing. (Aladdin).

—Dragons & Kings. 1998. (Dragonling Ser.: No. 6). (Illus.). 96p. (J). (gr. 2-5). per. 3.50 (0-671-01400-5, Aladdin) Simon & Schuster Children's Publishing.

—Dragons & Kings. 1998. (Dragonling Ser.). (J). 9.55 (0-606-12923-5) Turtleback Bks.

—Dragons of Krad. 1997. (Dragonling Ser.: Vol. 4). (Illus.). 96p. (YA). (gr. 2-5). per. 3.50 (0-671-00194-9, Aladdin) Simon & Schuster Children's Publishing.

—Dragons of Krad. 1997. (Dragonling Ser.). 8.60 o.p. (0-606-11280-4) Turtleback Bks.

Kubler, Annie. Daphne Dragon. 1985. (Illus.). 44p. (J). (ps-1). 4.99 (0-85953-260-7) Child's Play of England GBR. *Dist:* Child's Play-International.

Larranaga, Robert D. The King's Shadow. 1991. (Picture Bks.). (Illus.). 32p. (J). (ps-3). lib. bdg. 19.95 o.s.i (0-87614-688-4, Carolrhoda Bks.) Lerner Publishing Group.

Lawson, Julie. The Dragon's Pearl. 1993. (Illus.). 32p. (J). (ps-3). 15.95 o.p. (0-395-63623-X, Clarion Bks.) Houghton Mifflin Co. Trade & Reference Div.

Lawson, Julie & Morin, Paul. The Dragon's Pearl. 1992. 32p. (J). (0-19-540843-8) Oxford Univ. Pr., Inc.

Lukas, Sarah. Dragon Dance. 2003. (Illus.). (J). bds. 6.99 (0-375-82340-9) Random Hse. Children's Bks.

—Hand in Hand in Dragon Land. 2002. (Illus.). 32p. (J). (ps-1). 8.99 (0-375-81443-4) Random Hse., Inc.

Mahy, Margaret. The Dragon of an Ordinary Family. 1992. (Illus.). 480p. (J). (ps-3). 14.00 o.p. (0-8037-1062-3, Dial Bks. for Young Readers) Penguin Putnam Bks. for Young Readers.

Marquez, Desiree. Las Flores Felices de Max y Emmy. 2002. 24p. (J). pap. 3.25 (0-375-82284-4) Random Hse., Inc.

—Zak y Wheezie Hacen Limpieza. 2002. 24p. (J). pap. 3.25 (0-375-82282-8) Random Hse., Inc.

Marzollo, Jean. Baby Unicorn & Baby Dragon. 1989. (J). pap. 2.50 o.p. (0-590-42213-8) Scholastic, Inc.

Mayer, Mercer. Herbert the Timid Dragon. 1991. (Golden Star Reader Ser.: Level 3). (J). (gr. 1-3). pap. 3.25 o.s.i (0-307-11463-5, Golden Bks.) Random Hse. Children's Bks.

McCaffrey, Anne. A Diversity of Dragons. 1997. (Pern Ser.). (Illus.). 96p. (gr. 7-12). 35.00 (0-06-105531-X, Eos) Morrow/Avon.

—A Diversity of Dragons. 1995. (J). 19.95 (0-689-31868-5, Atheneum) Simon & Schuster Children's Publishing.

McLerran, Alice. Dragonfly. 142p. (J). (gr. 4-5). 2004. (Illus.). 15.95 (1-888842-15-6); 2000. pap. 11.45 (1-888842-22-9) Absey & Co.

McMullan, K. H. Class Trip to the Cave of Doom. 1998. (Dragon Slayers' Academy Ser.: No. 3). (Illus.). 96p. (J). (gr. 2-5). 13.89 o.s.i (0-448-41871-1, Grosset & Dunlap) Penguin Putnam Bks. for Young Readers.

—A Class Trip to the Cave of Doom. 1998. (Dragon Slayers' Academy Ser.: No. 3). (Illus.). 96p. (J). (gr. 2-5). 3.99 o.s.i (0-448-41594-1, Grosset & Dunlap) Penguin Putnam Bks. for Young Readers.

—Countdown to the Year 1000. 1999. (Dragon Slayers' Academy Ser.: No. 8). (Illus.). 96p. (J). (gr. 2-5). 13.89 o.p. (0-448-42054-6, Platt & Munk);Vol. 8. 3.99 o.p. (0-448-42033-3, Grosset & Dunlap) Penguin Putnam Bks. for Young Readers.

—The New Kid at School. 1997. (Dragon Slayers' Academy Ser.: No. 1). (Illus.). (J). (gr. 2-5). 92p. 13.89 o.s.i (0-448-41727-8); 96p. 3.99 o.s.i (0-448-41592-5) Penguin Putnam Bks. for Young Readers. (Grosset & Dunlap).

—Revenge of the Dragon Lady. 1997. (Dragon Slayers' Academy Ser.: No. 2). (Illus.). 96p. (J). (gr. 2-5). 13.89 o.p. (0-448-41728-6); 3.95 o.s.i (0-448-41593-3) Penguin Putnam Bks. for Young Readers. (Grosset & Dunlap).

—Revenge of the Dragon Lady, 2. 1997. (Dragon Slayers' Academy Ser.: No. 2). (Illus.). (J). (gr. 2-5). 10.10 (0-606-12920-0) Turtleback Bks.

McMullan, Kate. Class Trip to the Cave of Doom, Vol. 3. 2003. (Dragon Slayers' Academy Ser.: Vol. 3). (Illus.). 112p. mass mkt. 4.99 (0-448-43110-6, Grosset & Dunlap) Penguin Putnam Bks. for Young Readers.

—Countdown to the Year 1000. 2003. (Dragon Slayer's Academy Ser.). (Illus.). 112p. mass mkt. 4.99 (0-448-43508-X, Grosset & Dunlap) Penguin Putnam Bks. for Young Readers.

—Help! Its Parents Day at DSA. 2004. (Dragon Slayers' Academy Ser.: No. 10). (Illus.). 112p. (J). mass mkt. 4.99 (0-448-43220-X, Grosset & Dunlap) Penguin Putnam Bks. for Young Readers.

—New Kid at School. 2003. (Dragon Slayers' Academy Ser.). (Illus.). 112p. (J). mass mkt. 4.99 (0-448-43108-4, Grosset & Dunlap) Penguin Putnam Bks. for Young Readers.

—Wheel of Misfortune. 2003. (Dragon Slayer's Academy Ser.). (Illus.). 112p. mass mkt. 4.99 (0-448-43507-1, Grosset & Dunlap) Penguin Putnam Bks. for Young Readers.

—97 Ways to Train a Dragon. 2003. (Dragon Slayers' Academy Ser.). (Illus.). 112p. (J). mass mkt. 4.99 (0-448-43177-7, Grosset & Dunlap) Penguin Putnam Bks. for Young Readers.

McMullen, Eunice & McMullen, Nigel. Dragon for Breakfast. 1990. (Illus.). 28p. (J). (ps-3). lib. bdg. 7.95 o.p. (0-87614-650-7, Carolrhoda Bks.) Lerner Publishing Group.

Meddaugh, Susan. Harry on the Rocks. 2003. (Illus.). 32p. (J). (ps-3). lib. bdg., tchr. ed. 15.00 (0-618-27603-3) Houghton Mifflin Co.

Miles, Mary. Benjamin's Secret Sea Dragon: A Nantucket Adventure. 2002. pap. 17.50 (1-59109-320-1) Booksurge, LLC.

Murphy, Shirley Rousseau. Valentine for a Dragon. 1986. (Illus.). 48p. (J). (gr. k-3). pap. 3.95 o.s.i (0-689-71049-6, Simon & Schuster Children's Publishing) Simon & Schuster Children's Publishing.

Myers, Walter Dean. The Dragon Takes a Wife. (Illus.). (ps-3). 1995. 40p. (J). pap. 14.95 o.p. (0-590-46693-3); 2000. 32p. mass mkt. 5.99 (0-590-46694-1) Scholastic, Inc.

—The Dragon Takes a Wife. 2000. (Illus.). (J). 12.14 (0-606-18871-1) Turtleback Bks.

Nantus, Sheryl. The Dragon Who Was Bored. 2003. 41p. (J). pap. 12.95 (1-59286-126-1) PublishAmerica, Inc.

Nash, Ogden. Custard the Dragon. 1973. (Illus.). (J). (gr. k-3). lib. bdg. 14.95 o.p. (0-316-59841-0) Little Brown & Co.

—Custard the Dragon & the Wicked Knight. (J). 2003. bds. 6.95 (0-316-59760-0); 1999. (Illus.). 32p. pap. 5.95 (0-316-59905-0); 1996. (Illus.). 32p. 14.95 o.p. (0-316-59882-8) Little Brown & Co.

—Custard the Dragon & the Wicked Knight. 1999. (J). (gr. k up). pap., stu. ed. 25.20 incl. audio (0-7887-2986-1, 40868);Class set. pap. 91.30 incl. audio (0-7887-3016-9, 46833) Recorded Bks., LLC.

—The Tale of Custard the Dragon. (Illus.). 32p. (J). (ps-3). 1998. pap. 5.95 (0-316-59031-2); 1995. 14.95 o.p. (0-316-59880-1) Little Brown & Co.

—The Tale of Custard the Dragon. 1998. (J). 12.10 (0-606-13833-1) Turtleback Bks.

Nesbit, Edith. The Book of Beasts. 2001. (Illus.). 64p. (J). (gr. k up). 16.99 (0-7636-1579-X) Candlewick Pr.

—The Book of Dragons. 1990. 160p. (J). (gr. 4-6). pap. 3.50 o.s.i (0-440-40696-X) Dell Publishing.

—The Book of Dragons. 2001. (Peter Glassman Bk.). (Illus.). 256p. (J). 14.95 (1-58717-105-8); (gr. 3-7). pap. 9.95 (1-58717-106-6) North-South Bks., Inc.

—The Book of Dragons. 1991. (J). (gr. 5-8). 16.25 o.p. (0-8446-6454-5) Smith, Peter Pub., Inc.

Newhouse, Mark H. Dragons in the Neighborhood. 2001. (Illus.). 32p. (J). (ps-6). 14.95 (0-9704629-1-3); pap. 8.95 (0-9704629-2-1) Earthkids Publishing.

Nortung, Sandra. Voice from the Forest. 1999. (Illus.). 32p. (J). (gr. k-6). 11.95 (1-892885-50-6) Daring Child Pr.

Nunes, Susan Miho. The Last Dragon. (Illus.). 32p. (J). (ps-3). 1997. pap. 6.95 (0-395-84517-3); 1995. lib. bdg., tchr. ed. 16.00 (0-395-67020-9) Houghton Mifflin Co. Trade & Reference Div. (Clarion Bks.).

Paolini, Christopher. Eragon. unabr. ed. 2003. (Inheritance Trilogy: Bk. 1). (J). audio 39.95 (0-8072-1962-2, Listening Library) Random Hse. Audio Publishing Group.

—Eragon. 2003. (Inheritance Trilogy: Bk. 1). (Illus.). 528p. (J). (gr. 7). 18.95 (0-375-82668-8); lib. bdg. 20.99 (0-375-92668-2, Knopf Bks. for Young Readers) Random Hse. Children's Bks.

Patience, John. Dragon Tales. 1990. (Happy Ending Stories Ser.). (Illus.). 32p. (J). (gr. k-6). 3.99 o.s.i (0-517-02329-6) Random Hse. Value Publishing.

Pattison, Darcy. The River Dragon. 1991. (Illus.). 32p. (J). (gr. k up). 13.95 (0-688-10426-6); lib. bdg. 13.88 o.p. (0-688-10427-4) HarperCollins Children's Bk. Group.

—The River Dragon. (Illus.). 32p. (J). 3.98 o.p. (0-8317-3071-4) Smithmark Pubs., Inc.

Peet, Bill. How Droofus the Dragon Lost His Head. 2002. (Illus.). (J). 16.66 (0-7587-2761-5) Book Wholesalers, Inc.

—How Droofus the Dragon Lost His Head. 1999. (Illus.). (J). pap. 15.75 (0-8085-3078-X) Econo-Clad Bks.

—How Droofus the Dragon Lost His Head, 001. 1983. (Illus.). 48p. (J). (gr. k-3). 14.95 o.p. (0-395-15085-X); pap. 8.95 (0-395-34066-7) Houghton Mifflin Co.

—How Droofus the Dragon Lost His Head. 1971. (J). 14.10 (0-606-03769-1) Turtleback Bks.

Piebnkowski, Jan. Bel & Bub & the Black Hole. 2000. (Bel & Bub Stories Ser.). (Illus.). 32p. (J). (ps-k). pap. 9.95 o.p. (0-7894-6528-0) Dorling Kindersley Publishing, Inc.

Pilkey, Dav. Un Amigo para Dragon. 2000. (SPA., Illus.). 48p. (J). (gr. 1-3). pap. 6.99 (980-257-216-0) Ekare, Ediciones VEN. *Dist:* Kane/Miller Bk. Pubs., Lectorum Pubns., Inc.

—Dragon Gets By. 2002. (Illus.). (J). 13.79 (0-7587-4536-2) Book Wholesalers, Inc.

—Dragon Gets By. (Illus.). 48p. (J). 1996. (ps-3). mass mkt. 5.95 (0-531-07081-6); 1991. (gr. 1-3). mass mkt. 15.99 o.p. (0-531-08535-X); 1991. (gr. 1-3). mass mkt. 14.95 o.p. (0-531-05935-9) Scholastic, Inc. (Orchard Bks.).

—Dragon's Halloween. (J). 2003. 48p. mass mkt. 5.95 (0-439-54847-0); 1993. (Illus.). 48p. (gr. 1-3). mass mkt. 15.99 o.p. (0-531-08590-2); 1993. (Illus.). 48p. (gr. 1-3). pap. 15.95 (0-531-05990-1); 1989. (Illus.). 32p. (ps-3). mass mkt. 5.95 (0-531-07069-7) Scholastic, Inc. (Orchard Bks.).

—Dragon's Halloween. 1995. (Dragon Tales Ser.). 10.15 o.p. (0-606-09209-9) Turtleback Bks.

Prior, Natalie Jane. Lily Quench & the Black Mountains. 2004. (Illus.). 160p. (J). pap. 4.99 (0-14-240021-1, Puffin Bks.) Penguin Putnam Bks. for Young Readers.

—Lily Quench & the Dragon of Ashby. 2004. (Illus.). 160p. (J). pap. 4.99 (*0-14-240020-3*, Puffin Bks.) Penguin Putnam Bks. for Young Readers.

—Lily Quench & the Treasure of Mote Ely. 2004. (Illus.). 160p. (J). pap. 4.99 (*0-14-240022-X*, Puffin Bks.) Penguin Putnam Bks. for Young Readers.

Random House Beginners Books Staff. Hello, Dragons! (Hola, Dragones!) 2002. (Illus.). 12p. (J). (ps-1). bds. 9.99 (*0-375-81511-2*, Random Hse. Bks. for Young Readers) Random Hse. Children's Bks.

Random House Staff. Dragon Days. 2001. (Illus.). 80p. (J). (ps-3). pap. 2.99 (*0-375-81314-4*, Random Hse. Bks. for Young Readers) Random Hse. Children's Bks.

—Dragon Doodles. 2000. (Dragon Tales Ser.). (Illus.). 80p. (J). (ps-3). pap. 2.99 (*0-375-80636-9*, Random Hse. Bks. for Young Readers) Random Hse. Children's Bks.

—Magical Dragon Land. 2001. (Illus.). 8p. (J). bds. 10.99 (*0-375-81397-7*) Random Hse. Children's Bks.

—Wings & Tales & Dragon Scales. 2000. (Dragon Tales Ser.). (Illus.). 80p. (J). (ps-3). pap. 2.99 (*0-375-80637-7*, Random Hse. Bks. for Young Readers) Random Hse. Children's Bks.

Repchuk, Caroline. The Glitter Dragon. 1995. (Illus.). 32p. (J). (ps-k). 14.95 o.p. (*1-56924-838-9*, Marlowe & Co.) Avalon Publishing Group.

Richards, Maxwell J. George & the Dragon. 2000. 268p. (J). pap. 13.95 (*1-891929-36-4*) Four Seasons Pubs.

Robertson, M. P. The Egg. 2004. (Illus.). 32p. (J). 6.99 (*0-14-240038-6*, Puffin Bks.) Penguin Putnam Bks. for Young Readers.

—The Great Dragon Rescue. 2004. 32p. (J). 16.99 (*0-8037-2973-1*, Dial Bks. for Young Readers) Penguin Putnam Bks. for Young Readers.

Robertson, Mark. The Egg. 2001. (Illus.). 32p. (J). (ps-3). 15.99 (*0-8037-2546-9*, Fogelman, Phyllis Bks.) Penguin Putnam Bks. for Young Readers.

Robertson, Mark, illus. A Treasury of Dragon Stories. 1997. (Treasury of Stories Ser.). 160p. (J). (ps-4). pap. 6.95 (*0-7534-5114-X*) Larousse Kingfisher Chambers, Inc.

Rowe, John A. Jasper the Terror. 2001. (Illus.). 36p. (J). 15.95 (*0-7358-1476-7*); lib. bdg. 16.50 (*0-7358-1477-5*) North-South Bks., Inc.

Rupp, Rebecca. The Dragon of Lonely Island. 160p. (J). (gr. 3-6). 2002. (Illus.). bds. 5.99 (*0-7636-1661-3*); 1998. 16.99 (*0-7636-0408-9*) Candlewick Pr.

Ryan, Margaret. Littlest Dragon. 2003. (Roaring Good Reads Ser.). (Illus.). 64p. (J). pap. 6.95 (*0-00-714163-7*) HarperCollins Pubs. Ltd. GBR. *Dist:* Trafalgar Square.

Sandberg, Inger. Where Does All That Smoke Come from? 1972. (Illus.). 32p. (J). 3.95 o.s.i (*0-440-09651-0*); lib. bdg. 4.58 o.p. (*0-440-09652-9*, 9652) Dell Publishing. (Delacorte Pr.).

Schotter, Richard & Schotter, Roni. There's a Dragon About: A Winter's Revel. 1994. (Illus.). 32p. (J). (ps-2). mass mkt. 15.95 o.p. (*0-531-06858-7*); mass mkt. 16.99 o.p. (*0-531-08708-5*) Scholastic, Inc. (Orchard Bks.).

—There's a Dragon About: A Winter's Revel. 1994. E-Book (*1-58824-255-2*); E-Book (*1-59019-114-5*) ipicturebooks, LLC.

Seabrooke, Brenda. The Care & Feeding of Dragons. 1998. 128p. (J). (gr. 4-7). 15.99 o.s.i (*0-525-65252-3*, Dutton Children's Bks.) Penguin Putnam Bks. for Young Readers.

—The Dragon That Ate Summer. 1992. 112p. (J). (gr. 3-6). 14.95 o.s.i (*0-399-22115-8*, Philomel) Penguin Group (USA) Inc.

—The Dragon That Ate Summer. 1993. 112p. (J). (gr. 4-6). mass mkt. 2.95 (*0-590-46986-X*) Scholastic, Inc.

Seaton, Kristen, illus. Nine Dragons. 2003. 48p. (J). 15.95 (*0-8048-3481-4*) Tuttle Publishing.

Seo, Hong-Seock. Dragon Hunter, 9 vols. (Illus.). 192p. (YA). pap. 9.99 (*1-59182-437-0*); pap. 9.99 (*1-59182-436-2*); 2003. pap. 9.99 (*1-59182-163-0*);Vol. 4. 2004. pap. 9.99 (*1-59182-434-6*);Vol. 5. 2004. pap. 9.99 (*1-59182-435-4*) TOKYOPOP, Inc.

Siburt, Ruth. Dragon Charmer. 1996. 100p. (J). (gr. 4-8). pap. 9.99 (*0-88092-350-4*, 3504) Royal Fireworks Publishing Co.

Slote, Elizabeth. Nelly's Garden. 1991. (Illus.). 32p. (J). (ps-1). 13.95 o.p. (*0-688-10013-9*); lib. bdg. 13.88 o.p. (*0-688-10014-7*) Morrow/Avon. (Morrow, William & Co.).

—Nelly's Grannies. 1993. (Illus.). 32p. (J). (ps up). 14.00 o.p. (*0-688-11314-1*); lib. bdg. 13.93 o.p. (*0-688-11315-X*) Morrow/Avon. (Morrow, William & Co.).

Snyder, Margaret. Ord Makes a Wish. 2001. (Illus.). 24p. (J). 7.99 o.p. (*0-375-81338-1*) Random Hse. Children's Bks.

Snyder, Margaret & Albrect, Jeff. Race to the Finish. 2001. (Pictureback Bk.). (Illus.). 24p. (J). pap. 3.25 (*0-375-81388-8*, Random Hse. Bks. for Young Readers) Random Hse. Children's Bks.

Snyder, Margaret & Thompson Brothers Studio Staff. Dinosaurs & Dragons. 2001. (Pictureback Bk.). (Illus.). 24p. (J). pap. 3.25 (*0-375-81344-6*, Random Hse. Bks. for Young Readers) Random Hse. Children's Bks.

Spaulding, Mar. Kate Lynn's Fantastic Dream. 1999. (Illus.). 64p. (J). pap. 15.00 (*0-9674281-0-6*) Allen & Douglas Pubs.

Steck-Vaughn Staff. The Dragon Inside. 2003. audio 10.00 (*0-7398-8426-3*) Raintree Pubs.

Sterman, Betsy & Sterman, Samuel. Backyard Dragon. 1993. (Illus.). 192p. (J). (gr. 3-7). 15.95 (*0-06-020783-3*); lib. bdg. 13.89 o.p. (*0-06-020784-1*) HarperCollins Children's Bk. Group.

Stewart, Jennifer J. If That Breathes Fire, We're Toast! 1999. 117p. (J). (gr. 2-6). tchr. ed. 15.95 (*0-8234-1430-2*) Holiday Hse., Inc.

Summers, Lori. The Dragon Hunter's Handbook: Field Guides to the Paranormal. 2001. (Illus.). 96p. (J). mass mkt. 7.99 o.s.i (*0-8431-7704-7*, Price Stern Sloan) Penguin Putnam Bks. for Young Readers.

Sutcliff, Rosemary. The Minstrel & the Dragon Pup. 1993. (Illus.). 48p. (J). (ps up). 16.95 o.p. (*1-56402-098-3*) Candlewick Pr.

Thomas, Shelley Moore. Get Well, Good Knight. (Illus.). 48p. (J). 2004. pap. 3.99 (*0-14-240050-5*, Puffin Bks.); 2002. 13.99 (*0-525-46914-1*, Dutton Children's Bks.) Penguin Putnam Bks. for Young Readers.

—Good Night, Good Knight. 2002. 11.49 (*1-4046-1571-7*) Book Wholesalers, Inc.

—Good Night, Good Knight. 2002. (Easy-to-Read Ser.). (Illus.). 48p. (J). pap. 3.99 (*0-14-230201-5*, Puffin Bks.) Penguin Putnam Bks. for Young Readers.

Thomas, Shelley Moore & Plecas, Jennifer. Good Night, Good Knight. 2000. (Illus.). 48p. (J). (ps-2). 13.99 (*0-525-46326-7*, Dutton) Penguin Putnam Bks. for Young Readers.

Tolkien, J. R. R. Farmer Giles of Ham. (Illus.). 1978. 6.95 (*0-395-07121-6*); 1978. pap. 4.95 o.p. (*0-395-26799-4*); 1991. 96p. (J). reprint ed. 13.95 o.p. (*0-395-57645-8*) Houghton Mifflin Co.

—Farmer Giles of Ham: 50th Anniversary Edition. Scull, Christina & Hammond, Wayne G., eds. 50th anniv. ed. 1999. (Illus.). 128p. 17.00 (*0-618-00936-1*) Houghton Mifflin Co.

—Roverandom. abr. ed. 1998. (J). audio 16.85 (*0-00-105535-6*) HarperCollins Pubs. Ltd. GBR. *Dist:* Trafalgar Square.

—Roverandom. Scull, Christina & Hammond, Wayne G., eds. (Illus.). 106p. 1999. pap. 12.00 (*0-395-95799-0*); 1998. (gr. 3-5). 17.00 (*0-395-89871-4*) Houghton Mifflin Co.

—Roverandom. 1998. 18.05 (*0-606-16543-6*) Turtleback Bks.

Tolkien, J. R. R., et al. Roverandom. Scull, Christina & Hammond, Wayne G., eds. 783rd l.t. ed. 1998. (Science Fiction Ser.). (Illus.). 191p. (J). 25.95 (*0-7838-0299-4*) Thorndike Pr.

Townsend, Tom. The Dragon Trader, 8 vols., Vol. 3. 2000. (Fairie Ring Ser.: No. 3). 158p. (J). (gr. 6-12). pap. 9.99 (*0-88092-527-2*, 5272) Royal Fireworks Publishing Co.

Trimble, Irene. Down the Knuckerhole. 2001. (Illus.). 24p. (J). pap. 3.25 (*0-375-81340-3*, Random Hse. Bks. for Young Readers) Random Hse. Children's Bks.

—Ord Come Una Pizza! 2002. (SPA.). 32p. (J). lib. bdg. 11.99 (*0-375-92344-6*, Random Hse. Bks. for Young Readers) Random Hse. Children's Bks.

—Ord Come una Pizza! Ord Eats a Pizza. 2002. (SPA., Illus.). 32p. (J). pap. 3.99 (*0-375-82344-1*) Random Hse. Children's Bks.

Tucker, Kathy. The Seven Chinese Sisters. 2003. (Illus.). 32p. (J). (gr. k-3). 15.95 (*0-8075-7309-4*) Whitman, Albert & Co.

Ulmer, Mari P. Adventures of the Little Green Dragon. 1998. (Weewisdom Bks.). (Illus.). 64p. (J). (ps-3). 17.95 (*0-87159-228-2*) Unity Schl. of Christianity.

Ward, Helen. The Dragon Machine. 2003. (Illus.). 32p. (J). (ps-4). 15.99 (*0-525-47114-6*, Dutton Children's Bks.) Penguin Putnam Bks. for Young Readers.

Waterton, Betty. Orff, Twenty-Seven Dragons & a Snarkel. 1988. (Illus.). 32p. (ps-8). pap. 4.95 o.p. (*0-920303-03-X*) Annick Pr., Ltd. CAN. *Dist:* Firefly Bks., Ltd.

Waterton, Kulyn. Orff, Twenty-Seven Dragons & a Snarkel. 1984. (Illus.). 24p. (J). (ps-8). 12.95 (*0-920303-02-1*) Annick Pr., Ltd. CAN. *Dist:* Firefly Bks., Ltd.

Watt-Evans, Lawrence. The Dragon Society. 2001. 416p. 27.95 (*0-7653-0007-9*, Tor Bks.) Doherty, Tom Assocs., LLC.

Webb. Dragons of Kilve. 1993. pap. 6.95 (*0-7459-2747-5*) Lion Publishing PLC GBR. *Dist:* Trafalgar Square.

—Wanted One Dragon. 1999. (Illus.). 160p. pap. 6.95 (*0-7459-4069-2*) Lion Publishing PLC GBR. *Dist:* Trafalgar Square.

Weber, Bruce. The Quest for Camelot: The Search for Excalibur. rev. ed. 1979. (Quest for Camelot Ser.). (Illus.). 32p. (J). (gr. k-3). mass mkt. 3.50 (*0-590-12064-6*) Scholastic, Inc.

Weinberg, Jennifer Liberts. Slumberfairy Falls. 2003. (Illus.). 24p. (J). (ps-k). pap. 3.25 (*0-375-82166-X*) Random Hse., Inc.

West, Tracey. Jasper & the Mixed-Up Dragon. 2001. (Wee Wizards Ser.). 24p. (J). (ps-2). pap. 3.99 o.p. (*0-307-17145-0*, Golden Bks.) Random Hse. Children's Bks.

Wilson, Gina. Ignis. (Illus.). 40p. 2003. bds. 6.99 (*0-7636-2192-7*); 2001. (J). 16.99 (*0-7636-1623-0*) Candlewick Pr.

Woods, Tonita. Mystical Forest of Wise. 2001. pap. 10.95 (*0-595-19147-9*, Writers Club Pr.) iUniverse, Inc.

Wrede, Patricia C. Dealing with Dragons. (Enchanted Forest Chronicles: Bk. 1). (YA). 2002. (Illus.). 240p. (gr. 5 up). pap. 5.95 (*0-15-204566-X*, Magic Carpet Bks.); 1990. 224p. (gr. 7-12). 17.00 (*0-15-222900-0*) Harcourt Children's Bks.

—Dealing with Dragons. unabr. ed. 2001. (Enchanted Forest Ser.: Bk. 1). (J). (gr. 5 up). audio 25.00 (*0-8072-6190-4*, Listening Library) Random Hse. Audio Publishing Group.

—Dealing with Dragons. 1992. (Enchanted Forest Chronicles Ser.: Vol. 1). 212p. (YA). (gr. 7-12). mass mkt. 4.99 (*0-590-45722-5*, Scholastic Paperbacks) Scholastic, Inc.

—Dealing with Dragons. 1990. (Enchanted Forest Chronicles Ser.). (J). 11.04 (*0-606-01813-1*) Turtleback Bks.

—Searching for Dragons. 2002. (Enchanted Forest Chronicles: Bk. 2). (Illus.). 272p. (YA). (gr. 5 up). pap. 5.95 (*0-15-204565-1*, Magic Carpet Bks.) Harcourt Children's Bks.

—Searching for Dragons. unabr. ed. 2001. 242p. pap. 37.00 incl. audio (*0-8072-0670-9*);2. (Enchanted Forest Ser.: Bk. 2). (YA). (gr. 3 up). audio 26.00 (*0-8072-0632-6*) Random Hse. Audio Publishing Group. (Listening Library).

Wyllie, Stephen. The Red Dragon: A 3-D Picture Book. 1993. (Illus.). 208p. (J). (ps-2). 13.99 o.p. (*0-8037-1452-1*, Dial Bks. for Young Readers) Penguin Putnam Bks. for Young Readers.

Wynn, Thad & Wynn, Juliette. The Tale of a Dragon. 1999. (Illus.). 85p. (J). (gr. k-4). 15.95 o.p. (*1-57197-140-8*) Pentland Pr., Inc.

Yep, Laurence. Dragon War. 1992. 320p. (YA). (gr. 7 up). 15.00 o.p. (*0-06-020302-1*); lib. bdg. 14.89 o.p. (*0-06-020303-X*) HarperCollins Children's Bk. Group.

Yolen, Jane. Dragon's Blood Vol. 1: The Pit Dragon Trilogy. 2004. (Illus.). 320p. (YA). pap. 6.95 (*0-15-205126-0*, Magic Carpet Bks.) Harcourt Children's Bks.

—Heart's Blood: The Pit Dragon Trilogy, Volume Two. 2004. (Illus.). 368p. (YA). pap. 6.95 (*0-15-205118-X*, Magic Carpet Bks.) Harcourt Children's Bks.

—A Sending of Dragons: The Pit Dragon Trilogy, Volume Three. 2004. (Illus.). 320p. (YA). pap. 6.95 (*0-15-205128-7*, Magic Carpet Bks.) Harcourt Children's Bks.

Zhang, Song Nan. A Time of Golden Dragons. ed. 2001. (J). (gr. 1). spiral bd. (*0-616-07258-9*) Canadian National Institute for the Blind/Institut National Canadien pour les Aveugles.

E

EXTRATERRESTRIAL BEINGS—FICTION

Abbott, Tony & Coville, Bruce. There's an Alien in My Backpack! 2000. (I Was a Sixth Grade Alien Ser.: Vol. 9). (Illus.). 160p. (J). (gr. 3-6). pap. 3.99 (*0-671-02658-5*, Aladdin) Simon & Schuster Children's Publishing.

Albee, Sarah. Space Invaders! 1998. (Ready-to-Read Ser.). (Illus.). 32p. (J). (ps-3). pap. 3.99 (*0-689-82130-1*, Simon Spotlight/Nickelodeon) Simon & Schuster Children's Publishing.

Alexander, Alec. My Fantastic Dream of the Marshmallow Martians. 2000. (Marshmallow Martian Ser.: Vol. 1). (Illus.). 32p. (J). (ps-5). 5.95 (*0-9670091-0-3*) Smart Alec Toys Publishing.

—My Magical Christmas Dream of the Marshmallow Martians. 2000. (Marshmallow Martian Ser.: Vol. 2). (Illus.). 32p. (J). (ps-5). 5.95 (*0-9670091-1-1*) Smart Alec Toys Publishing.

Alf & Old Predictable. 1989. (Alf Storybooks Ser.: No. II). (Illus.). 24p. (J). (ps-3). pap. o.p. (*0-02-689219-7*) Checkerboard Pr., Inc.

Applegate, K. A. The Alien. 1997. (Animorphs Ser.: No. 8). 159p. (J). (gr. 3-7). mass mkt. 4.99 (*0-590-99728-9*) Scholastic, Inc.

—The Alien. 1997. (Animorphs Ser.: No. 8). (J). (gr. 3-7). 11.04 (*0-606-11050-X*) Turtleback Bks.

—The Android. 1997. (Animorphs Ser.: No. 10). (Illus.). 170p. (J). (gr. 3-7). mass mkt. 4.99 (*0-590-99730-0*) Scholastic, Inc.

—The Android. 1997. (Animorphs Ser.: No. 10). (J). (gr. 3-7). 11.04 (*0-606-11047-X*) Turtleback Bks.

—Animorphs Boxed Set No. 4: Books 13-16. 2001. (Animorphs Ser.). (J). (gr. 3-7). pap. 19.96 (*0-590-28434-7*, Scholastic Paperbacks) Scholastic, Inc.

—Animorphs Series Boxed Set. 1998. (Animorphs Ser.). (J). (gr. 3-7). pap. 143.64 (*0-590-51066-5*) Scholastic, Inc.

—Animorphs Series Boxed Set: The Threat; The Solution; The Pretender; The Suspicion, 4 vols., No. 6. 2001. (Animorphs Ser.: Nos. 21-24). (J). (gr. 3-7). pap. 19.96 (*0-590-28543-2*) Scholastic, Inc.

—Animorphs Series Boxed Set: The Weakness; The Arrival; The Hidden; The Other. 2000. (Animorphs Ser.: Nos. 37-40). (Illus.). (J). (gr. 3-7). pap. 19.96 (*0-439-10688-5*, Scholastic Paperbacks) Scholastic, Inc.

—The Arrival. 2000. (Animorphs Ser.: No. 38). (Illus.). 160p. (J). (gr. 3-7). mass mkt. 4.99 (*0-439-10677-X*, Scholastic Paperbacks) Scholastic, Inc.

—The Arrival. l.t. ed. 2001. (Animorphs Ser.: No. 38). 148p. (J). (gr. 4 up). lib. bdg. 22.60 (*0-8368-2771-6*) Stevens, Gareth Inc.

—The Arrival. 2000. (Animorphs Ser.: No. 38). (Illus.). (J). (gr. 3-7). 11.04 (*0-606-18509-7*) Turtleback Bks.

—The Attack, No. 26. 1999. (Animorphs Ser.: No. 26). 145p. (J). (gr. 3-7). mass mkt. 4.99 (*0-590-76259-1*) Scholastic, Inc.

—The Attack. 1999. (Animorphs Ser.: No. 26). (J). (gr. 3-7). 11.04 (*0-606-15834-0*) Turtleback Bks.

—Back to Before, No. 4. 2000. (Animorphs Ser.: No. 4). (Illus.). 240p. (J). (gr. 3-7). mass mkt. 5.99 (*0-439-17307-8*) Scholastic, Inc.

—The Capture. 1997. (Animorphs Ser.: No. 6). 154p. (J). (gr. 3-7). mass mkt. 4.99 (*0-590-62982-4*) Scholastic, Inc.

—The Capture. 1997. (Animorphs Ser.: No. 6). (J). (gr. 3-7). 11.04 (*0-606-10742-8*) Turtleback Bks.

—The Change. 1997. (Animorphs Ser.: No. 13). 162p. (J). (gr. 3-7). mass mkt. 4.99 (*0-590-49418-X*, Scholastic Paperbacks) Scholastic, Inc.

—The Conspiracy. 31st ed. 1999. (Animorphs Ser.: No. 31). 139p. (J). (gr. 3-7). mass mkt. 4.99 (*0-439-07031-7*) Scholastic, Inc.

—The Conspiracy. l.t. ed. 2000. (Animorphs Ser.: No. 31). 138p. (J). (gr. 4 up). lib. bdg. 22.60 (*0-8368-2754-6*) Stevens, Gareth Inc.

—The Conspiracy. 1999. (Animorphs Ser.: No. 31). (Illus.). (J). (gr. 3-7). 11.04 (*0-606-16928-8*) Turtleback Bks.

—The Decision. 1998. (Animorphs Ser.: No. 18). 168p. (J). (gr. 3-7). mass mkt. 4.99 (*0-590-49441-4*, Scholastic Paperbacks) Scholastic, Inc.

—The Decision. 1998. (Animorphs Ser.: No. 18). (J). (gr. 3-7). 11.04 (*0-606-13138-8*) Turtleback Bks.

—The Departure. 1998. (Animorphs Ser.: No. 19). 159p. (J). (gr. 3-7). mass mkt. 4.99 (*0-590-49451-1*, Scholastic Paperbacks) Scholastic, Inc.

—The Departure. 1998. (Animorphs Ser.: No. 19). (J). (gr. 3-7). 11.04 (*0-606-13139-6*) Turtleback Bks.

—The Discovery. 1998. (Animorphs Ser.: No. 20). 153p. (J). (gr. 3-7). mass mkt. 4.99 (*0-590-49637-9*, Scholastic Paperbacks) Scholastic, Inc.

—The Discovery. 1998. (Animorphs Ser.: No. 20). (J). (gr. 3-7). 11.04 (*0-606-13140-X*) Turtleback Bks.

—The Encounter. 1996. (Animorphs Ser.: No. 3). 157p. (J). (gr. 3-7). mass mkt. 4.99 (*0-590-62979-4*) Scholastic, Inc.

—The Encounter. 1996. (Animorphs Ser.: No. 3). (J). (gr. 3-7). 11.04 (*0-606-09004-5*) Turtleback Bks.

—The Experiment. 1999. (Animorphs Ser.: No. 28). 139p. (J). (gr. 3-7). mass mkt. 4.99 (*0-590-76261-3*) Scholastic, Inc.

—The Experiment. 1999. (Animorphs Ser.: No. 28). (J). (gr. 3-7). 11.04 (*0-606-16608-4*) Turtleback Bks.

—The Exposed. 1999. (Animorphs Ser.: No. 27). 154p. (J). (gr. 3-7). mass mkt. 4.99 (*0-590-76260-5*) Scholastic, Inc.

—The Exposed. 1999. (Animorphs Ser.: No. 27). (J). (gr. 3-7). 11.04 (*0-606-16589-4*) Turtleback Bks.

—The Extreme, No. 25. 1999. (Animorphs Ser.: No. 25). 146p. (J). (gr. 3-7). mass mkt. 4.99 (*0-590-76258-3*) Scholastic, Inc.

—The Familiar. l.t. ed. 2001. (Animorphs Ser.: No. 41). 143p. (J). (gr. 4 up). lib. bdg. 22.60 (*0-8368-2774-0*) Stevens, Gareth Inc.

—The Familiar. 2000. (Animorphs Ser.: No. 41). (Illus.). (J). (gr. 3-7). 11.04 (*0-606-18512-7*) Turtleback Bks.

—The First Journey. 1999. (Animorphs Ser.: No. 1). 115p. (J). (gr. 3-7). mass mkt. 4.99 (*0-439-06164-4*) Scholastic, Inc.

—The First Journey. 1999. (Animorphs: No. 1). (J). (gr. 3-7). 11.04 (*0-606-16606-8*) Turtleback Bks.

—The Forgotten. 1997. (Animorphs Ser.: No. 11). 162p. (J). (gr. 3-7). mass mkt. 4.99 (*0-590-99732-7*) Scholastic, Inc.

—The Forgotten. 1997. (Animorphs Ser.: No. 11). (J). (gr. 3-7). 11.04 (*0-606-11048-8*) Turtleback Bks.

—The Hidden. 2000. (Animorphs Ser.: No. 39). 160p. (J). (gr. 3-7). mass mkt. 4.99 (*0-439-10678-8*) Scholastic, Inc.

—The Hidden. l.t. ed. 2001. (Animorphs Ser.: No. 39). 121p. (J). (gr. 4 up). lib. bdg. 22.60 (*0-8368-2772-4*) Stevens, Gareth Inc.

—The Hork-Bajir Chronicles. (Animorphs Ser.). 206p. (J). (gr. 3-7). 1999. mass mkt. 5.99 (*0-590-03646-7*); 1998. pap. 13.95 (*0-439-04291-7*) Scholastic, Inc.

—The Hork-Bajir Chronicles. 1999. (Animorphs Ser.). (J). (gr. 3-7). 12.04 (*0-606-17284-X*) Turtleback Bks.

—The Illusion. 1999. (Animorphs Ser.: No. 33). 156p. (J). (gr. 3-7). mass mkt. 4.99 (*0-439-07033-3*) Scholastic, Inc.

—The Illusion. l.t. ed. 2000. (Animorphs Ser.: No. 33). 156p. (J). (gr. 4 up). lib. bdg. 22.60 (*0-8368-2755-4*) Stevens, Gareth Inc.

—The Illusion. 1999. (Animorphs Ser.: No. 33). (J). (gr. 3-7). 11.04 (*0-606-17287-4*) Turtleback Bks.

—In the Time of Dinosaurs. 1999. (Animorphs: No. 2). (J). (gr. 3-7). 12.40 (*0-613-07252-9*) Econo-Clad Bks.

—In the Time of Dinosaurs. 1998. (Animorphs Ser.: No. 2). 229p. (J). (gr. 3-7). mass mkt. 4.99 (*0-590-95615-9*, Scholastic Paperbacks) Scholastic, Inc.

—In the Time of Dinosaurs. 1998. (Animorphs: No. 2). (J). (gr. 3-7). 11.04 (*0-606-13142-6*) Turtleback Bks.

—The Invasion. 1996. (Animorphs Ser.: No. 1). (J). (gr. 3-7). 11.04 (*0-606-09002-9*) Turtleback Bks.

—L' Invasion. 1999. (Animorphs Ser.: No. 1). Tr. of Invasion. (FRE & SPA.). 128p. (J). (gr. 3-7). pap. text 4.99 (*0-439-05602-0*) Scholastic, Inc.

—The Journey. 42nd ed. 2000. (Animorphs Ser.: No. 42). (Illus.). 144p. (J). (gr. 3-7). mass mkt. 4.99 (*0-439-11516-7*) Scholastic, Inc.

—The Journey. l.t. ed. 2001. (Animorphs Ser.: No. 42). 139p. (J). (gr. 4 up). lib. bdg. 22.60 (*0-8368-2775-9*) Stevens, Gareth Inc.

—The Journey. 2000. (Animorphs Ser.: No. 42). (Illus.). (J). (gr. 3-7). 11.04 (*0-606-18860-6*) Turtleback Bks.

—El Mensaje. 1999. (Animorphs Ser.: No. 4). (SPA.). (J). (gr. 3-7). pap. text 4.99 (*0-439-08783-X*, SO5398) Scholastic, Inc.

—El Mensaje. 1999. No. 4. 11.04 (*0-606-17290-4*) Turtleback Bks.

—The Message. 1996. (Animorphs Ser.: No. 4). 151p. (J). (gr. 3-7). mass mkt. 4.99 (*0-590-62980-8*) Scholastic, Inc.

—The Message. 2000. (Animorphs Ser.: No. 4). (Illus.). (J). (gr. 3-7). 11.04 (*0-606-18510-0*) Turtleback Bks.

—Le Message. 1996. (Animorphs Ser.: No. 4). Tr. of Message. (FRE.). (J). (gr. 3-7). 11.04 (*0-606-10126-8*) Turtleback Bks.

—The Mutation. 36th ed. 1999. (Animorphs Ser.: No. 36). (Illus.). 142p. (J). (gr. 3-7). mass mkt. 4.99 (*0-439-10675-3*) Scholastic, Inc.

—The Mutation. l.t. ed. 2000. (Animorphs Ser.: No. 36). 142p. (J). (gr. 4 up). lib. bdg. 22.60 (*0-8368-2756-2*) Stevens, Gareth Inc.

—The Mutation. 1999. (Animorphs Ser.: No. 36). (Illus.). (J). (gr. 3-7). 11.04 (*0-606-18507-0*) Turtleback Bks.

—The Next Passage. 2000. (Animorphs Ser.: No. 2). (Illus.). 128p. (J). (gr. 3-7). mass mkt. 4.99 (*0-439-14263-6*) Scholastic, Inc.

—The Next Passage. 2000. (Animorphs: No. 2). (Illus.). (J). (gr. 3-7). 11.04 (*0-606-18506-2*) Turtleback Bks.

—The Other. 2000. (Animorphs Ser.: No. 40). (Illus.). 160p. (J). (gr. 3-7). mass mkt. 4.99 (*0-439-10679-6*) Scholastic, Inc.

—The Other. l.t. ed. 2001. (Animorphs Ser.: No. 40). 130p. (J). (gr. 4 up). lib. bdg. 22.60 (*0-8368-2773-2*) Stevens, Gareth Inc.

—The Other. 2000. (Animorphs Ser.: No. 40). (Illus.). (J). (gr. 3-7). 11.04 (*0-606-18511-9*) Turtleback Bks.

—The Predator. 1996. (Animorphs Ser.: No. 5). 152p. (J). (gr. 3-7). mass mkt. 4.99 (*0-590-62981-6*) Scholastic, Inc.

—The Predator. 1996. (Animorphs Ser.: No. 5). (J). (gr. 3-7). 11.04 (*0-606-10127-6*) Turtleback Bks.

—The Pretender. 1998. (Animorphs Ser.: No. 23). 154p. (J). (gr. 3-7). mass mkt. 4.99 (*0-590-76256-7*) Scholastic, Inc.

—The Pretender. 1998. (Animorphs Ser.: No. 23). (J). (gr. 3-7). 11.04 (*0-606-15435-3*) Turtleback Bks.

—The Prophecy. 1999. (Animorphs Ser.: No. 34). 141p. (J). (gr. 3-7). mass mkt. 4.99 (*0-439-07034-1*) Scholastic, Inc.

—The Prophecy. l.t. ed. 2000. (Animorphs Ser.: No. 34). 141p. (J). (gr. 4 up). lib. bdg. 22.60 (*0-8368-2757-0*) Stevens, Gareth Inc.

—The Prophecy. 1999. (Animorphs Ser.: No. 34). (J). (gr. 3-7). 11.04 (*0-606-17283-1*) Turtleback Bks.

—The Proposal. 1999. (Animorphs Ser.: No. 35). 147p. (J). (gr. 3-7). mass mkt. 4.99 (*0-439-07035-X*) Scholastic, Inc.

—The Proposal. l.t. ed. 2000. (Animorphs Ser.: No. 35). 147p. (J). (gr. 4 up). lib. bdg. 22.60 (*0-8368-2758-9*) Stevens, Gareth Inc.

—The Proposal. 1999. (Animorphs Ser.: No. 35). (J). (gr. 3-7). 11.04 (*0-606-17289-0*) Turtleback Bks.

—The Reaction. 1997. (Animorphs Ser.: No. 12). 152p. (J). (gr. 3-7). mass mkt. 4.99 (*0-590-99734-3*) Scholastic, Inc.

—The Revelation. 2000. (Animorphs Ser.: No. 45). (Illus.). 160p. (J). (gr. 3-7). mass mkt. 4.99 (*0-439-11519-1*) Scholastic, Inc.

—The Secret. 1997. (Animorphs Ser.: No. 9). (J). (gr. 3-7). 11.04 (*0-606-11051-8*) Turtleback Bks.

—The Separation. 1999. (Animorphs Ser.: No. 32). 158p. (J). (gr. 3-7). mass mkt. 4.99 (*0-439-07032-5*) Scholastic, Inc.

—The Separation. l.t. ed. 2000. (Animorphs Ser.: No. 32). 158p. (J). (gr. 4 up). lib. bdg. 22.60 (*0-8368-2759-7*) Stevens, Gareth Inc.

—The Separation. 1999. (Animorphs Ser.: No. 32). (J). (gr. 3-7). 11.04 (*0-606-17060-X*) Turtleback Bks.

—The Sickness. 1999. (Animorphs Ser.: No. 29). 152p. (J). (gr. 3-7). mass mkt. 4.99 (*0-590-76262-1*) Scholastic, Inc.

—The Sickness. 1999. (Animorphs Ser.: No. 29). 11.04 (*0-606-16618-1*) Turtleback Bks.

—The Solution. 1998. (Animorphs Ser.: No. 22). 152p. (J). (gr. 3-7). mass mkt. 4.99 (*0-590-76255-9*) Scholastic, Inc.

—The Solution. 1998. (Animorphs Ser.: No. 22). (J). (gr. 3-7). 11.04 (*0-606-15434-5*) Turtleback Bks.

—The Stranger. 1997. (Animorphs Ser.: No. 7). 163p. (J). (gr. 3-7). mass mkt. 4.99 (*0-590-99726-2*) Scholastic, Inc.

—The Stranger. 1997. (Animorphs Ser.: No. 7). (J). (gr. 3-7). 11.04 (*0-606-11049-6*) Turtleback Bks.

—The Suspicion, No. 24. 1998. (Animorphs Ser.: No. 24). 155p. (J). (gr. 3-7). mass mkt. 4.99 (*0-590-76257-5*) Scholastic, Inc.

—The Test. 2000. (Animorphs Ser.: No. 43). (Illus.). 144p. (J). (gr. 3-7). mass mkt. 4.99 (*0-439-11517-5*) Scholastic, Inc.

—The Test. 2000. (Animorphs Ser.: No. 43). (Illus.). (J). (gr. 3-7). 11.04 (*0-606-18861-4*) Turtleback Bks.

—The Threat. 1998. (Animorphs Ser.: No. 21). (J). (gr. 3-7). 11.04 (*0-606-13141-8*) Turtleback Bks.

—The Underground. 1998. (Animorphs Ser.: No. 17). 167p. (J). (gr. 3-7). mass mkt. 4.99 (*0-590-49436-8*, Scholastic Paperbacks) Scholastic, Inc.

—The Underground. 1998. (Animorphs Ser.: No. 17). (J). (gr. 3-7). 11.04 (*0-606-13137-X*) Turtleback Bks.

—The Unexpected. 2000. (Animorphs Ser.: No. 44). (Illus.). 160p. (J). (gr. 3-7). mass mkt. 4.99 (*0-439-11518-3*) Scholastic, Inc.

—The Unknown. 1998. (Animorphs Ser.: No. 14). 166p. (J). (gr. 3-7). mass mkt. 4.99 (*0-590-49423-6*, Scholastic Paperbacks) Scholastic, Inc.

—The Unknown. 1998. (Animorphs Ser.: No. 14). (J). (gr. 3-7). 11.04 (*0-606-12875-1*) Turtleback Bks.

—El Visitante. 1999. (Animorphs Ser.: No. 2). (SPA., Illus.). 192p. (J). (gr. 3-7). pap. 4.99 (*0-439-07163-1*, SO5396) Scholastic, Inc.

—El Visitante. 1999. (Animorphs Ser.: No. 2). (J). (gr. 3-7). 11.04 (*0-606-16929-6*) Turtleback Bks.

—The Visitor. 1996. (Animorphs Ser.: No. 2). (J). (gr. 3-7). 11.04 (*0-606-09003-7*) Turtleback Bks.

—The Warning. 1998. (Animorphs Ser.: No. 16). 151p. (J). (gr. 3-7). mass mkt. 4.99 (*0-590-49430-9*, Scholastic Paperbacks) Scholastic, Inc.

—The Warning. 1998. (Animorphs Ser.: No. 16). (J). (gr. 3-7). 11.04 (*0-606-13136-1*) Turtleback Bks.

—The Weakness. 37th ed. 2000. (Animorphs Ser.: No. 37). 160p. (J). (gr. 3-7). mass mkt. 4.99 (*0-439-10676-1*, Scholastic Paperbacks) Scholastic, Inc.

—The Weakness. l.t. ed. 2001. (Animorphs Ser.: No. 37). (Illus.). 129p. (J). (gr. 4 up). lib. bdg. 22.60 (*0-8368-2770-8*) Stevens, Gareth Inc.

—The Weakness. 2000. (Animorphs Ser.: No. 37). (Illus.). (J). (gr. 3-7). 11.04 (*0-606-18508-9*) Turtleback Bks.

Baltz, Terry & Baltz, Wayne. The Invisible Kid & the Intergalactic RV. 1997. (Invisible Kid Ser.: No. 3). 127p. (J). (gr. 2-6). pap. 6.95 (*1-884610-13-7*) Prairie Divide Productions.

Base, Graeme. The Worst Band in the Universe: A Totally Cosmic Musical Adventure. 1999. (Illus.). 48p. (J). (gr. 4-7). 19.95 o.p. incl. audio compact disk (*0-8109-3998-3*) Abrams, Harry N. , Inc.

Bellavia, Timothy D. We Are All the Same Inside. Bellavia, William D., ed. 2nd ed. 2000. (Illus.). 28p. (J). (ps-3). reprint ed. per. 10.95 (*0-615-11395-8*) T.I.M.M.-E. Co., Inc.

Biro, Val. Gumdrop & the Martians. (Illus.). 27p. (J). text 22.95 (*0-340-71485-9*); 1998. mass mkt. 11.95 (*0-340-71486-7*) Hodder & Stoughton, Ltd. GBR. *Dist:* Lubrecht & Cramer, Ltd., Trafalgar Square.

Blacker, Terence. The Angel Factory. (Illus.). 224p. (J). 2004. pap. 4.99 (*0-689-86413-2*, Aladdin); 2002. (gr. 6-9). 16.95 (*0-689-85171-5*, Simon & Schuster Children's Publishing) Simon & Schuster Children's Publishing.

Blackman, Malorie. Whizziwig Returns. l.t. unabr. ed. 2003. (Read-Along Ser.). 160p. (J). 24.95 incl. audio (*0-7540-6234-1*, RA035, Galaxy Children's Large Print) BBC Audiobooks America.

Brennan, Herbie. Zartog's Remote. 2001. (Middle Grade Fiction Ser.). (Illus.). 96p. (J). (gr. 3-6). lib. bdg. 14.95 (*1-57505-507-4*, Carolrhoda Bks.) Lerner Publishing Group.

Brooks, Walter R. Freddy & the Baseball Team from Mars. 1999. (Illus.). 256p. (YA). (gr. 3-7). 23.95 (*0-87951-942-8*) Overlook Pr., The.

—Freddy & the Baseball Team from Mars. 1963. (Illus.). (J). (gr. 3-7). 5.99 o.s.i (*0-394-90810-4*, Knopf Bks. for Young Readers) Random Hse. Children's Bks.

—Freddy & the Baseball Team from Mars. 2000. (J). pap. 67.95 incl. audio (*0-7887-4461-5*, 41150); pap. 67.95 incl. audio (*0-7887-4461-5*, 41150) Recorded Bks., LLC.

—Freddy & the Baseball Team From Mars. 1988. (Illus.). 256p. (J). (gr. 3-7). pap. 2.95 o.p. (*0-440-42724-X*) Dell Publishing.

—Freddy & the Men from Mars. 2002. (Illus.). 246p. (J). 23.95 (*1-58567-269-6*) Overlook Pr., The.

Buchanan, Paul. Uncle from Another Planet. 1999. (Heebie Jeebies Ser.: Vol. 4). 144p. (YA). pap. 5.99 (*0-8054-1650-1*) Broadman & Holman Pubs.

Bunting, Eve. Wanna Buy an Alien? 2000. (Illus.). 96p. (J). (gr. 4-6). tchr. ed. 14.00 (*0-395-69719-0*, Clarion Bks.) Houghton Mifflin Co. Trade & Reference Div.

Burnard, Damon. Burger! 1998. (Illus.). 118p. (J). (gr. 4-6). pap. 4.50 o.s.i (*0-395-91315-2*) Houghton Mifflin Co.

Butterfly, Atk. Dust Bunny. (J). E-Book 7.50 (*1-886420-77-7*); 1999. (Rust Bucket Universe Ser.: Vol. 3). E-Book 7.50 (*1-886420-61-0*) C&M Online Media, Inc. (Boson Bks.).

Butterworth, Nick. Q Pootle 5. 2001. (Illus.). 32p. (J). (ps-2). 13.95 (*0-689-84243-0*, Atheneum) Simon & Schuster Children's Publishing.

Calvert, Patricia. Picking up the Pieces. (YA). 1999. 176p. (gr. 5-9). pap. 4.99 (*0-689-82451-3*, Simon Pulse); 1993. 192p. (gr. 7 up). 15.00 (*0-684-19558-5*, Atheneum) Simon & Schuster Children's Publishing.

—Picking up the Pieces. 1999. 11.04 (*0-606-15922-3*) Turtleback Bks.

Campbell, Lucille C. Alien Logic. 1992. (J). (gr. 4-12). pap. text 7.97 (*0-937659-56-8*) GCT, Inc.

Cannon, Janell. Trupp: A Fuzzhead Tale. (Illus.). 48p. (J). 1998. pap. 7.00 (*0-15-201695-3*, Harcourt Paperbacks); 1995. 16.00 (*0-15-200130-1*) Harcourt Children's Bks.

—Trupp: A Fuzzhead Tale. 1998. (J). 13.15 (*0-606-13876-5*) Turtleback Bks.

Cazet, Denys. Minnie & Moo & the Potato from Planet X. (I Can Read Book Ser.). (Illus.). 48p. (J). (gr. k-3). 2003. pap. 3.99 (*0-06-444312-4*); 2002. 15.95 (*0-06-623750-5*); 2002. lib. bdg. 16.89 (*0-06-623751-3*) HarperCollins Children's Bk. Group.

—Minnie & Moo Save the Earth, Vol. 3. 1999. (Minnie & Moo Ser.: Vol. 3). (Illus.). 48p. (J). (gr. 1-3). pap. 3.99 (*0-7894-3929-8*); pap. 12.95 (*0-7894-2594-7*) Dorling Kindersley Publishing, Inc. (D K Ink).

Christopher, John. The Tripods Trilogy, 3 bks., Set. 1999. (Illus.). (YA). (gr. 7-12). 17.95 (*0-689-00852-X*, Simon Pulse) Simon & Schuster Children's Publishing.

Coffin, M. T. Student Exchange. 1997. (Spinetingler Ser.: No. 22). (J). (gr. 4-7). pap. 3.99 (*0-380-78804-7*, Avon Bks.) Morrow/Avon.

Collins, Terry. Boy Genius: Movie Storybook. 2001. (Jimmy Neutron Boy Genius Ser.). (Illus.). 32p. (J). (gr. 4-7). 8.99 (*0-689-84552-9*, Simon Spotlight/Nickelodeon) Simon & Schuster Children's Publishing.

—E. T. the Extra-Terrestrial. 2002. (E. T. the Extra-Terrestrial Ser.). (Illus.). 144p. (J). pap. 4.99 (*0-689-84367-4*, Simon Spotlight) Simon & Schuster Children's Publishing.

Conly, Jane Leslie. The Rudest Alien on Earth, ERS. 2002. 160p. (YA). (gr. 5-8). 16.95 (*0-8050-6069-3*, Holt, Henry & Co. Bks. For Young Readers) Holt, Henry & Co.

Corey, Shana. Nergal & the Great Space Race. 2002. (First Graders from Mars Ser.: No. 3). (Illus.). 32p. (J). (ps-2). pap. 15.95 (*0-439-26633-5*); mass mkt. 4.50 (*0-439-42443-7*) Scholastic, Inc. (Scholastic Pr.).

—Tera, Star Student. 2003. (First Graders from Mars Ser.: No. 4). (Illus.). 32p. (J). pap. 15.95 (*0-439-26634-3*); mass mkt. 4.50 (*0-439-45219-8*) Scholastic, Inc. (Scholastic Pr.).

Coville, Bruce. Aliens Stole My Body. 1998. (Bruce Coville's Alien Adventures Ser.). (J). (gr. 3-7). 10.04 (*0-606-13115-9*) Turtleback Bks.

—The Attack of the Two-Inch Teacher. unabr. ed. 2000. (I Was a Sixth Grade Alien Ser.). 165p. (J). (gr. 3-5). pap. 28.00 incl. audio (*0-8072-8354-1*, YA170SP, Listening Library) Random Hse. Audio Publishing Group.

—The Attack of the Two-Inch Teacher. 1999. (I Was a Sixth Grade Alien Ser.: Vol. 2). 176p. (J). (gr. 3-6). pap. 3.99 (*0-671-02651-8*, Aladdin) Simon & Schuster Children's Publishing.

—The Attack of the Two-Inch Teacher. 1999. (I Was a Sixth Grade Alien Ser.). (Illus.). (J). 10.04 (*0-606-18374-4*) Turtleback Bks.

—Bruce Coville's UFOs. 2000. (Bruce Coville Ser.). (Illus.). 224p. (J). (gr. 4-8). pap. 4.99 (*0-380-80257-0*) Morrow/Avon.

—Bruce Coville's UFOs. 2000. (Illus.). (J). 11.04 (*0-606-18679-4*) Turtleback Bks.

—Don't Fry My Veeblax! 2000. (Sixth Grade Alien Ser.: Vol. 6). (Illus.). 160p. (J). (gr. 3-6). pap. 3.99 (*0-671-02655-0*, Aladdin) Simon & Schuster Children's Publishing.

—I Lost My Grandfather's Brain. unabr. ed. 2000. (I Was a Sixth Grade Alien Ser.). 160p. (J). (gr. 3-5). pap. 28.00 incl. audio (*0-8072-8385-1*, YA180SP, Listening Library) Random Hse. Audio Publishing Group.

—I Lost My Grandfather's Brain. 1999. (I Was a Sixth Grade Alien Ser.: Vol. 3). 176p. (J). (gr. 3-7). pap. 3.99 (*0-671-02652-6*, Aladdin) Simon & Schuster Children's Publishing.

—I Lost My Grandfather's Brain. 1999. (I Was a Sixth Grade Alien Ser.). (Illus.). (J). 10.04 (*0-606-18306-X*) Turtleback Bks.

—I Was a Sixth Grade Alien. (I Was a Sixth Grade Alien Ser.). 170p. (J). (gr. 4-6). pap. 3.99 (*0-8072-8202-2*); 2000. (gr. 3-5). pap. 23.00 incl. audio (*0-8072-8201-4*, YYA138SP) Random Hse. Audio Publishing Group. (Listening Library).

—I Was a Sixth Grade Alien. 1999. (I Was a Sixth Grade Alien Ser.: Vol. 1). 192p. (J). (gr. 3-6). pap. 3.99 (*0-671-02650-X*, Aladdin); (Illus.). 16.00 (*0-671-03651-3*, Simon & Schuster Children's Publishing) Simon & Schuster Children's Publishing.

—I Was a Sixth Grade Alien. 1999. (I Was a Sixth Grade Alien Ser.). 10.04 (*0-606-17089-8*) Turtleback Bks.

—The Monsters of Morley Manor. 2002. (J). lib. bdg. 24.00 incl. audio (*0-9717540-3-9*, 02003L); lib. bdg. 24.00 incl. audio (*0-9717540-3-9*, 02003L) Full Cast Audio.

—The Monsters of Morley Manor. 240p. (YA). (gr. 3-6). 2003. (Illus.). pap. 5.95 (*0-15-204705-0*, Magic Carpet Bks.); 2001. 16.00 (*0-15-216382-4*) Harcourt Children's Bks.

—My Teacher Is an Alien. unabr. ed. 1998. (My Teacher Is an Alien Ser.). (J). (gr. 4-7). pap. 23.00 incl. audio (*0-8072-8029-1*, YA971SP, Listening Library) Random Hse. Audio Publishing Group.

—My Teacher Is an Alien. (J). 1990. (Illus.). mass mkt. 3.50 (*0-671-74177-2*); 1900. (gr. 4-7). mass mkt. (*0-671-03572-X*) Simon & Schuster Children's Publishing. (Aladdin).

—My Teacher Is an Alien. 1989. E-Book (*1-59019-038-6*); (J). (gr. 4-7). E-Book (*1-58824-026-6*) ipicturebooks, LLC.

—Peanut Butter Lover Boy. 2000. (I Was a Sixth Grade Alien Ser.: Vol. 4). (Illus.). 160p. (J). (gr. 3-6). pap. 3.99 (*0-671-02653-4*, Aladdin) Simon & Schuster Children's Publishing.

—Peanut Butter Lover Boy. 2000. (I Was a Sixth Grade Alien Ser.). (Illus.). (J). 10.04 (*0-606-18307-8*) Turtleback Bks.

—The Revolt of the Miniature Mutants. 2001. (I Was a Sixth Grade Alien Ser.: Vol. 10). (Illus.). 160p. (J). (gr. 3-6). pap. 3.99 (*0-671-02659-3*, Aladdin) Simon & Schuster Children's Publishing.

—The Revolt of the Miniature Mutants, No. 10. 2000. (I Was a Sixth Grade Alien Ser.). (Illus.). (J). 10.04 (*0-606-20716-3*) Turtleback Bks.

—Snatched from Earth! 2000. (I Was a Sixth Grade Alien Ser.: Vol. 8). (Illus.). 208p. (J). (gr. 3-6). pap. 3.99 (*0-671-02657-7*, Aladdin) Simon & Schuster Children's Publishing.

—There's an Alien in My Classroom! l.t. ed. 2000. pap. 16.95 (*0-7540-6108-6*, Galaxy Children's Large Print) BBC Audiobooks America.

—There's an Alien in My Classroom! (Illus.). 201p. pap. 8.95 (*0-340-73634-8*) Hodder & Stoughton, Ltd. GBR. *Dist:* Lubrecht & Cramer, Ltd., Trafalgar Square.

—There's an Alien in My Underwear! 2001. (I Was a Sixth Grade Alien Ser.: Vol. 11). (Illus.). 160p. (J). (gr. 3-6). pap. 3.99 (*0-671-02660-7*, Aladdin) Simon & Schuster Children's Publishing.

—Too Many Aliens! 2000. (I Was a Sixth Grade Alien Ser.: Vol. 7). (Illus.). 176p. (YA). (gr. 3-6). pap. 3.99 (*0-671-02656-9*, Aladdin) Simon & Schuster Children's Publishing.

—Zombies of the Science Fair. 5th ed. 2000. (I Was a Sixth Grade Alien Ser.: Vol. 5). (Illus.). 160p. (J). (gr. 3-6). pap. 3.99 (*0-671-02654-2*, Aladdin) Simon & Schuster Children's Publishing.

—Zombies of the Science Fair. 2000. (I Was a Sixth Grade Alien Ser.). (Illus.). (J). 10.04 (0-606-18308-6) Turtleback Bks.

Coville, Katherine. Aliens Stole My Body: Bring Back My Body! 1998. (J). (gr. 3-9). 14.00 (0-671-02414-0, Simon & Schuster Children's Publishing) Simon & Schuster Children's Publishing.

Crilley, Mark. Akiko & the Intergalactic Zoo. 2002. (Illus.). 160p. (J). (gr. 3-5). 9.95 (0-385-72968-5, Delacorte Pr.) Dell Publishing.

—Akiko & the Intergalactic Zoo. 2003. (Illus.). 160p. (gr. 3 up). pap. text 4.99 (0-440-41891-7, Yearling) Random Hse. Children's Bks.

Dadey, Debbie & Jones, Marcia Thornton. Aliens Don't Carve Jack-O-Lanterns. 2002. (Bailey School Kids Holiday Special Ser.). 112p. (J). mass mkt. 3.99 (0-439-40831-8, Scholastic Paperbacks) Scholastic, Inc.

De Darco, Alfredo. The Hoax- Files. 1998. 128p. (J). (gr. 7-12). pap. 4.50 (0-689-82185-9, Simon Pulse) Simon & Schuster Children's Publishing.

De Mejo, Oscar. Journey to Boc Boc: The Kidnapping of a Rock Star. 1987. (Illus.). 48p. (J). (gr. 3-7). 12.95 (0-06-021579-8); lib. bdg. 12.89 o.p. (0-06-021580-1) HarperCollins Children's Bk. Group.

Deacon, Alexis. Beegu, RS. 2003. (Illus.). 40p. (J). 16.00 (0-374-30667-2, Farrar, Straus & Giroux (BYR)) Farrar, Straus & Giroux.

DeAndrea, William L. & DeAndrea, Matthew. The Pizza That Time Forgot. 1999. (J). (gr. 3-7). pap. 3.99 (0-380-79155-2, Avon Bks.) Morrow/Avon.

Dereske, Jo. The Lone Sentinel. 1989. 176p. (J). (gr. 4-8). text 14.95 o.p. (0-689-31552-X, Atheneum) Simon & Schuster Children's Publishing.

Desrosiers, Sylvie. Ma Mere Est une Extraterrestre. 2002. (Premier Roman Ser.). (FRE., Illus.). 64p. (J). pap. 8.95 (2-89021-561-X) La Courte Echelle CAN. Dist: Firefly Bks., Ltd.

Dexter, Catherine. Alien Game. 208p. (YA). 1997. (gr. 5 up). pap. 4.95 (0-688-15290-2); 1995. (Illus.). (gr. 7 up). 15.00 o.p. (0-688-11332-X) Morrow/Avon. (Morrow, William & Co.).

Duey, Kathleen. Beware the Alien Invasion! 2000. (Alone in the Dark Ser.). (Illus.). 32p. (J). pap. 3.95 (1-891100-15-7) Smart Kids Publishing.

Duffey, Betsy. Alien for Rent. 1999. (Illus.). 80p. (gr. 2-5). text 14.95 o.s.i (0-385-32572-X, Delacorte Pr.) Dell Publishing.

—Alien for Rent. 2000. (Illus.). 80p. (gr. 2-5). pap. text 4.50 (0-440-41468-7, Yearling) Random Hse. Children's Bks.

—Alien for Rent. 2000. 10.65 (0-606-17889-9) Turtleback Bks.

Elections 2000 Set. 2000. (J). (gr. 2-4). 131.40 (0-7613-1243-9) Millbrook Pr., Inc.

Engle, Marty M. & Barnes, Johnny Ray, Jr. Fly the Unfriendly Skies. l.t. ed. 1996. (Strange Matter Ser.: No. 7). 124p. (J). (gr. 4-6). lib. bdg. 21.27 o.p. (0-8368-1673-0) Stevens, Gareth Inc.

Fallon, Joe. Quailman Battles the Giant Space Slug. 1999. (Golden Book Ser.). (Illus.). (J). pap. (0-307-13141-6, Golden Bks.) Random Hse. Children's Bks.

Falls, Gregory A. The Forgotten Door. 1986. (J). (gr. 4 up). pap. 6.50 (0-87602-242-5) Anchorage Pr.

Farber, Erica & Sansevere, J. R. The Alien. 1995. (Little Critter Ser.: No. 2). (Illus.). 32p. (J). (ps-3). bds. 3.99 o.s.i (0-307-16661-9, 16661, Golden Bks.) Random Hse. Children's Bks.

Gaarder, Jostein. Hello? Is Anybody There? l.t. ed. 2002. (Illus.). (J). 16.95 (0-7540-7814-0, Galaxy Children's Large Print) BBC Audiobooks America.

Gaarder, Jostein & Anderson, James. Hello? Is Anybody There?, RS. 1998. (Illus.). 144p. (J). (gr. 4-7). 15.00 o.p. (0-374-32948-6, Farrar, Straus & Giroux (BYR)) Farrar, Straus & Giroux.

Gaetz, Dayle Campbell. Night of the Aliens. 1995. (Out of This World Ser.). 72p. (J). (gr. 3-7). pap. 5.95 (1-896184-08-1) Roussan Pubs., Inc./Roussan Editeur, Inc. CAN. Dist: Orca Bk. Pubs.

Gauthier, Gail. Club Earth. 1999. (Illus.). 152p. (J). (gr. 3-7). 15.99 o.s.i (0-399-23373-3) Penguin Group (USA) Inc.

—My Life among the Aliens. 1996. (Illus.). 112p. (J). (gr. 3-7). 14.95 o.s.i (0-399-22945-0, G. P. Putnam's Sons) Penguin Group (USA) Inc.

—My Life among the Aliens. 1998. (Illus.). 112p. (J). (gr. 3-7). pap. 4.99 (0-698-11636-4, PaperStar) Penguin Putnam Bks. for Young Readers.

—My Life among the Aliens. l.t. ed. 2001. 126p. (J). 22.95 (0-7862-3604-3) Thorndike Pr.

—My Life among the Aliens. 1998. (J). 11.04 (0-606-12997-9) Turtleback Bks.

Gilden, Mel. The Pumpkins of Time. 1994. 192p. (YA). (gr. 6 up). 10.95 (0-15-276603-0) Harcourt Children's Bks.

—The Pumpkins of Time. 1994. 224p. (YA). (gr. 6 up). pap. 4.95 o.s.i (0-15-200889-6) Harcourt Trade Pubs.

Gilmore, Kate. The Exchange Student. 1999. 224p. (J). (gr. 5-9). tchr. ed. 15.00 (0-395-57511-7); E-Book 15.00 (0-618-15330-6) Houghton Mifflin Co.

Golden Books Staff. Eggstra-Terristrials: Jimmy Neutron. 2001. 32p. (J). (gr. k-3). pap. 4.99 (0-307-29955-4, Golden Bks.) Random Hse. Children's Bks.

—Jimmy Neutron: Alien Alert! 2001. 32p. pap. 4.99 (0-307-13930-1, Golden Bks.) Random Hse. Children's Bks.

—Jimmy Neutron: Intelligent Life? 2001. 16p. (J). (gr. k-3). pap. 4.99 (0-307-21835-X, Golden Bks.) Random Hse. Children's Bks.

Goldman, Leslie. The Return of Jay & Kay. movie tie-in ed. 2002. (Men in Black II Ser.). (Illus.). 64p. (J). pap. 4.99 (0-06-001179-3, Harper Festival) HarperCollins Children's Bk. Group.

Greenburg, Dan. Just Add Water & Scream. 2003. (Zack Files Ser.: No. 29). (Illus.). 64p. (J). mass mkt. 4.99 (0-448-42887-3, Grosset & Dunlap) Penguin Putnam Bks. for Young Readers.

Griffiths, Andy. Zombie Butts from Uranus. 2004. 128p. (J). mass mkt. 4.99 (0-439-42470-4) Scholastic, Inc.

Gutman, Dan. Funny Boy Takes on the Chit-Chatting Cheeses from Chattanooga. (L.A.F. Bks.). (Illus.). 114p. (J). (gr. 4-7). 2001. lib. bdg. 14.49 (0-7868-2578-2); No. 3. 2000. pap. 4.99 (0-7868-1445-4) Disney Pr.

Hall, Katy. The Great Halloween Alien Invasion. 1998. (Life with Louie Ser.: No. 1). (Illus.). 64p. (J). (gr. 2-5). mass mkt. 4.25 o.s.i (0-06-107129-3) HarperCollins Children's Bk. Group.

Hamilton, Virginia. Willie Bea & the Time the Martians Landed. 1983. 224p. (J). (gr. 5-9). 16.00 o.s.i (0-688-02390-8, Greenwillow Bks.) HarperCollins Children's Bk. Group.

—Willie Bea & the Time the Martians Landed. 1989. 224p. (J). (gr. 4-7). reprint ed. pap. 3.95 o.p. (0-689-71328-2, Simon Pulse) Simon & Schuster Children's Publishing.

Heintze, Ty. Valley of the Eels: A Science Fiction Mystery. 1993. (Illus.). 160p. (J). (gr. 5-6). 15.95 (0-89015-904-1) Eakin Pr.

Herman, Gail. Be Good, Gertie! 2002. (E. T. the Extra-Terrestrial Ser.). (Illus.). 24p. (J). pap. 3.50 (0-689-84364-X, Simon Spotlight) Simon & Schuster Children's Publishing.

—A Friend for E. T. 2002. (E. T. the Extra-Terrestrial Ser.). (Illus.). 24p. (J). (ps-3). pap. 3.50 (0-689-84363-1, Simon Spotlight) Simon & Schuster Children's Publishing.

—Scooby-Doo & Aliens Too! 2000. (Scooby-Doo Movie Storybooks). (Illus.). 32p. (J). (ps-3). mass mkt. 3.50 (0-439-17701-4) Scholastic, Inc.

Hess, Debra. Escape from Earth. 1994. (Spy from Outer Space Ser.: Vol. 3). (Illus.). 128p. (J). (gr. 3-6). pap. 3.50 o.p. (1-56282-682-4) Hyperion Bks. for Children.

—Spies, Incorporated. 1994. (Spy from Outer Space Ser.: Vol. 4). (Illus.). 128p. (J). (gr. 3-6). pap. 3.50 o.s.i (1-56282-683-2) Hyperion Bks. for Children.

Homzie, H. B. Alien Clones, No. 4. 2003. (Alien Clones from Outer Space Ser.). 80p. (J). pap. 3.99 (0-689-82345-2, Aladdin) Simon & Schuster Children's Publishing.

—Alien Clones Wore Diapers, No. 3. 2003. (Alien Clones from Outer Space Ser.). 80p. (J). pap. 3.99 (0-689-82344-4, Aladdin) Simon & Schuster Children's Publishing.

Homzie, Hillary, contrib. by. Two Heads Are Better Than One, Vol. 1. 2002. (Alien Clones from Outer Space Ser.). 80p. (J). pap. 3.99 (0-689-82342-8, Aladdin) Simon & Schuster Children's Publishing.

Hoopmann, Kathy. Of Mice & Aliens: An Asperger Adventure. 2001. (Illus.). 103p. (J). pap. (1-84310-007-X) Kingsley, Jessica Pubs.

Howe, James. Invasion of the Mind Swappers from Asteroid 6. (Tales from the House of Bunnicula Ser.). (J). 2003. 112p. pap. 3.99 (0-689-83950-2, Aladdin); 2002. (Illus.). 96p. (gr. 2-4). 9.95 (0-689-83949-9, Atheneum) Simon & Schuster Children's Publishing.

—It Came from Beneath the Bed! 2002. (Tales from the House of Bunnicula Ser.: Bk. 1). (Illus.). 96p. (J). (gr. 2-4). 9.95 (0-689-83947-2, Atheneum) Simon & Schuster Children's Publishing.

Hughes, Monica. The Golden Aquarians. 1995. 192p. (YA). (gr. 7). pap. 15.00 (0-671-50543-2, Simon & Schuster Children's Publishing) Simon & Schuster Children's Publishing.

Hulse, Shawna & Hulse, Dwight. The Bunky Family from Mars. 2000. (Illus.). 48p. pap. 9.00 (0-8059-4678-0) Dorrance Publishing Co., Inc.

James, Brian. Bad Dogs from Outer Space. 2003. (Supertwins Ser.: No. 1). (Illus.). 32p. (J). mass mkt. 3.99 (0-439-46623-7, Cartwheel Bks.) Scholastic, Inc.

Jeapes, Ben. The Ark. 2000. 352p. (YA). (gr. 8-12). mass mkt. 4.99 (0-439-21917-5) Scholastic, Inc.

Johnson, Pete. Eyes of the Alien. l.t. ed. 2000. pap. 16.95 (0-7540-6127-2); 2003. 184p. (J). 24.95 incl. audio (0-7540-6239-2, RA040) BBC Audiobooks America. (Galaxy Children's Large Print).

Johnston, Tony. Alien & Possum: Friends No Matter What. (Ready-to-Reads Ser.). 48p. (J). 2002. pap. 3.99 (0-689-85326-2, Aladdin); 2001. (Illus.). 15.00 (0-689-83835-2, Simon & Schuster Children's Publishing) Simon & Schuster Children's Publishing.

—Alien & Possum Hanging Out. (Ready-to-Reads Ser.). (Illus.). 48p. (J). 2003. pap. 3.99 (0-689-85771-3, Aladdin); 2002. (gr. 1-3). 15.00 (0-689-83836-0, Simon & Schuster Children's Publishing) Simon & Schuster Children's Publishing.

Joosse, Barbara M. Alien Brain Fryout. 2000. (Wild Willie Mystery Ser.). (Illus.). 96p. (J). (gr. 4-6). tchr. ed. 15.00 (0-395-68964-3, Clarion Bks.) Houghton Mifflin Co. Trade & Reference Div.

Katz, Z. L. Aliens Are Everywhere. movie tie-in ed. 2002. (Men in Black II Ser.). (Illus.). 32p. (J). (ps-2). pap. 3.99 (0-06-000189-5, Harper Festival) HarperCollins Children's Bk. Group.

Kendall, Benjamin. Alien Invasions. Thatch, Nancy R., ed. 1993. (Books for Students by Students). (Illus.). 29p. (J). (gr. 2-4). lib. bdg. 15.95 (0-933849-42-7) Landmark Editions, Inc.

Klause, Annette Curtis. Alien Secrets. 1999. 240p. (YA). (gr. 5-12). mass mkt. 5.50 (0-440-22851-4) Bantam Bks.

—Alien Secrets. 240p. 1994. (gr. 5-9). pap. text 4.99 o.s.i (0-440-41061-4); 1993. (J). (gr. 7-12). 15.95 o.s.i (0-385-30928-7, Delacorte Pr.) Dell Publishing.

—Alien Secrets. (J). 1995. pap. 4.99 (0-440-91038-2); 1994. pap. 4.99 (0-440-91023-4); 1993. o.s.i (0-385-30939-2) Random Hse. Children's Bks. (Dell Books for Young Readers).

—Alien Secrets. 1993. (J). 11.04 (0-606-07157-1) Turtleback Bks.

Korman, Gordon. Invasion of the Nose Pickers. 2001. (L.A.F. Ser.). (Illus.). 144p. (J). (gr. 4-7). pap. 4.99 (0-7868-1447-0) Hyperion Bks. for Children.

—Invasion of the Nose Pickers. 2000. (L.A.F. Bks.). (Illus.). 138p. (J). (gr. 2-6). lib. bdg. 14.49 (0-7868-2590-1) Hyperion Paperbacks for Children.

—Nose Pickers from Outer Space. 1999. 128p. (J). pap. 3.99 (0-7868-1413-6) Disney Pr.

—Nose Pickers from Outer Space. 1999. (L.A.F. Bks.). (Illus.). 137p. (J). (gr. 3-7). 13.49 (0-7868-2431-X) Hyperion Bks. for Children.

—Nosepickers from Outer Space. 1999. (Behind the Scenes Ser.). (Illus.). 128p. (J). (gr. 3-7). pap. 3.99 (0-7868-1343-1) Disney Pr.

—Planet of the Nose Pickers, No. 2. 2000. (Planet of the Nose Pickers Ser.: Vol. 2). 140p. (YA). lib. bdg. 14.49 (0-7868-2571-5) Hyperion Bks. for Children.

—Planet of the Nosepickers Vol. 2: Alien Exchange Student. 2000. (L.A.F. Bks.). (Illus.). 139p. (J). (gr. 2-6). pap. 3.99 (0-7868-1344-X) Disney Pr.

—Your Mummy Is a Nose Picker. 2000. (L.A.F. Bks.). (Illus.). 153p. (J). (gr. 4-7). pap. 4.99 (0-7868-1446-2) Disney Pr.

—Your Mummy Is a Nose Picker. 2000. (L.A.F. Bks.). (Illus.). 144p. (J). (gr. 4-7). pap. 14.49 (0-7868-2587-1) Hyperion Bks. for Children.

Krell, Robert. Sumo Baby, the Blade Brigade in the Big Earth Adventure. 1997. (1-880356-03-1) Emerald Bks.

Krull, Kathleen. The Night the Martians Landed. 2003. (Illus.). 80p. (J). (gr. 3 up). 4.25 (0-688-17246-6) HarperCollins Children's Bk. Group.

—The Night the Martians Landed: Just the Facts (Plus the Rumors)) about Invaders from Mars. 2003. (Illus.). 80p. (J). (gr. 2 up). lib. bdg. 15.89 (0-688-17247-4) HarperCollins Children's Bk. Group.

Kulling, Monica. Go, Stitch, Go! 2002. (Step into Reading Ser.). (Illus.). 32p. (J). (ps-1). pap. 3.99 (0-7364-1350-2); lib. bdg. 11.99 (0-7364-8010-2) Random Hse. Children's Bks. (RH/Disney).

Labatt, Mary. Aliens in Woodford. 2000. (Sam - Dog Detective Ser.). (Illus.). (J). (gr. 2-5). 110p. pap. 4.95 (1-55074-607-3); 210p. text 12.95 (1-55074-611-1) Kids Can Pr., Ltd.

Lantz, Francess L. Stepbaby from Planet Weird. 2001. (Illus.). (J). 3.99 (0-375-81259-8, Random Hse. Bks. for Young Readers) Random Hse. Children's Bks.

—Stepsister from the Planet Weird. (J). (gr. 3-7). 1997. 11.99 o.s.i (0-679-97330-3); 1996. 176p. pap. 3.99 o.s.i (0-679-87330-9) Random Hse. Children's Bks. (Random Hse. Bks. for Young Readers).

—Stepsister from the Planet Weird. 1997. 10.04 (0-606-13040-3) Turtleback Bks.

Lisle, Janet Taylor. Angela's Aliens. 1996. 128p. (J). (gr. 4-7). pap. 14.95 (0-531-09541-X); (Investigators of the Unknown Ser.: Bk. 4). lib. bdg. 15.99 (0-531-08891-X) Scholastic, Inc. (Orchard Bks.).

—Angela's Aliens. 1997. (Investigators of the Unknown Ser.). 10.04 (0-606-11043-7) Turtleback Bks.

Lytle, Casey. Alien in the Mirror Bk. 1: Homeworld. 2000. (Homeworld Ser.: Vol. 1). 218p. (YA). (gr. 4-9). mass mkt. 5.99 (0-9678933-0-5) Mcnarn Group, The.

Mackel, Kathy. Alien in a Bottle. 2004. 208p. (J). 15.99 (0-06-029281-4); lib. bdg. 16.89 (0-06-029282-2) HarperCollins Pubs.

—Can of Worms. 160p. (J). (gr. 3-7). 2000. (Illus.). pap. 3.99 (0-380-80050-0, Harper Trophy); 1999. 14.95 (0-380-97681-1); 1999. 14.95 (0-380-97681-1) HarperCollins Children's Bk. Group.

—Can of Worms. 2000. (Illus.). (J). 10.04 (0-606-17962-3) Turtleback Bks.

—Eggs in One Basket. 208p. (J). 2002. pap. 6.99 (0-380-81399-8); 2000. (gr. 5 up). lib. bdg. 17.89 (0-06-029213-X) HarperCollins Children's Bk. Group.

—Eggs in One Basket. 2000. 195p. (J). (gr. 5-7). 15.95 (0-380-97847-4) Morrow/Avon.

—From the Horse's Mouth. 2002. 224p. (J). lib. bdg. 15.89 (0-06-029415-9); (gr. 3-7). 15.95 (0-06-029414-0) HarperCollins Children's Bk. Group.

Manchester, Deborah M. & Davis, Madeline. Bula's Surprise Visit, 53 vols., Vol. 1. Manchester, Deborah M., ed. 1999. (Illus.). 32p. (J). 4.95 (0-9673099-0-5) Zula Ltd.

Mangels, Andy. Pursuit. 2003. (Roswell Ser.). (Illus.). 256p. (YA). mass mkt. 5.99 (0-689-85522-2, Simon Pulse) Simon & Schuster Children's Publishing.

Mason, Tom & Danko, Dan. Teenage Spaceland. 2002. (Butt-Ugly Martians Chapter Bks.: Bk. 4). 96p. (J). mass mkt. 4.50 (0-439-40791-5) Scholastic, Inc.

McCann, Jesse Leon. Scooby-Doo & the Alien Invaders. 2000. (Golden Book Ser.). (Illus.). 32p. (J). (ps-3). pap. text 3.99 (0-307-10474-5, 10474, Golden Bks.) Random Hse. Children's Bks.

—Scooby-Doo & the Alien Invaders. 2000. (Scooby-Doo Movie Storybooks). (Illus.). 32p. (J). (ps-3). mass mkt. 3.50 (0-439-17700-6) Scholastic, Inc.

McPhail, David M. Tinker & Tom & the Star Baby. (Illus.). 32p. (J). (ps-3). 2000. pap. 5.95 o.p. (0-316-56389-7); 1998. 14.95 o.p. (0-316-56349-8) Little Brown & Co.

—Tinker & Tom & the Star Baby. 1998. 12.10 (0-606-18268-3) Turtleback Bks.

—Tinker & Tom & the Star Baby. 1998. E-Book 4.99 (1-58824-897-6); E-Book (1-58824-681-7); E-Book (1-58824-680-9) ipicturebooks, LLC.

Meganck, Glenn. Big Deal. 1998. 67p. (J). (Illus.). (gr. 4-7). pap. 4.99 (1-892339-01-3); 11.99 (1-892339-00-5) Beachfront Publishing.

—No Big Deal. 2000. (Illus.). 76p. (J). (gr. 3-5). pap. 4.99 (1-892339-05-6) Beachfront Publishing.

Metz, Melinda. The Dark One. (Roswell High Ser.: No. 9). (YA). (gr. 6 up). 2000. 176p. mass mkt. 5.99 (0-671-03563-0); 2001. reprint ed. E-Book 5.90 (0-7434-3450-1) Simon & Schuster Children's Publishing. (Simon Pulse).

—The Intruder. (Roswell High Ser.: No. 5). (YA). (gr. 6 up). 2001. E-Book 4.99 (0-7434-3446-3); 2000. 160p. pap. 5.99 (0-671-77459-X); 1999. 176p. mass mkt. 4.50 (0-671-02378-0) Simon & Schuster Children's Publishing. (Simon Pulse).

—The Outsider. (Roswell High Ser.: No. 1). (YA). (gr. 6 up). 1999. 176p. pap. 5.99 (0-671-77466-2); 1998. 176p. mass mkt. 1.99 (0-671-02374-8); 2001. reprint ed. E-Book 5.99 (0-7434-3442-0) Simon & Schuster Children's Publishing. (Simon Pulse).

—The Rebel. (Roswell High Ser.: No. 8). (YA). (gr. 6 up). 2000. 176p. pap. 5.99 (0-671-03562-2); 2001. reprint ed. E-Book 5.99 (0-7434-3449-8) Simon & Schuster Children's Publishing. (Simon Pulse).

—The Salvation. (Roswell High Ser.: No. 10). (YA). (gr. 6 up). 2000. 176p. pap. 5.99 (0-671-03564-9); 2001. reprint ed. E-Book 5.99 (0-7434-3451-X) Simon & Schuster Children's Publishing. (Simon Pulse).

—The Seeker. (Roswell High Ser.: No. 3). (YA). (gr. 6 up). 2000. 176p. pap. 5.99 (0-671-77464-6); 1998. 176p. mass mkt. 4.50 (0-671-02376-4); 2001. reprint ed. E-Book 4.99 (0-7434-3444-7) Simon & Schuster Children's Publishing. (Simon Pulse).

—The Stowaway. (Roswell High Ser.: No. 6). (YA). (gr. 6 up). 2000. 176p. pap. 5.99 (0-671-02379-9); 2001. reprint ed. E-Book 4.99 (0-7434-3447-1) Simon & Schuster Children's Publishing. (Simon Pulse).

—The Vanished. (Roswell High Ser.: No. 7). (YA). (gr. 6 up). 2000. 176p. mass mkt. 5.99 (0-671-03561-4); 2001. reprint ed. E-Book 5.99 (0-7434-3448-X) Simon & Schuster Children's Publishing. (Simon Pulse).

—The Watcher. (Roswell High Ser.: No. 4). 176p. (YA). (gr. 6 up). 2000. pap. 5.99 (0-671-77463-8); 1999. per. 4.50 (0-671-02377-2); 2001. reprint ed. E-Book 5.99 (0-7434-3445-5) Simon & Schuster Children's Publishing. (Simon Pulse).

—The Wild One. (Roswell High Ser.: No. 2). (YA). (gr. 6 up). 1999. 176p. mass mkt. 5.99 (0-671-77465-4); 2001. reprint ed. E-Book 5.99 (0-7434-3443-9); No. 2. 1998. 176p. pap. 3.99 (0-671-02375-6) Simon & Schuster Children's Publishing. (Simon Pulse).

Mitchell, Richard, illus. The Man from Mars. 1999. (J). (0-7608-3201-3) Sundance Publishing.

F

FAIRIES—FICTION

—I Was a Teenage Fairy. 2000. (Illus.). (J). 14.00 (*0-606-18903-3*) Turtleback Bks.

Bottner, Barbara. Pish & Posh. 2004. (I Can Read Book Ser.). (Illus.). 48p. (J). 15.99 (*0-06-051416-7*); lib. bdg. 16.89 (*0-06-051417-5*) HarperCollins Pubs.

Bouchard, Dave. Fairy. 2001. (Illus.). 32p. (J). (gr. k-3). 16.95 (*1-55143-212-9*) Orca Bk. Pubs.

Bourgeois, Paulette. Benjamin et la Fee des Dents. ed. 1997. Tr. of Franklin & the Tooth Fairy. (FRE.). (J). (gr. 1). spiral bd. (*0-616-01825-8*) Canadian National Institute for the Blind/Institut National Canadien pour les Aveugles.

Boyd, William T. The Pumpkin Fairy. 2003. (Illus.). 32p. (J). (gr. k-1). 14.95 (*0-9718161-0-7*) Wyatt Pr.

Brennan, Herbie. Faerie Wars. 2003. (Illus.). 370p. (J). 17.95 (*1-58234-810-3*, Bloomsbury Children) Bloomsbury Publishing.

Brett, Jan. The Trouble with Trolls. 1992. (Illus.). 32p. (J). (ps-3). 16.99 (*0-399-22336-3*, G. P. Putnam's Sons) Penguin Group (USA) Inc.

—The Trouble with Trolls. 1999. (Illus.). 32p. (J). (ps-3). pap. 6.99 (*0-698-11791-3*, Puffin Bks.) Penguin Putnam Bks. for Young Readers.

—The Trouble with Trolls. 1999. 12.14 (*0-606-17433-8*) Turtleback Bks.

Bridwell, Norman & Lewison, Wendy Cheyette. Clifford's Loose Tooth. 2002. (Clifford Big Red Readers Ser.). (Illus.). 32p. (J). (ps-1). mass mkt. 3.99 (*0-439-33245-1*) Scholastic, Inc.

Brown, Rob. The Fairy Door, Only I Am. 1995. (Brown's Back-To-Back Children's Ser.: Vol. 1). (Illus.). 48p. (J). (gr. 4-7). 14.95 (*1-56313-744-5*) BrownTrout Pubs., Inc.

Carr, Jan. The Elf of Union Square. 2004. (J). 15.99 (*0-399-24180-9*) Penguin Putnam Bks. for Young Readers.

Carrier, Lark. Five Little Goblins. 2001. (Illus.). 18p. (J). (ps-1). 6.95 (*0-694-01576-8*, Harper Festival) HarperCollins Children's Bk. Group.

Cash, Rosanne. Penelope Jane: A Fairy's Tale. 2000. (Illus.). 32p. (J). (ps-3). 15.95 (*0-06-027543-X*, Cotler, Joanna Bks.) HarperCollins Children's Bk. Group.

Colfer, Eoin. The Arctic Incident. l.t. ed. 2003. (Artemis Fowl Ser.: Bk. 2). (J). (gr. 3-6). 16.95 (*0-7540-7839-6*, Galaxy Children's Large Print) BBC Audiobooks America.

—The Arctic Incident. (Artemis Fowl Ser.: Bk. 1). (J). (gr. 3-6). 2003. 304p. pap. 7.99 (*0-7868-1708-9*); 2002. 288p. 16.99 (*0-7868-0855-1*) Hyperion Bks. for Children.

—The Arctic Incident. l.t. ed. 2003. (Artemis Fowl Ser.: Bk. 2). 313p. (J). (gr. 3-6). 25.95 (*0-7862-4825-4*) Thorndike Pr.

—Artemis Fowl. 2002. (Artemis Fowl Ser.: Bk. 1). 288p. (J). (gr. 4-7). pap. 7.99 (*0-7868-1707-0*) Disney Pr.

—Artemis Fowl. l.t. ed. 2001. (Artemis Fowl Ser.: Bk. 1). 312p. (J). (gr. 3-6). 27.95 (*1-58724-092-0*, Wheeler Publishing, Inc.) Gale Group.

—Artemis Fowl. 2003. (Artemis Fowl Ser.: Bk. 1). (Illus.). 304p. (J). (gr. 3-6). mass mkt. 5.99 (*0-7868-1787-9*) Hyperion Bks. for Children.

—Artemis Fowl. 2001. (Artemis Fowl Ser.: Bk. 1). 288p. (gr. 4-7). 16.95 (*0-7868-0801-2*) Talk Miramax Bks.

—The Eternity Code. 2003. (Artemis Fowl Ser.: Bk. 3). 288p. (J). (gr. 3-6). 16.95 (*0-7868-1914-6*) Hyperion Bks. for Children.

Conroy, Stephen. The Must Be Magic in this House, Vol. 1. (J). (gr. 5-12). 14.95 (*0-944958-30-3*) Elfin Cove Pr.

Corbett, Terry. Nicholas & the Elves. 1999. (Illus.). 20p. (Orig.). (J). pap. 5.99 (*1-929731-03-5*) Rowfant Pr.

Cosgrove, Stephen. Gnome from Nome. (Serendipity Bks.). (Illus.). 32p. 2003. 4.99 (*0-8431-0585-2*); 1978. (J). (gr. 1-4). 3.95 o.p. (*0-8431-0555-0*) Penguin Putnam Bks. for Young Readers. (Price Stern Sloan).

—Gnome from Nome. 1986. (Serendipity Ser.). (J). 11.14 (*0-606-02388-7*) Turtleback Bks.

Cowley, Joy. The Wishing of Biddy Malone. 2004. (Illus.). 40p. (J). 15.99 (*0-399-23404-7*, Philomel) Penguin Putnam Bks. for Young Readers.

Dale, Penny. Pirate Diary. 2003. 128p. (J). pap. 6.99 (*0-7636-2169-2*) Candlewick Pr.

—Princess, Princess. 2003. 32p. (J). 14.99 (*0-7636-2212-5*) Candlewick Pr.

Dann, Penny, illus. Fairies All Year Long. 2003. (Secret Fairy Ser.). 24p. (J). bds. 5.95 (*0-439-44326-1*, Cartwheel Bks.) Scholastic, Inc.

Dann, Penny & Freedman, Claire. The Secret Fairy in Fairyland. 2002. (Secret Fairy Ser.). (Illus.). 96p. (YA). (gr. k up). pap. 15.95 (*0-439-35240-1*, Orchard Bks.) Scholastic, Inc.

Datlow, Ellen & Windling, Terri. The Faery Reel. 2004. 19.99 (*0-670-05914-5*, Viking) Viking Penguin.

Davis, Charles E. Creatures at My Feet. (Illus.). 32p. (J). (ps-1). 1999. pap. text 8.95 o.p. (*0-87358-739-1*, Rising Moon Bks. for Young Readers); 1993. 12.95 o.p. (*0-87358-560-7*) Northland Publishing.

Demers, Dominique. Old Thomas & the Little Fairy. ed. 2001. (J). (gr. 2). spiral bd. (*0-616-07229-5*) Canadian National Institute for the Blind/Institut National Canadien pour les Aveugles.

Dolan, Penny. Mary & the Fairy. 2002. (Read-It! Readers Ser.). (Illus.). 32p. (J). (ps-3). lib. bdg. 18.60 (*1-4048-0066-2*) Picture Window Bks.

Durant, Alan. Dear Tooth Fairy. 2004. (Illus.). 32p. (J). 14.99 (*0-7636-2175-7*) Candlewick Pr.

Elf: Buddys Little (S)elf Help Book. 2003. (Illus.). 112p. 3.99 (*0-8431-0799-5*, Price Stern Sloan) Penguin Putnam Bks. for Young Readers.

Erlbruch, Wolf. Leonard. 1996. (Illus.). 32p. (J). (ps-1). mass mkt. 15.95 o.p. (*0-531-09482-0*); mass mkt. 16.99 o.p. (*0-531-08782-4*) Scholastic, Inc. (Orchard Bks.).

Favreau, Jon & Berenbaum, David. Elf: A Short Story of a Tale. 2003. (Illus.). 32p. bds. 9.99 (*0-8431-0762-6*, Price Stern Sloan) Penguin Putnam Bks. for Young Readers.

Fields, Frever. Frumpy McDoogle: And the Legend of the Ruby Toad. 2003. 40p. 16.95 (*0-9632675-1-5*) Kimberlite Publishing Co.

Francour, Kathleen, illus. Counting. 2003. (Flitterbye Chunkie Board Bks.). (J). bds. 2.95 (*1-74047-359-0*) Book Co. Publishing Pty, Ltd., The AUS. *Dist:* Penton Overseas, Inc.

—Senses. 2003. (Flitterbye Chunkie Board Bks.). (J). bds. 2.95 (*1-74047-358-2*) Book Co. Publishing Pty, Ltd., The AUS. *Dist:* Penton Overseas, Inc.

Freedman, Claire. Fairy Dress-Up Fun. 2003. (Secret Fairy Ser.). (Illus.). 24p. (J). bds. 5.95 (*0-439-44327-X*, Cartwheel Bks.) Scholastic, Inc.

Gaudissart, Martine. Kanyon & the Rainbow Stone. 2000. (Illus.). 64p. (J). (gr. k-3). 17.95 (*0-9677547-0-4*) Black Orb.

Gelsey, James. Scooby-Doo & the Gruesome Goblin. 2004. (Scooby-Doo, Mysteries Ser.). 64p. (J). mass mkt. 3.99 (*0-439-42076-8*, Scholastic Paperbacks) Scholastic, Inc.

Gold, Carolyn J. Dragonfly Secret. 1997. (Illus.). 144p. (J). (gr. 3-7). 15.00 (*0-689-31938-X*, Atheneum) Simon & Schuster Children's Publishing.

Graham, Bob. Jethro Byrd, Fairy Child. 2002. (Illus.). 32p. (J). (ps-2). 15.99 (*0-7636-1772-5*) Candlewick Pr.

Grambling, Lois G. This Whole Tooth Fairy Thing's Nothing but a Big Rip-Off! 2002. (Illus.). (J). (gr. k-3). 15.95 (*0-7614-5104-8*) Cavendish, Marshall Corp.

Grayson, Linda. Butterbean Bunny: And a Fine Fairy Tea. 1996. (Illus.). 64p. (Orig.). (J). (gr. 3 up). pap. 6.95 (*0-9652076-1-7*) Printwick Papers.

—The Flutter Blossom Family: And the Spring Fairy Faire. 1996. (Illus.). 64p. (Orig.). (J). (gr. 3 up). pap. 6.95 (*0-9652076-0-9*) Printwick Papers.

Green, Isabel & Grissom, Martin L. Teresina: Adventures of a Tree Fairy. 1999. (Illus.). 16p. (J). (gr. k-6). pap. 10.00 o.p. (*0-8059-4643-8*) Dorrance Publishing Co., Inc.

Gregory, Dave & Puls, Grace. Theodore Was Here. 1997. (Illus.). 28p. (J). (ps-4). 15.95 (*0-9653798-0-9*) Theodore Publishing, Inc.

Grosset and Dunlap Staff. Jewel Fairies. 2000. (Jewel Sticker Stories Ser.). (Illus.). 24p. (J). (ps-3). mass mkt. 3.99 (*0-448-42192-5*, Planet Dexter) Penguin Putnam Bks. for Young Readers.

Gruelle, Johnny, ed. Raggedy Ann & the Magic Potion. 2001. (My First Raggedy Ann Ser.). (Illus.). 32p. (J). (ps-2). 15.00 (*0-689-83180-3*, Simon & Schuster Children's Publishing) Simon & Schuster Children's Publishing.

Hague, Kathleen. Good Night, Fairies. 2002. (Illus.). 40p. (J). (ps-2). 15.95 (*1-58717-134-1*) SeaStar Bks.

Hall, Kirsten. The Tooth Fairy. 2004. (My First Reader (Reissue) Ser.). (Illus.). 31p. (J). pap. 3.95 (*0-516-24640-2*, Children's Pr.) Scholastic Library Publishing.

Hanken, Sandra. Sky Castle. 1998. (Illus.). 32p. (J). (ps-3). 15.95 (*0-935699-14-7*) Illumination Arts Publishing Co., Inc.

Heneghan, James. Flood, RS. 2002. 192p. (YA). (gr. 7 up). 16.00 (*0-374-35057-4*, Farrar, Straus & Giroux (BYR)) Farrar, Straus & Giroux.

Herman, Gail. Hide & Peep. 2000. (Fairy School Ser.: Vol. 8). (Illus.). 80p. (gr. 1-4). pap. text 3.99 o.s.i (*0-553-48710-8*, Skylark) Random Hse. Children's Bks.

—Tooth Fairy Travels. 1999. (Fairy School Ser.: 1). (Illus.). 96p. (gr. 1-4). pap. text 3.99 o.s.i (*0-553-48679-9*, Dell Books for Young Readers) Random Hse. Children's Bks.

—When Wishes Come True. 2000. (Fairy School Ser.: Vol. 7). (Illus.). 80p. (gr. 1-4). pap. text 3.99 o.s.i (*0-553-48709-4*, Skylark) Random Hse. Children's Bks.

Hirt, Kelly K. Lucy & the Leprechaun Seekers. 2001. (Illus.). (J). (gr. k-4). pap. 14.95 (*0-9708027-0-6*, 14009) Passion Works, LLC.

Hughes, Carol. Toots & the Upside down House. Thomas, Jim, ed. 2000. (Illus.). 144p. (J). (gr. 3-5). pap. 4.50 (*0-679-88654-0*, Random Hse. Bks. for Young Readers) Random Hse. Children's Bks.

—Toots & the Upside down House. 1997. (J). (gr. 3-7). 143p. 17.00 o.s.i (*0-679-88653-2*); 18.99 o.s.i (*0-679-98653-7*) Random Hse. Children's Bks. (Random Hse. Bks. for Young Readers).

Hunter, Mollie. The Smartest Man in Ireland. 1996. 128p. (YA). (gr. 7 up). pap. 5.00 (*0-15-200993-0*, Magic Carpet Bks.) Harcourt Children's Bks.

—The Smartest Man in Ireland. 1996. 11.05 (*0-606-11852-7*) Turtleback Bks.

Inkpen, Deborah. Harriet & the Little Fat Fairy. 2002. (Illus.). 24p. (J). (gr. k-2). 11.95 (*0-7641-5562-8*) Barron's Educational Series, Inc.

James, Kari. Night for a Fairy Ball: With 3-D Glasses. 1997. (Golden Book Ser.). (Illus.). 16p. (J). (gr. 1-3). pap. 3.99 o.s.i (*0-307-14654-5*, Golden Bks.) Random Hse. Children's Bks.

Johnson, Paul Brett, tr. & illus. Little Bunny Foo Foo: A Cautionary Tale by the Good Fairy. 2004. (J). 15.95 (*0-439-37301-8*) Scholastic, Inc.

Joyce, Robert Dwyer. The Leaping Leprechaun. 2001. (Illus.). 10p. (J). 8.95 (*1-56554-915-5*) Pelican Publishing Co., Inc.

Kane, Tracy. Fairy Boat. 2nd ed. 2002. 40p. (J). per., act. bk. ed. 15.95 net. (*0-9708104-7-4*) Light-Beams Publishing.

—Fairy Flight. l.t. ed. 2003. (Fairy Houses Ser.). (Illus.). 40p. (J). (gr. k-3). per. 15.95 (*0-9708104-2-3*) Light-Beams Publishing.

Kendall, Cassie. Laurel & the Lost Treasure. 2nd ed. (Stardust Classics). (Illus.). 117p. (J). (gr. 2-6). 1998. pap. 5.95 (*1-889514-10-1*); 1997. 12.95 (*1-889514-09-8*) Dolls Corp.

—Laurel the Woodfairy. 2nd ed. 1998. (Stardust Classics). (Illus.). 114p. (J). (gr. 2-6). 12.95 (*1-889514-05-5*); pap. 5.95 (*1-889514-06-3*) Dolls Corp.

Kennedy, Kim. Mr. Bumble. 1997. (Illus.). 32p. (J). (ps-3). 15.95 (*0-7868-0263-4*); 16.49 (*0-7868-2293-7*) Hyperion Bks. for Children.

—Mr. Bumble. 1999. (Illus.). 32p. (J). (ps-3). pap. text 5.99 (*0-7868-1353-9*) Hyperion Pr.

Knudsen, Michelle. Fairy Freinds. 2003. (Board Books). (Illus.). 14p. (J). bds. 6.99 (*0-689-85629-6*, Little Simon) Simon & Schuster Children's Publishing.

Koski, Mary B. Stowaway Fairy Goes to Japan. 2002. (J). 12.99 (*0-89610-203-3*) Island Heritage Publishing.

Krensky, Stephen. The Youngest Fairy Godmother Ever. (Illus.). 32p. (J). 2003. pap. 5.99 (*0-689-86143-5*, Aladdin); 2000. 16.00 (*0-689-82011-9*, Simon & Schuster Children's Publishing) Simon & Schuster Children's Publishing.

Lehrer, Jamie. Magic Costumes: A Story with Pop-Ups, Foil & More. 1996. (Illus.). 24p. (J). (ps up). 14.99 o.s.i (*0-8037-1967-1*, Dial Bks. for Young Readers) Penguin Putnam Bks. for Young Readers.

LeMieux, Anne Connelly. The Fairy Lair: A Special Place. 1997. (J). (gr. 3-7). (Fairy Lair Ser.: Bk. 1). 158p. pap. 3.99 (*0-689-81725-8*, Aladdin); 144p. 16.00 (*0-689-81854-8*, Simon & Schuster Children's Publishing) Simon & Schuster Children's Publishing.

—A Magic Place. 1998. (Fairy Lair Ser.: 3). 160p. (J). (gr. 3-7). mass mkt. 4.50 (*0-689-81727-4*, Simon Pulse) Simon & Schuster Children's Publishing.

—A Safe Place. 1998. (Fairy Lair Ser.: 2). 160p. (J). (gr. 3-7). mass mkt. 4.50 (*0-689-81726-6*, Simon Pulse) Simon & Schuster Children's Publishing.

Leverich, Kathleen. Brigid, Bewitched. 1994. (First Stepping Stone Bks.). (Illus.). 80p. (J). (ps-3). pap. 2.99 o.s.i (*0-679-85433-9*, Random Hse. Bks. for Young Readers) Random Hse. Children's Bks.

—Brigid, Bewitched. 1994. 8.19 o.p. (*0-606-06252-1*) Turtleback Bks.

Lewis, Marian Moore. An Igloo on the Lake. 2002. 64p. pap. (*1-55369-689-1*) Trafford Publishing.

Lisle, Janet Taylor. Afternoon of the Elves. 1991. 128p. (J). (gr. 3-7). mass mkt. 3.99 o.p. (*0-590-43944-8*, Scholastic Paperbacks) Scholastic, Inc.

—Afternoon of the Elves. 1999. 11.04 (*0-606-16789-7*) Turtleback Bks.

Lyons, Mary E. Knockabeg: A Famine Tale. 2001. (Illus.). 128p. (J). (gr. 4-6). tchr. ed. 15.00 (*0-618-09283-8*) Houghton Mifflin Co.

Mackay, Stephen, illus. The Fairies' Ring: A Book of Fairy Stories & Poems. 1999. 96p. (J). (ps-3). 24.99 o.p. (*0-525-46045-4*, Dutton Children's Bks.) Penguin Putnam Bks. for Young Readers.

Madonna. The English Roses. 2003. (Illus.). 48p. (J). 19.95 (*0-670-03678-1*) Callaway Editions, Inc.

Mallen, Lisa. Elton the Elf. Pavanel, Jane, ed. 2000. (Illus.). 32p. (J). pap. (*1-894222-13-X*) Lobster Pr.

—Elton the Elf. 2nd adapted ed. 2001. (Illus.). 32p. (J). (ps-k). 12.95 (*1-894222-33-4*) Lobster Pr. CAN. *Dist:* Publishers Group West.

Mayne, William. The Book of Hob Stories. 1997. (Illus.). 96p. (J). (gr. 1-5). 17.99 o.p. (*0-7636-0390-2*) Candlewick Pr.

—Hob & the Peddler. 1997. (Illus.). 160p. (J). (gr. 3-6). pap. 15.95 o.p. (*0-7894-2462-2*) Dorling Kindersley Publishing, Inc.

—A Year & a Day. 2000. (Candlewick Treasures Ser.). (Illus.). 125p. (J). (gr. 3-7). 11.99 o.p. (*0-7636-0850-5*) Candlewick Pr.

—A Year & a Day. 1976. 112p. (J). (gr. 4-6). lib. bdg. 6.95 o.p. (*0-525-43450-X*, Dutton) Dutton/Plume.

—A Year & a Day. 1990. (J). (gr. 4-7). 19.25 (*0-8446-6431-6*) Smith, Peter Pub., Inc.

McGraw, Eloise Jarvis. The Moorchild. 2002. (Illus.). (J). 13.40 (*0-7587-4123-5*) Book Wholesalers, Inc.

—The Moorchild. (J). 1998. pap. 2.65 (*0-689-82164-6*, Aladdin); 1998. 256p. (gr. 4-7). pap. 4.99 (*0-689-82033-X*, Aladdin); 1996. 256p. (gr. 3-7). 17.00 (*0-689-80654-X*, McElderry, Margaret K.) Simon & Schuster Children's Publishing.

—The Moorchild. l.t. ed. 2002. (Young Adult Ser.). 291p. (YA). 24.95 (*0-7862-4787-8*) Thorndike Pr.

—The Moorchild. 1998. (J). 11.04 (*0-606-13621-5*) Turtleback Bks.

Mills, Lauren A. Fairy Wings. 1995. (Illus.). 32p. (J). (ps-3). 16.95 o.p. (*0-316-57397-3*) Little Brown & Co.

Mills, Lauren A. & Nolan, Dennis. Fairy Wings. 2001. (Illus.). 32p. (J). (gr. k-3). pap. 6.99 (*0-316-59078-9*) Little Brown & Co.

Milord, Susan. Willa the Wonderful. 2003. (Illus.). 32p. (J). (ps-3). tchr. ed. 15.00 (*0-618-27522-3*) Houghton Mifflin Co.

Minters, Frances. Princess Fishtail. 2002. (Illus.). 32p. (J). (ps-3). 15.99 (*0-670-03529-7*, Viking) Viking Penguin.

Misuraca, Thomas J. The Mystery of the Messy Room. 2003. (Scarytales Ser.: Vol. 1). (Illus.). (J). 7.95 (*1-932431-04-7*, Angel Gate) Left Field Ink.

Mueller, Martina. Pico the Gnome. 2001. (Illus.). 24p. (J). (gr. k-2). 16.95 (*0-86315-278-3*) Floris Bks. GBR. *Dist:* Gryphon Hse., Inc., SteinerBooks, Inc.

Namy, Verna. Ancient Secrets in the Garden. 2001. 32p. (J). 18.95 (*0-944851-18-5*) Earth Star Pubns.

Nesbit, Edith. Five Children & It. 207p. 20.95 (*0-8488-2523-3*) Amereon, Ltd.

—Five Children & It. 1981. 182p. (J). reprint ed. lib. bdg. 21.95 (*0-89967-036-9*, Harmony Raine & Co.) Buccaneer Bks., Inc.

—Five Children & It. 2002. (Dover Evergreen Classics Ser.). (Illus.). 160p. (J). pap. 2.50 (*0-486-42366-2*) Dover Pubns., Inc.

—Five Children & It. 1999. (Books of Wonder). (Illus.). 256p. (J). (gr. 4-7). 22.95 (*0-688-13545-5*); 22.95 (*0-688-13545-5*) HarperCollins Children's Bk. Group.

—Five Children & It. l.t. ed. 117p. pap. 16.00 (*0-7583-3201-7*); 160p. pap. 19.00 (*0-7583-3202-5*); 205p. pap. 22.00 (*0-7583-3203-3*); 397p. pap. 36.00 (*0-7583-3206-8*); 263p. pap. 26.00 (*0-7583-3204-1*); 461p. pap. 40.00 (*0-7583-3207-6*); 90p. pap. 14.00 (*0-7583-3200-9*); 90p. lib. bdg. 20.00 (*0-7583-3192-4*); 117p. lib. bdg. 23.00 (*0-7583-3193-2*); 160p. lib. bdg. 27.00 (*0-7583-3194-0*); 263p. lib. bdg. 37.00 (*0-7583-3196-7*); 397p. lib. bdg. 47.00 (*0-7583-3198-3*); 461p. lib. bdg. 51.00 (*0-7583-3199-1*); 323p. lib. bdg. 42.00 (*0-7583-3197-5*); 205p. lib. bdg. 33.00 (*0-7583-3195-9*) Huge Print Pr.

—Five Children & It. 2002. 160p. (gr. 4-7). per. 88.99 (*1-4043-0285-9*) IndyPublish.com.

—Five Children & It. Kemp, Sandra, ed. 1994. (Oxford World's Classics Ser.). (Illus.). 216p. (J). pap. 7.95 o.p. (*0-19-283163-1*) Oxford Univ. Pr., Inc.

—Five Children & It. 1959. 224p. (J). pap. 2.95 o.p. (*0-14-030128-3*, Puffin Bks.) Penguin Putnam Bks. for Young Readers.

—Five Children & It. 1988. 208p. (J). (gr. 4-7). mass mkt. 3.25 o.p. (*0-590-42146-8*, Scholastic Paperbacks) Scholastic, Inc.

—Five Children & It. 1989. (J). (gr. 4-6). 15.50 o.p. (*0-8446-6411-1*) Smith, Peter Pub., Inc.

—Five Children & It. E-Book 5.00 (*0-7410-0796-7*) SoftBook Pr.

—Five Children & It. 2002. 192p. pap. 14.95 (*1-59224-938-8*); lib. bdg. 24.95 (*1-59224-942-6*) Wildside Pr.

Nightingale, Sandy. Cider Apples. 1996. (Illus.). 32p. (J). (ps-3). 15.00 (*0-15-201244-3*) Harcourt Trade Pubs.

Nodelman, Perry. A Completely Different Place. 1997. 192p. (YA). (gr. 5-9). per. 16.00 (*0-689-80836-4*, Simon & Schuster Children's Publishing) Simon & Schuster Children's Publishing.

O'Connor, Jane. Dear Tooth Fairy, Vol. 2. 2002. (All Aboard Reading Ser.). (Illus.). 48p. (J). 3.99 (*0-448-42849-0*); 13.89 o.p. (*0-448-42881-4*) Penguin Putnam Bks. for Young Readers. (Grosset & Dunlap).

Ostrow, Kim. Up All Night. 2004. (Ready-to-Read Ser.: Vol. 1). (Illus.). 32p. (J). pap. 3.99 (*0-689-86320-9*, Simon Spotlight/Nickelodeon) Simon & Schuster Children's Publishing.

Pace, Mayme. The Fairy Godmother. 2000. E-Book 6.95 (*0-87714-567-9*) Denlingers Pubs., Ltd.

Palatini, Margie. Elf Help: http://www.falala.com. 1997. (Illus.). 32p. (J). (ps-2). 14.95 (*0-7868-0359-2*); lib. bdg. 15.49 (*0-7868-2304-6*) Hyperion Bks. for Children.

—The Sweet Tooth. 2004. (J). 15.95 (*0-689-85159-6*, Simon & Schuster Children's Publishing) Simon & Schuster Children's Publishing.

Park, Barbara. Junie B., First Grader: Toothless Wonder. (Illus.). 96p. (J). (gr. 1-4). 2003. pap. 3.99 (*0-375-82223-2*); 2002. 11.95 (*0-375-80295-9*) Random Hse., Inc.

—The Toothless Wonder. 2002. (Illus.). 96p. (J). (gr. 1-4). lib. bdg. 13.99 (*0-375-90295-3*) Random Hse., Inc.

Peterson, Janice & Peterson, Macy. The Sleep Fairy. 2003. (Illus.). 32p. (J). (ps-5). 16.95 (*0-9714405-0-6*) Behavenkids Pr.

Pickford, Susan B. The Fairy Houses of Monhegan Island. 1995. (Illus.). 8p. (Orig.). (J). (ps-6). pap. 5.95 (*1-889664-01-4*) SBP Collaboratioin Works.

Piscetta, Colleen McCauley. Dandelion Delilah: The Tale of the Dandelion Fairies. 2002. (Illus.). (J). 24.95 (*1-888683-87-2*) Wooster Bk. Co., The.

Powell, Stacy A. The Legend of Auggie the Awkard Elf. 2001. (Illus.). 120p. (J). (ps-8). pap. 12.50 (*0-9713551-0-X*) Candle Fly Pr.

Pratchett, Terry. The Wee Free Men. 2004. 279p. (J). pap. (*0-552-54905-3*, Corgi) Bantam Bks.

—The Wee Free Men. 2003. 279p. (*0-385-60533-1*) Doubleday Canada, Ltd. CAN. *Dist:* Random Hse. of Canada, Ltd., Random Hse., Inc.

—The Wee Free Men. 2003. 272p. (J). (gr. 7 up). 16.99 (*0-06-001236-6*); lib. bdg. 17.89 (*0-06-001237-4*) HarperCollins Pubs.

Random House Staff. Fairy Tale: A True Story. 1997. (Illus.). 128p. (J). mass mkt. 3.99 o.s.i (*0-679-88812-8*, Random Hse. Bks. for Young Readers) Random Hse. Children's Bks.

Random House Staff & Eng, Cynthia. Queen Mab. 1997. (Fairies of Cottingley GLN Ser.). (Illus.). 24p. (J). pap. 3.25 o.s.i (*0-679-88860-8*, Random Hse. Bks. for Young Readers) Random Hse. Children's Bks.

Random House Staff & Hall, Kirsten. Princess Florella. 1997. (Pictureback Shape Ser.). (Illus.). 24p. (J). pap. 3.25 o.s.i (*0-679-88861-6*, Random Hse. Bks. for Young Readers) Random Hse. Children's Bks.

Random House Staff & Kulling, Monica. Fairy Tale: A True Story: Storybook. 1997. (Illus.). 48p. (J). pap. 5.99 o.s.i (*0-679-88811-X*, Random Hse. Bks. for Young Readers) Random Hse. Children's Bks.

Rex, Michael. The Tooth Fairy. 2003. (Word-by-Word First Reader Ser.). (Illus.). 32p. (J). (ps-k). mass mkt. 3.99 (*0-439-33490-X*, Cartwheel Bks.) Scholastic, Inc.

Robin, Harry. I, Morgain: A Novella. Caso, Adolph, ed. 1995. 192p. 17.95 (*0-8283-2004-7*) Branden Bks.

Rodda, Emily. Fairy Realm. 2003. (Fairy Realm Ser.). (Illus.). 128p. (J). No. 1. (gr. 2-5). 8.99 (*0-06-009583-0*); No. 2. 8.99 (*0-06-009586-5*); No. 2. lib. bdg. 14.89 (*0-06-009587-3*); No. 3. lib. bdg. 14.89 (*0-06-009590-3*); No. 4. 8.99 (*0-06-009592-X*); No. 4. lib. bdg. 14.89 (*0-06-009593-8*) HarperCollins Pubs.

—Fairy Realm: The Charm Bracelet, No. 1. 2003. (Fairy Realm Ser.). (Illus.). 128p. (J). (gr. 2-5). lib. bdg. 14.89 (*0-06-009584-9*) HarperCollins Pubs.

—The Magic Key. 2004. (Fairy Realm Ser.). 128p. (J). 8.99 (*0-06-009595-4*); lib. bdg. 14.89 (*0-06-009596-2*) HarperCollins Pubs.

—The Unicorn. 2004. (J). (*0-06-009598-9*); lib. bdg. (*0-06-009599-7*) HarperCollins Pubs.

Romano, Ralph & Burke, Joe. Elbo Elf. 2nd ed. 2001. 26p. lib. bdg. 19.95 (*0-9704125-1-7*) Elbo Elf, Inc.

Scalora, Suza. The Fairies: Photographic Evidence of the Existence of Another World. 1999. (Illus.). 48p. (J). (gr. 5 up). 19.95 (*0-06-028234-7*, Cotler, Joanna Bks.) HarperCollins Children's Bk. Group.

Scheidl, Gerda Marie. Loretta & the Little Fairy. James, J. Alison, tr. from GER. 1945. (Illus.). 64p. (J). (gr. 2-3). 13.95 o.p. (*1-55858-185-5*); 13.88 o.p. (*1-55858-186-3*) North-South Bks., Inc.

—Loretta & the Little Fairy. 1994. 12.10 (*0-606-14136-7*) Turtleback Bks.

Schoberle, Cecile & Regan, Dana. The Tooth Fairies Night Time Visit. 1999. (Sparkle 'n' Twinkle Ser.). (Illus.). 16p. (J). (ps-2). pap. 4.99 (*0-689-82701-6*, Little Simon) Simon & Schuster Children's Publishing.

Sherman, Josepha. Windleaf. 1993. 128p. (YA). (gr. 7 up). 14.95 (*0-8027-8259-0*) Walker & Co.

Simmons, Jane. The Dreamtime Fairies. 2002. (Illus.). 32p. (J). (ps-1). 15.95 (*0-316-79523-2*) Little Brown Children's Bks.

—El Vuelo de las Hadas. 2002. Tr. of Where the Fairies Fly. (SPA.). 102p. (J). 17.95 (*84-488-1193-3*, BS31494) Beascoa, Ediciones S.A. ESP. *Dist:* Lectorum Pubns., Inc.

Sisk, Glenda. The Snow Fairy. 2000. (Illus.). (J). lib. bdg. 14.95 (*0-9705727-2-7*) Coastal Publishing Carolina, Inc.

Smith, Jane Denitz. Fairy Dust. 2002. (Illus.). 160p. (J). (gr. 3-7). 15.95 (*0-06-029279-2*); lib. bdg. 15.89 (*0-06-029280-6*) HarperCollins Children's Bk. Group.

—Fairy Dust. Date not set. (J). (gr. 3-7). mass mkt. 4.99 (*0-06-440961-9*) HarperCollins Pubs.

Springer, Nancy. I Am Morgan Le Fay: A Tale from Camelot. 2001. ix, 227p. (J). (gr. 7 up). 17.99 (*0-399-23451-9*, Philomel) Penguin Putnam Bks. for Young Readers.

—I Am Morgan le Fay: A Tale from Camelot. 2002. (Firebird Ser.). 240p. (J). pap. 5.99 (*0-698-11974-6*, Firebird) Penguin Putnam Bks. for Young Readers.

Steer, Dugald. Scary Fairies. 1997. 3. (Illus.). 24p. (J). (gr. k-3). 16.95 (*0-7613-0298-0*); 24.90 (*0-7613-0258-1*) Millbrook Pr., Inc.

Stein-Aubert, Danielle. The Blossoms' Ball. 2003. (Illus.). 34p. (J). 12.95 (*1-58246-096-5*) Tricycle Pr.

Story of the Christmas Elves. 2001. 26p. (J). 12.95 (*0-9712332-0-9*) G. D. Stewart Publishing.

Strauss, Linda Leopold. A Fairy Called Hilary. 1999. (Illus.). 113p. (J). (gr. 2-6). tchr. ed. 15.95 (*0-8234-1418-3*) Holiday Hse., Inc.

—A Fairy Called Hilary. 2001. (Illus.). 128p. (J). (gr. 2-5). mass mkt. 3.99 (*0-439-17519-4*) Scholastic, Inc.

Sullivan, Ellen. How Santa Got His Elves. 1998. (J). (*1-58173-148-5*) Sweetwater Pr.

Symes, Ruth Louise. The Sheep Fairy: When Wishes Have Wings. 2003. 32p. (J). 15.95 (*0-439-53168-3*) Scholastic, Inc.

Thompson, Corrynn. Angel Elf. 1978. (J). 4.50 o.p. (*0-533-03762-X*) Vantage Pr., Inc.

Thomson, Emma. Felicity Wishes Friendship & Fairy-school. 2002. 32p. (J). text 14.99 (*0-670-03593-9*) Penguin Putnam Bks. for Young Readers.

—Felicity Wishes Little Book of Birthdays. 2002. 20p. (J). 5.99 (*0-670-03592-0*) Penguin Putnam Bks. for Young Readers.

—Felicity Wishes Little Book of Friendship. 2002. 20p. (J). 5.99 (*0-670-03590-4*) Penguin Putnam Bks. for Young Readers.

—Felicity Wishes Little Book of Happiness. 2002. 20p. (J). 5.99 (*0-670-03591-2*) Penguin Putnam Bks. for Young Readers.

—Felicity Wishes Little Book of Wishes. 2002. 20p. (J). 5.99 (*0-670-03589-0*) Penguin Putnam Bks. for Young Readers.

Trondheim, Lewis. Happy Halloween, Li'l Santa. 2003. (Illus.). 48p. (J). 14.95 (*1-56163-361-5*) NBM Publishing Co.

Webb, Carla. The Magic in Believing: The Tooth Fairies. (Magic in Believing Ser.). (Illus.). 36p. (J). (gr. k-5). (*0-9705726-0-3*) Ageless Treasures.

Weinberg, Jennifer. Surprise for a Princess. 2003. (Step into Reading Ser.). (Illus.). 32p. (J). (ps-2). pap. 3.99 (*0-7364-2132-7*); lib. bdg. 11.99 (*0-7364-8022-6*) Random Hse., Inc.

Weninger, Brigitte, pseud. The Elf's Hat. James, J. Alison, tr. from GER. 2002. (Illus.). 36p. (J). pap. 6.95 (*0-7358-1568-2*, Michael Neugebauer Bks.) North-South Bks., Inc.

—The Elf's Hat. 2000. (Illus.). 36p. (J). (gr. k-3). lib. bdg. 16.50 (*0-7358-1255-1*) North-South Bks., Inc.

—The Elf's Hat. James, J. Alison, tr. from GER. 2000. (Illus.). 36p. (J). (gr. k-3). 15.95 (*0-7358-1254-3*) North-South Bks., Inc.

West, Tracey. The Angry Elf. 2000. (Pixie Tricks Ser.: No. 5). (Illus.). 80p. (J). (gr. 1-4). mass mkt. 3.99 (*0-439-17981-5*, Scholastic Paperbacks) Scholastic, Inc.

—The Greedy Gremlin. 2000. (Pixie Tricks Ser.: No. 2). (Illus.). 112p. (J). (gr. 1-4). mass mkt. 3.99 (*0-439-17219-5*) Scholastic, Inc.

Wilkins, Verna Allette. Toyin Fay. 1998. (Illus.). 24p. (J). (gr. 2 up). lib. bdg. 22.60 (*0-8368-2091-6*) Stevens, Gareth Inc.

Wolf, Tony. The Woodland Folk Meet the Giants. 1984. (Illus.). 42p. (J). (*0-528-82563-1*) Rand McNally.

Woods, Tonita. Mystical Forest of Wise. 2001. pap. 10.95 (*0-595-19147-9*, Writers Club Pr.) iUniverse, Inc.

Yagher, Kevin. Heverly. 2001. (Illus.). 48p. (J). (gr. 2-5). 15.95 o.p. (*1-58717-062-0*); (gr. 3-5). lib. bdg. 16.50 o.p. (*1-58717-063-9*) SeaStar Bks.

Yolen, Jane. Child of Faerie, Child of Earth. 1997. (Illus.). 32p. (J). (ps-3). 16.95 (*0-316-96897-8*) Little Brown & Co.

G

GHOSTS—FICTION

Adams, Pam & Jones, Ceri, illus. A Book of Ghosts. 1974. (Imagination Ser.). 32p. (Orig.). (J). (ps-2). pap. 5.50 o.p. (*0-85953-073-6*); pap. 3.99 (*0-85953-028-0*) Child's Play of England GBR. *Dist:* Random Hse. of Canada, Ltd., Child's Play-International.

Adler, C. S. Ghost Brother. 1990. 160p. (J). (ps-3). tchr. ed. 15.00 (*0-395-52592-6*, Clarion Bks.) Houghton Mifflin Co. Trade & Reference Div.

—Ghost Brother. 1992. 144p. (J). pap. 3.50 (*0-380-71386-1*, Avon Bks.) Morrow/Avon.

Ahlberg, Allan. Ghost Train. ALC Staff, ed. 1992. (Funnybones Ser.). (Illus.). 32p. (J). (ps-3). mass mkt. 3.95 (*0-688-11659-0*, Morrow, William & Co.) Morrow/Avon.

—Ghost Train. 1992. (Funnybones Ser.). (J). 10.10 (*0-606-01364-4*) Turtleback Bks.

—My Brother's Ghost. 2001. 87p. (J). (gr. 6 up). 9.99 o.s.i (*0-670-89290-4*, Viking Children's Bks.) Penguin Putnam Bks. for Young Readers.

Alexander, Wilma E. The William Ghost. 2001. (Illus.). 120p. (J). (gr. 3-7). pap. 6.95 (*1-896184-92-8*) Roussan Pubs., Inc./Roussan Editeur, Inc. CAN. *Dist:* Orca Bk. Pubs.

Almond, David. Kit's Wilderness. l.t. ed. 2000. pap. 16.95 (*0-7540-6115-9*, Galaxy Children's Large Print) BBC Audiobooks America.

—Kit's Wilderness. 2000. (J). audio 24.00 (*0-7366-9017-4*) Books on Tape, Inc.

—Kit's Wilderness. unabr. ed. 2000. (J). (gr. 4-6). 240p. pap. 35.00 incl. audio (*0-8072-8216-2*); audio 30.00 (*0-8072-8215-4*, LL0166) Random Hse. Audio Publishing Group. (Listening Library).

—Kit's Wilderness. (YA). (gr. 7). 2001. (Illus.). 256p. mass mkt. 4.99 (*0-440-41605-1*, Laurel Leaf); 2000. 240p. 15.95 (*0-385-32665-3*, Dell Books for Young Readers) Random Hse. Children's Bks.

—Kit's Wilderness. l.t. ed. 2001. (Illus.). 272p. (J). (gr. 4-7). 22.95 (*0-7862-2772-9*) Thorndike Pr.

Amsden, Janet. Grizzly Pete & the Ghosts. 2002. (Illus.). 32p. (J). (gr. k-2). lib. bdg. 19.95 (*1-55037-719-1*); per. 7.95 (*1-55037-718-3*) Annick Pr., Ltd. CAN. *Dist:* Firefly Bks., Ltd.

Asch, Frank. The Ghost of P. S. 42. 2002. (Class Pets Chapter Book Ser.). (Illus.). 96p. (J). (gr. 2-5). 14.95 (*0-689-84653-3*, Simon & Schuster Children's Publishing) Simon & Schuster Children's Publishing.

Avi. Midnight Magic. 2001. 11.04 (*0-606-22158-1*) Turtleback Bks.

Ballard, Mignon F. Aunt Matilda's Ghost. 2000. (Illus.). vii, 136p. (J). 22.50 (*1-57072-116-5*); pap. 12.50 (*1-57072-132-7*) Overmountain Pr.

Banks, Steven. The Big Halloween Scare. 2003. (SpongeBob SquarePants Ready-To-Read Ser.). 32p. (J). (gr. k-2). pap. 3.99 (*0-689-84196-5*, Simon Spotlight/Nickelodeon) Simon & Schuster Children's Publishing.

Barrett, Tracy. Cold in Summer, ERS. 2003. (Illus.). 208p. (J). (gr. 5-9). 16.95 (*0-8050-7052-4*, Holt, Henry & Co. Bks. For Young Readers) Holt, Henry & Co.

Bial, Raymond. The Ghost of Honeymoon Creek. (Illus.). 169p. (J). (gr. 4-7). 2000. 18.95 o.p. (*1-883953-28-6*); 1999. pap. 13.95 (*1-883953-27-8*) Midwest Traditions, Inc. (Face to Face Bks.).

Bianchi, John. In a Dark, Dark House. 2002. (Board Books). (Illus.). 14p. (J). bds. 4.99 (*0-448-42818-0*, Grosset & Dunlap) Penguin Putnam Bks. for Young Readers.

Black, Theodor, illus. Ghosts & Golems: Haunting Tales of the Supernatural. 2001. 128p. (J). (gr. 5-8). 14.95 (*0-8276-0733-4*) Jewish Pubn. Society.

Blackman, Malorie. Dead Gorgeous. 2003. 279p. (J). mass mkt. (*0-552-54633-X*, Corgi) Bantam Bks.

Bloor, Edward. Story Time: A Grim Fairy Tale. 2004. (Illus.). 432p. (YA). (*0-15-204670-4*) Harcourt Trade Pubs.

Bouton, Warren Hussey. The Ghost of Ichabod Paddack: A Spooky Tale from Nantucket. l.t. ed. 2002. 86p. (J). per. 5.95 (*0-9700555-2-8*) Hither Creek Pr.

Bright, Robert. Georgie. 1944. (Illus.). 44p. (J). (gr. k-1). mass mkt. 7.95 o.s.i (*0-385-07307-0*) Doubleday Publishing.

—Georgie, RS. 1999. (Illus.). 48p. (J). (ps-3). pap. 4.95 (*0-374-42539-6*, Sunburst) Farrar, Straus & Giroux.

—Georgie. (J). (gr. k-3). 9999. 48p. pap. 1.50 o.p. (*0-590-01617-2*); 2000. pap. 2.50 (*0-590-42126-3*) Scholastic, Inc.

—Georgie & the Baby Birds. 1983. (Balloon Bks.). (Illus.). 32p. (ps-2). 3.95 o.p. (*0-385-17246-X*) Doubleday Publishing.

—Georgie & the Ball of Yarn. 1983. (Balloon Bks.). (Illus.). 32p. (ps-2). 3.95 o.p. (*0-385-17244-3*) Doubleday Publishing.

—Georgie & the Buried Treasure. 1979. (Illus.). 40p. (J). lib. bdg. o.p. (*0-385-14627-2*) Doubleday Publishing.

—Georgie & the Little Dog. 1983. (Balloon Bks.). (Illus.). 32p. (ps-2). 3.95 o.p. (*0-385-17247-8*) Doubleday Publishing.

—Georgie & the Magician. 1966. (Illus.). 45p. (ps-1). 7.95 o.p. (*0-385-04824-6*); pap. 2.50 o.p. (*0-385-01021-4*); lib. bdg. 7.95 o.p. (*0-385-05948-5*) Doubleday Publishing.

—Georgie & the Noisy Ghost. 1971. (ps-1). 7.95 o.p. (*0-385-03103-3*); lib. bdg. o.p. (*0-385-05336-3*) Doubleday Publishing.

—Georgie & the Robbers. 1963. (Illus.). 28p. (J). (ps-1). 7.95 o.p. (*0-385-01470-8*); pap. 2.50 o.s.i (*0-385-13341-3*); mass mkt. 5.95 o.s.i (*0-385-04483-6*) Doubleday Publishing.

—Georgie & the Robbers, RS. 1999. (Illus.). 32p. (J). (ps-3). pap. 4.95 (*0-374-42542-6*, Sunburst) Farrar, Straus & Giroux.

—Georgie & the Robbers. 9999. pap. 1.50 o.p. (*0-590-08725-8*) Scholastic, Inc.

—Georgie & the Runaway Balloon. 1983. (Balloon Bks.). (Illus.). 32p. (ps-2). 3.95 o.p. (*0-385-17245-1*) Doubleday Publishing.

—Georgie Goes West. 1973. 48p. (gr. k-3). lib. bdg. o.p. (*0-385-05277-4*) Doubleday Publishing.

—Georgie to the Rescue. 1987. (ps-1). 7.95 o.p. (*0-385-07308-9*); lib. bdg. o.p. (*0-385-07613-4*) Doubleday Publishing.

—Georgie's Christmas Carol. 1985. (Illus.). 48p. (J). (ps). 9.95 o.s.i (*0-385-02344-8*) Doubleday Publishing.

—Georgie's Halloween. 1971. (Illus.). 28p. (ps-3). 7.95 o.p. (*0-385-07773-4*, 58-7154); pap. 2.95 o.p. (*0-385-01017-6*); lib. bdg. 7.95 o.p. (*0-385-07778-5*) Doubleday Publishing.

Brittain, Bill. Who Knew There'd Be Ghosts? 1985. (Illus.). 128p. (J). (gr. 4-7). 14.00 o.p. (*0-06-020699-3*); lib. bdg. 14.89 o.p. (*0-06-020700-0*) HarperCollins Children's Bk. Group.

—Who Knew There'd Be Ghosts? 1988. (J). 11.00 (*0-606-03677-6*) Turtleback Bks.

—Who Knew There'd Be Ghosts. 1988. (Trophy Bk.). (Illus.). 128p. (J). (gr. 4-7). pap. 4.95 (*0-06-440224-X*, Harper Trophy) HarperCollins Children's Bk. Group.

Brown, Marc. Arthur & the Goalie Ghost. 2001. (Arthur Good Sports Chapter Book Ser.: No. 5). (Illus.). 64p. (J). (gr. 3-6). 14.95 (*0-316-12042-1*); pap. 3.95 (*0-316-12146-0*) Little Brown Children's Bks.

Burgess, Melvin. The Ghost Behind the Wall, ERS. 2003. (Illus.). 176p. (YA). (gr. 4-7). 16.95 (*0-8050-7149-0*, Holt, Henry & Co. Bks. For Young Readers) Holt, Henry & Co.

—The Ghost Behind the Wall. l.t. ed. 2003. 160p. (J). 22.95 (*0-7862-5774-1*) Thorndike Pr.

Cabot, Meg. Haunted: A Tale of the Mediator. 2004. 288p. (J). pap. 6.99 (*0-06-447278-7*, Harper Trophy) HarperCollins Children's Bk. Group.

—Haunted: A Tale of the Mediator. 2003. 256p. (J). (gr. 7 up). 15.99 (*0-06-029471-X*); lib. bdg. 16.89 (*0-06-029472-8*) HarperCollins Pubs.

—Haunted: A Tale of the Mediator. abr. ed. 2003. (J). audio compact disk 19.99 (*0-8072-1622-4*, RH Audio) Random Hse. Audio Publishing Group.

Calmenson, Stephanie. The Teeny Tiny Teacher. 2002. (Illus.). 32p. (J). (ps-2). mass mkt. 5.99 (*0-439-40069-4*, Scholastic Paperbacks) Scholastic, Inc.

Carris, Joan Davenport. Ghost of a Chance. 2003. (Legends of the Carolinas Ser.). 155p. (J). 8.95 (*1-928556-40-X*) Coastal Carolina Pr.

Carroll, Jenny. Darkest Hour. 2001. (Mediator Ser.: Vol. 4). 256p. (YA). (gr. 7-10). mass mkt. 4.99 (*0-671-78847-7*, Simon Pulse) Simon & Schuster Children's Publishing.

—The Ninth Key. 2001. (Mediator Ser.: Vol. 2). (YA). E-Book 4.99 (*0-7434-2675-4*, Simon Pulse) Simon & Schuster Children's Publishing.

—Ninth Key. 2001. (Mediator Ser.: Vol. 2). (Illus.). 240p. (YA). (gr. 7 up). mass mkt. 4.99 (*0-671-78798-5*, Simon Pulse) Simon & Schuster Children's Publishing.

—Reunion. 2001. (Mediator Ser.: Vol. 3). 240p. (YA). (gr. 8). mass mkt. 4.99 (*0-671-78812-4*); reprint ed. E-Book 4.99 (*0-7434-2676-2*) Simon & Schuster Children's Publishing. (Simon Pulse).

—Shadowland. 2000. (Mediator Ser.: Vol. 1). 256p. (YA). mass mkt. 4.99 (*0-671-78791-8*, Simon Pulse) Simon & Schuster Children's Publishing.

Carus, Marianne, ed. That's Ghosts for You: 13 Scary Stories. 2000. (Illus.). viii, 134p. (J). (gr. 4-7). 15.95 (*0-8126-2675-3*) Cricket Bks.

Chase, Mary. The Wicked, Wicked Ladies in the Haunted House. 2003. (Illus.). 144p. (J). (gr. 2-5). 15.95 (*0-375-82572-X*); lib. bdg. 17.99 (*0-375-92572-4*) Knopf, Alfred A. Inc.

Clarke, Judith. Starry Nights. 2003. 152p. (J). 15.95 (*1-886910-82-0*, Front Street) Front Street, Inc.

Cohen, Daniel. There's a Ghost in the House. 1995. (Illus.). 64p. (J). (gr. 4-7). mass mkt. 2.99 (*0-590-54333-4*) Scholastic, Inc.

Cooper, Susan. The Boggart & the Monster. unabr. ed. 1997. 185p. (YA). (gr. 5 up). pap. 35.00 incl. audio (*0-8072-7821-1*, YA925SP, Listening Library) Random Hse. Audio Publishing Group.
—The Boggart & the Monster. 2001. 192p. (J). E-Book 6.99 (*0-689-84784-X*, McElderry, Margaret K.) Simon & Schuster Children's Publishing.
—The Boggart & the Monster. 1998. 11.04 (*0-606-14169-3*) Turtleback Bks.
Cox, Phil Roxbee. Ghost Train to Nowhere. 1994. (Spinechillers Ser.). (Illus.). 48p. (J). (gr. 4-7). pap. 5.95 (*0-7460-0677-2*); lib. bdg. 13.95 (*0-88110-519-8*) EDC Publishing. (Usborne).
Crowe, Carole. Sharp Horns on the Moon. 2003. 128p. (YA). 14.95 (*1-56397-671-4*) Boyds Mills Pr.
Cuyler, Margery. The Battlefield Ghost. (Illus.). (J). 2002. 112p. mass mkt. 3.99 (*0-590-10849-2*, Scholastic Paperbacks); 1999. 103p. (gr. 2-4). pap. 15.95 (*0-590-10848-4*) Scholastic, Inc.
—Skeleton Hiccups. 2002. (Illus.). 32p. (J). 14.95 (*0-689-84770-X*, McElderry, Margaret K.) Simon & Schuster Children's Publishing.
Dabcovich, Lydia, illus. The Ghost on the Hearth. 2003. (Family Heritage Ser.). 32p. (J). (gr. 1-5). 15.95 (*0-916718-18-2*) Vermont Folklife Ctr.
Dahl, Michael. The Ghost That Barked. (Scooter Spies Ser.: Vol. 2). 80p. 2000. (J). (gr. 2-5). pap. 3.99 (*0-7434-1878-6*); 2001. reprint ed. E-Book 3.99 (*0-7434-3460-9*) Simon & Schuster Children's Publishing. (Aladdin).
de Brunhoff, Laurent. Babar & the Ghost. 2001. (Babar Ser.). (Illus.). 40p. (J). (ps-3). 16.95 (*0-8109-4398-0*) Abrams, Harry N. , Inc.
—Babar & the Ghost. 2002. (Babar Ser.). (Illus.). (J). 26.13 (*0-7587-6816-8*) Book Wholesalers, Inc.
—Babar & the Ghost. ed. 2003. (gr. 1). spiral bd. (*0-616-14570-5*); (gr. 2). spiral bd. (*0-616-14571-3*) Canadian National Institute for the Blind/ Institut National Canadien pour les Aveugles.
DeFelice, Cynthia C. The Ghost & Mrs. Hobbs, RS. 2001. (Illus.). 180p. (J). (gr. 3-7). 16.00 (*0-374-38046-5*, Farrar, Straus & Giroux (BYR)) Farrar, Straus & Giroux.
—The Ghost & Mrs. Hobbs. 2003. 192p. (J). pap. 5.99 (*0-06-001172-6*, Harper Trophy) HarperCollins Children's Bk. Group.
—The Ghost of Cutler Creek, RS. 2004. (J). (*0-374-38058-9*, Farrar, Straus & Giroux (BYR)) Farrar, Straus & Giroux.
—The Ghost of Fossil Glen, RS. 1998. 176p. (J). (gr. 3-7). 16.00 (*0-374-31787-9*, Farrar, Straus & Giroux (BYR)) Farrar, Straus & Giroux.
—The Ghost of Fossil Glen. 1999. 160p. (J). (gr. 3-7). pap. 5.99 (*0-380-73175-4*, Harper Trophy) HarperCollins Children's Bk. Group.
—The Ghost of Fossil Glen. 2000. (YA). (gr. 6 up). pap. 52.00 incl. audio (*0-7887-4334-1*, 41129); pap. 52.00 incl. audio (*0-7887-4334-1*, 41129) Recorded Bks., LLC.
—The Ghost of Fossil Glen. l.t. ed. 2000. (Juvenile Ser.). (Illus.). 185p. (J). (gr. 4-7). 21.95 (*0-7862-2768-0*) Thorndike Pr.
—The Ghost of Fossil Glen. 1999. 11.00 (*0-606-16359-X*) Turtleback Bks.
DeGroat, Diane. Good Night, Sleep Tight, Don't Let the Bedbugs Bite! 2002. (Illus.). 32p. (J). (gr. k-3). 15.95 (*1-58717-128-7*); lib. bdg. 16.50 (*1-58717-129-5*) SeaStar Bks.
Dickens, Charles. A Christmas Carol. 1985. (Illus.). 80p. (J). (ps up). 1.50 o.p. (*0-8120-5705-8*) Barron's Educational Series, Inc.
—A Christmas Carol. reprint ed. 1981. (Illus.). 191p. (YA). lib. bdg. 15.95 (*0-89966-344-3*); 1980. 150p. (J). lib. bdg. 15.95 (*0-89967-017-2*, Harmony Raine & Co.) Buccaneer Bks., Inc.
—A Christmas Carol. 1993. (Illus.). 48p. (J). (ps-3). 15.95 o.p. (*1-56402-204-8*) Candlewick Pr.
—A Christmas Carol. 1988. mass mkt. 1.95 (*0-938819-20-8*, Aerie) Doherty, Tom Assocs., LLC.
—A Christmas Carol. 2001. (Illus.). 80p. (J). (gr. 1-5). 17.95 (*0-06-028577-X*); (gr. 2-5). lib. bdg. 17.89 (*0-06-028578-8*) HarperCollins Children's Bk. Group.
—A Christmas Carol. 1983. (Illus.). 128p. (J). (gr. 2-12). tchr. ed. 18.95 (*0-8234-0486-2*) Holiday Hse., Inc.
—A Christmas Carol. 1987. (Illus.). 88p. (J). 6.95 o.p. (*0-89783-046-6*) Larlin Corp.
—A Christmas Carol, Level 2. 2001. (Penguin Readers Lv. 2). (Illus.). (J). pap. 7.66 (*0-582-42120-9*) Longman Publishing Group.
—A Christmas Carol. 2001. (Illus.). 72p. (J). (ps up). 19.95 (*0-7358-1259-4*, Michael Neugebauer Bks.) North-South Bks., Inc.
—A Christmas Carol. 2001. (Illus.). 160p. pap. 8.95 (*1-86205-130-5*) Pavilion Bks., Ltd. GBR. *Dist:* Trafalgar Square.
—A Christmas Carol. Fagan, Tom, ed. 1978. (Now Age Illustrated IV Ser.). (Illus.). (gr. 4-12). (J). stu. ed. 1.25 (*0-88301-337-1*); (J). pap. text 2.95 (*0-88301-313-4*); (YA). text 7.50 o.p. (*0-88301-325-8*) Pendulum Pr., Inc.
—A Christmas Carol. (Classics for Young Readers Ser.). (J). 1984. 112p. (gr. 7). pap. 2.99 o.p. (*0-14-035027-6*, Puffin Bks.); 1983. (Illus.). 128p. (gr. 6). 12.95 o.p. (*0-8037-0032-6*, Dial Bks. for Young Readers) Penguin Putnam Bks. for Young Readers.
—A Christmas Carol. 1965. 96p. (J). (gr. 6 up). 6.95 o.p. (*0-88088-125-9*) Peter Pauper Pr. Inc.
—A Christmas Carol. (J). (gr. 4-7). 1986. pap. 1.95 o.p. (*0-590-02102-8*); 1987. (Illus.). 128p. reprint ed. pap. 2.50 o.p. (*0-590-41293-0*, Scholastic Paperbacks) Scholastic, Inc.
—A Christmas Carol. 1983. (Illus.). 240p. mass mkt. 3.99 (*0-671-47369-7*, Pocket) Simon & Schuster.
—A Christmas Carol. 1983. (Illus.). 128p. (J). pap. 16.00 o.p. (*0-671-45599-0*, Simon & Schuster Children's Publishing) Simon & Schuster Children's Publishing.
—A Christmas Carol. 1972. (J). pap. 5.95 o.p. incl. audio (*0-88142-364-5*, 364) Soundelux Audio Publishing.
—A Christmas Carol. 1999. (Saddleback Classics). (Illus.). (J). 13.10 (*0-606-21547-6*) Turtleback Bks.
—A Christmas Carol Book & Charm. 2002. (Charming Classics Ser.). 160p. (J). (ps-2). 6.99 (*0-694-01583-0*) HarperCollins Children's Bk. Group.
Dickens, Charles & Wheatcroft, Andrew. A Christmas Carol. 2001. (Classics Ser.). (Illus.). 64p. (J). pap. 9.99 (*0-7894-6246-X*, D K Ink) Dorling Kindersley Publishing, Inc.
Dolby, Karen. House of Shadows. 1993. (Spinechillers Ser.). (Illus.). 48p. (gr. 4 up). (J). lib. bdg. 13.95 (*0-88110-520-1*); (YA). pap. 5.95 (*0-7460-0679-9*) EDC Publishing. (Usborne).
Dower, Laura. The Powerpuff Girls Save Halloween. 2002. (Powerpuff Girls Ser.). (Illus.). 32p. (J). mass mkt. 5.99 (*0-439-42052-0*) Scholastic, Inc.
Duquennoy, Jacques. The Ghosts in the Cellar. (Illus.). (J). (ps-2). 2001. 48p. pap. 6.00 o.s.i (*0-15-216295-X*, Voyager Bks./Libros Viajeros); 1998. 56p. 12.00 o.s.i (*0-15-201775-5*) Harcourt Children's Bks.
—The Ghosts' Trip to Loch Ness. 2001. (Illus.). 48p. (J). (ps-2). pap. 6.00 (*0-15-216303-4*, Voyager Bks./Libros Viajeros) Harcourt Children's Bks.
—The Ghosts' Trip to Loch Ness. 1996. (Illus.). 52p. (J). (ps-3). 11.00 (*0-15-201440-3*) Harcourt Trade Pubs.
—Operation Ghost. 1999. (Illus.). 48p. (J). (ps-3). 13.00 (*0-15-202182-5*); pap. 6.00 o.s.i (*0-15-202203-1*) Harcourt Children's Bks.
—Operation Ghost. 1999. (J). 12.15 (*0-606-19002-3*) Turtleback Bks.
Durant. Team on Tour. 2003. (Illus.). 86p. (J). pap. (*0-330-35131-1*) Macmillan Children's Bks.
Ellerbee, Linda. Ghoul Reporter Digs up Zombies! 2000. (Get Real Ser.: No. 5). 208p. (J). (gr. 3-7). lib. bdg. 14.89 (*0-06-028249-5*);No. 5. pap. 4.99 (*0-06-440759-4*, Avon) HarperCollins Children's Bk. Group.
Engle, Marty M. & Barnes, Johnny Ray, Jr. Frozen Dinners. l.t. ed. 1996. (Strange Matter Ser.: No. 8). 144p. (J). (gr. 4-6). lib. bdg. 21.27 o.p. (*0-8368-1674-9*) Stevens, Gareth Inc.
Fantasma: Including Toy. 2001. (Jigsaw Ser.). (Illus.). 20p. (J). (ps-3). 7.95 (*968-5308-22-5*) Silver Dolphin Spanish Editions MEX. *Dist:* Publishers Group West.
Farley, Terri. Free Again. 2003. (Phantom Stallion Ser.: No. 5). 224p. (J). (gr. 5 up). pap. 4.99 (*0-06-441089-7*, Avon) HarperCollins Children's Bk. Group.
Fienberg, Anna & Fienberg, Barbara. The Big Big Big Book of Tashi. 2002. (Illus.). 448p. (J). (gr. 1-5). pap. 11.95 (*1-86508-563-4*) Allen & Unwin Pty., Ltd. AUS. *Dist:* Independent Pubs. Group.
Fischel, Emma. Midnight Ghosts. 1991. (Spinechillers Ser.). (Illus.). 48p. (J). (gr. 4-7). pap. 5.95 (*0-7460-0651-9*); lib. bdg. 13.95 (*0-88110-521-X*) EDC Publishing. (Usborne).
Fleischman, Sid. The 13th Floor: A Ghost Story. unabr. ed. 1996. (Illus.). 134p. (J). (gr. 3-5). pap. 28.00 (*0-8072-7615-4*, YA900SP, Listening Library) Random Hse. Audio Publishing Group.
Fuqua, Jonathon Scott. Catie & Josephine. 2003. (Illus.). 72p. (J). (gr. 2-5). 16.00 (*0-618-39403-6*) Houghton Mifflin Co.
Garland, Sherry. Cabin 102. 1995. (Illus.). 252p. (J). (gr. 4-7). 11.00 (*0-15-200663-X*); pap. 6.00 o.s.i (*0-15-200662-1*, Harcourt Paperbacks) Harcourt Children's Bks.
—Cabin 102. 1995. 12.05 (*0-606-09122-X*) Turtleback Bks.
Garretson, Jerri. The Secret of Whispering Springs. 2002. 208p. (J). per. 6.99 (*0-9659712-4-4*) Ravenstone Pr.
Geary, Rick. The Mask: The Mask in School Spirits. 1995. (Mask Children's Bks.). (Illus.). 32p. (J). (ps up). 10.95 (*1-56971-121-6*) Dark Horse Comics.
Gelsey, James. Scooby-Doo & the Sunken Ship: Scooby-Doo y el Barco Hundido. 2004. (Scooby-Doo Ser.). (ENG & SPA.). 64p. (J). pap. 3.99 (*0-439-55116-1*, Scholastic en Espanola) Scholastic, Inc.
The Ghost on Main Street: A Spooky Tale from Nantucket. 2001. 87p. (J). per. 5.95 (*0-9700555-1-X*) Hither Creek Pr.
Givens, Steven J. Stony Point: A Triangle Club Adventure. 2001. 101p. (J). pap. 5.95 (*1-889658-21-9*) New Canaan Publishing Co., Inc.
Golden Books Staff. Fright from Wrong. 2003. (Illus.). 32p. (J). (ps-2). pap. 3.99 (*0-375-82560-6*, Golden Bks.) Random Hse. Children's Bks.
Gordon, Lawrence. Haunted High Vol. 2: The Ghost Chronicles. 2000. 162p. (YA). (gr. 6-9). pap. 11.95 (*0-9653966-1-4*) Karmichael Pr.
Graham-Barber, Lynda. Say Boo. 2002. (Illus.). 16p. (J). (ps-k). bds. 4.99 (*0-7636-1890-X*) Candlewick Pr.
Griffin, Peni R. The Ghost Sitter. (J). 2002. 144p. pap. 5.99 (*0-14-230216-3*); 2001. 128p. (gr. 4-6). 14.99 (*0-525-46676-2*, Dutton Children's Bks.) Penguin Putnam Bks. for Young Readers.
Grow, Mary L. Chester Meets the Walker House Ghost, No. 1. 2000. (Illus.). 72p. (Orig.). (J). (gr. 8-12). pap. 12.00 (*0-9700777-0-X*) Studio 17.
Guillot, Claude. The Ghost of Shanghai. 1999. (Illus.). 48p. (ps-4). 16.95 o.p. (*0-8109-4129-5*) Abrams, Harry N. , Inc.
Harness, Cheryl. Ghosts of the Civil War. 2002. (Illus.). 48p. (J). 17.00 (*0-689-83135-8*, Simon & Schuster Children's Publishing) Simon & Schuster Children's Publishing.
Harris, Mark. Dario Figg & the Phantom of Murk. 2001. pap. 13.95 (*0-595-18933-4*, Writers Club Pr.) iUniverse, Inc.
Hawes, Louise. Rosey in the Present Tense. l.t. ed. 2002. (Young Adult Ser.). 186p. (J). 22.95 (*0-7862-4418-6*) Thorndike Pr.
—Rosey in the Present Tense. 1999. (Illus.). (J). 14.00 (*0-606-20488-1*) Turtleback Bks.
—Rosey in the Present Tense. 2000. (Illus.). 192p. (gr. 8-12). pap. 7.95 (*0-8027-7603-5*); 1999. 176p. (YA). (gr. 7). 15.95 (*0-8027-8685-5*) Walker & Co.
Hawthorne, Nathaniel. The House of the Seven Gables. abr. ed. 1994. (Illustrated Classics Collection). (Illus.). 64p. pap. 4.95 (*0-7854-0697-2*, 40453); (J). pap. 3.60 o.p. (*1-56103-531-9*) American Guidance Service, Inc.
—The House of the Seven Gables. (YA). reprint ed. 1999. pap. text 28.00 (*1-4047-1350-6*); 1851. pap. text 28.00 (*1-4047-3039-7*) Classic Textbooks.
—The House of the Seven Gables, Set. abr. ed. 1997. (Ultimate Classics Ser.). (YA). (gr. 9 up). 19.95 o.p. (*0-7871-0924-X*, 694868) NewStar Media, Inc.
—The House of the Seven Gables. Farr, Naunerle C., ed. abr. ed. 1977. (Now Age Illustrated III Ser.). (Illus.). (J). (gr. 4-12). text 7.50 o.p. (*0-88301-277-4*); pap. text 2.95 (*0-88301-265-0*) Pendulum Pr., Inc.
Hendry, Diana. Harvey Angell & the Ghost Child. 1999. 16.95 (*0-7540-6074-8*) BBC Audiobooks America.
—Harvey Angell & the Ghost Child. 2002. (Harvey Angell Ser.: Vol. 2). (Illus.). 160p. (YA). pap. 4.99 (*0-7434-2829-3*, Aladdin) Simon & Schuster Children's Publishing.
—Harvey Angell Beats Time. 2002. (Illus.). 160p. (J). (gr. 3-7). pap. 4.99 (*0-7434-2830-7*, Aladdin) Simon & Schuster Children's Publishing.
Herman, Gail. The Big White Ghost. 2003. (Big Red Reader Ser.). 32p. (J). mass mkt. 3.99 (*0-439-41682-5*, Cartwheel Bks.) Scholastic, Inc.
Hurst, Carol Otis. The Wrong One. 2003. 160p. (J). tchr. ed. 15.00 (*0-618-27599-1*) Houghton Mifflin Co.
Hutchens, Paul. The Secret Hideout. (Sugar Creek Gang Ser.: Vol. 5). 1968. (J). (gr. 3-7). mass mkt. 3.99 o.p. (*0-8024-4806-2*); rev. ed. 1989. (YA). pap. 4.99 o.p. (*0-8024-6960-4*); 6th rev. ed. 1997. 112p. (J). (gr. 4-7). mass mkt. 4.99 (*0-8024-7010-6*, 660) Moody Pr.
Hutchinson, Duane. A Storyteller's Ghost Stories. (J). 1987. 96p. (gr. 4 up). pap. 5.95 o.p. (*0-934988-07-2*); 2nd ed. 1989. (Illus.). 112p. (gr. 5-12). pap. 9.95 (*0-934988-32-3*); Bk. 2. 1990. (Illus.). 96p. (gr. 4 up). pap. 9.95 (*0-934988-18-8*); Bk. 3. 1992. (Illus.). 110p. (gr. 5-12). pap. 6.95 (*0-934988-25-0*) Foundation Bks., Inc.
Ibbotson, Eva. Dial-a-Ghost. l.t. ed. 2002. 212p. (J). 22.95 (*0-7862-3927-1*) Gale Group.
—Dial-a-Ghost. (Illus.). 2003. 224p. (J). pap. 5.99 (*0-14-250018-6*, Puffin Bks.); 2001. 256p. (YA). (gr. 3-7). 15.99 (*0-525-46693-2*, Dutton Children's Bks.) Penguin Putnam Bks. for Young Readers.
—The Great Ghost Rescue. 2002. (J). pap. 29.95 incl. audio (*0-7540-6253-8*) BBC Audiobooks America.
—The Great Ghost Rescue. 2003. 192p. (J). pap. 5.99 (*0-14-250087-9*, Puffin Bks.); 2002. (Illus.). 144p. (YA). (gr. 3-9). 15.99 (*0-525-46769-6*, Dutton Children's Bks.) Penguin Putnam Bks. for Young Readers.
—The Great Ghost Rescue. l.t. ed. 2002. (Illus.). 185p. (J). 22.95 (*0-7862-3967-0*) Thorndike Pr.
—Island of the Aunts. 2002. (Illus.). (YA). 13.19 (*1-4046-0936-9*) Book Wholesalers, Inc.
—Island of the Aunts. 2001. (J). 12.04 (*0-606-21782-7*) Turtleback Bks.
Inches, Alison. Ghost Town Trick or Treat. l.t. ed. 1998. (Lift-the-Flap Book Ser.). (Illus.). 16p. (J). (ps-1). pap. 6.99 o.s.i (*0-14-055863-2*) Penguin Putnam Bks. for Young Readers.
Ireland, Kenneth. A Treasury of Ghost Stories. 1996. 12.00 (*0-606-16563-0*) Turtleback Bks.
Irving, Washington. The Legend of Sleepy Hollow. 1990. 9.04 (*0-606-20311-7*) Turtleback Bks.
Irving, Washington, et al, contrib. by. The Legend of Sleepy Hollow. 1990. (Illus.). E-Book (*1-59019-783-6*) ipicturebooks, LLC.
Irving, Washington & Kelly, Gary. The Legend of Sleepy Hollow. 2002. 64p. (J). lib. bdg. 20.00 (*1-56846-145-3*) Creative Co., The.
James, Henry. The Turn of the Screw. 1998. (gr. 4-7). pap. 6.95 o.p. (*0-8114-6845-3*) Raintree Pubs.
Jan, Calamity. Shadow of Shaniko. 2002. (Ghostowners Ser.: 3). (Illus.). 100p. (Orig.). (J). pap. 10.00 (*0-9721800-2-8*) WildWest Publishing.
Jarman, Julia. Ollie & the Bogle. 2002. (Illus.). 135p. pap. 8.95 (*1-84270-039-1*) Trafalgar Square.
Jensen, Dorothea. The Riddle of Penncroft Farm. 2001. (Great Episodes Ser.). 272p. (YA). (gr. 5-9). pap. 6.00 (*0-15-216441-3*, Gulliver Bks.) Harcourt Children's Bks.
Johnson, Catherine. Sophie's Ghost. 2nd ed. 1997. 114p. (J). (gr. 4). reprint ed. pap. 11.95 (*0-8464-4812-2*) Beekman Pubs., Inc.
Johnson, Emily Rhoads. Write Me If You Dare! 2000. (Illus.). 208p. (J). (gr. 3-6). 15.95 (*0-8126-2944-2*) Cricket Bks.
Johnston, Norma. Feather in the Wind. 2001. (Illus.). 172p. (J). (gr. 5-9). 14.95 (*0-7614-5063-7*, Cavendish Children's Bks.) Cavendish, Marshall Corp.
Jones, Diana Wynne. The Time of the Ghost. 2002. 304p. (J). (gr. 7 up). 16.99 (*0-06-029887-1*); pap. 6.99 (*0-06-447354-6*) HarperCollins Children's Bk. Group.
Jones, Marcia Thornton & Dadey, Debbie. Ghost Game. 2003. (Ghostville Elementary Ser.). (Illus.). 96p. (J). mass mkt. 3.99 (*0-439-42438-0*, Scholastic Paperbacks) Scholastic, Inc.
—Happy Haunting! 2004. (Ghostville Elementary Ser.). 96p. (J). pap. 3.99 (*0-439-42440-2*, Scholastic Paperbacks) Scholastic, Inc.
—New Ghoul in School. 2004. (Ghostville Elementary Ser.). (Illus.). 96p. (J). mass mkt. 3.99 (*0-439-42439-9*, Scholastic Paperbacks) Scholastic, Inc.
Jones, Marcia Thornton, et al. Ghost Class. 2003. (Ghostville Elementary Ser.). 96p. (J). mass mkt. 3.99 (*0-439-42437-2*, 53616146, Scholastic Paperbacks) Scholastic, Inc.
Katchke, Judy, et al. Help! There's a Ghost in My Room. 2003. (Full House Ser.: No. 1). 96p. mass mkt. 4.99 (*0-06-054083-4*, 53751756, HarperEntertainment) Morrow/Avon.
Kehret, Peg. Horror at the Haunted House. 2002. 144p. (J). pap. 5.99 (*0-14-230146-9*, Puffin Bks.) Penguin Putnam Bks. for Young Readers.
King-Smith, Dick. The Roundhill. 2001. (Illus.). (J). 16.95 (*0-7540-6168-X*) BBC Audiobooks America.
—The Roundhill. 2002. (Illus.). 96p. (YA). (gr. 5-8). pap. 4.99 (*0-440-41844-5*) Random Hse., Inc.
Kipling, Rudyard. The Haunting of Holmescroft. 1998. (Classic Frights Ser.). Orig. Title: The House Surgeon. (Illus.). 64p. (J). (gr. 4-7). pap. 5.95 o.p. (*0-929605-81-0*, Classic Frights) Books of Wonder.
Kline, Trish. The Ghost Hunter & the Ghost of Gettysburg. 2002. 92p. (J). per. 7.50 (*0-9717234-0-0*) Ghost Hunter Productions.
Laing, Wendy. Captain Angus, the Lighthouse Ghost. (J). E-Book 5.95 (*1-930756-31-3*); 1999. E-Book 4.50 (*1-930364-16-4*) McGraw Publishing, Inc. (Bookmice).
Lassiter, Rhiannon. Ghosts. 2002. (Hex Ser.: Bk. 3). (Illus.). 288p. (J). (gr. 5 up). mass mkt. 4.99 (*0-7434-2213-9*, Simon Pulse) Simon & Schuster Children's Publishing.
Lawrence, Michael. The Poltergoose: A Jiggy McCue Story. 2002. 144p. (J). 14.99 (*0-525-46839-0*, Dutton Children's Bks.) Penguin Putnam Bks. for Young Readers.
The Legend of Sleepy Hollow. 1988. mass mkt. 1.95 (*0-938819-06-2*); 1987. mass mkt. 1.95 (*0-938819-42-9*) Doherty, Tom Assocs., LLC. (Aerie).
Lehr, Norma. Haunting at Black Water Cove. 2000. (Illus.). 119p. (J). (gr. 3-7). pap. 6.95 o.p. (*0-87358-750-2*, Rising Moon Bks. for Young Readers) Northland Publishing.
—Haunting at Black Water Cove. 2000. (Illus.). (J). 13.00 (*0-606-18311-6*) Turtleback Bks.
Lerangis, Peter & Talbot, Jim. Boo! Ghosts in School! 2002. (Abracadabra Ser.: No. 2). (Illus.). 96p. (J). mass mkt. 3.99 (*0-439-22231-1*, Scholastic Paperbacks) Scholastic, Inc.
Lowther, Joan Ellaine. The Ghosts of Brawnwyn's Castle. 2001. (Illus.). 96p. pap. (*1-55212-503-3*) Trafford Publishing.
MacPhail, Catherine. Dark Waters. 2003. 177p. (J). (gr. 5 up). 15.95 (*1-58234-846-4*, Bloomsbury Children) Bloomsbury Publishing.

Maguire, Gregory. Six Haunted Hairdos. 1999. (Hamlet Chronicles Ser.). (Illus.). 160p. (J). (gr. 3-7). pap. 4.95 (*0-06-440720-9*, Harper Trophy) HarperCollins Children's Bk. Group.

—Six Haunted Hairdos. 1997. (Illus.). 160p. (J). (gr. 4-6). tchr. ed. 15.00 (*0-395-78626-6*, Clarion Bks.) Houghton Mifflin Co. Trade & Reference Div.

—Six Haunted Hairdos. l.t. ed. 2002. 178p. (J). 21.95 (*0-7862-4421-6*) Thorndike Pr.

—Six Haunted Hairdos. 1999. 11.00 (*0-606-17470-2*) Turtleback Bks.

Maifair, Linda L. The Case of the Giggling Ghost. 1993. (Darcy J. Doyle, Daring Detective Ser.: Vol. 3). 64p. (J). (gr. 2-5). mass mkt. 3.99 (*0-310-57911-2*) Zondervan.

Manns, Nick. Operating Codes. 2001. (Illus.). 192p. (J). (gr. 5 up). 15.95 (*0-316-60465-8*) Little Brown Children's Bks.

Mantell, Paul. Shelter. Richardson, Julia, ed. 2000. (So Weird Ser.: No. 2). 141p. (J). (gr. 4-7). pap. 4.99 (*0-7868-1398-9*) Disney Pr.

Marquardt, Marsha, illus. Little Ghost Goes to the Zoo. 2001. 8p. (J). pap. text 3.00 (*1-882225-21-X*) Tott Pubns.

Mason, Janet, retold by. The Legend of Sleepy Hollow. 2002. (Scholastic Junior Classics Ser.). 80p. (J). mass mkt. 3.99 (*0-439-22510-8*) Scholastic, Inc.

Masters, Elaine. Kalani & the Night Marchers. 2002. pap. 4.99 (*0-89610-359-5*) Island Heritage Publishing.

McAllister, Margaret. Hold My Hand & Run. 2000. (Illus.). 160p. (J). (gr. 5-9). 15.99 o.p. (*0-525-46391-7*, Dutton Children's Bks.) Penguin Putnam Bks. for Young Readers.

McLean, Alan C. Ghost of the Glen. Date not set. (Knockout Ser.). text 44.77 (*0-582-25082-X*) Addison-Wesley Longman, Ltd. GBR. *Dist:* Trans-Atlantic Pubns., Inc.

McNicoll, Sylvia. Grave Secrets. l.t. ed. 1999. (Illus.). 176p. (J). (gr. 7-9). pap. 8.95 (*0-7737-6015-6*) Stoddart Kids CAN. *Dist:* Fitzhenry & Whiteside, Ltd.

—Grave Secrets. 1999. 15.00 (*0-606-19641-2*) Turtleback Bks.

McSherry, Frank D., Jr., et al, eds. Western Ghosts. 1990. (American Ghosts Ser.). 224p. (Orig.). (J). pap. 9.95 (*1-55853-069-X*) Rutledge Hill Pr.

Messer, Celeste M. The Ghost of Piper's Landing. 2002. (Illus.). (J). 4.95 (*0-9702171-7-X*) Ashley-Alan Enterprises.

Metzenthen, David. Gilbert's Ghost Train. 1998. 170 p. (J). o.p. (*1-86388-852-7*) Scholastic, Inc.

Montes, Marisa. Something Wicked's in Those Woods. 2000. 224p. (YA). (gr. 7-12). 17.00 (*0-15-202391-7*) Harcourt Children's Bks.

Montgomery, Raymond A. The Haunted House. 1983. (Choose Your Own Adventure Ser.: No. 2). 64p. (J). (gr. 2-4). pap. 2.25 o.s.i (*0-553-15428-1*); pap. 3.50 o.s.i (*0-553-15679-9*) Bantam Bks.

—The Haunted House. 1983. (Choose Your Own Adventure Ser.: No. 2). (J). (gr. 2-4). pap. 1.95 o.s.i (*0-553-15207-6*, Dell Books for Young Readers) Random Hse. Children's Bks.

—The Haunted House. 1981. (Choose Your Own Adventure Ser.: No. 2). (J). (gr. 2-4). 8.70 o.p. (*0-606-02400-X*) Turtleback Bks.

Morgan, Allen. Quackadack Duck. 2003. (Illus.). 32p. (J). (gr. k-2). 18.95 (*1-55037-761-2*) Annick Pr., Ltd. CAN. *Dist:* Firefly Bks., Ltd.

Morris, Tomy, illus. A Treasury of Ghost Stories. 1996. 160p. (J). (gr. k-4). pap. 6.95 o.s.i (*0-7534-5027-5*) Larousse Kingfisher Chambers, Inc.

Naylor, Phyllis Reynolds. Bernie Magruder & the Haunted Hotel. 2001. (Bernie Magruder Ser.). (Illus.). 176p. (J). (gr. 3-7). pap. 4.99 (*0-689-84126-4*, Aladdin) Simon & Schuster Children's Publishing.

—Bernie Magruder & the Haunted Hotel. l.t. ed. 2001. 127p. (J). 20.95 (*0-7862-3600-0*) Thorndike Pr.

—The Boys Return. 2003. 144p. (gr. 4-7). pap. text 4.99 (*0-440-41675-2*); 2001. (Illus.). 132p. (J). (*0-385-32734-X*, Delacorte Bks. for Young Readers); 2001. (Illus.). 144p. (gr. 4-6). text 15.95 (*0-385-32737-4*, Dell Books for Young Readers) Random Hse. Children's Bks.

—The Boys Return. l.t. ed. 2003. 170p. (J). 23.95 (*0-7862-5822-5*) Thorndike Pr.

—Jade Green: A Ghost Story. 176p. (YA). 2001. (gr. 4-7). mass mkt. 4.99 (*0-689-82002-X*, Simon Pulse); 2000. (gr. 5-9). 16.95 (*0-689-82005-4*, Atheneum) Simon & Schuster Children's Publishing.

—Jade Green: A Ghost Story. l.t. ed. 2000. 174p. (J). (gr. 4-7). 21.95 (*0-7862-2886-5*) Thorndike Pr.

Nguyen, Joe. The Demon in the Chain. 2001. 136p. pap. 10.95 o.p. (*0-595-19217-3*, Writers Club Pr.) iUniverse, Inc.

Nixon, Joan Lowery. Ghost Town: Seven Ghostly Stories. 2002. 160p. (gr. 3-7). pap. text 4.99 (*0-440-41603-5*) Random Hse. Children's Bks.

—Ghost Town: Seven Ghostly Stories. Horowitz, Beverly, ed. 2000. 160p. (gr. 3-7). text 14.95 (*0-385-32681-5*, Delacorte Bks. for Young Readers) Random Hse. Children's Bks.

—The Weekend Was Murder! 2003. 208p. (gr. 5). pap. text 4.99 (*0-440-41983-2*, Dell Books for Young Readers) Random Hse. Children's Bks.

O'Connell, Jennifer Barrett. Ten Timid Ghosts. 2000. (Read with Me Paperbacks Ser.). (Illus.). 32p. (J). (ps-3). mass mkt. 3.25 o.s.i (*0-439-15804-4*) Scholastic, Inc.

—Ten Timid Ghosts on a Christmas Night. 2002. (Illus.). 32p. (J). mass mkt. 3.25 (*0-439-39553-4*, Cartwheel Bks.) Scholastic, Inc.

Olsen, Ashley & Olsen, Mary-Kate. Dare to Scare. 2003. (Two of a Kind Ser.: No. 31). 112p. mass mkt. 4.99 (*0-06-009327-7*, HarperEntertainment) Morrow/Avon.

Olsen, Mary-Kate & Olsen, Ashley. The Case of the Giggling Ghost. 2002. (New Adventures of Mary-Kate & Ashley Ser.: No. 31). 96p. mass mkt. 4.50 (*0-06-106653-2*, Avon Bks.) Morrow/Avon.

Patneaude, David. Haunting at Home Plate. (J). 2003. 192p. pap. 6.95 (*0-8075-3182-0*); 2000. 181p. (gr. 5-8). lib. bdg. 14.95 (*0-8075-3181-2*) Whitman, Albert & Co.

Paton Walsh, Jill. Birdy & the Ghosties, RS. 48p. 1991. (Illus.). (gr. 4-7). pap. 4.95 o.p. (*0-374-40675-8*, Sunburst); 1989. 10.95 o.p. (*0-374-30716-4*, Farrar, Straus & Giroux (BYR)) Farrar, Straus & Giroux.

Patschke, Steve. The Spooky Book. 2001. (J). (gr. k-3). 26.90 incl. audio (*0-8045-6871-5*, 6871) Spoken Arts, Inc.

Peck, Richard. Ghosts I Have Been. November, S., ed. 2001. 224p. (J). (gr. 4-7). pap. 5.99 (*0-14-131096-0*, Puffin Bks.) Penguin Putnam Bks. for Young Readers.

—Ghosts I Have Been. 2002. (YA). 20.75 (*0-8446-7211-4*) Smith, Peter Pub., Inc.

—Ghosts I Have Been. 2001. (J). 12.04 (*0-606-21213-2*) Turtleback Bks.

Peyton, K. M. The Boy Who Wasn't There. 2000. pap. 5.95 (*0-552-52717-3*) Transworld Publishers Ltd. GBR. *Dist:* Trafalgar Square.

Pfeffer, Susan Beth & Ramsey, Marcy Dunn. Ghostly Tales. Bui, Francoise, ed. 2000. (Portraits of Little Women Ser.). (Illus.). 192p. (gr. 3-7). text 9.95 (*0-385-32741-2*, Delacorte Bks. for Young Readers) Random Hse. Children's Bks.

The Phantom. 1996. (YA). pap. text 5.99 (*0-934551-10-3*) Profile Entertainment, Inc.

Pike, Christopher, pseud. Remember Me 2: The Return. 1994. (Remember Me Ser.). 224p. (YA). (gr. 7 up). mass mkt. 5.99 (*0-671-87265-6*, Simon Pulse) Simon & Schuster Children's Publishing.

—Remember Me 2: The Return. MacDonald, Patricia, ed. 1994. (Remember Me Two Ser.). 224p. (YA). (gr. 9 up). 14.00 o.p. (*0-671-87257-5*, Simon & Schuster Children's Publishing) Simon & Schuster Children's Publishing.

Poe, Edgar Allan. The Raven & Other Writings. 2003. (Aladdin Classics Ser.). (Illus.). 448p. (J). pap. 4.99 (*0-689-86352-7*, Aladdin) Simon & Schuster Children's Publishing.

Preller, James. Case of the Ghost Writer. 2001. (Jigsaw Jones Mystery Ser.). (Illus.). (J). 10.14 (*0-606-20740-6*) Turtleback Bks.

Random House Disney Staff. Haunted Mansion: The Junior Novelization. 2003. (Illus.). 128p. (J). (gr. 3). pap. 4.99 (*0-7364-2175-0*, RH/Disney) Random Hse. Children's Bks.

Reiss, Kathryn. Sweet Miss Honeywell's Revenge. 2004. (Illus.). 448p. (YA). 17.00 (*0-15-216574-6*) Harcourt Children's Bks.

Rice, Bebe Faas. The Place at the Edge of the Earth. 2002. 192p. (J). (gr. 5-9). tchr. ed. 15.00 (*0-618-15978-9*) Houghton Mifflin Co.

Richardson, Bill. Sally Dog Little. 2002. (Illus.). 24p. (J). (ps-2). 14.95 (*1-55037-759-0*) Annick Pr., Ltd. CAN. *Dist:* Firefly Bks., Ltd.

Richardson, Julia, ed. Family Reunion. 2000. (So Weird Ser.: No. 1). (Illus.). 144p. (J). (gr. 4-7). pap. 4.99 (*0-7868-1397-0*) Disney Pr.

Roberts, Laura Peyton. Ghost of a Chance. 1997. 192p. (YA). (gr. 7-12). 14.95 o.s.i (*0-385-32508-8*, Delacorte Pr.) Dell Publishing.

—Ghost of a Chance. 1999. 192p. (gr. 5 up). pap. text 3.99 o.s.i (*0-440-41534-9*, Dell Books for Young Readers) Random Hse. Children's Bks.

—Ghost of a Chance. 1999. 10.04 (*0-606-16448-0*) Turtleback Bks.

Rochester & Merle: A Day at the Carnival. 2000. 32p. (J). pap. (*0-9701450-5-5*) Long Hill Productions, Inc.

Ruby, Laura. Lily's Ghost. 2003. 272p. (J). (gr. 5 up). 16.99 (*0-06-051829-4*); lib. bdg. 17.89 (*0-06-051830-8*) HarperCollins Children's Bk. Group.

Sauer, Cat. Gwendolyn the Ghost. (Brown Bag Bedtime Bks.). (ps-2). 2000. 22p. (J). pap. 16.50 o.p. incl. audio compact disk (*0-9704460-3-9*); 2003. (Illus.). 29p. (YA). spiral bd. 16.95 (*0-9704460-9-8*) Writer's Ink. Studios, Inc.

Saunders, Susan. The Chilling Tale of Crescent Pond. 1998. (Black Cat Club Ser.: Vol. 8). 96p. (J). (gr. 1-5). pap. 3.95 o.s.i (*0-06-442072-8*) HarperCollins Children's Bk. Group.

Scooby Doo & the Pirate Ghost. 2001. (Illus.). (J). 15.95 (*0-7853-4875-1*) Publications International, Ltd.

Seabrooke, Brenda. Haunting at Stratton Falls. 2000. (Illus.). 160p. (J). (gr. 5-7). 15.99 (*0-525-46389-5*, Dutton Children's Bks.) Penguin Putnam Bks. for Young Readers.

—The Haunting of Swain's Fancy. 2003. 160p. (J). (gr. 5 up). 16.99 (*0-525-46938-9*, Dutton Children's Bks.) Penguin Putnam Bks. for Young Readers.

Sefton, Catherine. The Ghost & Bertie Boggin. l.t. ed. 1991. 20.95 (*0-8161-9312-6*, Macmillan Reference USA) Gale Group.

—In a Blue Velvet Dress. l.t. ed. 1987. (J). 16.95 o.p. (*0-7451-0498-3*, Galaxy Children's Large Print) BBC Audiobooks America.

—In a Blue Velvet Dress, 2002. (Lost Treasures Ser.: No. 8). 128p. (J). pap. 4.99 (*0-7868-1693-7*) Disney Pr.

—In a Blue Velvet Dress. 1973. (Illus.). (J). (gr. 4-7). lib. bdg. 9.89 o.p. (*0-06-025263-4*) HarperCollins Pubs.

Showell, Ellen Harvey. The Ghost of Tillie Jean Cassaway. 2000. (Illus.). 128p. (gr. 4-7). pap. 9.95 (*0-595-14292-3*, Backinprint.com) iUniverse, Inc.

Shreve, Susan Richards. Ghost Cats. (J). 2001. 176p. mass mkt. 4.99 (*0-590-37132-0*); 1999. 162p. (gr. 3-7). pap. 14.95 (*0-590-37131-2*) Scholastic, Inc. (Levine, Arthur A. Bks.).

Slammin' Ghost of the Boy's Club. 2002. (J). pap. (*0-7868-1505-1*) Disney Pr.

Smith, Janice Lee. There's a Ghost in the Coatroom: Adam Joshua's Christmas. 1991. (Illus.). 96p. (J). (gr. 1-4). 13.95 (*0-06-022863-6*); lib. bdg. 13.89 o.p. (*0-06-022864-4*) HarperCollins Children's Bk. Group.

Snow Ghost. 2001. (Scooby-Doo Ser.: No. 9). 32p. mass mkt. 3.99 (*0-439-31845-9*) Scholastic, Inc.

Snyder, Zilpha Keatley. The Ghosts of Rathburn Park. 2002. 192p. lib. bdg. 17.99 (*0-385-90064-3*); (gr. 3-7). text 15.95 (*0-385-32767-6*) Random Hse., Inc.

Soto, Gary. The Afterlife: A Novel. 2003. 176p. (J). (gr. 6 up). 16.00 (*0-15-204774-3*, 53597422) Harcourt Children's Bks.

Spenceley, Annabel, illus. The Kingfisher Treasury of Spooky Stories. 2003. (Kingfisher Treasury of Stories Ser.). 160p. (J). pap. 5.95 (*0-7534-5634-6*, Kingfisher) Houghton Mifflin Co. Trade & Reference Div.

Stamper, Judith Bauer. Five Haunted Houses. 2001. (Hello Reader! Ser.). (Illus.). 48p. (J). (gr. 2-4). mass mkt. 3.99 o.s.i (*0-439-20546-8*, Cartwheel Bks.) Scholastic, Inc.

Stern, Jacqueline. The Ghosts of Goliad. 2003. iii, 165p. (J). 17.95 (*1-57168-785-8*, Eakin Pr.) Eakin Pr.

Stengel, Joyce A. Mystery of the Island Jewels. 2002. 208p. (J). (gr. 3-7). pap. 4.99 (*0-689-85049-2*, Aladdin) Simon & Schuster Children's Publishing.

Stine, R. L. Ghost Next Door. 2003. (Goosebumps Ser.). 144p. (J). mass mkt. 4.99 (*0-439-56832-3*, 53655426, Scholastic Paperbacks) Scholastic, Inc.

—When Good Ghouls Go Bad. 2001. (Nightmare Room Ser.: No. 11). 144p. (J). (gr. 4-6). pap. 3.99 (*0-06-441082-X*, Avon) HarperCollins Children's Bk. Group.

—Who's Been Sleeping in My Grave? 1995. (Ghosts of Fear Street Ser.: No. 2). 128p. (J). (gr. 4-7). pap. 3.99 (*0-671-52942-0*, Aladdin) Simon & Schuster Children's Publishing.

Stone, Tom B. There's a Ghost in the Boys' Bathroom. 1995. (Graveyard School Ser.: No. 10). 128p. (J). (gr. 3-7). pap. 3.50 o.s.i (*0-553-48345-5*, Skylark) Random Hse. Children's Bks.

—There's a Ghost in the Boys' Bathroom. 1996. (Graveyard School Ser.: No. 10). (J). (gr. 3-7). 8.60 o.p. (*0-606-08533-5*) Turtleback Bks.

Surrell, Jason. The Haunted Mansion: From the Magic Kingdom to the Movies. 2003. (Illus.). 132p. (J). pap. 20.00 (*0-7868-5419-7*) Disney Pr.

Sykes, Shelley & Szymanski, Lois. The Ghost Comes Out. 2001. (Gettysburg Ghost Gang Ser.: Vol. 1). 96p. (J). pap. 5.95 (*1-57249-266-X*, WM Kids) White Mane Publishing Co., Inc.

—Ghost on Board. 2001. (Gettysburg Ghost Gang Ser.: Vol. 2). (Illus.). 96p. (J). pap. 5.95 (*1-57249-267-8*, WM Kids) White Mane Publishing Co., Inc.

—The Soldier in the Cellar. 2002. (Gettysburg Ghost Gang Ser.: Vol. 5). 96p. (J). pap. 5.95 (*1-57249-299-6*, WM Kids) White Mane Publishing Co., Inc.

—A Whisper of War. 2003. (J). (*1-57249-327-5*, WM Kids) White Mane Publishing Co., Inc.

Terasaki, Stanley Todd. Ghosts for Breakfast. 2002. (Illus.). 32p. (J). (gr. k-4). 16.95 (*1-58430-046-9*) Lee & Low Bks., Inc.

Thompson, Julian F. Ghost Story, ERS. 1997. 224p. (J). 15.95 o.p. (*0-8050-4870-7*, Holt, Henry & Co. Bks. For Young Readers) Holt, Henry & Co.

Turner, Rosa M. The Ghost of Willow Hill. 2000. cd-rom 9.95 (*1-58338-390-5*) CrossroadsPub.com.

Van de Velde, Vivian. There's a Dead Person Following My Sister Around. 2001. (Illus.). (J). 11.04 (*0-606-21485-2*) Turtleback Bks.

Vande Velde, Vivian. A Coming Evil. 1998. 212p. (J). (gr. 5-9). tchr. ed. 17.00 (*0-395-90012-3*) Houghton Mifflin Co.

—Ghost of a Hanged Man. 1998. (Accelerated Reader Bks.). 95p. (J). (gr. 3-7). 14.95 (*0-7614-5015-7*, Cavendish Children's Bks.) Cavendish, Marshall Corp.

—There's a Dead Person Following My Sister Around. 2001. 160p. (J). pap. 4.99 (*0-14-131281-5*, Puffin Bks.) Penguin Putnam Bks. for Young Readers.

Vaughan, Marcia K. We're Going on a Ghost Hunt. 2001. (Illus.). 32p. (J). (gr. k-2). 15.00 (*0-15-202353-4*) Harcourt Children's Bks.

Velde, Vivian Vande. Ghost of a Hanged Man. 2003. (YA). pap. 5.95 (*0-7614-5154-4*, Cavendish Children's Bks.) Cavendish, Marshall Corp.

Warner, Gertrude Chandler. The Mystery of the Midnight Dog. 2001. (Boxcar Children Ser.: No. 81). (Illus.). 122p. (J). (gr. 2-7). pap. 3.95 (*0-8075-5476-6*); lib. bdg. 13.95 (*0-8075-5475-8*) Whitman, Albert & Co.

Warner, Gertrude Chandler, creator. The Mystery on Blizzard Mountain. 2002. (Boxcar Children Ser.: No. 86). (Illus.). 122p. (J). (gr. 2-7). lib. bdg. 13.95 (*0-8075-5493-6*); pap. 395.00 (*0-8075-5494-4*) Whitman, Albert & Co.

Wasserman, Robin, et al. Ghost School. 2003. (Scooby-Doo Ser.). 32p. (J). mass mkt. 3.99 (*0-439-44227-3*, Scholastic Paperbacks) Scholastic, Inc.

Weigelt, Udo. Miranda's Ghosts. 2002. (Illus.). 32p. (J). lib. bdg. 16.50 (*0-7358-1705-7*) North-South Bks., Inc.

—Miranda's Ghosts. Miller, Marisa, tr. from GER. 2002. (Illus.). 32p. (J). (gr. k-3). 15.95 (*0-7358-1704-9*) North-South Bks., Inc.

Weninger, Brigitte, pseud. Davy, Help! It's a Ghost! James, J. Alison, tr. from GER. 2002. (Illus.). 32p. (J). 15.95 (*0-7358-1687-5*); lib. bdg. 16.50 (*0-7358-1688-3*) North-South Bks., Inc.

West, Tracey. Hoothoot's Haunted Forest. 2001. (Pokemon Junior Chapter Bks.: No. 13). (Illus.). 48p. (J). (gr. k-4). pap. 3.99 (*0-439-32066-6*) Scholastic, Inc.

Whybrow, Ian. Little Wolf's Haunted Hall for Small Horrors. 2000. (Middle Grade Fiction Ser.). (Illus.). 125p. (J). (gr. 3-6). lib. bdg. 12.95 (*1-57505-412-4*, Carolrhoda Bks.) Lerner Publishing Group.

Wien, Hallie. Boo! to You, Too! 2002. (Peekaboo Bks.). (Illus.). 10p. (J). (ps). bds. 5.99 (*1-57584-949-6*, Reader's Digest Children's Bks.) Reader's Digest Children's Publishing, Inc.

Wilde, Oscar. The Canterville Ghost. Date not set. (Nelson Readers Ser.). (J). pap. text (*0-17-557035-3*) Addison-Wesley Longman, Inc.

—The Canterville Ghost. 1997. (Candlewick Treasures Ser.). (Illus.). 128p. (J). (gr. 3-9). 11.99 o.p. (*0-7636-0132-2*) Candlewick Pr.

—The Canterville Ghost. 2nd ed. 2000. (Reading & Training Ser.). 112p. (YA). pap. (*1-57159-012-9*) Los Andes Publishing Co.

—The Canterville Ghost. 1996. (Illus.). 44p. (J). (gr. 2-4). 16.95 o.p. (*1-55858-624-5*); (ps-3). pap. 6.95 (*1-55858-611-3*) North-South Bks., Inc.

—The Canterville Ghost. 1991. (Illus.). 36p. (J). (gr. 4 up). pap. 15.95 o.s.i (*0-88708-027-8*, Simon & Schuster Children's Publishing) Simon & Schuster Children's Publishing.

Wilhelm, Hans. The Boy Who Wasn't There. 1993. 32p. (J). (gr. 1-5). pap. 14.95 (*0-590-46635-6*) Scholastic, Inc.

Wilson, Jacqueline. Vicky Angel. 2001. (J). 16.95 (*0-7540-6165-5*) BBC Audiobooks America.

—Vicky Angel. 2002. 144p. (J). pap. (*0-440-86415-1*, Corgi) Bantam Bks.

—Vicky Angel. (Illus.). 176p. (gr. 3-7). 2003. pap. text 4.99 (*0-440-41808-9*, Yearling); 2001. text 15.95 (*0-385-72920-0*, Dell Books for Young Readers) Random Hse. Children's Bks.

Winters, Kay. Whooo's Haunting the Teeny Tiny Ghost? (Illus.). 32p. (J). (ps-3). 2001. pap. 5.95 (*0-06-443784-1*, Harper Trophy); Bk. 2. 2000. (Teeny Tiny Ghost Ser.: Vol. 2). lib. bdg. 14.89 (*0-06-027359-3*); Bk. 2. 1999. (Teeny Tiny Ghost Ser.: Vol. 2). 14.95 (*0-06-027358-5*) HarperCollins Children's Bk. Group.

Woodruff, Elvira. The Ghost of Lizard Light. 1999. (Illus.). 192p. (YA). (gr. 5-8). 14.95 (*0-679-89281-8*); lib. bdg. 16.99 (*0-679-99281-2*) Knopf, Alfred A. Inc.

—The Ghost of Lizard Light. 2001. (Illus.). 192p. (gr. 3-7). pap. text 4.99 (*0-440-41655-8*, Yearling) Random Hse. Children's Bks.

Woodson, Marion. My Brother's Keeper. 2002. (Illus.). 160p. (J). pap. 6.95 (*1-55192-488-9*) Raincoast Bk. Distribution CAN. *Dist:* Publishers Group West.

Wright, Betty Ren. Crandall's Castle. 2003. 192p. (J). tchr. ed. 16.95 (*0-8234-1726-3*) Holiday Hse., Inc.

—A Ghost in the Family. 2002. 96p. (J). (gr. 3-7). mass mkt. 3.99 (*0-590-02953-3*, Scholastic Paperbacks) Scholastic, Inc.

—The Moonlight Man. 2000. (Illus.). 181p. (J). (gr. 3-7). pap. 15.95 (*0-590-25237-2*, Scholastic Reference) Scholastic, Inc.

Yates, Dan. Angels Don't Knock! 1994. pap. 10.95 (*1-55503-711-9*, 019405) Covenant Communications, Inc.

Yolen, Jane. The Bagpiper's Ghost. (Tartan Magic Ser.: Bk. 3). 144p. 2003. (Illus.). (J). pap. 5.95 (*0-15-204913-4*, Magic Carpet Bks.); 2002. (YA). (gr. 4-7). 16.00 (*0-15-202310-0*) Harcourt Children's Bks.

GIANTS—FICTION

Ahlberg, Allan. Fee Fi Fo Fum. 1985. (Illus.). lib. bdg. 3.95 o.p. (*0-394-87193-6*); (J). 5.99 o.s.i (*0-394-97193-0*) Random Hse. Children's Bks. (Random Hse. Bks. for Young Readers).

—The Giant Baby. 1999. (J). pap. 3.99 (*0-14-038723-4*) Viking Penguin.

Allen, Linda, illus. & retold by. The Giant Who Had No Heart. 1988. 40p. (J). (ps-3). 13.95 o.s.i (*0-399-21446-1*, Philomel) Penguin Putnam Bks. for Young Readers.

Amstutz, Beverly. Too Big for the Bag. 1981. (Illus.). (J). (gr. k-7). pap. 3.50 (*0-937836-05-2*) Precious Resources.

Anholt, Laurence. Knee-High Norman. 1996. (Illus.). 32p. (Orig.). (J). (gr. k-3). bds. 4.99 o.p. (*1-56402-841-0*) Candlewick Pr.

Auer, Martin. Now, Now Markus. 1989. (Illus.). 48p. (J). (ps up). 12.95 o.p. (*0-688-08974-7*); lib. bdg. 12.88 o.p. (*0-688-08975-5*) HarperCollins Children's Bk. Group. (Greenwillow Bks.).

Bash, Barbara. Desert Giant Vol. 1: The World of the Saguaro Cactus. 1990. (Tree Tales Ser.). (Illus.). 32p. (J). (gr. 4-7). pap. 6.95 o.p. (*0-316-08307-0*) Little Brown & Co.

Beck, Ian. The Teddy Robber. 1993. (Illus.). 32p. (J). (ps-3). 12.95 o.p. (*0-8120-6401-1*); pap. text 5.95 o.p. (*0-8120-1711-0*) Barron's Educational Series, Inc.

—The Teddy Robber. 1989. 14.95 o.s.i (*0-385-26965-X*) Doubleday Publishing.

Bernal, Richard, illus. Jack & the Beanstalk. 1991. (Children's Classics Ser.). 32p. (J). 6.95 (*0-8362-4903-8*) Andrews McMeel Publishing.

Birdseye, Tom. Look Out Jack! Giant Is Back! 2003. (Illus.). (J). pap. 6.95 (*0-8234-1776-X*) Holiday Hse., Inc.

—Look Out, Jack! the Giant Is Back! 2001. (Illus.). 32p. (J). (ps-2). tchr. ed. 16.95 (*0-8234-1450-7*) Holiday Hse., Inc.

Bottner, Barbara. What Would You Do with a Giant? 1972. (Illus.). 32p. (J). (ps-3). 4.79 o.p. (*0-399-60738-2*) Putnam Publishing Group, The.

Briggs, Raymond, text. Ivor the Invisible. 2003. (Illus.). 40p. (J). 19.95 (*0-7522-2034-9*) Boxtree, Ltd. GBR. *Dist:* Trafalgar Square.

Brookes, Diane & Leonard, Marcia. A Novel Study for Grades One & Two Based on When the Giants Came to Town, 25 vols. 1998. pap., tchr. ed. (*0-9683234-5-6*) Raven Rock Publishing.

Burgess, Melvin. The Earth Giant. 1999. 154p. (gr. 3-7). pap. 4.99 o.p. (*0-698-11765-4*) Penguin Putnam Bks. for Young Readers.

Carle, Eric. Watch Out! A Giant! 1978. (Illus.). (J). (ps-3). 6.95 o.p. (*0-529-05455-8*); 6.99 o.p. (*0-529-05456-6*, 05456) Putnam Publishing Group, The.

—Watch Out! A Giant! 2002. (Illus.). 32p. (J). (ps-3). 14.95 (*0-689-84964-8*, Little Simon) Simon & Schuster Children's Publishing.

Carrick, Donald. Harald & the Giant Knight. 1982. 32p. (J). (gr. 1-3). 15.95 o.p. (*0-89919-060-X*, Clarion Bks.) Houghton Mifflin Co. Trade & Reference Div.

Carroll, John. Donkey Nina & the Giant. 1989. (Illus.). 32p. (J). (ps-2). 12.95 o.p. (*0-525-44478-5*, Dutton Children's Bks.) Penguin Putnam Bks. for Young Readers.

Christiana, David. A Tooth Fairy's Tale, RS. 1996. 32p. (J). (ps-3). pap. 6.95 o.p. (*0-374-47942-9*, Sunburst) Farrar, Straus & Giroux.

Cincerelli, Carol J. The Selfish Giant by Oscar Wilde. (Integrating Literature, Language, & the Arts Ser.). (Illus.). 96p. (J). (gr. 1-6). tchr. ed. 6.99 o.p. (*0-86653-537-3*, GA1158, Good Apple) McGraw-Hill Children's Publishing.

Clayton, Sandra. The Giant. 1994. (Voyages Ser.). (Illus.). (J). 4.25 (*0-383-03745-X*) SRA/McGraw-Hill.

Cole, Brock. The Giant's Toe, RS. 1986. 32p. (J). (ps up). 15.00 o.p. (*0-374-32559-6*, Farrar, Straus & Giroux (BYR)) Farrar, Straus & Giroux.

Compton, Kenn & Compton, Joanne. Jack the Giant Chaser: An Appalachian Tale. 1993. (Illus.). 32p. (J). (ps-3). lib. bdg. 14.95 o.p. (*0-8234-0998-8*) Holiday Hse., Inc.

Cote, Denis. Les Geants de Blizzard. 2002. (Roman Jeunesse Ser.). (FRE.). 96p. (YA). (gr. 4-7). pap. 8.95 (*2-89021-126-6*) La Courte Echelle CAN. *Dist:* Firefly Bks., Ltd.

Coville, Bruce & Coville, Katherine. The Foolish Giant. 1978. (Illus.). (J). (gr. k-2). lib. bdg. 13.89 (*0-397-31800-6*) HarperCollins Children's Bk. Group.

Cuneo, Mary Louise. What Can a Giant Do? 1994. (Illus.). 32p. (J). (ps-1). lib. bdg. 14.89 o.p. (*0-06-021217-9*); 15.00 o.p. (*0-06-021214-4*) HarperCollins Children's Bk. Group.

Cunliffe, John. The Giant Who Swallowed the Wind. 1980. (Illus.). (J). 8.95 o.p. (*0-233-96310-3*) Blackwell Publishing.

—Sara's Giant & the Upside-Down House. 1980. (Illus.). (J). 8.95 o.p. (*0-233-97202-1*) Blackwell Publishing.

Dadey, Debbie & Jones, Marcia Thornton. Giants Don't Go Snowboarding. 1998. (Adventures of the Bailey School Kids Ser.: No. 33). (Illus.). 76p. (J). (gr. 2-4). mass mkt. 3.99 (*0-590-18983-2*) Scholastic, Inc.

—Giants Don't Go Snowboarding. 1998. (Adventures of the Bailey School Kids Ser.: No. 33). (J). (gr. 2-4). 10.14 (*0-606-15547-3*) Turtleback Bks.

Dahl, Roald. The BFG. 1999. 16.95 (*0-7540-6054-3*) BBC Audiobooks America.

—The BFG, RS. 1982. (Illus.). 221p. (J). (gr. 1 up). 30.00 o.p. (*0-374-30471-8*); 32p. (YA). (gr. 4-7). 17.00 (*0-374-30469-6*) Farrar, Straus & Giroux. (Farrar, Straus & Giroux (BYR)).

—The BFG. 1993. (Children's Classics Ser.). 256p. (J). (gr. 2 up). 14.95 (*0-679-42813-5*, Everyman's Library) Knopf Publishing Group.

—The BFG. (Illus.). 208p. (J). 1998. (gr. 3-7). pap. 5.99 (*0-14-130105-8*); 1989. pap. 4.99 o.s.i (*0-14-034019-X*) Penguin Putnam Bks. for Young Readers. (Puffin Bks.).

—The BFG. 1984. (J). 12.04 (*0-606-00262-6*) Turtleback Bks.

—The BFG. 1984. (Illus.). 208p. (J). pap. 3.95 o.p. (*0-14-031597-7*) Viking Penguin.

Davis, Donna R. Tick Tock the Giant Who Hates Time. 1995. 20p. (J). (gr. k-5). pap. text 9.95 (*0-9644890-0-7*) Spirit Bks.

de Paola, Tomie. The Mysterious Giant of Barletta. 1988. (Illus.). 32p. (J). (ps-3). pap. 7.00 (*0-15-256349-0*, Voyager Bks./Libros Viajeros) Harcourt Children's Bks.

De Regniers, Beatrice. Boy Who Fooled the Giant. 1989. (Easy Reader Ser.). (J). (gr. k-3). 1.25 o.s.i (*0-8431-4307-X*, Price Stern Sloan) Penguin Putnam Bks. for Young Readers.

De Regniers, Beatrice Schenk. Jack the Giant Killer. 1987. (Illus.). 32p. (J). (gr. k-3). 13.95 o.p. (*0-689-31218-0*, Atheneum) Simon & Schuster Children's Publishing.

Desimini, Lisa. The Sun & Moon: A Giant Love Story. 1999. (Illus.). 40p. (YA). (ps-3). pap. 16.95 (*0-590-18720-1*, Blue Sky Pr., The) Scholastic, Inc.

Disney Staff. Giant's Journey. 2001. (Disney Dinosaur Ser.). (Illus.). 80p. (J). (ps-3). pap. 2.99 (*0-7364-1123-2*, RH/Disney) Random Hse. Children's Bks.

Donaldson, Julia. The Spiffiest Giant in Town. 2003. (Illus.). 32p. (J). 15.99 (*0-8037-2848-4*, Dial Bks. for Young Readers) Penguin Putnam Bks. for Young Readers.

Dubois, William P. The Giant. 1987. (J). (gr. k-6). pap. 4.95 o.s.i (*0-440-42994-3*) Dell Publishing.

—The Giant. 1979. (J). (gr. 3-6). 15.50 o.p. (*0-8446-6379-4*) Smith, Peter Pub., Inc.

Dunbar, Joyce. The Sand Children. 1999. (Illus.). 32p. (J). (ps-3). 15.95 (*1-56656-309-7*, Crocodile Bks.) Interlink Publishing Group, Inc.

Dussling, Jennifer. In a Dark Dark House. 1999. (Illus.). (J). (ps-k). pap. 11.05 (*0-613-12772-2*) Econo-Clad Bks.

Estes, Eleanor. Sleeping Giant & Other Stories. 1948. (Illus.). (J). (gr. 1-5). 4.50 o.p. (*0-15-275851-8*) Harcourt Children's Bks.

Farley, Jacqui. Giant Hiccups. 2001. (Selected Children's Multicultural Stories). (Illus.). 32p. (J). lib. bdg. 15.95 (*1-56674-312-5*) Forest Hse. Publishing Co., Inc.

—Giant Hiccups. 1998. (Illus.). 32p. (J). (gr. 2 up). lib. bdg. 22.60 (*0-8368-2090-8*) Stevens, Gareth Inc.

Farley, Jacqui & Venus, Pamela. Giant Hiccups. 1995. 32p. (ps-3). pap. 5.99 (*1-870516-27-3*) Child's Play-International.

Faulkner, Matt. Jack & the Beanstalk. 1965. (J). 9.40 (*0-606-02792-0*) Turtleback Bks.

Feldman, Eve B. A Giant Surprise. 1989. (Real Readers Ser.: Level Green). (Illus.). 32p. (J). (ps-3). pap. 4.95 (*0-8114-6724-4*); lib. bdg. 21.40 o.p. (*0-8172-3527-2*) Raintree Pubs.

Fienberg, Anna & Fienberg, Barbara. The Big Big Big Book of Tashi. 2002. (Illus.). 448p. (J). (gr. 1-5). pap. 11.95 (*1-86508-563-4*) Allen & Unwin Pty., Ltd. AUS. *Dist:* Independent Pubs. Group.

—Tashi & the Giants. 1996. (Illus.). 64p. (J). (gr. 1-4). pap. text 4.95 (*1-86373-945-9*) Independent Pubs. Group.

Finley-Day, Linda. The Brave Boy & the Giant. 1999. (My Little Camera Book Ser.). (Illus.). 12p. (J). (ps-2). 12.99 o.p. (*0-8054-1799-0*) Broadman & Holman Pubs.

Finnigan, Joan. Regarde, Il Y A Des Geants Partout. 1983. (ENG., Illus.). 40p. (J). (gr. 2 up). text 6.95 o.p. (*0-88776-154-2*) Tundra Bks. of Northern New York.

Fitzpatrick, Marie-Louise. The Sleeping Giant. 2001. (Illus.). 32p. (ps-3). pap. 7.95 (*0-86327-643-1*) Interlink Publishing Group, Inc.

Foreman, Michael. Two Giants. 1967. (Illus.). (J). (gr. k-4). lib. bdg. 5.99 o.p. (*0-394-91884-3*, Pantheon) Knopf Publishing Group.

Fowler, Richard. A Giant Problem! 1988. (Illus.). 32p. (J). (gr. 1-4). 0.50 o.p. (*0-8120-5950-6*) Barron's Educational Series, Inc.

Gaeddert, LouAnn. Gustav the Gourmet Giant. 1976. (Pied Piper Bks.). (Illus.). (J). (ps-3). reprint ed. 6.46 o.p. (*0-8037-3338-0*, Dial Bks. for Young Readers) Penguin Putnam Bks. for Young Readers.

Galdone, Paul. Jack & the Beanstalk. 1982. (Illus.). 32p. (J). (ps-3). pap. 6.95 (*0-89919-085-5*, Clarion Bks.) Houghton Mifflin Co. Trade & Reference Div.

Garcia Sanchez, J. L. El Nino Gigante (The Giant Child) 1994. (Derechos del Nino Ser.). (SPA., Illus.). 32p. (J). (ps-3). lib. bdg. 15.95 (*1-56014-580-3*) Santillana USA Publishing Co., Inc.

Geiss, Tony. David Braves the Giant. 1995. (Illus.). (J). pap. 3.25 o.s.i (*0-679-87518-2*) Random Hse., Inc.

Gerstein, Mordicai. The Giant. 1995. (Illus.). 40p. (J). (ps-2). 13.95 (*0-7868-0131-X*); lib. bdg. 14.49 (*0-7868-2104-3*) Hyperion Bks. for Children.

The Giant's Child (EV) Independent Reader 5-Pack, Unit 5. 1991. (Networks Ser.). (J). (gr. 2). pap. 21.25 o.p. (*0-88106-743-1*, N216) Charlesbridge Publishing, Inc.

Gill, Janie S. A Tall, Tall Giant. 1999. (Illus.). 23p. (J). pap. 3.95 (*0-89868-432-3*); lib. bdg. 10.95 (*0-89868-431-5*); 5.95 (*0-89868-433-1*) ARO Publishing Co.

Goffe, Toni. Giant That Sneezed. 1993. (Child's Play Library). (Illus.). 32p. (J). (gr. k-3). pap. 13.99 (*0-85953-927-X*) Child's Play of England GBR. *Dist:* Child's Play-International.

—Joe Giant's Missing Boot. 1990. 32p. (J). 12.95 o.p. (*0-688-09532-1*); lib. bdg. 12.88 o.p. (*0-688-09533-X*) HarperCollins Children's Bk. Group.

Gregory, Valiska. Kate's Giants. (Illus.). (J). (ps-3). 1995. 32p. 14.95 o.s.i (*1-56402-299-4*); 1997. 40p. reprint ed. bds. 5.99 o.p. (*0-7636-0151-9*) Candlewick Pr.

Haley, Patrick. The Little Person. 1981. (Illus.). 64p. (J). (gr. 2-3). lib. bdg. 9.00 (*0-9605738-0-1*) East Eagle Pr.

Hao, Kuang-ts'ai. The Giant & the Spring. (Illus.). 32p. (J). (gr. 2-4). 1997. 36.40 (*1-57227-017-9*); 1997. (CAM & ENG., 16.95 (*1-57227-015-2*); 1994. (CHI & ENG., 16.95 (*1-57227-009-8*); 1994. (ENG & KOR., 16.95 (*1-57227-012-8*); 1994. (ENG & TAG., 16.95 (*1-57227-014-4*); 1994. (ENG & LAO., 16.95 (*1-57227-016-0*); 1994. (ENG & THA., 16.95 (*1-57227-013-6*); 1994. (ENG & VIE., 16.95 (*1-57227-011-X*) Pan Asia Pubns. (USA), Inc.

—The Giant & the Spring: El Gigante y el Nino Primavera. Zeller, Beatriz, tr. 1994. (ENG & SPA., Illus.). 32p. (J). (gr. 2-4). 16.95 (*1-57227-010-1*) Pan Asia Pubns. (USA), Inc.

Hardy, Tad. Valley of the Giant. 1997. 216p. (J). (gr. 3-7). o.p. (*0-7814-3002-X*) Cook Communications Ministries.

Hasler, Eveline. The Giantess. McKenna, Laura, tr. from GER. 1997. Tr. of Riesin. (Illus.). 28p. (J). (ps-3). 12.95 (*0-916291-76-6*, Cranky Nell Bks.) Kane/Miller Bk. Pubs.

Hawkes, Kevin. His Royal Buckliness. 1992. (Illus.). 32p. (J). (ps up). 15.00 o.p. (*0-688-11062-2*); lib. bdg. 14.93 o.p. (*0-688-11063-0*) HarperCollins Children's Bk. Group.

Hearne, Betsy. South Star. 1977. (Illus.). 96p. (J). (gr. 3-7). 1.98 o.s.i (*0-689-50091-2*, McElderry, Margaret K.) Simon & Schuster Children's Publishing.

Heller, Nicholas. The Giant. 1997. (Illus.). 24p. (J). (gr. k-3). 15.00 o.s.i (*0-688-15224-4*); lib. bdg. 14.93 o.p. (*0-688-15225-2*) HarperCollins Children's Bk. Group. (Greenwillow Bks.).

The Helpful Giant Independent Reader 5-Pack, Unit 5. 1991. (Networks Ser.). (J). (gr. 2). pap. 21.25 o.p. (*0-88106-745-8*, N218) Charlesbridge Publishing, Inc.

Hogragian, Nonny. The Giant with 3 Golden Hairs. 1924. (J). o.s.i (*0-688-05183-9*); lib. bdg. o.s.i (*0-688-05184-7*) HarperCollins Children's Bk. Group. (Greenwillow Bks.).

Holub, Joan. Jack & the Jellybeanstalk. 2002. (Reading Railroad Bks.). (Illus.). 32p. mass mkt. 3.49 (*0-448-42657-9*) Penguin Putnam Bks. for Young Readers.

Houghton, Eric. A Giant Can Do Anything. 1980. (Illus.). 32p. (J). 8.95 o.p. (*0-233-96237-9*) Blackwell Publishing.

Huang, Benrei. Jack & the Beanstalk. 1995. (Pudgy Pal Board Bks.). (Illus.). 18p. (J). 3.95 o.s.i (*0-448-40857-0*, Grosset & Dunlap) Penguin Putnam Bks. for Young Readers.

Hughes, Ted. The Iron Giant. 1988. (Illus.). 64p. (J). (gr. 3-7). 11.95 (*0-06-022638-2*); lib. bdg. 12.89 o.p. (*0-06-022639-0*); mass mkt. 4.95 o.p. (*0-06-440214-2*, Harper Trophy) HarperCollins Children's Bk. Group.

—The Iron Giant. 1968. (Illus.). (J). (gr. 3-7). lib. bdg. 8.79 o.s.i (*0-06-022658-7*) HarperCollins Pubs.

—The Iron Giant. 1999. (Illus.). 96p. (gr. 3-5). pap. text 4.99 (*0-375-80153-7*) Knopf, Alfred A. Inc.

—The Iron Giant. 1999. (Illus.). 96p. (J). (gr. 3-5). 16.00 (*0-375-80167-7*, Knopf Bks. for Young Readers) Random Hse. Children's Bks.

Hutchins, Hazel J. Two So Small. 2000. (Illus.). 32p. (J). (ps-3). lib. bdg. 19.95 (*1-55037-651-9*); per. 7.95 (*1-55037-650-0*) Annick Pr., Ltd. CAN. *Dist:* Firefly Bks., Ltd.

Jacques et le Haricot Magique.Tr. of Jack & the Bean Stalk. (FRE.). 48p. (J). pap. 12.95 incl. audio compact disk (*2-89558-069-3*); pap. 12.95 incl. audio compact disk (*2-89558-069-3*); (Illus.). pap. 9.95 incl. audio (*2-921997-80-0*) Coffragants CAN. *Dist:* Penton Overseas, Inc.

Kanganas, Ethel & Sauer, Margaret. Orlif, the Friendly Giant. 1997. (Illus.). 40p. (J). 10.95 (*1-875560-79-3*) Univ. of Western Australia Pr. AUS. *Dist:* International Specialized Bk. Services.

Kasza, Keiko. The Mightiest. 2001. (Illus.). 32p. (J). 15.99 (*0-399-23586-8*) Penguin Group (USA) Inc.

—The Mightiest. 2003. (Picture Puffin Ser.). (Illus.). 32p. 5.99 (*0-14-250185-9*, Puffin Bks.) Penguin Putnam Bks. for Young Readers.

Kellogg, Steven, illus. & retold by. Jack & the Beanstalk. 1991. 48p. (J). (ps-3). 16.95 (*0-688-10250-6*); lib. bdg. 17.89 (*0-688-10251-4*) HarperCollins Children's Bk. Group.

Kennedy, Richard. Inside My Feet: The Story of a Giant. (Trophy Bk.). (Illus.). 80p. (J). 1991. (gr. 3-7). pap. 3.95 (*0-06-440409-9*, Harper Trophy); 1979. (gr. 2-6). o.p. (*0-06-023118-1*); 1979. (gr. 2-6). lib. bdg. 11.89 o.p. (*0-06-023119-X*) HarperCollins Children's Bk. Group.

Kielty, Derek. Back up the Beanstalk. 2003. (Illus.). 64p. (YA). pap. 8.95 (*1-901737-45-4*) Anvil Bks., Ltd. IRL. *Dist:* Dufour Editions, Inc.

Kirk, Daniel. Moondogs. 1999. (Illus.). 32p. (J). (ps-3). 15.99 (*0-399-23128-5*) Penguin Group (USA) Inc.

Krensky, Stephen. The Perils of Putney. 1978. (Illus.). (J). (gr. 4-6). 7.95 o.p. (*0-689-30657-1*, Atheneum) Simon & Schuster Children's Publishing.

Kreye, Walter. The Giant from the Little Island. 1945. (Illus.). 32p. (J). (ps-3). 13.95 o.p. (*1-55858-085-9*) North-South Bks., Inc.

Kroll, Steven. Big Jeremy. 1989. (Illus.). 32p. (J). (ps-3). 14.95 o.p. (*0-8234-0759-4*) Holiday Hse., Inc.

Larcombe, Jennifer Rees. The Terrible Giant. 1999. (Best Bible Stories Ser.). (Illus.). 24p. (J). (ps-3). pap. 2.99 (*1-58134-054-0*) Crossway Bks.

Leonard, Marcia. The Giant Baby & Other Giant Tales. 1994. (Hello Reader! Ser.: Level 4). (Illus.). 48p. (J). (ps-3). pap. 3.99 (*0-590-46892-8*) Scholastic, Inc.

Lesynski, Loris. Boy Soup: Or When Giant Caught Cold. 1996. (Illus.). 32p. (J). (ps-3). 16.95 (*1-55037-417-6*); pap. 5.95 (*1-55037-416-8*) Annick Pr., Ltd. CAN. *Dist:* Firefly Bks., Ltd.

Lewin, Ted & Lewin, Betsy. Elephant Quest. 2000. (Illus.). 48p. (J). (gr. 1 up). 15.95 (*0-688-14111-0*); 15.95 (*0-688-14111-0*); lib. bdg. 15.89 (*0-688-14112-9*); lib. bdg. 15.89 (*0-688-14112-9*) HarperCollins Children's Bk. Group.

Light, Steve. The Shoemaker Extraordinaire. 2003. (Illus.). 32p. (J). (gr. k-3). 14.95 (*0-8109-4236-4*) Abrams, Harry N. , Inc.

Little, Emily. David & the Giant. 1987. (Step into Reading Ser.). (Illus.). 32p. (ps-3). pap. 3.99 (*0-394-88867-7*, Random Hse. Bks. for Young Readers) Random Hse. Children's Bks.

Lobel, Anita. The Dwarf Giant. 1996. (Illus.). 32p. (J). (ps-3). pap. 4.95 (*0-688-14408-X*, Morrow, William & Co.) Morrow/Avon.

—Dwarf Giant. 1996. 11.10 (*0-606-09219-6*) Turtleback Bks.

Lomsky, Gerry. The Beanstalk Bandit: The Giant's Version of "Jack & the Beanstalk" 1993. (J). (gr. 2-7). 6.95 (*1-883499-01-1*); (Illus.). 30p. pap. 4.95 (*1-883499-00-3*) Princess Publishing.

Loredo, Elizabeth. Giant Steps. 2004. (Illus.). 32p. (J). 15.99 (*0-399-23491-8*) Penguin Putnam Bks. for Young Readers.

McConnell, Robert. Norbert Nipkin et la Pierre aux Enigmes. 1990. Tr. of Norbert Nipkin & the Magic Riddle Stone. (FRE., Illus.). 48p. (Orig.). (J). pap. *(0-929141-07-5)* Napoleon Publishing/Rendezvous Pr.

McMullan, Kate. Fluffy Plants a Jelly Bean. 2004. (Hello Reader! Ser.). (Illus.). (J). mass mkt. 16.95 *(0-439-31945-5)* Scholastic, Inc.

McMullan, Kate & McMullan, Jim. The Noisy Giants' Tea Party. 1992. (Michael di Capua Bks.). (Illus.). (J). (ps-3). 80p. 15.00 o.p. *(0-06-205017-6)*; 32p. lib. bdg. 14.89 o.p. *(0-06-205018-4)* HarperCollins Children's Bk. Group.

Messenger, Norman, illus. Jack & the Beanstalk. 1997. (Nursery Classics Ser.). 32p. (J). (ps-k). pap. 8.95 o.p. *(0-7894-1170-9)* Dorling Kindersley Publishing, Inc.

Moodie, Fiona. Boy & the Giants, RS. 1993. 32p. (J). (ps-3). 15.00 o.p. *(0-374-30927-2*, Farrar, Straus & Giroux (BYR)) Farrar, Straus & Giroux.

Morpurgo, Michael. The Sandman & the Turtles. 1994. 80p. (J). (gr. 3-7). 14.95 o.p. *(0-399-22672-9*, Philomel) Penguin Putnam Bks. for Young Readers.

Muller, Gerda. Jack & the Beanstalk. 1990. (Illus.). 48p. (J). (gr. 2-6). 2.99 o.p. *(0-517-02421-7)* Random Hse. Value Publishing.

Muller, Robin. Mollie Whuppie & the Giant. 1995. (Illus.). 36p. (J). (ps-3). 14.95 o.p. *(1-895565-84-7)* Firefly Bks., Ltd.

Muller, Robin, illus. & retold by. Mollie Whuppie & the Giant. 1995. 36p. (J). (ps-3). pap. 5.95 o.p. *(1-895565-79-0)* Firefly Bks., Ltd.

Munsch, Robert. Giant. 1989. (Illus.). 32p. (J). (gr. k-3). pap. 5.95 o.p. *(1-55037-070-7)*; text 15.95 o.p. *(1-55037-071-5)* Annick Pr., Ltd. CAN. *Dist:* Firefly Bks., Ltd.

Murphy, Chuck. Jack & the Beanstalk: Three-Dimensional Edition. 1998. (Classic Collectible Pop-Up Ser.). (Illus.). 14p. (J). (ps-3). 19.95 *(0-689-82207-3*, Little Simon) Simon & Schuster Children's Publishing.

Nolen, Jerdine. Hewitt Anderson's Big Life. 2005. (J). *(0-689-86866-9*, Simon & Schuster/Paula Wiseman Bks.) Simon & Schuster Children's Publishing.

Northland Publishing Staff, ed. Jack & the Giant/ Cowboy Billy. 1998. (J). pap. 15.95 *(0-87358-696-4*, Rising Moon Bks. for Young Readers) Northland Publishing.

Norton, Mary. Are All the Giants Dead? 1975. (Illus.). 159p. (J). (gr. 3-7). 6.50 o.s.i *(0-15-203810-8)* Harcourt Children's Bks.

—Are All the Giants Dead? 1997. 13.05 *(0-606-13147-7)* Turtleback Bks.

Oram, Hiawyn. Puddleglum to the Rescue. Date not set. (Step into Narnia Ser.). (Illus.). (J). 15.99 *(0-06-008361-1)*; lib. bdg. 16.89 *(0-06-001360-5)* HarperCollins Pubs.

Oram, Hiawyn & Brown, Ken. Little Giant & Jabber-Jabber. 1998. (Illus.). 32p. (J). (ps-3). 19.95 *(0-86264-798-3)* Andersen Pr., Ltd. GBR. *Dist:* Trafalgar Square.

O'Shea, Pat. Finn Mac Cool & the Small Men of Deeds. 1987. (Illus.). 96p. (J). (gr. 3 up). 12.95 o.p. *(0-8234-0651-2)* Holiday Hse., Inc.

Parkhurst, Ted. What Giants Eat. 1980. (Illus.). 32p. (J). (gr. k-5). pap. 2.95 o.p. *(0-935304-14-2)* August Hse. Pubs., Inc.

Pelley, Kathleen. The Giant King. Manning, Maurie, tr. & illus. by. 2003. 32p. (J). (ps-4). 14.95 *(0-87868-880-3*, Child & Family Pr.) Child Welfare League of America, Inc.

Pomerantz, Charlotte. Mangaboom. 1997. (Illus.). 40p. (J). (gr. k up). lib. bdg. 15.93 o.p. *(0-688-12957-9)*; (gr. 1 up). 16.00 *(0-688-12956-0)* HarperCollins Children's Bk. Group. (Greenwillow Bks.).

Porfirio, Guy, illus. Jack & the Beanstalk. 2001. (Brighter Child Keepsake Stories Ser.). 32p. (J). (ps-3). 3.99 *(1-57768-377-3)* McGraw-Hill Children's Publishing.

Porter, Sue. Little Wolf & the Giant. (J). (ps-6). 1993. (Illus.). 32p. pap. 7.95 o.s.i *(0-671-79853-7)*; 1990. pap. 13.95 *(0-671-70363-3)* Simon & Schuster Children's Publishing. (Simon & Schuster Children's Publishing).

Reeves, James. Giants & Warriors. 1978. (Illus.). pap. 2.95 o.p. *(0-8467-0540-0)* Hippocrene Bks., Inc.

Reinhardt, Jennifer B. The Giant's Toybox. 1995. (Illus.). 30p. (J). (ps-1). 13.95 *(0-941711-20-X)* Wyrick & Co.

Ringi, Kjell. Stranger. 1968. (Illus.). (J). (ps-2). 3.95 o.s.i *(0-394-81571-8*, Random Hse. Bks. for Young Readers) Random Hse. Children's Bks.

Roca, Empar. Saltapinos Ha Perdido los Calcetines. 1997. Tr. of Saltapinos Lost His Socks. (SPA., Illus.). 24p. (J). (gr. 2-4). 8.95 *(84-246-5406-4)* SM Ediciones ESP. *Dist:* i.b.d., Ltd.

Roddie, Shen. Animal Stew. 1992. (Illus.). 32p. (J). (ps). 13.95 o.p. *(0-395-57582-6)* Houghton Mifflin Co.

Rogers, Alan. Bright & Breezy. 1999. (Little Giants Ser.). (Illus.). 16p. (YA). (ps). pap. 2.95 *(0-7166-4417-7)* World Bk., Inc.

—Higher & Higher. 1999. (Little Giants Ser.). (Illus.). 16p. (J). (ps). pap. 2.95 o.p. *(0-7166-4419-3)*;Set. 8.00 o.p. *(0-7166-4418-5)* World Bk., Inc.

—Vacation Time. 1999. (Little Giants Ser.). (Illus.). 16p. (J). (ps). pap. 2.95 o.p. *(0-7166-4423-1)*;Set. 8.00 o.p. *(0-7166-4422-3)* World Bk., Inc.

Root, Phyllis. Soup for Supper. 1986. (Illus.). 32p. (J). (ps-2). 13.95 *(0-06-025070-4)*; lib. bdg. 13.89 o.p. *(0-06-025071-2)* HarperCollins Children's Bk. Group.

Ross, Tony. Jack the Giant Killer. 1987. (Illus.). 32p. (J). (gr. k-3). 12.95 o.p. *(0-86264-060-1)* Trafalgar Square.

Russell, P. Craig. Fairy Tales of Oscar Wilde: The Selfish Giant & the Star Child. 2003. (Fairy Tales of Oscar Wilde Ser.: 1). (Illus.). 48p. (J). pap. 8.95 *(1-56163-375-5)* NBM Publishing Co.

Ruzzier, Sergio. Dwarf Giant. 2004. (Illus.). 32p. (J). (ps-2). 15.99 *(0-06-052951-2)*; lib. bdg. 16.89 *(0-06-052952-0)* HarperCollins Children's Bk. Group. (Geringer, Laura Bk.).

Sherman, Ivan. I Am a Giant. 1975. (Illus.). (J). (gr. 5-8). 7.50 o.p. *(0-15-237983-5)* Harcourt Children's Bks.

Shlichta, Joe, illus. Strongheart Jack & the Beanstalk. 1995. (J). (gr. k-3). 15.95 *(0-87483-414-7)* August Hse. Pubs., Inc.

Slaton, Lana. Giants & Goblins. 1997. (Troubador Color & Story Ser.). (Illus.). 32p. (J). (ps up). reprint ed. 5.95 o.p. *(0-8431-7964-3*, Price Stern Sloan) Penguin Putnam Bks. for Young Readers.

Smith, Sherri L. Lucy the Giant. 2002. 224p. (YA). (gr. 9 up). 15.95 *(0-385-72940-5)*; lib. bdg. 17.99 *(0-385-90031-7)* Dell Publishing. (Delacorte Pr.).

—Lucy the Giant. Lt. ed. 2002. (Young Adult Ser.). 236p. 23.95 *(0-7862-4751-7)* Thorndike Pr.

Sorel, Edward & Sorel, Ed, illus. Jack & the Beanstalk. abr. adapted ed. 1991. (We All Have Tales Ser.). 40p. (J). (gr. k up). pap. 14.95 o.p. *(0-88708-188-6*, Simon & Schuster Children's Publishing) Simon & Schuster Children's Publishing.

Stanley, Diane. The Giant & the Beanstalk. 2004. (Illus.). (J). *(0-06-000010-4)* HarperCollins Pubs.

Stanley, Diane, illus. The Giant & the Beanstalk. 2004. (J). lib. bdg. *(0-06-000011-2)* HarperCollins Pubs.

Stickland, Paul. Machines As Tall As Giants. 1996. 32p. (J). pap. 4.99 o.s.i *(0-14-055911-6*, Puffin Bks.) Penguin Putnam Bks. for Young Readers.

Swift, Jonathan. Gulliver's Stories. 2001. (Junior Classics Ser.). (Illus.). 176p. (J). (gr. 8). mass mkt. 3.99 *(0-439-23620-7)* Scholastic, Inc.

—Gulliver's Travels. Marshall, Michael J., ed. abr. ed. 1997. (Core Classics Ser.: Vol. 1). (Illus.). 160p. (J). (gr. 4-6). pap. 5.95 *(1-890517-00-3)*; lib. bdg. 10.95 *(1-890517-01-1)* Core Knowledge Foundation.

Swift, Jonathan & Golden Books Staff. Tales of Gulliver's Travels. 1997. (Crayola Kids Adventures Ser.). 64p. (J). pap. 2.22 o.s.i *(0-307-20202-X*, Golden Bks.) Random Hse. Children's Bks.

Swope, Sam. Jack & the Seven Deadly Giants, RS. 2004. (J). 16.00 *(0-374-33670-9)* Farrar, Straus & Giroux.

Tegetthoff, Folke. Cuando los Gigantes Aman y Otros Cuentos (When Giants Fall in Love, & Other Stories) 1992. (SPA.). 104p. (YA). pap. 5.99 *(968-16-3914-6)* Fondo de Cultura Economica MEX. *Dist:* Continental Bk. Co., Inc.

Thoene, Jake & Thoene, Luke. The Giant Rat of Sumatra. 1998. (Baker Street Mysteries Ser.: Vol. 2). 168p. (J). (gr. 4-7). pap. 5.99 *(0-7852-7079-5)* Nelson, Thomas Pubs.

Torgersen, Don A. The Angry Giants of Troll Mountain. 1980. (Troll & Gnome Stories Ser.). (Illus.). 32p. (J). (gr. k-4). pap. 3.50 o.p. *(0-516-43409-8)*; lib. bdg. 9.95 o.p. *(0-516-03409-X)* Scholastic Library Publishing. (Children's Pr.).

Umansky, Kaye. Jealous Giant. (Illus.). 32p. (J). pap. 7.95 *(0-14-038840-0)* Penguin Bks., Ltd. GBR. *Dist:* Trafalgar Square.

—Romantic Giant. (Illus.). 32p. (J). pap. 7.95 *(0-14-038160-0)* Penguin Bks., Ltd. GBR. *Dist:* Trafalgar Square.

Ward, Nick. Don't Worry, Grandpa. 1995. (Illus.). 32p. (J). (ps-3). pap. 4.95 *(0-8120-9425-5)*; 12.95 o.p. *(0-8120-6533-6)* Barron's Educational Series, Inc.

—Giant. 1987. (Illus.). 24p. (J). 7.95 o.p. *(0-19-278201-0)* Oxford Univ. Pr., Inc.

Watkins, Peter. David & the Giant. 1982. (Blackbird Bks.). (Illus.). 48p. (J). (gr. k-3). lib. bdg. 5.95 o.p. *(0-531-04356-8*, Watts, Franklin) Scholastic Library Publishing.

Weesner, Stephen. The Shepherd Boy & the Giant. 1999. (Illus.). 24p. (J). (gr. 4-6). pap. 9.95 o.p. *(1-56167-471-0)* American Literary Pr., Inc.

White, Donal L. & Burrows, David. Me & the Jolly Green Giant. 1995. (J). (gr. 6-9). pap. 9.99 *(0-88092-293-1)*; lib. bdg. 15.00 o.p. *(0-88092-294-X)* Royal Fireworks Publishing Co.

Wilde, Oscar. The Selfish Giant. 1993. (Short Stories Ser.). 32p. (YA). (gr. 3 up). lib. bdg. 18.60 *(0-88682-068-5*, 1078-8, Creative Education) Creative Co., The.

—The Selfish Giant. unabr. ed. 1995. (Illus.). 32p. (J). (ps-1). 16.95 *(0-86315-212-0*, 26012) Floris Bks. GBR. *Dist:* Gryphon Hse., Inc., SteinerBooks, Inc.

—The Selfish Giant. 1979. (J). (gr. k-3). 9.95 o.p. *(0-07-070215-2)* McGraw-Hill Cos., The.

—The Selfish Giant. 1995. (Illus.). (J). (ps-3). 16.99 *(0-399-22448-3*, G. P. Putnam's Sons) Penguin Group (USA) Inc.

—The Selfish Giant. 1986. (Illus.). 24p. (J). (gr. 1-4). 10.95 o.p. *(0-13-803586-5)* Prentice Hall PTR.

—The Selfish Giant. 2001. (Illus.). 40p. (J). 12.99 *(0-517-22009-1)* Random Hse., Inc.

—The Selfish Giant. 1978. (Illus.). (J). (gr. k-3). 8.95 o.p. *(0-458-93420-8*, NO. 0062) Routledge.

—The Selfish Giant. 1991. (Illus.). 24p. (J). (ps-3). mass mkt. 4.95 *(0-590-44460-3)* Scholastic, Inc.

—The Selfish Giant. (Illus.). (J). (ps up). 1991. 28p. 16.00 *(0-907234-30-5)*; 1986. pap. 10.95 *(0-671-66847-1)* Simon & Schuster Children's Publishing. (Simon & Schuster Children's Publishing).

Willis, Jeanne. In Search of the Giant. 1994. (Illus.). 32p. (J). 13.99 o.p. *(0-525-45242-7*, Dutton Children's Bks.) Penguin Putnam Bks. for Young Readers.

Wilson, Budge. Duff the Giant Killer. 1997. (First Novels Ser.: Vol. 6). (Illus.). 64p. (J). (gr. 1-4). bds. *(0-88780-383-0)* Formac Publishing Co., Ltd.

—Duff the Giant Killer. 1998. (First Novels Ser.). (Illus.). 64p. (J). (gr. 1-4). pap. 3.99 *(0-88780-382-2)* Formac Publishing Co., Ltd. CAN. *Dist:* Formac Distributing, Ltd.

Wolf, Tony. The Woodland Folk Meet the Giants. 1984. (Illus.). 42p. (J). *(0-528-82563-1)* Rand McNally.

Wood, Audrey. Rude Giants. 2002. (Illus.). (J). 19.96 *(0-7587-3542-1)* Book Wholesalers, Inc.

—Rude Giants. (Illus.). 32p. (J). (ps-2). 1998. pap. 7.00 *(0-15-201889-1*, Voyager Bks./Libros Viajeros); 1993. 13.95 *(0-15-269412-9)* Harcourt Children's Bks.

—Rude Giants. 1998. (J). 12.15 *(0-606-13752-1)* Turtleback Bks.

Woodward, Sue, contrib. by. The Giant's Picnic. 1997. (Illus.). *(0-620-22003-1)* Kwagga Pubs.

Yep, Laurence. The City of Dragons. 1995. (Illus.). 32p. (J). (gr. k-4). pap. 14.95 *(0-590-47865-6)* Scholastic, Inc.

Yerkes, Lane, illus. Jenny & the Cornstalk. 1998. pap. 5.18 *(0-8172-7276-3)* Raintree Pubs.

Yolen, Jane. The Giants' Farm, 001. 1979. (Illus.). 48p. (J). (ps-3). 6.95 o.p. *(0-395-28834-7*, Clarion Bks.) Houghton Mifflin Co. Trade & Reference Div.

—The Giants Go Camping. 1979. (Illus.). (J). (gr. 1-3). 6.95 o.p. *(0-395-28955-6*, Clarion Bks.) Houghton Mifflin Co. Trade & Reference Div.

Yorinks, Arthur. The Miami Giant. 1999. (Illus.). 36p. (J). (gr. 5-8). text 16.00 *(0-7881-6464-3)* DIANE Publishing Co.

—The Miami Giant. 1995. (Michael di Capua Bks.). (Illus.). 40p. (J). (ps up). 15.95 o.p. *(0-06-205068-0)*; lib. bdg. 15.89 o.s.i *(0-06-205069-9)* HarperCollins Children's Bk. Group.

—Sid & Sol, RS. 1977. (Illus.). 32p. (J). (ps up). 14.00 o.p. *(0-374-36904-6*, Farrar, Straus & Giroux (BYR)) Farrar, Straus & Giroux.

Zeman, Ludmila, illus. & retold by. Sinbad's Secret: From the Tales of the Thousand & One Nights. 2003. 32p. (YA). (gr. 1 up). 17.95 *(0-88776-462-2)* Tundra Bks. of Northern New York.

Zeman, Ludmila & Levesque, Suzanne. Sinbad et les Geants. 2001. (FRE., Illus.). 32p. (J). (gr. 1). 19.95 *(0-88776-525-4)* Tundra Bks. of Northern New York.

Zimmerman, Arnold. Troll Island. 1977. (Children's Stories Ser.). (Illus.). 64p. 6.95 o.p. *(0-912278-67-6)*; pap. 3.95 o.p. *(0-912278-81-1)* Crossing Pr., Inc., The.

GRIFFINS—FICTION

Freeman, Barbara C. Timi. 1979. (Faber Fanfares Ser). (Illus.). (J). (gr. 1-4). pap. o.p. *(0-571-11350-8)* Faber & Faber Ltd.

Jones, Diana Wynne. Year of the Griffin. (J). 2001. 400p. (gr. 7 up). pap. 6.99 *(0-06-447335-X*, Harper Trophy); 2000. (Illus.). 272p. (gr. 5 up). 15.95 *(0-688-17898-7*, Greenwillow Bks.); 2000. (Illus.). 272p. (gr. 5 up). 15.95 *(0-688-17898-7*, Greenwillow Bks.); 2000. 272p. (gr. 5 up). 15.89 *(0-06-029158-3*, Greenwillow Bks.) HarperCollins Children's Bk. Group.

Marston, Elsa. A Griffin in the Garden. 1993. (Illus.). 32p. (J). (gr. k up). 15.00 o.p. *(0-688-10981-0)*; lib. bdg. 14.93 o.p. *(0-688-10982-9)* Morrow/Avon. (Morrow, William & Co.).

Pickford, Susan T. It's up to You, Griffin! 1993. (Illus.). 32p. (J). (ps-3). 10.95 *(0-87033-446-8*, Tidewater Pubs.) Cornell Maritime Pr., Inc.

Rodda, Emily. Fairy Realm, No. 2. 2003. (Fairy Realm Ser.). (Illus.). 128p. (J). 8.99 *(0-06-009586-5)*; lib. bdg. 14.89 *(0-06-009587-3)* HarperCollins Pubs.

Stanton, Mary. My Aunt, the Monster: A Magical Mystery Number One. 1997. (Magical Mystery Ser.: Vol. 1). 144p. (J). (gr. 3-7). mass mkt. 3.99 o.s.i *(0-425-15227-8)* Berkley Publishing Group.

Stockton, Frank Richard. The Griffin & the Minor Canon. 2004. (Sendak Reissues Ser.). (Illus.). 56p. (J). 15.95 *(0-06-029731-X)* HarperCollins Children's Bk. Group.

—The Griffin & the Minor Canon. 2003. (Sendak Reissues Ser.). (Illus.). 56p. (J). 17.89 *(0-06-029732-8)* HarperCollins Pubs.

M

MERMAIDS—FICTION

Ainsworth, Ruth. Mermaid's Tales. 1997. (Illus.). 124p. (J). 16.95 *(0-7188-2460-1)* Lutherworth Pr., The GBR. *Dist:* Parkwest Pubns., Inc.

Andersen, Hans Christian. Ariel & the Mysterious World Above. unabr. ed. 1997. (Disney Read-Alongs Ser.). (J). (ps-3). 7.99 incl. audio *(0-7634-0288-5)* Walt Disney Home Video.

—Ariel & the Secret Grotto. (Read-Along Ser.). (J). 7.99 incl. audio *(0-7634-0287-7)* Walt Disney Records.

—Disney's The Little Mermaid. 1991. (Big Golden Bks.). (J). (ps-3). o.p. *(0-307-12345-6*, Golden Bks.) Random Hse. Children's Bks.

—Disney's the Little Mermaid: Tales from under the Sea. 1991. (Illus.). 80p. (J). (gr. 2-7). 10.95 o.p. *(1-56282-014-1)* Disney Pr.

—The Little Mermaid. 1991. (Pop-Up Bks.). (Illus.). 12p. (J). (gr. 2-6). 9.95 o.p. *(1-56282-017-6)* Disney Pr.

—The Little Mermaid. 1992. (Children's Classics Ser.). (Illus.). 32p. (J). (ps-3). 6.95 *(0-8362-4918-6)* Andrews McMeel Publishing.

—The Little Mermaid. 1980. (J). pap. 2.95 *(0-88388-039-3)* Bellerophon Bks.

—The Little Mermaid. 1991. (Once upon a Time Children's Classics Retold in ASL Ser.: Vol. 1). 36p. (J). pap. 24.95 incl. VHS *(0-915035-39-1)* Dawn Sign Pr.

—The Little Mermaid. 2002. (Illus.). 48p. (J). pap. 12.95 incl. audio compact disk *(2-89558-085-5)* Editions Alexandre Stanke CAN. *Dist:* Penton Overseas, Inc.

—The Little Mermaid. James, M. R., tr. 1981. (Illus.). 26p. (J). o.p. *(0-571-11847-X)* Faber & Faber Ltd.

—The Little Mermaid. 1997. (J). pap. *(0-15-201561-2)* Harcourt Children's Bks.

—The Little Mermaid. 1989. (Illus.). 42p. (J). (gr. k-3). 15.95 *(0-15-246320-8)* Harcourt Trade Pubs.

—The Little Mermaid. 1997. (Illus.). 64p. (J). lib. bdg. 12.49 *(0-7868-2331-3)* Hyperion Bks. for Children.

—The Little Mermaid. 1997. (Illus.). 64p. (J). (gr. 4-7). 11.95 *(0-7868-0383-5)* Hyperion Pr.

—The Little Mermaid. 1992. (Fun-to-Read Fairy Tales Ser.). (Illus.). (J). 24p. pap. 2.50 *(1-56144-093-0)*; 32p. pap. 1.95 o.s.i *(1-56144-139-2*, Honey Bear Bks.) Modern Publishing.

—The Little Mermaid. (Classic Storybook Ser.). (J). 1997. 7.98 o.s.i *(1-57082-727-3)*; 1994. (Illus.). 96p. 7.98 o.p. *(1-57082-042-2)* Mouse Works.

—The Little Mermaid. (Illus.). (J). (ps-4). 9999. (Well-Loved Tales Ser.: Level 3, No. 606D-8). 3.50 o.p. *(0-7214-0627-0*, Ladybird Bks.); 1998. 32p. 15.99 o.s.i *(0-399-22813-6*, G. P. Putnam's Sons) Penguin Group (USA) Inc.

—The Little Mermaid. 1993. (Disney's Look & Find Ser.). (Illus.). 24p. (J). *(0-7853-0106-2)*; 12.98 *(0-7853-0133-X)* Publications International, Ltd.

—The Little Mermaid. (J). 1995. o.p. *(0-307-30074-9)*; 1993. (Illus.). 14p. bds. o.p. *(0-307-75301-8)*; 1993. (Illus.). 20p. 19.95 o.p. *(0-307-74304-7*, 64304); 1991. (Illus.). 24p. o.p. *(0-307-74014-5)* Random Hse. Children's Bks. (Golden Bks.).

—The Little Mermaid. 1991. (Illus.). (J). pap. 3.95 o.p. *(0-590-44456-5)* Scholastic, Inc.

—The Little Mermaid. 1994. (Little Library). 8p. (J). (ps-1). 4.98 o.p. *(0-8317-5527-X)* Smithmark Pubs., Inc.

—The Little Mermaid. 2000. (Illus.). (J). 13.14 *(0-606-18420-1)* Turtleback Bks.

—The Little Mermaid. 1987. (J). 3.99 o.p. *(0-8499-8530-7)* W Publishing Group.

—The Little Mermaid. 1997. (Disney Read-Alongs Ser.). (J). (ps-3). 7.99 incl. audio *(0-7634-0286-9)* Walt Disney Home Video.

—The Little Mermaid. Michel, Petra, tr. 1996. (Illus.). 32p. (J). (ps-3). 18.95 *(1-885394-17-9)* Amber Lotus Publishing.

—The Little Mermaid, ERS. 1994. (Illus.). (J). 16.95 o.p. *(0-8050-1010-6*, Holt, Henry & Co. Bks. For Young Readers) Holt, Henry & Co.

—The Little Mermaid: A Postcard Book. 1991. (Disney Postcard Bk.). (Illus.). 64p. (Orig.). (J). pap. 7.95 o.p. *(1-56138-042-3)* Running Pr. Bk. Pubs.

—The Little Mermaid: My Coloring Book. 1999. Tr. of Lille Havfrue. (J). pap. text 1.09 *(0-307-08630-5*, 08630, Golden Bks.) Random Hse. Children's Bks.

—The Little Mermaid: Underwater Adventure. 1995. (Illus.). 24p. (J). (ps-2). bds. o.p. *(0-307-00105-9*, Golden Bks.) Random Hse. Children's Bks.

—The Little Mermaid & Other Stories. 1997. (Illus.). 96p. (J). pap. 5.95 incl. audio (*0-486-29616-4*, 29616-4) Dover Pubns., Inc.

—The Little Mermaid & Other Tales. 1998. (Library of Folklore). (Illus.). 508p. (J). (gr. 4-7). 19.95 (*0-7818-0720-4*) Hippocrene Bks., Inc.

—The Little Mermaid Hunts for Treasure. 1992. (Surprise Lift-the-Flap Bk.). (Illus.). 18p. (J). (ps-k). 8.95 o.p. (*1-56282-146-6*) Disney Pr.

—The Little Mermaid Treasury Exclusive for AMS. 1997. 176p. (J). (ps-2). pap. 17.95 (*0-7868-3182-0*) Disney Pr.

—La Petite Sirene. 9999. (French Language Editions Ser.: No. 600-3). Tr. of Little Mermaid. (FRE., Illus.). (J). (gr. 3). 3.50 o.p. (*0-7214-1289-0*, Ladybird Bks.) Penguin Group (USA) Inc.

Andersen, Hans Christian & Hautzig, Deborah. The Little Mermaid. (Step into Reading Step 3 Bks.). (Illus.). 48p. (J). (gr. 2-4). 2004. 11.99 (*0-679-92241-5*); 1991. pap. 3.99 (*0-679-82241-0*) Random Hse. Children's Bks. (Random Hse. Bks. for Young Readers).

Andersen, Hans Christian & Isadora, Rachel. The Little Mermaid. 2000. (Picture Puffin Ser.). (Illus.). 32p. (J). (ps-3). pap. 6.99 (*0-698-11829-4*, Puffin Bks.) Penguin Putnam Bks. for Young Readers.

Andersen, Hans Christian & Santore, Charles. The Little Mermaid: The Original Story. 1993. (Illus.). 48p. (J). 14.00 o.s.i (*0-517-06495-2*) Random Hse. Value Publishing.

Andersen, Hans Christian & Weghorst, Suzanne J. The Little Mermaid Novels, 4 bks., Set. 1993. (Little Mermaid Novels Ser.). (Illus.). (J). (gr. 1-4). pap. 11.80 o.p. (*1-56282-562-3*) Disney Pr.

Anjelae, Samara. My Magical Mermaid. 2002. (Wonder Window Ser.). (Illus.). 32p. (J). 16.95 (*0-9634910-9-1*) BelleTress, Inc.

Applegate, K. A. The Boyfriend Mix-Up. 1994. (Little Mermaid Novels Ser.: No. 10). (Illus.). 80p. (J). (gr. 1-4). pap. 3.50 (*1-56282-642-5*) Disney Pr.

—The Haunted Palace. 1993. (Little Mermaid Novels Ser.). (Illus.). 80p. (J). (gr. 1-4). pap. 3.50 o.p. (*1-56282-503-8*) Disney Pr.

—King Triton, Beware! 1993. (Little Mermaid Novels Ser.). (Illus.). 80p. (J). (gr. 1-4). pap. 3.50 o.p. (*1-56282-502-X*) Disney Pr.

Ariel & Sebastian: Serpent Teen. 1992. (Illus.). 48p. (J). (ps-3). pap. o.p. (*1-56115-266-8*, 21807, Golden Bks.) Random Hse. Children's Bks.

Ariel's New Friend: The Little Mermaid. 1994. (Illus.). 24p. (J). (ps-3). pap. o.p. (*0-307-12817-2*, Golden Bks.) Random Hse. Children's Bks.

Balducci, Rita. Disney's The Little Mermaid Word Book. 1993. (Illus.). 28p. (J). (ps). bds. 3.50 o.p. (*0-307-12537-8*, Golden Bks.) Random Hse. Children's Bks.

Bateman, Teresa. The Merbaby. 2001. (Illus.). 32p. (J). (ps-2). tchr. ed. 16.95 (*0-8234-1531-7*) Holiday Hse., Inc.

Beckett, Sheilah, retold by. The Little Mermaid: Full-Color Sturdy Book. 1995. (Little Activity Bks.). (Illus.). 16p. (Orig.). (J). pap. text 1.00 (*0-486-28825-0*) Dover Pubns., Inc.

Blackaby, Susan. The Little Mermaid: A Retelling of the Hans Christian Andersen Fairy Tale. 2003. (Read-It! Readers Ser.). (Illus.). 32p. (J). (ps-3). lib. bdg. 18.60 (*1-4048-0221-5*) Picture Window Bks.

Blanco, Alberto. The Desert Mermaid (La Sirena del Desierto) 2002. (ENG & SPA., Illus.). 32p. (J). (gr. 1 up). pap. 7.95 (*0-89239-173-1*) Bellerophon Bks.

—The Desert Mermaid (La Sirena del Desierto) 1992. (ENG & SPA., Illus.). 32p. (J). (ps-3). 15.95 (*0-89239-106-5*, CBP1065) Children's Bk. Pr.

Brown, Christopher. Misty the Mermaid in Song of the Whales. 1985. (Illus.). 24p. (J). (gr. 3-7). pap. 1.95 o.p. (*0-89954-293-X*) Antioch Publishing Co.

Brown, Janet Allison & Andersen, Hans Christian. The Little Mermaid. 2004. (J). (*0-8037-2932-4*) Penguin Putnam Bks. for Young Readers.

Calder, Lyn. Ariel above the Sea: Walt Disney's The Little Mermaid. 1992. (Golden Book Ser.: Level 2). (Illus.). 32p. (J). (ps-2). pap. o.p. (*0-307-15965-5*, 15965, Golden Bks.) Random Hse. Children's Bks.

Carpenter, Mimi G. Mermaid in a Tidal Pool. 1985. (Illus.). 32p. (Orig.). (J). (ps-6). pap. 8.95 (*0-9614628-0-9*) Beachcomber Pr.

—Of Lucky Pebbles & Mermaids Tears. 1994. (Illus.). 32p. (J). (ps-5). pap. 9.95 (*0-9614628-2-5*) Beachcomber Pr.

Carr, Jan. The Little Mermaid M-TV. 1989. (J). pap. 2.50 o.p. (*0-590-42988-4*) Scholastic, Inc.

Carr, M. J. Ariel the Spy. 1993. (Little Mermaid Novels Ser.). (Illus.). 80p. (J). (gr. 1-4). pap. 3.50 o.p. (*1-56282-372-8*) Disney Pr.

—Arista's New Boyfriend. 1993. (Disney's the Little Mermaid Ser.). (Illus.). 80p. (J). (gr. 1-4). pap. 3.50 o.p. (*1-56282-371-X*) Disney Pr.

—Wave Dancer Is Missing: My Pretty Mermaid. 1993. (Illus.). 32p. (J). (ps-3). pap. 2.50 (*0-590-46604-6*) Scholastic, Inc.

Christopher, Jess. Alana's Secret Friend. 1994. (Disney's the Little Mermaid Ser.: No. 12). (Illus.). 80p. (J). (gr. 1-4). pap. 3.50 o.p. (*0-7868-4002-1*) Disney Pr.

Climo, Shirley. A Serenade of Mermaids: Mermaid Tales from Around the World. 1999. (Trophy Chapter Bks.). (Illus.). 112p. (J). (gr. 2-5). pap. 4.25 (*0-06-442103-1*, Harper Trophy) HarperCollins Children's Bk. Group.

—A Treasury of Mermaids: Mermaid Tales from Around the World. 1997. (Illus.). 80p. (J). (gr. 2 up). 17.95 (*0-06-023876-3*) HarperCollins Children's Bk. Group.

Clymer, Susan. The Glass Mermaid. 1986. (Illus.). 80p. (Orig.). (J). (gr. 2-5). pap. 2.25 o.p. (*0-590-32839-5*) Scholastic, Inc.

Colmenson, Stephanie. The Little Mermaid: Ariel above the Sea. 1991. (Golden Easy Readers Ser.). Orig. Title: Lille Hanfrue. (Illus.). (J). (gr. k-2). o.p. (*0-307-11697-2*, Golden Bks.) Random Hse. Children's Bks.

Dadey, Debbie & Jones, Marcia Thornton. Mermaids Don't Run Track. 1997. (Adventures of the Bailey School Kids Ser.: No. 26). (J). (gr. 2-4). 10.14 (*0-606-11620-6*) Turtleback Bks.

Dale, Nora. Nan & the Sea Monster. 1989. (Real Readers Ser.: Level Green). (Illus.). 32p. (J). pap. 4.95 o.p. (*0-8114-6728-7*); lib. bdg. 21.40 o.p. (*0-8172-3526-4*) Raintree Pubs.

Dann, Penny. The Secret Mermaid Handbook: or How to Be a Little Mermaid. 1998. (Illus.). 20p. (J). (ps-3). per. 14.95 (*0-689-82255-3*, Little Simon) Simon & Schuster Children's Publishing.

de la Mare, Walter. The Lord Fish. 1997. (Candlewick Treasures Ser.). (Illus.). 128p. (J). (gr. 3-9). 11.99 o.p. (*0-7636-0134-9*) Candlewick Pr.

Dias, Ron, illus. Disney's the Little Mermaid. 1993. (Illustrated Classics Ser.). (J). 96p. lib. bdg. 15.49 o.s.i (*1-56282-430-9*); 96p. 14.95 (*1-56282-429-5*); 64p. (gr. 2-6). pap. 3.50 o.p. (*1-56282-436-8*) Disney Pr.

Disney-Pixar The Little Mermaid. 2002. (J). spiral bd. (*0-9720651-9-9*) Story Reader, Inc.

Disney Staff. Ariel's Fishy Face Contest. 2002. (Illus.). (J). bds. 4.99 (*0-7364-2040-1*, RH/Disney) Random Hse. Children's Bks.

—Flounder the Fearless. 1997. (Disney's the Little Mermaid Ser.). (Illus.). 5p. (J). (ps). 7.98 o.p. (*1-57082-614-5*) Mouse Works.

—The Little Mermaid, Incl. toy. 1997. (Illus.). (J). pap. 16.95 (*0-7868-4201-6*) Disney Pr.

—The Little Mermaid, 4 vols. 1997. (Little Library). 5p. (J). 5.98 (*1-57082-072-4*) Mouse Works.

—The Little Mermaid: A Picture Book. 1997. (Illus.). 32p. (J). (ps-k). pap. 4.95 o.p. (*0-7868-4175-3*) Disney Pr.

—The Little Mermaid: Treasures of Old. 1997. (Disney's "Storytime Treasures" Library: Vol. 7). (Illus.). 44p. (J). (gr. 1-6). 3.49 o.p. (*1-57973-003-5*) Advance Pubs. LLC.

—The Little Mermaid Activity Pad. 1997. (J). (ps-3). o.p. (*0-307-09300-X*, 670239T, Golden Bks.) Random Hse. Children's Bks.

—The Little Mermaid Disney Little Libraries. 1992. (Illus.). (J). (ps-3). 5.98 o.p. (*0-453-03076-9*, Viking Children's Bks.) Penguin Putnam Bks. for Young Readers.

—The Little Mermaid under the Sea. 1991. (Illus.). (J). (ps-3). pap. o.p. (*0-307-21805-8*, Golden Bks.) Random Hse. Children's Bks.

—Sea Sayings: With Keychain. 1997. (Little Mermaid Ser.). 38p. (J). 2.98 o.p. (*1-57082-762-1*) Mouse Works.

—La Sirenita. 1992. (Penguin-Disney Ser.).Tr. of Little Mermaid. (SPA., Illus.). 96p. (J). (ps-3). 6.98 o.p. (*0-453-03017-3*) Viking Penguin.

Disney, Walter Elias. The Little Mermaid: A Visit with Friends Storyboard; Ariel's Story, Sebastian's Story. 1993. (J). (ps-3). 6.98 o.p. (*0-453-03127-7*) Mouse Works.

Doodle Art. Mermaid's Treasure. 2000. (Doodle Art Ser.). (J). 8.99 o.s.i (*0-8431-6634-7*, Price Stern Sloan) Penguin Putnam Bks. for Young Readers.

Douglas, Vincent. The Little Mermaid. 2001. (Disney Parent & Child Read Together Ser.). (Illus.). 32p. (J). pap. 4.99 (*1-57768-734-5*) McGraw-Hill Children's Publishing.

Edgar, Amy. The Little Mermaid. 2000. (Read-Aloud Storybook Ser.). (Illus.). 64p. (J). (ps-2). 8.99 (*0-7364-0161-X*) Mouse Works.

Estes, Kathleen. A Mermaid's Purse, Vol. 1. 1996. (Illus.). 40p. (J). (ps-1). 15.95 (*1-880851-24-5*) Greene Bark Pr., Inc.

Farber, Erica & Sansevere, J. R. Kiss of the Mermaid. 1996. (Mercer Mayer's Critters of the Night Ser.). (Illus.). (J). (ps-3). 11.99 o.s.i (*0-679-97381-8*); 48p. (gr. 2-3). pap. 3.99 o.s.i (*0-679-87381-3*) Random Hse., Inc.

Fienberg, Anna. Madeline the Mermaid: And Other Fishy Tales. 1996. (Illus.). 48p. (J). (gr. 1-5). 12.95 (*1-86373-838-X*); pap. text 6.95 o.p. (*1-86373-837-1*) Independent Pubs. Group.

Fontes, Justine. The Best Baby-Sitter under the Sea: The Little Mermaid. 1994. (Illus.). 24p. (J). (ps-3). pap. o.p. (*0-307-12818-0*, Golden Bks.) Random Hse. Children's Bks.

Foster, Evelyn. The Mermaid of Cafur. 1999. (Illus.). 32p. (J). (gr. k-3). 15.95 (*1-902283-40-6*) Barefoot Bks., Inc.

Frith, Margaret. Mermaid Island. 1997. (Eek! Stories to Make You Shriek Ser.). (Illus.). 48p. (J). (gr. 1-3). 13.89 o.s.i (*0-448-41725-1*); 3.95 o.s.i (*0-448-41618-2*) Penguin Putnam Bks. for Young Readers. (Grosset & Dunlap).

—Mermaid Island. 1997. (Eek! Stories to Make You Shriek Ser.). 9.15 o.p. (*0-606-11619-2*) Turtleback Bks.

Golden Books Staff. Ariel's Song: A Re-Telling of the Movie Story. 1997. (Tell-a-Story Sticker Ser.). (Illus.). 18p. (J). (ps-3). pap. text 4.99 o.p. (*0-307-05236-2*, 05236, Golden Bks.) Random Hse. Children's Bks.

—Fun & Games. 1997. (Disney Ser.). (Illus.). 84p. (J). (ps-4). pap. text 2.99 o.p. (*0-307-05666-X*, 05666, Golden Bks.) Random Hse. Children's Bks.

—The Little Mermaid. 1999. (Disney Ser.).Tr. of Lille havfrue. (Illus.). 24p. (J). (ps-3). 3.99 o.p. (*0-307-16234-6*, Golden Bks.) Random Hse. Children's Bks.

—The Little Mermaid: Film Fashion. 1999. (Disney Ser.).Tr. of Lille Havfrue. (Illus.). 12p. (J). (ps-3). pap. text 3.99 o.p. (*0-307-02016-9*, 02016, Golden Bks.) Random Hse. Children's Bks.

—The Little Mermaid: Flounder to the Rescue. 1995. (First Little Golden Bks.). (Illus.). 24p. (J). o.p. (*0-307-30204-0*, Golden Bks.) Random Hse. Children's Bks.

—The Little Mermaid II: A Princess in Two Worlds. 2000. (Illus.). 70p. (J). (ps-3). pap. text 2.99 (*0-307-25734-7*, 25734, Golden Bks.) Random Hse. Children's Bks.

—Under the Sea: Color Surprise. 1997. (Disney Ser.). (Illus.). (J). pap. text o.p. (*0-307-15282-0*, Golden Bks.) Random Hse. Children's Bks.

—Undersea ABC. 1999. (Disney Ser.). (Illus.). (J). pap. text 2.99 (*0-307-05664-3*, 05664, Golden Bks.) Random Hse. Children's Bks.

Gray, Nigel. Jake & the Mermaid. 1998. (Illus.). 32p. (J). pap. 9.95 (*1-86368-221-X*) Fremantle Arts Centre Pr. AUS. *Dist:* International Specialized Bk. Services.

Green Tiger Press Staff, ed. Mermaids. 1982. (Illus.). 12p. (Orig.). (J). pap. 2.50 o.p. (*0-88138-001-6*, Simon & Schuster Children's Publishing) Simon & Schuster Children's Publishing.

Grimes, Nikki, adapted by. Disney's Little Mermaid. 1992. (Disney Miniature Editions Ser.). (Illus.). 160p. (YA). (gr. 2 up). text 5.95 o.p. (*1-56138-154-3*) Running Pr. Bk. Pubs.

Grosset and Dunlap Staff. Mermaid World. 2001. (Glow Sticker Stories Ser.). (Illus.). 16p. (J). (ps-3). mass mkt. 4.99 (*0-448-42172-0*, Planet Dexter) Penguin Putnam Bks. for Young Readers.

Grossman, Patricia. Ariel's Treasure Hunt, Level 1. 1998. (Disney's First Readers Ser.: No. 7). (Illus.). 24p. (J). (gr. k-1). pap. 2.95 o.p. (*0-7868-4167-2*) Disney Pr.

Hapka, Catherine. How Ariel Met Flounder. 1998. (Illus.). 24p. (J). (ps-k). pap. o.p. (*0-307-10592-X*, Golden Bks.) Random Hse. Children's Bks.

Harris, Sarah, adapted by. La Petite Sirene. 1995. (Comes to Life Bks.).Tr. of Little Mermaid. (ENG & FRE.). 16p. (J). (ps-2). (*1-57234-038-X*) YES! Entertainment Corp.

Hassan & the Mermaids. 1997. (Scheherezade Children's Stories Ser.). (Illus.). 16p. (J). (*1-873938-82-9*, Ithaca Pr.) Garnet Publishing, Ltd.

Hazen, Lynn E. Mermaid Mary Margaret. 2003. (J). 15.95 (*1-58234-842-1*) Bloomsbury Publishing.

Hoffman, Alice. Aquamarine & Indigo. 2003. 128p. (J). (gr. 5 up). pap. 5.99 (*0-439-47414-0*, Scholastic Paperbacks) Scholastic, Inc.

How Does Your Garden Grow? 1982. (Dinosaur Wingate Ser.). 32p. pap. text o.p. (*0-521-27178-9*) Cambridge Univ. Pr.

Hughes, Linda. The Little Mermaid. 1993. (Illus.). 24p. (J). (ps-3). pap. o.p. (*0-307-12787-7*, Golden Bks.) Random Hse. Children's Bks.

Hunter, Mollie. Mermaid Summer. 1990. 11.00 (*0-606-12601-5*) Turtleback Bks.

Ives, Penny. Millie & the Mermaid. (Illus.). 32p. (J). pap. 9.95 o.p. (*0-14-055635-4*) Penguin Bks., Ltd. GBR. *Dist:* Trafalgar Square.

Izquierdo, Oriol & Andersen, Hans Christian. The Little Mermaid: La Sirenita. 2003. (ENG & SPA., Illus.). 32p. (J). 13.95 (*0-8118-3910-9*); pap. 6.95 (*0-8118-3911-7*) Chronicle Bks. LLC.

James, Robin. Maynard's Mermaid. (Serendipity Bks.). (Illus.). (J). 2001. mass mkt. 4.99 (*0-8431-7665-2*, Grosset & Dunlap); 1993. 32p. 3.95 o.p. (*0-8431-3495-X*, Price Stern Sloan) Penguin Putnam Bks. for Young Readers.

—Maynard's Mermaid. 1993. (Serendipity Ser.). (J). 10.10 (*0-606-05457-X*) Turtleback Bks.

Karr, Kathleen. The Lighthouse Mermaid. 1998. (Hyperion Chapters Ser.). (Illus.). 64p. (J). (gr. 3-4). pap. 3.95 (*0-7868-1232-X*); lib. bdg. 14.49 o.s.i (*0-7868-2297-X*) Disney Pr.

—The Lighthouse Mermaid. 1998. (Hyperion Chapters Ser.). 10.10 (*0-606-13570-7*) Turtleback Bks.

Kaye, Marilyn. Reflections of Arsulu. 1992. (Little Mermaid Novels Ser.). (Illus.). 80p. (J). (gr. 1-4). pap. 3.50 o.p. (*1-56282-248-9*) Disney Pr.

—The Same Old Song. 1992. (Little Mermaid Novels Ser.). (Illus.). 80p. (J). (gr. 1-4). pap. 3.50 o.p. (*1-56282-249-7*) Disney Pr.

King-Smith, Dick. The Merman. unabr. ed. 1999. 102p. (J). (gr. 3-5). pap. 28.00 incl. audio (*0-8072-8132-8*, Listening Library) Random Hse. Audio Publishing Group.

—The Merman. 2001. (J). 11.04 (*0-606-21328-7*) Turtleback Bks.

Kurtti, Jeff & Disney Staff. The Art of the Little Mermaid. 1997. (Disney Miniatures Ser.). (Illus.). 192p. (J). 10.95 o.p. (*0-7868-6335-8*) Hyperion Pr.

Little Golden Books Staff. The Little Mermaid. 9999. (Illus.). (J). (ps-3). pap. o.p. (*0-307-01747-8*, Golden Bks.) Random Hse. Children's Bks.

—The Little Mermaid: The Whole Story. 2000. (Illus.). 24p. (J). (ps-2). bds. 2.99 (*0-307-00106-7*, Golden Bks.) Random Hse. Children's Bks.

The Little Mermaid. 2002. (Classic Tales Mini Bks.). (Illus.). 32p. (J). (*1-59069-038-9*, T1007); incl. audio compact disk (*1-59069-105-9*, T1107) Studio Mouse LLC.

The Little Mermaid: The Whole Story. (Little Golden Bks.). (J). 4.99 o.s.i (*0-307-98275-0*, 98275, Golden Bks.) Random Hse. Children's Bks.

Ludier, Carol. Disney's Little Mermaid: What's under the Sea? 1993. (Golden Board Bks.). (Illus.). 12p. (J). (ps). bds. 1.95 o.p. (*0-307-06077-2*, Golden Bks.) Random Hse. Children's Bks.

Martin, Ann M. Karen's Mermaid. 1994. (Baby-Sitters Little Sister Ser.: No. 52). 112p. (J). (gr. 3-7). mass mkt. 2.95 (*0-590-48299-8*) Scholastic, Inc.

Mateu, Franc, et al, illus. The Little Mermaid. 1991. (Golden Super Shape Book Ser.). Orig. Title: Lille Havfrue. 24p. (J). (ps-k). pap. 14.99 o.p. (*0-307-10027-8*, 10027, Golden Bks.) Random Hse. Children's Bks.

McCafferty, Catherine. The Little Mermaid II: Return to the Sea. 2000. (Illus.). 24p. (J). (ps-2). pap. 1.69 o.p. (*0-307-13260-9*, 13260, Golden Bks.) Random Hse. Children's Bks.

McGuire, Leslie. Disney Little Q: The Little Mermaid's Treasure Hunt. 1990. (J). (ps). 4.95 o.p. (*0-8431-2865-8*, Price Stern Sloan) Penguin Putnam Bks. for Young Readers.

Melendez, Francisco. The Mermaid & the Major: or The True Story of the Invention of the Submarine. 1991. (Illus.). 64p. (J). 24.95 o.p. (*0-8109-3619-4*) Abrams, Harry N., Inc.

Mermaid Tales. 1993. (J). pap. o.p. (*0-590-28655-2*) Scholastic, Inc.

Minters, Frances. Princess Fishtail. 2002. (Illus.). 32p. (J). (ps-3). 15.99 (*0-670-03529-7*, Viking) Viking Penguin.

Misty the Mermaid: Mission of the Midnight Raiders. (J). (gr. 2-3). 1.95 o.p. (*0-89954-379-0*) Antioch Publishing Co.

Misty the Mermaid: The Pearl Lagoon Adventure. (J). (gr. 2-3). 1.95 o.p. (*0-89954-367-7*) Antioch Publishing Co.

Moore, Martha. Under Mermaid Angel. 1995. (J). 20.95 (*0-385-31000-5*, Dell Books for Young Readers) Random Hse. Children's Bks.

Moore, Martha A. Under the Mermaid Angel. 1997. (J). 9.09 o.p. (*0-606-12027-0*) Turtleback Bks.

Mouse Works Staff. Ariel's Sea. 1997. (Disney's the Little Mermaid Ser.). (J). (ps). 5.98 o.p. (*1-57082-629-3*) Mouse Works.

—The Little Mermaid. (Seek & See Book Ser.).Tr. of Lille Havfrue. (Illus.). (J). (gr. k-3). 1998. 24p. 3.98 o.p. (*1-57082-936-5*); 1997. (*1-57082-872-5*) Mouse Works.

—Little Mermaid: A Real Treasure. 1995. (Illus.). 7p. (J). (ps). 5.98 o.p. (*1-57082-276-X*) Mouse Works.

—Sleeping Beauty/The Little Mermaid, 2 vols. 75th anniv. ed. 1998. (Illus.). (ps-3). 9.99 (*0-7364-0091-5*) Mouse Works.

Napoli, Donna Jo. Sirena. (gr. 7-12). 2000. 224p. (J). mass mkt. 5.99 (*0-590-38389-2*); 1998. 256p. (YA). pap. 15.95 (*0-590-38388-4*) Scholastic, Inc.

Noble, Marty. The Little Mermaid Stained Glass Coloring Book. 1996. (Illus.). (J). pap. 1.00 (*0-486-29341-6*) Dover Pubns., Inc.

Noble, Trinka Hakes. Hansy's Mermaid. 1983. (Illus.). (J). (ps-2). 32p. 10.95 o.p. (*0-8037-3605-3*, 01063-320); 10.89 o.p. (*0-8037-3606-1*) Penguin Putnam Bks. for Young Readers. (Dial Bks. for Young Readers).

Null. Mermaid's Treasure. 2000. 10.99 o.s.i (*0-8431-6630-4*, Grosset & Dunlap) Penguin Putnam Bks. for Young Readers.

MONSTERS—FICTION

Miscellaneous

Benton, James Grant. Lunch Walks among Us. 2003. (Franny K. Stein, Mad Scientist Ser.). (Illus.). 112p. (J). 14.95 (*0-689-86291-1*, Simon & Schuster Children's Publishing) Simon & Schuster Children's Publishing.

Berenstain, Michael. The Creature Catalog: A Monster Watcher's Guide. 1982. (Illus.). 64p. (J). (gr. 3-7). lib. bdg. 3.95 o.s.i (*0-394-95277-4*, Random Hse. Bks. for Young Readers) Random Hse. Children's Bks.

—The Great Monster Party. 1983. (Texas Instruments Magic Wand Speaking Library). (Illus.). 49p. (J). (ps-3). text 7.30 o.p. (*0-89512-074-7*) Texas Instruments, Inc.

Berenstain, Stan & Berenstain, Jan. The Berenstain Bear Scouts & the Ice Monster. 1997. (Berenstain Bear Scouts Ser.). (Illus.). 32p. (J). (gr. 3-6). mass mkt. 3.99 (*0-590-94479-7*, Scholastic Paperbacks) Scholastic, Inc.

—The Berenstain Bear Scouts & the Ice Monster. 1997. (Berenstain Bear Scouts Ser.). (J). (gr. 3-6). 10.04 (*0-606-12627-9*) Turtleback Bks.

—Los Osos Scouts Berenstain & el Monstruo de Hielo. 1997. (Berenstain Bear Scouts Ser.).Tr. of Berenstain Bear Scouts & the Ice Monster. (SPA.). (J). (gr. 3-6). pap. text 3.50 (*0-590-94480-0*) Scholastic, Inc.

—Los Osos Scouts Berenstain & el Monstruo de Hielo. 1997. (Berenstain Bear Scouts Ser.).Tr. of Berenstain Bear Scouts & the Ice Monster. (SPA.). (J). (gr. 3-6). 9.55 (*0-606-12760-7*) Turtleback Bks.

Berlan, Kathryn H. Andrew's Amazing Monsters. 1993. (Illus.). 32p. (J). (ps-2). lib. bdg. 13.95 o.s.i (*0-689-31739-5*, Atheneum) Simon & Schuster Children's Publishing.

Bethancourt, T. Ernesto. Dr. Doom Superstar. 1980. 128p. (gr. 6-9). pap. 1.75 o.p. (*0-553-13929-0*) Bantam Bks.

Better Homes and Gardens Editors. Dandy Dragon Day. 1990. 32p. (J). 4.95 o.p. (*0-696-01902-7*) Meredith Bks.

—There's a Monster in My Soup. 1990. 32p. (J). 4.95 o.p. (*0-696-01903-5*) Meredith Bks.

Billings, Robert S. Adam & Mackie the Monster. 1997. (Illus.). 16p. (J). (gr. k-7). pap., per. 6.95 (*0-938911-12-0*) Individualized Education Systems/ Poppy Ln. Publishing.

Binder, Helga, illus. Wild Wicked Winifred & the Sea Serpent. 1999. (J). (*0-7608-3204-8*) Sundance Publishing.

Bird, Malcolm. The School in Murky Wood. 1993. (Illus.). 40p. (J). (ps-3). 10.95 o.p. (*0-8118-0544-1*) Chronicle Bks. LLC.

Biro, Val. Gumdrop & the Monster. (Illus.). 32p. (J). text 22.95 (*0-340-71446-8*); mass mkt. 11.95 (*0-340-71447-6*) Hodder & Stoughton, Ltd. GBR. *Dist:* Lubrecht & Cramer, Ltd., Trafalgar Square.

—The Hobyahs. (Illus.). (J). 1994. 32p. pap. o.p. (*0-19-272278-6*); 1987. 34p. (gr. 1-5). 12.95 o.p. (*0-19-279816-2*) Oxford Univ. Pr., Inc.

—The Hobyahs. 1998. (Illus.). 32p. (J). (gr. k-3). pap. 4.99 (*1-887734-44-9*) Star Bright Bks., Inc.

Blance, Ellen & Cook. Lady Monster Has a Plan. Date not set. pap. text 129.15 (*0-582-19312-5*) Addison-Wesley Longman, Ltd. GBR. *Dist:* Trans-Atlantic Pubns., Inc.

—Lady Monster Helps Out. Date not set. pap. text 129.15 (*0-582-19302-8*) Addison-Wesley Longman, Ltd. GBR. *Dist:* Trans-Atlantic Pubns., Inc.

—Monster & Magic Umbrella. Date not set. pap. text 129.15 (*0-582-18593-9*) Addison-Wesley Longman, Ltd. GBR. *Dist:* Trans-Atlantic Pubns., Inc.

—Monster & Surprise Cookie. Date not set. pap. text 129.15 (*0-582-19308-7*) Addison-Wesley Longman, Ltd. GBR. *Dist:* Trans-Atlantic Pubns., Inc.

—Monster at School. Date not set. pap. text 129.15 (*0-582-18597-1*) Addison-Wesley Longman, Ltd. GBR. *Dist:* Trans-Atlantic Pubns., Inc.

—Monster Buys a Pet. Date not set. pap. text 129.15 (*0-582-19311-7*) Addison-Wesley Longman, Ltd. GBR. *Dist:* Trans-Atlantic Pubns., Inc.

—Monster Cleans His House. Date not set. pap. text 129.15 (*0-582-18590-4*) Addison-Wesley Longman, Ltd. GBR. *Dist:* Trans-Atlantic Pubns., Inc.

—Monster Comes to the City. Date not set. pap. text 129.15 (*0-582-18588-2*) Addison-Wesley Longman, Ltd. GBR. *Dist:* Trans-Atlantic Pubns., Inc.

—Monster Gets a Job. Date not set. pap. text 129.15 (*0-582-19307-9*) Addison-Wesley Longman, Ltd. GBR. *Dist:* Trans-Atlantic Pubns., Inc.

—Monster Goes Around Town. Date not set. pap. text 129.15 (*0-582-19309-5*) Addison-Wesley Longman, Ltd. GBR. *Dist:* Trans-Atlantic Pubns., Inc.

—Monster Goes to Circus. Date not set. pap. text 129.15 (*0-582-19304-4*) Addison-Wesley Longman, Ltd. GBR. *Dist:* Trans-Atlantic Pubns., Inc.

—Monster Goes to School. Date not set. pap. text 129.15 (*0-582-18596-3*) Addison-Wesley Longman, Ltd. GBR. *Dist:* Trans-Atlantic Pubns., Inc.

—Monster Goes to the Beach. Date not set. pap. text 129.15 (*0-582-19306-0*) Addison-Wesley Longman, Ltd. GBR. *Dist:* Trans-Atlantic Pubns., Inc.

—Monster Goes to the Hospital. Date not set. pap. text 129.15 (*0-582-19305-2*) Addison-Wesley Longman, Ltd. GBR. *Dist:* Trans-Atlantic Pubns., Inc.

—Monster Goes to the Zoo. Date not set. pap. text 129.15 (*0-582-18599-8*) Addison-Wesley Longman, Ltd. GBR. *Dist:* Trans-Atlantic Pubns., Inc.

—Monster Looks for a House. Date not set. pap. text 129.15 (*0-582-18589-0*) Addison-Wesley Longman, Ltd. GBR. *Dist:* Trans-Atlantic Pubns., Inc.

—Monster Looks for Friend. Date not set. pap. text 129.15 (*0-582-18591-2*) Addison-Wesley Longman, Ltd. GBR. *Dist:* Trans-Atlantic Pubns., Inc.

—Monster Meets Lady Monster. Date not set. pap. text 129.15 (*0-582-18592-0*) Addison-Wesley Longman, Ltd. GBR. *Dist:* Trans-Atlantic Pubns., Inc.

—Monster on the Bus. Date not set. pap. text 129.15 (*0-582-18595-5*) Addison-Wesley Longman, Ltd. GBR. *Dist:* Trans-Atlantic Pubns., Inc.

Bloom, Hanya. Friendly Fangs. 1991. (Vic the Vampire Ser.: No. 4). 80p. (J). (gr. 4-7). mass mkt. 2.95 o.p. (*0-06-106032-1*, HarperTorch) Morrow/Avon.

Bloss, Janet A. Teeny Tiny Monster. 1989. (Illus.). 24p. (Orig.). (J). (gr. k-2). pap. text 1.95 o.p. (*0-87406-395-7*) Darby Creek Publishing.

Blundell, Tony. Oliver & the Monsters. 1995. (Illus.). 32p. (J). (ps up). lib. bdg. 22.60 (*0-8368-1293-X*) Stevens, Gareth Inc.

Boiko, Claire & Novick, Sandra. Left Over Dragon. 1977. (Play Bks.). (Illus.). (J). (gr. k-3). lib. bdg. 7.35 o.p. (*0-516-08752-5*, Children's Pr.) Scholastic Library Publishing.

Book Company Staff. It's a Monster Surprise. 2003. (Pop-up Bks.). (Illus.). (J). 14.95 (*1-74047-362-0*) Book Co. Publishing Pty, Ltd., The AUS. *Dist:* Penton Overseas, Inc.

—When I Grow Up. 2003. (Pop-up Bks.). (Illus.). (J). 14.95 (*1-74047-363-9*) Book Co. Publishing Pty, Ltd., The AUS. *Dist:* Penton Overseas, Inc.

Borovsky, Paul. The Strange Blue Creature. 1993. (Illus.). 32p. (J). (ps-2). 13.95 o.s.i (*1-56282-434-1*); lib. bdg. 13.89 o.s.i (*1-56282-435-X*) Hyperion Bks. for Children.

Bowen, Betsy, illus. The Troll with No Heart in His Body. 1999. 96p. (J). (gr. 4-6). tchr. ed. 18.00 (*0-395-91371-3*) Houghton Mifflin Co.

Boynton, Sandra. Birthday Monsters! 1993. (Boynton on Board Ser.). (Illus.). 48p. (J). (ps-k). bds. 6.95 (*1-56305-443-4*, 3443) Workman Publishing Co., Inc.

Brami, Elisabeth. Sweet Dreams, Scary Monsters. McGowan, Siobhan, tr. from FRE. 1999. (Illus.). 32p. (J). (ps-3). 14.95 (*1-55670-945-5*) Stewart, Tabori & Chang.

Branson, Dave. The Monster Encyclopedia. 1998. (Illus.). 40p. (J). (gr. k-3). 16.95 (*1-880851-35-0*) Greene Bark Pr., Inc.

Brennan, Herbie. Frankenstella & the Video Store Monster. 2002. (Illus.). (J). (ps up). 15.95 (*1-58234-752-2*, Bloomsbury Children) Bloomsbury Publishing.

Brett, Jan. Beauty & the Beast. 1989. (J). 13.10 (*0-606-04614-3*) Turtleback Bks.

Bridwell, Norman. How to Care for Your Monster. (Illus.). (J). 1972. pap. 1.50 o.p. (*0-590-09177-8*); 1988. 64p. (gr. 4-6). reprint ed. pap. 2.50 o.p. (*0-590-40782-1*) Scholastic, Inc.

—Monster Holidays. 1975. (Illus.). (J). pap. 1.75 o.p. (*0-590-09930-2*) Scholastic, Inc.

Briggs, Raymond. Fungus the Bogeyman. 1990. (Illus.). 48p. (J). pap. 11.95 o.p. (*0-14-054235-3*) Penguin Bks., Ltd. GBR. *Dist:* Trafalgar Square.

Broun, Heywood. The Fifty-First Dragon. Redpath, Ann A., ed. 1985. (Short Story Library). (Illus.). 32p. (YA). (gr. 5 up). lib. bdg. 13.95 o.p. (*0-88682-005-7*, 1076-C, Creative Education) Creative Co., The.

Brouwer, Sigmund. Creature of the Mists. 2003. (Accidental Detectives Ser.). (Illus.). 128p. (J). pap. 5.99 (*0-7642-2569-3*) Bethany Hse. Pubs.

—Creature of the Mists. (Accidental Detective Ser.: Vol. 6). 132p. (J). (gr. 3-7). 1995. pap. text 5.99 o.p. (*1-56476-375-7*, 6-3375); 1991. pap. text 4.99 o.p. (*0-89693-861-1*) Cook Communications Ministries.

Brown, Christopher. Whisper, Curse of the Dragon. 1985. (In Between Bks.). (Illus.). 32p. (J). (gr. 4). pap. 2.95 o.p. (*0-89954-401-0*) Antioch Publishing Co.

Brown, Marc. Monster's Lunchbox. 1995. 16p. (J). (ps-3). 14.95 (*0-316-11313-1*) Little Brown & Co.

Brown, Marc & Nelson, Judith A. 1, 2, 3 Monsters on Parade! 1998. (Arthur Ser.). 24p. (J). (ps-3). pap. 3.99 o.s.i (*0-679-89283-4*, Random Hse. Bks. for Young Readers) Random Hse. Children's Bks.

Bruce, Jill B. Mixed-Up Monsters. 1997. (Illus.). 32p. (J). (*0-86417-834-4*, Kangaroo Pr.) Simon & Schuster Australia.

Bulla, Clyde Robert. My Friend the Monster. (Trophy Bk.). (J). 1990. (Illus.). 96p. (gr. 2-5). pap. 3.50 (*0-06-440378-5*, Harper Trophy); 1981. (Illus.). 96p. (gr. 2-5). lib. bdg. 11.89 o.p. (*0-690-04087-3*); 1980. 12.95 (*0-690-04031-8*) HarperCollins Children's Bk. Group.

Byars, Betsy C. The Blossoms & the Green Phantom. 1988. (Illus.). 160p. (gr. 4-7). reprint ed. pap. text 3.99 o.s.i (*0-440-40069-4*) Dell Publishing.

Calmenson, Stephanie. Ten Furry Monsters. 1994. (Parents Magazine Press Read-Aloud Library). (J). lib. bdg. 17.27 o.p. (*0-8368-0989-0*) Stevens, Gareth Inc.

Carey, Valerie S. Harriet & William & the Terrible Creature. (Illus.). (J). 2000. pap. (*0-14-054758-4*, Puffin Bks.); 1990. 32p. pap. 3.95 o.s.i (*0-525-44652-4*, Dutton Children's Bks.) Penguin Putnam Bks. for Young Readers.

Carlson, JoAnne. Bethany's Monster. 1996. (J). (gr. 2-5). pap. 6.95 o.p. (*0-533-11952-9*) Vantage Pr., Inc.

Carrick, Malcolm. I Can Squash Elephants! A Masai Tale about Monsters. 1978. (Illus.). (J). (gr. k-3). 6.95 o.p. (*0-670-38983-8*) Viking Penguin.

Carroll, Colleen. Gerlach the Gargoyle, Incl. doll. 1996. (My Art Friends Ser.). (Illus.). 32p. (J). (ps-3). pap. 19.95 (*0-7892-0110-0*, Abbeville Kids) Abbeville Pr., Inc.

Carter, David A. Finger Bugs Dracubug. 1997. (Finger Bugs Ser.). (Illus.). (J). mass mkt. 5.99 (*0-689-81737-1*, Little Simon) Simon & Schuster Children's Publishing.

Cassinari, Ramon P. The Legend of Little Nessie. 1997. (Illus.). 24p. (J). (gr. k-4). 14.95 (*0-9654002-0-4*) Little Lochness Publishing.

Castle, Caroline. Phoebe & the Monster Maze. 1997. (Illus.). 32p. (J). (ps-2). o.p. (*0-09-176714-8*) Random Hse. of Canada, Ltd. CAN. *Dist:* Random Hse., Inc.

Cazet, Denys. Minnie & Moo Meet Frankenswine. 2002. (Minnie & Moo Ser.). (Illus.). 12.34 (*1-4046-1308-0*) Book Wholesalers, Inc.

—Minnie & Moo Meet Frankenswine. (I Can Read Bks.: Bk. 3). (Illus.). 48p. (J). 2002. pap. 3.99 (*0-06-444311-6*); 2001. 14.95 (*0-06-623748-3*); 2001. lib. bdg. 15.89 (*0-06-623749-1*) HarperCollins Children's Bk. Group.

Ceracini, Marc. Godzilla Saves America: A Monster Showdown in 3-D! 1996. (Illus.). (J). 11.99 o.s.i (*0-679-88079-8*) Random Hse., Inc.

Ceracini, Marc & Dwyer, Jacqueline. Godzilla on Monster Island. 1996. (Godzilla Ser.). (Illus.). 24p. (J). (gr. 1-4). pap. 3.25 o.s.i (*0-679-88080-1*) Random Hse., Inc.

Cerasini, Marc. Godzilla 2000. 1997. (Godzilla Ser.). (Illus.). 320p. (J). (gr. 3-7). mass mkt. 5.99 o.s.i (*0-679-88751-2*, Random Hse. Bks. for Young Readers) Random Hse. Children's Bks.

Cerasini, Marc A. Godzilla Returns. 1996. (Godzilla Ser.). (Illus.). 233p. (J). (gr. 9-12). mass mkt. 4.99 o.s.i (*0-679-88221-9*, Random Hse. Bks. for Young Readers) Random Hse. Children's Bks.

Charman, Andy. Monster Play. (Illus.). 96p. (J). 6.98 o.p. (*0-8317-1580-4*) Smithmark Pubs., Inc.

—Monster School. 1995. (Illus.). 96p. (J). (ps-1). 6.98 o.p. (*0-8317-5872-4*) Smithmark Pubs., Inc.

Cheron, Jeremy. The Googly-Eyed Monster. 1997. 16p. (J). (gr. k-4). pap. 6.00 o.p. (*0-8059-4102-9*) Dorrance Publishing Co., Inc.

Cherry, Lynne. The Dragon & the Unicorn. 1998. (Illus.). 40p. (J). (gr. 1-5). pap. 7.00 (*0-15-201888-3*, Harcourt Paperbacks) Harcourt Children's Bks.

Chetwin, Grace. Beauty & the Beast. 1998. (Illus.). 71p. (J). text 25.00 o.p. (*0-9649349-5-7*, Rivet Bks.) Feral Pr., Inc.

Chevalier, Christa. Spence & the Sleepytime Monster. Tucker, Kathleen, ed. 1984. (Just for Fun Bks.). (Illus.). 32p. (J). (ps-1). lib. bdg. 12.95 o.p. (*0-8075-7574-7*) Whitman, Albert & Co.

Chevat, Richie. Monster House. 1995. (Illus.). 96p. (J). (gr. 2 up). pap. 3.99 o.s.i (*0-553-48322-6*, Skylark) Random Hse. Children's Bks.

Christian, Mary Blount. Go West, Swamp Monsters. (Easy-to-Read Bks.). (Illus.). (J). (ps-3). 1987. 4p. pap. 4.95 o.p. (*0-8037-0438-0*); 1985. 4p. 8.95 o.p. (*0-8037-0091-1*); 1985. 48p. 8.89 o.p. (*0-8037-0144-6*) Penguin Putnam Bks. for Young Readers. (Dial Bks. for Young Readers).

—Swamp Monsters. (Puffin Easy-to-Read Ser.). (J). (ps-3). 1994. (Illus.). 48p. pap. 3.99 o.s.i (*0-14-036841-8*, Puffin Bks.); 1992. 40p. pap. 4.99 o.p. (*0-14-036211-8*, Puffin Bks.); 1983. (Illus.). 56p. 9.89 o.p. (*0-8037-7616-0*, Dial Bks. for Young Readers); 1983. (Illus.). 4p. pap. 4.95 o.p. (*0-8037-7614-4*, Dial Bks. for Young Readers) Penguin Putnam Bks. for Young Readers.

—Swamp Monsters. (J). (gr. 1-2). 48p. pap. 3.99 (*0-8072-1355-1*); 1985. pap. 17.00 incl. audio (*0-8072-0086-7*, FTR98SP) Random Hse. Audio Publishing Group. (Listening Library).

Christine, Mary L. Go West, Swamp Monsters Level 3, Yellow. 1996. (Puffin Easy-to-Read Ser.). (Illus.). 48p. (J). (gr. 1-4). pap. 3.50 o.p. (*0-14-036230-4*, Puffin Bks.) Penguin Putnam Bks. for Young Readers.

Ciencin, Scott. Godzilla: Journey to Monster Island, No. 2. 1998. (J). pap. 3.99 o.s.i (*0-679-88901-9*, Random Hse. Bks. for Young Readers) Random Hse. Children's Bks.

—Godzilla: King of the Monsters. 1996. (Godzilla Ser.). 97p. (J). (gr. 4-7). pap. 3.99 o.s.i (*0-679-88220-0*, Random Hse. Bks. for Young Readers) Random Hse. Children's Bks.

—Godzilla Invades America. 1997. (J). pap. 3.99 o.s.i (*0-679-88752-0*, Random Hse. Bks. for Young Readers) Random Hse. Children's Bks.

—Godzilla vs. the Space Monster, No. 3. 1998. (J). pap. 3.99 o.s.i (*0-679-88902-7*, Random Hse. Bks. for Young Readers) Random Hse. Children's Bks.

Ciencin, Scott & Jolley, Dan. Vengeance. 2002. (Angel Ser.: Bk. 14). 352p. (YA). (gr. 11 up). pap. 5.99 (*0-7434-2754-8*, Simon Pulse) Simon & Schuster Children's Publishing.

Clark, Ann Nolan. In the Land of Small Dragon. 1979. (Illus.). (J). (gr. k-3). 11.50 o.p. (*0-670-39697-4*) Viking Penguin.

Clarke, Gus. Ten Green Monsters: A Lift-the-Flap-and-See-Them-Fall Book. 1994. (Golden Book Ser.). (Illus.). 28p. (J). (ps-3). pap. 10.95 o.s.i (*0-307-17605-3*, Golden Bks.) Random Hse. Children's Bks.

Clarke, Judith & Egan, Caroline, illus. Monsters Inc. 2001. (J). 15.95 (*0-7853-4861-1*) Publications International, Ltd.

Clements, Andrew. Gromble's Haunted Halloween. 1998. (Real Monsters Ser.). (Illus.). 16p. (J). (ps-1). pap. 3.99 (*0-689-82052-6*, Simon Spotlight/ Nickelodeon) Simon & Schuster Children's Publishing.

—Real Monsters Go for the Mold. 1997. (Real Monsters Ser.). 16p. (J). (ps-2). mass mkt. 5.99 (*0-689-81609-X*, Simon Spotlight/Nickelodeon) Simon & Schuster Children's Publishing.

—Real Monsters Stage Fright. 1997. (Real Monsters Tattoo Bks.). (Illus.). 16p. (J). (ps-2). pap. 5.99 (*0-689-81610-3*, Simon Spotlight/Nickelodeon) Simon & Schuster Children's Publishing.

Coe, Frances. Monster Snuggles: Chomp Chomp! 2003. (Animal Snuggles Ser.). (Illus.). 8p. (J). bds. 7.95 (*0-8069-0637-5*) Sterling Publishing Co., Inc.

Coelho, Raquel. Monstrico (Little Monster) Matrangelo, Stella, tr. 1994. (SPA., Illus.). 41p. (J). (gr. 2). 5.99 (*968-16-4573-1*) Fondo de Cultura Economica MEX. *Dist:* Continental Bk. Co., Inc.

Coffin, M. T. Monster Channel. 1997. (Spinetingler Ser.: No. 17). (J). (gr. 4-7). pap. 3.50 (*0-380-78610-9*, Avon Bks.) Morrow/Avon.

—Monster Channel. 1997. (Spinetingler Ser.: No. 17). (J). (gr. 4-7). 8.60 o.p. (*0-606-10880-7*) Turtleback Bks.

Cohen, Daniel. Science Fiction's Greatest Monsters. 1980. (YA). (gr. 9-12). 8.95 o.p. (*0-396-07859-1*, G. P. Putnam's Sons) Penguin Putnam Bks. for Young Readers.

—Supermonsters. 1986. (Illus.). (J). (gr. 4 up). pap. (*0-671-62219-6*, HI-LO, Simon Pulse) Simon & Schuster Children's Publishing.

Cohen, Milton. Ilana & the Monsters. 1985. (Illus.). 40p. (Orig.). (J). (ps). pap. 4.00 (*0-9616076-0-2*) Jomilt Pubns.

Cohen, Miriam. Jim Meets the Thing. 1989. 49p. (J). (gr. k-6). pap. 2.95 o.s.i (*0-440-40149-6*, Yearling) Random Hse. Children's Bks.

—The Real-Skin Rubber Monster Mask. 1990. (Illus.). 32p. (J). (gr. k up). 12.95 o.p. (*0-688-09122-9*); lib. bdg. 12.88 o.p. (*0-688-09123-7*) HarperCollins Children's Bk. Group. (Greenwillow Bks.).

—The Real-Skin Rubber Monster Mask. 1995. (Illus.). 32p. (J). (gr. k-3). pap. 4.99 o.s.i (*0-440-40949-7*, Yearling) Random Hse. Children's Bks.

—The Real-Skin Rubber Monster Mask. 1995. (J). 10.44 o.p. (*0-606-08061-9*) Turtleback Bks.

Cole, Joanna. Monster & Muffin. 1996. (All Aboard Reading Ser.). (Illus.). 32p. (J). (ps-1). 3.95 o.p. (*0-448-41146-6*, Grosset & Dunlap) Penguin Putnam Bks. for Young Readers.

—Monster Manners. (Hello Reader! Ser.). (Illus.). (J). 1995. 56p. (gr. 1-2). mass mkt. 3.99 (*0-590-53951-5*, Cartwheel Bks.); 1985. 48p. (gr. k-3). pap. 2.50 o.p. (*0-590-40926-3*) Scholastic, Inc.

—Monster Movie. 1987. (Illus.). 48p. (Orig.). (J). (gr. k-3). pap. 2.50 o.p. (*0-590-41545-X*) Scholastic, Inc.

—Monster Valentines. 1990. (J). pap. 2.50 o.p. (*0-590-42216-2*) Scholastic, Inc.

Cole, William. Monster Knock Knocks. 1988. (Illus.). 96p. (Orig.). (J). (gr. 3-6). pap. (*0-671-63396-1*, Aladdin) Simon & Schuster Children's Publishing.

Colman, Hila. What's the Matter with the Dobsons? 1982. (J). (gr. 5-7). pap. (*0-671-43143-9*, Simon Pulse) Simon & Schuster Children's Publishing.

Conford, Ellen. Diary of a Monster's Son. 1999. (Illus.). 80p. (J). (gr. 3-7). 15.95 (*0-316-15245-5*) Little Brown & Co.

Cooney, Nancy Evans. Go Away Monsters, Lickety Split! 1990. (Illus.). 32p. (J). (ps-1). 13.95 o.p. (*0-399-21935-8*, G. P. Putnam's Sons) Penguin Putnam Bks. for Young Readers.

Miscellaneous

Cooper, Helen. Little Monster Did. 1996. (Illus.). 32p. (J). pap. 17.95 o.p. (*0-385-40620-7*) Doubleday Publishing.

—Little Monster Did It! 1999. (Illus.). 32p. (J). (ps-2). pap. 5.99 o.p. (*0-14-055883-7*, Puffin Bks.) Penguin Putnam Bks. for Young Readers.

Cooper, Stephen Roscoe. The Diary of Victor Frankenstein. 1997. (Illus.). 96p. (J). pap. 19.95 o.p. (*0-7894-2456-8*) Dorling Kindersley Publishing, Inc.

Cooper, Susan. The Boggart & the Monster. 192p. (J). (gr. 3-7). 1998. (Illus.). pap. 4.99 (*0-689-82286-3*, Aladdin); 1997. 16.00 (*0-689-81330-9*, McElderry, Margaret K.) Simon & Schuster Children's Publishing.

Corentin, Philipe. Papa! 1997. (Illus.). 32p. (J). (ps-1). 11.16 o.p. (*0-8118-1640-0*) Chronicle Bks. LLC.

Cosgrove, Stephen. Creole. 1978. (Serendipity Bks.). (Illus.). 32p. (J). (gr. 1-4). 3.95 o.s.i (*0-8431-0552-6*, Price Stern Sloan) Penguin Putnam Bks. for Young Readers.

—Serendipity. rev. ed. 1995. (Serendipity Bks.). (Illus.). 32p. (J). (ps-3). 4.99 (*0-8431-3819-X*, Price Stern Sloan) Penguin Putnam Bks. for Young Readers.

—Serendipity. 1995. 11.14 (*0-606-02428-X*) Turtleback Bks.

Cote, Denis. La Nuit du Vampire. 1990. (Roman Jeunesse Ser.). (FRE.). 96p. (YA). (gr. 4-7). pap. 8.95 o.p. (*2-89021-117-7*) La Courte Echelle CAN. *Dist:* Firefly Bks., Ltd.

—La Trahison du Vampire. 2002. (Roman Jeunesse Ser.). (FRE., Illus.). 96p. (YA). (gr. 4-7). pap. 8.95 (*2-89021-238-6*) La Courte Echelle CAN. *Dist:* Firefly Bks., Ltd.

Cote, Denis & Poulin, Stephane. La Nuit du Vampire. 2001. (FRE., Illus.). 96p. (J). pap. 10.95 (*2-89021-469-9*) La Courte Echelle CAN. *Dist:* Firefly Bks., Ltd.

Counsel, June. A Dragon in Class Four. 1984. (Illus.). 96p. (J). (gr. 1-4). o.p. (*0-571-13249-9*) Faber & Faber Ltd.

Courtney, Richard & Awdry, Wilbert V. The Monster under the Shed. 2001. (Pictureback Bk.). (Illus.). 24p. (J). pap. 3.25 (*0-375-81371-3*, Random Hse. Bks. for Young Readers) Random Hse. Children's Bks.

Coville, Bruce. Bruce Coville's Book of Monsters: Tales to Give You the Creeps. unabr. ed. 1996. (J). (gr. 3-6). pap. 23.00 incl. audio (*0-8072-7626-X*, YA903SP, Listening Library) Random Hse. Audio Publishing Group.

—Bruce Coville's Book of Monsters: Tales to Give You the Creeps. (Illus.). (J). 1993. 176p. (gr. 4-7). mass mkt. 3.99 (*0-590-46159-1*); No. 2. 1996. (gr. 3-7). mass mkt. 3.99 (*0-590-85292-2*) Scholastic, Inc.

—Bruce Coville's Book of Monsters: Tales to Give You the Creeps. 1993. 9.09 o.p. (*0-606-05173-2*) Turtleback Bks.

—Jeremy Thatcher, Dragon Hatcher. Yolen, Jane, ed. 1991. (Magic Book Shop Ser.). (Illus.). 160p. (YA). (gr. 4-7). 16.95 (*0-15-200748-2*) Harcourt Children's Bks.

—Monster of the Year. (J). 1990. mass mkt. 2.95 (*0-671-73357-5*); 1990. (gr. 4-7). pap. 3.99 (*0-671-73147-5*); 1989. (Illus.). 112p. (gr. 3-6). pap. 2.75 (*0-671-64749-0*); 1989. (Illus.). mass mkt. 2.75 (*0-671-69667-X*) Simon & Schuster Children's Publishing. (Aladdin).

—Monster of the Year. 1989. (J). 10.04 (*0-606-01968-5*) Turtleback Bks.

—The Monster's Ring. anniv. exp. ed. 2002. (Magic Shop Bks.). (Illus.). 128p. (YA). (gr. 3-7). 16.00 (*0-15-204618-6*) Harcourt Children's Bks.

—The Monster's Ring. 1982. (Illus.). 96p. (J). (gr. 8-11). 8.95 o.p. (*0-394-85320-2*, Pantheon) Knopf Publishing Group.

—The Monster's Ring. (Magic Shop Bks.). (J). 2003. (Illus.). 128p. pap. 4.99 (*0-689-85692-X*); 1989. (gr. 4-7). pap. 3.99 (*0-671-69389-1*); 1987. (Illus.). (gr. 3-7). pap. (*0-671-64441-6*) Simon & Schuster Children's Publishing. (Aladdin).

—The Monster's Ring. 1982. (J). 10.04 (*0-606-03620-2*) Turtleback Bks.

—Some of My Best Friends Are Monsters. (Camp Haunted Hills Ser.: Vol. 2). (J). 1989. (gr. 4-7). pap. 3.99 (*0-671-70652-7*); 1988. (Illus.). (gr. 3-6). pap. (*0-671-64747-4*) Simon & Schuster Children's Publishing. (Aladdin).

—Some of My Best Friends Are Monsters. 1988. (Camp Haunted Hills Ser.). (J). 10.04 (*0-606-03925-2*) Turtleback Bks.

Cowan, Bianca. Monster is Hiding (El Monstruo Escondido) 1999. (ENG & SPA., Illus.). 32p. (J). per. 7.95 (*0-9669645-3-5*, AlterLingo Bks.) O'Hollow Publishing.

Craig, Helen. The Night of the Paper Bag Monsters. (Illus.). 32p. 2003. bds. 4.99 (*0-7636-2037-8*); 1994. (J). reprint ed. bds. 4.95 o.p. (*1-56402-120-3*) Candlewick Pr.

Craig, M. Jean. Little Monsters. 1976. (J). (gr. k-3). pap. 1.95 o.p. (*0-590-10298-2*) Scholastic, Inc.

Crassy the Crude Beastie. 2001. (Beastie Buddies Ser.). (Illus.). 32p. (J). 6.95 (*1-891100-86-6*) Smart Kids Publishing.

Crebbin, June. Into the Castle. 1996. (Illus.). 32p. (J). 14.99 o.p. (*1-56402-822-4*) Candlewick Pr.

Creighton, J. Maybe a Monster. 1989. (Illus.). 24p. (ps-8). 12.95 (*1-55037-037-5*); pap. 4.95 (*1-55037-036-7*) Annick Pr., Ltd. CAN. *Dist:* Firefly Bks., Ltd.

Creighton, Jill. The Great Blue Grump. 1997. (Illus.). 32p. (J). (ps-2). pap. 5.95 (*1-55037-432-X*); lib. bdg. 15.95 (*1-55037-433-8*) Annick Pr., Ltd. CAN. *Dist:* Firefly Bks., Ltd.

Crider, Bill. Mike Gonzo & the Sewer Monster. 1996. 144p. (J). (gr. 2-4). mass mkt. 3.99 (*0-671-53651-6*, Aladdin) Simon & Schuster Children's Publishing.

Crowe, Robert L. Clyde Monster. (Illus.). 32p. (J). (ps-3). 1993. pap. 5.99 o.p. (*0-14-054743-6*, Puffin Bks.); 1987. pap. 3.95 o.p. (*0-525-44289-8*, Dutton Children's Bks.); 1976. 12.95 o.p. (*0-525-28025-1*, Dutton Children's Bks.) Penguin Putnam Bks. for Young Readers.

Cunliffe, John. Great Dragon Competition & Other Stories. 1980. (Illus.). (J). 7.95 o.p. (*0-233-96472-X*) Blackwell Publishing.

—Postman Pat & the Beast of Greendale, Bk. 12. (Illus.). 32p. (J). text 17.95 (*0-340-67816-X*) Hodder & Stoughton, Ltd. GBR. *Dist:* Lubrecht & Cramer, Ltd., Trafalgar Square.

—Postman Pat & the Beast of Greendale. 1997. (Postman Pat Ser.: Vol. 12). (J). text 12.95 incl. audio (*1-85998-919-5*) Hodder Headline Audiobooks GBR. *Dist:* Trafalgar Square.

Cushman, Doug. Giants. 1980. (Illus.). 48p. (J). (gr. 1-7). 5.29 o.p. (*0-448-13623-6*, Grosset & Dunlap) Penguin Putnam Bks. for Young Readers.

Dadey, Debbie. Swamp Monster in the Third Grade. 2003. (Illus.). 32p. (J). (gr. 2-5). mass mkt. 3.99 (*0-439-42441-0*, Scholastic Paperbacks) Scholastic, Inc.

Dadey, Debbie & Jones. Robots Don't Catch Chicken Pox. 2001. (Bailey School Kids Ser.). (Illus.). (J). 10.14 (*0-606-21402-X*) Turtleback Bks.

—Vikings Don't Wear Wrestling Belts. 2001. (Adventures of the Bailey School Kids Ser.). (Illus.). (J). 10.14 (*0-606-21504-2*) Turtleback Bks.

Dadey, Debbie & Jones, Marcia Thornton. Aliens Don't Wear Braces. 1993. (Adventures of the Bailey School Kids Ser.: No. 7). (J). (gr. 2-4). 10.14 (*0-606-05112-0*) Turtleback Bks.

—Dragons Don't Cook Pizza. 1997. (Adventures of the Bailey School Kids Ser.: No. 24). 80p. (J). (gr. 2-4). mass mkt. 3.99 (*0-590-84904-2*) Scholastic, Inc.

—Dragons Don't Cook Pizza. 1997. (Adventures of the Bailey School Kids Ser.: No. 24). (J). (gr. 2-4). 10.14 (*0-606-10790-8*) Turtleback Bks.

—Frankenstein Doesn't Plant Petunias. 1993. (Adventures of the Bailey School Kids Ser.: No. 6). 80p. (J). (gr. 2-4). mass mkt. 3.99 o.s.i (*0-590-47071-X*) Scholastic, Inc.

—Frankenstein Doesn't Plant Petunias. 1993. (Adventures of the Bailey School Kids Ser.: No. 6). (J). (gr. 2-4). 8.70 (*0-606-05298-4*) Turtleback Bks.

—Frankenstein Doesn't Slam Hockey Pucks. 1998. (Adventures of the Bailey School Kids Ser.: No. 34). (J). (gr. 2-4). 10.14 (*0-606-15898-7*) Turtleback Bks.

—Ghouls Don't Scoop Ice Cream. 1998. (Adventures of the Bailey School Kids Ser.: No. 31). (J). (gr. 2-4). 10.14 (*0-606-13426-3*) Turtleback Bks.

—Monsters Don't Scuba Dive. (Adventures of the Bailey School Kids Ser.: No. 14). (Illus.). (J). (gr. 2-4). (FRE.). 80p. pap. 5.99 (*0-590-24550-3*); 1995. 96p. mass mkt. 3.99 (*0-590-22635-5*) Scholastic, Inc.

—Swamp Monsters Don't Chase Wild Turkeys. 2001. (Bailey School Kids Ser.). (Illus.). 80p. (YA). (gr. 7). mass mkt. 3.99 (*0-439-33338-5*) Scholastic, Inc.

—Wolfmen Don't Hula Dance. 1999. (Adventures of the Bailey School Kids Ser.: No. 36). (Illus.). 71p. (J). (gr. 2-4). mass mkt. 3.99 (*0-590-18986-7*) Scholastic, Inc.

—Wolfmen Don't Hula Dance. 1999. (Adventures of the Bailey School Kids Ser.: No. 36). (J). (gr. 2-4). 10.14 (*0-606-16938-5*) Turtleback Bks.

—Zombies Don't Play Soccer. 1995. (Adventures of the Bailey School Kids Ser.: No. 15). (Illus.). 70p. (J). (gr. 2-4). mass mkt. 3.99 (*0-590-22636-3*, Scholastic Paperbacks) Scholastic, Inc.

Dadey, Debbie, et al. Aliens Don't Wear Braces. 1993. (Adventures of the Bailey School Kids Ser.: No. 7). (Illus.). 74p. (J). (gr. 2-4). mass mkt. 3.99 (*0-590-47070-1*) Scholastic, Inc.

Dague, Paige A. ScribbleMonster & the Crunchy, Crunchy Carrots. 2001. (Illus.). (J). (ps). pap. 5.50 (*0-9706406-0-9*) ScribbleBooks Co., The.

Dague, Paige A. & Dague, James. ScribbleMonster & the Broken TV. 2001. (Illus.). 32p. (J). (ps). pap. 5.50 (*0-9706406-1-7*) ScribbleBooks Co., The.

—ScribbleMonster Takes a Bath. 2001. (Illus.). 32p. (J). (ps). pap. 5.50 (*0-9706406-2-5*) ScribbleBooks Co., The.

David, Lawrence. The Cupcaked Crusader. 2002. (Halloween Ser.). (Illus.). (J). 144p. 14.99 (*0-525-46866-8*); 144p. pap. 4.99 (*0-14-230021-7*, Puffin Bks.);Vol. 1. 96p. (gr. 2-4). 14.99 (*0-525-46763-7*, Dutton Children's Bks.) Penguin Putnam Bks. for Young Readers.

—Invasion of the Shag Carpet Creature. 2004. (Illus.). 160p. pap. 4.99 (*0-14-240042-4*, Puffin Bks.) Penguin Putnam Bks. for Young Readers.

—To Catch a Clownosaurus. Gott, Barry, tr. & illus. by. 2003. (J). 160p. 14.99 (*0-525-47154-5*); 144p. pap. 4.99 (*0-14-250135-2*) Penguin Putnam Bks. for Young Readers. (Puffin Bks.).

DeCesare, Angelo. Anthony, the Perfect Monster. 1996. (I Can Read It All by Myself Ser.). (J). (ps-3). 11.99 o.s.i (*0-679-96845-8*, Random Hse. Bks. for Young Readers) Random Hse. Children's Bks.

DeGroat, Diane. Annie Pitts, Swamp Monster. 2001. (Illus.). 112p. (J). (gr. 3-7). 14.95 (*1-58717-044-2*); reprint ed. pap. 3.95 (*1-58717-045-0*) North-South Bks., Inc.

—Annie Pitts, Swamp Monster. 1994. (J). pap. 13.00 o.p. (*0-671-87004-1*, Simon & Schuster Children's Publishing) Simon & Schuster Children's Publishing.

Del Negro, Janice. Lucy Dove. (Illus.). 32p. (J). (gr. 3-6). 2001. pap. 6.95 (*0-7894-8084-0*, D K Ink); 1998. pap. 16.95 o.p. (*0-7894-2514-9*) Dorling Kindersley Publishing, Inc.

Del Negro, Janice & Gore, Leonid. Lucy Dove. 1999. (Illus.). 32p. (J). pap. 19.95 o.p. (*0-7737-3107-5*) Dorling Kindersley Publishing, Inc.

Delaney, Antoinette T. Monster Tracks? 1981. (Illus.). 32p. (J). (ps-1). 12.89 o.p. (*0-06-021588-7*); lib. bdg. 11.89 o.p. (*0-06-021589-5*) HarperCollins Children's Bk. Group.

Delaney, M. C. The Marigold Monster. 1983. (Illus.). 32p. (J). (ps-3). 9.95 o.p. (*0-525-44023-2*, Dutton) Dutton/Plume.

Delessert, Etienne. Dance! 1994. (Yok-Yok Ser.). (Illus.). 32p. (J). (gr. 1-8). 16.95 o.p. (*0-88682-627-6*, 97938-098, Creative Education) Creative Co., The.

—Dance! 1995. (Illus.). 32p. (J). (ps-3). 16.95 o.p. (*0-15-200964-7*) Harcourt Trade Pubs.

Demarest, Chris L. Morton & Sidney. (Illus.). 32p. (J). (ps-2). 1987. 13.95 o.s.i (*0-02-728450-6*, Simon & Schuster Children's Publishing); 1993. reprint ed. pap. 4.95 o.p. (*0-689-71740-7*, Aladdin) Simon & Schuster Children's Publishing.

Deschaine, Scott. Monster Love. 1993. (Illus.). 36p. (J). pap. 2.50 (*1-878181-05-X*) Discovery Comics.

Desrosiers, Sylvie. Mefiez-Vous des Monstres Marins. 2002. (Roman Jeunesse Ser.). (FRE.). 96p. (YA). (gr. 4-7). pap. 8.95 (*2-89021-146-0*) La Courte Echelle CAN. *Dist:* Firefly Bks., Ltd.

Dewey, Ariane. Dorin & the Dragon. 1982. (Illus.). 32p. (J). (gr. k-3). 12.95 o.p. (*0-688-00910-7*); lib. bdg. 12.88 o.p. (*0-688-00911-5*) HarperCollins Children's Bk. Group. (Greenwillow Bks.).

Dias, Ron & Gonzalez, Ric, illus. Disney's Beauty & the Beast. 1991. (Illustrated Classics Ser.). 96p. (J). lib. bdg. 15.49 o.s.i (*1-56282-050-8*); 14.95 o.p. (*1-56282-049-4*) Disney Pr.

Dickerson, Sharon. Jessica & the Tangle Monster. 2002. pap. 9.00 (*0-8059-5991-2*) Dorrance Publishing Co., Inc.

Dickins, Robert, illus. My Teacher Turns into a Tyrannosaurus. 1997. (*0-7608-0770-1*) Sundance Publishing.

Dickinson, Rebecca, tr. & illus. Over in the Hollow. 2002. (J). (*0-385-74620-2*, Doubleday Bks. for Young Readers) Random Hse. Children's Bks.

Dillon, Barbara. The Beast in the Bed. 1981. (Illus.). 32p. (J). (gr. k-3). 12.95 o.p. (*0-688-22254-4*); lib. bdg. 12.88 o.p. (*0-688-32254-9*) Morrow/Avon. (Morrow, William & Co.).

Dils, Tracey E. Whatever I Do, the Monster Does Too! 1991. (Really Reading Ser.: Level 1). (Illus.). 32p. (J). (gr. 1-2). pap. 2.99 o.p. (*0-87406-581-X*) Darby Creek Publishing.

Dinan, Carolyn. Goodnight, Monster. (Illus.). 32p. (J). pap. 7.95 (*0-14-038281-X*) Penguin Bks., Ltd. GBR. *Dist:* Trafalgar Square.

—The Lunch Box Monster. 1983. (Illus.). 32p. (J). (ps-1). pap. o.p. (*0-571-13153-0*) Faber & Faber Ltd.

Disney Staff. Beauty & the Beast: The Perfect Party. 1997. (Disney's "Storytime Treasures" Library: Vol. 4). (Illus.). 44p. (J). (gr. 1-6). 3.49 o.p. (*1-57973-000-0*) Advance Pubs. LLC.

—Big Monsters, Little Monsters. 2002. 12p. (J). bds. 7.99 (*0-7364-1324-3*, RH/Disney) Random Hse. Children's Bks.

—Employee Handbook: We Scare Because We Care. 2001. (Illus.). 64p. (J). (gr. 1-5). pap. 3.99 (*0-7364-1236-0*, RH/Disney) Random Hse. Children's Bks.

—Feel Better, Beast! 1998. (Illus.). (J). (ps-3). pap. text 0.99 o.p. (*0-307-15267-7*, 15267, Golden Bks.) Random Hse. Children's Bks.

—Lean, Mean, Monster Machine. 2001. 32p. (J). pap. 3.99 (*0-7364-1260-3*, RH/Disney) Random Hse. Children's Bks.

—M Is for Monster. 2001. (Illus.). 24p. (J). pap. 3.25 (*0-7364-1238-7*, RH/Disney) Random Hse. Children's Bks.

—May the Best Monster Win. 2001. 32p. (J). pap. 3.99 o.s.i (*0-7364-1257-3*, RH/Disney) Random Hse. Children's Bks.

—Monster Fun. 2001. (Illus.). 12p. (J). bds. 4.99 (*0-7364-1231-X*, RH/Disney) Random Hse. Children's Bks.

—Monsters in the Closet! 2001. (Illus.). 12p. (J). bds. 7.99 o.s.i (*0-7364-1276-X*, RH/Disney) Random Hse. Children's Bks.

—Monsters to Go. 2002. 12p. (J). bds. 9.99 (*0-7364-2058-4*, RH/Disney) Random Hse. Children's Bks.

—Monstruos en el Closet. 2001. (Illus.). 12p. (J). bds. 7.99 (*0-7364-1330-8*) Mouse Works.

—Ready, Set, Scare! 2001. (Illus.). 12p. (J). pap. 6.99 o.s.i (*0-7364-1273-5*, RH/Disney) Random Hse. Children's Bks.

—Welcome to Monstropolis. 2001. 12p. (J). bds. 7.99 o.s.i (*0-7364-1264-6*, RH/Disney) Random Hse. Children's Bks.

—Who's So Scary? 2001. 10p. (J). 7.99 o.s.i (*0-7364-1269-7*, RH/Disney) Random Hse. Children's Bks.

Disney Staff, illus. Monsters, Inc. 2001. (Read-Aloud Storybook Ser.). 72p. (J). 8.99 (*0-7364-1235-2*, RH/Disney) Random Hse. Children's Bks.

Dixon, Dorothy. The Night of the Green Dragon. 1996. (Illus.). 32p. (J). pap. text 4.95 (*0-19-421947-X*) Oxford Univ. Pr., Inc.

Dixon, Franklin W. The Monster in the Lake. 1999. (Hardy Boys Are: No. 11). (Illus.). 80p. (J). (gr. 2-4). pap. 3.99 (*0-671-02662-3*, Aladdin) Simon & Schuster Children's Publishing.

Dolby, Karen. Lucy & the Sea Monster to the Rescue. Bates, Michelle, ed. 1997. (Usborne Young Puzzle Adventures Ser.). (Illus.). 32p. (Orig.). (J). (ps-2). pap. 5.95 (*0-7460-2292-1*); lib. bdg. 13.95 (*0-88110-934-7*) EDC Publishing. (Usborne).

Dolby, Karen & Church, C. Lucy & the Sea Monster. 1994. (Puzzle Stories Ser.). (Illus.). 32p. (J). (ps-2). lib. bdg. 13.95 (*0-88110-679-8*, Usborne) EDC Publishing.

Donaldson, Julia. The Gruffalo. 2003. (Illus.). 24p. (J). pap. 9.95 (*0-333-71093-2*) Macmillan U.K. GBR. *Dist:* Trafalgar Square.

Dorling Kindersley Publishing Staff. Monsters, Inc. Sticker Book. 2001. (Ultimate Sticker Books Ser.). (Illus.). 16p. (J). pap. 6.95 (*0-7894-7942-7*) Dorling Kindersley Publishing, Inc.

Dos Santos, Joyce A. Henri & the Loup-Garou. 1982. (Illus.). 40p. (J). (ps-2). lib. bdg. 8.99 o.p. (*0-394-94950-1*, Pantheon) Knopf Publishing Group.

Dower, Laura. Three Girls & a Monster. 2002. (Powerpuff Girls Ser.). (Illus.). 32p. (J). (ps-3). mass mkt. 3.50 (*0-439-34432-8*, Cartwheel Bks.) Scholastic, Inc.

Downey, Lynn. Which Monster Do You Love Most? 2004. (Illus.). 32p. (J). 16.99 (*0-8037-2728-3*, Dial Bks. for Young Readers) Penguin Putnam Bks. for Young Readers.

Doyle, Debra & MacDonald, James D. Groogleman. 1996. 128p. (J). (gr. 7 up). 15.00 (*0-15-200235-9*) Harcourt Trade Pubs.

Doyle, Malachy. Hungry! Hungry! Hungry! 2001. (Illus.). 28p. (J). (ps-3). 15.95 (*1-56145-241-6*) Peachtree Pubs., Ltd.

Dracula. 1997. (Fx Packs Ser.). (Illus.). (J). (gr. 4-7). 6.95 o.p. (*0-7894-2284-0*) Dorling Kindersley Publishing, Inc.

Dracula. (J). 9.95 (*1-56156-373-0*) Kidsbooks, Inc.

Drescher, Henrik. The Boy Who Ate Around. 1994. (Illus.). 40p. (J). (ps-3). 14.95 (*0-7868-0014-3*); lib. bdg. 15.49 (*0-7868-2011-X*) Hyperion Bks. for Children.

—The Boy Who Ate Around. 1996. (Illus.). 40p. (J). (ps-3). pap. 4.95 (*0-7868-1128-5*) Hyperion Paperbacks for Children.

—The Boy Who Ate Around. 1996. 10.15 o.p. (*0-606-11164-6*) Turtleback Bks.

—Pat the Beastie: A Pull-&-Poke Book. 1993. (Illus.). 18p. (YA). (ps up). 9.95 (*1-56282-407-4*) Hyperion Bks. for Children.

—Pat the Beastie Book & Puppet. 1997. (Illus.). (J). (ps-3). pap. 10.95 (*0-7868-1228-1*) Disney Pr.

—Simon's Book. (Illus.). (J). (gr. k-3). 1983. 32p. 16.00 o.p. (*0-688-02085-2*); 1983. 32p. lib. bdg. 15.93 o.p. (*0-688-02086-0*); 1991. 40p. reprint ed. pap. 6.95 (*0-688-10484-3*, HarperTempest) HarperCollins Children's Bk. Group.

—Simon's Book. 1987. 40p. (J). (gr. k-3). 3.95 o.p. (*0-590-41934-X*) Scholastic, Inc.

Driscoll, Edwin. Alf & the Red-Eyed Yellow Monster. 1985. (J). (gr. k-4). 3.50 o.p. (*0-89536-942-7*, 7559) CSS Publishing Co.

Miscellaneous

Druce, Arden. Witch, Witch. 1991. (Child's Play Library). (Illus.). 32p. (J). (ps-3). 13.99 (*0-85953-780-3*) Child's Play of England GBR. *Dist:* Child's Play-International.

Duchesne, Christiane. Nox & Archimusse in the Monsters' Feast. Perkes, Carolyn, tr. 2000. (Illus.). (ps-3). pap. (*1-894363-20-5*) Dominique & Friends.

Duey, Kathleen. Boogeyman in the Basement! 2000. (Alone in the Dark Ser.). (Illus.). 32p. (J). pap. 3.95 (*1-891100-12-2*) Smart Kids Publishing.

—Nowhere to Run, Nowhere to Hide! 2000. (Alone in the Dark Ser.). (Illus.). 32p. (J). pap. 3.95 (*1-891100-14-9*) Smart Kids Publishing.

Duey, Kathleen & Berry, Ron. Crassy the Crude Beastie. 2000. (Beastie Buddies Ser.). (Illus.). 32p. (J). (ps-3). pap. 3.95 (*1-891100-28-9*) Smart Kids Publishing.

—Glumby the Grumbling Beastie. 2000. (Beastie Buddies Ser.). (Illus.). 32p. (J). (ps-3). mass mkt. 3.95 (*1-891100-27-0*) Smart Kids Publishing.

Duncan, Jane. Janet Reachfar & the Kelpie. 2002. (Illus.). 32p. (J). (gr. k-3). pap. 7.95 (*1-84158-210-7*) Birlinn, Ltd. GBR. *Dist:* Interlink Publishing Group, Inc.

Dussling, Jennifer. In a Dark Dark House. 1999. (Illus.). (J). (ps-k). pap. 11.05 (*0-613-12772-2*) Econo-Clad Bks.

—In a Dark, Dark House. 1995. (All Aboard Reading Ser.). (Illus.). 32p. (J). (ps-1). 3.99 (*0-448-40970-4*, Grosset & Dunlap) Penguin Putnam Bks. for Young Readers.

Dyer, Sarah. Five Little Fiends. 2002. (Illus.). (J). 15.95 (*1-58234-751-4*, Bloomsbury Children) Bloomsbury Publishing.

Eaton, Deborah. Monster Songs. 1999. (Real Kids Readers Ser.). (Illus.). 32p. (J). (gr. k-2). 18.90 (*0-7613-2054-7*); pap. 4.99 (*0-7613-2079-2*) Millbrook Pr., Inc.

—Monster Songs. 1999. (J). 10.14 (*0-606-19162-3*) Turtleback Bks.

—Monster Songs. 1999. E-Book (*1-58824-726-0*); E-Book (*1-58824-808-9*); E-Book (*1-58824-478-4*) ipicturebooks, LLC.

Eaton, Tom. Monster Mazes. 1981. (Pretzel Ser.). (Illus.). 64p. (Orig.). (J). (gr. 4-6). pap. 1.25 o.p. (*0-590-32117-X*) Scholastic, Inc.

Eccles, Jane. Maxwell's Birthday. 1992. (Illus.). 32p. (J). (ps-3). 14.00 o.p. (*0-688-11036-3*); lib. bdg. 13.93 o.p. (*0-688-11037-1*) Morrow/Avon. (Morrow, William & Co.).

Eifrig, Kate. Scary Monster. 1998. (Illus.). 8p. (J). (gr. k-1). pap. 4.95 (*1-879835-29-0*, Kaeden Bks.) Kaeden Corp.

Elec. In Search of Monsters. 1995. (J). pap. 12.95 (*0-689-71890-X*, Aladdin) Simon & Schuster Children's Publishing.

Elgar, Susan. The Brothers Gruesome. 2000. (Illus.). 32p. (J). (ps-3). 15.00 o.p. (*0-618-00515-3*) Houghton Mifflin Co.

Elliott, David. Hazel Nutt, Mad Scientist. 2003. (Illus.). (J). (gr. k-3). 16.95 (*0-8234-1711-5*) Holiday Hse., Inc.

Elmo & the Monsters. 2001. (J). text (*1-931312-39-7*) SoftPlay, Inc.

Elwod, Roger, ed. The Fifty-Meter Monsters & other Horrors. 1976. (J). (gr. 5-7). pap. (*0-671-29794-5*, Simon Pulse) Simon & Schuster Children's Publishing.

Emberley, Ed E. Glad Monster, Sad Monster: A Book about Feelings. 1997. (J). 14.95 o.p. (*0-316-23393-5*); (Illus.). 32p. 15.95 (*0-316-57395-7*) Little Brown & Co.

—Go Away, Big Green Monster! 1993. (Illus.). 32p. (J). (ps-3). 15.95 (*0-316-23653-5*) Little Brown & Co.

Emmett, Jonathan. Ten Little Monsters. 2001. (Illus.). 12p. (J). (ps-ps). tchr. ed., bds. 10.95 (*0-7534-5333-9*, Kingfisher) Houghton Mifflin Co. Trade & Reference Div.

—Ten Little Monsters. 2000. (Illus.). 12p. (J). (ps). tchr. ed. (*0-7534-0452-4*) Kingfisher Publications, plc.

—Ten Little Monsters Counting Box. 2002. (Illus.). 22p. (J). (-ps). tchr. ed. 16.95 (*0-7534-5562-5*, Kingfisher) Houghton Mifflin Co. Trade & Reference Div.

Emmett, Jonathan & Parker, Ant. Ten Little Monsters. 2000. (I Am Reading Bks.). (Illus.). 48p. (J). (gr. k-3). pap. 3.95 o.p. (*0-7534-5284-7*) Larousse Kingfisher Chambers, Inc.

Empty Scary, Spooky Monster Station. 1996. (J). (*0-8069-9589-0*) Sterling Publishing Co., Inc.

Engle, Marty M. & Barnes, Johnny Ray, Jr. The Last One In. l.t. ed. 1996. (Strange Matter Ser.: No. 5). 124p. (J). (gr. 4-6). lib. bdg. 21.27 o.p. (*0-8368-1671-4*) Stevens, Gareth Inc.

—A Place to Hide. l.t. ed. 1996. (Strange Matter Ser.: No. 4). 124p. (J). (gr. 4-6). lib. bdg. 21.27 o.p. (*0-8368-1670-6*) Stevens, Gareth Inc.

Ericksen, Claire, ed. A Monster Is Bigger Than 9. 1991. (Illus.). 48p. (J). pap. 8.95 o.s.i (*0-88138-099-7*, Aladdin) Simon & Schuster Children's Publishing.

Ering, Timothy B. The Story of Frog Belly Rat Bone. 2003. (Illus.). 48p. (J). 16.99 (*0-7636-1382-7*) Candlewick Pr.

Euvremer, Teryl. Triple Whammy. 1993. (Illus.). 32p. (J). (gr. k-4). 15.00 (*0-06-021060-5*); lib. bdg. 14.89 (*0-06-021061-3*) HarperCollins Children's Bk. Group.

Evans, Nate. Monster Maker. 1994. (Illus.). 8p. (J). (ps-3). mass mkt. 2.95 (*0-590-48393-5*, Cartwheel Bks.) Scholastic, Inc.

Evans, Nate, illus. Monster Party. 2000. (Glitter Tattoos Ser.). 24p. (ps-3). pap. 3.99 (*0-448-42185-2*) Penguin Putnam Bks. for Young Readers.

Everett, Felicity. Monster Gang. 1995. (Usborne Reading for Beginners Ser.). (Illus.). 24p. (J). (gr. k-4). pap. 4.95 (*0-7460-1460-0*); lib. bdg. 12.95 (*0-88110-728-X*) EDC Publishing. (Usborne).

Excuse Me, Are You a Dragon? 2002. (Illus.). 32p. (J). (gr. k-3). reprint ed. 16.95 (*1-880851-34-2*) Greene Bark Pr., Inc.

Eyen, Jennifer. Monster Stew. (Illus.). 64p. (Orig.). (J). (gr. 1-4). 1990. pap. text 0.99 o.p. (*0-87406-436-8*); 3rd ed. 1997. reprint ed. pap. 3.50 (*0-87406-834-7*, Willowisp Pr.) Darby Creek Publishing.

Farber, Erica. Headless Gargoyle. 1996. (Critters of the Night Ser.). 9.19 o.p. (*0-606-11448-3*) Turtleback Bks.

—Night of the Walking Dead. 1997. (Mercer Mayer's Critters of the Night Ser.). (J). Prt. 1. 10.19 o.p. (*0-606-13001-2*); Prt. 2. 10.19 o.p. (*0-606-13002-0*) Turtleback Bks.

Farber, Erica & Sansevere, J. R. The Headless Gargoyle. 1996. (Mercer Mayer's Critters of the Night Ser.). (Illus.). 72p. (ps-3). pap. 3.99 o.s.i (*0-679-87362-7*, Random Hse. Bks. for Young Readers) Random Hse. Children's Bks.

—The Vampire Brides. 1996. (Mercer Mayer's Critters of the Night Ser.). (Illus.). 72p. (J). (ps-3). pap. 3.99 o.s.i (*0-679-87360-0*, Random Hse. Bks. for Young Readers) Random Hse. Children's Bks.

Farber, Erica, et al. Zombies Don't Do Windows. 1996. (Creepy Critters Ser.). (Illus.). 80p. (J). (gr. 1-5). pap. 3.99 o.s.i (*0-679-87361-9*, Random Hse. Bks. for Young Readers) Random Hse. Children's Bks.

Farnsworth, Susan A. The Mogollon Monster: Arizona's Bigfoot. 1996. (Illus.). 130p. (YA). pap. text 14.95 (*1-881260-09-7*) Southwest Pubns.

Faulkner, Keith. Monster in My Bathroom. 1993. (Little Monsters Ser.). (Illus.). 16p. (J). (ps-3). 4.99 o.p. (*0-8431-3482-8*, Price Stern Sloan) Penguin Putnam Bks. for Young Readers.

—Monster in My Toybox. 1993. (Little Monsters Ser.). (Illus.). 16p. (J). (ps-3). 4.99 o.p. (*0-8431-3481-X*, Price Stern Sloan) Penguin Putnam Bks. for Young Readers.

—The Monster Who Loved Books. 2002. (Illus.). 16p. (J). (ps-k). pap. 10.95 (*0-439-34099-3*, Orchard Bks.) Scholastic, Inc.

Fisher, Leonard Everett. Cyclops. 1991. (Illus.). (J). (ps-3). pap. 5.95 (*0-8234-1062-5*) Holiday Hse., Inc.

Fisher, Lucretia. Two Monsters: A Fable. 1976. (Illus.). 48p. (J). (ps up). pap. 3.95 o.p. (*0-916144-08-9*) Stemmer Hse. Pubs., Inc.

Fisk, Nicholas. Monster Maker. l.t. ed. 1986. (J). (gr. 4-6). 16.95 o.p. (*0-7451-0301-4*, Galaxy Children's Large Print) BBC Audiobooks America.

Fleetwood, Tamela. Nellie Jelly & the Jelly Well, No. 1. 2000. 32p. (J). lib. bdg. 10.95 (*0-9702128-0-1*) Odditeas, Inc.

Flora, James. The Great Green Turkey Creek Monster. 1979. (Illus.). 32p. (J). (gr. k-4). pap. 1.95 o.s.i (*0-689-70459-3*, Simon & Schuster Children's Publishing) Simon & Schuster Children's Publishing.

Florian, Douglas. Monster Motel. 1996. (Illus.). 32p. (J). (ps-3). pap. 6.00 (*0-15-201386-5*, Harcourt Paperbacks) Harcourt Children's Bks.

—Monster Motel. 1996. 11.15 (*0-606-11632-X*) Turtleback Bks.

Flynn, Kieran. Monster Jam. 1998. (Screammates Ser.: Vol. 3). (J). mass mkt. 3.99 (*0-590-09896-9*, Scholastic Paperbacks) Scholastic, Inc.

Fontes, Justine & Fontes, Ron. The Wolf Man. 1992. (Illus.). 96p. (J). (gr. 3-7). pap. o.p. (*0-307-22336-1*, 22336, Golden Bks.) Random Hse. Children's Bks.

Ford, Barbara. Creature in Crestwood Park. 1996. 9.15 o.p. (*0-606-09169-6*) Turtleback Bks.

Forte, Imogene & MacKenzie, Joy. Monsters Come in Several Sizes. 1979. (Days of Wonder Ser.). (Illus.). 64p. (J). (gr. k-5). pap. 2.95 o.p. (*0-913916-91-9*, IP 91-9) Incentive Pubns., Inc.

Francis, Anna B. Pleasant Dreams, ERS. 1983. (Illus.). 32p. (J). (gr. k-2). o.p. (*0-03-060574-1*, Holt, Henry & Co. Bks. For Young Readers) Holt, Henry & Co.

Freedman, Sally. Monster Birthday Party. Tucker, Kathleen, ed. 1983. (Just for Fun Bks.). (Illus.). 32p. (J). (gr. k-3). lib. bdg. 12.95 o.p. (*0-8075-5259-3*) Whitman, Albert & Co.

Fromme, Charl. The Monster Costume Party. 1995. (Doll Book). (Illus.). 8p. (J). (ps-1). bds. 4.95 o.p. (*1-56293-805-3*, McClanahan Bk.) Learning Horizons, Inc.

Fry, Rosalie K. Mungo, RS. 1972. (Illus.). 128p. (J). (gr. 4 up). 4.95 o.p. (*0-374-35097-3*, Farrar, Straus & Giroux (BYR)) Farrar, Straus & Giroux.

Gackenbach, Dick. Harry y el Terrible Quiensabeque (Harry & the Terrible Whatzit) 1987. (J). pap. 1.95 o.p. (*0-590-12116-2*) Scholastic, Inc.

Galdone, Paul. The Monster & the Tailor. 1982. (Illus.). 32p. (J). (ps-3). 14.95 o.p. (*0-89919-116-9*, Clarion Bks.) Houghton Mifflin Co. Trade & Reference Div.

Galouchko, Annouchka Gravel. Sho & the Demons of the Deep. 1998. (Illus.). 32p. (J). (gr. 2-3). pap. 6.95 (*1-55037-393-5*) Annick Pr., Ltd. CAN. *Dist:* Firefly Bks., Ltd.

Gambill, Henrietta. Happy Times with the Lollipop Dragon. 1982. (Happy Day Bks.). (Illus.). 24p. (Orig.). (J). (ps-3). pap. 1.59 o.p. (*0-87239-538-3*, 3584) Standard Publishing.

Games, Sonia. Welcome to the Underground & Other Stories. 1996. 100p. (J). (gr. 3-8). mass mkt. 3.95 (*0-9650736-0-2*) Super Bks. & Tapes.

Gantos, Jack & Rubel, Nicole. Greedy Greeny. 1979. (Illus.). 8.95 o.p. (*0-385-14685-X*); lib. bdg. 8.95 o.p. (*0-385-14686-8*) Doubleday Publishing.

Garden, Nancy. Mystery of the Night Raiders. 1991. (Monster Hunters Ser.: Case 1). 176p. (J). pap. 2.99 (*0-671-70734-5*, Aladdin) Simon & Schuster Children's Publishing.

—Mystery of the Night Raiders. MacDonald, Patricia, ed. 1991. (Monster Hunters Ser.: No. 1). 176p. (J). reprint ed. per. 2.99 (*0-671-76064-5*, Aladdin) Simon & Schuster Children's Publishing.

—The Mystery of the Night Raiders, RS. 1987. (Monster Hunters Ser.: No. 1). 144p. (J). (gr. 4-7). 14.00 o.p. (*0-374-35221-6*, Farrar, Straus & Giroux (BYR)) Farrar, Straus & Giroux.

Gardner, Brandy. Monster Spray. Gardner, Greg, ed. & illus. by. 1998. 20p. (J). (ps-2). pap. 4.95 (*0-9667770-0-X*) New Horizons Pr.

Garmon, Larry Mike. Bride of Frankenstein: Vow of Vengence. 2002. (Universal Monsters Ser.: No. 6). 192p. (J). mass mkt. 4.50 (*0-439-40229-8*) Scholastic, Inc.

—Creature from the Black Lagoon: Black Water Horror. 2002. (Illus.). 192p. (J). mass mkt. 4.50 (*0-439-40228-X*) Scholastic, Inc.

—The Wolf Man: Blood Moon Rising. 2001. (Universal Monsters Ser.: No. 2). 160p. (J). (gr. 5 up). mass mkt. 4.50 (*0-439-20847-5*) Scholastic, Inc.

Gauch, Patricia L. Dragons on the Road. 1986. (YA). (gr. 7-10). pap. (*0-671-61775-3*, Simon Pulse) Simon & Schuster Children's Publishing.

Gelsey, James. Scooby-Doo & the Frankenstein Monster. 2000. (Scooby-Doo Mysteries Ser.: No. 12). (Illus.). 64p. (J). (ps-3). mass mkt. 3.99 (*0-439-18876-8*) Scholastic, Inc.

—Scooby-Doo & the Snow Monster. 1999. (Scooby-Doo Mysteries Ser.: No. 3). (Illus.). 57p. (J). (ps-3). mass mkt. 3.99 (*0-590-81914-3*, Scholastic Paperbacks) Scholastic, Inc.

Geoghegan, Adrienne. There's a Wardrobe in My Monster! 1999. (Picture Bks.). (Illus.). 28p. (J). (ps-3). lib. bdg. 15.95 (*1-57505-414-0*, Carolrhoda Bks.) Lerner Publishing Group.

Geringer, Laura. Look Out, Look Out, It's Coming! 1992. (Illus.). 40p. (J). (ps-2). 15.00 (*0-06-021711-1*); lib. bdg. 14.89 (*0-06-021712-X*) HarperCollins Children's Bk. Group.

Giants. 1980. (Illus.). 48p. (J). (gr. 1-7). 5.95 o.p. (*0-448-47486-7*, Grosset & Dunlap) Penguin Putnam Bks. for Young Readers.

Gifford, Griselda. Miranda's Monster. 1988. (Illus.). 28p. (J). (gr. k-2). text 15.95 o.p. (*0-340-41156-2*) Hodder & Stoughton, Ltd. GBR. *Dist:* Lubrecht & Cramer, Ltd., Trafalgar Square.

Gilden, Mel. Fifth Grade Monsters No. 12: Werewolf Come Home. 1990. (Camelot Bks.). (J). pap. 2.75 (*0-380-75908-X*, Avon Bks.) Morrow/Avon.

—Fifth Grade Monsters No. 13: Monster Boy. 1991. 96p. (J). pap. 2.95 (*0-380-76305-2*, Avon Bks.) Morrow/Avon.

—Fifth Grade Monsters No. 14: Troll Patrol. 1991. 96p. (Orig.). (J). pap. 2.95 (*0-380-76306-0*, Avon Bks.) Morrow/Avon.

—How to Be a Vampire in One Easy Lesson. 1990. (Fifth Grade Monsters Ser.: No. 10). (J). pap. 2.75 (*0-380-75906-3*, Avon Bks.) Morrow/Avon.

—Island of the Weird. 1990. (Fifth Grade Monsters Ser.: No. 11). 96p. (J). pap. 2.95 (*0-380-75907-1*, Avon Bks.) Morrow/Avon.

—M Is for Monster. 1987. 96p. (J). pap. 2.75 (*0-380-75423-1*, Avon Bks.) Morrow/Avon.

—The Monster in Creeps Head Bay. 1990. (Fifth Grade Monsters Ser.: No. 9). 96p. (J). pap. 2.75 (*0-380-75905-5*, Avon Bks.) Morrow/Avon.

—The Pet of Frankenstein. 1988. 96p. (J). (gr. 3-7). pap. 2.50 (*0-380-75185-2*, Avon Bks.) Morrow/Avon.

—Z Is for Zombie. 1988. (Fifth Grade Monsters Ser.: No. 5). 96p. (J). (gr. 3-7). pap. 2.75 (*0-380-75686-2*, Avon Bks.) Morrow/Avon.

Gill, Janice. Monster Stew. 1997. pap. 4.95 (*0-89868-370-X*) ARO Publishing Co.

Gilman, Phoebe. Jillian Jiggs to the Rescue. ed. 1996. (J). (gr. 2). spiral bd. (*0-616-01656-5*) Canadian National Institute for the Blind/Institut National Canadien pour les Aveugles.

Gilmour, H. B. Curse of Katana. 1996. (Real Monsters Ser.: 2). 64p. (J). (gr. 2-5). 3.99 (*0-689-80870-4*, Simon Spotlight) Simon & Schuster Children's Publishing.

—Godzilla: A Junior Novelization. novel ed. 1998. (Godzilla Ser.). 88p. (J). (gr. 1-4). mass mkt. 3.99 (*0-590-68091-9*) Scholastic, Inc.

Ginsberg, Ben. The Sibling Rivalry Monster. 1985. (Illus.). 48p. (Orig.). (J). (gr. 1-3). 6.95 o.p. (*0-89594-184-8*) Crossing Pr., Inc., The.

Glover, Susanne & Grewe, Georgeann. The Tax Monster. 1986. (J). (gr. 5-9). o.p. (*0-916456-94-3*, GA 185, Good Apple) McGraw-Hill Children's Publishing.

Glumby the Grumbling Beastie. 2001. (Beastie Buddies Ser.). (Illus.). 32p. (J). 6.95 (*1-891100-85-8*) Smart Kids Publishing.

Glusha, Laura & Muldrew, Karen. Sea Creature Kit: Shadow, Stick or Rod Puppet Workshop. 1997. (Illus.). 16p. (Orig.). (J). (gr. k-2). pap., wbk. ed. 8.00 (*1-890972-03-7*, KIN - SC) Nature's Shadows.

Godden, Rumer. The Dragon of Og. 1981. (Illus.). 64p. (J). (gr. 4-6). 9.95 o.p. (*0-670-28168-9*, Viking Children's Bks.) Penguin Putnam Bks. for Young Readers.

Godfrey, Martyn. More Monsters in School. 1999. (First Flight Ser.). (Illus.). (J). pap. (*1-55041-506-9*) Fitzhenry & Whiteside, Ltd.

Godfrey, Martyn N. Is It Ok If This Monster Stays for Lunch? unabr. ed. 1992. (Illus.). 32p. (J). (ps up). pap. (*0-19-540882-9*) Stoddart Kids.

Golden Books Family Entertainment Staff. Beauty & the Beast. 9999. (Illus.). (J). o.p. (*0-307-05535-3*, Golden Bks.) Random Hse. Children's Bks.

Golden Books Staff. I Am a Monster. 1999. (Golden Sturdy Bks.). (Illus.). 24p. (J). (ps-3). bds. 4.99 o.s.i (*0-307-12139-9*, Golden Bks.) Random Hse. Children's Bks.

—Me, Cookie! 1999. (Little Golden Bks.). (Illus.). 24p. (J). (ps-2). 2.29 o.s.i (*0-307-30218-0*, Golden Bks.) Random Hse. Children's Bks.

—Meet the Monsters. 2003. 32p. (J). pap. 3.99 (*0-307-10119-3*, Golden Bks.) Random Hse. Children's Bks.

—Monster Hunter's Guidebook. 2000. (Illus.). 32p. (J). (ps-3). pap. 3.99 o.s.i (*0-307-10476-1*, Golden Bks.) Random Hse. Children's Bks.

Golden Books Staff, ed. The Monsters' Picnic. 1997. (Golden's Sesame Street Ser.). 24p. (J). 2.29 o.s.i (*0-307-00109-1*, Golden Bks.) Random Hse. Children's Bks.

Gollub, Matthew. Ten Oni Drummers. 2000. (ENG & JPN., Illus.). 32p. (J). (ps-3). 15.95 (*1-58430-011-6*) Lee & Low Bks., Inc.

Gondosch, Linda. The Monsters of Marble Avenue. 1990. (J). (gr. 4-7). pap. 2.95 o.p. (*0-316-31992-9*, Joy Street Bks.) Little Brown & Co.

Goode, Molly. How the Grinch Got So Grinchy. 2000. (Step into Reading Step 2 Bks.). (Illus.). (J). pap. 3.99 (*0-375-81226-1*) Random Hse., Inc.

Goode, Molly, et al. How the Grinch Got So Grinchy. 2000. (Step into Reading Step 2 Bks.). (Illus.). 48p. (ps-3). 11.99 (*0-375-91226-6*) Random Hse., Inc.

Gordon, Sheila. A Monster in the Mailbox. 1978. (Illus.). (J). (gr. 2-4). 8.25 o.p. (*0-525-35150-7*, 0801-240, Dutton) Dutton/Plume.

Gordon, Wendy. I'm Safe! from Monsters. 1999. (I'm Safe! Ser.). (Illus.). 32p. (J). (ps-3). pap. 6.95 (*1-891596-02-0*) BackYard Bks.

—I'm Safe! from Monsters: Activity Book. 1999. 24p. (ps-3). pap. 2.95 (*1-891596-03-9*) Backyard Pub. Co., Inc.

Grabis, Bettina. Bobbo the Basement Monster. 1999. Tr. of Bobbo das Kellermonster. (Illus.). 100p. (J). (gr. 2-4). pap. 6.95 (*1-889658-09-X*) New Canaan Publishing Co., Inc.

Graham, Richard. Jack & the Monster. 1989. (Illus.). (J). (ps-3). 13.95 o.p. (*0-395-49680-2*) Houghton Mifflin Co.

Gramatky, Hardie & Gramatky, Dorothea C. Little Toot & the Loch Ness Monster. 1989. (Illus.). 48p. (J). (ps-3). 13.95 o.p. (*0-399-21684-7*, G. P. Putnam's Sons) Penguin Putnam Bks. for Young Readers.

Grant, Cynthia D. Uncle Vampire. 1995. (Illus.). (YA). (gr. 7 up). pap. 4.99 o.s.i (*0-679-86726-0*) Random Hse., Inc.

Grant, Joan. The Monster Who Grew Small. 1993. (Short Stories Ser.). 32p. (YA). (gr. 5 up). lib. bdg. 18.60 o.p. (*0-88682-343-9*, Creative Education) Creative Co., The.

Grant, John. Frankenstein. 1997. (Library of Fear, Fantasy & Adventure). (Illus.). 96p. (YA). (gr. 5 up). pap. 9.95 (*0-7460-2725-7*, Usborne) EDC Publishing.

Graves, Keith. Frank Was a Monster Who Wanted to Dance. 1999. (Illus.). 32p. (J). (ps-3). 13.95 (*0-8118-2169-2*) Chronicle Bks. LLC.

Greaves, Margaret. The Serpent Shell. 1993. (Illus.). 32p. (J). (ps-3). 13.95 o.p. (*0-8120-6350-3*) Barron's Educational Series, Inc.

Greenberg, Jan. No Dragons to Slay, RS. 1984. 152p. (J). (gr. 7 up). pap. 3.95 o.p. (*0-374-45509-0*, Sunburst) Farrar, Straus & Giroux.

Greenblat, Rodney A. Slombo the Gross. 1993. (Illus.). 32p. (J). (ps-3). 15.00 o.p. (*0-06-020775-2*); lib. bdg. 14.89 (*0-06-020776-0*) HarperCollins Children's Bk. Group.

Greene, Rhonda Gowler. Eek! Creak! Snicker, Sneak. 2002. (Illus.). 32p. (J). (ps-2). 16.00 (*0-689-83047-5*, Atheneum) Simon & Schuster Children's Publishing.

Greenleaf, Ann. The Halloween on Hawthorne Street: Too Many Monsters. 1993. (J). 2.99 o.s.i (*0-517-09158-5*) Random Hse. Value Publishing.

Greenlow, Jean. The Droopy Dragon. 1982. (Texas Instruments Magic Wand Speaking Library). (Illus.). 48p. (J). (ps-3). text 7.30 o.p. (*0-89512-063-1*) Texas Instruments, Inc.

Gresko, Marcia S. Monster Stew, Vol. 4474. Kupperstein, Joel, ed. 1998. (Learn to Read Math Ser.). (Illus.). 16p. (J). pap. 2.75 (*1-57471-381-7*, 4474) Creative Teaching Pr., Inc.

Groves. Pond Monster, Bk. 5A. Date not set. (J). pap. text 129.15 (*0-582-18796-6*) Addison-Wesley Longman, Ltd. GBR. *Dist:* Trans-Atlantic Pubns., Inc.

Gruesome, Gertrude. The Curse of Cleo Patrick's Mummy. 1996. (Monsterkids Ser.: No. 5). (Illus.). 64p. (J). mass mkt. 3.50 o.p. (*0-06-106310-X*) HarperCollins Pubs.

—Frank's Field Trip. 1995. (Monsterkids Ser.: No. 2). (Illus.). 64p. (J). mass mkt. 2.99 o.p. (*0-06-106237-5*, HarperTorch) Morrow/Avon.

—Zelda's Zombie Dance. 1996. (Monsterkids Ser.: No. 6). 64p. (J). mass mkt. 3.50 o.p. (*0-06-106311-8*) HarperCollins Pubs.

The Grumpus under Rug. 1991. (Illus.). (J). (ps-2). pap. 5.10 (*0-8136-5614-1*); lib. bdg. 7.95 (*0-8136-5114-X*) Modern Curriculum Pr.

Gutman, Dan. The Green Monster in Left Field. 1997. (Tales from the Sandlot Ser.: No. 2). (J). (gr. 3-7). 10.04 (*0-606-11967-1*) Turtleback Bks.

Hague, Michael. Beauty & the Beast, Vol. 1. 1983. (J). 12.95 o.p. (*0-03-064076-8*, Holt, Henry & Co. Bks. For Young Readers) Holt, Henry & Co.

Hahn, Jane E. & Mealy, Virginia T. The Monster Research Book. 1983. (Illus.). 32p. (J). (gr. 3-6). pap. 3.95 o.p. (*0-913839-07-8*) Pieces of Learning.

Hall, Katy & Eisenberg, Lisa. A Gallery of Monsters. 1981. (Illus.). 64p. (J). (gr. 2-5). pap. 2.95 o.p. (*0-394-84743-1*) Random Hse., Inc.

Hall, Kirsten. Boo! 1995. (My First Reader Ser.). (Illus.). 28p. (J). mass mkt. 16.00 o.p. (*0-516-05370-1*, Children's Pr.) Scholastic Library Publishing.

Hall, Lynn. A New Day for Dragons. 1976. (Illus.). (J). pap. 1.25 o.p. (*0-380-00763-0*, 30528, Avon Bks.) Morrow/Avon.

Hall, Starr. Jopalbers & Goodles: Face Your Fears. Hall, Grady, ed. 1998. (Monster Ser.). (Illus.). 62p. (J). (gr. k-4). 19.95 (*0-9651678-9-5*) Simply Angels Creative Pr. & Design.

Hamilton, John. Mission to Mars, 6 bks. Incl. Future Missions to Mars. lib. bdg. 24.21 (*1-56239-832-6*); Mariner Missions to Mars. lib. bdg. 24.21 (*1-56239-828-8*); Mars Myths & Legends. lib. bdg. 24.21 (*1-56239-827-X*); Pathfinder Mission to Mars. lib. bdg. 24.21 (*1-56239-831-8*); Search for Life on Mars. lib. bdg. 24.21 (*1-56239-830-X*); Viking Missions to Mars. lib. bdg. 24.21 (*1-56239-829-6*); 32p. (J). (gr. 5). 1998. (Illus.). Set lib. bdg. 136.68 (*1-57765-258-4*, ABDO & Daughters) ABDO Publishing Co.

Hardgrove, Micheal. The Ogre & the Angel: To Go & Tell Somebody. Hardgrove, J. Franklin, ed. 1998. (Illus.). 32p. (J). (ps-6). pap. 12.95 (*0-9660797-2-8*, OAA) Tiwinke Publishing, Inc.

Harrell, Janice. Blood Reunion. 1995. (Vampire Twins Ser.: No. 4). 240p. (J). mass mkt. 3.99 o.p. (*0-06-106283-9*, HarperTorch) Morrow/Avon.

—Blood Spell. 1995. (Vampire's Love Ser.: No. 2). (J). mass mkt. 3.99 (*0-590-60390-6*) Scholastic, Inc.

Harrington, Sean P. Patterson & the Great Green Greedy Galumpus. 2000. (Illus.). 20p. (J). (gr. k-4). pap. 10.95 (*0-9672290-2-2*) Harrington, Denis J. Pub.

Harris, Emma. Bedtime, Little Monsters! 2002. (Illus.). 20p. (J). tchr. ed. 14.95 (*1-58925-689-1*, Tiger Tales) ME Media LLC.

Harris, Sarah, adapted by. La Belle et la Bete - Beauty & the Beast. 1995. (Comes to Life Bks.). (ENG & FRE.). 16p. (J). (ps-2). (*1-57234-045-2*) YES! Entertainment Corp.

Harry & the Hendersons. 1987. (J). pap. 1.50 o.s.i (*0-440-82048-0*) Dell Publishing.

Hart, Tessa & Sergi, Frank. The Snarth Goes to School. 2000. (Illus.). 48p. (J). (gr. k-5). 18.95 (*0-9660172-0-X*) Brookfield Reader, Inc., The.

Hawcock, David. Frankenstein. 1999. (Illus.). (J). 15.99 (*0-7636-0888-2*) Candlewick Pr.

Hawkes, Kevin. Then the Troll Heard the Squeak. 1991. (J). (ps-3). lib. bdg. 13.88 o.p. (*0-688-09758-8*) HarperCollins Children's Bk. Group.

Hawkins, Colin & Hawkins, Jacqui. Snap! Snap! 1984. (Illus.). 32p. (J). (ps-3). 9.95 o.s.i (*0-399-21163-2*); 4.95 o.s.i (*0-399-21184-5*) Penguin Putnam Bks. for Young Readers. (G. P. Putnam's Sons).

Hayes, Geoffrey. The Night of the Circus Monsters. 1996. (Step into Reading Ser.). (Illus.). 48p. (gr. 2-3). pap. 3.99 (*0-679-87113-6*) McKay, David Co., Inc.

—Swamp of the Hideous Zombies. 1996. (Graveyard Creeper Mystery Ser.: No. 1). (J). (ps-3). 11.99 o.s.i (*0-679-97696-5*); 72p. (gr. 1-4). pap. 3.99 o.s.i (*0-679-87696-0*) Random Hse., Inc.

—Swamp of the Hideous Zombies. 1996. (Graveyard Creeper Mystery Ser.). 10.14 (*0-606-11415-7*) Turtleback Bks.

Hayward, Linda. The Biggest Cookie in the World. (Step into Reading Ser.). (Illus.). (J). (ps-3). 1995. 31p. 11.99 o.s.i (*0-679-97146-7*); 1995. 31p. pap. 3.99 (*0-679-87146-2*); 1989. 24p. 2.25 o.s.i (*0-394-84049-6*) Random Hse. Children's Bks. (Random Hse. Bks. for Young Readers).

—The Biggest Cookie in the World. 1995. (Step into Reading Step 1 Bks.). (J). (ps-1). 9.19 o.p. (*0-606-07288-8*) Turtleback Bks.

Heck, Elisabeth. Mirko y el Mamut (Mirko & the Mammoth) 1995. (SPA.). (J). (gr. 5-6). 5.99 (*968-16-4725-4*) Fondo de Cultura Economica MEX. *Dist:* Continental Bk. Co., Inc.

Heide, Florence P. & Heide, Roxanne. A Monster Is Coming! A Monster Is Coming! 1980. (gr. k-3). lib. bdg. 8.60 o.p. (*0-531-04136-0*, Watts, Franklin) Scholastic Library Publishing.

Heimberg, Justin. Shrek Scratch n' Stink Storybook. 2002. (Illus.). pap. 7.99 (*0-525-46937-0*, Dutton Children's Bks.) Penguin Putnam Bks. for Young Readers.

Heinz, Brian J. The Monsters' Test. 1996. (Single Titles Ser.). (Illus.). 32p. (gr. k-3). lib. bdg. 24.90 (*0-7613-0050-3*); (J). 14.95 o.p. (*0-7613-0095-3*) Millbrook Pr., Inc.

Heller, Nicholas. The Monster in the Cave. 1987. (Illus.). 32p. (J). (ps-3). 12.95 o.p. (*0-688-07313-1*); lib. bdg. 12.88 o.p. (*0-688-07314-X*) HarperCollins Children's Bk. Group. (Greenwillow Bks.).

—Ogres! Ogres! Ogres! A Feasting Frenzy from A to Z. 1999. (Illus.). 32p. (J). (gr. k-3). 16.95 (*0-688-16986-4*); 16.95 (*0-688-16986-4*); lib. bdg. 16.89 (*0-688-16987-2*) HarperCollins Children's Bk. Group. (Greenwillow Bks.).

Henderson Publishing Staff. Frankenstein. 1997. (FunFax Horror Ser.). (Illus.). (J). (gr. 3-9). 6.95 o.p. (*0-7894-2285-9*) Dorling Kindersley Publishing, Inc.

Henry, Lawrence. Disney's Gargoyles: Deadly Doubles. 1995. (Look-Look Bks.). (Illus.). 24p. (J). (ps-3). pap. o.p. (*0-307-12917-9*, Golden Bks.) Random Hse. Children's Bks.

Henry, Robert. Universal Monsters: Frankenstein. 1992. (Golden Star Reader Ser.). (Illus.). 48p. (J). (gr. 2-4). pap. 3.25 o.s.i (*0-307-11467-8*, 11467, Golden Bks.) Random Hse. Children's Bks.

Henson, Jim. 1, 2, 3 by Elmo. 2002. 32p. (J). 9.99 (*0-375-81390-X*) Random Hse. Children's Bks.

Here is Lunch with Taz, Bk. 2. 1999. (McGraw-Hill Junior Academic Ser.). (Illus.). 16p. (J). (gr. k-1). pap. 2.99 o.p. (*1-57768-520-2*) McGraw-Hill Children's Publishing.

Herman, Gail. Boo on the Loose. 2002. (Step into Reading Ser.). (Illus.). 48p. (J). (gr. 1-3). lib. bdg. 11.99 (*0-7364-8008-0*, RH/Disney) Random Hse. Children's Bks.

—Double-Header. (All Aboard Reading Ser.). (Illus.). 32p. (J). (ps-1). 2015. 7.99 (*0-448-40156-8*); 1993. 3.99 (*0-448-40157-6*) Penguin Putnam Bks. for Young Readers. (Grosset & Dunlap).

—Double-Header. 1993. (All Aboard Reading Ser.). (J). 10.14 (*0-606-05812-5*) Turtleback Bks.

—The Racecar Monster. 2001. (Scooby-Doo Ser.: No. 8). 32p. (J). (ps-3). mass mkt. 3.99 (*0-439-24236-3*) Scholastic, Inc.

Herman, Gail & Random House Disney Staff. Boo on the Loose! 2002. (Step into Reading Ser.). (Illus.). 48p. (J). (gr. 1-3). pap. 3.99 (*0-7364-1274-3*, RH/Disney) Random Hse. Children's Bks.

Herman, Hank. Monster Jam. 1996. (Super Hoops Ser.: No. 4). (gr. 4-6). (J). pap. 4.75 (*0-553-54251-6*, Dell Books for Young Readers); 96p. pap. text 3.50 o.s.i (*0-553-48276-9*, Skylark) Random Hse. Children's Bks.

—Monster Jam. 1996. (Super Hoops Ser.: No. 4). (J). (gr. 4-6). 8.60 o.p. (*0-606-09915-8*) Turtleback Bks.

Herrera, Juan G., illus. Ogros. 1994. Tr. of Ogres. (SPA.). 89p. (J). (gr. 4-6). 14.99 (*958-07-0314-0*) Santillana COL. *Dist:* T.R. Bks.

Hess, Debra. Are You a Monster? 1995. (Illus.). 32p. (J). (ps-4). 9.95 o.p. (*0-681-00755-9*) Borders Pr.

Hickox, Rebecca. Per & the Dala Horse. 1997. (Picture Yearling Ser.). (Illus.). 32p. (ps-3). pap. text 5.99 o.s.i (*0-440-41425-3*, Dell Books for Young Readers) Random Hse. Children's Bks.

Hiller, B. B. & Hiller, Neil W. Little Monsters. 1989. 96p. (J). (gr. 3 up). pap. 2.95 o.p. (*0-590-42741-5*) Scholastic, Inc.

Himmel, Roger J. How the Lollipop Dragon Got His Name. Manoni, Mary H., ed. 1978. (Adventures of the Lollipop Dragon Ser.). (Illus.). (J). (gr. k-3). pap. text 29.95 o.p. (*0-89290-043-1*) S V E & Churchill Media.

Hindley, Judy. The Perfect Little Monster. 2001. (Illus.). 24p. (J). (ps-1). 10.99 o.s.i (*0-7636-0902-1*); bds. 3.29 (*0-7636-0903-X*) Candlewick Pr.

Hird, Nancy E. Marty's Monster. 1993. (Really Reading! Bks.). (Illus.). 48p. (Orig.). (J). (gr. 1-3). pap. 4.49 o.p. (*0-7847-0098-2*, 03948) Standard Publishing.

Hitchcock, Alfred, ed. Alfred Hitchcock's Monster Museum. 1982. (Illus.). 224p. (J). (gr. 5 up). pap. 4.99 o.s.i (*0-394-84899-3*, Random Hse. Bks. for Young Readers) Random Hse. Children's Bks.

Hoban, Russell. Monsters. (Illus.). 32p. (J). 1993. (ps-2). 4.95 o.p. (*0-590-43421-7*); 1990. (gr. 1-4). 13.95 o.p. (*0-590-43422-5*) Scholastic, Inc.

Hodges, Margaret. Saint George & the Dragon. 1990. (Illus.). 32p. (J). (ps-3). pap. 6.99 (*0-316-36795-8*) Little Brown & Co.

Hogger the Hoarding Beastie. 2001. (Beastie Buddies Ser.). (Illus.). 32p. (J). 6.95 (*1-891100-83-1*) Smart Kids Publishing.

Hoh, Diane. Monster. 1994. (Nightmare Hall Ser.: No. 13). 176p. (YA). (gr. 7-9). mass mkt. 3.50 (*0-590-48321-8*) Scholastic, Inc.

—The Vampire's Kiss. 1995. (Nightmare Hall Ser.: No. 22). 176p. (J). (gr. 7-9). mass mkt. 3.50 (*0-590-25089-2*) Scholastic, Inc.

Hoke, Helen, ed. Weirdies, Weirdies, Weirdies. 1975. (Terrific Triple Titles Ser.). (Illus.). 244p. (gr. 6 up). lib. bdg. 7.90 o.p. (*0-531-02683-3*, Watts, Franklin) Scholastic Library Publishing.

Holden. One Hungry Monster. 2001. (Illus.). 10p. (J). 5.95 (*0-316-64185-5*) Little Brown & Co.

Holder, Bill & Dunn, Harry. Monster Wheels. 1987. (Winning Streak Ser.). (Illus.). 32p. (Orig.). (J). (gr. 3-8). pap. 0.50 o.p. (*0-87406-264-0*) Darby Creek Publishing.

Holland, Jeffrey. Chessie, the Sea Monster That Ate Annapolis. 1990. (Illus.). 32p. (J). (gr. k-4). 8.95 (*0-9618461-0-0*) BaySailor Bks.

Holland, Steve. Frankelstein. 1999. (Kenan & Kel Ser.: No. 6). 128p. (YA). (gr. 4-7). pap. 4.50 (*0-671-03590-8*, Simon Pulse) Simon & Schuster Children's Publishing.

Holub, Joan. Happy Monster Day! 1999. (Read with Me Ser.). (Illus.). 32p. (J). (ps-2). mass mkt. 3.25 (*0-439-06753-7*, Cartwheel Bks.) Scholastic, Inc.

—Happy Monster Day! 1999. (Illus.). (J). 9.40 (*0-606-18555-0*) Turtleback Bks.

Hooks, William H. The Monster from the Sea. 1992. (Bank Street Ready-to-Read Ser.). 32p. (J). (ps-3). 9.99 o.s.i (*0-553-08951-X*); (Illus.). pap. 3.99 o.s.i (*0-553-37024-3*) Bantam Bks.

—The Monster from the Sea. 1997. (Bank Street Reader Collection). (Illus.). 32p. (J). (gr. 1-3). lib. bdg. 21.26 (*0-8368-1694-3*) Stevens, Gareth Inc.

—The Monster from the Sea. (J). E-Book (*1-58824-170-X*); 1992. E-Book (*1-58824-123-8*); 1992. E-Book (*1-59019-308-3*) ipicturebooks, LLC.

—Mr. Monster, Level 3. 1990. (Bank Street Ready-to-Read Ser.). (Illus.). 48p. (J). 9.99 o.s.i (*0-553-05897-5*); pap. 3.99 o.s.i (*0-553-34927-9*) Random Hse. Children's Bks. (Dell Books for Young Readers).

—Mr. Monster. 1998. (Bank Street Reader Collection). (Illus.). 48p. (J). (gr. 2-4). lib. bdg. 21.26 (*0-8368-1774-5*) Stevens, Gareth Inc.

Hopkins, B. G. Kilroy Was Here. 2002. 20p. spiral bd. (*1-55369-029-X*) Trafford Publishing.

Houghton Mifflin Company Staff. The Great Sea Monster. 1990. (Literature Experience 1991 Ser.). (J). (gr. 1). pap. 8.72 (*0-395-55140-4*) Houghton Mifflin Co.

—Monster Tracks. (Literature Experience 1993 Ser.). (J). (gr. 1). 1992. pap. 8.72 (*0-395-61759-6*); 1990. pap. 8.72 (*0-395-55138-2*) Houghton Mifflin Co.

—Swamp Monsters. 1992. (Literature Experience 1993 Ser.). (J). (gr. 2). pap. 9.48 (*0-395-61772-3*) Houghton Mifflin Co.

Howe, David J. Doctor Who - A Book of Monsters: Meet the Monster & Their Makers. 1999. (Doctor Who Ser.). (Illus.). 118p. (J). 29.95 (*0-563-40562-7*) BBC Bk. Publishing GBR. *Dist:* Parkwest Pubns., Inc.

Howe, James. There's a Monster under My Bed. (Illus.). 32p. (J). (ps-3). 1986. 15.00 (*0-689-31178-8*, Atheneum); 1990. reprint ed. pap. 6.99 (*0-689-71409-2*, Aladdin) Simon & Schuster Children's Publishing.

—There's a Monster under My Bed. 1986. 12.14 (*0-606-04827-8*) Turtleback Bks.

Huntley, Chris. The Beast in the Bathroom. 1991. (Illus.). 32p. (J). (ps). (*0-9616679-2-3*) Aquarelle Pr.

Huriet, Genevieve. Aunt Zinnia & the Ogre. 1992. (Illus.). 32p. (J). (gr. k-3). lib. bdg. 21.27 o.p. (*0-8368-0910-6*) Stevens, Gareth Inc.

Hutchins, Pat. It's My Birthday! (Illus.). 32p. (J). (ps-3). 1999. 14.95 (*0-688-09663-8*); 1999. 14.95 (*0-688-09663-8*); 1950. lib. bdg. 14.89 (*0-688-09664-6*) HarperCollins Children's Bk. Group. (Greenwillow Bks.).

—Silly Billy! 1992. (Illus.). 32p. (J). (ps-6). 14.00 o.p. (*0-688-10817-2*); lib. bdg. 14.89 o.s.i (*0-688-10818-0*) HarperCollins Children's Bk. Group. (Greenwillow Bks.).

—Ten Red Apples. 2000. (Illus.). 32p. (J). (ps up). lib. bdg. 15.89 (*0-688-16798-5*, Greenwillow Bks.) HarperCollins Children's Bk. Group.

—Three-Star Billy. 1994. 32p. (J). 15.00 o.s.i (*0-688-13078-X*); (Illus.). lib. bdg. 14.93 o.p. (*0-688-13079-8*) HarperCollins Children's Bk. Group. (Greenwillow Bks.).

—The Very Worst Monster. (Illus.). 32p. (J). (ps-3). 1988. pap. 5.99 (*0-688-07816-8*, Harper Trophy); 1985. 16.00 o.p. (*0-688-04010-1*, Greenwillow Bks.); 1985. 16.89 (*0-688-04011-X*, Greenwillow Bks.) HarperCollins Children's Bk. Group.

—The Very Worst Monster. 1992. (Illus.). (J). pap., tchr. ed. 31.95 incl. audio (*0-87499-292-3*); (gr. 1-3). 24.95 incl. audio (*0-87499-291-5*); (gr. 1-3). 24.95 incl. audio (*0-87499-291-5*); (gr. 1-3). pap. 15.95 incl. audio (*0-87499-290-7*); (gr. 1-3). pap. 15.95 incl. audio (*0-87499-290-7*) Live Oak Media.

—The Very Worst Monster. 1989. (Read with Me Books & Cassettes). (Illus.). (YA). (gr. 1 up). pap. 7.95 o.p. incl. audio (*0-688-09038-9*); pap. 7.95 o.p. incl. audio (*0-688-09038-9*) Morrow/Avon. (Morrow, William & Co.).

—The Very Worst Monster. unabr. ed. 1991. (Illus.). 27p. (J). (ps-2). audio 17.00 (*0-8072-6035-5*, MR 26SP, Listening Library) Random Hse. Audio Publishing Group.

—The Very Worst Monster. 1985. (J). 9.15 o.p. (*0-606-03946-5*) Turtleback Bks.

—The Very Worst Monster. 2000. (J). (ps-k). pap. 12.95 incl. audio Weston Woods Studios, Inc.

Huygen, Wil & Poortvliet, Rien. The Pop-Up Book of Gnomes. 1979. (Illus.). 7.95 o.p. (*0-8109-0966-9*) Abrams, Harry N. , Inc.

Impey, Rose. The Ankle Grabber. 1998. (Creepies Ser.). (Illus.). 48p. (J). (gr. 1-3). lib. bdg. 22.60 (*1-57505-296-2*); pap. 6.95 (*1-57505-313-6*) Lerner Publishing Group. (Carolrhoda Bks.).

—The Flat Man. 1988. (Creepies Ser.). (Illus.). (J). (gr. k-3). 0.90 o.p. (*0-8120-5975-1*) Barron's Educational Series, Inc.

—The Flat Man. 1998. (Creepies Ser.). (Illus.). 48p. (J). (gr. k-3). pap. 6.95 (*1-57505-314-4*, Carolrhoda Bks.) Lerner Publishing Group.

—Jumble Joan. 1998. (Creepies Ser.). (Illus.). 48p. (J). (gr. 1-3). pap. 6.95 (*1-57505-315-2*, Carolrhoda Bks.) Lerner Publishing Group.

—Scare Yourself to Sleep. 1988. (Creepies Ser.). (Illus.). 42p. (J). (ps-3). 0.90 o.p. (*0-8120-5974-3*) Barron's Educational Series, Inc.

—Scare Yourself to Sleep. 1998. (Creepies Ser.). (Illus.). 48p. (J). (gr. k-3). lib. bdg. 22.60 o.s.i (*1-57505-297-0*); (gr. 1-3). pap. 6.95 (*1-57505-316-0*) Lerner Publishing Group. (Carolrhoda Bks.).

—Scare Yourself to Sleep. 1991. (J). pap. o.s.i (*0-440-80234-2*, Dell Books for Young Readers) Random Hse. Children's Bks.

Inches, Alison. The Thanksgiving Monster: A Lift-the-Flap Book. 1997. (Muppets Ser.). (Illus.). 16p. (J). (ps-k). pap. 5.99 o.s.i (*0-14-056239-7*) Penguin Putnam Bks. for Young Readers.

Inkpen, Mick. Kipper's Monster. 2002. (Kipper Ser.). (Illus.). 32p. (J). (ps-2). 13.95 (*0-15-216614-9*, Red Wagon Bks.) Harcourt Children's Bks.

Inman, Sue. There's a Monster in My Bed! 1997. (Illus.). 24p. (J). (ps-3). 3.98 (*1-85854-574-9*) Brimax Bks., Ltd.

Jackson, Daniel C. & Summers-Dawes, Kate. Monsters You've Never Heard of & Never Will Unless You Read This Book. 1991. (J). (gr. 1-5). pap. 5.95 (*1-880722-00-3*) Jackson, Stephan L. & Assocs.

Jackson, Ellen B. Monsters in My Mailbox. 1995. (J). 8.15 o.p. (*0-606-07885-1*) Turtleback Bks.

Jackson, Jean. Big Lips & Hairy Arms. 1998. (Illus.). 32p. (J). (ps-1). pap. 15.95 o.p. (*0-7894-2521-1*) Dorling Kindersley Publishing, Inc.

—Thorndike & Nelson: A Monster Story. 1997. (Illus.). 32p. (J). (ps-k). pap. 15.95 o.p. (*0-7894-2452-5*) Dorling Kindersley Publishing, Inc.

Jameson, Jon. Monsters of the Mountains. 1979. (Easy-Read Fact Bks.). (Illus.). (gr. 2-4). lib. bdg. 9.90 o.p. (*0-531-02269-2*, Watts, Franklin) Scholastic Library Publishing.

Jane, Pamela. Monster Countdown: A Spooky Counting Book. 2001. (Illus.). (J). (ps-2). 14.95 (*1-58653-857-8*) Mondo Publishing.

—Monster Mischief. 2001. (Illus.). 32p. (J). (ps-2). 16.00 (*0-689-80471-7*, Atheneum) Simon & Schuster Children's Publishing.

Jarvis, Robin. Thorn Ogres of Hagwood. 2002. (Hagwood Books: Bk. 1). (Illus.). 256p. (YA). (gr. 5 up). 16.00 (*0-15-216752-8*, Silver Whistle) Harcourt Children's Bks.

Johnson, Jane. Today I Thought I'd Run Away. 1986. (Illus.). 32p. (J). (ps-1). 9.95 o.p. (*0-525-44193-X*, Dutton) Dutton/Plume.

Johnson, William. Famous Monsters Funbook. 1989. (Illus.). 48p. (Orig.). (J). 2.95 o.s.i (*0-8431-1715-X*, Price Stern Sloan) Penguin Putnam Bks. for Young Readers.

Johnston, Tony. Big Foot Cinderrrrrella. 2000. (Illus.). 32p. (ps-3). pap. 6.99 (*0-698-11871-5*, Puffin Bks.) Penguin Putnam Bks. for Young Readers.

—Night Noises & Other Mole & Troll Stories. 1989. 64p. (J). (gr. k-6). pap. 2.95 o.s.i (*0-440-40232-8*, Yearling) Random Hse. Children's Bks.

Jones, Marcia Thornton & Dadey, Debbie. Double Trouble Monsters. 1999. (Bailey City Monsters Ser.: No. 5). (Illus.). 80p. (J). (gr. 2-4). mass mkt. 3.99 (*0-439-05870-8*) Scholastic, Inc.

—Double Trouble Monsters. 1999. (Bailey City Monsters Ser.: No. 5). (J). (gr. 2-4). 10.14 (*0-606-16604-1*) Turtleback Bks.

—Happy Boo Day. 2000. (Bailey City Monsters Ser.: No. 9). (Illus.). 80p. (J). (gr. 2-4). mass mkt. 3.99 (*0-439-15009-4*, Scholastic Paperbacks) Scholastic, Inc.

—The Hauntlys' Hairy Surprise. 1999. (Bailey City Monsters Super Special Ser.: No. 1). (Illus.). 112p. (J). (gr. 2-4). mass mkt. 3.99 (*0-590-04302-1*) Scholastic, Inc.

—The Hauntlys' Hairy Surprise. 1999. (Bailey City Monsters Super Special Ser.: No. 1). (J). (gr. 2-4). 10.14 (*0-606-19911-X*) Turtleback Bks.

—Howling at the Hauntlys' 1998. (Bailey City Monsters Ser.: No.2). (Illus.). (J). (gr. 2-4). mass mkt. 3.99 (*0-590-10845-X*) Scholastic, Inc.

—Howling at the Hauntlys' 1998. (Bailey City Monsters Ser.: No. 2). (Illus.). (J). (gr. 2-4). 10.14 (*0-606-15448-5*) Turtleback Bks.

—Kilmer's Pet Monster. 1999. (Bailey City Monsters Ser.: No. 4). (Illus.). 72p. (J). (gr. 2-4). mass mkt. 3.99 (*0-590-10847-6*) Scholastic, Inc.

—Kilmer's Pet Monster. 1998. (Bailey City Monsters Ser.: No. 4). (J). (gr. 2-4). 10.14 (*0-606-15899-5*) Turtleback Bks.

—The Monsters Next Door. 1998. (Bailey City Monsters Ser.: No. 1). (Illus.). 71p. (J). (gr. 2-4). mass mkt. 3.99 (*0-590-10787-9*) Scholastic, Inc.

—The Monsters Next Door. 1997. (Bailey City Monsters Ser.: No. 1). (J). (gr. 2-4). 10.14 (*0-606-15447-7*) Turtleback Bks.

—Snow Monster Mystery. 1999. (Bailey City Monsters Ser.: No. 8). (Illus.). (J). (gr. 2-4). 10.14 (*0-606-18514-3*) Turtleback Bks.

—The Snow Monster Mystery. 1999. (Bailey City Monsters Ser.: No. 8). (Illus.). 80p. (J). (gr. 2-4). mass mkt. 3.99 (*0-439-05873-2*) Scholastic, Inc.

—Spooky Spells. 1999. (Bailey City Monsters Ser.: No. 6). (Illus.). 80p. (J). (gr. 2-4). mass mkt. 3.99 (*0-439-05871-6*) Scholastic, Inc.

—Spooky Spells. 1999. (Bailey City Monsters Ser.: No. 6). (J). (gr. 2-4). 10.14 (*0-606-16656-4*) Turtleback Bks.

—Vampire Baby. 1999. (Bailey City Monsters Ser.: No. 7). (Illus.). 80p. (J). (gr. 2-4). mass mkt. 3.99 (*0-439-05872-4*) Scholastic, Inc.

—Vampire Baby. 1999. (Bailey City Monsters Ser.: No. 7). (J). (gr. 2-4). 10.14 (*0-606-17059-6*) Turtleback Bks.

—Vampire Trouble. 1998. (Bailey City Monsters Ser.: No. 3). (Illus.). 80p. (J). (gr. 2-4). mass mkt. 3.99 (*0-590-10846-8*) Scholastic, Inc.

—Vampire Trouble. 1998. (Bailey City Monsters Ser.: No. 3). (J). (gr. 2-4). 10.14 (*0-606-15449-3*) Turtleback Bks.

Jones, Terry. The Beast with a Thousand Teeth. (Illus.). 24p. (J). 3.98 o.p. (*0-7651-0175-0*) Smithmark Pubs., Inc.

—The Sea Tiger. (Illus.). 24p. (J). 3.98 o.p. (*0-7651-0179-3*) Smithmark Pubs., Inc.

Jonsen, George. Favorite Tales of Monsters & Trolls. Lerner, Sharon, ed. 1977. (Pictureback Library Editions). (Illus.). (J). (ps-2). pap. 1.95 o.s.i (*0-394-83477-1*, Random Hse. Bks. for Young Readers) Random Hse. Children's Bks.

Joy, Flora. The Blogg Beneath the Bed. 1995. (Storytelling in Education Funbooks Ser.). (Illus.). 48p. (J). (gr. k-6). pap. text 7.00 (*1-884624-05-7*) Storytelling World Pr.

Joy, Margaret. Gran's Dragon. 1980. (Illus.). 96p. (J). (gr. 4-8). o.p. (*0-571-11520-9*) Faber & Faber Ltd.

Joyce, John. Captain Cockle & the Loch Ness Monster. 1995. 136p. pap. 7.95 (*1-85371-464-X*) Poolbeg Pr. IRL. *Dist:* Dufour Editions, Inc.

JTG of Nashville Staff. Monster Club Handbook. 1994. (J). (ps-3). pap. 12.95 (*1-884832-04-0*) JTG of Nashville.

Jungman, Ann. Vlad the Drac. l.t. ed. 1994. (Illus.). (J). (gr. 1-8). 16.95 o.p. (*0-7451-2221-3*, Galaxy Children's Large Print) BBC Audiobooks America.

—Vlad the Drac Returns. l.t. ed. 1996. (Illus.). (J). 16.95 o.p. (*0-7451-4731-3*, Galaxy Children's Large Print) BBC Audiobooks America.

—Vlad the Drac Superstar. l.t. ed. (J). 1997. 16.95 o.p. (*0-7451-6970-8*, Galaxy Children's Large Print); 1998. pap. 24.95 incl. audio (*0-7540-6202-3*) BBC Audiobooks America.

Kaff, Frank. Monster for a Day: Or, the Monster in Gregory's Pajamas. 1979. (Illus.). (J). (ps-3). 1.95 o.p. (*0-525-69002-6*); lib. bdg. 5.95 o.p. (*0-525-69003-4*) Dutton/Plume. (Dutton).

Kamish, Daniel & Kamish, David. The Night the Scary Beasties Popped Out of My Head. 1998. (Illus.). 40p. (J). (gr. k-3). 14.00 o.s.i (*0-679-89039-4*); 15.99 o.s.i (*0-679-99039-9*) Random Hse. Children's Bks. (Random Hse. Bks. for Young Readers).

Kellogg, Steven. Mystery Beast of Ostergeest. 1985. (Illus.). (J). (ps-3). 9.95 o.p. (*0-8037-6237-2*); 9.89 o.p. (*0-8037-6238-0*) Penguin Putnam Bks. for Young Readers. (Dial Bks. for Young Readers).

Kemp, Gene. Matty's Midnight Monster. 1991. (Illus.). 32p. (J). (ps up). bds. 14.95 o.p. (*0-571-14336-9*) Faber & Faber, Inc.

Kent, Jack. The Once-upon-a-Time Dragon. 1982. (Illus.). 32p. (J). (ps-3). 11.95 o.p. (*0-15-257885-4*) Harcourt Children's Bks.

Kerr, Judith. Mog in the Garden. 2002. (Illus.). 16p. (J). 4.50 (*0-00-137476-1*) HarperCollins Pubs. Ltd. GBR. *Dist:* Trafalgar Square.

Kimura, Yasuko. Fergus & the Sea Monster. 1978. (Illus.). (J). (ps-3). o.p. (*0-07-034558-9*); lib. bdg. o.p. (*0-07-034559-7*) McGraw-Hill Cos., The.

King, Jane. The Monster Bash. 1996. (Ghoul School Ser.: No. 3). 80p. (J). (gr. 1-4). pap. 3.50 (*0-671-51025-8*, Aladdin) Simon & Schuster Children's Publishing.

King, Jerry. Cartoon Monsters. 1983. (Stick-Out-Your-Neck Ser.). (Illus.). 32p. (J). (gr. 3 up). pap. 1.98 o.p. (*0-88724-057-7*, CD-8018) Carson-Dellosa Publishing Co., Inc.

King-Smith, Dick. The Water Horse. 1998. (Illus.). 108p. (J). (gr. 2-5). 17.99 o.s.i (*0-517-80027-6*); (gr. 3-5). 16.00 o.s.i (*0-517-80026-8*) Crown Publishing Group.

Kingman, Lee. Goergina & the Dragon. 1978. (Illus.). (J). (gr. 3-5). pap. (*0-671-29892-5*, Simon Pulse) Simon & Schuster Children's Publishing.

Kingsley, Emily P. A Sitter for Baby Monster. 1987. (Sesame Street Growing-Up Bks.). (Illus.). 32p. (J). (gr. 2-5). o.p. (*0-307-12022-8*, Golden Bks.) Random Hse. Children's Bks.

Kingsley, Emily P. & Sesame Street Staff. Cookie Monster's Storybook. 1979. (Sesame Street Bks.). (Illus.). (J). (ps-2). 3.50 o.p. (*0-394-84242-1*); 4.99 o.s.i (*0-394-94242-6*) Random Hse. Children's Bks. (Random Hse. Bks. for Young Readers).

Kleinberg, Naomi. Another Monster at the End of This Book. 1999. (Jellybean Bks.). (Illus.). 32p. (ps-k). 3.99 o.s.i (*0-375-80415-3*) Random Hse., Inc.

Kleven, Elisa. Monster in the House. 1998. (Illus.). 32p. (J). (ps-3). 15.99 o.s.i (*0-525-45973-1*, Dutton Children's Bks.) Penguin Putnam Bks. for Young Readers.

Klevin, Elisa. Monster in the House. 2001. (Illus.). (J). 12.14 (*0-606-20808-9*) Turtleback Bks.

Klevin, Elisa & Markoe, Merrill. Monster in the House. Peskin, Joy, ed. 2001. (Illus.). 32p. (J). (ps-3). pap. 5.99 o.p. (*0-14-056813-1*, Puffin Bks.) Penguin Putnam Bks. for Young Readers.

Kline, Suzy. Horrible Harry in Room 2B. (Horrible Harry Ser.: No. 1). (Illus.). 64p. (J). (gr. 2-4). 1997. pap. 3.99 (*0-14-038552-5*, Puffin Bks.); 1988. 12.99 o.s.i (*0-670-82176-4*, Viking Children's Bks.) Penguin Putnam Bks. for Young Readers.

Knight, Amarantha. The Darker Passions: Dracula. 1993. (Darker Passions Ser.). pap. 4.95 (*1-56333-147-0*) Masquerade Bks., Inc.

Koller, Jackie. No Such Thing. 2003. (Illus.). 32p. (J). (ps-4). 14.95 (*1-56397-490-8*) Boyds Mills Pr.

Krensky, Stephen. The Monster Trap. 2004. (J). 15.99 (*0-06-052498-7*); 16.89 (*0-06-052499-5*) HarperCollins Pubs.

Kroll, Steven. Monster Birthday. 1980. (Illus.). 32p. (J). (gr. 1-3). 7.95 o.p. (*0-8234-0369-6*) Holiday Hse., Inc.

Kudalis, Eric. Dracula & Other Vampire Stories. 1994. (Classic Monster Stories Ser.). (Illus.). 48p. (J). (gr. 3-7). lib. bdg. 19.00 o.p. (*0-516-35212-1*, Children's Pr.) Scholastic Library Publishing.

—Frankenstein & Other Stories of Man-Made Monsters. 1994. (Classic Monster Stories Ser.). (Illus.). 48p. (J). (gr. 3-4). lib. bdg. 21.26 (*1-56065-213-6*, Capstone High-Interest Bks.) Capstone Pr., Inc.

—Frankenstein & Other Stories of Man-Made Monsters. 1994. (Classic Monster Stories Ser.). (Illus.). 48p. (J). (gr. 3-7). lib. bdg. 19.00 o.p. (*0-516-35213-X*, Children's Pr.) Scholastic Library Publishing.

—Stories of Mummies & the Living Dead. 1994. (Classic Monster Stories Ser.). (Illus.). 48p. (J). (gr. 3-7). lib. bdg. 19.00 o.p. (*0-516-35214-8*, Children's Pr.) Scholastic Library Publishing.

Lane, Barbara Donnelly. The Monster Boring. 2001. (Illus.). 14p. (J). (ps-4). pap. 7.95 (*0-9702985-0-1*) Shamrock Hse., The.

Larsen, Wendy. After Dark. 1999. (Illus.). 19p. (J). (ps-3). pap. 10.99 (*0-9665699-0-3*) Chase Pubns.

Laslett, Stephanie. Monster Party: A Spooky Story. 1996. (Illus.). 16p. (J). (gr. 1-4). 10.99 o.p. (*0-525-45691-0*) Penguin Putnam Bks. for Young Readers.

Lavette, Lavaille. The Adventures of Roopster Roux: The Monster All-Stars. 1998. (Adventures of Roopster Roux Ser.). (Illus.). 32p. (J). (ps-3). pap. text 5.95 (*1-56554-362-9*) Pelican Publishing Co., Inc.

Laybourn, Emma. Monster Shoes. 2000. (Illus.). 63p. (J). pap. 6.95 (*0-552-54634-8*) Transworld Publishers Ltd. GBR. *Dist:* Trafalgar Square.

Layne, Steven L. My Brother Dan's Delicious. 2003. (Illus.). 32p. (J). 14.95 (*1-58980-071-0*) Pelican Publishing Co., Inc.

Leach, Maria. Thing at the Foot of the Bed. 1987. (Illus.). 128p. (J). (gr. 3-5). 12.95 o.s.i (*0-399-21496-8*, Philomel) Penguin Putnam Bks. for Young Readers.

Lee, Stan. The Incredible Hulk. 1981. 64p. (J). pap. 2.95 o.p. (*0-8249-8013-1*) Ideals Pubns.

Leedy, Loreen. The Monster Money Book. (Illus.). (J). (ps-3). 2000. pap. 6.95 (*0-8234-1558-9*); 1992. 32p. tchr. ed. 16.95 (*0-8234-0922-8*) Holiday Hse., Inc.

Leetham, Helen. Sir Percy & the Dragon. 1994. (Illus.). 32p. (J). (ps-1). 17.95 (*0-86264-273-6*) Andersen Pr., Ltd. GBR. *Dist:* Trafalgar Square.

L'Engle, Madeleine. Dragons in the Waters. 1982. 336p. (YA). (gr. 4-7). mass mkt. 5.50 (*0-440-91719-0*, Laurel Leaf) Random Hse. Children's Bks.

Lerner, Sharon. Follow the Monsters! 1985. (Step into Reading Step 1 Bks.). (Illus.). 32p. (J). (ps-1). 7.99 o.s.i (*0-394-97126-4*); pap. 3.99 o.s.i (*0-394-87126-X*) Random Hse. Children's Bks. (Random Hse. Bks. for Young Readers).

—Follow the Monsters! l.t. ed. 1999. (Sesame Street Ser.). (Illus.). 24p. (J). (ps-1). bds. 4.99 (*0-375-80130-8*) Random Hse., Inc.

—Follow the Monsters! 1985. (Step into Reading Step 1 Bks.). (J). (ps-1). 10.14 (*0-606-12292-3*) Turtleback Bks.

Lester, Alison. Monsters Are Knocking. (Lift-the-Flap Ser.). (Illus.). 320p. (J). 2015. pap. 4.99 o.p. (*0-14-054477-1*); 1993. pap. 4.99 o.p. (*0-14-054967-6*) Penguin Putnam Bks. for Young Readers. (Puffin Bks.).

Lesynski, Loris. Ogre Fun. 1997. (Illus.). 32p. (J). (ps-2). pap. 5.95 (*1-55037-446-X*); lib. bdg. 15.95 (*1-55037-447-8*) Annick Pr., Ltd. CAN. *Dist:* Firefly Bks., Ltd.

—Ogre Fun. 1997. 12.10 (*0-606-12784-4*) Turtleback Bks.

Leuck, Laura. Goodnight, Baby Monster. 2002. (Illus.). 32p. (J). (ps-1). 14.99 (*0-06-029151-6*); lib. bdg. 16.89 (*0-06-029152-4*) HarperCollins Children's Bk. Group.

—Jeepers Creepers: A Monstrous ABC. 2003. (Illus.). 32p. (J). 15.95 (*0-8118-3509-X*, 53408263) Chronicle Bks. LLC.

—My Creature Teacher. (J). 2004. lib. bdg. 16.89 (*0-06-029695-X*); 2003. 15.99 (*0-06-029694-1*) HarperCollins Pubs.

—My Monster Mama Loves Me So. (Illus.). 24p. (J). (ps-3). 2002. pap. 5.99 (*0-06-008860-5*, Harper Trophy); 1999. 15.99 (*0-688-16866-3*); 1999. lib. bdg. 15.89 (*0-688-16867-1*) HarperCollins Children's Bk. Group.

Levin, Susan M. Harry the Hairy Monster. 1994. (Illus.). 16p. (Orig.). (J). (ps-2). pap. (*0-9642777-1-9*) Levin Family Publishing.

Levy, Elizabeth. The Bride: The Storybook Based on the Movie. 1985. (Illus.). 64p. (J). (gr. 3-7). 6.95 o.p. (*0-394-87371-8*); lib. bdg. 7.99 o.p. (*0-394-97371-2*) Random Hse. Children's Bks. (Random Hse. Bks. for Young Readers).

—Frankenstein Moved in on the Fourth Floor. (Trophy Chapter Bks.). (Illus.). (J). (gr. 1-5). 1981. 80p. pap. 4.99 (*0-06-440122-7*, Harper Trophy); 1979. lib. bdg. 13.89 o.p. (*0-06-023811-9*) HarperCollins Children's Bk. Group.

—Frankenstein Moved in on the Fourth Floor. 1990. (J). pap. 3.50 (*0-06-107013-0*, HarperTorch) Morrow/Avon.

—Frankenstein Moved in on the Fourth Floor. 1979. (J). 11.10 (*0-606-02115-9*) Turtleback Bks.

—Gorgonzola Zombies in the Park. 1993. (Illus.). 96p. (J). (gr. 2-5). 14.00 o.p. (*0-06-021461-9*); lib. bdg. 14.89 o.p. (*0-06-021460-0*) HarperCollins Children's Bk. Group.

Lewin, Betsy. Wiley Learns to Spell. 1998. (Hello Reader! Ser.). (Illus.). 32p. (J). (ps-1). mass mkt. 3.99 (*0-590-10835-2*) Scholastic, Inc.

—Wiley Learns to Spell. 1998. (Hello Reader! Ser.). (J). 10.14 (*0-606-13916-8*) Turtleback Bks.

Lia, Simone. Red's Great Chase. 2000. (Illus.). 32p. (J). (ps-2). 14.99 o.p. (*0-525-46213-9*) Penguin Putnam Bks. for Young Readers.

Lipton, Larry. Puff the Magic Dragon. 1994. (Sing-a-Song Storybooks Ser.). (Illus.). 24p. (J). 9.95 o.p. (*0-7935-3197-7*, HL00330702) Leonard, Hal Corp.

Little Monster at Home. 1978. (Golden Look-Look Bks.). (Illus.). (J). (ps-3). pap. o.p. (*0-307-11846-0*, Golden Bks.) Random Hse. Children's Bks.

Lively, Penelope. Dragon Trouble. 2002. (Yellow Bananas Ser.). (Illus.). 48p. (J). (gr. 3-4). pap. 4.95 (*0-7787-0987-6*); lib. bdg. 19.96 (*0-7787-0941-8*) Crabtree Publishing Co.

Lodge, Bernard. How Scary! Who Scares Who From One to Ten. 2001. (Illus.). 32p. (J). (ps-ps). tchr. ed. 15.00 (*0-618-11547-1*, Lorraine, A. Walter) Houghton Mifflin Co. Trade & Reference Div.

Lord, Suzanne. Count Morbida's Monster Quiz Book. 1980. 80p. (J). pap. 1.50 o.p. (*0-590-30621-9*) Scholastic, Inc.

Louise, T. Paula. The Baggage Comes to Town. 2002. (Illus.). 32p. (J). (gr. 1-5). pap. 7.99 (*0-9719775-0-X*) Idea & Design Works, LLC.

Lubar, David. The Accidental Vampire, Vol. 1. 1997. (Accidental Monsters Ser.: Vol. 1). 144p. (J). (gr. 3-7). mass mkt. 3.99 (*0-590-90718-2*) Scholastic, Inc.

—Gloomy Ghost, 4. 1998. (Accidental Monsters Ser.). 10.04 (*0-606-13108-6*) Turtleback Bks.

—The Wavering Werewolf. 1997. (Accidental Monsters Ser.: No. 3). (J). mass mkt. 3.99 (*0-590-90720-4*, Scholastic Paperbacks) Scholastic, Inc.

—The Wavering Werewolf, 3. 1997. (Accidental Monsters Ser.). 10.04 (*0-606-12867-0*) Turtleback Bks.

Lundgren, Mary Beth. Seven Scary Monsters. 2003. (Illus.). 32p. (J). (ps-3). lib. bdg., tchr. ed. 15.00 (*0-395-88913-8*, Clarion Bks.) Houghton Mifflin Co. Trade & Reference Div.

Maccarone, Grace. Monster Math. 2002. (Illus.). (J). 11.91 (*0-7587-1457-2*) Book Wholesalers, Inc.

—Monster Math. 1995. (Hello Reader! Math Ser.). (Illus.). 32p. (J). (ps-3). pap. 3.99 (*0-590-22712-2*, Cartwheel Bks.) Scholastic, Inc.

—Monster Math. 1995. (J). 10.14 (*0-606-07882-7*) Turtleback Bks.

—Monster Math Picnic. 1998. (J). 10.14 (*0-606-13617-7*) Turtleback Bks.

Maccarone, Grace & Burns, Marilyn. Monster Math Schooltime. 1997. (Hello Reader! Math Ser.). (Illus.). 32p. (J). (ps-1). pap. 3.99 (*0-590-30859-9*) Scholastic, Inc.

—Monster Money. 1998. (Hello Reader! Math Ser.: Level 1). (Illus.). 32p. (J). (ps-3). mass mkt. 3.99 (*0-590-12007-7*) Scholastic, Inc.

Maccarone, Grace, et al. Monster Math Picnic. 1998. (Hello Reader! Math Ser.). (Illus.). (J). (ps-4). mass mkt. 3.99 (*0-590-37127-4*) Scholastic, Inc.

MacDonald, Alan. Snarlyhissopus. 2002. (Illus.). (J). tchr. ed. 14.95 (*1-58925-021-4*); pap. 5.95 (*1-58925-370-1*) ME Media LLC. (Tiger Tales).

MacDonald, Marianne. Dragon for Sale. 1998. 9.10 (*0-606-17640-3*) Turtleback Bks.

Mackall, Dandi Daley. The Cinnamon Lake-Ness Monster. 1998. (Cinnamon Lake Mysteries Ser.: Vol. 7). 80p. (J). (gr. 1-4). 4.99 (*0-570-05336-6*, 12-3384) Concordia Publishing Hse.

Mahany, Patricia Shely. The Lollipop Dragon & Special Days. 1982. (Recolor Bks.). (Illus.). 16p. (Orig.). (J). (gr. k-3). pap. 2.50 o.p. (*0-87239-576-6*, 2392) Standard Publishing.

—The Lollipop Dragon & the Four Seasons. 1982. (Recolor Bks.). (Illus.). 16p. (Orig.). (J). (gr. k-3). pap. 2.50 o.p. (*0-87239-577-4*, 2393) Standard Publishing.

—The Lollipop Dragon Goes for a Walk. 1982. (Coloring Bks.). (Illus.). 16p. (Orig.). (J). (gr. k-3). pap. 0.89 o.p. (*0-87239-602-9*, 2391) Standard Publishing.

—Lollipop Keeps His Promise. 1983. (Happy Day Bks.). (Illus.). 24p. (J). (ps-2). 1.75 o.p. (*0-87239-638-X*, 3558) Standard Publishing.

Manes, Stephen. Monstra vs. Irving, ERS. (Illus.). 80p. (J). (gr. 2-4). 1991. pap. 4.95 o.p. (*0-8050-1642-2*); 1989. 12.95 o.p. (*0-8050-0836-5*) Holt, Henry & Co. (Holt, Henry & Co. Bks. For Young Readers).

Mann, Paul Z. Meet My Monster. 1999. (All-Star Readers: Level 2 Ser.). (Illus.). 32p. (J). (gr. k-2). pap. 3.99 (*1-57584-308-0*) Reader's Digest Children's Publishing, Inc.

Nolan, Dennis. Monster Bubbles: A Counting Book. 1976. (J). pap. o.p. (*0-13-600643-4*); lib. bdg. o.p. (*0-13-600635-3*) Prentice-Hall.

Nolan, Lucy. The Lizard Man of Crabtree County. (Illus.). 32p. (J). 2003. pap. 5.95 (*0-7614-5144-7*); 1999. 15.95 (*0-7614-5049-1*, Cavendish Children's Bks.) Cavendish, Marshall Corp.

Noonan, R. A. Beware the Claw! 1996. (Monsterville Ser.: 5). 144p. (J). pap. 3.95 o.p. (*0-689-71867-5*, Simon Pulse) Simon & Schuster Children's Publishing.

—Don't Go into the Graveyard! 1995. (Monsterville USA Ser.: No. 2). 144p. (J). (gr. 4-5). pap. 3.95 o.p. (*0-689-71864-0*, Simon Pulse) Simon & Schuster Children's Publishing.

—Enter at Your Own Risk. 1995. (Monsterville USA Ser.: 1). 160p. (J). (gr. 4-5). mass mkt. 3.95 o.p. (*0-689-71863-2*, Simon Pulse) Simon & Schuster Children's Publishing.

—My Teacher Is a Zombie. 1995. (Monsterville USA Ser.: No. 3). 144p. (J). pap. 3.95 o.p. (*0-689-71865-9*, Simon Pulse) Simon & Schuster Children's Publishing.

—New Grrrl in Town. 1996. (Monsterville USA Ser.: Vol. 6). (Illus.). 144p. (J). (gr. 3-7). pap. 3.99 (*0-689-71868-3*, Simon Pulse) Simon & Schuster Children's Publishing.

—Wild Ghost Chase. 1996. (Monsterville USA Ser.: 4). 144p. (J). pap. 3.95 o.p. (*0-689-71866-7*, Simon Pulse) Simon & Schuster Children's Publishing.

North Shuswap Elementary School Students. The Shoe Monster. 1994. 32p. (J). (gr. k-3). pap. 3.50 (*0-87406-687-5*) Darby Creek Publishing.

Numeroff, Laura Joffe. Laura Numeroff's 10 Step Guide to Living with Your Monster. 2002. (Illus.). 32p. (J). (ps-2). 15.95 (*0-06-623822-6*); lib. bdg. 15.89 (*0-06-623823-4*) HarperCollins Children's Bk. Group. (Geringer, Laura Bk.).

—Monster Munchies. 1998. (I Can Read It All by Myself: Beginner Books). (Illus.). 48p. (J). (gr. k-3). 7.99 (*0-679-89163-3*); lib. bdg. 11.99 o.p. (*0-679-99163-8*) Random Hse. Children's Bks. (Random Hse. Bks. for Young Readers).

O'Keefe, Susan H. One Hungry Monster: A Counting Book in Rhyme. (Illus.). 32p. (J). (ps-3). 1992. pap. 5.95 o.p. (*0-316-63388-7*); 1989. reprint ed. 12.95 (*0-316-63385-2*) Little Brown & Co. (Joy Street Bks.).

O'Keefe, Susan Heyboer. More Hungry Monsters. 2004. (Illus.). (J). 15.95 (*0-316-61061-5*) Little Brown & Co.

—One Hungry Monster: A Counting Book in Rhyme. 2001. (Illus.). 10p. (J). (ps-k). bds. 6.99 (*0-316-60804-1*) Little Brown & Co.

O'Keefe, Susan Heyboer. One Hungry Monster: A Counting Book in Rhyme. 1989. (J). 12.10 (*0-606-01417-9*) Turtleback Bks.

Osborne, Dwight A. The Squiggly Wiggly Head Family. 1992. (Illus.). 16p. (J). pap. 5.95 (*0-9632817-0-4*) Osborne Bks.

Ostheeren, Ingrid. The Blue Monster. Lanning, Rosemary, tr. from GER. 1996. (Illus.). 32p. (J). (gr. k-3). 15.95 o.p. (*1-55858-556-7*); 15.88 o.p. (*1-55858-557-5*) North-South Bks., Inc.

Otfinoski, Steven. Village of Vampires. 1979. (Pacesetters Ser.). (Illus.). (J). (gr. 4 up). lib. bdg. 9.25 o.p. (*0-516-02190-7*, Children's Pr.) Scholastic Library Publishing.

Otto, Carolyn B. Mighty Joe Young. 1998. (Junior Novelization Ser.). (Illus.). 96p. (J). (gr. 3-7). pap. 4.95 o.p. (*0-7868-4137-0*) Disney Pr.

Packard, Edward. Gorga, the Space Monster. 1983. (Choose Your Own Adventure Ser.: No. 5). 64p. (J). (gr. 2-4). pap. 2.25 o.s.i (*0-553-15507-5*) Bantam Bks.

—You Are a Monster. 1988. (Choose Your Own Adventure Ser.: No. 84). 128p. (J). (gr. 4-8). pap. 2.75 o.s.i (*0-553-27474-0*) Bantam Bks.

Packard, Mary. We Are Monsters. 1996. (My First Hello Reader! Ser.). (Illus.). 32p. (J). (ps-3). 3.99 (*0-590-68995-9*, Cartwheel Bks.) Scholastic, Inc.

Pantuso, Mike & Henson, Jim. 1,2,3 by Elmo. 2001. (Illus.). (J). lib. bdg. (*0-375-91390-4*, Random Hse. Bks. for Young Readers) Random Hse. Children's Bks.

Paraskevas, Betty. The Big Carrot. 2000. (Maggie & the Ferocious Beast Ser.). (Illus.). 40p. (J). (ps-3). 15.00 (*0-689-82490-4*, Simon & Schuster Children's Publishing) Simon & Schuster Children's Publishing.

—Maggie & the Ferocious Beast: The Big Scare! 1999. (Illus.). 40p. (J). (ps-1). 15.00 (*0-689-82489-0*, Simon & Schuster Children's Publishing) Simon & Schuster Children's Publishing.

—Monster Beach. 1995. (Illus.). 32p. (J). (ps-3). 15.00 o.s.i (*0-15-292882-0*) Harcourt Trade Pubs.

Parish, Peggy. No More Monsters for Me! 1987. (I Can Read Bks.). (Illus.). 64p. (J). (gr. k-3). pap. 3.99 (*0-06-444109-1*, Harper Trophy) HarperCollins Children's Bk. Group.

—Zed & the Monsters. 1979. 6.95 o.p. (*0-385-12948-3*); lib. bdg. 6.95 o.p. (*0-385-12949-1*) Doubleday Publishing.

Park, Barbara. Junie B. Jones Has a Monster under Her Bed. unabr. ed. 2001. (Junie B. Jones Ser.: No. 8). 69p. (J). (gr. k-4). pap. 17.00 incl. audio (*0-8072-0644-X*, Listening Library) Random Hse. Audio Publishing Group.

—Junie B. Jones Has a Monster under Her Bed. 1997. (Junie B. Jones Ser.: No. 8). (Illus.). (J). (gr. k-2). 10.14 (*0-606-11529-3*) Turtleback Bks.

—Psssst! It's Me... the Bogeyman. (Illus.). (J). (gr. k-3). 1999. 32p. per. 16.00 (*0-689-82742-3*, Simon & Schuster Children's Publishing); 1998. 40p. 16.00 o.s.i (*0-689-81667-7*, Atheneum/Anne Schwartz Bks.) Simon & Schuster Children's Publishing.

Parnell, Fran. The Barefoot Book of Monsters. 2003. (Illus.). 64p. (J). 19.99 (*1-84148-178-5*) Barefoot Bks., Inc.

Pascal, Francine, creator. Beware the Wolfman. 1994. (Sweet Valley High Ser.: No. 106). 240p. (YA). (gr. 7 up). mass mkt. 3.99 o.s.i (*0-553-56234-7*) Bantam Bks.

—Jessica's Monster Nightmare. 1993. (Sweet Valley Kids Ser.: No. 42). 80p. (J). (gr. 1-3). pap. 3.50 o.s.i (*0-553-48008-1*) Bantam Bks.

Paulsen, Gary. The Creature of Black Water Lake. 1997. (Mulberry Paperback Bks.= Un Libro Mulbe). 9.19 o.p. (*0-606-11224-3*) Turtleback Bks.

—The Gorgon Slayer. 1995. (World of Adventure Ser.). 80p. (J). (gr. 4-7). pap. 3.50 o.s.i (*0-440-41041-X*, Yearling) Random Hse. Children's Bks.

Peck, Richard. Monster Night at Grandma's House. 2003. (Illus.). 32p. (J). (gr. k-3). reprint ed. 12.99 (*0-8037-2904-9*, Dial Bks. for Young Readers) Penguin Putnam Bks. for Young Readers.

—Monster Night at Grandma's House. (Picture Puffin Ser.). (J). (gr. k-3). 1979. (Illus.). pap. 2.95 o.p. (*0-14-050330-7*, Penguin Bks.); 1977. 11.50 o.p. (*0-670-48680-9*) Viking Penguin.

Peet, Bill. Cyrus the Unsinkable Sea Serpent. (Carry-Along Book & Cassette Favorites Ser.). (Illus.). (J). (ps-3). 1995. 1p. pap. 10.95 incl. audio (*0-395-72025-7*, 492975); 1982. 48p. pap. 8.95 (*0-395-31389-9*); 1975. 48p. lib. bdg., tchr. ed. 16.00 (*0-395-20272-8*) Houghton Mifflin Co.

—Cyrus the Unsinkable Sea Serpent. 1975. (J). 14.10 (*0-606-03334-3*) Turtleback Bks.

—Jethro & Joel Were a Troll. (Illus.). 32p. (J). (ps-3). 1990. pap. 7.95 (*0-395-53968-4*); 1987. 14.95 o.p. (*0-395-43081-X*) Houghton Mifflin Co.

—Jethro & Joel Were a Troll. 1987. (J). 11.15 o.p. (*0-606-04450-7*) Turtleback Bks.

Penguin Books Staff, ed. The Dragon Den. 1990. (Illus.). (J). (ps-2). (Read with Me Key Words to Reading Ser.: No. 9010-2). 3.50 (*0-7214-1315-3*);Vol. 2. (Series 9011-2: No. 2). stu. ed. 2.95 (*0-7214-3221-2*) Penguin Group (USA) Inc. (Ladybird Bks.).

Percy, Graham. 24 Strange Little Animals: The Haunted House. 1996. (Illus.). 40p. (J). (ps-3). 12.95 o.p. (*0-8118-1035-6*) Chronicle Bks. LLC.

Peretti, Frank E. Cooper Kids Adventure Series. 1990. (Cooper Kids Adventure Ser.). (J). (gr. 5-7). pap. 23.96 (*0-89107-901-7*) Crossway Bks.

Perry, Janet & Gentle, Victor. Aliens. 1999. (Imagination Library). (Illus.). 24p. (J). (gr. 2 up). lib. bdg. 19.93 (*0-8368-2435-0*) Stevens, Gareth Inc.

—Giants & Wild, Hairy Monsters. 1999. (Imagination Library). (Illus.). 24p. (J). (gr. 2 up). lib. bdg. 19.93 (*0-8368-2437-7*) Stevens, Gareth Inc.

—Manmade Monsters. 1999. (Imagination Library). (Illus.). 24p. (J). (gr. 2 up). lib. bdg. 19.93 (*0-8368-2439-3*) Stevens, Gareth Inc.

—Monsters, 9 bks. Incl. Aliens. lib. bdg. 19.93 (*0-8368-2435-0*); Dragons & Dinosaurs. lib. bdg. 19.93 (*0-8368-2436-9*); Giants & Wild, Hairy Monsters. lib. bdg. 19.93 (*0-8368-2437-7*); Mad Scientists. lib. bdg. 19.93 (*0-8368-2438-5*); Manmade Monsters. lib. bdg. 19.93 (*0-8368-2439-3*); Monsters of the Deep. lib. bdg. 19.93 (*0-8368-2440-7*); Morph Monsters. lib. bdg. 19.93 (*0-8368-2441-5*); Vampires. lib. bdg. 19.93 (*0-8368-2442-3*); Zombies. lib. bdg. 19.93 (*0-8368-2443-1*); 24p. (J). (gr. 2 up). 1999. (Illus.). Set lib. bdg. 179.40 (*0-8368-2434-2*) Stevens, Gareth Inc.

—Monsters of the Deep. 1999. (Imagination Library). (Illus.). 24p. (J). (gr. 2 up). lib. bdg. 19.93 (*0-8368-2440-7*) Stevens, Gareth Inc.

—Morph Monsters. 1999. (Imagination Library). (Illus.). 24p. (J). (gr. 2 up). lib. bdg. 19.93 (*0-8368-2441-5*) Stevens, Gareth Inc.

Perry, Ritchie. The Runton Werewolf. l.t. ed. 1997. (J). 16.95 (*0-7451-6908-2*, Galaxy Children's Large Print) BBC Audiobooks America.

Peters, Catherine. Jackson's Monster. 1997. 16p. (J). pap. 2.49 o.p. (*0-395-88313-X*) Houghton Mifflin Co.

Peterson, Scott. Invasion of Mean Screen, the Computer Monster. 1996. (Power Rangers Zeo Ser.: No. 2). 80p. (J). (gr. k-3). 3.25 o.p. (*0-694-00989-X*, Harper Festival) HarperCollins Children's Bk. Group.

—The People Pitcher Strikes Out. 1996. (Power Rangers Zeo Ser.: No. 4). 80p. (J). (gr. k-3). 3.25 o.p. (*0-694-00991-1*, Harper Festival) HarperCollins Children's Bk. Group.

Pfister, Marcus & Weninger, Brigitte. It's Bedtime. 2002. (Illus.). 32p. (J). lib. bdg. 16.50 (*0-7358-1603-4*) North-South Bks., Inc.

Phinney, Margaret Y. We're off to Thunder Mountain. 1995. (Illus.). 16p. (J). (gr. k-3). pap. 4.00 (*1-57255-031-7*) Mondo Publishing.

Pienkowski, Jan. Little Monsters. (Pienkowski Mini Pop-Up Ser.). (Illus.). 10p. (J). (ps up). 1991. 6.99 o.p. (*0-8431-2964-6*); 1986. 10.95 o.s.i (*0-8431-1241-7*) Penguin Putnam Bks. for Young Readers. (Price Stern Sloan).

Pierce, Richard. Frankenstein's Children: The Creation. 1994. 208p. (Orig.). (YA). (gr. 7-12). mass mkt. 3.99 o.s.i (*0-425-14361-9*) Berkley Publishing Group.

Pike, Christopher, pseud. Black Blood. MacDonald, Pat, ed. 1994. (Last Vampire Ser.: No. 2). 208p. (YA). 14.00 o.p. (*0-671-87258-3*, Simon & Schuster Children's Publishing) Simon & Schuster Children's Publishing.

—Black Blood. MacDonald, Patricia, ed. 1994. (Last Vampire Ser.: No. 2). 208p. (YA). (gr. 7 up). pap. 3.99 (*0-671-87266-4*, Simon Pulse) Simon & Schuster Children's Publishing.

—Black Blood. 1994. (Last Vampire Ser.: Vol. 2). 10.04 (*0-606-07022-2*) Turtleback Bks.

—Creature in the Teacher. 1996. (Spooksville Ser.). 144p. (J). (gr. 4-6). pap. 3.99 (*0-671-00261-9*, Aladdin) Simon & Schuster Children's Publishing.

—Creatures of Forever. 1996. (Last Vampire Ser.: Vol. 6). 224p. (YA). (gr. 9 up). 14.00 o.p. (*0-671-55053-5*, Simon & Schuster Children's Publishing) Simon & Schuster Children's Publishing.

—The Creepy Creature. 1998. (Spooksville Ser.). (J). (gr. 4-6). 10.04 (*0-606-13798-X*) Turtleback Bks.

—The Last Vampire: Collector's Edition. 1998. (Last Vampire Ser.: No. 2). 560p. (J). (gr. 9 up). pap. 6.99 (*0-671-02290-3*, Simon Pulse) Simon & Schuster Children's Publishing.

—Monster. 2001. (Illus.). 240p. (J). pap. 5.99 (*0-7434-2800-5*, Simon Pulse) Simon & Schuster Children's Publishing.

—Monster. MacDonald, Pat, ed. 1992. 240p. (YA). (gr. 7 up). pap. 3.99 (*0-671-74507-7*, Simon Pulse) Simon & Schuster Children's Publishing.

—Monster. 1992. (J). 10.04 (*0-606-02203-1*) Turtleback Bks.

—The Thing in the Closet. 1997. (Spooksville Ser.). 128p. (J). (gr. 4-6). per. 3.99 (*0-671-00265-1*, Aladdin) Simon & Schuster Children's Publishing.

Pilkey, Dav. Dogzilla. 2002. (Illus.). (J). 14.04 (*0-7587-2405-5*) Book Wholesalers, Inc.

—Dogzilla. (Illus.). 32p. (J). 2003. 14.00 (*0-15-204948-7*); 2003. pap. 4.95 (*0-15-204949-5*, Harcourt Paperbacks); 1993. (gr. 4 up). 13.00 (*0-15-223944-8*); 1993. (ps-3). pap. 7.00 (*0-15-223945-6*) Harcourt Children's Bks.

—Dogzilla. 1993. 13.15 (*0-606-14197-9*) Turtleback Bks.

—Dragon's Fat Cat. 1992. (Illus.). 48p. (J). (gr. 1-3). mass mkt. 15.99 o.p. (*0-531-08582-1*); (ps-3). pap. 15.95 (*0-531-05982-0*) Scholastic, Inc. (Orchard Bks.).

—Dragon's Merry Christmas. 48p. (J). 2003. pap. 5.95 (*0-439-54848-9*); 1994. (Illus.). mass mkt. 5.95 (*0-531-07055-7*) Scholastic, Inc. (Orchard Bks.).

—Dragon's Merry Christmas. 1994. (Dragon Tales Ser.). 10.15 o.p. (*0-606-09210-2*) Turtleback Bks.

—A Friend for Dragon. 1994. (Illus.). 48p. (J). (ps-3). mass mkt. 4.95 (*0-531-07054-9*, Orchard Bks.) Scholastic, Inc.

—A Friend for Dragon. 1994. 10.15 o.p. (*0-606-08746-X*) Turtleback Bks.

Pinkwater, Daniel M. Around Fred's Bed. 1976. (Illus.). (J). (ps-2). o.p. (*0-13-046581-X*) Prentice-Hall.

—I Was a Second Grade Werewolf. 1983. (Illus.). 32p. (J). (ps-2). 12.95 o.s.i (*0-525-44038-0*) Live Oak Media.

—Yobgorgle: Mystery Monster of Lake Ontario, 001. 1979. 156p. (J). (gr. 3-6). 8.95 o.p. (*0-395-28970-X*, Clarion Bks.) Houghton Mifflin Co. Trade & Reference Div.

Platt, Kin. Frank & Stein & Me. 1982. (Triumph Bks.). 128p. (gr. 7 up). lib. bdg. 9.90 o.p. (*0-531-04169-7*, Watts, Franklin) Scholastic Library Publishing.

Polidori, John W. The Vampire. 1989. (Step-up Classic Chillers Ser.). (Illus.). 96p. (J). (gr. 4-7). pap. 3.50 o.s.i (*0-394-83844-0*, Random Hse. Bks. for Young Readers) Random Hse. Children's Bks.

Posner, Andrea. Helping Holiday Hands. 1999. (Rudolph Ser.). (Illus.). 18p. (J). (ps). bds. 3.99 (*0-307-14526-3*, Golden Bks.) Random Hse. Children's Bks.

Preller, James. Godzilla Deluxe Storybook. 1998. (Godzilla Ser.). 48p. (J). (gr. 2-5). mass mkt. 5.98 (*0-590-57213-X*) Scholastic, Inc.

—Maxx Trax II: Monster Truck Adventure. 1988. (Illus.). 32p. (Orig.). (J). (gr. k-3). pap. 2.50 o.p. (*0-590-41156-X*) Scholastic, Inc.

Prelutsky, Jack. Beauty of the Beast Promotion. 1997. audio o.p. (*0-676-76268-9*, Knopf Bks. for Young Readers) Random Hse. Children's Bks.

—Monday's Troll. 1996. (Illus.). 40p. (J). (ps up). 15.89 (*0-688-14373-3*, Greenwillow Bks.) HarperCollins Children's Bk. Group.

Pym, Tasha. It's a Monster Party! 2003. (Illus.). 32p. (J). 12.95 (*1-4027-0429-1*) Sterling Publishing Co., Inc.

Rae, Judy. Boogie Man, O Please. 1982. (Illus.). 44p. (J). (ps-5). 8.95 o.p. (*0-939728-07-9*); pap. 4.50 o.p. (*0-939728-08-7*) Steppingstone Enterprises, Inc.

Rainey, Richard. The Monster Factory. 1993. (Illus.). 128p. (YA). (gr. 6 up). lib. bdg. 19.00 (*0-02-775663-7*, Simon & Schuster Children's Publishing) Simon & Schuster Children's Publishing.

Random House Disney Staff. Monsters, Inc. 2001. (Read-Aloud Storybook Ser.). 72p. (J). 8.99 (*0-7364-1346-4*) Mouse Works.

Ratnett, Michael. Peter & the Bogeyman. 1989. (Illus.). 32p. (J). 9.95 o.p. (*0-8120-6104-7*) Barron's Educational Series, Inc.

Razzi, Jim. Dragons!, Vol. 16. 1984. (Choose Your Own Adventure Ser.: No. 16). 64p. (Orig.). (J). (gr. 2-4). pap. 2.25 o.s.i (*0-553-15465-6*, Skylark) Random Hse. Children's Bks.

—Monster of Lost Valley. 1986. (Double Dinomite Ser.: No. 1). (Illus.). (Orig.). (J). (gr. 1-3). pap. (*0-671-62091-6*, Aladdin) Simon & Schuster Children's Publishing.

Ready Reader Staff. Monster under Bed: R-Controlled Vowels, Level B. 2003. (J). 35.50 (*0-8136-0994-1*) Modern Curriculum Pr.

Reagan, Dian C. Home for the Howl-idays. 1994. 128p. (J). (gr. 4-6). mass mkt. 2.95 (*0-590-48772-8*) Scholastic, Inc.

Reed, Don C. The Kraken. 2003. (Illus.). 224p. (YA). (gr. 5-9). pap. 7.95 (*1-56397-693-5*) Boyds Mills Pr.

—The Kraken. 1997. lib. bdg. 14.00 (*0-606-14348-3*) Turtleback Bks.

Reeves, James. Heroes & Monsters. 1978. (Illus.). (J). pap. 2.95 o.p. (*0-8467-0539-7*) Hippocrene Bks., Inc.

Regan, Dian Curtis. Fangs-Giving. 1997. (J). (gr. 2-7). mass mkt. 3.99 (*0-590-96821-1*) Scholastic, Inc.

—Monster of the Month. 1997. 160p. (J). (gr. 3-7). mass mkt. 3.99 (*0-590-62391-5*) Scholastic, Inc.

—Monster of the Month Club, ERS. 1994. (Illus.). (J). 14.95 o.p. (*0-8050-3443-9*, Holt, Henry & Co. Bks. For Young Readers) Holt, Henry & Co.

—Monster of the Month Club. unabr. ed. 1998. (J). 38.24 incl. audio (*0-7887-2239-5*, 40723); 38.24 incl. audio (*0-7887-2239-5*, 40723); (gr. 4). 89.70 incl. audio (*0-7887-2544-0*, 46714) Recorded Bks., LLC.

—Monster of the Month Club. 1997. 10.04 (*0-606-11635-4*) Turtleback Bks.

—Monsters & My One True Love, ERS. 1998. (Illus.). 198p. (J). (gr. 4-7). 15.95 o.p. (*0-8050-4676-3*, Holt, Henry & Co. Bks. For Young Readers) Holt, Henry & Co.

—Monsters in Cyberspace, ERS. 1997. 192p. (J). (gr. 3-7). 14.95 o.p. (*0-8050-4677-1*, Holt, Henry & Co. Bks. For Young Readers) Holt, Henry & Co.

—Monsters in the Attic. 1999. (Illus.). 178p. (J). (gr. 4-6). reprint ed. text 15.00 (*0-7881-6676-X*) DIANE Publishing Co.

—Monsters in the Attic, ERS. 1995. (Illus.). 192p. (J). (gr. 3-7). 14.95 o.p. (*0-8050-3709-8*, Holt, Henry & Co. Bks. For Young Readers) Holt, Henry & Co.

—Monsters in the Attic. 1998. (J). pap. 4.50 (*0-590-84473-3*) Scholastic, Inc.

—Monsters in the Attic. 1998. 10.55 (*0-606-13620-7*) Turtleback Bks.

Regents. Monsters, Bk. 6. 1996. (J). (gr. 3-6). pap. text 8.20 (*0-13-349879-4*) Prentice Hall PTR.

Reimer, Ramon. Irene & the Big Red Monster. 2000. (Illus.). (J). (gr. k-5). lib. bdg. 14.95 (*0-9705727-0-0*) Coastal Publishing Carolina, Inc.

Reiner, Carl. Tell Me a Scary Story, but Not Too Scary. 2003. (Illus.). 32p. (J). (gr. k-5). 18.95 incl. audio compact disk (*0-316-83329-0*) Little Brown & Co.

Reitz, Mercedes M. & Reitz, Russell T. The Dreadful Monsters of Yellow Mountain. 1991. (Yellow Mountain Ser.). (Illus.). 216p. (Orig.). (J). (gr. 4 up). pap. 9.95 (*0-9625344-3-9*); text 19.95 (*0-9625344-2-0*) Creative Multi-Media.

Rex, Michael. The Mud Monster's Halloween. 2002. (Word-by-Word First Reader Ser.). (Illus.). 32p. (J). mass mkt. 3.99 (*0-439-33492-6*, Cartwheel Bks.) Scholastic, Inc.

RH Disney Staff. Monsters Get Scared of Dogs, Too. 2003. (Illus.). 16p. (J). pap. 3.99 (*0-7364-2163-7*, RH/Disney) Random Hse. Children's Bks.

—Monsters Get Scared of the Dark, Too. 2003. (Illus.). 16p. (J). 3.99 (*0-7364-2162-9*, 53528995, RH/Disney) Random Hse. Children's Bks.

—Monsters, Inc. 2003. (Illus.). 24p. (J). bds. 4.99 (*0-7364-2206-4*, RH/Disney) Random Hse. Children's Bks.

Richler, Mordecai. Jacob Two-Two Meets the Hooded Fang. 1994. (Illus.). (J). (gr. 4-7). pap. 3.50 o.s.i (*0-679-85403-7*, Knopf Bks. for Young Readers) Random Hse. Children's Bks.

Roberts, Bethany. Monster Manners. 1997. (Illus.). 32p. (J). (ps-3). pap. 5.95 (*0-395-86622-7*, Clarion Bks.) Houghton Mifflin Co. Trade & Reference Div.

—Monster Manners: A Guide to Monster Etiquette. 1996. (Illus.). 32p. (J). (ps-3). lib. bdg., tchr. ed. 15.00 (*0-395-69850-2*, Clarion Bks.) Houghton Mifflin Co. Trade & Reference Div.

Robins, Deri. Mystery of the Monster Party. 1998. (Gamebook Preschool Puzzles Ser.). (Illus.). 32p. (Orig.). (J). bds. 5.99 o.p. (*0-7636-0300-7*) Candlewick Pr.

Robison, Nancy. Ten Tall Soldiers, ERS. 1991. (Illus.). 32p. (J). (ps). 13.95 o.p. (*0-8050-0768-7*, Holt, Henry & Co. Bks. For Young Readers) Holt, Henry & Co.

—Ten Tall Soldiers. 2001. (Illus.). 40p. (ps-3). pap. 6.99 (*0-689-84325-9*, Aladdin) Simon & Schuster Children's Publishing.

—Ten Tall Soldiers. 1995. 4.98 o.p. (*0-8317-2271-1*) Smithmark Pubs., Inc.

Rockwell, Anne F. The One-Eyed Giant. 1996. (Illus.). 32p. (J). (ps-3). 16.00 (*0-688-13809-8*, Greenwillow Bks.) HarperCollins Children's Bk. Group.

—The One-Eyed Giant & Other Monsters from the Greek Myths. 1996. (Illus.). 32p. (J). (ps up). lib. bdg. 15.93 o.p. (*0-688-13810-1*, Greenwillow Bks.) HarperCollins Children's Bk. Group.

—Thump Thump Thump! 1981. (Smart Cat Bks.). (Illus.). (J). (ps-1). 8.25 o.p. (*0-525-41300-6*, Dutton) Dutton/Plume.

Rodda, Emily. Deltora Book of Monsters. 2002. (Deltora Quest Ser.). (Illus.). 48p. (J). (gr. 3-7). mass mkt. 7.99 o.s.i (*0-439-39084-2*) Scholastic, Inc.

Rodgers, Frank. Looking after Your First Monster. 1992. (J). (ps-3). mass mkt. 3.95 o.p. (*0-590-45695-4*) Scholastic, Inc.

Rojany, Lisa. Morty Monster. 1995. (Fuzzy Friends Ser.). (Illus.). 10p. (J). (ps up). 3.95 o.s.i (*0-8431-3788-6*, Price Stern Sloan) Penguin Putnam Bks. for Young Readers.

Roos, Stephen. Love Me, Love My Werewolf. 1993. (Pet Lovers Club Ser.: No. 1). 128p. (J). (gr. 4-7). pap. 3.50 o.s.i (*0-440-40812-1*) Dell Publishing.

Root, Phyllis. The Hungry Monster. 1997. (Illus.). 24p. (J). (ps up). 9.99 o.p. (*0-7636-0060-1*) Candlewick Pr.

—Hungry Monster. 1998. (Giggle Club Ser.). (Illus.). 24p. (J). (ps-1). bds. 3.29 o.s.i (*0-7636-0380-5*) Candlewick Pr.

Rosen, Winifred. Dragons Hate to Be Discreet. 1978. (Illus.). (J). (gr. 3-7). 4.95 o.p. (*0-394-83577-8*); lib. bdg. 4.99 o.p. (*0-394-93577-2*) Random Hse. Children's Bks. (Knopf Bks. for Young Readers).

Rosenberg, Liz. Monster Mama. 1997. (J). 13.14 (*0-606-11633-8*) Turtleback Bks.

Ross, Anna, et al. Elmo! 1997. (Sesame Street Furry Faces Ser.). (Illus.). 12p. (J). (ps). bds. 7.99 o.s.i (*0-679-88830-6*, Random Hse. Bks. for Young Readers) Random Hse. Children's Bks.

—Grover! 1997. (Sesame Street Furry Faces Ser.). (Illus.). 12p. (J). (ps). bds. 7.99 o.s.i (*0-679-88832-2*, Random Hse. Bks. for Young Readers) Random Hse. Children's Bks.

Ross, Dave. How to Prevent Monster Attacks. 1984. (Illus.). 64p. (J). (gr. 4 up). 10.00 o.p. (*0-688-03790-9*, Morrow, William & Co.) Morrow/Avon.

Ross, Katharine. Fuzzy Monsters. 1995. (J). (ps-k). bds. 0.99 o.s.i (*0-679-87274-4*) Random Hse., Inc.

Ross, Tony. I'm Coming to Get You! 1984. (Pied Piper Bks.). (Illus.). (J). (ps-2). 11.95 o.p. (*0-8037-0119-5*, Dial Bks. for Young Readers) Penguin Putnam Bks. for Young Readers.

Rostoker-Gruber, Karen. Food Fright: A Mouthwatering Novelty Book. 2003. (Illus.). 12p. (J). 11.99 (*0-8431-0456-2*, Price Stern Sloan) Penguin Putnam Bks. for Young Readers.

Rubel, Nicole. Sam & Violet's Bedtime Mystery. 1985. (J). (gr. k-3). pap. 2.50 o.p. (*0-380-89820-9*, Avon Bks.) Morrow/Avon.

Rudd, Elizabeth. Beauty & the Beast. 1988. (J). mass mkt. 15.93 o.p. (*0-516-08563-8*, Children's Pr.) Scholastic Library Publishing.

Ryan, John. Pugwash & the Sea Monster. 1993. (Illus.). 32p. (J). (gr. k-2). o.p. (*0-370-10793-4*) Random Hse., Inc.

S. I. International Staff, illus. The Green Monster. 2004. (Teenage Mutant Ninja Turtles Ser.). 32p. (J). pap. 3.99 (*0-689-86902-9*, Simon Spotlight) Simon & Schuster Children's Publishing.

Sabraw, John. I Wouldn't Be Scared. 1989. (Illus.). 32p. (J). (ps-1). 13.95 o.p. (*0-531-05818-2*); mass mkt. 13.99 o.p. (*0-531-08418-3*) Scholastic, Inc. (Orchard Bks.).

Sadler, Marilyn. Alistair Underwater. (J). (ps-3). 1992. pap. 5.95 (*0-671-79246-6*, Aladdin); 1990. pap. 15.00 o.s.i (*0-671-69406-5*, Simon & Schuster Children's Publishing) Simon & Schuster Children's Publishing.

Sage, Alison. Ogre's Banquet. 1978. (gr. 1-3). 5.95 o.p. (*0-385-14360-5*); lib. bdg. o.p. (*0-385-14462-8*) Doubleday Publishing.

Sampson, Fay. Pangur Ban, the White Cat, Vol. 2. 2003. 144p. (YA). (gr. 5-8). pap. 7.95 (*0-7459-4763-8*) Lion Publishing PLC GBR. *Dist:* Trafalgar Square.

Samton, Sheila White. Ten Tiny Monsters. 1997. (Illus.). 32p. (J). (ps-1). 18.99 o.s.i (*0-517-70942-2*) Crown Publishing Group.

Sanschagrin, Joceline. La Marque du Dragon. 2002. (Roman Jeunesse Ser.). (Illus.). 96p. (YA). (gr. 4-7). pap. 8.95 (*2-89021-355-2*) La Courte Echelle CAN. *Dist:* Firefly Bks., Ltd.

Sardegna, Jill. You Monsters Are in Charge. 2002. (Illus.). 12p. (J). 12.95 (*0-689-84675-4*, Little Simon) Simon & Schuster Children's Publishing.

Saunders, Susan. Attack of the Monster Plants. 1986. (Choose Your Own Adventure Ser.: No. 34). 64p. (J). (gr. 2-4). pap. 2.25 o.s.i (*0-553-15399-4*) Bantam Bks.

The Scary Monster House. 1993. (Play-a-Sound Ser.). (Illus.). 24p. (J). 12.98 (*0-7853-0139-9*) Publications International, Ltd.

Schaefer, Lola M. Out of the Night. (Illus.). 32p. (ps-k). 1999. pap. 6.95 (*1-58089-023-7*); 1995. (J). 14.95 (*1-879085-91-7*) Charlesbridge Publishing, Inc. (Whispering Coyote).

Schecter, Ellen. Murky Monster's Birthday Bash. 1999. (Bank Street Ready-to-Read Ser.). (Illus.). (J). trans. 20.01 (*0-553-37588-1*) Bantam Bks.

—Murky Monster's Birthday Bash. 1999. E-Book (*1-58824-972-7*); E-Book (*1-58824-974-3*); E-Book (*1-58824-973-5*) ipicturebooks, LLC.

—Real Live Monsters! 1996. (Bank Street Reader Collection). (Illus.). 32p. (J). (gr. 1-3). lib. bdg. 21.26 (*0-8368-1620-X*) Stevens, Gareth Inc.

—Real Live Monsters! 1995. (J). E-Book (*1-58824-185-8*) ipicturebooks, LLC.

—Real Live Monsters. 1995. (J). 19.95 (*0-553-53121-2*); mass mkt. 4.99 (*0-553-54203-6*) Random Hse. Children's Bks. (Dell Books for Young Readers).

—Real Live Monsters. 1995. E-Book (*1-59019-315-6*); E-Book (*1-58824-069-X*) ipicturebooks, LLC.

Schick, Joel & Schick, Alice. Mary Shelley's Frankenstein. 1981. (Illus.). 48p. (J). (gr. 4-6). lib. bdg. 11.95 o.s.i (*0-385-28302-4*, Delacorte Pr.) Dell Publishing.

Schnitzlein, Danny. The Monster Who Ate My Peas. 2001. (Illus.). 32p. (J). (gr. k-3). 15.95 (*1-56145-216-5*) Peachtree Pubs., Ltd.

Scholastic, Inc. Staff. Attack of the Baby Godzillas No. 2: Picture Book. 1998. (Godzilla Ser.). (Illus.). 32p. (J). (gr. k-3). mass mkt. 3.50 (*0-590-68112-5*) Scholastic, Inc.

—Godzilla: A Novelization. novel ed. 1998. (Godzilla Ser.). (Illus.). 152p. (J). (gr. 3-7). mass mkt. 3.99 (*0-590-28243-3*) Scholastic, Inc.

—Godzillas Scrapbook. 1998. (Godzilla Ser.). 32p. (J). (gr. 2-5). mass mkt. 8.98 (*0-590-57239-3*) Scholastic, Inc.

—Monsters Unleashed: Movie Scrapbook. 2004. (Scooby-Doo Ser.). 48p. (J). mass mkt. 5.99 (*0-439-56756-4*, Scholastic Paperbacks) Scholastic, Inc.

—Picture Book No. 1. 1998. (Godzilla Ser.). 32p. (J). (gr. k-3). mass mkt. 3.50 (*0-590-57212-1*) Scholastic, Inc.

Scholastic, Inc. Staff, ed. Monster Holidays. 9999. (J). pap. 2.25 o.s.i (*0-590-41534-4*) Scholastic, Inc.

Schreier, Joshua. Hank's Work. 1993. 320p. (J). (ps-2). 13.50 o.p. (*0-525-44970-1*, Dutton Children's Bks.) Penguin Putnam Bks. for Young Readers.

Seabrooke, Brenda. The Vampire in My Bathtub. 1999. 150p. (J). (gr. 3-7). tchr. ed. 15.95 (*0-8234-1505-8*) Holiday Hse., Inc.

Sendak, Maurice. Donde Viven los Monstruos, 2001. (SPA., Illus.). 40p. (J). (gr. k-3). 12.95 (*84-372-2185-4*) Altea, Ediciones, S.A. - Grupo Santillana ESP. *Dist:* Santillana USA Publishing Co., Inc.

—Donde Viven los Monstruos. 3rd ed. 1995. (SPA., Illus.). 40p. (J). (ps-3). 22.95 (*84-204-3022-6*, KZ226) Santillana USA Publishing Co., Inc.

—Seven Little Monsters. 1977. (Illus.). (J). (gr. 1 up). pap. 3.95 o.p. (*0-06-025501-3*); (gr. 1 up). lib. bdg. 14.89 o.s.i (*0-06-025478-5*); (ps-3). 11.95 o.p. (*0-06-025477-7*) HarperCollins Children's Bk. Group.

—Seven Little Monsters. 1986. (J). (ps-3). pap. 4.95 o.s.i (*0-06-443139-8*) HarperCollins Pubs.

—Seven Little Monsters. 1977. (J). 10.15 o.p. (*0-606-02851-X*) Turtleback Bks.

—Where the Wild Things Are. 2002. (Illus.). (J). 16.60 (*0-7587-0028-8*) Book Wholesalers, Inc.

—Where the Wild Things Are. 1995. (Illus.). reprint ed. lib. bdg. 29.95 (*1-56849-659-1*) Buccaneer Bks., Inc.

—Where the Wild Things Are. ed. 1984. (J). (gr. 1). spiral bd. (*0-616-01779-0*); (gr. 2). spiral bd. (*0-616-01780-4*) Canadian National Institute for the Blind/Institut National Canadien pour les Aveugles.

—Where the Wild Things Are. 2001. (Early Readers Ser.: Vol. 1). (J). lib. bdg. (*1-59054-500-1*) Fitzgerald Bks.

—Where the Wild Things Are. (J). 1998. 16.95 (*0-06-028223-1*); 1992. (Illus.). 48p. 16.95 o.s.i (*0-694-00431-6*, Harper Festival); 1992. (Illus.). 48p. 16.95 o.s.i (*0-694-00432-4*, Harper Festival); 1988. (Illus.). 48p. pap. 7.99 (*0-06-443178-9*, Harper Trophy); 1984. (Illus.). 48p. pap. 4.95 o.p. (*0-06-443055-3*, Harper Trophy); 1964. (SPA., Illus.). 48p. 11.95 o.p. (*0-06-025520-X*); 1964. (Illus.). 48p. lib. bdg. 11.89 o.p. (*0-06-025521-8*); 25th anniv. ed. 1988. (Illus.). 48p. 16.95 (*0-06-025492-0*); 25th anniv. ed. 1988. (Illus.). 48p. lib. bdg. 17.89 (*0-06-025493-9*); Vol. 2. 1985. (Illus.). 19.95 o.p. (*0-694-00096-5*) HarperCollins Children's Bk. Group.

—Where the Wild Things Are. 1999. (J). 9.95 (*1-56137-022-3*) Novel Units, Inc.

—Where the Wild Things Are. 9999. (Illus.). (J). pap. o.p. (*0-590-04537-7*); pap. 2.25 o.p. (*0-590-04513-X*) Scholastic, Inc.

—Where the Wild Things Are. 1984. (J). 13.10 (*0-606-03230-4*) Turtleback Bks.

—Where the Wild Things Are. (J). pap. text 12.95 incl. audio Weston Woods Studios, Inc.

Sensel, Joni. The Garbage Monster. 2001. (Illus.). 24p. (J). (ps up). 14.95 (*0-9701195-2-6*) Dream Factory Bks.

Sesame Street Staff. Monster at End of This Book. 2003. (Popular Characters/Author Collection). (Illus.). 24p. (J). (ps-k). 2.99 (*0-307-01085-6*, Golden Bks.) Random Hse. Children's Bks.

Sesame Street Staff & Ross, Anna. Cookie Monster! 1997. (Sesame Street Furry Faces Ser.). (Illus.). 12p. (J). (ps). bds. 7.99 o.s.i (*0-679-88831-4*, Random Hse. Bks. for Young Readers) Random Hse. Children's Bks.

Sesame Street Staff, et al. Monster Faces. 1996. (Chunky Shape Bks.). (Illus.). 22p. bds. 3.99 (*0-679-87761-4*, Random Hse. Bks. for Young Readers) Random Hse. Children's Bks.

Seymour, Peter. Milton the Monster. 1986. (Surprise Bks.). 22p. (J). (ps-1). 5.95 o.p. (*0-8431-1461-4*, Price Stern Sloan) Penguin Putnam Bks. for Young Readers.

Sfar, Joann. Little Vampire Does Kung Fu. 2003. (Illus.). 40p. (J). 12.95 (*0-689-85769-1*, Simon & Schuster Children's Publishing) Simon & Schuster Children's Publishing.

—Little Vampire Goes to School. Siegel, Mark & Siegel, Alexis, trs. from FRE. 2003. (Illus.). 40p. (J). 12.95 (*0-689-85717-9*, Simon & Schuster Children's Publishing) Simon & Schuster Children's Publishing.

Shannon, Margaret. Elvira. 1993. 11.15 o.p. (*0-606-08738-9*) Turtleback Bks.

—Gullible's Troubles. 1998. (Illus.). 32p. (J). (ps-3). lib. bdg., tchr. ed. 15.00 (*0-395-83933-5*) Houghton Mifflin Co.

—Gullible's Troubles. 2000. (Illus.). 32p. (J). (ps-3). pap. 5.95 (*0-618-07033-8*) Houghton Mifflin Co. Trade & Reference Div.

Shannon, Margaret, illus. & text. Elvira. 1993. 32p. (J). (ps-2). tchr. ed. 13.95 o.p. (*0-395-66597-3*) Houghton Mifflin Co.

Sharkey, Niamh. The Ravenous Beast. 2003. 32p. (J). 16.99 (*0-7636-2182-X*) Candlewick Pr.

Sharmat, Marjorie Weinman. Gila Monsters Meet You at the Airport. 1983. (Illus.). 32p. (J). (gr. k-3). pap. 3.95 o.p. (*0-14-050430-3*, Puffin Bks.) Penguin Putnam Bks. for Young Readers.

—Nate the Great & the Monster Mess. 2001. (Nate the Great Ser.). (Illus.). 48p. (gr. 1-4). pap. text 4.50 (*0-440-41662-0*, Dell Books for Young Readers) Random Hse. Children's Bks.

—Nate the Great & the Monster Mess. 2001. 10.65 (*0-606-22399-1*) Turtleback Bks.

—The Pizza Monster. 1989. (J). pap. 12.95 o.s.i (*0-440-50086-9*) Dell Publishing.

—Scarlet Monster Lives Here. (I Can Read Bks.). (Illus.). 64p. (J). (ps-1). 1986. pap. 3.50 o.p. (*0-06-444098-2*, Harper Trophy); 1979. lib. bdg. 11.89 o.p. (*0-06-025527-7*) HarperCollins Children's Bk. Group.

—Scarlet Monster Lives Here. 1986. (I Can Read Bks.). (J). (ps-1). 8.70 o.p. (*0-606-01938-3*) Turtleback Bks.

—The Trolls of Twelfth Street. 1979. (Break-of-Day Bks.). (Illus.). (J). (gr. k-3). 6.99 o.p. (*0-698-30716-X*) Putnam Publishing Group, The.

Sharmat, Marjorie Weinman & Sharmat, Mitchell. The Pizza Monster: Olivia Sharp, Agent for Secrets. 1990. 48p. (J). (gr. k-6). pap. 2.75 o.s.i (*0-440-40286-7*, Yearling) Random Hse. Children's Bks.

Shelley, Mary Wollstonecraft. Frankenstein. 2002. (Great Illustrated Classics). (Illus.). 240p. (J). (gr. 3-8). lib. bdg. 21.35 (*1-57765-686-5*, ABDO & Daughters) ABDO Publishing Co.

—Frankenstein. 1996. (Wishbone Classics Ser.: No. 7). (Illus.). 128p. (gr. 3-7). mass mkt. 3.99 (*0-06-106417-3*, HarperEntertainment) Morrow/Avon.

—Frankenstein. (J). 1999. (Saddleback Classics). (Illus.). 13.10 (*0-606-21551-4*); 1996. (Wishbone Classics Ser.: No.7). (gr. 3-7). 10.04 (*0-606-10370-8*) Turtleback Bks.

—Frankenstein: "The Modern Prometheus" Joseph, M. K., ed. & intro. by. 1998. (Oxford World's Classics Ser.). 264p. (YA). (gr. 7 up). pap. 6.95 (*0-19-283487-8*) Oxford Univ. Pr., Inc.

—Frankenstein: With a Discussion of Tolerance. Clift, Eva, tr. & illus. by. 2003. (Values in Action Illustrated Classics Ser.). (J). (*1-59203-048-3*) Learning Challenge, Inc.

Shelton, Ingrid. The Lollipop Dragon & the Writing Contest. 1983. (Tiny Tumtum Tales Ser.). (Illus.). 80p. (Orig.). (J). (gr. k-4). pap. 0.98 o.p. (*0-87239-698-3*, 2914) Standard Publishing.

—The Lollipop Dragon Finds the Missing Teddy Bear. 1983. (Tiny Tumtum Tales Ser.). (Illus.). 80p. (Orig.). (J). (gr. k-4). pap. 0.98 o.p. (*0-87239-697-5*, 2913) Standard Publishing.

—The Lollipop Dragon Helps the Flower Lady. 1983. (Tiny Tumtum Tales Ser.). (Illus.). 80p. (Orig.). (J). (gr. k-4). pap. 0.98 o.p. (*0-87239-696-7*, 2912) Standard Publishing.

—The Lollipop Dragon Plans a Potluck Picnic. 1983. (Tiny Tumtum Tales Ser.). (Illus.). 80p. (Orig.). (J). (gr. k-4). pap. 0.98 o.p. (*0-87239-695-9*, 2911) Standard Publishing.

Shi, Sharon. Monsters Get Scared Too. rev. ed. 2000. (Illus.). 24p. (J). mass mkt. 4.99 (*0-9678636-8-6*, B009, Tattoodles Bks.) Tattoo Manufacturing.

Shortsleeve, Kevin. 13 Monsters Who Should Be Avoided. 1998. (Illus.). 32p. (J). (gr. 1-5). 16.95 (*1-56145-146-0*) Peachtree Pubs., Ltd.

Sierra, Judy. The House That Drac Built. 1998. (Illus.). 32p. (J). (ps-2). pap. 6.00 (*0-15-201879-4*, Harcourt Paperbacks) Harcourt Children's Bks.

Silverman, Erica. Big Pumpkin. 1992. (Illus.). 32p. (J). (ps-3). 16.00 (*0-02-782683-X*, Simon & Schuster Children's Publishing) Simon & Schuster Children's Publishing.

—Big Pumpkin. 1995. 12.14 (*0-606-07286-1*) Turtleback Bks.

—The Halloween House. 1997. (Illus.). (J). (*0-374-16768-0*);RS. 32p. 16.00 o.p. (*0-374-33270-3*, Farrar, Straus & Giroux (BYR)) Farrar, Straus & Giroux.

Singer, A. L., adapted by. Disney's Beauty & the Beast. 1991. (Junior Novelization Ser.). (Illus.). 64p. (J). (gr. 2-6). pap. 3.50 o.p. (*1-56282-051-6*) Disney Pr.

Skolnick, Evan. Veiled Beauty. 1997. (Hunchback of Notre Dame Ser.). (J). pap. text 4.50 (*1-57840-156-9*) Acclaim Bks.

Skwarek, Skip. The Weirdies of Wailing Wood. 1992. (Mini Monster Pop-Up Bk.). (Illus.). 10p. (J). (gr. k-4). 4.95 o.p. (*0-8037-1188-3*, Dial Bks. for Young Readers) Penguin Putnam Bks. for Young Readers.

Slater, Jim. Big Nose. 1983. (A. Mazing Monsters Ser.). (Illus.). (J). (ps-3). pap. 1.25 o.p. (*0-394-84739-3*) Random Hse., Inc.

—The Great Gulper. 1981. (A. Mazing Monsters Ser.). (Illus.). (J). (gr. 3-6). pap. 1.25 o.p. (*0-394-84737-7*, Random Hse. Bks. for Young Readers) Random Hse. Children's Bks.

—The Tricky Troggle. 1981. (A. Mazing Monsters Ser.). (Illus.). (J). pap. 1.25 o.s.i (*0-394-84738-5*) Random Hse., Inc.

Slaton, Lana. Giants & Goblins. 1997. (Troubador Color & Story Ser.). (Illus.). 32p. (J). (ps up). reprint ed. 5.95 o.p. (*0-8431-7964-3*, Price Stern Sloan) Penguin Putnam Bks. for Young Readers.

Sleator, William. The Boxes. 1998. 208p. (J). (gr. 5-9). 15.99 (*0-525-46012-8*, Dutton Children's Bks.) Penguin Putnam Bks. for Young Readers.

Slepian, Jan. Hungry Thing. 1967. (J). 9.15 o.p. (*0-606-04007-2*) Turtleback Bks.

—Hungry Thing Returns. 1993. (J). (ps-3). pap. 3.95 o.p. (*0-590-42891-8*) Scholastic, Inc.

Slepian, Jan & Seidler, Ann. The Hungry Thing. 2001. (Illus.). 32p. (ps-1). mass mkt. 5.99 (*0-439-27598-9*) Scholastic, Inc.

Slime, R. U. Eat Cheese & Barf! 1995. (Gooflumps Ser.: Vol. 4). (Illus.). (J). (gr. 4-7). pap. 3.99 o.s.i (*0-679-87935-8*, Random Hse. Bks. for Young Readers) Random Hse. Children's Bks.

—Stay Out of the Bathroom. 1995. (Gooflumps Ser.: No. 2.5). (Illus.). (gr. 4-7). pap. 3.99 o.s.i (*0-679-87908-0*, Random Hse. Bks. for Young Readers) Random Hse. Children's Bks.

Smith, Alison. Come Away Home. 1991. (Illus.). 112p. (J). (gr. 3-5). lib. bdg. 12.95 o.p. (*0-684-19283-7*, Atheneum) Simon & Schuster Children's Publishing.

Smith, Dona. Shock Shots: Ghosts. 1993. 48p. (J). (gr. 4-6). pap. 1.25 (*0-590-47568-1*) Scholastic, Inc.

—Shock Shots: Monsters. 1993. (J). (gr. 4-7). pap. 1.25 (*0-590-47566-5*) Scholastic, Inc.

—Shock Shots: Mummies. 1993. 48p. (J). (gr. 4-6). pap. 1.25 (*0-590-47571-1*) Scholastic, Inc.

—Shock Shots: Vampires. 1993. 48p. (J). (gr. 4-6). pap. 1.25 o.p. (*0-590-47569-X*) Scholastic, Inc.

—Shock Shots: Zombies. 1993. 48p. (J). (gr. 4-6). pap. 1.25 (*0-590-47567-3*) Scholastic, Inc.

Smith, Dona, et al. Shock Shots: Werewolves. 1993. 48p. (J). (gr. 4-7). pap. 1.25 (*0-590-47570-3*) Scholastic, Inc.

Smith, Janice Lee. The Halloween Monster: And Other Stories about Adam Joshua. 1995. (Trophy Chapter Bk.: No. 5). (Illus.). 80p. (J). (gr. 2-5). pap. 3.95 o.s.i (*0-06-442007-8*, Harper Trophy) HarperCollins Children's Bk. Group.

—The Monster in the Third Dresser Drawer. 1981. (Illus.). 96p. (J). (gr. 1-4). 13.95 o.p. (*0-06-025734-2*); (ps-3). lib. bdg. 15.89 (*0-06-025739-3*) HarperCollins Children's Bk. Group.

—The Monster in the Third Dresser Drawer: And Other Stories about Adam Joshua. 1988. (Illus.). 96p. (J). (gr. 2-5). pap. 4.25 (*0-06-440223-1*, Harper Trophy) HarperCollins Children's Bk. Group.

—Monster in the Third Dresser Drawer & Otherstories about Adam Joshua. 1981. (J). 10.40 (*0-606-03863-9*) Turtleback Bks.

Smith, Parker. Universal Monsters: The Mummy. 1992. (Illus.). 96p. (J). (gr. 3-7). pap. o.p. (*0-307-22332-9*, 22332, Golden Bks.) Random Hse. Children's Bks.

Smithmark Staff. Dracula - Frankenstein. 1995. (Illus.). 498p. (J). 12.98 o.p. (*0-8317-6696-4*) Smithmark Pubs., Inc.

Snyder, Zilpha Keatley. Song of the Gargoyle. 93rd ed. 1993. pap. text 19.60 (*0-15-300378-2*) Harcourt Children's Bks.

Sommer-Bodenburg, Angela. The Vampire Takes a Trip. (J). 1990. mass mkt. 2.95 (*0-671-73699-X*); 1987. (Illus.). (gr. 3-7). pap. (*0-671-64822-5*) Simon & Schuster Children's Publishing. (Aladdin).

Spaht-Gill, Janie. Monster Stew. (Illus.). (J). 5.95 (*0-89868-307-6*); 1997. 23p. lib. bdg. 10.95 (*0-89868-306-8*) ARO Publishing Co.

Spencely, Annabel, illus. The Kingfisher Treasury of Giant & Monster Stories, Vol. 7. 2003. (Kingfisher Treasury of Stories Ser.). 160p. (J). pap. 5.95 (*0-7534-5667-2*, Kingfisher) Houghton Mifflin Co. Trade & Reference Div.

Spinelli, Eileen. Wanda's Monster. 2002. (Illus.). 32p. (J). (gr. k-3). lib. bdg. 15.95 (*0-8075-8656-0*) Whitman, Albert & Co.

Spinner, Stephanie. Monster in the Maze: The Story of the Minotaur. 2000. (All Aboard Reading Ser.). (Illus.). (J). 10.14 (*0-606-20404-0*) Turtleback Bks.

Sprecher, John. Jeffrey & the Despondent Dragon, Vol. SCPB1. l.t. ed. 1997. (Special Kids "Special Message" Bks.). (Illus.). 32p. (J). (gr. k-4). pap. 10.00 (*1-892186-00-4*) Anythings Possible, Inc.

St. Aubin, Bruno & Homel, David. My Favourite Monster. 2000. (Illus.). 32p. (gr. 1-4). pap. (*1-894363-41-8*) Dominique & Friends.

Stamper, Judith Bauer. Monster Phonics: Monster Town. 1998. (Hello Reader! Ser.). (J). (gr. 1-2). 10.14 (*0-606-13619-3*) Turtleback Bks.

Stamper, Judith Bauer & Blevins, Wiley. Monster Town, Level 1. 1997. (Hello Reader! Ser.). (Illus.). 32p. (J). (gr. 1-2). mass mkt. 3.99 (*0-590-76265-6*) Scholastic, Inc.

—Monster Town Fair. 1998. (Hello Reader! Ser.). (Illus.). 32p. (J). (gr. 1-2). pap. 3.99 (*0-590-76268-0*) Scholastic, Inc.

Stanley, George Edward. The Vampire Kittens of Count Dracula. 1997. (Scaredy Cats Ser.: No. 8). (Illus.). 80p. (J). (gr. 1-4). mass mkt. 3.99 (*0-689-81615-4*, Aladdin) Simon & Schuster Children's Publishing.

Staunton, Ted. The Monkey Mountain Monster. 2000. (Monkey Mountain Bks.). (Illus.). 64p. (J). (gr. 2-5). pap. 4.95 (*0-88995-206-X*) Red Deer Pr. CAN. *Dist:* General Distribution Services, Inc.

Steer, Dugald. Snappy Little Halloween. 2000. (Snappy Pop-Ups Ser.: 6). (Illus.). 20p. (ps-1). 12.95 o.p. (*0-7613-1433-4*) Millbrook Pr., Inc.

Steig, William. Shrek!, RS. (Illus.). 32p. (ps-3). 1993. (J). pap. 5.95 (*0-374-46623-8*, Sunburst); 1990. 10.95 (*0-374-36877-5*, Farrar, Straus & Giroux (BYR)) Farrar, Straus & Giroux.

—Shrek! 1990. 12.10 (*0-606-06000-6*) Turtleback Bks.

Stevens, Kathleen. The Beast in the Bathtub. 1985. (Illus.). 32p. (J). (gr. 2-3). lib. bdg. 19.93 o.p. (*0-918831-15-6*) Stevens, Gareth Inc.

—Bully for the Beast! 1990. (Illus.). 32p. (J). (gr. 2-3). lib. bdg. 18.60 o.p. (*0-8368-0020-6*) Stevens, Gareth Inc.

Stevenson, Robert Louis. Dr. Jekyll & Mr. Hyde Readalong. 1994. (Illustrated Classics Collection). 64p. (J). pap. 13.50 o.p. incl. audio (*1-56103-422-3*) American Guidance Service, Inc.

Stewart, Molly Mia. Jessica's Monster Nightmare. 1993. (Sweet Valley Kids Ser.: No. 42). (J). (gr. 1-3). 8.70 o.p. (*0-606-05645-9*) Turtleback Bks.

Stimson, Joan. Bad Ben & the Monster. 1990. (Scary Stories Ser.: No. S903-2). (J). (gr. k-2). pap. 3.95 (*0-7214-5266-3*, Ladybird Bks.) Penguin Group (USA) Inc.

—Monster Stories for under Fives. 1994. (Illus.). 32p. (J). text 3.50 (*0-7214-1639-X*, Ladybird Bks.) Penguin Group (USA) Inc.

—Monster Stories for under 5s. 1992. (Series 922). (Illus.). 44p. (J). (ps). pap. 3.50 (*0-7214-1505-9*, Ladybird Bks.) Penguin Group (USA) Inc.

Stine, Megan. The Girl Who Cried Monster. 1996. (Goosebumps Presents Ser.: No. 1). 57p. (J). (gr. 3-7). 9.19 o.p. (*0-606-08753-2*) Turtleback Bks.

Stine, Megan & Stine, H. William. Camp Zombie. 1994. (Bullseye Chillers Ser.). 108p. (J). (gr. 2-6). pap. 3.50 o.s.i (*0-679-85640-4*, Random Hse. Bks. for Young Readers) Random Hse. Children's Bks.

—Camp Zombie III: The Lake's Revenge. 1996. (Bullseye Chillers Ser.). 108p. (J). pap. 3.99 o.s.i (*0-679-87880-7*) Random Hse., Inc.

Stine, R. L. Attack of the Mutant. 1997. (Goosebumps Ser.: No. 25). (J). (gr. 3-7). 10.14 (*0-606-11406-8*) Turtleback Bks.

—Egg Monsters from Mars. 2003. (Goosebumps Ser.). 144p. (J). mass mkt. 4.99 (*0-439-56829-3*, 53655423, Scholastic Paperbacks) Scholastic, Inc.

—Egg Monsters from Mars. 1996. (Goosebumps Ser.: No. 42). (J). (gr. 3-7). 10.04 (*0-606-09230-7*) Turtleback Bks.

—The Girl Who Cried Monster. 1993. (Goosebumps Ser.: No. 8). 160p. (J). (gr. 3-7). mass mkt. 3.99 (*0-590-46618-6*) Scholastic, Inc.

—The Girl Who Cried Monster. l.t. ed. 1997. (Goosebumps Ser.: No. 8). 144p. (J). (gr. 3-7). lib. bdg. 21.27 o.p. (*0-8368-1980-2*) Stevens, Gareth Inc.

—The Girl Who Cried Monster. 1993. (Goosebumps Ser.: No. 8). (J). (gr. 3-7). 10.04 (*0-606-05318-2*) Turtleback Bks.

—Goosebumps Monster Edition 1: Welcome to Dead House; Stay out of the Basement; Say Cheese & Die!, 1995. (Goosebumps Ser.: Nos. 1, 2, 4). 400p. (J). (gr. 3-7). pap. 12.95 (*0-590-50995-0*) Scholastic, Inc.

—Goosebumps Monster Edition 3: The Ghost Next Door; Ghost Beach; The Barking Ghost, 3rd ed. 1997. (Goosebumps Ser.: Nos. 10, 22, 32). (Illus.). (J). (gr. 3-7). pap. 12.95 (*0-590-36673-4*) Scholastic, Inc.

—Monster Blood. 2003. (Goosebumps Ser.). 144p. (J). mass mkt. 4.99 (*0-439-56839-0*, 53655433, Scholastic Paperbacks) Scholastic, Inc.

—Monster Blood. 1997. (Goosebumps Presents Ser.: No. 15). (Illus.). 64p. (J). (gr. 3-7). mass mkt. 3.99 o.s.i (*0-590-30547-6*, Scholastic Paperbacks) Scholastic, Inc.

—Monster Blood. 1992. (Goosebumps Ser.: No. 3). 160p. (J). (gr. 3-7). mass mkt. 3.99 (*0-590-45367-X*, 061, Scholastic Paperbacks) Scholastic, Inc.

—Monster Blood. l.t. ed. 1997. (Goosebumps Ser.: No. 3). 128p. (J). (gr. 3-7). lib. bdg. 21.27 o.p. (*0-8368-1975-6*) Stevens, Gareth Inc.

—Monster Blood. 1997. (Goosebumps Presents Ser.: No. 3). (J). (gr. 3-7). 10.14 (*0-606-11409-2*) Turtleback Bks.

—Monster Blood. 1992. (Goosebumps Ser.: No. 3). (J). (gr. 3-7). 10.04 (*0-606-01910-3*) Turtleback Bks.

—Monster Blood II. 1994. (Goosebumps Ser.: No. 18). 160p. (J). (gr. 3-7). mass mkt. 3.99 o.s.i (*0-590-47740-4*) Scholastic, Inc.

—Monster Blood IV. 1997. (Goosebumps Ser.: No. 62). (J). (gr. 3-7). 10.04 (*0-606-12993-6*) Turtleback Bks.

—Please Don't Feed the Vampire! 1997. (Give Yourself Goosebumps Ser.: No. 15). (J). (gr. 3-7). 10.04 (*0-606-11391-6*) Turtleback Bks.

—Vampire Breath. 1996. (Goosebumps Ser.: No. 49). (J). (gr. 3-7). 10.04 (*0-606-10352-X*) Turtleback Bks.

—The Werewolf in the Living Room. 1999. (Goosebumps Series 2000: No. 17). (J). (gr. 3-7). mass mkt. 3.99 (*0-590-68521-X*) Scholastic, Inc.

—The Werewolf of Fever Swamp. 1993. (Goosebumps Ser.: No. 14). 160p. (J). (gr. 3-7). mass mkt. 3.99 o.s.i (*0-590-49449-X*) Scholastic, Inc.

Stoker, Bram. Bram Stoker's Dracula. 1980. (Illus.). 48p. (J). (gr. 3 up). lib. bdg. 10.89 o.s.i (*0-440-01349-6*, Delacorte Pr.) Dell Publishing.

—Dracula. Farr, Naunerle C., ed. 1973. (Now Age Illustrated Ser.). (Illus.). 64p. (J). (gr. 5-10). 7.50 o.p. (*0-88301-203-0*) Pendulum Pr., Inc.

—Dracula - Frankenstein. 1989. (J). 5.98 o.p. (*0-86136-606-9*) Smithmark Pubs., Inc.

Stone, Jon. Another Monster at the End of This Book. (Big Bird's Favorites Board Bks.). 24p. (J). (ps). 2000. (Illus.). bds. 4.99 (*0-375-80562-1*, Random Hse. Bks. for Young Readers); 1997. 3.99 o.s.i (*0-307-16088-2*, Golden Bks.) Random Hse. Children's Bks.

—Blue's Fruit Field Trip. 2003. (Illus.). 16p. (J). (ps-2). pap. 3.99 (*0-307-10506-7*, Golden Bks.) Random Hse. Children's Bks.

—The Monster at the End of This Book. (J). 2004. (Illus.). 32p. 8.99 (*0-375-82913-X*, Golden Bks.); 2004. (Illus.). lib. bdg. 10.99 (*0-375-92913-4*, Golden Bks.); 2000. (Illus.). 24p. bds. 4.99 (*0-375-80561-3*, Random Hse. Bks. for Young Readers); 1997. 24p. 3.99 o.s.i (*0-307-16025-4*, Golden Bks.) Random Hse. Children's Bks.

—The Monster at the End of This Book. 1999. 32p. 3.99 o.s.i (*0-375-80401-3*) Random Hse., Inc.

Summer Camp Adventure. 1987. (Alf Storybooks Ser.). (Illus.). 24p. (J). (ps-3). pap. 1.95 o.p. (*0-02-688553-0*) Checkerboard Pr., Inc.

Sutcliff, Rosemary. Beowulf: Dragon Slayer. 1984. (Illus.). (YA). (gr. 5-9). 20.75 (*0-8446-6165-1*) Smith, Peter Pub., Inc.

Sweeney, Jacqueline. Pond Monster. 2001. (We Can Read! Ser.). (Illus.). 32p. (J). (gr. 1-2). lib. bdg. 21.36 (*0-7614-1123-2*, Benchmark Bks.) Cavendish, Marshall Corp.

Tadjo, Veronique. Mamy Wata & the Monster. 2004. (Illus.). 24p. (Orig.). (J). (ARA, BEN, CHI, ENG & FRE.). pap. 9.95 (*1-84059-264-8*); (ARA, BEN, CHI, ENG & FRE., pap. 9.95 (*1-84059-268-0*); (ARA, BEN, CHI, ENG & FRE., pap. 9.95 (*1-84059-269-9*); (ARA, BEN, CHI, ENG & FRE., pap. 9.95 (*1-84059-271-0*); (ARA, BEN, CHI, ENG & FRE., pap. 9.95 (*1-84059-273-7*); pap. 7.95 (*1-84059-263-X*); (ARA, BEN, CHI, ENG & FRE., pap. 9.95 (*1-84059-272-9*); (ARA, BEN, CHI, ENG & FRE., pap. 9.95 (*1-84059-270-2*); (ARA, BEN, CHI, ENG & FRE., pap. 9.95 (*1-84059-265-6*); (ARA, BEN, CHI, ENG & FRE., pap. 9.95 (*1-84059-267-2*); (ARA, BEN, CHI, ENG & FRE., pap. 9.95 (*1-84059-266-4*) Milet Publishing, Ltd. GBR. *Dist:* Consortium Bk. Sales & Distribution.

Tallarico, Tony. Monster Hunt. 1982. (Tuffy Video Game Bks.). (Illus.). 16p. (J). (gr. 3-8). pap. 3.50 o.p. (*0-89828-327-2*, Tuffy Bks.) Putnam Publishing Group, The.

Tamchina, Jurgen. Dominique & the Dragon. 1969. (Illus.). (J). (gr. 3-6). 6.50 o.p. (*0-15-223972-3*) Harcourt Children's Bks.

Taniguchi, Kazuko. Monster Mary, Mischief Maker. 1976. (Illus.). (J). (ps-3). 6.95 o.p. (*0-07-062868-8*); text 7.95 o.p. (*0-07-062869-6*) McGraw-Hill Cos., The.

Tedrow, Thomas L. The Legend of the Missouri Mud Monster. 1996. (Younguns Ser.: Vol. 4). 224p. (J). (gr. 5-9). pap. 5.99 o.p. (*0-8407-4135-9*) Nelson, Thomas Inc.

Teitelbaum, Michael. Universal Monsters: Frankenstein. 1992. (Illus.). 96p. (J). (gr. 3-7). pap. o.p. (*0-307-22335-3*, 22335, Golden Bks.) Random Hse. Children's Bks.

—Universal Monsters: The Bride of Frankenstein. 1993. (J). (gr. 4-7). pap. o.p. (*0-307-22333-7*, Golden Bks.) Random Hse. Children's Bks.

Tester, Sylvia Root. Magic Monsters Around the Year. 1979. (Magic Monsters Ser.). (Illus.). 32p. (J). (ps-4). lib. bdg. 21.36 o.p. (*0-89565-059-2*) Child's World, Inc.

—Magic Monsters Learn about Safety. 1979. (Magic Monsters Ser.). (Illus.). 32p. (J). (ps-4). lib. bdg. 21.36 o.p. (*0-89565-060-6*) Child's World, Inc.

—What Is a Monster? 1979. (Magic Monsters Ser.). (Illus.). 32p. (J). (ps-4). lib. bdg. 21.36 o.p. (*0-89565-055-X*) Child's World, Inc.

Thaler, Mike. Bad Day at Monster Elementary. 1995. 32p. (Orig.). (J). pap. 3.99 (*0-380-77870-X*, Avon Bks.) Morrow/Avon.

—King Kong's Underwear. 1986. 96p. (Orig.). (YA). (gr. 7 up). pap. 2.50 (*0-380-89823-3*, Avon Bks.) Morrow/Avon.

Thomas, Frances. One Day, Daddy. 2001. (Illus.). 32p. (J). (ps-2). 15.99 (*0-7868-0732-6*) Hyperion Bks. for Children.

Thomas, Lenerd & Thomas, Janis. Sir Lacksalot & the Two Headed Dragon. 1990. (Illus.). (J). (gr. k-6). 16.95 (*1-879480-00-X*) L.T. Publishing.

Thomassie, Tynia. Feliciana Feydra LeRoux Meets d'Loup Garou: A Cajun Tall Tale. 1998. (Illus.). 32p. (J). (ps-3). 15.95 o.p. (*0-316-84133-1*) Little Brown & Co.

Thorpe, Kiki, adapted by. Monsters, Inc. novel ed. 2001. (Illus.). 128p. (J). (gr. 3-7). pap. 4.99 (*0-7364-1263-8*, RH/Disney) Random Hse. Children's Bks.

Timm, Stephen A. The Dragon & the Mouse: The Dream. 1982. (Illus.). 45p. (J). 12.95 (*0-939728-05-2*); pap. 4.95 (*0-939728-06-0*) Steppingstone Enterprises, Inc.

Todd, Mark. What Will You Be for Halloween? 2001. (Illus.). 32p. (J). (ps-3). tchr. ed. 9.95 (*0-618-08803-2*) Houghton Mifflin Co.

Torrey, Michele. The Case of the Mossy Lake Monster. 2002. (Illus.). 112p. (J). (gr. 3-6). 14.99 (*0-525-46815-3*, Dutton Children's Bks.) Penguin Putnam Bks. for Young Readers.

Trimble, Irene & Manders, John. Mommy's Monster. 1998. (Golden Super Shape Book Ser.). (Illus.). 24p. (J). (ps-k). pap. 3.29 o.s.i (*0-307-13308-7*, 13308, Golden Bks.) Random Hse. Children's Bks.

Trondhein, Lewis. Harum Scarum: The Spiffy Adventures of McConey, Vol. 1. (Illus.). 48p. (YA). (gr. 10 up). pap. 10.95 (*1-56097-288-2*) Fantagraphics Bks.

Trumbauer, Lisa. I Swear I Saw a Witch in Washington Square. 1994. (J). 6.95 o.p. (*0-681-00557-2*) Borders Pr.

Tunnell, Michael O. Halloween Pie. 1999. (Illus.). 24p. (J). (ps-3). 14.95 o.s.i (*0-688-16804-3*); lib. bdg. 14.89 o.p. (*0-688-16805-1*) HarperCollins Children's Bk. Group.

Tyrrell, Melissa. Beauty & the Beast. 2001. (Fairytale Friends Ser.). (Illus.). 12p. (J). bds. 5.95 (*1-58117-153-6*, Piggy Toes Pr.) Intervisual Bks., Inc.

Universal City Studios, Inc. Staff. Talking E. T. Wordbook. 1982. (Texas Insruments Magic Wand Speaking Library). (Illus.). 32p. (J). (ps-3). text 7.30 o.p. (*0-89512-065-8*) Texas Instruments, Inc.

Universal Monsters: Frightening Facts. 1992. (Illus.). 48p. (J). (gr. 3-7). pap. o.p. (*0-307-22281-0*, 22281, Golden Bks.) Random Hse. Children's Bks.

Universal Monsters: On the Loose. 1992. (Illus.). 48p. (J). (gr. 3-7). pap. o.p. (*0-307-22282-9*, 22282, Golden Bks.) Random Hse. Children's Bks.

Monster from the Sea. 1992. (J). mass mkt. o.s.i (*0-553-54092-0*, Dell Books for Young Readers) Random Hse. Children's Bks.

—Things That Go. 1978. (Platt & Munk Peggy Cloth Bks.). (Illus.). 8p. (J). (ps). 2.50 o.p. (*0-448-46809-3*, Grosset & Dunlap) Penguin Putnam Bks. for Young Readers.

Ury, Allen B. The Living Ghost. 1996. (Scary Stories for Sleep-Overs Ser.). 128p. (J). (gr. 3-7). pap. 4.95 o.s.i (*1-56565-520-6*, 05206W, Roxbury Park Juvenile) Lowell Hse. Juvenile.

Van der Meer, Mara. How Many Monsters? A Monster Counting Book. (Illus.). (J). (ps-3). 2001. 24p. pap. 8.99 (*0-7112-1500-6*); 2000. 35p. 19.99 (*0-7112-1499-9*) Lincoln, Frances Ltd. GBR. *Dist:* Antique Collectors' Club.

Van der Meer, Ron & Van der Meer, Atie. Jumping Monsters. 1989. 10p. (J). (ps-1). 4.99 (*0-85953-264-X*) Child's Play of England GBR. *Dist:* Child's Play-International.

Van Leeuwen, Jean. Amanda Pig & the Awful, Scary Monster. 2003. (Easy-to-Read Ser.: Vol. 2). (Illus.). 48p. (J). 13.99 (*0-8037-2766-6*, Fogelman, Phyllis Bks.) Penguin Putnam Bks. for Young Readers.

Van Woerkom, Dorothy. Alexandra the Rock-Eater. 1978. (Illus.). (J). (gr. k-3). 6.95 o.p. (*0-394-83536-0*, Knopf Bks. for Young Readers) Random Hse. Children's Bks.

Vande Velde, Vivian. Companions of the Night. 1995. 224p. (YA). (gr. 7 up). 17.00 (*0-15-200221-9*) Harcourt Children's Bks.

The Vanishing Monster. 9999. (Puddle Lane Reading Program Ser.: Stage 1, No. 855-5). (Illus.). (J). (ps-2). 3.50 o.p. (*0-7214-0914-8*, Ladybird Bks.) Penguin Group (USA) Inc.

Viorst, Judith. My Mama Says There Aren't Any Zombies, Ghosts, Vampires, Creatures, Demons, Monsters, Fiends, Goblins, or Things. (Illus.). 48p. (J). (ps-3). 1973. (My Mama Says There Arent Any CL Ser.: Vol. 1). 16.00 (*0-689-30102-2*, Atheneum); 2nd ed. 1987. reprint ed. pap. 6.99 (*0-689-71204-9*, Aladdin) Simon & Schuster Children's Publishing.

—My Mama Says There Aren't Any Zombies, Ghosts, Vampires, Creatures, Demons, Monsters, Fiends, Goblins, or Things. 1988. 12.14 (*0-606-00534-X*) Turtleback Bks.

Waddell, Martin. Little Dracula at the Seashore. 1992. (Illus.). 32p. (J). (ps up). bds. 3.95 o.p. (*1-56402-026-6*) Candlewick Pr.

—Little Dracula Goes to School. 1992. (Illus.). 32p. (J). (ps up). bds. 3.95 o.p. (*1-56402-027-4*) Candlewick Pr.

—Little Dracula's Christmas. 1986. (Picture Puffin Ser.). (Illus.). 32p. (J). (gr. k up). pap. 3.95 o.p. (*0-14-050658-6*, Puffin Bks.) Penguin Putnam Bks. for Young Readers.

—Little Dracula's First Bite. 1986. (Stoney McTavish Ser.). (Illus.). 32p. (J). (gr. k up). pap. 3.95 o.p. (*0-14-050657-8*, Viking Children's Bks.) Penguin Putnam Bks. for Young Readers.

Wagner, Jenny. Amy's Monster. 1991. (Illus.). 320p. (J). (ps-3). 12.95 o.p. (*0-670-82748-7*, Viking Children's Bks.) Penguin Putnam Bks. for Young Readers.

Wahl, Jan. Dracula's Cat & Frankenstein's Dog. 1990. (Illus.). (J). (ps-2). 13.95 o.p. (*0-671-70820-1*, Simon & Schuster Children's Publishing) Simon & Schuster Children's Publishing.

—Frankenstein's Dog. 1977. (Illus.). (J). (ps-2). lib. bdg. o.p. (*0-13-330522-8*) Prentice-Hall.

Waldron, Jan L. John Pig's Halloween. 1998. (Illus.). 32p. (J). (ps-3). 15.99 o.s.i (*0-525-45941-3*, Dutton Children's Bks.) Penguin Putnam Bks. for Young Readers.

Wallace, Daisy, ed. Monster Poems. 1976. (Illus.). 32p. (J). reprint ed. pap. 4.95 o.p. (*0-8234-0848-5*) Holiday Hse., Inc.

Ward, Jon H. Howard Wise & the Monster Mop. 1997. (Illus.). 34p. (J). (ps-4). 15.95 (*0-9658128-0-4*) Long Wind Publishing.

Waskey, Leah. Monsters. 1995. (Color & Story Bks.). (Illus.). 32p. (J). (gr. k-12). 5.95 o.p. (*0-8431-3880-7*, Price Stern Sloan) Penguin Putnam Bks. for Young Readers.

Watson, T. E. The Monster in the Mailbox. 2002. (Illus.). 32p. (J). (gr. 2-6). 16.95 (*1-58478-011-8*) Paw Prints Pr.

Weil, Lisl. The Riddle Monster, 001. 1981. (Illus.). 32p. (J). (ps-3). 7.95 o.p. (*0-395-31019-9*, Clarion Bks.) Houghton Mifflin Co. Trade & Reference Div.

Weinberg, Larry. Frankenstein. 2000. (Golden Star Reader Ser.). (Illus.). (J). 10.14 (*0-606-18854-1*) Turtleback Bks.

Weinberg, Larry, adapted by. Dragonslayer: The Storybook Based on the Movie. 1981. (Movie Storybooks Ser.). (Illus.). (J). (gr. 4-7). lib. bdg. 6.99 o.p. (*0-394-94849-1*, Random Hse. Bks. for Young Readers) Random Hse. Children's Bks.

Weinberg, Michael A. The Horrible Terrible Dragon: A Folktale. 1949. (Illus.). 10p. (J). (gr. 1-3). pap. 2.00 (*0-9601014-3-8*) Weinberg, Michael Aron.

Weis, Ellen. Shrek: The Novel. movie tie-in ed. 2001. (Movie Tie-Ins Ser.). 144p. (J). (gr. 3-6). pap. 4.99 o.s.i (*0-14-131249-1*, Puffin Bks.) Penguin Putnam Bks. for Young Readers.

Weiss, Ellen & Di Fiore, Larry. Jim Henson's Scary Scary Monsters. 1998. (Illus.). 10p. (J). (ps-3). bds. 14.95 o.s.i (*0-307-33200-4*, Golden Bks.) Random Hse. Children's Bks.

Wen, Zhang, ed. The Yellow Robe Monster. 1985. (Monkey Ser.: No. 8). (Illus.). 74p. (J). (gr. 4 up). pap. 7.95 o.p. (*0-8351-1368-X*) China Bks. & Periodicals, Inc.

Weninger, Brigitte, pseud. It's Bedtime. 2002. (Illus.). 25p. (J). 15.95 (*0-7358-1602-6*) North-South Bks., Inc.

West, Cathy, adapted by. Scream Team. 2001. (Illus.). 80p. (J). (gr. 1-5). pap. 3.99 (*0-7364-1262-X*, RH/Disney) Random Hse. Children's Bks.

West, Tracey. Pop Goes the Monster! 2001. (Powerpuff Girls Ser.). (Illus.). (J). (gr. 4). pap. 12.95 (*0-439-30548-9*) Scholastic, Inc.

—Three Strikes & You're a Monster. 2004. (Scream Shop Ser.). (Illus.). 144p. mass mkt. 4.99 (*0-448-43359-1*, Grosset & Dunlap) Penguin Putnam Bks. for Young Readers.

Weyn, Suzanne. Monsters Unleashed: Junior Novelization. 2004. (Scooby-Doo Ser.). 160p. (J). mass mkt. 4.99 (*0-439-56755-6*, Scholastic Paperbacks) Scholastic, Inc.

Whitlock, Susan L. Donovan Scares the Monsters. 1987. (Illus.). 24p. (J). (gr. k-3). 12.95 o.p. (*0-688-06438-8*); lib. bdg. 12.88 o.p. (*0-688-06439-6*) HarperCollins Children's Bk. Group. (Greenwillow Bks.).

Whittington, Don. Werewolf Tonight. 1995. 144p. (J). (gr. 3-7). pap. 3.50 (*0-380-77513-1*, Avon Bks.) Morrow/Avon.

Wickstrom, Lois June & Lorrah, Jean. Nessie & the Living Stone. 2001. pap. 13.80 (*1-58338-616-5*, CrossroadsPub.Org) CrossroadsPub.com.

Wigand, Molly. The Grombles Secret. 1996. (Ready-to-Read Ser.: 2). 32p. (J). (ps-3). pap. 3.99 (*0-689-80853-4*, Simon Spotlight/Nickelodeon) Simon & Schuster Children's Publishing.

—Monster Camp Out. 1997. (Real Monsters Ser.: No. 4). 32p. (J). (gr. k-3). pap. 3.99 (*0-689-81257-4*, Simon Spotlight/Nickelodeon) Simon & Schuster Children's Publishing.

—Real Monsters. 1997. (Real Monsters Ser.: No. 3). 32p. (J). (gr. k-3). 3.99 (*0-689-81256-6*, Simon Spotlight/Nickelodeon) Simon & Schuster Children's Publishing.

Wild, Margaret. Beast. (J). 1997. mass mkt. 3.99 (*0-590-47159-7*); 1995. 112p. (gr. 4-6). pap. 13.95 (*0-590-47158-9*) Scholastic, Inc.

—Beast. 1997. 10.04 (*0-606-11101-8*) Turtleback Bks.

Wild, Robin & Wild, Jocelyn. Dunmousie Monsters. 1975. (Illus.). 32p. (J). (gr. k-2). 5.95 o.p. (*0-698-20264-3*) Putnam Publishing Group, The.

William, Kate. Beware the Wolfman. 1994. (Sweet Valley High Ser.: No. 106). (YA). (gr. 7 up). 9.09 o.p. (*0-606-06779-5*) Turtleback Bks.

—A Date with a Werewolf. 1994. (Sweet Valley High Ser.: No. 105). (YA). (gr. 7 up). 9.09 o.p. (*0-606-06778-7*) Turtleback Bks.

Williams, Arlene. Tales from the Dragon's Cave: Peacemaking Stories for Everyone. 1995. (Illus.). 160p. (J). (gr. 2-6). 15.95 o.p. (*0-9605444-5-3*) Waking Light Pr., The.

Williams, Barbara. Gary & the Very Terrible Monster. 1973. (Easy Reading Picture Story Bks.). (Illus.). 32p. (J). (gr. k-3). lib. bdg. 7.95 o.p. (*0-516-03466-9*, Children's Pr.) Scholastic Library Publishing.

Williams, Don, illus. Beauty & the Beast: A Changing Pictures Book. 1992. (Changing Pictures Bk.). 12p. (J). (ps-3). 11.95 o.p. (*1-56282-131-8*) Disney Pr.

Williams, Jay & Abrashkin, Raymond. Danny Dunn & the Swamp Monster. 1971. (Illus.). (J). (gr. 5 up). lib. bdg. o.p. (*0-07-070539-9*) McGraw-Hill Cos., The.

—Danny Dunn & the Swamp Monster. 1981. (Danny Dunn Ser.: No. 6). (Illus.). (J). (gr. 4-6). pap. (*0-671-43404-7*, Simon Pulse) Simon & Schuster Children's Publishing.

Williams, Marcia. Fabulous Monsters. 1999. (Illus.). 29p. (J). (gr. k-5). 15.99 o.p. (*0-7636-0791-6*) Candlewick Pr.

Williams, Rozanne L. Donde Viven los Monstruos?, Vol. 4067. Hood, Christine, ed. Rancho Park Publishing Staff, tr. 1996. (Fun & Fantasy Spanish Learn to Read Ser.).Tr. of Where Do Monsters Live?. (SPA., Illus.). 8p. (J). (ps-2). pap. 1.75 (*1-57471-149-0*, 4067) Creative Teaching Pr., Inc.

—Five Little Monsters. (Emergent Reader Bks.). 16p. (J). (gr. k-2). Vol. 3727. 1995. pap. 2.75 (*0-916119-89-0*); Vol. 3970. 1996. (Illus.). pap. 12.98 (*1-57471-108-3*) Creative Teaching Pr., Inc.

—Ten Monsters in Bed. (Emergent Reader Bks.). 16p. (J). (gr. k-2). Vol. 3728. 1995. pap. 2.49 (*0-916119-90-4*); Vol. 3971. 1996. (Illus.). pap. 12.98 (*1-57471-109-1*) Creative Teaching Pr., Inc.

—There's a Monster in the Tree. (Emergent Reader Bks.). 16p. Vol. 3652. 1994. pap. 1.75 (*0-916119-66-1*); Vol. 3695. 1995. (Illus.). (J). pap. 11.98 (*1-57471-078-8*) Creative Teaching Pr., Inc.

—Where Do Monsters Live? (Emergent Reader Bks.). 8p. Vol. 3624. 1994. pap. 1.75 (*0-916119-52-1*); Vol. 3681. 1995. (Illus.). (J). pap. 8.98 (*1-57471-064-8*) Creative Teaching Pr., Inc.

Willis, Jeanne. The Monster Bed. 1987. (Illus.). (J). (ps-2). 112p. 15.00 (*0-688-06804-9*); 144p. 14.89 o.p. (*0-688-06805-7*) HarperCollins Children's Bk. Group.

—The Monster Storm. 1995. (Illus.). 176p. (J). (ps up). 14.00 (*0-688-13785-7*) HarperCollins Children's Bk. Group.

Willis, Jeanne & Varley, Susan. The Monster Bed. 1999. (Illus.). 32p. (J). (ps-3). mass mkt. 5.95 (*0-688-16707-1*, Harper Trophy) HarperCollins Children's Bk. Group.

Willis, Meredith Sue. Marco's Monster. 2nd ed. 2001. 118p. (J). pap. 7.95 (*0-9674477-5-5*) Montemayor Pr.

Willoughby, Elaine M. Boris & the Monsters. (Illus.). 32p. (J). (gr. k-3). 1986. pap. 4.95 o.p. (*0-395-42649-9*); 1980. 13.95 o.p. (*0-395-29067-8*) Houghton Mifflin Co.

Wilsdorf, Anne. Philomene. 1992. (J). 14.00 o.p. (*0-688-10369-3*); lib. bdg. 13.93 o.p. (*0-688-10370-7*) HarperCollins Children's Bk. Group. (Greenwillow Bks.).

Wilson. Monster Story-Teller. 2000. (Illus.). 59p. (J). 17.95 o.p. (*0-385-40857-9*); pap. 6.95 (*0-552-54529-5*) Transworld Publishers Ltd. GBR. *Dist:* Trafalgar Square.

Wilson, Trevor. Monster for Hire. 1994. (Illus.). 32p. (J). (gr. k-5). pap. 4.95 (*1-879531-61-5*) Mondo Publishing.

Windling, Terri. Goblins. 1996. (J). pap. 3.50 (*0-679-87404-6*) Random Hse., Inc.

Winn, Christine M. & Walsh, David. Monster Boy: Helping Kids Cope with Anger. 1996. (Illus.). 32p. (J). (gr. 1-4). 14.95 o.p. (*0-925190-87-X*) Fairview Pr.

Winthrop, Elizabeth. Maggie & the Monster. 1987. (Illus.). 32p. (J). (ps-3). pap. 5.95 (*0-8234-0698-9*); tchr. ed. 15.95 (*0-8234-0639-3*) Holiday Hse., Inc.

Wisniewski, David. The Wave of the Sea-Wolf. 1999. (Illus.). 32p. (J). (ps-3). pap. 5.95 (*0-395-96892-5*, Clarion Bks.) Houghton Mifflin Co. Trade & Reference Div.

Wolf, Jill, adapted by. The Bride Movie Storybook. 1985. (Collector Sticker Bks.). (Illus.). 22p. (J). (gr. 5-8). pap. 1.95 o.p. (*0-89954-384-7*) Antioch Publishing Co.

Wolff, Patricia Rae. Cackle Cook's Monster Stew. 2001. (Illus.). 32p. (J). 9.95 o.s.i (*0-307-10682-9*, Golden Bks.) Random Hse. Children's Bks.

Wolfson, Steve. Monster Cheese. 1985. (Illus.). 32p. (J). (ps-3). reprint ed. pap. 5.95 (*0-919926-43-6*) Coteau Bks. CAN. *Dist:* General Distribution Services, Inc.

Wood, Tim. Bertie Bones: Pop-Up Book. 1999. (Monster Madness Bks.). (Illus.). 12p. (J). (ps-2). pap. 4.95 o.p. (*0-7641-5165-7*) Barron's Educational Series, Inc.

Woodruff, Elvira. Dragon in My Backpack. 1996. 9.65 (*0-606-09206-4*) Turtleback Bks.

Wright, Cliff. The Tangleweed Troll. 1995. (Illus.). 32p. (J). (ps-3). 19.95 o.p. (*0-575-05491-3*) Gollancz, Victor GBR. *Dist:* Trafalgar Square.

Wylie, Joanne. Do You Know Where Your Monster Is Tonight: Learning about Time. 1984. (Many Monster Stories Ser.). (Illus.). 32p. (J). (ps-2). 15.00 o.p. (*0-516-04491-5*); pap. 3.95 o.p. (*0-516-44491-3*) Scholastic Library Publishing. (Children's Pr.).

—Have You Hugged Your Monster Today? A Manners's Story. 1984. (Many Monster Stories Ser.). (Illus.). 32p. (J). (ps-2). 14.60 o.p. (*0-516-04493-1*); pap. 3.95 o.p. (*0-516-44493-X*) Scholastic Library Publishing. (Children's Pr.).

—Sabes Donde Esta Tu Monstruo Esta Noche? Kratky, Lada J., tr. 1986. (Spanish Edition - Many Monsters Stories Ser.).Tr. of Do You Know Where Your Monster Is Tonight?: A Time Story. (SPA., Illus.). 32p. (J). (ps-2). pap. 3.95 o.p. (*0-516-54491-8*); lib. bdg. 15.27 o.p. (*0-516-34491-9*) Scholastic Library Publishing. (Children's Pr.).

Wylie, Joanne & Wylie, David. The Gumdrop Monster: Learning about Colors. 1984. (Many Monster Stories Ser.). (Illus.). 32p. (J). (ps-2). 14.60 o.p. (*0-516-04492-3*); pap. 3.95 o.p. (*0-516-44492-1*) Scholastic Library Publishing. (Children's Pr.).

—Has Abrazado Hoy a Tu Monstruo? Un Cuento de los Modales: Have You Hugged Your Monster Today? Learning about Manners. 1986. (Spanish Many Monster Stories Concept Bks.). (Illus.). 32p. (J). (ps-2). pap. 3.95 o.p. (*0-516-54493-4*); lib. bdg. 15.27 o.p. (*0-516-34493-5*) Scholastic Library Publishing. (Children's Pr.).

—Little Monster: Learning about Size. 1985. (Many Monster Learning about Bks.). (Illus.). 32p. (J). (ps-2). pap. 3.95 o.p. (*0-516-44495-6*); lib. bdg. 14.60 o.p. (*0-516-04495-8*) Scholastic Library Publishing. (Children's Pr.).

—So You Think You Saw a Monster? Learning about Make-Believe. 1985. (Many Monster Learning about Bks.). (Illus.). 32p. (J). (ps-2). pap. 3.95 o.p. (*0-516-44496-4*); lib. bdg. 14.50 o.p. (*0-516-04496-6*) Scholastic Library Publishing. (Children's Pr.).

—Y Tu Crees Que Viste un Monstruo? Un Cuento de Fantasia. 1986. (Spanish Many Monster Stories Concept Bks.).Tr. of So You Think You Saw a Monster? A Make Believe Story. (Illus.). 32p. (J). (ps-2). pap. 3.95 o.p. (*0-516-54496-9*); lib. bdg. 15.00 o.p. (*0-516-34496-X*) Scholastic Library Publishing. (Children's Pr.).

Wynne-Jones, Tim. On Tumbledown Hill. 1998. (Northern Lights Books for Children Ser.). (Illus.). 32p. (ps-3). 15.95 (*0-88995-186-1*) Red Deer Pr. CAN. *Dist:* General Distribution Services, Inc.

XYZ Group Staff. Funny Monsters. 1998. (Glow in Dark Posterbook Ser.). (Illus.). (J). (ps-2). pap. text 2.99 o.p. (*1-879332-78-7*) Futech Interactive Products, Inc.

Yaccarino, Dan. The Lima Bean Monster. 2001. (Illus.). 32p. (J). (ps-2). 15.95 (*0-8027-8776-2*); lib. bdg. 16.85 (*0-8027-8777-0*) Walker & Co.

YES! Entertainment Corporation Staff. Monster Talk. 1994. (Interactive Books Sound Ser.). 12p. (J). (ps-2). (*1-57234-042-8*) YES! Entertainment Corp.

Yolen, Jane. Commander Toad in Space. 1980. (Break-of-Day Bks.). (Illus.). 64p. (J). (gr. 1-5). 6.95 o.s.i (*0-698-20522-7*); (gr. 3-5). 10.99 o.s.i (*0-698-30724-0*) Putnam Publishing Group, The. (Coward-McCann).

—Dragon's Blood. 1996. 304p. (YA). (gr. 7 up). pap. 6.00 (*0-15-200866-7*, Magic Carpet Bks.) Harcourt Children's Bks.

—Dragon's Blood. 1996. (Pit Dragon Trilogy). 12.05 (*0-606-09208-0*) Turtleback Bks.

—The Dragon's Boy: A Tale of Young King Arthur. 1990. 128p. (J). (gr. 3-7). lib. bdg. 14.89 o.p. (*0-06-026790-9*); (ps-3). 15.95 (*0-06-026789-5*) HarperCollins Children's Bk. Group.

—Heart's Blood. 1984. 224p. (J). (gr. 7 up). 14.95 o.s.i (*0-385-29316-X*, Delacorte Pr.) Dell Publishing.

—Heart's Blood. 1996. (Pit Dragon Trilogy Ser.: Vol. 2). 352p. (YA). (gr. 7-12). pap. 6.00 (*0-15-200865-9*, Magic Carpet Bks.) Harcourt Children's Bks.

—Heart's Blood. 1996. (Pit Dragon Trilogy). 12.05 (*0-606-10211-6*) Turtleback Bks.

—Here There Be Dragons. 1998. 16.05 (*0-606-13477-8*) Turtleback Bks.

—A Sending of Dragons. (J). 1989. 208p. (gr. k up). mass mkt. 3.25 o.s.i (*0-440-20309-0*); 1987. 14.95 o.s.i (*0-440-50229-2*); 1987. (Illus.). 240p. (gr. 7 up). 14.95 o.s.i (*0-385-29587-1*, Delacorte Pr.) Dell Publishing.

—A Sending of Dragons. 1997. 304p. (YA). (gr. 6 up). pap. 6.00 (*0-15-200864-0*, Magic Carpet Bks.) Harcourt Children's Bks.

—A Sending of Dragons. 1997. (Pit Dragon Trilogy). 12.05 (*0-606-11829-2*) Turtleback Bks.

Yolen, Jane & Yolen-Stemple, Heidi Elizabet. Meet the Monsters. 1996. (Illus.). 32p. (J). (gr. 4-7). 15.95 (*0-8027-8441-0*); lib. bdg. 16.85 (*0-8027-8442-9*) Walker & Co.

Yorinks, Arthur. Seven Little Monsters 8 x 8: Monster in Space. 2003. 24p. (J). pap. 3.99 (*0-7868-1775-5*, Volo) Hyperion Bks. for Children.

—Seven Little Monsters 8 x 8: We Love You, Mama!, No. 2. 2003. 24p. (J). pap. 3.99 (*0-7868-1776-3*, Volo) Hyperion Bks. for Children.

Youseyah, You. When Hopi Children Were Bad: A Monster Story. 1989. (Illus.). 41p. (Orig.). (J). (gr. 4-7). pap. 46.95 (*0-940113-20-1*) Sierra Oaks Publishing Co.

Zach, Cheryl. The Mummy's Footsteps. 1997. (Mind over Matter Ser.: No. 1). 128p. (J). (gr. 4-6). 9.09 o.p. (*0-606-11623-0*) Turtleback Bks.

Los Zapatos Nuevos Del Herry. 1993. Tr. of Sesame Street: Herry's New Shoes. (SPA., Illus.). 24p. (J). (ps-3). pap. 3.50 o.p. (*0-307-52061-7*, Golden Bks.) Random Hse. Children's Bks.

Zemach, Harve. The Judge: An Untrue Tale, RS. 1969. (Illus.). 48p. (J). (ps-3). 17.00 o.p. (*0-374-33960-0*, Farrar, Straus & Giroux (BYR)) Farrar, Straus & Giroux.

Zimelman, Nathan. If I Were Strong Enough. 1982. (Illus.). 32p. (J). (gr. k-3). pap. text 9.95 o.p. (*0-687-18670-6*) Abingdon Pr.

Zindel, Paul. The Doom Stone. 1996. (Illus.). 192p. (J). (gr. 6-10). pap. 4.95 (*0-7868-1157-9*) Disney Pr.

—Loch. l.t. ed. 1997. (J). 16.95 o.p. (*0-7451-2859-9*, Galaxy Children's Large Print) BBC Audiobooks America.

—Loch. 1995. (Illus.). 224p. (J). (gr. 6-10). pap. 4.95 (*0-7868-1099-8*) Disney Pr.

—Loch. 1994. 224p. (gr. 6-10). (YA). lib. bdg. 15.89 (*0-06-024543-3*); (Illus.). (J). 15.95 (*0-06-024542-5*) HarperCollins Children's Bk. Group.

—Loch. 2004. (J). (-9). pap. 5.99 (*0-7868-5150-3*) Hyperion Bks. for Children.

—Loch, unabr. ed. 1997. (J). (gr. 5). audio 27.00 (*0-7887-0394-3*, 94586E7) Recorded Bks., LLC.

—Loch. 1995. (J). 11.00 (*0-606-08806-7*) Turtleback Bks.

—Night of the Bat. 144p. (J). 2003. pap. 5.99 (*0-7868-1226-5*); 2001. (gr. 5-9). lib. bdg. 16.49 (*0-7868-2554-5*); 2001. (gr. 6-10). trans. 15.99 (*0-7868-0340-1*) Hyperion Bks. for Children.

—Reef of Death. 1999. 192p. (J). pap. 5.99 (*0-7868-1408-X*) Disney Pr.

—Reef of Death. 1998. (Illus.). 192p. (J). (gr. 3 up). 15.95 (*0-06-024728-2*); (gr. 6-10). lib. bdg. 15.89 (*0-06-024733-9*) HarperCollins Children's Bk. Group.

—Reef of Death. 1999. 12.04 (*0-606-16669-6*) Turtleback Bks.

Zorn, Steven. Mostly Monsters: Eight Terrifying Tales to Tingle Your Spine. 2002. (Children's Illustrated Classics Ser.). (Illus.). 56p. (J). (gr. 4-7). 10.00 o.p. (*0-7624-0407-8*, Courage Bks.) Running Pr. Bk. Pubs.

5pc Box Set - Monsters (English), 5 bks. vols., Set. 2000. (*1-58805-100-5*) DS-Max USA, Inc.

MUMMIES—FICTION

Allen, Derek, retold by. Blood from the Mummy's Tomb. 1988. (Fleshcreepers Ser.). 160p. (J). (gr. 6 up). pap. 2.95 o.p. (*0-8120-4074-0*) Barron's Educational Series, Inc.

Bellairs, John. The Mummy, the Will & the Crypt. 1985. 176p. pap. 3.99 o.s.i (*0-553-15701-9*); (J). (gr. 6). pap. 2.75 o.s.i (*0-553-15498-2*) Bantam Bks.

—The Mummy, the Will & the Crypt. (Johnny Dixon Ser.). (Illus.). 1996. 176p. (J). (gr. 3-7). pap. 5.99 (*0-14-038007-8*, Puffin Bks.); 1983. 192p. (YA). (gr. 5 up). 12.89 o.p. (*0-8037-0030-X*, Dial Bks. for Young Readers) Penguin Putnam Bks. for Young Readers.

—The Mummy, the Will & the Crypt. 2001. (J). (gr. 4-8). 20.75 (*0-8446-7170-3*) Smith, Peter Pub., Inc.

—The Mummy, the Will & the Crypt. 1996. (J). 12.04 (*0-606-10883-1*) Turtleback Bks.

Bradman, Tony. The Magnificent Mummies. 2001. (Blue Bananas Ser.). (Illus.). 48p. (J). (gr. 1-2). pap. 4.95 (*0-7787-0889-6*); lib. bdg. 19.96 (*0-7787-0843-8*) Crabtree Publishing Co.

—The Magnificent Mummies. 1997. (Blue Bananas Ser.). (Illus.). 48p. pap. text 4.99 (*0-7497-2767-5*) London Bridge.

—Midnight in Memphis. 2001. (Blue Bananas Ser.). (Illus.). 48p. (J). (gr. 1-2). pap. 4.95 (*0-7787-0894-2*); lib. bdg. 19.96 (*0-7787-0848-9*) Crabtree Publishing Co.

Bunting, Eve. I Am the Mummy Heb-Nefert. 2000. (Illus.). 32p. (J). (ps-3). pap. 6.00 (*0-15-202464-6*, Harcourt Paperbacks) Harcourt Children's Bks.

—I Am the Mummy Heb-Nefert. 1997. (Illus.). 32p. (J). (gr. 2-7). 17.99 o.s.i (*0-88776-391-X*) Tundra Bks. of Northern New York.

Costain, Meredith. The Mummy's Curse. 1999. (Brains & Parker McGoohan Ser.). 64 p. (*0-7608-1938-6*) Sundance Publishing.

Dexter, Catherine. The Gilded Cat. 1992. 208p. (J). (gr. 4 up). 14.00 o.p. (*0-688-09425-2*, Morrow, William & Co.) Morrow/Avon.

Gelsey, James. Scooby-Doo y la Maldicion de la Momia. 2003. (Scooby-Doo Mysteries Ser.: No. 2). (SPA., Illus.). 48p. (J). (gr. 2-4). pap. 3.99 (*0-439-40985-3*, Scholastic en Espanola) Scholastic, Inc.

Gilmour, H. B. Curse of Katana. 1996. (Real Monsters Ser.: 2). 64p. (J). (gr. 2-5). 3.99 (*0-689-80870-4*, Simon Spotlight) Simon & Schuster Children's Publishing.

Herman, Gail. Mummies at the Mall. 2002. (Scooby-Doo! Reader Ser.: Vol. 11). (Illus.). 32p. (J). (ps-3). mass mkt. 3.99 (*0-439-34114-0*) Scholastic, Inc.

Jakab, E. A. M. The Mummy Who Wouldn't Die. 1996. (Choose Your Own Nightmare Ser.: No. 9). (Illus.). 96p. (J). (gr. 4-8). pap. 3.50 o.s.i (*0-553-48327-7*, Dell Books for Young Readers) Random Hse. Children's Bks.

—The Mummy Who Wouldn't Die. l.t. ed. 1997. (Illus.). 96p. (J). (gr. 4-8). lib. bdg. 21.27 o.p. (*0-8368-1721-4*) Stevens, Gareth Inc.

—The Mummy Who Wouldn't Die. 1996. (Choose Your Own Nightmare Ser.: No. 9). (J). (gr. 4-8). 8.60 o.p. (*0-606-09143-2*) Turtleback Bks.

Johnston, Tony. The Mummy's Mother. 2003. (Illus.). 160p. (J). pap. 15.95 (*0-439-32462-9*, Blue Sky Pr., The) Scholastic, Inc.

Karr, Kathleen. Gideon & the Mummy Professor, RS. 1993. 144p. (YA). (gr. 5 up). 16.00 o.p. (*0-374-32563-4*, Farrar, Straus & Giroux (BYR)) Farrar, Straus & Giroux.

Katz, Fred E. Tuck Me in, Mummy. 1997. (Spinechillers Mysteries Ser.: Vol. 9). (Illus.). 144p. (Orig.). (J). (gr. 3-7). pap. 4.99 (*0-8499-4052-4*) Nelson, Tommy.

Kudalis, Eric. Stories of Mummies & the Living Dead. 1994. (Classic Monster Stories Ser.). (Illus.). 48p. (J). (gr. 3-4). lib. bdg. 21.26 (*1-56065-214-4*, Capstone High-Interest Bks.) Capstone Pr., Inc.

—Stories of Mummies & the Living Dead. 1994. (Classic Monster Stories Ser.). (Illus.). 48p. (J). (gr. 3-7). lib. bdg. 19.00 o.p. (*0-516-35214-8*, Children's Pr.) Scholastic Library Publishing.

Lantz, Francess L. The Case of the Missing Mummy. 1998. (New Adventures of Mary-Kate & Ashley Ser.). (Illus.). 82p. (J). (gr. 2-7). mass mkt. 3.99 (*0-590-29404-0*) Scholastic, Inc.

Laybourn, Emma. Mummy Mania. 2003. 128p. (J). pap. 8.95 (*1-84270-167-3*) Andersen Pr., Ltd. GBR. *Dist:* Trafalgar Square.

Littke, Lael J. The Phantom Fair. 1996. (Bee There Ser.: Bk. 7). 156p. (J). (gr. 3-7). pap. 6.95 (*1-57345-200-9*, Cinnamon Tree) Deseret Bk. Co.

Mayer, Mercer. Mummy Pancakes. 1997. (Mercer Mayer's Critters of the Night Ser.). (Illus.). 24p. (J). (ps-1). pap. 5.99 o.s.i (*0-679-87378-3*, Random Hse. Bks. for Young Readers) Random Hse. Children's Bks.

McCrady, Lady. Mildred & the Mummy. 1980. (Illus.). 32p. (J). (gr. k-3). lib. bdg. 7.95 o.p. (*0-8234-0372-6*) Holiday Hse., Inc.

McMullan, Kate. The Mummy's Gold. 1996. (Eek! Stories to Make You Shriek Ser.). (Illus.). 48p. (J). (gr. 1-3). 13.99 o.s.i (*0-448-41345-0*); 3.99 (*0-448-41310-8*) Penguin Putnam Bks. for Young Readers. (Grosset & Dunlap).

—The Mummy's Gold. 1996. (Eek! Stories to Make You Shriek Ser.). 10.14 (*0-606-10884-X*) Turtleback Bks.

—Under the Mummy's Spell, RS. 1992. 176p. (J). (gr. 5 up). 16.00 o.p. (*0-374-38033-3*, Farrar, Straus & Giroux (BYR)) Farrar, Straus & Giroux.

—Under the Mummy's Spell. 1994. 224p. (J). (gr. 4-6). pap. 3.25 o.p. (*0-590-47897-4*) Scholastic, Inc.

Myers, Bill. I Want My Mummy. 2000. (Bloodhounds, Inc. Ser.: Vol. 8). (Illus.). 128p. (J). (gr. 3-8). pap. 5.99 (*1-55661-492-6*) Bethany Hse. Pubs.

Osborne, Mary Pope. Una Momia en la Manana. 2003. (SPA.). (J). pap. 4.95 (*1-930332-51-3*) Lectorum Pubns., Inc.

—Mummies in the Morning. unabr. ed. 2001. (Magic Tree House Ser. : No. 3). 65p. (J). (gr. 2-3). pap. 17.00 incl. audio (*0-8072-0332-7*, Listening Library) Random Hse. Audio Publishing Group.

—Mummies in the Morning. 1993. (Magic Tree House Ser.: No. 3). (Illus.). 80p. (J). (gr. k-3). lib. bdg. 11.99 (*0-679-92424-8*); pap. 3.99 (*0-679-82424-3*) Random Hse. Children's Bks. (Random Hse. Bks. for Young Readers).

—Mummies in the Morning. 1993. (Magic Tree House Ser.: No. 3). (Illus.). (J). (gr. k-3). 10.14 (*0-606-05932-6*) Turtleback Bks.

Preller, James. The Case of the Mummy Mystery. 2001. (Jigsaw Jones Mystery Ser.: No. 6). (Illus.). 80p. (J). (gr. 1-4). mass mkt. 3.99 (*0-439-08094-0*) Scholastic, Inc.

—The Case of the Mummy Mystery. 2000. (Jigsaw Jones Mystery Ser.: No. 6). (Illus.). (J). (gr. 1-4). 10.14 (*0-606-18528-3*) Turtleback Bks.

Ross, Pat. M & M & the Mummy Mess. (M & M Ser.). (J). 1986. (Illus.). 4p. (gr. 2-5). pap. 3.99 o.s.i (*0-14-032084-9*, Puffin Bks.); 1985. 48p. (ps-3). 9.95 o.p. (*0-670-80548-3*, Viking Children's Bks.) Penguin Putnam Bks. for Young Readers.

—M & M & the Mummy Mess. 1999. (Illus.). (J). 10.14 (*0-606-18424-4*) Turtleback Bks.

—The Mummy Mess. 1999. (Puffin Chapters Ser.). (Illus.). 48p. (gr. 2-5). pap. 3.99 (*0-14-130654-8*, Puffin Bks.) Penguin Putnam Bks. for Young Readers.

Roy, Ron. The Missing Mummy. 2001. (A to Z Mysteries Ser.: No. 13). (Illus.). 96p. (J). (gr. 2-5). pap. 3.99 (*0-375-80268-1*); lib. bdg. 11.99 (*0-375-90268-6*) Random Hse. Children's Bks. (Random Hse. Bks. for Young Readers).

Sabuda, Robert. The Mummy's Tomb: A Pop-Up Book. 1994. (Illus.). 12p. (J). (ps-3). o.p. (*0-307-17627-4*, Golden Bks.) Random Hse. Children's Bks.

Saunders, Susan. Curse of the Cat Mummy. 1997. (Black Cat Club Ser.: Vol. 3). (Illus.). 96p. (J). (gr. 1-5). pap. 3.95 o.s.i (*0-06-442037-X*, Harper Trophy) HarperCollins Children's Bk. Group.

—Curse of the Cat Mummy. 1997. (Black Cat Club Ser.). 9.15 (*0-606-11136-0*) Turtleback Bks.

Simon, Francesca. Horrid Henry & the Mummy's Curse. 2001. (Illus.). (J). 16.95 (*0-7540-6166-3*) BBC Audiobooks America.

Sommers, Stephen. The Mummy. novel ed. 1999. (Illus.). 142p. (J). mass mkt. 3.99 (*0-439-05015-4*) Scholastic, Inc.

Terry Deary's Dreadful Day in Ancient Egypt. 2004. 48p. (J). pap. 14.99 (*0-7894-9264-4*) Dorling Kindersley Publishing, Inc.

Warner, Gertrude Chandler. The Mystery of the Mummy's Curse. 2002. (Boxcar Children Ser.: Vol. 88). 128p. (J). lib. bdg. 13.95 (*0-8075-5503-7*);No. 88. pap. 3.95 (*0-8075-5504-5*) Whitman, Albert & Co.

Weiss, Ellen. Take the Mummy & Run. 1997. (Carmen Sandiego Mystery Ser.). (J). (gr. 4-6). 9.60 o.p. (*0-606-11192-1*) Turtleback Bks.

Weiss, Ellen & Friedman, Mel. Take the Mummy & Run. 1997. (Carmen Sandiego Mystery Ser.). (Illus.). 160p. (J). (gr. 4-6). pap. 4.50 o.s.i (*0-06-440664-4*, Harper Trophy) HarperCollins Children's Bk. Group.

Whitman, John. The Mummy Returns. 2001. (Illus.). 176p. (gr. 3-7). pap. text 4.99 (*0-553-48753-1*, Skylark) Random Hse. Children's Bks.

—The Mummy Returns Scrapbook: An Insider's Guide to the Movie & Ancient Egypt. 2001. (Illus.). 64p. (YA). (gr. 3-7). pap. 6.99 o.s.i (*0-553-37590-3*, Dell Books for Young Readers) Random Hse. Children's Bks.

Yates, Philip. Ten Little Mummies: An Egyptian Counting Book. 2003. (Illus.). 40p. (J). (ps-2). 15.99 (*0-670-03641-2*, Viking) Viking Penguin.

V

VAMPIRES—FICTION

Anderson, M. T. Thirsty. 2003. (Illus.). 256p. bds. 6.99 (*0-7636-2014-9*); 1998. 256p. (J). (gr. 9-12). bds. 4.99 o.s.i (*0-7636-0699-5*); 1997. (YA). (gr. 9-12). 17.99 o.p. (*0-7636-0048-2*) Candlewick Pr.

—Thirsty. 1998. 11.04 (*0-606-15734-4*) Turtleback Bks.

Atwater-Rhodes, Amelia. Demon in My View. 192p. (YA). (gr. 7). 2001. mass mkt. 4.99 (*0-440-22884-0*, Laurel Leaf); 2000. 9.95 (*0-385-32720-X*, Dell Books for Young Readers) Random Hse. Children's Bks.

—In the Forests of the Night. (Illus.). (YA). (gr. 7-12). 2000. 176p. mass mkt. 5.50 (*0-440-22816-6*, Laurel Leaf); 1999. 160p. 8.95 o.s.i (*0-385-32674-2*, Dell Books for Young Readers) Random Hse. Children's Bks.

—In the Forests of the Night. l.t. ed. 2002. (Young Adult Ser.). 120p. (YA). 22.95 (*0-7862-4761-4*) Thorndike Pr.

—In the Forests of the Night. 2000. (Illus.). (J). 11.04 (*0-606-17999-2*) Turtleback Bks.

—Shattered Mirror. 2001. E-Book 3.99 (*1-59061-571-9*) Adobe Systems, Inc.

—Shattered Mirror. 240p. (YA). (gr. 7). 2003. mass mkt. 5.50 (*0-440-22940-5*, Laurel Leaf); 2001. 9.95 (*0-385-32793-5*, Dell Books for Young Readers) Random Hse. Children's Bks.

Bianchi, John. A Vampire's Halloween. 2002. (Board Books). (Illus.). 14p. (J). bds. 4.99 (*0-448-42820-2*, Grosset & Dunlap) Penguin Putnam Bks. for Young Readers.

Bloom, Hanya. Science Spook. 1990. (Vic the Vampire Ser.: No. 2). 80p. (J). (gr. 4-7). mass mkt. 2.95 o.p. (*0-06-106020-8*, Perennial) HarperTrade.

—Vampire Cousins. 1990. (Vic the Vampire Ser.: No. 3). 80p. (J). (gr. 4-7). mass mkt. 2.95 o.p. (*0-06-106025-9*, Perennial) HarperTrade.

Boris, Cynthia. Pop Quiz. 1999. (Buffy the Vampire Slayer Ser.). (Illus.). 176p. (J). (gr. 7-12). mass mkt. 4.99 (*0-671-04258-0*, Simon Pulse) Simon & Schuster Children's Publishing.

Brereton, Dan & Ketcham, Rick. The Dust Waltz. 1998. (Buffy the Vampire Slayer Ser.). (Illus.). 80p. (YA). (gr. 7 up). pap. 9.95 (*1-56971-342-1*) Dark Horse Comics.

Buffy the Vampire Slayer. 1999. (Illus.). 144p. (YA). 10.95 o.p. (*0-7683-3639-2*) CEDCO Publishing.

Buffy the Vampire Slayer. 1998. pap. 12.99 o.p. (*1-56649-021-9*) Welcome Rain Pubs.

Buffy the Vampire Slayer: The Postcards. 1999. (Illus.). 44p. (J). pap. 8.00 (*0-671-03640-8*, Simon Pulse) Simon & Schuster Children's Publishing.

Buffy the Vampire Slayer Staff. The Script Book: Season Two. 2001. (Buffy the Vampire Slayer Ser.). 400p. (YA). pap. 14.00 (*0-7434-1014-9*, Simon Pulse) Simon & Schuster Children's Publishing.

Ciencin, Scott & Jolley, Dan. Vengeance. 2002. (Angel Ser.: Bk. 14). 352p. (YA). (gr. 11 up). pap. 5.99 (*0-7434-2754-8*, Simon Pulse) Simon & Schuster Children's Publishing.

Collins, Craig, et al. Visitors. 1999. (Buffy the Vampire Slayer Ser.: No. 9). 176p. (YA). (gr. 7 up). pap. 4.99 (*0-671-02628-3*, Simon Pulse) Simon & Schuster Children's Publishing.

Cooney, Caroline B. The Cheerleader. 1991. 192p. (YA). (gr. 7-9). mass mkt. 3.25 (*0-590-44316-X*, Scholastic Paperbacks) Scholastic, Inc.

—The Return of the Vampire. 1992. 176p. (YA). (gr. 7-9). mass mkt. 2.95 o.p. (*0-590-44884-6*, Scholastic Paperbacks) Scholastic, Inc.

Cooney, Caroline B., et al. Deadly Offer. 2003. (Vampire's Promise Ser.). 192p. (J). pap. 4.99 (*0-439-55395-4*, Scholastic Paperbacks) Scholastic, Inc.

—Evil Returns. 2003. (Vampire's Promise Ser.). 176p. (J). pap. 4.99 (*0-439-55396-2*, Scholastic Paperbacks) Scholastic, Inc.

—Fatal Bargain. 2003. (Vampire's Promise Ser.). 176p. (J). pap. 4.99 (*0-439-55397-0*, Scholastic Paperbacks) Scholastic, Inc.

Cover, Arthur Byron. Night of the Living Rerun. 1998. (Buffy the Vampire Slayer Ser.: No. 4). 192p. (YA). (gr. 7 up). mass mkt. 4.99 (*0-671-01715-2*, Simon Pulse) Simon & Schuster Children's Publishing.

Cusick, Richie Tankersley. Buffy the Vampire Slayer. 1997. 192p. (J). (gr. 8-12). mass mkt. 5.99 (*0-671-01700-4*, Simon Pulse) Simon & Schuster Children's Publishing.

—Buffy the Vampire Slayer. MacDonald, Patricia, ed. 1992. 192p. (J). (gr. 7 up). mass mkt. 3.99 (*0-671-79220-2*, Simon Pulse) Simon & Schuster Children's Publishing.

—The Harvest. 1997. (Buffy the Vampire Slayer Ser.: No. 1). 160p. (YA). (gr. 7 up). pap. 5.99 (*0-671-01712-8*, Simon Pulse) Simon & Schuster Children's Publishing.

—Vampire. MacDonald, Patricia, ed. 1991. 224p. (Orig.). (YA). (gr. 7 up). pap. 3.99 (*0-671-70956-9*, Simon Pulse) Simon & Schuster Children's Publishing.

Dadey, Debbie & Jones, Marcia Thornton. Mrs. Jeepers on Vampire Island. 2002. (Bailey School Kids Ser.: No. 6). (Illus.). 128p. (J). mass mkt. 3.99 (*0-439-30641-8*, Scholastic Paperbacks) Scholastic, Inc.

—Vampires Don't Wear Polka Dots. 1990. (Adventures of the Bailey School Kids Ser.: No. 1). Tr. of Vampires Ne Portent Pas de Robe a Pois. (Illus.). 78p. (J). (gr. 2-4). mass mkt. 3.99 (*0-590-43411-X*) Scholastic, Inc.

—Vampires Don't Wear Polka Dots. 1990. (Adventures of the Bailey School Kids Ser.: No. 1). Tr. of Vampires Ne Portent Pas de Robe a Pois. (J). (gr. 2-4). 10.14 (*0-606-04839-1*) Turtleback Bks.

DeCandido, Keith R. A. The Xander Years, 1999. (Buffy the Vampire Slayer Ser.: No. 1). (Illus.). 240p. (YA). (gr. 7 up). mass mkt. 4.99 (*0-671-02629-1*, Simon Pulse) Simon & Schuster Children's Publishing.

Dicks, Terrance. The MacMagics: My Brother the Vampire. 1992. (Arch Bks.). (Illus.). 64p. (J). (ps-3). pap. 3.50 o.p. (*0-8120-4883-0*) Barron's Educational Series, Inc.

Dokey, Cameron. Here Be Monsters. (Buffy the Vampire Slayer Ser.: No. 16). (YA). (gr. 7 up). 2000. 192p. mass mkt. 5.99 (*0-671-03921-0*); 2001. reprint ed. E-Book 5.99 (*0-7434-3125-1*) Simon & Schuster Children's Publishing. (Simon Pulse).

Dracula. abr. l.t. ed. 1996. (Great Illustrated Classics Ser.: Vol. 51). (Illus.). 240p. (J). (gr. 3-7). 9.95 (*0-86611-872-1*) Playmore, Inc., Pubs.

Durant, Alan. Vampire & Werewolf Stories. 1998. (Red Hot Reads Ser.). (Illus.). 224p. (J). (gr. 4-9). pap. 6.95 (*0-7534-5152-2*, Kingfisher) Houghton Mifflin Co. Trade & Reference Div.

—Vampire & Werewolf Stories. 1998. (Story Library). (Illus.). (J). (gr. 4-9). (*0-7534-5162-X*) Kingfisher Publications, plc.

—Vampire & Werewolf Stories. 1998. 13.00 (*0-606-17372-2*) Turtleback Bks.

Espenson, Jane. Haunted. 2002. (Buffy the Vampire Slayer Ser.). (Illus.). 96p. (YA). pap. 12.95 (*1-56971-737-0*) Dark Horse Comics.

Fassbender, Tom, et al. Buffy the Vampire Slayer: Creatures of Habit. Allie, Scott, ed. Fassbender, Tom, tr. 2002. (Illus.). 96p. pap. 17.95 (*1-56971-563-7*) Dark Horse Comics.

Gallagher, Diana G. Obsidian Fate. 1999. (Buffy the Vampire Slayer Ser.: No. 7). 304p. (YA). mass mkt. 5.99 (*0-671-03929-6*, Simon Pulse) Simon & Schuster Children's Publishing.

—Prime Evil. 2000. (Buffy the Vampire Slayer Ser.: No. 10). 272p. (YA). pap. 5.99 (*0-671-03930-X*, Simon Pulse) Simon & Schuster Children's Publishing.

Gardiner, Lindsey. When Poppy & Max Grow Up. 2001. (Illus.). 24p. (J). (gr. k-1). 12.95 (*0-316-60342-2*) Little Brown Children's Bks.

Gardner, Craig Shaw. Return to Chaos. 1998. (Buffy the Vampire Slayer Ser.: No. 2). 304p. (YA). pap. 5.99 (*0-671-02136-2*, Simon Pulse) Simon & Schuster Children's Publishing.

Garton, Ray. Resurrecting Ravana. 2000. (Buffy the Vampire Slayer Ser.: No. 9). 320p. (YA). pap. 5.99 (*0-671-02636-4*, Simon Pulse) Simon & Schuster Children's Publishing.

—Resurrecting Ravana. 1999. (Buffy the Vampire Slayer Ser.: No. 9). (Illus.). 12.04 (*0-606-18366-3*) Turtleback Bks.

Gilman, Laura Anne. Deep Water. 2000. (Buffy the Vampire Slayer Ser.: No. 14). (Illus.). (YA). (gr. 7 up). 11.04 (*0-606-18365-5*) Turtleback Bks.

Gilman, Laura Anne & Sherman, Josepha. Deep Water. 2000. (Buffy the Vampire Slayer Ser.: No. 14). 192p. (YA). (gr. 7 up). pap. 5.99 (*0-671-03919-9*, Simon Pulse) Simon & Schuster Children's Publishing.

Golden, Christopher. The Dark Times. 2001. (Buffy the Vampire Slayer Ser.: Vol. 2). 144p. (YA). pap. 2.99 (*0-7434-1186-2*, Simon Pulse) Simon & Schuster Children's Publishing.

—The King of the Dead. 2001. (Buffy the Vampire Slayer Ser.). E-Book 2.99 (*0-7434-3134-0*); 144p. (YA). pap. 2.99 (*0-7434-1187-0*) Simon & Schuster Children's Publishing. (Simon Pulse).

—Lost Slayer Pt. 1: The Prophecies. 2001. (Buffy the Vampire Slayer Ser.). reprint ed. E-Book 2.99 (*0-7434-3132-4*, Simon Pulse) Simon & Schuster Children's Publishing.

—The Lost Slayer Pt. 2: Dark Times. 2001. (Buffy the Vampire Slayer Ser.). reprint ed. E-Book 2.99 (*0-7434-3133-2*, Simon Pulse) Simon & Schuster Children's Publishing.

—The Original Sins. 2001. (Buffy the Vampire Slayer Ser.). E-Book 2.99 (*0-7434-3135-9*); 192p. (YA). pap. 2.99 (*0-7434-1188-9*) Simon & Schuster Children's Publishing. (Simon Pulse).

—Oz: Into the Wild. 2002. (Buffy the Vampire Slayer Ser.). 288p. pap. 6.99 (*0-7434-0038-0*, Simon Pulse) Simon & Schuster Children's Publishing.

—Prophecies. 2001. (Buffy the Vampire Slayer Ser.: Vol. 1). 144p. (YA). mass mkt. 2.99 (*0-7434-1185-4*, Simon Pulse) Simon & Schuster Children's Publishing.

—Sins of the Father. 1999. (Buffy the Vampire Slayer Ser.: No. 8). 304p. (YA). mass mkt. 5.99 (*0-671-03928-8*, Simon Pulse) Simon & Schuster Children's Publishing.

—Spike & Dru: Pretty Maids All in a Row. (Buffy the Vampire Slayer Ser.). (YA). (gr. 8-12). 2000. (Illus.). 320p. 22.95 (*0-7434-0046-1*); 2001. 368p. reprint ed. pap. 6.99 (*0-7434-1892-1*) Simon & Schuster Children's Publishing. (Simon Pulse).

—The Watcher's Guide. 1999. (YA). mass mkt. 29.99 incl. audio compact disk (*0-671-04219-X*, Simon Pulse) Simon & Schuster Children's Publishing.

—The Wisdom of War. 2002. (Buffy the Vampire Slayer Ser.). 416p. (YA). pap. 6.99 (*0-7434-2760-2*, Simon Pulse) Simon & Schuster Children's Publishing.

Golden, Christopher & Holder, Nancy. Child of the Hunt. 1998. (Buffy the Vampire Slayer Ser.: No. 1). 336p. (YA). mass mkt. 5.99 (*0-671-02135-4*, Simon Pulse) Simon & Schuster Children's Publishing.

—The Gatekeeper Trilogy Book 3: Sons of Entropy, 3 vols. 1999. (Buffy the Vampire Slayer Ser.: No. 5). 336p. (YA). pap. 6.99 (*0-671-02750-6*, Simon Pulse) Simon & Schuster Children's Publishing.

—Ghost Roads, 3 vols. 1999. (Buffy the Vampire Slayer Ser.: No. 2). 384p. (YA). mass mkt. 6.99 (*0-671-02749-2*, Simon Pulse) Simon & Schuster Children's Publishing.

—Halloween Rain. 1997. (Buffy the Vampire Slayer Ser.: No. 2). 176p. (YA). (gr. 7 up). mass mkt. 5.99 (*0-671-01713-6*, Simon Pulse) Simon & Schuster Children's Publishing.

—Immortal. 2000. (Buffy the Vampire Slayer Ser.). 320p. (YA). reprint ed. pap. 5.99 (*0-671-04175-4*, Simon Pulse) Simon & Schuster Children's Publishing.

—The Official Sunnydale High School Yearbook. 1999. (Buffy the Vampire Slayer Ser.). (Illus.). 112p. (YA). (gr. 7 up). 16.95 (*0-671-03541-X*, Simon Pulse) Simon & Schuster Children's Publishing.

Miscellaneous

Sfar, Joann. Little Vampire Does Kung Fu. 2003. (Illus.). 40p. (J). 12.95 (*0-689-85769-1*, Simon & Schuster Children's Publishing) Simon & Schuster Children's Publishing.

—Little Vampire Goes to School. Siegel, Mark & Siegel, Alexis, trs. from FRE. 2003. (Illus.). 40p. (J). 12.95 (*0-689-85717-9*, Simon & Schuster Children's Publishing) Simon & Schuster Children's Publishing.

Shan, Darren. Cirque du Freak: A Living Nightmare. l.t. ed. 2001. 253p. (J). 24.95 (*0-7862-3733-3*) Thorndike Pr.

—Cirque du Freak: The Vampire Prince. 2003. (Saga of Darren Shan Ser.: Vol. 6). 197p. (J). 15.95 (*0-316-60709-6*) Little Brown Children's Bks.

—Cirque du Freak: The Vampire's Assistant. 2004. (Darren Shan Saga: Bk. 2). (Illus.). pap. 5.99 (*0-316-90572-0*) Little Brown Children's Bks.

—Cirque du Freak: Vampire Mountain. 2003. (Saga of Darren Shan Ser.: Bk. 4). (J). (gr. 5 up). pap. 6.50 (*0-316-60542-5*) Little Brown Children's Bks.

—Cirque du Freak: The Vampire's Assistant. l.t. ed. 2002. (Young Adult Ser.). 240p. (J). 24.95 (*0-7862-3734-1*) Gale Group.

—Hunters of the Dusk. 2004. (Illus.). (J). 15.95 (*0-316-60596-4*) Little Brown Children's Bks.

—A Living Nightmare. 2001. (Saga of Darren Shan Ser.: Bk. 1). (gr. 5 up). (Illus.). viii, 279p. (YA). pap. (*0-316-64852-3*);Bk. 1. 272p. (J). 15.95 (*0-316-60340-6*) Little Brown Children's Bks.

—Trials of Death. (Saga of Darren Shan Ser.: Bk. 5). (J). (gr. 5 up). 2004. pap. 6.50 (*0-316-60395-3*); 2003. (Illus.). 224p. 15.95 (*0-316-60367-8*) Little Brown Children's Bks.

—Tunnels of Blood. (Saga of Darren Shan Ser.: Bk. 3). (J). (gr. 5 up). 2003. (Illus.). 240p. pap. 6.50 (*0-316-60608-1*); Bk. 3. 2002. 229p. 15.95 (*0-316-60763-0*) Little Brown Children's Bks.

—Vampire Mountain. 2002. (Saga of Darren Shan Ser.: Bk. 44). (Illus.). 208p. (J). (gr. 5 up). 15.95 (*0-316-60806-8*) Little Brown Children's Bks.

—The Vampire's Assistant. (Saga of Darren Shan Ser.: Bk. 2). 256p. (J). (gr. 5 up). 2002. (Illus.). pap. 6.50 (*0-316-60684-7*); Bk. 2. 2001. 15.95 (*0-316-60610-3*) Little Brown Children's Bks.

Simon and Schuster Children's Staff, ed. Tales of the Slayer. 2003. (Buffy the Vampire Slayer Ser.). (Illus.). (YA). Vol. II. 368p. pap. 9.99 (*0-7434-2744-0*); Vol. 3. 336p. pap. 9.99 (*0-689-86436-1*) Simon & Schuster Children's Publishing. (Simon Pulse).

Slonaker, Erin. The Vampire Hunter's Handbook. 2001. (Illus.). 96p. (YA). (gr. 5 up). mass mkt. 7.99 o.p. (*0-8431-7645-8*, Price Stern Sloan) Penguin Putnam Bks. for Young Readers.

Smith. The Fury. 1999. (Vampire Diaries Ser.: Vol. 3). 320p. (gr. 8-12). mass mkt. 4.99 (*0-06-105991-9*, Eos) Morrow/Avon.

Smith, L. J. The Awakening. (Vampire Diaries: No. 1). 320p. 1999. (gr. 7-12). mass mkt. 5.99 (*0-06-102000-1*, Eos); 1995. (J). mass mkt. 1.99 o.s.i (*0-06-106400-9*, HarperTorch); 1991. (YA). mass mkt. 3.99 (*0-06-106097-6*, HarperTorch) Morrow/ Avon.

—Dark Angel. 1996. (Night World Ser.: No. 4). 240p. (YA). (gr. 7 up). mass mkt. 3.99 (*0-671-55136-1*, Simon Pulse) Simon & Schuster Children's Publishing.

—Dark Reunion. (Vampire Diaries: Vol. IV). 320p. 1992. (YA). mass mkt. 3.99 (*0-06-106775-X*, HarperTorch); Vol. 4. 1999. (gr. 8-12). mass mkt. 5.99 (*0-06-105992-7*, Eos) Morrow/Avon.

—Daughters of Darkness, No. 2. 1996. (Daughters of Darkness Ser.: Vol. 2). 240p. (YA). (gr. 7 up). mass mkt. 4.50 (*0-671-55134-5*, Simon Pulse) Simon & Schuster Children's Publishing.

—The Fury. 1991. (Vampire Diaries: Vol. 3). 320p. (YA). mass mkt. 3.99 (*0-06-106099-2*, Harper-Torch) Morrow/Avon.

—The Secret Vampire. 1996. (Night World Ser.: Vol. 1). 240p. (YA). (gr. 7 up). pap. 3.99 (*0-671-55133-7*, Simon Pulse) Simon & Schuster Children's Publishing.

—The Struggle. (Vampire Diaries: 2). 320p. 1995. mass mkt. 1.99 o.s.i (*0-06-106393-2*, Harper-Torch); 1991. (YA). mass mkt. 3.99 (*0-06-106098-4*, HarperTorch); Bk. 2. 1999. (gr. 7-12). mass mkt. 5.99 (*0-06-102001-X*, Eos) Morrow/ Avon.

Sommer-Bodenburg, Angela. The Vampire in Love. 1991. (Illus.). (J). (gr. 2-6). 128p. 13.00 o.p. (*0-8037-0905-6*); 144p. 12.89 o.p. (*0-8037-0906-4*) Penguin Putnam Bks. for Young Readers. (Dial Bks. for Young Readers).

—The Vampire in Love. 1993. 144p. (J). (gr. 3-6). pap. 2.99 (*0-671-75877-2*, Aladdin) Simon & Schuster Children's Publishing.

—The Vampire in Love. 1986. (J). 8.09 o.p. (*0-606-05681-5*) Turtleback Bks.

—The Vampire on the Farm. 1989. (Illus.). 144p. (J). (gr. 2-6). 10.95 o.p. (*0-8037-0326-0*); 10.89 o.p. (*0-8037-0327-9*) Penguin Putnam Bks. for Young Readers. (Dial Bks. for Young Readers).

—The Vampire on the Farm. Greenberg, Ann, ed. 1990. (Illus.). 144p. (J). (gr. 3-6). reprint ed. pap. 2.95 (*0-671-70236-X*, Aladdin) Simon & Schuster Children's Publishing.

Stafford, Nikki. Bite Me! An Unofficial Guide to the World of Buffy the Vampire Slayer. 1998. (Illus.). 200p. (J). pap. 14.95 (*1-55022-361-5*) ECW Pr. CAN. *Dist:* LPC/InBook.

Stilton, Geronimo. Red Pizzas for Blue Count. 2004. (Geronimo Stilton Ser.: No. 7). (Illus.). 128p. (J). mass mkt. 5.99 (*0-439-55969-3*) Scholastic, Inc.

Stine, R. L. Dangerous Girls. 2003. 256p. (J). 111.92 (*0-06-056910-7*); 111.92 (*0-06-056909-3*); (Illus.). (gr. 7 up). 13.99 (*0-06-053080-4*) HarperCollins Children's Bk. Group.

—Ghosts of Fear Street Complete Vampire Kit: Vampire Fangs, Makeup, Makeup Applicator, Stage Blood, & Book. 1996. (Ghosts of Fear Street Ser.). 48p. pap. text 7.99 (*0-671-00345-3*, Aladdin) Simon & Schuster Children's Publishing.

—Horror Hotel Pt. 1: The Vampire Checks In. 1999. (Ghosts of Fear Street Ser.: No. 34). 128p. (J). (gr. 4-7). pap. 2.99 o.s.i (*0-307-24906-9*, Golden Bks.) Random Hse. Children's Bks.

—How to Be a Vampire. 1996. (Ghosts of Fear Street Ser.: No. 13). 144p. (J). (gr. 4-7). pap. 3.99 (*0-671-00185-X*, Aladdin) Simon & Schuster Children's Publishing.

—How to Be a Vampire. 1996. (Ghosts of Fear Street Ser.: No. 13). (J). (gr. 4-7). 10.04 (*0-606-10815-7*) Turtleback Bks.

Stine, R. L. & Hapka, Catherine. Attack of the Vampire Worms. 1998. (Ghosts of Fear Street Ser.: No. 33). 128p. (J). (gr. 4-7). pap. 3.99 o.s.i (*0-307-24905-0*, Golden Bks.) Random Hse. Children's Bks.

Stoker, Bram. Bram Stoker's Dracula. 1980. (Illus.). 48p. (J). (gr. 3 up). pap. 6.95 o.s.i (*0-440-01348-8*, Delacorte Pr.) Dell Publishing.

—Dracula. unabr. ed. 1965. (Classics Ser.). (YA). (gr. 7 up). mass mkt. 2.25 (*0-8049-0072-8*, CL-72) Airmont Publishing Co., Inc.

—Dracula. 1983. (Bantam Classics Ser.). 432p. (gr. 9-12). mass mkt. 4.95 (*0-553-21271-0*) Bantam Bks.

—Dracula. 1965. 416p. (YA). (gr. 7 up). pap. 2.50 o.s.i (*0-440-92148-1*, Laurel) Dell Publishing.

—Dracula. 1988. mass mkt. 2.25 (*0-938819-70-4*, Aerie) Doherty, Tom Assocs., LLC.

—Dracula. 1997. (Eyewitness Classics Ser.). (Illus.). 64p. (J). (gr. 3-6). pap. 14.95 o.p. (*0-7894-1489-9*) Dorling Kindersley Publishing, Inc.

—Dracula. 1997. (Children's Thrift Classics Ser.). (Illus.). 96p. (J). reprint ed. pap. text 1.00 (*0-486-29567-2*) Dover Pubns., Inc.

—Dracula. 1998. (Illustrated Classic Book Ser.). (Illus.). 61p. (J). (gr. 3 up). pap. text 4.95 (*1-56767-261-2*) Educational Insights, Inc.

—Dracula. unabr. ed. 1998. (Wordsworth Classics Ser.). (YA). (gr. 6-12). 5.27 o.p. (*0-89061-086-X*, R086XWW) Jamestown.

—Dracula. 2000. (Books of Wonder). (Illus.). 430p. (J). (gr. 7-12). 21.95 (*0-688-13921-3*) Morrow/ Avon.

—Dracula. 1986. (Signet Classics). 400p. (YA). (gr. 10). mass mkt. 4.95 (*0-451-52337-7*, Signet Classics) NAL.

—Dracula. Farr, Naunerle C., ed. 1973. (Now Age Illustrated Ser.). (Illus.). 64p. (J). (gr. 5-10). stu. ed. 1.25 (*0-88301-175-1*); pap. 2.95 (*0-88301-100-X*) Pendulum Pr., Inc.

—Dracula. (Puffin Classics Ser.). 1995. (Illus.). 528p. (YA). (gr. 4-7). pap. 3.99 (*0-14-036717-9*, Puffin Bks.); 1994. (Illus.). 432p. (J). 15.95 o.p. (*0-448-40559-8*, Grosset & Dunlap); 1986. 448p. (J). (gr. 4-6). pap. 3.50 o.p. (*0-14-035048-9*, Puffin Bks.) Penguin Putnam Bks. for Young Readers.

—Dracula. Lafreniere, Kenneth, ed. 1982. (Stepping Stone Bks.: No. 1). (Illus.). 96p. (J). (gr. 3-7). pap. 3.99 (*0-394-84828-4*, Random Hse. Bks. for Young Readers) Random Hse. Children's Bks.

—Dracula. 2000. 528p. (gr. 4-7). mass mkt. 4.99 (*0-439-15411-1*); 1992. (J). mass mkt. 3.99 (*0-590-46029-3*, 067, Scholastic Paperbacks) Scholastic, Inc.

—Dracula. 1999. (Saddleback Classics). (Illus.). (J). 13.10 (*0-606-21550-6*) Turtleback Bks.

—Dracula. 1985. (J). (ps-3). 19.95 o.p. (*0-88101-020-0*) Unicorn Publishing Hse., Inc., The.

Strasser, Todd. Help! I'm Trapped in a Vampire's Body. 2000. (Help! I'm Trapped Ser.). (Illus.). 144p. (J). (gr. 4-7). mass mkt. 4.50 o.s.i (*0-439-21034-8*) Scholastic, Inc.

—Help! I'm Trapped in a Vampire's Body. 2000. (Help! I'm Trapped Ser.). (J). (gr. 4-7). 10.55 (*0-606-19565-3*) Turtleback Bks.

Tankersley, Richie. The Angel Chronicles, Vol. 2. 1998. (Buffy the Vampire Slayer Ser.: No. 7). (Illus.). 240p. (YA). (gr. 7 up). mass mkt. 5.99 (*0-671-02627-5*, Simon Pulse) Simon & Schuster Children's Publishing.

Thompson, Kate. Midnight's Choice. 2000. 240p. (J). pap. 5.99 (*0-7868-1266-4*) Disney Pr.

—Midnight's Choice, No. 2. 1999. (Switchers Ser.: Vol. 2). 236p. (J). (gr. 5-9). lib. bdg. 16.49 (*0-7868-2329-1*) Hyperion Bks. for Children.

—Midnight's Choice, 1999. (Switchers Ser.: Vol. 2). 236p. (J). (gr. 5-9). 15.99 (*0-7868-0381-9*) Hyperion Pr.

—Midnight's Choice. unabr. ed. 2000. (Switchers Ser.: Vol. 2). 240p. (J). (gr. 4-7). pap. 37.00 incl. audio (*0-8072-8769-5*, Listening Library) Random Hse. Audio Publishing Group.

Tracy, Kathleen. The Girl's Got Bite: The Unofficial Guide to Buffy's World. 1998. (Illus.). 256p. pap. 14.95 o.p. (*1-58063-035-9*, Renaissance Bks.) St. Martin's Pr.

Vornholt, John. Coyote Moon. 1998. (Buffy the Vampire Slayer Ser.: No. 3). 176p. (YA). (gr. 7 up). pap. 4.99 (*0-671-01714-4*, Simon Pulse) Simon & Schuster Children's Publishing.

Watson, Andi, et al. Bad Blood. 2000. (Buffy the Vampire Slayer Ser.). (Illus.). 88p. (YA). (gr. 7 up). pap. 9.95 (*1-56971-445-2*) Dark Horse Comics.

—Crash Test Demons. 2000. (Buffy the Vampire Slayer Ser.). (Illus.). 80p. (YA). (gr. 7 up). pap. 9.95 (*1-56971-461-4*) Dark Horse Comics.

—The Remaining Sunlight. 1999. (Buffy the Vampire Slayer Ser.). (Illus.). 88p. (YA). (gr. 7 up). pap. 9.95 (*1-56971-354-5*) Dark Horse Comics.

—Uninvited Guests. 1999. (Buffy the Vampire Slayer Ser.). (Illus.). 96p. (YA). (gr. 7 up). pap. 10.95 (*1-56971-436-3*) Dark Horse Comics.

Williams, Tad & Crosby, Rodney. Child of an Ancient City. Hoffman, Nina Kiriki, ed. 1999. 288p. pap. text 6.99 (*0-8125-7211-4*, Tor Bks.) Doherty, Tom Assocs., LLC.

Williams, Tad & Hoffman, Nina K. Child of an Ancient City. 1994. 288p. reprint ed. mass mkt. 6.99 o.p. (*0-8125-3391-7*, Tor Bks.) Doherty, Tom Assocs., LLC.

—Child of an Ancient City. 1992. (Dragonflight Ser.). (Illus.). 144p. lib. bdg. 16.00 o.s.i (*0-689-31577-5*, Atheneum) Simon & Schuster Children's Publishing.

Williams, Tad & Hoffman, Nina Kiriki. Child of an Ancient City. 1992. E-Book (*1-58824-903-4*) ipicturebooks, LLC.

Wilson, Eric G. Vampires of Ottawa. 2001. (Liz Austen Mystery Ser.). (Illus.). 108p. (J). (gr. 3-7). 4.99 (*1-55143-228-5*) Orca Bk. Pubs.

Woo. Rebirth, 11 vols. 2004. (Illus.). (YA). Vol. 6. 192p. pap. 9.99 (*1-59182-524-5*); Vol. 7. 176p. pap. 9.99 (*1-59182-525-3*) TOKYOPOP, Inc.

Yolen, Jane & Greenberg, Martin H., eds. Vampires. (Trophy Chiller Bk.). (YA). (gr. 5 up). 1993. 208p. pap. 4.50 (*0-06-440485-4*, Harper Trophy); 1991. 240p. 15.00 (*0-06-026800-X*); 1991. 240p. lib. bdg. 14.89 o.p. (*0-06-026801-8*) HarperCollins Children's Bk. Group.

—Vampires. 1993. (Trophy Chiller Ser.). (YA). 9.60 o.p. (*0-606-05682-3*) Turtleback Bks.

Yolen, Jane & Greenberger, Martin H. Vampires: A Collection of Original Stories. 2002. 240p. (J). (gr. 5 up). pap. 5.99 (*0-06-050222-3*, Harper Trophy) HarperCollins Children's Bk. Group.

W

WEREWOLVES—FICTION

Amoss, Berthe. The Loup-Garou. 1979. (Illus.). 48p. (J). (gr. 5-7). 11.95 o.s.i (*0-88289-189-8*) Pelican Publishing Co., Inc.

Brennan, Herbie. Emily & the Werewolf. 1993. (Illus.). 96p. (J). (gr. 3-7). 16.95 o.p. (*0-689-50593-0*, McElderry, Margaret K.) Simon & Schuster Children's Publishing.

Buchanan, Paul. Dances with Werewolves, Vol. 8. 2000. (Heebie Jeebies Ser.: Vol. 6). 128p. (J). (gr. 3-7). pap. 5.99 (*0-8054-1982-9*) Broadman & Holman Pubs.

Conford, Ellen. Norman Newman & the Werewolf of Walnut Street. 1995. (Norman Newman Ser.). 8.15 o.p. (*0-606-07958-0*) Turtleback Bks.

Cuyler, Margery. Weird Wolf, ERS. (Illus.). 80p. (J). 1991. (gr. 4-7). pap. 6.95 (*0-8050-1643-0*); 1989. (gr. 2-4). 12.95 o.p. (*0-8050-0835-7*) Holt, Henry & Co. (Holt, Henry & Co. Bks. For Young Readers).

—Weird Wolf. 1991. (J). 13.10 (*0-606-12142-0*) Turtle-back Bks.

DeWeese, Gene. Adventures of a Two-Minute Werewolf. 1983. (Illus.). 132p. (gr. 5-8). 9.95 o.p. (*0-385-17453-5*) Doubleday Publishing.

—The Adventures of a Two-Minute Werewolf. 1984. 128p. (J). (gr. 5-9). reprint ed. 2.25 (*0-399-21082-2*) Putnam Publishing Group, The.

Dixon, Franklin W. Night of the Werewolf. Greenberg, Ann, ed. 1990. (Hardy Boys Mystery Stories Ser.: No. 59). 192p. (J). (gr. 3-6). pap. 3.99 (*0-671-70993-3*, Aladdin) Simon & Schuster Children's Publishing.

—Night of the Werewolf. 1979. (Hardy Boys Mystery Stories Ser.: No. 59). (Illus.). (J). (gr. 3-6). pap. (*0-671-95520-9*); pap. (*0-671-95498-9*) Simon & Schuster Children's Publishing. (Simon & Schuster Children's Publishing).

Durant, Alan. Vampire & Werewolf Stories. 1998. (Red Hot Reads Ser.). (Illus.). 224p. (J). (gr. 4-9). pap. 6.95 (*0-7534-5152-2*, Kingfisher) Houghton Mifflin Co. Trade & Reference Div.

—Vampire & Werewolf Stories. 1998. (Story Library). (Illus.). (J). (gr. 4-9). (*0-7534-5162-X*) Kingfisher Publications, plc.

—Vampire & Werewolf Stories. 1998. 13.00 (*0-606-17372-2*) Turtleback Bks.

Engle, Marty M. & Barnes, Johnny Ray, Jr. No Substitutions. l.t. ed. 1996. (Strange Matter Ser.: No. 1). (Illus.). 124p. (J). (gr. 4-6). lib. bdg. 21.27 o.p. (*0-8368-1667-6*) Stevens, Gareth Inc.

Farber, Erica. Werewolves for Lunch. 1996. (Critters of the Night Ser.). 9.19 o.p. (*0-606-10036-9*) Turtle-back Bks.

Farber, Erica, et al. Werewolves for Lunch. 1996. (Creepy Critters Ser.). (Illus.). 80p. (J). (gr. 1-5). pap. 3.99 o.s.i (*0-679-87359-7*, Random Hse. Bks. for Young Readers) Random Hse. Children's Bks.

Fontes, Justine & Fontes, Ron. The Wolf Man. 1992. (Illus.). 96p. (J). (gr. 3-7). pap. o.p. (*0-307-22336-1*, 22336, Golden Bks.) Random Hse. Children's Bks.

Gantos, Jack. The Werewolf Family, 001. 1980. (Illus.). (J). (gr. k-3). lib. bdg. 8.95 o.p. (*0-395-28760-X*) Houghton Mifflin Co.

Garden, Nancy. My Brother, the Werewolf. 1995. (J). lib. bdg. 7.99 o.p. (*0-679-95414-7*, Random Hse. Bks. for Young Readers) Random Hse. Children's Bks.

—My Brother, the Werewolf. 1995. (J). 9.60 o.p. (*0-606-09647-7*) Turtleback Bks.

Garfield, Henry. Tartabull's Throw. (Illus.). 2003. 304p. (YA). pap. 5.99 (*0-689-85671-7*, Simon Pulse); 2001. 272p. (J). (gr. 7 up). 16.00 (*0-689-83840-9*, Atheneum/Richard Jackson Bks.) Simon & Schuster Children's Publishing.

Garmon, Larry Mike. The Wolf Man: Blood Moon Rising. 2001. (Universal Monsters Ser.: No. 2). 160p. (J). (gr. 5 up). mass mkt. 4.50 (*0-439-20847-5*) Scholastic, Inc.

Greenburg, Dan. My Teacher Ate My Homework. 2002. (Zack Files Ser.: 27). (Illus.). 64p. (J). mass mkt. 4.99 (*0-448-42683-8*, Grosset & Dunlap) Penguin Putnam Bks. for Young Readers.

Halkin, John. Fangs of the Werewolf. 1988. (Flesh-creepers Ser.). 160p. (J). (gr. 6 up). pap. 2.95 o.p. (*0-8120-4071-6*) Barron's Educational Series, Inc.

Hill, Elizabeth S. Fangs Aren't Everything. 1985. (Illus.). 96p. (J). (gr. 3-7). 10.95 o.p. (*0-525-44152-2*, Dutton) Dutton/Plume.

Hodgman, Ann. Dark Dreams. 1993. (Children of the Night Ser.: No. 1). 224p. (J). (gr. 7 up). pap. 3.50 o.p. (*0-14-036374-2*, Puffin Bks.) Penguin Putnam Bks. for Young Readers.

—Dark Music. 1994. (Children of the Night Ser.). (J). 42.00 o.p. (*0-14-777166-8*);No. 2. 224p. (YA). (gr. 7 up). pap. 3.50 o.p. (*0-14-036375-0*) Penguin Putnam Bks. for Young Readers. (Puffin Bks.).

Jennings, Patrick. The Wolving Time. 2003. 208p. (J). 15.95 (*0-439-39555-0*) Scholastic, Inc.

Keene, Carolyn & Whelan, Patrick. Werewolf in a Winter Wonderland. 2003. (Nancy Drew Ser.). (Illus.). 160p. (J). pap. 4.99 (*0-689-86182-6*, Aladdin) Simon & Schuster Children's Publishing.

Klause, Annette Curtis. Blood & Chocolate. 1999. 288p. (YA). (gr. 7-12). mass mkt. 5.50 (*0-440-22668-6*) Dell Publishing.

—Blood & Chocolate. 1997. 272p. (YA). (gr. 9-12). 16.95 o.s.i (*0-385-32305-0*, Dell Books for Young Readers) Random Hse. Children's Bks.

Leroe, E. W. Revenge of the Hairy Horror. 1996. (Fiendly Corners Ser.: No. 3). (Illus.). 128p. (J). (gr. 4-7). pap. 3.95 (*0-7868-1097-1*) Disney Pr.

Levy, Elizabeth. Wolfman Sam. 1996. (Trophy Chapter Bks.). (Illus.). (J). (gr. 2-5). 80p. pap. 4.99 (*0-06-442048-5*, Harper Trophy);No. 4. 128p. lib. bdg. 13.89 o.p. (*0-06-024817-3*) HarperCollins Children's Bk. Group.

—Wolfman Sam. 1996. (J). 9.15 o.p. (*0-606-10081-4*) Turtleback Bks.

Martin, Les. Return of the Werewolf. 1993. (Bullseye Chillers Ser.). (Illus.). 96p. (J). (gr. 2-6). pap. 3.99 o.s.i (*0-679-84189-X*, Random Hse. Bks. for Young Readers) Random Hse. Children's Bks.

Noonan, R. A. New Grrrl in Town. 1996. (Monsterville USA Ser.: Vol. 6). (Illus.). 144p. (J). (gr. 3-7). pap. 3.99 (*0-689-71868-3*, Simon Pulse) Simon & Schuster Children's Publishing.

Ogburn, Jacqueline K. Scarlett Angelina Wolverton-Manning. 1994. (Illus.). 32p. (J). 14.99 o.p. (*0-8037-1376-2*); 14.89 o.s.i (*0-8037-1377-0*) Penguin Putnam Bks. for Young Readers. (Dial Bks. for Young Readers).

Packard, Edward. Night of the Werewolf. 1995. (Choose Your Own Nightmare Ser.: No. 1). (J). (gr. 4-8). 8.70 o.p. (*0-606-07365-5*) Turtleback Bks.

—The Night of the Werewolf. 1995. (Choose Your Own Nightmare Ser.: No. 1). 96p. (J). (gr. 4-8). pap. 3.50 o.s.i (*0-553-48229-7*) Bantam Bks.

—Night of the Werewolf. l.t. ed. 1996. (Illus.). 96p. (J). (gr. 4 up). lib. bdg. 22.60 o.p. (*0-8368-1510-6*) Stevens, Gareth Inc.

Pinkwater, Daniel M. I Was a Second Grade Werewolf. 1983. (Illus.). 32p. (J). (ps-2). 12.95 o.s.i (*0-525-44038-0*) Live Oak Media.

—The Magic Pretzel. 2000. (Werewolf Club Ready for Chapters Ser.: Bk. 1). (Illus.). 80p. (J). (gr. 2-4). pap. 3.99 (*0-689-83790-9*, Aladdin);Vol. 1. 15.00 (*0-689-83800-X*, Atheneum) Simon & Schuster Children's Publishing.

—The Magic Pretzel. 2001. (J). (gr. 2-5). 18.75 o.p. (*0-8446-7185-1*) Smith, Peter Pub., Inc.

—The Magic Pretzel. 2000. (Werewolf Club Ser.). 10.14 (*0-606-19734-6*); 10.14 (*0-606-17942-9*) Turtleback Bks.

—The Werewolf Club Meets Dorkula. 2001. (Werewolf Club Ready for Chapters Ser.: Vol. 3). (Illus.). 80p. (J). (gr. 4-7). 15.00 (*0-689-83848-4*, Atheneum); (gr. 2-5). pap. 3.99 (*0-689-83847-6*, Aladdin) Simon & Schuster Children's Publishing.

—The Werewolf Club Meets Oliver Twit. 2002. (Werewolf Club Ready for Chapters Ser.: No. 5). (Illus.). 64p. (J). pap. 3.99 (*0-689-84571-5*, Aladdin); 15.00 (*0-689-84574-X*, Atheneum) Simon & Schuster Children's Publishing.

—The Werewolf Club Meets the Hound of the Basketballs. 4th ed. 2001. (Werewolf Club Ser.: Vol. 4). (Illus.). 64p. (J). pap. 3.99 (*0-689-84473-5*, Aladdin); (gr. 2-4). 15.00 (*0-689-84575-8*, Atheneum) Simon & Schuster Children's Publishing.

—The Werewolf Club Meets the Hound of the Basketballs. 2001. 10.14 (*0-606-22089-5*) Turtleback Bks.

Rice, Bebe Faas. The Year the Wolves Came. 1994. 128p. (J). (gr. 3-7). 15.99 o.p. (*0-525-45209-5*, Dutton Children's Bks.) Penguin Putnam Bks. for Young Readers.

Skurzynski, Gloria. Manwolf. 1981. 192p. (J). (gr. 6 up). 10.95 o.p. (*0-395-30079-7*, Clarion Bks.) Houghton Mifflin Co. Trade & Reference Div.

Stanley, George Edward. A Werewolf Followed Me Home. 1997. (Scaredy Cats Ser.: No. 7). (Illus.). 80p. (J). (gr. 1-4). per. 3.99 (*0-689-81614-6*, Aladdin) Simon & Schuster Children's Publishing.

Stevenson, Drew. The Case of the Wandering Werewolf. 1987. (Illus.). 128p. (J). (gr. 3-7). 11.95 o.p. (*0-396-09154-7*, G. P. Putnam's Sons) Penguin Putnam Bks. for Young Readers.

—The Case of the Wandering Werewolf. MacDonald, Patricia, ed. 1991. (Illus.). 128p. (J). reprint ed. pap. 2.95 (*0-671-67238-X*, Aladdin) Simon & Schuster Children's Publishing.

Stewart, Mary. A Walk in Wolf Wood. 1987. 192p. mass mkt. 6.99 o.s.i (*0-449-21422-2*); 1984. 192p. mass mkt. 2.95 o.s.i (*0-449-20678-5*); 1982. mass mkt. 2.75 o.s.i (*0-449-20111-2*) Ballantine Bks. (Fawcett).

—A Walk in Wolf Wood. rev. ed. 1984. (Illus.). 160p. (J). (gr. 5). 11.95 o.p. (*0-688-03679-1*, Morrow, William & Co.) Morrow/Avon.

Sulzenko, J. C. Annabella & the Werewolves of Whale Cove. 2001. (Illus.). 48p. (J). pap. (*0-9685094-2-8*) Blue Poodle Bks.

Windsor, Patricia. The Blooding. (gr. 7-12). 1999. 288p. mass mkt. 4.50 (*0-590-43308-3*); 1996. 272p. (YA). pap. 15.95 (*0-590-43309-1*) Scholastic, Inc.

Yolen, Jane & Greenberg, Martin H., eds. Werewolves: A Collection of Original Stories. 1988. 288p. (YA). (gr. 5-9). 13.95 (*0-06-026798-4*); lib. bdg. 13.89 o.p. (*0-06-026799-2*) HarperCollins Children's Bk. Group.

WITCHES—FICTION

Akinyemi, Rowena. The Witches of Pendle, Level 1. Hedge, Tricia, ed. 2000. (Bookworms Ser.). (Illus.). 64p. (J). pap. text 5.95 (*0-19-422957-2*) Oxford Univ. Pr., Inc.

Alley, R. W., illus. There Once Was a Witch. 2003. 16p. (J). (ps up). 6.99 (*0-06-000795-8*) HarperCollins Children's Bk. Group.

Alton, Steve. The Malifex. 2002. (Middle Readers Ser.). (Illus.). 182p. (J). (gr. 3-7). lib. bdg. 14.95 (*0-8225-0959-8*, Carolrhoda Bks.) Lerner Publishing Group.

Asbury, Kelly. Witch Dot. 2001. (Illus.). 14p. (J). bds. 4.99 (*0-8431-7696-2*, Price Stern Sloan) Penguin Putnam Bks. for Young Readers.

Atwater-Rhodes, Amelia. Demon in My View. 192p. (YA). (gr. 7). 2001. mass mkt. 4.99 (*0-440-22884-0*, Laurel Leaf); 2000. 9.95 (*0-385-32720-X*, Dell Books for Young Readers) Random Hse. Children's Bks.

—Shattered Mirror. 2001. E-Book 3.99 (*1-59061-571-9*) Adobe Systems, Inc.

—Shattered Mirror. 240p. (YA). (gr. 7). 2003. mass mkt. 5.50 (*0-440-22940-5*, Laurel Leaf); 2001. 9.95 (*0-385-32793-5*, Dell Books for Young Readers) Random Hse. Children's Bks.

Baker, E. D. Dragon's Breath. 2003. 250p. (J). 15.95 (*1-58234-858-8*, Bloomsbury Children) Bloomsbury Publishing.

—The Frog Princess. 2002. 200p. (J). (gr. 3-9). 15.95 (*1-58234-799-9*, Bloomsbury Children) Bloomsbury Publishing.

Baltz, Terry & Baltz, Wayne. The Invisible Kid & the Killer Cat. 1994. (Invisible Kid Ser.: No. 2). 127p. (Orig.). (J). (gr. 2-6). pap. 6.95 (*1-884610-12-9*) Prairie Divide Productions.

Bell, Hilari. The Goblin Wood. 2003. (Illus.). 304p. (J). (gr. 5 up). 16.99 (*0-06-051371-3*); lib. bdg. 17.89 (*0-06-051372-1*) HarperCollins Children's Bk. Group.

Bird, Isobel. What the Cards Said, No. 4. 2001. (Circle of Three Ser.). (Illus.). 240p. (J). (gr. 7 up). pap. 4.99 (*0-06-447294-9*, Avon) HarperCollins Children's Bk. Group.

Bishop, Anne. The Black Jewels Trilogy. 2003. 1216p. pap. 18.00 (*0-451-52901-4*, ROC) NAL.

Blacker, Terence. Ms. Wiz Spells Trouble. 1990. (Arch Bks.). (Illus.). 64p. (J). (gr. 3-6). pap. 2.95 o.p. (*0-8120-4420-7*) Barron's Educational Series, Inc.

Brown, Marc. Witches Four. 1993. (Illus.). 42p. (J). (ps-3). lib. bdg. 19.93 o.p. (*0-8368-0893-2*) Stevens, Gareth Inc.

Bruja (Witch) 2001. (Jigsaw Ser.). 20p. (J). (ps-3). 7.95 (*1-57145-900-6*, Silver Dolphin Bks.) Advantage Pubs. Group.

Buck, Nola. The Littlest Witch. 1994. (Illus.). 16p. (J). (ps-2). 4.95 o.p. (*0-694-00647-5*, Harper Festival) HarperCollins Children's Bk. Group.

Buehner, Caralyn. A Job for Wittilda. 1993. (Illus.). 32p. (J). (ps-3). 13.89 o.p. (*0-8037-1150-6*, Dial Bks. for Young Readers) Penguin Putnam Bks. for Young Readers.

—A Job with Wittilda. 1993. (Illus.). 32p. (J). (ps-3). 15.99 o.p. (*0-8037-1149-2*, Dial Bks. for Young Readers) Penguin Putnam Bks. for Young Readers.

Calmenson, Stephanie. The Little Witch Sisters. 1990. (Illus.). (J). 2.95 o.s.i (*0-448-04336-X*, Grosset & Dunlap) Penguin Putnam Bks. for Young Readers.

—The Little Witch Sisters. 1993. (Illus.). 48p. (J). (gr. 1 up). lib. bdg. 19.93 o.p. (*0-8368-0970-X*) Stevens, Gareth Inc.

Canfield, Andrea. The Sassy Chronicles. 2003. Orig. Title: Sassy the Seahag. (Illus.). (J). per. (*0-9721327-3-2*) Eight Dog Publishing.

Comella, Maria Angeles. Donde Esta la Reina? 2001. (Illus.). (J). (gr. k-4). (CAT.). 32p. 14.95 (*84-8488-001-X*); (SPA., 126p. 14.95 (*84-95040-98-0*) Serres, Ediciones, S. L. ESP. *Dist:* Lectorum Pubns., Inc.

Coppinger, Tom. A Curse in Reverse. 2003. (Illus.). 40p. (J). (gr. k-3). 16.95 (*0-689-83096-3*, Atheneum) Simon & Schuster Children's Publishing.

Dahl, Roald. The Witches. 2002. (J). pap. 29.95 incl. audio (*0-7540-6247-3*) BBC Audiobooks America.

—The Witches. 1999. (gr. 3-7). pap. 13.55 (*0-8085-7491-4*) Econo-Clad Bks.

—The Witches, RS. 1983. (Illus.). 208p. (J). (gr. 3-7). 17.00 (*0-374-38457-6*); 35.00 o.p. (*0-374-38458-4*) Farrar, Straus & Giroux. (Farrar, Straus & Giroux (BYR)).

—The Witches. (Illus.). (J). 1999. 200p. (gr. 3-7). pap. 3.95 (*0-14-031730-9*, Viking Children's Bks.); 1998. 208p. (gr. 3-7). pap. 5.99 (*0-14-130110-4*, Puffin Bks.); 1989. 208p. pap. 4.99 o.s.i (*0-14-034020-3*, Puffin Bks.) Penguin Putnam Bks. for Young Readers.

—The Witches. 1985. (J). 11.04 (*0-606-00540-4*) Turtleback Bks.

D'Angelo, Alex. The Trouble with Sannie Langtand. 1997. (Illus.). (J). (*0-624-03546-8*) Tafelberg Pubs., Ltd. ZAF. *Dist:* Agora Publishing Consortium.

de Paola, Tomie. Strega Nona Takes a Vacation. 2000. (Illus.). 32p. (J). (ps-3). 16.99 (*0-399-23562-0*) Penguin Group (USA) Inc.

—Strega Nona Takes a Vacation. 2003. (Illus.). 32p. pap. 5.99 (*0-14-250076-3*, Puffin Bks.) Penguin Putnam Bks. for Young Readers.

Desmoinaux, Christel. Hallo-What? 2003. (Illus.). 32p. (J). (gr. k-3). 14.95 (*0-689-84795-5*, McElderry, Margaret K.) Simon & Schuster Children's Publishing.

Dexter, Catherine. A Is for Apple, W Is for Witch. 1996. (Illus.). 160p. (J). (gr. 4-7). 14.99 o.p. (*1-56402-541-1*) Candlewick Pr.

Dicks, Terrance. A Spell for My Sister. 1992. (Arch Bks.). (Illus.). 64p. (J). (gr. 3-6). pap. 3.50 o.p. (*0-8120-4881-4*) Barron's Educational Series, Inc.

Dokey, Cameron. Truth & Consequences. 2003. (Charmed Ser.). (Illus.). 208p. (YA). mass mkt. 5.99 (*0-689-85791-8*, Simon Pulse) Simon & Schuster Children's Publishing.

Donaldson, Julia. Room on the Broom. (Illus.). 32p. (J). (gr. k-2). 2003. pap. 6.99 (*0-14-250112-3*, Puffin Bks.); 2001. 15.99 (*0-8037-2657-0*, Dial Bks. for Young Readers) Penguin Putnam Bks. for Young Readers.

Estes, Eleanor. The Witch Family. 2000. (Illus.). 240p. (YA). (gr. 3 up). 17.00 (*0-15-202604-5*, Odyssey Classics) Harcourt Children's Bks.

—The Witch Family. 1990. (J). 12.10 o.p. (*0-606-02311-9*) Turtleback Bks.

Fienberg, Anna. The Witch in the Lake. 2002. 220p. (J). (gr. 5-9). pap. 7.95 (*1-55037-722-1*); lib. bdg. 18.95 (*1-55037-723-X*) Annick Pr., Ltd. CAN. *Dist:* Firefly Bks., Ltd.

Fontes, Justine. Hocus Pocus Halloween. 2003. (Magical Color Bks.). (Illus.). 10p. (J). bds. 5.95 (*1-4027-0992-7*, Sterling/Pinwheel) Sterling Publishing Co., Inc.

Forrester, Sandra. The Everyday Witch: A Tale of Magic & High Adventure. 2002. (Illus.). 186p. (J). (gr. 5-9). pap. 4.95 (*0-7641-2220-7*) Barron's Educational Series, Inc.

—The Witches of Friar's Lantern. 2003. (Illus.). 192p. (J). (gr. 5-9). pap. 4.95 (*0-7641-2436-6*) Barron's Educational Series, Inc.

—The Witches of Sea-Dragon Bay. 2003. 224p. (J). pap. 4.95 (*0-7641-2633-4*) Barron's Educational Series, Inc.

—The Witches of Winged-Horse Mountain. 2004. (Adventures of Beatrice Bailey Ser.). 224p. (J). pap. 4.95 (*0-7641-2784-5*) Barron's Educational Series, Inc.

Gallagher, Diana G. From the Horse's Mouth. 2001. (Sabrina, the Teenage Witch Ser.: Bk. 39). 176p. (YA). (gr. 5 up). mass mkt. 4.99 (*0-7434-1811-5*, Simon Pulse) Simon & Schuster Children's Publishing.

—Mist & Stone. 2003. (Charmed Ser.). (Illus.). 208p. (YA). mass mkt. 5.99 (*0-689-85789-6*, Simon Pulse) Simon & Schuster Children's Publishing.

—Spirit of the Wolf. 2002. (Charmed Ser.: bk. 12). (Illus.). 224p. (YA). (gr. 7 up). pap. 5.99 (*0-7434-4255-5*, Simon Pulse) Simon & Schuster Children's Publishing.

Gilleland, Rebecca. The Witch of Blackbird Pond: Study Guide. 2000. 72p. (J). (gr. 5-7). stu. ed., ring bd. 12.99 (*1-58609-171-9*) Progeny Pr.

Gilmour, H. B. Building a Mystery, No. 2. 2001. (T*Witches Ser.). (Illus.). (J). 10.55 (*0-606-21477-1*) Turtleback Bks.

—The Power of Two, No. 1. 2001. (T*Witches Ser.). (Illus.). (J). 10.55 (*0-606-21476-3*) Turtleback Bks.

Gilmour, H. B. & Reisfeld, Randi. Don't Think Twice. 2002. (T*Witches Ser.: No. 5). (Illus.). 160p. (J). mass mkt. 4.50 (*0-439-24074-3*) Scholastic, Inc.

—Double Jeopardy. 2002. (T*Witches Ser.: No. 6). 240p. (J). mass mkt. 4.50 (*0-439-24075-1*) Scholastic, Inc.

—Kindred Spirits. 2003. (T*Witches Ser.). 240p. (J). (gr. 4-8). mass mkt. 4.50 (*0-439-47219-9*) Scholastic, Inc.

Gilmour, H. B., et al. The Witch Hunters. 2003. (T*Witches Ser.: No. 8). 160p. (J). mass mkt. 4.50 o.s.i (*0-439-49227-0*, Scholastic Paperbacks) Scholastic, Inc.

Glassman, Miriam. Halloweena. 2002. (Illus.). 40p. (J). (gr. k-3). 15.95 (*0-689-82825-X*, Atheneum) Simon & Schuster Children's Publishing.

Glassman, Peter. My Working Mom. 1994. (Illus.). 32p. (J). (ps-3). 16.95 (*0-688-12259-0*) HarperCollins Children's Bk. Group.

—My Working Mom. 1994. (Illus.). (J). (ps-3). 15.89 (*0-688-12260-4*, Morrow, William & Co.) Morrow/Avon.

Gliori, Debi. Pure Dead Brilliant. 2003. 272p. (J). (gr. 5). 15.95 (*0-375-81412-4*); lib. bdg. 17.99 (*0-375-91412-9*) Random Hse. Children's Bks. (Knopf Bks. for Young Readers).

—Pure Dead Magic. 2001. 192p. (J). (gr. 5 up). 15.95 o.s.i (*0-375-81410-8*) Knopf, Alfred A. Inc.

—Pure Dead Magic. 2001. (Illus.). 192p. (J). (gr. 5). lib. bdg. 17.99 o.s.i (*0-375-91410-2*, Knopf Bks. for Young Readers) Random Hse. Children's Bks.

—Pure Dead Magic. 2002. 208p. (gr. 5). pap. 4.99 (*0-440-41849-6*) Random Hse., Inc.

—Pure Dead Magic. 2002. (Juvenile Ser.). (Illus.). (J). 21.95 (*0-7862-4869-6*) Thorndike Pr.

—Pure Dead Wicked. 224p. (gr. 5 up). 2003. pap. 4.99 (*0-440-41936-0*, Yearling); 2002. (J). lib. bdg. 17.99 (*0-375-91411-0*, Knopf Bks. for Young Readers); 2002. (Illus.). (J). 15.95 (*0-375-81411-6*, Knopf Bks. for Young Readers) Random Hse. Children's Bks.

—Pure Dead Wicked. 2003. (J). 22.95 (*0-7862-5225-1*) Thorndike Pr.

Goldman, Leslie. The Truth Hurts. 2003. (Sabrina, the Teenage Witch Ser.). (Illus.). 160p. (J). pap. 4.99 (*0-689-85579-6*, Simon Pulse) Simon & Schuster Children's Publishing.

Grambling, Lois G. The Witch Who Wanted to Be a Princess. 2002. (Illus.). 32p. (J). (ps-4). 15.95 (*1-58089-062-8*, Whispering Coyote) Charlesbridge Publishing, Inc.

Gray, Luli. Falcon & the Charles Street Witch. 2002. 144p. (J). (gr. 5-9). 15.00 (*0-618-16410-3*) Houghton Mifflin Co.

Griffin, Adele. Witch Twins. 2001. (Illus.). 160p. (J). (gr. 2-5). 14.99 (*0-7868-0739-3*, Volo) Hyperion Bks. for Children.

—Witch Twins. 2002. 160p. (J). (gr. 3-6). pap. 5.99 (*0-7868-1563-9*) Hyperion Paperbacks for Children.

—Witch Twins. l.t. ed. 2002. 174p. (J). 21.95 (*0-7862-4397-X*) Thorndike Pr.

—Witch Twins & Melody Malady. 2003. (Illus.). 160p. (J). 14.99 (*0-7868-1940-5*) Hyperion Bks. for Children.

—Witch Twins at Camp Bliss. (J). 2003. 144p. pap. 5.99 (*0-7868-1583-3*); 2002. (Illus.). 128p. (gr. 2-5). 15.99 (*0-7868-0763-6*) Hyperion Bks. for Children.

Gutteridge, Alex. Oven Chips for Tea. 2004. 149p. (J). (gr. 4-7). pap. (*0-440-86558-1*, Corgi) Bantam Bks.

Hamilton, Virginia. Wee Winnie Witch's Skinny: An Original Scare Tale for Halloween. 2001. (Illus.). (J). pap. 16.95 (*0-590-28880-6*, Blue Sky Pr., The) Scholastic, Inc.

Harrison, Emma. Garden of Evil. 2002. (Charmed Ser.: Bk. 13). 208p. (YA). (gr. 7 up). mass mkt. 5.99 (*0-689-85077-8*, Simon Pulse) Simon & Schuster Children's Publishing.

Harvey, Jayne. Great-Uncle Dracula. 1992. (Stepping Stone Bks.). (Illus.). 80p. (J). (gr. 2-4). pap. 2.50 o.s.i (*0-679-82448-0*, Random Hse. Bks. for Young Readers) Random Hse. Children's Bks.

Hautzig, Deborah. Little Witch & the Mean Kids. 2002. (Illus.). 24p. (J). pap. 3.25 (*0-679-87338-4*) Random Hse., Inc.

—Little Witch Learns to Read. 2003. (Illus.). 48p. (J). (gr. 1-3). pap. 3.99 (*0-375-82179-1*); lib. bdg. 11.99 (*0-375-92179-6*) Random Hse. Children's Bks. (Random Hse. Bks. for Young Readers).

—The Little Witch Takes Charge! 2002. (Random House Pictureback Book Ser.). (Illus.). 24p. (J). pap. 3.25 (*0-679-87337-6*) Random Hse. Children's Bks.

Heller, Nicholas. Elwood & the Witch. 2000. (Illus.). 32p. (J). (gr. k-3). 15.95 (*0-688-16945-7*); lib. bdg. 15.89 (*0-688-16946-5*) HarperCollins Children's Bk. Group. (Greenwillow Bks.).

Herman, Gail. When Wishes Come True. 2000. (Fairy School Ser.: Vol. 7). (Illus.). 80p. (gr. 1-4). pap. text 3.99 o.s.i (*0-553-48709-4*, Skylark) Random Hse. Children's Bks.

—When Wishes Come True. 2000. (Fairy School Ser.). (Illus.). (J). 10.14 (*0-606-21637-5*) Turtleback Bks.

Hillert, Margaret. Witch Who Went for a Walk. 2001. (Margaret Hillerts Fabulous Firsts Ser.). (J). lib. bdg. (*1-59054-178-2*) Fitzgerald Bks.

—Witch Who Went for a Walk. 1981. 12.20 (*0-606-14058-1*) Turtleback Bks.

Holder, Nancy. Curse. 2003. (Wicked Ser.). 304p. (YA). pap. 5.99 (*0-7434-2697-5*, Simon Pulse) Simon & Schuster Children's Publishing.

Horn, Emily. Excuse Me... Are You a Witch? 2003. (Illus.). 32p. (J). (gr. k-3). 15.95 (*1-58089-093-8*) Charlesbridge Publishing, Inc.

Horwood, Diane. The Wicked Witch of the West: And the Return of the Wicked Witch of the West. 2001. 116p. pap. 7.95 (*0-87714-508-3*) Denlingers Pubs., Ltd.

Howard, Arthur. Hoodwinked. 2001. (Illus.). 32p. (J). (ps-2). 16.00 (*0-15-202656-8*) Harcourt Children's Bks.

Hunter, Mollie. The Thirteenth Member. 2002. (Kelpies Ser.). (Illus.). 192p. (J). pap. (*0-86315-405-0*) Floris Bks. GBR. *Dist:* SteinerBooks, Inc.

Ibbotson, Eva. Not Just a Witch. 2003. (Illus.). 176p. (J). 15.99 (*0-525-47101-4*, Dutton Children's Bks.) Penguin Putnam Bks. for Young Readers.

—Secret of Platform 13/Island of the Aunts Flip-Over Book. 2002. pap. 5.99 (*0-14-230163-9*) Penguin Putnam Bks. for Young Readers.

—Which Witch? unabr. ed. 1993. (J). (gr. 1-8). audio 32.95 (*0-7451-4444-6*, CCA3210, Chivers Children's Audio Bks.) BBC Audiobooks America.

—Which Witch? 2002. (Illus.). 13.19 (*1-4046-1490-7*) Book Wholesalers, Inc.

—Which Witch? 2000. (Illus.). 256p. (J). (gr. 3-7). pap. 5.99 (*0-14-130427-8*, Puffin Bks.) Penguin Putnam Bks. for Young Readers.

—Which Witch? 1988. 208p. (J). (gr. 3-7). pap. 2.50 o.p. (*0-590-41926-9*, Scholastic Paperbacks) Scholastic, Inc.

—Which Witch? 2000. (J). 11.04 (*0-606-19882-2*) Turtleback Bks.

Ibbotson, Eva & Large, Annabel. Which Witch? l.t. ed. 2001. (Illus.). 249p. (J). 21.95 (*0-7862-3073-8*) Thorndike Pr.

Ibbotson, Eva. Which Witch? 1999. (Illus.). 224p. (J). (gr. 4-7). 15.99 (*0-525-46164-7*, Dutton Children's Bks.) Penguin Putnam Bks. for Young Readers.

Johnston, Tony. Alice Nizzy Nazzy, the Witch of Santa Fe. 1995. (Illus.). 32p. (J). (ps-3). 16.99 o.p. (*0-399-22788-1*, G. P. Putnam's Sons) Penguin Group (USA) Inc.

—Alice Nizzy Nazzy, the Witch of Santa Fe. 1998. (Illus.). 32p. (J). (ps-3). pap. 6.99 (*0-698-11650-X*, PaperStar) Penguin Putnam Bks. for Young Readers.

—Alice Nizzy Nazzy, the Witch of Santa Fe. 1998. 12.14 (*0-606-15430-2*) Turtleback Bks.

—Go Track a Yak! 2003. (Illus.). 40p. (J). (gr. k-2). 15.95 (*0-689-83789-5*, Simon & Schuster Children's Publishing) Simon & Schuster Children's Publishing.

Jones, Diana Wynne. Witch's Business. (J). 2004. 224p. pap. 5.99 (*0-06-008784-6*, Harper Trophy); 2002. 208p. (gr. 3 up). 15.99 (*0-06-008782-X*); 2002. 208p. (gr. 3 up). lib. bdg. 17.89 (*0-06-008783-8*) HarperCollins Children's Bk. Group.

Jones, Ursula. The Witch's Children. ERS. 2003. (Illus.). 32p. (J). (ps-2). 16.95 (*0-8050-7205-5*, Holt, Henry & Co. Bks. For Young Readers) Holt, Henry & Co.

Katz, Welwyn W. Come Like Shadows. 2001. (J). 14.00 (*0-606-21823-8*) Turtleback Bks.

Kellerhals-Stewart, Heather. Witch's Fang. 2000. (Illus.). 192p. (YA). (gr. 8 up). pap. 6.95 (*1-55192-368-8*) Raincoast Bk. Distribution CAN. *Dist:* Publishers Group West.

Kellogg, Steven. Christmas Witch. 2000. (Illus.). 40p. (J). (ps-3). pap. 6.99 (*0-14-056762-3*, Puffin Bks.) Penguin Putnam Bks. for Young Readers.

King-Smith, Dick. The Nine Lives of Aristotle. 2003. (Illus.). 80p. (J). 14.99 (*0-7636-2260-5*) Candlewick Pr.

—The Witch of Blackberry Bottom. l.t. unabr. ed. 2001. (Read-Along Ser.). 144p. (J). 29.95 incl. audio (*0-7540-6238-4*, RAO39, Chivers Children's Audio Bks.) BBC Audiobooks America.

Kitamura, Satoshi. Me & My Cat?. RS. 2000. (Illus.). 40p. (J). (ps-3). 16.00 (*0-374-34906-1*, Farrar, Straus & Giroux (BYR)) Farrar, Straus & Giroux.

Kreib, Richard. We're off to Find the Witch's House. 2005. 32p. 12.99 (*0-525-47003-4*, Dutton Children's Bks.) Penguin Putnam Bks. for Young Readers.

Krulik, Nancy E. Christmas Crisis. 2003. (Sabrina, the Teenage Witch Ser.). (Illus.). 160p. (J). mass mkt. 4.99 (*0-689-85582-6*, Simon Pulse) Simon & Schuster Children's Publishing.

Lachner, Dorothea. Meredith & Her Magical Book of Spells. James, J. Alison, tr. from GER. 2003. 32p. (J). lib. bdg. 16.50 (*0-7358-1846-0*); (Illus.). 15.95 (*0-7358-1845-2*) North-South Bks., Inc.

—Meredith's Mixed-Up Magic. James, J. Alison, tr. from GER. 2000. (Illus.). 32p. (J). (gr. k-3). 15.95 o.p. (*0-7358-1190-3*); 16.50 o.p. (*0-7358-1191-1*) North-South Bks., Inc.

Lagoon Books Staff, ed. Wanda the Witch & the Magical Maze. 2000. (Illus.). 20p. (J). (gr. 2-7). 9.95 (*1-902813-11-1*) Lagoon Bks. GBR. *Dist:* Midpoint Trade Bks., Inc.

Lattimore, Deborah Nourse. Cinderhazel: The Cinderella of Halloween. 2002. (Illus.). 32p. (J). (ps-3). mass mkt. 5.99 (*0-439-39471-6*) Scholastic, Inc.

Laughlin, Florence. The Little Leftover Witch. (Illus.). (J). 1971. 116p. (gr. 2-5). 10.95 o.s.i (*0-02-754560-1*, Simon & Schuster Children's Publishing); 2nd ed. 1988. 96p. (gr. 2-6). pap. 3.50 o.s.i (*0-689-71273-1*, Aladdin); 3rd ed. 1993. 96p. (gr. 1-4). reprint ed. pap. 3.95 o.s.i (*0-689-71742-3*, Aladdin) Simon & Schuster Children's Publishing.

Lenhard, Elizabeth. Soul of the Bride. 2001. (Charmed Ser.: Vol. 10). (Illus.). 192p. (YA). (gr. 7 up). pap. 5.99 (*0-7434-1237-0*, Simon Pulse) Simon & Schuster Children's Publishing.

Leuck, Laura. One Witch. 2003. (Illus.). (J). 16.85 (*0-8027-8861-0*); 15.95 (*0-8027-8860-2*) Walker & Co.

Lodge, Bernard. Mouldylocks. 1998. (Illus.). 32p. (J). (ps-3). 15.00 (*0-395-90945-7*) Houghton Mifflin Co.

Maguire, Gregory. The Dream Stealer. 2002. (Illus.). 144p. (J). (gr. 3-5). tchr. ed. 15.00 (*0-618-18188-1*, Clarion Bks.) Houghton Mifflin Co. Trade & Reference Div.

Mahy, Margaret. The Boy with Two Shadows. 1988. (Illus.). 32p. (J). (ps-3). 12.95 o.p. (*0-397-32270-4*); lib. bdg. 12.89 o.p. (*0-397-32271-2*) HarperCollins Children's Bk. Group.

Mariconda, Barbara. Witch Way to the Country. 1996. (Illus.). 48p. (J). pap. 3.99 o.s.i (*0-440-41100-9*) Dell Publishing.

Marshak, Suzanna. The Wizard's Promise. 1994. (Illus.). (J). pap. 15.00 o.s.i (*0-671-78431-5*, Simon & Schuster Children's Publishing) Simon & Schuster Children's Publishing.

McKee, Mel. Pike's Circus Day. 2002. 274p. pap. (*1-55212-812-1*) Trafford Publishing.

McMullan, K. H. Sir Lancelot, Where Are You? 1999. (Dragon Slayers' Academy Ser.: No. 6). (Illus.). 91p. (J). (gr. 2-5). 3.99 o.p. (*0-448-41979-3*, Grosset & Dunlap);Vol. 6. 13.89 o.p. (*0-448-42046-5*) Penguin Putnam Bks. for Young Readers.

McMullan, Kate. Sir Lancelot, Where Are You? 2003. (Dragon Slayers' Academy Ser.). (Illus.). 112p. mass mkt. 4.99 (*0-448-43278-1*, Grosset & Dunlap) Penguin Putnam Bks. for Young Readers.

Melmed, Laura Krauss. Fright Night Flight. 2002. (Illus.). 32p. (J). (ps-3). 15.99 (*0-06-029701-8*); lib. bdg. 17.89 (*0-06-029702-6*) HarperCollins Children's Bk. Group.

Molloy, Michael. The Time Witches. 2002. 256p. (YA). (gr. 5-8). pap. 4.99 (*0-439-42090-3*, Chicken Hse., The) Scholastic, Inc.

—Wild West Witches. 2003. 320p. (J). (gr. 3-6). pap. 4.99 (*0-439-54510-2*, Chicken Hse., The) Scholastic, Inc.

—The Witch Trade. (J). (gr. 3-7). 2002. 256p. pap. 4.99 (*0-439-43020-8*); 2001. (Illus.). 240p. pap. 15.95 (*0-439-29659-5*) Scholastic, Inc. (Chicken Hse., The).

Murphy, Jill. A Bad Spell for the Worst Witch. 2000. (Illus.). 112p. (J). (gr. 4-7). bds. 4.99 o.s.i (*0-7636-1256-1*) Candlewick Pr.

—A Bad Spell for the Worst Witch. 2000. (Worst Witch Ser.). 11.04 (*0-606-19310-3*) Turtleback Bks.

—The Worst Witch. l.t. ed. 1992. (Illus.). 96p. (J). 13.95 o.p. (*0-7451-1549-7*, Galaxy Children's Large Print) BBC Audiobooks America.

—The Worst Witch. 2000. (Illus.). 112p. (J). (gr. 4-7). bds. 4.99 o.s.i (*0-7636-1254-5*) Candlewick Pr.

—The Worst Witch. 1982. (Illus.). 80p. (J). (gr. 3-7). pap. 2.50 (*0-380-60665-8*, Avon Bks.) Morrow/Avon.

—The Worst Witch. (Illus.). 112p. (J). 1991. (gr. 4-7). pap. 3.95 o.p. (*0-14-031108-4*, Puffin Bks.); 1989. 9.95 o.p. (*0-670-82188-8*, Viking Children's Bks.) Penguin Putnam Bks. for Young Readers.

—The Worst Witch Strikes Again. l.t. ed. 1993. (Illus.). 96p. (J). 13.95 o.p. (*0-7451-1672-8*, Galaxy Children's Large Print) BBC Audiobooks America.

—The Worst Witch Strikes Again. 1982. 80p. (J). (gr. 3-7). pap. 2.50 (*0-380-60673-9*, Avon Bks.) Morrow/Avon.

—The Worst Witch Strikes Again. (Illus.). 96p. (J). 1991. (gr. 4-7). pap. 3.99 o.p. (*0-14-031348-6*, Puffin Bks.); 1989. (gr. 2-6). 9.95 o.p. (*0-670-82189-6*, Viking Children's Bks.) Penguin Putnam Bks. for Young Readers.

Naylor, Phyllis Reynolds. The Witch Herself. 2002. 176p. pap. 4.99 (*0-689-85317-3*, Aladdin) Simon & Schuster Children's Publishing.

—Witch's Sister. 2002. 160p. (J). pap. 4.99 (*0-689-85315-7*, Aladdin) Simon & Schuster Children's Publishing.

Nicoll, Helen. Owl at School. 1986. (Picture Puffin Ser.). (Illus.). 32p. (J). (ps). pap. 3.50 o.p. (*0-14-050496-6*, Penguin Bks.) Viking Penguin.

Nimmo, Jenny. Witch's Tears. 2003. (Roaring Good Reads Ser.). (Illus.). 96p. (J). pap. (*0-00-714162-9*) HarperCollins Pubs. Ltd. GBR. *Dist:* Trafalgar Square.

Norton, Mary. Bed-Knob & Broomstick. (Illus.). 2000. 240p. (YA). (gr. 3 up). 17.00 (*0-15-202450-6*); 1990. 189p. (J). (gr. 4-7). pap. 6.00 o.p. (*0-15-206231-9*) Harcourt Children's Bks. (Odyssey Classics).

—Bed-Knob & Broomstick. 2000. 12.05 (*0-606-20159-9*); 2000. 12.05 (*0-606-20322-2*); 1990. (J). 11.10 (*0-606-02277-5*) Turtleback Bks.

Palatini, Margie. Broom Mates. 2003. (J). 15.99 (*0-7868-0418-1*) Hyperion Bks. for Children.

—Piggie Pie! 1995. (Illus.). 32p. (J). (ps-3). lib. bdg., tchr. ed. 15.00 (*0-395-71691-8*) Houghton Mifflin Co.

—Piggie Pie! 1997. (J). 12.10 (*0-606-12792-5*) Turtleback Bks.

Peet, Bill. Big Bad Bruce, 001. (Illus.). (J). (ps-3). 1982. 40p. pap. 8.95 (*0-395-32922-1*); 1977. 48p. lib. bdg., tchr. ed. 17.00 (*0-395-25150-8*); 1987. 40p. pap. 10.95 incl. audio (*0-395-45741-6*, 493317) Houghton Mifflin Co.

—Big Bad Bruce. 1977. (J). 14.10 (*0-606-02722-X*) Turtleback Bks.

Petry, Ann. Tituba of Salem Village. 1991. (J). 12.00 (*0-606-01101-3*) Turtleback Bks.

Pike, Christopher, pseud. The Witch. MacDonald, Patricia, ed. 1990. 240p. (YA). (gr. 7 up). mass mkt. 4.99 (*0-671-69055-8*, Simon Pulse) Simon & Schuster Children's Publishing.

—The Witch. 2001. 240p. (YA). reprint ed. mass mkt. 5.99 (*0-7434-2799-8*, Simon Pulse) Simon & Schuster Children's Publishing.

—The Witch. 2001. (J). 12.04 (*0-606-21531-X*) Turtleback Bks.

Pratchett, Terry. The Wee Free Men. 2004. 279p. (J). pap. (*0-552-54905-3*, Corgi) Bantam Bks.

—The Wee Free Men. 2003. 279p. (*0-385-60533-1*) Doubleday Canada, Ltd. CAN. *Dist:* Random Hse. of Canada, Ltd., Random Hse., Inc.

—The Wee Free Men. 2003. 272p. (J). (gr. 7 up). 16.99 (*0-06-001236-6*); lib. bdg. 17.89 (*0-06-001237-4*) HarperCollins Pubs.

Rees, Celia. Witch Child. (gr. 7 up). 2002. 304p. (YA). bds. 8.99 (*0-7636-1829-2*); 2001. 272p. (J). 15.99 (*0-7636-1421-1*) Candlewick Pr.

—Witch Child. l.t. ed. 2002. (Young Adult Ser.). 284p. (J). 22.95 (*0-7862-3896-8*) Gale Group.

Reeves, Howard W. There Was An Old Witch. 1998. (Illus.). 24p. (J). (ps-3). 9.95 (*0-7868-0438-6*) Hyperion Pr.

—There Was an Old Witch. 2000. (Illus.). 32p. (J). (ps-3). pap. 5.99 (*0-7868-1492-6*) Disney Pr.

—There Was an Old Witch. 1998. (Illus.). 24p. (J). (ps-3). lib. bdg. 10.49 (*0-7868-2387-9*) Hyperion Pr.

Rex, Michael. Brooms Are for Flying. ERS. 2000. (Illus.). 32p. (J). (ps-2). 16.00 (*0-8050-6410-9*, Holt, Henry & Co. Bks. For Young Readers) Holt, Henry & Co.

Richardson, Julia, ed. Strangeling. 2000. (So Weird Ser.: 4). (Illus.). 128p. (J). (gr. 4-7). pap. 4.99 (*0-7868-1431-4*) Disney Pr.

Robertson, M. P. The Great Dragon Rescue. 2004. 32p. (J). 16.99 (*0-8037-2973-1*, Dial Bks. for Young Readers) Penguin Putnam Bks. for Young Readers.

Rowling, J. K. Harry Potter et la Chambre des Secrets. 1999. (Harry Potter Ser.: Year 2). Tr. of Harry Potter & the Chamber of Secrets. (FRE., Illus.). (YA). (gr. 3 up). pap. 14.95 (*2-07-052455-8*) Gallimard, Editions FRA. *Dist:* Distribooks, Inc.

—Harry Potter et le Prisonnier d'Azkaban. 1999. (Harry Potter Ser.: Year 3). Tr. of Harry Potter & the Prisoner of Azkaban. (FRE.). (YA). (gr. 3 up). pap. (*2-07-052818-9*) Gallimard, Editions.

—Harry Potter et l'Ecole des Sorciers. 3rd ed. 1998. (Harry Potter Ser.: Year 1). Tr. of Harry Potter & the Sorcerer's Stone. (FRE., Illus.). (YA). (gr. 3 up). pap. 14.95 (*2-07-050142-6*) Distribooks, Inc.

Ruditis, Paul. Where in the World Is Sabrina Spellman? 2003. (Sabrina, the Teenage Witch Ser.). (Illus.). 160p. (J). pap. 4.99 (*0-7434-4243-1*, Simon Pulse) Simon & Schuster Children's Publishing.

Sampson, Fay. Shape-Shifter: The Naming of Pangur Ban. 2003. 160p. (YA). (gr. 5-8). pap. 7.95 (*0-7459-4762-X*) Lion Publishing PLC GBR. *Dist:* Trafalgar Square.

Saunders, Kate. The Belfry Witches: Witch You Were Here. 2001. (J). 16.95 (*0-7540-6161-2*) BBC Audiobooks America.

Scalora, Suza. The Witches & Wizards of Oberin. 2001. (Ageless Bks.). (Illus.). 48p. (J). 19.95 (*0-06-029535-X*, Cotler, Joanna Bks.) HarperCollins Children's Bk. Group.

Simmons, Steven J. Alice & Greta's Color Magic. 32p. (J). 2003. pap. 6.99 (*0-440-41797-X*, Dell Books for Young Readers); 2001. (Illus.). 14.95 o.s.i (*0-375-81245-8*) Random Hse. Children's Bks.

—Alicia y Greta: Un Cuento de Dos Brujas. Mlawer, Teresa, tr. 1999. (SPA., Illus.). 32p. (J). (gr. k-2). pap. 7.95 (*0-88106-133-6*, CH5119) Charlesbridge Publishing, Inc.

Simon and Schuster Children's Staff, ed. Seasons of the Witch, Vol. 1. 2003. (Charmed Ser.). 192p. (YA). pap. 7.99 (*0-689-86545-7*, Simon Pulse) Simon & Schuster Children's Publishing.

Smalls, Irene. The Alphabet Witch. 1994. (Illus.). (J). 7.95 o.p. (*0-681-00542-4*) Borders Pr.

Smath, Jerry. Wee Witches' Halloween. 2002. (Read with Me Paperbacks Ser.). (Illus.). 32p. (J). mass mkt. 3.25 (*0-439-36740-9*, Cartwheel Bks.) Scholastic, Inc.

Smith, L. J. The Initiation. 1995. 79p. (J). mass mkt. 1.99 o.p. (*0-06-106399-1*, HarperTorch) Morrow/Avon.

—Secret Circle: The Initiation. 1992. (Secret Circle Ser.: Vol. 1). 320p. (gr. 7-12). mass mkt. 4.99 (*0-06-106712-1*, HarperTorch) Morrow/Avon.

Somers, Kevin. Meaner Than Meanest. 2001. (Illus.). 32p. (J). (ps-2). 15.99 (*0-7868-0577-3*); lib. bdg. 16.49 (*0-7868-2498-0*) Hyperion Bks. for Children.

Steig, William. Wizzil. RS. 2000. (Illus.). 32p. (J). (ps-3). 16.00 (*0-374-38466-5*, Farrar, Straus & Giroux (BYR)) Farrar, Straus & Giroux.

—Wizzil. unabr. ed. 2001. (J). (gr. k-3). audio 10.00 (*0-7887-5038-0*, 96532E7) Recorded Bks., LLC.

Stevenson, James. Emma. 1985. (Illus.). 32p. (J). (gr. k-3). 15.00 o.p. (*0-688-04020-9*, Greenwillow Bks.) HarperCollins Children's Bk. Group.

—Emma. 1987. (J). (gr. k up). reprint ed. pap. 3.95 o.p. (*0-688-07336-0*, Morrow, William & Co.) Morrow/Avon.

Stewart, Paul. The Weather Witch. 2002. 179p. pap. (*0-440-86504-2*, Corgi) Bantam Bks.

Thomas, Valerie. Winnie Flies Again. 2000. (Illus.). 28p. (J). (ps-3). 14.95 (*0-916291-94-4*, Cranky Nell Bks.) Kane/Miller Bk. Pubs.

—Winnie Flies Again. 2000. 14.10 (*0-606-19823-7*) Turtleback Bks.

Thomas, Valerie & Paul, Korky. Winnie Flies Again. 2000. (Illus.). 28p. (J). (ps-3). pap. 7.95 (*0-916291-95-2*, Cranky Nell Bks.) Kane/Miller Bk. Pubs.

Thompson. The Follower. 2003. 32p. (J). pap. (*1-55041-880-7*) Fitzhenry & Whiteside, Ltd.

Thompson, Richard. The Follower. 2000. (Illus.). 34p. (J). (gr. k-4). 15.95 (*1-55041-532-8*) Fitzhenry & Whiteside, Ltd. CAN. *Dist:* General Distribution Services, Inc.

Tiernan, Cate. The Blood Witch. 2001. (Sweep Ser.: Bk. 3). (Illus.). 192p. (YA). (gr. 7 up). pap. 4.99 (*0-14-131111-8*, Puffin Bks.) Penguin Putnam Bks. for Young Readers.

—The Reckoning, No. 13. 2002. (Sweep Ser.). 192p. (J). pap. 5.99 (*0-14-230086-1*, Puffin Bks.) Penguin Putnam Bks. for Young Readers.

—Super Special: Moira's Story. 2003. (Sweep Ser.). 384p. (YA). pap. 6.99 (*0-14-250119-0*, Puffin Bks.) Penguin Putnam Bks. for Young Readers.

Tunnell, Michael O. Halloween Pie. 1999. (Illus.). 24p. (J). (ps-3). 14.95 o.s.i (*0-688-16804-3*); lib. bdg. 14.89 o.p. (*0-688-16805-1*) HarperCollins Children's Bk. Group.

Tyrrell, Melissa. Hansel & Gretel. 2001. (Fairytale Friends Ser.). (Illus.). 12p. (J). bds. 5.95 (*1-58117-152-8*, Piggy Toes Pr.) Intervisual Bks., Inc.

Umansky, Kaye. Pongwiffy. 2001. (J). E-Book (*0-7434-2686-X*); (Illus.). 192p. mass mkt. 4.50 (*0-7434-1912-X*) Simon & Schuster Children's Publishing. (Aladdin).

—Pongwiffy: A Witch of Dirty Habits. l.t. ed. 1992. 208p. (J). 12.95 o.p. (*0-7451-1470-9*, Galaxy Children's Large Print) BBC Audiobooks America.

Vande Velde, Vivian. Witch's Wishes. 2003. (Illus.). (J). (gr. 2-5). tchr. ed. 15.95 (*0-8234-1789-1*) Holiday Hse., Inc.

Velde, Vivan V. Never Trust a Dead Man. 2001. (YA). 11.04 (*0-606-21346-5*) Turtleback Bks.

Villarreal Elizondo, Cesar. La Tierra de las Adivinanzas. Garcia, Nasario, tr. from SPA. & adapted by by. 2002. Tr. of Land of the Riddles. (ENG & SPA., Illus.). 32p. (J). (gr. 2-3). 14.95 (*1-55885-352-9*, Piñata Books) Arte Publico Pr.

Vornholt, John. Haunts in the House. 1999. (Sabrina, the Teenage Witch Ser.: No. 27). 144p. (YA). (gr. 5 up). mass mkt. 4.50 (*0-671-02819-7*, Simon Pulse) Simon & Schuster Children's Publishing.

Wallace, Barbara Brooks. Miss Switch Online. 192p. (J). 2003. (Illus.). pap. 4.99 (*0-689-86028-5*, Aladdin); 2002. (gr. 4-6). 16.00 (*0-689-84376-3*, Atheneum) Simon & Schuster Children's Publishing.

—Miss Switch to the Rescue. 2002. 176p. (YA). (gr. 5 up). reprint ed. pap. 4.99 (*0-689-85176-6*, Aladdin) Simon & Schuster Children's Publishing.

—Miss Switch to the Rescue. 2000. (Illus.). 158p. (gr. 4-7). pap. 10.95 o.p. (*0-595-15332-1*) iUniverse, Inc.

—The Trouble with Miss Switch. 1982. (Illus.). (J). (gr. 3-5). pap. (*0-671-46394-2*, Simon Pulse); 2002. 144p. (YA). (gr. 5 up). reprint ed. pap. 4.99 (*0-689-85177-4*, Aladdin) Simon & Schuster Children's Publishing.

—The Trouble with Miss Switch. 2000. 132p. (gr. 4-7). pap. 9.95 o.p. (*0-595-15330-5*, Backinprint.com) iUniverse, Inc.

Webb. Witch of Wookey Hole. 1998. 159p. (J). pap. 7.95 (*0-7459-3894-9*) Lion Publishing PLC GBR. *Dist:* Trafalgar Square.

Weiss, Bobbi J. G. & Wilson, Jacklyn. Between Worlds. 2003. (Charmed Ser.). (Illus.). 208p. (YA). mass mkt. 5.99 (*0-689-85792-6*, Simon Pulse) Simon & Schuster Children's Publishing.

Weiss, David Cody & Weiss, Bobbi J. G. Now & Again. 2003. (Sabrina, the Teenage Witch Ser.). (Illus.). 160p. (J). mass mkt. 4.99 (*0-689-85581-8*, Simon Pulse) Simon & Schuster Children's Publishing.

Whitcher, Susan. The Key to the Cupboard. RS. 1997. (Illus.). 32p. (J). (ps-3). 16.00 o.p. (*0-374-34127-3*, Farrar, Straus & Giroux (BYR)) Farrar, Straus & Giroux.

Wien, Hallie. Witchie's Surprise Treat. 2002. (Peekaboo Bks.). (Illus.). 10p. (J). (ps). bds. 5.99 (*1-57584-948-8*, Reader's Digest Children's Bks.) Reader's Digest Children's Publishing, Inc.

Wolff, Patricia Rae. Cackle Cook's Monster Stew. 2001. (Illus.). 32p. (J). 9.95 o.s.i (*0-307-10682-9*, Golden Bks.) Random Hse. Children's Bks.

Wrede, Patricia C. Searching for Dragons. 2002. (Enchanted Forest Chronicles: Bk. 2). (Illus.). 272p. (YA). (gr. 5 up). pap. 5.95 (*0-15-204565-1*, Magic Carpet Bks.) Harcourt Children's Bks.

—Searching for Dragons. unabr. ed. 2001. 242p. pap. 37.00 incl. audio (*0-8072-0670-9*);2. (Enchanted Forest Ser.: Bk. 2). (YA). (gr. 3 up). audio 26.00 (*0-8072-0632-6*) Random Hse. Audio Publishing Group. (Listening Library).

Yolen, Jane. Baba Yaga. Date not set. 32p. (J). (ps-1). pap. 5.99 (*0-06-443599-7*) HarperCollins Children's Bk. Group.

—The Flying Witch. 2003. (Illus.). 40p. (J). (ps-1). 15.99 (*0-06-028536-2*); lib. bdg. 16.89 (*0-06-028537-0*) HarperCollins Children's Bk. Group.

WIZARDS—FICTION

Abbott, Tony. Flight of the Genie. 2004. (Secrets of Droon Ser.). 128p. (J). pap. 3.99 (*0-439-56043-8*, Scholastic Paperbacks) Scholastic, Inc.

Alton, Steve. The Malifex. 2002. (Middle Readers Ser.). (Illus.). 182p. (J). (gr. 3-7). lib. bdg. 14.95 (0-8225-0959-8, Carolrhoda Bks.) Lerner Publishing Group.

Barron, T. A. The Lost Years of Merlin. unabr. ed. 2000. (gr. 5 up). (J). audio 30.00 (0-8072-6170-X); (J). audio 30.00 (0-8072-6170-X); 284p. (YA). pap. 46.00 incl. audio (0-8072-8766-0, YA261SP); 284p. (YA). pap. 46.00 incl. audio (0-8072-8766-0, YA261SP) Random Hse. Audio Publishing Group. (Listening Library).

—A T. A. Barron Collection: The Lost Years of Merlin; The Seven Songs of Merlin; The Fires of Merlin, 3 bks. in 1. 2001. (Illus.). (J). 14.98 (0-399-23734-8, Philomel) Penguin Putnam Bks. for Young Readers.

Baum, L. Frank. The Wonderful Wizard of Oz. 2000. (Classic Collectible Pop-Up Ser.). (Illus.). 16p. (J). (ps-3). 24.95 (0-689-81751-7, Little Simon) Simon & Schuster Children's Publishing.

Bergsma, Jody Lynn. The Little Wizard. l.t. ed. 2000. (Illus.). 32p. (J). (ps-7). 15.95 (0-935699-19-8) Illumination Arts Publishing Co., Inc.

Bouchard, David. The Mermaid's Muse. 2000. (Chinese Legends Trilogy). (Illus.). 223p. (J). (gr. 3-6). 15.95 (1-55192-248-7) Raincoast Bk. Distribution CAN. Dist: Publishers Group West.

Charles, Veronika Martenova. Stretch, Swallow & Stare. l.t. ed. 1999. (Illus.). 32p. (J). (ps-3). 16.95 (0-7737-3098-2) Stoddart Kids CAN. Dist: Fitzhenry & Whiteside, Ltd.

Charnas, Suzy McKee. The Silver Glove. 2001. 176p. pap. 14.95 (1-58715-479-X) Wildside Pr.

Clish, Marian L. You Choose the Way: A Book That Reads Like a Game - Mazash the Wizard. unabr. ed. 1999. (Illus.). (J). (gr. k-5). pap. 14.95 incl. audio compact disk (1-928632-09-2) Writers Marketplace:Consulting, Critiquing & Publishing.

—You Choose the Way: A Book That Reads Like a Game: Mazash the Wizard. 1999. (J). (gr. 2-7). 22.95 incl. cd-rom (1-928632-25-4); (Illus.). (gr. 2-7). 18.95 incl. audio (1-928632-24-6); (Illus.). (gr. 3-5). 15.95 (1-928632-23-8) Writers Marketplace:Consulting, Critiquing & Publishing.

de Brunhoff, Laurent. Babar & the Succotash Bird. 2000. (Babar Ser.). (Illus.). 38p. (J). (ps-3). 16.95 (0-8109-5700-0) Abrams, Harry N. , Inc.

Dicks, Terrance. A Spell for My Sister. 1992. (Arch Bks.). (Illus.). 64p. (J). (gr. 3-6). pap. 3.50 o.p. (0-8120-4881-4) Barron's Educational Series, Inc.

Downer, Ann. Hatching Magic. 2003. 256p. (J). 16.95 (0-689-02932-2, Simon & Schuster Children's Publishing); (Illus.). (gr. 7). 16.95 (0-689-83400-4, Atheneum) Simon & Schuster Children's Publishing.

Duane, Diane. Deep Wizardry. (Young Wizards Ser.: Bk. 2). 384p. (YA). 2003. (Illus.). pap. 6.95 (0-15-204942-8); 2001. (gr. 5 up). pap. 6.95 (0-15-216257-7) Harcourt Children's Bks. (Magic Carpet Bks.).

—Deep Wizardry. 1996. (Young Wizards Ser.: Bk. 2). 368p. (J). (gr. 5 up). pap. 6.00 o.p. (0-15-201240-0) Harcourt Trade Pubs.

—Deep Wizardry. 288p. (J). 1992. (gr. 4-7). pap. 3.50 o.s.i (0-440-40658-7, Yearling); 1988. (gr. 5 up). mass mkt. 3.25 o.s.i (0-440-20070-9, Laurel Leaf) Random Hse. Children's Bks.

—Deep Wizardry. 1996. (J). 12.05 (0-606-11248-0) Turtleback Bks.

—High Wizardry. (Young Wizards Ser.: Bk. 3). (YA). 2003. (Illus.). 372p. pap. 6.95 (0-15-204941-X); 2001. 368p. (gr. 5 up). pap. 6.50 (0-15-216244-5) Harcourt Children's Bks. (Magic Carpet Bks.).

—High Wizardry. 1997. (Young Wizards Ser.: Bk. 3). 352p. (YA). (gr. 5 up). reprint ed. pap. 6.00 o.p. (0-15-201241-9) Harcourt Trade Pubs.

—High Wizardry. 1992. 272p. (J). (gr. 5-9). pap. 3.50 o.s.i (0-440-40680-3, Yearling) Random Hse. Children's Bks.

—High Wizardry. 2000. (YA). (gr. 5 up). pap. 58.25 incl. audio (0-7887-3799-6, 41043) Recorded Bks., LLC.

—High Wizardry. 1997. (Magic Carpet Books Ser.). (J). 12.05 (0-606-11461-0) Turtleback Bks.

—So You Want to Be a Wizard. 1983. (Young Wizards Ser.: Bk. 1). 288p. (J). (gr. 5 up). reprint ed. 14.95 o.s.i (0-385-29305-4, Delacorte Pr.) Dell Publishing.

—So You Want to Be a Wizard. (Young Wizards Ser.). (YA). 2003. (Illus.). 408p. pap. 6.95 (0-15-204940-1, Magic Carpet Bks.); 2001. 400p. (gr. 5 up). pap. 6.95 (0-15-216250-X, Magic Carpet Bks.); 20th anniv. ed. 2003. (Illus.). 336p. 16.95 (0-15-204738-7) Harcourt Children's Bks.

—So You Want to Be a Wizard. 1996. (Young Wizards Ser.: Bk. 1). 384p. (J). (gr. 5 up). reprint ed. pap. 6.50 o.p. (0-15-201239-7) Harcourt Trade Pubs.

—So You Want to Be a Wizard. (J). (gr. 5 up). 1992. 240p. pap. 3.50 o.s.i (0-440-40638-2, Yearling); 1986. mass mkt. 2.75 o.s.i (0-440-98252-9, Laurel Leaf) Random Hse. Children's Bks.

—So You Want to Be a Wizard. 1996. (J). 12.55 (0-606-11854-3) Turtleback Bks.

—A Wizard Abroad. (Young Wizards Ser.: Bk. 4). (YA). (gr. 5 up). 2001. 368p. pap. 6.95 (0-15-216238-0, Magic Carpet Bks.); 1997. 352p. 15.00 o.s.i (0-15-201209-5) Harcourt Children's Bks.

—A Wizard Abroad. 1999. (Young Wizards Ser.: Bk. 4). 352p. (YA). (gr. 5 up). pap. 6.00 o.p. (0-15-201207-9) Harcourt Trade Pubs.

—A Wizard Abroad. 2001. (YA). pap., stu. ed. 71.25 incl. audio Recorded Bks., LLC.

—A Wizard Alone. (Young Wizards Ser.: Bk. 6). (Illus.). (YA). 2003. 352p. pap. 6.95 (0-15-204911-8, Magic Carpet Bks.); 2002. 336p. (gr. 7 up). 17.00 (0-15-204562-7) Harcourt Children's Bks.

—The Wizard's Dilemma. (Young Wizards Ser.: Bk. 5). (Illus.). (YA). (gr. 7 up). 2002. 432p. pap. 6.95 (0-15-202460-3, Magic Carpet Bks.); 2001. 416p. 17.00 (0-15-202551-0) Harcourt Children's Bks.

—The Wizard's Holiday. 2003. (Young Wizards Ser.: Bk. 7). (Illus.). 432p. (YA). 17.00 (0-15-204771-9) Harcourt Children's Bks.

Edmiston, Jim & Ellis, Andy. Mizzy & the Tigers. 1992. (Illus.). (J). (ps-3). pap. 5.95 o.p. (0-8120-4828-8) Barron's Educational Series, Inc.

Fienberg, Anna. The Witch in the Lake. 2002. 220p. (J). (gr. 5-9). pap. 7.95 (1-55037-722-1); lib. bdg. 18.95 (1-55037-723-X) Annick Pr., Ltd. CAN. Dist: Firefly Bks., Ltd.

Fox, Mem. The Magic Hat. 2002. (Illus.). 32p. (J). (ps-3). 16.00 (0-15-201025-4) Harcourt Children's Bks.

Gaiman, Neil. Books of Magic. 2004. (Books of Magic Ser.: No. 4). 192p. (J). pap. 5.99 (0-06-447382-1, Eos) Morrow/Avon.

—The Invitation. 2003. (Books of Magic: Vol. 1). (Illus.). 256p. (J). pap. 5.99 (0-06-447379-1, Eos) Morrow/Avon.

Gaydos, Nora. The Wizard Who Loved Black. 2002. (Magic Color Slide Ser.). (Illus.). 22p. (J). (ps-2). 14.99 (1-58476-131-8, IKIDS) Innovative Kids.

Haining, Peter, ed. The Wizards' Den: Spellbinding Stories of Magic & Magicians. 2003. (Illus.). 320p. (J). 22.95 (0-285-63628-6) Souvenir Pr. Ltd. GBR. Dist: Independent Pubs. Group.

Hansen, Ron. The Shadowmaker. (Trophy Bk.). (Illus.). 80p. (J). 1989. (gr. 5 up). pap. 4.95 (0-06-440287-8, Harper Trophy); 1987. (gr. 2-6). lib. bdg. 10.89 o.p. (0-06-022203-4) HarperCollins Children's Bk. Group.

—The Shadowmaker. 1987. (J). 11.10 (0-606-04036-6) Turtleback Bks.

Hayes, Sarah. Crumbling Castle. 80p. (J). (gr. 3-6). 1994. bds. 3.99 o.p. (1-56402-274-9); 1992. (Illus.). 13.95 o.p. (1-56402-108-4) Candlewick Pr.

Ibbotson, Eva. Which Witch? unabr. ed. 1993. (J). (gr. 1-8). audio 32.95 (0-7451-4444-6, CCA3210, Chivers Children's Audio Bks.) BBC Audiobooks America.

—Which Witch? 2002. (Illus.). 13.19 (1-4046-1490-7) Book Wholesalers, Inc.

—Which Witch? 2000. (Illus.). 256p. (J). (gr. 3-7). pap. 5.99 (0-14-130427-8, Puffin Bks.) Penguin Putnam Bks. for Young Readers.

—Which Witch? 1988. 208p. (J). (gr. 3-7). pap. 2.50 o.p. (0-590-41926-9, Scholastic Paperbacks) Scholastic, Inc.

—Which Witch? 2000. (J). 11.04 (0-606-19882-2) Turtleback Bks.

Ibbotson, Eva & Large, Annabel. Which Witch? l.t. ed. 2001. (Illus.). 249p. (J). 21.95 (0-7862-3073-8) Thorndike Pr.

Ibbotson, Eva, et al. Which Witch? 1999. (Illus.). 224p. (J). (gr. 4-7). 15.99 (0-525-46164-7, Dutton Children's Bks.) Penguin Putnam Bks. for Young Readers.

Jaffe, Rona. The Last of the Wizards. 2001. (Illus.). 12p. (J). (ps-2). bds. 12.99 o.s.i (0-307-10619-5, Golden Bks.) Random Hse. Children's Bks.

Jones, Diana Wynne. Archer's Goon. 1987. mass mkt. 2.95 o.s.i (0-441-02892-6) Ace Bks.

—Archer's Goon. 1987. 2.95 o.s.i (0-425-09888-5) Berkley Publishing Group.

Jones, Marcia Thornton & Dadey, Debbie. Spooky Spells. 1999. (Bailey City Monsters Ser.: No. 6). (Illus.). 80p. (J). (gr. 2-4). mass mkt. 3.99 (0-439-05871-6) Scholastic, Inc.

—Spooky Spells. 1999. (Bailey City Monsters Ser.: No. 6). (J). (gr. 2-4). 10.14 (0-606-16656-4) Turtleback Bks.

Koller, Jackie French. A Wizard Named Nell. 2003. 208p. (J). pap. 4.99 (0-689-85591-5, Aladdin) Simon & Schuster Children's Publishing.

—The Wizard's Apprentice. 2003. 192p. (J). pap. 4.99 (0-689-85592-3, Aladdin) Simon & Schuster Children's Publishing.

L' Homme, Erik. Quadehar the Sorcerer. 2003. (Book of Stars Ser.: Bk. 1). 224p. (J). (gr. 3-6). 16.95 (0-439-53643-X, Chicken Hse., The) Scholastic, Inc.

Levine, Gail Carson. The Two Princesses of Bamarre. 2001. 256p. (J). (gr. 5 up). 15.99 (0-06-029315-2); lib. bdg. 16.89 (0-06-029316-0) HarperCollins Children's Bk. Group.

—The Two Princesses of Bamarre. 2003. 256p. (J). (gr. 5 up). pap. 5.99 (0-06-440966-X) HarperCollins Pubs.

—The Two Princesses of Bamarre. 2004. (Illus.). 304p. (J). pap. 6.99 (0-06-057580-8, Eos) Morrow/Avon.

Levinson, Marilyn. Rufus & Magic Run Amok. 2001. (Illus.). 96p. (J). (gr. 2-6). 19.25 (0-7614-5102-1, Cavendish Children's Bks.) Cavendish, Marshall Corp.

Lubar, David. Wizards of the Game. 2003. 176p. (J). 16.99 (0-399-23706-2, Philomel) Penguin Putnam Bks. for Young Readers.

MacLachlan, Patricia. Tomorrow's Wizard. 1996. 80p. (J). (gr. 3 up). pap. 6.00 (0-15-201276-1, Magic Carpet Bks.) Harcourt Children's Bks.

—Tomorrow's Wizard. 1982. (Charlotte Zolotow Bk.). (Illus.). 96p. (J). (gr. 3-6). 12.95 (0-06-024073-3); lib. bdg. 13.89 o.s.i (0-06-024074-1) HarperCollins Children's Bk. Group.

Marshak, Suzanna. The Wizard's Promise. 1994. (Illus.). (J). pap. 15.00 o.s.i (0-671-78431-5, Simon & Schuster Children's Publishing) Simon & Schuster Children's Publishing.

McKillip, Patricia A. The Forgotten Beasts of Eld. 1986. 224p. (J). 2.95 o.p. (0-425-09452-9) Berkley Publishing Group.

—The Forgotten Beasts of Eld. 1996. (Jackson Friends Bk.). 352p. (YA). (gr. 7 up). pap. 6.00 (0-15-200869-1, Magic Carpet Bks.) Harcourt Children's Bks.

—The Forgotten Beasts of Eld. 1976. (J). (gr. 7 up). mass mkt. 2.50 o.p. (0-380-00480-1, 62505-9, Avon Bks.) Morrow/Avon.

—The Forgotten Beasts of Eld. 1974. 224p. (J). (gr. 6 up). 14.95 o.p. (0-689-30434-X, Atheneum) Simon & Schuster Children's Publishing.

McMullan, Kate. Dsa #11: Danger! Wizards at Work! 2004. (Dragon Slayer's Academy Ser.). (Illus.). 112p. mass mkt. 4.99 (0-448-43529-2, Grosset & Dunlap) Penguin Putnam Bks. for Young Readers.

McMylor, Phil. Trouble Brewing. 2002. (Wizard! Bks.). (Illus.). 16p. (J). (ps-2). bds. 4.95 (0-7641-5566-0) Barron's Educational Series, Inc.

—Twinkle's Treat. 2002. (Wizard! Bks.). (Illus.). 16p. (J). (ps-2). bds. 4.95 (0-7641-5567-9) Barron's Educational Series, Inc.

Nagy, Gloria & Chwast, Seymour. The Wizard Who Wanted to Be Santa. 2000. (Illus.). (J). (ps-3). 16.95 (0-9679436-0-4) Sheer Bliss Communications, LLC.

Nimbus Two Thousand, Vol. 5. 2001. (Harry Potter Ser.: No. 5). 29.94 (0-439-32356-8) Scholastic, Inc.

Pfister, Marcus. The Magic Book. 2003. (Illus.). 28p. (J). 12.95 (0-7358-1873-8) North-South Bks., Inc.

Rowling, J. K. Harri Potter Maen yr Athronydd. 2003. (WEL.). 300p. (J). pap. 21.95 (1-58234-827-8, Bloomsbury Children) Bloomsbury Publishing.

—Harrius Potter et Philosophi Lapis. 2003. (Harry Potter Ser.: Year 1). (LAT., Illus.). 300p. (J). 26.95 o.s.i (1-58234-825-1, Bloomsbury Children) Bloomsbury Publishing.

—Harry Potter & the Chamber of Secrets. 2003. 464p. (J). pap. 13.95 (1-59413-001-9, Wheeler Publishing, Inc.) Gale Group.

—Harry Potter & the Chamber of Secrets. braille ed. 1999. (Harry Potter Ser.: Year 2). 520p. (YA). (gr. 3 up). pap. 17.99 (0-939173-35-2) National Braille Pr.

—Harry Potter & the Chamber of Secrets. unabr. ed. 2000. (Harry Potter Ser.: Year 2). (YA). (gr. 3 up). audio 44.00 (0-8072-8207-3, YA137SP, Listening Library) Random Hse. Audio Publishing Group.

—Harry Potter & the Chamber of Secrets. (Harry Potter Ser.). 2003. 352p. (J). 24.95 (0-439-55489-6, Levine, Arthur A. Bks.); 2002. (Illus.). 352p. (J). pap. 6.99 (0-439-42010-5, Levine, Arthur A. Bks.); 2000. (Illus.). 352p. (YA). (gr. 3 up). pap. 6.99 (0-439-06487-2); 1999. (Illus.). viii, 341p. (J). (gr. 3 up). 19.95 (0-439-06486-4, Levine, Arthur A. Bks.) Scholastic, Inc.

—Harry Potter & the Chamber of Secrets. l.t. ed. 2000. (Harry Potter Ser.: Year 2). (Illus.). 464p. (J). (gr. 3 up). 24.95 (0-7862-2273-5) Thorndike Pr.

—Harry Potter & the Goblet of Fire. 2003. 936p. pap. 14.95 (1-59413-003-5, Wheeler Publishing, Inc.) Gale Group.

—Harry Potter & the Goblet of Fire. braille ed. 2000. (Harry Potter Ser.: Year 4). 650p. (YA). (gr. 3 up). pap. 25.95 (0-939173-37-9) National Braille Pr.

—Harry Potter & the Goblet of Fire. (Harry Potter Ser.). 2003. 752p. (J). 30.95 (0-439-55490-X); 2002. 752p. (J). (gr. 3 up). pap. 8.99 (0-439-13960-0); 2000. (Illus.). xi, 734p. (YA). (gr. 3 up). 25.95 (0-439-13959-7) Scholastic, Inc. (Levine, Arthur A. Bks.).

—Harry Potter & the Goblet of Fire. l.t. ed. 2000. (Harry Potter Ser.: Year 4). (Illus.). 936p. (J). (gr. 3 up). 25.95 (0-7862-2927-6) Thorndike Pr.

—Harry Potter & the Order of the Phoenix, 13 vols. braille ed. 2003. (Harry Potter Ser.: 5). (YA). 29.99 (0-939173-38-7) National Braille Pr.

—Harry Potter & the Order of the Phoenix. 2003. (Harry Potter Ser.: Year 5). (Illus.). 896p. (J). (gr. 3-6). 34.99 (0-439-56761-0); 29.99 (0-439-35806-X); 60.00 (0-439-56762-9) Scholastic, Inc.

—Harry Potter & the Order of the Phoenix. l.t. ed. 2003. (Sequel to Harry Potter & the Goblet of Fire Ser.). 1093p. 29.95 (0-7862-5778-4) Thorndike Pr.

—Harry Potter & the Prisoner of Azkaban. 2003. 592p. (J). pap. 13.95 (1-59413-002-7, Wheeler Publishing, Inc.) Gale Group.

—Harry Potter & the Prisoner of Azkaban. braille ed. 1999. (Harry Potter Ser.: Year 3). (YA). (gr. 3 up). pap. 19.95 (0-939173-36-0) National Braille Pr.

—Harry Potter & the Prisoner of Azkaban. 2000. tchr. ed. 9.95 (1-58130-656-3); stu. ed. 11.95 (1-58130-657-1) Novel Units, Inc.

—Harry Potter & the Prisoner of Azkaban. (Harry Potter Ser.: Year 3). (Illus.). (J). (gr. 3 up). 2001. 448p. pap. 7.99 (0-439-13636-9, Levine, Arthur A. Bks.); 1999. ix, 435p. 19.95 (0-439-13635-0) Scholastic, Inc.

—Harry Potter & the Prisoner of Azkaban. l.t. ed. 2000. (Harry Potter Ser.: Year 3). (Illus.). 592p. (YA). (gr. 3 up). 24.95 (0-7862-2274-3) Thorndike Pr.

—Harry Potter & the Sorcerer's Stone. 1997. (Harry Potter Ser.: Year 1). (Illus.). 223p. (YA). (gr. 3 up). pap. (0-7475-3274-5) Bloomsbury Publishing, Ltd. GBR. Dist: Raincoast Bk. Distribution.

—Harry Potter & the Sorcerer's Stone. 2003. 423p. pap. 13.95 (1-59413-000-0, Wheeler Publishing, Inc.) Gale Group.

—Harry Potter & the Sorcerer's Stone. unabr. ed. (Harry Potter Ser.: Year 1). (YA). (gr. 3 up). 320p. pap. 62.00 incl. audio (0-8072-1547-3); 320p. pap. 62.00 incl. audio (0-8072-1547-3); 2000. pap. 44.00 incl. audio (0-8072-8119-0, YYA108SP) Random Hse. Audio Publishing Group. (Listening Library).

—Harry Potter & the Sorcerer's Stone. (Harry Potter Ser.: Year 1). (YA). (gr. 3 up). 2001. 384p. mass mkt. 6.99 (0-439-36213-X); 1999. (Illus.). 312p. pap. 6.99 (0-590-35342-X); 1998. (Illus.). 320p. 19.95 (0-590-35340-3, Levine, Arthur A. Bks.); 2000. 320p. 75.00 (0-439-20352-X) Scholastic, Inc.

—Harry Potter & the Sorcerer's Stone. l.t. ed. 1999. (Harry Potter Ser.: Year 1). (Illus.). 422p. (YA). (gr. 3 up). 24.95 (0-7862-2272-7) Thorndike Pr.

—Harry Potter & the Sorcerer's Stone. 1999. (Harry Potter Ser.: Year 1). (Illus.). (YA). (gr. 3 up). 12.95 o.p. (0-606-17233-5) Turtleback Bks.

—Harry Potter Aur Paras Pathar. Khokhar, Darakhshanda Asghar, tr. from ENG. 2002. (URD.). 264p. (Orig.). pap. 12.95 (0-19-579858-9) Oxford Univ. Pr., Inc.

—Harry Potter Boxed Set: Harry Potter & the Sorcerer's Stone; Harry Potter & the Chamber of Secrets; Harry Potter & the Prisoner of Azkaban, 3 vols. (Harry Potter Ser.: Years 1-3). (Illus.). (YA). 2002. pap. 21.97 (0-439-32466-1); 1999. (gr. 3 up). 55.85 (0-439-13316-5) Scholastic, Inc. (Levine, Arthur A. Bks.).

—Harry Potter Boxed Set: Harry Potter & the Sorcerer's Stone; Harry Potter & the Chamber of Secrets; Harry Potter & the Prisoner of Azkaban; Harry Potter & the Goblet of Fire, 4 vols. (Harry Potter Ser.: Years 1-4). 2002. 752p. (YA). (gr. 3 up). pap. 30.96 (0-439-43486-6, Levine, Arthur A. Bks.); 2001. 85.80 (0-439-24954-6); 2000. (YA). (gr. 3 up). 85.80 (0-641-06631-7, Levine, Arthur A. Bks.) Scholastic, Inc.

—Harry Potter Boxed Set: Harry Potter & the Sorcerer's Stone; Harry Potter & the Chamber of Secrets; Harry Potter & the Prisoner of Azkaban; Harry Potter & the Goblet of Fire; Harry Potter & the Order of the Phoenix, 5 vols. ltd. ed. 2003. (Harry Potter Ser.). 2000p. (J). 99.95 (0-439-61255-1) Scholastic, Inc.

—Harry Potter Coffret: Harry Potter a l'Ecole des Sorciers; Harry Potter et la Chambre des Secrets; Harry Potter et le Prisonnier d'Azkaban. 1999. (Harry Potter Ser.: Years 1-3). Tr. of Harry Potter Boxed Set: Harry Potter & the Chamber of Secrets; Harry Potter & the Sorcerer's Stone; Harry Potter & the Prisoner of Azkaban. (FRE.). 1400p. (YA). (gr. 3 up). 34.95 (0-320-03843-2) French & European Pubns., Inc.

—Harry Potter Coffret: Harry Potter a l'Ecole des Sorciers; Harry Potter et la Chambre des Secrets; Harry Potter et le Prisonnier d'Azkaban. 1999. (Harry Potter Ser.: Years 1-3). Tr. of Harry Potter Boxed Set: Harry Potter & the Chamber of Secrets; Harry Potter & the Sorcerer's Stone; Harry Potter & the Prisoner of Azkaban. (FRE.). (YA). (gr. 3 up). pap. 43.95 (2-07-052929-0) Gallimard, Editions FRA. Dist: Distribooks, Inc.

—Harry Potter et la Chambre des Secrets. 1999. (Harry Potter Ser.: Year 2). Tr. of Harry Potter & the Chamber of Secrets. (FRE.). (YA). (gr. 3 up). pap. 13.95 (0-320-03778-9) French & European Pubns., Inc.

Miscellaneous

—Harry Potter et la Chambre des Secrets. 1999. (Harry Potter Ser.: Year 2). Tr. of Harry Potter & the Chamber of Secrets. (FRE., Illus.). (YA). (gr. 3 up). pap. 14.95 (*2-07-052455-8*) Gallimard, Editions FRA. *Dist:* Distribooks, Inc.

—Harry Potter et la Coupe de Feu. 2001. (Harry Potter Ser.: Year 4). Tr. of Harry Potter & the Goblet of Fire. (FRE.). (YA). (gr. 3 up). pap. 34.95 (*0-320-03932-3*) French & European Pubns., Inc.

—Harry Potter et le Prisonnier d'Azkaban. 1999. (Harry Potter Ser.: Year 3). Tr. of Harry Potter & the Prisoner of Azkaban. (FRE.). (YA). (gr. 3 up). pap. (*2-07-052818-9*) Gallimard, Editions.

—Harry Potter et l'Ecole des Sorciers. 3rd ed. 1998. (Harry Potter Ser.: Year 1). Tr. of Harry Potter & the Sorcerer's Stone. (FRE., Illus.). (YA). (gr. 3 up). pap. 14.95 (*2-07-050142-6*) Distribooks, Inc.

—Harry Potter et l'Ecole des Sorciers. 1999. (Harry Potter Ser.: Year 1). Tr. of Harry Potter & the Sorcerer's Stone. (FRE.). (YA). (gr. 3 up). pap. 16.95 (*0-320-03780-0*) French & European Pubns., Inc.

—Harry Potter et l'Ecole des Sorciers. 2000. Tr. of Harry Potter & the Sorcerer's Stone. (FRE.). (J). pap. 14.95 (*2-07-051426-9*) Gallimard, Editions FRA. *Dist:* Distribooks, Inc.

—Harry Potter und der Gefangene von Azkaban. 1999. (Harry Potter Ser.: Year 3). Tr. of Harry Potter & the Prisoner of Azkaban. (GER.). (YA). (gr. 3 up). 28.95 (*3-551-55169-3*) Carlsen Verlag DEU. *Dist:* Distribooks, Inc.

—Harry Potter und der Stein de Weisen. 1999. (Harry Potter Ser.: Year 1). Tr. of Harry Potter & the Sorcerer's Stone. (GER.). 335p. (YA). (gr. 3 up). 28.95 (*3-551-55167-7*) Carlsen Verlag DEU. *Dist:* Distribooks, Inc.

—Harry Potter und die Kammer des Schreckens. 1999. (Harry Potter Ser.: Year 2). Tr. of Harry Potter & Chamber of Secrets. (GER.). (YA). (gr. 3 up). 28.95 (*3-551-55168-5*) Carlsen Verlag DEU. *Dist:* Distribooks, Inc.

—Harry Potter y el Prisionero de Azkaban. 2000. (Harry Potter Ser.: Year 3). (SPA., Illus.). 360p. (YA). (gr. 3 up). 15.95 (*84-7888-519-6*, SAL1889) Emece Editores ESP. *Dist:* Lectorum Pubns., Inc.

—Harry Potter y el Prisionero de Azkaban. 2000. (Harry Potter Ser.: Year 3). (SPA.). (YA). (gr. 3 up). 16.95 (*0-320-03783-5*) French & European Pubns., Inc.

—Harry Potter y la Camara Secreta. (Harry Potter Ser.: Year 2). (SPA., Illus.). (YA). 2000. 288p. (gr. 3 up). (*84-7888-495-5*, SAL4595); 1999. 256p. (gr. 7 up). 15.95 (*84-7888-445-9*, SAL2819) Emece Editores ESP. *Dist:* Lectorum Pubns., Inc., Lectorum Pubns., Inc., Libros Sin Fronteras.

—Harry Potter y la Camara Secreta. 1999. (Harry Potter Ser.: Year 2). (SPA.). (YA). (gr. 3 up). 14.95 (*0-320-03781-9*) French & European Pubns., Inc.

—Harry Potter y la Piedra Filosofal. 1999. (Harry Potter Ser.: Year 1). (SPA.). (YA). (gr. 3 up). 14.95 (*0-320-03782-7*) French & European Pubns., Inc.

Satoru, Akahori. Sorcerer Hunter. 2001. (MIXX Manga Ser.). (Illus.). 195p. (YA). (gr. 8-12). pap. 12.95 (*1-892213-55-9*) TOKYOPOP, Inc.

—Sorcerer Hunter 13, 13 vols. 2003. (Illus.). 184p. (YA). (gr. 11 up). pap. 9.99 (*1-59182-066-9*) TOKYOPOP, Inc.

Satoru, Akahori & Omishi, Ray. Sorcerer Hunter. 1999. (MIXX Manga Ser.: Vol. 1). (Illus.). 192p. (YA). (gr. 7 up). pap. 11.95 (*1-892213-22-2*, Mixx Manga) Mixx Entertainment, Inc.

Scalora, Suza. The Witches & Wizards of Oberin. 2001. (Ageless Bks.). (Illus.). 48p. (J). 19.95 (*0-06-029535-X*, Cotler, Joanna Bks.) HarperCollins Children's Bk. Group.

Scholastic, Inc. Staff. Harry Potter & the Chamber of Secrets: A Deluxe Pop-Up Book. 2002. (Harry Potter Ser.). (Illus.). 5p. (J). pap. 17.95 (*0-439-45193-0*, Levine, Arthur A. Bks.) Scholastic, Inc.

School Crests: Harry Potter Journal. 2000. 144p. (J). pap. 8.99 (*0-439-20128-4*) Scholastic, Inc.

Scieszka, Jon. Knights of the Kitchen Table. (Time Warp Trio Ser.). (Illus.). 64p. (J). (gr. 4-7). 1993. pap. 4.99 (*0-14-034603-1*); 1991. 14.99 (*0-670-83622-2*, Viking Children's Bks.) Penguin Putnam Bks. for Young Readers.

—Knights of the Kitchen Table. unabr. ed. 1998. 55p. (J). (gr. 3-5). pap. 17.00 incl. audio (*0-8072-0391-2*, FTR193SP, Listening Library) Random Hse. Audio Publishing Group.

—Knights of the Kitchen Table. 1993. (Time Warp Trio Ser.). (J). 11.14 (*0-606-05399-9*) Turtleback Bks.

Smith, Janice Lee. Wizard & Wart in Trouble. (I Can Read Bks.). (Illus.). 48p. (J). (ps-3). 2000. pap. 3.99 (*0-06-444274-8*); 1998. lib. bdg. 15.89 (*0-06-027762-9*) HarperCollins Children's Bk. Group.

—Wizard & Wart in Trouble. 1998. (I Can Read Bks.). (Illus.). 48p. (J). (ps-3). 14.95 o.p. (*0-06-027761-0*) HarperCollins Pubs.

—Wizard & Wart in Trouble. 2000. (I Can Read Bks.). 10.10 (*0-606-18731-6*) Turtleback Bks.

Snyder, Zilpha Keatley. The Changing Maze. (Illus.). (J). (gr. k-4). 1985. 96p. lib. bdg. 12.95 o.s.i (*0-02-785900-2*, Simon & Schuster Children's Publishing); 1992. 32p. reprint ed. pap. 4.95 o.p. (*0-689-71618-4*, Aladdin) Simon & Schuster Children's Publishing.

Somtow, S. P. The Wizard's Apprentice. 1993. (Dragonflight Ser.: No. 7). (Illus.). 144p. (YA). (gr. 7 up). 14.95 o.s.i (*0-689-31576-7*, Atheneum) Simon & Schuster Children's Publishing.

—The Wizard's Apprentice. 2002. (J). E-Book (*1-58824-702-3*); 1993. E-Book (*1-58824-703-1*); 1993. E-Book (*1-58824-908-5*) ipicturebooks, LLC.

Strickland, Brad. The Beast under the Wizard's Bridge. (Lewis Barnavelt Ser.). 160p. 2002. pap. 5.99 (*0-14-230065-9*, Puffin Bks.); 2000. (Illus.). (J). (gr. 5-9). 16.99 o.p. (*0-8037-2220-6*, Dial Bks. for Young Readers) Penguin Putnam Bks. for Young Readers.

—The Bell, the Book & the Spellbinder. 2000. (John Bellairs Ser.). (Illus.). 160p. (gr. 3-7). pap. 5.99 (*0-14-130362-X*, Puffin Bks.) Penguin Putnam Bks. for Young Readers.

—The Hand of the Necromancer. (Johnny Dixon Mystery Ser.). 176p. 1998. (Illus.). (J). (gr. 3-7). pap. 4.99 o.p. (*0-14-038695-5*, Puffin Bks.); 1996. (YA). (gr. 5 up). 14.89 o.s.i (*0-8037-1830-6*, Dial Bks. for Young Readers); 1996. (YA). (gr. 5 up). 14.99 o.s.i (*0-8037-1829-2*, Dial Bks. for Young Readers) Penguin Putnam Bks. for Young Readers.

—The Tower at the End of the World. 2001. (Lewis Barnavelt Ser.). (Illus.). 160p. (YA). 16.99 (*0-8037-2620-1*, Dial Bks. for Young Readers) Penguin Putnam Bks. for Young Readers.

—Tower at the End of the World. 2003. (Lewis Barnavelt Ser.). (Illus.). 160p. pap. 5.99 (*0-14-250077-1*, Puffin Bks.) Penguin Putnam Bks. for Young Readers.

Strickland, Brad & Bellairs, John. The Bell, the Book & the Spellbinder. (J). 1999. (Illus.). pap. 14.89 (*0-8037-1832-2*); 1997. 160p. (gr. 5-9). 14.99 o.s.i (*0-8037-1831-4*) Penguin Putnam Bks. for Young Readers. (Dial Bks. for Young Readers).

Stroud, Jonathan. The Amulet of Samarkand. 2003. (Bartimaeus Trilogy: Bk. 1). (Illus.). 464p. (J). (gr. 5 up). 17.95 (*0-7868-1859-X*) Hyperion Bks. for Children.

—The Amulet of Samarkand, No. 1. unabr. ed. 2003. (J). audio 35.00 (*0-8072-1953-3*, Listening Library) Random Hse. Audio Publishing Group.

Tolkien, J. R. R. Roverandom. abr. ed. 1998. (J). audio 16.85 (*0-00-105535-6*) HarperCollins Pubs. Ltd. GBR. *Dist:* Trafalgar Square.

—Roverandom. Scull, Christina & Hammond, Wayne G., eds. (Illus.). 106p. 1999. pap. 12.00 (*0-395-95799-0*); 1998. (gr. 3-5). 17.00 (*0-395-89871-4*) Houghton Mifflin Co.

—Roverandom. 1998. 18.05 (*0-606-16543-6*) Turtleback Bks.

Tolkien, J. R. R., et al. Roverandom. Scull, Christina & Hammond, Wayne G., eds. 783rd l.t. ed. 1998. (Science Fiction Ser.). (Illus.). 191p. (J). 25.95 (*0-7838-0299-4*) Thorndike Pr.

Townsend, Tom. Never Trust a One-Eyed Wizard: The Fairie Ring. 2000. (Fairie Ring Ser.: Vol. 2). 171p. (YA). (gr. 8 up). pap. 9.99 (*0-88092-526-4*) Royal Fireworks Publishing Co.

Ure, Jean. The Wizard in the Woods. 1992. (Illus.). 176p. (J). (gr. 3-6). 14.95 o.p. (*1-56402-110-6*) Candlewick Pr.

Vande Velde, Vivian. Wizard at Work. 2003. (Illus.). 144p. (YA). 16.00 (*0-15-204559-7*) Harcourt Children's Bks.

Vrato, Elizabeth. The Wonderful Wizard of Oz. 2003. (Illus.). 64p. (J). 9.98 (*0-7624-1628-9*) Running Pr. Bk. Pubs.

Walsh, Ellen Stoll. Mouse Magic. 2000. (Illus.). 32p. (J). (ps-3). 14.00 o.s.i (*0-15-200326-6*) Harcourt Children's Bks.

Werner, Niels. The Wiley Wizard of Hveen. 1999. (Illus.). 64p. (Orig.). (J). (gr. k-8). pap. 9.95 (*0-9663019-7-8*) Pocket of Sanity.

West, Tracey. Windy Won't Practice. 2001. (Wee Wizards Ser.). (Illus.). 24p. (J). (ps-2). pap. 3.99 o.p. (*0-307-17143-4*, Golden Bks.) Random Hse. Children's Bks.

Whitcher, Susan. The Key to the Cupboard, RS. 1997. (Illus.). 32p. (J). (ps-3). 16.00 o.p. (*0-374-34127-3*, Farrar, Straus & Giroux (BYR)) Farrar, Straus & Giroux.

Wrede, Patricia C. Talking to Dragons. 1985. (Magic-Quest Ser.: No. 13). 240p. (J). 2.25 o.s.i (*0-441-79591-9*) Ace Bks.

—Talking to Dragons. (Enchanted Forest Chronicles: Bk. 4). 272p. 2003. (Illus.). (YA). pap. 5.95 (*0-15-204691-7*, Magic Carpet Bks.); 1993. (J). (gr. 7 up). 16.95 (*0-15-284247-0*) Harcourt Children's Bks.

—Talking to Dragons, 4. unabr. ed. 2002. (J). (gr. 3 up). audio 26.00 (*0-8072-0638-5*, Listening Library) Random Hse. Audio Publishing Group.

—Talking to Dragons. 1995. 272p. (J). (gr. 7-9). mass mkt. 4.99 (*0-590-48475-3*) Scholastic, Inc.

—Talking to Dragons. 1995. (Enchanted Forest Chronicles Ser.). (J). 11.04 (*0-606-08267-0*) Turtleback Bks.

Wrede, Patricia C. & Stevermer, Caroline. Sorcery & Cecelia: or the Enchanged Chocolate Pot: Magical Misadventures of Two Lady Cousins in Regency England. 2003. (Illus.). 336p. (YA). 17.00 (*0-15-204615-1*) Harcourt Children's Bks.

Wyllie, Stephen. The War of the Wizards. 1994. (Illus.). 24p. (J). 18.95 o.p. (*0-8037-1690-7*, Dial Bks. for Young Readers) Penguin Putnam Bks. for Young Readers.

Yolen, Jane. Wizard's Hall. 1999. 144p. (YA). pap. 6.00 (*0-15-202085-3*, Magic Carpet Bks.) Harcourt Children's Bks.

—Wizard's Hall. Ingber, Bonnie V., ed. 1991. 144p. (J). (gr. 3-7). 13.95 (*0-15-298132-2*) Harcourt Trade Pubs.

—Wizard's Hall. 144p. (J). (gr. 3-5). pap. 6.00 (*0-8072-1544-9*, Listening Library) Random Hse. Audio Publishing Group.

—Wizard's Hall. 1993. 144p. (J). (gr. 4-6). mass mkt. 3.50 o.p. (*0-590-45811-6*) Scholastic, Inc.

—Wizard's Hall. l.t. ed. 2001. 144p. (J). 21.95 (*0-7862-3605-1*) Thorndike Pr.

—Wizard's Hall. 1999. 12.05 (*0-606-16528-2*) Turtleback Bks.

Yolen, Jane, ed. & reader. Wizard's Hall. unabr. ed. 1995. 133p. (J). (gr. 3-5). pap. 28.00 incl. audio (*0-8072-7569-7*, YA882SP, Listening Library) Random Hse. Audio Publishing Group.

Youmans, Marly. The Curse of the Raven Mocker, RS. 2003. 288p. 18.00 (*0-374-31667-8*, Farrar, Straus & Giroux (BYR)) Farrar, Straus & Giroux.

Zambreno, Mary Frances. Journeyman Wizard: A Magical Mystery. abr. ed. 1994. 240p. (YA). (gr. 4-9). 16.95 (*0-15-200022-4*) Harcourt Children's Bks.

—Journeyman Wizard: A Magical Mystery. 1996. (Illus.). 272p. (YA). (gr. 5 up). pap. 5.95 o.p. (*0-7868-1127-7*) Hyperion Paperbacks for Children.

—Journeyman Wizard: A Magical Mystery. 1996. (YA). (gr. 5 up). 11.05 o.p. (*0-606-10234-5*) Turtleback Bks.

—A Plague of Sorcerers: A Magical Mystery. 1996. 288p. (J). (gr. 3-7). pap. 5.95 (*0-7868-1126-9*) Disney Pr.

—A Plague of Sorcerers: A Magical Mystery. abr. ed. 1991. 224p. (YA). (gr. 7 up). 16.95 o.s.i (*0-15-262430-9*) Harcourt Children's Bks.

—A Plague of Sorcerers: A Magical Mystery. 1996. (YA). 12.00 (*0-606-08846-6*) Turtleback Bks.

OCCUPATIONS

A

ACTORS AND ACTRESSES—FICTION

Bell, Cece. Sock Monkey Goes to Hollywood: A Star Is Bathed. 2003. (Illus.). 32p. (J). 13.99 (*0-7636-1962-0*) Candlewick Pr.

Blackwood, Gary L. The Shakespeare Stealer. 1998. 208p. (J). (gr. 4-6). 15.99 (*0-525-45863-8*, Dutton Children's Bks.) Penguin Putnam Bks. for Young Readers.

—The Shakespeare Stealer. 2000. 12.04 (*0-606-17870-8*) Turtleback Bks.

Collins, Suzanne. Fire Proof. 1999. (Mystery Files of Shelby Woo Ser.: No. 11). 144p. (J). (gr. 4-6). pap. 3.99 (*0-671-02695-X*, Aladdin) Simon & Schuster Children's Publishing.

Conford, Ellen. Annabel the Actress Starring in Gorilla My Dreams. (Annabel the Actress Ser.). (Illus.). 64p. (J). (gr. 2-5). 2000. pap. 3.99 (*0-689-83883-2*, Aladdin); 1999. 14.00 (*0-689-81404-6*, Simon & Schuster Children's Publishing) Simon & Schuster Children's Publishing.

—Annabel the Actress Starring in Gorilla My Dreams. 2000. (Ready-for-Chapters Ser.). 10.14 (*0-606-20029-0*) Turtleback Bks.

—Annabel the Actress Starring in Hound of the Barkervilles. 2002. (Annabel the Actress Ser.). (Illus.). 96p. (J). (gr. 2-5). 15.00 (*0-689-84734-3*, Simon & Schuster Children's Publishing) Simon & Schuster Children's Publishing.

—Annabel the Actress Starring in Just a Little Extra. 2000. (Annabel the Actress Ser.). (Illus.). 64p. (J). (gr. 4-5). 15.00 (*0-689-81405-4*, Simon & Schuster Children's Publishing) Simon & Schuster Children's Publishing.

Cooper, Susan. King of Shadows. (Illus.). 192p. (gr. 5-9). 2001. (J). pap. 4.99 (*0-689-84445-X*, Aladdin); 1999. (YA). 16.00 (*0-689-82817-9*, McElderry, Margaret K.) Simon & Schuster Children's Publishing.

—King of Shadows. l.t. ed. 2000. (Thorndike Press Large Print Juvenile Ser.). (Illus.). 246p. (J). (gr. 8-12). 21.95 (*0-7862-2706-0*) Thorndike Pr.

Garton, Ray. Lights, Camera, Action! 1998. (Secret World of Alex Mack Ser.: No. 33). 144p. (J). (gr. 4-7). pap. 3.99 (*0-671-02109-5*, Aladdin) Simon & Schuster Children's Publishing.

Greenfield, Eloise. Grandpa's Face. 1992. (Illus.). (J). o.p. (*0-09-174177-7*) Hutchinson Children's Bks, Ltd. GBR. *Dist:* Random Hse. of Canada, Ltd.

—Grandpa's Face. (Illus.). 32p. (J). (ps-3). 1996. pap. 6.99 (*0-698-11381-0*, PaperStar); 1993. (SPA., 5.95 o.p. (*0-399-22511-0*, Philomel); 1991. 5.95 o.s.i (*0-399-22106-9*, Sandcastle Bks.); 1988. 16.99 (*0-399-21525-5*, Philomel) Penguin Putnam Bks. for Young Readers.

—Grandpa's Face. 1996. 13.14 (*0-606-09349-4*) Turtleback Bks.

Heyes, Eileen. O'Dwyer & Grady Starring in Acting Innocents. 2002. 176p. (J). (gr. 4-7). pap. 4.99 (*0-689-84911-7*, Aladdin) Simon & Schuster Children's Publishing.

Hirsch, Odo. Antonio S. & the Mysterious Theodore Guzman. 1997. (Little Ark Book Ser.). (Illus.). 2024p. (J). (gr. 3-7). pap. (*1-86448-409-8*) Allen & Unwin Pty., Ltd.

—Antonio S. & the Mysterious Theodore Guzman. 2001. (Illus.). (J). 199p. lib. bdg. (*0-7868-2605-3*); 208p. (gr. 3-7). 15.99 (*0-7868-0747-4*) Hyperion Bks. for Children.

Howe, James. Stage Fright: A Sebastian Barth Mystery. 1991. 144p. (J). pap. 3.99 o.p. (*0-380-71331-4*); 1987. (YA). pap. 2.95 (*0-380-70173-1*) Morrow/Avon. (Avon Bks.).

—Stage Fright: A Sebastian Barth Mystery. (Sebastian Barth Mysteries Ser.). 160p. (J). 1995. (gr. 4-7). pap. 4.99 (*0-689-80338-9*, Aladdin); 1986. (gr. 3-7). 12.95 o.s.i (*0-689-31160-5*, Atheneum); 2nd ed. 1990. (gr. 3-7). 15.00 (*0-689-31701-8*, Atheneum) Simon & Schuster Children's Publishing.

—Stage Fright: A Sebastian Barth Mystery. 1995. 11.04 (*0-606-08193-3*) Turtleback Bks.

Littlesugar, Amy. The Tree of Hope. 2001. (Illus.). 40p. (J). pap. 6.99 (*0-698-11903-7*, Puffin Bks.) Penguin Putnam Bks. for Young Readers.

Marano, Lydia C. Rock 'n' Roll Robbery. 1997. (Mystery Files of Shelby Woo Ser.: No. 4). 144p. (J). (gr. 4-6). pap. 3.99 (*0-671-01155-3*, Aladdin) Simon & Schuster Children's Publishing.

Martin, Ann M. Maggie: Diary Three. (California Diaries). (YA). (gr. 6-8). 1999. 144p. mass mkt. 4.99 (*0-439-09547-6*); 1997. 160p. mass mkt. 3.99 (*0-590-29837-2*) Scholastic, Inc.

—Maggie: Diary Three. 1999. (California Diaries). (Illus.). (YA). (gr. 6-8). 11.04 (*0-606-18524-0*) Turtleback Bks.

Maxwell, Katie. The Year My Life Went down the Loo. (YA). 2004. mass mkt. 5.99 (*0-8439-5313-6*); 2003. mass mkt. 5.99 o.p. (*0-8439-5251-2*, SMOOCH) Dorchester Publishing Co., Inc.

McDonald, Megan. The Sisters Club. 2003. (Pleasant Company Publications). (Illus.). (J). pap. 15.95 (*1-58485-782-X*, American Girl) Pleasant Co. Pubns.

Miklowitz, Gloria D. Love Story, Take Three. 1987. (J). (gr. k-12). mass mkt. 2.75 o.s.i (*0-440-95084-8*, Laurel Leaf) Random Hse. Children's Bks.

Osborne, Mary Pope. Best Wishes, Joe Brady. 1984. (J). (gr. 5 up). 12.95 o.p. (*0-8037-0067-9*, 01258-370, Dial Bks. for Young Readers) Penguin Putnam Bks. for Young Readers.

—Best Wishes, Joe Brady. 1994. 192p. (YA). (gr. 7 up). pap. 4.99 (*0-679-84560-7*, Random Hse. Bks. for Young Readers) Random Hse. Children's Bks.

—Best Wishes, Joe Brady. 1985. 192p. (J). (gr. 7 up). reprint ed. pap. 2.25 o.p. (*0-590-33215-5*, Scholastic Paperbacks) Scholastic, Inc.

Palatini, Margie. Mary Had a Little Ham. 2003. (Illus.). 32p. (J). lib. bdg. 16.49 (*0-7868-2491-3*) Hyperion Bks. for Children.

Pfeffer, Susan Beth. Revenge of the Aztecs: A Story of the Jazz Age. (American Portraits Ser.). (Illus.). 114p. (YA). (gr. 5-8). 2001. 12.64 (*0-8092-0586-6*); 2000. pap. 5.95 (*0-8092-0627-7*, 06277E) Jamestown.

Ross, Rhea B. Hillbilly Choir. 1991. 186p. (YA). (gr. 7 up). 13.95 o.p. (*0-395-53356-2*) Houghton Mifflin Co.

Sones, Sonya. Miserably Yours, Ruby. 2004. (J). (*0-689-85820-5*, Simon & Schuster Children's Publishing) Simon & Schuster Children's Publishing.

Tripp, Valerie. Molly & the Movie Star. 2000. (American Girls Short Stories Ser.). (Illus.). 56p. (YA). (gr. 2 up). 3.95 (*1-58485-035-1*, American Girl) Pleasant Co. Pubns.

Occupations

Van Draanen, Wendelin. Sammy Keyes & the Hollywood Mummy. unabr. ed. 2001. (Sammy Keyes Ser.). (J). audio 23.95 (*0-87499-799-2*, OAK011) Live Oak Media.

—Sammy Keyes & the Hollywood Mummy. 2001. (Sammy Keyes Ser.). 272p. (gr. 5-8). text 15.95 (*0-375-80266-5*, Knopf Bks. for Young Readers); lib. bdg. 17.99 (*0-375-90266-X*, Random Hse. Bks. for Young Readers) Random Hse. Children's Bks.

Waber, Bernard. Evie & Margie. 2003. (Illus.). 32p. (J). (ps-3). 15.00 (*0-618-34124-2*) Houghton Mifflin Co. Trade & Reference Div.

Warner, Gertrude Chandler. The Movie Star Mystery. 1999. (Boxcar Children Ser.: No. 69). (J). (gr. 2-5). 10.00 (*0-606-18762-6*) Turtleback Bks.

Warner, Gertrude Chandler, creator. The Movie Star Mystery. 1999. (Boxcar Children Ser.: No. 69). (Illus.). 128p. (J). (gr. 2-5). lib. bdg. 13.95 (*0-8075-5303-4*); mass mkt. 3.95 (*0-8075-5304-2*) Whitman, Albert & Co.

AFRO-AMERICAN MUSICIANS—FICTION

Gregory, Deborah. Miss Cuchifrita, Ballerina. 2001. (Cheetah Girls Ser.: No. 10). 96p. (J). (gr. 3-7). pap. 3.99 (*0-7868-1476-4*, Jump at the Sun) Hyperion Bks. for Children.

Levine, Gail Carson. Dave at Night. 288p. (J). 2001. (gr. 3-7). pap. 5.99 (*0-06-440747-0*, Harper Trophy); 1999. (Illus.). (gr. k-3). lib. bdg. 16.89 (*0-06-028154-5*); 1999. (gr. k-4). 16.99 (*0-06-028153-7*) HarperCollins Children's Bk. Group.

—Dave at Night. unabr. ed. 2001. 278p. (J). (gr. 4-6). pap. 37.00 incl. audio (*0-8072-8379-7*, YA174SP, Listening Library) Random Hse. Audio Publishing Group.

—Dave at Night. 1999. (YA). pap., stu. ed. 69.95 incl. audio (*0-7887-3794-5*, 41038); pap., stu. ed. 69.95 incl. audio (*0-7887-3794-5*, 41038) Recorded Bks., LLC.

—Dave at Night. l.t. ed. 2001. (Illus.). 295p. (J). (gr. 4-7). 22.95 (*0-7862-2972-1*) Thorndike Pr.

APPRENTICES—FICTION

Cadnum, Michael. Ship of Fire. 2003. 208p. (YA). 16.99 (*0-670-89907-0*, Viking) Viking Penguin.

Cartwright, Pauline. The Bird Chain. 1994. (Illus.). (J). 4.25 (*0-383-03736-0*) SRA/McGraw-Hill.

Czernecki, Stefan. Paper Lanterns. 2001. (Illus.). (J). (ps-13). 15.95 (*1-57091-411-7*, Talewinds); 32p. 15.95 (*1-57091-410-9*) Charlesbridge Publishing, Inc.

—Paper Lanterns. 2002. (J). E-Book (*1-59019-575-2*); 2001. E-Book (*1-59019-576-0*); 2001. E-Book (*1-59019-577-9*) ipicturebooks, LLC.

DeFelice, Cynthia C. The Apprenticeship of Lucas Whitaker, RS. 1996. 160p. (YA). (gr. 5). 16.00 (*0-374-34669-0*, Farrar, Straus & Giroux (BYR)) Farrar, Straus & Giroux.

—The Apprenticeship of Lucas Whitaker. 1998. (J). 11.04 (*0-606-13078-0*) Turtleback Bks.

Garfield, Leon. The Apprentices. 1988. 320p. (J). (gr. 7 up). pap. 4.95 o.p. (*0-14-031595-0*, Puffin Bks.) Penguin Putnam Bks. for Young Readers.

—The Apprentices. 1978. (J). 10.00 o.p. (*0-670-12978-X*) Viking Penguin.

Hayner, Linda K. The Foundling. 1997. 352p. (YA). (gr. 10 up). pap. 9.95 (*0-89084-941-2*, 108951) Jones, Bob Univ. Pr.

Koller, Jackie French. The Wizard's Apprentice. 2003. 192p. (J). pap. 4.99 (*0-689-85592-3*, Aladdin) Simon & Schuster Children's Publishing.

Krensky, Stephen. The Printer's Apprentice. 1996. (Illus.). 112p. (J). pap. text 3.99 o.s.i (*0-440-41280-3*) Dell Publishing.

—The Printer's Apprentice. 1996. (J). pap. 4.99 (*0-440-91268-7*, Dell Books for Young Readers) Random Hse. Children's Bks.

—The Printer's Apprentice. 1996. (J). 9.09 o.p. (*0-606-11766-0*) Turtleback Bks.

Lantry, Kimberx. Uncle Uriah & Tad. 1980. (Trailblazers Ser.). (J). (gr. 4-8). pap. 1.99 o.p. (*0-8163-0361-4*) Pacific Pr. Publishing Assn.

Llorente, Pilar Molina. The Apprentice. 1994. 11.00 (*0-606-16136-8*) Turtleback Bks.

—Apprentice, RS. 1993. 112p. (J). (gr. 4-7). 13.00 o.p. (*0-374-30389-4*, Farrar, Straus & Giroux (BYR)) Farrar, Straus & Giroux.

—The Apprentice, RS. 1994. (Illus.). 112p. (YA). (gr. 4-7). pap. 4.95 (*0-374-40432-1*, Sunburst) Farrar, Straus & Giroux.

Ross, Andrea. To Touch the Sun. Davenport, May, ed. l.t. ed. 2000. 195p. (YA). (gr. 9-12). pap. text 15.95 (*0-943864-99-2*) Davenport, May Pubs.

Say, Allen. The Inn-Keeper's Apprentice. 1996. (J). 10.09 o.p. (*0-606-08554-8*) Turtleback Bks.

Stroud, Jonathan. The Amulet of Samarkand. 2003. (Bartimaeus Trilogy: Bk. 1). (Illus.). 464p. (J). (gr. 5 up). 17.95 (*0-7868-1859-X*) Hyperion Bks. for Children.

—The Amulet of Samarkand, No. 1. unabr. ed. 2003. (J). audio 35.00 (*0-8072-1953-3*, Listening Library) Random Hse. Audio Publishing Group.

Watts, Leander. Stonecutter. 2002. (Illus.). 224p. (J). (gr. 5-9). tchr. ed. 15.00 (*0-618-16474-X*) Houghton Mifflin Co.

ARCHITECTS—FICTION

Anholt, Laurence. Knee-High Norman. 1996. (Illus.). 32p. (Orig.). (J). (gr. k-3). bds. 4.99 o.p. (*1-56402-841-0*) Candlewick Pr.

Klee, Lucinda C. Lizzy the Architect Gift Set. 1997. (Career Girls & Company Ser.: No. 2A). (Illus.). 40p. (J). (gr. 2-6). pap. 19.95 (*1-891040-03-0*) LCK Pr.

Wells, Rosemary & Wells, Tom. The House in the Mail. (Illus.). 32p. 2004. 6.99 (*0-14-240061-0*, Puffin Bks.); 2002. (J). (gr. 1-5). text 16.99 (*0-670-03545-9*, Viking Children's Bks.) Penguin Putnam Bks. for Young Readers.

ARTISTS—FICTION

Alcock, Vivien. The Sylvia Game. 1997. 224p. (YA). (gr. 7-7). pap. 4.95 o.s.i (*0-395-81650-5*) Houghton Mifflin Co.

Alphin, Elaine Marie. Simon Says. 2002. (Illus.). 272p. (YA). (gr. 9 up). 17.00 (*0-15-216355-7*) Harcourt Children's Bks.

Anderson, Janet S. The Monkey Tree. 1998. (Illus.). 176p. (J). (gr. 7-12). 15.99 o.p. (*0-525-46032-2*, Dutton Children's Bks.) Penguin Putnam Bks. for Young Readers.

Anholt, Laurence. Camille & the Sunflowers. 1994. (Illus.). 32p. (J). (ps-2). 14.95 (*0-8120-6409-7*) Barron's Educational Series, Inc.

—The Child's Gift of Art, 4 vols. 2002. (Illus.). 128p. (J). (gr. k-3). 16.95 (*0-7641-7524-6*) Barron's Educational Series, Inc.

—Leonardo y el Aprendiz Volador: Un Cuento Sobre Leonardo Da Vinci. 2000. Tr. of Leonardo & the Flying Boy. (Illus.). 30p. (J). (gr. 3-5). (CAT.). 14.95 (*84-95040-79-4*); (SPA., 14.95 (*84-95040-78-6*) Serres, Ediciones, S. L. ESP. *Dist:* Lectorum Pubns., Inc.

—The Magical Garden of Claude Monet. 2003. (Illus.). 32p. (J). 14.95 (*0-7641-5574-1*) Barron's Educational Series, Inc.

—Picasso y Sylvette: Un Cuento Sobre Pablo Picasso. 2000. (Illus.). (J). (gr. 3-5). (CAT.). 32p. 14.95 (*84-8488-003-6*); (SPA., 200p. 14.95 (*84-95040-01-8*) Serres, Ediciones, S. L. ESP. *Dist:* Lectorum Pubns., Inc.

Ardizzone, Edward. Sarah & Simon & No Red Paint. 1966. (Illus.). (J). (ps-3). 4.95 o.p. (*0-440-07609-9*, Delacorte Pr.) Dell Publishing.

Auch, Mary Jane. Glass Slippers Give You Blisters. 1989. 176p. (J). (gr. 3-7). 14.95 o.p. (*0-8234-0752-7*) Holiday Hse., Inc.

Barrows, Allison. The Artist's Friends. 1997. (Picture Bks.). (Illus.). 32p. (J). (gr. k-3). lib. bdg. 15.95 o.s.i (*1-57505-054-4*, Carolrhoda Bks.) Lerner Publishing Group.

—The Artist's Model. 1996. (Illus.). 32p. (J). (ps-3). lib. bdg. 15.95 o.s.i (*0-87614-948-4*, Carolrhoda Bks.) Lerner Publishing Group.

Berenstain, Stan & Berenstain, Jan. The Berenstain Bears Draw-It! Drawing Lessons from Stan & Jan. 1996. (Berenstain Bears First Time Do-It! Bks.). (Illus.). (J). (ps-3). 8.99 o.s.i (*0-679-97314-1*); 23p. pap. 3.25 o.s.i (*0-679-87314-7*) Random Hse., Inc.

—The Berenstain Bears Draw-It! Drawing Lessons from Stan & Jan. 1996. (Berenstain Bears First Time Do-It! Bks.). (J). (ps-3). 9.40 (*0-606-10754-1*) Turtleback Bks.

Bolognese, Don. The War Horse. 2003. (Illus.). 176p. (J). (gr. 5-9). 16.95 (*0-689-85458-7*, Simon & Schuster Children's Publishing) Simon & Schuster Children's Publishing.

Bornstein, Ruth L. That's How It Is When We Draw. 1997. (Illus.). 32p. (J). (ps-2). 14.00 o.p. (*0-395-82509-1*) Houghton Mifflin Co.

Bowler, Tim. River Boy. (Illus.). 160p. (J). 2002. mass mkt. 4.99 (*0-689-84804-8*, Simon Pulse); 2000. (gr. 7 up). 16.00 (*0-689-82908-6*, McElderry, Margaret K.) Simon & Schuster Children's Publishing.

—River Boy. l.t. ed. 2001. 190p. (J). 22.95 (*0-7862-3507-1*) Thorndike Pr.

Bradford, Emma. Kat & the Missing Notebooks. 1999. (Stardust Classics: No. 4). (Illus.). 119p. (J). (gr. 2-5). 12.95 (*1-889514-27-6*); pap. 5.95 (*1-889514-28-4*) Dolls Corp.

Brokaw, Nancy Steele. Leaving Emma. 1999. 144p. (J). (gr. 4-6). tchr. ed. 15.00 (*0-395-90699-7*, Clarion Bks.) Houghton Mifflin Co. Trade & Reference Div.

Brown, Terry. Portrait of Lies. 2003. (Today's Girls Only Ser.: Bk. 2). 144p. (J). pap. 5.99 (*1-4003-0322-2*) Nelson, Tommy.

Browne, Anthony. Willy's Pictures. 2000. (Illus.). 32p. (J). (ps-3). 16.99 o.s.i (*0-7636-1323-1*) Candlewick Pr.

Buchholz, Quint. The Collector of Moments, RS. Neumeyer, Peter F., tr. from GER. 1999. (Illus.). 48p. (J). (gr. 4-7). 18.00 o.p. (*0-374-31520-5*, Farrar, Straus & Giroux (BYR)) Farrar, Straus & Giroux.

Bulla, Clyde Robert. The Paint Brush Kid. 1998. (Stepping Stone Bks.). (Illus.). 80p. (J). (gr. 4-7). pap. 3.99 (*0-679-89282-6*, Random Hse. Bks. for Young Readers) Random Hse. Children's Bks.

—The Paint Brush Kid. 1999. (Stepping Stone Bks.). 10.14 (*0-606-15668-2*) Turtleback Bks.

Butenhoff, Lisa K. Nina's Magic. Thatch, Nancy R., ed. 1992. (Books for Students by Students). (Illus.). 26p. (J). (ps-3). lib. bdg. 15.95 (*0-933849-40-0*) Landmark Editions, Inc.

Calders, Pere. Brush. Feitlowitz, Marguerite, tr. from SPA. 1988. Tr. of Cepillo. (Illus.). 32p. (J). (ps-3). reprint ed. pap. 6.95 (*0-916291-16-2*) Kane/Miller Bk. Pubs.

Carle, Eric. Draw Me a Star. 2002. (Illus.). (J). 14.04 (*0-7587-2416-0*) Book Wholesalers, Inc.

—Draw Me a Star. 1998. (J). 13.14 (*0-606-12924-3*) Turtleback Bks.

Carrick, Donald. Morgan & the Artist. 1991. (Illus.). 32p. (J). (gr. k-3). reprint ed. pap. 4.95 o.p. (*0-395-58176-1*, Clarion Bks.) Houghton Mifflin Co. Trade & Reference Div.

Catalanotto, Peter. Emily's Art. 2001. (Illus.). 32p. (J). (ps-4). 16.00 (*0-689-83831-X*, Atheneum/Richard Jackson Bks.) Simon & Schuster Children's Publishing.

—The Painter. (Illus.). 32p. (J). (ps-2). 1999. mass mkt. 5.95 (*0-531-07116-2*); 1996. pap. 15.95 (*0-531-09465-0*); 1996. lib. bdg. 16.99 (*0-531-08765-4*) Scholastic, Inc. (Orchard Bks.).

Clarke, J. Riffraff, ERS. 1992. 112p. (YA). (gr. 9-12). 14.95 o.p. (*0-8050-1774-7*, Holt, Henry & Co. Bks. For Young Readers) Holt, Henry & Co.

Cooney, Barbara. Hattie & the Wild Waves: A Story from Brooklyn. (Picture Puffins Ser.). (Illus.). (J). (ps-3). 1993. 40p. pap. 6.99 (*0-14-054193-4*, Puffin Bks.); 1990. 400p. 16.99 (*0-670-83056-9*, Viking Children's Bks.) Penguin Putnam Bks. for Young Readers.

—Hattie & the Wild Waves: A Story from Brooklyn. 1993. (Picture Puffin Ser.). (Illus.). (J). 12.14 (*0-606-05343-3*) Turtleback Bks.

Cormier, Robert. Tunes for Bears to Dance To. 1992. 112p. (J). (gr. 5 up). 15.00 o.s.i (*0-385-30818-3*, Delacorte Pr.) Dell Publishing.

Danziger, Paula. United Tates of America. 2002. (J). (gr. 4). lib. bdg. 28.00 incl. audio compact disk (*1-932076-03-4*, 02003CA) Full Cast Audio.

—United Tates of America. 2002. (Illus.). 144p. (J). (gr. 3-7). pap. 15.95 (*0-590-69221-6*, Scholastic Pr.) Scholastic, Inc.

de Paola, Tomie. The Art Lesson. 2002. (Illus.). (J). 13.19 (*0-7587-1969-8*) Book Wholesalers, Inc.

—The Art Lesson. (Illus.). 32p. (J). (ps-3). 1994. 5.95 o.s.i (*0-399-22761-X*); 1989. 16.99 (*0-399-21688-X*) Penguin Group (USA) Inc. (G. P. Putnam's Sons).

—The Art Lesson. 1997. (Illus.). 32p. (J). (ps-3). pap. 5.99 (*0-698-11572-4*, PaperStar) Penguin Putnam Bks. for Young Readers.

—The Art Lesson. unabr. ed. 1991. (Picture Book Read-Along Ser.). (Illus.). 29p. (J). (gr. k-2). pap. 17.00 incl. audio (*0-8072-6003-7*, PRA 809SP, Listening Library) Random Hse. Audio Publishing Group.

—The Art Lesson. 1997. 12.14 (*0-606-06184-3*) Turtleback Bks.

Deaver, Julie Reece. Chicago Blues. 1995. 192p. (J). (gr. 6-9). 15.95 (*0-06-024675-8*) HarperCollins Children's Bk. Group.

—Chicago Blues. 1995. 192p. (J). (gr. 6-9). lib. bdg. 14.89 o.p. (*0-06-024676-6*) HarperCollins Pubs.

Deeter, Catherine. Seymour Bleu: A Space Odyssey. 1998. (Illus.). 40p. (J). (ps-3). 16.00 (*0-689-80137-8*, Simon & Schuster Children's Publishing) Simon & Schuster Children's Publishing.

DeSantis, Anthony John & Namorato, Carmine, Jr. Vincent Van Mouse. 2001. 32p. (J). per. 16.50 (*0-9712994-0-4*) Black Cat Pubns., Inc.

Dunrea, Olivier. The Painter Who Loved Chickens, RS. 1995. (Illus.). 32p. (J). (ps-3). 15.00 o.p. (*0-374-35729-3*, Farrar, Straus & Giroux (BYR)) Farrar, Straus & Giroux.

Edwards, Michelle. A Baker's Portrait. 1991. (Illus.). 32p. (J). (gr. k up). lib. bdg. 13.88 o.p. (*0-688-09713-8*) HarperCollins Children's Bk. Group.

—Eve & Smithy. 1994. (J). (gr. 4 up). 15.00 o.p. (*0-688-11825-9*); (Illus.). 24p. lib. bdg. 14.93 o.p. (*0-688-11826-7*) HarperCollins Children's Bk. Group.

Ernst, Lisa Campbell. Hamilton's Art Show. 1986. (Illus.). 32p. (J). (ps-3). 12.95 o.p. (*0-688-04120-5*); lib. bdg. 12.88 o.p. (*0-688-04121-3*) HarperCollins Children's Bk. Group.

Fiorello, Frank. Frankie Big Head Becomes an Artist. 2002. 40p. (J). lib. bdg. 12.95 (*0-9708400-3-9*); per. 8.95 (*0-9708400-2-0*) Pumpkin Patch Publishing.

Foos, Laurie. Portrait of the Walrus by a Young Artist. 1997. 192p. 19.95 (*1-56689-057-8*) Coffee Hse. Pr.

Francis, Dorothy Brenner. The Jayhawk Horse Mystery. 2001. (Cover-to-Cover Novel Ser.). (Illus.). 80p. (J). (*0-7807-9728-0*); pap. (*0-7891-5349-1*) Perfection Learning Corp.

Gammell, Stephen. The Art Contest. 2001. (J). (*0-15-202048-9*) Harcourt Trade Pubs.

Garland, Michael. Dinner at Magritte's. 1995. (Young Readers' History of the Civil War Ser.). (Illus.). 32p. (J). (gr. 1-4). 14.99 o.s.i (*0-525-45336-9*, Dutton Children's Bks.) Penguin Putnam Bks. for Young Readers.

Geisert, Arthur. The Etcher's Studio. 1997. (Illus.). 32p. (J). (ps-3). lib. bdg., tchr. ed. 15.95 (*0-395-79754-3*) Houghton Mifflin Co.

Giff, Patricia Reilly. Pictures of Hollis Woods. unabr. ed. 2002. (gr. 4-7). audio 18.00 (*0-8072-0919-8*, Listening Library) Random Hse. Audio Publishing Group.

—Pictures of Hollis Woods. 2002. (Illus.). 176p. (gr. 3-8). text 15.95 (*0-385-32655-6*, Lamb, Wendy) Random Hse. Children's Bks.

—Pictures of Hollis Woods. 2002. 176p. lib. bdg. 17.99 (*0-385-90070-8*) Random Hse., Inc.

—Pictures of Hollis Woods. l.t. ed. 2003. 158p. (J). 23.95 (*0-7862-5094-1*) Thorndike Pr.

Gilchrist, Jan Spivey. Madelia. 1997. (Illus.). 32p. (J). (ps-3). 14.99 o.s.i (*0-8037-2052-1*); 14.89 o.s.i (*0-8037-2054-8*) Penguin Putnam Bks. for Young Readers. (Dial Bks. for Young Readers).

Giles, Gail. Breath of the Dragon. 1998. 10.04 (*0-606-15465-5*) Turtleback Bks.

—The Breath of the Dragon. 1997. (Illus.). 112p. (J). (gr. 4-6). tchr. ed. 14.95 (*0-395-76476-9*) Houghton Mifflin Co.

—Breath of the Dragon. 1998. (Illus.). 112p. (gr. 4-7). reprint ed. pap. text 3.99 o.s.i (*0-440-41496-2*) Dell Publishing.

Gilson, Jamie. Stink Alley. 2002. 192p. (J). (gr. 3 up). 15.95 (*0-688-17864-2*); lib. bdg. 15.89 (*0-06-029217-2*) HarperCollins Children's Bk. Group.

Glass, Andrew. Jackson Makes His Move. 1982. (Illus.). 48p. (J). (gr. 1-4). 9.95 o.p. (*0-7232-6207-1*, Warne, Frederick) Penguin Putnam Bks. for Young Readers.

Goffstein, M. B. Daisy Summerfield's Style. 1975. 112p. (J). (gr. 7 up). 6.95 o.p. (*0-440-05402-8*, Delacorte Pr.) Dell Publishing.

Goodman, Robert B. & Spicer, Robert A. The Magic Brush. Tabrah, Ruth, ed. 1974. (Illus.). (J). (gr. 1-7). 5.95 o.p. (*0-89610-007-3*) Island Heritage Publishing.

Green, Donna. My Little Artist. 1999. (Illus.). 32p. (J). (gr. 2-5). 11.98 (*0-7651-1742-8*) Smithmark Pubs., Inc.

—My Little Artist. 1999. (Illus.). 32p. (J). 12.95 (*1-883746-20-5*); 15.95 (*1-883746-21-3*) Vermilion.

Grove, Vicki. Destiny. 2000. (Illus.). 169p. (J). (gr. 5-9). 16.99 (*0-399-23449-7*, G. P. Putnam's Sons) Penguin Group (USA) Inc.

Guarnieri, Paolo. A Boy Named Giotto, RS. Galassi, Jonathan, tr. from ITA. 1999. (Illus.). 32p. (J). (gr. k-4). 17.00 (*0-374-30931-0*, Farrar, Straus & Giroux (BYR)) Farrar, Straus & Giroux.

Harding, William H. Alvin's Famous No-Horse. 1992. (Redfeather Bks.). (Illus.). 80p. (J). (gr. 2-4). 14.95 o.p. (*0-8050-2227-9*, Holt, Henry & Co. Bks. For Young Readers) Holt, Henry & Co.

Harris, Ruth Elwin. Frances' Story: Sisters of the Quantock Hills. 2002. 304p. (YA). (gr. 7 up). bds. 5.99 (*0-7636-1704-0*) Candlewick Pr.

—Gwen's Story. 2002. 304p. (YA). (gr. 7 up). bds. 5.99 (*0-7636-1705-9*) Candlewick Pr.

—Julia's Story. 2002. 304p. (YA). (gr. 7 up). bds. 5.99 (*0-7636-1706-7*) Candlewick Pr.

Hartfield, Claire. Me & Uncle Romie: A Story Inspired by the Life & Art of Romare Bearden. 2002. (Illus.). 40p. (J). 16.99 (*0-8037-2520-5*, Dial Bks. for Young Readers) Penguin Putnam Bks. for Young Readers.

Hassler, Jon. Jemmy. 1980. 180p. (J). (gr. 7 up). 10.95 o.s.i (*0-689-50130-7*, McElderry, Margaret K.) Simon & Schuster Children's Publishing.

Havill, Juanita. Sato & the Elephants. 1993. (Illus.). (J). (ps-3). 15.00 o.p. (*0-688-11155-6*); 32p. lib. bdg. 14.93 (*0-688-11156-4*) HarperCollins Children's Bk. Group.

Hayes, Daniel. Eye of the Beholder. 1998. 192p. (gr. 7-12). mass mkt. 6.99 (*0-449-00235-7*, Fawcett) Ballantine Bks.

—Eye of the Beholder. 1992. (Illus.). 192p. (J). (gr. 6 up). 14.95 o.p. (*0-87923-881-X*) Godine, David R. Pub.

—Eye of the Beholder. 1994. (YA). pap. 3.99 (*0-380-72285-2*, Avon Bks.) Morrow/Avon.

—Eye of the Beholder. 1998. 12.04 (*0-606-06365-X*) Turtleback Bks.

Heller, Nicholas. The Giant. 1997. (Illus.). 24p. (J). (gr. k-3). 15.00 o.s.i (*0-688-15224-4*); lib. bdg. 14.93 o.p. (*0-688-15225-2*) HarperCollins Children's Bk. Group. (Greenwillow Bks.).

Henkes, Kevin. The Birthday Room. 2001. 160p. (YA). (gr. 5-9). pap. 4.99 (*0-14-131093-6*, Puffin Bks.) Penguin Putnam Bks. for Young Readers.

Hest, Amy. Nana's Birthday Party. 1993. (Illus.). 32p. (J). (ps-3). 15.95 (*0-688-07497-9*) HarperCollins Children's Bk. Group.

—Nana's Birthday Party. 1993. (Illus.). 32p. (J). (gr. k up). lib. bdg. 14.93 o.p. (*0-688-07498-7*, Morrow, William & Co.) Morrow/Avon.

Hissey, Jane. Old Bear's Surprise Painting. 2001. (Illus.). 40p. (J). 15.99 o.s.i (*0-399-23709-7*, Philomel) Penguin Putnam Bks. for Young Readers.

Holmes, Barbara Ware. Following Fake Man. 2001. (Illus.). 240p. (gr. 5-9). text 15.95 (*0-375-81266-0*); lib. bdg. 17.99 (*0-375-91266-5*) Random Hse. Children's Bks. (Knopf Bks. for Young Readers).

Howker, Janni. The Topiary Garden. 1995. (Illus.). 64p. (YA). (gr. 2 up). mass mkt. 14.95 o.p. (*0-531-06891-9*, Orchard Bks.) Scholastic, Inc.

Hurd, Thacher. Art Dog. 1996. (Illus.). 32p. (J). (ps-3). 14.95 (*0-06-024424-0*); lib. bdg. 15.89 (*0-06-024425-9*) HarperCollins Children's Bk. Group.

Isom, Joan Shaddox. The First Starry Night. 1998. (Illus.). 32p. (J). (gr. k-7). 16.95 (*1-879085-96-8*, Whispering Coyote) Charlesbridge Publishing, Inc.

Jackson, Shelley. Sophia: The Alchemists Dog. 2002. (Illus.). 48p. (J). (gr. k-3). 17.95 (*0-689-84279-1*, Atheneum/Richard Jackson Bks.) Simon & Schuster Children's Publishing.

—Sophia, the Alchemist's Dog. 2000. (Illus.). (J). (*0-7894-2639-0*) Dorling Kindersley Publishing, Inc.

Jagtenberg, Yvonne. Jack's Rabbit. 2003. (Illus.). 32p. (ps-1). 15.95 (*0-7613-1844-5*); lib. bdg. 22.90 (*0-7613-2916-1*) Millbrook Pr., Inc. (Roaring Brook Pr.).

Jeffers, Susan. If I Had a Pony. (J). 2003. 15.99 (*0-7868-1995-2*); 2002. lib. bdg. (*0-7868-2673-8*) Hyperion Bks. for Children.

Johnson-Feelings, Dianne. The Painter Man. 1993. (Illus.). (J). 14.95 o.p. (*0-89334-220-3*) Humanics Publishing Group.

Karas, G. Brian. The Class Artist. 2001. (Illus.). 32p. (J). 15.95 (*0-688-17814-6*); 15.89 (*0-688-17815-4*) HarperCollins Children's Bk. Group. (Greenwillow Bks.).

Kingman, Lee. The Refiner's Fire, 001. 1981. (J). (gr. 7 up). 8.95 o.p. (*0-395-31606-5*) Houghton Mifflin Co.

Kinkade, Thomas. Girls of Lighthouse Lane. 2004. (Girls of Lighthouse Lane Ser.). (J). No. 1. 176p. 12.99 (*0-06-054341-8*); No. 1. 176p. lib. bdg. 13.89 (*0-06-054342-6*); No. 2. (*0-06-054344-2*); No. 2. lib. bdg. (*0-06-054345-0*) HarperCollins Pubs.

Knight, Joan. Charlotte Goes to Paris. 2003. (Illus.). 52p. (J). 16.95 (*0-8118-3766-1*) Chronicle Bks. LLC.

Knight, Joan MacPhail. Charlotte in Giverny. Rock, Victoria, ed. 2000. (Illus.). 64p. (J). (gr. 4-7). 15.95 (*0-8118-2383-0*) Chronicle Bks. LLC.

Koja, Kathe. The Blue Mirror, RS. 2004. (YA). 16.00 (*0-374-30849-7*, Farrar, Straus & Giroux (BYR)) Farrar, Straus & Giroux.

—Buddha Boy, RS. 2003. 128p. (YA). (gr. 7 up). 16.00 o.s.i (*0-374-30998-1*, Farrar, Straus & Giroux (BYR)) Farrar, Straus & Giroux.

—Buddha Boy. l.t. ed. 2003. 113p. (J). 24.95 (*0-7862-6012-2*) Gale Group.

Laden, Nina. When Pigasso Met Mootisse. 1998. (Illus.). 40p. (J). (ps-5). 16.95 (*0-8118-1121-2*) Chronicle Bks. LLC.

Laird, Elizabeth. Karen & the Artist. 1999. 144p. (J). pap. text 7.00 (*0-582-37174-0*) Addison-Wesley Longman, Inc.

Lakin, Pat. Subway Sonata. 2001. (Illus.). 32p. (J). (gr. k-4). 22.90 (*0-7613-1464-4*) Millbrook Pr., Inc.

Lamm, C. Drew. Bittersweet. 2003. 224p. (YA). (gr. 7 up). tchr. ed. 15.00 (*0-618-16443-X*, Clarion Bks.) Houghton Mifflin Co. Trade & Reference Div.

Lantz, Francess L. Fade Far Away. 176p. (YA). (gr. 7-12). 1999. mass mkt. 6.99 (*0-380-79372-5*); 1998. 14.00 o.p. (*0-380-97553-X*) Morrow/Avon. (Avon Bks.).

—Fade Far Away. 1999. 13.04 (*0-606-16361-1*) Turtleback Bks.

Lester, Julius. When Dad Killed Mom. (YA). 2003. 216p. pap. 6.95 (*0-15-204698-4*); 2003. (gr. 7-12). mass mkt. 6.95 (*0-15-524698-4*); 2001. (Illus.). 192p. (gr. 7-12). 17.00 (*0-15-216305-0*) Harcourt Children's Bks. (Silver Whistle).

Lewis, Beverly. Pickle Pizza. 1996. (Cul-de-Sac Kids Ser.: Vol. 8). 80p. (J). (gr. 2-5). pap. 3.99 (*1-55661-728-3*) Bethany Hse. Pubs.

Lisle, Janet Taylor. The Art of Keeping Cool. (Illus.). (J). (gr. 5-9). 2002. 256p. pap. 4.99 (*0-689-83788-7*, Aladdin); 2000. 216p. 17.00 (*0-689-83787-9*, Atheneum/Richard Jackson Bks.) Simon & Schuster Children's Publishing.

Lithgow, John. Micawber. 2003. mass mkt. 17.95 (*0-689-83542-6*, Aladdin) Simon & Schuster Children's Publishing.

—Micawber's Museum of Art. 2002. (Illus.). 44p. (J). (gr. k-3). 17.95 (*0-689-83341-5*, Simon & Schuster Children's Publishing) Simon & Schuster Children's Publishing.

Littlesugar, Amy. Jonkonnu: A Story from the Sketchbook of Winslow Homer. 1997. (Illus.). 32p. (J). (ps-3). 15.95 o.s.i (*0-399-22831-4*, Philomel) Penguin Putnam Bks. for Young Readers.

—A Portrait of Spotted Deer's Grandfather. 1997. (Illus.). 32p. (J). (gr. 2-6). lib. bdg. 15.95 (*0-8075-6622-5*) Whitman, Albert & Co.

Littlesugar, Amy & Garrison, Barbara. Josiah True & the Art Maker. 1995. (J). 15.00 o.s.i (*0-671-88354-2*, Simon & Schuster Children's Publishing) Simon & Schuster Children's Publishing.

Locker, Thomas. In Blue Mountains: An Artist's Return to America's First Wilderness. 2000. (Illus.). 32p. (J). (ps-3). 18.00 (*0-88010-471-6*, Bell Pond Bks.) SteinerBooks, Inc.

—Miranda's Smile. (J). 2000. (Illus.). pap. 4.99 (*0-14-055669-9*, Puffin Bks.); 1994. 32p. 15.99 o.s.i (*0-8037-1688-5*, Dial Bks. for Young Readers); 1994. 32p. 15.89 o.s.i (*0-8037-1689-3*, Dial Bks. for Young Readers) Penguin Putnam Bks. for Young Readers.

—The Young Artist. 1993. (Illus.). 32p. (J). pap. 4.99 o.s.i (*0-14-054923-4*, Puffin Bks.) Penguin Putnam Bks. for Young Readers.

Lowry, Lois. Gathering Blue. 2000. (Illus.). 224p. (YA). (gr. 7 up). tchr. ed. 15.00 (*0-618-05581-9*, Mariner Bks.) Houghton Mifflin Co. Trade & Reference Div.

—Gathering Blue. unabr. ed. 2000. (J). (gr. 4-7). audio 25.00 (*0-8072-6150-5*, Listening Library) Random Hse. Audio Publishing Group.

—Gathering Blue. 2002. 240p. (YA). (gr. 7-7). pap. 6.50 (*0-440-22949-9*) Random Hse., Inc.

—Gathering Blue. l.t. ed. 2000. (Young Adult Ser.). 256p. (J). (gr. 8-12). 22.95 (*0-7862-3048-7*) Thorndike Pr.

Luna, Rachel Nickerson. Darinka, the Little Artist Deer. 1999. (Illus.). 36p. (J). (gr. 3-4). 12.95 (*1-886551-06-5*) Howard, Emma Bks.

Lyons, Mary E. The Poison Palace. 1997. (Illus.). 160p. (J). (gr. 7 up). 16.00 (*0-689-81146-2*, Atheneum) Simon & Schuster Children's Publishing.

Mack, Tracy. Drawing Lessons. (Illus.). 176p. 2002. (YA). (gr. 5-9). mass mkt. 4.99 (*0-439-11203-6*, Scholastic Paperbacks); 2000. (J). (gr. 7-12). pap. 15.95 (*0-439-11202-8*, Scholastic Reference) Scholastic, Inc.

Mackett, Dandi. Portrait of Lies. 2000. (Todays-Girls.com Ser.: Vol. 2). (Illus.). 144p. (J). (gr. 5-9). pap. 5.99 o.s.i (*0-8499-7561-1*) Nelson, Tommy.

MacLachlan, Patricia. Summer. 2003. (Illus.). 40p. (J). (ps-3). lib. bdg. 16.89 (*0-06-029799-9*, Cotler, Joanna Bks.) HarperCollins Children's Bk. Group.

MacLachlan, Patricia & MacLachlan, Emily. Painting the Wind. 2003. (Illus.). 40p. (J). (ps-3). 15.99 (*0-06-029798-0*, Cotler, Joanna Bks.) HarperCollins Children's Bk. Group.

Magnier, Thierry. Isabelle & the Angel. 2000. (Illus.). 40p. (J). 14.95 (*0-8118-2526-4*) Chronicle Bks. LLC.

Mariconda, Barbara. Turn the Cup Around. 1997. 160p. (J). (gr. 3-7). text 15.95 o.s.i (*0-385-32292-5*, Delacorte Pr.) Dell Publishing.

—Turn the Cup Around. 1998. 10.04 (*0-606-13878-1*) Turtleback Bks.

Maynard, Bill. Incredible Ned. 1997. (Illus.). 40p. (J). (ps-3). 15.95 o.s.i (*0-399-23023-8*, G. P. Putnam's Sons) Penguin Group (USA) Inc.

McClintock, Barbara. The Fantastic Drawings of Danielle. (Illus.). 32p. (J). (ps-3). 2004. pap. 5.95 (*0-618-43230-2*); 1996. tchr. ed. 17.00 o.p. (*0-395-73980-2*) Houghton Mifflin Co.

McCully, Emily Arnold. Speak up, Blanche! 1991. (Illus.). 32p. (J). (gr. k-3). 15.00 (*0-06-024227-2*); lib. bdg. 14.89 (*0-06-024228-0*) HarperCollins Children's Bk. Group.

McKay, Hilary. Saffy's Angel. 2002. 160p. (J). (gr. 4-7). 16.00 (*0-689-84933-8*, McElderry, Margaret K.) Simon & Schuster Children's Publishing.

McPhail, David M. Drawing Lessons from a Bear. 2000. (Illus.). 32p. (J). (ps-3). 14.95 (*0-316-56345-5*) Little Brown & Co.

—Drawing Lessons from a Bear. E-Book (*1-58824-639-6*); E-Book (*1-58824-876-3*); E-Book (*1-58824-638-8*) ipicturebooks, LLC.

Merberg, Julie & Bober, Suzanne. In the Garden with Van Gogh. 2002. (Illus.). 22p. (J). (ps). 6.95 (*0-8118-3415-8*) Chronicle Bks. LLC.

—A Magical Day with Matisse. 2002. (Illus.). 22p. (J). (ps). bds. 6.95 (*0-8118-3414-X*) Chronicle Bks. LLC.

—Vinnie's Giant Roller Coaster Period Chart & Journal Sticker Book. 2002. (Illus.). 96p. (J). 15.95 (*0-8118-3440-9*) Chronicle Bks. LLC.

Miller, Mary J. Going the Distance. 1994. 160p. (J). 14.99 o.p. (*0-670-84815-8*) Penguin Putnam Bks. for Young Readers.

Molarsky, Osmond. A Sky Full of Kites. 1996. (Illus.). 32p. (J). (gr. k-2). 12.95 (*1-883672-26-0*) Tricycle Pr.

Moss, Marissa. Amelia Works It Out. 2000. (Amelia Ser.). (Illus.). 40p. (J). (gr. 3 up). 12.95 (*1-58485-081-7*); pap. 5.95 (*1-58485-080-9*) Pleasant Co. Pubns. (American Girl).

—Amelia Works It Out. 2000. (Amelia - American Girl Ser.). (J). 12.10 (*0-606-20544-6*) Turtleback Bks.

Nicholson, Nicholas B. & von Buhler, Cynthia. Little Girl in a Red Dress with Cat & Dog. 1998. 32p. (J). (gr. 1-4). 15.99 o.s.i (*0-670-87183-4*) Penguin Putnam Bks. for Young Readers.

Nixon, Joan Lowery. Who Are You? 2001. (Illus.). 192p. (YA). (gr. 7 up). mass mkt. 4.99 (*0-440-22757-7*, Delta) Dell Publishing.

—Who Are You? 2001. (YA). 11.04 (*0-606-21525-5*) Turtleback Bks.

Nolan, Han. Send Me down a Miracle. 1996. 256p. (YA). (gr. 7-12). pap. 6.00 o.s.i (*0-15-200978-7*, Harcourt Paperbacks) Harcourt Children's Bks.

—Send Me down a Miracle. 1996. 256p. (YA). (gr. 7 up). 13.00 o.s.i (*0-15-200979-5*) Harcourt Trade Pubs.

—Send Me Down a Miracle. 2003. 276p. (YA). pap. 6.95 (*0-15-204680-1*) Harcourt Children's Bks.

Nunes, Lygia Bojunga. My Friend the Painter. Pontiero, Giovanni, tr. from POR. 1991. 96p. (J). (gr. 3-7). 13.95 (*0-15-256340-7*) Harcourt Trade Pubs.

Pedersen, Janet. Millie in the Meadow. 2003. (Illus.). 32p. (J). 14.99 (*0-7636-1725-3*) Candlewick Pr.

Pilegard, Virginia Walton. The Warlord's Fish. 2002. (Illus.). 32p. (J). 14.95 (*1-56554-964-3*) Pelican Publishing Co., Inc.

Porte, Barbara Ann. Chickens! Chickens! 1995. (Illus.). 32p. (J). (ps-3). pap. 14.95 (*0-531-06877-3*, Orchard Bks.) Scholastic, Inc.

Pullman, Philip. The Broken Bridge. (gr. 7 up). 1994. (Illus.). 224p. mass mkt. 5.50 (*0-679-84715-4*, Random Hse. Bks. for Young Readers); 1992. 256p. (YA). 15.99 o.s.i (*0-679-91972-4*, Knopf Bks. for Young Readers) Random Hse. Children's Bks.

—The Broken Bridge. 2002. (YA). 20.25 (*0-8446-7229-7*) Smith, Peter Pub., Inc.

—The Broken Bridge. 1994. 11.04 (*0-606-06945-3*) Turtleback Bks.

Reeves, James. Mr. Horrox & the Gratch. 1991. (Illus.). 32p. (J). (gr. 1-6). 13.95 (*0-922984-08-5*) Wellington Publishing, Inc.

Rex, Michael. The Painting Gorilla. 1997. (Illus.). 32p. (J). (ps-2). 15.95 o.s.i (*0-8050-5020-5*, Holt, Henry & Co. Bks. For Young Readers) Holt, Henry & Co.

Ross, Tom. Eggbert, the Slightly Cracked Egg. 1994. (Illus.). 32p. (J). (ps-3). 16.99 o.p. (*0-399-22416-5*, G. P. Putnam's Sons) Penguin Group (USA) Inc.

Rylant, Cynthia. The Dreamer. 1993. (Illus.). 32p. (J). (ps-6). pap. 15.95 o.p. (*0-590-47341-7*, Blue Sky Pr., The) Scholastic, Inc.

Say, Allen. The Ink-Keeper's Apprentice. 1994. (Illus.). 160p. (YA). (gr. 7-7). tchr. ed. 13.95 (*0-395-70562-2*) Houghton Mifflin Co.

—The Sign Painter. 2000. (Illus.). 32p. (J). (ps-3). tchr. ed. 17.00 (*0-395-97974-9*, Lorraine, A. Walter) Houghton Mifflin Co. Trade & Reference Div.

Schmidt, Bernd. Our Friend the Sculptor. Young, Richard G., ed. 1989. (Illus.). 24p. (J). (gr. 1-3). lib. bdg. 14.60 o.p. (*0-944483-50-X*) Garrett Educational Corp.

Schreier, Joshua. Hank's Work. 1993. 320p. (J). (ps-2). 13.50 o.p. (*0-525-44970-1*, Dutton Children's Bks.) Penguin Putnam Bks. for Young Readers.

Seidler, Tor. Brothers below Zero. (Illus.). 144p. (J). 2003. (gr. 5 up). pap. 5.99 (*0-06-440936-8*, Harper Trophy); 2002. (gr. 3 up). 14.95 (*0-06-029179-6*, Geringer, Laura Bk.); 2002. (gr. 5 up). lib. bdg. 14.89 (*0-06-029180-X*, Geringer, Laura Bk.) HarperCollins Children's Bk. Group.

—A Rat's Tale, RS. 1990. 187p. pap. 6.95 o.p. (*0-374-46204-6*, Sunburst) Farrar, Straus & Giroux.

—A Rat's Tale. 1999. (Illus.). 192p. (J). (gr. 5 up). pap. 6.95 (*0-06-440779-9*, Harper Trophy) HarperCollins Children's Bk. Group.

Shafer, Anders C. The Fantastic Journey of Pieter Bruegel. 2002. (Illus.). 40p. (J). (gr. 3-6). 18.99 (*0-525-46986-9*, Dutton Children's Bks.) Penguin Putnam Bks. for Young Readers.

Shannon, Monica. Dobry. 1993. (Newbery Library). (Illus.). 192p. (J). (gr. 5 up). pap. 4.99 o.s.i (*0-14-036334-3*, Puffin Bks.) Penguin Putnam Bks. for Young Readers.

Slate, Joseph. Crossing the Trestle. 1999. (Accelerated Reader Bks.). 144p. (J). (gr. 3-7). 14.95 (*0-7614-5053-X*, Cavendish Children's Bks.) Cavendish, Marshall Corp.

Stadler, John. What's So Scary? 2000. (Illus.). (J). lib. bdg. 16.95 (*0-531-33301-9*); 32p. pap. 16.95 (*0-531-30301-2*) Scholastic, Inc. (Orchard Bks.).

Stahl, Hilda. Hannah & the Daring Escape. 1993. (Best Friends Ser.: Vol. 12). 160p. (J). (gr. 4-7). pap. 4.99 o.p. (*0-89107-714-6*) Crossway Bks.

Stewart, Celeste. Merry Berry. Weinberger, Jane & Black, Albert, eds. 1990. (Illus.). 88p. (J). (gr. 4-8). pap. 3.95 o.p. (*0-932433-53-7*) Windswept Hse. Pubs.

Stock, Catherine. Gugu's House. 2001. (Illus.). 32p. (J). (ps-3). lib. bdg., tchr. ed. 14.00 (*0-618-00389-4*, Clarion Bks.) Houghton Mifflin Co. Trade & Reference Div.

Strigenz, Geri K., illus. For Bread. 1992. (History's Children Ser.). 48p. (J). (gr. 4-5). pap. o.p. (*0-8114-6426-1*); lib. bdg. 21.36 o.p. (*0-8114-3501-6*) Raintree Pubs.

Sweeney, Joan. Bijou, Bonbon, & Beau: The Kittens Who Danced for Degas. 1998. (Illus.). 26p. (J). (ps-1). 12.95 (*0-8118-1975-2*) Chronicle Bks. LLC.

—Suzette & the Puppy: A Story about Mary Cassatt. 2000. (Illus.). 28p. (J). (ps-3). pap. 14.95 (*0-7641-5294-7*) Barron's Educational Series, Inc.

Tada, Joni Eareckson. I'll Be with You Always. 1998. (Illus.). 32p. (J). (gr. 8-12). 14.99 (*1-58134-000-1*) Crossway Bks.

Trottier, Maxine. A Circle of Silver. 2000. (Circle of Silver Chronicles Ser.). 220p. (J). (gr. 7-12). pap. 7.95 (*0-7737-6055-5*) Stoddart Kids CAN. *Dist:* Fitzhenry & Whiteside, Ltd.

—The Paint Box. (Illus.). 32p. (J). (*1-55041-804-1*) Fitzhenry & Whiteside, Ltd.

Tunnell, Michael O. The Joke's on George. 2003. (Illus.). 32p. (J). (gr. 1-3). 9.95 (*1-56397-970-5*) Boyds Mills Pr.

—The Joke's on George. 1993. (Illus.). 32p. (J). (gr. k up). 14.00 o.p. (*0-688-11758-9*); lib. bdg. 13.93 o.p. (*0-688-11759-7*) Morrow/Avon. (Morrow, William & Co.).

—The Joke's on George. 1995. 4.99 (*5-551-24172-6*) World Pr., Ltd.

Turner, Ann Warren. Time of the Bison. 1987. (Illus.). 64p. (J). (gr. 2-6). 13.95 o.p. (*0-02-789300-6*, Simon & Schuster Children's Publishing) Simon & Schuster Children's Publishing.

Van Draanen, Wendelin. Sammy Keyes & the Art of Deception. 2003. 288p. (gr. 5). text 15.95 (*0-375-81176-1*); lib. bdg. 17.99 (*0-375-91176-6*) Random Hse. Children's Bks. (Knopf Bks. for Young Readers).

Varvasovsky, Lazlo. Henry in Shadowland. 1989. (Illus.). 32p. (J). (gr. 2-7). 17.95 (*0-87923-785-6*) Godine, David R. Pub.

Velthuijs, Max. Crocodile's Masterpiece. 2001. (Illus.). 32p. pap. 9.95 (*1-84270-002-2*) Andersen Pr., Ltd. GBR. *Dist:* Trafalgar Square.

—Crocodile's Masterpiece, RS. 1992. (Illus.). 32p. (J). (ps-3). 14.00 o.p. (*0-374-31658-9*, Farrar, Straus & Giroux (BYR)) Farrar, Straus & Giroux.

Waldman, Neil. The Starry Night. 2003. (Illus.). 32p. (J). (ps-3). 15.95 (*1-56397-736-2*) Boyds Mills Pr.

Wallace, Ian. The Naked Lady. 2002. (Illus.). 40p. (J). (gr. k-3). 16.95 (*0-7613-1596-9*); 23.90 (*0-7613-2660-X*) Millbrook Pr., Inc. (Roaring Brook Pr.).

Walter, Mildred Pitts. Suitcase. 1999. (Illus.). 112p. (J). (gr. 3 up). 15.99 (*0-688-16547-8*) HarperCollins Children's Bk. Group.

Wheatley, Nadia. Luke's Way of Looking. 2001. (Illus.). 36p. (J). (gr. k up). 15.95 (*1-929132-18-2*, Cranky Nell Bks.) Kane/Miller Bk. Pubs.

Williams, Carol Lynch. Anna's Gift. 1995. (Latter-Day Daughters Ser.: Vol. 1). 80p. (J). (gr. 2 up). pap. 4.95 (*1-56236-501-0*) Aspen Bks.

Wilson, Jacqueline. Girls in Tears. 2003. 176p. (J). lib. bdg. 11.99 (*0-385-90104-6*); (gr. 7). 9.95 (*0-385-73082-9*) Dell Publishing. (Delacorte Pr.).

—Girls in Tears. 2004. 192p. (YA). (gr. 7). mass mkt. 4.99 (*0-440-23807-2*, Laurel Leaf) Random Hse. Children's Bks.

—Girls Out Late. 2003. 224p. (YA). (gr. 7). mass mkt. 4.99 (*0-440-22959-6*, Laurel Leaf) Random Hse. Children's Bks.

—Girls Out Late. 2002. 224p. (YA). (gr. 7). 9.95 (*0-385-72976-6*); lib. bdg. 11.99 (*0-385-90042-2*) Random Hse., Inc.

—Girls Out Late. 2003. (Illus.). 192p. (YA). mass mkt. (*0-552-54523-6*) Transworld Publishers Ltd. GBR. *Dist:* Random Hse. of Canada, Ltd.

Winter, Jeanette. Josefina. 1996. (Illus.). 36p. (J). (ps-3). 16.00 (*0-15-201091-2*) Harcourt Children's Bks.

Wojciechowski, Susan. The Christmas Miracle of Jonathan Toomey. (Illus.). 40p. (J). 2002. (gr. 1-6). 12.99 (*0-7636-1930-2*); 1995. (ps-3). 18.99 (*1-56402-320-6*) Candlewick Pr.

—The Christmas Miracle of Jonathan Toomey. 1998. (Illus.). 40p. (J). (ps-3). 18.99 incl. cd-rom (*0-8499-5905-5*) Nelson, Tommy.

Wooding, Sharon. The Painter's Cat. 1994. (Illus.). 32p. (J). (ps-3). 14.95 o.p. (*0-399-22414-9*) Penguin Group (USA) Inc.

Ziefert, Harriet. Lunchtime for a Purple Snake. 2003. (Illus.). 32p. (J). (ps-3). tchr. ed. 15.00 (*0-618-31133-5*) Houghton Mifflin Co.

ASTRONAUTS—FICTION

Agee, Jon. Dmitri the Astronaut. 1996. (Michael di Capua Bks.). (Illus.). 32p. (J). (ps up). 14.95 o.s.i *(0-06-205074-5)*; lib. bdg. 14.89 o.p. *(0-06-205075-3)* HarperCollins Children's Bk. Group.

—Dmitri the Astronaut. 1998. (Trophy Picture Book Ser.). (Illus.). 32p. (J). (ps up). pap. 5.95 o.s.i *(0-06-205925-4)* HarperCollins Pubs.

—Dmitri the Astronaut. 1998. (Trophy Picture Bks.). (J). 11.15 o.p. *(0-606-12916-2)* Turtleback Bks.

Barnes, Joyce Annette. The Baby Grand, the Moon in July, & Me. 1998. 10.09 o.p. *(0-606-13157-4)* Turtleback Bks.

—The Baby Grand, the Moon in July & Me. 144p. (J). (gr. 3-7). 1998. (Illus.). pap. 4.99 o.s.i *(0-14-130061-2*, Puffin Bks.); 1994. 15.99 o.s.i *(0-8037-1586-2*, Dial Bks. for Young Readers); 1994. 14.89 o.p. *(0-8037-1600-1*, Dial Bks. for Young Readers) Penguin Putnam Bks. for Young Readers.

Barton, Byron. I Want to Be an Astronaut. (Trophy Picture Bk.). (Illus.). 32p. (J). (ps-1). 1992. pap. 6.95 *(0-06-443280-7*, Harper Trophy); 1988. lib. bdg. 16.89 *(0-690-04744-4)*; 1988. 14.00 o.s.i *(0-694-00261-5)* HarperCollins Children's Bk. Group.

Bartram, Simon. Man on the Moon: A Day in the Life of Bob. 2002. (Illus.). 32p. (J). (gr. k-3). 16.99 *(0-7636-1897-7)* Candlewick Pr.

Benjamin, Cynthia. I Am an Astronaut. 1996. (I Am a . . . Ser.). (Illus.). (J). (ps-k). 24p. 7.95 *(0-8120-6539-5)*; 11.95 o.p. *(0-8120-6939-0)* Barron's Educational Series, Inc.

Carbin, Eddie. Arty the Part-Time Astronaut. 2000. 36p. (J). (gr. 1-7). pap. 19.95 *(0-9675299-0-5)* 3 Pounds Pr.

Cress, Michelle H. Annie the Astronaut Meets Gussie the Green Man. l.t. ed. 1999. (LB Ser.). (Illus.). 8p. (J). (ps-1). pap. text 10.95 *(1-57332-153-2)*; pap. text 10.95 *(1-57332-152-4)* HighReach Learning, Inc.

Dickens, Frank. Albert Herbert Hawkins, the Naughtiest Boy in the World, & the Space Rocket. 1978. 5.95 o.p. *(0-385-13327-8)*; lib. bdg. o.p. *(0-385-14416-4)* Doubleday Publishing.

Eco, Umberto. The Three Astronauts. 1989. (Illus.). 40p. (J). (gr. 5-9). 15.00 *(0-15-286383-4)* Harcourt Children's Bks.

Ewers, Joe. I Want to Be an Astronaut: Sesame Street. 1999. (Golden's Sesame Street Ser.). (Illus.). (J). (ps-k). pap. 3.29 o.s.i *(0-307-12624-2*, Golden Bks.) Random Hse. Children's Bks.

Fox, Christyan & Fox, Diane. Astronaut PiggyWiggy. 2002. (Illus.). 24p. (J). (ps-k). 9.95 *(1-929766-41-6)* Handprint Bks.

Gaffney, Timothy R. Grandpa Takes Me to the Moon. 1996. (Illus.). 32p. (J). 16.00 *(0-688-13937-X)*; lib. bdg. 15.93 o.p. *(0-688-13938-8)* Morrow/Avon. (Morrow, William & Co.).

George, David L. Freddie Freightliner Goes to Kennedy Space Center. Murphy, Carol, ed. 1982. (Illus.). (J). (gr. k-6). pap. 6.50 o.p. *(0-89868-133-2)* ARO Publishing Co.

Hart, Anne. Four Astronauts & a Kitten. 2001. 144p. pap. 11.95 *(0-595-19202-5*, Authors Choice Pr.) iUniverse, Inc.

Johnson, Larry D. & Mills, Jane L. Arnie the Astronaut. 1986. (Building Set Ser.: Level 3). (Illus.). 22p. (Orig.). (J). (ps-1). pap. 12.00 *(0-938155-02-4)* Read-A-Bol Group, The.

Kahn, Sharon. Kacy & the Space Shuttle Secret: A Space Adventure for Young Readers. 1996. (Illus.). 128p. (J). (gr. 6-7). 16.95 *(1-57168-025-X)* Eakin Pr.

Kirk, Daniel. Moondogs. 1999. (Illus.). 32p. (J). (ps-3). 15.99 *(0-399-23128-5)* Penguin Group (USA) Inc.

Lovejoy, Pamela. If I Were an Astronaut. 1994. (Illus.). 14p. (Orig.). (J). (ps-2). pap. *(1-880038-18-8)* Learn-Abouts.

Moche, Dinah L. & Golden Books Staff. If You Were an Astronaut. 1985. (Golden Look-Look Bks.). (Illus.). 24p. (J). (ps-3). pap. 3.29 o.s.i *(0-307-11896-7*, 11896-02, Golden Bks.) Random Hse. Children's Bks.

Murphy, Elspeth Campbell. Pug McConnell. 1986. (Kids from Apple Street Church Ser.). 107p. (J). (gr. 3-7). 4.99 o.p. *(0-89191-728-4)* Cook Communications Ministries.

North, Rick. Young Astronauts. 1990. (J). No. 2. mass mkt. 2.95 o.s.i *(0-8217-3173-4)*; No. 3. mass mkt. 2.95 o.s.i *(0-8217-3178-5)* Kensington Publishing Corp. (Zebra Bks.).

Reiser, Lynn W. Earthdance. 1999. (Illus.). 40p. (J). (gr. k-3). 15.95 *(0-688-16326-2)*; 15.95 *(0-688-16326-2)*; lib. bdg. 15.89 *(0-688-16327-0)* HarperCollins Children's Bk. Group. (Greenwillow Bks.).

Rouss, Sylvia. Reach for the Stars. 2004. 40p. (J). (gr. 3-7). 16.95 *(1-930143-82-6)*; pap. 9.95 *(1-930143-83-4)* Pitspopany Pr.

Rubinger, Michael. I Know an Astronaut. 1972. (Community Helper Bks.). (Illus.). 48p. (J). (gr. 1-3). 4.29 o.p. *(0-399-60713-7)* Putnam Publishing Group, The.

Smith, A. G. Glenn the Astronaut. 1999. (Little Activity Bks.). (J). pap. 1.00 *(0-486-40517-6)* Dover Pubns., Inc.

St. Pierre, Stephanie & Walz, Richard. Slimey to the Moon: Book & Finger Puppet. 1999. (Illus.). (J). (ps). 7.99 o.s.i *(0-679-89406-3*, Random Hse. Bks. for Young Readers) Random Hse. Children's Bks.

Standiford, Natalie. Astronauts Are Sleeping. 1996. (Illus.). (J). (ps-3). 2.99 o.s.i *(0-679-86999-9*, Knopf Bks. for Young Readers) Random Hse. Children's Bks.

Walters, Hugh. The Blue Aura. 1979. 128p. (J). (gr. 5-8). o.p. *(0-571-11423-7)* Faber & Faber Ltd.

AUTHORS—FICTION

Baker, Barbara. Anna's Book. 2004. (Illus.). 24p. (J). 8.99 *(0-525-47231-2*, Dutton Children's Bks.) Penguin Putnam Bks. for Young Readers.

Bedard, Michael. Glasstown. 1997. (Illus.). 40p. (J). (gr. 1-4). 16.00 *(0-689-81185-3*, Atheneum) Simon & Schuster Children's Publishing.

Blume, Judy. Places I Never Meant to Be: Original Stories by Censored Writers. 2001. (Illus.). (J). 16.05 *(0-606-20855-0)* Turtleback Bks.

Brown, Marc. Arthur Writes a Story. 2002. (Illus.). (J). 13.15 *(0-7587-1974-4)* Book Wholesalers, Inc.

—Arthur Writes a Story. ed. 2000. (J). (gr. 1). spiral bd. *(0-616-01604-2)*; (gr. 2). spiral bd. *(0-616-01605-0)* Canadian National Institute for the Blind/Institut National Canadien pour les Aveugles.

—Arthur Writes a Story. 2003. (Illus.). 14.95 *(1-59319-021-2)* LeapFrog Enterprises, Inc.

—Arthur Writes a Story. 1998. (Arthur Adventure Ser.). (J). (gr. k-3). pap. 5.95 o.s.i *(0-316-11973-3)* Little Brown Children's Bks.

Bunin, Sherry. Dear Great American Writers School. 1995. 176p. (YA). (gr. 7 up). tchr. ed. 15.00 *(0-395-71645-4)* Houghton Mifflin Co.

—Dear Great American Writers School. 1997. (J). 10.55 *(0-606-11245-6)* Turtleback Bks.

Christian, Mary Blount. Sebastian (Super Sleuth) & the Copycat Crime. 1993. (Sebastian Super Sleuth Ser.). (Illus.). 64p. (J). (gr. 2-6). lib. bdg. 13.00 *(0-02-718211-8*, Simon & Schuster Children's Publishing) Simon & Schuster Children's Publishing.

Christie, Amanda. Seventh Heaven: Nobody's Perfect. 1998. (7th Heaven Ser.). 126p. (J). (gr. 3-7). pap. 3.99 o.s.i *(0-679-89123-4)* Random Hse., Inc.

Clarke, J. Riffraff, ERS. 1992. 112p. (YA). (gr. 9-12). 14.95 o.p. *(0-8050-1774-7*, Holt, Henry & Co. Bks. For Young Readers) Holt, Henry & Co.

Clements, Andrew. The School Story Proprietary. 2002. (Illus.). 208p. (J). 4.99 *(0-689-85595-8*, Aladdin) Simon & Schuster Children's Publishing.

Coleman, Jane Candia. The Italian Quartet. 2001. (Five Star First Edition Women's Fiction Ser.). 197p. 25.95 *(0-7862-3379-6*, Five Star) Gale Group.

Dana, Barbara. Emily Dickinson: Fictionalized Biography. Date not set. (J). (gr. 3-7). 14.99 *(0-06-028704-7)*; lib. bdg. 15.89 *(0-06-028705-5)*; mass mkt. 4.99 *(0-06-440843-4)* HarperCollins Pubs.

Dawes, Claiborne. A Different Drummer: Thoreau & Will's Independence Day. 1998. (Illus.). 32p. (J). (gr. 2-5). pap. 7.95 *(1-57960-039-5)* Discovery Enterprises, Ltd.

Dufresne, John. Love Warps the Mind a Little. l.t. ed. 1997. (G. K. Hall Core Ser.). 553p. 26.95 *(0-7838-8127-4*, Macmillan Reference USA) Gale Group.

Edelman, Maurice. Disraeli Rising. 1984. 282p. pap. 3.95 o.p. *(0-8128-8058-7*, Scarborough Hse.) Madison Bks., Inc.

Garcia-Clairac, Santiago. El Libro Invisible (The Invisible Book) 10th ed. 2001. (SPA., Illus.). 140p. (J). (gr. 4-6). *(84-348-6556-4)* SM Ediciones.

Greenaway, Theresa, et al. The Absent Author. 1997. (Illus.). 96p. lib. bdg. 11.99 *(0-679-98168-3*, Knopf Bks. for Young Readers) Random Hse. Children's Bks.

Greenwald, Sheila. Write on, Rosy! A Young Author in Crisis. 1988. (Illus.). 128p. (J). (gr. 3-6). 13.95 o.p. *(0-316-32705-0*, Joy Street Bks.) Little Brown & Co.

Hershenhorn, Esther. The Confession$ & $ecret$ of Howard J. Fingerhut. 2002. (Illus.). 192p. (J). (gr. 3-7). tchr. ed. 16.95 *(0-8234-1642-9)* Holiday Hse., Inc.

Hest, Amy. Nana's Birthday Party. 1993. (Illus.). 32p. (J). (ps-3). 15.95 *(0-688-07497-9)* HarperCollins Children's Bk. Group.

—Nana's Birthday Party. 1993. (Illus.). 32p. (J). (gr. k up). lib. bdg. 14.93 o.p. *(0-688-07498-7*, Morrow, William & Co.) Morrow/Avon.

Jarrard, Kyle. Over There. unabr. ed. 1997. 283p. 21.00 *(1-880909-53-7)* Baskerville Pubs., Inc.

Manuel, Lynn. Lucy Maud & the Cavendish Cat. 1998. (Illus.). 32p. (J). (gr. 1-4). 15.95 *(0-88776-397-9)* Tundra Bks. of Northern New York.

McAlpine, Gordon. Mystery Box. 2003. 194p. (YA). 16.95 *(0-8126-2680-X)* Cricket Bks.

Nixon, Joan Lowery. The Name of the Game Was Murder. 192p. 1994. (YA). (gr. 7 up). mass mkt. 4.99 *(0-440-21916-7)*; 1993. (J). 15.00 o.s.i *(0-385-30864-7*, Delacorte Pr.) Dell Publishing.

Picano, Felice. A House on the Ocean, a House on the Bay. 2003. 270p. 17.95 *(1-56023-440-7*, Southern Tier Editions) Haworth Pr., Inc., The.

Pinkwater, Daniel M. Author's Day. (J). (gr. k-3). 1997. 3.99 *(0-689-81705-3*, Aladdin); 1993. (Illus.). 32p. lib. bdg. 14.00 *(0-02-774642-9*, Atheneum) Simon & Schuster Children's Publishing.

—Author's Day. 1997. 10.14 *(0-606-13156-6)* Turtleback Bks.

Roy, Ron, et al. A the Absent Author. 1997. (A to Z Mysteries Ser.: No. 1). (Illus.). 96p. (J). (gr. k-3). pap. 3.99 *(0-679-88168-9)* Random Hse. Children's Bks.

Sargent, Dave & Sargent, Pat. Charcoal (Charcoal Grey) Be Decisive #13. 2001. (Saddle Up Ser.). 36p. (J). pap. 6.95 *(1-56763-606-3)*; lib. bdg. 22.60 *(1-56763-605-5)* Ozark Publishing.

Sortland, Bjorn. The Story of the Search for the Story. 2000. (Picture Bks.). (Illus.). 40p. (J). (ps-3). lib. bdg. 15.95 *(1-57505-375-6*, Carolrhoda Bks.) Lerner Publishing Group.

Stefansson, Thorsteinn. The Golden Future. 1977. (J). (gr. 6-12). 6.95 o.p. *(0-8407-6520-7*, Dutton Children's Bks.) Penguin Putnam Bks. for Young Readers.

Van Raven, Pieter. The Great Man's Secret. 1989. 176p. (YA). (gr. 7 up). text 13.95 o.s.i *(0-684-19041-9*, Atheneum) Simon & Schuster Children's Publishing.

Whelan, Gloria. The Pathless Woods: Ernest Hemingway's Sixteenth Summer in Northern Michigan. 2nd rev. ed. 1998. (Illus.). (J). (gr. 6-10). 16.95 *(1-882376-63-3)*; 176p. (gr. 7-12). pap. 11.95 *(1-882376-44-7)* Thunder Bay Pr.

Wilkinson, Jack. Sunset over Craigie House: A Dramatized Novel about Henry W. Longfellow. 168p. 1985. (J). (gr. 5 up). 19.95 o.s.i *(0-931494-80-X)*; 1985. (J). (gr. 5 up). pap. 9.95 o.s.i *(0-931494-79-6)*; 2nd ed. 1986. (YA). (gr. 6 up). 19.95 o.p. *(0-931494-97-4)*; 2nd ed. 1986. (YA). (gr. 6 up). pap. 9.95 o.p. *(0-931494-96-6)* Brunswick Publishing Corp.

Williams, Barbara. Author & Squinty Gritt. 1990. 80p. (J). (gr. 2-5). 12.95 o.p. *(0-525-44655-9*, Dutton Children's Bks.) Penguin Putnam Bks. for Young Readers.

Woodhead, Richard. The Strange Case of R. L. Stevenson. 2002. 224p. pap. 26.95 *(0-946487-86-3)* Luath Pr. Ltd. GBR. *Dist:* Midpoint Trade Bks., Inc.

AUTOMOBILE DRIVERS—FICTION

Appleton, Victor. Tom Swift & His Electric Runabout. unabr. ed. 1992. (Tom Swift Original Ser.: No. 5). (J). (gr. 3-7). audio 26.95 *(1-55686-403-5*, 403) Books in Motion.

—Tom Swift & His Electric Runabout. (Tom Swift Original Ser.: No. 5). (J). (gr. 3-7). E-Book 1.95 *(1-57799-858-8)* Logos Research Systems, Inc.

—Tom Swift & His Electric Runabout. 1999. (Tom Swift Original Ser.: Vol. No. 5). (J). (gr. 3-7). E-Book 3.99 o.p. incl. cd-rom *(1-57646-025-8)* Quiet Vision Publishing.

Bauer, Joan. Rules of the Road. 1998. 208p. (YA). (gr. 7-12). 16.99 *(0-399-23140-4)* Penguin Group (USA) Inc.

—Rules of the Road. 2000. (Chapters Ser.). (Illus.). 208p. (YA). (gr. 7 up). reprint ed. pap. 6.99 *(0-698-11828-6*, Puffin Bks.) Penguin Putnam Bks. for Young Readers.

—Rules of the Road. 2000. 11.04 *(0-606-20370-2)*; (YA). 11.04 *(0-606-20252-8)* Turtleback Bks.

Buller, Jon & Schade, Susan. Toad on the Road. 2003. (Step into Reading Step 1 Bks.). (Illus.). 32p. (J). (ps-1). lib. bdg. 11.99 *(0-679-92689-5*, Random Hse. Bks. for Young Readers); 3.99 *(0-679-82689-0*, Golden Bks.) Random Hse. Children's Bks.

Burton, Terry, illus. Tiger's New Car. 1997. (My Big Little Fat Bks.). 20p. (J). (ps). bds. 3.49 *(1-85854-599-4)* Brimax Bks., Ltd.

Cooney, Caroline B. Driver's Ed. 1996. 208p. (YA). (gr. 7 up). mass mkt. 5.50 *(0-440-21981-7)* Dell Publishing.

—Driver's Ed. 1995. (J). 20.95 *(0-385-30974-0)* Doubleday Publishing.

—Driver's Ed. 2004. 192p. (YA). lib. bdg. 17.99 *(0-385-90236-0*, Delacorte Bks. for Young Readers); 1995. (J). mass mkt. 5.99 *(0-440-91078-1*, Dell Books for Young Readers); 1994. 192p. (YA). (gr. 7 up). 16.95 *(0-385-32087-6*, Delacorte Bks. for Young Readers) Random Hse. Children's Bks.

—Driver's Ed. 1996. (J). 11.55 *(0-606-08731-1)* Turtleback Bks.

Coy, John. Night Driving, ERS. (Illus.). 32p. (ps-3). 2001. pap. 6.95 *(0-8050-6708-6)*; 1996. (J). 14.95 *(0-8050-2931-1)* Holt, Henry & Co. (Holt, Henry & Co. Bks. For Young Readers).

Crowther, Terence G. The Very Dangerous Driver, Level 1. 1997. (Illus.). 30p. pap. text 3.95 *(0-19-434956-X)* Oxford Univ. Pr., Inc.

Curtis, Matt. Elliot Drives Away. 1996. (Rookie Readers Ser.). (J). pap. 3.50 o.p. *(0-516-26034-0*, Children's Pr.) Scholastic Library Publishing.

Douglas, James M. Hunger for Racing. 1967. (Putnam Sports Shelf Ser.). (Illus.). (J). (gr. 7-10). 4.97 o.p. *(0-399-60271-2)* Putnam Publishing Group, The.

Felsen, Henry G. Hot Rod. 1950. (J). (gr. 5 up). 8.50 o.p. *(0-525-32245-0*, 0826-240, Dutton) Dutton/Plume.

Fienberg, Anna. Minton Goes Driving. 2001. (Minton Ser.). (Illus.). 32p. (J). (ps-1). pap. 6.95 *(1-86448-594-9)* Allen & Unwin Pty., Ltd. AUS. *Dist:* Independent Pubs. Group.

Gackenbach, Dick. Binky Gets a Car. 1983. (Illus.). 32p. (J). (ps-2). 13.95 o.p. *(0-89919-144-4*, Clarion Bks.) Houghton Mifflin Co. Trade & Reference Div.

Hazen, Barbara Shook. Road Hog. 1998. (Road to Reading Ser.). (Illus.). 32p. (ps-3). pap. 3.99 *(0-307-26201-4*, 26201, Golden Bks.) Random Hse. Children's Bks.

—Road Hog. 1998. (Road to Reading Ser.). 10.14 *(0-606-16141-4)* Turtleback Bks.

Holy Cross School Kindergartners Staff. What's under Your Hood, Orson? 1993. (My First Library). (Illus.). (J). 14.95 o.p. *(0-590-72757-5)*; pap. 4.95 o.p. *(0-590-49247-0)* Scholastic, Inc.

Houghton Mifflin Company Staff. Houghton Mifflin Resource Book No. 4: License to Drive. 1993. (Literature Experience 1993 Ser.). pap., tchr. ed. 17.40 *(0-395-67235-X)* Houghton Mifflin Co.

Hyatt, Patricia Rusch. Coast to Coast with Alice. 1995. (Middle Grade Fiction Ser.). (Illus.). 72p. (J). (gr. 2-5). lib. bdg. 21.27 *(0-87614-789-9*, Carolrhoda Bks.) Lerner Publishing Group.

Mosher, Richard. The Taxi Navigator. 1998. 168p. (J). (gr. 3-7). pap. 4.99 o.s.i *(0-698-11658-5*, Paper-Star) Penguin Putnam Bks. for Young Readers.

Nick Drives the Car. Date not set. pap. *(1-58453-040-5)* Pioneer Valley Educational Pr., Inc.

Oxenbury, Helen. The Car Trip. 1994. (Out & About Bks.). (Illus.). 24p. (J). (ps-1). pap. 3.99 o.p. *(0-14-050377-3*, Puffin Bks.) Penguin Putnam Bks. for Young Readers.

—The Important Visitor. 1994. (Out & About Bks.). (Illus.). 24p. (J). (ps-1). pap. 3.99 o.p. *(0-14-050379-X*, Puffin Bks.) Penguin Putnam Bks. for Young Readers.

Parish, Herman. Good Driving, Amelia Bedelia. 1995. (Amelia Bedelia Ser.). (Illus.). 40p. (J). (ps-3). 15.99 *(0-688-13358-4)*; lib. bdg. 16.89 *(0-688-13359-2)* HarperCollins Children's Bk. Group. (Greenwillow Bks.).

—Good Driving, Amelia Bedelia. 1996. (Amelia Bedelia Ser.). (Illus.). 48p. (J). (gr. k-2). pap. 3.95 *(0-380-72510-X*, Avon Bks.) Morrow/Avon.

—Good Driving, Amelia Bedelia. 1996. (Amelia Bedelia Ser.). (J). (gr. k-2). 10.14 *(0-606-09341-9)* Turtleback Bks.

Powell, Richard. Formula Bunny. 2003. (Whizzy Wheels Bks.). (Illus.). 20p. (J). pap. 4.95 *(0-7641-5590-3)* Barron's Educational Series, Inc.

—GTI Kitten. 2003. (Whizzy Wheels Bks.). (Illus.). 20p. (J). pap. 4.95 *(0-7641-5588-1)* Barron's Educational Series, Inc.

—Race Bear. 2003. (Whizzy Wheels Bks.). (Illus.). 20p. (J). pap. 4.95 *(0-7641-5587-3)* Barron's Educational Series, Inc.

—Team Pig. 2003. (Whizzy Wheels Bks.). (Illus.). 20p. (J). pap. 4.95 *(0-7641-5586-5)* Barron's Educational Series, Inc.

Radlauer, Edward & Radlauer, Ruth S. Quarter Midget Challenge. 1969. (Illus.). 80p. (J). (gr. 4-8). lib. bdg. 9.25 o.p. *(0-516-07404-0*, Children's Pr.) Scholastic Library Publishing.

Steig, William. Grown-Ups Get to Do All the Driving. 1995. (Illus.). (J). 48p. (gr. 3-4). 15.00 o.s.i *(0-06-205080-X)*; 40p. (ps up). lib. bdg. 14.89 o.p. *(0-06-205081-8)* HarperCollins Children's Bk. Group.

Teitelbaum, Michael. If I Could Drive an Ambulance! 2003. (Tonka Ser.). (Illus.). 24p. (J). (ps-2). mass mkt. 3.50 *(0-439-43433-5)* Scholastic, Inc.

Temple, Charles. Cadillac. 1995. (Illus.). 32p. (J). (gr. k-2). 15.95 o.p. *(0-399-22654-0)* Penguin Group (USA) Inc.

Tomaselli, Doris. I Can Drive My Little Police Car. 1997. (I Can Do It Ser.). (Illus.). 12p. (J). (ps-1). bds. 24.99 o.p. *(1-57584-062-6)* Reader's Digest Children's Publishing, Inc.

Wood, Jakki. Bumper to Bumper: A Traffic Jam. 1999. (Illus.). 32p. (J). (ps-k). pap. *(0-7112-1031-4)* Lincoln, Frances Ltd.

—Bumper to Bumper: A Traffic Jam. 1996. (Illus.). 32p. (J). (ps-k). pap. 14.00 o.p. *(0-689-80391-5*, Simon & Schuster Children's Publishing) Simon & Schuster Children's Publishing.

B

BABYSITTERS—FICTION

Adams, Florence. Mushy Eggs. 1973. (Illus.). 32p. (J). (gr. k-3). 5.29 o.p. *(0-399-60854-0)* Putnam Publishing Group, The.

Albee, Sarah. Elmo's First Babysitter. 2001. (Illus.). 32p. (J). (ps-k). 3.99 o.s.i (*0-375-81149-4*, Random Hse. Bks. for Young Readers) Random Hse. Children's Bks.

Alexander, Martha. Nobody Asked Me If I Wanted a Baby Sister. 1993. (Illus.). 32p. (J). (ps-3). pap. 4.99 o.s.i (*0-14-054673-1*, Puffin Bks.) Penguin Putnam Bks. for Young Readers.

Anderson, Peggy Perry. Time for Bed, the Babysitter Said. 1995. (Illus.). 32p. (J). (ps-ps). pap. 4.95 (*0-395-74511-X*) Houghton Mifflin Co. Trade & Reference Div.

The Babysitter. 1999. 19.95 (*0-517-76278-1*, Random Hse. Bks. for Young Readers) Random Hse. Children's Bks.

Bates, Betty. Love Is Like Peanuts. 1980. 128p. (J). (gr. 6 up). 7.95 o.p. (*0-8234-0402-1*) Holiday Hse., Inc.

Benson, Rita. Looking after the Babysitter. 1994. (Voyages Ser.). (Illus.). (J). 4.25 (*0-383-03760-3*) SRA/McGraw-Hill.

Berenstain, Stan. Brown Brothers & Sitter. 1985. (J). 6.95 o.s.i incl. audio (*0-394-87662-8*) Random Hse., Inc.

Berk, Sheryl. Barney's Little Lessons: The New Babysitter. 2003. (Barney Ser.). 224p. (J). (ps-1). bds. 5.99 (*1-58668-302-0*) Lyrick Publishing.

Berman, Linda. The Goodbye Painting. 1982. (Illus.). 32p. (J). (ps-3). 16.95 (*0-89885-074-6*, Kluwer Academic/Human Science Pr.) Kluwer Academic Pubs.

Bird, Malcolm. The Sticky Child. 1981. (Illus.). 32p. (J). (gr. 4-8). 6.95 o.p. (*0-15-280338-6*) Harcourt Children's Bks.

Birney, Betty & Fulton, Mary J. Oh, Bother! Someone's Baby-Sitting. 1997. (Look-Look Bks.). (Illus.). 24p. (J). (ps-3). pap. 3.29 (*0-307-12634-X*, 12634, Golden Bks.) Random Hse. Children's Bks.

Black, Sonia W. & Brigandi, Pat. The Baby-Sitters Club Notebook. 1991. (Baby-Sitters Club Ser.). (Illus.). 64p. (J). (gr. 3-7). pap. 2.50 (*0-590-45074-3*) Scholastic, Inc.

Blair, Cynthia. Warning: Baby-Sitting May Be Hazardous to Your Health. 1993. (Bubble Gum Gang Ser.). (YA). mass mkt. 3.99 o.s.i (*0-449-70412-2*, Fawcett) Ballantine Bks.

Bourgeois, Paulette. Franklin & the Babysitter. 2002. (Franklin TV-Tie In Ser.: No. 10). (Illus.). 32p. (J). (ps-2). per. 4.50 (*0-439-24431-5*, Cartwheel Bks.) Scholastic, Inc.

Brandenberg, Franz. Leo & Emily & the Dragon. 1984. (Greenwillow Read-Alone Bks.). (Illus.). 56p. (J). (gr. 1-3). 15.00 o.p. (*0-688-02531-5*); lib. bdg. 12.88 o.p. (*0-688-02532-3*) HarperCollins Children's Bk. Group. (Greenwillow Bks.).

Braybrooks, Anne. Mercer Mayer's Little Critter: Just Me & the Babysitter. 1986. (Illus.). (J). (ps-3). lib. bdg. 1.99 o.p. (*0-307-13943-3*, Golden Bks.) Random Hse. Children's Bks.

Brown, Fern G. Baby-Sitter on Horseback. 1988. (J). (gr. 5 up). mass mkt. 2.95 o.s.i (*0-449-70283-9*, Fawcett) Ballantine Bks.

Brown, Marc. Arthur & the Babysitter. 2004. (J). 15.95 (*0-316-12128-2*) Little Brown & Co.

Brown, Marc. Arthur Babysits. (Arthur Adventure Ser.). 32p. (J). (gr. k-3). 1996. pap. 9.95 incl. audio (*0-316-11103-1*); 1996. pap. 9.95 incl. audio (*0-316-11103-1*); 1994. (Illus.). pap. 5.95 (*0-316-11442-1*); 1992. (Illus.). 15.95 (*0-316-11293-3*) Little Brown Children's Bks.

Bryant, Bonnie. Holiday Horse. 1997. (Saddle Club Ser.: No. 72). 160p. (Orig.). (gr. 4-6). pap. text 4.50 o.s.i (*0-553-48427-3*, Dell Books for Young Readers) Random Hse. Children's Bks.

Bush, Timothy. Benjamin McFadden & the Robot Babysitter. 1998. (Illus.). 32p. (gr. k-3). 18.99 o.s.i (*0-517-79985-5*, Crown) Crown Publishing Group.

Carlon, Patricia. Hush, It's a Game: Death by Demonstration. 2001. 189p. pap. 13.00 (*1-56947-245-9*) Soho Pr., Inc.

Carr, Jan & Martin, Ann M. The Baby-Sitters Club: The Movie Keepsake. 1995. (Baby-Sitters Club Ser.). 48p. (J). (gr. 2-5). pap. 12.95 (*0-590-60405-8*) Scholastic, Inc.

Carter, Dorothy. Bye, Mis' Lela, RS. 1998. (Frances Foster Bks.). (Illus.). 32p. (J). (gr. k-3). 16.00 (*0-374-31013-0*, Farrar, Straus & Giroux (BYR)) Farrar, Straus & Giroux.

Chalmers, Mary. Be Good, Harry. 1981. (Trophy Picture Bk.). (Illus.). 32p. (J). (ps-3). pap. 1.50 (*0-06-443027-8*, Harper Trophy) HarperCollins Children's Bk. Group.

Champion, Joyce & Stevenson, Supcie. Emily & Alice Baby-Sit Burton. 2001. (Emily & Alice: Bk. 3). (Illus.). 32p. (J). (gr. 1-3). 14.00 (*0-15-202184-1*, Gulliver Bks.) Harcourt Children's Bks.

Child, Lauren. Clarice Bean, Guess Who's Babysitting? 2001. (Illus.). 32p. (J). (gr. 1-4). 16.99 (*0-7636-1373-8*) Candlewick Pr.

Christelow, Eileen. Jerome & the Witchcraft Kids. (Illus.). 32p. (J). (ps-3). 1990. pap. 4.95 o.p. (*0-395-54428-9*); 1988. 13.95 o.p. (*0-89919-742-6*) Houghton Mifflin Co. Trade & Reference Div. (Clarion Bks.).

—Jerome the Babysitter. 1985. (Illus.). 32p. (J). (ps-3). 12.95 o.p. (*0-89919-331-5*) Clarion IND. *Dist:* Houghton Mifflin Co.

—Jerome the Babysitter. 1988. (J). pap. 6.95 o.p. (*0-89919-777-9*) Houghton Mifflin Co.

—Jerome the Babysitter. 1987. (Illus.). 32p. (J). (ps-3). pap. 4.95 o.p. (*0-89919-520-2*, Clarion Bks.) Houghton Mifflin Co. Trade & Reference Div.

Christopher, Matt. Operation Baby-Sitter. (Soccer Cats Ser.: No. 2). (Illus.). 64p. (J). 2001. (gr. 2-4). pap. 4.95 (*0-316-13556-9*); 1999. (ps-3). 13.95 (*0-316-13723-5*) Little Brown Children's Bks.

—Operation Baby-Sitter. 1999. (Soccer Cats Ser.: Vol. 2). E-Book (*1-58824-891-7*); E-Book (*1-58824-668-X*); E-Book (*1-58824-669-8*) ipicturebooks, LLC.

Cullen, Lynn. The Three Lives of Harris Harper. 1998. 160p. (J). pap. 3.99 (*0-380-72901-6*, Harper Trophy) HarperCollins Children's Bk. Group.

—The Three Lives of Harris Harper. 1996. (Illus.). 160p. (J). (gr. 4-7). tchr. ed. 14.95 o.p. (*0-395-73680-3*, Clarion Bks.) Houghton Mifflin Co. Trade & Reference Div.

—The Three Lives of Harris Harper. 1998. 10.04 (*0-606-13976-1*) Turtleback Bks.

Daniel, Kate. Baby-Sitter's Nightmare II. 1994. 224p. (YA). mass mkt. 3.99 o.p. (*0-06-106232-4*, Harper-Torch) Morrow/Avon.

—Babysitter's Nightmare. (YA). 1994. 79p. mass mkt. 1.99 o.p. (*0-06-106228-6*); 1992. (Thriller Ser.: No. 4). 224p. mass mkt. 3.99 o.p. (*0-06-106773-3*) Morrow/Avon. (HarperTorch).

Day, Alexandra. Carl Goes to Daycare. 2002. (Illus.). (J). 22.13 (*0-7587-2192-7*) Book Wholesalers, Inc.

—Carl Goes to Daycare, RS. 1995. (Carl Ser.). (J). (ps-1). (Illus.). 32p. 5.95 (*0-374-31145-5*); 71.40 o.p. (*0-374-31146-3*) Farrar, Straus & Giroux. (Farrar, Straus & Giroux (BYR)).

—Good Dog, Carl. (Carl Ser.). (Illus.). 40p. (J). (ps-3). 1997. pap. 4.99 (*0-689-81771-1*, Aladdin); 1991. 12.95 (*0-671-75204-9*, Simon & Schuster Children's Publishing) Simon & Schuster Children's Publishing.

de Paola, Tomie. The Baby Sister. 1996. (Illus.). 32p. (J). (ps-3). 16.99 (*0-399-22908-6*, G. P. Putnam's Sons) Penguin Group (USA) Inc.

Delton, Judy. Angel in Charge. (Illus.). (J). (gr. 4-6). 1999. 148p. pap. 4.95 (*0-395-96061-4*); 1985. 160p. tchr. ed. 16.00 (*0-395-37488-X*) Houghton Mifflin Co.

—Angel in Charge. 1990. 160p. (J). (gr. k-6). reprint ed. pap. 2.95 o.s.i (*0-440-40264-6*, Yearling) Random Hse. Children's Bks.

—Angel in Charge. 1999. (Illus.). (J). 11.00 (*0-606-18206-3*) Turtleback Bks.

Dubowski, Cathy. Baby-Sitters & Company. 2000. (Full House Sisters Ser.: No. 8). 160p. (J). (gr. 4-6). pap. 3.99 (*0-671-04087-1*, Simon Spotlight) Simon & Schuster Children's Publishing.

—The Baby-Sitting Boss. 1999. (Full House Michelle Ser.: No. 26). 96p. (J). (gr. 2-4). pap. 3.99 (*0-671-02156-7*, Simon Spotlight) Simon & Schuster Children's Publishing.

Endersby, Frank. The Baby Sitter. 1981. 12p. (J). (gr. 4 up). 3.99 (*0-85953-271-2*) Child's Play of England GBR. *Dist:* Child's Play-International.

Faucher, Elizabeth. Charles in Charge. 1984. 128p. (Orig.). (J). (gr. 7 up). pap. 2.25 (*0-590-33550-2*, Scholastic Paperbacks) Scholastic, Inc.

Fletcher, Susan. Anti-Babysitter Plot. 1994. 176p. (J). (gr. 4-7). pap. 2.95 (*0-590-46008-0*) Scholastic, Inc.

Fox, Paula. A Likely Place. (Illus.). (J). 1997. 80p. (*0-689-81401-1*, Simon & Schuster Children's Publishing); 1997. 80p. (gr. 1-4). per. 3.99 (*0-689-81402-X*, Aladdin); 1987. 64p. (gr. 2-6). reprint ed. text 15.00 o.s.i (*0-02-735761-9*, Simon & Schuster Children's Publishing) Simon & Schuster Children's Publishing.

—A Likely Place. 1997. (J). 10.14 (*0-606-11561-7*) Turtleback Bks.

Frankel, Alona. Prudence's Baby-Sitter Book. 2000. (Joshua & Prudence Bks.). (Illus.). 48p. (J). (ps-k). 6.95 (*0-694-01384-6*, Harper Festival) HarperCollins Children's Bk. Group.

Gardner, Sally. Mama, Don't Go Out Tonight. 2002. (Illus.). 32p. (J). (ps-k). 16.95 (*1-58234-790-5*, Bloomsbury Children) Bloomsbury Publishing.

Gershator, Phillis. The Babysitter Sings. 2004. (J). 16.95 (*0-8050-7199-7*, Holt, Henry & Co. Bks. For Young Readers) Holt, Henry & Co.

Gilson, Kristin. A Baby-Sitter's Nightmare: Tales Too Scary to Be True. 1998. (Illus.). 112p. (J). (gr. 3-7). pap. 4.95 (*0-06-440700-4*) HarperCollins Pubs.

Goldman, Lisa. A Day with a Dirtbike. 1998. (Doug Chronicles Ser.: No. 4). (Illus.). 64p. (J). (gr. 2-4). pap. 3.99 (*0-7868-4233-4*) Disney Pr.

—A Day with Dirtbike. 1998. (Doug Chronicles Ser.). (J). (gr. 2-4). pap. 3.95 o.s.i (*0-7868-4321-7*) Disney Pr.

Gorog, Judith. When Nobody's Home: Fifteen Baby-Sitting Tales of Terror. 1996. 95p. (YA). (gr. 7 up). pap. 15.95 (*0-590-46862-6*) Scholastic, Inc.

Gray, Genevieve. Alaska Woman. 1977. (Time of Danger, Time for Courage Ser.). (Illus.). (J). (gr. 3-9). pap. 3.95 o.p. (*0-88436-387-2*, 35300); lib. bdg. 6.95 o.p. (*0-88436-386-4*, 35482) Paradigm Publishing, Inc.

Green, Phyllis A. Eating Ice Cream with a Werewolf. 1983. (Illus.). 128p. (J). (gr. 3-7). 11.95 (*0-06-022140-2*); lib. bdg. 11.89 o.p. (*0-06-022141-0*) HarperCollins Children's Bk. Group.

Greenberg, Barbara. The Bravest Babysitter. 1977. (Illus.). (J). (gr. k-3). 6.95 o.p. (*0-8037-0363-5*); 6.46 o.p. (*0-8037-0364-3*) Penguin Putnam Bks. for Young Readers. (Dial Bks. for Young Readers).

—Bravest Babysitter. 1986. (Pied Piper Bks.). (Illus.). 32p. (J). (ps-3). pap. 3.95 o.p. (*0-8037-0309-0*, 0383-120, Dial Bks. for Young Readers) Penguin Putnam Bks. for Young Readers.

Gregory, Valiska. Babysitting for Benjamin. 1993. (Illus.). 32p. (J). (ps-3). 13.95 o.p. (*0-316-32785-9*) Little Brown & Co.

—Shirley's Wonderful Baby. 2002. (Illus.). 32p. (J). (ps-2). 14.99 (*0-06-028132-4*) HarperCollins Children's Bk. Group.

Guiberson, Brenda Z. Instant Soup. 1991. 112p. (J). (gr. 3-7). text 12.95 o.p. (*0-689-31688-7*, Atheneum) Simon & Schuster Children's Publishing.

Harris, Robie H. Don't Forget to Come Back. 1978. (Illus.). (J). (ps-2). 5.95 o.p. (*0-394-83849-1*); lib. bdg. 6.99 o.p. (*0-394-93849-6*) Random Hse. Children's Bks. (Knopf Bks. for Young Readers).

—Don't Forget to Come Back! 2004. (Illus.). 40p. (J). 15.99 (*0-7636-1782-2*) Candlewick Pr.

Hearne, Betsy. Who's in the Hall? A Mystery in Four Chapters. 2000. (Illus.). 32p. (J). (gr. k-5). 15.95 (*0-688-16261-4*); (gr. 2 up). lib. bdg. 16.89 (*0-688-16262-2*) HarperCollins Children's Bk. Group. (Greenwillow Bks.).

Hellard, Susan. Eleanor & the Babysitter. 1991. (J). (ps-3). 13.95 o.p. (*0-316-35459-7*) Little Brown & Co.

Hershenhorn, Esther. Chicken Soup by Heart. 2001. (Illus.). (J). (gr. k-3). 16.95 (*0-689-82665-6*, Simon & Schuster Children's Publishing) Simon & Schuster Children's Publishing.

Herzig, Alison C. & Mali, Jane L. The Ten Speed Babysitter. 1987. 144p. (J). (gr. 4-7). 11.95 o.p. (*0-525-44340-1*, 01160-350, Dutton Children's Bks.) Penguin Putnam Bks. for Young Readers.

Hest, Amy. Nannies for Hire. 1994. (Illus.). 48p. (J). (gr. 2 up). 15.00 o.p. (*0-688-12527-1*); lib. bdg. 14.93 o.p. (*0-688-12528-X*) Morrow/Avon. (Morrow, William & Co.).

Hodgman, Ann. My Babysitter Bites Again. Ashby, Ruth, ed. 1993. (Illus.). 144p. (Orig.). (J). (gr. 3-6). pap. 3.50 (*0-671-79378-0*, Aladdin) Simon & Schuster Children's Publishing.

—My Babysitter Has Fangs. Ashby, Ruth, ed. 1992. (Illus.). 128p. (Orig.). (J). pap. 3.50 (*0-671-75868-3*, Aladdin) Simon & Schuster Children's Publishing.

—My Babysitter Is a Movie Monster. 1995. (Illus.). 144p. (J). (gr. 3-6). pap. 3.50 (*0-671-88452-2*, Aladdin) Simon & Schuster Children's Publishing.

—My Babysitter Is a Movie Monster. 1995. (J). 8.60 o.p. (*0-606-07902-5*) Turtleback Bks.

—My Babysitter Is a Vampire. Ashby, Ruth, ed. 1991. (Illus.). 121p. (J). (gr. 4-7). per. 3.50 (*0-671-64751-2*, Aladdin) Simon & Schuster Children's Publishing.

Honeycutt, Natalie. Lydia Jane Bly & the Baby-Sitter Exchange. 1993. 128p. (J). (gr. 2-6). 13.95 o.p. (*0-02-744362-0*, Simon & Schuster Children's Publishing) Simon & Schuster Children's Publishing.

Horowitz, Ruth. Bat Time. 1991. (Illus.). 32p. (J). (ps-2). lib. bdg. 13.95 o.p. (*0-02-744541-0*, Simon & Schuster Children's Publishing) Simon & Schuster Children's Publishing.

Horvath, Polly. The Trolls, RS. 2001. (Sunburst Bks.). 144p. (J). (gr. 3-7). reprint ed. pap. 4.95 (*0-374-47991-7*, Sunburst) Farrar, Straus & Giroux.

Howe, James. The New Nick Kramer, or My Life As a Babysitter. 1997. 128p. (J). (gr. 5-9). pap. 4.50 (*0-7868-1017-3*) Disney Pr.

—The New Nick Kramer, or My Life As a Babysitter. 1995. (Illus.). 128p. (J). (gr. 5-9). 13.95 (*0-7868-0066-6*); lib. bdg. 14.49 (*0-7868-2053-5*) Hyperion Bks. for Children.

Hughes, Shirley. An Evening at Alfie's. 1985. (Illus.). 32p. (J). (ps-1). 16.00 o.p. (*0-688-04122-1*); lib. bdg. 15.93 o.p. (*0-688-04123-X*) HarperCollins Children's Bk. Group.

—George the Babysitter. 1978. (Illus.). (J). (ps-2). pap. o.p. (*0-13-352674-7*); lib. bdg. o.p. (*0-13-352682-8*) Prentice-Hall.

Jackson, Dave & Jackson, Neta. Secret Adventures Books Episode 2: Snap. 1994. 100p. (J). pap. 4.99 o.p. (*0-8054-4005-4*, 4240-05) Broadman & Holman Pubs.

James, Simon. Jake & the Babysitter. 2002. (Illus.). 32p. (J). bds. 4.99 (*0-7636-1800-4*) Candlewick Pr.

Johnson, Angela. Shoes Like Miss Alice's. 1995. (Illus.). 32p. (J). (ps-3). pap. 15.95 (*0-531-06814-5*); lib. bdg. 16.99 (*0-531-08664-X*) Scholastic, Inc. (Orchard Bks.).

Johnson, Dolores. What Kind of Baby-Sitter Is This? 1991. (Illus.). 32p. (J). (gr. k-3). lib. bdg. 15.00 (*0-02-747846-7*, Atheneum) Simon & Schuster Children's Publishing.

Johnson, Doug. Never Babysit the Hippopotamuses!, ERS. (J). 1997. (gr. 1-4). pap. 5.95 o.s.i (*0-8050-5029-9*); 1993. (Illus.). 32p. (ps-2). 14.95 o.p. (*0-8050-1873-5*) Holt, Henry & Co. (Holt, Henry & Co. Bks. For Young Readers).

—Never Babysit the Hippopotamuses! 1997. 12.10 (*0-606-11676-1*) Turtleback Bks.

Johnson, Lissa H. The Never-Ending Day. 1997. (China Tate Ser.: Bk. 7). (J). (gr. 6-11). pap. 5.99 o.p. (*1-56179-538-0*) Focus on the Family Publishing.

Johnson, Marion. Caillou Watches Rosie. 2002. (Illus.). 24p. (J). 12.95 (*2-89450-326-1*) Editions Chouette, Inc. CAN. *Dist:* Client Distribution Services.

Katschke, Judy. It's a Twin Thing. 1999. (Two of a Kind Ser.: No. 1). (Illus.). 112p. (gr. 3-7). mass mkt. 4.99 (*0-06-106571-4*) HarperCollins Pubs.

Kaye, Marilyn. The Best Babysitter in the World. 1987. (Hello Reader! Ser.). (Illus.). 48p. (J). (ps-2). pap. 2.50 o.p. (*0-590-40703-1*) Scholastic, Inc.

Keller, Beverly. Night the Baby-Sitter Didn't Come. 1994. 144p. (J). (gr. 4-7). pap. 3.25 (*0-590-43726-7*) Scholastic, Inc.

Keller, Holly. Geraldine & Mrs. Duffy. 2000. (Illus.). (J). (gr. k-3). 24p. 15.95 (*0-688-16887-6*); 24p. 15.95 (*0-688-16887-6*); 32p. lib. bdg. 15.89 (*0-688-16888-4*) HarperCollins Children's Bk. Group. (Greenwillow Bks.).

Kindig, Tess Eileen. Muggsy Makes an Assist. 2000. (Slam Dunk Ser.: Vol. 3). (J). (gr. 1-4). (Illus.). 94p. pap. 4.99 (*0-570-07018-X*);Vol. 4. 96p. pap. 4.99 (*0-570-07019-8*) Concordia Publishing Hse.

Kingsley, Emily P. A Sitter for Baby Monster. 1987. (Sesame Street Growing-Up Bks.). (Illus.). 32p. (J). (gr. 2-5). o.p. (*0-307-12022-8*, Golden Bks.) Random Hse. Children's Bks.

Klein, Leah. Babysitting Blues. 1994. (B. Y. Times Ser.: No. 16). 122p. (Orig.). (J). (gr. 6-8). pap. 8.95 o.p. (*1-56871-048-8*) Targum Pr., Inc.

Konigsburg, E. L. Silent to the Bone. unabr. ed. 2002. 272p. (YA). (gr. 10 up). pap. 35.00 incl. audio (*0-8072-8741-5*, LYA 253 SP); 2000. (J). (ps up). audio 25.00 (*0-8072-6165-3*) Random Hse. Audio Publishing Group. (Listening Library).

—Silent to the Bone. 272p. 2004. (YA). mass mkt. 5.99 (*0-689-86715-8*, Simon Pulse); 2002. (Illus.). (J). (gr. 5-9). pap. 5.99 (*0-689-83602-3*, Aladdin); 2000. (Illus.). (J). (gr. 5-9). 16.00 (*0-689-83601-5*, Atheneum) Simon & Schuster Children's Publishing.

—Silent to the Bone. l.t. ed. 2001. (Young Adult Ser.). 271p. (J). (gr. 4-7). 23.95 (*0-7862-3169-6*) Thorndike Pr.

Kraus, Robert. Spider's Baby-Sitting Job. 1990. (J). pap. 2.50 o.p. (*0-590-42445-9*) Scholastic, Inc.

Kubler, Annie. Baby-Sitter. 1999. (All in a Day Board-books Ser.). (Illus.). 14p. (J). (ps-k). 2.99 (*0-85953-588-6*) Child's Play of England GBR. *Dist:* Child's Play-International.

Levin, Betty. That'll Do, Moss. 2002. (Illus.). 128p. (J). (gr. 3 up). 15.89 (*0-06-000532-7*); 15.95 (*0-06-000531-9*) HarperCollins Children's Bk. Group. (Greenwillow Bks.).

Lipman, Ken. Bad News Babysitting! 1995. (Secret World of Alex Mack Ser.: No. 3). 144p. (J). (gr. 4-7). pap. 3.99 (*0-671-53446-7*, Aladdin) Simon & Schuster Children's Publishing.

Loomis, Christine. My New Baby-Sitter. (J). (ps up). 1991. (Illus.). 48p. 13.95 o.p. (*0-688-09625-5*); 1991. (Illus.). 48p. lib. bdg. 13.88 o.p. (*0-688-09626-3*); 1924. pap. o.s.i (*0-688-10197-6*) Morrow/Avon. (Morrow, William & Co.).

Lowry, Lois. Taking Care of Terrific. 001. 1983. 176p. (J). (gr. 4-6). 16.00 (*0-395-34070-5*) Houghton Mifflin Co.

—Taking Care of Terrific. l.t. ed. 1989. 208p. (YA). reprint ed. lib. bdg. 16.95 o.s.i (*1-55736-119-3*, Cornerstone Bks.) Pages, Inc.

—Taking Care of Terrific. 1983. (J). 10.55 (*0-606-03177-4*) Turtleback Bks.

Markel, Michelle. Gracias, Rosa. 1995. (Albert Whitman Concept Bks.). (Illus.). (J). (ps-3). lib. bdg. 14.95 (*0-8075-3024-7*) Whitman, Albert & Co.

Marshall, Val & Tester, Bronwyn. And Grandpa Sat on Friday. 1993. (Voyages Ser.). (Illus.). (J). 4.25 (*0-383-03610-0*) SRA/McGraw-Hill.

Martin, Ann M. Abby & the Best Kid Ever. 1998. (Baby-Sitters Club Ser.: No. 116). (J). (gr. 3-7). mass mkt. 3.99 (*0-590-05994-7*) Scholastic, Inc.

—Abby & the Best Kid Ever. 1998. (Baby-Sitters Club Ser.: No. 116). (J). (gr. 3-7). 10.04 (*0-606-13160-4*) Turtleback Bks.

—Abby & the Notorious Neighbor. 1998. (Baby-Sitters Club Mystery Ser.: No. 35). (Illus.). (J). (gr. 3-7). mass mkt. 3.99 (*0-590-05975-0*, Scholastic Paperbacks) Scholastic, Inc.

—Abby & the Secret Society. 1996. (Baby-Sitters Club Mystery Ser.: No. 23). (J). (gr. 3-7). mass mkt. 4.50 (*0-590-22867-6*) Scholastic, Inc.

—Abby & the Secret Society. 1996. (Baby-Sitters Club Mystery Ser.: No. 23). (J). (gr. 3-7). 10.04 (*0-606-09037-1*) Turtleback Bks.

—Abby in Wonderland. 1998. (Baby-Sitters Club Ser.: No. 121). (J). (gr. 3-7). mass mkt. 4.50 (*0-590-50063-5*, Scholastic Paperbacks) Scholastic, Inc.

—Abby in Wonderland. 1998. (Baby-Sitters Club Ser.: No. 121). (J). (gr. 3-7). 10.55 (*0-606-13165-5*) Turtleback Bks.

—Abby's Lucky Thirteen. 1996. (Baby-Sitters Club Ser.: No. 96). (J). (gr. 3-7). mass mkt. 3.99 (*0-590-22880-3*) Scholastic, Inc.

—Abby's Lucky Thirteen. 1996. (Baby-Sitters Club Ser.: No. 96). (J). (gr. 3-7). 9.09 o.p. (*0-606-09032-0*) Turtleback Bks.

—Abby's Twin. 1997. (Baby-Sitters Club Ser.: No. 104). 127p. (J). (gr. 3-7). mass mkt. 3.99 (*0-590-69210-0*) Scholastic, Inc.

—Abby's Twin. 1997. (Baby-Sitters Club Ser.: No. 104). (J). (gr. 3-7). 10.04 (*0-606-10744-4*) Turtleback Bks.

—Aloha, Baby-Sitters! 1996. (Baby-Sitters Club Super Special Ser.: No. 13). (J). (gr. 3-7). mass mkt. 4.50 (*0-590-22883-8*) Scholastic, Inc.

—Baby-Sitters at Shadow Lake. 1992. (Baby-Sitters Club Super Special Ser.: No. 8). 256p. (J). (gr. 3-7). mass mkt. 4.50 (*0-590-44962-1*) Scholastic, Inc.

—Baby-Sitters at Shadow Lake. 1992. (Baby-Sitters Club Super Special Ser.: No. 8). (J). (gr. 3-7). 9.05 o.p. (*0-606-01780-1*) Turtleback Bks.

—Baby-Sitters Beware. 1995. (Baby-Sitters Club Super Mystery Ser.: No. 2). (J). (gr. 3-7). mass mkt. 3.99 (*0-590-22871-4*) Scholastic, Inc.

—Baby-Sitters Beware. 1995. (Baby-Sitters Club Super Mystery Ser.: No. 2). (J). (gr. 3-7). 9.09 o.p. (*0-606-08483-5*) Turtleback Bks.

—Baby-Sitters' Christmas Chiller. 1997. (Baby-Sitters Club Super Mystery Ser.: No. 4). (J). (gr. 3-7). mass mkt. 4.50 (*0-590-05977-7*, Scholastic Paperbacks) Scholastic, Inc.

—Baby-Sitters' Christmas Chiller. 1997. (Baby-Sitters Club Super Mystery Ser.: No. 4). (J). (gr. 3-7). 10.55 (*0-606-12884-0*) Turtleback Bks.

—The Baby-Sitters Club, Set., No. 5. 1989. (Baby-Sitters Club Ser.). (J). (gr. 4 up). pap. 11.00 (*0-590-63344-9*) Scholastic, Inc.

—The Baby-Sitters Club, 40 vols. l.t. ed. (Baby-Sitters Club Ser.). 176p. (J). 1995. (gr. 4 up). lib. bdg. 637.20 o.p. (*0-8368-1445-2*); Set. 1994. lib. bdg. 318.60 o.p. (*0-8368-1267-0*); Vol. 2. 1994. lib. bdg. 159.30 o.p. (*0-8368-1241-7*) Stevens, Gareth Inc.

—The Baby-Sitters Club, 43 bks. l.t. ed. Incl. Boy-Crazy Stacey. 144p. 1995. lib. bdg. 21.27 o.p. (*0-8368-1321-9*); Claudia & Mean Janine. 176p. 1995. lib. bdg. 21.27 o.p. (*0-8368-1320-0*); Claudia & the Genius of Elm Street. 1996. lib. bdg. 21.27 o.p. (*0-8368-1573-4*); Claudia & the Great Search. 147p. 1995. lib. bdg. 21.27 o.p. (*0-8368-1413-4*); Claudia & the Middle School Mystery. 176p. 1995. lib. bdg. 21.27 o.p. (*0-8368-1420-7*); Claudia & the New Girl. 176p. 1993. lib. bdg. 21.27 o.p. (*0-8368-1016-3*); Claudia & the Phantom Phone Calls. 153p. 1995. lib. bdg. 21.27 o.p. (*0-8368-1315-4*); Claudia & the Sad Good-Bye. 176p. 1994. lib. bdg. 21.27 o.p. (*0-8368-1247-6*); Dawn & the Big Sleepover. 176p. 1996. lib. bdg. 21.27 o.p. (*0-8368-1568-8*); Dawn & the Impossible Three. 144p. 1995. lib. bdg. 21.27 o.p. (*0-8368-1318-9*); Dawn & the Older Boy. 144p. 1995. lib. bdg. 21.27 o.p. (*0-8368-1417-7*); Dawn on the Coast. 176p. 1994. lib. bdg. 21.27 o.p. (*0-8368-1244-1*); Dawn's Big Date. 176p. 1996. lib. bdg. 21.27 o.p. (*0-8368-1574-2*); Dawn's Wicked Stepsister. 144p. 1995. lib. bdg. 21.27 o.p. (*0-8368-1411-8*); Ghost at Dawn's House. 144p. 1995. lib. bdg. 21.27 o.p. (*0-8368-1322-7*); Hello, Mallory. 176p. 1993. lib. bdg. 21.27 o.p. (*0-8368-1018-X*); Jessi & the Dance School Phantom. 144p. 1996. lib. bdg. 21.27 o.p. (*0-8368-1566-1*); Jessi & the Superbrat. 176p. 1994. lib. bdg. 21.27 o.p. (*0-8368-1248-4*); Jessi Ramsey, Pet-Sitter. 144p. 1994. lib. bdg. 21.27 o.p. (*0-8368-1243-3*); Jessi's Baby-Sitter. 144p. 1995. lib. bdg. 21.27 o.p. (*0-8368-1416-9*); Jessi's Secret Language. 176p. 1993. lib. bdg. 21.27 o.p. (*0-8368-1020-1*); Jessi's Wish. 144p. 1996. lib. bdg. 21.27 o.p. (*0-8368-1572-6*); Kristy & the Baby Parade. 176p. 1996. lib. bdg. 21.27 o.p. (*0-8368-1569-6*); Kristy & the Mother's Day Surprise. 176p. 1994. lib. bdg. 21.27 o.p. (*0-8368-1245-X*); Kristy & the Secret of Susan. 144p. 1995. lib. bdg. 21.27 o.p. (*0-8368-1412-6*); Kristy & the Walking Disaster. 176p. 1993. lib. bdg. 21.27 o.p. (*0-8368-1024-4*); Kristy's Big Day. 144p. 1995. lib. bdg. 21.27 o.p. (*0-8368-1319-7*); Kristy's Mystery Admirer. 144p. 1995. lib. bdg. 21.27 o.p. (*0-8368-1418-5*); Little Miss Stoneybrook & Dawn. 176p. 1993. lib. bdg. 21.27 o.p. (*0-8368-1019-8*); Logan Likes Mary Anne! 144p. 1995. lib. bdg. 21.27 o.p. (*0-8368-1323-5*); Mallory & the Mystery Diary. 176p. 1994. lib. bdg. 21.27 o.p. (*0-8368-1250-6*); Mallory on Strike. 144p. 1996. lib. bdg. 21.27 o.p. (*0-8368-1571-8*); Mary Anne & the Great Romance. 176p. 1994. lib. bdg. 21.27 o.p. (*0-8368-1251-4*); Mary Anne & the Search for Tigger. 176p. 1994. lib. bdg. 23.95 o.p. (*0-8368-1246-8*); Mary Anne & Too Many Boys. 144p. 1995. lib. bdg. 21.27 o.p. (*0-8368-1414-2*); Mary Anne Misses Logan. 144p. 1996. lib. bdg. 21.27 o.p. (*0-8368-1570-X*); Mary Anne vs. Logan. 176p. 1996. lib. bdg. 21.27 o.p. (*0-8368-1565-3*); Mary Anne's Bad-Luck Mystery. 176p. 1993. lib. bdg. 21.27 o.p. (*0-8368-1021-X*); Poor Mallory! 144p. 1995. lib. bdg. 21.27 o.p. (*0-8368-1419-3*); Stacey & the Mystery of Stoneybrook. 144p. 1995. lib. bdg. 21.27 o.p. (*0-8368-1415-0*); Stacey's Emergency. 144p. 1996. lib. bdg. 21.27 o.p. (*0-8368-1567-X*); Truth about Stacey. 144p. 1995. lib. bdg. 21.27 o.p. (*0-8368-1316-2*); Welcome Back, Stacey! 176p. 1994. lib. bdg. 21.27 o.p. (*0-8368-1249-2*); (J). (gr. 3-7). 914.47 o.p. (*0-8368-1663-3*) Stevens, Gareth Inc.

—The Baby-Sitters Club Boxed Set. l.t. ed. 1993. (Baby-Sitters Club Ser.). (J). (gr. 4 up). pap. 159.30 o.p. (*0-8368-1025-2*) Stevens, Gareth Inc.

—The Baby-Sitters Club Boxed Set Bks. 1-10: Kristy's Great Idea; Claudia & the Phantom Phone Calls; The Truth about Stacey; Mary Anne Saves the Day; Dawn & the Impossible Three; Kristy's Big Day; Claudia & Mean Janine; Boy-Crazy Stacey; The Ghost at Dawn's House; Logan Likes Mary Anne! l.t. ed. 1995. (Baby-Sitters Club Ser.: Nos. 1-10). 144p. (J). (gr. 3-7). pap. 172.70 o.p. (*0-8368-1444-4*) Stevens, Gareth Inc.

—The Baby-Sitters Club Boxed Set Bks. 31-40: Dawn's Wicked Stepsister; Kristy & the Secret of Susan; Claudia & the Great Search; Mary Anne & Too Many Boys; Stacey & the Mystery of Stoneybrook; Jessi's Baby-Sitter; Dawn & the Older Boy; Kristy's Mystery Admirer; Poor Mallory!; Claudia & the Middle School Mystery. l.t. ed. 1995. (Baby-Sitters Club Ser.: Nos. 31-40). 144p. (J). (gr. 3-7). pap. 172.70 o.p. (*0-8368-1410-X*) Stevens, Gareth Inc.

—The Baby-Sitters Club Boxed Set Bks. 41-50: Mary Anne vs. Logan; Jessi & the Dance School Phantom; Stacey's Emergency; Dawn & the Big Sleepover; Kristy & the Baby Parade; Mary Anne Misses Logan; Mallory on Strike; Jessi's Wish; Claudia & the Genius of Elm Street; Dawn's Big Date. l.t. ed. 1995. (Baby-Sitters Club Ser.: Nos. 41-50). (J). (gr. 3-7). pap. 172.70 o.p. (*0-8368-1564-5*) Stevens, Gareth Inc.

—The Baby-Sitters Club Boxed Set No. 1: Kristy's Great Idea; Claudia & the Phantom Phone Calls; The Truth about Stacey; Mary Anne Saves the Day. (Baby-Sitters Club Ser.: Nos. 1-4). (J). (gr. 3-7). 1993. pap. 14.00 (*0-590-59887-2*); 1990. pap. 14.95 (*0-590-63673-1*); 1987. pap. 10.00 (*0-590-63218-3*) Scholastic, Inc.

—The Baby-Sitters Club Boxed Set No. 2: Dawn & the Impossible Three; Kristy's Big Day; Claudia & Mean Janine; Boy-Crazy Stacey. (Baby-Sitters Club Ser.: Nos. 5-8). (J). (gr. 3-7). 1987. pap. 10.00 (*0-590-63248-5*); Bks. 5-8. 1990. pap. 13.00 o.p. (*0-590-63672-3*); Bk.s 5-8. 1988. pap. 10.75 o.p. (*0-590-63319-8*) Scholastic, Inc.

—The Baby-Sitters Club Boxed Set No. 3: The Ghost at Dawn's House; Logan Likes Mary Anne!; Kristy & the Snobs; Claudia & the New Girl. (Baby-Sitters Club Ser.: Nos. 9-12). (J). (gr. 3-7). 1988. pap. 11.00 (*0-590-63288-4*); Bks. 9-12. 1991. pap. 13.00 o.p. (*0-590-63701-0*) Scholastic, Inc.

—The Baby-Sitters Club Boxed Set No. 4 Bks. 13-16: Good-Bye Stacey, Good-Bye; Hello, Mallory; Little Miss Stoneybrook & Dawn; Jessi's Secret Language. 1991. (Baby-Sitters Club Ser.: Nos. 13-16). (J). (gr. 3-7). pap. 13.00 (*0-590-63705-3*) Scholastic, Inc.

—The Baby-Sitters Club Boxed Set No. 5: Mary Anne's Bad Luck Mystery; Stacey's Mistake; Claudia & the Bad Joke; Kristy & the Walking Disaster. 1991. (Baby-Sitters Club Ser.: Nos. 17-20). (J). (gr. 3-7). pap. 13.00 (*0-590-63704-5*) Scholastic, Inc.

—The Baby-Sitters Club Boxed Set No. 6: Mallory & the Trouble with Twins; Jessi Ramsey, Pet-Sitter; Dawn on the Coast; Kristy & the Mother's Day Surprise, Bks. 21-24. 1989. (Baby-Sitters Club Ser.: Nos. 21-24). (J). (gr. 3-7). pap. 11.00 o.p. (*0-590-63404-6*) Scholastic, Inc.

—The Baby-Sitters Club Boxed Set No. 6 Bks. 21-24: Mallory & the Trouble with Twins; Jessi Ramsey, Pet-Sitter; Dawn on the Coast; Kristy & the Mother's Day Surprise. 1991. (Baby-Sitters Club Ser.: Nos. 21-24). (J). (gr. 3-7). pap. 13.00 o.p. (*0-590-63703-7*) Scholastic, Inc.

—The Baby-Sitters Club Boxed Set No. 7 Bks. 25-28: Mary Anne & the Search for Tigger; Claudia & the Sad Good-Bye; Jessi & the Superbrat; Welcome Back Stacey! 1991. (Baby-Sitters Club Ser.: Nos. 25-28). (J). (gr. 3-7). pap. 13.00 o.p. (*0-590-63702-9*) Scholastic, Inc.

—The Baby-Sitters Club Boxed Set No. 8: Dawn Saves the Planet; Stacey's Choice; Mallory Hates Boys; Mary Anne's Makeover. 1993. (Baby-Sitters Club Ser.: Nos. 57-60). (J). (gr. 3-7). pap. 14.00 (*0-590-66720-3*) Scholastic, Inc.

—The Baby-Sitters Club Boxed Set No. 8: Mallory & the Mystery Diary; Mary Anne & the Great Romance; Dawn's Wicked Stepsister; Kristy & the Secret of Susan. 1990. (Baby-Sitters Club Ser.: Nos. 29-32). (J). (gr. 3-7). pap. 13.00 (*0-590-63583-2*) Scholastic, Inc.

—The Baby-Sitters Club Boxed Set No. 9: Claudia & the Great Search; Mary Anne & Too Many Boys; Stacey & the Mystery of Stoneybrook; Jessi's Baby-Sitter. 1990. (Baby-Sitters Club Ser.: Nos. 33-36). (J). (gr. 3-7). pap. 13.00 (*0-590-63669-3*) Scholastic, Inc.

—The Baby-Sitters Club Boxed Set No. 10 Bks. 37-40: Dawn & the Older Boy; Kristy's Mystery Admirer; Poor Mallory!; Claudia & the Middle School Mystery. 1991. (J). (gr. k). 13.00 (*0-590-63828-9*) Scholastic, Inc.

—The Baby-Sitters Club Boxed Set No. 12: Kristy & the Baby Parade; Mary Anne Misses Logan; Mallory on Strike; Jessi's Wish. 1991. (Baby-Sitters Club Ser.: Nos. 45-48). (J). (gr. 3-7). pap. 13.00 (*0-590-63963-3*) Scholastic, Inc.

—The Baby-Sitters Club Boxed Set No. 16: Jessi & the Awful Secret; Kristy & the Worst Kid Ever; Claudia's Freind Friend; Dawn's Family Feud. 1993. (Baby-Sitters Club Ser.: Nos. 61-64). (J). (gr. 3-7). pap. text 14.00 (*0-590-66719-X*) Scholastic, Inc.

—The Baby-Sitters Club Boxed Set No. 16 Bks. 61-64: Jessi & the Awful Secret; Kristy & the Worst Kid Ever; Claudia's Freind Friend; Dawn's Family Feud. 1993. (J). 14.00 (*0-590-66213-9*) Scholastic, Inc.

—The Baby-Sitters Club Boxed Set No. 17: Stacey's Big Crush; Maid Mary Anne; Dawn's Big Move; Jessi & the Bad Baby-Sitter. 1993. (Baby-Sitters Club Ser.: Nos. 65-68). (J). (gr. 3-7). pap. 14.00 (*0-590-66718-1*) Scholastic, Inc.

—The Baby-Sitters Club Boxed Set No. 19 Bks. 73-76: Mary Anne & Miss Priss; Kristy & the Copycat; Jessi's Horrible Prank; Stacey's Lie. 1997. (Baby-Sitters Club Ser.: Nos. 73-76). (J). (gr. 3-7). 14.00 o.p. (*0-590-66934-6*) Scholastic, Inc.

—The Baby-Sitters Club Boxed Set No. 20: Dawn & Whitney, Friends Forever; Claudia & Crazy Peaches; Mary Anne Breaks the Rules; Mallory Pike #1 Fan. 1997. (Baby-Sitters Club Ser.: Nos. 77-80). (J). (gr. 3-7). pap. 14.00 (*0-590-66935-4*) Scholastic, Inc.

—The Baby-Sitters Club Boxed Set No. 21: Kristy & Mr. Mom; Jessi & the Troublemaker; Stacey vs. the BSC; Dawn & the School Spirit War. 1997. (Baby-Sitters Club Ser.: Nos. 81-84). (J). (gr. 3-7). pap. 14.00 (*0-590-25154-6*) Scholastic, Inc.

—The Baby-Sitters Club Boxed Set No. 22: Claudia Kishi, Live from WTSO!; Mary Anne & Camp BSC; Stacey & the Bad Girls; Farewell Dawn. 1997. (Baby-Sitters Club Ser.: Nos. 85-88). (J). (gr. 3-7). pap. 14.00 (*0-590-25155-4*) Scholastic, Inc.

—The Baby-Sitters Club Chain Letter. 1993. (Baby-Sitters Club Ser.). 40p. (J). (gr. 3-7). pap. 14.95 (*0-590-47151-1*) Scholastic, Inc.

—The Baby-Sitters Club in the U. S. A. 1997. (Baby-Sitters Club Super Special Ser.: No. 14). 246p. (J). (gr. 3-7). mass mkt. 4.50 (*0-590-69216-X*) Scholastic, Inc.

—The Baby-Sitters Club Mystery Boxed Set No. 1: Stacey & the Missing Ring; Beware, Dawn!; Mallory & the Ghost Cat; Kristy & the Missing Child. (Baby-Sitters Club Mystery Ser.: Nos. 1-4). (J). (gr. 3-7). 1993. pap. text 14.00 (*0-590-66714-9*); Bks. 1-4. 1992. pap. 13.00 o.p. (*0-590-66110-8*) Scholastic, Inc.

—The Baby-Sitters Club Mystery Boxed Set No. 2: Mary Anne & the Secret in the Attic; The Mystery at Claudia's House; Dawn & the Disappearing Dogs; Jessi & the Jewel Thieves. 1993. (J). 14.00 (*0-590-66214-7*) Scholastic, Inc.

—The Baby-Sitters Club Mystery Boxed Set No. 4: Mary Anne & the Library Mystery; Stacey & the Mystery at the Mall; Kristy & the Vampires; Claudia & the Clue in the Photograph. 1997. (Baby-Sitters Club Mystery Ser.: Nos. 13-16). (J). (gr. 3-7). pap. text 14.00 (*0-590-66961-3*) Scholastic, Inc.

—The Baby-Sitters Club Mystery Boxed Set No. 5: Dawn & the Halloween Mystery; Stacey & the Mystery at the Empty House; Kristy & the Missing Fortune; Mary Anne & the Zoo Mystery. 1997. (Baby-Sitters Club Mystery Ser.: Nos. 17-20). (J). (gr. 3-7). pap. 14.00 (*0-590-66962-1*) Scholastic, Inc.

—The Baby-Sitters Club Postcard Book. 1991. (Baby-Sitters Club Ser.). 64p. (J). (gr. 3-7). mass mkt. 4.95 (*0-590-44783-1*) Scholastic, Inc.

—The Baby-Sitters Club Super Summer Special, Bks. 1-3. 1991. (J). (gr. 3-7). 10.50 o.p. (*0-590-63714-2*) Scholastic, Inc.

—Baby-Sitters' European Vacation. 1998. (Baby-Sitters Club Super Special Ser.: No. 15). (J). (gr. 3-7). mass mkt. 4.50 (*0-590-06000-7*) Scholastic, Inc.

—Baby-Sitters' Fright Night. 1996. (Baby-Sitters Club Super Mystery Ser.: No. 3). (J). (gr. 3-7). mass mkt. 4.50 (*0-590-69180-5*) Scholastic, Inc.

—Baby-Sitters' Haunted House. 1995. (Baby-Sitters Club Super Mystery Ser.: No. 1). 256p. (J). (gr. 3-7). mass mkt. 3.99 (*0-590-48311-0*) Scholastic, Inc.

—Baby-Sitters' Haunted House. 1995. (Baby-Sitters Club Super Mystery Ser.: No. 1). (J). (gr. 3-7). 9.09 o.p. (*0-606-07237-3*) Turtleback Bks.

—Baby-Sitters' Island Adventure. 1990. (Baby-Sitters Club Super Special Ser.: No. 4). 240p. (J). (gr. 3-7). mass mkt. 4.50 (*0-590-42493-9*) Scholastic, Inc.

—Baby-Sitters' Island Adventure. 1990. (Baby-Sitters Club Super Special Ser.: No. 4). (J). (gr. 3-7). 9.05 o.p. (*0-606-03040-9*) Turtleback Bks.

—The Baby-Sitters Little Sister Boxed Set No. 1 Bks. 1-4: Karen's Witch; Karen's Roller Skates; Karen's Worst Day; Karen's Kittycat Club. (Baby-Sitters Little Sister Ser.). (J). (gr. 3-7). 1993. pap. 15.96 (*0-590-66717-3*); 1989. pap. 11.00 o.p. (*0-590-63403-8*) Scholastic, Inc.

—The Baby-Sitters Little Sister Boxed Set No. 10 Bks. 37-40: Karen's Tuba; Karen's Big Lie; Karen's Wedding; Karen's Newspaper. 1993. (Baby-Sitters Little Sister Ser.). (J). (gr. 3-7). pap. o.p. (*0-590-66715-7*) Scholastic, Inc.

—The Baby-Sitters Little Sister Boxed Set No. 14 Bks. 53-56: Karen's School Bus; Karen's Candy; Karen's Magician; Karen's Ice Skates. 1997. (Baby-Sitters Little Sister Ser.). (J). (gr. 3-7). pap. 11.80 (*0-590-66941-9*) Scholastic, Inc.

—The Baby-Sitters Little Sister Boxed Set No. 2 Bks. 5-8: Karen's School Picture; Karen's Little Sister; Karen's Birthday; Karen's Haircut. 1990. (Baby-Sitters Little Sister Ser.). (J). (gr. 3-7). pap. 11.00 o.p. (*0-590-63593-X*) Scholastic, Inc.

—The Baby-Sitters Little Sister Boxed Set No. 3 Bks. 9-12: Karen's Sleepover; Karen's Grandmothers; Karen's Prize; Karen's Ghost. 1990. (Baby-Sitters Little Sister Ser.). (J). (gr. 3-7). pap. 11.00 (*0-590-63668-5*) Scholastic, Inc.

—The Baby-Sitters Little Sister Boxed Set No. 4 Bks. 13-16: Karen's Surprise; Karen's New Year; Karen's In Love; Karen's Goldfish. 1991. (Baby-Sitters Little Sister Ser.). (J). (gr. 3-7). pap. 11.00 (*0-590-63827-0*) Scholastic, Inc.

—The Baby-Sitters Little Sister Boxed Set No. 5 Bks. 17-20: Karen's Brothers; Karen's Home Run; Karen's Good-Bye; Karen's Carnival. 1991. (Baby-Sitters Little Sister Ser.). (J). (gr. 3-7). pap. 11.00 (*0-590-63950-1*) Scholastic, Inc.

—The Baby-Sitters Little Sister Boxed Set No. 8 Bks. 29-32: Karen's Cartwheel; Karen's Kittens; Karen's Bully; Karen's Pumpkin Patch. 1992. (Baby-Sitters Little Sister Ser.). (J). (gr. 3-7). 11.00 (*0-590-66210-4*, Scholastic Paperbacks) Scholastic, Inc.

—The Baby-Sitters Little Sister Laugh Pack: Baby-Sitters Little Sister Book of Laughs. 1997. (Baby-Sitters Little Sister Ser.). 64p. (J). (gr. 3-7). 6.99 (*0-590-13801-4*, Scholastic Paperbacks) Scholastic, Inc.

—Baby-Sitters Little Sister Summer Fill-In Book. 1995. (Baby-Sitters Little Sister Ser.). 96p. (J). (gr. 3-7). mass mkt. 2.95 (*0-590-26467-2*) Scholastic, Inc.

—Baby-Sitters on Board! 1988. (Baby-Sitters Club Super Special Ser.: No. 1). 240p. (YA). (gr. 3-7). mass mkt. 4.50 (*0-590-44240-6*) Scholastic, Inc.

—Baby-Sitters on Board! 1988. (Baby-Sitters Club Super Special Ser.: No. 1). (J). (gr. 3-7). 10.55 (*0-606-03721-7*) Turtleback Bks.

—The Baby-Sitters Remember. 1994. (Baby-Sitters Club Super Special Ser.: No. 11). 256p. (J). (gr. 3-7). mass mkt. 3.95 (*0-590-47015-9*) Scholastic, Inc.

—The Baby-Sitters Remember. 1994. (Baby-Sitters Club Super Special Ser.: No. 11). (J). (gr. 3-7). 9.05 o.p. (*0-606-06211-4*) Turtleback Bks.

—The Baby-Sitters Special Edition Readers' Request Boxed Set: Logan's Story; Logan Bruno, Boy Baby-Sitter; Shannon's Story. 1992. (Baby-Sitters Club Special Edition Ser.). (gr. 3-7). mass mkt. 10.50 (*0-590-66273-2*) Scholastic, Inc.

—Baby-Sitters' Summer Vacation. 1989. (Baby-Sitters Club Super Special Ser.: No. 2). 256p. (J). (gr. 3-7). mass mkt. 4.50 (0-590-44239-2) Scholastic, Inc.

—Baby-Sitters' Summer Vacation. 1989. (Baby-Sitters Club Super Special Ser.: No. 2). (J). (gr. 3-7). 9.05 o.p. (0-606-04165-6) Turtleback Bks.

—Baby-Sitters' Winter Vacation. 1989. (Baby-Sitters Club Super Special Ser.: No. 3). (J). (gr. 3-7). pap. 3.50 o.p. (0-590-42499-8, Scholastic Paperbacks); 240p. mass mkt. 4.50 (0-590-43973-1) Scholastic, Inc.

—Baby-Sitters' Winter Vacation. 1989. (Baby-Sitters Club Super Special Ser.: No. 3). (J). (gr. 3-7). 9.05 o.p. (0-606-00391-6) Turtleback Bks.

—Beware, Dawn! 1991. (Baby-Sitters Club Mystery Ser.: No. 2). 176p. (J). (gr. 3-7). mass mkt. 3.99 (0-590-44085-3) Scholastic, Inc.

—Beware, Dawn! 1991. (Baby-Sitters Club Mystery Ser.: No. 2). (J). (gr. 3-7). 10.04 (0-606-00309-6) Turtleback Bks.

—Boy-Crazy Stacey. l.t. ed. 1988. (Baby-Sitters Club Ser.: No. 8). 138p. (J). (gr. 3-7). reprint ed. 9.50 o.p. (0-942545-69-9); lib. bdg. 10.50 o.p. (0-942545-79-6) Grey Castle Pr.

—Boy-Crazy Stacey. (Baby-Sitters Club Ser.: No. 8). (J). (gr. 3-7). 1995. mass mkt. 3.99 (0-590-25163-5); 1987. 160p. pap. 2.50 o.p. (0-590-41040-7, Scholastic Paperbacks); 1987. 192p. mass mkt. 3.50 (0-590-43509-4) Scholastic, Inc.

—Boy-Crazy Stacey. l.t. ed. 1995. (Baby-Sitters Club Ser.: No. 8). 144p. (J). (gr. 3-7). lib. bdg. 21.27 o.p. (0-8368-1321-9) Stevens, Gareth Inc.

—Boy-Crazy Stacey. 1987. (Baby-Sitters Club Ser.: No. 8). (J). (gr. 3-7). 10.04 (0-606-03548-6) Turtleback Bks.

—BSC in the USA. 1997. (Baby-Sitters Club Super Special Ser.: No. 14). (J). (gr. 3-7). 10.55 (0-606-11078-X) Turtleback Bks.

—Bsls Box Set # 9. 2003. (J). 11.80 (0-590-66716-5) Scholastic, Inc.

—Claudia & Crazy Peaches. (Baby-Sitters Club Ser.: No. 78). (J). (gr. 3-7). 1999. 138p. pap. 3.99 (0-590-92610-1); 1994. 192p. mass mkt. 3.50 (0-590-48222-X) Scholastic, Inc.

—Claudia & Crazy Peaches. 1994. (Baby-Sitters Club Ser.: No. 78). (J). (gr. 3-7). 10.04 (0-606-06204-1) Turtleback Bks.

—Claudia & Crazy Peaches. 1995. (Baby-Sitters Club Ser.: No. 78). (J). (gr. 3-7). 7.98 (1-57042-367-9) Warner Bks., Inc.

—Claudia & Mean Janine. l.t. ed. 1988. (Baby-Sitters Club Ser.: No. 7). 145p. (J). (gr. 3-7). reprint ed. 9.50 o.p. (0-942545-68-0); lib. bdg. 10.50 o.p. (0-942545-78-8) Grey Castle Pr.

—Claudia & Mean Janine. (Baby-Sitters Club Ser.: No. 7). (J). (gr. 3-7). 1995. mass mkt. 3.99 (0-590-25162-7); 1987. 160p. pap. 2.75 o.p. (0-590-41041-5, Scholastic Paperbacks); 1987. 192p. mass mkt. 3.50 (0-590-43719-4) Scholastic, Inc.

—Claudia & Mean Janine. 1995. (Baby-Sitters Club Ser.: No. 7). 176p. (J). (gr. 3-7). lib. bdg. 21.27 o.p. (0-8368-1320-0) Stevens, Gareth Inc.

—Claudia & Mean Janine. 1987. (Baby-Sitters Club Ser.: No. 7). (J). (gr. 3-7). 10.04 (0-606-00551-X) Turtleback Bks.

—Claudia & the Bad Joke. (Baby-Sitters Club Ser.: No. 19). (J). (gr. 3-7). 1996. mass mkt. 3.99 (0-590-60671-9); 1988. 192p. mass mkt. 3.50 (0-590-43510-8) Scholastic, Inc.

—Claudia & the Bad Joke. l.t. ed. 1993. (Baby-Sitters Club Ser.: No. 19). 176p. (J). (gr. 3-7). lib. bdg. 19.93 o.p. (0-8368-1023-6) Stevens, Gareth Inc.

—Claudia & the Bad Joke. 1988. (Baby-Sitters Club Ser.: No. 19). (J). (gr. 3-7). 10.04 (0-606-04084-6) Turtleback Bks.

—Claudia & the Clue in the Photograph. 1994. (Baby-Sitters Club Mystery Ser.: No. 16). 176p. (J). (gr. 3-7). mass mkt. 3.99 (0-590-47054-X) Scholastic, Inc.

—Claudia & the Clue in the Photograph. 1994. (Baby-Sitters Club Mystery Ser.: No. 16). (J). (gr. 3-7). 10.04 (0-606-06208-4) Turtleback Bks.

—Claudia & the First Thanksgiving. 1995. (Baby-Sitters Club Ser.: No. 91). (J). (gr. 3-7). mass mkt. 3.50 (0-590-22875-7) Scholastic, Inc.

—Claudia & the First Thanksgiving. 1995. (Baby-Sitters Club Ser.: No. 91). (J). (gr. 3-7). 8.60 o.p. (0-606-08480-0) Turtleback Bks.

—Claudia & the Genius of Elm Street. 1991. (Baby-Sitters Club Ser.: No. 49). 192p. (YA). (gr. 3-7). mass mkt. 3.25 (0-590-44970-2) Scholastic, Inc.

—Claudia & the Genius of Elm Street. 1996. (Baby-Sitters Club Ser.: No. 49). (J). (gr. 3-7). lib. bdg. 21.27 o.p. (0-8368-1573-4) Stevens, Gareth Inc.

—Claudia & the Genius of Elm Street. 1991. (Baby-Sitters Club Ser.: No. 49). (J). (gr. 3-7). 9.30 (0-606-00357-6) Turtleback Bks.

—Claudia & the Great Search. 1990. (Baby-Sitters Club Ser.: No. 33). 192p. (J). (gr. 3-7). mass mkt. 3.25 (0-590-42495-5); mass mkt. 3.99 (0-590-73190-4) Scholastic, Inc.

—Claudia & the Great Search. l.t. ed. 1995. (Baby-Sitters Club Ser.: No. 33). 147p. (J). (gr. 3-7). lib. bdg. 21.27 o.p. (0-8368-1413-4) Stevens, Gareth Inc.

—Claudia & the Great Search. 1990. (Baby-Sitters Club Ser.: No. 33). (J). (gr. 3-7). 10.04 (0-606-03158-8) Turtleback Bks.

—Claudia & the Lighthouse Ghost. 1996. (Baby-Sitters Club Mystery Ser.: No. 27). 154p. (J). (gr. 3-7). mass mkt. 3.99 (0-590-69175-9) Scholastic, Inc.

—Claudia & the Lighthouse Ghost. 1996. (Baby-Sitters Club Mystery Ser.: No. 27). (J). (gr. 3-7). 10.04 (0-606-10134-9) Turtleback Bks.

—Claudia & the Little Liar. 1999. (Baby-Sitters Club Ser.: No. 128). 114p. (J). (gr. 3-7). mass mkt. 4.50 (0-590-50351-0) Scholastic, Inc.

—Claudia & the Middle School Mystery. 1991. (Baby-Sitters Club Ser.: No. 40). 192p. (J). (gr. 3-7). mass mkt. 3.25 (0-590-44082-9) Scholastic, Inc.

—Claudia & the Middle School Mystery. l.t. ed. 1995. (Baby-Sitters Club Ser.: No. 40). 176p. (J). (gr. 3-7). lib. bdg. 21.27 o.p. (0-8368-1420-7) Stevens, Gareth Inc.

—Claudia & the Middle School Mystery. 1991. (Baby-Sitters Club Ser.: No. 40). (J). (gr. 3-7). 10.04 (0-606-04637-2) Turtleback Bks.

—Claudia & the Middle School Mystery: Collector's Edition. 1998. (Baby-Sitters Club Ser.: No. 40). (Illus.). 135p. (J). (gr. 3-7). mass mkt. 3.99 (0-590-73452-0) Scholastic, Inc.

—Claudia & the Mystery at the Museum. 1993. (Baby-Sitters Club Mystery Ser.: No. 11). 176p. (J). (gr. 3-7). mass mkt. 3.50 (0-590-47049-3) Scholastic, Inc.

—Claudia & the Mystery at the Museum. 1993. (Baby-Sitters Club Mystery Ser.: No. 11). (J). (gr. 3-7). 9.55 (0-606-05142-2) Turtleback Bks.

—Claudia & the Mystery in the Painting. 1997. (Baby-Sitters Club Mystery Ser.: No. 32). 144p. (J). (gr. 3-7). mass mkt. 3.99 (0-590-05972-6) Scholastic, Inc.

—Claudia & the Mystery in the Painting. 1997. (Baby-Sitters Club Mystery Ser.: No. 32). (J). (gr. 3-7). 10.04 (0-606-11076-3) Turtleback Bks.

—Claudia & the New Girl. (Baby-Sitters Club Ser.: No. 12). (J). (gr. 3-7). 1988. 160p. pap. 2.75 o.p. (0-590-41126-8, Scholastic Paperbacks); 1988. 192p. mass mkt. 3.50 (0-590-43721-6); 1996. 160p. mass mkt. 3.99 (0-590-25167-8) Scholastic, Inc.

—Claudia & the New Girl. l.t. ed. 1993. (Baby-Sitters Club Ser.: No. 12). 176p. (J). (gr. 3-7). lib. bdg. 21.27 o.p. (0-8368-1016-3) Stevens, Gareth Inc.

—Claudia & the New Girl. 1989. (Baby-Sitters Club Ser.: No. 12). (J). (gr. 3-7). 10.04 (0-606-03758-6) Turtleback Bks.

—Claudia & the Perfect Boy. 1994. (Baby-Sitters Club Ser.: No. 71). 192p. (J). (gr. 3-7). mass mkt. 3.99 (0-590-47009-4) Scholastic, Inc.

—Claudia & the Perfect Boy. 1994. (Baby-Sitters Club Ser.: No. 71). (J). (gr. 3-7). 10.04 (0-606-05736-6) Turtleback Bks.

—Claudia & the Phantom Phone Calls. l.t. ed. 1988. (Baby-Sitters Club Ser.: No. 2). 153p. (J). (gr. 3-7). reprint ed. 9.50 o.p. (0-942545-63-X); lib. bdg. 10.50 o.p. (0-942545-73-7) Grey Castle Pr.

—Claudia & the Phantom Phone Calls. (Baby-Sitters Club Ser.: No. 2). (J). (gr. 3-7). 1986. pap. 2.50 o.p. (0-590-33951-6); 1986. 160p. mass mkt. 3.50 (0-590-43513-2); 1995. 192p. mass mkt. 3.99 (0-590-22763-7) Scholastic, Inc.

—Claudia & the Phantom Phone Calls. l.t. ed. 1995. (Baby-Sitters Club Ser.: No. 2). 153p. (J). (gr. 3-5). lib. bdg. 21.27 o.p. (0-8368-1315-4) Stevens, Gareth Inc.

—Claudia & the Phantom Phone Calls. 1986. (Baby-Sitters Club Ser.: No. 2). (J). (gr. 3-7). 10.04 (0-606-03083-2) Turtleback Bks.

—Claudia & the Recipe for Danger. 1995. (Baby-Sitters Club Mystery Ser.: No. 21). 176p. (J). (gr. 3-7). mass mkt. 3.50 (0-590-48310-2) Scholastic, Inc.

—Claudia & the Recipe for Danger. 1995. (Baby-Sitters Club Mystery Ser.: No. 21). (J). (gr. 3-7). 9.55 (0-606-07235-7) Turtleback Bks.

—Claudia & the Sad Good-Bye. (Baby-Sitters Club Ser.: No. 26). (J). (gr. 3-7). 1997. mass mkt. 3.99 (0-590-67394-7); 1989. 192p. mass mkt. 3.50 (0-590-42503-X) Scholastic, Inc.

—Claudia & the Sad Good-Bye. l.t. ed. 1994. (Baby-Sitters Club Ser.: No. 26). 176p. (J). (gr. 3-7). lib. bdg. 21.27 o.p. (0-8368-1247-6) Stevens, Gareth Inc.

—Claudia & the Sad Good-Bye. 1989. (Baby-Sitters Club Ser.: No. 26). (J). (gr. 3-7). 10.04 (0-606-04187-7) Turtleback Bks.

—Claudia & the Terrible Truth. 1998. (Baby-Sitters Club Ser.: No. 117). (J). (gr. 3-7). mass mkt. 4.50 (0-590-05995-5, Scholastic Paperbacks) Scholastic, Inc.

—Claudia & the Terrible Truth. 1998. (Baby-Sitters Club Ser.: No. 117). (J). (gr. 3-7). 10.04 (0-606-13161-2) Turtleback Bks.

—Claudia & the World's Cutest Baby. 1996. (Baby-Sitters Club Ser.: No. 97). (J). (gr. 3-7). mass mkt. 3.99 (0-590-22881-1) Scholastic, Inc.

—Claudia & the World's Cutest Baby. 1996. (Baby-Sitters Club Ser.: No. 97). (J). (gr. 3-7). 9.09 o.p. (0-606-09033-9) Turtleback Bks.

—Claudia Kishi, Live from WSTO! 1995. (Baby-Sitters Club Ser.: No. 85). (J). (gr. 3-7). pap. text 3.99 (0-590-94784-2); 192p. mass mkt. 3.50 (0-590-48236-X) Scholastic, Inc.

—Claudia Kishi, Middle School Drop Out. 1996. (Baby-Sitters Club Ser.: No. 101). (J). (gr. 3-7). mass mkt. 3.99 (0-590-69207-0) Scholastic, Inc.

—Claudia Kishi, Middle School Drop Out. 1996. (Baby-Sitters Club Ser.: No. 101). (J). (gr. 3-7). 10.04 (0-606-10131-4) Turtleback Bks.

—Claudia Makes up Her Mind. 1997. (Baby-Sitters Club Ser.: No. 113). (J). (gr. 3-7). 9.09 o.p. (0-606-12882-4) Turtleback Bks.

—Claudia, Queen of the Seventh Grade. 1997. (Baby-Sitters Club Ser.: No. 106). (J). (gr. 3-7). mass mkt. 3.99 (0-590-69212-7) Scholastic, Inc.

—Claudia, Queen of the Seventh Grade. 1997. (Baby-Sitters Club Ser.: No. 106). (J). (gr. 3-7). 10.04 (0-606-11066-6) Turtleback Bks.

—Claudia's Big Party. 1998. (Baby-Sitters Club Ser.: No. 123). 140p. (J). (gr. 3-7). mass mkt. 3.99 (0-590-50174-7) Scholastic, Inc.

—Claudia's Book. 1995. (Baby-Sitters Club Portrait Collection). 160p. (J). (gr. 3-7). mass mkt. 3.50 (0-590-48400-1) Scholastic, Inc.

—Claudia's Book. 1995. (Baby-Sitters Club Portrait Collection). (J). (gr. 3-7). 8.60 o.p. (0-606-07242-X) Turtleback Bks.

—Claudia's Freind Friend. 1993. (Baby-Sitters Club Ser.: No. 63). 192p. (J). (gr. 3-7). mass mkt. 3.50 (0-590-45665-2) Scholastic, Inc.

—Claudia's Freind Friend. 1993. (Baby-Sitters Club Ser.: No. 63). (J). (gr. 3-7). 9.55 (0-606-05135-X) Turtleback Bks.

—The Complete Guide to the Baby-Sitters Club. 1996. (Baby-Sitters Club Ser.). 240p. (J). (gr. 3-7). mass mkt. 4.95 (0-590-92713-2) Scholastic, Inc.

—The Complete Guide to the Baby-Sitters Club. 1996. (Baby-Sitters Club Ser.). (J). (gr. 3-7). 10.05 o.p. (0-606-09036-3) Turtleback Bks.

—Dawn & the Disappearing Dogs. 1993. (Baby-Sitters Club Mystery Ser.: No. 7). 176p. (J). (gr. 3-7). mass mkt. 3.50 (0-590-44960-5) Scholastic, Inc.

—Dawn & the Disappearing Dogs. 1993. (Baby-Sitters Club Mystery Ser.: No. 7). (J). (gr. 3-7). 8.60 o.p. (0-606-02503-0) Turtleback Bks.

—Dawn & the Halloween Mystery. 1994. (Baby-Sitters Club Mystery Ser.: No. 17). 176p. (J). (gr. 3-7). mass mkt. 3.50 (0-590-48232-7) Scholastic, Inc.

—Dawn & the Impossible Three. (Baby-Sitters Club Ser.: No. 5). (J). (gr. 3-7). 1995. 192p. mass mkt. 4.50 (0-590-25160-0); 2nd ed. 1988. pap. 3.50 (0-590-42232-4) Scholastic, Inc.

—Dawn & the Impossible Three. l.t. ed. 1995. (Baby-Sitters Club Ser.: No. 5). 144p. (J). (gr. 3-7). lib. bdg. 21.27 o.p. (0-8368-1318-9) Stevens, Gareth Inc.

—Dawn & the Impossible Three. 1987. (Baby-Sitters Club Ser.: No. 5). (J). (gr. 3-7). 10.55 (0-606-00545-5) Turtleback Bks.

—Dawn & the Older Boy. 1997. (Baby-Sitters Club Ser.: No. 37). (J). (gr. 3-7). mass mkt. 3.99 (0-590-73337-0) Scholastic, Inc.

—Dawn & the Older Boy. l.t. ed. 1995. (Baby-Sitters Club Ser.: No. 37). 144p. (J). (gr. 3-7). lib. bdg. 21.27 o.p. (0-8368-1417-7) Stevens, Gareth Inc.

—Dawn & the Older Boy. 1990. (Baby-Sitters Club Ser.: No. 37). (J). (gr. 3-7). 10.04 (0-606-04650-X) Turtleback Bks.

—Dawn & the School Spirit War. 1995. (Baby-Sitters Club Ser.: No. 84). 192p. (J). (gr. 3-7). mass mkt. 3.50 (0-590-48228-9) Scholastic, Inc.

—Dawn & the We Love Kids Club. (Baby-Sitters Club Ser.: No. 72). (J). (gr. 3-7). 1997. pap. text 3.99 (0-590-92603-9); 1994. 192p. mass mkt. 3.99 (0-590-47010-8) Scholastic, Inc.

—Dawn & the We Love Kids Club. 1994. (Baby-Sitters Club Ser.: No. 72). (J). (gr. 3-7). 8.60 o.p. (0-606-05737-4) Turtleback Bks.

—Dawn & Too Many Sitters. 1996. (Baby-Sitters Club Ser.: No. 98). (J). (gr. 3-7). mass mkt. 3.99 (0-590-22882-X) Scholastic, Inc.

—Dawn & Too Many Sitters. 1996. (Baby-Sitters Club Ser.: No. 98). (J). (gr. 3-7). 9.09 o.p. (0-606-09034-7) Turtleback Bks.

—Dawn & Whitney, Friends Forever. 1994. (Baby-Sitters Club Ser.: No. 77). 192p. (J). (gr. 3-7). mass mkt. 3.99 (0-590-48221-1) Scholastic, Inc.

—Dawn & Whitney, Friends Forever. 1994. (Baby-Sitters Club Ser.: No. 77). (J). (gr. 3-7). 9.09 o.p. (0-606-06203-3) Turtleback Bks.

—Dawn on the Coast. (Baby-Sitters Club Ser.: No. 23). (J). (gr. 3-7). mass mkt. 3.95 (0-590-42007-0); 1997. 160p. mass mkt. 3.99 (0-590-67391-2); 1989. 192p. pap. 3.50 (0-590-43900-6) Scholastic, Inc.

—Dawn on the Coast. l.t. ed. 1994. (Baby-Sitters Club Ser.: No. 23). 176p. (J). (gr. 3-7). lib. bdg. 21.27 o.p. (0-8368-1244-1) Stevens, Gareth Inc.

—Dawn on the Coast. 1989. (Baby-Sitters Club Ser.: No. 23). (J). (gr. 3-7). 10.04 (0-606-04085-4) Turtleback Bks.

—Dawn Saves the Planet. 1992. (Baby-Sitters Club Ser.: No. 57). 192p. (J). (gr. 3-7). mass mkt. 3.50 (0-590-45658-X, 052) Scholastic, Inc.

—Dawn Saves the Planet. 1992. (Baby-Sitters Club Ser.: No. 57). (J). (gr. 3-7). 8.60 o.p. (0-606-01806-9) Turtleback Bks.

—Dawn Schafer, Undercover Baby-Sitter. 1996. (Baby-Sitters Club Mystery Ser.: No. 26). (J). (gr. 3-7). mass mkt. 3.99 (0-590-22870-6) Scholastic, Inc.

—Dawn Schafer, Undercover Baby-Sitter. 1996. (Baby-Sitters Club Mystery Ser.: No. 26). (J). (gr. 3-7). 9.09 o.p. (0-606-09040-1) Turtleback Bks.

—Dawn's Big Date. (Baby-Sitters Club Ser.: No. 50). (J). (gr. 3-7). 1992. 192p. mass mkt. 3.50 (0-590-44969-9); No. 50. 1997. mass mkt. 3.99 (0-590-98496-9) Scholastic, Inc.

—Dawn's Big Date. 1996. (Baby-Sitters Club Ser.: No. 50). 176p. (J). (gr. 3-7). lib. bdg. 21.27 o.p. (0-8368-1574-2) Stevens, Gareth Inc.

—Dawn's Big Date. 1992. (Baby-Sitters Club Ser.: No. 50). (J). (gr. 3-7). 9.09 o.p. (0-606-00382-7) Turtleback Bks.

—Dawn's Big Move. 1993. (Baby-Sitters Club Ser.: No. 67). 192p. (J). (gr. 3-7). mass mkt. 3.50 (0-590-47005-1) Scholastic, Inc.

—Dawn's Big Move. 1993. (Baby-Sitters Club Ser.: No. 67). (J). (gr. 3-7). 8.60 o.p. (0-606-05139-2) Turtleback Bks.

—Dawn's Book. 1995. (Baby-Sitters Club Portrait Collection). (J). (gr. 3-7). 8.60 o.p. (0-606-07243-8) Turtleback Bks.

—Dawn's Family Feud. 1993. (Baby-Sitters Club Ser.: No. 64). 192p. (J). (gr. 3-7). mass mkt. 3.50 (0-590-45666-0) Scholastic, Inc.

—Dawn's Family Feud. 1993. (Baby-Sitters Club Ser.: No. 64). (J). (gr. 3-7). 9.55 (0-606-05136-8) Turtleback Bks.

—Dawn's Wicked Stepsister. 1990. (Baby-Sitters Club Ser.: No. 31). 192p. (J). (gr. 3-7). mass mkt. 3.50 (0-590-42497-1) Scholastic, Inc.

—Dawn's Wicked Stepsister. l.t. ed. 1995. (Baby-Sitters Club Ser.: No. 31). 144p. (J). (gr. 3-7). lib. bdg. 21.27 o.p. (0-8368-1411-8) Stevens, Gareth Inc.

—Dawn's Wicked Stepsister. 1990. (Baby-Sitters Club Ser.: No. 31). (J). (gr. 3-7). 10.04 (0-606-00676-1) Turtleback Bks.

—Don't Give up, Mallory. 1997. (Baby-Sitters Club Ser.: No. 108). (J). (gr. 3-7). mass mkt. 3.99 o.p. (0-590-69214-3, Scholastic Paperbacks) Scholastic, Inc.

—Don't Give up, Mallory. 1997. (Baby-Sitters Club Ser.: No. 108). (J). (gr. 3-7). 10.04 (0-606-11068-2) Turtleback Bks.

—Everything Changes. 1999. (Baby-Sitters Club Friends Forever Special Ser.: No. 1). (J). (gr. 3-7). pap. 4.50 (0-590-50391-X); 5.50 (0-439-08324-9) Scholastic, Inc.

—Farewell, Dawn. 1995. (Baby-Sitters Club Ser.: No. 88). 192p. (J). (gr. 3-7). mass mkt. 3.50 (0-590-22872-2) Scholastic, Inc.

—Farewell, Dawn. 1995. (Baby-Sitters Club Ser.: No. 88). (J). (gr. 3-7). 8.60 o.p. (0-606-07230-6) Turtleback Bks.

—Get Well Soon, Mallory! 1993. (Baby-Sitters Club Ser.: No. 69). 192p. (J). (gr. 3-7). mass mkt. 3.50 (0-590-47007-8) Scholastic, Inc.

—Get Well Soon, Mallory! 1993. (Baby-Sitters Club Ser.: No. 69). (J). (gr. 3-7). 8.60 o.p. (0-606-05734-X) Turtleback Bks.

—Get Well Soon, Mallory! Collector's Edition. 1997. (Baby-Sitters Club Ser.: No. 69). (J). (gr. 3-7). pap. text 3.99 (0-590-92600-4) Scholastic, Inc.

—The Ghost at Dawn's House. 1988. (Baby-Sitters Club Ser.: No. 9). 192p. (J). (gr. 3-7). mass mkt. 3.50 (0-590-43508-6) Scholastic, Inc.

—The Ghost at Dawn's House. l.t. ed. 1995. (Baby-Sitters Club Ser.: No. 9). 144p. (J). (gr. 3-7). lib. bdg. 21.27 o.p. (0-8368-1322-7) Stevens, Gareth Inc.

—The Ghost at Dawn's House. 1988. (Baby-Sitters Club Ser.: No. 9). (J). (gr. 3-7). 10.04 (0-606-03549-4) Turtleback Bks.

—Good-Bye Stacey, Good-Bye. (Baby-Sitters Club Ser.: No. 13). (J). (gr. 3-7). 1996. 176p. mass mkt. 3.99 (0-590-25168-6); 1988. 192p. mass mkt. 3.50 (0-590-43386-5) Scholastic, Inc.

—Good-Bye Stacey, Good-Bye. l.t. ed. 1993. (Baby-Sitters Club Ser.: No. 13). 176p. (J). (gr. 3-7). lib. bdg. 19.93 o.p. (0-8368-1017-1) Stevens, Gareth Inc.

—Good-Bye Stacey, Good-Bye. 1988. (Baby-Sitters Club Ser.: No. 13). (J). (gr. 3-7). 10.04 (0-606-03794-2) Turtleback Bks.

—Graduation Day. 2000. (Baby-Sitters Club Friends Forever Special Ser.: No. 2). 192p. (J). (gr. 3-7). mass mkt. 4.50 (0-439-21918-3) Scholastic, Inc.

—Jessi & the Awful Secret. (Baby-Sitters Club Ser.: No. 61). (J). (gr. 3-7). 1997. pap. text 3.99 *(0-590-92589-X)*; 1993. 192p. mass mkt. 3.50 *(0-590-45663-6)* Scholastic, Inc.

—Jessi & the Awful Secret. 1993. (Baby-Sitters Club Ser.: No. 61). (J). (gr. 3-7). 10.04 *(0-606-02499-9)* Turtleback Bks.

—Jessi & the Bad Baby-Sitter. 1993. (Baby-Sitters Club Ser.: No. 68). 192p. (J). (gr. 3-7). mass mkt. 3.50 *(0-590-47006-X)* Scholastic, Inc.

—Jessi & the Bad Baby-Sitter. 1993. (Baby-Sitters Club Ser.: No. 68). (J). (gr. 3-7). 9.55 *(0-606-05140-6)* Turtleback Bks.

—Jessi & the Dance School Phantom. 1991. (Baby-Sitters Club Ser.: No. 42). (J). (gr. 3-7). mass mkt. 3.99 *(0-590-74242-6)*; 192p. mass mkt. 3.50 *(0-590-44083-7*, Scholastic Paperbacks) Scholastic, Inc.

—Jessi & the Dance School Phantom. 1991. (Baby-Sitters Club Ser.: No. 42). (J). (gr. 3-7). 10.04 *(0-606-04950-9)* Turtleback Bks.

—Jessi & the Jewel Thieves. 1993. (Baby-Sitters Club Mystery Ser.: No. 8). 176p. (J). (gr. 3-7). mass mkt. 3.50 *(0-590-44959-1)* Scholastic, Inc.

—Jessi & the Jewel Thieves. 1993. (Baby-Sitters Club Mystery Ser.: No. 8). (J). (gr. 3-7). 9.09 o.p. *(0-606-05143-0)* Turtleback Bks.

—Jessi & the Superbrat. (Baby-Sitters Club Ser.: No. 27). (gr. 3-7). 1997. 160p. (J). mass mkt. 3.99 *(0-590-67395-5)*; 1989. 192p. (YA). mass mkt. 3.50 *(0-590-42502-1*, Scholastic Paperbacks) Scholastic, Inc.

—Jessi & the Superbrat. l.t. ed. 1994. (Baby-Sitters Club Ser.: No. 27). 176p. (J). (gr. 3-7). lib. bdg. 21.27 o.p. *(0-8368-1248-4)* Stevens, Gareth Inc.

—Jessi & the Superbrat. 1989. (Baby-Sitters Club Ser.: No. 27). (J). (gr. 3-7). 8.60 o.p. *(0-606-01558-2)* Turtleback Bks.

—Jessi & the Troublemaker. (Baby-Sitters Club Ser.: No. 82). (J). (gr. 3-7). 1997. pap. text 3.99 *(0-590-94777-X)*; 1995. 192p. mass mkt. 3.99 *(0-590-48226-2)* Scholastic, Inc.

—Jessi & the Troublemaker. 1995. (Baby-Sitters Club Ser.: No. 82). (J). (gr. 3-7). 9.09 o.p. *(0-606-07224-1)* Turtleback Bks.

—Jessi Ramsey, Pet-Sitter. (Baby-Sitters Club Ser.: No. 22). (J). (gr. 3-7). 1997. mass mkt. 3.99 *(0-590-67390-4)*; 1989. 192p. mass mkt. 3.50 *(0-590-43658-9)*; 1989. lib. bdg. 2.75 o.p. *(0-590-42006-2*, BSC #22) Scholastic, Inc.

—Jessi Ramsey, Pet-Sitter. l.t. ed. 1994. (Baby-Sitters Club Ser.: No. 22). 144p. (J). (gr. 3-7). lib. bdg. 21.27 o.p. *(0-8368-1243-3)* Stevens, Gareth Inc.

—Jessi Ramsey, Pet-Sitter. 1989. (Baby-Sitters Club Ser.: No. 22). (J). (gr. 3-7). 10.04 *(0-606-04086-2)* Turtleback Bks.

—Jessi's Baby-Sitter. 1990. (Baby-Sitters Club Ser.: No. 36). (gr. 3-7). 192p. (J). mass mkt. 3.50 *(0-590-43565-5)*; mass mkt. 3.99 *(0-590-73285-4)* Scholastic, Inc.

—Jessi's Baby-Sitter. l.t. ed. 1995. (Baby-Sitters Club Ser.: No. 36). 144p. (J). (gr. 3-7). lib. bdg. 21.27 o.p. *(0-8368-1416-9)* Stevens, Gareth Inc.

—Jessi's Baby-Sitter. 1990. (Baby-Sitters Club Ser.: No. 36). (J). (gr. 3-7). 10.04 *(0-606-04444-2)* Turtleback Bks.

—Jessi's Big Break. 1998. (Baby-Sitters Club Ser.: No. 115). (J). (gr. 3-7). mass mkt. 3.99 *(0-590-05993-9*, Scholastic Paperbacks) Scholastic, Inc.

—Jessi's Big Break. 1998. (Baby-Sitters Club Ser.: No. 115). (J). (gr. 3-7). 10.04 *(0-606-13159-0)* Turtleback Bks.

—Jessi's Gold Medal. 1992. (Baby-Sitters Club Ser.: No. 55). (J). (gr. 3-7). 192p. mass mkt. 3.25 *(0-590-44964-8*, Scholastic Paperbacks); mass mkt. 3.99 *(0-590-92580-6)* Scholastic, Inc.

—Jessi's Gold Medal. 1992. (Baby-Sitters Club Ser.: No. 55). (J). (gr. 3-7). 9.09 o.p. *(0-606-01858-1)* Turtleback Bks.

—Jessi's Horrible Prank. 1994. (Baby-Sitters Club Ser.: No. 75). 192p. (J). (gr. 3-7). mass mkt. 3.50 *(0-590-47013-2)* Scholastic, Inc.

—Jessi's Horrible Prank. 1994. (Baby-Sitters Club Ser.: No. 75). (J). (gr. 3-7). 8.60 *(0-606-06201-7)* Turtleback Bks.

—Jessi's Secret Language. (Baby-Sitters Club Ser.: No. 16). (J). (gr. 3-7). 1996. mass mkt. 3.99 *(0-590-60410-4)*; 1988. 160p. pap. 2.75 o.p. *(0-590-41586-7*, Scholastic Paperbacks); 1988. 192p. mass mkt. 3.50 *(0-590-44234-1)* Scholastic, Inc.

—Jessi's Secret Language. l.t. ed. 1993. (Baby-Sitters Club Ser.: No. 16). 176p. (J). (gr. 3-7). lib. bdg. 21.27 o.p. *(0-8368-1020-1)* Stevens, Gareth Inc.

—Jessi's Secret Language. 1988. (Baby-Sitters Club Ser.: No. 16). (J). (gr. 3-7). 10.04 *(0-606-04087-0)* Turtleback Bks.

—Jessi's Wish. 1991. (Baby-Sitters Club Ser.: No. 48). 192p. (J). (gr. 3-7). mass mkt. 3.50 *(0-590-43571-X)* Scholastic, Inc.

—Jessi's Wish. 1996. (Baby-Sitters Club Ser.: No. 48). 144p. (J). (gr. 3-7). lib. bdg. 21.27 o.p. *(0-8368-1572-6)* Stevens, Gareth Inc.

—Jessi's Wish. 1991. (Baby-Sitters Club Ser.: No. 48). (J). (gr. 3-7). 8.60 o.p. *(0-606-00523-4)* Turtleback Bks.

—Karen, Hannie, & Nancy: The Three Musketeers. 1992. (Baby-Sitters Little Sister Super Special Ser.: No. 4). 128p. (J). (gr. 2-4). mass mkt. 2.95 *(0-590-45644-X*, Scholastic Paperbacks) Scholastic, Inc.

—Karen, Hannie, & Nancy: The Three Musketeers. 1992. (Baby-Sitters Little Sister Super Special Ser.: No. 4). (J). (gr. 2-4). 9.00 *(0-606-01859-X)* Turtleback Bks.

—Karen's Accident. 1997. (Baby-Sitters Little Sister Ser.: No. 81). 109p. (J). (gr. 3-7). mass mkt. 2.99 *(0-590-69189-9)* Scholastic, Inc.

—Karen's Accident. 1997. (Baby-Sitters Little Sister Ser.: No. 81). (J). (gr. 3-7). 8.09 o.p. *(0-606-10747-9)* Turtleback Bks.

—Karen's Angel. 1995. (Baby-Sitters Little Sister Ser.: No. 68). (J). (gr. 3-7). mass mkt. 2.95 *(0-590-26025-1)* Scholastic, Inc.

—Karen's Baby. 1992. (Baby-Sitters Little Sister Super Special Ser.: No. 5). 128p. (J). (gr. 2-4). mass mkt. 3.50 *(0-590-45649-0)* Scholastic, Inc.

—Karen's Baby. 1992. (Baby-Sitters Little Sister Super Special Ser.: No. 5). (J). (gr. 2-4). 8.60 o.p. *(0-606-02512-X)* Turtleback Bks.

—Karen's Baby-Sitter. 1994. (Baby-Sitters Little Sister Ser.: No. 46). 112p. (J). (gr. 3-7). mass mkt. 3.50 *(0-590-47045-0)* Scholastic, Inc.

—Karen's Baby-Sitter. 1994. (Baby-Sitters Little Sister Ser.: No. 46). (J). (gr. 3-7). 9.55 *(0-606-05744-7)* Turtleback Bks.

—Karen's Big City Mystery. 1998. (Baby-Sitters Little Sister Ser.: No. 99). (J). (gr. 3-7). mass mkt. 3.99 *(0-590-49760-X*, Scholastic Paperbacks) Scholastic, Inc.

—Karen's Big Job. 1997. (Baby-Sitters Little Sister Ser.: No. 84). (J). (gr. 3-7). mass mkt. 3.50 *(0-590-69192-9*, 691553) Scholastic, Inc.

—Karen's Big Job. 1997. (Baby-Sitters Little Sister Ser.: No. 84). (Illus.). (J). (gr. 3-7). 8.60 o.p. *(0-606-11081-X)* Turtleback Bks.

—Karen's Big Joke. 1992. (Baby-Sitters Little Sister Ser.: No. 27). 112p. (J). (gr. 3-7). mass mkt. 3.50 *(0-590-44829-3)* Scholastic, Inc.

—Karen's Big Joke. 1992. (Baby-Sitters Little Sister Ser.: No. 27). (J). (gr. 3-7). 9.55 *(0-606-01860-3)* Turtleback Bks.

—Karen's Big Lie. 1993. (Baby-Sitters Little Sister Ser.: No. 38). 112p. (J). (gr. 3-7). mass mkt. 3.50 *(0-590-45655-5)* Scholastic, Inc.

—Karen's Big Lie. 1993. (Baby-Sitters Little Sister Ser.: No. 38). (J). (gr. 3-7). 9.55 *(0-606-05149-X)* Turtleback Bks.

—Karen's Big Top. 1994. (Baby-Sitters Little Sister Ser.: No. 51). 112p. (J). (gr. 3-7). mass mkt. 3.50 *(0-590-48229-7)* Scholastic, Inc.

—Karen's Big Top. 1994. (Baby-Sitters Little Sister Ser.: No. 51). (J). (gr. 3-7). 8.05 o.p. *(0-606-06215-7)* Turtleback Bks.

—Karen's Big Weekend. 1993. (Baby-Sitters Little Sister Ser.: No. 44). 112p. (J). (gr. 3-7). mass mkt. 3.50 *(0-590-47043-4)* Scholastic, Inc.

—Karen's Big Weekend. 1993. (Baby-Sitters Little Sister Ser.: No. 44). (J). (gr. 3-7). 9.04 *(0-606-05742-0)* Turtleback Bks.

—Karen's Birthday. 1990. (Baby-Sitters Little Sister Ser.: No. 7). (J). (gr. 3-7). 112p. mass mkt. 3.99 *(0-590-44257-0)*; pap. 2.50 o.p. *(0-590-42671-0)* Scholastic, Inc.

—Karen's Birthday. 1990. (Baby-Sitters Little Sister Ser.: No. 7). (J). (gr. 3-7). 10.04 *(0-606-04456-6)* Turtleback Bks.

—Karen's Book. 1998. (Baby-Sitters Little Sister Ser.: No. 100). (J). (gr. 3-7). mass mkt. 4.50 *(0-590-50051-1*, Scholastic Paperbacks) Scholastic, Inc.

—Karen's Book. 1998. (Baby-Sitters Little Sister Ser.: No. 100). (J). (gr. 3-7). 8.60 o.p. *(0-606-13167-1)* Turtleback Bks.

—Karen's Brothers. 1991. (Baby-Sitters Little Sister Ser.: No. 17). 112p. (J). (gr. 3-7). mass mkt. 3.99 *(0-590-43643-0)* Scholastic, Inc.

—Karen's Brothers. 1991. (Baby-Sitters Little Sister Ser.: No. 17). (J). (gr. 3-7). 9.55 *(0-606-04953-3)* Turtleback Bks.

—Karen's Bully. 1992. (Baby-Sitters Little Sister Ser.: No. 31). 112p. (J). (gr. 3-7). mass mkt. 3.50 *(0-590-45646-6*, 053) Scholastic, Inc.

—Karen's Bully. 1992. (Baby-Sitters Little Sister Ser.: No. 31). (J). (gr. 3-7). 8.05 o.p. *(0-606-01862-X)* Turtleback Bks.

—Karen's Bunny. 1997. (Baby-Sitters Little Sister Ser.: No. 83). 112p. (J). (gr. 3-7). mass mkt. 3.50 *(0-590-69191-0*, Scholastic Paperbacks) Scholastic, Inc.

—Karen's Bunny. 1997. (Baby-Sitters Little Sister Ser.: No. 83). (J). (gr. 3-7). 8.60 o.p. *(0-606-11080-1)* Turtleback Bks.

—Karen's Campout. 1993. (Baby-Sitters Little Sister Super Special Ser.: No. 6). 128p. (J). (gr. 2-4). mass mkt. 3.99 *(0-590-46911-8)* Scholastic, Inc.

—Karen's Campout. 1993. (Baby-Sitters Little Sister Super Special Ser.: No. 6). (J). (gr. 2-4). 9.09 o.p. *(0-606-05147-3)* Turtleback Bks.

—Karen's Candy. 1994. (Baby-Sitters Little Sister Ser.: No. 54). 112p. (J). (gr. 3-7). mass mkt. 3.50 *(0-590-48301-3)* Scholastic, Inc.

—Karen's Candy. 1994. (Baby-Sitters Little Sister Ser.: No. 54). (J). (gr. 3-7). 8.60 o.p. *(0-606-06218-1)* Turtleback Bks.

—Karen's Carnival. 1991. (Baby-Sitters Little Sister Ser.: No. 20). 112p. (J). (gr. 3-7). mass mkt. 3.99 *(0-590-44823-4)* Scholastic, Inc.

—Karen's Carnival. 1991. (Baby-Sitters Little Sister Ser.: No. 20). (J). (gr. 3-7). 9.55 *(0-606-04954-1)* Turtleback Bks.

—Karen's Cartwheel. 1992. (Baby-Sitters Little Sister Ser.: No. 29). 112p. (J). (gr. 3-7). mass mkt. 3.50 *(0-590-44825-0)* Scholastic, Inc.

—Karen's Cartwheel. 1992. (Baby-Sitters Little Sister Ser.: No. 29). (J). (gr. 3-7). 9.55 *(0-606-01863-8)* Turtleback Bks.

—Karen's Chain Letter. 1998. (Baby-Sitters Little Sister Ser.: No. 101). (J). (gr. 3-7). 9.55 *(0-606-13168-X)* Turtleback Bks.

—Karen's Christmas Carol. 1998. (Baby-Sitters Little Sister Ser.: No. 104). 112p. (J). (gr. 3-7). mass mkt. 3.50 *(0-590-50056-2)* Scholastic, Inc.

—Karen's Cooking Contest. 1998. (Baby-Sitters Little Sister Ser.: No. 93). (J). (gr. 3-7). mass mkt. 3.99 *(0-590-06591-2*, Scholastic Paperbacks) Scholastic, Inc.

—Karen's Copycat. 1999. (Baby-Sitters Little Sister Ser.: No. 107). 112p. (J). (gr. 3-7). mass mkt. 3.99 *(0-590-50059-7)* Scholastic, Inc.

—Karen's County Fair. 1996. (Baby-Sitters Little Sister Ser.: No. 75). (J). (gr. 3-7). mass mkt. 2.95 *(0-590-69183-X)* Scholastic, Inc.

—Karen's County Fair. 1996. (Baby-Sitters Little Sister Ser.: No. 75). (J). (gr. 3-12). 8.05 o.p. *(0-606-09050-9)* Turtleback Bks.

—Karen's Dinosaur. 1996. (Baby-Sitters Little Sister Ser.: No. 73). (Illus.). 106p. (J). (gr. 3-7). mass mkt. 2.95 *(0-590-26301-3)* Scholastic, Inc.

—Karen's Dinosaur. 1996. (Baby-Sitters Little Sister Ser.: No. 73). (J). (gr. 3-7). 8.05 o.p. *(0-606-09048-7)* Turtleback Bks.

—Karen's Doll. 1991. (Baby-Sitters Little Sister Ser.: No. 23). (J). (gr. 3-7). 10.04 *(0-606-00530-7)* Turtleback Bks.

—Karen's Doll Hospital. 1993. (Baby-Sitters Little Sister Ser.: No. 35). 112p. (J). (gr. 3-7). mass mkt. 3.50 *(0-590-45652-0)* Scholastic, Inc.

—Karen's Doll Hospital. 1993. (Baby-Sitters Little Sister Ser.: No. 35). (J). (gr. 3-7). 8.05 o.p. *(0-606-02510-3)* Turtleback Bks.

—Karen's Ducklings. 1992. (Baby-Sitters Little Sister Ser.: No. 26). 112p. (J). (gr. 3-7). mass mkt. 3.50 *(0-590-44830-7)* Scholastic, Inc.

—Karen's Ducklings. 1992. (Baby-Sitters Little Sister Ser.: No. 26). (J). (gr. 3-7). 9.00 *(0-606-01864-6)* Turtleback Bks.

—Karen's Field Day. 1999. (Baby-Sitters Little Sister Ser.: No. 108). 112p. (J). (gr. 3-7). mass mkt. 3.99 *(0-590-50060-0)* Scholastic, Inc.

—Karen's Ghost. 1990. (Baby-Sitters Little Sister Ser.: No. 12). 112p. (J). (gr. 3-7). mass mkt. 3.50 *(0-590-43649-X)* Scholastic, Inc.

—Karen's Ghost. 1990. (Baby-Sitters Little Sister Ser.: No. 12). (J). (gr. 3-7). 9.55 *(0-606-04715-8)* Turtleback Bks.

—Karen's Goldfish. 1991. (Baby-Sitters Little Sister Ser.: No. 16). 112p. (J). (gr. 3-7). mass mkt. 3.99 *(0-590-43644-9)* Scholastic, Inc.

—Karen's Goldfish. 1991. (Baby-Sitters Little Sister Ser.: No. 16). (J). (gr. 3-7). 9.00 *(0-606-04955-X)* Turtleback Bks.

—Karen's Good-Bye. 1991. (Baby-Sitters Little Sister Ser.: No. 19). 112p. (J). (gr. 3-7). mass mkt. 3.50 *(0-590-43641-4)* Scholastic, Inc.

—Karen's Good-Bye. 1991. (Baby-Sitters Little Sister Ser.: No. 19). (J). (gr. 3-7). 9.55 *(0-606-04956-8)* Turtleback Bks.

—Karen's Grandad. 1996. (Baby-Sitters Little Sister Ser.: No. 70). (J). (gr. 3-7). mass mkt. 3.50 *(0-590-26280-7)* Scholastic, Inc.

—Karen's Grandad. 1996. (Baby-Sitters Little Sister Ser.: No. 70). (J). (gr. 3-7). 9.00 *(0-606-09045-2)* Turtleback Bks.

—Karen's Grandmothers. 1990. (Baby-Sitters Little Sister Ser.: No. 10). 112p. (J). (gr. 3-7). mass mkt. 3.50 *(0-590-43651-1)* Scholastic, Inc.

—Karen's Grandmothers. 1990. (Baby-Sitters Little Sister Ser.: No. 10). (J). (gr. 3-7). 9.55 *(0-606-04457-4)* Turtleback Bks.

—Karen's Haircut. 1990. (Baby-Sitters Little Sister Ser.: No. 8). 112p. (J). (gr. 3-7). mass mkt. 3.50 *(0-590-42670-2)* Scholastic, Inc.

—Karen's Haircut. 1990. (Baby-Sitters Little Sister Ser.: No. 8). (J). (gr. 3-7). 9.55 *(0-606-04458-2)* Turtleback Bks.

—Karen's Half Birthday. 1996. (Baby-Sitters Little Sister Ser.: No. 78). (J). (gr. 3-7). mass mkt. 2.95 *(0-590-69186-4)* Scholastic, Inc.

—Karen's Haunted House. 1997. (Baby-Sitters Little Sister Ser.: No. 90). 112p. (J). (gr. 3-7). mass mkt. 3.50 *(0-590-06588-2)* Scholastic, Inc.

—Karen's Haunted House. 1997. (Baby-Sitters Little Sister Ser.: No. 90). (J). (gr. 3-7). 9.55 *(0-606-11087-9)* Turtleback Bks.

—Karen's Home Run. 1991. (Baby-Sitters Little Sister Ser.: No. 18). 112p. (J). (gr. 3-7). mass mkt. 2.95 *(0-590-43642-2)* Scholastic, Inc.

—Karen's Home Run. 1991. (Baby-Sitters Little Sister Ser.: No. 18). (J). (gr. 3-7). 9.55 *(0-606-04957-6)* Turtleback Bks.

—Karen's Hurricane. 1999. (Baby-Sitters Little Sister Ser.: No. 113). (Illus.). 106p. (J). (gr. 3-7). mass mkt. 3.99 *(0-590-52379-1)* Scholastic, Inc.

—Karen's Ice Skates. 1994. (Baby-Sitters Little Sister Ser.: No. 56). 112p. (J). (gr. 3-7). mass mkt. 3.50 *(0-590-48302-1)* Scholastic, Inc.

—Karen's Ice Skates. 1994. (Baby-Sitters Little Sister Ser.: No. 56). (J). (gr. 3-7). 8.05 o.p. *(0-606-06925-9)* Turtleback Bks.

—Karen's in Love. 1991. (Baby-Sitters Little Sister Ser.: No. 15). 112p. (J). (gr. 3-7). mass mkt. 3.99 *(0-590-43645-7)* Scholastic, Inc.

—Karen's in Love. 1991. (Baby-Sitters Little Sister Ser.: No. 15). (J). (gr. 3-7). 10.04 *(0-606-04716-6)* Turtleback Bks.

—Karen's Island Adventure. 1996. (Baby-Sitters Little Sister Ser.: No. 71). (J). (gr. 3-7). mass mkt. 2.95 *(0-590-26194-0)* Scholastic, Inc.

—Karen's Island Adventure. 1996. (Baby-Sitters Little Sister Ser.: No. 71). (J). (gr. 3-7). 8.60 o.p. *(0-606-09046-0)* Turtleback Bks.

—Karen's Kite. 1994. (Baby-Sitters Little Sister Ser.: No. 47). 112p. (J). (gr. 3-7). mass mkt. 2.95 *(0-590-46913-4)* Scholastic, Inc.

—Karen's Kite. 1994. (Baby-Sitters Little Sister Ser.: No. 47). (J). (gr. 3-7). 8.05 o.p. *(0-606-05745-5)* Turtleback Bks.

—Karen's Kittens. 1992. (Baby-Sitters Little Sister Ser.: No. 30). 112p. (J). (gr. 3-7). mass mkt. 3.50 *(0-590-45645-8)* Scholastic, Inc.

—Karen's Kittens. 1992. (Baby-Sitters Little Sister Ser.: No. 30). (J). (gr. 3-7). 8.05 o.p. *(0-606-01865-4)* Turtleback Bks.

—Karen's Kittycat Club. 1989. (Baby-Sitters Little Sister Ser.: No. 4). (J). (gr. 3-7). pap. 2.95 o.p. *(0-590-41782-7)*; 112p. mass mkt. 3.99 *(0-590-44264-3)* Scholastic, Inc.

—Karen's Kittycat Club. 1989. (Baby-Sitters Little Sister Ser.: No. 4). (J). (gr. 3-7). 10.04 *(0-606-04259-8)* Turtleback Bks.

—Karen's Lemonade Stand. 1995. (Baby-Sitters Little Sister Ser.: No. 64). 112p. (J). (gr. 3-7). mass mkt. 3.50 *(0-590-25997-0)* Scholastic, Inc.

—Karen's Lemonade Stand. 1995. (Baby-Sitters Little Sister Ser.: No. 64). (J). (gr. 3-7). 8.05 o.p. *(0-606-07251-9)* Turtleback Bks.

—Karen's Leprechaun. 1995. (Baby-Sitters Little Sister Ser.: No. 59). 112p. (J). (gr. 3-7). mass mkt. 3.50 *(0-590-48231-9)* Scholastic, Inc.

—Karen's Leprechaun. 1995. (Baby-Sitters Little Sister Ser.: No. 59). (J). (gr. 3-7). 8.05 o.p. *(0-606-07246-2)* Turtleback Bks.

—Karen's Little Sister. 1989. (Baby-Sitters Little Sister Ser.: No. 6). (J). (gr. 3-7). mass mkt. 2.50 o.p. *(0-590-42692-3*, Scholastic Paperbacks) Scholastic, Inc.

—Karen's Little Witch. 1991. (Baby-Sitters Little Sister Ser.: No. 22). (J). (gr. 3-7). 8.60 o.p. *(0-606-00531-5)* Turtleback Bks.

—Karen's Lucky Penny. abr. ed. 1994. (Baby-Sitters Little Sister Ser.: No. 50). 112p. (J). (gr. 3-7). mass mkt. 3.50 *(0-590-47048-5)* Scholastic, Inc.

—Karen's Lucky Penny. 1994. (Baby-Sitters Little Sister Ser.: No. 50). (J). (gr. 3-7). 9.55 *(0-606-06214-9)* Turtleback Bks.

—Karen's Magic Garden. 1996. (Baby-Sitters Little Sister Ser.: No. 76). (J). (gr. 3-7). mass mkt. 2.95 *(0-590-69184-8)* Scholastic, Inc.

—Karen's Magic Garden. 1996. (Baby-Sitters Little Sister Ser.: No. 76). (J). (gr. 3-7). 8.05 o.p. *(0-606-09051-7)* Turtleback Bks.

—Karen's Magician. 1994. (Baby-Sitters Little Sister Ser.: No. 55). 112p. (J). (gr. 3-7). mass mkt. 3.50 *(0-590-48230-0)* Scholastic, Inc.

—Karen's Magician. 1994. (Baby-Sitters Little Sister Ser.: No. 54). (J). (gr. 3-7). 8.05 o.p. *(0-606-06924-0)* Turtleback Bks.

—Karen's Mermaid. 1994. (Baby-Sitters Little Sister Ser.: No. 52). 112p. (J). (gr. 3-7). mass mkt. 2.95 *(0-590-48299-8)* Scholastic, Inc.

—Karen's Mermaid. 1994. (Baby-Sitters Little Sister Ser.: No. 52). (J). (gr. 3-7). 8.05 o.p. *(0-606-06216-5)* Turtleback Bks.

—Karen's Monsters. 1995. (Baby-Sitters Little Sister Ser.: No. 66). (J). (gr. 3-7). mass mkt. 3.50 *(0-590-26279-3)* Scholastic, Inc.

—Karen's Monsters. 1995. (Baby-Sitters Little Sister Ser.: No. 66). (J). (gr. 3-7). 8.05 o.p. *(0-606-07253-5)* Turtleback Bks.

—Karen's Movie. 1995. (Baby-Sitters Little Sister Ser.: No. 63). 112p. (J). (gr. 3-7). mass mkt. 3.50 (*0-590-25996-2*) Scholastic, Inc.
—Karen's Movie. 1995. (Baby-Sitters Little Sister Ser.: No. 63). (J). (gr. 3-7). 8.05 o.p. (*0-606-07250-0*) Turtleback Bks.
—Karen's Movie Star. 1998. (Baby-Sitters Little Sister Ser.: No. 103). 112p. (J). (gr. 3-7). mass mkt. 3.99 (*0-590-50055-4*) Scholastic, Inc.
—Karen's Mystery. 1991. (Baby-Sitters Little Sister Super Special Ser.: No. 3). (J). (gr. 2-4). 8.35 o.p. (*0-606-00532-3*) Turtleback Bks.
—Karen's New Bike. abr. ed. 1995. (Baby-Sitters Little Sister Ser.: No. 62). 112p. (J). (gr. 3-7). mass mkt. 3.50 (*0-590-48307-2*) Scholastic, Inc.
—Karen's New Bike. 1995. (Baby-Sitters Little Sister Ser.: No. 62). (J). (gr. 3-7). 8.05 o.p. (*0-606-07249-7*) Turtleback Bks.
—Karen's New Friend. 1993. (Baby-Sitters Little Sister Ser.: No. 36). 112p. (J). (gr. 3-7). mass mkt. 3.50 (*0-590-45651-2*) Scholastic, Inc.
—Karen's New Friend. 1993. (Baby-Sitters Little Sister Ser.: No. 36). (J). (gr. 3-7). 8.05 o.p. (*0-606-02511-1*) Turtleback Bks.
—Karen's New Puppy. 1996. (Baby-Sitters Little Sister Ser.: No. 72). (J). (gr. 3-7). mass mkt. 3.50 (*0-590-26195-9*) Scholastic, Inc.
—Karen's New Teacher. 1991. (Baby-Sitters Little Sister Ser.: No. 21). (J). (gr. 3-7). 9.55 (*0-606-00537-4*) Turtleback Bks.
—Karen's New Year. 1991. (Baby-Sitters Little Sister Ser.: No. 14). 112p. (J). (gr. 3-7). mass mkt. 3.99 (*0-590-43646-5*) Scholastic, Inc.
—Karen's New Year. 1991. (Baby-Sitters Little Sister Ser.: No. 15). (J). (gr. 3-7). 10.04 (*0-606-04717-4*) Turtleback Bks.
—Karen's Newspaper. 1993. (Baby-Sitters Little Sister Ser.: No. 40). 112p. (J). (gr. 3-7). mass mkt. 3.50 (*0-590-47040-X*) Scholastic, Inc.
—Karen's Newspaper. 1993. (Baby-Sitters Little Sister Ser.: No. 40). (J). (gr. 3-7). 9.55 (*0-606-05151-1*) Turtleback Bks.
—Karen's Paper Route. 1997. (Baby-Sitters Little Sister Ser.: No. 97). (Illus.). (J). (gr. 3-7). mass mkt. 3.50 (*0-590-06595-5*) Scholastic, Inc.
—Karen's Pen Pal. 1992. (Baby-Sitters Little Sister Ser.: No. 25). (J). (gr. 3-7). 9.55 (*0-606-00538-2*) Turtleback Bks.
—Karen's Pizza Party. 1993. (Baby-Sitters Little Sister Ser.: No. 42). 112p. (J). (gr. 3-7). mass mkt. 3.50 (*0-590-47042-6*) Scholastic, Inc.
—Karen's Pizza Party. 1993. (Baby-Sitters Little Sister Ser.: No. 42). (J). (gr. 3-7). 9.55 (*0-606-05153-8*) Turtleback Bks.
—Karen's Plane Trip. 1991. (Baby-Sitters Little Sister Super Special Ser.: No. 2). 128p. (J). (gr. 2-4). mass mkt. 3.25 (*0-590-44834-X*) Scholastic, Inc.
—Karen's Plane Trip. 1991. (Baby-Sitters Little Sister Super Special Ser.: No. 2). (J). (gr. 2-4). 8.35 o.p. (*0-606-04958-4*) Turtleback Bks.
—Karen's Pony. 1995. (Baby-Sitters Little Sister Ser.: No. 60). 112p. (J). (gr. 3-7). mass mkt. 3.50 (*0-590-48305-6*) Scholastic, Inc.
—Karen's Pony. 1995. (Baby-Sitters Little Sister Ser.: No. 60). (J). (gr. 3-7). 8.05 o.p. (*0-606-07247-0*) Turtleback Bks.
—Karen's Pony Camp. 1997. (Baby-Sitters Little Sister Ser.: No. 87). 112p. (J). (gr. 3-7). mass mkt. 3.50 (*0-590-06585-8*) Scholastic, Inc.
—Karen's Pony Camp. 1997. (Baby-Sitters Little Sister Ser.: No. 87). (J). (gr. 3-7). 9.55 (*0-606-11084-4*) Turtleback Bks.
—Karen's Prize. 1990. (Baby-Sitters Little Sister Ser.: No. 11). 112p. (J). (gr. 3-7). mass mkt. 3.50 (*0-590-43650-3*) Scholastic, Inc.
—Karen's Prize. 1990. (Baby-Sitters Little Sister Ser.: No. 11). (J). (gr. 3-7). 9.55 (*0-606-04718-2*) Turtleback Bks.
—Karen's Promise. 1998. (Baby-Sitters Little Sister Ser.: No. 95). (J). (gr. 3-7). mass mkt. 3.99 (*0-590-06593-9*, Scholastic Paperbacks) Scholastic, Inc.
—Karen's Promise. 1998. (Baby-Sitters Little Sister Ser.: No. 95). (J). (gr. 3-7). 10.04 (*0-606-13171-X*) Turtleback Bks.
—Karen's Pumpkin Patch. 1992. (Baby-Sitters Little Sister Ser.: No. 32). 112p. (J). (gr. 3-7). mass mkt. 3.50 (*0-590-45647-4*) Scholastic, Inc.
—Karen's Pumpkin Patch. 1992. (Baby-Sitters Little Sister Ser.: No. 32). (J). (gr. 3-7). 9.55 (*0-606-01866-2*) Turtleback Bks.
—Karen's Puppet Show. 1997. (Baby-Sitters Little Sister Ser.: No. 88). (J). (gr. 3-7). mass mkt. 3.50 (*0-590-06586-6*) Scholastic, Inc.
—Karen's Puppet Show. 1997. (Baby-Sitters Little Sister Ser.: No. 88). (J). (gr. 3-7). 9.55 (*0-606-11085-2*) Turtleback Bks.
—Karen's Roller Skates. 1988. (Baby-Sitters Little Sister Ser.: No. 2). (J). (gr. 3-7). 112p. mass mkt. 3.99 (*0-590-44259-7*); (Illus.). 80p. pap. 2.50 o.p. (*0-590-41781-9*) Scholastic, Inc.
—Karen's Roller Skates. 1988. (Baby-Sitters Little Sister Ser.: No. 2). (J). (gr. 3-7). 10.04 (*0-606-04061-7*) Turtleback Bks.
—Karen's School. (Baby-Sitters Little Sister Ser.: No. 41). 112p. (J). (gr. 3-7). 1994. mass mkt. 3.50 (*0-590-48300-5*); 1993. mass mkt. 2.95 (*0-590-47041-8*) Scholastic, Inc.
—Karen's School. 1993. (Baby-Sitters Little Sister Ser.: No. 41). (J). (gr. 3-7). 8.09 o.p. (*0-606-05152-X*) Turtleback Bks.
—Karen's School Bus. 1994. (Baby-Sitters Little Sister Ser.: No. 53). (J). (gr. 3-7). 8.05 o.p. (*0-606-06217-3*) Turtleback Bks.
—Karen's School Mystery. 1995. (Baby-Sitters Little Sister Ser.: No. 57). 112p. (J). (gr. 3-7). mass mkt. 3.99 (*0-590-48303-X*) Scholastic, Inc.
—Karen's School Mystery. 1995. (Baby-Sitters Little Sister Ser.: No. 57). (J). (gr. 3-7). 9.55 (*0-606-07244-6*) Turtleback Bks.
—Karen's School Mystery; Karen's Ski Trip; Karen's Leprechaun; Karen's Pony Bks. 57-60. 1997. (Baby-Sitters Little Sister Ser.). (J). (gr. 3-7). pap. 11.80 (*0-590-66958-3*) Scholastic, Inc.
—Karen's School Picture. 1989. (Baby-Sitters Little Sister Ser.: No. 5). (J). (gr. 3-7). 10.04 (*0-606-01609-0*) Turtleback Bks.
—Karen's School Surprise. 1996. (Baby-Sitters Little Sister Ser.: No. 77). (J). (gr. 3-7). mass mkt. 2.95 (*0-590-69185-6*) Scholastic, Inc.
—Karen's School Surprise. 1996. (Baby-Sitters Little Sister Ser.: No. 77). (J). (gr. 3-7). 8.05 o.p. (*0-606-09052-5*) Turtleback Bks.
—Karen's School Trip. 1992. (Baby-Sitters Little Sister Ser.: No. 24). (J). (gr. 3-7). mass mkt. 3.50 (*0-590-44859-5*) Scholastic, Inc.
—Karen's School Trip. 1992. (Baby-Sitters Little Sister Ser.: No. 24). (J). (gr. 3-7). 8.05 o.p. (*0-606-00539-0*) Turtleback Bks.
—Karen's Secret. (Baby-Sitters Little Sister Ser.: No. 33). (J). (gr. 3-7). 1997. 106p. mass mkt. 3.50 (*0-590-69190-2*); 1992. 112p. mass mkt. 3.50 (*0-590-45648-2*) Scholastic, Inc.
—Karen's Secret. 1992. (Baby-Sitters Little Sister Ser.: No. 33). (J). (gr. 3-7). 8.05 o.p. (*0-606-02508-1*) Turtleback Bks.
—Karen's Ski Trip. 1995. (Baby-Sitters Little Sister Ser.: No. 58). 112p. (J). (gr. 3-7). mass mkt. 3.50 (*0-590-48304-8*) Scholastic, Inc.
—Karen's Ski Trip. 1995. (Baby-Sitters Little Sister Ser.: No. 58). (J). (gr. 3-7). 8.05 o.p. (*0-606-07245-4*) Turtleback Bks.
—Karen's Sleepover. 1990. (Baby-Sitters Little Sister Ser.: No. 9). 112p. (J). (gr. 3-7). mass mkt. 3.99 (*0-590-43652-X*) Scholastic, Inc.
—Karen's Sleepover. 1990. (Baby-Sitters Little Sister Ser.: No. 9). (J). (gr. 3-7). 10.04 (*0-606-04459-0*) Turtleback Bks.
—Karen's Sleigh Ride. 1997. (Baby-Sitters Little Sister Ser.: No. 92). (J). (gr. 3-7). mass mkt. 3.99 (*0-590-06590-4*, Scholastic Paperbacks) Scholastic, Inc.
—Karen's Snow Day. 1993. (Baby-Sitters Little Sister Ser.: No. 34). 112p. (J). (gr. 3-7). mass mkt. 3.50 (*0-590-45650-4*) Scholastic, Inc.
—Karen's Snow Day. 1993. (Baby-Sitters Little Sister Ser.: No. 34). (J). (gr. 3-7). 8.05 o.p. (*0-606-02509-X*) Turtleback Bks.
—Karen's Snow Princess. 1998. (Baby-Sitters Little Sister Ser.: No. 94). (J). (gr. 3-7). mass mkt. 3.99 (*0-590-06592-0*) Scholastic, Inc.
—Karen's Softball Mystery. 1996. (Baby-Sitters Little Sister Ser.: No. 74). (J). (gr. 3-7). mass mkt. 2.95 (*0-590-26214-9*) Scholastic, Inc.
—Karen's Softball Mystery. 1996. (Baby-Sitters Little Sister Ser.: No. 74). (J). (gr. 3-7). 8.05 o.p. (*0-606-09049-5*) Turtleback Bks.
—Karen's Spy Mystery. 1999. (Babysitters Little Sister Ser.: No. 111). (Illus.). 109p. (J). (gr. 3-7). mass mkt. 3.99 (*0-590-52356-2*) Scholastic, Inc.
—Karen's Stepmother. 1994. (Baby-Sitters Little Sister Ser.: No. 49). 112p. (J). (gr. 3-7). mass mkt. 3.50 (*0-590-47047-7*) Scholastic, Inc.
—Karen's Stepmother. 1994. (Baby-Sitters Little Sister Ser.: No. 49). (J). (gr. 3-7). 9.00 (*0-606-06213-0*) Turtleback Bks.
—Karen's Surprise. 1990. (Baby-Sitters Little Sister Ser.: No. 13). 112p. (J). (gr. 3-7). mass mkt. 3.99 (*0-590-43648-1*) Scholastic, Inc.
—Karen's Surprise. 1990. (Baby-Sitters Little Sister Ser.: No. 13). (J). (gr. 3-7). 8.05 o.p. (*0-606-04719-0*) Turtleback Bks.
—Karen's Tattletale. 1995. (Baby-Sitters Little Sister Ser.: No. 61). 112p. (J). (gr. 3-7). mass mkt. 3.50 (*0-590-48306-4*) Scholastic, Inc.
—Karen's Tattletale. 1995. (Baby-Sitters Little Sister Ser.: No. 61). (J). (gr. 3-7). 8.05 o.p. (*0-606-07248-9*) Turtleback Bks.
—Karen's Tattletale; Karen's New Bike; Karen's Movie; Karen's Lemonade Stand Bks. 61-64. 1997. (Baby-Sitters Little Sister Ser.). (J). (gr. 3-7). pap. 11.80 (*0-590-66959-1*) Scholastic, Inc.
—Karen's Tea Party. 1992. (Baby-Sitters Little Sister Ser.: No. 28). 112p. (J). (gr. 3-7). mass mkt. 3.50 (*0-590-44828-5*) Scholastic, Inc.
—Karen's Tea Party. 1992. (Baby-Sitters Little Sister Ser.: No. 28). (J). (gr. 3-7). 9.55 (*0-606-01868-9*) Turtleback Bks.
—Karen's Telephone Trouble. 1997. (Baby-Sitters Little Sister Ser.: No. 86). (J). (gr. 3-7). mass mkt. 3.50 (*0-590-69194-5*, Scholastic Paperbacks) Scholastic, Inc.
—Karen's Telephone Trouble. 1997. (Baby-Sitters Little Sister Ser.: No. 86). (J). (gr. 3-7). 8.60 o.p. (*0-606-11083-6*) Turtleback Bks.
—Karen's Toothache. 1993. (Baby-Sitters Little Sister Ser.: No. 43). 112p. (J). (gr. 3-7). mass mkt. 3.50 (*0-590-46912-6*) Scholastic, Inc.
—Karen's Toothache. 1993. (Baby-Sitters Little Sister Ser.: No. 43). (J). (gr. 3-7). 9.55 (*0-606-05741-2*) Turtleback Bks.
—Karen's Toys. 1995. (Baby-Sitters Little Sister Ser.: No. 65). (J). (gr. 3-7). mass mkt. 3.50 (*0-590-25998-9*) Scholastic, Inc.
—Karen's Toys. 1995. (Baby-Sitters Little Sister Ser.: No. 65). (J). (gr. 3-7). 8.05 o.p. (*0-606-07252-7*) Turtleback Bks.
—Karen's Treasure. 1997. (Baby-Sitters Little Sister Ser.: No. 85). 112p. (J). (gr. 3-7). mass mkt. 3.50 (*0-590-69193-7*, Scholastic Paperbacks) Scholastic, Inc.
—Karen's Treasure. 1997. (Baby-Sitters Little Sister Ser.: No. 85). (J). (gr. 3-7). 9.55 (*0-606-11082-8*) Turtleback Bks.
—Karen's Tuba. 1993. (Baby-Sitters Little Sister Ser.: No. 37). 112p. (J). (gr. 3-7). mass mkt. 3.50 (*0-590-45653-9*) Scholastic, Inc.
—Karen's Tuba. 1993. (Baby-Sitters Little Sister Ser.: No. 37). (J). (gr. 3-7). 8.05 o.p. (*0-606-05148-1*) Turtleback Bks.
—Karen's Turkey Day. 1995. (Baby-Sitters Little Sister Ser.: No. 67). (J). (gr. 3-7). mass mkt. 2.95 (*0-590-26024-3*) Scholastic, Inc.
—Karen's Twin. 1994. (Baby-Sitters Little Sister Ser.: No. 45). 112p. (J). (gr. 3-7). mass mkt. 3.50 (*0-590-47044-2*) Scholastic, Inc.
—Karen's Twin. 1994. (Baby-Sitters Little Sister Ser.: No. 45). (J). (gr. 3-7). 9.55 (*0-606-05743-9*) Turtleback Bks.
—Karen's Two Families. 1994. (Baby-Sitters Little Sister Ser.: No. 48). 112p. (J). (gr. 3-7). mass mkt. 3.50 (*0-590-47046-9*) Scholastic, Inc.
—Karen's Two Families. 1994. (Baby-Sitters Little Sister Ser.: No. 48). (J). (gr. 3-7). 9.55 (*0-606-06212-2*) Turtleback Bks.
—Karen's Unicorn. 1997. (Baby-Sitters Little Sister Ser.: No. 89). (Illus.). 112p. (J). (gr. 3-7). mass mkt. 3.50 (*0-590-06587-4*) Scholastic, Inc.
—Karen's Unicorn. 1997. (Baby-Sitters Little Sister Ser.: No. 89). (J). (gr. 3-7). 9.55 (*0-606-11086-0*) Turtleback Bks.
—Karen's Wedding. 1993. (Baby-Sitters Little Sister Ser.: No. 39). 112p. (J). (gr. 3-7). mass mkt. 3.50 (*0-590-45654-7*) Scholastic, Inc.
—Karen's Wedding. 1993. (Baby-Sitters Little Sister Ser.: No. 39). (J). (gr. 3-7). 9.55 (*0-606-05150-3*) Turtleback Bks.
—Karen's Wish. 1990. (Baby-Sitters Little Sister Super Special Ser.: No. 1). (J). (gr. 2-4). 8.35 o.p. (*0-606-04720-4*) Turtleback Bks.
—Karen's Witch. 1988. (Baby-Sitters Little Sister Ser.: No. 1). 112p. (J). (gr. 3-7). pap. 2.50 o.p. (*0-590-41783-5*); mass mkt. 3.99 (*0-590-44300-3*) Scholastic, Inc.
—Karen's Witch. 1988. (Baby-Sitters Little Sister Ser.: No. 1). (J). (gr. 3-7). 10.04 (*0-606-03838-8*) Turtleback Bks.
—Karen's Worst Day. 1989. (Baby-Sitters Little Sister Ser.: No. 3). 112p. (J). (gr. 3-7). mass mkt. 3.99 (*0-590-44299-6*) Scholastic, Inc.
—Karen's Worst Day. 1989. (Baby-Sitters Little Sister Ser.: No. 3). (J). (gr. 3-7). 10.04 (*0-606-04062-5*) Turtleback Bks.
—Karen's Yo-Yo. 2000. (Baby-Sitters Little Sister Ser.: No. 119). (Illus.). 144p. (J). (gr. 3-7). mass mkt. 3.99 (*0-590-52511-5*) Scholastic, Inc.
—Keep Out, Claudia! 1992. (Baby-Sitters Club Ser.: No. 56). 192p. (J). (gr. 3-7). mass mkt. 3.50 (*0-590-45657-1*, Scholastic Paperbacks) Scholastic, Inc.
—Keep Out, Claudia! 1992. (Baby-Sitters Club Ser.: No. 56). (J). (gr. 3-7). 8.60 o.p. (*0-606-01870-0*) Turtleback Bks.
—Kristy + Bart = ? 1996. (Baby-Sitters Club Ser.: No. 95). (J). (gr. 3-7). mass mkt. 3.99 (*0-590-22879-X*) Scholastic, Inc.
—Kristy + Bart = ? 1996. (Baby-Sitters Club Ser.: No. 95). (J). (gr. 3-7). 9.09 o.p. (*0-606-09031-2*) Turtleback Bks.
—Kristy & Mr. Mom. 1995. (Baby-Sitters Club Ser.: No. 81). 192p. (J). (gr. 3-7). mass mkt. 3.50 (*0-590-48225-4*) Scholastic, Inc.
—Kristy & Mr. Mom. 1995. (Baby-Sitters Club Ser.: No. 81). (J). (gr. 3-7). 8.60 (*0-606-07223-3*) Turtleback Bks.
—Kristy & Mr. Mom. 1995. (Baby-Sitters Club Ser.: No. 81). (J). (gr. 3-7). 7.98 (*1-57042-368-7*) Warner Bks., Inc.
—Kristy & the Baby Parade. 1991. (Baby-Sitters Club Ser.: No. 45). 192p. (J). (gr. 3-7). mass mkt. 3.50 (*0-590-43574-4*) Scholastic, Inc.
—Kristy & the Baby Parade. 1996. (Baby-Sitters Club Ser.: No. 45). 176p. (J). (gr. 3-7). lib. bdg. 21.27 o.p. (*0-8368-1569-6*) Stevens, Gareth Inc.
—Kristy & the Baby Parade. 1991. (Baby-Sitters Club Ser.: No. 45). (J). (gr. 3-7). 9.55 (*0-606-04960-6*) Turtleback Bks.
—Kristy & the Cat Burglar. 1998. (Baby-Sitters Club Mystery Ser.: No. 36). (J). (gr. 3-7). mass mkt. 4.50 (*0-590-05976-9*, Scholastic Paperbacks) Scholastic, Inc.
—Kristy & the Copycat. 1994. (Baby-Sitters Club Ser.: No. 74). 192p. (J). (gr. 3-7). mass mkt. 3.99 (*0-590-47012-4*) Scholastic, Inc.
—Kristy & the Copycat. 1994. (Baby-Sitters Club Ser.: No. 74). (J). (gr. 3-7). 9.09 o.p. (*0-606-06200-9*) Turtleback Bks.
—Kristy & the Dirty Diapers. 1995. (Baby-Sitters Club Ser.: No. 89). 192p. (gr. 3-7). mass mkt. 3.50 (*0-590-22873-0*) Scholastic, Inc.
—Kristy & the Dirty Diapers. 1995. (Baby-Sitters Club Ser.: No. 89). (J). (gr. 3-7). 8.60 o.p. (*0-606-07231-4*) Turtleback Bks.
—Kristy & the Haunted Mansion. 1993. (Baby-Sitters Club Mystery Ser.: No. 9). 176p. (J). (gr. 3-7). mass mkt. 3.50 (*0-590-44958-3*) Scholastic, Inc.
—Kristy & the Haunted Mansion. 1993. (Baby-Sitters Club Mystery Ser.: No. 9). (J). (gr. 3-7). 8.60 o.p. (*0-606-05144-9*) Turtleback Bks.
—Kristy & the Middle School Vandal. 1996. (Baby-Sitters Club Mystery Ser.: No. 25). (J). (gr. 3-7). mass mkt. 3.99 (*0-590-22869-2*) Scholastic, Inc.
—Kristy & the Middle School Vandal. 1996. (Baby-Sitters Club Mystery Ser.: No. 25). (J). (gr. 3-7). 9.09 o.p. (*0-606-09039-8*) Turtleback Bks.
—Kristy & the Missing Child. 1992. (Baby-Sitters Club Mystery Ser.: No. 4). 176p. (J). (gr. 3-7). mass mkt. 3.99 (*0-590-44800-5*) Scholastic, Inc.
—Kristy & the Missing Child. 1992. (Baby-Sitters Club Mystery Ser.: No. 4). (J). (gr. 3-7). 9.55 (*0-606-01879-4*) Turtleback Bks.
—Kristy & the Missing Fortune. 1995. (Baby-Sitters Club Mystery Ser.: No. 19). 176p. (J). (gr. 3-7). mass mkt. 3.50 (*0-590-48234-3*) Scholastic, Inc.
—Kristy & the Missing Fortune. 1995. (Baby-Sitters Club Mystery Ser.: No. 19). (J). (gr. 3-7). 8.60 (*0-606-07233-0*) Turtleback Bks.
—Kristy & the Mother's Day Surprise. (Baby-Sitters Club Ser.: No. 24). (J). (gr. 3-7). 1997. 160p. mass mkt. 3.99 (*0-590-67392-0*); 1989. 192p. pap. 3.50 (*0-590-43506-X*); 1989. mass mkt. 2.75 o.p. (*0-590-42002-X*) Scholastic, Inc.
—Kristy & the Mother's Day Surprise. l.t. ed. 1994. (Baby-Sitters Club Ser.: No. 24). 176p. (J). (gr. 3-7). lib. bdg. 21.27 o.p. (*0-8368-1245-X*) Stevens, Gareth Inc.
—Kristy & the Mother's Day Surprise. 1989. (Baby-Sitters Club Ser.: No. 24). (J). (gr. 3-7). 10.04 (*0-606-04260-1*) Turtleback Bks.
—Kristy & the Mystery Train. 1997. (Baby-Sitters Club Mystery Ser.: No. 30). 160p. (J). (gr. 3-7). mass mkt. 3.99 (*0-590-69178-3*, Scholastic Paperbacks) Scholastic, Inc.
—Kristy & the Mystery Train. 1997. (Baby-Sitters Club Mystery Ser.: No. 30). (J). (gr. 3-7). 10.04 (*0-606-11074-7*) Turtleback Bks.
—Kristy & the Secret of Susan. 1990. (Baby-Sitters Club Ser.: No. 32). (J). (gr. 3-7). 192p. mass mkt. 3.50 (*0-590-42496-3*); mass mkt. 3.99 (*0-590-73189-0*) Scholastic, Inc.
—Kristy & the Secret of Susan. 1995. (Baby-Sitters Club Ser.: No. 32). 144p. (J). (gr. 3-7). lib. bdg. 21.27 o.p. (*0-8368-1412-6*) Stevens, Gareth Inc.
—Kristy & the Secret of Susan. 1990. (Baby-Sitters Club Ser.: No. 32). (J). (gr. 3-7). 10.04 (*0-606-04462-0*) Turtleback Bks.
—Kristy & the Sister War. 1997. (Baby-Sitters Club Ser.: No. 112). 160p. (J). (gr. 3-7). mass mkt. 3.99 (*0-590-05990-4*) Scholastic, Inc.
—Kristy & the Sister War. 1997. (Baby-Sitters Club Ser.: No. 112). (J). (gr. 3-7). 10.04 (*0-606-11072-0*) Turtleback Bks.
—Kristy & the Snobs. (Baby-Sitters Club Ser.: No. 11). (J). (gr. 3-7). 1996. 176p. mass mkt. 3.99 (*0-590-25166-X*); 1988. 160p. pap. 2.75 o.p. (*0-590-41125-X*, Scholastic Paperbacks); 1988. 192p. mass mkt. 3.50 (*0-590-43660-0*) Scholastic, Inc.
—Kristy & the Snobs. l.t. ed. 1993. (Baby-Sitters Club Ser.: No. 11). 176p. (J). (gr. 3-7). lib. bdg. 19.93 o.p. (*0-8368-1015-5*) Stevens, Gareth Inc.
—Kristy & the Snobs. 1988. (Baby-Sitters Club Ser.: No. 11). (J). (gr. 3-7). 10.55 (*0-606-03547-8*) Turtleback Bks.
—Kristy & the Vampires. 1994. (Baby-Sitters Club Mystery Ser.: No. 15). 176p. (J). (gr. 3-7). mass mkt. 3.50 (*0-590-47053-1*) Scholastic, Inc.
—Kristy & the Vampires. 1994. (Baby-Sitters Club Mystery Ser.: No. 14). (J). (gr. 3-7). 10.04 (*0-606-06207-6*) Turtleback Bks.

Occupations

—The Secret Life of Mary Anne Spier. 1997. (Baby-Sitters Club Ser.: No. 114). (J). (gr. 3-7). mass mkt. 3.99 (*0-590-05992-0*, Scholastic Paperbacks) Scholastic, Inc.

—The Secret Life of Mary Anne Spier. 1997. (Baby-Sitters Club Ser.: No. 114). (J). (gr. 3-7). 10.04 (*0-606-12883-2*) Turtleback Bks.

—Secret Santa. 1994. (Baby-Sitters Club Ser.). 40p. (J). (gr. 3-7). pap. 14.95 (*0-590-48295-5*) Scholastic, Inc.

—Snowbound. 1991. (Baby-Sitters Club Super Special Ser.: No. 7). 256p. (J). (gr. 3-7). mass mkt. 4.50 (*0-590-44963-X*) Scholastic, Inc.

—Stacey & the Bad Girls. 1995. (Baby-Sitters Club Ser.: No. 87). (J). (gr. 3-7). 192p. mass mkt. 3.50 (*0-590-48237-8*); 139p. pap. text 3.99 (*0-590-94786-9*) Scholastic, Inc.

—Stacey & the Bad Girls. 1995. (Baby-Sitters Club Ser.: No. 87). (J). (gr. 3-7). 9.09 o.p. (*0-606-07229-2*) Turtleback Bks.

—Stacey & the Cheerleaders. (Baby-Sitters Club Ser.: No. 70). (J). (gr. 3-7). 1997. pap. text 3.99 (*0-590-92601-2*); 1993. 192p. mass mkt. 3.50 (*0-590-47008-6*) Scholastic, Inc.

—Stacey & the Cheerleaders. 1993. (Baby-Sitters Club Ser.: No. 70). (J). (gr. 3-7). 9.09 o.p. (*0-606-05735-8*) Turtleback Bks.

—Stacey & the Fashion Victim. 1997. (Baby-Sitters Club Mystery Ser.: No. 29). 144p. (J). (gr. 3-7). mass mkt. 3.99 (*0-590-69177-5*, 691540) Scholastic, Inc.

—Stacey & the Fashion Victim. 1997. (Baby-Sitters Club Mystery Ser.: No. 29). (J). (gr. 3-7). 10.04 (*0-606-11073-9*) Turtleback Bks.

—Stacey & the Haunted Masquerade. 1995. (Baby-Sitters Club Mystery Ser.: No. 22). 176p. (J). (gr. 3-7). mass mkt. 3.50 (*0-590-22866-8*) Scholastic, Inc.

—Stacey & the Haunted Masquerade. 1995. (Baby-Sitters Club Mystery Ser.: No. 22). (J). (gr. 3-7). 9.55 (*0-606-07236-5*) Turtleback Bks.

—Stacey & the Mystery at the Empty House. 1994. (Baby-Sitters Club Mystery Ser.: No. 18). 176p. (J). (gr. 3-7). mass mkt. 3.50 (*0-590-48233-5*) Scholastic, Inc.

—Stacey & the Mystery at the Empty House. 1994. (Baby-Sitters Club Mystery Ser.: No. 18). (J). (gr. 3-7). 8.60 o.p. (*0-606-06921-6*) Turtleback Bks.

—Stacey & the Mystery at the Mall. 1994. (Baby-Sitters Club Mystery Ser.: No. 14). 176p. (J). (gr. 3-7). mass mkt. 3.99 (*0-590-47052-3*) Scholastic, Inc.

—Stacey & the Mystery at the Mall. 1994. (Baby-Sitters Club Mystery Ser.: No. 14). (J). (gr. 3-7). 9.09 o.p. (*0-606-06206-8*) Turtleback Bks.

—Stacey & the Mystery Money. 1993. (Baby-Sitters Club Mystery Ser.: No. 10). 176p. (J). (gr. 3-7). mass mkt. 3.50 (*0-590-45696-2*) Scholastic, Inc.

—Stacey & the Mystery Money. 1993. (Baby-Sitters Club Mystery Ser.: No. 10). (J). (gr. 3-7). 8.60 o.p. (*0-606-05141-4*) Turtleback Bks.

—Stacey & the Mystery of Stoneybrook. 1990. (Baby-Sitters Club Ser.: No. 35). 192p. (J). (gr. 3-7). mass mkt. 3.50 (*0-590-42508-0*) Scholastic, Inc.

—Stacey & the Stolen Hearts. 1998. (Baby-Sitters Club Mystery Ser.: No. 33). (J). (gr. 3-7). mass mkt. 3.99 (*0-590-05973-4*) Scholastic, Inc.

—Stacey McGill... Matchmaker? 1998. (Baby-Sitters Club Ser.: No. 124). 160p. (J). (gr. 3-7). mass mkt. 3.99 (*0-590-50175-5*) Scholastic, Inc.

—Stacey McGill, Super Sitter. 1996. (Baby-Sitters Club Ser.: No. 94). (J). (gr. 3-7). mass mkt. 3.99 (*0-590-22878-1*) Scholastic, Inc.

—Stacey McGill, Super Sitter. 1996. (Baby-Sitters Club Ser.: No. 94). (J). (gr. 3-7). 10.04 (*0-606-09030-4*) Turtleback Bks.

—Stacey the Math Whiz. 1997. (Baby-Sitters Club Ser.: No. 105). 143p. (J). (gr. 3-7). mass mkt. 3.99 (*0-590-69211-9*) Scholastic, Inc.

—Stacey the Math Whiz. 1997. (Baby-Sitters Club Ser.: No. 105). (J). (gr. 3-7). 10.04 (*0-606-10745-2*) Turtleback Bks.

—Stacey vs. the BSC. 1995. (Baby-Sitters Club Ser.: No. 83). 192p. (J). (gr. 3-7). mass mkt. 3.99 (*0-590-48235-1*) Scholastic, Inc.

—Stacey vs. the BSC. 1995. (Baby-Sitters Club Ser.: No. 83). (J). (gr. 3-7). 8.60 o.p. (*0-606-07225-X*) Turtleback Bks.

—Stacey's Big Crush. 1993. (Baby-Sitters Club Ser.: No. 65). 192p. (J). (gr. 3-7). mass mkt. 3.50 (*0-590-45667-9*) Scholastic, Inc.

—Stacey's Big Crush. 1993. (Baby-Sitters Club Ser.: No. 65). (J). (gr. 3-7). 9.55 (*0-606-05137-6*) Turtleback Bks.

—Stacey's Book. 1994. (Baby-Sitters Club Portrait Collection). 160p. (J). (gr. 3-7). mass mkt. 3.50 (*0-590-48399-4*) Scholastic, Inc.

—Stacey's Broken Heart. 1996. (Baby-Sitters Club Ser.: No. 99). (J). (gr. 3-7). mass mkt. 3.99 (*0-590-69205-4*) Scholastic, Inc.

—Stacey's Choice. (Baby-Sitters Club Ser.: No. 58). (gr. 3-7). 1997. pap. text 3.99 (*0-590-92584-9*); 1992. 192p. (J). mass mkt. 3.50 (*0-590-45659-8*) Scholastic, Inc.

—Stacey's Choice. 1992. (Baby-Sitters Club Ser.: No. 58). (J). (gr. 3-7). 9.09 o.p. (*0-606-01948-0*) Turtleback Bks.

—Stacey's Emergency. 1991. (Baby-Sitters Club Ser.: No. 43). (J). (gr. 3-7). 192p. mass mkt. 3.50 (*0-590-43572-8*);No. 4. mass mkt. 3.99 (*0-590-74243-4*) Scholastic, Inc.

—Stacey's Emergency. 1996. (Baby-Sitters Club Ser.: No. 43). 144p. (J). (gr. 3-7). lib. bdg. 21.27 o.p. (*0-8368-1567-X*) Stevens, Gareth Inc.

—Stacey's Emergency. 1991. (Baby-Sitters Club Ser.: No. 43). (J). (gr. 3-7). 10.04 (*0-606-05021-3*) Turtleback Bks.

—Stacey's Ex-Best Friend. 1992. (Baby-Sitters Club Ser.: No. 51). 192p. (J). (gr. 3-7). mass mkt. 3.50 (*0-590-44968-0*) Scholastic, Inc.

—Stacey's Ex-Best Friend. 1992. (Baby-Sitters Club Ser.: No. 51). (J). (gr. 3-7). 8.60 o.p. (*0-606-00770-9*) Turtleback Bks.

—Stacey's Ex-Boyfriend. 1998. (Baby-Sitters Club Ser.: No. 119). (J). (gr. 3-7). mass mkt. 3.99 (*0-590-05997-1*) Scholastic, Inc.

—Stacey's Ex-Boyfriend. 1998. (Baby-Sitters Club Ser.: No. 119). (J). (gr. 3-7). 10.04 (*0-606-13163-9*) Turtleback Bks.

—Stacey's Lie. (Baby-Sitters Club Ser.: No. 76). (J). (gr. 3-7). 1997. pap. text 3.99 (*0-590-92608-X*); 1994. 192p. mass mkt. 3.50 (*0-590-47014-0*) Scholastic, Inc.

—Stacey's Lie. 1994. (Baby-Sitters Club Ser.: No. 76). (J). (gr. 3-7). 9.09 o.p. (*0-606-06202-5*) Turtleback Bks.

—Stacey's Mistake. (Baby-Sitters Club Ser.: No. 18). (J). (gr. 3-7). 1996. mass mkt. 3.99 (*0-590-60534-8*); 1988. 192p. mass mkt. 3.99 (*0-590-43718-6*); 1988. pap. 2.75 o.p. (*0-590-41584-0*) Scholastic, Inc.

—Stacey's Mistake. l.t. ed. 1993. (Baby-Sitters Club Ser.: No. 18). 176p. (J). (gr. 3-7). lib. bdg. 19.93 o.p. (*0-8368-1022-8*) Stevens, Gareth Inc.

—Stacey's Mistake. 1987. (Baby-Sitters Club Ser.: No. 18). (J). (gr. 3-7). 10.04 (*0-606-04091-9*) Turtleback Bks.

—Stacey's Problem. 2000. (Baby-Sitters Club Friends Forever Ser.: No. 10). (Illus.). 144p. (J). (gr. 3-7). mass mkt. 4.50 (*0-590-52345-7*) Scholastic, Inc.

—Stacey's Secret Friend. 1997. (Baby-Sitters Club Ser.: No. 111). (Illus.). 160p. (J). (gr. 3-7). mass mkt. 3.99 (*0-590-05989-0*) Scholastic, Inc.

—Starring the Baby-Sitters Club! 1992. (Baby-Sitters Club Super Special Ser.: No. 9). 256p. (J). (gr. 3-7). mass mkt. 3.95 (*0-590-45661-X*) Scholastic, Inc.

—The Truth about Stacey. (Baby-Sitters Club Ser.: No. 3). (J). (gr. 3-7). 1995. 192p. mass mkt. 3.99 (*0-590-25158-9*); 1986. 144p. pap. 2.75 o.p. (*0-590-42124-7*, Scholastic Paperbacks); 1986. pap. 2.50 o.p. (*0-590-33952-4*); 1986. mass mkt. 3.50 (*0-590-43511-6*) Scholastic, Inc.

—The Truth about Stacey. l.t. ed. 1995. (Baby-Sitters Club Ser.: No. 3). 144p. (J). (gr. 3-7). lib. bdg. 21.27 o.p. (*0-8368-1316-2*) Stevens, Gareth Inc.

—The Truth about Stacey. 1986. (Baby-Sitters Club Ser.: No. 3). (J). (gr. 3-7). 10.04 (*0-606-03084-0*) Turtleback Bks.

—Welcome Back, Stacey! 1989. (Baby-Sitters Club Ser.: No. 28). 192p. (J). (gr. 3-7). mass mkt. 3.50 (*0-590-42501-3*, Scholastic Paperbacks) Scholastic, Inc.

—Welcome Back, Stacey! l.t. ed. 1994. (Baby-Sitters Club Ser.: No. 28). 176p. (J). (gr. 3-7). lib. bdg. 21.27 o.p. (*0-8368-1249-2*) Stevens, Gareth Inc.

—Welcome Back, Stacey! 1989. (Baby-Sitters Club Ser.: No. 28). (J). (gr. 3-7). 9.09 o.p. (*0-606-04419-1*) Turtleback Bks.

—Welcome Home, Mary Anne! 2000. (Baby-Sitters Club Friends Forever Ser.: No. 11). (Illus.). 144p. (J). (gr. 3-7). mass mkt. 4.50 (*0-590-52346-5*) Scholastic, Inc.

—Welcome to the BSC, Abby. 1995. (Baby-Sitters Club Ser.: No. 90). 192p. (J). (gr. 3-7). mass mkt. 3.99 (*0-590-22874-9*) Scholastic, Inc.

Martin, Ann M. & Singer, A. L. The Baby-Sitters Club: The Movie. 1995. 144p. (gr. 4-7). mass mkt. 3.50 (*0-590-60404-X*); 32p. (ps-3). mass mkt. 2.95 (*0-590-60403-1*) Scholastic, Inc.

Masurel, Claire. Emily & Her Baby-Sitter: A Lift-the-Flap Book. 2001. (Lift-the-Flap Ser.). (Illus.). 16p. pap. 6.99 (*0-14-056847-6*, Puffin Bks.) Penguin Putnam Bks. for Young Readers.

Mayer, Mercer. Just Me & My Babysitter. 1986. (Little Critter Ser.). (J). (ps-3). 9.44 (*0-606-12376-8*) Turtleback Bks.

Mazer, Anne. Out of Sight, Out of Mind. 2002. (Amazing Days of Abby Hayes Ser.: No. 9). 144p. (J). (gr. 1-4). pap. 4.50 o.s.i (*0-439-35368-8*) Scholastic, Inc.

McAllister, Angela. The Babies of Cockle Bay. 1994. (Illus.). 32p. (J). (ps-3). 13.95 o.p. (*0-8120-6424-0*); pap. 5.95 o.p. (*0-8120-1952-0*) Barron's Educational Series, Inc.

McAllister, Angela & Archbold, Tim. Be Good Gordon. 2003. (Illus.). 25p. (J). pap. 8.95 (*0-7475-5580-X*) Bloomsbury Publishing, Ltd. GBR. *Dist:* Trafalgar Square.

McCourt, Lisa. Chicken Soup for Little Souls: The Never-Forgotten Doll. 1997. (Chicken Soup for Little Souls Ser.). (Illus.). 32p. (J). (ps-3). tchr. ed. 14.95 (*1-55874-507-6*) Health Communications, Inc.

McKenna, Colleen O'Shaughnessy. The Brightest Light. 1992. 208p. (YA). (gr. 7-9). pap. 13.95 (*0-590-45347-5*) Scholastic, Inc.

Mills, Claudia. You're a Brave Man, Julius Zimmerman, RS. 1999. 160p. (J). (gr. 3-7). 16.00 (*0-374-38708-7*, Farrar, Straus & Giroux (BYR)) Farrar, Straus & Giroux.

—You're a Brave Man, Julius Zimmerman. 2001. 160p. (J). (gr. 4-7). pap. 5.99 (*0-7868-1448-9*) Hyperion Bks. for Children.

Minsky, Terri, creator. Lizzie McGuire Vol. 3: When Moms Attack & Misadventures in Babysitting. 2003. (Illus.). 192p. (J). pap. 7.99 (*1-59182-245-9*) TOKYOPOP, Inc.

Miranda, Anne. Baby-Sit, Vol. 1. 1990. (J). (ps). 9.95 (*0-316-57454-6*, Joy Street Bks.) Little Brown & Co.

Morton, Elizabeth. Anne's Baby Sitting Blues: The Animated Series. 2001. 96p. (J). (gr. 2-5). pap. 4.99 (*0-06-442159-7*, Avon) HarperCollins Children's Bk. Group.

Nixon, Joan Lowery. Gloria Chipmunk, Star! 1980. (Illus.). 48p. (J). pap. 1.50 o.p. (*0-590-31920-5*) Scholastic, Inc.

Okeane, Bernard. Lights Out. 1995. (Baby-Sitter's Nightmares Ser.: No. 7). 160p. mass mkt. 3.50 o.p. (*0-06-106297-9*) HarperCollins Pubs.

Orgel, Doris. My War with Mrs. Galloway. (Novels Ser.). (Illus.). 80p. (J). 1986. (gr. 2-5). pap. 3.95 o.p. (*0-14-032171-3*, Puffin Bks.); 1985. (gr. 4-6). 9.95 o.p. (*0-670-50217-0*, Viking Children's Bks.) Penguin Putnam Bks. for Young Readers.

Ostrow, Kim. Up All Night. 2004. (Ready-to-Read Ser.: Vol. 1). (Illus.). 32p. (J). pap. 3.99 (*0-689-86320-9*, Simon Spotlight/Nickelodeon) Simon & Schuster Children's Publishing.

Packard, Edward. The Haunted Baby. l.t. ed. 1998. (Choose Your Own Nightmare Ser.: No. 13). (Illus.). 96p. (J). (gr. 4 up). lib. bdg. 22.60 (*0-8368-2070-3*) Stevens, Gareth Inc.

Packard, Mary. Disney's Bambi: Opossum Problems. 1997. (Little Super Shape Bks.). (Illus.). 24p. (J). (ps). pap. text 2.79 o.p. (*0-307-10581-4*, 10581, Golden Bks.) Random Hse. Children's Bks.

Parker, Daniel. Alone in the Dark. 1995. (Baby-Sitter's Nightmares Ser.: No. 1). 176p. mass mkt. 3.50 o.p. (*0-06-106302-9*, HarperTorch) Morrow/Avon.

Pascal, Francine. Elizabeth's First Kiss. 1990. (J). pap. o.s.i (*0-553-16981-5*) Bantam Bks.

Pascal, Francine, creator. Beware the Babysitter. 1996. (Sweet Valley High Ser.: No. 99). 224p. (YA). (gr. 7 up). mass mkt. 2.49 o.s.i (*0-553-57034-X*) Bantam Bks.

—Jessica the Baby-Sitter. 1990. (Sweet Valley Kids Ser.: No. 14). 80p. (gr. 1-3). pap. text 3.50 o.s.i (*0-553-15838-4*) Bantam Bks.

Paterson, Bettina. Bun & Mrs. Tubby. 1987. (Illus.). 32p. (J). (ps-1). 11.95 o.p. (*0-531-05700-3*); mass mkt. 11.99 o.p. (*0-531-08300-4*) Scholastic, Inc. (Orchard Bks.).

Paton, Priscilla. Howard & the Sitter Surprise. 1996. (Illus.). 32p. (J). (ps-3). 15.95 o.p. (*0-395-71814-7*) Houghton Mifflin Co.

Pryor, Bonnie & Baird, Anne. Jenny's New Baby Sitter. 1987. (Next Step Ser.). (Illus.). (J). (ps). 3.95 o.p. (*0-671-63758-4*, Atheneum) Simon & Schuster Children's Publishing.

Quackenbush, Robert. Henry Babysits. 1990. (Gold Banner Bks.). (Illus.). 48p. (J). (ps-2). 2.95 o.p. (*0-448-04338-6*, Grosset & Dunlap) Penguin Putnam Bks. for Young Readers.

—Henry Babysits. 1993. 48p. (J). (gr. 1 up). lib. bdg. 19.93 o.p. (*0-8368-0968-8*) Stevens, Gareth Inc.

Random House Staff. Cassie's Babysitting Surprise. Angelilli, Chris, ed. 2000. (Sticker Time Ser.). (Illus.). 16p. (J). (ps-3). pap. 2.99 (*0-375-81065-X*, Random Hse. Bks. for Young Readers) Random Hse. Children's Bks.

Robbins, Beth. Tom, Ally & the Babysitter. 2001. (It's OK! Ser.). (Illus.). 32p. (J). (ps-k). pap. 3.95 (*0-7894-7426-3*, D K Ink) Dorling Kindersley Publishing, Inc.

Roberts, Willo Davis. Baby-Sitting is a Dangerous Job. 1985. 192p. (J). (gr. 4-6). text 14.95 o.s.i (*0-689-31100-1*, Atheneum) Simon & Schuster Children's Publishing.

—Baby-Sitting is a Dangerous Job. 1996. 10.55 (*0-606-09044-4*) Turtleback Bks.

—Baby-Sitting Is a Dangerous Job. 1987. 144p. (gr. 4-7). mass mkt. 6.50 (*0-449-70177-8*, Fawcett) Ballantine Bks.

—Baby-Sitting Is a Dangerous Job. 1996. 192p. (J). (gr. 3-7). pap. 4.99 (*0-689-80657-4*, Aladdin) Simon & Schuster Children's Publishing.

—Baby-Sitting Is a Dangerous Job. 1987. (J). 9.60 (*0-606-01206-0*) Turtleback Bks.

Ross, Pat. M & M & the Bad News Babies. 1999. (Illus.). (J). pap. 12.40 (*0-8085-3696-6*) Econo-Clad Bks.

—M & M & the Bad News Babies. 1985. (Picture Puffin Bks.). (Illus.). 48p. (J). (ps-3). pap. 4.99 (*0-14-031851-8*, Puffin Bks.) Penguin Putnam Bks. for Young Readers.

—M & M & the Bad News Babies. 1983. (I Am Reading Bks.). (Illus.). 48p. (J). (gr. 6-9). pap. 6.95 o.p. (*0-394-84532-3*); 7.99 o.s.i (*0-394-94532-8*) Random Hse. Children's Bks. (Knopf Bks. for Young Readers).

—M & M & the Bad News Babies. 1985. (Picture Puffin Ser.). (Illus.). (J). 11.14 (*0-606-01684-8*) Turtleback Bks.

Rubel, Nicole. Uncle Henry & Aunt Henrietta's Honeymoon. 1986. (Pied Piper Bks.). (Illus.). 32p. (J). (ps-2). 10.95 o.p. (*0-8037-0246-9*); 10.89 o.p. (*0-8037-0247-7*) Penguin Putnam Bks. for Young Readers. (Dial Bks. for Young Readers).

Rylant, Cynthia. Henry & Mudge & Mrs. Hopper's House. (Henry & Mudge Ser.). (J). 2004. 40p. pap. 3.99 (*0-689-83446-2*, Aladdin); 2003. (Illus.). 40p. 14.95 (*0-689-81153-5*, Simon & Schuster Children's Publishing); 1999. 12.95 (*0-689-81320-1*, Simon & Schuster Children's Publishing) Simon & Schuster Children's Publishing.

Saunders, Susan. Patti's New Look. 1988. (Sleepover Friends Ser.: No. 4). 80p. (Orig.). (J). (gr. 4-6). mass mkt. 2.50 o.p. (*0-590-40644-2*, Scholastic Paperbacks) Scholastic, Inc.

Scarry, Richard. The Best Baby-Sitter Ever. 1995. (J). mass mkt. 2.95 (*0-689-80742-2*); (Illus.). 32p. 3.25 (*0-689-80366-4*) Simon & Schuster Children's Publishing. (Simon Spotlight).

Scholastic, Inc. Staff. Baby-Sitter's Club. 1998. pap. 45.92 o.p. (*0-590-63077-6*) Scholastic, Inc.

Schulte, Elaine L. Cara & the Terrible Teeners. 1995. (Twelve Candles Club Ser.: Vol. 8). 128p. (J). (gr. 3-7). pap. 5.99 o.p. (*1-55661-536-1*) Bethany Hse. Pubs.

Shahan, Sherry. Baby-Sitting Crack-Up. 1988. (Treetop Tales Ser.). (Illus.). 112p. (J). (gr. 3-6). pap. 1.00 o.p. (*0-87406-326-4*) Darby Creek Publishing.

Siburt, Ruth. The Trouble with Alex. 1998. 93p. (J). (gr. 5-8). pap. 9.99 (*0-88092-366-0*, 3660) Royal Fireworks Publishing Co.

Simon, Charnan. Click & the Kids Go Sailing. 2000. (Illus.). 32p. (J). (gr. 1 up). 12.95 (*1-57768-885-6*, Cricket) McGraw-Hill Children's Publishing.

Simon, Francesca. The Topsy-Turvies. 1996. (Illus.). 28p. (J). (ps-3). 14.99 o.s.i (*0-8037-1969-8*, Dial Bks. for Young Readers) Penguin Putnam Bks. for Young Readers.

Singer, A. L. The Baby-Sitters Club: Based on the Movie. 1995. (Baby-Sitters Club Ser.). 40p. (gr. 1-3). mass mkt. 2.95 (*0-590-54085-8*) Scholastic, Inc.

—The Baby-Sitters Club: Based on The Movie. 1995. (Baby-Sitters Club Ser.). (J). 8.60 o.p. (*0-606-07238-1*) Turtleback Bks.

Singleton, Linda Joy. Babysitter Beware. 1996. (My Sister, the Ghost Ser.: No. 4). (J). (gr. 3-5). 9.09 o.p. (*0-606-09655-8*) Turtleback Bks.

Smith, Jane Denitz. Fairy Dust. 2002. (Illus.). 160p. (J). (gr. 3-7). 15.95 (*0-06-029279-2*); lib. bdg. 15.89 (*0-06-029280-6*) HarperCollins Children's Bk. Group.

—Fairy Dust. Date not set. (J). (gr. 3-7). mass mkt. 4.99 (*0-06-440961-9*) HarperCollins Pubs.

Smith, Susan. Monster-Sitter. 1987. (Samantha Slade Ser.: No. 1). (J). (gr. 5 up). pap. (*0-671-63713-4*, Simon Pulse) Simon & Schuster Children's Publishing.

Stahl, Hilda. Kathy's Baby-Sitting Hassle. 1992. (Best Friends Ser.: No. 3). 160p. (J). (gr. 4-7). pap. 4.99 o.p. (*0-89107-659-X*) Crossway Bks.

Steel, Danielle. Max & the Babysitter. 1989. (Illus.). 32p. (J). (ps-3). 8.95 (*0-385-29796-3*, Delacorte Pr.) Dell Publishing.

Stevens, Kathleen. The Beast & the Babysitter. 1989. (Illus.). 32p. (J). (gr. 2-3). lib. bdg. 18.60 o.p. (*1-55532-929-2*) Stevens, Gareth Inc.

Stewart, Molly Mia. Jessica the Baby-Sitter. 1990. (Sweet Valley Kids Ser.: No. 14). (J). (gr. 1-3). 8.70 o.p. (*0-606-04711-5*) Turtleback Bks.

Stine, R. L. Attack of the Beastly Babysitter. 1997. (Give Yourself Goosebumps Ser.: No. 18). (J). (gr. 3-7). mass mkt. 3.99 (*0-590-93485-6*, Scholastic Paperbacks) Scholastic, Inc.

—Attack of the Beastly Babysitter. 1997. (Give Yourself Goosebumps Ser.: No. 18). (J). (gr. 3-7). 9.09 o.p. (*0-606-11063-1*) Turtleback Bks.

—The Baby-Sitter. (Babysitter Ser.: Vol. 4). 1995. (Illus.). 176p. (gr. 8-12). mass mkt. 3.99 (*0-590-48744-2*); 1989. 167p. (YA). (gr. 7-12). mass mkt. 3.99 (*0-590-44236-8*, Scholastic Paperbacks) Scholastic, Inc.

Strasser, Todd. Here Comes Heavenly, No. 1. 1999. (Here Comes Heavenly Ser.). 192p. (YA). (gr. 7-12). pap. 4.99 (*0-671-03626-2*, Simon Pulse) Simon & Schuster Children's Publishing.

Stuart, Jon, illus. Newton & the Babysitter. 2001. (It's OK! Ser.). 32p. (J). (ps-k). pap. 12.95 (*0-7894-7427-1*, D K Ink) Dorling Kindersley Publishing, Inc.

Summer, M. C. The Evil Child. 1995. (Baby-Sitter's Nightmares Ser.: No. 2). 176p. mass mkt. 3.50 o.p. (*0-06-106301-0*, HarperTorch) Morrow/Avon.

Suzanne, Jamie. Boys Against Girls. 1988. (Sweet Valley Twins Ser.: No. 17). (J). (gr. 3-7). 112p. pap. 3.50 o.s.i (*0-553-15666-7*); mass mkt. o.s.i (*0-553-16826-6*) Bantam Bks.

—Boys Against Girls. 1987. (Sweet Valley Twins Ser.: No. 17). (J). (gr. 3-7). pap. o.p. (*0-553-16806-1*, Dell Books for Young Readers) Random Hse. Children's Bks.

—The Bully. 1988. (Sweet Valley Twins Ser.: No. 19). (J). (gr. 3-7). pap. 3.25 (*0-553-16827-4*) Bantam Bks.

—Center of Attention. 1988. (Sweet Valley Twins Ser.: No. 18). (J). (gr. 3-7). 112p. pap. 3.25 o.s.i (*0-553-15668-3*); pap. 3.25 (*0-553-16823-1*) Bantam Bks.

—Don't Go in the Basement. 1997. (Sweet Valley Twins Ser.: No. 109). 144p. (gr. 3-7). pap. text 3.50 o.s.i (*0-553-48440-0*, Sweet Valley) Random Hse. Children's Bks.

Teague, Mark. The Baby Tamer. 1997. (Illus.). 32p. (J). (ps-2). pap. 15.95 (*0-590-67712-8*) Scholastic, Inc.

Tolles, Martha. Katie's Baby-Sitting Job. 1985. (Orig.). pap. 2.50 o.p. (*0-590-32523-X*); 128p. (J). (gr. 3-7). mass mkt. 2.75 o.p. (*0-590-42608-7*); 128p. (J). (gr. 4-7). pap. 2.50 o.p. (*0-590-40724-4*, Scholastic Paperbacks) Scholastic, Inc.

Travers, Pamela L. Mary Poppins. 1981. (J). (gr. 4-7). reprint ed. lib. bdg. 27.95 (*0-89966-390-7*) Buccaneer Bks., Inc.

—Mary Poppins. 1997. (Illus.). 224p. (YA). (gr. 3-7). rev. ed. 18.00 (*0-15-252595-5*); 2nd rev. ed. pap. 6.00 (*0-15-201717-8*, Odyssey Classics) Harcourt Children's Bks.

—Mary Poppins. (J). 1997. 100.00 o.s.i (*0-15-252596-3*); 1981. (Illus.). 206p. (gr. 3-7). 14.95 (*0-15-252408-8*) Harcourt Trade Pubs.

—Mary Poppins. 202p. (J). (gr. 3-5). pap. 6.00 (*0-8072-1536-8*, Listening Library) Random Hse. Audio Publishing Group.

—Mary Poppins. 1997. 12.05 (*0-606-12418-7*) Turtleback Bks.

—Mary Poppins Comes Back. 1981. (J). reprint ed. lib. bdg. 17.95 (*0-89966-392-3*) Buccaneer Bks., Inc.

—Mary Poppins Comes Back. 1997. (Illus.). 320p. (J). (gr. 3-7). 18.00 (*0-15-201718-6*); pap. 6.00 (*0-15-201719-4*, Odyssey Classics) Harcourt Children's Bks.

—Mary Poppins in Cherry Tree Lane. 1982. (J). 10.95 (*0-440-05137-1*, Delacorte Pr.) Dell Publishing.

—Mary Poppins in Cherry Tree Lane. 1992. 96p. (J). (gr. 3-7). pap. 3.50 o.s.i (*0-440-40637-4*, Yearling) Random Hse. Children's Bks.

—Mary Poppins in the Park. (Illus.). (J). 1997. 288p. (gr. 3-7). 18.00 (*0-15-201716-X*); 1952. 265 p. 11.95 (*0-15-252947-0*); 2nd ed. 1997. 288p. (gr. 3-7). pap. 6.00 (*0-15-201721-6*, Odyssey Classics) Harcourt Children's Bks.

—Mary Poppins Opens the Door. 1981. (J). reprint ed. lib. bdg. 27.95 (*0-89966-391-5*) Buccaneer Bks., Inc.

—Mary Poppins Opens the Door. 1997. (Illus.). 272p. (YA). (gr. 3-7). 18.00 (*0-15-201720-8*); 2nd ed. pap. 6.00 (*0-15-201722-4*, Odyssey Classics) Harcourt Children's Bks.

Tulloch, Richard. Being Bad for the Baby-Sitter. 1994. 56p. (J). (gr. 4-7). pap. 2.95 o.p. (*0-590-46061-7*) Scholastic, Inc.

Venn, Cecilia. On with the Show! 1998. (Real Kids Readers Ser.). (Illus.). 48p. (J). (gr. 1-3). 18.90 (*0-7613-2011-3*); pap. 4.99 (*0-7613-2036-9*) Millbrook Pr., Inc.

—On with the Show! 1998. (Real Kids Readers Ser.). 10.14 (*0-606-15805-7*) Turtleback Bks.

—On with the Show! 2001. (J). E-Book (*1-58824-734-1*); 1998. E-Book (*1-58824-817-8*); 1998. E-Book (*1-58824-486-5*) ipicturebooks, LLC.

Vestly, Anne-Catherine. Aurora & Socrates. 1977. (Illus.). (J). (gr. 3-7). 12.95 (*0-690-01293-4*) HarperCollins Children's Bk. Group.

Waggoner, Karen. Lemonade Babysitter. 1992. (J). (ps-3). 14.95 o.p. (*0-316-91711-7*, Joy Street Bks.) Little Brown & Co.

Wardlaw, Lee. Saturday Night Jamboree. 2000. (Illus.). 32p. (J). (ps-3). 15.99 o.p. (*0-8037-2189-7*, Dial Bks. for Young Readers) Penguin Putnam Bks. for Young Readers.

Wells, Rosemary. Shy Charles. (Illus.). (J). (ps-2). 2001. 32p. 15.99 (*0-670-88729-3*); 1992. 320p. pap. 17.99 o.s.i (*0-14-054570-0*, Puffin Bks.); 1992. 32p. pap. 5.99 o.p. (*0-14-054537-9*, Puffin Bks.); 1988. (*0-8037-0511-5*, Dial Bks. for Young Readers); 1988. 32p. 13.99 o.s.i (*0-8037-0563-8*, Dial Bks. for Young Readers); 1988. 32p. 11.89 o.p. (*0-8037-0564-6*, Dial Bks. for Young Readers) Penguin Putnam Bks. for Young Readers.

—Shy Charles. 1988. (Picture Puffin Ser.). (Illus.). (J). 12.14 (*0-606-01745-3*) Turtleback Bks.

Weyn, Suzanne. Baby-Sitter Go Home. 1992. (Baker's Dozen Ser.: No. 4). 96p. (J). pap. 2.75 o.p. (*0-590-43561-2*) Scholastic, Inc.

White, Susan. Bad Baby-Sitter's Handbook. 1992. 64p. (J). (gr. 4-7). pap. 2.99 o.s.i (*0-440-40633-1*, Yearling) Random Hse. Children's Bks.

William, Kate. Beware the Babysitter. 1993. (Sweet Valley High Ser.: No. 99). (YA). (gr. 7 up). 8.60 o.p. (*0-606-06028-6*) Turtleback Bks.

—The Ghost of Tricia Martin. 1990. (Sweet Valley High Ser.: No. 64). (YA). (gr. 7 up). 8.35 o.p. (*0-606-03370-X*) Turtleback Bks.

Wilson, Pauline Hutchens & Dengler, Sandy. The Case of the Monster in the Creek. 2001. (New Sugar Creek Gang Ser.: Vol. 6). 144p. (J). mass mkt. 5.99 (*0-8024-8666-5*) Moody Pr.

Winthrop, Elizabeth. Bear's Christmas Surprise. 1999. (Illus.). (ps-3). pap. 5.99 (*0-440-41492-X*) Dell Publishing.

—Bear's Christmas Surprise. 1991. (Illus.). 32p. (J). (ps-3). tchr. ed. 14.95 (*0-8234-0888-4*) Holiday Hse., Inc.

Wolff, Virginia Euwer. Make Lemonade, ERS. 1993. 208p. (YA). (gr. 5-9). 17.95 (*0-8050-2228-7*, Holt, Henry & Co. Bks. For Young Readers) Holt, Henry & Co.

—Make Lemonade. 2003. 208p. (J). (gr. 5 up). mass mkt. 5.99 (*0-590-48141-X*, Scholastic Paperbacks) Scholastic, Inc.

—Make Lemonade. l.t. ed. 1993. (Teen Scene Ser.). (YA). (gr. 9-12). 17.95 (*0-7862-0056-1*) Thorndike Pr.

—Make Lemonade. 1993. (Point Signature Ser.). (J). 11.04 (*0-606-06555-5*) Turtleback Bks.

Wright, Betty Ren. Haunted Summer. 1996. 99p. (J). (gr. 4-7). pap. 14.95 (*0-590-47355-7*) Scholastic, Inc.

Zoehfeld, Kathleen Weidner. Roo's New Babysitter. 1999. (My Very First Winnie the Pooh Ser.). (Illus.). 32p. (J). (ps-k). 11.99 (*0-7868-3215-0*) Disney Pr.

BUCCANEERS—FICTION

Pyle, Howard. Tales of Pirates & Buccaneers. Suriano, Gregory R., ed. 1998. (Illus.). 207p. (J). text 15.00 o.p. (*0-7881-5277-7*) DIANE Publishing Co.

—Tales of Pirates & Buccaneers. 1994. (Illus.). (J). 12.99 o.s.i (*0-517-10162-9*) Random Hse. Value Publishing.

BUS DRIVERS—FICTION

Bland, Geneva F. Herman & the Mini-Bus with Soul. 1994. (Illus.). 22p. (J). 14.95 (*0-9638969-0-3*) GBL Publishing Co.

Gray, Genevieve. I Know a Bus Driver. 1972. (Community Helper Bks.). (Illus.). 48p. (J). (gr. 1-3). 4.29 o.p. (*0-399-60703-X*) Putnam Publishing Group, The.

Helakoski, Leslie. The Smushy Bus. 2002. (Illus.). 32p. (J). (gr. k-3). 22.90 (*0-7613-1398-2*); 15.95 (*0-7613-1917-4*) Millbrook Pr., Inc.

Lakin, Patricia. Up a Tree. 1994. (My School Ser.). (Illus.). (J). lib. bdg. 21.40 o.p. (*0-8114-3868-6*) Raintree Pubs.

Morris, Deborah. Runaway Bus & other True Stories: Real Kids Real Adventures. 2003. (Juvenile Ser.). (Illus.). (J). 21.95 (*0-7862-5095-X*) Thorndike Pr.

Nichols, Paul. Big Paul's School Bus. 1981. (Illus.). 32p. (J). (ps-3). 8.95 o.s.i (*0-13-076091-9*) Prentice Hall PTR.

Pulver, Robin. Axle Annie. 1999. (Illus.). (J). lib. bdg. 16.01 (*0-8037-2097-1*, Dial Bks. for Young Readers) Penguin Putnam Bks. for Young Readers.

—Axle Annie. Kane, Cindy, ed. 1999. (Illus.). 32p. (J). (ps-3). 15.99 (*0-8037-2096-3*, Dial Bks. for Young Readers) Penguin Putnam Bks. for Young Readers.

Willner-Pardo, Gina. Spider Storch's Fumbled Field Trip. 1998. 10.10 (*0-606-17183-5*) Turtleback Bks.

—Spider Storch's Fumbled Field Trip. 1998. (Illus.). (J). (gr. 2-5). 68p. pap. 3.95 (*0-8075-7582-8*); 80p. lib. bdg. 11.95 (*0-8075-7581-X*) Whitman, Albert & Co.

C

CANADA—ROYAL CANADIAN MOUNTED POLICE—FICTION

Freedman, Benedict. Mrs. Mike. 1981. (J). (gr. 8-12). reprint ed. lib. bdg. 35.95 (*0-89966-396-6*) Buccaneer Bks., Inc.

Freedman, Benedict, et al. Mrs. Mike. 1987. 288p. (YA). (gr. 8-12). mass mkt. 4.99 (*0-425-10328-5*) Berkley Publishing Group.

Freedman, Nancy. Mrs. Mike. 9999. (J). pap. 1.95 o.s.i (*0-590-03445-6*) Scholastic, Inc.

CLERGY—FICTION

Barrie, J. M. The Little Minister. 1968. (Airmont Classics Ser.). (J). (gr. 10 up). mass mkt. 0.75 o.p. (*0-8049-0187-2*, CL-187) Airmont Publishing Co., Inc.

Christie, Amanda. Nobody's Perfect. 1999. (7th Heaven Ser.). (Illus.). 176p. (J). (gr. 5-8). mass mkt. 4.99 (*0-375-80433-1*) Random Hse., Inc.

—Seventh Heaven: Nobody's Perfect. 1998. (7th Heaven Ser.). 126p. (J). (gr. 3-7). pap. 3.99 o.s.i (*0-679-89123-4*) Random Hse., Inc.

Dahl, Roald. The Vicar of Nibbleswicke. (Illus.). 1994. 48p. (YA). (gr. 4-7). pap. 6.99 (*0-14-036837-X*, Puffin Bks.); 1992. 240p. (J). 12.50 o.s.i (*0-670-84384-9*, Viking Children's Bks.) Penguin Putnam Bks. for Young Readers.

—The Vicar of Nibbleswicke. 1993. 12.14 (*0-606-06849-X*) Turtleback Bks.

Father Murphy's Promise. 1982. (Illus.). 128p. (J). (gr. 4-7). pap. 1.95 o.p. (*0-394-85318-0*, Random Hse. Bks. for Young Readers) Random Hse. Children's Bks.

Goldsmith, Oliver. The Vicar of Wakefield. 1964. (Airmont Classics Ser.). (YA). (gr. 10 up). mass mkt. 1.25 o.p. (*0-8049-0052-3*, CL-52) Airmont Publishing Co., Inc.

—The Vicar of Wakefield. 1981. (gr. 10 up). pap. 0.95 o.s.i (*0-671-47869-9*, Pocket) Simon & Schuster.

Hernandez, Natalie A. Las Aventuras con Padre Serra. Hernandez, Tony Y., tr. 1999. (ENG & SPA., Illus.). 112p. (Orig.). (J). (gr. 3-8). pap. 9.95 (*0-9644386-1-5*) Santa Ines Pubns.

Jackson, Dave & Jackson, Neta. Abandoned on the Wild Frontier: Peter Cartwright. 1995. (Trailblazer Bks.: Vol. 15). (Illus.). 144p. (J). (gr. 3-7). pap. 5.99 (*1-55661-468-3*) Bethany Hse. Pubs.

Roseman, Kenneth D. The Cardinal's Snuffbox. 1982. (Do-It-Yourself Jewish Adventure Ser.). (Illus.). 128p. (J). (gr. 4-7). pap. text 8.95 (*0-8074-0059-9*, 140060) UAHC Pr.

Seago, Kate. Matthew Unstrung. 1998. 240p. (J). (gr. 6-12). 16.99 o.s.i (*0-8037-2230-3*, Dial Bks. for Young Readers) Penguin Putnam Bks. for Young Readers.

Tompert, Ann. The Pied Piper of Peru. 2003. (Illus.). 32p. (J). (gr. 1 up). 15.95 (*1-56397-949-7*) Boyds Mills Pr.

Van Heerde, Gerrit. The Man with the Red Beard. 2002. (J). (*0-9579517-0-1*) Inheritance Pubns.

Vernon, Louise A. A Heart Strangely Warmed. (Illus.). 128p. (J). (gr. 4-9). 2002. pap. 7.99 (*0-8361-1769-7*); 1975. 4.95 o.p. (*0-8361-1768-9*) Herald Pr.

Voigt, Cynthia. Come a Stranger. 1987. 240p. (YA). (gr. 6 up). mass mkt. 3.95 o.s.i (*0-449-70246-4*, Fawcett) Ballantine Bks.

—Come a Stranger. 1995. 256p. (J). (gr. 7 up). mass mkt. 5.99 (*0-689-80444-X*, Simon Pulse); 1986. 208p. (YA). (gr. 6 up). 15.95 (*0-689-31289-X*, Atheneum) Simon & Schuster Children's Publishing.

—Come a Stranger. 1995. (J). 11.04 (*0-606-07384-1*) Turtleback Bks.

Weisheit, Eldon. The Preacher's Yellow Pants. 1973. (Illus.). 48p. (J). (gr. k-4). 4.95 o.p. (*0-570-03420-5*, 56-1149) Concordia Publishing Hse.

Whelan, Gloria. A Time to Keep Silent. 1993. 124p. (J). (gr. 4-9). pap. 6.00 (*0-8028-0118-8*, Eerdmans Bks For Young Readers) Eerdmans, William B. Publishing Co.

—A Time to Keep Silent. 1979. (J). (gr. 7-12). 7.95 o.p. (*0-399-20693-0*) Putnam Publishing Group, The.

Wilson, Mike. The Warrior Priest: The Story of Father Roy Bourgeois. 2002. (Contemporary Profiles & Policy Series for the Younger Reader). (Illus.). (YA). (gr. 8 up). pap. 28.00 (*0-934272-68-9*) Burke, John Gordon Pub., Inc.

Wilson, Miles. The Warrior Priest: The Story of Father Roy Bourgeois. 2001. (Contemporary Profiles & Policy Series for the Younger Reader). (Illus.). (YA). (gr. 8 up). (*0-934272-69-7*) Burke, John Gordon Pub., Inc.

Wolcott, Leonard T. & Wolcott, Carolyn E. Wilderness Rider. 1984. 144p. (Orig.). (J). (gr. 5 up). pap. text 4.00 o.p. (*0-687-45570-7*) Abingdon Pr.

CLOWNS—FICTION

Abels, Harriette S. Call Me Clown. 1977. (Jobs for Juniors Ser.). (Illus.). 48p. (J). (gr. 3-6). lib. bdg. 9.25 o.p. (*0-516-03205-4*, Children's Pr.) Scholastic Library Publishing.

Adler, David A. You Think It's Fun to Be a Clown. 1980. (Illus.). (gr. 2). 9.95 o.p. (*0-385-14459-8*); lib. bdg. o.p. (*0-385-14460-1*) Doubleday Publishing.

Benjamin, Cynthia. What's Going On? 1999. (Real Kids Readers Ser.). (Illus.). 32p. (J). (gr. k-2). 18.90 (*0-7613-2070-9*); pap. 4.99 (*0-7613-2095-4*) Millbrook Pr., Inc.

—What's Going On? 1999. (J). 10.14 (*0-606-19180-1*) Turtleback Bks.

—What's Going On? 1999. E-Book (*1-58824-750-3*); E-Book (*1-58824-833-X*); E-Book (*1-58824-503-9*) ipicturebooks, LLC.

Big Comfy Couch Company. Dress-Up Day. 1997. (Big Comfy Couch Ser.). 24p. (J). (ps). 3.99 o.s.i (*0-448-41640-9*, Grosset & Dunlap) Penguin Putnam Bks. for Young Readers.

Blake. Clown, ERS. 1996. (J). 15.95 o.p. (*0-8050-4583-X*, Holt, Henry & Co. Bks. For Young Readers) Holt, Henry & Co.

Boll, Heinrich. The Clown. 1982. (J). mass mkt. 3.95 o.p. (*0-380-00333-3*, 69534, Avon Bks.) Morrow/Avon.

Bozo. 2004. 32p. pap. text 8.95 (*0-7624-1862-1*) Running Pr. Bk. Pubs.

Brouwer, Sigmund. The Jester's Quest. 1994. (Winds of Light Ser.: No. 7). 132p. (Orig.). (J). pap. 5.99 o.p. (*1-56476-273-4*, 6-3273) Cook Communications Ministries.

But You Promised! A Book about Keeping Your Word. 1998. (Big Comfy Couch Ser.). (Illus.). 32p. (J). 5.95 (*0-7370-1001-0*) Time-Life Inc.

Caring Clowns. 1997. (Big Comfy Couch Huge Coloring & Activity Ser.). (Illus.). 96p. (J). (ps-1). pap. (*0-7666-0016-5*, Honey Bear Bks.) Modern Publishing.

Cline, Paul. Fools, Clowns & Jesters. 1991. (Illus.). 58p. (J). (gr. 3-10). pap. 12.95 o.p. (*0-914676-88-1*, Simon & Schuster Children's Publishing) Simon & Schuster Children's Publishing.

Clowns. Date not set. 9.95 (*0-89868-287-8*) ARO Publishing Co.

Clowntown Fun. 1997. (Big Comfy Couch Digest Ser.). (Illus.). 32p. (J). (ps-1). pap. (*0-7666-0010-6*, Honey Bear Bks.) Modern Publishing.

Coco, Eugene. The Magic Clown. 1993. (Storytime Bks.). (Illus.). 24p. (J). (ps-2). pap. 1.29 o.p. (*1-56293-348-5*, McClanahan Bk.) Learning Horizons, Inc.

Cole, Joanna. The Clown-Arounds. 1992. (Sunny Day Bks.). (Illus.). 48p. (J). (ps-2). 2.95 o.p. (*0-448-40321-8*, Grosset & Dunlap) Penguin Putnam Bks. for Young Readers.

—The Clown-Arounds. 1994. (Illus.). 48p. (J). (gr. 1 up). lib. bdg. 19.93 o.p. (*0-8368-0995-5*) Stevens, Gareth Inc.

—The Clown-Arounds Go on Vacation. 1993. (Illus.). 48p. (J). lib. bdg. 19.93 o.p. (*0-8368-0966-1*) Stevens, Gareth Inc.

—The Clown-Arounds Have a Party. 1995. (Illus.). (J). (gr. 1 up). lib. bdg. 19.93 o.p. (*0-8368-0999-8*) Stevens, Gareth Inc.

—Get Well, Clown-Arounds! 1993. (Parents Magazine Press Read-Aloud Library). (Illus.). 42p. (J). (ps-3). lib. bdg. 17.27 o.p. (*0-8368-0895-9*) Stevens, Gareth Inc.

—Sweet Dreams, Clown-Arounds. 1994. (Illus.). 36p. (J). (gr. 1 up). lib. bdg. 18.60 o.p. (*0-8368-0976-9*) Stevens, Gareth Inc.

Coleman, Sheila. McHappy, the Unhappy Clown. 1986. (Appleseed Ser.). 24p. (J). pap. 2.95 o.p. (*0-8407-6692-0*) Nelson, Thomas Inc.

Corcoran, Barbara. The Clown. 1975. 192p. (J). (gr. 5-9). 8.95 o.s.i (*0-689-30465-X*, Atheneum) Simon & Schuster Children's Publishing.

Dale, Nora. The Best Trick of All. 1989. (Real Readers Ser.). (Illus.). 32p. (J). (ps-3). pap. 4.95 (*0-8114-6700-7*); lib. bdg. 21.40 o.p. (*0-8172-3505-1*); lib. bdg. 21.40 o.p. (*0-8172-3505-1*) Raintree Pubs.

Daly, Niki. Bravo, Zan Angelo! A Comedia Dell'Arte Tale with Story & Pictures, RS. 1998. (Illus.). 36p. (J). (ps-3). 16.00 (*0-374-30953-1*, Farrar, Straus & Giroux (BYR)) Farrar, Straus & Giroux.

de Paola, Tomie. Jingle, the Christmas Clown. 1992. (Illus.). 40p. (J). (ps-3). 16.95 o.s.i (*0-399-22338-X*, G. P. Putnam's Sons) Penguin Group (USA) Inc.

—Jingle, the Christmas Clown. 1998. (Illus.). 40p. (J). (ps-3). pap. 6.99 o.s.i (*0-698-11669-0*, PaperStar) Penguin Putnam Bks. for Young Readers.

Dedieu, Thierry. Baby Clown: A Pull-the-Tab Book. l.t. ed. 1995. (Illus.). 16p. (J). (ps-1). 12.95 (*0-7868-0075-5*) Hyperion Bks. for Children.

Dumas, Alexandre. When Pierrot Was Young. Munro, Douglas, tr. from FRE. 1978. (Illus.). (J). (gr. 6-9). 10.95 o.p. (*0-19-271373-6*) Oxford Univ. Pr., Inc.

Falwell, Cathryn. Clowning Around. 1991. (Illus.). 32p. (J). (ps-1). 13.95 o.p. (*0-531-05952-9*); mass mkt. 13.99 o.p. (*0-531-08552-X*) Scholastic, Inc. (Orchard Bks.).

Fedorova, Mariana. The Smallest Circus in the World. James, J. Alison, tr. from GER. 2003. 32p. (J). lib. bdg. 16.50 (*0-7358-1788-X*); (Illus.). 15.95 (*0-7358-1787-1*) North-South Bks., Inc.

Fischel, Sharon H. The Day-Night Circus Clowns. 1986. (J). (gr. 1-3). 4.95 o.p. (*0-533-07105-4*) Vantage Pr., Inc.

Occupations

Fishwick, Marshall W. Ronald Revisited: The World of Ronald McDonald. 1983. 19.95 o.p. (*0-87972-247-9*); (J). pap. 10.95 o.p. (*0-87972-248-7*) Univ. of Wisconsin Pr. (Popular Pr.).

Fox, Diane. What Color Is That, Piggywiggy? 2001. (Illus.). 20p. (J). (ps-k). bds. 5.95 (*1-929766-17-3*) Handprint Bks.

Ganly, Helen. The Wolfman & the Clown. 1991. (Illus.). 32p. (J). (gr. k-2). pap. 13.95 o.p. (*0-233-98504-2*) Andre Deutsch GBR. *Dist:* Trafalgar Square, Trans-Atlantic Pubns., Inc.

Gill, Janie S. Clowns. 1997. pap. 3.95 (*0-89868-286-X*) ARO Publishing Co.

Gipson, Morrell & Hansson, Peter. Clumsy Clown Willie. Stefoff, Rebecca, ed. 1990. (Magic Mountain Fables Ser.). (Illus.). 24p. (J). (gr. k-3). lib. bdg. 14.60 (*0-944483-90-9*) Garrett Educational Corp.

Goofy the Clown. 1981. (Disney Puppet Bks.). pap. 4.95 o.p. (*0-531-05153-6*, Watts, Franklin) Scholastic Library Publishing.

Gutelle, Andrew M. I Can Do That! A Book about Confidence. 1999. (Big Comfy Couch Ser.). (Illus.). 32p. (J). (ps-1). 4.95 o.s.i (*0-7835-4894-X*) Time-Life, Inc.

Harper, Jo. Ollie Jolly, Rodeo Clown. 2002. (Illus.). 32p. (J). (gr. k-3). 15.95 (*1-55868-552-9*); pap. 8.95 (*1-55868-553-7*) Graphic Arts Ctr. Publishing Co. (West Winds Pr.).

Hayes, Geoffrey, illus. & text. Patrick at the Circus. 2002. (Adventures of Patrick Brown Ser.). (J). (gr. k-3). 48p. 15.99 (*0-7868-0716-4*); lib. bdg. (*0-7868-2595-2*) Hyperion Bks. for Children.

Huser, Glen. Touch of the Clown. (YA). (gr. 7-12). 2001. 224p. pap. 5.95 (*0-88899-357-9*); 1999. 223p. 15.95 (*0-88899-343-9*) Groundwood Bks. CAN. *Dist:* Publishers Group West.

Jackson, Gavin. Night Owl Loonette: A Book about Sleep. 1999. (Big Comfy Couch Ser.). (Illus.). 32p. (J). (ps-1). 4.95 o.p. (*0-7835-4885-0*) Time-Life Education, Inc.

Johnson, Lois Walfrid. The Runaway Clown. 1993. (Adventure of the Northwoods Ser.: Vol. 8). 160p. (Orig.). (J). (gr. 4-7). pap. 5.99 (*1-55661-240-0*) Bethany Hse. Pubs.

Johnson, Sharon Sliter. I Want to Be a Clown, Level 1. Gregorich, Barbara, ed. 1985. (Start to Read! Ser.). (Illus.). (J). (ps-2). 16p. 2.29 (*0-88743-014-7*, 06014); 32p. pap. 3.95 (*0-88743-412-6*, 06064) School Zone Publishing Co.

Krahn, Fernando. A Funny Friend from Heaven. 1977. (J). (gr. 2 up). 11.95 (*0-397-31760-3*) HarperCollins Children's Bk. Group.

Lacome, Julie. Funny Business. 1991. (Illus.). (J). (ps up). 11.95 o.p. (*0-688-10159-3*, Morrow, William & Co.) Morrow/Avon.

Laden, Nina. Clowns on Vacation. 2002. (Illus.). 32p. (J). (gr. k-3). 16.95 (*0-8027-8780-0*) Walker & Co.

Laden, Nina, illus. Clowns on Vacation. 2002. (J). (ps-3). 17.85 (*0-8027-8781-9*) Walker & Co.

Lake, Mary Dixon. My Circus Family. (Illus.). 8p. (J). (gr. k-1). pap. 15.90 (*1-57255-064-3*); 1995. pap. 3.00 (*1-57255-034-1*) Mondo Publishing.

Littlesugar, Amy. Clown Child. 2015. (J). 15.95 (*0-399-23106-4*, Philomel) Penguin Putnam Bks. for Young Readers.

Long, Kathy. Hallelujah the Clown: A Story of Blessing & Discovery. 1992. (Illus.). 32p. (J). (ps). pap. 4.99 o.p. (*0-8066-2560-0*, 9-2560, Augsburg Bks.) Augsburg Fortress, Pubs.

Lubar, David. Dunk. 2002. 256p. (YA). (gr. 7-10). tchr. ed. 15.00 (*0-618-19455-X*, Clarion Bks.) Houghton Mifflin Co. Trade & Reference Div.

Lyon, Leslie Connell & Lyon, Charles. Surf Clowns. 2000. (Illus.). 176p. (gr. 3-10). pap. 29.95 (*0-9675214-4-0*) Bad Cat Bks.

MacDonald, Steven. Just Clowning Around: Two Stories. 2000. (Green Light Readers Ser.). (Illus.). 20p. (J). (gr. k-2). 10.95 o.s.i (*0-15-202512-X*); pap. 3.95 o.s.i (*0-15-202518-9*) Harcourt Children's Bks. (Green Light Readers).

—Just Clowning Around: Two Stories. 2000. (Illus.). (J). 10.10 (*0-606-18180-6*) Turtleback Bks.

Marceau, Marcel. The Story of Bip. 1976. (Illus.). 32p. (J). (ps-3). o.p. (*0-06-024052-0*); lib. bdg. 6.79 o.p. (*0-06-024053-9*) HarperCollins Pubs.

Moncure, Jane Belk. Con el Payaso de Colores las Cosas Lucen Mejores. 1989. (Castillo Magico Ser.).Tr. of Color Clown Comes to Town. (SPA., Illus.). 32p. (J). (ps-3). lib. bdg. 21.36 o.p. (*0-89565-926-3*) Child's World, Inc.

Parish, Peggy. Clues in the Woods. 1980. 160p. (gr. 4-7). pap. text 3.99 (*0-440-41461-X*, Yearling) Random Hse. Children's Bks.

—Clues in the Woods. 1968. (J). 10.04 (*0-606-02328-3*) Turtleback Bks.

Pennell, Kathleen. Circus of Fear. 2002. (Pony Investigators Ser.: Vol. III). (Illus.). 96p. (J). (gr. 3-6). pap. 5.95 (*1-930353-47-2*) Masthof Pr.

Pennington, Lillian B. Snafu: The Littlest Clown. 1972. (Illus.). 32p. (J). (gr. 1-6). pap. 7.94 incl. audio (*0-87783-225-0*); lib. bdg. 9.95 (*0-913532-00-2*) Oddo Publishing, Inc.

Pfister, Marcus. El Sol y la Luna. Clements, Andrew, tr. 1994. (SPA., Illus.). 32p. (J). (gr. k-3). 15.95 (*1-55858-341-6*) North-South Bks., Inc.

Rau, Dana Meachen. Clown Around, Level B. 2001. (Early Reader Ser.). (Illus.). 32p. (J). (gr. 1). lib. bdg. 18.60 (*0-7565-0074-5*) Compass Point Bks.

Rockwell, Anne F. Gogo's Car Breaks Down. 1979. (J). reprint ed. pap. 1.25 o.p. (*0-590-05740-5*) Scholastic, Inc.

—Gogo's Pay Day. 1978. (ps-3). 5.95 o.p. (*0-385-13045-7*); lib. bdg. o.p. (*0-385-13046-5*) Doubleday Publishing.

Rodriguez, Lisa M. Bopo Joins the Circus (Bop Se Une al Circo) Rodriguez, David A., ed. 1998. (Illus.). 34p. (J). (ps-3). 14.95 (*0-9665575-0-6*) BOPO Biligual Bks.

Roffey, Maureen, illus. Clown's Vacation. 1995. (Duplo Playbooks Ser.). 14p. (J). (ps up). bds. 7.50 o.p. (*0-316-72383-5*) Little Brown & Co.

Sawyer, Joan. Oafie the Clown. 1993. (J). (gr. k-2). pap. 8.95 o.p. incl. audio (*0-7608-0496-6*); pap. 4.95 o.p. (*1-56801-173-3*);Big bk. pap. 17.95 o.p. (*1-56801-172-5*) Sundance Publishing.

Spencer, Ladonna, ed. Happy the King's Clown. 1985. 30p. (J). pap. 3.50 (*0-88144-057-4*) Christian Publishing Services, Inc.

Tassell, Brad. Billy Fustertag Learns Comedy. 2000. 32p. (J). pap. 8.00 (*0-89708-226-5*) And Bks.

Thompson, Ruth. Joey the Clown: Play With Us. 1989. (J). 1.99 o.s.i (*0-517-67197-2*, Random Hse. Bks. for Young Readers) Random Hse. Children's Bks.

Time-Life Books Editors. Hello Molly! A Book about Friendship. 1999. (Big Comfy Couch Ser.). (Illus.). 32p. (J). (ps-1). 4.95 o.p. (*0-7835-4504-5*) Time-Life Education, Inc.

—Scaredy Cat: A Book about Being Brave. 1998. (Big Comfy Couch Ser.). (Illus.). 32p. (J). 5.95 (*0-7370-1000-2*) Time-Life Inc.

—What Did Loonette Forget? A Book about Thoughtfulness. 1999. (Big Comfy Couch Ser.). (Illus.). 32p. (J). (ps-1). 5.95 o.p. (*0-7835-4883-4*) Time-Life Education, Inc.

—Who Made This Big Mess? 1999. (Big Comfy Couch Ser.). (Illus.). 32p. (J). (ps-1). 4.95 o.p. (*0-7835-4505-3*) Time-Life Education, Inc.

Tsutsui, Keisuk, et al. D. B. Kabelevsky's Joey the Clown (the Comedians) 1974. (Fantasia Pictorial Ser.). 27p. (J). (*0-7232-1783-1*, Warne, Frederick) Penguin Putnam Bks. for Young Readers.

Urmston, Kathleen & Evans, Karen. The Clown. Kaeden Corp. Staff, ed. 1991. (Illus.). 8p. (J). (gr. k-2). pap. text 4.50 (*1-879835-06-1*) Kaeden Corp.

Van der Meer, Ron & Van der Meer, Atie. Jumping Clowns. 1989. 10p. (J). (gr. 4 up). 4.99 o.p. (*0-85953-263-1*) Child's Play of England GBR. *Dist:* Child's Play-International.

Wagner, Cheryl. The Big Comfy Couch Potato: A Book about Get-up-and-Go. 1999. (Big Comfy Couch Ser.). (Illus.). 32p. (J). (gr. 2-5). 4.95 o.s.i (*0-7835-5294-7*) Time-Life, Inc.

—It's Taking Too Long! A Book about Patience. 1999. (Big Comfy Couch Ser.). (Illus.). 32p. (J). (ps-1). 4.95 o.s.i (*0-7835-4893-1*) Time-Life, Inc.

—Molly's Bad Hair Day: A Book about Looking Good, Feeling Special. 1999. (Big Comfy Couch Ser.). (Illus.). 32p. (J). (gr. 2-5). 4.95 o.s.i (*0-7835-5295-5*) Time-Life, Inc.

Zeplin, Zeno. Clowns to the Rescue. 1993. (Katy & Beth Mysteries Ser.: No. II). (Illus.). 48p. (J). (gr. k-3). 11.95 (*1-877740-12-8*); pap. 6.95 (*1-877740-13-6*) Nel-Mar Publishing.

Ziefert, Harriet. Clown Games. (Illus.). 32p. (J). (ps-2). 1998. pap. 3.99 (*0-14-038962-8*); 1993. pap. 3.50 o.p. (*0-14-054581-6*); 1993. 9.00 o.s.i (*0-670-84652-X*, Viking Children's Bks.) Penguin Putnam Bks. for Young Readers.

—Where's Bobo? 1993. (Illus.). 24p. (J). (ps up). 10.95 o.p. (*0-688-12327-9*, Morrow, William & Co.) Morrow/Avon.

COMPOSERS—FICTION

Anderson, Matthew T. Handel, Who Knew What He Liked. 2001. (Illus.). 48p. (J). (gr. 2-6). 16.99 (*0-7636-1046-1*) Candlewick Pr.

Aurum Press & Van der Meer, Frank. The Phantom of the Opera Pop-Up Book. 1989. 19.95 o.p. (*0-06-016012-8*) HarperTrade.

Celenza, Anna Harwell. The Farewell Symphony. 2000. (Illus.). 32p. (J). (ps-3). 19.95 (*1-57091-406-0*) Charlesbridge Publishing, Inc.

—The Heroic Symphony. 2004. (J). (*1-57091-509-1*) Charlesbridge Publishing, Inc.

—Pictures at an Exhibition. 2003. (Illus.). 32p. (J). (gr. 3-6). 19.95 (*1-57091-492-3*) Charlesbridge Publishing, Inc.

Fraser, Julia. Musical Discoveries: A Story about Music, History & Friendship, Bk. 1. 1995. (Grammy Musical Discoveries Ser.: Bk. 1). (Illus.). (J). (gr. 6-8). 6.95 (*0-88284-656-6*, 4707) Alfred Publishing Co., Inc.

Leroux, Gaston. The Phantom of the Opera. l.t. ed. 1999. (Large Print Heritage Ser.). 420p. (J). (gr. 7-12). lib. bdg. 35.95 (*1-58118-043-8*, 22512) LRS.

—The Phantom of the Opera. 1994. (Classics for Young Readers Ser.). (Illus.). 336p. (YA). (gr. 4-7). pap. 4.99 (*0-14-036813-2*, Puffin Bks.) Penguin Putnam Bks. for Young Readers.

—The Phantom of the Opera. 1989. (Step-up Classic Chillers Ser.). (Illus.). 96p. (J). (gr. 2-5). pap. 3.99 (*0-394-83847-5*, Random Hse. Bks. for Young Readers) Random Hse. Children's Bks.

—The Phantom of the Opera. Bair, Lowell, tr. abr. ed. 1998. 336p. (YA). (gr. 7-12). mass mkt. 3.99 (*0-440-22774-7*, Dell Books for Young Readers) Random Hse. Children's Bks.

—The Phantom of the Opera. abr. ed. 1998. 10.04 (*0-606-15677-1*) Turtleback Bks.

—The Phantom of the Opera. 1988. (Illus.). (J). (gr. 4 up). 14.95 o.p. (*0-88101-082-0*); 208p. (YA). (gr. 7 up). 9.95 o.p. (*0-88101-121-5*) Unicorn Publishing Hse., Inc., The.

Neumeyer, Peter. The Phantom of the Opera. abr. ed. 1988. (Illus.). 48p. (J). 14.95 o.p. (*0-87905-330-5*) Smith, Gibbs Pub.

Swain, Gwenyth. I Wonder As I Wander. 2003. (Illus.). 32p. (J). 16.00 (*0-8028-5214-9*, Eerdmans Bks For Young Readers) Eerdmans, William B. Publishing Co.

Weinberg, Larry. Universal Monsters: The Phantom of the Opera. 1993. (J). (gr. 4-7). pap. o.p. (*0-307-22334-5*, Golden Bks.) Random Hse. Children's Bks.

COWBOYS—FICTION

Alpers, Jody. Cowboy's Christmas. 1996. (Illus.). 24p. (Orig.). (J). (gr. k-6). pap. 6.95 (*0-9640533-1-4*) Libros de Ninos.

Anglund, Joan Walsh. The Brave Cowboy. 2000. (Illus.). 40p. (J). (ps-3). 6.95 (*0-7407-0649-7*) Andrews McMeel Publishing.

—The Brave Cowboy. 1959. (Illus.). (J). (ps-2). 6.95 o.p. (*0-15-211956-6*) Harcourt Children's Bks.

—Cowboy & His Friend. 2002. (Illus.). 40p. (J). 6.95 (*0-7407-2211-5*) Andrews McMeel Publishing.

—Cowboy & His Friend. 1901. (Illus.). (J). (ps-2). 3.95 o.p. (*0-15-220369-9*) Harcourt Children's Bks.

—The Cowboy's Christmas. 1972. (Illus.). (J). (ps-2). 2.95 o.p. (*0-689-30301-7*, McElderry, Margaret K.) Simon & Schuster Children's Publishing.

—Cowboy's Secret Life. 1901. (Illus.). (J). (ps-2). 3.95 o.p. (*0-15-220565-9*) Harcourt Children's Bks.

—A Cowboy's Secret Life. anniv. ed. 2002. (Illus.). 40p. (J). (gr. k-3). 6.95 (*0-7407-2680-3*) Andrews McMeel Publishing.

Antle, Nancy. Sam's Wild West Show. 1995. (Easy-to-Read Ser.). (Illus.). 40p. (J). (ps-3). 12.99 o.s.i (*0-8037-1532-3*); 12.89 o.s.i (*0-8037-1533-1*) Penguin Putnam Bks. for Young Readers. (Dial Bks. for Young Readers).

Appelt, Kathi A. Cowboy Dreams: Sleep Tight, Little Buckaroo. 1999. (Illus.). 32p. (J). (gr. k-2). 14.95 o.s.i (*0-06-027763-7*, Harper Trophy); lib. bdg. 14.89 o.p. (*0-06-027764-5*) HarperCollins Children's Bk. Group.

Beecham, Tom, illus. The Lone Ranger. 1984. (Rocking Bks.). (J). (ps-3). 2.95 o.p. (*0-394-84690-7*) Random Hse., Inc.

Bethancourt, T. Ernesto. The Concrete Cowboy. 1924. (J). o.s.i (*0-688-05158-8*); lib. bdg. o.s.i (*0-688-05161-8*) HarperCollins Children's Bk. Group. (Greenwillow Bks.).

Birney, Betty G. Tyrannosaurus Tex. 1994. (Illus.). 32p. (J). (ps-3). tchr. ed. 14.95 o.p. (*0-395-67648-7*) Houghton Mifflin Co.

—Tyrannosaurus Tex. 1994. 11.15 (*0-606-10960-9*) Turtleback Bks.

Blackmore, Richard D. Lorna Doone. 1981. 378p. (J). reprint ed. lib. bdg. 24.95 o.s.i (*0-89967-024-5*, Harmony Raine & Co.) Buccaneer Bks., Inc.

Bly, Stephen A. Hawks Don't Say Goodbye. 1994. (Nathan T. Riggins Adventure Ser.: Vol. 6). 128p. (J). (gr. 4-7). pap. 4.99 (*0-89107-782-0*) Crossway Bks.

Bond, Michael. Paddington Rides On! 1993. (Paddington Ser.). (Illus.). 32p. (J). (ps-3). 3.95 (*0-694-00461-8*, Harper Festival) HarperCollins Children's Bk. Group.

Brimner, Larry Dane. Cowboy Up! 1999. (Rookie Readers Ser.). (Illus.). 32p. (J). (gr. 1-2). pap. 4.95 (*0-516-26475-3*); lib. bdg. 19.00 (*0-516-21199-4*) Scholastic Library Publishing. (Children's Pr.).

Brooks, Walter R. Freddy the Cowboy. 2002. (Freddy the Pig Ser.). (Illus.). 233p. (J). (gr. 3). 23.95 (*1-58567-225-4*) Overlook Pr., The.

Brownlow, Mike. Way Out West... With a Baby! 2000. (Illus.). 32p. (J). (ps-2). 13.95 (*1-929927-04-5*) Ragged Bears USA.

Bulla, Clyde Robert. Surprise for a Cowboy. 1950. (Illus.). (J). (gr. 2-5). 11.74 (*0-690-79837-7*) HarperCollins Children's Bk. Group.

Burton, Virginia Lee. Calico the Wonder Horse, or the Saga of Stewy Stinker. (Illus.). 64p. (J). (ps-3). 1997. tchr. ed. 18.00 (*0-395-85735-X*); 1996. pap. 5.95 (*0-395-84541-6*) Houghton Mifflin Co.

Carter, Anne. Tall in the Saddle. 1999. (Illus.). 32p. (J). (ps-3). 8.95 (*1-55143-154-8*) Orca Bk. Pubs.

Carter, Peter. Borderlands, RS. 432p. 1993. (YA). pap. 4.95 o.p. (*0-374-40883-1*, Aerial); 1990. 17.00 o.p. (*0-374-30895-0*, Farrar, Straus & Giroux (BYR)) Farrar, Straus & Giroux.

—Borderlands. 1993. (Aerial Fiction Ser.). (J). 10.05 o.p. (*0-606-05764-1*) Turtleback Bks.

Censoni, Robert. Cowgirl Kate. 1977. (Illus.). 32p. (J). (gr. k-3). lib. bdg. 4.95 o.p. (*0-8234-0299-1*) Holiday Hse., Inc.

Charlip, Remy & Rettenmund, Tamara, illus. Little Old Big Beard & Big Young Little Beard: A Short & Tall Tale. 2003. 32p. (J). 16.95 (*0-7614-5142-0*, Cavendish Children's Bks.) Cavendish, Marshall Corp.

—Little Old Big Beard & Big Young Little Beard: A Short & Tall Tale. 2002. (J). (*1-58837-000-3*) Winslow Pr.

Chrismer, Melanie. Phoebe Clappsaddle & the Tumbleweed Gang. 2002. (Illus.). 32p. (J). 14.95 (*1-56554-966-X*) Pelican Publishing Co., Inc.

Cowboys & Cowgirls Coloring Book. 1982. 48p. (J). pap. 2.50 o.p. (*0-8431-0686-7*, Price Stern Sloan) Penguin Putnam Bks. for Young Readers.

Crawford, Diane M. Cowboy Kisses. 1993. (Sweet Dreams Ser.: No. 205). 144p. (YA). pap. 2.99 o.s.i (*0-553-29984-0*) Bantam Bks.

Crogin Herzig, Alison. Bronco Busters. 1998. (Illus.). 32p. (J). (ps-3). 15.99 o.s.i (*0-399-22917-5*, G. P. Putnam's Sons) Penguin Group (USA) Inc.

Dadey, Debbie & Jones, Marcia Thornton. Ghosts Don't Ride Wild Horses. 2002. (Bailey School Kids Ser.: No. 44). (Illus.). 96p. (J). (gr. 2-5). mass mkt. 3.99 (*0-439-21584-6*, Scholastic Paperbacks) Scholastic, Inc.

Davidson, Sara. Cowboy: A Novel. 2001. 288p. mass mkt. 7.50 (*0-380-81933-3*) Morrow/Avon.

Dearen, Patrick. On the Pecos Trail. 2001. (Lone Star Heroes Ser.). 128p. (J). (gr. 4-7). pap. 8.95 (*1-55622-830-9*, Republic of Texas Pr.) Wordware Publishing, Inc.

Denslow, Sharon Phillips. On the Trail with Miss Pace. 1995. (Illus.). 40p. (J). (ps-3). pap. 15.00 (*0-02-728688-6*, Simon & Schuster Children's Publishing) Simon & Schuster Children's Publishing.

Disney Staff. Woody the Cowboy. 2001. (Illus.). 12p. (J). bds. 5.99 (*0-7364-1270-0*, RH/Disney) Random Hse. Children's Bks.

Downing, Warwick. Kid Curry's Last Ride. 1992. (Trophy Bk.). 176p. (J). (gr. 5-7). pap. 3.95 (*0-06-440421-8*, Harper Trophy) HarperCollins Children's Bk. Group.

—Kid Curry's Last Ride. 1989. 176p. (J). (gr. 5-7). 12.95 o.p. (*0-531-05802-6*); mass mkt. 12.99 o.p. (*0-531-08402-7*) Scholastic, Inc. (Orchard Bks.).

Dubowski, Cathy. Cowboy Roy. 2000. (All Aboard Reading Ser.). (Illus.). 32p. (J). (ps-1). mass mkt. 3.99 (*0-448-41568-2*, Grosset & Dunlap) Penguin Putnam Bks. for Young Readers.

Dukore, Jesse. Never Love a Cowboy. 1983. (Sweet Dreams Ser.). 163p. (gr. 6-12). pap. 2.25 o.p. (*0-553-24313-6*) Bantam Bks.

Eilenberg, Max. Cowboy Kid. 2000. (Illus.). 32p. (J). (ps-3). 15.99 (*0-7636-1058-5*) Candlewick Pr.

Ellis, Patricia. Rodeo Hearts. 2000. (Zebra Bouquet Ser.: Vol. 63). 256p. mass mkt. 4.99 o.s.i (*0-8217-6686-4*, Zebra Bks.) Kensington Publishing Corp.

Erickson, John R. The Case of the Vanishing Fishhook. 1999. (Hank the Cowdog Ser.: No. 31). (Illus.). (J). (gr. 2-5). 11.04 (*0-606-16826-5*) Turtleback Bks.

—Cowboys Are Partly Human. 1983. (Illus.). (Orig.). (J). (gr. 3 up). 110p. 9.95 (*0-9608612-6-2*); 100p. pap. 6.95 o.p. (*0-9608612-4-6*, 6124) Maverick Bks., Inc.

—Slim's Good-Bye. 2000. (Hank the Cowdog Ser.: No. 34). (Illus.). 144p. (J). (gr. 2-5). 14.99 (*0-670-88889-3*); pap. 4.99 (*0-14-130677-7*) Penguin Putnam Bks. for Young Readers. (Puffin Bks.).

—Slim's Good-Bye. 2000. (Hank the Cowdog Ser.: No. 34). (Illus.). (J). (gr. 2-5). 11.04 (*0-606-18408-2*) Turtleback Bks.

Evans, Max. My Pardner. 1972. (Illus.). 104p. (J). (gr. 5-9). 3.95 (*0-395-13725-X*) Houghton Mifflin Co.

—My Pardner. 1984. (Zia Bks.). (Illus.). 111p. (J). reprint ed. pap. 5.95 o.p. (*0-8263-0699-3*) Univ. of New Mexico Pr.

Everett, Percival. The One That Got Away. 1992. (Illus.). 32p. (J). (ps-3). tchr. ed. 14.95 o.p. (*0-395-56437-9*, Clarion Bks.) Houghton Mifflin Co. Trade & Reference Div.

Failing, Barbara Larmon. Lasso Lou & Cowboy Mccoy. 2003. (Illus.). 40p. (J). 16.99 (*0-8037-2578-7*, Dial Bks. for Young Readers) Penguin Putnam Bks. for Young Readers.

Fontes, Ron & Fontes, Justine. Wild Bill Hickok & the Rebel Raiders. 1993. (Disney's American Frontier Ser.: Bk. 10). (Illus.). 80p. (J). (gr. 1-4). lib. bdg. 12.89 o.s.i (*1-56282-494-5*); pap. 3.50 o.p. (*1-56282-493-7*) Disney Pr.

Frank, John. The Toughest Cowboy. 2006. (gr. 4-6). per. 6.99 (*0-689-83462-4*, Aladdin); 2002. (J). (gr. k-3). per. 16.00 (*0-689-83461-6*, Simon & Schuster Children's Publishing) Simon & Schuster Children's Publishing.

Garland, Sarah. Tex the Cowboy. 1995. 32p. (J). 12.99 o.s.i (*0-525-45418-7*, Dutton Children's Bks.) Penguin Putnam Bks. for Young Readers.

Garland, Sherry. Goodnight, Cowboy. 1998. (Illus.). (J). 15.95 (*0-590-98831-X*) Scholastic, Inc.

Givens, Shirley. Adventures in Violinland Bk. 1E: Meet Tex Neek, the Fiddling Cowboy. 1994. (Illus.). 36p. (J). (gr. k-6). pap. text 12.00 (*0-937205-11-7*) Seesaw Music Corp.

Gonzalez, Gloria. Gaucho. 1986. 144p. (gr. 5 up). pap. 1.25 o.p. (*0-440-92803-6*) Dell Publishing.

—Gaucho. 1977. (Illus.). (J). (gr. 4-7). 5.95 o.p. (*0-394-83389-9*); lib. bdg. 6.99 o.p. (*0-394-93389-3*) Random Hse. Children's Bks. (Knopf Bks. for Young Readers).

Gramling, Lee. Ninety-Mile Praire. 2002. (Cracker Western Ser.). (Illus.). 280p. pap. 8.95 (*1-56164-257-6*); 279p. 14.95 (*1-56164-255-X*) Pineapple Pr., Inc.

Greene, Carla. Cowboys: What Do They Do? 1972. (I Can Read Bks.). (Illus.). 64p. (J). (ps-3). 5.95 o.p. (*0-06-022081-3*); lib. bdg. 8.89 o.p. (*0-06-022082-1*) HarperCollins Pubs.

Guthrie, A. B., Jr. The Last Valley, 001. 1975. 304p. 8.95 o.p. (*0-395-21899-3*) Houghton Mifflin Co.

Hafen, Lyman. Over the Joshua Slope. 1994. 160p. (J). (gr. 4-8). mass mkt. 14.95 o.p. (*0-02-741100-1*, Simon & Schuster Children's Publishing) Simon & Schuster Children's Publishing.

Halvorson, Marilyn. Cowboys Don't Cry. 1985. 169p. (J). (gr. 7 up). 13.95 o.p. (*0-385-29374-7*, Delacorte Pr.) Dell Publishing.

—Cowboys Don't Cry. 1986. 176p. (J). (gr. 6 up). mass mkt. 3.50 o.s.i (*0-440-91303-9*, Laurel Leaf) Random Hse. Children's Bks.

—Cowboys Don't Cry. unabr. ed. 1998. 160p. (YA). (gr. 7-9). mass mkt. 5.95 (*0-7736-7429-2*) Stoddart Kids CAN. *Dist:* Fitzhenry & Whiteside, Ltd.

—Cowboys Don't Quit. unabr. ed. 1998. (Gemini Bks.). 160p. (YA). (gr. 7-9). mass mkt. 5.95 (*0-7736-7425-X*) Stoddart Kids CAN. *Dist:* Fitzhenry & Whiteside, Ltd.

Hancock, Sibyl. Old Blue. 1980. (See & Read Book). (Illus.). 48p. (J). (gr. 1-4). 6.99 o.p. (*0-399-61141-X*, G. P. Putnam's Sons) Penguin Putnam Bks. for Young Readers.

Hardman, Ric L. Sunshine Rider: The First Vegetarian Western. 1999. (Laurel-Leaf Bks.). 352p. (YA). (gr. 7-12). mass mkt. 4.99 (*0-440-22812-3*, Dell Books for Young Readers) Random Hse. Children's Bks.

Hardman, Ric Lynden. Sunshine Rider: The First Vegetarian Western. 1998. 352p. (YA). (gr. 7-12). 15.95 o.s.i (*0-385-32543-6*, Delacorte Pr.) Dell Publishing.

Harper, Jo. Jalapeno Hal. Date not set. (Illus.). 40p. (J). (gr. 4). pap. 7.95 (*1-57168-206-6*) Eakin Pr.

—Jalapeno Hal. 1993. (Illus.). 40p. (J). (ps-2). 14.95 o.p. (*0-02-742645-9*, Simon & Schuster Children's Publishing) Simon & Schuster Children's Publishing.

—Mayor Jalapeno Hal from Presidio, Texas. 2003. (Illus.). (J). (*1-57168-767-X*, Eakin Pr.) Eakin Pr.

—Ollie Jolly, Rodeo Clown. 2002. (Illus.). 32p. (J). (gr. k-3). 15.95 (*1-55868-552-9*); pap. 8.95 (*1-55868-553-7*) Graphic Arts Ctr. Publishing Co. (West Winds Pr.).

Heap, Sue, illus. Cowboy Baby. 1998. 32p. (J). (ps-k). 15.99 o.p. (*0-7636-0437-2*) Candlewick Pr.

Heath, Lorraine. Samantha & the Cowboy. 2002. (True Romance Ser.). 256p. (J). pap. 4.99 (*0-06-447341-4*, Avon Bks.) Morrow/Avon.

Hedstrom, Deborah. From Ranch to Railhead with Charles Goodnight. 1998. (My American Journey Ser.: No. 6). 19.99 o.p. (*1-57673-261-4*) Multnomah Pubs., Inc.

Helberg, Kristin. Cowboys. 1997. (Troubador Color & Story Ser.). (Illus.). 32p. (Orig.). (J). (ps up). reprint ed. 5.95 o.p. (*0-8431-8226-1*, Price Stern Sloan) Penguin Putnam Bks. for Young Readers.

Hillert, Margaret. Little Cowboy & Big... 1981. (Illus.). (J). (ps). pap. 5.10 (*0-8136-5576-5*, TK2327); lib. bdg. 7.95 (*0-8136-5076-3*, TK2326) Modern Curriculum Pr.

Hindley, Judy. Does a Cowboy Say Boo. 2003. (Illus.). 32p. bds. 6.99 (*0-7636-2156-0*) Candlewick Pr.

Holub, Joan. Cinderdog & the Wicked Stepcat. 2001. (Illus.). 32p. (J). (ps-3). lib. bdg. 14.95 (*0-8075-1178-1*) Whitman, Albert & Co.

Hooker, Ruth. Matthew the Cowboy. 1994. (Albert Whitman Prairie Book Ser.). (Illus.). 32p. (J). (ps-2). pap. 5.95 o.p. (*0-8075-4998-3*) Whitman, Albert & Co.

—Matthew the Cowboy. Tucker, Kathy, ed. 1990. (Illus.). 32p. (J). (ps-3). lib. bdg. 14.95 o.p. (*0-8075-4999-1*) Whitman, Albert & Co.

Hopkins, Jacqueline. Tumbleweed Tom on the Texas Trail. 1994. 12.15 o.p. (*0-606-06830-9*) Turtleback Bks.

Hutchens, Paul. Battle of the Bees. (Sugar Creek Gang Ser.: No. 30). 128p. (J). (gr. 3-7). mass mkt. 3.99 o.p. (*0-8024-4830-5*, 622) Moody Pr.

James, Will. Cowboy in the Making. 2001. (Illus.). 92p. (J). 15.00 (*0-87842-439-3*) Mountain Pr. Publishing Co., Inc.

—Look-See with Uncle Bill. 2002. (Illus.). 190p. (J). 26.00 (*0-87842-459-8*); pap. 14.00 (*0-87842-458-X*) Mountain Pr. Publishing Co., Inc.

—Scorpion: A Good Bad Horse. 2001. (Illus.). ix, 242p. (YA). 30.00 (*0-87842-436-9*); pap. 15.00 (*0-87842-435-0*) Mountain Pr. Publishing Co., Inc.

—Smoky, the Cow Horse. (Library of Contemporary Classics). (YA). 1981. (gr. 12 up). 5.95 o.s.i (*0-684-17145-7*); 1972. (gr. 7-11). 12.95 o.s.i (*0-684-12875-6*) Simon & Schuster Children's Publishing. (Atheneum).

—Uncle Bill. Carey, Jennifer, ed. 1998. (Tumbleweed Ser.). (Illus.). 198p. (YA). (gr. 4 up). reprint ed. 16.00 (*0-87842-379-6*, 695) Mountain Pr. Publishing Co., Inc.

—Uncle Bill: A Tale of Two Kids & a Cowboy. 1998. (Tumbleweed Ser.). 183p. (gr. 9-12). pap. 14.00 (*0-87842-380-X*, 694) Mountain Pr. Publishing Co., Inc.

—Young Cowboy. 1993. reprint ed. lib. bdg. 31.95 (*1-56849-173-5*) Buccaneer Bks., Inc.

—Young Cowboy. 2000. (Tumbleweed Ser.). (Illus.). 72p. (J). (*0-87842-444-X*); 80p. (gr. 4-7). 15.00 (*0-87842-419-9*) Mountain Pr. Publishing Co., Inc.

Johnston, Tony. The Cowboy & the Black-Eyed Pea. 1992. (Illus.). 32p. (J). (ps-3). 15.99 o.s.i (*0-399-22330-4*, G. P. Putnam's Sons) Penguin Group (USA) Inc.

—The Cowboy & the Black-Eyed Pea. 1996. (Illus.). 32p. (J). (ps-3). pap. 5.99 (*0-698-11356-X*, Paper-Star) Penguin Putnam Bks. for Young Readers.

—The Cowboy & the Black-Eyed Pea. 1996. 11.10 (*0-606-09165-3*) Turtleback Bks.

—Sparky & Eddie: The Rodeo. 1997. (Sparky & Eddie Ser.). (Illus.). 40p. (J). (gr. 1-3). pap. 13.95 (*0-590-47984-9*) Scholastic, Inc.

—Sparky & Eddie: The Rodeo. 1997. (Illus.). (J). mass mkt. 3.99 (*0-590-47985-7*) Scholastic, Inc.

Karas, G. Brian. Home on the Bayou: A Cowboy's Story. 1996. (Illus.). 32p. (J). (ps-3). 15.00 o.p. (*0-689-80156-4*, Simon & Schuster Children's Publishing) Simon & Schuster Children's Publishing.

Keith, Harold. Chico & Dan. 1998. (Illus.). 120p. (YA). (gr. 4-7). 16.95 (*1-57168-216-3*) Eakin Pr.

Keith, Harold & Arbuckle, Scott. Chico & Dan. 1998. E-Book 16.95 (*0-585-23231-8*) netLibrary, Inc.

Kellogg, Steven. Pecos Bill. 1986. (Illus.). 48p. (J). (ps-3). 16.95 (*0-688-05871-X*) HarperCollins Children's Bk. Group.

—Pecos Bill. 1986. (Illus.). 32p. (J). (ps up). lib. bdg. 15.93 o.p. (*0-688-05872-8*, Morrow, William & Co.) Morrow/Avon.

Kelsey, Avonelle. Cosmic Cowboy. 1995. (Illus.). 400p. (YA). pap. text 22.95 (*0-9640610-3-1*) Cheval International.

Kerr, Rita. The Texas Cowboy. 1996. (Illus.). 96p. (J). (gr. 2-4). 13.95 (*1-57168-105-1*) Eakin Pr.

Ketteman, Helen. Bubba the Cowboy Prince: A Fractured Texas Tale. 1997. (Illus.). 32p. (J). (gr. k-3). pap. 15.95 (*0-590-25506-1*) Scholastic, Inc.

Khalsa, Dayal Kaur. Cowboy Dreams. 1990. (Illus.). 32p. (J). (gr. k-4). 16.00 o.s.i (*0-517-57490-X*, Clarkson Potter) Crown Publishing Group.

—Cowboy Dreams. (Illus.). (J). (gr. 1-3). 1999. 32p. pap. 7.95 (*0-88776-377-4*); 1990. 24p. 17.95 o.p. (*0-88776-245-X*) Tundra Bks. of Northern New York.

—Cowboy Dreams. 1990. 11.19 o.p. (*0-606-09166-1*) Turtleback Bks.

Kimmel, Eric A. Four Dollars & Fifty Cents. 1990. (Illus.). 32p. (J). (ps-3). tchr. ed. 16.95 o.p. (*0-8234-0817-5*) Holiday Hse., Inc.

Kincaid, Beth. Back in the Saddle. 1994. (Silver Creek Riders Ser.: Vol. 1). 192p. (Orig.). (J). (gr. 4-7). mass mkt. 3.99 o.s.i (*0-515-11480-4*, Jove) Berkley Publishing Group.

Kinerk, Robert. Slim & Miss Prim. (J). pap. 7.95 (*0-87358-792-8*); (Illus.). pap. 7.95 (*0-87358-819-3*); 1998. (Illus.). 32p. 15.95 o.p. (*0-87358-689-1*) Northland Publishing. (Rising Moon Bks. for Young Readers).

Knowlton, Laurie Lazzaro. Why Cowboys Need a Brand. 1996. (Illus.). 32p. (J). (gr. 1-4). 14.95 (*1-56554-228-2*) Pelican Publishing Co., Inc.

—Why Cowboys Need a Pardner. 200th ed. 1998. (Illus.). 32p. (J). (gr. k-3). 14.95 (*1-56554-336-X*) Pelican Publishing Co., Inc.

—Why Cowgirls Are Such Sweet Talkers. 2000. (Illus.). 32p. (J). (ps-3). 14.95 (*1-56554-698-9*) Pelican Publishing Co., Inc.

Legrand. Why Cowboys Sing in Texas. 1984. (Illus.). (J). (gr. 1-5). 3.25 o.p. (*0-687-45424-7*) Abingdon Pr.

Lenski, Lois. Cowboy Small. 2001. (Illus.). 56p. (J). (gr. k-3). 11.95 (*0-375-81075-7*); lib. bdg. 13.99 (*0-375-91075-1*) Random Hse. Children's Bks. (Random Hse. Bks. for Young Readers).

—The Cowboy Small. 1980. (Mr. Small Bks.). (Illus.). (J). (gr. k-3). 5.25 o.s.i (*0-8098-1021-2*) McKay, David Co., Inc.

Lentz, Alice B. Tweetsie Adventure. 1995. (Illus.). 32p. (J). (ps-3). 9.95 (*1-57072-025-8*) Overmountain Pr.

Lester, Julius. Black Cowboy Wild Horses. 1998. (Illus.). 32p. (J). (gr. k-3). 18.99 (*0-8037-1787-3*, Dial Bks. for Young Readers) Penguin Putnam Bks. for Young Readers.

—The Man Who Was Horse. 1998. (Illus.). 40p. (J). (gr. k-3). 16.89 o.s.i (*0-8037-1788-1*, Dial Bks. for Young Readers) Penguin Putnam Bks. for Young Readers.

Liles, Maurine W. The Littlest Vaquero: A Story of the First Texas Cowboys, Longhorns, & the American Revolution. 1996. (Illus.). 120p. (J). (gr. 4-6). 15.95 (*1-57168-103-5*) Eakin Pr.

Loesch, Joe. Saving the Badlands Adventure: With Buffalo Biff & Farley's Raiders. Hutchinson, Cheryl J., ed. unabr. ed. 1995. (Backyard Adventure Ser.: Vol. 2). (Illus.). 54p. (J). (gr. 1-5). pap. 16.95 incl. audio compact disk (*1-887729-03-8*) Toy Box Productions.

Loomis, Christine. Cowboy Bunnies. 1997. (Illus.). 32p. (J). (ps-1). 15.99 (*0-399-22625-7*, G. P. Putnam's Sons) Penguin Group (USA) Inc.

—Cowboy Bunnies. 2000. (Illus.). (J). 12.14 (*0-606-18397-3*) Turtleback Bks.

—The Cowboy Bunnies. 2000. (Illus.). 32p. (J). (ps-3). pap. 5.99 o.s.i (*0-698-11831-6*, Puffin Bks.) Penguin Putnam Bks. for Young Readers.

Martin, Ann M. Karen's Cowboy. 2000. (Baby-Sitters Little Sister Ser.: No. 122). (Illus.). 112p. (J). (gr. 3-7). mass mkt. 3.99 (*0-590-52528-X*) Scholastic, Inc.

McAllister, Angela. Clever Cowboy. 1998. (Illus.). 32p. (J). (ps-2). pap. 15.95 o.p. (*0-7894-3491-1*) Dorling Kindersley Publishing, Inc.

—Clever Cowboy. 2000. 12.10 (*0-606-17801-5*) Turtleback Bks.

—The Clever Cowboy. 2000. 32p. (J). (gr. k-2). pap. text 5.95 (*0-7894-2659-5*, D K Ink) Dorling Kindersley Publishing, Inc.

McAllister, Anne. Do You Take This Cowboy? The Seduction of Jake Tallman; Cowboys Don't Cry, 2 vols. in 1. 2000. 384p. mass mkt. (*0-373-21708-0*, 1-21708-2, Harlequin Bks.) Harlequin Enterprises, Ltd.

McBride, Earvin, Jr. The Bowdery Rodeo Cowboys of Texas. 2nd unabr. ed. 2003. (Earvin MacBride's Amazing Sci-Fi & Adventure Heroes Ser.). (Illus.). 329p. (J). (gr. 7-12). pap. 4.95 (*1-892511-07-X*) MacBride, E. J. Pubn., Inc.

Mitchell, Marianne. Joe Cinders, ERS. 2002. (Illus.). 48p. (J). (ps-3). 16.95 (*0-8050-6529-6*, Holt, Henry & Co. Bks. For Young Readers) Holt, Henry & Co.

Mora, Jo. Budgee Budgee Cottontail. 2000. (Illus.). 60p. (YA). (gr. 2 up). pap. 15.00 (*0-922029-23-7*) Stoecklein Publishing.

Morck, Irene. Tiger's New Cowboy Boots. 1996. (Northern Lights Books for Children Ser.). (Illus.). 32p. (J). (gr. k-3). 15.95 (*0-88995-153-5*) Red Deer Pr. CAN. *Dist:* Fitzhenry & Whiteside, Ltd.

—Tyler's New Boots. 1998. (Illus.). 40p. (J). (ps-3). 14.95 o.p. (*0-8118-2248-6*) Chronicle Bks. LLC.

Morris, Neil. Longhorn on the Move. 1989. (Tales of the Old West Ser.). (Illus.). 32p. (J). (gr. 3-8). lib. bdg. 9.95 o.p. (*1-85435-166-4*) Cavendish, Marshall Corp.

Muldrow, Diane. Woody's Round-Up. 1999. (Disney Ser.). (Illus.). 24p. (J). (ps-k). pap. 3.29 (*0-307-13326-5*, Golden Bks.) Random Hse. Children's Bks.

Myers, Walter Dean. The Journal of Joshua Loper: A Black Cowboy: The Chisholm Trail, 1871. 1999. (My Name Is America Ser.). (Illus.). 158p. (J). (gr. 4-8). pap. 10.95 (*0-590-02691-7*) Scholastic, Inc.

Naylor, Phyllis Reynolds. Walker's Crossing. 240p. (YA). (gr. 5-9). 2001. pap. 4.99 (*0-689-84261-9*, Aladdin); 1999. (Illus.). 16.00 (*0-689-82939-6*, Atheneum) Simon & Schuster Children's Publishing.

Northland Publishing Staff, ed. Jack & the Giant/Cowboy Billy. 1998. (J). pap. 15.95 (*0-87358-696-4*, Rising Moon Bks. for Young Readers) Northland Publishing.

Patrick, Denise Lewis. The Adventures of Midnight Son, ERS. 1997. 128p. (J). (gr. 4-7). 16.00 (*0-8050-4714-X*, Holt, Henry & Co. Bks. For Young Readers) Holt, Henry & Co.

Peck, Robert Newton. Cowboy Ghost. 208p. (gr. 7 up). 2000. (J). pap. 4.95 (*0-06-447228-0*, Harper Trophy); 1999. (J). lib. bdg. 15.89 (*0-06-028211-8*); 1999. (YA). 15.95 (*0-06-028168-5*, Harper Trophy) HarperCollins Children's Bk. Group.

—Cowboy Ghost. 1999. (YA). pap., stu. ed. 52.95 incl. audio (*0-7887-3189-0*, 40924); pap., stu. ed. 52.95 incl. audio (*0-7887-3189-0*, 40924); (gr. 5). audio 30.00 (*0-7887-3208-0*, 95795E7);Class set. audio 197.80 (*0-7887-3235-8*, 46891) Recorded Bks., LLC.

—Cowboy Ghost. 2000. (Illus.). (J). 11.00 (*0-606-18684-0*) Turtleback Bks.

Poulsen, David A. Cowboy Cool. 2002. (Lawrence High Yearbook Ser.). 106p. (YA). 3.99 (*1-55305-028-2*) Cygnet Publishing Group, Inc./Coolreading.com CAN. *Dist:* Orca Bk. Pubs.

Proimos, James. Cowboy Boy. 2003. 96p. (J). 14.95 (*0-439-41681-7*, Scholastic Pr.) Scholastic, Inc.

Pryor, Bonnie. Mr. Munday & the Rustlers. 1991. (J). (gr. k-3). pap. 4.95 o.p. (*0-671-73619-1*, Aladdin) Simon & Schuster Children's Publishing.

Reeves, Greg. Judy Ford: World Champion Cowgirl. 1992. (Illus.). 46p. (J). (gr. 4-7). pap. 5.95 (*0-938349-88-0*) State Hse. Pr.

Reid, Ace. Cowpokes Comin' Yore Way. 5th ed. 1966. (Illus.). 64p. reprint ed. pap. 7.50 (*0-917207-05-X*) Cowpokes Cartoon Bks.

—Cowpokes Cookbook & Cartoons. 12th ed. 1969. (Illus.). 64p. reprint ed. pap. 7.50 (*0-917207-06-8*) Cowpokes Cartoon Bks.

—Cowpokes Cow Country Cartoons. 14th ed. 1958. (Illus.). 56p. reprint ed. pap. 7.50 (*0-917207-00-9*) Cowpokes Cartoon Bks.

—Cowpokes Rarin' to Go. 2nd ed. 1978. (Illus.). 74p. reprint ed. pap. 7.50 (*0-917207-09-2*) Cowpokes Cartoon Bks.

—Cowpokes Ride Again. 4th ed. 1974. (Illus.). 64p. reprint ed. pap. 7.50 (*0-917207-08-4*) Cowpokes Cartoon Bks.

—Cowpokes Tales & Cartoons. 2nd ed. 1981. (Illus.). 64p. reprint ed. pap. 7.50 (*0-917207-10-6*) Cowpokes Cartoon Bks.

—Cowpokes Wanted. 12th ed. 1964. (Illus.). 62p. reprint ed. pap. 7.50 (*0-917207-02-5*) Cowpokes Cartoon Bks.

—Draggin' S Ranch Cowpokes. 14th ed. 1966. (Illus.). 65p. reprint ed. pap. 7.50 (*0-917207-04-1*) Cowpokes Cartoon Bks.

—More Cowpokes. 14th ed. 1960. (Illus.). 60p. reprint ed. pap. 7.50 (*0-917207-01-7*) Cowpokes Cartoon Bks.

Rice, James, tr. & illus. Trail Boss: J. M. Daugherty. 2003. (J). (*1-57168-769-6*, Eakin Pr.) Eakin Pr.

Riosley, Lane. Pecos Bill's Wild West Show. 1992. (Illus.). 22p. (J). (gr. k-8). pap. 4.00 (*1-57514-256-2*, 1060) Encore Performance Publishing.

Roach, Joyce Gibson. Horned Toad Canyon. 2003. 48p. (J). 17.95 (*1-931721-01-7*) Bright Sky Pr.

Robinson, David. The Australian Cowboy & the Big Storm. 2002. (Illus.). 20p. (J). pap. 7.95 (*0-9718091-0-0*) Robinson Pubs.

Rogers, Lisa Waller. Get along Little Dogies: The Chisholm Trail Diary of Hallie Lou Wells. 2001. (Lone Star Journals: Vol. 1). (Illus.). 174p. (J). (gr. 4-7). 14.50 (*0-89672-446-8*) Texas Tech Univ. Pr.

—Get along, Little Dogies: The Chisholm Trail Diary of Hallie Lou Wells, South Texas 1878. 2001. (Lone Star Journals). (Illus.). 174p. (J). (gr. 4-7). 8.95 (*0-89672-448-4*) Texas Tech Univ. Pr.

Rossi, Joyce. The Gullywasher. 1995. (Illus.). 32p. (J). (gr. k-3). lib. bdg. 14.95 o.p. (*0-87358-607-7*, Rising Moon Bks. for Young Readers) Northland Publishing.

—The Gullywasher (El Chaparron Torrencial) 1998. (ENG & SPA., Illus.). 32p. (J). (gr. k-3). pap. 7.95 (*0-87358-728-6*, Rising Moon Bks. for Young Readers) Northland Publishing.

Rounds, Glen. Cowboys. 1991. (J). (ps-3). pap. 5.95 (*0-8234-1061-7*); (Illus.). 32p. tchr. ed. 16.95 (*0-8234-0867-1*) Holiday Hse., Inc.

—Whitey Ropes & Rides. 1956. (Illus.). 90p. (J). (gr. 4-6). 3.95 o.p. (*0-8234-0139-1*) Holiday Hse., Inc.

Rubel, Nicole. A Cowboy Named Ernestine. 2001. (Illus.). 32p. (J). (ps-3). 15.99 (*0-8037-2152-8*, Dial Bks. for Young Readers) Penguin Putnam Bks. for Young Readers.

Rushmore, Helen. Cowboy Joe of the Circle S. 1966. (Illus.). (J). (gr. 4-6). pap. 3.95 o.p. (*0-15-622720-7*, Voyager Bks./Libros Viajeros) Harcourt Children's Bks.

Saltzberg, Barney. Backyard Cowboy: A Pop-up Book. 1996. (Illus.). 12p. (J). (ps-3). 11.95 (*0-7868-0204-9*) Hyperion Bks. for Children.

Sanfield, Steve. The Great Turtle Drive. 1996. (Illus.). 40p. (J). (ps-3). 12.00 o.s.i (*0-679-85834-2*); 13.99 o.s.i (*0-679-95834-7*) Knopf, Alfred A. Inc.

Sargent, Dave & Sargent, Pat. Rusty (Red Roan) Be Strong & Brave. 2003. (Saddle Up Ser.: Vol. 52). (Illus.). 42p. (J). lib. bdg. 22.60 (*1-56763-803-1*); mass mkt. 6.95 (*1-56763-804-X*) Ozark Publishing.

Sathre, Vivian. Leroy Potts Meets the McCrooks. 1997. (First Choice Chapter Book Ser.). (Illus.). 48p. (J). (gr. k-3). pap. 3.99 o.s.i (*0-440-41137-8*, Dell Books for Young Readers) Random Hse. Children's Bks.

Saxon, Nancy. Panky in the Saddle. 1985. (Illus.). 128p. (J). (gr. 4-6). reprint ed. pap. 2.25 o.p. (*0-590-33616-9*, Scholastic Paperbacks) Scholastic, Inc.

Schaefer, Jack. Shane: An Illustrated American Classic. 2001. (Illustrated American Classic Ser.). (Illus.). 224p. (YA). (gr. 7-9). tchr. ed. 22.00 (*0-395-94116-4*) Houghton Mifflin Co.

Schertle, Alice. How Now, Brown Cow. 1998. 12.65 (*0-606-13496-4*) Turtleback Bks.

Schnetzler, Pattie L. Widdermaker. 2002. (Illus.). 32p. (J). (gr. k-3). lib. bdg. 15.95 (*0-87614-647-7*, Carolrhoda Bks.) Lerner Publishing Group.

Scieszka, Jon. The Good, the Bad & the Goofy. 1992. (Time Warp Trio Ser.). (Illus.). 80p. (J). (gr. 4-7). 14.99 (*0-670-84380-6*, Viking Children's Bks.) Penguin Putnam Bks. for Young Readers.

—The Good, the Bad & the Goofy. 1993. (Time Warp Trio Ser.). (J). 10.14 (*0-606-05847-8*) Turtleback Bks.

—The Good, the Bad, & the Goofy. 2004. (Time Warp Trio Ser.). (Illus.). 80p. pap. 4.99 (*0-14-240046-7*, Puffin Bks.) Penguin Putnam Bks. for Young Readers.

—The Good, the Bad & the Goofy. 1993. (Time Warp Trio Ser.). (Illus.). 80p. (J). (gr. 4-7). reprint ed. pap. 4.99 (*0-14-036170-7*) Penguin Putnam Bks. for Young Readers.

—The Good, the Bad, & the Goofy Twt Promo. 2003. (Time Warp Trio Ser.). (Illus.). 76p. pap. 2.66 (*0-14-250132-8*, Puffin Bks.) Penguin Putnam Bks. for Young Readers.

Sewall, Marcia. Riding That Strawberry Roan. 1985. (Illus.). 32p. (J). (ps-2). 9.95 o.p. (*0-670-80623-4*, Viking Children's Bks.) Penguin Putnam Bks. for Young Readers.

Smith, Dana Kessimakis. A Wild Cowboy. 2003. (Illus.). 32p. (J). 14.99 (*0-7868-1931-6*, Disney Editions) Disney Pr.

Smith, George S. The Christmas Eve Cattle Drive. 1991. (Illus.). 32p. (J). (gr. 3-4). pap. 3.95 (*0-89015-820-7*) Eakin Pr.

Smith, Janice Lee. Jess & the Stinky Cowboys. 2004. (Dial Easy-To-Read Ser.). (Illus.). 48p. (J). 14.99 (*0-8037-2641-4*, Dial Bks. for Young Readers) Penguin Putnam Bks. for Young Readers.

Stamaty, Mark A. Small in the Saddle. 1974. (J). (gr. k-5). 5.95 o.p. (*0-525-61525-3*, Dutton) Dutton/ Plume.

Stanley, George Edward. Adam Sharp, the Spy Who Barked. 2002. (Road to Reading Ser.). (Illus.). 48p. (J). (gr. 2-4). pap. 3.99 (*0-307-26412-2*); lib. bdg. 11.99 (*0-307-46412-1*) Random Hse. Children's Bks. (Golden Bks.).

Steig, Jeanne. Tales from Gizzards Grill. 2004. (J). (*0-06-000959-4*); lib. bdg. (*0-06-000960-8*) HarperCollins Children's Bk. Group. (Cotler, Joanna Bks.).

Stillerman, Robbie. Jake, the Cowboy: With 21 Stickers. 2001. (Illus.). (J). 1.00 (*0-486-41633-X*) Dover Pubns., Inc.

Stuart, Kelly. Cowboys Can Do! Amazing Things, Too! 2002. (Can Do! Bks.). (Illus.). 32p. (J). 14.95 (*0-9709987-3-2*) Yorkville Pr.

—Cowgirls Can Do! Amazing Things, Too! 2002. (Can Do! Bks.). (Illus.). 32p. 14.95 (*0-9709987-4-0*) Bright Sky Pr.

Stutson, Caroline. CowPokes. 1999. (Illus.). 24p. (J). (ps-1). lib. bdg. 14.89 (*0-688-13974-4*) HarperCollins Children's Bk. Group.

—Cowpokes. 1999. (Illus.). 24p. (J). (ps up). 15.95 (*0-688-13973-6*) HarperCollins Children's Bk. Group.

Sullivan, Silky. Grandpa Was a Cowboy. 1996. (Illus.). 32p. (J). (ps-3). pap. 15.95 (*0-531-09511-8*); lib. bdg. 16.99 (*0-531-08861-8*) Scholastic, Inc. (Orchard Bks.).

Taylor, Bonnie Highsmith. To Be a Cowboy. 1999. (Cover-to-Cover Bks.). (Illus.). 54p. (J). (*0-7807-8155-4*); pap. (*0-7891-2901-9*) Perfection Learning Corp.

Teague, Mark. How I Spent My Summer Vacation. 1995. (Illus.). 32p. (J). 16.00 o.s.i (*0-517-59998-8*); 17.99 o.s.i (*0-517-59999-6*) Random Hse. Children's Bks. (Random Hse. Bks. for Young Readers).

Thorpe, Kiki. Cowboy Christmas. 2001. (Woody's Roundup Ser.: 9). (Illus.). 64p. (J). (gr. 2-5). pap. 4.99 (*0-7868-4482-5*) Disney Pr.

Tibo, Gilles. L' Enfant Cowboy. 2000. (FRE., Illus.). 32p. (J). (gr. k-2). 16.95 (*0-88776-511-4*) Tundra Bks. of Northern New York.

Timberlake, Amy. The Dirty Cowboy, RS. 2003. (Illus.). 32p. 16.00 (*0-374-31791-7*, Farrar, Straus & Giroux (BYR)) Farrar, Straus & Giroux.

Tucker, Kathy. Do Cowboys Ride Bikes? (Illus.). 32p. (J). 1999. (ps-1). pap. 6.95 (*0-8075-1694-5*); 1997. (gr. 1-4). lib. bdg. 15.95 o.p. (*0-8075-1693-7*) Whitman, Albert & Co.

Ulmer, Wendy K. A Campfire for Cowboy Billy. 1997. (Illus.). 32p. (J). (gr. k-3). lib. bdg. 15.95 o.p. (*0-87358-681-6*, Rising Moon Bks. for Young Readers) Northland Publishing.

Von Mason, Stephen, illus. Brother Anansi & the Cattle Ranch - El Hermano Anansi y el Rancho de Ganado. 1996. (ENG & SPA.). 32p. (J). (gr. 1 up). reprint ed. pap. 7.95 (*0-89239-142-1*) Children's Bk. Pr.

Ward, Jon. The Clash of the Cowasorouses: Where the Cowboys Came From. 1997. (Illus.). 32p. (J). (gr. k-4). 15.95 (*0-9658128-1-2*) Long Wind Publishing.

Whatley, Bruce. Cowboy Pirate. 2002. (Illus.). 32p. 14.95 (*0-207-19891-8*) HarperCollins Pubs.

Wheeler, Lisa. Avalanche Annie: A Not-So-Tall Tale. 2003. (Illus.). 32p. (J). 16.00 (*0-15-216735-8*) Harcourt Children's Bks.

—Sixteen Cows. 2002. (Illus.). 32p. (J). (ps-2). 16.00 (*0-15-202676-2*) Harcourt Children's Bks.

Wilson, Sarah. Christmas Cowboy. 1993. (J). (ps-6). 14.00 o.p. (*0-671-74780-0*, Simon & Schuster Children's Publishing) Simon & Schuster Children's Publishing.

Wister, Owen. Virginian. 1964. (Airmont Classics Ser.). (J). (gr. 8 up). mass mkt. 2.95 o.p. (*0-8049-0046-9*, CL-46) Airmont Publishing Co., Inc.

Wolf, Bernard. Cowboy. 1985. (Illus.). 80p. (J). (gr. 5 up). 13.00 o.p. (*0-688-03877-8*); lib. bdg. 12.88 o.p. (*0-688-03878-6*) Morrow/Avon. (Morrow, William & Co.).

Wood, Audrey. A Cowboy Christmas: The Miracle at Lone Pine Ridge. 2001. (Illus.). 48p. (J). (gr. 2-4). 19.95 (*0-689-82190-5*, Simon & Schuster Children's Publishing) Simon & Schuster Children's Publishing.

Worcester, Donald E. Cowboy with a Camera: Erwin E. Smith, Cowboy Photograph. 1999. (Illus.). 48p. (J). (gr. 4-7). 18.95 (*0-88360-091-9*) Amon Carter Museum.

D

DANCERS—FICTION

Andersen, Hans Christian. The Red Shoes. 1997. (Illus.). 40p. (J). (gr. 1-5). 10.95 (*1-879085-56-9*, Whispering Coyote) Charlesbridge Publishing, Inc.

Anholt, Laurence. Degas & the Little Dancer. 1996. (Illus.). 32p. (J). (ps-3). 14.95 (*0-8120-6583-2*) Barron's Educational Series, Inc.

—Degas y la Pequena Bailarina. 1998. Tr. of Degas & the Little Dancer. (SPA., Illus.). 30p. (J). (ps-2). pap. 15.95 (*1-58105-122-0*, SAN1220) Santillana USA Publishing Co., Inc.

Beylon, Cathy, illus. We Are Ballerinas. 1997. (Sticker Stories Ser.). 16p. (J). (ps-k). 4.99 (*0-448-41723-5*, Grosset & Dunlap) Penguin Putnam Bks. for Young Readers.

Bornstein, Ruth Lercher. The Dancing Man. rev. ed. 1998. (Illus.). 32p. (J). (ps-3). tchr. ed. 16.00 (*0-395-83429-5*) Houghton Mifflin Co.

Brenner, Summer. Dancers & the Dance. 1990. 160p. (Orig.). (YA). (ps up). pap. 9.95 (*0-918273-75-7*) Coffee Hse. Pr.

Coombs, Karen Mueller. Samantha Gill, Belly Dancer. 1989. 128p. (J). pap. 2.75 (*0-380-75737-0*, Avon Bks.) Morrow/Avon.

Cowley, Joy. Agapanthus Hum & the Eyeglasses. 1999. (YA). pap. 30.99 incl. audio (*0-7887-3788-0*, 41032) Recorded Bks., LLC.

Di Laura, Dennis, illus. Barbie. 1999. (J). (*0-7853-3595-1*) Publications International, Ltd.

Dillon, Leo & Dillon, Diane. Rap a Tap Tap: Here's Bojangles - Think of That! 2002. (Illus.). 32p. (J). pap. 15.95 (*0-590-47883-4*, Blue Sky Pr., The) Scholastic, Inc.

Dominguez, Barbara. La Hija de la Manaa. 2001. Tr. of Child of the Morning. (SPA.). 152p. (J). 7.95 (*84-348-1979-1*) SM Ediciones ESP. *Dist:* AIMS International Bks., Inc.

Drayton, Kat, illus. Nantucket's Night Magic. 1998. 32p. (J). 14.95 (*0-9667090-0-4*) Dionis Bound Publishing.

Estoril, Jean. Drina Dances Again, No. 5. 1989. (J). pap. 2.95 o.p. (*0-590-42557-9*) Scholastic, Inc.

—Drina Dances Alone, No. 3. 1989. (J). pap. 2.75 o.p. (*0-590-42559-5*); pap. 2.75 o.p. (*0-590-43081-5*) Scholastic, Inc.

—Drina Dances on Stage, No. 4. 1989. (J). pap. 2.75 o.p. (*0-590-42558-7*) Scholastic, Inc.

—Drina's Dancing Year, No. 2. 1989. (J). pap. 2.75 o.p. (*0-590-42192-1*) Scholastic, Inc.

Fox, Paula. The Slave Dancer. 2002. (Illus.). (J). 14.47 (*0-7587-0214-0*) Book Wholesalers, Inc.

—The Slave Dancer. 1997. mass mkt. 2.69 o.p. (*0-440-22739-9*); 1990. 160p. (gr. 5-9). pap. text 5.99 (*0-440-40402-9*); 1990. (J). mass mkt. o.p. (*0-440-80203-2*) Dell Publishing.

—The Slave Dancer. 1998. (Assessment Packs Ser.). 15p. pap. text, tchr.'s training gde. ed. 15.95 (*1-58303-061-1*) Pathways Publishing.

—The Slave Dancer. unabr. ed. 2000. 152p. (J). (gr. 4-6). pap. 37.00 incl. audio (*0-8072-0458-7*, Listening Library) Random Hse. Audio Publishing Group.

—The Slave Dancer. (Laurel-Leaf Historical Fiction Ser.). 1974. 144p. (YA). (gr. 4-7). mass mkt. 5.50 (*0-440-96132-7*); 1988. (J). (gr. 3-7). reprint ed. lib. bdg. 15.95 o.p. (*1-55736-029-4*) Random Hse. Children's Bks. (Laurel Leaf).

—The Slave Dancer. (Illus.). 192p. (YA). 2001. 17.95 (*0-689-84505-7*); 1982. (gr. 5-9). lib. bdg. 16.95 (*0-02-735560-8*) Simon & Schuster Children's Publishing. (Atheneum/Richard Jackson Bks.).

—The Slave Dancer. 1973. (Laurel-Leaf Historical Fiction Ser.). 11.55 (*0-606-04914-2*) Turtleback Bks.

Freydont, Shelley. High Seas Murder: A Lindy Haggerty Mystery. 2001. 336p. mass mkt. 5.99 (*1-57566-676-6*) Kensington Publishing Corp.

Gauch, Patricia L. Dance, Tanya. 1989. (Illus.). 32p. (J). (ps-3). 16.99 (*0-399-21521-2*, Philomel) Penguin Putnam Bks. for Young Readers.

—Dance, Tanya: Mini Book & Doll Set. 1994. (Illus.). 32p. (J). (ps). 21.95 o.p. (*0-399-22795-4*, Philomel) Penguin Putnam Bks. for Young Readers.

Gauch, Patricia Lee. Tanya & the Red Shoes. 2002. (Illus.). 40p. (J). 16.99 (*0-399-23314-8*, Philomel) Penguin Putnam Bks. for Young Readers.

Giff, Patricia Reilly. Ballet Slippers No. 4: Not-So-Perfect Rosie. 1998. (Ballet Slippers Ser.: Vol. 4). (Illus.). 80p. (J). (gr. 2-5). pap. 4.99 (*0-14-130060-4*, Puffin Bks.) Penguin Putnam Bks. for Young Readers.

—Dance with Rosie. 1996. (Ballet Slippers Ser.: Vol. 1). (Illus.). 64p. (J). (gr. 4-7). 13.99 o.s.i (*0-670-86864-7*, Viking) Penguin Putnam Bks. for Young Readers.

—A Glass Slipper for Rosie. 1997. (Ballet Slippers Ser.: Vol. 5). (Illus.). 96p. (J). (gr. 2-5). 13.99 o.s.i (*0-670-87469-8*) Penguin Putnam Bks. for Young Readers.

—Not-So Perfect Rosie. 1997. (Ballet Slippers Ser.: No. 4). (Illus.). 80p. (J). (gr. 2-6). 13.99 o.p. (*0-670-86968-6*) Penguin Putnam Bks. for Young Readers.

—Rosie's Nutcracker Dreams. 1996. (Ballet Slippers Ser.: Vol. 2). (Illus.). 80p. (J). (gr. 4-7). 13.99 o.s.i (*0-670-86865-5*, Viking Children's Bks.) Penguin Putnam Bks. for Young Readers.

—Starring Rosie. 1997. (Ballet Slippers Ser.: Vol. 3). (Illus.). 80p. (J). (gr. 5-7). 13.99 o.s.i (*0-670-86967-8*) Penguin Putnam Bks. for Young Readers.

Hall, Kirsten. I'm a Ballerina! 2001. (Fantasy Tales Ser.). (Illus.). 24p. (J). (ps-k). 14.95 (*0-439-27904-6*, Cartwheel Bks.) Scholastic, Inc.

Hannert, Todd. The Morning Dance. 2001. (Illus.). 32p. (J). (ps-1). 12.95 o.p. (*0-8118-2812-3*) Chronicle Bks. LLC.

Hest, Amy. Mabel Dancing. 2000. (Illus.). 40p. (J). (ps-3). 15.99 (*0-7636-0746-0*) Candlewick Pr.

Hewett, Lorri. Dancer: Everybody Has a Dream. 2001. 224p. (YA). (gr. 8-12). pap. 5.99 (*0-14-131085-5*) Penguin Putnam Bks. for Young Readers.

Hill, Elizabeth S. The Street Dancers. 1991. 192p. (J). (gr. 3-7). 13.95 o.p. (*0-670-83435-1*, Viking Children's Bks.) Penguin Putnam Bks. for Young Readers.

Holabird, Katharine. Angelina & the Princess. 1988. (Angelina Ballerina Ser.). (Illus.). 24p. (J). (ps-3). 16.00 o.p. (*0-517-55273-6*, Clarkson Potter) Crown Publishing Group.

—Angelina & the Princess. (Angelina Ballerina Ser.). (Illus.). 24p. (J). (ps-3). 2002. 12.95 (*1-58485-653-X*); 2000. 9.95 (*1-58485-148-1*) Pleasant Co. Pubns.

—Angelina Ballerina. (Angelina Ballerina Ser.). (Illus.). (J). (ps-3). 1990. 24p. 5.99 o.p. (*0-517-57668-6*); 1988. 16.00 o.p. (*0-517-55083-0*) Crown Publishing Group. (Clarkson Potter).

—Angelina Ballerina. (Angelina Ballerina Ser.). (Illus.). 24p. (J). (ps-3). 2002. 12.95 (*1-58485-655-6*); 2000. 9.95 (*1-58485-135-X*) Pleasant Co. Pubns.

—My Memory Book. 2003. (Angelina Ballerina Ser.). (Illus.). 32p. (J). 14.95 (*1-58485-715-3*) Pleasant Co. Pubns.

Houghton Mifflin Company Staff. Dance Away. 1992. (Literature Experience 1993 Ser.). (J). (gr. 1). pap. 8.72 (*0-395-61764-2*) Houghton Mifflin Co.

Isadora, Rachel. Lili on Stage. 2002. (Illus.). (J). 14.04 (*0-7587-2988-X*) Book Wholesalers, Inc.

—Lili on Stage. 1995. (Illus.). 32p. (J). (ps-3). 16.99 o.p. (*0-399-22637-0*, G. P. Putnam's Sons) Penguin Group (USA) Inc.

—Lili on Stage. 1998. (Illus.). 32p. (J). (ps-3). pap. 6.99 o.p. (*0-698-11651-8*, PaperStar) Penguin Putnam Bks. for Young Readers.

Kamaiko & Mathers. Aunt Elaine Dance. 1992. (J). o.s.i (*0-385-44565-2*, Dell Books for Young Readers) Random Hse. Children's Bks.

The Katy Moon Chronicles: Dark Dances. 2000. 265p. (YA). pap. (*0-9687719-0-4*) Lambert, Julie D.

King, Sandra. Shannon: An Ojibway Dancer. 1993. (We Are Still Here Ser.). (Illus.). 48p. (J). (gr. 4-6). pap. 6.95 (*0-8225-9643-1*, Lerner Pubns.) Lerner Publishing Group.

Krementz, Jill. A Very Young Dancer. 1992. (J). 18.50 o.p. (*0-8446-6601-7*) Smith, Peter Pub., Inc.

Magnuson, Diana, illus. Dancin' down. 1997. (*0-7802-8029-6*) Wright Group, The.

Marshall, James. Swine Lake. ed. 2000. (J). (gr. 2). spiral bd. (*0-616-01712-X*) Canadian National Institute for the Blind/Institut National Canadien pour les Aveugles.

—Swine Lake. 2002. (Illus.). 45p. (YA). (gr. 6-8). 16.00 (*0-7567-5267-1*) DIANE Publishing Co.

—Swine Lake. 1999. (Illus.). (J). (ps-3). 15.95 (*0-06-028430-7*) HarperCollins Children's Bk. Group.

—Swine Lake. 1999. (Michael di Capua Bks.). (Illus.). 40p. (J). (ps-3). lib. bdg. 15.89 (*0-06-205172-5*); 15.95 (*0-06-205171-7*) Morrow/Avon. (Avon Bks.).

Morrison, Lillian. The Break Dance Kids. 1924. (J). o.s.i (*0-688-04264-3*); lib. bdg. o.s.i (*0-688-04265-1*) HarperCollins Children's Bk. Group.

Murphy, Kelly. The Boll Weevil Ball, ERS. 2002. (Illus.). 32p. (J). (ps-2). 15.95 (*0-8050-6712-4*, Holt, Henry & Co. Bks. For Young Readers) Holt, Henry & Co.

Plante, Raymond. Une Curieuse Invasion de Picots-les-Bains par les Zhbres. 2002. (Itait une Fois Ser.). (FRE., Illus.). 24p. (J). (ps up). pap. 7.95 (*2-89021-597-0*) La Courte Echelle CAN. *Dist:* Firefly Bks., Ltd.

Prior, Natalie Jane. Dance Crazy: Star Turns from Ballet to Belly Dancing. 1997. (Illus.). 96p. (Orig.). (J). (gr. 3-7). pap. 6.95 o.p. (*1-86448-390-3*) Allen & Unwin Pty., Ltd. AUS. *Dist:* Independent Pubs. Group.

Sachs, Albert. Filbert P. Emmette - Philbrech Hugelmann: The Aunt Who Loved to Dance - Die Ameise, Dig Vom Tanzen Schwarmte. Sachs, Albert, tr. 1994. (GER., Illus.). 106p. (Orig.). (J). pap. 9.95 (*1-886902-04-6*) Wildcat Pr.

Singer, Marilyn. The Case of the Sabotaged School Play. 1984. (Sam & Dave Mystery Ser.). (Illus.). 64p. (J). (gr. 3-7). lib. bdg. 10.89 o.p. (*0-06-025795-4*) HarperCollins Children's Bk. Group.

Smith, Charles R., Jr. Dance with Me. 2004. (J). (*0-7636-2246-X*) Candlewick Pr.

Smith, Doris B. Karate Dancer. 1987. 208p. (J). (gr. 6-9). 14.95 o.s.i (*0-399-21464-X*, G. P. Putnam's Sons) Penguin Putnam Bks. for Young Readers.

Staples, Suzanne Fisher. Shiva's Fire. l.t. ed. 2000. (Young Adult Ser.). 316p. (J). (gr. 8-12). 21.95 (*0-7862-2902-0*) Thorndike Pr.

Stout, Roxanne E. Sabrina the Dancer. 1993. (Illus.). 30p. (Orig.). (J). (gr. 4-5). pap. 3.00 (*0-88092-048-3*) Royal Fireworks Publishing Co.

Sutton, Elizabeth H. The Pony Champions. 1992. 45p. (J). (ps-3). 13.95 o.p. (*1-56566-019-6*) Lickle Publishing, Inc.

Tolles, Martha. Darci & the Dance Contest. 1987. 112p. (J). (gr. 4-6). reprint ed. pap. 2.50 o.p. (*0-590-33824-2*, Scholastic Paperbacks) Scholastic, Inc.

Winthrop, Elizabeth. Dumpy La Rue. 2004. (J). pap. 6.95 (*0-8050-7535-6*, Holt, Henry & Co. Bks. For Young Readers) Holt, Henry & Co.

DETECTIVES—FICTION

Adler, David A. My Dog & the Key Mystery. 1982. (Easy-Read Story Bks.). (Illus.). (gr. k-3). 3.95 o.p. (*0-531-03555-7*); lib. bdg. 9.40 o.p. (*0-531-04449-1*) Scholastic Library Publishing. (Watts, Franklin).

The Annette Mysteries. 2003. (Illus.). 288p. (J). 15.99 (*0-7868-3461-7*) Disney Pr.

Armstrong, Beverly. Dinosaur Detective. 1979. (Skill Builder Ser.). (Illus.). 32p. (J). (gr. k-3). pap. 4.95 o.p. (*0-88160-075-X*, LW808) Creative Teaching Pr., Inc.

Avi. The Man Who Was Poe. 1989. 224p. (J). (gr. 6-8). 13.95 o.p. (*0-531-05833-6*); mass mkt. 13.99 o.p. (*0-531-08433-7*) Scholastic, Inc. (Orchard Bks.).

Bailey, Linda. How Can a Brilliant Detective Shine in the Dark? (Stevie Diamond Mystery Ser.). 1999. 174p. (J). pap. (*1-55074-750-9*); No. 6. 2003. 200p. (YA). 14.95 (*1-55074-896-3*) Kids Can Pr., Ltd.

Baker, Eugene. At the Scene of the Crime. 1980. (Junior Detective Bks.). (Illus.). 32p. (J). (gr. 2-6). lib. bdg. 9.95 o.p. (*0-516-06470-3*, Children's Pr.) Scholastic Library Publishing.

—In the Detective's Lab. 1980. (Junior Detective Bks.). (Illus.). 32p. (J). (gr. 2-6). 9.95 o.p. (*0-516-06471-1*, Children's Pr.) Scholastic Library Publishing.

—Master of Disguise. 1980. (Junior Detective Bks.). (Illus.). 32p. (J). (gr. 2-6). 9.95 o.p. (*0-516-06472-X*, Children's Pr.) Scholastic Library Publishing.

—Shadowing the Suspect. 1980. (Junior Detective Bks.). (Illus.). 32p. (J). (gr. 2-6). 9.25 o.p. (*0-516-06474-6*, Children's Pr.) Scholastic Library Publishing.

Block, Judy R. The World's First Police Detective. 1978. (Famous Firsts Ser.). (Illus.). (J). lib. bdg. 10.76 o.p. (*0-89547-041-1*) Silver, Burdett & Ginn, Inc.

Brooks, Walter R. Freddy & Mr. Camphor. 2000. (Illus.). 234p. (J). (gr. 3-7). 23.95 (*1-58567-027-8*) Overlook Pr., The.

—Freddy & Mr. Camphor. 2003. (Illus.). 256p. (J). pap. 7.99 (*0-14-230248-1*, Puffin Bks.) Penguin Putnam Bks. for Young Readers.

—Freddy & the Baseball Team from Mars. 1999. (Illus.). 256p. (YA). (gr. 3-7). 23.95 (*0-87951-942-8*) Overlook Pr., The.

—Freddy & the Baseball Team from Mars. 1963. (Illus.). (J). (gr. 3-7). 5.99 o.s.i (*0-394-90810-4*, Knopf Bks. for Young Readers) Random Hse. Children's Bks.

—Freddy & the Baseball Team from Mars. 2000. (J). pap. 67.95 incl. audio (*0-7887-4461-5*, 41150); pap. 67.95 incl. audio (*0-7887-4461-5*, 41150) Recorded Bks., LLC.

—Freddy & the Baseball Team From Mars. 1988. (Illus.). 256p. (J). (gr. 3-7). pap. 2.95 o.p. (*0-440-42724-X*) Dell Publishing.

—Freddy & the Dragon. 2000. (Illus.). 239p. (J). (gr. 3 up). 23.95 (*1-58567-026-X*) Overlook Pr., The.

—Freddy & the Flying Saucer Plans. 248p. (J). 22.95 o.s.i (*0-8488-2441-5*) Amereon, Ltd.

—Freddy & the Flying Saucer Plans. 1998. (Freddy Ser.). (Illus.). 256p. (J). (gr. 3-7). 23.95 (*0-87951-883-9*) Overlook Pr., The.

—Freddy & the Flying Saucer Plans. unabr. ed. 2000. (J). pap. 66.95 incl. audio (*0-7887-3639-6*, 41004X4) Recorded Bks., LLC.

—Freddy & the Ignormus. 288p. (J). 23.95 o.s.i (*0-8488-2440-7*) Amereon, Ltd.

—Freddy & the Ignormus. 1998. (Freddy Ser.). (Illus.). 288p. (J). (gr. 3-7). 23.95 (*0-87951-882-0*) Overlook Pr., The.

—Freddy & the Ignormus. 1999. (J). pap. 66.95 incl. audio (*0-7887-2996-9*, 40878) Recorded Bks., LLC.

—Freddy & the Men from Mars. 1987. (Knopf Children's Paperbacks Ser.). (Illus.). 256p. (J). (gr. 3-7). 3.95 o.s.i (*0-394-88887-1*, Knopf Bks. for Young Readers) Random Hse. Children's Bks.

—Freddy & the Perilous Adventure. 1986. (Freddy the Pig Bks.). (Illus.). 256p. (J). (gr. 3-7). 9.99 o.s.i (*0-394-97601-0*, Knopf Bks. for Young Readers) Random Hse. Children's Bks.

—Freddy the Detective. 1997. (Freddy Ser.). (Illus.). 256p. (J). (gr. 3-7). 23.95 (*0-87951-809-X*) Overlook Pr., The.

—Freddy the Detective. 1987. (Knopf Children's Paperbacks Ser.). (Illus.). 272p. (J). (gr. 3-7). 4.95 o.s.i (*0-394-88885-5*, Knopf Bks. for Young Readers) Random Hse. Children's Bks.

Caufield, Don & Caufield, Joan. The Incredible Detectives. 1966. 88p. (J). (gr. 2-6). lib. bdg. 10.89 o.p. (*0-06-021169-5*) HarperCollins Pubs.

Caufield, Don & Caulfield, Joan. The Incredible Detectives. 1983. (Illus.). (J). (gr. 4-6). pap. 0.95 o.p. (*0-380-01282-0*, 50443, Avon Bks.) Morrow/Avon.

Childrens Press Staff. Solve a Mystery: From the Casebook of J. P. Landers, Master Detective, Vol. 3. 1982. (J). 10.60 o.p. (*0-516-01993-7*, Children's Pr.) Scholastic Library Publishing.

Christian, Mary Blount. The Phantom of the Operetta. 1986. (Determined Detectives Ser.). (Illus.). 80p. (J). (gr. 2-5). 10.95 o.p. (*0-525-44272-3*, Dutton Children's Bks.) Penguin Putnam Bks. for Young Readers.

Cormier, Robert. The Rag & Bone Shop. 2001. 160p. (YA). (gr. 7 up). lib. bdg. 17.99 (*0-385-90027-9*, Delacorte Pr.) Dell Publishing.

—The Rag & Bone Shop. l.t. ed. 2002. 141p. (J). 24.95 (*0-7862-3873-9*) Gale Group.

—The Rag & Bone Shop. 2001. (Illus.). 160p. (YA). (gr. 7 up). 15.95 (*0-385-72962-6*, Delacorte Bks. for Young Readers) Random Hse. Children's Bks.

Dautrich, Jack & Huff, Vivian. Big City Detective. 1986. (Illus.). 128p. (YA). (gr. 7 up). 13.95 o.p. (*0-525-67183-8*, Dutton Children's Bks.) Penguin Putnam Bks. for Young Readers.

Ehrlich, Amy. Where It Stops, Nobody Knows. 1988. 192p. (YA). (gr. 6 up). 14.95 o.p. (*0-8037-0575-1*, Dial Bks. for Young Readers) Penguin Putnam Bks. for Young Readers.

Eisenberg, Lisa. Mystery at Bluff Point Dunes. 1988. 176p. (J). (gr. 5 up). 14.95 o.p. (*0-8037-0527-1*, Dial Bks. for Young Readers) Penguin Putnam Bks. for Young Readers.

Ferguson, Dwayne J. The Werewolf of PS 40. 1998. (Kid Caramel, Private Investigator Ser.: Vol. 2). 68p. (J). (gr. 4-7). pap. 4.50 (*0-940975-82-3*) Just Us Bks., Inc.

—The Werewolf of PS 40. 1998. (Kid Caramel, Private Investigator Ser.: Vol. 2). E-Book (*1-59019-131-5*); E-Book (*1-59019-130-7*); E-Book (*1-59019-132-3*) ipicturebooks, LLC.

Fleischman, Paul. Phoebe Danger, Detective, in the Case of the Two-Minute Cough, 001. 1983. (Illus.). 64p. (J). (gr. 2-5). 8.95 o.p. (*0-395-33226-5*) Houghton Mifflin Co.

Franzen, Nils Olof. Agaton Sax & the Big Rig. 1981. (Illus.). 128p. (J). 8.95 o.p. (*0-233-96754-0*) Blackwell Publishing.

Funke, Cornelia. The Thief Lord. Latsch, Oliver, tr. from GER. 2002. (Illus.). 352p. (J). (gr. 4-7). pap. 16.95 (*0-439-40437-1*, Chicken Hse., The) Scholastic, Inc.

—The Thief Lord. 2003. 376p. (J). (gr. 3-6). reprint ed. pap. 6.99 (*0-439-42089-X*, Chicken Hse., The) Scholastic, Inc.

Hardy, Robin. Sammy: Dallas Detective. 1997. 224p. (YA). pap. 9.99 o.p. (*1-56384-134-7*, Vital Issue Pr.) Huntington Hse. Pubs.

Heisler, Edith. Mystery at the Old Estate. 2002. 129p. pap. 17.95 (*1-59129-275-1*) PublishAmerica, Inc.

Henry, Marguerite. Marguerite Henry's Misty Treasury. 1982. (Illus.). 570p. (gr. 3-6). 14.95 o.p. (*0-528-82423-6*) Rand McNally.

Johnson, Larry D. & Mills, Jane L. Arnie the Detective. 1986. (Search & Find Set Ser.: Level 3). (Illus.). 24p. (J). (ps). pap. 12.00 (*0-938155-06-7*) Read-A-Bol Group, The.

Joosse, Barbara M. The Losers Fight Back: A Wild Willie Mystery. 9999. pap. 4.99 o.s.i (*0-440-91140-0*) Bantam Bks.

—The Losers Fight Back: A Wild Willie Mystery. 1994. (Illus.). 112p. (J). (gr. 4-6). tchr. ed. 15.00 (*0-395-62335-9*, Clarion Bks.) Houghton Mifflin Co. Trade & Reference Div.

—The Losers Fight Back: A Wild Willie Mystery. 1996. (Illus.). 112p. (J). (gr. 2-6). pap. 3.99 o.s.i (*0-440-41110-6*, Yearling) Random Hse. Children's Bks.

—The Losers Fight Back: A Wild Willie Mystery. 1996. 9.09 o.p. (*0-606-09578-0*) Turtleback Bks.

—Wild Willie & King Kyle Detectives. 1996. (Illus.). 80p. (J). (gr. 2-5). pap. 3.50 o.s.i (*0-440-41107-6*, Yearling) Random Hse. Children's Bks.

Kelso, Mary J. Sierra Summer. 1992. (Lynne Garrett Adventure Ser.: No. 3). (Illus.). 120p. (Orig.). (YA). (gr. 6 up). pap. 4.95 (*0-9621406-3-5*) MarKel Pr.

Kwitz, Mary D. Gumshoe Goose, Private Eye. 1988. (Easy-to-Read Bks.). (Illus.). 48p. (J). (ps-3). 9.95 o.p. (*0-8037-0423-2*); 9.89 o.p. (*0-8037-0424-0*) Penguin Putnam Bks. for Young Readers. (Dial Bks. for Young Readers).

Miller, Marvin. Who Dunnit? How to Be a Detective in Ten Easy Lessons. 1992. (J). (gr. 4-7). mass mkt. 2.75 o.p. (*0-590-44717-3*) Scholastic, Inc.

Obrist, Jurg. Case Closed?! 40 Mini-Mysteries for You to Solve. 2003. (Single Titles Ser.). 96p. pap. 6.95 (*0-7613-1999-9*); 22.90 (*0-7613-2739-8*) Millbrook Pr., Inc.

Paulsen. Spitball Gang. 1980. (J). 7.95 o.p. (*0-525-66695-8*) NAL.

Platt, Kin. Big Max. 1978. (I Can Read Bks.). (Illus.). 64p. (J). (gr. k-3). pap. 3.99 (*0-06-444006-0*, Harper Trophy) HarperCollins Children's Bk. Group.

Pomerantz, Charlotte. Detective Poufy's First Case. 1976. (Illus.). 64p. (J). (gr. 3-7). lib. bdg. 5.95 o.p. (*0-201-05853-7*) Addison-Wesley Longman, Inc.

Quackenbush, Robert. Piet Potter Returns. 1980. (J). (gr. 4-6). text 7.95 o.p. (*0-07-051022-9*) McGraw-Hill Cos., The.

Rosenberg, Amye & Mason, Patrice G. Sam the Detective & the Alef Bet Mystery. Rossel, Seymour, ed. 1980. (Illus.). 64p. (Orig.). (J). (gr. 1-3). pap. text 5.50 (*0-87441-328-1*) Behrman Hse., Inc.

Sobol, Donald J. Encyclopedia Brown Lends a Hand. 1993. (Encyclopedia Brown Ser.: No. 11). 96p. (gr. 2-6). pap. text 4.50 (*0-553-48133-9*) Bantam Bks.

—Encyclopedia Brown's Book of Wacky Animals. 1985. (Encyclopedia Brown Ser.). 128p. (J). (gr. 2-6). pap. 2.25 o.s.i (*0-553-15346-3*, Skylark) Random Hse. Children's Bks.

—Encyclopedia Brown's Third Record Book of Weird & Wonderful Facts. 1985. (Encyclopedia Brown Ser.). 144p. (J). (gr. 2-6). pap. 2.50 o.s.i (*0-553-15372-2*, Skylark) Random Hse. Children's Bks.

Spillane, Mickey. Kiss Me Deadly. 1953. (Mike Hammer Ser.). reprint ed. mass mkt. 3.95 o.p. (*0-451-16593-4*, Signet Bks.) NAL.

Stanley, George Edward. The Clue of the Left-Handed Envelope. 2000. (Third Grade Detectives Ser.: No. 1). (Illus.). 64p. (J). (gr. 1-4). pap. 3.99 (*0-689-82194-8*, Aladdin) Simon & Schuster Children's Publishing.

—The Cobweb Confession. 2001. (Third Grade Detectives Ser.: No. 4). (Illus.). 80p. (J). (gr. 1-4). pap. 3.99 (*0-689-82197-2*, Aladdin) Simon & Schuster Children's Publishing.

—The Puzzle of the Pretty Pink Handkerchief. 2000. (Third Grade Detectives Ser.: No. 2). (Illus.). 64p. (J). (gr. 1-4). pap. 3.99 (*0-689-82232-4*, Aladdin) Simon & Schuster Children's Publishing.

Stevenson, James. Mud Flat Mystery. 2003. (Illus.). 64p. (J). pap. 4.25 (*0-06-051181-8*, Harper Trophy) HarperCollins Children's Bk. Group.

Talbert, Marc. The Paper Knife. 1988. 176p. (J). (gr. 4 up). 14.95 o.p. (*0-8037-0571-9*, Dial Bks. for Young Readers) Penguin Putnam Bks. for Young Readers.

Tashjian, Janet. Marty Frye, Private Eye, ERS. 1998. (Redfeather Bks.). (Illus.). 80p. (J). (gr. 1-3). 15.95 (*0-8050-5888-5*, Holt, Henry & Co. Bks. For Young Readers) Holt, Henry & Co.

—Marty Frye, Private Eye. 2000. (Illus.). 80p. (J). (gr. 1-3). mass mkt. 3.99 (*0-439-09557-3*) Scholastic, Inc.

—Marty Frye, Private Eye. 2000. 10.14 (*0-606-18880-0*) Turtleback Bks.

Taylor, Andrew. The Private Nose. 1995. (Illus.). (J). bds. 3.99 o.p. (*1-56402-518-7*) Candlewick Pr.

Tracy, Jack. The Encyclopaedia Sherlockiana. 1979. pap. 7.95 o.p. (*0-380-46490-X*, 46490, Avon Bks.) Morrow/Avon.

Van Draanen, Wendelin. Sammy Keyes & the Hotel Thief. 1998. (Sammy Keyes Ser.). 176p. (gr. 5-8). text 15.00 (*0-679-88839-X*, Knopf Bks. for Young Readers) Random Hse. Children's Bks.

Weiner, Eric. Booby-Trapped! 1994. (Clue Ser.: No. 6). 112p. (J). (gr. 3-6). mass mkt. 3.99 (*0-590-47805-2*) Scholastic, Inc.

—Booby-Trapped! 1994. (Clue Ser.: No. 6). (J). (gr. 3-6). 9.09 o.p. (*0-606-09094-0*) Turtleback Bks.

Whatley, Bruce & Smith, Rosie. Detective Donut & the Wild Goose Chase. 1997. (Illus.). 40p. (J). (ps-3). 14.95 (*0-06-026604-X*) HarperCollins Children's Bk. Group.

Whybrow, Ian. Little Wolf, Forest Detective. 2001. (Middle Grade Fiction Ser.). (Illus.). 112p. (J). (gr. 3-6). lib. bdg. 12.95 (*1-57505-413-2*, Carolrhoda Bks.) Lerner Publishing Group.

Williams, Jay & Abrashkin, Raymond. Danny Dunn, Scientific Detective. 1981. (Danny Dunn Ser.: No. 3). (Illus.). (J). (gr. 4-6). pap. (*0-671-44382-8*, Simon Pulse) Simon & Schuster Children's Publishing.

Wyatt. Amazing Investigations Twins. 1998. (J). 12.95 (*0-13-023649-7*, Simon & Schuster Children's Publishing) Simon & Schuster Children's Publishing.

E

EVANGELISTS—FICTION

Paulsen, Gary. The Tent: A Parable in One Sitting. 1995. 96p. (YA). (gr. 7 up). 15.00 (*0-15-292879-0*) Harcourt Children's Bks.

Whalen, Terry. When I Grow up, I Can Go Anywhere for Jesus. 1992. 32p. (J). (ps-3). pap. 8.99 o.p. (*1-55513-488-2*) Cook Communications Ministries.

EXPLORERS—FICTION

Abbott, Tony. Danger Guys & the Golden Lizard. 1996. (Trophy Chapter Bks.). (Illus.). 96p. (J). (gr. 2-5). pap. 3.95 o.s.i (*0-06-442011-6*, Harper Trophy) HarperCollins Children's Bk. Group.

—Danger Guys & the Golden Lizard. 1996. (Danger Guys Ser.). 9.15 o.p. (*0-606-09178-5*) Turtleback Bks.

Beinstein, Phoebe. Dora's Color Adventure! 2002. (Dora the Explorer Ser.). (Illus.). 20p. (J). bds. 6.99 (*0-689-84663-0*, Simon Spotlight/Nickelodeon) Simon & Schuster Children's Publishing.

Christian, Mary Blount. Who'd Believe John Colter? 1993. (Illus.). 64p. (J). (gr. 2-6). lib. bdg. 13.95 o.s.i (*0-02-718477-3*, Simon & Schuster Children's Publishing) Simon & Schuster Children's Publishing.

Cleary, Beverly. The Real Hole. 1996. (Illus.). 32p. (J). (ps-3). pap. 4.95 (*0-688-14741-0*, Harper Trophy) HarperCollins Children's Bk. Group.

—The Real Hole. rev. ed. 1986. (Illus.). 32p. (J). (ps-1). 11.95 o.p. (*0-688-05850-7*); lib. bdg. 11.88 o.p. (*0-688-05851-5*) Morrow/Avon. (Morrow, William & Co.).

—The Real Hole. 1990. (J). pap. o.s.i (*0-440-80185-0*, Dell Books for Young Readers) Random Hse. Children's Bks.

—The Real Hole. 1996. 11.10 (*0-606-09780-5*) Turtleback Bks.

Cowan, Mary M. Ice Country. 1995. (Illus.). (J). (gr. 6-8). 18.95 (*0-89725-220-9*, 1597, Cricketfield Pr.) Picton Pr.

Ellis, Terry. Explorers from Willow Wood Springs. 1989. (Willow Wood Springs Ser.: No. 2). (Illus.). 180p. (Orig.). (J). (gr. 4 up). pap. 4.75 (*0-915677-31-8*) Roundtable Publishing.

Garfield, Henry. The Lost Voyage of John Cabot. 2004. (YA). (*0-689-85173-1*, Atheneum/Richard Jackson Bks.) Simon & Schuster Children's Publishing.

Hedstrom, Debbie. From East to West with Lewis & Clark. 1997. (My American Journey Ser.). (J). (gr. 4-7). 19.99 o.p. (*1-57673-066-2*) Questar, Inc.

Karwoski, Gail Langer. Seaman: The Dog Who Explored the West with Lewis & Clark. 2003. (Illus.). 192p. (J). (gr. 3-7). pap. 8.95 (*1-56145-190-8*, 51908) Peachtree Pubs., Ltd.

—Seaman: The Dog Who Explored the West with Lewis & Clark. 1999. 15.00 (*0-606-17742-6*) Turtleback Bks.

—Surviving Jamestown: The Adventures of Young Sam Collier. 2001. (Illus.). 192p. (J). (gr. 3-7). 14.95 (*1-56145-239-4*); pap. 8.95 (*1-56145-245-9*) Peachtree Pubs., Ltd.

Lasky, Kathryn. The Journal of Augustus Pelletier: The Lewis & Clark Expedition, 1804. 2000. (My Name Is America Ser.). (Illus.). 171p. (J). (gr. 4-8). pap. 10.95 (*0-590-68489-2*) Scholastic, Inc.

Lee, Rebecca L. Kori & the Island of Enchantment. 1990. 80p. (Orig.). (YA). (gr. 8 up). pap. 6.95 o.p. (*0-931832-46-2*) Fithian Pr.

Luna, Rachel Nickerson. The Haunting of Captain Snow. 2003. (Eel Grass Girls Mystery Ser.: No. 2). (Illus.). 332p. (YA). pap. 11.95 (*1-886551-08-1*) Howard, Emma Bks.

Mayhew, James. Miranda the Explorer: A Magical-Round-the-World Adventure. 2003. (Illus.). 32p. (J). pap. 8.95 (*1-84255-280-5*); 16.95 (*1-84255-000-4*) Orion Publishing Group, Ltd. GBR. (Dolphin Paperbacks). *Dist:* Trafalgar Square.

McAndrews, Anita. Blessed Be the Light of Day. 2001. 48p. (J). (gr. 2-5). 14.95 (*1-930093-02-0*) Brookfield Reader, Inc., The.

Moses, Amy. I Am an Explorer. 1990. (Rookie Readers Ser.). (Illus.). 32p. (J). (ps-2). mass mkt. 16.00 o.p. (*0-516-02059-5*); mass mkt. 4.95 o.p. (*0-516-42059-3*) Scholastic Library Publishing. (Children's Pr.).

—I Am an Explorer Big Book. 1991. (Rookie Readers Big Bks.). (Illus.). 32p. (J). (ps-2). mass mkt. 33.70 o.p. (*0-516-49517-8*, Children's Pr.) Scholastic Library Publishing.

O'Dell, Scott. Streams to the River, River to the Sea: A Novel of Sacagawea. 1987. 176p. (gr. 7-12). mass mkt. 5.99 (*0-449-70244-8*, Fawcett) Ballantine Bks.

—Streams to the River, River to the Sea: A Novel of Sacagawea. l.t. ed. 1989. 312p. (YA). (gr. 7 up). lib. bdg. 14.95 (*0-8161-4811-2*, Macmillan Reference USA) Gale Group.

—Streams to the River, River to the Sea: A Novel of Sacagawea. 1986. 208p. (YA). (gr. 7 up). tchr. ed. 16.00 (*0-395-40430-4*) Houghton Mifflin Co.

—Streams to the River, River to the Sea: A Novel of Sacagawea. 1986. (J). 12.04 (*0-606-03695-4*) Turtleback Bks.

Pepper Bird Staff. Frozen Fury: Adventures of Matthew Henson. 1993. (Multicultural Historical Fiction Ser.). (Illus.). 48p. (Orig.). (J). (gr. 4-7). pap. 4.95 (*1-56817-001-7*) Pepper Bird Publishing.

Peterson, John. The Littles Go Exploring. (Littles Ser.). (Illus.). (J). (gr. 1-5). 9999. 96p. 2.25 o.p. (*0-590-40140-8*); 1993. 96p. mass mkt. 3.99 (*0-590-46596-1*); 1987. 96p. mass mkt. 2.50 o.p. (*0-590-44012-8*); 1978. pap. 2.25 o.p. (*0-590-32005-X*) Scholastic, Inc.

—The Littles Go Exploring. 1978. (Littles Ser.). (Illus.). (J). (gr. 1-5). 10.14 (*0-606-05436-7*) Turtleback Bks.

Place, Francois. The Last Giants. Rodarmor, William, tr. from FRE. 1993. (Illus.). 78p. (J). 15.95 (*0-87923-990-5*) Godine, David R. Pub.

—The Last Giants. 2001. (Illus.). 74p. (J). pap. 11.00 (*1-86205-289-1*) Pavilion Bks., Ltd. GBR. *Dist:* Trafalgar Square.

—Los Ultimos Gigantes. 1999. (SPA., Illus.). 78p. (J). (gr. 3 up). 16.95 (*980-257-235-7*, EK2575) Ekare, Ediciones VEN. *Dist:* Kane/Miller Bk. Pubs., Lectorum Pubns., Inc.

—A Voyage of Discovery Vol. 1: From the Land of the Amazons to the Indigo Isles. 2001. (Illus.). 144p. (YA). (gr. 3 up). 22.95 (*1-86205-213-1*) Pavilion Bks., Ltd. GBR. *Dist:* Trafalgar Square.

Primavera, Elise. Ralph's Frozen Tale. 1991. (Illus.). 32p. (J). 14.95 o.p. (*0-399-22252-9*, G. P. Putnam's Sons) Penguin Group (USA) Inc.

Sargent, Dave & Sargent, Pat. Chalky (Chalky Grullo) I'm Forgotten #12: I'm Forgetful #12. 2001. (Saddle Up Ser.). 36p. (J). lib. bdg. 22.60 (*1-56763-603-9*) Ozark Publishing.

—Chalky (Chalky Grullo) No. 12: I'm Forgetful. 2001. (Saddle Up Ser.). 36p. (J). pap. 6.95 (*1-56763-604-7*) Ozark Publishing.

Sheldon, Dyan. Harry the Explorer. 1994. (Illus.). 80p. (J). (gr. 3-6). bds. 3.99 o.p. (*1-56402-393-1*) Candlewick Pr.

Smith, Roland. The Captain's Dog: My Journey with the Lewis & Clark Tribe. (Great Episodes Ser.). 296p. 2000. (Illus.). (J). (gr. 4-7). pap. 6.00 (*0-15-202696-7*, Harcourt Paperbacks); 1999. (YA). (gr. 5-9). 17.00 (*0-15-201989-8*, Gulliver Bks.) Harcourt Children's Bks.

—The Captain's Dog: My Journey with the Lewis & Clark Tribe. 2000. (J). 12.05 (*0-606-19000-7*) Turtleback Bks.

Occupations

Stoddart, Matthew. Chelli the Great Explorer. 1996. (Big Bag Ser.). (Illus.). 24p. (J). (ps-k). pap. 3.29 o.s.i (*0-307-13011-8*, Golden Bks.) Random Hse. Children's Bks.

Thomas, Frances. One Day, Daddy. 2001. (Illus.). 32p. (J). (ps-2). 15.99 (*0-7868-0732-6*) Hyperion Bks. for Children.

Villoldo, Alberto. The First Story Ever Told. 1996. (Illus.). (J). (ps-3). 40p. 16.00 (*0-689-80515-2*); 16.00 (*0-671-89729-2*) Simon & Schuster Children's Publishing. (Simon & Schuster Children's Publishing).

Vollmann, William T. Argall: The True Story of Pocahontas & Captain John Smith. 2001. (Seven Dreams Ser.: Vol. 3). (Illus.). 736p. 40.00 o.s.i (*0-670-91030-9*, Viking) Viking Penguin.

F

FIRE FIGHTERS—FICTION

Appleton, Victor. Tom Swift among the Fire Fighters. (Tom Swift Original Ser.: No. 24). (J). (gr. 3-7). E-Book 2.49 (*1-58627-071-0*) Electric Umbrella Publishing.

—Tom Swift among the Fire Fighters. (Tom Swift Original Ser.: No. 24). (J). (gr. 3-7). E-Book 1.95 (*1-57799-871-5*) Logos Research Systems, Inc.

—Tom Swift among the Fire Fighters. 1999. (Tom Swift Original Ser.: Vol. No. 24). (J). (gr. 3-7). E-Book 3.99 o.p. incl. cd-rom (*1-57646-037-1*) Quiet Vision Publishing.

—Tom Swift among the Fire Fighters. (J). E-Book 5.00 (*0-7410-0646-4*) SoftBook Pr.

Arceneaux, Marc, illus. The Little Fire Engine. 1984. (Beep Beep Board Bks.). 14p. (J). 2.85 o.p. (*0-671-47338-7*, Atheneum) Simon & Schuster Children's Publishing.

Barbaresi, Nina. Firemouse. 2002. (Illus.). 40p. (J). (gr. k-3). 12.95 (*0-375-82294-1*) Knopf, Alfred A. Inc.

—Firemouse. (Illus.). 40p. (J). 2002. lib. bdg. 14.99 (*0-375-92294-6*); 1987. 10.95 o.s.i (*0-517-56337-1*) Random Hse. Children's Bks. (Random Hse. Bks. for Young Readers).

Barkan, Joanne. Whiskerville Firestation. 1990. (J). (GRE.). 5.99 (*0-85953-858-3*); (ITA.). 5.99 (*0-85953-646-7*) Child's Play of England GBR. *Dist:* Child's Play-International.

Baumann, Kurt. Piro & the Fire Brigade. Koenig, Marion, tr. 1981. (Illus.). 30p. (J). o.p. (*0-571-11843-7*) Faber & Faber Ltd.

Boelts, Maribeth. The Firefighters' Thanksgiving. 2004. (Illus.). 32p. (J). 16.99 (*0-399-23600-7*) Putnam Publishing Group, The.

Bond, Felicia. Poinsettia & the Firefighters. (J). 2003. (Illus.). 32p. 14.99 (*0-06-053509-1*, Geringer, Laura Bk.); 2003. (Illus.). 32p. lib. bdg. 15.89 (*0-06-053510-5*, Geringer, Laura Bk.); 1984. 12.95 (*0-690-04400-3*); 1984. (Illus.). 32p. lib. bdg. 16.89 o.s.i (*0-690-04401-1*); 1988. (Illus.). 32p. reprint ed. pap. 4.95 o.p. (*0-06-443160-6*, Harper Trophy) HarperCollins Children's Bk. Group.

Brown, Margaret Wise. The Little Fireman. (Trophy Picture Bk.). (Illus.). 40p. (J). (ps-3). 1995. pap. 4.95 o.p. (*0-06-443389-7*, Harper Trophy); 1993. 12.95 o.p. (*0-06-021476-7*); 1993. lib. bdg. 12.89 o.s.i (*0-06-021477-5*); 1952. 11.95 (*0-201-09261-1*) HarperCollins Children's Bk. Group.

Desimini, Lisa. Dot the Fire Dog. 2001. (Illus.). 40p. (J). (ps up). pap. 15.95 (*0-439-23322-4*, Blue Sky Pr., The) Scholastic, Inc.

Dotty the Dalmatian: Has Epilepsy. 1996. (Dr. Wellbook Collection). (Illus.). 24p. (J). (ps-3). reprint ed. pap. 7.95 (*1-879874-35-0*) Peters, Tim & Co., Inc.

Edwards, Julie Andrews. Dumpy & the Firefighters. 2003. (Julie Andrews Collection). (Illus.). 32p. (J). lib. bdg. 16.89 (*0-06-052682-3*) HarperCollins Pubs.

Edwards, Julie Andrews & Hamilton, Emma Walton. Dumpy & the Firefighters. 2003. (Julie Andrews Collection). (Illus.). 32p. (J). 15.99 (*0-06-052681-5*) HarperCollins Pubs.

Fireman & Pilot Jane No. 2, Bk. 2. 1998. (Playmobile Bks.). (Illus.). (J). 13.98 (*1-57584-305-6*, Reader's Digest Children's Bks.) Reader's Digest Children's Publishing, Inc.

Fisher-Price Staff & Hood, Susan. Firefighter Sam Finds a Friend. 1997. (Fisher-Price Take-Me-Out Playbook Ser.). (Illus.). 14p. (J). (ps-k). bds. 9.99 (*1-57584-182-7*) Reader's Digest Children's Publishing, Inc.

Fox, Diane. Fire Fighter PiggyWiggy. 2001. (Illus.). 24p. (J). (ps-k). 9.95 (*1-929766-16-5*) Handprint Bks.

Froeb, Lori. Emergency Rescue! 2002. (Tonka Mighty Movers Ser.). (Illus.). 8p. (J). bds. 14.99 (*1-57584-999-2*, Reader's Digest Children's Bks.) Reader's Digest Children's Publishing, Inc.

Gergely, Tibor, illus. The Fire Engine Book. 2001. (Little Golden Bks.). 24p. (J). (ps-k). 2.99 (*0-307-96024-2*, Golden Bks.) Random Hse. Children's Bks.

Hedger, Jack. The Volunteers: Firefighters. unabr. ed. 1994. (Illus.). (J). 19.95 (*1-882416-01-5*) Akela West Pubs.

Hill, Mary L. My Dad's a Smokejumper. 1978. (Career Adventures Ser.). (Illus.). 32p. (J). (gr. 2-4). lib. bdg. 9.25 o.p. (*0-516-07636-1*, Children's Pr.) Scholastic Library Publishing.

Horowitz, Jordan. Working Hard with the Busy Fire Truck. 1993. 32p. (J). (ps-3). mass mkt. 3.50 (*0-590-46602-X*) Scholastic, Inc.

Ladybird Books Staff. Forgetful Little Fireman. 1998. (Little People Stories Ser.). (Illus.). 32p. (J). text 2.50 o.p. (*0-7214-1926-7*, Ladybird Bks.) Penguin Group (USA) Inc.

Lippman, Peter. Firehouse Co. No. 1. 1994. (Mini House Book Ser.). (Illus.). 20p. (J). (ps up). bds. 9.95 (*1-56305-663-1*, 3663) Workman Publishing Co., Inc.

Lukasewich, Lori. The Night Fire. 2001. (Illus.). 32p. (J). (ps-3). 15.95 (*0-7737-3296-9*) Stoddart Kids CAN. *Dist:* Fitzhenry & Whiteside, Ltd.

MacAulay, Craig. Ten Men on a Ladder. (Illus.). 32p. (J). (ps up). 1996. pap. 4.95 (*1-55037-340-4*); 1993. lib. bdg. 14.95 (*1-55037-341-2*) Annick Pr., Ltd. CAN. *Dist:* Firefly Bks., Ltd.

Maifair, Linda L. & Cooke, Tom. I Want to Be a Fire Fighter: Sesame Street. 1999. (Golden's Sesame Street Ser.). (Illus.). 24p. (J). (ps). pap. 3.29 o.s.i (*0-307-12626-9*, Golden Bks.) Random Hse. Children's Bks.

Marion, Kenneth P. Volunteer Firefighter. 1990. (Illus.). 32p. (J). (ps-2). pap. 4.00 (*0-945878-00-1*) JK Publishing.

Marsh, Carole. The Adventure Diaries of Felipe, the Fearless Firefighter!, 12 vols. 2002. 48p. (J). per. 5.95 (*0-635-01096-8*); (Illus.). lib. bdg. 9.95 (*0-635-01270-7*) Gallopade International.

McMullan, Kate & Smith, Mavis, illus. Fluffy & the Fire Fighters. 2001. (Hello Reader! Ser.). 40p. (J). (gr. 1-3). mass mkt. 3.99 (*0-439-12917-6*, Cartwheel Bks.) Scholastic, Inc.

Metaxas, Eric & Peck, Everett. Mose the Fireman. 1996. (Illus.). 48p. (J). (ps up). pap. 19.95 o.p. incl. audio (*0-689-80227-7*, Simon & Schuster Children's Publishing) Simon & Schuster Children's Publishing.

Miglis, Jenny. Fire Engine Evan. 2002. (Jay Jay the Jet Plane Ser.). 192p. mass mkt. 3.49 (*0-8431-4575-7*, Price Stern Sloan) Penguin Putnam Bks. for Young Readers.

Mitter, Matt. Billy Blazes, Firefighter. 1999. (Fisher-Price Rescue Heroes Ser.). (Illus.). 12p. (J). (ps-1). bds. 6.99 (*1-57584-307-2*) Reader's Digest Children's Publishing, Inc.

Morgan, Allen. Matthew & the Midnight Firefighter. Martchenko, Michael, tr. & illus. by. 2003. (Wild Midnight Adventure Ser.). 40p. (J). pap. (*1-55041-877-7*); lib. bdg. (*1-55041-875-0*) Fitzhenry & Whiteside, Ltd.

—Matthew & the Midnight Firefighter. 2000. (Matthew's Midnight Adventures Ser.). (Illus.). 32p. (J). (ps-3). pap. 6.99 (*0-7737-6090-3*) Stoddart Kids CAN. *Dist:* Fitzhenry & Whiteside, Ltd.

—Matthew & the Midnight Firefighters. ed. 1999. (J). (gr. 2). spiral bd. (*0-616-07242-2*) Canadian National Institute for the Blind/Institut National Canadien pour les Aveugles.

Osborne, Mary Pope. New York's Bravest. 2002. (Illus.). 32p. (J). (gr. k-3). 15.95 (*0-375-82196-1*); lib. bdg. 17.99 (*0-375-92196-6*) Random Hse. Children's Bks. (Knopf Bks. for Young Readers).

Rabley, Stephen. The Fireboy. Date not set. pap. text 73.13 (*0-582-06072-9*) Addison-Wesley Longman, Ltd. GBR. *Dist:* Trans-Atlantic Pubns., Inc.

Rex, Michael, illus. Firefighter! 2003. (Word-by-Word First Reader Ser.). 32p. (J). mass mkt. 3.99 (*0-439-52785-6*) Scholastic, Inc.

Rockwell, Anne F. Come to the Firehouse. 2003. (Illus.). 40p. (J). (ps-1). 15.99 (*0-06-029815-4*) HarperCollins Pubs.

Rockwell, Anne F., illus. & text. Come to the Firehouse! 2003. 40p. (J). lib. bdg. 16.89 (*0-06-029816-2*) HarperCollins Pubs.

Rucker, Mike. Terry The Smoke Jumper. pap. (*0-9711650-4-1*) Aegina Pr., Inc.

—Terry the Smokejumper. 2001. (Terry the Tractor Ser.: Vol. 9). (Illus.). (J). (ps-5). pap. 3.95 (*0-9711659-0-4*) Univ. Editions.

Scarry, Richard. Richard Scarry's Busiest Fire Fighters Ever! 1997. (Richard Scarry Ser.). 24p. (J). (ps-3). 3.99 o.s.i (*0-307-16054-8*, 16054, Golden Bks.) Random Hse. Children's Bks.

Sierra, Judy. Coco & Cavendish: Fire Dogs. 2004. (Illus.). 48p. (J). (gr. 1-3). pap. 3.99 (*0-375-82238-0*); lib. bdg. 11.99 (*0-375-92238-5*) Random Hse., Inc.

Smyth, Iain. Zoom, Zoom, Fire Engine! 1997. 12p. (J). (ps-3). 2.99 o.s.i (*0-517-70956-2*) Crown Publishing Group.

Yee, Wong Herbert. Fireman Small. 1994. (Illus.). 32p. (J). (ps-3). lib. bdg., tchr. ed. 16.00 (*0-395-68987-2*) Houghton Mifflin Co.

—Fireman Small - Fire down Below! 2001. (Illus.). 32p. (J). (ps-3). tchr. ed. 15.00 (*0-618-00707-5*) Houghton Mifflin Co.

Yoder, Karen L. Fire Kids! The Adventures of Hose Company. 2nd Lt. ed. 2002. 124p. (J). pap. 6.95 (*0-9700487-3-4*) Stoney Creek Pr.

Zimmerman, Andrea Griffing & Clemesha, David. Fire! Fire! 2003. (Illus.). 32p. (J). lib. bdg. 16.89 (*0-06-029760-3*, Greenwillow Bks.) HarperCollins Children's Bk. Group.

—Fire! Fire! Hurry! Hurry! 2003. (Illus.). 32p. (J). 15.99 (*0-06-029759-X*, Greenwillow Bks.) HarperCollins Children's Bk. Group.

Zokeisha. Firehouse. Klimo, Kate, ed. 1983. (Chubby Shape Bks.). (Illus.). 16p. (J). (ps). pap. 3.50 (*0-671-46128-1*, Little Simon) Simon & Schuster Children's Publishing.

Zytman, Leah. The Bravest Fireman. 1998. (Illus.). 32p. (J). (ps-1). 9.95 (*0-922613-88-5*) Hachai Publishing.

FUR TRADERS—FICTION

Durbin, William. The Broken Blade. 176p. (gr. 5-9). 1997. text 14.95 o.s.i (*0-385-32224-0*, Dell Books for Young Readers); 1998. (Illus.). reprint ed. pap. text 4.99 (*0-440-41184-X*, Yearling) Random Hse. Children's Bks.

—The Broken Blade. 1998. (J). 10.55 (*0-606-13228-7*) Turtleback Bks.

—Wintering. 208p. (YA). (gr. 5-7). 2000. (Illus.). pap. 4.50 (*0-440-22759-3*, Yearling); 1999. 14.95 (*0-385-32598-3*, Dell Books for Young Readers) Random Hse. Children's Bks.

Ernst, Kathleen. Trouble at Fort la Pointe. 2000. (American Girl Collection: Bk. 7). (Illus.). 176p. (J). (gr. 5-9). pap. 5.95 (*1-58485-086-8*); 9.95 (*1-58485-087-6*) Pleasant Co. Pubns. (American Girl).

—Trouble at Fort la Pointe. 2000. (American Girl Collection). (Illus.). (J). 12.00 (*0-606-20956-5*) Turtleback Bks.

Panagopoulos, Janie Lynn. Traders in Time: A Dream-Quest Adventure. (J). (gr. 3-6). 1994. pap. 7.95 (*0-938682-27-X*); 1993. 200p. 14.95 o.p. (*0-938682-24-5*) River Road Pubns., Inc.

H

HOUSEHOLD EMPLOYEES—FICTION

Adams, Phylliss, et al. Pippin Cleans Up: Group III. 1983. (Double Scoop Bks.). (Illus.). 32p. (J). (gr. k-2). 6.60 o.p. (*0-516-09725-3*, Children's Pr.) Scholastic Library Publishing.

Adler, Susan S. Meet Samantha: An American Girl. Thieme, Jeanne, ed. 1986. (American Girls Collection: Bk. 1). (Illus.). 72p. (YA). (gr. 2 up). pap. 5.95 (*0-937295-04-3*, American Girl); lib. bdg. 12.95 (*0-937295-80-9*, American Girl); 12.95 o.p. (*0-937295-03-5*) Pleasant Co. Pubns.

—Meet Samantha: An American Girl. 1986. (American Girls Collection: Bk. 1). (YA). (gr. 2 up). 12.10 (*0-606-02770-X*) Turtleback Bks.

Armstrong, Jennifer. Little Salt Lick & the Sun King. 1994. (Illus.). 32p. (J). (ps-3). 15.99 o.s.i (*0-517-59621-0*, Random Hse. Bks. for Young Readers) Random Hse. Children's Bks.

Dabcovich, Lydia, illus. The Ghost on the Hearth. 2003. (Family Heritage Ser.). 32p. (J). (gr. 1-5). 15.95 (*0-916718-18-2*) Vermont Folklife Ctr.

Delton, Judy. Hired Help for Rabbit. 1992. (Illus.). 32p. (J). (gr. k-3). pap. 4.50 o.s.i (*0-689-71522-6*, Aladdin) Simon & Schuster Children's Publishing.

Fine, Anne. Alias Madame Doubtfire. 1989. (Young Adults Ser.). 208p. (YA). mass mkt. 3.99 o.p. (*0-553-56615-6*) Bantam Bks.

—Alias Madame Doubtfire. 1988. (YA). (gr. 7 up). 12.95 o.p. (*0-316-28313-4*, Joy Street Bks.) Little Brown & Co.

—Senora Doubtfire. Pena, Flora, tr. 1992. Tr. of Mrs. Doubtfire. (SPA.). 165p. (J). (gr. 7 up). pap. 12.95 (*84-204-4680-7*) Santillana USA Publishing Co., Inc.

—Senora Doubtfire. 1992. Tr. of Mrs. Doubtfire. 19.00 (*0-606-17745-0*) Turtleback Bks.

Hutchins, Pat. King Henry's Palace. 1983. (Illus.). 56p. (J). (gr. 1-3). 11.95 o.p. (*0-688-02294-4*); lib. bdg. 11.88 o.p. (*0-688-02295-2*) HarperCollins Children's Bk. Group. (Greenwillow Bks.).

Lowry, Lois. Anastasia "Asusordenes"Tr. of Anastasia at Your Order. (SPA.). 120p. (J). 9.95 (*84-239-7073-6*) Espasa Calpe, S.A. ESP. *Dist:* Planeta Publishing Corp.

—Anastasia at Your Service. l.t. ed. 1988. 224p. (J). lib. bdg. 15.95 o.p. (*1-55736-101-0*) Bantam Doubleday Dell Large Print Group, Inc.

—Anastasia at Your Service. 1982. (Illus.). 160p. (J). (gr. 4-6). 16.00 (*0-395-32865-9*) Houghton Mifflin Co.

—Anastasia at Your Service. 149p. (J). (gr. 4-6). pap. 3.99 (*0-8072-1409-4*, Listening Library) Random Hse. Audio Publishing Group.

—Anastasia at Your Service. 1983. 160p. (gr. 4-7). pap. text 4.50 (*0-440-40290-5*, Yearling) Random Hse. Children's Bks.

—Anastasia at Your Service. 1984. (J). 10.55 (*0-606-02648-7*) Turtleback Bks.

Marino, Jan. For the Love of Pete: A Novel. 1993. (J). 14.95 o.p. (*0-316-54627-5*) Little Brown & Co.

Maugham, W. Somerset. Appointment. 1993. (Illus.). (J). (ps-3). pap. 16.00 o.p. (*0-671-75887-X*, Simon & Schuster Children's Publishing) Simon & Schuster Children's Publishing.

Parish, Herman. Amelia Bedelia 4 Mayor. (I Can Read Bks.). (Illus.). (J). (gr. k-2). 2001. 64p. pap. 3.99 (*0-06-444309-4*, Harper Trophy); No. 2. 2003. 8.99 incl. audio (*0-06-009345-5*) HarperCollins Children's Bk. Group.

—Calling Doctor Amelia Bedelia. 2002. (Illus.). 64p. (J). (gr. 1-2). 15.99 (*0-06-001421-0*); lib. bdg. 17.89 (*0-06-001422-9*) HarperCollins Children's Bk. Group. (Greenwillow Bks.).

—Good Driving, Amelia Bedelia. 1995. (Amelia Bedelia Ser.). (Illus.). 40p. (J). (ps-3). 15.99 (*0-688-13358-4*); lib. bdg. 16.89 (*0-688-13359-2*) HarperCollins Children's Bk. Group. (Greenwillow Bks.).

—Good Driving, Amelia Bedelia. 1996. (Amelia Bedelia Ser.). (Illus.). 48p. (J). (gr. k-2). pap. 3.95 (*0-380-72510-X*, Avon Bks.) Morrow/Avon.

—Good Driving, Amelia Bedelia. 1996. (Amelia Bedelia Ser.). (J). (gr. k-2). 10.14 (*0-606-09341-9*) Turtleback Bks.

Parish, Peggy. Amelia Bedelia. 1999. (I Can Read Bks.). (J). (gr. 1-3). 11.50 (*0-88103-916-0*); (SPA.). (*0-613-09959-1*) Econo-Clad Bks.

—Amelia Bedelia. 1999. (I Can Read Bks.). (Illus.). 64p. (J). (ps-3). 15.99 (*0-694-01296-3*); 15.99 (*0-694-01296-3*) HarperCollins Children's Bk. Group. (Harper Festival).

—Amelia Bedelia. Canetti, Yanitzia, tr. 1996. (I Can Read Bks.). (SPA., Illus.). 64p. (J). (gr. 1-3). 15.95 o.s.i (*0-06-026247-8*); pap. 4.95 o.p. (*0-06-444200-4*) HarperCollins Children's Bk. Group.

—Amelia Bedelia. (I Can Read Bks.). (Illus.). (J). 1992. 64p. (gr. k-3). 15.99 (*0-06-020186-X*); 1992. 64p. (gr. k-3). pap. 3.99 (*0-06-444155-5*, Harper Trophy); 1992. 64p. (gr. k-3). lib. bdg. 16.89 (*0-06-020187-8*); 1983. 32p. (gr. 1-3). pap. 3.50 o.p. (*0-06-443036-7*, Harper Trophy); 1963. 80p. (gr. 1-3). 13.00 o.p. (*0-06-024640-5*); 1963. 80p. (gr. 1-3). lib. bdg. 12.89 o.p. (*0-06-024641-3*) HarperCollins Children's Bk. Group.

—Amelia Bedelia. 1993. (I Can Read Bks.). (Illus.). 64p. (J). (gr. k-3). 8.99 incl. audio (*1-55994-782-9*, HarperAudio) HarperTrade.

—Amelia Bedelia. 2000. (Coleccion Ya Se Leer). (SPA., Illus.). (J). (gr. 1-3). 15.95 (*1-880507-76-5*, LC0355); pap. 6.95 (*1-880507-75-7*, LC0360) Lectorum Pubns., Inc.

—Amelia Bedelia. 1999. (J). (gr. 1-3). 9.95 (*1-56137-023-1*) Novel Units, Inc.

—Amelia Bedelia. (J). 2001. (SPA., Illus.). 12.10 (*0-606-21546-8*); 1996. (gr. 1-3). 10.15 o.p. (*0-606-10377-5*); 1963. (gr. 1-3). 10.10 (*0-606-01041-6*) Turtleback Bks.

—Amelia Bedelia & the Baby. 1999. (Amelia Bedelia Ser.). (J). (gr. k-2). 11.50 (*0-88103-914-4*) Econo-Clad Bks.

—Amelia Bedelia & the Baby. (I Can Read Book 2 Ser.). (Illus.). 64p. (J). 2004. pap. 3.99 (*0-06-051105-2*, Harper Trophy); 1981. 16.00 (*0-688-00316-8*, Greenwillow Bks.); 1981. lib. bdg. 16.89 (*0-688-00321-4*, Greenwillow Bks.) HarperCollins Children's Bk. Group.

—Amelia Bedelia & the Baby. (Amelia Bedelia Ser.). (Illus.). 64p. (J). (gr. k-2). 1996. pap. 3.99 (*0-380-72795-1*); 1982. pap. 3.99 (*0-380-57067-X*) Morrow/Avon. (Avon Bks.).

—Amelia Bedelia & the Baby. unabr. ed. 2001. (Amelia Bedelia Ser.). (J). (gr. k-2). audio 10.00 (*0-7887-0369-2*, 94561E7) Recorded Bks., LLC.

—Amelia Bedelia & the Baby. 1986. (Amelia Bedelia Ser.). (J). (gr. k-2). 31.99 incl. audio (*0-394-69327-2*) SRA/McGraw-Hill.

—Amelia Bedelia & the Baby. 1996. (Amelia Bedelia Ser.). (J). (gr. k-2). 10.10 (*0-606-00368-1*) Turtleback Bks.

—Amelia Bedelia & the Surprise Shower. (I Can Read Bks.). (Illus.). 64p. (J). 9999. (gr. 1-3). 5.98 o.p. incl. audio (*0-694-00161-9*, JC-144, Harper Trophy); 9999. (gr. 1-3). 5.98 o.p. incl. audio (*0-694-00161-9*, JC-144, Harper Trophy); 1979. (ps-3). pap. 3.99 (*0-06-444019-2*, Harper Trophy); 1966. (gr. k-3). 15.95 (*0-06-024642-1*) HarperCollins Children's Bk. Group.

I

INVENTORS—FICTION

J

JOB HUNTING—FICTION

K

KINGS, QUEENS, RULERS, ETC.—FICTION

Occupations

(J). (gr. k up). 15.95 o.s.i (*0-06-205044-3*); 1994. (YA). (gr. k up). lib. bdg. 15.89 o.p. (*0-06-205045-1*) HarperCollins Children's Bk. Group.

—Bub: Or the Very Best Thing. 1998. (Illus.). (J). (gr. k-3). pap., tchr. ed. 37.95 incl. audio (*0-87499-467-5*); pap. 15.95 incl. audio (*0-87499-465-9*); 24.95 o.p. incl. audio (*0-87499-466-7*) Live Oak Media.

—Bub: Or the Very Best Thing. 1994. 13.10 (*0-606-09113-0*) Turtleback Bks.

Bacon, Joy. Oliver Bean Visits the Queen. 1998. (Illus.). 48p. (J). (gr. k-5). pap. 8.95 (*1-883650-45-3*) Windswept Hse. Pubs.

Badoe, Adwoa A. The Queen's New Shoes. 1998. (Illus.). 24p. (J). (gr. 3-7). pap. 7.95 (*0-88961-232-3*) Women's Pr. CAN. *Dist:* Univ. of Toronto Pr.

Balmain, Julianne. The Queen's Amulet. 1999. (Star Wars). (Illus.). 24p. 12.95 o.p. (*0-8118-2462-4*) Chronicle Bks. LLC.

Banks, Lynne Reid. The Adventures of King Midas. 1976. (Illus.). (J). 9.00 o.p. (*0-460-06752-4*) Biblio Distribution.

—The Adventures of King Midas. 1992. (Illus.). 160p. (J). (gr. 4-7). 14.00 (*0-688-10894-6*, Morrow, William & Co.) Morrow/Avon.

Baranski, Joan. Round Is a Pancake. Monfried, Lucia, ed. 2000. (Illus.). 32p. (J). (ps-1). 14.99 o.p. (*0-525-46173-6*, Dutton Children's Bks.) Penguin Putnam Bks. for Young Readers.

Barrett, Tracy. Anna of Byzantium. 224p. (YA). (gr. 7-12). 2000. mass mkt. 4.50 (*0-440-41536-5*, Laurel Leaf); 1999. (Illus.). 14.95 (*0-385-32626-2*, Dell Books for Young Readers) Random Hse. Children's Bks.

—Anna of Byzantium. 2000. 10.55 (*0-606-19742-7*) Turtleback Bks.

Bauer, Marion Dane. A Dream of Queens & Castles. 1991. 128p. (J). (gr. 4-7). pap. 3.25 o.s.i (*0-440-40554-8*) Dell Publishing.

Baum, L. Frank. The Magical Monarch of Mo. 1982. (Illus.). (J). (gr. 4-8). 23.25 (*0-8446-1609-5*) Smith, Peter Pub., Inc.

—Queen Zixi of Ix: The Story of the Magic Cloak. 1971. (Illus.). 231p. (J). (gr. 1-3). reprint ed. pap. 8.95 (*0-486-22691-3*) Dover Pubns., Inc.

—Queen Zixi of Ix: The Story of the Magic Cloak. 1990. (Illus.). (J). (gr. 2-6). 19.25 o.p. (*0-8446-0026-1*) Smith, Peter Pub., Inc.

Benson, Patrick, illus. The Baron All at Sea. 1987. (Baron Bks.). 32p. (J). (gr. 3 up). 12.95 o.s.i (*0-399-21387-2*, Philomel) Penguin Putnam Bks. for Young Readers.

Bentheim, Rozelle. King Kid, ERS. 1991. (Illus.). 128p. (J). (gr. 4-7). 13.95 o.p. (*0-8050-1633-3*, Holt, Henry & Co. Bks. For Young Readers) Holt, Henry & Co.

Berenguer, Carmen. El Rey Mocho. 2000. (SPA., Illus.). 24p. (J). (ps-3). pap. 6.95 (*980-257-068-0*) Ekare, Ediciones VEN. *Dist:* Kane/Miller Bk. Pubs., Lectorum Pubns., Inc.

Birch, David. King's Chessboard. 1988. (Picture Puffin Ser.). (Illus.). (J). 12.14 (*0-606-05394-8*) Turtleback Bks.

Black, Charles C. The Royal Nap. 1995. (Illus.). 32p. (J). (ps-3). 14.99 o.p. (*0-670-85863-3*, Viking Children's Bks.) Penguin Putnam Bks. for Young Readers.

Bober, Natalie S. Countdown to Independence. 2001. (Illus.). 368p. (J). (gr. 7 up). 26.95 (*0-689-81329-5*, Atheneum) Simon & Schuster Children's Publishing.

Bolognese, Don. The War Horse. 2003. (Illus.). 176p. (J). (gr. 5-9). 16.95 (*0-689-85458-7*, Simon & Schuster Children's Publishing) Simon & Schuster Children's Publishing.

Bolton, Michael. The Secret of the Lost Kingdom. 1997. (Illus.). 48p. (J). 15.95 (*0-7868-0286-3*) Hyperion Bks. for Children.

Bond, Michael. Paddington Meets the Queen. 1993. (Paddington Ser.). (Illus.). 32p. (J). (ps-3). 3.95 (*0-694-00460-X*, Harper Festival) HarperCollins Children's Bk. Group.

Bosca, Francesca. The Apple King. James, J. Alison, tr. from GER. 2001. (Illus.). 32p. (J). (ps-1). 15.95 (*0-7358-1397-3*, Michael Neugebauer Bks.) North-South Bks., Inc.

Bosca, Francesca & Ferri, Giuliano. The Apple King. 2001. (Illus.). 32p. (J). (ps-6). lib. bdg. 16.50 (*0-7358-1398-1*, Michael Neugebauer Bks.) North-South Bks., Inc.

Brennan, Herbie. Fairy Nuff. 2002. (Illus.). 121p. (J). (gr. 2-4). 13.95 (*1-58234-770-0*, Bloomsbury Children) Bloomsbury Publishing.

Brenner, Peter. King for One Day. (Illus.). 36p. (J). (ps-3). 12.95 (*0-87592-027-6*) Scroll Pr., Inc.

Brittain, Bill. My Buddy, the King. 1989. 144p. (J). (gr. 5-8). 13.00 o.p. (*0-06-020724-8*); lib. bdg. 12.89 o.p. (*0-06-020725-6*) HarperCollins Children's Bk. Group.

—The Wish Giver: Three Tales of Coven Tree. 1986. (Trophy Bk.). (Illus.). 192p. (J). (gr. 4-7). pap. 5.99 (*0-06-440168-5*, Harper Trophy) HarperCollins Children's Bk. Group.

Brumbeau, Jeff. The Quiltmaker's Gift. 1999. (Illus.). 48p. (J). (ps-3). 17.95 o.p. (*1-57025-199-1*) Scholastic, Inc.

Bruna, Dick. The King. 1975. (Bruna Books). (Illus.). 28p. (J). (ps-2). 3.50 o.p. (*0-416-30371-4*, NO. 0025) Routledge.

Bunting, Eve. Demetrius & the Golden Goblet. 1980. (Illus.). (J). (gr. k-4). pap. 3.95 o.p. (*0-15-625282-1*, Voyager Bks./Libros Viajeros) Harcourt Children's Bks.

Burnett, Frances Hodgson. The Lost Prince. 1997. (Illus.). 336p. (YA). (gr. 5 up). pap. 3.99 o.s.i (*0-14-036754-3*, Puffin Bks.) Penguin Putnam Bks. for Young Readers.

Burton, Virginia Lee, illus. The Emperor's New Clothes. 2004. 48p. (J). (ps-3). 16.00 (*0-618-34421-7*); pap. 6.95 (*0-618-34420-9*) Houghton Mifflin Co.

Busser, Marianne & Schroder, Ron. King Bobble. 1999. (Easy-To-Read Bks.). (Illus.). 64p. (J). (gr. 2-4). pap. 5.95 o.p. (*0-7358-1202-0*) North-South Bks., Inc.

—King Bobble. James, J. Alison, tr. from GER. 1996. (Illus.). 64p. (J). (gr. 2-4). 13.95 o.p. (*1-55858-591-5*); 14.50 o.p. (*1-55858-592-3*) North-South Bks., Inc.

Cave, K. & Riddell. Emperor's Grucklehound. 1996. (Illus.). 127p. (J). pap. text 8.95 (*0-340-65599-2*) Hodder & Stoughton, Ltd. GBR. *Dist:* Lubrecht & Cramer, Ltd., Trafalgar Square.

Charnas, Suzy M. The Bronze King, 001. 1985. 208p. (J). (gr. 5 up). 12.95 o.p. (*0-395-38394-3*) Houghton Mifflin Co.

—The Bronze King. 1987. 208p. (J). pap. 2.95 o.s.i (*0-553-15493-1*, Skylark) Random Hse. Children's Bks.

Chew, Ruth. Royal Magic. 1991. 128p. (J). mass mkt. 2.75 o.p. (*0-590-44742-4*) Scholastic, Inc.

Christian, Mary Blount. Penrod Again. 1987. (Ready-to-Read Ser.). (Illus.). 56p. (J). (gr. 1-4). lib. bdg. 11.95 o.s.i (*0-02-718550-8*, Simon & Schuster Children's Publishing) Simon & Schuster Children's Publishing.

Cleaver, Vera & Cleaver, Bill. Queen of Hearts. 1987. (Trophy Bk.). 160p. (YA). (gr. 5 up). reprint ed. pap. 3.50 o.p. (*0-06-440196-0*, Harper Trophy) HarperCollins Children's Bk. Group.

Cole, Brock. The King at the Door. 1979. (Illus.). 32p. (gr. k-3). 8.95 o.p. (*0-385-14718-X*); lib. bdg. o.p. (*0-385-14719-8*) Doubleday Publishing.

—King at the Door, RS. 1992. 32p. (J). (ps-3). pap. 4.95 o.p. (*0-374-44041-7*, Sunburst) Farrar, Straus & Giroux.

Comrie, Margaret S. The Heroes of Castle Bretten. 2003. (Illus.). 229p. (J). (*1-894666-65-8*) Inheritance Pubns.

Croutier, Alev Lytle. Leyla: The Black Tulip. 2003. (Girls of Many Lands Ser.). (Illus.). 196p. (J). pap. 15.95 (*1-58485-831-1*); pap. 7.95 (*1-58485-749-8*) Pleasant Co. Pubns. (American Girl).

Cunliffe, John. King's Birthday Cake. 1979. (Illus.). (J). 9.95 o.p. (*0-233-96453-3*) Blackwell Publishing.

Daily, Renee, illus. King Midas & the Golden Touch. 1996. (Little Golden Bks.). 24p. (J). (ps-k). 2.29 o.s.i (*0-307-30302-0*, 98810, Golden Bks.) Random Hse. Children's Bks.

Daniels, Edmond F. The King That Never Was. 1998. 160p. E-Book 8.00 (*0-7388-7989-4*) Xlibris Corp.

Davis, Kathryn. Versailles. l.t. ed. 2003. 25.95 (*1-58724-394-6*, Wheeler Publishing, Inc.) Gale Group.

—Versailles. 2003. 240p. pap. 13.95 (*0-316-73761-5*, Back Bay) Little Brown & Co.

De Angeli, Marguerite. The Door in the Wall. 1996. (J). pap. 4.99 (*0-440-91164-8*, Dell Books for Young Readers); 1998. (Illus.). 128p. (YA). (gr. 5-9). reprint ed. mass mkt. 4.99 (*0-440-22779-8*, Laurel Leaf) Random Hse. Children's Bks.

—The Door in the Wall. 1984. (J). mass mkt. 2.50 o.p. (*0-590-40968-9*) Scholastic, Inc.

—The Door in the Wall. 1995. (J). (gr. 3-6). 20.25 (*0-8446-6834-6*) Smith, Peter Pub., Inc.

—The Door in the Wall. 1998. 11.04 (*0-606-13344-5*); 1977. (J). 11.04 (*0-606-03234-7*) Turtleback Bks.

—The Door in the Wall: Story of Medieval London. 1990. (Yearling Newbery Ser.). (Illus.). 128p. (J). (gr. 5-9). reprint ed. pap. text 5.50 (*0-440-40283-2*) Dell Publishing.

—The Door in the Wall: Story of Medieval London. 1989. (Illus.). 128p. (gr. 4-7). text 16.95 (*0-385-07283-X*) Doubleday Publishing.

De Haan, Linda & Nijland, Stern. King & King. 2003. (Illus.). 32p. (J). 14.95 (*1-58246-061-2*) Tricycle Pr.

de Paola, Tomie. The Story of the Three Wise Kings. (Illus.). (J). 13.99 (*0-399-61259-9*) Penguin Group (USA) Inc.

Deedy, Carmen Agra. The Yellow Star: The Legend of King Christian X of Denmark. 2000. (Illus.). 32p. (J). (gr. 3-7). 16.95 (*1-56145-208-4*) Peachtree Pubs., Ltd.

DeLuise, Dom. Dom Deluise's The Nightingale. 1998. Orig. Title: Nattergalen. (Illus.). 40p. (J). (ps-3). per. 15.00 (*0-689-81749-5*, Simon & Schuster Children's Publishing) Simon & Schuster Children's Publishing.

—King Bob's New Clothes. (Illus.). (J). (ps-3). 1999. 40p. pap. 5.99 (*0-689-83050-5*, Aladdin); 1996. 40p. 15.00 (*0-689-80520-9*, Simon & Schuster Children's Publishing); 1996. 14.00 (*0-671-89727-6*, Simon & Schuster Children's Publishing) Simon & Schuster Children's Publishing.

—King Bob's New Clothes. 1999. (J). 12.14 (*0-606-18949-1*) Turtleback Bks.

Demi. King Midas: The Golden Touch. 2002. (Illus.). 48p. (J). (gr. 2-5). 19.95 (*0-689-83297-4*, McElderry, Margaret K.) Simon & Schuster Children's Publishing.

Derby, Sally. King Kenrick's Splinter. 1994. (Illus.). (J). lib. bdg. 15.85 (*0-8027-8323-6*); 32p. 14.95 (*0-8027-8322-8*) Walker & Co.

Deskis, Jane. Brielle & the Castle Siege. 2003. (YA). per. 11.95 (*1-932133-48-8*) Writers' Collective, The.

Di Girolamo, Vittorio. Bo & the Sad King. Eagleson, John & Gray, Rockwell, trs. 1972. (Illus.). 32p. (J). (gr. 1-5). pap. 2.95 o.p. (*0-88344-039-3*) Orbis Bks.

Dieterle', Nathalie. I Am the King! American Edition. 2001. (Illus.). 32p. (J). (ps-k). pap. 15.95 (*0-531-30324-1*, Orchard Bks.) Scholastic, Inc.

Disney Staff. Here Comes the Bride. 2001. (Illus.). 10p. (J). bds. 10.99 (*0-7364-1198-4*, RH/Disney) Random Hse. Children's Bks.

Dixon, Franklin W. King for a Day. 1999. (Hardy Boys Are: No. 12). (Illus.). 80p. (J). (gr. 2-4). per. 3.99 (*0-671-02719-0*, Aladdin) Simon & Schuster Children's Publishing.

Doodle Art. King's Feast. 2000. (Doodle Art Ser.). (J). 10.99 o.s.i (*0-8431-6629-0*, Price Stern Sloan) Penguin Putnam Bks. for Young Readers.

D'Ottari, Francesca. The Legend of King Arthur: A Young Reader's Edition of the Classic Story by Howard Pyle. 1996. (Illus.). 56p. (J). text 9.98 o.p. (*1-56138-503-4*, Courage Bks.) Running Pr. Bk. Pubs.

Dulcken, H. W., tr. The Emperor's New Clothes. 1982. Tr. of Kejserens nye klaeder. (J). 9.95 (*0-690-04150-0*) HarperCollins Children's Bk. Group.

Dunbar, Joyce. Magic Lemonade. 2001. (Blue Bananas Ser.). (Illus.). 48p. (J). (gr. 1-2). pap. 4.95 (*0-7787-0885-3*); lib. bdg. 19.96 (*0-7787-0839-X*) Crabtree Publishing Co.

Dunn, Carolyn. A Pie Went By. 32p. (J). (ps-1). Date not set. pap. 4.99 (*0-06-443649-7*); 2000. (Illus.). 14.95 (*0-06-028807-8*); 2000. (Illus.). lib. bdg. 14.89 (*0-06-028808-6*) HarperCollins Children's Bk. Group.

—Real Kings Don't Do Ballet. 2001. (J). 15.95 (*0-688-16176-6*); lib. bdg. 15.89 (*0-688-16177-4*) HarperCollins Children's Bk. Group. (Greenwillow Bks.).

Dunsmuir, Tom & Silva, David. The Queen's New Clothes, No. 1. 1998. (Queen's New Clothes Ser.: Vol. 1). (Illus.). 24p. (J). (ps-3). pap. 3.25 o.s.i (*0-679-89120-X*, Random Hse. Bks. for Young Readers) Random Hse. Children's Bks.

Durkee, Noura. The King, the Prince & the Naughty Sheep. 1999. (Illus.). 24p. (J). (gr. 1-5). 16.00 (*1-879402-58-0*) Tahrike Tarsile Quran, Inc.

Eaton, Deborah. The Cheerful King: Big Book. l.t. ed. 1996. (Sadlier Phonics Reading Program). (Illus.). 16p. (J). (gr. 1-3). (*0-8215-0983-7*, Sadlier-Oxford) Sadlier, William H. Inc.

—Little Book:The Cheerful King. 1997. (Sadlier Phonics Reading Program). (Illus.). 16p. (J). (*0-8215-0963-2*, Sadlier-Oxford) Sadlier, William H. Inc.

Edmiston, Jim, illus. The Emperor Who Forgot His Birthday. 1999. 32p. (J). (ps-3). 14.95 (*1-84148-015-0*) Barefoot Bks., Inc.

—The Emperor Who Hated Yellow. 1999. 32p. (J). (ps-k). 14.95 (*1-902283-39-2*) Barefoot Bks., Inc.

Ekwensi, Cyprian O. King Forever! 1992. (Junior African Writers Ser.). (Illus.). 80p. (J). (gr. 3 up). pap. 4.99 (*0-7910-2921-2*) Chelsea Hse. Pubs.

Elkin, Benjamin. King's Wish & Other Stories. 1960. (Illus.). (J). (gr. 1-2). 5.99 o.s.i (*0-394-90014-6*) Beginner Bks.

Engelbreit, Mary. Queen of the Class. 2004. (J). (*0-06-008178-3*); lib. bdg. (*0-06-008179-1*) HarperCollins Pubs.

Evans, Richard Paul. The Spyglass: A Book about Faith. 2000. (Illus.). 32p. (J). (ps-3). 16.00 (*0-689-83466-7*, Simon & Schuster Children's Publishing) Simon & Schuster Children's Publishing.

Farley, Carol. The King's Secret. 2001. (Illus.). 32p. (J). (gr. 1 up). 15.95 (*0-688-12776-2*); lib. bdg. 15.89 (*0-688-12777-0*) HarperCollins Children's Bk. Group.

Faulkner, Keith. King Leo. 2002. (Slot-to-Slot Model Ser.). (Illus.). 16p. (J). 9.95 (*1-931411-01-8*) CPG Publishing, Inc.

Ferris, Jean. Once upon a Marigold. 2004. 288p. (J). pap. 5.95 (*0-15-205084-1*, Harcourt Paperbacks); 2002. 272p. (YA). (gr. 5 up). 17.00 (*0-15-216791-9*) Harcourt Children's Bks.

Fine, Judith & Bazilian, Barbara. Princess Lily. 1998. (Illus.). 32p. (J). (gr. 1-5). 15.95 (*1-58089-006-7*); 6.99 (*1-58089-010-5*) Charlesbridge Publishing, Inc. (Whispering Coyote).

Finley-Day, Linda. The Beautiful Queen. 1999. (My Little Camera Book Ser.). (Illus.). 12p. (J). (ps-2). 12.99 o.p. (*0-8054-1811-3*) Broadman & Holman Pubs.

Fletcher, Susan. Flight of the Dragon Kyn. 224p. (gr. 5-9). 1997. (J). pap. 4.99 (*0-689-81515-8*, Aladdin); 1993. (YA). 17.00 (*0-689-31880-4*, Atheneum) Simon & Schuster Children's Publishing.

—Flight of the Dragon Kyn. 1997. 11.04 (*0-606-12701-1*) Turtleback Bks.

Foster, Cheryl L. A Song Pleases the King. 1994. 32p. (J). pap. 7.95 (*0-9639270-4-3*) Light Rain Communications.

French, Allen. The Lost Baron. 2001. (Illus.). 320p. (YA). (gr. 5-12). reprint ed. pap. 14.95 (*1-883937-53-1*, 53-1) Bethlehem Bks.

French, Fiona. King of Another Country. 1992. (Illus.). 32p. (J). o.p. (*0-19-279918-5*) Oxford Univ. Pr., Inc.

—King of Another Country. 1993. (Illus.). 32p. (J). (ps-3). 14.95 o.p. (*0-590-46369-1*) Scholastic, Inc.

Friedman, Aileen. The King's Commissioners. 1995. (Brainy Day Bks.). (Illus.). 36p. (J). (gr. 1-4). pap. 16.95 (*0-590-48989-5*) Scholastic, Inc.

Gackenbach, Dick. King Wacky. 1986. (Illus.). 32p. (J). (ps-2). 8.95 o.s.i (*0-517-55265-5*, Random Hse. Bks. for Young Readers) Random Hse. Children's Bks.

Galloway, Priscilla. Aleta et Penelope: Un Recit de la Grece Antique. Asselin, Michelle, tr. 1997. Tr. of Aleta & the Queen. (FRE., Illus.). 160p. (J). (gr. 5 up). pap. 19.95 (*1-55037-420-6*) Annick Pr., Ltd. CAN. *Dist:* Firefly Bks., Ltd.

Gill, Janice. King of the Mountain. 1997. (ps-3). pap. 4.95 (*0-89868-411-0*) ARO Publishing Co.

Ginsburg, Mirra. The King Who Tried to Fry an Egg on His Head. 1994. (Illus.). 32p. (J). (gr. k-3). lib. bdg. 14.95 o.s.i (*0-02-736242-6*, Simon & Schuster Children's Publishing) Simon & Schuster Children's Publishing.

Gleitzman, Morris. Two Weeks with the Queen. l.t. ed. 2002. (J). 16.95 (*0-7540-7816-7*, Galaxy Children's Large Print) BBC Audiobooks America.

—Two Weeks with the Queen. 1993. (Illus.). 144p. (J). (gr. 3-7). pap. 3.95 o.p. (*0-06-440482-X*, Harper Trophy) HarperCollins Children's Bk. Group.

Gopnick, Adam. King in the Window. 2003. (Illus.). 512p. (J). 22.95 (*0-7868-1862-X*) Hyperion Bks. for Children.

Granados, Antonio. El Rey Que Se Equivoco de Cuento. 1995. (SPA.). (J). (gr. 5-6). 5.99 (*968-16-4571-5*) Fondo de Cultura Economica MEX. *Dist:* Continental Bk. Co., Inc.

Green, Roger Lancelyn. King Arthur & His Knights of the Round Table. 1993. (Everyman's Library Children's Classics Ser.). 368p. (gr. 2 up). 14.95 (*0-679-42311-7*) Knopf, Alfred A. Inc.

—King Arthur & His Knights of the Round Table. (Puffin Classics Ser.). (J). 1995. (Illus.). 352p. (gr. 4-7). pap. 4.99 (*0-14-036670-9*, Puffin Bks.); 1990. 288p. (gr. 5 up). pap. 3.99 o.p. (*0-14-035100-0*, Puffin Bks.); 1974. 288p. (gr. 5-7). pap. 2.95 o.p. (*0-14-030073-2*, Viking Children's Bks.) Penguin Putnam Bks. for Young Readers.

—King Arthur & His Knights of the Round Table. abr. ed. 1997. (Children's Classics Ser.). 2p. (J). pap. 10.95 o.s.i incl. audio (*0-14-086369-9*, Penguin AudioBooks) Viking Penguin.

Gregory, Kristiana. Eleanor: Crown Jewel of Aquitaine. 2002. (Royal Diaries Ser.). 112p. (YA). (gr. 4-9). 10.95 (*0-439-16484-2*, Scholastic Pr.) Scholastic, Inc.

Groves, Richard. Surprise, Surprise, Queen Loonia! 1992. (Illus.). 32p. (J). (ps-1). pap. 5.95 o.p. (*0-8120-4582-3*) Barron's Educational Series, Inc.

Gwynne, Fred. The King Who Rained. 1979. (Illus.). 40p. (J). (gr. 1 up). 3.95 o.s.i (*0-671-96070-9*, Simon & Schuster Children's Publishing) Simon & Schuster Children's Publishing.

Hao, Kuang-ts'ai. The Emperor & the Nightingale. (Illus.). 32p. (J). (gr. 2-4). 1997. 36.40 (*1-57227-026-8*); 1997. (CAM & ENG., 36.40 (*1-57227-024-1*); 1994. (ENG & VIE., 16.95 (*1-57227-020-9*); 1994. (ENG & KOR., 16.95 (*1-57227-021-7*); 1994. (CHI & ENG., 16.95 (*1-57227-018-7*); 1994. (ENG & LAO., 16.95 (*1-57227-025-X*); 1994. (ENG & TAG., 16.95 (*1-57227-023-3*); 1994. (ENG & THA., 16.95 (*1-57227-022-5*) Pan Asia Pubns. (USA), Inc.

Occupations

—The Emperor & the Nightingale: El Emperador y el Ruisenor. Zeller, Beatriz, tr. from CHI. 1994. (ENG & SPA., Illus.). 32p. (J). (gr. 2-4). 16.95 (*1-57227-019-5*) Pan Asia Pubns. (USA), Inc.

Harris, Geraldine. Prince of the Godborn. 1987. (Seven Citadels Ser.: No. 1). (J). (gr. k-12). reprint ed. mass mkt. 2.50 o.s.i (*0-440-95407-X*, Laurel Leaf) Random Hse. Children's Bks.

Hartman, Bob & McGuire, Michael. The Birthday of a King. 1994. (J). (ps-3). 11.99 incl. audio (*7-900882-48-0*, 3-1215) Cook Communications Ministries.

Haugaard, Erik Christian. Prince Boghole. 1987. (Illus.). 32p. (J). (gr. k-3). lib. bdg. 14.95 o.s.i (*0-02-743440-0*, Simon & Schuster Children's Publishing) Simon & Schuster Children's Publishing.

Hawkes, Kevin. His Royal Buckliness. (Illus.). 32p. (J). 3.98 o.p. (*0-8317-3051-X*) Smithmark Pubs., Inc.

Helprin, Mark. A City in Winter. 1999. (J). pap. 6.99 (*0-14-038743-9*, Puffin Bks.) Penguin Putnam Bks. for Young Readers.

—The Veil of Snows. 1997. (Illus.). 128p. (J). 24.00 o.p. (*0-670-87491-4*, Viking Children's Bks.) Penguin Putnam Bks. for Young Readers.

Henderson, Lois T. The Touch of the Golden Scepter. 1981. (gr. 5 up). pap. 2.50 o.p. (*0-89191-375-0*, 53751) Cook, David C. Publishing Co.

Henley, Karyn. King for a Day. 2000. (Tails Ser.). (Illus.). 28p. (J). (ps-5). 9.99 (*0-8054-2285-4*) Broadman & Holman Pubs.

Hennessy, B. G. The Missing Tarts. 1991. (Illus.). 320p. (J). (ps-3). pap. 3.95 o.s.i (*0-14-050815-5*, Puffin Bks.) Penguin Putnam Bks. for Young Readers.

Henry, Maeve. The Witch King. 1988. 128p. (J). (gr. 4-7). 12.95 o.p. (*0-531-05738-0*); mass mkt. 12.99 o.p. (*0-531-08338-1*) Scholastic, Inc. (Orchard Bks.).

Henty, G. A. The Dragon & the Raven: Or the Days of King Alfred. 2000. (Illus.). 238p. (J). pap. 14.99 (*1-887159-31-2*) Preston-Speed Pubns.

Heym, Stefan. The King David Report: A Novel. 1973. 254 P. ;p. (J). (*0-340-17272-X*) St. Martin's Pr.

Hiatt, Fred. If I Were Queen of the World. 1997. (Illus.). 32p. (J). (ps-3). pap. 16.00 (*0-689-80700-7*, McElderry, Margaret K.) Simon & Schuster Children's Publishing.

Hicks, Linda. What Could Be Better Than This? 2005. (Illus.). 32p. (J). 15.99 (*0-525-46954-0*, Dutton Children's Bks.) Penguin Putnam Bks. for Young Readers.

Hillard, Cecelia. The Rescuers. 2001. 60p. pap. 9.00 (*0-8059-5424-4*) Dorrance Publishing Co., Inc.

Hillig, Chuck. The Magic King. 1984. (Illus.). 32p. (J). (ps-2). 12.95 o.p. (*0-913299-07-3*) Stillpoint Publishing.

Hilton, Nette. Prince Lachlan. 1990. (Illus.). 32p. (J). (ps-1). 13.95 o.p. (*0-531-05863-8*); lib. bdg. 13.99 o.p. (*0-531-08463-9*) Scholastic, Inc. (Orchard Bks.).

Hirsch, Odo. Bartlett & the Ice Voyage. 2003. (Illus.). 175p. (J). (gr. 3-9). 14.95 (*1-58234-797-2*, Bloomsbury Children) Bloomsbury Publishing.

Hoelscher, Gwen. Prince Skippy's Quest. 1986. (Illus.). 64p. (Orig.). (J). (gr. 6 up). pap. 7.95 (*0-9617597-0-4*) Wright/Monday Pr.

Hoosier, Wanda M. Princess Mandisa. 1999. (Illus.). 34p. (J). 15.00 (*1-56469-070-9*) Harmony Hse. Pubs.

Hopkins, Andrea. Harald the Ruthless: The Saga of the Last Viking, ERS. 1996. (Illus.). 64p. (YA). (gr. 7 up). 16.95 o.p. (*0-8050-3176-6*, Holt, Henry & Co. Bks. For Young Readers) Holt, Henry & Co.

Houser, Shauna. The Goblin King. Gerl, Clara, ed. 1999. 117p. (YA). pap. 12.95 (*0-9663820-6-4*) Gerl Publishing.

Hutchins, Pat. King Henry's Palace. 1983. (Illus.). 56p. (J). (gr. 1-3). 11.95 o.p. (*0-688-02294-4*); lib. bdg. 11.88 o.p. (*0-688-02295-2*) HarperCollins Children's Bk. Group. (Greenwillow Bks.).

Ihimaera, Witi. The Whale Rider. 2003. (YA). (gr. 3-6). 152p. 17.00 (*0-15-205017-5*); 168p. pap. 8.00 (*0-15-205016-7*, Harcourt Paperbacks) Harcourt Children's Bks.

Jackson, Ellen B. The Impossible Riddle. 1995. (Illus.). 32p. (J). (gr. 1-5). 14.95 (*1-879085-93-3*, Whispering Coyote) Charlesbridge Publishing, Inc.

—A Tale of Two Turkeys. 1996. (J). 7.70 (*0-606-08262-X*) Turtleback Bks.

Johnson, David. The Perfect Cartoon. 1992. (J). 7.95 o.p. (*0-533-09529-8*) Vantage Pr., Inc.

Johnson, Michael. The Most Special Person. 1999. (Illus.). 24p. (J). (gr. k-6). 12.95 (*1-893672-00-X*) Johnson, Michael Presentations.

Johnston, Johanna. Kings, Lovers & Fools. 1981. 114p. (Orig.). (J). (gr. k-3). pap. 2.50 o.p. (*0-590-41705-3*) Scholastic, Inc.

Kane, Andrea. The Last Duke. 1995. (Illus.). 400p. mass mkt. 7.50 (*0-671-86508-0*, Pocket) Simon & Schuster.

Kase, Judith B. The Emperor's New Clothes. 1978. (J). (gr. k up). 6.00 (*0-87602-125-9*) Anchorage Pr.

Kimmel, Eric A. Squash It! A True & Ridiculous Tale. 1997. (Illus.). 32p. (J). (ps-3). tchr. ed. 15.95 (*0-8234-1299-7*) Holiday Hse., Inc.

Kindl, Patrice. Goose Chase. 2002. 224p. (J). pap. 5.99 (*0-14-230208-2*, Puffin Bks.) Penguin Putnam Bks. for Young Readers.

—Goose Chase: A Novel. 2001. 224p. (J). (gr. 5-9). tchr. ed. 15.00 (*0-618-03377-7*) Houghton Mifflin Co.

King of the Mountain. Date not set. 5.95 (*0-89868-357-2*); lib. bdg. 10.95 (*0-89868-356-4*) ARO Publishing Co.

King-Smith, Dick. The Queen's Nose. l.t. ed. 2002. (J). 16.95 (*0-7540-7832-9*, Galaxy Children's Large Print) BBC Audiobooks America.

—The Queen's Nose. 1994. (Trophy Bk.). (Illus.). 128p. (J). (gr. 3-7). pap. 3.95 o.p. (*0-06-440450-1*, Harper Trophy) HarperCollins Children's Bk. Group.

The King's Three Children. 1997. (Scheherezade Children's Stories Ser.). (Illus.). 16p. (J). (*1-85964-001-X*, Ithaca Pr.) Garnet Publishing, Ltd.

The King's 50 Sons. 1997. (Scheherezade Children's Stories Ser.). (Illus.). 16p. (J). (*1-85964-024-9*, Ithaca Pr.) Garnet Publishing, Ltd.

Kisling, Lee. The Fools' War. 1992. 176p. (gr. 5 up). (J). lib. bdg. 13.89 o.p. (*0-06-020837-6*); (YA). 14.00 o.p. (*0-06-020836-8*) HarperCollins Children's Bk. Group.

Korczak, Janusz. King Matt I. Lourie, Richard, tr. from POL. 1986. 332p. (J). (gr. 1 up). 15.95 o.p. (*0-374-34139-7*) Farrar, Straus & Giroux.

Kraus, Robert. The King's Trousers. 1981. (Illus.). 40p. (J). (gr. 1-4). 9.95 o.p. (*0-671-42259-6*, Simon & Schuster Children's Publishing) Simon & Schuster Children's Publishing.

Kroll, Steven. Queen of the May. 1993. (Illus.). 32p. (J). (ps-3). tchr. ed. 15.95 (*0-8234-1004-8*) Holiday Hse., Inc.

Kulling, Monica. Queen in Disguise. 2000. (Star Wars: Step. 2). (Illus.). 48p. (J). (ps-3). lib. bdg. 11.99 o.s.i (*0-375-90429-8*) Random Hse., Inc.

Kurtz, Jane. Saba: Under the Hyena's Foot. 2003. (Girls of Many Lands Ser.). (Illus.). 207p. (J). pap. 15.95 (*1-58485-829-X*); pap. 7.95 (*1-58485-747-1*) Pleasant Co. Pubns. (American Girl).

La Rochelle, David. Evening King. (Illus.). 28p. (J). 4.98 o.p. (*0-7651-0066-5*) Smithmark Pubs., Inc.

Lamb, Sherry. A Royal Storybook. 1999. (Illus.). 50p. (J). (gr. 5-8). 10.95 o.p. (*0-533-12883-8*) Vantage Pr., Inc.

Lasky, Kathryn. Marie Antoinette: Princess of Versailles, Austria-France, 1544. 2000. (Royal Diaries Ser.). (Illus.). 236p. (J). (gr. 4-8). 10.95 (*0-439-07666-8*) Scholastic, Inc.

—Mary, Queen of Scots: Queen Without a Country, France, 1553. 2002. (Royal Diaries Ser.). (Illus.). 208p. (J). (gr. 4-8). 10.95 (*0-439-19404-0*, Scholastic Pr.) Scholastic, Inc.

Lebowitz Cader, Lisa. When I Wear My Crown. 2002. 24p. (J). (ps-3). 14.95 (*0-8118-3484-0*) Chronicle Bks. LLC.

—When I Wear My Tiara. 2002. 24p. (J). (ps-3). 14.95 (*0-8118-3485-9*) Chronicle Bks. LLC.

Leonard, Marcia. King Lionheart's Castle. 1992. (What Belongs? Ser.). (Illus.). 24p. (J). (ps-1). 5.95 (*0-382-72974-9*); lib. bdg. 9.98 (*0-382-72973-0*) Silver, Burdett & Ginn, Inc.

Levine, Gail Carson. The Princess Test. 1999. (Princess Tales Ser.). (Illus.). 96p. (J). (ps-k). lib. bdg. 14.89 (*0-06-028063-8*); (gr. 2-7). 9.99 (*0-06-028062-X*) HarperCollins Children's Bk. Group.

Lindgren, Astrid. Mio, My Son. 2003. Tr. of Mio, Min Mio. (Illus.). 179p. (J). 17.95 (*1-930900-23-6*) Purple Hse. Pr.

Littledale, Freya. King Midas & the Golden Touch. 1989. (Illus.). (J). (gr. k-3). pap. 2.50 o.p. (*0-590-42262-6*) Scholastic, Inc.

Llywelyn, Morgan. Brian Boru: Emperor of the Irish. 1997. 192p. (gr. 7-12). mass mkt. 4.99 (*0-8125-4461-7*); 1995. (Illus.). 160p. (J). (gr. 5-10). 14.95 o.p. (*0-312-85623-7*) Doherty, Tom Assocs., LLC. (Tor Bks.).

Lobel, Anita. Sven's Bridge. 1992. (Illus.). 32p. (J). (ps-4). 14.00 o.p. (*0-688-11251-X*); lib. bdg. 13.93 o.p. (*0-688-11252-8*) HarperCollins Children's Bk. Group. (Greenwillow Bks.).

Love, Ann. The Prince Who Wrote a Letter. 1992. (Child's Play Library). (Illus.). 32p. (J). (ps-3). 13.99 (*0-85953-398-0*); pap. 6.99 (*0-85953-399-9*) Child's Play of England GBR. *Dist:* Child's Play-International.

Lucado, Max. The Children of the King. 1994. (Illus.). 32p. (J). (gr. 3-6). 12.99 o.p. (*0-89107-823-1*) Crossway Bks.

—Just the Way You Are. 1999. Orig. Title: Children of the King. (Illus.). 31p. (J). (ps-5). reprint ed. 15.99 (*1-58134-114-8*) Crossway Bks.

—The Song of the King. 1995. (Illus.). 32p. (J). (ps-3). 12.99 o.p. (*0-89107-827-4*) Crossway Bks.

Luttrell, Ida. The Star Counters. 1994. (Illus.). 32p. (J). 15.00 o.p. (*0-688-12149-7*); lib. bdg. 14.93 o.p. (*0-688-12150-0*) Morrow/Avon. (Morrow, William & Co.).

Lyon, Justice. The King of Meat-Yuk-Land. 2002. 20p. (J). 4.95 (*0-9716596-0-5*) 7 Heads Publishing.

Maccarone, Grace. The Sword in the Stone. 1992. (Hello Reader! Ser.). (J). 10.14 (*0-606-01957-X*) Turtleback Bks.

Maddern, Eric. The King with Horse's Ears. 2003. (Illus.). 36p. (J). 14.95 (*0-7112-1957-5*) Lincoln, Frances Ltd. GBR. *Dist:* Publishers Group West.

Mahy, Margaret. Seventeen Kings & Forty-Two Elephants. Fogelman, Phyllis J., ed. 1990. (Illus.). 32p. (J). (ps-3). pap. 4.95 o.p. (*0-8037-0781-9*, Dial Bks. for Young Readers) Penguin Putnam Bks. for Young Readers.

—When the King Rides By. 1995. (Illus.). 16p. (Orig.). (J). (ps-2). pap. 4.95 (*1-57255-002-3*) Mondo Publishing.

Manning-Sanders, Ruth. A Book of Kings & Queens. 1978. (Illus.). (J). (gr. 2-6). lib. bdg. 7.95 o.p. (*0-525-26925-8*, Dutton) Dutton/Plume.

Marriott, Michelle. Old King Cole & Friends. 1990. (Soap Opera Ser.). (Illus.). 8p. (J). (ps-1). 6.99 (*0-85953-446-4*) Child's Play of England GBR. *Dist:* Child's Play-International.

Martel, Suzanne. King's Daughter. 1998. 232p. (gr. 5-9). 14.95 (*0-88899-323-4*) Publishers Group West.

—The King's Daughter. rev. ed. 1998. 192p. (YA). (gr. 5-9). pap. 6.95 (*0-88899-218-1*) Groundwood Bks. CAN. *Dist:* Publishers Group West.

Martin, Rafe & Amiri, Fahimeh. The Monkey Bridge. 1997. (Illus.). (J). (gr. 1-4). 17.00 o.s.i (*0-679-88106-9*) Random Hse., Inc.

Mathias, B. J. Jeffrey William & The Little Prince. 2002. 10.00 (*0-9711320-9-7*) Electronic Publishing Services.

Matsuura, Richard & Matsuura, Ruth. King Who Wanted to See God. (Illus.). (J). 8.95 (*1-887916-00-8*) Orchid Isle Publishing Co.

Maugham, W. Somerset. Princess September & the Nightingale. 1998. (Iona & Peter Opie Library of Children's Literature). (Illus.). 48p. (YA). (gr. k-6). 16.95 o.p. (*0-19-512480-4*) Oxford Univ. Pr., Inc.

Mayne, William. All the King's Men. 1988. 192p. (J). (gr. 3-7). 14.95 o.s.i (*0-385-29626-6*, Delacorte Pr.) Dell Publishing.

Mazer, Anne. A Kid in King Arthur's Court: Junior Novelization. 1995. (Illus.). 112p. (J). (gr. 2-6). pap. 4.95 (*0-7868-4069-2*) Disney Pr.

McAllister, Angela. The King Who Sneezed. 1988. (Illus.). 32p. (J). (gr. k-3). 12.95 o.p. (*0-688-08327-7*); lib. bdg. 12.88 o.p. (*0-688-08328-5*) Morrow/Avon. (Morrow, William & Co.).

McCafferty, Catherine. Quest for Camelot. 1998. (J). (*0-7853-2383-X*) Publications International, Ltd.

McCaughrean, Geraldine. Casting the Gods Adrift: A Tale of Ancient Egypt. 2003. (Illus.). 112p. (J). (gr. 4-7). 15.95 (*0-8126-2684-2*) Cricket Bks.

McConnell, Robert. Fraises en Deconfiture. 1990. Tr. of Strawberry Jam. (FRE., Illus.). 48p. (Orig.). (J). pap. (*0-929141-06-7*) Napoleon Publishing/Rendezvous Pr.

McCully, Emily Arnold. The Pirate Queen. 1998. (Illus.). 32p. (J). (gr. k-3). pap. 6.99 o.s.i (*0-698-11629-1*, PaperStar) Penguin Putnam Bks. for Young Readers.

McEvoy, Greg. The Ice Cream King. (Illus.). 32p. (J). (ps-3). 1999. pap. 7.95 (*0-7737-6024-5*); 1998. 13.95 (*0-7737-3069-9*) Stoddart Kids CAN. *Dist:* Fitzhenry & Whiteside, Ltd.

McGuire, Leslie. Dragonheart Movie Storybook. 1996. (Dragonheart Ser.). (Illus.). (J). (gr. k up). 8.95 o.p. (*0-8431-3961-7*, Price Stern Sloan) Penguin Putnam Bks. for Young Readers.

McKee, David. The Adventures of King Rollo. 1986. (Picture Puffin Ser.). (Illus.). 32p. (J). (ps-3). pap. 3.95 o.p. (*0-14-050625-X*, Penguin Bks.) Viking Penguin.

—King Rollo: King Rollo & the New Shoes; King Rollo & the Birthday; King Rollo & the Bread. 1980. (J). (gr. 1-3). 6.95 o.p. (*0-316-56044-8*) Little Brown & Co.

—King Rollo & King Frank. 1982. (King Rollo Ser.). (Illus.). 32p. (J). (ps up). lib. bdg. 6.95 o.p. (*0-87191-834-X*, Creative Education) Creative Co., The.

—King Rollo & the Bath. 1982. (King Rollo Ser.). (Illus.). 32p. (J). (ps up). lib. bdg. 6.95 o.p. (*0-87191-833-1*, Creative Education) Creative Co., The.

—King Rollo & the Breakfast. 1982. (King Rollo Ser.). 32p. (J). (ps up). lib. bdg. 6.95 o.p. (*0-87191-902-8*, Creative Education) Creative Co., The.

—King Rollo & the Dishes. 1982. (King Rollo Ser.). (Illus.). 32p. (J). (ps up). lib. bdg. 6.95 o.p. (*0-87191-832-3*, Creative Education) Creative Co., The.

—King Rollo & the Dog. 1982. (King Rollo Ser.). 32p. (J). (ps up). lib. bdg. 6.95 o.p. (*0-87191-901-X*, Creative Education) Creative Co., The.

—King Rollo & the Masks. 1982. (King Rollo Ser.). 32p. (J). (ps up). lib. bdg. 6.95 o.p. (*0-87191-900-1*, Creative Education) Creative Co., The.

—King Rollo & the New Stockings. 2002. (Illus.). 32p. 17.95 (*0-86264-953-6*) Trafalgar Square.

—King Rollo & the New Stockings. 2001. (J). E-Book (*1-59019-406-3*); E-Book (*1-59019-407-1*); (J). E-Book 5.99 (*1-59019-408-X*) ipicturebooks, LLC.

—King Rollo & the Playroom. 1982. (King Rollo Ser.). 32p. (J). (ps up). lib. bdg. 6.95 o.p. (*0-87191-899-4*, Creative Education) Creative Co., The.

—King Rollo & the Search. 1982. (King Rollo Ser.). (Illus.). 32p. (J). (ps up). lib. bdg. 6.95 o.p. (*0-87191-835-8*, Creative Education) Creative Co., The.

—King Rollo's Spring. 1987. (J). (ps). 2.95 o.p. (*0-670-81612-4*, Viking Children's Bks.) Penguin Putnam Bks. for Young Readers.

—King Rollo's Winter. 1987. (J). (ps). 2.95 o.p. (*0-670-81611-6*, Viking Children's Bks.) Penguin Putnam Bks. for Young Readers.

—Minilibros - Rey Rollo. (SPA., Illus.). (J). (ps-1). 7.99 (*980-257-191-1*) Ekare, Ediciones VEN. *Dist:* Kane/Miller Bk. Pubs.

McKenzie, Ellen K. The King, the Princess, & the Tinker, ERS. 1993. (Illus.). 64p. (J). (gr. 2-4). 14.95 o.p. (*0-8050-1773-9*); pap. 4.95 o.p. (*0-8050-2951-6*) Holt, Henry & Co. (Holt, Henry & Co. Bks. For Young Readers).

McKillip, Patricia A. The Changeling Sea. 1989. 160p. mass mkt. 4.99 o.s.i (*0-345-36040-0*, Del Rey) Ballantine Bks.

—The Changeling Sea. 2003. (Firebird Ser.). (Illus.). 144p. (J). pap. 5.99 (*0-14-131262-9*) Penguin Putnam Bks. for Young Readers.

—The Changeling Sea. 1988. 144p. (YA). (gr. 5 up). lib. bdg. 13.95 o.p. (*0-689-31436-1*, Atheneum) Simon & Schuster Children's Publishing.

McKissack, Patricia C. Nzingha: Warrior Queen of Matamba, Angola, Africa, 1595. 2000. (Royal Diaries Ser.). (Illus.). 144p. (J). (gr. 4-8). 10.95 (*0-439-11210-9*) Scholastic, Inc.

McMullen, Eunice & McMullen, Nigel. Dragon for Breakfast. 1990. (Illus.). 28p. (J). (ps-3). lib. bdg. 7.95 o.p. (*0-87614-650-7*, Carolrhoda Bks.) Lerner Publishing Group.

McNeill, Janet. The Three Crowns of King Hullabaloo. 1976. (Stepping Stones Ser.). (Illus.). 24p. (J). (gr. k-3). 7.00 o.p. (*0-516-03593-2*, Children's Pr.) Scholastic Library Publishing.

Melling, David. The Kiss That Missed. 2002. (Illus.). 32p. (J). (gr. k-2). 14.95 (*0-7641-5451-6*) Barron's Educational Series, Inc.

Mendelson, Steve, illus. & retold by. The Emperor's New Clothes. 1992. 32p. (J). (gr. k-3). 7.50 o.p. (*1-55670-232-9*) Stewart, Tabori & Chang.

Meyer, Carolyn. Anastasia: Last Grand Duchess, Russia, 1914. 2000. (Royal Diaries Ser.). (Illus.). 220p. (J). (gr. 4-8). 10.95 (*0-439-12908-7*) Scholastic, Inc.

—Doomed Queen Anne. (Young Royals Ser.). (Illus.). 2004. 256p. (J). pap. 5.95 (*0-15-205086-8*); 2002. 240p. (YA). (gr. 7 up). 17.00 (*0-15-216523-1*) Harcourt Children's Bks. (Gulliver Bks.).

—Kristina, the Girl King. 2003. (Royal Diaries Ser.). 176p. (J). 10.95 (*0-439-24976-7*, Scholastic Pr.) Scholastic, Inc.

Meyer, Carolyn, contrib. by. Isabel: Jewel of Castilla, Spain, 1466. 2000. (Royal Diaries Ser.). (Illus.). 204p. (J). (gr. 4-8). 10.95 (*0-439-07805-9*) Scholastic, Inc.

Miller, M. L. The Enormous Snore. 1995. (Illus.). 32p. (J). (ps-3). 15.95 o.p. (*0-399-22650-8*, G. P. Putnam's Sons) Penguin Group (USA) Inc.

Mitchell, Mark S. The Curious Kingship of Sir George. 1998. (Chronicles of the House of Chax Ser.: Bk. 3). 89p. (J). (gr. 3-6). pap. 9.99 (*0-88092-355-5*, 3555) Royal Fireworks Publishing Co.

Molarsky, Osmond. The Peasant & the Fly. 1980. (Illus.). (J). (gr. k-3). 7.95 o.p. (*0-15-260152-X*); 48p. pap. 3.95 o.p. (*0-15-260153-8*, Voyager Bks./Libros Viajeros) Harcourt Children's Bks.

Mollel, Tololwa M. The King & the Tortoise. 1993. (Illus.). 30p. (J). (ps-3). 14.95 (*0-395-64480-1*, Clarion Bks.) Houghton Mifflin Co. Trade & Reference Div.

Morgan Creek Productions Staff. King & I. 1999. (Illus.). 31p. (J). mass mkt. 3.50 (*0-590-68064-1*) Scholastic, Inc.

—King & I: Deluxe Edition. 1999. mass mkt. 5.99 (*0-590-68066-8*) Scholastic, Inc.

Morpurgo, Michael. Jo-Jo, & the Melon Donkey. 2002. (Yellow Bananas Ser.). (Illus.). 48p. (J). (gr. 3-4). pap. 4.95 (*0-7787-0988-4*); lib. bdg. 19.96 (*0-7787-0942-6*) Crabtree Publishing Co.

—King of the Cloud Forests. 1991. (Illus.). 160p. (J). pap. 3.95 o.p. (*0-14-032586-7*, Puffin Bks.) Penguin Putnam Bks. for Young Readers.

Muntean, Michaela & Golden Books Staff. Imagine If Ernie Is King: Sesame Street Storybook. 1999. (Illus.). 24p. (J). (ps-3). pap. 3.29 o.s.i (*0-307-13123-8*, Golden Bks.) Random Hse. Children's Bks.

Newby, Robert. King Midas: With Selected Sentences in American Sign Language. 1990. (Awareness & Caring Ser.). (Illus.). 64p. (J). (gr. 1-6). lib. bdg. 16.95 (*1-878363-25-5*) Forest Hse. Publishing Co., Inc.

Newman, Marjorie. The King & the Cuddly. 2000. (Illus.). 32p. (J). (ps-1). (*0-09-176932-9*) Random Hse. of Canada, Ltd. CAN. *Dist:* Random Hse., Inc.

Newman, Matt H., ed. Thanksgiving for King. 1980. (Children's Stories Book Cassettes). (Illus.). (J). (gr. k-3). 29.95 o.p. (*0-89290-087-3*, BC13-4) S V E & Churchill Media.

Newton, Michael. The King Conspiracy: Unexplained Facts Behind the M. L. K. Murder. 1991. 256p. (J). mass mkt. 3.25 (*0-87067-729-2*) Holloway Hse. Publishing Co.

Nobisso, Josephine. El Peso de Una Misa: Un Relato de Fe. 2003. Orig. Title: The Weight of a Mass a Tale of Faith. (SPA., Illus.). 32p. (J). 17.95 (*0-940112-15-9*); pap. 9.95 (*0-940112-17-5*) Gingerbread Hse.

—The Weight of a Mass: A Tale of Faith. 2002. (SPA., Illus.). 32p. (J). (gr. k-5). 17.95 (*0-940112-09-4*); pap. 9.95 (*0-940112-10-8*) Gingerbread Hse.

Noble, Trinka Hakes. The King's Tea. 1979. (Illus.). 32p. (J). (ps-2). 7.50 o.p. (*0-8037-4529-X*); 7.50 o.p. (*0-8037-4530-3*); 3.25 o.p. (*0-8037-4540-0*) Penguin Putnam Bks. for Young Readers. (Dial Bks. for Young Readers).

Noonan, Janet & Calvert, Jacquelyn. Berries for the Queen. 1994. 32p. (J). (ps-2). 8.99 (*0-7814-0903-9*) Cook Communications Ministries.

Olofsson, Helena-Adapt. The Little Jester. 2002. (Illus.). 28p. (J). (gr. k-3). 16.00 (*91-29-65499-8*) R & S Bks. SWE. *Dist:* Farrar, Straus & Giroux, Holtzbrinck Pubs.

Oppenheim, Joanne F. The Story Book Prince. 1987. (Illus.). 32p. (J). (ps-3). 12.95 o.p. (*0-15-200590-0*, Gulliver Bks.) Harcourt Children's Bks.

Osuchowska, Isia. The Gift: A Magical Story about Caring for the Earth. 1996. (Illus.). 32p. (J). (gr. 5-7). 14.95 (*0-86171-116-5*) Wisdom Pubns.

Packard, Mary. I Am King! (My First Reader (Reissue) Ser.). 2004. pap. 3.95 (*0-516-24629-1*); 2003. (Illus.). 31p. (J). lib. bdg. 17.50 (*0-516-22927-3*); 1995. (Illus.). 28p. (J). pap. 3.95 (*0-516-45365-3*); 1994. (Illus.). 28p. (J). mass mkt. 15.50 o.p. (*0-516-05365-5*) Scholastic Library Publishing. (Children's Pr.).

Paterson, Katherine. The King's Equal. (Trophy Picture Bk.). (Illus.). 64p. (J). (gr. 2-5). 1996. pap. 7.99 (*0-06-443396-X*, Harper Trophy); 1992. 17.00 (*0-06-022496-7*); 1992. lib. bdg. 18.89 (*0-06-022497-5*) HarperCollins Children's Bk. Group.

—The King's Equal. 1992. 13.10 (*0-606-08791-5*) Turtleback Bks.

—The Wide-Awake Princess. 2000. (Illus.). 48p. (J). (ps-3). lib. bdg., tchr. ed. 15.00 (*0-395-53777-0*, Clarion Bks.) Houghton Mifflin Co. Trade & Reference Div.

Paton Walsh, Jill. The Emperor's Winding Sheet, RS. 1992. 288p. (YA). (gr. 7 up). pap. 4.95 o.p. (*0-374-42121-8*, Sunburst) Farrar, Straus & Giroux.

—The Emperor's Winding Sheet. 1993. (J). (gr. 4-9). 18.00 o.p. (*0-8446-6665-3*) Smith, Peter Pub., Inc.

Peck, Richard. Princess Ashley. 1987. 208p. (J). (gr. 7 up). 14.95 o.p. (*0-385-29561-8*, Delacorte Pr.) Dell Publishing.

Pelta, Kathy. The Blue Empress, ERS. 1988. (Illus.). 160p. (J). (gr. 3-7). 12.95 o.p. (*0-8050-0406-8*, Holt, Henry & Co. Bks. For Young Readers) Holt, Henry & Co.

Pfister, Marcus. How Leo Learned to Be King. 1998. (Illus.). 32p. (J). (ps-3). 15.95 (*1-55858-913-9*); 15.88 o.p. (*1-55858-914-7*) North-South Bks., Inc.

Pierce, Tamora. Emperor Mage. 2003. (Immortals Ser.). (Illus.). 320p. (YA). 10.95 (*0-689-85613-X*, Atheneum) Simon & Schuster Children's Publishing.

—Emperor Mage. 2002. (YA). 20.50 (*0-8446-7227-0*) Smith, Peter Pub., Inc.

Platt, Chris. Willow King: Race the Wind! 2002. 256p. (YA). (gr. 5-8). pap. 4.99 (*0-679-88658-3*, Random Hse. Bks. for Young Readers) Random Hse. Children's Bks.

Pohl, Linda P. The Grumpy Queen. 1998. (Illus.). 16p. (J). (ps-1). pap. text 4.95 (*0-9625453-3-3*) Pohl, Linda Perelman.

Poor Little Rich King. 1973. (Illus.). 96p. (gr. 1-3). pap. 1.25 o.p. (*0-912692-26-X*) Cook, David C. Publishing Co.

Pray, Ralph. Jingu: The Hidden Princess. 2002. (Illus.). 80p. (J). 14.95 (*1-885008-21-X*, 188500821x) Shen's Bks.

Price, Stern, Sloan Publishing Staff. Feast Fit for a King. 2015. (Doodle Art Ser.). (J). (gr. k up). pap. 8.99 (*0-8431-6585-5*); pap. 10.99 (*0-8431-6588-X*) Penguin Putnam Bks. for Young Readers. (Price Stern Sloan).

Priest, Robert. The Old Pirate of Central Park. 1999. (Illus.). 30p. (J). (ps-3). tchr. ed. 16.00 (*0-395-90505-2*) Houghton Mifflin Co.

Pushkin, Alexandr. The Tale of the Golden Cockerel. Lowe, Patrica T., tr. 1975. (Illus.). (J). (gr. 1-5). 5.95 o.p. (*0-690-00790-6*) HarperCollins Children's Bk. Group.

Pyle, Howard. Bearskin. 1997. (Books of Wonder). (Illus.). 48p. (J). (gr. k-3). 16.00 (*0-688-09837-1*); 15.89 (*0-688-09838-X*) Morrow/Avon. (Morrow, William & Co.).

—The Story of King Arthur & His Knights. 1986. (Signet Classics Ser.). (J). 12.00 (*0-606-01952-9*) Turtleback Bks.

Quin-Harkin, Janet. The King & I. novel ed. 1999. (J). mass mkt. 3.99 (*0-590-68065-X*) Scholastic, Inc.

Quintana, Anton. The Baboon King. 2001. 192p. (YA). (gr. 7 up). mass mkt. 4.99 (*0-440-22907-3*, Laurel Leaf) Random Hse. Children's Bks.

—The Baboon King. Nieuwenhuizen, John, tr. 1999. (DUT.). 192p. (YA). (gr. 7-12). 16.95 (*0-8027-8711-8*) Walker & Co.

Rabe, Tish, et al. The King's Beard. 1997. (Wubbulous World of Reading Ser.). (Illus.). 48p. (J). pap. 14.00 o.s.i (*0-679-88633-8*, Random Hse. Bks. for Young Readers) Random Hse. Children's Bks.

Rabley, Stephen. Billy & the Queen. 1996. (Easystarts Ser.). (J). pap. text 7.00 (*0-582-09694-4*) Addison-Wesley Longman, Ltd. GBR. *Dist:* Trans-Atlantic Pubns., Inc.

Radunsky, Vladimir. The Mighty Asparagus. 2004. (Illus.). 34p. (J). 16.00 (*0-15-216743-9*) Harcourt Trade Pubs.

Robbins, Ruth. Baboushka & the Three Kings. (Illus.). (J). (ps-3). 1986. 32p. pap. 6.95 (*0-395-42647-2*); 1960. 28p. reprint ed. lib. bdg. 4.95 o.p. (*0-395-27672-1*) Houghton Mifflin Co.

—L' Empereur et le Tambour, 001. 1962. (FRE., Illus.). (J). (gr. k-3). reprint ed. 4.95 o.p. (*0-395-27708-6*) Houghton Mifflin Co.

Robison, Nancy. Ten Tall Soldiers, ERS. 1991. (Illus.). 32p. (J). (ps). 13.95 o.p. (*0-8050-0768-7*, Holt, Henry & Co. Bks. For Young Readers) Holt, Henry & Co.

—Ten Tall Soldiers. 1995. 4.98 o.p. (*0-8317-2271-1*) Smithmark Pubs., Inc.

Rogerson, James. King Wilbur the Third & the Bath. 1976. (Illus.). (J). 1.95 o.p. (*0-460-06706-0*) Biblio Distribution.

—King Wilbur the Third & the Bicycle. 1976. (Illus.). (J). 1.95 o.p. (*0-460-06708-7*) Biblio Distribution.

—King Wilbur the Third Rebuilds His Palace. 1976. (Illus.). (J). 1.95 o.p. (*0-460-06705-2*) Biblio Distribution.

Ron, Kare. The Adventures of Sir Noodlefish: The Cake Wars. 2000. (Illus.). 32p. (J). (gr. 1-3). pap. (*1-931179-00-X*) Long Hill Productions, Inc.

Rosenberg, Amye. Jewels for Josephine. 1993. (Illus.). 28p. (J). (ps-2). 12.95 o.s.i (*0-448-40457-5*, Grosset & Dunlap) Penguin Putnam Bks. for Young Readers.

Ross, Jillian. Alissa & the Castle Ghost. 2nd ed. 1998. (Stardust Classics). (Illus.). (J). (gr. 2-6). 113p. 12.95 (*1-889514-07-1*); 119p. pap. 5.95 (*1-889514-08-X*) Dolls Corp.

Ross, Stewart. Beware of the King. 1996. (Illus.). 62p. (J). 17.95 (*0-237-51636-5*); pap. 8.95 (*0-237-51637-3*) Evans Brothers, Ltd. GBR. *Dist:* Trafalgar Square.

Rothsteis, Shmuel. Heir to the Throne. 1990. (Illus.). 224p. (J). (gr. 5-8). 16.95 (*1-56062-043-9*, CFR106H); pap. 13.95 (*1-56062-044-7*, CFR106S) CIS Communications, Inc.

Rowe, William. King Fulgreed & Other Tales for Happiness & Wisdom. 2000. 180p. E-Book 8.00 (*0-7388-8996-2*) Xlibris Corp.

Rukstalis, Susan. How Many Steps Before the Queen? 1992. (Illus.). 32p. (J). (ps-4). 14.95 (*0-9628914-2-8*) Padakami Pr.

Ruskin, John. The King of the Golden River. 2000. (Candlewick Treasures Ser.). (Illus.). 96p. (J). (gr. 3-7). 11.99 o.p. (*0-7636-0845-9*) Candlewick Pr.

—The King of the Golden River or the Black Brothers. 1974. (Illus.). 56p. (J). (gr. 1 up). reprint ed. pap. 3.50 (*0-486-20066-3*) Dover Pubns., Inc.

Rust, Patricia. King of Skittledeedoo. 1998. 32p. (J). (gr. k-3). 15.00 (*0-9655890-5-6*) Markowitz Publishing.

—The King of Skittledeedoo. 2nd rev. ed. 2000. (Illus.). 32p. (J). (ps-3). lib. bdg. 12.95 (*1-885848-00-5*, Power for Kids Pr.) Rust Foundation for Literacy, Inc., The.

Saddler, Allen. The King Gets Fit. 1987. (Illus.). 32p. (J). 4.95 o.p. (*0-19-279761-1*) Oxford Univ. Pr., Inc.

Santore, Charles. William the Curious: Knight of the Water Lilies. 1997. (Illus.). 40p. (J). (ps-1). 18.00 (*0-679-88742-3*, Random Hse. Bks. for Young Readers) Random Hse. Children's Bks.

Sanzari, Sylvester. The King of Pizza: A Magical Story about the World's Favorite Food. 1995. (Illus.). 32p. (J). (ps-4). pap. 14.95 (*0-7611-0107-1*, 10107) Workman Publishing Co., Inc.

Sargent, Dave & Sargent, Pat. Whiskers (Roan) Pride & Peace. (Saddle Up Ser.: Vol. 59). (Illus.). 42p. (J). 2003. mass mkt. 6.95 (*1-56763-806-6*); 2002. lib. bdg. 22.60 (*1-56763-805-8*) Ozark Publishing.

Saunders, Susan. A Sniff in Time. 1982. (Illus.). 32p. (J). (ps-3). 10.95 o.s.i (*0-689-30890-6*, Atheneum) Simon & Schuster Children's Publishing.

Schneegans, Nicole. The King's Twins. 1992. (I Love to Read Collections). (Illus.). 46p. (J). (gr. 1-5). lib. bdg. 8.50 o.p. (*0-89565-813-5*) Child's World, Inc.

Service, Pamela F. Being of Two Minds. 1991. 176p. (J). (gr. 3-7). lib. bdg. 14.95 o.s.i (*0-689-31524-4*, Atheneum) Simon & Schuster Children's Publishing.

Shankar, Alaka. The Seven Queens. 1980. (Illus.). 16p. (Orig.). (J). (gr. k-3). pap. 2.50 o.p. (*0-89744-217-2*) Children's Bk. Trust IND. *Dist:* Random Hse. of Canada, Ltd.

Sharratt, Nick. The Green Queen. 1992. (Illus.). 24p. (J). (ps up). 5.95 o.p. (*1-56402-093-2*) Candlewick Pr.

Sharrett, Nick. The Green Queen. 1995. (Illus.). (J). bds. 2.99 o.p. (*1-56402-441-5*) Candlewick Pr.

Sheehan, Patty. Gwendolyn's Gifts. 1991. (Illus.). 32p. (J). (ps-3). 14.95 (*0-88289-845-0*) Pelican Publishing Co., Inc.

Shulevitz, Uri. One Monday Morning, RS. 2003. (Illus.). 48p. (J). reprint ed. pap. 6.95 (*0-374-45648-8*, Sunburst) Farrar, Straus & Giroux.

—One Monday Morning. (Illus.). (J). (ps-4). 1974. 48p. text 14.95 o.s.i (*0-684-13195-1*, Atheneum); 1986. 32p. reprint ed. pap. 4.95 o.s.i (*0-689-71062-3*, Aladdin) Simon & Schuster Children's Publishing.

—What Is a Wise Bird Like You Doing in a Silly Tale Like This, RS. 2000. (Illus.). 40p. (J). (ps-3). 16.00 (*0-374-38300-6*, Farrar, Straus & Giroux (BYR)) Farrar, Straus & Giroux.

Simon, Les. The Secret of the Red Silk Pouch. 1998. 157p. (J). (gr. 5-8). pap. 9.99 (*0-88092-362-8*, 3628) Royal Fireworks Publishing Co.

Singer, Isaac Bashevis. Naftali the Storyteller & His Horse, Sus: And Other Stories, RS. 1987. (Sunburst Ser.). (Illus.). 144p. (J). (gr. 4-7). pap. 3.50 o.s.i (*0-374-45487-6*, Sunburst) Farrar, Straus & Giroux.

Slightly Off-Center Writers Group Staff. King Saurus' Big Decision. 1994. (Under Twenty Writing Society Ser.). (Illus.). 48p. (J). (gr. 3-5). pap. 6.95 o.p. (*1-56721-064-3*) 25th Century Pr.

Snyder, Zilpha Keatley. The Box & the Bone. 1995. (Castle Court Kids Ser.: No. 2). 128p. (J). pap. 3.50 o.s.i (*0-440-40986-1*) Dell Publishing.

Sommer, Carl. The Great Royal Race. 1997. (Another Sommer-Time Story Ser.). (Illus.). 48p. (J). (gr. 1-4). 9.95 (*1-57537-008-5*); lib. bdg. 16.95 (*1-57537-054-9*) Advance Publishing, Inc.

—The Great Royal Race Read-Along. 2003. (Another Sommer-Time Story Ser.). (Illus.). 48p. (J). (gr. 1-4). 16.95 incl. audio compact disk (*1-57537-508-7*); 16.95 incl. audio (*1-57537-557-5*); 16.95 incl. audio compact disk (*1-57537-508-7*) Advance Publishing, Inc.

Spencer, Ladonna, ed. Happy the King's Clown. 1985. 30p. (J). pap. 3.50 (*0-88144-057-4*) Christian Publishing Services, Inc.

Spongberg, Emily. Hannibal & the King. l.t. ed. 1999. (Illus.). 32p. (J). (gr. k-4). 15.95 (*1-893659-00-3*) Rainbow Hse. Publishing.

Sprague, Gilbert M. The Nome King's Shadow in Oz. 1992. (Oz Ser.). (Illus.). 120p. (YA). (gr. 2-7). pap. 9.95 o.p. (*0-929605-18-7*); (gr. 5 up). 39.95 o.p. (*0-929605-19-5*) Books of Wonder.

Springer, Nancy. I Am Mordred: A Tale from Camelot. 1998. 184p. (YA). (gr. 7-12). 16.99 (*0-399-23143-9*, Philomel) Penguin Putnam Bks. for Young Readers.

—Outlaw Princess of Sherwood, a Tale of Rowan Hood. 2003. 160p. (J). 16.99 (*0-399-23721-6*, Philomel) Penguin Putnam Bks. for Young Readers.

Sproul, R. C. The King Without a Shadow. 1996. (Illus.). 32p. (J). 16.99 o.p. (*0-7814-0257-3*) Cook Communications Ministries.

—The King Without a Shadow. 2000. (Illus.). 32p. (J). (ps-3). 16.99 (*0-87552-700-0*) P&R Publishing.

Stevenson, Sucie, illus. & reader. The Emperor's New Clothes. 1998. 10.14 (*0-606-13367-4*) Turtleback Bks.

Stewart, Josie & Salem, Lynn. The King's Surprise. 1995. (Illus.). 8p. (J). (gr. k-2). pap. 3.75 (*1-880612-38-0*) Seedling Pubns., Inc.

Stolz, Mary. King Emmett II. 1993. (Illus.). 64p. (J). (gr. 4-7). pap. 3.25 o.s.i (*0-440-40777-X*) Dell Publishing.

—King Emmett II. 1924. (J). lib. bdg. 99.98 o.p. (*0-688-09521-6*, Greenwillow Bks.) HarperCollins Children's Bk. Group.

Stoner, Laura M. Prophets, Priests & Kings: A Story Color Book. Huskey, Freeda, ed. & illus. by. 1994. 85p. (Orig.). (J). (gr. k-6). pap., stu. ed. 5.95 o.p. (*0-934426-58-9*) NAPSAC Reproductions.

Storr, Catherine. King Midas. 1993. (J). (ps-3). pap. 4.95 o.p. (*0-8114-7148-9*) Raintree Pubs.

Sula, Sondra. Gopher World: The Sleazy Snakes. 2000. (Illus.). 32p. (J). (gr. 1-3). pap. (*0-9701450-7-1*) Long Hill Productions, Inc.

The Sword in the Stone. 1994. (Classics Ser.). (Illus.). 96p. (J). (ps-4). 7.98 o.p. (*1-57082-052-X*) Mouse Works.

Taylor, Glenn. Emperor of Time. 1991. (Star Shows Ser.). (J). lib. bdg. 15.93 o.p. (*0-516-35013-7*, Children's Pr.) Scholastic Library Publishing.

Thomson, Peggy. The King Has Horse's Ears. (J). 1991. (gr. k-3). pap. 4.95 o.p. (*0-671-74055-5*, Aladdin); 1988. (Illus.). (gr. 2 up). pap. 12.95 o.s.i (*0-671-64953-1*, Simon & Schuster Children's Publishing) Simon & Schuster Children's Publishing.

Thomson, Peter. The Palace of Cards. 1994. (Illus.). 32p. (J). (gr. 1-3). o.p. (*0-370-31863-3*) Random Hse., Inc.

Tingle, Rebecca. The Edge on the Sword. 2001. (Illus.). 288p. (J). (gr. 7 up). 18.99 (*0-399-23580-9*) Penguin Group (USA) Inc.

—The Edge on the Sword. 2003. (Sailing Mystery Ser.). 288p. (J). pap. 6.99 (*0-14-250058-5*, Puffin Bks.) Penguin Putnam Bks. for Young Readers.

Tournier, Michel. Rois Mages. 1978. (Folio - Junior Ser.: No. 280). (FRE., Illus.). 160p. (J). (gr. 5-10). pap. 7.95 (*2-07-033280-2*) Schoenhof's Foreign Bks., Inc.

Trudel, Sylvain. Le Roi Qui Venait du Bout du Monde. 2002. (Premier Roman Ser.). (FRE., Illus.). 64p. (J). (gr. 2-5). pap. 8.95 (*2-89021-279-3*) La Courte Echelle CAN. *Dist:* Firefly Bks., Ltd.

—Le Royaume de Bruno. 1998. (Premier Roman Ser.). (FRE., Illus.). 64p. (J). (gr. 2-5). pap. 8.95 (*2-89021-326-9*) La Courte Echelle CAN. *Dist:* Firefly Bks., Ltd.

Turnbull, Ann. The Wolf King, 001. 1979. 144p. (J). (gr. 6 up). 5.95 o.p. (*0-395-28927-0*, Clarion Bks.) Houghton Mifflin Co. Trade & Reference Div.

Turner, Megan Whalen. The Queen of Attolia. (J). (gr. 5 up). 2001. 416p. pap. 6.95 (*0-380-73304-8*, Harper Trophy); 2000. 288p. 15.95 (*0-688-17423-X*, Greenwillow Bks.) HarperCollins Children's Bk. Group.

—The Queen of Attolia. 2001. 13.00 (*0-606-22313-4*) Turtleback Bks.

Utz. The King, the Queen, & the Lima Bean. 1974. (Illus.). 32p. (J). (gr. k-3). lib. bdg. 9.95 (*0-87783-121-1*); pap. 3.94 (*0-87783-122-X*) Oddo Publishing, Inc.

Van Jacobs, Gregory. The Polka Dot Queen. 1992. (J). 7.95 o.p. (*0-533-09669-3*) Vantage Pr., Inc.

Voigt, Cynthia. Elske. 256p. 2001. (YA). pap. 10.00 (*0-689-84444-1*, Simon Pulse); 1999. (Illus.). (J). (gr. 7-12). 18.00 (*0-689-82472-6*, Atheneum/Anne Schwartz Bks.) Simon & Schuster Children's Publishing.

Walker, Jan. The Kingdom of Neep. 1993. (Illus.). 32p. (J). (gr. k-12). 14.95 (*0-9636190-0-4*) Children's Gallery Pubns.

Walt Disney Productions Staff. King for a Day. 1998. (J). (ps-3). 2.99 (*0-307-08726-3*, 08726, Golden Bks.) Random Hse. Children's Bks.

Wasserman, Mira. Too Much of a Good Thing. 2003. (Illus.). (J). 6.95 (*1-58013-066-6*); lib. bdg. 14.95 (*1-58013-082-8*) Kar-Ben Publishing.

Watson, Jude. Queen Amidala. 1999. (Star Wars Ser.). (Illus.). 111p. (J). (gr. 4-7). mass mkt. 5.99 (*0-590-52101-2*) Scholastic, Inc.

Weaver, Patricia. Ashaki, African Princess. 2001. 164p. pap. 12.95 (*0-595-18283-6*, Writer's Showcase Pr.) iUniverse, Inc.

Weiss, Ellen & de Brunhoff, Laurent. Babar & the Christmas House. 2003. 32p. (J). 9.95 (*0-8109-4583-5*, 53604968) Abrams, Harry N. , Inc.

—Babar Goes to School. 2003. (Illus.). 32p. (J). 9.95 (*0-8109-4582-7*) Abrams, Harry N. , Inc.

Werner, Jerry. Sunny Kingdom. 1989. (J). o.p. (*0-89081-761-8*) Harvest Hse. Pubs.

West, Colin. The King's Toothache. 1990. (Trophy Picture Bk.). (Illus.). 24p. (J). (ps-2). reprint ed. pap. 3.95 o.p. (*0-06-443168-1*, Harper Trophy) HarperCollins Children's Bk. Group.

West, Steven H. Nobody's King. 1996. (Illus.). x, 54p. (Orig.). (J). (gr. 3-5). pap. 5.95 (*0-9652042-1-9*) PageWorthy Bks.

Wheeler, Cindy. The Emperor's Birthday Suit. 1996. (Step into Reading Step 2 Bks.). (J). (gr. 1-3). 10.14 (*0-606-11297-9*) Turtleback Bks.

White, Ellen E. Long Live the Queen. 1990. (YA). mass mkt. 2.95 o.p. (*0-590-40851-8*) Scholastic, Inc.

White, T. H. The Sword in the Stone. 1978. 288p. (YA). (gr. 5-12). mass mkt. 5.99 (*0-440-98445-9*, Laurel) Dell Publishing.

—The Sword in the Stone. (Illus.). 1993. 256p. (J). (gr. 2 up). 22.99 (*0-399-22502-1*, Philomel); 1972. 11.95 o.s.i (*0-399-10783-5*, G. P. Putnam's Sons) Penguin Putnam Bks. for Young Readers.

—The Sword in the Stone. 1963. 11.55 (*0-606-05065-5*) Turtleback Bks.

Wild, Margaret. The Queen's Holiday. 1992. (Illus.). 32p. (J). (ps-1). 13.95 o.p. (*0-531-05973-1*); mass mkt. 13.99 o.p. (*0-531-08573-2*) Scholastic, Inc. (Orchard Bks.).

Wilkes, Larry. The King's Egg Dance. 1990. (Illus.). 32p. (J). (ps-3). lib. bdg. 7.95 o.s.i (*0-87614-446-6*, Carolrhoda Bks.) Lerner Publishing Group.

Winston, Helena. Royal Treasures. 2001. (Illus.). 32p. (J). (ps-3). pap. 3.99 (*0-7364-1130-5*, RH/Disney) Random Hse. Children's Bks.

Winterson, Jeanette. The King of Capri. 2003. (Illus.). 32p. (J). 16.95 (*1-58234-830-8*, Bloomsbury Children) Bloomsbury Publishing.

Wise, William. Perfect Pancakes, If You Please. 1997. (Illus.). 32p. (J). (ps-3). 14.99 o.s.i (*0-8037-1446-7*); 14.89 o.s.i (*0-8037-1447-5*) Penguin Putnam Bks. for Young Readers. (Dial Bks. for Young Readers).

Wisniewski, David. Sundiata: Lion King of Mali. 1992. 12.10 (*0-606-16428-6*) Turtleback Bks.

—Sundiata, Lion King of Mali. 1999. (Illus.). 32p. (J). (ps-3). pap. 6.95 (*0-395-76481-5*, Clarion Bks.) Houghton Mifflin Co. Trade & Reference Div.

Wolff, Ferida. The Emperor's Garden. 1994. (Illus.). (J). 15.00 o.p. (*0-688-11651-5*); 32p. lib. bdg. 14.93 o.p. (*0-688-11652-3*) Morrow/Avon. (Morrow, William & Co.).

Wood, Audrey. King Bidgood's in the Bathtub. 1985. (Illus.). 32p. (J). (ps-3). 16.00 (*0-15-242730-9*) Harcourt Children's Bks.

—King Bidgood's in the Bathtub. 1993. (Brace Big Bks.). (Illus.). 32p. (J). (ps-3). pap. 24.95 (*0-15-242732-5*) Harcourt Trade Pubs.

—King Bidgood's in the Bathtub: The Musical. unabr. ed. 1993. (Bks. & Musical Cassettes). (Illus.). (J). (ps-3). 9.95 incl. audio (*0-15-242733-3*) Harcourt Children's Bks.

Wood, Audrey & Wood, Don. King Bidgood's in the Bathtub: The Musical. Shaylen, Carl, ed. unabr. ed. 1991. (Bks. & Musical Cassettes). (Illus.). (C). (ps-2). 20.00 o.s.i incl. audio (*0-15-242731-7*) Harcourt Children's Bks.

Wrede, Patricia C. Calling on Dragons. (Enchanted Forest Chronicles: Bk. 3). (YA). 2003. (Illus.). 272p. pap. 5.95 (*0-15-204692-5*, Magic Carpet Bks.); Vol. 3. 1993. 240p. (gr. 7 up). 16.95 o.s.i (*0-15-200950-7*) Harcourt Children's Bks.

—Calling on Dragons. unabr. ed. 2002. (Enchanted Forest Ser.: Vol 3). (YA). 244p. pap. 37.00 incl. audio (*0-8072-0792-6*, LYA 347 SP);3. (gr. 5 up). audio 26.00 (*0-8072-0635-0*) Random Hse. Audio Publishing Group. (Listening Library).

—Calling on Dragons. 1994. 256p. (YA). (gr. 7-9). mass mkt. 4.99 (*0-590-48467-2*) Scholastic, Inc.

—Calling on Dragons. 1993. (Enchanted Forest Chronicles Ser.). 11.04 (*0-606-06950-X*) Turtleback Bks.

—Talking to Dragons. 1985. (MagicQuest Ser.: No. 13). 240p. (J). 2.25 o.s.i (*0-441-79591-9*) Ace Bks.

—Talking to Dragons. (Enchanted Forest Chronicles: Bk. 4). 272p. 2003. (Illus.). (YA). pap. 5.95 (*0-15-204691-7*, Magic Carpet Bks.); 1993. (J). (gr. 7 up). 16.95 (*0-15-284247-0*) Harcourt Children's Bks.

—Talking to Dragons, 4. unabr. ed. 2002. (J). (gr. 3 up). audio 26.00 (*0-8072-0638-5*, Listening Library) Random Hse. Audio Publishing Group.

—Talking to Dragons. 1995. 272p. (J). (gr. 7-9). mass mkt. 4.99 (*0-590-48475-3*) Scholastic, Inc.

—Talking to Dragons. 1995. (Enchanted Forest Chronicles Ser.). (J). 11.04 (*0-606-08267-0*) Turtleback Bks.

Wright, Randall. Hunchback. 2004. (J). 16.95 (*0-8050-7232-2*) Holt, Henry & Co.

Wyatt, Melissa. Raising the Griffin. 2004. 208p. (YA). (gr. 7). 16.95 (*0-385-73095-0*); lib. bdg. 18.99 (*0-385-90115-1*) Random Hse. Children's Bks. (Lamb, Wendy).

Yang, Jwing-Ming. The Mask of the King. Dougall, Alan, ed. 1990. (Ymaa Storybook Ser.: No. 2). (Illus.). 32p. (J). (gr. 4-7). pap. 3.50 (*0-940871-11-4*, CB002/114) YMAA Pubn. Ctr.

Yolen, Jane. The Emperor & the Kite. (Illus.). 32p. (J). (ps-3). 1998. pap. 6.99 (*0-698-11644-5*, PaperStar); 1988. 16.99 (*0-399-21499-2*, Philomel) Penguin Putnam Bks. for Young Readers.

—The Emperor & the Kite. 1998. (J). (ps-3). 12.14 (*0-606-13366-6*) Turtleback Bks.

—The Queen's Own Fool. 2001. 14.04 (*0-606-22526-9*) Turtleback Bks.

—Travelers Rose. 2015. (J). 14.95 (*0-399-21985-4*) Penguin Putnam Bks. for Young Readers.

Yolen, Jane & Harris, Robert J. The Queen's Own Fool. (Illus.). (J). 2001. 400p. pap. 7.99 (*0-698-11918-5*, Puffin Bks.); 2000. viii, 390p. (gr. 5-9). 19.99 (*0-399-23380-6*, Philomel) Penguin Putnam Bks. for Young Readers.

KNIGHTS AND KNIGHTHOOD—FICTION

Ardizzone, Edward, illus. Exploits of Don Quixote. 1985. (Children's Classics from World Literature Ser.). (YA). (gr. 5 up). 12.95 o.p. (*0-87226-025-9*); pap. 5.95 o.p. (*0-87226-026-7*) McGraw-Hill Children's Publishing. (Bedrick, Peter Bks.).

Asala, Joanne. The Green Knight: A Tale of Ancient Britain - Arthurian Romance about Sir Gawain & the Green Knight. 1992. (Illus.). 64p. (J). (gr. 3). pap. 6.95 (*1-880954-00-1*) Kalevala Bks.

Barkan, Joanne. A Pup in King Arthur's Court. 1998. (Adventures of Wishbone Ser.: No. 15). (Illus.). 164p. (J). (gr. 2-5). pap. 3.99 o.p. (*1-57064-325-3*) Lyrick Publishing.

—A Pup in King Arthur's Court. l.t. ed. 1999. (Adventures of Wishbone Ser.: No. 15). (Illus.). 164p. (J). (gr. 2-5). lib. bdg. 22.60 (*0-8368-2593-4*) Stevens, Gareth Inc.

Bell, Hilari. The Goblin Wood. 2003. (Illus.). 304p. (J). (gr. 5 up). 16.99 (*0-06-051371-3*); lib. bdg. 17.89 (*0-06-051372-1*) HarperCollins Children's Bk. Group.

Bellairs, John. The Secret of the Underground Room. (Johnny Dixon Ser.). (Illus.). (J). 1992. 144p. (gr. 3-7). pap. 4.99 o.p. (*0-14-034932-4*, Puffin Bks.); 1990. 160p. (ps-3). 14.00 o.s.i (*0-8037-0863-7*, Dial Bks. for Young Readers); 1990. 12p. (ps-3). 13.89 o.p. (*0-8037-0864-5*, Dial Bks. for Young Readers) Penguin Putnam Bks. for Young Readers.

—The Secret of the Underground Room. 1992. (J). 9.09 (*0-606-01744-5*) Turtleback Bks.

Blake, Quentin. Simpkin. 1994. (Illus.). 32p. (J). (ps-1). 14.99 o.p. (*0-670-85371-2*, Viking Children's Bks.) Penguin Putnam Bks. for Young Readers.

Bradley, Marion Zimmer. Sword & Sorceress, Vol. 14. 1997. (Sword & Sorceress Ser.). 352p. (J). mass mkt. 5.99 o.s.i (*0-88677-741-0*) DAW Bks., Inc.

Brandon, Mary. Sir Wimpy. 2000. (J). 10.95 o.p. (*0-533-13355-6*) Vantage Pr., Inc.

Brett, Simon. The Three Detectives & the Knight in Armor. 1987. 176p. (J). (gr. 5-9). 13.95 o.p. (*0-684-18895-3*, Atheneum) Simon & Schuster Children's Publishing.

Bulla, Clyde Robert. The Sword in the Tree. (Illus.). (J). 1962. 128p. (gr. 4-7). lib. bdg. 15.89 (*0-690-79909-8*); 1956. (gr. 2-5). 12.95 (*0-690-79908-X*) HarperCollins Children's Bk. Group.

Los Caballeros del Rey Arturo. (SPA., Illus.). (YA). 14.95 (*84-7281-107-7*, AF1107) Auriga, Ediciones S.A. ESP. *Dist:* Continental Bk. Co., Inc.

Cadnum, Michael. The Leopard Sword. 2002. 224p. (J). (gr. 7 up). 15.99 (*0-670-89908-9*, Viking) Viking Penguin.

Cain, Michael. The Legend of Sir Miguel. Thatch, Nancy R., ed. 1990. (Books for Students by Students). (Illus.). 26p. (J). (gr. 4-7). lib. bdg. 15.95 (*0-933849-26-5*) Landmark Editions, Inc.

Cervantes Saavedra, Miguel de. Don Quijote de la Mancha. 2002. (Classics for Young Readers Ser.). (SPA.). (YA). 14.95 (*84-392-0926-6*, EV30621) Lectorum Pubns., Inc.

—Don Quijote de la Mancha, Pt. 2. 1971. (SPA., Illus.). (YA). (gr. 11-12). pap. 3.95 o.p. (*0-88345-138-7*) Prentice Hall, ESL Dept.

—Don Quixote. Harrison, Michael, ed. 1999. (Oxford Illustrated Classics Ser.). (Illus.). 96p. (YA). pap. 12.95 o.p. (*0-19-274182-9*) Oxford Univ. Pr., Inc.

—Don Quixote. 1979. (Now Age Illustrated V Ser.). (Illus.). 64p. (J). (gr. 4-12). text 7.50 o.p. (*0-88301-399-1*); pap. text 2.95 (*0-88301-387-8*); stu. ed. 1.25 (*0-88301-411-4*) Pendulum Pr., Inc.

—Don Quixote. 1972. (Enriched Classics Ser.). (J). (gr. 9 up). pap. 0.95 o.s.i (*0-671-47873-7*, Washington Square Pr.) Simon & Schuster.

—Don Quixote. 1993. (Illus.). 32p. (J). (gr. 2 up). 13.95 o.p. (*1-56402-174-2*) Candlewick Pr.

—Don Quixote. 1995. (Oxford Illustrated Classics Ser.). (Illus.). 96p. (J). (gr. 4 up). 22.95 o.p. (*0-19-274165-9*) Oxford Univ. Pr., Inc.

—Don Quixote. Marshall, Michael J., ed. abr. ed. 1999. (Core Classics Ser.: Vol. 6). (Illus.). (J). (gr. 4-6). 264p. pap. 7.95 (*1-890517-10-0*); 256p. lib. bdg. 9.95 o.p. (*1-890517-11-9*) Core Knowledge Foundation.

—Don Quixote: Illustrated Classics. 1994. (Illustrated Classics Collection). 64p. (J). pap. 3.60 o.p. (*1-56103-621-8*) American Guidance Service, Inc.

—Don Quixote: Wishbone Classics. 1996. (Wishbone Classics Ser.: No. 1). (Illus.). 128p. (gr. 3-7). mass mkt. 4.25 (*0-06-106416-5*, HarperEntertainment) Morrow/Avon.

—Don Quixote: Wishbone Classics. 1996. (Wishbone Classics Ser.: No. 1). (J). (gr. 3-7). 10.30 (*0-606-10364-3*) Turtleback Bks.

—Don Quixote of Mancha. 1999. (Everyman's Library Children's Classics). (Illus.). 256p. (gr. 8-12). 14.95 (*0-375-40659-X*) Random Hse., Inc.

Ciencin, Scott. Return to Lost City. Alfonsi, Alice, ed. 2000. (Dinotopia Ser.: No. 12). (Illus.). 176p. (J). (gr. 3-7). pap. 3.99 (*0-375-81018-8*, Random Hse. Bks. for Young Readers) Random Hse. Children's Bks.

—Return to Lost City. 2000. (Dinotopia Ser.). (Illus.). (J). 10.04 (*0-606-20466-0*) Turtleback Bks.

CLAMP Staff. Magic Knight Rayearth. 1999. (Magic Knight Rayearth Ser.: Vol. 3). (Illus.). 208p. (YA). (gr. 8-12). pap. 12.95 (*1-892213-16-8*, Mixx Manga) Mixx Entertainment, Inc.

Comrie, Margaret S. The Heroes of Castle Bretten. 2003. (Illus.). 229p. (J). (*1-894666-65-8*) Inheritance Pubns.

Dadey, Debbie & Jones, Marcia Thornton. Knights Don't Teach Piano. 1998. (Adventures of the Bailey School Kids Ser.: No. 29). (Illus.). 66p. (J). (gr. 2-4). mass mkt. 3.99 (*0-590-25804-4*, Scholastic Paperbacks) Scholastic, Inc.

—Knights Don't Teach Piano. 1998. (Adventures of the Bailey School Kids Ser.: No. 29). (J). (gr. 2-4). 10.14 (*0-606-12975-8*) Turtleback Bks.

De France, Marie. Shadow of the Hawk & Other Stories, 001. Reeves, James, ed. 1979. (J). (gr. 6 up). 7.95 o.p. (*0-395-28820-7*, Clarion Bks.) Houghton Mifflin Co. Trade & Reference Div.

de Paola, Tomie. The Knight & the Dragon. 2002. (Illus.). (J). 13.19 (*0-7587-2938-3*) Book Wholesalers, Inc.

—The Knight & the Dragon. 1980. (Illus.). 32p. (J). (ps-3). 16.99 (*0-399-20707-4*, G. P. Putnam's Sons) Penguin Group (USA) Inc.

—The Knight & the Dragon. 1998. (Illus.). 32p. (J). (ps-3). pap. 5.99 (*0-698-11623-2*, PaperStar) Penguin Putnam Bks. for Young Readers.

—The Knight & the Dragon. 1980. (Illus.). 32p. (J). (gr. k-2). 6.95 o.s.i (*0-399-20708-2*, Sandcastle Bks.) Putnam Publishing Group, The.

—The Knight & the Dragon. 1980. (J). (ps-2). 12.14 (*0-606-03327-0*) Turtleback Bks.

Dixon, Andy. Los Caballeros del Rey Arturo. 2001. (SPA., Illus.). 32p. (YA). (gr. 3 up). pap. 8.95 (*0-7460-3896-8*); lib. bdg. 16.95 (*1-58086-318-3*) EDC Publishing. (Usborne).

Dodds, Dayle Ann. The Great Divide: A Mathematical Marathon. 1999. (Illus.). 32p. (J). (gr. k-5). 15.99 o.s.i (*0-7636-0442-9*) Candlewick Pr.

Doyle, Arthur Conan. The White Company. 1988. (Books of Wonder). (Illus.). 362p. (J). (gr. 2 up). 24.99 (*0-688-07817-6*) HarperCollins Children's Bk. Group.

Doyle, Debra. The Knight's Wyrd. 1997. (Magic Carpet Books Ser.). (J). 12.05 (*0-606-11539-0*) Turtleback Bks.

Doyle, Debra & MacDonald, James D. The Knight's Wyrd. 1992. 176p. (YA). (gr. 7 up). 16.95 o.s.i (*0-15-200764-4*) Harcourt Children's Bks.

Doyle, Debra & McDonald, James D. The Knight's Wyrd. 1997. 320p. (YA). pap. 6.00 (*0-15-201520-5*, Magic Carpet Bks.) Harcourt Children's Bks.

Engle, Marty M. & Barnes, Johnny Ray, Jr. Knightmare. l.t. ed. 1996. (Strange Matter Ser.: No. 10). 124p. (J). (gr. 4-6). lib. bdg. 21.27 o.p. (*0-8368-1676-5*) Stevens, Gareth Inc.

Farber, Erica & Sansevere, J. R. If You Dream a Dragon. 1996. (Critters of the Night Ser.). (Illus.). 24p. (J). pap. 3.25 o.s.i (*0-679-87374-0*) Random Hse., Inc.

Fisher, Leonard Everett, illus. Don Quixote & the Windmills, RS. 2004. (J). 16.00 (*0-374-31825-5*, Farrar, Straus & Giroux (BYR)) Farrar, Straus & Giroux.

Fisher, Robert. Knight in Rusty Armor. 1987. (Illus.). 88p. (J). pap. 5.00 (*0-87980-421-1*) Wilshire Bk. Co.

Foote, Daniel H. A Knight in the Forest. (Illus.). 32p. (J). pap. 8.99 (*0-7814-3796-2*) Cook Communications Ministries.

Funke, Cornelia. The Princess Knight. 2004. 32p. (J). 15.95 (*0-439-53630-8*, Chicken Hse., The) Scholastic, Inc.

Garrick, Liz. Quest for King Arthur, Vol. 23. 1988. (Time Machine Ser.). (Illus.). 144p. (J). (ps-6). mass mkt. 2.50 o.s.i (*0-553-27126-1*) Bantam Bks.

George, Jim. Knight-Time for Brigitte. 1994. (Illus.). 72p. (J). (gr. 1 up). 12.95 (*1-56844-040-5*) Enchante Publishing.

Gerrard, Roy. Sir Cedric, RS. (Sunburst Ser.). (Illus.). 32p. (J). 1986. (ps-3). pap. 4.95 o.p. (*0-374-46659-9*, Sunburst); 1984. (gr. 2 up). 14.95 o.p. (*0-374-36959-3*, Farrar, Straus & Giroux (BYR)) Farrar, Straus & Giroux.

Gerver, Jane E. Lucky Little Knight. 1997. (Illus.). (J). (ps-1). pap. 3.25 o.p. (*0-679-88048-8*) Random Hse., Inc.

Goodman, Joan Elizabeth. The Winter Hare. 1996. (Illus.). 272p. (YA). (gr. 7-7). tchr. ed. 17.00 (*0-395-78569-3*) Houghton Mifflin Co.

Green, Roger Lancelyn. King Arthur & His Knights of the Round Table. 1993. (Everyman's Library Children's Classics Ser.). 368p. (gr. 2 up). 14.95 (*0-679-42311-7*) Knopf, Alfred A. Inc.

—King Arthur & His Knights of the Round Table. (Puffin Classics Ser.). (J). 1995. (Illus.). 352p. (gr. 4-7). pap. 4.99 (*0-14-036670-9*, Puffin Bks.); 1990. 288p. (gr. 5 up). pap. 3.99 o.p. (*0-14-035100-0*, Puffin Bks.); 1974. 288p. (gr. 5-7). pap. 2.95 o.p. (*0-14-030073-2*, Viking Children's Bks.) Penguin Putnam Bks. for Young Readers.

—King Arthur & His Knights of the Round Table. abr. ed. 1997. (Children's Classics Ser.). 2p. (J). pap. 10.95 o.s.i incl. audio (*0-14-086369-9*, Penguin AudioBooks) Viking Penguin.

Grey, Patrick. Five Days till Dawn. 2002. (YA). pap. (*1-894869-51-6*, PO 00033) Zumaya Pubns.

Gross, Gwen. Knights of the Round Table. 1985. (Bullseye Step into Classics Ser.). (Illus.). 112p. (J). (gr. 2-5). lib. bdg. 5.99 o.s.i (*0-394-97579-0*); (gr. 3-5). pap. 3.99 (*0-394-87579-6*) Random Hse. Children's Bks. (Random Hse. Bks. for Young Readers).

Hastings, Selina. Sir Gawain & the Loathly Lady. 1985. (Illus.). 32p. (J). 15.00 o.p. (*0-688-05823-X*) HarperCollins Children's Bk. Group.

Hastings, Selina & Wijngaard, Juan. Sir Gawain & the Loathly Lady - Sir Gawain y la Abominable Dama. (SPA., Illus.). 32p. (J). (gr. 1-5). 14.95 o.p. (*84-372-6604-1*) Santillana USA Publishing Co., Inc.

Hazen, Barbara Shook. The Knight Who Was Afraid of the Dark. (Illus.). 32p. (J). (ps-3). 1992. pap. 6.99 (*0-14-054545-X*, Puffin Bks.); 1989. 12.95 o.p. (*0-8037-0667-7*, Dial Bks. for Young Readers); 1989. 12.89 o.s.i (*0-8037-0668-5*, Dial Bks. for Young Readers) Penguin Putnam Bks. for Young Readers.

—The Knight Who Was Afraid of the Dark. 1989. (J). 12.14 (*0-606-01710-0*) Turtleback Bks.

—The Knight Who Was Afraid to Fight. 1994. 32p. (YA). 14.89 o.p. (*0-8037-1592-7*); (Illus.). (J). 14.99 o.p. (*0-8037-1591-9*) Penguin Putnam Bks. for Young Readers. (Dial Bks. for Young Readers).

Hildick, E. W. The Case of the Dragon in Distress. 1991. (McGurk Mystery Ser.). 160p. (J). (gr. 4-7). 13.95 o.p. (*0-02-743931-3*, Simon & Schuster Children's Publishing) Simon & Schuster Children's Publishing.

Hodges, Margaret. Saint George & the Dragon: A Golden Legend. 1984. 12.85 (*0-606-04790-5*) Turtleback Bks.

Hoffman, Mary. Women of Camelot: Queens & Enchantresses at the Court of King Arthur. 2000. (Illus.). 72p. (J). 19.95 (*0-7892-0646-3*) Abbeville Pr., Inc.

Hughes, Robert Don. Gabriel's Trumpet. 1993. (Orig.). (J). pap. 6.99 o.p. (*0-8054-6059-4*) Broadman & Holman Pubs.

Hunter, Mollie. Day of the Unicorn. 1994. (Illus.). 64p. (J). (gr. 2-5). lib. bdg. 13.89 o.p. (*0-06-021063-X*) HarperCollins Pubs.

—Day of the Unicorn. 1994. (Illus.). 96p. (J). (gr. 2-5). 14.00 o.p. (*0-06-021062-1*) HarperTrade.

—Knight of the Golden Plain. 1983. (Charlotte Zolotow Bk.). (Illus.). 48p. (J). (gr. k-4). 12.95 o.p. (*0-06-022685-4*); lib. bdg. 12.89 o.p. (*0-06-022686-2*) HarperCollins Children's Bk. Group.

Jinks, Catherine. Pagan's Crusade. 2003. (Illus.). 256p. (J). 15.99 (*0-7636-2019-X*) Candlewick Pr.

Johnson, Annie F. Two Little Knights of Kentucky: The Little Colonel's Neighbors. 2004. (Little Colonel Ser.). (Illus.). 192p. (J). (gr. 4-7). reprint ed. pap. 9.95 (*1-55709-316-4*) Applewood Bks.

Klein-Gousseff, Catherine. The Perfect Knight. Negrin, Fabian, tr. from FRE. & illus. by. 2004. (J). (*0-89236-739-3*) Getty Pubns.

Koller, Jackie French. Horace the Horrible: A Knight Meets His Match. 2003. (J). 16.95 (*0-7614-5150-1*, Cavendish Children's Bks.) Cavendish, Marshall Corp.

Lasker, Joe. Tournament of Knights. 1986. (Illus.). 32p. (J). (gr. 3 up). 12.95 o.p. (*0-690-04541-7*); lib. bdg. 14.89 o.p. (*0-690-04542-5*) HarperCollins Children's Bk. Group.

Lister, Robin. The Story of King Arthur. 1996. (Kingfisher Classics Ser.). (Illus.). 96p. (J). (gr. 4 up). pap. 15.95 (*0-7534-5101-8*, Kingfisher) Houghton Mifflin Co. Trade & Reference Div.

Lively, Penelope. The Whispering Knights. l.t. ed. 1990. 248p. (J). (gr. 3 up). 16.95 o.p. (*0-7451-1153-X*, Galaxy Children's Large Print) BBC Audiobooks America.

Lofgren, Ulf. Alvin the Knight. 1992. (J). (ps-3). lib. bdg. 19.95 o.p. (*0-87614-698-1*) Lerner Publishing Group.

Madinaveitia, Horacio. Sir Robert's Little Outing. 1991. (Illus.). 32p. (J). (gr. k-4). pap. text 7.95 (*1-879567-00-8*); lib. bdg. 13.95 (*1-879567-01-6*) Wonder Well Pubs. (Valeria Bks.).

Maidment, Stella. A Brave Knight to the Rescue! 1998. (Gamebook Ser.). (Illus.). 32p. (J). (gr. k-3). bds. 5.99 o.p. (*0-7636-0325-2*) Candlewick Pr.

Marchesi, Stephen, illus. Don Quixote & Sancho Panza. 1992. 80p. (YA). (gr. 6 up). 16.95 (*0-684-19235-7*, Atheneum) Simon & Schuster Children's Publishing.

Matthews, John. The Barefoot Book of Knights. 2002. (Illus.). 80p. (J). (gr. 4-7). 19.99 (*1-84148-064-9*) Barefoot Bks., Inc.

Mayer, Marianna. Ivanhoe. 2003. (Illus.). 48p. (J). 16.95 (*1-58717-248-8*); lib. bdg. 17.50 (*1-58717-249-6*) SeaStar Bks.

Mayer, Mercer. Herbert the Timid Dragon. 1991. (Golden Star Reader Ser.: Level 3). (J). (gr. 1-3). pap. 3.25 o.s.i (*0-307-11463-5*, Golden Bks.) Random Hse. Children's Bks.

—Whinnie the Lovesick Dragon. 1986. (Illus.). 32p. (J). (gr. k-3). lib. bdg. 14.95 (*0-02-765180-0*, Simon & Schuster Children's Publishing) Simon & Schuster Children's Publishing.

McCafferty, Catherine. Quest for Camelot. 1998. (J). (*0-7853-2383-X*) Publications International, Ltd.

McMullan, K. H. Knight for a Day. 1999. (Dragon Slayers' Academy Ser.: No. 5). (Illus.). 96p. (J). (gr. 2-5). 3.99 o.s.i (*0-448-41974-2*, Grosset & Dunlap);Vol. 5. 13.89 o.p. (*0-448-42045-7*) Penguin Putnam Bks. for Young Readers.

—Sir Lancelot, Where Are You? 1999. (Dragon Slayers' Academy Ser.: No. 6). (Illus.). 91p. (J). (gr. 2-5). 3.99 o.p. (*0-448-41979-3*, Grosset & Dunlap);Vol. 6. 13.89 o.p. (*0-448-42046-5*) Penguin Putnam Bks. for Young Readers.

McMullan, Kate. Knight for a Day. 2003. (Dragon Slayers' Academy Ser.). (Illus.). 112p. mass mkt. 4.99 (*0-448-43277-3*, Grosset & Dunlap) Penguin Putnam Bks. for Young Readers.

—Sir Lancelot, Where Are You? 2003. (Dragon Slayers' Academy Ser.). (Illus.). 112p. mass mkt. 4.99 (*0-448-43278-1*, Grosset & Dunlap) Penguin Putnam Bks. for Young Readers.

Mitchell, Mark. The Curious Knighthood of Sir Pellimore. Kemnitz, Myrna, ed. 1996. (Chronicles of the House of Chax Ser.: Bk. 1). 62p. (J). (gr. 3-6). pap. 9.99 (*0-88092-139-0*, 1390) Royal Fireworks Publishing Co.

Mitgutsch, Ali. A Knight's Book. Crawford, Elizabeth D., tr. 1991. (Illus.). 40p. (J). (gr. 2-5). 16.95 o.p. (*0-395-58103-6*, Clarion Bks.) Houghton Mifflin Co. Trade & Reference Div.

Mitter, Matt & Reader's Digest Editors. Brave Knights to the Rescue. 1998. (Fisher-Price Great Adventures Lift-The-Flap Playbooks Ser.). (Illus.). 10p. (J). (ps-3). bds. 7.99 o.p. (*1-57584-219-X*, Reader's Digest Children's Bks.) Reader's Digest Children's Publishing, Inc.

Moore, Margaret. The Maiden & Her Knight. 2001. 384p. mass mkt. 5.99 (*0-380-81336-X*, Avon Bks.) Morrow/Avon.

Morpurgo, Michael. Arthur, High King of Britain. 1995. (Illus.). 144p. (YA). (gr. 4-7). 22.00 (*0-15-200080-1*) Harcourt Children's Bks.

Morris, Gerald. The Ballad of Sir Dinadan. 2003. 256p. (J). (gr. 5-9). tchr. ed. 15.00 (*0-618-19099-6*) Houghton Mifflin Co.

—The Savage Damsel & the Dwarf. 224p. (gr. 5-9). 2004. (YA). pap. 5.95 (*0-618-19681-1*); 2000. (J). tchr. ed. 16.00 (*0-395-97126-8*) Houghton Mifflin Co.

—The Savage Damsel & the Dwarf. l.t. ed. 2001. (Illus.). 248p. (J). 22.95 (*0-7862-3037-1*) Thorndike Pr.

—The Savage Damsel & the Dwarf. 2000. E-Book 15.00 (*0-585-36843-0*) netLibrary, Inc.

—The Squire & His Knight. l.t. ed. 2001. (Young Adult Ser.). (Illus.). 257p. (J). (gr. 4-7). 21.95 (*0-7862-3039-8*) Thorndike Pr.

—The Squire, His Knight & His Lady. 2001. (Illus.). (J). 11.04 (*0-606-21454-2*) Turtleback Bks.

—The Squire, His Knight, & His Lady. 1999. 232p. (J). (gr. 5-9). tchr. ed. 15.00 (*0-395-91211-3*) Houghton Mifflin Co.

—The Squire, His Knight & His Lady. 2001. 240p. (YA). (gr. 7 up). reprint ed. mass mkt. 4.99 o.s.i (*0-440-22885-9*, Laurel Leaf) Random Hse. Children's Bks.

—The Squire's Tale. 1998. 224p. (J). (gr. 5-9). tchr. ed. 15.00 (*0-395-86959-5*) Houghton Mifflin Co.

—The Squire's Tale. 2000. (Sister Frevisse Medieval Mysteries Ser.). (Illus.). 224p. (YA). (gr. 5 up). mass mkt. 4.99 (*0-440-22823-9*, Laurel Leaf) Random Hse. Children's Bks.

—The Squire's Tale. l.t. ed. 2000. (Young Adult Ser.). (Illus.). 213p. (J). 19.95 (*0-7862-3038-X*) Thorndike Pr.

Murdocca, Sal. The Hero of Hamblett. 1980. (Illus.). 48p. (J). (gr. 3 up). pap. 4.95 o.s.i (*0-440-04457-X*); lib. bdg. 8.44 o.s.i (*0-440-04458-8*) Dell Publishing. (Delacorte Pr.).

Murphy, Jill. Jeffrey Strangeways. (Illus.). 144p. (J). (gr. 3-6). 1994. bds. 4.50 o.p. (*1-56402-283-8*); 1992. 14.95 o.p. (*1-56402-018-5*) Candlewick Pr.

—Jeffrey Strangeways. 1994. (J). 9.60 o.p. (*0-606-05891-5*) Turtleback Bks.

Nash, Ogden. Custard the Dragon & the Wicked Knight. (J). 2003. bds. 6.95 (*0-316-59760-0*); 1999. (Illus.). 32p. pap. 5.95 (*0-316-59905-0*); 1996. (Illus.). 32p. 14.95 o.p. (*0-316-59882-8*) Little Brown & Co.

—Custard the Dragon & the Wicked Knight. 1999. (J). (gr. k up). pap., stu. ed. 25.20 incl. audio (*0-7887-2986-1*, 40868);Class set. pap. 91.30 incl. audio (*0-7887-3016-9*, 46833) Recorded Bks., LLC.

Newman, Robert. Merlin's Mistake. 2001. (Lost Treasures Ser.: No. 5). (Illus.). 352p. (J). pap. 4.99 (*0-7868-1546-9*); (gr. 3-7). pap. 1.99 (*0-7868-1545-0*) Hyperion Bks. for Children. (Volo).

—Merlin's Mistake. 1990. (Illus.). (J). (gr. 5-9). 18.75 (*0-8446-6187-2*) Smith, Peter Pub., Inc.

Noonan, Janet & Calvert, Jacquelyn. A Crown for Sir Conrad. 1992. 32p. (J). 8.99 o.p. (*0-7814-0317-0*) Cook Communications Ministries.

Oakeshott, R. Ewart. A Knight & His Castle. 2nd ed. 1997. (Illus.). 128p. (J). (gr. 5-12). pap. 12.95 (*0-8023-1294-2*) Dufour Editions, Inc.

O'Brien, Patrick. The Making of a Knight: How Sir James Earned His Armor. 1998. (Illus.). 32p. (J). (gr. 1-4). 15.95 (*0-88106-354-1*) Charlesbridge Publishing, Inc.

Osborne, Mary Pope. El Caballero del Alba. 2003. (SPA.). (J). pap. 4.95 (*1-930332-50-5*) Lectorum Pubns., Inc.

—The Knight at Dawn. unabr. ed. 2001. (Magic Tree House Ser. : No. 2). 66p. (J). (gr. k-4). pap. 17.00 incl. audio (*0-8072-0331-9*, Listening Library) Random Hse. Audio Publishing Group.

—The Knight at Dawn. 1993. (Magic Tree House Ser.: No. 2). (Illus.). 80p. (gr. k-3). lib. bdg. 11.99 (*0-679-92412-4*); (J). pap. 3.99 (*0-679-82412-X*) Random Hse. Children's Bks. (Random Hse. Bks. for Young Readers).

—The Knight at Dawn. 1993. (Magic Tree House Ser.: No. 2). (Illus.). (J). (gr. k-3). 10.14 (*0-606-09518-7*) Turtleback Bks.

Palacios, Argentina. The Adventures of Don Quixote de la Mancha. 1999. (Children's Thrift Classics Ser.). (Illus.). 80p. (J). pap. text 1.00 (*0-486-40791-8*) Dover Pubns., Inc.

—The Knight & the Squire. 1979. (Illus.). (gr. 4-5). 7.95 o.p. (*0-385-12433-3*); lib. bdg. o.p. (*0-385-12434-1*) Doubleday Publishing.

Paterson, Katherine, retold by. Parzival: The Quest of the Grail Knight. 1998. 144p. (J). (gr. 5-9). 15.99 o.s.i (*0-525-67579-5*, Dutton Children's Bks.) Penguin Putnam Bks. for Young Readers.

Peet, Bill. Cowardly Clyde. 1999. (Illus.). (J). (ps-3). pap. 15.65 (*0-8085-3560-9*) Econo-Clad Bks.

—Cowardly Clyde. (Illus.). 48p. (J). (ps-3). 1984. pap. 8.95 (*0-395-36171-0*); 1979. 14.95 o.p. (*0-395-27802-3*) Houghton Mifflin Co.

—Cowardly Clyde. 1979. (J). 14.10 (*0-606-03196-0*) Turtleback Bks.

Pierce, Tamora. Alanna. 2002. 240p. (YA). 10.95 (*0-689-85323-8*, Atheneum) Simon & Schuster Children's Publishing.

—First Test. l.t. ed. 2002. 261p. (J). 23.95 (*0-7862-3632-9*) Gale Group.

—First Test. (Protector of the Small Ser.: Vol. 1). (Illus.). (gr. 5-9). 2000. 256p. pap. 5.99 (*0-679-88917-5*); 1. 1999. 224p. (J). 16.00 (*0-679-88914-0*) Random Hse. Children's Bks. (Random Hse. Bks. for Young Readers).

—In the Hand of the Goddess. 1990. (Song of the Lioness Ser.: Vol. 2). 240p. (gr. 4-7). reprint ed. mass mkt. 5.50 (*0-679-80111-1*, Random Hse. Bks. for Young Readers) Random Hse. Children's Bks.

—In the Hand of the Goddess: Song of the Lioness, Bk. Two. 1984. 240p. (YA). (gr. 7 up). lib. bdg. 16.95 o.s.i (*0-689-31054-4*, Atheneum) Simon & Schuster Children's Publishing.

—Page. (Protector of the Small Ser.: No. 2). (gr. 5-9). 2000. 272p. text 16.00 (*0-679-88915-9*); 2000. (Illus.). 272p. lib. bdg. 17.99 (*0-679-98915-3*); Bk. 2. 2001. 288p. (YA). pap. 5.99 (*0-679-88918-3*) Random Hse. Children's Bks. (Random Hse. Bks. for Young Readers).

—Page: Protector of the Small. l.t. ed. 2002. 321p. (J). 23.95 (*0-7862-3631-0*) Gale Group.

—Squire: Companion. 2002. 432p. (YA). (gr. 7). pap. 5.99 (*0-679-88919-1*, Random Hse. Bks. for Young Readers) Random Hse. Children's Bks.

—Squire: Protector of the Small, Bk. 3. 2001. (Protector of the Small Ser.: Vol. 3). (Illus.). 416p. (gr. 5-8). (J). lib. bdg. 17.99 (*0-679-98916-1*); text 15.95 (*0-679-88916-7*) Random Hse. Children's Bks. (Random Hse. Bks. for Young Readers).

—Squire: Protector of the Small. l.t. ed. 2002. 526p. (J). 23.95 (*0-7862-3630-2*) Thorndike Pr.

—The Woman Who Rides Like a Man: Song of the Lioness, Book Three. 1986. 288p. (YA). (gr. 7 up). lib. bdg. 16.95 o.s.i (*0-689-31117-6*, Atheneum) Simon & Schuster Children's Publishing.

Preiss, Byron & Gasperini, Jim. Secret of the Knights. 1984. (Time Machine Ser.: No. 1). (Illus.). 144p. (J). (gr. 4 up). mass mkt. 2.25 o.s.i (*0-553-25368-9*) Bantam Bks.

Pyle, Howard. King Arthur & the Knights of the Round Table. Hanft, Joshua, ed. 1993. (Great Illustrated Classics Ser.: Vol. 31). (Illus.). 240p. (J). (gr. 3-6). 9.95 (*0-86611-982-5*) Playmore, Inc., Pubs.

—Men of Iron. 1965. (Airmont Classics Ser.). (Illus.). (J). (gr. 6 up). mass mkt. 3.50 (*0-8049-0093-0*, CL-93) Airmont Publishing Co., Inc.

—Men of Iron. 2003. (General Juvenile Ser.). 224p. (J). pap. 8.95 (*0-486-42841-9*) Dover Pubns., Inc.

—Men of Iron. (J). E-Book 2.49 (*1-58627-667-0*) Electric Umbrella Publishing.

—Men of Iron. (Illus.). (J). (gr. 5 up). 8.95 o.p. (*0-06-024800-9*); lib. bdg. 10.89 o.p. (*0-06-024801-7*) HarperCollins Pubs.

—Men of Iron. 1993. 220p. (YA). (gr. 7 up). pap. 6.49 (*0-89084-694-4*, 070466) Jones, Bob Univ. Pr.

—Men of Iron. 1965. (Illus.). (J). 10.00 (*0-606-17899-6*) Turtleback Bks.

—The Story of King Arthur & His Knights. 1986. (Signet Classics Ser.). (J). 12.00 (*0-606-01952-9*) Turtleback Bks.

Rescue of Sir Clyde the Clumsy. 1991. (J). pap. 1.97 (*1-56297-114-X*) Lee Pubns.

Robins, Deri & Robins, Jim. Stone in the Sword: The Quest for the Missing Emerald. 1998. (Gamebook Ser.). (Illus.). 32p. (J). (gr. 2-5). 12.99 o.p. (*0-7636-0313-9*) Candlewick Pr.

Ron, Kare. The Adventures of Sir Noodlefish: The Cake Wars. 2000. (Illus.). 32p. (J). (gr. 1-3). pap. (*1-931179-00-X*) Long Hill Productions, Inc.

Rutland, Jonathan & All-About Books Staff. Knights & Castles. 1987. (All about Bks.). (Illus.). 24p. (J). (gr. 2-5). 5.99 o.s.i (*0-394-98973-2*); 2.95 o.s.i (*0-394-88973-8*) Random Hse. Children's Bks. (Random Hse. Bks. for Young Readers).

Ryan, John. A Bad Year for Dragons: The Legend of Saint George. 1989. (Illus.). 28p. (J). (gr. k-4). 8.95 o.p. (*0-8192-1512-0*) Morehouse Publishing.

Sabuda, Robert. The Knight's Castle: A Pop-Up Book. 1994. (Illus.). 12p. (J). o.p. (*0-307-17626-6*, Golden Bks.) Random Hse. Children's Bks.

San Souci, Robert D. Young Lancelot. 1998. (Illus.). 32p. (gr. 1-5). pap. text 6.99 o.s.i (*0-440-41459-8*, Yearling) Random Hse. Children's Bks.

—Young Lancelot. 1998. (J). 13.14 (*0-606-13937-0*) Turtleback Bks.

Schurch, Maylan. The Sword of Denis Anwyck. 1992. (J). pap. 7.99 o.p. (*0-8280-0658-X*) Review & Herald Publishing Assn.

Scieszka, Jon. Kight of the Kitchen Table Twt Promo. 2003. (Time Warp Trio Ser.). (Illus.). 76p. pap. 2.66 (*0-14-250130-1*, Puffin Bks.) Penguin Putnam Bks. for Young Readers.

—Knights of the Kitchen Table. (Illus.). 64p. (J). 2004. (Time Warp Trio Ser.: Bk. 1). pap. 4.99 (*0-14-240043-2*, Puffin Bks.); 1993. (Time Warp Trio Ser.). (gr. 4-7). pap. 4.99 (*0-14-034603-1*); 1991. (Time Warp Trio Ser.). (gr. 4-7). 14.99 (*0-670-83622-2*, Viking Children's Bks.) Penguin Putnam Bks. for Young Readers.

—Knights of the Kitchen Table. (Time Warp Trio Ser.). 55p. (J). (gr. 2-4). pap. 3.99 (*0-8072-1301-2*); 1998. (gr. 3-5). pap. 17.00 incl. audio (*0-8072-0391-2*, FTR193SP) Random Hse. Audio Publishing Group. (Listening Library).

—Knights of the Kitchen Table. 1993. (Time Warp Trio Ser.). (J). 11.14 (*0-606-05399-9*) Turtleback Bks.

Scott, Dennis. Sir Gawain & the Green Knight. 1978. (J). (gr. k up). 7.00 (*0-87602-202-6*) Anchorage Pr.

Scott, Walter, Sr. Ivanhoe. 2002. (Great Illustrated Classics). (Illus.). 240p. (J). (gr. 3-8). lib. bdg. 21.35 (*1-57765-811-6*, ABDO & Daughters) ABDO Publishing Co.

—Ivanhoe. (SPA., Illus.). 176p. (YA). 14.95 (*84-7281-096-8*, AF1096) Auriga, Ediciones S.A. ESP. *Dist:* Continental Bk. Co., Inc.

—Ivanhoe. 1991. (Wishbone Classics Ser.: No. 12). (J). (gr. 3-7). 13.00 (*0-606-17587-3*) Turtleback Bks.

Sharoff, Victor. The Heart of the Wood. 1972. (Break-of-Day Bks.). (Illus.). (J). (gr. k-3). 4.69 o.p. (*0-698-30187-0*) Putnam Publishing Group, The.

Siegel, Scott. Revenge of the Falcon Knight. 1985. (Wizards, Warriors & You Ser.: Bk. 6). 112p. (J). (gr. 4 up). pap. 2.25 o.p. (*0-380-89524-2*, Avon Bks.) Morrow/Avon.

Smith, Linda. Sir Cassie to the Rescue. Patkau, Karen, tr. & illus. by. 2003. 32p. (J). (ps-3). 16.95 (*1-55143-243-9*) Orca Bk. Pubs.

Springer, Nancy. I Am Mordred: A Tale from Camelot. 1998. 184p. (YA). (gr. 7-12). 16.99 (*0-399-23143-9*, Philomel) Penguin Putnam Bks. for Young Readers.

—I Am Morgan Le Fay: A Tale from Camelot. 2001. ix, 227p. (J). (gr. 7 up). 17.99 (*0-399-23451-9*, Philomel) Penguin Putnam Bks. for Young Readers.

—I Am Morgan le Fay: A Tale from Camelot. 2002. (Firebird Ser.). 240p. (J). pap. 5.99 (*0-698-11974-6*, Firebird) Penguin Putnam Bks. for Young Readers.

Storr, Catherine. Sword & the Stone. 1993. (Legends & Folktales Ser.). (J). (ps-3). pap. 4.95 o.p. (*0-8114-7147-0*) Raintree Pubs.

Sutcliff, Rosemary. The Sword & the Circle: King Arthur & the Knights of the Round Table. 1981. 26p. (J). (gr. 4-7). 14.99 o.s.i (*0-525-40585-2*, Dutton Children's Bks.) Penguin Putnam Bks. for Young Readers.

Talbott, Hudson. The Sword in the Stone. 1991. (Books of Wonder). (Illus.). 56p. (J). (gr. 5 up). lib. bdg. 16.89 o.s.i (*0-688-09404-X*, Morrow, William & Co.) Morrow/Avon.

—Tales of King Arthur: The Sword in the Stone. 1991. (Books of Wonder). (Illus.). 48p. (J). (gr. k-3). 18.95 (*0-688-09403-1*) HarperCollins Children's Bk. Group.

Thomas, Shelley Moore. Get Well, Good Knight. (Illus.). 48p. (J). 2004. pap. 3.99 (*0-14-240050-5*, Puffin Bks.); 2002. 13.99 (*0-525-46914-1*, Dutton Children's Bks.) Penguin Putnam Bks. for Young Readers.

—Good Night, Good Knight. 2002. 11.49 (*1-4046-1571-7*) Book Wholesalers, Inc.

—Good Night, Good Knight. 2002. (Easy-to-Read Ser.). (Illus.). 48p. (J). pap. 3.99 (*0-14-230201-5*, Puffin Bks.) Penguin Putnam Bks. for Young Readers.

—Happy Birthday, Good Knight. 2004. (Illus.). 48p. 13.99 (*0-525-47184-7*, Dutton Children's Bks.) Penguin Putnam Bks. for Young Readers.

Thomas, Shelley Moore & Plecas, Jennifer. Good Night, Good Knight. 2000. (Illus.). 48p. (J). (ps-2). 13.99 (*0-525-46326-7*, Dutton) Penguin Putnam Bks. for Young Readers.

Tolhurst, Marilyn. Knights Treasure Chest: The Age of Adventure, to Unlock & Discover. 2001. (Treasure Chest Ser.). (Illus.). 32p. (J). (gr. 4-7). pap. text 19.95 (*1-56138-545-X*) Running Pr. Bk. Pubs.

Tolkien, J. R. R. Sir Gawain & the Green Knight, Pearl & Sir Orfeo. 1975. (J). 13.04 (*0-606-00575-7*) Turtleback Bks.

Tompert, Ann. The Errant Knight. 2003. (Illus.). 32p. (J). 15.95 (*0-9701907-6-X*) Illumination Arts Publishing Co., Inc.

Twain, Mark. A Connecticut Yankee in King Arthur's Court. 1997. (Classics Illustrated Study Guides). (Illus.). 64p. (YA). (gr. 7 up). mass mkt., stu. ed. 4.99 o.p. (*1-57840-016-3*) Acclaim Bks.

—A Connecticut Yankee in King Arthur's Court. 1964. (Airmont Classics Ser.). (J). (gr. 5 up). mass mkt. 3.25 (*0-8049-0029-9*, CL-29) Airmont Publishing Co., Inc.

—A Connecticut Yankee in King Arthur's Court. 1999. (YA). reprint ed. pap. text 28.00 (*1-4047-1121-X*) Classic Textbooks.

—A Connecticut Yankee in King Arthur's Court. 1991. 333p. (gr. 4-7). mass mkt. 3.99 (*0-8125-0436-4*, Tor Classics) Doherty, Tom Assocs., LLC.

—A Connecticut Yankee in King Arthur's Court. 1988. (Books of Wonder). (Illus.). 384p. (J). (ps-3). 24.99 (*0-688-06346-2*) HarperCollins Children's Bk. Group.

—A Connecticut Yankee in King Arthur's Court. deluxe ltd. ed. 1988. (Books of Wonder). (Illus.). 384p. (YA). (gr. 5 up). 100.00 o.p. (*0-688-08258-0*, Morrow, William & Co.) Morrow/Avon.

—A Connecticut Yankee in King Arthur's Court. 1963. (Signet Classics). 336p. (YA). mass mkt. 4.95 (*0-451-52475-6*, Signet Classics) NAL.

—A Connecticut Yankee in King Arthur's Court. Fago, John N., ed. abr. ed. 1977. (Now Age Illustrated III Ser.). (Illus.). (gr. 4-12). (J). pap. text 2.95 (*0-88301-263-4*); (YA). text 7.50 o.p. (*0-88301-275-8*) Pendulum Pr., Inc.

Weber, Bruce. The Quest for Camelot: The Search for Excalibur. rev. ed. 1979. (Quest for Camelot Ser.). (Illus.). 32p. (J). (gr. k-3). mass mkt. 3.50 (*0-590-12064-6*) Scholastic, Inc.

Wein, Elizabeth. Winter Prince. 2003. (Firebird Ser.). (Illus.). 224p. (YA). pap. 6.99 (*0-14-250014-3*, Puffin Bks.) Penguin Putnam Bks. for Young Readers.

White, T. H. The Sword in the Stone. 1978. 288p. (YA). (gr. 5-12). mass mkt. 5.99 (*0-440-98445-9*, Laurel) Dell Publishing.

—The Sword in the Stone. (Illus.). 1993. 256p. (J). (gr. 2 up). 22.99 (*0-399-22502-1*, Philomel); 1972. 11.95 o.s.i (*0-399-10783-5*, G. P. Putnam's Sons) Penguin Putnam Bks. for Young Readers.

—The Sword in the Stone. 1963. 11.55 (*0-606-05065-5*) Turtleback Bks.

Williams, Marcia, illus. & retold by. Don Quixote. 1995. (J). (gr. 2 up). bds. 5.99 o.p. (*1-56402-070-3*) Candlewick Pr.

Winthrop, Elizabeth. The Battle for the Castle. 1994. 224p. (J). (gr. 4-7). pap. text 5.50 (*0-440-40942-X*) Dell Publishing.

—The Battle for the Castle. 1993. 160p. (J). (gr. 4-7). tchr. ed. 15.95 (*0-8234-1010-2*) Holiday Hse., Inc.

—The Battle for the Castle. 1994. (J). pap. o.s.i (*0-440-82255-6*, Dell Books for Young Readers) Random Hse. Children's Bks.

—The Battle for the Castle. 1994. (J). 11.55 (*0-606-06928-3*) Turtleback Bks.

—The Castle in the Attic. 1985. (Illus.). 192p. (J). (gr. 4-7). tchr. ed. 16.95 (*0-8234-0579-6*) Holiday Hse., Inc.

Winthrop, Elizabeth, ed. The Battle for the Castle. unabr. ed. 1997. 211p. (J). (gr. 3-5). pap. 35.00 incl. audio (*0-8072-7794-0*, YA9195P, Listening Library) Random Hse. Audio Publishing Group.

Yolen, Jane. Sword of the Rightful King: A Novel of King Arthur. 2003. (Illus.). 368p. (J). 17.00 (*0-15-202527-8*) Harcourt Children's Bks.

L

LAWYERS—FICTION

Brown, Drollene p. Belva Lockwood Wins Her Case. Levine, Abby, ed. 1987. (Albert Whitman Biography Ser.). (Illus.). 48p. (J). (gr. 4-7). lib. bdg. 13.95 (*0-8075-0630-3*) Whitman, Albert & Co.

Holder, Nancy & Mariotte, Jeff. Endangered Species. 2002. (Angel Ser.). 384p. (YA). 17.95 (*0-7434-2782-3*, Simon Pulse) Simon & Schuster Children's Publishing.

Killien, Christi. Artie's Brief: The Whole Truth & Nothing But. 1990. 112p. (J). pap. 2.95 (*0-380-71108-7*, Avon Bks.) Morrow/Avon.

Lazewnik, Libby. Baker's Dozen: Baker's Best. 1996. 150p. (J). (gr. 4-8). pap. 9.95 o.p. (*1-56871-107-7*) Targum Pr., Inc.

Vaughan, Bridget & Moore, Larry. Grand Jury Connections. 2001. 264p. (YA). pap. 14.95 (*0-9678436-0-X*) Gayle Publishing Co.

Zemach, Harve. Judge: An Untrue Tale. 1988. (J). 13.10 (*0-606-04455-8*) Turtleback Bks.

LIBRARIANS—FICTION

Barr, Terri. Lillian: The Librarain. 1999. (Illus.). 16p. (J). (ps-2). pap. 3.75 (*1-880612-86-0*) Seedling Pubns., Inc.

Bellairs, John. The Dark Secret of Weatherend. 1986. 192p. (J). pap. 3.50 o.s.i (*0-553-15621-7*) Bantam Bks.

—The Dark Secret of Weatherend. (Anthony Monday Mystery Ser.). 1997. 192p. (J). (gr. 3-7). pap. 3.99 o.p. (*0-14-038006-X*); 1984. (Illus.). 208p. (YA). (gr. 5 up). 13.89 o.p. (*0-8037-0074-1*, Dial Bks. for Young Readers); 1984. (Illus.). 208p. (YA). (gr. 5 up). 13.95 o.p. (*0-8037-0072-5*, Dial Bks. for Young Readers) Penguin Putnam Bks. for Young Readers.

—The Dark Secret of Weatherend. 1986. 192p. (J). pap. 2.50 o.s.i (*0-553-15375-7*, Skylark) Random Hse. Children's Bks.

—The Dark Secret of Weatherend. 1997. (Anthony Monday Mystery Ser.). 9.09 (*0-606-11238-3*) Turtleback Bks.

Bloor, Thomas. The Memory Prisoner. 2001. (Illus.). 144p. (J). (gr. 5-7). 15.99 (*0-8037-2687-2*, Dial Bks. for Young Readers) Penguin Putnam Bks. for Young Readers.

Dadey, Debbie. Wizards Don't Need Computers. 1996. (Adventures of the Bailey School Kids Ser.: No. 20). (Illus.). 63p. (J). (gr. 2-4). mass mkt. 3.99 (*0-590-50962-4*) Scholastic, Inc.

Deedy, Carmen Agra. The Library Dragon. 1994. (Illus.). 32p. (J). (gr. 4-7). 16.95 (*1-56145-091-X*) Peachtree Pubs., Ltd.

Ernst, Lisa Campbell. Stella Louella's Runaway Book. (Illus.). 40p. (J). 2001. pap. 6.99 (*0-689-84460-3*, Aladdin); 1998. 16.00 (*0-689-81883-1*, Simon & Schuster Children's Publishing) Simon & Schuster Children's Publishing.

Friesinger, Alison. Eaglewood: Save the Manatee. 1998. (Eaglewood Ser.: Vol. 3). (J). (gr. 4-7). 11.99 o.s.i (*0-679-99040-2*, Random Hse. Bks. for Young Readers) Random Hse. Children's Bks.

—Friends in Deed: Save the Manatee. 1998. (Stepping Stone Bks.). (Illus.). 80p. (J). pap. 3.99 o.s.i (*0-679-89040-8*) Random Hse., Inc.

Furtado, Jo. Sorry, Miss Folio! 1988. (Illus.). 32p. (J). (ps-3). 10.95 o.p. (*0-916291-18-9*) Kane/Miller Bk. Pubs.

Lakin, Patricia. Information, Please. 1995. (My Community Ser.). (Illus.). 32p. (J). (ps-4). lib. bdg. 21.40 o.p. (*0-8114-8260-X*) Raintree Pubs.

Mahy, Margaret. Great Piratical Rumbustification & the Librarian & the Robbers. 1986. (Illus.). 32p. (J). 11.95 o.s.i (*0-87923-629-9*) Godine, David R. Pub.

Mann, Pamela. The Frog Princess? (J). 2002. (ENG & TUR.). 15.95 (*1-85269-324-X*); 2000. (ENG & PAN.). 17.95 (*1-85269-323-1*); 2000. (BEN & ENG.). 19.95 (*1-85269-317-7*); 2000. (ENG & SOM.). 15.95 (*1-85269-319-3*); 2000. (ENG & URD.). 17.95 (*1-85269-321-5*); 2000. (ENG & GUJ., Illus.). 25p. 19.95 (*1-85269-322-3*) Mantra Publishing, Ltd. GBR. *Dist:* AIMS International Bks., Inc.

—The Frog Princess? 1995. (Illus.). 32p. (J). (gr. 2 up). lib. bdg. 19.93 o.p. (*0-8368-1352-9*) Stevens, Gareth Inc.

Mora, Pat. Tomas & the Library Lady. 1997. (Illus.). 40p. (J). (ps-3). 17.00 (*0-679-80401-3*) Random Hse., Inc.

Pascal, Francine. R for Revenge. 1997. (Sweet Valley High Super Thriller Ser.). (YA). (gr. 7 up). 10.55 (*0-606-14340-8*) Turtleback Bks.

Pascal, Francine, creator. R for Revenge. 1997. (Sweet Valley High Super Thriller Ser.). 240p. (gr. 7 up). mass mkt. 4.50 o.s.i (*0-553-57072-2*, Dell Books for Young Readers) Random Hse. Children's Bks.

Pinkwater, Daniel M. Aunt Lulu. (Illus.). 32p. (J). (gr. k-3). 1988. 13.95 o.p. (*0-02-774661-5*, Atheneum); 1991. reprint ed. pap. 3.95 o.s.i (*0-689-71413-0*, Aladdin) Simon & Schuster Children's Publishing.

Robinson, Nancy K. Countess Veronica. (J). 1996. pap. text 3.50 (*0-590-44486-7*); 1994. 176p. (gr. 4-6). pap. 13.95 (*0-590-44485-9*) Scholastic, Inc.

—Countess Veronica. 1994. (J). 8.60 o.p. (*0-606-09163-7*) Turtleback Bks.

Rockwell, Norman. Willie Was Different. 1994. (Illus.). 32p. (J). (gr. 1-5). 16.95 (*0-936399-61-9*, Berkshire Hse.) Countryman Pr.

—Willie Was Different. 1997. (Illus.). 27p. (J). pap. 5.99 o.s.i (*0-679-88262-6*) McKay, David Co., Inc.

—Willie Was Different. 1997. 12.14 (*0-606-12101-3*) Turtleback Bks.

Stadler, Alexander. Beverly Billingsly Borrows a Book. 2002. (Illus.). 32p. (J). (ps-2). 16.00 (*0-15-202510-3*, Silver Whistle) Harcourt Children's Bks.

—Beverly Billingsly Can't Catch. 2004. (Illus.). 32p. (J). 16.00 (*0-15-204906-1*) Harcourt Trade Pubs.

Stine, Megan. The Girl Who Cried Monster. 1996. (Goosebumps Presents Ser.: No. 1). 57p. (J). (gr. 3-7). 9.19 o.p. (*0-606-08753-2*) Turtleback Bks.

Stine, R. L. The Girl Who Cried Monster. 1993. (Goosebumps Ser.: No. 8). 160p. (J). (gr. 3-7). mass mkt. 3.99 (*0-590-46618-6*) Scholastic, Inc.

—The Girl Who Cried Monster. l.t. ed. 1997. (Goosebumps Ser.: No. 8). 144p. (J). (gr. 3-7). lib. bdg. 21.27 o.p. (*0-8368-1980-2*) Stevens, Gareth Inc.

—The Girl Who Cried Monster. 1993. (Goosebumps Ser.: No. 8). (J). (gr. 3-7). 10.04 (*0-606-05318-2*) Turtleback Bks.

Thaler, Mike. Cannon the Librarian. 1993. (Illus.). 32p. (Orig.). (J). pap. 3.50 (*0-380-76964-6*, Avon Bks.) Morrow/Avon.

—The Librarian from the Black Lagoon. 1997. (Black Lagoon Ser.). 32p. (J). (ps-3). mass mkt. 3.25 (*0-590-50311-1*, Cartwheel Bks.) Scholastic, Inc.

—The Librarian from the Black Lagoon. 1997. (Black Lagoon Ser.). (J). (ps-3). 9.40 (*0-606-11559-5*) Turtleback Bks.

Williams, Suzanne. Library Lil. 1997. (Illus.). 32p. (J). (ps-3). 16.99 (*0-8037-1698-2*); 15.89 o.s.i (*0-8037-1699-0*) Penguin Putnam Bks. for Young Readers. (Dial Bks. for Young Readers).

M

MAGICIANS—FICTION

Alexander, Lloyd. The Rope Trick. 2002. 256p. (J). (gr. 3-6). 16.99 (*0-525-47020-4*) Penguin Putnam Bks. for Young Readers.

—The Wizard in the Tree. 1974. (Illus.). 144p. (J). (gr. 4-7). 14.95 o.s.i (*0-525-43128-4*, Dutton Children's Bks.) Penguin Putnam Bks. for Young Readers.

Alexander, Nina. Rose's Magic Touch. 1997. (Magic Attic Club Ser.). (Illus.). 80p. (J). (gr. 2-6). 18.90 (*1-57513-184-6*, Magic Attic Pr.) Millbrook Pr., Inc.

—Rose's Magic Touch. 1997. (Magic Attic Club Ser.). (J). (gr. 2-6). 12.10 (*0-606-18797-9*) Turtleback Bks.

Alexander, Nina & Williams, Laura E. Rose's Magic Touch. Korman, Susan, ed. 1997. (Magic Attic Club Ser.). (Illus.). 80p. (J). (gr. 2-6). pap. 5.95 (*1-57513-105-6*, Magic Attic Pr.) Millbrook Pr., Inc.

Alexander, Sue. Marc the Magnificent. 1978. (Illus.). (J). (gr. k-3). 4.95 o.p. (*0-394-83728-2*); lib. bdg. 5.99 o.p. (*0-394-93728-7*) Knopf Publishing Group. (Pantheon).

Avi. Midnight Magic. 2001. 11.04 (*0-606-22158-1*) Turtleback Bks.

Babbitt, Samuel. Forty-Ninth Magician. 1966. (Illus.). (J). (gr. 1-3). lib. bdg. 4.99 o.p. (*0-394-91167-9*, Pantheon) Knopf Publishing Group.

Balian, Lorna. The Sweet Touch. 1976. (Illus.). (J). (gr. k-3). 8.95 o.p. (*0-687-40773-7*) Abingdon Pr.

Bardill, Linard. The Great Golden Thing. James, J. Alison, tr. from GER. 2002. (Illus.). 32p. (J). 16.50 (*0-7358-1594-1*); 15.95 (*0-7358-1593-3*) North-South Bks., Inc. (Michael Neugebauer Bks.).

Barron, T. A. The Lost Years of Merlin, Bk. 1. 1999. (Lost Years of Merlin Ser.). 304p. (J). (gr. 4-7). reprint ed. mass mkt. 6.99 (*0-441-00668-X*) Ace Bks.

—The Lost Years of Merlin. 1998. (J). (gr. 4-7). mass mkt. 4.99 (*0-8125-7777-9*, Tor Bks.) Doherty, Tom Assocs., LLC.

—The Lost Years of Merlin. 1996. (Lost Years of Merlin Ser.: No. 1). 336p. (J). (gr. 5-9). 19.99 (*0-399-23018-1*, Philomel) Penguin Putnam Bks. for Young Readers.

Bates, Martine. The Taker's Key. 1998. 208p. pap. 8.95 (*0-88995-184-5*) Red Deer Pr. CAN. *Dist:* General Distribution Services, Inc.

Bazaldua, Barbara. Monkey Business: Disney's Aladdin. 1993. (Illus.). 24p. (J). (ps-3). pap. o.p. (*0-307-12788-5*, Golden Bks.) Random Hse. Children's Bks.

Binato, Leonardo. What's in the Magician's Hat? 1992. (Turn & Learn Ser.). (Illus.). 12p. (J). (ps-3). 4.95 o.p. (*1-56566-008-0*) LegacyWords Publishing.

Braybrooks, Ann. The Cave of Wonders: Disney's Aladdin. 1993. (Illus.). (J). (ps-3). o.p. (*0-307-11565-8*); pap. o.p. (*0-307-15974-4*) Random Hse. Children's Bks. (Golden Bks.).

Bright, Robert. Georgie & the Magician. 1966. (Illus.). 45p. (ps-1). 7.95 o.p. (*0-385-04824-6*); pap. 2.50 o.p. (*0-385-01021-4*); lib. bdg. 7.95 o.p. (*0-385-05948-5*) Doubleday Publishing.

Burleigh, Robert. The Secrets of the Great Houdini. 2002. (Illus.). 40p. (J). (gr. 2-5). 16.95 (*0-689-83267-2*, Atheneum) Simon & Schuster Children's Publishing.

Chwast, Seymour. Mr. Merlin & the Turtle. 1996. (Illus.). 24p. (J). (ps up). 11.95 o.p. (*0-688-14632-5*, Greenwillow Bks.) HarperCollins Children's Bk. Group.

Coombs, Patricia. Dorrie & the Witches' Camp. 1983. (Illus.). 48p. (J). (gr. 1-5). 11.95 o.p. (*0-688-01507-7*); lib. bdg. 12.88 o.p. (*0-688-01508-5*) HarperCollins Children's Bk. Group.

—The Magician & McTree. 1984. (Illus.). (J). (gr. 1-4). 11.95 o.p. (*0-688-02109-3*); lib. bdg. 11.88 o.p. (*0-688-02111-5*) HarperCollins Children's Bk. Group.

Dadey, Debbie & Jones, Marcia Thornton. Sorciers/Ne Croient/Ordinateur. (Adventures of the Bailey School Kids Ser.). (FRE., Illus.). 88p. (J). mass mkt. 5.99 (*0-590-16024-9*) Scholastic, Inc.

Emberley, Ed E. The Wizard of Op. 1975. (Illus.). 32p. (J). (gr. 1-3). 6.95 o.p. (*0-316-23610-1*) Little Brown & Co.

Evans, Dilys. Looking for Merlyn. 1997. (Illus.). (J). 14.95 (*0-590-60191-1*) Scholastic, Inc.

Fagan, Cary. Daughter of the Great Zandini. 2001. (Illus.). 64p. (J). (gr. 3-7). 16.95 (*0-88776-534-3*) Tundra Bks. of Northern New York.

Frost-Snyder, M. G. The Hallu Realm. 2001. (Illus.). 80p. pap. 9.00 (*0-8059-5418-X*) Dorrance Publishing Co., Inc.

Fujikawa, Gyo. The Magic Show. 1981. (Gyo Fujikawa Ser.). (Illus.). 32p. (J). (ps-1). 3.95 o.p. (*0-448-11750-9*, Grosset & Dunlap) Penguin Putnam Bks. for Young Readers.

Gauthier, Bertrand & Sylvestre, Daniel. Le Grand Magicien. 1998. (J). 7.95 (*2-89021-333-1*) La Courte Echelle CAN. *Dist:* Firefly Bks., Ltd.

Graham, Bob. Benny: An Adventure Story. (Illus.). 32p. (J). 2003. bds. 5.99 (*0-7636-1703-2*); 1999. 16.99 (*0-7636-0813-0*) Candlewick Pr.

Green, Marion. The Magician Who Lived on the Mountain. 1978. (Illus.). (J). (gr. k-3). lib. bdg. 8.65 o.p. (*0-516-03539-8*, Children's Pr.) Scholastic Library Publishing.

Houghton, Eric. The Mouse & the Magician. 1979. (Illus.). (J). 9.95 o.p. (*0-233-96777-X*) Blackwell Publishing.

Howe, James. Harold & Chester in Rabbit-Cadabra. (Bunnicula Ser.). (Illus.). 48p. (J). (gr. k-3). 1999. pap. 5.95 (*0-688-16699-7*, Morrow, William & Co.); 1994. pap. 5.99 (*0-380-71336-5*, Avon Bks.); 1993. 15.00 (*0-688-10402-9*, Morrow, William & Co.); 1993. lib. bdg. 14.93 o.p. (*0-688-10403-7*, Morrow, William & Co.) Morrow/Avon.

Hoye, Regena. Ala Voom, Vol. 1. 1998. (Illus.). 65p. (J). (ps-6). 12.00 (*0-9636906-0-4*) Ishnuvu Publishing Co.

Hyman, Trina Schart, illus. Comus. 1996. Orig. Title: A Mask at Ludlow Castle. 32p. (J). (ps-3). tchr. ed. 16.95 (*0-8234-1146-X*) Holiday Hse., Inc.

Jones, Diana Wynne. Archer's Goon. (J). 2003. (Illus.). 336p. (gr. 5 up). 16.99 (*0-06-029889-8*, Greenwillow Bks.); 2003. (Illus.). 336p. (gr. 5 up). pap. 5.99 (*0-06-447356-2*, Harper Trophy); 1984. 256p. (gr. 7 up). 16.00 o.p. (*0-688-02582-X*, Greenwillow Bks.) HarperCollins Children's Bk. Group.

—The Lives of Christopher Chant. 2001. (J). 16.95 (*0-7540-6163-9*) BBC Audiobooks America.

—The Lives of Christopher Chant. 1988. (YA). (gr. 7 up). 15.00 o.p. (*0-688-07806-0*, Greenwillow Bks.) HarperCollins Children's Bk. Group.

—The Lives of Christopher Chant. 1990. 240p. (J). (gr. 4-7). reprint ed. pap. 3.50 o.s.i (*0-394-82205-6*, Random Hse. Bks. for Young Readers) Random Hse. Children's Bks.

—The Magicians of Caprona. (MagicQuest Ser.: No. 12). (YA). pap. 2.25 o.s.i (*0-441-51556-8*) Ace Bks.

—The Magicians of Caprona. 1999. 12.00 (*0-606-22058-5*) Turtleback Bks.

King-Smith, Dick. Clever Lollipop. 2003. (Illus.). 144p. (J). 15.99 (*0-7636-2174-9*) Candlewick Pr.

Kurt, Kemal. The Mixed-Up Journey to Magic Mountain. Martens, Marianne, tr. from GER. 2002. (Illus.). 64p. (J). (gr. 2-4). 13.95 (*0-7358-1632-8*); lib. bdg. 14.50 (*0-7358-1633-6*) North-South Bks., Inc.

Lacome, Julie. Hocus Pocus. 1991. (Illus.). (J). (ps up). 11.95 o.p. (*0-688-10158-5*, Morrow, William & Co.) Morrow/Avon.

Langstaff, John M. The Two Magicians. 1973. (Illus.). 32p. (J). (ps-3). 4.95 o.p. (*0-689-30319-X*, McElderry, Margaret K.) Simon & Schuster Children's Publishing.

Laurin, Anne. Perfect Crane. 1981. (Illus.). 32p. (J). (gr. 1-4). lib. bdg. 14.89 o.p. (*0-06-023744-9*) HarperCollins Children's Bk. Group.

Levy, Elizabeth. Running Out of Magic with Houdini. 1981. (Illus.). 128p. (J). (gr. 3-6). lib. bdg. 4.99 o.p. (*0-394-94685-5*, Knopf Bks. for Young Readers) Random Hse. Children's Bks.

Lovitt, Chip, et al. Batman & the Magician. 1996. (Golden Book Ser.). (Illus.). 24p. (J). (ps-3). pap. 3.29 o.s.i (*0-307-12880-6*, Golden Bks.) Random Hse. Children's Bks.

Mahy, Margaret. Alchemy. 2003. (Illus.). 224p. (YA). (gr. 7-12). 16.95 (*0-689-85053-0*, McElderry, Margaret K.) Simon & Schuster Children's Publishing.

Many, Paul. The Great Pancake Escape. 2002. (Illus.). 32p. (J). (gr. k-3). 16.95 (*0-8027-8795-9*); lib. bdg. 17.85 (*0-8027-8796-7*) Walker & Co.

McEwan, Chris. The 9 Tasks of Mistry: An Adventure in the World of Illusion, Vol. 1. 1996. (Illus.). 32p. (J). (gr. 3 up). 14.95 o.p. (*0-316-55523-1*) Little Brown & Co.

McGowen, Tom. Magician's Apprentice. 1987. 128p. (J). (gr. 5-9). 12.95 o.p. (*0-525-67189-7*, Dutton Children's Bks.) Penguin Putnam Bks. for Young Readers.

—The Magicians' Challenge. 1989. 144p. (J). (gr. 5-9). 13.95 o.p. (*0-525-67289-3*, Dutton Children's Bks.) Penguin Putnam Bks. for Young Readers.

—The Magician's Company. 1988. 128p. (J). (gr. 5-9). 13.95 o.p. (*0-525-67261-3*, Dutton Children's Bks.) Penguin Putnam Bks. for Young Readers.

McGraw, Eloise Jarvis. Joel & the Great Merlini. 1979. (Illus.). (J). (gr. 3-5). 5.95 o.p. (*0-394-84193-X*); lib. bdg. 5.99 o.p. (*0-394-94193-4*) Knopf Publishing Group. (Pantheon).

McKee, David. The Magician & the Balloon. 1986. (Illus.). 26p. (J). (gr. k-3). 10.95 o.p. (*0-87226-087-9*, Bedrick, Peter Bks.) McGraw-Hill Children's Publishing.

—The Magician & the Petnapping, 001. 1977. (Illus.). (J). (gr. k-3). 5.95 o.p. (*0-395-24916-3*) Houghton Mifflin Co.

Meddaugh, Susan. Lulu's Hat. 2002. (Illus.). 64p. (J). (gr. 2-4). 15.00 (*0-618-15277-6*) Houghton Mifflin Co.

Newman, Patti. As If by Magic. 1985. 31p. (J). (gr. 3-5). 4.95 o.p. (*0-533-06323-X*) Vantage Pr., Inc.

Pearson, Susan. The Green Magician Puzzle. 1991. (Eagle-Eye Ernie Mysteries Ser.). (Illus.). (J). pap. 11.95 (*0-671-74054-7*, Simon & Schuster Children's Publishing); pap. 2.95 o.p. (*0-671-74053-9*, Aladdin) Simon & Schuster Children's Publishing.

Roessler, Mark. The Last Magician in Blue Haven. 1994. (Illus.). 52p. (Orig.). (J). (gr. 4-8). pap. 10.00 (*0-9638293-0-0*) Hundelrut Studio.

Romey, Elizabeth A. Lera of Tymoria: The Dragonmage. 2002. (Illus.). 252p. (YA). (gr. 5 up). pap. 9.99 (*0-88092-570-1*, 5701) Royal Fireworks Publishing Co.

Rosenberg, Liz. Eli & Uncle Dawn. 1997. (Illus.). 32p. (J). (ps-3). 15.00 o.s.i (*0-15-200947-7*) Harcourt Trade Pubs.

Schneider, Christine M. Horace P. Tuttle, Magican Extraordinaire! 2001. (Illus.). 32p. (J). (gr. k-2). lib. bdg. 16.85 (*0-8027-8789-4*); 15.95 (*0-8027-8788-6*) Walker & Co.

Schubert, Ingrid. Abracadabra. 1997. (Illus.). 25p. (J). (ps-3). 15.95 (*1-886910-17-0*, Front Street) Front Street, Inc.

Selznick, Brian. The Houdini Box. (Illus.). 64p. (J). (gr. 1-6). 1994. pap. 2.99 o.s.i (*0-679-85448-7*, Random Hse. Bks. for Young Readers); 1991. 13.99 o.s.i (*0-679-91429-3*, Knopf Bks. for Young Readers); 1991. 13.00 o.s.i (*0-679-81429-9*, Knopf Bks. for Young Readers) Random Hse. Children's Bks.

—The Houdini Box. 2001. (Illus.). 64p. (J). 17.00 (*0-689-84488-3*, Atheneum/Anne Schwartz Bks.); pap. 4.99 (*0-689-84451-4*, Aladdin) Simon & Schuster Children's Publishing.

Springer, Nancy. I Am Mordred: A Tale from Camelot. 1998. 184p. (YA). (gr. 7-12). 16.99 (*0-399-23143-9*, Philomel) Penguin Putnam Bks. for Young Readers.

Taylor, Theodore. The Boy Who Could Fly Without a Motor. (Illus.). 2004. 168p. (J). pap. 5.95 (*0-15-204767-0*, Harcourt Paperbacks); 2002. 144p. (YA). (gr. 3-6). 15.00 (*0-15-216529-0*) Harcourt Children's Bks.

Tomasol, el Mago del Color (Balderdash the Brilliant) 1996. (SPA., Illus.). 64p. (J). (gr. k-2). 16.95 (*0-7835-3529-5*) Time-Life, Inc.

Van Der Essen. The Magician & Three Other Stories. 1983. (Yok-Yok Ser.). (Illus.). 32p. (J). (gr. k-3). 6.95 o.p. (*0-87191-928-1*, Creative Education) Creative Co., The.

Wayne, Jennifer. Sprout & the Magician. 1977. (Illus.). (J). (gr. 4-6). lib. bdg. o.p. (*0-07-068705-6*) McGraw-Hill Cos., The.

Willard, Nancy. The Sorcerer's Apprentice. Dillon, Leo et al, eds. 1993. (Illus.). 32p. (J). (gr. 2 up). pap. 16.95 (*0-590-47329-8*) Scholastic, Inc.

Willever, Lisa Funari & Funari, Lorraine. Maximilian the Great. 2000. (Illus.). 32p. (J). (ps-2). 9.95 (*0-9679227-3-9*) Franklin Mason Pr.

Wrede, Patricia C. Searching for Dragons. abr. ed. 1991. (Enchanted Forest Chronicles Ser.: Bk. 2). 256p. (YA). (gr. 7-12). 16.95 (*0-15-200898-5*) Harcourt Children's Bks.

—Searching for Dragons. 1992. (Enchanted Forest Chronicles Ser.). 242p. (YA). (gr. 7-12). mass mkt. 4.99 (*0-590-45721-7*, 071, Scholastic Paperbacks) Scholastic, Inc.

—Searching for Dragons. 1991. (Enchanted Forest Chronicles Ser.). (J). 11.04 (*0-606-01941-3*) Turtleback Bks.

Wynne-Jones, Diana. The Lives of Christopher Chant. 1998. 12.00 (*0-606-15619-4*) Turtleback Bks.

Yolen, Jane. The Hobby. 1996. (Young Merlin Trilogy Ser.: Bk. 2). 104p. (YA). (gr. 2-5). 16.00 (*0-15-200815-2*) Harcourt Children's Bks.

MIGRANT LABOR—FICTION

Altman, Linda Jacobs. Amelia's Road. (Illus.). 32p. (J). (gr. k-5). 1995. pap. 6.95 (*1-880000-27-X*); 1993. (ENG & SPA., 15.95 (*1-880000-04-0*, LLB040) Lee & Low Bks., Inc.

—Amelia's Road. 1993. 13.10 (*0-606-08913-6*) Turtleback Bks.

—El Camino de Amelia. Santacruz, Daniel M., tr. from ENG. 1994. (Illus.). 32p. (J). (gr. 3-5). (ENG & SPA.). 15.95 (*1-880000-07-5*, LC075); (SPA., pap. 5.56 (*1-880000-10-5*) Lee & Low Bks., Inc.

Bridgers, Sue E. Home Before Dark. 1985. 160p. (YA). mass mkt. 2.95 o.s.i (*0-553-27338-8*) Bantam Bks.

—Home Before Dark. 1976. (Illus.). (YA). (gr. 6 up). 10.95 o.s.i (*0-394-83299-X*, Knopf Bks. for Young Readers) Random Hse. Children's Bks.

—Home Before Dark. 1998. 186p. (J). reprint ed. lib. bdg. 29.95 (*0-7351-0053-5*) Replica Bks.

Bunting, Eve. Going Home. 1996. (Trophy Picture Book Ser.). (Illus.). 32p. (J). (ps-3). 15.99 (*0-06-026296-6*, Cotler, Joanna Bks.); lib. bdg. 15.89 (*0-06-026297-4*) HarperCollins Children's Bk. Group.

Cochrane, Patricia A. Purely Rosie Pearl. 1996. 136p. (J). (gr. 4-7). 14.95 o.s.i (*0-385-32193-7*, Dell Books for Young Readers) Random Hse. Children's Bks.

Covault, Ruth M. Pablo & Pimienta (Pablo y Pimienta) 1994. (ENG & SPA., Illus.). 32p. (J). (gr. 1-3). lib. bdg. 14.95 o.p. (*0-87358-588-7*, NP887, Rising Moon Bks. for Young Readers) Northland Publishing.

Dorros, Arthur. Radio Man: Don Radio: A Story in English & Spanish. Dorros, Sandra M., tr. 1993. (ENG & SPA., Illus.). 40p. (J). (gr. 1-5). lib. bdg. 15.89 o.p. (*0-06-021548-8*) HarperCollins Children's Bk. Group.

—Radio Man: Don Radio: A Story in English & Spanish. Dorros, Sandra, tr. 1995. (ENG & SPA.). (J). (gr. 4). 9.00 (*0-395-73244-1*) Houghton Mifflin Co.

—Radio Man: Don Radio: A Story in English & Spanish. 1997. (Trophy Picture Bks.). 13.10 (*0-606-11777-6*) Turtleback Bks.

—Radio Man (Don Radio) A Story in English & Spanish. 1997. (Harper Arco Iris Ser.). (SPA., Illus.). 40p. (J). (gr. 1-5). reprint ed. pap. 6.99 (*0-06-443482-6*, Rayo) HarperTrade.

—Radio Man/Don Radio: A Story. Dorros, Sandra M., tr. 1993. (ENG & SPA., Illus.). 40p. (J). (gr. 1-5). 16.00 o.p. (*0-06-021547-X*, L-38181-00) HarperCollins Children's Bk. Group.

Durbin, William. The Journal of C. J. Jackson: A Dust Bowl Migrant, Oklahoma to California, 1935. 2002. (My Name Is America Ser.). (Illus.). 144p. (J). (gr. 4-9). pap. 10.95 (*0-439-15306-9*, Scholastic Pr.) Scholastic, Inc.

Forbes, Tom. Quincy's Harvest. 1976. (J). (gr. 5-8). o.p. (*0-397-31688-7*) HarperCollins Children's Bk. Group.

Gates, Doris. Blue Willow. (Puffin Newbery Library). (Illus.). 176p. (J). (gr. 4-7). 1976. pap. 5.99 (*0-14-030924-1*, VS30, Puffin Bks.); 1940. 14.99 o.s.i (*0-670-17557-9*, Viking Children's Bks.) Penguin Putnam Bks. for Young Readers.

—Blue Willow. 2000. (J). (gr. 3-7). 20.75 (*0-8446-7143-6*) Smith, Peter Pub., Inc.

—Blue Willow. 1976. (Puffin Newbery Library). (J). 12.04 (*0-606-02396-8*) Turtleback Bks.

Jiménez, Francisco. The Christmas Gift. 2000. Tr. of Regalo de Navidad. (ENG & SPA., Illus.). 32p. (J). (ps-3). lib. bdg., tchr. ed. 15.00 (*0-395-92869-9*) Houghton Mifflin Co. Trade & Reference Div.

Lenski, Lois. Judy's Journey. 1947. (Regional Stories Ser.). (Illus.). (J). (gr. 4-6). lib. bdg. 13.89 (*0-397-30131-6*) HarperCollins Children's Bk. Group.

Montgomery, Bobbie. Fruit Tramp Kids. 2000. (Pathfinder Junior Book Club Ser.). 143p. (J). (gr. 4-7). pap. 6.99 (*0-8280-1422-1*) Review & Herald Publishing Assn.

Mora, Pat. Tomas & the Library Lady. 2000. (Illus.). 32p. (gr. k-3). pap. 6.99 (*0-375-80349-1*) Knopf, Alfred A. Inc.

—Tomas & the Library Lady. 1997. (Illus.). 40p. (ps-3). (J). 17.00 (*0-679-80401-3*); lib. bdg. 18.99 (*0-679-90401-8*) Random Hse., Inc.

—Tomas & the Library Lady. 2000. 13.14 (*0-606-18093-1*) Turtleback Bks.

—Tomas y la Senora de la Biblioteca. ed. 2000. (J). (gr. 1). spiral bd. (*0-616-03092-4*) Canadian National Institute for the Blind/Institut National Canadien pour les Aveugles.

—Tomas y la Senora de la Biblioteca. 1997. (SPA., Illus.). 40p. (J). (gr. 1-3). pap. 7.99 (*0-679-84173-3*); (ps-3). 18.99 o.s.i (*0-679-94173-8*) Random Hse. Children's Bks. (Knopf Bks. for Young Readers).

—Tomas y la Senora de la Biblioteca/Tomas & the Library Lady. 1997. (J). 14.14 (*0-606-11996-5*) Turtleback Bks.

Peck, Robert Newton. Arly's Run. 1991. 160p. (J). (gr. 4-7). 16.95 (*0-8027-8120-9*) Walker & Co.

Perez, L. King. First Day in Grapes. 2002. (Illus.). 32p. (J). (gr. 1-3). 16.95 (*1-58430-045-0*) Lee & Low Bks., Inc.

Shotwell, Louisa Roosevelt Grady. 1963. (Illus.). 152p. (J). (gr. 4-6). 5.99 o.p. (*0-529-03781-5*) Penguin Putnam Bks. for Young Readers.

Shotwell, Louisa. Roosevelt Grady. 1977. (gr. 4-8). pap. 1.25 o.p. (*0-440-47487-6*) Dell Publishing.

Smothers, Ethel. The Hard Times Jar, RS. 2003. (Illus.). 32p. (J). 16.00 (*0-374-32852-8*, Farrar, Straus & Giroux (BYR)) Farrar, Straus & Giroux.

Strang, Celia. Foster Mary. 1979. (J). (gr. 7-9). text 9.95 o.p. (*0-07-061996-4*) McGraw-Hill Cos., The.

Taylor, Florance W. From Texas to Illinois. 1971. (Felipe Adventure Stories Ser.). (Illus.). (J). (gr. 2-4). lib. bdg. 3.95 o.p. (*0-8225-0141-4*) Lerner Publishing Group.

—What Is a Migrant? 1971. (Felipe Adventure Stories Ser.). (Illus.). (J). (gr. 2-4). lib. bdg. 3.95 o.p. (*0-8225-0142-2*) Lerner Publishing Group.

Thomas, Jane Resh. Lights on the River. 1994. (Illus.). 32p. (J). (ps-3). 15.95 (*0-7868-0004-6*); lib. bdg. 16.49 (*0-7868-2003-9*) Hyperion Bks. for Children.

—Lights on the River. 1996. (Illus.). 32p. (J). (ps-3). pap. 4.95 o.p. (*0-7868-1132-3*) Hyperion Paperbacks for Children.

Wier, Ester. Loner. 1963. (Illus.). (J). (gr. 7-9). 5.95 o.p. (*0-679-20097-5*) McKay, David Co., Inc.

—Loner. 1992. 160p. (J). (gr. 4-7). pap. 4.50 (*0-590-44352-6*) Scholastic, Inc.

Williams, Sherley Anne. Working Cotton. 2002. (Illus.). (J). 14.04 (*0-7587-0168-3*) Book Wholesalers, Inc.

—Working Cotton. (Illus.). 32p. (J). 1997. pap. 7.00 (*0-15-201482-9*, Harcourt Paperbacks); 1992. 17.00 (*0-15-299624-9*) Harcourt Children's Bks.

—Working Cotton. 1997. 13.15 (*0-606-12114-5*) Turtleback Bks.

MINERS—FICTION

Cochran, Laura J. The Old Miner & the Spider. 1998. (J). (gr. 6-8). 8.95 o.p. (*0-533-12151-5*) Vantage Pr., Inc.

Leppard, Lois Gladys. Mandie & the Abandoned Mine. 1987. (Mandie Bks.: No. 8). 160p. (J). (gr. 4-7). pap. 4.99 (*0-87123-932-9*) Bethany Hse. Pubs.

—Mandie & the Abandoned Mine. 1987. (Mandie Bks.: No. 8). (J). (gr. 4-7). 11.04 (*0-606-06123-1*) Turtleback Bks.

Lyon, George Ella. Mama Is a Miner. 1994. (Illus.). 32p. (J). (gr. k-3). pap. 15.95 (*0-531-06853-6*); lib. bdg. 16.99 o.p. (*0-531-08703-4*) Scholastic, Inc. (Orchard Bks.).

Perez, N. A. Breaker. 2002. 216p. (YA). pap. 9.95 (*0-8229-5778-7*, Golden Triangle Bks.) Univ. of Pittsburgh Pr.

Perez, N. A. The Breaker. 1988. 216p. (YA). (gr. 7 up). 16.00 (*0-395-45537-5*) Houghton Mifflin Co.

Rappaport, Doreen. Trouble at the Mines. 1987. (Illus.). 96p. (J). (gr. 3-7). 11.95 o.p. (*0-690-04445-3*); lib. bdg. 14.89 o.p. (*0-690-04446-1*) HarperCollins Children's Bk. Group.

Turner, Philip. Devil's Nob. 1973. 190p. (J). (gr. 6-9). 6.95 o.p. (*0-525-66270-7*, Dutton Children's Bks.) Penguin Putnam Bks. for Young Readers.

Vazquez, Diana. Hannah. l.t. ed. 1998. 144p. (YA). (gr. 4-7). pap. 5.95 (*1-55050-149-6*) Coteau Bks. CAN. *Dist:* Fitzhenry & Whiteside, Ltd.

Weber, Kathryn. Molly Moonshine & Timothy. 1990. (Illus.). 44p. (J). (gr. 2-4). pap. 2.95 (*1-878438-01-8*) Ranch Hse. Pr.

MISSIONARIES—FICTION

Arensen, Sheldon. Kenyan Chronicles Bk. 1: The Secret Oath. 2000. 108p. (gr. 4-7). pap. 9.95 o.p. (*0-595-15844-7*) iUniverse, Inc.

Barth, Jeff. The Missionary Adventures of Bob & Arty Vol. 1: In Search of the Lost Missionary. Barth, Marge, ed. 1997. (Illus.). 240p. (J). (gr. 4-12). pap. 10.00 (*0-9624067-6-7*) Barth Family Ministries.

—The Missionary Adventures of Bob & Arty Vol. 2: Trapped in an Abandoned Mine. Barth, Marge, ed. 1997. (Illus.). 192p. (J). (gr. 4-12). pap. 10.00 (*0-9624067-7-5*) Barth Family Ministries.

—The Missionary Adventures of Bob & Arty Vol. 3: Mission Alaska. Barth, Marge, ed. 1998. (Illus.). 293p. (J). (gr. 4-12). pap. 10.00 (*0-9624067-8-3*) Barth Family Ministries.

—The Missionary Adventures of Bob & Arty Vol. 4: The Storm! Barth, Marge, ed. 1999. (Illus.). 392p. (J). (gr. 4-12). pap. 10.00 (*1-891484-01-X*) Barth Family Ministries.

Berry, Eileen. Roses on Baker Street. 1998. (Illus.). 48p. (J). (gr. k-4). pap. 5.49 (*0-89084-934-X*, 106401) Jones, Bob Univ. Pr.

Boehr, Karren. Ants in the Sugar Bowl. 1986. 165p. (J). (gr. 4-6). pap. 3.99 o.s.i (*0-570-03638-0*, 39-1122) Concordia Publishing Hse.

Brammer, Deb. Peanut Butter Friends in a Chop Suey World. 1994. 177p. (J). (gr. 4-7). pap. 6.49 (*0-89084-751-7*, 082685) Jones, Bob Univ. Pr.

Branyon, Beth. Miss Alma: Friend of Missions. 1996. (Little MISSionary Bks.). (Illus.). 32p. (Orig.). (J). (gr. 5-8). pap. 8.95 (*1-57736-012-5*) Providence Hse. Pubs.

—Miss Eloise: First Lady of Foreign Missions. 1996. (Little Missionary Ser.: Vol. 1). (Illus.). 32p. (Orig.). (J). (gr. 4-7). pap. 8.95 (*1-881576-78-7*) Providence Hse. Pubs.

—Miss Henrietta: Lady of Many Firsts. 1996. (Little Missionary Bks.). (Illus.). 32p. (Orig.). (J). (gr. 3-5). pap. 8.95 (*1-57736-013-3*) Providence Hse. Pubs.

Buckwalter, Leoda A. The Road to Chumba. 1994. 187p. (YA). pap. 7.95 (*0-916035-60-3*) Evangel Publishing Hse.

Carlson, Melody. It's My Life. 2000. (Diary of a Teenage Girl Ser.). 252p. (J). (gr. 7 up). pap. 12.99 o.p. (*1-57673-772-1*) Multnomah Pubs., Inc.

Crawford, Kenneth C. Yuki. 1998. 96p. (J). (ps up). pap. 7.99 o.p. (*0-8280-1051-X*) Review & Herald Publishing Assn.

Dewey, Jennifer Owings. Minik's Story. 2003. (J). 15.95 (*0-7614-5134-X*) Cavendish, Marshall Corp.

Farnes, Catherine. Out of Hiding. 2000. 174p. (YA). (gr. 9 up). pap. 6.49 (*1-57924-329-0*, 122085) Jones, Bob Univ. Pr.

Gostick, Adrian R. Jessica's Search: The Secret of Ballycater Cove. 1998. (J). 1.99 (*1-57345-436-2*) Deseret Bk. Co.

Haislip, Phyllis Hall. Lottie's Courage: A Contraband Slave's Story. 2003. (Illus.). 120p. (J). pap. 7.95 (*1-57249-311-9*, WM Kids) White Mane Publishing Co., Inc.

Hardy, LeAnne. The Outsiders. 2003. 160p. (J). pap. 6.99 (*0-8254-2793-2*) Kregel Pubns.

—The Wooden Ox: A Novel. 2002. 192p. (J). (gr. 4-8). 6.99 (*0-8254-2794-0*) Kregel Pubns.

Hart, Laverne. You May Wear Your Shoes in Church. 1981. (J). (gr. k-3). 5.95 o.p. (*0-8054-4275-8*, 4242-75) Broadman & Holman Pubs.

Hernandez, Natalie A. Las Aventuras con Padre Serra. Hernandez, Tony Y., tr. 1999. (ENG & SPA., Illus.). 112p. (Orig.). (J). (gr. 3-8). pap. 9.95 (*0-9644386-1-5*) Santa Ines Pubns.

Hibschman, Barbara, et al. Yo Quiero Ser un Misionero (Want to Be a Missionary), Vol. 4. 1994. (Missionary-That's Me! Ser.).Tr. of I Want to Be a Missionary. (SPA., Illus.). 23p. (J). (ps-3). pap. 4.99 (*0-87509-540-2*, 0015402) Christian Pubns., Inc.

Hill, Anthony. The Burnt Stick. 1995. (Illus.). 64p. (J). (gr. 4-7). 12.95 o.p. (*0-395-73974-8*) Houghton Mifflin Co.

Hill, Kirkpatrick. Minuk: Ashes in the Pathway. 2002. (Girls of Many Lands Ser.). (Illus.). 196p. (J). (gr. 4-7). 12.95 (*1-58485-596-7*); pap. 7.95 (*1-58485-520-7*) Pleasant Co. Pubns. (American Girl).

Jackson, Dave & Jackson, Meta. The Warrior's Challenge: David Zeisberger. 1996. (Trailblazer Bks.: Vol. 20). (Illus.). 144p. (J). (gr. 3-7). pap. 5.99 (*1-55661-473-X*) Bethany Hse. Pubs.

Jackson, Dave & Jackson, Neta. Drawn by a China Moon: Lottie Moon. 2000. (Trailblazer Bks.: Vol. 34). (Illus.). 160p. (J). (gr. 3-7). pap. 5.99 o.s.i (*0-7642-2267-8*) Bethany Hse. Pubs.

—Race for the Record: Joy Ridderhof. 1999. (Trailblazer Bks.: Vol. 29). 144p. (J). (gr. 3-7). pap. 5.99 (*0-7642-2013-6*) Bethany Hse. Pubs.

—Sinking the Dayspring: John G. Paton. 2001. (Trailblazer Bks.: Vol. 35). (Illus.). 144p. (J). (gr. 3-7). pap. 5.99 (*0-7642-2268-6*) Bethany Hse. Pubs.

Johnson, Lissa Halls & Wierenga, Kathy. Croutons for Breakfast. 2003. (Brio Girls Ser.). (Illus.). 192p. (J). (gr. 6-11). pap. 6.99 (*1-58997-080-2*) Focus on the Family Publishing.

Kent, Renee Holmes. Mollie's Miracle. 1997. (Illus.). 112p. (J). (gr. 4-6). pap. text 6.95 (*1-56309-207-7*, N977105, New Hope) Woman's Missionary Union.

Linam, Gail. Kind Doctor, Missionary Friend. 1981. (J). (gr. 1-3). 5.95 o.p. (*0-8054-4274-X*) Broadman & Holman Pubs.

Linford, Richard & Linford, Marilynne T. I Hope They Call Me on a Mission Too. 1984. (J). (ps-5). pap. 3.95 o.p. (*0-87747-991-7*) Deseret Bk. Co.

Little, Jean. His Banner over Me. 1999. 224p. mass mkt. 4.99 (*0-14-037761-1*) Viking Penguin.

London, Carolyn. Cat-Alog. 1971. (Children's Bks.). (Illus.). 128p. (J). (gr. 5 up). pap. 1.50 o.p. (*0-8024-1120-7*) Moody Pr.

Martin, Mildred A. Missionary Stories & the Millers. 1993. (Miller Family Ser.). (Illus.). 208p. (J). (gr. 3 up). 9.50 (*0-9627643-7-X*) Green Pastures Pr.

Matchette, Katharine E. Walk Safe Through the Jungle. 1996. (Illus.). 140p. (J). (gr. 4-9). pap. 8.75 (*0-9645045-1-0*) Deka Pr.

Matchette, Katharine E. Walk Safe Through the Jungle. 1974. (Illus.). 144p. (J). (gr. 4-9). 4.95 o.p. (*0-8361-1736-0*) Herald Pr.

McDaniel, Lurlene. Angel of Hope. 2000. (Mercy Trilogy Ser.). 240p. (YA). (gr. 7-12). mass mkt. 4.99 (*0-553-57148-6*, Starfire) Random Hse. Children's Bks.

—Angel of Hope. 2000. (Illus.). (J). 11.04 (*0-606-17991-7*) Turtleback Bks.

—Angel of Mercy. 1999. (Mercy Trilogy Ser.). 224p. (YA). (gr. 7-12). 8.95 (*0-553-57145-1*, Dell Books for Young Readers) Random Hse. Children's Bks.

—Angel of Mercy. 2001. 11.04 (*0-606-21031-8*); 1999. (Illus.). (J). 14.30 o.p. (*0-606-17992-5*) Turtleback Bks.

Myers, Bill. My Life as Crocodile Junk Food. 1993. (Incredible Worlds of Wally McDoogle Ser.: No. 4). 128p. (J). (gr. 3-7). 5.99 (*0-8499-3405-2*) Nelson, Tommy.

Nelson-Hernandez, Natalie. Stowaway to California: Adventures with Father Serra. 1994. (Illus.). 136p. (Orig.). (J). (gr. 3-8). pap. 9.95 (*0-9644386-0-7*) Santa Ines Pubns.

Repp, Gloria. Charlie. 2002. (Illus.). 147p. (J). (*1-57924-817-9*) Jones, Bob Univ. Pr.

—Mik-Shrok. 1998. 133p. (J). (gr. 4-7). pap. 6.49 (*1-57924-069-0*, 113902) Jones, Bob Univ. Pr.

—A Question of Yams. 1992. 67p. (J). (gr. 1-2). pap. 6.49 (*0-89084-614-6*, 057885) Jones, Bob Univ. Pr.

—Zebra 77. 2002. (Adventures of an Arctic Missionary Ser.). (Illus.). 156p. (J). (gr. 4-6). 6.49 (*1-57924-930-2*) Jones, Bob Univ. Pr.

Rispin, Karen. Sabrina the Schemer. 1994. (Anika Scott Ser.: Vol. 5). 130p. (J). (gr. 3-7). pap. 4.99 o.p. (*0-8423-1296-X*) Tyndale Hse. Pubs.

—Tianna, the Terrible. 1992. (Anika Scott Ser.: No. 2). (J). (gr. 3-7). 4.99 o.p. (*0-8423-2031-8*) Tyndale Hse. Pubs.

Ross, Uta O. The Boy Who Wanted to Be a Missionary. 1984. (Illus.). 48p. (Orig.). (J). (gr. 1-3). pap. text 6.95 o.p. (*0-687-03910-X*) Abingdon Pr.

Smith, Goerky. Danger Follows. 1999. 98p. (YA). (gr. 7 up). pap. 6.49 (*1-57924-070-4*, 109835) Jones, Bob Univ. Pr.

St. John, Patricia M. Star of Light. 2002. (Illus.). 256p. (J). pap. 6.99 (*0-8024-6577-3*) Moody Pr.

Stinetorf, Louise A. White Witch Doctor. 1950. (Illus.). 286p. (J). (gr. 7 up). o.p. (*0-664-30034-0*) Westminster John Knox Pr.

Tada, Joni Eareckson & Jensen, Steve. The Mission Adventure. 2001. 143p. (J). (gr. 3-6). pap. 5.99 (*1-58134-257-8*) Crossway Bks.

Vogelaar-Van Amersfoort, Alie. Tekko Returns. 1997. (Tekko Ser.). (Illus.). (J). pap. 6.90 (*0-921100-75-2*) Inheritance Pubns.

—Tekko the Fugitive. Van Brugge, Jean, tr. from DUT. 1995. (Tekko Ser.: No. 2). (Illus.). 93p. (Orig.). pap. 6.90 (*0-921100-74-4*) Inheritance Pubns.

Wilkinson, Barbara. Apples for the Missionaries. 1989. (Illus.). 32p. (J). (gr. 1-3). pap. text 2.95 (*0-936625-67-8*, W897108) Woman's Missionary Union.

Youngberg, Norma R. Jungle Thorn. 2000. (Illus.). 128p. (J). reprint ed. pap. 8.95 (*1-57258-157-3*) TEACH Services, Inc.

Zook, Mary R. Little Missionaries & Other Stories. 1979. (Illus.). 180p. (J). (gr. 3-6). 8.50 (*0-7399-0087-0*, 2315) Rod & Staff Pubs., Inc.

MODELS (PERSONS)—FICTION

Alexander, Nina. And the Winner Is.... 1999. (Full House Sisters Ser.: No. 3). 160p. (J). (gr. 4-6). pap. 3.99 (*0-671-04055-3*, Simon Spotlight) Simon & Schuster Children's Publishing.

Anderson, Marcie. Your're Really a Model Now! 1985. 96p. (J). (gr. 5-8). 2.25 o.p. (*0-87406-042-7*) Darby Creek Publishing.

Barrows, Allison. The Artist's Model. 1996. (Illus.). 32p. (J). (ps-3). lib. bdg. 15.95 o.s.i (*0-87614-948-4*, Carolrhoda Bks.) Lerner Publishing Group.

Blacker, Terence. Ms Wiz, Supermodel. 2003. (Illus.). 58p. (J). pap. (*0-330-35312-8*) Macmillan Children's Bks.

Byrd, Sandra. Picture Perfect. 2000. (Secret Sisters Ser.: Vol. 11). 112p. (J). (gr. 3-7). pap. 4.95 o.s.i (*1-57856-063-2*) WaterBrook Pr.

Farrell, Mame. Bradley & the Billboard, RS. 224p. (J). 2002. pap. 5.95 (*0-374-40912-9*, Sunburst); 1998. (gr. 5-9). 16.00 (*0-374-30949-3*, Farrar, Straus & Giroux (BYR)) Farrar, Straus & Giroux.

—Bradley & the Billboard. 1999. (YA). pap., stu. ed. 58.00 incl. audio (*0-7887-3060-6*, 40894) Recorded Bks., LLC.

Green, Yvonne. Rising Star: Kelly Blake, Teen Model, Vol. 2. 1986. 176p. (YA). (gr. 7-12). mass mkt. 2.50 o.s.i (*0-553-25639-4*) Bantam Bks.

Greene, Yvonne. Double Trouble. 1986. (Kelly Blake, Teen Model Ser.: No. 5). 160p. (Orig.). (YA). (gr. 7-12). mass mkt. 2.50 o.s.i (*0-553-26154-1*) Bantam Bks.

—Hard to Get: Kelly Blake. 1986. (Teen Model Ser.: No. 3). 176p. (Orig.). (YA). (gr. 7-12). mass mkt. 2.50 o.s.i (*0-553-26037-5*) Bantam Bks.

—Kelly Blake: Headliners. 1986. (Teen Model Ser.: No. 4). 160p. (Orig.). (YA). (gr. 7-12). mass mkt. 2.50 o.s.i (*0-553-26112-6*) Bantam Bks.

—Paris Nights, Vol.. 6. 1986. (Kelly Blake, Teen Model Ser.). 160p. (Orig.). (YA). (gr. 7-12). mass mkt. 2.50 o.s.i (*0-553-26199-1*) Bantam Bks.

Hunt, Angela Elwell. Star Light, Star Bright. 1993. (Cassie Perkins Ser.: Vol. 7). (YA). pap. 4.99 o.p. (*0-8423-1117-3*) Tyndale Hse. Pubs.

—Star Light, Star Bright. 2000. (Cassie Perkins Ser.: Vol. 7). 180p. (gr. 4-7). pap. 11.95 (*0-595-08996-8*, Backinprint.com) iUniverse, Inc.

Lehman, Yvonne. Picture Perfect. 1997. (White Dove Romances Ser.: No. 4). 176p. (J). (gr. 7-12). mass mkt. 4.99 o.p. (*1-55661-708-9*) Bethany Hse. Pubs.

Myers, Walter Dean. Crystal. 2002. 208p. (J). (gr. 7 up). lib. bdg. 15.89 (*0-06-008350-6*); reprint ed. pap. 5.95 (*0-06-447312-0*) HarperCollins Children's Bk. Group. (Harper Trophy).

—Crystal. 1987. (J). (gr. 5-9). 14.95 o.p. (*0-670-80426-6*, Viking Children's Bks.) Penguin Putnam Bks. for Young Readers.

—Crystal. (J). 1990. (Illus.). mass mkt. 5.95 (*0-440-80157-5*, Dell Books for Young Readers); 1989. 208p. mass mkt. 3.25 o.s.i (*0-440-20538-7*, Laurel Leaf) Random Hse. Children's Bks.

Rayban, C. Street to Stardom. 1997. (Model Ser.: Bk 4). (Illus.). 140p. (J). mass mkt. 7.95 (*0-340-68165-9*) Hodder & Stoughton, Ltd. GBR. *Dist:* Lubrecht & Cramer, Ltd., Trafalgar Square.

Thompson, Julian F. Ghost Story, ERS. 1997. 224p. (J). 15.95 o.p. (*0-8050-4870-7*, Holt, Henry & Co. Bks. For Young Readers) Holt, Henry & Co.

MUSICIANS—FICTION

Anderson, Ken. Nessie & the Little Blind Boy of Loch Ness. deluxe ed. 1992. (Illus.). 72p. (J). 49.95 o.p. (*0-941613-27-5*) Stabur Pr., Inc.

Appelt, Kathi A. Piggies in a Polka. 2003. (Illus.). 40p. (J). 16.00 (*0-15-216483-9*) Harcourt Trade Pubs.

Arrhenius, Peter. The Penguin Quartet. 1998. (Picture Bks.). (Illus.). 28p. (J). (ps-3). lib. bdg. 15.95 (*1-57505-252-0*, Carolrhoda Bks.) Lerner Publishing Group.

Base, Graeme. The Worst Band in the Universe: A Totally Cosmic Musical Adventure. 1999. (Illus.). 48p. (J). (gr. 4-7). 19.95 o.p. incl. audio compact disk (*0-8109-3998-3*) Abrams, Harry N. , Inc.

Bateman, Teresa. Red, White, Blue & Uncle Who? The Story Behind Some of America's Patriotic Symbols. 2001. (Illus.). 64p. (J). (gr. 1-5). tchr. ed. 15.95 (*0-8234-1285-7*) Holiday Hse., Inc.

Battle-Lavert, Gwendolyn. The Music in Derrick's Heart. 2000. (Illus.). 32p. (J). (ps-3). tchr. ed. 16.95 (*0-8234-1353-5*) Holiday Hse., Inc.

Bell, Madison Smartt. Anything Goes: A Novel. 2002. 320p. 24.00 (*0-375-42125-4*, Pantheon) Knopf Publishing Group.

Bell, Mary S. Sonata for Mind & Heart. 1992. 224p. (YA). (gr. 7 up). lib. bdg. 14.95 o.s.i (*0-689-31734-4*, Atheneum) Simon & Schuster Children's Publishing.

Bennett, Cherie. Sunset Fling. 1995. 224p. mass mkt. 3.99 o.s.i (*0-425-15026-7*) Berkley Publishing Group.

—Sunset Holiday. 1995. 224p. (Orig.). mass mkt. 3.99 o.s.i (*0-425-15109-3*) Berkley Publishing Group.

Berry, Liz. Easy Connections. 1984. 180p. (J). (gr. 7-9). 12.95 o.p. (*0-670-28694-X*, Viking Children's Bks.) Penguin Putnam Bks. for Young Readers.

Birchman, David F. A Green Horn Blowing. 1997. (Illus.). 32p. (J). lib. bdg. 14.93 o.p. (*0-688-12389-9*); 15.00 (*0-688-12388-0*) HarperCollins Children's Bk. Group.

Bontemps, Arna. Lonesome Boy. 1988. (Night Lights Ser.). (Illus.). 32p. (J). (gr. k-3). reprint ed. pap. 4.95 o.p. (*0-8070-8307-0*, NL 2); lib. bdg. 12.95 o.p. (*0-8070-8306-2*) Beacon Pr.

Brett, Jan. Berlioz the Bear. (Illus.). (J). (ps-3). 2015. 5.95 o.s.i (*0-399-22846-2*, Sandcastle Bks.); 1991. 32p. 15.95 (*0-399-22248-0*, G. P. Putnam's Sons) Penguin Group (USA) Inc.

—Berlioz the Bear. 1996. (Illus.). 32p. (J). (ps-3). pap. 6.99 (*0-698-11399-3*, PaperStar) Penguin Putnam Bks. for Young Readers.

—Berlioz the Bear. 1996. 13.14 (*0-606-11114-X*) Turtleback Bks.

Bridgman, Herb. Songs for School with the Bandimals. 2002. (Illus.). 44p. (J). (gr. 2-6). pap. 15.95 (*0-9700757-0-7*) Stirling, H. Publishing.

Brooks, Bruce. Cody. 1997. (Wolfbay Wings Ser.: No. 3). (Illus.). 128p. (J). (gr. 5 up). pap. 4.50 o.s.i (*0-06-440599-0*, Harper Trophy) HarperCollins Children's Bk. Group.

Brooks, Walter R. Freddy the Pied Piper. 2002. (Illus.). 253p. (J). (gr. 3). 23.95 (*1-58567-226-2*) Overlook Pr., The.

Burleigh, Robert. Lookin' for Bird in the Big City. 2001. (Illus.). 32p. (J). (gr. 1-4). 16.00 (*0-15-202031-4*, Silver Whistle) Harcourt Children's Bks.

Campbell, Louisa & Taylor, Bridget S. Phoebe's Fabulous Father. 1996. (Illus.). 32p. (J). (ps-3). 14.00 (*0-15-200996-5*) Harcourt Trade Pubs.

Carlson, Nancy. Harriet's Recital. unabr. ed. 1985. (Illus.). (J). (gr. k-3). 24.95 incl. audio (*0-941078-69-8*); 24.95 incl. audio (*0-941078-69-8*); pap. 31.95 incl. audio (*0-941078-68-X*); pap. 15.95 incl. audio (*0-941078-67-1*) Live Oak Media.

Cartwright, Pauline. Jimmy Parker's New Job. 1994. (Illus.). (J). pap. (*0-383-03679-8*) SRA/McGraw-Hill.

Chocolate, Deborah M. Newton. The Piano Man. 1998. (Illus.). 32p. (J). (gr. k-3). 15.95 (*0-8027-8646-4*); lib. bdg. 16.85 (*0-8027-8647-2*) Walker & Co.

—Piano Man. 2000. 13.10 (*0-606-17886-4*) Turtleback Bks.

—Piano Man. 2000. (Illus.). 32p. (J). (gr. k-3). pap. 6.95 (*0-8027-7578-0*) Walker & Co.

Christian, Mary Blount. Singin' Somebody Else's Song. 1990. 192p. (J). (gr. 5 up). pap. 3.95 o.p. (*0-14-034169-2*, Puffin Bks.) Penguin Putnam Bks. for Young Readers.

Coco, Eugene B. The Fiddler's Son. 1991. (Illus.). 32p. (J). pap. 5.95 (*0-88138-111-X*, Simon & Schuster Children's Publishing) Simon & Schuster Children's Publishing.

Collier, James Lincoln. The Jazz Kid. 1996. 224p. (YA). (gr. 6 up). pap. 4.99 o.s.i (*0-14-037778-6*, Puffin Bks.) Penguin Putnam Bks. for Young Readers.

—The Jazz Kid. 1996. (YA). (gr. 6 up). 10.09 o.p. (*0-606-09485-7*) Turtleback Bks.

Constable, Kate. The Singer of All Songs. 2004. (YA). (*0-439-55479-9*, Levine, Arthur A. Bks.) Scholastic, Inc.

—Singer of All Songs. 2004. 304p. (J). 16.95 (*0-439-55478-0*, Levine, Arthur A. Bks.) Scholastic, Inc.

Cooner, Donna D. Barney Makes Music. Davis, Guy, ed. 1999. (Barney Ser.). (Illus.). 24p. (J). (ps-k). 4.95 (*1-57064-461-6*) Scholastic, Inc.

Corbet, Robert. Fifteen Love. 2003. 192p. (J). (gr. 7 up). 16.95 (*0-8027-8851-3*) Walker & Co.

Cosgrove, Stephen. Fiddler. Brown, Jane, ed. 1988. (Barely There Ser.). (Illus.). (J). (gr. 4-9). 12.99 o.p. (*0-88070-211-7*); 8.99 o.p. (*0-88070-235-4*) Zonderkidz.

Cowling, Douglas. Hallelujah Handel. 2003. (Illus.). 48p. (J). pap. 16.95 (*0-439-05850-3*) Scholastic, Inc.

Cox, Judy. My Family Plays Music. 2003. (Illus.). (J). (gr. k-3). tchr. ed. 16.95 (*0-8234-1591-0*) Holiday Hse., Inc.

Crozon, Alain. What Am I? Music! (J). 7.95 (*2-02-061210-0*) Chronicle Bks. LLC.

Cutler, Jane. The Cello of Mr. O. 1999. (Illus.). 32p. (J). (gr. k-4). 15.99 (*0-525-46119-1*, Dutton Children's Bks.) Penguin Putnam Bks. for Young Readers.

Davol, Marguerite W. The Loudest, Fastest, Best Drummer in Kansas. 2000. (Illus.). 32p. (J). (gr. k-4). pap. 15.95 (*0-531-30191-5*); lib. bdg. 16.99 (*0-531-33191-1*) Scholastic, Inc. (Orchard Bks.).

Day, Betsy. Stefan & Olga. 1991. (Illus.). 320p. (J). (ps-3). 12.95 o.p. (*0-8037-0816-5*); 12.89 o.p. (*0-8037-0817-3*) Penguin Putnam Bks. for Young Readers. (Dial Bks. for Young Readers).

Delaney, Mark. Growler's Horn. 2000. (Misfits, Inc. Ser.: No. 3). 192p. (YA). (gr. 6-10). pap. 5.95 (*1-56145-206-8*) Peachtree Pubs., Ltd.

—Growler's Horn. 2000. (Illus.). (J). 12.00 (*0-606-18339-6*) Turtleback Bks.

Dennis, Jeanne Gowen & Seifert, Sheila. Attack! Hohn, David, tr. & illus. by. 2003. (Strive to Thrive Ser.). (J). pap. 4.99 (*0-7814-3894-2*) Cook Communications Ministries.

Edwards, Julie Andrews. Simeon's Gift. 2003. (Julie Andrews Collection). (J). 169.90 (*0-06-056905-0*); 169.90 (*0-06-056906-9*) HarperCollins Children's Bk. Group.

Edwards, Julie Andrews & Hamilton, Emma Walton. Simeon's Gift. 2003. (Julie Andrews Collection). 40p. (J). lib. bdg. 17.89 (*0-06-008915-6*); (Illus.). 16.99 incl. audio compact disk (*0-06-008914-8*); (Illus.). 16.99 incl. audio compact disk (*0-06-008914-8*) HarperCollins Pubs.

Egland, Linda. 3 Kids Dreamin' 1997. (Illus.). 32p. (J). (gr. 2-5). 16.00 (*0-689-80866-6*, McElderry, Margaret K.) Simon & Schuster Children's Publishing.

Eisenberg, Lisa. The Case of the Rock & Roll Mystery. 1998. (New Adventures of Mary-Kate & Ashley Ser.). 87p. (J). (gr. 2-7). mass mkt. 3.99 (*0-590-29402-4*) Scholastic, Inc.

England, Linda. The Old Cotton Blues. 1998. (Illus.). 32p. (J). (ps-2). 16.00 (*0-689-81074-1*, McElderry, Margaret K.) Simon & Schuster Children's Publishing.

Fenner, Carol. Yolonda's Genius. 2002. (Illus.). (J). 14.47 (*0-7587-0333-3*) Book Wholesalers, Inc.

—Yolonda's Genius. (J). 2002. 224p. E-Book 6.99 (*0-689-84785-8*, McElderry, Margaret K.); 1998. pap. 2.65 (*0-689-82172-7*, Aladdin); 1997. 224p. (gr. 3-7). pap. 5.99 (*0-689-81327-9*, Aladdin); 1995. 224p. (gr. 3-7). 17.00 (*0-689-80001-0*, McElderry, Margaret K.) Simon & Schuster Children's Publishing.

—Yolonda's Genius. 1997. (J). 12.04 (*0-606-12122-6*) Turtleback Bks.

First, Julia. Move Over, Beethoven. 1978. (gr. 5 up). lib. bdg. 7.90 o.p. (*0-531-01472-X*, Watts, Franklin) Scholastic Library Publishing.

Fleming, Candace. Gabriella's Song. 2001. (Illus.). (J). 12.14 (*0-606-21206-X*) Turtleback Bks.

Fox, Paula. The Slave Dancer. 2002. (Illus.). (J). 14.47 (*0-7587-0214-0*) Book Wholesalers, Inc.

—The Slave Dancer. 1997. mass mkt. 2.69 o.p. (*0-440-22739-9*); 1990. 160p. (gr. 5-9). pap. text 5.99 (*0-440-40402-9*); 1990. (J). mass mkt. o.p. (*0-440-80203-2*) Dell Publishing.

—The Slave Dancer. 1998. (Assessment Packs Ser.). 15p. pap. text, tchr.'s training gde. ed. 15.95 (*1-58303-061-1*) Pathways Publishing.

—The Slave Dancer. unabr. ed. 2000. 152p. (J). (gr. 4-6). pap. 37.00 incl. audio (*0-8072-0458-7*, Listening Library) Random Hse. Audio Publishing Group.

—The Slave Dancer. (Laurel-Leaf Historical Fiction Ser.). 1974. 144p. (YA). (gr. 4-7). mass mkt. 5.50 (*0-440-96132-7*); 1988. (J). (gr. 3-7). reprint ed. lib. bdg. 15.95 o.p. (*1-55736-029-4*) Random Hse. Children's Bks. (Laurel Leaf).

—The Slave Dancer. (Illus.). 192p. (YA). 2001. 17.95 (*0-689-84505-7*); 1982. (gr. 5-9). lib. bdg. 16.95 (*0-02-735560-8*) Simon & Schuster Children's Publishing. (Atheneum/Richard Jackson Bks.).

—The Slave Dancer. 1973. (Laurel-Leaf Historical Fiction Ser.). 11.55 (*0-606-04914-2*) Turtleback Bks.

Francis, Panama & Reiser, Bob. David Gets His Drum. 2002. (Illus.). 32p. (J). (gr. k-3). 16.95 (*0-7614-5088-2*) Cavendish, Marshall Corp.

—David Gets His Drum. 2015. (Illus.). 32p. (J). 15.99 (*0-525-65240-X*, Dutton Children's Bks.) Penguin Putnam Bks. for Young Readers.

Frank, Lucy. Will You Be My Brussels Sprout? 1996. 160p. (YA). (gr. 7-12). tchr. ed. 15.95 (*0-8234-1220-2*) Holiday Hse., Inc.

Fraser, Julia. Musical Discoveries: A Story about Music, History & Friendship, Bk. 1. 1995. (Grammy Musical Discoveries Ser.: Bk. 1). (Illus.). (J). (gr. 6-8). 6.95 (*0-88284-656-6*, 4707) Alfred Publishing Co., Inc.

Gibbons, Faye. Emma Jo's Song. 2003. (Illus.). 32p. (J). (gr. k-3). 15.95 (*1-56397-935-7*) Boyds Mills Pr.

Gibson, William. Idoru. 1997. 400p. mass mkt. 7.50 (*0-425-15864-0*) Berkley Publishing Group.

—Idoru. 1996. 304p. 24.95 o.s.i (*0-399-14130-8*, G. P. Putnam's Sons) Penguin Group (USA) Inc.

—Idoru. 1998. 4.98 o.p. (*0-7651-0900-X*) Smithmark Pubs., Inc.

Gillmor, Don. The Fabulous Song. (J). 2003. pap. 7.95 (*1-929132-48-4*); 1998. (Illus.). 32p. 12.95 (*0-916291-80-4*) Kane/Miller Bk. Pubs.

Going, Kelly. Fat Kid Rules the World. 2003. 192p. (YA). 17.99 (*0-399-23990-1*, G. P. Putnam's Sons) Penguin Putnam Bks. for Young Readers.

Goodman, Joan Elizabeth. Songs from Home. 1994. 224p. (YA). (gr. 5 up). pap. 4.95 (*0-15-203591-5*); (Illus.). 10.95 o.s.i (*0-15-203590-7*) Harcourt Trade Pubs.

—Songs from Home. 1994. 10.10 o.p. (*0-606-09875-5*) Turtleback Bks.

Greenwald, Sheila. Here's Hermione: A Rosy Cole Production. 1991. (Illus.). (J). (gr. 3-7). 13.95 o.p. (*0-316-32715-8*) Little Brown & Co.

Gregory, Deborah. Dorinda's Secret. 2000. (Cheetah Girls Ser.: No. 7). 141p. (J). (gr. 3-7). pap. 3.99 (*0-7868-1426-8*, Jump at the Sun) Hyperion Bks. for Children.

—Growl Power. 2000. (Cheetah Girls Ser.: No. 8). 143p. (J). (gr. 3-7). pap. 3.99 (*0-7868-1427-6*, Jump at the Sun) Hyperion Bks. for Children.

—It's Raining Benjamins! 2000. (Cheetah Girls Ser.: No. 6). 150p. (J). (gr. 3-7). pap. 3.99 (*0-7868-1425-X*) Disney Pr.

Griffith, Helen V. Alex & the Cat. 1982. (Greenwillow Read-Alone Bks.). (Illus.). 64p. (J). (gr. 1-3). 13.95 o.p. (*0-688-00420-2*); lib. bdg. 13.88 o.p. (*0-688-00421-0*) HarperCollins Children's Bk. Group. (Greenwillow Bks.).

Grimm, Jacob W. The Bremen Town Musicians. 1998. 13.14 (*0-606-13226-0*) Turtleback Bks.

Gross, Ruth Belov. The Bremen Town Musicians. 1985. (Illus.). 32p. (J). (ps-3). pap. 3.25 (*0-590-42364-9*) Scholastic, Inc.

—The Bremen Town Musicians. 1974. 9.40 (*0-606-10149-7*) Turtleback Bks.

Haas, Jessie. Keeping Barney. 1982. 160p. (J). (gr. 5-9). 12.95 o.p. (*0-688-00859-3*, Greenwillow Bks.) HarperCollins Children's Bk. Group.

—Keeping Barney. 1998. 160p. (J). (gr. 3 up). pap. 4.50 (*0-688-15859-5*, Morrow, William & Co.) Morrow/Avon.

—Keeping Barney. 1998. 10.55 (*0-606-16829-X*) Turtleback Bks.

Hall, Pat. The Kona Town Musicians. 1998. (Illus.). 32p. (J). (ps-5). 9.95 (*0-9633493-6-8*) Pacific Greetings.

Harranth, Wolf. The Flute Concert. 1998. Tr. of Flotenkonzert. (Illus.). 32p. (J). (ps-3). 16.95 o.p. (*1-56711-803-8*, Blackbirch Pr., Inc.) Gale Group.

Hentoff, Nat. Jazz Country. 1965. 160p. (YA). (gr. 7 up). lib. bdg. 12.89 o.p. (*0-06-022306-5*) HarperCollins Children's Bk. Group.

—Jazz Country. 1976. (J). (gr. 7-12). pap. 1.25 o.p. (*0-06-080355-X*, P355) HarperCollins Pubs.

—Jazz Country. 1983. 144p. (YA). (gr. 7 up). mass mkt. 2.25 o.s.i (*0-440-94203-9*, Laurel Leaf) Random Hse. Children's Bks.

Hill, Elizabeth S. The Banjo Player. 1993. 208p. (J). (gr. 5-9). 14.99 o.p. (*0-670-84967-7*, Viking Children's Bks.) Penguin Putnam Bks. for Young Readers.

—The Banjo Player. 1999. pap. 4.99 (*0-14-036422-6*) Viking Penguin.

Hoban, Brom. Skunk Lane. 1983. (Illus.). 64p. (J). (gr. 2-4). o.p. (*0-06-022347-2*); lib. bdg. 10.89 o.p. (*0-06-022348-0*) HarperCollins Children's Bk. Group.

Hopper, Nancy J. Cassandra Live at Carnegie Hall! 1998. 160p. (J). (gr. 5-8). 15.99 o.s.i (*0-8037-2329-6*, Dial Bks. for Young Readers) Penguin Putnam Bks. for Young Readers.

—Hang on, Harvey! 1983. 128p. (J). (gr. 4-8). 9.95 o.p. (*0-525-44045-3*, Dutton Children's Bks.) Penguin Putnam Bks. for Young Readers.

Houghton Mifflin Company Staff. Ty's One-Man Band. 1992. (Literature Experience 1993 Ser.). (J). (gr. 4). pap. 10.24 (*0-395-61801-0*) Houghton Mifflin Co.

Isadora, Rachel. Ben's Trumpet. (Illus.). 40p. (J). (ps-3). 1979. 17.99 (*0-688-80194-3*, Greenwillow Bks.); 1991. reprint ed. pap. 6.99 (*0-688-10988-8*, Harper Trophy) HarperCollins Children's Bk. Group.

—Ben's Trumpet. 1998. (Illus.). (J). (gr. k-3). pap., tchr. ed. 33.95 incl. audio (*0-87499-435-7*); 24.95 incl. audio (*0-87499-434-9*); 24.95 incl. audio (*0-87499-434-9*); pap. 15.95 incl. audio (*0-87499-433-0*); pap. 15.95 incl. audio (*0-87499-433-0*) Live Oak Media.

Janover, Caroline. Zipper, the Kid with ADHD. 1997. (Illus.). 164p. (J). (gr. 3-6). pap. 11.95 (*0-933149-95-6*) Woodbine Hse.

Johnson, Allen, Jr. Picker McClikker. 1996. (Illus.). 48p. (J). (gr. 1-4). pap. text 6.95 (*1-887654-14-3*) Premium Pr. America.

Johnson, Angela. Violet's Music. 2004. (Illus.). 32p. (J). 16.99 (*0-8037-2740-2*, Dial Bks. for Young Readers) Penguin Putnam Bks. for Young Readers.

Jones, Melanie Davis. Pigs Rock! 2003. (Illus.). 32p. (J). 15.99 (*0-670-03581-5*, Viking) Viking Penguin.

Kassirer, Sue. Math Fair Blues. 2001. (Math Matters Ser.). (Illus.). 32p. (J). (gr. k-2). pap. 4.95 (*1-57565-104-1*) Kane Pr., The.

Keller, Holly. Cromwell's Glasses. 1982. (Illus.). 32p. (J). (gr. k-3). 14.00 o.p. (*0-688-00834-8*); lib. bdg. 11.88 o.p. (*0-688-00835-6*) HarperCollins Children's Bk. Group. (Greenwillow Bks.).

Kennedy, Pagan. The Exes. 1998. 208p. (YA). (gr. 10 up). 23.00 o.s.i (*0-684-83481-2*, Simon & Schuster) Simon & Schuster.

Kennedy, Richard. Oliver Hyde's Dishcloth Concert. 1977. (J). (gr. 2-5). 6.95 o.p. (*0-316-48902-6*) Little Brown & Co.

Kerner, Charlotte. Blueprint. Crawford, Elizabeth D., tr. from GER. 2000. (Young Adult Fiction Ser.). 192p. (YA). (gr. 9-12). lib. bdg. 16.95 (*0-8225-0080-9*, Lerner Pubns.) Lerner Publishing Group.

Ketcham, Sallie. Bach's Big Adventure. 1999. (Illus.). 32p. (J). (gr. k-4). pap. 16.95 (*0-531-30140-0*); lib. bdg. 17.99 (*0-531-33140-7*) Scholastic, Inc. (Orchard Bks.).

Kinsey-Warnock, Natalie. The Fiddler of the Northern Lights. 1996. (J). (ps-3). 14.99 (*0-525-65125-X*); (Illus.). 32p. 16.99 (*0-525-65215-9*) Penguin Putnam Bks. for Young Readers. (Dutton Children's Bks.).

Kovacs, Deborah. Brewster's Courage. 1992. (Illus.). 112p. (J). (gr. 2-6). pap. 14.00 o.p. (*0-671-74016-4*, Simon & Schuster Children's Publishing) Simon & Schuster Children's Publishing.

Kraus, Robert. Musical Max. 1992. (J). (ps-3). pap. 5.95 o.s.i (*0-671-79250-4*, Aladdin) Simon & Schuster Children's Publishing.

Krementz, Jill. A Very Young Musician. 48p. (J). 1992. (gr. 4-7). pap. 5.95 o.s.i (*0-671-79251-2*, Aladdin); 1991. (Illus.). (gr. 3-7). pap. 14.95 o.s.i (*0-671-72687-0*, Simon & Schuster Children's Publishing) Simon & Schuster Children's Publishing.

Kuskin, Karla. The Philharmonic Gets Dressed. (Trophy Picture Bk.). (Illus.). (J). (ps-3). 1986. 48p. pap. 5.99 (*0-06-443124-X*, Harper Trophy); 1982. 80p. lib. bdg. 14.89 o.p. (*0-06-023623-X*); 1982. 48p. 15.99 (*0-06-023622-1*) HarperCollins Children's Bk. Group.

—The Philharmonic Gets Dressed. 1986. (J). 12.10 (*0-606-03257-6*) Turtleback Bks.

Landis, James D. The Band Never Dances. 1989. 288p. (YA). (gr. 7 up). 13.95 (*0-06-023721-X*); lib. bdg. 13.89 o.p. (*0-06-023722-8*) HarperCollins Children's Bk. Group.

Lawlor, Laurie. George on His Own. Tucker, Kathleen, ed. 1993. (Illus.). 144p. (J). (gr. 3-7). lib. bdg. 13.95 o.p. (*0-8075-2823-4*) Whitman, Albert & Co.

Lems, Kristin. Piano Teacher's Daughter. 2002. (Illus.). pap. 18.00 (*0-9637048-2-6*) Lems-Dworkin, Carol Pubs.

Leonard, Marcia. Big Ben. 1998. (Real Kids Readers Ser.). (Illus.). 32p. (J). (ps-1). 18.90 (*0-7613-2013-X*); pap. 4.99 (*0-7613-2038-5*) Millbrook Pr., Inc.

—Big Ben. 1998. 10.14 (*0-606-15793-X*) Turtleback Bks.

—Big Ben. 1998. E-Book (*1-58824-789-9*); (Illus.). E-Book (*1-58824-458-X*); (Illus.). E-Book (*1-58824-706-6*) ipicturebooks, LLC.

Levinson, Nancy S. Sweet Notes, Sour Notes. 1993. (Illus.). 64p. (J). (gr. 2-5). 12.99 o.p. (*0-525-67379-2*) NAL.

Levoy, Myron. Kelly 'n' Me. 1992. (Charlotte Zolotow Bk.). 208p. (YA). (gr. 7 up). 15.00 (*0-06-020838-4*); lib. bdg. 14.89 o.p. (*0-06-020839-2*) HarperCollins Children's Bk. Group.

—Kelly 'n' Me. 2000. 202p. (gr. 7-12). pap. 13.95 (*0-595-09356-6*) iUniverse, Inc.

Linscott, Jody. Once upon A to Z: An Alphabet Odyssey. 1991. 64p. (J). (ps up). 15.99 o.s.i (*0-385-41907-4*) Doubleday Publishing.

Lithgow, John. The Remarkable Farkle McBride. 2000. (Illus.). 40p. (J). (ps-3). 16.00 (*0-689-83340-7*, Simon & Schuster Children's Publishing) Simon & Schuster Children's Publishing.

Littlesugar, Amy. Shake Rag: From the Life of Elvis Presley. 2001. 13.14 (*0-606-21428-3*) Turtleback Bks.

London, Jonathan. Hip Cat. 1993. (Illus.). 40p. (J). (ps-9). 14.95 o.p. (*0-8118-0315-5*) Chronicle Bks. LLC.

MacLean, Mrs. Alistair, pseud. Here Comes Buddy. 1996. (Yesterday & Tomorrow Fantasy Cartoon Ser.). (Illus.). 75p. (YA). spiral bd. 5.00 o.p. (*0-940178-88-5*) Sitare, Ltd.

—Hollywood. l.t. ed. 1999. (Yesterday & Tomorrow Fantasy Cartoon Ser.). (FRE., Illus.). 75p. (YA). 10.00 (*0-940178-89-3*) Sitare, Ltd.

Major, Kevin. Dear Bruce Springsteen. 1989. 144p. (J). (gr. k-12). reprint ed. mass mkt. 3.25 o.s.i (*0-440-20410-0*) Dell Publishing.

Marino, Jan. Day That Elvis Came to Town, Vol. 1. 1991. (YA). (gr. 9-12). 15.95 o.p. (*0-316-54618-6*) Little Brown & Co.

Markas, Jenny. Scooby Doo & the Legend of Vampire Rock. 2003. (Scooby-Doo Ser.). (Illus.). 64p. (J). mass mkt. 3.99 (*0-439-45521-9*) Scholastic, Inc.

Martin, Bill, Jr. The Maestro Plays. 1996. (Illus.). 48p. (J). (ps-3). reprint ed. pap. 6.00 (*0-15-201217-6*, Voyager Bks./Libros Viajeros) Harcourt Children's Bks.

McKee, David. The Sad Story of Veronica Who Played the Violin. 1991. (Illus.). 32p. (J). (ps-3). 10.95 o.p. (*0-916291-37-5*) Kane/Miller Bk. Pubs.

Metz, Melinda. The Case of the Rock Star's Secret. 2000. (New Adventures of Mary-Kate & Ashley Ser.). (Illus.). 96p. (gr. 2-7). mass mkt. 4.50 (*0-06-106589-7*, HarperEntertainment) Morrow/Avon.

Millman, Isaac. Moses Goes to a Concert, RS. (Illus.). 40p. (J). 2002. pap. 5.95 (*0-374-45366-7*, Sunburst); 1998. 16.00 (*0-374-35067-1*, Farrar, Straus & Giroux (BYR)) Farrar, Straus & Giroux.

Mutchnick, Brenda & Casden, Ron. A Noteworthy Tale. 1997. (Illus.). 32p. (J). (ps-3). 17.95 o.p. (*0-8109-1386-0*) Abrams, Harry N. , Inc.

Namioka, Lensey. Yang the Eldest & His Odd Jobs. 2000. (Illus.). 128p. (J). (gr. 3-7). 15.95 (*0-316-59011-8*) Little Brown & Co.

Napoli, Donna Jo. Changing Tunes. 160p. (gr. 3-7). 2000. (Illus.). (YA). pap. 4.99 o.s.i (*0-14-130811-7*, Puffin Bks.); 1998. (J). 15.99 o.s.i (*0-525-45861-1*, Dutton Children's Bks.) Penguin Putnam Bks. for Young Readers.

—Changing Tunes. 2000. (Illus.). (J). 11.04 (*0-606-18394-9*) Turtleback Bks.

Okimoto, Jean Davies. Talent Night. 1995. 176p. (YA). (gr. 7-9). pap. 14.95 (*0-590-47809-5*) Scholastic, Inc.

Ostrow, Kim. Rock-and-Roll Bob. 2003. (Bob the Builder Ser.). (Illus.). 24p. (J). pap. 3.99 (*0-689-85832-9*, Simon Spotlight) Simon & Schuster Children's Publishing.

Palmer, Bernard. Felicia Cartright & the Hungry Fiddler. 1962. (J). (gr. 8 up). pap. 1.50 o.p. (*0-8024-7410-1*) Moody Pr.

Paul, Sherry. Two-B & the Rock 'n Roll Band. 1981. (See How I Read Bks.). (Illus.). 32p. (J). (gr. k-3). 9.95 o.p. (*0-516-02355-1*, Children's Pr.) Scholastic Library Publishing.

Percy, Graham, illus. The Pied Piper of Hamelin. l.t. ed. 2001. 28p. (J). (ps-3). 8.99 incl. audio compact disk (*84-8214-085-X*); 8.99 incl. audio (*84-86154-38-3*); 8.99 incl. audio compact disk (*84-8214-085-X*); 8.99 incl. audio (*84-86154-38-3*) Peralt Montagut ESP. *Dist:* imaJen, Inc.

Pinkwater, Daniel M. Bongo Larry. 1998. (Accelerated Reader Bks.). (Illus.). 32p. (J). (ps up). 14.95 (*0-7614-5020-3*, Cavendish Children's Bks.) Cavendish, Marshall Corp.

—Mush, a Dog from Space. (Ready-for-Chapters Ser.). (Illus.). (J). 2002. 64p. pap. 3.99 (*0-689-84572-3*, Aladdin); 2002. 64p. pap. 11.89 (*0-689-84576-6*, Aladdin Library); 1995. 40p. 15.00 (*0-689-80317-6*, Atheneum) Simon & Schuster Children's Publishing.

Plemons, Marti. Scott & the Ogre. 1992. (Grace Street Kids Ser.). (Illus.). 128p. (J). (gr. 3-6). pap. 4.99 o.p. (*0-87403-688-7*, 24-03728) Standard Publishing.

Plume, Ilse. The Bremen-Town Musicians. 1998. (Illus.). 32p. (ps-3). reprint ed. pap. text 6.99 (*0-440-41456-3*, Yearling) Random Hse. Children's Bks.

Poole, Valerie. Obadiah Coffee & the Music Contest. 1991. (Illus.). 32p. (J). (ps-3). 14.95 (*0-06-021619-0*); lib. bdg. 14.89 (*0-06-021620-4*) HarperCollins Children's Bk. Group.

Pratchett, Terry. The Amazing Maurice & His Educated Rodents. (J). (gr. 7 up). 2003. (Illus.). 368p. pap. 6.99 (*0-06-001235-8*); 2001. 256p. lib. bdg. 17.89 (*0-06-001234-X*); 2001. (Illus.). 256p. 16.95 (*0-06-001233-1*) HarperCollins Children's Bk. Group.

Rayner, Mary. Garth Pig Steals the Show. 1993. (Illus.). 32p. (J). (ps-3). 13.99 o.p. (*0-525-45023-8*, Dutton Children's Bks.) Penguin Putnam Bks. for Young Readers.

Rice, Anne. The Violin. unabr. ed. 1997. audio 64.00 (*0-7366-3771-0*, 4444) Books on Tape, Inc.

—The Violin, Set. abr. ed. 1997. audio 24.00 (*0-679-46038-1*, 495973); audio compact disk 27.50 (*0-679-46065-9*) Random Hse. Audio Publishing Group. (RH Audio).

Schroeder, Alan. Satchmo's Blues. 1996. (Illus.). 32p. (J). (gr. k-3). 15.95 o.s.i (*0-385-32046-9*) Doubleday Publishing.

Sebastian, John. J. B.'s Harmonica. 1993. (Illus.). 32p. (J). (ps-3). 13.95 (*0-15-240091-5*) Harcourt Trade Pubs.

Shyer, Marlene Fanta. Me & Joey Pinstripe, the King of Rock. 1988. 224p. (YA). (gr. 7 up). 13.95 o.s.i (*0-684-18941-0*, Atheneum) Simon & Schuster Children's Publishing.

Sinykin, Sheri Cooper. The Buddy Trap. 1991. 144p. (J). (gr. 3-7). lib. bdg. 13.95 o.p. (*0-689-31674-7*, Atheneum) Simon & Schuster Children's Publishing.

Sitare Ltd. Staff. Almost Elvis (Out of Print) MacLean, Alistair, ed. l.t. ed. 1998. (Yesterday & Tomorrow Fantasy Cartoon Ser.). (Illus.). 72p. (YA). 10.00 o.p. (*0-940178-87-7*) Sitare, Ltd.

Skurzynski, Gloria. Minstrel in the Tower. 1992. (Illus.). (J). 1.99 o.p. (*0-517-08953-X*) Random Hse. Value Publishing.

—Minstrel in the Tower. 1988. 10.14 (*0-606-12424-1*) Turtleback Bks.

Smith, Wendy. Haddock McCraddock. 1979. 5.95 o.p. (*0-385-14656-6*); lib. bdg. o.p. (*0-385-14657-4*) Doubleday Publishing.

Strong, Stacie. Barbie Rockin' Rappin' Dancin' World Tour Pop-Up Book. 1992. (Illus.). 12p. (J). (ps-3). pap. 2.22 o.s.i (*0-307-16560-4*, 16560, Golden Bks.) Random Hse. Children's Bks.

Sullivan, Mary W. Bluegrass Iggy. 1975. 150p. (gr. 5 up). 6.95 o.p. (*0-525-66475-0*, Dutton Children's Bks.) Penguin Putnam Bks. for Young Readers.

—The Indestructible Old Time String Band. 1975. (J). (gr. 6 up). 6.95 o.p. (*0-8407-6426-X*, Dutton Children's Bks.) Penguin Putnam Bks. for Young Readers.

Sweeney, Joyce. Piano Man. 1992. 18.95 (*0-385-30724-1*) Doubleday Publishing.

—Piano Man. 1994. (J). mass mkt. o.p. (*0-440-90127-8*, Dell Books for Young Readers) Random Hse. Children's Bks.

Tate, Eleanora E. The Minstrel's Melody. 2001. (American Girl Collection: Bk. 11). (Illus.). 160p. (J). (gr. 5-9). 9.95 (*1-58485-311-5*); pap. 5.95 (*1-58485-310-7*) Pleasant Co. Pubns. (American Girl).

—The Minstrel's Melody. 2001. (American Girl Collection). (Illus.). (J). 12.00 (*0-606-21331-7*) Turtleback Bks.

Taylor, Debbie. A Special Day in Harlem. Morrison, Frank, tr. & illus. by. 2004. (J). (*1-58430-165-1*) Lee & Low Bks., Inc.

Thomas, Ianthe. Willie Blows a Mean Horn. 1981. (Illus.). 24p. (J). (gr. k-3). lib. bdg. 11.89 o.p. (*0-06-026107-2*) HarperCollins Children's Bk. Group.

Tornqvist, Rita. The Old Musician. 1994. Tr. of Den Gamle Musikanten. (Illus.). 40p. (J). (ps-3). reprint ed. 13.00 o.p. (*91-29-62244-1*) R & S Bks. SWE. *Dist:* Farrar, Straus & Giroux, Holtzbrinck Pubs.

Trist, Alan. The Water of Life: A Tale of the Grateful Dead. 1990. (Illus.). 52p. (J). (gr. 2-12). lib. bdg. 12.95 o.p. (*0-938493-12-4*) Hulogosi Communications, Inc.

Ungerer, Tomi. Tortoni Tremolo the Cursed Magician. 1998. (Illus.). 32p. (J). (gr. 1-5). 16.95 (*1-57098-226-0*) Rinehart, Roberts Pubs.

Velasquez, Eric. Grandma's Records. 2001. (Illus.). 32p. (J). (gr. k-3). 16.95 (*0-8027-8760-6*) Walker & Co.

Vincent, Gabrielle. Bravo, Ernest & Celestine! 1982. Tr. of Ernest et Celestine, Musiciens Des Rues. (Illus.). 24p. (J). (gr. k-3). 10.75 o.p. (*0-688-00857-7*); lib. bdg. 11.88 o.p. (*0-688-00858-5*) HarperCollins Children's Bk. Group. (Greenwillow Bks.).

—Ernest & Celestine. 1982. (Illus.). 24p. (J). (gr. k-3). 10.75 o.p. (*0-688-00855-0*); lib. bdg. 11.88 o.p. (*0-688-00856-9*) HarperCollins Children's Bk. Group. (Greenwillow Bks.).

Voigt, Cynthia. Orfe. 1994. 128p. (J). (gr. 7-9). mass mkt. 3.95 (*0-590-47442-1*) Scholastic, Inc.

—Orfe. 2002. (Illus.). 160p. (J). pap. 4.99 (*0-689-84868-4*, Simon Pulse); 1992. 128p. (YA). (gr. 9 up). 12.95 (*0-689-31771-9*, Atheneum) Simon & Schuster Children's Publishing.

—Orfe. 1992. (Point Signature Ser.). 9.05 o.p. (*0-606-06641-1*) Turtleback Bks.

Ward Weller, Frances. The Angel of Mill Street. 1998. (Illus.). 32p. (J). (ps-3). 15.99 o.p. (*0-399-23133-1*, G. P. Putnam's Sons) Penguin Putnam Bks. for Young Readers.

Weik, Mary H. The Jazz Man. 2nd ed. 1993. (Illus.). 48p. (J). (gr. 3-7). reprint ed. pap. 4.99 (*0-689-71767-9*, Aladdin) Simon & Schuster Children's Publishing.

—The Jazz Man. 1996. 20.25 (*0-8446-6882-6*) Smith, Peter Pub., Inc.

The Wiggles in Concert. 2004. (Wiggles Ser.). 10p. bds. 8.99 (*0-448-43527-6*, Grosset & Dunlap) Penguin Putnam Bks. for Young Readers.

Willett, Edward. The Dark Unicorn. 18th ed. 1998. 158p. (J). pap. 9.99 (*0-88092-414-4*, 4144) Royal Fireworks Publishing Co.

Williams, Laura E. Rose Faces the Music. 1997. (Magic Attic Club Ser.). (Illus.). 80p. (J). (gr. 2-6). 18.90 (*1-57513-183-8*, Magic Attic Pr.) Millbrook Pr., Inc.

—Rose Faces the Music. Korman, Susan, ed. 1997. (Magic Attic Club Ser.). (Illus.). 80p. (J). (gr. 2-6). 13.95 (*1-57513-108-0*, Magic Attic Pr.) Millbrook Pr., Inc.

—Rose Faces the Music. 1997. 12.10 (*0-606-18796-0*) Turtleback Bks.

Williams, Laura E. & Alexander, Nina. Rose Faces the Music. Korman, Susan, ed. 1997. (Magic Attic Club Ser.). (Illus.). 80p. (J). (gr. 2-6). pap. 5.95 (*1-57513-107-2*, Magic Attic Pr.) Millbrook Pr., Inc.

Willner-Pardo, Gina. Spider Storch's Music Mess. 1998. 10.10 (*0-606-17180-0*) Turtleback Bks.

—Spider Storch's Music Mess. 1998. (Illus.). 80p. (J). (gr. 2-5). lib. bdg. 11.95 (*0-8075-7583-6*) Whitman, Albert & Co.

Wolff, Virginia Euwer. The Mozart Season, ERS. 1991. 88p. (J). (gr. 6 up). 15.95 o.p. (*0-8050-1571-X*, Holt, Henry & Co. Bks. For Young Readers) Holt, Henry & Co.

—The Mozart Season. 1993. 256p. (J). (gr. 7-9). mass mkt. 3.25 o.p. (*0-590-45445-5*, Scholastic Paperbacks) Scholastic, Inc.

Woodbury, Mary. Brad's Universe. 1998. 192p. (YA). (gr. 7-11). pap. 7.95 (*1-55143-120-3*) Orca Bk. Pubs.

Wynne-Jones, Tim. The Maestro. 1996. 224p. (YA). (gr. 4-9). pap. 6.95 o.p. (*0-88899-263-7*) Firefly Bks., Ltd.

Yockey, R. Paul. Peace Out. Ashby, Ruth, ed. 1992. (New Kids on the Block Ser.). 144p. (J). pap. 3.50 (*0-671-73943-3*, Simon Pulse) Simon & Schuster Children's Publishing.

Yolen, Jane. The Musicians of Bremen: A Tale from Germany. 1996. (Illus.). 32p. (J). (ps-3). 14.00 (*0-689-80501-2*, Simon & Schuster Children's Publishing) Simon & Schuster Children's Publishing.

N

NURSES AND NURSING—FICTION

Belloc, Hilaire. Jim, Who Ran Away from His Nurse, & Was Eaten by a Lion. 1987. (Joy Street Bks.). (Illus.). (J). (gr. 2 up). 12.95 o.s.i (*0-316-13815-0*); mass mkt. 4.95 o.p. (*0-316-13816-9*) Little Brown & Co.

Blatter, Dorothy. Cap & Candle. 1961. (J). (gr. 7-10). 3.95 o.s.i (*0-664-32255-7*) Westminster John Knox Pr.

Boylston, Helen D. Sue Barton, Neighborhood Nurse. 1940. (Sue Barton Ser.). (Illus.). (J). (gr. 7-12). 5.95 o.p. (*0-316-10475-2*) Little Brown & Co.

—Sue Barton, Student Nurse. 1936. (Sue Barton Ser.). (Illus.). (J). (gr. 7 up). 5.95 o.p. (*0-316-10479-5*) Little Brown & Co.

Brand, Christianna. Nurse Matilda. 1980. (J). lib. bdg. 8.50 o.p. (*0-8398-2604-4*, Macmillan Reference USA) Gale Group.

Carlyle, Carolyn. Mercy Hospital: Crisis! 1993. 128p. (Orig.). (J). (gr. 5). pap. 3.50 (*0-380-76846-1*, Avon Bks.) Morrow/Avon.

—Mercy Hospital: Don't Tell Mrs. Harris. 1993. 128p. (Orig.). (YA). pap. 3.50 (*0-380-76848-8*, Avon Bks.) Morrow/Avon.

—Mercy Hospital: Dr. Cute. 1993. 128p. (Orig.). (YA). pap. 3.50 (*0-380-76849-6*, Avon Bks.) Morrow/Avon.

—Mercy Hospital: The Best Medicine. 1993. 128p. (Orig.). (J). pap. 3.50 (*0-380-76847-X*, Avon Bks.) Morrow/Avon.

Carney, Karen L. Everything Changes, but Love Endures: Explaining Hospice to Children. 2000. (Barklay & Eve Ser.: Bk. 6). (Illus.). (J). pap. 6.95 (*0-9667820-5-4*) Dragonfly Publishing.

Cavanna, Betty. Catchpenny Street. 1975. (Illus.). 222p. (J). (gr. 6 up). 7.50 o.p. (*0-664-32574-2*) Westminster John Knox Pr.

Dicks, Terrance. Nurse Sally Ann. 1994. (Illus.). (J). pap. 14.00 o.p. (*0-671-79428-0*, Simon & Schuster Children's Publishing) Simon & Schuster Children's Publishing.

Ellis, Joyce. Tiffany. (Springsong Ser.). 176p. (Orig.). (YA). 1996. mass mkt. 4.99 o.p. (*1-55661-734-8*, Bethany Backyard); 1986. (gr. 9-12). mass mkt. 3.99 o.p. (*0-87123-893-4*) Bethany Hse. Pubs.

Flanagan, Alice K. Ask Nurse Pfaff, She'll Help You! 1998. (Our Neighborhood Ser.). (Illus.). 32p. (J). (gr. 1-2). pap. 6.95 (*0-516-26245-9*, Children's Pr.) Scholastic Library Publishing.

Hall, Marjory. The Carved Wooden Ring. 1972. 176p. (J). (gr. 6 up). 4.75 o.s.i (*0-664-32506-8*) Westminster John Knox Pr.

Jackson, Dave & Jackson, Neta. The Drummer Boy's Battle: Florence Nightingale. 1997. (Trailblazer Bks.: Vol. 21). (Illus.). 144p. (J). (gr. 3-7). pap. 5.99 (*1-55661-740-2*) Bethany Hse. Pubs.

Lakin, Patricia. The Mystery Illness. 1994. (My School Ser.). (Illus.). (J). lib. bdg. 21.40 o.p. (*0-8114-3867-8*) Raintree Pubs.

Laklan, Carli. Nancy Kimball, Nurse's Aide. 1984. (Signal Bks.). (gr. 6-9). 7.95 o.p. (*0-385-01950-5*) Doubleday Publishing.

—Nurse in Training. 1984. 5.95 o.p. (*0-385-05816-0*) Doubleday Publishing.

—Second Year Nurse: Nancy Kimball at City Hospital. 1967. (gr. 5-9). 5.95 o.p. (*0-385-06288-5*) Doubleday Publishing.

Lyon, George Ella. Here & Then. 1994. 128p. (J). (gr. 4-7). pap. 15.95 (*0-531-06866-8*); (gr. 5-7). mass mkt. 16.99 o.p. (*0-531-08716-6*) Scholastic, Inc. (Orchard Bks.).

McDonnell, Virginia. Trouble at Mercy Hospital. 1968. (gr. 7-8). 5.95 o.p. (*0-385-08948-1*) Doubleday Publishing.

Newell, Hope. Cap for Mary Ellis. 1953. (YA). (gr. 7 up). lib. bdg. 12.89 o.p. (*0-06-024526-3*) HarperCollins Children's Bk. Group.

O

OCEANOGRAPHY—FICTION

P

PAINTERS—FICTION

PHYSICIANS—FICTION

Robbins, Beth. Tom & Ally Visit the Doctor: American Edition. 2001. (It's OK! Ser.). (Illus.). 32p. (J). (ps-k). pap. 3.95 (*0-7894-7428-X*, D K Ink) Dorling Kindersley Publishing, Inc.

Roessler, Mark. The Last Magician in Blue Haven. 1994. (Illus.). 52p. (Orig.). (J). (gr. 4-8). pap. 10.00 (*0-9638293-0-0*) Hundelrut Studio.

Sanschagrin, Joceline. Caillou: La Visita al Doctor. 2004. Tr. of A Visit to the Doctor. (SPA.). (J). 5.95 (*1-58728-337-9*) Creative Publishing international, Inc.

Sargent, Dave & Sargent, Pat. Gus (Slate Grullo) Be Thankful. 2003. (Saddle Up Ser.: Vol.32). (Illus.). 42p. (J). mass mkt. 6.95 (*1-56763-694-2*); lib. bdg. 22.60 (*1-56763-693-4*) Ozark Publishing.

Scarry, Richard & Golden Books Staff. Nicky Goes to the Doctor. 1990. (Richard Scarry's Ser.). (Illus.). 24p. (J). (ps-3). pap. 3.29 o.s.i (*0-307-11842-8*) Random Hse. Children's Bks.

Schwartz, Joel L. Shrink. 1986. (J). (gr. 3-6). pap. 2.75 o.s.i (*0-440-47687-9*, Yearling) Random Hse. Children's Bks.

Shulman, Neil & Fleming, Sibley. What's in a Doctor's Bag. 1994. (Illus.). (J). (ps-3). pap. 8.95 (*0-9639002-3-4*) Rx Humor.

Sirken, Michael L. Mr. Fine Goes to the Eye Doctor. 1993. 28p. (J). (ps-4). pap. 2.95 (*0-9635483-0-1*) Sirken Pubns.

Smee, Nicola. Freddie Visits the Doctor. 1999. 20p. pap. 4.95 o.p. (*0-7641-0866-2*) Barron's Educational Series, Inc.

Sommers, Tish. Big Bird Goes to the Doctor. 1986. (Sesame Street Growing-Up Bks.). (Illus.). 32p. (J). (ps). o.p. (*0-307-12019-8*, Golden Bks.) Random Hse. Children's Bks.

Steel, Danielle. Freddie & the Doctor. 1992. (Illus.). 32p. (J). (gr. 1-3). pap. 2.99 o.s.i (*0-440-40575-0*, Yearling) Random Hse. Children's Bks.

Steig, William. Doctor De Soto. (Picture Books Collection). (SPA.). 32p. (J). (gr. k-3). 16.95 (*84-372-6616-5*) Altea, Ediciones, S.A. - Grupo Santillana ESP. *Dist:* Santillana USA Publishing Co., Inc.

—Doctor De Soto. 1982. (Illus.). 32p. (J). (ps-3). 17.00 (*0-374-31803-4*, Farrar, Straus & Giroux (BYR)) Farrar, Straus & Giroux.

—Doctor De Soto. 1997. (J). 12.10 (*0-606-12675-9*) Turtleback Bks.

—Doctor De Soto. 2001. (Foreign Language Media Collection). (ENG & SPA.). (J). (gr. k-4). tchr. ed. 29.95 o.s.i incl. VHS (*0-7882-0185-9*, WW3571) Weston Woods Studios, Inc.

Stevenson, Robert Louis. Dr. Jekyll & Mr. Hyde. (Illus.). 72p. (YA). (gr. 4 up). pap. 7.95 (*0-931334-50-0*, EDN402B) AV Concepts Corp.

—Dr. Jekyll & Mr. Hyde. 1981. (Tempo Classics Ser.). 176p. (J). 1.95 o.s.i (*0-448-17015-9*) Ace Bks.

—Dr. Jekyll & Mr. Hyde. 1964. (Airmont Classics Ser.). (YA). (gr. 8 up). mass mkt. 2.25 (*0-8049-0042-6*, CL-42) Airmont Publishing Co., Inc.

—Dr. Jekyll & Mr. Hyde. 1995. 32p. (YA). (gr. 6-12). pap. 3.95 (*0-7854-1117-8*, 40205) American Guidance Service, Inc.

—Dr. Jekyll & Mr. Hyde. 1996. (Andre Deutsch Classics). 107p. (J). (gr. 5-8). 11.95 (*0-233-99078-X*) Andre Deutsch GBR. *Dist:* Trafalgar Square, Trans-Atlantic Pubns., Inc.

—Dr. Jekyll & Mr. Hyde. 1981. 128p. (YA). (gr. 7-12). pap. 1.95 o.s.i (*0-553-21087-4*, Bantam Classics) Bantam Bks.

—Dr. Jekyll & Mr. Hyde. (Classics Illustrated Ser.). (Illus.). 52p. (YA). pap. 4.95 (*1-57209-008-1*) Classics International Entertainment, Inc.

—Dr. Jekyll & Mr. Hyde. 1990. 82p. (J). mass mkt. 2.99 (*0-8125-0448-8*, Tor Classics) Doherty, Tom Assocs., LLC.

—Dr. Jekyll & Mr. Hyde. 2nd ed. 1998. (Illustrated Classic Book Ser.). (Illus.). 61p. (J). (gr. 3 up). reprint ed. pap. text 4.95 (*1-56767-237-X*) Educational Insights, Inc.

—Dr. Jekyll & Mr. Hyde. (YA). (gr. 5-12). pap. 7.95 (*0-8224-9255-5*) Globe Fearon Educational Publishing.

—Dr. Jekyll & Mr. Hyde, Level 4. Hedge, Tricia, ed. 2000. (Bookworms Ser.). (Illus.). 96p. (J). pap. text 5.95 (*0-19-423032-5*) Oxford Univ. Pr., Inc.

—Dr. Jekyll & Mr. Hyde. Platt, Kin, ed. 1973. (Now Age Illustrated Ser.). (Illus.). 64p. (J). (gr. 5-10). 7.50 o.p. (*0-88301-202-2*); pap. 2.95 (*0-88301-096-8*) Pendulum Pr., Inc.

—Dr. Jekyll & Mr. Hyde. (YA). (gr. 5 up). 1997. (Illus.). 240p. pap. 3.99 o.s.i (*0-14-036764-0*); 1978. 6.95 o.p. (*0-448-41110-5*, Grosset & Dunlap) Penguin Putnam Bks. for Young Readers.

—Dr. Jekyll & Mr. Hyde. Vogel, Malvina, ed. 1990. (Great Illustrated Classics Ser.: Vol. 10). (Illus.). 240p. (J). (gr. 3-6). 9.95 (*0-86611-961-2*) Playmore, Inc., Pubs.

—Dr. Jekyll & Mr. Hyde. 1987. (Regents Illustrated Classics Ser.). (Illus.). (YA). (gr. 7-12). pap. text 5.25 net. o.p. (*0-13-216680-1*, 20432) Prentice Hall, ESL Dept.

—Dr. Jekyll & Mr. Hyde. Lafreniere, Kenneth, ed. 1984. (Stepping Stone Bks.: No. 9). (Illus.). 96p. (J). (gr. 3-7). reprint ed. pap. 3.99 (*0-394-86365-8*, Random Hse. Bks. for Young Readers) Random Hse. Children's Bks.

—Dr. Jekyll & Mr. Hyde. 208p. 2002. (YA). mass mkt. 3.99 (*0-439-29575-0*); 1991. (J). mass mkt. 3.25 o.p. (*0-590-45169-3*) Scholastic, Inc.

—Dr. Jekyll & Mr. Hyde. 1990. (Illus.). (J). 9.04 (*0-606-18639-5*) Turtleback Bks.

—The Strange Case of Dr. Jekyll & Mr. Hyde. 1997. (Eyewitness Classics Ser.). (Illus.). 64p. (J). (gr. 3-6). pap. 14.95 o.p. (*0-7894-2069-4*) Dorling Kindersley Publishing, Inc.

—The Strange Case of Dr. Jekyll & Mr. Hyde. (J). E-Book 2.49 (*1-58627-524-0*) Electric Umbrella Publishing.

—The Strange Case of Dr. Jekyll & Mr. Hyde. Harris, Raymond, ed. 1982. (Classics Ser.). (Illus.). 48p. (YA). (gr. 6-12). tchr. ed. 7.32 (*0-89061-254-4*, 453); pap. text 5.99 (*0-89061-253-6*, 451) Jamestown.

—The Strange Case of Dr. Jekyll & Mr. Hyde. (Young Collector's Illustrated Classics Ser.). (Illus.). 192p. (J). (gr. 3-7). 9.95 (*1-56156-460-5*) Kidsbooks, Inc.

—The Strange Case of Dr. Jekyll & Mr. Hyde. 1993. (Fiction Ser.). (YA). pap. text 6.50 (*0-582-08484-9*, 79829) Longman Publishing Group.

—The Strange Case of Dr. Jekyll & Mr. Hyde. 1996. (Wishbone Classics Ser.: No. 8). 128p. (J). (gr. 4-7). mass mkt. 3.99 (*0-06-106414-9*, HarperEntertainment) Morrow/Avon.

—The Strange Case of Dr. Jekyll & Mr. Hyde. 2000. (Dr. Jekyll & Mr. Hyde Ser.). (Illus.). (J). (gr. 7-12). 105p. 25.99 o.s.i (*0-670-88865-6*); 112p. pap. 17.99 (*0-670-88871-0*) Penguin Putnam Bks. for Young Readers. (Viking Children's Bks.).

—The Strange Case of Dr. Jekyll & Mr. Hyde. 1996. (Wishbone Classics Ser.: No. 8). (J). (gr. 3-7). 10.04 (*0-606-10371-6*) Turtleback Bks.

—The Strange Case of Dr. Jekyll & Mr. Hyde & the Suicide Club. 1986. (Classics for Young Readers Ser.). 176p. (J). (gr. 5 up). pap. 3.99 o.p. (*0-14-035047-0*, Puffin Bks.) Penguin Putnam Bks. for Young Readers.

—Treasure Island, The Master of Balantrae, Dr. Jekyll & Mr. Hyde, Kidnapped. 1985. (J). 15.45 (*0-671-52760-6*, Atheneum) Simon & Schuster Children's Publishing.

—The Works of Robert Louis Stevenson: Treasure Island, Kidnapped, The Strange Case of Dr. Jekyll & Mr. Hyde. 1995. (Classic Bonded Leather Ser.). 800p. (YA). 24.95 o.p. (*0-681-10373-6*) Borders Pr.

Stoker, Bram, et al. Dracula, Frankenstein, Dr. Jekyll & Mr. Hyde. 1978. 672p. (J). (gr. 7). mass mkt. 6.95 (*0-451-52363-6*, Signet Classics) NAL.

Stuart, Jon, illus. Tom & Ally Visit the Doctor. 2001. (It's OK! Ser.). 32p. (J). (ps-k). pap. 12.95 (*0-7894-7429-8*, D K Ink) Dorling Kindersley Publishing, Inc.

Swenson, David. The Interfacers. Zygarlicke, Eileen, ed. 1997. 250p. pap. 14.95 (*1-890939-03-X*) Century Creations, Inc.

Tannenbaum, D. Leb. A Visit to the Doctor. 1981. (New Feelings Activity Bks.). (Illus.). 64p. (J). (ps-2). pap. 3.95 o.s.i (*0-671-43205-2*, Atheneum) Simon & Schuster Children's Publishing.

Teddy Goes to the Doctor. 1973. (Puppet Story Bks.). (J). 1.95 o.p. (*0-448-00778-9*) Putnam Publishing Group, The.

Tirotta, Christopher F. & Tirotta, Conni S. A Day Surgery Trip with Dr. Bip. 2nd rev. ed. 1995. (Illus.). i, 23p. (J). (ps-6). pap. text 1.50 (*1-891359-03-7*) Kidz-Med, Inc.

—A Hospital Trip with Dr. Bip. 3rd rev. ed. 1994. (Illus.). iii, 29p. (J). (ps-6). pap. text 1.50 (*1-891359-02-9*) Kidz-Med, Inc.

—Una Operacion Con el Dr. Bip - A Hospital Trip with Dr. Bip. 2nd rev. ed. 1995. (SPA., Illus.). iii, 29p. (J). (ps-6). pap. text 1.50 (*1-891359-04-5*) Kidz-Med, Inc.

Toby Turtle: Takes a Tumble. 1996. (Dr. Wellbook Collection). (Illus.). 20p. (J). (ps-3). reprint ed. pap. 7.95 (*1-879874-29-6*) Peters, Tim & Co., Inc.

Twinn, Michael, illus. A Visit to the Doctor. 1977. (Nursery Ser.). 12p. (Orig.). (J). (ps-1). 2.00 o.p. (*0-85953-067-1*) Child's Play of England GBR. *Dist:* Random Hse. of Canada, Ltd.

Vernon, Louise A. Doctor in Rags. 1973. (Illus.). (J). (gr. 4-9). 160p. 5.95 o.p. (*0-8361-1697-6*); 2nd ed. 152p. pap. 7.99 (*0-8361-1698-4*) Herald Pr.

Williams, David P. & Williams, Helen R. The Doctor's Mouse: A Read-with-Me Story for Grown-Ups & Others. 1991. (Read-with-Me Mouse Stories Ser. Vol. 1). (Illus.). 27p. (J). pap. 5.00 (*1-886058-01-6*) Williams, David Park.

Wiseman, Bernard. Doctor Duck & Nurse Swan. 1984. (Illus.). 32p. (J). (ps-1). 9.95 o.p. (*0-525-44095-X*, Dutton) Dutton/Plume.

Wolde, Gunilla. Betsy & the Doctor. 1982. (Betsy Bks.). (Illus.). (J). (ps). 1.75 o.s.i (*0-394-85382-2*); lib. bdg. 4.99 o.s.i (*0-394-95382-7*) Random Hse. Children's Bks. (Random Hse. Bks. for Young Readers).

Zoehfeld, Kathleen Weidner. Pooh Plays Doctor. (My Very First Winnie the Pooh Ser.). (Illus.). 32p. (J). (ps-k). 1999. pap. 4.99 (*0-7868-4341-1*); 1997. 11.95 o.p. (*0-7868-3124-3*) Disney Pr.

PIANISTS—FICTION

Barrett, Mary Brigid. Sing to the Stars. 1994. (Illus.). (J). 15.95 o.p. (*0-316-08224-4*) Little Brown & Co.

Bottner, Barbara. Nana Hannah's Piano. 1996. (Illus.). 32p. (J). (ps-3). 15.95 o.s.i (*0-399-22656-7*, G. P. Putnam's Sons) Penguin Group (USA) Inc.

de Brunhoff, Laurent. Babar Raconte le Pianiste. (Babar Ser.). (FRE., Illus.). 48p. (J). (ps-3). 19.95 (*0-7859-8822-X*) French & European Pubns., Inc.

Gilbert, Barbara Snow. Broken Chords. 1998. (Illus.). 188p. (YA). (gr. 5-7). 15.95 (*1-886910-23-5*) Front Street, Inc.

—Broken Chords. 2001. 192p. (YA). (gr. 7 up). reprint ed. mass mkt. 5.50 (*0-440-22887-5*, Laurel Leaf) Random Hse. Children's Bks.

Goffstein, M. B. Two Piano Tuners, RS. 1977. (Illus.). 72p. (J). (ps-3). 12.95 o.s.i (*0-374-38019-8*, Farrar, Straus & Giroux (BYR)) Farrar, Straus & Giroux.

Johnson, Nora. The World of Henry Orient. 2002. 224p. (YA). 12.95 (*0-9714612-0-1*, 01-GMP-001) Green Mansion Pr. LLC.

—The World of Henry Orient. 1998. lib. bdg. 18.95 (*1-56723-068-7*) Yestermorrow, Inc.

Levine, Evan. Not the Piano, Mrs. Medley! 1995. (Illus.). 32p. (J). (ps-3). mass mkt. 5.95 (*0-531-07062-X*, Orchard Bks.) Scholastic, Inc.

McPeak-Bailey, Bobbi. Emma's Happy Birthday Piano. 1991. (Illus.). 36p. (J). (gr. k-4). pap. 5.95 (*0-9625005-1-8*) Wee Pr.

Pascal, Francine, creator. Elizabeth's Piano Lessons. 1993. (Sweet Valley Kids Ser.: No. 45). 80p. (J). (gr. 1-3). pap. 3.50 o.s.i (*0-553-48102-9*) Bantam Bks.

Peyton, K. M. The Beethoven Medal. 1972. (Illus.). (J). (gr. 6-9). 12.45 o.p. (*0-690-12846-0*) HarperCollins Children's Bk. Group.

Ray, Mary L. Pianna. 1994. (Illus.). 32p. (J). (ps-3). 14.95 o.s.i (*0-15-261357-9*) Harcourt Children's Bks.

Schick, Eleanor. A Piano for Julie. 1984. (Illus.). 32p. (J). (gr. k-3). 11.95 o.p. (*0-688-01818-1*); lib. bdg. 11.88 o.p. (*0-688-01819-X*) HarperCollins Children's Bk. Group. (Greenwillow Bks.).

Sweeney, Joyce. Piano Man. 1994. 240p. (YA). mass mkt. 3.99 o.s.i (*0-440-21915-9*) Dell Publishing.

PIRATES—FICTION

Adkins, Jan E. What If You Met a Pirate? 2004. (Single Titles Ser.: Vol. 4). 32p. (gr. 2). 15.95 (*0-7613-1678-7*); lib. bdg. 22.90 (*0-7613-2764-9*) Millbrook Pr., Inc.

Albee, Sarah. Ahoy, Uncle Roy! 2001. (Road to Reading Ser.). (Illus.). 32p. (J). 11.99 (*0-307-46216-1*); pap. 3.99 (*0-307-26216-2*) Random Hse. Children's Bks. (Golden Bks.).

Albert, Burton. The Pirates of Bat Cave Island. 1997. (Illus.). 24p. (J). per. 12.95 (*0-689-81284-1*, Little Simon) Simon & Schuster Children's Publishing.

Allen, Pamela. I Wish I Had a Pirate Suit. 1993. (Illus.). 32p. (J). (gr. 4 up). pap. 3.99 o.s.i (*0-14-050988-7*, Puffin Bks.) Penguin Putnam Bks. for Young Readers.

Allen, Tom & Allen, Patsy. Captain Scruffy. 1993. (Illus.). 32p. (J). (ps-1). 15.95 o.p. (*0-460-88104-3*) Dent, J.M. & Sons GBR. *Dist:* Trafalgar Square.

Ambrus, Victor G. Blackbeard the Pirate. (Illus.). 32p. (J). 1987. (gr. 1-3). 12.95 o.p. (*0-19-279771-9*); 1990. (gr. 2 up). reprint ed. pap. 8.95 o.p. (*0-19-272220-4*) Oxford Univ. Pr., Inc.

Amoss, Berthe. The Secret of Pirate's Manor. 1995. (Illus.). 24p. (J). 14.95 o.p. (*0-8362-4245-9*) Andrews McMeel Publishing.

Andrews, J. S. Cargo for a King. 1973. 176p. (J). (gr. 4-7). 6.95 o.p. (*0-525-27460-X*, Dutton) Dutton/Plume.

Applegate, K. A. Climb Aboard If You Dare! Stories from the Pirates of the Caribbean. 1996. (Illus.). 80p. (J). (gr. 2-6). pap. 3.50 o.s.i (*0-7868-4061-7*); lib. bdg. 14.49 (*0-7868-5033-7*) Disney Pr.

Arden, William. The Mystery of the Purple Pirate. 1982. (Three Investigators Ser.: No. 33). (Illus.). 192p. (J). (gr. 3-7). 6.99 o.s.i (*0-394-94951-X*); pap. 2.95 o.s.i (*0-394-84951-5*) Random Hse. Children's Bks. (Random Hse. Bks. for Young Readers).

Asch, Frank. Pearl's Pirates. 1989. 176p. (J). (gr. k-6). pap. 3.25 o.s.i (*0-440-40245-X*, Yearling) Random Hse. Children's Bks.

Augarde, Steve. Barnaby Shrew, Black Dan & the Mighty Wedgwood. 1980. (Illus.). (J). (ps-3). 7.95 o.p. (*0-233-97104-1*) Blackwell Publishing.

Avi. Captain Grey. 1977. (Illus.). (J). (gr. 5 up). 5.95 o.p. (*0-394-83484-4*); lib. bdg. 6.99 o.s.i (*0-394-93484-9*) Knopf Publishing Group. (Pantheon).

—Captain Grey. 1993. 160p. (YA). (gr. 5-9). pap. 4.95 (*0-688-12234-5*, Morrow, William & Co.) Morrow/Avon.

—Captain Grey. 1993. (J). 11.00 (*0-606-05780-3*) Turtleback Bks.

—Captain Grey. 1993. (Illus.). 160p. (J). (ps-3). 16.00 o.p. (*0-688-12233-7*, Morrow, William & Co.) Morrow/Avon.

Baker, Roberta. Olive's Pirate Party. 2004. (Illus.). (J). 14.95 (*0-316-16792-4*) Little Brown & Co.

Baum, Louis. Juju & the Pirate. 1984. (Illus.). 25p. (J). (gr. k-3). 9.95 o.p. (*0-911745-14-9*, Bedrick, Peter Bks.) McGraw-Hill Children's Publishing.

Bennett, Gertrude. Juan, Carmela & the Pirates. 1978. (Illus.). (J). 4.95 o.p. (*0-533-03108-7*) Vantage Pr., Inc.

Bethlen, Julianna. The Ghost Pirate: A Spirited Hologram Book. 1996. (Illus.). 24p. (J). (gr. k up). 18.95 o.s.i (*0-8037-1958-2*, Dial Bks. for Young Readers) Penguin Putnam Bks. for Young Readers.

Binato, Leonardo. What's Hidden in the Pirate's Chest? 1992. (Turn & Learn Ser.). (Illus.). 12p. (J). (ps-3). 4.95 o.p. (*1-56566-009-9*) LegacyWords Publishing.

Binder, Helga, illus. Wild Wicked Winifred & Horrible Hank. 1999. (J). (*0-7608-3206-4*) Sundance Publishing.

—Wild Wicked Winifred & the Pirates. 1999. (J). (*0-7608-3207-2*) Sundance Publishing.

—Wild Wicked Winifred & the Sea Serpent. 1999. (J). (*0-7608-3204-8*) Sundance Publishing.

—Wild Wicked Winifred & the Treasure Map. 1999. (*0-7608-3205-6*) Sundance Publishing.

Bradman, Tony. The Bluebeards: Revenge at Ryan's Reef. 1992. (Arch Bks.). (Illus.). 64p. (J). (ps-3). pap. 3.50 o.p. (*0-8120-4903-9*) Barron's Educational Series, Inc.

—A Treasury of Pirate Stories. 1999. (Illus.). 160p. (J). (gr. k-4). pap. 6.95 (*0-7534-5190-5*) Larousse Kingfisher Chambers, Inc.

Brouillet, Chrystine. Les Pirates. 1992. (Roman Jeunesse Ser.). (FRE.). 96p. (YA). (gr. 4-7). pap. 8.95 o.p. (*2-89021-180-0*) La Courte Echelle CAN. *Dist:* Firefly Bks., Ltd.

Brouillet, Chrystine & Brochard, Philippe. Les Pirates. 2001. (Roman Jeunesse Ser.). (FRE., Illus.). 96p. (J). pap. 10.95 (*2-89021-474-5*) La Courte Echelle CAN. *Dist:* Firefly Bks., Ltd.

Brouwer, Sigmund. The Missing Map of Pirate's Haven. (Accidental Detective Ser.: Vol. 5). 132p. (J). 1995. (gr. 4-7). pap. text 5.99 (*1-56476-374-9*, 6-3374); 1991. (gr. 3-7). pap. text 4.99 o.p. (*0-89693-858-1*) Cook Communications Ministries.

—Pirate's Cross. 1997. (Cyberquest Ser.: Vol. 3). 64p. (Orig.). (J). (gr. 5-9). mass mkt. 3.50 o.p. (*0-8499-4036-2*) Nelson, Tommy.

Brown, Edi. A Pirate Treasure. 2000. ii, 232p. (YA). (gr. 5-10). 5.95 (*0-9677953-0-3*) Red Fox Publishing Co.

Brown, Jo. Pirate Jam. 2002. (Illus.). 32p. (J). 15.95 (*1-57768-442-7*, American Education Publishing) McGraw-Hill Children's Publishing.

Bulla, Clyde Robert. Pirate's Promise. (Trophy Chapter Bks.). (Illus.). (J). (gr. 2-5). 1994. 96p. pap. 4.95 (*0-06-440457-9*, Harper Trophy); 1958. lib. bdg. o.p. (*0-690-62656-8*) HarperCollins Children's Bk. Group.

Burningham, John. Come Away from the Water, Shirley. 1983. (Trophy Picture Bk.). (Illus.). 32p. (J). (ps-3). pap. 5.95 o.p. (*0-06-443039-1*, Harper Trophy) HarperCollins Children's Bk. Group.

Burston, Patrick. The Pirates of Doom: A Choose-Your-Challenge Gamebook. 1996. (Gamebooks Ser.). (Illus.). 48p. (J). (gr. k-3). bds. 5.99 o.p. (*1-56402-855-0*) Candlewick Pr.

Cannon, A. E. On the Go with Pirate Pete & Pirate Joe! 2002. (Easy-to-Read Ser.). (Illus.). 32p. (J). 13.99 (*0-670-03550-5*); pap. 3.99 (*0-14-230136-1*, Viking) Penguin Putnam Bks. for Young Readers.

Carris, Joan D. A Ghost of a Chance. 1992. (Illus.). 160p. (J). (gr. 3-7). 14.95 o.p. (*0-316-13016-8*) Little Brown & Co.

Carris, Joan Davenport. A Ghost of a Chance. 2003. (Legends of the Carolinas Ser.). 155p. (J). 8.95 (*1-928556-40-X*) Coastal Carolina Pr.

Cartwright, Pauline. Jake Was a Pirate. 1994. (Illus.). (J). 4.25 (*0-383-03754-9*) SRA/McGraw-Hill.

Cerda, Alfredo G. La Princesa y el Pirata (The Princess & the Pirate) 1991. (SPA.). 32p. (J). (gr. 1-3). 12.99 (*968-16-3654-6*) Fondo de Cultura Economica MEX. *Dist:* Continental Bk. Co., Inc.

Chaparro, John E. Pirates Island. 2000. 170p. (J). (gr. 4-7). pap. 11.95 (*1-891929-32-1*) Four Seasons Pubs.

Coerr, Eleanor. The Bell Ringer & the Pirates. 1983. (I Can Read Bks.). (Illus.). 64p. (J). (ps-3). 9.95 (*0-06-021354-X*); lib. bdg. 10.89 o.p. (*0-06-021355-8*) HarperCollins Children's Bk. Group.

Cole, Babette. The Trouble with Uncle. 1992. (Illus.). (J). (ps-3). 14.95 o.p. (*0-316-15190-4*) Little Brown & Co.

Corbett, Scott. Captain Butcher's Body. 1976. (Illus.). 144p. (J). (gr. 4-6). o.p. (*0-316-15727-9*) Little Brown & Co.

Cox, David. Captain Ding, the Double-Decker Pirate. 1992. (Illus.). 32p. (J). (ps-1). o.p. (*0-09-176365-7*) Random Hse. of Canada, Ltd. CAN. *Dist:* Random Hse., Inc.

Cox, Greg. The Pirate Paradox. 1991. (Time Tours Ser.: No. 05). 160p. (YA). mass mkt. 3.50 o.p. (*0-06-106016-X*, HarperTorch) Morrow/Avon.

Dadey, Debbie & Jones, Marcia Thornton. Pirates Don't Wear Pink Sunglasses. 1994. (Adventures of the Bailey School Kids Ser.: No. 9). (Illus.). 80p. (J). (gr. 2-4). mass mkt. 3.99 (*0-590-47298-4*) Scholastic, Inc.

—Pirates Don't Wear Pink Sunglasses. 1994. (Adventures of the Bailey School Kids Ser.: No. 9). (J). (gr. 2-4). 10.14 (*0-606-06671-3*) Turtleback Bks.

Davis, Guy. Freddi Fish & the Pirate's Treasure. 2001. (Humongous Ser.). 12p. (J). bds. 9.99 incl. cd-rom (*1-58668-066-8*) Lyrick Studios.

Davis, Tim. Mice of the Nine Lives. 1994. 86p. (J). (gr. 1-2). pap. 6.49 (*0-89084-755-X*, 080556) Jones, Bob Univ. Pr.

—Mice of the Seven Seas. 1995. 138p. (J). (gr. 1-2). pap. 6.49 (*0-89084-845-9*, 092312) Jones, Bob Univ. Pr.

Day, Jan. The Pirate, Pink. 2001. (Illus.). 32p. (J). (gr. k-3). 14.95 (*1-56554-879-5*) Pelican Publishing Co., Inc.

—Pirate Pink & Treasures of the Reef. 2003. (Illus.). 32p. (J). 14.95 (*1-58980-086-9*) Pelican Publishing Co., Inc.

Dewey, Ariane. Lafitte, the Pirate. 1985. (Illus.). 48p. (J). (gr. 1-4). 12.95 o.p. (*0-688-04229-5*); lib. bdg. 12.88 o.p. (*0-688-04230-9*) HarperCollins Children's Bk. Group. (Greenwillow Bks.).

—Lafitte, the Pirate. 1993. (Illus.). 48p. (J). (gr. 1 up). pap. 4.95 o.p. (*0-688-04578-2*, Morrow, William & Co.) Morrow/Avon.

Dickens, Charles. Captain Murderer. 1986. (Illus.). 32p. (J). (ps-2). 12.95 o.p. (*0-688-06306-3*); lib. bdg. 12.88 o.p. (*0-688-06307-1*) HarperCollins Children's Bk. Group.

Disney Staff. Peter Pan. 2002. (Illus.). 24p. (J). (gr. k-3). pap. 3.25 (*0-7364-1295-6*, RH/Disney) Random Hse. Children's Bks.

—Pirate's Cove: Paint with Water. 1998. (Disney Ser.). (Illus.). 32p. (J). (ps-3). pap. text 3.99 o.p. (*0-307-27000-9*, 27000, Golden Bks.) Random Hse. Children's Bks.

Dixon, Franklin W. Pirates Ahoy! 1999. (Hardy Boys Are: No. 13). (Illus.). 80p. (J). (gr. 2-4). pap. 3.99 (*0-671-02786-7*, Aladdin) Simon & Schuster Children's Publishing.

Doodle Art Staff. Pirates Ahoy. 2002. (Doodle Art Mini Tubes Ser.). (Illus.). (J). 6.99 (*0-8431-6661-4*, Price Stern Sloan) Penguin Putnam Bks. for Young Readers.

Downer, Maggie, illus. The Treasure Hunt. 1992. 32p. (J). (ps-4). 6.98 o.p. (*1-56566-018-8*) LegacyWords Publishing.

Drake, David. Pirates. 2002. (Cricket of Dew Drop Dell Ser.). (Illus.). 32p. (J). 3.49 (*1-885631-59-6*, Family Of Man Pr., The) Hutchison, G.F. Pr.

Drew, David. Ah, Treasure! 1993. (Voyages Ser.). (Illus.). (J). 3.75 (*0-383-03611-9*) SRA/McGraw-Hill.

Dubowski, Cathy. Pirate School. 1996. (All Aboard Reading Ser.). (J). 10.14 (*0-606-11751-2*) Turtleback Bks.

Dubowski, Cathy & Dubowski, Mark. Pirate School. 1996. (All Aboard Reading Ser.: Level 2). (Illus.). 48p. (J). (gr. 1-3). 13.99 o.s.i (*0-448-41133-4*); (ps-3). 3.99 (*0-448-41132-6*) Penguin Putnam Bks. for Young Readers. (Grosset & Dunlap).

Dupasquier, Philippe. Andy's Pirate Ship, ERS. 1994. 32p. (J). 11.95 o.p. (*0-8050-3154-5*, Holt, Henry & Co. Bks. For Young Readers) Holt, Henry & Co.

Engle, Marty M. & Barnes, Johnny Ray, Jr. Driven to Death. l.t. ed. 1996. (Strange Matter Ser.: No. 3). 124p. (J). (gr. 4-6). lib. bdg. 21.27 o.p. (*0-8368-1669-2*) Stevens, Gareth Inc.

Fangface: A Time Machine Trip to the Pirate's Ship. 1980. 96p. (J). (gr. 3-9). 1.25 o.s.i (*0-448-17172-4*) Ace Bks.

Ferguson, Virginia & Durkin, Peter. Yo Ho! Yo Ho! 1994. (Illus.). (J). (*0-383-03729-8*) SRA/McGraw-Hill.

Ferrone, John M. Gus & the Pirate Treasure. Date not set. (Illus.). 36p. (J). (ps-5). pap. 16.95 (*1-928811-01-9*) Story Stuff, Inc.

Fienberg, Anna. Dead Sailors Don't Bite. 1997. (Illus.). 128p. (Orig.). (J). (gr. 3-6). pap. 6.95 o.p. (*1-86448-088-2*) Allen & Unwin Pty., Ltd. AUS. *Dist:* Independent Pubs. Group.

—Horrendo's Curse. 2002. (Illus.). 160p. (J). 18.95 (*1-55037-773-6*); pap. 6.95 (*1-55037-772-8*) Annick Pr., Ltd. CAN. *Dist:* Firefly Bks., Ltd.

—Pirate Trouble for Wiggy & Boa. 1997. (Illus.). 128p. (Orig.). (J). (gr. 3-6). pap. 6.95 o.p. (*1-86448-253-2*) Allen & Unwin Pty., Ltd. AUS. *Dist:* Independent Pubs. Group.

Finn, Felicity. Jeremy & the Air Pirates. 1998. (Illus.). 219p. (J). (gr. 3-8). pap. 5.95 (*1-896764-02-9*) Second Story Pr. CAN. *Dist:* Orca Bk. Pubs., Univ. of Toronto Pr.

Fleischman, Sid. The Ghost in the Noonday Sun. 1999. 144p. (gr. 4-7). pap. text 4.50 o.s.i (*0-440-41583-7*) Bantam Bks.

—The Ghost in the Noonday Sun. 1989. (Illus.). (YA). (gr. 4-7). 16.00 (*0-688-08410-9*, Greenwillow Bks.) HarperCollins Children's Bk. Group.

—The Ghost in the Noonday Sun. 1995. 144p. (J). (gr. 3-7). mass mkt. 3.50 (*0-590-43662-7*, Scholastic Paperbacks) Scholastic, Inc.

—The Ghost in the Noonday Sun. 1999. (J). 10.55 (*0-606-18960-2*) Turtleback Bks.

—The 13th Floor: A Ghost Story. 1995. (Illus.). 144p. (J). (gr. 3 up). 15.99 (*0-688-14216-8*, Greenwillow Bks.) HarperCollins Children's Bk. Group.

—The 13th Floor: A Ghost Story. unabr. ed. 1996. (Illus.). 134p. (J). (gr. 3-5). pap. 28.00 (*0-8072-7615-4*, YA900SP, Listening Library) Random Hse. Audio Publishing Group.

—The 13th Floor: A Ghost Story. 1997. (Illus.). 176p. (gr. 3-7). pap. text 4.99 (*0-440-41243-9*, Yearling) Random Hse. Children's Bks.

—The 13th Floor: A Ghost Story. 1997. (J). 10.55 (*0-606-11011-9*) Turtleback Bks.

Flemming, Paul. Bowbeard Walks the Plank. Reader's Digest Editors, ed. 1998. (Playmobil Play Feet Ser.: Vol. 1). (Illus.). 14p. (J). (ps-3). bds. 6.99 (*1-57584-232-7*) Reader's Digest Children's Publishing, Inc.

Fox, Christyan & Fox, Diane. Pirate PiggyWiggy. 2003. (Illus.). 24p. (J). 11.95 o.s.i (*1-929766-76-9*) Handprint Bks.

Fox, Mem. Tough Boris. abr. ed. 1994. (Illus.). 32p. (J). (ps-3). 16.00 (*0-15-289612-0*) Harcourt Children's Bks.

Freeman, Maggie. Danger! Space Pirates. 1988. (Illus.). 112p. (J). (gr. 5-7). 13.95 o.p. (*0-340-39307-6*) Hodder & Stoughton, Ltd. GBR. *Dist:* Lubrecht & Cramer, Ltd., Trafalgar Square.

Gale, Cathy. Pirates! Puzzles, Jokes, & Things to Make & Do. 1994. (Illus.). 32p. (J). (ps-3). bds. 2.99 o.p. (*1-56402-406-7*) Candlewick Pr.

Gardner, Cliff. Black Caesar, Pirate. 1980. (Illus.). 96p. (J). (gr. 4 up). 6.95 o.p. (*0-931948-09-6*) Peachtree Pubs., Ltd.

Gelsey, James. Scooby-Doo & the Sunken Ship: Scooby-Doo y el Barco Hundido. 2004. (Scooby-Doo Ser.). (ENG & SPA.). 64p. (J). pap. 3.99 (*0-439-55116-1*, Scholastic en Espanola) Scholastic, Inc.

Giff, Patricia Reilly. The Gift of the Pirate Queen. (Illus.). (gr. 4-6). 1982. 160p. (J). lib. bdg. 11.95 o.s.i (*0-385-28339-3*, Delacorte Pr.); 1982. 160p. (J). 9.95 o.s.i (*0-440-02970-8*, Delacorte Pr.); 1982. 160p. (J). lib. bdg. 9.89 o.s.i (*0-440-02972-4*, Delacorte Pr.); 1983. 192p. reprint ed. pap. text 4.99 (*0-440-43046-1*) Dell Publishing.

—The Gift of the Pirate Queen. 1982. (J). 10.55 (*0-606-04681-X*) Turtleback Bks.

Gilman, Phoebe. Grandma & the Pirates. ed. 1993. (J). (gr. 2). spiral bd. (*0-616-01651-4*) Canadian National Institute for the Blind/Institut National Canadien pour les Aveugles.

—Grandma & the Pirates. (J). (gr. k-3). 1992. 32p. pap. 4.99 (*0-590-43425-X*); 1990. 12.95 o.p. (*0-590-43426-8*) Scholastic, Inc.

—Grandma & the Pirates. 1990. (J). 10.19 o.p. (*0-606-01846-8*) Turtleback Bks.

Gliori, Debi. The Princess & the Pirate King. 1996. (Illus.). 32p. (J). (ps-2). tchr. ed. o.s.i (*0-7534-5023-2*) Kingfisher Publications, plc.

Gregory, Kristiana. The Stowaway: A Tale of California Pirates. 144p. (J). (gr. 4-7). 2003. mass mkt. 4.50 (*0-590-48823-6*, Scholastic Paperbacks); 1995. (Illus.). pap. 3.99 (*0-590-48822-8*) Scholastic, Inc.

—The Stowaway: A Tale of California Pirates. 1997. 10.55 (*0-606-13045-4*) Turtleback Bks.

Griffin, Nicholas. The Requiem Shark: A Novel. 2001. 384p. reprint ed. pap. 14.00 o.s.i (*0-425-18158-8*) Berkley Publishing Group.

Hagen, Michael. Sail to Caribee. 1998. 157p. (J). (gr. 5 up). pap. 9.99 (*0-88092-410-1*, 4101) Royal Fireworks Publishing Co.

Hamilton, Richard. Violet & the Mean & Rotten Pirates. 2003. (Illus.). (J). 127p. 4.99 (*1-58234-848-0*); 96p. (gr. 1-5). pap. 6.95 (*1-58234-866-9*, Bloomsbury Children) Bloomsbury Publishing.

Hapka, Catherine. Pirates Need Sleep, Too! A Bedtime Book. 1998. (Illus.). 32p. (J). (ps up). pap. text 3.99 (*0-307-10433-8*, Golden Bks.) Random Hse. Children's Bks.

Haseley, Dennis. The Pirate Who Tried to Capture the Moon. 1983. (Illus.). 48p. (J). (gr. k-4). lib. bdg. 11.89 o.p. (*0-06-022227-1*) HarperCollins Children's Bk. Group.

Hausman, Gerald. Tom Cringle: Battle on the High Seas. 2000. (Illus.). 224p. (J). (gr. 4-6). 16.95 (*0-689-82810-1*, Simon & Schuster Children's Publishing) Simon & Schuster Children's Publishing.

—Tom Cringle: The Pirate & the Patriot. 2001. (Illus.). 160p. (J). 16.00 (*0-689-82811-X*, Simon & Schuster Children's Publishing) Simon & Schuster Children's Publishing.

Hawes, Charles Boardman. The Dark Frigate. (J). E-Book 3.95 (*0-594-02339-4*) 1873 Pr.

Hawthorn, P. Pirate McGrew & His Nautical Crew. 1995. (Rhyming Stories Ser.). (Illus.). 24p. (gr. 2 up). (J). lib. bdg. 12.95 (*0-88110-778-6*); (YA). pap. 4.95 (*0-7460-1646-8*) EDC Publishing. (Usborne).

Haynes. The Ghost of Gravstone Hearth. 1977. (J). 6.95 o.p. (*0-525-66544-7*) NAL.

Hellsing, Lennart. The Pirate Book. Smith, William J., tr. 1972. (Illus.). 166p. (J). (gr. k-2). 4.95 o.p. (*0-440-07221-2*); lib. bdg. 4.58 o.p. (*0-440-07222-0*) Dell Publishing. (Delacorte Pr.).

Helquist, Brett. Jolly Roger. 2004. 40p. (J). 15.99 (*0-06-623805-6*); lib. bdg. 16.89 (*0-06-623806-4*) HarperCollins Pubs.

Hilz, Tammy. Jewels of the Sea: Once a Pirate. 2000. (Jewels of the Sea Ser.). 32p. mass mkt. 5.50 o.s.i (*0-8217-6697-X*, Zebra Bks.) Kensington Publishing Corp.

—Once a Rebel. 2001. (Jewels of the Sea Ser.). 32p. mass mkt. 5.50 o.s.i (*0-8217-6779-8*, Zebra Bks.) Kensington Publishing Corp.

Hooks, William H. Lo-Jack & Pirates. 1990. (J). mass mkt. o.p. (*0-553-53059-3*, Dell Books for Young Readers) Random Hse. Children's Bks.

—Lo-Jack & the Pirates. 1991. (Bank Street Ready-to-Read Ser.). 48p. (J). (ps-3). 9.99 o.s.i (*0-553-07092-4*); pap. 3.99 o.p. (*0-553-35210-5*) Bantam Bks.

—Lo-Jack & the Pirates. 1999. (Bank Street Reader Collection). (Illus.). 48p. (J). (gr. 2-4). lib. bdg. 21.26 (*0-8368-1782-6*) Stevens, Gareth Inc.

—Lo-Jack & the Pirates. 1991. E-Book (*1-58824-238-2*); E-Book (*1-59019-310-5*); E-Book (*1-59019-311-3*) ipicturebooks, LLC.

Hughes, Carol. Jack Black & Ship of Thieves. 2001. 240p. (J). (gr. 3-8). pap. 4.99 (*0-375-80473-0*, Random Hse. Bks. for Young Readers) Random Hse. Children's Bks.

Hutchins, Pat. One-Eyed Jake. 1994. (Illus.). 32p. (J). (ps up). reprint ed. pap. 4.95 (*0-688-13113-1*, Morrow, William & Co.) Morrow/Avon.

—One-Eyed Jake. 1994. 10.15 o.p. (*0-606-06638-1*) Turtleback Bks.

Impey, Rose. Who's a Clever Girl? 2003. (Yellow Bananas Ser.). (Illus.). 48p. (J). (gr. 3-4). pap. 4.95 (*0-7787-0976-0*) Crabtree Publishing Co.

Isadora, Rachel. The Pirates of Bedford Street. 1988. (Illus.). 32p. (J). (ps-3). 12.95 o.p. (*0-688-05206-1*); lib. bdg. 12.88 o.p. (*0-688-05208-8*) HarperCollins Children's Bk. Group. (Greenwillow Bks.).

Jackson, Dave & Jackson, Neta. Hostage on the Nighthawk: William Penn. 2000. (Trailblazer Bks.: Vol. 32). (Illus.). 144p. (J). (gr. 3-7). pap. 5.99 (*0-7642-2265-1*) Bethany Hse. Pubs.

Jacques, Brian. The Angel's Command. 2003. (Illus.). 448p. (J). (gr. 3-6). 23.99 (*0-399-23999-5*, G. P. Putnam's Sons) Penguin Putnam Bks. for Young Readers.

Jaggi, Jean-Pierre. Pirate Pete Sets Sail. James, J. Alison, tr. from GER. 2003. 32p. (J). lib. bdg. 16.50 (*0-7358-1833-9*); (Illus.). 15.95 (*0-7358-1832-0*) North-South Bks., Inc.

Jaspersohn, William. The Scrimshaw Ring. 2002. (Family Heritage Ser.). (Illus.). 32p. (J). (gr. 4-7). text 15.95 (*0-916718-19-0*) Vermont Folklife Ctr.

Johnson, Charles. Pieces of Eight. 1989. (Footprints in Time Ser.). (Illus.). 110p. (J). (gr. 3-6). 9.95 (*0-944770-00-2*) Discovery Pr., Inc.

Jones, Elizabeth McDavid. Mystery on Skull Island. 2001. (American Girl Collection: Bk. 15). (Illus.). 192p. (J). 9.95 (*1-58485-342-5*); pap. 5.95 (*1-58485-341-7*) Pleasant Co. Pubns. (American Girl).

Karen Poth. Three Pirates & Me. 2004. (Illus.). 32p. 7.99 (*0-310-70725-0*) Zondervan.

Kaserman, James F. & Kaserman, Sarah Jane. The Legend of Gasparilla: A Tale for All Ages. 2000. 304p. (YA). pap. 14.95 (*0-9674081-1-3*) Pirate Publishing International.

Kassirer, Sue. Lazy Bones the Pirate. 1996. (Illus.). pap. 3.25 o.p. (*0-679-88049-6*) Random Hse., Inc.

Kennedy, Kim & Kennedy, Doug, illus. Pirate Pete: "Where There's Gold I'm a Goin'" 2002. 40p. (J). 15.95 (*0-8109-4356-5*) Abrams, Harry N., Inc.

Kennedy, Richard. Amy's Eyes. 1985. (Illus.). 448p. (J). (ps up). 15.00 o.s.i (*0-06-023219-6*); lib. bdg. 14.89 o.p. (*0-06-023220-X*) HarperCollins Children's Bk. Group.

Ketchersid, Sarah. Bloodthirsty Pirates. 2000. (Illus.). 32p. (J). (gr. 2-3). pap. 3.49 o.p. (*0-525-46357-7*, Dutton Children's Bks.) Penguin Putnam Bks. for Young Readers.

Kimmel, Eric A. The Erie Canal Pirates. 2002. (Illus.). 32p. (J). (gr. k-3). tchr. ed. 16.95 (*0-8234-1657-7*) Holiday Hse., Inc.

—Robin Hook, Pirate Hunter! 2001. (Illus.). 32p. (J). (gr. k-4). pap. 15.95 (*0-590-68199-0*) Scholastic, Inc.

Kimmel, Eric A. & Dooling, Michael. Robin Hook, Pirate Hunter! 2001. (Illus.). pap. (*0-590-68219-9*) Scholastic, Inc.

Kraske, Robert. The Sea Robbers. 1977. (Illus.). 147p. (J). (gr. 5 up). 6.95 o.p. (*0-15-271170-8*) Harcourt Children's Bks.

Kroll, Steven. The Pigrates Clean Up, ERS. 1993. (Illus.). 32p. (J). (ps). 14.95 o.p. (*0-8050-2368-2*, Holt, Henry & Co. Bks. For Young Readers) Holt, Henry & Co.

—The Pirates Clean Up. (Illus.). 32p. (J). 3.98 o.p. (*0-8317-9888-2*) Smithmark Pubs., Inc.

Krosoczka, Jarrett J. Bubble Bath Pirates. 2003. (Illus.). 40p. (J). (ps-k). 15.99 (*0-670-03599-8*, Puffin Bks.) Penguin Putnam Bks. for Young Readers.

Ladybird Books Staff, ed. Treasure Island. 1998. (Ladybird Picture Classics Ser.). (Illus.). 32p. (J). (gr. 2 up). pap. 4.99 o.p. (*0-7214-7377-6*, Ladybird Bks.) Penguin Group (USA) Inc.

Laird, Marnie. Water Rat. 1998. (Illus.). 196p. (J). (gr. 4-7). 15.95 (*1-890817-08-2*) Winslow Pr.

Lamm, C. Drew. Pirates. (J). 2001. (Illus.). 40p. (gr. 1-4). 15.99 (*0-7868-0392-4*); 2000. 32p. lib. bdg. 15.49 (*0-7868-2343-7*) Hyperion Bks. for Children.

Lamut, Sonja. Pirates. 1999. (Sticker Stories Ser.). 16p. (J). (ps-3). 4.99 (*0-448-41988-2*) Penguin Putnam Bks. for Young Readers.

Lasky, Kathryn. Grace the Pirate. 1997. (Hyperion Chapters Ser.). (Illus.). 64p. (J). (gr. 3-4). pap. 3.95 (*0-7868-1147-1*) Disney Pr.

—Grace the Pirate. 1997. (Chapters Ser.). (Illus.). 64p. (J). (gr. 3-4). lib. bdg. 14.49 (*0-7868-2236-8*) Hyperion Paperbacks for Children.

—Grace the Pirate. 1997. (Hyperion Chapters Ser.). 10.10 (*0-606-13448-4*) Turtleback Bks.

Laurence, Daniel. Captain & Matey Set Sail, Bk. 2. 2001. (I Can Read Bks.). (Illus.). 64p. (J). (gr. k-3). 15.99 (*0-06-028956-2*); lib. bdg. 15.89 (*0-06-028957-0*) HarperCollins Children's Bk. Group.

—Captain & Matey Set Sail. 2003. (I Can Read Book 2 Ser.). (Illus.). 64p. (J). (ps-3). pap. 3.99 (*0-06-444285-3*) HarperCollins Pubs.

Lawrence, Caroline. The Pirates of Pompeii. 2003. (Roman Mysteries Ser.: Bk. III). 160p. (gr. 6-9). lib. bdg. 22.90 (*0-7613-2604-9*); (YA). 15.95 (*0-7613-1584-5*) Millbrook Pr., Inc. (Roaring Brook Pr.).

Lawrence, Iain. The Buccaneers. (Illus.). 256p. (gr. 5-9). 2003. pap. 5.50 (*0-440-41671-X*, Yearling); 2001. text 15.95 (*0-385-32736-6*, Dell Books for Young Readers) Random Hse. Children's Bks.

—The Buccaneers. l.t. ed. 2001. (Illus.). 320p. (J). 23.95 (*0-7862-3464-4*) Thorndike Pr.

—Ghost Boy. (YA). (gr. 7-12). 2000. (Illus.). 336p. 15.95 (*0-385-32739-0*, Dell Books for Young Readers); 2002. 352p. reprint ed. mass mkt. 5.99 (*0-440-41668-X*, Laurel Leaf) Random Hse. Children's Bks.

—Ghost Boy. l.t. ed. 2001. (Young Adult Ser.). 413p. (J). (gr. 8-12). 23.95 (*0-7862-3243-9*) Thorndike Pr.

Lawson, Robert. Captain Kidd's Cat. 1984. (Illus.). (J). (gr. 2-4). mass mkt. 7.95 (*0-316-51735-6*) Little Brown & Co.

Leigh, Susannah. Uncle Pete the Pirate. 1994. (Usborne Young Puzzle Adventures Ser.). (Illus.). 32p. (J). (ps-2). pap. 5.95 (*0-7460-1529-1*); lib. bdg. 13.95 (*0-88110-713-1*) EDC Publishing. (Usborne).

Leonard, Marcia. Violet & the Pirates. 1992. (What Belongs? Ser.). (Illus.). 24p. (J). (ps-1). 4.95 o.p. (*0-671-72976-4*); lib. bdg. 6.95 o.p. (*0-671-72975-6*) Silver, Burdett & Ginn, Inc.

Little Golden Books Staff. Disney's Ghostship Little Gold. 9999. (J). (ps-2). o.p. (*0-307-00112-1*, Golden Bks.) Random Hse. Children's Bks.

Lofgren, Ulf. Alvin the Pirate. 1990. (Illus.). 32p. (J). (ps-3). lib. bdg. 19.95 o.p. (*0-87614-402-4*, Carolrhoda Bks.) Lerner Publishing Group.

—Alvin the Pirate: Picture Book. 1991. (J). (ps-3). pap. 5.95 o.p. (*0-87614-551-9*, Carolrhoda Bks.) Lerner Publishing Group.

London, Jack. La Expedicion del Pirata. 3rd ed. 1988. (Punto Juvenil Ser.). (SPA.). (J). 10.05 o.p. (*0-606-05401-4*) Turtleback Bks.

Long, Melinda. How I Became a Pirate. 2003. (Illus.). 44p. (J). 16.00 (*0-15-201848-4*) Harcourt Children's Bks.

MacDonald, Marianne. The Pirate Queen. 1992. (Illus.). 32p. (J). (ps-3). 12.95 o.p. (*0-8120-6288-4*); pap. 5.95 o.p. (*0-8120-4952-7*) Barron's Educational Series, Inc.

MacGill-Callahan, Sheila. How the Boats Got Their Sails. 1997. (Illus.). (J). (ps-3). 14.89 o.s.i (*0-8037-1542-0*, Dial Bks. for Young Readers) Penguin Putnam Bks. for Young Readers.

—To Capture the Wind. 1997. (Illus.). 32p. (J). (ps-3). 14.99 o.s.i (0-8037-1541-2, Dial Bks. for Young Readers) Penguin Putnam Bks. for Young Readers.

Maden, Mary. The Great Shark Adventure. 1999. (Earth/Ocean Adventures Ser.: Vol. 1). (Illus.). (J). (gr. 1-7). pap. 5.95 (1-890479-60-8) Dog & Pony Publishing.

—The Secret of Blackbeard's Treasure: A Pony's Tale. 1995. (Outer Banks Animal Ser.). (Illus.). 20p. (Orig.). (J). (gr. 1-4). pap. 5.95 (0-9646970-1-7) Dog & Pony Publishing.

Mahy, Margaret. The Horrendous Hullabaloo. 1992. (Illus.). 320p. (J). (ps-3). 13.00 o.p. (0-670-84547-7, Viking Children's Bks.) Penguin Putnam Bks. for Young Readers.

—The Pirate Uncle. 1994. (Illus.). 128p. (J). (gr. 4-7). 14.95 (0-87951-555-4) Overlook Pr., The.

—The Pirates' Mixed-Up Voyage. 1995. (Illus.). 192p. (YA). (gr. 7 up). pap. 3.99 o.p. (0-14-037128-1, Puffin Bks.) Penguin Putnam Bks. for Young Readers.

—Pirates Mixed up Voyage. 1993. (Illus.). 192p. (J). (gr. 4-8). 13.99 o.p. (0-8037-1350-9, Dial Bks. for Young Readers) Penguin Putnam Bks. for Young Readers.

—Tingleberries, Tuckertubs & Telephones. (Illus.). 96p. (gr. 3-7). 1998. (YA). pap. 4.99 o.p. (0-14-038973-3); 1996. (J). 12.99 o.s.i (0-670-86331-9, Viking Children's Bks.) Penguin Putnam Bks. for Young Readers.

—Tingleberries, Tuckertubs & Telephones. 1998. 11.14 (0-606-13052-7) Turtleback Bks.

Mahy, Margaret & Chamberlain, Margaret. The Man Whose Mother Was a Pirate. 1987. (Illus.). 32p. (J). (gr. 3-7). reprint ed. pap. 4.99 o.p. (0-14-050624-1, Puffin Bks.) Penguin Putnam Bks. for Young Readers.

Marston, Elsa. Cynthia & the Runaway Gazebo. 1992. (Illus.). 32p. (J). (gr. k-4). 14.00 o.p. (0-688-10282-4); lib. bdg. 13.93 o.p. (0-688-10283-2) Morrow/Avon. (Morrow, William & Co.).

Marzollo, Dan, et al. I Spy Pirate Treasure. 2003. (I Spy Ser.). (Illus.). 24p. (J). pap. 3.50 (0-439-45525-1) Scholastic, Inc.

Masefield, John. Jim Davis: A High-Sea Adventure. 2002. 160p. (YA). (gr. 4-7). pap. 15.95 (0-439-40436-3, Chicken Hse., The) Scholastic, Inc.

Mayhar, Ardath & Dunn, Marylois. Timber Pirates. Richards, Jerri S., ed. ltd. ed. 1998. (YA). (gr. 6-12). pap. (1-887303-19-7) Blue Lantern Publishing.

McAllister, Angela. The Babies of Cockle Bay. 1994. (Illus.). 32p. (J). (ps-3). 13.95 o.p. (0-8120-6424-0); pap. 5.95 o.p. (0-8120-1952-0) Barron's Educational Series, Inc.

McCafferty, Catherine. Pirate Candy Treasure. 1998. (Illus.). 10p. (J). (ps-3). bds. 4.99 (1-57151-607-7, Nibble Me Bks.) Playhouse Publishing.

McCaughrean, Geraldine. The Pirate's Son. (gr. 5-9). 1999. 304p. mass mkt. 4.99 (0-590-20348-7); 1998. 224p. (YA). 16.95 o.s.i (0-590-20344-4) Scholastic, Inc.

McCulley, Johnston. Zorro & the Pirate Raiders. 1986. 176p. pap. 2.50 o.p. (0-553-24670-4) Bantam Bks.

McCully, Emily Arnold. The Pirate Queen. 1998. (Illus.). 32p. (J). (gr. k-3). pap. 6.99 o.s.i (0-698-11629-1, PaperStar) Penguin Putnam Bks. for Young Readers.

—The Pirate Queen. 1998. 12.19 (0-606-13709-2) Turtleback Bks.

McNaughton, Colin. Anton B. Stanton & the Pirates. 1980. (Benn Bk.). 32p. (ps-3). 8.95 o.p. (0-385-15759-2); lib. bdg. 8.95 o.p. (0-385-15760-6) Doubleday Publishing.

—Captain Abdul's Pirate School. (Illus.). 40p. (J). 1994. (ps-3). 16.99 o.s.i (1-56402-429-6); 1996. (gr. 4-7). reprint ed. bds. 7.99 (1-56402-843-7) Candlewick Pr.

—Jolly Roger. 1988. (J). pap. 14.95 o.p. (0-671-66843-9, Simon & Schuster Children's Publishing) Simon & Schuster Children's Publishing.

—Jolly Roger: And the Pirates of Captain Abdul. 2nd ed. 1995. (Illus.). 48p. (J). (gr. 1-5). bds. 7.99 o.p. (1-56402-512-8) Candlewick Pr.

McPhail, David M. Edward & the Pirates. 1997. (J). (ps-3). 15.95 (0-316-56885-8); (Illus.). 32p. 16.95 (0-316-56344-7) Little Brown & Co.

Metaxas, Eric & Kenney, Cindy. Jonah & the Pirates Who Usually Don't Do Anything. 2002. (Illus.). 32p. (J). 12.99 (0-310-70460-X) Zondervan.

Meyer, Louis. Bloody Jack: Being an Account of the Curios Adventures of Mary Jacky Faber, Ship's Boy. 2002. (Illus.). 336p. (YA). (gr. 6-9). 17.00 (0-15-216731-5) Harcourt Children's Bks.

Mezek, Karen. Katie Lost in the South Seas. 1991. (J). 4.99 o.p. (0-89081-900-9) Harvest Hse. Pubs.

Miles, Patricia. Mind Pirates. 1984. 160p. (J). (gr. 5-9). 13.95 o.p. (0-241-10989-2) Trafalgar Square.

Mitter, Matt. Treasure of Pirate Island: A Lift-the-Flap PlayBook. Reader's Digest Editors, ed. 1998. (Fisher-Price Great Adventures Lift-The-Flap Playbooks Ser.). (Illus.). 10p. (J). (ps-3). bds. 7.99 o.p. (1-57584-218-1, Reader's Digest Young Families, Inc.) Reader's Digest Children's Publishing, Inc.

Moerbeek, Kees. When the Wild Pirates Go Sailing. 1997. 9.95 o.p. (1-888443-43-X) Intervisual Bks., Inc.

—When the Wild Pirates Go Sailing. (Triangle Pop-up Ser.). (Illus.). 12p. (J). (ps up). 1992. 4.95 o.p. (0-8431-3450-X); 1989. 9.95 o.p. (0-8431-2731-7) Penguin Putnam Bks. for Young Readers. (Price Stern Sloan).

Montgomery, Hugh. The Voyage of the Arctic Tern. 2002. (Illus.). 216p. (J). (gr. 5-7). 16.99 (0-7636-1902-7) Candlewick Pr.

Moore, Robin. The Man with the Silver Oar. 2002. 192p. (J). (gr. 5 up). 15.95 (0-380-97877-6) HarperCollins Children's Bk. Group.

—The Man with the Silver Oar. 2002. 192p. (J). (gr. 5 up). lib. bdg. 15.89 (0-06-000048-1) HarperCollins Pubs.

Morgan, Allen. Matthew & the Midnight Pirates. 1998. (Matthew's Midnight Adventures Ser.). (Illus.). 32p. (J). (ps-3). pap. 6.99 (0-7737-5940-9) Stoddart Kids CAN. Dist: Fitzhenry & Whiteside, Ltd.

Mundy, Talbot. Purple Pirate. 2001. 377p. 26.95 (0-8488-2767-8) Amereon, Ltd.

Muppet Treasure Island. 1996. 40p. pap. 12.95 (0-7935-6713-0) Leonard, Hal Corp.

Muppet Treasure Island. 1995. (Deluxe Sound Story Bks.). (Illus.). 24p. (YA). bds. o.p. (0-307-74039-0, Golden Bks.) Random Hse. Children's Bks.

Nelson, Ginger K. Pirate's Revenge. Kratoville, Betty Lou, ed. 1989. (Meridian Bks.). (Illus.). 64p. (J). (gr. 3-9). lib. bdg. 4.95 o.p. (0-87879-654-1) High Noon Bks.

Newman, Marjorie. Hornpipe's Hunt for Pirate Gold. 1998. (Gamebook Preschool Puzzles Ser.). (Illus.). 32p. (J). (gr. k-3). bds. 5.99 o.p. (0-7636-0419-4) Candlewick Pr.

Nick, Sharratt. Ahoy Pirate Pete. 2004. 14p. (J). 8.99 (0-7636-2197-8) Candlewick Pr.

Nickles, Greg. Pirates. 1996. (Crabapples Ser.). 12.10 (0-606-12793-3) Turtleback Bks.

O'Dell, Scott. The Black Pearl. 1996. 112p. (J). mass mkt. 2.49 o.s.i (0-440-22028-9); 96p. (gr. 5-9). pap. text 4.99 (0-440-41146-7) Dell Publishing.

—The Black Pearl. 1977. 96p. (YA). (gr. 7-12). mass mkt. 4.99 (0-440-90803-5, Laurel Leaf) Random Hse. Children's Bks.

Oleksy, Walter. The Pirates of Deadman's Cay. 1982. (Hiway Book). (Illus.). 112p. (J). (gr. 7-9). 9.95 o.p. (0-664-32693-5) Westminster John Knox Pr.

Osborne, Mary Pope. Piratas Despues del Medio Dia. 2003. (SPA.). (J). pap. 4.95 (1-930332-52-1) Lectorum Pubns., Inc.

—Pirates Past Noon. unabr. ed. 2000. (Magic Tree House Ser. : No. 4). (J). (gr. k-3). pap. 17.00 incl. audio Random Hse. Audio Publishing Group.

—Pirates Past Noon. 1994. (Magic Tree House Ser.: No. 4). (Illus.). 80p. (J). (gr. k-3). lib. bdg. 11.99 (0-679-92425-6); pap. 3.99 (0-679-82425-1) Random Hse., Inc.

—Pirates Past Noon. 1994. (Magic Tree House Ser.: No. 4). (Illus.). (J). (gr. k-3). 10.14 (0-606-07068-0) Turtleback Bks.

Parker, Beth. Thomas Knew There Were Pirates Living in the Bathroom. 1990. (Illus.). 28p. (J). (ps-3). (0-88753-224-1); pap. (0-88753-201-2) Black Moss Pr.

Peake, Mervyn Laurence, illus. Captain Slaughterboard Drops Anchor. 2nd ed. 2001. 48p. (J). 16.99 (0-7636-1625-7) Candlewick Pr.

Perego, Maria. Comes to Life Storyplayer & Topo Gigio & the Friends of the Forest Book Set: Comes to Life Storyplayer & Topo Gigio e Gli Animaletti del Bosco. Preziosi, Giochi, tr. from ENG. 1994. (Comes to Life Bks.). (ITA.). 16p. (J). (ps-2). (1-57234-004-5) YES! Entertainment Corp.

—Topo Gigio e il Pirata (Topo Gigio & the Pirate with the Beard) Preziosi, Giochi, tr. from ENG. 1994. (Comes to Life Bks.). (ITA.). 16p. (J). (ps-2). (1-57234-005-3) YES! Entertainment Corp.

Peter Pan. 2003. (Illus.). 12.99 (0-7868-3479-X) Disney Pr.

Petrie, Glen. Lucy & the Pirates. 2001. (Illus.). 32p. (J). (gr. k-5). pap. 6.95 (1-896580-38-6) Interlink Publishing Group, Inc.

—Lucy & the Pirates. 2000. (Illus.). 32p. (J). (gr. k-4). text 14.95 (1-896580-02-5) Tradewind Bks. CAN. Dist: Tricycle Pr.

Pirata (Pirate) 2001. (Jigsaw Ser.). 20p. (J). (ps-3). 7.95 (1-57145-901-4, Silver Dolphin Bks.) Advantage Pubs. Group.

Platt, Richard. Pirate Diary: The Journal of Jake Carpenter. 2001. (Illus.). 64p. (J). (gr. 4-7). 17.99 (0-7636-0848-3) Candlewick Pr.

Preminger, Victoria. Barkley Unleashed: A Pirate's Tail. abr. ed. 1997. (Illus.). 32p. (J). (ps-2). 14.95 o.p. incl. audio (0-7871-1027-2, NewStar Pr.) NewStar Media, Inc.

Priest, Robert. The Old Pirate of Central Park. 1999. (Illus.). 30p. (J). (ps-3). tchr. ed. 16.00 (0-395-90505-2) Houghton Mifflin Co.

Pyle, Howard. Tales of Pirates & Buccaneers. Suriano, Gregory R., ed. 1998. (Illus.). 207p. (J). text 15.00 o.p. (0-7881-5277-7) DIANE Publishing Co.

—Tales of Pirates & Buccaneers. 1994. (Illus.). (J). 12.99 o.s.i (0-517-10162-9) Random Hse. Value Publishing.

Random House Disney Staff. Treasure Planet SIR Step 3. 2002. (Step into Reading Ser.). 48p. (J). (gr. 1-3). pap. 3.99 (0-7364-2021-5, RH/Disney) Random Hse. Children's Bks.

—Treasure Planet Sir 3. 2002. (Step into Reading Ser.). 48p. (J). lib. bdg. 11.99 (0-7364-8014-5, RH/Disney) Random Hse. Children's Bks.

Random House Disney Staff & Trimble, Irene. Pirates of the Caribbean: The Curse of the Black Pearl. novel ed. 2003. (Illus.). 128p. (J). (gr. 4-7). pap. 4.99 (0-7364-2171-8, RH/Disney) Random Hse. Children's Bks.

Ransome, Arthur. Missee Lee: The Swallows & Amazons in the China Seas. 2002. (Godine Storyteller Ser.). (Illus.). 352p. (J). pap. 14.95 (1-56792-196-5) Godine, David R. Pub.

Reed, Neil, illus. Treasure Island. 1996. 96p. (J). (gr. 1-6). 9.98 (1-85854-190-5) Brimax Bks., Ltd.

Rees, Celia. Pirates. 2003. (Illus.). 300p. (0-7475-5950-3) Bloomsbury Publishing, Ltd. GBR. Dist: Trafalgar Square.

Reuter, Bjarne. Ring of the Slave Prince. 2003. 384p. 22.99 (0-525-47146-4, Dutton Children's Bks.) Penguin Putnam Bks. for Young Readers.

Richards, Kitty. Yo Ho Ho & a Bottle of Milk: A Time Travel Adventure. 2000. (Rugrats Files: Bk. 2). (Illus.). 144p. (J). (gr. 1-5). pap. 3.99 (0-689-83335-0, Simon Spotlight) Simon & Schuster Children's Publishing.

Roberts, Dannel. Me & Uncle Mike & the Pirate Ship. Lt. ed. 2001. (Me & Uncle Mike Children's Book Series: Bk. 2). (Illus.). 36p. (J). (ps-3). per. 14.95 (1-893459-01-2) Lions & Tigers & Bears Publishing, Inc.

Roberts, Nancy. Blackbeard's Cat. 1998. (Cat of Nine Tales Ser.: Vol. I). (Illus.). 96p. (J). pap. 9.95 (1-886391-41-6, Shipwreck Pr.) Narwhal Pr., Inc.

Robinet, Harriette Gillem. The Twins, the Pirates & the Battle of New Orleans. 1997. 144p. (J). (gr. 3-7). 15.00 o.s.i (0-689-81208-6, Atheneum) Simon & Schuster Children's Publishing.

Rodgers, Frank. Pirate & the Pig. (Illus.). 32p. (J). pap. 9.95 (0-14-055561-7) Penguin Bks., Ltd. GBR. Dist: Trafalgar Square.

Rosen, Michael J. William Shakespeare: His Work & His World. 2001. (Illus.). 104p. (J). (gr. 6 up). 19.99 (0-7636-1568-4) Candlewick Pr.

Ross, Tony, illus. The Kingfisher Treasury of Pirate Stories. 2003. (Kingfisher Treasury of Stories Ser.). 160p. (J). pap. 5.95 (0-7534-5632-X, Kingfisher) Houghton Mifflin Co. Trade & Reference Div.

Rossiter-McFarland, Lyn. The Pirate's Parrot. 2003. (Illus.). 40p. (J). (gr. k-2). 14.95 (1-58246-014-0) Tricycle Pr.

Rossman, Parker. Pirate Slave. 1976. (J). (gr. 6-12). 6.95 o.p. (0-8407-6517-7, Dutton Children's Bks.) Penguin Putnam Bks. for Young Readers.

Rotsler, William. The Pirate Movie. Schneider, Meg F., ed. 1982. (Illus.). 192p. (J). (gr. 3 up). pap. 2.85 o.s.i (0-671-45999-6, Simon & Schuster Children's Publishing) Simon & Schuster Children's Publishing.

Rubel, Nicole. Pirate Jupiter & the Moondogs. 1987. (Pied Piper Bks.). (Illus.). 32p. (J). (ps-3). pap. 4.95 o.p. (0-8037-0164-0, Dial Bks. for Young Readers) Penguin Putnam Bks. for Young Readers.

Ryan, John. Pugwash & the Ghost Ship. 1968. (Illus.). (J). (gr. k-3). 22.95 o.p. (0-87599-146-7) Phillips, S.G. Inc.

—Pugwash in the Pacific. 1973. (Illus.). 32p. (J). (gr. k-3). 16.95 o.p. (0-87599-199-8) Phillips, S.G. Inc.

Saponaro, Dominic, et al. Heart of Steele. 2003. (Pirate Hunter Ser.). (Illus.). 208p. (J). pap. 4.99 (0-689-85298-3, Aladdin) Simon & Schuster Children's Publishing.

Saunders, Susan. The Revenge of the Pirate Ghost. 1997. (Black Cat Club Ser.: No. 5). (Illus.). 80p. (J). (gr. 1-5). pap. 3.95 o.p. (0-06-442065-5, Harper Trophy) HarperCollins Children's Bk. Group.

—The Revenge of the Pirate Ghost. 1997. (Black Cat Club Ser.). 9.15 o.p. (0-606-11138-7) Turtleback Bks.

Scarry, Richard. Pie Rats Ahoy! 2002. (Illus.). (J). 11.91 (0-7587-6251-8) Book Wholesalers, Inc.

—Pie Rats Ahoy! 1994. (Step into Reading Ser.). (Illus.). 32p. (J). (ps-3). lib. bdg. 11.99 (0-679-94760-4, Random Hse. Bks. for Young Readers) Random Hse. Children's Bks.

—Richard Scarry's Pie Rats Ahoy! 1994. (Step into Reading Ser.). (Illus.). 32p. (ps-1). pap. 3.99 (0-679-84760-X, Random Hse. Bks. for Young Readers) Random Hse. Children's Bks.

Schaad, Hans P. Rhine Pirates. Crawford, Elizabeth D., tr. 1968. (Illus.). (J). (gr. k-3). 4.75 o.p. (0-15-266680-X) Harcourt Children's Bks.

Schubert, Ingrid & Schubert, Dieter. Wild Will. 1994. (J). (ps-3). lib. bdg. 14.95 (0-87614-816-X, Carolrhoda Bks.) Lerner Publishing Group.

Scieszka, Jon. The Not-So-Jolly Roger. (Illus.). 64p. (J). 1993. (Time Warp Trio Ser.: Vol. 2). (gr. 2-6). pap. 4.99 (0-14-034684-8); 1991. (Time Warp Trio Ser.). (gr. 4-7). 14.99 (0-670-83754-7, Viking Children's Bks.) Penguin Putnam Bks. for Young Readers.

—Not-So-Jolly Roger Twt Promo. 2003. (Time Warp Trio Ser.). (Illus.). 76p. pap. 2.66 (0-14-250131-X, Puffin Bks.) Penguin Putnam Bks. for Young Readers.

Sharratt, Nick. Mrs. Pirate. (Illus.). (J). 1996. bds. 2.99 o.p. (1-56402-684-1); 1994. 24p. 8.95 o.p. (1-56402-249-8) Candlewick Pr.

Shub, Elizabeth. Cutlass in the Snow. 1986. (Illus.). 48p. (J). (gr. 1-4). 12.95 o.p. (0-688-05927-9); lib. bdg. 14.93 o.p. (0-688-05928-7) HarperCollins Children's Bk. Group. (Greenwillow Bks.).

Slote, Elizabeth. Nana & Bold Berto. 1924. (J). o.s.i (0-688-12980-3); lib. bdg. o.s.i (0-688-12981-1) Morrow/Avon. (Morrow, William & Co.).

Smallcomb, Pam. Camp Buccaneer. 2002. (Ready-for-Chapters Ser.). (Illus.). 64p. (J). (gr. 1-3). lib. bdg. 11.89 (0-689-84383-6, Aladdin Library); (gr. 2-5). pap. 3.99 (0-689-84384-4, Aladdin) Simon & Schuster Children's Publishing.

Smith, Duncan. Fred the Pirate. (Fred the Ted Ser.). (Illus.). (J). o.p. (1-85435-248-2) Cavendish, Marshall Corp.

—Fred the Pirate. 1991. (Fred the Ted Ser.). (Illus.). 25p. (J). (gr. k-2). 11.95 o.p. (0-237-51144-4) Evans Brothers, Ltd. GBR. Dist: Trafalgar Square.

Smyth, Iain. Pirate Plunder's Treasure Hunt: A Pop-Up Whodunit. 1996. (Illus.). 12p. (J). (gr. 4-7). 16.99 o.s.i (0-525-45693-7, Dutton Children's Bks.) Penguin Putnam Bks. for Young Readers.

Sohl, Marcia & Dackerman, Gerald. Treasure Island. 1976. (Now Age Illustrated Ser.). 16p. (J). (gr. 4-10). pap. 2.95 (0-88301-106-9); pap., stu. ed. 1.25 (0-88301-185-9) Pendulum Pr., Inc.

Sprenger. Pirates in Petticoats. 1996. (J). pap. o.p. (0-679-87645-6) Random Hse., Inc.

Stashko, Ilona K. Secret Treasures of Coco Island. 1995. (Illus.). 24p. (J). (ps-4). pap. 4.95 (1-882651-00-6) Come Alive Pubns., Inc.

Stevenson, Robert Louis. La Isla del Tesoro. (Coleccion Clasicos de la Juventud). (SPA., Illus.). 188p. (J). 12.95 (84-7189-017-8, ORT301) Ortells, Alfredo Editorial S.L. ESP. Dist: Continental Bk. Co., Inc.

—La Isla del Tesoro. (Coleccion Estrella). (SPA., Illus.). 64p. (J). 14.95 (950-11-0009-X, SGM009) Sigmar ARG. Dist: Continental Bk. Co., Inc.

—La Isla del Tesoro. 1999. (Coleccion "Clasicos Juveniles" Ser.). (SPA., Illus.). 188p. (J). (gr. 4-7). pap. 9.95 (1-58348-832-4) iUniverse, Inc.

—Kidnapped & Treasure Island. 1981. 464p. (YA). (gr. 9-12). mass mkt. 3.50 o.p. (0-451-52206-0, Signet Classics) NAL.

—Secuestrado. 3rd ed. (Coleccion Clasicos en Accion). (SPA., Illus.). 80p. (YA). (gr. 5-8). 15.95 (84-241-5781-8, EV1487) Everest de Ediciones y Distribucion, S.L. ESP. Dist: Lectorum Pubns., Inc.

—Secuestrado. 2002. (Clover Ser.). (SPA., Illus.). 156p. (YA). 11.50 (84-392-8006-8, EV5548) Lectorum Pubns., Inc.

—Treasure Island. 2002. (Great Illustrated Classics). (Illus.). 240p. (J). (gr. 3-8). lib. bdg. 21.35 (1-57765-805-1, ABDO & Daughters) ABDO Publishing Co.

—Treasure Island. 1979. (Illus.). (J). 35.00 o.p. (0-913870-78-1) Abaris Bks.

—Treasure Island. 1999. (Abbeville Classics Ser.). (Illus.). 176p. (J). pap. 7.95 (0-7892-0551-3, Abbeville Kids) Abbeville Pr., Inc.

—Treasure Island. 1962. (Classics Ser.). (YA). (gr. 7 up). mass mkt. 2.95 (0-8049-0002-7, CL-2) Airmont Publishing Co., Inc.

—Treasure Island. 1996. (Andre Deutsch Classics). 253p. (J). (gr. 5-8). 11.95 (0-233-99038-0) Andre Deutsch GBR. Dist: Trafalgar Square, Trans-Atlantic Pubns., Inc.

—Treasure Island. 1982. 208p. (J). mass mkt. 1.75 o.s.i (0-553-21099-8, Bantam Classics) Bantam Bks.

—Treasure Island. 1991. (Illus.). 45p. (J). 3.75 (0-425-12335-9, Classics Illustrated) Berkley Publishing Group.

—Treasure Island. 1975. (Dent's Illustrated Children's Classics Ser.). 281p. (J). reprint ed. text 11.00 o.p. (0-460-05001-X) Biblio Distribution.

—Treasure Island. 2002. (YA). 12.34 (0-7587-7947-X) Book Wholesalers, Inc.

—Treasure Island. 1995. (Longmeadow Press Children's Library). (Illus.). 224p. (J). (gr. 2-5). 10.95 o.p. (0-681-00769-9) Borders Pr.

—Treasure Island. McGuinn, Nicholas, ed. 1995. (Literature Ser.). (Illus.). 256p. pap. text 9.95 (0-521-48568-1) Cambridge Univ. Pr.

—Treasure Island. Marshall, Michael J., ed. abr. ed. 1997. (Core Classics Ser.). (Illus.). 160p. (J). (gr. 4-6). lib. bdg. 10.95 (1-890517-05-4); pap. 5.95 (1-890517-04-6) Core Knowledge Foundation.

—Treasure Island. 1988. mass mkt. 2.25 (0-938819-26-7, Aerie) Doherty, Tom Assocs., LLC.

—Treasure Island. 1993. (Thrift Editions Ser.). 160p. (J). reprint ed. pap. 1.50 (0-486-27559-0) Dover Pubns., Inc.

—Treasure Island. 1996. 304p. (YA). (gr. 10 up). pap. 14.95 (0-9652952-3-0) Doyle Studio Pr.

—Treasure Island. 2nd ed. 1998. (Illustrated Classic Book Ser.). (Illus.). 61p. (J). (gr. 3 up). reprint ed. pap. text 4.95 (1-56767-239-6) Educational Insights, Inc.

—Treasure Island. 2001. (YA). (gr. 5-12). pap. text 9.95 (0-8359-0234-X) Globe Fearon Educational Publishing.

—Treasure Island. 1980. (Pocket Pop-Ups Ser.). (Illus.). 16p. (J). (ps-5). 2.95 o.s.i (0-89346-143-1) Heian International Publishing, Inc.

—Treasure Island. abr. ed. 2001. (YA). (gr. 7 up). audio 13.95 (1-84032-412-0) Hodder Headline Audiobooks GBR. *Dist:* Trafalgar Square.

—Treasure Island, ERS. 1993. (Little Classics Ser.). (Illus.). xx, 379p. (J). (gr. 4-8). 15.95 o.p. (0-8050-2773-4, Holt, Henry & Co. Bks. For Young Readers) Holt, Henry & Co.

—Treasure Island. 1997. text 8.25 (0-03-051503-3) Holt, Rinehart & Winston.

—Treasure Island. 2001. (Kingfisher Classics Ser.). 352p. (J). (gr. 4-6). tchr. ed. 15.95 (0-7534-5380-0, Kingfisher) Houghton Mifflin Co. Trade & Reference Div.

—Treasure Island. unabr. ed. 1998. (Wordsworth Classics Ser.). (YA). (gr. 6-12). 5.27 (0-89061-103-3, R1033WW) Jamestown.

—Treasure Island. (Young Collector's Illustrated Classics Ser.). (Illus.). 192p. (J). (gr. 3-7). 9.95 (1-56156-456-7) Kidsbooks, Inc.

—Treasure Island. 1992. (Everyman's Library Children's Classics Ser.). (Illus.). 320p. (gr. 2 up). 14.95 (0-679-41800-8, Everyman's Library) Knopf Publishing Group.

—Treasure Island. 1999. (Illus.). 240p. (YA). (gr. 3 up). reprint ed. 7.95 (1-56852-233-9, Konecky & Konecky) Konecky, William S. Assocs., Inc.

—Treasure Island. 1998. (Cloth Bound Pocket Ser.). 240p. 7.95 (3-89508-458-1, 521307) Konemann.

—Treasure Island. l.t. ed. 1997. (Large Print Heritage Ser.). 323p. (YA). (gr. 7-12). lib. bdg. 30.95 (1-58118-008-X, 21494) LRS.

—Treasure Island. 1977. (McKay Illustrated Classics Ser.). (J). (gr. 7 up). 7.95 o.p. (0-679-20393-1) McKay, David Co., Inc.

—Treasure Island. 1993. (Illus.). 24p. (J). (gr. k up). pap. 2.50 o.s.i (1-56144-103-1, Honey Bear Bks.) Modern Publishing.

—Treasure Island. 1998. (Signet Classic Shakespeare Ser.). 224p. (J). mass mkt. 3.95 (0-451-52704-6) NAL.

—Treasure Island. abr. ed. 1996. pap. 19.95 o.s.i incl. audio (0-7871-0016-1, NewStar Pr.) NewStar Media, Inc.

—Treasure Island. 1998. (Twelve-Point Ser.). 204p. reprint ed. lib. bdg. 25.00 (1-58287-075-6) North Bks.

—Treasure Island. 1994. (Read-Along Ser.). (YA). pap., stu. ed. 34.95 incl. audio (0-88432-972-0, S23919) Norton Pubs., Inc., Jeffrey /Audio-Forum.

—Treasure Island. 1993. (Illus.). 80p. (J). pap. text 5.95 o.p. (0-19-422722-7) Oxford Univ. Pr., Inc.

—Treasure Island. Letley, Emma, ed. & intro. by. 1985. (WC-P Ser.). 240p. (YA). (gr. 7-12). pap. 5.95 o.p. (0-19-281681-0) Oxford Univ. Pr., Inc.

—Treasure Island. 1996. (Classic Ser.). (J). (Illus.). 56p. (gr. 2-4). 2.99 o.s.i (0-7214-5609-X, Ladybird Bks.); (gr. 4-7). pap. 6.95 o.p. incl. audio (0-7871-1071-X, 651804) Penguin Group (USA) Inc.

—Treasure Island. (Whole Story Ser.). 1996. (Illus.). 304p. (YA). (gr. 7 up). 23.99 o.s.i (0-670-86920-1, Viking Children's Bks.); 1994. (Illus.). 342p. (J). (gr. 4-7). 17.99 (0-448-40562-8, Grosset & Dunlap); 1975. (J). pap. 2.25 o.p. (0-14-030036-8, Puffin Bks.) Penguin Putnam Bks. for Young Readers.

—Treasure Island. Vogel, Malvina, ed. 1989. (Great Illustrated Classics Ser.: Vol. 7). (Illus.). 240p. (J). (gr. 3-6). 9.95 (0-86611-958-2) Playmore, Inc., Pubs.

—Treasure Island. (Short Classics Learning Files Ser.). (J). (gr. 4 up). 1988. 22.00 o.p. (0-8172-2196-4); 1983. (Illus.). lib. bdg. 22.80 o.p. (0-8172-1655-3) Raintree Pubs.

—Treasure Island. (Illustrated Library for Children). (Illus.). (J). 2002. 272p. 12.99 (0-517-22114-4); 1990. 96p. (gr. 3-5). pap. 3.99 (0-679-80402-1) Random Hse. Children's Bks. (Random Hse. Bks. for Young Readers).

—Treasure Island. 1995. (Children's Library Ser.). (J). 1.10 o.s.i (0-517-14145-0) Random Hse. Value Publishing.

—Treasure Island. (Courage Unabridged Classics Ser.). (YA). 2001. 208p. pap. 6.00 o.p. (0-7624-0555-4); 1989. (Illus.). 273p. reprint ed. text 12.98 o.p. (0-89471-778-2) Running Pr. Bk. Pubs. (Courage Bks.).

—Treasure Island. (Aladdin Classics Ser.). 2000. 368p. (J). (gr. 3-7). pap. 3.99 (0-689-83212-5, Aladdin); 1981. (Illus.). 273p. (YA). (gr. 4-7). 28.00 (0-684-17160-0, Atheneum) Simon & Schuster Children's Publishing.

—Treasure Island. 1999. (Saddleback Classics). (Illus.). (J). 13.10 (0-606-21576-X) Turtleback Bks.

—Treasure Island. Seelye, John, ed. & intro. by. 1999. (Classics Ser.). (Illus.). 224p. (J). pap. 5.95 (0-14-043768-1, Penguin Classics) Viking Penguin.

—Treasure Island. 1998. (Children's Classics). 224p. (J). (gr. 3-7). pap. 3.95 (1-85326-103-3, 1033WW) Wordsworth Editions, Ltd. GBR. *Dist:* Advanced Global Distribution Services.

—Treasure Island: With a Discussion of Courage. 2003. (Values in Action Illustrated Classics Ser.). (J). (1-59203-054-8) Learning Challenge, Inc.

—Treasure Island: With Story of the Treasure of Normon Island. Date not set. (J). (gr. 5-6). reprint ed. lib. bdg. 22.95 (0-89190-236-8, American Reprint Co.) Amereon, Ltd.

—Treasure Island: With Story of the Treasure of Normon Island. 1982. (Bantam Classics Ser.). (Illus.). 208p. (gr. 7-12). mass mkt. 3.95 (0-553-21249-4, Bantam Classics) Bantam Bks.

—Treasure Island: With Story of the Treasure of Normon Island. 1989. (Illus.). 192p. (J). (gr. 4 up). 1.50 o.p. (0-8120-5942-5) Barron's Educational Series, Inc.

—Treasure Island: With Story of the Treasure of Normon Island. 1986. (Children's Classics Ser.). (Illus.). 258p. (J). (gr. 4 up). 11.95 o.p. (0-681-40059-5) Borders Pr.

—Treasure Island: With Story of the Treasure of Normon Island. 1990. 252p. (YA). (gr. 4-7). mass mkt. 3.99 (0-8125-0508-5, Tor Classics) Doherty, Tom Assocs., LLC.

—Treasure Island: With Story of the Treasure of Normon Island. 1988. 224p. (J). (gr. 4-7). pap. 2.50 o.p. (0-590-41617-0) Dramatists Play Service, Inc.

—Treasure Island: With Story of the Treasure of Normon Island. 1992. (Illus.). (J). (0-89434-128-6, Ferguson Publishing Co.) Facts on File Inc.

—Treasure Island: With Story of the Treasure of Normon Island. 1987. (Illus.). (J). (gr. 5-12). reprint ed. lib. bdg. 9.95 o.s.i (0-8052-3707-0, Schocken) Knopf Publishing Group.

—Treasure Island: With Story of the Treasure of Normon Island. 1965. 224p. (J). (gr. 6). mass mkt. 3.95 o.s.i (0-451-52189-7); (YA). (gr. 7 up). mass mkt. 1.75 o.p. (0-451-51917-5) NAL. (Signet Classics).

—Treasure Island: With Story of the Treasure of Normon Island. 1982. (Oxford Progressive English Readers Ser.). (Illus.). (YA). (gr. 7-12). pap. 4.95 o.p. (0-19-581379-0) Oxford Univ. Pr., Inc.

—Treasure Island: With Story of the Treasure of Normon Island. (Illus.). 192p. 1995. (YA). (gr. 5 up). pap. 19.95 (1-85793-488-1); 1994. (J). (gr. 4 up). 24.95 (1-85145-962-6) Pavilion Bks., Ltd. GBR. *Dist:* Trafalgar Square.

—Treasure Island: With Story of the Treasure of Normon Island. (Illus.). (J). 9999. (Children's Classics Ser.: No. 740-1). (gr. 3-5). pap. 3.50 o.p. (0-7214-0597-5); 1994. (Classics Ser.). 56p. text 3.50 (0-7214-1658-6) Penguin Group (USA) Inc. (Ladybird Bks.).

—Treasure Island: With Story of the Treasure of Normon Island. (Puffin Classics Ser.). 1994. (Illus.). 320p. (YA). (gr. 4-7). pap. 4.99 (0-14-036672-5, Puffin Bks.); 1992. (Illus.). 176p. (J). 20.00 o.p. (0-670-84685-6, Viking Children's Bks.); 1984. 240p. (J). (gr. 2-5). pap. 3.50 o.p. (0-14-035016-0, Puffin Bks.); 1996. (Illus.). 304p. (J). (gr. 7-12). 19.99 (0-670-86795-0, Viking Children's Bks.); 1947. (Illus.). 352p. (J). (gr. 1-9). 13.95 o.p. (0-448-06025-6, Grosset & Dunlap) Penguin Putnam Bks. for Young Readers.

—Treasure Island: With Story of the Treasure of Normon Island. 1978. (Illus.). (J). (gr. 6-9). 2.95 o.p. (0-448-14920-6) Putnam Publishing Group, The.

—Treasure Island: With Story of the Treasure of Normon Island. (J). (gr. 4-7). 1993. 32p. pap. 4.95 (0-8114-6844-5); 1983. (Illus.). pap. 9.27 o.p. (0-8172-2026-7) Raintree Pubs.

—Treasure Island: With Story of the Treasure of Normon Island. 1988. (Illustrated Classics Ser.). (Illus.). (J). 3.99 o.s.i (0-517-65587-X, Random Hse. Bks. for Young Readers) Random Hse. Children's Bks.

—Treasure Island: With Story of the Treasure of Normon Island. 1989. (Children's Classics Ser.). 272p. (J). 12.99 o.s.i (0-517-61816-8) Random Hse. Value Publishing.

—Treasure Island: With Story of the Treasure of Normon Island. 1987. (Illus.). 224p. (YA). (gr. 5 up). 12.95 o.p. (0-89577-262-0) Reader's Digest Assn., Inc., The.

—Treasure Island: With Story of the Treasure of Normon Island. 1993. (N. C. Wyeth Illustrated Classics Ser.). (Illus.). 274p. (YA). (gr. 5 up). reprint ed. text 16.95 o.p. (1-56138-264-7) Running Pr. Bk. Pubs.

—Treasure Island: With Story of the Treasure of Normon Island. 1988. 224p. (J). (gr. 4-7). mass mkt. 4.50 (0-590-44501-4, Scholastic Paperbacks); 1972. (YA). (gr. 7-12). reprint ed. pap. 2.25 o.p. (0-590-40105-X) Scholastic, Inc.

—Treasure Island: With Story of the Treasure of Normon Island. 1994. (Classic Story Bks.). (J). (gr. 4 up). 4.98 o.p. (0-8317-1649-5) Smithmark Pubs., Inc.

—Treasure Island: With Story of the Treasure of Normon Island. 1989. (Kelpie Ser.). (Illus.). 256p. (J). (gr. 5-8). pap. 5.95 o.p. (0-86241-190-4) Trafalgar Square.

—Treasure Island Coloring Book. 1997. (Illus.). (J). pap. 2.95 (0-486-29566-4) Dover Pubns., Inc.

—Treasure Island Promotion. 2003. 224p. (J). pap. 3.99 o.p. (0-14-250091-7, Puffin Bks.) Penguin Putnam Bks. for Young Readers.

Stevenson, Robert Louis & Hitchner, Earle. Treasure Island. 1999. (Illus.). 245p. (J). (0-03-054463-7) Holt, Rinehart & Winston.

Strickland, Brad. Salty Dog. 1997. (Adventures of Wishbone Ser.: No. 2). (Illus.). 144p. (J). (gr. 2-5). mass mkt. 3.99 o.p. (1-57064-194-3, Big Red Chair Bks.) Lyrick Publishing.

—Salty Dog. l.t. ed. 1999. (Adventures of Wishbone Ser.: No. 2). (Illus.). 140p. (J). (gr. 4 up). lib. bdg. 22.60 (0-8368-2298-6) Stevens, Gareth Inc.

—Salty Dog. 1997. E-Book (1-58824-430-X); E-Book (1-58824-399-0) ipicturebooks, LLC.

Strong, Jeremy. The Indoor Pirates. l.t. ed. 1997. (Illus.). (J). 16.95 o.p. (0-7451-8928-8, Galaxy Children's Large Print) BBC Audiobooks America.

—Indoor Pirates on Treasure Island. (Illus.). 96p. (J). pap. 7.95 (0-14-038637-8) Penguin Bks., Ltd. GBR. *Dist:* Trafalgar Square.

—Pirate Pandemonium. l.t. ed. 2002. (Illus.). (J). 16.95 (0-7540-7807-8, Galaxy Children's Large Print) BBC Audiobooks America.

Stroud, Jonathan. The Lost Treasure of Captain Blood: A Pirate Puzzle Adventure. 1996. (Illus.). 32p. (J). (gr. 4-7). 14.99 o.p. (1-56402-875-5) Candlewick Pr.

Sturges, Philomen. This Little Pirate. 2005. (Illus.). 15.99 (0-525-46440-9, Dutton Children's Bks.) Penguin Putnam Bks. for Young Readers.

Thompson, Julian F. Terry & the Pirates. (YA). (gr. 7 up). 2002. 320p. pap. 5.99 (0-689-85085-9, Simon Pulse); 2000. (Illus.). 272p. 17.00 (0-689-83076-9, Atheneum) Simon & Schuster Children's Publishing.

Thompson, Lynaire. Red Pirate. 1998. (Adventure Zone Ser.). pap. text 4.50 (1-57840-212-3) Acclaim Bks.

Torrey, Michele. Bottles of Eight & Pieces of Rum. 1998. 138p. (J). (gr. 4-7). pap. 9.99 (0-88092-321-0, 3210) Royal Fireworks Publishing Co.

Townsend, Tom. Powderhorn Passage: Sequel to Where the Pirates Are, Vol. 3. Roberts, Melissa, ed. 1988. 112p. (J). (gr. 4-5). 11.95 o.p. (0-89015-642-5) Eakin Pr.

Tucker, Kathy. Do Pirates Take Baths? Levine, Abby, ed. 1994. (Illus.). 32p. (J). (ps-3). lib. bdg. 15.95 o.p. (0-8075-1696-1) Whitman, Albert & Co.

Valerius, Sandra. Rumbeard. 1985. 76p. (J). (gr. 3-5). 6.45 o.p. (0-533-06211-X) Vantage Pr., Inc.

Vinton, Iris. Look Out for Pirates. 1961. (Illus.). 72p. (J). (gr. 1-2). 9.99 o.s.i (0-394-90022-7) Beginner Bks.

Vischer, Lisa. Three Pirates & You. 2004. (Illus.). 32p. 7.99 (0-310-70724-2) Zondervan.

Walker, Richard. The Barefoot Book of Pirates. 1998. (Illus.). 64p. (J). (gr. 4-7). reprint ed. 18.95 (1-901223-79-5) Barefoot Bks., Inc.

Wallace, John. Pirate Boy. 2002. (Illus.). 32p. (J). 17.95 (0-00-198421-7); pap. 9.95 (0-00-664776-6) HarperCollins Pubs. Ltd. GBR. *Dist:* Trafalgar Square.

Wallace, Lew. Blackbeard & the Topsail Island Pirate. 1999. 112p. (J). (gr. 3-7). pap. 6.95 (1-889062-03-0) Artel Publishing.

—The Pirate of Topsail Island. 1997. 80p. (J). (gr. 1-6). pap. 5.95 (1-889062-05-7) Artel Publishing.

—The Pirate Strikes Again. 1998. 80p. (J). (gr. 3-7). pap. 5.95 (1-889062-06-5) Artel Publishing.

Wechter, Nell W. & Tucker, Bruce. Teach's Light. 1999. (Chapel Hill Book Ser.). (Illus.). 160p. (J). (gr. 4-7). pap. 9.95 (0-8078-4793-3) Univ. of North Carolina Pr.

Weise, Selene H. C. Gold for a Boat. 2001. (Illus.). 68p. (J). (gr. 1-6). 5.95 (1-57249-270-8, Burd Street Pr.) White Mane Publishing Co., Inc.

Weiss, Ellen. The Pirates of Tarnoonga. Spinner, Stephanie, ed. 1986. (Droid Adventure Ser.). (Illus.). 32p. (J). (gr. k-4). 4.95 o.p. (0-394-87926-0, Random Hse. Bks. for Young Readers) Random Hse. Children's Bks.

West, Jerry. The Happy Hollisters at Sea Gull Beach. 1979. (Happy Hollisters Ser.: No. 3). (Illus.). (J). (gr. 1-5). reprint ed. 2.95 o.p. (0-448-16872-3) Putnam Publishing Group, The.

Whatley, Bruce. Cowboy Pirate. 2002. (Illus.). 32p. 14.95 (0-207-19891-8) HarperCollins Pubs.

Wibberley, Leonard. Flint's Island. 1995. (Adventure Library). 176p. (J). (gr. 4-7). reprint ed. pap. 11.95 (1-883937-11-6, 11-6) Bethlehem Bks.

—Flint's Island, RS. 1972. 176p. (J). (gr. 7 up). 4.95 o.p. (0-374-32331-3, Farrar, Straus & Giroux (BYR)) Farrar, Straus & Giroux.

Wickstrom, Lois June & Lorrah, Jean. Nessie & the Living Stone. 2001. pap. 13.80 (1-58338-616-5, CrossroadsPub.Org) CrossroadsPub.com.

Wilhelm, Hans. Pirates Ahoy! 1990. (Gold Banner Bks.). (Illus.). 48p. (J). (ps-2). 2.95 o.s.i (0-448-04340-8, Grosset & Dunlap) Penguin Putnam Bks. for Young Readers.

Williams, Marcia, illus. & retold by. Sinbad the Sailor. 1996. 40p. (J). (gr. 2-6). reprint ed. bds. 7.99 o.p. (1-56402-814-3) Candlewick Pr.

Willson, Sarah. Up & Away, Reptar! 2000. (Ready-to-Read Ser.). (Illus.). 32p. (J). (ps-3). per. 3.99 (0-671-77315-1, Simon & Schuster Children's Publishing) Simon & Schuster Children's Publishing.

Wolcott, Patty. Pirates, Pirates over the Salt, Salt Sea. 1981. (Illus.). 24p. (J). (ps-1). 8.95 (0-201-08335-3) HarperCollins Children's Bk. Group.

Woychuk, Denis. Mimi & Gustov in Pirates! (Illus.). 32p. (J). 3.98 o.p. (0-8317-3066-8) Smithmark Pubs., Inc.

—Pirates! 1992. (Illus.). (J). (ps-3). 14.00 o.p. (0-688-10336-7); lib. bdg. 13.93 o.p. (0-688-10337-5) HarperCollins Children's Bk. Group.

Yolen, Jane. The Ballad of the Pirate Queens. ed. 1999. (J). (gr. 2). spiral bd. (0-616-01821-5) Canadian National Institute for the Blind/Institut National Canadien pour les Aveugles.

—The Ballad of the Pirate Queens. 1998. (Illus.). 32p. (J). (gr. k-7). pap. 7.00 (0-15-201885-9, Voyager Bks./Libros Viajeros) Harcourt Children's Bks.

—The Ballad of the Pirate Queens. 1995. (Illus.). 32p. (J). (ps-3). 16.00 o.s.i (0-15-200710-5) Harcourt Trade Pubs.

—The Ballad of the Pirate Queens. 1998. 12.15 (0-606-13178-7) Turtleback Bks.

—Commander Toad & the Space Pirates. 1997. (Illus.). 64p. (J). (gr. 2-5). pap. 5.99 (0-698-11419-1, PaperStar) Penguin Putnam Bks. for Young Readers.

—Commander Toad & the Space Pirates. 1987. (Illus.). 64p. (J). (gr. 1-4). 11.99 o.s.i (0-698-30749-6); 6.95 o.s.i (0-698-20633-9) Putnam Publishing Group, The. (Coward-McCann).

Young, Joseph R. Legend of the Lost Josephine Mine: A Fascinating Adventure. 2001. 221p. (J). pap. 13.95 (1-55517-550-3, Bonneville Bks.) Cedar Fort, Inc./CFI Distribution.

Zakon, Miriam S. Floating Minyan of Pirate's Cove. 1986. (Judaica Youth Ser.). (Illus.). 152p. (J). (gr. 3-9). 8.95 (0-910818-62-2); pap. 6.95 (0-910818-63-0) Judaica Pr., Inc., The.

POETS—FICTION

Barnes, Henry. Percy MacKaye: Poet of Old Worlds & New. 2000. (Illus.). 127p. pap. 12.50 (0-932776-26-4) Adonis Pr.

Bedard, Michael. Emily. 1992. (Illus.). 40p. (J). (ps-3). 16.95 (0-385-30697-0) Doubleday Publishing.

Bellow, Saul. Humboldt's Gift. 1984. 496p. pap. 12.95 o.p. (0-14-007271-3, Penguin Bks.); 1975. 416p. 12.95 o.p. (0-670-38655-3) Viking Penguin.

Burleigh, Robert, et al. Edna. 2000. (Illus.). 32p. (J). (gr. k-4). pap. 15.95 (0-531-30246-6, Orchard Bks.) Scholastic, Inc.

Byars, Betsy C. Keeper of the Doves. 2004. (Illus.). 112p. (J). pap. 5.99 (0-14-240063-7, Puffin Bks.) Penguin Putnam Bks. for Young Readers.

—Keeper of the Doves. 2002. 112p. (J). (gr. 3-7). 14.99 (0-670-03576-9, Viking) Viking Penguin.

Dana, Barbara. Emily Dickinson: Fictionalized Biography. Date not set. (J). (gr. 3-7). 14.99 (0-06-028704-7); lib. bdg. 15.89 (0-06-028705-5); mass mkt. 4.99 (0-06-440843-4) HarperCollins Pubs.

Hayward, Linda & Seuss, Dr. Oh, Say Can You Rhyme. 1998. (J). pap. (0-679-87084-9, Random Hse. Bks. for Young Readers) Random Hse. Children's Bks.

Kleinbaum, N. H. Dead Poets Society. 1989. 176p. (YA). mass mkt. 5.50 o.s.i (0-553-28298-0); mass mkt. 4.99 o.s.i (0-553-56612-1) Bantam Bks.

—Dead Poets Society. 1989. 10.09 o.p. (0-606-04196-6) Turtleback Bks.

Mitchell, Minnie Belle & Dunham, Montrew. James Whitcomb Riley, Young Poet. Underdown, Harold, ed. 2003. (Young Patriots Ser.: 5). (Illus.). 116p. (J). E-Book 7.95 (1-882859-30-8); E-Book 7.95 (1-882859-31-6) Patria Pr., Inc.

—James Whitcomb Riley, Young Poet, 6. Mitchell, Minnie Belle & Underdown, Harold, eds. 2nd ed. 2002. (Young Patriots Ser.: Vol. 5). (Illus.). 112p. (J). (gr. 3-7). 14.95 (1-882859-10-3) Patria Pr., Inc.

—James Whitcomb Riley, Young Poet. Underdown, Harold, ed. 2nd ed. 2002. (Young Patriots Ser.: Vol. 5). (Illus.). 112p. (J). (gr. 3-7). pap. 9.95 (1-882859-11-1) Patria Pr., Inc.

Moulton, Mark K. The Visit. 2003. (Illus.). (J). 14.95 (0-8249-5475-0, Candy Cane Pr.) Ideals Pubns.

Myers, Tim. Basho & the Fox. 2000. (Illus.). 32p. (J). (gr. k-3). 15.95 (0-7614-5068-8, Cavendish Children's Bks.) Cavendish, Marshall Corp.

Rodriguez, Luis J. America Is Her Name. 2004. (Illus.). 32p. (J). (gr. 4-7). 15.95 (1-880684-40-3) Curbstone Pr.

—La Llaman America. Villanueva, Tino, tr. 2004. (SPA., Illus.). 32p. (J). (gr. 4-7). 15.95 (1-880684-41-1) Curbstone Pr.

Siebert, Diane. Heartland. 1989. (Illus.). 32p. (J). (ps-3). 17.99 (0-690-04730-4); lib. bdg. 15.89 o.p. (0-690-04732-0) HarperCollins Children's Bk. Group.

Tashjian, Janet. Marty Frye, Private Eye. ERS. 1998. (Redfeather Bks.). (Illus.). 80p. (J). (gr. 1-3). 15.95 (0-8050-5888-5, Holt, Henry & Co. Bks. For Young Readers) Holt, Henry & Co.

—Marty Frye, Private Eye. 2000. (Illus.). 80p. (J). (gr. 1-3). mass mkt. 3.99 (0-439-09557-3) Scholastic, Inc.

—Marty Frye, Private Eye. 2000. 10.14 (0-606-18880-0) Turtleback Bks.

Yolen, Jane. The Stone Silences. 1984. 128p. (J). (gr. 7 up). 10.95 o.s.i (0-399-20971-9, Philomel) Penguin Putnam Bks. for Young Readers.

POLICE—FICTION

Alexander, Liza. I Want to Be a Police Officer: Sesame Street. 1999. (Illus.). 24p. (J). (ps-3). pap. 3.29 o.s.i (0-307-13124-6, Golden Bks.) Random Hse. Children's Bks.

Auerbach, Annie. Police on Patrol. 2003. (Matchbox Ser.). (Illus.). 24p. (J). pap. 3.50 (0-689-85896-5, Little Simon) Simon & Schuster Children's Publishing.

Bailer, Darice. Motor Cop. 2003. (Matchbox Ser.). (Illus.). 16p. (J). bds. 6.99 (0-689-85971-6, 53545784, Little Simon) Simon & Schuster Children's Publishing.

Bantam Books Inc. Editors. Cop & a Half. 1993. 144p. (J). (gr. 4-6). mass mkt. 3.50 o.s.i (0-553-48138-X) Bantam Bks.

Barney & BJ Go to the Police Station. 2002. (Barney's Go to Ser.). 32p. (J). (ps-k). bds. 5.95 (1-58668-231-8) Lyrick Studios.

Baum, L. Frank. Policeman Bluejay. 1981. 152p. (J). (gr. 1-6). reprint ed. 50.00 (0-8201-1367-0) Scholars' Facsimiles & Reprints.

Benjamin, Cynthia. I Am a Police Officer. 1995. (I Am a . . . Ser.). (Illus.). 24p. (J). 7.95 (0-8120-6438-0) Barron's Educational Series, Inc.

Carter, Anne. Under a Prairie Sky. 2001. (Illus.). 30p. (J). (ps-3). trans. 16.95 (1-55143-226-9) Orca Bk. Pubs.

Cook, Fred J. City Cop. 1979. (Signal Bks.). (gr. 9 up). 7.95 o.p. (0-385-13460-6) Doubleday Publishing.

Corbett, Scott. Cop's Kid. 1968. (Illus.). (J). (gr. 4-6). 13.95 o.s.i (0-316-15660-4, Joy Street Bks.) Little Brown & Co.

Cormier, Robert. The Rag & Bone Shop. 2001. 160p. (YA). (gr. 7 up). lib. bdg. 17.99 (0-385-90027-9, Delacorte Pr.) Dell Publishing.

—The Rag & Bone Shop. l.t. ed. 2002. 141p. (J). 24.95 (0-7862-3873-9) Gale Group.

—The Rag & Bone Shop. 2001. (Illus.). 160p. (YA). (gr. 7 up). 15.95 (0-385-72962-6, Delacorte Bks. for Young Readers) Random Hse. Children's Bks.

Derwent, Lavinia. Tale of Greyfriar's Bobby. 1986. (Illus.). 80p. (J). (gr. 3-6). pap. 7.95 (0-14-031181-5) Penguin Bks., Ltd. GBR. *Dist:* Trafalgar Square.

Desimini, Lisa, et al. Policeman Lou & Policewoman Sue. 2003. (Illus.). 40p. (J). pap. 15.95 (0-439-40888-1) Scholastic, Inc.

Dubois, William P. Three Policemen. 1960. (Illus.). (J). (gr. 2-5). 8.95 o.p. (0-670-70912-3) Viking Penguin.

Flanagan, Alice K. Officer Brown Keeps Neighborhoods Safe. 1999. (Our Neighborhood Ser.). (Illus.). 32p. (J). (gr. 1-2). pap. 6.95 (0-516-26407-9, Children's Pr.) Scholastic Library Publishing.

Gruelle, Johnny. Raggedy Ann & Andy & the Nice Police Officer. 2002. (My First Raggedy Ann Ser.). (Illus.). 40p. (J). pap. 6.99 (0-689-85344-0, Aladdin) Simon & Schuster Children's Publishing.

Hart, Alison. Hostage. 2002. (Police Work Bks.). (Illus.). 96p. (gr. 3-5). lib. bdg. 11.99 (0-679-99366-5, Random Hse. Bks. for Young Readers) Random Hse. Children's Bks.

Hayler, Kate. Tough Stuff Police Chase! (Policia en Accion! Emergencia) 2003. (SPA., Illus.). 10p. (J). 12.99 (0-7868-1947-2) Hyperion Bks. for Children.

Hunter, David. A Sonnet for Shasta. 2001. iii, 186p. pap. 13.95 (1-57072-181-5) Overmountain Pr.

Jeffries, Roderic. Patrol Car. (J). (gr. 5-9). 1981. 192p. pap. 2.95 o.p. (0-06-440123-5); 1967. lib. bdg. 8.79 o.p. (0-06-022818-0) HarperCollins Pubs.

Jezard, Alison. Albert Police Bear. 1975. o.p. (0-575-01939-5) David & Charles Pubs.

Kunhardt, Edith. I'm Going to Be a Police Officer. 1995. (I'm Going to Be Ser.). (Illus.). 32p. (J). (ps-3). pap. 3.25 (0-590-25485-5, Cartwheel Bks.) Scholastic, Inc.

Lakin, Patricia. Aware & Alert. 1995. (My Community Ser.). (Illus.). 32p. (J). (ps-4). lib. bdg. 21.40 o.p. (0-8114-8261-8) Raintree Pubs.

Lenski, Lois. Policeman Small. 2001. (Lois Lenski Bks.). (Illus.). 56p. (J). (gr. k-3). 11.95 (0-375-81072-2); lib. bdg. 13.99 (0-375-91072-7) Random Hse. Children's Bks. (Random Hse. Bks. for Young Readers).

Levy, Elizabeth. Dani Trap. 1986. 112p. (YA). (gr. 7 up). pap. 2.50 o.p. (0-380-69995-8, Avon Bks.) Morrow/Avon.

Marsh, Carole. The Adventure Diaries of the Perils of Pauline, the Police Officer!, 2 vols. 2002. 48p. (J). per. 5.95 (0-635-01144-1); (Illus.). lib. bdg. 9.95 (0-635-01271-5) Gallopade International.

McClanahan, Frank. The Little Policeman. 1992. (Storytime Bks.). (Illus.). 24p. (Orig.). (J). (ps-2). pap. 1.29 o.p. (1-878624-38-5, McClanahan Bk.) Learning Horizons, Inc.

McKay, Hilary. Dog Friday. 1995. 144p. (J). (gr. 4-7). 15.00 (0-689-80383-4, McElderry, Margaret K.) Simon & Schuster Children's Publishing.

Minstrel Books Staff. Dudley Do-Right. 1999. (Illus.). 160p. (J). (gr. 4-7). pap. 4.99 (0-671-03934-2, Aladdin) Simon & Schuster Children's Publishing.

Morey, Walt. The Lemon Meringue Dog. 1980. 176p. (J). (gr. 4-7). 13.95 o.p. (0-525-33455-6, Dutton Children's Bks.) Penguin Putnam Bks. for Young Readers.

Murphy, Barbara Beasley. Tripping the Runner. 2000. 192p. (gr. 4-7). pap. 12.95 (0-595-15398-4, Backinprint.com) iUniverse, Inc.

Numeroff, Laura Joffe & Evans, Nate. Sherman Crunchley. 2003. (Illus.). 32p. (J). (gr. k-3). 15.99 (0-525-47130-8, Dutton) Dutton/Plume.

Oakley, Graham. The Foxbury Force. 1994. (Illus.). 32p. (J). 13.95 o.s.i (0-689-31898-7, Atheneum) Simon & Schuster Children's Publishing.

Off Goes Officer Pat. 1995. (J). 3.99 o.p. (0-88705-433-1) Reader's Digest Children's Publishing, Inc.

Paulsen. Spitball Gang. 1980. (J). 7.95 o.p. (0-525-66695-8) NAL.

Paulsen, Gary. The Glass Cafe: Or the Stripper & the State; How My Mother Started a War with the System That Made Us Kind of Rich & a Little Bit Famous. 2003. 112p. lib. bdg. 14.99 (0-385-90121-6, Delacorte Pr.) Dell Publishing.

—The Glass Cafe: or The Stripper & the State: How My Mother Started a War with the System That Made Us Kind of Rich & a Little Bit Famous. 2003. 112p. (J). text 12.95 (0-385-32499-5, Delacorte Pr.) Dell Publishing.

Pinkston, Ronald. A Police Officer That's What I'll Be! 1999. (Illus.). 26p. (J). (gr. k-2). 12.99 (0-9671708-0-X) Pinkston Publishing.

Prescott, Jerry. Deadly Sweet in Ann Arbor. 1996. (Illus.). 380p. 22.50 (1-882792-33-5) Proctor Pubns.

Radlauer, Ed & Radlauer, Dan. Pursuit School. 1975. (Schools for Action Ser.). (Illus.). 48p. (gr. 3 up). lib. bdg. 7.90 o.p. (0-531-02098-3, Watts, Franklin) Scholastic Library Publishing.

Rathmann, Peggy. Officer Buckle & Gloria. 2002. (Illus.). (J). 23.64 (0-7587-0061-X) Book Wholesalers, Inc.

Rathmann, Peggy, illus. Officer Buckle & Gloria. 1995. 32p. (J). (ps-3). 16.99 (0-399-22616-8, G. P. Putnam's Sons) Penguin Group (USA) Inc.

Rosenbloom, Joseph. Deputy Dan Gets His Man. 1985. (Step into Reading Step 3 Bks.). (Illus.). 48p. (J). (gr. 2-3). 6.99 o.s.i (0-394-97250-3); (ps-3). pap. 3.99 o.s.i (0-394-87250-9) Random Hse. Children's Bks. (Random Hse. Bks. for Young Readers).

—Deputy Dan Gets His Man. 1985. (Step into Reading Step 3 Bks.). (J). (gr. 2-3). 10.14 (0-606-06119-3) Turtleback Bks.

Scarry, Huck. A Day at the Police Station. 2004. (Illus.). (J). pap. (0-375-82822-2, Golden Bks.) Random Hse. Children's Bks.

Scarry, Richard. Bananas Gorilla: Richard Scarry's Smallest Pop-Up Book Ever! 1992. (Illus.). 10p. (J). (ps-3). bds. 4.95 o.s.i (0-307-12462-2, 12462, Golden Bks.) Random Hse. Children's Bks.

—Sergeant Murphy's Busiest Day Ever: Richard Scarry. 1992. (Golden Sound Story Bks.). (Illus.). 20p. (J). (ps-2). o.p. (0-307-74710-7, 64710, Golden Bks.) Random Hse. Children's Bks.

Schleier, Curt. You'd Better Not Tell. 1979. 94p. (J). 7.50 o.p. (0-664-32646-3) Westminster John Knox Pr.

Sheely, Robert. Police Lab: Using Science to Solve Crimes. 1993. (Science Lab Ser.). (Illus.). 64p. (J). (gr. 4-8). 14.95 (1-881889-40-8) Silver Moon Pr.

Sherrard, Raymond H., et al. The Centurions Shield: Badges of the LAPD. deluxe unabr. ed. 1996. (Illus.). 320p. (YA). lthr. 129.95 (0-914503-06-5); 49.95 (0-914503-05-7); pap. 29.95 (0-914503-04-9) RHS Enterprises.

Strickland, Brad & Strickland, Barbara. Frame-Up. 1998. (Mystery Files of Shelby Woo Ser.: No. 8). 144p. (J). (gr. 4-6). pap. 3.99 (0-671-02008-0, Aladdin) Simon & Schuster Children's Publishing.

Thomson, Andy. Booklinks, Level 1. 1987. 126p. (J). (gr. 4). pap. 6.49 (0-89084-371-6, 031443) Jones, Bob Univ. Pr.

Turner Sinnenburg, Kris, illus. Aero & Officer Mike: Police Partners. 2003. 32p. (J). 15.95 (1-56397-931-4) Boyds Mills Pr.

Yee, Wong Herbert. The Officers' Ball. 1997. (Illus.). 32p. (J). (ps-3). lib. bdg. 14.95 (0-395-81182-1) Houghton Mifflin Co.

Yorinks, Arthur. Whitefish Will Rides Again! 1996. (Michael di Capua Bks.). (Illus.). 32p. (YA). pap. 5.95 o.s.i (0-06-205921-1, Harper Trophy) HarperCollins Children's Bk. Group.

911: Includes Ambulance. 2001. (Matchbox Bks.). (Illus.). 14p. (J). bds. 6.95 o.p. (1-58485-407-3) Pleasant Co. Pubns.

POTTERS—FICTION

Johnston, Norma. The Potter's Wheel. 1988. 256p. (J). (gr. 7 up). 12.95 o.p. (0-688-06463-9, Morrow, William & Co.) Morrow/Avon.

PRESIDENTS—UNITED STATES—FICTION

Adams, Laurie & Coudert, Allison. Who Wants a Turnip for President, Anyway? 1986. 96p. (Orig.). (J). pap. 2.25 o.s.i (0-553-15432-X) Bantam Bks.

Brown, Marc. Arthur Meets the President. (Arthur Adventure Ser.). (Illus.). (J). (gr. k-3). 1997. pap. 5.95 (0-316-11578-9); 1992. 32p. pap. 5.95 (0-316-11291-7) Little Brown Children's Bks.

—Arthur Meets the President. 1991. (Arthur Adventure Ser.). (J). (gr. k-3). 12.10 (0-606-02222-8) Turtleback Bks.

Brown, Marc, et al. Arthur Meets the President. (Arthur Adventure Ser.). 32p. (J). (gr. k-3). 1996. pap. 9.95 incl. audio (0-316-11044-2); 1996. pap. 9.95 incl. audio (0-316-11044-2); 1991. 15.95 (0-316-11265-8) Little Brown Children's Bks.

Craig, Millie. Mr. Peanut & Mr. Jellybean. 1983. (Illus.). (J). 4.95 o.p. (0-533-05480-X) Vantage Pr., Inc.

Davis, Mary L. Polly & the President. 1967. (Illus.). (J). (gr. k-5). lib. bdg. 3.95 o.p. (0-8225-0264-X) Lerner Publishing Group.

Farley, Karin. Canal Boy. 1978. (Illus.). (gr. 5-8). pap. 1.95 o.p. (0-89191-106-5) Cook, David C. Publishing Co.

Fritz, Jean. The Great Little Madison. 1998. (J). 12.04 (0-606-12956-1) Turtleback Bks.

Garland, Michael. The President & Mom's Apple Pie. 2002. (Illus.). 32p. (J). (ps-3). 15.99 (0-525-46887-0, Dutton Children's Bks.) Penguin Putnam Bks. for Young Readers.

Goffe, Toni. The President. 1992. (Illus.). 32p. (J). (ps-3). 5.99 (0-85953-787-0); pap. 3.99 (0-85953-788-9) Child's Play of England GBR. *Dist:* Child's Play-International.

Goffe, Toni, illus. No Smoking. 1992. 32p. (J). (ps-3). 5.99 (0-85953-368-9); pap. 3.99 (0-85953-369-7) Child's Play of England GBR. *Dist:* Child's Play-International.

Griest, Lisa. Lost at the White House: A 1909 Easter Story. 1993. (Carolrhoda on My Own Bks.). (Illus.). (J). (gr. 1-3). lib. bdg. 21.27 o.p. (0-87614-726-0, Carolrhoda Bks.) Lerner Publishing Group.

Gross, Virginia T. The President Is Dead: A Story of the Kennedy Assassination. 1993. (Once upon America Ser.). (Illus.). 64p. (J). (gr. 2-6). 12.99 o.p. (0-670-85156-6, Viking Children's Bks.) Penguin Putnam Bks. for Young Readers.

Heberlein, L. A. Sixteen Reasons Why I Killed Richard M. Nixon: A Novel. 1996. 160p. (C). 23.95 (0-942979-29-X); pap. 9.95 (0-942979-30-3) Livingston Pr.

Henrick, Richard P. Nightwatch. 2001. 384p. mass mkt. 6.99 (0-380-79028-9) HarperCollins Pubs.

Hoobler, Dorothy & Hoobler, Thomas. The 1960s: Rebels, 2001. (Century Kids Ser.). (Illus.). 160p. (J). (gr. 5-8). 22.90 (0-7613-1606-X) Millbrook Pr., Inc.

Kanehl, Robert. Murder in the Newsroom: Or Andrew Gates, Reporter. Weinberger, Jane, ed. 1998. 164p. (J). (gr. 3-10). pap. 8.00 (1-883650-52-6) Windswept Hse. Pubs.

Peck, Robert Newton. Soup for President. 1998. (Illus.). 112p. (J). (gr. 4-7). pap. 4.99 o.s.i (0-679-89259-1, Knopf Bks. for Young Readers) Random Hse. Children's Bks.

—Soup for President. 1978. (Dell Yearling Bks.). (J). 9.09 o.p. (0-606-03073-5) Turtleback Bks.

Sachar, Louis. Marvin Redpost: Class President. 1999. (Marvin Redpost Ser.: No. 5). (Illus.). 80p. (J). (gr. k-3). 11.99 (0-679-98999-4); (gr. 1-4). pap. 3.99 (0-679-88999-X) Random Hse. Children's Bks. (Random Hse. Bks. for Young Readers).

—Marvin Redpost: Class President. 1999. 10.14 (0-606-16895-8) Turtleback Bks.

Service, Pamela F. A Question of Destiny. 1986. 168p. (J). (gr. 5-9). 13.95 o.s.i (0-689-31181-8, Atheneum) Simon & Schuster Children's Publishing.

Sinnott, Trip. President Clinton Visits Hyde Park: Story & Coloring Book. 1993. (Illus.). 52p. (Orig.). (J). (gr. k-5). pap. 4.95 (1-883551-00-5) Attic Studio Publishing Hse.

Strasser, Todd. Help! I'm Trapped in the President's Body. 1997. (Help! I'm Trapped Ser.). 144p. (J). (gr. 4-7). mass mkt. 4.50 (0-590-92166-5) Scholastic, Inc.

—Help! I'm Trapped in the President's Body. 1996. (Help! I'm Trapped Ser.). (J). (gr. 4-7). 10.55 (0-606-10839-4) Turtleback Bks.

Twinn, Michael. President Citizen. 1996. (J). lib. bdg. 11.95 (0-85953-844-3) Child's Play of England GBR. *Dist:* Child's Play-International.

White, Ellen E. The President's Daughter. 1984. 304p. pap. 2.95 (0-380-88740-1, Avon Bks.) Morrow/Avon.

—The President's Daughter. 1994. 256p. (J). (gr. 7-9). pap. 3.25 (0-590-47799-4) Scholastic, Inc.

PSYCHIATRISTS—FICTION

Barker, Pat. The Eye in the Door. unabr. ed. 1997. audio 51.00 (0-7887-0819-8, 94969E7) Recorded Bks., LLC.

Galvin, Matthew R. Ignatius Finds Help: A Story about Psychotherapy for Children. 1988. (Illus.). 48p. (J). (ps-3). 16.95 o.p. (0-945354-01-0) American Psychological Assn.

Kraus, Robert. Boris Bad Enough. 1976. 32p. (J). (gr. k-2). 7.95 o.p. (0-525-61541-5); pap. 2.95 o.p. (0-525-62345-0) Dutton/Plume. (Dutton).

—Boris Bad Enough. 1976. (Illus.). E-Book (1-58824-230-7) ipicturebooks, LLC.

Miller, Mary Beth. Aimee. 2002. (Illus.). 308p. (YA). (gr. 9 up). 16.99 (0-525-46894-3) Dutton/Plume.

—Aimee. 2004. (Illus.). 288p. pap. 6.99 (0-14-240025-4, Puffin Bks.) Penguin Putnam Bks. for Young Readers.

Neufeld, John. Lisa, Bright & Dark. 1970. 144p. (YA). (gr. 7-12). mass mkt. 5.99 (0-451-16684-1) NAL.

Zindel, Bonnie. Dr. Adriana Earthlight, Student Shrink. 1988. 144p. (YA). (gr. 7 up). 11.95 o.p. (0-670-81647-7, Viking Children's Bks.) Penguin Putnam Bks. for Young Readers.

R

RADIO OPERATORS—FICTION

Parkinson, Ethelyn. Today I Am a Ham. 1977. (J). (gr. 5-8). pap. (0-671-29871-2, Simon Pulse) Simon & Schuster Children's Publishing.

Wall, Cynthia. A Spark to the Past. 1998. 184p. (J). (gr. 5-8). pap. 6.95 (0-931625-34-3) DIMI Pr.

REPORTERS AND REPORTING—FICTION

Bazaldua, Barbara. The Jewel Thief. 1998. (Barbie, Television Reporter Ser.). (Illus.). 24p. (J). (ps-k). 2.99 o.s.i (0-307-98864-3, 98864, Golden Bks.) Random Hse. Children's Bks.

Gohman, Fred. Spider Webb Mysteries. 1969. (Illus.). (J). (gr. 5-10). lib. bdg. 6.19 o.p. (0-8313-0063-9) Lantern Pr., Inc., Pubs.

Hiser, Constance. Scoop Snoops. 1993. (Illus.). 112p. (J). (gr. 3-7). 13.95 o.p. (0-8234-1011-0) Holiday Hse., Inc.

Hudgins, Lynne. Wanda Water, the Traveling Reporter. 1996. (Illus.). 32p. (J). (gr. 3-6). text 5.50 (1-889203-08-4) Hudgins, Lynne.

Lasky, Kathryn. Alice Rose & Sam. 1999. 208p. (J). (gr. 3-7). pap. 5.99 (0-7868-1222-2) Disney Pr.

—Alice Rose & Sam. 1998. (Illus.). 208p. (J). (gr. 3-7). 15.95 (0-7868-0336-3); lib. bdg. 16.49 (0-7868-2277-5) Hyperion Bks. for Children.

—Alice Rose & Sam. 1999. 12.04 (0-606-17380-3) Turtleback Bks.

Morreale, Marie. In the Spotlight. 1998. (Barbie, Television Reporter Ser.). (Illus.). 24p. (J). 3.99 o.s.i (0-307-16008-4, 16008); 2.99 (0-307-98863-5, 98863) Random Hse. Children's Bks. (Golden Bks.).

Pageler, Elaine. The Riddle Street Mystery, 5 bks., Set. Kratoville, Betty Lou, ed. 1994. (Riddle Street Mystery Ser.: Set 1). (Illus.). 48p. (YA). (gr. 4-11). pap. 19.00 (*0-87879-983-4*, HN9834) High Noon Bks.

Schmidt, Annie M. Minnie. Salway, Lance, tr. from DUT. 1994. (J). 14.95 o.p. (*0-915943-94-8*); pap. 6.95 o.p. (*0-915943-95-6*) Milkweed Editions.

Steel, Elizabeth. Danger in the Air. 1986. (Starlight Adventure Ser.). (Illus.). 300p. (Orig.). (J). (gr. 5-9). pap. 2.95 o.p. (*0-14-031893-3*, Penguin Bks.) Viking Penguin.

Steele, Alexander. Case of the Breaking Story. 2000. (Wishbone Mysteries Ser.: No. 20). (Illus.). 144p. (J). (gr. 2-5). mass mkt. 3.99 o.p. (*1-57064-771-2*, Big Red Chair Bks.) Lyrick Publishing.

—Case of the Breaking Story. l.t. ed. 2000. (Wishbone Mysteries Ser.: No. 20). 144p. (J). (gr. 4 up). lib. bdg. 22.60 (*0-8368-2703-1*) Stevens, Gareth Inc.

S

SALES PERSONNEL—FICTION

Bond, Michael. Paddington Goes to the Sales. 1981. (Paddington Ser.). (Illus.). 48p. (J). (ps-3). pap. 1.50 o.p. (*0-8431-0733-2*, Price Stern Sloan) Penguin Putnam Bks. for Young Readers.

Brittain, Bill. Professor Popkin's Prodigious Polish. 1991. (Trophy Bk.). (Illus.). 160p. (J). (gr. 3-7). pap. 3.95 o.p. (*0-06-440386-6*, Harper Trophy) HarperCollins Children's Bk. Group.

Calder, Lyn. Minnie 'n Me: Lemonade for Sale. 1992. (Golden Little Look-Look Bks.). (Illus.). 24p. (J). (ps). pap. o.p. (*0-307-11649-2*, 11649, Golden Bks.) Random Hse. Children's Bks.

Field, Rachel. General Store. 1988. (Illus.). (J). (ps-3). 15.95 (*0-316-28163-8*) Little Brown & Co.

The Greedy Merchant. 1997. (Scheherezade Children's Stories Ser.). (Illus.). 16p. (J). (*1-873938-91-8*, Ithaca Pr.) Garnet Publishing, Ltd.

Heap, Jonathon. Joha & the Three Merchants. 1991. (J). 8.95 (*0-86685-569-6*, LDL48E) Librairie du Liban Pubns. FRA. *Dist:* International Bk. Ctr., Inc.

The Honest Merchant. 1997. (Scheherezade Children's Stories Ser.). (Illus.). 16p. (J). (*1-85964-033-8*, Ithaca Pr.) Garnet Publishing, Ltd.

Lee, Etrulia R. Mel. 1994. (Illus.). 20p. (J). (ps-2). pap. text (*1-884876-07-2*) Chamike Pubs.

—Mel Is Back. 1994. (Illus.). 32p. (J). (gr. k-2). pap. text (*1-884876-13-7*) Chamike Pubs.

—Mel's Store. 1994. (Illus.). 36p. (J). (gr. k-2). pap. text (*1-884876-21-8*) Chamike Pubs.

London, Jonathan. The Candystore Man. 1998. (Illus.). 24p. (J). (gr. k-3). 16.00 (*0-688-13241-3*); lib. bdg. 15.89 (*0-688-13242-1*) HarperCollins Children's Bk. Group.

Mattingly, Christobel. Rummage. 1992. (J). (gr. 4-7). pap. 7.00 o.p. (*0-207-17135-1*) HarperCollins Pubs.

McOmber, Rachel B., ed. McOmber Phonics Storybooks: The Lemonade Sale. rev. ed. (Illus.). (J). (*0-944991-41-6*) Swift Learning Resources.

Merrill, Jean. The Pushcart War. 1992. (Illus.). 224p. (J). (gr. 5-8). lib. bdg. 14.89 o.p. (*0-06-020822-8*) HarperCollins Children's Bk. Group.

Newbery, F. Cries of London. Lurie, Alison & Schiller, Justin G., eds. 1977. (J). lib. bdg. 46.00 o.p. (*0-8240-2258-0*) Garland Publishing, Inc.

O'Neill, Alexis. Estela's Swap. 2002. (Illus.). 32p. (J). (ps-2). 16.95 (*1-58430-044-2*) Lee & Low Bks., Inc.

Peters, Catherine. Yard Sale. 1997. 16p. (J). pap. 2.49 o.p. (*0-395-88300-8*) Houghton Mifflin Co.

Slawson, Michele Benoit. Signs for Sale. 2002. (Illus.). 40p. (J). (gr. k-3). 16.99 (*0-670-03568-8*) Penguin Putnam Bks. for Young Readers.

Williams-Garcia, Rita. Fast Talk on a Slow Track. 1992. 192p. (YA). mass mkt. 3.99 o.p. (*0-553-29594-2*) Bantam Bks.

—Fast Talk on a Slow Track. (YA). (gr. 7-12). 1998. 190p. 5.99 (*0-14-130231-3*, Puffin Bks.); 1991. 176p. 15.00 o.s.i (*0-525-67334-2*, Dutton Children's Bks.) Penguin Putnam Bks. for Young Readers.

SAMURAI—FICTION

Giblin, James C. The Truth about Unicorns. 1991. (Illus.). 128p. (J). (gr. 3-7). 15.00 o.p. (*0-06-022478-9*); lib. bdg. 14.89 o.p. (*0-06-022479-7*) HarperCollins Children's Bk. Group.

Haugaard, Erik Christian. The Boy & the Samurai. 1991. 256p. (YA). (gr. 7-7). tchr. ed. 16.00 (*0-395-56398-4*) Houghton Mifflin Co.

—The Boy & the Samurai. 2000. (Illus.). 256p. (YA). (gr. 7-9). pap. 7.95 (*0-618-07039-7*) Houghton Mifflin Co. Trade & Reference Div.

—The Revenge of the Forty-Seven Samurai. 1995. 240p. (YA). (gr. 7 up). tchr. ed. 16.00 (*0-395-70809-5*) Houghton Mifflin Co.

—The Samurai's Tale, 001. 1984. 256p. (J). (gr. 7 up). 14.95 o.p. (*0-395-34559-6*, 5-87439) Houghton Mifflin Co.

Hoobler, Dorothy & Hoobler, Thomas. The Demon in the Teahouse. (J). 2002. 192p. pap. 5.99 (*0-698-11971-1*, PaperStar); 2001. 181p. (gr. 5-8). 17.99 (*0-399-23499-3*, G. P. Putnam's Sons) Penguin Putnam Bks. for Young Readers.

—The Ghost in the Tokaido Inn. 1999. 214p. (J). (gr. 5-9). 17.99 (*0-399-23330-X*, G. P. Putnam's Sons) Penguin Putnam Bks. for Young Readers.

Kimmel, Eric A. Sword of the Samurai: Adventure Stories from Japan. 1999. 128p. (J). 15.00 (*0-15-201985-5*) Harcourt Children's Bks.

—Sword of the Samurai: Adventure Stories from Japan. 2000. (Trophy Chapter Bks.). (Illus.). 112p. (J). (gr. 2-5). pap. 4.25 (*0-06-442131-7*, Harper Trophy) HarperCollins Children's Bk. Group.

—Sword of the Samurai: Adventure Stories from Japan. 2000. 10.30 (*0-606-19999-3*) Turtleback Bks.

Konzak, Burt. Samurai Spirit: Ancient Wisdom for Modern Life. 2002. 144p. (YA). (gr. 6 up). pap. 8.95 (*0-88776-611-0*) Tundra Bks. of Northern New York.

Namioka, Lensey. The Coming of the Bear. 1992. 192p. (YA). (gr. 7 up). 14.00 (*0-06-020288-2*); lib. bdg. 14.89 o.p. (*0-06-020289-0*) HarperCollins Children's Bk. Group.

—Den of the White Fox. 1997. 256p. (YA). 14.00 o.s.i (*0-15-201282-6*); (J). pap. 6.00 (*0-15-201283-4*) Harcourt Trade Pubs.

—Den of the White Fox. 1997. 12.05 (*0-606-11250-2*) Turtleback Bks.

—Island of Ogres. 1989. 208p. (YA). (gr. 7 up). 13.95 (*0-06-024372-4*); lib. bdg. 13.89 o.p. (*0-06-024373-2*) HarperCollins Children's Bk. Group.

—Valley of the Broken Cherry Trees. 176p. (YA). (gr. 6 up). reprint ed. pap. 8.95 o.p. (*0-936085-32-0*) Blue Heron Publishing.

—Valley of the Broken Cherry Trees. 1980. (YA). (gr. 7 up). 8.95 o.s.i (*0-440-09325-2*, Delacorte Pr.) Dell Publishing.

—Village of the Vampire Cat: A Novel. 1995. 192p. (YA). pap. 8.95 o.p. (*0-936085-29-0*) Blue Heron Publishing.

—Village of the Vampire Cat: A Novel. 1981. 224p. (YA). (gr. 8-12). 9.95 o.s.i (*0-440-09377-5*, Delacorte Pr.) Dell Publishing.

—White Serpent Castle. 1976. (J). (gr. 7 up). 6.95 o.p. (*0-679-20362-1*) McKay, David Co., Inc.

Paterson, Katherine. Of Nightingales That Weep. 1974. (Illus.). (J). (gr. 5 up). 14.00 o.s.i (*0-690-00485-0*) HarperCollins Children's Bk. Group.

Scieszka, Jon. Sam Samurai. (Time Warp Trio Ser.). (Illus.). 2004. 112p. pap. 4.99 (*0-14-240088-2*); Vol. 10. 2002. 112p. (J). pap. 4.99 (*0-14-230213-9*); Vol. 10. 2001. 80p. (J). (gr. 2-5). 14.99 (*0-670-89915-1*) Penguin Putnam Bks. for Young Readers. (Puffin Bks.).

Siefken, Paul, et al. Fighting Blind. 2003. (Samurai Jack Chapter Bks.: No. 4). 80p. (J). mass mkt. 4.50 (*0-439-44920-0*) Scholastic, Inc.

Steiber, Ellen. Shadow of the Fox. 1994. (Bullseye Chillers Ser.). 108p. (J). (gr. 2-6). pap. 3.50 o.s.i (*0-679-86667-1*, Random Hse. Bks. for Young Readers) Random Hse. Children's Bks.

Teitelbaum, Michael. The Legend Begins. 2002. (Samurai Jack Ser.). (Illus.). 32p. (J). (gr. 3-7). mass mkt. 4.50 (*0-439-40972-1*) Scholastic, Inc.

West, Tracey. Code of the Samurai. 2003. (Samurai Jack Ser.). 48p. (J). mass mkt. 5.99 (*0-439-45555-3*) Scholastic, Inc.

—Jack & the Wanderers. 2004. (Samurai Jack Ser.). (Illus.). 80p. (J). mass mkt. 4.50 (*0-439-44945-6*, Scholastic Paperbacks) Scholastic, Inc.

—Journey to the Impossible Islands. 2003. (Samurai Jack Chapter Bks.: No. 3). 80p. (J). mass mkt. 4.50 (*0-439-45554-5*) Scholastic, Inc.

—Mountain of Mayhem. 2002. (Samurai Jack Chapter Bks.: No. 1). 80p. (J). (gr. 3-7). mass mkt. 3.99 (*0-439-40975-6*) Scholastic, Inc.

—The Seven Labors of Jack. 2003. (Samurai Jack Chapter Bks.: No. 2). (Illus.). 80p. (J). (gr. 3-7). mass mkt. 4.50 (*0-439-40974-8*) Scholastic, Inc.

SCULPTORS—FICTION

Bedard, Michael. The Clay Ladies. braille ed. 2000. (J). (gr. 2). spiral bd. (*0-616-01544-5*) Canadian National Institute for the Blind/Institut National Canadien pour les Aveugles.

—The Clay Ladies. 1999. 16.00 (*0-689-81184-5*, Atheneum) Simon & Schuster Children's Publishing.

—The Clay Ladies. (Illus.). 40p. (J). (gr. 3-7). 2001. pap. 7.95 (*0-88776-573-4*); 1999. 16.95 (*0-88776-385-5*) Tundra Bks. of Northern New York.

—The Clay Ladies. 2001. 14.10 (*0-606-21845-9*) Turtleback Bks.

SECRETARIES—FICTION

Pearson, Susan. Lenore's Big Break. 1992. (Illus.). 32p. (J). (gr. k up). 14.00 o.p. (*0-670-83474-2*, Viking Children's Bks.) Penguin Putnam Bks. for Young Readers.

SHEPHERDS—FICTION

Ada, Alma Flor. Jordi's Star. 1996. (Illus.). 32p. (J). (ps-3). 15.95 o.s.i (*0-399-22832-2*, G. P. Putnam's Sons) Penguin Group (USA) Inc.

Ben-Ezer, Ehud. Hosni the Dreamer: An Arabian Tale, RS. 1997. (Illus.). 32p. (J). (ps-3). 16.00 (*0-374-33340-8*, Farrar, Straus & Giroux (BYR)) Farrar, Straus & Giroux.

Calhoun, Mary. A Shepherd Boy's Christmas. 2001. (Illus.). 32p. (J). (ps-4). 15.95 (*0-688-15176-0*); 15.89 (*0-688-15177-9*) HarperCollins Children's Bk. Group.

—A Shepherd's Gift: El Regalo del Pastor. 2001. 32p. (J). (ps-4). 15.89 (*0-06-029786-7*) HarperCollins Children's Bk. Group.

Caudill, Rebecca. A Certain Small Shepherd. 1987. 48p. (J). (gr. k-6). pap. 2.99 o.s.i (*0-440-41194-7*, Yearling) Random Hse. Children's Bks.

—A Certain Small Shepherd. 1971. (J). 9.05 o.p. (*0-606-12217-6*) Turtleback Bks.

Caudill, Rebecca & Caudill, Gertrude. A Certain Small Shepherd. 1997. (Illus.). 48p. (J). (ps-3). pap. 6.95 (*0-8050-5392-1*, Holt, Henry & Co. Bks. For Young Readers) Holt, Henry & Co.

Dennis, Jeanne Gowen & Seifert, Sheila. Attack! Hohn, David, tr. & illus. by. 2003. (Strive to Thrive Ser.). (J). pap. 4.99 (*0-7814-3894-2*) Cook Communications Ministries.

Dijs, Carla. Boy Who Cried Wolf. 1997. (My First Book of Fables Ser.: Vol. 4). (Illus.). 10p. (J). (ps-2). 5.99 (*0-689-81483-6*, Little Simon) Simon & Schuster Children's Publishing.

Flinn, Lisa & Younger, Barbara. The Christmas Garland. Corvino, Lucy, tr. & illus. by. 2003. 32p. (J). 14.95 (*0-8249-5460-2*, Ideals Pr.) Ideals Pubns.

—That's What a Friend Is! Corvino, Lucy, tr. & illus. by. 2003. 26p. (J). 6.95 (*0-8249-5468-8*, Ideals Pr.) Ideals Pubns.

Franklin, Kristine L. The Shepherd Boy - El Nino Pastor. Ada, Alma Flor, tr. 1994. (Illus.). 32p. (J). (ps-1). (ENG & SPA.). 14.95 (*0-689-31809-X*); (SPA., 14.95 (*0-689-31918-5*) Simon & Schuster Children's Publishing. (Atheneum).

Gantschev, Ivan. El Lago de la Luna. 1996. (SPA., Illus.). 32p. (J). (gr. k-3). 19.95 o.p. (*1-55858-600-8*, NSB008, Ediciones Norte-Sur) North-South Bks., Inc.

—Moon Lake. Martens, Marianne, tr. 1996. (Illus.). 32p. (J). (gr. k-3). 18.95 o.p. (*1-55858-598-2*); 18.88 o.p. (*1-55858-599-0*) North-South Bks., Inc.

—Moon Lake. 1991. (J). (ps-3). pap. 14.95 (*0-907234-08-9*, Simon & Schuster Children's Publishing) Simon & Schuster Children's Publishing.

—La Pietra di Luna. 1998. (ITA., Illus.). (J). (ps-3). 18.95 (*88-8203-054-7*) North-South Bks., Inc.

Garaway, Margaret K. Ashkii & His Grandfather - Ashkii y el Abuelo. Cartes, Marie R., tr. (ENG & SPA., Illus.). 32p. (Orig.). (J). (gr. 2-10). 1996. pap. 8.95 (*0-9638851-6-2*); 1995. pap. 14.95 (*0-9638851-7-0*) Old Hogan Publishing Co.

Good, Joyce. A Shepherd Boy. 1978. (Say It Again Ser.). (Illus.). 22p. (J). pap. 2.50 (*0-7399-0002-1*, 2392) Rod & Staff Pubs., Inc.

Hackman, Martha. Komo the Shepherd Boy. 1991. (Envelope Library Ser.). (Illus.). 12p. (Orig.). (YA). (gr. 7-9). pap. 2.50 o.p. (*0-88138-002-4*, Simon & Schuster Children's Publishing) Simon & Schuster Children's Publishing.

Haseley, Dennis. The Cave of Snores. 1987. (Illus.). 40p. (J). (gr. k-4). 11.95 (*0-06-022214-X*); lib. bdg. 11.89 o.p. (*0-06-022215-8*) HarperCollins Children's Bk. Group.

Hort, Lenny. Goatherd & the Shepherdess. 1995. (Illus.). 32p. (J). 15.99 o.p. (*0-8037-1352-5*); 15.89 o.p. (*0-8037-1353-3*) Penguin Putnam Bks. for Young Readers. (Dial Bks. for Young Readers).

Hunt, Angela Elwell. Singing Shepherd. 1992. (Illus.). 32p. (J). (ps-6). 13.95 o.p. (*0-7459-2224-4*) Lion Publishing.

Irigaray, Louis & Taylor, Theodore. A Shepherd Watches, a Shepherd Sings. 1977. 8.95 o.p. (*0-385-11652-7*) Doubleday Publishing.

Jennings, Patrick. The Wolving Time. 2003. 208p. (J). 15.95 (*0-439-39555-0*) Scholastic, Inc.

Krenzer, Rolf. Christmas Bell. 2003. (Illus.). 32p. (J). 15.95 (*1-57768-410-9*, Gingham Dog Pr.) McGraw-Hill Children's Publishing.

Laughlin, Charlotte. Where's the Lost Sheep? 1992. (J). 9.99 o.p. (*0-8499-0919-8*) W Publishing Group.

Lazy Shepherd. 1992. (YA). pap. o.p. (*0-7327-0263-1*) Prentice Hall PTR.

Lewis, Kim. The Shepherd Boy. 1990. (Illus.). 32p. (J). (ps-1). lib. bdg. 13.95 (*0-02-758581-6*, Simon & Schuster Children's Publishing) Simon & Schuster Children's Publishing.

Mehl, Ron, Jr. & Gundersen, Sandy. The Littlest Shepherd. 1991. (Illus.). 40p. (ps-3). 10.99 o.p. (*0-88070-449-7*) Zonderkidz.

Mills, Claudia. One Small Lost Sheep, RS. 1997. (Illus.). 32p. (J). (ps-3). 16.00 o.p. (*0-374-35649-1*, Farrar, Straus & Giroux (BYR)) Farrar, Straus & Giroux.

Novak, Matt. While the Shepherd Slept. (Illus.). 32p. (J). 3.98 o.p. (*0-8317-6778-2*) Smithmark Pubs., Inc.

Pearson, Tracey Campbell. Little Bo Peep, RS. 2004. bds. (*0-374-30859-4*) Farrar, Straus & Giroux.

Rowzee, Janet Z. & Watson, James A. The Song of the Shepherd Boy. 1993. 20p. (J). (gr. 4-8). pap. 6.95 (*0-9638941-0-2*) Eagles 3 Productions.

Schaefer, Jack. Old Ramon. 1975. (Illus.). (J). (gr. 6-10). 7.95 o.p. (*0-395-07087-2*) Houghton Mifflin Co.

—Old Ramon. 1973. (Sandpipers Ser.). (Illus.). 102p. (J). (gr. 6 up). reprint ed. pap. 2.95 o.p. (*0-395-15056-6*) Houghton Mifflin Co. Trade & Reference Div.

—Old Ramon. 1993. (Newbery Honor Roll Ser.). 13.00 (*0-606-05959-8*) Turtleback Bks.

Schaeffer, Jack. Old Ramon. 1993. (Newbery Honor Roll Ser.). (Illus.). 112p. (J). (gr. 4-7). reprint ed. pap. 6.95 (*0-8027-7403-2*) Walker & Co.

The Shepherd Boy's Story. 2001. (Illus.). 20p. (J). (ps-k). 4.99 (*0-8499-5932-2*) Nelson, Tommy.

Snyder, Zilpha Keatley. The Changing Maze. (Illus.). (J). (gr. k-4). 1985. 96p. lib. bdg. 12.95 o.s.i (*0-02-785900-2*, Simon & Schuster Children's Publishing); 1992. 32p. reprint ed. pap. 4.95 o.p. (*0-689-71618-4*, Aladdin) Simon & Schuster Children's Publishing.

Spyri, Johanna. Moni, the Goat Boy: And Other Stories. (Illus.). (J). 1993. 218p. pap. 5.95 (*1-883453-00-3*); 2000. 219p. reprint ed. pap. 6.95 (*1-883453-09-7*) Deutsche Buchhandlung-James Lowry.

Tabb, Mark A. Song of the Shepherd: Psalm 23. 1999. (Foundations of the Faith Ser.). 160p. pap. 8.99 (*0-8024-6190-5*) Moody Pr.

Tharlet, Eve, pseud. Simon & the Holy Night. 1993. (Pixies Ser.: Vol. 26). (Illus.). (J). 4.95 (*0-88708-324-2*, Simon & Schuster Children's Publishing) Simon & Schuster Children's Publishing.

—Simon & the Holy Night. Clements, Andrew, tr. 1991. (Illus.). 28p. (J). (ps up). pap. 14.95 (*0-88708-185-1*, Simon & Schuster Children's Publishing) Simon & Schuster Children's Publishing.

Tripp, Valerie. Josefina's Song. 2001. (American Girls Short Stories Ser.). (Illus.). 56p. (YA). (gr. 2 up). 3.95 (*1-58485-272-0*, American Girl) Pleasant Co. Pubns.

Weesner, Stephen. The Shepherd Boy & the Giant. 1999. (Illus.). 24p. (J). (gr. 4-6). pap. 9.95 o.p. (*1-56167-471-0*) American Literary Pr., Inc.

Westphal, Arnold C. Alibiography - The Children's Shepherd: His Fears, Frenzies, Faith & Fun. 1985. 400p. (J). 8.95 (*0-915398-23-0*) Visual Evangels Publishing Co.

Wier, Ester. Loner. 1963. (Illus.). (J). (gr. 7-9). 5.95 o.p. (*0-679-20097-5*) McKay, David Co., Inc.

—Loner. 1992. 160p. (J). (gr. 4-7). pap. 4.50 (*0-590-44352-6*) Scholastic, Inc.

Witmer, Edith. Miguel, the Shepherd Boy. De Mejia, Maria Juana, tr. 1995. (SPA., Illus.). 220p. (J). (gr. 3-6). 8.10 (*0-7399-0090-0*, 2237.1) Rod & Staff Pubs., Inc.

—Miguel, the Shepherd Boy. 1992. (Illus.). 189p. (J). (gr. 3-6). 8.55 (*0-7399-0089-7*, 2237) Rod & Staff Pubs., Inc.

SOLDIERS—FICTION

Adams, Pam, illus. Oh, Soldier! Soldier! (J). 1990. 16p. (ps-3). pap. 6.99 (*0-85953-092-2*); 1978. 16p. (ps-3). 13.99 (*0-85953-093-0*); 1975. (ITA.). (gr. 4-7). pap. 6.99 (*0-85953-594-0*) Child's Play of England GBR. *Dist:* Child's Play-International.

Andersen, Hans Christian. The Steadfast Tin Soldier. 1997. (Michael di Capua Bks.).Tr. of Standhaftige Tinsoldat. (Illus.). 32p. (J). reprint ed. pap. 6.95 (*0-06-205900-9*, Harper Trophy) HarperCollins Children's Bk. Group.

—The Steadfast Tin Soldier. 1983. Tr. of Standhaftige Tinsoldat. (Illus.). 32p. (J). (gr. 1-3). 14.95 o.p. (*0-316-03949-7*) Little Brown & Co.

Bosse, Malcolm. Tusk & Stone. 1995. 244p. (YA). (gr. 4-7). 15.95 (*1-886910-01-4*) Front Street, Inc.

—Tusk & Stone. 1996. 256p. (J). (gr. 5-9). pap. 4.99 o.s.i (*0-14-038217-8*) Penguin Putnam Bks. for Young Readers.

Brouwer, Sigmund. Soldier's Aim. 1998. (Cyberquest Ser.: Vol. 5). 64p. (Orig.). (J). (gr. 5-9). mass mkt. 3.50 o.p. (*0-8499-4038-9*) Nelson, Tommy.

Brown, Marcia. Sopa de Piedras. Mlawer, Teresa, tr. 1991. (SPA., Illus.). (J). (gr. k-3). lib. bdg. 12.95 (*0-9625162-1-X*, LC3847) Lectorum Pubns., Inc.

—Sopa de Piedras. unabr. ed. 1992. (SPA., Illus.). (J). (gr. k-3). pap. 15.95 incl. audio (*0-87499-278-8*, LK4670); (gr. 1-3). 24.95 incl. audio (*0-87499-279-6*) Live Oak Media.

—Sopa de Piedras. Mlawer, Teresa, tr. 2001. (SPA., Illus.). (J). (gr. k-3). 7.96 net. (*1-56137-559-4*, NU5657) Novel Units, Inc.

—Sopa de Piedras, Grades 1-3. 1992. Tr. of Stone Soup. (SPA., Illus.). (J). pap., tchr. ed. 33.95 incl. audio (*0-87499-280-X*) Live Oak Media.

—Stone Soup: An Old Tale. 1997. (Aladdin Picture Bks.). (Illus.). 48p. (J). (ps-3). reprint ed. pap. 5.99 (*0-689-71103-4*, Aladdin) Simon & Schuster Children's Publishing.

—Stone Soup: An Old Tale. 1986. (J). 12.14 (*0-606-03331-9*) Turtleback Bks.

Chambers, John W. The Colonel & Me. 1985. 192p. (J). (gr. 5-9). 11.95 o.s.i (*0-689-31087-0*, Atheneum) Simon & Schuster Children's Publishing.

Chetkowski, Emily. Gooseman. 2001. (J). 11.95 (*1-880158-32-9*) Townsend Pr.

Collington, Peter. The Angel & the Soldier Boy. Schulman, Janet, ed. 1994. (Illus.). 32p. (J). (ps-3). lib. bdg. 10.99 o.p. (*0-394-98626-1*, Knopf Bks. for Young Readers) Random Hse. Children's Bks.

—The Angel & the Soldier Boy. 1988. (Illus.). 32p. (J). (ps-2). reprint ed. 4.95 o.s.i (*0-394-81967-5*, Knopf Bks. for Young Readers) Random Hse. Children's Bks.

Connell, Kate. Yankee Blue or Rebel Grey: The Civil War Adventures of Sam Shaw. 2003. (I Am American Ser.). (Illus.). 40p. (J). pap. 6.99 (*0-7922-5179-2*) National Geographic Society.

Cooney, Caroline B. Operation: Homefront. 1992. 224p. (J). mass mkt. 3.99 o.s.i (*0-440-22689-9*, Dell Books for Young Readers) Random Hse. Children's Bks.

Davoll, Barbara. Ashley's Yellow Ribbon. 1991. (J). (gr. 4-7). pap. 5.99 o.p. (*0-8024-0815-X*) Moody Pr.

Denslow, Sharon Phillips. All Their Names Were Courage. 2003. 144p. (J). 15.99 (*0-06-623810-2*, Greenwillow Bks.) HarperCollins Children's Bk. Group.

Dixon, Franklin W. & Walker, Jeff. The Secret of the Soldier's Gold. 2003. (Hardy Boys Ser.). (Illus.). 160p. (J). pap. 4.99 (*0-689-85885-X*, Aladdin) Simon & Schuster Children's Publishing.

Earbooker, Mo & Carey, Craig Robert. Keeping the Peace. 2004. (G. I. Joe Ser.). (Illus.). 32p. (J). mass mkt. 3.99 (*0-439-55143-9*) Scholastic, Inc.

Ellis, Caroljean. The Soldier. 1996. (Tales of Little Angels: Bk. 2). (Illus.). 40p. (Orig.). (J). (gr. k-4). pap. 8.95 (*1-889383-01-5*) Angel Pubns.

Etherington, Frank. The General. 1996. (Young Novels Ser.). (Illus.). 64p. (J). (gr. 4-6). pap. 5.95 (*0-920236-55-3*) Annick Pr., Ltd. CAN. *Dist:* Firefly Bks., Ltd.

Evans, George Brinley. Boys of Gold. 2001. 78p. pap. 12.95 (*1-902638-12-3*) Parthian Bks. GBR. *Dist:* Dufour Editions, Inc.

Fedor, Janis M. Girl Lieutenant in Blue, Vol. 2. 2002. 166p. (YA). (gr. 5-6). pap. 9.95 (*0-936369-38-8*) Son-Rise Pubns. & Distribution Co.

Forstchen, William R. We Look Like Men of War. 2001. 192p. 21.95 (*0-7653-0114-8*, Forge Bks.) Doherty, Tom Assocs., LLC.

French, Michael. Soldier Boy. 1986. 173p. (J). (gr. 8 up). 13.95 o.p. (*0-448-47768-8*, Grosset & Dunlap) Penguin Putnam Bks. for Young Readers.

Gardiner, John Reynolds. General Butterfingers. 1993. (J). 10.14 (*0-606-05304-2*) Turtleback Bks.

Garland, Sherry. In the Shadow of the Alamo. 2001. (Great Episodes Ser.). 288p. (YA). (gr. 5-8). 17.00 (*0-15-201744-5*, Gulliver Bks.) Harcourt Children's Bks.

Greene, Bette. Summer of My German Soldier. 1984. 208p. (YA). (gr. 7-12). mass mkt. 2.95 o.s.i (*0-553-27247-0*) Bantam Bks.

—Summer of My German Soldier. 1993. 208p. (YA). mass mkt. 5.50 o.s.i (*0-440-21892-6*) Dell Publishing.

—Summer of My German Soldier. l.t. ed. 2000. (LRS Large Print Cornerstone Ser.). 305p. (YA). (gr. 6-12). lib. bdg. 29.95 (*1-58118-059-4*, 23473) LRS.

—Summer of My German Soldier. l.t. ed. 1989. 272p. (YA). reprint ed. lib. bdg. 16.95 o.s.i (*1-55736-134-7*, Cornerstone Bks.) Pages, Inc.

—Summer of My German Soldier. 2003. (Illus.). 256p. (J). 16.99 (*0-8037-2869-7*, Dial Bks. for Young Readers); 1999. (Illus.). 208p. (J). (gr. 5-9). pap. 6.99 (*0-14-130636-X*, Puffin Bks.); 1973. 240p. (YA). (gr. 7 up). 14.99 o.s.i (*0-8037-8321-3*, Dial Bks. for Young Readers) Penguin Putnam Bks. for Young Readers.

—Summer of My German Soldier. 1993. (YA). mass mkt. o.p. (*0-440-90056-5*, Dell Books for Young Readers) Random Hse. Children's Bks.

—Summer of My German Soldier. 2000. (YA). (gr. 6 up). 20.50 (*0-8446-7144-4*) Smith, Peter Pub., Inc.

—Summer of My German Soldier. 1999. 11.04 (*0-606-17432-X*); 1975. (YA). 10.09 o.p. (*0-606-05063-9*) Turtleback Bks.

Greene, Carla. Soldiers & Sailors: What Do They Do? 1963. (I Can Read Bks.). (Illus.). (J). (ps-3). lib. bdg. 9.89 o.p. (*0-06-022096-1*) HarperCollins Pubs.

Greeson, Janet. An American Army of Two. 1992. (On My Own History Ser.). (Illus.). 48p. (J). (gr. 1-3). lib. bdg. 21.27 (*0-87614-664-7*, Carolrhoda Bks.) Lerner Publishing Group.

Hahn, Stephen. Pike McCallister. 1998. 253p. (YA). (gr. 6 up). per. 14.95 (*1-888125-29-2*) Publication Consultants.

Hayes, Richard. The Secret Army. 1979. (J). (gr. 5-9). 8.95 o.p. (*0-670-62839-5*) Viking Penguin.

Hilbrecht, Kirk & Hilbrecht, Sharron. My Daddy Is a Soldier. 1996. (Illus.). 30p. (J). (ps-3). reprint ed. pap. 5.75 (*1-889658-01-4*) New Canaan Publishing Co., Inc.

Hopkinson, Deborah. Billy & the Rebel. 2001. (Ready-to-Read Ser.). (Illus.). (J). lib. bdg. 15.00 (*0-689-83964-2*, Atheneum) Simon & Schuster Children's Publishing.

Johnson, Guy. Standing at the Scratch Line. 2001. E-Book 11.95 (*1-58945-866-4*) Adobe Systems, Inc.

—Standing at the Scratch Line. 2001. E-Book 11.95 (*0-375-50656-X*) Random Hse., Inc.

—Standing at the Scratch Line: A Novel. 1998. 432p. 24.95 o.s.i (*0-375-50158-4*) Random Hse. Information Group.

Johnston, Annie F. The Little Colonel: Maid of Honor. 1982. (YA). (gr. 5 up). 16.95 (*0-89201-034-7*) Zenger Publishing Co., Inc.

—The Little Colonel Stories. 1982. (YA). (gr. 5 up). First Series. 16.95 (*0-89201-070-3*); Second Series. 16.95 (*0-89201-071-1*) Zenger Publishing Co., Inc.

—The Little Colonel's Chum: Mary Ware. 1982. (YA). (gr. 5 up). 16.95 (*0-89201-036-3*) Zenger Publishing Co., Inc.

—The Little Colonel's Hero. 1982. (YA). (gr. 5 up). 16.95 (*0-89201-037-1*) Zenger Publishing Co., Inc.

—The Little Colonel's Knight Comes Riding. 1982. (YA). (gr. 5 up). 18.95 (*0-89201-072-X*) Zenger Publishing Co., Inc.

Jorgensen, Norman. In Flanders Fields. Gray, Peter, ed. 2002. (Illus.). 36p. 22.95 (*1-86368-369-0*) Fremantle Arts Centre Pr. AUS. *Dist:* International Specialized Bk. Services.

—In Flanders Fields. 2003. (Illus.). (J). (*1-894965-01-9*) Simply Read Bks.

Le Feuvre, Amy. Teddy's Button. 2002. (Golden Inheritance Ser.: Vol. 6). (Illus.). 93p. (J). 6.90 (*0-921100-83-3*) Inheritance Pubns.

—Teddy's Button. 1997. (Classic Ser.). 128p. (J). (gr. 4-7). pap. 6.00 (*0-7188-2803-8*) Lutherworth Pr., The GBR. *Dist:* Parkwest Pubns., Inc.

Lerangis, Peter. The Sultan's Secret. 1988. (G. I. Joe Ser.). (YA). (gr. 8 up). mass mkt. 2.95 o.s.i (*0-345-35099-5*) Ballantine Bks.

Marsh, Carole. The Adventure Diaries of Jack, the U. S. Army Special Forces Solider!, 4 vols. 2002. 48p. (J). per. 5.95 (*0-635-01147-6*); (Illus.). lib. bdg. 9.95 (*0-635-01273-1*) Gallopade International.

Morgan, Alison. At Willy Tucker's Place. 1976. (Illus.). (J). 5.95 o.p. (*0-525-66515-3*, Dutton Children's Bks.) Penguin Putnam Bks. for Young Readers.

Myers, Walter Dean. Patrol: An American Soldier in Vietnam. 2002. (Illus.). 40p. (J). (gr. 4 up). lib. bdg. 17.89 (*0-06-028364-5*); (ps-1). 16.95 (*0-06-028363-7*) HarperCollins Children's Bk. Group.

Nimmo, Jenny. The Chestnut Soldier. 1991. 160p. (J). (gr. 6 up). 14.95 o.p. (*0-525-44656-7*, Dutton Children's Bks.) Penguin Putnam Bks. for Young Readers.

Paulsen, Gary. A Soldier's Heart. 2001. 128p. (YA). (gr. 5 up). pap. 28.00 incl. audio (*0-8072-8301-0*); 1999. (J). (gr. 7-12). audio 18.00 (*0-553-52611-1*) Random Hse. Audio Publishing Group. (Listening Library).

—A Soldier's Heart. 2000. (J). 11.55 (*0-606-19222-0*) Turtleback Bks.

—A Soldier's Heart: Being the Story of the Enlistment & Due Service of the Boy Charley Goddard in the First Minnesota Volunteers. 1998. 128p. (YA). (gr. 7-12). 15.95 (*0-385-32498-7*) Doubleday Publishing.

Pratte, Francois. L' Armee Rose D'Awa. 1996. (Premier Roman Ser.). (FRE., Illus.). 64p. (J). (gr. 2-5). pap. (*2-89021-130-4*) Nelson Thomson Learning.

Reit, Seymour V. Guns for General Washington: A Story of the American Revolution. 2001. (Great Episodes Ser.). 160p. (YA). (gr. 5-9). pap. 6.00 (*0-15-216435-9*, Gulliver Bks.) Harcourt Children's Bks.

Remarque, Erich Maria. All Quiet on the Western Front: With Related Readings. Wheen, A. W., tr. from GER. 2002. (EMC Masterpiece Series Access Editions). (Illus.). xxv, 249p. (YA). 14.60 (*0-8219-2420-6*) EMC/Paradigm Publishing.

Ritchie, Jo-An. Jonie & Her Soldier. Wheeler, Gerald, ed. 1985. 128p. (YA). (gr. 8 up). pap. 5.50 o.p. (*0-8280-0249-5*) Review & Herald Publishing Assn.

Robison, Nancy. Ten Tall Soldiers. 2001. (Illus.). 40p. (ps-3). pap. 6.99 (*0-689-84325-9*, Aladdin) Simon & Schuster Children's Publishing.

—Ten Tall Soldiers. 1995. 4.98 o.p. (*0-8317-2271-1*) Smithmark Pubs., Inc.

Schmidt, Gary D. Anson's Way. 2001. 224p. (J). pap. 5.99 (*0-14-131229-7*, Puffin Bks.) Penguin Putnam Bks. for Young Readers.

Schulman, Lester. An Original Adventure Story: Small Soldiers Gorgonites. 1998. (Small Soldiers Ser.). 128p. (J). (gr. 3-7). 3.99 o.s.i (*0-448-41882-7*, Grosset & Dunlap) Penguin Putnam Bks. for Young Readers.

Scott, Gavin. Small Soldiers, Level 2. 1999. (J). pap. 7.66 (*0-582-38099-5*) Longman Publishing Group.

—Small Soldiers. novel ed. 1998. 128p. (J). (gr. 2-6). 4.99 o.s.i (*0-448-41880-0*, Grosset & Dunlap) Penguin Putnam Bks. for Young Readers.

Sergeant Murphy's Busiest Day Ever. 1995. (Favorite Sound Story Bks.). (Illus.). 24p. (J). bds. o.p. (*0-307-70901-9*, Golden Bks.) Random Hse. Children's Bks.

Summer of My German Soldier. 1999. (YA). 9.95 (*1-56137-113-0*) Novel Units, Inc.

Sutcliff, Rosemary. The Eagle of the Ninth, RS. 1993. 264p. (J). (gr. 7 up). pap. 5.95 (*0-374-41930-2*, Sunburst) Farrar, Straus & Giroux.

—The Eagle of the Ninth. 1987. (Illus.). 264p. (J). 20.00 o.p. (*0-19-271037-0*) Oxford Univ. Pr., Inc.

—The Lantern Bearers, RS. 1994. 40p. (J). (gr. 7 up). pap. 6.95 (*0-374-44302-5*, Sunburst) Farrar, Straus & Giroux.

—The Lantern Bearers. 1979. (New Oxford Library Ser.). (Illus.). (J). (gr. 4 up). reprint ed. 4.95 o.p. (*0-19-277082-9*) Oxford Univ. Pr., Inc.

—The Lantern Bearers. 1995. (J). 20.00 (*0-8446-6837-0*) Smith, Peter Pub., Inc.

—The Lantern Bearers. 1994. 12.00 (*0-606-17793-0*) Turtleback Bks.

—The Silver Branch, RS. 1993. 228p. (J). (gr. 7 up). pap. 6.95 (*0-374-46648-3*, Sunburst) Farrar, Straus & Giroux.

—The Silver Branch. 1994. (J). 20.25 (*0-8446-6780-3*) Smith, Peter Pub., Inc.

Sykes, Shelley & Szymanski, Lois. The Ghost Comes Out. 2001. (Gettysburg Ghost Gang Ser.: Vol. 1). 96p. (J). pap. 5.95 (*1-57249-266-X*, WM Kids) White Mane Publishing Co., Inc.

—The Soldier in the Cellar. 2002. (Gettysburg Ghost Gang Ser.: Vol. 5). 96p. (J). pap. 5.95 (*1-57249-299-6*, WM Kids) White Mane Publishing Co., Inc.

Taylor, C. J. Guerrier Solitaire et le Fantome: An Arapaho Legend, Vol. 2. 1993. (Native Legends Ser.). (FRE., Illus.). 24p. (YA). (gr. 3 up). pap. 6.95 (*0-88776-309-X*) Tundra Bks. of Northern New York.

Teitelbaum, Michael. Venom of Cobra. 2003. (G. I. Joe Ser.). 32p. (J). mass mkt. 3.99 (*0-439-45541-3*, Scholastic Paperbacks) Scholastic, Inc.

Ultimate Sticker Book: G. I. Joe Valor vs. Venom. 2004. (Ultimate Sticker Books Ser.). 16p. (J). pap. 6.99 (*0-7566-0367-6*) Dorling Kindersley Publishing, Inc.

Van Stockum, Hilda. The Mitchells: Five for Victory. 1995. (Mitchells Ser.: Vol. 1). (Illus.). 250p. (J). (gr. 4-7). reprint ed. pap. 12.95 (*1-883937-05-1*, 05-1) Bethlehem Bks.

Walker, Mort. I've Got You on My List, Beetle Bailey. 1981. (Beetle Bailey Ser.: No. 11). 128p. (J). (gr. 1 up). 1.75 o.s.i (*0-448-17002-7*) Ace Bks.

—Take a Walk, Beetle Bailey. 1981. (Beetle Bailey Ser.). 128p. (J). 1.75 o.s.i (*0-448-17001-9*) Ace Bks.

Wartski, Maureen C. A Long Way from Home. 1980. 156p. (J). (gr. 6 up). 9.95 o.p. (*0-664-32674-9*) Westminster John Knox Pr.

Windrow, Martin & Hook, Richard. The Footsoldier. 1988. (Illus.). 80p. (J). (ps-5). bds. 17.95 o.p. (*0-19-273147-5*) Oxford Univ. Pr., Inc.

—The Horse Soldier. 1988. (Illus.). 80p. (J). (ps-5). bds. 17.95 o.p. (*0-19-273157-2*) Oxford Univ. Pr., Inc.

Winston, Stan. Small Soldiers. 1998. (J). 261.62 o.p. (*0-448-41926-2*, Grosset & Dunlap) Penguin Putnam Bks. for Young Readers.

—Small Soldiers: The Movie Storybook. 1998. (Small Soldiers Ser.). 40p. (J). (gr. 3-7). 9.99 o.p. (*0-448-41877-0*, Grosset & Dunlap) Penguin Putnam Bks. for Young Readers.

Wisler, G. Clifton. Red Cap. 176p. (gr. 5 up). 1994. (YA). pap. 5.99 (*0-14-036936-8*, Puffin Bks.); 1991. (J). 15.99 o.p. (*0-525-67337-7*, Dutton Children's Bks.) Penguin Putnam Bks. for Young Readers.

—Red Cap, 2000. (YA). pap., stu. ed. 41.24 incl. audio (*0-7887-3629-9*, 41018X4); pap., stu. ed. 41.24 incl. audio (*0-7887-3629-9*, 41018X4) Recorded Bks., LLC.

—Red Cap. 2001. (YA). 20.25 (*0-8446-7196-7*) Smith, Peter Pub., Inc.

—Red Cap. 1994. 11.04 (*0-606-06691-8*) Turtleback Bks.

Wulffson, Don. Soldier X. 2003. 240p. (YA). pap. 6.99 (*0-14-250073-9*, Puffin Bks.) Penguin Putnam Bks. for Young Readers.

SPIES—FICTION

Aaron, Chester. Out of Sight, Out of Mind. 1986. 192p. pap. 2.95 o.p. (*0-553-26027-8*) Bantam Bks.

Allan, Mabel E. The Formidable Enemy. 1975. 160p. (J). (gr. 6 up). 6.95 o.p. (*0-8407-6443-X*, Dutton Children's Bks.) Penguin Putnam Bks. for Young Readers.

Archer, Chris. The Last Clue. 2003. (Pyrates Ser.: No. 4). 176p. (J). pap. 4.50 (*0-439-36854-5*, Scholastic Paperbacks) Scholastic, Inc.

Arthur, Robert, ed. Spies & More Spies. 1972. (Illus.). (J). (gr. 7-11). pap. 0.95 o.p. (*0-394-82190-4*, Random Hse. Bks. for Young Readers) Random Hse. Children's Bks.

Bader, Bonnie. Highway Robbery. 1997. (Carmen Sandiego Mystery Ser.). (J). (gr. 4-6). 9.60 o.p. (*0-606-11193-X*) Turtleback Bks.

—One T. Rex over Easy. 1997. (Carmen Sandiego Mystery Ser.). (Illus.). 144p. (J). (gr. 4-6). pap. 4.50 o.p. (*0-06-440679-2*, Harper Trophy) HarperCollins Children's Bk. Group.

—One T. Rex over Easy. 1997. (Carmen Sandiego Mystery Ser.). (J). (gr. 4-6). 9.60 o.p. (*0-606-11190-5*) Turtleback Bks.

Bader, Bonnie & West, Tracey. Highway Robbery. 1997. (Carmen Sandiego Mystery Ser.). (Illus.). 144p. (J). (gr. 4-6). pap. 4.50 o.s.i (*0-06-440685-7*, Harper Trophy) HarperCollins Children's Bk. Group.

Bakeless, Katherine & Bakeless, John. Confederate Spy Stories. 1973. 160p. (J). (gr. 7 up). o.p. (*0-397-31230-X*) HarperCollins Children's Bk. Group.

Ball, Duncan. Emily Eyefinger, Secret Agent. 1994. pap. 3.95 o.p. (*0-671-89906-6*, Aladdin); 1993. (Illus.). 96p. (J). (gr. 2-5). pap. 13.00 o.p. (*0-671-79827-8*, Simon & Schuster Children's Publishing) Simon & Schuster Children's Publishing.

—Spy Code Handbook. 1992. (J). (gr. 4-7). pap. 3.95 o.p. (*0-207-17718-X*) HarperCollins Pubs.

Bell, Mary Reeves. Secret of Mezuzah. 1999. (Passport to Danger Ser.: Vol. 1). 208p. (J). (gr. 7-12). pap. 5.99 o.p. (*1-55661-549-3*) Bethany Hse. Pubs.

—Secret of Mezuzah. 1999. (J). 12.04 (*0-606-18974-2*) Turtleback Bks.

Bennett, Dorothea. The Jigsaw Man. 1976. 256p. 8.95 o.p. (*0-698-10729-2*) Putnam Publishing Group, The.

Bethancourt, T. Ernesto. Doris Fein: Quartz Boyar. 1980. 160p. (YA). (gr. 7 up). 10.95 o.p. (*0-8234-0378-5*) Holiday Hse., Inc.

—Doris Fein: Superspy. 1980. 160p. (gr. 9 up). 10.95 o.p. (*0-8234-0407-2*) Holiday Hse., Inc.

Blair, Margaret W. House of Spies: Danger in the Civil War. 1999. (White Mane Kids Ser.: Vol. 7). (Illus.). 169p. (YA). (ps up). pap. 8.95 (*1-57249-161-2*, WM Kids) White Mane Publishing Co., Inc.

Bradley, Kimberly Brubaker. For Freedom: The Story of a French Spy. 2003. 192p. lib. bdg. 17.99 (*0-385-90087-2*); (gr. 5-9). text 15.95 (*0-385-72961-8*) Random Hse. Children's Bks.

Bruchac, Joseph. A Code Talker's Story. 2004. 16.99 (*0-8037-2921-9*, Dial Bks. for Young Readers) Penguin Putnam Bks. for Young Readers.

Bryant-Mole, Karen. Mortimer Plays I-Spy. 2000. (Mortimer's Fun with Words Ser.). (Illus.). 24p. (J). (ps up). lib. bdg. 19.93 (*0-8368-2749-X*) Stevens, Gareth Inc.

Burrows, Geraldine. Miss Sedgewick & the Spy. 2000. (Five Star First Edition Romance Ser.). 263p. (J). 25.95 (*0-7862-2215-8*, Five Star) Gale Group.

Butcher, A. J. The Frankenstein Factory. 2004. (J). 15.95 (*0-316-73759-3*); pap. 6.50 (*0-316-73760-7*) Little Brown Children's Bks.

—Spy High No. 2: The Chaos Connection. 2004. (Illus.). (J). pap. 6.50 (*0-316-73765-8*); (gr. 5-8). 15.95 (*0-316-73762-3*) Little Brown Children's Bks.

Cage, Elizabeth. Dial V for Vengeance. 1999. (Spy Girls Ser.: No. 5). 192p. (YA). (gr. 7 up). mass mkt. 4.50 (*0-671-03565-7*, Simon Pulse) Simon & Schuster Children's Publishing.

—License to Thrill. 1998. (Spy Girls Ser.: No. 1). 192p. (YA). (gr. 7 up). mass mkt. 4.50 (*0-671-02286-5*, Simon Pulse) Simon & Schuster Children's Publishing.

—Live & Let Spy. 1998. (Spy Girls Ser.: No. 2). (YA). (gr. 7 up). 10.55 (*0-606-16817-6*) Turtleback Bks.

—Nobody Does It Better. 1999. (Spy Girls Ser.: No. 3). 176p. (YA). (gr. 7 up). mass mkt. 4.50 (*0-671-02288-1*, Simon Pulse) Simon & Schuster Children's Publishing.

—Spy Girls. Date not set. (Spy Girls Ser.: No. 7). (YA). (gr. 7 up). mass mkt. (*0-671-03637-8*); mass mkt. (*0-671-03638-6*) Simon & Schuster Children's Publishing. (Simon Pulse).

—Spy Girls are Forever. 1999. (Spy Girls Ser.: No. 4). 192p. (YA). (gr. 7 up). per. 4.50 (*0-671-02289-X*, Simon Pulse) Simon & Schuster Children's Publishing.

—Hasta la Vista, Blarney. 1997. (Carmen Sandiego Mystery Ser.). (J). (gr. 4-6). 10.55 (*0-606-11189-1*) Turtleback Bks.

Platt, Richard. Spy. 2000. (Eyewitness Bks.). (Illus.). 64p. (J). (gr. 4-7). pap. 19.99 (*0-7894-6616-3*, D K Ink) Dorling Kindersley Publishing, Inc.

—Spy. 2001. (Dorling Kindersley Eyewitness Bks.). (J). lib. bdg. (*1-59054-645-8*) Fitzgerald Bks.

Rash, Andy. Agent A to Agent Z. 2004. (Illus.). (J). (*0-439-36883-9*); pap. 16.95 (*0-439-36882-0*) Scholastic, Inc. (Levine, Arthur A. Bks.).

Richardson, Bill. Sally Dog Little, Undercover Agent. 2003. (Illus.). 24p. (J). pap. 6.95 (*1-55037-824-4*); lib. bdg. 18.95 (*1-55037-825-2*) Annick Pr., Ltd. CAN. *Dist:* Firefly Bks., Ltd.

Richler, Mordecai. Jacob Two-Two's First Spy Case, RS. 1997. (Illus.). 152p. (J). (gr. 2-5). 16.00 o.p. (*0-374-33659-8*, Farrar, Straus & Giroux (BYR)) Farrar, Straus & Giroux.

Rieman, Barbara & Rieman, Roy. Where in America's Past Is Carmen Sandiego? 1992. (Carmen Sandiego). (Illus.). (J). (gr. 4-6). 14.95 o.p. (*0-672-48527-3*, Hayden) New Riders Publishing.

—Where in the World Is Carmen Sandiego? 1992. (Carmen Sandiego). (Illus.). (J). (gr. 4-6). 14.95 o.p. (*0-672-48525-7*, Hayden) New Riders Publishing.

—Where in Time Is Carmen Sandiego? 1992. (Carmen Sandiego). (Illus.). (J). (gr. 4-6). 14.95 o.p. (*0-672-48524-9*, Hayden) New Riders Publishing.

Rinaldi, Ann. Finishing Becca: A Story about Peggy Shippen & Benedict Arnold. (Great Episodes Ser.). 384p. (YA). 2004. pap. (*0-15-205079-5*); 1994. (gr. 7 up). 12.00 (*0-15-200880-2*); 1994. (gr. 7 up). pap. 6.00 o.s.i (*0-15-200879-9*) Harcourt Children's Bks. (Gulliver Bks.).

—Finishing Becca: A Story about Peggy Shippen & Benedict Arnold. 1994. 12.05 (*0-606-14207-X*) Turtleback Bks.

—Girl in Blue. 2001. (Illus.). 272p. (J). (gr. 4-9). pap. 15.95 (*0-439-07336-7*) Scholastic, Inc.

—The Secret of Sarah Revere. (Great Episodes Ser.). 336p. (YA). 2003. pap. 6.95 (*0-15-204684-4*); 1995. (gr. 7 up). 13.00 (*0-15-200393-2*, Gulliver Bks.); 1995. (gr. 7 up). pap. 6.00 o.s.i (*0-15-200392-4*, Gulliver Bks.) Harcourt Children's Bks.

Rodriguez, Robert & Willard, Eliza. Spy Kids. movie tie-in ed. 2001. 32p. (J). (gr. 3-6). pap. 5.99 (*0-7868-1626-0*) Hyperion Bks. for Children.

Rogers, Kirby. Operation Dewey. 2002. (Illus.). ix, 100p. (J). pap. (*1-877633-65-8*) Luthers.

Rylant, Cynthia. Henry & Mudge & the Sneaky Crackers. (Henry & Mudge Ser.). (Illus.). (J). (gr. k-3). 1999. 48p. pap. 3.99 (*0-689-82525-0*, Aladdin); 1998. 40p. 15.00 (*0-689-81176-4*, Simon & Schuster Children's Publishing) Simon & Schuster Children's Publishing.

Sappey, Maureen S. Yankee Spy. 1999. (Young American Ser.: Vol. 3). (Illus.). 140p. (J). (gr. 4-7). 5.99 (*1-57249-135-3*) White Mane Publishing Co., Inc.

Scheffler, Ursel. The Spy in the Attic. 1998. (Illus.). 64p. (J). (gr. 1-4). pap. 5.95 (*1-55858-991-0*) North-South Bks., Inc.

—The Spy in the Attic. 1998. (Easy to Read Chapter Bks.). 12.10 (*0-606-15717-4*) Turtleback Bks.

Schmidt, Suzy. Spy Master. 2002. (Illus.). 32p. (J). (gr. 3-7). 12.95 (*0-439-32540-4*) Scholastic, Inc.

Scholastic, Inc. Staff, ed. Spy in My Mouth. 9999. (J). pap. 2.50 o.s.i (*0-590-40444-X*) Scholastic, Inc.

Sharmat, Marjorie Weinman. Spy in the Neighborhood. 1989. (J). mass mkt. 2.75 o.p. (*0-590-42633-8*) Scholastic, Inc.

Skurnick, Elizabeth. Alias - Pursuit: A Michael Vaughn Novel. 2003. (Alias Ser.: Bk. 5). 208p. (YA). (gr. 7). mass mkt. 5.99 (*0-553-49402-3*, Bantam Bks. for Young Readers) Random Hse. Children's Bks.

Sobol, Donald J. Encyclopedia Brown & the Case of the Two Spies. 1995. (Encyclopedia Brown Ser.: No. 19). 80p. (gr. 2-6). pap. text 4.50 (*0-553-48297-1*) Bantam Bks.

—Encyclopedia Brown's Book of Wacky Spies. 1984. (Encyclopedia Brown Ser.). (Illus.). 112p. (J). (gr. 2-6). pap. 2.25 o.s.i (*0-553-15369-2*, Skylark) Random Hse. Children's Bks.

—Secret Agents Four. 2003. (Adventure Library). (Illus.). 140p. (J). pap. 10.95 (*1-883937-65-5*) Bethlehem Bks.

—Secret Agents Four. 1988. (Illus.). 144p. (J). (gr. 3-7). pap. 2.50 o.p. (*0-590-40565-9*) Scholastic, Inc.

Stanley, George Edward. Adam Sharp, Operation Spy School. 2003. (Stepping Stone Book Ser.). (Illus.). 48p. (J). (gr. 1-4). lib. bdg. 11.99 (*0-375-92404-3*);No. 4. pap. 3.99 (*0-375-82404-9*) Random Hse., Inc.

—Adam Sharp, Swimming with Sharks. 2003. (Illus.). 48p. (J). (gr. 2-4). pap. 3.99 (*0-307-26418-1*); lib. bdg. 11.99 (*0-307-46418-0*) Random Hse., Inc.

—Adam Sharp, the Spy Who Barked. 2002. (Road to Reading Ser.). (Illus.). 48p. (J). (gr. 2-4). pap. 3.99 (*0-307-26412-2*); lib. bdg. 11.99 (*0-307-46412-1*) Random Hse. Children's Bks. (Golden Bks.).

—Moose Master: Adam Sharp Spy School. 2004. (Illus.). (J). (gr. 1-4). 48p. pap. 3.99 (*0-375-82688-2*); lib. bdg. 11.99 (*0-375-92688-7*) Random Hse. Children's Bks. (Random Hse. Bks. for Young Readers).

Stine, Megan. Spy Kids. novel ed. 2001. 128p. (J). (gr. 3-6). pap. 4.99 (*0-7868-1627-9*) Hyperion Bks. for Children.

Teague, Bob. Agent K-Thirteen the Super-Spy. 1974. 48p. (gr. 1-3). 7.95 o.p. (*0-385-08704-7*); lib. bdg. o.p. (*0-385-03186-6*) Doubleday Publishing.

—Super-Spy K-Thirteen in Outer Space. 1980. (Illus.). (gr. 1-3). 9.95 o.p. (*0-385-14314-1*); lib. bdg. o.p. (*0-385-14315-X*) Doubleday Publishing.

Travis, Lucille. Jeanmarie & the FBI. 2000. (Apple Valley Mysteries Ser.: Vol. 1). (Illus.). 160p. (J). (gr. 3-7). pap. 5.99 o.p. (*0-8010-4471-5*) Baker Bks.

Vincent, John. High Stakes. 1992. (James Bond Adventure Ser.: No. 6). (Illus.). 128p. (J). (gr. 3-7). mass mkt. 2.99 o.p. (*0-14-036048-4*, Puffin Bks.) Penguin Putnam Bks. for Young Readers.

Walden, Amelia. A Spy Case Built for Two. 1969. (J). (gr. 7 up). 3.95 o.p. (*0-664-32433-9*) Westminster John Knox Pr.

—The Spy on Danger Island. 1965. (J). (gr. 7-10). 3.50 o.p. (*0-664-32364-2*) Westminster John Knox Pr.

—To Catch a Spy. 1964. (J). (gr. 7-10). 5.50 o.p. (*0-664-32329-4*) Westminster John Knox Pr.

Wayfair, Irwin. Top-Secret Dossier: Small Soldiers. 1998. (Small Soldiers Ser.). 80p. (YA). (gr. 3 up). 8.99 o.p. (*0-448-41879-7*, Grosset & Dunlap) Penguin Putnam Bks. for Young Readers.

Weiss, Ellen. Color Me Criminal. 1997. (Carmen Sandiego Mystery Ser.). (J). (gr. 4-6). 10.55 (*0-606-11188-3*) Turtleback Bks.

—Take the Mummy & Run. 1997. (Carmen Sandiego Mystery Ser.). (J). (gr. 4-6). 9.60 o.p. (*0-606-11192-1*) Turtleback Bks.

Weiss, Ellen & Friedman, Mel. Color Me Criminal. 1997. (Carmen Sandiego Mystery Ser.). (Illus.). 144p. (J). (gr. 4-6). pap. 4.50 o.s.i (*0-06-440663-6*, Harper Trophy) HarperCollins Children's Bk. Group.

—Take the Mummy & Run. 1997. (Carmen Sandiego Mystery Ser.). (Illus.). 160p. (J). (gr. 4-6). pap. 4.50 o.s.i (*0-06-440664-4*, Harper Trophy) HarperCollins Children's Bk. Group.

West, Anna. Revenge at the Spy-Catchers' Picnic. 1981. 64p. (J). (gr. 6-9). 8.95 o.s.i (*0-201-08498-8*) Addison-Wesley Longman, Inc.

West, Tracey. Eye Spy Aliens. 2003. (Scream Shop Ser.: Vol. 3). (Illus.). 144p. (J). mass mkt. 4.99 (*0-448-43226-9*, Grosset & Dunlap) Penguin Putnam Bks. for Young Readers.

Westall, Robert. Fathom Five. 1990. (YA). 17.25 o.p. (*0-8446-6664-5*) Smith, Peter Pub., Inc.

Whelan, Gerard. A Winter of Spies. 1999. 191p. (YA). (gr. 5 up). pap. 6.95 (*0-86278-566-9*) O'Brien Pr., Ltd., The IRL. *Dist:* Independent Pubs. Group.

Wilson, Linda Miller. Summer Spy. 1996. 93 p. (J). lib. bdg. o.p. (*0-88092-173-0*) Royal Fireworks Publishing Co.

Windle, Jeanette. Escape to Deer Island. 1996. (Twin Pursuits Ser.). 128p. pap. 4.99 o.p. (*0-88070-906-5*, Multnomah Bks.) Multnomah Pubs., Inc.

Yolen, Jane. Commander Toad & the Intergalactic Spy. 1997. (Illus.). 64p. (J). (gr. 2-5). pap. 5.99 (*0-698-11418-3*, PaperStar) Penguin Putnam Bks. for Young Readers.

—Commander Toad & the Intergalactic Spy. 1986. (Commander Toad Bks.). (Illus.). 64p. (J). (ps-4). 10.99 o.s.i (*0-698-30747-X*); 6.95 o.s.i (*0-698-20623-1*) Putnam Publishing Group, The. (Coward-McCann).

—Commander Toad & the Intergalactic Spy. 1997. (J). 12.14 (*0-606-11220-0*) Turtleback Bks.

Younger, Marshal, et al. Mystery of the Hooded Horseman. 2002. (Mysteries in Odyssey Ser.: Bk. 2). (Illus.). 128p. (J). (gr. 3-7). 5.99 (*1-56179-973-4*) Focus on the Family Publishing.

Zindel, Paul. The Gadget. 2001. 192p. (J). (gr. 6 up). lib. bdg. 16.89 (*0-06-028255-X*) HarperCollins Children's Bk. Group.

—The Gadget. 2003. (Illus.). 192p. (YA). (gr. 7). mass mkt. 5.50 (*0-440-22951-0*, Laurel Leaf) Random Hse. Children's Bks.

T

TAILORS—FICTION

Anholt, Laurence. The Emperor's New Underwear. 1999. (Illus.). (J). (ps-7). 64p. 3.95 (*0-689-83073-4*); pap. text (*0-88166-347-6*) Meadowbrook Pr.

Bunting, Eve. Clancy's Coat. (J). 1985. 12.95 o.p. (*0-670-80698-6*, Viking Children's Bks.); 1984. (Illus.). 48p. (gr. 1-5). 11.95 o.p. (*0-7232-6252-7*, Warne, Frederick) Penguin Putnam Bks. for Young Readers.

Calmenson, Stephanie. The Principal's New Clothes. (J). (ps-3). 1991. pap. 3.95 o.p. (*0-590-41824-6*); 1991. (Illus.). 40p. mass mkt. 5.99 (*0-590-44778-5*, Scholastic Paperbacks); 1989. (Illus.). pap. 13.95 (*0-590-41822-X*) Scholastic, Inc.

—The Principal's New Clothes. 1991. 12.14 (*0-606-12490-X*) Turtleback Bks.

Dugina, Olga & Dugin, Andrej, illus. The Brave Little Tailor. 2000. 32p. (J). (ps-3). 15.95 (*0-8109-4113-9*) Abrams, Harry N. , Inc.

Friedman, Aileen. A Cloak for the Dreamer. 1995. (Brainy Day Bks.). (Illus.). 36p. (J). (ps-3). pap. (*0-590-48987-9*) Scholastic, Inc.

Grimm, Jacob W. & Grimm, Wilhelm K. The Brave Little Tailor. Moncure, Jane Belk, tr. 1988. (Classic Tales Ser.). (Illus.). 32p. (J). (ps-3). lib. bdg. 19.93 o.p. (*0-89565-460-1*) Child's World, Inc.

Kimmel, Eric A. A Cloak for the Moon: A Tale of Rabbi Nachman of Bratslav. 2001. (Illus.). 32p. (J). (ps-3). tchr. ed. 16.95 (*0-8234-1493-0*) Holiday Hse., Inc.

Klinting, Lars. Bruno the Tailor, ERS. 1996. (Illus.). 40p. (J). (ps-3). 14.95 o.s.i (*0-8050-4500-7*, Holt, Henry & Co. Bks. For Young Readers) Holt, Henry & Co.

Krahn, Fernando. Who's Seen the Scissors? 1975. (J). (ps-1). 6.95 o.p. (*0-525-42710-4*, Dutton) Dutton/Plume.

Littledale, Freya. Brave Little Tailor. 1990. 32p. (J). (gr. k-3). pap. 2.50 o.p. (*0-590-42797-0*) Scholastic, Inc.

Obrist, Jurg. The Miser Who Wanted the Sun. 1984. (Illus.). 32p. (J). (gr. k-3). 14.95 o.s.i (*0-689-50294-X*, McElderry, Margaret K.) Simon & Schuster Children's Publishing.

Potter, Beatrix. Tailleur de Gloucester. 1991. (FRE., Illus.). 58p. (J). 9.95 (*0-7859-3630-0*, 2070560767) French & European Pubns., Inc.

—Tailleur de Gloucester. 1991. (Gallimard Ser.). (FRE.). 58p. (J). 10.95 (*2-07-056076-7*) Schoenhof's Foreign Bks., Inc.

—The Tailor of Gloucester. 2002. (Illus.). 64p. (J). 6.99 (*0-7232-4772-2*, Warne, Frederick) Penguin Putnam Bks. for Young Readers.

—The Tailor of Gloucester. (J). (ps-3). 1995. (Illus.). 40p. pap. 10.95 o.p. incl. audio (*0-689-80362-1*); 1995. (Illus.). 40p. pap. 10.95 o.p. incl. audio (*0-689-80362-1*); 1988. pap. 19.95 o.p. incl. audio (*0-88708-085-5*, LC 88-11510) Simon & Schuster Children's Publishing. (Simon & Schuster Children's Publishing).

—Tailor of Gloucester. 1991. (Potter 23 Tales Ser.). (Illus.). 64p. (J). (ps). pap. 2.50 o.p. (*0-7232-3767-0*, Warne, Frederick) Penguin Putnam Bks. for Young Readers.

—The Tailor of Gloucester: Lift-the-Flap Book. 1994. (Lift-the-Flap Ser.). (Illus.). 24p. (J). (ps-1). 11.99 o.p. (*0-7232-4147-3*, Warne, Frederick) Penguin Putnam Bks. for Young Readers.

—The Tale of the Tailor of Gloucester. 1987. (Illus.). 64p. (J). (ps-3). 3.95 o.s.i (*0-671-63234-5*, Little Simon) Simon & Schuster Children's Publishing.

San Souci, Daniel, illus. The Brave Little Tailor. 1982. 32p. (gr. k-3). lib. bdg. o.p. (*0-385-17569-8*) Doubleday Publishing.

San Souci, Robert D. The Brave Little Taylor. Ryan, Kevin, ed. 2000. (Wishbone Ser.: No. 4). (Illus.). 104p. (J). (ps-3). mass mkt. 3.99 o.p. (*1-57064-742-9*, Big Red Chair Bks.) Lyrick Publishing.

Schotter, Roni. Dreamland. 1996. (Illus.). 40p. (J). (ps-3). pap. 15.95 (*0-531-09508-8*); lib. bdg. 16.99 (*0-531-08858-8*) Scholastic, Inc. (Orchard Bks.).

The Tailor's Passion. 1997. (Scheherezade Children's Stories Ser.). (Illus.). 16p. (J). (*1-85964-013-3*, Ithaca Pr.) Garnet Publishing, Ltd.

TEACHERS—FICTION

Abbott, Tony. The Fake Teacher. 1999. (Don't Touch That Remote Ser.: No. 2). 160p. (J). (gr. 3-6). pap. 3.99 (*0-671-02782-4*, Aladdin) Simon & Schuster Children's Publishing.

Abdo Publishing Staff, contrib. by. Flower Girl Friends. 2000. (Faithful Friends Ser.). (Illus.). 64p. (J). (gr. 4). lib. bdg. 21.35 (*1-57765-229-0*, ABDO & Daughters) ABDO Publishing Co.

Adams, W. Royce. Teacher, Teacher, I Declare! & Other Little Tattle Tales. 2nd ed. 2001. 228p. pap. 14.95 (*0-9712206-1-1*) Rairarubia Bks.

Adler, C. S. Not Just a Summer Crush. 1998. (Illus.). 118p. (J). (gr. 5-9). tchr. ed. 15.00 (*0-395-88532-9*, Clarion Bks.) Houghton Mifflin Co. Trade & Reference Div.

Adler, David A. Cam Jansen & the Tennis Trophy Mystery. Natti, Susanna, tr. & illus. by. 2003. 64p. (J). 13.99 (*0-670-03643-9*, Viking) Viking Penguin.

—School Trouble for Andy Russell. (Andy Russell Ser.). (Illus.). 128p. (YA). (gr. 2-5). 2000. pap. 4.95 (*0-15-202496-4*); 1999. 14.00 (*0-15-202190-6*) Harcourt Children's Bks. (Gulliver Bks.).

—School Trouble for Andy Russell. 2000. (J). 11.00 (*0-606-19004-X*) Turtleback Bks.

Ahlberg, Allan. Mr. Tick the Teacher. 1981. 24p. (J). (gr. 3-6). pap. 6.95 (*0-14-031245-5*) Penguin Bks., Ltd. GBR. *Dist:* Trafalgar Square.

Allard, Harry G. Miss Nelson Has a Field Day. (Miss Nelson Ser.). (Illus.). (J). (ps-3). 1989. 1p. pap. 9.95 incl. audio (*0-395-52138-6*, 480440); 1989. 1p. pap. 9.95 incl. audio (*0-395-52138-6*, 480440); 1985. 32p. lib. bdg., tchr. ed. 16.00 (*0-395-36690-9*) Houghton Mifflin Co.

—Miss Nelson Has a Field Day. 1988. (Miss Nelson Ser.). (Illus.). 32p. (J). (ps-3). pap. 5.95 (*0-395-48654-8*) Houghton Mifflin Co. Trade & Reference Div.

—Miss Nelson Has a Field Day. 1985. (Miss Nelson Ser.). (Illus.). (J). (ps-3). 12.10 (*0-606-04276-8*) Turtleback Bks.

—Miss Nelson Is Back. (Miss Nelson Ser.). (Illus.). 32p. (J). (ps-3). 1986. pap. 5.95 (*0-395-41668-X*); 1982. lib. bdg., tchr. ed. 16.00 (*0-395-32956-6*) Houghton Mifflin Co.

—Miss Nelson Is Missing! (Miss Nelson Ser.). (Illus.). (J). (ps-3). 1987. pap. 7.95 o.p. incl. audio (*0-395-45737-8*); 1985. 32p. pap. 5.95 (*0-395-40146-1*) Houghton Mifflin Co.

—Miss Nelson Is Missing! 1978. (Miss Nelson Ser.). (Illus.). (J). (ps-3). pap. 1.95 o.p. (*0-590-11877-3*) Scholastic, Inc.

—Miss Nelson Is Missing! 1977. (Miss Nelson Ser.). (Illus.). (J). (ps-3). 12.10 (*0-606-04400-0*) Turtleback Bks.

—Miss Nelson Is Missing! 2000. (Miss Nelson Ser.). (Illus.). (J). (ps-3). pap. 12.95 incl. audio Weston Woods Studios, Inc.

—Miss Nelson Is Missing. (Miss Nelson Ser.). (J). (ps-3). audio 8.95 Weston Woods Studios, Inc.

—La Senorita Nelson Ha Desaparecido! Canetti, Yanitzia, tr. 1998. (SPA., Illus.). 32p. (J). (ps-3). pap. 5.95 (*0-395-90008-5*, HM8029) Houghton Mifflin Co.

—La Senorita Nelson Ha Desaparecido! 1998. (Miss Nelson Ser.). (SPA., Illus.). 32p. (J). (ps-3). lib. bdg. 16.00 (*0-395-90009-3*) Houghton Mifflin Co.

Allard, Harry G., ed. Miss Nelson Is Back. 1988. (Miss Nelson Ser.). (Illus.). 1p. (J). (ps-3). pap. 9.95 incl. audio (*0-395-48872-9*, 480436); pap. 9.95 incl. audio (*0-395-48872-9*, 480436) Houghton Mifflin Co.

—Miss Nelson Is Back. 1982. (Miss Nelson Ser.). (Illus.). (J). (ps-3). 12.10 (*0-606-02538-3*) Turtleback Bks.

Allard, Harry G. & Marshall, James. Miss Nelson Is Missing! 1977. (Miss Nelson Ser.). (Illus.). 32p. (J). (ps-3). lib. bdg., tchr. ed. 16.00 (*0-395-25296-2*) Houghton Mifflin Co.

Anderson, Janet. Going Through the Gate. 2000. 144p. (YA). (gr. 3-7). pap. 4.99 o.s.i (*0-14-130698-X*, Puffin Bks.) Penguin Putnam Bks. for Young Readers.

—Going Through the Gate. 2000. (Illus.). (J). 11.04 (*0-606-18407-4*) Turtleback Bks.

—Going Through the Gate: Graduation. 1997. 144p. (J). (gr. 4-7). 15.99 o.s.i (*0-525-45836-0*) Penguin Putnam Bks. for Young Readers.

Angell, Judie. The Adventures of Shirley Holmes: The Case of the Blazing Star & the Case of the King of Hearts. 1999. (Adventures of Shirley Holmes Ser.). 96p. (gr. 3-7). pap. text 3.99 o.s.i (*0-440-41503-9*, Dell Books for Young Readers) Random Hse. Children's Bks.

Arter, Jim. Gruel & Unusual Punishment. 1991. 112p. (J). (gr. 3-7). 13.95 o.s.i (*0-385-30298-3*, Delacorte Pr.) Dell Publishing.

Arthur's Teacher Moves In. (Illus.). (J). 2001. pap. 5.95 (*0-316-12206-8*); 2000. 15.95 (*0-316-11809-5*) Little Brown & Co.

Avery, Gillian. Maria Escapes. 1992. (Illus.). 272p. (J). (gr. 4-8). pap. 15.00 (*0-671-77074-8*, Simon & Schuster Children's Publishing) Simon & Schuster Children's Publishing.

Avi. The Secret School. 2001. 160p. (J). (gr. 3-7). 16.00 (*0-15-216375-1*) Harcourt Children's Bks.

—Who Was That Masked Man, Anyway? 1994. (Avon Camelot Bks.). 176p. (J). (gr. 5 up). pap. 5.99 (*0-380-72113-9*) Morrow/Avon.

—Who Was That Masked Man, Anyway? 1992. 176p. (YA). (gr. 4-7). pap. 16.95 (*0-531-05457-8*); lib. bdg. 17.99 (*0-531-08607-0*) Scholastic, Inc. (Orchard Bks.).

—Who Was That Masked Man, Anyway? 1992. (J). 10.04 (*0-606-06097-9*) Turtleback Bks.

Baker, Keri. Once in a Green Room. l.t. ed. 2001. 200p. per. 18.95 (*1-888725-61-3*, MacroPrint-Books) Science & Humanities Pr.

—Once in a Green Room: A Novel. 2001. 145p. (YA). per. 14.95 (*1-888725-38-9*) Science & Humanities Pr.

Bartlett, Susan. Seal Island School. Bonnell, J., ed. 2001. (Chapter Ser.). (Illus.). 80p. (J). (gr. 2-5). pap. 4.99 (*0-14-131104-5*, Puffin Bks.) Penguin Putnam Bks. for Young Readers.

—Seal Island School. 1999. (Illus.). 80p. (J). (gr. 2-5). 15.99 (*0-670-88349-2*) Penguin Putnam Bks. for Young Readers.

Occupations

Bellingham, Brenda. Lilly in the Middle. 2003. (Illus.). 64p. (J). pap. 3.99 (*0-88780-589-2*) Orca Bk. Pubs.

Benjamin, Saragail K. My Dog Ate It. 1994. 176p. (J). (gr. 4-7). 14.95 (*0-8234-1047-1*) Holiday Hse., Inc.

—My Dog Ate It. 1996. (J). (gr. 3-7). mass mkt. 3.50 o.p. (*0-590-22286-4*) Scholastic, Inc.

Berenstain, Stan & Berenstain, Jan. The Berenstain Bears & the Red-Handed Thief. 1993. (Berenstain Bears Big Chapter Bks.). (Illus.). (gr. 2-6). 102p. (J). 11.99 o.s.i (*0-679-94033-2*); 112p. pap. 3.99 (*0-679-84033-8*) Random Hse. Children's Bks. (Random Hse. Bks. for Young Readers).

Bertrand, Diane Gonzales. Lessons of the Game. 1998. 192p. (YA). (gr. 6-12). pap. 9.95 (*1-55885-245-X*, Piñata Books) Arte Publico Pr.

Blacker, Terence. Ms. Wiz Spells Trouble. 1990. (Arch Bks.). (Illus.). 64p. (J). (gr. 3-6). pap. 2.95 o.p. (*0-8120-4420-7*) Barron's Educational Series, Inc.

Boies, Janice. Love on Strike. 1990. (Sweet Dreams Ser.: No. 174). 176p. (YA). (gr. 9-12). pap. 2.75 o.s.i (*0-553-28633-1*) Bantam Bks.

Boonstra, Jean Elizabeth. Miss Button & the School-board: Sarah 1842-1844. 2002. 95p. (J). (*0-8163-1874-3*) Pacific Pr. Publishing Assn.

Borden, Louise. Good Luck, Mrs. K.! (Illus.). 32p. (J). 2002. (gr. 1-5). pap. 6.99 (*0-689-85119-7*, Aladdin); 1999. (gr. k-3). 15.00 (*0-689-82147-6*, McElderry, Margaret K.) Simon & Schuster Children's Publishing.

Bottner, Barbara. Let Me Tell You Everything: Memoirs of a Lovesick Intellectual. 1989. 160p. (YA). (gr. 7 up). 12.95 (*0-06-020596-2*) Harper-Collins Children's Bk. Group.

—Let Me Tell You Everything: Memoirs of a Lovesick Intellectual. MacDonald, Patricia, ed. 1991. 160p. (YA). reprint ed. pap. 2.95 (*0-671-72323-5*, Simon Pulse) Simon & Schuster Children's Publishing.

Bradman, Tony. Ghost Teacher. 2000. (Illus.). 60p. (J). pap. 6.95 (*0-552-52976-1*) Transworld Publishers Ltd. GBR. *Dist:* Trafalgar Square.

Brandt, Amy. When Katie Was Our Teacher. de la Vega, Eida, tr. 2004. (Child Care Bks. for Kids).Tr. of Cuando Katie Era Nuestra Maestra. (ENG & SPA., Illus.). 32p. (J). (ps-2). pap. 11.95 (*1-884834-78-7*, 709901) Redleaf Pr.

Brenner, Emily. On the First Day of Grade School. 2004. (J). lib. bdg. (*0-06-051041-2*) HarperCollins Pubs.

Brillhart, Julie. Anna's Goodbye Apron. Mathews, Judith, ed. 1990. (Illus.). 32p. (J). (ps-1). lib. bdg. 14.95 o.p. (*0-8075-0375-4*) Whitman, Albert & Co.

Brooks, Jerome. Knee Holes. 1992. 144p. (gr. 7 up). (J). 14.95 o.p. (*0-531-05994-4*); (YA). mass mkt. 14.99 o.p. (*0-531-08594-5*) Scholastic, Inc. (Orchard Bks.).

Brown, Marc. Arthur's Adventures Four Book Set: Arthur's Computer Disaster, Arthur's TV Troubles, Arthur's Teacher Troubles, Arthur's New Puppy. 2002. pap. 23.80 (*0-316-16961-7*) Little Brown & Co.

—Arthur's Teacher Moves In. 2000. (Arthur Adventure Ser.). (J). (gr. k-3). (Illus.). 32p. 15.95 (*0-316-11979-2*); 15.95 (*0-316-11856-7*) Little Brown Children's Bks.

—Arthur's Teacher Trouble. (Arthur Adventure Ser.). (J). (gr. k-3). 1995. lib. bdg. 99.95 (*1-57135-019-5*); 1994. pap. 23.75 net. incl. cd-rom (*1-57135-017-9*) Broderbund Software, Inc.

—Arthur's Teacher Trouble. ed. 1999. (J). (gr. 1). spiral bd. (*0-616-01603-4*); (gr. 2). spiral bd. (*0-616-00406-0*) Canadian National Institute for the Blind/Institut National Canadien pour les Aveugles.

—Arthur's Teacher Trouble. 1986. (Arthur Adventure Ser.). (J). (gr. k-3). 12.10 (*0-606-04161-3*) Turtle-back Bks.

—Arthur's Teacher Trouble Class Set. 1995. (Arthur Adventure Ser.). (J). (gr. k-3). pap. 79.95 (*1-57135-018-7*) Broderbund Software, Inc.

—Arturo y Sus Problemas con el Profesor. 1994. (Arthur Adventure Ser.). (SPA.). (J). (gr. k-3). 15.95 o.p. (*0-316-11379-4*) Little Brown Children's Bks.

—La Visita del Señor Rataquemada. Sarfatti, Esther, tr. from ENG. 2003. (SPA.). (J). (gr. k-2). pap. 6.95 (*1-930332-41-6*) Lectorum Pubns., Inc.

Brown, Marc, reader. Arthur's Teacher Trouble. 1994. (Arthur Adventure Ser.). (Illus.). (J). (gr. k-3). pap. 9.95 incl. audio (*0-316-11389-1*) Little Brown Children's Bks.

Brown, Marc, et al. Arthur's Teacher Trouble. (Arthur Adventure Ser.). (Illus.). (J). (gr. k-3). 1989. 30p. pap. 5.95 (*0-316-11186-4*); 1987. 32p. 16.95 (*0-316-11244-5*) Little Brown Children's Bks.

Bunt, Sandra K. The Other Side of the Desk. 1992. (Illus.). 135p. (Orig.). (J). (gr. 3-6). pap. 7.95 (*0-932433-80-4*) Windswept Hse. Pubs.

Bunting, Eve. Our Teacher's Having a Baby. (Illus.). 32p. (J). (ps-3). 2001. pap. 5.95 (*0-618-11138-7*); 1992. lib. bdg., tchr. ed. 15.00 (*0-395-60470-2*) Houghton Mifflin Co. Trade & Reference Div. (Clarion Bks.).

—Our Teacher's Having a Baby. 2001. (Illus.). (J). 12.10 (*0-606-21372-4*) Turtleback Bks.

Burkett, Kathy & Korman, Gordon. Clue Me In! The Detective Work of Ethan Flask & Professor Von Offel. 2003. (Mad Science Ser.: No. 5). 112p. (J). (gr. 3-7). mass mkt. 4.50 (*0-439-20727-4*) Scholastic, Inc.

Butler, Elizabeth. Surprise! 1997. (Let Me Read Ser.). (Illus.). (J). (ps-3). pap. 2.95 o.p. (*0-673-36342-2*, Good Year Bks.) Celebration Pr.

Butterfield, Moira. School Mouse: Village Mouse Stories. 1992. (J). (ps-3). 3.95 o.p. (*0-8431-3424-0*, Price Stern Sloan) Penguin Putnam Bks. for Young Readers.

Calamari, Barbara. The Trouble with Teachers. 2001. (Angela Anaconda Ser.: Vol. 1). (Illus.). 64p. (J). (gr. 4-7). pap. 3.99 (*0-689-83996-0*, Simon Spotlight) Simon & Schuster Children's Publishing.

Calmenson, Stephanie. The Teeny Tiny Teacher. (Illus.). 32p. (J). (ps-2). 2002. mass mkt. 5.99 (*0-439-40069-4*, Scholastic Paperbacks); 1998. pap. 15.95 (*0-590-37123-1*) Scholastic, Inc.

Capeci, Anne. Watch Out! The Daring Disasters of Ethan Flask & Professor Con Offel. 2002. (Mad Science Ser.: No. 4). 32p. (J). mass mkt. 4.50 (*0-439-20726-6*) Scholastic, Inc.

Carabine, Sue. A Teacher's Night Before Christmas. 1996. (Night Before Christmas Ser.). (Illus.). 60p. 5.95 (*0-87905-764-5*) Smith, Gibbs Pub.

Carpenter, Humphrey. Mr. Majeika. 1985. (Illus.). 96p. (J). (gr. 3-6). pap. 7.95 (*0-14-031677-9*) Penguin Bks., Ltd. GBR. *Dist:* Trafalgar Square.

—Mr. Majeika & the School Inspector. 1993. (Illus.). 96p. (J). (gr. 3-6). pap. 7.95 (*0-14-036288-6*) Penguin Bks., Ltd. GBR. *Dist:* Trafalgar Square.

—Mr. Majeika & the School Play. 1993. (Illus.). 96p. (J). (gr. 3-6). pap. 7.95 (*0-14-034358-X*) Penguin Bks., Ltd. GBR. *Dist:* Trafalgar Square.

Chardiet, Bernice. The Best Teacher in the World. 1990. (J). (ps-3). 11.95 o.p. (*0-590-44108-6*) Scholastic, Inc.

—The Best Teacher in the World. 1996. (Hello Reader! Ser.). 10.14 (*0-606-09070-3*) Turtleback Bks.

Chardiet, Bernice & Maccarone, Grace. The Best Teacher in the World. (Illus.). 32p. (J). (ps-3). 1996. (Hello Reader! Ser.: Level 3). pap. 3.99 (*0-590-68158-3*, Cartwheel Bks.); 1991. (School Friends Ser.). reprint ed. pap. 2.50 (*0-590-43307-5*) Scholastic, Inc.

Chardiet, Bernice. The Best Teacher in the World. 1996. (Hello Reader! Ser.). (FRE., Illus.). 32p. (J). pap. 5.99 (*0-590-16029-X*) Scholastic, Inc.

Chesely, Mary. Miss Purdy's Problem. Weinberger, Jane, ed. 1994. (Illus.). 48p. (J). (ps-4). pap. 7.95 (*0-932433-75-8*) Windswept Hse. Pubs.

Christian, Mary Blount. Swamp Monsters. (Puffin Easy-to-Read Ser.). (J). (ps-3). 1994. (Illus.). 48p. pap. 3.99 o.s.i (*0-14-036841-8*); 1992. 40p. pap. 4.99 o.p. (*0-14-036211-8*) Penguin Putnam Bks. for Young Readers. (Puffin Bks.).

—Swamp Monsters. unabr. ed. 1985. (Follow the Reader Ser.). (J). (gr. 1-2). pap. 17.00 incl. audio (*0-8072-0086-7*, FTR98SP, Listening Library) Random Hse. Audio Publishing Group.

Clarke, Gus. What Would We Do Without Missus Mac? 2001. (J). E-Book (*1-59019-418-7*); 1999. E-Book (*1-59019-419-5*); 1999. (J). E-Book 5.99 (*1-59019-420-9*) ipicturebooks, LLC.

—What Would We Do Without Missus Mac. 1999. (Illus.). 24p. (J). 19.95 (*0-86264-884-X*) Andersen Pr., Ltd. GBR. *Dist:* Trafalgar Square.

Cleary, Beverly. Dear Mr. Henshaw. 1992. 144p. (J). (gr. 4-7). mass mkt. 1.99 o.s.i (*0-440-21366-5*) Dell Publishing.

Clements, Andrew. Billy & the Bad Teacher. 1992. (Illus.). 28p. (J). (ps up). pap. 15.00 o.p. (*0-88708-244-0*, Simon & Schuster Children's Publishing) Simon & Schuster Children's Publishing.

—Frindle. l.t. ed. 2000. (LRS Large Print Cornerstone Ser.). (Illus.). 116p. (YA). (gr. 4-10). lib. bdg. 24.95 (*1-58118-062-4*, 23476) LRS.

—Frindle. 105p. (J). (gr. 3-5). pap. 4.50 (*0-8072-1522-8*); 2000. (YA). (gr. 4-7). audio 18.00 (*0-8072-8276-6*); 2000. (YA). (gr. 4-7). audio 18.00 (*0-8072-8276-6*); 1998. 105p. (J). (gr. 3-5). pap. 23.00 incl. audio (*0-8072-7994-3*, YA961SP) Random Hse. Audio Publishing Group. (Listening Library).

—Frindle. (Two Thousand Kids Picks Ser.). (Illus.). (J). 2000. 112p. (gr. 4-6). mass mkt. 2.99 (*0-689-83861-1*, Aladdin); 1999. (gr. 3-7). E-Book 6.99 (*0-689-83250-8*, Aladdin); 1998. 112p. (gr. 3-7). pap. 4.99 (*0-689-81876-9*, Aladdin); 1996. 112p. (gr. 4-7). 15.95 (*0-689-80669-8*, Simon & Schuster Children's Publishing) Simon & Schuster Children's Publishing.

—Frindle. 1998. (J). 10.55 (*0-606-12939-1*) Turtleback Bks.

—The Landry News. 2002. (Illus.). (J). 13.40 (*0-7587-6519-3*) Book Wholesalers, Inc.

—The Landry News. unabr. ed. 2000. 128p. (J). pap. 23.00 incl. audio (*0-8072-8782-2*, YA266SP); (gr. 4-7). audio 18.00 (*0-8072-6155-6*) Random Hse. Audio Publishing Group. (Listening Library).

—The Landry News. (Illus.). (J). (gr. 3-7). 2002. E-Book 6.99 (*0-689-85052-2*, Simon & Schuster Children's Publishing); 2000. 144p. pap. 4.99 (*0-689-82868-3*, Aladdin); 1999. 123p. 15.00 (*0-689-81817-3*, Simon & Schuster Children's Publishing) Simon & Schuster Children's Publishing.

—The Landry News. l.t. ed. 2000. (Juvenile Ser.). (Illus.). 138p. (J). (gr. 4-7). 21.95 (*0-7862-2707-9*) Thorndike Pr.

—The Landry News. 1999. (J). 11.04 (*0-606-19720-6*) Turtleback Bks.

Coffin, M. T. My Teacher's a Bug. 1995. (Spinetingler Ser.: No. 3). (J). (gr. 4-7). pap. 3.50 (*0-380-77785-1*, Avon Bks.) Morrow/Avon.

—My Teacher's a Bug. 1995. (Spinetingler Ser.: No. 3). (J). (gr. 4-7). 8.60 o.p. (*0-606-07911-4*) Turtle-back Bks.

—The Substitute Creature. 1995. (Spinetingler Ser.: No. 1). (J). (gr. 4-7). pap. 3.50 (*0-380-77829-7*, Avon Bks.) Morrow/Avon.

Cone, Molly. Mishmash & the Substitute Teacher. 1984. (Illus.). (J). (gr. 3-5). pap. (*0-671-54315-6*, Simon Pulse) Simon & Schuster Children's Publishing.

Cooper, Ilene. The Winning of Miss Lynn Ryan. 1989. (Illus.). 128p. (J). (gr. 3-7). pap. 3.95 o.p. (*0-14-032755-X*, Puffin Bks.) Penguin Putnam Bks. for Young Readers.

Corcoran, Barbara. Strike! 1983. 168p. (YA). (gr. 6-9). 12.95 o.p. (*0-689-30952-X*, Atheneum) Simon & Schuster Children's Publishing.

Coryell, Susan. Eaglebait. 1989. 187p. (YA). (gr. 7 up). 14.95 (*0-15-200442-4*, Gulliver Bks.) Harcourt Children's Bks.

Coville, Bruce. The Attack of the Two-Inch Teacher. unabr. ed. 2000. (I Was a Sixth Grade Alien Ser.). 165p. (J). (gr. 3-5). pap. 28.00 incl. audio (*0-8072-8354-1*, YA170SP, Listening Library) Random Hse. Audio Publishing Group.

—The Attack of the Two-Inch Teacher. 1999. (I Was a Sixth Grade Alien Ser.). (Illus.). (J). 10.04 (*0-606-18374-4*) Turtleback Bks.

—My Teacher Flunked the Planet. MacDonald, Pat, ed. 1992. (My Teacher Is an Alien Ser.). (Illus.). 176p. (J). (gr. 4-7). pap. 3.99 (*0-671-79199-0*, Aladdin) Simon & Schuster Children's Publishing.

—My Teacher Flunked the Planet. 1992. (My Teacher Is an Alien Ser.). (Illus.). (J). (gr. 4-7). 10.04 (*0-606-02087-X*) Turtleback Bks.

—My Teacher Flunked the Planet. (My Teacher is an Alien Ser.). (J). (gr. 4-7). E-Book (*1-58824-028-2*) ipicturebooks, LLC.

—My Teacher Fried My Brains. MacDonald, Patricia, ed. 1991. (My Teacher Is an Alien Ser.). 144p. (J). (gr. 4-7). pap. 4.99 (*0-671-72710-9*, Aladdin) Simon & Schuster Children's Publishing.

—My Teacher Fried My Brains. 1991. (My Teacher Is an Alien Ser.). (J). (gr. 4-7). pap. 2.99 (*0-671-74610-3*, Aladdin) Simon & Schuster Children's Publishing.

—My Teacher Fried My Brains. 1991. (My Teacher Is an Alien Ser.). (J). (gr. 4-7). 10.55 (*0-606-04984-3*) Turtleback Bks.

—My Teacher Fried My Brains. 1991. E-Book (*1-59019-044-0*); E-Book (*1-59019-045-9*); (J). (gr. 4-7). E-Book (*1-58824-027-4*) ipicturebooks, LLC.

—My Teacher Glows in the Dark. MacDonald, Patricia, ed. 1991. (My Teacher Is an Alien Ser.). (Illus.). 144p. (J). (gr. 4-7). pap. 4.50 (*0-671-72709-5*, Aladdin) Simon & Schuster Children's Publishing.

—My Teacher Glows in the Dark. 1991. (Illus.). mass mkt. 3.99 (*0-671-75425-4*, Aladdin) Simon & Schuster Children's Publishing.

—My Teacher Glows in the Dark. 1991. (My Teacher Is an Alien Ser.). (Illus.). (J). (gr. 4-7). 10.55 (*0-606-04985-1*) Turtleback Bks.

—My Teacher Glows in the Dark. 1991. E-Book (*1-59019-042-4*); E-Book (*1-59019-041-6*); (J). (gr. 4-7). E-Book (*1-58824-029-0*) ipicturebooks, LLC.

—My Teacher Is an Alien. (My Teacher Is an Alien Ser.). (J). (gr. 4-7). (Illus.). 123p. pap. 4.50 (*0-8072-1528-7*); 1998. pap. 23.00 incl. audio (*0-8072-8029-1*, YA971SP) Random Hse. Audio Publishing Group. (Listening Library).

—My Teacher Is an Alien. (My Teacher Is an Alien Ser.). (J). 1999. (Illus.). 592p. (gr. 4-7). pap. 16.00 (*0-671-03571-1*, Simon & Schuster Children's Publishing); 1990. (Illus.). mass mkt. 3.50 (*0-671-74177-2*, Aladdin); 1990. (Illus.). 128p. (gr. 4-7). pap. 4.99 (*0-671-73729-5*, Aladdin); 1989. (Illus.). (gr. 4-7). pap. 2.75 (*0-671-64748-2*, Aladdin); 1900. (gr. 4-7). mass mkt. (*0-671-03572-X*, Aladdin); 1900. (Illus.). (gr. 4-7). per. 3.99 (*0-671-31189-1*, Aladdin) Simon & Schuster Children's Publishing.

—My Teacher Is an Alien. 1989. (My Teacher Is an Alien Ser.). (Illus.). (J). (gr. 4-7). 10.55 (*0-606-04280-6*) Turtleback Bks.

—My Teacher Is an Alien. 1998. E-Book (*1-59019-039-4*); 1989. E-Book (*1-59019-038-6*); 1989. (J). (gr. 4-7). E-Book (*1-58824-026-6*) ipicturebooks, LLC.

Crawford, Charles P. Letter Perfect. 1977. (J). (gr. 7 up). 9.95 o.p. (*0-525-33635-4*, Dutton) Dutton/Plume.

Creech, Sharon. A Fine, Fine School. ed. 2001. (YA). (gr. 2 up). spiral bd. (*0-616-11107-X*) Canadian National Institute for the Blind/Institut National Canadien pour les Aveugles.

—A Fine, Fine School. 32p. (J). 2004. pap. 6.99 (*0-06-000728-1*, Harper Trophy); 2001. (Illus.). 15.99 (*0-06-027736-X*, Cotler, Joanna Bks.) HarperCollins Children's Bk. Group.

Cupo, Hortense. No Way Out but Through. 1994. 150p. (J). pap. 4.95 (*0-8198-5130-2*) Pauline Bks. & Media.

Curry, Peter. You & Me-Me. 1984. (Peter Curry Board Bks.). 12p. (Orig.). (J). (ps). 3.95 o.p. (*0-8431-1048-1*, Price Stern Sloan) Penguin Putnam Bks. for Young Readers.

Cusick, Richie Tankersley. Teacher's Pet. 1990. 224p. (Orig.). (YA). (gr. 7-9). mass mkt. 3.50 (*0-590-43114-5*) Scholastic, Inc.

Cutler, Jane. Spaceman. 144p. (J). (gr. 3-7). 1999. (Illus.). pap. 4.99 o.s.i (*0-14-038150-3*); 1997. 14.99 o.s.i (*0-525-45636-8*) Penguin Putnam Bks. for Young Readers.

—Spaceman. 1999. 11.04 (*0-606-16980-6*) Turtleback Bks.

Dadey, Debbie & Jones, Marcia Thornton. Bogeymen Don't Play Football. 1997. (Adventures of the Bailey School Kids Ser.: No. 27). (Illus.). 80p. (J). (gr. 2-4). mass mkt. 3.99 (*0-590-25701-3*) Scholastic, Inc.

—Knights Don't Teach Piano. 1998. (Adventures of the Bailey School Kids Ser.: No. 29). (J). (gr. 2-4). 10.14 (*0-606-12975-8*) Turtleback Bks.

—Vampires Don't Wear Polka Dots. 1990. (Adventures of the Bailey School Kids Ser.: No. 1). Tr. of Vampires Ne Portent Pas de Robe a Pois. (Illus.). 78p. (J). (gr. 2-4). mass mkt. 3.99 (*0-590-43411-X*) Scholastic, Inc.

—Vampires Don't Wear Polka Dots. 1990. (Adventures of the Bailey School Kids Ser.: No. 1). Tr. of Vampires Ne Portent Pas de Robe a Pois. (J). (gr. 2-4). 10.14 (*0-606-04839-1*) Turtleback Bks.

Dagg, Stephanie. Oh Teacher! 2001. (J). (gr. 1-4). per. (*1-84210-130-7*) Mentor Bks.

Dahl, Roald. Matilda. 1995. (SPA.). (J). (gr. 4-7). lib. bdg. 15.95 (*84-204-4638-6*) Alfaguara, Ediciones, S.A.- Grupo Santillana ESP. *Dist:* Santillana USA Publishing Co., Inc.

—Matilda. (Illus.). 240p. (J). (gr. 3-7). 1998. pap. 5.99 (*0-14-130106-6*, Puffin Bks.); 1988. 15.99 (*0-670-82439-9*, Viking Children's Bks.) Penguin Putnam Bks. for Young Readers.

Dalgliesh, Alice. The Silver Pencil. 1991. (Newbery Library Ser.). (Illus.). 256p. (YA). (gr. 7 up). pap. 5.99 (*0-14-034792-5*, Puffin Bks.) Penguin Putnam Bks. for Young Readers.

Danneberg, Julie. First Day Jitters. 2000. (Illus.). 32p. (J). (gr. k-4). 16.95 (*1-58089-054-7*); pap. 6.95 (*1-58089-061-X*) Charlesbridge Publishing, Inc. (Whispering Coyote).

—First Day Jitters. 2000. (Illus.). (J). 13.10 (*0-606-18748-0*) Turtleback Bks.

—First Day Jitters. 2000. (Illus.). E-Book (*1-59019-570-1*); E-Book (*1-59019-571-X*); (J). E-Book 12.99 (*1-59019-572-8*) ipicturebooks, LLC.

—First Year Letters. 2003. (Illus.). 32p. (J). (gr. k-4). 16.95 (*1-58089-084-9*) Charlesbridge Publishing, Inc.

Danziger, Paula. The Cat Ate My Gymsuit. l.t. ed. 1987. 184p. (J). (gr. 3-7). reprint ed. lib. bdg. 14.95 o.p. (*1-55736-068-5*) Bantam Doubleday Dell Large Print Group, Inc.

—The Cat Ate My Gymsuit. 1974. 160p. (YA). (gr. 7 up). 14.95 o.s.i (*0-385-28183-8*, Delacorte Pr.) Dell Publishing.

—The Cat Ate My Gymsuit. 1998. (Illus.). 147p. (J). (gr. 4-7). pap. 5.99 (*0-698-11684-4*, PaperStar) Penguin Putnam Bks. for Young Readers.

—The Cat Ate My Gymsuit. 1980. 160p. (YA). (gr. 5 up). pap. 4.50 o.p. (*0-440-41612-4*, Dell Books for Young Readers) Random Hse. Children's Bks.

—The Cat Ate My Gymsuit & There's a Bat in Bunk Five Flip-Over Book. 2002. pap. 4.99 o.p. (*0-698-11955-X*) Penguin Putnam Bks. for Young Readers.

De Pressense, Domitille. Natalie: The Scribbles. 1990. (Illus.). 28p. (J). (ps-1). pap. 0.30 o.p. (*0-8120-4508-4*) Barron's Educational Series, Inc.

DeFord, Diane E. The Day Miss Francie Got Skunked. 1997. (Illus.). (J). (*1-56270-878-3*) Dominie Pr., Inc.

Demuth, Patricia B. In Trouble with Teacher. 1995. (Illus.). 80p. (J). (gr. 2-4). 13.99 o.s.i (*0-525-45286-9*, Dutton Children's Bks.) Penguin Putnam Bks. for Young Readers.

Denslow, Sharon Phillips. On the Trail with Miss Pace. 1995. (Illus.). 40p. (J). (ps-3). pap. 15.00 (0-02-728688-6, Simon & Schuster Children's Publishing) Simon & Schuster Children's Publishing.

Dicks, Terrance. Teacher's Pet. 1992. (Adventures of Goliath Ser.). (Illus.). 52p. (J). (gr. 2-5). pap. 3.50 o.p. (0-8120-4820-2) Barron's Educational Series, Inc.

Dower, Laura. Teacher's Pets: Blossom. 2001. (Illus.). 32p. (ps-3). mass mkt. 4.95 (0-439-16455-9) Scholastic, Inc.

—Teacher's Pets: Bubbles. 2001. (Illus.). 32p. (ps-3). pap. 4.95 (0-439-20734-7) Scholastic, Inc.

—Teacher's Pets: Buttercup. 2001. (Illus.). 32p. (ps-3). mass mkt. 4.95 (0-439-27640-3) Scholastic, Inc.

—Teacher's Pets: Mojo Jojo. 2001. (Illus.). 32p. (ps-3). mass mkt. 4.95 (0-439-22613-9) Scholastic, Inc.

Dubowski, Cathy. I've Got a Secret. 1997. (Full House Michelle Ser.: No. 14). 96p. (J). (gr. 2-4). per. 3.99 (0-671-00366-6, Simon Spotlight) Simon & Schuster Children's Publishing.

Duey, Kathleen. Mr. Stumpguss Is a Third Grader. 1992. (Illus.). 80p. (Orig.). (J). pap. 3.50 (0-380-76939-5, Avon Bks.) Morrow/Avon.

Dugan, Barbara. Good-Bye, Hello. 1994. 160p. (J). (gr. 5 up). 13.00 (0-688-12447-X, Greenwillow Bks.) HarperCollins Children's Bk. Group.

Dumbleton, Mike. Mr. Knuckles. (Illus.). 32p. (J). (ps-3). 14.95 o.p. (1-86373-584-4) Allen & Unwin Pty., Ltd. AUS. *Dist:* Independent Pubs. Group.

—Mr. Knuckles. 1994. (Illus.). 32p. (J). (ps-3). pap. 6.95 o.p. (1-86373-595-X) Independent Pubs. Group.

Edwards, Sally. George Midgett's War. 1985. 144p. (J). (gr. 5-7). 12.95 o.p. (0-684-18315-3, Atheneum) Simon & Schuster Children's Publishing.

Ehrlich, Fred. A Class Play with Ms. Vanilla Level 1, Blue. (Hello Reading! Ser.: Vol. 34). (Illus.). (J). (ps-2). 1994. 32p. pap. 3.99 o.s.i (0-14-037142-7, Puffin Bks.); 1992. 320p. 9.00 o.p. (0-670-84651-1, Viking Children's Bks.); 1992. 320p. pap. 3.50 o.p. (0-14-054580-8) Penguin Putnam Bks. for Young Readers.

—A Valentine for Ms. Vanilla. 1992. (Hello Reading! Ser.). (Illus.). 32p. (J). (ps-3). 8.95 o.p. (0-670-84274-5, Viking Children's Bks.) Penguin Putnam Bks. for Young Readers.

El-Hendi, Mary A. Mona the Teacher. 1996. (Illus.). 64p. (Orig.). (J). pap. 7.95 (1-56002-539-5, University Editions) Aegina Pr., Inc.

Engle, Marty M. & Barnes, Johnny Ray, Jr. No Substitutions. l.t. ed. 1996. (Strange Matter Ser.: No. 1). (Illus.). 124p. (J). (gr. 4-6). lib. bdg. 21.27 o.p. (0-8368-1667-6) Stevens, Gareth Inc.

Evans, Douglas. Apple Island, or the Truth about Teachers. 1998. (Illus.). 144p. (J). (gr. 3-7). 14.95 o.p. (1-886910-25-1) Front Street, Inc.

—So What Do You Do? 1997. 124p. (J). (gr. 5 up). 14.95 (1-886910-20-0) Front Street, Inc.

Feder, Paula K. Where Does the Teacher Live? 1999. 48p. pap. 3.50 (0-14-054854-8) NAL.

—Where Does the Teacher Live? (Illus.). 48p. (J). 1996. (Puffin Easy-to-Read Ser.). (ps-3). pap. 3.99 o.s.i (0-14-038119-8); 1992. (Unicorn Paperbacks Ser.). (gr. 1-3). pap. 3.99 o.p. (0-525-44889-6, Dutton Children's Bks.); 1979. (Smart Cat Bks.: Vol. 1). (ps-3). 12.95 o.s.i (0-525-42586-1, Dutton Children's Bks.) Penguin Putnam Bks. for Young Readers.

—Where Does the Teacher Live? 1996. (Puffin Easy-to-Read Ser.). (J). 9.19 o.p. (0-606-12085-8) Turtleback Bks.

Fienberg, Anna. Dead Sailors Don't Bite. 1997. (Illus.). 128p. (Orig.). (J). (gr. 3-6). pap. 6.95 o.p. (1-86448-088-2) Allen & Unwin Pty., Ltd. AUS. *Dist:* Independent Pubs. Group.

Figley, Marty Rhodes. The Schoolchildren's Blizzard. 2004. (On My Own History Ser.). (J). pap. 5.95 (1-57505-619-4); lib. bdg. 22.60 (1-57505-586-4) Lerner Publishing Group. (Carolrhoda Bks.).

Finchler, Judy. Miss Malarkey Doesn't Live in Room 10. 1996. (J). 12.10 (0-606-10879-3) Turtleback Bks.

—Miss Malarkey Doesn't Live in Room 10. (Illus.). 32p. (J). (gr. k-4). 1996. pap. 6.95 (0-8027-7498-9); 1995. 16.95 (0-8027-8386-4); 1995. lib. bdg. 15.85 (0-8027-8387-2) Walker & Co.

—Miss Malarkey Won't Be in Today. (Illus.). 32p. (J). 1998. 15.95 (0-8027-8652-9); 1998. lib. bdg. 16.85 (0-8027-8653-7); 2000. reprint ed. pap. 6.95 (0-8027-7591-8) Walker & Co.

Flake, Sharon G. The Skin I'm In. 1998. 171p. (J). 14.95 (0-7868-0444-0); (YA). pap. 15.49 (0-7868-2392-5) Hyperion Pr.

—The Skin I'm In. l.t. ed. 1999. (Young Adult Ser.). 173p. (J). (gr. 7-12). 20.95 (0-7862-2179-8) Thorndike Pr.

—The Skin I'm In. 2000. 12.04 (0-606-17605-5) Turtleback Bks.

Fletcher, Ralph J. Flying Solo. 1998. (Illus.). 138p. (J). (gr. 4-6). tchr. ed. 15.00 (0-395-87323-1, Clarion Bks.) Houghton Mifflin Co. Trade & Reference Div.

Foley, June. It's No Crush, I'm in Love. 1982. 224p. (J). (gr. 7 up). 13.95 o.s.i (0-385-28465-9, Delacorte Pr.) Dell Publishing.

Foley, Louise Munro. My Substitute Teacher's Gone Batty! 1996. (Vampire Cat Ser.: No. 1). 96p. (J). (gr. 4-7). mass mkt. 4.50 (0-8125-5366-7, Tor Bks.) Doherty, Tom Assocs., LLC.

Fourth Graders at Rio Bravo-Greeley Elementary School Staff. Where's Our Teacher? 1995. (Kids Are Authors Picture Bks.). (Illus.). 24p. 5.99 (0-87406-742-1) Darby Creek Publishing.

Frank, E. R. Friction. 2003. (Illus.). 208p. (YA). 16.95 (0-689-85384-X, Atheneum/Richard Jackson Bks.) Simon & Schuster Children's Publishing.

Friedrich, Joachim. 4 1/2 Friends & the Disappearing Bio Teacher. Crawford, Elizabeth D., tr. from GER. 2001. 156p. (J). (0-7868-2588-X, Volo) Hyperion Bks. for Children.

—4 1/2 Friends & the Disappearing Bio Teacher, Bk. 2. 2001. (Illus.). 156p. (J). (gr. 3-7). 15.99 (0-7868-0698-2, Volo) Hyperion Bks. for Children.

Garaway, Margaret K. Dezbah & the Dancing Tumbleweeds. 2nd ed. 1990. (Illus.). 83p. (J). (gr. 3-10). reprint ed. pap. 7.95 (0-9638851-2-X) Old Hogan Publishing Co.

Garland, Michael. Miss Smith's Incredible Storybook. 2003. (Illus.). 32p. (J). (gr. k-6). 16.99 (0-525-47133-2, Dutton Children's Bks.) Penguin Putnam Bks. for Young Readers.

Gibson, Kathleen & Dillard, Kristine. Where Does the Teacher Sleep? 1994. (Illus.). 8p. (J). (gr. k-2). pap. text 3.75 (1-880612-45-3) Seedling Pubns., Inc.

Gilson, Jamie. Thirteen Ways to Sink a Sub. 1982. (Illus.). 144p. (J). (ps up). 15.95 (0-688-01304-X) HarperCollins Children's Bk. Group.

Glassman, Miriam. Box Top Dreams. 1998. 192p. (gr. 2-6). text 14.95 o.s.i (0-385-32532-0, Dell Books for Young Readers) Random Hse. Children's Bks.

Glennon, Karen M. Miss Eva & the Red Balloon. 1990. (Illus.). 32p. (J). (ps-3). pap. 13.95 o.s.i (0-671-68854-5, Simon & Schuster Children's Publishing) Simon & Schuster Children's Publishing.

Gold, Sharlya. Time to Take Sides, 001. 1979. 176p. (J). (gr. 6 up). 6.95 o.p. (0-395-28905-X, Clarion Bks.) Houghton Mifflin Co. Trade & Reference Div.

Golden Books Staff. The Best Teacher Ever. 1996. (Tell-a-Story Sticker Ser.). 16p. (J). pap. 3.29 o.s.i (0-307-07606-7, 07606, Golden Bks.) Random Hse. Children's Bks.

Granger, Michele. Fifth Grade Fever. 144p. (J). (gr. 3-7). 1998. pap. 4.99 o.p. (0-14-037972-X); 1995. 14.99 o.s.i (0-525-45279-6, Dutton Children's Bks.) Penguin Putnam Bks. for Young Readers.

Grant, Cynthia D. The White Horse. 160p. (gr. 7-12). 2000. (Illus.). (J). mass mkt. 4.99 (0-689-83263-X, Simon Pulse); 1998. (YA). 16.00 (0-689-82127-1, Atheneum) Simon & Schuster Children's Publishing.

Greenburg, Dan. My Teacher Ate My Homework. 2002. (Zack Files Ser.: 27). (Illus.). 64p. (J). mass mkt. 4.99 (0-448-42683-8, Grosset & Dunlap) Penguin Putnam Bks. for Young Readers.

Greene, Stephanie. Show & Tell. 1998. (Illus.). 84p. (J). (ps-3). tchr. ed. 15.00 (0-395-88898-0, Clarion Bks.) Houghton Mifflin Co. Trade & Reference Div.

Groch, Judith. Play the Bach, Dear! 1978. (gr. 4-7). 6.95 o.p. (0-385-13228-X); lib. bdg. o.p. (0-385-13229-8) Doubleday Publishing.

Hagen, Michael. The African Term. Kemnitz, Myrna, ed. 1998. 81p. (YA). (gr. 7 up). pap. 9.99 (0-88092-368-7) Royal Fireworks Publishing Co.

Hall, Kirsten. First Day of School: All about Shapes & Sizes. 2003. (Beastieville Ser.). (Illus.). 31p. (J). lib. bdg. 18.50 (0-516-22893-5, Children's Pr.) Scholastic Library Publishing.

Hallinan, P. K. My Teacher's My Friend. 24p. (J). pap. 5.95 (0-8249-5308-8, Ideals) Ideals Pubns.

—My Teacher's My Friend. 1990. (P. K. Books Values for Life). (Illus.). 32p. (J). (ps-3). lib. bdg. 13.27 o.p. (0-516-09217-0, Children's Pr.) Scholastic Library Publishing.

—My Teacher's My Friend. 1999. (Illus.). 24p. (ps-3). 6.95 (1-57102-155-8) Warehousing & Fulfillment Specialists, LLC (WFS, LLC).

Hallinan, P. K., illus. My Teacher's My Friend. 2001. 24p. (J). 7.95 (0-8249-5309-6, Ideals) Ideals Pubns.

Haugaard, Erik Christian. The Death of Mr. Angel. 1992. 167p. (YA). (gr. 7-12). 13.95 o.p. (1-879373-26-2) Rinehart, Roberts Pubs.

Havill, Juanita. Jamaica & the Substitute Teacher. 2001. (Illus.). 32p. (J). (ps-3). pap. 6.95 (0-618-15242-3) Houghton Mifflin Co. Trade & Reference Div.

Hawks, Robert. The Substitute. 1995. 192p. (Orig.). (YA). mass mkt. 3.99 (0-380-77622-7, Avon Bks.) Morrow/Avon.

Hayes, Daniel. No Effect. 1995. (YA). pap. 3.99 (0-380-72392-1, Avon Bks.) Morrow/Avon.

Haynes, Betsy. The Scapegoat. 1991. (Fabulous Five Ser.: No. 27). 128p. (J). (gr. 4-7). pap. 2.99 o.s.i (0-553-15872-4) Bantam Bks.

—Teacher Creature. 1995. (Bone Chillers Ser.: No. 6). 144p. (J). (gr. 4-7). mass mkt. 3.99 o.s.i (0-06-106314-2) HarperTrade.

Hemmeter, Karla. Teacher's Remarkable Secret. l.t. ed. 2003. (Illus.). 16p. (J). (ps-6). pap. 5.00 (1-891452-09-6, 2) Heart Arbor Bks.

Henderson, Lyndsey. Dino. 2001. (Teacher's Pet Ser.). 48p. (J). 4.95 (0-439-17344-2) Scholastic, Inc.

Hendry, Diana. Kid Kibble. 1994. (J). (ps-3). 14.95 o.p. (1-56402-413-X) Candlewick Pr.

Henkes, Kevin. Lilly Book & Doll Package. 1998. (Illus.). 160p. (J). 24.95 (0-688-16437-4, Harper Festival) HarperCollins Children's Bk. Group.

—Lilly's Purple Plastic Purse. 1996. (Illus.). (J). (ps-3). 40p. 15.99 (0-688-12897-1); 32p. lib. bdg. 16.89 (0-688-12898-X) HarperCollins Children's Bk. Group. (Greenwillow Bks.).

—Lily y Su Bolso de Plastico Morado. Mlawer, Teresa, tr. 2001. (SPA., Illus.). 32p. (J). (gr. k-2). 6.95 (84-241-7984-6, EV3112) Everest de Ediciones y Distribucion, S.L. ESP. *Dist:* Lectorum Pubns., Inc.

—Lily y Su Bolso de Plastico Morado. 2001. (Illus.). (J). 13.10 (0-606-20767-8) Turtleback Bks.

Herman, Gail. I've Got the Back-to-School Blues. 2002. (All Aboard Reading Ser.). (Illus.). 48p. (J). 13.89 (0-448-42833-4); mass mkt. 3.99 (0-448-42832-6) Penguin Putnam Bks. for Young Readers. (Grosset & Dunlap).

Herman, Hank. Hang Time. 1997. (Super Hoops Ser.: No. 9). 96p. (gr. 4-6). pap. text 3.50 o.s.i (0-553-48431-1, Skylark) Random Hse. Children's Bks.

Hill, Kirkpatrick. The Year of Miss Agnes. 128p. (J). (gr. 3-7). 2002. pap. 4.99 (0-689-85124-3, Aladdin); 2000. 16.00 (0-689-82933-7, McElderry, Margaret K.) Simon & Schuster Children's Publishing.

Hilton, James. Goodbye, Mr. Chips. 1976. 124p. (YA). 17.95 (0-8488-0364-7) Amereon, Ltd.

—Goodbye, Mr. Chips. 1982. (YA). (gr. 7 up). mass mkt. 2.75 o.s.i (0-553-25613-0); 144p. mass mkt. 4.99 o.s.i (0-553-27321-3) Bantam Bks.

—Goodbye, Mr. Chips. 1982. (YA). reprint ed. lib. bdg. 21.95 (0-89966-413-X) Buccaneer Bks., Inc.

—Goodbye, Mr. Chips. 1962. (Illus.). 132p. (gr. 4-7). 22.00 (0-316-36420-7) Little Brown & Co.

—Goodbye, Mr. Chips. 1986. (J). mass mkt. o.p. (0-553-16698-0, Dell Books for Young Readers) Random Hse. Children's Bks.

—Goodbye, Mr. Chips. 1957. (YA). 10.55 (0-606-00727-X) Turtleback Bks.

—Goodbye, Mr. Chips & to You, Mr. Chips. l.t. ed. 1995. 266p. (YA). 22.95 (0-7838-1231-0) Thorndike Pr.

Hoffman, James. The Fabulous Principal Pie, Level 3. Hoffman, Joan, ed. 1993. (Start to Read! Ser.). (Illus.). (J). (ps-2). 16p. 2.29 (0-88743-266-2, 06033); 32p. pap. 3.95 (0-88743-427-4, 06079) School Zone Publishing Co.

Holland, Margaret & McKee, Craig B. The Teacher Who Could Not Count. 1990. (Illus.). 24p. (Orig.). (J). (gr. k-4). pap. text 1.95 o.p. (0-87406-125-3) Darby Creek Publishing.

Hollingsworth, Mary. Christmas in Happy Forest. 1990. (God's Happy Forest Ser.). (Illus.). (J). (ps-2). 6.99 o.p. (1-877719-05-6) Brownlow Publishing Co., Inc.

Honey, Elizabeth. Don't Pat the Wombat! (Illus.). 144p. 2001. (gr. 5-9). pap. text 4.99 (0-440-41652-3, Yearling); 2000. (YA). (gr. 4-9). lib. bdg. 16.99 (0-375-90578-2, Knopf Bks. for Young Readers) Random Hse. Children's Bks.

Howe, James. The Day the Teacher Went Bananas. (Illus.). 32p. (ps-3). 1992. pap. 5.99 (0-14-054744-4, Puffin Bks.); 1987. (J). pap. 3.95 o.p. (0-525-44321-5, Dutton Children's Bks.); 1984. (J). 13.99 o.s.i (0-525-44107-7, Dutton Children's Bks.) Penguin Putnam Bks. for Young Readers.

—The Day the Teacher Went Bananas. 1987. (J). 11.14 (0-606-03765-9) Turtleback Bks.

Hurwitz, Johanna. Teacher's Pet. (J). 1988. (Illus.). 128p. (gr. 2-5). 16.00 o.s.i (0-688-07506-1); 1924. lib. bdg. o.p. (0-688-07507-X) Morrow/Avon. (Morrow, William & Co.).

—Teacher's Pet. 1989. 128p. (J). (gr. 2-5). pap. 2.99 (0-590-42031-3, Scholastic Paperbacks) Scholastic, Inc.

Hutchens, Paul. Teacher Trouble. rev. ed. 1997. (Sugar Creek Gang Ser.: Vol. 11). (Illus.). 98p. (J). (gr. 4-7). mass mkt. 4.99 (0-8024-7015-7) Moody Pr.

I Thought My Soul Would Rise & Fly: The Diary of Patsy, a Freed Girl. 2003. (J). lib. bdg. 12.95 (0-439-55505-1) Scholastic, Inc.

James, Simon. Dear Mr. Blueberry. (Illus.). 32p. (J). (ps-3). 1996. pap. 5.99 (0-689-80768-6, Aladdin); 1991. 15.00 (0-689-50529-9, McElderry, Margaret K.) Simon & Schuster Children's Publishing.

Jane, Pamela. Milo & the Flapjack Fiasco! Johnson, Meredith, ed. & tr. by. 2004. (J). (1-59336-113-0); pap. (1-59336-114-9) Mondo Publishing.

Jeffs, Stephanie. It's Mine, Christopher Bear! 2004. (Christopher Bear Ser.). (Illus.). 32p. (J). 5.99 (0-8066-4400-1, Augsburg Bks.) Augsburg Fortress, Pubs.

Johnson, Doug. Substitute Teacher Plans, ERS. 2002. (Illus.). 32p. (J). (gr. k-3). 16.95 (0-8050-6520-2, Holt, Henry & Co. Bks. For Young Readers) Holt, Henry & Co.

Johnson, Janet. Ellie Brader Hates Mr. G. 1995. 144p. (J). reprint ed. pap. 3.50 (0-671-78506-0, Aladdin) Simon & Schuster Children's Publishing.

Johnson, Michael. The Most Special Person. 1999. (Illus.). 24p. (J). (gr. k-6). 12.95 (1-893672-00-X) Johnson, Michael Presentations.

Johnston, Janet. Ellie Brader Hates Mr. G. 1991. 144p. (J). (gr. 3-6). 13.95 o.p. (0-395-58195-8, Clarion Bks.) Houghton Mifflin Co. Trade & Reference Div.

Keene, Carolyn. Alien in the Classroom. 1998. (Nancy Drew Notebooks Ser.: No. 23). 80p. (J). (gr. k-3). pap. 3.99 (0-671-00818-8, Aladdin) Simon & Schuster Children's Publishing.

—Alien in the Classroom. 1998. (Nancy Drew Notebooks Ser.: No. 23). (J). (gr. k-3). 10.04 (0-606-13653-3) Turtleback Bks.

Kindl, Patrice. Owl in Love. 1993. 208p. (YA). (gr. 7-7). tchr. ed. 16.00 (0-395-66162-5) Houghton Mifflin Co.

—Owl in Love. 1994. 208p. (J). (gr. 7 up). pap. 5.99 (0-14-037129-X, Puffin Bks.) Penguin Putnam Bks. for Young Readers.

—Owl in Love. unabr. ed. 1998. (J). Class Set. 102.80 incl. audio (0-7887-2562-9, 46732); Homework Set. 49.75 incl. audio (0-7887-2106-2, 40701) Recorded Bks., LLC.

—Owl in Love. 1994. 12.04 (0-606-06653-5) Turtleback Bks.

Klass, Sheila S. Kool Ada. (J). (gr. 4-7). 1993. pap. 2.95 o.p. (0-590-43903-0); 1991. pap. 13.95 (0-590-43902-2) Scholastic, Inc.

Kline, Suzy. Horrible Harry & the Dungeon. (Horrible Harry Ser.: No. 7). (Illus.). 64p. (J). (gr. 2-4). 1998. pap. 3.99 (0-14-038620-3, Puffin Bks.); 1996. 13.99 (0-670-86862-0, Viking Children's Bks.) Penguin Putnam Bks. for Young Readers.

—Marvin & the Mean Words. 1997. (Illus.). 80p. (J). (gr. 1-4). 14.99 o.s.i (0-399-23009-2, G. P. Putnam's Sons) Penguin Group (USA) Inc.

—Marvin & the Mean Words. 1998. (Illus.). 96p. (J). (gr. 4-7). pap. 4.99 (0-698-11657-7, PaperStar) Penguin Putnam Bks. for Young Readers.

—Marvin & the Mean Words. 1998. (J). 11.14 (0-606-13599-5) Turtleback Bks.

—Mary Marony & the Chocolate Surprise. 1995. (Illus.). 80p. (J). (gr. 4-7). 14.99 (0-399-22829-2, G. P. Putnam's Sons) Penguin Group (USA) Inc.

—Mary Marony & the Chocolate Surprise. 1997. (Illus.). 96p. (J). (gr. 2-5). pap. text 3.99 o.s.i (0-440-41326-5, Yearling) Random Hse. Children's Bks.

—Mary Marony & the Chocolate Surprise. 1997. 9.19 o.p. (0-606-11002-X) Turtleback Bks.

Konigsburg, E. L. The View from Saturday. 2002. (Illus.). (J). 25.11 (0-7587-0221-3) Book Wholesalers, Inc.

—The View from Saturday. 2000. (J). 11.95 (1-56137-936-0) Novel Units, Inc.

—The View from Saturday. (YA). (gr. 5 up). 280p. pap. 4.95 (0-8072-1511-2); 2001. audio 25.00 (0-8072-0469-2) Random Hse. Audio Publishing Group. (Listening Library).

—The View from Saturday. (J). 1999. pap. 2.99 (0-689-82964-7, Aladdin); 1998. 176p. (gr. 4-6). pap. 2.65 o.s.i (0-689-82163-8, Aladdin); 1998. 160p. (gr. 5-9). pap. 4.99 (0-689-82120-4, Aladdin); 1996. 128p. (gr. 3-7). 16.00 (0-689-80993-X, Atheneum); 1998. 176p. (gr. 3-7). reprint ed. pap. 4.99 (0-689-81721-5, Aladdin) Simon & Schuster Children's Publishing.

—The View from Saturday. l.t. ed. 2000. (Young Adult Ser.). 227p. (YA). (gr. 8-12). 20.95 (0-7862-2691-9) Thorndike Pr.

—The View from Saturday. 1998. (J). 11.04 (0-606-13063-2) Turtleback Bks.

Krailing, Tessa. Scruncher Goes Wandering, Vol. 5. 1998. (Petsitters Club Ser.: No. 5). (Illus.). 96p. (J). (gr. 1-4). pap. 3.95 (0-7641-0574-4) Barron's Educational Series, Inc.

Kraus, Robert. Good Morning, Miss Gator. 1989. 8.05 o.p. (0-606-12317-2) Turtleback Bks.

Krensky, Stephen. My Teacher's Secret Life. (Illus.). 32p. (J). (ps-1). 1999. pap. 5.99 (0-689-82982-5, Aladdin); 1996. 15.00 (0-689-80271-4, Simon & Schuster Children's Publishing) Simon & Schuster Children's Publishing.

—My Teacher's Secret Life. 1999. 12.14 (0-606-17317-X) Turtleback Bks.

Krulik, Nancy E. Doggone It! 2003. (Katie Kazoo Switcheroo Ser.: No. 8). (Illus.). 80p. (J). mass mkt. 3.99 (0-448-43172-6, Grosset & Dunlap) Penguin Putnam Bks. for Young Readers.

—No Messin with My Lesson. 2004. (Katie Kazoo Switcheroo Ser.: Vol. 11). (Illus.). 80p. (J). mass mkt. 3.99 (*0-448-43357-5*, Grosset & Dunlap) Penguin Putnam Bks. for Young Readers.

Lawrence, Jan. Revenge of the Substitute Teacher. 1998. 10.55 (*0-606-13739-4*) Turtleback Bks.

—The Revenge of the Substitute Teacher. 1998. (J). (gr. 3-7). mass mkt. 4.50 (*0-590-05902-5*, Scholastic Paperbacks) Scholastic, Inc.

Lems, Kristin. Piano Teacher's Daughter. 2002. (Illus.). pap. 18.00 (*0-9637048-2-6*) Lems-Dworkin, Carol Pubs.

Leuck, Laura. My Creature Teacher. (J). 2004. lib. bdg. 16.89 (*0-06-029695-X*); 2003. 15.99 (*0-06-029694-1*) HarperCollins Pubs.

Levy, Elizabeth. The Great Laugh Off. 1997. 192p. (J). (gr. 3-7). lib. bdg. 14.89 (*0-06-026603-1*) HarperCollins Children's Bk. Group.

—Keep Ms. Sugarman in the Fourth Grade. (Trophy Bk.). (Illus.). 96p. (J). (gr. 3-6). 1993. pap. 4.99 (*0-06-440487-0*, Harper Trophy); 1992. 13.95 (*0-06-020426-5*); 1992. lib. bdg. 14.89 (*0-06-020427-3*) HarperCollins Children's Bk. Group.

—Keep Ms. Sugarman in the Fourth Grade. 1993. (J). 11.10 (*0-606-05390-5*) Turtleback Bks.

Lewis, Beverly. Creepy Sleep-Over. 1998. (Cul-de-Sac Kids Ser.: Vol. 17). (Illus.). 80p. (J). (gr. 2-5). pap. 3.99 (*1-55661-988-X*) Bethany Hse. Pubs.

—Straight - A Teacher. 1994. (Holly's Heart Ser.: Vol. 8). 160p. (J). pap. 6.99 (*0-310-46111-1*) Zondervan.

—Straight-A Teacher. 2002. (Hollys Heart Ser.). 160p. (J). pap. 5.99 (*0-7642-2615-0*) Bethany Hse. Pubs.

Lisle, Janet Taylor. Sirens & Spies. 2002. (Illus.). 224p. (YA). (gr. 5 up). pap. 4.99 (*0-689-84457-3*, Aladdin); 1985. 192p. (J). (gr. 7 up). lib. bdg. 14.95 o.p. (*0-02-759150-6*, Simon & Schuster Children's Publishing) Simon & Schuster Children's Publishing.

Lopez, Arcadia. Barrio Teacher. 1992. 96p. (YA). (gr. 6-12). pap. text 9.50 (*1-55885-051-1*) Arte Publico Pr.

MacDonald, Amy. No More Nasty, RS. 2001. (Illus.). 176p. (J). (gr. 3-7). 16.00 (*0-374-35529-0*, Farrar, Straus & Giroux (BYR)) Farrar, Straus & Giroux.

Madonna. Las Manzanas del Sr. Peabody. 2003. Tr. of Mr. Peabody's Apples. (SPA., Illus.). 32p. (J). 19.95 (*0-439-62279-4*, Scholastic en Espanola) Scholastic, Inc.

—Mr. Peabody's Apples. 2003. (Illus.). 40p. (J). 19.95 (*0-670-05883-1*) Callaway Editions, Inc.

Maguire, Gregory. Four Stupid Cupids. 2001. (Hamlet Chronicles Ser.). 192p. (J). (gr. 5 up). pap. 4.95 (*0-06-441072-2*, Harper Trophy) HarperCollins Children's Bk. Group.

—Four Stupid Cupids. 2001. (Illus.). 160p. (J). (gr. 4-6). tchr. ed. 15.00 (*0-395-83895-9*, Clarion Bks.) Houghton Mifflin Co. Trade & Reference Div.

—Four Stupid Cupids. l.t. ed. 2001. 225p. (J). 21.95 (*0-7862-3547-0*) Thorndike Pr.

Mallett, Jerry & Bartch, Marian. Close the Curtains. 1986. (Tumtwit Ser.). (Illus.). 54p. (J). (gr. 2-5). lib. bdg. 7.50 o.p. (*0-8479-9927-0*, 056115) Perma-Bound Bks.

Marney, Dean. The Valentine That Ate My Teacher. 1998. (J). mass mkt. 3.99 (*0-590-93943-2*, Scholastic Paperbacks) Scholastic, Inc.

—The Valentine That Ate My Teacher. 1998. (J). 10.04 (*0-606-13062-4*) Turtleback Bks.

Marshall, Catherine. The Angry Intruder. 1995. (Christy Fiction Ser.: No. 3). 128p. (J). (gr. 4-8). pap. 4.99 o.s.i (*0-8499-3688-8*) Nelson, Tommy.

—The Bridge to Cutter Gap. 1995. (Christy Fiction Ser.: No. 1). 128p. (J). (gr. 4-8). mass mkt. 4.99 (*0-8499-3686-1*) Nelson, Tommy.

—Brotherly Love. 1997. (Christy Fiction Ser.: No. 12). 128p. (Orig.). (J). (gr. 4-8). mass mkt. 4.99 (*0-8499-3963-1*) Nelson, Tommy.

—Family Secrets. 1996. (Christy Fiction Ser.: No. 8). (Illus.). 128p. (Orig.). (J). (gr. 4-8). mass mkt. 4.99 (*0-8499-3959-3*) Nelson, Tommy.

—Goodbye, Sweet Prince. 1997. (Christy Fiction Ser.: No. 11). 128p. (Orig.). (J). (gr. 4-8). pap. 4.99 (*0-8499-3962-3*) Nelson, Tommy.

—Midnight Rescue. 1995. (Christy Fiction Ser.: No. 4). 128p. (J). (gr. 4-8). pap. 4.99 o.s.i (*0-8499-3689-6*) Nelson, Tommy.

—Mountain Madness. adapted ed. 1997. (Christy Fiction Ser.: No. 9). 128p. (Orig.). (J). (gr. 4-8). mass mkt. 4.99 (*0-8499-3960-7*) Nelson, Tommy.

—The Princess Club. 1996. (Christy Fiction Ser.: No. 7). 128p. (J). (gr. 4-8). pap. text 4.99 (*0-8499-3958-5*) Nelson, Tommy.

—The Proposal. 1995. (Christy Fiction Ser.: No. 5). 128p. (J). (gr. 4-8). mass mkt. 4.99 (*0-8499-3918-6*) Nelson, Tommy.

—Silent Superstitions. 1995. (Christy Fiction Ser.: No. 2). 128p. (J). (gr. 4-8). pap. 4.99 o.s.i (*0-8499-3687-X*) Nelson, Tommy.

—Stage Fright. 1997. (Christy Fiction Ser.: No. 10). (Illus.). 128p. (J). (gr. 4-8). mass mkt. 4.99 (*0-8499-3961-5*) Nelson, Tommy.

Martin, Ann M. Karen's New Teacher. 1991. (Baby-Sitters Little Sister Ser.: No. 21). 112p. (J). (gr. 3-7). mass mkt. 3.50 (*0-590-44824-2*) Scholastic, Inc.

—Stacey's Big Crush. 1993. (Baby-Sitters Club Ser.: No. 65). 192p. (J). (gr. 3-7). mass mkt. 3.50 (*0-590-45667-9*) Scholastic, Inc.

—Stacey's Big Crush. 1993. (Baby-Sitters Club Ser.: No. 65). (J). (gr. 3-7). 9.55 (*0-606-05137-6*) Turtleback Bks.

—Teacher's Pet. 1995. (Kids in Ms. Colman's Class Ser.: No. 1). (J). (gr. 1-4). 9.65 (*0-606-07761-8*) Turtleback Bks.

Marzollo, Jean. Shanna's Teacher Show. (Illus.). 24p. (J). 2003. pap. 3.50 (*0-7868-1759-3*); 2002. 7.99 (*0-7868-0635-4*) Hyperion Bks. for Children. (Jump at the Sun).

Mason, Jane B. Animaniacs Adventures: Two Wacky Tales in One Cool Book. 1995. 48p. (J). (gr. k-2). mass mkt. 3.95 (*0-590-53528-5*) Scholastic, Inc.

Matsuura, Richard & Matsuura, Ruth. Angels Masquerading on Earth. (Illus.). (J). 7.95 (*1-887916-07-5*) Orchid Isle Publishing Co.

McKenna, Colleen O'Shaughnessy. Merry Christmas Miss McConnell. 1990. 160p. (J). (gr. 4-6). 12.95 o.p. (*0-590-43554-X*) Scholastic, Inc.

—Merry Christmas, Miss McConnell. 1991. (Illus.). 160p. (J). (gr. 4-6). mass mkt. 2.95 o.p. (*0-590-43555-8*, Scholastic Paperbacks) Scholastic, Inc.

—The Truth about Sixth Grade. 192p. (J). (gr. 4-6). 1992. pap. 3.50 (*0-590-44392-5*, Scholastic Paperbacks); 1991. pap. 12.95 o.p. (*0-590-44388-7*) Scholastic, Inc.

McKenzie, Ellen K. A Bowl of Mischief, ERS. 1992. 144p. (J). (gr. 4-7). 14.95 o.p. (*0-8050-2090-X*, Holt, Henry & Co. Bks. For Young Readers) Holt, Henry & Co.

—Stargone John, ERS. (Illus.). 80p. (J). 1992. (ps-3). pap. 7.95 (*0-8050-2069-1*); 1990. (gr. 3-7). 13.95 o.s.i (*0-8050-1451-9*) Holt, Henry & Co. (Holt, Henry & Co. Bks. For Young Readers).

—Stargone John. 1992. (Redfeather Bks.). (J). 13.10 (*0-606-02256-2*) Turtleback Bks.

McKissack, Patricia C. & McKissack, Fredrick L. Miami Sees It Through. 2002. (Road to Reading Ser.). (Illus.). 96p. (J). (gr. 2-4). pap. 3.99 (*0-307-26513-7*); lib. bdg. 11.99 (*0-307-46513-6*) Random Hse. Children's Bks. (Golden Bks.).

Meganck, Glenn. Big Deal at the Center of the Earth. 1999. (Illus.). 67p. (J). 11.99 (*1-892339-02-1*); (gr. 4-7). pap. 4.99 (*1-892339-03-X*) Beachfront Publishing.

Mills, Claudia. After Fifth Grade, the World! 1991. 128p. (J). (gr. 3-7). reprint ed. pap. 2.95 (*0-380-70894-9*, Avon Bks.) Morrow/Avon.

—After Fifth Grade, the World! 1989. 128p. (J). (gr. 3-7). 13.95 o.s.i (*0-02-767041-4*, Simon & Schuster Children's Publishing) Simon & Schuster Children's Publishing.

—Standing up to Mr. O., RS. 1998. 176p. (J). (gr. 4-7). 16.00 (*0-374-34721-2*, Farrar, Straus & Giroux (BYR)) Farrar, Straus & Giroux.

—Standing up to Mr. O. 2000. 165p. (J). (gr. 3-7). pap. 5.99 (*0-7868-1404-7*) Hyperion Bks. for Children.

Mills, Reita. Don't Dump the Teacher. 1987. (J). 8.95 o.p. (*0-533-07345-6*) Vantage Pr., Inc.

Miner, Jane C. Margaret. 1988. (Sunfire Ser.: No. 27). 224p. (Orig.). (J). (gr. 7 up). pap. 2.75 o.p. (*0-590-41191-8*) Scholastic, Inc.

Miss Nelson Is Back; Miss Nelson Is Missing. 1999. (Miss Nelson Ser.). (J). (ps-3). 9.95 (*1-56137-032-0*) Novel Units, Inc.

Mitchell, Carolyn B., et al. Mzungu. 1995. (Junior African Writers Ser.). (Illus.). 80p. (J). (ps-3). pap. 4.95 (*0-7910-3017-2*) Chelsea Hse. Pubs.

Montgomery, L. M. Anne of Avonlea. 1984. (Avonlea Ser.: No. 2). (YA). (gr. 5-8). mass mkt. 2.95 o.p. (*0-8049-0219-4*, CL219) Airmont Publishing Co., Inc.

—Anne of Avonlea. 1976. (Avonlea Ser.: No. 2). 376p. (YA). (gr. 5-8). 22.95 (*0-89190-155-8*) Amereon, Ltd.

—Anne of Avonlea. (Avonlea Ser.: No. 2). (gr. 5-8). 1992. 288p. (YA). pap. 3.25 o.s.i (*0-553-15114-2*); 1984. 288p. (J). mass mkt. 2.95 o.s.i (*0-553-24740-9*); 1984. 288p. (YA). mass mkt. 3.95 (*0-7704-2206-3*); No. 2. 1984. 304p. (YA). mass mkt. 4.50 (*0-553-21314-8*) Bantam Bks.

—Anne of Avonlea. (Avonlea Ser.: No. 2). (YA). (gr. 5-8). 2001. per. 12.50 (*1-891355-33-3*); 2000. per. 15.50 (*1-58396-201-8*) Blue Unicorn Editions.

—Anne of Avonlea. 1992. (Avonlea Ser.: No. 2). (Illus.). xiv, 204p. (YA). (gr. 5-8). 12.99 o.s.i (*0-517-08127-X*) Crown Publishing Group.

—Anne of Avonlea. 1995. (Avonlea Ser.: No. 2). 291p. (YA). (gr. 5-8). mass mkt. 2.99 (*0-8125-5196-6*, Tor Classics) Doherty, Tom Assocs., LLC.

—Anne of Avonlea. unabr. ed. 2002. (Juvenile Classics). 272p. (J). pap. 3.00 (*0-486-42239-9*) Dover Pubns., Inc.

—Anne of Avonlea. 1997. (Avonlea Ser.: No. 2). (YA). (gr. 5-8). pap. 5.60 (*0-87129-791-4*, A72) Dramatic Publishing Co.

—Anne of Avonlea. (Avonlea Ser.: No. 2). (YA). (gr. 5-8). E-Book 2.49 (*0-7574-3111-9*) Electric Umbrella Publishing.

—Anne of Avonlea, RS. 1950. (Avonlea Ser.: No. 2). (YA). (gr. 5-8). o.p. (*0-374-30354-1*, Farrar, Straus & Giroux (BYR)) Farrar, Straus & Giroux.

—Anne of Avonlea. 2002. (Charming Classics Ser.). 256p. (J). (ps-1). pap. 6.99 (*0-694-01584-9*, Harper Festival) HarperCollins Children's Bk. Group.

—Anne of Avonlea, unabr. ed. 1999. (Avonlea Ser.: No. 2). (YA). (gr. 5-8). audio 49.95 Highsmith Inc.

—Anne of Avonlea. l.t. ed. (Avonlea Ser.: No. 2). (YA). (gr. 5-8). 545p. pap. 43.82 (*0-7583-0219-3*); 426p. pap. 35.52 (*0-7583-0218-5*); 249p. pap. 23.08 (*0-7583-0216-9*); 859p. pap. 68.25 (*0-7583-0221-5*); 1056p. pap. 82.79 (*0-7583-0222-3*); 311p. pap. 28.60 (*0-7583-0217-7*); 698p. pap. 53.79 (*0-7583-0220-7*); 1225p. pap. 92.89 (*0-7583-0223-1*); 1225p. lib. bdg. 104.89 (*0-7583-0215-0*); 1056p. lib. bdg. 94.79 (*0-7583-0214-2*); 859p. lib. bdg. 84.25 (*0-7583-0213-4*); 311p. lib. bdg. 34.60 (*0-7583-0209-6*); 698p. lib. bdg. 59.79 (*0-7583-0212-6*); 545p. lib. bdg. 49.82 (*0-7583-0211-8*); 426p. lib. bdg. 41.52 (*0-7583-0210-X*); 249p. lib. bdg. 29.08 (*0-7583-0208-8*) Huge Print Pr.

—Anne of Avonlea. 2001. 248p. (gr. 8-12). 24.99 (*1-58827-590-6*); per. 20.99 (*1-58827-591-4*) IndyPublish.com.

—Anne of Avonlea. l.t. ed. 1998. (Avonlea Ser.: No. 2). 401p. (YA). (gr. 5-8). lib. bdg. 35.95 (*1-58118-039-X*, 22507) LRS.

—Anne of Avonlea. (Avonlea Ser.: No. 2). (YA). (gr. 5-8). E-Book 1.95 (*1-57799-878-2*) Logos Research Systems, Inc.

—Anne of Avonlea. 1987. (Avonlea Ser.: No. 2). 288p. (YA). (gr. 5-8). mass mkt. 3.95 o.s.i (*0-451-52113-7*, Signet Classics) NAL.

—Anne of Avonlea. l.t. ed. (Avonlea Ser.: No. 2). (YA). (gr. 5-8). reprint ed. 1993. 435p. lib. bdg. 26.00 (*0-939495-26-0*); 1998. 270p. lib. bdg. 25.00 (*1-58287-013-6*) North Bks.

—Anne of Avonlea. (Avonlea Ser.: No. 2). (YA). (gr. 5-8). 1997. (Illus.). 336p. pap. 4.99 (*0-14-036798-5*); 1992. 240p. pap. 2.99 o.p. (*0-14-032565-4*, Puffin Bks.); 1990. (Illus.). 320p. 15.99 (*0-448-40063-4*, Grosset & Dunlap) Penguin Putnam Bks. for Young Readers.

—Anne of Avonlea. (YA). (gr. 5-8). 1999. (Avonlea Ser.: No. 2). E-Book 8.99 o.p. incl. cd-rom (*1-57646-053-3*); 2000. (Anne of Green Gables Ser.: Vol. 2). 366p. pap. 24.99 (*1-57646-306-0*); 2000. (Anne of Green Gables Ser.: Vol. No. 2). 366p. lib. bdg. 34.99 (*1-57646-307-9*) Quiet Vision Publishing.

—Anne of Avonlea. (Avonlea Ser.: No. 2). (YA). (gr. 5-8). 1994. pap. o.s.i (*0-553-85021-0*); 1993. pap. o.s.i (*0-553-56709-8*) Random Hse. Children's Bks. (Dell Books for Young Readers).

—Anne of Avonlea. 1994. (Avonlea Ser.: No. 2). 256p. (YA). (gr. 5-8). text 5.98 o.p. (*1-56138-368-6*, Courage Bks.) Running Pr. Bk. Pubs.

—Anne of Avonlea. 1991. (Avonlea Ser.: No. 2). 336p. (YA). (gr. 5-8). mass mkt. 4.50 (*0-590-44556-1*, Scholastic Paperbacks) Scholastic, Inc.

—Anne of Avonlea. 1976. (Avonlea Ser.: No. 2). (YA). (gr. 5-8). 10.04 (*0-606-00791-1*) Turtleback Bks.

—Anne of Avonlea. 2002. (Children's Classics). 288p. (J). pap. 3.95 (*1-85326-162-9*) Wordsworth Editions, Ltd. GBR. *Dist:* Advanced Global Distribution Services.

—Anne of Windy Poplars. 1976. (Avonlea Ser.: No. 9). 268p. (YA). (gr. 5-8). 22.95 (*0-8488-0586-0*) Amereon, Ltd.

—Anne of Windy Poplars. (Avonlea Ser.: No. 9). (YA). (gr. 5-8). 1992. 288p. pap. 3.99 o.s.i (*0-553-48065-0*); 1983. 288p. mass mkt. 4.50 (*0-553-21316-4*, Bantam Classics); 1983. 272p. mass mkt. 2.95 o.s.i (*0-553-24397-7*); 4th ed. 1983. 288p. mass mkt. 3.95 (*0-7704-2167-9*) Bantam Bks.

—Anne of Windy Poplars. (Avonlea Ser.: No. 9). 274p. (YA). (gr. 5-8). pap. 4.98 o.p. (*0-7710-6164-1*) McClelland & Stewart/Tundra Bks.

—Anne of Windy Poplars, Vol. 4. 1999. 336p. (J). pap. 3.99 (*0-14-036800-0*, Puffin Bks.) Penguin Putnam Bks. for Young Readers.

—Anne of Windy Poplars. 1970. (Avonlea Ser.: No. 9). (YA). (gr. 5-8). 6.95 o.p. (*0-448-02548-5*) Putnam Publishing Group, The.

—Anne of Windy Poplars. 1987. (Avonlea Ser.: No. 9). (YA). (gr. 5-8). 10.04 (*0-606-02371-2*) Turtleback Bks.

Moore, Elaine. The Trouble with Valentines. 1998. (J). (gr. 2-5). mass mkt. 3.50 (*0-590-37234-3*, Scholastic Paperbacks) Scholastic, Inc.

Moore, Lilian & Adelson, Leone. The Terrible Mr. Twitmeyer. 1988. (Illus.). 64p. (J). (gr. 2-6). pap. 2.50 o.p. (*0-590-41595-6*) Scholastic, Inc.

Moore, Raymond S. & Moore, Dorothy N. Oh, No! Miss Dent Is Coming to Dinner: A Story of Manners. 2nd ed. 1985. (Illus.). 32p. (J). (gr. 3-5). 5.95 (*0-8407-6654-8*) Moore Foundation, The.

Morgenstern, Susie. A Book of Coupons. Rosner, Gill, tr. from FRE. 2001. (Illus.). 64p. (J). (gr. 3-6). 13.99 (*0-670-89970-4*, Viking Children's Bks.) Penguin Putnam Bks. for Young Readers.

—The Book of Coupons. 2003. (Illus.). 80p. pap. 5.99 (*0-14-250115-8*, Puffin Bks.) Penguin Putnam Bks. for Young Readers.

Moses, B. More Secret Lives of Teachers. 2003. (Illus.). 62p. (J). pap. (*0-330-34994-5*) Macmillan Children's Bks.

Munro-Foley, Louise. My Substitute Treacher's Gone Batty! 1996. (Vampire Cat Ser.). (J). 10.65 (*0-606-12032-7*) Turtleback Bks.

Muntean, Michaela. I Want to Be a Teacher: Sesame Street. 1999. (Golden's Sesame Street Ser.). (Illus.). (J). (ps). pap. 3.29 o.s.i (*0-307-12627-7*, Golden Bks.) Random Hse. Children's Bks.

Murphy, Jim. My Face to the Wind: The Diary of Sarah Jane Price, a Prairie Teacher. 2001. (Dear America Ser.). (Illus.). 208p. (J). (gr. 4-9). pap. 10.95 (*0-590-43810-7*) Scholastic, Inc.

My Little Red Book. 1993. (Little Color Library). (Illus.). 24p. (J). (ps). pap. 2.95 o.p. (*1-56458-313-9*) Dorling Kindersley Publishing, Inc.

My Principal Lives Next Door! 1992. (Kids Are Authors Picture Bks.). (Illus.). 24p. (J). (gr. 3). pap. 3.50 (*0-87406-598-4*) Darby Creek Publishing.

Myers, Bernice. It Happens to Everyone. 1990. (J). 12.95 o.p. (*0-688-09081-8*) HarperCollins Children's Bk. Group.

Myers, Christopher. Wings. 2001. (YA). (gr. 2-4). 27.90 incl. audio (*0-8045-6880-4*, 6880) Spoken Arts, Inc.

Myers, Laurie. Earthquake in the Third Grade. (Illus.). 64p. (J). 1998. (gr. 4-6). pap. 5.95 (*0-395-92866-4*); 1993. (gr. 2-4). tchr. ed. 15.00 o.s.i (*0-395-65360-6*) Houghton Mifflin Co. Trade & Reference Div. (Clarion Bks.).

—Earthquake in the Third Grade. 1998. 12.10 (*0-606-14199-5*) Turtleback Bks.

Nastick, Sharon. Mr. Radagast Makes an Unexpected Journey. 1981. (Illus.). 96p. (J). (gr. 3-7). 10.95 (*0-690-04050-4*); lib. bdg. 11.89 (*0-690-04051-2*) HarperCollins Children's Bk. Group.

Noonan, R. A. My Teacher Is a Zombie. 1995. (Monsterville USA Ser.: No. 3). 144p. (J). pap. 3.95 o.p. (*0-689-71865-9*, Simon Pulse) Simon & Schuster Children's Publishing.

Oliver, Lin. The Mighty Mogul. 1999. (Great Railway Adventures Ser.: Vol. 2;1). (Illus.). 32p. (J). (gr. k-4). 14.95 (*1-890647-56-X*); pap. 14.99 incl. audio (*1-890647-57-8*) Learning Curve International, LLC.

Oppenheim, Joanne F. Mrs. Peloki's Class Play. 1983. (Illus.). 32p. (J). (ps-3). 10.95 o.p. (*0-396-08178-9*, G. P. Putnam's Sons) Penguin Putnam Bks. for Young Readers.

—Mrs. Peloki's Substitute. 1987. (Illus.). 32p. (J). (ps-3). 12.95 o.p. (*0-396-08918-6*, G. P. Putnam's Sons) Penguin Putnam Bks. for Young Readers.

Ormerod, Jan. Ms. MacDonald Has a Class. 2002. (Illus.). (J). 23.36 (*0-7587-3197-3*) Book Wholesalers, Inc.

—Ms. MacDonald Has a Class. 2001. (Illus.). 32p. (J). (ps-3). pap. 6.95 (*0-618-13056-X*, Clarion Bks.) Houghton Mifflin Co. Trade & Reference Div.

Parish, Peggy. Teach Us, Amelia Bedelia. 1999. (Amelia Bedelia Ser.). (J). (gr. k-2). 11.55 (*0-88103-912-8*) Econo-Clad Bks.

—Teach Us, Amelia Bedelia. 1977. (Illus.). 56p. (J). (gr. k-3). (Amelia Bedelia Ser.). 15.99 (*0-688-80069-6*); (Greenwillow Read-Alone Bks.: Vol. 1). lib. bdg. 16.89 (*0-688-84069-8*) HarperCollins Children's Bk. Group. (Greenwillow Bks.).

—Teach Us, Amelia Bedelia. (Hello Reader! Ser.). (Illus.). (J). 1995. 56p. (gr. 2-3). mass mkt. 3.99 (*0-590-53773-3*, Cartwheel Bks.); 1987. 64p. (gr. k-2). mass mkt. 2.95 o.p. (*0-590-43345-8*); 1980. (gr. k-2). pap. 1.95 o.p. (*0-590-05797-9*); 1980. (gr. k-2). pap. 2.50 o.p. (*0-590-33362-3*); 1987. 64p. (gr. k-2). reprint ed. pap. 2.50 o.p. (*0-590-40940-9*) Scholastic, Inc.

Pascal, Francine, creator. Get the Teacher! 1994. (Sweet Valley Kids Ser.: No. 46). 80p. (J). (gr. 1-3). pap. 3.50 o.s.i (*0-553-48106-1*) Bantam Bks.

—Good-Bye, Mrs. Otis. 1997. (Sweet Valley Kids Ser.: No. 70). 96p. (gr. 1-3). pap. text 3.50 o.s.i (*0-553-48336-6*, Sweet Valley) Random Hse. Children's Bks.

—The Twin's Mystery Teacher. 1989. (Sweet Valley Kids Ser.: No. 3). 80p. (gr. 1-3). pap. text 3.50 o.s.i (*0-553-15760-4*, Skylark) Random Hse. Children's Bks.

Passen, Lisa. The Abominable Snow Teacher. 2004. (J). 15.95 (*0-8050-7379-5*, Holt, Henry & Co. Bks. For Young Readers) Holt, Henry & Co.

—Attack of the Fifty-Foot Teacher, ERS. 2000. (Illus.). 32p. (J). (gr. k-3). 16.00 (*0-8050-6100-2*, Holt, Henry & Co. Bks. For Young Readers) Holt, Henry & Co.

—The Attack of the 50-Foot Teacher, ERS. 2003. (Illus.). 32p. (J). (gr. 1-3). pap. 6.95 (*0-8050-7260-8*, Holt, Henry & Co. Bks. For Young Readers) Holt, Henry & Co.

—The Incredible Shrinking Teacher, 2002. (Illus.). 32p. (J). (gr. k-3). 15.95 (*0-8050-6452-4*, Holt, Henry & Co. Bks. For Young Readers) Holt, Henry & Co.

Patneaude, David. The Last Man's Reward. 1996. 192p. (J). (gr. 4-8). lib. bdg. 14.95 (*0-8075-4370-5*) Whitman, Albert & Co.

Pearson, Mary E. Donde Esta Max? Córdova, Jacqueline, tr. (Rookie Espanol Ser.). (SPA., Illus.). 24p. (gr. k-1). 2001. pap. 4.95 (*0-516-27011-7*); 2000. (J). lib. bdg. 15.00 (*0-516-22023-3*) Scholastic Library Publishing. (Children's Pr.).

Peck, Robert Newton. Arly. 1991. 160p. (YA). mass mkt. 2.95 o.p. (*0-590-43469-1*, Scholastic Paperbacks) Scholastic, Inc.

—Arly. 1989. (History Series for Young People). 160p. (J). (gr. 5 up). 16.95 (*0-8027-6856-3*) Walker & Co.

Petersen, P. J. The Sub. 96p. (J). 1995. pap. 4.99 o.s.i (*0-14-037442-6*); 1993. (Illus.). (gr. 2-5). 13.99 o.p. (*0-525-45059-9*, Dutton Children's Bks.) Penguin Putnam Bks. for Young Readers.

Pfeffer, Susan Beth. Head of the Class. 1989. 128p. (YA). mass mkt. 2.95 o.s.i (*0-553-28190-9*) Bantam Bks.

Piasecki, Jerry. Teacher Vic Is a Vampire... Retired. 1995. 128p. (J). (gr. 3-7). pap. 3.50 o.s.i (*0-553-48281-5*, Skylark) Random Hse. Children's Bks.

—They're Torturing Teachers in Room 104. 1997. 144p. (YA). pap. 3.50 o.s.i (*0-553-48024-3*) Bantam Bks.

—What Is the Teacher's Toupe Doing in the Fish Tank? 1994. 128p. (J). (gr. 3-7). pap. 3.50 o.s.i (*0-553-48171-1*) Bantam Bks.

Pilkey, Dav. Captain Underpants & the Attack of the Talking Toilets. 1999. (Captain Underpants Ser.: No. 2). (Illus.). (J). (gr. 2-5). 144p. pap. 16.95 (*0-590-63136-5*); 139p. pap. 4.99 (*0-590-63427-5*) Scholastic, Inc. (Blue Sky Pr., The).

—Captain Underpants & the Attack of the Talking Toilets. 1999. (Captain Underpants Ser.: No. 2). (Illus.). (J). (gr. 2-5). 10.04 (*0-606-15830-8*) Turtleback Bks.

—Captain Underpants & the Invasion of the Incredibly Naughty Cafeteria Ladies from Outer Space: And the Subsequent Assault of the Equally Evil Lunchroom Zombie Nerds. 1999. (Captain Underpants Ser.: No. 3). (Illus.). (J). (gr. 2-5). 134p. pap. 16.95 (*0-439-04995-4*); 112p. pap. 4.99 (*0-439-04996-2*) Scholastic, Inc. (Blue Sky Pr., The).

—Captain Underpants & the Perilous Plot of Professor Poopypants. 2000. (Captain Underpants Ser.: No. 4). (Illus.). 160p. (J). (gr. 2-5). pap. 3.99 (*0-439-04998-9*); pap. 16.95 (*0-439-04997-0*) Scholastic, Inc. (Blue Sky Pr., The).

—Captain Underpants & the Perilous Plot of Professor Poopypants. 2000. (Captain Underpants Ser.: No. 4). (Illus.). (J). (gr. 2-5). 10.04 (*0-606-18526-7*) Turtleback Bks.

—Captain Underpants & the Wrath of the Wicked Wedgie Woman. 2001. (Adventures of Captain Underpants Ser.). (Illus.). (J). 11.04 (*0-606-21101-2*) Turtleback Bks.

Pinkwater, Jill. Mister Fred. 1994. 224p. (J). (gr. 5-8). 15.99 o.s.i (*0-525-44778-4*, Dutton Children's Bks.) Penguin Putnam Bks. for Young Readers.

Plourde, Lynn. Teacher Appreciation Day. 2003. (Illus.). 40p. (J). 16.99 (*0-525-47113-8*, Dutton Children's Bks.) Penguin Putnam Bks. for Young Readers.

Polacco, Patricia. Gracias, Senor Falker. Mlawer, Teresa, tr. from ENG. 2001. (SPA., Illus.). (J). (gr. 1-3). lib. bdg. 17.00 (*1-930332-03-3*, LC30185) Lectorum Pubns., Inc.

—Thank You, Mr. Falker. 2002. (Illus.). (J). 23.64 (*0-7587-3779-3*) Book Wholesalers, Inc.

—Thank You, Mr. Falker. 1998. (Illus.). 40p. (J). (gr. k-4). 16.99 (*0-399-23166-8*, Philomel) Penguin Putnam Bks. for Young Readers.

—Thank You, Mr. Falker. 2001. (J). (gr. k-4). 27.95 incl. audio (*0-8045-6854-5*, 6854) Spoken Arts, Inc.

Priceman, Marjorie. Emeline at the Circus. (J). (gr. k-3). 2000. pap. 6.99 (*0-375-80351-3*, Random Hse. Bks. for Young Readers); 1999. (Illus.). 40p. 15.00 (*0-679-87685-5*, Random Hse. Bks. for Young Readers); 1999. (Illus.). 40p. lib. bdg. 16.99 (*0-679-97685-X*, Random Hse. Bks. for Young Readers); 2001. (Illus.). 36p. reprint ed. pap. 6.99 o.s.i (*0-440-41732-5*, Dragonfly Bks.) Random Hse. Children's Bks.

Pulver, Robin. Mrs. Toggle's Beautiful Blue Shoe. 1994. (Illus.). 32p. (J). (ps-2). 13.95 o.p. (*0-02-775456-1*, Simon & Schuster Children's Publishing) Simon & Schuster Children's Publishing.

Pyne, Patricia P. The Magic Chopsticks. l.t. ed. 1996. (Illus.). 24p. (J). (gr. 1-8). lib. bdg. 14.95 (*0-9655465-9-4*) Pelican Publishing.

Quin-Harkin, Janet. Friday Night Fright. 1995. (TGIF Ser.: No. 2). (Illus.). 128p. (J). (gr. 3-6). pap. 3.50 (*0-671-51018-5*, Aladdin) Simon & Schuster Children's Publishing.

Rathmann, Peggy. Ruby the Copycat. 32p. (J). (ps-2). 1997. (Illus.). pap. 9.95 (*0-590-76715-1*); 1993. (Illus.). mass mkt. 4.95 (*0-590-47423-5*); 1991. pap. 14.95 (*0-590-43747-X*) Scholastic, Inc.

—Ruby the Copycat. 1991. (Blue Ribbon Bks.). (J). 12.14 (*0-606-05573-8*) Turtleback Bks.

Ray, Delia. Ghost Girl: A Blue Ridge Mountain Story. 2003. (Illus.). 224p. (YA). (gr. 5-9). tchr. ed. 15.00 (*0-618-33377-0*, Clarion Bks.) Houghton Mifflin Co. Trade & Reference Div.

Rexroad, Zoe. 'Miz Liz Do You Dye Your Hair? 1997. 140p. (Orig.). (J). (gr. 5-6). pap. 6.95 (*1-57502-490-X*, P01457) Morris Publishing.

Reynolds, Marilynn. The Magnificent Piano Recital. 2001. (Illus.). 32p. (J). (ps-3). 15.95 (*1-55143-180-7*) Orca Bk. Pubs.

Richardson, Arleta. Eighteen & on Her Own. 1986. (Grandma's Attic Ser.). 173p. (J). (gr. 3-7). pap. 3.99 o.p. (*0-89191-512-5*) Cook Communications Ministries.

—A School of Her Own. 1995. (Grandma's Attic Ser.). 173p. (J). (gr. 3-7). pap. 3.99 (*1-55513-670-2*) Cook Communications Ministries.

Rocklin, Joanne. For Your Eyes Only! 1997. 112p. (J). (gr. 3-7). pap. 14.95 (*0-590-67447-1*) Scholastic, Inc.

Rogers, Amy Keating. Powerpuff Professor. 2000. (Powerpuff Girls Ser.: No. 1). (Illus.). 64p. (J). (gr. 1-4). mass mkt. 3.99 (*0-439-16019-7*) Scholastic, Inc.

Sachar, Louis. Marvin Redpost: Alone in His Teacher's House. 1994. (Illus.). 96p. (J). (First Stepping Stone Bks.). (gr. k-4). lib. bdg. 11.99 (*0-679-91949-X*); (Marvin Redpost Ser.: Vol. 4). (gr. 1-4). pap. 3.99 (*0-679-81949-5*) Random Hse. Children's Bks. (Random Hse. Bks. for Young Readers).

Sachs, Marilyn. The Bears' House. 1989. 80p. (J). (gr. 3-7). pap. 2.99 (*0-380-70582-6*, Avon Bks.) Morrow/Avon.

—The Bears' House. (J). (gr. 4-7). 1996. 78p. pap. 4.99 (*0-14-038321-2*); 1987. 80p. 10.95 o.s.i (*0-525-44286-3*, Dutton Children's Bks.) Penguin Putnam Bks. for Young Readers.

—A Summer's Lease. 1979. 12p. (J). (gr. 5-9). 13.95 o.p. (*0-525-40480-5*, 0898-270, Dutton Children's Bks.) Penguin Putnam Bks. for Young Readers.

Salant, Sherry Ann. Skipping School. l.t. ed. 2001. 24p. 6.95 (*0-9712952-0-4*) Storywriter Pr.

Schick, Eleanor. Art Lessons. 1987. (Illus.). 48p. (J). (gr. k-3). 12.95 o.p. (*0-688-05120-0*); lib. bdg. 12.88 o.p. (*0-688-05121-9*) HarperCollins Children's Bk. Group. (Greenwillow Bks.).

Schraff, Anne. The Vanished One. rev. ed. 1999. (Standing Tall Mysteries Ser.). 49p. (YA). (gr. 4 up). pap. 3.95 o.p. (*1-58659-100-2*) Artesian Pr.

—The Vanished One. Newell, Carol, ed. 1995. (Standing Tall Mystery Ser.). 49p. (J). (gr. 5-9). pap. 4.95 o.p. (*1-56254-159-5*, SP1595) Saddleback Publishing, Inc.

—The Vanished One. 1995. (Standing Tall Mystery Ser.). 11.10 (*0-606-12036-X*) Turtleback Bks.

Schwandt, Stephen. A Risky Game, ERS. 1986. 128p. (YA). (gr. 7 up). 11.95 o.p. (*0-8050-0091-7*, Holt, Henry & Co. Bks. For Young Readers) Holt, Henry & Co.

Seuss, Dr. & Prelutsky, Jack. Hooray for Diffendoofer Day! 1998. (Illus.). 56p. (gr. k-3). (J). 18.99 (*0-679-99008-9*); 17.00 (*0-679-89008-4*) Random Hse. Children's Bks. (Random Hse. Bks. for Young Readers).

Shannon, Jacqueline. Why Would Anyone Have a Crush on Horace Beemis? 1992. 144p. (J). mass mkt. 2.75 o.p. (*0-590-43743-7*, Scholastic Paperbacks) Scholastic, Inc.

Shura, Mary Francis. Our Teacher Is Missing. 1993. (J). (gr. 4-6). 176p. pap. 2.99 o.p. (*0-590-44597-9*); 128p. mass mkt. 2.95 o.p. (*0-590-44677-0*) Scholastic, Inc.

Singleton, Linda Joy. Teacher Trouble. 1996. (My Sister, the Ghost Ser.: No. 3). 128p. (J). (gr. 3-5). pap. 3.50 o.p. (*0-380-77895-5*, Avon Bks.) Morrow/Avon.

—Teacher Trouble. 1996. (My Sister, the Ghost Ser.: No. 3). (J). (gr. 3-5). 8.60 o.p. (*0-606-09654-X*) Turtleback Bks.

Slack, Thomas, ed. The Pleasing Instructor. 1973. (Children's Books from the Past: Vol. 6). 368p. (YA). reprint ed. 66.75 o.p. (*3-261-01008-8*) Lang, Peter Publishing, Inc.

Slate, Joseph. Miss Bindergarten Gets Ready for Kindergarten. 2001. (Illus.). 40p. (J). pap. 6.99 (*0-14-056273-7*, Puffin Bks.) Penguin Putnam Bks. for Young Readers.

—Miss Bindergarten's Craft Center. 1999. (Illus.). 12p. (J). (ps-3). bds. 17.99 o.s.i (*0-525-46257-0*) Penguin Putnam Bks. for Young Readers.

Smith. Teacher Trouble. 2000. pap. 6.95 o.p. (*0-552-52803-X*) Transworld Publishers Ltd. GBR. *Dist:* Trafalgar Square.

Spinner, Stephanie. Bird Is the Word, 5. 1997. (Weebie Zone Ser.). (J). 9.15 o.p. (*0-606-12058-0*) Turtleback Bks.

Spinner, Stephanie & Weiss, Ellen. Bird Is the Word. 1997. (Weebie Zone Ser.: No. 5). (Illus.). 80p. (J). (gr. 2-4). lib. bdg. 13.89 (*0-06-027590-1*) HarperCollins Children's Bk. Group.

Stewart, Molly Mia. Get the Teacher! 1994. (Sweet Valley Kids Ser.: No. 46). (J). (gr. 1-3). 8.70 o.p. (*0-606-06031-6*) Turtleback Bks.

—Good-Bye, Mrs. Otis. 1997. (Sweet Valley Kids Ser.: No. 70). (J). (gr. 1-3). 9.55 (*0-606-11950-7*) Turtleback Bks.

—The Twin's Mystery Teacher. 1989. (Sweet Valley Kids Ser.: No. 3). (J). (gr. 1-3). 8.70 o.p. (*0-606-04416-7*) Turtleback Bks.

Stine, R. L. Creature Teacher. 1998. (Goosebumps Series 2000: No. 3). (J). (gr. 3-7). mass mkt. 3.99 (*0-590-39989-6*, Scholastic Paperbacks) Scholastic, Inc.

—Creature Teacher. 1998. (Goosebumps Series 2000: No. 3). (J). (gr. 3-7). 10.04 (*0-606-13440-9*) Turtleback Bks.

—Who's Been Sleeping in My Grave? 1995. (Ghosts of Fear Street Ser.: No. 2). 128p. (J). (gr. 4-7). pap. 3.99 (*0-671-52942-0*, Aladdin) Simon & Schuster Children's Publishing.

Stone, Tom B. The Creature Teacher. 1997. (Graveyard School Ser.: No. 20). 96p. (gr. 3-7). pap. text 3.99 o.s.i (*0-553-48520-2*, Dell Books for Young Readers) Random Hse. Children's Bks.

—Let's Scare the Teacher to Death! 1995. (Graveyard School Ser.: No. 8). (J). (gr. 3-7). pap. 4.75 (*0-553-54232-X*, Dell Books for Young Readers); 128p. pap. 3.50 o.s.i (*0-553-48337-4*, Skylark) Random Hse. Children's Bks.

—Let's Scare the Teacher to Death! 1995. (Graveyard School Ser.: No. 8). (J). (gr. 3-7). 8.60 o.p. (*0-606-07597-6*) Turtleback Bks.

Strasser, Todd. Help! I'm Trapped in My Gym Teacher's Body. 1997. (Help! I'm Trapped Ser.). (J). (gr. 4-7). mass mkt. 4.50 (*0-590-67987-2*, Scholastic Paperbacks) Scholastic, Inc.

—Help! I'm Trapped in My Gym Teacher's Body. 1997. (Help! I'm Trapped Ser.). (J). (gr. 4-7). 10.55 (*0-606-11453-X*) Turtleback Bks.

Strauch, Eileen W. Hey You, Sister Rose. 1993. 160p. (J). (gr. 3 up). 13.00 o.p. (*0-688-11829-1*, Morrow, William & Co.) Morrow/Avon.

Stretton, Barbara. The Truth of the Matter. 1983. 256p. (J). (gr. 7-12). 10.95 o.p. (*0-394-86144-2*, Knopf Bks. for Young Readers) Random Hse. Children's Bks.

Sustrin, Sheila & Sustrin, Letty. The Teacher Who Would Not Retire. unabr. ed. 2002. (Illus.). 32p. (J). (ps-3). 16.00 (*0-9674602-3-9*) Blue Marlin Pubns.

Suzanne, Jamie. Cammi's Crush. 1997. (Sweet Valley Twins Ser.: No. 108). 144p. (gr. 3-7). pap. text 3.50 o.s.i (*0-553-48439-7*, Sweet Valley) Random Hse. Children's Bks.

—Teacher's Pet. 1986. (Sweet Valley Twins Ser.: No. 2). (Illus.). (J). (gr. 3-7). pap. 7.95 (*0-553-16654-9*, Dell Books for Young Readers) Random Hse. Children's Bks.

Suzanne Staples the Teacher. 1998. (J). o.s.i (*0-06-449423-3*) HarperCollins Children's Bk. Group.

Syverson-Stork, Jill, tr. Arturo y Sus Problemas con el Profesor. 1994. (Arthur Adventure Ser.). (SPA.). 32p. (J). (gr. k-3). pap. 5.95 (*0-316-11380-8*) Little Brown Children's Bks.

Thaler, Mike. A Hippopotamus Ate the Teacher! 1981. (Camelot Bks.). (Illus.). 32p. (J). (gr. k-3). pap. 3.95 (*0-380-78048-8*, Harper Trophy) HarperCollins Children's Bk. Group.

—A Hippopotamus Ate the Teacher! 1981. (J). 10.14 (*0-606-02133-7*) Turtleback Bks.

—Miss Yonkers Goes Bonkers. 1994. (Illus.). (J). (gr. 2). pap. 3.99 (*0-380-77510-7*, Avon Bks.) Morrow/Avon.

—Miss Yonkers Goes Bonkers. 1994. (Young Camelot Bks.). (YA). 9.19 o.p. (*0-606-06573-3*) Turtleback Bks.

—The Music Teacher from the Black Lagoon. 2000. (Black Lagoon Ser.). (Illus.). 32p. (J). (ps-3). mass mkt. 3.25 (*0-439-18873-3*) Scholastic, Inc.

—The Music Teacher from the Black Lagoon. 2000. (Black Lagoon Ser.). (J). (ps-3). 9.40 (*0-606-18882-7*) Turtleback Bks.

—The Teacher from the Black Lagoon. 1989. (Black Lagoon Ser.). (Illus.). 31p. (J). (ps-3). mass mkt. 3.25 (*0-590-41962-5*) Scholastic, Inc.

—The Teacher from the Black Lagoon. 1989. (Black Lagoon Ser.). (J). (ps-3). 9.40 (*0-606-02723-8*) Turtleback Bks.

Thompson, Cliff. The Meteor Man. 1993. (J). (gr. 7 up). mass mkt. 3.25 o.p. (*0-590-47300-X*) Scholastic, Inc.

Van Raven, Pieter. Harpoon Island. 1989. 160p. (J). (gr. 6-9). 13.95 o.s.i (*0-684-19092-3*, Atheneum) Simon & Schuster Children's Publishing.

Vande Velde, Vivian. Troll Teacher. 2000. (Illus.). 32p. (J). (ps-3). tchr. ed. 16.95 (*0-8234-1503-1*) Holiday Hse., Inc.

Vaughan, Marcia K. Up the Learning Tree. 2003. (Illus.). (J). 16.96 (*1-58430-049-3*) Lee & Low Bks., Inc.

Vivelo, Jackie. Mr. Scatter's Magic Spell. 1993. (Teachers Secrets Ser.). (Illus.). 32p. (J). (gr. 2-5). pap. 10.95 o.p. (*1-56458-201-9*) Dorling Kindersley Publishing, Inc.

Walden, Amelia. Where Is My Heart? 1960. (J). (gr. 9 up). 4.95 o.p. (*0-664-32228-X*) Westminster John Knox Pr.

Wardlaw, Lee. 101 Ways to Bug Your Teacher. 2004. (Illus.). (J). 16.99 (*0-8037-2658-9*, Dial Bks. for Young Readers) Penguin Putnam Bks. for Young Readers.

Waricha, Jean & Dubowski, Cathy. The Substitute Teacher. 1997. (Full House Michelle Ser.: No. 12). 96p. (J). (gr. 2-4). pap. 3.99 (*0-671-00364-X*, Simon Spotlight) Simon & Schuster Children's Publishing.

Warner, Gertrude Chandler. Benny's Saturday Surprise. 2001. (Adventures of Benny & Watch: Vol. 8). (Illus.). 32p. (J). (gr. 1-3). pap. 3.95 (*0-8075-0642-7*) Whitman, Albert & Co.

Weber, Susan. Seal Island School. 2001. (Puffin Chapters Ser.). (Illus.). (J). 11.14 (*0-606-21423-2*) Turtleback Bks.

Weiss, Leatie. My Teacher Sleeps in School. (J). 1986. 13.95 o.p. (*0-670-81095-9*, Viking Children's Bks.); 1985. (Illus.). 32p. pap. 5.99 (*0-14-050559-8*, Puffin Bks.) Penguin Putnam Bks. for Young Readers.

—My Teacher Sleeps in School. 1985. (Picture Puffin Ser.). (J). 12.14 (*0-606-00344-4*) Turtleback Bks.

Whalen, Sharla Scannell. Flower Girl Friends. 1997. (Illus.). 64p. (J). pap. 5.95 o.p. (*1-56239-840-7*) ABDO Publishing Co.

Wheatley, Nadia. Luke's Way of Looking. 2001. (Illus.). 36p. (J). (gr. k up). 15.95 (*1-929132-18-2*, Cranky Nell Bks.) Kane/Miller Bk. Pubs.

Wiggin, Eric. Maggie's Secret Longing. 1995. (Maggie's World Ser.: Vol. 3). 165p. (Orig.). (J). (gr. 5-9). mass mkt. 3.99 o.p. (*1-56507-266-9*) Harvest Hse. Pubs.

Willner-Pardo, Gina. Spider Storch's Fumbled Field Trip. 1998. 10.10 (*0-606-17183-5*) Turtleback Bks.

—Spider Storch's Fumbled Field Trip. 1998. (Illus.). (J). (gr. 2-5). 68p. pap. 3.95 (*0-8075-7582-8*); 80p. lib. bdg. 11.95 (*0-8075-7581-X*) Whitman, Albert & Co.

—Spider Storch's Music Mess. 1998. 10.10 (*0-606-17180-0*) Turtleback Bks.

—Spider Storch's Music Mess. 1998. (Illus.). 80p. (J). (gr. 2-5). lib. bdg. 11.95 (*0-8075-7583-6*) Whitman, Albert & Co.

—Spider Storch's Teacher Torture. 1997. 10.10 (*0-606-17181-9*) Turtleback Bks.

—Spider Storch's Teacher Torture. 1997. (Illus.). 56p. (J). (gr. 3-5). pap. 3.95 (*0-8075-7578-X*); (gr. 4-5). lib. bdg. 11.95 (*0-8075-7577-1*) Whitman, Albert & Co.

Winfrey, Michelle Whitaker. It's My Birthday... Finally! A Leap Year Story. 2003. (Illus.). (J). per. 11.95 (*0-9727179-0-0*) Hobby Hse. Publishing Group.

Winters, Kay. My Teacher for President. 2004. (Illus.). 32p. (J). 12.99 (*0-525-47186-3*, Dutton Children's Bks.) Penguin Putnam Bks. for Young Readers.

Wittman, Sally. The Wonderful Mrs. Trumbly. 1982. (Illus.). 40p. (J). (gr. k-3). 11.95 (*0-06-026511-6*) HarperCollins Children's Bk. Group.

Wolitzer, Meg. Operation: Save the Teacher: Tuesday Night Pie. 1993. 128p. (Orig.). (J). pap. 3.50 (*0-380-76460-1*, Avon Bks.) Morrow/Avon.

—Operation: Save the Teacher: Saturday Night Toast. 1993. 128p. (Orig.). (J). pap. 3.50 (*0-380-76462-8*, Avon Bks.) Morrow/Avon.

—Operation: Save the Teacher: Wednesday Night Match. 1993. (Wednesday Night Match Ser.). 128p. (Orig.). (J). (gr. 4-8). pap. 3.50 (*0-380-76461-X*, Avon Bks.) Morrow/Avon.

Wood, Douglas. What Teachers Can't Do. 2002. (Illus.). 32p. (J). (ps-3). 14.95 (*0-689-84644-4*, Simon & Schuster Children's Publishing) Simon & Schuster Children's Publishing.

Wood, Kenneth. Shining Armour. 1982. (Julia MacRae Blackbird Bks.). 144p. (J). (gr. 7). 9.95 o.p. (*0-531-04434-3*, Watts, Franklin) Scholastic Library Publishing.

Yates, Elizabeth. Prudence Crandall: Woman of Courage. 1955. (Illus.). (J). (gr. 7 up). 8.50 o.p. (*0-525-37883-9*, Dutton) Dutton/Plume.

Yorke, Malcolm. Miss Butterpat Goes Wild! 1993. (Teachers Secrets Ser.). (Illus.). 32p. (J). (gr. 1-5). pap. 10.95 o.p. (*1-56458-200-0*) Dorling Kindersley Publishing, Inc.

RELATIONSHIPS

A

Greene, Carol. The Old Ladies Who Liked Cats. 1991. (Illus.). 32p. (J). (gr. k-3). 15.00 o.p. (*0-06-022104-6*); lib. bdg. 14.89 o.p. (*0-06-022105-4*) HarperCollins Children's Bk. Group.

Hart, Bruce & Hart, Carole. Sooner or Later. 1983. (YA). (gr. 7 up). pap. 2.50 o.p. (*0-380-64717-6*, 64717-6, Avon Bks.) Morrow/Avon.

Herman, Charlotte. Our Snowman Had Olive Eyes. 1977. (J). (gr. 4-6). 7.95 o.p. (*0-525-36490-0*, Dutton) Dutton/Plume.

Hickman, Janet. Jericho. 1994. 144p. (J). (gr. 3 up). 15.00 (*0-688-13398-3*, Greenwillow Bks.) HarperCollins Children's Bk. Group.

—Jericho. 1996. 144p. (YA). (gr. 4-7). pap. 3.99 (*0-380-72693-9*, Avon Bks.) Morrow/Avon.

—Jericho. 1996. 9.09 o.p. (*0-606-09488-1*) Turtleback Bks.

Houghton Mifflin Company Staff. Rocking Chair Rebel. 1992. (Literature Experience 1993 Ser.). (J). (gr. 7). pap. 11.04 (*0-395-61852-5*) Houghton Mifflin Co.

Hughes, Shirley. The Snow Lady. 1990. (Illus.). 32p. (J). 13.95 o.p. (*0-688-09874-6*); lib. bdg. 13.88 o.p. (*0-688-09875-4*) HarperCollins Children's Bk. Group.

Komaiko, Leah. Leonora O'Grady. 1992. (Laura Geringer Bks.). (Illus.). 32p. (J). (gr. k-3). 15.00 (*0-06-021766-9*); lib. bdg. 14.89 (*0-06-021767-7*) HarperCollins Children's Bk. Group.

Krulik, Nancy E. Mr. Magoo. 1997. (Illus.). 96p. (J). (gr. 3-7). pap. 4.95 o.p. (*0-7868-4174-5*) Disney Pr.

Leedahl, Shelley A. The Bone Talker. 2000. (Northern Lights Books for Children Ser.). (Illus.). 32p. (J). (ps-3). 15.95 (*0-88995-214-0*) Red Deer Pr. CAN. *Dist:* General Distribution Services, Inc.

Lindgren, Barbro & Eriksson, Eva. The Story of the Little Old Man. 1992. (Illus.). (J). (gr. k-5). 6.00 o.p. (*91-29-59942-3*, 575320) R & S Bks. SWE. *Dist:* Farrar, Straus & Giroux, Holtzbrinck Pubs.

Marsoli, Lisa A. Mother Hubbard's Empty Cupboard. 1997. (Puzzle Board Bks.). (Illus.). 5p. (J). 6.95 o.p. (*0-8118-1702-4*) Chronicle Bks. LLC.

Masterson, Linda. We Love America. 2003. (Illus.). 24p. (J). pap. 3.25 (*0-307-10427-3*, Golden Bks.) Random Hse. Children's Bks.

Newman, Leslea. Remember That. 1996. (Illus.). 32p. (J). (ps-3). tchr. ed. 14.95 o.s.i (*0-395-66156-0*, Clarion Bks.) Houghton Mifflin Co. Trade & Reference Div.

Nystrom, Carolyn. Jenny & Grandpa: A Child's Guide to Growing Older. 1994. 48p. (J). (gr. 4-7). pap. 4.99 o.p. (*0-7459-2922-2*) Lion Publishing.

O'Malley, Kevin, illus. There Was a Crooked Man. 1995. (J). (ps). 9.95 (*0-671-89477-3*, Little Simon) Simon & Schuster Children's Publishing.

Palmer, Michele. Zoup Soup. 1978. (Illus.). (J). (ps-1). pap. 1.95 (*0-932306-00-4*) Rocking Horse Pr.

Pfeffer, Susan Beth & Alcott, Louisa May. Jo's Story. 1997. (Portraits of Little Women Ser.). 112p. (gr. 3-7). text 9.95 o.s.i (*0-385-32523-1*, Dell Books for Young Readers) Random Hse. Children's Bks.

Porter-Gaylord, Laurel. I Love My Mommy Because. 2004. 20p. bds. 6.99 (*0-525-47248-7*, Dutton Children's Bks.) Penguin Putnam Bks. for Young Readers.

Quirk, Anne. Dancing with Great-Aunt Cornelia. 1997. 160p. (J). (gr. 3-7). 14.95 o.p. (*0-06-027332-1*) HarperCollins Children's Bk. Group.

Ruby, Lois. This Old Man. 1986. (J). mass mkt. 2.50 o.s.i (*0-449-70152-2*, Fawcett) Ballantine Bks.

—This Old Man, 001. 1984. 192p. (J). (gr. 7 up). 11.95 o.p. (*0-395-36563-5*) Houghton Mifflin Co.

Rylant, Cynthia. Mr. Putter & Tabby Row the Boat. 1997. (Mr. Putter & Tabby Ser.). (Illus.). 44p. (J). (gr. 1-5). 14.00 (*0-15-256257-5*); pap. 5.95 (*0-15-201059-9*, Harcourt Paperbacks) Harcourt Children's Bks.

—Mr. Putter & Tabby Row the Boat. 1997. 12.10 (*0-606-12774-7*) Turtleback Bks.

Scott, Cynthia A. Old Jake's Skirts. (Illus.). (J). 2003. pap. 7.95 (*0-87358-839-8*); 1998. 36p. lib. bdg. 15.95 (*0-87358-615-8*) Northland Publishing. (Rising Moon Bks. for Young Readers).

Shawver, Margaret. What's Wrong with Grandma? A Family's Experience with Alzheimer's. 1996. (Young Readers Ser.). (Illus.). 62p. (YA). (gr. 2 up). 17.00 (*1-57392-107-6*) Prometheus Bks., Pubs.

Shecter, Ben. Great-Uncle Alfred Forgets. (Illus.). (J). (gr. k-3). 1996. 80p. lib. bdg. 14.89 o.p. (*0-06-026219-2*); 1995. 32p. 14.95 o.p. (*0-06-026218-4*) HarperCollins Children's Bk. Group.

Simmons, Lynn Sheffield. Bo, the Famous Retriever. 1997. (Illus.). 117p. (J). (gr. 4-8). 9.95 (*0-9642573-1-9*) Argyle Bks.

Singer, Isaac Bashevis, et al. The Safe Deposit & Other Stories about Grandparents, Old Lovers & Crazy Old Men. 1989. (Masterworks of Modern Jewish Writings Ser.). 360p. (J). 19.95 (*1-55876-013-X*) Wiener, Markus Pubs., Inc.

Skorpen, Liesel M. Grace. 1984. 128p. (J). (gr. 5 up). 12.95 (*0-06-025798-9*); lib. bdg. 12.89 o.p. (*0-06-025799-7*) HarperCollins Children's Bk. Group.

Snow, Pegeen. Mrs. Periwinkle's Groceries. 1981. (Easy Reading Picture Story Bks.). (Illus.). 48p. (J). (gr. k-3). pap. 2.95 o.s.i (*0-516-43558-2*); lib. bdg. 9.65 o.p. (*0-516-03558-4*) Scholastic Library Publishing. (Children's Pr.).

Soto, Gary. The Old Man & His Door. 1996. (Illus.). 32p. (J). (ps-3). 15.99 o.p. (*0-399-22700-8*, G. P. Putnam's Sons) Penguin Group (USA) Inc.

Stark, Ulf. Can You Whistle, Johanna? A Boy's Search for a Grandfather. Segerberg, Ebba, tr. from SWE. 1999. (Illus.). 47p. (J). (gr. 2-5). 16.95 (*1-57143-057-1*, Wetlands Pr.) RDR Bks.

Stevens, Diane. Liza's Star Wish. 1997. (Illus.). 320p. (YA). (gr. 5 up). 15.00 o.s.i (*0-688-15310-0*, Greenwillow Bks.) HarperCollins Children's Bk. Group.

Stobbs, William. I Know an Old Lady Who Swallowed a Fly. 1987. (Illus.). 26p. (J). (ps-1). 15.00 o.p. (*0-19-279837-5*) Oxford Univ. Pr., Inc.

Sullivan, Silky. Grandpa Was a Cowboy. 1996. (Illus.). 32p. (J). (ps-3). pap. 15.95 (*0-531-09511-8*); lib. bdg. 16.99 (*0-531-08861-8*) Scholastic, Inc. (Orchard Bks.).

Thurston, Dorie. Thank-You for the Thistle. 2001. (Illus.). 36p. (J). (ps-3). pap. 9.95 (*0-9703326-0-2*) Dorie Bks.

Van Trease, Alice. The Rabbit in the Moon: A Garden Tale for the Young & the Young at Heart. 1996. (Illus.). 80p. (J). (gr. k-8). pap. 12.00 (*0-9651578-0-6*) Pele Publishing.

Waggoner, Karen. Lemonade Babysitter. 1992. (J). (ps-3). 14.95 o.p. (*0-316-91711-7*, Joy Street Bks.) Little Brown & Co.

Wakeman, Cheryl A. Johnnie Ollie Carri III & His Friend. 1985. (Illus.). 32p. (J). (ps-3). 5.95 (*0-9614819-0-0*) Moen, R.E.

White, Linda. Too Many Pumpkins. 1996. (Illus.). 32p. (J). (ps-3). reprint ed. pap. 6.95 (*0-8234-1320-9*) Holiday Hse., Inc.

Winch, John. Old Man Who Loved to Sing. 1998. mass mkt. 5.99 (*0-590-22641-X*) Scholastic, Inc.

—The Old Woman Who Loved to Read. 1997. (Illus.). (J). (ps-3). pap. 6.95 (*0-8234-1348-9*) Holiday Hse., Inc.

Wisenfeld, Vicki. Old Man & the Tree. 2003. (Illus.). 32p. (J). (ps-3). 17.95 o.p. (*0-7459-4231-8*) Lion Publishing PLC GBR. *Dist:* Trafalgar Square.

Ziefert, Harriet. This Old Man. 1995. (Illus.). (J). 8.95 (*0-689-80054-1*, Little Simon) Simon & Schuster Children's Publishing.

B

BROTHERS AND SISTERS—FICTION

Aarrestad, Thomas. The Potter Giselle. 2001. (Illus.). (J). (ps-3). 14.95 (*0-8249-5403-3*) Ideals Pubns.

Abish, Walter. How German Is It=Wie Deutsch Ist Es. 1980. 256p. pap. 10.95 (*0-8112-0776-5*, NDP508); 14.95 o.p. (*0-8112-0775-7*) New Directions Publishing Corp.

Acker, Rick. The Case of the Autumn Rose. 2003. (Davis Detective Mysteries Ser.). 204p. (J). pap. 6.99 (*0-8254-2004-0*) Kregel Pubns.

Adams, Edward B., ed. Two Brothers & Their Magic Gourds. 1981. (Korean Folk Story for Children Ser.). (Illus.). 32p. (J). (gr. 3). 10.95 (*0-8048-1474-0*) Seoul International Tourist Publishing Co. KOR. *Dist:* Tuttle Publishing.

Adams, Michelle Medlock. Sister for Sale. 2004. (Illus.). 28p. (J). pap. 4.99 (*0-310-70820-6*); 2002. 32p. 7.99 (*0-310-70254-2*) Zondervan.

Adler, C. S. The Courtyard Cat. 1995. 128p. (J). 13.95 o.s.i (*0-395-71126-6*, Clarion Bks.) Houghton Mifflin Co. Trade & Reference Div.

—Get Lost, Little Brother. 1983. 144p. (J). (gr. 4-7). 11.95 o.p. (*0-89919-154-1*, Clarion Bks.) Houghton Mifflin Co. Trade & Reference Div.

—In Our House Scott Is My Brother. 1982. (gr. 5 up). pap. 1.95 o.p. (*0-553-20910-8*) Bantam Bks.

—In Our House Scott Is My Brother. 1980. 144p. (J). (gr. 5-9). lib. bdg. 13.95 o.p. (*0-02-700140-7*, Simon & Schuster Children's Publishing) Simon & Schuster Children's Publishing.

—Tuna Fish Thanksgiving. 1992. 160p. (J). (gr. 5-9). 13.95 o.p. (*0-395-58829-4*, Clarion Bks.) Houghton Mifflin Co. Trade & Reference Div.

—Youn Hee & Me. 1995. 192p. (YA). (gr. 3-7). 12.00 o.s.i (*0-15-200073-9*) Harcourt Children's Bks.

Adler, David A. Andy & Tamika. 1999. (Andy Russell Ser.). (Illus.). 144p. (YA). (gr. 2-5). 14.00 (*0-15-201735-6*, Gulliver Bks.) Harcourt Children's Bks.

Adler, Katie & McBride, Rachael. For Sale: One Sister—Cheap! 1986. (Childhood Fantasies & Fears Ser.). (Illus.). 32p. (J). (ps-2). mass mkt. 3.95 o.p. (*0-516-43476-4*); lib. bdg. 14.60 o.p. (*0-516-03476-6*) Scholastic Library Publishing. (Children's Pr.).

Adoff, Arnold. Big Sister Tells Me That I'm Black. ERS. 1976. (Illus.). 32p. (J). (gr. k-4). o.p. (*0-03-014546-5*, Holt, Henry & Co. Bks. For Young Readers) Holt, Henry & Co.

Ahlberg, Allan. My Brother's Ghost. 2001. 87p. (J). (gr. 6 up). 9.99 o.s.i (*0-670-89290-4*, Viking Children's Bks.) Penguin Putnam Bks. for Young Readers.

Albee, Sarah. My Baby Brother Is a Little Monster. 2001. (Jellybean Bks.). (Illus.). 32p. (J). (ps-k). 3.99 (*0-375-81148-6*, Random Hse. Bks. for Young Readers) Random Hse. Children's Bks.

Alcock, Deborah. The Spanish Brothers. 2001. (Reformation Trail Ser.). (Illus.). 326p. (YA). pap. 12.90 (*1-894666-02-X*) Inheritance Pubns.

Alcock, Vivien. The Cuckoo Sister. l.t. ed. 1987. 256p. (J). (gr. 3-7). 16.95 o.p. (*0-7451-0586-6*, Galaxy Children's Large Print) BBC Audiobooks America.

—The Cuckoo Sister. 1986. 158p. (J). (gr. 4-6). 14.95 o.s.i (*0-385-29467-0*, Delacorte Pr.) Dell Publishing.

—The Cuckoo Sister. 1997. 240p. (YA). (gr. 7-7). pap. 4.95 (*0-395-81651-3*) Houghton Mifflin Co.

Alcott, Louisa May. Les Quatre Filles du Docteur March. 1993. (Folio - Junior Ser.: No. 413). Tr. of Little Women. (FRE., Illus.). (J). (gr. 5-10). 10.95 (*2-07-033413-9*) Schoenhof's Foreign Bks., Inc.

Aldridge, Melanie. Paula's Feeling Angry. rev. ed. 1979. (Values to Live By Ser.). (Illus.). (J). (ps-3). lib. bdg. 4.95 o.p. (*0-89565-076-2*) Child's World, Inc.

Alexander, Martha. Good Night, Lily. 1993. (Illus.). 14p. (J). (ps). bds. 4.95 o.p. (*1-56402-164-5*) Candlewick Pr.

—I'll Be the Horse If You'll Play with Me. 1975. (Illus.). (J). (ps-2). 32p. 5.95 o.p. (*0-8037-5458-2*, 0869-260); 32p. 5.47 o.p. (*0-8037-5511-2*); 1.95 o.p. (*0-8037-5459-0*) Penguin Putnam Bks. for Young Readers. (Dial Bks. for Young Readers).

—Lily & Willy. 1993. (Illus.). 14p. (J). (ps). bds. 0.05 o.p. (*1-56402-163-7*) Candlewick Pr.

—Nobody Asked Me If I Wanted a Baby Sister. 1971. (Pied Piper Bks.). (Illus.). (J). (ps-2). 10.95 o.p. (*0-8037-6401-4*); 10.89 o.p. (*0-8037-6402-2*) Penguin Putnam Bks. for Young Readers. (Dial Bks. for Young Readers).

—Where's Willy? 1993. (Illus.). 14p. (J). (ps). bds. 4.95 o.p. (*1-56402-161-0*) Candlewick Pr.

—Willy's Boot. 1993. (Illus.). 14p. (J). (ps). bds. 4.95 o.p. (*1-56402-162-9*) Candlewick Pr.

Aliki. Jack & Jake. 1986. (Illus.). 32p. (J). (ps-1). 12.95 o.p. (*0-688-06099-4*); lib. bdg. 12.88 o.p. (*0-688-06100-1*) HarperCollins Children's Bk. Group. (Greenwillow Bks.).

Allen, Eric. The Latchkey Children. 1987. (Illus.). 158p. (J). 8.95 o.p. (*0-19-277111-6*) Oxford Univ. Pr., Inc.

Allen, Pamela. I Wish I Had a Pirate Suit. 1993. (Illus.). 32p. (J). (gr. 4 up). pap. 3.99 o.s.i (*0-14-050988-7*, Puffin Bks.) Penguin Putnam Bks. for Young Readers.

Alpert, Lou. Max & the Great Blueness. 1993. (Illus.). 32p. (J). (ps-3). 13.95 (*1-879085-38-0*, Whispering Coyote) Charlesbridge Publishing, Inc.

Amato, Mary. The Riot Brothers. Long, Ethan, tr. & illus. by. 2003. (J). (*0-8234-1750-6*) Holiday Hse., Inc.

Ames, Mildred. The Dancing Madness: A Novel. 1980. 144p. (J). (gr. 7 up). 8.95 o.s.i (*0-385-28113-7*, Delacorte Pr.) Dell Publishing.

Andersen, C. B. The Book of Mormon Sleuth Vol. 3: The Hidden Path. 2003. ix, 214p. (J). pap. (*1-57008-988-4*) Deseret Bk. Co.

Anderson, Bendix. Quetzal & the Cool School. 2000. (Dragon Tales Ser.). (Illus.). 24p. (J). (ps-k). pap. 3.25 o.p. (*0-375-80634-2*, Random Hse. Bks. for Young Readers) Random Hse. Children's Bks.

Anderson, Launi K. Gracie's Angel. Utley, Jennifer, ed. 1996. (Latter-Day Daughters Ser.). (Illus.). 80p. (J). (gr. 3-9). pap. 4.95 (*1-56236-508-8*) Aspen Bks.

—Sadie's Trade. 1998. (Latter-Day Daughters Ser.). (J). o.p. (*1-57345-415-X*) Deseret Bk. Co.

Anderson, Myra. A Tail of a Different Color. 1992. (Illus.). 32p. (J). (gr. k-4). 13.95 o.p. (*0-9625620-3-3*) DOT Garnet.

Andres, Katherine. Humphrey & Ralph. 1994. (Illus.). (J). 14.00 o.p. (*0-671-88129-9*, Simon & Schuster Children's Publishing) Simon & Schuster Children's Publishing.

Angell, Judie. A Home Is to Share... & Share... & Share. 1984. 112p. (J). (gr. 4-6). lib. bdg. 13.95 o.s.i (*0-02-705830-1*, Simon & Schuster Children's Publishing) Simon & Schuster Children's Publishing.

Anholt, Catherine & Anholt, Laurence. Come Back, Jack! (Illus.). 32p. (J). (ps up). 1996. bds. 5.99 o.p. (*1-56402-686-8*); 1994. 13.95 o.p. (*1-56402-313-3*) Candlewick Pr.

—Sophie & the New Baby. 2000. (Concept Book Ser.). (Illus.). 32p. (J). (ps-k). lib. bdg. 15.95 (*0-8075-7550-X*) Whitman, Albert & Co.

Anno, Mitsumasa. All in a Day. 1999. 13.14 (*0-606-16797-8*) Turtleback Bks.

Anno, Mitsumasa, ed. All in a Day. 1999. (Illus.). 24p. (J). (ps-3). pap. 6.99 (*0-698-11772-7*, PaperStar) Penguin Putnam Bks. for Young Readers.

Anno, Mitsumasa, et al. All in a Day. 1986. (Illus.). 32p. (YA). (ps up). 15.89 o.s.i (*0-399-61292-0*, Philomel) Penguin Putnam Bks. for Young Readers.

Antle, Nancy. Touch Choices: A Story of the Vietnam War. 1993. (Once upon America Ser.). (Illus.). 64p. (J). (gr. 2-6). 12.99 o.p. (*0-670-84879-4*, Viking Children's Bks.) Penguin Putnam Bks. for Young Readers.

Apperley, Dawn. Flip & Flop. 2001. (Illus.). 32p. (J). (ps-k). pap. 12.95 (*0-439-28892-4*, Orchard Bks.) Scholastic, Inc.

Applegate, K. A. My Sister's Boyfriend. 1992. (Changes Romance Ser.: No. 9). 240p. (YA). mass mkt. 3.50 o.p. (*0-06-106717-2*, HarperTorch) Morrow/Avon.

Ardagh, Philip. The Fall of Fergal, or, Not So Dingly in the Dell. Roberts, David, tr. & illus. by. 2004. (J). 9.95 (*0-8050-7476-7*, Holt, Henry & Co. Bks. For Young Readers) Holt, Henry & Co.

Armstrong, Jennifer. That Terrible Baby. 1994. (Illus.). 32p. (J). 14.00 o.p. (*0-688-11832-1*); lib. bdg. 13.93 o.p. (*0-688-11833-X*) Morrow/Avon. (Morrow, William & Co.).

Armstrong, Robb. Drew & the Bub Daddy Showdown. 1996. (Trophy Chapter Bks.). (Illus.). (J). (gr. 2-5). 64p. pap. 4.25 o.p. (*0-06-442030-2*, Harper Trophy); 96p. lib. bdg. 13.89 o.p. (*0-06-027275-9*) HarperCollins Children's Bk. Group.

—Drew & the Bub Daddy Showdown. 1996. 9.15 o.p. (*0-606-09217-X*) Turtleback Bks.

Arnaud, Rayne. Getaway. (J). E-Book (*1-84045-034-7*) Online Originals.

Arnold, Marsha Diane. Edward G. & the Beautiful Pink Hairbow. 2002. (Road to Reading Ser.). (Illus.). 48p. (J). (gr. 1-3). 11.99 (*0-307-46337-0*); pap. 3.99 (*0-307-26337-1*) Random Hse. Children's Bks. (Golden Bks.).

Arnold, Tedd. More Parts. 32p. 2003. pap. 5.99 (*0-14-250149-2*, Puffin Bks.); 2001. (Illus.). (J). 15.99 (*0-8037-1417-3*, Dial Bks. for Young Readers) Penguin Putnam Bks. for Young Readers.

Arnosky, Jim. Little Champ. 1995. (Illus.). 69p. (J). (ps-3). 13.95 o.s.i (*0-399-22759-8*, G. P. Putnam's Sons) Penguin Group (USA) Inc.

Arnosky, Jim, illus. Little Champ. 2001. (J). pap. 6.95 (*0-9657144-5-4*) Onion River Pr.

Arthur, Catherine. My Sister's Silent World. 1979. (Social Values Ser.). (Illus.). 32p. (J). (gr. 3). pap. 3.95 o.p. (*0-516-42022-4*); lib. bdg. 13.27 o.p. (*0-516-02022-6*) Scholastic Library Publishing. (Children's Pr.).

Asch, Frank & Vagin, Vladimir. Dear Brother. 1992. 32p. (J). (gr. 1-4). pap. 13.95 (*0-590-43107-2*) Scholastic, Inc.

Ash, Russell. Henry & Caroline at Home. 1991. (Illus.). 32p. (J). (gr. 2-4). 17.95 o.p. (*1-85145-358-X*) Pavilion Bks., Ltd. GBR. *Dist:* Trafalgar Square.

Atkins, Jeannine. Dessert First. 1997. (Illus.). (J). 16.00 (*0-689-80345-1*, Atheneum) Simon & Schuster Children's Publishing.

Auch, Mary Jane. Pick of the Litter. 1988. 160p. (J). (gr. 3-7). 14.95 o.p. (*0-8234-0692-X*) Holiday Hse., Inc.

—The Road to Home, ERS. 2000. 224p. (YA). (gr. 5-8). 16.95 (*0-8050-4921-5*, Holt, Henry & Co. Bks. For Young Readers) Holt, Henry & Co.

—The Road to Home. 2002. 224p. (gr. 5). pap. text 4.99 (*0-440-41805-4*, Random Hse. Bks. for Young Readers) Random Hse. Children's Bks.

Aver, Kate. Joey's Way. 1992. (Illus.). 48p. (J). (gr. 1-4). 13.95 o.s.i (*0-689-50552-3*, McElderry, Margaret K.) Simon & Schuster Children's Publishing.

Avery, Gillian. Maria Escapes. 1992. (Illus.). 272p. (J). (gr. 4-8). pap. 15.00 (*0-671-77074-8*, Simon & Schuster Children's Publishing) Simon & Schuster Children's Publishing.

—To Tame a Sister. 1973. (Illus.). 256p. (J). (gr. 4-6). 5.95 o.p. (*0-670-71777-0*) Viking Penguin.

Axelsen, Stephen & Axelsen, Jenny. Little Sisters. 1993. (Voyages Ser.). (Illus.). (J). 4.25 (*0-383-03637-2*) SRA/McGraw-Hill.

Bacon, Katharine J. Pip & Emma. 1986. 128p. (J). (gr. 4-7). 11.95 o.s.i (*0-689-50385-7*, McElderry, Margaret K.) Simon & Schuster Children's Publishing.

Baczewski, Paul C. Just for Kicks. 1990. 192p. (gr. 6 up). (J). 13.95 (*0-397-32465-0*); (YA). lib. bdg. 14.89 o.p. (*0-397-32466-9*) HarperCollins Children's Bk. Group.

Baer, Judy. Never Too Late. 1993. (Cedar River Daydreams Ser.: No. 19). 128p. (Orig.). (YA). (gr. 7-10). mass mkt. 4.99 o.p. (*1-55661-329-6*) Bethany Hse. Pubs.

Bradman, Tony. Billy & the Baby. 1992. (J). (ps-3). 11.95 o.p. (*0-8120-6328-7*); pap. 5.95 o.p. (*0-8120-1387-5*) Barron's Educational Series, Inc.

—The Bluebeards: Peril at the Pirate School. 1990. (Arch Bks.). (Illus.). 64p. (J). (gr. 2-5). pap. 2.95 o.p. (*0-8120-4502-5*) Barron's Educational Series, Inc.

Brandenberg, Franz. I Wish I Was Sick, Too! 1976. (Illus.). 32p. (J). (gr. k-3). 8.25 o.p. (*0-688-80047-5*); lib. bdg. 15.93 o.p. (*0-688-84047-7*) HarperCollins Children's Bk. Group. (Greenwillow Bks.).

—I Wish I Was Sick, Too! 1990. (Illus.). 32p. (J). (ps up). reprint ed. pap. 3.95 o.p. (*0-688-09354-X*, Morrow, William & Co.) Morrow/Avon.

—I Wish I Was Sick, Too! 1978. (Illus.). (J). (ps-3). pap. 3.95 o.p. (*0-14-050292-0*, Puffin Bks.) Penguin Putnam Bks. for Young Readers.

Bravo, E. G. Alexandria the Great! The Magical Story of Adopting a Sister Through the Eyes of Her Brother. 2000. (Illus.). 17p. (J). (ps-3). E-Book 6.95 (*0-9704384-0-0*); E-Book 6.95 (*0-9704384-1-9*) Zander eBooks.

Breathed, Berkeley. Edwurd Fudwupper Fibbed Big. 2000. (Illus.). 48p. (J). (ps-3). 15.95 (*0-316-10675-5*) Little Brown & Co.

—Edwurd Fudwupper Fibbed Big. 2003. (Illus.). 40p. (J). (gr. 1-3). pap. 6.99 (*0-316-14425-8*) Little Brown Children's Bks.

—Edwurd Fudwupper Fibbed Big: Scholastic Edition. 2000. (J). pap. 15.95 (*0-316-14291-3*) Little Brown & Co.

Breaux, Shane. Sudden Turn, Vol. 1. 2002. (Rollercoaster Tycoon Ser.). 128p. (J). mass mkt. 4.99 (*0-448-42863-6*, Grosset & Dunlap) Penguin Putnam Bks. for Young Readers.

Brenneman, Tim. Jimmie Boogie Learns about Smoking. LaFlamme, Nicole & Davidson, Don, eds. 2000. (Illus.). 12p. (J). (gr. k-7). pap. text 5.99 o.p. (*0-9700453-0-1*) Grand Unification Pr., Inc.

—Jimmie Boogie Learns about Smoking. Hedrick, Bonnie & Canning, Robert, eds. 3rd ed. 2002. 12p. (J). 5.99 (*0-9700453-2-8*) Grand Unification Pr., Inc.

Brenner, Barbara. Rosa & Marco & the Three Wishes. 1992. (Illus.). 32p. (J). (gr. 1-3). lib. bdg. 12.95 o.p. (*0-02-712315-4*, Simon & Schuster Children's Publishing) Simon & Schuster Children's Publishing.

Breslin, Paul. The Grandpa Stories. 1996. (Orig.). (J). (gr. 3-6). pap. 6.95 o.p. (*0-533-12048-9*) Vantage Pr., Inc.

Bridwell, Norman. A Tiny Family. 1999. (Hello Reader! Ser.). 32p. (J). (ps-1). mass mkt. 3.99 (*0-439-04019-1*) Scholastic, Inc.

Brink, Carol R. Caddie Woodlawn. l.t. ed. 1988. (YA). (gr. 5 up). reprint ed. lib. bdg. 16.95 o.s.i (*1-55736-043-X*, Cornerstone Bks.) Pages, Inc.

—Caddie Woodlawn. (J). 9999. pap. 2.50 o.s.i (*0-590-10121-8*); 1997. (Illus.). 16p. mass mkt. 3.95 (*0-590-37359-5*) Scholastic, Inc.

—Caddie Woodlawn. 1990. (Illus.). 288p. (J). (gr. 3-7). pap. 5.99 (*0-689-71370-3*, Aladdin); 1973. (Illus.). 288p. (J). (gr. 3-7). 17.00 (*0-02-713670-1*, Simon & Schuster Children's Publishing); 2nd ed. 1997. 288p. (YA). (gr. 3-7). mass mkt. 5.50 (*0-689-81521-2*, Simon Pulse); Vol. 1. 1999. pap. 2.99 (*0-689-82969-8*, Aladdin) Simon & Schuster Children's Publishing.

—Caddie Woodlawn. 1970. (J). 11.04 (*0-606-02490-5*) Turtleback Bks.

—Magical Melons. 1990. (Illus.). 208p. (J). (gr. 4-7). reprint ed. pap. 4.99 (*0-689-71416-5*, Aladdin) Simon & Schuster Children's Publishing.

—Magical Melons. 1990. (J). 10.00 (*0-606-04473-6*) Turtleback Bks.

Brisson, Pat. Your Best Friend, Kate. 1992. (Illus.). 40p. (J). (gr. 1-7). reprint ed. pap. 4.50 o.p. (*0-689-71545-5*, Aladdin) Simon & Schuster Children's Publishing.

Broach, Elise. What the No-Good Baby Is Good For. Carter, Abby, tr. & illus. by. 2005. (J). (*0-399-23877-8*, G. P. Putnam's Sons) Penguin Putnam Bks. for Young Readers.

Brooks, Bruce. The Dolores Stories: Seven Stories about Her. 2002. 144p. (J). (gr. 5 up). 15.95 (*0-06-027818-8*); lib. bdg. 15.89 (*0-06-029473-6*) HarperCollins Children's Bk. Group.

Brouwer, Sigmund. Bad Bug Blues. 2002. (Watch Out for Joel Ser.). (Illus.). 32p. (J). (gr. 1-3). pap. 3.99 (*0-7642-2580-4*) Bethany Hse. Pubs.

Brown, Alan. I Am a Dog. 2002. 28p. (J). pap. 7.95 (*1-929132-37-9*) Kane/Miller Bk. Pubs.

Brown, Jeff. Invisible Stanley. (Stanley Lambchop Adventure Ser.). (Illus.). 96p. (J). 2003. pap. 4.99 (*0-06-009792-2*); 1996. (gr. 2-5). pap. 4.25 (*0-06-442029-9*, Harper Trophy) HarperCollins Children's Bk. Group.

—Invisible Stanley. 1996. 10.40 (*0-606-09475-X*) Turtleback Bks.

Brown, Laurene Krasny. Rex & Lilly Family Time. (Rex & Lilly Ser.). (Illus.). 32p. (J). (ps-1). 1997. pap. 3.95 o.p. (*0-316-11109-0*); 1995. 12.95 o.p. (*0-316-11385-9*) Little Brown & Co.

—Rex & Lilly Playtime. 1997. (Rex & Lilly Ser.). (Illus.). 32p. (J). (ps-1). pap. 3.95 (*0-316-11110-4*) Little Brown & Co.

—Rex & Lilly Schooltime. 1997. (Rex & Lilly Ser.). (Illus.). 32p. (J). (ps-1). 13.95 o.p. (*0-316-10920-7*) Little Brown & Co.

Brown, Marc. Arthur Breaks the Bank. 2005. (J). (*0-375-81002-1*); lib. bdg. (*0-375-91002-6*) Random Hse., Inc.

—Arthur's Back-to-School Surprise. 2002. (Illus.). 24p. (J). pap. 3.99 (*0-375-81000-5*); lib. bdg. 11.99 (*0-375-91000-X*) Random Hse., Inc.

—Arthur's First Kiss. 2001. (Step into Reading Sticker Bks.). (Illus.). 24p. (J). (ps-3). pap. 3.99 (*0-375-80602-4*); lib. bdg. 11.99 (*0-375-90602-9*) Random Hse. Children's Bks. (Random Hse. Bks. for Young Readers).

—Arthur's Messy Room. 1999. (Step into Reading Ser.). (Illus.). 24p. (J). (ps-3). pap. 3.99 (*0-679-88467-X*) Random Hse., Inc.

—Arthur's Reading Race. 1996. (Step into Reading Sticker Bks.). 24p. (J). (ps-3). lib. bdg. 11.99 (*0-679-96738-9*, Random Hse. Bks. for Young Readers) Random Hse. Children's Bks.

—Arthur's Reading Race. 1996. (Step into Reading Sticker Bks.). (Illus.). (J). (ps-3). 24p. pap. 3.99 (*0-679-86738-4*); o.p. (*0-679-88042-9*); lib. bdg. o.p. (*0-679-98042-3*) Random Hse., Inc.

—Arthur's TV Trouble. 2002. (Arthur Picture Bks.). (Illus.). (J). 13.15 (*0-7587-1990-6*) Book Wholesalers, Inc.

—Arthur's TV Trouble. (Arthur Adventure Ser.). (J). (gr. k-3). 1999. (Illus.). 32p. 9.95 incl. audio (*0-316-11594-0*); 1997. (Illus.). 32p. reprint ed. pap. 5.95 (*0-316-11047-7*); 1997. pap. 5.95 (*0-316-11959-8*) Little Brown Children's Bks.

—Arthur's TV Trouble. 1997. (Arthur Adventure Ser.). (J). (gr. k-3). 12.10 (*0-606-12620-1*) Turtleback Bks.

—D. W. Rides Again! 1993. (D. W. Ser.). (Illus.). 24p. (J). (gr. k-2). 15.95 (*0-316-11356-5*) Little Brown Children's Bks.

—D. W. Thinks Big. 1998. (D. W. Ser.). (Illus.). 52p. (J). (gr. k-2). 5.95 (*0-316-11112-0*) Little Brown Children's Bks.

—Glasses for D. W. 1996. (Step into Reading Sticker Bks.). (Illus.). (J). (ps-3). 24p. pap. 3.99 (*0-679-86740-6*); o.p. (*0-679-98043-1*) Random Hse., Inc.

—Rex & Lilly Schooltime: A Dino Easy Reader. 2001. (Illus.). 32p. (J). (gr. k-1). pap. 4.95 (*0-316-13535-6*) Little Brown Children's Bks.

Brown, Marc & Sarfatti, Esther. D.W. y el Carne de Biblioteca. 2003. (ENG & SPA., Illus.). (J). pap. 6.95 (*1-930332-47-5*) Lectorum Pubns., Inc.

Brown, Marc, et al. Arthur's TV Trouble. 1995. (Arthur Adventure Ser.). (Illus.). 32p. (J). (gr. k-3). 16.95 (*0-316-10919-3*) Little Brown Children's Bks.

Brown, Margery W. Baby Jesus Like My Brother. 1995. (Illus.). 32p. (J). (ps-3). 15.95 (*0-940975-53-X*); pap. 7.95 (*0-940975-54-8*) Just Us Bks., Inc.

—Baby Jesus Like My Brother. 1995. (J). 13.20 o.p. (*0-606-09028-2*) Turtleback Bks.

—Baby Jesus Like My Brother. (Illus.). 2001. (J). E-Book (*1-59019-146-3*); 1995. E-Book 5.99 (*1-59019-148-X*); 1995. E-Book (*1-59019-147-1*) ipicturebooks, LLC.

Brown, Ruth. Cry Baby. 1997. 32p. (J). (ps-1). 15.99 o.s.i (*0-525-45902-2*) Penguin Putnam Bks. for Young Readers.

Bryant, Jennifer. Into Enchanted Woods. 2001. (Winterthur Book for Children Ser.). (Illus.). (J). (*0-912724-59-5*) Winterthur, Henry Francis duPont Museum, Inc.

Buchen, Kathryn. Rainmaker. 1995. 153p. (Orig.). (J). pap. 7.50 (*0-9645405-0-9*) Beson, Kathryn.

Buck, Nola. Hey, Little Baby! 1999. (Growing Tree Ser.). (Illus.). 24p. (J). (ps up). 9.95 (*0-694-01200-9*, Harper Festival) HarperCollins Children's Bk. Group.

Buckley, Helen E. Take Care of Things, Edward Said. 1991. (Illus.). 32p. (J). (ps up). 13.95 o.p. (*0-688-07731-5*); lib. bdg. 13.88 o.p. (*0-688-07732-3*) HarperCollins Children's Bk. Group.

Budnick, Leslie. It Takes Two. 2002. 24p. (J). pap. 3.25 (*0-375-81604-6*) Random Hse., Inc.

Bulla, Clyde Robert. The Christmas Coat. 1990. (Illus.). 48p. (J). (gr. 2-4). 13.95 o.s.i (*0-394-89385-9*); 14.99 o.s.i (*0-394-99385-3*) Random Hse. Children's Bks. (Knopf Bks. for Young Readers).

—Keep Running, Allen! (J). 1985. 8.95 o.p. (*0-690-01374-4*); 1978. (Illus.). lib. bdg. 14.89 o.p. (*0-690-01375-2*) HarperCollins Children's Bk. Group.

Bulla, Dale. My Brother's a Pain in the Back Seat. 1995. (Illus.). 28p. (J). (gr. 2-6). 16.95 (*1-884197-05-1*); pap. 7.95 (*1-884197-06-X*) New Horizon Educational Services Pr.

Bunting, Eve. Twinnies. 1997. (Illus.). 32p. (J). (gr. 1-5). 15.00 (*0-15-291592-3*) Harcourt Children's Bks.

—Your Move. 1998. (Illus.). 32p. (J). (gr. 1-5). 16.00 (*0-15-200181-6*) Harcourt Children's Bks.

Burgess, Barbara H. Oren Bell. 192p. (J). (ps-3). 1992. pap. 3.50 o.s.i (*0-440-40747-8*); 1991. 15.00 o.s.i (*0-385-30325-4*, Delacorte Pr.) Dell Publishing.

Burgess, Melvin. The Earth Giant. 1997. 160p. (J). (gr. 3-7). 15.95 o.s.i (*0-399-23187-0*, G. P. Putnam's Sons) Penguin Group (USA) Inc.

Burkett, Larry, et al. What If I Owned Everything? 1997. (Illus.). 32p. (ps-3). 12.99 o.s.i (*0-8499-1509-0*) Nelson, Tommy.

Burnett, Frances Hodgson. The Pretty Sister of Jose. 2000. 252p. (J). E-Book 3.95 (*0-594-04833-8*) 1873 Pr.

Burningham, John. The Baby. 2nd ed. 1994. (Illus.). 24p. (J). (ps). 6.95 o.p. (*1-56402-334-6*) Candlewick Pr.

—The Baby. 1975. (J). 3.95 (*0-690-00900-3*); (Illus.). lib. bdg. 11.89 o.p. (*0-690-00901-1*) HarperCollins Children's Bk. Group.

Busby, Cylin. Chicken-Fried Rat: Tales Too Gross to Be True. 1998. (Illus.). 112p. (J). (gr. 3-7). pap. 4.95 o.p. (*0-06-440701-2*) HarperCollins Pubs.

Butler, Beverly. My Sister's Keeper. 224p. (YA). (gr. 7-11). 1985. 3.95 o.p. (*0-396-08744-2*); 1980. 8.95 o.p. (*0-396-07803-6*) Penguin Putnam Bks. for Young Readers. (G. P. Putnam's Sons).

Butler, Charles. Timon's Tide. 2000. (Illus.). 192p. (YA). (gr. 7-12). 16.00 (*0-689-82593-5*, McElderry, Margaret K.) Simon & Schuster Children's Publishing.

Byars, Betsy C. Bingo Brown, Gypsy Lover. l.t. ed. 1992. 152p. (J). (gr. 1-8). 13.95 o.p. (*0-7451-1499-7*, Galaxy Children's Large Print) BBC Audiobooks America.

—Bingo Brown, Gypsy Lover. (Bingo Brown Ser.). (J). 1992. (Illus.). 128p. (gr. 4-7). pap. 4.99 (*0-14-034518-3*, Puffin Bks.); 1990. 160p. (gr. 3 up). 12.95 o.s.i (*0-670-83322-3*, Viking Children's Bks.) Penguin Putnam Bks. for Young Readers.

—Go & Hush the Baby. unabr. ed. 1974. (J). pap. o.p. incl. audio (*0-670-05083-0*) Live Oak Media.

—Go & Hush the Baby. (Illus.). (J). (ps-3). 1982. 32p. pap. 4.99 o.s.i (*0-14-050396-X*, Puffin Bks.); 1971. 11.95 o.p. (*0-670-34270-X*, Viking Children's Bks.) Penguin Putnam Bks. for Young Readers.

—The Joy Boys. (Illus.). (J). 1996. 48p. (gr. 1-3). pap. 3.99 o.s.i (*0-440-41094-0*); 1995. o.p. (*0-440-41097-5*) Random Hse. Children's Bks. (Yearling).

—My Brother, Ant. (Easy-to-Read Ser.). (Illus.). 32p. (J). 1998. (gr. 1-4). pap. 3.99 (*0-14-038345-X*); 1996. (gr. k-3). 13.99 (*0-670-86664-4*, Viking Children's Bks.) Penguin Putnam Bks. for Young Readers.

—The Night Swimmers. 1981. 144p. (J). (gr. 5-9). mass mkt. 2.75 o.s.i (*0-440-96766-X*, Laurel) Dell Publishing.

—The Not-Just-Anybody Family. l.t. ed. 1988. 176p. (J). 13.95 o.p. (*0-7451-0756-7*, Galaxy Children's Large Print) BBC Audiobooks America.

—The Not-Just-Anybody Family. 1986. (Illus.). 160p. (J). (gr. 4-6). 13.95 o.s.i (*0-385-29443-3*, Delacorte Pr.) Dell Publishing.

—The Not-Just-Anybody Family. 1987. (J). 10.55 (*0-606-03059-X*) Turtleback Bks.

—The Summer of the Swans. 2002. (Illus.). (J). 13.19 (*0-7587-0217-5*) Book Wholesalers, Inc.

—The Summer of the Swans. l.t. ed. 2000. (LRS Large Print Cornerstone Ser.). (Illus.). 176p. (YA). (gr. 5-12). lib. bdg. 27.95 (*1-58118-060-8*, 23474) LRS.

—The Summer of the Swans. 1978. (J). pap. 1.50 o.p. (*0-380-00098-9*, 50526, Avon Bks.) Morrow/Avon.

—The Summer of the Swans. l.t. ed. 1988. 185p. (J). (gr. 5 up). reprint ed. lib. bdg. 16.95 o.s.i (*1-55736-030-8*, Cornerstone Bks.) Pages, Inc.

—The Summer of the Swans. (Illus.). 144p. 2004. pap. 5.99 (*0-14-240114-5*, Puffin Bks.); 1981. (J). (gr. 4-7). pap. 5.99 (*0-14-031420-2*, Puffin Bks.); 1970. (J). (gr. 4-7). 15.99 (*0-670-68190-3*, Viking Children's Bks.) Penguin Putnam Bks. for Young Readers.

—The Summer of the Swans. 1981. (J). 11.04 (*0-606-01838-7*) Turtleback Bks.

Byrd, Sandra. War Paint. 1998. (Secret Sisters Ser.: Vol. 6). 112p. (gr. 3-7). pap. 4.95 (*1-57856-020-9*) WaterBrook Pr.

Callahan, Thera S. All Wrapped Up. (Rookie Reader Level C Ser.). (Illus.). 31p. (J). 2004. pap. 4.95 (*0-516-21949-9*); 2003. lib. bdg. 19.00 (*0-516-22844-7*) Scholastic Library Publishing. (Children's Pr.).

Callen, Larry. Contrary Imaginations. 1991. (Illus.). 128p. (J). (gr. 6 up). 12.95 o.p. (*0-688-09961-0*, Greenwillow Bks.) HarperCollins Children's Bk. Group.

Calvert, Patricia. Writing to Richie. 1994. 128p. (J). (gr. 4-6). 13.95 (*0-684-19764-2*, Atheneum) Simon & Schuster Children's Publishing.

Cameron, Ann. More Stories Huey Tells, RS. 1997. (Illus.). 128p. (J). (gr. 3-5). 14.00 (*0-374-35065-5*, Farrar, Straus & Giroux (BYR)) Farrar, Straus & Giroux.

—More Stories Huey Tells. 1999. (Illus.). 128p. (J). (gr. k-4). pap. 4.99 (*0-679-88363-0*) Knopf, Alfred A. Inc.

—More Stories Huey Tells. 1998. (J). pap. 4.99 (*0-679-88576-5*, Knopf Bks. for Young Readers) Random Hse. Children's Bks.

—More Stories Huey Tells. 1999. 11.04 (*0-606-16567-3*) Turtleback Bks.

—The Stories Huey Tells. (Illus.). 112p. (J). 1995. (gr. k-4). 17.99 o.s.i (*0-679-96732-X*); 1995. (gr. 3-5). 16.00 o.s.i (*0-679-86732-5*); 1997. (gr. k-4). reprint ed. pap. 4.99 (*0-679-88559-5*) Random Hse. Children's Bks. (Knopf Bks. for Young Readers).

—The Stories Huey Tells. 1997. 11.04 (*0-606-13042-X*) Turtleback Bks.

Cannon, A. E. Shadow Brothers. 1992. mass mkt. 3.99 (*0-440-80328-4*) Bantam Bks.

—Shadow Brothers. 1990. 192p. (J). 14.95 o.s.i (*0-385-29982-6*) Doubleday Publishing.

—Shadow Brothers. 1990. 9.09 (*0-606-00748-2*) Turtleback Bks.

—The Shadow Brothers. 1992. 192p. (YA). (gr. 7 up). mass mkt. 3.99 o.s.i (*0-440-21167-0*) Dell Publishing.

Caple, Kathy. The Coolest Place in Town. 1990. (Illus.). 32p. (J). (gr. k-3). 13.95 o.p. (*0-395-51523-8*) Houghton Mifflin Co.

—The Wimp. (Illus.). 32p. (J). (ps-3). 2000. pap. 5.95 (*0-618-05577-0*); 1994. tchr. ed. 14.95 o.p. (*0-395-63115-7*) Houghton Mifflin Co.

Caraher, Kim. There's a Bat on the Balcony. 1993. (Voyages Ser.). (Illus.). (J). 4.25 (*0-383-03660-7*) SRA/McGraw-Hill.

Carey, Janet Lee. Wenny Has Wings. 2002. 240p. (J). (gr. 4-6). 15.95 (*0-689-84294-5*, Atheneum) Simon & Schuster Children's Publishing.

Carey, Mary. A Place for Allie. 1985. (J). (gr. 3-7). 12.95 o.p. (*0-396-08583-0*, G. P. Putnam's Sons) Penguin Putnam Bks. for Young Readers.

Carlson, Judy. Life with Max. 1989. (Real Reading Ser.: Level Green). 32p. (J). pap. 4.95 o.p. (*0-8114-6727-9*); (Illus.). lib. bdg. 21.40 o.p. (*0-8172-3525-6*) Raintree Pubs.

Carlson, Nancy, tr. & illus. Louanne Pig in the Perfect Family. 2nd rev. ed. 2004. (Nancy Carlson's Neighborhood Ser.). (J). pap. 6.95 (*1-57505-616-X*); lib. bdg. 15.95 (*1-57505-611-9*) Lerner Publishing Group. (Carolrhoda Bks.).

Carlson, Natalie S. A Brother for the Orphelines. 1969. (J). (gr. k-6). pap. 2.75 o.s.i (*0-440-40827-X*, Yearling) Random Hse. Children's Bks.

—The Half Sisters. 1974. (Illus.). (J). (gr. 5 up). pap. 2.95 o.p. (*0-06-440017-4*) HarperCollins Pubs.

Carlstrom, Nancy White. Heather Hiding. 1990. (Illus.). 32p. (J). (ps-1). lib. bdg. 13.95 o.p. (*0-02-717370-4*, Simon & Schuster Children's Publishing) Simon & Schuster Children's Publishing.

—Wishing at Dawn in Summer. 1993. (Illus.). (J). (ps-2). 14.95 o.p. (*0-316-12854-6*) Little Brown & Co.

Carmi, Daniella. Samir & Yonatan. Lotan, Yael, tr. from HEB. 2002. 160p. (J). (gr. 3-7). mass mkt. 4.99 (*0-439-13523-0*, Scholastic Paperbacks) Scholastic, Inc.

—Samir & Yonatan. 2000. (Illus.). 183p. (J). (gr. 3-7). pap. 15.95 (*0-439-13504-4*, Levine, Arthur A. Bks.) Scholastic, Inc.

Carter, Alden R. Big Brother Dustin. 1997. (Illus.). 32p. (J). (gr. 1-4). lib. bdg. 14.95 (*0-8075-0715-6*) Whitman, Albert & Co.

Carter, Dorothy. Grandma's General Store: The Ark, RS. 2004. (J). (*0-374-32766-1*, Farrar, Straus & Giroux (BYR)) Farrar, Straus & Giroux.

—Wilhemina Miles: After the Stork Night, RS. 1999. (Illus.). 32p. (J). (gr. k-3). 16.00 o.p. (*0-374-33551-6*, Farrar, Straus & Giroux (BYR)) Farrar, Straus & Giroux.

Casanova, Mary. Curse of a Winter Moon. 2000. 137p. (J). 15.99 (*0-7868-0547-1*); 144p. (YA). lib. bdg. 16.49 (*0-7868-2475-1*) Hyperion Bks. for Children.

—Curse of a Winter Moon. 2002. (Illus.). 144p. (J). pap. 5.99 (*0-7868-1602-3*) Hyperion Paperbacks for Children.

Caseley, Judith. Harry & Arney. 1994. 138p. (J). (ps-3). 14.00 o.s.i (*0-688-12140-3*, Greenwillow Bks.) HarperCollins Children's Bk. Group.

—My Sister Celia. 1986. (Illus.). 32p. (J). (gr. k-3). 12.95 o.p. (*0-688-06483-3*); lib. bdg. 12.88 o.p. (*0-688-06484-1*) HarperCollins Children's Bk. Group. (Greenwillow Bks.).

—Sophie & Sammy's Library Sleepover. 1993. (Illus.). 32p. (J). (ps-3). 16.95 (*0-688-10615-3*); lib. bdg. 15.93 o.p. (*0-688-10616-1*) HarperCollins Children's Bk. Group. (Greenwillow Bks.).

—Witch Mama. 1996. (Illus.). 32p. (J). (ps-3). 15.00 (*0-688-14457-8*); lib. bdg. 14.93 (*0-688-14458-6*) HarperCollins Children's Bk. Group. (Greenwillow Bks.).

Cawley, Rhya N. Pongee Goes to Paris. 1996. (Illus.). 70p. (Orig.). (J). pap. 4.95 (*1-57502-282-6*, PO985) Morris Publishing.

Celsi, Teresa. Fourth Little Pig. 1993. (J). (ps-3). pap. 4.95 (*0-8114-6740-6*) Raintree Pubs.

—Rats!, RS. abr. ed. 1996. (Illus.). 114p. (J). (gr. 4-7). 14.00 o.p. (*0-374-36181-9*, Farrar, Straus & Giroux (BYR)) Farrar, Straus & Giroux.

Cyrkozuch, Alonda. Queenie's Pond: The Barker Brothers Arrive. 1999. 24p. (J). (ps-12). pap. 5.95 (*1-929098-01-4*, 02) Story Teller, The.

Czuchna-Curl, Ardyce. Days of Gold. 2002. (Illus.). 128p. (J). pap. text 12.95 (*0-88196-012-8*) Oak Woods Media.

Dadey, Debbie & Jones, Marcia Thornton. Triplet Trouble & the Bicycle Race. 1997. (Triplet Trouble Ser.: No. 8). (J). (gr. 2-4). 8.70 o.p. (*0-606-12007-6*) Turtleback Bks.

—Triplet Trouble & the Class Trip. 1997. (Triplet Trouble Ser.: No. 7). (J). (gr. 2-4). 10.14 (*0-606-12008-4*) Turtleback Bks.

—Triplet Trouble & the Cookie Contest. 1996. (Triplet Trouble Ser.: No. 5). (J). (gr. 2-4). 8.70 o.p. (*0-606-12009-2*) Turtleback Bks.

—Triplet Trouble & the Field Day Disaster. 1996. (Triplet Trouble Ser.: No. 4). (Illus.). 64p. (J). (gr. 2-4). pap. text 3.99 (*0-590-58107-4*) Scholastic, Inc.

—Triplet Trouble & the Pizza Party. 1996. (Triplet Trouble Ser.: No. 6). (J). (gr. 2-4). 8.70 o.p. (*0-606-12010-6*) Turtleback Bks.

Dale, Penny. Bet You Can't. 1988. (Illus.). 32p. (J). (ps-1). 12.95 (*0-397-32235-6*); lib. bdg. 12.89 (*0-397-32256-9*) HarperCollins Children's Bk. Group.

—Bet You Can't. 1991. 3.99 o.p. (*0-517-07099-5*); 3.99 o.p. (*0-517-07100-2*) Random Hse. Value Publishing.

—Big Brother, Little Brother. 1997. (Illus.). 32p. (J). (ps-2). 15.99 o.p. (*0-7636-0146-2*) Candlewick Pr.

Dale, Penny, illus. Big Brother, Little Brother. 2000. 32p. (J). (ps-2). bds. 5.99 o.p. (*0-7636-1249-9*) Candlewick Pr.

Daly, Kathleen N. Little Sister. 1986. (Big Little Golden Bks.). (Illus.). 24p. (J). (gr. k-3). o.p. (*0-307-10256-4*, Golden Bks.) Random Hse. Children's Bks.

Dana, Martha. No Talk! No Baby! 2001. (Illus.). 48p. (J). (ps-3). pap. 11.95 (*1-880158-31-0*) Townsend, J.N. Publishing.

Daniels, Teri. G-Rex. 2000. (Illus.). 32p. (J). (gr. k-4). pap. 16.95 (*0-531-30243-1*); lib. bdg. 17.99 (*0-531-33243-8*) Scholastic, Inc. (Orchard Bks.).

Dannhauss, Dianne. Big Brother, Big Sister, Big Deal. Bowen, Debbie, ed. 1998. (Professional Mom Ser.). (Illus.). 14p. (J). (gr. 1-4). pap. text 6.95 o.p. (*1-56763-152-5*); lib. bdg. 19.95 (*1-56763-151-7*) Ozark Publishing.

Danziger, Paula. Barfburger Baby, I Was Here First! Karas, G. Brian, tr. & illus. by. 2015. (J). 15.95 (*0-399-23204-4*, G. P. Putnam's Sons) Penguin Putnam Bks. for Young Readers.

David, Lawrence. The Cupcaked Crusader. 2002. (Halloween Ser.). (Illus.). (J). 144p. 14.99 (*0-525-46866-8*); 144p. pap. 4.99 (*0-14-230021-7*, Puffin Bks.);Vol. 1. 96p. (gr. 2-4). 14.99 (*0-525-46763-7*, Dutton Children's Bks.) Penguin Putnam Bks. for Young Readers.

—Terror of the Pink Dodo Balloons. 3rd ed. 2003. (Horace Splattly Ser.: No. 3). (Illus.). 160p. (YA). pap. 4.99 (*0-14-250001-1*, Puffin Bks.) Penguin Putnam Bks. for Young Readers.

—To Catch a Clownosaurus. Gott, Barry, tr. & illus. by. 2003. (J). 160p. 14.99 (*0-525-47154-5*); 144p. pap. 4.99 (*0-14-250135-2*) Penguin Putnam Bks. for Young Readers. (Puffin Bks.).

—When Second Graders Attack. 2nd ed. 2002. (Horace Splattly Ser.). (Illus.). 144p. (YA). pap. 4.99 (*0-14-230118-3*, Puffin Bks.) Penguin Putnam Bks. for Young Readers.

David, Luke. Oh, Brother! 1999. (Rugrats Ser.). (Illus.). 24p. (J). (ps-2). pap. 3.50 (*0-689-82440-8*, 076714003507, Simon Spotlight/Nickelodeon) Simon & Schuster Children's Publishing.

Davies, Gill. Wilbur Waited. 2001. (Growing Pains Ser.). (Illus.). 32p. (J). (ps-1). 12.95 (*0-8069-7843-0*) Sterling Publishing Co., Inc.

Davis, Deborah. My Brother Has AIDS. 1994. 192p. (J). (gr. 4-8). 15.00 (*0-689-31922-3*, Atheneum) Simon & Schuster Children's Publishing.

Davis, Jenny. Anchovy Breath to Zoo Food: One Hundred Seventy-Five Names I Call My Brother When I'm Mad. 1994. (Illus.). 80p. (Orig.). (YA). pap. 3.50 (*0-380-77135-7*, Avon Bks.) Morrow/ Avon.

Davoll, Barbara. Ashley's Yellow Ribbon. 1991. (J). (gr. 4-7). pap. 5.99 o.p. (*0-8024-0815-X*) Moody Pr.

Day, Lara. My Brother & I. 1992. (Foundations Ser.). 15p. (J). (ps). pap. text 4.50 (*1-56843-054-X*) EMG Networks.

—My Brother & I: Big Book. 1992. (Foundations Ser.). 15p. (J). (ps). pap. text 23.00 (*1-56843-004-3*) EMG Networks.

de Paola, Tomie. The Baby Sister. 1996. (Illus.). 32p. (J). (ps-3). 16.99 (*0-399-22908-6*, G. P. Putnam's Sons) Penguin Group (USA) Inc.

—The Baby Sister. 1999. (Illus.). 32p. (J). (ps-3). pap. 5.99 (*0-698-11773-5*, PaperStar) Penguin Putnam Bks. for Young Readers.

—Kit & Kat. 1994. (All Aboard Reading Ser.). (Illus.). 32p. (J). (ps-1). 7.99 o.s.i (*0-448-40749-3*); 3.99 (*0-448-40748-5*) Penguin Putnam Bks. for Young Readers. (Grosset & Dunlap).

—Meet the Barkers: Morgan & Moffat Go to School. 2001. (Illus.). (J). (ps-1). 13.99 (*0-399-23708-9*, G. P. Putnam's Sons) Penguin Group (USA) Inc.

—Meet the Barkers: Morgan & Moffat Go to School. 2003. (Barkers Ser.). 32p. pap. 5.99 (*0-14-250083-6*, Puffin Bks.) Penguin Putnam Bks. for Young Readers.

—A New Barker in the House. 2002. (Illus.). 32p. (J). (ps-3). 13.99 (*0-399-23865-4*) Putnam Publishing Group, The.

De Rolf, Shane. The Cut-Up Sisters. 1998. (*0-679-88451-3*, Random Hse. Bks. for Young Readers) Random Hse. Children's Bks.

De Saint Mars, Dominique. Lily Fights with Her Mother. 1993. (About Me Ser.). (Illus.). 24p. (J). (gr. 2-4). lib. bdg. 12.79 o.p. (*0-89565-980-8*) Child's World, Inc.

—Max Doesn't Like to Read. 1993. (About Me Ser.). (Illus.). 24p. (J). (gr. 2-4). lib. bdg. 12.79 o.p. (*0-89565-979-4*) Child's World, Inc.

Dealey, Erin. Goldie Locks Has Chicken Pox. ed. 2003. spiral bd. (*0-616-14573-X*); (gr. 1). spiral bd. (*0-616-14572-1*) Canadian National Institute for the Blind/Institut National Canadien pour les Aveugles.

—Goldie Locks Has Chicken Pox. 2002. (Illus.). 40p. (J). 16.00 (*0-689-82981-7*, Atheneum) Simon & Schuster Children's Publishing.

Deans, Sis B. Racing the Past, ERS. 2001. (Illus.). 160p. (YA). (gr. 5-10). 15.95 (*0-8050-6635-7*, Holt, Henry & Co. Bks. For Young Readers) Holt, Henry & Co.

Deans, Sis Boulos. Every Day & All the Time, ERS. 2003. 240p. (J). 16.95 (*0-8050-7337-X*, Holt, Henry & Co. Bks. For Young Readers) Holt, Henry & Co.

Deaver, Julie Reece. First Wedding, Once Removed. (Charlotte Zolotow Bk.). 224p. (gr. 5-9). 1993. (YA). pap. 4.95 o.p. (*0-06-440402-1*, Harper Trophy); 1990. (J). 13.95 (*0-06-021426-0*); 1990. (J). lib. bdg. 13.89 o.p. (*0-06-021427-9*) Harper-Collins Children's Bk. Group.

Degen, Bruce. Teddy Bear Towers. 1991. (Illus.). 32p. (J). (ps-1). 14.00 (*0-06-021420-1*); lib. bdg. 13.89 (*0-06-021430-9*) HarperCollins Children's Bk. Group.

DeGroat, Diane. Trick or Treat, Smell My Feet. (Illus.). 32p. (J). (ps-3). 1999. pap. 4.95 (*0-688-17061-7*, Harper Trophy); 1998. 14.95 (*0-688-15766-1*); 1998. 14.95 (*0-688-15766-1*); 1998. 14.89 (*0-688-15767-X*) HarperCollins Children's Bk. Group.

—Trick or Treat, Smell My Feet. 1999. 11.10 (*0-606-17241-6*) Turtleback Bks.

Delace, Lulu. Rafi & Rosi Coqui. 2004. (I Can Read Book 3 Ser.). 64p. (J). lib. bdg. 16.89 (*0-06-009896-1*) HarperCollins Pubs.

Delacre, Lulu. Rafi & Rosi Coqui. 2004. (I Can Read Book 3 Ser.). 64p. (J). 15.99 (*0-06-009895-3*) HarperCollins Pubs.

Delton, Judy. Angel in Charge. (Illus.). (J). (gr. 4-6). 1999. 148p. pap. 4.95 (*0-395-96061-4*); 1985. 160p. tchr. ed. 16.00 (*0-395-37488-X*) Houghton Mifflin Co.

—Angel in Charge. 1990. 160p. (J). (gr. k-6). reprint ed. pap. 2.95 o.s.i (*0-440-40264-6*, Yearling) Random Hse. Children's Bks.

—Angel in Charge. 1999. (Illus.). (J). 11.00 (*0-606-18206-3*) Turtleback Bks.

—Angel's Mother's Baby. 1992. 144p. (J). (gr. 4-7). pap. 3.25 o.s.i (*0-440-40586-6*) Dell Publishing.

Denchfield, Nick. Desmond the Dog. 1998. (Illus.). 20p. (J). (ps). bds. 12.95 o.s.i (*0-15-201340-7*, Red Wagon Bks.) Harcourt Children's Bks.

Denslow, Sharon Phillips. All Their Names Were Courage. 2003. 144p. (J). 15.99 (*0-06-623810-2*); pap. 16.89 (*0-06-623809-9*) HarperCollins Children's Bk. Group. (Greenwillow Bks.).

DeSaix, Deborah D. In the Back Seat, RS. 1993. 32p. (J). (ps-3). 14.00 o.p. (*0-374-33639-3*, Farrar, Straus & Giroux (BYR)) Farrar, Straus & Giroux.

Devlin, Wende & Devlin, Harry. Tales from Cranberryport: A New Baby in Cranberryport. 1994. (Tales from Cranberryport Ser.). (Illus.). 24p. (J). pap. 2.95 o.p. (*0-689-71780-6*, Little Simon) Simon & Schuster Children's Publishing.

Dewan, Ted. Crispin & the 3 Little Piglets. 2003. (Illus.). (J). lib. bdg. 17.99 (*0-385-90859-8*); 32p. 15.95 (*0-385-74633-4*) Random Hse. Children's Bks. (Doubleday Bks. for Young Readers).

Dickens, Lucy. At the Beach. 1991. (My Sister & Me Ser.). (Illus.). 10p. (J). (ps-1). 4.95 o.p. (*0-670-83927-2*, Viking Children's Bks.) Penguin Putnam Bks. for Young Readers.

—Our Day. 1991. (My Sister & Me Ser.). (Illus.). 10p. (J). (ps-1). 4.95 o.p. (*0-670-83929-9*, Viking Children's Bks.) Penguin Putnam Bks. for Young Readers.

—Outside. 1991. (My Sister & Me Ser.). (Illus.). 10p. (J). (ps-1). 4.95 o.p. (*0-670-83928-0*, Viking Children's Bks.) Penguin Putnam Bks. for Young Readers.

—Playtime. 1991. (My Sister & Me Ser.). (Illus.). 10p. (J). (ps-1). 4.95 o.p. (*0-670-83926-4*, Viking Children's Bks.) Penguin Putnam Bks. for Young Readers.

Dickinson, Mike. My Brother's Silly. 1983. (Illus.). 32p. (J). (ps-1). 9.95 o.p. (*0-233-97531-4*) Andre Deutsch GBR. *Dist:* Trafalgar Square, Trans-Atlantic Pubns., Inc.

DiTerlizzi, Tony & Black, Holly. The Ironweed Tree. 2003. (Spiderwick Chronicles: No. 4). (Illus.). 128p. (J). 9.95 (*0-689-85939-2*, Simon & Schuster Children's Publishing) Simon & Schuster Children's Publishing.

Dixon, Franklin W. Brother Against Brother. 1989. (Hardy Boys Casefiles Ser.: No. 11). 160p. (Orig.). (YA). (gr. 6 up). mass mkt. 2.95 (*0-671-70712-4*, Simon Pulse) Simon & Schuster Children's Publishing.

Dodds, Bill. My Sister Annie. 2003. (Illus.). 96p. (J). (gr. 5-7). pap. 7.95 (*1-56397-554-8*) Boyds Mills Pr.

Dodge, Mary Mapes. Hans Brinker & the Silver Skates. 2002. (Great Illustrated Classics). (Illus.). 240p. (J). (gr. 3-8). lib. bdg. 21.35 (*1-57765-814-0*, ABDO & Daughters) ABDO Publishing Co.

—Hans Brinker or the Silver Skates. Lindskoog, Kathryn, ed. 2001. (Classics for Young Readers Ser.). (Illus.). 224p. (J). (gr. 3-6). pap. 7.99 (*0-87552-725-6*) P&R Publishing.

—Hans Brinker, or the Silver Skates. Kopito, Janet Baine, ed. 2003. (Dover Evergreen Classics Ser.). 240p. (J). pap. 3.00 (*0-486-42842-7*) Dover Pubns., Inc.

Dow, Unity. Far & Beyon' 2002. 208p. (YA). (gr. 7 up). pap. 11.95 (*1-879960-64-8*) Aunt Lute Bks.

Dowell, Frances O'Roark. Dovey Coe. 192p. (J). 2001. (Illus.). pap. 4.99 (*0-689-84667-3*, Aladdin); 2000. (gr. 4-7). 16.00 (*0-689-83174-9*, Atheneum) Simon & Schuster Children's Publishing.

—Dovey Coe. l.t. ed. 2001. 171p. (J). 22.95 (*0-7862-3590-X*) Thorndike Pr.

—Dovey Coe. 2001. 11.04 (*0-606-22127-1*) Turtleback Bks.

Doyle, Peter R. Ambushed in Africa. 1993. (Daring Adventure Ser.: Vol. 1). (J). (gr. 4). pap. 5.99 o.p. (*1-56179-142-3*) Focus on the Family Publishing.

—Chased by the Jewel Thieves. 1997. (Daring Adventure Ser.: Bk. 11). (J). (gr. 4). pap. 5.99 o.p. (*1-56179-547-X*) Focus on the Family Publishing.

—Kidnapped in Rome. 1996. (Daring Adventure Ser.: Vol. 9). (J). (gr. 4). pap. 5.99 o.p. (*1-56179-480-5*) Focus on the Family Publishing.

—Lost in the Secret Cave. 1996. (Daring Adventure Ser.: Bk. 10). (J). (gr. 4). pap. 5.99 o.p. (*1-56179-481-3*) Focus on the Family Publishing.

Doyon, Stephanie. Buying Time. 1999. (On the Road Ser.: Vol. 2). 235p. (J). (gr. 7-12). pap. 4.50 (*0-689-82108-5*, 076714004504, Simon Pulse) Simon & Schuster Children's Publishing.

—Buying Time. 1999. (On the Road Ser.: No. 2). 10.55 (*0-606-18898-3*) Turtleback Bks.

Dragonwagon, Crescent. I Hate My Brother Harry. (Trophy Picture Bk.). (Illus.). 32p. (J). (gr. k-3). 1989. pap. 3.50 o.p. (*0-06-443193-2*, Harper Trophy); 1983. lib. bdg. 12.89 o.p. (*0-06-021758-8*) HarperCollins Children's Bk. Group.

Draper, Sharon M. Forged by Fire. 2002. (Illus.). (J). 13.40 (*0-7587-0354-6*) Book Wholesalers, Inc.

—Forged by Fire. (Hazelwood High Trilogy: Bk. 2). 160p. (YA). (gr. 7 up). 1998. mass mkt. 4.99 (*0-689-81851-3*, Simon Pulse); 1997. 16.95 (*0-689-80699-X*, Atheneum) Simon & Schuster Children's Publishing.

—Forged by Fire. 1998. 11.04 (*0-606-13397-6*) Turtleback Bks.

Drescher, Joan. The Birth-Order Blues. 1993. (Illus.). 32p. (J). (ps-3). 13.99 o.p. (*0-670-83621-4*, Viking Children's Bks.) Penguin Putnam Bks. for Young Readers.

Drew, David. Something Silver, Something Blue. 1993. (Voyages Ser.). (Illus.). (J). 4.25 (*0-383-03654-2*) SRA/McGraw-Hill.

Dubois, Claude K. He's My Jumbo! 1990. (Illus.). 320p. (J). (ps-1). 9.95 o.p. (*0-670-83029-1*, Viking Children's Bks.) Penguin Putnam Bks. for Young Readers.

—Looking for Ginny. 1990. (Illus.). 320p. (J). (ps-1). 9.95 o.p. (*0-670-83030-5*, Viking Children's Bks.) Penguin Putnam Bks. for Young Readers.

Duffey, Betsy. Fur-Ever Yours, Booker Jones. 128p. 2002. (YA). (gr. 5-9). pap. 4.99 (*0-14-230215-5*, Puffin Bks.); 2001. (J). (gr. 4-6). 15.99 (*0-670-89287-4*, Viking Children's Bks.) Penguin Putnam Bks. for Young Readers.

Duffy, Daniel M., illus. Meet the Boxcar Children. 1998. (Adventures of Benny & Watch: Vol. No. 1). 46p. (J). (gr. 1-3). pap. 3.95 (*0-8075-5034-5*) Whitman, Albert & Co.

Dunbar, Fiona. My Secret Brother. 1992. (Illus.). 32p. (J). (ps-1). o.p. (*0-09-176402-5*) Random Hse. of Canada, Ltd. CAN. *Dist:* Random Hse., Inc.

Dunbar, Joyce. Tell Me Something Happy Before I Go to Sleep. 1998. (Illus.). 32p. (J). (ps-3). 16.00 (*0-15-201795-X*) Harcourt Children's Bks.

—Tell Me What It's Like to Be Big. 2001. (Illus.). 32p. (J). (ps-2). 16.00 (*0-15-202564-2*) Harcourt Children's Bks.

Duncan, Alice F. Willie Jerome. 1995. (Illus.). 32p. (J). (ps-3). 15.00 o.p. (*0-02-733208-X*, Atheneum) Simon & Schuster Children's Publishing.

Duncan, Debbie. When Molly Was in the Hospital: A Book for Brothers & Sisters of Hospitalized Children. 1994. (Minimed Ser.: Vol. 1). (Illus.). 40p. (J). (ps-7). 12.95 (*1-877810-44-4*, MOLL) Rayve Productions, Inc.

Dunlop, Eileen. Websters' Leap. 1995. (Illus.). 176p. (J). (gr. 4-7). 15.95 (*0-8234-1193-1*) Holiday Hse., Inc.

Dunmore, Helen. Brother Brother, Sister Sister. 2000. (Illus.). 116p. (J). (gr. 3-7). mass mkt. 4.50 (*0-439-11322-9*) Scholastic, Inc.

Durrant, Lynda, illus. Echohawk. 1996. 192p. (J). (gr. 4-6). tchr. ed. 16.00 (*0-395-74430-X*, Clarion Bks.) Houghton Mifflin Co. Trade & Reference Div.

Easton, Kelly. The Life History of a Star. 208p. (YA). 2002. pap. 6.99 (*0-689-85270-3*, Simon Pulse); 2001. (Illus.). (gr. 7 up). 16.00 (*0-689-83134-X*, McElderry, Margaret K.) Simon & Schuster Children's Publishing.

—The Life History of a Star. l.t. ed. 2002. (Young Adult Ser.). 200p. 22.95 (*0-7862-4786-X*) Thorndike Pr.

Eaton, Deborah. Monster Songs. 1999. (Real Kids Readers Ser.). (Illus.). 32p. (J). (gr. k-2). 18.90 (*0-7613-2054-7*); pap. 4.99 (*0-7613-2079-2*) Millbrook Pr., Inc.

—Monster Songs. 1999. (J). 10.14 (*0-606-19162-3*) Turtleback Bks.

—Monster Songs. 1999. E-Book (*1-58824-808-9*); E-Book (*1-58824-478-4*); E-Book (*1-58824-726-0*) ipicturebooks, LLC.

—The Rainy Day Grump. 1998. (Real Kids Readers Ser.). (Illus.). 32p. (J). (gr. k-2). 18.90 (*0-7613-2018-0*); pap. 4.99 (*0-7613-2043-1*) Millbrook Pr., Inc.

—The Rainy Day Grump. 1998. (Real Kids Readers Ser.). 10.14 (*0-606-15806-5*) Turtleback Bks.

—The Rainy Day Grump. 1998. E-Book (*1-58824-736-8*); E-Book (*1-58824-819-4*); E-Book (*1-58824-488-1*) ipicturebooks, LLC.

Edelman, Elaine. I Love My Baby Sister: Most of the Time. 1985. (Illus.). 32p. (J). (ps-3). pap. 3.95 o.s.i (*0-14-050547-4*, Puffin Bks.) Penguin Putnam Bks. for Young Readers.

Edwards, Becky. My Brother Sammy. 1999. (Illus.). 32p. (J). (gr. k-3). 23.90 (*0-7613-1417-2*); 14.95 (*0-7613-0439-8*) Millbrook Pr., Inc.

Elgar, Susan. The Brothers Gruesome. 2000. (Illus.). 32p. (J). (ps-3). 15.00 o.p. (*0-618-00515-3*) Houghton Mifflin Co.

Eliot, George. The Mill on the Floss, 001. Haight, G. S., ed. 1972. (YA). (gr. 9 up). pap. 14.76 o.p. (*0-395-05151-7*, Riverside Editions) Houghton Mifflin Co.

Ellis, Sarah. Big Ben. 2001. (Illus.). 32p. (J). (ps-1). (*1-55041-679-0*) Fitzhenry & Whiteside, Ltd.

Elmer, Robert. Far from the Storm. 1995. (Young Underground Ser.: Bk. 4). 176p. (J). (gr. 3-8). pap. 5.99 (*1-55661-377-6*) Bethany Hse. Pubs.

—Follow the Star. 1997. (Young Underground Ser.: Vol. 7). 176p. (J). (gr. 3-8). pap. 5.99 (*1-55661-660-0*) Bethany Hse. Pubs.

—Into the Flames. 1995. (Young Underground Ser.: Bk. 3). 192p. (J). (gr. 3-8). pap. 5.99 (*1-55661-376-8*) Bethany Hse. Pubs.

Elwood, Roger. The Frankenstein Project. 1991. (J). (gr. 3-7). pap. 5.99 o.p. (*0-8499-3303-X*) W Publishing Group.

Enderle, Judith R. & Tessler, Stephanie G. What's the Matter, Kelly Beans? 1996. (Illus.). 112p. (J). (gr. 1-3). 14.99 o.p. (*1-56402-534-9*) Candlewick Pr.

Enderle, Judith Ross & Gordon, Stephanie Jacob. School Stinks! 2001. (Illus.). 148p. (J). pap. (*0-439-32852-7*) Scholastic, Inc.

Engelbreit, Mary. Because You're My Sister. 2003. (Illus.). 32p. 6.95 (*0-8362-3676-9*) Andrews McMeel Publishing.

Engle, Marty M. & Barnes, Johnny Ray, Jr. Deadly Delivery. l.t. ed. 1996. (Strange Matter Ser.: No. 9). 124p. (J). (gr. 4-6). lib. bdg. 21.27 o.p. (*0-8368-1675-7*) Stevens, Gareth Inc.

—Driven to Death. l.t. ed. 1996. (Strange Matter Ser.: No. 3). 124p. (J). (gr. 4-6). lib. bdg. 21.27 o.p. (*0-8368-1669-2*) Stevens, Gareth Inc.

Relationships

Enright, Elizabeth. The Four-Story Mistake, ERS. 2002. (Melendy Quartet Ser.: Bk. 2). (Illus.). 176p. (J). (gr. 3-7). 16.95 (*0-8050-7061-3*, Holt, Henry & Co. Bks. For Young Readers) Holt, Henry & Co.

—The Saturdays. (Illus.). 1941. (gr. 4-6). 5.95 o.p. (*0-03-089690-8*); ERS. 2002. (Melendy Quartet Ser.: Bk. 1). 176p. (J). (gr. 3-6). 16.95 (*0-8050-7060-5*, Holt, Henry & Co. Bks. For Young Readers); ERS. 1988. 196p. (YA). (gr. 4-7). 12.95 o.s.i (*0-8050-0291-X*, Holt, Henry & Co. Bks. For Young Readers) Holt, Henry & Co.

—Spiderweb for Two: A Melendy Mystery. 1997. (Melendy Family Ser.). (Illus.). 224p. (J). (gr. 3-7). pap. 4.99 o.s.i (*0-14-038396-4*) Penguin Putnam Bks. for Young Readers.

—Then There Were Five. 1996. o.p. (*0-03-032835-7*); ERS. 2002. (Melendy Quartet Ser.: Bk. 3). (Illus.). 176p. (J). (gr. 3-7). 16.95 (*0-8050-7062-1*, Holt, Henry & Co. Bks. For Young Readers) Holt, Henry & Co.

—Then There Were Five. 1997. (Melendy Family Ser.). (Illus.). 256p. (J). (gr. 3-7). pap. 4.99 o.s.i (*0-14-038397-2*) Penguin Putnam Bks. for Young Readers.

—Then There Were Five. 1987. (Illus.). (J). (gr. k-6). pap. 2.95 o.s.i (*0-440-48806-0*, Yearling) Random Hse. Children's Bks.

Ephron, Delia. The Girl Who Changed the World. 1993. 160p. (J). (gr. 3-6). tchr. ed. 13.95 (*0-395-66139-0*) Houghton Mifflin Co.

Erickson, Gina Clegg. Bat's Surprise. 1993. (Get Ready...Get Set...Read! Ser.). (Illus.). 24p. (J). (ps-2). pap. 4.50 (*0-8120-1735-8*) Barron's Educational Series, Inc.

Erkel, Cynthia R. Sarah's Rocking Chair. 1999. (Illus.). (J). pap. 15.99 (*0-525-65234-5*, Dutton Children's Bks.) Penguin Putnam Bks. for Young Readers.

Esbaum, Jill. Stink Soup, RS. 2004. (J). 16.00 (*0-374-37252-7*, Farrar, Straus & Giroux (BYR)) Farrar, Straus & Giroux.

Estes, Eleanor. Ginger Pye. 2000. (Illus.). 320p. (YA). (gr. 3 up). 17.00 (*0-15-202499-9*, Odyssey Classics); (gr. 4-7). pap. 6.00 (*0-15-202505-7*) Harcourt Children's Bks.

—Ginger Pye. l.t. ed. 1987. (Illus.). 300p. (J). (gr. 3-7). reprint ed. lib. bdg. 16.95 o.s.i (*1-55736-056-1*, Cornerstone Bks.) Pages, Inc.

—Rufus M. 2001. (Young Classics). (Illus.). 256p. (YA). (gr. 3 up). 17.00 (*0-15-202571-5*, Odyssey Classics); pap. 6.00 (*0-15-202577-4*) Harcourt Children's Bks.

Etchemendy, Nancy. The Power of UN. 2000. 160p. (J). (gr. 3-7). 15.95 (*0-8126-2850-0*) Cricket Bks.

Evans, David. The Famous Hooper Brothers. 1988. (Illus.). 101p. (Orig.). (J). pap. 15.95 (*0-929422-00-7*) Jonah Pr.

Ewing, Lynne. Drive-By. 96p. (J). (gr. 5 up). 1998. pap. 4.99 (*0-06-440649-0*, Harper Trophy); 1996. 13.95 o.p. (*0-06-027125-6*) HarperCollins Children's Bk. Group.

—Tito. 1996. 96p. (J). (gr. 5 up). lib. bdg. 13.89 o.p. (*0-06-027126-4*) HarperCollins Children's Bk. Group.

Fallon, Joan & Feltenstein, Arlene. Will the New Baby Be Bigger Than Me? 1998. (Illus.). (J). (ps-3). 9.95 (*1-56492-252-9*) Laredo Publishing Co., Inc.

Falwell, Cathryn. Nicky & Alex. 1992. (Illus.). 32p. (J). (ps). 5.95 o.p. (*0-395-56915-X*, Clarion Bks.) Houghton Mifflin Co. Trade & Reference Div.

Farrer, Frances. Charlie & Elly Stories. 1989. (Illus.). 96p. (J). (gr. 3-5). 15.95 o.s.i (*0-575-03966-3*) Gollancz, Victor GBR. *Dist:* Trafalgar Square.

Feldman, Eve B. That Cat! 1994. (Illus.). 112p. (J). 14.00 (*0-688-13310-X*, Morrow, William & Co.) Morrow/Avon.

Fenner, Carol. Yolonda's Genius. 2002. (Illus.). (J). 14.47 (*0-7587-0333-3*) Book Wholesalers, Inc.

—Yolonda's Genius. unabr. ed. 2002. 211p. pap. 37.00 incl. audio (*0-8072-0462-5*, Listening Library) Random Hse. Audio Publishing Group.

—Yolonda's Genius. (J). 2002. 224p. E-Book 6.99 (*0-689-84785-8*, McElderry, Margaret K.); 1998. pap. 2.65 (*0-689-82172-7*, Aladdin); 1997. 224p. (gr. 3-7). pap. 5.99 (*0-689-81327-9*, Aladdin); 1995. 224p. (gr. 3-7). 17.00 (*0-689-80001-0*, McElderry, Margaret K.) Simon & Schuster Children's Publishing.

—Yolonda's Genius. 1997. (J). 12.04 (*0-606-12122-6*) Turtleback Bks.

Ferguson, Alane. The Practical Joke War. 1991. 144p. (J). (gr. 3-7). lib. bdg. 13.95 o.s.i (*0-02-734526-2*, Simon & Schuster Children's Publishing) Simon & Schuster Children's Publishing.

Fields, T. S. Danger in the Desert. 1997. (Illus.). 136p. (J). (gr. 3-7). 12.95 (*0-87358-666-2*); pap. 6.95 (*0-87358-664-6*) Northland Publishing. (Rising Moon Bks. for Young Readers).

—Danger in the Desert. 1997. 13.00 (*0-606-16007-8*) Turtleback Bks.

Figler, Jeanie. Majestic Blue Horses. 1999. (Illus.). (J). 9.95 (*1-56492-273-1*) Laredo Publishing Co., Inc.

Fine, Anne. The Book of the Banshee. 1992. (YA). (gr. 7 up). 13.95 (*0-316-28315-0*) Little Brown & Co.

—The Book of the Banshee. 1994. 176p. (J). (gr. 4-7). pap. 2.95 o.p. (*0-590-46926-6*) Scholastic, Inc.

Finkelstein, Ruth. Big Like Me. 2001. (Illus.). 32p. (J). 9.95 (*1-929628-04-8*) Hachai Publishing.

Finley, Mary Peace. Meadow Lark. 2003. (YA). 15.95 (*0-86541-070-4*) Filter Pr., LLC.

Fisher, Melanie. Nathan & Lou: The Finders. 1995. (Illus.). 36p. (Orig.). (J). (gr. k-4). mass mkt. 4.95 (*0-9649664-0-9*) Jermel Visuals.

Fisher, Valorie. My Big Brother. 2002. (Illus.). 40p. (J). (ps-2). 14.95 (*0-689-84327-5*, Atheneum/Anne Schwartz Bks.) Simon & Schuster Children's Publishing.

Fitzgerald, John. The Baby Brother. 1994. (Illus.). (J). 64.00 (*0-383-03677-1*) SRA/McGraw-Hill.

Fleischman, Sid. Disappearing Act. 2003. (Illus.). 144p. (J). (gr. 3-7). 15.99 (*0-06-051962-2*); lib. bdg. 16.89 (*0-06-051963-0*) HarperCollins Children's Bk. Group. (Greenwillow Bks.).

—The 13th Floor: A Ghost Story. 1995. (Illus.). 144p. (J). (gr. 3 up). 15.99 (*0-688-14216-8*, Greenwillow Bks.) HarperCollins Children's Bk. Group.

—The 13th Floor: A Ghost Story. 1997. (Illus.). 176p. (gr. 3-7). pap. text 4.99 (*0-440-41243-9*, Yearling) Random Hse. Children's Bks.

—The 13th Floor: A Ghost Story. 1997. (J). 10.55 (*0-606-11011-9*) Turtleback Bks.

Fleming, Leanne, illus. The Quiet World. 1994. (J). (*0-383-03671-2*) SRA/McGraw-Hill.

Flieger, Pat. The Fog's Net. 1994. (Illus.). 32p. (J). tchr. ed. 14.95 o.p. (*0-395-68194-4*) Houghton Mifflin Co.

Flournoy, Valerie. The Twins Strike Back. 1994. (Illus.). 32p. (J). (gr. 2 up). 13.00 o.p. (*0-940975-51-3*); (gr. 4-7). pap. 5.00 (*0-940975-52-1*) Just Us Bks., Inc.

—The Twins Strike Back. 1980. (Illus.). (J). (ps-4). 7.95 o.p. (*0-8037-8691-3*); 7.45 o.p. (*0-8037-8692-1*) Penguin Putnam Bks. for Young Readers. (Dial Bks. for Young Readers).

Floyer, Edith S. The Young Huguenots. 1998. (Huguenots Inheritance Ser.). 9.95 (*0-921100-65-5*) Inheritance Pubns.

Flynn, Mary Jane. If a Seahorse Wore a Saddle. 1991. (Illus.). 48p. (J). (ps-1). pap. 10.95 (*0-9623072-3-8*) Storytellers Ink, Inc.

Foley, Louise Munro. Tackle Twenty-Two. 1978. (Illus.). (J). (gr. 1-3). 6.95 o.s.i (*0-440-08464-4*); lib. bdg. 6.46 o.s.i (*0-440-08465-2*) Dell Publishing. (Delacorte Pr.).

Fontes, Justine. The Cat in the Hat Movie Storybook. 2003. (Illus.). 48p. (J). (gr. 1-6). 8.99 (*0-375-82502-9*, 53534399) Random Hse., Inc.

Fontes, Ron. To Fly with Dragons. Kleinberg, Naomi, ed. 2000. (Sparkle Storybook Ser.). (Illus.). 32p. (J). (ps-3). 8.99 (*0-375-80661-X*, Random Hse. Bks. for Young Readers) Random Hse. Children's Bks.

Forsberg, Crystal. Michael's Brothers. 1998. (Illus.). 16p. (J). (ps-k). pap. 5.95 (*0-9655442-3-0*) Business Word, The.

Foster, Evelyn. The Mermaid of Cafur. 1999. (Illus.). 32p. (J). (gr. k-3). 15.95 (*1-902283-40-6*) Barefoot Bks., Inc.

Foster, Scarlett R. Secret of the Viking Dagger. Qualben, James D., ed. 1997. 144p. (J). (gr. 4-7). pap. 7.95 (*1-880292-55-6*); lib. bdg. 15.95 (*1-880292-56-4*) LangMarc Publishing. (North Sea Pr.).

Fox, Nancy. Clarence When You Are Sleeping. 1997. (Illus.). 32p. (Orig.). (J). (gr. k-2). pap. 7.95 (*1-884242-88-X*) Multicultural Pubns.

Fox, Paula. Lily & the Lost Boy. l.t. unabr. ed. 1989. 230p. (J). (gr. 5-7). lib. bdg. 13.95 o.p. (*0-8161-4725-6*, Macmillan Reference USA) Gale Group.

—Lily & the Lost Boy. 1987. 160p. (J). (gr. 6-8). lib. bdg. 17.99 (*0-531-08320-9*); (YA). (gr. 7-12). pap. 16.95 (*0-531-05720-8*) Scholastic, Inc. (Orchard Bks.).

—Radiance Descending. 1999. 112p. (YA). (gr. 5-7). mass mkt. 4.99 o.s.i (*0-440-22748-8*) Bantam Bks.

—Radiance Descending. 1997. (Illus.). 112p. (J). (gr. 4-7). pap. 14.95 o.p. (*0-7894-2467-3*) Dorling Kindersley Publishing, Inc.

—Radiance Descending. 1999. 11.04 (*0-606-17838-4*) Turtleback Bks.

—Western Wind. 1993. 208p. (YA). (gr. 4-7). lib. bdg. 17.99 (*0-531-08652-6*); (gr. 5 up). pap. 16.95 (*0-531-06802-1*) Scholastic, Inc. (Orchard Bks.).

Fran, Renee. What Happened to Mommy? 1994. (Illus.). 32p. (Orig.). (J). (ps-6). pap. 7.95 (*0-9640250-0-0*) D. R. Eastman.

Francesca, Lia. Wasteland. 2003. 160p. (J). lib. bdg. 16.89 (*0-06-028645-8*, Cotler, Joanna Bks.) HarperCollins Children's Bk. Group.

Franco, Betsy. Silly Sally Level 3. 2002. (Rookie Readers Ser.). (Illus.). 24p. (J). (gr. k-1). lib. bdg. 16.00 (*0-516-22492-1*, Children's Pr.) Scholastic Library Publishing.

Franklin, Jonathan. Don't Wake the Baby, RS. 1991. (Illus.). 32p. (J). (ps-1). 13.95 o.p. (*0-374-31826-3*, Farrar, Straus & Giroux (BYR)) Farrar, Straus & Giroux.

Franklin, Kristine L. Dove Song. 1999. (Illus.). 192p. (J). (gr. 5-9). 16.99 (*0-7636-0409-7*) Candlewick Pr.

Fraustino, Lisa Rowe. Ash. 1995. (Illus.). 176p. (YA). (gr. 7 up). pap. 16.95 (*0-531-06889-7*); lib. bdg. 17.99 (*0-531-08739-5*) Scholastic, Inc. (Orchard Bks.).

Freeman, Becky. Secrets of Thief Cave. 2001. 96p. (J). (gr. 2-5). pap. 4.95 o.s.i (*1-57856-350-X*) Water-Brook Pr.

—The Wild Rattle in the Woods. 2001. (Camp Wanna Banana Mysteries Ser.). (Illus.). 96p. (J). (gr. 2-5). pap. 3.99 o.s.i (*1-57856-349-6*) WaterBrook Pr.

French, Vivian. A Christmas Star Called Hannah. (Illus.). 32p. (J). (ps-3). 2000. bds. 3.99 (*0-7636-1198-0*); 1997. 9.99 o.s.i (*0-7636-0397-X*) Candlewick Pr.

Freymann-Weyr, Garret. My Heartbeat. 2002. 160p. (J). (gr. 7-12). 15.00 (*0-618-14181-2*) Houghton Mifflin Co.

—My Heartbeat. unabr. ed. 2003. (J). (gr. 7). audio 25.00 (*0-8072-1199-0*, Listening Library) Random Hse. Audio Publishing Group.

—When I Was Older. 2000. (Illus.). 176p. (YA). (gr. 5-9). tchr. ed. 15.00 (*0-618-05545-2*) Houghton Mifflin Co. Trade & Reference Div.

—When I Was Older. 2002. 176p. (J). pap. 5.99 (*0-14-230093-4*, Puffin Bks.) Penguin Putnam Bks. for Young Readers.

—When I Was Older. l.t. ed. 2001. 159p. (J). 22.95 (*0-7862-3546-2*) Thorndike Pr.

Friedrich, Joachim. 4 1/2 Friends & the Secret Cave, Bk. 1. Crawford, Elizabeth D., tr. from GER. 2001. (Illus.). 154p. (J). (gr. 3-7). 14.99 (*0-7868-0648-6*) Hyperion Bks. for Children.

Friend, Catherine. The Sawfin Stickleback: A Very Fishy Story. 1994. (Illus.). 32p. (J). 13.95 o.p. (*1-56282-473-2*); lib. bdg. 14.49 (*1-56282-474-0*) Hyperion Bks. for Children.

Fries, Chloe. No Place to Hide. 1979. (Challenge Bks.). (Illus.). (J). (gr. 4-8). lib. bdg. 7.95 o.p. (*0-87191-678-9*, Creative Education) Creative Co., The.

Fromm, Pete. Monkey Tag. 1994. 352p. (J). (gr. 4-7). pap. 14.95 (*0-590-46525-2*) Scholastic, Inc.

Fuqua, Jonathon Scott. The Willoughby Spit Wonder. 2004. 160p. (J). 15.99 (*0-7636-1776-8*) Candlewick Pr.

Gaberman, Judith. A Home Is to Share...and Share...and Share... 2001. 164p. (gr. 4-7). pap. 11.95 (*0-595-15796-3*, Backinprint.com) iUniverse, Inc.

Gaeddert, LouAnn Bigge. Hope. 160p. (J). 1997. (gr. 3-7). pap. 3.99 (*0-689-80382-6*, Aladdin); 1995. (gr. 4-7). 14.00 (*0-689-80128-9*, Atheneum) Simon & Schuster Children's Publishing.

Galbraith, Kathryn O. Roommates & Rachel. 1991. (Illus.). 48p. (J). (ps-3). 14.00 (*0-689-50520-5*, McElderry, Margaret K.) Simon & Schuster Children's Publishing.

Gantos, Jack. Jack on the Tracks: Four Seasons of Fifth Grade, RS. 1999. (J). E-Book 4.95 (*0-374-70043-5*); E-Book 4.95 o.p. (*0-374-70045-1*); (Illus.). 192p. (gr. 5-9). 16.00 (*0-374-33665-2*) Farrar, Straus & Giroux. (Farrar, Straus & Giroux (BYR)).

—Jack on the Tracks: Four Seasons of Fifth Grade. l.t. ed. 2002. 210p. (J). 22.95 (*0-7862-4394-5*) Thorndike Pr.

Garland, Sarah. Billy & Belle. 1992. (Illus.). 320p. (J). (ps-3). 13.00 o.p. (*0-670-84396-2*, Viking Children's Bks.) Penguin Putnam Bks. for Young Readers.

Garren, Devorah-Leah. Shabbos Is Coming! We're Lost in the Zoo! 1999. (Illus.). 32p. (J). (ps-3). 12.95 (*1-880582-32-5*) Judaica Pr., Inc., The.

Gay, Marie-Louise. Good Morning, Sam. 2003. (Illus.). 32p. (J). (ps-k). 14.95 (*0-88899-528-8*, Libros Tigrillo) Groundwood Bks. CAN. *Dist:* Publishers Group West.

—Stella, Fairy of the Forest. ed. 2003. (gr. 1). spiral bd. (*0-616-14580-2*); (gr. 2). spiral bd. (*0-616-14581-0*) Canadian National Institute for the Blind/Institut National Canadien pour les Aveugles.

—Stella, Fairy of the Forest. 2002. (Illus.). 32p. (J). (ps-3). 15.95 (*0-88899-448-6*) Groundwood Bks. CAN. *Dist:* Publishers Group West.

—Stella, Star of the Sea. 2000. (Illus.). 32p. (J). (ps-k). 15.95 (*0-88899-337-4*) Groundwood Bks. CAN. *Dist:* Publishers Group West.

Geller, Mark. Who's on First? 1992. (Charlotte Zolotow Bk.). 64p. (J). (gr. 6 up). 14.00 (*0-06-021084-2*); lib. bdg. 14.89 o.p. (*0-06-021085-0*) HarperCollins Children's Bk. Group.

George, Jean Craighead. On the Far Side of the Mountain. (J). 1999. (Illus.). 144p. (gr. 4-7). 15.99 (*0-525-46348-8*, Dutton Children's Bks.); 1991. (Illus.). 176p. (gr. 3-7). pap. 4.99 o.s.i (*0-14-034248-6*, Puffin Bks.); 1990. 176p. (gr. 3-7). 15.99 o.s.i (*0-525-44563-3*, Dutton Children's Bks.) Penguin Putnam Bks. for Young Readers.

—On the Far Side of the Mountain. 2001. 12.04 (*0-606-21366-X*); 1991. (J). 11.04 (*0-606-04996-7*) Turtleback Bks.

—The Wolf Pup Named Nutik. (J). (gr. k-3). 2001. (Illus.). 40p. 15.99 (*0-06-028164-2*); 2001. (Illus.). 40p. lib. bdg. 16.89 (*0-06-028165-0*); 2000. 32p. pap. 5.95 (*0-06-443522-9*) HarperCollins Children's Bk. Group.

George, Jim. Holey Moley. 1996. (Ha! Ser.). (Illus.). 64p. (Orig.). (J). (ps up). pap. (*1-56844-047-2*) Enchante Publishing.

Geras, Adele. Little Swan. 1995. (Illus.). 62p. (J). (ps-3). 11.99 (*0-679-97000-2*); pap. 3.99 o.s.i (*0-679-87000-8*) Random Hse., Inc.

—Little Swan. 1995. 9.19 o.p. (*0-606-07801-0*) Turtleback Bks.

Gerstein, Mordicai. The Gigantic Baby. 1991. (Illus.). 32p. (J). (gr. k-3). 14.95 (*0-06-022074-0*); lib. bdg. 14.89 o.p. (*0-06-022106-2*) HarperCollins Children's Bk. Group.

Getz, David. Thin Air. 1992. (Trophy Bk.). 128p. (J). (gr. 3-7). pap. 3.95 o.p. (*0-06-440422-6*, Harper Trophy) HarperCollins Children's Bk. Group.

—Thin Air, ERS. 1990. 128p. (J). (gr. 6 up). 14.95 o.p. (*0-8050-1379-2*, Holt, Henry & Co. Bks. For Young Readers) Holt, Henry & Co.

Gifaldi, David. Ben, King of the River. 2001. (Concept Book Ser.). (Illus.). 32p. (J). (gr. 1-3). lib. bdg. 14.95 (*0-8075-0635-4*) Whitman, Albert & Co.

Giff, Patricia Reilly. Nory Ryan's Song. unabr. ed. 2000. (J). (gr. 3-7). audio 22.00 (*0-8072-6163-7*, Listening Library) Random Hse. Audio Publishing Group.

—Nory Ryan's Song. Lamb, Wendy, ed. 2000. 160p. (gr. 5-9). text 15.95 (*0-385-32141-4*, Dell Books for Young Readers) Random Hse. Children's Bks.

—Nory Ryan's Song. 2002. 176p. (gr. 3-7). pap. text 5.99 (*0-440-41829-1*) Random Hse., Inc.

—Nory Ryan's Song. l.t. ed. 2001. 176p. (J). 23.95 (*0-7862-3459-8*) Thorndike Pr.

Gikow, Louise & Cooke, Tom. Mom's Having a Baby. 1991. (Muppet Kids Ser.). (Illus.). 24p. (J). (ps-3). pap. 3.29 o.s.i (*0-307-12661-7*, Golden Bks.) Random Hse. Children's Bks.

Gilden, Mel. My Brother Blubb. 1994. 144p. (J). (gr. 3-6). pap. 3.50 (*0-671-79898-7*, Aladdin) Simon & Schuster Children's Publishing.

Gilson, Jamie. You Cheat! 1992. (Illus.). 64p. (J). (gr. 1-4). text 13.95 o.p. (*0-02-735993-X*, Simon & Schuster Children's Publishing) Simon & Schuster Children's Publishing.

Givens, Terryl L. Dragon Scales & Willow Leaves. 1997. (Illus.). 32p. (J). (ps-3). 12.95 o.s.i (*0-399-22619-2*, G. P. Putnam's Sons) Penguin Group (USA) Inc.

Glaser, Linda. Keep Your Socks on, Albert! 1992. (Illus.). 4p. (J). (ps-2). 11.99 o.p. (*0-525-44838-1*, Dutton Children's Bks.) Penguin Putnam Bks. for Young Readers.

Glass, Andrew. My Brother Tries to Make Me Laugh. 1984. (Illus.). 32p. (J). (ps-1). 12.95 o.p. (*0-688-02257-X*); lib. bdg. 12.88 o.p. (*0-688-02259-6*) HarperCollins Children's Bk. Group.

Gleitzman, Morris. Two Weeks with the Queen. 1991. 144p. (YA). 14.95 o.p. (*0-399-22249-9*, G. P. Putnam's Sons) Penguin Group (USA) Inc.

Gliori, Debi. My Little Brother. (Illus.). (J). (ps up). 1995. bds. 4.99 o.p. (*1-56402-455-5*); 1992. 32p. 13.95 o.p. (*1-56402-079-7*) Candlewick Pr.

—My Little Brother. 1995. 10.19 o.p. (*0-606-08829-6*) Turtleback Bks.

—New Big Sister. 1991. (Illus.). 32p. (J). (ps-3). lib. bdg. 13.95 o.p. (*0-02-735995-6*, Simon & Schuster Children's Publishing) Simon & Schuster Children's Publishing.

Godden, Rumer. The Fairy Doll. 2015. (Illus.). (J). 14.95 (*0-399-21962-5*, Philomel) Penguin Putnam Bks. for Young Readers.

Goffstein, M. B. My Crazy Sister. 1976. (Illus.). (J). (gr. k-3). 5.95 o.p. (*0-8037-6198-8*); 5.47 o.p. (*0-8037-6199-6*) Penguin Putnam Bks. for Young Readers. (Dial Bks. for Young Readers).

Golant, Galina & Grant, Lisa. Play Checkers with Me. 2003. (Illus.). (J). pap. 9.95 (*1-932133-01-1*) Writers' Collective, The.

The Golden Brothers. 1981. 48p. (J). pap. 1.50 o.p. (*0-8431-0731-6*, Price Stern Sloan) Penguin Putnam Bks. for Young Readers.

Goldowsky, Jill. Lost & Found Puppy. Fitchwell, Jennifer, tr. & illus. by. 2004. (All-Star Readers Ser.). 32p. (J). pap. (*0-7944-0383-2*, Reader's Digest Children's Bks.) Reader's Digest Children's Publishing, Inc.

Gondosch, Linda. Who Needs a Bratty Brother? 1985. (Illus.). 112p. (J). (gr. 4-6). 11.95 o.p. (*0-525-67170-6*, Dutton Children's Bks.) Penguin Putnam Bks. for Young Readers.

Goodman, Louise. Ida's Doll. 1989. (Illus.). 32p. (J). (ps-3). 12.95 (*0-06-022275-1*); lib. bdg. 12.89 o.p. (*0-06-022276-X*) HarperCollins Children's Bk. Group.

—Ida's Doll. 1992. (Illus.). (J). 3.99 o.p. (*0-517-08507-0*) Random Hse. Value Publishing.

Goodman, Louise & Carter, D. Ida's Doll. 1991. 3.99 o.p. (*0-517-07120-7*) Random Hse. Value Publishing.

Gorbachev, Valeri. Nicky & the Rainy Day. 2002. (Illus.). 32p. (J). (ps-2). 15.95 (*0-7358-1644-1*); lib. bdg. 16.50 (*0-7358-1645-X*) North-South Bks., Inc.

Gordon, David, tr. & illus. The Ugly Truckling. 2004. (J). (*0-06-054600-X*); lib. bdg. (*0-06-054601-8*) HarperCollins Children's Bk. Group. (Geringer, Laura Bk.).

Gorman, Carol. Brian's Footsteps. 1994. (I Witness Ser.). (Illus.). 96p. (Orig.). (J). (gr. 4-7). pap. 4.99 o.p. (*0-570-04629-7*, 12-3210) Concordia Publishing Hse.

Got, Yves. Sam's Little Sister. 2002. (Illus.). 18p. (J). (ps-1). bds. 6.95 (*0-8118-3504-9*) Chronicle Bks. LLC.

Goudge, Elizabeth. Linnets & Valerians. 1981. (J). lib. bdg. 12.95 o.p. (*0-8398-2750-4*, Macmillan Reference USA) Gale Group.

—Linnets & Valerians. 1985. (YA). (gr. 7 up). pap. 1.75 o.p. (*0-380-01934-5*, 37838, Avon Bks.) Morrow/Avon.

—Linnets & Valerians. 2001. 256p. (J). pap. 5.99 (*0-14-230026-8*, Puffin Bks.) Penguin Putnam Bks. for Young Readers.

Graeber, Charlotte Towner & Boddy, Joe. The Hand-Me-Down Cap. 1986. (Mr. T & Me Ser.). (Illus.). 24p. (ps-4). pap. 1.95 o.p. (*0-8407-6637-8*) Nelson, Thomas Inc.

Graef, Renee, illus. Pioneer Sisters. 1997. (Little House Ser.: No. 2). 80p. (J). (gr. 3-6). pap. 4.25 (*0-06-442046-9*, Harper Trophy); (gr. 2-5). lib. bdg. 14.89 o.p. (*0-06-027132-9*) HarperCollins Children's Bk. Group.

—Pioneer Sisters. 1997. (Little House Chapter Bks.: No. 2). (J). (gr. 3-6). 10.40 (*0-606-10905-6*) Turtleback Bks.

Graham, Bob. Crusher Is Coming! 1990. (Illus.). 320p. (J). (ps-3). pap. 3.95 o.p. (*0-14-050826-0*, Puffin Bks.) Penguin Putnam Bks. for Young Readers.

Grahame, Kenneth. Dream Days. 1993. (Illus.). 240p. (YA). (gr. 5 up). 18.95 o.s.i (*0-89815-546-0*) Ten Speed Pr.

—The Golden Age. 2000. (J). E-Book 2.49 (*1-58744-126-8*) Electric Umbrella Publishing.

—The Golden Age. l.t. ed. 99p. pap. 14.50 (*0-7583-0936-8*); 421p. pap. 37.29 (*0-7583-0942-2*); 488p. pap. 42.06 (*0-7583-0943-0*); 342p. pap. 31.72 (*0-7583-0941-4*); 278p. pap. 27.19 (*0-7583-0940-6*); 217p. pap. 22.88 (*0-7583-0939-2*); 170p. pap. 19.52 (*0-7583-0938-4*); 124p. pap. 16.27 (*0-7583-0937-6*); 99p. lib. bdg. 20.60 (*0-7583-0928-7*); 278p. lib. bdg. 38.44 (*0-7583-0932-5*); 488p. lib. bdg. 53.31 (*0-7583-0935-X*); 421p. lib. bdg. 48.54 (*0-7583-0934-1*); 342p. lib. bdg. 42.97 (*0-7583-0933-3*); 170p. lib. bdg. 27.81 (*0-7583-0930-9*); 217p. lib. bdg. 33.37 (*0-7583-0931-7*); 124p. lib. bdg. 23.18 (*0-7583-0929-5*) Huge Print Pr.

—The Golden Age. 2002. 124p. (gr. 4-7). 22.99 (*1-4043-0572-6*); per. 18.99 (*1-4043-0573-4*) IndyPublish.com.

—The Golden Age. 1993. (Illus.). 264p. (YA). (gr. 5 up). 18.95 o.s.i (*0-89815-545-2*) Ten Speed Pr.

Grant, Eva. Will I Ever Be Older? 1981. (Life & Living from a Child's Point of View Ser.). (Illus.). (J). (gr. k-6). lib. bdg. 21.40 o.p. (*0-8172-1363-5*) Raintree Pubs.

Grant, Eva H. Will I Ever Be Older? (Good Days-Bad Days Ser.). (Illus.). 32p. (J). (gr. 1-3). 4.95 o.p. (*0-89191-206-1*) Cook Communications Ministries.

Graves, Kimberlee. I Have a New Baby Brother, Vol. 4154. 1997. (Science Ser.). (Illus.). 16p. (J). (gr. k-1). pap. 2.75 (*1-57471-317-5*, 4154) Creative Teaching Pr., Inc.

Gray, Luli. The Timespinners. 2003. 160p. (J). (gr. 5-9). tchr. ed. 15.00 (*0-618-16412-X*) Houghton Mifflin Co.

Greene, Constance C. I & Sproggy. 1990. (J). (gr. 4 up). pap. 3.95 o.p. (*0-14-034542-6*, Puffin Bks.) Penguin Putnam Bks. for Young Readers.

—I & Sproggy. 1978. (Illus.). (J). (gr. 3-7). 11.50 o.p. (*0-670-38980-3*, Viking Children's Bks.) Penguin Putnam Bks. for Young Readers.

Greene, Vivian. Chip, Oh Brother! 1979. (Illus.). (gr. 3-5). 2.95 o.p. (*0-531-02510-1*); lib. bdg. 5.90 o.p. (*0-531-04089-5*) Scholastic Library Publishing. (Watts, Franklin).

Greenfield, Eloise. Good News. 1977. (Illus.). 32p. (J). (gr. k-3). 5.95 o.p. (*0-698-20406-9*) Putnam Publishing Group, The.

—She Come Bringing Me That Little Baby Girl. 1999. (Illus.). (J). 13.35 (*0-7857-0466-3*) Econo-Clad Bks.

—She Come Bringing Me That Little Baby Girl. (Trophy Picture Bk.). (Illus.). 32p. (J). (ps-3). 1993. pap. 6.95 (*0-06-443296-3*, Harper Trophy); 1990. lib. bdg. 15.89 o.p. (*0-397-32478-2*); 1974. 16.00 o.p. (*0-397-31586-4*) HarperCollins Children's Bk. Group.

—She Come Bringing Me That Little Baby Girl. 1993. (J). 13.10 (*0-606-02891-9*) Turtleback Bks.

—Talk about a Family. (Trophy Bk.). (J). 1993. (Illus.). 64p. (gr. 4 up). pap. 4.99 (*0-06-440444-7*, Harper Trophy); 1991. (Illus.). 64p. (gr. 2-5). lib. bdg. 16.89 o.p. (*0-397-32504-5*); 1978. 12.95 o.p. (*0-397-31789-1*) HarperCollins Children's Bk. Group.

—Talk about a Family. 64p. (J). 1989. (gr. 3-7). mass mkt. 2.50 o.p. (*0-590-42247-2*, Scholastic Paperbacks); 1980. (Illus.). reprint ed. pap. 1.25 o.p. (*0-590-31268-5*) Scholastic, Inc.

—Talk about a Family. 1993. (J). 11.10 (*0-606-02943-5*) Turtleback Bks.

Gregory, Valiska. Shirley's Wonderful Baby. 2002. (Illus.). 32p. (J). (ps-2). 14.99 (*0-06-028132-4*) HarperCollins Children's Bk. Group.

Gretz, Susanna & Sage, Alison. Teddy Bears Cure a Cold. 1986. (Illus.). 32p. (J). (gr. k-3). reprint ed. pap. 2.95 o.p. (*0-590-42132-8*) Scholastic, Inc.

Griffin, Adele. Rainy Season. 1998. 208p. (J). (gr. 5-9). reprint ed. pap. 5.95 (*0-7868-1241-9*) Disney Pr.

—Rainy Season. 1996. (Illus.). 208p. (J). (gr. 4-7). tchr. ed. 14.95 o.p. (*0-395-81181-3*) Houghton Mifflin Co.

—Rainy Season. 1998. 12.00 (*0-606-13726-2*) Turtleback Bks.

Griffin, Andrew. Stanley Goes Ape. 2001. (Illus.). 32p. (J). (ps-2). 13.99 (*0-7868-0684-2*) Hyperion Bks. for Children.

Griffin, Claire Janosik. Kidding Around. 2000. (Rollicking Rhymes Ser.). (Illus.). 20p. (J). (gr. k-1). 3.99 (*1-56822-978-X*, IF40212-E4, Instructional Fair * T S Dension) McGraw-Hill Children's Publishing.

Griffin, Peni R. The Ghost Sitter. (J). 2002. 144p. pap. 5.99 (*0-14-230216-3*); 2001. 128p. (gr. 4-6). 14.99 (*0-525-46676-2*, Dutton Children's Bks.) Penguin Putnam Bks. for Young Readers.

—Vikki Vanishes. 1995. 160p. (J). (gr. 7 up). pap. 15.00 (*0-689-80028-2*, McElderry, Margaret K.) Simon & Schuster Children's Publishing.

Griffith, Helen V. Dinosaur Habitat. 1998. (Illus.). 112p. (J). (gr. 2 up). 15.99 (*0-688-15324-0*, Greenwillow Bks.) HarperCollins Children's Bk. Group.

—Dinosaur Habitat. 1999. (Avon Camelot Bks.). (Illus.). 112p. (J). (gr. 3-7). pap. 4.95 (*0-380-73225-4*, Avon Bks.) Morrow/Avon.

—Dinosaur Habitat. 1999. 10.04 (*0-606-17327-7*) Turtleback Bks.

Grimm, Jacob W. & Grimm, Wilhelm K. The Four Clever Brothers: A Story by the Brothers Grimm. 1967. (Illus.). 32p. (J). (gr. k-3). 6.95 o.p. (*0-15-229100-8*) Harcourt Children's Bks.

—Hansel & Gretel. 1986. (Pied Piper Bks.). (Illus.). 32p. (J). (gr. k up). pap. 4.95 o.p. (*0-8037-0318-X*, Dial Bks. for Young Readers) Penguin Putnam Bks. for Young Readers.

Grove, Vicki. Destiny. 2000. (Illus.). 169p. (J). (gr. 5-9). 16.99 (*0-399-23449-7*, G. P. Putnam's Sons) Penguin Group (USA) Inc.

Gruber, Wilhelm. The Upside-Down Reader. 1998. (Illus.). 60p. (J). (gr. 1-4). 13.95 o.p. (*1-55858-974-0*); 13.88 o.p. (*1-55858-975-9*) North-South Bks., Inc.

Gunn, Robin Jones. Without a Doubt. 1998. (Sierra Jensen Ser.: No. 5). 160p. (YA). (gr. 7-11). pap. 6.99 (*1-56179-519-4*) Focus on the Family Publishing.

Gutman, Dan. The Edison Mystery. 2001. (Qwerty Stevens Ser.). (Illus.). 208p. (J). (gr. 4-8). 16.00 (*0-689-84124-8*, Simon & Schuster Children's Publishing) Simon & Schuster Children's Publishing.

Haarhoff, Dorian. Desert December. 1992. (Illus.). 32p. (J). (ps-3). 13.95 o.s.i (*0-395-61300-0*, Clarion Bks.) Houghton Mifflin Co. Trade & Reference Div.

Haas, Dan. You Can Call Me Worm. 1998. 176p. (J). (gr. 5-9). 15.00 o.p. (*0-395-85783-X*) Houghton Mifflin Co.

—You Can Call Me Worm. 1999. (Illus.). 176p. (gr. 5-9). pap. 5.99 o.p. (*0-698-11751-4*, PaperStar) Penguin Putnam Bks. for Young Readers.

—You Can Call Me Worm. 1999. 12.04 (*0-606-16790-0*) Turtleback Bks.

Haas, Irene. The Maggie B. 1975. (Maggie B. Ser.: Vol. 1). (Illus.). 32p. (J). (ps-3). 18.00 (*0-689-50021-1*, McElderry, Margaret K.) Simon & Schuster Children's Publishing.

Haddix, Margaret Peterson. Among the Barons. 2003. (Shadow Children Ser.). 192p. (J). (gr. 4-7). 16.95 (*0-689-83906-5*, Simon & Schuster Children's Publishing) Simon & Schuster Children's Publishing.

Hager, Betty. Marcie & the Shrimp Boat Adventure. 1994. (Tales from the Bayou Ser.: Bk. 3). 128p. (J). (gr. 3-7). 5.99 o.p. (*0-310-38421-4*) Zondervan.

Hahn, Mary Downing. As Ever, Gordy. 1998. 192p. (YA). (gr. 7-9). tchr. ed. 15.00 (*0-395-83627-1*, Clarion Bks.) Houghton Mifflin Co. Trade & Reference Div.

—Hear the Wind Blow. 2003. (Illus.). 224p. (J). (gr. 5-9). tchr. ed. 15.00 (*0-618-18190-3*, Clarion Bks.) Houghton Mifflin Co. Trade & Reference Div.

Hahn, Mary Downing & Hansen, Joyce. One True Friend. Giblin, James Cross, ed. 2001. 160p. (J). (gr. 5-9). tchr. ed. 14.00 (*0-395-84983-7*, Clarion Bks.) Houghton Mifflin Co. Trade & Reference Div.

Halam, Ann. Taylor Five. 2004. (YA). (gr. 5). 208p. 15.95 (*0-385-73094-2*); 120892p. lib. bdg. 17.99 (*0-385-90114-3*) Random Hse. Children's Bks. (Lamb, Wendy).

Hall, Kirsten. My Brother, the Brat. 1995. (My First Hello Reader! Ser.). (Illus.). 32p. (J). (ps-1). 3.99 (*0-590-48504-0*, Cartwheel Bks.) Scholastic, Inc.

—Our Tea Party. 1997. (My First Hello Reader! Ser.). (Illus.). 32p. (J). (ps-1). 3.99 o.s.i (*0-590-68996-7*) Scholastic, Inc.

Hall, Lynn. Half the Battle. 1982. 160p. (YA). (gr. 7 up). 10.95 o.s.i (*0-684-17348-4*, Macmillan Reference USA) Gale Group.

Hallinan, P. K. We're Very Good Friends, My Brother & I. 2001. (Illus.). 24p. (J). (ps-3). pap. 5.95 (*0-8249-5387-8*, Ideals) Ideals Pubns.

—We're Very Good Friends, My Brother & I. 1973. (P. K. Books Values for Life). (Illus.). 32p. (J). (gr. k-3). lib. bdg. 13.27 o.p. (*0-516-03659-9*, Children's Pr.) Scholastic Library Publishing.

Hallinan, P. K., tr. & illus. My Brother & I. 2003. 26p. (J). 7.95 (*0-8249-5455-6*, Candy Cane Pr.) Ideals Pubns.

Halvorson, Marilyn. Brothers & Strangers. unabr. ed. 1996. (Gemini Bks.). 192p. (YA). (gr. 7-12). mass mkt. 5.95 (*0-7736-7452-7*) Stoddart Kids CAN. *Dist:* Fitzhenry & Whiteside, Ltd.

Hamilton, Gail. Family Rivalry. 1993. (Road to Avonlea Ser.: No. 16). 128p. (J). (gr. 4-6). pap. 3.99 o.p. (*0-553-48042-1*) Bantam Bks.

Hamilton, Virginia. Justice & Her Brothers. 1989. (Justice Cycle Ser.: Vol. 1). 290p. (YA). (gr. 7 up). pap. 3.95 o.p. (*0-15-241640-4*, Odyssey Classics) Harcourt Children's Bks.

—Justice & Her Brothers. 1998. (Justice Cycle Ser.: Vol. 1). 214p. (J). (gr. 6-12). mass mkt. 4.99 (*0-590-36214-3*, Scholastic Paperbacks) Scholastic, Inc.

—Justice & Her Brothers. 1992. (J). (gr. 4-7). 17.55 o.p. (*0-8446-6577-0*) Smith, Peter Pub., Inc.

—Justice & Her Brothers. (Justice Cycle Ser.: Vol. 1). 1998. 11.04 (*0-606-12973-1*); 1989. 9.05 o.p. (*0-606-01602-3*) Turtleback Bks.

Hamner, Genie L. Kitten for Julie & Christopher. 1998. (Illus.). 23p. (J). (ps). pap. 6.95 o.p. (*1-887650-10-5*) Factor Pr.

Hanel, Wolfram. Little Elephant Runs Away. James, J. Alison, tr. from GER. 2001. (Illus.). 32p. (J). (ps-2). 15.95 (*0-7358-1444-9*); lib. bdg. 16.50 (*0-7358-1445-7*) North-South Bks., Inc.

Hanrahan, Brendan. My Sisters Love My Clothes. 1992. (Illus.). 32p. (J). (gr. 1-4). 12.95 (*0-9630181-0-8*) Perry Heights Pr.

Hansel et Gretel. (Best-Sellers Ser.).Tr. of Hansel & Gretel. (FRE., Illus.). 48p. (J). (gr. k-3). pap. 9.95 incl. audio (*2-921997-79-7*) Coffragants CAN. *Dist:* Penton Overseas, Inc.

Harber, Frances. The Brothers' Promise. 1998. (Illus.). 32p. (J). (gr. 1-5). lib. bdg. 15.95 o.p. (*0-8075-0900-0*) Whitman, Albert & Co.

Harlan, Elizabeth. Watershed. 1986. (Viking Kestrel Novels Ser.). 224p. (J). (gr. 5-9). 12.95 o.p. (*0-670-80824-5*, Viking Children's Bks.) Penguin Putnam Bks. for Young Readers.

Harper, Anita. It's Not Fair. 1986. (Illus.). 24p. (J). (ps). 10.95 o.s.i (*0-399-21365-1*, Philomel) Penguin Putnam Bks. for Young Readers.

Harper, Charise Mericle. Yes, No, Maybe So. 2004. 32p. (J). bds. 9.99 (*0-8037-2956-1*, Dial Bks. for Young Readers) Penguin Putnam Bks. for Young Readers.

Harris, Dorothy Joan. Cameron & Me. ed. 1999. (J). (gr. 1). spiral bd. (*0-616-01667-0*); (gr. 2). spiral bd. (*0-616-01668-9*) Canadian National Institute for the Blind/Institut National Canadien pour les Aveugles.

—Cameron & Me. 1997. (Illus.). 32p. (J). (ps-3). 13.95 (*0-7737-3004-4*) Stoddart Kids CAN. *Dist:* Fitzhenry & Whiteside, Ltd.

Harrison, Dorothy L. Operation Morningstar. 1997. (Chronicles of Courage Ser.). 128p. (J). (gr. 3-7). pap. 4.99 o.p. (*0-7814-0242-5*) Cook Communications Ministries.

Harvey, Jayne. Great-Uncle Dracula & the Dirty Rat. 1993. (Stepping Stone Book Ser.). (Illus.). 64p. (J). (gr. 2-4). pap. 2.50 o.s.i (*0-679-83457-5*, Random Hse. Bks. for Young Readers) Random Hse. Children's Bks.

Hassett, John & Hassett, Ann. We Got My Brother at the Zoo. 1993. 32p. (J). (ps-3). 14.95 o.p. (*0-395-62429-0*) Houghton Mifflin Co.

Hathaway, Lucinda. Takashi's Voyage: The Wreck of the Sindia. 1995. (Illus.). 107p. (J). (gr. 4-7). 12.00 (*0-945582-24-2*) Down The Shore Publishing.

Hatrick, Gloria. Masks. 1996. 128p. (YA). (gr. 7 up). pap. 15.95 (*0-531-09514-2*); lib. bdg. 16.99 (*0-531-08864-2*) Scholastic, Inc. (Orchard Bks.).

Hatton, Caroline K. Vero & Philippe. 2001. (Illus.). 120p. (J). (gr. 3-7). 14.95 (*0-8126-2940-X*) Cricket Bks.

Hauger, Torill Thorstad. Escape from the Vikings. Hannes, Lisa, ed. Born, Anne, tr. from NOR. 2000. Orig. Title: Flukten Fra Vikingene. (Illus.). 175p. (J). (gr. 4-12). pap. (*1-57534-013-5*) Skandisk, Inc.

Havill, Juanita. It Always Happens to Leona. 1989. (Illus.). (J). (gr. 2 up). 12.95 o.s.i (*0-517-57227-3*, Random Hse. Bks. for Young Readers) Random Hse. Children's Bks.

—Jamaica Tag-Along. (Carry-Along Book & Cassette Favorites Ser.). (J). 1996. (Illus.). 1p. (ps-3). pap. 9.95 incl. audio (*0-395-77941-3*, 4-95859); 1996. (Illus.). 1p. (ps-3). pap. 9.95 incl. audio (*0-395-77941-3*, 4-95859); 1994. pap. 44.32 (*0-395-70375-1*); 1992. (gr. 1). pap. 8.72 (*0-395-61768-5*); 1990. (Illus.). 32p. (ps-3). pap. 6.95 (*0-395-54949-3*); 1989. (Illus.). 32p. (ps-3). lib. bdg., tchr. ed. 16.00 (*0-395-49602-0*) Houghton Mifflin Co.

—Jamaica Tag-Along. 1990. 12.10 (*0-606-17136-3*) Turtleback Bks.

—Jennifer, Too. 1995. (Hyperion Chapters Ser.: Vol. 1). (Illus.). 64p. (J). (ps-3). pap. 3.95 o.s.i (*0-7868-1072-6*) Disney Pr.

—Jennifer, Too. 1994. (Illus.). (J). (gr. 2-4). 64p. 11.95 o.s.i (*1-56282-618-2*); 56p. lib. bdg. 12.49 o.s.i (*1-56282-619-0*) Hyperion Bks. for Children.

—Jennifer, Too. 1994. 10.10 (*0-606-09486-5*) Turtleback Bks.

—Saving Owen's Toad. 1994. (Illus.). 128p. (J). (gr. 3-6). 14.95 o.p. (*0-7868-0029-1*); lib. bdg. 15.49 o.s.i (*0-7868-2024-1*) Hyperion Bks. for Children.

Hawkins, Colin. Foxy & His Naughty Little Sister. (Illus.). 24p. pap. 8.95 (*0-00-664564-X*) Collins Willow GBR. *Dist:* Trafalgar Square.

Hazen, Barbara Shook. It Isn't Fair: A Book about Sibling Rivalry. 1986. (Golden Learn About Living Bks.). (Illus.). 32p. (J). (gr. k-3). o.p. (*0-307-12489-4*, Golden Bks.) Random Hse. Children's Bks.

HB Staff. Two of Everything. 95th ed. 1995. (J). (gr. 2). lib. bdg. 9.25 (*0-15-305200-7*) Harcourt College Pubs.

Hearne, Betsy. Wishes, Kisses, & Pigs. 144p. (J). 2003. pap. 4.99 (*0-689-86347-0*, Aladdin); 2001. (Illus.). (gr. 3-7). 16.00 (*0-689-84122-1*, McElderry, Margaret K.) Simon & Schuster Children's Publishing.

—Wishes, Kisses & Pigs. l.t. ed. 2001. (Juvenile Ser.). 133p. (J). 20.95 (*0-7862-3470-9*) Thorndike Pr.

Heckmsn, Philip. Waking Upside Down. 1996. (Illus.). 40p. (J). (ps-3). 16.00 (*0-689-31930-4*, Atheneum) Simon & Schuster Children's Publishing.

Hedger, Jack. The Seven Cartons of Love: Do Siblings Care? unabr. ed. 1996. (Illus.). 58p. (J). 19.95 (*1-882416-18-X*) Akela West Pubs.

Heesakkers, Wim. My Little Brother. 1985. (First Step Ser.). 24p. (J). (ps-1). 3.95 o.p. (*0-8120-5643-4*) Barron's Educational Series, Inc.

Hegeman, Andrew. The Last Dinosaur Egg. 1998. (Illus.). 36p. (J). (ps-3). 15.95 (*1-890817-04-X*) Winslow Pr.

Hell, John. Dear Sister. 1994. 224p. (YA). mass mkt. 3.99 o.p. (*0-06-106282-0*) HarperCollins Children's Bk. Group.

Helldorfer, Mary-Claire. The Darling Boys. 1992. (Illus.). 32p. (J). (gr. k-3). lib. bdg. 14.95 o.p. (*0-02-743516-4*, Atheneum) Simon & Schuster Children's Publishing.

Helmering, Doris Wild & Helmering, John. We're Going to Have a Baby. 1978. (Illus.). (J). (gr. k-3). 6.95 o.p. (*0-687-44446-2*) Abingdon Pr.

Henderson, Garnet, illus. Joseph & His Brothers. 1995. 40p. (J). (gr. 1-4). 19.95 o.p. incl. audio (*0-689-80064-9*, Simon & Schuster Children's Publishing) Simon & Schuster Children's Publishing.

Henkes, Kevin. Julius, the Baby of the World. 1990. (Illus.). 32p. (J). (ps-3). 15.99 (*0-688-08943-7*); lib. bdg. 16.89 (*0-688-08944-5*) HarperCollins Children's Bk. Group. (Greenwillow Bks.).

—Julius, the Baby of the World. 1995. (Illus.). 32p. (J). (ps-3). pap. 5.99 (*0-688-14388-1*, Morrow, William & Co.) Morrow/Avon.

—Julius, the Baby of the World. 1995. 12.10 (*0-606-07754-5*) Turtleback Bks.

—Margaret & Taylor. 1983. (Illus.). 64p. (J). (gr. 1-3). 11.95 o.p. (*0-688-01425-9*); lib. bdg. 11.88 o.p. (*0-688-01426-7*) HarperCollins Children's Bk. Group. (Greenwillow Bks.).

—Sheila Rae's Peppermint Stick. (Illus.). 24p. (J). 2003. bds. 10.99 (*0-06-054078-8*); 2001. 6.95 (*0-06-029451-5*) HarperCollins Children's Bk. Group. (Harper Festival).

Henry, Marguerite. Misty of Chincoteague. 1991. pap. 3.95 o.p. (*0-689-71483-1*) Aladdin Paperbacks.

—Misty of Chincoteague. 2002. (Illus.). (J). 13.40 (*0-7587-0291-4*) Book Wholesalers, Inc.

—Misty of Chincoteague. 1995. (Illus.). (J). (gr. 4). 9.00 (*0-395-73241-7*) Houghton Mifflin Co.

Relationships

—Misty of Chincoteague. 1986. (J). 19.95 o.p. (*0-516-09863-2*, Children's Pr.) Scholastic Library Publishing.
—Misty of Chincoteague. 9999. 160p. (J). (gr. 4-6). pap. 1.75 o.s.i (*0-590-02388-8*) Scholastic, Inc.
—Misty of Chincoteague. 2003. 176p. (J). pap. o.s.i (*0-689-86224-5*, Aladdin); 2001. 176p. mass mkt. 2.99 (*0-689-84512-X*, Aladdin); 1998. (J). pap. 2.65 (*0-689-82170-0*, Aladdin); 1997. (J). 100.00 (*0-689-81377-5*, Simon & Schuster Children's Publishing); 1995. (J). 3.95 o.s.i (*0-689-80407-5*, Aladdin); 1990. (Illus.). 176p. (J). (gr. 3-7). 17.95 (*0-02-743622-5*, Simon & Schuster Children's Publishing); 2000. (Illus.). 176p. (J). (gr. 3-7). 21.95 o.s.i (*0-689-83926-X*, Simon & Schuster Children's Publishing); 1991. (Illus.). 176p. (J). (gr. 3-7). reprint ed. pap. 4.99 (*0-689-71492-0*, Aladdin); Vol. 1. 1999. pap. 2.99 (*0-689-82993-0*, Aladdin) Simon & Schuster Children's Publishing.
—Misty of Chincoteague. l.t. ed. 2001. (Illus.). 195p. (J). (gr. 4-7). 21.95 (*0-7862-2847-4*) Thorndike Pr.
—Misty of Chincoteague. 1991. (J). 11.04 (*0-606-04009-9*) Turtleback Bks.
Hering, Marianne. Mockingbird Mystery. (White House Adventures Ser.: Vol. 1). 64p. (J). (gr. 2-5). pap. 4.99 (*0-7814-3065-8*) Cook Communications Ministries.
Herman, Charlotte. On the Way to the Movies. 1980. (Illus.). 32p. (J). (gr. k-3). 7.95 o.p. (*0-525-36400-5*, Dutton) Dutton/Plume.
Herman, Emily. The Missing Fossil Mystery. 1996. (Hyperion Chapters Ser.). (Illus.). 64p. (J). (gr. 2-4). pap. 3.95 o.s.i (*0-7868-1091-2*) Disney Pr.
—The Missing Fossil Mystery. 1996. (Chapters Ser.). (Illus.). 64p. (J). (gr. 2-4). 13.95 o.s.i (*0-7868-0145-X*) Hyperion Bks. for Children.
Herman, Gail. Buried in the Back Yard. 2003. (Science Solves It! Ser.). (Illus.). 32p. (J). 4.99 (*1-57565-126-2*) Kane Pr., The.
—The Creeping Tide. 2003. (Science Solves It! Ser.). (Illus.). 32p. (J). 4.99 (*1-57565-128-9*) Kane Pr., The.
—Spike at Halloween. 2002. (All Aboard Reading Ser.). (Illus.). 32p. (J). mass mkt. 3.99 (*0-448-42692-7*, Grosset & Dunlap) Penguin Putnam Bks. for Young Readers.
Hermes, Patricia. Cheat the Moon: A Novel. 1998. (Illus.). 176p. (J). (gr. 3-7). 15.95 o.p. (*0-316-35929-7*) Little Brown & Co.
—Everything Stinks. MacDonald, Pat, ed. (Cousins' Club Ser.). (J). 1999. 176p. 14.00 (*0-671-89653-9*, Simon & Schuster Children's Publishing); 1995. 160p. (gr. 4-7). pap. 3.50 (*0-671-87967-7*, Aladdin) Simon & Schuster Children's Publishing.
—Everything Stinks. 1995. (Cousins' Club Ser.). (YA). 8.60 o.p. (*0-606-07392-2*) Turtleback Bks.
—Mama, Let's Dance. 1991. (YA). (gr. 5 up). 15.95 o.p. (*0-316-35861-4*) Little Brown & Co.
Hernandez, Irene B. The Secret of Two Brothers. 1995. 182p. (YA). (gr. 7-12). pap. 9.95 (*1-55885-142-9*, Piñata Books) Arte Publico Pr.
—The Secret of Two Brothers. 1995. 16.00 (*0-606-16039-6*) Turtleback Bks.
Herrick, Amy. Kimbo's Marble. 1993. (Laura Geringer Bks.). (Illus.). 48p. (J). (gr. 1-5). 16.00 o.p. (*0-06-020373-0*); lib. bdg. 15.89 o.p. (*0-06-020374-9*) HarperCollins Children's Bk. Group.
Hersom, Kathleen. The Half Child. 1991. 176p. (YA). (gr. 5-9). ring bd. 15.00 o.s.i (*0-671-74225-6*, Simon & Schuster Children's Publishing) Simon & Schuster Children's Publishing.
Herzig, Alison C. & Mali, Jane L. A Season of Secrets. 1982. 192p. (J). (gr. 5-7). 14.95 o.p. (*0-316-35889-4*) Little Brown & Co.
—A Season of Secrets. 1985. 284p. (J). (gr. 4-6). reprint ed. pap. 2.25 o.p. (*0-590-32818-2*, Scholastic Paperbacks) Scholastic, Inc.
Hest, Amy. You're the Boss, Baby Duck! 1997. (Illus.). 32p. (J). (ps-1). 16.99 o.s.i (*1-56402-667-1*) Candlewick Pr.
Heymans, Annemie & Heymans, Margriet. The Princess in the Kitchen Garden, RS. 1993. (Illus.). 48p. (J). (ps-3). 16.00 o.p. (*0-374-36122-3*, Farrar, Straus & Giroux (BYR)) Farrar, Straus & Giroux.
Hiatt, Fred. Baby Talk. 1999. (Illus.). 32p. (J). (ps-2). 14.00 o.s.i (*0-689-82146-8*, McElderry, Margaret K.) Simon & Schuster Children's Publishing.
Hickox, Rebecca. Per & the Dala Horse. 1995. (Illus.). 32p. (J). (ps-3). 15.95 o.s.i (*0-385-32075-2*, Doubleday Bks. for Young Readers) Random Hse. Children's Bks.
Hill, Kirkpatrick. Toughboy & Sister. 128p. (J). (gr. 3-7). 2000. pap. 4.99 (*0-689-83978-2*, Aladdin); 1990. mass mkt. 15.00 o.s.i (*0-689-50506-X*, McElderry, Margaret K.) Simon & Schuster Children's Publishing.
—Toughboy & Sister. 1992. (J). 9.09 (*0-606-00808-X*) Turtleback Bks.
Hill, Kirkpatrick & Greene, Douglas G. Toughboy & Sister. 1992. (Illus.). 128p. (J). (gr. 3-7). pap. 5.99 (*0-14-034866-2*, Puffin Bks.) Penguin Putnam Bks. for Young Readers.
Hill, Sue K. Night Travelers. 1994. (Illus.). 64p. (J). (gr. 4 up). pap. 9.00 (*1-56002-335-X*, University Editions) Aegina Pr., Inc.
Hines, Anna Grossnickle. Big Help! 1995. (Illus.). 32p. (J). (ps-3). tchr. ed. 13.95 o.p. (*0-395-68702-0*, Clarion Bks.) Houghton Mifflin Co. Trade & Reference Div.
—Big Like Me. 1989. (Illus.). 32p. (J). (ps-3). 16.99 (*0-688-08354-4*); lib. bdg. 15.93 o.p. (*0-688-08355-2*) HarperCollins Children's Bk. Group. (Greenwillow Bks.).
—Got You! 2001. (Rookie Readers Ser.). (Illus.). 32p. (J). (gr. 1-2). pap. 4.95 (*0-516-27294-2*); lib. bdg. 19.00 (*0-516-22176-0*) Scholastic Library Publishing. (Children's Pr.).
—They Really Like Me! 1989. (Illus.). 24p. (J). (ps up). 11.95 o.p. (*0-688-07733-1*); lib. bdg. 11.88 o.p. (*0-688-07734-X*) HarperCollins Children's Bk. Group. (Greenwillow Bks.).
Hinton, S. E. The Puppy Sister. 1997. (Illus.). 128p. (J). (gr. 2-6). pap. text 4.50 (*0-440-41384-2*) Dell Publishing.
—The Puppy Sister. 1995. (Illus.). 96p. (J). (gr. 2-6). 14.95 o.s.i (*0-385-32060-4*, Dell Books for Young Readers) Random Hse. Children's Bks.
—Rumble Fish. 1989. (J). mass mkt. o.s.i (*0-440-80139-7*, Dell Books for Young Readers); 144p. (YA). (gr. 7-12). mass mkt. 5.99 (*0-440-97534-4*, Laurel Leaf) Random Hse. Children's Bks.
Hoban, Lillian. Arthur's Back to School Day. 1996. (I Can Read Bks.). (Illus.). 48p. (J). (gr. k-3). lib. bdg. 16.89 (*0-06-024956-0*); 15.95 o.p. (*0-06-024955-2*) HarperCollins Children's Bk. Group.
—Arthur's Birthday Party. 1999. (I Can Read Bks.). (Illus.). 64p. (J). (ps-3). 14.95 (*0-06-027798-X*) HarperCollins Children's Bk. Group.
Hoban, Russell. La Nueva Hermanita de Francisca. González, Tomás, tr. 1997. (SPA., Illus.). 32p. (J). (ps-3). pap. 5.95 o.p. (*0-06-443461-3*) HarperCollins Children's Bk. Group.
—La Nueva Hermanita de Francisca. 1997. 11.15 o.p. (*0-606-10859-9*) Turtleback Bks.
Hobbs, Valerie. Sonny's War, RS. 2002. 224p. (YA). (gr. 7 up). 16.00 (*0-374-37136-9*, Farrar, Straus & Giroux (BYR)) Farrar, Straus & Giroux.
Hobbs, William. Jackie's Wild Seattle. (J). 2004. 208p. pap. 5.99 (*0-380-73311-0*, Harper Trophy); 2003. 192p. (gr. 5 up). 15.99 (*0-688-17474-4*); 2003. 192p. (gr. 5 up). lib. bdg. 16.89 (*0-06-051631-3*) HarperCollins Children's Bk. Group.
Hoberman, Mary Ann. And to Think That We Thought That We'd Never be Friends. 1999. (Illus.). 40p. (J). (gr. k-3). 15.95 (*0-517-80068-3*, Crown) Crown Publishing Group.
—The Seven Silly Eaters. (J). (ps-3). 2000. (Illus.). 40p. pap. 6.00 (*0-15-202440-9*, Voyager Bks./Libros Viajeros); 1997. 15.00 o.s.i (*0-15-201742-9*); 1997. (Illus.). 40p. 16.00 (*0-15-200096-8*, Gulliver Bks.) Harcourt Children's Bks.
Holabird, Katharine. Angelina's Baby Sister. 1991. (Angelina Ballerina Ser.). (J). (ps-3). 16.00 o.p. (*0-517-58600-2*, Clarkson Potter) Crown Publishing Group.
—Angelina's Baby Sister. (Angelina Ballerina Ser.). (Illus.). 24p. (J). (ps-3). 2002. 12.95 (*1-58485-657-2*); 2000. 9.95 (*1-58485-132-5*) Pleasant Co. Pubns.
—Angelina's Baby Sister: Includes Polly Doll. 2002. (Angelina Ballerina Ser.). (Illus.). (J). (ps-3). 24.95 (*1-58485-590-8*) Pleasant Co. Pubns.
Holcomb, Jerry K. The Chinquapin Tree. 1998. (Accelerated Reader Bks.). 192p. (J). (gr. 3-7). 14.95 (*0-7614-5028-9*, Cavendish Children's Bks.) Cavendish, Marshall Corp.
Holeman, Linda. Search of the Moon King's Daughter. 320p. (YA). (gr. 6). 2003. pap. 9.95 (*0-88776-609-9*); 2002. 17.95 o.s.i (*0-88776-592-0*) Tundra Bks. of Northern New York.
Holm, Jennifer L. Our Only May Amelia. (Harper Trophy Bks.). (Illus.). 272p. (gr. 4 up). 2001. (J). pap. 5.99 (*0-06-440856-6*, Harper Trophy); 1999. (J). 16.99 (*0-06-027822-6*); 1999. (YA). lib. bdg. 15.89 (*0-06-028354-8*) HarperCollins Children's Bk. Group.
—Our Only May Amelia. unabr. ed. 2001. 253p. (J). (gr. 4-6). pap. 35.00 incl. audio (*0-8072-8366-5*, YA191SP, Listening Library) Random Hse. Audio Publishing Group.
—Our Only May Amelia. l.t. ed. 2000. (Illus.). 261p. (J). (ps up). 21.95 (*0-7862-2742-7*) Thorndike Pr.
Holm-McHenry, Janet. The Chosen Ones. 1995. (Golden Rule Duo Ser.). 48p. (J). pap. 3.99 o.p. (*0-7814-0172-0*) Cook Communications Ministries.
Holmes, Sarah. I'm Somebody Too. 1996. 50p. pap., tchr. ed. 10.95 (*1-884281-13-3*) Verbal Images Pr.
Hooks, William H. Gruff Brothers. 1989. (J). o.p. (*0-553-53021-6*, Dell Books for Young Readers) Random Hse. Children's Bks.
—The Legend of the Christmas Rose. 1999. (Illus.). 32p. (J). (gr. k-4). 14.95 (*0-06-027102-7*); lib. bdg. 14.89 (*0-06-027103-5*) HarperCollins Children's Bk. Group.
—Mr. Baseball. 1991. 48p. (J). (ps-3). 9.99 o.s.i (*0-553-07315-X*); pap. 4.50 o.s.i (*0-553-35303-9*) Bantam Bks.
—Mr. Baseball. 1998. (Bank Street Reader Collection). (Illus.). 48p. (J). (gr. 2-4). lib. bdg. 21.26 (*0-8368-1765-6*) Stevens, Gareth Inc.
—Mr. Baseball. (J). E-Book (*1-58824-172-6*); 1991. E-Book (*1-59019-346-6*) ipicturebooks, LLC.
—Mr. Big Brother. 1999. (Bank Street Ready-to-Read Ser.). (Illus.). 32p. (J). (ps-3). pap. 4.50 o.s.i (*0-553-37586-5*) Bantam Bks.
—Mr. Big Brother. 1999. (Bank Street Reader Collection). (Illus.). (J). (ps-2). lib. bdg. 21.26 (*0-8368-2417-2*) Stevens, Gareth Inc.
—Mr. Big Brother. (J). E-Book (*1-58824-173-4*); 1999. E-Book (*1-58824-376-1*) ipicturebooks, LLC.
—Mr. Bubble Gum. 1997. (Bank Street Reader Collection). (Illus.). 48p. (J). (gr. 2-4). lib. bdg. 21.26 (*0-8368-1754-0*) Stevens, Gareth Inc.
—Mr. Bubble Gum. 2000. (J). E-Book (*1-58824-174-2*); 1989. E-Book (*1-58824-078-9*); 1989. E-Book (*1-59019-306-7*) ipicturebooks, LLC.
—Mr. Dinosaur. 1994. (Bank Street Ready-to-Read Ser.). (Illus.). (J). 32p. 10.95 o.s.i (*0-553-09042-9*); 48p. pap. 4.50 o.s.i (*0-553-37234-3*) Random Hse. Children's Bks. (Dell Books for Young Readers).
—Mr. Dinosaur. 1997. (Bank Street Reader Collection). (Illus.). 48p. (J). (gr. 2-4). lib. bdg. 21.26 (*0-8368-1755-9*) Stevens, Gareth Inc.
—Mr. Garbage Level 3: Bank Street Ready-to-Read. 1996. (J). (gr. 2-3). E-Book (*1-58824-176-9*) ipicturebooks, LLC.
—Mr. Monster. 1998. (Bank Street Reader Collection). (Illus.). 48p. (J). (gr. 2-4). lib. bdg. 21.26 (*0-8368-1774-5*) Stevens, Gareth Inc.
Hooks, William H. & Meisel, Paul. Mr. Baseball. 1991. E-Book (*1-58824-103-3*) ipicturebooks, LLC.
Hope, Laura Lee. The Bobbsey Twins & the Weird Science Mystery. 1990. (New Bobbsey Twins Ser.: No. 20). (Illus.). 96p. (Orig.). (J). (gr. 3-5). pap. 2.95 (*0-671-69292-5*, Aladdin) Simon & Schuster Children's Publishing.
Horgan, Dorothy. Tom & Maggie. 1988. (Illus.). 124p. (J). (gr. 4 up). 13.95 o.p. (*0-19-271544-5*) Oxford Univ. Pr., Inc.
Horowitz, Ruth. Mommy's Lap. 1993. (J). (ps-3). 13.00 o.p. (*0-688-07235-6*); lib. bdg. 12.93 o.p. (*0-688-07236-4*) HarperCollins Children's Bk. Group.
Horrocks, Anita. Topher. 2000. 192p. (YA). (gr. 5-9). pap. 7.95 (*0-7737-6092-X*) Stoddart Kids CAN. *Dist:* Fitzhenry & Whiteside, Ltd.
Horvath, Polly. The Trolls, RS. 1999. 144p. (J). (gr. 3-7). 16.00 (*0-374-37787-1*, Farrar, Straus & Giroux (BYR)) Farrar, Straus & Giroux.
Howard, Elizabeth Fitzgerald. Mac & Marie & the Train Toss Surprise. 1993. (Illus.). 32p. (J). (ps-2). 14.95 o.s.i (*0-02-744640-9*, Simon & Schuster Children's Publishing) Simon & Schuster Children's Publishing.
—When Will Sarah Come. 1999. (Illus.). 24p. (J). (ps-3). 16.00 (*0-688-16180-4*); lib. bdg. 15.89 (*0-688-16181-2*) HarperCollins Children's Bk. Group. (Greenwillow Bks.).
Howard, Ellen. The Cellar. 1992. (Illus.). 64p. (J). (gr. 2-4). lib. bdg. 12.95 o.p. (*0-689-31724-7*, Atheneum) Simon & Schuster Children's Publishing.
Howard, Megan. My Sister Stole My Boyfriend, Bk. 3. 1994. (Diary S. O. S. Ser.: No. 3). 144p. (Orig.). (J). (gr. 3-9). pap. 3.99 o.s.i (*0-679-85703-6*, Random Hse. Bks. for Young Readers) Random Hse. Children's Bks.
Howe, James. Pinky & Rex Get Married. 1990. (Pinky & Rex Ser.). (Illus.). 48p. (J). (gr. 1-4). text 12.95 o.s.i (*0-689-31453-1*, Atheneum) Simon & Schuster Children's Publishing.
—There's a Dragon in My Sleeping Bag. 1994. (Illus.). 40p. (J). (ps-2). 15.00 o.s.i (*0-689-31873-1*, Atheneum) Simon & Schuster Children's Publishing.
Howland, Ethan. The Lobster War. 2001. (Illus.). 146p. (J). (gr. 7 up). 15.95 (*0-8126-2800-4*) Cricket Bks.
Hughes, Dean. Brothers. 1989. 105p. (YA). (gr. 7-12). pap. 4.95 o.p. (*0-87579-232-4*) Deseret Bk. Co.
Hughes, Pat. The Breaker Boys, RS. 2004. (J). (*0-374-30956-6*) Farrar, Straus & Giroux.
Hughes, Shirley. Alfie's ABC. 1998. (Illus.). 32p. (J). (ps-k). 16.00 (*0-688-16126-X*, Morrow, William & Co.) Morrow/Avon.
—Annie Rose Is My Little Sister. 2003. (Illus.). 32p. (J). (ps-2). 15.99 (*0-7636-1959-0*) Candlewick Pr.
—The Big Alfie & Annie Rose Storybook. 1989. (Illus.). 64p. (J). (ps-1). lib. bdg. 14.88 o.p. (*0-688-07673-4*); 18.00 (*0-688-07672-6*) HarperCollins Children's Bk. Group.
—Olly & Me. 2004. 32p. (J). 15.99 (*0-7636-2374-1*) Candlewick Pr.
Hunt, L. J. The Abernathy Boys. 2004. (Abernathy Boys Ser.). 208p. (J). 15.99 (*0-06-440953-8*); (Illus.). lib. bdg. 16.89 (*0-06-029259-8*) HarperCollins Pubs.
Hunter, Sally M. Humphrey's Bedtime, ERS. (Illus.). 32p. (J). 2003. pap. 5.95 (*0-8050-7398-1*); 2001. 14.95 (*0-8050-6903-8*) Holt, Henry & Co. (Holt, Henry & Co. Bks. For Young Readers).
Huriet, Genevieve. Violette's Daring Adventure. 1992. (Beechwood Bunny Tales Ser.). (Illus.). 32p. (J). (gr. k-3). lib. bdg. 19.93 o.p. (*0-8368-0912-2*) Stevens, Gareth Inc.
Hurst, Carol Otis. The Wrong One. 2003. 160p. (J). tchr. ed. 15.00 (*0-618-27599-1*) Houghton Mifflin Co.
Hurwitz, Johanna. Aldo Ice Cream. 1981. (Illus.). 128p. (J). (gr. 4-6). 15.00 o.p. (*0-688-00375-3*); lib. bdg. 15.93 o.p. (*0-688-00374-5*) Morrow/Avon. (Morrow, William & Co.).
—Aldo Ice Cream. 1989. (Illus.). 128p. (J). (gr. 4-7). pap. 4.99 o.s.i (*0-14-034084-X*, Puffin Bks.) Penguin Putnam Bks. for Young Readers.
—Aldo Ice Cream. (J). (gr. 3-5). 1984. pap. (*0-671-52762-2*); 1982. (Illus.). reprint ed. pap. (*0-671-43940-5*) Simon & Schuster Children's Publishing. (Simon Pulse).
—Aldo Ice Cream. 1981. (J). 9.09 o.p. (*0-606-00308-8*) Turtleback Bks.
—Elisa in the Middle. 1995. (Illus.). 96p. (J). (ps-3). 14.95 (*0-688-14050-5*, Morrow, William & Co.) Morrow/Avon.
—Even Stephen. 1996. (Illus.). 104p. (J). (gr. 4-7). 15.00 (*0-688-14197-8*, Morrow, William & Co.) Morrow/Avon.
—Make Room for Elisa. 1993. (Illus.). 80p. (J). (gr. k up). 15.00 o.s.i (*0-688-12404-6*, Morrow, William & Co.) Morrow/Avon.
—Make Room for Elisa. 1995. (Illus.). 96p. (J). pap. 3.99 o.s.i (*0-14-037034-X*, Puffin Bks.) Penguin Putnam Bks. for Young Readers.
—New Neighbors for Nora. 2001. (Riverside Kids Ser.). (Illus.). 96p. (J). (gr. 1-8). pap. 4.25 (*0-06-442169-4*, Harper Trophy) HarperCollins Children's Bk. Group.
—New Neighbors for Nora. (Illus.). 80p. (J). (gr. k-3). 1979. 11.95 o.p. (*0-688-22173-4*); 1991. reprint ed. 12.95 o.p. (*0-688-09947-5*); 1991. reprint ed. lib. bdg. 12.88 (*0-688-09948-3*) Morrow/Avon. (Morrow, William & Co.).
—Nora & Mrs. Mind-Your-Own-Business. 1981. (Illus.). 96p. (gr. 1-5). pap. 1.25 o.p. (*0-440-45668-1*) Dell Publishing.
—Nora & Mrs. Mind-Your-Own-Business. 2001. (Riverside Kids Ser.). (Illus.). 96p. (J). (gr. 1-4). pap. 4.25 (*0-06-442156-2*, Harper Trophy) HarperCollins Children's Bk. Group.
—Nora & Mrs. Mind-Your-Own-Business. 1982. (Illus.). 64p. (J). (gr. k-3). 11.95 o.p. (*0-688-22097-5*, Morrow, William & Co.) Morrow/Avon.
—Nora & Mrs. Mind-Your-Own-Business. 1991. (Illus.). 80p. (J). (gr. 2-5). pap. 3.99 o.s.i (*0-14-034595-7*, Puffin Bks.) Penguin Putnam Bks. for Young Readers.
—Nora & Mrs. Mind-Your-Own Business. 1991. (Illus.). 80p. (J). (ps up). reprint ed. 12.95 o.p. (*0-688-09945-9*); lib. bdg. 12.88 o.p. (*0-688-09946-7*) Morrow/Avon. (Morrow, William & Co.).
—Rip-Roaring Russell. 2001. (Riverside Kids Ser.). (Illus.). 112p. (J). (gr. 1-4). pap. 4.25 (*0-06-442155-4*, Harper Trophy) HarperCollins Children's Bk. Group.
—Rip-Roaring Russell. (Beech Tree Chapter Bks.). (Illus.). 96p. (gr. k-4). 1999. mass mkt. 4.95 (*0-688-16664-4*); 1983. (J). 16.00 o.p. (*0-688-02347-9*); 1983. (J). lib. bdg. 15.93 o.p. (*0-688-02348-7*) Morrow/Avon. (Morrow, William & Co.).
—Rip-Roaring Russell. (Puffin Chapters Ser.). (Illus.). 96p. (J). (gr. 2-5). 1997. pap. 3.99 o.s.i (*0-14-038729-3*); 1989. pap. 3.99 o.s.i (*0-14-032939-0*) Penguin Putnam Bks. for Young Readers. (Puffin Bks.).
—Roz & Ozzie. 1924. (J). lib. bdg. o.p. (*0-688-10946-2*, Morrow, William & Co.) Morrow/Avon.
—Russell & Elisa. rev. ed. 2001. (Riverside Kids Ser.). (Illus.). 128p. (J). (ps-3). pap. 4.25 (*0-06-442150-3*, Harper Trophy) HarperCollins Children's Bk. Group.
—Russell & Elisa. (Beech Tree Chapter Bks.). (Illus.). 96p. (J). (gr. k-4). 1999. mass mkt. 4.95 (*0-688-16666-0*); 1989. 15.00 o.p. (*0-688-08792-2*); 1989. lib. bdg. 14.93 o.p. (*0-688-08793-0*) Morrow/Avon. (Morrow, William & Co.).
—Russell & Elisa. 1990. (Illus.). 96p. (J). (gr. 4 up). pap. 3.99 o.s.i (*0-14-034406-3*, Puffin Bks.) Penguin Putnam Bks. for Young Readers.
—Russell & Elisa. (Beech Tree Chapter Bks.). 1999. (Illus.). (J). 11.00 (*0-606-21759-2*); 1990. 9.09 o.p. (*0-606-04788-3*) Turtleback Bks.
—School's Out. 1991. (Illus.). 128p. (J). (gr. 2 up). 14.95 (*0-688-09938-6*) HarperCollins Children's Bk. Group.
—School's Out. 1992. (Illus.). 96p. (J). (ps up). mass mkt. 3.99 (*0-590-45053-0*, Scholastic Paperbacks) Scholastic, Inc.
—School's Out. 1991. (J). 8.60 o.p. (*0-606-01940-5*) Turtleback Bks.

—Superduper Teddy. 1982. (Illus.). 80p. (gr. k-6). pap. 1.75 o.p. (*0-440-48001-9*) Dell Publishing.

—Superduper Teddy. (Illus.). 80p. (J). 1980. 11.95 o.p. (*0-688-22234-X*); 1980. lib. bdg. 11.88 o.p. (*0-688-32234-4*); 1990. 12.95 o.p. (*0-688-09094-X*); 1990. lib. bdg. 12.88 o.p. (*0-688-09095-8*) Morrow/Avon. (Morrow, William & Co.).

—Superduper Teddy. 1991. (Illus.). 80p. (J). (gr. 2-5). pap. 4.50 o.s.i (*0-14-034593-0*, Puffin Bks.) Penguin Putnam Bks. for Young Readers.

—Superduper Teddy. 2001. (Illus.). (J). 10.30 (*0-606-22039-9*) Turtleback Bks.

Hurwitz, Johanna & Hoban, Lillian. Superduper Teddy. 2001. (Riverside Kids Ser.). (Illus.). 96p. (J). (gr. 1-4). pap. 4.99 (*0-06-442146-5*, Harper Trophy) HarperCollins Children's Bk. Group.

Hutchins, Hazel J. Katie's Babbling Brother. (Illus.). 24p. (J). (ps-2). 2003. (Annikins Ser.: Vol. 15). pap. 1.25 (*1-55037-496-6*); 1991. pap. 4.95 (*1-55037-156-8*); 1991. lib. bdg. 15.95 (*1-55037-153-3*) Annick Pr., Ltd. CAN. *Dist:* Firefly Bks., Ltd.

Hutchins, Pat. Silly Billy! 1992. (Illus.). 32p. (J). (ps-6). 14.00 o.p. (*0-688-10817-2*); lib. bdg. 14.89 o.s.i (*0-688-10818-0*) HarperCollins Children's Bk. Group. (Greenwillow Bks.).

—Tidy Titch. 1991. (Illus.). 32p. (J). (ps up). 16.00 o.p. (*0-688-09963-7*); lib. bdg. 15.93 o.p. (*0-688-09964-5*) HarperCollins Children's Bk. Group. (Greenwillow Bks.).

—Titch. 2002. (Illus.). (J). 14.47 (*0-7587-3818-8*) Book Wholesalers, Inc.

—Titch. 1993. (Illus.). 32p. (J). (ps-3). reprint ed. pap. 9.60 (*0-689-71688-5*, Aladdin) Simon & Schuster Children's Publishing.

—Titch. 1971. (J). 12.14 (*0-606-02948-6*) Turtleback Bks.

—The Very Worst Monster. 1988. (Illus.). 32p. (J). (ps-3). pap. 5.99 (*0-688-07816-8*, Harper Trophy) HarperCollins Children's Bk. Group.

Hyland, Betty. The Girl with the Crazy Brother. 1987. 137p. (YA). (gr. 7-12). lib. bdg. 13.90 o.p. (*0-531-10345-5*, Watts, Franklin) Scholastic Library Publishing.

Hyman, Trina Schart, illus. Comus. 1996. Orig. Title: A Mask at Ludlow Castle. 32p. (J). (ps-3). tchr. ed. 16.95 (*0-8234-1146-X*) Holiday Hse., Inc.

Ichikawa, Satomi. Suzette & Nicholas in the Garden. 1986. (Illus.). 32p. (J). (ps-2). 7.95 o.p. (*0-312-77982-8*) St. Martin's Pr.

Imai, Miko. Sebastian's Trumpet. 1995. (Illus.). 32p. (J). (ps up). 14.95 o.p. (*1-56402-359-1*) Candlewick Pr.

Impey, Rose. Jumble Joan. 1998. (Creepies Ser.). (Illus.). 48p. (J). (gr. 1-3). lib. bdg. 22.60 (*1-57505-295-4*, Carolrhoda Bks.) Lerner Publishing Group.

—Scare Yourself to Sleep. 1988. (Creepies Ser.). (Illus.). 42p. (J). (ps-3). 0.90 o.p. (*0-8120-5974-3*) Barron's Educational Series, Inc.

—Scare Yourself to Sleep. 1998. (Creepies Ser.). (Illus.). 48p. (J). (gr. k-3). lib. bdg. 22.60 o.s.i (*1-57505-297-0*); (gr. 1-3). pap. 6.95 (*1-57505-316-0*) Lerner Publishing Group. (Carolrhoda Bks.).

—Scare Yourself to Sleep. 1991. (J). pap. o.s.i (*0-440-80234-2*, Dell Books for Young Readers) Random Hse. Children's Bks.

Inches, Alison. In the Mushroom Meadow. 2002. (Illus.). 24p. (J). (gr. k-3). pap. 3.25 (*0-375-81479-5*) Random Hse., Inc.

Inkiow, Dimiter. Me & Clara & Baldwin the Pony. McGuire, Paul, tr. from GER. 1980. (Me-and-Clara Storybook Ser.). (Illus.). 96p. (J). (gr. k-4). 3.95 o.p. (*0-394-84434-3*); lib. bdg. 4.99 o.p. (*0-394-94434-8*) Knopf Publishing Group. (Pantheon).

—Me & Clara & Casimir the Cat. 1979. (Illus.). (J). (gr. 1-4). lib. bdg. 3.99 o.p. (*0-394-94124-1*, Pantheon) Knopf Publishing Group.

—Me & Clara & Snuffy the Dog. McGuire, Paul, tr. from GER. 1980. (Me-and-Clara Storybook Ser.). (Illus.). 96p. (J). (gr. k-4). 3.95 o.p. (*0-394-84433-5*); lib. bdg. 4.99 o.p. (*0-394-94433-X*) Knopf Publishing Group. (Pantheon).

—Me & My Sister Clara. 1979. (Illus.). (J). (gr. 1-4). 2.95 o.p. (*0-394-84123-9*); lib. bdg. 3.99 o.p. (*0-394-94123-3*) Knopf Publishing Group. (Pantheon).

Ireland, Shep. Wesley & Wendell: At Home. 1991. (Illus.). 40p. (J). (gr. 1). lib. bdg. 4.75 (*0-8378-0330-6*) Gibson, C. R. Co.

—Wesley & Wendell: Happy Birthday. 1991. (Illus.). 40p. (J). (gr. 1). lib. bdg. 4.75 (*0-8378-0333-0*) Gibson, C. R. Co.

—Wesley & Wendell: In the Garden. 1991. (Illus.). 40p. (J). (gr. 1). lib. bdg. 4.75 (*0-8378-0331-4*) Gibson, C. R. Co.

—Wesley & Wendell: Vacation. 1991. (Illus.). 40p. (J). (gr. 1). lib. bdg. 4.75 (*0-8378-0332-2*) Gibson, C. R. Co.

Isaacs, Anne. Treehouse Tales. 96p. (J). 1999. (gr. 2-6). pap. 4.99 o.p. (*0-14-038738-2*, Puffin Bks.); 1997. (Illus.). (gr. 3-5). 14.99 o.s.i (*0-525-45611-2*) Penguin Putnam Bks. for Young Readers.

Itaya, Satoshi. Buttons & Bo. (J). 15.95 (*0-7358-1883-5*); 16.50 (*0-7358-1884-3*) North-South Bks., Inc.

Jackson, Dave & Jackson, Neta. Thieves of Tyburn Square: Elizabeth Fry. 1995. (Trailblazer Bks.: Vol. 17). (Illus.). 144p. (J). (gr. 3-7). pap. 5.99 (*1-55661-470-5*) Bethany Hse. Pubs.

Jacobs, Kate. A Sister's Wish. 1996. (Illus.). 32p. (J). (ps-3). 14.95 (*0-7868-0138-7*); lib. bdg. 15.49 (*0-7868-2112-4*) Hyperion Bks. for Children.

Jaffe, Nina. Older Brother, Younger Brother, a Koren Folktale. 1997. (Picture Puffin Ser.). (J). 11.19 o.p. (*0-606-11701-6*) Turtleback Bks.

James, B. J., et al. Supertwins Meet the Dangerous Dinobots. 2003. (Scholastic Reader Ser.). 32p. (J). mass mkt. 3.99 (*0-439-46625-3*, Cartwheel Bks.) Scholastic, Inc.

James, Brian. Bad Dogs from Outer Space. 2003. (Supertwins Ser.: No. 1). (Illus.). 32p. (J). mass mkt. 3.99 (*0-439-46623-7*, Cartwheel Bks.) Scholastic, Inc.

—Supertwins & Tooth Trouble. 2003. (Supertwins Ser.: Vol. 2). (Illus.). 32p. (J). mass mkt. 3.99 (*0-439-46624-5*, Cartwheel Bks.) Scholastic, Inc.

James, Will. In the Saddle with Uncle Bill. 2001. (Illus.). xii, 188p. (J). (gr. 4-7). 26.00 (*0-87842-427-X*); pap. 14.00 (*0-87842-428-8*) Mountain Pr. Publishing Co., Inc.

Jane, Pamela. Milo & the Flapjack Fiasco! Johnson, Meredith, ed. & tr. by. 2004. (J). (*1-59336-113-0*); pap. (*1-59336-114-9*) Mondo Publishing.

Janover, Caroline. How Many Days until Tomorrow? 2000. (Illus.). 173p. (J). (gr. 4-8). pap. 11.95 (*1-890627-22-4*) Woodbine Hse.

Jarrell, Mary. The Knee-Baby, RS. 1973. (Illus.). 32p. (J). (ps up). 10.95 o.p. (*0-374-34246-6*, Farrar, Straus & Giroux (BYR)) Farrar, Straus & Giroux.

Jaspersohn, William. The Two Brothers. 2000. (Family Heritage Ser.). (Illus.). 32p. (J). (gr. 1-5). text 14.95 (*0-916718-16-6*) Vermont Folklife Ctr.

Jaworski, Anna M. My Brother Needs an Operation. 1998. (Illus.). 57p. (J). (ps-5). 20.00 (*0-9652508-2-2*) Baby Hearts Pr.

Jennings, Patrick. The Bird Shadow: An Ike & Mem Story. 2001. (Illus.). 56p. (J). (ps-3). tchr. ed. 15.95 (*0-8234-1670-4*) Holiday Hse., Inc.

—The Weeping Willow. 2002. (Ike & Mem Story Ser.: No. 3). (Illus.). 56p. (J). (gr. 1-4). tchr. ed. 15.95 (*0-8234-1671-2*) Holiday Hse., Inc.

Jewell, Nancy. Two Silly Trolls. (I Can Read Bks.). (Illus.). 64p. (J). 1994. (ps-3). pap. 3.99 (*0-06-444173-3*, Harper Trophy); 1992. (gr. 1-3). 14.00 o.p. (*0-06-022829-6*); 1992. (gr. 1-3). lib. bdg. 14.89 o.p. (*0-06-022830-X*) HarperCollins Children's Bk. Group.

—Two Silly Trolls. 1994. (I Can Read Bks.). (J). (gr. 1-3). 8.95 o.p. (*0-606-06071-5*) Turtleback Bks.

Jinkins, Jim. Pinky Dinky Doo: Polka-Dot Pox. 2004. (Illus.). 48p. (J). (gr. 1-3). pap. 3.99 (*0-375-82713-7*); lib. bdg. 11.99 (*0-375-92713-1*) Random Hse., Inc.

—Pinky Dinky Doo: Polka Dot Pox. 2004. (Illus.). 48p. (J). (gr. 1-3). 12.95 (*0-375-82915-6*) Random Hse., Inc.

—Pinky Dinky Doo: Where Are My Shoes? 2004. (Illus.). 48p. (J). (gr. 1-3). 12.95 (*0-375-82914-8*); pap. 3.99 (*0-375-82712-9*); lib. bdg. 11.99 (*0-375-92712-3*) Random Hse., Inc.

Johns, Michael-Anne. Zac Attack: Hanson's Little Brother. 1998. (J). (gr. 4-7). mass mkt. 3.99 (*0-590-03488-X*) Scholastic, Inc.

Johnson, Angela. Looking for Red. 128p. 2003. (Illus.). (YA). mass mkt. 4.99 (*0-689-86388-8*, Simon Pulse); 2002. (J). (gr. 7 up). 15.95 (*0-689-83253-2*, Simon & Schuster Children's Publishing) Simon & Schuster Children's Publishing.

—Looking for Red. l.t. ed. 2003. 117p. (J). 24.95 (*0-7862-5603-6*) Thorndike Pr.

—One of Three. 1991. (Illus.). 32p. (J). (ps-1). pap. 15.95 (*0-531-05955-3*); mass mkt. 15.99 o.p. (*0-531-08555-4*) Scholastic, Inc. (Orchard Bks.).

Johnson, Audrey P. Sisters. 1982. 160p. (J). pap. 1.95 o.p. (*0-590-32183-8*) Scholastic, Inc.

Johnson, Lissa H. The Never-Ending Day. 1997. (China Tate Ser.: Bk. 7). (J). (gr. 6-11). pap. 5.99 o.p. (*1-56179-538-0*) Focus on the Family Publishing.

Johnson, Lissa Halls. The Worst Wish. 2000. (Kidwitness Tales Ser.). (Illus.). 128p. (J). (gr. 3-7). pap. 5.99 (*1-56179-882-7*) Bethany Hse. Pubs.

Johnson, Marion. Caillou Watches Rosie. 2002. (Illus.). 24p. (J). 12.95 (*2-89450-326-1*) Editions Chouette, Inc. CAN. *Dist:* Client Distribution Services.

Johnson, Terry C. & Johnston, Tony. Slither McCreep & His Brother, Joe. 1992. (Illus.). 32p. (J). (ps-3). 13.95 (*0-15-276100-4*) Harcourt Children's Bks.

Johnston, Julie. The Only Outcast. (YA). (gr. 6-9). 1998. 232p. 14.95 (*0-88776-441-X*); 1999. 248p. reprint ed. pap. 6.95 (*0-88776-488-6*) Tundra Bks. of Northern New York.

—The Only Outcast. 1999. (J). 13.00 (*0-606-19122-4*) Turtleback Bks.

Johnston, Tony. The Iguana Brothers: A Tale of Two Lizards. 1995. (Illus.). 32p. (J). (ps-3). pap. 15.95 (*0-590-47468-5*, Blue Sky Pr., The) Scholastic, Inc.

Jonell, Lynne. It's My Birthday, Too! 1999. (Illus.). 32p. (J). (ps-3). 13.99 o.s.i (*0-399-23323-7*) Penguin Group (USA) Inc.

Jones, Allan Frewin. Yo Soy Mi Hermana. Ortega, Emilio, tr. 1997. (SPA.). 106p. (J). (gr. 4-6). 10.95 (*84-348-5582-8*, SM3993) SM Ediciones ESP. *Dist:* Lectorum Pubns., Inc., i.b.d., Ltd.

Jones, Lara. Fun at the Park. 2003. (Lola & Binky Bks.). (Illus.). 8p. (J). bds. 5.95 (*0-7641-5689-6*) Barron's Educational Series, Inc.

—Fun on the Farm. 2003. (Lola & Binky Bks.). (Illus.). 8p. (J). bds. 5.95 (*0-7641-5688-8*) Barron's Educational Series, Inc.

Joosse, Barbara M. Hot City. Gauch, Patricia Lee, ed. 2004. (Illus.). (J). 16.99 (*0-399-23640-6*, Philomel) Penguin Putnam Bks. for Young Readers.

—I Love You the Purplest. 1996. (Illus.). 32p. (J). (ps-3). 15.95 (*0-8118-0718-5*) Chronicle Bks. LLC.

—Stars in the Darkness. 2001. (Illus.). 36p. (J). (gr. k-3). 14.95 (*0-8118-2168-4*) Chronicle Bks. LLC.

Joseph, Lynn. The Color of My Words. 144p. (J). 2002. (gr. 5 up). pap. 5.99 (*0-06-447204-3*, Harper Trophy); 2000. (Illus.). (gr. 3-7). 14.99 (*0-06-028232-0*, Cotler, Joanna Bks.); 2000. (Illus.). (gr. 3-7). lib. bdg. 15.89 (*0-06-028233-9*, Cotler, Joanna Bks.) HarperCollins Children's Bk. Group.

Joyce, Bill. Billy. 2001. (Rolie Polie Olie Ser.). (Illus.). 10p. (J). (ps-k). bds. 3.99 (*0-7868-3321-1*) Disney Pr.

—Zowie. 2001. (Rolie Polie Olie Ser.). (Illus.). 10p. (J). (ps-k). bds. 3.99 (*0-7868-3323-8*) Disney Pr.

Joyce, Bill & Zoefeld, Kathy. Be My Pal Olie, Vol.1. 2000. (Rolie Polie Olie Ser.). 18p. (J). (ps-k). 5.99 o.s.i (*0-7364-0180-6*) Mouse Works.

Joyce, William. Be My Pal. 2001. (Rolie Polie Olie Ser.). (Illus.). 18p. (J). (ps). bds. 5.99 (*0-7868-3318-1*) Disney Pr.

—Santa Calls. 1993. (Illus.). (J). 40p. (gr. 5 up). 16.95 (*0-06-021133-4*, Geringer, Laura Bk.); 10p. (ps-3). 6.95 (*0-694-00841-9*, Harper Festival); 40p. (ps up). lib. bdg. 17.89 o.s.i (*0-06-021134-2*); 40p. (ps up). 125.00 (*0-06-023355-9*) HarperCollins Children's Bk. Group.

—Santa Calls Board Book. 1998. (Illus.). 36p. (J). (ps-k). 6.95 (*0-694-01212-2*, Harper Festival) HarperCollins Children's Bk. Group.

—Santa Calls Gift Box. 1996. (Laura Geringer Bks.). (Illus.). 40p. (J). (ps-3). 15.95 o.p. (*0-694-00902-4*, Harper Festival) HarperCollins Children's Bk. Group.

Jukes, Mavis. Expecting the Unexpected. 1996. 144p. (J). (gr. 4-7). 15.95 o.s.i (*0-385-32242-9*, Delacorte Pr.) Dell Publishing.

Kalman, Maira. Hey Willy, See the Pyramids. 1990. 400p. (J). (ps-3). pap. 4.99 o.p. (*0-14-050840-6*, Puffin Bks.) Penguin Putnam Bks. for Young Readers.

Kane, Cindy, ed. The Goblin Baby. 1999. (Illus.). 32p. (J). (ps-3). 15.99 o.s.i (*0-8037-2172-2*, Dial Bks. for Young Readers) Penguin Putnam Bks. for Young Readers.

Karr, Kathleen. In the Kaiser's Clutch, RS. 1995. 182p. (J). (gr. 4-7). 16.00 o.p. (*0-374-33638-5*, Farrar, Straus & Giroux (BYR)) Farrar, Straus & Giroux.

—The Seventh Knot. 2003. (J). 15.95 (*0-7614-5135-8*, Cavendish Children's Bks.) Cavendish, Marshall Corp.

Katz, Illana & Ritvo, Edward. Joey & Sam: A Heartwarming Storybook about Autism, a Family, & a Brother's Love. 1993. (Illus.). 40p. (J). (gr. k-6). 16.95 (*1-882388-00-3*) Real Life Storybooks.

Kaye, Geraldine. Tim & the Red Indian Headdress. 1976. (Stepping Stones Ser.). (Illus.). 24p. (J). (gr. k-3). 7.00 o.p. (*0-516-03594-0*, Children's Pr.) Scholastic Library Publishing.

Keats, Ezra Jack. Peter's Chair. (Illus.). (J). (gr. k-3). 1995. 16p. 14.95 o.p. (*0-694-00685-8*, Harper Festival); 1983. 32p. pap. 4.95 o.p. (*0-06-443040-5*, Harper Trophy); 1967. 15.00 o.p. (*0-06-023111-4*) HarperCollins Children's Bk. Group.

—Peter's Chair. 2001. (Illus.). 40p. (J). (gr. k-3). pap. 6.95 (*1-931016-07-0*, MHC-07-0) Minnesota Humanities Commission.

—Peter's Chair. 1998. (Illus.). 40p. (J). (ps-3). 15.99 (*0-670-88064-7*); pap. 6.99 (*0-14-056441-1*, Puffin Bks.) Penguin Putnam Bks. for Young Readers.

—Peter's Chair. 1998. (Picture Puffin Ser.). (Illus.). 12.14 (*0-606-13701-7*) Turtleback Bks.

—Peter's Chair. (J). (ps-3). pap. text 12.95 incl. audio Weston Woods Studios, Inc.

—Peter's Chair Big Book. 1993. (Trophy Picture Bk.). (Illus.). 32p. (J). (ps-3). pap. 19.95 o.p. (*0-06-443325-0*, Harper Trophy) HarperCollins Children's Bk. Group.

—La Silla de Pedro. Fiol, Maria A., tr. from ENG. 1996. (SPA., Illus.). 32p. (J). (ps-3). 15.95 o.p. (*0-06-026655-4*); pap. 5.95 o.p. (*0-06-443433-8*) HarperCollins Children's Bk. Group.

—La Silla de Pedro. Fiol, Maria A., tr. from ENG. 1999. (SPA., Illus.). 32p. (J). (ps-3). 15.99 (*0-670-88815-X*) Penguin Putnam Bks. for Young Readers.

—La Silla de Pedro. 1999. 12.14 (*0-606-17430-3*) Turtleback Bks.

Kehret, Peg. Danger at the Fair. 1995. 144p. (J). 15.99 o.s.i (*0-525-65182-9*, Dutton Children's Bks.) Penguin Putnam Bks. for Young Readers.

—Earthquake Terror. (Puffin Novel Ser.). 144p. (J). (gr. 3-7). 1998. pap. 4.99 (*0-14-038343-3*); 1996. 14.99 o.p. (*0-525-65226-4*, Dutton Children's Bks.) Penguin Putnam Bks. for Young Readers.

—Earthquake Terror. 1998. (Puffin Novel Ser.). (J). 11.04 (*0-606-13073-X*) Turtleback Bks.

—Escaping the Giant Wave. 2003. (Illus.). 160p. (J). 15.95 (*0-689-85272-X*, Simon & Schuster Children's Publishing) Simon & Schuster Children's Publishing.

—Escaping the Giant Wave. l.t. ed. 2003. 152p. (J). 21.95 (*0-7862-5985-X*) Thorndike Pr.

—My Brother Made Me Do It. 144p. (J). 2001. pap. 4.99 (*0-671-03419-7*, Aladdin); 2000. (gr. 3-6). 16.00 (*0-671-03418-9*, Simon & Schuster Children's Publishing) Simon & Schuster Children's Publishing.

Kelleher, Victor. Del-Del. 1992. (YA). (gr. 7-10). 17.95 (*0-8027-8154-3*) Walker & Co.

Keller, Holly. Geraldine & Mrs. Duffy. 2000. (Illus.). (J). (gr. k-3). 24p. 15.95 (*0-688-16887-6*); 32p. lib. bdg. 15.89 (*0-688-16888-4*) HarperCollins Children's Bk. Group. (Greenwillow Bks.).

—Geraldine First. 1996. (Illus.). 24p. (J). (ps-3). 15.00 o.s.i (*0-688-14149-8*); lib. bdg. 14.93 o.p. (*0-688-14150-1*) HarperCollins Children's Bk. Group. (Greenwillow Bks.).

—Geraldine's Baby Brother. 1994. (J). (ps up). 15.00 o.s.i (*0-688-12005-9*); (Illus.). 32p. lib. bdg. 14.93 o.p. (*0-688-12006-7*) HarperCollins Children's Bk. Group. (Greenwillow Bks.).

—Harry & Tuck. 1993. (Illus.). 24p. (J). (ps up). lib. bdg. 13.93 o.s.i (*0-688-11463-6*, Greenwillow Bks.) HarperCollins Children's Bk. Group.

—Too Big. 1983. (Illus.). 32p. (J). (gr. k-3). 11.95 o.p. (*0-688-01998-6*); lib. bdg. 11.93 o.p. (*0-688-01999-4*) HarperCollins Children's Bk. Group. (Greenwillow Bks.).

—What Alvin Wanted. 1990. (Illus.). 32p. (J). (ps up). 12.95 o.p. (*0-688-08933-X*); lib. bdg. 12.88 o.p. (*0-688-08934-8*) HarperCollins Children's Bk. Group. (Greenwillow Bks.).

Kellogg, Steven. Much Bigger Than Martin. (Pied Piper Bks.). (Illus.). 32p. (J). (ps-3). 1985. 11.89 o.p. (*0-8037-5810-3*); 1976. 16.99 o.s.i (*0-8037-5809-X*) Penguin Putnam Bks. for Young Readers. (Dial Bks. for Young Readers).

Kelly, Irene. Ebbie & Flo. 1998. (Illus.). 32p. (J). (ps-2). 16.95 (*1-57525-115-9*) Smith & Kraus Pubs., Inc.

Kennedy, X. J. The Eagle As Wide As the World. 1997. 192p. (J). (gr. 3-7). 16.00 (*0-689-81157-8*, McElderry, Margaret K.) Simon & Schuster Children's Publishing.

Kennemore, Tim. Circle of Doom, RS. 2003. 208p. (J). 16.00 (*0-374-31284-2*, Farrar, Straus & Giroux (BYR)) Farrar, Straus & Giroux.

Kerr, M. E. Linger. (Trophy Bk.). 224p. (YA). (gr. 7 up). 1995. pap. 4.95 o.s.i (*0-06-447102-0*, Harper Trophy); 1993. 15.00 o.p. (*0-06-022879-2*); 1993. lib. bdg. 14.89 o.p. (*0-06-022882-2*) HarperCollins Children's Bk. Group.

—Linger. 1995. (J). 10.30 o.p. (*0-606-07790-1*) Turtleback Bks.

—Love Is a Missing Person. 1975. (Ursula Nordstrom Bk.). 176p. (YA). (gr. 7 up). lib. bdg. 13.89 o.p. (*0-06-023162-9*) HarperCollins Children's Bk. Group.

—Night Kites. (Trophy Keypoint Bks.). (gr. 7 up). 1987. 256p. (J). mass mkt. 5.99 (*0-06-447035-0*, Harper Trophy); 1986. 192p. (YA). 12.95 o.p. (*0-06-023253-6*); 1986. 192p. (YA). lib. bdg. 14.89 o.p. (*0-06-023254-4*) HarperCollins Children's Bk. Group.

—Night Kites. 1987. 11.00 (*0-606-03523-0*) Turtleback Bks.

Khalsa, Dayal Kaur. Green Cat. 2002. (Illus.). 24p. (J). (gr. k-3). 14.95 (*0-88776-586-6*) Tundra Bks. of Northern New York.

Kidder, Judy. The Special Brother. 1999. 16p. (J). pap. (*0-9663764-1-2*) Reivers Pr.

Kimball, K. M. The Star Spangled Secret. 2001. (Mystery Ser.). 240p. (J). (gr. 5-7). pap. 4.99 (*0-689-84550-2*, Aladdin) Simon & Schuster Children's Publishing.

Kindley, Jeff. Choco-Louie. 1996. (Bank Street Reader Collection). (Illus.). 48p. (J). (gr. 1-3). lib. bdg. 21.26 (*0-8368-1618-8*) Stevens, Gareth Inc.

Kindley, Jeffrey. Choco-Louie. 1996. (Bank Street Ready-to-Read Ser.). (Illus.). 32p. (J). (gr. 1-3). 13.95 o.s.i (*0-553-09744-X*); pap. 3.99 o.s.i (*0-553-37576-8*) Bantam Bks.

King-Smith, Dick. George Speaks. 2002. (Illus.). 96p. (gr. 2-4). lib. bdg. 21.90 (*0-7613-2519-0*); (J). 14.95 (*0-7613-1544-6*) Millbrook Pr., Inc. (Roaring Brook Pr.).

—The Terrible Trins. l.t. ed. 1995. (Illus.). (J). 16.95 o.p. (*0-7451-3147-6*, Galaxy Children's Large Print) BBC Audiobooks America.

Kinsey-Warnock, Natalie. The Summer of Stanley. 1997. (Illus.). 32p. (J). (ps-3). 14.99 (*0-525-65177-2*, Dutton Children's Bks.) Penguin Putnam Bks. for Young Readers.

Kirksey, M. E. This Week I Got a Sister. 1995. (Illus.). (J). 12.95 o.p. (*1-56790-536-6*) C&O Research.

Kjelle, Marylou M. Sometimes I Wish My Mom Was Two People. 1996. (Illus.). 14p. (J). (ps-4). pap. text 7.95 (*0-9648855-5-7*) MoranoCo, Inc.

Klein, Lee. Are There Stripes in Heaven. 1994. 32p. (J). (ps-3). pap. 4.95 o.p. (*0-8091-6618-6*) Paulist Pr.

Kleinhenz, Sydnie M., et al. More for Me. 1997. (Hello Reader! Ser.). (Illus.). (J). (gr. k-2). mass mkt. 3.99 (*0-590-30877-7*) Scholastic, Inc.

Kleven, Elisa. Ernst. 2003. 32p. pap. 6.95 (*1-58246-053-1*) Tricycle Pr.

—Puddle Pail. 1997. (Illus.). 32p. (J). (ps-3). 16.99 o.p. (*0-525-45803-4*, Dutton Children's Bks.) Penguin Putnam Bks. for Young Readers.

—The Puddle Pail. 1999. (J). pap. 14.99 (*0-525-45741-0*, Dutton Children's Bks.) Penguin Putnam Bks. for Young Readers.

Klimowicz, Barbara. Ha, Ha, Ha, Henrietta. 1975. (Illus.). 32p. (J). (gr. k-3). lib. bdg. 4.95 o.p. (*0-687-16469-9*) Abingdon Pr.

Kline, Suzy. Orp & the FBI. 1995. 100p. (J). (gr. 4-7). 14.99 o.p. (*0-399-22664-8*, G. P. Putnam's Sons) Penguin Group (USA) Inc.

Klingel/Noyed. The Amazing Letter B. 2003. (Alphaphonics Ser.). (Illus.). 24p. (J). (ps-3). lib. bdg. 24.21 (*1-59296-092-8*) Child's World, Inc.

Klise, Kate. Letters from Camp. (Illus.). 192p. (J). 2000. (gr. 4-7). pap. 5.99 (*0-380-79348-2*, Harper Trophy); 1999. (gr. 3-7). 15.99 (*0-380-97539-4*) HarperCollins Children's Bk. Group.

Koller, Jackie French. Baby for Sale. 2002. (Illus.). 32p. (J). (ps-2). 16.95 (*0-7614-5106-4*) Cavendish, Marshall Corp.

Komaiko, Leah. Annie Bananie & the Pain Sisters. 2000. (Illus.). 80p. (gr. 2-6). pap. text 4.50 (*0-440-41038-X*, Yearling) Random Hse. Children's Bks.

—Annie Bananie & the Pain Sisters. 2000. 10.14 (*0-606-17890-2*) Turtleback Bks.

—Where Can Daniel Be? 1994. (Illus.). 32p. (J). (ps-1). 15.95 o.p. (*0-531-06850-1*); mass mkt. 16.99 o.p. (*0-531-08700-X*) Scholastic, Inc. (Orchard Bks.).

—Where Can Daniel Be. 9999. (J). 15.00 o.s.i (*0-06-023263-3*) HarperCollins Children's Bk. Group.

Konigsburg, E. L. Father's Arcane Daughter. 1986. 128p. (gr. 5-8). pap. text 3.99 o.s.i (*0-440-42496-8*, Yearling) Random Hse. Children's Bks.

—Father's Arcane Daughter. 128p. (J). 1999. (gr. 5-9). pap. 4.99 (*0-689-82680-X*, 076714004993, Aladdin); 1976. (gr. 4-8). lib. bdg. 15.00 (*0-689-30524-9*, Atheneum) Simon & Schuster Children's Publishing.

—Father's Arcane Daughter. 1999. (J). 11.04 (*0-606-19131-3*) Turtleback Bks.

—From the Mixed-Up Files of Mrs. Basil E. Frankweiler. 1998. (Illus.). 168p. (J). (gr. 3-7). pap. 5.99 (*0-689-71181-6*, Aladdin) Simon & Schuster Children's Publishing.

—From the Mixed up Files of Mrs. Basil E. Frankweiler. 2002. 208p. (YA). mass mkt. 5.99 (*0-689-85354-8*, Simon Pulse) Simon & Schuster Children's Publishing.

—From the Mixed up Files of Mrs. Basil E. Frankweiler: 35th Anniversary Edition. anniv. ed. 2002. (Illus.). 176p. (J). (gr. 3-7). 16.95 (*0-689-85322-X*, Atheneum) Simon & Schuster Children's Publishing.

—Silent to the Bone. unabr. ed. 2002. 272p. (YA). (gr. 10 up). pap. 35.00 incl. audio (*0-8072-8741-5*, LYA 253 SP); 2000. (J). (ps up). audio 25.00 (*0-8072-6165-3*) Random Hse. Audio Publishing Group. (Listening Library).

—Silent to the Bone. 272p. 2004. (YA). mass mkt. 5.99 (*0-689-86715-8*, Simon Pulse); 2002. (Illus.). (J). (gr. 5-9). pap. 5.99 (*0-689-83602-3*, Aladdin); 2000. (Illus.). (J). (gr. 5-9). 16.00 (*0-689-83601-5*, Atheneum) Simon & Schuster Children's Publishing.

—Silent to the Bone. l.t. ed. 2001. (Young Adult Ser.). 271p. (J). (gr. 4-7). 23.95 (*0-7862-3169-6*) Thorndike Pr.

Kordon, Klaus. Brothers Like Friends. 2015. (Illus.). (J). 14.95 (*0-399-22100-X*, Philomel) Penguin Putnam Bks. for Young Readers.

—Brothers Like Friends. Crawford, Elizabeth D., tr. from GER. 1992. 192p. (J). (gr. 5 up). 14.95 o.s.i (*0-399-22137-9*, Philomel) Penguin Putnam Bks. for Young Readers.

Kraft, Erik P. Lenny & Mel's Summer Vacation. 2003. (Illus.). 64p. (J). 14.95 (*0-689-85108-1*, Simon & Schuster Children's Publishing) Simon & Schuster Children's Publishing.

Kramer, Sydelle A. At the Ball Game. 1994. (Pictureback Ser.). (Illus.). 32p. (Orig.). (J). (ps-3). pap. 3.25 o.s.i (*0-679-85291-3*, Random Hse. Bks. for Young Readers) Random Hse. Children's Bks.

Krasilovsky, Phyllis. The Very Little Boy. 1992. (Illus.). 32p. (J). (ps-3). pap. 4.95 (*0-590-44762-9*, 030, Cartwheel Bks.) Scholastic, Inc.

—The Very Little Girl. 1992. (Illus.). 32p. (J). (ps). pap. 4.95 o.p. (*0-590-44761-0*, 029, Cartwheel Bks.) Scholastic, Inc.

Kraus, Robert. Little Louie the Baby Bloomer. 1998. (Illus.). 32p. (J). (ps-3). 15.95 (*0-06-026293-1*) HarperCollins Children's Bk. Group.

—Little Louie the Baby Bloomer. 1998. (Illus.). 32p. (J). (ps-3). lib. bdg. 15.89 (*0-06-026294-X*) HarperCollins Pubs.

—Little Louie the Baby Bloomer. 2000. (Illus.). (J). 12.10 (*0-606-18702-2*) Turtleback Bks.

—Little Louie the Baby Bloomer. 2000. (Illus.). 32p. (J). (ps-3). pap. 5.95 (*0-06-443656-X*, Harper Trophy) HarperCollins Children's Bk. Group.

Krensky, Stephen. Lionel & Louise. 1997. (Easy-to-Read Ser.). (Illus.). 48p. (J). (gr. 1-4). pap. 3.50 o.s.i (*0-14-038617-3*) Penguin Putnam Bks. for Young Readers.

—Lionel's Birthday. 2003. (Easy-to-Read Ser.). (Illus.). 48p. (J). 13.99 (*0-8037-2752-6*, Dial Bks. for Young Readers) Penguin Putnam Bks. for Young Readers.

Kritlow, William. Backfire: A Novel. 1995. (Virtual Reality Bks.: Vol. 3). 168p. (J). (gr. 3-7). pap. 5.99 o.p. (*0-7852-7925-3*) Nelson, Tommy.

—The Deadly Maze: A Novel. 1995. (Virtual Reality Bks.: Bk. 2). 168p. (J). (gr. 3-7). pap. 5.99 o.p. (*0-7852-7924-5*) Nelson, Tommy.

Kroll, Steven. Loose Tooth. 1984. (Illus.). 32p. (J). (ps-3). 13.95 o.p. (*0-8234-0518-4*) Holiday Hse., Inc.

—Loose Tooth. 1992. (Illus.). 32p. (J). (ps-3). mass mkt. 4.99 o.p. (*0-590-45713-6*) Scholastic, Inc.

—Loose Tooth. 1984. (J). 10.19 o.p. (*0-606-02729-7*) Turtleback Bks.

—The Squirrels' Thanksgiving. 1991. (Illus.). 32p. (J). tchr. ed. 15.95 o.p. (*0-8234-0823-X*) Holiday Hse., Inc.

Kroll, Virginia L. Helen the Fish. Mathews, Judith, ed. 1992. (Albert Whitman Concept Bks.). (Illus.). 32p. (J). (ps-3). lib. bdg. 14.95 (*0-8075-3194-4*) Whitman, Albert & Co.

Kubler, Annie. When I Grow Up. 1992. (Illus.). 12p. (J). (ps-3). 5.99 (*0-85953-505-3*) Child's Play of England GBR. *Dist:* Child's Play-International.

Kubler, Annie, illus. Waiting for Baby. 2000. 14p. (ps-k). bds. 2.99 (*0-85953-973-3*) Child's Play-International.

Kudler, David. The Seven Gods of Luck. 1997. (Illus.). 32p. (J). (ps-3). tchr. ed. 15.00 o.p. (*0-395-78830-7*) Houghton Mifflin Co.

Kurtz, Jane. Saba: Under the Hyena's Foot. 2003. (Girls of Many Lands Ser.). (Illus.). 207p. (J). pap. 15.95 (*1-58485-829-X*); pap. 7.95 (*1-58485-747-1*) Pleasant Co. Pubns. (American Girl).

Lachtman, Ofelia D. The Girl from Playa Blanca. 1995. 259p. (YA). (gr. 6 up). 14.95 o.p. (*1-55885-148-8*, Piñata Books) Arte Publico Pr.

Lachtman, Ofelia Dumas. The Girl from Playa Blanca. 1995. 259p. (YA). (gr. 4-7). pap. 9.95 (*1-55885-149-6*, Piñata Books) Arte Publico Pr.

Laing, Kate. Best Kind of Baby. 2003. (Illus.). 32p. (J). 15.99 (*0-8037-2662-7*, Dial Bks. for Young Readers) Penguin Putnam Bks. for Young Readers.

Lakin, Patricia. Just Like Me, Vol. 1. 1989. (J). 14.95 o.p. (*0-316-51233-8*) Little Brown & Co.

—Oh, Brother! 1987. (Illus.). 32p. (J). (gr. 1 up). 12.95 o.s.i (*0-316-51231-1*) Little Brown & Co.

Lamm, C. Drew. Pirates. (J). 2001. (Illus.). 40p. (gr. 1-4). 15.99 (*0-7868-0392-4*); 2000. 32p. lib. bdg. 15.49 (*0-7868-2343-7*) Hyperion Bks. for Children.

Landis, James D. The Sisters Impossible. 1984. 160p. (J). mass mkt. 2.50 o.s.i (*0-553-26013-8*) Bantam Bks.

—The Sisters Impossible. 1979. (J). (gr. 4-7). 6.95 o.p. (*0-394-84190-5*); 6.99 o.s.i (*0-394-94190-X*) Random Hse. Children's Bks. (Knopf Bks. for Young Readers).

Landrey, Wanda A. The Ghost of Spindletop Hill. 2000. (Illus.). xiii, 140p. (J). 15.95 (*1-57168-449-2*) Eakin Pr.

Lane, Carolyn & Shortall, Leonard. The Winnemah Spirit, 001. 1975. (Illus.). 128p. (J). (gr. 2-5). 5.95 o.p. (*0-395-20490-9*) Houghton Mifflin Co.

Langreuter, Jutta. Little Bear Is a Big Brother. 1998. (Little Bear Collection). (Illus.). 32p. (ps-k). 22.90 o.p. (*0-7613-0404-5*); pap. 7.95 o.p. (*0-7613-0376-6*) Millbrook Pr., Inc.

Lansky, Bruce. When I'm a Big Brother. 2003. 22p. mass mkt. 9.95 (*0-684-01868-3*) Meadowbrook Pr.

—When I'm a Big Sister. 2003. 22p. mass mkt. 9.95 (*0-684-01865-9*) Meadowbrook Pr.

LaReau, Kara & LaReau, Jenna, trs. Rocko & Spanky Go to a Party. 2004. (Rocko & Spanky Ser.). (Illus.). 40p. (J). 15.00 (*0-15-216624-6*) Harcourt Trade Pubs.

Lashbrook, Marilyn. Get Lost Little Brother. (*0-87973-863-4*, 863) Our Sunday Visitor, Publishing Div.

Laskin, Pamela L. Getting to Know You. 2003. (YA). (*0-936389-92-3*) Tudor Pubs., Inc.

Lasky, Kathryn. Lucille Camps In. 2003. (Illus.). 32p. (J). (ps-2). 14.95 (*0-517-80041-1*); lib. bdg. 16.99 (*0-517-80042-X*) Random Hse. Children's Bks. (Knopf Bks. for Young Readers).

—Lucille's Snowsuit. Cascardi, Andrea, ed. 2000. (Illus.). 32p. (J). (gr. k-3). lib. bdg. 16.99 (*0-517-80038-1*); 14.95 o.s.i (*0-517-80037-3*) Random Hse. Children's Bks. (Random Hse. Bks. for Young Readers).

—Lucille's Snowsuit. 2002. 32p. (J). pap. 6.99 (*0-440-41750-3*) Random Hse., Inc.

—Prank. 1986. (J). (gr. 6 up). mass mkt. 2.75 o.s.i (*0-440-97144-6*, Laurel Leaf) Random Hse. Children's Bks.

—Show & Tell Bunnies. (Illus.). 32p. (J). (ps-3). 2001. bds. 5.99 (*0-7636-1050-X*); 1998. 15.99 o.s.i (*0-7636-0396-1*) Candlewick Pr.

—Voice in the Wind: A Starbuck Family Adventure. 1993. (Illus.). 224p. (J). (gr. 3-7). 10.95 (*0-15-294102-9*); pap. 3.95 o.s.i (*0-15-294103-7*) Harcourt Children's Bks.

Lassie Hayloft Hideout, No. 4. 1996. 144p. (J). mass mkt. 5.99 (*0-7814-0265-4*) Cook Communications Ministries.

Lawler, Pat. My Brother's Place. 1978. (YA). 6.95 o.p. (*0-394-83846-7*); lib. bdg. 6.99 o.p. (*0-394-93846-1*) Knopf Publishing Group. (Pantheon).

Lawlor, Laurie. Addie's Forever Friend. 1997. (Illus.). 128p. (J). (gr. 2-5). lib. bdg. 13.95 (*0-8075-0164-6*) Whitman, Albert & Co.

—The Biggest Pest on Eighth Avenue. 1997. (Holiday House Reader Ser.). (Illus.). 48p. (J). (gr. k-3). tchr. ed. 14.95 (*0-8234-1321-7*) Holiday Hse., Inc.

—Crooked Creek. Himler, Ronald, tr. & illus. by. 2004. (J). (*0-8234-1812-X*) Holiday Hse., Inc.

—Gold in the Hills. 1995. 196p. (J). (gr. 4-7). 15.95 (*0-8027-8371-6*) Walker & Co.

—West along the Wagon Road 1852. 1998. (American Sisters Ser.: Vol. 1). 192p. (J). (gr. 4-7). pap. 9.00 (*0-671-01551-6*, Aladdin) Simon & Schuster Children's Publishing.

Lawrence, Iain. The Lightkeeper's Daughter. 256p. (YA). 2004. (gr. 9). pap. 7.95 (*0-385-73127-2*, Delacorte Bks. for Young Readers); 2002. lib. bdg. 18.99 (*0-385-90062-7*); 2002. (gr. 9-12). 16.95 (*0-385-72925-1*, Delacorte Bks. for Young Readers) Random Hse. Children's Bks.

Lawrence, James. Binky Brothers & the Fearless Four. 1983. (I Can Read Bks.). (Illus.). 64p. (J). (ps-3). pap. 3.50 o.p. (*0-06-444039-7*, Harper Trophy) HarperCollins Children's Bk. Group.

—Binky Brothers, Detectives. 1978. (I Can Read Bks.). (Illus.). (J). (ps-3). reprint ed. pap. 3.50 o.p. (*0-06-444003-6*, Harper Trophy) HarperCollins Children's Bk. Group.

Lawson, A. Star Baby. 1992. (Illus.). 72p. (J). 15.95 (*0-15-200905-1*) Harcourt Children's Bks.

Le Guin, Ursula K. A Ride on the Red Mare's Back. (Illus.). 48p. (J). 1996. (ps-3). mass mkt. 6.95 (*0-531-07079-4*); 1992. (gr. 4-7). lib. bdg. 17.99 (*0-531-08591-0*); 1992. (ps-3). pap. 16.95 (*0-531-05991-X*) Scholastic, Inc. (Orchard Bks.).

—A Ride on the Red Mare's Back. 1996. 13.10 (*0-606-10910-2*) Turtleback Bks.

Lears, Laurie. Ian's Walk: A Story about Autism. (Illus.). 32p. (J). 2003. pap. 6.95 (*0-8075-3481-1*); 1998. (gr. 1-4). lib. bdg. 14.95 (*0-8075-3480-3*) Whitman, Albert & Co.

Leech, Jay & Spencer, Zane. Bright Fawn & Me. 1979. (Illus.). (J). (ps-3). 12.95 o.p. (*0-690-03937-9*) HarperCollins Children's Bk. Group.

Leeuwen, Jean Van. Oliver & Amanda & the Big Snow. 2001. (Franklin & Friends Ser.). lib. bdg. (*1-59054-260-6*) Fitzgerald Bks.

Leigh, Frances. The Lost Boy. 1976. (J). (gr. 3-5). 6.95 o.p. (*0-525-34221-4*, Dutton) Dutton/Plume.

L'Engle, Madeleine. A Wrinkle in Time. 1996. 224p. mass mkt. 2.49 o.s.i (*0-440-22039-4*) Dell Publishing.

Leonard, Marcia. Get the Ball, Slim. 1998. (Real Kids Readers Ser.). (Illus.). 32p. (ps-1). (J). 18.90 (*0-7613-2000-8*); pap. 4.99 (*0-7613-2025-3*) Millbrook Pr., Inc.

—Get the Ball, Slim. 1998. 10.14 (*0-606-15795-6*) Turtleback Bks.

—Get the Ball, Slim. 1998. (Illus.). E-Book (*1-58824-464-4*); E-Book (*1-58824-712-0*); E-Book (*1-58824-794-5*) ipicturebooks, LLC.

Leroe, Ellen. Leap Frog Friday. 1992. (Illus.). 64p. (J). (gr. 2-5). 12.00 o.p. (*0-525-67370-9*, Dutton Children's Bks.) Penguin Putnam Bks. for Young Readers.

LeRoy, Gen. Billy's Shoes. Higginbottom, J. Winslow, tr. 1981. (Illus.). (J). (gr. 1-3). text 9.95 o.p. (*0-07-037201-2*) McGraw-Hill Cos., The.

—Lucky Stiff! 1981. (Illus.). 48p. (J). (gr. 1-3). text 9.95 o.p. (*0-07-037203-9*) McGraw-Hill Cos., The.

Lester, Alison. The Journey Home. 1995. (Illus.). 32p. (J). (gr. k-3). pap. 4.95 o.p. (*0-395-74517-9*) Houghton Mifflin Co. Trade & Reference Div.

Lester, Julius. When Dad Killed Mom. (YA). 2003. 216p. pap. 6.95 (*0-15-204698-4*); 2003. (gr. 7-12). mass mkt. 6.95 (*0-15-524698-4*); 2001. (Illus.). 192p. (gr. 7-12). 17.00 (*0-15-216305-0*) Harcourt Children's Bks. (Silver Whistle).

Leuck, Laura. My Baby Brother Has Ten Tiny Toes. 1997. (Illus.). 24p. (J). (gr. 1-4). lib. bdg. 14.95 (*0-8075-5310-7*) Whitman, Albert & Co.

—My Beastly Brother. 2003. (Illus.). 32p. (J). (ps-1). 15.99 (*0-06-029547-3*); lib. bdg. 16.89 (*0-06-029548-1*) HarperCollins Children's Bk. Group.

Levin, Betty. Fire in the Wind. (J). 1997. (Illus.). 144p. (gr. 3-7). pap. 4.95 (*0-688-15495-6*, Harper Trophy); 1995. 176p. (gr. 7 up). 15.00 o.s.i (*0-688-14299-0*, Greenwillow Bks.) HarperCollins Children's Bk. Group.

—Fire in the Wind. 1997. 11.00 (*0-606-11327-4*) Turtleback Bks.

—Shoddy Cove. 2003. 208p. (J). (gr. 5 up). 15.99 (*0-06-052271-2*); lib. bdg. 16.89 (*0-06-052272-0*) HarperCollins Children's Bk. Group. (Greenwillow Bks.).

Levine, Abby. Ollie Knows Everything. (Illus.). 32p. (J). (ps-2). 1994. lib. bdg. 15.95 o.p. (*0-8075-6020-0*); 1996. reprint ed. pap. 6.95 (*0-8075-6021-9*) Whitman, Albert & Co.

Levine, Arthur A. All the Lights in the Night. 1991. (Illus.). 32p. (J). (ps-3). 16.00 o.p. (*0-688-10107-0*); lib. bdg. 15.93 o.p. (*0-688-10108-9*) Morrow/Avon. (Morrow, William & Co.).

Levinson, Marilyn. And Don't Bring Jeremy, ERS. 1985. (Illus.). 128p. (J). (gr. 4-6). 10.95 o.p. (*0-8050-0554-4*, Holt, Henry & Co. Bks. For Young Readers) Holt, Henry & Co.

—And Don't Bring Jeremy. 2000. (Illus.). 122p. (gr. 4-7). pap. 9.95 (*0-595-16919-8*) iUniverse, Inc.

Levinson, Riki. Me Baby! 1991. (Illus.). 32p. (J). (ps-1). 13.95 o.p. (*0-525-44693-1*, Dutton Children's Bks.) Penguin Putnam Bks. for Young Readers.

—Watch the Stars Come Out. 1987. (Reading Rainbow Bks.). (Illus.). 64p. (J). (gr. 1-5). pap. 4.95 o.p. (*0-02-688766-5*) Checkerboard Pr., Inc.

Levy, Elizabeth. A Mammoth Mix-Up. (Brian & Pea Brain Mystery Ser.). (Illus.). 96p. (J). (gr. 2-5). 1996. pap. 3.95 o.p. (*0-06-442043-4*, Harper Trophy); 1995. 12.95 o.p. (*0-06-024814-9*); 1995. lib. bdg. 12.89 o.s.i (*0-06-024815-7*) HarperCollins Children's Bk. Group.

—School Spirit Sabotage. 1994. (Brian & Pea Brain Mystery Ser.). (Illus.). 96p. (J). (gr. 2-5). 14.00 o.p. (*0-06-023407-5*); lib. bdg. 13.89 o.p. (*0-06-023408-3*) HarperCollins Children's Bk. Group.

Lewis, Beverly. The Chicken Pox Panic. 1995. (Cul-de-Sac Kids Ser.: Vol. 2). 80p. (J). (gr. 2-5). pap. 3.99 (*1-55661-626-0*) Bethany Hse. Pubs.

—The Double Dabble Surprise. 1995. (Cul-de-Sac Kids Ser.: Vol. 1). 80p. (J). (gr. 2-5). pap. 3.99 (*1-55661-625-2*) Bethany Hse. Pubs.

—Photo Perfect. 2001. (Girls Only Go Ser.: Vol. 7). 128p. (J). (gr. 4-7). pap. 5.99 (*1-55661-642-2*) Bethany Hse. Pubs.

Lewis, C. S. The Complete Chronicles of Narnia. 2002. (Chronicles of Narnia Ser.). pap. 29.99 (*0-06-051758-1*) HarperCollins Pubs.

Lewis, Kim. The Last Train. 1994. (Illus.). 32p. (J). (ps up). 14.95 o.p. (*1-56402-343-5*) Candlewick Pr.

Lewis, Linda. Want to Trade Two Brothers for a Cat? 1989. (Orig.). (J). (gr. 3-6). pap. 2.75 (*0-671-66605-3*); (Illus.). mass mkt. 2.75 (*0-671-69666-1*) Simon & Schuster Children's Publishing. (Aladdin).

Lewison, Wendy. My Baby Brother. 1990. (J). 7.95 o.s.i (*1-55782-102-X*) Warner Bks., Inc.

Lewison, Wendy Cheyette. Our New Baby. 1996. (All Aboard Bks.). (Illus.). 32p. (J). (ps-3). 3.49 (*0-448-41147-4*, Grosset & Dunlap) Penguin Putnam Bks. for Young Readers.

Lillington, Kenneth. Full Moon. 1986. 175p. o.p. (*0-571-13792-X*) Faber & Faber Ltd.

Lindbergh, Anne M. The Shadow on the Dial. 1987. 160p. (J). (gr. 5-8). 12.95 (*0-06-023882-8*); lib. bdg. 12.89 o.p. (*0-06-023883-6*) HarperCollins Children's Bk. Group.

Linde, Gunnel. Trust in the Unexpected. Crampton, Patricia, tr. from SWE. 1984. (Illus.). 144p. (J). (gr. 4-7). 10.95 o.s.i (*0-689-50300-8*, McElderry, Margaret K.) Simon & Schuster Children's Publishing.

Relationships

Lindgren, Astrid. The Children on Troublemaker Street. (Ready-for-Chapters Ser.). (Illus.). (J). 2001. 96p. pap. 3.99 (0-689-84674-6); 1991. 112p. (gr. 1-4). reprint ed. pap. 3.50 o.s.i (0-689-71515-3) Simon & Schuster Children's Publishing. (Aladdin).

—I Want a Brother or Sister. Lucas, Barbara, tr. from SWE. 1981. (Illus.). 32p. (J). (ps-3). 9.95 o.p. (0-15-239387-0) Harcourt Children's Bks.

Lindman, Maj. Snipp, Snapp, Snurr & the Big Farm. 1993. (Illus.). 32p. (J). reprint ed. lib. bdg. 14.95 (1-56849-004-6) Buccaneer Bks., Inc.

—Snipp, Snapp, Snurr & the Big Surprise. 1993. (Illus.). 32p. (J). reprint ed. lib. bdg. 14.95 (1-56849-003-8) Buccaneer Bks., Inc.

—Snipp, Snapp, Snurr & the Buttered Bread. 1993. (Illus.). 32p. (J). reprint ed. lib. bdg. 14.95 (1-56849-002-X) Buccaneer Bks., Inc.

—Snipp, Snapp, Snurr & the Buttered Bread. 1995. (J). (ps-2). pap. 6.95 o.p. (0-8075-7504-6); pap. 6.95 (0-8075-7491-0) Whitman, Albert & Co.

—Snipp, Snapp, Snurr & the Gingerbread. 1991. (Illus.). 30p. (J). reprint ed. pap. 10.95 (0-89966-829-1) Buccaneer Bks., Inc.

—Snipp, Snapp, Snurr & the Magic Horse. 1993. (Illus.). 32p. (J). reprint ed. lib. bdg. 14.95 (1-56849-001-1) Buccaneer Bks., Inc.

—Snipp, Snapp, Snurr & the Red Shoes. 1993. (Illus.). 32p. (J). reprint ed. lib. bdg. 14.95 (1-56849-000-3) Buccaneer Bks., Inc.

—Snipp, Snapp, Snurr & the Reindeer. 1993. (Illus.). 32p. (J). reprint ed. lib. bdg. 14.95 (1-56849-005-4) Buccaneer Bks., Inc.

—Snipp, Snapp, Snurr & the Seven Dogs. 1993. (Illus.). 32p. (J). reprint ed. lib. bdg. 14.95 (1-56849-007-0) Buccaneer Bks., Inc.

—Snipp, Snapp, Snurr & the Yellow Sled. 1991. (Illus.). 30p. (J). reprint ed. pap. 10.95 (0-89966-828-3) Buccaneer Bks., Inc.

—Snipp, Snapp, Snurr & the Yellow Sled. 1995. (J). (ps-3). pap. 6.95 (0-8075-7499-6) Whitman, Albert & Co.

—Snipp, Snapp, Snurr Learn to Swim. 1993. (Illus.). 32p. (J). reprint ed. lib. bdg. 14.95 (1-56849-006-2) Buccaneer Bks., Inc.

—Snipp, Snapp, Snurr Learn to Swim. 1995. (J). (ps-3). pap. 6.95 (0-8075-7494-5) Whitman, Albert & Co.

Linko, Gina. Ben's Big Break. 2004. (Seekers Ser.: No. 4). 108p. (J). pap. 5.99 (0-8066-4185-1, Augsburg Bks.) Augsburg Fortress, Pubs.

Lipniacka, Ewa. Asleep at Last. 1993. (Jamie & Luke Ser.). (Illus.). (J). 6.95 o.p. (1-56656-118-3, Crocodile Bks.) Interlink Publishing Group, Inc.

—It's Mine! 1993. (Jamie & Luke Ser.). (Illus.). 20p. (J). (ps-1). 6.95 o.p. (1-56656-119-1, Crocodile Bks.) Interlink Publishing Group, Inc.

—Who Shares? 2003. (Illus.). 24p. (J). 14.99 (0-8037-2889-1, Dial Bks. for Young Readers) Penguin Putnam Bks. for Young Readers.

Lisle, Janet Taylor. The Forest. November, S., ed. 2001. (Illus.). 160p. (J). (gr. 4-7). pap. 4.99 o.s.i (0-14-131095-2, Puffin Bks.) Penguin Putnam Bks. for Young Readers.

—How I Became a Writer & Oggie Learned to Drive. (Illus.). 160p. 2003. pap. 5.99 (0-14-250167-0, Puffin Bks.); 2002. (J). (gr. 4-7). 16.99 (0-399-23394-6, Philomel) Penguin Putnam Bks. for Young Readers.

Little, Jean. Emma's Strange Pet. 2003. (I Can Read Bks.). (Illus.). 64p. (J). 15.99 (0-06-028350-5); lib. bdg. 16.89 (0-06-028351-3) HarperCollins Pubs.

—Emma's Yucky Brother. 2001. (I Can Read Bks.). (Illus.). 64p. (J). (gr. k-3). 14.95 (0-06-028348-3); lib. bdg. 16.89 (0-06-028349-1) HarperCollins Children's Bk. Group.

—Emma's Yucky Brother. 2002. (I Can Read Book 3 Ser.). (Illus.). 64p. (J). pap. 3.99 (0-06-444258-6) HarperCollins Pubs.

—Listen for the Singing. 1991. (Trophy Bk.). 272p. (J). (gr. 4-7). pap. 3.95 o.p. (0-06-440394-7, Harper Trophy); lib. bdg. 14.89 o.p. (0-06-023910-7) HarperCollins Children's Bk. Group.

—Stand in the Wind. 1975. (Illus.). 256p. (J). (gr. 4-6). lib. bdg. 12.89 o.p. (0-06-023904-2) HarperCollins Children's Bk. Group.

Lively, Penelope. Fanny's Sister. 1980. (Illus.). 64p. (J). (gr. 3-5). 7.95 o.p. (0-525-29618-2, Dutton) Dutton/Plume.

Lloyd, David. The Stopwatch. 1986. (Illus.). 32p. (J). (ps-2). lib. bdg. 11.89 (0-397-32193-7); reprint ed. pap. 2.50 o.p. (0-06-443107-X, Harper Trophy) HarperCollins Children's Bk. Group.

Loehr, Mallory. Earth Magic. 1999. (Magic Elements Quartet Ser.: Vol. 2). 128p. (J). (gr. 3-5). lib. bdg. 11.99 o.s.i (0-679-99218-9);3. pap. 3.99 (0-679-89218-4) Random Hse., Inc.

—Earth Magic. 1999. (J). 10.04 (0-606-19081-3) Turtleback Bks.

—Water Wishes. 1999. (J). (gr. 3-5). (Stepping Stone Bks.). (Illus.). 117p. lib. bdg. 11.99 (0-679-99216-2);No. 1. (Magic Elements Quartet Ser.: Vol. 1). 128p. pap. 3.99 (0-679-89216-8) Random Hse. Children's Bks. (Random Hse. Bks. for Young Readers).

—Water Wishes. 1999. 10.04 (0-606-19085-6) Turtleback Bks.

Loesch, Joe. The Abraham Lincoln Logues. Hutchinson, Cheryl, ed. unabr. ed. 2000. (Backyard Adventure Ser.). (Illus.). 60p. (J). (gr. k-5). reprint ed. 16.95 incl. audio compact disk (1-932332-03-0) Toy Box Productions.

—The Abraham Lincoln Logues. Hutchinson, Cheryl J., ed. unabr. ed. 2000. (Backyard Adventure Ser.). (Illus.). (J). (gr. k-6). pap. 16.95 incl. audio compact disk (1-887729-77-1); pap. 14.95 incl. audio (1-887729-76-3) Toy Box Productions.

London, Jonathan. Froggy's Baby Sister. 2003. (Illus.). 32p. (J). 15.99 (0-670-03659-5, Viking) Viking Penguin.

—Moshi Moshi. 1998. (Around the World Ser.). (Illus.). 32p. (gr. k-4). lib. bdg. 23.90 o.p. (0-7613-0110-0) Millbrook Pr., Inc.

Long, D. J. I Wish I Was the Baby. (Illus.). (J). 2002. 32p. pap. 5.95 (0-8249-5441-6); 1995. lib. bdg. 12.95 (0-8249-5427-0, Ideals Children's Bks.) Ideals Pubns.

Look, Lenore. Henry's First-Moon Birthday. 2001. (Illus.). 40p. (J). (ps-2). 16.00 (0-689-82294-4, Atheneum/Anne Schwartz Bks.) Simon & Schuster Children's Publishing.

Lord, Athena V. The Luck of Z. A. P. & Zoe. 1987. (Illus.). 160p. (J). (gr. 4-7). lib. bdg. 13.95 o.s.i (0-02-759560-9, Simon & Schuster Children's Publishing) Simon & Schuster Children's Publishing.

—Z. A. P., Zoe, & the Musketeers. 1992. 160p. (J). (gr. 3-7). text 13.95 o.p. (0-02-759561-7, Simon & Schuster Children's Publishing) Simon & Schuster Children's Publishing.

Love, D. Anne. Three Against the Tide. 1998. 162p. (J). (gr. 4-7). tchr. ed. 15.95 (0-8234-1400-0) Holiday Hse., Inc.

—Three Against the Tide. 2000. (Illus.). 192p. (gr. 4-7). pap. text 4.50 (0-440-41634-5, Yearling) Random Hse. Children's Bks.

—Three Against the Tide. 2000. 10.55 (0-606-18909-2) Turtleback Bks.

Low, Alice. The Witch Who Was Afraid of Witches. 1999. (I Can Read Bks.). (Illus.). 48p. (J). (gr. 3-4). 14.95 (0-06-028305-X); lib. bdg. 14.89 (0-06-028306-8) HarperCollins Children's Bk. Group.

—The Witch Who Was Afraid of Witches. 1978. (I Can Read Chapter Bks.). (Illus.). (J). (gr. 3-5). 5.95 o.p. (0-394-83718-5); lib. bdg. 6.99 o.p. (0-394-93718-X) Knopf Publishing Group. (Pantheon).

Lowery, Linda. Somebody Somewhere Knows My Name. 1995. (First Person Ser.). (Illus.). 40p. (J). (gr. 2-4). lib. bdg. 19.93 o.s.i (0-87614-946-8, Carolrhoda Bks.) Lerner Publishing Group.

Lowry, Lois. All about Sam. l.t. ed. 1993. 152p. (J). 13.95 o.p. (0-7451-1659-0, Galaxy Children's Large Print) BBC Audiobooks America.

—All about Sam. 1989. (Illus.). 160p. (gr. 3-7). pap. text 4.99 (0-440-40221-2, Yearling) Random Hse. Children's Bks.

—Anastasia, Ask Your Analyst. 1984. 128p. (J). (gr. 4-6). tchr. ed. 16.00 (0-395-36011-0, 5-90388) Houghton Mifflin Co.

—Anastasia, Ask Your Analyst. l.t. ed. 1989. 176p. (YA). reprint ed. lib. bdg. 16.95 o.s.i (1-55736-133-9, Cornerstone Bks.) Pages, Inc.

—Anastasia, Ask Your Analyst. 1992. 128p. (gr. 4-7). pap. text 4.50 (0-440-40289-1, Yearling) Random Hse. Children's Bks.

—Anastasia, Ask Your Analyst. 1992. (J). 10.55 (0-606-00251-0) Turtleback Bks.

—The One Hundredth Thing about Caroline. 1983. 160p. (J). (gr. 4-6). tchr. ed. 16.00 (0-395-34829-3) Houghton Mifflin Co.

—The One Hundredth Thing about Caroline. 1985. 160p. (J). (gr. 4-7). pap. 4.50 (0-440-46625-3, Yearling) Random Hse. Children's Bks.

—The Silent Boy. 2003. (Illus.). 192p. (YA). (gr. 5-12). tchr. ed. 15.00 (0-618-28231-9) Houghton Mifflin Co.

—A Summer to Die. 1983. (YA). 128p. mass mkt. 3.50 o.s.i (0-553-27395-7); 160p. (gr. 7-12). mass mkt. 5.50 (0-440-21917-5) Bantam Bks.

—A Summer to Die. 1999. mass mkt. (0-553-24389-6); mass mkt. (0-553-25447-2); mass mkt. (0-553-14304-2) Random Hse., Inc.

—A Summer to Die. 1977. 11.04 (0-606-01656-2) Turtleback Bks.

Lunney, Linda Hayward. Monster Bug. Palmisciano, Diane, tr. & illus. by. 2004. (Science Solves It! Ser.). (J). pap. (1-57565-135-1) Kane Pr., The.

Lynch, Chris. Dog Eat Dog. 1996. (Blue-Eyed Son Ser.: Vol. 3). (Illus.). 144p. (YA). (gr. 12 up). pap. 4.50 o.s.i (0-06-447123-3); lib. bdg. 13.89 o.p. (0-06-027210-4) HarperCollins Children's Bk. Group. (Harper Trophy).

—Dog Eat Dog. 1996. (Blue-Eyed Son Ser.). (J). 9.60 o.p. (0-606-09091-6) Turtleback Bks.

—Elvin No. 3. 2004. (J). (0-06-623940-0) HarperCollins Pubs.

—Gypsy Davey. 1994. 160p. (YA). (gr. 12 up). 14.00 o.s.i (0-06-023586-1); (gr. 7 up). lib. bdg. 13.89 o.p. (0-06-023587-X) HarperCollins Children's Bk. Group.

—Shadow Boxer. (Trophy Bk.). 224p. (J). (gr. 5 up). 1995. pap. 5.95 (0-06-447112-8, Harper Trophy); 1993. 14.95 o.p. (0-06-023027-4); 1993. lib. bdg. 14.89 o.s.i (0-06-023028-2) HarperCollins Children's Bk. Group.

—Shadow Boxer. 1996. (YA). (gr. 9-12). 20.75 (0-8446-6886-9) Smith, Peter Pub., Inc.

—Shadow Boxer. 1995. 11.00 (0-606-08147-X) Turtleback Bks.

Maccarone, Grace. Sharing Time Troubles. 1997. (Hello Reader! Ser.: Level 1). (Illus.). 32p. (J). (ps-1). pap. 3.99 o.p. (0-590-73879-8) Scholastic, Inc.

—Sharing Time Troubles. 1997. (First-Grade Friends Ser.). (J). 10.14 (0-606-11331-2) Turtleback Bks.

MacDonald, Maryann. No Room for Francie, No. 2. 1995. (Hyperion Chapters Ser.). (Illus.). 64p. (J). (gr. 2-4). pap. 3.95 o.s.i (0-7868-1081-5) Disney Pr.

—No Room for Francie, No. 2. 1995. (Lots of O'Learys Ser.). (Illus.). 64p. (J). (gr. 2-4). 13.95 (0-7868-0032-1) Hyperion Bks. for Children.

—No Room for Francie. 1995. (Lots of O'Leary's Ser.). (J). 9.15 o.p. (0-606-09693-0) Turtleback Bks.

Mackall, Dandi Daley. Horsefeathers Mystery. 2001. (Horsefeathers Ser.: Vol. 7). (Illus.). 191p. (J). (gr. 7-12). pap. 5.99 (0-570-07128-3) Concordia Publishing Hse.

—Kyra's Story. 2003. (Degrees of Guilt Ser.). 225p. (YA). pap. 12.99 (0-8423-8284-4) Tyndale Hse. Pubs.

MacKenzie, Carine. El Secreto de la Hermana Mayor, el Maria.Tr. of Big Sister's Secret. (SPA.). (J). 1.99 (1-56063-700-5, 497731) Editorial Unilit.

Mackinnon, Debbie. Tom's Train. 1997. (Surprise Board Book Ser.). 8p. (J). (ps-k). 4.99 o.s.i (0-8037-2105-6, Dial Bks. for Young Readers) Penguin Putnam Bks. for Young Readers.

Mader, Jan. My Brother Wants to Be Like Me. l.t. ed. 1998. (Illus.). 16p. (J). (gr. k-2). pap. 4.95 (1-879835-27-4, Kaeden Bks.) Kaeden Corp.

Maher, Mickle Brandt. Master Stitchum & the Moon. 2003. (Illus.). (J). 19.99 (1-932188-01-0) Bollix Bks.

Mahy, Margaret. The Changeover: A Supernatural Romance. l.t. unabr. ed. 1988. (Illus.). (YA). 13.95 o.p. (0-8161-4440-0, Macmillan Reference USA) Gale Group.

—The Changeover: A Supernatural Romance. 1985. (YA). pap. 2.25 o.p. (0-590-33798-X); 264p. (gr. 7 up). reprint ed. pap. 2.50 o.p. (0-590-41289-2, Scholastic Paperbacks) Scholastic, Inc.

—The Changeover: A Supernatural Romance. 1984. 224p. (YA). (gr. 7 up). 16.00 (0-689-50303-2, McElderry, Margaret K.) Simon & Schuster Children's Publishing.

—The Changeover: A Supernatural Romance. 1994. (YA). 10.09 o.p. (0-606-05784-6) Turtleback Bks.

—The Seven Chinese Brothers. (Blue Ribbon Book Ser.). 40p. (J). (ps-3). 1997. mass mkt. 7.60 (0-590-42057-7); 1994. (SPA., Illus.). pap. 3.95 (0-590-25211-9); 1990. (Illus.). pap. 15.95 o.p. (0-590-42055-0) Scholastic, Inc.

—Seven Chinese Brothers. 1989. (Blue Ribbon Bks.). (J). 12.14 (0-606-01945-6) Turtleback Bks.

—Tangled Fortunes. (Cousins Quartet Ser.: Bk. 4). 112p. (J). 1996. (gr. 4-7). pap. 3.99 o.s.i (0-440-41163-7); 1994. (Illus.). (gr. 3-6). 14.95 (0-385-32066-3, Delacorte Pr.) Dell Publishing.

—Tangled Fortunes. 1995. 18.95 (0-385-30979-1) Doubleday Publishing.

Maifair, Linda L. Brothers Don't Know Everything. 1993. (Illus.). 64p. (J). pap. 3.99 o.p. (0-8066-2635-6, 9-2635, Augsburg Bks.) Augsburg Fortress, Pubs.

Mallat, Kathy. Oh, Brother. 2003. (Illus.). (J). 15.95 (0-8027-8875-0); lib. bdg. 16.85 (0-8027-8876-9) Walker & Co.

Manes, Stephen. An Almost Perfect Game. 1995. 176p. (J). (gr. 4-7). pap. 14.95 (0-590-44432-8) Scholastic, Inc.

—Chocolate-Covered Ants. 1990. (J). (gr. 4-7). 13.95 o.p. (0-590-40960-3) Scholastic, Inc.

—Monstra vs. Irving, ERS. 1989. (Illus.). 80p. (J). (gr. 2-4). 12.95 o.p. (0-8050-0836-5, Holt, Henry & Co. Bks. For Young Readers) Holt, Henry & Co.

Mango, Karin N. Somewhere Green. 1987. 208p. (J). (gr. 5-9). 13.95 o.s.i (0-02-762270-3, Simon & Schuster Children's Publishing) Simon & Schuster Children's Publishing.

Manson, Ainslie. Ballerinas Don't Wear Glasses. 2001. (Illus.). 32p. (J). (gr. k-3). pap. 6.95 (1-55143-176-9) Orca Bk. Pubs.

Mantell, Paul. Shelter. Richardson, Julia, ed. 2000. (So Weird Ser.: No. 2). 141p. (J). (gr. 4-7). pap. 4.99 (0-7868-1398-9) Disney Pr.

Marcus, Irene W. & Marcus, Paul. Scary Night Visitors: A Story for Children with Bedtime Fears. 1990. (Illus.). 32p. (J). (ps-2). 11.95 (0-945354-26-6); pap. 8.95 o.p. (0-945354-25-8) American Psychological Assn.

—Scary Night Visitors: A Story for Children with Bedtime Fears. 1993. (Books to Help Children Ser.). (Illus.). 32p. (J). (ps up). lib. bdg. 18.60 o.p. (0-8368-0935-1) Stevens, Gareth Inc.

Margolis, Richard J. Secrets of a Small Brother. 1984. (Illus.). 40p. (J). (gr. 1-4). lib. bdg. 12.95 o.s.i (0-02-762280-0, Simon & Schuster Children's Publishing) Simon & Schuster Children's Publishing.

Mariconda, Barbara. Turn the Cup Around. 1997. 160p. (J). (gr. 3-7). text 15.95 o.s.i (0-385-32292-5, Delacorte Pr.) Dell Publishing.

—Turn the Cup Around. 1998. 160p. (gr. 3-7). reprint ed. pap. text 3.99 o.s.i (0-440-41311-7, Yearling) Random Hse. Children's Bks.

—Turn the Cup Around. 1998. 10.04 (0-606-13878-1) Turtleback Bks.

Marino, Jan. The Mona Lisa of Salem Street: A Novel. 1995. 176p. (J). 14.95 o.p. (0-316-54614-3) Little Brown & Co.

Mario, Heidi S. I'd Rather Have an Iguana. 1999. (Illus.). 32p. (J). (ps-3). 14.95 (0-88106-357-6, Talewinds) Charlesbridge Publishing, Inc.

Marshall, Catherine. Brotherly Love. 1997. (Christy Fiction Ser.: No. 12). 128p. (Orig.). (J). (gr. 4-8). mass mkt. 4.99 (0-8499-3963-1) Nelson, Tommy.

Marshall, James. The Cut-Ups. 1984. (Cut-Ups Ser.). (Illus.). 32p. (J). (gr. 3-8). 15.99 o.p. (0-670-25195-X, Viking Children's Bks.) Penguin Putnam Bks. for Young Readers.

Martin, Ann M. The Baby-Sitters Little Sister Boxed Set No. 1 Bks. 1-4: Karen's Witch; Karen's Roller Skates; Karen's Worst Day; Karen's Kittycat Club. 1989. (Baby-Sitters Little Sister Ser.). (J). (gr. 3-7). pap. 11.00 o.p. (0-590-63403-8) Scholastic, Inc.

—The Baby-Sitters Little Sister Boxed Set No. 14 Bks. 53-56: Karen's School Bus; Karen's Candy; Karen's Magician; Karen's Ice Skates. 1997. (Baby-Sitters Little Sister Ser.). (J). (gr. 3-7). pap. 11.80 (0-590-66941-9) Scholastic, Inc.

—Dawn's Wicked Stepsister. 1990. (Baby-Sitters Club Ser.: No. 31). (J). (gr. 3-7). 10.04 (0-606-00676-1) Turtleback Bks.

—Inside Out. 1984. 160p. (J). (gr. 4-9). 13.95 o.p. (0-8234-0512-5) Holiday Hse., Inc.

—Inside Out. 1990. (J). (gr. 5-7). pap. 2.95 o.p. (0-590-43621-X); 1985. pap. 2.25 o.p. (0-590-33552-9); 1985. 160p. (J). (gr. 4-6). reprint ed. pap. 2.50 o.p. (0-590-40883-6, Scholastic Paperbacks) Scholastic, Inc.

—Karen's Big Sister. 1996. (Baby-Sitters Little Sister Ser.: No. 69). (J). (gr. 3-7). mass mkt. 2.95 (0-590-26193-2) Scholastic, Inc.

—Karen's Big Sister. 1996. (Baby-Sitters Little Sister Ser.: No. 69). (J). (gr. 3-7). 9.00 (0-606-08486-X) Turtleback Bks.

—Karen's Copycat. 1999. (Baby-Sitters Little Sister Ser.: No. 107). 112p. (J). (gr. 3-7). mass mkt. 3.99 (0-590-50059-7) Scholastic, Inc.

—Karen's Grandad. 1996. (Baby-Sitters Little Sister Ser.: No. 70). (J). (gr. 3-7). mass mkt. 3.50 (0-590-26280-7) Scholastic, Inc.

—Karen's Little Sister. 1989. (Baby-Sitters Little Sister Ser.: No. 6). (J). (gr. 3-7). 9.55 (0-606-01608-2) Turtleback Bks.

—Karen's New Year. 1991. (Baby-Sitters Little Sister Ser.: No. 15). (J). (gr. 3-7). 10.04 (0-606-04717-4) Turtleback Bks.

—Karen's Pilgrim. 1997. (Baby-Sitters Little Sister Ser.: No. 91). (J). (gr. 3-7). mass mkt. 3.50 (0-590-06589-0) Scholastic, Inc.

—Karen's Prize. 1990. (Baby-Sitters Little Sister Ser.: No. 11). (J). (gr. 3-7). 9.55 (0-606-04718-2) Turtleback Bks.

—Karen's School Mystery; Karen's Ski Trip; Karen's Leprechaun; Karen's Pony Bks. 57-60. 1997. (Baby-Sitters Little Sister Ser.). (J). (gr. 3-7). pap. 11.80 (0-590-66958-3) Scholastic, Inc.

—Karen's Sleepover. 1990. (Baby-Sitters Little Sister Ser.: No. 9). (J). (gr. 3-7). 10.04 (0-606-04459-0) Turtleback Bks.

—Karen's Surprise. 1990. (Baby-Sitters Little Sister Ser.: No. 13). (J). (gr. 3-7). 8.05 o.p. (0-606-04719-0) Turtleback Bks.

—Karen's Tattletale; Karen's New Bike; Karen's Movie; Karen's Lemonade Stand Bks. 61-64. 1997. (Baby-Sitters Little Sister Ser.). (J). (gr. 3-7). pap. 11.80 (0-590-66959-1) Scholastic, Inc.

—Karen's Unicorn. 1997. (Baby-Sitters Little Sister Ser.: No. 89). (Illus.). 112p. (J). (gr. 3-7). mass mkt. 3.50 (*0-590-06587-4*) Scholastic, Inc.

—Karen's Wish. 1990. (Baby-Sitters Little Sister Super Special Ser.: No. 1). (J). (gr. 2-4). 8.35 o.p. (*0-606-04720-4*) Turtleback Bks.

—Karen's Yo-Yo. 2000. (Baby-Sitters Little Sister Ser.: No. 119). (Illus.). 144p. (J). (gr. 3-7). mass mkt. 3.99 (*0-590-52511-5*) Scholastic, Inc.

—Missing since Monday. 1986. 176p. (YA). (gr. 7 up). 14.95 o.p. (*0-8234-0626-1*) Holiday Hse., Inc.

Martin, Patricia. Travels with Rainie Marie. 1997. 192p. (J). (gr. 4-8). 15.95 (*0-7868-0257-X*) Hyperion Bks. for Children.

Martin, Patricia M. Travels with Rainie Marie. 1997. 192p. (J). (gr. 4-8). lib. bdg. 16.49 (*0-7868-2212-0*) Hyperion Bks. for Children.

Martini, Teri. All Because of Jill. 1976. 154p. (J). (gr. 7-9). 6.95 o.p. (*0-664-32589-0*) Westminster John Knox Pr.

Marx, David F. Baby in the House. 2000. (Rookie Readers Ser.). (Illus.). 32p. (J). (gr. 1-2). lib. bdg. 19.00 (*0-516-21688-0*, Children's Pr.) Scholastic Library Publishing.

Mason, Babbie. A Sister for Sam. 1985. (Care Bear Ser.). (J). pap. 11.95 o.p. (*0-516-09003-8*, Children's Pr.) Scholastic Library Publishing.

Mason, Margo C. Are We There Yet? 1990. 32p. (J). (ps-3). pap. 3.50 o.s.i (*0-553-34886-8*) Bantam Bks.

Massey, Jane. Count Your Cookies. 2003. (Illus.). 32p. (J). 14.95 (*1-57768-661-6*, Gingham Dog Pr.) McGraw-Hill Children's Publishing.

Massi, Jeri. The Lesser Brother. 1989. 124p. (Orig.). (YA). (gr. 11). pap. 5.95 (*1-877778-02-8*) Llama Bks.

Masters, Susan Rowan. Night Journey to Vicksburg. Killcoyne, Hope L., ed. 2003. (J). 14.95 (*1-893110-30-3*) Silver Moon Pr.

Matarasso, Janet. Angela's New Sister. 1988. (Illus.). 24p. text 11.95 o.p. (*0-521-35640-7*) Cambridge Univ. Pr.

Matthews, Ellen. Getting Rid of Roger. 1978. (Illus.). 96p. (J). (gr. 3-7). 7.50 o.p. (*0-664-32622-6*) Westminster John Knox Pr.

—The Trouble with Leslie. 1979. (Illus.). 110p. (J). (gr. 3-6). 8.95 o.p. (*0-664-32653-6*) Westminster John Knox Pr.

Matthews, Kezi. Scorpio's Child. 2001. 160p. (J). (gr. 6-8). 15.95 (*0-8126-2890-X*) Cricket Bks.

—Scorpio's Child. 2004. 160p. (J). 6.99 (*0-14-240079-3*, Puffin Bks.) Penguin Putnam Bks. for Young Readers.

May, Kara. Big Brave Brother Ben. 1992. (Illus.). (J). (ps-3). 14.00 o.p. (*0-688-11234-X*); 32p. lib. bdg. 13.93 o.p. (*0-688-11235-8*) HarperCollins Children's Bk. Group.

Mayer, Mercer. Goodnight, Little Critter, Level 3. 2001. (First Readers, Skills & Practice Ser.). (Illus.). 24p. (J). (gr. 1-2). pap. 3.95 (*1-57768-834-1*) McGraw-Hill Children's Publishing.

—Grandma's Garden. 2001. (First Readers, Skills & Practice Ser.). (Illus.). 24p. (J). (gr. k-1). 3.95 (*1-57768-846-5*) McGraw-Hill Children's Publishing.

—Just Me & My Little Brother. 1998. (Little Critter Ser.). (Illus.). 24p. (J). (ps-3). pap. 3.29 (*0-307-12628-5*, 12628, Golden Bks.) Random Hse. Children's Bks.

—Just Me & My Little Brother. 1991. (Little Critter Ser.). (J). (ps-3). 9.44 (*0-606-12378-4*) Turtleback Bks.

—Little Critter's the Best Present. 2000. (Little Critter Ser.). (Illus.). 32p. (J). (ps-3). pap. 3.99 (*0-307-26215-4*); lib. bdg. 11.99 (*0-307-46215-3*, 46215) Random Hse. Children's Bks. (Golden Bks.).

—Little Critter's the Best Present. 2000. (Little Critter Ser.). (J). (ps-3). 10.14 (*0-606-18923-8*) Turtleback Bks.

—Me Too! 1985. (Little Critter Ser.). (J). (ps-3). 9.44 (*0-606-12422-5*) Turtleback Bks.

—The New Potty. 2003. (Illus.). 24p. 3.25 (*0-375-82631-9*) Random Hse. Children's Bks.

—Our Tree House, Level 3. 2001. (First Readers, Skills & Practice Ser.). (Illus.). 24p. (J). (gr. 1-2). pap. 3.95 (*1-57768-833-3*) McGraw-Hill Children's Publishing.

Mayer, Mercer & Mayer, Gina. Just a Bully. 1999. (Little Critter Ser.). (Illus.). 24p. (J). (ps-3). pap. 3.29 (*0-307-13200-5*, Golden Bks.) Random Hse. Children's Bks.

—Just a Bully. 1999. (Little Critter Ser.). (J). (ps-3). 9.44 (*0-606-19800-8*) Turtleback Bks.

Mayer, Mercer, et al. My Big Sister. 1995. (Little Critter Ser.). (Illus.). 24p. (J). (ps-3). pap. 1.79 (*0-307-11619-0*, 11619, Golden Bks.) Random Hse. Children's Bks.

—The New Potty. 1992. (Little Critter Ser.). (Illus.). 24p. (J). (ps-3). pap. 1.79 o.s.i (*0-307-11523-2*, 11523, Golden Bks.) Random Hse. Children's Bks.

Mayfield, Julie. The Magical First Day. 1998. (Illus.). (J). 17.25 (*1-56763-336-6*); pap. (*1-56763-337-4*) Ozark Publishing.

Maynard, Bill. Rock River. 1998. 104p. (J). (gr. 3-7). 15.99 o.s.i (*0-399-23224-9*) Penguin Group (USA) Inc.

Mazer, Anne. The Fixits. 1999. (Illus.). 24p. (J). (ps-3). 12.99 (*0-7868-0213-8*); lib. bdg. 13.89 (*0-7868-2202-3*) Hyperion Bks. for Children.

Mazer, Norma Fox. D, My Name Is Danita. 1991. 176p. (J). (gr. 4-6). 13.95 (*0-590-43655-4*) Scholastic, Inc.

—Three Sisters. (YA). (gr. 7 up). 1991. pap. 2.95 o.p. (*0-590-43817-4*, Scholastic Paperbacks); 1986. 240p. pap. 12.95 o.p. (*0-590-33774-2*) Scholastic, Inc.

Mbuthia, Waithira. My Sister's Wedding: A Story of Kenya. 2002. (Make Friends Around the World Ser.). (Illus.). 32p. (J). (gr. k-3). 15.95 (*1-56899-896-1*, B8006); 19.95 incl. audio (*1-56899-898-8*, BC8006); pap. 5.95 (*1-56899-897-X*, S8006) Soundprints.

McAllister, Angela. The Snow Angel. 1993. (Illus.). (J). 14.00 o.p. (*0-688-04569-3*) HarperCollins Children's Bk. Group.

McCaffrey, Mary. My Brother Ange. 1982. (Illus.). 96p. (J). (gr. 3-6). lib. bdg. 11.89 o.p. (*0-690-04195-0*) HarperCollins Children's Bk. Group.

McCann, Yvette B. Eddie Pasghetti. Damerest, Nancy & Lea, Judy, eds. 1994. (Eddie Pasghetti Collection: Bk. 1). (Illus.). 64p. (J). (gr. 4 up). 14.95 (*0-9639486-5-2*) Rhyme Tyme Pubns.

McClintock, Barbara. Adele & Simon, RS. 2005. (J). (*0-374-38044-9*, Farrar, Straus & Giroux (BYR)) Farrar, Straus & Giroux.

McColley, Kevin. Switch. 1997. 224p. (gr. 7 up). (J). 16.00 (*0-689-81122-5*, Simon & Schuster Children's Publishing); (YA). pap. 4.50 (*0-689-81527-1*, Simon Pulse) Simon & Schuster Children's Publishing.

McCormick, Wendy. The Night You Were Born. 2000. (Illus.). 32p. (J). (ps-2). 15.95 (*1-56145-225-4*) Peachtree Pubs., Ltd.

McCullough, Sharon Pierce. Bunbun at the Fair. 2002. (Bunbun Ser.). (Illus.). 24p. (J). (gr. k-2). 14.99 (*1-84148-900-X*) Barefoot Bks., Inc.

—Bunbun, the Middle One. 2002. (Bunbun Ser.). (Illus.). 24p. (J). (gr. k-2). bds. 6.99 (*1-84148-377-X*) Barefoot Bks., Inc.

McCusker, Paul. Voice & Protector. 1999. (Passages Ser.: Vol. 1). 190p. (J). (gr. 5-9). 6.99 (*1-56179-773-1*) Nelson, Tommy.

McDaniel, Becky B. Katie Did It. 1983. (Rookie Readers Ser.). (Illus.). 32p. (J). (ps-3). pap. 4.95 (*0-516-42043-7*, Children's Pr.) Scholastic Library Publishing.

McDaniel, Becky Bring. Katie Couldn't. 1985. (Rookie Readers Ser.). (Illus.). 32p. (J). (gr. 1-2). pap. 4.95 (*0-516-42069-0*); lib. bdg. 19.00 (*0-516-02069-2*) Scholastic Library Publishing. (Children's Pr.).

—Katie Did It. (Rookie Readers Ser.). (Illus.). 32p. (J). 1983. (gr. 1-2). lib. bdg. 19.00 o.p. (*0-516-02043-9*); 2003. lib. bdg. 19.00 (*0-516-22848-X*) Scholastic Library Publishing. (Children's Pr.).

McDaniel, Lurlene. The Time Capsule. 2003. 224p. (YA). (gr. 7). 9.95 (*0-553-57096-X*, Bantam Bks. for Young Readers) Random Hse. Children's Bks.

—The Time Capsule. 2003. 224p. (YA). (gr. 7). lib. bdg. 11.99 (*0-553-13051-X*) Random Hse., Inc.

McDonald, Megan. The Great Pumpkin Switch. 1992. (Illus.). 32p. (J). (ps-2). mass mkt. 15.95 o.p. (*0-531-05450-0*); mass mkt. 16.99 o.p. (*0-531-08600-3*) Scholastic, Inc. (Orchard Bks.).

—Judy Moody Gets Famous! (Illus.). 144p. (J). (gr. 1-5). 2003. pap. 5.99 (*0-7636-1931-0*); 2001. 15.99 (*0-7636-0849-1*) Candlewick Pr.

—Judy Moody Saves the World. (Illus.). 160p. (J). 2004. pap. 5.99 (*0-7636-2087-4*); 2002. (gr. 1-5). 15.99 (*0-7636-1446-7*) Candlewick Pr.

McElfresh, Lynn E. Can You Feel the Thunder? 1999. (YA). pap., stu. ed. 52.00 incl. audio (*0-7887-3837-2*, 41031) Recorded Bks., LLC.

—Can You Feel the Thunder? 1999. 144p. (J). (gr. 5-9). 16.00 (*0-689-82324-X*, Atheneum) Simon & Schuster Children's Publishing.

McEvoy, Seth. Between Brothers. 1991. (New Kids on the Block Ser.). (YA). pap. 3.50 (*0-671-73941-7*, Simon Pulse) Simon & Schuster Children's Publishing.

McGeorge, Constance W. Snow Riders. 1995. (Illus.). 32p. (J). (ps-1). 13.95 o.p. (*0-8118-0873-4*) Chronicle Bks. LLC.

McGraw, Al. Timmie & His Little Brother. 1977. (Illus.). (J). 5.95 o.p. (*0-533-02872-8*) Vantage Pr., Inc.

McGugan, Jim. Bridge 6. ed. 1999. (J). (gr. 2). spiral bd. (*0-616-01721-9*) Canadian National Institute for the Blind/Institut National Canadien pour les Aveugles.

—Bridge 6. 1999. (Illus.). 32p. (J). (ps-3). 16.95 (*0-7737-3137-7*) Stoddart Kids CAN. *Dist:* Fitzhenry & Whiteside, Ltd.

McGuigan, Mary Ann. Cloud Dancer. 1994. 128p. (J). (gr. 6-8). pap. 14.95 (*0-684-19632-8*, Atheneum) Simon & Schuster Children's Publishing.

McHenry, Janet Holm. And the Winner Is.... Reck, Sue, ed. 1994. (Golden Rule Duo Ser.). 48p. (J). (gr. 2-4). pap. 3.99 (*0-7814-0170-4*) Cook Communications Ministries.

—Trick 'n Trouble. Reck, Sue, ed. 1994. (Golden Rule Duo Ser.). 48p. (J). (gr. 2-4). pap. 3.99 (*0-7814-0171-2*) Cook Communications Ministries.

McHugh, Elisabet. Karen's Sister. 1983. 160p. (J). (gr. 5-9). 11.95 o.p. (*0-688-02472-6*, Greenwillow Bks.) HarperCollins Children's Bk. Group.

McKay, Hilary. Dolphin Luck. l.t. ed. 2003. (Illus.). (J). pap. 16.95 incl. audio (*0-7540-7865-5*, Galaxy Children's Large Print) BBC Audiobooks America.

—Dolphin Luck. 160p. (J). (gr. 3-7). 2000. (Illus.). pap. 4.99 o.s.i (*0-689-83889-1*, Aladdin); 1999. 16.00 (*0-689-82376-2*, McElderry, Margaret K.) Simon & Schuster Children's Publishing.

—Dolphin Luck. l.t. ed. 2001. (Illus.). 198p. (J). (gr. 4-7). 21.95 (*0-7862-2703-6*) Thorndike Pr.

—Dolphin Luck. 2000. (J). 11.04 (*0-606-20086-X*) Turtleback Bks.

—The Exiles. 1992. (Illus.). 208p. (J). (gr. 3-7). 17.99 o.s.i (*0-689-50555-8*, McElderry, Margaret K.) Simon & Schuster Children's Publishing.

—Indigo's Star. 2004. (J). 15.95 (*0-689-86563-5*, McElderry, Margaret K.) Simon & Schuster Children's Publishing.

—Saffy's Angel. unabr. ed. 2002. (J). (gr. 13 up). audio 25.00 (*0-8072-0823-X*, Listening Library) Random Hse. Audio Publishing Group.

—Saffy's Angel. 160p. (J). 2003. (Illus.). pap. 4.99 (*0-689-84934-6*, Aladdin); 2002. (gr. 4-7). 16.00 (*0-689-84933-8*, McElderry, Margaret K.) Simon & Schuster Children's Publishing.

—Saffy's Angel. 2003. (Juvenile Ser.). 227p. (J). 21.95 (*0-7862-5500-5*) Thorndike Pr.

McKay, Sindy. Ben & Becky Get a Pet. (We Both Read Ser.). (Illus.). 48p. (J). 1999. (gr. 1-3). pap. 3.99 (*1-891327-10-0*); 1998. (ps-3). 7.99 (*1-891327-06-2*) Treasure Bay, Inc.

McKillip, Patricia A. The Night Gift. 1976. (Illus.). 192p. (J). (gr. 5-9). 6.95 o.p. (*0-689-30508-7*, Atheneum) Simon & Schuster Children's Publishing.

McManis, Margaret Olivia. Ima & the Great Texas Ostrich Race. 2002. (Illus.). (J). pap. (*1-57168-671-1*); 32p. 15.95 (*1-57168-605-3*) Eakin Pr. (Eakin Pr.).

McMullan, Kate. The Mummy's Gold. 1996. (Eek! Stories to Make You Shriek Ser.). (Illus.). 48p. (J). (gr. 1-3). 13.99 o.s.i (*0-448-41345-0*); 3.99 (*0-448-41310-8*) Penguin Putnam Bks. for Young Readers. (Grosset & Dunlap).

—The Mummy's Gold. 1996. (Eek! Stories to Make You Shriek Ser.). 10.14 (*0-606-10884-X*) Turtleback Bks.

McNichols, Ann. Falling from Grace. 2000. 164p. (J). (gr. 6-9). 16.95 (*0-8027-8750-9*) Walker & Co.

McPeak-Bailey, Bobbi. Chicken Pox Christmas. 1994. (Illus.). 64p. (Orig.). (J). (gr. k-4). pap. 8.95 (*0-9625005-2-6*) Wee Pr.

McPhail, David, tr. & illus. My Little Brother. 2004. 32p. (J). 16.00 (*0-15-204900-2*) Harcourt Trade Pubs.

McPhail, David M. Sisters. (Illus.). 32p. (J). (ps-2). 2003. 9.95 (*0-15-204659-3*); 1990. pap. 5.00 (*0-15-275320-6*, Voyager Bks./Libros Viajeros) Harcourt Children's Bks.

Mead, Alice. Adem's Cross, RS. 1996. 160p. (YA). (gr. 7-12). 15.00 o.p. (*0-374-30057-7*, Farrar, Straus & Giroux (BYR)) Farrar, Straus & Giroux.

—Adem's Cross. 1998. (Laurel-Leaf Bks.). 144p. (YA). (gr. 5-9). mass mkt. 4.50 o.s.i (*0-440-22735-6*, Laurel Leaf) Random Hse. Children's Bks.

—Adem's Cross. 1998. 10.55 (*0-606-13110-8*) Turtleback Bks.

—Girl of Kosovo, RS. 2001. 113p. (J). (gr. 4-7). 16.00 (*0-374-32620-7*, Farrar, Straus & Giroux (BYR)) Farrar, Straus & Giroux.

—Girl of Kosovo. 2003. (Illus.). 128p. (gr. 5). pap. text 4.99 (*0-440-41853-4*, Yearling) Random Hse. Children's Bks.

—Junebug, RS. 1995. 112p. (J). (gr. 3-7). 16.00 (*0-374-33964-3*, Farrar, Straus & Giroux (BYR)) Farrar, Straus & Giroux.

—Junebug. 1997. 112p. (gr. 3-7). pap. text 4.50 (*0-440-41245-5*, Yearling); 1996. (J). pap. 4.99 (*0-440-91275-X*, Dell Books for Young Readers) Random Hse. Children's Bks.

—Junebug. 1997. (J). 10.55 (*0-606-11528-5*) Turtleback Bks.

Meddaugh, Susan. Cinderella's Rat. (Illus.). 32p. (J). (ps-3). 2002. pap. 5.95 (*0-618-12540-X*); 1997. lib. bdg., tchr. ed. 16.00 (*0-395-86833-5*) Houghton Mifflin Co. Trade & Reference Div. (Lorraine, A. Walter).

Medearis, Angela Shelf. Seven Spools of Thread: A Kwanzaa Story. 2000. (Illus.). 40p. (J). (gr. 2-5). lib. bdg. 15.95 (*0-8075-7315-9*) Whitman, Albert & Co.

—What Did I Do to Deserve a Sister Like You? 2002. (Illus.). 123p. (J). (gr. 3-5). 12.95 (*1-57168-471-9*); pap. 7.95 (*1-57168-642-8*) Eakin Pr. (Eakin Pr.).

Mendes, Valerie. Look at Me, Grandma! 2001. (Illus.). 32p. (J). (ps-1). pap. 15.95 (*0-439-29654-4*, Chicken Hse., The) Scholastic, Inc.

Merritt, Kate, illus. My Family: My Sister. 2003. 10p. bds. 3.95 (*0-8069-8581-X*, Sterling/Pinwheel) Sterling Publishing Co., Inc.

Merritt, William E. She-Ra the Mammoth Rider & Her Sister Emily. (YA). E-Book 4.50 (*1-929120-02-8*) Electric Umbrella Publishing.

Metzger, Lois. Barry's Sister. 1993. 240p. (J). (gr. 5 up). pap. 4.50 o.p. (*0-14-036484-6*, Puffin Bks.) Penguin Putnam Bks. for Young Readers.

—Barry's Sister. 1992. 240p. (YA). (gr. 5 up). 15.95 (*0-689-31521-X*, Atheneum) Simon & Schuster Children's Publishing.

—Ellen's Case. 1997. 208p. (J). pap. 4.99 o.s.i (*0-14-038372-7*) Penguin Putnam Bks. for Young Readers.

—Ellen's Case. 1995. 208p. (YA). (gr. 7 up). 16.00 (*0-689-31934-7*, Atheneum) Simon & Schuster Children's Publishing.

Michels-Gualtieri, Akaela S. I Was Born to Be a Sister. 2001. (Illus.). 32p. (J). (ps-1). 16.95 (*1-930775-03-2*) Platypus Media, L.L.C.

Michels-Gualtieri, Zaydek G. & Michels, Dia L. I Was Born to Be a Brother. Liegey, Daniel, tr. & illus. by. 2003. (J). (*1-930775-09-1*) Platypus Media, L.L.C.

Miklowitz, Gloria D. The Love Bombers. 1980. 160p. (J). (gr. 7 up). pap. 8.95 o.s.i (*0-385-28545-0*, Delacorte Pr.) Dell Publishing.

Miller, Roselyn Ogden. Poor As Church Mice. 2000. (Illus.). (J). 13.98 o.s.i (*1-886225-57-5*) Dageforde Publishing, Inc.

Mills, Charles. Voyager. 157p. (J). reprint ed. pap. 48.70 (*0-7837-6401-4*, 204611700010) Bks. on Demand.

—Voyager. Johnson, Jeannette, ed. 1989. 160p. (J). pap. 7.95 o.p. (*0-8280-0491-9*) Review & Herald Publishing Assn.

—Voyager, II. 1991. 192p. (Orig.). (J). (gr. 5-8). pap. 7.99 o.p. (*0-8280-0595-8*) Review & Herald Publishing Assn.

Mills, Claudia. Boardwalk with Hotel. 1986. 144p. (YA). (gr. 7-12). reprint ed. pap. 2.50 o.s.i (*0-553-15397-8*, Skylark) Random Hse. Children's Bks.

—Losers, Inc., RS. 1997. 160p. (J). (gr. 3-7). 16.00 (*0-374-34661-5*, Farrar, Straus & Giroux (BYR)) Farrar, Straus & Giroux.

—Losers, Inc. 1998. 160p. (J). pap. 4.95 (*0-7868-1364-4*) Hyperion Paperbacks for Children.

—Losers, Inc. 1998. 96p. (J). (gr. 3-7). pap. 4.95 (*0-7868-1274-5*) Hyperion Pr.

—Losers, Inc. 1998. 11.00 (*0-606-14259-2*) Turtleback Bks.

—A Visit to Amy-Claire. 1992. (Illus.). 32p. (J). (gr. k-3). 14.95 o.s.i (*0-02-766991-2*, Simon & Schuster Children's Publishing) Simon & Schuster Children's Publishing.

Mitton, Tony & Sutcliffe, Mandy. Goodnight Me, Goodnight You. 2003. (Illus.). 32p. (J). 14.95 (*0-316-73880-8*) Little Brown & Co.

Moers, Hermann. Hugo's Baby Brother. Lanning, Rosemary, tr. from GER. 1945. (Illus.). 32p. (J). (gr. k-3). 14.95 o.p. (*1-55858-137-5*); 15.50 o.p. (*1-55858-146-4*) North-South Bks., Inc.

Mohr, Carole. Freud & Freud, Inc. 1991. 128p. (J). (gr. 4-7). pap. 2.75 o.s.i (*0-553-15915-1*) Bantam Bks.

Moll, Linda J. A Poison Tree: A Children's Fairy Tale. 1994. (Illus.). 40p. (J). (gr. 1). 12.95 (*0-9641641-1-6*) Punking Pr.

Moncure, Jane Belk. Caring for My Baby Sister. 1990. (Growing Responsible Ser.). (Illus.). 32p. (J). (ps-3). lib. bdg. 18.50 o.p. (*0-89565-669-8*) Child's World, Inc.

—My Baby Brother Needs a Friend. 1979. (Understanding Myself Picture Books Ser.). (Illus.). 24p. (J). (ps-3). lib. bdg. 21.36 o.p. (*0-89565-019-3*) Child's World, Inc.

—What's So Special about Lauren? She's My Baby Sister. 1987. (What's So Special Ser.). (Illus.). 32p. (J). (ps-3). lib. bdg. 21.36 o.p. (*0-89565-413-X*) Child's World, Inc.

Montgomery, Bobbie. Donkey Cart Kids. 2000. (Pathfinder Junior Book Club Ser.). 110p. (J). pap. 6.99 (*0-8280-1442-6*) Review & Herald Publishing Assn.

Montgomery, L. M. Rainbow Valley. 1976. (Avonlea Ser.: No. 6). 234p. (YA). (gr. 5-8). 21.95 (*0-8488-0591-7*) Amereon, Ltd.

—Rainbow Valley. (Avonlea Ser.: No. 6). (gr. 5-8). 1987. 256p. (J). mass mkt. 4.99 (*0-7704-2268-3*); 1985. 240p. (YA). mass mkt. 2.95 o.s.i (*0-553-25213-5*) Bantam Bks.

—Rainbow Valley. unabr. ed. 1995. (Avonlea Ser.: No. 6). (YA). (gr. 5-8). audio 44.95 (*0-7861-0913-0*, 1704) Blackstone Audio Bks., Inc.

—Rainbow Valley. unabr. ed. 1999. (Avonlea Ser.: No. 6). (YA). (gr. 5-8). audio 44.95 Highsmith Inc.

—Rainbow Valley. 1985. (Avonlea Ser.: No. 6). 256p. (YA). (gr. 5-8). mass mkt. 4.50 (*0-553-26921-6*, Dell Books for Young Readers) Random Hse. Children's Bks.

—Rainbow Valley. 1985. (Avonlea Ser.: No. 6). (YA). (gr. 5-8). 10.04 (*0-606-02613-4*) Turtleback Bks.

Montgomery, L. M. & Outlet Book Company Staff. Rainbow Valley. 1995. (Avonlea Ser.: No. 6). (Illus.). xi, 256p. (YA). (gr. 5-8). 7.99 o.s.i (*0-517-10192-0*) Random Hse. Value Publishing.

Moon, Nicola. Something Special. 1997. (Illus.). 32p. (J). (ps-1). 14.95 (*1-56145-137-1*) Peachtree Pubs., Ltd.

Moore, Eva. Good Children Get Rewards: A Story of Colonial Times. 2001. (Hello Reader! Ser.). (J). 10.14 (*0-606-19563-7*) Turtleback Bks.

Moore, Martha A. Under the Mermaid Angel. (YA). (gr. 7 up). 1997. 176p. mass mkt. 3.99 o.s.i (*0-440-22682-1*, Laurel Leaf); 1995. 192p. 14.95 o.s.i (*0-385-32160-0*, Dell Books for Young Readers) Random Hse. Children's Bks.

Moore, Miriam. The Kwanzaa Contest. 1996. (Hyperion Chapters Ser.). (Illus.). 64p. (J). (gr. 4-7). pap. 3.95 (*0-7868-1122-6*) Disney Pr.

—The Kwanzaa Contest. 1996. 10.10 (*0-606-10245-0*) Turtleback Bks.

Moore, Miriam & Taylor, Penny. The Kwanzaa Contest. 1997. (Illus.). 64p. (J). lib. bdg. 14.49 (*0-7868-2336-4*) Disney Pr.

—The Kwanzaa Contest. 1996. (Illus.). 64p. (J). (gr. 3-4). 13.95 (*0-7868-0261-8*) Hyperion Bks. for Children.

Moore, Robin. The Bread Sister of Sinking Creek. 1992. (Trophy Bk.). 160p. (J). (gr. 4-7). pap. 4.95 (*0-06-440357-2*, Harper Trophy) HarperCollins Children's Bk. Group.

Morck, Irene. Between Brothers. 2003. (Young Adult Ser.). 160p. (J). (gr. 3-6). pap. 7.95 (*0-7737-5530-6*) Stoddart Kids CAN. *Dist:* Fitzhenry & Whiteside, Ltd.

Morpurgo, Michael. Twist of Gold. 1993. 224p. (J). (gr. 5-9). 14.99 o.p. (*0-670-84851-4*, Viking Children's Bks.) Penguin Putnam Bks. for Young Readers.

Morris, Gilbert. Buckingham Palace & the Crown Jewels - Travels in England Vol. 2: Adventures of the Kerrigan Kids. 2001. (Illus.). 128p. (J). (gr. 3-7). pap. 5.99 (*0-8024-1579-2*) Moody Pr.

—The Bucks of Goober Hollow. 1994. (Ozark Adventures Ser.: Vol. 1). 225p. (J). (gr. 3-7). pap. 3.99 o.p. (*0-8423-4392-X*) Tyndale Hse. Pubs.

—The Dangerous Voyage. 1995. (Time Navigators Ser.: Vol. 1). 160p. (J). (gr. 6-9). pap. 5.99 o.p. (*1-55661-395-4*) Bethany Hse. Pubs.

—Kangaroos & the Outback - Travels in Australia No. 3: Adventures of the Kerrigan Kids. 2001. (Illus.). 144p. (J). (gr. 3-7). pap. 5.99 (*0-8024-1580-6*) Moody Pr.

—Painted Warriors & Wild Lions - Travels in Africa. 2001. (Adventures of the Kerrigan Kids Ser.). (Illus.). 128p. (J). (gr. 3-7). pap. 5.99 (*0-8024-1578-4*) Moody Pr.

—Vanishing Clues. 1996. (Time Navigators Ser.: Vol. 2). 144p. (J). (gr. 4-7). pap. 5.99 o.p. (*1-55661-396-2*) Bethany Hse. Pubs.

Morton, Daniel. Marti & the Mango. 1996. (Illus.). 32p. (J). 4.50 (*1-55670-264-7*) Stewart, Tabori & Chang.

Mulford, Philippa G. The World Is My Eggshell. 1986. (J). (gr. 7 up). pap. 14.95 o.s.i (*0-385-29432-8*, Delacorte Pr.) Dell Publishing.

Murdocca, Sal. Baby Wants the Moon. 1995. (Illus.). 32p. (J). lib. bdg. 14.93 o.p. (*0-688-13665-6*); (gr. 4 up). 15.00 o.p. (*0-688-13664-8*) HarperCollins Children's Bk. Group.

Murphy, Catherine F. Songs in the Silence. 1994. 192p. (J). (gr. 3-7). 14.95 o.p. (*0-02-767730-3*, Simon & Schuster Children's Publishing) Simon & Schuster Children's Publishing.

Murphy, Claire Rudolf. Gold Star Sister. 1996. 10.09 o.p. (*0-606-11400-9*) Turtleback Bks.

Myers, Anna. Rosie's Tiger. 1994. 128p. (J). (gr. 4-7). 14.95 (*0-8027-8305-8*) Walker & Co.

—Spotting the Leopard. 1997. (Illus.). 224p. (J). (gr. 3-7). pap. 4.50 o.s.i (*0-14-038728-5*, Puffin Bks.) Penguin Putnam Bks. for Young Readers.

—Spotting the Leopard. 1996. 176p. (J). (gr. 4-7). 15.95 (*0-8027-8459-3*) Walker & Co.

Myers, Bernice. Crybaby. 1990. (Illus.). 32p. (J). (ps-2). 12.95 o.p. (*0-688-09083-4*); lib. bdg. 12.88 o.p. (*0-688-09084-2*) HarperCollins Children's Bk. Group.

Myers, Bill. The Curse of the Horrible Hair Day. 2001. (Bloodhounds, Inc. Ser.: Vol. 9). 128p. (J). (gr. 4-7). pap. 5.99 (*0-7642-2437-9*) Bethany Hse. Pubs.

—Phantom of the Haunted Church. 1998. (Bloodhounds, Inc. Ser.: Vol. 3). (Illus.). 128p. (J). (gr. 3-8). pap. 5.99 (*1-55661-892-1*) Bethany Hse. Pubs.

—The Scam of the Screwball Wizards. 2001. (Bloodhounds, Inc. Ser.). 128p. (J). (gr. 3-8). pap. 5.99 (*0-7642-2438-7*) Bethany Hse. Pubs.

Myers, Bill & Wimbish, David. Mystery of the Melodies from Mars. 2002. (Bloodhounds, Inc. Ser.: No. 11). 128p. (J). pap. 5.99 (*0-7642-2623-1*) Bethany Hse. Pubs.

—Room with a Boo. 2002. (Bloodhounds Inc Ser.). 128p. (J). pap. 5.99 (*0-7642-2624-X*) Bethany Hse. Pubs.

Myers, Edward. Climb or Die. 192p. (J). 1996. pap. 4.95 (*0-7868-1181-1*); 1994. (gr. 5-9). 14.95 (*0-7868-0026-7*); 1994. (gr. 5-9). lib. bdg. 14.89 o.p. (*0-7868-2021-7*) Hyperion Bks. for Children.

—Climb or Die. 1997. 180p. (J). (gr. 5-9). lib. bdg. 14.49 (*0-7868-2350-X*) Hyperion Pr.

—Climb or Die. 1996. (J). 11.00 (*0-606-10162-4*) Turtleback Bks.

—Climb or Die: A Test of Survival. 1996. 192p. (J). (gr. 4-7). pap. 4.95 (*0-7868-1129-3*) Disney Pr.

Myers, Laurie. Surviving Brick Johnson. 2000. (Illus.). 96p. (J). (gr. 4-6). tchr. ed. 15.00 (*0-395-98031-3*, Clarion Bks.) Houghton Mifflin Co. Trade & Reference Div.

Myers, Walter Dean. Darnell Rock Reporting. 144p. 1996. (Illus.). (gr. 4-7). pap. text 4.99 (*0-440-41157-2*); 1994. (J). 14.95 o.s.i (*0-385-32096-5*, Delacorte Pr.) Dell Publishing.

Naidoo, Beverley. The Other Side of Truth. 272p. (J). (gr. 5 up). 2003. pap. 5.99 (*0-06-441002-1*); 2001. 16.99 (*0-06-029628-3*); 2001. lib. bdg. 17.89 (*0-06-029629-1*) HarperCollins Children's Bk. Group.

—The Other Side of Truth. 2000. 208p. (J). pap. (*0-14-130476-6*, Puffin Bks.) Penguin Putnam Bks. for Young Readers.

Namioka, Lensey. Yang the Second. 1998. (Illus.). 144p. (J). (gr. 3-7). 15.95 (*0-316-59731-7*) Little Brown & Co.

Napoli, Donna J. Shark Shock. 1994. (Illus.). 176p. (J). (gr. 3-7). 13.99 o.p. (*0-525-45267-2*, Dutton Children's Bks.) Penguin Putnam Bks. for Young Readers.

Napoli, Donna Jo. No Fair! 2000. (Aladdin Angelwings Ser.: Vol. 6). (Illus.). 96p. (J). (gr. 2-5). pap. 3.99 (*0-689-83206-0*, Aladdin) Simon & Schuster Children's Publishing.

—No Fair! 2000. (Illus.). (J). 10.14 (*0-606-17909-7*) Turtleback Bks.

—Playing Games. 2000. (Aladdin Angelwings Ser.: No. 8). (Illus.). 80p. (J). (gr. 2-5). pap. 3.99 (*0-689-83208-7*, Aladdin) Simon & Schuster Children's Publishing.

—Playing Games. 2000. (Angelwings Ser.). (Illus.). (J). 10.14 (*0-606-20386-9*) Turtleback Bks.

Nash, Bruce. So You Think You Know Your Brother-Sister? Schneider, Meg, ed. 1982. (Flip-Overs Ser.). 64p. (Orig.). (J). (gr. 3-7). pap. 2.85 o.p. (*0-671-45549-4*, Simon & Schuster Children's Publishing) Simon & Schuster Children's Publishing.

Nash, Mary. Mrs. Coverlet's Magicians. 2001. (Lost Treasures Ser.: No. 2). 192p. (J). (gr. 3-7). pap. 4.99 (*0-7868-1517-5*); (Illus.). (gr. 4-7). pap. 4.99 (*0-7868-1518-3*, Volo) Hyperion Bks. for Children.

Naylor, Phyllis Reynolds. Alice in Blunderland. 2003. (Alice Ser.). (Illus.). 208p. (J). 15.95 (*0-689-84397-6*, Atheneum) Simon & Schuster Children's Publishing.

—Being Danny's Dog. 160p. (J). (gr. 4-7). 1997. (Illus.). pap. 4.50 (*0-689-81472-0*, Aladdin); 1995. 15.00 (*0-689-31756-5*, Atheneum) Simon & Schuster Children's Publishing.

—Being Danny's Dog. 1997. 10.04 (*0-606-11105-0*) Turtleback Bks.

—Bernie Magruder & the Bus Station Blow-Up. l.t. ed. 2002. 156p. (J). 21.95 (*0-7862-3599-3*) Gale Group.

—Bernie Magruder & the Parachute Peril. 2001. (Illus.). (J). 11.04 (*0-606-21061-X*) Turtleback Bks.

—The Bomb in the Bessledorf Bus Depot. 144p. (J). 1997. (gr. 3-7). pap. 4.99 (*0-689-80599-3*, Aladdin); 1996. (gr. 4-7). 16.00 (*0-689-80461-X*, Atheneum) Simon & Schuster Children's Publishing.

—The Bomb in the Bessledorf Bus Depot. 1997. 10.04 (*0-606-11147-6*) Turtleback Bks.

—Boys Against Girls. 1994. (Illus.). 160p. (J). 14.95 (*0-385-32081-7*, Delacorte Pr.) Dell Publishing.

—Boys Against Girls. 1995. (J). 18.95 (*0-385-30982-1*) Doubleday Publishing.

—Boys Against Girls. 2000. (Illus.). 160p. (gr. 3-7). mass mkt. 2.99 o.s.i (*0-375-80673-3*, Random Hse. Bks. for Young Readers); 1995. 160p. (gr. 4-7). pap. text 4.99 (*0-440-41123-8*, Yearling); 1995. (J). pap. 4.99 (*0-440-91052-8*, Dell Books for Young Readers) Random Hse. Children's Bks.

—Boys Against Girls. 2003. (Juvenile Ser.). (Illus.). (J). 23.95 (*0-7862-5017-8*) Thorndike Pr.

—Boys Against Girls. 1995. (J). 11.04 (*0-606-09101-7*) Turtleback Bks.

—Boys in Control. 2003. 160p. (gr. 4-7). text 15.95 (*0-385-32740-4*); lib. bdg. 17.99 (*0-385-90154-2*) Random Hse. Children's Bks. (Delacorte Bks. for Young Readers).

—The Boys Return. 2003. 144p. (gr. 4-7). pap. text 4.99 (*0-440-41675-2*); 2001. (Illus.). 132p. (J). (*0-385-32734-X*, Delacorte Bks. for Young Readers); 2001. (Illus.). 144p. (gr. 4-6). text 15.95 (*0-385-32737-4*, Dell Books for Young Readers) Random Hse. Children's Bks.

—The Boys Return. l.t. ed. 2003. 170p. (J). 23.95 (*0-7862-5822-5*) Thorndike Pr.

—The Boys Start the War. 1993. 144p. (J). (gr. 4-7). 15.95 o.s.i (*0-385-30814-0*) Doubleday Publishing.

—The Boys Start the War. l.t. ed. 2002. (Thorndike Press Large Print Juvenile Ser.). 144p. (J). 22.95 (*0-7862-4651-0*) Thorndike Pr.

—The Boys Start the War. 1993. (J). 12.04 (*0-606-06248-3*) Turtleback Bks.

—The Fear Place. 128p. 1996. (YA). (gr. 4-9). pap. 4.50 (*0-689-80442-3*, Aladdin); 1994. (J). (gr. 3-7). 16.95 (*0-689-31866-9*, Atheneum) Simon & Schuster Children's Publishing.

—The Fear Place. 1996. 10.00 (*0-606-09269-2*) Turtleback Bks.

—The Girls Get Even. 1993. 144p. (J). 14.95 o.s.i (*0-385-31029-3*, Delacorte Pr.) Dell Publishing.

—The Girls' Revenge. 1998. 160p. (gr. 4-7). text 15.95 o.s.i (*0-385-32334-4*, Dell Books for Young Readers) Random Hse. Children's Bks.

—The Girls' Revenge. l.t. ed. 2003. (Thorndike Press Large Print Juvenile Ser.). 172p. (J). 23.95 (*0-7862-5180-8*) Thorndike Pr.

—The Great Chicken Debacle. (J). 2003. 48p. (gr. 4-8). pap. 5.95 (*0-7614-5148-X*); 2001. (Illus.). 96p. (gr. 3-7). 14.95 (*0-7614-5095-5*, Cavendish Children's Bks.) Cavendish, Marshall Corp.

—Simply Alice. 2002. (Alice Ser.). 240p. (YA). (gr. 6-9). 16.00 (*0-689-82635-4*, Atheneum) Simon & Schuster Children's Publishing.

—The Solomon System. (J). (gr. 5-9). 1983. 210p. lib. bdg. 13.95 o.s.i (*0-689-30991-0*, Atheneum); 1987. 216p. reprint ed. pap. 3.95 o.s.i (*0-689-71128-X*, Aladdin) Simon & Schuster Children's Publishing.

—A Spy among the Girls. Poploff, Michelle, ed. 2000. (Illus.). 144p. (gr. 4-7). text 15.95 (*0-385-32336-0*, Delacorte Bks. for Young Readers) Random Hse. Children's Bks.

—A Traitor among the Boys. 2003. 152p. (J). 23.95 (*0-7862-5471-8*) Thorndike Pr.

—A Traitor among the Boys. 2001. (J). 11.04 (*0-606-20953-0*) Turtleback Bks.

—Walker's Crossing. 240p. (YA). (gr. 5-9). 2001. pap. 4.99 (*0-689-84261-9*, Aladdin); 1999. (Illus.). 16.00 (*0-689-82939-6*, Atheneum) Simon & Schuster Children's Publishing.

Neale, Jonathan. Lost at Sea. 112p. (J). (gr. 5-9). 2004. pap. 5.95 (*0-618-43236-1*); 2002. (Illus.). 15.00 (*0-618-13920-6*) Houghton Mifflin Co.

Neenan, Colin. In Your Dreams. 1995. 256p. (YA). (gr. 7 up). 11.00 (*0-15-200885-3*); pap. 5.00 (*0-15-200884-5*, Harcourt Paperbacks) Harcourt Children's Bks.

Nelson, S. D. The Star People. 2003. (Illus.). 40p. (J). (gr. k-3). 14.95 (*0-8109-4584-3*) Abrams, Harry N. , Inc.

Nelson, Theresa. The Empress of Elsewhere. 1998. (Illus.). 224p. (J). (gr. 5-9). pap. 17.95 o.p. (*0-7894-2498-3*) Dorling Kindersley Publishing, Inc.

—Empress of Elsewhere. 2000. (Illus.). 224p. (J). (gr. 5-9). pap. 5.99 o.s.i (*0-14-130813-3*, Puffin Bks.) Penguin Putnam Bks. for Young Readers.

—Ruby Electric. 2003. (Illus.). 272p. (J). 16.95 (*0-689-83852-2*, Atheneum/Richard Jackson Bks.) Simon & Schuster Children's Publishing.

Nesbit, Edith. The Deliverers of Their Country. 1996. (Illus.). 32p. (J). (ps-3). pap. 6.95 o.p. (*1-55858-612-1*); 16.95 o.p. (*1-55858-623-7*) North-South Bks., Inc.

—Five Children & It. 207p. 20.95 (*0-8488-2523-3*) Amereon, Ltd.

—Five Children & It. 1981. 182p. (J). reprint ed. lib. bdg. 21.95 (*0-89967-036-9*, Harmony Raine & Co.) Buccaneer Bks., Inc.

—Five Children & It. 2002. (Dover Evergreen Classics Ser.). (Illus.). 160p. (J). pap. 2.50 (*0-486-42366-2*) Dover Pubns., Inc.

—Five Children & It. 1999. (Books of Wonder). (Illus.). 256p. (J). (gr. 4-7). 22.95 (*0-688-13545-5*) HarperCollins Children's Bk. Group.

—Five Children & It. l.t. ed. 461p. pap. 40.00 (*0-7583-3207-6*); 397p. pap. 36.00 (*0-7583-3206-8*); 323p. pap. 30.00 (*0-7583-3205-X*); 263p. pap. 26.00 (*0-7583-3204-1*); 205p. pap. 22.00 (*0-7583-3203-3*); 117p. pap. 16.00 (*0-7583-3201-7*); 160p. pap. 19.00 (*0-7583-3202-5*); 90p. pap. 14.00 (*0-7583-3200-9*); 117p. lib. bdg. 23.00 (*0-7583-3193-2*); 160p. lib. bdg. 27.00 (*0-7583-3194-0*); 205p. lib. bdg. 33.00 (*0-7583-3195-9*); 323p. lib. bdg. 42.00 (*0-7583-3197-5*); 397p. lib. bdg. 47.00 (*0-7583-3198-3*); 461p. lib. bdg. 51.00 (*0-7583-3199-1*); 90p. lib. bdg. 20.00 (*0-7583-3192-4*); 263p. lib. bdg. 37.00 (*0-7583-3196-7*) Huge Print Pr.

—Five Children & It. 2002. 160p. (gr. 4-7). per. 88.99 (*1-4043-0285-9*) IndyPublish.com.

—Five Children & It. 1996. (Illus.). 256p. (YA). (gr. 4-7). pap. 4.99 (*0-14-036735-7*); 1959. 224p. (J). pap. 2.95 o.p. (*0-14-030128-3*, Puffin Bks.) Penguin Putnam Bks. for Young Readers.

—Five Children & It. E-Book 5.00 (*0-7410-0796-7*) SoftBook Pr.

—Five Children & It. 2002. 192p. pap. 14.95 (*1-59224-938-8*); lib. bdg. 24.95 (*1-59224-942-6*) Wildside Pr.

—The Railway Children. 1998. (J). pap. text 7.00 o.p. (*0-582-40140-2*) Addison-Wesley Longman, Inc.

—The Railway Children. 1996. (Andre Deutsch Classics). 223p. (J). (gr. 5-8). 11.95 (*0-233-99037-2*) Andre Deutsch GBR. *Dist:* Trafalgar Square, Trans-Atlantic Pubns., Inc.

—The Railway Children. 1993. 272p. (J). (gr. 4 up). mass mkt. 3.25 o.s.i (*0-553-21415-2*, Bantam Classics) Bantam Bks.

—The Railway Children. 1975. (Dent's Illustrated Children's Classics Ser.). (Illus.). 208p. (J). 9.00 o.p. (*0-460-05094-X*) Biblio Distribution.

—The Railway Children. 1994. (Classics for Young Readers Ser.). 64p. (J). 5.98 o.p. (*0-86112-983-0*) Brimax Bks., Ltd.

—The Railway Children. 1992. 224p. (J). (gr. 4-7). pap. 3.50 o.s.i (*0-440-40602-1*) Dell Publishing.

—The Railway Children. (J). E-Book 2.49 (*1-58627-659-X*) Electric Umbrella Publishing.

—The Railway Children. Dryhurst, Dinah, tr. & illus. by. 2003. (J). 18.95 (*1-56792-261-9*) Godine, David R. Pub.

—The Railway Children. 1999. (Chapter Book Charmers Ser.). (Illus.). 80p. (J). (gr. 2-5). 2.99 o.p. (*0-694-01285-8*) HarperCollins Children's Bk. Group.

—The Railway Children. 1993. (Children's Classics Ser.). (J). (gr. 2-7). 12.95 (*0-679-42534-9*, Everyman's Library) Knopf Publishing Group.

—The Railway Children. 1992. 256p. mass mkt. 2.95 o.s.i (*0-451-52561-2*, Signet Classics) NAL.

—The Railway Children. 1991. (Oxford World's Classics Ser.). (Illus.). 224p. (J). pap. 4.95 o.p. (*0-19-282659-X*, 11912) Oxford Univ. Pr., Inc.

—The Railway Children. 2000. (Illus.). 224p. pap. 8.95 (*1-86205-235-2*) Pavilion Bks., Ltd. GBR. *Dist:* Trafalgar Square.

—The Railway Children. (Illus.). (J). (gr. 3-5). 9999. (Children's Classics Ser.: No. 740-19). pap. 3.50 o.p. (*0-7214-0824-9*); 1997. (Classic Ser.). 54p. 2.99 o.s.i (*0-7214-5708-8*) Penguin Group (USA) Inc. (Ladybird Bks.).

—The Railway Children. (Classics for Young Readers Ser.). (Illus.). 1994. 288p. (J). (gr. 4-7). pap. 3.99 (*0-14-036671-7*, Puffin Bks.); 1991. 192p. (YA). 16.95 o.s.i (*0-399-21819-X*, Philomel); 1983. 240p. (J). (gr. 3-7). pap. 3.50 o.p. (*0-14-035005-5*, Puffin Bks.) Penguin Putnam Bks. for Young Readers.

—The Railway Children. (Children's Library Ser.). 1996. (J). 1.10 o.s.i (*0-517-14153-1*); 1991. (Illus.). 192p. (YA). 9.99 o.s.i (*0-517-07011-1*) Random Hse. Value Publishing.

—The Railway Children. 9999. (Illus.). (J). 19.95 o.p. (*0-590-74000-8*) Scholastic, Inc.

—The Railway Children. 1988. (J). (gr. 5-8). 16.30 o.p. (*0-8446-6345-X*) Smith, Peter Pub., Inc.

—The Railway Children. E-Book 5.00 (*0-7410-0817-3*) SoftBook Pr.

—The Railway Children. 1961. (Illus.). (J). (gr. 2-5). pap. 1.95 o.p. (*0-14-030147-X*, Penguin Bks.) Viking Penguin.

—The Railway Children. 1998. (Children's Classics). 208p. (J). (gr. 4-7). pap. 3.95 (*1-85326-107-6*, 1076WW) Wordsworth Editions, Ltd. GBR. *Dist:* Advanced Global Distribution Services.

—Railway Children. 2000. (Juvenile Classics). (Illus.). iii, 188p. (J). pap. 2.50 (*0-486-41022-6*) Dover Pubns., Inc.

—Railway Children. (J). 3.50 (*0-340-71497-2*) Hodder & Stoughton, Ltd. GBR. *Dist:* Lubrecht & Cramer, Ltd., Trafalgar Square.

—The Railway Children, ERS. 1994. (J). 14.95 o.p. (*0-8050-3129-4*, Holt, Henry & Co. Bks. For Young Readers) Holt, Henry & Co.

—The Railway Children, Level 2. 2000. (C). pap. 7.66 (*0-582-41790-2*) Longman Publishing Group.

—The Railway Children. abr. ed. 1996. (J). audio 13.98 (*962-634-585-3*, NA208514, Naxos AudioBooks) Naxos of America, Inc.

—The Railway Children, Level 3. Hedge, Tricia, ed. 2000. (Bookworms Ser.). (Illus.). 74p. pap. text 5.95 (*0-19-423013-9*) Oxford Univ. Pr., Inc.

—The Railway Children. l.t. ed. 1987. (Charnwood Large Print Ser.). 288p. 29.99 o.p. (*0-7089-8382-0*, Charnwood) Thorpe, F. A. Pubs. GBR. *Dist:* Ulverscroft Large Print Bks., Ltd., Ulverscroft Large Print Canada, Ltd.

—The Railway Children. abr. ed. (Children's Classics Ser.). (J). 1997. pap. 15.95 o.p. incl. audio (*1-85998-750-8*); 1994. audio 14.95 (*1-85998-081-3*) Trafalgar Square.

Nesbit, Jeffrey A. The Puzzled Prodigy. 1992. (Capital Crew Ser.). (Orig.). (J). (gr. 3-6). pap. 1.00 (*0-89693-075-0*) Cook Communications Ministries.

Price, M. & Le Cain, Errol. Have You Seen My Sister? 1991. (Illus.). 28p. (J). (ps-2). 12.95 o.p. (*0-15-200467-X*) Harcourt Children's Bks.

Price, Olive. Three Golden Rivers. l.t. ed. 1999. (Golden Triangle Bks.). 272p. (YA). (gr. 4-7). pap. 9.95 (*0-8229-5707-8*) Univ. of Pittsburgh Pr.

Pryor, Bonnie. Jumping Jenny. 1992. (Illus.). 192p. (J). (gr. 2 up). 14.00 o.p. (*0-688-09684-0*, Morrow, William & Co.) Morrow/Avon.

—Louie & Dan Are Friends. 1997. (Illus.). 32p. (J). lib. bdg. 15.93 o.p. (*0-688-08561-X*); 16.00 (*0-688-08560-1*) Morrow/Avon. (Morrow, William & Co.).

—The Porcupine Mouse. 2002. (Illus.). (J). (ps-4). 32p. 15.95 (*1-58717-185-6*); 40p. pap. 5.95 (*1-58717-186-4*) North-South Bks., Inc.

Pyrnelle, Louise Clarke. Diddie, Dumps & Tot. 1963. (Illus.). 240p. (J). (gr. 4-8). 15.95 (*0-911116-17-6*) Pelican Publishing Co., Inc.

Qualey, Marsha. Thin Ice. 1997. 272p. (YA). (gr. 7-12). 14.95 o.s.i (*0-385-32298-4*, Delacorte Pr.) Dell Publishing.

—Thin Ice. 1999. 272p. (YA). (gr. 7-7). mass mkt. 4.99 (*0-440-22037-8*, Dell Books for Young Readers) Random Hse. Children's Bks.

—Thin Ice. 1999. 11.04 (*0-606-17348-X*) Turtleback Bks.

Quarles, Heather. A Door Near Here. 1998. 240p. (YA). (gr. 7-10). 13.95 o.s.i (*0-385-32595-9*) Doubleday Publishing.

—A Door Near Here. 2000. (Illus.). 240p. (YA). (gr. 7 up). mass mkt. 4.99 (*0-440-22761-5*, Laurel Leaf) Random Hse. Children's Bks.

—A Door Near Here. l.t. ed. 2000. (Young Adult Ser.). 323p. (J). (gr. 8-12). 21.95 (*0-7862-2884-9*) Thorndike Pr.

—A Door Near Here. 2000. 10.55 (*0-606-17796-5*) Turtleback Bks.

Quin-Harkin, Janet. Cool in School. 1996. (Sister Sister Ser.). 144p. (J). (gr. 4-7). pap. 3.99 (*0-671-00176-0*, Aladdin) Simon & Schuster Children's Publishing.

Rabin, Staton. Casey over There. 1994. (Illus.). 32p. (J). (ps-3). 14.95 (*0-15-253186-6*) Harcourt Trade Pubs.

Radley, Gail. Zahra's Search. 1982. (Illus.). 32p. (Orig.). (J). (gr. 2-6). pap. 3.95 o.s.i (*0-87743-161-2*) Baha'i Distribution Service.

Ramirez, Linda M. & Salcines, Maria Luisa. Playtime for Molly: A Story about Filial Therapy: How a Parent & Child Play to Improve Their Relationship. 2001. (Illus.). 24p. pap. text 8.95 (*0-9713839-0-1*) MarLin Bks.

Randall, Rod. Along Came a Spider. 2000. (Heebie Jeebies Ser.: Vol. 7). 138p. (J). (gr. 3-7). pap. 5.99 (*0-8054-1981-0*) Broadman & Holman Pubs.

Random House Books for Young Readers Staff. Cat in the Hat Novelization. 2003. (Illus.). 128p. (J). (gr. 2-4). pap. 4.99 (*0-375-82470-7*, 53578056) Random Hse. Children's Bks.

Ransom, Candice F. My Sister the Meanie. (J). 1989. pap. 2.50 o.p. (*0-590-41527-1*); 1989. 160p. (gr. 4-7). pap. 2.75 o.p. (*0-590-44116-7*); 1988. 176p. (gr. 5-8). pap. 12.95 o.p. (*0-590-41982-X*) Scholastic, Inc.

Raschka, Chris. The Blushful Hippopotamus. 1996. (Illus.). 32p. (J). (ps-3). pap. 14.95 (*0-531-09532-0*); lib. bdg. 15.99 (*0-531-08882-0*) Scholastic, Inc. (Orchard Bks.).

Ray, Deborah Kogan. Sunday Morning We Went to the Zoo. 1981. (Illus.). 32p. (J). (ps-2). 8.95 o.p. (*0-06-024841-6*); lib. bdg. 10.89 o.p. (*0-06-024842-4*) HarperCollins Children's Bk. Group.

Read, Elfreida. Brothers by Choice, RS. 1974. 160p. (J). (gr. 7 up). 9.95 o.p. (*0-374-30996-5*, Farrar, Straus & Giroux (BYR)) Farrar, Straus & Giroux.

Recheis, Kathe. Little Raccoon Always Knows Best. 2002. Tr. of Kleiner Waschbar Weiss Alles Besser. 24p. (J). 14.95 (*0-7940-0009-6*); (Illus.). lib. bdg. 15.95 (*0-7940-0010-X*) Munchweiler Pr.

Recorvits, Helen. Goodbye, Walter Malinski, RS. 1999. (Illus.). 96p. (J). (gr. 4-7). 15.00 o.p. (*0-374-32747-5*, Farrar, Straus & Giroux (BYR)) Farrar, Straus & Giroux.

Reece, Colleen L. Plymouth Pioneers. 1998. (American Adventure Ser.: No. 2). (Illus.). 142p. (J). (gr. 3-7). lib. bdg. 15.95 (*0-7910-5042-4*) Chelsea Hse. Pubs.

Reeder, Carolyn. Captain Kate. 2002. 210p. (J). (gr. 4-7). reprint ed. pap. 6.50 (*1-890920-14-2*) Children's Literature.

—Captain Kate. 224p. (J). 2000. (gr. 3-7). pap. 4.99 (*0-380-79668-6*); 1999. (gr. 4-7). 15.00 (*0-380-97628-5*, Avon Bks.) Morrow/Avon.

—Captain Kate. 1999. (Illus.). (J). 11.04 (*0-606-17963-1*) Turtleback Bks.

Reiss, Kathryn. The Glass House People. 1992. 288p. (YA). (gr. 7 up). 16.95 (*0-15-231040-1*) Harcourt Children's Bks.

Remkiewicz, Frank. GreedyAnna. 1992. (J). (ps-3). 14.00 o.p. (*0-688-10294-8*); lib. bdg. 13.93 o.p. (*0-688-10295-6*) HarperCollins Children's Bk. Group.

Renner, Beverly H. The Hideaway Summer. 1978. (Illus.). (J). (gr. 4-6). o.p. (*0-06-024862-9*); lib. bdg. 12.89 o.p. (*0-06-024863-7*) HarperCollins Children's Bk. Group.

Rheingrover, Jean S. Veronica's First Year. 1996. (Illus.). 24p. (J). (ps-3). lib. bdg. 13.95 o.p. (*0-8075-8474-6*) Whitman, Albert & Co.

Richard, Adrienne. Into the Road. 1976. (J). (gr. 7-12). 7.95 o.p. (*0-316-74318-6*) Little Brown & Co.

Richardson, Julia, ed. Escape. 2000. (So Weird Ser.: No. 3). (Illus.). 160p. (J). (gr. 4-7). 4.99 (*0-7868-1399-7*) Disney Pr.

—Family Reunion. 2000. (So Weird Ser.: No. 1). (Illus.). 144p. (J). (gr. 4-7). pap. 4.99 (*0-7868-1397-0*) Disney Pr.

Richler, Mordecai. Jacob Two-Two Meets the Hooded Fang. 1975. (Illus.). 96p. (J). (gr. 3-6). 5.50 o.p. (*0-394-82992-1*); lib. bdg. 5.99 o.p. (*0-394-92992-6*) Random Hse. Children's Bks. (Knopf Bks. for Young Readers).

Rinaldi, Ann. Promises Are for Keeping. 1984. 224p. pap. 2.25 o.p. (*0-553-24049-8*) Bantam Bks.

—Term Paper. 1980. 202p. (J). (gr. 5 up). 9.95 o.s.i (*0-8027-6395-2*) Walker & Co.

Ringgold, Faith. Aunt Harriet's Underground Railroad in the Sky. 1995. (Illus.). 32p. (ps-3). pap. 6.99 (*0-517-88543-3*) Crown Publishing Group.

—Aunt Harriet's Underground Railroad in the Sky. 1992. (Illus.). 32p. (J). (ps-3). lib. bdg. 17.99 o.s.i (*0-517-58768-8*); 16.00 o.s.i (*0-517-58767-X*) Random Hse. Children's Bks. (Random Hse. Bks. for Young Readers).

—Aunt Harriet's Underground Railroad in the Sky. 1995. (J). 13.14 (*0-606-08478-9*) Turtleback Bks.

Rispin, Karen. Ambush at Amboseli. 1994. (Anika Scott Ser.: Vol. 4). 136p. (J). (gr. 5-7). 4.99 o.p. (*0-8423-1295-1*) Tyndale Hse. Pubs.

Rix, Jamie. The War Diaries of Alistair Fury: Bugs on the Brain, Vol. 1. 2003. (Illus.). 160p. (J). (gr. 3). pap. (*0-440-86476-3*, Corgi) Bantam Bks.

Robbins, Beth. Tom, Ally, & the New Baby. 2001. (It's OK! Ser.). (Illus.). 32p. (J). (ps-k). pap. 3.95 (*0-7894-7430-1*, D K Ink) Dorling Kindersley Publishing, Inc.

Roberts, Willo Davis. The Absolutely True Story . . . How I Visited Yellowstone Park with the Terrible Rupes. 1994. 160p. (J). (gr. 3-7). 15.00 (*0-689-31939-8*, Atheneum) Simon & Schuster Children's Publishing.

—To Grandmother's House We Go. 1990. 192p. (J). (gr. 3-7). lib. bdg. 16.00 o.s.i (*0-689-31594-5*, Atheneum) Simon & Schuster Children's Publishing.

Robinson, Joan (Maurice). The Dark House of the Sea Witch. 1979. (J). (gr. 3-6). 7.50 o.p. (*0-698-20494-8*) Putnam Publishing Group, The.

Roche, P. K. Webster & Arnold Go Camping. 1991. (Illus.). 320p. (J). (ps-3). pap. 3.95 o.s.i (*0-14-050806-6*, Puffin Bks.) Penguin Putnam Bks. for Young Readers.

Rocklin, Joanne. Jake & the Copycats. 1998. (Illus.). 48p. (J). (gr. k-3). 13.95 o.s.i (*0-385-32530-4*, Dell Books for Young Readers); pap. 4.50 o.s.i (*0-440-41408-3*, Yearling) Random Hse. Children's Bks.

—Jake & the Copycats. 1998. 10.65 (*0-606-16623-8*) Turtleback Bks.

Rockwell, Anne F. Porker Twins Play Basketball. 2005. (J). (*0-06-028443-9*); lib. bdg. (*0-06-028447-1*) HarperCollins Pubs.

Rockwell, Lizzy. Hello Baby! 2002. (Illus.). (J). 14.79 (*0-7587-4439-0*) Book Wholesalers, Inc.

—Hello Baby! (Illus.). (J). (ps-k). 2000. 32p. pap. 6.99 (*0-517-80074-8*); 1999. 40p. 15.00 o.s.i (*0-517-80011-X*) Random Hse. Children's Bks. (Random Hse. Bks. for Young Readers).

—Hello Baby! 2000. (J). 13.14 (*0-606-18980-7*) Turtleback Bks.

—Hello, Baby! 1999. 40p. (J). (ps-3). lib. bdg. 16.99 o.s.i (*0-517-80012-8*, Random Hse. Bks. for Young Readers) Random Hse. Children's Bks.

Rodda, Emily. The Timekeeper. 1993. (Illus.). 160p. (J). (gr. 5 up). 14.00 o.p. (*0-688-12448-8*, Greenwillow Bks.) HarperCollins Children's Bk. Group.

Roddie, Shen. Toes Are to Tickle. 1997. (Illus.). 24p. (J). (ps-k). 13.95 (*1-883672-49-X*) Tricycle Pr.

Roddy, Lee. Eye of the Hurricane. 1994. (Ladd Family Adventure Ser.: Vol. 9). 170p. (J). (gr. 3-7). pap. 5.99 o.p. (*1-56179-220-9*) Focus on the Family Publishing.

Rodell, Susanna. Dear Fred. 1995. (Illus.). 32p. (J). (ps-3). 14.95 (*0-395-71544-X*) Houghton Mifflin Co.

Rodowski, Colby F. What About Me. 1976. 160p. (gr. 6 up). lib. bdg. 7.90 o.p. (*0-531-01209-3*, Watts, Franklin) Scholastic Library Publishing.

Rodowsky, Colby. Clay, RS. 2001. 176p. (J). (gr. 3-7). 16.00 (*0-374-31338-5*, Farrar, Straus & Giroux (BYR)) Farrar, Straus & Giroux.

—Clay. 2004. 160p. (J). pap. 5.99 (*0-06-000618-8*, Harper Trophy) HarperCollins Children's Bk. Group.

—Not Quite a Stranger, RS. 2003. 192p. (gr. 5 up). 16.00 (*0-374-35548-7*, Farrar, Straus & Giroux (BYR)) Farrar, Straus & Giroux.

Roe. Con Me Hermano. 1998. Tr. of With My Brother. (J). pap. 5.99 (*0-87628-126-9*) Ctr. for Applied Research in Education, The.

Roe, Eileen. Con Mi Hermano (With My Brother) 1994. (ENG & SPA., Illus.). 32p. (J). (gr. k-3). pap. 6.99 (*0-689-71855-1*, Aladdin) Simon & Schuster Children's Publishing.

—Con Mi Hermano/With My Brother. 1991. (Illus.). 32p. (J). (ps-3). lib. bdg. 14.00 (*0-02-777373-6*, Simon & Schuster Children's Publishing) Simon & Schuster Children's Publishing.

Rogers, Mary. Big Brother. 1992. (Foundations Ser.). 19p. (J). pap. text 23.00 (*1-56843-010-8*); pap. text 4.50 (*1-56843-060-4*) EMG Networks.

Rojany, Lisa. Leave It to Beaver. novel ed. 1997. 144p. (J). (gr. 3 up). 4.95 o.s.i (*0-8431-7858-2*, Price Stern Sloan) Penguin Putnam Bks. for Young Readers.

Roland, Christopher P., Jr. The Two Brothers That Aren't the Same. Bey, Malik R., ed. 1997. (Illus.). (Orig.). (J). (gr. k-4). pap. 1.99 (*0-9656137-8-X*) Bey, Malik Rasul.

Roop, Peter & Roop, Connie. An Eye for an Eye: A Story of the American Revolution. 2001. (Jamestown Classics Ser.). (Illus.). 168p. (YA). (gr. 5-8). 12.64 (*0-8092-0587-4*) Jamestown.

Roos & Degroat. Never Trust a Sister. 1993. o.s.i (*0-385-30955-4*, Dell Books for Young Readers) Random Hse. Children's Bks.

Roos, Stephen. My Horrible Secret. 1983. (Illus.). 128p. (J). (gr. 4-6). pap. 10.95 o.s.i (*0-385-29246-5*, Delacorte Pr.) Dell Publishing.

—Never Trust a Sister over Twelve. 1995. (Illus.). 160p. (J). (gr. 3-7). pap. 3.99 o.s.i (*0-440-41105-X*, Dell Books for Young Readers) Random Hse. Children's Bks.

—Never Trust a Sister over Twelve. 1995. (J). 9.09 o.p. (*0-606-09679-5*) Turtleback Bks.

Root, Phyllis. Moon Tiger, ERS. 1985. (Illus.). 32p. (J). (ps-2). 14.95 o.p. (*0-8050-0896-9*, Holt, Henry & Co. Bks. For Young Readers) Holt, Henry & Co.

Rosenberg, Liz. The Carousel. 1995. (Illus.). 32p. (J). (ps-3). 16.00 (*0-15-200853-5*) Harcourt Children's Bks.

Rosenblum, Richard. My Sister's Wedding. 1987. (Illus.). 32p. (J). (gr. 2-5). 11.95 o.p. (*0-688-05955-4*); lib. bdg. 11.88 o.p. (*0-688-05956-2*) Morrow/Avon. (Morrow, William & Co.).

Ross, Christine. Lily & the Present. 1992. (Illus.). 28p. (J). (ps-3). 13.95 o.p. (*0-395-61127-X*) Houghton Mifflin Co.

Ross, Helen. The Adventures of Dip & Dee Darrow. 1984. (J). 5.95 o.p. (*0-533-05987-9*) Vantage Pr., Inc.

Ross, Rhea B. The Bet's on Lizzie Bingman! 1992. (YA). pap. 4.95 o.p. (*0-395-64375-9*); 1988. 192p. (J). (gr. 5-9). 13.95 o.p. (*0-395-44472-1*) Houghton Mifflin Co.

Ross, Tony. I Want a Sister. 2002. (Illus.). 10p. (J). 8.95 (*1-84270-103-7*) Andersen Pr., Ltd. GBR. *Dist:* Trafalgar Square.

Rottman, S. L. Rough Waters. 1998. (Illus.). 192p. (YA). (gr. 7-11). 14.95 (*1-56145-172-X*) Peachtree Pubs., Ltd.

—Rough Waters. 2000. (Illus.). 224p. (YA). (gr. 7-12). pap. 6.99 (*0-14-130703-X*) Penguin Putnam Bks. for Young Readers.

—Stetson. 2002. 256p. (YA). (gr. 9 up). 16.99 (*0-670-03542-4*, Viking Children's Bks.) Penguin Putnam Bks. for Young Readers.

Rottman, S.L. Rough Waters. 2000. 12.04 (*0-606-17869-4*) Turtleback Bks.

Rottman, Susan. Stetson. 2003. 224p. pap. 5.99 (*0-14-250194-8*, Puffin Bks.) Penguin Putnam Bks. for Young Readers.

Rouss, Sylvia A. Aaron's Bar Mitzvah. Dubois, Liz Goulet, tr. & illus. by. 2003. (J). 14.95 (*0-8246-0447-4*) Jonathan David Pubs., Inc.

—My Baby Brother: What a Miracle! 2002. (J). 14.95 (*0-8246-0445-8*) Jonathan David Pubs., Inc.

Rowinski, Kate. Cats in the Dark. 1998. (Illus.). 32p. (J). (ps-3). 14.95 (*0-89272-427-7*) Down East Bks.

Roy, J. Soul Daddy. 1992. 224p. (YA). (gr. 7 up). 16.95 o.s.i (*0-15-277193-X*, Gulliver Bks.) Harcourt Children's Bks.

Roy, Ronald. Where's Buddy? 1986. (Illus.). 96p. (J). (gr. 4-6). reprint ed. pap. 2.50 o.p. (*0-590-41120-9*, Scholastic Paperbacks) Scholastic, Inc.

Rubin, Vicky. Careful Around Eggs. 2004. (J). (*0-8050-6836-8*, Holt, Henry & Co. Bks. For Young Readers) Holt, Henry & Co.

Rue, Nancy. The Secret. 1998. (Christian Heritage Ser.). 192p. (Orig.). (J). (gr. 3-7). pap. 5.99 (*1-56179-443-0*) Focus on the Family Publishing.

—The Thief. 1998. (Christian Heritage Ser.). 192p. (J). (gr. 3-7). pap. 5.99 (*1-56179-479-1*) Focus on the Family Publishing.

Ruelle, Karen G. April Fool! 2003. (Illus.). pap. 4.95 (*0-8234-1780-8*) Holiday Hse., Inc.

Ruelle, Karen Gray. April Fool! A Holiday House Reader. 2002. (Reader Level 2 Ser.). (Illus.). 32p. (J). (gr. k-3). tchr. ed. 14.95 (*0-8234-1686-0*) Holiday Hse., Inc.

—Easter Egg Disaster. 2004. (J). (*0-8234-1806-5*) Holiday Hse., Inc.

—The Monster in Harry's Backyard. 2003. (Illus.). pap. 4.95 (*0-8234-1783-2*) Holiday Hse., Inc.

—Monster in Harry's Backyard. 1999. (Holiday House Reader Ser.). (Illus.). 32p. (J). (ps-3). tchr. ed. 14.95 (*0-8234-1417-5*) Holiday Hse., Inc.

—Mother's Day. 2003. (Illus.). 32p. (J). tchr. ed. 14.95 (*0-8234-1773-5*) Holiday Hse., Inc.

—Spookier Than a Ghost. 2001. (Illus.). 32p. (J). (ps-3). tchr. ed. 15.95 (*0-8234-1667-4*) Holiday Hse., Inc.

—The Thanksgiving Beast Feast Level 2: A Holiday House Reader. 1999. (Illus.). 32p. (J). (gr. k-3). tchr. ed. 14.95 (*0-8234-1511-2*) Holiday Hse., Inc.

Rumford, James. The Island-below-the-Star. 1998. (Illus.). 32p. (J). (ps-3). tchr. ed. 16.00 (*0-395-85159-9*) Houghton Mifflin Co.

Rupp, Rebecca. The Dragon of Lonely Island. 160p. (J). (gr. 3-6). 2002. (Illus.). bds. 5.99 (*0-7636-1661-3*); 1998. 16.99 (*0-7636-0408-9*) Candlewick Pr.

Russell, Barbara T. Last Left Standing. 1998. 144p. (J). (gr. 3-7). pap. 4.50 o.s.i (*0-14-038686-6*, Puffin Bks.) Penguin Putnam Bks. for Young Readers.

Russo, Marisabina. I Don't Want to Go Back to School. 1994. (Illus.). 32p. (J). (ps-3). 16.99 (*0-688-04601-0*); lib. bdg. 15.89 (*0-688-04602-9*) HarperCollins Children's Bk. Group. (Greenwillow Bks.).

—Only Six More Days. 1992. (Illus.). 320p. (J). (ps-3). pap. 3.99 o.p. (*0-14-054473-9*, Puffin Bks.) Penguin Putnam Bks. for Young Readers.

—The Trouble with Baby. 2003. (Illus.). 32p. (J). (ps up). lib. bdg. 16.89 (*0-06-008925-3*); 15.99 (*0-06-008924-5*) HarperCollins Children's Bk. Group. (Greenwillow Bks.).

Ryan, Mary E. Me, My Sister, & I. 1992. 160p. (YA). (gr. 5-9). pap. 15.00 (*0-671-73851-8*, Simon & Schuster Children's Publishing) Simon & Schuster Children's Publishing.

—My Sister Is Driving Me Crazy. 224p. (J). (gr. 5-9). 1993. pap. 3.95 o.s.i (*0-671-86694-X*, Aladdin); 1991. pap. 15.00 o.p. (*0-671-73203-X*, Simon & Schuster Children's Publishing) Simon & Schuster Children's Publishing.

Sachs, Marilyn. Jojo & Winnie Again: More Sister Stories. 2000. (Illus.). 80p. (J). (gr. 2-5). 15.99 (*0-525-46393-3*, Dutton Children's Bks.) Penguin Putnam Bks. for Young Readers.

—What My Sister Remembered. (J). (gr. 5 up). 1994. 128p. pap. 3.99 o.s.i (*0-14-036944-9*, Puffin Bks.); 1992. 120p. 15.00 o.p. (*0-525-44953-1*, Dutton Children's Bks.) Penguin Putnam Bks. for Young Readers.

—What My Sister Remembered. 1994. 9.09 o.p. (*0-606-06865-1*) Turtleback Bks.

Sadler, Marilyn. Honey Bunny Funnybunny. 1997. 48p. (J). (ps-3). 8.99 (*0-679-88181-6*) McKay, David Co., Inc.

—The PJ Funnybunny Beginner Book. 1997. (J). (ps-3). 11.99 (*0-679-98181-0*) McKay, David Co., Inc.

Saint Mars, Dominique de. Max Is Shy. 1993. (About Me Ser.). (Illus.). 24p. (J). (-4). lib. bdg. 12.79 o.p. (*0-89565-977-8*, 59778) Child's World, Inc.

Salisbury, Graham. Jungle Dogs. 1999. 192p. (gr. 4-8). pap. text 4.99 (*0-440-41573-X*) Bantam Bks.

—Jungle Dogs. 1998. 192p. (gr. 4-8). text 15.95 o.s.i (*0-385-32187-2*) Doubleday Publishing.

—Jungle Dogs. 2000. (YA). (gr. 5 up). pap., stu. ed. 59.95 incl. audio (*0-7887-4336-8*, 41131) Recorded Bks., LLC.

—Jungle Dogs. 1999. 11.04 (*0-606-17837-6*) Turtleback Bks.

Samuels, Barbara. Faye & Dolores. 1987. (Illus.). 40p. (J). (ps-3). reprint ed. pap. 4.95 o.s.i (*0-689-71154-9*, Aladdin) Simon & Schuster Children's Publishing.

Sanders, Scott Russell. Crawdad Creek. 1999. (Illus.). 32p. (J). (ps-3). 15.95 (*0-7922-7097-5*) National Geographic Society.

Sandoval, Dolores. Be Patient, Abdul. 1996. (Illus.). 32p. (J). (gr. k-4). mass mkt. 15.00 o.p. (*0-689-50607-4*, McElderry, Margaret K.) Simon & Schuster Children's Publishing.

Sathre, Vivian. J. B. Wigglebottom & the Parade of Pets. 1993. (Illus.). 96p. (J). (gr. 2-6). 12.95 (*0-689-31811-1*, Atheneum) Simon & Schuster Children's Publishing.

Saunders, Susan. Big Sister Stephanie. 1990. (Sleepover Friends Ser.: No. 30). 128p. (J). mass mkt. 2.75 o.p. (*0-590-43929-4*) Scholastic, Inc.

Savage, Cindy. Just Between Sisters. 1987. (Impressions Ser.). 128p. (Orig.). (J). (gr. 5-8). pap. 2.50 o.p. (*0-87406-260-8*) Darby Creek Publishing.

—My Sister, the Pig, & Me. 1992. (Illus.). 142p. (J). (gr. 3-5). pap. 2.50 o.p. (*0-87406-638-7*) Darby Creek Publishing.

Scarboro, Elizabeth. The Secret Language of the SB. 1990. 144p. (J). (gr. 3-7). 11.95 o.p. (*0-670-83087-9*, Viking Children's Bks.) Penguin Putnam Bks. for Young Readers.

Schaller, Bob. Adventure in Wyoming. 2000. (X-Country Adventures Ser.). (Illus.). 128p. (J). (gr. 3-6). pap. 5.99 o.p. (*0-8010-4452-9*) Baker Bks.

—Crime in a Colorado Cave. 2000. (X-Country Adventures Ser.). (Illus.). 128p. (J). (gr. 3-6). pap. 5.99 o.p. (*0-8010-4453-7*) Baker Bks.

—Treasure in Texas. 2001. (X-Country Adventures Ser.). 128p. (J). (gr. 3-6). pap. 5.99 o.p. (*0-8010-4492-8*) Baker Bks.

Scheidl, Gerda Marie. Tommy's New Sister. (Illus.). 32p. (J). (ps-2). 2002. pap. 6.95 (*0-7358-1700-6*); 1999. 15.95 (*0-7358-1056-7*); 1999. 16.50 o.p. (*0-7358-1057-5*) North-South Bks., Inc.

Schietinger-Cachina, Daryl A. Hey New Baby in There. 1999. (Illus.). 8p. (J). (ps-5). pap. 5.00 (*1-928641-02-4*) Daryl Ann Pubns.

Schneider, Christine M. Saxophone Sam & His Snazzy Jazz Band. 2002. (Illus.). 32p. (J). (gr. k-3). 17.85 (*0-8027-8810-6*); trans. 16.95 (*0-8027-8809-2*) Walker & Co.

Schneider, Mical. Annie Quinn in America. 2001. (J). 6.95 (*1-57505-535-X*) Carolrhoda Bks.

—Annie Quinn in America. 2001. (Adventures in Time Ser.). (Illus.). 252p. (J). (gr. 4-7). lib. bdg. 15.95 (*1-57505-510-4*, Carolrhoda Bks.) Lerner Publishing Group.

Schnitter, Jane T. William Is My Brother. 1990. (Illus.). 32p. (J). (ps-3). 12.00 o.p. (*0-944934-03-X*) Perspectives Pr., Inc.

Scholastic, Inc. Staff. Franklin Forgives. 2004. (Franklin Ser.). 32p. (J). pap. 4.50 (*0-439-62054-6*) Scholastic, Inc.

Schreiber, Anne. Slower Than a Snail. 1995. (Hello Reader! Math Ser.). (Illus.). (J). (ps-3). mass mkt. 3.50 (*0-590-18074-6*); 32p. mass mkt. 2.95 o.p. (*0-590-26599-7*, Cartwheel Bks.) Scholastic, Inc.

Schulz, Charles M. Happy Valentine's Day, Sweet Babboo! 1997. (Peanuts Ser.). (Illus.). 24p. (J). (ps-1). 11.95 o.p. (*0-694-00961-X*, Harper Festival) HarperCollins Children's Bk. Group.

—Lose the Blanket, Linus! 2003. (Peanuts Ready-to-Read Ser.). (Illus.). 32p. (J). pap. 3.99 (*0-689-85472-2*); lib. bdg. 11.89 (*0-689-85474-9*) Simon & Schuster Children's Publishing. (Little Simon).

—Mischief on Daisy Hill. (Illus.). 32p. (J). (ps-3). 12.95 (*0-915696-15-0*) Determined Productions, Inc.

Schwartz, Joel L. How to Get Rid of Your Older Brother. 1992. 128p. (J). (gr. 4-7). pap. 3.25 o.s.i (*0-440-40623-4*) Dell Publishing.

Schwartz, Roslyn. The Mole Sisters & the Piece of Moss. 1999. (Mole Sisters Ser.). (Illus.). 32p. (J). (ps-k). lib. bdg. 14.95 (*1-55037-583-0*) Annick Pr., Ltd. CAN. *Dist:* Firefly Bks., Ltd.

—The Mole Sisters & the Rainy Day. 1999. (Mole Sisters Ser.). (Illus.). 32p. (J). (ps-k). lib. bdg. 14.95 (*1-55037-611-X*) Annick Pr., Ltd. CAN. *Dist:* Firefly Bks., Ltd.

Schwarz, Eugene. Two Brothers. Hapgood, Elizabeth, tr. 1973. (ENG & RUS., Illus.). 48p. (J). (gr. 1-5). 4.95 o.p. (*0-06-025248-0*); lib. bdg. 4.79 o.p. (*0-06-025249-9*) HarperCollins Pubs.

Scott, Michael. Gemini Game. 1994. 160p. (J). (gr. 7 up). 14.95 o.p. (*0-8234-1092-7*) Holiday Hse., Inc.

—Gemini Game. 1996. 10.00 (*0-606-14213-4*) Turtleback Bks.

Seabrooke, Brenda. The Haunting of Holroyd Hill. 144p. 1997. (YA). (gr. 5-9). pap. 4.99 o.s.i (*0-14-038540-1*); 1995. (J). (ps-3). 14.99 o.p. (*0-525-65167-5*, Dutton Children's Bks.) Penguin Putnam Bks. for Young Readers.

—The Haunting of Holroyd Hill. 1997. (J). 11.04 (*0-606-10987-0*) Turtleback Bks.

Seidler, Tor. The Dulcimer Boy. 2003. (Illus.). 160p. (J). lib. bdg. 16.89 (*0-06-623610-X*, Geringer, Laura Bk.) HarperCollins Children's Bk. Group.

—The Dulcimer Boy. 2003. (Illus.). 160p. (J). reprint ed. 15.99 (*0-06-623609-6*) HarperCollins Pubs.

—The Dulcimer Boy. 1979. (Illus.). (J). 8.95 o.p. (*0-670-28609-5*) Viking Penguin.

Selznick, Brian. The Robot King. 1995. (Laura Geringer Bks.). (Illus.). 80p. (J). (gr. k up). 13.95 o.s.i (*0-06-024493-3*); lib. bdg. 13.89 o.p. (*0-06-024494-1*) HarperCollins Children's Bk. Group.

Sensenig, Janet. Daryl Borrows a Brother. 1989. (Illus.). 166p. (J). (gr. 3-6). 8.20 (*0-7399-0081-1*, 2182) Rod & Staff Pubs., Inc.

Service, Pamela F. Stinker from Space. 1989. 96p. (gr. 4-7). mass mkt. 5.99 (*0-449-70330-4*, Fawcett) Ballantine Bks.

Seuss, Dr. Viene de Nuevo el Gato del Sombrero. Canetti, Yanitzia, tr. from ENG. (SPA., Illus.). (J). 9.95 (*1-930332-43-2*) Lectorum Pubns., Inc.

Shahan, Sherry. One Sister Too Many. 1987. (Treetop Tales Ser.). (Illus.). 112p. (Orig.). (J). (gr. 3-5). pap. 2.25 o.p. (*0-87406-254-3*) Darby Creek Publishing.

Shands, Linda I. Blind Fury. 2001. (Wakara of Eagle Lodge Ser.: Vol. 2). (Illus.). 176p. (YA). (gr. 7-9). pap. 5.99 (*0-8007-5747-5*) Revell, Fleming H. Co.

Shea, Pegi Deitz. New Moon. (Illus.). 32p. (J). (ps-3). 2003. pap. 8.95 (*1-56397-922-5*); 1996. 14.95 (*1-56397-410-X*) Boyds Mills Pr.

Shearer, Alex. The Summer Sisters & the Dance Disaster. 1998. (Illus.). 103p. (J). (gr. 3-7). pap. 14.95 (*0-531-30080-3*); lib. bdg. 15.99 (*0-531-33080-X*) Scholastic, Inc. (Orchard Bks.).

Sheldon, Dyan. My Brother Is a Superhero. (J). 1998. 128p. (gr. 3-6). bds. 4.99 (*0-7636-0383-X*); 1996. (Illus.). 123p. (gr. 4-7). 15.99 o.p. (*1-56402-624-8*) Candlewick Pr.

—My Brother Is a Visitor from Another Planet. (Illus.). (J). 1995. (gr. 4-7). bds. 3.99 o.p. (*1-56402-517-9*); 1993. 96p. (gr. 3-6). 14.95 o.p. (*1-56402-141-6*) Candlewick Pr.

—My Brother is a Visitor from Another Planet. 1995. (J). 9.09 o.p. (*0-606-07904-1*) Turtleback Bks.

Shelton, Rick. Hoggle's Christmas. 1993. (Illus.). 80p. (J). (gr. 2-6). 12.99 o.p. (*0-525-65129-2*, Dutton Children's Bks.) Penguin Putnam Bks. for Young Readers.

Shenk De Regniers, Beatrice. Little Sister & the Month Brothers. 1994. 10.15 o.p. (*0-606-06539-3*) Turtleback Bks.

Shields, Carol Diggory. I Wish My Brother Was a Dog. 1999. (Illus.). 32p. (J). (ps-3). pap. 6.99 (*0-14-056191-9*, Puffin Bks.) Penguin Putnam Bks. for Young Readers.

Shreve, Susan Richards. The Formerly Great Alexander Family. 1995. (Illus.). 128p. (J). (gr. 3 up). 13.00 o.s.i (*0-688-13551-X*, Morrow, William & Co.) Morrow/Avon.

—Ghost Cats. (J). 2001. 176p. mass mkt. 4.99 (*0-590-37132-0*); 1999. 162p. (gr. 3-7). pap. 14.95 (*0-590-37131-2*) Scholastic, Inc. (Levine, Arthur A. Bks.).

—Wait for Me. 1992. (Illus.). 112p. (J). (gr. 3 up). 13.00 o.p. (*0-688-11120-3*, Morrow, William & Co.) Morrow/Avon.

Shulman, Dee. Dora's New Brother. 1993. (Illus.). 32p. (J). (ps-1). o.p. (*0-370-31814-5*) Random Hse., Inc.

Shusterman, Neal. Full Tilt. 2003. (Illus.). 208p. (J). 16.95 (*0-689-80374-5*, Simon & Schuster Children's Publishing) Simon & Schuster Children's Publishing.

—Full Tilt. l.t. ed. 2003. 243p. (J). 22.95 (*0-7862-5886-1*) Thorndike Pr.

Shyer, Marlene Fanta. The Rainbow Kite. 2002. 208p. (J). (gr. 7-10). 14.95 (*0-7614-5122-6*) Cavendish, Marshall Corp.

—Welcome Home, Jellybean. 1980. (J). (gr. 3-5). pap. 2.50 o.p. (*0-590-40841-0*, Scholastic Paperbacks); pap. 1.95 o.p. (*0-590-30902-1*); pap. 2.25 o.p. (*0-590-40174-2*) Scholastic, Inc.

—Welcome Home, Jellybean. 1988. 160p. (J). (gr. 4-7). reprint ed. pap. 4.99 (*0-689-71213-8*, Aladdin) Simon & Schuster Children's Publishing.

—Welcome Home, Jellybean. 1996. (J). (gr. 5-10). 20.25 (*0-8446-6884-2*) Smith, Peter Pub., Inc.

—Welcome Home, Jellybean. 1988. (J). 11.04 (*0-606-03674-1*) Turtleback Bks.

Sidney, Margaret. Five Little Peppers & Their Friends. 2001. (YA). reprint ed. lib. bdg. 29.95 (*0-89966-970-0*) Buccaneer Bks., Inc.

—Five Little Peppers in the Little Brown House. 1992. (YA). reprint ed. lib. bdg. 25.95 (*0-89966-968-9*) Buccaneer Bks., Inc.

Silberman, Shoshana. A Family Haggadah II. (Illus.). 64p. 1997. (gr. 5). pap. 4.95 (*0-929371-96-8*); 2003. (J). pap. 9.95 (*1-58013-014-3*) Kar-Ben Publishing.

Silverman, Erica. Follow the Leader, RS. 2003. (Illus.). 32p. (J). pap. 6.95 (*0-374-42403-9*, Sunburst) Farrar, Straus & Giroux.

Silverman, Manuel S. Rosie & the Mole: The Story of a Bris. 1999. (Illus.). 48p. (J). (gr. 1-4). 16.95 (*0-943706-22-X*); pap. 9.95 (*0-943706-20-3*) Pitspopany Pr.

Simmons, Jane. Daisy & the Beastie. 2002. (Illus.). (J). 19.11 (*0-7587-2334-2*) Book Wholesalers, Inc.

—Daisy & the Beastie. 2000. (Illus.). 32p. (J). (ps-2). 12.95 (*0-316-79785-5*) Little Brown & Co.

—Daisy & the Egg. 2002. (Illus.). (J). 19.96 (*0-7587-2335-0*) Book Wholesalers, Inc.

—Daisy & the Egg. 1999. (Illus.). 32p. (J). (ps-2). 13.95 (*0-316-79747-2*) Little Brown & Co.

—Daisy & the Egg. 2003. (Illus.). 32p. (J). (ps-3). pap. 6.99 (*0-316-73872-7*) Little Brown Children's Bks.

—Daisy & the Egg. 2004. (ALB, ARA, BEN, CHI & ENG., Illus.). 36p. (J). (ps-1). pap. 11.95 (*1-84059-172-2*); pap. 11.95 (*1-84059-216-8*); pap. 11.95 (*1-84059-170-6*); pap. 11.95 (*1-84059-171-4*); pap. 11.95 (*1-84059-173-0*); pap. 11.95 (*1-84059-174-9*); pap. 11.95 (*1-84059-175-7*); pap. 11.95 (*1-84059-176-5*) Milet Publishing, Ltd. GBR. *Dist:* Consortium Bk. Sales & Distribution.

—Little Fern's First Winter. 2001. (Illus.). 32p. (J). (gr. k-1). 13.95 (*0-316-79667-0*) Little Brown Children's Bks.

Simoen, Jan. What about Anna? Nieuwenhuizen, John, tr. from DUT. 2002. (Illus.). 264p. (J). (gr. 7 up). 16.95 (*0-8027-8808-4*) Walker & Co.

Simon, Charnan. Click & the Kids Go Sailing. 2000. (Illus.). 32p. (J). (gr. 1 up). 12.95 (*1-57768-885-6*, Cricket) McGraw-Hill Children's Publishing.

—I Like to Win! 1999. (Real Kids Readers Ser.). (Illus.). 32p. (ps-1). (J). pap. 4.99 (*0-7613-2087-3*); lib. bdg. 18.90 (*0-7613-2062-8*) Millbrook Pr., Inc.

Simon, Francesca. Horrid Henry. 1999. (Wisecracks Ser.). (Illus.). 96p. (J). (gr. 2-5). lib. bdg. 13.49 (*0-7868-2451-4*) Disney Pr.

Simon, Shirley. Benny's Baby Brother. Gregorich, Barbara, ed. (Start to Read! Ser.). (Illus.). (J). (gr. k-2). 1992. 32p. pap. 3.95 o.p. (*0-88743-414-2*, 06066); Level 2. 1985. 16p. 2.29 (*0-88743-016-3*, 06016) School Zone Publishing Co.

Singleton, Joy. Almost Twins. 1991. (Illus.). 128p. (Orig.). (J). (gr. 3-6). pap. text 2.50 o.p. (*0-87406-452-X*) Darby Creek Publishing.

Singleton, Linda Joy. Babysitter Beware. 1996. (My Sister, the Ghost Ser.: No. 4). (J). (gr. 3-5). pap. 3.99 o.p. (*0-380-78346-0*, Avon Bks.) Morrow/Avon.

Siracusa, Catherine. Bingo, the Best Dog in the World. 1991. (I Can Read Bks.). (Illus.). 64p. (J). (ps-3). 11.95 o.p. (*0-06-025812-8*); lib. bdg. 14.89 o.p. (*0-06-025813-6*) HarperCollins Children's Bk. Group.

Skillings Prigger, Mary. Aunt Minnie McGranahan. 1999. (Illus.). 40p. (J). (ps-3). lib. bdg., tchr. ed. 15.00 (*0-395-82270-X*, Clarion Bks.) Houghton Mifflin Co. Trade & Reference Div.

Skinner, Daphne. Henry Keeps Score. 2001. (Math Matters Ser.). (Illus.). 32p. (J). (ps-2). pap. 4.95 (*1-57565-102-5*) Kane Pr., The.

Skurzynski, Gloria. Caught in the Moving Mountains. 1984. (Illus.). 144p. (J). (ps up). 11.00 o.p. (*0-688-01635-9*) HarperCollins Children's Bk. Group.

—Caught in the Moving Mountains. 1994. (Illus.). 144p. (J). (gr. 7 up). reprint ed. pap. 4.95 (*0-688-12945-5*, Morrow, William & Co.) Morrow/Avon.

—Caught in the Moving Mountains. 1994. 10.05 o.p. (*0-606-06269-6*) Turtleback Bks.

Sleator, William. The Beasties. 208p. (J). 1997. (gr. 5-9). 15.99 (*0-525-45598-1*); Vol. 1. 1999. (Illus.). (gr. 3-7). pap. 6.99 (*0-14-130639-4*, Puffin Bks.) Penguin Putnam Bks. for Young Readers.

—The Beasties. 1999. 12.04 (*0-606-17410-9*) Turtleback Bks.

—Fingers. 1990. 208p. (J). (gr. 7). mass mkt. 3.50 o.s.i (*0-553-25004-3*, Starfire) Random Hse. Children's Bks.

—Marco's Millions. (J). 2002. 176p. (gr. 4-7). pap. 5.99 (*0-14-230217-1*, Puffin Bks.); 2001. 160p. (gr. 5-9). 16.99 (*0-525-46441-7*, Dutton Children's Bks.) Penguin Putnam Bks. for Young Readers.

Slier, Debby. Brothers & Sisters. 1989. (Hello Baby Bks.). 12p. (J). (ps). 2.95 (*1-56288-146-9*) Checkerboard Pr., Inc.

Slote, Alfred. Moving In. 1989. (Trophy Bk.). 176p. (J). (gr. 3-6). reprint ed. pap. 3.50 o.p. (*0-06-440294-0*, Harper Trophy) HarperCollins Children's Bk. Group.

Slote, Elizabeth. Nana & Bold Berto. 1924. (J). o.s.i (*0-688-12980-3*); lib. bdg. o.s.i (*0-688-12981-1*) Morrow/Avon. (Morrow, William & Co.).

Smith, Anne W. Sister in the Shadow. 1986. 180p. (J). (gr. 5-9). 11.95 o.s.i (*0-689-31185-0*, Atheneum) Simon & Schuster Children's Publishing.

Smith, Helene. Children of Morwena. 2002. 256p. (J). pap. 14.95 (*1-86368-356-9*) Fremantle Arts Centre Pr. AUS. *Dist:* International Specialized Bk. Services.

Smith, Janice Lee. The Monster in the Third Dresser Drawer. 1999. (Adam Joshua Capers Ser.). (J). (gr. 2 up). pap., stu. ed. 22.50 incl. audio (*0-7887-3850-X*, 41048X4) Recorded Bks., LLC.

Smith, Lucia B. A Special Kind of Sister, ERS. 1979. (Illus.). (J). (gr. 1-3). o.p. (*0-03-047121-4*, Holt, Henry & Co. Bks. For Young Readers) Holt, Henry & Co.

Smith, Peter. Jenny's Baby Brother. 1988. (Illus.). (J). (ps-3). pap. 3.95 o.p. (*0-14-050798-1*, Puffin Bks.) Penguin Putnam Bks. for Young Readers.

Smothers, Ethel Footman. Down in the Piney Woods. 2003. 128p. (J). 6.00 (*0-8028-5248-3*, Eerdmans Bks For Young Readers) Eerdmans, William B. Publishing Co.

—Down in the Piney Woods. (J). 1994. 156p. (gr. 3-7). pap. 4.99 o.s.i (*0-679-84714-6*, Random Hse. Bks. for Young Readers); 1992. 144p. (gr. 5-9). 14.00 o.s.i (*0-679-80360-2*, Knopf Bks. for Young Readers); 1992. 144p. (gr. 5-9). 14.99 o.s.i (*0-679-90360-7*, Knopf Bks. for Young Readers) Random Hse. Children's Bks.

—Down in the Piney Woods. 1992. (J). 9.09 (*0-606-05813-3*) Turtleback Bks.

Snell, Nigel. Clare's New Baby Brother. 1982. (Illus.). 32p. (J). (ps-1). text 7.95 o.p. (*0-241-10790-3*) Trafalgar Square.

Snicket, Lemony, pseud. The Austere Academy. 2000. (Series of Unfortunate Events: Bk. 5). (Illus.). 240p. (J). (gr. 5 up). 10.99 (*0-06-440863-9*); lib. bdg. 14.89 (*0-06-028888-4*) HarperCollins Children's Bk. Group.

—The Bad Beginning. l.t. ed. 2002. (Series of Unfortunate Events: Bk. 1). (Illus.). (J). 16.95 (*0-7540-7812-4*, Galaxy Children's Large Print) BBC Audiobooks America.

—The Bad Beginning. (Series of Unfortunate Events: Bk. 1). (Illus.). (J). (gr. 5 up). 1999. 176p. lib. bdg. 14.89 (*0-06-028312-2*); 2003. 192p. 14.99 (*0-06-051828-6*) HarperCollins Children's Bk. Group.

—The Bad Beginning. 1999. (Series of Unfortunate Events: Bk. 1). (Illus.). 176p. (J). (gr. 5 up). 10.99 (*0-06-440766-7*) HarperCollins Pubs.

—The Bad Beginning. unabr. ed. 2001. (Series of Unfortunate Events : Bk. 1). (J). (gr. 4-7). audio 18.00 (*0-8072-6178-5*, Listening Library) Random Hse. Audio Publishing Group.

—The Bad Beginning. l.t. ed. 2000. (Series of Unfortunate Events : Bk. 1). (Illus.). 144p. (J). (gr. 4-7). 22.95 o.p. (*0-7862-2974-8*) Thorndike Pr.

—The Carnivorous Carnival. 2002. (Series of Unfortunate Events: Bk. 9). (Illus.). 304p. (J). (gr. 4-7). 10.99 (*0-06-441012-9*, Harper Trophy); (ps-3). lib. bdg. 14.89 (*0-06-029640-2*) HarperCollins Children's Bk. Group.

—The Ersatz Elevator. 2001. (Series of Unfortunate Events: Bk. 6). (Illus.). 272p. (J). (gr. 5 up). 10.99 (*0-06-440864-7*); 6th ed. lib. bdg. 14.89 (*0-06-028889-2*) HarperCollins Children's Bk. Group.

—La Habitacion de los Reptiles. 2002. (Series of Unfortunate Events). (SPA.). 208p. (J). (gr. 4-6). 10.95 (*84-264-3741-9*, LM31164) Editorial Lumen ESP. *Dist:* Lectorum Pubns., Inc.

—The Hostile Hospital. 8th ed. 2001. (Series of Unfortunate Events: Bk. 8). (Illus.). 272p. (J). (gr. 5 up). lib. bdg. 14.89 (*0-06-028891-4*) HarperCollins Children's Bk. Group.

—The Hostile Hospital. 2001. (Series of Unfortunate Events: Bk. 8). (Illus.). (J). 272p. (gr. 5 up). 10.99 (*0-06-440866-3*); 255p. (gr. 4-7). lib. bdg. (*0-06-623919-2*) HarperCollins Pubs.

—Un Mal Principio. 2002. (Series of Unfortunate Events). (SPA.). 224p. (J). (gr. 4-6). 10.95 (*84-264-3740-0*, LM31162) Editorial Lumen ESP. *Dist:* Lectorum Pubns., Inc.

—The Reptile Room. l.t. ed. 2002. (Series of Unfortunate Events: Bk. 2). (Illus.). (J). pap. 16.95 (*0-7540-7823-X*, Galaxy Children's Large Print) BBC Audiobooks America.

—The Reptile Room. 1999. (Series of Unfortunate Events: Bk. 2). (Illus.). 208p. (J). (gr. 5 up). 10.99 (*0-06-440767-5*); lib. bdg. 14.89 (*0-06-028313-0*) HarperCollins Children's Bk. Group.

—The Reptile Room. unabr. ed. 2001. (Series of Unfortunate Events : Bk. 2). (J). (gr. 4-7). audio 18.00 (*0-8072-6179-3*, Listening Library) Random Hse. Audio Publishing Group.

—The Slippery Slope. 2003. (Series of Unfortunate Events: Bk. 10). (Illus.). (J). 197.82 (*0-06-057743-6*); (Illus.). 352p. (J). (gr. 3-6). 10.99 (*0-06-441013-7*); (Illus.). 352p. (J). (gr. 3-6). lib. bdg. 14.89 (*0-06-029641-0*); (gr. 3-6). audio compact disk 25.95 (*0-06-056441-5*) HarperCollins Children's Bk. Group.

—The Slippery Slope. unabr. ed. 2003. (Series of Unfortunate Events : Bk. 10). (gr. 3-6). audio 20.00 (*0-06-051439-6*, HarperAudio) HarperTrade.

—The Vile Village. 2001. (Series of Unfortunate Events: Bk. 7). (Illus.). 272p. (J). (gr. 5 up). 10.99 (*0-06-440865-5*); 7th ed. lib. bdg. 14.89 (*0-06-028890-6*) HarperCollins Children's Bk. Group.

—The Wide Window. l.t. ed. 2003. (Series of Unfortunate Events: Bk. 3). (J). 16.95 (*0-7540-7850-7*, Galaxy Children's Large Print) BBC Audiobooks America.

—The Wide Window. 2000. (Series of Unfortunate Events: Bk. 3). (Illus.). 224p. (J). (gr. 5 up). 10.99 (*0-06-440768-3*); (ps-2). lib. bdg. 14.89 (*0-06-028314-9*) HarperCollins Children's Bk. Group.

Snicket, Lemony, pseud & Helquist, Brett. The Miserable Mill. 2000. (Series of Unfortunate Events: Bk. 4). (Illus.). 208p. (J). (gr. 3-6). 10.99 (*0-06-440769-1*); (ps-2). lib. bdg. 14.89 (*0-06-028315-7*) HarperCollins Children's Bk. Group.

Snyder, Carol. One up, One down. 1995. (Illus.). 32p. (J). (ps-3). 15.00 (*0-689-31828-6*, Atheneum) Simon & Schuster Children's Publishing.

Snyder, Melissa. Souvenirs. 1995. 192p. (YA). (gr. 6 up). pap. 3.50 (*0-380-77805-X*, Avon Bks.) Morrow/Avon.

—Souvenirs. 1995. 8.60 o.p. (*0-606-08187-9*) Turtleback Bks.

Snyder, Zilpha Keatley. Blair's Nightmare. 1984. 204p. (J). (gr. 4-6). lib. bdg. 14.95 o.p. (*0-689-31022-6*, Atheneum) Simon & Schuster Children's Publishing.

—The Unseen. 2004. (J). 208p. text 15.95 (*0-385-73084-5*); 192p. lib. bdg. (*0-385-90106-2*) Dell Publishing. (Delacorte Pr.).

Sorenson, Jane B. The New Pete. 1986. (Jennifer Bks.). (Illus.). 128p. (J). (gr. 5-8). 4.99 o.p. (*0-87403-086-2*, 2986) Standard Publishing.

Spinelli, Jerry. Who Put That Hair in My Toothbrush? (J). 2000. 225p. (gr. 4-7). pap. 6.99 (*0-316-80687-0*); 1984. (gr. 5-9). 15.95 o.p. (*0-316-80712-5*); 1994. 220p. (gr. 4-7). reprint ed. pap. 5.95 o.p. (*0-316-80841-5*) Little Brown & Co.

—Who Put That Hair in My Toothbrush? 1986. 224p. (J). (gr. 5-9). mass mkt. 3.50 o.s.i (*0-440-99485-3*, Laurel Leaf) Random Hse. Children's Bks.

—Who Put That Hair in My Toothbrush? 1984. (J). 12.00 (*0-606-06149-5*) Turtleback Bks.

Springer, Nancy. Toughing It. 1994. 144p. (YA). (gr. 7 up). 10.95 (*0-15-200008-9*) Harcourt Children's Bks.

—Toughing It. 1994. 144p. (YA). (gr. 7 up). pap. 4.95 o.s.i (*0-15-200011-9*) Harcourt Trade Pubs.

—Toughing It. 1994. 11.00 (*0-606-08680-3*) Turtleback Bks.

St. John, Patricia. Treasures of the Snow. 2002. 64p. 12.99 (*0-8024-1418-4*) Moody Pr.

Stahl, Hilda. Kathy's New Brother. 1992. (Best Friends Ser.: Vol. 6). 160p. (J). (gr. 4-7). pap. 4.99 o.p. (*0-89107-682-4*) Crossway Bks.

—Roxie's Mall Madness. 1993. (Best Friends Ser.: Vol. 15). 160p. (J). (gr. 4-7). pap. 4.99 (*0-89107-753-7*) Crossway Bks.

Stark, Ken, illus. Oh, Brother! 2003. 32p. (J). 15.99 (*0-399-23766-6*) Putnam Publishing Group, The.

Steig, William. The Toy Brother. (Trophy Picture Book Ser.). (Illus.). 32p. 1998. (J). (ps-3). pap. 7.99 (*0-06-205927-0*, Harper Trophy); 1996. (YA). (gr. 2 up). lib. bdg. 14.89 o.p. (*0-06-205079-6*); 1996. (YA). (gr. 2 up). 14.95 o.p. (*0-06-205078-8*) HarperCollins Children's Bk. Group.

—The Toy Brother. 1998. (Trophy Picture Bks.). (J). 12.10 (*0-606-13054-3*) Turtleback Bks.

Stein, Aidel. The Do-Gooders. 1994. (Baker's Dozen Ser.: No. 11). 162p. (J). (gr. 6-8). pap. 8.95 o.p. (*1-56871-049-6*) Targum Pr., Inc.

Steptoe, John L. Baby Says. 1988. (Illus.). 32p. (J). (ps). 15.00 o.p. (*0-688-07423-5*); lib. bdg. 16.89 (*0-688-07424-3*) HarperCollins Children's Bk. Group.

—Baby Says. ALC Staff, ed. 1992. (Illus.). 28p. (J). (ps up). pap. 3.95 o.p. (*0-688-11855-0*, Morrow, William & Co.) Morrow/Avon.

Stevenson, James. Worse Than Willy! 1984. (Illus.). 32p. (J). (gr. k-3). 11.95 o.p. (*0-688-02596-X*); 11.88 o.s.i (*0-688-02597-8*) HarperCollins Children's Bk. Group. (Greenwillow Bks.).

Stevenson, Sucie. Do I Have to Take Violet? 1992. (Illus.). 32p. (J). (ps-3). pap. 3.99 o.s.i (*0-440-40682-X*, Yearling) Random Hse. Children's Bks.

Stimson, Joan. Big Panda, Little Panda. 1994. (Illus.). 32p. (J). (ps-2). 12.95 o.p. (*0-8120-6404-6*); pap. 5.95 o.p. (*0-8120-1691-2*) Barron's Educational Series, Inc.

—Big Panda, Little Panda. 1994. (J). 10.15 o.p. (*0-606-06230-0*) Turtleback Bks.

Stoehr, Shelley. Wannabe. 1997. 176p. (YA). (gr. 9 up). 15.95 o.s.i (*0-385-32223-2*, Dell Books for Young Readers) Random Hse. Children's Bks.

Stonesifer, Gertrude. Sister & Me. 2003. (Illus.). 98p. pap. 7.95 (*1-878044-62-1*) Mayhaven Publishing.

Strasser, Todd. Help! I'm Trapped in My Sister's Body! 1997. (Help! I'm Trapped Ser.). (J). (gr. 4-7). mass mkt. 4.50 (*0-590-92167-3*, Scholastic Paperbacks) Scholastic, Inc.

—Help! I'm Trapped in My Sister's Body! 1997. (Help! I'm Trapped Ser.). (J). (gr. 4-7). 10.55 (*0-606-11454-8*) Turtleback Bks.

Strauch, Eileen W. Hey You, Sister Rose. 1993. 160p. (J). (gr. 3 up). 13.00 o.p. (*0-688-11829-1*, Morrow, William & Co.) Morrow/Avon.

Streatfeild, Noel. Gemma & Sisters. 1986. (Orig.). (J). (gr. k-6). pap. 3.25 o.s.i (*0-440-42862-9*, Yearling) Random Hse. Children's Bks.

Stren, Patti. For Sale: One Brother. 1993. (Illus.). 32p. (J). (gr. k-4). 13.95 o.s.i (*1-56282-126-1*); lib. bdg. 13.89 o.s.i (*1-56282-127-X*) Hyperion Bks. for Children.

Stretton, Hesba. Little Meg's Children. 2000. (Golden Inheritance Ser.: Vol. 5). (Illus.). 88p. (J). pap. 7.90 (*0-921100-92-2*) Inheritance Pubns.

—Lost Gip. 2003. (Golden Inheritance Ser.: Vol. 7). (Illus.). 121p. (J). (*0-921100-93-0*) Inheritance Pubns.

—Pilgrim Street. 1996. (Golden Inheritance Ser.). (J). 7.90 (*0-921100-91-4*) Inheritance Pubns.

Strickland, Michael R. Haircuts at Sleepy Sam's. 2003. (Illus.). 32p. (J). (ps-3). 15.95 (*1-56397-562-9*) Boyds Mills Pr.

Strub, Susanne. My Dog, My Sister, & I (Mon Chien, Ma Soeur, et Moi) 1993. (ENG & FRE., Illus.). 32p. (J). (ps up). 14.00 o.p. (*0-688-12010-5*); lib. bdg. 13.93 o.p. (*0-688-12011-3*) Morrow/Avon. (Morrow, William & Co.).

Stuart, Jon, illus. Tom, Ally, & the New Baby. 2001. (It's OK! Ser.). 32p. (J). (ps-k). pap. 12.95 (*0-7894-7431-X*, D K Ink) Dorling Kindersley Publishing, Inc.

Sturges, Philemon. I Love School! 2004. (J). (*0-06-009284-X*); lib. bdg. (*0-06-009285-8*) HarperCollins Pubs.

Stuve-Bodeen, Stephanie. Mama Elizabeti. 2000. (Illus.). 32p. (J). (ps up). 12.76 (*1-58430-002-7*) Lee & Low Bks., Inc.

—We'll Paint the Octopus Red. 1998. (Illus.). 25p. (J). (ps-2). 14.95 (*1-890627-06-2*) Woodbine Hse.

Sullivan, Silky. Henry & Melinda. 1982. (Henry & Melinda Sports Stories Ser). (Illus.). 32p. (J). (gr. k-4). pap. 2.50 o.p. (*0-516-41916-1*); lib. bdg. 10.35 o.p. (*0-516-01916-3*) Scholastic Library Publishing. (Children's Pr.).

Supraner, Robyn. It's Not Fair! 1976. (Illus.). (J). (ps-3). 6.95 o.p. (*0-7232-6133-4*, Warne, Frederick) Penguin Putnam Bks. for Young Readers.

Susi, Geraldine Lee. Looking for Pa: A Civil War Journey from Catlett to Manassas, 1861. 2nd ed. 2001. (Illus.). 127p. (J). (gr. 4-7). pap. 10.95 (*1-880664-33-X*) E. M. Productions.

—Looking for Pa: A Civil War Journey from Catlett to Manassas, 1861. 1995. (Illus.). 128p. (J). (gr. 5-7). pap. 9.95 (*0-939009-87-0*, EPM Pubns.) Howell Pr.

Sutton, Esther. Growing Up. (B. Y. Times Kid Sisters Ser.: No. 7). 136p. (Orig.). (J). (gr. 4-7). pap. 7.95 o.p. (*1-56871-035-6*) Targum Pr., Inc.

Suzanne, Jamie. Big Brother's in Love. 1992. (Sweet Valley Twins Ser.: No. 57). (J). (gr. 3-7). pap. o.s.i (*0-553-54051-3*, Dell Books for Young Readers) Random Hse. Children's Bks.

—Pumpkin Fever. 1997. (Sweet Valley Twins Ser.: No. 110). 144p. (Orig.). (gr. 3-7). pap. text 3.50 o.s.i (*0-553-48441-9*, Dell Books for Young Readers) Random Hse. Children's Bks.

Sweeney, Jacqueline. Lou Goes Too! 1999. (We Can Read! Ser.). (Illus.). 32p. (J). (gr. 1-2). lib. bdg. 21.36 (*0-7614-0921-1*, Benchmark Bks.) Cavendish, Marshall Corp.

—What about Bettie? 2000. (We Can Read! Ser.). (Illus.). 32p. (J). (gr. 1-2). lib. bdg. 21.36 (*0-7614-1118-6*, Benchmark Bks.) Cavendish, Marshall Corp.

Sweeney, Joyce. Free Fall. 1996. 240p. (YA). 15.95 (*0-385-32211-9*, Delacorte Pr.) Dell Publishing.

Swindells, Robert. Fallout. ALC Staff, ed. 1992. 160p. (J). (gr. 7 up). pap. 3.95 o.p. (*0-688-11778-3*, Morrow, William & Co.) Morrow/Avon.

—Hermano en la Tierra. Dominguez, Catalina, tr. 1994. Tr. of Brother in the Land. (SPA., Illus.). (YA). 6.99 (*968-16-4590-1*) Fondo de Cultura Economica MEX. *Dist:* Continental Bk. Co., Inc.

Sykes, Julie. Wait for Me, Little Tiger! 2001. (Illus.). 32p. (J). (ps-k). tchr. ed. 14.95 (*1-58925-009-5*, Tiger Tales) ME Media LLC.

Szekeres, Cyndy. Toby's New Brother. 2000. (Toby Ser.: Vol. 8). (Illus.). 32p. (J). (ps-k). 6.99 o.s.i (*0-689-82651-6*, Little Simon) Simon & Schuster Children's Publishing.

Tada, Joni Eareckson. Ryan & the Circus Wheels. 1988. 32p. (J). (ps-1). 8.99 o.p. (*1-55513-154-9*) Cook Communications Ministries.

Taggart, Misty. Sister, Stay Out! 1994. (Angel Academy Ser.: Vol. 2). (Illus.). 32p. (J). (ps-3). pap. 3.99 o.p. (*0-8499-5017-1*) Nelson, Tommy.

Tamar, Erika. Alphabet City Ballet. 176p. (J). (gr. 3-7). 1996. lib. bdg. 14.89 o.p. (*0-06-027329-1*); 1996. 14.95 o.p. (*0-06-027328-3*); 1997. (Illus.). reprint ed. pap. 5.99 (*0-06-440668-7*, Harper Trophy) HarperCollins Children's Bk. Group.

—Alphabet City Ballet. 1997. (J). 11.00 (*0-606-11032-1*) Turtleback Bks.

—The Midnight Train Home. 2000. (Illus.). 208p. (YA). (gr. 5-8). lib. bdg. 18.99 (*0-375-90159-0*, Knopf Bks. for Young Readers) Random Hse. Children's Bks.

Tang, Charles, illus. The Basketball Mystery. 1999. (Boxcar Children Ser.: No. 68). 128p. (J). (gr. 2-5). pap. 3.95 (*0-8075-0576-5*) Whitman, Albert & Co.

—The Chocolate Sundae Mystery. 1995. (Boxcar Children Ser.: No. 46). 120p. (J). (gr. 2-5). pap. 3.95 (*0-8075-1145-5*); lib. bdg. 13.95 (*0-8075-1146-3*) Whitman, Albert & Co.

—The Mystery in New York. 1999. (Boxcar Children Special Ser.: No. 13). 121p. (J). (gr. 2-5). lib. bdg. 13.95 (*0-8075-5459-6*); mass mkt. 3.95 (*0-8075-5460-X*) Whitman, Albert & Co.

—The Mystery in the Cave. 1996. (Boxcar Children Ser.: No. 50). (J). (gr. 2-5). lib. bdg. 13.95 (*0-8075-5411-1*) Whitman, Albert & Co.

—The Mystery of the Empty Safe. 2000. (Boxcar Children Ser.: No. 75). (J). (gr. 2-5). 10.00 (*0-606-18768-5*) Turtleback Bks.

—The Mystery of the Empty Safe. 2000. (Boxcar Children Ser.: No. 75). 120p. (J). (gr. 2-5). mass mkt. 3.95 (*0-8075-5463-4*) Whitman, Albert & Co.

—The Mystery of the Stolen Music. 1995. (Boxcar Children Ser.: No. 45). 118p. (J). (gr. 2-5). lib. bdg. 13.95 (*0-8075-5415-4*); mass mkt. 3.95 (*0-8075-5416-2*) Whitman, Albert & Co.

Tapp, Kathy K. Den Four Meets the Jinx. 1988. 128p. (J). (gr. 3-6). lib. bdg. 12.95 o.s.i (*0-689-50453-5*, McElderry, Margaret K.) Simon & Schuster Children's Publishing.

Tashjian, Janet. Tru Confessions, ERS. 1997. 161p. (J). (gr. 4-7). 15.95 (*0-8050-5254-2*, Holt, Henry & Co. Bks. For Young Readers) Holt, Henry & Co.

—Tru Confessions. 1999. (J). mass mkt. 4.99 (*0-590-96047-4*) Scholastic, Inc.

—Tru Confessions. 1999. 11.04 (*0-606-16611-4*) Turtleback Bks.

Tatham, Sara. Because of Thomas. 1995. (Light Line Ser.). 132p. (YA). (gr. 7 up). pap. 6.49 (*0-89084-794-0*, 083824) Jones, Bob Univ. Pr.

Taylor, Bonnie Highsmith. Simon Can't Say Hippopotamus. Hornung, Phyllis, tr. & illus. by. 2003. 24p. (J). 14.95 (*1-59336-017-7*); pap. (*1-59336-018-5*) Mondo Publishing.

Tea, Joyce W. The Point System. 1998. (Illus.). (J). pap. (*1-56763-399-4*) Ozark Publishing.

Teal, Joyce W. The Point System. 1998. (Illus.). (J). lib. bdg. 25.25 (*1-56763-398-6*) Ozark Publishing.

Telesco, Patricia. Brother Wind, Sister Rain. 1996. (Illus.). 96p. (Orig.). (J). (gr. 1-7). pap. 9.95 (*1-880090-32-5*) Galde Pr., Inc.

Terris, Susan. The Latchkey Kids, RS. 1986. 167p. (J). (gr. 7 up). 15.00 o.p. (*0-374-34363-2*, Farrar, Straus & Giroux (BYR)) Farrar, Straus & Giroux.

—No Boys Allowed. 1976. 48p. (gr. 1-5). 5.95 o.p. (*0-385-04887-4*); lib. bdg. o.p. (*0-385-05749-0*) Doubleday Publishing.

Testa, Maria. Thumbs Up, Rico! 1994. (Illus.). 40p. (J). (gr. 4-7). lib. bdg. 14.95 (*0-8075-7906-8*) Whitman, Albert & Co.

Tester, Sylvia R. Feeling Angry. 1976. (Values to Live By Ser.). (Illus.). (J). (ps-3). 5.95 o.p. (*0-913778-49-4*) Child's World, Inc.

Thaler, Mike. Bully Brothers. 1996. (Illus.). (J). (gr. k-3). mass mkt. 3.50 (*0-590-47802-8*) Scholastic, Inc.

—The Bully Brothers: Gobblin' Halloween. 1993. (All Aboard Bks.). (Illus.). 32p. (J). (ps-3). 2.25 o.p. (*0-448-40158-4*, Grosset & Dunlap) Penguin Putnam Bks. for Young Readers.

Thesman, Jean. Between. 2002. 224p. (J). (gr. 5-7). 15.99 (*0-670-03561-0*) Penguin Putnam Bks. for Young Readers.

Thomas, Jane Resh. Elizabeth Catches a Fish, 001. 1979. (Illus.). (J). (gr. 1-4). 6.95 o.p. (*0-395-28827-4*, Clarion Bks.) Houghton Mifflin Co. Trade & Reference Div.

Thomas, Pat. My Brother, My Sister & Me: A First Look at Sibling Rivalry. 2000. (First Look at Bks.). (Illus.). 29p. (J). (ps-3). pap. 5.95 o.p. (*0-7641-1460-3*) Barron's Educational Series, Inc.

Thompson, Julian F. Brothers. 2000. (Illus.). 224p. (YA). (gr. 7 up). mass mkt. 4.99 o.s.i (*0-375-80353-X*, Knopf Bks. for Young Readers) Random Hse. Children's Bks.

Thompson, Mary. Andy & His Yellow Frisbee. 1996. (Illus.). 19p. (J). (gr. k-5). 14.95 (*0-933149-83-2*) Woodbine Hse.

—My Brother, Matthew. 1992. (Illus.). 26p. (J). (gr. k-5). 14.95 (*0-933149-47-6*) Woodbine Hse.

Three Sisters. 1997. (Scheherezade Children's Stories Ser.). (Illus.). 16p. (J). (*1-873938-80-2*, Ithaca Pr.) Garnet Publishing, Ltd.

Tierney, Hanne. Where's Your Baby Brother, Becky Bunting? 1979. (gr. 1-3). 7.95 o.p. (*0-385-08653-9*); lib. bdg. o.p. (*0-385-08654-7*) Doubleday Publishing.

Tolan, Stephanie S. Who's There? 1994. 192p. (YA). (gr. 7 up). 15.00 (*0-688-04611-8*) HarperCollins Children's Bk. Group.

—Who's There? 1997. 240p. (gr. 5-9). mass mkt. 4.95 (*0-688-15289-9*, Morrow, William & Co.) Morrow/Avon.

Tomaszewski, Blanche L. The Not-So-Scary Night. 1997. (J). (*1-56763-316-1*); pap. 4.95 (*1-56763-317-X*) Ozark Publishing.

Tomioka, Chiyoko. Rise & Shine, Mariko-Chan! 1992. (Illus.). 32p. (J). (ps-1). pap. 3.95 (*0-590-45507-9*) Scholastic, Inc.

—Rise & Shine, Mariko-Chan! 1992. (J). 10.19 o.p. (*0-606-01931-6*) Turtleback Bks.

Topek, Susan R. A Costume for Noah: A Purim Story. (Illus.). 24p. (J). (ps-1). 1996. 13.95 (*0-929371-91-7*); 1995. pap. 5.95 (*0-929371-90-9*) Kar-Ben Publishing.

Torrey, Michele. Voyage of Ice. 2004. (J). (gr. 5). 192p. 15.95 (*0-375-82381-6*); 208p. lib. bdg. 17.99 (*0-375-92381-0*) Random Hse. Children's Bks. (Knopf Bks. for Young Readers).

Tripp, Valerie. Molly's Puppy Tale. 2003. (American Girls Collection). (Illus.). 40p. (J). pap. 4.95 (*1-58485-695-5*, American Girl) Pleasant Co. Pubns.

Tsutsui, Yoriko. Anna in Charge. 1989. (Illus.). 320p. (J). (ps-1). 11.95 o.p. (*0-670-81672-8*, Viking Children's Bks.) Penguin Putnam Bks. for Young Readers.

—Anna's Special Present. 1990. (Illus.). 32p. (J). (ps-3). pap. 3.95 o.s.i (*0-14-054219-1*, Puffin Bks.) Penguin Putnam Bks. for Young Readers.

Turner, Barbara. Treasure in Ghost Town. 2001. 126p. (J). pap. 11.95 (*1-55517-540-6*, Bonneville Bks.) Cedar Fort, Inc./CFI Distribution.

Turner, Barbara J. A Little Bit of Rob. 1996. (Illus.). 32p. (J). (ps-3). lib. bdg. 14.95 (*0-8075-4577-5*) Whitman, Albert & Co.

Tyler, Linda W. My Brother Oscar Thinks He Knows It All. 1991. (Illus.). 320p. (J). (ps-3). pap. 3.95 o.p. (*0-14-050947-X*, Puffin Bks.) Penguin Putnam Bks. for Young Readers.

Tyrrell, Melissa. Hansel & Gretel. 2001. (Fairytale Friends Ser.). (Illus.). 12p. (J). bds. 5.95 (*1-58117-152-8*, Piggy Toes Pr.) Intervisual Bks., Inc.

Udry, Janice May. Thump & Plunk. 1981. (My First I Can Read Bks.). (Illus.). 32p. (J). (ps-k). 14.00 (*0-06-026149-8*) HarperCollins Children's Bk. Group.

—Thump & Plunk. 2001. (Illus.). (J). 10.10 (*0-606-20479-2*) Turtleback Bks.

Ungerer, Tomi. Christmas Eve at the Mellops' 1998. (Illus.). 32p. (J). (gr. k-4). pap. 5.95 (*1-57098-227-9*) Rinehart, Roberts Pubs.

Van der Meer, Ron & Van der Meer, Atie. My Brother Sammy. 1980. (Illus.). 32p. o.p. (*0-241-10053-4*) David & Charles Pubs.

Van Draanen, Wendelin. How I Survived Being a Girl. 1997. (J). 176p. (gr. k-3). 15.99 (*0-06-026671-6*); 80p. (gr. 3-7). lib. bdg. 14.89 o.p. (*0-06-026672-4*) HarperCollins Children's Bk. Group.

Van Leeuwen, Jean. Oliver & Amanda & the Big Snow. 1995. (Dial Easy-to-Read Ser.). (Illus.). 48p. (J). (gr. k-3). 13.99 o.p. (*0-8037-1762-8*); 12.89 o.s.i (*0-8037-1763-6*) Penguin Putnam Bks. for Young Readers. (Dial Bks. for Young Readers).

—Oliver & Amanda & the Big Snow. 1998. 10.14 (*0-606-18439-2*) Turtleback Bks.

—Oliver & Amanda's Halloween. 1992. (Dial Easy-to-Read Ser.). (Illus.). 48p. (J). (ps-3). 14.99 (*0-8037-1237-5*); 10.89 o.p. (*0-8037-1238-3*) Penguin Putnam Bks. for Young Readers. (Dial Bks. for Young Readers).

—Too Hot for Ice Cream. (Illus.). 40p. (J). (ps-3). 1985. 5.47 o.p. (*0-8037-6077-9*); 1974. 5.95 o.p. (*0-8037-6076-0*) Penguin Putnam Bks. for Young Readers. (Dial Bks. for Young Readers).

Van Stockum, Hilda. Friendly Gables. 1996. (Mitchells Ser.: Vol. 3). (Illus.). 192p. (J). (gr. 4-7). pap. 11.95 o.p. (*1-883937-19-1*, 19-1) Bethlehem Bks.

Vanasse, Debra. Out of the Wilderness. 1999. 176p. (J). (gr. 5-9). tchr. ed. 15.00 (*0-395-91421-3*, Clarion Bks.) Houghton Mifflin Co. Trade & Reference Div.

Vande Velde, Vivian. There's a Dead Person Following My Sister Around. 2001. 160p. (J). pap. 4.99 (*0-14-131281-5*, Puffin Bks.) Penguin Putnam Bks. for Young Readers.

Venezia, Mike. How to Be an Older Brother or Sister. 1986. (Childhood Fantasies & Fears Ser.). (Illus.). 32p. (J). (ps-3). pap. 3.95 o.p. (*0-516-43494-2*); mass mkt. 15.50 o.p. (*0-516-03494-4*) Scholastic Library Publishing. (Children's Pr.).

Vigna, Judith. Couldn't We Have a Turtle Instead. 1975. (Self-Starter Bks.). 32p. (J). (gr. k-2). lib. bdg. 8.75 o.p. (*0-8075-1312-1*) Whitman, Albert & Co.

Vigor, John. Danger, Dolphins & Ginger Beer. 1993. (Illus.). 192p. (J). (gr. 3-7). 16.00 o.p. (*0-689-31817-0*, Atheneum) Simon & Schuster Children's Publishing.

Viorst, Judith. I'll Fix Anthony. 1969. (Illus.). (J). (ps-3). 14.00 o.s.i (*0-06-026306-7*); lib. bdg. 14.89 o.s.i (*0-06-026307-5*) HarperCollins Children's Bk. Group.

—Sunday Morning. 2nd ed. (Illus.). 32p. (J). (ps-3). 1992. 16.95 (*0-689-31794-8*, Atheneum); 1993. reprint ed. pap. 4.99 (*0-689-71702-4*, Aladdin) Simon & Schuster Children's Publishing.

Voigt, Cynthia. Dicey's Song. 1987. 224p. (gr. 7-12). mass mkt. 5.99 o.s.i (*0-449-70276-6*, Fawcett) Ballantine Bks.

—Dicey's Song. l.t. ed. 1990. 334p. (J). reprint ed. lib. bdg. 16.95 o.s.i (*1-55736-166-5*, Cornerstone Bks.) Pages, Inc.

—Dicey's Song. 1997. (Pathways to Critical Thinking Ser.). 32p. (YA). (gr. 9-12). pap. text, stu. ed., tchr.'s training gde. ed. 19.95 (*1-58303-024-7*) Pathways Publishing.

—Dicey's Song. 2003. (Tillerman Ser.). (Illus.). 368p. (J). pap. 5.99 (*0-689-86362-4*, Aladdin); 2002. (Tillerman Saga: Bk. 2). 368p. (YA). (gr. 7 up). mass mkt. 5.99 (*0-689-85131-6*, Simon Pulse); 2001. 204p. (J). E-Book 6.99 (*0-689-84798-X*, Atheneum); 1982. (Tillerman Saga: Bk. 2). 204p. (YA). (gr. 7 up). 17.95 (*0-689-30944-9*, Atheneum) Simon & Schuster Children's Publishing.

—Dicey's Song. 1982. (J). 12.04 (*0-606-03279-7*) Turtleback Bks.

—The Vandemark Mummy. 1992. 224p. (gr. 7 up). mass mkt. 4.50 o.s.i (*0-449-70417-3*, Fawcett) Ballantine Bks.

Relationships

—Max's Dragon Shirt. 1991. (Max & Ruby Ser.). (Illus.). 32p. (J). (gr. k-2). 14.99 o.p. (*0-8037-0944-7*); 10.89 o.p. (*0-8037-0945-5*) Penguin Putnam Bks. for Young Readers. (Dial Bks. for Young Readers).

—Max's First Word. 1998. (Max & Ruby Ser.). (Illus.). 12p. (J). (gr. k-2). bds. 5.99 o.s.i (*0-8037-2269-9*, Dial Bks. for Young Readers) Penguin Putnam Bks. for Young Readers.

—Max's New Suit. 1998. (Max & Ruby Ser.). (Illus.). 12p. (J). (gr. k-2). bds. 5.99 o.p. (*0-8037-2270-2*, Dial Bks. for Young Readers) Penguin Putnam Bks. for Young Readers.

—Max's Ride. 1998. (Max & Ruby Ser.). (Illus.). 12p. (J). (gr. k-2). bds. 5.99 o.s.i (*0-8037-2272-9*, Dial Bks. for Young Readers) Penguin Putnam Bks. for Young Readers.

—Max's Toys: A Counting Book. 1998. (Max & Ruby Ser.). (Illus.). 12p. (J). (gr. k-2). bds. 5.99 o.p. (*0-8037-2271-0*, Dial Bks. for Young Readers) Penguin Putnam Bks. for Young Readers.

—Ruby's Beauty Shop. 2002. (Max & Ruby Ser.). (Illus.). 32p. (J). (ps-3). 15.99 (*0-670-03553-X*, Viking Children's Bks.) Penguin Putnam Bks. for Young Readers.

—Waiting for the Evening Star. 1993. (Illus.). (J). (gr. k-3). 400p. 15.00 o.s.i (*0-8037-1398-3*); 32p. 14.89 o.p. (*0-8037-1399-1*) Penguin Putnam Bks. for Young Readers. (Dial Bks. for Young Readers).

Weninger, Brigitte, pseud. A Baby for Davy. 2002. (Illus.). 16p. (J). (ps). bds. 6.95 (*0-7358-1746-4*, Michael Neugebauer Bks.) North-South Bks., Inc.

—Dany, Quieres Cuidar a Tu Hermanita? Acevedo, Pilar, tr. 2000. (SPA., Illus.). 32p. (J). (gr. k-3). 15.95 (*0-7358-1310-8*); pap. 6.95 (*0-7358-1311-6*) North-South Bks., Inc.

—Davy, Help! It's a Ghost! James, J. Alison, tr. from GER. 2002. (Illus.). 32p. (J). 15.95 (*0-7358-1687-5*); lib. bdg. 16.50 (*0-7358-1688-3*) North-South Bks., Inc.

—Une Petite Soeur pour Fenouil. 1998. Tr. of Will You Mind the Baby, Davy?. (FRE., Illus.). (J). (gr. k-3). 15.95 (*3-314-21063-9*) North-South Bks., Inc.

—Una Sorellina Per Paolino. 1998. Tr. of Will You Mind the Baby, Davy?. (ITA., Illus.). (J). (gr. k-3). 15.95 (*88-8203-036-9*) North-South Bks., Inc.

—Will You Mind the Baby, Davy? (Illus.). (J). (gr. k-3). 2000. 32p. pap. 6.95 o.s.i (*0-7358-1309-4*); 1998. (JPN., 15.95 (*4-06-261976-8*) North-South Bks., Inc.

—Will You Mind the Baby, Davy? Lanning, Rosemary, tr. from GER. 1997. (Illus.). 32p. (J). (gr. k-3). 15.95 o.s.i (*1-55858-731-4*); 16.50 (*1-55858-732-2*) North-South Bks., Inc.

Wersba, Barbara. You'll Never Guess the End. 1992. (Charlotte Zolotow Bk.). 144p. (YA). (gr. 7 up). 14.00 (*0-06-020448-6*); lib. bdg. 13.89 o.p. (*0-06-020449-4*) HarperCollins Children's Bk. Group.

West, Kipling. A Rattle of Bones: A Halloween Book of Collective Nouns. 1999. (Illus.). 32p. (J). (ps-1). pap. 15.95 (*0-531-30196-6*, Orchard Bks.) Scholastic, Inc.

West, Tracey. Fire in the Valley. 1993. (Stories of the States Ser.). 80p. (J). (gr. 4-7). lib. bdg. 14.95 (*1-881889-32-7*) Silver Moon Pr.

Westall, Robert. Gulf. 1996. 96p. (YA). (gr. 5 up). pap. 14.95 (*0-590-22218-X*) Scholastic, Inc.

Weston, Carol. Melanie Martin Goes Dutch: The Private Diary of My Almost Bummer Summer with Cecily, Matt the Brat, & Vincent van Go Go Go. 2002. (Illus.). 240p. (J). (gr. 3-7). 15.95 (*0-375-82195-3*); lib. bdg. 17.99 (*0-375-92195-8*) Knopf, Alfred A. Inc.

—Melanie Martin Goes Dutch: The Private Diary of My Almost Bummer Summer with Cecily, Matt the Brat, & Vincent van Go Go Go. 2003. (Illus.). 240p. (J). (gr. 3-7). pap. 4.99 (*0-440-41899-2*, Yearling) Random Hse. Children's Bks.

Weston, Martha. Bad Baby Brother. 1997. (Illus.). 32p. (J). (ps-1). tchr. ed. 14.95 o.s.i (*0-395-72103-2*, Clarion Bks.) Houghton Mifflin Co. Trade & Reference Div.

—Tuck's Haunted House. 2002. (Illus.). 32p. (J). (gr. k-2). lib. bdg., tchr. ed. 14.00 (*0-618-15966-5*, Clarion Bks.) Houghton Mifflin Co. Trade & Reference Div.

Whelan, Gloria. The Impossible Journey. 2004. 256p. (J). pap. 5.99 (*0-06-441083-8*, Harper Trophy) HarperCollins Children's Bk. Group.

—The Impossible Journey. 2003. 256p. (J). (gr. 5 up). 15.99 (*0-06-623811-0*); lib. bdg. 16.89 (*0-06-623812-9*) HarperCollins Pubs.

Whitaker, Alexander. Dream Sister, 001. 1986. (J). (gr. 5 up). pap. 12.95 o.p. (*0-395-39377-9*) Houghton Mifflin Co.

—Dream Sister. 1989. 160p. (J). (gr. k-6). reprint ed. pap. 2.95 o.s.i (*0-440-40156-9*, Yearling) Random Hse. Children's Bks.

White, Ellen Emerson. Where Have All the Flowers Gone? The Diary of Molly Mackenzie Flaherty, Boston, Massachusetts, 1968. 2002. (Dear America Ser.). (Illus.). 176p. (J). (gr. 4-9). pap. 10.95 (*0-439-14889-8*, Scholastic Pr.) Scholastic, Inc.

Whitethorne, Baje, Sr. Father's Boots: Azhe'e bikenidoots'osii. Marvin, Yellowhair & Jerrold, Johnson, eds. Darlene, Redhair, tr. 2001. (ENG & NAV., Illus.). 42p. (J). (gr. 1-6). text 17.95 (*1-893354-29-6*) Salina Bookshelf.

Whybrow, Ian. Harry & the Snow King. 1999. (Illus.). 32p. (J). (ps-1). pap. 6.95 (*1-86233-032-8*) Gullane Children's Bks. GBR. *Dist:* Sterling Publishing Co., Inc.

—Harry & the Snow King Book & Plush Set. 1999. (Illus.). 32p. (J). (ps-2). pap. 19.95 (*1-86233-132-4*) David & Charles Children's Bks. GBR. *Dist:* Sterling Publishing Co., Inc.

—Little Wolf's Diary of Daring Deeds. (Illus.). (J). 2003. pap. 6.95 (*0-87614-536-5*); 2000. 132p. (gr. 3-6). lib. bdg. 12.95 (*1-57505-411-6*) Lerner Publishing Group. (Carolrhoda Bks.).

Whybrow, Ian & Reynolds, Adrian. Harry & the Snow King. 1998. (Illus.). 32p. (J). (ps-3). 14.95 (*1-899607-85-4*) Sterling Publishing Co., Inc.

Wiesner, David. Hurricane. 1990. (Illus.). 32p. (J). (ps-3). lib. bdg., tchr. ed. 16.00 (*0-395-54382-7*, Clarion Bks.) Houghton Mifflin Co. Trade & Reference Div.

Wiggins, Darius. The Sword of Tobago. 2000. (Justin's & Kevin's Great Backyard Adventures Ser.). (Illus.). 57p. (J). (gr. 2-5). 12.95 (*1-58141-018-2*) Rivercross Publishing, Inc.

Wilde, Nicholas. The Eye of the Storm. 1996. (J). 288p. (gr. 4-7). pap. 4.95 o.p. (*0-8120-9708-4*); 12.95 o.p. (*0-8120-6601-4*) Barron's Educational Series, Inc.

—The Eye of the Storm. 1996. 10.05 o.p. (*0-606-11307-X*) Turtleback Bks.

Wilder, Laura Ingalls. Little House Sisters: Collected Stories from the Little House Books. 1997. (Little House Ser.). (Illus.). 96p. (J). (gr. 3-6). lib. bdg. 19.89 o.p. (*0-06-027670-3*) HarperCollins Pubs.

Wilkes, Maria D. Caroline & Her Sister. 2000. (Little House Chapter Bks.: No. 2). (Illus.). 80p. (J). (gr. 3-6). pap. 4.25 (*0-06-442092-2*, Harper Trophy); lib. bdg. 14.89 (*0-06-028155-3*) HarperCollins Children's Bk. Group.

—Caroline & Her Sister. 2000. (Little House Chapter Bks.: No. 2). (J). (gr. 3-6). 10.40 (*0-606-20285-4*) Turtleback Bks.

Willey, Margaret. Facing the Music. 1997. 192p. (YA). (gr. 7 up). mass mkt. 3.99 o.s.i (*0-440-22680-5*) Dell Publishing.

—Facing the Music. 1996. 256p. (YA). (gr. 7 up). 14.95 o.p. (*0-385-32104-X*, Dell Books for Young Readers) Random Hse. Children's Bks.

—Facing the Music. 1997. 10.04 (*0-606-11310-X*) Turtleback Bks.

Williams, Barbara. Jeremy Isn't Hungry. 1989. (Unicorn Paperbacks Ser.). (Illus.). (J). (ps-1). 4p. 10.95 o.p. (*0-525-32760-6*); 32p. 3.95 o.p. (*0-525-44536-6*) Penguin Putnam Bks. for Young Readers. (Dutton Children's Bks.).

—Mitzi & Frederick the Great. 1984. (Illus.). 128p. (J). (gr. 2-4). 9.95 o.p. (*0-525-44099-2*, Dutton Children's Bks.) Penguin Putnam Bks. for Young Readers.

—Mitzi & the Terrible Tyrannosaurus Rex. 1982. (Illus.). 112p. (J). (gr. 2-4). 10.95 o.p. (*0-525-45105-6*, 0966-290, Dutton) Dutton/Plume.

—Mitzi & the Terrible Tyrannosaurus Rex. 1983. (Illus.). 112p. (J). (gr. 3-7). pap. 1.95 o.s.i (*0-440-45673-8*, Yearling) Random Hse. Children's Bks.

—Titanic Crossing. 1995. 176p. (J). (gr. 4-7). 15.99 o.s.i (*0-8037-1790-3*); 15.89 o.p. (*0-8037-1791-1*) Penguin Putnam Bks. for Young Readers. (Dial Bks. for Young Readers).

—Titanic Crossing. 1997. 167p. (J). (gr. 3-7). mass mkt. 4.50 (*0-590-94464-9*) Scholastic, Inc.

—Titanic Crossing. 1997. 10.55 (*0-606-12829-8*) Turtleback Bks.

Williams, Carol Lynch. Laurel's Flight. 1995. (Latter-Day Daughters Ser.). (Illus.). 80p. (J). pap. 4.95 (*1-56236-502-9*) Aspen Bks.

—The True Colors of Caitlynne Jackson. 1998. 176p. (gr. 5-9). pap. text 4.50 o.s.i (*0-440-41235-8*, Yearling) Random Hse. Children's Bks.

—The True Colors of Caitlynne Jackson. 1998. (J). 10.55 (*0-606-13873-0*) Turtleback Bks.

Williams, Jeanne. To Buy a Dream. 2001. 164p. pap. 11.95 (*0-595-16527-3*, Backinprint.com) iUniverse, Inc.

Williams, Karen L. A Real Christmas This Year. 1995. 176p. (J). (gr. 4-7). tchr. ed. 15.00 o.p. (*0-395-70117-1*) Houghton Mifflin Co.

Williams, Suzanne. Edwin & Emily. 1995. (Illus.). 48p. (J). (ps-3). 13.95 o.s.i (*0-7868-0129-8*) Hyperion Bks. for Children.

—Edwin & Emily. 1995. (Hyperion Chapters Ser.). 9.15 o.p. (*0-606-09228-5*) Turtleback Bks.

—Edwin & Emily in Winter. 1995. (Hyperion Chapters Ser.). (Illus.). 48p. (J). (gr. 1-3). pap. 3.95 o.s.i (*0-7868-1065-3*) Disney Pr.

Williams, Vera. Amber Was Brave, Essie Was Smart: The Story of Amber & Essie Told Here in Poems & Pictures. 2004. 72p. (J). pap. 6.99 (*0-06-057182-9*, Harper Trophy) HarperCollins Children's Bk. Group.

Willis, Meredith S. Marco's Monster. 1996. (J). (gr. 3-7). 128p. lib. bdg. 13.89 o.p. (*0-06-027196-5*); (Illus.). 80p. 13.95 o.p. (*0-06-027195-7*) HarperCollins Children's Bk. Group.

Wilmer, Diane. Counting. 1988. (Step by Step Bks.). (Illus.). 32p. (J). (ps). pap. 4.95 o.s.i (*0-689-71244-8*, Simon & Schuster Children's Publishing) Simon & Schuster Children's Publishing.

—Shopping. 1988. (Step by Step Bks.). (Illus.). 10p. (J). (ps). pap. 3.95 o.s.i (*0-689-71242-1*, Simon & Schuster Children's Publishing) Simon & Schuster Children's Publishing.

—There & Back Again. 1988. (Step by Step Bks.). (Illus.). 32p. (J). (ps-2). pap. 4.95 o.s.i (*0-689-71250-2*, Simon & Schuster Children's Publishing) Simon & Schuster Children's Publishing.

Wilson, Jacqueline. Lola Rose. 2004. 99p. (J). (gr. 5). pap. (*0-552-54712-3*, Corgi) Bantam Bks.

—My Brother Bernadette. 2002. (Yellow Bananas Ser.). (Illus.). 48p. (J). (gr. 3-4). pap. 4.95 (*0-7787-0986-8*); lib. bdg. 19.96 (*0-7787-0940-X*) Crabtree Publishing Co.

Wilson, Jodi L. When I Grow Up. (Illus.). 32p. (Orig.). (J). (gr. 1-3). pap. 4.95 (*0-9628335-0-9*) Wilander Publishing Co.

Wilson, Johnniece M. Oh, Brother. 128p. (J). (gr. 4-7). 1989. pap. 4.50 (*0-590-41001-6*, Scholastic Paperbacks); 1988. pap. 10.95 o.p. (*0-590-41363-5*) Scholastic, Inc.

—Oh, Brother. 1989. (J). 10.55 (*0-606-12457-8*) Turtleback Bks.

Wilson, Linda Miller. A Few Days Journey. 1998. 124p. (J). (gr. 6-9). pap. 9.99 (*0-88092-402-0*, 4020) Royal Fireworks Publishing Co.

Wilson, Nancy Hope. Bringing Nettie Back. 1994. (J). pap. 3.99 o.p. (*0-380-72256-9*, Avon Bks.) Morrow/Avon.

—Bringing Nettie Back. 1992. 9.09 o.p. (*0-606-06253-X*) Turtleback Bks.

—Flapjack Waltzes, RS. 1998. 144p. (J). (gr. 3-7). 16.00 o.p. (*0-374-32345-3*, Farrar, Straus & Giroux (BYR)) Farrar, Straus & Giroux.

Winter, Susan. I Can. 1993. (Illus.). 24p. (J). (ps-1). pap. 9.95 o.p. (*1-56458-197-7*) Dorling Kindersley Publishing, Inc.

—Me Too. 1993. (Illus.). 24p. (J). (ps-1). pap. 9.95 o.p. (*1-56458-198-5*) Dorling Kindersley Publishing, Inc.

Winthrop, Elizabeth. Bear & Roly-Poly. 1996. (Illus.). 32p. (J). (ps-3). tchr. ed. 15.95 (*0-8234-1197-4*) Holiday Hse., Inc.

—A Little Demonstration of Affection. 1975. 160p. (YA). (gr. 7 up). 7.95 o.p. (*0-06-026557-4*); lib. bdg. 11.89 o.p. (*0-06-026558-2*) HarperCollins Children's Bk. Group.

—Potbellied Possums. 1977. (Illus.). 32p. (J). (ps-3). 4.95 o.p. (*0-8234-0289-4*) Holiday Hse., Inc.

—The Red-Hot Rattoons, ERS. 2003. (Illus.). 224p. (J). 15.95 (*0-8050-7229-2*, Holt, Henry & Co. Bks. For Young Readers) Holt, Henry & Co.

Wishinsky, Frieda. Oonga Boonga, Vol. 1. 1990. (J). (ps-3). 13.95 o.p. (*0-316-94872-1*, Joy Street Bks.) Little Brown & Co.

—Oonga Boonga. (Illus.). 32p. (J). (gr. k-1). 2001. pap. 5.99 o.p. (*0-14-056840-9*); 1999. 15.99 o.s.i (*0-525-46095-0*, Dutton Children's Bks.) Penguin Putnam Bks. for Young Readers.

Wisler, G. Clifton. Jericho's Journey. 144p. (J). 1995. (gr. 4-7). pap. 5.99 (*0-14-037065-X*, Puffin Bks.); 1993. (gr. 5-9). 13.99 o.s.i (*0-525-67428-4*, Dutton Children's Bks.) Penguin Putnam Bks. for Young Readers.

—Jericho's Journey. 1995. 11.04 (*0-606-07737-5*) Turtleback Bks.

Wittman, Sally. Stepbrother Sabotage. (Trophy Bk.). (Illus.). (J). (gr. 2-5). 1991. 80p. mass mkt. 3.95 o.p. (*0-06-440408-0*, Harper Trophy); 1990. 64p. 13.95 o.p. (*0-06-026561-2*); 1990. 80p. lib. bdg. 12.89 o.p. (*0-06-026562-0*) HarperCollins Children's Bk. Group.

Wodehouse, P. G. Mike at Wrykyn. reprint ed. lib. bdg. 98.00 (*0-7426-3265-2*); 2001. pap. text 28.00 (*0-7426-8265-X*) Classic Bks.

—Mike at Wrykyn. 1998. 192p. pap. 9.95 o.s.i (*0-14-012454-3*) Penguin Group (USA) Inc.

Wolde, Gunilla. Betsy's Baby Brother. (Betsy Bks.). (ps). 1982. (Illus.). 24p. (J). 1.95 o.s.i (*0-394-85380-6*); 1982. (Illus.). 24p. (J). lib. bdg. 4.99 o.s.i (*0-394-95380-0*); 1975. 3.99 o.s.i (*0-394-93162-9*) Random Hse. Children's Bks. (Random Hse. Bks. for Young Readers).

—Betsy's Baby Brother. 1992. (Illus.). (J). 1.99 o.p. (*0-517-08317-5*) Random Hse. Value Publishing.

Wolff, Virginia Euwer. Probably Still Nick Swansen. 1997. (Point Signature Ser.). 175p. (YA). (gr. 7-12). mass mkt. 4.50 (*0-590-43146-3*) Scholastic, Inc.

—Probably Still Nick Swanson, ERS. 1988. 160p. (YA). (gr. 7 up). 14.95 o.s.i (*0-8050-0701-6*, Holt, Henry & Co. Bks. For Young Readers) Holt, Henry & Co.

Wood, Brian. The Cramp Twins. 2001. (J). pap. 9.95 (*0-385-32714-5*, Random Hse. Bks. for Young Readers) Random Hse. Children's Bks.

—Opposites Attack: Swamp Fever. 2002. (Cramp Twins Ser.: Bk. 1). (Illus.). 96p. (J). (gr. 2-7). pap. 7.95 (*1-58234-765-4*, Bloomsbury Children) Bloomsbury Publishing.

—Swamp Fever. 2001. (Cramp Twins Ser.). (J). pap. (*0-385-32717-X*, Dell Books for Young Readers) Random Hse. Children's Bks.

Wood, Brian, creator. Swamp Fever. 2002. (Cramp Twins Ser.: Bk. 2). (Illus.). (J). (gr. 4-9). pap. 7.95 (*1-58234-766-2*, Bloomsbury Children) Bloomsbury Publishing.

Wood, June Rae. A Share of Freedom. 1996. 256p. (J). (gr. 4-8). pap. 4.95 o.s.i (*0-7868-1085-8*) Disney Pr.

—A Share of Freedom. 1994. 256p. (YA). 15.95 o.s.i (*0-399-22767-9*, G. P. Putnam's Sons) Penguin Group (USA) Inc.

—When Pigs Fly. 1995. 224p. (J). (gr. 4-7). 16.95 o.s.i (*0-399-22911-6*, G. P. Putnam's Sons) Penguin Group (USA) Inc.

—When Pigs Fly. 1997. (Illus.). 272p. (J). (gr. 3-7). pap. 5.99 (*0-698-11570-8*, PaperStar) Penguin Putnam Bks. for Young Readers.

—When Pigs Fly. 1997. 12.04 (*0-606-10990-0*) Turtleback Bks.

Woodruff, Elvira. Ghosts Don't Get Goosebumps. 1995. 176p. (J). (gr. 3-7). pap. text 3.99 o.s.i (*0-440-41033-9*) Dell Publishing.

—Ghosts Don't Get Goosebumps. 1993. 96p. (J). (gr. 4-7). tchr. ed. 16.95 (*0-8234-1035-8*) Holiday Hse., Inc.

—Ghosts Don't Get Goosebumps. 1995. (J). 9.09 o.p. (*0-606-07566-6*) Turtleback Bks.

—Magnificent Mummy Maker. 1994. (Illus.). 160p. (J). (gr. 4-6). pap. 13.95 (*0-590-45742-X*) Scholastic, Inc.

—Magnificent Mummy Maker. 1994. (J). 10.55 (*0-606-07828-2*) Turtleback Bks.

—The Magnificent Mummy Maker. 1995. 160p. (J). (gr. 4-7). 4.50 (*0-590-45743-8*) Scholastic, Inc.

—Tubtime. 1990. (Illus.). 32p. (J). (ps-3). lib. bdg. 14.95 o.p. (*0-8234-0777-2*) Holiday Hse., Inc.

Wright, Betty R. The Scariest Night. 1991. 166p. (J). (gr. 4-7). tchr. ed. 15.95 o.p. (*0-8234-0904-X*) Holiday Hse., Inc.

Wright, Betty Ren. Ghost of Popcorn Hill. 1993. (Illus.). 96p. (J). (gr. 4-7). tchr. ed. 15.95 (*0-8234-1009-9*) Holiday Hse., Inc.

—Ghosts Beneath Our Feet. 1986. 144p. (J). (gr. 4-6). reprint ed. pap. 2.50 o.p. (*0-590-40755-4*, Scholastic Paperbacks) Scholastic, Inc.

—Haunted Summer. 1996. 99p. (J). (gr. 4-7). pap. 14.95 (*0-590-47355-7*) Scholastic, Inc.

Wyeth, Sharon Dennis. Lisa, We Miss You. 1990. (Pen Pals Ser.: No. 13). 144p. (J). pap. 2.95 o.s.i (*0-440-40393-6*) Dell Publishing.

Yaccarino, Dan. Big Brother Mike. 1993. (Illus.). 32p. (J). (ps-2). 13.95 o.s.i (*1-56282-329-9*); lib. bdg. 13.89 o.s.i (*1-56282-330-2*) Hyperion Bks. for Children.

—Where the Four Winds Blow. 2003. (Illus.). 104p. (J). 16.99 (*0-06-623626-6*); lib. bdg. 17.89 (*0-06-623627-4*) HarperCollins Children's Bk. Group. (Cotler, Joanna Bks.).

Yarbough, Camille. The Little Tree Growing in the Shade. 1996. (Illus.). 64p. (J). (gr. 2-5). 18.95 o.s.i (*0-399-21204-3*, G. P. Putnam's Sons) Penguin Group (USA) Inc.

Yates, Dan. An Angel in the Family. 1998. (J). 12.95 (*1-57734-302-6*) Covenant Communications, Inc.

—An Angel in the Family: A Novel. 1999. (Illus.). 188 p. pap. 12.95 (*1-57734-282-8*, 01113461) Covenant Communications, Inc.

Yates, Elizabeth. American Haven. 2002. (Illus.). 112p. (J). (*1-57924-896-9*) Jones, Bob Univ. Pr.

Yep, Laurence. Later, Gator. 1997. (Illus.). 128p. (J). (gr. 3-7). pap. 4.50 (*0-7868-1160-9*) Disney Pr.

—Later, Gator. (J). 1997. pap. 4.50 (*0-7868-1277-X*); 1995. (Illus.). 128p. (gr. 3-7). 13.95 o.p. (*0-7868-0059-3*); 1995. (Illus.). 128p. (ps-7). lib. bdg. 13.89 (*0-7868-2083-7*) Hyperion Bks. for Children.

—Later, Gator. 1997. (J). 10.55 (*0-606-11001-1*) Turtleback Bks.

Yorinks, Arthur. Oh, Brother, RS. 1991. (Illus.). 40p. (J). (gr. 2 up). pap. 5.95 o.p. (*0-374-45598-8*, Sunburst) Farrar, Straus & Giroux.

Young, Alida E. Is My Sister Dying? 1991. 144p. (Orig.). (J). (gr. 5-8). pap. 2.99 o.p. (*0-87406-541-0*) Darby Creek Publishing.

Yumoto, Kazumi. The Spring Tone, RS. 1999. (JPN.). 176p. (J). (gr. 7-12). 16.00 o.p. (*0-374-37153-9*, Farrar, Straus & Giroux (BYR)) Farrar, Straus & Giroux.

—The Spring Tone. Hirano, Cathy, tr. 2001. 176p. (YA). (gr. 7 up). mass mkt. 4.99 (*0-440-22855-7*, Laurel Leaf) Random Hse. Children's Bks.

—The Spring Tone. Hirano, Cathy, tr. 2000. (YA). pap., stu. ed. 52.00 incl. audio (*0-7887-4189-6*, 41112) Recorded Bks., LLC.

—The Spring Tone. 2002. (YA). 20.25 (*0-8446-7233-5*) Smith, Peter Pub., Inc.

—The Spring Tone. 2001. (J). 11.04 (*0-606-21453-4*) Turtleback Bks.

Zacharias, Ravi K. The Forgiveness Jar. (Illus.). (J). 17.99 (*0-7814-3451-3*) Cook Communications Ministries.

Zafris, Nancy. The Metal Shredders: A Novel. 2003. 320p. reprint ed. pap. 13.00 (*0-425-19080-3*, BlueHen Bks.) Putnam Publishing Group, The.

Zakutinsky, Ruth. Judah & Yoni. 1975. (Illus.). 32p. (J). (ps-4). o.p. (*0-911643-03-6*) Aura Printing, Inc.

Zalben, Jane Breskin. Buster Gets Braces, ERS. 1992. (Illus.). 32p. (J). (ps-2). 15.95 o.p. (*0-8050-1682-1*, Holt, Henry & Co. Bks. For Young Readers) Holt, Henry & Co.

Zeises, Lara M. Contents under Pressure. 2004. (YA). 256p. 15.95 (*0-385-73047-0*); 192p. lib. bdg. (*0-385-90162-3*) Dell Publishing. (Delacorte Pr.).

Ziefert, Harriet. My Sister Says Nothing Ever Happens When We Go Sailing. 1986. (Illus.). 12p. (J). (ps-2). 5.95 o.p. (*0-694-00081-7*) HarperCollins Children's Bk. Group.

—Sisters Are for Making Sand Castles. 2001. (Illus.). 16p. (ps-k). pap. 6.99 (*0-14-056850-6*) Penguin Putnam Bks. for Young Readers.

—Sometimes I Share. 1991. (Stickerbook Reader Ser.). (Illus.). 24p. (J). (ps-3). mass mkt. 3.95 (*0-06-107425-X*) HarperCollins Children's Bk. Group.

Ziefert, Harriet & Boon, Emilie. Little Hippo & the New Baby. 1998. (Little Hippo Board Books Ser.). (Illus.). 18p. (J). pap. 12.95 o.p. (*0-7894-2191-7*) Dorling Kindersley Publishing, Inc.

Zimmerman, Andrea Griffing & Clemesha, David. Digger Man, ERS. 2003. (Illus.). 32p. (J). 15.95 (*0-8050-6628-4*, Holt, Henry & Co. Bks. For Young Readers) Holt, Henry & Co.

Zindel, Paul. Loch. l.t. ed. 1997. (J). 16.95 o.p. (*0-7451-2859-9*, Galaxy Children's Large Print) BBC Audiobooks America.

—Loch. 1995. (Illus.). 224p. (J). (gr. 6-10). pap. 4.95 (*0-7868-1099-8*) Disney Pr.

—Loch. 1994. 224p. (gr. 6-10). (YA). lib. bdg. 15.89 (*0-06-024543-3*); (Illus.). (J). 15.95 (*0-06-024542-5*) HarperCollins Children's Bk. Group.

—Loch. 2004. (J). (-9). pap. 5.99 (*0-7868-5150-3*) Hyperion Bks. for Children.

—Loch, unabr. ed. 1997. (J). (gr. 5). audio 27.00 (*0-7887-0394-3*, 94586E7) Recorded Bks., LLC.

—Loch. 1995. (J). 11.00 (*0-606-08806-7*) Turtleback Bks.

Zitelman, Jem. Ventures Tested: One Teenager's Story . . . to Happiness. 2000. viii, 206p. (J). pap. 15.95 (*1-891612-01-8*, 9701); lib. bdg. 24.95 (*1-891612-02-6*, 9701) Celjon Bks.

Zoller, Bob. My Sister Is an Only Child. 1983. (J). (gr. 4-8). pap. 3.95 o.p. (*0-8307-0887-1*, 5900045, Regal Bks.) Gospel Light Pubns.

Zollman, Pam. Don't Bug Me! 2001. (Illus.). 134p. (J). (gr. 2-6). tchr. ed. 15.95 (*0-8234-1584-8*) Holiday Hse., Inc.

Zolotow, Charlotte. Big Brother. 1982. (Trophy Picture Bk.). (Illus.). 32p. (J). (gr. k-3). pap. 1.95 (*0-06-443033-2*, Harper Trophy) HarperCollins Children's Bk. Group.

—Big Sister & Little Sister. 1990. (Trophy Picture Bk.). (Illus.). 32p. (J). (gr. k-3). pap. 5.99 (*0-06-443217-3*, Harper Trophy) HarperCollins Children's Bk. Group.

—Do You Know What I'll Do? (Illus.). (J). (ps-2). 2000. 32p. lib. bdg. 15.89 (*0-06-027880-3*); 1958. 32p. 14.00 (*0-06-026930-8*); 1958. 48p. 14.89 (*0-06-026940-5*); 2000. 32p. 15.99 (*0-06-027879-X*) HarperCollins Children's Bk. Group.

Zusak, Markus. Fighting Ruben Wolfe. 2001. (Illus.). 208p. (YA). (gr. 5-10). pap. 15.95 (*0-439-24188-X*, Levine, Arthur A. Bks.) Scholastic, Inc.

D

DATING (SOCIAL CUSTOMS)—FICTION

Abrams, Liesa. His Other Girlfriend. 1999. (Love Stories Ser.). 192p. (gr. 7-12). mass mkt. 4.50 o.s.i (*0-553-49295-0*) Bantam Bks.

—Stolen Kisses. 1999. (Love Stories Ser.). 192p. (gr. 7-12). mass mkt. 3.99 o.s.i (*0-553-49288-8*, Dell Books for Young Readers) Random Hse. Children's Bks.

Aks, Patricia. Junior Prom. 1982. 176p. (Orig.). (J). (gr. 7 up). pap. 2.25 o.p. (*0-590-40970-0*) Scholastic, Inc.

Anderson, Mary. Do You Call That a Dream Date? 1989. 176p. (J). (gr. 6 up). mass mkt. 2.95 o.s.i (*0-440-20350-3*, Laurel Leaf) Random Hse. Children's Bks.

Appelt, Kathi A. Kissing Tennessee: And Other Stories from the Stardust Dance. 2004. (Illus.). 132p. (YA). pap. (*0-15-205127-9*, Harcourt Paperbacks) Harcourt Children's Bks.

Applegate, K. A. Aisha Goes Wild. 1994. (Making Out Ser.: No. 8). 240p. (YA). (gr. 7-12). mass mkt. 3.99 o.p. (*0-06-106251-0*) HarperCollins Children's Bk. Group.

—Aisha Goes Wild, No. 8. 1999. (Making Out Ser.: No. 8). 192p. (YA). (gr. 7-12). pap. 3.99 (*0-380-80219-8*, Avon Bks.) Morrow/Avon.

—Always Loving Zoey. 2000. (Making Out Ser.: No. 22). 192p. (YA). (gr. 7-12). pap. 3.99 (*0-380-81311-4*, Avon Bks.) Morrow/Avon.

—Don't Tell Zoey. 1999. (Making Out Ser.: No. 13). 176p. (YA). (gr. 7 up). pap. 3.99 (*0-380-80869-2*, Avon Bks.) Morrow/Avon.

—Falling for Claire. 2000. (Making Out Ser.: No. 27). 176p. (YA). (gr. 7-12). pap. 3.99 (*0-380-81531-1*, Avon Bks.) Morrow/Avon.

—Jake Finds Out. (Making Out Ser.: No. 2). (YA). (gr. 7-12). 1994. 240p. mass mkt. 3.99 o.p. (*0-06-106203-0*, HarperTorch); 1998. 224p. reprint ed. pap. 3.99 (*0-380-80212-0*, Avon Bks.) Morrow/Avon.

—Lara Gets Even. 1999. (Making Out Ser.: No. 16). (Illus.). 176p. (YA). (gr. 7-12). pap. 3.99 (*0-380-80872-2*, Avon Bks.) Morrow/Avon.

—Nina Won't Tell, No. 3. 1998. (Making Out Ser.: No. 3). 224p. (YA). (gr. 7-12). reprint ed. mass mkt. 3.99 (*0-380-80213-9*, Avon Bks.) Morrow/Avon.

—True Love No. 1: Off Limits. 2001. 240p. mass mkt. 4.99 (*1-931497-34-6*) 17th Street Productions, An Alloy Online Inc. Co.

—Zoey Comes Home. 2000. (Making Out Ser.: No. 28). 176p. (YA). (gr. 7-12). pap. 3.99 (*0-380-81532-X*) Morrow/Avon.

—Zoey Fools Around, No. 1. 1998. (Making Out Ser.: No. 1). 272p. (J). (gr. 7-12). reprint ed. pap. 3.99 (*0-380-80211-2*, Avon Bks.) Morrow/Avon.

Baker, Camy. Camy Baker's It Must Be Love: 15 Cool Rules for Choosing a Better Boyfriend. 1999. (Camy Baker Ser.). 144p. (gr. 4-7). pap. text 3.99 o.s.i (*0-553-48657-8*, Dell Books for Young Readers) Random Hse. Children's Bks.

Bennett, Cherie & Gottesfeld, Jeff. Flirt in the Mirror, 2000. (Mirror Image Ser.: Vol. 4). 176p. (YA). (gr. 6-9). pap. 4.50 (*0-671-03633-5*, Simon Pulse) Simon & Schuster Children's Publishing.

Berenstain, Stan & Berenstain, Jan. The Berenstain Bears & Queenie's Crazy Crush. 1997. (Berenstain Bears Big Chapter Bks.). (J). (gr. 2-6). 11.99 o.s.i (*0-679-98745-2*); (Illus.). 112p. pap. 3.99 o.s.i (*0-679-88745-8*) Random Hse. Children's Bks. (Random Hse. Bks. for Young Readers).

—The Berenstain Bears & Queenie's Crazy Crush. 1997. (Berenstain Bears Big Chapter Bks.). (J). (gr. 2-6). 9.09 (*0-606-12628-7*) Turtleback Bks.

—The Berenstain Bears & the Big Date. 1998. (Berenstain Bears Big Chapter Bks.). (J). (gr. 2-6). 10.04 (*0-606-13951-6*) Turtleback Bks.

Bethancourt, T. Ernesto. The Great Computer Dating Caper. 1985. 160p. (J). (gr. 7 up). 1.99 o.p. (*0-517-55213-2*) Random Hse. Value Publishing.

Black, Jonah. Black Book Diary of a Teenage Stud: Stop, Don't Stop, Vol. II. 2001. (Black Books). 240p. (J). (gr. 9 up). pap. 4.99 (*0-06-440799-3*, Avon) HarperCollins Children's Bk. Group.

Brian, Kate. The V Club. 2004. 288p. (J). 14.95 (*0-689-86764-6*, Simon & Schuster Children's Publishing) Simon & Schuster Children's Publishing.

Brown, Marc. Muffy's Secret Admirer. 1999. (Arthur Chapter Book Ser.: No. 17). (J). (gr. 3-6). pap. 3.95 (*0-316-12047-2*); (Illus.). 64p. 13.95 (*0-316-12017-0*); (Illus.). 64p. pap. 3.95 (*0-316-12230-0*) Little Brown Children's Bks.

—Muffy's Secret Admirer. 1999. (Arthur Chapter Book Ser.: No. 17). (J). (gr. 3-6). 10.10 (*0-606-17237-8*) Turtleback Bks.

Bryant, Bonnie. The Long Ride. 1998. (Pine Hollow Ser.: No. 1). 192p. (gr. 7 up). mass mkt. 4.50 o.s.i (*0-553-49242-X*, Dell Books for Young Readers) Random Hse. Children's Bks.

—Reining In. 1998. (Pine Hollow Ser.: No. 3). 240p. (gr. 7 up). mass mkt. 4.50 o.s.i (*0-553-49244-6*) Bantam Bks.

Bunting, Eve. The Girl in the Painting. 1978. (Creative's Young Romance Ser.). (Illus.). (J). (gr. 3-9). pap. 3.25 o.p. (*0-89812-069-1*); lib. bdg. 7.95 o.p. (*0-87191-639-8*) Creative Co., The. (Creative Education).

Byars, Betsy C. The Cybil War. l.t. ed. 1991. (Lythway Ser.). 136p. (J). 14.95 o.p. (*0-7451-1403-2*, Galaxy Children's Large Print) BBC Audiobooks America.

—The Cybil War. (Illus.). 1990. 128p. (J). (gr. 3-7). pap. 4.99 (*0-14-034356-3*, Puffin Bks.); 1981. 14p. (YA). (gr. 8-12). 13.99 o.s.i (*0-670-25248-4*, Viking Children's Bks.) Penguin Putnam Bks. for Young Readers.

—The Cybil War. (J). 1988. pap. 2.75 o.p. (*0-590-42609-5*); 1982. pap. 2.25 o.p. (*0-590-33750-5*); 1982. pap. 1.95 o.p. (*0-590-32500-0*); 1987. pap. 2.50 o.p. (*0-590-40466-0*) Scholastic, Inc.

—The Cybil War. 1981. (J). 11.04 (*0-606-03178-2*) Turtleback Bks.

Cabot, Meg. Princess in Waiting. 2004. (Princess Diaries). (Illus.). 288p. (J). pap. 6.99 (*0-06-009609-8*, Harper Trophy) HarperCollins Children's Bk. Group.

—Princess in Waiting. 2003. (Princess Diaries: Vol. IV). (YA). (gr. 7 up). mass mkt. 6.99 (*0-06-054065-6*) HarperCollins Pubs.

—Princess in Waiting. unabr. ed. 2003. (Princess Diaries: Vol. IV). (J). (gr. 3 up). audio 26.00 (*0-8072-1561-9*, Listening Library) Random Hse. Audio Publishing Group.

Cajio, Linda. Dancing in the Dark. 1995. 192p. (J). mass mkt. 3.50 o.s.i (*0-553-25244-5*) Bantam Bks.

Chandler, Elizabeth. Love Happens. 1997. (Love Stories Super Edition Ser.). 208p. (Orig.). (YA). (gr. 7-12). mass mkt. 4.50 o.s.i (*0-553-49217-9*, Dell Books for Young Readers) Random Hse. Children's Bks.

Chandler, Elizabeth & Mason, Lynn. I Do. 1999. (Love Stories Ser.). 208p. (gr. 7-12). mass mkt. 4.50 o.s.i (*0-553-49275-6*, Dell Books for Young Readers) Random Hse. Children's Bks.

Clark, Catherine. Frozen Rodeo. 2004. 304p. (J). pap. 6.99 (*0-06-447385-6*, HarperTempest) HarperCollins Children's Bk. Group.

—Frozen Rodeo. 2003. 304p. (J). (gr. 8 up). 15.99 (*0-06-009070-7*) HarperCollins Pubs.

—Frozen Rodeo, or a Summer on Ice. 2003. 304p. (J). lib. bdg. 16.89 (*0-06-624008-5*) HarperCollins Pubs.

—True Love No. 3: Star-Crossed. 2001. 240p. mass mkt. 4.99 (*1-931497-36-2*) 17th Street Productions, An Alloy Online Inc. Co.

Clark, Kathy. He's the One. 2001. (Full House Club Stephanie Ser.: No.15). 144p. (J). (gr. 4-6). pap. 3.99 (*0-671-04208-4*, Simon Spotlight) Simon & Schuster Children's Publishing.

—Truth or Dare. 2000. (Full House Club Stephanie Ser.: No. 10). 160p. (J). (gr. 4-6). pap. 3.99 (*0-671-04126-6*, Simon Spotlight) Simon & Schuster Children's Publishing.

Conford, Ellen. Crush. 1998. (Illus.). 144p. (J). (gr. 7 up). 15.95 (*0-06-025414-9*, Harper Trophy) HarperCollins Children's Bk. Group.

—Crush. 1998. (Illus.). 144p. (J). (gr. 12). lib. bdg. 14.89 o.p. (*0-06-025415-7*) HarperCollins Pubs.

—We Interrupt This Semester for an Important Bulletin. 1979. 192p. (YA). (gr. 7 up). pap. 1.95 o.p. (*0-590-32830-1*) Scholastic, Inc.

Craft, Elisabeth. Cafe 2: I'll Have What He's Having. 1997. (Cafe Ser.: Vol. 2). 208p. (J). (gr. 2-12). pap. 3.99 (*0-671-00446-8*, Simon Pulse) Simon & Schuster Children's Publishing.

Craft, Elizabeth. Love Bytes. 1997. (Cafe Ser.: Vol. 1). (Illus.). 192p. (J). (gr. 7-12). per. 3.99 (*0-671-00445-X*, Simon Pulse) Simon & Schuster Children's Publishing.

—Show Me Love. 2000. (Turning Seventeen Ser.: No. 4). 208p. (YA). (gr. 7 up). pap. 4.95 (*0-06-447240-X*, Harper Trophy) HarperCollins Children's Bk. Group.

Cruise, Beth. Going, Going, Gone! 1994. (Saved by the Bell: No. 3). 128p. (YA). (gr. 5-8). pap. 3.95 (*0-689-71852-7*, Aladdin) Simon & Schuster Children's Publishing.

Dessen, Sarah. Dreamland. 2000. (Illus.). 280p. (J). (gr. 7-12). 15.99 (*0-670-89122-3*, Viking Children's Bks.) Penguin Putnam Bks. for Young Readers.

—Someone Like You. 2004. 288p. pap. 7.99 (*0-14-240177-3*, Puffin Bks.) Penguin Putnam Bks. for Young Readers.

—This Lullaby. 2002. 352p. (YA). text 16.99 (*0-670-03530-0*) Penguin Putnam Bks. for Young Readers.

Dickenson, Celia. Too Many Boys. 1984. (Loveswept Ser.: No. 71). 160p. (Orig.). (J). (gr. 5-6). mass mkt. 2.50 o.s.i (*0-553-26615-2*) Bantam Bks.

Dickerson, Karle. Just My Type. 1989. 111p. (Orig.). (J). (gr. 5-8). pap. text 2.75 o.p. (*0-87406-404-X*) Darby Creek Publishing.

Du Jardin, Rosamond. Class Ring. 1951. (J). (gr. 4-9). 14.95 (*0-397-30184-7*) HarperCollins Children's Bk. Group.

—Double Date. 1952. (J). (gr. 4-9). 9.89 o.p. (*0-397-30208-8*) HarperCollins Children's Bk. Group.

—Someone to Count On. 1962. (J). (gr. 4-9). lib. bdg. 6.95 o.p. (*0-397-30636-9*) HarperCollins Children's Bk. Group.

Ellerbee, Linda. Girl Reporter Snags Crush! 2000. (Get Real Ser.: No. 4). (Illus.). (J). (gr. 3-7). 229p. lib. bdg. 14.89 (*0-06-028248-7*);No. 4. 240p. pap. 4.50 (*0-06-440758-6*, Avon) HarperCollins Children's Bk. Group.

Fiedler, Lisa. Lucky Me. 1998. 172p. (YA). (gr. 7-9). tchr. ed. 15.00 o.s.i (*0-395-89131-0*, Clarion Bks.) Houghton Mifflin Co. Trade & Reference Div.

Fleming, Maria. Where Do Kisses Come From? 1999. (Little Golden Bks.). (Illus.). 16p. (J). (ps-3). 2.99 (*0-307-99503-8*, Golden Bks.) Random Hse. Children's Bks.

Flinn, Alex. Breathing Underwater. 2001. (J). (gr. 8 up). 224p. lib. bdg. 16.89 (*0-06-029199-0*); (Illus.). 272p. 15.99 (*0-06-029198-2*) HarperCollins Children's Bk. Group.

—Breathing Underwater. 2002. 272p. (J). (gr. 5 up). pap. 7.99 (*0-06-447257-4*) HarperCollins Pubs.

Foley, June. Susanna Siegelbaum Gives up Guys. 1992. 8.35 o.p. (*0-606-12529-9*) Turtleback Bks.

Friedman, Ina R. How My Parents Learned to Eat. (Carry-Along Book & Cassette Favorites Ser.). (J). (ps-3). 1993. 1p. pap. 9.95 incl. audio (*0-395-66488-8*, 485871); 1993. 1p. pap. 9.95 incl. audio (*0-395-66488-8*, 485871); 1987. (Illus.). 32p. pap. 5.95 (*0-395-44235-4*); 1984. (Illus.). 32p. lib. bdg., tchr. ed. 15.00 (*0-395-35379-3*) Houghton Mifflin Co.

—How My Parents Learned to Eat. 1984. (J). 12.10 (*0-606-03692-X*) Turtleback Bks.

Garfield, Valerie. Sergeant Sniff's Secret Valentine Mystery. 2001. (Sergeant Sniff Scratch-and-Sniff Mystery Ser.). (Illus.). 16p. (J). (ps-k). 6.95 (*0-694-01507-5*, Harper Festival) HarperCollins Children's Bk. Group.

Gelman, Jan. Marci's Secret Book of Dating. 1993. (Illus.). (Orig.). (J). 3.49 o.p. (*0-517-10455-5*) Random Hse. Value Publishing.

Gershon, A. A. You're Dating Him? 2001. (Love Stories Ser.). 192p. (YA). (gr. 7-12). mass mkt. 4.50 o.s.i (*0-553-49373-6*, Dell Books for Young Readers) Random Hse. Children's Bks.

Giles, Gail. Playing in Traffic. 2004. 176p. 16.95 (*0-7613-1895-X*); lib. bdg. 23.90 (*0-7613-2781-9*) Millbrook Pr., Inc. (Roaring Brook Pr.).

Golden Books Staff. Prom Night. 1994. 8p. pap. 3.29 o.s.i (*0-307-30238-5*, Golden Bks.) Random Hse. Children's Bks.

Gordon, Margaret, illus. A Paper of Pins, 001. 1979. 32p. (J). (ps-3). 6.95 o.p. (*0-395-28814-2*, Clarion Bks.) Houghton Mifflin Co. Trade & Reference Div.

Greene, Bette. Philip Hall Likes Me, I Reckon, Maybe. 1975. (Illus.). 144p. (gr. 3-7). pap. text 4.99 o.s.i (*0-440-45755-6*, Yearling) Random Hse. Children's Bks.

Greene, Constance C. Al's Blind Date. 128p. (J). (gr. 5-9). 1991. (Illus.). pap. 3.95 o.p. (*0-14-034171-4*, Puffin Bks.); 1989. 12.95 o.p. (*0-670-82815-7*, Viking Children's Bks.) Penguin Putnam Bks. for Young Readers.

Haft, Erin. A Kiss Between Friends. 1997. (Love Stories Ser.). 192p. (YA). (gr. 7-12). mass mkt. 3.99 o.s.i (*0-553-57078-1*, Dell Books for Young Readers) Random Hse. Children's Bks.

Hall, John. Where the Boys Are. 1998. 208p. (J). (gr. 5-9). mass mkt. 4.50 (*0-590-05960-2*) Scholastic, Inc.

Hall, Lynn. Dagmar Schultz & the Angel Edna. 1989. (Dagmar Schultz Ser.). 96p. (J). (gr. 5-8). lib. bdg. 13.95 o.s.i (*0-684-19097-4*, Atheneum) Simon & Schuster Children's Publishing.

Hamilton, Linda J. The Saturday Night Bash. 1994. (Pick Your Own Dream Date Ser.). 128p. (J). 3.95 o.p. (*1-56565-143-X*) Lowell Hse. Juvenile.

HarperEntertainment Staff. Bye-Bye Boyfriend. 2000. (Two of a Kind Ser.: No. 14). 112p. (gr. 3-7). mass mkt. 4.99 (*0-06-106637-0*, HarperEntertainment) Morrow/Avon.

Harrison, Emma. Never Been Kissed. 2002. (Mary-Kate & Ashley Sweet 16 Ser.: Vol. 1). 144p. mass mkt. 4.99 (*0-06-009209-2*) HarperCollins Children's Bk. Group.

Haynes, Betsy. Great Dad Disaster. 1994. 8.60 o.p. (*0-606-06426-5*) Turtleback Bks.

—The Great Dad Disaster. 1994. 176p. (J). (gr. 4-7). pap. 3.50 o.s.i (*0-553-48169-X*) Bantam Bks.

Henry, Emma. The Nine-Hour Date. 2001. (Love Stories Ser.). 192p. (YA). (gr. 7-12). mass mkt. 4.50 (*0-553-49370-1*, Dell Books for Young Readers) Random Hse. Children's Bks.

Hewett, Lorri. Lives of Our Own. (gr. 7-12). 1998. 192p. (J). 15.99 (*0-525-45959-6*); 2000. (Illus.). 196p. (YA). reprint ed. pap. 5.99 o.s.i (*0-14-130589-4*, Puffin Bks.) Penguin Putnam Bks. for Young Readers.

—Lives of Our Own. 2000. 12.04 (*0-606-19695-1*) Turtleback Bks.

Hoh, Diane. Last Date. 1994. (Nightmare Hall Ser.: No. 11). 176p. (YA). (gr. 7-9). mass mkt. 3.50 (*0-590-48133-9*) Scholastic, Inc.

—Prom Date. 1996. 274p. (J). (gr. 6-10). mass mkt. 4.50 (*0-590-54429-2*) Scholastic, Inc.

Hopkins, Cathy. Mates, Dates & Cosmic Kisses. 2003. (Illus.). 208p. (YA). mass mkt. 4.99 (*0-689-85545-1*, Simon Pulse) Simon & Schuster Children's Publishing.

—Mates, Dates & Inflatable Bras. 2003. (Illus.). 176p. (YA). mass mkt. 4.99 (*0-689-85544-3*, Simon Pulse) Simon & Schuster Children's Publishing.

—Mates, Dates, & Sleepover Secrets. 2003. (Illus.). 208p. (YA). pap. 4.99 (*0-689-85991-0*, Simon Pulse) Simon & Schuster Children's Publishing.

James, Dean. Three's a Crowd. 1993. (Melrose Place Ser.: No. 4). 79p. (YA). mass mkt. 3.99 o.p. (*0-06-106205-7*, HarperTorch) Morrow/Avon.

Johansson, Alice Nicole. In Love with Mandy. 1997. (Unicorn Club Ser.: No. 20). 144p. (gr. 3-7). pap. text 3.50 o.s.i (*0-553-48448-6*, Dell Books for Young Readers) Random Hse. Children's Bks.

—Jessica's Dream Date. 1998. (Unicorn Club Ser.: No. 22). 144p. (gr. 3-7). pap. text 3.50 o.s.i (*0-553-48608-X*, Sweet Valley) Random Hse. Children's Bks.

—Trapped in the Mall. 1998. (Unicorn Club Ser.: No. 23). 144p. (gr. 3-7). pap. text 3.50 o.s.i (*0-553-48609-8*, Sweet Valley) Random Hse. Children's Bks.

John, Laurie. The Other Woman. 1995. (Sweet Valley University Ser.: No. 16). (YA). (gr. 7 up). 9.09 o.p. (*0-606-08636-6*) Turtleback Bks.

Johnson, Lissa Halls. Opportunity Knocks Twice. 2002. (Brio Girls Ser.). 192p. (J). pap. 6.99 (*1-56179-953-X*) Bethany Hse. Pubs.

Kenyon, Kate. The Big Date. 1988. (Junior High Ser.: No. 10). 160p. (J). (gr. 5-9). pap. 2.50 o.p. (*0-590-41389-9*) Scholastic, Inc.

Kinoian, Vartkis & Costello, Emily. A Boy Friend Is Not a "Boyfriend" 1997. (Party of Five: No. 3). 144p. (Orig.). (J). (gr. 3-6). pap. 3.99 (*0-671-00678-9*, Aladdin) Simon & Schuster Children's Publishing.

Kornreich, Leron. Ivory Towers. 2001. (YA). 7.99 (*0-9707509-0-0*) Banana Peel Bks.

Krulik, Nancy E. Who Do You Love? Your Complete Guide to Romance. 2001. 112p. (gr. 7-12). pap. 3.99 (*0-689-84301-1*, Aladdin) Simon & Schuster Children's Publishing.

Landesman, Peter. Ten Ways to Wreck a Date. 1996. (Full House Stephanie Ser.: No. 15). 144p. (J). (gr. 4-6). pap. 3.99 (*0-671-53548-X*, Simon Spotlight) Simon & Schuster Children's Publishing.

Lane, Dakota. Johnny Voodoo. 1997. 208p. (YA). (gr. 7-12). mass mkt. 4.50 o.s.i (*0-440-21998-1*, Dell Books for Young Readers) Random Hse. Children's Bks.

Levy, Elizabeth. Double Standard. 1984. 160p. (YA). (gr. 7 up). pap. 2.25 (*0-380-87379-6*, 87379-6, Avon Bks.) Morrow/Avon.

Lundell, Margo. Dream Date. 1998. (Sabrina, the Teenage Witch Ser.: No. 2). (Illus.). 32p. (J). (gr. 2-4). pap. 3.99 (*0-689-82124-7*, Simon Pulse) Simon & Schuster Children's Publishing.

Lynch, Chris. Ladies' Choice, 4. 1997. (He-Man Women Haters Club Ser.). 9.60 o.p. (*0-606-11447-5*) Turtleback Bks.

Mackler, Carolyn. Love & Other Four-Letter Words. 2002. (Laurel-Leaf Books). 256p. (YA). (gr. 7). mass mkt. 5.50 (*0-440-22831-X*, Random Hse. Bks. for Young Readers) Random Hse. Children's Bks.

Mannarino, Melanie. Seventeen: The Boyfriend Clinic: The Final Word on Flirting, Dating, Guys & Love. 2000. (Seventeen Ser.). (Illus.). 128p. (YA). (gr. 7 up). pap. 6.95 (*0-06-447235-3*, Harper Trophy) HarperCollins Children's Bk. Group.

Martin, Ann M. Dawn's Big Date, No. 50. 1997. (Baby-Sitters Club Ser.: No. 50). (J). (gr. 3-7). mass mkt. 3.99 (*0-590-98496-9*) Scholastic, Inc.

—Mary Anne & Too Many Boys. 1990. (Baby-Sitters Club Ser.: No. 34). (J). (gr. 3-7). mass mkt. 3.99 (*0-590-73283-8*); 192p. mass mkt. 3.50 (*0-590-42494-7*) Scholastic, Inc.

—Mary Anne & Too Many Boys. l.t. ed. 1995. (Baby-Sitters Club Ser.: No. 34). 144p. (J). (gr. 3-7). lib. bdg. 21.27 o.p. (*0-8368-1414-2*) Stevens, Gareth Inc.

—Mary Anne & Too Many Boys. 1990. (Baby-Sitters Club Ser.: No. 34). (J). (gr. 3-7). 8.60 (*0-606-04475-2*) Turtleback Bks.

—Mary Anne's Big Breakup. 1999. (Baby-Sitters Club Friends Forever Ser.: No. 3). 144p. (J). (gr. 3-7). mass mkt. 4.50 (*0-590-52326-0*) Scholastic, Inc.

—Stacey's Ex-Boyfriend. 1998. (Baby-Sitters Club Ser.: No. 119). (J). (gr. 3-7). mass mkt. 3.99 (*0-590-05997-1*) Scholastic, Inc.

—Stacey's Ex-Boyfriend. 1998. (Baby-Sitters Club Ser.: No. 119). (J). (gr. 3-7). 10.04 (*0-606-13163-9*) Turtleback Bks.

Mason, Lynn. As I Am. 1999. (Love Stories Ser.). 192p. (gr. 7-12). mass mkt. 3.99 o.s.i (*0-553-49274-8*, Dell Books for Young Readers) Random Hse. Children's Bks.

Matson, Nancy & Chesworth, Michael. The Boy Trap. 2001. 112p. (YA). (gr. 5 up). mass mkt. 4.50 (*0-439-22365-2*, Scholastic Paperbacks) Scholastic, Inc.

McCants, William D. Much Ado about Prom Night. 1995. 240p. (YA). (gr. 7 up). 11.00 o.p. (*0-15-200083-6*); pap. 5.00 o.p. (*0-15-200081-X*) Harcourt Children's Bks.

—Much Ado about Prom Night. 1995. 11.05 (*0-606-14276-2*) Turtleback Bks.

McDaniel, Lurlene. My Secret Boyfriend. 1988. (Impressions Ser.). 128p. (J). (gr. 6-8). pap. 2.50 o.p. (*0-87406-310-8*) Darby Creek Publishing.

McFann, Jane. Nothing More, Nothing Less. 1993. 176p. (Orig.). (YA). (gr. 5 up). pap. 3.50 (*0-380-76636-1*, Avon Bks.) Morrow/Avon.

Milcsik, Margie. Cupid Computer. 1992. 128p. (J). (gr. 3-7). reprint ed. pap. 3.95 o.s.i (*0-689-71569-2*, Aladdin) Simon & Schuster Children's Publishing.

Moore, Sheila. Samson Svenson's Baby. 1983. (Illus.). 48p. (J). (gr. 1-4). 11.95 (*0-06-022612-9*) Harper-Collins Children's Bk. Group.

Moore, Stephanie Perry. Purity Reigns. 2002. (Laurel Shadrach Ser.: Vol. 1). 239p. (YA). 6.99 (*0-8024-4035-5*) Moody Pr.

Musgrave, Florence. Two Dates for Mike. 1964. (Illus.). (J). (gr. 6-9). 6.95 o.p. (*0-8038-7083-3*) Hastings Hse. Daytrips Pubs.

Noonan, Rosalind. Can't Let Go. 2000. (Turning Seventeen Ser.: No. 5). 208p. (J). (gr. 7 up). pap. 4.95 (*0-06-447241-8*, Harper Trophy) HarperCollins Children's Bk. Group.

—Turning Seventeen: Any Guy You Want, Bk. 1. 2000. (Turning Seventeen Ser.: No. 1). 208p. (YA). (gr. 7 up). pap. 4.95 (*0-06-447237-X*) HarperCollins Children's Bk. Group.

Novak, Barbara. Down with Love. 2003. 288p. pap. 14.95 (*0-06-054162-8*, HarperEntertainment) Morrow/Avon.

Olsen, Mary-Kate & Olsen, Ashley. Beauty & the Beach. 2004. (Mary-Kate & Ashley Sweet 16 Ser.: No. 15). mass mkt. 4.99 (*0-06-059522-1*, HarperEntertainment) Morrow/Avon.

—Boy Crazy. 2003. (So Little Time Ser.: No. 11). 128p. mass mkt. 4.99 (*0-06-009315-3*, HarperEntertainment) Morrow/Avon.

—How to Flunk Your First Date. 1999. (Two of a Kind Ser.: No. 2). (Illus.). 112p. (gr. 3-7). mass mkt. 4.99 (*0-06-106572-2*, HarperEntertainment) Morrow/Avon.

—Instant Boyfriend. l.t. ed. 2002. (So Little Time Ser.: Vol. 2). 128p. mass mkt. 4.99 (*0-06-008369-7*) HarperCollins Pubs.

—Love & Kisses. 2004. (Mary-Kate & Ashley Sweet 16 Ser.: No. 13). 144p. mass mkt. 4.99 (*0-06-059066-1*, HarperEntertainment) Morrow/Avon.

—Love Is in the Air. 2004. (So Little Time Ser.: No. 13). 128p. mass mkt. 4.99 (*0-06-059068-8*, Harper-Entertainment) Morrow/Avon.

—Prom Princess. 2004. (Two of a Kind Ser.: No. 34). 112p. mass mkt. 4.99 (*0-06-009330-7*, HarperEntertainment) Morrow/Avon.

—School Dance Party. 2001. (Mary-Kate & Ashley Starring In Ser.: No. 3). (Illus.). 96p. mass mkt. 4.99 (*0-06-106667-2*) HarperCollins Pubs.

Osburn, Jesse. Prom Night. 1995. (Orig.). pap. 3.99 (*0-380-77318-X*, Avon Bks.) Morrow/Avon.

Pascal, Francine. Cheating on Anna. 1999. (Sweet Valley Junior High Ser.: No. 8). 160p. (gr. 3-7). pap. text 3.99 o.s.i (*0-553-48666-7*) Bantam Bks.

—Lila's New Flame. 1997. (Sweet Valley High Ser.: No. 135). (YA). (gr. 7 up). 10.04 (*0-606-14331-9*) Turtleback Bks.

—Too Hot to Handle. 1997. (Sweet Valley High Ser.: No. 136). (YA). (gr. 7 up). 10.04 (*0-606-14338-6*) Turtleback Bks.

Pascal, Francine, creator. The Big Night. 1998. (Sweet Valley High Ser.: No. 142). 208p. (gr. 7 up). mass mkt. 3.99 o.s.i (*0-553-49232-2*, Sweet Valley) Random Hse. Children's Bks.

—The Boyfriend War. 1996. (Sweet Valley High Ser.: No. 101). 224p. (YA). (gr. 7 up). mass mkt. 2.49 o.s.i (*0-553-57035-8*) Bantam Bks.

—The Broken Angel. 1999. (Sweet Valley High Senior Year Ser.: No. 10). 192p. (gr. 7 up). mass mkt. 4.50 o.s.i (*0-553-49282-9*) Bantam Bks.

—Brokenhearted. 1989. (Sweet Valley High Ser.: No. 58). 144p. (YA). (gr. 7 up). mass mkt. 3.25 o.s.i (*0-553-28156-9*) Bantam Bks.

—California Love. 1995. (Sweet Valley High TV Ser.: No. 1). (YA). (gr. 7 up). 9.60 o.p. (*0-606-08228-X*) Turtleback Bks.

—The Dreaded Ex. 2000. (Sweet Valley University Ser.: No. 58). 240p. (YA). (gr. 9 up). mass mkt. 4.50 o.s.i (*0-553-49310-8*, Sweet Valley) Random Hse. Children's Bks.

—Elizabeth in Love. 2000. (Sweet Valley University Ser.: No. 59). 240p. (YA). (gr. 9 up). mass mkt. 4.50 o.s.i (*0-553-49347-7*, Sweet Valley) Random Hse. Children's Bks.

—Fight Fire with Fire. 1997. (Sweet Valley High Ser.: No. 137). 208p. (Orig.). (gr. 7 up). mass mkt. 3.99 o.s.i (*0-553-57071-4*, Dell Books for Young Readers) Random Hse. Children's Bks.

—I've Got a Secret. 1999. (Sweet Valley High Senior Year Ser.: No. 4). 192p. (gr. 7 up). mass mkt. 4.50 (*0-553-49278-0*, Dell Books for Young Readers) Random Hse. Children's Bks.

—Lacey's Crush. 1999. (Sweet Valley Junior High Ser.: No. 6). 160p. (gr. 3-7). pap. text 4.50 o.s.i (*0-553-48665-9*) Bantam Bks.

—Lila's New Flame. 1997. (Sweet Valley High Ser.: No. 135). 208p. (gr. 7 up). mass mkt. 3.99 o.s.i (*0-553-57069-2*, Dell Books for Young Readers) Random Hse. Children's Bks.

—Maria Who? 1999. (Sweet Valley High Senior Year Ser.: No. 8). 192p. (gr. 7 up). mass mkt. 4.50 o.s.i (*0-553-49280-2*) Bantam Bks.

—The Morning After, Vol. 95. 1996. (Sweet Valley High Ser.: No. 95). 224p. (YA). (gr. 7 up). mass mkt. 2.49 o.s.i (*0-553-57033-1*) Bantam Bks.

—Mystery Date. 1998. (Sweet Valley High Super Edition Ser.). 240p. (gr. 7 up). mass mkt. 4.50 o.s.i (*0-553-57073-0*, Sweet Valley) Random Hse. Children's Bks.

—One Last Kiss. 1997. (Sweet Valley University Ser.: No. 29). 240p. (gr. 7 up). mass mkt. 3.99 o.s.i (*0-553-57053-6*, Sweet Valley) Random Hse. Children's Bks.

—The One that Got Away. 1999. (Sweet Valley High Senior Year Ser.: No. 9). 192p. (gr. 7 up). mass mkt. 4.50 o.s.i (*0-553-49281-0*) Bantam Bks.

—Out of the Picture. 1997. (Sweet Valley University Ser.: No. 33). 240p. (Orig.). (gr. 7 up). mass mkt. 3.99 o.s.i (*0-553-57057-9*, Dell Books for Young Readers) Random Hse. Children's Bks.

—A Picture-Perfect Prom? 1998. (Sweet Valley High Ser.: No. 141). 208p. (gr. 7 up). mass mkt. 3.99 o.s.i (*0-553-49231-4*, Sweet Valley) Random Hse. Children's Bks.

—She Loves Me... Not. 2000. (Sweet Valley Junior High Ser.: No. 19). 160p. (gr. 3-7). pap. text 4.50 o.s.i (*0-553-48721-3*, Sweet Valley) Random Hse. Children's Bks.

—So Cool. 1999. (Sweet Valley High Senior Year Ser.: No. 3). 192p. (gr. 7 up). mass mkt. 4.50 (*0-553-57028-5*, Sweet Valley) Random Hse. Children's Bks.

—Third Wheel. 1999. (Sweet Valley Junior High Ser.: No. 12). 160p. (gr. 3-7). pap. text 4.50 o.s.i (*0-553-48670-5*) Bantam Bks.

—Too Hot to Handle. 1997. (Sweet Valley High Ser.: No. 136). 208p. (gr. 7 up). mass mkt. 3.99 o.s.i (*0-553-57070-6*, Dell Books for Young Readers) Random Hse. Children's Bks.

—Truth or Dare. 1999. (Sweet Valley University Ser.: No. 53). 240p. (gr. 9 up). mass mkt. 4.50 (*0-553-49273-X*) Bantam Bks.

—Twin Hearts. 1996. (Sweet Valley High TV Ser.: No. 2). (YA). (gr. 7 up). 9.60 o.p. (*0-606-08629-3*) Turtleback Bks.

Pellowski, Michael J. One Last Date with Archie, No. 3. 1991. (Riverdale High Ser.). (Illus.). 128p. (J). (gr. 4-8). pap. 2.99 o.p. (*1-56282-109-1*) Hyperion Bks. for Children.

Perez, Marlene. Unexpected Development. 2004. 176p. (J). 16.95 (*0-7613-2425-9*); lib. bdg. 23.90 (*0-7613-2948-X*) Millbrook Pr., Inc. (Roaring Brook Pr.).

Plante, Edmund. Last Date. 1993. 176p. (Orig.). (YA). (gr. 5 up). pap. 3.50 (*0-380-77154-3*, Avon Bks.) Morrow/Avon.

Plummer, Louise. The Unlikely Romance of Kate Bjorkman. 1997. 192p. (YA). pap. 15.00 (*0-375-89521-3*, Laurel Leaf); (gr. 7-12). mass mkt. 4.50 o.s.i (*0-440-22704-6*, Dell Books for Young Readers) Random Hse. Children's Bks.

—The Unlikely Romance of Kate Bjorkman. 1997. (J). 10.55 (*0-606-12838-7*) Turtleback Bks.

Pohlmann, Lillian. Love Can Say No. 1966. (J). (gr. 7-10). 5.50 o.p. (*0-664-32365-0*) Westminster John Knox Pr.

Poulsen, David A. Blind Date. 2002. (Lawrence High Yearbook Ser.). (Illus.). 106p. (YA). pap. 3.99 (*1-55305-010-X*) Cygnet Publishing Group, Inc./Coolreading.com CAN. *Dist:* Orca Bk. Pubs.

Powell, Randy. Is Kissing a Girl Who Smokes Like Licking an Ashtray?, RS. 2003. 208p. (YA). pap. 5.95 (*0-374-43628-2*, Sunburst) Farrar, Straus & Giroux.

Quin-Harkin, Janet. The Great Boy Chase. 1985. (Sweet Dreams Ser.: No. 93). 192p. (YA). (gr. 7-12). pap. 2.50 o.s.i (*0-553-26743-4*) Bantam Bks.

—Love Potion. 1999. (Enchanted Hearts Ser.: No. 4). (Illus.). 192p. (YA). (gr. 7 up). pap. 4.50 (*0-380-80122-1*, Avon Bks.) Morrow/Avon.

—Love Potion. 1999. (Enchanted Hearts Ser.). (Illus.). (J). 10.55 (*0-606-17966-6*) Turtleback Bks.

—Torn Apart. 1999. (Love Stories Ser.). 192p. (gr. 7-12). mass mkt. 3.99 o.s.i (*0-553-49289-6*, Dell Books for Young Readers) Random Hse. Children's Bks.

—True Love No. 2: Secrets. 2001. 240p. mass mkt. 4.99 (*1-931497-35-4*) 17th Street Productions, An Alloy Online Inc. Co.

—True Love No. 4: Kiss & Lie. 2001. 240p. mass mkt. 4.99 (*1-931497-37-0*) 17th Street Productions, An Alloy Online Inc. Co.

—Wanted: A Date for Saturday Night. 1985. 160p. (J). (gr. 5 up). 11.95 (*0-448-47752-1*) Putnam Publishing Group, The.

Raine, Allison. Sweet Sixteen. 2000. (Love Stories Super Edition Ser.). 224p. (YA). (gr. 7-12). mass mkt. 4.99 o.s.i (*0-553-49325-6*, Dell Books for Young Readers) Random Hse. Children's Bks.

Rennison, Louise. Dancing in My Nuddy-Pants: Even Further Confessions of Georgia Nicolson. (J). 2004. (Illus.). 240p. pap. 6.99 (*0-06-009748-5*); 2003. 224p. 15.99 (*0-06-009746-9*); 2003. 224p. lib. bdg. 16.89 (*0-06-009747-7*) HarperCollins Children's Bk. Group. (HarperTempest).

—On the Bright Side, I'm Now the Girlfriend of a Sex God: Further Confessions of Georgia Nicolson. 2001. 256p. (J). (gr. 7 up). 15.99 (*0-06-028813-2*) HarperCollins Children's Bk. Group.

—On the Bright Side, I'm Now the Girlfriend of a Sex God: Further Confessions of Georgia Nicolson. 2002. 272p. (J). pap. 6.99 (*0-06-447226-4*) Harper-Collins Pubs.

—On the Bright Side, I'm Now the Girlfriend of a Sex God: Further Confessions of Georgia Nicolson. 2003. 256p. (J). mass mkt. 6.99 (*0-06-052185-6*, Avon Bks.) Morrow/Avon.

Roberts, Christa. Turning Seventeen: For Real, Bk. 3. 2000. (Turning Seventeen Ser.: No. 3). 208p. (J). (gr. 7 up). pap. 4.95 (*0-06-447239-6*, Harper Trophy) HarperCollins Children's Bk. Group.

Roberts, Laura Peyton. Now & Always. 2001. 224p. (YA). (gr. 7). mass mkt. 4.50 o.s.i (*0-553-49378-7*, Dell Books for Young Readers) Random Hse. Children's Bks.

Rottman, S. L. Head above Water. 2003. 224p. pap. 6.95 (*1-56145-238-6*); 1999. 192p. (YA). (gr. 7-11). 14.95 (*1-56145-185-1*) Peachtree Pubs., Ltd.

Rushton, Rosie. How Could You Do This to Me, Mum? 1999. (Fab Five Ser.). 224p. (J). (gr. 5-9). pap. 3.99 (*0-7868-1388-1*) Disney Pr.

—What a Week to Fall in Love. (Illus.). 144p. (J). pap. 7.95 (*0-14-038760-9*) Penguin Bks., Ltd. GBR. *Dist:* Trafalgar Square.

—Where Do We Go from Here? 1999. (Fab Five Ser.: 3). 224p. (J). (gr. 5-9). pap. text 3.99 (*0-7868-1390-3*) Hyperion Pr.

Santori, Helen. The Perfect Couple. 1988. (First Kiss Ser.: No. 4). (YA). (gr. 5 up). mass mkt. 2.95 o.s.i (*0-8041-0238-4*, Ivy Bks.) Ballantine Bks.

Schwemm, Diane. Don't Say Good-Bye. 1997. (Love Stories Ser.). 192p. (YA). (gr. 7-12). mass mkt. 3.99 o.s.i (*0-553-49219-5*, Dell Books for Young Readers) Random Hse. Children's Bks.

Scott, Kieran. Boy Crazy! 2nd ed. 2001. pap. 4.99 (*0-06-441050-1*, Avon Bks.) Morrow/Avon.

—How Do I Tell? 1999. (Love Stories Ser.). 192p. (gr. 7-12). mass mkt. 4.50 (*0-553-49293-4*) Bantam Bks.

Sherman, Eileen B. The Violin Players. 1998. 130p. (YA). (gr. 5 up). 14.95 (*0-8276-0595-1*) Jewish Pubn. Society.

Sinclair, Stephanie. The Rumor about Julia. 1997. (Love Stories Ser.). 192p. (Orig.). (YA). (gr. 7-12). mass mkt. 3.99 o.s.i (*0-553-49218-7*, Dell Books for Young Readers) Random Hse. Children's Bks.

Singleton, Linda Joy. Opposites Attract. 1991. (Sweet Dreams Ser.: No. 180). 144p. (YA). pap. 2.99 o.s.i (*0-553-29021-5*) Bantam Bks.

—Spring Break. 1994. (Pick Your Own Dream Date Ser.). 128p. (YA). (gr. 7 up). 3.95 o.p. (*1-56565-144-8*) Lowell Hse. Juvenile.

Smith, Nancy C. Apple Valley: The Proposal, Bk. 2. 1994. (Apple Valley Ser.). (Orig.). (YA). (gr. 6 up). pap. 3.50 (*0-380-77391-0*, Avon Bks.) Morrow/Avon.

Smith, Sinclair. Dream Date. 1993. 160p. (J). (gr. 7-9). mass mkt. 3.25 (*0-590-46126-5*) Scholastic, Inc.

Smurthwaite, Don. Do You Like Me, Julie Sloan? 1997. (J). pap. 10.95 (*1-57008-302-9*, Bookcraft, Inc.) Deseret Bk. Co.

Sorenson, Jane B. Boy Friend. 1985. (Jennifer Bks.). 128p. (J). (gr. 5-8). 4.99 o.p. (*0-87239-931-1*, 2981) Standard Publishing.

Steiner, Barbara. Love Match. 1988. 128p. (J). (gr. 5-8). 1.00 o.p. (*0-87406-312-4*, 31-16381-3) Darby Creek Publishing.

Stewart, Molly Mia. Jessica Plays Cupid. 1995. (Sweet Valley Kids Ser.: No. 56). (J). (gr. 1-3). 8.70 o.p. (*0-606-08230-1*) Turtleback Bks.

Stine, Megan. One Twin Too Many. 1999. (Two of a Kind Ser.: No. 4). (Illus.). 112p. (gr. 3-7). mass mkt. 4.99 (*0-06-106574-9*, HarperEntertainment) Morrow/Avon.

Stine, R. L. Blind Date. 1986. (J). 10.55 (*0-606-01807-7*) Turtleback Bks.

—Broken Date. 1988. (YA). (gr. 7 up). mass mkt. (*0-373-98021-3*, Harlequin Bks.) Harlequin Enterprises, Ltd.

—Broken Date. MacDonald, Patricia, ed. 1991. (Fear Street Ser.: No. 8). 224p. (YA). (gr. 7 up). reprint ed. pap. 3.99 (*0-671-69322-0*, Simon Pulse) Simon & Schuster Children's Publishing.

—Broken Date. 1988. (Fear Street Ser.: No. 8). (YA). (gr. 7 up). 10.04 (*0-606-04881-2*) Turtleback Bks.

—How I Broke up with Ernie. 1990. 160p. (YA). (gr. 7 up). mass mkt. 3.99 (*0-671-69496-0*, Simon Pulse) Simon & Schuster Children's Publishing.

—How I Broke up with Ernie. 1990. (J). 10.04 (*0-606-03777-2*) Turtleback Bks.

Stoks, Peggy. Sonido de las Aguas. 2000. (Reunited Ser.: Vol. 4). (SPA.). (J). (gr. 8-12). mass mkt. 3.99 (*0-7899-0805-0*) Spanish Hse. Distributors.

Stowe, Aurelia, ed. When Boy Dates Girl. 1965. (J). (gr. 10-12). lib. bdg. 4.99 o.s.i (*0-394-91810-X*, Random Hse. Bks. for Young Readers) Random Hse. Children's Bks.

Strasser, Todd. Girl Gives Birth to Own Prom Date. 1996. 208p. (YA). (gr. 7 up). lib. bdg. 16.00 (*0-689-80482-2*, Simon & Schuster Children's Publishing) Simon & Schuster Children's Publishing.

Suzanne, Jamie. Boys Against Girls. 1988. (Sweet Valley Twins Ser.: No. 17). (J). (gr. 3-7). 8.60 o.p. (*0-606-03554-0*) Turtleback Bks.

—Jessica's Blind Date. 1994. (Sweet Valley Twins Ser.: No. 79). (J). (gr. 3-7). 8.60 o.p. (*0-606-06786-8*) Turtleback Bks.

—The Older Boy. 1987. (Sweet Valley Twins Ser.: No. 15). (J). (gr. 3-7). pap. o.s.i (*0-553-16804-5*, Dell Books for Young Readers) Random Hse. Children's Bks.

—Pumpkin Fever. 1997. (Sweet Valley Twins Ser.: No. 110). 144p. (Orig.). (gr. 3-7). pap. text 3.50 o.s.i (*0-553-48441-9*, Dell Books for Young Readers) Random Hse. Children's Bks.

—Romeo & 2 Juliets. 1994. (Sweet Valley Twins Ser.: No. 84). (J). (gr. 3-7). pap. 4.50 (*0-553-54180-3*, Dell Books for Young Readers) Random Hse. Children's Bks.

Tashjian, Janet. Fault Line, ERS. 2003. (Illus.). 256p. (J). 16.95 (*0-8050-7200-4*, Holt, Henry & Co. Bks. For Young Readers) Holt, Henry & Co.

Truth or Dairy Bound Galley. 2000. (J). pap. (*0-06-029055-2*, Harper Trophy) HarperCollins Children's Bk. Group.

Various. The Big Book of Summer Love. 2001. 480p. pap. (*0-09-941758-8*) Random Hse. of Canada, Ltd. CAN. *Dist:* Random Hse., Inc.

Vogel, Jane. Goodbye to All That. 2002. (Brio Girls Ser.). 192p. (J). pap. 6.99 (*1-58997-051-9*) Bethany Hse. Pubs.

Von Ziegesar, Cecily. Gossip Girl Collection, 3 vols. 2003. (Gossip Girl Ser.). (J). pap. 26.99 (*0-316-72271-5*, 53605112) Little Brown Children's Bks.

Weber, Judith. Dating, No. 47. 1988. (Cheerleaders Ser.). (YA). (gr. 7-12). pap. 2.50 o.p. (*0-590-41918-8*) Scholastic, Inc.

Wierenga, Kathy. Double Exposure. 2002. (Brio Girls Ser.). 192p. (J). pap. 6.99 (*1-56179-954-8*) Bethany Hse. Pubs.

Wilensky, Amy S. 24/7. 1997. (Love Stories Ser.). 192p. (YA). (gr. 7-12). mass mkt. 4.50 o.s.i (*0-553-57074-9*, Dell Books for Young Readers) Random Hse. Children's Bks.

William, Kate. All Night Long. 1984. (Sweet Valley High Ser.: No. 5). (YA). (gr. 7 up). 9.09 o.p. (*0-606-01144-7*) Turtleback Bks.

—Are We in Love. 1993. (Sweet Valley High Ser.: No. 94). (YA). (gr. 7 up). 8.35 o.p. (*0-606-05635-1*) Turtleback Bks.

—Brokenhearted. 1989. (Sweet Valley High Ser.: No. 58). (YA). (gr. 7 up). 8.35 o.p. (*0-606-02453-0*) Turtleback Bks.

—Dangerous Love. 1984. (Sweet Valley High Ser.: No. 6). (YA). (gr. 7 up). 9.09 o.p. (*0-606-01159-5*) Turtleback Bks.

—Deceptions. 1984. (Sweet Valley High Ser.: No. 14). (YA). (gr. 7 up). 9.09 o.p. (*0-606-01157-9*) Turtleback Bks.

—Heartbreaker. 1984. (Sweet Valley High Ser.: No. 8). (YA). (gr. 7 up). 9.09 o.p. (*0-606-01185-4*) Turtleback Bks.

—Jessica's Older Guy. 1995. (Sweet Valley High Ser.: No. 119). (YA). (gr. 7 up). 9.09 (*0-606-08224-7*) Turtleback Bks.

—The Morning After. 1993. (Sweet Valley High Ser.: No. 95). (YA). (gr. 7 up). 8.60 o.p. (*0-606-05636-X*) Turtleback Bks.

—Racing Hearts. 1984. (Sweet Valley High Ser.: No. 9). (YA). (gr. 7 up). 8.35 o.p. (*0-606-02451-4*) Turtleback Bks.

Wilson, Jacqueline. Girls in Love. 2002. 192p. (YA). (gr. 6-9). 9.95 (*0-385-72974-X*); (gr. 7-9). lib. bdg. 11.99 (*0-385-90040-6*) Dell Publishing. (Delacorte Pr.).

—Girls in Love. l.t. ed. 2000. 192p. pap. 18.99 (*0-7089-9503-9*) Harlequin Mills & Boon, Ltd. GBR. *Dist:* Ulverscroft Large Print Bks., Ltd., Ulverscroft Large Print Canada, Ltd.

—Girls in Love. 2002. 192p. (YA). (gr. 7). mass mkt. 4.99 (*0-440-22957-X*) Random Hse., Inc.

—Girls in Love. (Illus.). (J). 2003. 160p. mass mkt. (*0-552-54521-X*); 2000. 156p. 17.95 (*0-385-40804-8*) Transworld Publishers Ltd. GBR. *Dist:* Random Hse. of Canada, Ltd., Trafalgar Square.

Wolitzer, Meg. Operation: Save the Teacher: Wednesday Night Match. 1993. (Wednesday Night Match Ser.). 128p. (Orig.). (J). (gr. 4-8). pap. 3.50 (*0-380-76461-X*, Avon Bks.) Morrow/Avon.

Wyeth, Sharon Dennis. Too Cute for Words. 1989. (Pen Pals Ser.: No. 2). 128p. (J). (gr. k-6). pap. 2.95 o.s.i (*0-440-40225-5*, Yearling) Random Hse. Children's Bks.

Yolen, Jane. The Gift of Sarah Barker. 1981. 156p. (J). (gr. 7 up). 12.50 o.p. (*0-670-64580-X*) Viking Penguin.

Zach, Cheryl. Secret Admirer. 1999. (Dear Diary Ser.). 192p. (YA). (gr. 7-12). mass mkt. 4.50 o.s.i (*0-425-17114-0*, JAM) Berkley Publishing Group.

Zeises, Lara M. Bringing up the Bones. 2004. 224p. (YA). (gr. 9). mass mkt. 5.99 (*0-440-22974-X*, Laurel Leaf) Random Hse. Children's Bks.

—Bringing up the Bones. 2002. 224p. (YA). (gr. 9). 12.95 (*0-385-73001-2*) Random Hse., Inc.

Zimmerman, Zoe. Danny. 2000. (Love Stories). (Illus.). 192p. (YA). (gr. 7-12). mass mkt. 4.50 o.s.i (*0-553-49322-1*, Skylark) Random Hse. Children's Bks.

—Johnny. 2000. (Love Stories). 192p. (YA). (gr. 7-12). mass mkt. 4.50 (*0-553-49324-8*, Dell Books for Young Readers) Random Hse. Children's Bks.

—Kevin. 2000. (Love Stories). 192p. (YA). (gr. 7-12). mass mkt. 4.50 o.s.i (*0-553-49323-X*, Dell Books for Young Readers) Random Hse. Children's Bks.

DIVORCE—FICTION

Abercrombie, Barbara. Cat-Man's Daughter. 1981. 160p. (J). (gr. 6-9). 11.95 (*0-06-020030-8*); lib. bdg. 12.89 o.p. (*0-06-020031-6*) HarperCollins Children's Bk. Group.

Adams, Eric J. & Adams, Kathleen. On the Day His Daddy Left. (Illus.). 24p. (J). 2003. pap. 6.95 (*0-8075-6073-1*); 2000. lib. bdg. 14.95 (*0-8075-6072-3*) Whitman, Albert & Co.

Adler, C. S. The Silver Coach. 1979. (J). (gr. 4-7). 8.95 o.p. (*0-698-20504-9*) Putnam Publishing Group, The.

—Tuna Fish Thanksgiving. 1992. 160p. (J). (gr. 5-9). 13.95 o.p. (*0-395-58829-4*, Clarion Bks.) Houghton Mifflin Co. Trade & Reference Div.

Agle, Nan H. Susan's Magic. 1973. (Illus.). 140p. (J). (gr. 3-6). 6.95 o.p. (*0-8164-3108-6*) Houghton Mifflin Co.

Aiello, Barbara & Shulman, Jeffrey. On with the Show! Featuring Brenda Dubrowski. 1995. (Kids on the Block Bks.). (Illus.). 56p. (J). (gr. 5-8). 13.95 (*0-941477-06-1*, 21st Century Bks., Inc.) Millbrook Pr., Inc.

Alexander, Anne. To Live a Lie. 1975. (Illus.). 176p. (J). (gr. 3-7). 8.95 o.p. (*0-689-30470-6*, Atheneum) Simon & Schuster Children's Publishing.

Alvarez, Julia. How Tia Lola Came to (Visit) Stay. 160p. (gr. 3-7). 2004. (J). lib. bdg. 17.99 (*0-375-91552-4*, Knopf Bks. for Young Readers); 2004. (SPA., Illus.). pap. text 5.50 (*0-375-81552-X*, Yearling); 2002. (Illus.). pap. text 5.50 (*0-440-41870-4*, Laurel Leaf) Random Hse. Children's Bks.

—How Tia Lola Came to (Visit) Stay. Cascardi, Andrea, ed. 2001. (Illus.). 160p. (gr. 3-5). text 15.95 (*0-375-80215-0*); lib. bdg. 17.99 (*0-375-90215-5*) Random Hse. Children's Bks. (Knopf Bks. for Young Readers).

Anderson, Penny S. A Pretty Good Team. 1979. (Handling Difficult Times Ser.). (Illus.). (J). (gr. 1-4). lib. bdg. 5.95 o.p. (*0-89565-097-5*) Child's World, Inc.

Andrews, V. C. Jade. l.t. ed. 1999. (Core Ser.). 176p. (YA). 29.95 (*0-7838-8804-X*, Macmillan Reference USA) Gale Group.

—Jade. 1999. (Wildflowers Ser.: No. 3). (Illus.). 192p. mass mkt. 3.99 o.s.i (*0-671-02802-2*, Pocket) Simon & Schuster.

—Jade. 1999. (Wildflower Ser.). 10.04 (*0-606-17531-8*) Turtleback Bks.

—Misty. 1999. (Wildflowers Ser.: No. 1). (Illus.). 176p. mass mkt. 3.99 o.s.i (*0-671-02800-6*, Pocket) Simon & Schuster.

—Misty. l.t. ed. 1999. (Core Ser.). 164p. 27.95 (*0-7838-8802-3*) Thorndike Pr.

—Misty. 1999. (Wildflower Ser.). 10.04 (*0-606-17532-6*) Turtleback Bks.

—Star. l.t. ed. 1999. (Core Ser.). 161p. (YA). 28.95 o.p. (*0-7838-8803-1*, Macmillan Reference USA) Gale Group.

—Star. 1999. (Wildflowers Ser.: No. 2). 176p. pap. 3.99 o.s.i (*0-671-02801-4*, Pocket) Simon & Schuster.

—Star. 1999. 10.04 (*0-606-17533-4*) Turtleback Bks.

Angell, Judie. Yours Truly: A Novel. 1993. 192p. (YA). (gr. 7 up). mass mkt. 15.95 o.p. (*0-531-05472-1*); mass mkt. 15.99 o.p. (*0-531-08622-4*) Scholastic, Inc. (Orchard Bks.).

Atkins, Jeannine. Dessert First. 1997. (Illus.). (J). 16.00 (*0-689-80345-1*, Atheneum) Simon & Schuster Children's Publishing.

Ballard, Robin. Gracie. 1993. (Illus.). 24p. (J). (ps up). lib. bdg. 13.93 o.p. (*0-688-11807-0*, Greenwillow Bks.) HarperCollins Children's Bk. Group.

Bauer, Joan. Stand Tall. 2002. 192p. (J). (gr. 6-9). 16.99 (*0-399-23473-X*, G. P. Putnam's Sons) Penguin Putnam Bks. for Young Readers.

Bernhard, Durga. To & Fro, Fast & Slow. 2001. (Illus.). 32p. (J). (ps-2). 15.95 (*0-8027-8782-7*); lib. bdg. 16.85 (*0-8027-8783-5*) Walker & Co.

Betancourt, Jeanne. The Rainbow Kid. 1983. 112p. (Orig.). (J). (gr. 3-7). pap. 2.50 (*0-380-84665-9*, Avon Bks.) Morrow/Avon.

Binch, Caroline. Since Dad Left. 1998. 5. (Illus.). 32p. (gr. k-4). 15.95 o.p. (*0-7613-0290-5*) Millbrook Pr., Inc.

Blue, Rose. A Month of Sundays. 1972. (Illus.). 64p. (gr. 3-5). lib. bdg. 6.90 o.p. (*0-531-02037-1*, Watts, Franklin) Scholastic Library Publishing.

Blume, Judy. It's Not the End of the World. l.t. ed. 1986. (J). 13.95 o.p. (*0-7451-0329-4*, Galaxy Children's Large Print) BBC Audiobooks America.

—It's Not the End of the World. 1979. (YA). mass mkt. 1.95 o.s.i (*0-553-13628-3*) Bantam Bks.

—It's Not the End of the World. 2002. (Illus.). (J). 13.94 (*0-7587-9132-1*) Book Wholesalers, Inc.

—It's Not the End of the World. 1982. 176p. (YA). (gr. 4-7). mass mkt. 5.50 (*0-440-94140-7*) Dell Publishing.

—It's Not the End of the World. 174p. (YA). (gr. 5 up). pap. 4.50 (*0-8072-1365-9*, Listening Library) Random Hse. Audio Publishing Group.

—It's Not the End of the World. 1986. 176p. (gr. 4-7). pap. text 5.50 (*0-440-44158-7*, Yearling) Random Hse. Children's Bks.

—It's Not the End of the World. 176p. (J). 2002. 17.00 (*0-689-84293-7*); 1982. (gr. 4-7). lib. bdg. 17.00 (*0-02-711050-8*) Simon & Schuster Children's Publishing. (Atheneum/Richard Jackson Bks.).

—It's Not the End of the World. 1986. (J). 11.55 (*0-606-03964-3*) Turtleback Bks.

Boulden, Jim & Boulden, Joan. Divorce Happens. Ward, Evelyn M., ed. 1994. (Illus.). 16p. (Orig.). (J). (gr. k-2). pap., act. bk. ed. 5.95 (*1-878076-34-5*) Boulden Publishing.

Boyd, Candy Dawson. Chevrolet Saturdays. 1995. 192p. (J). (gr. 3-7). pap. 5.99 (*0-14-036859-0*, Puffin Bks.) Penguin Putnam Bks. for Young Readers.

—Chevrolet Saturdays. 1993. 192p. (J). (gr. 3-7). 16.00 (*0-02-711765-0*, Simon & Schuster Children's Publishing) Simon & Schuster Children's Publishing.

—Chevrolet Saturdays. 1995. (J). 11.04 (*0-606-07361-2*) Turtleback Bks.

Bradley, Kimberly Brubaker. Halfway to the Sky. 2003. 176p. (YA). pap. text 4.99 (*0-440-41830-5*, Yearling) Dell Bks. for Young Readers CAN. *Dist:* Random Hse. of Canada, Ltd.

—Halfway to the Sky. 2002. 176p. (gr. 3-7). text 15.95 (*0-385-72960-X*, Delacorte Pr.) Dell Publishing.

—Halfway to the Sky: The Story of a French Spy. 2002. 176p. (gr. 3-7). lib. bdg. 17.99 (*0-385-90029-5*, Delacorte Pr.) Dell Publishing.

Briggs-Bunting, Jane. Laddie of the Light, Grades 3-6. 1997. (Barnyard Tales Ser.). (Illus.). 48p. tchr. ed. 17.00 (*0-9649083-1-X*) Black River Trading Co.

Brinkerhoff, Shirley. Tangled Web, 2000. (Nikki Sheridan Ser.: Vol. 5). 176p. (J). (gr. 9-12). pap. 5.99 (*1-56179-737-5*) Bethany Hse. Pubs.

Brown, Marc. Arthur & the 1,001 Dads. 2003. (Arthur Chapter Book Ser.: No. 28). (Illus.). 64p. (J). (gr. 2-4). 14.95 (*0-316-12516-4*); pap. 4.25 (*0-316-12280-7*) Little Brown Children's Bks.

Bunting, Eve. Days of Summer. 2001. (Illus.). 40p. (J). (gr. k-3). 16.00 (*0-15-201840-9*) Harcourt Children's Bks.

—A Part of the Dream. 1992. (Eve Bunting Collection). (Illus.). 48p. (J). (gr. 2-6). lib. bdg. 12.79 o.p. (*0-89565-771-6*) Child's World, Inc.

—Some Frog! 1998. (Illus.). 48p. (J). (gr. 1). 15.00 o.s.i (*0-15-277082-8*) Harcourt Children's Bks.

Burns, Peggy. The Splitting Image of Rosie Brown. 1989. 128p. (Orig.). (YA). (gr. 7-10). pap. 4.99 o.p. (*0-7459-1831-X*) Lion Publishing.

Carlson, Melody. Cherished Wish. 1998. (Allison Chronicles Ser.: Vol. 2). 160p. (J). (gr. 6-9). pap. 5.99 o.p. (*1-55661-958-8*) Bethany Hse. Pubs.

Carney, Karen L. Together, We'll Get Through This! Learning to Cope with Loss & Transition. 1999. (Barklay & Eve Ser.: Bk. 1). (Illus.). (J). pap. 6.95 (*0-9667820-0-3*) Dragonfly Publishing.

Caseley, Judith. Losing Louisa, RS. 1999. 240p. (YA). (gr. 7-12). 17.00 (*0-374-34665-8*, Farrar, Straus & Giroux (BYR)) Farrar, Straus & Giroux.

—Priscilla Twice. 1995. (Illus.). 32p. (J). (gr. k up). 15.00 o.s.i (*0-688-13305-3*); lib. bdg. 14.93 (*0-688-13306-1*) HarperCollins Children's Bk. Group. (Greenwillow Bks.).

Christiansen, C. B. My Mother's House, My Father's House. 1990. 32p. (J). (ps-3). pap. 3.95 o.p. (*0-14-054210-8*, Puffin Bks.) Penguin Putnam Bks. for Young Readers.

Christopher, Matt. The Comeback Challenge. 1996. (Illus.). 176p. (J). (gr. 3-7). 15.95 (*0-316-14090-2*) Little Brown & Co.

—The Comeback Challenge. 1996. (Matt Christopher Sports Classics Ser.). (Illus.). 176p. (J). (gr. 3-7). pap. 4.50 (*0-316-14152-6*) Little Brown Children's Bks.

—The Comeback Challenge. 1996. 10.55 (*0-606-08716-8*) Turtleback Bks.

—The Fox Steals Home. 1978. (Illus.). (J). (gr. 4-6). 15.95 o.p. (*0-316-13976-9*) Little Brown & Co.

—The Fox Steals Home. 1985. (Matt Christopher Sports Classics Ser.). (Illus.). 178p. (J). (gr. 3-7). pap. 4.50 (*0-316-13986-6*) Little Brown Children's Bks.

—The Fox Steals Home. 1978. (J). 10.55 (*0-606-04068-4*) Turtleback Bks.

—Windmill Windup. 2002. (J). (gr. 3-7). 140p. 15.95 (*0-316-14531-9*); 144p. pap. 4.50 (*0-316-14432-0*) Little Brown Children's Bks.

Cleary, Beverly. Dear Mr. Henshaw. l.t. ed. 1987. (Illus.). 141p. (J). (gr. 2-6). reprint ed. lib. bdg. 14.95 o.s.i (*1-55736-001-4*) Bantam Doubleday Dell Large Print Group, Inc.

—Dear Mr. Henshaw. 2002. (Illus.). (J). 13.83 (*0-7587-9140-2*) Book Wholesalers, Inc.

—Dear Mr. Henshaw. 1994. 128p. (J). (gr. 4-7). pap. 1.99 o.s.i (*0-440-21934-5*) Dell Publishing.

—Dear Mr. Henshaw. 2000. (Cleary Reissue Ser.). (Illus.). 160p. (J). (gr. 5 up). pap. 5.99 (*0-380-70958-9*, Harper Trophy) HarperCollins Children's Bk. Group.

—Dear Mr. Henshaw. 1995. (Illus.). (J). 9.32 (*0-395-73255-7*) Houghton Mifflin Co.

—Dear Mr. Henshaw. (J). 1996. pap. 4.99 (*0-380-72798-6*, Avon Bks.); 1983. (Illus.). 144p. (gr. 4-7). 15.99 (*0-688-02405-X*, Morrow, William & Co.); 1983. (Illus.). 144p. (gr. 4-7). lib. bdg. 16.89 (*0-688-02406-8*, Morrow, William & Co.) Morrow/Avon.

—Dear Mr. Henshaw. (J). 1992. pap. o.s.i (*0-440-80308-X*, Dell Books for Young Readers); 1984. (Illus.). 144p. pap. 4.50 o.s.i (*0-440-41794-5*, Yearling) Random Hse. Children's Bks.

—Dear Mr. Henshaw. (J). 1996. 9.60 o.p. (*0-606-09187-4*); 1983. 11.00 (*0-606-06315-3*) Turtleback Bks.

—Querido Senor Henshaw. 1996. (SPA.). 144p. (J). (gr. 4-7). 9.50 (*84-239-2766-0*) Espasa Calpe, S.A. ESP. *Dist:* AIMS International Bks., Inc.

—Strider. (Cleary Reissue Ser.). (Illus.). (J). 1992. 176p. (gr. 4-7). pap. 5.99 (*0-380-71236-9*, Harper Trophy); 1991. 192p. (gr. 3 up). 15.95 (*0-688-09900-9*); 1991. 192p. (ps-3). lib. bdg. 16.89 (*0-688-09901-7*) HarperCollins Children's Bk. Group.

—Strider. 1995. (Illus.). (YA). (gr. 6 up). 9.28 (*0-395-73264-6*) Houghton Mifflin Co.

—Strider. (gr. 4-7). 1996. 176p. (J). pap. 4.50 (*0-380-72802-8*); Set. 1992. pap. 18.00 (*0-380-72125-2*) Morrow/Avon. (Avon Bks.).

—Strider. l.t. ed. 1995. 176p. (J). (gr. 4-8). lib. bdg. 16.95 o.p. (*1-885885-13-X*, Cornerstone Bks.) Pages, Inc.

—Strider. 1996. 10.55 (*0-606-09908-5*); 1991. 11.04 (*0-606-00402-5*) Turtleback Bks.

Clewes, Dorothy. Missing from Home. 1978. (J). (gr. 7 up). 6.95 o.p. (*0-15-254882-3*) Harcourt Children's Bks.

Comor-Jacobs, Annie. Reesy: A Little Girl Learning Life's Lessons: Reesy Learning about Divorce; Reesy Learning about the Deep South; Reesy Learning about Deafness; Reesy Learning about Death, 4 vols. 2000. (Illus.). 40p. (J). (gr. 2-5). pap. 30.00 (*1-889743-18-6*) Robbie Dean Pr.

Cooney, Caroline B. Tune in Anytime. 192p. (YA). (gr. 7). 2001. (Illus.). mass mkt. 4.99 (*0-440-22798-4*, Laurel Leaf); 1999. 8.95 o.s.i (*0-385-32649-1*, Dell Books for Young Readers) Random Hse. Children's Bks.

—Tune in Anytime. 2001. (J). 11.04 (*0-606-21495-X*) Turtleback Bks.

Coy, John. Two Old Potatoes & Me. 2003. (Illus.). 40p. (J). lib. bdg. 17.99 (*0-375-92180-X*); 15.95 (*0-375-82180-5*) Random Hse. Children's Bks. (Knopf Bks. for Young Readers).

Cruise, Robin. The Top-Secret Journal of Fiona Claire Jardin. 1998. 160p. (J). (gr. 4-7). 13.00 (*0-15-201383-0*) Harcourt Children's Bks.

Danziger, Paula. Amber Brown Goes Fourth. 1995. (Amber Brown Ser.: No. 3). (Illus.). 112p. (J). (gr. 3-6). 15.99 (*0-399-22849-7*, G. P. Putnam's Sons) Penguin Group (USA) Inc.

—Amber Brown Is Feeling Blue. 1998. (Amber Brown Ser.: No. 7). (Illus.). 128p. (J). (gr. 3-6). 14.99 (*0-399-23179-X*, G. P. Putnam's Sons) Penguin Putnam Bks. for Young Readers.

—Amber Brown is Green with Envy. 2003. (Illus.). 160p. (J). 15.99 (*0-399-23181-1*, G. P. Putnam's Sons) Penguin Putnam Bks. for Young Readers.

—Amber Brown Sees Red. 1997. (Amber Brown Ser.: No. 6). (Illus.). 112p. (J). (gr. 3-6). 15.99 (*0-399-22901-9*, G. P. Putnam's Sons) Penguin Group (USA) Inc.

—Amber Brown Wants Extra Credit. 1996. (Amber Brown Ser.: No. 4). (Illus.). 120p. (J). (gr. 3-6). 15.99 (*0-399-22900-0*, G. P. Putnam's Sons) Penguin Group (USA) Inc.

Relationships

—Amber Brown Wants Extra Credit. 1997. (Amber Brown Ser.: No. 4). (Illus.). 120p. (J). (gr. 3-6). mass mkt. 3.99 (*0-590-94716-8*, Scholastic Paperbacks) Scholastic, Inc.

—Amber Brown Wants Extra Credit. 1997. (Amber Brown Ser.: No. 4). (J). (gr. 3-6). 10.04 (*0-606-11035-6*) Turtleback Bks.

—The Divorce Express. 1991. (J). mass mkt. o.s.i (*0-440-80278-4*) Bantam Bks.

—The Divorce Express. l.t. ed. 1988. (Children's Ser.). 183p. (YA). (gr. 7 up). 13.95 o.p. (*0-8161-4413-3*, Macmillan Reference USA) Gale Group.

—The Divorce Express. 1998. 160p. (J). (gr. 5-9). pap. 5.99 (*0-698-11685-2*, PaperStar) Penguin Putnam Bks. for Young Readers.

—The Divorce Express. 160p. pap. 3.99 (*0-8072-1376-4*, Listening Library) Random Hse. Audio Publishing Group.

—The Divorce Express. 1983. 160p. (YA). (gr. 7 up). mass mkt. 3.99 o.p. (*0-440-92062-0*, Laurel Leaf) Random Hse. Children's Bks.

—The Divorce Express. 1998. 11.04 (*0-606-15504-X*) Turtleback Bks.

—Forever Amber Brown. 1996. (Amber Brown Ser.: No.5). (Illus.). 112p. (J). (gr. 3-6). 14.99 (*0-399-22932-9*, G. P. Putnam's Sons) Penguin Group (USA) Inc.

—Forever Amber Brown. 1997. (Amber Brown Ser.: No.5). (J). (gr. 3-6). 10.04 (*0-606-11345-2*) Turtleback Bks.

—I, Amber Brown. 1999. (Amber Brown Ser.: No. 8). (Illus.). 144p. (J). (gr. 3-6). 14.99 (*0-399-23180-3*, Ace/Putnam) Penguin Group (USA) Inc.

—It's an Aardvark-Eat-Turtle World. 1985. 144p. (J). (gr. 7 up). 12.95 o.s.i (*0-385-29371-2*, Delacorte Pr.) Dell Publishing.

—It's an Aardvark-Eat-Turtle World. l.t. unabr. ed. 1989. 145p. (J). (gr. 4 up). 13.95 o.p. (*0-8161-4704-3*, Macmillan Reference USA) Gale Group.

—It's an Aardvark-Eat-Turtle World. 2000. 144p. (YA). (gr. 5-9). pap. 4.99 (*0-698-11691-7*, Puffin Bks.) Penguin Putnam Bks. for Young Readers.

—It's an Aardvark-Eat-Turtle World. 144p. 1996. (J). pap. 3.99 o.s.i (*0-440-41399-0*, Dell Books for Young Readers); 1986. (YA). (gr. 5 up). mass mkt. 3.99 o.p. (*0-440-94028-1*, Laurel Leaf) Random Hse. Children's Bks.

—It's an Aardvark-Eat-Turtle World. 2000. (Illus.). (J). 11.04 (*0-606-18469-4*); 1996. 9.09 o.p. (*0-606-00305-3*) Turtleback Bks.

—You Can't Eat Your Chicken Pox, Amber Brown. 1995. (Amber Brown Ser.: No. 2). (Illus.). 80p. (J). (gr. 3-6). 14.99 (*0-399-22702-4*, G. P. Putnam's Sons) Penguin Group (USA) Inc.

—You Can't Eat Your Chicken Pox, Amber Brown. 1996. (Amber Brown Ser.: No. 2). (Illus.). 101p. (J). (gr. 3-6). mass mkt. 4.50 (*0-590-50207-7*, Scholastic Paperbacks) Scholastic, Inc.

—You Can't Eat Your Chicken Pox, Amber Brown. 1996. (Amber Brown Ser.: No. 2). (J). (gr. 3-6). 10.04 (*0-606-08911-X*) Turtleback Bks.

Davitt, Kristi. Aftershocks. 2001. E-Book 4.75 incl. disk (*1-58749-036-6*); E-Book 4.75 (*1-58749-037-4*) Awe-Struck E-Bks.

De Guzman, Michael. Melonhead, RS. 2002. 224p. (J). (gr. 5 up). 17.00 (*0-374-34944-4*, Farrar, Straus & Giroux (BYR)) Farrar, Straus & Giroux.

Deuker, Carl. Night Hoops. 2001. 256p. (J). (gr. 7 up). pap. 5.99 (*0-06-447275-2*, Harper Trophy) HarperCollins Children's Bk. Group.

—Night Hoops. 2000. (Illus.). 256p. (J). (gr. 7-12). tchr. ed. 15.00 (*0-395-97936-6*) Houghton Mifflin Co.

—Night Hoops. 2001. 12.00 (*0-606-22927-2*) Turtleback Bks.

—Night Hoops. 2000. E-Book 15.00 (*0-585-36795-7*) netLibrary, Inc.

Devore, Cynthia D. Breakfast for Dinner. 1993. (Children of Courage Ser.). 32p. (J). (gr. 5 up). lib. bdg. 21.95 o.p. (*1-56239-245-X*) ABDO Publishing Co.

Dhami, Narinder. Genius Games. 2001. (J). 160p. (gr. 3-7). 15.99 (*0-7868-0616-8*); 32p. (gr. 4-6). lib. bdg. 16.49 (*0-7868-2528-6*) Hyperion Bks. for Children.

DiSanto, Mark. My Parents Are Divorced. 1997. (J). (gr. 3-6). 8.95 o.p. (*0-533-12371-2*) Vantage Pr., Inc.

Doherty, Berlie. Holly Starcross. 2002. 192p. (J). (gr. 7 up). 15.99 (*0-06-001341-9*); 17.89 (*0-06-001342-7*) HarperCollins Children's Bk. Group. (Greenwillow Bks.).

Donnelly, Elfie. Tina into Two Won't Go. Bell, Anthea, tr. from GER. 1984. 128p. (J). (gr. 8-11). 8.95 o.p. (*0-02-733140-7*, Simon & Schuster Children's Publishing) Simon & Schuster Children's Publishing.

Dower, Laura. Sink or Swim. 2003. (From the Files of Madison Finn Ser.: No. 13). 176p. (J). pap. 4.99 (*0-7868-1735-6*, Volo) Hyperion Bks. for Children.

Duffey, Betsy. Coaster. 1994. 128p. (J). (gr. 5 up). 13.99 o.s.i (*0-670-85480-8*, Viking Children's Bks.) Penguin Putnam Bks. for Young Readers.

Ellis, Joyce. The Big Split. rev. ed. 1983. 128p. pap. 3.95 o.p. (*0-8024-0190-2*) Moody Pr.

Engel, Diana. Holding On. 1997. (Accelerated Reader Bks.). (Illus.). 96p. (J). (gr. 3-7). 14.95 (*0-7614-5016-5*, Cavendish Children's Bks.) Cavendish, Marshall Corp.

Eulo, Elena Yates. Mixed-up Doubles. 2003. 208p. (J). tchr. ed. 16.95 (*0-8234-1706-9*) Holiday Hse., Inc.

Eyerly, Jeannette. World of Ellen March. 1964. (J). (gr. 7-9). o.p. (*0-397-30793-4*) HarperCollins Children's Bk. Group.

Fattah, Michel. Lacey. 1990. 40p. (J). 12.95 (*0-915677-47-4*) Roundtable Publishing.

Ferris, Jean. Relative Strangers, RS. 1993. 240p. (YA). 16.00 o.p. (*0-374-36243-2*, Farrar, Straus & Giroux (BYR)) Farrar, Straus & Giroux.

Fine, Anne. Alias Madame Doubtfire. 1989. (Young Adults Ser.). 208p. (YA). mass mkt. 3.99 o.p. (*0-553-56615-6*) Bantam Bks.

—Alias Madame Doubtfire. 1988. (YA). (gr. 7 up). 12.95 o.p. (*0-316-28313-4*, Joy Street Bks.) Little Brown & Co.

—Senora Doubtfire. Pena, Flora, tr. 1992. Tr. of Mrs. Doubtfire. (SPA.). 165p. (J). (gr. 7 up). pap. 12.95 (*84-204-4680-7*) Santillana USA Publishing Co., Inc.

—Senora Doubtfire. 1992. Tr. of Mrs. Doubtfire. 19.00 (*0-606-17745-0*) Turtleback Bks.

—Step by Wicked Step: A Novel. 1997. 144p. (gr. 4-7). pap. text 3.99 o.s.i (*0-440-41329-X*) Dell Publishing.

—Step by Wicked Step: A Novel. 1996. 144p. (J). (gr. 4-7). 15.95 o.p. (*0-316-28345-2*) Little Brown & Co.

—Step by Wicked Step: A Novel. 1997. 10.04 (*0-606-11910-8*) Turtleback Bks.

Fitch, Sheree. One More Step. 2002. 96p. (YA). pap. 9.95 (*1-55143-248-X*) Orca Bk. Pubs.

Fitzhugh, Louise. Sport. 1980. 224p. (J). (gr. 7 up). mass mkt. 3.25 o.s.i (*0-440-98350-9*, Laurel Leaf) Random Hse. Children's Bks.

Fleming, Alice. Welcome to Grossville. 1985. 112p. (J). (gr. 5-7). 12.95 o.s.i (*0-684-18289-0*, Atheneum) Simon & Schuster Children's Publishing.

Francis, Dorothy B. The Flint Hills Foal. 1976. (Illus.). 128p. (J). (gr. 3-7). lib. bdg. 4.50 o.p. (*0-687-13189-8*) Abingdon Pr.

Franklin, Kristine L. Lone Wolf. (J). 1998. 224p. (gr. 3-7). bds. 4.99 o.s.i (*0-7636-0480-1*); 1997. (gr. 4-8). 17.99 o.s.i (*1-56402-935-2*) Candlewick Pr.

—Lone Wolf. 1998. (J). 11.04 (*0-606-13578-2*) Turtleback Bks.

Fritz, T. J. Katey's Dream List. 1999. 90p. (J). (gr. 4-7). pap. 7.95 (*1-56315-084-0*) SterlingHouse Pubs., Inc.

Garon, Risa J. Snowman. 2000. (Illus.). 5p. (J). pap. 5.00 (*0-9729415-0-9*) National Family Resiliency Ctr., Inc.

George, J. Carroll & Eaton, Joi. Divorcing Daddy. 1992. 125p. (YA). (gr. 7-12). pap. 5.95 (*1-881223-01-9*) Zulema Enterprises.

Gleitzman, Morris. Puppy Fat. 1996. 192p. (YA). (gr. 3-7). pap. 5.00 o.s.i (*0-15-200052-6*, Harcourt Paperbacks); (gr. 4-7). 11.00 o.s.i (*0-15-200047-X*) Harcourt Children's Bks.

—Puppy Fat. 1995. 10.10 o.p. (*0-606-09771-6*) Turtleback Bks.

Goff, Beth Twiggar. Where Is Daddy? The Story of a Divorce. 1969. (Illus.). 32p. (J). (ps). 8.95 o.p. (*0-8070-2388-4*, NL1); pap. 5.95 o.p. (*0-8070-2305-1*, BP 694) Beacon Pr.

Goldman, Katie. In the Wings. 1982. 176p. (J). (gr. 6 up). 10.95 o.p. (*0-8037-3968-0*, Dial Bks. for Young Readers) Penguin Putnam Bks. for Young Readers.

Graham, Rosemary. My Not-So-Terrible Time at the Hippie Hotel. 2003. 224p. (J). (gr. 5-9). 16.99 (*0-670-03611-0*, Viking) Viking Penguin.

Gray, Juliette, ed. Cherubic Children's New Classic Storybook Vol. 2: Teaching & Healing Stories to Help Children Learn, Understand & Cope. 1997. (Illus.). 384p. (J). (gr. k up). 24.95 (*1-889590-24-X*) Cherubic Pr.

Green, Phyllis. Ice River. 1975. (Illus.). 48p. (J). (gr. 3-6). lib. bdg. 5.95 o.p. (*0-201-02582-5*, 2582) Addison-Wesley Longman, Inc.

Grindley, Sally. A New Room for William. 2000. (Illus.). 32p. (J). (ps-3). 15.99 o.s.i (*0-7636-1196-4*) Candlewick Pr.

Haas, Dan. You Can Call Me Worm. 1998. 176p. (J). (gr. 5-9). 15.00 o.p. (*0-395-85783-X*) Houghton Mifflin Co.

—You Can Call Me Worm. 1999. (Illus.). 176p. (gr. 5-9). pap. 5.99 o.p. (*0-698-11751-4*, PaperStar) Penguin Putnam Bks. for Young Readers.

—You Can Call Me Worm. 1999. 12.04 (*0-606-16790-0*) Turtleback Bks.

Hamm, Diane J. Second Family. 1992. 128p. (J). (gr. 5-7). 13.95 o.p. (*0-684-19436-8*, Atheneum) Simon & Schuster Children's Publishing.

Hare, Sharon C. Now I Have Two Homes. 1995. (Illus.). 20p. (Orig.). (J). (ps-3). pap. 5.00 (*0-9639450-2-5*) Joy Enterprises.

Harrison, Michael. It's My Life. 1998. 144p. (J). (gr. 4-7). 15.95 (*0-8234-1363-2*) Holiday Hse., Inc.

Hawkins, Laura. Valentine to a Flying Mouse. 1993. (J). (ps-7). 13.95 o.s.i (*0-395-61628-X*) Houghton Mifflin Co.

Heide, Florence P. When the Sad One Comes to Stay. 1975. (YA). (gr. 5-8). 12.95 o.p. (*0-397-31651-8*) HarperCollins Children's Bk. Group.

Helmering, Doris Wild. I Have Two Families. 1981. (Illus.). 48p. (J). (gr. 1-3). 8.95 o.p. (*0-687-18507-6*) Abingdon Pr.

High, Linda O. The Summer of the Great Divide. 1996. 188p. (J). (gr. 4-7). 15.95 (*0-8234-1228-8*) Holiday Hse., Inc.

Hillman, Carole D. It's Different Now... A New Beginning. 1990. (Illus.). 10p. (J). pap. text (*0-9624257-1-0*) Early Child Consultants.

Hobbs, Valerie. Charlie's Run, RS. 2000. (Illus.). 176p. (J). (gr. 4-7). 16.00 (*0-374-34994-0*, Farrar, Straus & Giroux (BYR)) Farrar, Straus & Giroux.

—Charlie's Run. 2002. 176p. (J). (gr. 3-7). pap. 5.99 (*0-14-230204-X*) Penguin Putnam Bks. for Young Readers.

—Charlie's Run. l.t. ed. 2001. (Illus.). 166p. (J). (gr. 4-7). 21.95 (*0-7862-3104-1*) Thorndike Pr.

Hogan, Paula Z. Will Dad Ever Move Back Home? 1980. (Life & Living from a Child's Point of View Ser.). (Illus.). 32p. (J). (gr. k-6). lib. bdg. 21.40 o.p. (*0-8172-1356-2*) Raintree Pubs.

Holl, Kristi D. For Every Joy That Passes. 1997. (J). (gr. 7-9). pap. 9.99 (*0-88092-341-5*) Royal Fireworks Publishing Co.

Homer, Larona. Julie & the Marigold Boy. 1997. 144p. (YA). pap. 7.95 (*0-912608-98-6*) Middle Atlantic Pr.

Hrdlitschka, Shelly. Beans on Toast. 1998. 128p. (YA). (gr. 6 up). pap. 6.95 (*1-55143-116-5*) Orca Bk. Pubs.

Hunter, Evan & McBain, Ed. Me & Mr. Stenner. 1976. (J). (gr. 4-7). 11.95 (*0-397-31689-5*) HarperCollins Children's Bk. Group.

—Me & Mr. Stenner. 1978. 128p. (J). (gr. 5-9). pap. 1.25 o.s.i (*0-440-95551-3*, Laurel Leaf) Random Hse. Children's Bks.

Hurwitz, Johanna. One Small Dog. 2000. (Illus.). 128p. (J). (gr. 2 up). lib. bdg. 15.89 (*0-06-029220-2*); 15.95 (*0-688-17382-9*) HarperCollins Children's Bk. Group.

—One Small Dog. 2002. (Illus.). 112p. (J). (gr. 2 up). pap. 4.99 (*0-380-73293-9*) Morrow/Avon.

Irwin, Hadley. Bring to a Boil & Separate. 1988. (J). (gr. 5 up). mass mkt. 2.50 o.p. (*0-451-14825-8*, Signet Bks.) NAL.

Johnson, Angela. Songs of Faith. 1999. 108p. (YA). (gr. 5-8). reprint ed. pap. 4.99 (*0-679-89488-8*, Knopf Bks. for Young Readers) Random Hse. Children's Bks.

—Songs of Faith. 1998. (Illus.). 112p. (J). (gr. 3-7). pap. 15.95 (*0-531-30023-4*); lib. bdg. 16.99 (*0-531-33023-0*) Scholastic, Inc. (Orchard Bks.).

Johnson, Patricia P. & Williams, Donna R. Our Family Is Divorcing, Grades 4-7: A Read-Aloud Book for Families Experiencing Divorce. 1996. (Helping Children Who Hurt Ser.). (Illus.). 80p. (Orig.). (J). pap., tchr. ed. 11.95 (*0-89390-391-4*) Resource Pubns., Inc.

Jones, Cordelia. Cat Called Camouflage. 1971. (Illus.). (J). (gr. 7 up). 26.95 (*0-87599-189-0*) Phillips, S.G. Inc.

Jones, Jennifer B. Dear Mrs. Ryan, You're Ruining My Life. 2000. 122p. (J). (gr. 5-9). 15.95 (*0-8027-8728-2*) Walker & Co.

Jones, Rebecca C. Madeline & the Great (Old) Escape Artist. 1983. (Madeline Ser.). 112p. (J). (ps-3). 9.95 o.p. (*0-525-44074-7*, 0966-290, Dutton) Dutton/Plume.

Jones, Robin D. The Beginning of Unbelief. 1993. 160p. (YA). (gr. 7 up). lib. bdg. 13.95 o.s.i (*0-689-31781-6*, Atheneum) Simon & Schuster Children's Publishing.

Jong, Erica. Megan's Two Houses. 1996. (J). (ps-3). (Illus.). 64p. pap. 14.95 o.p. (*0-7871-0405-1*); 6.95 o.p. (*0-7871-0993-2*) NewStar Media, Inc.

Kent, Lisa. Love Is Always There. 1993. (Illus.). 32p. (J). (ps-3). pap. 4.95 o.p. (*0-8091-6611-9*) Paulist Pr.

Klass, Sheila S. Next Stop: Nowhere. 1995. (Illus.). 176p. (YA). (gr. 7-9). pap. 14.95 (*0-590-46686-0*) Scholastic, Inc.

Klein, Norma. Angel Face. 1984. 228p. (J). (gr. 7 up). 13.95 o.p. (*0-670-12517-2*, Viking Children's Bks.) Penguin Putnam Bks. for Young Readers.

—What It's All About. 1975. 192p. (J). (gr. 5 up). 5.95 o.p. (*0-8037-5028-5*, Dial Bks. for Young Readers) Penguin Putnam Bks. for Young Readers.

Koss, Amy Goldman. A Stranger in Dadland. Hornik, Lauri, ed. 2001. (Illus.). 128p. (J). (gr. 5 up). 16.99 (*0-8037-2563-9*, Dial Bks. for Young Readers) Penguin Putnam Bks. for Young Readers.

Krishnaswami, Uma. Naming Maya, RS. 2004. (J). 16.00 (*0-374-35485-5*, Farrar, Straus & Giroux (BYR)) Farrar, Straus & Giroux.

Kropp, Paul. Moonkid & Liberty. 1990. (J). (gr. 3-6). 13.95 (*0-316-50485-8*, Joy Street Bks.) Little Brown & Co.

LaFaye, A. The Year of the Sawdust Man. 224p. (J). (gr. 3-7). 1999. (Illus.). pap. 4.99 (*0-689-83106-4*, Aladdin); 1998. 16.00 (*0-689-81513-1*, Simon & Schuster Children's Publishing) Simon & Schuster Children's Publishing.

—The Year of the Sawdust Man. 1999. 11.04 (*0-606-17947-X*) Turtleback Bks.

Lapka, Fay S. The Sea, the Song & the Trumpetfish. 1991. (Young Adult Fiction Ser.). 160p. (Orig.). (YA). (gr. 7-12). pap. 6.99 o.p. (*0-87788-754-3*, Shaw) WaterBrook Pr.

Larson, Rodger. What I Know Now, ERS. 1997. 272p. (J). (gr. 7-12). 15.95 o.s.i (*0-8050-4869-3*, Holt, Henry & Co. Bks. For Young Readers) Holt, Henry & Co.

Laskin, Pamela L. Getting to Know You. 2003. (YA). (*0-936389-92-3*) Tudor Pubs., Inc.

Lawson, Julie. Danger Game: A Novel. 1996. 214p. (YA). (gr. 5 up). 15.95 o.p. (*0-316-51728-3*) Little Brown & Co.

Lehrman, Robert. Separations. 1993. 224p. (J). (gr. 5-9). pap. 3.99 o.p. (*0-14-032322-8*, Puffin Bks.) Penguin Putnam Bks. for Young Readers.

LeMieux, A. C. The TV Guidance Counselor. 1993. 240p. (YA). (gr. 7 up). 13.00 o.p. (*0-688-12402-X*, Morrow, William & Co.) Morrow/Avon.

Lems, Kristin. Piano Teacher's Daughter. 2002. (Illus.). pap. 18.00 (*0-9637048-2-6*) Lems-Dworkin, Carol Pubs.

Levinson, Marilyn. No Boys Allowed. 1993. 8.05 o.p. (*0-606-07059-1*) Turtleback Bks.

Lewis, Beverly. Secret Summer Dreams. 1993. (Holly's Heart Ser.: Vol. 2). 160p. (J). (gr. 6-9). pap. 6.99 o.p. (*0-310-38061-8*) Zondervan.

—Secret Summer Dreams: Holly's Heart. 2001. (Hollys Heart Ser.). 144p. (J). (gr. 6-9). pap. 5.99 (*0-7642-2501-4*) Bethany Hse. Pubs.

Lieberg, Carolyn. West with Hopeless. 2004. 176p. (J). 16.99 (*0-525-47194-4*, Dutton Children's Bks.) Penguin Putnam Bks. for Young Readers.

Linko, Gina. Holden's Heart. 2004. (Seekers Ser.). (J). pap. 5.99 (*0-8066-4180-0*, Augsburg Bks.) Augsburg Fortress, Pubs.

Lisker, Sonia O. & Dean, Leigh. Two Special Cards. 1976. (Illus.). (J). (gr. k-2). 4.95 o.p. (*0-15-292222-9*) Harcourt Children's Bks.

Lisle, Janet Taylor. The Gold Dust Letters. 1994. (Investigators of the Unknown Ser.: Vol. 1). 128p. (J). (gr. 4-7). pap. 15.95 (*0-531-06830-7*); lib. bdg. 16.99 (*0-531-08680-1*) Scholastic, Inc. (Orchard Bks.).

Littleton, Mark. Winter Thunder. 1993. (Crista Chronicles Ser.: Bk. 2). (J). mass mkt. 3.99 o.p. (*1-56507-008-9*) Harvest Hse. Pubs.

Lorenzo, Carol L. The White Sand Road. 1978. (J). lib. bdg. 6.79 o.p. (*0-06-024012-1*) HarperCollins Pubs.

Losier, Dave. Fred's Prayer Machine. 2002. (Illus.). 152p. (J). pap. 11.95 (*1-929039-07-7*) Ambassador Bks., Inc.

Lowry, Danielle. What Can I Do? A Book for Children of Divorce. 2001. (Illus.). 46p. (J). (gr. 3-7). 14.95 (*1-55798-769-6*); pap. 8.95 (*1-55798-770-X*) American Psychological Assn. (Magination Pr.).

Mack, Tracy. Drawing Lessons. (Illus.). 176p. 2002. (YA). (gr. 5-9). mass mkt. 4.99 (*0-439-11203-6*, Scholastic Paperbacks); 2000. (J). (gr. 7-12). pap. 15.95 (*0-439-11202-8*, Scholastic Reference) Scholastic, Inc.

Madison, Winifred. The Genessee Queen. 1977. (J). (gr. 7 up). 6.95 o.p. (*0-440-02809-4*, Delacorte Pr.) Dell Publishing.

Mann, Peggy. My Dad Lives in a Downtown Hotel. 1973. 96p. (gr. k-5). 7.95 o.p. (*0-385-07080-2*) Doubleday Publishing.

—My Dad Lives in a Downtown Hotel. 1976. (J). pap. 1.75 o.p. (*0-380-00096-2*, 55038-5, Avon Bks.) Morrow/Avon.

Margolis, Bette S. A Heart Full of Love: With Workshop for Children of Divorce. 1999. 80p. (J). (gr. 1-4). pap. 14.95 (*0-9676360-0-0*) Bette's Bks.

Marshall, Hallie. Parent Trap Jr. 1998. 96p. (J). pap. 4.95 o.p. (*0-7868-4234-2*) Little Brown & Co.

Marshall, Linda D. What Is a Step? 1992. (Illus.). 48p. (Orig.). (J). (ps-5). pap. 10.00 (*1-879289-00-8*) Native Sun Pubs., Inc.

Martin, Ann M. Dawn on the Coast. (Baby-Sitters Club Ser.: No. 23). (J). (gr. 3-7). mass mkt. 3.95 (*0-590-42007-0*); 1997. 160p. mass mkt. 3.99 (*0-590-67391-2*); 1989. 192p. pap. 3.50 (*0-590-43900-6*) Scholastic, Inc.

—Dawn on the Coast. l.t. ed. 1994. (Baby-Sitters Club Ser.: No. 23). 176p. (J). (gr. 3-7). lib. bdg. 21.27 o.p. (*0-8368-1244-1*) Stevens, Gareth Inc.

—Dawn on the Coast. 1989. (Baby-Sitters Club Ser.: No. 23). (J). (gr. 3-7). 10.04 (*0-606-04085-4*) Turtleback Bks.

—Welcome Back, Stacey! l.t. ed. 1994. (Baby-Sitters Club Ser.: No. 28). 176p. (J). (gr. 3-7). lib. bdg. 21.27 o.p. (*0-8368-1249-2*) Stevens, Gareth Inc.

Relationships

—Welcome Back, Stacey! 1989. (Baby-Sitters Club Ser.: No. 28). (J). (gr. 3-7). 9.09 o.p. (*0-606-04419-1*) Turtleback Bks.

Mazer, Harry. Guy Lenny. 1971. (J). (gr. 4-7). 4.95 o.p. (*0-440-03316-0*); lib. bdg. 4.58 o.s.i (*0-440-03313-6*) Dell Publishing. (Delacorte Pr.).

—Guy Lenny. 1977. 96p. (J). (gr. 4-8). mass mkt. 2.95 o.s.i (*0-440-93311-0*, Laurel Leaf) Random Hse. Children's Bks.

—Guy Lenny. 1989. (J). (gr. 4-8). 15.00 o.p. (*0-8446-6369-7*) Smith, Peter Pub., Inc.

Mazer, Norma. I, Trissy. 1971. (J). (gr. 4-7). 6.95 o.s.i (*0-440-03986-X*); lib. bdg. 6.46 o.s.i (*0-440-03997-5*) Dell Publishing. (Delacorte Pr.).

Mazer, Norma Fox. E, My Name Is Emily. 1991. 176p. (J). pap. 13.95 o.p. (*0-590-43653-8*) Scholastic, Inc.

—Taking Terri Mueller. 1983. 224p. (YA). (gr. 7 up). 16.00 o.p. (*0-688-01732-0*, Morrow, William & Co.) Morrow/Avon.

McAfee, Annalena & Browne, A. Visitors Who Came to Stay. 1985. 32p. (J). (gr. 4-6). 11.95 o.p. (*0-670-74714-9*, Viking Children's Bks.) Penguin Putnam Bks. for Young Readers.

McEwan, Elaine K. Murphy's Mansion. Norton, LoraBeth, ed. 1994. (Josh McIntire Ser.). 96p. (J). (gr. 3-6). pap. 4.99 (*0-7814-0160-7*) Cook Communications Ministries.

—Operation Garbage. 1993. (Josh McIntire Ser.). 96p. (J). pap. 4.99 o.p. (*0-7814-0121-6*) Cook Communications Ministries.

—Underground Hero. 1993. 96p. (J). (gr. 3-6). pap. 4.99 (*0-7814-0113-5*) Cook Communications Ministries.

McGinnis, Lila S. If Daddy Only Knew Me. 1995. (Albert Whitman Concept Bks.). (Illus.). 32p. (J). (ps-3). lib. bdg. 14.95 o.p. (*0-8075-3537-0*) Whitman, Albert & Co.

Mead, Alice. Walking the Edge. 1995. 192p. (J). (gr. 4-7). lib. bdg. 14.95 (*0-8075-8649-8*) Whitman, Albert & Co.

Miller, Judi. Purple Is My Game, Morgan Is My Name. 1998. 128p. (J). (gr. 4-7). per. 3.99 (*0-671-00280-5*, Aladdin) Simon & Schuster Children's Publishing.

Morrison, Dannell C. Pee Yew Bartholomew: A Story about Divorce. 1997. 16p. (Orig.). (J). (gr. 5-8). pap. 5.95 o.p. (*1-57543-028-2*) MAR*CO Products, Inc.

Moss, Marissa. Amelia's Family Ties. 2000. (Amelia Ser.). (Illus.). (J). (gr. 3 up). 38p. 12.95 (*1-58485-079-5*); 40p. 5.95 (*1-58485-078-7*) Pleasant Co. Pubns. (American Girl).

—Amelia's Family Ties. 2000. (Amelia Ser.). (Illus.). (J). (gr. 3-5). 12.10 (*0-606-18352-3*) Turtleback Bks.

—Max's Logbook. 2003. (Illus.). 48p. (J). pap. 12.95 (*0-439-46660-1*) Scholastic, Inc.

Murphy, Claire Rudolf. To the Summit. 1998. 208p. pap. 3.99 (*0-380-79537-X*, Avon Bks.) Morrow/Avon.

—To the Summit. 1998. (J). 9.09 o.p. (*0-606-13853-6*) Turtleback Bks.

Napoli, Donna Jo. Changing Tunes. 160p. (gr. 3-7). 2000. (Illus.). (YA). pap. 4.99 o.s.i (*0-14-130811-7*, Puffin Bks.); 1998. (J). 15.99 o.s.i (*0-525-45861-1*, Dutton Children's Bks.) Penguin Putnam Bks. for Young Readers.

—Changing Tunes. 2000. (Illus.). (J). 11.04 (*0-606-18394-9*) Turtleback Bks.

Naylor, Phyllis Reynolds. Being Danny's Dog. 160p. (J). (gr. 4-7). 1997. (Illus.). pap. 4.50 (*0-689-81472-0*, Aladdin); 1995. 15.00 (*0-689-31756-5*, Atheneum) Simon & Schuster Children's Publishing.

—Being Danny's Dog. 1997. 10.04 (*0-606-11105-0*) Turtleback Bks.

Nelson, Carol. Dear Angie: Your Family Is Getting a Divorce. 1901. (J). (gr. 5-8). pap. 2.95 o.p. (*0-89191-246-0*) Cook Communications Ministries.

Nightingale, Lois V. My Parents Still Love Me, Even Though They're Getting Divorced: An Interactive Tale for Children. 1996. (Illus.). 128p. (J). (gr. k-6). pap. 14.95 (*1-889755-00-1*) Nightingale Rose Pubns.

Nixon, Joan Lowery. Casey & the Great Idea. 1982. (Illus.). 144p. (J). (gr. 4-6). pap. 2.50 o.p. (*0-590-32337-7*, Scholastic Paperbacks) Scholastic, Inc.

—Nobody's There. 2000. (Illus.). 208p. (YA). (gr. 7-9). 15.95 o.s.i (*0-385-32567-3*, Dell Books for Young Readers) Random Hse. Children's Bks.

Noble, June. Two Homes for Lynn, ERS. 1979. (Illus.). (J). (gr. k-3). o.p. (*0-03-046186-3*, Holt, Henry & Co. Bks. For Young Readers) Holt, Henry & Co.

Norris, Lori P. D Is for Divorce. 1991. (Little Books for Big Feelings Ser.). (Illus.). (J). (ps-4). 3.95 o.p. (*1-55874-140-2*) Health Communications, Inc.

Okimoto, Jean Davies. My Mother Is Not Married to My Father. 1979. (J). (gr. 5 up). 8.95 o.p. (*0-399-20664-7*) Putnam Publishing Group, The.

Orenstein, Denise G. When the Wind Blows Hard. 1982. (Illus.). (J). 11.95 (*0-201-10740-6*) HarperCollins Children's Bk. Group.

Orgel, Doris. Risking Love. 1984. 192p. (YA). (gr. 7 up). 12.95 o.p. (*0-8037-0131-4*, Dial Bks. for Young Readers) Penguin Putnam Bks. for Young Readers.

Orlev, Uri. Lydia: Queen of Palestine. Halkin, Hillel, tr. from HEB. 1993. Tr. of Lidyah: Malkat Erest Yisrael. 176p. (J). 13.95 o.p. (*0-395-65660-5*) Houghton Mifflin Co.

—Lydia, Queen of Palestine. Halkin, Hillel, tr. 1995. (Illus.). 176p. (J). (gr. 5-9). pap. 4.99 o.s.i (*0-14-037089-7*, Puffin Bks.) Penguin Putnam Bks. for Young Readers.

—Lydia, Queen of Palestine. 1995. 9.09 o.p. (*0-606-07817-7*) Turtleback Bks.

Park, Barbara. Don't Make Me Smile. 1983. 132p. (J). (gr. 4-7). pap. 2.95 (*0-380-61994-6*, Avon Bks.) Morrow/Avon.

—Don't Make Me Smile. 2002. 144p. (J). (gr. 3-7). pap. 4.99 (*0-375-81555-4*, Random Hse. Bks. for Young Readers); 1981. 128p. (J). (gr. 4-7). 8.95 o.s.i (*0-394-84978-7*, Knopf Bks. for Young Readers); 1981. 128p. (J). (gr. 4-7). lib. bdg. 10.99 (*0-394-94978-1*, Knopf Bks. for Young Readers); 1990. 128p. (gr. 4-7). reprint ed. pap. 4.50 o.s.i (*0-394-84745-8*, Random Hse. Bks. for Young Readers) Random Hse. Children's Bks.

—Don't Make Me Smile. 1981. 10.55 (*0-606-03233-9*) Turtleback Bks.

Paulsen, Gary. Hatchet. l.t. ed. 1989. 232p. (YA). reprint ed. lib. bdg. 15.95 o.p. (*1-55736-117-7*) Bantam Doubleday Dell Large Print Group, Inc.

—Hatchet. 2002. (Illus.). (J). 14.47 (*0-7587-0017-2*) Book Wholesalers, Inc.

—Hatchet. 1999. 235p. (J). (*0-03-054626-5*) Holt, Rinehart & Winston.

—Hatchet. 1995. (YA). (gr. 6 up). 9.28 (*0-395-73261-1*) Houghton Mifflin Co.

—Hatchet. l.t. ed. 2000. (LRS Large Print Cornerstone Ser.). 205p. (YA). (gr. 4-12). lib. bdg. 28.95 (*1-58118-055-1*, 23469) LRS.

—Hatchet. 2003. 151p. (J). pap. (*0-330-31045-3*) Macmillan Children's Bks.

—Hatchet. 208p. 1989. (J). (gr. 4-7). pap. 4.99 o.s.i (*0-14-034371-7*); 1988. (YA). (gr. 5-9). pap. 4.99 o.p. (*0-14-032724-X*) Penguin Putnam Bks. for Young Readers. (Puffin Bks.).

—Hatchet. 195p. (J). (gr. 4-6). pap. 4.99 (*0-8072-8320-7*, Listening Library) Random Hse. Audio Publishing Group.

—Hatchet. 2000. (Illus.). (J). 16.95 (*0-689-84092-6*, Atheneum/Richard Jackson Bks.); 1999. 208p. (YA). (gr. 5-9). mass mkt. 5.99 (*0-689-82699-0*, 076714004993, Simon Pulse); 1999. (J). pap. 2.99 o.p. (*0-689-82965-5*, Aladdin); 1998. 208p. (J). pap. 2.65 (*0-689-82167-0*, Aladdin); 1996. 208p. (YA). (gr. 5-9). pap. 5.99 (*0-689-80882-8*, Aladdin); 1987. 208p. (YA). (gr. 5-9). text 16.95 (*0-02-770130-1*, Atheneum/Richard Jackson Bks.) Simon & Schuster Children's Publishing.

—Hatchet. 1996. (J). 11.04 (*0-606-10206-X*) Turtleback Bks.

Paulsen, Gary, et al. Hatchet/Robinson Crusoe: Curriculum Unit — Novel Series — Grades 6-12. 1996. (Novel Ser.). 79p. tchr. ed., spiral bd. 18.95 (*1-56077-457-6*) Ctr. for Learning, The.

Peck, Richard. Voices after Midnight. 1990. (J). pap. o.p. (*0-440-80209-1*); 192p. (YA). (gr. 4-7). reprint ed. pap. text 4.50 o.s.i (*0-440-40378-2*) Dell Publishing.

—Voices after Midnight. 1989. 9.60 o.p. (*0-606-04840-5*) Turtleback Bks.

Pennebaker, Ruth. Conditions of Love, ERS. 1999. (Illus.). 256p. (J). (gr. 9-12). 16.95 o.s.i (*0-8050-6104-5*, Holt, Henry & Co. Bks. For Young Readers) Holt, Henry & Co.

—Conditions of Love. 2000. 272p. (YA). (gr. 9-12). mass mkt. 4.99 o.s.i (*0-440-22834-4*, Laurel Leaf) Random Hse. Children's Bks.

Perry, Patricia & Lynch, Marietta. Mommy & Daddy Are Divorced. 1985. (Pied Piper Bks.). (Illus.). 27p. (J). (ps-3). pap. 3.95 o.p. (*0-8037-0233-7*, Dial Bks. for Young Readers) Penguin Putnam Bks. for Young Readers.

Peters, Julie Anne. How Do You Spell G-E-E-K? 1997. 144p. (J). (gr. 3-7). pap. 3.99 o.p. (*0-380-73053-7*, Avon Bks.) Morrow/Avon.

Petersen, P. J. I Want Answers & a Parachute. 1993. (Illus.). 64p. (YA). (gr. 2-6). mass mkt. 13.00 (*0-671-86577-3*, Simon & Schuster Children's Publishing) Simon & Schuster Children's Publishing.

Pevsner, Stella. A Smart Kid Like You, 001. 1979. 192p. (J). (gr. 4-8). 14.95 o.p. (*0-395-28876-2*, Clarion Bks.) Houghton Mifflin Co. Trade & Reference Div.

Pfeffer, Susan Beth. Dear Dad, Love Laurie. 1989. (J). (gr. 4-7). pap. 10.95 o.p. (*0-590-41681-2*) Scholastic, Inc.

Phillips, Carolyn. Our Family Got a Divorce. 1979. (Illus.). 112p. (J). (gr. k-6). pap. 5.95 o.p. (*0-8307-0677-1*, 5419212, Regal Bks.) Gospel Light Pubns.

Pickhardt, Carl E. The Case of the Scary Divorce. 1997. (Jackson Skye Mystery Ser.). (Illus.). 96p. (YA). (gr. 3-10). pap. 14.95 o.p. (*0-945354-80-0*) American Psychological Assn.

Prestine, Joan Singleton. Mom & Dad Break Up. (Illus.). 32p. (J). 2002. pap. 6.95 (*1-57768-656-X*); 1996. (Kids Have Feelings, Too Ser.: Vol. 3857). 8.99 o.p. (*0-86653-857-7*, FE3857, Fearon Teacher Aids) McGraw-Hill Children's Publishing.

—Mom & Dad Break Up: Resource Guide. 2001. (Illus.). 32p. (J). (ps-3). 15.00 (*1-57768-683-7*) McGraw-Hill Children's Publishing.

Price, Reynolds. Michael Egerton. 1993. (J). (gr. 6 up). o.p. (*0-88682-591-1*, Creative Education) Creative Co., The.

Qualey, Marsha. Close to a Killer. (YA). (gr. 7-12). 2000. 208p. mass mkt. 4.99 (*0-440-22763-1*, Laurel Leaf); 1999. 192p. 15.95 o.s.i (*0-385-32597-5*, Dell Books for Young Readers) Random Hse. Children's Bks.

Quarles, Heather. A Door Near Here. 1998. 240p. (YA). (gr. 7-10). 13.95 o.s.i (*0-385-32595-9*) Doubleday Publishing.

—A Door Near Here. 2000. (Illus.). 240p. (YA). (gr. 7 up). mass mkt. 4.99 (*0-440-22761-5*, Laurel Leaf) Random Hse. Children's Bks.

—A Door Near Here. l.t. ed. 2000. (Young Adult Ser.). 323p. (J). (gr. 8-12). 21.95 (*0-7862-2884-9*) Thorndike Pr.

—A Door Near Here. 2000. 10.55 (*0-606-17796-5*) Turtleback Bks.

Ransom, Jeanie Franz. I Don't Want to Talk about It. 2000. (Illus.). 28p. (J). (ps-3). (*1-55798-664-9*, 441-6649); pap. (*1-55798-703-3*, 441-7033) American Psychological Assn. (Magination Pr.).

Reilly, Natalie & Pavese, Brandi J. My Stick Family: Helping Children Cope with Divorce. 2002. (Illus.). 48p. (J). mass mkt. 12.95 (*0-88282-207-1*, Small Horizons) New Horizon Pr. Pubs., Inc.

Richardson, Grace. Apples Every Day. 1973. 224p. (J). (gr. 7 up). reprint ed. pap. 1.95 o.p. (*0-06-440045-X*) HarperCollins Pubs.

Robinson, Lee. Gateway. 1996. 176p. (J). (gr. 7-12). tchr. ed. 14.95 o.p. (*0-395-72772-3*) Houghton Mifflin Co.

Robinson, Nancy K. Countess Veronica. (J). 1996. pap. text 3.50 (*0-590-44486-7*); 1994. 176p. (gr. 4-6). pap. 13.95 (*0-590-44485-9*) Scholastic, Inc.

—Countess Veronica. 1994. (J). 8.60 o.p. (*0-606-09163-7*) Turtleback Bks.

Rodell, Susanna. Dear Fred. 1995. (Illus.). 32p. (J). (ps-3). 14.95 (*0-395-71544-X*) Houghton Mifflin Co.

Rodowsky, Colby. Clay, RS. 2001. 176p. (J). (gr. 3-7). 16.00 (*0-374-31338-5*, Farrar, Straus & Giroux (BYR)) Farrar, Straus & Giroux.

—Clay. 2004. 160p. (J). pap. 5.99 (*0-06-000618-8*, Harper Trophy) HarperCollins Children's Bk. Group.

—Spindrift, RS. 2000. (Illus.). 144p. (J). (gr. 4-7). 16.00 (*0-374-37155-5*, Farrar, Straus & Giroux (BYR)) Farrar, Straus & Giroux.

—Spindrift. 2002. 144p. (J). (gr. 4-7). pap. 5.95 (*0-06-440991-0*, Harper Trophy) HarperCollins Children's Bk. Group.

Rogers, Helen S. Morris & His Brave Lion. 1975. (Illus.). 48p. (J). (ps-3). lib. bdg. o.p. (*0-07-053502-7*) McGraw-Hill Cos., The.

Sachs, Elizabeth-Ann. Shyster. 1985. (Illus.). 128p. (J). (gr. 2-5). 11.95 o.p. (*0-689-31161-3*, Atheneum) Simon & Schuster Children's Publishing.

Sachs, Marilyn. Another Day. 1997. 176p. (J). (gr. 5-9). 15.99 o.p. (*0-525-45787-9*) Penguin Putnam Bks. for Young Readers.

—At the Sound of the Beep. (J). 1991. 160p. (gr. 3-7). pap. 3.95 o.s.i (*0-14-034681-3*, Puffin Bks.); 1990. 16p. (gr. 4-7). 14.99 o.s.i (*0-525-44571-4*, Dutton Children's Bks.) Penguin Putnam Bks. for Young Readers.

Sanford, Doris. Please Come Home: A Child's Book about Divorce. 1985. (Hurts of Childhood Ser.). (Illus.). 24p. (J). (ps-5). 7.99 o.p. (*0-88070-138-2*) Zonderkidz.

Santucci, Barbara. Loon Summer. 2001. (Illus.). 16p. (J). (gr. k-3). 16.00 (*0-8028-5182-7*, Eerdmans Bks For Young Readers) Eerdmans, William B. Publishing Co.

Schindel, John. Dear Daddy. 1995. (Illus.). 24p. (J). (ps-3). lib. bdg. 13.95 (*0-8075-1531-0*) Whitman, Albert & Co.

Schnur, Steven. The Koufax Dilemma. 1997. (Illus.). 186p. (J). (gr. 5 up). 15.00 (*0-688-14221-4*, Morrow, William & Co.) Morrow/Avon.

—The Koufax Dilemma. 2001. 196p. pap. 14.95 (*0-595-19998-4*, Backinprint.com) iUniverse, Inc.

Shalant, Phyllis. The Great Eye. 1996. 160p. (J). (gr. 5-9). 15.99 o.s.i (*0-525-45695-3*) Penguin Putnam Bks. for Young Readers.

Shoup, Barbara. Wish You Were Here. 1994. 288p. (J). (gr. 7 up). 16.95 o.p. (*0-7868-0028-3*) Hyperion Bks. for Children.

Shreve, Susan Richards. The Formerly Great Alexander Family. 1995. (Illus.). 128p. (J). (gr. 3 up). 13.00 o.s.i (*0-688-13551-X*, Morrow, William & Co.) Morrow/Avon.

Siebold, Jan. Rope Burn. 1998. 80p. (J). (gr. 4-7). lib. bdg. 13.95 (*0-8075-7109-1*) Whitman, Albert & Co.

Silsbee, Peter. The Temptation of Kate. 1990. 160p. (J). (gr. 6-9). lib. bdg. 13.95 o.p. (*0-02-782761-5*, Simon & Schuster Children's Publishing) Simon & Schuster Children's Publishing.

Singer, Nicky. Feather Boy. 2002. 272p. (gr. 5-8). text 15.95 (*0-385-72980-4*); (gr. 6-8). lib. bdg. 17.99 (*0-385-90043-0*) Dell Publishing. (Delacorte Pr.).

—Feather Boy. 2003. (Illus.). 272p. (gr. 5). pap. text 4.99 (*0-440-41858-5*, Dell Books for Young Readers) Random Hse. Children's Bks.

Skinner, Daphne. Santa Clause Jr. 1994. (J). pap. 1.00 o.p. (*0-7868-1058-0*) Hyperion Bks. for Children.

Skinner, Daphne, adapted by. The Santa Clause. 1994. (Junior Novel Ser.). (Illus.). 80p. (J). (gr. 3-7). pap. 3.95 (*0-7868-1011-4*) Disney Pr.

Smith, Doris B. Kick a Stone Home. 1974. 192p. (J). (gr. 5 up). 12.95 o.p. (*0-690-00535-0*) HarperCollins Children's Bk. Group.

Sommer, Karen. Satch & the Motormouth. 1987. (Satch Ser.). (J). (gr. 3-7). pap. 4.99 o.p. (*1-55513-063-1*) Cook Communications Ministries.

Southgate, Martha. Another Way to Dance. 1996. 192p. (YA). (gr. 7-12). 15.95 o.s.i (*0-385-32191-0*, Delacorte Pr.) Dell Publishing.

—Another Way to Dance. 1998. 208p. (YA). (gr. 7-12). reprint ed. mass mkt. 4.99 o.s.i (*0-440-21968-X*, Laurel Leaf) Random Hse. Children's Bks.

—Another Way to Dance. 1998. 10.55 (*0-606-12878-6*) Turtleback Bks.

Spelman, Cornelia Maude. Mama & Daddy Bear's Divorce. (Concept Book Ser.). (Illus.). (J). (ps-1). 2001. 24p. pap. 5.95 (*0-8075-5222-4*); 1998. 32p. lib. bdg. 13.95 (*0-8075-5221-6*) Whitman, Albert & Co.

Springer, Nancy. Separate Sisters. 2001. 160p. (J). (gr. 5-7). tchr. ed. 16.95 (*0-8234-1544-9*) Holiday Hse., Inc.

Steindal, Yvonne L. D. Holden's Heart. ldr.'s ed. 2004. (Seekers Ser.). 3.99 (*0-8066-4183-5*, Augsburg Bks.) Augsburg Fortress, Pubs.

Steiner, Barbara. Tessa. 1988. 224p. (J). (gr. 7 up). 12.95 o.p. (*0-688-07232-1*, Morrow, William & Co.) Morrow/Avon.

Still-Chapman, Ann. Kids' Play. 1995. (Illus.). 49p. (J). text 14.50 (*0-930329-93-7*) Kabel Pubs.

Stinson, Kathy. Mom & Dad Don't Live Together Anymore. 2003. (Illus.). 32p. (J). (gr. k-3). pap. 5.95 (*0-920236-87-1*); lib. bdg. 15.95 (*0-920236-92-8*) Annick Pr., Ltd. CAN. *Dist:* Firefly Bks., Ltd.

Stolz, Mary. Go & Catch a Flying Fish. 1979. (Ursula Nordstrom Bk.). (YA). (gr. 6 up). lib. bdg. 12.89 o.p. (*0-06-025868-3*) HarperCollins Children's Bk. Group.

Stowe, Cynthia. Home Sweet Home, Good-bye. 1990. (J). (gr. 4-7). pap. 10.95 o.p. (*0-590-43001-7*) Scholastic, Inc.

Talbert, Marc. Thin Ice. 1986. (J). (gr. 3 up). 13.95 o.s.i (*0-316-83133-6*) Little Brown & Co.

—Thin Ice. 2001. 216p. pap. 15.95 (*0-595-20019-2*, Backinprint.com) iUniverse, Inc.

Thomas, Ianthe. Eliza's Daddy. 1976. (Let Me Read Ser.). (Illus.). (J). (gr. 1-5). 4.95 o.p. (*0-15-225400-5*); pap. 1.65 o.p. (*0-15-225401-3*) Harcourt Children's Bks.

Thomas, Rob. Rats Saw God: A Comic Emotionally Charged Tale. 1996. (Illus.). 224p. (YA). (gr. 7 up). per. 17.00 (*0-689-80207-2*, Simon & Schuster Children's Publishing) Simon & Schuster Children's Publishing.

Tobesman, Rachmiel. The Magic Glasses: Stories & Other Activities for Children of Separation & Divorce. 1998. (Illus.). 38p. (J). (ps-12). spiral bd. 12.95 (*0-9677266-0-3*) Child Access Ctr. of Maryland,The.

Van Leeuwen, Jean. Blue Sky, Butterfly. 1996. (Illus.). 128p. (J). (gr. 4-7). 14.99 o.s.i (*0-8037-1972-8*, Dial Bks. for Young Readers) Penguin Putnam Bks. for Young Readers.

Velasquez, Gloria. Maya's Divided World. 1995. (Roosevelt High School Series Bks.). 125p. (YA). (gr. 4-7). 12.95 (*1-55885-126-7*); pap. 9.95 (*1-55885-131-3*) Arte Publico Pr. (Piñata Books).

Venable, Leslie Allgood. The Not So Wicked Stepmother. 1999. (Illus.). 24p. (J). (gr. 1-7). per. 9.95 (*0-9666817-0-3*) Venable, L.A. Publishing Co.

Vigna, Judith. Daddy's New Baby. Fay, Ann, ed. 1982. (Albert Whitman Concept Bks.). (Illus.). 32p. (J). (ps-3). lib. bdg. 11.95 o.p. (*0-8075-1435-7*) Whitman, Albert & Co.

—I Live with Daddy. 1997. 32p. (J). (gr. 1-4). lib. bdg. 14.95 (*0-8075-3512-5*) Whitman, Albert & Co.

Voigt, Cynthia. Bad, Badder, Baddest. (J). (gr. 4-7). 1999. 272p. mass mkt. 4.99 (*0-439-08096-7*, Scholastic Paperbacks); 1997. 176p. pap. 16.95 (*0-590-60136-9*) Scholastic, Inc.

Relationships

—Bad, Badder, Baddest. 1999. 11.04 (*0-606-17038-3*) Turtleback Bks.

—A Solitary Blue. 1987. (YA). (gr. 6 up). mass mkt. 3.95 o.s.i (*0-449-70268-5*, Fawcett) Ballantine Bks.

—A Solitary Blue. l.t. ed. 2001. 369p. (J). lib. bdg. 33.95 net. (*1-58118-085-3*) LRS.

—A Solitary Blue. 1993. (Point Ser.). 320p. (J). (gr. 7 up). mass mkt. 4.99 (*0-590-47157-0*) Scholastic, Inc.

—A Solitary Blue. (Tillerman Ser.). 2003. 256p. (J). pap. 5.99 (*0-689-86360-8*, Aladdin); 2003. (Illus.). 256p. (YA). mass mkt. 5.99 (*0-689-86434-5*, Simon Pulse); 2001. 204p. (J). E-Book 6.99 (*0-689-84799-8*, Atheneum); 1983. 204p. (YA). (gr. 7 up). 18.00 (*0-689-31008-0*, Atheneum) Simon & Schuster Children's Publishing.

—A Solitary Blue. 1983. (Point Ser.). (J). 11.04 (*0-606-05611-4*) Turtleback Bks.

Warner, Sally. Sister Split. 2001. (American Girls Collection Ser.). 156p. (J). 14.95 (*1-58485-373-5*); pap. 5.95 (*1-58485-372-7*) Pleasant Co. Pubns. (American Girl).

Weatherly, Lee. Child X. 2003. 224p. (gr. 4-9). pap. text 5.50 (*0-440-41904-2*, Dell Books for Young Readers) Random Hse. Children's Bks.

Weeks, Sarah. Guy Time. 176p. (J). (gr. 3-7). 2001. pap. 5.99 (*0-06-440783-7*, Harper Trophy); 2000. (Illus.). 14.95 (*0-06-028365-3*, Geringer, Laura Bk.); 2000. (Illus.). lib. bdg. 15.89 (*0-06-028366-1*, Geringer, Laura Bk.) HarperCollins Children's Bk. Group.

—Guy Time. 2001. (J). 11.00 (*0-606-21222-1*) Turtleback Bks.

Weiss, Ellen & Cooke, Tom. Worried about Divorce. 1991. (Muppet Kids Ser.). (Illus.). 24p. (J). (ps-3). pap. 3.29 o.s.i (*0-307-12657-9*, Golden Bks.) Random Hse. Children's Bks.

Weninger, Brigitte, pseud. Good-Bye, Daddy! (Illus.). 32p. (J). (gr. k-3). 1997. pap. 6.95 (*1-55858-770-5*); 1995. 14.95 (*1-55858-383-1*); 1995. 15.50 o.p. (*1-55858-384-X*) North-South Bks., Inc.

Wiggins, VeraLee. LeeAnne, the Disposable Kid. 1994. (J). (gr. 7-10). pap. 5.99 o.p. (*0-8280-0791-8*) Review & Herald Publishing Assn.

Williams, Vera B. Scooter. 1993. (Illus.). 160p. (J). (gr. 2 up). 17.95 (*0-688-09376-0*); (ps-3). 14.89 o.p. (*0-688-09377-9*) HarperCollins Children's Bk. Group. (Greenwillow Bks.).

Willner-Pardo, Gina. Jason & the Losers. 1995. 128p. (J). 14.95 o.p. (*0-395-70160-0*, Clarion Bks.) Houghton Mifflin Co. Trade & Reference Div.

—What I'll Remember When I Am a Grownup. 1994. (Illus.). (J). (gr. 2-4). 13.95 o.s.i (*0-395-63310-9*, Clarion Bks.) Houghton Mifflin Co. Trade & Reference Div.

Willson, Sarah. I Have Two Homes: A Sesame Solutions Book about Divorce. 2001. (J). 12.99 (*0-375-81395-0*); (*0-375-91395-5*) Random Hse., Inc.

Wilson, Jacqueline. The Bed & Breakfast Star. l.t. ed. 2000. (J). (Illus.). pap. (*0-7540-6090-X*); 242p. pap. 29.95 incl. audio (*0-7540-6231-7*, RA032, Chivers Children's Audio Bks.) BBC Audiobooks America.

—The Bed & Breakfast Star. 2000. 32p. (J). pap. 6.95 (*0-440-86324-4*, Delacorte Pr.) Dell Publishing.

—The Suitcase Kid. l.t. ed. 1993. (J). (gr. 1-8). 19.95 o.p. (*0-7451-1703-1*, Galaxy Children's Large Print) BBC Audiobooks America.

—The Suitcase Kid. 1998. (Illus.). 144p. (gr. 3-7). pap. text 4.50 (*0-440-41371-0*, Dell Books for Young Readers) Random Hse. Children's Bks.

Wilson, Nancy Hope. The Reason for Janey. 1994. 176p. (J). (gr. 5 up). 15.00 (*0-02-793127-7*, Atheneum) Simon & Schuster Children's Publishing.

Winkler, David. The Return of Calico Bright, RS. 2003. 352p. 19.00 (*0-374-38048-1*, Farrar, Straus & Giroux (BYR)) Farrar, Straus & Giroux.

Winthrop, Elizabeth. As the Crow Flies. 1998. (Illus.). 32p. (J). (gr. k-4). tchr. ed. 15.00 o.p. (*0-395-77612-0*, Clarion Bks.) Houghton Mifflin Co. Trade & Reference Div.

Wittlinger, Ellen. Hard Love. (YA). 1999. (Illus.). 224p. (gr. 7 up). 16.95 (*0-689-82134-4*, Simon & Schuster Children's Publishing); 2001. 240p. (gr. 8-12). reprint ed. pap. 8.00 (*0-689-84154-X*, Simon Pulse) Simon & Schuster Children's Publishing.

Wolitzer, Hilma. Out of Love, RS. (Illus.). 160p. (J). (gr. 5 up). 1984. pap. 3.50 o.p. (*0-374-45685-2*, Sunburst); 1976. 14.00 o.p. (*0-374-35675-0*, Farrar, Straus & Giroux (BYR)) Farrar, Straus & Giroux.

Wood, Phyllis A. Song of the Shaggy Canary. 1974. (Hiway Book). 156p. (J). (gr. 6 up). 9.00 o.p. (*0-664-32543-2*) Westminster John Knox Pr.

—Win Me & You Lose. 1977. (Hiway Book). 136p. (J). (gr. 7 up). 8.95 o.p. (*0-664-32605-6*) Westminster John Knox Pr.

Wyeth, Sharon Dennis. Ginger Brown: Too Many Houses. 1996. (Illus.). 80p. (J). (ps-3). 11.99 o.s.i (*0-679-95437-6*); (gr. 1-4). pap. 3.99 o.s.i (*0-679-85437-1*) Random Hse. Children's Bks. (Random Hse. Bks. for Young Readers).

—Ginger Brown: Too Many Houses. 1996. 9.19 o.p. (*0-606-09327-3*) Turtleback Bks.

Zach, Cheryl. Secret Admirer. 1999. (Dear Diary Ser.). 192p. (YA). (gr. 7-12). mass mkt. 4.50 o.s.i (*0-425-17114-0*, JAM) Berkley Publishing Group.

DOMESTIC RELATIONS—FICTION

Brennan, Herbie. Faerie Wars. 2003. (Illus.). 370p. (J). 17.95 (*1-58234-810-3*, Bloomsbury Children) Bloomsbury Publishing.

Brooks, Kevin. Martyn Pig. 240p. (J). 2003. pap. 6.99 o.s.i (*0-439-50752-9*); 2002. (gr. 5 up). pap. 15.95 (*0-439-29595-5*, Chicken Hse., The) Scholastic, Inc.

Brown, Terry. Tangled Web. 2003. (Today's Girls Only Ser.: Bk. 3). 128p. (J). pap. 5.99 (*1-4003-0323-0*) Nelson, Tommy.

Brown, Terry, creator. Tangled Web. 2000. (Todays-Girls.com Ser.: Vol. 3). 128p. (J). (gr. 5-9). pap. 5.99 o.s.i (*0-8499-7562-X*) Nelson, Tommy.

Christopher, Matt. Windmill Windup. 2002. (J). (gr. 3-7). 140p. 15.95 (*0-316-14531-9*); 144p. pap. 4.50 (*0-316-14432-0*) Little Brown Children's Bks.

Cross, Gillian. Tightrope. 2001. (Harper Trophy Bks.). 304p. (J). (gr. 7 up). pap. 5.95 (*0-06-447272-8*, Harper Trophy) HarperCollins Children's Bk. Group.

—Tightrope. 1999. 208p. (YA). (gr. 7-12). 16.95 (*0-8234-1512-0*) Holiday Hse., Inc.

—Tightrope. 1999. 210p. (YA). (*0-19-271804-5*) Oxford Univ. Pr., Inc.

Dean, Carolee. Comfort. 2002. 240p. (J). (gr. 7 up). 15.00 (*0-618-13846-3*) Houghton Mifflin Co.

Dewey, Jennifer Owings. Borderlands. 2002. 159p. (J). 14.95 (*0-7614-5114-5*) Cavendish, Marshall Corp.

Fisk, Pauline. Midnight Blue. 2003. 250p. (J). 16.95 (*1-58234-829-4*, Bloomsbury Children) Bloomsbury Publishing.

—Midnight Blue. (YA). 1992. 220p. (gr. 6-10). pap. text 4.99 o.p. (*0-7459-1925-1*); 1990. 224p. (gr. 7-12). 11.95 o.p. (*0-7459-1848-4*) Lion Publishing.

—Telling the Sea. 1992. 256p. (YA). (gr. 6-10). text 11.95 o.p. (*0-7459-2061-6*) Lion Publishing.

—Telling the Sea. 2003. 252p. (J). pap. 8.95 (*0-7459-4740-9*) Lion Publishing PLC GBR. *Dist:* Trafalgar Square.

Frank, E. R. Life Is Funny. 2002. 272p. (J). pap. 7.99 (*0-14-230083-7*, Puffin Bks.) Penguin Putnam Bks. for Young Readers.

Gray, Nigel. A Balloon for Grandad. 1988. (Illus.). 32p. (J). (ps-2). 13.95 o.p. (*0-531-05755-0*); mass mkt. 13.99 o.p. (*0-531-08355-1*) Scholastic, Inc. (Orchard Bks.).

Greenwald, Sheila. All the Way to Wit's End. 1981. 144p. (J). (gr. k-6). pap. 1.75 o.s.i (*0-440-40188-7*, Yearling) Random Hse. Children's Bks.

Gripe, Maria. The Night Daddy. 1973. (gr. 3 up). pap. 1.25 o.p. (*0-440-46683-0*) Dell Publishing.

Head, Ann. Mr. & Mrs. Bo Jo Jones. 1985. mass mkt. 0.95 o.p. (*0-451-05230-7*); 1968. mass mkt. 1.25 o.p. (*0-451-06440-2*); 1968. mass mkt. 1.75 o.p. (*0-451-11255-5*); 1968. mass mkt. 2.25 o.p. (*0-451-14140-7*); 1968. mass mkt. 1.95 o.p. (*0-451-12375-1*); 1968. mass mkt. 1.50 o.p. (*0-451-07869-1*) NAL. (Signet Bks.).

—Mr. & Mrs. Bo Jo Jones. 1967. 9.95 o.p. (*0-399-10562-X*, G. P. Putnam's Sons) Penguin Putnam Bks. for Young Readers.

—Mr. & Mrs. Bo Jo Jones. 9999. (J). pap. 1.95 o.s.i (*0-590-03201-1*) Scholastic, Inc.

Holl, Kristi. 4Give & 4Get. 2001. (TodaysGirls.com Ser.: Vol. 9). (Illus.). 144p. (J). (gr. 5-9). pap. 5.99 o.s.i (*0-8499-7712-6*) Nelson, Tommy.

Lisle, Janet Taylor. How I Became a Writer & Oggie Learned to Drive. (Illus.). 160p. 2003. pap. 5.99 (*0-14-250167-0*, Puffin Bks.); 2002. (J). (gr. 4-7). 16.99 (*0-399-23394-6*, Philomel) Penguin Putnam Bks. for Young Readers.

Lynch, Chris. Babes in the Woods. 1997. (He-Man Women Haters Club Ser.: Vol. 2). 128p. (J). pap. 4.50 o.p. (*0-06-440656-3*, Harper Trophy) HarperCollins Children's Bk. Group.

Lyon, George Ella. Gina, Jamie, Father, Bear. 2002. 144p. (J). (gr. 6-9). 15.95 (*0-689-84370-4*, Atheneum/Richard Jackson Bks.) Simon & Schuster Children's Publishing.

Matthews, Kezi. Scorpio's Child. 2001. 160p. (J). (gr. 6-8). 15.95 (*0-8126-2890-X*) Cricket Bks.

—Scorpio's Child. 2004. 160p. (J). 6.99 (*0-14-240079-3*, Puffin Bks.) Penguin Putnam Bks. for Young Readers.

Montes, Marisa. A Circle of Time. 2002. (Time Travel Mystery Ser.). 272p. (YA). (gr. 6-10). 17.00 (*0-15-202626-6*) Harcourt Children's Bks.

Neufeld, John. Edgar Allan. 1969. mass mkt. 0.60 o.p. (*0-451-04113-5*, Signet Bks.); mass mkt. 0.95 o.p. (*0-451-06278-7*, Signet Bks.); mass mkt. 1.25 o.p. (*0-451-06628-6*, Signet Bks.); mass mkt. 1.75 o.p. (*0-451-11801-4*, Signet Bks.); mass mkt. 2.25 o.p. (*0-451-14469-4*, Signet Bks.); mass mkt. 2.95 o.p. (*0-451-15870-9*, Signet Bks.); mass mkt. 2.75 o.p. (*0-451-15381-2*, Signet Bks.); mass mkt. 1.95 o.p. (*0-451-13355-2*, Signet Bks.); mass mkt. 1.50 o.p. (*0-451-11179-6*, Signet Bks.); 128p. (YA). mass mkt. 4.99 o.s.i (*0-451-16775-9*) NAL.

—Edgar Allan. 1999. 128p. (J). (gr. 5-9). pap. 5.99 (*0-14-130432-4*, Puffin Bks.) Penguin Putnam Bks. for Young Readers.

—Edgar Allan. 1968. (J). 10.09 o.p. (*0-606-03122-7*) Turtleback Bks.

Perl, Lila. The Telltale Summer of Tina C, 001. 1979. 160p. (J). (gr. 4-8). tchr. ed. 6.95 o.p. (*0-395-28872-X*, Clarion Bks.) Houghton Mifflin Co. Trade & Reference Div.

Rapp, Adam. Missing the Piano. 2002. (Illus.). 256p. (J). (gr. 7 up). pap. 5.95 (*0-06-447369-4*, Harper Trophy) HarperCollins Children's Bk. Group.

—Missing the Piano. (YA). (gr. 7 up). 1996. 208p. pap. 4.99 o.s.i (*0-14-036833-7*, Puffin Bks.); 1994. 160p. 14.99 (*0-670-95340-7*, Viking Children's Bks.) Penguin Putnam Bks. for Young Readers.

—Missing the Piano. 1996. (J). 10.09 o.p. (*0-606-09621-3*) Turtleback Bks.

Rinaldi, Ann. Millicent's Gift. 224p. (J). 2004. pap. 5.99 (*0-06-441009-9*, Harper Trophy); 2002. lib. bdg. 15.89 (*0-06-029637-2*); 2002. (Illus.). 15.95 (*0-06-029636-4*) HarperCollins Children's Bk. Group.

Roth, David. River Runaways, 001. 1981. (J). (gr. 5-9). 7.95 o.p. (*0-395-31678-2*) Houghton Mifflin Co.

Saksena, Kate. Hang on in There, Shelley. 2003. 219p. (J). 16.95 (*1-58234-822-7*, Bloomsbury Children) Bloomsbury Publishing.

Taylor, Kim. Cissy Funk. 2001. 224p. (J). (gr. 5 up). 15.95 (*0-06-029041-2*); lib. bdg. 15.89 (*0-06-029042-0*) HarperCollins Children's Bk. Group.

Wells, Rosemary. None of the Above. 1974. 192p. (J). (gr. 8 up). 5.95 o.p. (*0-8037-6148-1*, Dial Bks. for Young Readers) Penguin Putnam Bks. for Young Readers.

F

FAMILY—FICTION

Abolafia, Yossi. My Three Uncles. 1985. (Illus.). 32p. (J). (gr. k-3). 12.95 o.p. (*0-688-04024-1*); lib. bdg. 12.88 o.p. (*0-688-04025-X*) HarperCollins Children's Bk. Group. (Greenwillow Bks.).

Abramov, Yirmiyohu & Abramo, Tehilla. Harmony in the Home: An Educational Program for the Jewish Family. 1996. (Illus.). (J). (ps-5). pap. 12.95 o.p. (*1-56871-114-X*) Targum Pr., Inc.

Ackerman, Karen. The Leaves in October. 1993. (J). pap. o.s.i (*0-440-90049-2*); 128p. (gr. 3-7). pap. 3.99 o.s.i (*0-440-40868-7*) Dell Publishing.

—The Leaves in October. 1991. 128p. (J). (gr. 3-7). 13.95 (*0-689-31583-X*, Atheneum) Simon & Schuster Children's Publishing.

—The Leaves in October. 1991. (J). 9.09 o.p. (*0-606-05420-0*) Turtleback Bks.

Ada, Alma Flor. El Arbol de Navidad. 1997. Tr. of Christmas Tree. (SPA., Illus.). 32p. (J). (ps-1). 14.95 (*0-7868-0151-4*) Hyperion Bks. for Children.

Adams, Pam. Ups & Downs. 1985. (Illus.). 44p. (J). (ps-1). 4.99 (*0-85953-257-7*) Child's Play of England GBR. *Dist:* Child's Play-International.

Adams-Treska, Lucille. The Twig Tops: Thunder in the Woods. 2002. 32p. pap. 8.00 (*0-8059-5650-6*) Dorrance Publishing Co., Inc.

Adler, C. S. Youn Hee & Me. 1995. 192p. (YA). (gr. 3-7). 12.00 o.s.i (*0-15-200073-9*) Harcourt Children's Bks.

Ahlberg, Allan. Happy Familie's Master Tracks Train. (Illus.). 24p. (J). pap. 6.95 (*0-14-037881-2*) Penguin Bks., Ltd. GBR. *Dist:* Trafalgar Square.

—My Brother's Ghost. 2001. 87p. (J). (gr. 6 up). 9.99 o.s.i (*0-670-89290-4*, Viking Children's Bks.) Penguin Putnam Bks. for Young Readers.

Aks, Patricia. Who Needs a Stepsister? 1982. 176p. (J). pap. 1.95 o.p. (*0-590-32358-X*) Scholastic, Inc.

Albee, Sarah. Ahoy, Uncle Roy! 2001. (Road to Reading Ser.). (Illus.). 32p. (J). 11.99 (*0-307-46216-1*); pap. 3.99 (*0-307-26216-2*) Random Hse. Children's Bks. (Golden Bks.).

Alcock, Vivien. A Kind of Thief. 1992. 192p. (J). (gr. 4-7). 14.00 o.s.i (*0-385-30564-8*, Delacorte Pr.) Dell Publishing.

Alcott, Louisa May. Jo's Boys. 2001. (YA). pap., stu. ed. 87.20 incl. audio Recorded Bks., LLC.

—Rose in Bloom. 1876. 344p. (YA). reprint ed. pap. text 28.00 (*1-4047-1634-3*) Classic Textbooks.

—Rose in Bloom. 312p. (J). 1995. (gr. 5 up). pap. 9.99 (*0-316-03089-9*); Vol. 1. 1996. 17.95 o.p. (*0-316-03782-6*) Little Brown & Co.

Alexander, Nina. And the Winner Is.... 1999. (Full House Sisters Ser.: No. 3). 160p. (J). (gr. 4-6). pap. 3.99 (*0-671-04055-3*, Simon Spotlight) Simon & Schuster Children's Publishing.

Aliki. Go Tell Aunt Rhody. 1996. (Illus.). 40p. (J). (ps-3). mass mkt. 5.99 (*0-689-80765-1*, Aladdin) Simon & Schuster Children's Publishing.

—Go Tell Aunt Rhody. 1996. 12.14 (*0-606-09330-3*) Turtleback Bks.

Allan, Jay. Blocks. 1993. (My New Bk.). (Illus.). (J). (ps). pap. 5.95 (*0-9631798-1-0*) Silver Seahorse Pr.

Allan, Nicholas. The Thing That Ate Aunt Julia. 1991. (Illus.). 320p. (J). (ps-3). 11.95 o.p. (*0-8037-0872-6*, Dial Bks. for Young Readers) Penguin Putnam Bks. for Young Readers.

Alphin, Elaine Marie. Counterfeit Son. 2000. (Illus.). 192p. (YA). (gr. 9 up). 17.00 (*0-15-202645-2*) Harcourt Children's Bks.

Alvarez, Julia. Antes de Ser Libre. 2004. (SPA.). 176p. (YA). (gr. 7). mass mkt. 5.99 (*0-375-81545-7*, Laurel Leaf) Random Hse. Children's Bks.

—How Tia Lola Came to (Visit) Stay. 160p. (gr. 3-7). 2004. (J). lib. bdg. 17.99 (*0-375-91552-4*, Knopf Bks. for Young Readers); 2004. (SPA., Illus.). pap. text 5.50 (*0-375-81552-X*, Yearling); 2002. (Illus.). pap. text 5.50 (*0-440-41870-4*, Laurel Leaf) Random Hse. Children's Bks.

—How Tia Lola Came to (Visit) Stay. Cascardi, Andrea, ed. 2001. (Illus.). 160p. (gr. 3-5). text 15.95 (*0-375-80215-0*); lib. bdg. 17.99 (*0-375-90215-5*) Random Hse. Children's Bks. (Knopf Bks. for Young Readers).

Amedick, Deborah. A Cat Named Wellington: His Lessons for Life. 1998. (Animal Ser.). (Illus.). 52p. (J). (ps-1). pap. 6.95 (*1-891210-87-4*, CNW01) Bartlett Publishing.

Andersen, C. B. The Book of Mormon Sleuth. 2000. v, 279p. (J). pap. 9.95 (*1-57345-664-0*) Deseret Bk. Co.

Andrews, Jan & Carrier, Ephrem. Pa's Harvest: A True Story Told by Ephrem Carrier. 2000. (Illus.). 39p. (J). (ps-3). 12.95 (*0-88899-405-2*) Groundwood Bks. CAN. *Dist:* Publishers Group West.

Angell, Judie. Don't Rent My Room. 1991. 144p. (YA). mass mkt. 3.50 o.s.i (*0-553-29142-4*) Bantam Bks.

Anshaw, Carol. Latchkey Kids. 1991. (J). (ps-3). mass mkt. 2.75 o.p. (*0-590-43188-9*) Scholastic, Inc.

Antle, Nancy. Playing Solitaire. 2000. (Illus.). 112p. (YA). (gr. 7 up). 16.99 o.p. (*0-8037-2406-3*, Dial Bks. for Young Readers) Penguin Putnam Bks. for Young Readers.

Applegate, Cathy. Red Sand, Blue Sky. 2004. (Girls First! Ser.). 142p. (J). (gr. 4-7). pap. 13.50 (*1-55861-278-5*) Feminist Pr. at The City Univ. of New York.

Arter, Jim. Gruel & Unusual Punishment. 1991. 112p. (J). (gr. 3-7). 13.95 o.s.i (*0-385-30298-3*, Delacorte Pr.) Dell Publishing.

Atkins, Jeannine. Becoming Little Women: Louisa May at Fruitlands. 2001. (Illus.). 176p. (J). (gr. 4-7). 16.99 (*0-399-23619-8*, G. P. Putnam's Sons) Penguin Group (USA) Inc.

—A Name on the Quilt: A Story of Remembrance. 1999. (Illus.). 32p. (J). (gr. k-3). 16.00 (*0-689-81592-1*, Atheneum) Simon & Schuster Children's Publishing.

—A Name on the Quilt: A Story of Remembrance. 2003. (Illus.). 32p. (J). pap. 6.99 (*0-689-85998-8*, Aladdin) Simon & Schuster Children's Publishing.

Auvil, Peggy A. We Bought a Bird That Said Dirty Words. 1999. (Illus.). 24p. (J). (gr. k-6). pap. 8.00 o.p. (*0-8059-4656-X*) Dorrance Publishing Co., Inc.

Avi. Blue Heron. 1993. 192p. (J). (gr. 4-7). pap. 5.99 (*0-380-72043-4*, Avon Bks.) Morrow/Avon.

—Blue Heron. 1992. 192p. (J). (gr. 7 up). lib. bdg. 17.00 (*0-02-707751-9*, Simon & Schuster Children's Publishing) Simon & Schuster Children's Publishing.

—Blue Heron. 1992. 10.55 (*0-606-05163-5*) Turtleback Bks.

—Prairie School. 2001. (I Can Read Chapter Bks.). (Illus.). 48p. (J). (gr. 3-4). 15.99 (*0-06-027664-9*) HarperCollins Children's Bk. Group.

Ayres, Katherine. Family Tree. 1996. 144p. (J). (gr. 3-7). 15.95 o.s.i (*0-385-32227-5*, Delacorte Pr.) Dell Publishing.

—Family Tree. 1997. (Yearling Ser.). 176p. (gr. 3-7). pap. text 4.50 (*0-440-41193-9*, Dell Books for Young Readers) Random Hse. Children's Bks.

—Family Tree. 1997. (J). 10.04 (*0-606-13074-8*) Turtleback Bks.

Bahr, Howard. Home for Christmas. 1997. (J). 9.95 (*1-877853-51-8*) Nautical & Aviation Publishing Co. of America, Inc., The.

Bailey, Debbie. My Family, No. 11. 1998. (Talk-about-Books: Vol. 11). (Illus.). 14p. (J). (ps). 5.95 (*1-55037-510-5*) Annick Pr., Ltd. CAN. *Dist:* Firefly Bks., Ltd.

Baltz, Terry & Baltz, Wayne. The Invisible Kid & the Killer Cat. 1994. (Invisible Kid Ser.: No. 2). 127p. (Orig.). (J). (gr. 2-6). pap. 6.95 (*1-884610-12-9*) Prairie Divide Productions.

Banks, Kate. Dillon Dillon, RS. 2002. 160p. (J). (gr. 3-6). 16.00 (*0-374-31786-0*, Farrar, Straus & Giroux (BYR)) Farrar, Straus & Giroux.

Banks, Sarah Harrell. A Net to Catch Time. 1996. (Illus.). 32p. (J). (ps-3). 17.99 o.s.i (*0-679-96673-0*) Random Hse., Inc.

Relationships

Bardi, Carol A. & Bates, Georgia. Who Loves You. 1997. (Illus.). 34p. (J). (ps-k). pap. 9.95 (*0-9660498-0-2*, Bardi Pr.) Bardi Consulting.

Bauer, Joan. Rules of the Road. 2000. 11.04 (*0-606-20370-2*) Turtleback Bks.

Bauer, Marion Dane. Land of the Buffalo Bones: The Diary of Mary Elizabeth Rodgers, an English Girl in Minnesota. 2003. (Dear America Ser.). (Illus.). 240p. (J). pap. 12.95 (*0-439-22027-0*) Scholastic, Inc.

Baylor, Byrd. The Table Where Rich People Sit. 1998. 12.14 (*0-606-13832-3*) Turtleback Bks.

Bechard, Margaret E. Tory & Me & the Spirit of True Love. 1992. 160p. (J). (gr. 3-7). 14.00 o.p. (*0-670-84688-0*, Viking Children's Bks.) Penguin Putnam Bks. for Young Readers.

Beers, V. Gilbert. Preschooler's Family Story. 1995. (Preschoolers Bible Ser.). 256p. (J). 16.99 (*1-56476-492-3*, 6-3492) Cook Communications Ministries.

Belle Prater's Boy. 1999. (Pathways to Critical Thinking Ser.). 32p. (YA). pap. text, stu. ed., tchr.'s training gde. ed. 19.95 (*1-58303-081-6*) Pathways Publishing.

Belton, Sandra. McKendree. 2000. 272p. (J). (gr. 5 up). 16.99 (*0-688-15950-8*, Greenwillow Bks.) HarperCollins Children's Bk. Group.

Bennett, Cherie. The Fall of the the Perfect Girl. 1993. (Surviving Sixteen Ser.: No. 2). 224p. (J). (gr. 7 up). pap. 3.50 o.p. (*0-14-036319-X*, Puffin Bks.) Penguin Putnam Bks. for Young Readers.

Bennett, James W. The Squared Circle. 1995. 288p. (YA). (gr. 7 up). pap. 14.95 o.p. (*0-590-48671-3*) Scholastic, Inc.

Berenstain, Stan & Berenstain, Jan. The Berenstain Bears, 7 vols., Date not set. (Early Childhood First Bks.). (Illus.). (J). (ps-2). lib. bdg. 97.65 (*1-56674-942-5*) Forest Hse. Publishing Co., Inc.

Bertrand, Diane Gonzales. Sweet Fifteen. 1996. 296p. (YA). (gr. 6-12). pap. text 7.95 o.p. (*1-55885-184-4*) Arte Publico Pr.

Black, Judith. Adult Children of ... Parents. (J). 12.00 (*0-9701073-2-3*) Black, Judith Storyteller.

Blackstone, Stella. Bear's Busy Family. 2000. (Illus.). 24p. (J). (ps). reprint ed. bds. 6.99 (*1-84148-391-5*) Barefoot Bks., Inc.

Blair, L. E. Family Affair. 1991. (Girl Talk Ser.: No. 19). 128p. (J). (gr. 4-7). pap. 2.95 o.s.i (*0-307-22019-2*, 22019, Golden Bks.) Random Hse. Children's Bks.

Blanchett, Warwick. Mrs. Rochester: A Sequel to Jane Eyre. 2000. 288p. (YA). pap. 24.95 (*1-86950-365-1*) HarperCollins NZL. *Dist:* Antipodes Bks. & Beyond.

Bloom, Hanya. Science Spook. 1990. (Vic the Vampire Ser.: No. 2). 80p. (J). (gr. 4-7). mass mkt. 2.95 o.p. (*0-06-106020-8*, Perennial) HarperTrade.

—Vampire Cousins. 1990. (Vic the Vampire Ser.: No. 3). 80p. (J). (gr. 4-7). mass mkt. 2.95 o.p. (*0-06-106025-9*, Perennial) HarperTrade.

Bloor, Edward. The Crusader. 2001. 608p. (J). (gr. 7 up). mass mkt. 7.50 (*0-439-22160-9*) Scholastic, Inc.

Blos, Joan W. A Gathering of Days: A New England Girl's Journal, 1830-1832, Vol. 1. 1999. pap. 2.99 (*0-689-82991-4*, Aladdin) Simon & Schuster Children's Publishing.

Bloss, Janet A. One Hundred & One Ways to a Perfect Family. 1990. (Illus.). 128p. (Orig.). (J). (gr. 3-6). pap. text 2.50 o.p. (*0-87406-462-7*) Darby Creek Publishing.

Bodner, Elizabeth L. Uncompromising Vol. 1: Family Style. 1997. 235p. (Orig.). pap. 14.95 (*0-9657162-0-1*) EBW Assocs.

Bond, Rebecca. Bravo, Maurice! 2000. (Illus.). 32p. (J). (ps-3). 14.95 (*0-316-10545-7*) Little Brown & Co.

—Bravo, Maurice! 2000. E-Book (*1-58824-628-0*); E-Book (*1-58824-629-9*); E-Book 11.99 (*1-58824-871-2*) ipicturebooks, LLC.

—Just Like a Baby. 1999. (Illus.). 32p. (J). (ps-3). 15.95 (*0-316-10416-7*) Little Brown & Co.

—Just Like a Baby. 1999. (Illus.). (J). E-Book (*1-58824-647-7*) ipicturebooks, LLC.

Bonners, Susan. Edwina Victorious, RS. 2000. (Illus.). 144p. (J). (gr. 2-5). 16.00 (*0-374-31968-5*, Farrar, Straus & Giroux (BYR)) Farrar, Straus & Giroux.

Borntrager, Mary Christner. Rebecca. 1989. (Ellie's People Ser.: Vol. 2). 176p. (J). (gr. 4-7). pap. 8.99 (*0-8361-3500-8*) Herald Pr.

Bos, Burny. Leave It to the Molesons! 1998. (Illus.). 48p. (J). (gr. 1-4). pap. 5.95 (*1-55858-993-7*) North-South Bks., Inc.

Bosak, Susan V. Something to Remember Me By: A Story about Love & Legacies. 2003. (Illus.). 32p. (gr. 1-6). (*1-896232-01-9*) Communication Project, The.

Bowen, Elizabeth. Friends & Relations. 1980. 192p. (YA). (gr. 7 up). pap. 2.25 (*0-380-49601-1*, 49601-1, Avon Bks.) Morrow/Avon.

Boyd, Lizi. The Not-So-Wicked Stepmother. 1987. (J). (ps-4). 11.95 o.p. (*0-670-81589-6*, Viking Children's Bks.) Penguin Putnam Bks. for Young Readers.

—Sam Is My Half Brother. 1992. (Picture Puffin Ser.). (Illus.). 32p. (J). (ps-3). pap. 3.99 o.s.i (*0-14-054190-X*, Puffin Bks.) Penguin Putnam Bks. for Young Readers.

Brandenberg, Franz. Aunt Nina & Her Nephews & Nieces. 1983. (Illus.). 32p. (J). (gr. k-3). 16.00 o.p. (*0-688-01869-6*); lib. bdg. 15.93 o.p. (*0-688-01870-X*) HarperCollins Children's Bk. Group. (Greenwillow Bks.).

—Aunt Nina, Good Night. 1989. (Illus.). 32p. (J). (ps up). 12.95 o.p. (*0-688-07463-4*); lib. bdg. 12.88 o.p. (*0-688-07464-2*) HarperCollins Children's Bk. Group. (Greenwillow Bks.).

Brayfield, Celia. Getting Home. 1998. (Illus.). 391p. o.s.i (*0-316-64246-0*) Little Brown & Co.

Breakthrough Publishing Staff, ed. Horse Family's Busy Day. 1996. (Illus.). 48p. (J). (ps-3). pap. 7.50 o.p. (*0-914327-63-1*) Breakthrough Pubns., Inc.

Bridgers, Sue E. Notes for Another Life. 1998. 258p. (YA). lib. bdg. 29.95 (*0-7351-0044-6*) Replica Bks.

Briggs, Raymond, text. Ivor the Invisible. 2003. (Illus.). 40p. (J). 19.95 (*0-7522-2034-9*) Boxtree, Ltd. GBR. *Dist:* Trafalgar Square.

Brisley, Joyce Lakester. Milly-Molly-Mandy Storybook. 2001. (Milly-Molly-Mandy Ser.). (Illus.). 224p. (J). (gr. k-3). tchr. ed. 13.95 (*0-7534-5332-0*, Kingfisher) Houghton Mifflin Co. Trade & Reference Div.

—Milly-Molly-Mandy Storybook. 1998. (Milly-Molly-Mandy Ser.). (Illus.). 224p. (J). (gr. k-3). tchr. ed. 13.95 o.p. (*1-85697-493-6*) Larousse Kingfisher Chambers, Inc.

Brisson, Pat. Star Blanket. 2003. (Illus.). 32p. (J). 15.95 (*1-56397-889-X*) Boyds Mills Pr.

Brokaw, Nancy Steele. Leaving Emma. 1999. 144p. (J). (gr. 4-6). tchr. ed. 15.00 (*0-395-90699-7*, Clarion Bks.) Houghton Mifflin Co. Trade & Reference Div.

Brown, Laurene Krasny. Rex & Lilly Family Time. 1997. (Rex & Lilly Ser.). (Illus.). 32p. (J). (ps-1). 10.10 (*0-606-11793-8*) Turtleback Bks.

Bruna, Dick. Auntie Alice's Party: A Miffy Storybook. 2000. (Miffy Ser.). (Illus.). 28p. (J). (ps-k). 4.95 (*1-56836-304-4*) Kodansha America, Inc.

Brundige, Patricia. Traveling with Aunt Patty: Aunt Patty Visits London. Wright, Cindy, ed. Date not set. (Illus.). (J). (gr. 1-4). text 12.95 (*0-9659668-0-1*) Aunt Patty's Travels-London.

Buechner, Frederick. The Wizard's Tide: A Story. 1990. 15.00 o.p. (*0-06-061160-X*) HarperSanFrancisco.

Bullard, Lisa. My Family: Love & Care, Give & Share. 2002. (All about Me Ser.). (Illus.). 24p. (J). (ps-1). lib. bdg. 19.90 (*1-4048-0044-1*) Picture Window Bks.

Bunn, Scott. Just Hold On. 1982. 160p. (J). (gr. 7 up). pap. 9.95 o.s.i (*0-385-28490-X*, Delacorte Pr.) Dell Publishing.

Bunting, Eve. I Have an Olive Tree. 1999. (YA). stu. ed. 167.80 incl. audio (*0-7887-3674-4*, 46977); 2000. (YA). pap. 31.95 incl. audio (*0-7887-3644-2*, 41010X4); 2000. (YA). pap. 31.95 incl. audio (*0-7887-3644-2*, 41010X4); 2000. (J). 10.00 incl. audio (*0-7887-3512-8*, 95865E7); 2000. (J). 10.00 incl. audio (*0-7887-3512-8*, 95865E7) Recorded Bks., LLC.

—My Backpack. 2003. (Illus.). 32p. (J). (gr. 1-3). 15.95 (*1-56397-433-9*) Boyds Mills Pr.

—Our Teacher's Having a Baby. 1992. (Illus.). 32p. (J). (ps-3). lib. bdg., tchr. ed. 15.00 (*0-395-60470-2*, Clarion Bks.) Houghton Mifflin Co. Trade & Reference Div.

Burgess, Lynn. Family Reunion. 1998. (Illus.). 16p. (J). (ps-k). pap. 5.95 (*0-9655442-7-3*) Business Word, The.

Burke, Diana. Matchmakers. 2000. (Full House Sisters Ser.: No. 11). (Illus.). 176p. (J). (gr. 4-6). pap. 3.99 (*0-671-04091-X*, Simon Spotlight) Simon & Schuster Children's Publishing.

Busselle, Rebecca. A Frog's-Eye View. 1990. 208p. (J). (gr. 7 up). 14.95 o.p. (*0-531-05907-3*); mass mkt. 14.99 o.p. (*0-531-08507-4*) Scholastic, Inc. (Orchard Bks.).

Butterworth, Bill. Butterworth Takes a Vacation: But Wishes He Could Give It Back. 1997. 160p. pap. 10.99 o.p. (*1-57673-046-8*, Multnomah Bks.) Multnomah Pubs., Inc.

Byars, Betsy C. The Cartoonist. 1987. (Illus.). 128p. (J). (gr. 4-7). reprint ed. pap. 5.99 (*0-14-032309-0*, Puffin Bks.) Penguin Putnam Bks. for Young Readers.

—The Cartoonist. 1980. 128p. (J). (gr. k-6). pap. 1.25 o.s.i (*0-440-41046-0*, Yearling) Random Hse. Children's Bks.

—The Night Swimmers. 1981. 144p. (J). (gr. 5-9). mass mkt. 2.75 o.s.i (*0-440-96766-X*, Laurel) Dell Publishing.

—The Not-Just-Anybody Family. (gr. 4-6). 149p. (J). pap. 4.50 (*0-8072-1429-9*); 1987. (YA). pap. 29.00 incl. audio (*0-8072-7324-4*, YA-805 SP) Random Hse. Audio Publishing Group. (Listening Library).

—The Not-Just-Anybody Family. 1986. (J). 13.95 o.s.i (*0-440-50211-X*, Dell Books for Young Readers) Random Hse. Children's Bks.

Calvert, Patricia. Sooner. 1998. 176p. (J). (gr. 4-7). 16.00 (*0-689-81114-4*, Atheneum) Simon & Schuster Children's Publishing.

Camp, Lindsay. Why? 1999. (Illus.). 32p. (J). (ps-3). 15.99 o.p. (*0-399-23396-2*, G. P. Putnam's Sons) Penguin Group (USA) Inc.

Canady, Pat. Boots the World's Best Kid-Sitter: Springtime Adventures. 2000. (Illus.). 6p. (J). (ps-4). pap. 10.00 (*1-929889-02-X*) Canady SW Publishing.

Canfield, Dorothy. The Bent Twig. 1997. 400p. (ps up). reprint ed. pap. 20.00 (*0-8214-1185-3*) Ohio Univ. Pr.

Cann, Kate. Hard Cash. 2003. (Illus.). 336p. (YA). mass mkt. 5.99 (*0-689-85905-8*, Simon Pulse) Simon & Schuster Children's Publishing.

Cano, Robin B. Lucita Regresa a Oaxaca (Lucita Comes Home to Oaxaca) Ricardez, Rafael E., tr. 1998. (ENG & SPA., Illus.). 32p. (J). (gr. 3-6). 16.95 (*1-56492-111-5*) Laredo Publishing Co., Inc.

Carlson, Mary E. Cousins. 1994. (J). pap. 7.95 o.p. (*0-533-10803-9*) Vantage Pr., Inc.

Carlson, Melody. Benjamin's Box: A Resurrection Story. 1997. (Illus.). 40p. (J). (gr. k-5). 10.99 o.p. (*1-57673-139-1*) Zonderkidz.

—A Tale of Two Houses. 1998. (Illus.). 40p. (ps-13). 14.99 o.p. (*1-57673-314-9*) Zonderkidz.

Carlson, Nancy L. My Family Is Forever. 2004. (J). 15.99 (*0-670-03650-1*, Viking) Viking Penguin.

Carlson, Natalie S. Family under the Bridge. 1989. (J). 12.00 (*0-606-04031-5*) Turtleback Bks.

—The Family under the Bridge. 1989. (Trophy Bk.). (Illus.). 112p. (J). (gr. 2-6). pap. 5.99 (*0-06-440250-9*, Harper Trophy) HarperCollins Children's Bk. Group.

Carmody, Isobelle. The Gathering. 288p. (J). 1996. pap. 4.99 o.s.i (*0-14-038538-X*); 1994. 15.99 o.s.i (*0-8037-1716-4*, Dial Bks. for Young Readers) Penguin Putnam Bks. for Young Readers.

—The Gathering. 1996. (J). 10.09 o.p. (*0-606-10191-8*) Turtleback Bks.

—The Gathering. 1996. 288p. (J). (gr. 7). pap. 4.99 o.p. (*0-14-036059-X*) Viking Penguin.

Carney, Mary L. Too Tough to Hurt. 1991. 128p. (J). pap. 6.99 (*0-310-28621-2*) Zondervan.

Carr, Jan. Dark Day, Light Night. 1996. (Illus.). 32p. (J). (ps-3). 14.95 (*0-7868-0018-6*) Hyperion Bks. for Children.

Carris, Joan D. Aunt Morbelia & the Screaming Skulls. 1990. (Illus.). (J). (gr. 3-7). 14.95 o.p. (*0-316-12945-3*) Little Brown & Co.

Carroll, Jacqueline. For the Birds. 2001. (Full House Michelle Ser.: No. 37). (Illus.). 96p. (J). (gr. 2-4). pap. 3.99 (*0-671-04202-5*, Simon Spotlight) Simon & Schuster Children's Publishing.

Cart, Michael, ed. Necessary Noise: Stories about Our Families As They Really Are. 2003. (Illus.). 256p. (J). (gr. 12 up). 15.99 (*0-06-027499-9*) HarperCollins Pubs.

Carter, Alden R. Crescent Moon. 1999. 153p. (J). (gr. 5-9). tchr. ed. 16.95 (*0-8234-1521-X*) Holiday Hse., Inc.

Case, Susan. Aunt Charles' Surprise Visit. 1995. 96p. (J). (gr. 2-9). pap. 1.00 (*1-56722-026-6*) Word Aflame Pr.

Casson, Les. My Uncle Max. 2003. (Annikins Ser.: Vol. 10). (Illus.). 15p. (Orig.). (J). (ps-2). pap. 1.25 (*1-55037-130-4*) Annick Pr., Ltd. CAN. *Dist:* Firefly Bks., Ltd.

Castillo, Ana. Mi Hija, Mi Hijo, el Aguila, la Paloma. 2000. (SPA., Illus.). 48p. (J). (gr. 3-5). 12.99 (*0-525-45867-0*, DT4486, Dutton Children's Bks.) Penguin Putnam Bks. for Young Readers.

Cazet, Denys. Great-Uncle Felix. 1988. (Illus.). 32p. (J). (ps-1). 14.95 o.p. (*0-531-05750-X*); mass mkt. 15.99 o.p. (*0-531-08350-0*) Scholastic, Inc. (Orchard Bks.).

Cerasini, Marc. Sister Trouble. Alfonsi, Alice, ed. 2000. (Seventh Heaven Ser.: Vol. 4). (Illus.). 160p. (gr. 3-7). pap. text 3.99 o.s.i (*0-375-81158-3*, Random Hse. Bks. for Young Readers) Random Hse. Children's Bks.

Chaconas, Doris J. On a Wintry Morning. (Illus.). 32p. (J). 2002. pap. 5.99 (*0-14-250006-2*, Puffin Bks.); 2000. 15.99 (*0-670-89245-9*, Viking Children's Bks.) Penguin Putnam Bks. for Young Readers.

Charles, Norma. Sophie Sea to Sea: Star Girl's Cross-Canada Adventures! 2000. 130p. (J). (gr. 3-8). pap. 5.95 (*0-88878-404-X*, Sandcastle Bks.) Beach Holme Pubs., Ltd. CAN. *Dist:* Strauss Consultants.

Charlip, Remy. I Love You. 1999. (Illus.). 32p. (J). (ps-1). pap. 4.95 (*0-590-02315-2*, Cartwheel Bks.) Scholastic, Inc.

Charnas, Suzy McKee. The Silver Glove. 2001. 176p. pap. 14.95 (*1-58715-479-X*) Wildside Pr.

Cheng, Andrea. Anna the Bookbinder. 2003. (Illus.). 32p. (J). (gr. k-4). 16.95 (*0-8027-8831-9*); lib. bdg. 17.85 (*0-8027-8832-7*) Walker & Co.

Cherrington, Janelle. Drawing the Line. 2000. (Wild Thornberrys Ready-to-Read Ser. : Vol. 2). (Illus.). 32p. (J). (gr. 4-6). pap. 3.99 (*0-689-83231-1*, Simon Spotlight/Nickelodeon) Simon & Schuster Children's Publishing.

Child, Lauren. Clarice Bean, Guess Who's Babysitting? 2001. (Illus.). 32p. (J). (gr. 1-4). 16.99 (*0-7636-1373-8*) Candlewick Pr.

Choldenko, Gennifer. Notes from a Liar & Her Dog. 2003. 224p. pap. 5.99 (*0-14-250068-2*, Puffin Bks.) Penguin Putnam Bks. for Young Readers.

Christian, Mary Blount. Linc. 1991. 128p. (YA). (gr. 7 up). text 13.95 o.p. (*0-02-718580-X*, Simon & Schuster Children's Publishing) Simon & Schuster Children's Publishing.

Christie, Amanda. The New Me. Lafreniere, Kenneth, ed. 2000. (7th Heaven Ser.). (Illus.). 128p. (J). (gr. 3-7). pap. 3.99 o.s.i (*0-375-81161-3*, Random Hse. Bks. for Young Readers) Random Hse. Children's Bks.

Chumbley, Peggy Lucinda. Mommy & Daddy Take Me to Church. 1999. (Illus.). 32p. (J). pap. 9.95 (*0-9672309-0-X*) PLC Publishing.

Clark, David F. The First Mission. 1997. (Ammon Adventures Ser.: Vol. 2). 96p. (J). (gr. 6-12). pap. 7.95 (*1-890830-57-7*) Riplah Publishing.

Clark, Emma C. Lunch with Aunt Augusta. 1992. (Illus.). 320p. (J). (ps-3). 14.00 o.p. (*0-8037-1104-2*, Dial Bks. for Young Readers) Penguin Putnam Bks. for Young Readers.

Clary, Margie Willis. A Sweet, Sweet Basket. Stone, Barbara, ed. 1995. (Illus.). 40p. (J). (gr. k-7). 15.95 (*0-87844-127-1*) Sandlapper Publishing Co., Inc.

Cleary, Beverly. Ramona Empieza el Curso. 1997. (Ramona Ser.). (SPA., Illus.). 192p. (J). (gr. 3-7). 15.00 (*0-688-15467-0*, MR7552, Greenwillow Bks.) HarperCollins Children's Bk. Group.

Cleary, Brian P. It Looks a Lot Like Reindeer. 1995. (It Could Be Verse Ser.). (Illus.). 32p. (J). (gr. 3-6). lib. bdg. 12.95 (*0-8225-2117-2*, Lerner Pubns.) Lerner Publishing Group.

—You Never Sausage Love. 1996. (It Could Be Verse Ser.). (Illus.). 32p. (J). (gr. 3-6). lib. bdg. 12.95 (*0-8225-2115-6*) Lerner Publishing Group.

Cleaver, Vera. Where the Lilies Bloom. 1986. pap. 1.25 o.s.i (*0-440-82197-5*) Dell Publishing.

Cleaver, Vera & Cleaver, Bill. Where the Lilies Bloom. (Illus.). (J). (gr. 7 up). 1991. 176p. lib. bdg. 14.89 o.p. (*0-397-32500-2*); 1989. 224p. pap. 5.99 (*0-06-447005-9*, Harper Trophy); 1969. 176p. 15.95 (*0-397-31111-7*) HarperCollins Children's Bk. Group.

—Where the Lilies Bloom. 1982. 175p. (J). mass mkt. 2.25 o.p. (*0-451-15203-4*, Signet Bks.) NAL.

—Where the Lilies Bloom. 1989. (J). 11.00 (*0-606-04364-0*) Turtleback Bks.

Cochrane, Shirley G. & Townsend, Betsy B. The Jones Family. 1992. (Illus.). 50p. (Orig.). (J). pap. 10.00 (*0-9609062-2-3*) Washington Expatriates Pr.

Coerr, Eleanor. Josefina y la Colcha de Retazos. Marcuse, Aida E., tr. unabr. ed. 1995. (I Can Read Bks.).Tr. of Josefina Story Quilt. (SPA., Illus.). 80p. (J). (gr. 2-4). pap. 10.95 o.p. incl. audio (*0-694-70023-1*) HarperCollins Children's Bk. Group.

Cogan, Karen. Mi Hermanito Ben. Romo, Alberto, tr. 1999. (Books for Young Learners).Tr. of My Little Brother Ben. (SPA., Illus.). 12p. (J). (gr. k-2). pap. text 5.00 (*1-57274-343-3*, A2878) Owen, Richard C. Pubs., Inc.

Cohen, Miriam. Say Hi, Backpack Baby. l.t. ed. 2001. (Backpack Baby Stories Ser.). (Illus.). 12p. (J). (ps). bds. 5.95 (*1-887734-82-1*) Star Bright Bks., Inc.

—Wah! Wah! A Backpack Baby Story. l.t. ed. 2001. (Backpack Baby Stories Ser.). (Illus.). 12p. (J). (ps). bds. 5.95 (*1-887734-81-3*) Star Bright Bks., Inc.

Collier, James Lincoln. Rich & Famous. 2001. (Lost Treasures Ser.: No. 6). (Illus.). 240p. (J). pap. 4.99 (*0-7868-1520-5*); (gr. 3-7). pap. 1.99 (*0-7868-1519-1*) Hyperion Bks. for Children. (Volo).

Colman, Hila. Diary of a Frantic Kid Sister. 1985. (J). (gr. 4-7). pap. 2.95 (*0-671-61926-8*, Simon Pulse) Simon & Schuster Children's Publishing.

—Diary of a Frantic Kid Sister. 1973. (J). 8.05 o.p. (*0-606-03060-3*) Turtleback Bks.

Colrus, Bill. I Got Your Nose! 1996. (Uncle Louie Ser.). (Illus.). 6p. (Orig.). (J). (ps up). pap. 1.99 o.p. (*1-56293-836-3*, McClanahan Bk.) Learning Horizons, Inc.

Combs, Bobbie. 1-2-3 Family Counting Book. 2001. 32p. (J). pap. 8.95 (*0-9674468-0-5*) Two Lives Publishing.

Conrad, Pam. This Mess. 1998. (Illus.). 32p. (J). (ps-3). 14.95 (*0-7868-0159-X*); lib. bdg. 15.49 (*0-7868-2131-0*) Hyperion Bks. for Children.

—What I Did for Roman. (Trophy Bk.). 224p. (YA). (gr. 7 up). 1996. pap. 4.50 o.p. (*0-06-447164-0*, Harper Trophy); 1987. lib. bdg. 14.89 o.p. (*0-06-021332-9*) HarperCollins Children's Bk. Group.

Coombs, Corinne. My Brother Sam Is Dead. 1999. (Literature Units Ser.). (Illus.). 48p. (J). pap., tchr. ed. 7.99 (*1-57690-507-1*, TCA2507) Teacher Created Materials, Inc.

Cooney, Caroline B. Family Reunion. 1990. 176p. (YA). mass mkt. 2.95 o.s.i (*0-553-28573-4*) Bantam Bks.

—Family Reunion. 2004. lib. bdg. 11.99 (*0-385-90167-4*, Delacorte Bks. for Young Readers); 2004. 208p. (gr. 5). text 9.95 (*0-385-73136-1*, Delacorte Bks. for Young Readers); 1989. 176p. (YA). (gr. 7 up). 14.95 o.s.i (*0-553-05836-3*, Starfire) Random Hse. Children's Bks.

—Tune in Anytime. 192p. (YA). (gr. 7). 2001. (Illus.). mass mkt. 4.99 (*0-440-22798-4*, Laurel Leaf); 1999. 8.95 o.s.i (*0-385-32649-1*, Dell Books for Young Readers) Random Hse. Children's Bks.

Cooper, Melrose. I Got a Family, ERS. (Illus.). (J). (ps-2). 1993. 88p. 14.95 o.p. (*0-8050-1965-0*); 1997. 32p. reprint ed. pap. 6.95 (*0-8050-5542-8*) Holt, Henry & Co. (Holt, Henry & Co. Bks. For Young Readers).

—I Got a Family. 1997. 12.10 (*0-606-13503-0*) Turtleback Bks.

Coran, Pierre. Family Tree. 1999. (Picture Bks.). (Illus.). 32p. (J). (ps-3). lib. bdg. 15.95 o.s.i (*1-57505-219-9*, Carolrhoda Bks.) Lerner Publishing Group.

Corbet, Robert. Fifteen Love. 2003. 192p. (J). (gr. 7 up). 16.95 (*0-8027-8851-3*) Walker & Co.

Cormier, Robert. Eight Plus One. 1985. 192p. (YA). mass mkt. 2.75 o.s.i (*0-553-26815-5*) Bantam Bks.

—Eight Plus One. 1991. 208p. (YA). (gr. 7 up). mass mkt. 5.50 (*0-440-20838-6*, Laurel Leaf) Random Hse. Children's Bks.

Cory, Kim Delmar. Lilly's Way. Austin, Jane G., ed. 1998. 187p. (J). (gr. 4 up). pap. 9.99 (*0-88092-363-6*, 3636) Royal Fireworks Publishing Co.

Costella, Deborah. Cooking with Granddad. Morisson, Connie, ed. 2002. 42p. pap. 14.95 (*0-9718155-5-0*, 14) Inkwell Productions.

Couloumbis, Audrey. Getting near to Baby. 1999. 224p. (J). (gr. 5-9). 17.99 (*0-399-23389-X*, G. P. Putnam's Sons) Penguin Group (USA) Inc.

—Getting near to Baby. 2001. 224p. (YA). (gr. 5-9). pap. 5.99 (*0-698-11892-8*, Puffin Bks.) Penguin Putnam Bks. for Young Readers.

—Getting near to Baby. l.t. ed. 2000. (Juvenile Ser.). (Illus.). 215p. (J). (gr. 4-7). 22.95 (*0-7862-2705-2*) Thorndike Pr.

Courtney, Vincent. Virtual Fred. 1996. (Stepping Stone Bks.). (Illus.). 90p. (gr. 1-4). pap. 3.99 o.s.i (*0-679-88214-6*) McKay, David Co., Inc.

Covey, Stephen R. & Butcher, Samuel J. Little Blessings. 1996. (Super Shape Bks.). (Illus.). 24p. (J). (ps-3). pap. 3.29 o.s.i (*0-307-10001-4*, 10001, Golden Bks.) Random Hse. Children's Bks.

Cox, Sophie O. Yewka & the Two Pear Trees: A Family Story. 1995. (Illus.). 24p. (YA). (gr. 7-12). spiral bd. 15.00 (*0-9641138-1-3*) Beach Pebbles Pr.

The Crayon Box Family: A Story about Responsibility. 1998. (Excellence in Character Series Storybks.). (Illus.). 30p. (J). (gr. k-8). pap. 6.00 (*1-58259-025-7*) Global Classroom, The.

Creech, Sharon. Pleasing the Ghost. (Illus.). 96p. (J). (gr. 3-7). 1996. 14.95 (*0-06-026985-5*); 1996. 14.89 (*0-06-026986-3*); 1997. reprint ed. pap. 4.99 (*0-06-440686-5*, Harper Trophy) HarperCollins Children's Bk. Group.

Cresswell, Helen. Bagthorpes Unlimited: Being the Third Part of the Bagthorpe Saga. 1985. 182p. (J). pap. 1.75 o.p. (*0-380-49296-2*, 49296-2, Avon Bks.) Morrow/Avon.

Cristaldi, Kathryn. Even Steven & Odd Todd. 1996. (Hello Reader! Math Ser.: Level 3). (Illus.). 32p. (J). (gr. 1-3). mass mkt. 3.99 (*0-590-22715-7*, Cartwheel Bks.) Scholastic, Inc.

Crowe, Carole. Groover's Heart. 2003. (Illus.). 144p. (J). (gr. 4-6). 15.95 (*1-56397-953-5*) Boyds Mills Pr.

Crutcher, Chris. Chinese Handcuffs. 1989. 208p. (J). (gr. 7 up). 16.95 (*0-688-08345-5*, Greenwillow Bks.) HarperCollins Children's Bk. Group.

—Chinese Handcuffs. 1991. (Laurel-Leaf Bks.). 224p. (YA). (gr. 7 up). mass mkt. 4.99 o.s.i (*0-440-20837-8*, Laurel Leaf) Random Hse. Children's Bks.

—Chinese Handcuffs. 1991. 11.04 (*0-606-04892-8*) Turtleback Bks.

Cummings, Priscilla. Autumn Journey. (J). 1999. (Illus.). pap. 4.99 (*0-14-130361-1*, Puffin Bks.); 1997. 144p. (gr. 5-9). 14.99 o.p. (*0-525-65238-8*) Penguin Putnam Bks. for Young Readers.

Curry, Jane Louise. The Big Smith Snatch. 1989. 224p. (J). (gr. 4-7). lib. bdg. 16.00 (*0-689-50478-0*, McElderry, Margaret K.) Simon & Schuster Children's Publishing.

Curtis, Sandra R. Gabriel's Ark. 1998. (Illus.). 64p. (J). (gr. 3-6). pap. 7.95 (*1-881283-23-2*) Alef Design Group.

Dadey, Debbie. Whistler's Stump. 2002. 111p. (J). 14.95 (*1-58234-789-1*, Bloomsbury Children) Bloomsbury Publishing.

Dahl, Roald. The Minpins. 1991. 48p. (J). (ps-3). text 17.00 (*0-670-84168-4*, Viking Children's Bks.) Penguin Putnam Bks. for Young Readers.

Daly, Niki. Mama, Papa & Baby Joe. (J). 1999. (Illus.). 32p. pap. 4.99 (*0-14-054969-2*, Puffin Bks.); 1991. 14.95 o.p. (*0-670-84161-7*, Viking Children's Bks.) Penguin Putnam Bks. for Young Readers.

Dann, Colin. Just Nuffin. 1994. 248p. (J). mass mkt. (*0-09-966900-5*) Random Hse. of Canada, Ltd. CAN. *Dist:* Random Hse., Inc.

Danziger, Paula. Can You Sue Your Parents for Malpractice? 1998. 160p. (J). (gr. 5-9). pap. 4.99 (*0-698-11688-7*, PaperStar) Penguin Putnam Bks. for Young Readers.

—Everyone Else's Parents Said Yes. 1996. (J). pap. 4.99 (*0-440-91119-2*, Dell Books for Young Readers) Random Hse. Children's Bks.

—United Tates of America. 2002. (Illus.). 144p. (J). (gr. 3-7). pap. 15.95 (*0-590-69221-6*, Scholastic Pr.) Scholastic, Inc.

Darden, Hunter D. The Everlasting Snowman. 1996. (Illus.). 37p. (J). (gr. k-5). 16.95 (*0-9653729-0-1*) Sunfleur Pubns., Inc.

de Brunhoff, Jean. Babar en Famille. 1975. (Babar Ser.).Tr. of Babar & His Children. (FRE., Illus.). 26p. (J). (ps-3). 15.95 (*0-7859-0672-X*, FC589) French & European Pubns., Inc.

de Brunhoff, Jean & de Brunhoff, Laurent. Babar en Famille. 1999. (Babar Ser.).Tr. of Babar & His Children. (FRE., Illus.). (J). (ps-3). 13.95 (*2-01-002516-4*) Distribooks, Inc.

de Paola, Tomie. Tomie's Family. 2000. (Illus.). (J). (*0-698-11718-2*, Puffin Bks.) Penguin Putnam Bks. for Young Readers.

—Too Many Hopkins. 1989. (Illus.). 24p. (J). (ps-1). 5.95 o.s.i (*0-399-21661-8*, G. P. Putnam's Sons) Penguin Putnam Bks. for Young Readers.

Deaver, Julie Reece. Chicago Blues. 1995. 192p. (J). (gr. 6-9). 15.95 (*0-06-024675-8*) HarperCollins Children's Bk. Group.

—Chicago Blues. 1995. 192p. (J). (gr. 6-9). lib. bdg. 14.89 o.p. (*0-06-024676-6*) HarperCollins Pubs.

Deedy, Carmen Agra. The Secret of Old Zeb. (Illus.). 36p. (J). (gr. 1-5). 2002. pap. 8.95 (*1-56145-280-7*); 1997. 16.95 (*1-56145-115-0*) Peachtree Pubs., Ltd.

DeFelice, Cynthia C. The Real, True Dulcie Campbell, RS. 2002. (Illus.). 32p. (J). (gr. k-3). 16.00 (*0-374-36220-3*, Farrar, Straus & Giroux (BYR)) Farrar, Straus & Giroux.

Delaney, Mary. Mabel O Leary Puts Peas in Her Ear-Y. 2005. (J). 15.95 (*0-316-13506-2*) Little Brown & Co.

Delavan, Elizabeth. Peter & George & Uncle Henry. 1988. (Illus.). 48p. (J). (gr. 3-4). reprint ed. pap. 2.95 o.p. (*1-55787-020-9*, NY75041) Heart of the Lakes Publishing.

Delton, Judy. Angel Bites the Bullet. 2003. (Illus.). 144p. (J). pap. 4.95 (*0-618-36920-1*) Houghton Mifflin Co.

Dessen, Sarah. Keeping the Moon. (Illus.). (gr. 7 up). 2000. 240p. (YA). pap. 6.99 (*0-14-131007-3*, Puffin Bks.); 1999. 288p. (J). 15.99 (*0-670-88549-5*, Viking) Penguin Putnam Bks. for Young Readers.

Devine, Pauline. Riders by the Grey Lake. 1997. 144p. pap. 8.95 (*0-947962-99-9*) Dufour Editions, Inc.

Devoto, Pat Cunningham. Out of the Night That Covers Me. 2001. 432p. 23.95 o.p. (*0-446-52751-3*) Warner Bks., Inc.

Dexter, Catherine. Safe Return. (Illus.). 96p. (J). (gr. 4-7). 1998. bds. 4.99 o.s.i (*0-7636-0486-0*); 1996. 16.99 (*0-7636-0005-9*) Candlewick Pr.

Dickinson, Peter. The Ropemaker. 2003. 384p. (YA). (gr. 7). pap. 7.95 (*0-385-73063-2*, Delacorte Bks. for Young Readers) Random Hse. Children's Bks.

DiSalvo-Ryan, DyAnne. Uncle Willie & the Soup Kitchen. 1991. (Illus.). 32p. (J). (gr. 1 up). 16.00 o.p. (*0-688-09165-2*); lib. bdg. 15.93 o.p. (*0-688-09166-0*) Morrow/Avon. (Morrow, William & Co.).

—Uncle Willie & the Soup Kitchen. 1997. (J). 11.10 (*0-606-12026-2*) Turtleback Bks.

Dixon, Paige. Skipper. 1979. 132p. (J). (gr. 5-9). 8.95 o.s.i (*0-689-30706-3*, Atheneum) Simon & Schuster Children's Publishing.

Dodds, Dayle Ann. Sing, Sophie! 1997. (Illus.). 32p. (J). (gr. k-3). 15.99 o.s.i (*0-7636-0131-4*) Candlewick Pr.

Dokey, Cameron. Winning Is Everything. 1998. (Full House Stephanie Ser.: No. 29). 144p. (J). (gr. 4-6). pap. 3.99 (*0-671-01728-4*, Simon Spotlight) Simon & Schuster Children's Publishing.

Dorris, Michael. The Window. 1999. 112p. (J). (gr. 4 up). pap. 4.99 (*0-7868-1317-2*) Disney Pr.

—The Window. 1997. (Illus.). 112p. (J). (gr. 4 up). 16.95 (*0-7868-0301-0*); lib. bdg. 17.49 (*0-7868-2240-6*) Hyperion Bks. for Children.

—The Window. 1999. 112p. (J). (gr. 4 up). pap. 4.99 (*0-7868-1373-3*) Hyperion Pr.

Douglas, Erin. Get That Pest! 2003. (Green Light Readers Level 2 Ser.). (Illus.). 24p. (J). 11.95 (*0-15-204873-1*); pap. 3.95 (*0-15-204833-2*) Harcourt Children's Bks. (Green Light Readers).

Doyle, Brian. Uncle Ronald. 1997. (J). text 16.95 (*0-88899-266-1*) Douglas & McIntyre, Ltd. CAN. *Dist:* Publishers Group West.

—Uncle Ronald. 1998. 144p. (J). (gr. 4-7). pap. 4.95 (*0-88899-309-9*) Groundwood Bks. CAN. *Dist:* Publishers Group West.

—Uncle Ronald. 1997. 144p. (J). pap. (*0-88899-267-X*) Publishers Group West.

Drake, John W. Just Another Day. 1994. (Illus.). 40p. (J). (gr. k-4). 16.95 (*0-9633574-1-7*) Little Turtle Pr.

Draper, Sharon M. The Battle of Jericho. 2003. (Illus.). 304p. (YA). 16.95 (*0-689-84232-5*, Atheneum) Simon & Schuster Children's Publishing.

Dreibrodt, Stacie Champlin. Where the Lilies Bloom. 2000. (YA). 9.95 (*1-58130-634-2*); 11.95 (*1-58130-635-0*) Novel Units, Inc.

Drescher, Joan. The Birth-Order Blues. 1993. (Illus.). 32p. (J). (ps-3). 13.99 o.p. (*0-670-83621-4*, Viking Children's Bks.) Penguin Putnam Bks. for Young Readers.

Dubowski, Cathy. Substitute Sister. 2000. (Full House Sisters Ser.: No. 9). (Illus.). 160p. (J). (gr. 4-6). pap. 3.99 (*0-671-04089-8*, Simon Spotlight) Simon & Schuster Children's Publishing.

Duey, Kathleen. Agnes May Gleason: Walsenburg, Colorado, 1933. 1998. (American Diaries Ser.: No. 11). 144p. (J). (gr. 3-7). pap. 4.50 (*0-689-82329-0*, Aladdin) Simon & Schuster Children's Publishing.

—Agnes May Gleason: Walsenburg, Colorado, 1933. 1998. (American Diaries Ser.: No. 11). (J). (gr. 3-7). 10.04 (*0-606-16133-3*) Turtleback Bks.

Duey, Kathleen & Bale, Karen A. Blizzard, Estes Park, Colorado, 1886. 1998. (Survival! Ser.: No. 3). (J). (gr. 4-7). 10.55 (*0-606-13827-7*) Turtleback Bks.

Duffey, Betsy. Utterly Yours, Booker Jones. 1997. (Illus.). 128p. (J). (gr. 5-9). pap. 4.99 o.p. (*0-14-037496-5*) Penguin Putnam Bks. for Young Readers.

Dugan, Barbara. Leaving Home with a Pickle Jar. (Illus.). 32p. (J). 3.98 o.p. (*0-8317-3385-3*) Smithmark Pubs., Inc.

Dumas, Bianca Cowan. Tia Luisa, the Magical Cook: A Tale in English & Spanish. 2000. (ENG & SPA., Illus.). 32p. (J). (gr. k-4). per. 7.95 (*0-9669645-4-3*, AlterLingo Bks.) O'Hollow Publishing.

Dunlop, Eileen. The House on Mayferry Street, ERS. 1977. (gr. 5 up). o.p. (*0-03-020686-3*, Holt, Henry & Co. Bks. For Young Readers) Holt, Henry & Co.

Dygard, Thomas J. River Danger. 1998. 160p. (J). (gr. 7 up). 15.99 (*0-688-14852-2*) HarperCollins Children's Bk. Group.

Earls, Nick. 48 Shades of Brown. 1999. 288p. (YA). (*0-14-028769-8*) Penguin Group (USA) Inc.

Eastman, P. D. Eres Mi Mama? 2001. (ENG & SPA., Illus.). 24p. (J). bds. 4.99 (*0-375-81505-8*) Random Hse. Children's Bks.

Edens, Cooper & Day, Alexandra. Taffy's Family. 1997. (Michael di Capua Bks.). (Illus.). 32p. (J). (ps up). lib. bdg. 12.89 (*0-06-205150-4*) HarperCollins Children's Bk. Group.

Edwards, Pamela Duncan. Rosie's Roses. 2003. (Illus.). 32p. (J). (ps-1). 15.99 (*0-06-028997-X*); lib. bdg. 16.89 (*0-06-028998-8*) HarperCollins Pubs.

Edwards, Pat. A Visit to Cousin Boris. 1999. (Illus.). 24p. (J). (*0-7608-3196-3*) Sundance Publishing.

Ellis, Sarah. A Family Project. 1990. 144p. (J). (gr. k-6). pap. 3.25 o.s.i (*0-440-40397-9*) Dell Publishing.

—A Family Project. 1988. 144p. (J). (gr. 4-7). lib. bdg. 15.00 o.p. (*0-689-50444-6*, McElderry, Margaret K.) Simon & Schuster Children's Publishing.

—Out of the Blue. 2001. 120p. (YA). (gr. 5-9). pap. 5.95 (*0-88899-236-X*) Groundwood Bks. CAN. *Dist:* Publishers Group West.

—Out of the Blue. 1996. 128p. (J). (gr. 5-9). pap. 3.99 o.s.i (*0-14-038066-3*) Penguin Putnam Bks. for Young Readers.

—Out of the Blue. 1995. 144p. (YA). (gr. 5-9). pap. 15.00 (*0-689-80025-8*, McElderry, Margaret K.) Simon & Schuster Children's Publishing.

—Out of the Blue. 1996. (J). 9.09 o.p. (*0-606-10278-7*) Turtleback Bks.

Enderle, Judith R. & Tessler, Stephanie G. Dear Timothy Tibbits. 1995. (Illus.). (J). (gr. 3 up). text 14.00 (*0-02-733384-1*, Simon & Schuster Children's Publishing) Simon & Schuster Children's Publishing.

Enderle, Judith R., et al. Dear Timothy Tibbetts. 1997. (Illus.). 32p. (J). (gr. k-3). lib. bdg. 14.95 o.p. (*0-7614-5009-2*) Cavendish, Marshall Corp.

Engel, Diana. Holding On. 1997. (Accelerated Reader Bks.). (Illus.). 96p. (J). (gr. 3-7). 14.95 (*0-7614-5016-5*, Cavendish Children's Bks.) Cavendish, Marshall Corp.

English, Karen. Strawberry Moon, RS. 2001. 128p. (J). (gr. 4-6). 16.00 (*0-374-47122-3*, Farrar, Straus & Giroux (BYR)) Farrar, Straus & Giroux.

Enright, Elizabeth. The Saturdays. 1941. (Illus.). (gr. 4-6). 5.95 o.p. (*0-03-089690-8*) Holt, Henry & Co.

—Spiderweb for Two: A Melendy Mystery. 1997. (Melendy Family Ser.). (Illus.). 224p. (J). (gr. 3-7). pap. 4.99 o.s.i (*0-14-038396-4*) Penguin Putnam Bks. for Young Readers.

—Then There Were Five. 1997. (Melendy Family Ser.). (Illus.). 256p. (J). (gr. 3-7). pap. 4.99 o.s.i (*0-14-038397-2*) Penguin Putnam Bks. for Young Readers.

—Then There Were Five. 1987. (Illus.). (J). (gr. k-6). pap. 2.95 o.s.i (*0-440-48806-0*, Yearling) Random Hse. Children's Bks.

Erdrich, Louise. The Range Eternal. 2002. (Illus.). 32p. (J). (ps-2). 15.99 (*0-7868-0220-0*) Hyperion Bks. for Children.

Ernst, Donna B. Sundance, My Uncle. 1992. (Illus.). 170p. (YA). (gr. 9). 21.95 o.p. (*0-932702-96-1*) Creative Publishing Co., Inc.

Estes, Eleanor. The Moffat Museum. 1983. (Illus.). 262p. (YA). (gr. 3). 10.95 o.s.i (*0-15-255086-0*) Harcourt Children's Bks.

Fairweather, Eileen. French Leave: Maxine Harrison Moves Out! 1997. (Livewire Ser.). 132p. (YA). (gr. 7-11). pap. 7.95 (*0-7043-4916-7*) Women's Pr., Ltd., The GBR. *Dist:* Trafalgar Square.

Falwell, Cathryn. We Have a Baby. 2002. (Illus.). (J). 13.79 (*0-7587-3939-7*) Book Wholesalers, Inc.

—We Have a Baby. 1999. (Illus.). 32p. (J). (ps-ps). pap. 5.95 (*0-395-73970-5*) Houghton Mifflin Co.

—We Have a Baby. 1993. (Illus.). 32p. (J). (ps-ps). lib. bdg., tchr. ed. 15.00 (*0-395-62038-4*, Clarion Bks.) Houghton Mifflin Co. Trade & Reference Div.

Family Matters Scrapbook. 1992. 64p. (J). (gr. 4-7). pap. 2.95 o.s.i (*1-56144-150-3*, Honey Bear Bks.) Modern Publishing.

Family Ties Set. (Illus.). (J). (gr. 1-3). 74.75 (*1-881889-82-3*) Silver Moon Pr.

Family Tree. 1993. (J). (gr. 4-7). 16.95 o.p. (*0-8094-9325-X*) Time-Life, Inc.

Farber, Erica & Sansevere, J. R. The Vampire Brides. 1996. (Mercer Mayer's Critters of the Night Ser.). (Illus.). 72p. (J). (ps-3). pap. 3.99 o.s.i (*0-679-87360-0*, Random Hse. Bks. for Young Readers) Random Hse. Children's Bks.

Fassler, Joan. All Alone with Daddy: A Young Girl Plays the Role of Mother. 1975. (Illus.). 32p. (J). (ps-3). 16.95 (*0-87705-009-0*, Kluwer Academic/Human Science Pr.) Kluwer Academic Pubs.

—One Little Girl. 1969. (Illus.). 32p. (J). (ps-3). 16.95 o.p. (*0-87705-008-2*, Kluwer Academic/Human Science Pr.) Kluwer Academic Pubs.

Favorite, Deborah. The Tush People. (J). 11.95 (*0-9722514-0-5*) Tush People, The.

Feldman, Eve B. Seymour, the Formerly Fearful. 2000. 164p. (gr. 4-7). pap. 11.95 (*0-595-00391-5*, Backinprint.com) iUniverse, Inc.

Ferguson, Alane. Secrets. 1997. 160p. (J). (gr. 3-7). 16.00 (*0-689-80313-3*, Simon & Schuster Children's Publishing) Simon & Schuster Children's Publishing.

Ferris, Jean. Of Sound Mind, RS. (YA). 2004. pap. 5.95 (*0-374-45584-8*); 2001. 224p. (gr. 8 up). 16.00 (*0-374-35580-0*, Farrar, Straus & Giroux (BYR)) Farrar, Straus & Giroux.

—Signs of Life, RS. 1995. 160p. (J). (gr. 7 up). 14.00 o.p. (*0-374-36909-7*, Farrar, Straus & Giroux (BYR)) Farrar, Straus & Giroux.

Finley, Martha. Elsie's New Relations, Bk. 9. 2001. (J). pap. 5.99 (*1-931343-00-4*) Hibbard Pubns., Inc.

Fitzhugh, Louise. Nobody's Family Is Going to Change, RS. 1986. (Sunburst Ser.). (Illus.). 40p. (J). (gr. 4-7). pap. 5.95 (*0-374-45523-6*, Sunburst) Farrar, Straus & Giroux.

—Sport. 1979. 250p. (J). (gr. 4-6). pap. 8.95 o.s.i (*0-385-28908-1*, Delacorte Pr.) Dell Publishing.

—Sport. unabr. ed. 2003. (J). (gr. 5). audio 25.00 (*0-8072-1023-4*, Listening Library) Random Hse. Audio Publishing Group.

—Sport. 2002. 240p. (gr. 5). pap. text 5.99 (*0-440-41818-6*, Yearling); 2001. (Illus.). 224p. (gr. 5-9). lib. bdg. 17.99 (*0-385-90011-2*, Delacorte Bks. for Young Readers); 1980. 224p. (J). (gr. 7 up). mass mkt. 3.25 o.s.i (*0-440-98350-9*, Laurel Leaf); 1982. 224p. (YA). reprint ed. pap. 3.25 o.s.i (*0-440-48221-6*, Yearling) Random Hse. Children's Bks.

Fletcher, Ralph J. Uncle Daddy, ERS. 2001. (Illus.). 133p. (J). (gr. 4-6). 15.95 (*0-8050-6663-2*, Holt, Henry & Co. Bks. For Young Readers) Holt, Henry & Co.

Flood, Pansie Hart. Secret Holes. 2003. (Illus.). 122p. (J). 15.95 (*0-87614-923-9*, Carolrhoda Bks.) Lerner Publishing Group.

Flournoy, Valerie. Tanya's Reunion. 1995. (Illus.). 40p. (J). (ps-3). 16.99 (*0-8037-1604-4*, Dial Bks. for Young Readers) Penguin Putnam Bks. for Young Readers.

Focus on the Family Staff. Sibling Rivalry. 2001. (Adventures in Odyssey Ser.). (J). (gr. 1-7). audio 9.99 (*1-58997-021-7*) Focus on the Family Publishing.

Forbes, Kathryn. Mama's Bank Account. 1968. 154p. reprint ed. pap. 10.00 (*0-15-656377-0*, Harvest Bks.) Harcourt Trade Pubs.

Ford, Juwanda G. Kenya's Family Reunion. 1996. (Illus.). 32p. (J). mass mkt. 2.99 (*0-590-53736-9*) Scholastic, Inc.

—Kenya's Family Reunion. 1996. 8.19 o.p. (*0-606-09511-X*) Turtleback Bks.

Forman, James D. The Pumpkin Shell, RS. 1981. 160p. (J). (gr. 7 up). 10.95 o.p. (*0-374-36159-2*, Farrar, Straus & Giroux (BYR)) Farrar, Straus & Giroux.

Forney, Melissa. Oonawassee Summer: Something is Lurking Beneath the Surface... 2000. (Illus.). 126p. (J). (gr. 4-8). pap. 14.95 (*1-928961-04-5*) Barker Creek Publishing, Inc.

Fox, Robert. Inherited Family. 1999. 188p. E-Book 8.00 (*0-7388-7039-0*) Xlibris Corp.

Frank, E. R. Life Is Funny. 2000. (Richard Jackson Bks.). (Illus.). 272p. (J). (gr. 7-12). pap. 19.99 (*0-7894-2634-X*, D K Ink) Dorling Kindersley Publishing, Inc.

Frank, Lucy. I Am an Artichoke. 1995. 192p. (J). (gr. 7 up). tchr. ed. 14.95 o.p. (*0-8234-1150-8*) Holiday Hse., Inc.

Franklin, Kristine L. Dove Song. 1999. (Illus.). 192p. (J). (gr. 5-9). 16.99 (*0-7636-0409-7*) Candlewick Pr.

Frantz, Evelyn. A Bonnet for Virginia. 1978. (J). pap. 1.95 o.p. (*0-87178-101-8*) Brethren Pr.

Friedlander, Eleanor. Mrs. Digger's Roots. 1999. (Illus.). 44p. (J). (ps-3). 17.95 (*0-9672124-0-5*) Jadeda Pr.

Friesen, Gayle. Men of Stone. 2000. (Illus.). 286p. (YA). (gr. 6 up). text 16.95 (*1-55074-781-9*) Kids Can Pr., Ltd.

Fritz, T. J. Katey's Dream List. 1999. 90p. (J). (gr. 4-7). pap. 7.95 (*1-56315-084-0*) SterlingHouse Pubs., Inc.

Froissart, Benedicte. La Cena Con el Tio Enrique. Segovia, Francisco, tr. 1992. Tr. of Uncle Henry's Dinner Guests. (SPA., Illus.). 33p. (J). (gr. 1-3). 12.99 (*968-16-3942-1*) Fondo de Cultura Economica MEX. *Dist:* Continental Bk. Co., Inc.

—Uncle Henry's Dinner Guests. 1990. (Illus.). 32p. (J). (ps-2). pap. 4.95 (*1-55037-140-1*); lib. bdg. 15.95 (*1-55037-141-X*) Annick Pr., Ltd. CAN. *Dist:* Firefly Bks., Ltd.

—Uncle Henry's Dinner Guests. ed. 2000. (J). (gr. 2). spiral bd. (*0-616-01644-1*) Canadian National Institute for the Blind/Institut National Canadien pour les Aveugles.

Fuller, Jill. John's Book. 2002. (Illus.). 88p. (J). 20.00 (*0-7188-2870-4*) Lutherworth Pr., The GBR. *Dist:* Parkwest Pubns., Inc.

Gaines, Isabel. Pooh's Family Tree, Vol. 20. 2000. (Winnie the Pooh Ser.). (Illus.). 34p. (J). (gr. k-3). pap. 3.99 (*0-7868-4367-5*) Disney Pr.

Gallacher, Marcie. Amaryllis Lilies. 1996. (Values for Young Women Ser.). pap. 7.95 (*0-15-623645-1*) Aspen Bks.

Gallagher, Diane G. A Dog's Life. 2001. (Full House Sisters Ser.: No. 13). (Illus.). 176p. (J). (gr. 4-6). pap. 3.99 (*0-671-04093-6*, Simon Spotlight) Simon & Schuster Children's Publishing.

Galvin, Kim. RJ's Farm. 2000. 208p. (gr. 4-7). pap. 12.95 (*0-595-13989-2*, Writers Club Pr.) iUniverse, Inc.

Gantos, Jack. The Werewolf Family, 001. 1980. (Illus.). (J). (gr. k-3). lib. bdg. 8.95 o.p. (*0-395-28760-X*) Houghton Mifflin Co.

Garaway, Margaret K. Dezbah & the Dancing Tumbleweeds. 2nd ed. 1990. (Illus.). 83p. (J). (gr. 3-10). reprint ed. pap. 7.95 (*0-9638851-2-X*) Old Hogan Publishing Co.

Garis, Howard R. Uncle Wiggily's Happy Days. Date not set. 226p. (J). 21.95 (*0-8488-2650-7*) Amereon, Ltd.

Garland, Michael. Mystery Mansion: A Look Again Book. 2001. (Illus.). 32p. (J). 15.99 (*0-525-46675-4*, Dutton Children's Bks.) Penguin Putnam Bks. for Young Readers.

Garon, Risa J. Snowman. 2000. (Illus.). 5p. (J). pap. 5.00 (*0-9729415-0-9*) National Family Resiliency Ctr., Inc.

Gauch, Patricia L. Christina Katerina & the Time She Quit the Family. 1992. (Sandcastle Ser.). (Illus.). 32p. (J). (ps-3). 5.99 o.s.i (*0-399-22405-X*, Philomel) Penguin Group (USA) Inc.

—Christina Katerina & the Time She Quit the Family. 1987. (Illus.). 32p. (J). (ps-3). 14.95 o.s.i (*0-399-21408-9*, G. P. Putnam's Sons) Penguin Putnam Bks. for Young Readers.

—Uncle Magic. 1992. (Illus.). 32p. (J). (ps-3). lib. bdg. 14.95 o.p. (*0-8234-0937-6*) Holiday Hse., Inc.

Geras, Adele. Family Files. 1999. (Fabulous Fantoras Ser.: Vol. 1). 144p. (J). (gr. 4-7). mass mkt. 3.99 (*0-380-79359-8*, Avon Bks.) Morrow/Avon.

—Watching the Roses. Stearns, Michael, ed. 1998. (Egerton Hall Trilogy Ser.: Vol. 2). (Illus.). 192p. (gr. 7-12). pap. 6.00 o.s.i (*0-15-201517-5*, Harcourt Paperbacks) Harcourt Children's Bks.

—Watching the Roses. 1992. 192p. (YA). (gr. 9 up). 16.95 (*0-15-294816-3*) Harcourt Children's Bks.

Gerrard, Roy. The Favershams, RS. 1983. (Illus.). 32p. (J). (gr. 2 up). 15.00 o.p. (*0-374-32292-9*, Farrar, Straus & Giroux (BYR)) Farrar, Straus & Giroux.

Gibbons, Faye. Emma Jo's Song. 2003. (Illus.). 32p. (J). (gr. k-3). 15.95 (*1-56397-935-7*) Boyds Mills Pr.

Giff, Patricia Reilly. Pictures of Hollis Woods. unabr. ed. 2002. (gr. 4-7). audio 18.00 (*0-8072-0919-8*, Listening Library) Random Hse. Audio Publishing Group.

—Pictures of Hollis Woods. 2002. (Illus.). 176p. (gr. 3-8). text 15.95 (*0-385-32655-6*, Lamb, Wendy) Random Hse. Children's Bks.

—Pictures of Hollis Woods. 2002. 176p. lib. bdg. 17.99 (*0-385-90070-8*) Random Hse., Inc.

—Pictures of Hollis Woods. l.t. ed. 2003. 158p. (J). 23.95 (*0-7862-5094-1*) Thorndike Pr.

—The Winter Worm Business. 1981. (Illus.). (J). (gr. 4-6). pap. 8.95 o.s.i (*0-385-29152-3*); pap. 8.89 o.s.i (*0-385-29154-X*) Dell Publishing. (Delacorte Pr.).

Giordenello, Jennifer. Here Come the Bubbles. 1997. (Illus.). 16p. (J). (gr. k-3). pap. 6.00 o.p. (*0-8059-4139-8*) Dorrance Publishing Co., Inc.

Gipson, Morrell, et al. Walkers Go Hiking. 1990. (Magic Mountain Fables Ser.). (Illus.). 24p. (J). (gr. k-3). lib. bdg. 14.60 (*0-944483-91-7*) Garrett Educational Corp.

Girlhood Journeys, Inc., Staff. Marie: Summer in the Country, Paris, 1775. 1997. (Girlhood Journeys Ser.: 3). (Illus.). 69p. (J). (gr. 2-6). per. 5.99 (*0-689-81562-X*, Simon Pulse) Simon & Schuster Children's Publishing.

Glassman, Miriam. Box Top Dreams. 1999. (Illus.). 192p. (gr. 4-7). pap. text 3.99 (*0-440-41417-2*, Dell Books for Young Readers) Random Hse. Children's Bks.

—Box Top Dreams. 1999. 10.04 (*0-606-15910-X*) Turtleback Bks.

Godden, Rumer. Miss Happiness & Miss Flower. 2002. (Illus.). 128p. (J). (gr. 3-7). lib. bdg. 14.89 (*0-06-029193-1*); pap. 4.95 (*0-06-440938-4*, Harper Trophy) HarperCollins Children's Bk. Group.

—Miss Happiness & Miss Flower. 1987. (Illus.). 112p. (J). (gr. 2-6). pap. 3.95 o.p. (*0-14-030273-5*, Puffin Bks.) Penguin Putnam Bks. for Young Readers.

Goehring, Sherri K. Katelyn Begins Day Care at Luv-n-Hugs Day Care, Vol. 5. 1998. (Illus.). 28p. (Orig.). (J). (ps-6). pap. 6.95 (*0-9658824-3-8*) Luv-n-Hugs Bks.

Goldman, Susan. Cousins Are Special. Rubin, Caroline, ed. 1978. (Self-Starter Bks.). (Illus.). (J). (ps-2). lib. bdg. 9.75 o.p. (*0-8075-1317-2*) Whitman, Albert & Co.

Gordon, Shirley. The Boy Who Wanted a Family. 1982. 96p. (J). (gr. 1-4). pap. 2.75 o.s.i (*0-440-40786-9*, Yearling) Random Hse. Children's Bks.

Goudge, Elizabeth. Linnets & Valerians. 1981. (J). lib. bdg. 12.95 o.p. (*0-8398-2750-4*, Macmillan Reference USA) Gale Group.

—Linnets & Valerians. 1985. (YA). (gr. 7 up). pap. 1.75 o.p. (*0-380-01934-5*, 37838, Avon Bks.) Morrow/Avon.

—Linnets & Valerians. 2001. 256p. (J). pap. 5.99 (*0-14-230026-8*, Puffin Bks.) Penguin Putnam Bks. for Young Readers.

Graef, Renee, illus. Little House Farm Days. 1998. (Little House Chapter Bks.: No. 7). (J). (gr. 3-6). 10.40 (*0-606-13576-6*) Turtleback Bks.

Granowsky, Alvin. My Family. 2001. 24p. 1. (J). pap. 4.99 (*0-7613-2326-0*); (My World Ser.). (Illus.). 16.90 (*0-7613-2169-1*) Millbrook Pr., Inc. (Copper Beech Bks.).

Grant, Cynthia D. Mary Wolf. 1997. pap. 4.50 (*0-689-81292-2*, Simon Pulse); 1997. 224p. (J). (gr. 7 up). per. 4.99 (*0-689-81251-5*, Simon Pulse); 1995. 176p. (YA). (gr. 7 up). 16.00 (*0-689-80007-X*, Atheneum) Simon & Schuster Children's Publishing.

—Mary Wolf. 1997. (YA). 11.04 (*0-606-11600-1*) Turtleback Bks.

—Uncle Vampire. 1993. 160p. (YA). (gr. 8 up). 14.00 o.p. (*0-689-31852-9*, Atheneum) Simon & Schuster Children's Publishing.

Grattan-Dominguez, Alejandro. Breaking Even. 1997. 250p. (YA). (gr. 9 up). pap. 11.95 (*1-55885-213-1*) Arte Publico Pr.

Gray, Juliette, ed. Cherubic Children's New Classic Storybook Vol. 2: Teaching & Healing Stories to Help Children Learn, Understand & Cope. 1997. (Illus.). 384p. (J). (gr. k up). 24.95 (*1-889590-24-X*) Cherubic Pr.

Gray, Nigel. Full House. 2002. (Illus.). 20p. (J). 9.95 (*0-85091-879-0*) Lothian Bks. AUS. *Dist:* Star Bright Bks., Inc.

—Full House. 1999. (Illus.). 20p. (J). (ps-k). 8.95 (*1-887734-68-6*) Star Bright Bks., Inc.

Green, Connie J. Emmy. 1992. (Illus.). 160p. (J). (gr. 5-9). 13.95 (*0-689-50556-6*, McElderry, Margaret K.) Simon & Schuster Children's Publishing.

Greenburg, J. C. Andrew Lost: In the Kitchen. 2002. (Illus.). 96p. (J). (gr. 2-5). pap. 3.99 (*0-375-81279-2*) Random Hse., Inc.

—Andrew Lost: Under Water. 2003. (Illus.). 96p. (J). (gr. 2-5). lib. bdg. 11.99 (*0-375-92523-6*); pap. 3.99 (*0-375-82523-1*) Random Hse. Children's Bks.

—Andrew Lost #1: On the Dog. 2004. 96p. (J). (gr. 1-4). pap. 0.99 (*0-375-83000-6*, Random Hse. Bks. for Young Readers) Random Hse. Children's Bks.

—Andrew Lost #8: In the Deep. 2004. (Illus.). 96p. (J). (gr. 2-5). pap. 3.99 (*0-375-82526-6*); lib. bdg. 11.99 (*0-375-92526-0*) Random Hse. Children's Bks. (Random Hse. Bks. for Young Readers).

Greene, Constance C. Getting Nowhere. 1977. (J). 11.50 o.p. (*0-670-33762-5*) Viking Penguin.

Greenfield, Eloise. Easter Parade. 1998. (Illus.). 64p. (J). (gr. 1-5). 13.95 (*0-7868-0326-6*); lib. bdg. 14.49 (*0-7868-2271-6*) Hyperion Bks. for Children.

Greenwald, Sheila. Move over, Columbus, Rosy Cole Discovers America! 1992. (J). 13.95 o.p. (*0-316-32721-2*, Joy Street Bks.) Little Brown & Co.

—Rosy Cole's Official (and Completely Accidental) Tour of New York City. 2003. (Illus.). 128p. 16.00 (*0-374-36349-8*, Farrar, Straus & Giroux (BYR)) Farrar, Straus & Giroux.

—Will the Real Gertrude Hollings Please Stand Up? 1983. 168p. (J). (gr. 3-7). 12.95 o.s.i (*0-316-32707-7*, Joy Street Bks.) Little Brown & Co.

Griffith, Helen V. Alex Remembers. 1983. (Illus.). 32p. (J). (gr. k-3). 11.95 o.p. (*0-688-01800-9*); lib. bdg. 11.88 o.p. (*0-688-01801-7*) HarperCollins Children's Bk. Group. (Greenwillow Bks.).

Guest, Elissa Haden. Iris & Walter & Cousin Howie. 2003. (Iris & Walter Ser.). (Illus.). 44p. (J). (gr. 1-3). 15.00 (*0-15-216695-5*, Gulliver Bks.) Harcourt Children's Bks.

Gunn, Robin Jones. A Promise Is Forever. rev. ed. 1999. (Christy Miller Ser.: Vol. 12). 160p. (J). (gr. 7-12). pap. 6.99 (*1-56179-733-2*) Focus on the Family Publishing.

—Seventeen Wishes. rev. ed. 1999. (Christy Miller Ser.: Vol. 9). 160p. (J). (gr. 7-12). pap. 6.99 (*1-56179-730-8*) Focus on the Family Publishing.

—Sweet Dreams, rev. ed. 1999. (Christy Miller Ser.: Vol. 11). 160p. (J). (gr. 7-12). pap. 6.99 (*1-56179-732-4*) Focus on the Family Publishing.

—A Time to Cherish. rev. ed. 1999. (Christy Miller Ser.: Vol. 10). 176p. (J). (gr. 7-12). pap. 6.99 (*1-56179-731-6*) Focus on the Family Publishing.

Gutman, Anne. Lisa in New York. 2002. (Illus.). 32p. (J). (gr. k-3). 9.95 (*0-375-81119-2*, Knopf Bks. for Young Readers) Random Hse. Children's Bks.

Haas, Jessie. Keeping Barney. 1982. 160p. (J). (gr. 5-9). 12.95 o.p. (*0-688-00859-3*, Greenwillow Bks.) HarperCollins Children's Bk. Group.

—Keeping Barney. 1998. 160p. (J). (gr. 3 up). pap. 4.50 (*0-688-15859-5*, Morrow, William & Co.) Morrow/Avon.

—Keeping Barney. 1998. 10.55 (*0-606-16829-X*) Turtleback Bks.

Haddix, Margaret Peterson. Takoffs & Landings. 2003. (Illus.). 208p. (J). pap. 4.99 (*0-689-85543-5*, Aladdin) Simon & Schuster Children's Publishing.

Hafen, Marie F. Queridos Ma Ma' y Pa Pa' 1997. Tr. of Dear Mommy & Daddy. (ENG & SPA., Illus.). 152p. (Orig.). pap. 14.95 (*1-886990-02-6*) CareMORE.

Hafner, Marylin. Emmett's Dream. 2001. (Molly & Emmett Ser.). (Illus.). 32p. (J). 12.95 (*1-57768-896-1*, Cricket) McGraw-Hill Children's Publishing.

Hahn, Mary Downing. Following My Own Footsteps. 1998. (Camelot Bks.). 192p. (J). (gr. 3-7). reprint ed. mass mkt. 4.95 (*0-380-72990-3*, Avon Bks.) Morrow/Avon.

—Time for Andrew: A Ghost Story. 1994. 176p. (YA). (gr. 7-7). tchr. ed. 15.00 (*0-395-66556-6*, Clarion Bks.) Houghton Mifflin Co. Trade & Reference Div.

—Time for Andrew: A Ghost Story. 1995. (Avon Camelot Bks.). 176p. (J). (gr. 4 up). pap. 5.99 (*0-380-72469-3*, Avon Bks.) Morrow/Avon.

Hale, Lucretia P. Complete Peterkin Papers, 001. 1960. (Illus.). 302p. (J). (gr. 5-7). 8.95 o.p. (*0-395-06792-8*) Houghton Mifflin Co.

Haley, Lin. Finn Meets Sharlena's Cousins. 1996. (Illus.). 28p. pap. 3.95 (*1-56763-203-3*); text 12.95 o.p. (*1-56763-202-5*) Ozark Publishing.

Hall, Barbara. Dixie Storms. 1991. 208p. (YA). mass mkt. 3.50 o.s.i (*0-553-29047-9*) Bantam Bks.

—Dixie Storms. 1991. (J). mass mkt. o.s.i (*0-553-54037-8*, Dell Books for Young Readers) Random Hse. Children's Bks.

Hall, Kirsten. Who Loves Me Best?, Level 1. 1999. (All-Star Readers Ser.: Vol. 2). (Illus.). 32p. (J). (ps-1). mass mkt. 3.99 (*1-57584-293-9*, Reader's Digest Children's Bks.) Reader's Digest Children's Publishing, Inc.

Hamilton, Dorothy. The Gift of a Home. 1974. 120p. (YA). (gr. 9-11). pap. 3.95 o.p. (*0-8361-1727-1*) Herald Pr.

—Ken's Bright Room. 1982. (Illus.). 88p. (Orig.). (J). (gr. 7-10). 6.95 o.p. (*0-8361-3327-7*); pap. 3.95 o.p. (*0-8361-3328-5*) Herald Pr.

Hamilton, Virginia. Cousins. 1990. 128p. (J). (gr. 3-7). 17.99 (*0-399-22164-6*, Philomel) Penguin Putnam Bks. for Young Readers.

—Cousins. 1997. (J). mass mkt. 3.99 (*0-590-05377-9*) Scholastic, Inc.

—Cousins. 1990. (J). 10.55 (*0-606-02570-7*) Turtleback Bks.

—Primos. 2002. Tr. of Cousins. (SPA., Illus.). 126p. (YA). (gr. 5-8). pap. 12.95 (*968-19-0787-6*) Aguilar Editorial MEX. *Dist:* Santillana USA Publishing Co., Inc.

—Primos. 1995. Tr. of Cousins. (SPA., Illus.). 128p. (J). (gr. 4-7). 15.95 (*84-204-4747-1*, LEC7471) Alfaguara, Ediciones, S.A.- Grupo Santillana ESP. *Dist:* Santillana USA Publishing Co., Inc.

—Primos. 1993. Tr. of Cousins. 16.00 (*0-606-10491-7*) Turtleback Bks.

—Second Cousins. 2000. (Illus.). 176p. (YA). (gr. 4-8). mass mkt. 4.99 (*0-590-47369-7*, Scholastic Reference) Scholastic, Inc.

—Second Cousins. 2000. 11.04 (*0-606-18602-6*) Turtleback Bks.

—Zeely. 93rd ed. 1993. pap. text 17.40 (*0-15-300358-8*) Harcourt Children's Bks.

—Zeely. 1998. (C). pap. 3.95 (*0-87628-345-8*) Simon & Schuster.

—Zeely. (Illus.). 128p. (J). 1968. (gr. 4-7). 17.95 (*0-02-742470-7*, Simon & Schuster Children's Publishing); 1987. (gr. 5-7). reprint ed. pap. 3.95 o.s.i (*0-689-71110-7*, Aladdin); 2nd ed. 1993. (gr. 4-7). reprint ed. pap. 4.99 (*0-689-71695-8*, Aladdin) Simon & Schuster Children's Publishing.

—Zeely. 1986. 11.04 (*0-606-03513-3*) Turtleback Bks.

Hands, Cynthia. Odd Couples. 2001. 70p. (J). (ps-3). pap. 2.99 (*0-307-33771-5*, Golden Bks.) Random Hse. Children's Bks.

Harding, Donal. The Leaving Summer. 1996. 192p. (YA). (gr. 5 up). 15.00 (*0-688-13893-4*, Morrow, William & Co.) Morrow/Avon.

—The Leaving Summer. 1998. 9.09 o.p. (*0-606-13566-9*) Turtleback Bks.

Harmon, Lyn. Clyde's Clam Farm. 2001. (Illus.). 132p. (gr. 4-7). pap. 9.95 (*0-595-16339-4*, Backinprint-.com) iUniverse, Inc.

Harper, Jo. Delfino's Journey. 2000. viii, 184p. (J). (gr. 8-12). 15.95 (*0-89672-437-9*) Texas Tech Univ. Pr.

—Delfino's Journey, Grades 8-12. 2000. (Illus.). viii, 184p. (J). tchr. ed. 5.95 (*0-89672-442-5*) Texas Tech Univ. Pr.

Harper, Jo & Harper, Josephine. Como los Perros de la Pradera. Gutiérrez, Guillermo, tr. 2000. (SPA.). 48p. (J). (ps-3). pap. 8.95 (*1-890515-24-8*) Turtle Bks.

—Prairie Dog Pioneers. 2000. (Illus.). 48p. (J). (ps-3). pap. 8.95 (*1-890515-23-X*) Turtle Bks.

HarperEntertainment Staff. War of the Wardrobes. 2000. (Two of a Kind Ser.: No. 13). (Illus.). 112p. (gr. 3-7). mass mkt. 4.99 (*0-06-106636-2*, HarperEntertainment) Morrow/Avon.

Harriott, Ted & Kopper, Lisa. Coming Home. 1985. (Illus.). 32p. (J). (gr. 1-4). 13.95 o.p. (*0-575-03583-8*) Gollancz, Victor GBR. *Dist:* Trafalgar Square.

Harris, Brad. My Brother & I. 2003. (Illus.). 24p. (J). 15.95 (*0-9710278-6-2*) All About Kids Publishing.

Hartfield, Claire. Me & Uncle Romie: A Story Inspired by the Life & Art of Romare Bearden. 2002. (Illus.). 40p. (J). 16.99 (*0-8037-2520-5*, Dial Bks. for Young Readers) Penguin Putnam Bks. for Young Readers.

Hartling, Peter. Old John. Crawford, Elizabeth D., tr. from GER. 1990. 128p. (J). (gr. 4-9). 11.95 o.p. (*0-688-08734-5*) HarperCollins Children's Bk. Group.

Hautman, Pete. Mr. Was. (YA). (gr. 7-12). 1998. 256p. pap. 4.99 (*0-689-81914-5*, Simon Pulse); 1996. 224p. 16.00 (*0-689-81068-7*, Simon & Schuster Children's Publishing) Simon & Schuster Children's Publishing.

Havill, Juanita. Treasure Map. 1992. (Illus.). 32p. (J). (ps-3). lib. bdg., tchr. ed. 16.00 (*0-395-57817-5*) Houghton Mifflin Co.

Hayashi, Nancy. Cosmic Cousin. 1988. (Illus.). 80p. (J). (gr. 2-5). 10.95 o.p. (*0-525-44387-8*, Dutton Children's Bks.) Penguin Putnam Bks. for Young Readers.

—Cosmic Cousin. 1990. (Illus.). 96p. (J). (gr. 2-5). pap. 2.95 o.s.i (*0-553-15841-4*, Skylark) Random Hse. Children's Bks.

Haynes, David. Right by My Side. 1993. (Minnesota Voices Project Ser.). 190p. pap. 12.95 o.p. (*0-89823-147-7*) New Rivers Pr.

Helldorfer, Mary-Claire. Harmonica Night. 1997. (Illus.). 32p. (J). (gr. k-4). 16.00 (*0-689-80532-2*, Atheneum) Simon & Schuster Children's Publishing.

Heller, Andrew. A Mouthful of Teeth. 2002. (Illus.). 16p. (J). 7.99 (0-9722038-4-2) Mr Do It All, Inc.

Henderson, Kathy. And the Good Brown Earth. 2004. 40p. (J). 15.99 (0-7636-2301-6) Candlewick Pr.

Hendry, Diana. Dog Donovan. (Illus.). (J). (ps-3). 1995. 13.95 o.p. (1-56402-537-3); 1996. 32p. reprint ed. bds. 5.99 o.p. (1-56402-699-X) Candlewick Pr.

—Dog Donovan. 1996. 11.19 o.p. (0-606-09199-8) Turtleback Bks.

Henkes, Kevin. Chester's Way. 1989. (Illus.). 32p. (J). (ps-3). pap. 4.99 o.p. (0-14-054053-9, Puffin Bks.) Penguin Putnam Bks. for Young Readers.

—Two under Par. 1987. (Illus.). 128p. (J). (gr. 2 up). pap. 15.95 (0-688-06708-5, Greenwillow Bks.) HarperCollins Children's Bk. Group.

Hensley, Amy. Abandon Indiana. 2001. 233p. pap. 21.99 (0-7388-4086-6); text 31.99 (0-7388-4085-8) Xlibris Corp.

Hensley, Sam, Jr. Family Portrait. FS Staff, ed. 1988. 256p. (YA). (gr. 9-12). 12.90 o.p. (0-531-10611-X, Watts, Franklin) Scholastic Library Publishing.

Herman, Charlotte. The Memory Cupboard: A Thanksgiving Story. 2003. (Illus.). 32p. (J). (gr. 1-4). 15.95 (0-8075-5055-8) Whitman, Albert & Co.

Herman, Hank. Out of Bounds! 1997. (Super Hoops Ser.: No. 13). (Illus.). 96p. (gr. 4-6). pap. text 3.50 o.s.i (0-553-48476-1, Skylark) Random Hse. Children's Bks.

Herman, John. Labyrinth. 2001. (Illus.). 188p. (J). (gr. 7 up). 17.99 (0-399-23571-X, Philomel) Penguin Putnam Bks. for Young Readers.

Hesse, Karen. Lavender, ERS. (Illus.). (J). 1995. 64p. (ps-3). pap. 7.95 (0-8050-4257-1); 1993. 48p. (gr. 2-4). 14.95 o.p. (0-8050-2528-6) Holt, Henry & Co. (Holt, Henry & Co. Bks. For Young Readers).

Hest, Amy. Fancy Aunt Jess. 1990. (Illus.). (J). lib. bdg. 12.88 o.p. (0-688-08097-9, Morrow, William & Co.) Morrow/Avon.

—Guess Who Baby Duck. Barton, Jill, tr. & illus. by. 2004. 32p. (J). 14.99 (0-7636-1981-7) Candlewick Pr.

—Pete & Lily. 1993. 128p. (J). (gr. 6 up). pap. 4.95 o.p. (0-688-12490-9, Morrow, William & Co.) Morrow/Avon.

—Where in the World Is the Perfect Family? 1989. 112p. (J). (gr. 4-7). 12.95 o.p. (0-89919-659-4, Clarion Bks.) Houghton Mifflin Co. Trade & Reference Div.

Hewett, Lorri. Soulfire. 1998. 240p. (gr. 7-12). pap. 5.99 o.s.i (0-14-038960-1, Puffin Bks.) Penguin Putnam Bks. for Young Readers.

Heynen, Jim. Being Youngest. 2000. 272p. (J). (gr. 3-7). pap. 4.95 (0-380-73204-1, Harper Trophy) HarperCollins Children's Bk. Group.

—Being Youngest. 2000. 11.00 (0-606-17829-5) Turtleback Bks.

Hicks, Betty. Animal House & Iz. 2003. 176p. (gr. 3-7). 15.95 (0-7613-1891-7); lib. bdg. 22.90 (0-7613-2746-0) Millbrook Pr., Inc. (Roaring Brook Pr.).

Hill, Elizabeth S. When Christmas Comes. 1989. 208p. (J). (gr. 5-7). 11.95 o.p. (0-670-82201-9, Viking Children's Bks.) Penguin Putnam Bks. for Young Readers.

Hinds, P. Mignon. King's Daughters. 1997. 24p. o.p. (0-307-16162-5, Golden Bks.) Random Hse. Children's Bks.

Hines, Anna Grossnickle. Mean Old Uncle Jack. 1990. (Illus.). 32p. (J). 13.95 o.p. (0-395-52137-8) Houghton Mifflin Co.

Hinton, S. E. Tex. 1989. (Illus.). (J). (gr. 7-13). 12.25 (0-88103-050-3) Econo-Clad Bks.

Hippely, Hilary Horder. The Crimson Ribbon. 1994. (Illus.). 32p. (J). (ps-3). 15.95 o.p. (0-399-22542-0, G. P. Putnam's Sons) Penguin Group (USA) Inc.

Hite, Sid. Those Darn Dithers, ERS. 1996. 192p. (YA). (gr. 7-12). 15.95 o.s.i (0-8050-3838-8, Holt, Henry & Co. Bks. For Young Readers) Holt, Henry & Co.

—Those Darn Dithers. 1998. (Laurel-Leaf Bks.). 192p. (YA). (gr. 7-12). reprint ed. mass mkt. 4.50 o.s.i (0-440-22671-6, Laurel Leaf) Random Hse. Children's Bks.

—Those Darn Dithers. 1998. (J). 10.55 (0-606-13846-3) Turtleback Bks.

Hoban, Russell. Sorely Trying Day. 1964. (Illus.). (J). (gr. k-3). lib. bdg. 12.89 o.p. (0-06-022421-5) HarperCollins Children's Bk. Group.

Hobbs, Lois Z., et al. Family Reunion. 2nd ed. 1997. (John Deere Storybook for Little Folks Ser.). (Illus.). iii, 17p. (J). (gr. 2 up). reprint ed. 6.95 (1-887327-18-5) Ertl Co., Inc.

Hobbs, William. Jackie's Wild Seattle. (J). 2004. 208p. pap. 5.99 (0-380-73311-0, Harper Trophy); 2003. 192p. (gr. 5 up). 15.99 (0-688-17474-4); 2003. 192p. (gr. 5 up). lib. bdg. 16.89 (0-06-051631-3) HarperCollins Children's Bk. Group.

Hodge, Deborah. Emma's Story. 2003. (Illus.). 24p. (J). (gr. k-3). 17.95 (0-88776-632-3) Tundra Bks. of Northern New York.

Hogan, Mary. Tigger's Family. 2000. (Winnie the Pooh Ser.). (Illus.). 10p. (J). (ps-k). bds. 4.99 (0-7364-1062-7) Mouse Works.

Hoguet, Susan R. I Unpacked My Grandmother's Trunk. 1983. (Illus.). 58p. (J). (ps-3). 13.95 o.p. (0-525-44069-0, Dutton Children's Bks.) Penguin Putnam Bks. for Young Readers.

Hoobler, Dorothy & Hoobler, Thomas. The 1970s: Arguments. 2002. (Century Kids Ser.). (Illus.). 160p. (YA). (gr. 5-8). 22.90 (0-7613-1607-8) Millbrook Pr., Inc.

—The 1990s: Families. 2002. (Century Kids Ser.). (Illus.). 160p. (J). (gr. 5-8). 22.90 (0-7613-1609-4) Millbrook Pr., Inc.

Hopper, Nancy J. Cassandra Live at Carnegie Hall! 1998. 160p. (J). (gr. 5-8). 15.99 o.s.i (0-8037-2329-6, Dial Bks. for Young Readers) Penguin Putnam Bks. for Young Readers.

Horn, Peter. Cuando Sea Grande... 2001. (SPA., Illus.). 32p. (J). (gr. k-3). pap. 6.95 (0-7358-1435-X, NS30340) North-South Bks., Inc.

—Cuando Sea Grande... Almohar, Ariel, tr. 2001. (SPA., Illus.). 32p. (J). (gr. k-3). 15.95 (0-7358-1434-1, NS30341) North-South Bks., Inc.

—When I Grow Up... Cuando Sea Grande. Almohar, Ariel, tr. from GER. 2001. (Illus.). 32p. (J). (ps-3). pap. 6.95 (0-7358-1418-X, Michael Neugebauer Bks.) North-South Bks., Inc.

Horvath, Betty F. Sir Galahad, Mr. Longfellow & Me. 1998. 144p. (J). (gr. 4-6). 15.00 (0-689-81470-4, Atheneum) Simon & Schuster Children's Publishing.

Houghton Mifflin Company Staff. Family Reunion. 1992. (Literature Experience 1993 Ser.). (J). (gr. 8). pap. 11.04 (0-395-61878-9) Houghton Mifflin Co.

—Speaking English for Mom. 1992. (Literature Experience 1993 Ser.). (J). (gr. 2). pap. 9.48 (0-395-61776-6) Houghton Mifflin Co.

Houston, Gloria M. My Great-Aunt Arizona. 1997. 12.10 (0-606-11656-7) Turtleback Bks.

Howard, Elizabeth Fitzgerald. What's in Aunt Mary's Room? 2002. (Illus.). 32p. (J). (ps-3). pap. 5.95 (0-618-24621-5, Clarion Bks.) Houghton Mifflin Co. Trade & Reference Div.

Howard, Elizabeth Fitzgerald & Lucas, Cedric. What's in Aunt Mary's Room? 1996. (Illus.). 32p. (J). (ps-3). lib. bdg., tchr. ed. 16.00 (0-395-69845-6, Clarion Bks.) Houghton Mifflin Co. Trade & Reference Div.

Howe, James. Pinky & Rex & the Perfect Pumpkin. 2000. (Pinky & Rex Ser.). (J). (gr. 1-4). pap., stu. ed. 23.24 incl. audio (0-7887-4459-3, 41149); pap., stu. ed. 23.24 incl. audio (0-7887-4459-3, 41149) Recorded Bks., LLC.

—Pinky & Rex & the Perfect Pumpkin. 1998. (Pinky & Rex Ser.). (J). (gr. 1-4). 10.14 (0-606-17958-5) Turtleback Bks.

Hudson, Wade. I Love My Family. 1995. (Illus.). 32p. (J). (ps-3). pap. 2.50 o.p. (0-590-45764-0) Scholastic, Inc.

—I Love My Family: An African-American Family Reunion. (Illus.). 32p. (J). (ps-2). 1995. mass mkt. 4.95 (0-590-47325-5); 1993. pap. 12.95 o.p. (0-590-45763-2) Scholastic, Inc.

Hughes, Dean. Family Picture. 1990. (J). pap. 2.75 o.p. (0-590-43356-3) Scholastic, Inc.

Hughes, Shirley. An Evening at Alfie's. 1985. (Illus.). 32p. (J). (ps-1). 16.00 o.p. (0-688-04122-1); lib. bdg. 15.93 o.p. (0-688-04123-X) HarperCollins Children's Bk. Group.

Hunt, Angela Elwell. A Dream to Cherish. 1992. (Cassie Perkins Ser.: Vol. 4). 176p. (J). (gr. 4-8). pap. 4.99 o.p. (0-8423-1064-9) Tyndale Hse. Pubs.

—A Dream to Cherish. 2000. (Cassie Perkins Ser.: Vol. 4). 196p. (gr. 5-9). pap. 12.95 (0-595-08995-X) iUniverse, Inc.

—The Much-Adored Sandy Shore. 1992. (Cassie Perkins Ser.). 176p. (J). (gr. 4-8). pap. 4.99 o.p. (0-8423-1065-7) Tyndale Hse. Pubs.

Hunt, Nancy. Families Are Funny. 1992. (Illus.). 32p. (J). (ps-1). 13.95 o.p. (0-531-05969-3); mass mkt. 13.99 o.p. (0-531-08569-4) Scholastic, Inc. (Orchard Bks.).

Hunter, Lynn, et al. Meet the Dooples. 1997. (The Dooples & the Shapes). (Illus.). 32p. (J). (ps-2). lib. bdg. 19.95 (0-9656279-1-8) Educational Media Enterprises, Inc.

Hutchins, Pat. There's Only One of Me. 2003. (Illus.). 24p. (J). 15.99 (0-06-029819-7); lib. bdg. 16.89 (0-06-029820-0) HarperCollins Children's Bk. Group. (Greenwillow Bks.).

I Love Grandpa. 1990. 16p. (J). pap. (1-55513-981-7) Cook Communications Ministries.

Impey, Rose. My Mom & Our Dad. 1991. (Illus.). 32p. (J). (ps-3). 12.95 o.p. (0-670-83663-X, Viking Children's Bks.) Penguin Putnam Bks. for Young Readers.

Inches, Alison. Blue's First Holiday. 2003. (Blue's Clues Ser.). (Illus.). 24p. (J). 9.99 (0-689-86167-2, Simon Spotlight/Nickelodeon) Simon & Schuster Children's Publishing.

Inman, Sue. Coconut's Rainbow Aunties. 1997. (Toddlers' First Stories Ser.). (Illus.). 16p. (J). (ps). bds. 2.98 (1-85854-525-0) Brimax Bks., Ltd.

Inserra, Rose. Wedding Day Disaster. 1999. (Supa Doopers Ser.). (Illus.). 64p. (J). (0-7608-3288-9) Sundance Publishing.

Inteli, Nancy. The Tutter Family Reunion. 2001. (Bear in the Big Blue House Ser.). (Illus.). 32p. (J). (ps-3). pap. 5.99 (0-689-84022-5, Simon Spotlight) Simon & Schuster Children's Publishing.

Irwin, Hadley. The Original Freddie Ackerman. (Illus.). 192p. (YA). 1996. (gr. 4-7). pap. 4.50 (0-689-80389-3, Simon Pulse); 1992. (gr. 5 up). 15.00 (0-689-50562-0, McElderry, Margaret K.) Simon & Schuster Children's Publishing.

Jacob, Lucinda. Good Morning. 1998. (Illus.). 32p. (ps). pap. 7.95 (1-85371-752-5) Poolbeg Pr. IRL. *Dist:* Dufour Editions, Inc.

James, Betsy. The Mud Family. 1998. (Illus.). 32p. (J). pap. 10.95 (0-19-512479-0) Oxford Univ. Pr., Inc.

James, Henry. Washington Square. unabr. ed. 1970. (Classics Ser.). (YA). (gr. 10 up). mass mkt. 1.50 o.p. (0-8049-0210-0, CL-210) Airmont Publishing Co., Inc.

—Washington Square. 1880. 270p. (YA). reprint ed. pap. text 28.00 (1-4047-3377-9) Classic Textbooks.

—Washington Square, Level 2. 1999. 144p. (J). pap. 7.66 (0-582-40162-3) Longman Publishing Group.

—Washington Square, Level 4. Hedge, Tricia, ed. 2000. (Bookworms Ser.). (Illus.). 96p. (YA). pap. text 5.95 (0-19-423052-X) Oxford Univ. Pr., Inc.

—Washington Square. 2001. (Washington Square Press Enriched Classic Ser.). (Illus.). (J). 13.04 (0-606-21510-7) Turtleback Bks.

James, Simon. Jake & His Cousin Sidney. 2002. (Illus.). 32p. (J). bds. 4.99 (0-7636-1801-2) Candlewick Pr.

—Little One Step. 2003. (Illus.). 32p. (J). (gr. k-3). 15.99 (0-7636-2070-X) Candlewick Pr.

James, Will. Uncle Bill. Carey, Jennifer, ed. 1998. (Tumbleweed Ser.). (Illus.). 198p. (YA). (gr. 4 up). reprint ed. 26.00 (0-87842-379-6, 695) Mountain Pr. Publishing Co., Inc.

Javernick, Ellen. Where's Brooke? 1993. (Rookie Readers Ser.). (Illus.). 32p. (J). (gr. 1-2). pap. 4.95 o.p. (0-516-42012-7, Children's Pr.) Scholastic Library Publishing.

Jennings, Sharon. The Bye-Bye Pie. 1999. (Illus.). 32p. (J). (gr. k-3). (1-55041-405-4) Fitzhenry & Whiteside, Ltd.

—Into My Mother's Arms. 2000. (Illus.). 32p. (J). (ps-k). (1-55041-533-6) Fitzhenry & Whiteside, Ltd.

—Into My Mother's Arms: With Sticker & Card. 2001. (Illus.). 32p. (J). (ps-k). (1-55041-669-3) Fitzhenry & Whiteside, Ltd.

Jewell, Nancy. The Family under the Moon. 1976. (Illus.). (J). (ps-3). lib. bdg. 11.89 o.p. (0-06-022828-8) HarperCollins Children's Bk. Group.

Johns, Linda. To Pee or Not to Pee. 1998. (All by Myself Bks.). (Illus.). 16p. (J). (ps). 6.95 (1-58260-003-1) Infinity Plus One, LLC.

Johnson, Angela. The Aunt in Our House. 1996. (Illus.). 32p. (J). (ps-3). pap. 15.95 (0-531-09502-9); lib. bdg. 16.99 (0-531-08852-9) Scholastic, Inc. (Orchard Bks.).

—The Wedding. 1999. (Illus.). 32p. (J). (ps-2). pap. 16.95 (0-531-30139-7); lib. bdg. 17.99 (0-531-33139-3) Scholastic, Inc. (Orchard Bks.).

Johnson, Annabel & Johnson, Edgar. The Grizzly. 1964. (Illus.). 194p. (J). (gr. 5-9). lib. bdg. 13.89 o.p. (0-06-022871-7) HarperCollins Children's Bk. Group.

Johnston, Julie. In Spite of Killer Bees. 264p. (YA). (gr. 6 up). 2002. pap. 9.95 (0-88776-601-3); 2001. 17.95 o.s.i (0-88776-537-8) Tundra Bks. of Northern New York.

Johnston, Tony & Vanden Broeck, Fabrizio. Uncle Rain Cloud. 2003. pap. 6.95 (0-88106-372-X) Charlesbridge Publishing, Inc.

Jones, Diana Wynne. Aunt Maria. (J). 2003. 288p. 16.99 (0-06-623742-4); 1991. (Illus.). (gr. 7 up). 13.95 o.p. (0-688-10611-0) HarperCollins Children's Bk. Group. (Greenwillow Bks.).

—Yes Dear. 9999. (J). lib. bdg. 99.98 o.p. (0-688-11196-3, Greenwillow Bks.) HarperCollins Children's Bk. Group.

Jones, Jennifer B. Dear Mrs. Ryan, You're Ruining My Life. 2000. 122p. (J). (gr. 5-9). 15.95 (0-8027-8728-2) Walker & Co.

Jones, Lara. I Love Hugs. 2002. (Illus.). 16p. (J). bds. 6.95 (0-439-36767-0, Cartwheel Bks.) Scholastic, Inc.

Joosse, Barbara M. The Pitiful Life of Simon Schultz. 1991. 192p. (J). (gr. 5-9). 13.95 (0-06-022486-X); lib. bdg. 13.89 (0-06-022487-8) HarperCollins Children's Bk. Group.

Julian, Alison. Brave as a Bunny Can Be. 2001. (Illus.). 40p. (J). (gr. 2 up). 15.95 (0-931674-46-8) Waldman Hse. Pr., Inc.

Julik, Edie. Sailing Through the Storm: To the Ocean of Peace. 1998. (Illus.). 42p. (J). (gr. k-2). 16.95 (1-880090-70-8) Galde Pr., Inc.

Kalish, Ginny. Rachel Rude Rowdy. 2001. (Illus.). 128p. (J). pap. 15.95 (1-56976-127-2, 1148, Zephyr Pr.) Chicago Review Pr., Inc.

Karr, Kathleen. Man of the Family, RS. 1999. (Illus.). 192p. (J). (gr. 5 up). 16.00 (0-374-34764-6, Farrar, Straus & Giroux (BYR)) Farrar, Straus & Giroux.

Kata, Elizabeth. A Patch of Blue. 1981. 144p. (J). (gr. 7 up). mass mkt. 2.25 o.p. (0-449-70015-1, Fawcett) Ballantine Bks.

Katschke, Judy. If I Were President. 1999. (Full House Michelle Ser.: No. 29). 96p. (J). (gr. 2-4). pap. 3.99 (0-671-02153-2, Simon Spotlight) Simon & Schuster Children's Publishing.

—The Penguin Skates. 2001. (Full House Michelle Ser.: No. 36). 96p. (J). (gr. 2-4). pap. 3.99 o.s.i (0-671-04201-7, Simon Spotlight) Simon & Schuster Children's Publishing.

—Smile & Say "Woof!" 2000. (Full House Michelle Ser.: No. 34). 96p. (J). (gr. 2-4). pap. 3.99 (0-671-04199-1, Simon Spotlight) Simon & Schuster Children's Publishing.

Katz, Illana. Uncle Jimmy. 1994. (Illus.). 40p. (J). (gr. k-6). 16.95 (1-882388-03-8) Real Life Storybooks.

Katz, Susan. Snowdrops for Cousin Ruth. 1998. (Illus.). 183p. (J). (gr. 3-7). per. 16.00 (0-689-81391-0, 866182, Simon & Schuster Children's Publishing) Simon & Schuster Children's Publishing.

Katzakian, Norma. Naomi - A First Generation American. Chidester, Ardis & Folchi, Robert A., eds. Lt. ed. 2000. (Illus.). (J). (gr. 4-7). pap. 12.95 (0-9662228-1-4) Dab Publishing Co.

Kay, Alan N. On the Trail of John Brown's Body. 2001. (Young Heroes of History Ser.: Vol. 2). (Illus.). 175p. (J). (gr. 4-7). pap. 5.95 (1-57249-239-2, 1572492406, Burd Street Pr.) White Mane Publishing Co., Inc.

Keane, Bil. I Can't Untie My Shoes. 1983. (Family Circus Ser.). (Illus.). 128p. (J). (gr. 3). mass mkt. 1.95 o.p. (0-449-12557-2, Fawcett) Ballantine Bks.

Keats, Ezra Jack. Louie's Search. 2002. (Illus.). (J). 13.19 (0-7587-5737-9) Book Wholesalers, Inc.

—Louie's Search. 2001. (Illus.). 40p. (J). (ps-3). 15.99 (0-670-89224-6, Viking Children's Bks.) Penguin Putnam Bks. for Young Readers.

Keith, Harold. Chico & Dan. 1998. (Illus.). 120p. (YA). (gr. 4-7). 16.95 (1-57168-216-3) Eakin Pr.

Keith, Harold & Arbuckle, Scott. Chico & Dan. 1998. E-Book 16.95 (0-585-23231-8) netLibrary, Inc.

Keller, Beverly. Desdemona Moves On. 1992. 176p. (J). (gr. 3-7). 13.95 o.p. (0-02-749751-8, Simon & Schuster Children's Publishing) Simon & Schuster Children's Publishing.

Keller, Holly. Cromwell's Glasses. 1982. (Illus.). 32p. (J). (gr. k-3). 14.00 o.p. (0-688-00834-8); lib. bdg. 11.88 o.p. (0-688-00835-6) HarperCollins Children's Bk. Group. (Greenwillow Bks.).

—Newton's Hat. 2003. (Illus.). 24p. (J). 15.99 (0-06-051479-5); lib. bdg. 16.89 (0-06-051480-9) HarperCollins Children's Bk. Group. (Greenwillow Bks.).

Kelly, Sean. Becky Makes a Wish. 1993. (Shining Time Station Classics Ser.). 40p. (J). (ps-3). pap. 5.95 (1-884336-03-5) Quality Family Entertainment, Inc.

Kennedy, Shannon. A Day at a Time. 2nd rev. ed. 1997. Orig. Title: There's No Cure. 100p. (YA). (gr. 5 up). reprint ed. pap. 5.99 (0-9653703-2-1) Copalis Publishing.

Kern, Jennifer A. & Elliott, Bill. Cindy Snake in the Adventure of Skull Mountain. Lt. ed. 1994. (Jimmy Roo Adventure Ser.: No. 2). (Illus.). 100p. (J). (gr. k-6). 14.95 (1-888086-00-9, 1-A) New Era Publishing Co.

—Golly Cricket in the Adventure of the Spider King. Lt. ed. 1994. (Jimmy Roo Adventure Ser.: No. 3). (Illus.). 110p. (J). (gr. k-6). 14.95 (1-888086-01-7, 1-B) New Era Publishing Co.

Kerr, M. E. I'll Love You When You're More Like Me. 1977. 160p. (YA). (gr. 7 up). lib. bdg. 14.89 o.p. (0-06-023137-8) HarperCollins Children's Bk. Group.

Kessler, Jascha. Tataga's Children: Fairy Tales by Grozdana Olujic. 2000. 144p. E-Book 8.00 (0-7388-7429-9) Xlibris Corp.

Ketteman, Hellen. Aunt Hilarity's Bustle. 1992. (J). (ps-3). pap. 14.00 o.p. (0-671-77861-7, Simon & Schuster Children's Publishing) Simon & Schuster Children's Publishing.

Kherdian, David. A Song for Uncle Harry. 1989. (Illus.). 80p. (J). (gr. 3-7). 13.95 o.s.i (0-399-21895-5, Philomel) Penguin Putnam Bks. for Young Readers.

Kidd, Ronald. Doug's Trading Places. 1997. (Illus.). (1-57759-026-0) Dalmatian Pr.

Kim, Helen S. The Long Season of Rain. 1997. 256p. (gr. 7-12). mass mkt. 6.50 o.s.i (0-449-70462-9, Fawcett) Ballantine Bks.

—The Long Season of Rain, ERS. 1996. 288p. (YA). (gr. 7 up). 15.95 o.s.i (0-8050-4758-1, Holt, Henry & Co. Bks. For Young Readers) Holt, Henry & Co.

—Mi Mimo y Yo (Just Me & My Cousin) 1997. (Spanish Golden Look-Look Bks.). (SPA., Illus.). 24p. (J). pap. 3.29 o.s.i (0-307-72688-6, Golden Bks.) Random Hse. Children's Bks.

Mayer, Mercer & Mayer, Gina. This Is My Family. 1997. (Little Critter Ser.). 24p. (J). (ps-3). 3.99 o.s.i (0-307-16068-8, 16068, Golden Bks.) Random Hse. Children's Bks.

Mazer, Anne. Have Wheels, Will Travel. 2001. (Amazing Days of Abby Hayes Ser.: No. 4). (Illus.). 144p. (J). (gr. 4-7). pap. 4.50 (0-439-17878-9) Scholastic, Inc.

Mazer, Norma Fox. Missing Pieces. 1995. (Illus.). 208p. (YA). (gr. 7 up). 16.00 (0-688-13349-5, Morrow, William & Co.) Morrow/Avon.

—When She Was Good. 240p. (J). (gr. 7 up). 2003. (Illus.). mass mkt. 5.99 (0-590-31990-6, Scholastic Paperbacks); 2000. pap. 16.95 (0-590-13506-6) Scholastic, Inc.

—When She Was Good. 2000. 11.04 (0-606-18615-8) Turtleback Bks.

—When We First Met. 1984. (J). (gr. 7 up). 9.95 o.s.i (0-02-767080-5, Simon & Schuster Children's Publishing) Simon & Schuster Children's Publishing.

McCaughrean, Geraldine. The Kite Rider. (J). (gr. 7 up). 2003. (Illus.). 320p. pap. 6.99 (0-06-441091-9); 2002. 288p. lib. bdg. 16.89 (0-06-623875-7) HarperCollins Children's Bk. Group.

—The Kite Rider. 2002. (Illus.). 288p. (J). (gr. 7 up). 15.95 (0-06-623874-9) HarperCollins Pubs.

—My Grandmother's Clock. 2002. (Illus.). 32p. (J). (ps-3). 15.00 (0-618-21695-2, Clarion Bks.) Houghton Mifflin Co. Trade & Reference Div.

McCloskey, Robert. One Morning in Maine. (Picture Puffin Bks.). (J). (ps-3). 1976. 62p. pap. 6.99 (0-14-050174-6, Puffin Bks.); 1952. (Illus.). 64p. 17.99 (0-670-52627-4, Viking Children's Bks.) Penguin Putnam Bks. for Young Readers.

—One Morning in Maine. 1976. (Picture Puffin Ser.). (Illus.). (J). 12.14 (0-606-04247-4) Turtleback Bks.

McCully, Emily Arnold. My Real Family. 1999. (Illus.). 32p. (J). (gr. k-3). pap. 6.00 (0-15-201957-X, Harcourt Paperbacks) Harcourt Children's Bks.

McElligott, Matthew. Uncle Frank's Pit. 1998. (Illus.). 32p. (J). (gr. k-3). 15.99 o.s.i (0-670-87737-9, Viking Children's Bks.) Penguin Putnam Bks. for Young Readers.

McGrail, Anna. Mrs. Einstein: A Novel. 1998. 320p. 24.95 (0-393-04611-7) Norton, W. W. & Co., Inc.

McKee, David. The Hill & the Rock. 1999. (Illus.). 25p. pap. 9.95 (0-86264-784-3) Andersen Pr., Ltd. GBR. *Dist:* Trafalgar Square.

—The Hill & the Rock. 1985. (Illus.). 32p. (J). (ps-4). 10.95 o.p. (0-89919-341-2, Clarion Bks.) Houghton Mifflin Co. Trade & Reference Div.

—The Hill & the Rock. 1986. (Picture Puffin Ser.). (Illus.). 32p. (J). (ps-3). pap. 3.95 o.p. (0-14-050621-7, Puffin Bks.) Penguin Putnam Bks. for Young Readers.

—Prince Peter & the Teddy Bear, RS. 1997. (Illus.). 32p. (J). (ps-1). 15.00 o.p. (0-374-36123-1, Farrar, Straus & Giroux (BYR)) Farrar, Straus & Giroux.

McKenna, Colleen O'Shaughnessy. Cousins: Not Quite Sisters. 1993. 160p. (J). (gr. 4-6). mass mkt. 2.95 (0-590-49428-7) Scholastic, Inc.

—Cousins: Stuck in the Middle. 1993. 160p. (J). (gr. 4-6). pap. 2.95 (0-590-49429-5) Scholastic, Inc.

McMullen, Nigel. Not Me! 2001. (Illus.). 24p. (J). 12.99 o.s.i (0-525-46789-0, Dutton Children's Bks.) Penguin Putnam Bks. for Young Readers.

McMurtrey, Martin. Loose to the Wilds. 2nd ed. 162p. (YA). reprint ed. pap. 6.00 (0-9623961-0-9) McMurtrey, Martin A.

Mendes, Valerie. Look at Me, Grandma! 2001. (Illus.). 32p. (J). (ps-1). pap. 15.95 (0-439-29654-4, Chicken Hse., The) Scholastic, Inc.

Menning, Lori. One Was Not Enough. 2000. (Illus.). 16p. (J). pap. 5.95 (1-891846-18-3) Business Word, The.

Merrill, Susan. Washday, 001. 1979. (Illus.). 32p. (J). (ps-4). 6.95 o.p. (0-395-28817-7, Clarion Bks.) Houghton Mifflin Co. Trade & Reference Div.

Mildred at Home. 2001. (Mildred Classics Ser.: Vol. 5). 288p. pap. 5.95 (1-58182-231-6) Cumberland Hse. Publishing.

Mildred Keith. 2001. (Mildred Classics Ser.: Vol. 1). 288p. pap. 5.95 (1-58182-227-8) Cumberland Hse. Publishing.

Mildred's Boys & Girls. 2001. (Mildred Classics Ser.: Vol. 6). 288p. pap. 5.95 (1-58182-232-4) Cumberland Hse. Publishing.

Mildred's New Daughter, 7 Vols., 7. 2001. (Mildred Classics: Vol. 7). 288p. pap. 5.95 (1-58182-233-2) Cumberland Hse. Publishing.

Miller, Judi. My Crazy Cousin Courtney Comes Back. 1994. 8.60 o.p. (0-606-11651-6); 1993. 8.09 o.p. (0-606-11650-8) Turtleback Bks.

—My Crazy Cousin Courtney Gets Crazier. 1997. (Crazy Courtney Ser.). 8.60 o.p. (0-606-11652-4) Turtleback Bks.

—My Crazy Cousin Courtney Returns Again. MacDonald, Pat, ed. 1995. 160p. (Orig.). (J). pap. 3.50 o.p. (0-671-88733-5, Aladdin) Simon & Schuster Children's Publishing.

—My Crazy Cousin Courtney Returns Again. 1995. (Orig.). 8.60 (0-606-11653-2) Turtleback Bks.

Modarressi, Mitra. The Parent Thief. 1996. (Illus.). 32p. (J). (ps-3). mass mkt. 16.99 o.p. (0-531-08776-X, Orchard Bks.) Scholastic, Inc.

Monk, Isabell. Family. 2001. (Picture Bks.). (Illus.). 32p. (J). (ps-3). lib. bdg. 15.95 (1-57505-485-X, Carolrhoda Bks.) Lerner Publishing Group.

—Hope. 1998. (Picture Bks.). (Illus.). 32p. (J). (ps-3). lib. bdg. 15.95 (1-57505-230-X, Carolrhoda Bks.) Lerner Publishing Group.

Montgomery. Story Girl of Avonlea: Dreams Scheme. 2004. 96p. pap. 4.99 (0-310-70601-7) Zondervan.

Montgomery Buvens, Norma O'Rene. A Salute for Trixey. 2001. 40p. (J). 16.95 (1-57168-943-5, Eakin Pr.) Eakin Pr.

Montgomery, L. M. The King Cousins. 2004. (Story Girl Ser.). 96p. (J). pap. 4.99 (0-310-70598-3) Zondervan.

—Measles, Mischief, & Mishaps. 2004. (Story Girl Ser.). 96p. (J). pap. 4.99 (0-310-70599-1) Zondervan.

Moore, Ishbel L. Daughter. (YA). 1999. 288p. (gr. 6-8). text (1-55074-535-2); 2002. (Illus.). 216p. (gr. 5-9). pap. 6.95 (1-55074-537-9) Kids Can Pr., Ltd.

Moore, Martha. Angels on the Roof. 1997. 192p. (YA). (gr. 7 up). 15.95 o.s.i (0-385-32278-X, Delacorte Pr.) Dell Publishing.

Moore, Yvette. Freedom Songs. 1992. 176p. (YA). (gr. 7 up). pap. 5.99 (0-14-036017-4, Puffin Bks.) Penguin Putnam Bks. for Young Readers.

—Freedom Songs. 1991. 176p. (YA). (gr. 7 up). mass mkt. 15.99 o.p. (0-531-08412-4); mass mkt. 15.95 o.p. (0-531-05812-3) Scholastic, Inc. (Orchard Bks.).

—Freedom Songs. 1992. (J). 12.04 (0-606-01693-7) Turtleback Bks.

Moorhead, Ileen. The Pretzel Family. 1996. (Illus.). 64p. (Orig.). (J). (gr. k-1). pap. 7.00 (1-56002-541-7, University Editions) Aegina Pr., Inc.

Mora, Eddy G. Toby & Dad at Work. deluxe ed. 2000. (Toby & Tig Ser.). (Illus.). (J). (gr. 3-8). 13.99 (0-9671753-1-3) Mora Art Studio.

Mora, Pat. A Birthday Basket for Tia. 1992. (Illus.). 32p. (J). (ps-3). 16.00 (0-02-767400-2, Simon & Schuster Children's Publishing) Simon & Schuster Children's Publishing.

—Una Canasta de Cumpleanos Para Tia. 1997. (J). 11.19 o.p. (0-606-12024-6) Turtleback Bks.

Morris, Rosie. The Lilly Pond Family. 2000. (Illus.). (J). (gr. 3-6). pap. 6.95 o.p. (0-533-12309-7) Vantage Pr., Inc.

Morrow, Liza K. Allergic to My Family. 1995. 160p. (J). (gr. 3-6). reprint ed. per. 3.50 (0-671-86505-6, Aladdin) Simon & Schuster Children's Publishing.

Moses, Will. Silent Night. (Illus.). 40p. (J). 2002. pap. 6.99 (0-698-11964-9); 1997. 16.99 (0-399-23100-5, Philomel) Penguin Putnam Bks. for Young Readers.

Mosher, Richard. The Taxi Navigator. 1996. 144p. (J). (gr. 4-7). 15.95 o.s.i (0-399-23104-8, Philomel) Penguin Putnam Bks. for Young Readers.

Mother Branch & Her Leaf Children: A Story about Assertiveness. 1998. (Excellence in Character Series Storybks.). (Illus.). 30p. (J). (gr. k-8). pap. 6.00 (1-58259-015-X) Global Classroom, The.

Mufaro's Beautiful Daughters. 2001. (J). (ps-3). 24.95 incl. audio (0-87499-656-2); pap. 33.95 incl. audio (0-87499-657-0); pap. text 15.95 incl. audio (0-87499-655-4) Live Oak Media.

Mullican, Judy. Families - Familias. Loomis, Linda, tr. 1995. (Big Bks.). (SPA., Illus.). 8p. (Orig.). (J). (ps-k). pap. text 10.95 (1-57332-055-2) HighReach Learning, Inc.

Munsil, Janet. Dinner at Auntie Rose's. 2003. (Annikins Ser.: Vol 8). (Illus.). 32p. (J). (ps-2). pap. 1.25 (1-55037-047-2) Annick Pr., Ltd. CAN. *Dist:* Firefly Bks., Ltd.

Muntean, Michaela. Kermit & Robin's Scary Story. 1995. (Easy-to-Read Ser.). (Illus.). 32p. (J). (gr. k-3). 11.99 o.s.i (0-670-86106-5, Viking Children's Bks.) Penguin Putnam Bks. for Young Readers.

Murail, Marie-Aude. Uncle Giorgio. 1992. (I Love to Read Collections). (Illus.). 46p. (J). (gr. 1-5). lib. bdg. 8.50 o.p. (0-89565-809-7) Child's World, Inc.

Murphy, Barbara B. Eagles in Their Flight. 1994. 192p. (J). (gr. 6 up). 14.95 o.s.i (0-385-32035-3, Delacorte Pr.) Dell Publishing.

Murphy, Elspeth Campbell. The Birthday Present Mystery. 2001. (Young Cousins Mysteries Ser.). (Illus.). 32p. (J). (gr. 1-3). pap. 4.99 (0-7642-2494-8) Bethany Hse. Pubs.

—The Chalk Drawings Mystery. 2002. (Young Cousins Mysteries Ser.: Vol. 4). (Illus.). 32p. (J). (gr. 1-3). pap. 4.99 (0-7642-2497-2) Bethany Hse. Pubs.

—The Flying Pigs Mystery. 2002. (Young Cousins Mysteries Ser.). (Illus.). 32p. (J). (gr. 1-3). pap. 4.99 (0-7642-2499-9) Bethany Hse. Pubs.

—The Giant Chicken Mystery. 2002. (Young Cousins Mysteries Ser.: Vol. 3). (Illus.). 32p. (J). (gr. 1-3). pap. 4.99 (0-7642-2496-4) Bethany Hse. Pubs.

—Mystery of the Candy Box. 1989. 48p. (J). pap. text 2.79 o.p. (1-55513-570-6) Cook, David C. Publishing Co.

—The Mystery of the Gingerbread House. 1997. (Three Cousins Detective Club Ser.: No. 13). (Illus.). 64p. (J). (gr. 2-5). pap. 3.99 (1-55661-851-4) Bethany Hse. Pubs.

—The Mystery of the Golden Reindeer. 2000. (Three Cousins Detective Club Ser.: No. 30). (Illus.). 64p. (J). (gr. 2-5). pap. 3.99 (0-7642-2138-8) Bethany Hse. Pubs.

—Mystery of the Princess Doll. 1990. 48p. (J). pap. text 2.79 o.p. (1-55513-913-2) Cook, David C. Publishing Co.

—The Mystery of the Zoo Camp. 1997. (Three Cousins Detective Club Ser.: No. 14). (Illus.). 64p. (J). (gr. 2-5). pap. 3.99 (1-55661-852-2) Bethany Hse. Pubs.

—The Purple Cow Mystery. 2002. (Young Cousins Mysteries Ser.). (Illus.). 32p. (J). (gr. 1-3). pap. 4.99 (0-7642-2498-0) Bethany Hse. Pubs.

Murphy, Shirley Rousseau. Silver Woven in My Hair. 1992. (Illus.). 128p. (J). (gr. 3-7). reprint ed. pap. 3.95 o.s.i (0-689-71525-0, Aladdin) Simon & Schuster Children's Publishing.

Murray, Martine. The Slightly True Story of Cedar B. Hartley: (Who Planned to Live an Unusual Life) 2003. (Illus.). 240p. (J). (gr. 3-9). 15.95 (0-439-48622-X, Levine, Arthur A. Bks.) Scholastic, Inc.

My Wonderful Aunt. 1988. (J). 12.34 o.p. (0-516-08913-7); 12.34 o.p. (0-516-08914-5) Scholastic Library Publishing. (Children's Pr.).

Myers, Anna. When the Bough Breaks. 2000. 170p. (J). 16.95 (0-8027-8725-8) Walker & Co.

Myers, Bernice. Company's Coming. 1994. (Whole-Language Big Bks.). (Illus.). 16p. (Orig.). (J). (ps-2). pap. 16.95 (1-56784-064-7) Newbridge Educational Publishing.

Myers, Walter Dean. The Glory Field. 1999. 420p. (J). 15.60 (0-03-054616-8) Holt, Rinehart & Winston.

—The Glory Field. 288p. (gr. 7-12). 1996. (YA). mass mkt. 4.99 (0-590-45898-1); 1994. (J). pap. 14.95 (0-590-45897-3) Scholastic, Inc.

—The Glory Field. 1994. (J). 11.04 (0-606-08527-0) Turtleback Bks.

Namioka, Lensey. Yang the Eldest & His Odd Jobs. 2000. (Illus.). 128p. (J). (gr. 3-7). 15.95 (0-316-59011-8) Little Brown & Co.

—Yang the Third & Her Impossible Family. 1996. (Illus.). 144p. (gr. 4-7). pap. text 4.50 (0-440-41231-5, Yearling) Random Hse. Children's Bks.

Nash, Mary. While Mrs. Coverlet Was Away. 2002. (Lost Treasures Ser.: No. 10). 128p. (J). (gr. 4-7). pap. 4.99 (0-7868-1695-3) Disney Pr.

Naylor, Phyllis Reynolds. Alice the Brave. 1995. (Alice Ser.). 144p. (YA). (gr. 5-9). 15.95 (0-689-80095-9, Atheneum) Simon & Schuster Children's Publishing.

—Beetles, Lightly Toasted. 1987. 144p. (J). (gr. 3-7). 16.95 (0-689-31355-1, Atheneum) Simon & Schuster Children's Publishing.

—I Can't Take You Anywhere. (Illus.). 32p. (J). (ps-3). 2001. pap. 5.99 (0-689-84116-7, Aladdin); 1997. 16.00 (0-689-31966-5, Atheneum) Simon & Schuster Children's Publishing.

Neeley, Gwen C. Miss Ima & the Hogg Family. 1992. (Illus.). 96p. (J). (gr. 7 up). pap. 10.95 (0-937460-79-6) Hendrick-Long Publishing Co.

Nelson, Lynda M. The Little Red Buckets. 1995. (Illus.). 91p. (Orig.). (J). (gr. 1 up). pap. 5.95 o.p. (0-9645810-4-3) Galleon Pubns.

—The Little Red Buckets. Florence, Giles et al, eds. 1995. (Illus.). 91p. (Orig.). (J). (gr. 1 up). pap. 5.95 o.p. (0-9645810-9-4) Galleon Pubns.

Newberger, Devra. A Full House Family Scrapbook. 1993. 40p. (J). (gr. 1-7). pap. 2.95 (0-590-46640-2, SC12) Scholastic, Inc.

Newberger-Speregen, Devra. Phone Call from a Flamingo. 1993. (Full House Stephanie Ser.: No. 1). 128p. (J). (gr. 4-6). per. 3.99 (0-671-88004-7, Aladdin) Simon & Schuster Children's Publishing.

Nixon, Joan Lowery. A Family Apart. 1997. 176p. (J). mass mkt. 4.50 (0-440-91309-8); 1996. (Orphan Train Adventures Ser.: Bk. 1). (J). mass mkt. 5.99 (0-440-91116-8); 1995. (Orphan Train Adventures Ser.: Vol. 1). 176p. (YA). (gr. 4-7). mass mkt. 5.50 (0-440-22676-7) Random Hse. Children's Bks. (Dell Books for Young Readers).

—The Haunting. 1998. 192p. (YA). (gr. 7-12). 15.95 o.s.i (0-385-32247-X) Doubleday Publishing.

—The Haunting. Horowitz, Beverly, ed. 2000. 192p. (YA). (gr. 7-12). mass mkt. 4.99 (0-440-22008-4, Laurel Leaf) Random Hse. Children's Bks.

—The Haunting. l.t. ed. 2000. (Illus.). 224p. (J). (ps up). 21.95 (0-7862-2739-7) Thorndike Pr.

—The Haunting. 2000. (YA). 11.04 (0-606-19191-7) Turtleback Bks.

Nolan, Han. Dancing on the Edge. 1999. 256p. (J). (gr. 7-12). pap. 5.99 (0-14-130203-8, Puffin Bks.) Penguin Putnam Bks. for Young Readers.

—Dancing on the Edge. 1999. 11.04 (0-606-16836-2) Turtleback Bks.

Noonan, Rosalind. Sarah: Don't Say You Love Me. 1998. (Party of Five: No. 5). 160p. (J). (gr. 3-6). pap. 4.50 (0-671-02452-3, Simon Pulse) Simon & Schuster Children's Publishing.

Norman, Hilary. The Pact. 1997. 432p. (YA). 24.95 o.p. (0-525-94256-4) Dutton/Plume.

Norris, Carolyn. In Our House: Story for Young Children in Sign Language. 1984. (Illus.). 32p. (Orig.). (J). (ps-3). pap. 3.95 o.p. (0-916708-11-X) Modern Signs Pr., Inc.

Norton, Mary. The Borrowers Aloft: Plus the Short Tale, Poor Stainless. 2003. (Illus.). 224p. (YA). (gr. 3-7). pap. 5.95 (0-15-204734-4, Odyssey Classics) Harcourt Children's Bks.

Oates, Joyce Carol. Little Reynard. 2003. (Illus.). 32p. (J). lib. bdg. 16.89 (0-06-029583-X) HarperCollins Pubs.

Oates, Joyce Carol & Graham, Mark. Little Reynard. 2003. (Illus.). 32p. (J). 15.99 (0-06-029559-7) HarperCollins Pubs.

O'Connor, Barbara. Moonpie & Ivy, RS. 2004. (Illus.). pap. (0-374-45320-9); 2001. 160p. (YA). (gr. 5 up). 16.00 (0-374-35059-0, Farrar, Straus & Giroux (BYR)) Farrar, Straus & Giroux.

O'Connor, Ilett. A Born Leader - Our Francine. 2002. 32p. pap. 10.00 (0-9717003-1-1) O'Connor, Ilett K.

Oliver, Lin. The Mighty Mogul. 1999. (Great Railway Adventures Ser.: Vol. 2;1). (Illus.). 32p. (J). (gr. k-4). 14.95 (1-890647-56-X); pap. 14.99 incl. audio (1-890647-57-8) Learning Curve International, LLC.

O'Neil, Laura. Hello Birthday, Goodbye Friend. 1999. (Full House Stephanie Ser.: No. 30). 144p. (J). (gr. 4-6). pap. 3.99 (0-671-02160-5, Simon Spotlight) Simon & Schuster Children's Publishing.

—Second Noah. 1996. (J). (gr. 4-7). mass mkt. 3.99 (0-590-93710-3) Scholastic, Inc.

Optic, Oliver. Through by Daylight: The Young Engineer. unabr. ed. 1998. (Lakeshore Ser.: Vol. 1). 312p. reprint ed. 15.00 (1-889128-50-3) Mantle Ministries.

Orgel, Doris. Midnight Soup & a Witch's Hat. 1989. (Illus.). 96p. (J). (gr. 2-5). pap. 3.95 o.p. (0-14-032212-4, Puffin Bks.) Penguin Putnam Bks. for Young Readers.

Osmond, Alan. If the Shoe Fits. 1998. (Twice Upon a Time Ser.). (Illus.). 32p. (J). (ps-2). 11.95 (1-57102-133-7) Warehousing & Fulfillment Specialists, LLC (WFS, LLC).

Osmond, Alan & Osmond, Suzanne. If the Shoe Fits. 1998. (Illus.). 32p. (J). (ps-2). per. (1-59093-012-6, Eager Minds Pr.) Warehousing & Fulfillment Specialists, LLC (WFS, LLC).

Osmond, Hazel M. Mollie & Company: And Gussie Too. 1996. (Illus.). (J). (ps up). (1-86106-083-1) Minerva Pr. GBR. *Dist:* Unity Distribution.

Otto, Maryleah. Tom Doesn't Visit Us Anymore. 1987. (Illus.). 24p. (J). reprint ed. pap. 4.95 (0-88961-117-3) Women's Pr. CAN. *Dist:* Univ. of Toronto Pr.

Oughton, Jerrie. Music from a Place Called Half Moon. 1995. 176p. (YA). (gr. 7-7). 16.00 (0-395-70737-4) Houghton Mifflin Co.

—Music from a Place Called Half Moon. 1997. 176p. (YA). (gr. 5-9). mass mkt. 3.99 o.s.i (0-440-21999-X, Yearling) Random Hse. Children's Bks.

—Music from a Place Called Half Moon. 1997. 10.04 (0-606-11003-8) Turtleback Bks.

Parish, Peggy. Amelia Bedelia's Family Album. (I Can Read Bks.). (Illus.). 48p. (J). (gr. k-3). 2003. pap. 3.99 (0-06-051116-8, Harper Trophy); 1997. pap. 3.95 (0-380-72860-5, Harper Trophy); 1988. 15.99 (0-688-07676-9, Greenwillow Bks.); 1988. lib. bdg. 16.89 (0-688-07677-7, Greenwillow Bks.) HarperCollins Children's Bk. Group.

—Amelia Bedelia's Family Album. (Amelia Bedelia Ser.). (J). (gr. k-2). 1991. (Illus.). pap. 3.99 (0-380-71698-4); 1989. 48p. mass mkt. 3.99 o.p. (0-380-70760-8) Morrow/Avon. (Avon Bks.).

—Amelia Bedelia's Family Album. 1988. (Amelia Bedelia Ser.). (J). (gr. k-2). 10.14 (0-606-04154-0) Turtleback Bks.

Park, Linda Sue. The Kite Fighters. 2000. (Illus.). 144p. (J). (gr. 5-9). tchr. ed. 15.00 (0-395-94041-9, Clarion Bks.) Houghton Mifflin Co. Trade & Reference Div.

Parker, Nancy Winslow. Love from Aunt Betty. 1983. (Illus.). 32p. (J). (gr. k-3). 11.95 o.p. (0-396-08135-5, G. P. Putnam's Sons) Penguin Putnam Bks. for Young Readers.

Parker, Richard. The Runaway. 1977. (J). 7.95 o.p. (0-525-66568-4, Dutton Children's Bks.) Penguin Putnam Bks. for Young Readers.

Parkinson, Curtis. Emily's Eighteen Aunts. ed. 2002. (YA). (gr. 1 up). spiral bd. (0-616-11134-7); (gr. 2). spiral bd. (0-616-11135-5) Canadian National Institute for the Blind/Institut National Canadien pour les Aveugles.

—Emily's Eighteen Aunts. 2002. (Illus.). 32p. (J). 15.95 (*0-7737-3336-1*) Stoddart Kids CAN. *Dist:* Fitzhenry & Whiteside, Ltd.

Parkinson, Siobhan. Four Kids, Three Cats, Two Cows, One Witch (Maybe) 2002. 192p. (YA). (gr. 5-9). pap. 7.95 (*0-86278-515-4*) O'Brien Pr., Ltd., The IRL. *Dist:* Independent Pubs. Group, Irish American Bk. Co.

Parr, Todd. The Family Book. 2003. (Illus.). 32p. (J). (gr. k-3). 15.95 (*0-316-73896-4*) Little Brown & Co.

Partridge, Elizabeth. Oranges on Golden Mountain. (Illus.). 40p. 2003. (YA). pap. 6.99 (*0-14-250033-X*, Puffin Bks.); 2001. (J). (gr. 1-4). 16.99 (*0-525-46453-0*, Dutton Children's Bks.) Penguin Putnam Bks. for Young Readers.

Pascal, Francine, creator. The Wakefields of Sweet Valley. 1991. (Sweet Valley Saga Ser.). 352p. (gr. 7 up). mass mkt. 4.50 o.s.i (*0-553-29278-1*) Bantam Bks.

Passen, Lisa. Uncle's New Suit, ERS. 1992. (Illus.). 32p. (J). (gr. 1-3). 14.95 o.p. (*0-8050-1652-X*, Holt, Henry & Co. Bks. For Young Readers) Holt, Henry & Co.

Paterson, Katherine. Park's Quest. 2000. (J). (gr. 5-8). pap., stu. ed. 42.24 incl. audio (*0-7887-4345-7*, 41139) Recorded Bks., LLC.

Paulsen, Gary. Father Water, Mother Woods: Essays on Fishing & Hunting in the North Woods. 1995. (J). mass mkt. 6.99 (*0-440-91088-9*, Dell Books for Young Readers) Random Hse. Children's Bks.

—The Schernoff Discoveries. 1997. 112p. (gr. 5-9). text 15.95 o.s.i (*0-385-32194-5*, Delacorte Pr.) Dell Publishing.

—The Schernoff Discoveries. 1998. 112p. (gr. 5-9). pap. text 4.50 (*0-440-41463-6*, Dell Books for Young Readers) Random Hse. Children's Bks.

—The Schernoff Discoveries. 1998. 10.55 (*0-606-13761-0*) Turtleback Bks.

Pearson, Gayle. Fish Friday. 1989. 192p. (J). (gr. 3-7). reprint ed. pap. 3.95 o.s.i (*0-689-71324-X*, Aladdin) Simon & Schuster Children's Publishing.

Peck, Robert Newton. Extra Innings. 2001. 192p. (J). (gr. 7 up). 16.99 (*0-06-028867-1*) HarperCollins Children's Bk. Group.

—Extra Innings. 2003. 224p. (J). (gr. 7 up). pap. 5.99 (*0-06-447229-9*) HarperCollins Pubs.

Pelgrom, Els. The Acorn Eaters, RS. Prins, Johanna H. & Prins, Johanna W., trs. from DUT. 1997. Tr. of Eikelvreters. 224p. (J). (gr. 7-12). 16.00 o.p. (*0-374-30029-1*, Farrar, Straus & Giroux (BYR)) Farrar, Straus & Giroux.

Pellegrini, Nina. Families Are Different. 1991. (Illus.). 32p. (J). (gr. k-3). tchr. ed. 16.95 (*0-8234-0887-6*) Holiday Hse., Inc.

Penn, Ruth B. Mommies Are for Loving. 1962. (Illus.). (J). (gr. k-3). 4.99 o.p. (*0-399-60468-5*) Putnam Publishing Group, The.

Perrault, Charles. Contes de ma Mere l'Oye. 1988. (Folio - Junior Ser.: No. 443). (FRE., Illus.). 223p. (J). (gr. 5-10). pap. 8.95 (*2-07-033443-0*) Schoenhof's Foreign Bks., Inc.

Perry, Michael. Daniel's Ride. 2001. (Illus.). 32p. (J). (gr. 2-5). 16.00 (*0-9701771-9-4*) Free Will Pr.

Peters, Julie Anne. Define "Normal" 2000. 208p. (J). (gr. 7-10). 16.95 (*0-316-70631-0*) Little Brown & Co.

—Define "Normal" 2003. (Illus.). 208p. (J). (gr. 3-7). pap. 5.95 (*0-316-73489-6*) Little Brown Children's Bks.

Peterson, John. The Littles & the Trash Tinies. 1977. (Littles Ser.). (Illus.). (J). (gr. 1-5). 10.14 (*0-606-02713-0*) Turtleback Bks.

—The Littles Have a Merry Christmas. 2003. (Littles First Readers Ser.). (Illus.). 32p. (J). pap. 3.99 (*0-439-42498-4*, Scholastic Paperbacks) Scholastic, Inc.

—The Littles to the Rescue. 1981. (Littles Ser.). (Illus.). 48p. (J). (gr. 1-5). 6.95 o.p. (*0-448-47491-3*, Grosset & Dunlap) Penguin Putnam Bks. for Young Readers.

Petertyl, Mary E. Seeds of Love: For Brothers & Sisters of International Adoption. 1997. (Illus.). 32p. (J). (ps-4). 15.95 (*0-9655753-1-4*) Folio One Publishing.

Pevsner, Stella. Jon, Flora, & the Odd-Eyed Cat. 1997. 192p. (J). per. 3.99 (*0-671-56105-7*, Aladdin) Simon & Schuster Children's Publishing.

—Sister of the Quints. 1987. 192p. (J). (gr. 5-9). 13.95 o.p. (*0-89919-498-2*, Clarion Bks.) Houghton Mifflin Co. Trade & Reference Div.

Pfeffer, Susan Beth. Claire at Sixteen. 1989. (Sebastian Sisters Quintet Ser.: No. 3). 192p. (YA). 13.95 o.s.i (*0-553-05819-3*, Starfire) Random Hse. Children's Bks.

—Family of Strangers. 1993. 176p. (YA). mass mkt. 3.99 o.s.i (*0-440-21895-0*) Dell Publishing.

—Family of Strangers. 1991. (J). o.s.i (*0-553-53091-7*, Dell Books for Young Readers) Random Hse. Children's Bks.

Plemons, Marti. Josh & the Guinea Pig. 1992. (Grace Street Kids Ser.). (Illus.). 128p. (J). (gr. 3-6). pap. 4.99 o.p. (*0-87403-686-0*, 24-03726) Standard Publishing.

Plummer, Louise. A Dance for Three. 2000. 240p. (YA). (gr. 9 up). 15.95 o.s.i (*0-385-32511-8*, Dell Books for Young Readers) Random Hse. Children's Bks.

Polacco, Patricia. Uncle Vova's Tree. 1998. (Illus.). 32p. (J). (ps-3). pap. 6.99 o.s.i (*0-698-11643-7*, PaperStar) Penguin Putnam Bks. for Young Readers.

Pople, Maureen. The Other Side of the Family, ERS. 1988. 176p. (J). (gr. 6 up). 13.95 o.p. (*0-8050-0758-X*, Holt, Henry & Co. Bks. For Young Readers) Holt, Henry & Co.

Prager, Annabelle. The Four Getsys & What They Forgot. 1982. (Illus.). 48p. (J). (gr. 1-4). 6.95 o.p. (*0-394-84833-0*); lib. bdg. 7.99 o.p. (*0-394-94833-5*) Knopf Publishing Group. (Pantheon).

Prigger, Mary Skillings. Aunt Minnie & the Twister. 2002. (Illus.). 32p. (J). (ps-3). lib. bdg. 15.00 (*0-618-11136-0*, Clarion Bks.) Houghton Mifflin Co. Trade & Reference Div.

Pullman, Philip. Count Karlstein. 2000. (Illus.). 256p. (YA). (gr. 5-8). pap. 5.99 (*0-375-80348-3*) Knopf, Alfred A. Inc.

—Count Karlstein. 1998. 176p. (J). (gr. 3-7). 18.99 o.s.i (*0-679-99255-3*); (gr. 5-8). 17.00 (*0-679-89255-9*) Random Hse. Children's Bks. (Random Hse. Bks. for Young Readers).

—Count Karlstein. 2000. 11.04 (*0-606-17845-7*) Turtleback Bks.

Pushker, Gloria T. A Belfer Bar Mitzvah. 1995. (Illus.). 32p. (J). (gr. 4-7). 14.95 (*1-56554-095-6*) Pelican Publishing Co., Inc.

Pyke, Helen G. Father Take Me Home. Wheeler, Gerald, ed. 1991. 160p. (Orig.). (J). pap. 8.95 o.p. (*0-8280-0596-6*) Review & Herald Publishing Assn.

Qualey, Marsha. One Night. 176p. 2003. (YA). pap. 5.99 (*0-14-250150-6*, Puffin Bks.); 2002. (Illus.). (J). 16.99 (*0-8037-2602-3*, Dial Bks. for Young Readers) Penguin Putnam Bks. for Young Readers.

—Thin Ice. 1997. 272p. (YA). (gr. 7-12). 14.95 o.s.i (*0-385-32298-4*, Delacorte Pr.) Dell Publishing.

—Thin Ice. 1999. 272p. (YA). (gr. 7-7). mass mkt. 4.99 (*0-440-22037-8*, Dell Books for Young Readers) Random Hse. Children's Bks.

—Thin Ice. 1999. 11.04 (*0-606-17348-X*) Turtleback Bks.

Quirk, Anne. Dancing with Great-Aunt Cornelia. 1997. 160p. (J). (gr. 3-7). 14.95 o.p. (*0-06-027332-1*) HarperCollins Children's Bk. Group.

Rada, James R., Jr. Logan's Fire. 1996. (YA). o.p. (*1-55503-841-7*) Covenant Communications, Inc.

Raintree Steck-Vaughn Staff. A Picnic in October. 2000. 32p. (gr. k-5). 16.98 (*0-7398-1367-6*) Raintree Pubs.

Rand, Ted, illus. Sailing Home: A Story of a Childhood at Sea. 2001. (Cheshire Studio Bk.). 32p. (J). (gr. k-3). 15.95 (*0-7358-1539-9*); (gr. 2-5). lib. bdg. 16.50 (*0-7358-1540-2*) North-South Bks., Inc.

Ransom, Candice F. The Promise Quilt. 2002. (Illus.). 32p. (J). (gr. k-3). pap. 6.95 (*0-8027-7648-5*) Walker & Co.

Rattigan, Jama Kim. Truman's Aunt Farm. 1994. (Illus.). 32p. (J). (ps-3). tchr. ed. 14.95 (*0-395-65661-3*) Houghton Mifflin Co.

Reddekopp, Sharon. A New Baby for Paige. 2000. (Illus.). 16p. (ps-3). pap. (*1-894303-07-5*) Raven Rock Publishing.

Regan, Dian Curtis. Dirty Laundry: Stories about Family Secrets. Fraustino, Lisa Rowe, ed. 1998. 160p. (YA). (gr. 4-7). 16.99 (*0-670-87911-8*) Penguin Putnam Bks. for Young Readers.

Reid, Mary C. Too Many Treasures. 1996. (Backpack Mystery Ser.: No. 1). (Illus.). 80p. (J). (gr. 2-5). pap. 3.99 o.p. (*1-55661-715-1*) Bethany Hse. Pubs.

Reiser, Lynn W. Cherry Pies & Lullabies. 1998. (Illus.). 40p. (J). (ps-3). 16.99 (*0-688-13391-6*, Greenwillow Bks.) HarperCollins Children's Bk. Group.

—The Surprise Family. 1997. (Illus.). 32p. (J). pap. 4.95 o.p. (*0-688-15476-X*, Morrow, William & Co.) Morrow/Avon.

—The Surprise Family. 1997. (J). 10.15 o.p. (*0-606-11947-7*) Turtleback Bks.

Reudor Staff. Are Pigeons Kosher? 1998. (Reudor's the Doodle Family Ser.). (Illus.). 96p. (J). (gr. 3-12). pap. 5.95 (*1-886611-05-X*) Atara Publishing.

—My Bubbe's Arms: Reudor's the Doodle Family. 1998. (Rhyme Time Doodles Ser.). (Illus.). 24p. (J). (gr. 1-12). 7.95 (*1-886611-00-9*) Atara Publishing.

—My Runaway Matzah Ball: Reudor's the Doodle Family. 1998. (Rhyme Time Doodles Ser.). (Illus.). 24p. (J). (gr. 1-12). 7.95 o.p. (*1-886611-02-5*) Atara Publishing.

—My Shabbat Palace: Reudor's the Doodle Family. (Rhyme Time Doodles Ser.). (Illus.). 24p. (J). (gr. 1-12). 7.95 o.p. (*1-886611-04-1*) Atara Publishing.

—The Young Maccabees. 1998. (Reudor's the Doodle Family Ser.). (Illus.). 22p. (J). (gr. 3-12). 8.95 (*1-886611-07-6*) Atara Publishing.

Rice, David. Crazy Loco. 2003. (Illus.). 144p. pap. 5.99 (*0-14-250056-9*, Puffin Bks.) Penguin Putnam Bks. for Young Readers.

Rice, James. The Ghost of Pont Diable. 1996. (Illus.). 176p. (J). (gr. 5-8). 14.95 o.p. (*1-57168-109-4*); pap. 8.95 o.p. (*1-57168-130-2*) Eakin Pr.

Richards, Kitty. Have Yourself a Thornberry Little Christmas. 2000. (Wild Thornberrys Ser.). (Illus.). 32p. (J). (gr. k-3). pap. 5.99 (*0-689-83229-X*, Simon Spotlight/Nickelodeon) Simon & Schuster Children's Publishing.

Richter, Conrad. Elements of Literature: The Light in the Forest. 1989. pap., stu. ed. 15.33 (*0-03-023439-5*) Holt, Rinehart & Winston.

—The Light in the Forest. (YA). (gr. 7 up). 21.95 (*0-89190-333-X*) Amereon, Ltd.

—The Light in the Forest. 1994. 128p. (gr. 7-12). mass mkt. 6.50 (*0-449-70437-8*, Fawcett) Ballantine Bks.

—The Light in the Forest. 1990. 128p. (J). (gr. 5-12). mass mkt. 3.99 o.s.i (*0-553-26878-3*); 1986. mass mkt. o.s.i (*0-553-16642-5*) Bantam Bks.

—The Light in the Forest. 1991. (YA). (gr. 7 up). lib. bdg. 21.95 (*1-56849-064-X*) Buccaneer Bks., Inc.

—The Light in the Forest. 1953. (Illus.). (J). 23.00 o.s.i (*0-394-43314-9*); (YA). (gr. 7 up). lib. bdg. 5.99 o.p. (*0-394-91404-X*) Knopf, Alfred A. Inc.

—The Light in the Forest. 1986. (J). mass mkt. o.s.i (*0-553-16679-4*, Dell Books for Young Readers) Random Hse. Children's Bks.

—The Light in the Forest. 9999. pap. 1.95 o.p. (*0-590-02336-5*) Scholastic, Inc.

—The Light in the Forest. 1994. (YA). (gr. 7 up). 12.04 (*0-606-06903-8*) Turtleback Bks.

Riley, Dorothy W. & Riley, Tiaudra. Dorothy Mae's Cornbread. 1992. 25p. (YA). pap. (*1-880234-05-X*) Winbush Publishing Co.

Ringgold, Faith. Bonjour, Lonnie. 1996. (Illus.). 32p. (J). (gr. k-4). 15.95 (*0-7868-0076-3*); (gr. 4-7). lib. bdg. 16.49 (*0-7868-2062-4*) Hyperion Bks. for Children.

Rispin, Karen. Anika's Mountain. 1994. (Anika Scott Ser.: No. 3). (Illus.). (J). pap. 4.99 o.p. (*0-8423-1219-6*) Tyndale Hse. Pubs.

Robben, Robert F. Petro Pals - Getting Lost in Petropolis. Robben, Margaret B., ed. 1998. (Illus.). 24p. (J). (ps-3). pap. 5.95 (*0-9653562-1-3*) Petro Pals, Inc.

Robbins, Terrie C. Bushtail Is Our Cousin. 2002. (Illus.). 32p. (J). (gr. 3-6). pap. 7.99 (*0-9711577-0-7*) Possibilities Unlimited.

Roberts, Dannel. Me & Uncle Mike & the 3-Toed Bear. l.t. ed. 1999. (Me & Uncle Mike Children's Book Series: Bk. 1). 36p. (J). (gr. k-5). per. 14.95 (*1-893459-00-4*) Lions & Tigers & Bears Publishing, Inc.

Roberts, Laura Peyton. Ghost of a Chance. 1997. 192p. (YA). (gr. 7-12). 14.95 o.s.i (*0-385-32508-8*, Delacorte Pr.) Dell Publishing.

Roberts, Willo Davis. Buddy Is a Stupid Name for a Girl. (Illus.). 224p. (J). 2002. pap. 4.99 (*0-689-85164-2*, Aladdin); 2001. (gr. 3-7). 16.00 (*0-689-81670-7*, Atheneum) Simon & Schuster Children's Publishing.

—Undercurrents. (Illus.). 240p. (J). 2003. pap. 4.99 (*0-689-85994-5*, Aladdin); 2002. (gr. 5-8). 16.00 (*0-689-81671-5*, Atheneum) Simon & Schuster Children's Publishing.

Robertson, Barbara. Rosemary in Paris: Back to 1889. 2001. (Hourglass Adventures Ser.: Bk. 2). (Illus.). 121p. (J). (gr. 4-7). pap. 4.95 (*1-890817-56-2*) Winslow Pr.

—Rosemary Meets Rosemarie Book #1: Berlin in 1870. 2001. (Hourglass Adventures Ser.: Bk. 1). (Illus.). 128p. (J). (gr. 4-6). pap. 5.95 (*1-890817-55-4*) Winslow Pr.

Robinson, W. Heath. The Adventures of Uncle Lubin. 2000. (Illus.). 128p. 9.95 (*1-56792-173-6*, Pocket Paragon) Godine, David R. Pub.

Roca, Nuria. Your Family: From the Youngest to the Oldest. 2001. (From ... to Ser.). (Illus.). 36p. (J). (ps-1). pap. 6.95 (*0-7641-1687-8*) Barron's Educational Series, Inc.

Rodowsky, Colby. Jenny & the Grand Old Great-Aunts. 1992. (Illus.). 40p. (J). (gr. 1-4). lib. bdg. 13.95 o.p. (*0-02-777785-5*, Simon & Schuster Children's Publishing) Simon & Schuster Children's Publishing.

—Not My Dog, RS. 1999. (Illus.). 80p. (J). (gr. 2-5). 15.00 (*0-374-35531-2*, Farrar, Straus & Giroux (BYR)) Farrar, Straus & Giroux.

Rodriguez, Bobbie. Sarah's Sleepover. 2000. (Illus.). 32p. (J). (gr. k-4). 15.99 (*0-670-87750-6*, Viking Children's Bks.) Penguin Putnam Bks. for Young Readers.

Rodriguez, Robert. One Agent Too Many. 2nd ed. 2003. (Spy Kids 2 Ser.: Bk. 1). 144p. (J). (gr. 3-7). pap. 4.99 (*0-7868-1715-1*, Volo) Hyperion Bks. for Children.

Romain, Trevor. Stuck in the Middle. 1995. (Illus.). 64p. (J). (gr. k-5). 13.95 o.p. (*1-880092-33-6*) Bright Bks.

Romanelli, Serena. Little Bobo Saves the Day. 1997. (Illus.). 32p. (J). (gr. k-3). 15.95 o.p. (*1-55858-786-1*); 16.50 o.p. (*1-55858-787-X*) North-South Bks., Inc.

Roos, Stepehn. Silver Secrets. 1991. (Maple Street Kids Ser.). (Illus.). 96p. (J). (gr. 2-6). per. 1.50 o.p. (*0-89486-777-6*, T5171) Hazelden Publishing & Educational Services.

Roos, Stephen. Dear Santa, Make Me a Star. 1993. (Maple Street Kids Ser.). (Illus.). 96p. (J). (gr. 2-6). pap. 1.95 o.p. (*0-89486-764-4*, 5174A) Hazelden Publishing & Educational Services.

—Leave It to Augie. 1993. (Maple Street Kids Ser.). (Illus.). 96p. (J). (gr. 2-6). per. 1.50 o.p. (*0-89486-774-1*, T5172) Hazelden Publishing & Educational Services.

—My Blue Tongue. 1991. (Maple Street Kids Ser.). (Illus.). 96p. (J). (gr. 2-6). pap. 1.50 o.p. (*0-89486-784-9*, T5173) Hazelden Publishing & Educational Services.

Root, Phyllis. Aunt Nancy & Cousin Lazybones. 1998. (Illus.). 32p. (J). (gr. k-3). 16.99 o.s.i (*1-56402-425-3*) Candlewick Pr.

—Aunt Nancy & Old Man Trouble. ed. 2000. (J). (gr. 2). spiral bd. (*0-616-01775-8*) Canadian National Institute for the Blind/Institut National Canadien pour les Aveugles.

—Aunt Nancy & Old Man Trouble. 1998. (Illus.). 32p. (J). (gr. k-3). bds. 6.99 (*0-7636-0650-2*) Candlewick Pr.

—Aunt Nancy & Old Man Trouble. 1998. 13.14 (*0-606-15445-0*) Turtleback Bks.

Rose, Miriam. Baker's Dozen No. 12: The Baker Family Circus. 1994. 172p. (J). (gr. 6-8). pap. 9.95 o.p. (*1-56871-062-3*) Targum Pr., Inc.

Rosenberg, Liz. Eli & Uncle Dawn. 1997. (Illus.). 32p. (J). (ps-3). 15.00 o.s.i (*0-15-200947-7*) Harcourt Trade Pubs.

—Heart & Soul. 1996. 224p. (YA). (gr. 7 up). pap. 5.00 o.s.i (*0-15-201270-2*, Harcourt Paperbacks) Harcourt Children's Bks.

—Heart & Soul. 1996. 224p. (YA). (gr. 7 up). 11.00 (*0-15-200942-6*) Harcourt Trade Pubs.

—Moonbathing. 1996. (Illus.). 32p. (J). 14.00 o.s.i (*0-15-200945-0*) Harcourt Trade Pubs.

Rosenberry, Vera. The Growing up Tree. 2003. (Illus.). (J). tchr. ed. 16.95 (*0-8234-1718-2*) Holiday Hse., Inc.

Rosenfeld, Dina. Peanut Butter & Jelly for Shabbos. 1995. (Illus.). 32p. (J). (ps-1). 9.95 (*0-922613-69-9*) Hachai Publishing.

Rosner, Ruth. My Super Best Friend. 1997. (Illus.). (J). pap. o.p. (*0-7868-1130-7*) Hyperion Paperbacks for Children.

Rosofsky, Iris. My Aunt Ruth. 1991. (Charlotte Zolotow Bk.). 224p. (YA). (gr. 7 up). 13.95 (*0-06-025087-9*); lib. bdg. 13.89 o.p. (*0-06-025088-7*) HarperCollins Children's Bk. Group.

Ross, Christine. The Whirlys & the West Wind. 1993. (J). 13.95 o.p. (*0-395-65379-7*) Houghton Mifflin Co.

Ross, Sandra B. The Nicelies Series, 4 vols. 1994. (Nicelies Ser.). (Illus.). (J). (ps-1). per. 19.95 (*1-881235-04-1*) Creative Opportunities, Inc.

Rottman, S. L. Rough Waters. 1998. (Illus.). 192p. (YA). (gr. 7-11). 14.95 (*1-56145-172-X*) Peachtree Pubs., Ltd.

—Shadow of a Doubt. 2003. 224p. (J). (gr. 6-10). 14.95 (*1-56145-291-2*) Peachtree Pubs., Ltd.

Rouss, Sylvia. Tali's Jerusalem Scrapbook. 2003. (Illus.). 32p. (J). 14.95 (*1-930143-68-0*); pap. 9.95 (*1-930143-69-9*) Pitspopany Pr.

Rubin, C. M. Eleanor, Ellatony, Ellencake, & Me. 2003. (Illus.). 32p. (J). (gr. k-3). 14.95 (*1-57768-412-5*, Gingham Dog Pr.) McGraw-Hill Children's Publishing.

Rue, Nancy. The Chase. 1999. (Christian Heritage Ser.). 192p. (J). (gr. 3-7). pap. 5.99 (*1-56179-735-9*) Focus on the Family Publishing.

—The Trick. 1999. (Christian Heritage Ser.). 208p. (J). (gr. 3-7). pap. 5.99 (*1-56179-734-0*) Focus on the Family Publishing.

Rugrats Back to School Riser. 1998. (*0-689-00701-9*, Simon & Schuster Children's Publishing) Simon & Schuster Children's Publishing.

Ruiz, Art, illus. The Weirdest Fun Book, Ever! 2015. (Addams Family Ser.). (J). 7.95 (*0-448-40503-2*, Grosset & Dunlap) Penguin Putnam Bks. for Young Readers.

Rundle, Vesta M. Snow Calf. 1993. (Illus.). 36p. (Orig.). (J). (gr. 4-8). pap. 4.50 (*1-882672-01-1*) Rundle, Vesta M.

Rush, Alison. The Last of Danu's Children, 001. 1982. (J). (gr. 7 up). 9.95 o.p. (*0-395-32270-7*) Houghton Mifflin Co.

Rushton, Rosie. How Could You Do This to Me, Mum? 1999. (Fab Five Ser.). 224p. (J). (gr. 5-9). pap. 3.99 (*0-7868-1388-1*) Disney Pr.

Ryan, Pam Muñoz. One Hundred Is a Family. 1996. (Illus.). 32p. (J). (ps-3). pap. 4.95 (*0-7868-1120-X*) Disney Pr.
—One Hundred Is a Family. 1994. (Illus.). 32p. (J). (gr. k-3). 13.95 o.s.i (*1-56282-672-7*); lib. bdg. 14.49 (*1-56282-673-5*) Hyperion Bks. for Children.
—One Hundred Is a Family. 1998. (Illus.). 24p. (J). (ps). 5.95 (*0-7868-0405-X*) Hyperion Pr.
—One Hundred Is a Family. 1996. (J). 11.10 (*0-606-09715-5*) Turtleback Bks.
Rylant, Cynthia. The Cobble Street Cousins: In Aunt Lucy's Kitchen. 1998. (Cobble Street Cousins Ser.). (Illus.). 64p. (J). (gr. 2-5). 14.00 (*0-689-81711-8*, Simon & Schuster Children's Publishing) Simon & Schuster Children's Publishing.
—The Cobble Street Cousins Book 3: Special Gifts. 1999. (Cobble Street Cousins Ser.). (Illus.). 64p. (J). (gr. 2-5). 14.00 (*0-689-81714-2*, Simon & Schuster Children's Publishing) Simon & Schuster Children's Publishing.
—Henry & Mudge & the Tall Tree House. 2003. (Henry & Mudge Ser.). 40p. (J). pap. 3.99 (*0-689-83445-4*, Aladdin) Simon & Schuster Children's Publishing.
—Henry & Mudge in the Family Trees. 1998. (Henry & Mudge Ser.). (Illus.). 48p. (J). (gr. k-3). pap. 3.99 (*0-689-82317-7*, Aladdin) Simon & Schuster Children's Publishing.
—In Aunt Lucy's Kitchen: A Little Shopping. 2000. (Cobble Street Cousins Ser.: Vol. 1). (Illus.). 64p. (J). (gr. 2-5). pap. 3.99 (*0-689-81708-8*, Aladdin) Simon & Schuster Children's Publishing.
—A Little Shopping. 1998. (Cobble Street Cousins Ser.: No. 2). (Illus.). 64p. (J). (gr. 2-5). 14.00 (*0-689-81710-X*, Simon & Schuster Children's Publishing) Simon & Schuster Children's Publishing.
—Some Good News. 2001. (Cobble Street Cousins Ser.: Vol. 4). (Illus.). 64p. (J). (gr. 4-7). pap. 3.99 (*0-689-81712-6*, Aladdin) Simon & Schuster Children's Publishing.
—The Special Gifts. 2000. (Cobble Street Cousins Ser.: Vol. 3). (Illus.). 64p. (J). pap. 3.99 (*0-689-81715-0*, Aladdin) Simon & Schuster Children's Publishing.
—The Special Gifts. 2000. 10.14 (*0-606-20026-6*) Turtleback Bks.
—Summer Party. (Cobble Street Cousins Ser.: No. 5). (Illus.). 64p. (J). (gr. 2-5). 2002. pap. 3.99 (*0-689-83417-9*, Aladdin); 2001. 15.00 (*0-689-83241-9*, Simon & Schuster Children's Publishing) Simon & Schuster Children's Publishing.
Sachs, Marilyn. Ghosts in the Family. 1995. 176p. (J). (gr. 3-6). 15.99 o.s.i (*0-525-45421-7*, Dutton Children's Bks.) Penguin Putnam Bks. for Young Readers.
—Surprise Party. 1998. 192p. (J). (gr. 5-9). 15.99 (*0-525-45962-6*) Penguin Putnam Bks. for Young Readers.
—What My Sister Remembered. (J). (gr. 5 up). 1994. 128p. pap. 3.99 o.s.i (*0-14-036944-9*, Puffin Bks.); 1992. 120p. 15.00 o.p. (*0-525-44953-1*, Dutton Children's Bks.) Penguin Putnam Bks. for Young Readers.
—What My Sister Remembered. 1994. 9.09 o.p. (*0-606-06865-1*) Turtleback Bks.
Salzman, Yuri. Happy Families Bears-Barnie. 1991. (J). 1.95 o.p. (*0-8431-2953-0*, Price Stern Sloan) Penguin Putnam Bks. for Young Readers.
—Happy Families Bears-Bonnie. 1991. (J). 1.95 o.p. (*0-8431-2951-4*, Price Stern Sloan) Penguin Putnam Bks. for Young Readers.
—Happy Families Bunnies-Billy. 1991. (J). 1.95 o.s.i (*0-8431-2947-6*, Price Stern Sloan) Penguin Putnam Bks. for Young Readers.
—Happy Families Bunnies-Milly. 1991. (J). 1.95 o.p. (*0-8431-2948-4*, Price Stern Sloan) Penguin Putnam Bks. for Young Readers.
—Happy Families Kittens-Muffy. 1991. (J). 1.95 o.p. (*0-8431-2962-X*, Price Stern Sloan) Penguin Putnam Bks. for Young Readers.
—Happy Families Kittens-Tuffy. 1991. (J). 1.95 o.p. (*0-8431-2960-3*, Price Stern Sloan) Penguin Putnam Bks. for Young Readers.
—Happy Families Playful Pups-Dipper. 1991. (J). 1.95 o.p. (*0-8431-2955-7*, Price Stern Sloan) Penguin Putnam Bks. for Young Readers.
—Happy Families Playful Pups-Tipper. 1991. (J). 1.95 o.p. (*0-8431-2957-3*, Price Stern Sloan) Penguin Putnam Bks. for Young Readers.
Sammy & Sara's First Day. 1993. (J). mass mkt. o.s.i (*0-553-20397-5*, Dell Books for Young Readers) Random Hse. Children's Bks.
Samuel, Lynette M. The Middle is the Best Part. Baker, Patty, ed. & creator by. 1997. (Illus.). 32p. (J). (gr. 2-5). per. 15.95 (*0-9651270-2-8*) Bright Lamb Pubs., Inc.
—Mommy's Hat. 1997. (Illus.). 32p. (J). (gr. 2-5). per. 15.95 (*0-9651270-4-4*) Bright Lamb Pubs., Inc.
Sandburg, Carl. The Huckabuck Family: And How They Raised Popcorn in Nebraska & Quit & Came Back, RS. 1999. (Illus.). 40p. (J). (ps-3). 16.00 (*0-374-33511-7*, Farrar, Straus & Giroux (BYR)) Farrar, Straus & Giroux.
Saroyan, William. The Human Comedy. rev. ed. 1943. (Illus.). 246p. 10.95 o.p. (*0-15-142299-0*) Harcourt Trade Pubs.
Sasloff, Jackie. Mommy Got Bigger: And So Did Our Family. 2001. (Illus.). 24p. (J). (ps-5). 12.95 (*0-9712942-0-8*) Terrapin Pubns.
Satterfield, Barbara. The Story Dance. 1997. (Illus.). 32p. (J). (gr. 1-4). 14.95 o.p. (*1-57749-022-3*) Fairview Pr.
Savage, Deborah. Kotuku. 2002. 304p. (YA). (gr. 7 up). 16.00 (*0-618-04756-5*) Houghton Mifflin Co.
Sawyer, Ruth. Maggie Rose. 1952. (Illus.). (J). (gr. 3-6). lib. bdg. 10.89 o.p. (*0-06-025201-4*) Harper-Collins Pubs.
Saylor, Melissa, illus. My Aunt Came Back Big Book: Black & White Nellie Edge I Can Read & Sing Big Book. 1988. (J). (ps-2). pap. text 21.00 (*0-922053-12-X*) Nellie Edge Resources, Inc.
Schachner, Judith Byron. Willy & May. 1995. (Illus.). 32p. (J). (ps-3). 14.99 (*0-525-45347-4*, Dutton Children's Bks.) Penguin Putnam Bks. for Young Readers.
Schaefer, Carole Lexa. Two Scarlet Songbirds: A Story of Anton Dvorak. 2001. (Illus.). 40p. (J). lib. bdg. 18.99 (*0-375-91022-0*); (gr. 1-4). 16.95 (*0-375-81022-6*, Knopf Bks. for Young Readers) Random Hse. Children's Bks.
Schaller, Bob. Arlington Family Adventures, 4 vols. 2000. (J). (gr. 4-7). pap. 19.95 (*0-8010-8493-8*) Baker Bks.
Schietinger-Cachina, Daryl A. Hey New Baby in There. 1999. (Illus.). 8p. (J). (ps-5). pap. 5.00 (*1-928641-02-4*) Daryl Ann Pubns.
Schlein, Miriam. My House. 1971. (Illus.). (ps-2). 5.50 o.p. (*0-8075-5357-3*) Whitman, Albert & Co.
Scholastic, Inc. Staff. The Moffatts. 1999. (gr. 2-9). mass mkt. 5.99 (*0-439-13552-4*) Scholastic, Inc.
Schotter, Roni. Dreamland. 1996. (Illus.). 40p. (J). (ps-3). pap. 15.95 (*0-531-09508-8*); lib. bdg. 16.99 (*0-531-08858-8*) Scholastic, Inc. (Orchard Bks.).
Schreck, Karen Halvorsen. Lucy's Family Tree. 2001. (Illus.). 40p. (J). (gr. 1-5). text 16.95 (*0-88448-225-1*, Harpswell Pr.) Tilbury Hse. Pubs.
Schultz, Jan Neubert. Horse Sense: The Story of Will Sasse, His Horse Star & the Outlaw Jesse James. 2001. (Adventures in Time Ser.). 180p. (J). (gr. 4-7). lib. bdg. 15.95 (*1-57505-998-3*, Carolrhoda Bks.) Lerner Publishing Group.
Schwartz, Alvin. There Is a Carrot in My Ear & Other Noodle Tales. 1982. (I Can Read Bks.). (Illus.). 64p. (J). (gr. k-3). lib. bdg. 15.89 (*0-06-025234-0*); 10.95 (*0-06-025233-2*) HarperCollins Children's Bk. Group.
Schwartz, Amy. What James Likes Best. 2003. (Illus.). 32p. (J). 16.95 (*0-689-84059-4*, Atheneum/Richard Jackson Bks.) Simon & Schuster Children's Publishing.
Schwartz, Noa. Old Timers: The One That Got Away. 1998. (J). pap. text 5.95 (*0-9683303-1-2*) Tumbleweed Pr.
Scott, Stefanie. House Party! 1998. (Moesha Ser.:). 176p. (YA). (gr. 7 up). mass mkt. 4.50 (*0-671-02593-7*, Simon Pulse) Simon & Schuster Children's Publishing.
Sebestyen, Ouida. Far from Home. 1980. 192p. (J). (gr. 7 up). 15.95 (*0-316-77932-6*, Joy Street Bks.) Little Brown & Co.
Senn. In the Castle of the Bear. 1985. (J). 11.95 o.s.i (*0-689-31167-2*, Atheneum) Simon & Schuster Children's Publishing.
Serres, Alain. Du Commerce de la Souris. 1989. (Folio - Cadet Bleu Ser.: No. 195). (FRE., Illus.). 55p. (J). (gr. 1-5). pap. 8.95 (*2-07-031195-3*) Schoenhof's Foreign Bks., Inc.
Shahan, Sherry. Frozen Stiff. 1998. 160p. (gr. 4-7). text 14.95 o.s.i (*0-385-32303-4*, Delacorte Pr.) Dell Publishing.
Sharmat, Marjorie Weinman. He Noticed I'm Alive... & Other Hopeful Signs. 1984. 160p. (J). (gr. 7 up). 14.95 o.p. (*0-385-29351-8*, Delacorte Pr.) Dell Publishing.
Sharratt, Nick. Snazzy Aunties. (Illus.). (J). 1996. bds. 2.99 o.p. (*1-56402-685-X*); 1994. 24p. 8.95 o.p. (*1-56402-214-5*) Candlewick Pr.
Shaw, Janet Beeler. Kaya Shows the Way: A Sister Story. 2002. (American Girls Collection: Bk. 5). (Illus.). 88p. (J). (gr. 2-7). 12.95 (*1-58485-432-4*); pap. 5.95 (*1-58485-431-6*) Pleasant Co. Pubns. (American Girl).
Shaw, Susan. Black-Eyed Suzie. 2004. (J). pap. 9.95 (*1-59078-257-7*) Boyds Mills Pr.
Shecter, Ben. Great-Uncle Alfred Forgets. (Illus.). (J). (gr. k-3). 1996. 80p. lib. bdg. 14.89 o.p. (*0-06-026219-2*); 1995. 32p. 14.95 o.p. (*0-06-026218-4*) HarperCollins Children's Bk. Group.
Shemin, Craig. Families Are Forever. l.t. ed. 2003. (Illus.). 34p. (J). per. 16.95 (*0-9728666-1-2*, 1) As Simple As That.
Sherman, Allan & Busch, Lou. Hello Muddah, Hello Faddah. 2004. (Illus.). 32p. 12.99 (*0-525-46942-7*, Dutton Children's Bks.) Penguin Putnam Bks. for Young Readers.
Shuster, Bud. Double Buckeyes: A Story of the Way America Used to Be. (Illus.). vi, 149p. (J). (gr. 4-7). 2000. pap. 7.95 (*1-57249-177-9*, WM Kids); 1999. 19.95 (*1-57249-176-0*, White Mane Bks.) White Mane Publishing Co., Inc.
Siburt, Ruth. The Trouble with Alex. 1998. 93p. (J). (gr. 5-8). pap. 9.99 (*0-88092-366-0*, 3660) Royal Fireworks Publishing Co.
Sidney, Margaret. Five Little Peppers & How They Grew. 1989. 276p. (J). (gr. 4-6). pap. 3.99 o.p. (*0-590-42520-X*) Scholastic, Inc.
—The Five Little Peppers & How They Grew. 1981. 302p. (J). (gr. 4-7). reprint ed. lib. bdg. 27.95 (*0-89966-340-0*) Buccaneer Bks., Inc.
—Five Little Peppers Grown Up. 1981. 334p. (J). (ps up). reprint ed. lib. bdg. 27.95 (*0-89966-341-9*) Buccaneer Bks., Inc.
Simon, Norma. All Families Are Special. 2003. (Illus.). 32p. (J). (gr. k-3). 15.95 (*0-8075-2175-2*) Whitman, Albert & Co.
Simont, Marc. The Stray Dog. 2001. (Illus.). 32p. (J). (gr. k-3). 15.95 (*0-06-028933-3*) HarperCollins Children's Bk. Group.
—The Stray Dog. 2003. (Illus.). 32p. (J). (ps-3). pap. 6.99 (*0-06-443669-1*) HarperCollins Pubs.
Simpson, Lesley B. The Hug. 2003. (Annikins Ser.: Vol. 4). (Illus.). 32p. (J). (ps-1). pap. 1.25 (*0-920303-23-4*) Annick Pr., Ltd. CAN. *Dist:* Firefly Bks., Ltd.
Singer, Marilyn. Didi & Daddy on the Promenade. 2001. (Illus.). 32p. (J). (ps-3). tchr. ed. 14.00 (*0-618-04640-2*, Clarion Bks.) Houghton Mifflin Co. Trade & Reference Div.
Skolsky, Mindy Warshaw. Hannah Is a Palindrome. 1980. (Illus.). 128p. (J). (gr. 3-6). lib. bdg. 12.89 o.p. (*0-06-025727-X*) HarperCollins Children's Bk. Group.
Skurzynski, Gloria. Trapped in Sliprock Canyon. 1984. (Mountain West Adventure Ser.). (Illus.). 32p. (J). (ps up). 16.00 (*0-688-02688-5*) HarperCollins Children's Bk. Group.
Skutch, Robert. Who's in a Family? 1995. (Illus.). 32p. (J). (ps-2). 12.95 o.p. (*1-883672-13-9*) Tricycle Pr.
Smith, Alexander M. The Five Lost Aunts of Harriet Bean. l.t. ed. 1997. (Illus.). (J). 16.95 (*0-7451-8927-X*, Galaxy Children's Large Print) BBC Audiobooks America.
Smith-Ayala, Emilie. Clouds on the Mountain. 1996. (Illus.). 32p. (J). (ps-2). pap. 5.95 (*1-55037-472-9*); lib. bdg. 16.95 (*1-55037-473-7*) Annick Pr., Ltd. CAN. *Dist:* Firefly Bks., Ltd.
Smith, Doris B. The First Hard Times. 1984. 144p. (J). (gr. 5-9). pap. 2.50 o.s.i (*0-440-42532-8*, Yearling) Random Hse. Children's Bks.
Smith, Lane. Happy Hocky Family. 1996. (Illus.). 64p. (J). (ps-3). pap. 6.99 (*0-14-055771-7*) Penguin Putnam Bks. for Young Readers.
Smith, Miriam. Kimi & the Watermelon. 1989. (Illus.). 320p. (J). (ps-3). pap. 3.95 o.p. (*0-14-050950-X*, Puffin Bks.) Penguin Putnam Bks. for Young Readers.
Smothers, Ethel Footman. Auntee Edna. (Illus.). 32p. 2002. pap. 8.00 (*0-8028-5246-7*); 2001. (J). 16.00 (*0-8028-5154-1*) Eerdmans, William B. Publishing Co. (Eerdmans Bks For Young Readers).
Snyder, Midori. Hannah's Garden. 2002. 208p. (J). text 16.99 (*0-670-03577-7*) Penguin Putnam Bks. for Young Readers.
Snyder, Zilpha Keatley. Spyhole Secrets. 2001. 192p. (gr. 3-7). text 15.95 (*0-385-32764-1*); lib. bdg. 17.99 (*0-385-90016-3*) Random Hse. Children's Bks. (Dell Books for Young Readers).
—Spyhole Secrets. 2002. 192p. (gr. 3-7). pap. text 4.99 (*0-440-41708-2*) Random Hse., Inc.
Sobol, Harriet L. We Don't Look Like Our Mom & Dad. 1984. (Illus.). 32p. (J). (gr. 4-7). 11.95 o.s.i (*0-698-20608-8*, Coward-McCann) Putnam Publishing Group, The.
Soto, Gary. If the Shoe Fits. 2002. (Illus.). 32p. (J). (gr. 4-8). 15.99 (*0-399-23420-9*) Penguin Group (USA) Inc.
Spalding, Andrea. The Keeper & the Crows. 2000. (Young Reader Ser.). (Illus.). 112p. (J). (gr. 3-4). pap. 4.99 (*1-55143-141-6*) Orca Bk. Pubs.
Speregen, Devra Newberger. One Boss Too Many. 1998. (Full House Sisters Ser.: No. 2). 160p. (J). (gr. 4-6). pap. 3.99 (*0-671-02150-8*, Simon Spotlight) Simon & Schuster Children's Publishing.
—Two on the Town. 1998. (Full House Sisters Ser.: No. 1). 160p. (J). (gr. 4-6). pap. 3.99 (*0-671-02149-4*, Simon Spotlight) Simon & Schuster Children's Publishing.
Spurr, Elizabeth. The Long, Long Letter. 1997. (Illus.). 32p. (J). (ps-3). reprint ed. pap. 5.95 (*0-7868-1202-8*) Disney Pr.
—The Long, Long Letter. 1996. (Illus.). 32p. (J). (ps-3). 14.95 o.p. (*0-7868-0127-1*); lib. bdg. 15.49 (*0-7868-2100-0*) Hyperion Bks. for Children.
St. John, Patricia M. The Tanglewoods' Secret. 2001. (Illus.). 167p. (J). 6.99 (*0-8024-6576-5*) Moody Pr.
St. Peter, Joyce. Always Abigail. 1981. (Illus.). 128p. (J). (gr. 3-5). o.p. (*0-397-31934-7*); lib. bdg. 11.89 (*0-397-31935-5*) HarperCollins Children's Bk. Group.
Starr, Claire. They Called Me Beautiful: Based on the Classic Story of a Dog's Search for Love & the Family That Rescued Him. 2002. (Illus.). 128p. (J). (ps-4). pap. 10.95 (*0-9706377-1-3*) Lucky Pr., LLC.
Staunton, Ted. Two False Moves. 2000. (Monkey Mountain Bks.). (Illus.). 64p. (J). (gr. 2-5). pap. 4.95 (*0-88995-205-1*) Red Deer Pr. CAN. *Dist:* General Distribution Services, Inc.
Steptoe, Javaka. The Jones Family Express. 2003. (Illus.). 40p. (J). (ps-4). 17.95 (*1-58430-047-7*) Lee & Low Bks., Inc.
Steptoe, John L. Shawn & Uncle John. 1924. (J). o.s.i (*0-688-05600-8*); lib. bdg. o.s.i (*0-688-05601-6*) HarperCollins Children's Bk. Group.
Stern, Ricki. Beryl E. Bean. 2nd ed. 2002. (Beryl E. Bean Ser.). (Illus.). 64p. (J). lib. bdg. 14.89 (*0-06-028772-1*) HarperCollins Children's Bk. Group.
Stern, Ricki & Worcester, Heidi P. Beryl E. Bean: Expedition Sleepaway Camp. 2nd ed. 2002. (Beryl E. Bean Ser.). (Illus.). 64p. (J). pap. 5.95 (*0-06-442121-X*) HarperCollins Pubs.
Stewart, Sarah. The Gardener. 2002. (Illus.). (J). 15.49 (*0-7587-2567-1*) Book Wholesalers, Inc.
—The Gardener. 2000. (J). pap. 19.97 incl. audio (*0-7366-9203-7*) Books on Tape, Inc.
—The Gardener, RS. (Sunburst Bks.). (Illus.). 40p. (J). (gr. k-4). 2000. pap. 6.95 (*0-374-42518-3*, Sunburst); 1997. 16.00 (*0-374-32517-0*, Farrar, Straus & Giroux (BYR)) Farrar, Straus & Giroux.
—The Gardener. (J). (gr. k-3). 1999. (Illus.). pap., tchr. ed. 33.95 incl. audio (*0-87499-432-2*); 1998. pap. 9.95 incl. audio (*0-87499-428-4*); 1998. (Illus.). 24.95 incl. audio (*0-87499-430-6*) Live Oak Media.
—The Gardener. 2000. 12.10 (*0-606-17840-6*) Turtleback Bks.
Stinson, Kathy. Those Green Things. 2003. (Illus.). 32p. (J). (ps-1). pap. 4.95 (*1-55037-376-5*) Annick Pr., Ltd. CAN. *Dist:* Firefly Bks., Ltd.
—Those Green Things. ed. 1997. (J). (gr. 1). spiral bd. (*0-616-01786-3*); (gr. 2). spiral bd. (*0-616-01787-1*) Canadian National Institute for the Blind/Institut National Canadien pour les Aveugles.
Stoltz, Donald R. Penelope Pen-Pal. 1994. (Illus.). 38p. (J). pap. 12.50 (*0-930329-81-3*) Kabel Pubs.
Stolz, Mary. Ready or Not. 2000. 256p. pap. 15.95 (*0-595-15119-1*, Backinprint.com) iUniverse, Inc.
—What Time of Night Is It? 1993. (Ursula Nordstrom Bk.). 224p. (YA). (gr. 6 up). pap. 3.95 o.p. (*0-06-447093-8*, Harper Trophy) HarperCollins Children's Bk. Group.
Stone, Miriam R. At the End of Words: A Daughters Memoir. 2003. 64p. (J). 14.00 (*0-7636-1854-3*) Candlewick Pr.
Stone, Tom B. Here Comes Santa Claws. 1998. (Graveyard School Ser.: No. 27). 96p. (gr. 3-7). pap. text 2.99 o.s.i (*0-553-48548-2*, Skylark) Random Hse. Children's Bks.
—Here Comes Santa Claws. 1998. (Graveyard School Ser.: No. 27). (J). (gr. 3-7). 9.04 (*0-606-16158-9*) Turtleback Bks.
Strasser, Todd. Hey Dad, Get a Life! 1996. 160p. (J). (gr. 4-7). tchr. ed. 15.95 (*0-8234-1278-4*) Holiday Hse., Inc.
—Spell Danger. 4th ed. 2000. (Here Comes Heavenly Ser.: No. 4). 176p. (J). (gr. 7-12). mass mkt. 4.99 (*0-671-03629-7*, Simon Pulse) Simon & Schuster Children's Publishing.
Strather, Gracie L. Mom's Milk Spilling Monster & More. 2001. 108p. pap. 14.95 (*0-7596-4566-3*) 1stBooks Library.
Stretton, Barbara. The Truth of the Matter. 1984. 256p. (J). reprint ed. (*0-399-21147-0*) Putnam Publishing Group, The.
Super, Gretchen. Family Traditions. (Illus.). 48p. (J). 3.98 o.p. (*0-8317-9880-7*) Smithmark Pubs., Inc.
Suzanne, Jamie. The Cousin War. 1995. (Sweet Valley Twins Ser.: No. 90). (J). (gr. 3-7). 144p. pap. 3.50 o.s.i (*0-553-48192-4*, Sweet Valley); pap. 4.75 (*0-553-54215-X*, Dell Books for Young Readers) Random Hse. Children's Bks.
—The Cousin War. 1995. (Sweet Valley Twins Ser.: No. 90). (J). (gr. 3-7). 8.60 o.p. (*0-606-08245-X*) Turtleback Bks.
—The Mother-Daughter Switch. 1995. (Sweet Valley Twins Ser.: No. 86). (J). (gr. 3-7). 8.60 o.p. (*0-606-08242-5*) Turtleback Bks.
—The Wakefields Strike it Rich. 1992. (Sweet Valley Twins Ser.: No. 56). 144p. (J). (gr. 3-7). pap. 3.25 o.s.i (*0-553-15950-X*) Bantam Bks.
Swift, Carolyn. Bugsy Goes to Cork. 1990. 190p. (J). (gr. 3-7). pap. 7.95 (*1-85371-071-7*) Poolbeg Pr. IRL. *Dist:* Dufour Editions, Inc.
Sykes, Shelley & Szymanski, Lois. The Soldier in the Cellar. 2002. (Gettysburg Ghost Gang Ser.: Vol. 5). 96p. (J). pap. 5.95 (*1-57249-299-6*, WM Kids) White Mane Publishing Co., Inc.

—The Pumpkin Blanket. 1997. 13.10 (*0-606-16988-1*) Turtleback Bks.

—The Sea House. 2003. (Illus.). 32p. (J). (gr. k-3). 15.95 (*1-58246-030-2*) Tricycle Pr.

Zamorano, Ana. Let's Eat! 1997. (Illus.). 32p. (J). (ps-2). pap. 15.95 (*0-590-13444-2*) Scholastic, Inc.

Zemser, Amy Bronwen. Beyond the Mango Tree. (Illus.). (gr. 5 up). 2000. 176p. (J). pap. 5.99 (*0-06-440786-1*, Harper Trophy); 1998. 156p. (YA). 14.95 (*0-688-16005-0*, Greenwillow Bks.) HarperCollins Children's Bk. Group.

Zirkel, Lynn. Amazing Maisy's Family Tree. 1987. (Illus.). 32p. (J). 12.95 o.p. (*0-19-279830-8*) Oxford Univ. Pr., Inc.

Zoehfeld, Kathleen Weidner. Billy. 2001. (Rolie Polie Olie Ser.). (Illus.). 12p. (J). (gr. k-2). bds. 3.99 (*0-7364-1023-6*) Mouse Works.

Zolotow, Charlotte. The Quarreling Book. 1963. (Charlotte Zolotow Bk.). (Illus.). 32p. (J). (gr. k-3). 13.00 (*0-06-026975-8*); lib. bdg. 13.89 o.p. (*0-06-026976-6*) HarperCollins Children's Bk. Group.

—The Sky Was Blue. 1963. (Charlotte Zolotow Bk.). (Illus.). (J). (gr. k-3). lib. bdg. 14.89 o.s.i (*0-06-027001-2*) HarperCollins Children's Bk. Group.

—This Quiet Lady. (Illus.). 24p. (ps-3). 2000. (J). pap. 5.95 (*0-688-17527-9*, Harper Trophy); 1992. (J). 15.95 (*0-688-09305-1*, Greenwillow Bks.); 1992. (YA). lib. bdg. 13.93 o.p. (*0-688-09306-X*, Greenwillow Bks.) HarperCollins Children's Bk. Group.

FAMILY LIFE—FICTION

Abelove, Joan. Saying It Out Loud. 2001. (YA). 12.04 (*0-606-21410-0*) Turtleback Bks.

Aboff, Marcie. Giant Jelly Bean Jar. 2004. (Easy-to-Read, Puffin Ser.). (Illus.). 32p. pap. 3.99 (*0-14-240049-1*, Puffin Bks.) Penguin Putnam Bks. for Young Readers.

—Uncle Willy's Tickles. 1996. (Illus.). 32p. (J). (ps-3). pap. 8.95 (*0-945354-67-3*) American Psychological Assn.

Abraham, Michelle Shapiro. Good Morning, Boker Tov. 2002. (Illus.). (J). pap. 6.00 (*0-8074-0783-6*) UAHC Pr.

—Good Night, Lilah Tov. 2002. (Illus.). (J). pap. 6.00 (*0-8074-0784-4*) UAHC Pr.

Abramchik, Lois. Is Your Family Like Mine? 2nd ed. 2002. (Illus.). 36p. (Orig.). (J). pap. 9.95 (*0-9674468-9-9*) Two Lives Publishing.

Ackerman, Karen. In the Park with Dad. 1996. (Illus.). 29p. (J). (ps-2). pap. 5.95 (*0-8198-3669-9*) Pauline Bks. & Media.

Adams, Jeanie. Going for Oysters. 1993. (J). (gr. 2-6). lib. bdg. 15.95 (*0-8075-2978-8*) Whitman, Albert & Co.

Adler, C. S. In Our House Scott Is My Brother. 1982. (gr. 5 up). pap. 1.95 o.p. (*0-553-20910-8*) Bantam Bks.

—In Our House Scott Is My Brother. 1980. 144p. (J). (gr. 5-9). lib. bdg. 13.95 o.p. (*0-02-700140-7*, Simon & Schuster Children's Publishing) Simon & Schuster Children's Publishing.

—The No Place Cat. 2002. 160p. (YA). (gr. 5-9). 15.00 (*0-618-09644-2*, Clarion Bks.) Houghton Mifflin Co. Trade & Reference Div.

—Not Just a Summer Crush. 1998. (Illus.). 118p. (J). (gr. 5-9). tchr. ed. 15.00 (*0-395-88532-9*, Clarion Bks.) Houghton Mifflin Co. Trade & Reference Div.

—One Sister Too Many. 1991. 176p. (J). (gr. 4-7). reprint ed. pap. 3.95 (*0-689-71521-8*, Aladdin) Simon & Schuster Children's Publishing.

—One Sister Too Many (A Sequel to Split Sisters) 1989. 176p. (J). (gr. 4-8). text 13.95 o.s.i (*0-02-700271-3*, Simon & Schuster Children's Publishing) Simon & Schuster Children's Publishing.

—The Silver Coach. 1979. (J). (gr. 4-7). 8.95 o.p. (*0-698-20504-9*) Putnam Publishing Group, The.

—Split Sisters. (J). (gr. 4-7). 1990. 176p. pap. 3.95 o.s.i (*0-689-71369-X*, Aladdin); 1986. (Illus.). 156p. 12.95 o.s.i (*0-02-700380-9*, Simon & Schuster Children's Publishing) Simon & Schuster Children's Publishing.

—Tuna Fish Thanksgiving. 1992. 160p. (J). (gr. 5-9). 13.95 o.p. (*0-395-58829-4*, Clarion Bks.) Houghton Mifflin Co. Trade & Reference Div.

Adler, David A. Andy & Tamika. 1999. (Andy Russell Ser.). (Illus.). 144p. (YA). (gr. 2-5). 14.00 (*0-15-201735-6*, Gulliver Bks.) Harcourt Children's Bks.

—Mama Played Baseball. 2003. (Illus.). 32p. (J). 16.00 (*0-15-202196-5*) Harcourt Children's Bks.

—The Many Troubles of Andy Russell. (Andy Russell Ser.). (Illus.). 144p. (YA). (gr. 2-5). 1999. pap. 4.95 (*0-15-201900-6*); 1998. 14.00 (*0-15-201295-8*) Harcourt Children's Bks. (Gulliver Bks.).

—The Many Troubles of Andy Russell. 1998. 11.00 (*0-606-18183-0*) Turtleback Bks.

Adoff, Arnold. Black Is Brown Is Tan. (Illus.). (J). (ps-3). 2002. 40p. 15.95 (*0-06-028776-4*); 2002. 40p. lib. bdg. 15.89 (*0-06-028777-2*); 1992. 32p. pap. 5.95 (*0-06-443269-6*, Harper Trophy); 1973. 32p. 15.95 (*0-06-020083-9*); 1973. 80p. lib. bdg. 14.89 o.p. (*0-06-020084-7*) HarperCollins Children's Bk. Group.

—Black Is Brown Is Tan. 2004. (Illus.). 40p. (J). (gr. k-3). reprint ed. pap. 5.99 (*0-06-443644-6*) HarperCollins Pubs.

—Mandala. 1971. (Illus.). (J). (gr. k-2). 6.95 o.p. (*0-06-020085-5*); lib. bdg. 7.89 o.p. (*0-06-020086-3*) HarperCollins Pubs.

Adshead, Paul S. Incredible Reversing Peppermints. (Child's Play Library). (J). (gr. k-7). 1999. (Illus.). 120p. pap. text 5.99 (*0-85953-629-7*); 1993. 128p. 7.99 (*0-85953-514-2*) Child's Play of England GBR. *Dist:* Child's Play-International.

Agell, Charlotte. Mud Makes Me Dance in the Spring. 1994. (Illus.). 32p. (J). (ps-4). 7.95 (*0-88448-112-3*) Tilbury Hse. Pubs.

Ahlberg, Allan. The Cat Who Got Carried Away. 2003. (Illus.). 96p. (J). 15.99 (*0-7636-2073-4*) Candlewick Pr.

Al-Chokhachy, Elissa. How Can I Help, Papa? A Child's Journey Through Loss & Healing. 2002. (Illus.). 32p. (J). (ps-7). 15.95 (*0-9712481-0-9*) Works of Hope Publishing.

Al-Huda, Bint. Prosperous Ending. Talebian, Fatemeh, tr. 1997. 156p. (J). pap. 12.95 (*1-871031-72-9*) Kazi Pubns., Inc.

Alan, Lloyd. Aunt Weird. 1995. (Trophy Chiller). 144p. (J). (gr. 3-7). pap. 3.95 o.p. (*0-06-440560-5*, Harper Trophy) HarperCollins Children's Bk. Group.

Albee, Sarah. My Baby Brother Is a Little Monster. 2001. (Jellybean Bks.). (Illus.). 32p. (J). (ps-k). 3.99 (*0-375-81148-6*, Random Hse. Bks. for Young Readers) Random Hse. Children's Bks.

Alborough, Jez. Cuddly Dudley. 1993. (Illus.). 32p. (J). (ps up). 14.95 o.p. (*1-56402-095-9*) Candlewick Pr.

Alcock, Vivien. The Stranger at the Window. 1998. 208p. (YA). (gr. 7-9). 16.00 (*0-395-81661-0*) Houghton Mifflin Co.

—The Stranger at the Window. 1999. 208p. (J). (gr. 5-9). pap. 4.95 (*0-395-94329-9*) Houghton Mifflin Co. Trade & Reference Div.

Alcott, Louisa May. Eight Cousins. 2000. 252p. (J). pap. 9.95 (*0-594-06118-0*); E-Book 3.95 (*0-594-06121-0*) 1873 Pr.

—Eight Cousins. 1874. 291p. (YA). reprint ed. pap. text 28.00 (*1-4047-1633-5*) Classic Textbooks.

—Eight Cousins. 1985. 272p. (gr. 4-7). pap. text 3.99 o.s.i (*0-440-42231-0*) Dell Publishing.

—Eight Cousins. 1996. (Illus.). 256p. (J). (gr. 4-7). pap. 9.99 (*0-316-03086-4*); 1996. (Illus.). 256p. (J). (gr. 5 up). 17.95 o.p. (*0-316-03779-6*); 1974. (YA). (gr. 7 up). 19.95 o.p. (*0-316-03091-0*) Little Brown & Co.

—Eight Cousins. (Puffin Classics Ser.). (J). 1995. (Illus.). 320p. (gr. 4-7). pap. 5.99 (*0-14-037456-6*); 1989. 304p. (gr. 5 up). pap. 3.99 o.p. (*0-14-035112-4*) Penguin Putnam Bks. for Young Readers. (Puffin Bks.).

—Eight Cousins. 1995. 288p. (J). 8.99 o.s.i (*0-517-14810-2*) Random Hse. Value Publishing.

—Eight Cousins. 1989. (Works of Louisa May Alcott). (J). reprint ed. lib. bdg. 79.00 (*0-7812-1633-8*) Reprint Services Corp.

—Good Wives Book & Charm. 2004. (Charming Classics Ser.). 416p. (J). pap. 6.99 (*0-06-055991-8*, Harper Festival) HarperCollins Children's Bk. Group.

—The Inheritance. l.t. ed. 1997. 26.95 o.p. (*1-56895-505-7*, Wheeler Publishing, Inc.) Gale Group.

—The Inheritance. 1998. 192p. mass mkt. 5.99 o.s.i (*0-14-027729-3*) Penguin Group (USA) Inc.

—The Inheritance. Myerson, Joel & Shealy, Daniel, eds. 1997. 160p. (YA). 18.00 o.s.i (*0-525-45756-9*) Penguin Putnam Bks. for Young Readers.

—The Inheritance. 1998. (Illus.). (J). 12.04 (*0-606-18412-0*) Turtleback Bks.

—The Inheritance. Myerson, Joel & Shealy, Daniel, eds. 1998. (Classics Ser.). 192p. 13.00 (*0-14-043666-9*, Penguin Classics) Viking Penguin.

—Jack & Jill. (J). E-Book 3.95 (*0-594-06550-X*) 1873 Pr.

—Jack & Jill. Date not set. 352p. (YA). 25.95 (*0-8488-2671-X*) Amereon, Ltd.

—Jack & Jill. 1880. (YA). reprint ed. pap. text 28.00 (*1-4047-1638-6*) Classic Textbooks.

—Jack & Jill. 2002. 248p. (gr. 4-7). 24.99 (*1-4043-1058-4*); per. 20.99 (*1-4043-1059-2*) IndyPublish.com.

—Jack & Jill. 1999. (Illus.). 304p. (J). (gr. 5-9). pap. 9.95 (*0-316-03084-8*); 1997. (YA). (*0-316-03778-8*); 1979. (YA). (gr. 5 up). 17.95 o.s.i (*0-316-03092-9*) Little Brown & Co.

—Jack & Jill. 1991. (Illus.). 352p. (YA). (gr. 5 up). pap. 3.50 o.s.i (*0-14-035128-0*, Puffin Bks.) Penguin Putnam Bks. for Young Readers.

—Jack & Jill. 1971. (Louisa May Alcott Library). (YA). (gr. 5-9). reprint ed. 5.95 o.p. (*0-448-02361-X*) Putnam Publishing Group, The.

—Jack & Jill. 1989. (Works of Louisa May Alcott). (YA). reprint ed. lib. bdg. 79.00 (*0-7812-1638-9*) Reprint Services Corp.

—Jo's Boys. 1988. (J). 23.95 (*0-8488-0411-2*) Amereon, Ltd.

—Jo's Boys. 1995. 336p. mass mkt. 4.95 (*0-553-21449-7*) Bantam Bks.

—Jo's Boys. 1886. 366p. (YA). reprint ed. pap. text 28.00 (*1-4047-1642-4*) Classic Textbooks.

—Jo's Boys. (Juvenile Classics). (J). 2002. 292p. 3.00 (*0-486-42226-7*); 1999. (Illus.). 80p. pap. 1.00 (*0-486-40789-6*) Dover Pubns., Inc.

—Jo's Boys. 1987. 304p. (YA). (gr. 7-12). mass mkt. 2.25 o.p. (*0-451-52089-0*, Signet Classics) NAL.

—Jo's Boys. (gr. 4-7). 1996. (Illus.). 350p. (YA). 4.99 (*0-14-036714-4*); 1984. 352p. (J). pap. 3.99 o.p. (*0-14-035015-2*, Puffin Bks.) Penguin Putnam Bks. for Young Readers.

—Jo's Boys. 1949. (Illustrated Junior Library). (J). (gr. 4-6). 5.95 o.p. (*0-448-05813-8*); 8.95 o.p. (*0-448-06013-2*) Putnam Publishing Group, The.

—Jo's Boys. 1994. 320p. (J). (gr. 4-8). 8.99 o.s.i (*0-517-11830-0*) Random Hse. Value Publishing.

—Jo's Boys. 1989. (Works of Louisa May Alcott). (J). reprint ed. lib. bdg. 79.00 (*0-7812-1642-7*) Reprint Services Corp.

—Jo's Boys. 1992. 344p. (J). mass mkt. 3.25 o.p. (*0-590-45178-2*, Scholastic Paperbacks) Scholastic, Inc.

—Jo's Boys & How They Turned Out. 2000. 252p. (J). pap. 9.95 (*0-594-05147-9*); E-Book 3.95 (*0-594-05150-9*) 1873 Pr.

—Jo's Boys & How They Turned Out. 1994. 336p. (J). (gr. 4-7). pap. 8.95 (*0-316-03103-8*); 1994. 316p. (J). (gr. 7-10). 16.95 o.p. (*0-316-03110-0*); 1986. (YA). (gr. 7 up). 19.95 o.s.i (*0-316-03093-7*) Little Brown & Co.

—Little Men: Life at Plumfield with Jo's Boys. E-Book 3.95 (*0-594-06146-6*) 1873 Pr.

—Little Men: Life at Plumfield with Jo's Boys. 1871. 292p. (YA). reprint ed. pap. text 28.00 (*1-4047-1629-7*) Classic Textbooks.

—Little Men: Life at Plumfield with Jo's Boys. 2001. (Juvenile Classics). 304p. (J). pap. 3.00 (*0-486-41808-1*) Dover Pubns., Inc.

—Little Men: Life at Plumfield with Jo's Boys. 1991. o.s.i (*0-517-06050-7*); 224p. (J). 12.99 o.s.i (*0-517-03088-8*) Random Hse. Value Publishing.

—Little Men: Life at Plumfield with Jo's Boys. 1995. (Illus.). 816p. (J). (gr. 3-5). 12.98 o.p. (*0-8317-1212-0*) Smithmark Pubs., Inc.

—Little Men: Life at Plumfield with Jo's Boys. l.t. ed. 1995. 460p. (J). 23.95 (*0-7838-1468-2*) Thorndike Pr.

—Little Women. 2002. (Great Illustrated Classics). (Illus.). 240p. (J). (gr. 3-8). lib. bdg. 21.35 (*1-57765-693-8*, ABDO & Daughters) ABDO Publishing Co.

—Little Women. 1998. (Keepsake Collection Bks.). (J). 3.99 o.p. (*1-57145-101-3*, Thunder Bay Pr.) Advantage Pubs. Group.

—Little Women. 1966. (Airmont Classics Ser.). (Illus.). (YA). (gr. 6 up). pap. 2.95 o.p. (*0-8049-0106-6*, CL-106) Airmont Publishing Co., Inc.

—Little Women. 1996. (Andre Deutsch Classics). 264p. (J). (gr. 5-8). 11.95 (*0-233-99040-2*) Andre Deutsch GBR. *Dist:* Trafalgar Square, Trans-Atlantic Pubns., Inc.

—Little Women. 1983. 480p. (ps up). mass mkt. 3.95 (*0-553-21275-3*, Bantam Classics) Bantam Bks.

—Little Women. 1998. (Young Reader's Christian Library). (Illus.). 192p. (J). (gr. 3-7). pap. 1.39 o.p. (*1-57748-229-8*) Barbour Publishing, Inc.

—Little Women. (Paperback Classics Ser.). (J). 1995. 294p. pap. 2.95 o.p. (*0-681-10333-7*); 1994. (Illus.). 10.95 o.p. (*0-681-00767-2*); 1986. (Illus.). 388p. (gr. 4 up). 12.95 o.p. (*0-681-40055-2*) Borders Pr.

—Little Women. 1995. (Illus.). 93p. (J). 7.98 o.p. (*1-85854-176-X*) Brimax Bks., Ltd.

—Little Women. 1987. 608p. (gr. k-6). pap. text 4.99 o.s.i (*0-440-44768-2*) Dell Publishing.

—Little Women. Gerver, Jane E., ed. 1999. (Eyewitness Classics Ser.). (Illus.). 64p. (J). (gr. 2 up). pap. 14.95 (*0-7894-4767-3*, D K Ink) Dorling Kindersley Publishing, Inc.

—Little Women. 2000. (Juvenile Classics). (Illus.). 608p. (J). pap. 3.00 (*0-486-41023-4*) Dover Pubns., Inc.

—Little Women. 1999. (Focus on the Family Great Stories Ser.). (Illus.). 576p. (J). pap. 9.99 o.p. (*1-56179-744-8*) Focus on the Family Publishing.

—Little Women. 2001. (Young Reader's Classics Ser.). 94p. (J). pap. 9.95 (*1-55013-783-2*, Key Porter kids) Key Porter Bks. CAN. *Dist:* Firefly Bks., Ltd.

—Little Women. (Illus.). 192p. (J). 9.95 (*1-56156-371-4*) Kidsbooks, Inc.

—Little Women. 1994. (Everyman's Library Children's Classics Ser.). 530p. (gr. 4 up). 14.95 (*0-679-43642-1*, Everyman's Library) Knopf Publishing Group.

—Little Women. 1988. (Knopf Book & Cassette Classics Ser.). (Illus.). 512p. (J). 18.95 o.s.i (*0-394-56279-8*) Knopf, Alfred A. Inc.

—Little Women. 1994. 512p. (J). (gr. 4-7). 19.95 (*0-316-03107-0*); 1994. 512p. (J). (gr. 4-7). pap. 9.99 (*0-316-03105-4*); 1968. (Illus.). 524p. (YA). (gr. 7 up). 19.95 (*0-316-03095-3*) Little Brown & Co.

—Little Women. (J). E-Book 1.95 (*1-58515-196-3*) MesaView, Inc.

—Little Women. 1924. (Books of Wonder). (J). 22.99 o.s.i (*0-688-14090-4*, Morrow, William & Co.) Morrow/Avon.

—Little Women. 1983. 480p. (J). (gr. 3 up). mass mkt. 3.95 (*0-451-52341-5*, Signet Classics) NAL.

—Little Women. Bassett, Jennifer, ed. 1995. (Illus.). 78p. (J). pap. text 5.95 o.p. (*0-19-422756-1*) Oxford Univ. Pr., Inc.

—Little Women. 1982. (Oxford Graded Readers Ser.). (Illus.). 48p. (YA). (gr. 7-12). pap. text 3.25 o.p. (*0-19-421804-X*) Oxford Univ. Pr., Inc.

—Little Women. 2000. (Illus.). 288p. pap. 8.95 (*1-86205-220-4*) Pavilion Bks., Ltd. GBR. *Dist:* Trafalgar Square.

—Little Women. 9999. (Children's Classics Ser.: No. 740-25). (Illus.). (J). (gr. 3-5). 3.50 o.p. (*0-7214-5005-9*, Ladybird Bks.) Penguin Group (USA) Inc.

—Little Women. (Whole Story Ser.). 1997. 288p. (J). (gr. 7-12). 23.99 o.s.i (*0-670-87705-0*, Viking Children's Bks.); 1997. (Illus.). 696p. (J). (gr. 5-9). pap. 6.99 (*0-14-038022-1*, Puffin Bks.); 1995. (Illus.). 336p. (YA). (gr. 5 up). pap. 4.99 o.p. (*0-14-036668-7*); 1983. 304p. (J). (gr. 3-7). pap. 3.50 o.p. (*0-14-035008-X*, Puffin Bks.); 1981. (Illus.). (J). (gr. 4-6). 9.95 o.s.i (*0-448-11019-9*, Grosset & Dunlap); 1963. (Illus.). (J). (gr. 4-6). 3.95 o.p. (*0-448-05466-3*, Grosset & Dunlap) Penguin Putnam Bks. for Young Readers.

—Little Women. Vogel, Malvina, ed. 1989. (Great Illustrated Classics Ser.: Vol. 4). (Illus.). 240p. (J). (gr. 3-6). 9.95 (*0-86611-955-8*) Playmore, Inc., Pubs.

—Little Women. (Louisa May Alcott Library). (J). 1971. (gr. 4-6). 5.95 o.p. (*0-448-02364-4*); 1969. (Illus.). (gr. 5 up). 15.00 o.s.i (*0-529-00529-8*) Putnam Publishing Group, The.

—Little Women. (Illustrated Library for Children). (J). 2002. (Illus.). 400p. 9.99 (*0-517-22116-0*); 1994. 112p. (gr. 3-5). pap. 3.99 (*0-679-86175-0*) Random Hse. Children's Bks. (Random Hse. Bks. for Young Readers).

—Little Women. (Children's Classics Ser.). (J). 1998. (Illus.). 400p. 5.99 (*0-517-18954-2*); 1995. 4.99 o.s.i (*0-517-14144-2*); 1988. (Illus.). 400p. (gr. 2 up). 12.99 o.s.i (*0-517-63489-9*) Random Hse. Value Publishing.

—Little Women. 1985. (Illus.). 432p. (J). (gr. 4-12). 12.95 o.p. (*0-89577-209-4*) Reader's Digest Assn., Inc., The.

—Little Women. 1999. (Giant Courage Classics Ser.). 688p. (YA). 9.00 o.p. (*0-7624-0565-1*, Courage Bks.) Running Pr. Bk. Pubs.

—Little Women. 1996. (YA). 37.50 (*0-87557-135-2*) Saphrograph Corp.

—Little Women. 9999. (Illus.). (J). pap. 19.95 o.p. (*0-590-74470-4*); 2000. 608p. (gr. 4-7). mass mkt. 6.99 (*0-439-10136-0*); 1994. 510p. (J). (gr. 4-7). mass mkt. 4.50 o.s.i (*0-590-20350-9*); 1994. 32p. (J). (ps-3). mass mkt. 2.95 o.s.i (*0-590-22537-5*); 1986. 256p. (J). (gr. 3-7). pap. 2.50 o.p. (*0-590-40498-9*, Scholastic Paperbacks) Scholastic, Inc.

—Little Women. 1988. (Illustrated Classics Ser.). (J). 2.98 (*0-671-09222-7*) Simon & Schuster.

—Little Women. Barish, Wendy, ed. 1982. (Illus.). 576p. (J). 15.95 o.p. (*0-671-44447-6*, Atheneum) Simon & Schuster Children's Publishing.

—Little Women. 2000. (Signature Classics Ser.). (Illus.). 544p. (J). 24.95 (*1-58279-069-8*) Trident Pr. International.

—Little Women. 1994. 13.00 (*0-606-16009-4*) Turtleback Bks.

—Little Women. Showalter, Elaine, ed. & intro. by. 1989. (Classics Ser.). 544p. (J). pap. 7.95 (*0-14-039069-3*, Penguin Classics) Viking Penguin.

—Little Women. 1998. (Children's Classics). 224p. (J). (gr. 4-7). pap. 3.95 (*1-85326-116-5*, 1165WW) Wordsworth Editions, Ltd. GBR. *Dist:* Advanced Global Distribution Services.

—Little Women. 1994. 144p. (YA). pap. 3.99 (*0-671-51902-6*, Aladdin) Simon & Schuster Children's Publishing.

—Little Women. adapted ed. 1997. (Living Classics Ser.). (Illus.). 32p. (J). (gr. 3-7). 14.95 (*0-7641-7047-3*) Barron's Educational Series, Inc.

—Little Women. 1983. (YA). (gr. 6 up). reprint ed. lib. bdg. 18.95 (*0-89966-408-3*) Buccaneer Bks., Inc.

—Little Women. 1867. 451p. (YA). reprint ed. pap. text 28.00 (*1-4047-1627-0*) Classic Textbooks.

—Little Women. 1997. (Children's Thrift Classics Ser.). (Illus.). 96p. (J). reprint ed. pap. text 1.00 (*0-486-29634-2*) Dover Pubns., Inc.

—Little Women, ERS. 1993. (Little Classics Ser.). (Illus.). 308p. (J). (gr. 4-8). 15.95 o.p. (*0-8050-2767-X*, Holt, Henry & Co. Bks. For Young Readers) Holt, Henry & Co.

—Little Women. 1993. (Illus.). 352p. (J). reprint ed. 25.00 (*0-88363-203-9*) Levin, Hugh Lauter Assocs.
—Little Women. abr. l.t. ed. 1995. (Illus.). 32p. (J). (gr. k up). pap. 14.95 (*1-886201-05-6*) Nana Banana Classics.
—Little Women. 1998. 559p. (J). reprint ed. lib. bdg. 25.00 (*1-58287-046-2*) North Bks.
—Little Women, Level 4. Hedge, Tricia, ed. 2000. (Bookworms Ser.). (Illus.). 96p. (J). pap. text 5.95 (*0-19-423036-8*) Oxford Univ. Pr., Inc.
—Little Women. deluxe ed. (Whole Story Ser.). (Illus.). 288p. (J). 1997. (gr. 7-12). pap. 18.99 (*0-670-87706-9*, Viking Children's Bks.); 1947. (gr. 2 up). 19.99 (*0-448-06019-1*, Grosset & Dunlap) Penguin Putnam Bks. for Young Readers.
—Little Women. 1989. (Works of Louisa May Alcott). (J). reprint ed. lib. bdg. 79.00 (*0-7812-1627-3*) Reprint Services Corp.
—Little Women. abr. ed. 1986. 256p. (J). (gr. 4-7). mass mkt. 4.50 (*0-590-43797-6*, Scholastic Paperbacks) Scholastic, Inc.
—Little Women. l.t. ed. 1987. (Charnwood Large Print Ser.). 400p. 29.99 o.p. (*0-7089-8384-7*, Charnwood) Thorpe, F. A. Pubs. GBR. *Dist:* Ulverscroft Large Print Bks., Ltd., Ulverscroft Large Print Canada, Ltd.
—Little Women. deluxe ed. 2000. (Signature Classics Ser.). (Illus.). 544p. (J). (*1-58279-075-2*) Trident Pr. International.
—Little Women: Book & Charm. 2003. (Charming Classics Ser.). (Illus.). 384p. (J). pap. 6.99 (*0-06-051180-X*, Harper Festival) HarperCollins Children's Bk. Group.
—Little Women: Book & Charm Keepsake. 1994. 48p. (J). (gr. 4-7). pap. 12.95 (*0-590-22538-3*) Scholastic, Inc.
—Little Women: Four Funny Sisters. Lindskoog, Kathryn, ed. 1991. (Young Reader's Library). (Illus.). (J). (gr. 3-7). pap. 12.99 o.p. (*0-88070-437-3*) Zonderkidz.
—Little Women: The Children's Picture Book. 1995. (Illus.). 96p. (J). (gr. 2 up). pap. 9.95 o.p. (*1-55704-252-7*) Newmarket Pr.
—Little Women: With a Discussion of Family. 2003. (Values in Action Illustrated Classics Ser.). (Illus.). 191p. (J). (*1-59203-032-7*) Learning Challenge, Inc.
—Little Women Vol. 2: The Sisters Grow Up. Lindskoog, Kathryn, ed. 1991. (Illus.). (J). (gr. 3-7). pap. 4.99 o.p. (*0-88070-463-2*) Zonderkidz.
—Little Women & The Secret Garden. 2002. 4.99 (*0-14-230170-1*) Penguin Putnam Bks. for Young Readers.
—The Little Women Pop-Up Dollhouse. 2000. (Illus.). 8p. (J). 21.95 (*1-55263-290-3*) Key Porter Bks. CAN. *Dist:* Firefly Bks., Ltd.
—Marmee's Surprise: A Little Women Story. 1997. (Step into Reading Step 3 Bks.). (J). (gr. 2-3). 10.14 (*0-606-12765-8*) Turtleback Bks.
—A Modern Mephistopheles. Date not set. (J). lib. bdg. 16.95 (*0-8488-0412-0*) Amereon, Ltd.
—A Modern Mephistopheles. 1877. (YA). reprint ed. pap. text 28.00 (*1-4047-1636-X*) Classic Textbooks.
—Mujercitas. (SPA., Illus.). 192p. (YA). 11.95 (*84-7281-101-8*, AF1101) Auriga, Ediciones S.A. ESP. *Dist:* Continental Bk. Co., Inc.
—Mujercitas. 2002. (Classics for Young Readers Ser.). (SPA.). (YA). 14.95 (*84-392-0901-0*, EV30608) Lectorum Pubns., Inc.
—Mujercitas. 1998. (SPA., Illus.). 304p. (J). (*84-01-46257-6*) Plaza & Janés Editories, S.A.
—Mujercitas. (Coleccion Estrella). (SPA., Illus.). 64p. 14.95 (*950-11-0010-3*, SGM010) Sigmar ARG. *Dist:* Continental Bk. Co., Inc.
—Mujercitas. 1999. (Coleccion "Clasicos Juveniles" Ser.). (SPA., Illus.). 290p. (J). (gr. 4-7). pap. 12.95 (*1-58348-784-0*) iUniverse, Inc.
—Trudel's Siege. 1976. (Illus.). (J). (gr. 4-6). o.p. (*0-07-057791-9*) McGraw-Hill Cos., The.
—The Works of Louisa May Alcott. (J). (gr. 5-6). 40.95 (*0-88411-173-3*) Amereon, Ltd.
—The Works of Louisa May Alcott. 1995. (Classic Bonded Leather Ser.). 888p. (YA). 24.95 o.p. (*0-681-10371-X*) Borders Pr.
Alcott, Louisa May, photos by. Little Men: Life at Plumfield with Jo's Boys. 1969. (Classics Ser.). (Illus.). (YA). (gr. 5 up). mass mkt. 1.95 o.p. (*0-8049-0194-5*, CL-194) Airmont Publishing Co., Inc.
—Little Men: Life at Plumfield with Jo's Boys. 1983. (J). reprint ed. lib. bdg. 18.95 o.s.i (*0-89966-409-1*) Buccaneer Bks., Inc.
—Little Men: Life at Plumfield with Jo's Boys. 1991. 320p. (J). (gr. 4-7). pap. 3.99 o.s.i (*0-440-40152-6*) Dell Publishing.
—Little Men: Life at Plumfield with Jo's Boys. 1994. (J). 344p. (gr. 4-7). pap. 9.99 (*0-316-03104-6*); (gr. 7-10). 16.95 (*0-316-03108-9*) Little Brown & Co.
—Little Men: Life at Plumfield with Jo's Boys. (Puffin Classics Ser.). (J). (gr. 4-7). 1995. (Illus.). 369p. 4.99 (*0-14-036713-6*); 1984. 368p. pap. 2.99 o.p. (*0-14-035018-7*, Puffin Bks.); 1982. (Illus.). 384p. 6.95 o.s.i (*0-448-11018-0*, Grosset & Dunlap); 1971. 5.95 o.p. (*0-448-02363-6*, Grosset & Dunlap); 1963. (Illus.). 2.95 o.p. (*0-448-05465-5*, Grosset & Dunlap); 1947. (Illus.). 5.95 o.p. (*0-448-05818-9*, Grosset & Dunlap) Penguin Putnam Bks. for Young Readers.
—Little Men: Life at Plumfield with Jo's Boys. 1989. (Works of Louisa May Alcott). (J). reprint ed. lib. bdg. 79.00 (*0-7812-1629-X*) Reprint Services Corp.
—Little Men: Life at Plumfield with Jo's Boys. 1987. 384p. (J). (gr. 4-7). pap. 3.99 (*0-590-41279-5*, Scholastic Paperbacks) Scholastic, Inc.
—Little Men: Life at Plumfield with Jo's Boys. 1994. (Puffin Classics). (J). 11.04 (*0-606-07797-9*) Turtleback Bks.
Alcott, Louisa May & Golden Books Staff. Little Women. 1987. (Golden Classics Ser.). (Illus.). 128p. (J). (gr. 3-7). pap. 8.95 o.s.i (*0-307-17116-7*, Golden Bks.) Random Hse. Children's Bks.
Alcott, Louisa May & Thorne, Jenny. Little Women. 1978. (Illustrated Classics). (J). (*0-8393-6210-2*) Raintree Pubs.
Alcott, Louisa May, et al. Mujercitas. Prunier, James, tr. 2002. (SPA., Illus.). 268p. (J). 29.95 (*84-348-5324-8*) SM Ediciones ESP. *Dist:* AIMS International Bks., Inc.
Alda, Arlene. Morning Glory Monday. 2003. (Illus.). 32p. (J). (gr. k-3). 17.95 (*0-88776-620-X*) Tundra Bks. of Northern New York.
Aldrich, Bess S. A Lantern in Her Hand. 1997. 256p. (YA). (gr. 8 up). pap. 6.99 (*0-14-038428-6*) Penguin Putnam Bks. for Young Readers.
Aldridge, Ruth. I Remember When. 1994. (Voyages Ser.). (Illus.). (J). 4.25 (*0-383-03750-6*) SRA/McGraw-Hill.
Aleichem, Sholem. Around the Table: Family Stories of Sholom Aleichem. Shevrin, Aliza, tr. from YID. & selected by. 1991. (Illus.). 96p. (J). (gr. 5-8). lib. bdg. 12.95 o.s.i (*0-684-19237-3*, Atheneum) Simon & Schuster Children's Publishing.
Alexander, Anne. Connie. 1976. (Illus.). 208p. (J). (gr. 5-8). 6.95 o.p. (*0-689-30534-6*, Atheneum) Simon & Schuster Children's Publishing.
Alexander, Harry. Sleepy Surprise. 2003. (Illus.). 6p. (J). 6.95 (*0-8069-2949-9*) Sterling Publishing Co., Inc.
Alexander, Marge. Adventures at the Grandparents' House. 2001. 96p. 9.95 (*1-58169-064-9*, Evergreen Pr.) Genesis Communications, Inc.
Alexander, Martha. Nobody Asked Me If I Wanted a Baby Sister. 1971. (Pied Piper Bks.). (Illus.). (J). (ps-2). 10.95 o.p. (*0-8037-6401-4*); 10.89 o.p. (*0-8037-6402-2*) Penguin Putnam Bks. for Young Readers. (Dial Bks. for Young Readers).
Alexander, Sue. Dear Phoebe. 1984. (Illus.). 32p. (J). (ps-3). 12.95 o.p. (*0-316-03132-1*) Little Brown & Co.
—One More Time, Mama. 1999. (Accelerated Reader Bks.). (Illus.). 32p. (J). (ps-k). 15.95 (*0-7614-5051-3*, Cavendish Children's Bks.) Cavendish, Marshall Corp.
—World Famous Muriel. 1984. (Illus.). (J). (ps-3). 14.95 o.s.i (*0-316-03131-3*) Little Brown & Co.
Alford, Katherine. Home Again, Home Again. 1996. (Illus.). 31p. (Orig.). (J). (gr. 2-7). pap. 12.00 (*0-9652438-0-X*) Little City Bks.
Aliki, Susan. One Little Spoonful. 2001. (Growing Tree Ser.). (Illus.). 24p. (J). (ps-k). 9.95 (*0-694-01502-4*, Harper Festival) HarperCollins Children's Bk. Group.
Allard, Harry G. The Stupids Have a Ball. 1984. (Illus.). 32p. (J). (ps-3). pap. 5.95 (*0-395-36169-9*) Houghton Mifflin Co.
—The Stupids Step Out. 1989. (Book & Cassette Favorites Ser.). (Illus.). 1p. (J). (ps-3). pap. 9.95 incl. audio (*0-395-52139-4*, 490926, Clarion Bks.) Houghton Mifflin Co. Trade & Reference Div.
Allard, Harry G., ed. The Stupids Have a Ball. 1978. (Illus.). 32p. (J). (ps-3). tchr. ed. 18.00 (*0-395-26497-9*) Houghton Mifflin Co.
—The Stupids Have a Ball. 1978. (J). 12.10 (*0-606-03207-X*) Turtleback Bks.
—The Stupids Step Out, 001. (Illus.). 32p. (J). (ps-3). 1977. pap. 5.95 (*0-395-25377-2*); 1974. tchr. ed. 16.00 (*0-395-18513-0*) Houghton Mifflin Co.
Allen, Eric. The Latchkey Children. 1987. (Illus.). 158p. (J). 8.95 o.p. (*0-19-277111-6*) Oxford Univ. Pr., Inc.
Allison, Diane W. In Window Eight, the Moon Is Late. 1988. (Illus.). (J). (ps-3). 12.95 o.p. (*0-316-03435-5*) Little Brown & Co.
Alma, Ann. Summer of Adventures. 2003. (Summer Ser.). 144p. pap. 5.95 (*1-55039-122-4*) Sono Nis Pr. CAN. *Dist:* Orca Bk. Pubs.
Almond, David. Counting Stars. 2002. 224p. (gr. 7 up). text 16.95 (*0-385-72946-4*); lib. bdg. 18.99 (*0-385-90034-1*) Dell Publishing. (Delacorte Pr.).
—Skellig. 2001. E-Book 3.99 (*1-59061-419-4*) Adobe Systems, Inc.
—Skellig. 1999. (J). 16.95 (*0-7540-6066-7*) BBC Audiobooks America.
—Skellig. 2000. (J). audio 18.00 (*0-7366-9025-5*) Books on Tape, Inc.
—Skellig. 1999. 192p. (gr. 3 up). text 16.95 (*0-385-32653-X*, Delacorte Pr.) Dell Publishing.
—Skellig. 2001. (Illus.). 208p. (gr. 5). mass mkt. 5.99 (*0-440-22908-1*, Laurel Leaf) Random Hse. Children's Bks.
—Skellig. Wojtyla, Karen, ed. 2000. (Illus.). 192p. (gr. 5-7). pap. text 4.99 (*0-440-41602-7*, Yearling) Random Hse. Children's Bks.
—Skellig. l.t. ed. 2000. (Young Adult Ser.). 205p. (J). 21.95 o.p. (*0-7862-2344-8*) Thorndike Pr.
—Skellig. 2000. 11.04 (*0-606-19192-5*) Turtleback Bks.
—Skellig. abr. ed. 1999. (J). audio 15.00 (*1-84032-224-1*) Ulverscroft Audio (U.S.A.).
Alphin, Elaine Marie. Tournament of Time. 1994. 125p. (Orig.). (J). (gr. 4-6). pap. 3.95 (*0-9643683-0-7*) Bluegrass Bks.
Altman, Linda Jacobs. Amelia's Road. (Illus.). 32p. (J). (gr. k-5). 1995. pap. 6.95 (*1-880000-27-X*); 1993. (ENG & SPA., 15.95 (*1-880000-04-0*, LLB040) Lee & Low Bks., Inc.
—Amelia's Road. 1993. 13.10 (*0-606-08913-6*) Turtleback Bks.
—El Camino de Amelia. Santacruz, Daniel M., tr. from ENG. 1994. (Illus.). 32p. (J). (gr. 3-5). (ENG & SPA.). 15.95 (*1-880000-07-5*, LC075); (SPA., pap. 5.56 (*1-880000-10-5*) Lee & Low Bks., Inc.
Ames, Elizabeth S. Morning Dew. l.t. ed. 1997. (Illus.). 24p. (Orig.). (J). (gr. 3-5). pap. (*0-9647244-3-X*, 46141) Cortland Pr.
Amoss, Berthe. The Mockingbird Song. 1988. 128p. (J). (gr. 4-7). 12.95 (*0-06-020061-8*); lib. bdg. 13.89 o.p. (*0-06-020062-6*) HarperCollins Children's Bk. Group.
Anderson, Janet S. The Last Treasure. 2003. (Illus.). 256p. (YA). 17.99 (*0-525-46919-2*, Dutton Children's Bks.) Penguin Putnam Bks. for Young Readers.
—The Monkey Tree. 1998. (Illus.). 176p. (J). (gr. 7-12). 15.99 o.p. (*0-525-46032-2*, Dutton Children's Bks.) Penguin Putnam Bks. for Young Readers.
Anderson, Launi K. Violet's Garden. 1996. (Latter-Day Daughters Ser.). (Illus.). 80p. (J). (gr. 3-9). pap. 4.95 (*1-56236-506-1*) Aspen Bks.
Anderson, Laurie Halse. Fear of Falling. 2001. (American Girl Wild at Heart Ser.: Bk. 9). (Illus.). 144p. (J). pap. 4.95 (*1-58485-059-0*, American Girl) Pleasant Co. Pubns.
—Fever 1793. unabr. ed. 2002. 256p. (YA). (gr. 5 up). pap. 37.00 incl. audio (*0-8072-8719-9*, LYA 246 SP); 2000. (gr. 7 up). audio 22.00 (*0-8072-6158-0*, YA246CX) Random Hse. Audio Publishing Group. (Listening Library).
—Turkey Pox. 1996. 13.10 (*0-606-15748-4*) Turtleback Bks.
—Turkey Pox. (Illus.). 32p. (J). (ps-2). 1998. pap. 6.95 (*0-8075-8128-3*); 1996. lib. bdg. 14.95 (*0-8075-8127-5*) Whitman, Albert & Co.
Anderson, Mary Elizabeth. Forget-Me-Not. (J). pap. 6.99 o.p. (*0-7814-3902-7*) Cook Communications Ministries.
Anderson, Peggy K. Safe at Home! 1992. 128p. (J). (gr. 3-7). lib. bdg. 13.95 o.s.i (*0-689-31686-0*, Atheneum) Simon & Schuster Children's Publishing.
Andrew, Prudence. Close Within My Own Circle. 1980. (J). 6.95 o.p. (*0-525-66650-8*, Dutton Children's Bks.) Penguin Putnam Bks. for Young Readers.
Angell, Judi. Don't Rent My Room! 1991. (J). mass mkt. o.s.i (*0-553-54016-5*, Dell Books for Young Readers) Random Hse. Children's Bks.
Angier, Bradford & Corcoran, Barbara. Ask for Love & They Give You Rice Pudding. 1977. 160p. (J). (gr. 7 up). 6.95 o.p. (*0-395-25300-4*) Houghton Mifflin Co.
Anholt, Catherine. Good Days, Bad Days. 1991. (Illus.). 32p. (J). 14.95 o.s.i (*0-399-22283-9*, G. P. Putnam's Sons) Penguin Group (USA) Inc.
Appelt, Kathi A. Oh My Baby, Little One. 2002. (Illus.). (J). 23.40 (*0-7587-3298-8*) Book Wholesalers, Inc.
—Oh My Baby, Little One. 2000. (Illus.). 32p. (J). (ps-k). 16.00 (*0-15-200041-0*) Harcourt Children's Bks.
—Someone's Come to Our House. 1999. (Illus.). 24p. (J). (ps-3). 16.00 o.p. (*0-8028-5144-4*, Eerdmans Bks For Young Readers) Eerdmans, William B. Publishing Co.
April Morning. 1999. (YA). 9.95 (*1-56137-119-X*) Novel Units, Inc.
Arcellana, Francisco. The Mats. 1999. (Illus.). 24p. (J). (ps-3). 13.95 (*0-916291-86-3*) Kane/Miller Bk. Pubs.
Armstrong, William H. Sounder. (Trophy Bk.). (Illus.). 128p. 1996. (YA). (gr. 7 up). pap. 2.25 o.p. (*0-06-447153-5*, Harper Trophy); 1969. (J). (gr. 5 up). 15.99 (*0-06-020143-6*); 1969. (J). (gr. 5 up). lib. bdg. 16.89 (*0-06-020144-4*); 1972. (J). (gr. 5 up). reprint ed. pap. 5.99 (*0-06-440020-4*, Harper Trophy) HarperCollins Children's Bk. Group.
—Sounder. (Perennial Classics Ser.). 2001. 96p. (gr. 4-7). pap. 7.00 (*0-06-093548-0*); 1978. pap. 4.50 o.p. (*0-06-080379-7*, P379) HarperTrade. (Perennial).
—Sounder. l.t. ed. 1999. (LRS Large Print Cornerstone Ser.). (Illus.). 230p. (YA). (gr. 6-12). lib. bdg. 27.95 (*1-58118-054-3*, 22768) LRS.
—Sounder. l.t. ed. 1987. (Illus.). 99p. (J). (gr. 2-6). reprint ed. lib. bdg. 16.95 o.s.i (*1-55736-003-0*, Cornerstone Bks.) Pages, Inc.
—Sounder. 9999. 116p. (YA). (gr. 7 up). pap. 2.50 o.p. (*0-590-40212-9*) Scholastic, Inc.
—Sounder. 1972. (J). 12.00 (*0-606-04962-2*) Turtleback Bks.
—Sounder Ri. 1989. 128p. (YA). (gr. 4-7). reprint ed. pap. 6.00 (*0-06-080975-2*, P 975, Perennial) HarperTrade.
Arnold, Chirley. The Bet. 1996. (Values for Young Women Ser.). 170p. (YA). pap. 7.95 (*1-56236-450-2*) Aspen Bks.
Arrington, Frances. Prairie Whispers. 2003. 176p. (YA). (gr. 5-9). 17.99 (*0-399-23975-8*, Philomel) Penguin Putnam Bks. for Young Readers.
Arter, Jim. Cruel & Unusual Punishment. 1993. 112p. (J). pap. 3.50 o.s.i (*0-440-40891-1*) Dell Publishing.
Arundel, Honor. A Family Failing. 1972. 160p. (J). 7.95 o.p. (*0-525-66256-1*, Dutton Children's Bks.) Penguin Putnam Bks. for Young Readers.
Ashley, Bernard. All My Men. 1978. (J). (gr. 6 up). 26.95 (*0-87599-228-5*) Phillips, S.G. Inc.
—Seeing off Uncle Jack. l.t. ed. 1997. (J). 16.95 (*0-7451-6907-4*, Galaxy Children's Large Print) BBC Audiobooks America.
Atkins, Catherine. When Jeff Comes Home. 2001. (Illus.). 240p. (J). pap. 6.99 (*0-698-11915-0*, Puffin Bks.) Penguin Putnam Bks. for Young Readers.
Atkins, Jeannine. Dessert First. 1997. (Illus.). (J). 16.00 (*0-689-80345-1*, Atheneum) Simon & Schuster Children's Publishing.
Atkinson, Chryssa. Lindsey. 2001. (American Girl Today Ser.). (Illus.). 123p. (J). pap. 6.95 (*1-58485-450-2*) Pleasant Co. Pubns.
Atwell, Debby. Pearl. 2001. (Illus.). 32p. (J). (ps-3). tchr. ed. 16.00 (*0-395-88416-0*) Houghton Mifflin Co.
Auch, Mary Jane. Cry Uncle! 1987. 224p. (J). (gr. 4-7). 15.95 o.p. (*0-8234-0660-1*) Holiday Hse., Inc.
—Journey to Nowhere, ERS. 1997. 128p. (J). (gr. 4-7). 16.95 (*0-8050-4922-3*, Holt, Henry & Co. Bks. For Young Readers) Holt, Henry & Co.
Austad, Julie. Uncle's Trunk: A Shadows in the Dark Book. 2001. 134p. pap. 20.99 (*0-7388-9943-7*) Xlibris Corp.
Auster, Benjamin. I Like It When. . . 1990. (Ready-Set-Read Ser.). (Illus.). 32p. (J). (ps-3). lib. bdg. 21.40 o.p. (*0-8172-3578-7*) Raintree Pubs.
—I Like It When... 1990. (Ready-Set-Read Ser.). (Illus.). 24p. (J). (ps-2). lib. bdg. 17.10 o.p. (*0-8114-2933-4*) Raintree Pubs.
Avery, Gillian. A Likely Lad. 1994. (YA). 16.00 o.p. (*0-671-79867-7*, Simon & Schuster Children's Publishing) Simon & Schuster Children's Publishing.
Avi. The True Confessions of Charlotte Doyle. 2003. 224p. (J). pap. 9.95 (*0-439-32731-8*, Orchard Bks.) Scholastic, Inc.
Axelrod, Amy. They'll Believe Me When I'm Gone. 2003. (Illus.). 32p. (J). (gr. k-3). 15.99 (*0-525-46660-6*) Penguin Group (USA) Inc.
Ayad, Graciela & Panzer, Richard. Mami, Papi, de Donde Vienen los Bebes? Makowski, Nancy, ed. 1997. (Maravilloso Mundo del Amor Verdadero Ser.). (ENG & SPA., Illus.). 24p. (Orig.). (J). (gr. k-3). pap. 12.95 (*1-888933-08-9*) Ctr. for Educational Media.
Ayres, Katherine. Family Tree. 1997. (Yearling Ser.). 176p. (gr. 3-7). pap. text 4.50 (*0-440-41193-9*, Dell Books for Young Readers) Random Hse. Children's Bks.
—Macaroni Boy. 2003. (Illus.). 192p. (gr. 3-7). text 15.95 (*0-385-73016-0*); lib. bdg. 17.99 (*0-385-90085-6*) Random Hse. Children's Bks. (Delacorte Bks. for Young Readers).
Bach, Alice. A Father Every Few Years. 1977. 144p. (YA). (gr. 7 up). 12.95 o.p. (*0-06-020342-0*); lib. bdg. 6.89 o.p. (*0-06-020343-9*) HarperCollins Children's Bk. Group.
Baer, Judy. A Special Kind of Love. 1993. (Cedar River Daydreams Ser.: No. 21). 128p. (YA). (gr. 7-10). mass mkt. 4.99 o.p. (*1-55661-367-9*) Bethany Hse. Pubs.
Baggette, Susan K. Jonathan Goes to the Grocery Store. 1998. (Jonathan Adventures Ser.). (Illus.). 16p. (J). (ps-k). bds. 5.95 (*0-9660172-2-6*) Brookfield Reader, Inc., The.
Baicker, Karen. I Can Do It Too! 2003. 24p. (J). 13.95 (*1-929766-83-1*) Handprint Bks.
Bailey, Anne. Burn Up. 1992. 144p. (YA). (gr. 7 up). pap. 4.95 o.p. (*0-571-16504-4*) Faber & Faber, Inc.
Bailey, Barbara. When I Get Older I'll Understand. 2000. 192p. (YA). (gr. 7-12). pap. 7.95 (*1-56315-211-8*) SterlingHouse Pubs., Inc.

Baker, Barbara. Oh, Emma. (Young Puffin Ser.). (Illus.). (J). (gr. 2-5). 1993. 144p. pap. 3.99 o.s.i (*0-14-036357-2*, Puffin Bks.); 1991. 96p. 12.95 o.p. (*0-525-44771-7*, Dutton Children's Bks.) Penguin Putnam Bks. for Young Readers.

—One Saturday Afternoon. (Easy-to-Read Ser.). (Illus.). 48p. 2001. (ps-3). pap. 3.99 o.s.i (*0-14-038756-0*); 1999. (J). (gr. 1-4). 13.99 o.p. (*0-525-45882-4*) Penguin Putnam Bks. for Young Readers.

—One Saturday Morning. (Puffin Easy-to-Read Ser.). (Illus.). 48p. (J). (gr. k-3). 1997. pap. 3.50 o.p. (*0-14-038605-X*); 1994. 12.99 o.s.i (*0-525-45262-1*, Dutton Children's Bks.) Penguin Putnam Bks. for Young Readers.

—One Saturday Morning. 1997. (Puffin Easy-To-Read. Level 2 Ser.). (J). 9.65 (*0-606-11709-1*) Turtleback Bks.

Baker, Carin G. Families, Phooey! No. 6. 1996. (Gullah Gullah Island Ser.). (Illus.). 24p. (ps-3). mass mkt. 3.25 (*0-689-80826-7*, Simon Spotlight/ Nickelodeon) Simon & Schuster Children's Publishing.

—Karate Club No. 5: Out of Control. 1992. (High Flyer Ser.). 144p. (J). (gr. 3-7). pap. 3.99 o.p. (*0-14-036264-9*, Puffin Bks.) Penguin Putnam Bks. for Young Readers.

Baker, Jennifer. At Midnight a Novel Based on Cinderella. 1995. (Once Upon a Dream Ser.). (J). 9.09 o.p. (*0-606-07968-8*) Turtleback Bks.

Ballard, Robin. When We Get Home. 1999. lib. bdg. (*0-688-16169-3*); (Illus.). 24p. (J). 16.00 (*0-688-16168-5*) HarperCollins Children's Bk. Group. (Greenwillow Bks.).

Banks, Kate. Howie Bowles & Uncle Sam, RS. 2000. (Illus.). 96p. (J). (gr. 2-4). 15.00 (*0-374-35116-3*, Farrar, Straus & Giroux (BYR)) Farrar, Straus & Giroux.

—Mama's Coming Home, RS. 2003. (Illus.). 32p. (J). (ps-1). 16.00 (*0-374-34747-6*, Farrar, Straus & Giroux (BYR)) Farrar, Straus & Giroux.

Banks, Lynne Reid. The Mystery of the Cupboard. 1993. (Indian in the Cupboard Ser.: No. 4). (Illus.). 256p. (J). (gr. 5 up). 16.95 (*0-688-12138-1*) HarperCollins Children's Bk. Group.

—The Mystery of the Cupboard. (Indian in the Cupboard Ser.: No. 4). (J). (gr. 4-7). 1994. (Illus.). 256p. pap. 5.99 (*0-380-72013-2*, Avon Bks.); 1993. (Illus.). 256p. 15.89 o.p. (*0-688-12635-9*, Morrow, William & Co.); 1995. 224p. reprint ed. mass mkt. 4.50 (*0-380-72595-9*, Avon Bks.) Morrow/Avon.

Barbour, Karen. Mr. Bow Tie. 1991. (Illus.). 32p. (J). (ps-3). 13.95 o.s.i (*0-15-256165-X*) Harcourt Children's Bks.

Barnes, Emma. Jessica Haggerthwaite: Witch Dispatcher. 2001. (Illus.). 160p. (J). (gr. 3-7). 16.95 (*0-8027-8794-0*) Walker & Co.

Barnes, Joyce Annette. The Baby Grand, the Moon in July, & Me. 1998. 10.09 o.p. (*0-606-13157-4*) Turtleback Bks.

—The Baby Grand, the Moon in July & Me. 144p. (J). (gr. 3-7). 1998. (Illus.). pap. 4.99 o.s.i (*0-14-130061-2*, Puffin Bks.); 1994. 15.99 o.s.i (*0-8037-1586-2*, Dial Bks. for Young Readers); 1994. 14.89 o.p. (*0-8037-1600-1*, Dial Bks. for Young Readers) Penguin Putnam Bks. for Young Readers.

Barrett, Joyce D. Willie's Not the Hugging Kind. 1991. (Trophy Picture Bk.). (Illus.). 32p. (J). (gr. k-3). pap. 6.95 (*0-06-443264-5*, Harper Trophy) HarperCollins Children's Bk. Group.

Barrett, Mary Brigid. Day Care Days. 1999. (Illus.). 32p. (J). (ps-1). 12.95 o.p. (*0-316-08456-5*) Little Brown & Co.

Barrington, Margaret. My Cousin Justin. 1990. Orig. Title: Turn Ever Northward. 288p. (Orig.). (YA). (gr. 10-12). pap. 11.95 (*0-85640-456-X*) Blackstaff Pr., The IRL. *Dist:* Dufour Editions, Inc.

Bartek, Mary. Stanislawski the Great. 2004. (J). 16.95 (*0-8050-7409-0*, Holt, Henry & Co. Bks. For Young Readers) Holt, Henry & Co.

Bassett, Katie. Don't Give Up. 1996. (Illus.). 20p. (Orig.). (J). (gr. k-5). pap. 7.00 (*0-9654492-0-3*) Numbers Unlimited.

Bat-Ami, Miriam. When the Frost Is Gone. 1994. (Illus.). 80p. (YA). (gr. 5 up). lib. bdg. 13.95 o.s.i (*0-02-708497-3*, Simon & Schuster Children's Publishing) Simon & Schuster Children's Publishing.

Bateman, Teresa. Red, White, Blue & Uncle Who? The Story Behind Some of America's Patriotic Symbols. 2001. (Illus.). 64p. (J). (gr. 1-5). tchr. ed. 15.95 (*0-8234-1285-7*) Holiday Hse., Inc.

Bauer, Joan. Rules of the Road. 1998. 208p. (YA). (gr. 7-12). 16.99 (*0-399-23140-4*) Penguin Group (USA) Inc.

—Rules of the Road. 2000. (Chapters Ser.). (Illus.). 208p. (YA). (gr. 7 up). reprint ed. pap. 6.99 (*0-698-11828-6*, Puffin Bks.) Penguin Putnam Bks. for Young Readers.

—Rules of the Road. 2000. (YA). 11.04 (*0-606-20252-8*) Turtleback Bks.

Bauer, Marion Dane. The Kissing Monster: A Lift-the-Flap Story. 2002. (Illus.). 16p. (J). (ps-1). pap. 5.99 (*0-689-84899-4*, Little Simon) Simon & Schuster Children's Publishing.

Baum, Betty. New Home for Theresa. 1968. (Illus.). (J). (gr. 4-8). lib. bdg. 5.39 o.p. (*0-394-91472-4*, Knopf Bks. for Young Readers) Random Hse. Children's Bks.

Bawden, Nina. The Peppermint Pig. l.t. ed. 1987. (J). 16.95 o.p. (*0-7451-0447-9*, Galaxy Children's Large Print) BBC Audiobooks America.

—The Peppermint Pig. 1988. 160p. (J). (gr. 5 up). pap. 4.95 o.s.i (*0-440-40122-4*) Dell Publishing.

—The Peppermint Pig. 1975. 192p. (J). (gr. 3-6). lib. bdg. 13.89 (*0-397-31618-6*) HarperCollins Children's Bk. Group.

—The Peppermint Pig. 1977. (Story Bks.). 160p. (J). (gr. 2-7). pap. 2.95 o.p. (*0-14-030944-6*, Penguin Bks.) Viking Penguin.

—Robbers. l.t. ed. 1986. (J). 16.95 o.p. (*0-7451-0328-6*, Galaxy Children's Large Print) BBC Audiobooks America.

Baxter, Linda. River of Ice. 2001. (J). 104p. 11.90 (*0-7891-5392-0*); pap. 5.90 (*0-7807-9805-8*) Perfection Learning Corp.

Baylor, Byrd. The Table Where Rich People Sit. 1994. (Illus.). 32p. (J). (gr. 2-5). 17.95 (*0-684-19653-0*, Atheneum) Simon & Schuster Children's Publishing.

Beake, Lesley. Song of Be. 1995. (J). 9.09 o.p. (*0-606-08183-6*) Turtleback Bks.

Beard, Darleen Bailey. Operation Clean Sweep, RS. 2004. (*0-374-38034-1*) Farrar, Straus & Giroux.

Beatty, Patricia. Lupita Manana. 1992. (J). 11.00 (*0-606-01376-8*) Turtleback Bks.

—The Nickel-Plated Beauty. 1993. 272p. (YA). (gr. 5 up). 16.00 o.p. (*0-688-12360-0*, Morrow, William & Co.) Morrow/Avon.

—8 Mules From Monterey. 1993. 224p. (J). reprint ed. mass mkt. 4.95 o.p. (*0-688-12281-7*, Morrow, William & Co.) Morrow/Avon.

Beers, V. Gilbert. A Birthday Gift for Mommi. 1994. (Muffin Family Ser.). (Illus.). 32p. (Orig.). (J). pap. 3.50 (*1-56476-311-0*, 6-3311) Cook Communications Ministries.

—It's Not Fair. 1994. (Muffin Family Ser.). (Illus.). 32p. (Orig.). (J). pap. 3.50 (*1-56476-312-9*, 6-3312) Cook Communications Ministries.

—Toddy Bear's Good Morning Book. 1994. (Toddy Bear Bks.). (Illus.). 24p. (J). 5.99 (*1-56476-166-5*, 6-3166) Cook Communications Ministries.

—Toyland Tales. 1984. (Muffin Family Ser.). (Illus.). (J). (ps). 11.95 o.p. (*0-8024-9574-5*) Moody Pr.

Beiler, Edna. Mattie Mae. (Illus.). (J). 1967. 128p. (gr. 4-7). pap. 5.99 (*0-8361-1789-1*); 2nd ed. 2000. 112p. (ps-4). pap. 6.99 (*0-8361-9141-2*) Herald Pr.

Belden, Wilanne Schneider. Frankie! 1987. (Illus.). 163p. (YA). (gr. 4-7). 14.95 o.s.i (*0-15-229380-9*) Harcourt Children's Bks.

Belton, Sandra. Ernestine & Amanda. (Ernestine & Amanda Ser.: Vol. 1). 160p. (J). 1996. (gr. 4-7). 16.00 o.p. (*0-689-80848-8*, Simon & Schuster Children's Publishing); Bk. 1. 1998. (gr. 3-7). pap. 4.50 (*0-689-80847-X*, Aladdin) Simon & Schuster Children's Publishing.

Ben-Moring, Alvin L. Quadrus & Goliath. 1976. (Illus.). (J). (gr. 6-9). 6.95 o.p. (*0-664-32590-4*) Westminster John Knox Pr.

Bender, Carrie. Hemlock Hill Hideaway. 2000. (Whispering Brook Ser.: Bk. 4). (Illus.). 168p. (J). (gr. 4-8). pap. 8.99 (*0-8361-9128-5*) Herald Pr.

—Summerville Days. 2001. (Whispering Brook Ser.). (Illus.). 183p. (J). 24.95 (*0-7862-3081-9*, Five Star) Gale Group.

—Summerville Days. 1996. (Whispering Brook Ser.: Vol. 2). (Illus.). 224p. (J). (gr. 4-8). pap. 8.99 (*0-8361-9040-8*) Herald Pr.

—Summerville Days. 1996. E-Book 7.99 (*0-585-22774-8*) netLibrary, Inc.

—Whispering Brook Farm. 2000. (Whispering Brook Ser.). (Illus.). 168p. (J). (gr. 4-7). 23.95 o.p. (*0-7862-2549-1*, Five Star) Gale Group.

—Whispering Brook Farm. 1995. (Whispering Brook Ser.: Vol. 1). (Illus.). 184p. (J). (gr. 4-7). pap. 8.99 (*0-8361-9011-4*) Herald Pr.

—Whispering Brook Farm. 1995. E-Book 7.99 (*0-585-26293-4*) netLibrary, Inc.

—Whispering Brook Series, 3 vols., Set. 1997. (Illus.). (gr. 4-8). pap. 35.95 (*0-8361-9068-8*) Herald Pr.

Bender, Esther. Elisabeth & the Windmill. 2003. (Lemon Tree Ser.). 112p. (J). (gr. 3-7). pap. 6.99 (*0-8361-9204-4*) Herald Pr.

—Virginia & the Tiny One. 1998. (Lemon Tree Ser.: Vol. 2). (Illus.). 104p. (J). (gr. 3-7). pap. 6.99 (*0-8361-9090-4*) Herald Pr.

Beni, Ruth. The Family Next Door. 1990. (Sparklers Ser.). (Illus.). 48p. (J). (gr. 2-4). pap. 6.95 o.p. (*0-233-98383-X*) Andre Deutsch GBR. *Dist:* Trafalgar Square, Trans-Atlantic Pubns., Inc.

Benjamin, A. H. It Could Have Been Worse. (Illus.). (J). (ps-k). 2000. 28p. 6.95 (*1-58431-015-4*); 1999. 32p. pap. 5.95 (*1-58431-006-5*) Little Tiger Pr.

Benjamin, Carolea. Nobody's Baby Now. 1991. (J). mass mkt. o.s.i (*0-553-54020-3*, Dell Books for Young Readers) Random Hse. Children's Bks.

Bennett, Jill. Grandad's Tree: Poems about Families. 2003. (Illus.). 32p. (J). 16.99 (*1-84148-541-1*) Barefoot Bks., Inc.

Benton-Borghi, Beatrice Hope. A Thousand Lights. 1996. (Illus.). 95p. (J). (gr. 3-8). 14.95 (*1-888927-03-8*, ATLB); pap. 4.50 (*1-888927-81-X*, ATLB) Open Minds, Inc.

Berenstain, Stan. The Berenstain Bears' Report Card Trouble. ed. 2002. (YA). (gr. 1). spiral bd. (*0-616-11095-2*); (gr. 2). spiral bd. (*0-616-11096-0*) Canadian National Institute for the Blind/Institut National Canadien pour les Aveugles.

Berenstain, Stan & Berenstain, Jan. The Berenstain Bears & Baby Makes Five. 2000. (Berenstain Bears First Time Bks.). (Illus.). 32p. (J). (gr. k-1). pap. 3.25 (*0-679-88960-4*); lib. bdg. 8.99 (*0-679-98960-9*) Random Hse. Children's Bks. (Random Hse. Bks. for Young Readers).

—The Berenstain Bears & Baby Makes Five. 2000. (Berenstain Bears First Time Bks.). (Illus.). (J). (gr. k-2). 9.40 (*0-606-18485-6*) Turtleback Bks.

—The Berenstain Bears & Baby Makes Five. 2002. (J). E-Book (*1-59019-222-2*); 2002. (J). E-Book (*1-59019-223-0*); 2000. E-Book (*1-59019-224-9*) ipicturebooks, LLC.

—The Berenstain Bears Are a Family. 1996. (Berenstain Bears Toddler Bks.). 23p. (J). (ps). bds. 3.99 o.s.i (*0-679-88185-9*, Random Hse. Bks. for Young Readers) Random Hse. Children's Bks.

—The Berenstain Bears Count Their Blessings. 1995. (Berenstain Bears First Time Bks.). (Illus.). 32p. (gr. k-2). (J). lib. bdg. 8.99 (*0-679-97707-4*); pap. 3.25 (*0-679-87707-X*) Random Hse., Inc.

—The Berenstain Bears Get the Don't Haftas. 1998. (Library of American Biography). (J). (ps-3). 7.99 o.s.i (*0-679-99236-7*, Random Hse. Bks. for Young Readers) Random Hse. Children's Bks.

—The Berenstain Bears Get the Screamies. 1998. (Library of American Biography). (J). (ps-3). 7.99 o.s.i (*0-679-99235-9*, Random Hse. Bks. for Young Readers) Random Hse. Children's Bks.

—The Berenstain Bears' Report Card Trouble. 2002. (Illus.). 32p. (J). (gr. k-3). lib. bdg. 8.99 (*0-375-91127-8*, Random Hse. Bks. for Young Readers) Random Hse. Children's Bks.

—The Berenstain Bears' Report Card Trouble. 2002. (Illus.). 32p. (J). pap. 3.25 (*0-375-81127-3*) Random Hse., Inc.

Bernstein, Sharon C. A Family That Fights. Levine, Abby, ed. 1991. (Illus.). 32p. (J). (ps-3). lib. bdg. 13.95 (*0-8075-2248-1*) Whitman, Albert & Co.

Bertrand, Diane Gonzales. Sweet Fifteen. 1995. 224p. (YA). (gr. 6-12). 12.95 o.p. (*1-55885-122-4*); 2nd ed. (gr. 7 up). pap. 9.95 o.p. (*1-55885-133-X*) Arte Publico Pr.

Best, Cari. Getting Used to Harry. 1996. (Illus.). 32p. (J). (ps-3). pap. 15.95 o.p. (*0-531-09494-4*); lib. bdg. 16.99 (*0-531-08794-8*) Scholastic, Inc. (Orchard Bks.).

Beukema, George D. Stories from Below the Poverty Line: Urban Lessons for Today's Mission. 2000. 112p. (J). pap. 9.99 (*0-8361-9143-9*) Herald Pr.

Birch, Reginald Bathurst, et al, illus. Little Men: Life at Plumfield with Jo's Boys. 1971. (YA). (gr. 7 up). 19.95 o.p. (*0-316-03094-5*) Little Brown & Co.

Bird & Falk. Go Home, Kid! 1993. (New Trend Fiction B Ser.). (J). pap. text 9.95 (*0-582-80030-7*) Addison-Wesley Longman, Ltd. GBR. *Dist:* Trans-Atlantic Pubns., Inc.

Bird, Isobel. The Written in the Stars. 2001. (Circle of Three Ser.). 224p. (J). (gr. 7 up). pap. 4.99 (*0-06-000604-8*) HarperCollins Children's Bk. Group.

Birdseye, Tom. A Regular Flood of Mishap. 1994. (Illus.). 32p. (J). (gr. k-3). 16.95 (*0-8234-1070-6*) Holiday Hse., Inc.

Bittner, Wolfgang. Despierta, Osogris! 1999. (SPA., Illus.). 32p. (J). (gr. k-3). 15.95 (*0-7358-1125-3*, NSB253, Ediciones Norte-Sur) North-South Bks., Inc.

—Despierta, Osogris! Antresyan, Augustin, tr. from GER. 1999. (SPA., Illus.). 32p. (J). (gr. k-3). pap. 6.95 (*0-7358-1126-1*, NS5941) North-South Bks., Inc.

—Despierta, Osogris! 1999. 13.10 (*0-606-17635-7*) Turtleback Bks.

Black, Jonah. Black Book Diary of a Teenage Stud: Girls, Girls, Girls, Vol. 1. 2001. (Black Books). 240p. (J). (gr. 10 up). pap. 4.99 (*0-06-440798-5*, Avon) HarperCollins Children's Bk. Group.

Black, Judith. OOPS Ma! (YA). audio 10.00 (*0-9701073-8-2*) Black, Judith Storyteller.

Blacker, Terence. The Angel Factory. (Illus.). 224p. (J). 2004. pap. 4.99 (*0-689-86413-2*, Aladdin); 2002. (gr. 6-9). 16.95 (*0-689-85171-5*, Simon & Schuster Children's Publishing) Simon & Schuster Children's Publishing.

—Homebird. 1993. 144p. (J). (gr. 7 up). text 13.95 o.s.i (*0-02-710685-3*, Simon & Schuster Children's Publishing) Simon & Schuster Children's Publishing.

Blackwell, Muriel F. The Secret Dream. 1981. (J). (gr. 5-9). 7.95 o.p. (*0-8054-4804-7*, 4248-04) Broadman & Holman Pubs.

Blades, Ann. Too Small. 2000. (Illus.). 32p. (J). (ps-3). 15.95 (*0-88899-400-1*) Groundwood Bks. CAN. *Dist:* Publishers Group West.

Blaine, Marge. The Terrible Thing That Happened at Our House. 1984. (Illus.). 40p. (J). (ps-3). reprint ed. 13.95 o.p. (*0-02-710720-5*, Simon & Schuster Children's Publishing) Simon & Schuster Children's Publishing.

Blaisdell, Robert. Little Men: Life at Plumfield with Jo's Boys. 1997. (Children's Thrift Classics Ser.). (Illus.). (J). pap. 1.00 (*0-486-29805-1*) Dover Pubns., Inc.

Blake, Claire, et al. The Paper Chain. 1999. (Illus.). 32p. (J). (gr. k-6). pap. 8.95 (*0-929173-28-7*) Health Pr. NA, Inc.

Blakeslee, Ann R. After the Fortune Cookies. 1989. 128p. (J). (gr. 3-7). 13.95 o.s.i (*0-399-21562-X*, G. P. Putnam's Sons) Penguin Putnam Bks. for Young Readers.

Blegvad, Lenore. A Sound of Leaves. 1996. (Illus.). 64p. (J). (ps-3). 15.00 (*0-689-80038-X*, McElderry, Margaret K.) Simon & Schuster Children's Publishing.

Blos, Bringing Jackson Home. 1997. (J). 16.00 (*0-689-80357-5*, Atheneum) Simon & Schuster Children's Publishing.

Blos, Joan W. Brooklyn Doesn't Rhyme. (Illus.). 96p. (gr. 3-7). 2000. pap. 4.50 (*0-689-83557-4*, Aladdin); 1994. (J). 16.00 o.s.i (*0-684-19694-8*, Atheneum) Simon & Schuster Children's Publishing.

Bloss, Janet A. Thirty Ways to Dump a Sister. 1996. (Treetop Tales Ser.). (Illus.). 144p. (J). (gr. 3-6). 3.99 (*0-87406-805-3*) Darby Creek Publishing.

Blue, Rose. Cold Rain on the Water. 1979. (J). (gr. 7 up). text 7.95 o.p. (*0-07-006168-8*) McGraw-Hill Cos., The.

—Grandma Didn't Wave Back. 1972. (Illus.). 64p. (gr. 3-5). lib. bdg. 9.90 o.p. (*0-531-02557-8*, Watts, Franklin) Scholastic Library Publishing.

—Quiet Place. 1969. (Illus.). (gr. 4-6). lib. bdg. 4.33 o.p. (*0-531-01773-7*, Watts, Franklin) Scholastic Library Publishing.

Blume, Judy. The Best of Judy Blume, 4 vols., Set. 2004. (J). 23.47 (*0-440-42022-9*, Yearling) Random Hse. Children's Bks.

—Double Fudge. 2004. 208p. mass mkt. 5.99 (*0-425-19647-X*) Berkley Publishing Group.

—Double Fudge. 2003. (Illus.). 224p. pap. 5.99 (*0-14-250111-5*, Puffin Bks.); 2002. 160p. (J). (gr. 3-7). 15.99 (*0-525-46926-5*, Dutton Children's Bks.) Penguin Putnam Bks. for Young Readers.

—Estas Ahi Dios? Soy Yo, Margaret. rev. ed. 2001. Tr. of Are You There God? It's Me, Margaret. (SPA.). 176p. (J). (gr. 4-6). 17.00 (*0-689-84688-6*, Atheneum/Richard Jackson Bks.) Simon & Schuster Children's Publishing.

—Fudge-a-Mania. 2004. 176p. (J). mass mkt. 5.99 (*0-425-19382-9*) Berkley Publishing Group.

—Fudge-a-Mania. 1990. 160p. (J). (gr. 4-7). 14.99 o.s.i (*0-525-44672-9*, Dutton Children's Bks.) Penguin Putnam Bks. for Young Readers.

—It's Not the End of the World. l.t. ed. 1986. (J). 13.95 o.p. (*0-7451-0329-4*, Galaxy Children's Large Print) BBC Audiobooks America.

—It's Not the End of the World. 1979. (YA). mass mkt. 1.95 o.s.i (*0-553-13628-3*) Bantam Bks.

—It's Not the End of the World. 2002. (Illus.). (J). 13.94 (*0-7587-9132-1*) Book Wholesalers, Inc.

—It's Not the End of the World. 1982. 176p. (YA). (gr. 4-7). mass mkt. 5.50 (*0-440-94140-7*) Dell Publishing.

—It's Not the End of the World. 174p. (YA). (gr. 5 up). pap. 4.50 (*0-8072-1365-9*, Listening Library) Random Hse. Audio Publishing Group.

—It's Not the End of the World. 1986. 176p. (gr. 4-7). pap. text 5.50 (*0-440-44158-7*, Yearling) Random Hse. Children's Bks.

—It's Not the End of the World. 176p. (J). 2002. 17.00 (*0-689-84293-7*); 1982. (gr. 4-7). lib. bdg. 17.00 (*0-02-711050-8*) Simon & Schuster Children's Publishing. (Atheneum/Richard Jackson Bks.).

—It's Not the End of the World. 1986. (J). 11.55 (*0-606-03964-3*) Turtleback Bks.

—The One in the Middle Is the Green Kangaroo. 1982. (Illus.). 40p. (J). (gr. k-3). 12.95 o.s.i (*0-02-711060-5*, Atheneum/Richard Jackson Bks.) Simon & Schuster Children's Publishing.

—Starring Sally J. Freedman As Herself. 1982. 296p. (J). (gr. 4-7). 17.00 (*0-02-711070-2*, Atheneum/ Richard Jackson Bks.) Simon & Schuster Children's Publishing.

—Superfudge. 2004. 192p. (J). mass mkt. 5.99 (*0-425-19381-0*) Berkley Publishing Group.

—Superfudge. 2002. (Illus.). (J). 13.40 (*0-7587-6668-8*) Book Wholesalers, Inc.

—Superfudge. (J). 1993. 176p. (gr. 4-7). pap. 1.99 o.s.i (*0-440-21619-2*); 1923. pap. 2.95 o.s.i (*0-440-78433-6*) Dell Publishing.

—Superfudge. l.t. ed. 2000. (LRS Large Print Cornerstone Ser.). 216p. (YA). (gr. 5-10). lib. bdg. 28.95 (*1-58118-061-6*, 23475) LRS.

—Superfudge. 1999. 9.95 (*1-56137-175-0*) Novel Units, Inc.

—Superfudge. l.t. ed. 1987. 239p. (J). (gr. 2-6). reprint ed. lib. bdg. 16.95 o.s.i (*1-55736-014-6*, Cornerstone Bks.) Pages, Inc.

—Superfudge. 2003. 192p. pap. 5.99 (*0-14-240098-X*, Puffin Bks.); 2003. (Illus.). 192p. pap. 5.99 (*0-14-230229-5*, Puffin Bks.); 2002. (Illus.). 176p. (YA). 15.99 (*0-525-46930-3*, Dutton Children's Bks.); 1980. 176p. (J). (gr. 4-7). 15.99 o.s.i (*0-525-40522-4*, Dutton Children's Bks.) Penguin Putnam Bks. for Young Readers.

—Superfudge. 166p. (J). (gr. 2-4). pap. 4.99 (*0-8072-1457-4*); 1993. pap. 28.00 incl. audio (*0-8072-7407-0*, YA842SP) Random Hse. Audio Publishing Group. (Listening Library).

—Superfudge. 1994. (J). pap. 4.99 (*0-440-91028-5*, Dell Books for Young Readers); 1988. (J). pap. o.s.i (*0-440-80039-0*, Dell Books for Young Readers); 1988. (J). mass mkt. o.s.i (*0-440-80007-2*, Dell Books for Young Readers); 1986. 176p. (gr. 3-7). pap. text 4.99 o.s.i (*0-440-48433-2*, Yearling); 1981. (J). mass mkt. o.s.i (*0-440-70006-X*, Dell Books for Young Readers) Random Hse. Children's Bks.

—Superfudge. 1996. (SPA.). (YA). (gr. 5-8). pap. 11.95 (*1-56014-665-6*) Santillana USA Publishing Co., Inc.

—Superfudge. (J). 1996. 16.00 (*0-606-10512-3*); 1980. 11.04 (*0-606-02659-2*) Turtleback Bks.

—Tales of a Fourth Grade Nothing. l.t. ed. 1991. (J). (gr. 1-8). 13.95 o.p. (*0-7451-0722-2*, Galaxy Children's Large Print) BBC Audiobooks America.

—Tales of a Fourth Grade Nothing. l.t. ed. 1987. (Illus.). 174p. (J). (gr. 2-6). reprint ed. lib. bdg. 14.95 o.p. (*1-55736-015-4*) Bantam Doubleday Dell Large Print Group, Inc.

—Tales of a Fourth Grade Nothing. 1972. (Illus.). 128p. (J). (gr. 4-7). 15.99 o.s.i (*0-525-40720-0*, Dutton Children's Bks.) Penguin Putnam Bks. for Young Readers.

—Tales of a Fourth Grade Nothing. unabr. ed. 1996. 120p. (J). (gr. 3-5). pap. 28.00 incl. audio (*0-8072-7760-6*, YA911SP, Listening Library) Random Hse. Audio Publishing Group.

—Tales of a Fourth Grade Nothing. 1976. (Illus.). 128p. (gr. 3-7). pap. text 4.99 o.s.i (*0-440-48474-X*, Yearling) Random Hse. Children's Bks.

—Then Again, Maybe I Won't. 1975. 128p. (YA). (gr. 4-7). mass mkt. 5.50 (*0-440-98659-1*, Laurel Leaf) Random Hse. Children's Bks.

—Then Again, Maybe I Won't. 1982. 176p. (J). (gr. 5-9). 16.95 (*0-02-711090-7*, Atheneum/Richard Jackson Bks.) Simon & Schuster Children's Publishing.

Bodger, Joan. The Forest Family. (Illus.). 112p. (J). (gr. 3-7). 2001. pap. 7.95 (*0-88776-579-3*); 1999. 16.95 (*0-88776-485-1*) Tundra Bks. of Northern New York.

Bolden, Tonya. Doing It for Yourself: A Tammy & Owen Adventure with Madame C. J. Walker. 1997. (America's Family Bks.). (Illus.). 48p. (J). (gr. 2-5). 15.95 (*1-885053-01-0*) Corporation for Cultural Literacy.

—Just Family. 1996. 160p. (J). (gr. 4-7). 14.99 o.s.i (*0-525-65192-6*, Dutton Children's Bks.) Penguin Putnam Bks. for Young Readers.

Bond, Felicia. Poinsettia & Her Family. 1985. (Trophy Picture Bk.). (Illus.). 32p. (J). (ps-3). reprint ed. pap. 4.95 o.s.i (*0-06-443076-6*, Harper Trophy) HarperCollins Children's Bk. Group.

Bond, Michael. More about Paddington. 1979. (Paddington Ser.). (Illus.). 128p. (J). (ps-3). pap. 2.95 o.s.i (*0-440-45825-0*, Yearling) Random Hse. Children's Bks.

—Paddington at Large. 1970. (Paddington Ser.). (Illus.). 128p. (J). (ps-3). pap. 0.65 o.s.i (*0-440-46801-9*, Yearling) Random Hse. Children's Bks.

—Paddington at Work. 1971. (Paddington Ser.). (Illus.). 128p. (J). (ps-3). pap. 0.75 o.s.i (*0-440-40797-4*, Yearling) Random Hse. Children's Bks.

Bonsall, Crosby N. The Day I Had to Play with My Sister. 1972. (I Can Read Bks.). (Illus.). 32p. (J). (ps-2). lib. bdg. 14.89 o.p. (*0-06-020576-8*) HarperCollins Children's Bk. Group.

Bontemps, Arna W. & Hughes, Langston. Popo & Fifina. 1993. (Iona & Peter Opie Library of Children's Literature). (Illus.). 128p. (YA). (gr. 3 up). 16.95 o.p. (*0-19-508765-8*) Oxford Univ. Pr., Inc.

Boonstra, Jean Elizabeth. Secret in the Family A: Sarah 1842-1844. 2002. 95p. (J). (*0-8163-1887-5*) Pacific Pr. Publishing Assn.

Boorman, Linda. Montana Bride. 1994. 196p. (Orig.). pap. 6.95 o.p. (*0-89636-180-2*) Cook Communications Ministries.

Borden, Louise. Just in Time for Christmas. (J). 2000. mass mkt. 5.99 (*0-590-45356-4*); 1994. (Illus.). 32p. pap. 14.95 (*0-590-45355-6*) Scholastic, Inc.

Borntrager, Mary Christner. Andy. 1993. (Ellie's People Ser.: Vol. 6). 144p. (J). (gr. 7 up). pap. 8.99 (*0-8361-3633-0*); (gr. 5-7). pap. 8.99 o.p. (*0-8361-3641-1*) Herald Pr.

—Annie. 1997. (Ellie's People Ser.: Vol. 10). 144p. (J). (gr. 7-12). pap. 8.99 (*0-8361-9070-X*); (gr. 5-7). pap. 8.99 o.p. (*0-8361-9071-8*) Herald Pr.

—Ellie. (Ellie's People Ser.: Vol. 1). 168p. (J). 1988. (gr. 3-7). pap. 8.99 (*0-8361-3468-0*); 1993. (gr. 4-7). pap. 8.99 o.p. (*0-8361-3636-5*) Herald Pr.

—Ellie's People Series. (J). (ps up). 1995. pap. 89.90 (*0-8361-9003-3*); 1993. pap. 89.90 o.p. (*0-8361-9004-1*) Herald Pr.

—Mandy. 1996. (Ellie's People Ser.: Vol. 9). 144p. (Orig.). (J). (gr. 4-7). pap. 8.99 (*0-8361-9046-7*); (gr. 5-7). pap. 8.99 o.p. (*0-8361-9048-3*) Herald Pr.

—Rebecca. l.t. ed. 1993. (Ellie's People Ser.: Vol. 2). 176p. (J). (gr. 7 up). pap. 8.99 o.p. (*0-8361-3637-3*) Herald Pr.

—Reuben. (Ellie's People Ser.: Vol. 5). 160p. (J). 1992. (gr. 7 up). pap. 8.99 (*0-8361-3593-8*); 1993. (gr. 5-7). pap. 8.99 o.p. (*0-8361-3640-3*) Herald Pr.

—Reuben. l.t. ed. 2001. (Christian Fiction Ser.). 193p. 23.95 (*0-7862-3596-9*) Thorndike Pr.

—Sarah. 1995. (Ellie's People Ser.: Vol. 8). 144p. (J). (gr. 4-7). pap. 8.99 (*0-8361-9019-X*); pap. 8.99 o.p. (*0-8361-9020-3*) Herald Pr.

Bos, Burny. Good Times with the Molesons. James, J. Alison, tr. from GER. 2001. (Illus.). 48p. (J). 13.95 (*0-7358-1519-4*); (gr. 1-4). lib. bdg. 14.50 (*0-7358-1520-8*) North-South Bks., Inc.

—Leave It to the Molesons! James, J. Alison, tr. from GER. 1995. (Illus.). 48p. (J). (gr. 2-4). 13.95 o.p. (*1-55858-431-5*); (ps-3). lib. bdg. 14.50 (*1-55858-432-3*) North-South Bks., Inc.

—More from the Molesons. 1945. (Illus.). 48p. (J). (gr. 1-4). 14.95 o.p. (*1-55858-407-2*); (gr. 2-4). 15.50 o.p. (*1-55858-408-0*) North-South Bks., Inc.

Bosworth, Michael. My Own Place. 1994. (Voyages Ser.). (Illus.). (J). 4.25 (*0-383-03766-2*) SRA/McGraw-Hill.

Bourgeois, Paulette. The Franklin Annual, Vol. 2. 2003. (Franklin Ser.). (Illus.). 96p. (J). 14.95 (*1-55337-531-9*) Kids Can Pr., Ltd.

Bousman, Cindy. Pete & P. J. Sing, Dance & Read with Me, Read-Along with Small Book & Cassette. 2000. 12p. (J). (ps-3). pap. 9.95 incl. audio (*1-931127-37-9*, 986-004) Kindermusik International.

Bowler, Tim. Storm Catchers. 2003. (Illus.). 208p. (J). 16.95 (*0-689-84573-1*, McElderry, Margaret K.) Simon & Schuster Children's Publishing.

Bowman, Crystal. Jonathan James Says, "I Can Help" 1995. (Jonathan James Ser.: Bk. 3). (Illus.). 48p. (J). (ps-3). pap. 4.99 (*0-310-49611-X*) Zondervan.

Boyce, Julia G. Not Very Messy, Unless... 1998. (Illus.). 8p. (J). (gr. k-2). pap. 3.75 (*1-880612-79-8*) Seedling Pubns., Inc.

Boylston, Helen D. Sue Barton, Neighborhood Nurse. 1940. (Sue Barton Ser.). (Illus.). (J). (gr. 7-12). 5.95 o.p. (*0-316-10475-2*) Little Brown & Co.

Braby, Marie. The Longest Wait. 1995. (Illus.). 32p. (J). (ps-2). pap. 15.95 o.p. (*0-531-06871-4*); lib. bdg. 16.99 o.p. (*0-531-08721-2*) Scholastic, Inc. (Orchard Bks.).

Bradburne, Elizabeth & Voller, Katheen. Happy Families. 1989. (J). (gr. 4-7). 4.25 o.s.i (*0-901269-20-4*) Grosvenor U.S.A.

Bradbury, Bianca. In Her Father's Footsteps, 001. 1976. (Illus.). 176p. (J). (gr. 5-9). 6.95 o.p. (*0-395-24381-5*) Houghton Mifflin Co.

—Those Traver Kids, 001. 1972. (Illus.). 208p. (J). (gr. 3-7). 5.95 o.p. (*0-395-14330-6*) Houghton Mifflin Co.

—Three Keys. 1967. (J). (gr. 4-6). 3.25 o.p. (*0-395-06653-0*) Houghton Mifflin Co.

Bradfield, Carl. Getting in Shape with Wendell & Myrtle: The Wendells Family, at It Again. 1994. (Illus.). 247p. (Orig.). (YA). (gr. 8-12). pap. 4.99 (*0-9632319-4-4*) ASDA Publishing, Inc.

—Hawaii Calls Wendell & Myrtle: The Wendells Family Make It to the Big Island. (Illus.). 196p. (Orig.). (YA). (gr. 8-12). pap. (*0-9632319-5-2*) ASDA Publishing, Inc.

Bradley, Kimberly Brubaker. Ruthie's Gift. 1998. (Illus.). 160p. (gr. 2-7). text 14.95 o.s.i (*0-385-32525-8*, Dell Books for Young Readers) Random Hse. Children's Bks.

Bradley-McBeth, Anna E. & Bradley-McBeth, Nilaja A. I Eat at Mommy's. 1999. (Illus.). v, 41p. (J). 14.99 (*0-9670636-4-7*) Big Brain Publishing, LLC.

Bradman, Tony. A Goodnight Kind of Feeling. 1998. (Illus.). 32p. (J). (ps-k). tchr. ed. 15.95 (*0-8234-1351-9*) Holiday Hse., Inc.

Branscum, Robbie. The Saving of P.S. 1977. (gr. 5-7). o.p. (*0-385-11270-X*); lib. bdg. 5.95 o.p. (*0-385-11271-8*) Doubleday Publishing.

—To the Tune of a Hickory Stick. 1978. (gr. 3-7). 7.95 o.p. (*0-385-13037-6*); lib. bdg. o.p. (*0-385-13038-4*) Doubleday Publishing.

Breckler, Rosemary K. Hoang Breaks the Lucky Teapot. 1992. (Illus.). 32p. (J). (gr. k-3). tchr. ed. 13.95 o.s.i (*0-395-57031-X*) Houghton Mifflin Co.

Brenner, Barbara. Year in the Life of Rosie Bernard. 1971. (Illus.). 170p. (J). (gr. 3-7). lib. bdg. 11.89 o.p. (*0-06-020657-8*) HarperCollins Pubs.

Bridwell, Norman. Clifford's Family. 2002. (Clifford Bks.). (Illus.). (J). 11.45 (*0-7587-6708-0*) Book Wholesalers, Inc.

—La Familia de Clifford. 1989. (Clifford, the Big Red Dog Ser.). (SPA.). 32p. (J). (gr. k-2). pap. 3.50 (*0-590-41992-7*, SO2844, Scholastic en Espanola) Scholastic, Inc.

Brimner, Larry Dane. Elliot Fry's Goodbye. 2003. (Illus.). 32p. (J). (ps-3). 8.95 (*1-56397-715-X*) Boyds Mills Pr.

Britton, Anna. Fike's Point. 1979. (J). (gr. 6-12). 7.50 o.p. (*0-698-20474-3*) Putnam Publishing Group, The.

Brochmann, Elizabeth. What's the Matter, Girl? 1980. 128p. (YA). (gr. 7 up). 8.95 o.p. (*0-06-020677-2*); lib. bdg. 12.89 o.p. (*0-06-020678-0*) HarperCollins Children's Bk. Group.

Brokaw, Nancy Steele. Leaving Emma. 1999. 144p. (J). (gr. 4-6). tchr. ed. 15.00 (*0-395-90699-7*, Clarion Bks.) Houghton Mifflin Co. Trade & Reference Div.

Bronin, Andrew. Gus & Buster Work Things Out. 1975. (Break-of-Day Bks.). (Illus.). 64p. (J). (gr. k-3). 6.59 o.p. (*0-698-30561-2*) Putnam Publishing Group, The.

Brooke, Lauren. Out of the Darkness. 2002. (Heartland Ser.: No. 7). 160p. (J). (gr. 3-7). mass mkt. 4.50 (*0-439-31714-2*) Scholastic, Inc.

Brooks, Bruce. Asylum for Nightface. 1996. 144p. (gr. 7 up). (J). 13.95 o.p. (*0-06-027060-8*); (YA). lib. bdg. 13.89 o.p. (*0-06-027061-6*) HarperCollins Children's Bk. Group.

—Vanishing. 2000. (Laura Geringer Bks.). 112p. (J). (gr. 5 up). pap. 6.95 (*0-06-447234-5*, HarperTempest) HarperCollins Children's Bk. Group.

Brooks, Jerome. Naked in Winter. 1990. 224p. (J). (gr. 7 up). 14.95 o.p. (*0-531-05866-2*); lib. bdg. 14.99 o.p. (*0-531-08466-3*) Scholastic, Inc. (Orchard Bks.).

Brooks, Martha. Two Moons in August. (YA). (gr. 7-12). 1998. 160p. pap. text 4.95 (*0-88899-170-3*); 1990. 14.95 (*0-88899-123-1*) Groundwood Bks. CAN. *Dist:* Publishers Group West.

—Two Moons in August. 1992. (YA). (gr. 7 up). 15.95 (*0-316-10979-7*) Little Brown & Co.

—Two Moons in August. 1993. 208p. (J). (gr. 7-9). pap. 3.25 o.p. (*0-590-45923-6*, Scholastic Paperbacks) Scholastic, Inc.

Brown, Elizabeth Ferguson. Coal Country Christmas. 2003. (Illus.). 32p. (J). 15.95 (*1-59078-020-5*) Boyds Mills Pr.

—Coal Country Christmas. 2000. (J). 16.00 (*0-689-80705-8*, Atheneum) Simon & Schuster Children's Publishing.

Brown, Jane C., illus. George Washington's Ghost. 1994. 96p. (J). 13.95 o.p. (*0-395-69452-3*) Houghton Mifflin Co.

Brown, Janet Allison, retold by. Little Women. 2001. (Storytime Classics Ser.). (Illus.). 32p. (J). (ps-3). pap. 5.99 (*0-14-131202-5*, Puffin Bks.) Penguin Putnam Bks. for Young Readers.

Brown, Janet Allison & Alcott, Louisa May. Little Women. 2001. (Storytime Classics Ser.). (Illus.). 32p. (J). (ps-3). 15.99 o.p. (*0-670-89912-7*, Puffin Bks.) Penguin Putnam Bks. for Young Readers.

Brown, Marc. Arthur's Family Treasury. 2000. (Illus.). 112p. (J). (ps-3). 18.95 (*0-316-12147-9*) Little Brown & Co.

—D. W., Go to Your Room! 2001. (D. W. Ser.). (Illus.). 24p. (J). (gr. k-2). pap. 5.95 (*0-316-10670-4*) Little Brown Children's Bks.

—D. W., Go to Your Room! 2001. (Illus.). (J). 12.10 (*0-606-21133-0*) Turtleback Bks.

—D. W.'s Lost Blankie. 2002. (D.W. Ser.). (Illus.). (J). 13.15 (*0-7587-2330-X*) Book Wholesalers, Inc.

—D. W.'s Lost Blankie. (D. W. Ser.). (Illus.). (J). (gr. k-2). 2000. 24p. pap. 5.95 (*0-316-11595-9*); 1998. 32p. 13.95 (*0-316-10914-2*) Little Brown Children's Bks.

—D. W.'s Lost Blankie. 1998. (D. W. Ser.). (J). (gr. k-2). 12.10 (*0-606-17848-1*) Turtleback Bks.

Brown, Marc, et al. Arthur's Family Vacation. 1993. (Arthur Adventure Ser.). 32p. (J). (gr. k-3). 15.95 (*0-316-11312-3*) Little Brown Children's Bks.

Brown, Margaret Wise. A Child's Good Morning Book. 1996. (Illus.). 32p. (J). (ps-3). 6.95 (*0-694-00882-6*, Harper Festival) HarperCollins Children's Bk. Group.

—My World: A Companion to Goodnight Moon. (Illus.). (J). 2004. 40p. pap. 5.99 (*0-694-01660-8*, Harper Trophy); 2003. 36p. bds. 7.99 (*0-694-00862-1*, Harper Festival); 2001. 32p. 15.95 (*0-06-024798-3*, Harper Festival); 2001. 32p. lib. bdg. 15.89 (*0-06-024799-1*, Harper Festival) HarperCollins Children's Bk. Group.

—Where Have You Been? Date not set. 32p. (J). (ps-1). 15.99 (*0-06-028378-5*); pap. 6.99 (*0-06-443569-5*) HarperCollins Children's Bk. Group.

Brown, Ruth. The Big Sneeze. Date not set. (J). pap. text (*0-05-004391-9*) Addison-Wesley Longman, Inc.

Browne, Anthony. Piggybook. 1986. (Illus.). 32p. (J). (ps-3). 14.99 o.s.i (*0-394-98416-1*, Knopf Bks. for Young Readers) Random Hse. Children's Bks.

—Piggybook. 1986. (J). 14.14 (*0-606-04771-9*) Turtleback Bks.

Bruchac, Joseph. Eagle Song. 1997. (Illus.). 80p. (J). (gr. 2-5). 14.99 o.p. (*0-8037-1918-3*, Dial Bks. for Young Readers) Penguin Putnam Bks. for Young Readers.

—Hidden Roots. 2004. (J). pap. 16.95 (*0-439-35358-0*) Scholastic, Inc.

Brummett, Nancy Parker. Journey of Elisa: From Switzerland to America. (Immigrants Chronicles Ser.). 132p. (J). (gr. 3-7). pap. 5.99 (*0-7814-3286-3*) Cook Communications Ministries.

Bryant, Bonnie. Corey's Christmas Wish. 1997. (Pony Tails Ser.: No. 15). (Illus.). 96p. (Orig.). (gr. 3-5). pap. text 3.99 o.s.i (*0-553-48485-0*, Dell Books for Young Readers) Random Hse. Children's Bks.

Buchanan, Dawna L. The Falcon's Wing. 1992. 144p. (YA). (gr. 4-7). pap. 15.95 (*0-531-05986-3*); pap. 16.99 (*0-531-08586-4*) Scholastic, Inc. (Orchard Bks.).

Buchanan, Paul & Randall, Rod. A House Divided. 2001. (Misadventures of Willie Plummett Ser.: Vol. 20). (Illus.). 124p. (J). (gr. 3-7). pap. 5.99 (*0-570-07131-3*) Concordia Publishing Hse.

Budnick, Leslie. It Takes Two. 2002. 24p. (J). pap. 3.25 (*0-375-81604-6*) Random Hse., Inc.

Bulla, Clyde Robert. Open the Door & See All the People. 1972. (Illus.). (J). (gr. 2-5). lib. bdg. o.p. (*0-690-60046-1*) HarperCollins Children's Bk. Group.

Bullard, Lisa. My Day: Morning, Noon & Night. 2002. (All about Me Ser.). (Illus.). 24p. (J). (ps-1). lib. bdg. 19.90 (*1-4048-0045-X*) Picture Window Bks.

Bundrum, Ken. The Fighting Stevensons: Honor & War. 1998. 48p. (YA). (gr. 8 up). pap. 8.00 o.p. (*0-8059-4460-5*) Dorrance Publishing Co., Inc.

Bunting, Eve. The Big Red Barn. 1979. (Let Me Read Ser.). (Illus.). 32p. (J). (ps-3). 4.95 o.p. (*0-15-207145-8*) Harcourt Children's Bks.

—The In-Between Days. (Illus.). 128p. (J). 1996. (gr. 3-7). pap. 5.99 (*0-06-440563-X*, Harper Trophy); 1994. (gr. 4-7). lib. bdg. 13.89 o.p. (*0-06-023612-4*); 1994. (gr. 3-7). 14.95 o.p. (*0-06-023609-4*) HarperCollins Children's Bk. Group.

—The In-Between Days. 1996. (YA). (gr. 4 up). 11.00 (*0-606-08782-6*) Turtleback Bks.

Burch, Robert. D. J.'s Worst Enemy: A Novel by Robert Burch. 1993. (Brown Thrasher Bks.). (Illus.). 144p. (J). (gr. 4-6). reprint ed. 19.95 (*0-8203-1554-0*) Univ. of Georgia Pr.

—Queenie Peavy. 1984. (Illus.). 160p. (J). (gr. 5-9). pap. 1.50 o.p. (*0-440-47505-8*) Dell Publishing.

—Queenie Peavy. 1987. 160p. (J). (gr. 4-7). pap. 5.99 (*0-14-032305-8*, Puffin Bks.) Penguin Putnam Bks. for Young Readers.

—Queenie Peavy. 9999. (J). pap. 1.95 o.s.i (*0-590-08754-1*) Scholastic, Inc.

—Queenie Peavy. 1993. (J). (gr. 3-7). 16.75 o.p. (*0-8446-6651-3*) Smith, Peter Pub., Inc.

—Queenie Peavy. 1966. (J). 11.04 (*0-606-04394-2*) Turtleback Bks.

—Queenie Peavy. 1966. (Illus.). (J). (gr. 4-7). 13.95 o.p. (*0-670-58422-3*) Viking Penguin.

Burke, Diana. Will You Be My Valentine? 2000. (Full House Sisters Ser.: No. 6). 160p. (J). (gr. 4-6). pap. 3.99 (*0-671-04086-3*, Simon Spotlight) Simon & Schuster Children's Publishing.

Burnett, Frances Hodgson. El Jardin Secreto. 2002. (Classics for Young Readers Ser.). (SPA.). (YA). 14.95 (*84-392-0906-1*, EV30589) Lectorum Pubns., Inc.

—The Secret Garden. 1988. mass mkt. 4.95 (*1-55902-009-1*); mass mkt. 2.25 (*0-938819-58-5*) Doherty, Tom Assocs., LLC. (Aerie).

—The Secret Garden. 1999. 10.04 (*0-606-17320-X*) Turtleback Bks.

Burningham, John. The Blanket. (Illus.). 24p. (J). (ps). 1996. reprint ed. bds. 2.99 o.p. (*1-56402-927-1*); 2nd ed. 1994. 6.95 o.p. (*1-56402-337-0*) Candlewick Pr.

Butcher, Kristin. The Gramma War. 2001. (Illus.). 176p. (J). (gr. 4-7). pap. 6.95 (*1-55143-183-1*) Orca Bk. Pubs.

Butterworth, Nick. My Grandpa Is Amazing. 2003. (Illus.). 32p. (J). 5.99 (*0-7636-2057-2*) Candlewick Pr.

Butterworth, Oliver. Visiting the Big House. Cohn, Amy, ed. 1995. Orig. Title: A Visit to the Big House. (Illus.). 48p. (J). reprint ed. pap. 3.95 o.p. (*0-688-13303-7*, Morrow, William & Co.) Morrow/Avon.

Byalick, Marcia. Quit It. 2004. 176p. (gr. 3-7). pap. text 5.50 (*0-440-41865-8*, Yearling) Random Hse. Children's Bks.

—Quit It. 2002. 176p. (gr. 3-7). lib. bdg. 17.99 (*0-385-90061-9*); (gr. 4-8). text 15.95 (*0-385-72997-9*) Random Hse., Inc.

Byars, Betsy C. The Cartoonist. 1978. (Illus.). 128p. (J). (gr. 3-7). 13.95 o.s.i (*0-670-20556-7*, Viking Children's Bks.) Penguin Putnam Bks. for Young Readers.

—The Glory Girl. (J). 1985. (Illus.). 128p. (gr. 4-7). pap. 4.99 (*0-14-031785-6*, Puffin Bks.); 1983. 132p. (gr. 5-9). 12.95 o.p. (*0-670-34261-0*, Viking Children's Bks.) Penguin Putnam Bks. for Young Readers.

—The Glory Girl. 1985. 11.04 (*0-606-12311-3*) Turtleback Bks.

—Goodbye, Chicken Little. 1979. 112p. (J). (gr. 5 up). lib. bdg. 14.89 o.s.i (*0-06-020911-9*) HarperCollins Children's Bk. Group.

—Keeper of the Doves. 2004. (Illus.). 112p. (J). pap. 5.99 (*0-14-240063-7*, Puffin Bks.) Penguin Putnam Bks. for Young Readers.

—Keeper of the Doves. 2002. 112p. (J). (gr. 3-7). 14.99 (*0-670-03576-9*, Viking) Viking Penguin.

—The Night Swimmers. 1980. (Illus.). 160p. (J). (gr. 4-6). pap. 11.95 o.s.i (*0-385-28709-7*, Delacorte Pr.) Dell Publishing.

—The Not-Just-Anybody Family. 1987. 160p. (gr. 4-7). pap. text 4.99 (*0-440-45951-6*, Yearling) Random Hse. Children's Bks.

—The Summer of the Swans. 2002. (Illus.). (J). 13.19 (*0-7587-0217-5*) Book Wholesalers, Inc.

—The Summer of the Swans. l.t. ed. 2000. (LRS Large Print Cornerstone Ser.). (Illus.). 176p. (YA). (gr. 5-12). lib. bdg. 27.95 (*1-58118-060-8*, 23474) LRS.

—The Summer of the Swans. 1978. (J). pap. 1.50 o.p. (*0-380-00098-9*, 50526, Avon Bks.) Morrow/Avon.

—The Summer of the Swans. l.t. ed. 1988. 185p. (J). (gr. 5 up). reprint ed. lib. bdg. 16.95 o.s.i (*1-55736-030-8*, Cornerstone Bks.) Pages, Inc.

—The Summer of the Swans. (Illus.). 144p. 2004. pap. 5.99 (*0-14-240114-5*, Puffin Bks.); 1981. (J). (gr. 4-7). pap. 5.99 (*0-14-031420-2*, Puffin Bks.); 1970. (J). (gr. 4-7). 15.99 (*0-670-68190-3*, Viking Children's Bks.) Penguin Putnam Bks. for Young Readers.

—The Summer of the Swans. 1981. (J). 11.04 (*0-606-01838-7*) Turtleback Bks.

—Wanted... Mud Blossom. 1991. (Illus.). 160p. (J). (gr. 4-8). 15.95 o.s.i (*0-385-30428-5*, Delacorte Pr.) Dell Publishing.

Byers, Rinda M. Mycca's Baby. 1990. (Illus.). 32p. (J). (ps-2). 13.95 o.p. (*0-531-05828-X*); mass mkt. 13.99 o.p. (*0-531-08428-0*) Scholastic, Inc. (Orchard Bks.).

Cadnum, Michael. Zero at the Bone. 1996. 224p. (YA). (gr. 7 up). 15.99 o.s.i (*0-670-86725-X*, Viking Children's Bks.) Penguin Putnam Bks. for Young Readers.

Caffrey, Jaye A. First Star I See. 1997. (Illus.). 128p. (J). (gr. 3-6). pap. 9.95 (*1-884281-17-6*) Verbal Images Pr.

Caines, Jeannette F. Abby. (Trophy Picture Bk.). (Illus.). 32p. (J). (ps-3). 1984. pap. 5.95 (*0-06-443049-9*, Harper Trophy); 1973. lib. bdg. 13.89 o.p. (*0-06-020922-4*) HarperCollins Children's Bk. Group.

—Abby. 1996. (Illus.). (J). (ps-3). 7.66 (*0-06-020921-6*, 180875) HarperCollins Pubs.

—Abby. 1984. (J). 12.10 (*0-606-03369-6*) Turtleback Bks.

—Window Wishing. 1980. (Illus.). 32p. (J). (gr. k-3). lib. bdg. 13.89 o.p. (*0-06-020934-8*) HarperCollins Children's Bk. Group.

Caldwell, Jan Lister. Cousin Clash. 2001. (Illus.). 90p. pap. (*1-55212-716-8*) Trafford Publishing.

Caldwell, V. M. The Ocean Within. 1999. (Illus.). (J). (gr. 3-8). 273p. 15.95 (*1-57131-623-X*); 275p. pap. 6.95 (*1-57131-624-8*) Milkweed Editions.

—The Ocean Within. 1999. (J). (gr. 3-9). 13.00 (*0-606-19035-X*) Turtleback Bks.

—Tides. 2001. (Illus.). 311p. (J). (gr. 3-8). pap. 6.95 (*1-57131-629-9*); (gr. 4-7). 16.95 (*1-57131-628-0*) Milkweed Editions.

Callahan, Thera S. All Wrapped Up. 2004. (Rookie Reader Level C Ser.). (Illus.). 31p. (J). pap. 4.95 (*0-516-21949-9*, Children's Pr.) Scholastic Library Publishing.

Calmenson, Stephanie. Marigold & Grandma on the Town. 1997. (I Can Read Bks.). (J). (gr. 1-3). 8.95 o.p. (*0-606-10871-8*) Turtleback Bks.

Calvert, Patricia. Glennis, Before & After. 1999. 144p. (J). (gr. 3-7). pap. 3.99 (*0-380-73132-0*, Avon Bks.) Morrow/Avon.

—Glennis, Before & After. 1999. 10.04 (*0-606-15932-0*) Turtleback Bks.

Cameron, Ann. Gloria's Way. 2001. 11.04 (*0-606-22055-0*) Turtleback Bks.

—Julian, Dream Doctor. 2002. (J). 12.32 (*0-7587-6155-4*) Book Wholesalers, Inc.

—Julian, Dream Doctor. 1995. (Illus.). (J). (gr. 3). 8.60 (*0-395-73237-9*) Houghton Mifflin Co.

—Julian, Dream Doctor. (Stepping Stone Bks.). (Illus.). 64p. 1993. (J). (gr. 4-7). pap. 4.50 (*0-679-80524-9*); 1990. (ps-3). lib. bdg. 11.99 (*0-679-90524-3*) Random Hse. Children's Bks. (Random Hse. Bks. for Young Readers).

—Julian, Dream Doctor. 1990. (Stepping Stone Bks.). 10.14 (*0-606-09497-0*) Turtleback Bks.

—More Stories Huey Tells, RS. 1997. (Illus.). 128p. (J). (gr. 3-5). 14.00 (*0-374-35065-5*, Farrar, Straus & Giroux (BYR)) Farrar, Straus & Giroux.

—More Stories Huey Tells. 1999. (Illus.). 128p. (J). (gr. k-4). pap. 4.99 (*0-679-88363-0*) Knopf, Alfred A. Inc.

—More Stories Huey Tells. 1998. (J). pap. 4.99 (*0-679-88576-5*, Knopf Bks. for Young Readers) Random Hse. Children's Bks.

—More Stories Huey Tells. 1999. 11.04 (*0-606-16567-3*) Turtleback Bks.

—More Stories Julian Tells. (Illus.). 96p. (J). (gr. k-4). 1986. 13.95 o.s.i (*0-394-86969-9*); 1986. 14.99 o.s.i (*0-394-96969-3*); 1989. reprint ed. pap. 4.99 (*0-394-82454-7*) Random Hse. Children's Bks. (Knopf Bks. for Young Readers).

—More Stories Julian Tells. 1986. (J). 11.04 (*0-606-04278-4*) Turtleback Bks.

—The Secret Life of Amanda K. Woods, RS. 1998. 208p. (J). (gr. 5 up). 16.00 (*0-374-36702-7*, Farrar, Straus & Giroux (BYR)) Farrar, Straus & Giroux.

—The Secret Life of Amanda K. Woods. 1999. (Illus.). 208p. (YA). (gr. 5-9). pap. 5.99 (*0-14-130642-4*, Puffin Bks.) Penguin Putnam Bks. for Young Readers.

—The Stories Huey Tells. (Illus.). 112p. (J). 1995. (gr. k-4). 17.99 o.s.i (*0-679-96732-X*); 1995. (gr. 3-5). 16.00 o.s.i (*0-679-86732-5*); 1997. (gr. k-4). reprint ed. pap. 4.99 (*0-679-88559-5*) Random Hse. Children's Bks. (Knopf Bks. for Young Readers).

—The Stories Huey Tells. 1997. 11.04 (*0-606-13042-X*) Turtleback Bks.

—The Stories Julian Tells. 1995. (J). pap. text 15.40 (*0-15-305580-4*) Harcourt Trade Pubs.

—The Stories Julian Tells. 1999. (J). 9.95 (*1-56137-671-X*) Novel Units, Inc.

—The Stories Julian Tells. (J). 1996. pap. 3.99 o.p. (*0-679-88125-5*, Random Hse. Bks. for Young Readers); 1989. (Illus.). 80p. reprint ed. pap. 4.99 (*0-394-82892-5*, Knopf Bks. for Young Readers) Random Hse. Children's Bks.

—The Stories Julian Tells. 1981. (J). 11.14 (*0-606-03480-3*) Turtleback Bks.

Cameron, Ann & Strugnell, Ann. The Stories Julian Tells. 1981. (Illus.). 96p. (J). (gr. k-5). 15.99 o.s.i (*0-394-94301-5*, Pantheon) Knopf Publishing Group.

Cameron, Eleanor. Julia & the Hand of God. 1977. (Illus.). (J). (gr. 4-7). 12.95 o.p. (*0-525-32910-2*, Dutton Children's Bks.) Penguin Putnam Bks. for Young Readers.

—Julia's Magic. 1984. (Illus.). 144p. (J). (gr. 2-5). 13.95 o.p. (*0-525-44114-X*, Dutton Children's Bks.) Penguin Putnam Bks. for Young Readers.

—The Private World of Julia Redfern. 1990. 224p. (J). (gr. 5 up). pap. 4.95 o.p. (*0-14-034043-2*, Puffin Bks.) Penguin Putnam Bks. for Young Readers.

—A Room Made of Windows. 1971. (YA). (gr. 7 up). 15.95 o.p. (*0-316-12523-7*, Joy Street Bks.) Little Brown & Co.

—That Julia Redfern. 1982. (Illus.). 14p. (J). (gr. 2-5). 12.95 o.p. (*0-525-44015-1*, Dutton Children's Bks.) Penguin Putnam Bks. for Young Readers.

Camp, Lindsay. The Biggest Bed in the World. 2000. (Illus.). 40p. (J). (ps-1). 14.95 (*0-06-028687-3*) HarperCollins Children's Bk. Group.

Campbell, Louisa & Taylor, Bridget S. Phoebe's Fabulous Father. 1996. (Illus.). 32p. (J). (ps-3). 14.00 (*0-15-200996-5*) Harcourt Trade Pubs.

Canals, Sonia. Castanets. 1999. (Music Time Ser.). (Illus.). 8p. (J). (ps). 6.95 (*1-899607-75-7*) Levinson Bks. Ltd. GBR. *Dist:* Sterling Publishing Co., Inc.

Cannon, A. E. Sam's Gift. 1997. 97p. (J). pap. 7.95 (*1-57345-289-0*, Shadow Mountain) Deseret Bk. Co.

Cao, Glen. Beijinger in New York. 1994. 220p. (J). (gr. 10-12). pap. 14.95 (*0-8351-2526-2*) China Bks. & Periodicals, Inc.

Carbone, Elisa L. Corey's Story. 1997. 116p. (J). (gr. 4-9). pap. 9.95 (*0-914525-30-1*); 12.95 o.p. (*0-914525-31-X*) Waterfront Bks.

Card, Orson Scott, ed. Future on Ice. 1998. 432p. (YA). (gr. 7 up). 24.95 (*0-312-86694-1*, Tor Bks.) Doherty, Tom Assocs., LLC.

Carlson, Carole C. & ten Boom, Corrie. In My Father's House. 2000. (Corrie Ten Boom Library Ser.). 272p. (gr. 13 up). 14.99 (*0-8007-1771-6*) Revell, Fleming H. Co.

Carlson, Dale. A Wild Heart. 1977. (Triumph Bks.). lib. bdg. 7.90 o.p. (*0-531-01326-X*, Watts, Franklin) Scholastic Library Publishing.

Carlson, Melody. Cherished Wish. 1998. (Allison Chronicles Ser.: Vol. 2). 160p. (J). (gr. 6-9). pap. 5.99 o.p. (*1-55661-958-8*) Bethany Hse. Pubs.

Carlson, Nancy. Louanne Pig in the Perfect Family. 1985. (Nancy Carlson's Neighborhood Ser.). (Illus.). 32p. (J). (ps-1). lib. bdg. 15.95 (*0-87614-280-3*); pap. 4.95 (*0-87614-854-2*) Lerner Publishing Group. (Carolrhoda Bks.).

—Louanne Pig in the Perfect Family. 1987. (Illus.). (J). (gr. k-3). pap., tchr. ed. 31.95 incl. audio (*0-87499-036-X*); 24.95 incl. audio (*0-87499-037-8*); pap. 15.95 incl. audio (*0-87499-035-1*) Live Oak Media.

—Louanne Pig in the Perfect Family. 1986. (Louanne Pig Ser.). (Illus.). 32p. (J). (ps-3). pap. 3.95 o.p. (*0-14-050600-4*, Puffin Bks.) Penguin Putnam Bks. for Young Readers.

—Take Time to Relax. 320p. (J). 1993. pap. 4.99 o.s.i (*0-14-054242-6*, Puffin Bks.); 1991. 14.00 o.p. (*0-670-83287-1*, Viking Children's Bks.) Penguin Putnam Bks. for Young Readers.

Carlson, Nancy, tr. & illus. Louanne Pig in the Perfect Family. 2nd rev. ed. 2004. (Nancy Carlson's Neighborhood Ser.). (J). pap. 6.95 (*1-57505-616-X*); lib. bdg. 15.95 (*1-57505-611-9*) Lerner Publishing Group. (Carolrhoda Bks.).

Carlson, Natalie S. The Half Sisters. 1970. (Illus.). (J). (gr. 5 up). lib. bdg. 6.89 o.p. (*0-06-021004-4*) HarperCollins Pubs.

Carlson, Ron. The Speed of Light. 288p. (J). 2004. pap. 6.99 (*0-380-81312-2*); 2003. 15.99 (*0-380-97837-7*) HarperCollins Children's Bk. Group. (HarperTempest).

Carlstrom, Nancy White. Giggle-Wiggle Wake-Up! 2003. (Illus.). 32p. (J). 15.95 (*0-375-81350-0*); lib. bdg. 17.99 (*0-375-91350-5*) Random Hse. Children's Bks.

Carpelan, Bo. Bow Island. LaFarge, Shiela, tr. 1971. (J). (gr. 6 up). 4.95 o.p. (*0-440-00743-7*); lib. bdg. 4.58 o.p. (*0-440-00843-3*) Dell Publishing. (Delacorte Pr.).

Carr, Jan. Dark Day, Light Night. 1996. (Illus.). 32p. (J). (ps-3). lib. bdg. 15.49 (*0-7868-2014-4*) Hyperion Bks. for Children.

Carrick, Carol. Left Behind. 1991. (Illus.). 32p. (J). (ps-3). reprint ed. pap. 4.95 o.p. (*0-395-54380-0*, Clarion Bks.) Houghton Mifflin Co. Trade & Reference Div.

Carris, Joan D. Just a Little Ham. MacDonald, Pat, ed. 1993. (Illus.). 144p. (J). (gr. 4-7). reprint ed. pap. 3.99 (*0-671-74783-5*, Aladdin) Simon & Schuster Children's Publishing.

Cartoon Network Staff, contrib. by. Attack of the 50 Foot Sister: Dexter's Laboratory. 2000. (Illus.). 16p. (ps-3). pap. 4.99 (*0-307-29952-X*, Golden Bks.) Random Hse. Children's Bks.

Cartwright, Pauline. Taking Our Photo. 1993. (Voyages Ser.). (Illus.). (J). 3.75 (*0-383-03595-3*) SRA/McGraw-Hill.

Case, Dianne. Ninety-Two Queens Road, RS. 1995. 176p. (J). (gr. 4-7). 16.00 o.p. (*0-374-35518-5*, Farrar, Straus & Giroux (BYR)) Farrar, Straus & Giroux.

Caseley, Judith. Harry & Arney. 1994. 138p. (J). (ps-3). 14.00 o.s.i (*0-688-12140-3*, Greenwillow Bks.) HarperCollins Children's Bk. Group.

—Hurricane Harry. (Illus.). (J). 1994. 112p. (gr. 4-7). pap. 5.95 (*0-688-12549-2*, Harper Trophy); 1991. 128p. (gr. 1 up). 13.95 o.p. (*0-688-10027-9*, Greenwillow Bks.) HarperCollins Children's Bk. Group.

—Hurricane Harry. 1994. 10.05 o.p. (*0-606-06484-2*) Turtleback Bks.

—Starring Dorothy Kane. 1992. 154p. (J). (ps-3). 13.00 o.s.i (*0-688-10182-8*, Greenwillow Bks.) HarperCollins Children's Bk. Group.

—Starring Dorothy Kane. 1994. (Illus.). 160p. (J). (gr. 4-7). mass mkt. 4.95 o.p. (*0-688-12548-4*, Morrow, William & Co.) Morrow/Avon.

Casey, Maude. Over the Water. 1990. (Wildfire Bks.). 224p. text 13.95 o.p. (*0-521-38557-1*) Cambridge Univ. Pr.

—Over the Water, ERS. 1994. 88p. (J). 15.95 o.p. (*0-8050-3276-2*, Holt, Henry & Co. Bks. For Young Readers) Holt, Henry & Co.

—Over the Water. 1996. 10.09 o.p. (*0-606-08841-5*) Turtleback Bks.

Casey, Maude & Paterson, Katherine. Over the Water. 1996. 256p. (YA). (gr. 7 up). pap. 4.99 o.s.i (*0-14-037589-9*, Puffin Bks.) Penguin Putnam Bks. for Young Readers.

Castle, Caroline. Rosie Pugh & the Great Clothes War. 1995. (Illus.). 128p. (J). (gr. 4-7). pap. 3.50 o.p. (*0-8120-9181-7*) Barron's Educational Series, Inc.

Cate, Dick. Nice Day Out? 1981. (Illus.). (J). 7.95 o.p. (*0-525-66700-8*, Dutton Children's Bks.) Penguin Putnam Bks. for Young Readers.

Caudill, Rebecca. Happy Little Family. 1989. 128p. (J). (gr. k-6). pap. 2.75 o.s.i (*0-440-40164-X*, Yearling) Random Hse. Children's Bks.

—Saturday Cousins. 1989. 128p. (J). (gr. k-6). pap. 2.75 o.s.i (*0-440-40208-5*, Yearling) Random Hse. Children's Bks.

—Somebody Go & Bang a Drum. 1974. (Illus.). 144p. (J). (gr. 1-4). 7.95 o.p. (*0-525-39575-X*, Dutton) Dutton/Plume.

Cauley, Lorinda Bryan. The New House. 1981. (Let Me Read Ser.). (Illus.). 48p. (J). (gr. 1-5). pap. 3.50 o.p. (*0-15-257041-X*, Voyager Bks./Libros Viajeros); (gr. 6 up). 7.95 o.p. (*0-15-257040-3*) Harcourt Children's Bks.

Cavanna, Betty. Love, Laurie. 1953. (J). (gr. 5-9). 5.50 o.p. (*0-664-32101-1*) Westminster John Knox Pr.

Cave, Hugh B. The Voyage. 1988. 192p. (J). (gr. 3-7). 13.95 o.s.i (*0-02-717780-7*, Simon & Schuster Children's Publishing) Simon & Schuster Children's Publishing.

Center for Learning Network Staff. Belle Prater's Boy/My Louisiana Sky: Curriculum Unit — Novel Series. 2001. (Novel Ser.). 77p. tchr. ed., spiral bd. 18.95 (*1-56077-662-5*) Ctr. for Learning, The.

Cerasini, Marc A., et al. Sisters Through the Seasons. 2002. 256p. (YA). (gr. 5). mass mkt. 4.99 (*0-375-82290-9*) Random Hse., Inc.

Chaikin, Miriam. Finders Weepers. 2001. 136p. pap. 11.95 (*0-595-19878-3*, Backinprint.com) iUniverse, Inc.

—I Should Worry, I Should Care. 1979. (Illus.). (J). (gr. 3-6). 12.89 o.p. (*0-06-021174-1*); lib. bdg. 11.89 o.p. (*0-06-021175-X*) HarperCollins Children's Bk. Group.

—I Should Worry, I Should Care. 2000. (Illus.). 116p. (gr. 4-7). pap. 9.95 (*0-595-09011-7*, Backinprint.com) iUniverse, Inc.

Chall, Marsha W. Happy Birthday, America! 2000. (Illus.). 32p. (J). (ps-3). lib. bdg. 16.89 (*0-688-13052-6*) HarperCollins Children's Bk. Group.

—Happy Birthday, America! 2000. (Illus.). 32p. (J). (ps-3). 15.99 (*0-688-13051-8*) Morrow/Avon.

—Sugarbush Spring. 2000. (Illus.). 24p. (J). (gr. 1 up). 16.99 (*0-688-14907-3*); lib. bdg. 16.89 (*0-688-14908-1*) HarperCollins Children's Bk. Group.

Chang, Margaret S. & Chang, Raymond. In the Eye of War. 1990. 208p. (J). (gr. 4-7). 14.95 (*0-689-50503-5*, McElderry, Margaret K.) Simon & Schuster Children's Publishing.

Child, Lauren. Clarice Bean, Guess Who's Babysitting? 2001. (Illus.). 32p. (J). (gr. 1-4). 16.99 (*0-7636-1373-8*) Candlewick Pr.

—Para Tio el Mio, Dice Ana Tarambana. 2001. (CAT., Illus.). 28p. (J). (gr. 2-4). 17.95 (*84-95040-85-9*) Serres, Ediciones, S. L. ESP. *Dist:* Lectorum Pubns., Inc.

—Para Tio el Mio, Dice Ana Tarambana. Rubio, Esther, tr. & adapted by by. 2001. (SPA., Illus.). 146p. (J). (ps-3). 17.95 (*84-95040-84-0*) Serres, Ediciones, S. L. ESP. *Dist:* Lectorum Pubns., Inc.

—Utterly Me, Clarice Bean. 2003. (Illus.). 192p. (J). 15.99 (*0-7636-2186-2*) Candlewick Pr.

—What Planet Are You from Clarice Bean? 2002. (Illus.). 32p. (J). (gr. 1-5). 16.99 (*0-7636-1696-6*) Candlewick Pr.

Chocolate, Deborah M. Newton. On the Day I Was Born. 1995. (Illus.). 32p. (J). (gr. k-4). pap. 12.95 o.p. (*0-590-47609-2*, Cartwheel Bks.) Scholastic, Inc.

Choi, Sook-Nyul. Yunmi & Halmoni's Trip. 1997. (Illus.). 32p. (J). (ps-3). tchr. ed. 15.00 o.s.i (*0-395-81180-5*) Houghton Mifflin Co.

Choldenko, Gennifer. Notes from a Liar & Her Dog. 2001. (Illus.). 216p. (J). (gr. 5-9). 16.99 (*0-399-23591-4*, Philomel) Penguin Group (USA) Inc.

Chorao, Kay. Here Comes Kate. (Easy-to-Read Ser.). 48p. 2002. pap. 3.99 (*0-14-230081-0*); 2000. (Illus.). (J). 13.99 o.s.i (*0-525-46443-3*, Dutton Children's Bks.) Penguin Putnam Bks. for Young Readers.

—Up & down with Kate. 2002. (Dutton Easy Reader Ser.). (Illus.). 48p. (J). 13.99 (*0-525-46891-9*, Dutton Children's Bks.) Penguin Putnam Bks. for Young Readers.

Christiansen, C. B. I See the Moon. (Illus.). 128p. (gr. 5 up). 1996. (YA). mass mkt. 3.99 (*0-689-80441-5*, Aladdin); 1994. (J). 14.95 (*0-689-31928-2*, Atheneum) Simon & Schuster Children's Publishing.

—I See the Moon. 1996. 9.09 o.p. (*0-606-09450-4*) Turtleback Bks.

—A Small Pleasure. 1988. 144p. (YA). (gr. 7 up). 13.95 (*0-689-31369-1*, Atheneum) Simon & Schuster Children's Publishing.

Christie, Amanda. Mary's Rescue. 2003. 176p. (YA). (gr. 4-7). mass mkt. 4.99 (*0-375-82409-X*) Random Hse. Children's Bks.

—Nobody's Perfect. 1999. (7th Heaven Ser.). (Illus.). 176p. (J). (gr. 5-8). mass mkt. 4.99 (*0-375-80433-1*) Random Hse., Inc.

—Rivals. 2000. (7th Heaven Ser.). 176p. (YA). (gr. 3-8). mass mkt. 4.99 (*0-375-80337-8*, Random Hse. Bks. for Young Readers) Random Hse. Children's Bks.

Christopher, Doris A. Curious Jessica & Her Weird Family Album. 1997. 64p. (J). pap. 8.00 (*1-56002-678-2*, University Editions) Aegina Pr., Inc.

Christopher, Matt. Tight End. 1981. 128p. (J). (gr. 3 up). 15.95 o.p. (*0-316-14017-1*) Little Brown & Co.

Cisneros, Phil. Gabriela Gecko, the Story of Belonging. 1996. (Illus.). 22p. (J). (gr. 1-6). pap. 8.00 (*0-9651804-1-7*, 102) New Horizons, Unlimited.

Clark, Catherine. Frozen Rodeo. 2004. 304p. (J). pap. 6.99 (*0-06-447385-6*, HarperTempest) HarperCollins Children's Bk. Group.

—Frozen Rodeo. 2003. 304p. (J). (gr. 8 up). 15.99 (*0-06-009070-7*) HarperCollins Pubs.

—Frozen Rodeo, or a Summer on Ice. 2003. 304p. (J). lib. bdg. 16.89 (*0-06-624008-5*) HarperCollins Pubs.

—I Do, Don't I? 2002. (Gilmore Girls Ser.: No. 3). 176p. mass mkt. 5.99 (*0-06-009757-4*, HarperEntertainment) Morrow/Avon.

Clark, Emma Chichester. Up in Heaven. 2004. (Illus.). (J). pap. 15.95 (*0-385-74638-5*) Doubleday Publishing.

Claro, Joe. Family Ties: Alex Gets the Business. 1986. 112p. (Orig.). (YA). (gr. 7 up). pap. 2.95 o.p. (*0-380-75235-2*, Avon Bks.) Morrow/Avon.

Cleary, Beverly. Beezus & Ramona. 1989. (Ramona Ser.). (J). (gr. 3-5). mass mkt. o.p. (*0-440-80144-3*) Dell Publishing.

—Beezus & Ramona. 1988. (Ramona Ser.). (J). (gr. 3-5). mass mkt. o.s.i (*0-440-80009-9*) Doubleday Publishing.

—Beezus & Ramona. 1955. (Ramona Ser.). (Illus.). 160p. (J). (gr. 4-7). 15.95 (*0-688-21076-7*) HarperCollins Children's Bk. Group.

—Beezus & Ramona. 1990. (Ramona Ser.). (Illus.). 176p. (J). (gr. 3-7). pap. 5.99 (*0-380-70918-X*, Avon Bks.) Morrow/Avon.

—Beezus & Ramona. (Ramona Ser.). 142p. (J). (gr. 3-5). pap. 4.99 (*0-8072-1441-8*); 1990. pap. 28.00 incl. audio (*0-8072-7317-1*, YA 822 SP) Random Hse. Audio Publishing Group. (Listening Library).

—Beezus & Ramona. 1979. (Ramona Ser.). (J). (gr. 3-5). pap. 3.25 o.s.i (*0-440-70665-3*, Dell Books for Young Readers); (Illus.). 160p. pap. 1.75 o.s.i (*0-440-40665-X*, Yearling) Random Hse. Children's Bks.

—Beezus & Ramona. 9999. (Ramona Ser.). (J). (gr. 3-5). pap. 1.95 o.s.i (*0-590-11828-5*) Scholastic, Inc.

—The Beezus & Ramona Diary. 1986. (Ramona Ser.). (Illus.). 224p. (J). (gr. 3-5). pap. 11.95 (*0-688-06353-5*, Morrow, William & Co.) Morrow/Avon.

—The Growing up Feet. 1997. (Illus.). 32p. (J). (ps-3). pap. 5.95 (*0-688-15470-0*, Harper Trophy) HarperCollins Children's Bk. Group.

—The Growing up Feet. 1987. (Illus.). 32p. (J). (ps-1). lib. bdg. 11.88 o.p. (*0-688-06620-8*, Morrow, William & Co.) Morrow/Avon.

—The Growing-Up Feet. 1987. (Illus.). 32p. (J). (ps-3). 16.00 (*0-688-06619-4*) HarperCollins Children's Bk. Group.

—Mitch & Amy. 1967. (Illus.). 224p. (J). (gr. 3-7). 16.00 o.p. (*0-688-21688-9*); lib. bdg. 15.93 o.p. (*0-688-31688-3*) Morrow/Avon. (Morrow, William & Co.).

—Petey's Bedtime Story. 1995. (J). 11.10 (*0-606-08011-2*) Turtleback Bks.

—Ramona & Her Family. (J). Dell Publishing.

—Ramona & Her Father. 2002. (Illus.). (J). 13.83 (*0-7587-5636-4*) Book Wholesalers, Inc.

—Ramona & Her Father. (Ramona Ser.). (J). (gr. 3-5). 1983. pap.; 1923. pap. 2.95 o.s.i (*0-440-77241-9*) Dell Publishing.

—Ramona & Her Father. 1977. (Ramona Ser.). (Illus.). 192p. (J). (gr. 3-5). 15.95 (*0-688-22114-9*); lib. bdg. 16.89 (*0-688-32114-3*) HarperCollins Children's Bk. Group.

—Ramona & Her Father. 1990. (Ramona Ser.). (Illus.). 208p. (J). (gr. 3-5). pap. 5.99 (*0-380-70916-3*, Avon Bks.) Morrow/Avon.

—Ramona & Her Father. l.t. ed. 1988. (Ramona Ser.). 155p. (J). (gr. 3-5). reprint ed. lib. bdg. 16.95 o.s.i (*1-55736-076-6*, Cornerstone Bks.) Pages, Inc.

—Ramona & Her Father. (Ramona Ser.). (J). 186p. (gr. 3-5). pap. 4.99 (*0-8072-1439-6*); 2003. (gr. 2). audio 18.00 (*0-8072-1032-3*) Random Hse. Audio Publishing Group. (Listening Library).

—Ramona & Her Father. 1979. (Ramona Ser.). (Illus.). 196p. (J). (gr. 3-5). pap. 1.75 o.s.i (*0-440-47241-5*, Yearling) Random Hse. Children's Bks.

—Ramona & Her Father. 1977. (Ramona Ser.). (J). (gr. 3-5). 11.00 (*0-606-04522-8*) Turtleback Bks.

—Ramona & Her Mother. (Ramona Ser.). (J). (gr. 3-5). 1988. pap. o.p. (*0-440-80004-8*); 1980. 208p. pap. 3.25 o.s.i (*0-440-47243-1*); 1923. pap. 3.25 o.s.i (*0-440-77243-5*) Dell Publishing.

—Ramona & Her Mother. 1979. (Ramona Ser.). (Illus.). 208p. (J). (gr. 3-5). 16.99 (*0-688-22195-5*); (ps-3). lib. bdg. 17.89 (*0-688-32195-X*) HarperCollins Children's Bk. Group.

—Ramona & Her Mother. 1990. (Ramona Ser.). (Illus.). 224p. (J). (gr. 3-5). reprint ed. pap. 5.99 (*0-380-70952-X*) Morrow/Avon.

—Ramona & Her Mother. (Ramona Ser.). 208p. (J). (gr. 3-5). pap. 4.99 (*0-8072-1435-3*); 2003. (J). (gr. 2). audio 18.00 (*0-8072-1030-7*); 1990. 186p. (J). (gr. 3-5). pap. 28.00 incl. audio (*0-8072-7314-7*, YA 820 SP); 1989. 208p. pap. 28.00 incl. audio (*0-8072-7319-8*, YA815SP) Random Hse. Audio Publishing Group. (Listening Library).

—Ramona & Her Mother. 1980. (Ramona Ser.). (J). (gr. 3-5). pap. 4.50 (*0-440-70007-8*, Dell Books for Young Readers) Random Hse. Children's Bks.

—Ramona & Her Mother. 1979. (Ramona Ser.). (J). (gr. 3-5). 11.00 (*0-606-04781-6*) Turtleback Bks.

—Ramona Empieza el Curso. 1996. (Ramona Ser.). (SPA.). 176p. (J). (gr. 3-5). 9.95 o.p. (*84-239-2791-1*) Espasa Calpe, S.A. ESP. *Dist:* AIMS International Bks., Inc.

—Ramona Empieza el Curso. Bustelo, Gabriela, tr. 1997. (Ramona Ser.). (SPA., Illus.). 224p. (J). (gr. 2-6). pap. 6.99 (*0-688-15487-5*, MR7554, Morrow, William & Co.) Morrow/Avon.

—Ramona Empieza el Curso. 1997. (J). 13.00 (*0-606-11779-2*) Turtleback Bks.

—Ramona Forever. unabr. ed. 1999. (Ramona Ser.). (J). (gr. 3-5). audio 23.00 BBC Audiobooks America.

—Ramona Forever. unabr. ed. 1999. (Ramona Ser.). (J). (gr. 3-5). audio 17.95 Blackstone Audio Bks., Inc.

—Ramona Forever. (Ramona Ser.). (J). (gr. 3-5). 1994. 192p. pap. 1.99 o.s.i (*0-440-21937-X*); 1993. 192p. pap. 1.99 o.s.i (*0-440-21616-8*); 1985. pap. 2.95 o.s.i (*0-440-77210-9*) Dell Publishing.

—Ramona Forever. (Ramona Ser.). (Illus.). (J). 1984. 192p. (gr. 3-5). lib. bdg. 16.89 (*0-688-03786-0*); 1984. 192p. (ps-3). 15.99 (*0-688-03785-2*); 1995. 208p. (gr. 3-5). reprint ed. pap. 5.99 (*0-380-70960-0*, Harper Trophy) HarperCollins Children's Bk. Group.

—Ramona Forever. 1996. (Ramona Ser.). (J). (gr. 3-5). pap. 4.50 (*0-380-72801-X*, Avon Bks.) Morrow/Avon.

—Ramona Forever. 2001. (Ramona Ser.). (J). (gr. 3-5). pap., wbk. ed. (*1-58130-690-3*); pap., wbk. ed. (*1-58130-691-1*) Novel Units, Inc.

—Ramona Forever. l.t. ed. 1989. (Ramona Ser.). 192p. (J). (gr. 3-5). reprint ed. lib. bdg. 16.95 o.s.i (*1-55736-139-8*, Cornerstone Bks.) Pages, Inc.

—Ramona Forever. (Ramona Ser.). (J). 182p. (gr. 3-5). pap. 4.99 (*0-8072-1437-X*); 2003. (gr. 2). audio 18.00 (*0-8072-1028-5*); 1988. 182p. (gr. 3-5). pap. 28.00 incl. audio (*0-8072-7318-X*, YA817SP); 1988. (gr. 3-5). audio 23.00 (*0-8072-7265-5*, YA 817 CX) Random Hse. Audio Publishing Group. (Listening Library).

—Ramona Forever. (Ramona Ser.). (J). (gr. 3-5). 1988. pap. o.s.i (*0-440-80005-6*, Dell Books for Young Readers); 1985. 192p. pap. 4.50 o.p. (*0-440-47210-5*, Yearling) Random Hse. Children's Bks.

—Ramona Forever. (Ramona Ser.). (J). (gr. 3-5). 1996. 8.60 o.p. (*0-606-09778-3*); 1995. 11.00 (*0-606-08054-6*) Turtleback Bks.

—Ramona la Chinche. 1996. Tr. of Ramona the Pest. (SPA., Illus.). 192p. (J). (ps-3). pap. 5.99 (*0-688-14888-3*, MR2295, Rayo) HarperTrade.

—Ramona la Chinche. Palacios, Argentina, tr. 1984. Tr. of Ramona the Pest. (SPA., Illus.). 192p. (J). (ps-3). 16.95 (*0-688-02783-0*, MR1442, Rayo) HarperTrade.

—Ramona la Chinche. 1996. Tr. of Ramona the Pest. 12.00 (*0-606-10495-X*) Turtleback Bks.

—Ramona Quimby, 4 vols., Set. 1993. (Ramona Ser.). (J). (gr. 3-5). pap. 19.96 (*0-380-72123-6*, Avon Bks.) Morrow/Avon.

—Ramona Quimby, Age 8. l.t. ed. 1987. (Ramona Ser.). (Illus.). 142p. (J). (gr. 3-5). reprint ed. lib. bdg. 14.95 o.p. (*1-55736-000-6*) Bantam Doubleday Dell Large Print Group, Inc.

—Ramona Quimby, Age 8. (Ramona Ser.). (J). (gr. 3-5). 1983. pap. Dell Publishing.

—Ramona Quimby, Age 8. 1988. (Ramona Ser.). (J). (gr. 3-5). pap. o.s.i (*0-440-80012-9*) Doubleday Publishing.

—Ramona Quimby, Age 8. 1994. (Ramona Ser.). (J). (gr. 3-5). pap. 5.60 (*0-87129-330-7*, R54) Dramatic Publishing Co.

—Ramona Quimby, Age 8. 95th ed. 1995. (Ramona Ser.). (J). (gr. 3-5). lib. bdg. 13.25 (*0-15-305205-8*) Harcourt College Pubs.

—Ramona Quimby, Age 8, 4 vols. (Ramona Ser.). (gr. 3-7). 1999. 19.80 (*0-380-81468-4*); 1992. (Illus.). 208p. (J). pap. 5.99 (*0-380-70956-2*, Avon Bks.); 1981. (Illus.). 192p. (J). 16.99 (*0-688-00477-6*, Morrow, William & Co.); 1981. (Illus.). 192p. (J). lib. bdg. 16.89 (*0-688-00478-4*, Morrow, William & Co.) Morrow/Avon.

—Ramona Quimby, Age 8. (Ramona Ser.). (J). (gr. 3-5). 1999. 9.95 (*1-56137-448-2*); 1998. 44p. 11.95 (*1-56137-708-2*, NU7082SP) Novel Units, Inc.

—Ramona Quimby, Age 8. (Ramona Ser.). (J). (gr. 3-5). 190p. pap. 4.99 (*0-8072-1436-1*); 2000. audio 18.00 (*0-8072-7403-8*); 1989. 190p. pap. 28.00 incl. audio (*0-8072-7320-1*, YA816SP) Random Hse. Audio Publishing Group. (Listening Library).

—Ramona Quimby, Age 8. 1981. (Ramona Ser.). (J). (gr. 3-5). 11.00 (*0-606-01002-5*) Turtleback Bks.

—Ramona the Brave. unabr. ed. 1997. (Ramona Ser.). (J). (gr. 3-5). audio 23.00 BBC Audiobooks America.

—Ramona the Brave. unabr. ed. 1999. (Ramona Ser.). (J). (gr. 3-5). audio 17.95 Blackstone Audio Bks., Inc.

—Ramona the Brave. 1984. (Ramona Ser.). (J). (gr. 3-5). pap. 2.95 o.s.i (*0-440-77351-2*) Dell Publishing.

—Ramona the Brave. (Ramona Ser.). (Illus.). 192p. (J). (gr. 3-5). 1995. pap. 5.99 (*0-380-70959-7*, Harper Trophy); 1975. 15.99 (*0-688-22015-0*); 1975. lib. bdg. 17.89 (*0-688-32015-5*) HarperCollins Children's Bk. Group.

—Ramona the Brave. 2000. (Ramona Ser.). (J). (gr. 3-5). 9.95 (*1-56137-444-X*) Novel Units, Inc.

—Ramona the Brave. l.t. ed. 1989. (Ramona Ser.). (Illus.). 143p. (J). (gr. 3-5). reprint ed. lib. bdg. 16.95 o.s.i (*1-55736-159-2*, Cornerstone Bks.) Pages, Inc.

—Ramona the Brave. (Ramona Ser.). (J). (gr. 3-5). 190p. pap. 4.99 (*0-8072-1440-X*); 2000. audio 18.00 (*0-8072-7418-6*, YA 821 CXR); 1990. pap. 28.00 incl. audio (*0-8072-7315-5*, YA 821 SP); 1990. audio 23.00 (*0-8072-7277-9*, YA 821 CX) Random Hse. Audio Publishing Group. (Listening Library).

—Ramona the Brave. 1995. (Ramona Ser.). (J). (gr. 3-5). 11.00 (*0-606-08055-4*) Turtleback Bks.

—Ramona the Pest. (Ramona Ser.). (J). (gr. 3-5). 1988. pap. o.p. (*0-440-80051-X*); 1983. pap. 1923. pap. 2.25 o.s.i (*0-440-77209-5*) Dell Publishing.

—Ramona the Pest. 1968. (Ramona Ser.). (Illus.). 192p. (J). (gr. 3-5). 15.99 (*0-688-21721-4*); lib. bdg. 16.89 (*0-688-31721-9*) HarperCollins Children's Bk. Group.

—Ramona the Pest. 1992. (Ramona Ser.). (Illus.). 192p. (J). (gr. 3-5). pap. 5.99 (*0-380-70954-6*, Avon Bks.) Morrow/Avon.

—Ramona the Pest. l.t. ed. 1990. (Ramona Ser.). (Illus.). 175p. (J). (gr. 3-5). reprint ed. lib. bdg. 16.95 o.s.i (*1-55736-158-4*, Cornerstone Bks.) Pages, Inc.

—Ramona the Pest. (Ramona Ser.). 192p. (J). (gr. 3-5). pap. 4.99 (*0-8072-1438-8*); 1991. pap. 28.00 incl. audio (*0-8072-7316-3*, YA 819SP) Random Hse. Audio Publishing Group. (Listening Library).

—Ramona the Pest. 1968. (Ramona Ser.). (J). (gr. 3-5). 11.04 (*0-606-00711-3*) Turtleback Bks.

—Ramona y Su Madre. 1996. (Ramona Ser.). (SPA.). 184p. (J). (gr. 4-7). 9.95 (*84-239-2803-9*) Espasa Calpe, S.A. ESP. *Dist:* AIMS International Bks., Inc.

—Ramona y su Madre. 1997. Orig. Title: Ramona & Her Mother. (SPA., Illus.). 184p. (J). (gr. 2-6). pap. 5.95 (*0-688-15486-7*, Morrow, William & Co.) Morrow/Avon.

—Ramona's World. 1999. (Ramona Ser.). (Illus.). 192p. (J). (gr. 3-5). lib. bdg. 15.89 (*0-688-16818-3*) HarperCollins Children's Bk. Group.

—Ramona's World. (Ramona Ser.). (Illus.). (J). (gr. 3-5). 2001. 208p. pap. 5.99 (*0-380-73272-6*); 1999. 192p. 15.99 (*0-688-16816-7*, Morrow, William & Co.) Morrow/Avon.

—Sister of the Bride. 1963. (Illus.). 288p. (J). (gr. 5 up). 19.89 (*0-688-31742-1*) HarperCollins Children's Bk. Group.

—Viva Ramona. 1996. (Ramona Ser). (SPA.). 192p. (J). (gr. 4-7). 11.95 (*84-239-7120-1*) Espasa Calpe, S.A. ESP. *Dist:* AIMS International Bks., Inc.

Cleary, Jon. The Sundowners. 25.95 (*0-88411-467-8*) Amereon, Ltd.

—The Sundowners. 1973. 382p. pap. 7.95 o.p. (*0-684-13364-4*, Scribner Paper Fiction) Simon & Schuster.

Cleaver, Vera. Belle Pruitt. 1988. 176p. (J). (gr. 4-7). 12.95 (*0-397-32304-2*); lib. bdg. 13.89 (*0-397-32305-0*) HarperCollins Children's Bk. Group.

—Sugar Blue. 1984. (Illus.). 160p. (J). (gr. 5 up). 13.00 o.p. (*0-688-02720-2*) HarperCollins Children's Bk. Group.

—Sweetly Sings the Donkey. 1985. 160p. (J). (gr. 5-9). 12.95 (*0-397-32156-2*); lib. bdg. 12.89 (*0-397-32157-0*) HarperCollins Children's Bk. Group.

Cleaver, Vera & Cleaver, Bill. Delpha Green & Company. 1972. 144p. (J). (gr. 6 up). pap. 2.95 o.p. (*0-397-31236-9*); pap. 2.95 (*0-397-31344-6*, LSC-8) HarperCollins Children's Bk. Group.

—Dust of the Earth. 1975. 160p. (YA). (gr. 7 up). 13.95 (*0-397-31650-X*) HarperCollins Children's Bk. Group.

—A Little Destiny. 1979. (J). (gr. 5 up). 12.95 o.p. (*0-688-41904-6*); lib. bdg. 12.88 o.p. (*0-688-51904-0*) HarperCollins Children's Bk. Group.

—Mock Revolt. 1971. 160p. (J). (gr. 6 up). pap. 1.95 o.p. (*0-397-31237-7*); lib. bdg. 12.89 (*0-397-31238-5*) HarperCollins Children's Bk. Group.

Clements, Andrew. Hey Dad, Could I Borrow Your Hammer? 1999. (J). lib. bdg. (*0-7613-1312-5*) Millbrook Pr., Inc.

Clewes, Dorothy. The End of Summer. 1971. (J). (gr. 7-11). 5.95 o.p. (*0-698-20041-1*) Putnam Publishing Group, The.

—Missing from Home. 1978. (J). (gr. 7 up). 6.95 o.p. (*0-15-254882-3*) Harcourt Children's Bks.

Clifford, Eth. Family for Sale. 1996. 112p. (J). (gr. 4-6). tchr. ed. 15.00 o.s.i (*0-395-73571-8*) Houghton Mifflin Co.

Clifton, Lucille. Everett Anderson's Year, ERS. rev. ed. 1992. (Illus.). 32p. (J). (ps-3). 14.95 o.s.i (*0-8050-2247-3*, Holt, Henry & Co. Bks. For Young Readers) Holt, Henry & Co.

Clough, Brenda W. An Impossumble Summer. 1992. 160p. (J). (gr. 3-6). 14.95 (*0-8027-8150-0*) Walker & Co.

Clymer, Eleanor. Me & the Eggman. 1972. (Illus.). 64p. (J). (gr. 3-6). 7.95 o.p. (*0-525-34775-5*, Dutton) Dutton/Plume.

—A Search for Two Bad Mice. (Illus.). 80p. (J). 1980. (gr. 2-5). 9.95 o.s.i (*0-689-30771-3*, Atheneum); 1991. (gr. 1-4). reprint ed. pap. 3.50 o.s.i (*0-689-71537-4*, Aladdin) Simon & Schuster Children's Publishing.

Cochin, Ira. Love & Life. 2001. 233p. (J). E-Book 8.00 (*1-4010-0350-8*) Xlibris Corp.

Cohen, Barbara. The Orphan Game. 1988. (Illus.). (J). (gr. 3-6). 12.95 o.p. (*0-688-07615-7*) HarperCollins Children's Bk. Group.

Cohen, Laura A., et al. One Family under the Same Sky. 1997. (Illus.). 88p. (J). pap. 13.95 (*1-882801-04-0*) Feelings Factory, Inc.

Cohn, Rachel. The Steps. unabr. ed. 2003. (J). (gr. 3-7). audio 18.00 (*0-8072-1558-9*, Listening Library) Random Hse. Audio Publishing Group.

—The Steps. 2003. (Illus.). 137p. (J). (gr. 3-7). 16.95 (*0-689-84549-9*, Simon & Schuster Children's Publishing) Simon & Schuster Children's Publishing.

Cole, Brock. No More Baths. 1980. (Illus.). 32p. (gr. 1-3). 10.95 o.p. (*0-385-14714-7*); lib. bdg. o.p. (*0-385-14715-5*) Doubleday Publishing.

Cole, Joanna. This Is the Place for Me. l.t. ed. 1993. (J). (ps-2). bds. 19.95 (*0-590-71917-3*) Scholastic, Inc.

Colfer, Eoin. Benny & Omar. 2001. 240p. (YA). (gr. 5 up). pap. 7.95 (*0-86278-567-7*) O'Brien Pr., Ltd., The IRL. *Dist:* Independent Pubs. Group.

Collier, James Lincoln. My Brother Sam Is Dead. 1999. (YA). 9.95 (*1-56137-380-X*) Novel Units, Inc.

—My Brother Sam Is Dead. 2000. (Pathways to Critical Thinking Ser.). 32p. pap. text, stu. ed., tchr.'s training gde. ed. 19.95 (*1-58303-086-7*) Pathways Publishing.

—The Winchesters. 1988. 176p. (YA). (gr. 5 up). lib. bdg. 14.95 o.s.i (*0-02-722831-2*, Simon & Schuster Children's Publishing) Simon & Schuster Children's Publishing.

Collier, James Lincoln & Collier, Christopher. My Brother Sam Is Dead. 1999. 11.95 (*1-56137-823-2*) Novel Units, Inc.

Collins, Pat Lowery. Just Imagine. 2001. (Illus.). 244p. (J). (gr. 5-9). tchr. ed. 15.00 (*0-618-05603-3*) Houghton Mifflin Co.

Colman, Hila. The Family Trap. 1982. 192p. 11.95 o.p. (*0-688-01472-0*, Morrow, William & Co.) Morrow/Avon.

—Nobody Told Me What I Need to Know. 1987. 128p. (J). mass mkt. 2.95 o.s.i (*0-449-70136-0*, Fawcett) Ballantine Bks.

—Suddenly. 1987. 160p. (YA). (gr. 7 up). 12.95 o.p. (*0-688-05865-5*, Morrow, William & Co.) Morrow/Avon.

—Tell Me No Lies. 1978. (Illus.). (J). (gr. 6 up). 6.95 o.p. (*0-517-53229-8*, Crown) Crown Publishing Group.

Coman, Carolyn. Many Stones. 2000. (Illus.). 158p. (J). (gr. 7-12). 15.95 (*1-886910-55-3*, Front Street) Front Street, Inc.

—Many Stones. 2002. 160p. (J). pap. 5.99 (*0-14-230148-5*, Puffin Bks.) Penguin Putnam Bks. for Young Readers.

—Many Stones. l.t. ed. 2001. 24.95 (*0-7862-3399-0*) Thorndike Pr.

—What Jamie Saw. 2002. (Illus.). (J). 12.81 (*0-7587-0330-9*) Book Wholesalers, Inc.

—What Jamie Saw. unabr. ed. 2000. (J). (gr. 4-7). audio 18.00 (*0-8072-6157-2*); 128p. (YA). (gr. 6 up). pap. 28.00 incl. audio (*0-8072-8788-1*, YA268SP) Random Hse. Audio Publishing Group. (Listening Library).

Compestine, Ying Chang. The Story of Noodles. 2002. (Illus.). 32p. (J). (gr. k-3). tchr. ed. 16.95 (*0-8234-1600-3*) Holiday Hse., Inc.

Condra, Estelle. See the Ocean. 2002. (Illus.). 32p. (J). (gr. k-3). (*1-59093-067-3*, Eager Minds Pr.) Warehousing & Fulfillment Specialists, LLC (WFS, LLC).

Cone, Molly. Annie Annie, 001. 1973. (Illus.). (J). (gr. 5-9). 8.95 o.p. (*0-395-06705-7*) Houghton Mifflin Co.

Conford, Ellen. And This Is Laura. (J). (gr. 4-7). 1992. (Illus.). 192p. mass mkt. 4.95 (*0-316-15354-0*); 1977. 14.95 o.s.i (*0-316-15300-1*) Little Brown & Co.

—And This Is Laura. (J). (gr. 4-7). 1990. per. 2.95 (*0-671-72771-0*); 1987. pap. (*0-671-63712-6*); 1984. pap. (*0-671-55504-9*); 1982. pap. (*0-671-46526-0*); 1988. reprint ed. pap. 2.75 (*0-671-67879-5*) Simon & Schuster Children's Publishing. (Simon Pulse).

—Norman Newman & the Werewolf of Walnut Street. 1995. (Norman Newman Ser.). 8.15 o.p. (*0-606-07958-0*) Turtleback Bks.

Conlon-McKenna, Marita. Fields of Home. 1997. (Illus.). 192p. (J). (gr. 3-7). pap. 15.95 (*0-8234-1295-4*) Holiday Hse., Inc.

Connelly, Neil O. St. Michael's Scales. 2002. (Illus.). 320p. (J). (gr. 8 up). pap. 16.95 (*0-439-19445-8*, Levine, Arthur A. Bks.) Scholastic, Inc.

Conrad, Pam. Prairie Songs. (Trophy Book Ser.). (Illus.). 176p. (gr. 5 up). 1987. (YA). pap. 5.99 (*0-06-440206-1*, Harper Trophy); 1985. (J). lib. bdg. 15.89 (*0-06-021337-X*) HarperCollins Children's Bk. Group.

—Prairie Songs. 1985. (Illus.). (J). (gr. 4-7). 14.00 o.s.i (*0-06-021336-1*, 236070) HarperCollins Pubs.

—Prairie Songs. 1995. 19.50 (*0-8446-6812-5*) Smith, Peter Pub., Inc.

—Prairie Songs. 1987. (J). 11.00 (*0-606-03639-3*) Turtleback Bks.

—Prairie Visions: The Life & Times of Solomon Butcher. 1991. (Illus.). 96p. (gr. 5 up). (J). lib. bdg. 16.89 o.p. (*0-06-021375-2*); (YA). 17.00 o.p. (*0-06-021373-6*) HarperCollins Children's Bk. Group.

Cook, Jean T. Room for a Stepdaddy. 1995. (Albert Whitman Concept Bks.). (Illus.). 32p. (J). (ps-3). lib. bdg. 14.95 (*0-8075-7106-7*) Whitman, Albert & Co.

Cooke, Trish. So Much. 1997. (Illus.). 48p. (J). (ps-1). reprint ed. bds. 6.99 (*0-7636-0296-5*) Candlewick Pr.

Cooney, Barbara. The Kellyhorns. 2001. (Lost Treasures Ser.: No. 1). 352p. (J). (Illus.). (gr. 3-7). reprint ed. pap. 1.99 (*0-7868-1522-1*);Bk. 3. pap. 4.99 (*0-7868-1523-X*) Hyperion Bks. for Children. (Volo).

Cooney, Caroline B. Family Reunion. 1990. 176p. (YA). mass mkt. 2.95 o.s.i (*0-553-28573-4*) Bantam Bks.

—Family Reunion. 2004. lib. bdg. 11.99 (*0-385-90167-4*); 208p. (gr. 5). text 9.95 (*0-385-73136-1*) Random Hse. Children's Bks. (Delacorte Bks. for Young Readers).

—Tune in Anytime. 2001. (J). 11.04 (*0-606-21495-X*) Turtleback Bks.

Cooper, Helen. Little Monster Did It! 1996. (Illus.). 32p. (J). (ps-2). 12.99 o.s.i (*0-8037-1993-0*, Dial Bks. for Young Readers) Penguin Putnam Bks. for Young Readers.

Cooper, Ilene. Buddy Love - Now on Video. 1995. 192p. (J). (gr. 5 up). lib. bdg. 13.89 o.p. (*0-06-024664-2*); 13.95 o.p. (*0-06-024663-4*) HarperCollins Children's Bk. Group.

—Buddy Love - Now on Video. 1998. 11.00 (*0-606-15466-3*) Turtleback Bks.

Cooper, Melrose. Gettin' Through Thursday. 2000. (Illus.). 32p. (J). (ps-5). 15.95 (*1-880000-67-9*); pap. 6.95 (*1-58430-014-0*) Lee & Low Bks., Inc.

—Life Magic, ERS. 1996. 128p. (J). (gr. 4-7). 14.95 o.p. (*0-8050-4114-1*, Holt, Henry & Co. Bks. For Young Readers) Holt, Henry & Co.

—Life Riddles. 1995. mass mkt. 4.50 o.s.i (*0-449-70446-7*, Fawcett) Ballantine Bks.

—Life Riddles, ERS. 1994. 88p. (J). (gr. 5-7). 14.95 o.p. (*0-8050-2613-4*, Holt, Henry & Co. Bks. For Young Readers) Holt, Henry & Co.

Corcoran, Barbara. Family Secrets. 1992. 176p. (J). (gr. 3-7). lib. bdg. 13.95 (*0-689-31744-1*, Atheneum) Simon & Schuster Children's Publishing.

—I Am the Universe. 1986. 144p. (J). (gr. 4-8). lib. bdg. 13.95 o.s.i (*0-689-31208-3*, Atheneum) Simon & Schuster Children's Publishing.

Corey, Dorothy. Will There Be a Lap for Me? Levine, Abby, ed. 1992. (Illus.). 24p. (J). (gr. k-2). lib. bdg. 13.95 (*0-8075-9109-2*); pap. 5.95 (*0-8075-9110-6*) Whitman, Albert & Co.

Corey, Shana & Alvarez, Cynthia. Babe: Oops, Pig. 1998. (Early Step into Reading Ser.). (Illus.). (J). (ps-3). pap. 3.99 o.s.i (*0-679-88967-1*) Random Hse., Inc.

Corlett, William. The Bloxworth Blue. 1985. 192p. (YA). (gr. 7 up). 12.95 (*0-06-021343-4*); lib. bdg. 12.89 o.p. (*0-06-021344-2*) HarperCollins Children's Bk. Group.

Cormier, Robert. Eight Plus One. 1985. mass mkt. 2.50 o.s.i (*0-553-25153-8*) Bantam Bks.

—Eight Plus One. 1980. 7.99 o.s.i (*0-394-94595-6*, Pantheon) Knopf Publishing Group.

Corpi, Lucha. Where Fireflies Dance (Ahi, Donde Bailan las Luciernagas) (Illus.). 32p. (J). (gr. 1 up). 2002. pap. 7.95 (*0-89239-177-4*); 1997. (ENG & SPA., 15.95 (*0-89239-145-6*) Children's Bk. Pr.

Cosby, Bill. Shipwreck Saturday. 1998. (Little Bill Books for Beginning Readers Ser.). (Illus.). 40p. (J). (gr. k-3). mass mkt. 3.99 o.s.i (*0-590-95620-5*) Scholastic, Inc.

—The Treasure Hunt. 1997. (Little Bill Books for Beginning Readers Ser.). (Illus.). 40p. (J). (gr. k-3). pap. 13.95 (*0-590-16399-X*); (gr. 1-5). mass mkt. 3.99 (*0-590-95618-3*) Scholastic, Inc.

—The Treasure Hunt. 1997. (Little Bill Books for Beginning Readers Ser.). (J). (gr. k-3). 10.14 (*0-606-12002-5*) Turtleback Bks.

Cotton, Cynthia. Abbie in Stitches, RS. 2005. (*0-374-30004-6*, Farrar, Straus & Giroux (BYR)) Farrar, Straus & Giroux.

Coulter, Hope N. Uncle Chuck's Truck. 1993. (Illus.). 32p. (J). (ps-1). lib. bdg. 13.95 (*0-02-724825-9*, Simon & Schuster Children's Publishing) Simon & Schuster Children's Publishing.

Cousain, Hattie M. When I Was Little. (J). 8.95 (*0-9640459-0-7*) Cole's, C. Consultant & Pubns.

Cousins, Lucy. Maisy Takes a Bath. 2000. (Maisy Bks.). (Illus.). 24p. (J). (ps). bds. 3.29 (*0-7636-1084-4*); 9.99 o.s.i (*0-7636-1082-8*) Candlewick Pr.

—Za-Za's Baby Brother. 2002. (Illus.). (J). 15.74 (*0-7587-4072-7*) Book Wholesalers, Inc.

—Za-Za's Baby Brother. 1997. (Illus.). 32p. (J). (ps-3). reprint ed. bds. 7.99 o.s.i (*0-7636-0337-6*) Candlewick Pr.

Coutler, Hope N. Uncle Chuck's Truck. (Illus.). 32p. (J). 3.98 o.p. (*0-7651-0030-4*) Smithmark Pubs., Inc.

Coville, Bruce. The Skull of Truth. 1997. (Magic Book Shop Ser.). (Illus.). 208p. (YA). (gr. 3-7). 17.00 (*0-15-275457-1*) Harcourt Children's Bks.

Cowley, Joy, contrib. by. Bow Down, Shadrach. 1997. (J). (*0-7802-8307-4*) Wright Group, The.

Cox, Judy. My Family Plays Music. 2003. (Illus.). (J). (gr. k-3). tchr. ed. 16.95 (*0-8234-1591-0*) Holiday Hse., Inc.

Cox, Suzy. Suzanne's 10th Birthday. 1995. 64p. (Orig.). (J). (gr. 1-6). per. 9.95 (*0-9645042-0-0*) Cox, Suzy.

Crawford, Ann Fears. Vangie: The Ghost of the Pines. 2002. 142p. (J). 17.95 (*1-57168-710-6*, Eakin Pr.) Eakin Pr.

The Crayon Box Family: A Story about Responsibility. 1998. (Excellence in Character Series Storybks.). (Illus.). 30p. (J). (gr. k-8). pap. 6.00 (*1-58259-025-7*) Global Classroom, The.

Creech, Sharon. Absolutely Normal Chaos. 240p. (J). (gr. 4 up). 1997. (Illus.). pap. 5.99 (*0-06-440632-6*, Harper Trophy); 1995. 16.99 (*0-06-026989-8*); 1995. lib. bdg. 16.89 (*0-06-026992-8*, Harper Trophy) HarperCollins Children's Bk. Group.

—Absolutely Normal Chaos. 1997. 12.00 (*0-606-10734-7*) Turtleback Bks.

—Bloomability. unabr. ed. 2000. (J). pap. 37.00 incl. audio (*0-8072-8754-7*, YA257SP); (gr. 4-7). audio 25.00 (*0-8072-6152-1*) Random Hse. Audio Publishing Group. (Listening Library).

—Bloomability. 1999. 12.00 (*0-606-17460-5*) Turtleback Bks.

—Walk Two Moons. 2002. (Illus.). (J). 15.00 (*0-7587-0223-X*) Book Wholesalers, Inc.

—Walk Two Moons. (J). 2004. 304p. pap. 6.50 (*0-06-056013-4*, Harper Trophy); 1994. 288p. (gr. 7 up). 16.99 (*0-06-023334-6*); 1994. 288p. (gr. 7 up). lib. bdg. 17.89 (*0-06-023337-0*) HarperCollins Children's Bk. Group.

—Walk Two Moons. 1999. (J). 9.95 (*1-56137-770-8*); 11.95 (*1-56137-771-6*) Novel Units, Inc.

—Walk Two Moons. (Assessment Packs Ser.). (J). 1998. 15p. pap. text, tchr.'s training gde. ed. 15.95 (*1-58303-067-0*); 1997. 32p. (gr. 5 up). pap. text, stu. ed., tchr.'s training gde. ed. 19.95 (*1-58303-030-1*) Pathways Publishing.

—Walk Two Moons. 280p. (J). (gr. 4-6). pap. 4.95 (*0-8072-1509-0*); 1997. pap. 37.00 incl. audio (*0-8072-7872-6*, YA 938 SP) Random Hse. Audio Publishing Group. (Listening Library).

—Walk Two Moons. l.t. ed. 2000. (Illus.). 287p. (J). 21.95 (*0-7862-2773-7*) Thorndike Pr.

—Walk Two Moons. 1996. (J). (gr. 5 up). 12.00 (*0-606-10018-0*) Turtleback Bks.

—Walk Two Moons: Chasing Redbird. 1999. (J). (gr. 3-7). pap. text o.p. (*0-06-449366-0*) HarperCollins Pubs.

—The Wanderer. 2000. (Illus.). 320p. (J). (ps-3). 16.99 (*0-06-027730-0*); lib. bdg. 16.89 (*0-06-027731-9*) HarperCollins Children's Bk. Group. (Cotler, Joanna Bks.).

—The Wanderer. 2002. (Illus.). 320p. (J). (gr. 3-7). pap. 5.99 (*0-06-441032-3*) HarperCollins Pubs.

—The Wanderer. unabr. ed. 2000. (YA). (gr. 4-7). audio 22.00 (*0-8072-8243-X*, Listening Library) Random Hse. Audio Publishing Group.

—The Wanderer. l.t. ed. 2002. (Illus.). 263p. (J). 24.95 (*0-7862-4125-X*) Thorndike Pr.

Cresswell, Helen. Absolute Zero: Being the Second Part of the Bagthorpe Saga. 1978. 180p. (YA). (gr. 5 up). lib. bdg. 14.95 o.p. (*0-02-725550-6*, Simon & Schuster Children's Publishing) Simon & Schuster Children's Publishing.

—Bagthorpes Abroad. 1987. (Bagthorpes Ser.). 192p. (J). (gr. 3-7). reprint ed. pap. 3.95 o.p. (*0-14-031972-7*, Puffin Bks.) Penguin Putnam Bks. for Young Readers.

—The Bagthorpes vs the World: Being the Fourth Part of the Bagthorpe Saga. 1980. (Illus.). 196p. (J). (gr. 1 up). pap. 1.95 o.p. (*0-380-51102-9*, 51102-9, Avon Bks.) Morrow/Avon.

—The Bagthorpes vs. the World: Being the Fourth Part of the Bagthorpe Saga. 1979. 204p. (YA). (gr. 5 up). lib. bdg. 14.95 o.p. (*0-02-725420-8*, Simon & Schuster Children's Publishing) Simon & Schuster Children's Publishing.

—Ordinary Jack: Being the First Part of the Bagthorpe Saga. 1977. 192p. (YA). (gr. 5 up). lib. bdg. 14.95 o.p. (*0-02-725540-9*, Simon & Schuster Children's Publishing) Simon & Schuster Children's Publishing.

—Posy Bates, Again! 1994. (Illus.). 112p. (J). (gr. k-4). mass mkt. 13.95 o.s.i (*0-02-725372-4*, Simon & Schuster Children's Publishing) Simon & Schuster Children's Publishing.

Crew, Linda. Nekomah Creek. (Illus.). 192p. (gr. 4-7). 1993. pap. text 3.99 o.s.i (*0-440-40788-5*); 1991. (J). 14.00 o.s.i (*0-385-30442-0*, Delacorte Pr.) Dell Publishing.

—Nekomah Creek. 2001. (Illus.). 192p. (gr. 4-7). pap. text 12.00 (*0-375-89506-X*, Random Hse. Bks. for Young Readers); 1991. (J). o.s.i (*0-385-30379-3*, Dell Books for Young Readers) Random Hse. Children's Bks.

—Nekomah Creek. 1991. 9.09 (*0-606-05506-1*) Turtleback Bks.

—Nekomah Creek Christmas. 1995. (Illus.). 160p. (J). (gr. 4-7). pap. 3.99 o.s.i (*0-440-41099-1*, Yearling) Random Hse. Children's Bks.

—Nekomah Creek Christmas. 1995. (J). 9.34 o.p. (*0-606-07940-8*) Turtleback Bks.

—Someday I'll Laugh about This. 1990. 176p. (YA). 14.95 o.s.i (*0-385-30083-2*) Doubleday Publishing.

Crews, Donald. Bigmama's. 2001. (J). (gr. k-3). pap. 16.90 incl. audio (*0-8045-6840-5*, 6840) Spoken Arts, Inc.

Crofford, Emily. Stories from the Blue Road. 1981. (Good Time Library). (Illus.). 168p. (J). (gr. 2-5). lib. bdg. 13.50 o.p. (*0-87614-189-0*, Carolrhoda Bks.) Lerner Publishing Group.

Cruise, Robin. The Top-Secret Journal of Fiona Claire Jardin. 1998. 160p. (J). (gr. 4-7). 13.00 (*0-15-201383-0*) Harcourt Children's Bks.

Crum, Shutta. Spitting Image. 2003. 224p. (J). tchr. ed. 15.00 (*0-618-23477-2*, Clarion Bks.) Houghton Mifflin Co. Trade & Reference Div.

Cry, the Beloved Country. 1999. (YA). 11.95 (*1-56137-355-9*) Novel Units, Inc.

Cullen, Lynn. The Three Lives of Harris Harper. 1998. 160p. (J). pap. 3.99 (*0-380-72901-6*, Harper Trophy) HarperCollins Children's Bk. Group.

—The Three Lives of Harris Harper. 1996. (Illus.). 160p. (J). (gr. 4-7). tchr. ed. 14.95 o.p. (*0-395-73680-3*, Clarion Bks.) Houghton Mifflin Co. Trade & Reference Div.

—The Three Lives of Harris Harper. 1998. 10.04 (*0-606-13976-1*) Turtleback Bks.

Curtis, Christopher Paul. The Watsons Go to Birmingham - 1963. 1999. 240p. (gr. 5-8). mass mkt. 2.99 o.s.i (*0-440-22836-0*) Bantam Bks.

—The Watsons Go to Birmingham - 1963. 1998. 15p. pap., stu. ed., tchr.'s training gde. ed. 15.95 (*1-58303-068-9*) Pathways Publishing.

—The Watsons Go to Birmingham - 1963. 210p. (YA). (gr. 5 up). pap. 5.50 (*0-8072-8336-3*); 2000. (J). pap. 37.00 incl. audio (*0-8072-8335-5*, YA166SP) Random Hse. Audio Publishing Group. (Listening Library).

—The Watsons Go to Birmingham - 1963. 2000. 224p. (YA). (gr. 5-7). mass mkt. 5.99 (*0-440-22800-X*, Laurel Leaf); 1997. 224p. (gr. 4-10). pap. text 6.50 (*0-440-41412-1*, Dell Books for Young Readers); 1997. (YA). pap. o.s.i (*0-440-41431-8*, Dell Books for Young Readers) Random Hse. Children's Bks.

—The Watsons Go to Birmingham - 1963. l.t. ed. 2000. (Illus.). 260p. (J). (ps up). 22.95 (*0-7862-2741-9*) Thorndike Pr.

—The Watsons Go to Birmingham - 1963. 1997. (YA). 12.04 (*0-606-10993-5*) Turtleback Bks.

—The Watsons Go to Birmingham—1963. 1995. 224p. (gr. 4-7). text 16.95 (*0-385-32175-9*, Dell Books for Young Readers) Random Hse. Children's Bks.

Curtis, Marci. Big Sister, Little Sister. 2002. 40p. pap. 6.99 (*0-14-230078-0*) Penguin Putnam Bks. for Young Readers.

Cushman, Karen. The Ballad of Lucy Whipple. 1996. 208p. (YA). (gr. 7-9). tchr. ed. 15.00 (*0-395-72806-1*, Clarion Bks.) Houghton Mifflin Co. Trade & Reference Div.

Cutler, Jane. Family Dinner, RS. (Sunburst Ser.). 112p. (J). 1995. (gr. 4-7). pap. 5.95 (*0-374-42258-3*, Sunburst); 1992. (Illus.). (gr. 3 up). 14.00 o.p. (*0-374-32267-8*, Farrar, Straus & Giroux (BYR)) Farrar, Straus & Giroux.

—Family Dinner. 1995. (ANTA Series of Distinguished Plays). (J). 11.00 (*0-606-07496-1*) Turtleback Bks.

—Rats!, RS. abr. ed. 1996. (Illus.). 114p. (J). (gr. 4-7). 14.00 o.p. (*0-374-36181-9*, Farrar, Straus & Giroux (BYR)) Farrar, Straus & Giroux.

Cuyler, Margery. Daisy's Crazy Thanksgiving, ERS. 1990. (Illus.). 32p. (J). (ps-3). 14.95 o.s.i (*0-8050-0559-5*, Holt, Henry & Co. Bks. For Young Readers) Holt, Henry & Co.

Czernecki, Stefan. Don't Forget Winona. 2004. 32p. (J). (ps-2). 14.99 (*0-06-027197-3*) HarperCollins Children's Bk. Group.

Dabney, Colleen. A View from Saturday. 1997. (Literature Unit Ser.). (Illus.). 48p. (YA). (gr. 5-8). pap., tchr. ed. 7.99 (*1-57690-348-6*, TCM2348) Teacher Created Materials, Inc.

Dadey, Debbie & Jones, Marcia Thornton. Triplet Trouble & the Cookie Contest. 1996. (Triplet Trouble Ser.: No. 5). (J). (gr. 2-4). 8.70 o.p. (*0-606-12009-2*) Turtleback Bks.

—Triplet Trouble & the Red Heart Race. 1996. (Triplet Trouble Ser.: No. 3). (Illus.). (J). (gr. 2-4). mass mkt. 2.99 (*0-590-58106-6*) Scholastic, Inc.

—Triplet Trouble & the Red Heart Race. 1996. (Triplet Trouble Ser.: No. 3). (J). (gr. 2-4). 8.70 o.p. (*0-606-08650-1*) Turtleback Bks.

Dahl, Borghild. Under This Roof. 1985. (J). (gr. 7 up). 5.95 o.p. (*0-525-41868-7*, Dutton) Dutton/Plume.

Dahl, Roald. Matilda. 1996. (J). 11.04 (*0-606-02745-9*) Turtleback Bks.

Dahlstedt, Marden. The Stopping Place. 1976. (Illus.). 160p. (J). (gr. 5 up). 6.95 o.p. (*0-399-20496-2*) Putnam Publishing Group, The.

Dana, Barbara. Necessary Parties. (J). 1991. mass mkt. o.s.i (*0-553-54043-2*, Dell Books for Young Readers); 1987. 320p. mass mkt. 3.50 o.s.i (*0-553-26984-4*, Starfire) Random Hse. Children's Bks.

Daniel, Alan & Munsch, Robert. Good Families Don't. 1991. (Illus.). 32p. (ps-3). pap. text 5.99 (*0-440-40565-3*) Dell Publishing.

Daniels, Lucy. In Good Faith, Vol. 4. 2003. (Horseshoe Trilogies). (Illus.). 144p. (J). pap. 4.99 (*0-7868-1747-X*, Volo) Hyperion Bks. for Children.

Danziger, Paula. Amber Brown is Green with Envy. 2003. (Illus.). 160p. (J). 15.99 (*0-399-23181-1*, G. P. Putnam's Sons) Penguin Putnam Bks. for Young Readers.

—Can You Sue Your Parents for Malpractice? 1979. 266p. (J). (gr. 7 up). 6.95 o.s.i (*0-385-28112-9*, Delacorte Pr.) Dell Publishing.

—Can You Sue Your Parents for Malpractice? 1998. 160p. (J). (gr. 5-9). pap. 4.99 (*0-698-11688-7*, PaperStar) Penguin Putnam Bks. for Young Readers.

—Can You Sue Your Parents for Malpractice? 1980. 144p. (YA). (gr. 7 up). mass mkt. 3.99 o.p. (*0-440-91066-8*, Laurel Leaf) Random Hse. Children's Bks.

—Everyone Else's Parents Said Yes. 1989. 128p. (J). (gr. 3-7). 13.95 o.s.i (*0-385-29805-6*, Delacorte Pr.) Dell Publishing.

—Everyone Else's Parents Said Yes. 1990. (J). pap. o.s.i (*0-440-80180-X*, Dell Books for Young Readers) Random Hse. Children's Bks.

—Forever Amber Brown. 1996. (Amber Brown Ser.: No.5). (Illus.). 112p. (J). (gr. 3-6). 14.99 (*0-399-22932-9*, G. P. Putnam's Sons) Penguin Group (USA) Inc.

—Forever Amber Brown. 1997. (Amber Brown Ser.: No.5). (J). (gr. 3-6). 10.04 (*0-606-11345-2*) Turtleback Bks.

—Make Like a Tree & Leave. l.t. ed. 1993. (J). (gr. 1-8). 16.95 o.p. (*0-7451-1912-3*, Galaxy Children's Large Print) BBC Audiobooks America.

—Make Like a Tree & Leave. 128p. (J). (gr. 4-7). 1992. pap. 3.99 o.p. (*0-440-40577-7*); 1990. 13.95 o.s.i (*0-385-30151-0*, Delacorte Pr.) Dell Publishing.

—Make Like a Tree & Leave. 1998. 126p. (J). (gr. 4-7). pap. 4.99 (*0-698-11686-0*, PaperStar) Penguin Putnam Bks. for Young Readers.

—Make Like a Tree & Leave. (J). 1992. pap. o.s.i (*0-440-80305-5*); 1990. o.s.i (*0-385-30195-2*) Random Hse. Children's Bks. (Dell Books for Young Readers).

—Make Like a Tree & Leave. 1998. (J). 11.04 (*0-606-13593-6*) Turtleback Bks.

—P. S. Longer Letter Later: A Novel in Letters. 1999. 11.04 (*0-606-17062-6*) Turtleback Bks.

—United Tates of America. 2002. (J). (gr. 4-7). lib. bdg. 20.00 incl. audio (*0-9717540-5-5*, 02002) Full Cast Audio.

Danziger, Paula & Martin, Ann M. P. S. Longer Letter Later: A Novel in Letters. unabr. ed. 1999. 240p. (J). pap. 35.00 incl. audio (*0-8072-8085-2*, YA998SP, Listening Library) Random Hse. Audio Publishing Group.

—Snail Mail No More. unabr. ed. 2000. (J). (gr. 3-6). audio 30.00 (*0-8072-8412-2*, YA194CX); 307p. (gr. 4-6). pap. 35.00 incl. audio (*0-8072-8413-0*) Random Hse. Audio Publishing Group. (Listening Library).

—Snail Mail No More. (Illus.). (J). 2001. 320p. (gr. 3-7). mass mkt. 4.99 (*0-439-06336-1*); 2000. 307p. (gr. 4-7). pap. 16.95 (*0-439-06335-3*, Scholastic Reference) Scholastic, Inc.

Danziger, Paula, et al. United Tates of America. 2003. 144p. (J). mass mkt. 5.99 *(0-590-69222-4,* Scholastic Paperbacks) Scholastic, Inc.

Daringer, Helen F. Stepsister Sally. 1966. (Illus.). (J). (gr. 3-7). pap. 1.45 o.p. *(0-15-684951-8,* Voyager Bks./Libros Viajeros) Harcourt Children's Bks.

Darrow, Sharon. The Painters of Lexieville. 2003. 192p. (YA). 16.99 *(0-7636-1437-8)* Candlewick Pr.

Davidson, Alice Joyce. Charlie Helps His Mother. 1996. (Charlie the Gentle Bear Ser.). (Illus.). 16p. (J). (ps-k). 5.95 *(0-88271-531-3,* 10118) Regina Pr., Malhame & Co.

Davidson, Neil. The Sweet Revenge of Melissa Chavez: A Novel. 1995. 178p. (YA). (gr. 9 up). lib. bdg. 18.95 o.p. *(0-936389-39-7)* Tudor Pubs., Inc.

Davies, Nicola. Everything Happens on Mondays. 1995. 64p. (J). (gr. 4). pap. 9.95 *(0-8464-4835-1)* Beekman Pubs., Inc.

Davis, C. L. The Christmas Barn. 2001. 200p. (J). 12.95 *(1-58485-414-6,* American Girl) Pleasant Co. Pubns.

Davis, Deborah. My Brother Has AIDS. 1994. 192p. (J). (gr. 4-8). 15.00 *(0-689-31922-3,* Atheneum) Simon & Schuster Children's Publishing.

Davis, Jenny. Good-Bye & Keep Cold. 1987. 224p. (J). (gr. 7 up). pap. 16.95 o.p. *(0-531-05715-1,* Orchard Bks.) Scholastic, Inc.

—Goodbye & Keep Cold. 1987. 224p. (YA). (gr. 7 up). mass mkt. 15.99 o.p. *(0-531-08315-2,* Orchard Bks.) Scholastic, Inc.

Davoll, Barbara. Christopher & His Family. 2003. (Christopher Churchmouse Ser.). (Illus.). 128p. (J). 14.99 *(0-8423-5735-1)* Tyndale Hse. Pubs.

Day, Alexandra. Carl, RS. 2005. (Carl Ser.). (J). (ps-1). *(0-374-31088-2,* Farrar, Straus & Giroux (BYR)) Farrar, Straus & Giroux.

Day, Clarence. Life with Father. 1972. (Enriched Classics Ser.). (J). (gr. 9 up). mass mkt. 1.50 o.s.i *(0-671-48806-6,* Pocket) Simon & Schuster.

de Brunhoff, Laurent. Babar Learns to Cook. 1989. (Babar Ser.). (Illus.). (J). (ps-3). 8.45 o.p. *(0-606-12173-0)* Turtleback Bks.

De Jong, Dola. By Marvelous Agreement. 1962. (J). (gr. 7-11). lib. bdg. 4.99 o.p. *(0-394-90992-5,* Knopf Bks. for Young Readers) Random Hse. Children's Bks.

De Lint, Charles. The Dreaming Place. 2002. (Firebird Ser.). 160p. (J). pap. 5.99 *(0-14-230218-X)* Penguin Putnam Bks. for Young Readers.

—The Dreaming Place. 1990. (Dragonflight Ser.). (Illus.). 144p. (YA). (gr. 7 up). 14.95 *(0-689-31571-6,* Atheneum) Simon & Schuster Children's Publishing.

De Messieres, Nicole. Reina the Galgo. 1981. 224p. (J). (gr. 7 up). 9.95 o.p. *(0-525-66749-0,* Dutton Children's Bks.) Penguin Putnam Bks. for Young Readers.

de Paola, Tomie. Big Anthony: His Story. 2002. (Illus.). (J). 23.64 *(0-7587-2090-4)* Book Wholesalers, Inc.

—Big Anthony: His Story. 2001. (Illus.). 32p. (ps-3). pap. 5.99 *(0-698-11893-6)* Penguin Putnam Bks. for Young Readers.

—Things Will Never Be the Same. 2004. pap. 5.99 *(0-14-240155-2,* Puffin Bks.) Penguin Putnam Bks. for Young Readers.

De Saint Mars, Dominique. Lily Doesn't Want to Sleep. 1993. (About Me Ser.). (Illus.). 24p. (J). (gr. 1-4). lib. bdg. 12.79 o.p. *(0-89565-978-6)* Child's World, Inc.

—Lily Fights with Her Mother. 1993. (About Me Ser.). (Illus.). 24p. (J). (gr. 2-4). lib. bdg. 12.79 o.p. *(0-89565-980-8)* Child's World, Inc.

De Vries, Anke. Bruises. 1997. 176p. (YA). (gr. 9-12). mass mkt. 4.50 o.s.i *(0-440-22694-5,* Dell Books for Young Readers) Random Hse. Children's Bks.

De Vries, David. Home at Last. 1992. 160p. (J). (gr. 4-7). pap. 3.25 o.s.i *(0-440-40621-8)* Dell Publishing.

De Young, C. Coco. A Letter to Mrs. Roosevelt. 112p. (gr. 3-7). 2000. pap. text 4.50 *(0-440-41529-2,* Yearling); 1999. text 14.95 o.s.i *(0-385-32633-5,* Dell Books for Young Readers) Random Hse. Children's Bks.

DeClements, Barthe. Liar, Liar. 1998. (Accelerated Reader Bks.). 144p. (J). (gr. 3-7). lib. bdg. 14.95 *(0-7614-5021-1,* Cavendish Children's Bks.) Cavendish, Marshall Corp.

Deem, James M. Three NBs of Julian Drew. 1994. 224p. (J). (gr. 7 up). tchr. ed. 16.00 o.s.i *(0-395-69453-1)* Houghton Mifflin Co.

Degens, T. Freya on the Wall. 1997. 288p. (J). 19.00 o.s.i *(0-15-200210-3)* Harcourt Trade Pubs.

DeJong, Meindert. Hurry Home, Candy. 1972. (Harper Trophy Bks.). 13.00 *(0-606-12348-2)* Turtleback Bks.

Delaney, Michael. Deep Doo-Doo. 1996. 176p. (J). (gr. 3-6). 14.99 o.s.i *(0-525-45647-3,* Dutton Children's Bks.) Penguin Putnam Bks. for Young Readers.

Delton, Judy. Angel Bites the Bullet. 2000. (Illus.). 112p. (J). (gr. 4-6). tchr. ed. 15.00 *(0-618-04085-4)* Houghton Mifflin Co. Trade & Reference Div.

—Angel in Charge. (Illus.). (J). (gr. 4-6). 1999. 148p. pap. 4.95 *(0-395-96061-4)*; 1985. 160p. tchr. ed. 16.00 *(0-395-37488-X)* Houghton Mifflin Co.

—Angel in Charge. 1990. 160p. (J). (gr. k-6). reprint ed. pap. 2.95 o.s.i *(0-440-40264-6,* Yearling) Random Hse. Children's Bks.

—Angel in Charge. 1999. (Illus.). (J). 11.00 *(0-606-18206-3)* Turtleback Bks.

—Moving Up. 1995. (Lottery Luck Ser.: Bk. 4). (Illus.). 96p. (J). (gr. 4-7). pap. 3.95 *(0-7868-1021-1)* Hyperion Paperbacks for Children.

—Next Stop, the White House! 1995. (Lottery Luck Ser.: No. 6). (Illus.). 96p. (J). (gr. 2-5). pap. 3.95 *(0-7868-1023-8)* Hyperion Paperbacks for Children.

—Ship Ahoy! 1995. (Lottery Luck Ser.: Bk. 5). (Illus.). 96p. (J). (gr. 2-5). pap. 3.95 *(0-7868-1022-X)* Hyperion Paperbacks for Children.

—Ten's a Crowd! 1995. (Lottery Luck Ser.: Bk. 3). (Illus.). 96p. (J). (gr. 2-5). pap. 3.95 *(0-7868-1020-3)* Hyperion Paperbacks for Children.

—Winning Ticket! 1995. (Lottery Luck Ser.: Bk. 1). (Illus.). 96p. (J). (gr. 2-5). pap. 3.95 *(0-7868-1018-1)* Hyperion Paperbacks for Children.

Delton, Julie. My Uncle Nikos. 1983. (Illus.). 32p. (J). (gr. 1-4). o.p. *(0-690-04164-0)*; lib. bdg. 11.89 *(0-690-04165-9)* HarperCollins Children's Bk. Group.

Dennis-Wyeth, Sharon. Something Beautiful. 2002. 32p. (J). pap. 6.99 *(0-440-41210-2,* Random Hse. Bks. for Young Readers) Random Hse. Children's Bks.

D'Erasmo, Stacey. Tea: A Novel. 2001. (Washington Square Press Enriched Classic Ser.). (Illus.). (J). 20.00 *(0-606-20936-0)* Turtleback Bks.

Derby, Pat. Grams, Her Boyfriend, My Family, & Me. 1997. 12.00 *(0-606-11413-0)* Turtleback Bks.

—Grams, Her Boyfriend, My Family & Me, RS. 256p. (YA). (gr. 5 up). 1997. pap. 7.95 *(0-374-42790-9,* Sunburst); 1994. 16.00 o.p. *(0-374-38131-3,* Farrar, Straus & Giroux (BYR)) Farrar, Straus & Giroux.

Derman, Martha. And Philippa Makes Four. 1984. 128p. (J). (gr. 3-6). 8.95 o.p. *(0-02-728670-3,* Simon & Schuster Children's Publishing) Simon & Schuster Children's Publishing.

Desai Hidier, Tanuja. Born Confused. 2003. 512p. (J). pap. 7.99 *(0-439-51011-2,* PUSH) Scholastic, Inc.

Desbarats, Peter. Gabrielle & Selena. 1968. (Illus.). (J). (gr. k-3). 5.50 o.p. *(0-15-230514-9)* Harcourt Children's Bks.

Desnick, Chaim. The Little Room. 2004. (Illus.). 32p. (J). (ps-1). 14.95 *(1-930143-81-8)*; pap. 9.95 *(1-930143-86-9)* Pitspopany Pr.

Dewan, Ted. Top Secret. 1997. 32p. (J). 15.95 o.s.i *(0-385-32324-7,* Doubleday Bks. for Young Readers) Random Hse. Children's Bks.

Dewees, Eleanor. Those Four & Plenty More. Van Dolson, Bobbie J., ed. 1981. (J). (gr. 2-5). pap. 6.95 o.p. *(0-8280-0092-1)* Review & Herald Publishing Assn.

Dickinson, Mary & Charlotte. Alex's Bed. Date not set. (J). pap. text *(0-05-004389-7)* Addison-Wesley Longman, Inc.

DiMarco, Carol. Alchemy. 2nd rev. ed. 2002. (Illus.). 25p. (J). pap. 11.95 *(1-886383-65-0,* Little Blue Works) Windstorm Creative Ltd.

Dines, Carol. Talk to Me: Stories & a Novella. 1999. (Laurel-Leaf Bks.). 240p. (YA). (gr. 7 up). mass mkt. 4.50 o.s.i *(0-440-22026-2,* Dell Books for Young Readers) Random Hse. Children's Bks.

—Talk to Me: Stories & a Novella. 1999. 10.55 *(0-606-16451-0)* Turtleback Bks.

Dionetti, Michelle V. Coal Mine Peaches. 1991. (Illus.). 32p. (J). (ps-2). 14.95 o.p. *(0-531-05948-0)*; mass mkt. 14.99 o.p. *(0-531-08548-1)* Scholastic, Inc. (Orchard Bks.).

DiPucchio, Kelly S. Bed Hogs. Date not set. (J). 15.99 *(0-7868-1884-0)* Hyperion Bks. for Children.

DiSalvo-Ryan, DyAnne. Spaghetti Park. 2002. (Illus.). (J). (gr. 3). tchr. ed. 16.95 *(0-8234-1682-8)* Holiday Hse., Inc.

Disney Staff. The Lion King. 1999. (Disney's Read-Aloud Storybooks Ser.). (SPA., Illus.). 64p. (J). (ps-2). 4.99 o.p. *(0-7364-0130-X)* Mouse Works.

Distribution Media Staff & Rylant, Cynthia. The Relatives Came. 1986. (J). 14.00 incl. audio *(0-676-31727-8)* Random Hse., Inc.

Dixon, Sylvia W. Sug Learns How to Cook. Angaza, Mai T., ed. 1991. (Illus.). 28p. (Orig.). (J). (gr. 3-10). pap. 5.00 *(0-9652951-0-9)* Dixon, S. W.

Dorris, Michael. Morning Girl. 80p. 1994. (YA). (gr. 4-7). pap. 4.95 *(1-56282-661-1)*; 1992. (J). 12.95 o.p. *(1-56282-284-5)*; 1992. (YA). (gr. 3 up). lib. bdg. 13.49 o.s.i *(1-56282-285-3)* Hyperion Bks. for Children.

—Morning Girl. 1999. 80p. (J). (gr. 4 up). pap. text 4.99 *(0-7868-1372-5)*; mass mkt. 4.99 *(0-7868-1358-X)* Hyperion Pr.

—Morning Girl. 1994. (J). 11.14 *(0-606-06583-0)* Turtleback Bks.

Dorros, Arthur. La Isla. 1995. (SPA., Illus.). 48p. (J). (gr. k-3). 16.99 *(0-525-45422-5,* DT0992, Dutton Children's Bks.) Penguin Putnam Bks. for Young Readers.

Dotlich, Rebecca Kai. Mama Loves. 2004. (Illus.). 32p. (J). 14.99 *(0-06-029407-8)*; lib. bdg. 15.89 *(0-06-029408-6)* HarperCollins Pubs.

Doucet, Sharon Arms. Fiddle Fever. l.t. ed. 2001. 174p. (J). 20.95 *(0-7862-3548-9)* Gale Group.

—Fiddle Fever. 2000. (Illus.). 176p. (J). (gr. 5-9). tchr. ed. 15.00 *(0-618-04324-1,* Clarion Bks.) Houghton Mifflin Co. Trade & Reference Div.

Dowell, Ruth I. Pollyanna Herself. 1988. (Illus.). 44p. (J). (ps-6). pap. 6.00 *(0-945842-08-2)* Pollyanna Productions.

Dower, Laura. Sink or Swim. 2003. (From the Files of Madison Finn Ser.: No. 13). 176p. (J). pap. 4.99 *(0-7868-1735-6,* Volo) Hyperion Bks. for Children.

Dragonwagon, Crescent. The Sun Begun. 1999. (J). 16.00 *(0-689-81159-4,* Atheneum) Simon & Schuster Children's Publishing.

Draper, C. G. A Holiday Year. 1988. (J). (gr. 5-9). 12.95 o.p. *(0-316-19203-1)* Little Brown & Co.

Ducey, Jean S. The Bittersweet Time. 1995. 115p. (J). (gr. 5-8). 13.00 o.p. *(0-8028-5096-0)* Eerdmans, William B. Publishing Co.

Duder, Tessa. Jellybean. 112p. (J). (gr. 3-7). 1988. pap. 3.95 o.p. *(0-14-032114-4,* Puffin Bks.); 1986. 10.95 o.p. *(0-670-81235-8,* Viking Children's Bks.) Penguin Putnam Bks. for Young Readers.

Duey, Kathleen. The Silver Thread. 2001. (Unicorn's Secret Ser.: No. 2). (Illus.). 80p. (J). pap. 3.99 *(0-689-84270-8,* Aladdin) Simon & Schuster Children's Publishing.

Duffey, Betsy. Fur-Ever Yours, Booker Jones. 128p. 2002. (YA). (gr. 5-9). pap. 4.99 *(0-14-230215-5,* Puffin Bks.); 2001. (J). (gr. 4-6). 15.99 *(0-670-89287-4,* Viking Children's Bks.) Penguin Putnam Bks. for Young Readers.

—Utterly Yours, Booker Jones. 1995. (Illus.). 128p. (YA). (gr. 3 up). 14.99 o.p. *(0-670-86007-7,* Viking Children's Bks.) Penguin Putnam Bks. for Young Readers.

Duffy, Daniel M., illus. Meet the Boxcar Children. 1998. (Adventures of Benny & Watch: Vol. No. 1). 46p. (J). (gr. 1-3). pap. 3.95 *(0-8075-5034-5)* Whitman, Albert & Co.

Duffy, James. Cleaver & Company. 1991. 144p. (J). (gr. 4-6). lib. bdg. 13.95 o.s.i *(0-684-19371-X,* Atheneum) Simon & Schuster Children's Publishing.

Dunbar, James. When I Was Young. 1999. (Picture Bks.). (Illus.). 32p. (J). (ps-3). lib. bdg. 15.95 *(1-57505-359-4,* Carolrhoda Bks.) Lerner Publishing Group.

Dunlop, Eileen. The Ghost by the Sea. 1996. 192p. (J). (gr. 4-7). tchr. ed. 15.95 *(0-8234-1264-4)* Holiday Hse., Inc.

—Websters' Leap. 1995. (Illus.). 176p. (J). (gr. 4-7). 15.95 *(0-8234-1193-1)* Holiday Hse., Inc.

Dupasquier, Philippe. I Can't Sleep. 1990. (Illus.). 40p. (J). (ps-1). 13.95 o.p. *(0-531-05874-3)*; lib. bdg. 13.99 o.p. *(0-531-08474-4)* Scholastic, Inc. (Orchard Bks.).

Durbin, William. The Journal of C. J. Jackson: A Dust Bowl Migrant, Oklahoma to California, 1935. 2002. (My Name Is America Ser.). (Illus.). 144p. (J). (gr. 4-9). pap. 10.95 *(0-439-15306-9,* Scholastic Pr.) Scholastic, Inc.

—Song of Sampo Lake. 2002. 224p. (gr. 4-7). lib. bdg. 17.99 *(0-385-90055-4)*; (gr. 5 up). text 15.95 *(0-385-32731-5)* Dell Publishing. (Delacorte Pr.).

—Song of Sampo Lake. 2004. 224p. (gr. 5). pap. text 5.50 *(0-440-22899-9,* Yearling) Random Hse. Children's Bks.

Dutton, Cheryl. Not in Here, Dad! 1989. (Illus.). 32p. (J). (ps-2). 10.95 o.p. *(0-8120-6105-5)* Barron's Educational Series, Inc.

Eason, Cassandra. Benjamin Helps Mommy & Daddy. 1998. (Illus.). 16p. (J). (ps-k). 4.95 *(0-8069-9516-5)* Sterling Publishing Co., Inc.

Eastern, Anne G. The Picolinis. 1988. 160p. (Orig.). (J). (gr. 2-5). pap. 2.75 o.s.i *(0-553-15566-0,* Skylark) Random Hse. Children's Bks.

Easton, Kelly. The Life History of a Star. 208p. (YA). 2002. pap. 6.99 *(0-689-85270-3,* Simon Pulse); 2001. (Illus.). (gr. 7 up). 16.00 *(0-689-83134-X,* McElderry, Margaret K.) Simon & Schuster Children's Publishing.

—The Life History of a Star. l.t. ed. 2002. (Young Adult Ser.). 200p. 22.95 *(0-7862-4786-X)* Thorndike Pr.

—Walking on Air. 2004. (Illus.). 240p. (J). 16.95 *(0-689-84875-7,* McElderry, Margaret K.) Simon & Schuster Children's Publishing.

Eccles, Mary. By Lizzie. 128p. (J). 2003. (Illus.). pap. 4.99 *(0-14-250036-4,* Puffin Bks.); 2001. (gr. 3-5). 15.99 o.s.i *(0-8037-2608-2,* Dial Bks. for Young Readers) Penguin Putnam Bks. for Young Readers.

Eckert, Allan W. Incident at Hawk's Hill. l.t. ed. 1974. lib. bdg. 7.95 o.p. *(0-8161-6176-3,* Macmillan Reference USA) Gale Group.

—Incident at Hawk's Hill. (Illus.). 1995. 224p. (J). (gr. 5-9). pap. 6.99 *(0-316-20948-1)*; 1971. 173p. (YA). (gr. 7 up). 15.95 o.p. *(0-316-20866-3)* Little Brown & Co.

—Incident at Hawk's Hill. 1972. 192p. (J). (gr. 7 up). mass mkt. 0.75 o.s.i *(0-440-94020-6,* Laurel Leaf) Random Hse. Children's Bks.

—Incident at Hawk's Hill. 1996. (YA). (gr. 7 up). 19.50 o.p. *(0-8446-6848-6)* Smith, Peter Pub., Inc.

—Incident at Hawk's Hill. 1971. 13.00 *(0-606-07163-6)* Turtleback Bks.

Ehrlich, Amy. Parents in the Pigpen, Pigs in the Tub. 1997. (Illus.). 40p. (J). (ps-3). pap. 6.99 *(0-14-056297-4,* Puffin Bks.) Penguin Putnam Bks. for Young Readers.

—When I Was Your Age: Original Stories about Growing Up. 2001. (Illus.). (J). 14.04 *(0-606-20988-3)* Turtleback Bks.

—Zeek Silver Moon. 1972. (Illus.). 32p. (J). (ps-3). 7.95 o.p. *(0-8037-9825-3)*; 7.89 o.p. *(0-8037-9826-1)* Penguin Putnam Bks. for Young Readers. (Dial Bks. for Young Readers).

Ehrlich, Amy, ed. When I Was Your Age: Original Stories about Growing Up, Vol. 2. 2002. 192p. (YA). (gr. 4-9). bds. 7.99 *(0-7636-1734-2)* Candlewick Pr.

Eilenberg, Max. Cowboy Kid. 2000. (Illus.). 32p. (J). (ps-3). 15.99 *(0-7636-1058-5)* Candlewick Pr.

Eisch, Beverly. In the Woods. 2002. 12p. (J). pap. 5.00 *(0-9724517-0-6)* Eisch, Beverly.

Eisenberg, Lisa. Lexie on Her Own. 1992. 128p. (J). (gr. 3-7). 13.00 o.p. *(0-670-84489-6,* Viking Children's Bks.) Penguin Putnam Bks. for Young Readers.

Ellis, Carol. Once upon a Mix-Up. 2001. (Full House Sisters Ser.: No. 14). 160p. (J). (gr. 4-6). pap. 3.99 *(0-671-04094-4,* Simon Spotlight) Simon & Schuster Children's Publishing.

—Stepdaughter. 1993. 176p. (J). (gr. 7-9). mass mkt. 3.25 o.p. *(0-590-46044-7)* Scholastic, Inc.

Ellis, Caroljean. The Picnic. 1996. (Tales of Little Angels: Bk. 4). (Illus.). 40p. (Orig.). (J). (gr. k-4). pap. 8.95 *(1-889383-03-1)* Angel Pubns.

Ellis, Mel. An Eagle to the Wind, ERS. 1978. (J). o.p. *(0-03-022766-6,* Holt, Henry & Co. Bks. For Young Readers) Holt, Henry & Co.

Ellis, Sarah. Next-Door Neighbors. 1992. 160p. (J). (gr. 4-7). pap. 3.25 o.s.i *(0-440-40620-X)* Dell Publishing.

—Next-Door Neighbors. 1990. 160p. (J). (gr. 4-7). 16.00 *(0-689-50495-0,* McElderry, Margaret K.) Simon & Schuster Children's Publishing.

Elwin, Rosamund & Paulse, Michele. Asha's Mums. 1990. (Illus.). 24p. (J). (ps-3). pap. 7.95 *(0-88961-143-2)* Women's Pr. CAN. *Dist:* Univ. of Toronto Pr.

Emerson, Charlotte. Amy's True Prize. 1999. (Little Women Journals Ser.). 10.04 *(0-606-16348-4)* Turtleback Bks.

—Beth's Snow Dancer. 1999. (Little Women Journals Ser.). 10.04 *(0-606-16347-6)* Turtleback Bks.

—Meg's Dearest Wish. 1999. (Little Women Journals). 10.04 *(0-606-16350-6)* Turtleback Bks.

Emerson, Charlotte & Alcott, Louisa May. Amy's True Prize. (Little Women Journals). (Illus.). (J). 1999. 128p. (gr. 3-7). mass mkt. 3.99 *(0-380-79706-2)*; 1998. 144p. 10.00 o.p. *(0-380-97634-X)* Morrow/Avon. (Avon Bks.).

—Beth's Snow Dancer. (Little Women Journals). (J). 1999. (Illus.). 128p. (gr. 3-7). mass mkt. 3.99 *(0-380-79704-6)*; 1998. 144p. 10.00 o.p. *(0-380-97632-3)* Morrow/Avon. (Avon Bks.).

—Jo's Troubled Heart. (Little Women Journals). (J). 1999. (Illus.). 128p. (gr. 3-7). pap. 3.99 *(0-380-79669-4)*; 1998. 119p. (gr. 4-7). 10.00 o.p. *(0-380-97629-3)* Morrow/Avon. (Avon Bks.).

—Meg's Dearest Wish. (Little Women Journals). (Illus.). (J). 1999. 128p. (gr. 3-7). pap. 3.99 *(0-380-79705-4)*; 1998. 144p. mass mkt. 10.00 o.p. *(0-380-97633-1)* Morrow/Avon. (Avon Bks.).

Enderle, Judith R. & Tessler, Stephanie G. What's the Matter, Kelly Beans? 1996. (Illus.). 112p. (J). (gr. 1-3). 14.99 o.p. *(1-56402-534-9)* Candlewick Pr.

Endersby, Frank. The Nuisance. 1981. 12p. (J). (ps-3). 2.99 *(0-85953-233-X)* Child's Play of England GBR. *Dist:* Child's Play-International.

—What about Me? 1981. 12p. (J). (ps-k). 3.99 *(0-85953-232-1)* Child's Play of England GBR. *Dist:* Child's Play-International.

Engel, Diana. Gino Badino. 1991. (Illus.). 32p. (J). (ps up). 13.95 o.p. *(0-688-09502-X)*; lib. bdg. 13.88 o.p. *(0-688-09503-8)* Morrow/Avon. (Morrow, William & Co.).

Engelbreit, Mary. Baby Booky: Honey Bunny. 2004. (Illus.). 14p. (J). bds. 6.99 *(0-06-008135-X,* Harper Festival) HarperCollins Children's Bk. Group.

English, Karen. Big Wind Coming! 1996. (Illus.). 32p. (J). (ps-3). lib. bdg. 14.95 *(0-8075-0726-1)* Whitman, Albert & Co.

—Just Right Stew. (Illus.). 32p. (J). pap. 8.95 *(1-59078-168-6)*; 2003. 15.95 *(1-56397-487-8)* Boyds Mills Pr.

Relationships

—Neeny Coming, Neeny Going. 1998. 12.10 (*0-606-13656-8*) Turtleback Bks.

Enright, Elizabeth. The Four-Story Mistake. (J). 1996. o.p. (*0-03-032830-6*); ERS. 2002. (Melendy Quartet Ser.: Bk. 2). (Illus.). 176p. (gr. 3-7). 16.95 (*0-8050-7061-3*, Holt, Henry & Co. Bks. For Young Readers) Holt, Henry & Co.

—The Four-Story Mistake. 1997. (Melendy Family Ser.). (Illus.). 176p. (J). (gr. 3-7). pap. 5.99 (*0-14-038394-8*) Penguin Putnam Bks. for Young Readers.

—The Four-Story Mistake. 1987. 192p. (J). (gr. k-6). pap. 3.25 o.s.i (*0-440-42514-X*, Yearling) Random Hse. Children's Bks.

—The Saturdays, ERS. 1988. (Illus.). 196p. (YA). (gr. 4-7). 12.95 o.s.i (*0-8050-0291-X*, Holt, Henry & Co. Bks. For Young Readers) Holt, Henry & Co.

—The Saturdays. 1997. (Melendy Family Ser.). (Illus.). 192p. (J). (gr. 3-7). pap. 4.99 o.s.i (*0-14-038395-6*) Penguin Putnam Bks. for Young Readers.

—The Saturdays. 1923. (Illus.). 176p. (J). (gr. k-6). pap. 0.65 o.p. (*0-440-47615-1*, Yearling) Random Hse. Children's Bks.

—Spiderweb for Two: A Melendy Maze, ERS. 2002. (Melendy Quartet Ser.: Bk. 4). (Illus.). 224p. (J). (gr. 3-7). 16.95 (*0-8050-7063-X*, Holt, Henry & Co. Bks. For Young Readers) Holt, Henry & Co.

Epperley, Mike. Buckethead Bunch: Bossy, Loser, Show-off & Angry. 1992. (Illus.). 40p. (Orig.). (J). (gr. k-6). pap. 5.98 (*1-882183-24-X*) Page, Andrea.

—The Buckethead Families: Givers & Takers. rev. ed. 1992. (Buckethead Ser.). (Illus.). 32p. (J). (gr. k-6). pap. 5.98 (*1-882183-23-1*) Page, Andrea.

Estes, Eleanor. The Middle Moffat. 1989. (J). pap. 3.25 o.s.i (*0-440-70028-0*) Dell Publishing.

—The Middle Moffat. 1943. (Illus.). (J). (gr. 3-7). 12.95 o.p. (*0-15-253663-9*) Harcourt Children's Bks.

—The Middle Moffat. 1989. 288p. (J). (gr. k-6). pap. 3.25 o.s.i (*0-440-40180-1*, Yearling) Random Hse. Children's Bks.

—The Moffat Museum. 1989. (J). pap. 3.25 o.s.i (*0-440-70029-9*) Dell Publishing.

—The Moffat Museum. 2001. (Young Classics). (Illus.). 256p. (YA). (gr. 3 up). 17.00 (*0-15-202547-2*); pap. 6.00 (*0-15-202553-7*) Harcourt Children's Bks.

—The Moffat Museum. 1989. 272p. (J). (gr. k-6). pap. 3.25 o.s.i (*0-440-40201-8*, Yearling) Random Hse. Children's Bks.

—The Moffat Museum. 2001. (J). 12.05 (*0-606-20805-4*) Turtleback Bks.

—Moffats. (Illus.). (J). (gr. 4-6). 1968. pap. 5.95 o.p. (*0-15-661850-8*, Voyager Bks./Libros Viajeros); 1941. 290p. 17.00 o.s.i (*0-15-255095-X*) Harcourt Children's Bks.

—The Moffats. 1989. (J). pap. 3.25 o.s.i (*0-440-70026-4*) Dell Publishing.

—The Moffats. 2001. (Young Classics). (Illus.). 224p. (YA). (gr. 3 up). 17.00 (*0-15-202535-9*, Odyssey Classics) Harcourt Children's Bks.

—The Moffats. 1989. 272p. (J). (gr. k-6). pap. 3.25 o.s.i (*0-440-40177-1*, Yearling) Random Hse. Children's Bks.

—The Moffats. 2001. (J). 12.05 (*0-606-20806-2*) Turtleback Bks.

—Pinky Pye. (Illus.). 2000. 272p. (YA). (gr. 3-7). pap. 6.00 (*0-15-202565-0*); 2000. 272p. (YA). (gr. 4-7). 17.00 (*0-15-202559-6*); 1958. 192p. (J). (gr. 3-7). 12.95 o.s.i (*0-15-262076-1*) Harcourt Children's Bks.

—Rufus M. 1989. (J). pap. 3.25 o.s.i (*0-440-70027-2*) Dell Publishing.

—Rufus M. 1943. (Illus.). 320p. (YA). (gr. 3). 15.95 o.s.i (*0-15-269415-3*) Harcourt Children's Bks.

—Rufus M. 2001. (Young Classics). (Illus.). 256p. (YA). (gr. 3 up). 17.00 (*0-15-202571-5*, Odyssey Classics); pap. 6.00 (*0-15-202577-4*) Harcourt Children's Bks.

—Rufus M. 2001. (Illus.). (J). 12.05 (*0-606-20893-3*) Turtleback Bks.

—The Witch Family. 1965. (Illus.). 223p. (J). (gr. 3-7). pap. 3.95 o.p. (*0-15-697645-5*, Voyager Bks./Libros Viajeros) Harcourt Children's Bks.

Estes, Eleanor & Slobodkin, Louis. The Moffats. 2001. (Odyssey Classics). (Illus.). 224p. (YA). (gr. 3 up). pap. 6.00 (*0-15-202541-3*, Odyssey Classics) Harcourt Children's Bks.

ETR Associates Staff. A Family That Fits. 1992. (Contemporary Health Ser.). (Illus.). (YA). 2.00 (*1-56071-103-5*) ETR Assocs.

Evans, Douglas. The Elevator Family. 2001. (J). 10.55 (*0-606-21173-X*) Turtleback Bks.

Everett, Gwen. Li'l Sis & Uncle Willie: A Story Based on the Life & Paintings of William H. Johnson. 1994. (Illus.). 32p. (J). (ps-3). pap. 4.95 o.s.i (*1-56282-593-3*) Hyperion Bks. for Children.

Ewing, Juliana H. A Great Emergency & A Very Ill-Tempered Family. (Victorian Revival Ser.). (Illus.). (J). 1988. 7.50 o.s.i (*0-8052-3087-4*); 1969. pap. 1.75 o.p. (*0-8052-0225-0*) Knopf Publishing Group. (Schocken).

Ewing, Kathryn. A Private Matter. 1975. (J). (gr. 4-8). 7.95 o.p. (*0-15-263576-9*) Harcourt Children's Bks.

Faine, Edward Allan. Little Ned Stories. 1999. (Illus.). 128p. (J). (gr. k-3). pap. 9.99 (*0-9654651-5-2*) IM Pr.

Fakih, Kimberly O. High on the Hog, RS. 1994. 160p. (J). (gr. 5-7). 16.00 o.p. (*0-374-33209-6*, Farrar, Straus & Giroux (BYR)) Farrar, Straus & Giroux.

Falconer, Elizabeth. La Casa Que Jack Construyo. 2002. (SPA.). 28p. 10.95 (*1-4000-0119-6*) Random Hse., Inc.

Fallon, Joan & Feltenstein, Arlene. Will the New Baby Be Bigger Than Me? 1998. (Illus.). (J). (ps-3). 9.95 (*1-56492-252-9*) Laredo Publishing Co., Inc.

Falwell, Cathryn. Feast for Ten. 1995. (J). pap. text 5.95 o.p. (*0-590-48466-4*) Scholastic, Inc.

—Feast for 10. 2002. (Illus.). (J). 14.74 (*0-7587-2485-3*) Book Wholesalers, Inc.

—Feast for 10. (Illus.). (J). 2003. 30p. bds. 4.95 (*0-618-38226-7*); 1996. 1p. pap. 9.95 incl. audio (*0-395-72082-6*, 1-11762); 1995. 32p. pap. 6.95 (*0-395-72081-8*); 1993. 32p. lib. bdg., tchr. ed. 16.00 (*0-395-62037-6*) Houghton Mifflin Co. Trade & Reference Div. (Clarion Bks.).

Families, Pack C. 1992. (ENG & SPA., Illus.). (J). (gr. 1-3). 184.95 o.p. (*1-56334-242-1*) Hampton-Brown Bks.

Family under the Bridge. 1999. (J). 9.95 (*1-56137-368-0*) Novel Units, Inc.

Farish, Terry. Talking in Animal. 1996. 160p. (YA). (gr. 5 up). 15.00 o.s.i (*0-688-14671-6*, Greenwillow Bks.) HarperCollins Children's Bk. Group.

Farley, Carol. Sergeant Finney's Family. 1969. (Illus.). (gr. 4-6). lib. bdg. 4.90 o.p. (*0-531-01915-2*, Watts, Franklin) Scholastic Library Publishing.

Farmer, Nancy. Do You Know Me? 1994. (Illus.). 112p. (J). (gr. 3-7). pap. 5.99 (*0-14-036946-5*, Puffin Bks.) Penguin Putnam Bks. for Young Readers.

—Do You Know Me? 1993. (Illus.). 112p. (J). (gr. 3-5). pap. 15.95 (*0-531-05474-8*); (gr. 4-7). lib. bdg. 16.99 (*0-531-08624-0*) Scholastic, Inc. (Orchard Bks.).

Farmer, Patti. What's He Doing Now? 2003. (Illus.). 32p. (J). (ps-3). 15.95 (*1-55209-220-8*); pap. 5.95 (*1-55209-218-6*) Firefly Bks., Ltd.

Farmer, Penelope. Thicker Than Water. 1995. (J). (gr. 6-10). bds. 4.99 o.p. (*1-56402-519-5*) Candlewick Pr.

—Thicker Than Water. 1995. (J). 10.09 o.p. (*0-606-08282-4*) Turtleback Bks.

Favorite Friends Set, 6 bks. Incl. Bonnie on the Beach. Peters, Catherine. pap. 2.49 o.p. (*0-395-88312-1*); Class Play. Newell, Robert. pap. 2.49 o.p. (*0-395-88301-6*); Hand-Me-Downs. Peters, Catherine. pap. 2.49 o.p. (*0-395-88314-8*); Jackson's Monster. Peters, Catherine. pap. 2.49 o.p. (*0-395-88313-X*); Lola & Miss Kitty. (Illus.). pap. 2.49 o.p. (*0-395-88932-4*); Yard Sale. Peters, Catherine. pap. 2.49 o.p. (*0-395-88300-8*); 16p. (J). (Little Readers Book Bag Ser.). 1997. 15.00 o.p. (*0-395-88308-3*) Houghton Mifflin Co.

Fearnley, Jan. Billy Tibbles Moves Out! 2004. 32p. (J). 15.99 (*0-06-054650-6*) HarperCollins Pubs.

Feiffer, Jules. The House Across the Street. 2002. (Illus.). 32p. (J). 15.95 (*0-7868-0910-8*, Di Capua, Michael Bks.) Hyperion Bks. for Children.

—I Lost My Bear. 2002. (Illus.). (J). 14.43 (*0-7587-4249-5*) Book Wholesalers, Inc.

—I Lost My Bear. (Illus.). 40p. (J). (ps-2). 2000. pap. 5.99 (*0-688-17722-0*, Harper Trophy); 1998. 16.00 (*0-688-15147-7*); 1998. 15.89 (*0-688-15148-5*) HarperCollins Children's Bk. Group.

—I Lost My Bear. 2000. (YA). pap. 34.25 incl. audio (*0-7887-4095-4*, 41091) Recorded Bks., LLC.

Fenner, Carol. Yolonda's Genius. unabr. ed. 2002. 211p. pap. 37.00 incl. audio (*0-8072-0462-5*, Listening Library) Random Hse. Audio Publishing Group.

Fernandes, Eugenie. A Difficult Day. 2002. (Illus.). 32p. (J). (ps-2). pap. (*0-921103-80-8*) Kids Can Pr., Ltd.

—Waves in the Bathtub. 1996. (Illus.). 32p. (ps-3). pap. 5.95 (*1-55209-147-3*) Firefly Bks., Ltd.

Ferris, Jean. Love among the Walnuts. 1998. 224p. (YA). (gr. 5-9). 16.00 (*0-15-201590-6*) Harcourt Children's Bks.

—Love among the Walnuts. 2001. (Illus.). (J). 12.04 (*0-606-20776-7*) Turtleback Bks.

—Love among the Walnuts: Or How I Saved My Entire Family from Being Poisoned. November, S., ed. 2001. 272p. (YA). (gr. 5-9). pap. 5.99 (*0-14-131099-5*) Penguin Putnam Bks. for Young Readers.

—Once upon a Marigold. 2004. 288p. (J). pap. 5.95 (*0-15-205084-1*, Harcourt Paperbacks); 2002. 272p. (YA). (gr. 5 up). 17.00 (*0-15-216791-9*) Harcourt Children's Bks.

Fidler, Mark. Pond Puckster. 2nd ed. 2003. 148p. (J). (gr. 4-8). reprint ed. pap. 11.95 (*0-9721839-0-6*) BLR Bks.

—Pond Puckster. 2000. 141p. (gr. 4-7). pap. 9.95 o.p. (*0-595-12998-6*) iUniverse, Inc.

Fine, Anne. The Book of the Banshee. 1992. (YA). (gr. 7 up). 13.95 (*0-316-28315-0*) Little Brown & Co.

—The Book of the Banshee. 1994. 176p. (J). (gr. 4-7). pap. 2.95 o.p. (*0-590-46926-6*) Scholastic, Inc.

—Crummy Mummy & Me. l.t. ed. 2002. (Illus.). (J). 16.95 (*0-7540-7813-2*, Galaxy Children's Large Print) BBC Audiobooks America.

Finley, Martha. Elsie's Endless Wait. 1999. (Elsie Dinsmore: Bk. 1). (Illus.). 224p. (J). (gr. 5-9). 9.99 (*1-928749-01-1*) Mission City Pr., Inc.

—Elsie's Stolen Heart. 1999. (Elsie Dinsmore: Bk. 4). (Illus.). 224p. (J). (gr. 5-9). 9.99 (*1-928749-04-6*) Mission City Pr., Inc.

Finn, Felicity. Jeremy & the Aunties. 1998. (Illus.). 134p. (J). (gr. 4-8). pap. 4.95 (*0-929005-40-6*) Second Story Pr. CAN. *Dist:* Orca Bk. Pubs.

Finney, Patricia. I Jack. 2004. 192p. (J). 15.99 (*0-06-052207-0*); lib. bdg. 16.89 (*0-06-052208-9*) HarperCollins Pubs.

Fish, Dorothy & Cohen, Betty. My Busy Little Dreidel. 1997. (Illus.). 20p. (J). (ps-3). 5.99 (*0-914080-08-3*) Shulsinger Sales, Inc.

Fisher, Melanie. Nathan & Lou: The Finders. 1995. (Illus.). 36p. (Orig.). (J). (gr. k-4). mass mkt. 4.95 (*0-9649664-0-9*) Jermel Visuals.

Fishman, Cathy Goldberg. Soup Level B. 2001. (Rookie Readers Ser.). (Illus.). 32p. (J). (gr. 1-2). lib. bdg. 19.00 (*0-516-22536-7*, Children's Pr.) Scholastic Library Publishing.

Fitch, Sheree. One More Step. 2002. 96p. (YA). pap. 9.95 (*1-55143-248-X*) Orca Bk. Pubs.

Fitzhugh, Louise. Nobody's Family Is Going to Change. 1975. 224p. (J). (gr. 3-7). pap. 2.95 o.s.i (*0-440-46454-4*, Yearling) Random Hse. Children's Bks.

Flam, Chanie. Good Night. (Goldie Gold Board Book Ser.: Vol. 6). (Illus.). (J). (ps-1). bds. 4.95 (*1-58330-030-9*) Feldheim, Philipp Inc.

Fleischman, Paul. A Fate Totally Worse Than Death. 2004. 128p. pap. 5.99 (*0-7636-2189-7*) Candlewick Pr.

—A Fate Totally Worse Than Death. 1997. 10.09 o.p. (*0-606-12695-3*) Turtleback Bks.

Fleischman, Sid. Humbug Mountain. 1978. (Illus.). (J). (gr. 4-6). 14.95 o.s.i (*0-316-28569-2*) Scholastic, Inc.

—McBroom Tells a Lie. 1976. (Adventures of McBroom Ser.). (Illus.). 64p. (J). (gr. 4-6). 13.95 o.s.i (*0-316-28572-2*, Joy Street Bks.) Little Brown & Co.

—McBroom Tells a Lie. (Adventures of McBroom Ser.). (J). 2015. 13.89 (*0-8431-7519-2*); 1999. (Illus.). 64p. (gr. 2-5). 4.99 (*0-8431-7497-8*) Penguin Putnam Bks. for Young Readers. (Price Stern Sloan).

—McBroom Tells a Lie. 1999. 10.14 (*0-606-19073-2*) Turtleback Bks.

—McBroom Tells the Truth. 1981. (Illus.). 48p. (J). (gr. 2-5). reprint ed. (*0-316-28550-1*); mass mkt. 3.95 o.p. (*0-316-28552-8*) Little Brown & Co.

—McBroom Tells the Truth. 1998. (Adventures of McBroom Ser.). (Illus.). (J). (gr. 2-5). 64p. 13.89 o.s.i (*0-8431-7898-1*); 62p. 4.99 (*0-8431-7947-3*) Penguin Putnam Bks. for Young Readers. (Price Stern Sloan).

—McBroom Tells the Truth. 1998. 10.14 (*0-606-15962-2*) Turtleback Bks.

—Mr. Mysterious & Company. 1962. (Illus.). (J). (gr. 4-6). 14.95 o.s.i (*0-316-28578-1*, Joy Street Bks.) Little Brown & Co.

—The Whipping Boy. 93rd ed. 1993. pap. text 15.80 (*0-15-300357-X*) Harcourt Children's Bks.

Fleischman, Sid & Von Schmidt, Eric. Humbug Mountain. 9999. (J). pap. 1.75 o.p. (*0-590-30096-2*) Scholastic, Inc.

Fletcher, Ralph J. Fig Pudding. 1996. (Illus.). 160p. (gr. 3-7). pap. text 5.50 (*0-440-41203-X*) Dell Publishing.

—Fig Pudding. 1995. (Illus.). 144p. (J). (gr. 4-6). tchr. ed. 15.00 (*0-395-71125-8*, Clarion Bks.) Houghton Mifflin Co. Trade & Reference Div.

—Fig Pudding. unabr. ed. 2000. (YA). (gr. 5 up). pap. 39.75 incl. audio (*0-7887-3181-5*, 40916X4) Recorded Bks., LLC.

—Fig Pudding. 1996. (J). 10.55 (*0-606-10810-6*) Turtleback Bks.

Flood, Pansie Hart. Secret Holes. 2003. (Illus.). 122p. (J). 15.95 (*0-87614-923-9*, Carolrhoda Bks.) Lerner Publishing Group.

—Sylvia & Miz Lula Maye. 2002. (Middle Grade Fiction Ser.). (Illus.). 120p. (J). (gr. 3-6). lib. bdg. 15.95 (*0-87614-204-8*, Carolrhoda Bks.) Lerner Publishing Group.

Flory, Jane. It Was a Pretty Good Year, 001. 1977. (Illus.). (J). (gr. 3-7). 6.95 o.p. (*0-395-25835-9*) Houghton Mifflin Co.

Flournoy, Valerie. The Patchwork Quilt. 1985. (Illus.). 32p. (J). (gr. 4-8). 14.89 o.p. (*0-8037-0098-9*); (ps-3). 16.99 (*0-8037-0097-0*) Penguin Putnam Bks. for Young Readers. (Dial Bks. for Young Readers).

Flynn, Mary. Cornelius in Charge. 1990. (Illus.). (Orig.). (J). (gr. 1-6). 10.95 o.p. (*0-947962-53-0*); pap. 7.95 o.p. (*0-947962-54-9*) Anvil Bks., Ltd. IRL. *Dist:* Irish Bks. & Media, Inc.

Flynn, Pat. Alex Jackson: Grommet. Grommett, Gary, ed. 2001. 132p. (YA). pap. 13.95 o.s.i (*0-7022-3223-8*) Univ. of Queensland Pr. AUS. *Dist:* International Specialized Bk. Services.

Fogelin, Adrian. My Brother's Hero. 2002. (Peachtree Junior Publication Ser.). 224p. (J). (gr. 3-7). 14.95 (*1-56145-274-2*, Peachtree Junior) Peachtree Pubs., Ltd.

Foland, Constance M. Flying High, Pogo! 2002. (American Girls Collection Ser.). (Illus.). 144p. (J). (gr. 5 up). pap. 5.95 (*1-58485-535-5*); trans. 14.95 (*1-58485-624-6*) Pleasant Co. Pubns. (American Girl).

Forbes, Kathryn. Mama's Bank Account. 1975. (J). pap. 1.95 o.p. (*0-590-09927-2*) Scholastic, Inc.

Forbing, Shirley E. Sylvester: A Squirrel for Suzie. 2001. (YA). pap. 21.95 incl. audio compact disk Wild Animal XPress.

Foreman, Wilmoth. Summer of the Skunks. 2003. 156p. (J). 15.95 (*1-886910-80-4*, Front Street) Front Street, Inc.

Forest, Antonia. The Attic Term. 1976. (J). (gr. 5 up). o.p. (*0-571-10970-5*) Faber & Faber Ltd.

—The Cricket Term. 1982. (J). (gr. 5 up). o.s.i (*0-571-10632-3*) Faber & Faber Ltd.

—End of Term. 1972. 238p. (J). (gr. 5 up). o.p. (*0-571-05707-1*); (Illus.). pap. o.p. (*0-571-10131-3*) Faber & Faber Ltd.

—The Ready-Made Family. 1980. (Fanfares Ser.). 194p. (J). (gr. 4 up). pap. o.p. (*0-571-11494-6*) Faber & Faber Ltd.

Forrester, Maureen. Joy to the World. unabr. ed. 1992. (Illus.). 32p. (J). 15.95 (*1-895555-19-1*) Stoddart Kids CAN. *Dist:* General Distribution Services, Inc.

Forrester, Sandra. My Home Is over Jordan: Sequel to "Sound the Jubilee" 1997. Orig. Title: Fire & Shadow. 160p. (J). (gr. 5-9). 15.99 o.s.i (*0-525-67568-X*, Dutton Children's Bks.) Penguin Putnam Bks. for Young Readers.

Forsberg, Crystal. Michael's Brothers. 1998. (Illus.). 16p. (J). (ps-k). pap. 5.95 (*0-9655442-3-0*) Business Word, The.

Foster, Kelli C. Mop for Pop. 1991. (Get Ready...Get Set...Read! Ser.). (J). 9.65 (*0-606-01641-4*) Turtleback Bks.

Foster, Kelli C. & Erickson, Gina Clegg. The Tan Can. 1997. (Get Ready...Get Set...Read! Ser.: Set 2). (Illus.). 24p. (J). lib. bdg. 11.95 (*1-56674-137-8*) Forest Hse. Publishing Co., Inc.

Fowler, Susi Gregg. Fog. 1992. (Illus.). 32p. (J). (ps-8). 14.00 o.p. (*0-688-10593-9*); lib. bdg. 13.93 o.p. (*0-688-10594-7*) HarperCollins Children's Bk. Group. (Greenwillow Bks.).

Fox, Paula. Ivan. 2002. (SPA.). (YA). pap. 8.50 (*84-279-3245-6*, NG31202) Molino, Editorial ESP. *Dist:* Lectorum Pubns., Inc.

—Maurice's Room. 3rd ed. 1985. (Illus.). 64p. (J). (gr. 2-6). lib. bdg. 13.95 (*0-02-735490-3*, Simon & Schuster Children's Publishing) Simon & Schuster Children's Publishing.

Frame, Jeron Ashford. Yesterday I Had the Blues. 2003. (Illus.). 30p. (J). (gr. k-3). 14.95 (*1-58246-084-1*) Tricycle Pr.

Francis, Dorothy B. Run of the Sea Witch. 1978. (Illus.). (J). (gr. 3-7). 5.95 o.p. (*0-687-36648-8*) Abingdon Pr.

Frank, Lucy. I Am an Artichoke. 1996. 192p. (J). (gr. 7-12). mass mkt. 3.99 o.s.i (*0-440-21990-6*) Dell Publishing.

—Oy, Joy! 1999. (Illus.). 288p. (J). (gr. 6-9). pap. 16.95 o.p. (*0-7894-2538-6*) Dorling Kindersley Publishing, Inc.

Frank, Penny. Ruth's New Family. 1994. 24p. (J). (ps-3). pap. 1.99 o.p. (*0-7459-1760-7*) Lion Publishing.

Frantz, Jennifer. My Smelly Family. 2002. (Illus.). 16p. (J). bds. 7.99 (*0-8431-7720-9*, Price Stern Sloan) Penguin Putnam Bks. for Young Readers.

Fraser, Alan. Fiddlesticks. 2004. 69p. (J). (gr. 2-4). pap. (*0-440-86606-5*, Corgi) Bantam Bks.

Frasier, Debra. El Dia en Que Tu Naciste. 1998. 13.15 (*0-606-13363-1*) Turtleback Bks.

Fraustino, Lisa Rowe. Ash. 1995. (Illus.). 176p. (YA). (gr. 7 up). pap. 16.95 (*0-531-06889-7*); lib. bdg. 17.99 (*0-531-08739-5*) Scholastic, Inc. (Orchard Bks.).

Freeman, Martha. The Polyester Grandpa. 1998. 160p. (J). (gr. 4-7). tchr. ed. 15.95 (*0-8234-1398-5*) Holiday Hse., Inc.

French, Renee. The Soap Lady. unabr. ed. 2001. (Illus.). 112p. 19.95 (*1-891830-24-4*) Top Shelf Productions.

Freymann-Weyr, Garret. My Heartbeat. 2002. 160p. (J). (gr. 7-12). 15.00 (*0-618-14181-2*) Houghton Mifflin Co.

—My Heartbeat. unabr. ed. 2003. (J). (gr. 7). audio 25.00 (*0-8072-1199-0*, Listening Library) Random Hse. Audio Publishing Group.

Fuqua, Jonathon Scott. The Reappearance of Sam Webber. 2001. 15.04 *(0-606-21397-X)* Turtleback Bks.

Furgang, Kathy. Flower Girl. 2003. (Illus.). 32p. (J). (gr. k-3). 15.99 *(0-670-88950-4*, Viking Children's Bks.) Penguin Putnam Bks. for Young Readers.

Gackenbach, Dick. Where Are Momma, Poppa, & Sister June. 1994. (Illus.). 32p. (J). (ps-3). tchr. ed. 13.95 o.p. *(0-395-67323-2)* Houghton Mifflin Co.

Gaeddert, LouAnn Bigge. Breaking Free. 1996. 9.09 o.p. *(0-606-10148-9)* Turtleback Bks.

Galbraith, Kathryn O. Come Spring. 1979. 216p. (J). (gr. 4-7). 8.95 o.s.i *(0-689-50142-0*, McElderry, Margaret K.) Simon & Schuster Children's Publishing.

Gale, Elizabeth W. My Two Families. 1985. (Illus.). (J). pap. 0.59 o.p. *(0-8170-0426-2)* Judson Pr.

Galloway, Priscilla. The Courtesan's Daughter. 2004. 272p. (YA). (gr. 7). mass mkt. 5.50 *(0-440-22902-2*, Laurel Leaf) Random Hse. Children's Bks.

—The Courtesan's Daughter. 2002. 272p. (YA). lib. bdg. 18.99 *(0-385-90052-X)*; (gr. 7-12). 16.95 *(0-385-72907-3)* Random Hse., Inc.

Gantos, Jack. Aunt Bernice. 1978. (Illus.). (J). (gr. k-3). 6.95 o.p. *(0-395-26461-8)* Houghton Mifflin Co.

—Heads or Tails: Stories from the Sixth Grade, RS. 1995. 160p. (J). (gr. 4-7). pap. 5.95 *(0-374-42923-5*, Sunburst); 1994. (J). E-Book 4.95 *(0-374-70049-4*, Farrar, Straus & Giroux (BYR)); 1994. E-Book 4.95 o.p. *(0-374-70050-8*, Farrar, Straus & Giroux (BYR)); 1994. 160p. (J). (gr. 5-9). 16.00 *(0-374-32909-5*, Farrar, Straus & Giroux (BYR)) Farrar, Straus & Giroux.

—Heads or Tails: Stories from the Sixth Grade. 1995. (J). 11.00 *(0-606-09397-4)* Turtleback Bks.

—Jacks New Power, RS. 1995. (J). E-Book 16.00 o.p. *(0-374-70055-9*, Farrar, Straus & Giroux (BYR)) Farrar, Straus & Giroux.

—Jack's New Power: Stories from a Caribbean Year, RS. (J). 1997. 224p. (gr. 5-9). pap. 5.95 *(0-374-43715-7*, Sunburst); 1995. E-Book 4.95 *(0-374-70052-4*, Farrar, Straus & Giroux (BYR)); 1995. E-Book 4.95 *(0-374-70053-2*, Farrar, Straus & Giroux (BYR)); 1995. E-Book 4.95 o.p. *(0-374-70054-0*, Farrar, Straus & Giroux (BYR)); 1995. 224p. (gr. 5-9). 16.00 *(0-374-33657-1*, Farrar, Straus & Giroux (BYR)) Farrar, Straus & Giroux.

—Jack's New Power: Stories from a Caribbean Year. 1997. 11.00 *(0-606-13532-4)* Turtleback Bks.

—What Would Joey Do?, RS. 2002. 240p. (J). (gr. 5-9). 16.00 *(0-374-39986-7*, Farrar, Straus & Giroux (BYR)) Farrar, Straus & Giroux.

—What Would Joey Do? 2004. (Illus.). 240p. (J). pap. 5.99 *(0-06-054403-1*, Harper Trophy) HarperCollins Children's Bk. Group.

—What Would Joey Do? 2002. (J). (gr. 4-8). 30.00 *(0-8072-0949-X)*; audio 25.00 *(0-8072-0948-1)* Random Hse. Audio Publishing Group. (Listening Library).

—What Would Joey Do? 2003. (Juvenile Ser.). 264p. (J). 22.95 *(0-7862-5468-8)* Thorndike Pr.

Ganz, Yaffa. Savta Simcha, Uncle Nechemya & the Very Strange Stone in the Garden. 1992. (Illus.). (J). 14.95 *(0-87306-618-9)* Feldheim, Philipp Inc.

Garber, Linda. Don't Leave the Lawn! l.t. ed. 1999. (Illus.). (J). (gr. 1-4). spiral bd. 9.95 *(1-892218-04-6)* Murlin Pubns.

Garden, Nancy. Molly's Family, RS. 2004. (J). 16.00 *(0-374-35002-7*, Farrar, Straus & Giroux (BYR)) Farrar, Straus & Giroux.

Gardner, Richard A. The Boys & Girls Book about Stepfamilies. 1985. (Illus.). 180p. (J). (gr. 3-10). reprint ed. pap. 6.50 *(0-933812-13-2)* Creative Therapeutics, Inc.

Garis, Howard R. Uncle Wiggily's Fortune. Date not set. 192p. (J). 20.95 *(0-8488-2280-3)* Amereon, Ltd.

Garland, Sherry. A Line in the Sand: The Alamo Diary of Lucinda Lawrence, Gonzales, Texas, 1836. 1998. (Dear America Ser.). (Illus.). 201p. (YA). (gr. 4-9). pap. 10.95 *(0-590-39466-5*, Scholastic Pr.) Scholastic, Inc.

—Shadow of the Dragon. 1993. (Illus.). (YA). (gr. 7 up). 368p. 10.95 *(0-15-273530-5)*; 320p. pap. 6.00 *(0-15-273532-1*, Harcourt Paperbacks) Harcourt Children's Bks.

Garnett, Eve. The Family from One End Street. 1976. 176p. (J). pap. 1.50 o.p. *(0-14-030007-4*, Penguin Classics) Viking Penguin.

Garrett, Ann. What's for Dinner? 2000. (Illus.). 10p. (J). (ps-k). 9.99 *(0-525-46377-1*, Dutton Children's Bks.) Penguin Putnam Bks. for Young Readers.

Gates, Eleanor. The Poor Little Rich Girl. 1976. (Classics of Children's Literature, 1621-1932: Vol. 64). (Illus.). (J). reprint ed. lib. bdg. 42.00 o.p. *(0-8240-2313-7)* Garland Publishing, Inc.

Gehret, Jeanne. Eagle Eyes: A Child's View of Attention Deficit Disorder. 1991. (Illus.). 32p. (Orig.). (J). (gr. 1-5). pap. 7.95 o.p. *(0-9625136-1-X)* Verbal Images Pr.

—I'm Somebody Too. 1992. 170p. (J). (gr. 4-7). 16.00 o.p. *(0-9625136-6-0)*; 16.00 *(0-9625136-7-9)*; reprint ed. pap. 13.00 o.p. *(1-884281-12-5)* Verbal Images Pr.

Gelsanliter, Wendy & Christian, Frank. Dancin' in the Kitchen. 1998. (Illus.). 32p. (J). (ps-3). 15.99 o.s.i *(0-399-23035-1*, G. P. Putnam's Sons) Penguin Group (USA) Inc.

George, Jean Craighead. The Cry of the Crow. 1980. 160p. (YA). (gr. 5 up). lib. bdg. 13.89 o.p. *(0-06-021957-2)* HarperCollins Children's Bk. Group.

—There's an Owl in the Shower. 1997. (Illus.). 144p. (J). (gr. 2-5). pap. 5.99 *(0-06-440682-2*, Harper Trophy) HarperCollins Children's Bk. Group.

Gerber, Merrill J. Please Don't Kiss Me Now. 1981. 224p. (gr. 8 up). 9.95 o.p. *(0-8037-6792-7*, Dial Bks. for Young Readers) Penguin Putnam Bks. for Young Readers.

Gerson, Corinne. Tread Softly. (J). (gr. 4-7). 1985. 7.45 o.p. *(0-8037-9059-7)*; 1979. 7.95 o.p. *(0-8037-9058-9)* Penguin Putnam Bks. for Young Readers. (Dial Bks. for Young Readers).

Gewing, Lisa. Mama, Daddy, Baby & Me. 1989. (Illus.). 30p. (J). (ps). 14.95 *(0-944296-04-1)* Spirit Pr.

Gibala-Broxholm, Scott. Scary Fright, Are You All Right? 2002. (Illus.). 48p. (J). 14.99 *(0-8037-2588-4*, Dial Bks. for Young Readers) Penguin Putnam Bks. for Young Readers.

Gibbons, Alan. Jaws of the Dragon. 1994. 156p. (J). (gr. 4-7). lib. bdg. 19.93 o.p. *(0-8225-0737-4*, Lerner Pubns.) Lerner Publishing Group.

Gibbons, Faye. Mighty Close to Heaven. 1985. 192p. (J). (gr. 5-9). 11.95 o.p. *(0-688-04147-7*, Morrow, William & Co.) Morrow/Avon.

—Mountain Wedding. 1996. (Illus.). 40p. (J). (ps-3). 16.00 *(0-688-11348-6)* HarperCollins Children's Bk. Group.

—Mountain Wedding. 1996. (Illus.). 40p. (J). (ps-3). 16.89 *(0-688-11349-4*, Morrow, William & Co.) Morrow/Avon.

—Some Glad Morning. 1982. 240p. (J). (gr. 4-6). 12.95 o.p. *(0-688-01068-7*, Morrow, William & Co.) Morrow/Avon.

Gibson, Ray, ed. Que Hacemos Hoy? 1995. (SPA., Illus.). 96p. (J). (gr. k-7). 18.95 *(0-7460-3436-9*, EU6315, Usborne) EDC Publishing.

Giff, Patricia Reilly. Next Year I'll Be Special. 1996. (J). 10.19 o.p. *(0-606-09680-9)* Turtleback Bks.

—Rosie's Nutcracker Dreams. 1996. (Ballet Slippers Ser.: Vol. 2). (Illus.). 80p. (J). (gr. 4-7). 13.99 o.s.i *(0-670-86865-5*, Viking Children's Bks.) Penguin Putnam Bks. for Young Readers.

—Today Was a Terrible Day. 1984. (Picture Puffin Ser.). (Illus.). (J). 12.14 *(0-606-01750-X)* Turtleback Bks.

Gillmor, Don. The Fabulous Song. (J). 2003. pap. 7.95 *(1-929132-48-4)*; 1998. (Illus.). 32p. 12.95 *(0-916291-80-4)* Kane/Miller Bk. Pubs.

Gilmore, Rachna. Mina's Spring of Colors. 2000. 150p. (J). (gr. 4-7). *(1-55041-549-2)*; pap. *(1-55041-534-4)* Fitzhenry & Whiteside, Ltd.

Gipson, Fred. Old Yeller. Date not set. 192p. (J). 20.95 *(0-8488-2273-0)* Amereon, Ltd.

—Old Yeller. abr. ed. 1995. (J). audio 16.95 *(1-55927-347-X*, 393873) Audio Renaissance.

—Old Yeller. unabr. ed. 1989. (J). (gr. 4-7). audio 30.00 *(0-7366-1648-9*, 2500) Books on Tape, Inc.

—Old Yeller. 1992. 192p. (YA). (gr. 8-12). reprint ed. 25.95 *(0-89966-906-9)* Buccaneer Bks., Inc.

—Old Yeller. 1990. (Trophy Bk.). (Illus.). 192p. (J). (gr. 5 up). pap. 5.99 *(0-06-440382-3*, Harper Trophy) HarperCollins Children's Bk. Group.

—Old Yeller. 1956. (Illus.). 176p. (gr. 7 up). 23.00 *(0-06-011545-9)*; 1956. (Illus.). (J). (gr. 7-9). lib. bdg. 14.89 o.p. *(0-06-011546-7)*; 1942. (YA). mass mkt. 4.50 o.p. *(0-06-080002-X*, Perennial) HarperTrade.

—Old Yeller. 1995. (J). (gr. 5). 9.32 *(0-395-73259-X)* Houghton Mifflin Co.

—Old Yeller. 1990. (YA). pap. 3.50 o.p. *(0-06-107008-4*, HarperTorch) Morrow/Avon.

—Old Yeller, unabr. ed. 1991. (J). (gr. 5). audio 27.00 *(1-55690-389-8*, 91104E7) Recorded Bks., LLC.

—Old Yeller. 9999. (J). pap. 1.75 o.p. *(0-590-02310-1)* Scholastic, Inc.

—Old Yeller. 1989. (J). 11.55 *(0-606-01189-7)* Turtleback Bks.

—Old Yeller. 1999. (J). lib. bdg. 21.95 *(1-56723-204-3)* Yestermorrow, Inc.

—Old Yeller Reissue. 1989. 192p. (J). (gr. 4-7). reprint ed. pap. 5.50 *(0-06-080971-X*, P 971, Perennial) HarperTrade.

—Savage Sam. 1962. (Illus.). (J). o.p. *(0-06-011560-2)*; lib. bdg. o.p. *(0-06-011561-0)* HarperCollins Pubs.

—Savage Sam. 1962. (Perennial Library). 160p. (gr. 4-7). mass mkt. 6.00 *(0-06-080377-0*, P377, Perennial) HarperTrade.

—Savage Sam. Date not set. pap. 371.40 *(0-671-75819-5*, Atria) Simon & Schuster.

—Savage Sam. 1962. (Perennial Library). (J). 12.05 *(0-606-04373-X)* Turtleback Bks.

Glass, Esther E. Aunt Nan & the Miller Five. 1961. (Illus.). (J). (gr. 4-9). 2.50 o.p. *(0-8361-1309-8)* Herald Pr.

Glassman, Jackie. Don't Wake Daddy! 2001. (My First Games Readers Ser.). (Illus.). 32p. (J). (ps-1). mass mkt. 3.99 *(0-439-26464-2)* Scholastic, Inc.

Gleeson, Libby. Hurry Up! 1993. (Voyages Ser.). (Illus.). (J). 3.75 *(0-383-03632-1)* SRA/McGraw-Hill.

Gleitzman, Morris. Worry Warts. 1995. 176p. (J). (gr. 4-7). pap. 5.00 o.s.i *(0-15-200871-3)* Harcourt Trade Pubs.

Glencoe McGraw-Hill Staff. Topics from the Restless, Bk. 1. unabr. ed. 1999. (Wordsworth Classics Ser.). (YA). (gr. 10 up). pap. 21.00 *(0-89061-116-5*, R1165WW) Jamestown.

Glenn, Mel. One Order to Go. 1984. 192p. (J). (gr. 7 up). 11.95 o.p. *(0-89919-257-2*, Clarion Bks.) Houghton Mifflin Co. Trade & Reference Div.

Gliori, Debi. Mr. Bear's New Baby. 1999. (Illus.). 32p. (J). (ps-1). pap. 15.95 *(0-531-30152-4*, Orchard Bks.) Scholastic, Inc.

—Pure Dead Magic. 2001. 192p. (J). (gr. 5 up). 15.95 o.s.i *(0-375-81410-8)* Knopf, Alfred A. Inc.

—Pure Dead Magic. 2001. (Illus.). 192p. (J). (gr. 5). lib. bdg. 17.99 o.s.i *(0-375-91410-2*, Knopf Bks. for Young Readers) Random Hse. Children's Bks.

—Pure Dead Magic. 2002. 208p. (gr. 5). pap. 4.99 *(0-440-41849-6)* Random Hse., Inc.

—Pure Dead Magic. 2002. (Juvenile Ser.). (Illus.). (J). 21.95 *(0-7862-4869-6)* Thorndike Pr.

—Pure Dead Wicked. 224p. (gr. 5 up). 2003. pap. 4.99 *(0-440-41936-0*, Yearling); 2002. (J). lib. bdg. 17.99 *(0-375-91411-0*, Knopf Bks. for Young Readers); 2002. (Illus.). (J). 15.95 *(0-375-81411-6*, Knopf Bks. for Young Readers) Random Hse. Children's Bks.

Godden, Rumer. Thursday's Children. 1987. (J). (gr. k-12). mass mkt. 3.25 o.s.i *(0-440-98790-3*, Laurel Leaf) Random Hse. Children's Bks.

Goffstein, Brooke. Our Prairie Home: A Picture Album. 1988. (Charlotte Zolotow Bk.). (Illus.). 32p. (J). (ps up). 12.95 *(0-06-022290-5)*; lib. bdg. 12.89 o.p. *(0-06-022291-3)* HarperCollins Children's Bk. Group.

Golden Books Staff. Baby Is Born. 2001. 36p. pap. 2.22 o.s.i *(0-307-13811-9*, Golden Bks.) Random Hse. Children's Bks.

—Colorful Tale, Special ed. 1999. (Disney Ser.). 84p. (ps-3). pap. text 0.88 o.p. *(0-307-25719-3*, Golden Bks.) Random Hse. Children's Bks.

—I Love You, Mommy. 2001. 16p. 3.99 o.s.i *(0-307-16047-5*, Golden Bks.) Random Hse. Children's Bks.

—Lost & Found. 2002. (Illus.). 32p. (J). (ps-2). pap. 3.99 *(0-307-21693-4*, Golden Bks.) Random Hse. Children's Bks.

—My Family & Me. 2004. (Illus.). 64p. (J). pap. 2.99 *(0-375-82790-0*, Golden Bks.) Random Hse. Children's Bks.

—Snacktime with Blue. 2001. 32p. (J). (ps-k). pap. 4.99 *(0-307-29953-8*, Golden Bks.) Random Hse. Children's Bks.

—We Help Daddy. 2001. (Illus.). 2.22 o.s.i *(0-307-34014-7*, Golden Bks.) Random Hse. Children's Bks.

—We Help Mommy. 2001. (Illus.). 2.22 o.s.i *(0-307-34011-2*, Golden Bks.) Random Hse. Children's Bks.

Goldman, E. Maureen. Shrinking Pains. 1996. 160p. (J). (gr. 4-8). 14.99 o.s.i *(0-670-86321-1)* Penguin Putnam Bks. for Young Readers.

Goldman-Rubin, Susan. Emily in Love. 1997. 176p. (J). 14.00 o.s.i *(0-15-200961-2)* Harcourt Trade Pubs.

Gonzales Bertrand, Diane. Family, Familia. Castilla, Julia Mercedes, tr. 1999. (SPA., Illus.). 32p. (J). (ps-3). 14.95 *(1-55885-269-7*, Piñata Books) Arte Publico Pr.

—Sip, Slurp, Soup, Soup. 1997. (SPA., Illus.). 32p. (J). (ps-2). 14.95 *(1-55885-183-6*, Piñata Books) Arte Publico Pr.

Goode, Diane. Thanksgiving Is Here! 2003. (Illus.). 32p. (J). 15.99 *(0-06-051588-0)*; lib. bdg. 16.89 *(0-06-051589-9)* HarperCollins Pubs.

Gorman, Carol. Brian's Footsteps. 1994. (I Witness Ser.). (Illus.). 96p. (Orig.). (J). (gr. 4-7). pap. 4.99 o.p. *(0-570-04629-7*, 12-3210) Concordia Publishing Hse.

Gorsline, Douglas, illus. Little Men: Life at Plumfield with Jo's Boys. 1947. (Illustrated Junior Library). 400p. (J). (gr. 4 up). 16.95 o.s.i *(0-448-06018-3*, Grosset & Dunlap) Penguin Putnam Bks. for Young Readers.

Graber, Richard. A Little Breathing Room. 1978. (J). 6.95 o.p. *(0-06-022059-7)*; lib. bdg. 8.89 o.p. *(0-06-022060-0)* HarperCollins Pubs.

Graef, Renee, illus. Farmer Boy Days. 1998. (Little House Ser.: No. 6). 80p. (J). (gr. 2-5). pap. 4.25 *(0-06-442061-2*, Harper Trophy) HarperCollins Children's Bk. Group.

—Farmer Boy Days. 1998. (Little House Chapter Bks.: No. 6). 80p. (J). (gr. 3-6). lib. bdg. 13.89 o.p. *(0-06-027497-2)* HarperCollins Pubs.

—Hard Times on the Prairie. adapted ed. 1998. (Little House Ser.: No. 8). 80p. (J). (gr. 3-6). pap. 4.25 *(0-06-442077-9*, Harper Trophy); lib. bdg. 15.89 *(0-06-027792-0)* HarperCollins Children's Bk. Group.

—Hard Times on the Prairie. 1998. (Little House Chapter Bks.: No. 8). (J). (gr. 3-6). 10.40 *(0-606-13458-1)* Turtleback Bks.

—Laura & Nellie. 1998. (Little House Chapter Bks.: No. 5). (J). (gr. 3-6). 10.40 *(0-606-12979-0)* Turtleback Bks.

—Laura's Ma. 1999. (Little House Ser.: No. 11). 80p. (J). (gr. 3-6). lib. bdg. 14.89 *(0-06-027897-8)* HarperCollins Children's Bk. Group.

—Pioneer Sisters. 1997. (Little House Ser.: No. 2). 80p. (J). (gr. 3-6). pap. 4.25 *(0-06-442046-9*, Harper Trophy); (gr. 2-5). lib. bdg. 14.89 o.p. *(0-06-027132-9)* HarperCollins Children's Bk. Group.

—Pioneer Sisters. 1997. (Little House Chapter Bks.: No. 2). (J). (gr. 3-6). 10.40 *(0-606-10905-6)* Turtleback Bks.

Graham, Bob. Has Anyone Here Seen William? 2nd ed. 2001. (Illus.). 32p. (J). (ps-k). bds. 4.99 *(0-7636-1551-X)* Candlewick Pr.

—Has Anyone Here Seen William? 1989. (Illus.). 32p. (J). (ps-3). 11.95 o.p. *(0-316-32313-6)* Little Brown & Co.

—Queenie, One of the Family. (Illus.). 32p. (J). (gr. k-3). 2001. bds. 5.99 *(0-7636-1400-9)*; 1997. 15.99 o.p. *(0-7636-0359-7)* Candlewick Pr.

—Spirit of Hope. 1996. (Illus.). 32p. (J). (gr. 2-6). 14.95 *(1-57255-202-6)* Mondo Publishing.

Graham, Brenda K. The Pattersons & the Mysterious Airplane. 1980. (J). (gr. 5-9). 6.50 o.p. *(0-8054-4802-0)* Broadman & Holman Pubs.

Grant, Cynthia D. Mary Wolf. 1997. pap. 4.50 *(0-689-81292-2*, Simon Pulse); 1997. 224p. (J). (gr. 7 up). per. 4.99 *(0-689-81251-5*, Simon Pulse); 1995. 176p. (YA). (gr. 7 up). 16.00 *(0-689-80007-X*, Atheneum) Simon & Schuster Children's Publishing.

—Mary Wolf. 1997. (YA). 11.04 *(0-606-11600-1)* Turtleback Bks.

Graves, Bonnie. Taking Care of Trouble. 2002. (Illus.). 70p. (J). (gr. 3-6). 14.99 *(0-525-46830-7*, Dutton Children's Bks.) Penguin Putnam Bks. for Young Readers.

Gray, Genevieve. Send Wendell. 1974. (Illus.). 40p. (J). (ps-4). o.p. *(0-07-024195-3)* McGraw-Hill Cos., The.

Gray, Libba Moore. Little Lil & the Swing-Singing Sax. 1996. (Illus.). 32p. (J). (gr. k-2). 16.00 o.p. *(0-689-80681-7*, Simon & Schuster Children's Publishing) Simon & Schuster Children's Publishing.

Gray, Nigel. A Country Far Away. 1999. (Illus.). 32p. (J). (ps-3). pap. 11.95 *(0-86264-860-2)* Andersen Pr., Ltd. GBR. *Dist:* Trafalgar Square.

The Great Follywood Fizzle. 2003. (J). 14.99 *(0-310-70586-X)* Zonderkidz.

Green, David W. The Backyard. 1996. (Illus.). 16p. (J). (gr. 2-6). 19.50 *(1-57529-008-1)* Kabel Pubs.

Green, Kate. Everything a Dinosaur Could Want: Asking for Your Needs to Be Met. 1991. (Fossil Family Tales Ser.). (Illus.). 32p. (J). (gr. 1-5). lib. bdg. 22.79 o.p. *(0-89565-739-2)* Child's World, Inc.

Green, Mary M. Everybody Has a House & Everybody Eats. 1961. (Young Scott Bks.). (Illus.). (J). 8.95 o.p. *(0-201-09179-8)* HarperCollins Children's Bk. Group.

Green, Phyllis. Uncle Roland, the Perfect Guest. 1984. (Illus.). 32p. (J). (ps-2). 10.95 o.p. *(0-02-737330-4*, Simon & Schuster Children's Publishing) Simon & Schuster Children's Publishing.

Green, Sylvia. The Best Christmas Ever. 2001. 128p. mass mkt. 3.99 *(0-439-34013-6)* Scholastic, Inc.

Greenberg, Polly. Oh Lord, I Wish I Was a Buzzard. (Illus.). 32p. (J). (gr. k-3). 2003. pap. 5.95 *(1-58717-220-8)*; 2002. 15.95 *(1-58717-122-8)*; 2002. lib. bdg. 16.50 *(1-58717-123-6)* North-South Bks., Inc.

Greenblat, Rodney A. Aunt Ippy's Museum of Junk. 1991. (Illus.). 32p. (J). (gr. k-4). 14.95 o.p. *(0-06-022511-4)*; lib. bdg. 14.89 o.p. *(0-06-022512-2)* HarperCollins Children's Bk. Group.

Greenburg, Dan. How I Went from Bad to Verse. 2000. (Zack Files Ser.). (Illus.). (J). 2.66 o.p. *(0-448-42577-7)*; 64p. (gr. 2-5). mass mkt. 4.99 *(0-448-42042-2)* Penguin Putnam Bks. for Young Readers. (Grosset & Dunlap).

Greene, Constance C. Beat the Turtle Drum. l.t. ed. 1988. 215p. (J). (gr. 5 up). reprint ed. 16.95 o.s.i *(1-55736-039-1*, Cornerstone Bks.) Pages, Inc.

—Beat the Turtle Drum. 1976. (Illus.). 128p. (J). (gr. 4-6). 13.95 o.p. *(0-670-15241-2*, Viking Children's Bks.) Penguin Putnam Bks. for Young Readers.

—Beat the Turtle Drum. 128p. (J). (gr. 4-6). pap. 3.99 (*0-8072-1411-6*, Listening Library) Random Hse. Audio Publishing Group.

—Beat the Turtle Drum. 1994. (J). 11.04 (*0-606-05751-X*) Turtleback Bks.

Greene, Stephanie. Falling into Place. 2002. (Illus.). 128p. (J). (gr. 4-7). tchr. ed. 15.00 (*0-618-17744-2*, Clarion Bks.) Houghton Mifflin Co. Trade & Reference Div.

—Owen Foote, Money Man. (Illus.). 96p. (J). 2003. (ps-3). pap. 4.95 (*0-618-37837-5*); 2000. (gr. 5-9). tchr. ed. 14.00 (*0-618-02369-0*) Houghton Mifflin Co. Trade & Reference Div. (Clarion Bks.).

Greenfield, Eloise. First Pink Light. 1976. (Illus.). 40p. (J). (gr. k-3). lib. bdg. 7.89 o.p. (*0-690-01087-7*) HarperCollins Children's Bk. Group.

—First Pink Light. 1979. (J). pap. 1.50 o.p. (*0-590-12083-2*) Scholastic, Inc.

—First Pink Light. (Illus.). 32p. (J). (ps-4). 1993. pap. 6.95 (*0-86316-212-6*); 1991. 13.95 (*0-86316-207-X*) Writers & Readers Publishing, Inc.

—Sister. 1987. (Trophy Bk.). (Illus.). 96p. (J). (gr. 6 up). reprint ed. pap. 4.99 (*0-06-440199-5*, Harper Trophy) HarperCollins Children's Bk. Group.

—Sister. 1974. (Illus.). 96p. (J). (gr. 5-12). 15.99 (*0-690-00497-4*) HarperCollins Pubs.

—Sister. 1987. (J). 11.10 (*0-606-03469-2*) Turtleback Bks.

Greenwald, Sheila. All the Way to Wit's End. 1979. (Illus.). (J). (gr. 3-7). 12.95 o.s.i (*0-316-32670-4*, Joy Street Bks.) Little Brown & Co.

Greenwood, Barbara. Secret Garden. 2001. (Young Reader's Classics Ser.). (Illus.). 94p. (J). 16.95 (*1-55013-548-1*, Key Porter kids) Key Porter Bks. CAN. *Dist:* Firefly Bks., Ltd.

Gregory, Helen I. A Blanket for Svea: Story Book - Coloring Book - Pattern Book. 1998. (Illus.). 32p. pap. 6.95 (*0-941973-15-8*) Pinstripe Publishing.

Griffin, Adele. Hannah, Divided. (J). 2004. (gr. 3-7). pap. 5.99 (*0-7868-1727-5*); 2002. (Illus.). 272p. (gr. 4-7). 15.99 (*0-7868-0879-9*) Hyperion Bks. for Children.

—The Other Shepards. (J). 2000. 224p. pap. o.s.i (*0-7868-1600-7*); 1998. 224p. (gr. 4-9). 14.95 (*0-7868-0423-8*); 1998. 218p. (gr. 4-9). lib. bdg. 15.49 (*0-7868-2370-4*) Disney Pr.

—The Other Shepards. 1999. 224p. (J). (gr. 5-9). pap. 5.99 (*0-7868-1333-4*) Hyperion Bks. for Children.

—The Other Shepards. l.t. ed. 2000. (Illus.). 209p. (J). (gr. 4-7). 20.95 (*0-7862-2914-4*) Thorndike Pr.

—The Other Shepards. 1999. 12.04 (*0-606-17144-4*) Turtleback Bks.

—Rainy Season. 1998. 208p. (J). (gr. 5-9). reprint ed. pap. 5.95 (*0-7868-1241-9*) Disney Pr.

—Rainy Season. 1996. (Illus.). 208p. (J). (gr. 4-7). tchr. ed. 14.95 o.p. (*0-395-81181-3*) Houghton Mifflin Co.

—Rainy Season. 1998. 12.00 (*0-606-13726-2*) Turtleback Bks.

—Sons of Liberty. 1998. 230p. (J). (gr. 5-9). pap. 4.95 (*0-7868-1300-8*) Disney Pr.

—Sons of Liberty. 1997. (Illus.). 240p. (J). (gr. 5-12). 14.95 (*0-7868-0351-7*); lib. bdg. 15.49 (*0-7868-2292-9*) Hyperion Bks. for Children.

—Sons of Liberty. 1998. 11.00 (*0-606-15709-3*) Turtleback Bks.

—Witch Twins. 2001. (Illus.). 160p. (J). (gr. 2-5). 14.99 (*0-7868-0739-3*, Volo) Hyperion Bks. for Children.

—Witch Twins. 2002. 160p. (J). (gr. 3-6). pap. 5.99 (*0-7868-1563-9*) Hyperion Paperbacks for Children.

—Witch Twins. l.t. ed. 2002. 174p. (J). 21.95 (*0-7862-4397-X*) Thorndike Pr.

Griffin, Peni R. A Dig in Time. 1992. 160p. (J). (gr. 3-7). pap. 3.99 o.p. (*0-14-036001-8*, Puffin Bks.) Penguin Putnam Bks. for Young Readers.

—A Dig in Time. 1991. 192p. (J). (gr. 4-7). 14.95 (*0-689-50525-6*, McElderry, Margaret K.) Simon & Schuster Children's Publishing.

—The Music Thief, ERS. 2002. 160p. (YA). (gr. 5-8). 16.95 (*0-8050-7055-9*, Holt, Henry & Co. Bks. For Young Readers) Holt, Henry & Co.

—The Music Thief. l.t. ed. 2003. 190p. (J). 21.95 (*0-7862-5606-0*) Thorndike Pr.

Griffith, Clay. The Stupids. 1995. (J). pap. 4.99 (*0-553-54223-0*, Dell Books for Young Readers) Random Hse. Children's Bks.

Griffith, Connie. Mysterious Rescuer. 1994. (Tootie McCarthy Ser.: Bk. 4). 128p. (Orig.). (J). (gr. 6-9). pap. 6.99 o.p. (*0-8010-3865-0*) Baker Bks.

—Secret Behind Locked Doors. 1994. (Tootie McCarthy Ser.: Bk. 3). 128p. (J). (gr. 6-9). pap. 6.99 o.p. (*0-8010-3864-2*) Baker Bks.

Griffiths, Helen. Grip, a Dog Story. 1981. (Illus.). (J). (gr. 5-7). pap. (*0-671-56034-4*, Simon Pulse) Simon & Schuster Children's Publishing.

Grimes, Nikki. My Man Blue. 2002. (Illus.). 32p. (J). (ps-3). pap. 6.99 (*0-14-230197-3*, Puffin Bks.) Penguin Putnam Bks. for Young Readers.

Grossman, Linda Sky. A Tale Worth Telling. 2002. (I'm a Great Little Kid Ser.). (Illus.). 24p. (YA). (gr. 3 up). 12.95 (*1-896764-62-2*); (J). pap. 4.95 (*1-896764-60-6*) Second Story Pr. CAN. *Dist:* Orca Bk. Pubs.

Grote, JoAnn A. Queen Anne's War. 1999. (American Adventure Ser.: No. 5). 144p. (J). (gr. 3-7). lib. bdg. 15.95 (*0-7910-5045-9*) Chelsea Hse. Pubs.

Grove, Vicki. Reaching Dustin. 2000. (Illus.). 208p. (YA). (gr. 4-9). pap. 5.99 (*0-698-11839-1*, Puffin Bks.) Penguin Putnam Bks. for Young Readers.

—Reaching Dustin. 2000. 12.04 (*0-606-18844-4*) Turtleback Bks.

Groves. Best Duster Bk. 5. Date not set. (J). pap. text 129.15 (*0-582-18766-4*) Addison-Wesley Longman, Ltd. GBR. *Dist:* Trans-Atlantic Pubns., Inc.

—Sticky Trousers. Date not set. (J). pap. text 129.15 (*0-582-18304-9*) Addison-Wesley Longman, Ltd. GBR. *Dist:* Trans-Atlantic Pubns., Inc.

Guenter, Clarence A. God's Children. 1998. (Illus.). 106p. (J). (gr. 5-7). pap. text 8.00 (*1-58345-027-0*) Domhan Bks.

Gugler, Laurel Dee. Facing the Day. 1999. (Illus.). 24p. (J). lib. bdg. 15.95 (*1-55037-577-6*) Annick Pr., Ltd. CAN. *Dist:* Firefly Bks., Ltd.

Guiberson, Brenda Z. Turtle People. 1990. 112p. (J). (gr. 3-6). lib. bdg. 13.95 o.p. (*0-689-31647-X*, Atheneum) Simon & Schuster Children's Publishing.

Guinn, Jeff. Sometimes a Fantasy: Midlife Misadventures with Baseball Heroes. Swindell, Larry & Towle, Mike, eds. 1993. (Illus.). 349p. (J). 22.95 (*1-56530-042-4*) Summit Publishing Group - Legacy Bks.

Gunn, Robin Jones. Only You - Sierra. 1998. (Sierra Jensen Ser.: No. 1). 176p. (J). (gr. 7-11). pap. 6.99 (*1-56179-370-1*) Focus on the Family Publishing.

—Time Will Tell. 1998. (Sierra Jensen Ser.: No. 8). 160p. (YA). (gr. 7-11). pap. 6.99 (*1-56179-568-2*) Focus on the Family Publishing.

Gunning, Monica. Under the Breadfruit Tree. 2004. (Illus.). (J). pap. 8.95 (*1-59078-258-5*) Boyds Mills Pr.

Gusman, Annie, illus. Small Cloud. 1996. 24p. (J). (ps-3). reprint ed. pap. 5.95 (*0-8027-7490-3*) Walker & Co.

Gutman, Dan. The Edison Mystery. 2001. (Qwerty Stevens Ser.). (Illus.). 208p. (J). (gr. 4-8). 16.00 (*0-689-84124-8*, Simon & Schuster Children's Publishing) Simon & Schuster Children's Publishing.

Guy, Rosa. Edith Jackson. 1981. 192p. pap. 1.95 o.p. (*0-553-20109-3*) Bantam Bks.

—Edith Jackson. 1992. 192p. (YA). (gr. 7 up). mass mkt. 3.50 o.s.i (*0-440-21137-9*) Dell Publishing.

—Edith Jackson. 1993. (J). (gr. 7 up). 17.00 o.p. (*0-8446-6690-4*) Smith, Peter Pub., Inc.

—Edith Jackson. 1978. 180p. (J). (gr. 7 up). 11.50 o.p. (*0-670-28906-X*) Viking Penguin.

Haas, Jessie. Clean House. 1996. (Illus.). 56p. (J). (ps-3). 15.00 (*0-688-14079-3*, Greenwillow Bks.) HarperCollins Children's Bk. Group.

—Skipping School. 1992. (J). (gr. 6-12). 14.00 o.s.i (*0-688-10179-8*, Greenwillow Bks.) HarperCollins Children's Bk. Group.

—Unbroken: A Novel. 2001. 208p. (J). (gr. 5 up). pap. 5.95 (*0-380-73313-7*, Harper Trophy) HarperCollins Children's Bk. Group.

Hafner, Marylin. Mommies Don't Get Sick! (Illus.). 32p. (J). (gr. k-3). 1995. 14.95 o.p. (*1-56402-287-0*); 1997. reprint ed. bds. 5.99 (*0-7636-0154-3*) Candlewick Pr.

Hahn, Mary Downing. Anna All Year Round. 2001. (Illus.). 144p. (J). (gr. 4-7). pap. 4.95 (*0-380-73317-X*, Harper Trophy) HarperCollins Children's Bk. Group.

—Anna All Year Round. 2001. (Illus.). (J). 11.00 (*0-606-21037-7*) Turtleback Bks.

—Anna All Year Round. 1999. (Illus.). 144p. (J). (gr. 4-6). tchr. ed. 15.00 (*0-395-86975-7*, Clarion Bks.) Houghton Mifflin Co. Trade & Reference Div.

—Stepping on the Cracks. 1991. 224p. (YA). (gr. 7-7). tchr. ed. 16.00 (*0-395-58507-4*, Clarion Bks.) Houghton Mifflin Co. Trade & Reference Div.

—Stepping on the Cracks. 1992. 224p. (J). (gr. 3-7). pap. 5.99 (*0-380-71900-2*, Avon Bks.) Morrow/Avon.

—Stepping on the Cracks. 1991. (J). 11.00 (*0-606-00435-1*) Turtleback Bks.

Hall, Barbara. Dixie Storms. 1990. 197p. (YA). (gr. 7 up). 15.95 (*0-15-223825-5*) Harcourt Trade Pubs.

Hall, Elizabeth. Stand up, Lucy. 1971. (Illus.). (J). (gr. 3-7). 5.95 o.p. (*0-395-12365-8*) Houghton Mifflin Co.

Hall, Kirsten. Oops! 2004. (Beastieville-Pb Ser.). pap. 3.95 (*0-516-24657-7*, Children's Pr.) Scholastic Library Publishing.

Hall, Lynn. Flyaway. 1987. 128p. (YA). (gr. 7 up). 12.95 o.s.i (*0-684-18888-0*, Atheneum) Simon & Schuster Children's Publishing.

—Windsong. 1992. 80p. (J). (gr. 6-8). mass mkt. 12.95 (*0-684-19439-2*, Atheneum) Simon & Schuster Children's Publishing.

Halperin, Wendy Anderson. Once upon a Company. 1998. (Illus.). 40p. (J). (gr. k-4). pap. 16.95 (*0-531-30089-7*); lib. bdg. 17.99 (*0-531-33089-3*) Scholastic, Inc. (Orchard Bks.).

Hamalainen, Marilyn. What's Wrong with Melissa? 1983. (Illus.). 96p. (Orig.). (YA). (gr. 7-11). pap. 1.95 o.p. (*0-88243-641-4*, 02-0641) Gospel Publishing Hse.

Hambrick, Sharon. Arby Jenkins. 1996. 117p. (J). (gr. 4-7). pap. 6.49 (*0-89084-879-3*, 099622) Jones, Bob Univ. Pr.

—Booklinks, Level 1. 1997. 128p. (J). (gr. 6). pap. 6.49 (*0-89084-932-3*, 106138) Jones, Bob Univ. Pr.

Hamilton, Dorothy. The Eagle. 1974. 168p. 6.95 o.p. (*0-8361-1748-4*) Herald Pr.

—Linda's Rain Tree. 1975. (Illus.). 120p. (J). (gr. 4-8). 4.95 o.p. (*0-8361-1777-8*); pap. 3.95 o.p. (*0-8361-1778-6*) Herald Pr.

—Rosalie. 1977. (Illus.). 128p. (J). (gr. 3-10). text 4.95 o.p. (*0-8361-1806-5*); pap. text 3.95 o.p. (*0-8361-1807-3*) Herald Pr.

Hamilton, Gail. Family Rivalry. 1993. (Road to Avonlea Ser.: No. 16). 128p. (J). (gr. 4-6). pap. 3.99 o.p. (*0-553-48042-1*) Bantam Bks.

—Titantia's Lodestone. 1975. 240p. (J). (gr. 5-9). 1.98 o.p. (*0-689-30449-8*, Atheneum) Simon & Schuster Children's Publishing.

Hamilton, Kersten. Adam Straight to the Rescue. Norton, LoraBeth, ed. 1991. (Adam Straight Ser.). 96p. (J). (gr. 4-6). pap. 4.99 o.p. (*1-55513-386-X*) Cook Communications Ministries.

Hamilton, Virginia. Arilla Sun Down. 1976. 256p. (J). (gr. 7 up). 12.50 o.p. (*0-688-80058-0*); lib. bdg. 14.88 o.p. (*0-688-84058-2*) HarperCollins Children's Bk. Group. (Greenwillow Bks.).

—The Great M. C. Higgins, 6 vols. 3rd ed. (J). pap. text 23.70 (*0-13-620220-9*); pap. text 3.95 (*0-13-800137-5*) Prentice Hall (Schl. Div.).

—M. C. Higgins, the Great. l.t. ed. 1988. 320p. (J). (gr. 3-7). reprint ed. lib. bdg. 15.95 o.p. (*1-55736-075-8*) Bantam Doubleday Dell Large Print Group, Inc.

—M. C. Higgins, the Great. 1998. (J). pap. 4.50 (*0-87628-568-X*) Ctr. for Applied Research in Education, The.

—M. C. Higgins, the Great. l.t. ed. 1976. 400 p. lib. bdg. 10.95 o.p. (*0-8161-6356-1*, Macmillan Reference USA) Gale Group.

—M. C. Higgins, the Great. pap. text, stu. ed. (*0-13-620246-2*) Prentice Hall (Schl. Div.).

—M. C. Higgins, the Great. 1976. 240p. (J). (gr. 7 up). pap. 2.50 o.s.i (*0-440-95598-X*, Laurel Leaf) Random Hse. Children's Bks.

—M. C. Higgins, the Great. 2003. (J). E-Book 6.99 (*0-689-84806-4*, Simon & Schuster Children's Publishing); 1998. (J). pap. 2.65 o.p. (*0-689-82168-9*, Aladdin); 1974. 288p. (YA). (gr. 7 up). lib. bdg. 17.00 (*0-02-742480-4*, Simon & Schuster Children's Publishing); 1987. 288p. (YA). (gr. 5-9). reprint ed. pap. 4.99 (*0-02-043490-1*, Simon Pulse); 2nd ed. 1993. 288p. (J). (gr. 4-7). reprint ed. mass mkt. 4.99 (*0-689-71694-X*, Simon Pulse); 25th anniv. ed. 1999. (Illus.). 240p. (J). (gr. 7). 18.00 (*0-689-83074-2*, Simon & Schuster Children's Publishing) Simon & Schuster Children's Publishing.

—M. C. Higgins, the Great. 1987. (J). 11.04 (*0-606-02497-2*) Turtleback Bks.

—M. C. Higgins, the Great & Newbery Summer. 2003. 288p. (J). pap. 2.99 (*0-689-86228-8*, Aladdin) Simon & Schuster Children's Publishing.

Hamm, Diane J. Daughter of Suqua. 1997. 160p. (J). (gr. 5-7). lib. bdg. 14.95 o.p. (*0-8075-1477-2*) Whitman, Albert & Co.

—Second Family. 1992. 128p. (J). (gr. 5-7). 13.95 o.p. (*0-684-19436-8*, Atheneum) Simon & Schuster Children's Publishing.

Harder Tangvald, Christine. My Family Is Special. 1987. (God Made Me Special Bks.). (J). (ps). bds. 5.88 o.p. (*1-55513-169-7*) Cook Communications Ministries.

Hare, Sharon C. Now I Have Two Homes. 1995. (Illus.). 20p. (Orig.). (J). (ps-3). pap. 5.00 (*0-9639450-2-5*) Joy Enterprises.

Hargreaves, Roger. Mr. Tickle. 1998. (Mr. Men & Little Miss Ser.). (Illus.). 32p. (J). (gr. k up). 2.99 (*0-8431-7422-6*) Putnam Publishing Group, The.

Harlan, Elizabeth. Watershed. 1986. (Viking Kestrel Novels Ser.). 224p. (J). (gr. 5-9). 12.95 o.p. (*0-670-80824-5*, Viking Children's Bks.) Penguin Putnam Bks. for Young Readers.

Harris, Mark J. Come the Morning. 1989. 176p. (J). (gr. 5-9). lib. bdg. 14.95 o.s.i (*0-02-742750-1*, Simon & Schuster Children's Publishing) Simon & Schuster Children's Publishing.

Harris, Robie H. Hi New Baby. 2003. (Illus.). 32p. (J). bds. 6.99 (*0-7636-1826-8*) Candlewick Pr.

Harris, Ruth Elwin. Frances' Story: Sisters of the Quantock Hills. 2002. 304p. (YA). (gr. 7 up). bds. 5.99 (*0-7636-1704-0*) Candlewick Pr.

—Gwen's Story. 2002. 304p. (YA). (gr. 7 up). bds. 5.99 (*0-7636-1705-9*) Candlewick Pr.

—Julia's Story. 2002. 304p. (YA). (gr. 7 up). bds. 5.99 (*0-7636-1706-7*) Candlewick Pr.

—Sarah's Story. 2002. 304p. (YA). (gr. 7 up). bds. 5.99 (*0-7636-1707-5*) Candlewick Pr.

Harrison, Pam & Worthinglon, Denise. Snuggle Up. 1998. (Illus.). 8p. (J). (gr. k-2). pap. 3.75 (*1-880612-75-5*) Seedling Pubns., Inc.

Harrison, Troon. A Bushel of Light. 2001. 224p. (YA). (gr. 7-9). pap. 7.95 (*0-7737-6140-3*) Stoddart Kids CAN. *Dist:* Fitzhenry & Whiteside, Ltd.

Harry Moore Family. Sad Dad. 1985. (Illus.). (J). pap. 0.59 o.p. (*0-8170-0432-7*) Judson Pr.

Hart, Carole. Delilah. 1983. (Illus.). 64p. (J). (gr. 2-5). pap. 1.95 o.p. (*0-380-62729-9*, 62729-9, Avon Bks.) Morrow/Avon.

Hart, Jan S. The Many Adventures of Minnie. 1992. (Illus.). 96p. (J). (gr. 4-7). 12.95 o.p. (*0-89015-859-2*) Eakin Pr.

—The Many Adventures of Minnie. 1997. (Illus.). 111p. (J). (gr. 3-6). reprint ed. 12.95 (*0-9644559-2-7*) Hart Publishing.

Hart, Laverne. Billy Bentson & His Family. 1981. (J). (gr. k-3). bds. 5.95 o.p. (*0-8054-4270-7*) Broadman & Holman Pubs.

Hartman, Bob. Granny Mae's Christmas Play. 2004. (Illus.). 40p. (J). (gr. k-5). 16.99 (*0-8066-4063-4*, Augsburg Bks.) Augsburg Fortress, Pubs.

Hartnett, Sonya. Thursday's Child. 272p. 2003. (Illus.). pap. 7.99 (*0-7636-2203-6*); 2002. (YA). (gr. 9 up). 15.99 (*0-7636-1620-6*) Candlewick Pr.

—Thursday's Child. 2000. 223p. (*0-14-029732-4*) Penguin Group (USA) Inc.

Harvey, Jayne. Great-Uncle Dracula & the Dirty Rat. 1993. (Stepping Stone Book Ser.). (Illus.). 64p. (J). (gr. 2-4). pap. 2.50 o.s.i (*0-679-83457-5*, Random Hse. Bks. for Young Readers) Random Hse. Children's Bks.

Harwood, Pearl A. Mr. Bumba Keeps House. 1964. (Mr. Bumba Bks.). (Illus.). 32p. (J). (gr. k-3). lib. bdg. 5.95 o.p. (*0-8225-0103-1*, Lerner Pubns.) Lerner Publishing Group.

Haskins, James. The March on Washington. 2003. 192p. (YA). (gr. 5 up). pap. 10.95 (*0-940975-93-9*) Just Us Bks., Inc.

Hassler, Kurt. Hannah & the Homunculus. 2001. (Illus.). 28p. (J). 15.95 (*1-58536-043-0*) Sleeping Bear Pr.

Hatton, Caroline K. Vero & Philippe. 2001. (Illus.). 120p. (J). (gr. 3-7). 14.95 (*0-8126-2940-X*) Cricket Bks.

Hausman, Gerald & Hinds, Uton. The Jacob Ladder. 2001. (Illus.). 120p. (J). (gr. 5-8). pap. 15.95 (*0-531-30331-4*, Orchard Bks.) Scholastic, Inc.

Hautzig, Deborah. Little Witch Learns to Read. 2003. (Illus.). 48p. (J). (gr. 1-3). pap. 3.99 (*0-375-82179-1*); lib. bdg. 11.99 (*0-375-92179-6*) Random Hse. Children's Bks. (Random Hse. Bks. for Young Readers).

Hautzig, Esther. A Gift for Mama. 1981. (Illus.). 64p. (J). (gr. 3-7). 8.95 o.p. (*0-670-33976-8*) Viking Penguin.

Hautzig, Esther Rudomin. A Picture of Grandmother, RS. 2002. (Illus.). 80p. (J). (gr. 2-5). 15.00 (*0-374-35920-2*, Farrar, Straus & Giroux (BYR)) Farrar, Straus & Giroux.

Haven, Susan P. Maybe I'll Move to the Lost & Found. 1988. 160p. (YA). (gr. 5 up). 14.95 o.p. (*0-399-21509-3*, G. P. Putnam's Sons) Penguin Putnam Bks. for Young Readers.

Hayes, Joe. Little Gold Star (Estrellita de Oro) A Cinderella Cuento. 2000. (ENG & SPA., Illus.). 32p. (J). (ps-3). 15.95 (*0-938317-49-0*, CPP7490) Cinco Puntos Pr.

Haynes, Betsy. The Great Mom Swap. 1990. (J). pap. o.s.i (*0-553-54003-3*, Dell Books for Young Readers) Random Hse. Children's Bks.

Haynes, David. The Gumma Wars. 1997. (West 7th Wildcats Ser.). (Illus.). 128p. (J). (gr. 2-6). pap. 6.95 o.p. (*1-57131-610-8*) Milkweed Editions.

Hazen, Barbara Shook. Tiempos Duros: Tight Times. 1993. (Illus.). 32p. (J). (ps-3). 12.99 o.p. (*0-670-84841-7*, Viking Children's Bks.) Penguin Putnam Bks. for Young Readers.

—Why Couldn't I Be an Only Kid Like You, Wigger. (Illus.). (J). (ps-2). 1979. pap. 1.95 o.s.i (*0-689-70460-7*, Simon & Schuster Children's Publishing); 1975. 32p. 7.95 o.s.i (*0-689-30488-9*, Atheneum) Simon & Schuster Children's Publishing.

Hazen, Nancy. Grown-Ups Cry Too: Los Adultos Tambien Lloran-English-Spanish Text. Cotera, Martha P., tr. 2nd ed. 1978. (Illus.). 25p. (J). (ps-1). pap. 4.95 (*0-914996-19-3*) Lollipop Power Bks.

Head, Ann. Mr. & Mrs. Bo Jo Jones. 1968. (Illus.). 192p. (YA). (gr. 7 up). mass mkt. 4.99 (*0-451-16319-2*, Signet Bks.) NAL.

Heal, Gillian. The Halfpennys Find a Home. 1995. (Illus.). 32p. (J). (ps-3). 12.95 o.p. (*1-885223-04-8*) Beyond Words Publishing, Inc.

—Twilight in Grace Falls. 1999. 192p. (J). (gr. 3-7). pap. 4.50 (*0-380-73128-2*, Avon Bks.) Morrow/Avon.

—Twilight in Grace Falls. 1997. 192p. (YA). (gr. 6-9). pap. 16.95 o.p. (*0-531-30007-2*); lib. bdg. 17.99 (*0-531-33007-9*) Scholastic, Inc. (Orchard Bks.).

—Twilight in Grace Falls. 1999. 10.55 (*0-606-15928-2*) Turtleback Bks.

Hoobler, Dorothy & Hoobler, Thomas. The Second Decade: Voyages. 2000. E-Book 21.90 (*0-585-35349-2*) netLibrary, Inc.

—The 1910s: Voyages. 2000. (Century Kids Ser.). (Illus.). 160p. (YA). (gr. 5-8). 22.90 (*0-7613-1601-9*) Millbrook Pr., Inc.

—The 1970s: Arguments. 2002. (Century Kids Ser.). (Illus.). 160p. (YA). (gr. 5-8). 22.90 (*0-7613-1607-8*) Millbrook Pr., Inc.

hooks, bell. Homemade Love. 2001. (Illus.). 32p. (J). lib. bdg. 16.49 (*0-7868-2553-7*) Hyperion Bks. for Children.

Hooks, William H. Crossing the Line. 1978. (YA). 6.95 o.p. (*0-394-83938-2*); lib. bdg. 6.99 o.p. (*0-394-93938-7*) Random Hse. Children's Bks. (Knopf Bks. for Young Readers).

—A Flight of Dazzle Angels. 1988. 176p. (YA). (gr. 7 up). lib. bdg. 13.95 o.p. (*0-02-744430-9*, Simon & Schuster Children's Publishing) Simon & Schuster Children's Publishing.

—Where's Lulu? 1998. (Bank Street Reader Collection). (Illus.). 48p. (J). (ps-2). lib. bdg. 21.26 (*0-8368-1768-0*) Stevens, Gareth Inc.

Horvath, Polly. The Happy Yellow Car, RS. (J). 2004. (Illus.). pap. 5.95 (*0-374-42879-4*); 1994. 128p. (gr. 4-7). 15.00 o.p. (*0-374-32845-5*, Farrar, Straus & Giroux (BYR)) Farrar, Straus & Giroux.

—The Trolls, RS. 144p. (J). (gr. 3-7). 1999. 16.00 (*0-374-37787-1*, Farrar, Straus & Giroux (BYR)); 2001. reprint ed. pap. 4.95 (*0-374-47991-7*, Sunburst) Farrar, Straus & Giroux.

—When the Circus Comes to Town. 1969. (Americana Books Ser.). (Illus.). (J). 2.00 o.p. (*0-911410-23-6*) Applied Arts Pubs.

—When the Circus Comes to Town, RS. 1996. 112p. (J). (gr. 3-7). 15.00 o.p. (*0-374-38308-1*, Farrar, Straus & Giroux (BYR)) Farrar, Straus & Giroux.

Houghton Mifflin Company Staff. Daddy Wore Striped Shorts. 1992. (Literature Experience 1993 Ser.). (J). (gr. 1). pap. 8.72 (*0-395-61758-8*) Houghton Mifflin Co.

Houston, Gloria M. Littlejim's Gift: An Appalachian Christmas Story. 1994. (Illus.). 32p. (J). (gr. 1-5). 16.99 o.s.i (*0-399-22696-6*, Philomel) Penguin Putnam Bks. for Young Readers.

Howard, Elizabeth Fitzgerald. Flower Girl Butterflies. 2004. 32p. (J). 15.99 (*0-688-17809-X*, Greenwillow Bks.) HarperCollins Children's Bk. Group.

Howard, Ellen. The Log Cabin Quilt. 1996. (Illus.). 32p. (J). (ps-3). tchr. ed. 16.95 (*0-8234-1247-4*) Holiday Hse., Inc.

—Sister. 1990. 160p. (J). (gr. 3-7). lib. bdg. 13.95 o.p. (*0-689-31653-4*, Atheneum) Simon & Schuster Children's Publishing.

Howe, James. Hay un Dragon en Mi Bolsa de Dormir. 1998. Tr. of There's a Dragon in My Sleeping Bag. (SPA., Illus.). 40p. (J). (ps-2). pap. 6.99 (*0-689-81923-4*, Aladdin) Simon & Schuster Children's Publishing.

—There's a Dragon in My Sleeping Bag. 1998. (Illus.). 40p. (J). (ps-2). pap. 5.99 (*0-689-81922-6*, Aladdin) Simon & Schuster Children's Publishing.

—The Watcher. (YA). (gr. 7-12). 1999. 192p. pap. 8.00 (*0-689-82662-1*, 076714008007, Simon Pulse); 1997. 184p. 16.00 (*0-689-80186-6*, Atheneum) Simon & Schuster Children's Publishing.

—The Watcher. 1999. 14.05 (*0-606-16319-0*) Turtleback Bks.

Howell, Troy, illus. Little Men: Life at Plumfield with Jo's Boys. 1991. (Children's Classics Ser.). 202p. (J). (gr. 4 up). 11.95 o.p. (*0-681-41080-9*) Borders Pr.

Howker, Janni. The Topiary Garden. 1995. (Illus.). 64p. (YA). (gr. 2 up). mass mkt. 14.95 o.p. (*0-531-06891-9*, Orchard Bks.) Scholastic, Inc.

Hrdlitschka, Shelley. Disconnected. 1999. 144p. (YA). (gr. 7-9). pap. 6.95 (*1-55143-105-X*) Orca Bk. Pubs.

Hubbell, Patricia. Bouncing Time. 2000. (Illus.). 32p. (ps up). (J). lib. bdg. 15.89 (*0-688-17377-2*); (YA). 15.95 (*0-688-17376-4*) HarperCollins Children's Bk. Group.

Hudson, Jan. Sweetgrass. 1991. 160p. (YA). (gr. 7-9). pap. 3.99 (*0-590-43486-1*) Scholastic, Inc.

—Sweetgrass. 1984. 9.09 o.p. (*0-606-04820-0*) Turtleback Bks.

Hughes, Pat. The Breaker Boys, RS. 2004. (J). (*0-374-30956-6*) Farrar, Straus & Giroux.

Hughes, Shirley. The Big Alfie Out of Doors Storybook. 1992. (Illus.). 64p. (J). (ps-3). 17.00 (*0-688-11428-8*) HarperCollins Children's Bk. Group.

The Hundred Penny Box. 1999. (J). 9.95 (*1-56137-386-9*) Novel Units, Inc.

Hunt, Irene. Up a Road Slowly. 1966. (J). (gr. 7 up). 4.95 o.p. (*0-695-89009-3*); lib. bdg. 4.98 o.p. (*0-695-49009-5*) Modern Curriculum Pr.

—Up a Road Slowly. 9999. (J). pap. 1.95 o.s.i (*0-590-03171-6*) Scholastic, Inc.

—William. 1977. (J). (gr. 5 up). 11.95 o.s.i (*0-684-14902-8*, Atheneum) Simon & Schuster Children's Publishing.

Hunter, Janer N. It's a Terrible Age to Be. 1989. 172p. (J). (gr. 5-8). pap. 2.95 o.p. (*0-87406-388-4*) Darby Creek Publishing.

Hunter, Lynn, et al. Meet the Dooples, Set. 1997. (Illus.). (J). (ps-2). 24.95 incl. audio (*0-9656279-2-6*); 32p. lib. bdg. 19.95 (*0-9656279-1-8*) Educational Media Enterprises, Inc.

Hurst, James. The Scarlet Ibis: A Classic Story of Brotherhood. 1993. (Creative Short Stories Ser.). (Illus.). 32p. (YA). (gr. 4-12). lib. bdg. 18.60 (*0-88682-000-6*, Creative Education) Creative Co., The.

Hurwitz, Johanna. Aldo Peanut Butter. 1992. (Illus.). 128p. (J). (gr. 4-7). pap. 4.99 o.s.i (*0-14-036020-4*, Puffin Bks.) Penguin Putnam Bks. for Young Readers.

—E Is for Elisa. 2003. (Riverside Kids Ser.). (Illus.). 96p. (J). (gr. 1-4). pap. 4.25 (*0-06-054374-4*) HarperCollins Children's Bk. Group.

—E Is for Elisa. 1991. (Illus.). 80p. (J). (ps-3). 12.89 (*0-688-10440-1*); 12.95 (*0-688-10439-8*) Morrow/Avon. (Morrow, William & Co.).

—E Is for Elisa. 1993. (Young Puffin Ser.). (Illus.). 96p. (J). (gr. 4-7). pap. 4.99 o.p. (*0-14-036033-6*, Puffin Bks.) Penguin Putnam Bks. for Young Readers.

—E Is for Elisa. 1993. 11.04 (*0-606-02608-8*) Turtleback Bks.

—Elisa in the Middle. 1995. (Illus.). 96p. (J). (ps-3). 14.95 (*0-688-14050-5*, Morrow, William & Co.) Morrow/Avon.

—Ethan at Home. 2003. (Illus.). 8p. (J). bds. 5.99 (*0-7636-1092-5*) Candlewick Pr.

—Ever Clever Elisa. 1997. (Illus.). 64p. (J). (gr. k-3). 15.00 (*0-688-15189-2*, Morrow, William & Co.) Morrow/Avon.

—Make Room for Elisa. 1993. (Illus.). 80p. (J). (gr. k up). 15.00 o.s.i (*0-688-12404-6*, Morrow, William & Co.) Morrow/Avon.

—Make Room for Elisa. 1995. (Illus.). 96p. (J). pap. 3.99 o.s.i (*0-14-037034-X*, Puffin Bks.) Penguin Putnam Bks. for Young Readers.

—Oh No, Noah! (J). (gr. 2-4). 2003. 144p. pap. 4.95 (*1-58717-231-3*); 2002. (Illus.). 128p. 14.95 (*1-58717-133-3*) North-South Bks., Inc.

—Ozzie on His Own. 1995. (Illus.). 128p. (J). (gr. 4-7). 15.99 (*0-688-13742-3*) HarperCollins Children's Bk. Group.

—The Rabbi's Girls. 2002. Orig. Title: The Diddakoi. (Illus.). 144p. (J). pap. 5.95 (*0-06-447370-8*, Harper Trophy) HarperCollins Children's Bk. Group.

—The Rabbi's Girls. 1982. Orig. Title: The Diddakoi. (Illus.). 192p. (J). (gr. 4-6). 15.00 o.p. (*0-688-01089-X*, Morrow, William & Co.) Morrow/Avon.

—Roz & Ozzie. 1992. (Illus.). 128p. (J). (gr. 2 up). 13.00 o.p. (*0-688-10945-4*, Morrow, William & Co.) Morrow/Avon.

—Summer with Elisa. (Riverside Kids Ser.). (Illus.). (J). 2002. 128p. pap. 4.25 (*0-06-000480-0*, Harper Trophy); 2000. 96p. 15.95 (*0-688-17095-1*) HarperCollins Children's Bk. Group.

—Superduper Teddy. 2001. (Illus.). (J). 10.30 (*0-606-22039-9*) Turtleback Bks.

—Tough-Luck Karen. 1982. (Illus.). 160p. (J). (gr. 4-6). 15.95 (*0-688-01485-2*, Morrow, William & Co.) Morrow/Avon.

Hurwitz, Johanna & Hafner, Marylin. Ethan at Home. 2003. (Brand New Readers Ser.). (Illus.). 8p. (J). 12.99 (*0-7636-1093-3*) Candlewick Pr.

Hutchins, Pat. The Doorbell Rang. 1989. (Illus.). 24p. (J). (ps-3). pap. 5.99 (*0-688-09234-9*, Harper Trophy) HarperCollins Children's Bk. Group.

—Llaman a la Puerta. 1996. (SPA., Illus.). pap., tchr. ed. 31.95 incl. audio (*0-87499-372-5*); (J). 24.95 incl. audio (*0-87499-371-7*); (J). pap. 15.95 incl. audio (*0-87499-370-9*, LK1625) Live Oak Media.

—Llaman a la Puerta. 1994. 13.10 (*0-606-06544-X*) Turtleback Bks.

—Titch. 1971. (Illus.). 40p. (J). (ps-1). lib. bdg. 14.95 o.s.i (*0-02-745880-6*, Simon & Schuster Children's Publishing) Simon & Schuster Children's Publishing.

—You'll Soon Grow into Them, Titch. 1992. (J). 12.10 (*0-606-01325-3*) Turtleback Bks.

Hyppolite, Joanne. Ola Shakes It Up. 1998. (Illus.). 176p. (gr. 2-6). text 14.95 o.s.i (*0-385-32235-6*, Delacorte Pr.) Dell Publishing.

—Ola Shakes It Up. 1999. (Illus.). 176p. (gr. 4-7). pap. text 4.50 o.s.i (*0-440-41204-8*, Dell Books for Young Readers) Random Hse. Children's Bks.

—Seth & Samona. 1996. (Illus.). 128p. pap. text 3.99 o.s.i (*0-440-41272-2*) Dell Publishing.

—Seth & Samona. 2001. 128p. (gr. 3-7). pap. text 12.00 (*0-375-89508-6*, Random Hse. Bks. for Young Readers); 1995. (J). 18.95 (*0-385-44630-6*, Dell Books for Young Readers) Random Hse. Children's Bks.

—Seth & Samona. 1997. 9.09 o.p. (*0-606-10928-5*) Turtleback Bks.

Hébert, Marie-Francine & Perkes, Carolyn. Daddy, Can I Have the Moon? 2001. (Illus.). 32p. (J). (ps up). (*1-894363-79-5*) Dominique & Friends.

I Know Why the Caged Bird Sings. 1998. 44p. (YA). 11.95 (*1-56137-634-5*, NU6345SP) Novel Units, Inc.

I Love You Like Crazy Cakes. 2002. (J). 24.95 incl. audio (*1-55592-095-0*); 29.95 incl. audio compact disk (*1-55592-135-3*) Weston Woods Studios, Inc.

Ihimaera, Witi. The Whale Rider. 2003. (YA). (gr. 3-6). 152p. 17.00 (*0-15-205017-5*); 168p. pap. 8.00 (*0-15-205016-7*, Harcourt Paperbacks) Harcourt Children's Bks.

Ingman, Bruce. Lost Property. 1998. (Illus.). 22p. (J). (ps-3). 15.00 o.s.i (*0-395-88900-6*) Houghton Mifflin Co.

Ingold, Jeanette. Airfield. 2001. (J). 12.04 (*0-606-21017-2*) Turtleback Bks.

—Mountain Solo. 2003. 320p. (J). 17.00 (*0-15-202670-3*) Harcourt Children's Bks.

—The Window. 1996. 192p. (YA). (gr. 7 up). 13.00 o.s.i (*0-15-201265-6*); pap. 6.00 o.s.i (*0-15-201264-8*, Harcourt Paperbacks) Harcourt Children's Bks.

—The Window. 2003. 208p. (YA). pap. 6.95 (*0-15-204926-6*) Harcourt Trade Pubs.

—The Window. 1996. (YA). 12.05 (*0-606-13075-6*) Turtleback Bks.

Inman, Sue. Coconut's Week. 1997. (Tofflers' First Stories Ser.). (Illus.). 16p. (J). (ps). bds. 2.98 (*1-85854-524-2*) Brimax Bks., Ltd.

Ireland, Shep. Wesley & Wendell: At Home. 1991. (Illus.). 40p. (J). (gr. 1). lib. bdg. 4.75 (*0-8378-0330-6*) Gibson, C. R. Co.

Irgens, Barbara E. Finding the Way. 2001. 187p. (YA). pap. 14.95 (*1-930580-06-1*, Luminary Media Group) Pine Orchard, Inc.

Irwin, Hadley. Abby, My Love. 1985. 168p. (YA). (gr. 7 up). 13.95 o.s.i (*0-689-50323-7*, McElderry, Margaret K.) Simon & Schuster Children's Publishing.

It's Time for Dinner. 2002. 12p. (J). bds. 7.95 (*1-84250-495-9*, Bright Sparks) Parragon, Inc.

Iwasaki, Chihiro. A New Baby Is Coming to My House. 1972. (Illus.). 32p. (J). (gr. k-3). lib. bdg. o.p. (*0-07-032075-6*) McGraw-Hill Cos., The.

Jackson, Chris. Edmund for Short: A Tale from China Plate Farm. 2000. (J). pap. 6.99 (*0-00-648165-5*) HarperCollins Children's Bk. Group.

—Edmund for Short: A Tale from China Plate Farm. 1998. (Illus.). 24p. (J). 12.00 (*0-00-224553-1*) HarperCollins Pubs.

Jackson, Dave & Jackson, Neta. Journey to the End of the Earth: William Seymour. 2000. (Trailblazer Bks.: Vol. 33). (Illus.). 160p. (J). (gr. 3-7). pap. 5.99 (*0-7642-2266-X*) Bethany Hse. Pubs.

Jackson, Isaac. Somebody's New Pajamas. 1996. (Illus.). 32p. (J). (gr. 1-5). 14.89 o.s.i (*0-8037-1549-8*); (ps-3). 14.99 o.s.i (*0-8037-1570-6*) Penguin Putnam Bks. for Young Readers. (Dial Bks. for Young Readers).

Jackson, Jill L. Fine Feathers Don't Make a Peacock. 2000. (Lessons for Lucile Ser.). (Illus.). 79p. (J). 24.95 (*0-9700692-0-0*) Noble Endeavor.

—How Dan Patch Got His Name. deluxe ed. 2001. (Lessons for Lucile Ser.). (Illus.). 104p. (YA). (gr. 2-7). 24.95 (*0-9700692-2-7*) Noble Endeavor.

Jackson, Kamichi. You're Too Much, Reggie Brown. l.t. ed. 2000. (Illus.). 110p. (J). (gr. 2-5). pap. 5.95 (*0-615-11287-0*) Shug' n Spice Pr.

James, Simon. The Day Jake Vacuumed. 1989. 32p. (J). (ps-3). 7.95 o.s.i (*0-553-05840-1*) Bantam Bks.

Janke, Katelan. Survival in the Storm: The Dust Bowl Diary of Grace Edwards. 2002. (Dear America Ser.). (Illus.). 192p. (J). (gr. 4-9). pap. 10.95 (*0-439-21599-4*, Scholastic Pr.) Scholastic, Inc.

Janover, Caroline. The Worst Speller in Jr. High. Wallner, Rosemary, ed. 1994. 208p. (YA). (gr. 5 up). pap. 4.95 o.p. (*0-915793-76-8*, FS301) Free Spirit Publishing, Inc.

—Zipper, the Kid with ADHD. 1997. (Illus.). 164p. (J). (gr. 3-6). pap. 11.95 (*0-933149-95-6*) Woodbine Hse.

Janover, Caroline D. The Worst Speller in Jr. High. 2000. 208p. (gr. 4-7). pap. 13.95 (*0-595-15328-3*, Backinprint.com) iUniverse, Inc.

Jaques, Faith. Kidnap in Willowbank Wood. 1983. (Illus.). 40p. (ps-2). o.p. (*0-434-94442-4*) David & Charles Pubs.

Jarrell, Pamela R. The Big Surprise! 1994. (Big Bks.). (Illus.). 8p. (J). (ps-k). pap. text 10.95 (*1-57332-007-2*) HighReach Learning, Inc.

Jenkins, A. M. Breaking Boxes. 192p. (YA). (gr. 9-12). 2000. mass mkt. 4.99 o.s.i (*0-440-22717-8*); 1997. 15.95 o.s.i (*0-385-32513-4*, Delacorte Pr.) Dell Publishing.

—Breaking Boxes. 2000. 11.04 (*0-606-17834-1*) Turtleback Bks.

Jenness, Aylette. Families. 1990. (J). pap. 13.95 o.p. (*0-395-51973-X*) Houghton Mifflin Co.

Jensen, Patricia. My House. 2004. (My First Reader (Reissue) Ser.). pap. 3.95 (*0-516-24636-4*, Children's Pr.) Scholastic Library Publishing.

Jerman, Jerry. The Long Way Home. 1995. (Journeys of Jessie Land Ser.). 132p. (J). (gr. 3-8). pap. 5.99 o.p. (*1-56476-272-6*, 6-3272) Cook Communications Ministries.

Johansson, Alice Nicole. Ellen's Family Secret. 1995. (Unicorn Club Ser.: No. 9). 144p. (Orig.). (J). (gr. 3-7). pap. 3.50 o.s.i (*0-553-48354-4*, Sweet Valley) Random Hse. Children's Bks.

Johnson, Allen, Jr. Picker McClikker. 1996. (Illus.). 48p. (J). (gr. 1-4). pap. text 6.95 (*1-887654-14-3*) Premium Pr. America.

Johnson, Anabel & Johnson, Edgar. Count Me Gone. 1968. (J). (gr. 7 up). lib. bdg. 4.73 o.p. (*0-671-65007-6*, Simon & Schuster Children's Publishing) Simon & Schuster Children's Publishing.

Johnson, Angela. Daddy Calls Me Man. 1997. (Illus.). 32p. (J). (ps-k). pap. 15.95 (*0-531-30042-0*); lib. bdg. 16.99 o.p. (*0-531-33042-7*) Scholastic, Inc. (Orchard Bks.).

—Gone from Home. 2001. 112p. (gr. 5-8). mass mkt. 4.99 o.s.i (*0-440-22942-1*, Dell Books for Young Readers) Random Hse. Children's Bks.

—One of Three. 1991. (Illus.). 32p. (J). (ps-1). pap. 15.95 (*0-531-05955-3*); mass mkt. 15.99 o.p. (*0-531-08555-4*) Scholastic, Inc. (Orchard Bks.).

—Songs of Faith. (YA). (gr. 5-8). 2001. 112p. mass mkt. 4.99 (*0-440-22944-8*, Dell Books for Young Readers); 1999. 108p. reprint ed. pap. 4.99 (*0-679-89488-8*, Knopf Bks. for Young Readers) Random Hse. Children's Bks.

—Songs of Faith. 1998. (Illus.). 112p. (J). (gr. 3-7). pap. 15.95 (*0-531-30023-4*); lib. bdg. 16.99 (*0-531-33023-0*) Scholastic, Inc. (Orchard Bks.).

—Songs of Faith. 1999. 11.04 (*0-606-17374-9*) Turtleback Bks.

—Toning the Sweep. 2002. (J). 13.19 (*0-7587-0401-1*) Book Wholesalers, Inc.

—Toning the Sweep. 112p. 2003. (J). (gr. 7 up). mass mkt. 5.99 (*0-590-48142-8*, Scholastic Paperbacks); 1993. (YA). (gr. 6 up). mass mkt. 15.99 o.p. (*0-531-08626-7*, Orchard Bks.); 1993. (YA). (gr. 6 up). pap. 15.95 (*0-531-05476-4*, Orchard Bks.) Scholastic, Inc.

—Toning The Sweep. 1993. (Point Signature Ser.). 11.04 (*0-606-06817-1*) Turtleback Bks.

—The Wedding. 1999. (Illus.). 32p. (J). (ps-2). pap. 16.95 (*0-531-30139-7*); lib. bdg. 17.99 (*0-531-33139-3*) Scholastic, Inc. (Orchard Bks.).

Johnson, Emily R. A House Full of Strangers. 1992. 176p. (J). (gr. 5 up). 14.00 o.p. (*0-525-65091-1*, Dutton Children's Bks.) Penguin Putnam Bks. for Young Readers.

Johnson, Lee K. & Johnson, Sue K. If I Ran the Family. Espeland, Pamela, ed. 1992. (Illus.). 32p. (J). (ps-4). 14.95 o.p. (*0-915793-41-5*) Free Spirit Publishing, Inc.

Johnson, Patricia P. & Williams, Donna R. Morgan's Baby Sister: A Read-Aloud Book for Families Who Have Experienced the Death of a Newborn. 1993. (Helping Children Who Hurt Ser.). (Illus.). 64p. (J). (ps-2). pap. 11.95 o.p. (*0-89390-257-8*) Resource Pubns., Inc.

Johnson, Ruth I. Joy Sparton & the Money Mix-Up. 1960. (Joy Sparton Ser.: No. 3). (J). (gr. 5-8). pap. 3.50 o.p. (*0-8024-4403-2*) Moody Pr.

—Joy Sparton of Parsonage Hill. 1958. (Joy Sparton Ser.: No. 1). (J). (gr. 5-8). pap. 3.50 o.p. (*0-8024-4401-6*) Moody Pr.

Johnston, Norma. Carlisle's Hope. 1999. (Carlisle Chronicles Series). 168p. (YA). (gr. 9 up). reprint ed. pap. 16.00 (*1-892323-34-6*, Pierce Harris Press) Vivisphere Publishing.

—Feather in the Wind. 2001. (Illus.). 172p. (J). (gr. 5-9). 14.95 (*0-7614-5063-7*, Cavendish Children's Bks.) Cavendish, Marshall Corp.

—Glory in the Flower. 1990. (Keeping Days Ser.). 200p. (J). (gr. 4 up). pap. 3.95 o.s.i (*0-14-034292-3*, Puffin Bks.) Penguin Putnam Bks. for Young Readers.

—The Keeping Days. 1981. 256p. (J). (gr. 6-12). pap. 2.50 o.s.i (*0-441-43276-X*) Ace Bks.

—The Keeping Days. 1990. (Keeping Days Ser.). 240p. (J). (gr. 4 up). pap. 3.95 o.s.i (*0-14-034291-5*, Puffin Bks.) Penguin Putnam Bks. for Young Readers.

—The Keeping Days. 1993. (J). (gr. 7 up). 17.05 o.p. (*0-8446-6653-X*) Smith, Peter Pub., Inc.

—The Keeping Days. 1999. (Keeping Days Ser.). 233p. (YA). reprint ed. pap. 16.00 (*1-892323-28-1*, Pierce Harris Press) Vivisphere Publishing.

—To Jess, With Love & Memories. 1999. (Carlisle Chronicles Series). 168p. (YA). (gr. 9 up). reprint ed. pap. 16.00 (*1-892323-35-4*, Pierce Harris Press) Vivisphere Publishing.

—Milton the Early Riser. 1972. (J). 13.14 (0-606-02795-5) Turtleback Bks.

Krauss, Ruth. Un Dia Feliz. 1995. (J). 13.10 (0-606-08652-8) Turtleback Bks.

—Happy Day. 1949. (J). 12.10 (0-606-03976-7) Turtleback Bks.

Kray. A Way of Life. 2002. (Illus.). 322p. mass mkt. 11.95 (0-330-48511-3) Pan Bks. Ltd. GBR. *Dist:* Trafalgar Square.

Krensky, Stephen. Lionel at Large. (Easy-to-Read Bks.). (Illus.). (J). (ps-3). 1988. 56p. pap. 4.95 o.p. (0-8037-0556-5); 1986. 480p. 9.89 o.p. (0-8037-0241-8); 1986. 480p. 9.95 o.p. (0-8037-0240-X) Penguin Putnam Bks. for Young Readers. (Dial Bks. for Young Readers).

—Lionel at Large. 1986. (Dial Easy-to-Read Ser.). (J). 10.14 (0-606-01661-9) Turtleback Bks.

—Lionel at Large Level 3: Yellow. 1993. (Puffin Easy-to-Read Ser.). (Illus.). 56p. (J). (ps-3). pap. 3.99 (0-14-036542-7, Puffin Bks.) Penguin Putnam Bks. for Young Readers.

—Lionel in Spring. 1997. (Puffin Easy-to-Read Ser.). (Illus.). 48p. (J). (gr. 1-4). pap. 3.99 o.p. (0-14-038463-4) Penguin Putnam Bks. for Young Readers.

Krisher, Trudy B. Kinship. 1997. 304p. (YA). (gr. 7). 15.95 o.s.i (0-385-32272-0, Delacorte Pr.) Dell Publishing.

—Kinship. 1997. mass mkt. 15.95 (0-385-44695-0) Doubleday Publishing.

—Kinship. 1999. 304p. (YA). (gr. 7 up). mass mkt. 4.50 o.s.i (0-440-22023-8, Dell Books for Young Readers) Random Hse. Children's Bks.

—Kinship. 1999. 10.55 (0-606-16170-8) Turtleback Bks.

Krishnaswami, Uma. Chachaji's Cup. 2003. (Illus.). 32p. (J). (gr. 1 up). 16.95 (0-89239-178-2) Children's Bk. Pr.

—Naming Maya, RS. 2004. (J). 16.00 (0-374-35485-5, Farrar, Straus & Giroux (BYR)) Farrar, Straus & Giroux.

Kroeber, Theodora. Ishi, Last of His Tribe. 1992. (J). mass mkt. o.s.i (0-553-54066-1, Dell Books for Young Readers) Random Hse. Children's Bks.

Kroll, Virginia L. Beginnings: How Families Come to Be. 1994. (Albert Whitman Concept Bks.). (Illus.). 32p. (J). (ps-4). lib. bdg. 14.95 (0-8075-0602-8) Whitman, Albert & Co.

—A Carp for Kimiko. 1993. (Illus.). 32p. (J). (ps-3). 14.95 (0-88106-412-2, Talewinds); lib. bdg. 15.88 o.p. (0-88106-413-0) Charlesbridge Publishing, Inc.

—Fireflies, Peach Pies, & Lullabies. 1995. (Illus.). 32p. (J). (gr. k-4). 15.00 o.s.i (0-689-80291-9, Simon & Schuster Children's Publishing) Simon & Schuster Children's Publishing.

Kuhn, Betsy. Not Exactly Nashville. 1998. 144p. (gr. 3-7). text 14.95 o.s.i (0-385-32589-4, Delacorte Pr.) Dell Publishing.

—Not Exactly Nashville. 1999. 144p. (gr. 3-7). pap. text 3.99 o.s.i (0-440-41478-4, Dell Books for Young Readers) Random Hse. Children's Bks.

—Not Exactly Nashville. 1999. 10.04 (0-606-16708-0) Turtleback Bks.

Kurtis-Kleinman, Eileen. When Aunt Lena Did the Rhumba. 1997. (Illus.). 32p. (J). (gr. k-4). 14.95 o.p. (0-7868-0082-8); lib. bdg. 15.49 (0-7868-2067-5) Hyperion Bks. for Children.

Kurtz, Jane. Jakarta Missing. 2001. 272p. (J). (gr. 5 up). 15.99 (0-06-029401-9); lib. bdg. 16.89 (0-06-029402-7) HarperCollins Children's Bk. Group. (Greenwillow Bks.).

Kuskin, Karla. Something Sleeping in the Hall. 1985. (Charlotte Zolotow Bk.). (Illus.). 64p. (J). (gr. k-3). 13.00 o.p. (0-06-023633-7); lib. bdg. 14.89 o.p. (0-06-023634-5) HarperCollins Children's Bk. Group.

Kwasney, Michelle D. Baby Blue. 2004. (J). 16.95 (0-8050-7050-8) Holt, Henry & Co.

Kwitz, Mary Deball. Little Vampire & the Midnight Bear. 1995. (Easy-to-Read Ser.). (Illus.). 48p. (J). 12.99 o.s.i (0-8037-1528-5); 12.89 o.s.i (0-8037-1529-3) Penguin Putnam Bks. for Young Readers. (Dial Bks. for Young Readers).

Lachtman, Ofelia Dumas. Pepita Finds Out - Lo Que Pepita Descubre. Villarroel, Carolina, tr. 2002. (ENG & SPA., Illus.). 32p. (J). 14.95 (1-55885-375-8, Piñata Books) Arte Publico Pr.

LaFaye, A. Nissa's Place. 2001. (J). 11.04 (0-606-21355-4) Turtleback Bks.

—Strawberry Hill. (Illus.). 272p. (J). 2000. (gr. 4-5). pap. 5.99 (0-689-82961-2, Aladdin); 1999. (gr. 3-7). 16.95 (0-689-82441-6, Simon & Schuster Children's Publishing) Simon & Schuster Children's Publishing.

—Strawberry Hill. 2000. 11.04 (0-606-19953-5) Turtleback Bks.

Laird, Elizabeth. Jake's Tower. 2002. (Illus.). 154p. (J). (gr. 4-7). pap. 4.95 (0-7641-2231-2) Barron's Educational Series, Inc.

Lakin, Patricia. A Summer Job. 1995. (My Community Ser.). (Illus.). 32p. (J). (ps-4). lib. bdg. 21.40 o.p. (0-8114-8259-6) Raintree Pubs.

Lambregtse, Cornelius. He Gathers the Lambs. 1996. (J). 12.90 (0-921100-77-9) Inheritance Pubns.

Laminack, Lester. Saturdays & Tea Cakes. 2004. 32p. (J). (gr. 1-2). 16.95 (1-56145-303-X) Peachtree Pubs., Ltd.

Lane, Dakota. Johnny Voodoo. 1997. 208p. (YA). (gr. 7-12). mass mkt. 4.50 o.s.i (0-440-21998-1, Dell Books for Young Readers) Random Hse. Children's Bks.

Lane, Rose Wilder. Young Pioneers. 1998. (Little House Ser.). (Illus.). 192p. (J). (gr. 3 up). pap. 5.99 (0-06-440698-9, Harper Trophy) HarperCollins Children's Bk. Group.

—Young Pioneers. 1998. (Little House Ser.). (YA). (gr. 3 up). 12.00 (0-606-17778-7) Turtleback Bks.

Lankester-Brisley, Joyce. Milly-Molly-Mandy Stories. 2002. (Kingfisher Modern Classics Ser.). (Illus.). 224p. (J). tchr. ed. 15.95 (0-7534-5559-5, Kingfisher) Houghton Mifflin Co. Trade & Reference Div.

Lansing, Karen E. Time to Fly. 1991. 104p. (Orig.). (J). (gr. 4-7). pap. 5.99 (0-8361-3560-1) Herald Pr.

Lantz, Francess L. Someone to Love. 1997. 224p. (J). (gr. 5). 14.00 (0-380-97477-0, Avon Bks.) Morrow/Avon.

Larson, Rodger. What I Know Now, ERS. 1997. 272p. (J). (gr. 7-12). 15.95 o.s.i (0-8050-4869-3, Holt, Henry & Co. Bks. For Young Readers) Holt, Henry & Co.

Lasker, Joe. The Do-Something Day. 1982. (Illus.). 32p. (J). (ps-3). 12.95 o.p. (0-670-27503-4, Viking Children's Bks.) Penguin Putnam Bks. for Young Readers.

Lasky, Kathryn. Christmas after All: The Great Depression Diary of Minnie Swift, Indianapolis, Indiana, 1932. 2001. (Dear America Ser.). (Illus.). 192p. (J). (gr. 4-9). pap. 10.95 (0-439-21943-4) Scholastic, Inc.

—Dreams in the Golden Country: The Diary of Zipporah Feldman, a Jewish Immigrant Girl, New York City, 1903. (Dear America Ser.). (YA). 2002. E-Book 9.95 (0-439-42539-5); 1998. (Illus.). 188p. (gr. 4-9). pap. 10.95 (0-590-02973-8) Scholastic, Inc.

Lathan, Tamala. Black Butterflies. 2000. 250p. (J). 7.99 (0-9700599-0-6) Sybrell Publishing.

Lattimore, Eleanor F. Adam's Key. 1976. (Illus.). (J). (gr. 2-5). lib. bdg. 12.88 o.p. (0-688-32089-9, Morrow, William & Co.) Morrow/Avon.

Lawlor, Laurie. Addie's Forever Friend. 1997. (Illus.). 128p. (J). (gr. 2-5). lib. bdg. 13.95 (0-8075-0164-6) Whitman, Albert & Co.

—Come Away with Me. 1996. (Heartland Ser.). 9.09 o.p. (0-606-10163-2) Turtleback Bks.

Lawrence, Iain. B for Buster. 2004. (YA). 320p. lib. bdg. 17.99 (0-385-90108-9); 336p. (gr. 7). 15.95 (0-385-73086-1) Random Hse. Children's Bks. (Delacorte Bks. for Young Readers).

Lawrence, Louise. Sing & Scatter Daisies. 1977. (J). (gr. 7 up). 8.95 o.p. (0-06-023772-4); lib. bdg. 11.89 o.p. (0-06-023773-2) HarperCollins Children's Bk. Group.

Lawson, Julie. A Morning to Polish & Keep. 1992. (Illus.). 32p. (J). (ps-3). pap. 7.95 (0-88995-179-9) Red Deer Pr. CAN. *Dist:* General Distribution Services, Inc.

Le Feuvre, Amy. Probable Sons, No. 2. 1996. (Golden Inheritance Ser.). (J). pap. 5.90 (0-921100-81-7) Inheritance Pubns.

—Probable Sons. 1997. (Classic Ser.). 128p. (J). (gr. 4-7). pap. 6.00 (0-7188-2818-6) Lutherworth Pr., The GBR. *Dist:* Parkwest Pubns., Inc.

Lee, Benjamin. It Can't Be Helped, RS. 1979. 152p. (J). (gr. 7 up). 7.95 o.p. (0-374-33648-2, Farrar, Straus & Giroux (BYR)) Farrar, Straus & Giroux.

Lee, Lauren. Stella: On the Edge of Popularity. 1994. 184p. (J). (gr. 4-8). 10.95 (1-879965-08-9) Polychrome Publishing Corp.

Lee, Marie G. Necessary Roughness. 1998. 240p. (J). (gr. 7 up). pap. 5.99 (0-06-447169-1, Harper Trophy) HarperCollins Children's Bk. Group.

—Necessary Roughness. 1998. (J). 11.00 (0-606-13000-4) Turtleback Bks.

Legge, David. Bamboozled. 1995. (Illus.). 32p. (J). (ps-2). pap. 14.95 (0-590-47989-X) Scholastic, Inc.

Lehman, Yvonne. Tornado Alley. 1995. (White Dove Romances Ser.: Vol. 1). 176p. (Orig.). (J). (gr. 7-12). mass mkt. 4.99 o.p. (1-55661-705-4, Bethany Backyard) Bethany Hse. Pubs.

Lehri, R. M. Cut & Make Festival Masks from India: 6 Full-Color Designs. 2001. (Illus.). (J). 5.95 (0-486-41667-4) Dover Pubns., Inc.

Leithart, Peter J. Wise Words: Family Stories that Bring the Proverbs to Life. 1996. (Illus.). 169p. pap. text 9.99 (1-880692-23-6) Holly Hall Pubns., Inc.

LeMieux, Anne Connelly. Fruit Flies, Fish & Fortune Cookies. 1995. (J). 9.09 o.p. (0-606-07553-4) Turtleback Bks.

L'Engle, Madeleine. Camilla. 1981. 288p. (J). (gr. 7 up). 14.95 o.p. (0-385-28110-2, Delacorte Pr.) Dell Publishing.

—Meet the Austins. 2002. (Illus.). (J). 13.94 (0-7587-8955-6) Book Wholesalers, Inc.

—Meet the Austins. 1981. 192p. (YA). (gr. 4-7). mass mkt. 5.50 (0-440-95777-X, Laurel) Dell Publishing.

—Meet the Austins, RS. 1997. (Austin Family Ser.). (Illus.). 224p. (J). (gr. 5-9). 17.00 (0-374-34929-0, Farrar, Straus & Giroux (BYR)) Farrar, Straus & Giroux.

—Meet the Austins. 1960. (J). 10.55 (0-606-02172-8) Turtleback Bks.

—The Twenty-Four Days Before Christmas: An Austin Family Story. 1987. (Young Yearling Ser.). 80p. (ps-3). pap. text 3.99 o.s.i (0-440-40105-4, Yearling) Random Hse. Children's Bks.

—The Twenty-Four Days Before Christmas: An Austin Family Story. 1984. (Dell Young Yearling Ser.). (J). 10.14 (0-606-04059-5) Turtleback Bks.

Lenski, Lois. The Little Family: A Little Book. 2002. (Illus.). 56p. (J). (ps-1). 9.95 (0-375-81077-3); lib. bdg. 11.99 (0-375-91077-8) Random Hse. Children's Bks. (Random Hse. Bks. for Young Readers).

—Papa Small. 2004. (J). 11.95 (0-375-82749-8); lib. bdg. 11.95 (0-375-92749-2) Random Hse., Inc.

Lentz, Alice B. Mountain Magic. 1998. (Illus.). 32p. (J). (ps-3). 12.99 (0-8499-5841-5) Nelson, Tommy.

Leodhas, Sorche N. Always Room for One More, ERS. 1972. (J). pap. 3.95 o.p. (0-03-088507-8, Holt, Henry & Co. Bks. For Young Readers) Holt, Henry & Co.

Leppard, Lois Gladys. Mandie & the Unwanted Gift, 29. 1997. (Mandie Bks.: No. 29). 176p. (J). (gr. 4-7). pap. 4.99 (1-55661-556-6) Bethany Hse. Pubs.

—Mandie & the Unwanted Gift. 1998. (Mandie Bks.: No. 29). (J). (gr. 4-7). 11.04 (0-606-18916-5) Turtleback Bks.

Leppard, Shannon M. The Ballet Class Mystery. 1997. (Adventures of Callie Ann Ser.: Vol. 2). 80p. (J). (gr. 2-5). pap. 3.99 o.p. (1-55661-814-X) Bethany Hse. Pubs.

Leroy, Gen. Hotheads. 1977. (J). (gr. 5 up). lib. bdg. 9.89 o.p. (0-06-023787-2) HarperCollins Pubs.

Lester, Alison. Bumping & Bouncing. 1989. (Illus.). 16p. (J). (ps). 3.50 o.p. (0-670-81991-3, Viking Children's Bks.) Penguin Putnam Bks. for Young Readers.

Let's Get Ready! (Illus.). (J). pap. 2.79 (0-88743-713-3) School Zone Publishing Co.

Levene, Nancy S. Chocolate Chips & Trumpet Tricks. Reck, Sue, ed. 1994. 192p. (J). (gr. 3-6). pap. 5.99 (0-7814-0103-8) Cook Communications Ministries.

Levin, Betty. Fire in the Wind. (J). 1997. (Illus.). 144p. (gr. 3-7). pap. 4.95 (0-688-15495-6, Harper Trophy); 1995. 176p. (gr. 7 up). 15.00 o.s.i (0-688-14299-0, Greenwillow Bks.) HarperCollins Children's Bk. Group.

—Fire in the Wind. 1997. 11.00 (0-606-11327-4) Turtleback Bks.

—The Keeping Room. 1981. (J). lib. bdg. o.p. (0-688-00680-9, Greenwillow Bks.) HarperCollins Children's Bk. Group.

—Mercy's Mill. 1992. (J). (gr. 7 up). 14.00 o.p. (0-688-11122-X, Greenwillow Bks.) HarperCollins Children's Bk. Group.

—The Trouble with Gramary. 1988. 192p. (YA). (gr. 5 up). 16.00 o.p. (0-688-07372-7, Greenwillow Bks.) HarperCollins Children's Bk. Group.

Levine, Abby. This Is the Turkey. (Illus.). 32p. (J). 2003. pap. 6.95 (0-8075-7889-4); 2000. lib. bdg. 14.95 (0-8075-7888-6) Whitman, Albert & Co.

Levine, Joan G. Bedtime Story. 1975. (Illus.). (J). (gr. 7 up). 5.50 o.p. (0-525-26290-3, Dutton) Dutton/Plume.

Levinson, Marilyn. No Boys Allowed. 1993. 8.05 o.p. (0-606-07059-1) Turtleback Bks.

Levinson, Riki. Boys Here - Girls There. 1993. (Illus.). 112p. (J). 13.00 o.p. (0-525-67374-1, Dutton Children's Bks.) Penguin Putnam Bks. for Young Readers.

—Grandpa's Hotel. 1995. (Illus.). 32p. (J). (gr. k-3). mass mkt. 15.95 o.p. (0-531-09475-8); mass mkt. 16.99 o.p. (0-531-08775-1) Scholastic, Inc. (Orchard Bks.).

Levit, Rose. With Secrets to Keep. 1991. 160p. (YA). (gr. 12 up). pap. 12.95 o.p. (1-55870-197-4, Betterway Bks.) F&W Pubns., Inc.

Levithan, David. 101 Ways to Get Away with Anything! 2002. (Malcolm in the Middle Ser.). (Illus.). 96p. (J). (gr. 3-7). mass mkt. 4.50 (0-439-35132-4) Scholastic, Inc.

Levitin, Sonia. Dream Freedom. 2000. 192p. (J). (gr. 4-7). 17.00 (0-15-202404-2, Silver Whistle) Harcourt Children's Bks.

—The Golem & the Dragon Girl. 1994. 176p. (YA). mass mkt. 3.99 o.s.i (0-449-70441-6, Fawcett) Ballantine Bks.

—The Golem & the Dragon Girl. 1993. 192p. (J). (gr. 3-7). 14.89 o.p. (0-8037-1281-2); 14.99 o.p. (0-8037-1280-4) Penguin Putnam Bks. for Young Readers. (Dial Bks. for Young Readers).

—Nine for California. 1996. (Illus.). 32p. (J). (ps-3). pap. 15.95 (0-531-09527-4); mass mkt. 16.99 o.p. (0-531-08877-4) Scholastic, Inc. (Orchard Bks.).

—Silver Days. 1989. 192p. (YA). (gr. 5 up). lib. bdg. 16.00 o.s.i (0-689-31563-5, Atheneum) Simon & Schuster Children's Publishing.

—The Singing Mountain. (YA). (gr. 7-12). 1998. 272p. 17.00 (0-689-80809-7, Simon & Schuster Children's Publishing); 2000. 304p. reprint ed. mass mkt. 4.99 (0-689-83523-X, Simon Pulse) Simon & Schuster Children's Publishing.

Levy, Elizabeth, adapted by. Mom or Pop. 1988. (gr. 1-4). pap. 1.95 o.p. (0-440-45779-3) Dell Publishing.

Lewis, Maggie. Morgy Makes His Move. (Illus.). (J). 2002. 80p. (gr. 1-4). pap. 4.95 (0-618-19680-3); 1999. 74p. (gr. 4-6). tchr. ed. 15.00 (0-395-92284-4) Houghton Mifflin Co.

Lewis, Naomi. The Stepsister. 1987. (Illus.). 32p. (J). (ps-3). 11.95 o.p. (0-8037-0430-5, Dial Bks. for Young Readers) Penguin Putnam Bks. for Young Readers.

Lewison, Wendy Cheyette. Our New Baby. 1996. (All Aboard Bks.). (J). 9.14 (0-606-11714-8) Turtleback Bks.

Lexau, Joan M. Benjie. 1964. (Illus.). 40p. (J). (ps-3). 6.45 o.p. (0-8037-0536-0, Dial Bks. for Young Readers) Penguin Putnam Bks. for Young Readers.

—Benjie on His Own. 1970. (Illus.). (J). (ps-3). 9.89 o.p. (0-8037-0713-4, Dial Bks. for Young Readers) Penguin Putnam Bks. for Young Readers.

—Me Day. (Illus.). (J). (ps-3). 1985. 7.45 o.p. (0-8037-5573-2); 1971. 4.95 o.p. (0-8037-5572-4) Penguin Putnam Bks. for Young Readers. (Dial Bks. for Young Readers).

—Striped Ice Cream. 1968. (Illus.). 96p. (J). (gr. k-3). 15.89 (0-397-31047-1) HarperCollins Children's Bk. Group.

—Striped Ice Cream. 1968. (J). (gr. 1-6). 12.89 o.p. (0-397-31046-3) HarperCollins Pubs.

—Striped Ice Cream. (J). (gr. 2-5). 1992. 128p. 3.99 (0-590-45729-2, Scholastic Paperbacks); 1985. 128p. pap. 2.75 o.p. (0-590-42903-5); 1971. (Illus.). pap. 2.50 o.p. (0-590-41307-4) Scholastic, Inc.

—Striped Ice Cream. 1968. (J). 10.04 (0-606-04060-9) Turtleback Bks.

Light, John. Beachcombers. 1991. (Light Reading Ser.). (Illus.). 24p. (J). (ps-1). 1.99 (0-85953-502-9) Child's Play of England GBR. *Dist:* Child's Play-International.

—It's Great Outdoors. 1991. (ITA.). (J). (gr. 4-7). pap. 3.99 (0-85953-602-5); (Illus.). 24p. (YA). (ps-1). 1.99 (0-85953-338-7) Child's Play of England GBR. *Dist:* Child's Play-International.

—Race Ace Roger. 1991. (J). (ITA.). (gr. 4-7). pap. 3.99 (0-85953-604-1); (Illus.). 24p. (ps-1). 1.99 (0-85953-501-0) Child's Play of England GBR. *Dist:* Child's Play-International.

—Snap Happy. 1991. (Light Reading Ser.). (Illus.). 24p. (J). (ps-1). 1.99 (0-85953-504-5) Child's Play of England GBR. *Dist:* Child's Play-International.

—What's Cooking. 1991. (Light Reading Ser.). (Illus.). 24p. (J). (ps-1). 1.99 (0-85953-337-9) Child's Play of England GBR. *Dist:* Child's Play-International.

Lightburn, Ron & Lightburn, Sandra. Driftwood Cove. 1998. (Illus.). 32p. (J). 19.95 o.s.i (0-385-25626-4) Doubleday Publishing.

Lin, Grace. Dim Sum for Everyone! 2003. 32p. (J). pap. 6.99 (0-440-41770-8, Dell Books for Young Readers) Random Hse. Children's Bks.

Lindbergh, Anne M. Bailey's Window. 1991. 144p. (YA). pap. 3.50 (0-380-70767-5, Avon Bks.) Morrow/Avon.

Lindgren, Astrid. The Children on Troublemaker Street. (Ready-for-Chapters Ser.). (Illus.). (J). 2001. 96p. pap. 3.99 (0-689-84674-6); 1991. 112p. (gr. 1-4). reprint ed. pap. 3.50 o.s.i (0-689-71515-3) Simon & Schuster Children's Publishing. (Aladdin).

Lindman, Maj. Snipp, Snapp, Snurr & the Reindeer. 1995. (Illus.). (J). (ps-3). pap. 6.95 (0-8075-7497-X) Whitman, Albert & Co.

—Snipp, Snapp, Snurr & the Yellow Sled. 1995. (J). (ps-3). pap. 6.95 (0-8075-7499-6) Whitman, Albert & Co.

Lindsey, Kathleen D. Sweet Potato Pie. 2003. (Illus.). (J). 16.95 (1-58430-061-2) Lee & Low Bks., Inc.

Lingard, Joan. A Proper Place. 1975. (J). 7.95 o.p. (0-525-66425-4, Dutton Children's Bks.) Penguin Putnam Bks. for Young Readers.

—The Resettling. 1976. 176p. (J). 7.95 o.p. (0-525-66485-8, Dutton Children's Bks.) Penguin Putnam Bks. for Young Readers.

—Snake Among the Sunflowers. 1977. (J). 6.95 o.p. (0-525-66570-6, Dutton Children's Bks.) Penguin Putnam Bks. for Young Readers.

Lish, Ted. Ese No Es Mi Trabajo. 2002. (J). lib. bdg. 15.95 (0-7940-0011-8) Munchweiler Pr.

—It's Not My Job! 2002. 24p. (J). 14.95 (0-7940-0004-5); lib. bdg. 15.95 (0-7940-0005-3) Munchweiler Pr.

Relationships

Lisle, Janet Taylor. Afternoon of the Elves. 1989. 128p. (YA). (gr. 4-9). pap. 15.95 o.s.i (*0-531-05837-9*); (J). (gr. 5-9). lib. bdg. 16.99 (*0-531-08437-X*) Scholastic, Inc. (Orchard Bks.).

Litchfield, Ada B. Making Room for Uncle Joe. Tucker, Kathleen, ed. 1984. (Albert Whitman Concept Bks.). (Illus.). 32p. (J). (gr. 3-5). 12.95 o.p. (*0-8075-4952-5*) Whitman, Albert & Co.

Littke, Lael. Searching for Selene. 2003. 203p. (J). pap. 13.95 (*1-59038-179-3*) Deseret Bk. Co.

Little, Jean. Home from Far. 1965. (Illus.). (YA). (gr. 5 up). 14.95 o.p. (*0-316-52792-0*); mass mkt. 4.95 o.p. (*0-316-52802-1*) Little Brown & Co.

—Look Through My Window. 1970. (Illus.). 270p. (J). (gr. 4-7). lib. bdg. 14.89 o.p. (*0-06-023924-7*) HarperCollins Children's Bk. Group.

—Look Through My Window. 1970. (J). (gr. 4-7). pap. 2.95 o.p. (*0-06-440010-7*) HarperCollins Pubs.

—One to Grow On. 1969. (Illus.). (J). (gr. 4-6). 12.95 o.p. (*0-316-52796-3*) Little Brown & Co.

—Revenge of the Small Small. 1993. (Illus.). 320p. (J). (ps-3). 14.00 o.p. (*0-670-84471-3*, Viking Children's Bks.) Penguin Putnam Bks. for Young Readers.

—Spring Begins in March. 1966. (Illus.). (J). (gr. 4-6). 7.95 o.p. (*0-316-52785-8*) Little Brown & Co.

—Stand in the Wind. 1975. (Illus.). 256p. (J). (gr. 4-6). lib. bdg. 12.89 o.p. (*0-06-023904-2*) HarperCollins Children's Bk. Group.

Littman, Jennifer. Matzo Ball Soup: The Balls That Bobbed in the Broth That Bubbe Brewed. 1997. (Illus.). 32p. (Orig.). (J). (ps-2). pap. 7.95 (*0-9656431-0-7*) Brickford Lane Pubs.

Llewellyn, Richard. How Green Was My Valley. 1997. 20.05 (*0-606-12728-3*) Turtleback Bks.

Lo Tempio, T. C. 93 Crane Street. (J). E-Book 7.95 (*1-930756-29-1*); 2000. E-Book 4.95 (*1-930364-70-9*) McGraw Publishing, Inc. (Bookmice).

Lola & Miss Kitty. 1997. (Illus.). 16p. (J). (ps-2). pap. 2.49 o.p. (*0-395-88932-4*) Houghton Mifflin Co.

Lomas Garza, Carmen. Family Pictures (Cuadros de Familia) 1993. (ENG & SPA., Illus.). 32p. (J). (gr. 1 up). pap. 7.95 (*0-89239-108-1*) Children's Bk. Pr.

Look, Lenore. Ruby Lu, Brave & True. Wilsdorf, Anne, tr. & illus. by. 2004. 112p. (J). 15.95 (*0-689-84907-9*, Atheneum/Anne Schwartz Bks.) Simon & Schuster Children's Publishing.

Lord, Wendy. Pickle Stew. 1994. (Tabitha Sarah Bigbee Book). 96p. (J). pap. 4.99 (*0-7814-0886-5*) Cook Communications Ministries.

Loree, Sharron. The Sunshine Family & the Pony, 001. 1979. (Illus.). 48p. (J). (ps-2). 5.95 o.p. (*0-395-28816-9*, Clarion Bks.) Houghton Mifflin Co. Trade & Reference Div.

Lothrop, Harriet M. The Five Little Peppers & How They Grew. 1985. 288p. (J). (gr. 4-7). pap. text 3.99 o.s.i (*0-440-42505-0*) Dell Publishing.

—Five Little Peppers & How They Grew. 1976. (Classics of Children's Literature, 1621-1932: Vol. 47). (Illus.). (J). reprint ed. lib. bdg. 42.00 o.p. (*0-8240-2296-3*) Garland Publishing, Inc.

Lotz, Karen E. Can't Sit Still. (Picture Puffins Ser.). (Illus.). (J). (ps-3). 1998. 40p. pap. 5.99 o.p. (*0-14-056361-X*); 1993. 480p. 13.99 o.p. (*0-525-45066-1*, Dutton Children's Bks.) Penguin Putnam Bks. for Young Readers.

Lough, Loree. Fire by Night: The Great Fire Devastates Boston. 1999. (American Adventure Ser.: No. 4). 144p. (J). (gr. 3-7). lib. bdg. 15.95 (*0-7910-5044-0*) Chelsea Hse. Pubs.

Love, D. Anne. A Year Without Rain. 2000. (Illus.). vii, 118p. (J). (gr. 3-7). tchr. ed. 15.95 (*0-8234-1488-4*) Holiday Hse., Inc.

Lowry, Lois. Anastasia Again! l.t. ed. 1988. (Illus.). 200p. (J). (gr. 3-8). reprint ed. lib. bdg. 15.95 o.p. (*1-55736-074-X*) Bantam Doubleday Dell Large Print Group, Inc.

—Anastasia Again! 1981. (Illus.). 160p. (J). (gr. 4-6). tchr. ed. 16.00 (*0-395-31147-0*) Houghton Mifflin Co.

—Anastasia Again! 1982. 160p. (gr. 4-7). pap. text 4.50 (*0-440-40009-0*, Yearling) Random Hse. Children's Bks.

—Anastasia Again! 1981. (J). 10.04 (*0-606-02808-0*) Turtleback Bks.

—Anastasia de Nuevo. 1999. (Juvenil Ser.: Vol. 77). Tr. of Anastasia Again. (SPA., Illus.). 112p. (J). (gr. 5-7). 9.95 (*84-239-9047-8*) Espasa Calpe, S.A. ESP. *Dist:* Lectorum Pubns., Inc., Planeta Publishing Corp.

—Anastasia de Nuevo. 1996. Tr. of Anastasia Again. (SPA.). 232p. (J). (gr. 4-7). 9.75 (*84-239-2793-8*) Lectorum Pubns., Inc.

—Anastasia de Nuevo. 1988. Tr. of Anastasia Again. 16.00 (*0-606-16062-0*) Turtleback Bks.

—Anastasia Esta al Mando.Tr. of Anastasia on Her Own. (SPA.). 168p. (J). 9.95 (*84-239-7095-7*) Espasa Calpe, S.A. ESP. *Dist:* Lectorum Pubns., Inc., Planeta Publishing Corp.

—Anastasia Has the Answers. l.t. ed. 1991. (Lythway Ser.). 176p. (J). (gr. 3-7). lib. bdg. 16.95 o.p. (*0-7451-1292-7*, Macmillan Reference USA) Gale Group.

—Anastasia Krupnik. 1984. (Skylark Ser.). 128p. (J). pap. 2.75 o.s.i (*0-553-15534-2*) Bantam Bks.

—Anastasia Krupnik. 1984. (Illus.). 144p. (gr. 4-7). pap. text 4.99 (*0-440-40852-0*) Dell Publishing.

—Anastasia Krupnik. 7th ed. 2001. (SPA., Illus.). 140p. (gr. 4-7). 9.95 (*84-239-7061-2*) Espasa Calpe, S.A. ESP. *Dist:* Lectorum Pubns., Inc.

—Anastasia Krupnik. 1979. 128p. (J). (gr. 4-6). tchr. ed. 16.00 (*0-395-28629-8*) Houghton Mifflin Co.

—Anastasia Krupnik. 1996. (SPA.). (J). (gr. 4-7). pap. (*84-395-1092-6*) Lectorum Pubns., Inc.

—Anastasia Krupnik. l.t. ed. 1988. 144p. (J). (gr. 3-7). reprint ed. lib. bdg. 16.95 o.s.i (*1-55736-073-1*, Cornerstone Bks.) Pages, Inc.

—Anastasia Krupnik. 1998. 144p. mass mkt. 2.99 o.s.i (*0-440-22784-4*, Yearling) Random Hse. Children's Bks.

—Anastasia Krupnik. (J). 2001. 16.00 (*0-606-22686-9*); 1987. 16.00 (*0-606-17006-5*); 1979. 8.04 (*0-606-05118-X*) Turtleback Bks.

—Anastasia on Her Own. 1985. 144p. (J). (gr. 4-6). tchr. ed. 16.00 (*0-395-38133-9*) Houghton Mifflin Co.

—Anastasia on Her Own. l.t. ed. 1989. 184p. (YA). reprint ed. lib. bdg. 16.95 o.s.i (*1-55736-135-5*, Cornerstone Bks.) Pages, Inc.

—Anastasia on Her Own. 1986. 160p. (gr. 4-7). pap. text 4.50 (*0-440-40291-3*, Yearling) Random Hse. Children's Bks.

—Anastasia on Her Own. 1985. (J). 10.55 (*0-606-02375-5*) Turtleback Bks.

—Attaboy, Sam! 1992. (Illus.). 128p. (J). (gr. 4-6). tchr. ed. 16.00 (*0-395-61588-7*) Houghton Mifflin Co.

—Attaboy, Sam! 1992. (J). 10.55 (*0-606-05129-5*) Turtleback Bks.

—Us & Uncle Fraud, 001. 1984. 160p. (J). (gr. 4-6). 16.00 (*0-395-36633-X*) Houghton Mifflin Co.

—Us & Uncle Fraud. 1985. (J). (gr. k-6). pap. 3.25 o.s.i (*0-440-49185-1*, Yearling) Random Hse. Children's Bks.

Lowry, Lois & Oliver, Jenni. A Summer to Die. 1977. (Illus.). 160p. (YA). (gr. 7 up). tchr. ed. 16.00 (*0-395-25338-1*) Houghton Mifflin Co.

Lucado, Max, creator. Rock, Roll & Run. 2003. (Hermie & Freinds Ser.). (Illus.). 20p. (J). pap. 5.99 (*1-4003-0291-9*) Nelson, Tommy.

Luetke-Stahlman, Barbara. Hannie. 1996. (Illus.). 192p. (Orig.). (J). pap. 9.95 (*1-884362-15-X*) Butte Pubns., Inc.

Luger, Harriett. Bye, Bye, Bali Kai. 1996. 192p. (J). (gr. 3-7). pap. 5.00 (*0-15-200863-2*) Harcourt Children's Bks.

Lukas, Sarah. Good Morning, Kiki. 2002. (Illus.). 12p. (J). bds. 3.99 (*0-375-81533-3*, Random Hse. Bks. for Young Readers) Random Hse. Children's Bks.

Luke, Deanna. Marky & the Cat. 2000. (Marky Ser.: Vol. No. 2). (Illus.). 40p. (J). (gr. 2-7). 8.95 (*1-928777-06-6*, BOW Bks.) Blessing Our World, Inc.

Lundell, Margo. The Kissenbear Picture Album No. 2: Bear for All Seasons. 2004. 40p. (J). pap. 14.95 (*0-439-13079-4*, Cartwheel Bks.) Scholastic, Inc.

Lunn, Janet. One Hundred Shining Candles. 1991. (Illus.). 32p. (J). (gr. 2-4). text 13.95 o.p. (*0-684-19280-2*, Atheneum) Simon & Schuster Children's Publishing.

Luth, Sophie A. The Special Princess. 1990. (Illus.). 36p. (J). 3.95 (*0-9626153-0-7*) Luth & Assocs.

Luttrell, Chuck, illus. Everything's Going Wrong. 1986. 74p. (Orig.). (J). (gr. 3-6). pap. 6.95 (*0-9617609-0-7*) Shade Tree Bks.

Luvaas, William. Going Under. 1994. 352p. 23.95 o.p. (*0-399-13968-0*, G. P. Putnam's Sons) Penguin Group (USA) Inc.

Lynch, Chris. Elvin No. 3. 2004. (J). (*0-06-623940-0*) HarperCollins Pubs.

Lynch, Patricia. Back of Beyond. 1993. 180p. (J). (gr. 4 up). pap. 9.95 (*1-85371-206-X*) Poolbeg Pr. IRL. *Dist:* Dufour Editions, Inc.

Lyon, George Ella. Borrowed Children. 1990. 176p. (YA). mass mkt. 3.99 o.p. (*0-553-28380-4*) Bantam Bks.

—Borrowed Children. 1988. 160p. (J). (gr. 5-7). 15.95 o.p. (*0-531-05751-8*); mass mkt. 16.99 o.p. (*0-531-08351-9*) Scholastic, Inc. (Orchard Bks.).

—One Lucky Girl. 2000. (Richard Jackson Bks.). (Illus.). 32p. (J). (gr. k-3). pap. 15.95 o.p. (*0-7894-2613-7*, D K Ink) Dorling Kindersley Publishing, Inc.

MacBride, Roger Lea. The Adventures of Rose & Swiney. 2000. (Little House Chapter Bks.: No. 4). (Illus.). 80p. (J). (gr. 2-5). lib. bdg. 14.89 (*0-06-028553-2*) HarperCollins Children's Bk. Group.

MacDonald, Marianne. Secondhand Star. 1998. (Lots of O'Leary's Ser.). 10.10 (*0-606-13769-6*) Turtleback Bks.

MacDonald, Maryann. No Room for Francie, No. 2. 1995. (Hyperion Chapters Ser.). (Illus.). 64p. (J). (gr. 2-4). pap. 3.95 o.s.i (*0-7868-1081-5*) Disney Pr.

—No Room for Francie, No. 2. 1995. (Lots of O'Learys Ser.). (Illus.). 64p. (J). (gr. 2-4). 13.95 (*0-7868-0032-1*) Hyperion Bks. for Children.

—No Room for Francie. 1995. (Lots of O'Leary's Ser.). (J). 9.15 o.p. (*0-606-09693-0*) Turtleback Bks.

—Rosie Runs Away. 1990. (Illus.). 32p. (J). (ps-2). lib. bdg. 12.95 o.p. (*0-689-31625-9*, Atheneum) Simon & Schuster Children's Publishing.

—Secondhand Star. 1994. (Lots of O'Learys Ser.). (Illus.). 64p. (J). (gr. 2-5). 11.95 (*1-56282-616-6*); lib. bdg. 12.49 o.p. (*1-56282-617-4*) Hyperion Bks. for Children.

—Secondhand Star. 1997. (Lots of O'Leary's Ser.). (J). 19.50 (*0-7868-2316-X*) Hyperion Pr.

MacDonald, Steven. Just Clowning Around: Two Stories. 2003. (Green Light Readers Level 1 Ser.). (Illus.). 24p. (J). 11.95 (*0-15-204816-2*); pap. 3.95 (*0-15-204856-1*) Harcourt Children's Bks. (Green Light Readers).

Mackey, Samatha. Today's a Good Day. 1997. (Illus.). 16p. (J). (gr. k-3). pap. 7.00 o.p. (*0-8059-4125-8*) Dorrance Publishing Co., Inc.

Mackler, Carolyn. Love & Other Four-Letter Words. (Laurel-Leaf Books). (YA). (gr. 7). 2002. 256p. mass mkt. 5.50 (*0-440-22831-X*, Random Hse. Bks. for Young Readers); 2000. 240p. 14.95 o.s.i (*0-385-32743-9*, Dell Books for Young Readers) Random Hse. Children's Bks.

MacLachlan, Patricia. Caleb: Caleb's Story. 2002. (SPA., Illus.). 112p. 8.50 (*84-279-3252-9*, NG31208) Noguer y Caralt Editores, S. A. ESP. *Dist:* Lectorum Pubns., Inc.

—Sarah, Plain & Tall. 1985. (Charlotte Zolotow Bk.). 64p. (J). (gr. k-4). lib. bdg. 15.89 (*0-06-024102-0*); (gr. 3-7). 14.99 (*0-06-024101-2*) HarperCollins Children's Bk. Group.

—Seven Kisses in a Row. 1983. (Charlotte Zolotow Bk.). (Illus.). 64p. (J). (gr. k-3). lib. bdg. 16.89 (*0-06-024084-9*); (gr. 2-5). 13.00 o.p. (*0-06-024083-0*) HarperCollins Children's Bk. Group.

—Three Names. 1994. (Illus.). 32p. (J). (gr. k-4). pap. 5.99 (*0-06-443360-9*, Harper Trophy) HarperCollins Children's Bk. Group.

—What You Know First. 1998. (Trophy Picture Book Ser.). (Illus.). 32p. (J). (ps-3). pap. 6.99 (*0-06-443492-3*, Harper Trophy) HarperCollins Children's Bk. Group.

MacLeod, Charlotte. Maid of Honor. 1985. 144p. (J). mass mkt. 2.50 o.s.i (*0-449-70124-7*, Fawcett) Ballantine Bks.

Mahy, Margaret. The Good Fortunes Gang No. 1: The Cousins Quartet. 1994. 112p. (J). (gr. 4-7). pap. 3.50 o.s.i (*0-440-41060-6*) Dell Publishing.

—The Other Side of Silence. 1997. 10.09 (*0-606-13010-1*) Turtleback Bks.

—Tangled Fortunes. 1996. (Cousins Quartet Ser.: Bk. 4). 112p. (J). (gr. 4-7). pap. 3.99 o.s.i (*0-440-41163-7*) Dell Publishing.

—Tangled Fortunes. 1995. 18.95 (*0-385-30979-1*) Doubleday Publishing.

Maine, Margarita. Un Gran Resfrio. 2002. (SPA.). 32p. pap. 8.95 (*1-4000-0033-5*) Random Hse., Inc.

Major, Kevin. Hold Fast. 1981. 176p. (J). (gr. 7 up). mass mkt. 3.50 o.s.i (*0-440-93756-6*) Dell Publishing.

Maloney, Peter & Zekauskas, Felicia. His Mother's Nose. 2001. (Illus.). 40p. (J). (ps-3). 15.99 (*0-8037-2545-0*, Dial Bks. for Young Readers) Penguin Putnam Bks. for Young Readers.

Mama's Little Bears. 2004. (J). bds. 7.99 (*0-439-57357-2*) Scholastic, Inc.

Man Who Didn't Wash Dishes. 9999. (J). pap. 1.75 o.p. (*0-590-00498-0*) Scholastic, Inc.

Mantell, Paul, text. Stealing Home. 2004. (Illus.). 128p. (J). 15.99 (*0-316-60739-8*) Little Brown & Co.

—Stealing Home. 2004. (Illus.). 144p. (J). pap. 4.50 (*0-316-60742-8*) Time Warner Bk. Group.

Marino, Jan. Eighty-Eight Steps to September. 1991. 160p. (J). (gr. 3-7). pap. 2.95 (*0-380-71001-3*, Avon Bks.) Morrow/Avon.

Markus, Julia. Uncle. 1987. (J). mass mkt. 3.95 o.s.i (*0-440-39187-3*, Laurel) Dell Publishing.

Marron, Carol A. Just One of the Family. 1993. (Use Your Imagination Ser.). (J). pap. 4.95 o.p. (*0-8114-8404-1*) Raintree Pubs.

—When Great Aunt Zelda Comes. 1985. (Family Bks.). (Illus.). 32p. (J). (gr. 3-6). lib. bdg. 14.65 o.p. (*0-940742-42-X*) Raintree Pubs.

Marron, Carol A. & Root, Phyllis. Just One of the Family. 1985. (Imagination Clippers Ser.). (Illus.). 32p. (J). (gr. 3-6). lib. bdg. 27.99 o.p. (*0-8172-2287-1*); lib. bdg. 14.65 o.p. (*0-940742-47-0*) Raintree Pubs.

Marsden, Carolyn. Silk Umbrellas. 2004. 144p. (J). 15.99 (*0-7636-2257-5*) Candlewick Pr.

Marsden, John. Checkers. 1998. 122p. (YA). (gr. 7-12). 15.00 o.s.i (*0-395-85754-6*) Houghton Mifflin Co.

—Checkers. 2000. 128p. (YA). (gr. 7-12). mass mkt. 4.99 (*0-440-22860-3*, Laurel Leaf) Random Hse. Children's Bks.

Marshall, Catherine. Family Secrets. 1996. (Christy Fiction Ser.: No. 8). (Illus.). 128p. (Orig.). (J). (gr. 4-8). mass mkt. 4.99 (*0-8499-3959-3*) Nelson, Tommy.

Marshall, Edward. Zorro en la Escuela. 1996. (Libro Puffin Facil-de-Leer Ser.). 8.70 o.p. (*0-606-10110-1*) Turtleback Bks.

Marshall, Janet. A Honey of a Day. 2000. (Illus.). 24p. (J). (ps up). 15.95 (*0-688-16917-1*, Greenwillow Bks.) HarperCollins Children's Bk. Group.

Marshall, Linda D. What Is a Step? 1992. (Illus.). 48p. (Orig.). (J). (ps-5). pap. 10.00 (*1-879289-00-8*) Native Sun Pubs., Inc.

Marshall, Robert T. & Arbuckle, Wendall S. Ice Cream. 5th ed. 1996. (Illus.). 349p. (C). 83.00 o.p. (*0-412-99491-7*); 2000. reprint ed. 87.00 (*0-8342-1917-4*) Aspen Pubs., Inc.

Marsoli, Lisa A. Mother Hubbard's Empty Cupboard. 1997. (Puzzle Board Bks.). (Illus.). 5p. (J). 6.95 o.p. (*0-8118-1702-4*) Chronicle Bks. LLC.

Martin, Ann M. Belle Teal. 2004. 224p. (J). pap. 4.99 (*0-439-09824-6*, Scholastic Paperbacks) Scholastic, Inc.

—Claudia & the Genius of Elm Street. 1996. (Baby-Sitters Club Ser.: No. 49). (J). (gr. 3-7). lib. bdg. 21.27 o.p. (*0-8368-1573-4*) Stevens, Gareth Inc.

—Claudia & the Genius of Elm Street. 1991. (Baby-Sitters Club Ser.: No. 49). (J). (gr. 3-7). 9.30 (*0-606-00357-6*) Turtleback Bks.

—Claudia Makes up Her Mind. 1997. (Baby-Sitters Club Ser.: No. 113). (J). (gr. 3-7). 9.09 o.p. (*0-606-12882-4*) Turtleback Bks.

—A Corner of the Universe. 208p. 2004. (YA). pap. 5.99 (*0-439-38881-3*, Scholastic Paperbacks); 2002. (J). (gr. 5-8). pap. 15.95 (*0-439-38880-5*, Scholastic Pr.) Scholastic, Inc.

—Dawn on the Coast. (Baby-Sitters Club Ser.: No. 23). (J). (gr. 3-7). mass mkt. 3.95 (*0-590-42007-0*); 1997. 160p. mass mkt. 3.99 (*0-590-67391-2*); 1989. 192p. pap. 3.50 (*0-590-43900-6*) Scholastic, Inc.

—Dawn on the Coast. l.t. ed. 1994. (Baby-Sitters Club Ser.: No. 23). 176p. (J). (gr. 3-7). lib. bdg. 21.27 o.p. (*0-8368-1244-1*) Stevens, Gareth Inc.

—Dawn on the Coast. 1989. (Baby-Sitters Club Ser.: No. 23). (J). (gr. 3-7). 10.04 (*0-606-04085-4*) Turtleback Bks.

—Eleven Kids, One Summer. 1991. 160p. (J). (gr. 3-7). 15.95 o.p. (*0-8234-0912-0*) Holiday Hse., Inc.

—Karen's Promise. 1998. (Baby-Sitters Little Sister Ser.: No. 95). (J). (gr. 3-7). 10.04 (*0-606-13171-X*) Turtleback Bks.

—Karen's Snow Princess. 1998. (Baby-Sitters Little Sister Ser.: No. 94). (J). (gr. 3-7). 9.55 (*0-606-13170-1*) Turtleback Bks.

—Little Miss Stoneybrook & Dawn. l.t. ed. 1993. (Baby-Sitters Club Ser.: No. 15). 176p. (J). (gr. 3-7). lib. bdg. 21.27 o.p. (*0-8368-1019-8*) Stevens, Gareth Inc.

—Mallory on Strike. 1991. (Baby-Sitters Club Ser.: No. 47). 192p. (J). (gr. 3-7). mass mkt. 3.25 (*0-590-44971-0*) Scholastic, Inc.

—Mallory on Strike. 1996. (Baby-Sitters Club Ser.: No. 47). 144p. (J). (gr. 3-7). lib. bdg. 21.27 o.p. (*0-8368-1571-8*) Stevens, Gareth Inc.

—Mallory on Strike. 1991. (Baby-Sitters Club Ser.: No. 47). (J). (gr. 3-7). 8.35 o.p. (*0-606-00586-2*) Turtleback Bks.

—Mary Anne vs. Logan. (Baby-Sitters Club Ser.: No. 41). (J). (gr. 3-7). 1997. mass mkt. 3.99 (*0-590-74241-8*, Scholastic Reference); 1991. 192p. mass mkt. 3.50 (*0-590-43570-1*) Scholastic, Inc.

—Mary Anne vs. Logan. 1996. (Baby-Sitters Club Ser.: No. 41). 176p. (J). (gr. 3-7). lib. bdg. 21.27 o.p. (*0-8368-1565-3*) Stevens, Gareth Inc.

—Mary Anne vs. Logan. 1991. (Baby-Sitters Club Ser.: No. 41). (J). (gr. 3-7). 10.04 (*0-606-04743-3*) Turtleback Bks.

—Me & Katie (The Pest) 1985. (Illus.). 160p. (J). (gr. 4-7). tchr. ed. 13.95 o.p. (*0-8234-0580-X*) Holiday Hse., Inc.

—Me & Katie (The Pest) 1990. (J). mass mkt. 3.25 o.p. (*0-590-43618-X*) Scholastic, Inc.

—Sunny: Diary Three, 1999. (California Diaries). 160p. (YA). (gr. 6-8). mass mkt. 4.50 (*0-590-02390-X*) Scholastic, Inc.

—Ten Kids, No Pets. 1988. 184p. (J). 15.95 o.p. (*0-8234-0691-1*) Holiday Hse., Inc.

—Ten Kids, No Pets. 1990. 176p. (J). (gr. 3-7). mass mkt. 3.50 (*0-590-43620-1*) Scholastic, Inc.

Martin, Antoinette T. Famous Seaweed Soup. 1993. 11.15 o.p. (*0-606-08741-9*) Turtleback Bks.

—Famous Seaweed Soup. 1996. (Illus.). 32p. (J). (ps-2). reprint ed. pap. 5.95 (*0-8075-2264-3*) Whitman, Albert & Co.

Martin, David. Five Little Piggies. 2002. (Illus.). (J). 14.79 (*0-7587-2513-2*) Book Wholesalers, Inc.

—Five Little Piggies. (Illus.). 40p. (J). (ps-1). 2000. bds. 6.99 (*0-7636-1081-X*); 1998. 16.99 o.s.i (*1-56402-918-2*) Candlewick Pr.

—I, Piggy & Dad. 2000. (Brand New Readers Ser.). (Illus.). (J). *(0-7636-1328-2)* Candlewick Pr.

Martin, Dorothy. Prayer Answered for Peggy. 1976. (Peggy Bks.). 128p. pap. 2.95 o.p. *(0-8024-7610-4)* Moody Pr.

Martin, Mildred A. Prudence & the Millers. 2nd rev. ed. 1996. (Miller Family Ser.). (Illus.). 192p. (J). (gr. 3-8). pap. 6.00 *(1-884377-03-3)* Green Pastures Pr.

—School Days with the Millers. 1995. (Miller Family Ser.). 160p. (J). (gr. 3-8). pap. text 6.00 *(1-884377-01-7)* Green Pastures Pr.

—Working with Wisdom. 1996. (Miller Family Ser.). (J). (gr. 3-4). pap. text 4.00 *(1-884377-02-5)* Green Pastures Pr.

Martinez, Victor. Parrot in the Oven. 1998. 224p. (gr. 7 up). (Illus.). (J). pap. 5.99 *(0-06-447186-1*, Harper Trophy); audio 16.95 *(0-694-70093-2)* HarperCollins Children's Bk. Group.

—Parrot in the Oven: Mi Vida: A Novel. 1996. (Joanna Cotler Bks.). (Illus.). 224p. (J). (gr. 7 up). 16.99 *(0-06-026704-6)*; lib. bdg. 16.89 *(0-06-026706-2)* HarperCollins Children's Bk. Group. (Cotler, Joanna Bks.).

—Parrot in the Oven: Mi Vida: A Novel. 1998. 12.00 *(0-606-13695-9)* Turtleback Bks.

Marvin, Isabel R. Josefina & the Hanging Tree. 1992. (Chaparral Book Ser.). 128p. (YA). (gr. 7 up). pap. 9.95 *(0-87565-103-8)* Texas Christian Univ. Pr.

Marx, Trish. Hanna's Cold Winter. 1993. (Illus.). 32p. (J). (ps-3). lib. bdg. 15.95 o.s.i *(0-87614-772-4*, Carolrhoda Bks.) Lerner Publishing Group.

Marzollo, Jean. Uproar on Holler Cat Hill. 1981. (Illus.). (J). (ps-2). 8.95 o.p. *(0-8037-9027-9)*; 8.89 o.p. *(0-8037-9028-7)* Penguin Putnam Bks. for Young Readers. (Dial Bks. for Young Readers).

Masilela, Johnny. We Shall Not Weep. 2003. 132p. pap. 9.95 *(0-7957-0147-0)* Kwela Bks. ZAF. *Dist:* Independent Pubs. Group.

Mason, Simon. The Quigleys. 160p. 2003. (YA). pap. 4.99 *(0-440-41898-4*, Dell Books for Young Readers); 2002. (Illus.). (J). 14.95 *(0-385-75006-4*, Fickling, David Bks.) Random Hse. Children's Bks.

Mass, Wendy. A Mango-Shaped Space. 2003. 224p. (J). (gr. 5-9). 16.95 *(0-316-52388-7)* Little Brown Children's Bks.

Masters, Susan Rowan. The Secret Life of Hubie Hartzel. 1990. (Illus.). 144p. (J). (gr. 3-7). 11.95 *(0-397-32399-9)*; lib. bdg. 11.89 *(0-397-32400-6)* HarperCollins Children's Bk. Group.

—The Secret Life of Hubie Hartzel. 2000. 101p. (gr. 4-7). pap. 9.95 *(0-595-08893-7)* iUniverse, Inc.

Masterton, David S. Get Out of My Face. 1991. 160p. (J). (gr. 5-9). lib. bdg. 13.95 o.s.i *(0-689-31675-5*, Atheneum) Simon & Schuster Children's Publishing.

Masurel, Claire. Emily's Busy Day. (Giant Lift-the-Flap Ser.). (Illus.). (J). 2003. 16p. (gr. 4-7). text 4.99 *(0-448-42527-0)*; 2002. 12p. 10.99 *(0-448-42609-9)* Penguin Putnam Bks. for Young Readers. (Grosset & Dunlap).

—Two Homes. (Illus.). 40p. 2003. bds. 6.99 *(0-7636-1984-1)*; 2001. (J). 14.99 *(0-7636-0511-5)* Candlewick Pr.

Matas, Carol. Rebecca. 2000. (Illus.). 160p. (J). mass mkt. *(0-439-98718-0)* Scholastic, Inc.

—Sparks Fly Upward. 2002. 192p. (YA). (gr. 5-9). 15.00 *(0-618-15964-9*, Clarion Bks.) Houghton Mifflin Co. Trade & Reference Div.

Mathis, Sharon Bell. The Hundred Penny Box. 1995. (Illus.). (J). (gr. 5). 9.32 *(0-395-73254-9)* Houghton Mifflin Co.

—The Hundred Penny Box. 1986. (Puffin Newbery Library). (Illus.). 48p. (J). (gr. 1-4). pap. 5.99 *(0-14-032169-1*, Puffin Bks.) Penguin Putnam Bks. for Young Readers.

—The Hundred Penny Box. Dillon, Leo, ed. 1975. (Illus.). 48p. (J). (gr. k-3). 16.99 o.s.i *(0-670-38787-8*, Viking Children's Bks.) Penguin Putnam Bks. for Young Readers.

—The Hundred Penny Box. 1986. (J). 12.14 *(0-606-01280-X)* Turtleback Bks.

—Listen for the Fig Tree. 1990. 176p. (J). (gr. 7 up). pap. 4.99 o.s.i *(0-14-034364-4*, Puffin Bks.) Penguin Putnam Bks. for Young Readers.

—Listen for the Fig Tree. 1974. 176p. (J). (gr. 7 up). 9.95 o.p. *(0-670-43016-1)* Viking Penguin.

—Teacup Full of Roses. Lt. ed. 1973. (J). lib. bdg. 5.95 o.p. *(0-8161-6121-6*, Macmillan Reference USA) Gale Group.

—Teacup Full of Roses. 1979. (YA). (gr. 7 up). pap. 1.50 o.p. *(0-380-00780-0*, 54312, Avon Bks.) Morrow/Avon.

—Teacup Full of Roses. 1987. (Novels Ser.). 128p. (J). (gr. 4-7). pap. 4.99 *(0-14-032328-7*, Puffin Bks.) Penguin Putnam Bks. for Young Readers.

—Teacup Full of Roses. 9999. pap. 1.75 o.s.i *(0-590-03178-3)* Scholastic, Inc.

—Teacup Full of Roses. 1993. (J). (gr. 5-9). 17.05 o.p. *(0-8446-6650-5)* Smith, Peter Pub., Inc.

—Teacup Full of Roses. 1987. 11.04 *(0-606-03482-X)* Turtleback Bks.

—Teacup Full of Roses. 1972. 128p. (YA). (gr. 7 up). 10.95 o.p. *(0-670-69434-7)* Viking Penguin.

Matthews, Ellen. Getting Rid of Roger. 1978. (Illus.). 96p. (J). (gr. 3-7). 7.50 o.p. *(0-664-32622-6)* Westminster John Knox Pr.

Matute, Ana M. Polizon del Ulises. 2002. (SPA.). 8.95 *(1-4000-0139-0)* Random Hse., Inc.

Mayer, Mercer. I Am Helping. 1995. (Little Critter Ser.). (Illus.). (J). (ps-3). 4.99 o.s.i *(0-679-87348-1)* Random Hse., Inc.

—No Dancing in the Bathtub. 1998. (Pictureback Ser.). (J). pap. 3.25 *(0-679-88708-3*, Random Hse. Bks. for Young Readers) Random Hse. Children's Bks.

—There's Something in My Attic. 2002. (Illus.). (J). 13.19 *(0-7587-3785-8)* Book Wholesalers, Inc.

—There's Something in My Attic. 1988. (J). 12.14 *(0-606-01749-6)* Turtleback Bks.

Mayer, Mercer & Mayer, Gina. This Is My Family. 1999. (Little Critter Ser.). (Illus.). 24p. (J). (ps-3). 2.99 *(0-307-00137-7*, 98089, Golden Bks.) Random Hse. Children's Bks.

Mazer, Anne. Everything New under the Sun. 2003. (Amazing Days of Abby Hayes Ser.). 112p. (J). pap. 4.50 *(0-439-35369-6)* Scholastic, Inc.

Mazer, Anne & Gesue, Monica. Two Heads Are Better Than One. 2002. (Amazing Days of Abby Hayes Ser.: No. 7). 144p. (J). (gr. 4-7). pap. 4.50 *(0-439-35366-1)* Scholastic, Inc.

Mazer, Norma Fox. Mrs. Fish, Ape, & Me, the Dump Queen. 1981. 140p. (J). (gr. 4-7). pap. 2.25 o.p. *(0-380-57042-4*, Avon Bks.) Morrow/Avon.

McBrier, Page. Confessions of a Reluctant Elf. 1994. 144p. (J). (gr. 3-7). pap. 3.95 o.s.i *(0-7868-1010-6)* Hyperion Paperbacks for Children.

McClintock, Norah E. The Stepfather Game. 1991. 192p. (YA). pap. 2.95 o.p. *(0-590-43971-5*, Scholastic Paperbacks) Scholastic, Inc.

McCloskey, Robert. Time of Wonder. 2002. (Illus.). (J). 14.04 *(0-7587-0079-2)* Book Wholesalers, Inc.

—Time of Wonder. 1985. (J). 13.14 *(0-606-03977-5)* Turtleback Bks.

McCormick, Patricia. Cut. 2000. 168p. (J). (gr. 7-12). trans. 16.95 *(1-886910-61-8*, Front Street) Front Street, Inc.

McCue, Delton. My Mom Made Me Take Out the Garbage. 1993. (J). o.s.i *(0-385-44600-4)* Doubleday Publishing.

McCusker, Paul. Danger Lies Ahead. 1995. (Adventures in Odyssey Ser.: No. 7). 99p. (J). (gr. 3-7). pap. 4.99 *(1-56179-369-8)* Focus on the Family Publishing.

—The Point of No Return. 1995. (Adventures in Odyssey Ser.: No. 8). 125p. (J). (gr. 3-7). 4.99 *(1-56179-401-5)* Focus on the Family Publishing.

McDaniel, Lurlene. Garden of Angels. 2003. (Illus.). 288p. (YA). (gr. 7). 9.95 *(0-553-57093-5*, Starfire) Random Hse. Children's Bks.

—Season for Goodbye. 1994. (J). mass mkt. 4.50 *(0-553-54177-3*, Dell Books for Young Readers) Random Hse. Children's Bks.

McDonald, Joyce. Comfort Creek. 1996. 192p. (J). (gr. 3-7). 15.95 o.s.i *(0-385-32232-1*, Delacorte Pr.) Dell Publishing.

—Comfort Creek. 1998. 208p. (gr. 3-7). reprint ed. pap. text 3.99 o.s.i *(0-440-41198-X*, Yearling) Random Hse. Children's Bks.

—Comfort Creek. 1998. 10.04 *(0-606-13289-9)* Turtleback Bks.

—Mail-Order Kid. 1988. 128p. (J). (gr. 3-7). 13.95 o.s.i *(0-399-21513-1*, G. P. Putnam's Sons) Penguin Putnam Bks. for Young Readers.

—Swallowing Stones. 1999. 256p. (YA). (gr. 7-12). mass mkt. 5.50 *(0-440-22672-4*, Dell Books for Young Readers) Random Hse. Children's Bks.

—Swallowing Stones. 1999. 11.04 *(0-606-16721-8)* Turtleback Bks.

McDonald, Megan. Insects Are My Life. 1995. (Illus.). 32p. (J). (ps-3). pap. 15.95 *(0-531-06874-9)*; lib. bdg. 16.99 *(0-531-08724-7)* Scholastic, Inc. (Orchard Bks.).

—The Sisters Club. 2003. (Pleasant Company Publications). (Illus.). (J). pap. 15.95 *(1-58485-782-X*, American Girl) Pleasant Co. Pubns.

McElligott, Matthew. The Truth about Cousin Ernie's Head. 1996. (Illus.). 32p. (J). (gr. k-3). lib. bdg. 15.00 *(0-689-80179-3*, Simon & Schuster Children's Publishing) Simon & Schuster Children's Publishing.

McEwan, Ian. The Daydreamer. 2000. 160p. (gr. 4-7). pap. 10.00 *(0-385-49805-5)* Doubleday Publishing.

—The Daydreamer. (Illus.). (J). (gr. 3 up). 2002. 208p. pap. 5.99 *(0-06-053015-4*, Harper Trophy); 1996. 208p. pap. 5.95 *(0-06-440576-1*, Harper Trophy); 1994. 208p. 15.95 *(0-06-024426-7*, Cotler, Joanna Bks.); 1994. 80p. lib. bdg. 13.89 o.p. *(0-06-024427-5)* HarperCollins Children's Bk. Group.

—The Daydreamer. 1996. 11.05 o.p. *(0-606-09184-X)* Turtleback Bks.

McFann, Jane. Hide & Seek. 1995. 176p. (J). (gr. 7-9). mass mkt. 3.99 *(0-590-60387-6)* Scholastic, Inc.

McGill, Alice. Mile's Song. 2002. (Illus.). 224p. (YA). (gr. 6-8). mass mkt. 4.99 *(0-439-28070-2*, Scholastic Pr.) Scholastic, Inc.

McHenry, Janet Holm. Secret of the Locked Trunk. 1997. (Annie Shepard Mysteries Ser.). (J). pap. 4.99 *(1-56476-567-9)* Cook Communications Ministries.

McHugh, Elisabet. Karen & Vicki. 1984. 160p. (J). (gr. 5-9). 11.95 o.p. *(0-688-02543-9*, Greenwillow Bks.) HarperCollins Children's Bk. Group.

McKade, Maureen. His Unexpected Wife. 2001. 384p. mass mkt. 5.99 *(0-380-81567-2*, Avon Bks.) Morrow/Avon.

McKaughan, Larry. Why Are Your Fingers Cold? 1992. (Illus.). 32p. (J). (ps up). 14.99 *(0-8361-3604-7)* Herald Pr.

McKay, Hilary. The Exiles at Home. 208p. (J). (gr. 4-8). 1997. (Illus.). pap. 3.99 *(0-689-81403-8*, Aladdin); 1994. 15.95 *(0-689-50610-4*, McElderry, Margaret K.) Simon & Schuster Children's Publishing.

—Indigo's Star. 2004. (J). 15.95 *(0-689-86563-5*, McElderry, Margaret K.) Simon & Schuster Children's Publishing.

—Saffy's Angel. unabr. ed. 2002. (J). (gr. 13 up). audio 25.00 *(0-8072-0823-X*, Listening Library) Random Hse. Audio Publishing Group.

—Saffy's Angel. 160p. (J). 2003. (Illus.). pap. 4.99 *(0-689-84934-6*, Aladdin); 2002. (gr. 4-7). 16.00 *(0-689-84933-8*, McElderry, Margaret K.) Simon & Schuster Children's Publishing.

—Saffy's Angel. 2003. (Juvenile Ser.). 227p. (J). 21.95 *(0-7862-5500-5)* Thorndike Pr.

McKean, Thomas. Secret of the Seven Willows. 160p. (J). 1993. (gr. 4-7). pap. 2.95 o.s.i *(0-671-86690-7*, Aladdin); 1991. pap. 12.95 *(0-671-72997-7*, Simon & Schuster Children's Publishing) Simon & Schuster Children's Publishing.

McKee, David. Not Now Bernard. 1991. (J). pap. text *(0-05-004559-8)* Addison-Wesley Longman, Inc.

McKenna, Colleen O'Shaughnessy. Mother Murphy. 160p. (J). (gr. 4-6). 1993. mass mkt. 2.95 *(0-590-44856-0)*; 1992. 13.95 o.p. *(0-590-44820-X)* Scholastic, Inc.

—Murphy's Island. 1990. (J). (gr. 4-7). 12.95 o.p. *(0-590-43552-3)* Scholastic, Inc.

—Too Many Murphys. 144p. (J). 1989. (gr. 4-6). pap. 3.50 o.p. *(0-590-41732-0)*; 1988. (gr. 3-7). pap. 13.95 o.p. *(0-590-41731-2)* Scholastic, Inc.

McKissack. One Family's Story. 1995. (J). 19.95 *(0-8050-1671-6*, Holt, Henry & Co. Bks. For Young Readers) Holt, Henry & Co.

McKissack, Patricia C. Color Me Dark: The Diary of Nellie Lee Love, the Great Migration North, Chicago, Illinois, 1919. 2000. (Dear America Ser.). (Illus.). 218p. (J). (gr. 4-9). pap. 10.95 *(0-590-51159-9*, Scholastic Pr.) Scholastic, Inc.

McKissack, Patricia C. & McKissack, Fredrick L. Messy Bessey's Family Reunion. 2000. (Rookie Readers Ser.). (Illus.). 32p. (J). (gr. 1-2). pap. 4.95 *(0-516-26552-0*, Children's Pr.) Scholastic Library Publishing.

McKissack, Patricia C., et al. Messy Bessey's Closet, Level C. rev. ed. 2001. (Rookie Readers Ser.). (Illus.). 32p. (J). (gr. 1-2). lib. bdg. 19.00 *(0-516-21659-7*, Children's Pr.) Scholastic Library Publishing.

—Messy Bessey's Family Reunion. 2000. (Rookie Readers Ser.). (Illus.). 32p. (J). (gr. 1-2). lib. bdg. 19.00 *(0-516-20830-6*, Children's Pr.) Scholastic Library Publishing.

McLaren, Clemence. Aphrodite's Blessings: Love Stories from the Greek Myth. 2002. 208p. (J). (gr. 8 up). 16.00 *(0-689-84377-1*, Atheneum) Simon & Schuster Children's Publishing.

—Dance for the Land. 1999. 128p. (J). (gr. 5-9). 16.00 *(0-689-82393-2*, Atheneum) Simon & Schuster Children's Publishing.

McMahen, Chris. Buddy Concrackle's Amazing Adventure. 1997. 144p. (J). (gr. 3-7). pap. 5.95 *(1-55050-101-1)* Coteau Bks. CAN. *Dist:* General Distribution Services, Inc.

McMurtrey, Martin. Loose to the Wilds. 1976. (J). (gr. 7 up). 5.95 o.p. *(0-06-024158-6)*; lib. bdg. 5.79 o.p. *(0-06-024159-4)* HarperCollins Pubs.

McNamara, John. Model Behavior. 1985. (Illus.). 168p. (J). (gr. 7 up). 14.95 o.p. *(0-385-29419-0*, Delacorte Pr.) Dell Publishing.

McNamee, Graham. Hate You. 2000. 128p. (YA). (gr. 7-12). mass mkt. 5.50 *(0-440-22762-3*, Laurel Leaf) Random Hse. Children's Bks.

—Hate You. 2000. (Illus.). (J). 11.04 *(0-606-18803-7)* Turtleback Bks.

McNeal, Laura & McNeal, Tom. Crooked. 1999. 352p. (YA). (gr. 9-11). lib. bdg. 18.99 o.s.i *(0-679-99300-2)* Knopf, Alfred A. Inc.

McNeal, Tom & McNeal, Laura. Crooked. 2002. 352p. (YA). (gr. 9-11). mass mkt. 5.50 *(0-440-22946-4)* Random Hse., Inc.

McNeill, Joyce Darling. The Last Codfish. 2004. 16.95 *(0-8050-7489-9*, Holt, Henry & Co. Bks. For Young Readers) Holt, Henry & Co.

McPhail, David M. Sisters. 1984. (Illus.). 32p. (J). (ps-3). 14.00 o.s.i *(0-15-275319-2)* Harcourt Children's Bks.

Mead, Alice. Isabella's Above-Ground Pool, RS. 2006. *(0-374-33617-2*, Farrar, Straus & Giroux (BYR)) Farrar, Straus & Giroux.

Mearian, Judy F. Two Ways About It. 1985. (J). (gr. 5 up). 7.45 o.p. *(0-8037-8796-0*, Dial Bks. for Young Readers) Penguin Putnam Bks. for Young Readers.

—Two Ways about It. 1985. (J). (gr. 5 up). 7.95 o.p. *(0-8037-8797-9*, Dial Bks. for Young Readers) Penguin Putnam Bks. for Young Readers.

Meckley, Stephanie R., et al. Just Like Mom. 1998. (Illus.). 24p. (J). (gr. k-2). pap. 3.00 *(1-892464-03-9)* Meckley Publishing Co.

Meddaugh, Susan, illus. Beast. 1985. 32p. (J). (ps-3). pap. 6.95 *(0-395-38366-8)* Houghton Mifflin Co.

Merrell, Mar'ce. Trading Riley. 2001. (Middle Readers Ser.). (Illus.). 96p. (J). (gr. 3-7). pap. 6.95 *(1-896184-88-X)* Roussan Pubs., Inc./Roussan Editeur, Inc. CAN. *Dist:* Orca Bk. Pubs.

Merrifield, Margaret. Come Sit by Me. 2nd ed. 1998. (Illus.). 30p. (J). (ps-3). reprint ed. pap. 5.50 *(0-7737-5958-1)* Stoddart Kids CAN. *Dist:* Fitzhenry & Whiteside, Ltd.

Merrill, Frank T., illus. Little Men: Life at Plumfield with Jo's Boys. 1995. (Everyman's Library Children's Classics Ser.). (J). 13.95 o.s.i *(0-679-44503-X*, Everyman's Library) Knopf Publishing Group.

Merritt, Susan E. The Stone Orchard. 1999. 168p. (J). (gr. 3-7). pap. *(1-55125-030-6)* Vanwell Publishing, Ltd.

Messer, Celeste M. Three Miracles, 5 vols., Set. Howey, Paul M., ed. 2001. (Adventures of Andi O'Malley Ser.: Vol. 5). 82p. (YA). (gr. 3 up). E-Book *(1-877749-69-9)* Five Star Pubns., Inc.

Metzger, Lois. Barry's Sister. 1993. 240p. (J). (gr. 5 up). pap. 4.50 o.p. *(0-14-036484-6*, Puffin Bks.) Penguin Putnam Bks. for Young Readers.

Meyer, Carolyn. Gideon's People. 1996. (Gulliver Bks.). 304p. (J). (gr. 4-7). 12.00 *(0-15-200303-7)*; pap. 6.00 *(0-15-200304-5)* Harcourt Children's Bks. (Gulliver Bks.).

—Gideon's People. 1996. 12.05 *(0-606-15548-1)* Turtleback Bks.

—Killing the Kudu. 1990. 208p. (YA). (gr. 9 up). lib. bdg. 14.95 o.s.i *(0-689-50508-6*, McElderry, Margaret K.) Simon & Schuster Children's Publishing.

Michels, Dia L. At Home. 2002. (Look What I See! Where Can I Be? Ser.). (Illus.). (J). 16.95 *(1-930775-06-7)* Platypus Media, L.L.C.

—With My Animal Friends. 2002. (Illus.). (J). 16.95 *(1-930775-08-3)*; (Look What I See! Where Can I Be? Ser.: Vol. 3). 32p. lib. bdg. 16.95 *(1-930775-07-5)* Platypus Media, L.L.C.

Miklowitz, Gloria D. Close to the Edge. 1983. 160p. (J). (gr. 7 up). 13.95 o.p. *(0-385-29240-6*, Delacorte Pr.) Dell Publishing.

—Suddenly Super Rich. 1989. 160p. (YA). (gr. 7 up). 13.95 o.s.i *(0-553-05845-2*, Starfire) Random Hse. Children's Bks.

Milam, June M. Rainy Days. Daley, Charlotte C., ed. Miranda, Carmen, tr. 1997. (Drugless Douglass Tales Ser.). (SPA., Illus.). 24p. (Orig.). (J). (ps). pap. 32.95 *(1-884307-30-2)*; pap. 6.95 *(1-884307-31-0)* Developing Resources for Education in America, Inc. (DREAM).

Mildred's Married Life. 2001. (Mildred Classics Ser.: Vol. 4). 288p. pap. 5.95 *(1-58182-230-8)* Cumberland Hse. Publishing.

Miles, Betty. Just the Beginning. (Illus.). 152p. (J). (gr. 4-8). 1988. 5.95 o.s.i *(0-394-83226-4)*; 1976. 10.99 o.s.i *(0-394-93226-9)* Random Hse. Children's Bks. (Knopf Bks. for Young Readers).

Miles, Patricia. The Gods in Winter. 1978. (J). (gr. 4-7). 10.50 o.p. *(0-525-30748-6*, Dutton) Dutton/Plume.

Miller, Judi. Courtney Gets Crazier. 1997. (My Crazy Cousin Ser.). 128p. (Orig.). (YA). mass mkt. 3.50 o.p. *(0-671-00279-1*, Aladdin) Simon & Schuster Children's Publishing.

Miller, Mary J. Upside Down. 1992. 128p. (J). (gr. 3-7). 13.00 o.p. *(0-670-83648-6*, Viking Children's Bks.) Penguin Putnam Bks. for Young Readers.

Miller, Wayne H. Ellie. Smith, Denise M., ed. 1995. (Sandy Dallas Series of Books for Children, Parents, & Teachers). (Illus.). 100p. (Orig.). (YA). (gr. 6-12). pap. text 4.95 *(0-9634735-7-3)* Hiram Charles Publishing.

—The Family Budget. Smith, Denise M., ed. 1995. (Sandy Dallas Series of Books for Children, Parents, & Teachers). (Illus.). 100p. (Orig.). (YA). (gr. 6-12). pap. text 4.95 *(0-9634735-2-2)* Hiram Charles Publishing.

—Sandy Dallas. Smith, Denise M., ed. 1995. (Sandy Dallas Series of Books for Children, Parents, & Teachers). (Illus.). 100p. (Orig.). (YA). (gr. 6-12). pap. text 4.95 *(0-9634735-4-9)* Hiram Charles Publishing.

—Why Don't I Listen to My Parents? Smith, Denise M., ed. 1995. (Sandy Dallas Series of Books for Children, Parents, & Teachers). (Illus.). 100p. (Orig.). (YA). (gr. 6-12). pap. text 4.95 *(0-9634735-1-4)* Hiram Charles Publishing.

Milstein, Linda B. Miami-Nanny Stories. 1994. (Illus.). (J). 16.00 o.p. (*0-688-11151-3*); lib. bdg. 15.93 o.p. (*0-688-11152-1*) Morrow/Avon. (Morrow, William & Co.).

Minarik, Else Holmelund. Lost in Little Bears Room. 2004. (Festival Reader Ser.). (Illus.). 32p. (J). pap. 3.99 (*0-694-01706-X*, Harper Festival) HarperCollins Children's Bk. Group.

Mitchell, Greg. Simply Sam. 1993. (Voyages Ser.). (Illus.). (J). 3.75 (*0-383-03652-6*) SRA/McGraw-Hill.

Mitchell, Rhonda. The Talking Cloth. (Illus.). 32p. (J). (ps-2). 2001. mass mkt. 6.95 (*0-531-07182-0*); 1997. pap. 15.95 (*0-531-30004-8*); 1997. lib. bdg. 16.99 (*0-531-33004-4*) Scholastic, Inc. (Orchard Bks.).

Mitchell, Tracy, illus. What Do Fish Have to Do with Anything? And Other Stories. 1997. 208p. (J). (gr. 5-9). 16.99 o.s.i (*0-7636-0329-5*); bds. 6.99 o.s.i (*0-7636-0412-7*) Candlewick Pr.

Modarressi, Mitra. The Parent Thief. 1996. (Illus.). 32p. (J). (ps-3). mass mkt. 15.95 o.p. (*0-531-09476-6*, Orchard Bks.) Scholastic, Inc.

Mogdics, Teresa. Jimmy Johnson. 2001. 117p. (YA). pap. 16.95 (*1-58851-574-5*) PublishAmerica, Inc.

Mohr, Nicholasa. Felita. 1990. 112p. (J). pap. 3.99 o.s.i (*0-553-15792-2*) Bantam Bks.

—Felita. 1979. (Illus.). (J). (gr. 3-6). 6.95 o.p. (*0-8037-3143-4*); 12.89 o.p. (*0-8037-3144-2*) Penguin Putnam Bks. for Young Readers. (Dial Bks. for Young Readers).

—Felita. 1995. 112p. (gr. 3-7). pap. text 4.50 o.s.i (*0-440-41295-1*); 1991. (J). pap. o.s.i (*0-553-54034-3*) Random Hse. Children's Bks. (Dell Books for Young Readers).

—Felita. 1990. (J). 9.09 o.p. (*0-606-03280-0*) Turtleback Bks.

—Going Home. 1989. 208p. (J). pap. 4.50 o.s.i (*0-440-41434-2*, Dell Books for Young Readers); (gr. 4-7). pap. 3.99 o.s.i (*0-553-15699-3*, Skylark) Random Hse. Children's Bks.

Molloy, Michael. House on Falling Star Hill. 2004. 384p. (J). pap. 16.95 (*0-439-57740-3*) Scholastic, Inc.

Molzahn, Arlene Bourgeois. The Goat Who Wouldn't Come Home. 1998. (Illus.). 12p. (J). (gr. k-2). pap. 3.75 (*1-880612-82-8*) Seedling Pubns., Inc.

Moncure, Jane Belk. I Never Say I'm Thankful, But I Am. 1979. (Understanding Myself Picture Books Ser.). (Illus.). 24p. (J). (ps-3). lib. bdg. 21.36 o.p. (*0-89565-023-1*) Child's World, Inc.

—Where Things Belong. 1976. (Illus.). (J). (ps-2). 4.95 o.p. (*0-913778-44-3*) Child's World, Inc.

Montes, Marisa. A Crazy Mixed-Up Spanglish Day. 2003. (Get Ready for Gabi Ser.). (Illus.). 96p. (J). pap. 12.95 (*0-439-51710-9*, Scholastic Paperbacks) Scholastic, Inc.

Montgomery, L. M. After Many Days: Tales of Time Passed. 1992. 320p. (YA). (gr. 4-7). mass mkt. 4.99 o.s.i (*0-553-29184-X*, Dell Books for Young Readers) Random Hse. Children's Bks.

—Akin to Anne: Tales of Other Orphans. (YA). 22.95 (*0-8488-2656-6*) Amereon, Ltd.

—Akin to Anne: Tales of Other Orphans. Wilmshurst, Rea, ed. 1988. (J). o.p. (*0-7710-6156-0*) McClelland & Stewart/Tundra Bks.

—Akin to Anne: Tales of Other Orphans. 9999. (YA). pap. 2.50 o.p. (*0-451-52345-8*, Signet Classics) NAL.

—Akin to Anne: Tales of Other Orphans. 1990. 224p. (YA). (gr. 4-7). mass mkt. 4.99 o.s.i (*0-553-28387-1*, Dell Books for Young Readers) Random Hse. Children's Bks.

—Among the Shadows. 1991. 304p. (YA). mass mkt. 4.99 o.s.i (*0-553-28959-4*) Bantam Bks.

—Anne of Ingleside. (Avonlea Ser.: No. 10). (YA). (gr. 5-8). 23.95 (*0-8488-0890-8*); 1976. 286p. 23.95 (*0-8488-1101-1*) Amereon, Ltd.

—Anne of Ingleside. 1984. (Avonlea Ser.: No. 10). (YA). (gr. 5-8). 288p. mass mkt. 2.95 o.s.i (*0-553-24648-8*); mass mkt. 3.50 o.s.i (*0-7704-2144-X*); 6th ed. 304p. mass mkt. 3.95 (*0-7704-2207-1*);No. 6. 304p. mass mkt. 4.50 (*0-553-21315-6*, Bantam Classics) Bantam Bks.

—Anne of Ingleside. (Avonlea Ser.: No. 10). (Illus.). 341p. (YA). (gr. 5-8). 6.98 (*0-7710-6180-3*) McClelland & Stewart/Tundra Bks.

—Anne of Ingleside. 1999. (Avonlea Ser.: No. 10). 320p. (YA). (gr. 5-8). mass mkt. 3.95 (*0-451-52643-0*, Signet Classics) NAL.

—Anne of Ingleside, Vol. 6. 1999. 384p. (J). pap. 3.99 (*0-14-036801-9*, Puffin Bks.) Penguin Putnam Bks. for Young Readers.

—Anne of Ingleside. 1970. (Avonlea Ser.: No. 10). (YA). (gr. 5-8). 6.95 o.p. (*0-448-02546-9*) Putnam Publishing Group, The.

—Anne of Ingleside. 1967. (Avonlea Ser.: No. 10). (YA). (gr. 5-8). 10.55 (*0-606-00375-4*) Turtleback Bks.

—Chronicles of Avonlea. 1976. (Avonlea Ser.: No. 3). 318p. (YA). (gr. 5-8). 24.95 (*0-8488-0719-7*) Amereon, Ltd.

—Chronicles of Avonlea. (Avonlea Ser.: No. 3). (YA). (gr. 5-8). E-Book 2.49 (*0-7574-3262-X*) Electric Umbrella Publishing.

—Chronicles of Avonlea. 1970. (Avonlea Ser.: No. 3). (YA). (gr. 5-8). 6.95 o.p. (*0-448-02550-7*, Grosset & Dunlap) Penguin Putnam Bks. for Young Readers.

—Chronicles of Avonlea. 1988. (Avonlea Ser.: No. 3). 192p. (YA). (gr. 5-8). mass mkt. 3.99 (*0-553-21378-4*, Dell Books for Young Readers) Random Hse. Children's Bks.

—Chronicles of Avonlea. 1988. (Avonlea Ser.: No. 3). (YA). (gr. 5-8). 10.04 (*0-606-03755-1*) Turtleback Bks.

—The Complete Anne of Green Gables: Anne of Green Gables; Anne of the Island; Anne of Avonlea; Anne of Windy Poplars; Anne's House of Dreams; Anne of Ingleside; Rainbow Valley; Rilla of Ingleside, 8 vols. gif. ed. 1997. (J). (gr. 4-7). mass mkt. 36.00 (*0-553-60941-6*) Bantam Bks.

—Further Chronicles of Avonlea. 1989. (Avonlea Ser.: No. 7). 208p. (YA). (gr. 5-8). mass mkt. 3.99 (*0-553-21381-4*, Starfire) Random Hse. Children's Bks.

—Magic for Marigold. 1989. 288p. (YA). (gr. 5-9). mass mkt. 4.99 (*0-553-28046-5*, Dell Books for Young Readers) Random Hse. Children's Bks.

—Rainbow Valley. 1976. (Avonlea Ser.: No. 6). 234p. (YA). (gr. 5-8). 21.95 (*0-8488-0591-7*) Amereon, Ltd.

—Rainbow Valley. (Avonlea Ser.: No. 6). (gr. 5-8). 1987. 256p. (J). mass mkt. 4.99 (*0-7704-2268-3*); 1985. 240p. (YA). mass mkt. 2.95 o.s.i (*0-553-25213-5*) Bantam Bks.

—Rainbow Valley, unabr. ed. 1995. (Avonlea Ser.: No. 6). (YA). (gr. 5-8). audio 44.95 (*0-7861-0913-0*, 1704) Blackstone Audio Bks., Inc.

—Rainbow Valley. unabr. ed. 1999. (Avonlea Ser.: No. 6). (YA). (gr. 5-8). audio 44.95 Highsmith Inc.

—Rainbow Valley. (Avonlea Ser.: No. 6). (YA). (gr. 5-8). E-Book 1.95 (*1-57799-881-2*) Logos Research Systems, Inc.

—Rainbow Valley. 1985. (Avonlea Ser.: No. 6). 256p. (YA). (gr. 5-8). mass mkt. 4.50 (*0-553-26921-6*, Dell Books for Young Readers) Random Hse. Children's Bks.

—Rainbow Valley. 1985. (Avonlea Ser.: No. 6). (YA). (gr. 5-8). 10.04 (*0-606-02613-4*) Turtleback Bks.

—The Road to Yesterday. 1993. 416p. (YA). (gr. 4-7). mass mkt. 4.99 (*0-553-56068-9*) Bantam Bks.

—The Road to Yesterday. 1974. 251p. (J). o.p. (*0-07-077721-7*) McGraw-Hill Cos., The.

—The Story Girl. Date not set. 22.95 (*0-8488-2372-9*) Amereon, Ltd.

—The Story Girl. 272p. 1988. (J). mass mkt. 4.50 o.s.i (*0-553-21366-0*, Bantam Classics); 1987. (YA). mass mkt. 4.99 (*0-7704-2285-3*) Bantam Bks.

—The Story Girl. unabr. ed. 1997. audio 49.95 Blackstone Audio Bks., Inc.

—The Story Girl, Set. unabr. ed. 1999. (J). audio 49.95 Highsmith Inc.

—The Story Girl. 1991. 288p. (YA). mass mkt. 3.95 o.s.i (*0-451-52532-9*, Signet Classics) NAL.

—The Story Girl. 2000. (Sara Stanley of Avonlea Series: Vol. vol 1). (YA). 178p. pap. 10.99 (*1-57646-321-4*); 178p. lib. bdg. 19.99 (*1-57646-322-2*); 453p. E-Book 3.99 incl. cd-rom (*1-57646-320-6*); 370p. pap. 24.99 (*1-57646-323-0*); 370p. lib. bdg. 34.99 (*1-57646-324-9*) Quiet Vision Publishing.

—The Story Girl. 1996. vi, 231p. 8.99 o.s.i (*0-517-14818-8*) Random Hse., Inc.

Montgomery, L. M., text. The Avonlea Album. 1991. (Avonlea Ser.). (Illus.). 72p. (YA). (gr. 5-8). pap. 9.95 (*0-920668-97-6*); lib. bdg. 16.95 o.p. (*0-920668-96-8*) Firefly Bks., Ltd.

Montgomery, L. M. & Outlet Book Company Staff. Rainbow Valley. 1995. (Avonlea Ser.: No. 6). (Illus.). xi, 256p. (YA). (gr. 5-8). 7.99 o.s.i (*0-517-10192-0*) Random Hse. Value Publishing.

Mooney, Bel. Voices of Silence. 1997. 192p. text 14.95 o.s.i (*0-385-32326-3*, Dell Books for Young Readers) Random Hse. Children's Bks.

—Voices of Silence. 1998. 11.04 (*0-606-13887-0*) Turtleback Bks.

Moore, Elaine. The Peanut Butter Trap. 1996. (Orig.). (J). 9.15 (*0-606-09732-5*) Turtleback Bks.

Moore, Emily. Something to Count On. 1980. 112p. (J). (gr. 5 up). 9.95 o.p. (*0-525-39595-4*, Dutton) Dutton/Plume.

Moore, Eugenia. In a Minute! Leiper, Esther M., ed. 1988. 32p. (Orig.). (YA). (gr. 9 up). pap. 3.95 (*0-9617284-9-3*) Sand & Silk.

Moore, Martha. Angels on the Roof. 1997. 192p. (YA). (gr. 7 up). 15.95 o.s.i (*0-385-32278-X*, Delacorte Pr.) Dell Publishing.

Moore, Peggy S. The Case of the Missing Bike & Other Things. 2nd rev. ed. 1992. (Illus.). 40p. (Orig.). (J). (gr. 4-6). pap. 5.95 (*0-9613078-1-1*) Detroit Black Writer's Guild.

Mora, Pat. A Birthday Basket for Tia. unabr. ed. 2001. (J). (gr. k-3). pap. 15.95 incl. audio (*0-8045-6841-3*, 6841) Spoken Arts, Inc.

—Maria Paints the Hills. 2002. (J). 19.95 o.p. (*0-89013-401-4*); pap. 9.95 (*0-89013-410-3*) Museum of New Mexico Pr.

Morales, Maximino. Juan & the Three Wise Men/Juan y los Tres Reyes Mogos. (ENG & SPA., Illus.). 28p. (J). 6.95 (*0-9740308-1-3*) Maximum Publishing Co.

Moran, Alex. Six Silly Foxes. 2000. (Green Light Readers Ser.). (Illus.). 20p. (J). (gr. k-2). pap. 3.95 o.s.i (*0-15-202566-9*, Green Light Readers) Harcourt Children's Bks.

Moranville, Sharelle Byars. Over the River, ERS. 2002. 192p. (YA). (gr. 4-9). 16.95 (*0-8050-7049-4*, Holt, Henry & Co. Bks. For Young Readers) Holt, Henry & Co.

—The Purple Ribbon, ERS. 2003. (Illus.). 80p. (J). (gr. 1-4). 17.95 (*0-8050-6659-4*, Holt, Henry & Co. Bks. For Young Readers) Holt, Henry & Co.

Morgan, Mary, illus. Guess Who I Love? 1992. (Pudgy Board Bks.). 18p. (J). (ps). 3.50 o.s.i (*0-448-40313-7*, Grosset & Dunlap) Penguin Putnam Bks. for Young Readers.

Morgan, Stacy Towle. The Cuddlers. 1993. (Illus.). 32p. 9.95 (*0-912500-41-7*, 155-12) La Leche League International.

Morganstern, Mimi. The House at Hemlock Farms. 2000. (Illus.). vi, 54p. (J). (gr. 3-6). pap. 6.95 (*0-9700522-3-5*) Morganstern, Mimi.

—The House at Hemlock Farms-"Read-Along with Mimi" A Cool Chapterbook-Package. 2000. (Illus.). vi, 54p. (J). (gr. 3-6). per. 9.99 incl. audio (*0-9700522-4-3*) Morganstern, Mimi.

Morrison, Dannell C. Pee Yew Bartholomew: A Story about Divorce. 1997. 16p. (Orig.). (J). (gr. 5-8). pap. 5.95 o.p. (*1-57543-028-2*) MAR*CO Products, Inc.

Morrison, Toni & Morrison, Slade. La Gran Caja. 2001. (SPA., Illus.). 56p. (YA). (gr. 3 up). 15.16 (*84-406-9535-7*) B Ediciones S.A. ESP. *Dist:* Lectorum Pubns., Inc.

Morton, Lone. Get Dressed, Robbie. Jansen, Jacqueline, tr. 1998. Tr. of Habille-Toi, Robbie. (ENG & FRE., Illus.). 28p. (J). (ps-3). 6.95 o.p. (*0-7641-5128-2*) Barron's Educational Series, Inc.

Morton, Lone & Risk, Mary. Get Dressed, Roberto. 1998. (Language Learning Story Bks.).Tr. of Vistete, Roberto. (ENG & SPA., Illus.). 28p. (J). (ps-3). 7.95 (*0-7641-5129-0*, BA290) Barron's Educational Series, Inc.

Moses, Shelia P. The Legend of Buddy Bush. 2004. (Illus.). 224p. (YA). 15.95 (*0-689-85839-6*, McElderry, Margaret K.) Simon & Schuster Children's Publishing.

Mosher, Richard. The Taxi Navigator. 1996. 144p. (J). (gr. 4-7). 15.95 o.s.i (*0-399-23104-8*, Philomel) Penguin Putnam Bks. for Young Readers.

Moss, Marissa. Amelia Writes Again! 1999. (Amelia Ser.). (Illus.). 32p. (YA). (gr. 3 up). 12.95 (*1-56247-787-0*); pap. 5.95 (*1-56247-786-2*) Pleasant Co. Pubns. (American Girl).

—Amelia Writes Again! 1996. (Amelia Ser.). (Illus.). 32p. (J). (gr. 3-5). 14.00 o.p. (*1-883672-42-2*) Tricycle Pr.

—Amelia Writes Again. 1999. (Amelia Ser.). (J). (gr. 3-5). 12.10 (*0-606-17252-1*) Turtleback Bks.

—Rose's Journal: The Story of a Girl in the Great Depression. (Young American Voices Ser.). (Illus.). 56p. (J). 2003. pap. 7.00 (*0-15-204605-4*); 2001. (gr. 3-7). 15.00 (*0-15-202423-9*) Harcourt Children's Bks. (Silver Whistle).

Muchmore, Jo Ann. Johnny Rides Again. 1995. 128p. (J). (gr. 4-7). tchr. ed. 14.95 o.p. (*0-8234-1156-7*) Holiday Hse., Inc.

Munsch, Robert. On Partage Tout. ed. 2000. (J). (gr. 1). spiral bd. (*0-616-01838-X*) Canadian National Institute for the Blind/Institut National Canadien pour les Aveugles.

—Tengo Que Ir! 2003. (Hablemos Ser.). (SPA., Illus.). 24p. (J). (gr. k-2). per. 5.95 (*1-55037-682-9*, AP30494) Annick Pr., Ltd. CAN. *Dist:* Firefly Bks., Ltd., Lectorum Pubns., Inc.

Munsch, Robert & Martchenko, Michael. Up, up, Down. 2002. 32p. (J). pap. 3.99 (*0-439-31796-7*) Scholastic, Inc.

Munsil, Janet. Dinner at Auntie Rose's. 1984. (Illus.). 32p. (J). (ps-3). pap. 4.95 (*0-920236-63-4*) Annick Pr., Ltd. CAN. *Dist:* Firefly Bks., Ltd.

Munsil, Ritchie. Dinner at Auntie Rose's. 1984. (Illus.). 24p. (J). (ps-8). 12.95 o.p. (*0-920236-66-9*) Annick Pr., Ltd. CAN. *Dist:* Firefly Bks., Ltd.

Murphy, Mary. I Like It When... 1997. (Illus.). 32p. (J). (ps). 11.95 (*0-15-200039-9*, Red Wagon Bks.) Harcourt Children's Bks.

Murphy, Rita. Night Flying. 2002. 144p. (YA). (gr. 7 up). mass mkt. 4.99 (*0-440-22837-9*, Laurel Leaf) Random Hse. Children's Bks.

Murphy, Shirley Rousseau. Poor Jenny, Bright As a Penny. 1974. 176p. (J). (gr. 7 up). 5.95 o.p. (*0-670-56433-8*) Viking Penguin.

Murphy, Stuart J. Chicken Sunday. 1998. (Illus.). 32p. (J). (gr. k-3). reprint ed. pap. 6.99 (*0-698-11615-1*) Putnam Publishing Group, The.

Murray, Brendan. Tev. Rubin, Barry & Veremis, Thanos, eds. 2002. 152p. (J). pap. 13.95 (*1-86368-334-8*) Fremantle Arts Centre Pr. AUS. *Dist:* International Specialized Bk. Services.

Murray, Carol. Hurry Up! 2003. (Rookie Reader Ser.). (Illus.). pap. 4.95 (*0-516-27831-2*, Children's Pr.) Scholastic Library Publishing.

Murrow, Liza K. Allergic to My Family. 1992. (Illus.). 160p. (J). 13.95 o.p. (*0-8234-0959-7*) Holiday Hse., Inc.

Muzik, Katy. At Home in the Coral Reef. Dworkin Wright, Elena, ed. 1992. (Illus.). 32p. (J). (ps-3). pap. 14.95 (*0-88106-487-4*, CB4874) Charlesbridge Publishing, Inc.

—At Home in the Coral Reef. 1992. (Illus.). 32p. (J). (ps-3). pap. 6.95 (*0-88106-486-6*) Charlesbridge Publishing, Inc.

—At Home in the Coral Reef. unabr. ed. 1994. (J). (gr. k-4). pap. 17.90 incl. audio (*0-8045-6814-6*, 6814) Spoken Arts, Inc.

Myers, Anna. Captain's Command. 2001. 144p. (gr. 4-7). pap. text 4.50 (*0-440-41699-X*, Yearling) Random Hse. Children's Bks.

—Captain's Command. 1999. 144p. (YA). (gr. 5-9). 15.95 (*0-8027-8706-1*) Walker & Co.

—Fire in the Hills. 1996. 192p. (YA). (gr. 7 up). 15.95 (*0-8027-8421-6*) Walker & Co.

—The Fire in the Hills. 1998. (Puffin Novel Ser.). 176p. (J). (gr. 7-12). pap. 5.99 o.s.i (*0-14-130074-4*, Puffin Bks.) Penguin Putnam Bks. for Young Readers.

—Red Dirt Jessie. 1997. (Illus.). 128p. (J). (gr. 3-7). pap. 4.99 (*0-14-038734-X*, Puffin Bks.) Penguin Putnam Bks. for Young Readers.

—Spotting the Leopard. 1997. (Illus.). 224p. (J). (gr. 3-7). pap. 4.50 o.s.i (*0-14-038728-5*, Puffin Bks.) Penguin Putnam Bks. for Young Readers.

—Spotting the Leopard. 1996. 176p. (J). (gr. 4-7). 15.95 (*0-8027-8459-3*) Walker & Co.

Myers, Walter Dean. Bearer Of Dreams. 2003. 192p. (J). (gr. 5 up). lib. bdg. 16.89 (*0-06-029522-8*, Amistad Pr.) HarperTrade.

—The Dream Bearer. 2003. 192p. (J). (gr. 5 up). 15.99 (*0-06-029521-X*, Amistad Pr.) HarperTrade.

—The Dream Bearer. l.t. ed. 2003. 207p. (J). 25.95 (*0-7862-5923-X*) Thorndike Pr.

—It Ain't All for Nothin' 2003. (Amistad Ser.). 240p. (J). (gr. 7 up). pap. 5.99 (*0-06-447311-2*, Harper Trophy) HarperCollins Children's Bk. Group.

Myracle, Lauren. Eleven. 2004. 160p. (J). 16.99 (*0-525-47165-0*, Dutton Children's Bks.) Penguin Putnam Bks. for Young Readers.

Na, An. A Step from Heaven. 2001. 176p. (J). (gr. 7 up). 15.95 (*1-886910-58-8*, Front Street) Front Street, Inc.

—A Step from Heaven. l.t. ed. 2002. 193p. (J). 22.95 (*0-7862-4126-8*) Gale Group.

—A Step from Heaven. 2003. (Illus.). 160p. (YA). pap. 7.99 (*0-14-250027-5*, Puffin Bks.) Penguin Putnam Bks. for Young Readers.

—A Step from Heaven. unabr. ed. 2002. (YA). (gr. 3 up). audio 25.00 (*0-8072-0721-7*, Listening Library) Random Hse. Audio Publishing Group.

Namioka, Lensey. Half & Half. 2003. 144p. lib. bdg. 17.99 (*0-385-90072-4*); (gr. 3-7). text 15.95 (*0-385-73038-1*) Random Hse. Children's Bks. (Delacorte Bks. for Young Readers).

—Yang the Eldest & His Odd Jobs. 2002. (Illus.). 128p. (gr. 4-7). pap. text 4.50 (*0-440-41802-X*, Yearling) Random Hse. Children's Bks.

—Yang the Third & Her Impossible Family. 1995. (Illus.). 160p. (J). 15.95 o.p. (*0-316-59726-0*) Little Brown & Co.

—Yang the Third & Her Impossible Family. 1996. (J). 10.55 (*0-606-10096-2*) Turtleback Bks.

Napoli, Donna Jo. Crazy Jack. 2001. 11.55 (*0-606-20617-5*) Turtleback Bks.

—The Daughter of Venice. 2002. 288p. (YA). lib. bdg. 18.99 (*0-385-90036-8*); (gr. 7-7). 16.95 (*0-385-32780-3*) Dell Publishing. (Delacorte Pr.).

—Daughter of Venice. 2003. 288p. (YA). (gr. 7). mass mkt. 5.50 (*0-440-22928-6*, Dell Books for Young Readers) Random Hse. Children's Bks.

—When the Water Closes over My Head. (Illus.). 144p. (J). 1996. (gr. 3-7). pap. 3.99 o.s.i (*0-14-037996-7*, Puffin Bks.); 1994. (gr. 2-5). 13.99 o.s.i (*0-525-45083-1*, Dutton Children's Bks.) Penguin Putnam Bks. for Young Readers.

—When the Water Closes over My Head. 1996. 9.09 (*0-606-10058-X*) Turtleback Bks.

Napoli, Donna Jo & Tchen, Richard. Spinners. November, S., ed. 2001. 208p. (YA). pap. 5.99 (*0-14-131110-X*, Puffin Bks.) Penguin Putnam Bks. for Young Readers.

Narahashi, Keiko. Ouch! 2004. (J). (*0-689-84978-8*, McElderry, Margaret K.) Simon & Schuster Children's Publishing.

Nash, Mary. Mrs. Coverlet's Magicians. 2001. (Lost Treasures Ser.: No. 2). 192p. (J). (gr. 3-7). pap. 4.99 (*0-7868-1517-5*); (Illus.). (gr. 4-7). pap. 4.99 (*0-7868-1518-3*, Volo) Hyperion Bks. for Children.

Relationships

Naylor, Phyllis Reynolds. Alice in April. 1993. (Alice Ser.). 176p. (J). (gr. 5-9). 16.00 (*0-689-31805-7*, Atheneum) Simon & Schuster Children's Publishing.

—Alice in April. 1995. (Alice Ser.). (YA). (gr. 5-9). 10.04 (*0-606-07181-4*) Turtleback Bks.

—Alice In-Between. 1996. (Alice Ser.). 160p. (YA). (gr. 5-9). pap. text 4.50 (*0-440-41064-9*) Dell Publishing.

—Alice In-Between. 1994. (Alice Ser.). 160p. (YA). (gr. 5-9). 16.95 (*0-689-31890-1*, Atheneum) Simon & Schuster Children's Publishing.

—Alice In-Between. 1996. (Alice Ser.). (YA). (gr. 5-9). 10.55 (*0-606-08976-4*) Turtleback Bks.

—Alice in Lace. (Alice Ser.). 144p. (YA). (gr. 5-9). 1997. pap. 4.99 (*0-689-80597-7*, Aladdin); 1996. 17.00 (*0-689-80358-3*, Atheneum) Simon & Schuster Children's Publishing.

—Alice in Lace. 1997. (Alice Ser.). (YA). (gr. 5-9). 11.04 (*0-606-13114-0*) Turtleback Bks.

—Alice the Brave. 1996. (Alice Ser.). 144p. (YA). (gr. 5-9). pap. 4.99 (*0-689-80598-5*, Aladdin) Simon & Schuster Children's Publishing.

—Alice the Brave. 1995. (Alice Ser.). (YA). (gr. 5-9). 10.55 (*0-606-10737-1*) Turtleback Bks.

—I Can't Take You Anywhere. 2001. (J). 12.14 (*0-606-20714-7*) Turtleback Bks.

—The Keeper. 1987. 192p. (YA). (gr. 6 up). mass mkt. 2.95 o.s.i (*0-553-26882-1*, Starfire) Random Hse. Children's Bks.

—Outrageously Alice. (Alice Ser.). 144p. (gr. 5-9). 1998. (YA). pap. 4.99 (*0-689-80596-9*, Aladdin); 1997. (J). 15.95 (*0-689-80354-0*, Atheneum) Simon & Schuster Children's Publishing.

—Outrageously Alice. 1998. (Alice Ser.). (YA). (gr. 5-9). 11.04 (*0-606-14288-6*) Turtleback Bks.

—Patiently Alice. 2003. (Alice Ser.). (Illus.). 256p. (YA). 15.95 (*0-689-82636-2*, Atheneum) Simon & Schuster Children's Publishing.

—Peril in the Besseldorf Parachute Factory. 2000. (Illus.). 160p. (J). (gr. 3-7). 16.00 (*0-689-82539-0*, Atheneum) Simon & Schuster Children's Publishing.

—Saving Shiloh. 1999. (Shiloh Ser.: No. 3). (J). (gr. 4-7). pap. 12.40 (*0-613-12073-6*) Econo-Clad Bks.

—Saving Shiloh. (Shiloh Ser.: No. 3). 144p. (J). (gr. 4-7). 1997. 15.00 (*0-689-81460-7*, Atheneum); 1999. reprint ed. pap. 5.50 (*0-689-81461-5*, Aladdin) Simon & Schuster Children's Publishing.

—Saving Shiloh. l.t. ed. 2002. 193p. (J). 22.95 (*0-7862-3713-9*) Thorndike Pr.

—Saving Shiloh. 1999. 11.04 (*0-606-14310-6*) Turtleback Bks.

—Send No Blessings. 1992. 240p. (YA). (gr. 5 up). pap. 3.99 o.s.i (*0-14-034859-X*, Puffin Bks.) Penguin Putnam Bks. for Young Readers.

—Send No Blessings. 1990. 240p. (YA). (gr. 7 up). 16.00 (*0-689-31582-1*, Atheneum) Simon & Schuster Children's Publishing.

—Send No Blessings. 1992. 10.09 o.p. (*0-606-00744-X*) Turtleback Bks.

—Shiloh. 1996. (Shiloh Ser.: No. 1). 144p. (J). (gr. 4-7). mass mkt. 2.49 o.s.i (*0-440-21991-4*) Dell Publishing.

—Shiloh. (SPA.). (YA). (gr. 5-8). (*968-16-5805-1*, FC0086) Fondo de Cultura Economica MEX. *Dist:* Lectorum Pubns., Inc.

—Shiloh. l.t. ed. 2000. (Shiloh Ser.: No. 1). 155p. (J). (gr. 4-7). lib. bdg. 27.95 (*1-58118-058-6*, 23472) LRS.

—Shiloh. l.t. ed. 1995. (Shiloh Ser.: No. 1). 160p. (J). (gr. 4-7). lib. bdg. 16.95 o.p. (*1-885885-10-5*, Cornerstone Bks.) Pages, Inc.

—Shiloh. 144p. (J). (gr. 4-7). (Shiloh Ser.: No. 1). pap. 4.99 (*0-8072-8330-4*);No. 1. 2000. pap. 28.00 incl. audio (*0-8072-8329-0*, YA164SP) Random Hse. Audio Publishing Group. (Listening Library).

—Shiloh. (Shiloh Ser.: No. 1). (gr. 4-7). 1998. 160p. mass mkt. 2.99 o.s.i (*0-440-22811-5*, Yearling); 1992. 160p. pap. text 5.50 o.s.i (*0-440-40752-4*, Yearling); 1992. (J). pap. 3.50 (*0-440-80297-0*, Dell Books for Young Readers) Random Hse. Children's Bks.

—Shiloh. (Shiloh Ser.: No. 1). 144p. (J). 2000. (gr. 3-7). pap. 5.99 (*0-689-83582-5*, Aladdin); 1991. (gr. 4-7). 16.00 (*0-689-31614-3*, Atheneum) Simon & Schuster Children's Publishing.

—Shiloh. (J). 2000. 11.55 (*0-606-19724-9*); 1991. (Shiloh Ser.: No. 1). (gr. 4-7). 10.09 (*0-606-01016-5*) Turtleback Bks.

—Shiloh Movie Tie-In. 2000. (Shiloh Ser.: No. 6). (Illus.). 144p. (J). (gr. 4-7). pap. 5.50 (*0-689-83583-3*, Aladdin) Simon & Schuster Children's Publishing.

—Shiloh Season. unabr. ed. 2000. (Shiloh Ser.: No. 2). 120p. (J). (gr. 4-7). pap. 28.00 incl. audio (*0-8072-8707-5*, YA242SP, Listening Library) Random Hse. Audio Publishing Group.

—Shiloh Season. (Shiloh Ser.: No. 2). 128p. (J). (gr. 4-7). 2000. mass mkt. 2.99 (*0-689-83862-X*, Aladdin); 1999. (Illus.). pap. 5.50 (*0-689-82931-0*, Aladdin); 1998. pap. 4.99 (*0-689-80646-9*, Aladdin); 1996. 15.00 (*0-689-80647-7*, Atheneum) Simon & Schuster Children's Publishing.

—Shiloh Season. l.t. ed. 2000. (Juvenile Ser.). (Illus.). 164p. (J). (gr. 4-7). 21.95 o.p. (*0-7862-2702-8*) Thorndike Pr.

—Shiloh Season. 1998. (Shiloh Ser.: No. 2). (J). (gr. 4-7). 11.04 (*0-606-13085-3*) Turtleback Bks.

—Shiloh Trilogy: Shiloh; Shiloh Season; Saving Shiloh. (J). 2000. (gr. 3-7). 14.99 (*0-689-01525-9*, Aladdin); 1998. (Shiloh Ser.: Nos. 1-3). (gr. 4-7). 35.00 (*0-689-82327-4*, Atheneum) Simon & Schuster Children's Publishing.

—Starting with Alice. (Alice Ser.). (J). 2004. (Illus.). 208p. pap. 4.99 (*0-689-84396-8*, Aladdin); 2002. 192p. 15.95 (*0-689-84395-X*, Atheneum) Simon & Schuster Children's Publishing.

—Starting with Alice. l.t. ed. 2003. 199p. (J). 22.95 (*0-7862-5091-7*) Thorndike Pr.

—A String of Chances. 1983. (J). mass mkt. 2.25 o.s.i (*0-449-70075-5*, Fawcett) Ballantine Bks.

—Walker's Crossing. unabr. ed. 2001. 232p. (YA). (gr. 6 up). pap. 35.00 incl. audio (*0-8072-8410-6*, Listening Library) Random Hse. Audio Publishing Group.

—Walker's Crossing. 2001. (J). 11.04 (*0-606-21506-9*) Turtleback Bks.

Naylor, Phyllis Reynolds & Reynolds, Lura Schield. Maudie in the Middle. 1988. (Illus.). 176p. (J). (gr. 2-6). lib. bdg. 16.00 (*0-689-31395-0*, Atheneum) Simon & Schuster Children's Publishing.

Neenan, Colin. Live a Little. 1996. 264p. (J). (gr. 7-12). pap. 6.00 (*0-15-201243-5*, Harcourt Paperbacks) Harcourt Children's Bks.

Neigoff, Mike. It Will Never Be the Same Again, ERS. 1979. (Illus.). (J). (gr. 5-9). o.p. (*0-03-047106-0*, Holt, Henry & Co. Bks. For Young Readers) Holt, Henry & Co.

Nelson, Theresa. The Empress of Elsewhere. 1998. (Illus.). 224p. (J). (gr. 5-9). pap. 17.95 o.p. (*0-7894-2498-3*) Dorling Kindersley Publishing, Inc.

—Empress of Elsewhere. 2000. (Illus.). 224p. (J). (gr. 5-9). pap. 5.99 o.s.i (*0-14-130813-3*, Puffin Bks.) Penguin Putnam Bks. for Young Readers.

—Empress of Elsewhere. 2000. (Illus.). (J). 12.04 (*0-606-18836-3*) Turtleback Bks.

Nesbit, Edith. Five Children & It. 1990. 208p. (J). (gr. 4-6). pap. 3.50 o.s.i (*0-440-42586-7*) Dell Publishing.

—Five Children & It. 2002. (Children's Classics). 192p. (J). pap. 3.95 (*1-85326-124-6*) Wordsworth Editions, Ltd. GBR. *Dist:* Advanced Global Distribution Services.

—The Railway Children. 1998. (J). pap. text 7.00 o.p. (*0-582-40140-2*) Addison-Wesley Longman, Inc.

—The Railway Children. 1996. (Andre Deutsch Classics). 223p. (J). (gr. 5-8). 11.95 (*0-233-99037-2*) Andre Deutsch GBR. *Dist:* Trafalgar Square, Trans-Atlantic Pubns., Inc.

—The Railway Children. 1993. 272p. (J). (gr. 4 up). mass mkt. 3.25 o.s.i (*0-553-21415-2*, Bantam Classics) Bantam Bks.

—The Railway Children. 1975. (Dent's Illustrated Children's Classics Ser.). (Illus.). 208p. (J). 9.00 o.p. (*0-460-05094-X*) Biblio Distribution.

—The Railway Children. 1994. (Classics for Young Readers Ser.). 64p. (J). 5.98 o.p. (*0-86112-983-0*) Brimax Bks., Ltd.

—The Railway Children. 1992. 224p. (J). (gr. 4-7). pap. 3.50 o.s.i (*0-440-40602-1*) Dell Publishing.

—The Railway Children. (J). E-Book 2.49 (*1-58627-659-X*) Electric Umbrella Publishing.

—The Railway Children. Dryhurst, Dinah, tr. & illus. by. 2003. (J). 18.95 (*1-56792-261-9*) Godine, David R. Pub.

—The Railway Children. 1999. (Chapter Book Charmers Ser.). (Illus.). 80p. (J). (gr. 2-5). 2.99 o.p. (*0-694-01285-8*) HarperCollins Children's Bk. Group.

—The Railway Children. 1993. (Children's Classics Ser.). (J). (gr. 2-7). 12.95 (*0-679-42534-9*, Everyman's Library) Knopf Publishing Group.

—The Railway Children. 1992. 256p. mass mkt. 2.95 o.s.i (*0-451-52561-2*, Signet Classics) NAL.

—The Railway Children. 1991. (Oxford World's Classics Ser.). (Illus.). 224p. (J). pap. 4.95 o.p. (*0-19-282659-X*, 11912) Oxford Univ. Pr., Inc.

—The Railway Children. 2000. (Illus.). 224p. pap. 8.95 (*1-86205-235-2*) Pavilion Bks., Ltd. GBR. *Dist:* Trafalgar Square.

—The Railway Children. (Illus.). (J). (gr. 3-5). 9999. (Children's Classics Ser.: No. 740-19). pap. 3.50 o.p. (*0-7214-0824-9*); 1997. (Classic Ser.). 54p. 2.99 o.s.i (*0-7214-5708-8*) Penguin Group (USA) Inc. (Ladybird Bks.).

—The Railway Children. (Classics for Young Readers Ser.). (Illus.). 1994. 288p. (J). (gr. 4-7). pap. 3.99 (*0-14-036671-7*, Puffin Bks.); 1991. 192p. (YA). 16.95 o.s.i (*0-399-21819-X*, Philomel); 1983. 240p. (J). (gr. 3-7). pap. 3.50 o.p. (*0-14-035005-5*, Puffin Bks.) Penguin Putnam Bks. for Young Readers.

—The Railway Children. (Children's Library Ser.). 1996. (J). 1.10 o.s.i (*0-517-14153-1*); 1991. (Illus.). 192p. (YA). 9.99 o.s.i (*0-517-07011-1*) Random Hse. Value Publishing.

—The Railway Children. 9999. (Illus.). (J). 19.95 o.p. (*0-590-74000-8*) Scholastic, Inc.

—The Railway Children. 1988. (J). (gr. 5-8). 16.30 o.p. (*0-8446-6345-X*) Smith, Peter Pub., Inc.

—The Railway Children. E-Book 5.00 (*0-7410-0817-3*) SoftBook Pr.

—The Railway Children. 1961. (Illus.). (J). (gr. 2-5). pap. 1.95 o.p. (*0-14-030147-X*, Penguin Bks.) Viking Penguin.

—The Railway Children. 1998. (Children's Classics). 208p. (J). (gr. 4-7). pap. 3.95 (*1-85326-107-6*, 1076WW) Wordsworth Editions, Ltd. GBR. *Dist:* Advanced Global Distribution Services.

—Railway Children. 2000. (Juvenile Classics). (Illus.). iii, 188p. (J). pap. 2.50 (*0-486-41022-6*) Dover Pubns., Inc.

—Railway Children. (J). 3.50 (*0-340-71497-2*) Hodder & Stoughton, Ltd. GBR. *Dist:* Lubrecht & Cramer, Ltd., Trafalgar Square.

—The Railway Children, ERS. 1994. (J). 14.95 o.p. (*0-8050-3129-4*, Holt, Henry & Co. Bks. For Young Readers) Holt, Henry & Co.

—The Railway Children, Level 2. 2000. (C). pap. 7.66 (*0-582-41790-2*) Longman Publishing Group.

—The Railway Children. abr. ed. 1996. (J). audio 13.98 (*962-634-585-3*, NA208514, Naxos AudioBooks) Naxos of America, Inc.

—The Railway Children, Level 3. Hedge, Tricia, ed. 2000. (Bookworms Ser.). (Illus.). 74p. pap. text 5.95 (*0-19-423013-9*) Oxford Univ. Pr., Inc.

—The Railway Children. l.t. ed. 1987. (Charnwood Large Print Ser.). 288p. 29.99 o.p. (*0-7089-8382-0*, Charnwood) Thorpe, F. A. Pubs. GBR. *Dist:* Ulverscroft Large Print Bks., Ltd., Ulverscroft Large Print Canada, Ltd.

—The Railway Children. abr. ed. (Children's Classics Ser.). (J). 1997. pap. 15.95 o.p. incl. audio (*1-85998-750-8*); 1994. audio 14.95 (*1-85998-081-3*) Trafalgar Square.

Nesbit, Jeffrey A. The Reluctant Runaway. 1991. (Capital Crew Ser.). 120p. (J). pap. 4.99 o.p. (*0-89693-131-5*) Scripture Pr. Pubs., Inc.

Neville, Emily C. Garden of Broken Glass. 1975. 228p. (J). (gr. 5-9). 6.95 o.s.i (*0-440-04839-7*); lib. bdg. 6.46 o.s.i (*0-440-04842-7*) Dell Publishing. (Delacorte Pr.).

Newberger, Devra. A Full House Family Scrapbook. 1992. 40p. (J). (gr. 4-7). pap. 3.95 o.p. (*0-590-45706-3*) Scholastic, Inc.

Newman, James A. Making a Living. 1991. (Illus.). 120p. (Orig.). (J). (gr. 2-8). pap. 7.95 (*0-9642980-0-7*) Newman, James A.

Newman, Leslea. Remember That. 1996. (Illus.). 32p. (J). (ps-3). tchr. ed. 14.95 o.s.i (*0-395-66156-0*, Clarion Bks.) Houghton Mifflin Co. Trade & Reference Div.

Newton, Jill. Don't Sit There! 1994. (Illus.). 32p. (J). 15.00 o.p. (*0-688-13309-6*) HarperCollins Children's Bk. Group.

Newton, Suzanne. I Will Call It Georgie's Blues. 1983. 204p. (J). (gr. 6 up). 12.95 o.p. (*0-670-39131-X*, Viking Children's Bks.) Penguin Putnam Bks. for Young Readers.

Nicholson, Nicholas B. & von Buhler, Cynthia. Little Girl in a Red Dress with Cat & Dog. 1998. 32p. (J). (gr. 1-4). 15.99 o.s.i (*0-670-87183-4*) Penguin Putnam Bks. for Young Readers.

Nicholson, Peggy & Warner, John F. The Case of the Squeaky Thief. 1994. (Kerry Hill Casecrackers Ser.: No. 3). 120p. (J). (gr. 3-6). lib. bdg. 13.27 (*0-8225-0711-0*, Lerner Pubns.) Lerner Publishing Group.

Nickerson, Sara. How to Disappear Completely & Never Be Found. (Illus.). 288p. (J). (gr. 5 up). 2003. pap. 5.99 (*0-06-441027-7*); 2002. 15.95 (*0-06-029771-9*); 2002. lib. bdg. 15.89 (*0-06-029772-7*) HarperCollins Children's Bk. Group.

Nielsen, Shelly. Take a Bow, Victoria. 1986. (Victoria Ser.). 130p. (J). (gr. 3-7). pap. 4.99 o.p. (*0-89191-470-6*) Cook Communications Ministries.

Nixon, Joan Lowery. Land of Promise. l.t. ed. 2001. (Ellis Island Stories Ser.). 169p. (J). (gr. 4 up). lib. bdg. 22.60 (*0-8368-2812-7*) Stevens, Gareth Inc.

—Search for the Shadowman. 1996. 160p. (gr. 3-7). text 15.95 o.s.i (*0-385-32203-8*, Delacorte Pr.) Dell Publishing.

Nixon-Weaver, Elizabeth. Rooster. 2001. (Illus.). 320p. (J). (gr. 7 up). 16.95 (*1-58837-001-1*) Winslow Pr.

Nobens, Cheryl A. Montgomery's Time Zone. 1990. (J). (ps-2). lib. bdg. 7.95 o.p. (*0-87614-398-2*) Lerner Publishing Group.

Noble, June. Where Do I Fit In?, ERS. 1981. (Illus.). 32p. (gr. k-2). o.p. (*0-03-046181-2*, Holt, Henry & Co. Bks. For Young Readers) Holt, Henry & Co.

Noble, Sheilagh. Uh Oh! 2001. (Toddler Ser.). (Illus.). 24p. (J). (ps up). 9.95 o.p. (*1-84089-182-3*) Zero to Ten, Ltd. GBR. *Dist:* Independent Pubs. Group.

Noises in the Attic. 1997. (Illus.). 24p. (J). (gr. 1-3). 3.98 (*1-890095-04-4*) Nesak International.

Nolan, Han. Dancing on the Edge. 1997. 256p. (YA). (gr. 7-12). 16.00 (*0-15-201648-1*) Harcourt Children's Bks.

—A Face in Every Window. 2001. 264p. (J). 5.99 (*0-14-131218-1*, Puffin Bks.) Penguin Putnam Bks. for Young Readers.

—A Face in Every Window. 2001. (J). 12.04 (*0-606-21184-5*) Turtleback Bks.

Nolan, Madeena S. My Daddy Don't Go to Work. 1978. (Illus.). (J). (gr. k-3). lib. bdg. 5.95 o.p. (*0-87614-093-2*, Carolrhoda Bks.) Lerner Publishing Group.

Nolen-Harold, Jerdine. In My Momma's Kitchen. 1999. (Amistad Ser.). (Illus.). 32p. (J). (ps-3). lib. bdg. 15.89 (*0-688-12761-4*); 15.95 (*0-688-12760-6*) HarperTrade. (Amistad Pr.).

Nolen, Jerdine. In My Momma's Kitchen. 2001. (Illus.). (J). 12.10 (*0-606-21246-9*) Turtleback Bks.

Norris, Gunilla B. Take My Waking Slow. 1970. (Illus.). (J). (gr. 5-9). 1.59 o.p. (*0-689-20608-9*, Atheneum) Simon & Schuster Children's Publishing.

Northway, Jennifer. Get Lost, Laura! 1995. (Illus.). 32p. (J). (ps-2). pap. 10.95 o.s.i (*0-307-17520-0*, Golden Bks.) Random Hse. Children's Bks.

Norton, Andre & Miller, Phyllis. House of Shadows. 1984. 216p. (J). (gr. 5-9). 14.95 o.s.i (*0-689-50298-2*, McElderry, Margaret K.) Simon & Schuster Children's Publishing.

Nostlinger, Christine. Girl Missing. Bell, Anthea, tr. 1976. (ENG & GER.). 144p. (gr. 6 up). lib. bdg. 5.90 o.p. (*0-531-00346-9*, Watts, Franklin) Scholastic Library Publishing.

Novak, Matt. Mouse TV. 1994. (Illus.). 32p. (J). (ps-1). pap. 16.95 (*0-531-06856-0*); lib. bdg. 17.99 (*0-531-08706-9*) Scholastic, Inc. (Orchard Bks.).

Nye, Naomi S. Sitti's Secrets. 1997. 32p. (J). (gr. k-3). pap. 6.99 (*0-689-81706-1*, Aladdin) Simon & Schuster Children's Publishing.

Nye, Naomi Shihab. Habibi. unabr. ed. 2000. (YA). pap. 49.24 incl. audio (*0-7887-3642-6*, 41008X4) Recorded Bks., LLC.

—Habibi. 272p. (YA). (gr. 5 up). 1999. mass mkt. 5.99 (*0-689-82523-4*, Simon Pulse); 1997. 16.00 (*0-689-80149-1*, Simon & Schuster Children's Publishing) Simon & Schuster Children's Publishing.

—Sitti's Secrets. 1997. (J). 12.14 (*0-606-13029-2*) Turtleback Bks.

Nygren, Tord. Fiddler & His Brothers. 1987. Tr. of Spelevink Och Hans Broder. (Illus.). 32p. (J). (gr. k-3). 12.95 o.p. (*0-688-07145-7*); lib. bdg. 12.88 o.p. (*0-688-07146-5*) Morrow/Avon. (Morrow, William & Co.).

Nystrom, Carolyn. Mike's Lonely Summer. 1986. (Lion Care Ser.). (Illus.). 48p. (J). (gr. 1-6). 7.99 o.p. (*0-7459-1016-5*) Lion Publishing.

O'Brien, Anne Sibley. It Hurts!, ERS. 1986. (Busy Day Board Bks.). (Illus.). 14p. (J). (ps-2). pap. 3.95 o.p. (*0-8050-0048-8*, Holt, Henry & Co. Bks. For Young Readers) Holt, Henry & Co.

O'Connor, Barbara. Taking Care of Moses, RS. 2004. (*0-374-38038-4*) Farrar, Straus & Giroux.

O'Dell, Scott. Zia. 2002. (J). 13.94 (*0-7587-5209-1*) Book Wholesalers, Inc.

—Zia. 1995. (J). 11.55 (*0-606-01279-6*); 11.14 (*0-606-08414-2*) Turtleback Bks.

Oden, Fay G. Where Is Calvin? 1994. (Illus.). 48p. (J). (gr. 2-6). per. 6.95 (*0-9638946-0-9*) Tennedo Pubs.

Offerman, Lynn. Where Is It? Hers. 1998. (Nuk Bks.). (Illus.). 8p. (J). 6.95 (*0-7641-7233-6*) Barron's Educational Series, Inc.

Okimoto, Jean Davies. My Mother Is Not Married to My Father. 1981. (J). (gr. 7-9). reprint ed. pap. (*0-671-56079-4*, Simon Pulse) Simon & Schuster Children's Publishing.

Oldfield, J. Susie Orphan. 1996. (Home Farm Twins Ser.: No. 4). (Illus.). 120p. (J). mass mkt. 7.95 (*0-340-66130-5*) Hodder & Stoughton, Ltd. GBR. *Dist:* Lubrecht & Cramer, Ltd., Trafalgar Square.

Oldfield, Pamela. Melanie Brown & the Jar of Sweets. 1974. (Illus.). 64p. (J). (ps-5). o.p. (*0-571-10619-6*) Faber & Faber Ltd.

O'Leary, Patsy Baker. With Wings As Eagles. 1997. 272p. (YA). (gr. 7-12). tchr. ed. 15.00 (*0-395-70557-6*) Houghton Mifflin Co.

Oliker, Elena. B4me. 2001. 156p. E-Book 8.00 (*0-7388-6550-8*) Xlibris Corp.

O'Malley, Kevin. Roller Coaster. 1995. (Illus.). 24p. (J). (ps up). lib. bdg. 15.93 o.p. (*0-688-13972-8*) HarperCollins Children's Bk. Group.

Once upon a Time. Date not set. (*0-517-80128-0*) Random Hse. Value Publishing.

Oppenheim, Joanne F. Could It Be? 1998. (Bank Street Reader Collection). (Illus.). 48p. (J). (gr. 1-3). lib. bdg. 21.26 (*0-8368-1770-2*) Stevens, Gareth Inc.

—Could It Be? 1990. (Illus.). E-Book (*1-58824-117-3*); E-Book (*1-59019-340-7*) ipicturebooks, LLC.

Orgel, Doris. Mulberry Music. 1971. (Illus.). (J). (gr. 4-7). lib. bdg. 7.89 o.p. (*0-06-024612-X*) HarperCollins Pubs.

Relationships

Ormerod, Jan. Sunshine. 1984. (Picture Puffin Ser.). (Illus.). 32p. (J). (ps). pap. 3.50 o.p. (*0-14-050362-5*, Puffin Bks.) Penguin Putnam Bks. for Young Readers.

—Who's Whose. 1998. (Illus.). 40p. (J). (gr. k-3). 16.00 (*0-688-14678-3*) HarperCollins Children's Bk. Group.

—Who's Whose? 1998. (Illus.). 32p. (J). (gr. k-3). 15.89 (*0-688-14679-1*) HarperCollins Children's Bk. Group.

Osborne, Mary Pope. Happy Birthday, America. 2003. (Illus.). 32p. (ps-3). (J). 15.95 (*0-7613-1675-2*); lib. bdg. 22.90 (*0-7613-2761-4*) Millbrook Pr., Inc. (Roaring Brook Pr.).

Osofsky, Audrey. Dreamcatcher. 1992. (Illus.). 32p. (J). (ps-3). pap. 14.95 (*0-531-05988-X*); lib. bdg. 16.99 (*0-531-08588-0*) Scholastic, Inc. (Orchard Bks.).

Oughton, Jerrie. The War in Georgia. 1997. 192p. (J). (gr. 7-10). tchr. ed. 14.95 o.p. (*0-395-81568-1*) Houghton Mifflin Co.

—The War in Georgia. 1999. 192p. (YA). (gr. 7 up). mass mkt. 4.50 o.s.i (*0-440-22752-6*, Dell Books for Young Readers) Random Hse. Children's Bks.

—The War in Georgia. 1999. 10.55 (*0-606-16444-8*) Turtleback Bks.

Owens, Vivian W. The Rosebush Witch. 1996. (Illus.). 96p. (J). (gr. 3-9). pap. 8.95 (*0-9623839-4-5*) Eschar Pubns.

Palangi, Paula. Last Straw. 1992. 32p. (J). (ps-3). pap. 9.99 (*0-7814-0562-9*) Cook Communications Ministries.

Palatini, Margie. The Wonder Worm Wars. 1997. (Illus.). 176p. (J). (gr. 3-7). 14.95 (*0-7868-0321-5*); lib. bdg. 15.49 (*0-7868-2295-3*) Hyperion Bks. for Children.

—The Wonder Worm Wars. 1999. 196p. (J). (gr. 3-7). pap. 4.99 (*0-7868-1352-0*) Hyperion Pr.

Paley, Nina, illus. What about Me? 1993. (Contemporary Health Ser.). (J). 3.00 (*1-56071-314-3*) ETR Assocs.

Palmer, Kate S. A Gracious Plenty. 1991. (Illus.). 40p. (J). pap. 13.95 o.p. (*0-671-73566-7*, Simon & Schuster Children's Publishing) Simon & Schuster Children's Publishing.

—A Gracious Plenty. 1998. (Illus.). 32p. (J). (gr. 1-4). reprint ed. pap. 7.95 (*0-9667114-0-8*) Warbranch Pr., Inc.

Pals. Early in Morning Big Book. 1995. 16p. (J). pap. 25.65 (*0-201-85303-5*) Longman Publishing Group.

Panagopoulos, Janie Lynn. A Place Called Home: Michigan's Mill Creek Story. 2001. (Illus.). 48p. (J). 18.95 (*1-58536-054-6*) Sleeping Bear Pr.

Papagapitos, Karen. Jose's Basket. Kleinman, Estelle, ed. 2nd ed. 1993. (JB Ser.). (Illus.). 32p. (J). (gr. 1-3). 6.95 (*0-9637328-1-1*) Kapa Hse. Pr.

—Socorro, Daughter of the Desert. Kleinman, Estelle, ed. 1993. (JB Ser.). (Illus.). 64p. (J). (gr. 3-6). 6.95 (*0-9637328-0-3*) Kapa Hse. Pr.

Parenteau, Shirley. Blue Hands, Blue Cloth. 2nd ed. 1998. (Illus.). (J). (gr. 3-5). E-Book 4.50 incl. disk (*1-58200-042-5*) Hard Shell Word Factory.

Park, Barbara. My Mother Got Married: And Other Disasters. 1989. 128p. (J). (gr. 3-7). 13.99 o.s.i (*0-394-92149-6*); 1990. 144p. (gr. 4-7). reprint ed. pap. 4.99 (*0-394-85059-9*) Random Hse. Children's Bks. (Knopf Bks. for Young Readers).

Park, Linda Sue. When My Name Was Keoko. 2002. 208p. (YA). (gr. 5-9). 16.00 (*0-618-13335-6*, Clarion Bks.) Houghton Mifflin Co. Trade & Reference Div.

—When My Name Was Keoko. 2004. (Illus.). 208p. (gr. 5). pap. 5.50 (*0-440-41944-1*, Yearling) Random Hse. Children's Bks.

Partridge, Elizabeth & Weston, Martha. Annie & Bo & the Big Surprise. 2002. (Easy-to-Read Ser.). (Illus.). 48p. (J). pap. 3.99 (*0-14-230071-3*, Puffin Bks.) Penguin Putnam Bks. for Young Readers.

Pascal, Francine. Hangin' Out with Cici. 1977. (J). (gr. 5-9). 12.95 o.p. (*0-670-36045-7*, Viking Children's Bks.) Penguin Putnam Bks. for Young Readers.

—Twins, 2 vols. 1992. (J). 3.50 o.s.i (*0-553-62855-0*, Dell Books for Young Readers) Random Hse. Children's Bks.

Pascal, Francine, creator. Cousin Kelly's Family Secret. 1991. (Sweet Valley Kids Ser.: No. 24). 80p. (J). (gr. 1-3). pap. 3.50 o.s.i (*0-553-15920-8*) Bantam Bks.

—The Evil Twin. 1993. (Sweet Valley High Ser.: No. 100). (YA). (gr. 7 up). mass mkt. o.s.i (*0-553-54130-7*, Dell Books for Young Readers) Random Hse. Children's Bks.

—Jessica the Baby-Sitter. 1990. (Sweet Valley Kids Ser.: No. 14). (J). (gr. 1-3). pap. o.s.i (*0-553-16990-4*, Dell Books for Young Readers) Random Hse. Children's Bks.

—The Parent Plot. 1990. (Sweet Valley High Ser.: No. 67). 144p. (YA). (gr. 7 up). mass mkt. 3.50 o.s.i (*0-553-28611-0*) Bantam Bks.

—Take Me On. 1999. (Sweet Valley High Senior Year Ser.: No. 11). 192p. (gr. 7 up). mass mkt. 4.50 o.s.i (*0-553-49283-7*) Bantam Bks.

—The Wakefields of Sweet Valley. 1991. (Sweet Valley Saga Ser.). (YA). (gr. 7 up). mass mkt. o.s.i (*0-553-54018-1*, Dell Books for Young Readers) Random Hse. Children's Bks.

Paterson, Katherine. Preacher's Boy. 2001. 192p. (J). (gr. 5 up). pap. 4.95 (*0-06-447233-7*, Harper Trophy) HarperCollins Children's Bk. Group.

—Preacher's Boy. 1999. (Illus.). 160p. (J). (gr. 5-9). tchr. ed. 15.00 (*0-395-83897-5*, Clarion Bks.) Houghton Mifflin Co. Trade & Reference Div.

—Preacher's Boy. l.t. ed. 2000. (Juvenile Ser.). 228p. (J). (gr. 4-7). 21.95 (*0-7862-2717-6*) Thorndike Pr.

—Preacher's Boy. 2001. (J). 11.00 (*0-606-20861-5*) Turtleback Bks.

—The Same Stuff as Stars. 2004. 288p. (J). pap. 5.99 (*0-06-055712-5*, Harper Trophy) HarperCollins Children's Bk. Group.

Paton Walsh, Jill. Goldengrove, RS. (Sunburst Ser.). 130p. 1985. (YA). (gr. 7 up). pap. 3.50 o.p. (*0-374-42587-6*, Sunburst); 1972. (J). (gr. 6 up). 4.50 o.p. (*0-374-32696-7*, Farrar, Straus & Giroux (BYR)) Farrar, Straus & Giroux.

—Goldengrove. l.t. ed. 1973. (J). lib. bdg. 6.50 o.p. (*0-8161-6104-6*, Macmillan Reference USA) Gale Group.

Paulsen, Gary. Father Water, Mother Woods: Essays on Fishing & Hunting in the North Woods. 1995. 21.95 (*0-385-30984-8*) Doubleday Publishing.

Pearce, Philippa. Here Comes Tod! 1994. (Illus.). 96p. (J). (gr. k-3). 14.95 o.p. (*1-56402-328-1*) Candlewick Pr.

Pearce, Q. L. Weekend Territory. 1993. (Clipper Fiction Ser.). 128p. (J). pap. text 9.95 (*0-582-80053-6*) Addison-Wesley Longman, Ltd. GBR. *Dist:* Trans-Atlantic Pubns., Inc.

Pearson, Gayle. The Fog Doggies & Me. 1993. 128p. (J). (gr. 4-8). lib. bdg. 13.95 o.s.i (*0-689-31845-6*, Atheneum) Simon & Schuster Children's Publishing.

—One Potato, Tu: Seven Stories. 1992. 128p. (J). (gr. 5-9). 13.95 o.p. (*0-689-31706-9*, Atheneum) Simon & Schuster Children's Publishing.

Pearson, Kit. Awake & Dreaming. 1999. (J). 11.04 (*0-606-21048-2*) Turtleback Bks.

Peck, Richard. Don't Look & It Won't Hurt, ERS. 1999. 176p. (J). (gr. 7-12). 16.95 (*0-8050-6316-1*, Holt, Henry & Co. Bks. For Young Readers) Holt, Henry & Co.

—Fair Weather. l.t. ed. 2002. (Young Adult Ser.). 161p. (YA). 24.95 (*0-7862-3922-0*) Gale Group.

—Fair Weather. 160p. 2003. (YA). pap. 5.99 (*0-14-250034-8*, Puffin Bks.); 2001. (Illus.). (J). (gr. 4-8). 16.99 (*0-8037-2516-7*, Dial Bks. for Young Readers) Penguin Putnam Bks. for Young Readers.

—Fair Weather. unabr. ed. 2002. (J). (gr. 4-7). audio 25.00 (*0-8072-0951-1*, Listening Library) Random Hse. Audio Publishing Group.

—The Last Safe Place on Earth. 1995. 176p. (J). 15.95 o.s.i (*0-385-32052-3*, Delacorte Pr.) Dell Publishing.

—The Last Safe Place on Earth. 1996. (Laurel-Leaf Bks.). 176p. (YA). (gr. 7 up). mass mkt. 5.50 (*0-440-22007-6*, Laurel Leaf) Random Hse. Children's Bks.

—The Last Safe Place on Earth. 1996. 11.04 (*0-606-09528-4*) Turtleback Bks.

—The River Between Us. 2003. 176p. (J). 16.99 (*0-8037-2735-6*, Dial Bks. for Young Readers) Penguin Putnam Bks. for Young Readers.

Peck, Robert Newton. Extra Innings. 2001. 192p. (J). (gr. 7 up). 16.99 (*0-06-028867-1*) HarperCollins Children's Bk. Group.

—Extra Innings. 2003. 224p. (J). (gr. 7 up). pap. 5.99 (*0-06-447229-9*) HarperCollins Pubs.

—Soup's Uncle. 1990. (J). pap. o.p. (*0-440-80166-4*) Dell Publishing.

Pedersen, Ted & Gilden, Mel. Ghost on the Net. 1996. (Cybersurfers Ser.: Vol. 3). (J). (gr. 4-7). 3.95 o.s.i (*0-8431-3978-1*, Price Stern Sloan) Penguin Putnam Bks. for Young Readers.

Pellowski, Anne. Betsy's Up-and-Down Year, Vol. 5. rev. ed. 1997. (Polish American Girls Ser.). (Illus.). 160p. (J). (gr. 3-5). pap. 9.95 (*0-88489-539-4*) St. Mary's Pr.

Pellowski, Michael J. Double Trouble on Vacation. 1996. (Illus.). 128p. (Orig.). (J). (gr. 3-6). pap. text 3.99 (*0-87406-807-X*) Darby Creek Publishing.

Pennebaker, Ruth. Conditions of Love, ERS. 1999. (Illus.). 256p. (J). (gr. 9-12). 16.95 o.s.i (*0-8050-6104-5*, Holt, Henry & Co. Bks. For Young Readers) Holt, Henry & Co.

—Conditions of Love. 2000. 272p. (YA). (gr. 9-12). mass mkt. 4.99 o.s.i (*0-440-22834-4*, Laurel Leaf) Random Hse. Children's Bks.

Perez, Amada Irma. My Diary from Here to There / Mi Diario de Aqui Hasta Alla. 2002. Tr. of Mi Diario de Aqui Hasta Alla. (ENG & SPA., Illus.). 32p. (J). (gr. 2-5). 16.95 (*0-89239-175-8*) Children's Bk. Pr.

—My Very Own Room (Mi Propio Cuartito) 2000. (ENG & SPA., Illus.). 32p. (J). (gr. 1 up). 15.95 (*0-89239-164-2*) Children's Bk. Pr.

Perez-Mercado, Mary Margaret. Zas! 2000. (Rookie Espanol Ser.). (SPA., Illus.). 24p. (J). (gr. k-2). lib. bdg. 15.00 (*0-516-21692-9*, Children's Pr.) Scholastic Library Publishing.

Perez, N. A. Breaker. 2002. 216p. (YA). pap. 9.95 (*0-8229-5778-7*, Golden Triangle Bks.) Univ. of Pittsburgh Pr.

Perez, Norah A. The Breaker. 1988. 216p. (YA). (gr. 7 up). 16.00 (*0-395-45537-5*) Houghton Mifflin Co.

Perkins, Lynne Rae. All Alone in the Universe. 2001. (Illus.). 160p. (J). (gr. 5 up). reprint ed. pap. 5.99 (*0-380-73302-1*, Harper Trophy) HarperCollins Children's Bk. Group.

Perkins, Mitali. The Sunita Experiment. 1994. (Illus.). 192p. (J). (gr. 5-9). pap. 4.50 o.p. (*1-56282-671-9*) Hyperion Bks. for Children.

—The Sunita Experiment. 1993. 144p. (J). (gr. 1-6). 15.95 o.p. (*0-316-69943-8*, Joy Street Bks.) Little Brown & Co.

Perrin, Randy, et al. Time Like a River. 1999. 144p. (YA). (gr. 5 up). 14.95 (*1-57143-061-X*) RDR Bks.

Perry, Katy. The Laughing Lighthouse. Lyons Graphic Design Staff, ed. 1995. (Illus.). 16p. (Orig.). (J). (gr. 1-4). pap. 7.50 (*0-9626823-6-5*) Perry Publishing.

Peters, Catherine. Special Time Set, 6 bks. Incl. Grandpa's Cookies. 16p. pap. 2.49 o.p. (*0-395-88292-3*); Here We Go Round the Mulberry Bush. 16p. pap. 2.49 o.p. (*0-395-88305-9*); Rosie's Pool. (Illus.). pap. 2.49 o.p. (*0-395-88930-8*); Smile, Baby! 16p. pap. 2.49 o.p. (*0-395-88311-3*); Tooth Race. 16p. pap. 2.49 o.p. (*0-395-88306-7*); Who Ate the Broccoli? pap. 2.49 o.p. (*0-395-88290-7*); (J). (Little Readers Book Bag Ser.). 1997. 15.00 o.p. (*0-395-88296-6*) Houghton Mifflin Co.

Petersen, John. The Littles Go on a Hike. 2002. (Littles First Readers Ser.: No. 9). (Illus.). 32p. (J). mass mkt. 3.99 o.s.i (*0-439-31718-5*, Scholastic Paperbacks) Scholastic, Inc.

Peterson, Jeanne Whitehouse. Don't Forget Winona. 2004. 32p. (J). (ps-2). lib. bdg. 15.89 (*0-06-027198-1*) HarperCollins Children's Bk. Group.

Peterson, John. The Littles. 1970. (Littles Ser.). (Illus.). (J). (gr. 1-5). pap. 1.95 o.p. (*0-590-32006-8*) Scholastic, Inc.

Peterson, P. J. Some Days, Other Days. 1994. (Illus.). 32p. (J). (gr. k-2). mass mkt. 14.95 (*0-684-19595-X*, Atheneum) Simon & Schuster Children's Publishing.

Pevsner, Stella. Is Everyone Moonburned but Me? 2000. (Illus.). 208p. (J). (gr. 5-9). tchr. ed. 15.00 (*0-395-95770-2*, Clarion Bks.) Houghton Mifflin Co. Trade & Reference Div.

—Keep Stompin' till the Music Stops, 001. 1979. 144p. (J). (gr. 4-7). 13.95 o.p. (*0-395-28875-4*, Clarion Bks.) Houghton Mifflin Co. Trade & Reference Div.

—Would My Fortune Cookie Lie? 1996. 192p. (J). (gr. 4-6). 14.95 (*0-395-73082-1*, Clarion Bks.) Houghton Mifflin Co. Trade & Reference Div.

—Would My Fortune Cookie Lie? 1999. 10.04 (*0-606-14369-6*) Turtleback Bks.

Pevsner, Stella & Tang, Fay. Sing for Your Father, Su Phan. 1997. (Illus.). 112p. (J). (gr. 4-6). 14.00 o.s.i (*0-395-82267-X*, Clarion Bks.) Houghton Mifflin Co. Trade & Reference Div.

—Sing for Your Father, Su Phan. 1999. 10.55 (*0-606-16709-9*) Turtleback Bks.

Peyton, K. M. Darkling. 1989. 16.95 o.p. (*0-385-26963-3*) Doubleday Publishing.

Pfeffer, Susan Beth. Amy's Story. 2001. (Portraits of Little Women Ser.). (Illus.). (J). 10.55 (*0-606-21030-X*) Turtleback Bks.

—Amy's Story: Portraits of Little Women. 2001. (Portraits of Little Women Ser.: Vol. 4). 112p. (gr. 3-7). pap. text 4.50 (*0-440-41354-0*, Yearling) Random Hse. Children's Bks.

—A Gift for Jo. 1999. (Portraits of Little Women Ser.: No. 10). (Illus.). 112p. (gr. 3-7). text 9.95 o.s.i (*0-385-32668-8*, Dell Books for Young Readers) Random Hse. Children's Bks.

—Jo's Story. 2001. (Portraits of Little Women Ser.). (Illus.). (J). 10.55 (*0-606-21270-1*) Turtleback Bks.

—Kid Power. 1977. (J). (gr. 4-6). lib. bdg. 12.90 o.p. (*0-531-00123-7*, Watts, Franklin) Scholastic Library Publishing.

—Kid Power Strikes Back. 1984. (Illus.). 128p. (J). (gr. k-8). lib. bdg. 12.90 o.p. (*0-531-04839-X*, Watts, Franklin) Scholastic Library Publishing.

—Twin Troubles, ERS. 1992. (Illus.). (J). 14.95 o.p. (*0-8050-2146-9*, Holt, Henry & Co. Bks. For Young Readers) Holt, Henry & Co.

Pfeffer, Susan Beth & Alcott, Louisa May. Amy Makes a Friend. 1998. (Portraits of Little Women Ser.). (Illus.). 112p. (gr. 3-7). text 9.95 o.s.i (*0-385-32584-3*, Dell Books for Young Readers) Random Hse. Children's Bks.

—Amy's Story. 1997. (Portraits of Little Women Ser.). 112p. (gr. 3-7). text 9.95 o.s.i (*0-385-32529-0*, Delacorte Pr.) Dell Publishing.

—Beth's Story. 1997. (Portraits of Little Women Ser.). 112p. (gr. 3-7). text 9.95 o.s.i (*0-385-32526-6*, Delacorte Pr.) Dell Publishing.

—A Gift for Beth. 1999. (Portraits of Little Women Ser.: No. 11). (Illus.). 112p. (gr. 3-7). text 9.95 o.s.i (*0-385-32667-X*, Dell Books for Young Readers) Random Hse. Children's Bks.

—Jo Makes a Friend. 1998. (Portraits of Little Women Ser.). (Illus.). 112p. (gr. 3-7). text 9.95 (*0-385-32581-9*, Dell Books for Young Readers) Random Hse. Children's Bks.

—Jo's Story. 1997. (Portraits of Little Women Ser.). 112p. (gr. 3-7). text 9.95 o.s.i (*0-385-32523-1*, Dell Books for Young Readers) Random Hse. Children's Bks.

—Meg Makes a Friend. 1998. (Portraits of Little Women Ser.). (Illus.). 112p. (gr. 3-7). text 9.95 (*0-385-32580-0*, Delacorte Pr.) Dell Publishing.

Pfeffer, Susan Beth & Ramsey, Marcy Dunn. Ghostly Tales. Bui, Francoise, ed. 2000. (Portraits of Little Women Ser.). (Illus.). 192p. (gr. 3-7). text 9.95 (*0-385-32741-2*, Delacorte Bks. for Young Readers) Random Hse. Children's Bks.

Phillips, Robert B. Through My Picture Window. 1988. (Illus.). 256p. (YA). (gr. 9-12). 9.95 (*0-9620577-1-1*) Phillips, Robert B. Pub.

Pinkney, Andrea Davis. Mim's Christmas Jam. 2001. (Illus.). 32p. (J). (ps-2). 16.00 (*0-15-201918-9*, Gulliver Bks.) Harcourt Children's Bks.

—Raven in a Dove House. 1998. 224p. (J). (gr. 6). 16.00 o.s.i (*0-15-201461-6*, Gulliver Bks.) Harcourt Children's Bks.

—Raven in a Dove House. 1999. 208p. (J). pap. 6.99 (*0-7868-1349-0*) Hyperion Bks. for Children.

—Raven in a Dove House. 1999. 13.04 (*0-606-17789-2*) Turtleback Bks.

Pittman, Helena Clare. Sunrise. 1998. (Illus.). 32p. (J). (ps-1). 12.00 o.s.i (*0-15-201684-8*, Silver Whistle) Harcourt Children's Bks.

Pitts, Paul. Crossroads. 1994. 160p. (J). (gr. 5). pap. 3.99 o.p. (*0-380-77606-5*, Avon Bks.) Morrow/Avon.

—Crossroads. 1994. 9.09 o.p. (*0-606-06297-1*) Turtleback Bks.

—Racing the Sun. 1988. 160p. (J). (gr. 4-7). pap. 5.99 (*0-380-75496-7*, Harper Trophy) HarperCollins Children's Bk. Group.

—Racing the Sun. 1988. 11.00 (*0-606-03897-3*) Turtleback Bks.

Platt, Kin. Crocker. 1983. (Lippincott Page-Turner Ser.). 128p. (YA). (gr. 7 up). 11.95 (*0-397-32025-6*); lib. bdg. 11.89 (*0-397-32026-4*) HarperCollins Children's Bk. Group.

Plummer, Louise. The Unlikely Romance of Kate Bjorkman. 1995. 176p. (YA). (gr. 7 up). 15.95 o.s.i (*0-385-32049-3*, Dell Books for Young Readers) Random Hse. Children's Bks.

Polacco, Patricia. The Butterfly. 2002. (Illus.). (J). 23.64 (*0-7587-2166-8*) Book Wholesalers, Inc.

—The Butterfly. unabr. ed. 2001. (J). (gr. 1-6). 27.95 incl. audio (*0-8045-6875-8*, 6875) Spoken Arts, Inc.

—When Lightning Comes in a Jar: Come to a Family Reunion. 2002. (Illus.). 40p. (J). 16.99 (*0-399-23164-1*, Philomel) Penguin Putnam Bks. for Young Readers.

Poploff, Michelle. Splash-a-Roo & Snowflakes. 1996. (Illus.). 48p. (J). (ps-3). pap. 3.99 o.s.i (*0-440-41119-X*, Yearling) Random Hse. Children's Bks.

—Tea Party for Two. 1997. (Yearling First Choice Chapter Book Ser.). (Illus.). 48p. (J). (gr. k-3). pap. 3.99 o.s.i (*0-440-41334-6*); (gr. 2-3). 13.95 o.s.i (*0-385-32260-7*) Dell Publishing. (Delacorte Pr.).

Porte, Barbara Ann. I Only Made up the Roses. 1987. 128p. (YA). (gr. 7 up). 15.00 o.p. (*0-688-05216-9*, Greenwillow Bks.) HarperCollins Children's Bk. Group.

—If You Ever Get Lost: The Adventures of Julia & Evan. 2000. (Illus.). 80p. (J). (gr. 2 up). 15.95 (*0-688-16947-3*, Greenwillow Bks.) HarperCollins Children's Bk. Group.

—The Kidnapping of Aunt Elizabeth. 1985. 145p. (J). (gr. 7 up). 11.95 o.p. (*0-688-04302-X*, Greenwillow Bks.) HarperCollins Children's Bk. Group.

—Surprise! Surprise! It's Grandfather's Birthday! 1997. (Illus.). 32p. (J). (gr. k up). lib. bdg. 14.93 o.p. (*0-688-14158-7*); 15.00 (*0-688-14157-9*) HarperCollins Children's Bk. Group. (Greenwillow Bks.).

—Taxicab Tales. 1992. (Illus.). 56p. (J). 13.00 o.p. (*0-688-09908-4*, Greenwillow Bks.) HarperCollins Children's Bk. Group.

—When Aunt Lucy Rode a Mule & Other Stories. 1994. (Illus.). 32p. (J). (gr. k-2). 15.95 o.p. (*0-531-06816-1*); mass mkt. 16.99 o.p. (*0-531-08666-6*) Scholastic, Inc. (Orchard Bks.).

—When Grandma Almost Fell off the Mountain & Other Stories. 1993. (Illus.). 32p. (J). (ps-2). 15.95 o.p. (*0-531-05965-0*); mass mkt. 16.99 o.p. (*0-531-08565-1*) Scholastic, Inc. (Orchard Bks.).

Porter, Connie Rose. Changes for Addy: A Winter Story. Johnson, Roberta, ed. 1994. (American Girls Collection: Bk. 6). (Illus.). 72p. (YA). (gr. 2 up). 12.95 (*1-56247-086-8*); pap. 5.95 (*1-56247-085-X*) Pleasant Co. Pubns. (American Girl).

—Changes for Addy: A Winter Story. 1994. (American Girls Collection: Bk. 6). (Illus.). (YA). (gr. 2 up). 12.10 (*0-606-06272-6*) Turtleback Bks.

Porter, Eleanor H. Pollyanna. 2000. (Historias de Siempre Ser.). (SPA., Illus.). 198p. (YA). (gr. 4-7). 15.95 (*84-204-5730-2*) Alfaguara, Ediciones, S.A.-Grupo Santillana ESP. *Dist:* Santillana USA Publishing Co., Inc.

—Pollyanna. (J). 21.95 (*0-8488-1445-2*) Amereon, Ltd.

—Pollyanna. 1996. (Andre Deutsch Classics). 224p. (J). (gr. 5-8). 11.95 (*0-233-99094-1*) Andre Deutsch GBR. *Dist:* Trafalgar Square, Trans-Atlantic Pubns., Inc.

—Pollyanna. (Young Reader's Christian Library). 1994. (Illus.). 224p. (J). (gr. 3-7). pap. text 1.39 o.p. (*1-55748-660-3*); 1993. 176p. (YA). (gr. 6 up). pap. 2.97 o.p. (*1-55748-296-9*) Barbour Publishing, Inc.

—Pollyanna. (J). E-Book 5.00 (*0-7607-1285-9*) Barnes & Noble, Inc.

—Pollyanna. 2002. 256p. pap. 7.95 (*1-84222-615-0*) Carlton Bks., Ltd. GBR. *Dist:* Trafalgar Square.

—Pollyanna. Marshall, Michael J., ed. abr. ed. 1997. (Core Classics Ser.: Vol. 4). (Illus.). 160p. (J). (gr. 4-6). pap. 5.95 (*1-890517-06-2*); lib. bdg. 10.95 (*1-890517-07-0*) Core Knowledge Foundation.

—Pollyanna. 1990. 224p. (J). (gr. 4-7). pap. text 4.50 o.s.i (*0-440-45985-0*) Dell Publishing.

—Pollyanna. (J). E-Book 2.49 (*1-58627-760-X*) Electric Umbrella Publishing.

—Pollyanna. Date not set. (J). 14.99 (*0-06-028226-6*); 32p. pap. 4.99 (*0-06-443536-9*) HarperCollins Children's Bk. Group.

—Pollyanna. l.t. ed. 2000. (Large Print Heritage Ser.). 310p. (J). (gr. 7-12). lib. bdg. 29.95 (*1-58118-069-1*, 23663) LRS.

—Pollyanna. (YA). E-Book 1.95 (*1-58515-092-4*) MesaView, Inc.

—Pollyanna. (Puffin Classics Ser.). (J). 1996. (Illus.). 288p. (gr. 5-9). pap. 4.99 (*0-14-036682-2*); 1988. 208p. pap. 3.50 o.p. (*0-14-035023-3*) Penguin Putnam Bks. for Young Readers. (Puffin Bks.).

—Pollyanna. Hanft, Joshua, ed. 1995. (Great Illustrated Classics Ser.: Vol. 43). (Illus.). 240p. (J). (gr. 3-6). 9.95 (*0-86611-994-9*) Playmore, Inc., Pubs.

—Pollyanna. 1994. (J). (gr. 2-8). 12.99 o.s.i (*0-517-11987-0*) Random Hse. Value Publishing.

—Pollyanna. 1987. (Apple Classics Ser.). (J). (gr. 4-7). pap. 2.50 o.p. (*0-590-41269-8*, Scholastic Paperbacks); 240p. pap. 2.75 o.p. (*0-590-43405-5*); (Illus.). 240p. mass mkt. 3.50 o.p. (*0-590-44769-6*) Scholastic, Inc.

—Pollyanna. (J). (ps-3). 1989. 6.95 o.p. (*0-88101-089-8*); 1988. 18.95 o.p. (*0-88101-084-7*) Unicorn Publishing Hse., Inc., The.

—Pollyanna Grows Up. Date not set. 216p. (J). 21.95 (*0-8488-1447-9*) Amereon, Ltd.

—Pollyanna Grows Up. 1994. 208p. (J). pap. 2.97 o.p. (*1-55748-297-7*) Barbour Publishing, Inc.

—Pollyanna Grows Up. 1996. (Illus.). 304p. (J). (gr. 4-7). pap. 4.99 (*0-14-036758-6*); 1989. 272p. (YA). (gr. 5 up). pap. 3.50 o.p. (*0-14-035024-1*, Puffin Bks.) Penguin Putnam Bks. for Young Readers.

—Pollyanna Grows up. 1990. 240p. (J). pap. 3.50 o.s.i (*0-440-40354-5*) Dell Publishing.

Porter, Eleanor H. & Falkoff, Marc D. Pollyanna. 1999. (Chapter Book Charmers Ser.). 70p. (J). (gr. 2-5). 2.99 o.p. (*0-694-01289-0*) HarperCollins Children's Bk. Group.

Poupeney, Mollie. Her Father's Daughter. 2002. 272p. (YA). (gr. 9). mass mkt. 5.50 (*0-440-22879-4*, Random Hse. Bks. for Young Readers) Random Hse. Children's Bks.

Prater, John. Once upon a Time. 1995. (J). 11.44 o.p. (*0-606-07969-6*) Turtleback Bks.

Pray, Ralph. Jingu: The Hidden Princess. 2002. (Illus.). 80p. (J). 14.95 (*1-885008-21-X*, 188500821x) Shen's Bks.

Price, Mathew. Are You Awake? 2003. (Tommy Board Bks.). (Illus.). 10p. (J). bds. 4.99 (*0-7696-2942-3*, Gingham Dog Pr.) McGraw-Hill Children's Publishing.

Priddy, Roger. It's My Day. 2002. bds. 8.95 (*0-312-49093-3*, Priddy Bks.) St. Martin's Pr.

The Prince & the Pauper. 1988. mass mkt. 2.25 (*0-938819-24-0*, Aerie) Doherty, Tom Assocs., LLC.

Probasco, Teri. Imprints. 1994. 177p. (J). (gr. 3-8). pap. 10.95 (*0-932970-99-0*) Prinit Pr.

Pryor, Bonnie. The Dream Jar. 1996. (Illus.). (J). (gr. k-3). 32p. 16.00 o.p. (*0-688-13061-5*); lib. bdg. 15.89 (*0-688-13062-3*) Morrow/Avon. (Morrow, William & Co.).

—Horses in the Garage. 1992. 160p. (J). (gr. 4 up). 14.00 o.p. (*0-688-10567-X*, Morrow, William & Co.) Morrow/Avon.

—Jumping Jenny. 1992. (Illus.). 192p. (J). (gr. 2 up). 14.00 o.p. (*0-688-09684-0*, Morrow, William & Co.) Morrow/Avon.

—Louie & Dan Are Friends. 1997. (Illus.). 32p. (J). lib. bdg. 15.93 o.p. (*0-688-08561-X*); 16.00 (*0-688-08560-1*) Morrow/Avon. (Morrow, William & Co.).

—The Plum Tree War. 1989. (Illus.). 128p. (J). (gr. 4-7). 15.99 (*0-688-08142-8*) HarperCollins Children's Bk. Group.

—Poison Ivy & Eyebrow Wigs. 1993. (Illus.). 176p. (J). (gr. 3 up). 15.00 (*0-688-11200-5*, Morrow, William & Co.) Morrow/Avon.

—Poison Ivy & Eyebrow Wigs. 1995. (J). 10.30 o.p. (*0-606-08026-0*) Turtleback Bks.

—Toenails, Tonsils, Tornadoes. 1997. (Illus.). 160p. (J). (gr. 3 up). 15.00 (*0-688-14885-9*, Morrow, William & Co.) Morrow/Avon.

—Vinegar Pancakes & Vanishing Cream. 1987. (Illus.). 128p. (J). (gr. 4-7). 16.00 (*0-688-06728-X*, Morrow, William & Co.) Morrow/Avon.

Pullman, Philip. The Broken Bridge. (gr. 7 up). 1994. (Illus.). 224p. mass mkt. 5.50 (*0-679-84715-4*, Random Hse. Bks. for Young Readers); 1992. 256p. (YA). 15.99 o.s.i (*0-679-91972-4*, Knopf Bks. for Young Readers) Random Hse. Children's Bks.

—The Broken Bridge. 2002. (YA). 20.25 (*0-8446-7229-7*) Smith, Peter Pub., Inc.

—The Broken Bridge. 1994. 11.04 (*0-606-06945-3*) Turtleback Bks.

—The Firework-Maker's Daughter. 2001. (Illus.). 112p. (gr. 3-7). mass mkt. 4.99 (*0-439-22420-9*) Scholastic, Inc.

Pulver, Robin. Alicia's Tutu. (Illus.). (J). 2004. pap. 5.99 (*0-14-056525-6*, Puffin Bks.); 1997. 32p. 14.89 o.s.i (*0-8037-1933-7*, Dial Bks. for Young Readers); 1997. 32p. 14.99 o.s.i (*0-8037-1932-9*, Dial Bks. for Young Readers) Penguin Putnam Bks. for Young Readers.

Qualey, Marsha. Revolutions of the Heart. 1993. 192p. (YA). (gr. 7 up). 16.00 (*0-395-64168-3*) Houghton Mifflin Co.

Quarles, Heather. A Door Near Here. 1998. 240p. (YA). (gr. 7-10). 13.95 o.s.i (*0-385-32595-9*) Doubleday Publishing.

—A Door Near Here. 2000. (Illus.). 240p. (YA). (gr. 7 up). mass mkt. 4.99 (*0-440-22761-5*, Laurel Leaf) Random Hse. Children's Bks.

—A Door Near Here. l.t. ed. 2000. (Young Adult Ser.). 323p. (J). (gr. 8-12). 21.95 (*0-7862-2884-9*) Thorndike Pr.

—A Door Near Here. 2000. 10.55 (*0-606-17796-5*) Turtleback Bks.

Quindlen, Anna. The Tree That Came to Stay. 1997. (Illus.). 32p. (J). 14.99 o.p. (*0-670-87704-2*) Penguin Putnam Bks. for Young Readers.

—The Tree That Came to Stay. 1992. (Illus.). 32p. (J). (ps-4). 13.99 o.s.i (*0-517-58146-9*); 14.00 o.s.i (*0-517-58145-0*) Random Hse. Children's Bks. (Random Hse. Bks. for Young Readers).

Rabe, Bernice. Rass. 1973. 192p. (J). (gr. 5-9). 6.95 o.p. (*0-8407-6284-4*, Dutton Children's Bks.) Penguin Putnam Bks. for Young Readers.

Radlauer, Ruth S. Breakfast by Molly. 1987. (Illus.). (J). (ps-2). 8.95 o.s.i (*0-13-081506-3*, Simon & Schuster Children's Publishing) Simon & Schuster Children's Publishing.

Rand, Ted, illus. Sailing Home: A Story of a Childhood at Sea. 2001. (Cheshire Studio Bk.). 32p. (J). (gr. k-3). 15.95 (*0-7358-1539-9*); (gr. 2-5). lib. bdg. 16.50 (*0-7358-1540-2*) North-South Bks., Inc.

Randall, Florence E. The Almost Year. 1975. (J). pap. 1.50 o.p. (*0-590-05209-8*) Scholastic, Inc.

Random House Beginners Books Staff. All about Cassie. 2002. 48p. (J). pap. 2.99 (*0-375-81483-3*, Random Hse. Bks. for Young Readers) Random Hse. Children's Bks.

—Everybodee Loves. 2002. 80p. (J). pap. 2.99 (*0-375-81456-6*, Random Hse. Bks. for Young Readers) Random Hse. Children's Bks.

Random House Books for Young Readers Staff. Fix It Day. 2003. (Illus.). 12p. (J). bds. 4.99 (*0-375-82219-4*, Random Hse. Bks. for Young Readers) Random Hse. Children's Bks.

Random House Staff. Big Enough for a Bed. 2002. (Illus.). 12p. (J). bds. 4.99 (*0-375-82270-4*, Random Hse. Bks. for Young Readers) Random Hse. Children's Bks.

Ransom, Candice F. We're Growing Together. 1993. (Illus.). 32p. (J). (ps-2). lib. bdg. 14.95 (*0-02-775666-1*, Simon & Schuster Children's Publishing) Simon & Schuster Children's Publishing.

Ra'Oof, Mae O. & Ra'Oof, Jum. The Friends of Rainbow Forest Series, 5 bks. unabr. ed. 1995. (Illus.). 246p. (J). (ps-2). pap. 39.99 (*1-888527-05-6*) A + Children's Bks. and Music.

Raphael, Taffy E. Missing May. (Book Club Novel Guide Ser.). 48p. 2002. 17.95 (*1-931376-08-5*); 2001. E-Book 9.95 (*0-965621l-3-8*) Small Planet Communications, Inc.

Raskin, Ellen. Figgs & Phantoms. (Illus.). (J). (gr. 4 up). 1977. 160p. 1.95 o.p. (*0-525-45035-1*); 1974. 16p. 15.95 o.s.i (*0-525-29680-8*, 01063-320) Penguin Putnam Bks. for Young Readers. (Dutton Children's Bks.).

Rattigan, Jama K. Dumpling Soup. 1993. (Illus.). 32p. (J). (gr. 4-8). 16.95 o.p. (*0-316-73445-4*) Little Brown & Co.

Rawlings, Marjorie Kinnan. The Yearling. 50th annot. ed. 1988. (Scribner Classics Ser.). (Illus.). 416p. (YA). (gr. 7-12). mass mkt. 5.95 (*0-02-044931-3*, Simon Pulse) Simon & Schuster Children's Publishing.

—The Yearling. 1988. (YA). 12.00 (*0-606-00109-3*) Turtleback Bks.

Rayner, Mary. Garth Pig Steals the Show. 1993. (Illus.). 32p. (J). (ps-3). 13.99 o.p. (*0-525-45023-8*, Dutton Children's Bks.) Penguin Putnam Bks. for Young Readers.

Reaney, James. Take the Big Picture. 1986. 176p. pap. (*0-88984-087-3*) Porcupine's Quill, Inc.

Recorvits, Helen. Goodbye, Walter Malinski, RS. 1999. (Illus.). 96p. (J). (gr. 4-7). 15.00 o.p. (*0-374-32747-5*, Farrar, Straus & Giroux (BYR)) Farrar, Straus & Giroux.

Reeder, Carolyn. Foster's War. 2000. 272p. (J). (gr. 4-7). pap. 4.50 (*0-590-09856-X*); 1998. 224p. (YA). (gr. 5-9). pap. 16.95 o.p. (*0-590-09846-2*) Scholastic, Inc.

—Moonshiner's Son. 1995. 208p. (J). (gr. 4-7). pap. 4.99 (*0-380-72251-8*, Avon Bks.) Morrow/Avon.

—Moonshiner's Son. 1993. 208p. (J). (gr. 3-7). lib. bdg. 14.95 (*0-02-775805-2*, Simon & Schuster Children's Publishing) Simon & Schuster Children's Publishing.

—Moonshiner's Son. 1995. (J). 10.55 (*0-606-07887-8*) Turtleback Bks.

Reiser, Lynn W. Tortillas & Lullabies, Tortillas y Cancioncitas. 1998. (ENG & SPA., Illus.). 48p. (J). (ps-3). lib. bdg. 17.89 (*0-688-14629-5*) HarperCollins Children's Bk. Group.

—Tortillas & Lullabies, Tortillas y Cancioncitas. 1998. (ENG & SPA., Illus.). 48p. (J). (ps-3). 16.99 (*0-688-14628-7*, Rayo) HarperTrade.

Reiss, Johanna. The Journey Back. 1976. 128p. (YA). (gr. 5 up). 12.95 o.p. (*0-690-01252-7*) HarperCollins Children's Bk. Group.

—The Upstairs Room. 2002. (Illus.). (J). 14.47 (*0-7587-0326-0*) Book Wholesalers, Inc.

—The Upstairs Room. 1999. (J). 9.95 (*1-56137-657-4*) Novel Units, Inc.

Reiss, Kathryn. The Glass House People. 1992. 288p. (YA). (gr. 7 up). 16.95 (*0-15-231040-1*) Harcourt Children's Bks.

—Riddle of the Prairie Bride. 2001. (American Girl Collection: Bk. 12). (Illus.). 176p. (J). (gr. 3-6). pap. 5.95 (*1-58485-308-5*); 9.95 o.p. (*1-58485-309-3*) Pleasant Co. Pubns. (American Girl).

—Riddle of the Prairie Bride. 2001. (American Girl Collection). (Illus.). (J). 12.00 (*0-606-21400-3*) Turtleback Bks.

Renken, Aleda. Never the Same Again. 1971. (J). (gr. 6-9). 4.50 o.p. (*0-664-32487-8*) Westminster John Knox Pr.

Rennison, Louise. Dancing in My Nuddy-Pants: Even Further Confessions of Georgia Nicolson. (J). 2004. (Illus.). 240p. pap. 6.99 (*0-06-009748-5*); 2003. 224p. 15.99 (*0-06-009746-9*); 2003. 224p. lib. bdg. 16.89 (*0-06-009747-7*) HarperCollins Children's Bk. Group. (HarperTempest).

—On the Bright Side, I'm Now the Girlfriend of a Sex God: Further Confessions of Georgia Nicolson. 2001. 256p. (J). (gr. 7 up). 15.99 (*0-06-028813-2*) HarperCollins Children's Bk. Group.

—On the Bright Side, I'm Now the Girlfriend of a Sex God: Further Confessions of Georgia Nicolson. 2002. 272p. (J). pap. 6.99 (*0-06-447226-4*) HarperCollins Pubs.

—On the Bright Side, I'm Now the Girlfriend of a Sex God: Further Confessions of Georgia Nicolson. 2003. 256p. (J). mass mkt. 6.99 (*0-06-052185-6*, Avon Bks.) Morrow/Avon.

Repp, Gloria. The Stolen Years. 1989. 152p. (YA). (gr. 7 up). pap. 6.49 (*0-89084-481-X*, 044412) Jones, Bob Univ. Pr.

Retana, Maria L. Nacer en la Manada. Retana, Guillermo, tr. 1997. (SPA., Illus.). 32p. (Orig.). (J). (gr. k-3). pap. 6.95 (*0-9652920-4-5*) High Desert Productions.

RH Disney Staff. One Wacky Family. 2004. (Illus.). (J). pap. 3.99 (*0-7364-2211-0*, RH/Disney) Random Hse. Children's Bks.

Rice, Alice H. Mrs. Wiggs of the Cabbage Patch. 1984. 96p. (J). pap. 3.95 o.s.i (*0-671-52476-3*, Pocket) Simon & Schuster.

Rice, David L. Because Brian Hugged His Mother. 1999. (Sharing Nature with Children Book Ser.). (Illus.). 32p. (ps-3). (J). 16.95 (*1-883220-90-4*); (YA). pap. 7.95 (*1-883220-89-0*) Dawn Pubns.

Richardson, I. M. Charles Dickens' A Christmas Carol. 1988. (J). 10.10 (*0-606-03559-1*) Turtleback Bks.

Richardson, Sandy. The Girl Who Ate Chicken Feet & Other Stories. (J). 1999. pap. 14.89 (*0-8037-2255-9*); 1998. 144p. (gr. 5-9). 16.99 o.s.i (*0-8037-2254-0*) Penguin Putnam Bks. for Young Readers. (Dial Bks. for Young Readers).

Riecken, Nancy. Andrew's Own Place. 1993. (Illus.). (J). 14.95 o.p. (*0-395-64723-1*) Houghton Mifflin Co.

Rigby, Shirley L. Smaller Than Most. 1985. (Illus.). 32p. (J). (gr. k-3). 11.50 (*0-06-025027-5*); lib. bdg. 11.89 o.p. (*0-06-025028-3*) HarperCollins Children's Bk. Group.

Riggio, Anita. Smack Dab in the Middle. 2002. (Illus.). 32p. (J). (gr. k-3). 15.99 (*0-399-23700-3*) Penguin Group (USA) Inc.

Riley, Jocelyn. Only My Mouth Is Smiling. 1982. 224p. (J). (gr. 7-9). 12.95 o.p. (*0-688-01087-3*, Morrow, William & Co.) Morrow/Avon.

Rinaldi, Ann. Broken Days. (Quilt Trilogy Ser.: Vol. 2). 288p. 1997. (J). mass mkt. 5.99 o.s.i (*0-590-46054-4*, Scholastic Paperbacks); 1995. (YA). (gr. 7 up). pap. 14.95 (*0-590-46053-6*) Scholastic, Inc.

—Broken Days. 1997. (Quilt Trilogy Ser.). 11.04 (*0-606-11167-0*) Turtleback Bks.

—The Coffin Quilt: The Feud Between the Hatfields & the McCoys. 2001. (J). 12.05 (*0-606-20507-1*) Turtleback Bks.

—The Last Silk Dress. 1990. 352p. (YA). mass mkt. 4.99 o.s.i (*0-553-28315-4*) Bantam Bks.

—The Last Silk Dress. 1988. 368p. (YA). (gr. 5 up). 15.95 o.p. (*0-8234-0690-3*) Holiday Hse., Inc.

—The Last Silk Dress. 1988. (J). 11.55 (*0-606-04464-7*) Turtleback Bks.

—Millicent's Gift. 224p. (J). 2004. pap. 5.99 (*0-06-441009-9*, Harper Trophy); 2002. lib. bdg. 15.89 (*0-06-029637-2*); 2002. (Illus.). 15.95 (*0-06-029636-4*) HarperCollins Children's Bk. Group.

—Or Give Me Death: A Novel of Patrick Henry's Family. 2003. (Great Episodes Ser.). 240p. (J). 17.00 (*0-15-216687-4*) Harcourt Children's Bks.

—A Stitch in Time. (Quilt Trilogy Ser.: Vol. 1). 320p. (J). (gr. 7 up). 1995. mass mkt. 5.99 (*0-590-46056-0*); 1994. pap. 13.95 (*0-590-46055-2*) Scholastic, Inc.

—A Stitch in Time. 1994. (Quilt Trilogy Ser.). (J). 11.04 (*0-606-08206-9*) Turtleback Bks.

Ringgold, Faith. Dinner at Aunt Connie's House. 1996. (Illus.). 32p. (J). (ps-3). pap. 4.95 (*0-7868-1150-1*) Disney Pr.

—Dinner at Aunt Connie's House. 1993. (Illus.). 32p. (J). (gr. k-4). 16.95 (*1-56282-425-2*); lib. bdg. 15.49 (*1-56282-426-0*) Hyperion Bks. for Children.

—Dinner at Aunt Connie's House. 1996. (J). 11.10 (*0-606-10782-7*) Turtleback Bks.

Ripa, Kelly. Thanks Mom! 2004. pap. 13.00 (*0-7868-8852-0*) Hyperion Pr.

Risk, Mary. Qu'est-ce Qu'on Mange ce Soir? 1998. (ENG & FRE., Illus.). 28p. (J). (ps-3). pap. 6.95 o.p. (*0-7641-5126-6*) Barron's Educational Series, Inc.

Risk, Mary & Morton, Lone. Que Hay de Almuerzo? 1998. (Language Learning Story Bks.). (ENG & SPA., Illus.). 28p. (YA). (ps up). 7.95 (*0-7641-5127-4*, BA274) Barron's Educational Series, Inc.

Risk, Mary, et al. Hurry up, Molly. 2000. (I Can Read Bks.). (ENG & FRE., Illus.). 28p. (J). (ps-2). 6.95 (*0-7641-5287-4*) Barron's Educational Series, Inc.

Rispin, Karen. Tianna, the Terrible. 1992. (Anika Scott Ser.: No. 2). (J). (gr. 3-7). 4.99 o.p. (*0-8423-2031-8*) Tyndale Hse. Pubs.

Ritter, John H. Choosing up Sides. 2001. (J). 11.04 (*0-606-20603-5*) Turtleback Bks.

—Over the Wall. 2002. 320p. pap. 6.99 (*0-698-11931-2*, Puffin Bks.) Penguin Putnam Bks. for Young Readers.

Rivers, Karen. Surviving Sam. 2002. (Illus.). 176p. (YA). (gr. 9 up). pap. 6.95 (*1-55192-506-0*, Polestar Book Pubs.) Raincoast Bk. Distribution CAN. *Dist:* Advanced Global Distribution Services, Publishers Group West.

Rivers, Nancy F. A New Life for Toby. 1997. 80p. (Orig.). (J). (ps-3). pap. 9.95 (*1-57736-052-4*, Hillsboro Pr.) Providence Hse. Pubs.

Rix, Jamie. Dead Dad Dog. 2003. (Illus.). 169p. (J). (gr. 3). pap. (*0-440-86477-1*, Corgi) Bantam Bks.

Roberts, Ken. Past Tense. 2002. (Illus.). 112p. (J). (gr. 3-5). pap. 6.95 (*0-88899-214-9*) Groundwood Bks. CAN. *Dist:* Publishers Group West.

Roberts, Laura Peyton. More Than This. 1999. (Clearwater Crossing Ser.: No. 11). 224p. (gr. 7-8). mass mkt. 3.99 o.s.i (*0-553-49296-9*) Bantam Bks.

—Reality Check. 1998. (Clearwater Crossing Ser.: No. 2). (YA). (gr. 5-8). 10.04 (*0-606-13283-X*) Turtleback Bks.

Roberts, Willo Davis. Megan's Island. (Kids' Picks Ser.). 192p. (J). 2000. (gr. 4-6). pap. 2.99 (*0-689-83867-0*, Aladdin); 1990. (gr. 4-7). pap. 4.99 (*0-689-71387-8*, Aladdin); 1988. (gr. 3-7). lib. bdg. 14.95 (*0-689-31397-7*, Atheneum) Simon & Schuster Children's Publishing.

Robinet, Harriette Gillem. Walking to the Bus Rider Blues. 2002. (Illus.). 160p. (J). pap. 4.99 (*0-689-83886-7*, Aladdin) Simon & Schuster Children's Publishing.

Robinson, Barbara. My Brother Louis Measures Worms: And Other Louis Stories. (Charlotte Zolotow Bk.). 160p. (J). (gr. 3 up). 1991. pap. 4.95 (*0-06-440362-9*, Harper Trophy); 1988. 13.00 o.p. (*0-06-025082-8*); 1988. lib. bdg. 15.89 (*0-06-025083-6*) HarperCollins Children's Bk. Group.

Robinson, Nancy K. Angela & the Broken Heart. 144p. (J). 1992. pap. 2.95 o.p. (*0-590-43211-7*, Scholastic Paperbacks); 1991. (gr. 4-6). 12.95 (*0-590-43212-5*) Scholastic, Inc.
—Angela, Private Citizen. 1989. 146p. (J). (gr. 3-6). pap. 10.95 o.p. (*0-590-41726-6*) Scholastic, Inc.
—Just Plain Cat. 1984. 128p. (Orig.). (J). (gr. 3-6). lib. bdg. 13.95 (*0-02-777350-7*, Simon & Schuster Children's Publishing) Simon & Schuster Children's Publishing.
—Oh Honestly, Angela! 1985. 128p. (J). (gr. 3-6). 9.95 o.p. (*0-590-32983-9*) Scholastic, Inc.
—Veronica Knows Best. 1989. 160p. (J). (gr. 3-7). pap. 2.75 o.p. (*0-590-40510-1*, Scholastic Paperbacks) Scholastic, Inc.
Roche, P. K. Goodbye, Arnold. 1979. (Illus.). (J). (ps-2). 8.50 o.p. (*0-8037-3031-4*); 8.23 o.p. (*0-8037-3032-2*) Penguin Putnam Bks. for Young Readers. (Dial Bks. for Young Readers).
Rock, Gail. A Dream for Addie. 1975. (Illus.). 96p. (J). (gr. 4 up). lib. bdg. 5.99 o.p. (*0-394-93076-2*, Knopf Bks. for Young Readers) Random Hse. Children's Bks.
Rocklin, Joanne. Strudel Stories. 1999. 144p. (gr. 3-7). text 14.95 (*0-385-32602-5*, Delacorte Pr.) Dell Publishing.
—Strudel Stories. 2000. (Illus.). 144p. (gr. 3-7). pap. text 4.50 o.s.i (*0-440-41509-8*, Yearling) Random Hse. Children's Bks.
—Strudel Stories. l.t. ed. 2000. (Illus.). 102p. (J). (gr. 4-7). 21.95 (*0-7862-2770-2*) Thorndike Pr.
Roddy, Lee. Eye of the Hurricane. 1994. (Ladd Family Adventure Ser.: Vol. 9). 170p. (J). (gr. 3-7). pap. 5.99 o.p. (*1-56179-220-9*) Focus on the Family Publishing.
—Stranded on Terror Island, No. 14. 1996. (Ladd Family Adventure Ser.). (J). (gr. 3-7). pap. 6.00 o.p. (*1-56179-482-1*) Focus on the Family Publishing.
Rodowsky, Colby. Not Quite a Stranger, RS. 2003. 192p. (gr. 5 up). 16.00 (*0-374-35548-7*, Farrar, Straus & Giroux (BYR)) Farrar, Straus & Giroux.
—Remembering Mog, RS. 1996. 144p. (YA). (gr. 7 up). 14.00 o.p. (*0-374-34663-1*, Farrar, Straus & Giroux (BYR)) Farrar, Straus & Giroux.
Rogers, Kenny & Davenport, Donald. Christmas in Canaan. 2002. 336p. (J). (gr. 6-9). 15.99 (*0-06-000746-X*) HarperCollins Children's Bk. Group.
Rogers, Paul & Rogers, Emma. Our House. 1993. (Illus.). 40p. (J). (ps up). 14.95 o.p. (*1-56402-134-3*) Candlewick Pr.
Rojany, Lisa. Leave It to Beaver. novel ed. 1997. 144p. (J). (gr. 3 up). 4.95 o.s.i (*0-8431-7858-2*, Price Stern Sloan) Penguin Putnam Bks. for Young Readers.
Romanelli, Serena. Little Bobo. 1999. (Illus.). 32p. (J). (gr. k-3). pap. 6.95 (*0-7358-1097-4*) North-South Bks., Inc.
—Little Bobo. 1999. 13.10 (*0-606-16194-5*) Turtleback Bks.
Roop, Peter & Roop, Connie. An Eye for an Eye: A Story of the American Revolution. 2001. (Jamestown Classics Ser.). (Illus.). 168p. (YA). (gr. 5-8). 12.64 (*0-8092-0587-4*) Jamestown.
Root, Phyllis. Bump, Thump, Splat. 2000. (Brand New Readers Ser.). (Illus.). (J). 4.99 o.p. (*0-7636-1024-0*) Candlewick Pr.
—Hidden Places. 1983. (Adventure Diaries). (Illus.). 32p. (J). (gr. 3-6). lib. bdg. 14.65 o.p. (*0-940742-30-6*) Raintree Pubs.
—My Cousin Charlie. 1985. (Family Bks.). (Illus.). 32p. (J). (gr. 3-6). lib. bdg. 14.65 o.p. (*0-940742-40-3*) Raintree Pubs.
Rosa-Casanova, Sylvia. Mama Provi & the Pot of Rice. ed. 2001. (J). (gr. 1). spiral bd. (*0-616-07257-0*) Canadian National Institute for the Blind/Institut National Canadien pour les Aveugles.
—Mama Provi & the Pot of Rice. 2001. (Illus.). (J). 12.14 (*0-606-20782-1*) Turtleback Bks.
Rosado, Maria. Armando's Great Big Surprise No. 5. 1996. (Gullah Gullah Island Ser.). (Illus.). 24p. (ps-3). mass mkt. 3.25 (*0-689-80825-9*, Simon Spotlight/Nickelodeon) Simon & Schuster Children's Publishing.
Rosenberg, Liz. The Silence in the Mountains. (Illus.). 32p. (J). (gr. k-4). 1999. lib. bdg. 16.99 (*0-531-33084-2*); 1998. pap. 15.95 (*0-531-30084-6*) Scholastic, Inc. (Orchard Bks.).
Rosenberry, Vera. Vera Runs Away, ERS. 2000. (Illus.). 32p. (J). (ps-2). 16.00 (*0-8050-6267-X*, Holt, Henry & Co. Bks. For Young Readers) Holt, Henry & Co.
Rosie's Pool. 1997. (Illus.). (J). (ps-2). pap. 2.49 o.p. (*0-395-88930-8*) Houghton Mifflin Co.
Ross, Tony. Happy Rag. 2002. (Illus.). 28p. (Orig.). pap. 8.95 (*1-84270-053-7*) Trafalgar Square.
Rosselson, Leon. Rosa & Her Singing Grandfather. 1996. (Illus.). 96p. (J). (gr. k-3). 12.95 o.s.i (*0-399-22733-4*, Philomel) Penguin Putnam Bks. for Young Readers.
Roth, David. Best of Friends, 001. 1983. 208p. (J). (gr. 7 up). 10.95 o.p. (*0-395-33889-1*) Houghton Mifflin Co.
Roth, Susan L. & Phang, Ruth. Patchwork Tales. 1984. (Illus.). 32p. (J). (gr. k-3). 10.95 o.s.i (*0-689-31053-6*, Atheneum) Simon & Schuster Children's Publishing.
Rowe, Gordon J. The Magic Spectacles. 1998. (Illus.). 32p. (J). pap. 8.95 o.p. (*1-56167-444-3*) American Literary Pr., Inc.
Rowlands, Avril. Animals to the Rescue & Other Stories. 2002. (Illus.). 128p. pap. 7.50 (*0-7459-4764-6*) Lion Publishing PLC GBR. *Dist:* Trafalgar Square.
Roy, Ron. The Empty Envelope. 1998. (Stepping Stone Book Ser.: No. 5). (Illus.). 96p. (gr. 2-5). lib. bdg. 11.99 (*0-679-99054-2*, Random Hse. Bks. for Young Readers) Random Hse. Children's Bks.
Rubinstein, Gillian. Foxspell. 1996. 224p. (YA). (gr. 7 up). 16.00 (*0-689-80602-7*, Simon & Schuster Children's Publishing) Simon & Schuster Children's Publishing.
Ruckman, Ivy. In Care of Cassie Tucker. 1998. 176p. (gr. 5-8). text 14.95 o.s.i (*0-385-32514-2*, Dell Books for Young Readers) Random Hse. Children's Bks.
Rue, Nancy. The Pursuit. 2000. (Christian Heritage Ser.). 192p. (J). (gr. 3-7). pap. 5.99 (*1-56179-856-8*) Bethany Hse. Pubs.
—The Trap. 1998. (Christian Heritage Ser.). 208p. (J). (gr. 3-7). pap. 5.99 (*1-56179-567-4*) Focus on the Family Publishing.
Ruelle, Karen Gray. Spookier Than a Ghost. 2001. (Illus.). 32p. (J). (ps-3). tchr. ed. 15.95 (*0-8234-1667-4*) Holiday Hse., Inc.
Russ, Lavinia. Over the Hills & Far Away. 1968. (J). (gr. 5 up). 5.50 o.p. (*0-15-258946-5*) Harcourt Children's Bks.
Russell, Anne. Discoveries in God's Family. 1991. (50-Day Spiritual Adventure Ser.). (Illus.). 64p. (Orig.). (J). (gr. 3-6). pap. text, stu. ed. 4.95 (*1-879050-05-6*) Chapel of the Air.
Russo, Marisabina. House of Sports. 2002. 192p. (J). (gr. 3 up). 15.95 (*0-06-623803-X*); lib. bdg. 16.89 (*0-06-623804-8*) HarperCollins Children's Bk. Group. (Greenwillow Bks.).
Rylant, Cynthia. A Blue-Eyed Daisy. 1986. 112p. (J). (gr. 3-7). pap. 3.50 o.s.i (*0-440-40927-6*, Yearling) Random Hse. Children's Bks.
—A Blue-Eyed Daisy. 112p. (J). (gr. 4-7). 2001. pap. 4.99 (*0-689-84495-6*, Aladdin); 2000. 15.00 (*0-689-84217-1*, Atheneum/Richard Jackson Bks.); 1985. lib. bdg. 15.00 (*0-02-777960-2*, Atheneum/Richard Jackson Bks.) Simon & Schuster Children's Publishing.
—A Blue-Eyed Daisy. 2001. (J). 11.04 (*0-606-21074-1*) Turtleback Bks.
—The Blue Hill Meadows. 1997. (Illus.). 48p. (J). (gr. 3-7). 16.00 (*0-15-201404-7*) Harcourt Children's Bks.
—The Blue Hill Meadows. 2001. (Illus.). (J). 12.15 (*0-606-21075-X*) Turtleback Bks.
—Bunny Bungalow. (Illus.). 32p. (J). (ps-k). 2002. pap. 6.00 (*0-15-216316-6*, Voyager Bks./Libros Viajeros); 1999. 13.00 (*0-15-201092-0*) Harcourt Children's Bks.
—The Cobble Street Cousins Bk. 4: Some Good News. 1999. (Cobble Street Cousins Ser.: Vol. 4). (Illus.). 55p. (J). (gr. 2-5). 14.00 (*0-689-81713-4*, Simon & Schuster Children's Publishing) Simon & Schuster Children's Publishing.
—The Cobble Street Cousins Bk. 4: Some Good News. 2001. (Illus.). (J). 10.14 (*0-606-21115-2*) Turtleback Bks.
—Henry & Mudge in the Family Trees. 1997. (Henry & Mudge Ser.: V). (Illus.). 48p. (J). (gr. k-3). 15.00 (*0-689-81179-9*, Simon & Schuster Children's Publishing) Simon & Schuster Children's Publishing.
—Henry y Mudge y el Mejor Dia del Ano. 1997. (Henry & Mudge Ser.).Tr. of Henry & Mudge & the Best Day of All. (SPA.). (J). (gr. k-3). 12.14 (*0-606-12724-0*) Turtleback Bks.
—Old Town in the Green Groves: Laura Ingalls Wilder's Lost Little House Years. 2002. (Little House Ser.). (Illus.). 176p. (J). (gr. 3-7). lib. bdg. 16.89 (*0-06-029562-7*); (ps-1). 15.99 (*0-06-029561-9*) HarperCollins Children's Bk. Group.
—The Relatives Came. 2000. (J). pap. 19.97 incl. audio (*0-7366-9212-6*) Books on Tape, Inc.
—The Relatives Came. 2001. (J). (gr. k-4). 15.95 incl. audio Kimbo Educational.
—The Relatives Came. 1999. (Illus.). (J). (gr. k-3). pap., tchr. ed. 33.95 incl. audio (*0-87499-534-5*); 24.95 incl. audio (*0-87499-533-7*); pap. 15.95 incl. audio (*0-87499-532-9*) Live Oak Media.
—The Relatives Came. 32p. (J). 2002. mass mkt. 1.00 (*0-689-85586-9*, Aladdin); 2001. 16.95 (*0-689-84508-1*, Atheneum/Richard Jackson Bks.); 1985. (Illus.). lib. bdg. 16.00 (*0-02-777220-9*, Atheneum/Richard Jackson Bks.); 1993. (Illus.). reprint ed. pap. 6.99 (*0-689-71738-5*, Aladdin) Simon & Schuster Children's Publishing.
—The Relatives Came. 1993. (J). 12.14 (*0-606-05565-7*) Turtleback Bks.
Saban, Vera. The Westering: Joanna. 1994. (This Is America Ser.). (J). 15.95 (*0-914565-43-5*) Capstan Pubns.
Sachar, Louis. Marvin Redpost: Kidnapped at Birth? 1992. (Marvin Redpost Ser.: Vol. 1). (Illus.). 80p. (J). (gr. k-3). pap. 3.99 (*0-679-81946-0*); lib. bdg. 11.99 o.s.i (*0-679-91946-5*) Random Hse. Children's Bks. (Random Hse. Bks. for Young Readers).
—Marvin Redpost: Kidnapped at Birth? 1992. (J). 10.14 (*0-606-02323-2*) Turtleback Bks.
Sachs, Marilyn. Baby Sister. 1987. (J). pap. 3.50 (*0-380-70358-0*, Avon Bks.) Morrow/Avon.
—The Bears' House. 1989. 80p. (J). (gr. 3-7). pap. 2.99 (*0-380-70582-6*, Avon Bks.) Morrow/Avon.
—The Bears' House. (J). (gr. 4-7). 1996. 78p. pap. 4.99 (*0-14-038321-2*); 1987. 80p. 10.95 o.s.i (*0-525-44286-3*, Dutton Children's Bks.) Penguin Putnam Bks. for Young Readers.
—Dorrie's Book. 1975. (Illus.). 144p. (J). (gr. 4-6). 7.95 o.p. (*0-385-03350-8*) Doubleday Publishing.
—Fran Ellen's House. 1989. (J). pap. 2.75 (*0-380-70583-4*, Avon Bks.) Morrow/Avon.
—Fran Ellen's House. 1997. 96p. pap. 3.99 o.s.i (*0-14-038553-3*) Penguin Putnam Bks. for Young Readers.
—Marv. 1970. (gr. 4-7). lib. bdg. 5.95 o.p. (*0-385-00009-X*) Doubleday Publishing.
—The Truth about Mary Rose. 1973. 160p. (gr. 4-7). lib. bdg. 5.95 o.p. (*0-385-09449-3*) Doubleday Publishing.
—Veronica Ganz. 1968. (gr. 4-7). lib. bdg. 6.95 o.p. (*0-385-01436-8*) Doubleday Publishing.
—Veronica Ganz. 1995. 144p. (J). (gr. 3-7). pap. 5.99 (*0-14-037078-1*, Puffin Bks.) Penguin Putnam Bks. for Young Readers.
—Veronica Ganz. 1996. (J). (gr. 4-8). 19.00 (*0-8446-6896-6*) Smith, Peter Pub., Inc.
—Veronica Ganz. 1995. 11.04 (*0-606-08344-8*) Turtleback Bks.
Saldana, Rene, Jr. The Jumping Tree. 2002. (Illus.). 192p. (YA). (gr. 5). mass mkt. 5.50 (*0-440-22881-6*, Laurel Leaf) Random Hse. Children's Bks.
—The Jumping Tree: A Novel. 2001. (Illus.). 192p. (YA). (gr. 5-9). 14.95 (*0-385-32725-0*, Delacorte Bks. for Young Readers) Random Hse. Children's Bks.
Salmansohn, Karen. Wherever I Go, There I Am. 2002. (Illus.). 70p. (J). (gr. 4-7). 12.95 (*1-58246-079-5*) Tricycle Pr.
Sams, Rebeca A. Under the Bed. 2001. (Illus.). 28p. (J). (ps-k). 9.99 (*0-689-84009-8*, Little Simon) Simon & Schuster Children's Publishing.
Samuels, Gertrude. Yours, Brett. 1988. 192p. (YA). (gr. 7 up). 13.95 o.p. (*0-525-67255-9*, Dutton Children's Bks.) Penguin Putnam Bks. for Young Readers.
—Yours, Brett. 2000. 165p. (gr. 4-7). pap. 13.95 (*0-595-00806-2*) iUniverse, Inc.
Sandberg, Inger. Come on Out, Daddy. 1971. (Illus.). (J). (ps-3). 4.95 o.p. (*0-440-01522-7*); lib. bdg. 4.58 o.p. (*0-440-01523-5*) Dell Publishing. (Delacorte Pr.).
Sandin, Joan. The Long Way to a New Land. 1986. (I Can Read Bks.). (Illus.). 64p. (J). (gr. k-3). pap. 3.99 (*0-06-444100-8*, Harper Trophy) HarperCollins Children's Bk. Group.
—The Long Way to a New Land. 1991. (I Can Read Bks.). (Illus.). 64p. (J). (gr. k-3). pap. 8.99 incl. audio (*1-55994-494-3*, HarperAudio) HarperTrade.
Sandoval, Victor. Roll over, Big Toben. 2003. 160p. (J). pap. 9.95 (*1-55885-401-0*, Piñata Books) Arte Publico Pr.
Sanford, Doris. I Know the World's Worst Secret: A Child's Book about Living with an Alcoholic Parent. 1988. (Hurts of Childhood Ser.). (Illus.). 24p. (J). (gr. k-6). 7.99 o.p. (*0-88070-212-5*) Zonderkidz.
Sanroman, Susana. Senora Reganona: A Mexican Bedtime Story. ed. 2001. (J). (gr. 1). spiral bd. (*0-616-07280-5*) Canadian National Institute for the Blind/Institut National Canadien pour les Aveugles.
Santana, Patricia. Motorcycle Ride on the Sea of Tranquillity. 2002. 276p. (YA). 19.95 (*0-8263-2435-5*) Univ. of New Mexico Pr.
Santos, Rosario. Play Date. 2001. (Math Matters Ser.). (Illus.). 32p. (J). (ps-1). pap. 4.95 (*1-57565-105-X*) Kane Pr., The.
—Play Date. 2001. (Math Matters Ser.). (Illus.). (J). 11.10 (*0-606-20857-7*) Turtleback Bks.
Santucci, Barbara. Anna's Corn. 2002. (Illus.). 32p. (J). (gr. 1 up). 16.00 (*0-8028-5119-3*, Eerdmans Bks For Young Readers) Eerdmans, William B. Publishing Co.
Saul, Carol P. Someplace Else. 1997. 12.14 (*0-606-13031-4*) Turtleback Bks.
Saunders, Susan. Stephanie's Family Secret. 1989. (Sleepover Friends Ser.: No. 11). (J). mass mkt. 2.50 o.p. (*0-590-41845-9*) Scholastic, Inc.
Savage, Cindy. The Popularity Secret. 1988. 112p. (J). (gr. 5-8). 2.75 o.p. (*0-87406-315-9*, 37-16478-9) Darby Creek Publishing.
Scanlon. It Happened on Saturday. 1993. (New Trend Fiction B Ser.). (J). pap. text 9.95 (*0-582-80035-8*) Addison-Wesley Longman, Ltd. GBR. *Dist:* Trans-Atlantic Pubns., Inc.
Schaefer, Carole Lexa. The Copper Tin Cup. 2000. (Illus.). 32p. (J). (ps-3). 15.99 o.s.i (*0-7636-0471-2*) Candlewick Pr.
Schecter, Ellen. My Worst Days Diary. 1995. (J). 19.95 (*0-553-53120-4*, Dell Books for Young Readers) Random Hse. Children's Bks.
Scheidl, Gerda Marie. Tommy's New Sister. (Illus.). 32p. (J). (ps-2). 2002. pap. 6.95 (*0-7358-1700-6*); 1999. 16.50 o.p. (*0-7358-1057-5*) North-South Bks., Inc.
Schertle, Alice. Maisie. 1995. (Illus.). 32p. (J). (ps-3). 16.00 (*0-688-09310-8*) HarperCollins Children's Bk. Group.
Schick, Eleanor. Home Alone. 1969. (J). o.s.i (*0-688-05244-4*); lib. bdg. o.s.i (*0-688-05245-2*) HarperCollins Children's Bk. Group. (Greenwillow Bks.).
—Rainy Sunday. 1981. (Easy-to-Read Bks.). (Illus.). 56p. (J). (ps-3). 5.99 o.p. (*0-8037-7369-2*); 2.50 o.p. (*0-8037-7371-4*) Penguin Putnam Bks. for Young Readers. (Dial Bks. for Young Readers).
Schickling, Wanda. Chipper Picks a Family. 1952. (J). (gr. 4-6). pap. 1.25 o.p. (*0-8024-1135-5*) Moody Pr.
Schneider, Rex. That's Not All!, Level 2. Gregorich, Barbara, ed. 1985. (Start to Read! Ser.). (Illus.). 16p. (J). (ps-2). 2.29 (*0-88743-019-8*, 06019) School Zone Publishing Co.
Schnur, Steven. The Koufax Dilemma. 1997. (Illus.). 186p. (J). (gr. 5 up). 15.00 (*0-688-14221-4*, Morrow, William & Co.) Morrow/Avon.
—The Koufax Dilemma. 2001. 196p. pap. 14.95 (*0-595-19998-4*, Backinprint.com) iUniverse, Inc.
Schnurr, Constance B. Crazy Lady. 1969. (Illus.). (J). (gr. 3-6). 4.50 o.p. (*0-15-220864-X*); 4.50 o.p. (*0-15-220865-8*) Harcourt Children's Bks.
Schotter, Roni. Warm at Home. (Illus.). 28p. (J). 3.98 o.p. (*0-7651-0032-0*) Smithmark Pubs., Inc.
—Warm at Home. 2002. (J). E-Book (*1-58824-280-3*); 1993. E-Book (*1-59019-600-7*); 1993. E-Book (*1-59019-601-5*) ipicturebooks, LLC.
Schraff, Anne. The Greatest Heroes. 2000. 143p. (J). (*0-7807-9271-8*); pap. (*0-7891-5133-2*) Perfection Learning Corp.
Schultz, Betty K. Mom of Mystery. Diehl, Diana, ed. num. ed. 2002. (Illus.). 158p. (Orig.). (J). (gr. 6-8). lib. bdg. 18.95 (*0-929568-02-8*) Raspberry Pr., Ltd.
Schulz, Charles M. Hello, World! 2003. (Baby Snoopy Ser.). (Illus.). 8p. (J). 7.99 (*0-689-86365-9*, Little Simon) Simon & Schuster Children's Publishing.
Schumacher, Julie. Grass Angel. 2004. 144p. lib. bdg. 17.99 (*0-385-90163-1*); 208p. (gr. 5-9). text 15.95 (*0-385-73073-X*) Dell Publishing. (Delacorte Pr.).
Schur, Maxine R. Samantha's Surprise: A Christmas Story. Thieme, Jeanne, ed. 1986. (American Girls Collection: Bk. 3). (Illus.). (YA). (gr. 2 up). 80p. 12.95 (*0-937295-86-8*, American Girl); 80p. pap. 5.95 (*0-937295-22-1*, American Girl); 72p. 12.95 o.p. (*0-937295-21-3*) Pleasant Co. Pubns.
—Samantha's Surprise: A Christmas Story. 1986. (American Girls Collection: Bk. 3). (Illus.). (YA). (gr. 2 up). 12.10 (*0-606-03452-8*) Turtleback Bks.
Schwandt, Stephen. Holding Steady. 1996. 184p. (J). (gr. 7-9). reprint ed. pap. 5.95 o.p. (*0-915793-94-6*) Free Spirit Publishing, Inc.
Schwartz, Amy. Her Majesty, Aunt Essie. 1984. (Illus.). 32p. (J). (gr. k-2). lib. bdg. 14.95 o.p. (*0-02-781450-5*, Simon & Schuster Children's Publishing) Simon & Schuster Children's Publishing.
Schwartz, Virginia Frances. Messenger. 2002. vii, 277p. (J). tchr. ed. 17.95 (*0-8234-1716-6*) Holiday Hse., Inc.
Schweninger, Ann. On My Way to Grandpa's. 1981. (Illus.). 32p. (J). (ps-2). 7.50 o.p. (*0-8037-6741-2*); 7.50 o.p. (*0-8037-6752-8*) Penguin Putnam Bks. for Young Readers. (Dial Bks. for Young Readers).
Scott, Adam. Joe Moves In: A First-Week Scrapbook. 2002. (Blue's Clues Ser.). (Illus.). 24p. (J). (ps-1). pap. 3.50 (*0-689-84943-5*, 12, Simon Spotlight/Nickelodeon) Simon & Schuster Children's Publishing.
Scott, Ann Herbert. Sam. 1967. (Illus.). (J). (ps-3). text 14.95 o.p. (*0-07-055803-5*) McGraw-Hill Cos., The.
—Sam. (Illus.). 40p. (J). (ps-3). 1996. pap. 5.95 o.s.i (*0-698-11387-X*, PaperStar); 1992. 14.95 o.s.i (*0-399-22104-2*, Philomel) Penguin Putnam Bks. for Young Readers.
—Sam. 1996. (J). 11.15 o.p. (*0-606-09817-8*) Turtleback Bks.
Scribner, Toni. The Best Place in the World: A Wrinkles Storybook. 1986. 12p. (J). (ps-1). 4.95 o.s.i (*0-394-88431-0*, Random Hse. Bks. for Young Readers) Random Hse. Children's Bks.

Seabrooke, Brenda. Home Is Where They Take You In. 1980. 192p. (J). (gr. 7-9). 12.95 o.p. (*0-688-22221-8*); lib. bdg. 12.88 o.p. (*0-688-32221-2*) Morrow/Avon. (Morrow, William & Co.).

—The Swan's Gift. 1996. (Illus.). 32p. (J). (gr. k-3). reprint ed. bds. 5.99 o.p. (*1-56402-970-0*) Candlewick Pr.

Seckar, Alvena Vajdak. Misko. 1999. (Illus.). 159p. (J). pap. 15.00 (*0-86516-465-7*) Bolchazy-Carducci Pubs.

—Trapped in the Old Mine. 1999. (Illus.). 224p. (J). pap. 15.00 (*0-86516-466-5*) Bolchazy-Carducci Pubs.

Segal, Lore. Tell Me a Mitzi, RS. 1982. (Illus.). 40p. (J). (ps-3). 17.00 o.p. (*0-374-37392-2*, Farrar, Straus & Giroux (BYR)) Farrar, Straus & Giroux.

—Tell Me a Story, RS. 1977. (Illus.). 40p. (J). (ps-3). 15.00 o.p. (*0-374-37395-7*, Farrar, Straus & Giroux (BYR)) Farrar, Straus & Giroux.

Segal, Lore & Pincus, Harriet. Tell Me a Mitzi. 9999. (J). pap. 7.50 o.s.i (*0-590-20039-9*) Scholastic, Inc.

Seldomridge, Ray, ed. The Clubhouse Collection. 1993. (J). (gr. 3-7). pap. 5.99 o.p. (*1-56179-161-X*) Focus on the Family Publishing.

Seredy, Kate. The Good Master. 1986. (Puffin Newbery Library). (Illus.). 192p. (J). (gr. 4-7). pap. 5.99 (*0-14-030133-X*, Puffin Bks.) Penguin Putnam Bks. for Young Readers.

Seuling, Barbara. Robert & the Lemming Problem. 2003. (Illus.). 120p. (J). 15.95 (*0-8126-2686-9*) Cricket Bks.

Sharmat, Marjorie Weinman. Get Rich Mitch! 1986. 96p. (J). (gr. 3-7). pap. 2.50 (*0-380-70170-7*, Avon Bks.) Morrow/Avon.

—Mitchell Is Moving. 1978. (Ready-to-Read Ser.). (Illus.). 48p. (J). (gr. 1-4). lib. bdg. 13.00 o.s.i (*0-02-782410-1*, Simon & Schuster Children's Publishing) Simon & Schuster Children's Publishing.

—Sometimes Mama & Papa Fight. 1980. (Illus.). (J). (gr. k-3). 9.38 (*0-06-025611-7*); lib. bdg. 11.89 o.p. (*0-06-025612-5*) HarperCollins Children's Bk. Group.

Shavers Gayle, Sharon. Family Picnic. 1997. (Stickers 'n' Shapes Ser.). (Illus.). 24p. (J). (gr. k-3). mass mkt. 3.99 (*0-689-81318-X*, Simon Spotlight/Nickelodeon) Simon & Schuster Children's Publishing.

Shaw, Richard. The Hard Way Home. 1977. (J). (gr. 6 up). reprint ed. 6.95 o.p. (*0-525-66529-3*, Dutton Children's Bks.) Penguin Putnam Bks. for Young Readers.

Shawver, Margaret. What's Wrong with Grandma? A Family's Experience with Alzheimer's. 1996. (Young Readers Ser.). (Illus.). 62p. (YA). (gr. 2 up). 17.00 (*1-57392-107-6*) Prometheus Bks., Pubs.

Shecter, Ben. Someplace Else. 1971. (Illus.). (J). (gr. 3-7). lib. bdg. 8.89 o.p. (*0-06-025577-3*) HarperCollins Pubs.

Shelby, Anne. Homeplace. 1995. (Illus.). 32p. (J). (ps-3). pap. 16.95 (*0-531-06882-X*); lib. bdg. 17.99 (*0-531-08732-8*) Scholastic, Inc. (Orchard Bks.).

Sherwood, Mary. The History of the Fairchild Family. 1977. (Classics of Children's Literature, 1621-1932: Vol. 22). (J). reprint ed. lib. bdg. 46.00 o.p. (*0-8240-2271-8*) Garland Publishing, Inc.

Shields, Carol Diggory. Lucky Pennies & Hot Chocolate. 2002. (Illus.). 32p. (J). pap. 5.99 (*0-14-230190-6*) Penguin Putnam Bks. for Young Readers.

Shore, June L. Summer Storm. 1977. (J). (gr. 7 up). 4.95 o.p. (*0-687-40609-9*) Abingdon Pr.

Shreve, Susan Richards. The Bad Dreams of a Good Girl. (J). 1983. 92p. (gr. 2-5). pap. 2.25 o.p. (*0-380-63966-1*, 63966-1, Avon Bks.); 1993. (Illus.). 96p. (gr. 4 up). reprint ed. mass mkt. 3.95 o.p. (*0-688-12113-6*, Morrow, William & Co.) Morrow/Avon.

—Blister. (Illus.). 160p. (J). (gr. 3-7). 2003. pap. 4.99 (*0-439-19314-1*, Scholastic Paperbacks); 2001. pap. 15.95 (*0-439-19313-3*, Levine, Arthur A. Bks.) Scholastic, Inc.

—Family Secrets: Five Very Important Stories. 1979. (Illus.). (J). (gr. 4-7). 5.95 o.s.i (*0-394-83896-3*, Knopf Bks. for Young Readers) Random Hse. Children's Bks.

—Joshua T. Bates in Trouble Again. (Illus.). (gr. 3-7). 2000. 128p. mass mkt. 2.99 o.s.i (*0-375-80675-X*); 1998. 112p. (J). pap. 4.99 o.s.i (*0-679-89263-X*) Random Hse. Children's Bks. (Random Hse. Bks. for Young Readers).

—Joshua T. Bates in Trouble Again. 1998. 11.04 (*0-606-14243-6*) Turtleback Bks.

—Wait for Me. 1992. (Illus.). 112p. (J). (gr. 3 up). 13.00 o.p. (*0-688-11120-3*, Morrow, William & Co.) Morrow/Avon.

—Warts. 1996. (Illus.). 96p. (J). (gr. 2). 15.00 o.s.i (*0-688-14378-4*, Morrow, William & Co.) Morrow/Avon.

Shull, Megan Elisabeth. Yours Truly, Skye O'Shea. 2003. (Pleasant Company Publications). (J). pap. 6.95 (*1-58485-768-4*, American Girl) Pleasant Co. Pubns.

Sidney, Margaret. Five Little Peppers & How They Grew. (J). 23.95 (*0-8488-0629-8*) Amereon, Ltd.

—Five Little Peppers & How They Grew. (Illus.). (J). (gr. 4-6). reprint ed. 1981. 5.95 o.p. (*0-448-11008-3*); 1978. 2.95 o.p. (*0-448-16303-9*); 1948. 12.95 o.s.i (*0-448-06008-6*) Penguin Putnam Bks. for Young Readers. (Grosset & Dunlap).

—Five Little Peppers & How They Grew Book & Charm. 2002. (Charming Classics Ser.). 304p. (J). pap. 6.99 (*0-694-01582-2*, Harper Festival) HarperCollins Children's Bk. Group.

—Five Little Peppers Midway. 1987. (J). (gr. 5-7). reprint ed. lib. bdg. 27.95 (*0-89966-550-0*) Buccaneer Bks., Inc.

Silver, Norman. Cloud Nine. 1995. (Illus.). 32p. (J). (gr. k-3). 15.95 o.p. (*0-395-73545-9*, Clarion Bks.) Houghton Mifflin Co. Trade & Reference Div.

—An Eye for Color. 1993. 192p. (YA). (gr. 8 up). 14.99 o.p. (*0-525-44859-4*, Dutton Children's Bks.) Penguin Putnam Bks. for Young Readers.

Silverman, Maida. The Glass Menorah & Other Stories for Jewish Holidays. 1992. (Illus.). 64p. (J). (gr. 1-4). 14.95 o.p. (*0-02-782682-1*, Simon & Schuster Children's Publishing) Simon & Schuster Children's Publishing.

Simmons, Michael. Pool Boy. 2003. 176p. (gr. 7 up). 15.95 (*0-7613-1885-2*); lib. bdg. 22.90 (*0-7613-2924-2*) Millbrook Pr., Inc. (Roaring Brook Pr.).

Simon, Shirley. Get Lost, Becka!, Level 1. Gregorich, Barbara, ed. 1985. (Start to Read! Ser.). (Illus.). 16p. (J). (gr. k-2). 2.29 (*0-88743-013-9*, 06013) School Zone Publishing Co.

Sinclair, Catherine. Holiday House. 1976. (Classics of Children's Literature, 1621-1932: Vol. 24). (J). reprint ed. lib. bdg. 46.00 o.p. (*0-8240-2273-4*) Garland Publishing, Inc.

Singer, A. L. Little Monsters. 1989. (J). mass mkt. 2.95 o.p. (*0-590-42742-3*) Scholastic, Inc.

Skillings Prigger, Mary. Aunt Minnie McGranahan. 1999. (Illus.). 40p. (J). (ps-3). lib. bdg., tchr. ed. 15.00 (*0-395-82270-X*, Clarion Bks.) Houghton Mifflin Co. Trade & Reference Div.

Skolsky, Mindy Warshaw. Carnival & Kopeck & More about Hannah. 1979. (Illus.). 80p. (J). (gr. 2-5). lib. bdg. 12.89 o.p. (*0-06-025692-3*) HarperCollins Children's Bk. Group.

Skurzynski, Gloria. Cliff Hanger. 2001. (National Parks Mystery Ser.). (Illus.). (J). 12.00 (*0-606-21111-X*) Turtleback Bks.

—Deadly Waters. 2001. (National Parks Mystery Ser.). (Illus.). (J). 12.00 (*0-606-21142-X*) Turtleback Bks.

Skutch, Robert. Who's in a Family? 1995. (Illus.). 32p. (J). (ps-2). 12.95 o.p. (*1-883672-13-9*) Tricycle Pr.

Sleator, William. Oddballs. 1993. 144p. (J). (gr. 7 up). 14.99 o.p. (*0-525-45057-2*, Dutton Children's Bks.) Penguin Putnam Bks. for Young Readers.

Sleep Tight. 1994. (J). mass mkt. 4.99 (*0-553-54164-1*, Dell Books for Young Readers) Random Hse. Children's Bks.

Sloan, Glenna. A Year on the Dot. 2001. 91p. (YA). (gr. 5-8). pap. 9.99 (*0-88092-545-0*, 5450) Royal Fireworks Publishing Co.

Smalls, Irene. Because You're Lucky. 1997. (Illus.). 32p. (J). (ps-3). 15.95 (*0-316-79867-3*) Little Brown & Co.

—Because You're Lucky. 2003. (Illus.). 32p. (J). (ps-1). pap. 5.99 (*0-316-76425-6*) Little Brown Children's Bks.

—Dawn & the Round-to-It. 1994. (Illus.). 40p. (J). (ps-3). pap. 15.00 (*0-671-87166-8*, Simon & Schuster Children's Publishing) Simon & Schuster Children's Publishing.

—Louise's Gift. 1996. (Illus.). 36p. (J). (ps-3). 15.95 o.p. (*0-316-79877-0*) Little Brown & Co.

Smith, Alison. Help! There's a Cat Washing in Here! 1981. (Illus.). (J). (gr. 4-6). 10.25 o.p. (*0-525-31630-2*, Dutton) Dutton/Plume.

Smith, Anne Warren. Turkey Monster Thanksgiving. 2003. 112p. (J). lib. bdg. 13.95 (*0-8075-8125-9*) Whitman, Albert & Co.

Smith, Barbara A. Somewhere Just Beyond. 1993. 96p. (J). (gr. 3-7). 12.95 o.s.i (*0-689-31877-4*, Atheneum) Simon & Schuster Children's Publishing.

Smith, Beth Esh. What's Cooking. l.t. ed. 1996. (Big Bks.). (Illus.). 8p. (Orig.). (J). (ps-1). pap. text 10.95 (*1-57332-036-6*) HighReach Learning, Inc.

Smith, Betty. Joy in the Morning. 1976. 19.05 (*0-606-12368-7*) Turtleback Bks.

Smith, Debra. Hattie Marshall & the Prowling Panther. 1995. (Hattie Marshall Frontier Adventure Ser.: Vol. 1). 144p. (J). (gr. 3-7). pap. 4.99 o.p. (*0-89107-831-2*) Crossway Bks.

Smith, Debra West. Hattie Marshall & the Prowling Panther. 2002. (J). 6.95 (*1-56554-940-6*) Pelican Publishing Co., Inc.

—Yankees on the Doorstep: The Story of Sarah Morgan. 2001. (Illus.). 176p. (J). (gr. 3-7). pap. 10.95 (*1-56554-872-8*) Pelican Publishing Co., Inc.

Smith, Doris B. The First Hard Times. 1990. 144p. (J). (gr. 4 up). pap. 3.95 o.p. (*0-14-034538-8*, Puffin Bks.) Penguin Putnam Bks. for Young Readers.

—Tough Chauncey. 1986. (Novels Ser.). 224p. (J). (gr. 3-7). pap. 3.95 o.p. (*0-14-031928-X*, Puffin Bks.) Penguin Putnam Bks. for Young Readers.

Smith, Doris Buchanan. Return to Bitter Creek. 2002. (J). (gr. 3-7). 19.75 (*0-8446-7212-2*) Smith, Peter Pub., Inc.

Smith, Greg Leitich. Ninjas, Piranhas, & Galileo. 2003. 192p. (J). (gr. 3-6). 15.95 (*0-316-77854-0*) Little Brown & Co.

Smith, Jane D. And Baby & Kitty & Mommy & Daddy. 1994. (Illus.). (J). (ps). bds. 9.95 o.s.i (*1-56305-668-2*, 3668) Workman Publishing Co., Inc.

Smith, Joan. The Gift of Umtal. 1983. (Julia MacRae Blackbird Bks.). 144p. (gr. 5 up). 8.95 o.p. (*0-531-04580-3*, Watts, Franklin) Scholastic Library Publishing.

Smith, Lane. The Happy Hocky Family. 1993. (Illus.). 64p. (J). (ps-3). 16.99 (*0-670-85206-6*, Viking Children's Bks.) Penguin Putnam Bks. for Young Readers.

—The Happy Hocky Family. 1996. 11.14 (*0-606-14061-1*) Turtleback Bks.

—The Happy Hocky Family Moves to the Country! 2003. (Illus.). 64p. (J). 16.99 (*0-670-03594-7*, Viking) Viking Penguin.

Smith, Lucia B. My Mom Got a Job, ERS. 1979. (Illus.). (J). (gr. k-3). o.p. (*0-03-048321-2*, Holt, Henry & Co. Bks. For Young Readers) Holt, Henry & Co.

Smith, Patrick D. A Land Remembered, 2 vols. 2001. (Illus.). Vol. 1. 235p. (J). (gr. 5-12). pap., stu. ed. 7.95 (*1-56164-223-1*); Vol. 1. 240p. (YA). (gr. 5-12). stu. ed. 14.95 (*1-56164-230-4*); Vol. 2. 235p. (J). pap., stu. ed. 7.95 (*1-56164-224-X*); Vol. 2. 200p. (YA). (gr. 5-12). 14.95 (*1-56164-231-2*) Pineapple Pr., Inc.

Smith, Robert Kimmel. The War with Grandpa. 1984. (Illus.). 128p. (J). (gr. 4-8). pap. 12.95 o.s.i (*0-385-29314-3*); 12.95 o.p. (*0-385-29312-7*) Dell Publishing. (Delacorte Pr.).

Smith, Rukshana. Sumitra's Story. 1983. 168p. (J). (gr. 6). 10.95 o.p. (*0-698-20579-0*, Coward-McCann) Putnam Publishing Group, The.

Smothers, Ethel Footman. Down in the Piney Woods. 2003. 128p. (J). 6.00 (*0-8028-5248-3*, Eerdmans Bks For Young Readers) Eerdmans, William B. Publishing Co.

—Down in the Piney Woods. (J). 1994. 156p. (gr. 3-7). pap. 4.99 o.s.i (*0-679-84714-6*, Random Hse. Bks. for Young Readers); 1992. 144p. (gr. 5-9). 14.00 o.s.i (*0-679-80360-2*, Knopf Bks. for Young Readers); 1992. 144p. (gr. 5-9). 14.99 o.s.i (*0-679-90360-7*, Knopf Bks. for Young Readers) Random Hse. Children's Bks.

—Down in the Piney Woods. 1992. (J). 9.09 (*0-606-05813-3*) Turtleback Bks.

Snapshot Staff. Rise & Shine - Block Book. 1996. (Block Books Ser.). (Illus.). 20p. (J). bds. 3.95 o.p. (*0-7894-0624-1*) Dorling Kindersley Publishing, Inc.

Snelling, Lauraine. Class Act. 2000. (High Hurdles Ser.: No. 10). 176p. (J). (gr. 6-9). pap. 5.99 (*0-7642-2038-1*) Bethany Hse. Pubs.

Snyder, Carol. Dear Mom & Dad, Don't Worry. 1992. 160p. (YA). mass mkt. 3.50 o.s.i (*0-553-29646-9*) Bantam Bks.

—The Leftover Kid. 1987. 160p. (J). 2.50 o.p. (*0-425-09709-9*) Berkley Publishing Group.

—The Leftover Kid. 1986. 160p. (J). (gr. 6 up). 13.95 o.p. (*0-448-47773-4*, G. P. Putnam's Sons) Penguin Putnam Bks. for Young Readers.

Snyder, Dianne. George & the Dragon Word. 1991. (Illus.). 56p. (J). (gr. 2-4). 13.95 o.p. (*0-395-55129-3*) Houghton Mifflin Co. Trade & Reference Div.

—George & the Dragon Word. 1994. 64p. (YA). (gr. 4-7). mass mkt. 2.99 (*0-671-79393-4*, Aladdin) Simon & Schuster Children's Publishing.

—George & the Dragon Word. 1991. (J). 8.19 o.p. (*0-606-06404-4*) Turtleback Bks.

Snyder, Zilpha Keatley. Cat Running. 176p. 1996. (gr. 4-7). pap. text 4.99 (*0-440-41152-1*); 1994. (gr. 5 up). text 15.95 o.s.i (*0-385-31056-0*, Delacorte Pr.) Dell Publishing.

—Cat Running. 1995. (YA). (gr. 5 up). 18.95 (*0-385-30987-2*, Dell Books for Young Readers) Random Hse. Children's Bks.

—Cat Running. 1996. (YA). (gr. 5 up). 11.04 (*0-606-08710-9*) Turtleback Bks.

—The Ghosts of Rathburn Park. 2002. 192p. lib. bdg. 17.99 (*0-385-90064-3*); (gr. 3-7). text 15.95 (*0-385-32767-6*) Random Hse., Inc.

—The Headless Cupid. 1999. 224p. mass mkt. 2.99 o.s.i (*0-440-22895-6*) Bantam Bks.

—The Headless Cupid. 2002. (Illus.). (J). 13.38 (*0-7587-0269-8*) Book Wholesalers, Inc.

—The Headless Cupid. 1992. pap. o.p. (*0-440-80350-0*) Dell Publishing.

—The Headless Cupid. 1985. (Illus.). 208p. (gr. 4-7). pap. text 4.99 (*0-440-43507-2*, Yearling) Random Hse. Children's Bks.

—The Headless Cupid, Set. 1996. (J). (gr. 6). pap. 47.75 incl. audio (*0-7887-1546-1*, 40344) Recorded Bks., LLC.

—The Headless Cupid. 1971. (Illus.). 208p. (J). (gr. 3-7). 17.00 (*0-689-20687-9*, Atheneum) Simon & Schuster Children's Publishing.

—The Unseen. 2004. 208p. (J). text 15.95 (*0-385-73084-5*, Delacorte Pr.) Dell Publishing.

Somer, Mesa. Night of the Five Aunties. 1996. (Illus.). 32p. (J). (gr. k-4). lib. bdg. 14.95 (*0-8075-5631-9*) Whitman, Albert & Co.

Sommer, Carl. No Longer a Dilly Dally. 1997. (Another Sommer-Time Story Ser.). (Illus.). 48p. (J). (gr. k-3). 9.95 (*1-57537-001-8*); (gr. 1-4). lib. bdg. 16.95 (*1-57537-053-0*) Advance Publishing, Inc.

—No Longer a Dilly Dally Read-along Cassette, 1 bk. 2003. (Another Sommer-Time Story Ser.). (Illus.). 48p. (J). 16.95 incl. audio (*1-57537-550-8*) Advance Publishing, Inc.

—No Longer a Dilly Dally Read-along CD, 11 vols. 2003. (Another Sommer-Time Story Ser.). (Illus.). 48p. (J). (gr. 1-4). 16.95 incl. audio compact disk (*1-57537-501-X*) Advance Publishing, Inc.

Son, John. Finding My Hat. 2003. (First Person Fiction Ser.). 192p. (J). pap. 16.95 (*0-439-43538-2*, Orchard Bks.) Scholastic, Inc.

Sonenklar, Carol. My Own Worst Enemy. 1999. 144p. (YA). (gr. 5-9). tchr. ed. 15.95 (*0-8234-1456-6*) Holiday Hse., Inc.

Sonneborn, Ruth A. Friday Night Is Papa Night. 1987. (Picture Puffin Ser.). (Illus.). (J). 10.19 o.p. (*0-606-01810-7*) Turtleback Bks.

—Friday Night Is Papa Night. 1970. (Illus.). (J). (gr. k-3). 6.95 o.p. (*0-670-32938-X*) Viking Penguin.

—Seven in a Bed. 1968. (Illus.). (J). (gr. k-2). 3.95 o.p. (*0-670-63507-3*) Viking Penguin.

Sorensen, Henri. New Hope. 1995. (Illus.). 32p. (J). (gr. k up). lib. bdg. 14.93 o.p. (*0-688-13926-4*) HarperCollins Children's Bk. Group.

Sorensen, Virginia. Miracles on Maple Hill. 2002. (Illus.). (J). 13.19 (*0-7587-0203-5*) Book Wholesalers, Inc.

—Miracles on Maple Hill. 2003. (Illus.). 256p. (J). 17.00 (*0-15-204719-0*, Harcourt Young Classics); (YA). pap. 5.95 (*0-15-204718-2*, Odyssey Classics) Harcourt Children's Bks.

—Miracles on Maple Hill. 1956. (Odyssey Classic Ser.). (J). 12.05 (*0-606-04005-6*) Turtleback Bks.

Sorenson, Jane B. Family Crisis. 1986. (Jennifer Bks.). (Illus.). 144p. (J). (gr. 5-8). 4.99 o.p. (*0-87403-089-7*, 2989) Standard Publishing.

Soto, Gary. The Pool Party. 1993. (Illus.). 112p. (J). 13.95 (*0-385-30890-6*, Delacorte Pr.) Dell Publishing.

Spalding, Andrea. Me & Mr. Mah. (Illus.). 32p. (ps-3). 2001. pap. 7.95 (*1-55143-177-7*); 2000. (J). 14.95 (*1-55143-168-8*) Orca Bk. Pubs.

Speare, Elizabeth George. Calico Captive. 1973. 288p. (gr. 4-7). pap. text 4.99 o.s.i (*0-440-41156-4*, Yearling) Random Hse. Children's Bks.

Speregen, Devra Newberger. Blossom's Family Album. 1993. 40p. (J). (gr. 4-7). pap. 4.95 o.p. (*0-590-47234-8*) Scholastic, Inc.

Spinelli, Eileen. Thanksgiving Tappletons Reill. 2003. (Illus.). 32p. (J). 14.99 (*0-06-008670-X*); lib. bdg. 15.89 (*0-06-008671-8*) HarperCollins Pubs.

—When Mama Comes Home Tonight. (Illus.). (J). (gr. k-3). 1999. 30p. bds. 14.00 (*0-689-82714-8*, Simon & Schuster Children's Publishing); 2002. 32p. reprint ed. pap. 6.99 (*0-689-84897-8*, Aladdin) Simon & Schuster Children's Publishing.

Spinelli, Eileen & Lisker, Emily, illus. Summerhouse Time. 2001. (J). 16.00 (*0-689-82418-1*, Simon & Schuster Children's Publishing) Simon & Schuster Children's Publishing.

Spinelli, Jerry. Blue Ribbon Blues. 1998. (Tooter Tale Ser.: Vol. 2). (Illus.). 80p. (gr. k-3). pap. 3.99 (*0-679-88753-9*); (gr. 2-5). lib. bdg. 11.99 (*0-679-98753-3*) Random Hse. Children's Bks. (Random Hse. Bks. for Young Readers).

—Crash. 1996. 176p. (gr. 3-9). (J). 16.00 (*0-679-87957-9*); lib. bdg. 17.99 (*0-679-97957-3*) Knopf, Alfred A. Inc.

—Loser. 224p. (J). 2003. pap. 6.99 (*0-06-054074-5*); 2002. (gr. 4-7). 15.99 (*0-06-000193-3*, Cotler, Joanna Bks.); 2002. (Illus.). (gr. 4-6). lib. bdg. 15.89 (*0-06-000483-5*, Cotler, Joanna Bks.) HarperCollins Children's Bk. Group.

Springer, Nancy. Not on a White Horse. 1988. 192p. (YA). (gr. 5 up). lib. bdg. 14.95 o.s.i (*0-689-31366-7*, Atheneum) Simon & Schuster Children's Publishing.

Springfield Capitals Professional Baseball Junior Team Staff. Cappy's Crazy Day. 1997. (WeWrite Kids! Ser.: No. 37). (Illus.). 50p. (J). (ps-4). pap. 3.95 (*1-57635-013-4*) WeWrite Corp.

Spurr, Elizabeth. Mama's Birthday Surprise. 1996. (Hyperion Chapters Ser.). (Illus.). 64p. (J). (gr. 1-4). pap. 3.95 (*0-7868-1124-2*) Disney Pr.

Relationships

Thomas, Jane Resh. Celebration! 1997. (Illus.). 32p. (J). (ps-3). lib. bdg. 15.49 (*0-7868-2160-4*); (Maggie Stories Ser.: Vol. 2). 14.95 (*0-7868-0189-1*) Hyperion Bks. for Children.

—Daddy Doesn't Have to Be a Giant Anymore. 1996. (Illus.). 48p. (J). (gr. k-3). tchr. ed. 14.95 o.p. (*0-395-69427-2*, Clarion Bks.) Houghton Mifflin Co. Trade & Reference Div.

—Elizabeth Catches a Fish, 001. 1979. (Illus.). (J). (gr. 1-4). 6.95 o.p. (*0-395-28827-4*, Clarion Bks.) Houghton Mifflin Co. Trade & Reference Div.

—Lights on the River. 1994. (Illus.). 32p. (J). (ps-3). 15.95 (*0-7868-0004-6*); lib. bdg. 16.49 (*0-7868-2003-9*) Hyperion Bks. for Children.

—Lights on the River. 1996. (Illus.). 32p. (J). (ps-3). pap. 4.95 o.p. (*0-7868-1132-3*) Hyperion Paperbacks for Children.

Thomas Young, Ronder. Moving Mama to Town. 1997. 224p. (J). (gr. 3-8). pap. 17.95 (*0-531-30025-0*, Orchard Bks.) Scholastic, Inc.

Thompson, Jean. Don't Forget Michael. 1979. (Illus.). 64p. (J). (gr. k-3). 11.95 o.p. (*0-688-22196-3*); lib. bdg. 11.88 o.p. (*0-688-32196-8*) Morrow/Avon. (Morrow, William & Co.).

—I'm Going to Run Away. 1975. (Illus.). 32p. (J). (gr. k-3). lib. bdg. 4.95 o.p. (*0-687-18676-5*) Abingdon Pr.

Thompson, Julian F. Brothers. 2000. (Illus.). 224p. (YA). (gr. 7 up). mass mkt. 4.99 o.s.i (*0-375-80353-X*, Knopf Bks. for Young Readers) Random Hse. Children's Bks.

—The Trials of Molly Sheldon, ERS. 1995. 176p. (YA). (gr. 7 up). 16.95 o.p. (*0-8050-3382-3*, Holt, Henry & Co. Bks. For Young Readers) Holt, Henry & Co.

—The Trials of Molly Sheldon. 1997. 192p. (gr. 7 up). pap. 4.99 o.s.i (*0-14-038425-1*) Penguin Putnam Bks. for Young Readers.

—The Trials of Molly Sheldon. 1997. (J). 10.09 o.p. (*0-606-12006-8*) Turtleback Bks.

Thorne-Thomsen, Kathleen & Rocheleau, Paul. A Shakers Dozen. 1999. (Illus.). 40p. (J). (ps-3). 15.95 o.p. (*0-8118-2299-0*) Chronicle Bks. LLC.

Thrasher, Crystal. A Taste of Daylight. 1984. 228p. (YA). (gr. 7 up). 12.95 o.s.i (*0-689-50313-X*, McElderry, Margaret K.) Simon & Schuster Children's Publishing.

Thurman Runs Away from Home. 1996. (Little Twirps: Understanding People Storybooks: No. 62). 40p. (J). (gr. k-5). pap. 4.98 (*0-89544-062-8*) Silbert & Bress Pubns.

Tildes, Phyllis Limbacher. Billy's Big-Boy Bed. 2003. 32p. pap. 6.95 (*1-57091-606-3*) Charlesbridge Publishing, Inc.

Tobesman, Rachmiel. The Magic Glasses: Stories & Other Activities for Children of Separation & Divorce. 1998. (Illus.). 38p. (J). (ps-12). spiral bd. 12.95 (*0-9677266-0-3*) Child Access Ctr. of Maryland,The.

Tobias, Tobi. At the Beach. 1978. (J). (ps-4). pap. 5.95 o.p. (*0-679-20447-4*) McKay, David Co., Inc.

—How Your Mother & Father Met. 1978. (Illus.). (J). (gr. k-5). text 6.95 o.p. (*0-07-064957-X*) McGraw-Hill Cos., The.

—Jane, Wishing. 1977. (Illus.). (J). (gr. 1-4). 8.95 o.p. (*0-670-40565-5*) Viking Penguin.

—Jane, Wishing. 2001. (Illus.). (J). E-Book (*1-59019-447-0*); 1977. E-Book (*1-59019-448-9*) ipicturebooks, LLC.

—The Man Who Played Accordian Music. 1979. (Illus.). (J). (gr. 1-4). 5.95 o.p. (*0-394-83663-4*); lib. bdg. 5.99 o.p. (*0-394-93663-9*) Random Hse. Children's Bks. (Knopf Bks. for Young Readers).

Tolan, Stephanie S. The Great Skinner Getaway. 1988. 208p. (J). (gr. 5 up). pap. 3.95 o.p. (*0-14-032653-7*, Puffin Bks.) Penguin Putnam Bks. for Young Readers.

—The Great Skinner Getaway. 1987. (Great Skinner Ser.). 204p. (YA). (gr. 7 up). 14.95 o.p. (*0-02-789361-8*, Simon & Schuster Children's Publishing) Simon & Schuster Children's Publishing.

—Ordinary Miracles. 2002. 240p. (J). pap. 5.95 (*0-380-73322-6*, Morrow, William & Co.) Morrow/Avon.

—Surviving the Applewhites. 2002. 224p. (J). (gr. 6-9). 15.99 (*0-06-623602-9*); lib. bdg. 17.89 (*0-06-623603-7*) HarperCollins Children's Bk. Group.

—Welcome to the Ark. 1996. 240p. (YA). (gr. 5 up). 15.00 (*0-688-13724-5*, Morrow, William & Co.) Morrow/Avon.

Tomlinson, Sylvia. Maddie. 2002. (Illus.). 124p. (J). (gr. 3-7). 12.95 (*0-9720293-0-3*) Redbud Publishing Co.

Tomlinson, Theresa. Dancing Through the Shadows. 1997. (Illus.). 128p. (J). (gr. 4 up). pap. 14.95 o.p. (*0-7894-2459-2*) Dorling Kindersley Publishing, Inc.

Tondreau Levert, Louise & Perkes, Carolyn. Parents Do the Weirdest Things! 2001. (Little Wolf Bks.: Level 2). (Illus.). 32p. (J). (gr. 1 up). (*1-894363-75-2*) Dominique & Friends.

Too Many Tamales. 2002. (J). (ps-3). 24.95 incl. audio (*1-55592-098-5*); 29.95 incl. audio compact disk (*1-55592-137-X*) Weston Woods Studios, Inc.

Torres, Leyla. The Kite Festival, RS. 2004. (J). 16.00 (*0-374-38054-6*, Farrar, Straus & Giroux (BYR)) Farrar, Straus & Giroux.

Towne, Mary. Supercouple. 1984. 192p. 14.95 o.s.i (*0-385-29379-8*, Delacorte Pr.) Dell Publishing.

Townsend, John R. Noah's Castle. 1976. (YA). (gr. 6 up). 12.95 o.p. (*0-397-31654-2*) HarperCollins Children's Bk. Group.

Townzen, L. Carl. Peter Slade. 1996. (Orig.). (J). pap. 8.95 o.p. (*0-533-11959-6*) Vantage Pr., Inc.

Travers, Pamela L. Mary Poppins. 1981. (J). (gr. 4-7). reprint ed. lib. bdg. 27.95 (*0-89966-390-7*) Buccaneer Bks., Inc.

—Mary Poppins. 1997. (Illus.). 224p. (YA). (gr. 3-7). rev. ed. 18.00 (*0-15-252595-5*); 2nd rev. ed. pap. 6.00 (*0-15-201717-8*, Odyssey Classics) Harcourt Children's Bks.

—Mary Poppins. (J). 1997. 100.00 o.s.i (*0-15-252596-3*); 1981. (Illus.). 206p. (gr. 3-7). 14.95 (*0-15-252408-8*) Harcourt Trade Pubs.

—Mary Poppins. 202p. (J). (gr. 3-5). pap. 6.00 (*0-8072-1536-8*, Listening Library) Random Hse. Audio Publishing Group.

—Mary Poppins. 1997. 12.05 (*0-606-12418-7*) Turtleback Bks.

—Mary Poppins Comes Back. 1981. (J). reprint ed. lib. bdg. 17.95 (*0-89966-392-3*) Buccaneer Bks., Inc.

—Mary Poppins Comes Back. 1997. (Illus.). 320p. (J). (gr. 3-7). 18.00 (*0-15-201718-6*); pap. 6.00 (*0-15-201719-4*, Odyssey Classics) Harcourt Children's Bks.

—Mary Poppins in Cherry Tree Lane. 1982. (J). 10.95 (*0-440-05137-1*, Delacorte Pr.) Dell Publishing.

—Mary Poppins in the Park. (Illus.). (J). 1997. 288p. (gr. 3-7). 18.00 (*0-15-201716-X*); 1952. 265 p. 11.95 (*0-15-252947-0*); 2nd ed. 1997. 288p. (gr. 3-7). pap. 6.00 (*0-15-201721-6*, Odyssey Classics) Harcourt Children's Bks.

—Mary Poppins Opens the Door. 1981. (J). reprint ed. lib. bdg. 27.95 (*0-89966-391-5*) Buccaneer Bks., Inc.

—Mary Poppins Opens the Door. 1997. (Illus.). 272p. (YA). (gr. 3-7). 18.00 (*0-15-201720-8*); 2nd ed. pap. 6.00 (*0-15-201722-4*, Odyssey Classics) Harcourt Children's Bks.

Treasure in the Attic. Date not set. (Illus.). 12p. (J). (gr. k-2). pap. 3.75 (*1-58323-024-6*) Seedling Pubns., Inc.

Trimble, Irene. Zak & Wheezie Clean Up. 2000. (Dragon Tales Ser.). (Illus.). 24p. (J). (ps-k). pap. 3.25 (*0-375-80635-0*, Random Hse. Bks. for Young Readers) Random Hse. Children's Bks.

Tripp, Valerie. Josefina Aprende une Leccion: Un Cuento de la Escuela. Moreno, Jose, tr. 1997. (American Girls Collection: Bk. 2). (SPA., Illus.). 80p. (J). (gr. 2 up). pap. 5.95 (*1-56247-497-9*, BT4979, American Girl) Pleasant Co. Pubns.

—Josefina Learns a Lesson: A School Story. 1997. (American Girls Collection: Bk. 2). (Illus.). 80p. (J). (gr. 2 up). lib. bdg. 12.95 (*1-56247-518-5*, American Girl) Pleasant Co. Pubns.

—Josefina Learns a Lesson: A School Story. 1997. (American Girls Collection: Bk. 2). (Illus.). (YA). (gr. 2 up). 12.10 (*0-606-11524-2*) Turtleback Bks.

—Meet Josefina: An American Girl. 1997. (American Girls Collection: Bk. 1). (Illus.). 96p. (J). (gr. 2 up). pap. 5.95 (*1-56247-515-0*); lib. bdg. 12.95 (*1-56247-516-9*) Pleasant Co. Pubns. (American Girl).

—Meet Josefina: An American Girl. 1997. (American Girls Collection: Bk. 1). (Illus.). (YA). (gr. 2 up). 12.10 (*0-606-11614-1*) Turtleback Bks.

—Molly's Surprise: A Christmas Story. Thieme, Jeanne, ed. 1986. (American Girls Collection: Bk. 3). (Illus.). (gr. 2 up). 80p. (J). lib. bdg. 12.95 (*0-937295-87-6*, American Girl); 80p. (YA). pap. 5.95 (*0-937295-25-6*, American Girl); 72p. (YA). 12.95 o.p. (*0-937295-24-8*) Pleasant Co. Pubns.

—Molly's Surprise: A Christmas Story. 1986. (American Girls Collection: Bk. 3). (Illus.). (YA). (gr. 2 up). 12.10 (*0-606-02827-7*) Turtleback Bks.

—A Reward for Josefina. 1999. (American Girls Short Stories Ser.). (Illus.). 56p. (YA). (gr. 2 up). 3.95 (*1-56247-763-3*, American Girl) Pleasant Co. Pubns.

Trottier, Maxine. Alison's House. unabr. ed. 1993. (Illus.). 32p. (J). (ps-3). pap. 5.95 (*0-19-540968-X*) Oxford Univ. Pr., Inc.

—Prairie Willow. 2000. (Illus.). 24p. (J). (gr. k-5). pap. 7.95 (*0-7737-6100-4*) Stoddart Kids CAN. *Dist:* Fitzhenry & Whiteside, Ltd.

Trudel, Sylvain. L' Ange de Monsieur Chose. 1999. (Premier Roman Ser.). (Illus.). 64p. (J). (gr. 2-5). pap. 8.95 (*2-89021-347-1*) La Courte Echelle CAN. *Dist:* Firefly Bks., Ltd.

Tulloch, Richard. Stories from Our House. 1987. (Illus.). 32p. (ps-3). text 12.95 o.p. (*0-521-33485-3*) Cambridge Univ. Pr.

Turner, Ann. Finding Walter. 1997. 176p. (J). (gr. 3-7). 16.00 (*0-15-200212-X*) Harcourt Children's Bks.

Turner, Ann Warren. Dust for Dinner. (I Can Read Bks.). (Illus.). 64p. (J). 1997. (gr. k-3). pap. 3.95 (*0-06-444225-X*, Harper Trophy); 1995. (gr. k-3). lib. bdg. 15.89 (*0-06-023377-X*); 1995. (gr. 2-4). 13.95 o.p. (*0-06-023376-1*) HarperCollins Children's Bk. Group.

—Dust for Dinner. 1997. (I Can Read Bks.). (J). (gr. 2-4). 10.10 (*0-606-10794-0*) Turtleback Bks.

—Red Flower Goes West. 1999. (Illus.). 32p. (J). (gr. k-4). lib. bdg. 15.49 (*0-7868-2253-8*) Disney Pr.

—Red Flower Goes West. Date not set. (Illus.). 32p. (J). pap. 15.49 (*0-7868-1177-3*) Hyperion Bks. for Children.

—Red Flower Goes West: Book Club Edition. 1999. 32p. (J). pap. 14.99 (*0-7868-0575-7*) Disney Pr.

Tusa, Tricia. Family Reunion, RS. 1993. 32p. (J). 15.00 o.p. (*0-374-32268-6*, Farrar, Straus & Giroux (BYR)) Farrar, Straus & Giroux.

Uchida, Yoshiko. The Best Bad Thing. 1986. 136p. (J). (gr. 4-7). reprint ed. pap. 4.95 o.s.i (*0-689-71069-0*, Aladdin) Simon & Schuster Children's Publishing.

Udry, Janice May. Mary Jo's Grandmother. 1970. (Mary Jo Stories Ser.). (Illus.). 32p. (J). (gr. k-3). 8.75 o.p. (*0-8075-4984-3*) Whitman, Albert & Co.

Uff, Caroline. Hello, Lulu. 1999. (Illus.). 24p. (J). (ps-3). 14.95 (*0-8027-8712-6*) Walker & Co.

Ugolini, Lydia. The Story of a Rich Dog & a Poor Dog. Hall, Susan R., ed. Taraboletti-Segre, Anna, tr. from ITA. 1997. (Illus.). 115p. (J). (gr. 3-7). pap. 12.95 (*0-912339-04-7*, Beacon Hill Bks.) Meridian Hse.

Uk. The Quilt. 93rd ed. 1993. pap. text 12.40 (*0-15-300316-2*) Harcourt Children's Bks.

Uncle Walt's Christmas Box. 2001. 32p. (J). (gr. k-3). pap. 10.99 (*0-8254-7243-1*) Kregel Pubns.

Ungerer, Tomi. The Mellops Go Spelunking. 1998. (Illus.). 32p. (J). (gr. k-4). pap. 5.95 (*1-57098-228-7*) Rinehart, Roberts Pubs.

Unstead, Sue. Say Hello. 2004. (J). 14.95 (*1-58728-438-3*) Creative Publishing international, Inc.

Ure, Jean. If It Weren't For Sebastian. 1985. 192p. (J). (gr. 7 up). 14.95 o.s.i (*0-385-29380-1*, Delacorte Pr.) Dell Publishing.

—If It Weren't for Sebastian. 1987. (J). (gr. k-12). reprint ed. mass mkt. 2.95 o.s.i (*0-440-93996-8*, Laurel Leaf) Random Hse. Children's Bks.

Usher, Frances. The Hermit Shell. 1998. (Cambridge Reading Ser.). (Illus.). 160p. pap. text 10.25 (*0-521-55666-X*);Set. 6p. 53.00 (*0-521-64914-5*) Cambridge Univ. Pr.

Vail, Rachel. Daring to Be Abigail. 1997. 11.04 (*0-606-11237-5*) Turtleback Bks.

—If You Only Knew: Zoe. 1998. (Friendship Ring Ser.: No. 1). 240p. (J). (gr. 4-8). pap. 14.95 (*0-590-03370-0*); mass mkt. 4.99 (*0-590-37451-6*) Scholastic, Inc.

—Not That I Care: Morgan. 1998. (Friendship Ring Ser.: No. 3). (J). (gr. 4-8). 240p. pap. 14.95 (*0-590-03476-6*); 240p. mass mkt. 4.99 (*0-590-37453-2*); 59.88 (*0-590-95214-5*) Scholastic, Inc.

Valgardson, W. D. Garbage Creek: And Other Stories. 1998. (Illus.). 136p. (J). (gr. 3-7). pap. 5.95 (*0-88899-339-0*) Groundwood Bks. CAN. *Dist:* Publishers Group West.

—Garbage Creek & Other Stories. 1997. 96p. (J). (gr. 3-7). text 15.95 (*0-88899-297-1*) Groundwood Bks. CAN. *Dist:* Publishers Group West.

Valley, MaryJo. Please Don't Go. 1996. (Illus.). 93p. (J). (gr. 5-7). pap. 9.99 (*0-88092-097-1*) Royal Fireworks Publishing Co.

Van Draanen, Wendelin. Flipped. 2001. 224p. (gr. 5-9). (J). 14.95 (*0-375-81174-5*); lib. bdg. 16.99 (*0-375-91174-X*) Knopf, Alfred A. Inc.

—Flipped. 2003. (Illus.). 224p. (J). (gr. 5-9). pap. 8.95 (*0-375-82544-4*, Knopf Bks. for Young Readers) Random Hse. Children's Bks.

—Flipped! 2003. (Young Adult Ser.). (YA). 24.95 (*0-7862-4798-3*) Thorndike Pr.

—How I Survived Being a Girl. 1997. (J). 176p. (gr. k-3). 15.99 (*0-06-026671-6*); 80p. (gr. 3-7). lib. bdg. 14.89 o.p. (*0-06-026672-4*) HarperCollins Children's Bk. Group.

Van Leeuwen, Jean. Amanda Pig & Her Big Brother Oliver. 1994. (Puffin Easy-to-Read Ser.). (J). 10.14 (*0-606-01658-9*) Turtleback Bks.

—Amanda Pig & the Really Hot Day. 2005. (J). (*0-8037-2887-5*, Dial Bks. for Young Readers) Penguin Putnam Bks. for Young Readers.

—Blue Sky, Butterfly. 1996. (Illus.). 128p. (J). (gr. 4-7). 14.99 o.s.i (*0-8037-1972-8*, Dial Bks. for Young Readers) Penguin Putnam Bks. for Young Readers.

—Going West. (Picture Puffin Bks.). (Illus.). (J). (gr. k-3). 1997. 48p. pap. 5.99 (*0-14-056096-3*); 1992. 48p. 17.99 o.s.i (*0-8037-1027-5*, Dial Bks. for Young Readers); 1992. 4p. 14.89 o.p. (*0-8037-1028-3*, Dial Bks. for Young Readers) Penguin Putnam Bks. for Young Readers.

—Hannah of Fairfield. Fogelman, Phyllis, ed. 1999. (Pioneer Daughters Ser.: No. 1). (Illus.). 96p. (J). (gr. 2-5). 14.89 (*0-8037-2336-9*, Dial Bks. for Young Readers) Penguin Putnam Bks. for Young Readers.

—Hannah's Helping Hands. Fogelman, Phyllis, ed. 1999. (Pioneer Daughters Ser.: No. 2). (Illus.). 96p. (J). (gr. 2-5). 13.99 o.p. (*0-8037-2447-0*, Dial Bks. for Young Readers) Penguin Putnam Bks. for Young Readers.

—More Tales of Amanda Pig. 1995. (Puffin Easy-to-Read Ser.). (Illus.). 56p. (J). (ps-3). pap. 3.99 (*0-14-037603-8*, Puffin Bks.) Penguin Putnam Bks. for Young Readers.

—Oliver & Amanda & the Big Snow. 1995. (Dial Easy-to-Read Ser.). (Illus.). 48p. (J). (gr. k-3). 13.99 o.p. (*0-8037-1762-8*); 12.89 o.s.i (*0-8037-1763-6*) Penguin Putnam Bks. for Young Readers. (Dial Bks. for Young Readers).

—Oliver & Amanda & the Big Snow. 1998. 10.14 (*0-606-18439-2*) Turtleback Bks.

—Seems Like This Road Goes on Forever. 1979. (YA). (gr. 8 up). 8.95 o.p. (*0-8037-7687-X*, Dial Bks. for Young Readers) Penguin Putnam Bks. for Young Readers.

—Tales of Amanda Pig. (Easy-to-Read Ser.). (Illus.). 56p. (J). 1992. pap. 4.99 o.p. (*0-14-036212-6*, Puffin Bks.); 1983. 9.89 o.p. (*0-8037-8450-3*, Dial Bks. for Young Readers); 1983. pap. 4.95 o.p. (*0-8037-8443-0*, Dial Bks. for Young Readers) Penguin Putnam Bks. for Young Readers.

—Tales of Amanda Pig. 1994. (Puffin Easy-to-Read Ser.). (J). 10.14 (*0-606-01670-8*) Turtleback Bks.

—Tales of Amanda Pig Level 2, Red. 1994. (Puffin Easy-to-Read Ser.). (Illus.). 56p. (J). (ps-3). pap. 3.99 (*0-14-036840-X*, Puffin Bks.) Penguin Putnam Bks. for Young Readers.

Van Steenwyk, Elizabeth. Maggie in the Morning. 144p. (gr. 4-9). 2002. (YA). pap. 6.00 (*0-8028-5219-X*); 2001. (J). 16.00 (*0-8028-5222-X*) Eerdmans, William B. Publishing Co. (Eerdmans Bks For Young Readers).

Van Stockum, Hilda. Friendly Gables. 1996. (Mitchells Ser.: Vol. 3). (Illus.). 192p. (J). (gr. 4-7). pap. 11.95 o.p. (*1-883937-19-1*, 19-1) Bethlehem Bks.

—The Mitchells: Five for Victory. 1995. (Mitchells Ser.: Vol. 1). (Illus.). 250p. (J). (gr. 4-7). reprint ed. pap. 12.95 (*1-883937-05-1*, 05-1) Bethlehem Bks.

Various. Family Stories You Can Relate To. 2001. (Reading Rainbow Readers Ser.). (Illus.). 64p. (J). 14.95 (*1-58717-103-1*); pap. 3.99 (*1-58717-104-X*) North-South Bks., Inc.

Vaughn, Margaret Britton, et al. The Birthday Dolly. 2000. (Illus.). 47p. (J). pap. (*1-882845-09-9*) Bell Buckle Pr.

Velasquez, Gloria. Rina's Family Secret. 1998. 112p. (J). 16.95 o.p. (*1-55885-236-0*, Piñata Books) Arte Publico Pr.

—Tommy Stands Alone. 1995. (Roosevelt High School Series Bks.). 135p. (YA). (gr. 7 up). pap. 9.95 (*1-55885-147-X*); 14.95 (*1-55885-146-1*) Arte Publico Pr. (Piñata Books).

—Tommy Stands Alone. 1995. (Roosevelt High School Ser.). 16.00 (*0-606-16337-9*) Turtleback Bks.

Venokur, Ross. The Amazing Frecktacle. 1998. 144p. (gr. 3-7). text 14.95 o.s.i (*0-385-32621-1*, Delacorte Pr.) Dell Publishing.

Verderame, Mark. Strawberry Junction. 1997. (Illus.). 16p. (J). (gr. 1-3). pap. 7.00 o.p. (*0-8059-3959-8*) Dorrance Publishing Co., Inc.

Vestly, Anne-Catherine. Aurora & Socrates. 1977. (Illus.). (J). (gr. 3-7). 12.95 (*0-690-01293-4*) HarperCollins Children's Bk. Group.

View from Saturday. 1999. 9.95 (*1-56137-935-2*) Novel Units, Inc.

Villasenor, Victor. Los Trece Sentidos. 2001. 512p. 26.00 (*0-06-621297-9*, Rayo) HarperTrade.

Voake, Charlotte. Here Comes the Train. 1998. (Illus.). 32p. (J). (ps-k). 15.99 o.p. (*0-7636-0438-0*) Candlewick Pr.

Vogel, Ilse-Margret. My Summer Brother. 1981. (Illus.). 96p. (J). (gr. 2-5). o.p. (*0-06-026324-5*); lib. bdg. 10.89 o.p. (*0-06-026325-3*) HarperCollins Children's Bk. Group.

Voigt, Cynthia. Dicey's Song. 1987. 224p. (gr. 7-12). mass mkt. 5.99 o.s.i (*0-449-70276-6*, Fawcett) Ballantine Bks.

—Dicey's Song. l.t. ed. 2002. (LRS Large Print Cornerstone Ser.). 370p. (YA). lib. bdg. 35.95 (*1-58118-106-X*, 25790) LRS.

—Dicey's Song. l.t. ed. 1990. 334p. (J). reprint ed. lib. bdg. 16.95 o.s.i (*1-55736-166-5*, Cornerstone Bks.) Pages, Inc.

—Dicey's Song. 1997. (Pathways to Critical Thinking Ser.). 32p. (YA). (gr. 9-12). pap. text, stu. ed., tchr.'s training gde. ed. 19.95 (*1-58303-024-7*) Pathways Publishing.

—Dicey's Song. 2003. (Tillerman Ser.). (Illus.). 368p. (J). pap. 5.99 (*0-689-86362-4*, Aladdin); 2002. (Tillerman Saga: Bk. 2). 368p. (YA). (gr. 7 up). mass mkt. 5.99 (*0-689-85131-6*, Simon Pulse);

2001. 204p. (J). E-Book 6.99 (*0-689-84798-X*, Atheneum); 1982. (Tillerman Saga: Bk. 2). 204p. (YA). (gr. 7 up). 17.95 (*0-689-30944-9*, Atheneum) Simon & Schuster Children's Publishing.

—Dicey's Song. 1982. (J). 12.04 (*0-606-03279-7*) Turtleback Bks.

—Homecoming. (Tillerman Saga: Bk. 1). (YA). (gr. 7 up). 2002. (Illus.). 416p. mass mkt. 5.99 (*0-689-85132-4*, Simon Pulse); 1981. 320p. 18.00 (*0-689-30833-7*, Atheneum) Simon & Schuster Children's Publishing.

—Homecoming. 1981. (J). 12.04 (*0-606-03026-3*) Turtleback Bks.

—The Homecoming. 1987. 384p. (gr. 7-12). mass mkt. 5.99 o.s.i (*0-449-70254-5*, Fawcett) Ballantine Bks.

—Homecoming. l.t. ed. 2002. (LRS Large Print Cornerstone Ser.). (J). lib. bdg. 35.95 (*1-58118-090-X*) LRS.

—Seventeen Against the Dealer. 1990. 224p. (gr. 7 up). mass mkt. 5.50 o.s.i (*0-449-70375-4*, Fawcett) Ballantine Bks.

—Seventeen Against the Dealer. (Tillerman Saga: Bk. 3). (YA). (gr. 7 up). 2002. (Illus.). 352p. mass mkt. 5.99 (*0-689-85133-2*, Simon Pulse); 1989. 192p. 18.00 (*0-689-31497-3*, Atheneum) Simon & Schuster Children's Publishing.

—Seventeen Against the Dealer. 1990. 10.55 (*0-606-12512-4*) Turtleback Bks.

—Tree by Leaf. 1989. 176p. (J). (gr. 7 up). mass mkt. 4.50 o.s.i (*0-449-70334-7*, Fawcett) Ballantine Bks.

—Tree by Leaf. (J). (gr. 4-7). 2000. 240p. pap. 4.99 (*0-689-83527-2*, Aladdin); 1988. 208p. 15.95 (*0-689-31403-5*, Atheneum) Simon & Schuster Children's Publishing.

—Tree by Leaf. 1989. (J). 9.60 o.p. (*0-606-01223-0*) Turtleback Bks.

Voigt, Hannelore. Not Now, Sara! James, J. Alison, tr. from GER. 1945. Tr. of Sara Will erz Ahlen. (Illus.). 32p. (J). (gr. k-3). 14.95 o.p. (*1-55858-393-9*); 15.50 o.p. (*1-55858-394-7*) North-South Bks., Inc.

Von Hippel, Ursula. Toute Ma Famille. 1967. (Illus.). (J). (gr. k-3). 3.49 o.p. (*0-698-30373-3*) Putnam Publishing Group, The.

Vulliamy, Clara. Ellen & Penguin & the New Baby. 1997. (Illus.). 32p. (J). (ps-k). reprint ed. bds. 5.99 o.p. (*0-7636-0268-X*) Candlewick Pr.

Waber, Bernard. Funny, Funny Lyle. 2002. (Lyle the Crocodile Ser.). (Illus.). (J). 14.74 (*0-7587-2559-0*) Book Wholesalers, Inc.

—Funny, Funny Lyle. 1987. (Lyle Ser.). (Illus.). 40p. (J). (ps-3). lib. bdg., tchr. ed. 16.00 (*0-395-43619-2*) Houghton Mifflin Co.

—Funny, Funny Lyle. 1991. (Lyle Ser.). (Illus.). 40p. (J). (ps-3). pap. 6.95 (*0-395-60287-4*) Houghton Mifflin Co. Trade & Reference Div.

—Funny, Funny Lyle. 1987. (Lyle Ser.). (J). (ps-3). 12.10 (*0-606-16122-8*) Turtleback Bks.

—Goodbye, Funny Dumpy-Lumpy, 001. 1977. (Illus.). (J). (gr. 1-4). 6.95 o.p. (*0-395-24735-7*) Houghton Mifflin Co.

Waddell, Martin. Little Obie & the Kidnap. 1994. (Illus.). 80p. (J). (gr. 3-6). 14.95 o.p. (*1-56402-352-4*) Candlewick Pr.

—Night Night, Cuddly Bear. 2000. (Illus.). 32p. (J). (ps-3). 14.99 o.p. (*0-7636-1195-6*) Candlewick Pr.

—Once There Were Giants. (Illus.). 32p. (J). (ps-3). 1997. reprint ed. bds. 5.99 o.s.i (*0-7636-0286-8*); 2nd ed. 1995. 15.99 o.p. (*1-56402-612-4*) Candlewick Pr.

—Tango's Baby. 1995. 207p. (YA). (gr. 9-12). 16.95 o.p. (*1-56402-615-9*) Candlewick Pr.

Wagener, Gerda. A Mouse in the House! Lanning, Rosemary, tr. 1995. (Illus.). 47p. (J). (gr. 2-4). 15.50 o.p. (*1-55858-507-9*); (ps-3). 13.95 o.p. (*1-55858-506-0*) North-South Bks., Inc.

Waggoner, Karen. Dad Gummit & Ma Foot. 1990. (Illus.). 32p. (J). (ps-3). 14.95 o.p. (*0-531-05891-3*); mass mkt. 14.99 o.p. (*0-531-08491-4*) Scholastic, Inc. (Orchard Bks.).

Wahl, Jan. More Room for the Pipkins. 1983. (Illus.). 29p. (J). (ps-3). lib. bdg. o.p. (*0-13-601146-2*) Prentice-Hall.

Wake up, Jeff! the Wiggles. 2004. (Wiggles Ser.). 12p. bds. 8.99 (*0-448-43528-4*, Grosset & Dunlap) Penguin Putnam Bks. for Young Readers.

Walker, Barbara M., ed. The Little House Diary. 1985. (Illus.). 160p. (J). (ps up). pap. 9.95 o.p. (*0-06-446006-1*) HarperCollins Children's Bk. Group.

Walker, Diana. Mother Wants a Horse. 1978. 186p. (J). lib. bdg. 6.79 o.p. (*0-200-00181-7*) Criterion Bks., Inc.

Walker, Mary A. Brad's Box. 1988. 128p. (J). (gr. 6-9). lib. bdg. 13.95 o.s.i (*0-689-31426-4*, Atheneum) Simon & Schuster Children's Publishing.

The Walkman. 1995. (Young Dragon Readers 3 Ser.). (J). pap. text (*962-359-536-0*) Addison-Wesley Longman, Inc.

Wallace, Bill. Eye of the Great Bear. 1999. 176p. (J). (gr. 3-6). pap. 4.99 (*0-671-02502-3*, Aladdin); (Illus.). 16.00 (*0-671-02504-X*, Simon & Schuster Children's Publishing) Simon & Schuster Children's Publishing.

—Eye of the Great Bear. 1999. (J). 11.04 (*0-606-19050-3*) Turtleback Bks.

—True Friends. 1996. 176p. (J). (gr. 4-7). pap. 3.99 (*0-671-53036-4*, Aladdin) Simon & Schuster Children's Publishing.

—True Friends. 1996. (J). 10.04 (*0-606-09994-8*) Turtleback Bks.

Wallace, Ian & Wood, Angela. The Sandwich. 1975. (Illus.). 80p. (J). pap. (*0-919964-02-8*) Kids Can Pr., Ltd.

Wallace, Karen. Colour Young Puffin Developing Reader's Freaky Families. (Illus.). 64p. (J). pap. 7.95 (*0-14-038499-5*) Penguin Bks., Ltd. GBR. *Dist:* Trafalgar Square.

Wallace, Rich. Losing Is Not an Option: Stories. 2003. 144p. (YA). (gr. 5-9). 15.95 (*0-375-81351-9*); lib. bdg. 17.99 (*0-375-91351-3*) Knopf, Alfred A. Inc.

Wallner, Alexandra. An Alcott Family Christmas. 1996. (Illus.). 32p. (J). (gr. k-3). tchr. ed. 15.95 (*0-8234-1265-2*) Holiday Hse., Inc.

Walter, Mildred Pitts. Justin & the Best Biscuits in the World. 2002. (Illus.). (J). 13.40 (*0-7587-0371-6*) Book Wholesalers, Inc.

—Justin & the Best Biscuits in the World. 1986. (Illus.). 128p. (J). (gr. 4-7). 15.95 (*0-688-06645-3*) HarperCollins Children's Bk. Group.

—Justin & the Best Biscuits in the World. 1995. (Illus.). (J). (gr. 4). 9.00 (*0-395-73245-X*) Houghton Mifflin Co.

—Justin & the Best Biscuits in the World. 1999. (Illus.). 128p. (J). (gr. 3-5). pap. 4.99 (*0-679-89448-9*) Knopf, Alfred A. Inc.

—Justin & the Best Biscuits in the World. 1986. (J). 11.04 (*0-606-04714-X*) Turtleback Bks.

—Mariah Keeps Cool. 1990. 144p. (J). (gr. 3-7). lib. bdg. 15.00 (*0-02-792295-2*, Simon & Schuster Children's Publishing) Simon & Schuster Children's Publishing.

—Mariah Loves Rock. 1988. 128p. (J). (gr. 3-7). lib. bdg. 13.95 o.p. (*0-02-792511-0*, Simon & Schuster Children's Publishing) Simon & Schuster Children's Publishing.

Walton, Marilyn J. Those Terrible Terwilliger Twins. 1985. (Family Bks.). (Illus.). 32p. (J). (gr. 3-6). lib. bdg. 14.65 o.p. (*0-940742-39-X*) Raintree Pubs.

Walton, Rick. Bunny Day. 2002. (Illus.). 32p. (J). (gr. 2 up). 15.95 (*0-06-029183-4*); (ps up). lib. bdg. 16.89 (*0-06-029184-2*) HarperCollins Children's Bk. Group.

—Bunny Xmas. 2003. (J). 15.99 (*0-06-008415-4*); (Illus.). lib. bdg. 16.89 (*0-06-008416-2*) HarperCollins Pubs.

Wangerin, Walter, Jr. Thistle. 1983. (Illus.). 48p. (J). (gr. 2-4). lib. bdg. 11.89 o.p. (*0-06-026352-0*) HarperCollins Children's Bk. Group.

Warburg, Sandol Stoddard. Hooray for Us, 001. 1970. (Illus.). 48p. (J). (gr. 1-3). 1.95 o.p. (*0-395-10927-2*); 2.20 o.p. (*0-395-10928-0*) Houghton Mifflin Co.

Wardlaw, Lee. 101 Ways to Bug Your Parents. (gr. 4-7). 1999. (J). pap. 14.89 (*0-8037-1902-7*); 1996. 208p. (YA). 16.99 (*0-8037-1901-9*) Penguin Putnam Bks. for Young Readers. (Dial Bks. for Young Readers).

Warner, Gertrude Chandler. The Boxcar Children. Date not set. (Boxcar Children Ser.: No. 1). (J). (gr. 2-5). lib. bdg. 18.95 (*0-8488-1712-5*) Amereon, Ltd.

—The Boxcar Children. 1977. (Boxcar Children Ser.: No. 1). (J). (gr. 2-5). 10.00 (*0-606-04176-1*) Turtleback Bks.

—The Boxcar Children. 1942. (Boxcar Children Ser.: No. 1). (J). (gr. 2-5). reprint ed. lib. bdg. 13.95 (*0-8075-0851-9*); (Illus.). 154p. pap. 3.95 (*0-8075-0852-7*) Whitman, Albert & Co.

—The Boxcar Children Vol. 1-4: The Boxcar Children; Surprise Island; The Yellow House Mystery; Mystery Ranch. 1942. (Boxcar Children Ser.). (J). (gr. 2-5). reprint ed. pap. 15.80 (*0-8075-0854-3*) Whitman, Albert & Co.

—The Boxcar Children Vol. 5-8: Mike's Mystery; Blue Bay Mystery; The Woodshed Mystery; The Lighthouse Mystery. 1942. (Boxcar Children Ser.). (J). (gr. 2-5). reprint ed. pap. 15.80 (*0-8075-0857-8*) Whitman, Albert & Co.

—The Mystery of the Midnight Dog. 2001. (Boxcar Children Ser.). (Illus.). (J). 10.00 (*0-606-21080-6*) Turtleback Bks.

—The Mystery of the Screech Owl. 2001. (Boxcar Children Special Ser.). (Illus.). (J). 10.00 (*0-606-21085-7*) Turtleback Bks.

Warner, Gertrude Chandler, creator. Meet the Boxcar Children. 1998. (Adventures of Benny & Watch: No. 1). (J). (gr. 1-3). 10.10 (*0-606-13215-5*) Turtleback Bks.

Warner, Sally. Sister Split. 2001. (American Girls Collection Ser.). 156p. (J). 14.95 (*1-58485-373-5*); pap. 5.95 (*1-58485-372-7*) Pleasant Co. Pubns. (American Girl).

—Some Friend. 1997. 160p. (J). (gr. 3-9). pap. 4.99 o.s.i (*0-679-87619-7*) Random Hse., Inc.

—Some Friend. 1997. 10.09 o.p. (*0-606-11857-8*) Turtleback Bks.

Wash Day Mix-Up. 2001. (Noddy Soft Tabs Ser.). (Illus.). 10p. (J). (ps). bds. 7.99 (*1-57584-719-1*, Reader's Digest Children's Bks.) Reader's Digest Children's Publishing, Inc.

Watson, Kim. Just Like Dad. 2001. (Little Bill Ser.). (Illus.). 32p. (J). (gr. k-3). pap. 5.99 (*0-689-83999-5*, Simon Spotlight/Nickelodeon) Simon & Schuster Children's Publishing.

—Just Like Dad. 2001. (Little Bill Books for Beginning Readers Ser.). (Illus.). (J). 12.14 (*0-606-21276-0*) Turtleback Bks.

Watson, Wendy. Thanksgiving at Our House. 1991. (Illus.). 32p. (J). (ps-1). 14.95 o.p. (*0-395-53626-X*, Clarion Bks.) Houghton Mifflin Co. Trade & Reference Div.

Watts, Margaret. Trouble with Hairgrow. 1994. (Illus.). (J). 4.25 (*0-383-03782-4*) SRA/McGraw-Hill.

Waugh, Sylvia. The Mennyms. (Illus.). (gr. 5-7). 1994. 32p. (YA). 16.00 (*0-688-13070-4*, Greenwillow Bks.); 1995. 224p. (J). reprint ed. pap. 4.99 (*0-380-72528-2*, Harper Trophy) HarperCollins Children's Bk. Group.

—The Mennyms. 1995. (J). 11.04 (*0-606-07858-4*) Turtleback Bks.

—Mennyms in the Wilderness. 1995. (Illus.). 32p. (YA). (ps-3). 15.00 o.s.i (*0-688-13820-9*, Greenwillow Bks.) HarperCollins Children's Bk. Group.

—Mennyms in the Wilderness. 1996. 272p. (J). (gr. 5-7). mass mkt. 4.50 (*0-380-72529-0*, Avon Bks.) Morrow/Avon.

—Mennyms in the Wilderness. 1996. (J). 10.55 (*0-606-08821-0*) Turtleback Bks.

—Mennyms under Seige. 1997. 256p. (J). (gr. 5-7). pap. 4.50 (*0-380-72584-3*, Harper Trophy) HarperCollins Children's Bk. Group.

—Mennyms under Siege. 1996. 224p. (J). (gr. 3-7). 16.00 o.p. (*0-688-14372-5*, Greenwillow Bks.) HarperCollins Children's Bk. Group.

—Mennyms under Siege. 1997. 10.55 (*0-606-11617-6*) Turtleback Bks.

Wayland, April Halprin. It's Not My Turn to Look for Grandma. 1995. (Illus.). 132p. (J). 15.00 o.s.i (*0-679-84491-0*) Knopf, Alfred A. Inc.

—It's Not My Turn to Look for Grandma. 1995. (Illus.). (J). 15.99 o.s.i (*0-679-94491-5*) Knopf, Alfred A. Inc.

Weatherford, Carole Boston. Me & My Family Tree. 1996. (Illus.). 12p. (J). (ps-k). bds. 5.95 (*0-86316-251-7*) Writers & Readers Publishing, Inc.

Weatherly, Lee. Child X. 2003. 224p. (gr. 4-9). pap. text 5.50 (*0-440-41904-2*, Dell Books for Young Readers) Random Hse. Children's Bks.

Weathers, Anah D. Secrets of the Cave. unabr. ed. 2000. (Treasures from the Past Ser.). (Illus.). x, 104p. (J). (gr. 4-8). pap. 7.98 (*0-9702584-0-2*) Creative Services.

Weber, Judith E. Lights, Camera, Cats! 1984. (Illus.). (J). (gr. 4-6). pap. (*0-671-46858-8*, Simon Pulse) Simon & Schuster Children's Publishing.

Weber, Lenora Mattingly. Beany Has a Secret Life. 1955. (J). (gr. 5 up). 10.95 o.p. (*0-690-12384-1*) HarperCollins Children's Bk. Group.

—Beany Has a Secret Life. 1999. (Beany Malone Ser.). 296p. (J). pap. 12.95 (*0-9639607-7-6*) Image Cascade Publishing.

—Beany Malone. 1948. (J). (gr. 5 up). o.p. (*0-690-12455-4*) HarperCollins Children's Bk. Group.

—A Bright Star Falls. 1959. (J). (gr. 5 up). 10.95 o.p. (*0-690-16005-4*) HarperCollins Children's Bk. Group.

—A Bright Star Falls. 1999. (Beany Malone Ser.). 278p. (J). reprint ed. pap. 12.95 (*1-930009-01-1*) Image Cascade Publishing.

—Come Back, Wherever You Are. 1969. (YA). (gr. 7 up). 14.95 o.p. (*0-690-20123-0*) HarperCollins Children's Bk. Group.

—Come Back, Wherever You Are. 1999. (Beany Malone Ser.). 259p. (J). pap. 12.95 (*1-930009-06-2*) Image Cascade Publishing.

—Don't Call Me Katie Rose. 1964. (J). (gr. 5 up). 13.75 (*0-690-24241-7*) HarperCollins Children's Bk. Group.

—New & Different Summer. 1966. (J). (gr. 5 up). 13.50 o.p. (*0-690-58040-1*) HarperCollins Children's Bk. Group.

Weddle, Ferris. Tall Like a Pine. 1974. (Illus.). 128p. (gr. 4-7). 5.95 o.p. (*0-8075-7757-X*) Whitman, Albert & Co.

Weedn, Flavia M. Flavia & the Dream Maker. 1999. (Illus.). 48p. (J). (ps-3). 14.95 (*0-7683-2102-6*) CEDCO Publishing.

Weinberg, Lawrence. The Forgetfuls Give a Wedding. 1984. (Illus.). 40p. (Orig.). (J). (ps-3). pap. 1.95 o.p. (*0-590-31716-4*) Scholastic, Inc.

Weiss, Ellen. Peek-a-Boo! 2000. (Fisher-Price First Steps Ser.). (Illus.). 12p. (ps up). bds. 6.99 (*1-57584-391-9*, Reader's Digest Children's Bks.) Reader's Digest Children's Publishing, Inc.

—Voting Rights Days. 2002. (Hitty's Travels Ser.: No. 3). (Illus.). 64p. (J). pap. 3.99 (*0-689-84912-5*, Aladdin) Simon & Schuster Children's Publishing.

Weiss, Ellen & Lucas, Margeaux. The Nose Knows. 2002. (Science Solves It! Ser.). (Illus.). 32p. (J). 4.99 (*1-57565-120-3*) Kane Pr., The.

Welber, Robert. The Train. 1972. (Illus.). (J). (gr. 1-4). lib. bdg. 5.99 o.p. (*0-394-92430-4*, Pantheon) Knopf Publishing Group.

Wells, Rosemary. Julieta Estate Quieta. Orig. Title: Noisy Nora. (SPA.). 43p. (J). 5.50 (*84-372-1523-4*) Santillana USA Publishing Co., Inc.

—Max & Ruby's Busy Week. 2002. (Sticker Stories Ser.). 16p. (J). mass mkt. 4.99 (*0-448-42853-9*) Penguin Putnam Bks. for Young Readers.

—McDuff & the Baby. 1996. (Illus.). 24p. (J). (ps-k). pap. 4.99 (*0-7868-1191-9*) Hyperion Paperbacks for Children.

—Noisy Nora. 1997. (Illus.). 32p. (J). 15.99 o.s.i (*0-8037-1835-7*); 15.89 o.s.i (*0-8037-1836-5*) Penguin Putnam Bks. for Young Readers. (Dial Bks. for Young Readers).

—None of the Above. 1974. 192p. (J). (gr. 8 up). 5.95 o.p. (*0-8037-6148-1*, Dial Bks. for Young Readers) Penguin Putnam Bks. for Young Readers.

—Nora la Revoltosa. 1997. (SPA., Illus.). 32p. (J). 15.99 o.p. (*0-8037-2065-3*, Dial Bks. for Young Readers) Penguin Putnam Bks. for Young Readers.

—Unfortunately Harriet. (Illus.). 32p. (J). (ps-3). 1985. 4.95 o.p. (*0-8037-9168-2*); 1972. 4.58 o.p. (*0-8037-9169-0*) Penguin Putnam Bks. for Young Readers. (Dial Bks. for Young Readers).

Weltner, Linda. Beginning to Feel the Magic. 1981. 168p. (J). (gr. 6 up). 8.95 o.p. (*0-316-93052-0*) Little Brown & Co.

Weninger, Brigitte, pseud. Dany, Mira lo Que Has Hecho! Petit, Susana, tr. from GER. 1999. (SPA., Illus.). 32p. (J). (gr. k-3). 15.95 (*0-7358-1075-3*, NSB753, Ediciones Norte-Sur); pap. 6.95 (*0-7358-1076-1*) North-South Bks., Inc.

—Dany, Mira lo Que Has Hecho! 1999. 13.10 (*0-606-17631-4*) Turtleback Bks.

—What Have You Done, Davy? 1996. (Illus.). 32p. (J). (gr. k-3). 15.95 (*1-55858-581-8*); lib. bdg. 16.50 (*1-55858-582-6*) North-South Bks., Inc.

Werlin, Nancy. Are You Alone on Purpose? 1995. (J). (gr. 7 up). mass mkt. 4.50 o.s.i (*0-449-70445-9*, Fawcett) Ballantine Bks.

—Are You Alone on Purpose? 1994. 208p. (YA). (gr. 7-7). tchr. ed. 16.00 (*0-395-67350-X*) Houghton Mifflin Co.

Wesley, Mary. Haphazard House. Date not set. (Sky Bks.). pap. text 54.75 (*0-582-08108-4*) Addison-Wesley Longman, Ltd. GBR. *Dist:* Trans-Atlantic Pubns., Inc.

—Haphazard House. 1993. 156p. (YA). (gr. 7 up). 14.95 (*0-87951-470-1*) Overlook Pr., The.

West, Jerry. Happy Hollisters. 1979. (Happy Hollisters Ser.: No. 1). (Illus.). (J). (gr. 2-6). reprint ed. 2.95 o.p. (*0-448-16870-7*) Putnam Publishing Group, The.

—The Happy Hollisters & the Ice Carnival Mystery. 1979. (Happy Hollisters Ser.: No. 4). (Illus.). (J). (gr. 1-5). reprint ed. 2.95 o.p. (*0-448-16873-1*) Putnam Publishing Group, The.

—The Happy Hollisters at Sea Gull Beach. 1979. (Happy Hollisters Ser.: No. 3). (Illus.). (J). (gr. 1-5). reprint ed. 2.95 o.p. (*0-448-16872-3*) Putnam Publishing Group, The.

—Happy Hollisters on a River Trip. 1979. (Happy Hollisters Ser.: No. 2). (Illus.). (J). (gr. 1-5). reprint ed. 2.95 o.p. (*0-448-16871-5*) Putnam Publishing Group, The.

West, Tracey. Cubix Tattoo Book: Connor's Guide to Bubble Town. 2002. 24p. (J). (ps). mass mkt. 4.99 (*0-439-38056-1*) Scholastic, Inc.

Westall, Robert. A Place for Me. 1994. (J). 13.95 (*0-590-47747-1*) Scholastic, Inc.

Weston, Carol. The Diary of Melanie Martin: How I Survived Matt the Brat, Michelangelo & the Leaning Tower of Pizza. 2000. (Illus.). 160p. (gr. 3-5). lib. bdg. 17.99 o.s.i (*0-375-90509-X*, Knopf Bks. for Young Readers) Random Hse. Children's Bks.

—The Diary of Melanie Martin: Or How I Survived Matt the Brat, Michelangelo & the Leaning Tower of Pizza. (Illus.). 160p. (gr. 3-7). 2001. pap. text 4.99 (*0-440-41667-1*, Yearling); 2000. text 15.95 o.s.i (*0-375-80509-5*, Knopf Bks. for Young Readers) Random Hse. Children's Bks.

—With Love from Spain, Melanie Martin. 2004. (Illus.). 256p. (J). (gr. 3-7). 15.95 (*0-375-82646-7*); lib. bdg. 17.99 (*0-375-92646-1*) Random Hse. Children's Bks. (Knopf Bks. for Young Readers).

Weston, Martha. Act I, Act II, Act Normal. 2003. 160p. (gr. 5-9). lib. bdg. 22.90 (*0-7613-2859-9*); (YA). 15.95 (*0-7613-1779-1*) Millbrook Pr., Inc. (Roaring Brook Pr.).

Weston, Tamson. Hey, Pancakes! 2003. (Illus.). 32p. (J). 16.00 (*0-15-216502-9*) Harcourt Trade Pubs.

Wetter, Bruce. The Boy with the Lampshade on His Head. 2004. (J). (*0-689-85032-8*, Atheneum) Simon & Schuster Children's Publishing.

Relationships

Weyn, Suzanne. Ask Miss Know-It-All. 2000. (Full House Sisters Ser.: No. 10). (Illus.). 144p. (J). (gr. 4-6). pap. 3.99 (*0-671-04090-1*, Aladdin) Simon & Schuster Children's Publishing.

Whelan, Gloria. Farewell to the Island. 208p. (gr. 4 up). 1999. (Illus.). (YA). pap. 5.99 (*0-06-440821-3*, Harper Trophy); 1998. (J). 16.95 (*0-06-027751-3*) HarperCollins Children's Bk. Group.

—Fruitlands: Louisa May Alcott Made Perfect. 2002. 128p. (J). (gr. 5-7). lib. bdg. 17.89 (*0-06-623816-1*) HarperCollins Children's Bk. Group.

—Fruitlands: Louisa May Alcott Made Perfect. 2002. 128p. (J). (gr. 4-7). 15.99 (*0-06-623815-3*) HarperCollins Pubs.

When I Go. 2003. (Illus.). (J). bds. 7.98 (*0-7525-8657-2*) Parragon, Inc.

White, Jack N. The Canebrake Kids: The Trip to Texas. 1996. (Illus.). 120p. (J). (gr. 4-6). 12.95 o.p. (*1-57168-111-6*) Eakin Pr.

Whitney, Kim Ablon. See You down the Road: A Novel. 2004. (J). (gr. 7). 192p. 15.95 (*0-375-82467-7*); 176p. lib. bdg. 17.99 (*0-375-92467-1*) Random Hse. Children's Bks. (Knopf Bks. for Young Readers).

Wickham, Martha. A Golden Age: The Golden Age of Radio. 1996. (Smithsonian Odyssey Ser.). (Illus.). 32p. (J). (gr. 2-5). 19.95 incl. audio (*1-56899-373-0*, BC6004); (gr. 4-7). 14.95 (*1-56899-371-4*); (gr. 4-7). pap. 5.95 (*1-56899-372-2*);Incl. toy. (gr. 2-5). 29.95 (*1-56899-375-7*);Incl. toy. (gr. 2-5). pap. 17.95 (*1-56899-376-5*) Soundprints.

Wickstrom, Lois. Oliver: A Story about Adoption. 1991. (Illus.). 32p. (J). 14.95 (*0-9611872-5-5*) Our Child Pr.

Wiggins, Evelyn M. Jake's First Year. 1998. (Illus.). 48p. (J). pap. 4.95 o.p. (*1-56167-419-2*) American Literary Pr., Inc.

Wikler, Linda. Alfonse, Where Are You? 1998. (J). 13.14 (*0-606-13113-2*) Turtleback Bks.

Wilcox, Jessie. Pisces Times 2. 1985. (Zodiac Club Ser.). 160p. (Orig.). (YA). (gr. 7 up). 2.25 (*0-448-47731-9*) Putnam Publishing Group, The.

Wild, Margaret. One Night. 2004. 240p. (J). (gr. 7). 15.95 (*0-375-82920-2*); lib. bdg. 17.99 (*0-375-92920-7*) Random Hse. Children's Bks. (Knopf Bks. for Young Readers).

Wilder, Laura Ingalls. Christmas in the Big Woods. (My First Little House Bks.). (Illus.). (J). (ps-1). 1996. 80p. 3.25 o.p. (*0-694-00877-X*, Harper Festival); 1995. 40p. 14.99 (*0-06-024752-5*); 1995. 40p. lib. bdg. 12.89 o.p. (*0-06-024753-3*) HarperCollins Children's Bk. Group.

—Christmas in the Big Woods. 1995. (My First Little House Bks.). (Illus.). (J). (ps-1). 12.10 (*0-606-10772-X*) Turtleback Bks.

—Dance at Grandpa's. 1994. (My First Little House Bks.). (Illus.). 40p. (J). (ps-1). lib. bdg. 11.89 o.p. (*0-06-023879-8*); 12.95 o.p. (*0-06-023878-X*) HarperCollins Children's Bk. Group.

—The Deer in the Wood. (My First Little House Bks.). (Illus.). (J). (ps-3). 1999. 32p. pap. 5.99 (*0-06-443498-2*, Harper Trophy); 1996. 32p. pap. 3.25 (*0-694-00879-6*, Harper Festival); 1995. 40p. 11.95 o.p. (*0-06-024881-5*); 1995. 40p. lib. bdg. 11.89 o.p. (*0-06-024882-3*) HarperCollins Children's Bk. Group.

—The Deer in the Wood. (My First Little House Bks.). 1999. 12.10 (*0-606-15841-3*); 1996. (Illus.). (J). 8.20 o.p. (*0-606-10780-0*) Turtleback Bks.

—Farmer Boy. (Little House Ser.). (J). 2003. 304p. pap. 5.99 (*0-06-052238-0*); 1953. (Illus.). 384p. (gr. 5 up). pap. 6.99 (*0-06-440003-4*, Harper Trophy); 1953. (Illus.). 384p. (gr. 5 up). 16.99 (*0-06-026425-X*); 1953. (Illus.). 384p. (gr. 5 up). lib. bdg. 17.89 (*0-06-026421-7*) HarperCollins Children's Bk. Group.

—Farmer Boy. l.t. ed. 2000. (Little House Ser.). (Illus.). 400p. (J). (gr. 3-6). lib. bdg. 33.95 (*1-58118-079-9*, 24071) LRS.

—Farmer Boy. 9999. (Little House Ser.). (J). (gr. 3-6). pap. 1.75 o.s.i (*0-590-32787-9*) Scholastic, Inc.

—Farmer Boy. 1971. (Little House Ser.). 12.00 (*0-606-03209-6*) Turtleback Bks.

—A Farmer Boy Christmas. 1999. (My First Little House Bks.). (Illus.). (J). (ps-1). 12.95 (*0-06-025940-X*); lib. bdg. 12.89 (*0-06-025941-8*) HarperCollins Pubs.

—Going to Town. (My First Little House Bks.). (Illus.). (J). (ps-1). 1997. 12p. 3.25 (*0-694-00955-5*, Harper Festival); 1996. 32p. pap. 5.95 (*0-06-443452-4*, Harper Trophy); 1995. 40p. 11.95 o.p. (*0-06-023012-6*); 1995. 40p. lib. bdg. 11.89 o.p. (*0-06-023013-4*) HarperCollins Children's Bk. Group.

—Going to Town. 1995. (My First Little House Bks.). (Illus.). (J). (ps-1). 12.10 (*0-606-09335-4*) Turtleback Bks.

—Laura's Ma. 1999. (Little House Chapter Bks.: No. 11). (J). (gr. 3-6). 10.40 (*0-606-15839-1*) Turtleback Bks.

—Laura's Pa. 1999. (Little House Ser.: No. 12). (Illus.). 80p. (J). (gr. 3-6). pap. 4.25 (*0-06-442082-5*, Harper Trophy) HarperCollins Children's Bk. Group.

—Laura's Pa. 1999. (Little House Chapter Bks.: No. 12). (J). (gr. 3-6). 10.40 (*0-606-15840-5*) Turtleback Bks.

—A Little House Birthday. 1997. (My First Little House Bks.). (Illus.). 40p. (J). (ps-3). 13.99 (*0-06-025928-0*) HarperCollins Children's Bk. Group.

—A Little House Christmas: Holiday Stories from the Little House Books. 1994. (Little House Ser.). (Illus.). (J). (gr. 3-6). 96p. lib. bdg. 18.89 o.p. (*0-06-024270-1*); 80p. 18.95 o.p. (*0-06-024269-8*) HarperCollins Children's Bk. Group.

—The Little House Collection, 9 bks., Set. 2003. (YA). pap. 49.99 (*0-06-052996-2*, Avon Bks.) Morrow/Avon.

—Little House "History Comes to Life" Event Kit. 2000. (J). (*0-06-028839-6*) HarperCollins Children's Bk. Group.

—Little House in the Big Woods. (Little House Ser.). (J). 2003. 176p. pap. 5.99 (*0-06-052236-4*); 1953. (Illus.). 256p. (gr. 3-6). pap. 6.99 (*0-06-440001-8*, Harper Trophy); 1953. (Illus.). 256p. (gr. 3-6). 16.99 (*0-06-026430-6*); 1953. (Illus.). 256p. (gr. 3-6). lib. bdg. 17.89 (*0-06-026431-4*) HarperCollins Children's Bk. Group.

—Little House in the Big Woods. l.t. ed. 1987. (Little House Ser.). 161p. (J). (gr. 3-6). reprint ed. lib. bdg. 14.95 o.p. (*1-85089-913-4*) ISIS Large Print Bks. GBR. *Dist:* Transaction Pubs.

—Little House in the Big Woods. l.t. ed. 2000. (Little House Ser.). (Illus.). 244p. (J). (gr. 3-6). lib. bdg. 28.95 (*1-58118-078-0*, 24070) LRS.

—Little House in the Big Woods. 2003. audio compact disk 25.95 (*0-06-054398-1*, HarperEntertainment); 1990. (J). (gr. 3-6). pap. 3.50 o.p. (*0-06-107005-X*, HarperTorch) Morrow/Avon.

—Little House in the Big Woods. 1971. (Little House). (J). (gr. 3-6). 12.00 (*0-606-03811-6*) Turtleback Bks.

—Little House in the Big Woods A Special Read Aloud Edition. 2001. (Little House Ser.). (Illus.). 256p. (J). (gr. k-4). 19.95 (*0-06-029647-X*) HarperCollins Children's Bk. Group.

—Little House in the Big Woods A Special Read Aloud Edition. 2001. (Little House Ser.). (Illus.). 256p. (J). (gr. 3-5). lib. bdg. 19.89 (*0-06-029648-8*) HarperCollins Pubs.

—Little House on the Prairie. 2003. audio compact disk 25.95 (*0-06-054399-X*, Access Pr.) HarperInformation.

—Little House on the Prairie. 1981. (Little House). (J). (gr. 3-6). 12.00 (*0-606-03812-4*) Turtleback Bks.

—Little House Sisters: Collected Stories from the Little House Books. 1997. (Little House Ser.). (Illus.). 96p. (J). (gr. 3-7). 19.95 (*0-06-027587-1*) HarperCollins Children's Bk. Group.

—A Little Prairie House. (My First Little House Bks.). (Illus.). (J). (ps-3). 1999. 32p. pap. 5.99 (*0-06-443526-1*, Harper Trophy); 1998. 40p. 14.99 (*0-06-025907-8*); 1998. 40p. lib. bdg. 13.89 (*0-06-025908-6*) HarperCollins Children's Bk. Group.

—A Little Prairie House. 1998. (My First Little House Bks.). 12.10 (*0-606-16687-4*) Turtleback Bks.

—The Long Winter. (Little House Ser.). (J). 2003. 368p. pap. 5.99 (*0-06-052241-0*); 1953. (Illus.). 352p. (gr. 3-7). pap. 6.99 (*0-06-440006-9*, Harper Trophy); 1953. (Illus.). 352p. (gr. k-3). lib. bdg. 17.89 (*0-06-026461-6*); 1953. (Illus.). 352p. (ps-2). 16.99 (*0-06-026460-8*) HarperCollins Children's Bk. Group.

—The Long Winter. l.t. ed. 2002. (LRS Large Print Cornerstone Ser.). (Illus.). (J). lib. bdg. 35.95 (*1-58118-100-0*) LRS.

—The Long Winter. 1995. (Little House Ser.). (J). (gr. 3-6). pap. 2.50 (*0-590-30094-6*) Scholastic, Inc.

—The Long Winter. 1981. (Little House Ser.). (J). (gr. 3-6). 12.00 (*0-606-03846-9*) Turtleback Bks.

—My Little House Book of Family. 1998. (My First Little House Bks.). (Illus.). (J). (ps). lib. bdg. (*0-06-025989-2*) HarperCollins Children's Bk. Group.

—My Little House 123. 1997. (My First Little House Bks.). (Illus.). 24p. (J). (ps). 7.95 o.p. (*0-06-025986-8*); lib. bdg. 7.89 o.p. (*0-06-025987-6*) HarperCollins Children's Bk. Group.

—On the Banks of Plum Creek. 2003. 96p. audio compact disk 25.95 (*0-06-054400-7*, Access Pr.) HarperInformation.

—Prairie Day. 1997. (My First Little House Bks.). (Illus.). 40p. (J). (ps-1). lib. bdg. 11.89 o.p. (*0-06-025906-X*); 12.95 o.p. (*0-06-025905-1*) HarperCollins Children's Bk. Group.

—Santa Comes to Little House. 2001. (Little House Picture Bks.). (Illus.). 32p. (J). (ps-3). 15.95 (*0-06-025938-8*); lib. bdg. 15.89 (*0-06-025939-6*) HarperCollins Children's Bk. Group.

—Winter Days in the Big Woods. 1994. (My First Little House Bks.). (Illus.). 40p. (J). (ps-1). lib. bdg. 11.89 o.p. (*0-06-023022-3*); 12.00 (*0-06-023014-2*) HarperCollins Children's Bk. Group.

—Winter on the Farm. 1996. (My First Little House Bks.). (Illus.). 40p. (J). (ps-1). lib. bdg. 11.89 o.p. (*0-06-027170-1*); 12.95 o.p. (*0-06-027169-8*) HarperCollins Children's Bk. Group.

Wilder, Laura Ingalls & Graef, Renee. My Little House Book of Family. 1998. (My First Little House Bks.). (Illus.). 24p. (J). (ps). 7.95 o.p. (*0-06-025988-4*) HarperCollins Pubs.

Wilder, Thornton. Our Town. 1971. (Keith Jennison Large Type Bks.). (gr. 7 up). 9.95 o.p. (*0-531-00315-9*, Watts, Franklin) Scholastic Library Publishing.

Wiley, Melissa. Charlotte Novel, No. 4. 2004. (J). pap. (*0-06-440740-3*) HarperCollins Pubs.

—The Far Side of the Loch. (Little House). (Illus.). (J). (gr. 3-6). 2001. lib. bdg. (*0-06-028556-7*); 2000. 256p. pap. 5.99 (*0-06-440713-6*, Harper Trophy); 2000. 256p. 15.95 (*0-06-027984-2*); 2000. 256p. lib. bdg. 15.89 (*0-06-028203-7*) HarperCollins Children's Bk. Group.

—The Far Side of the Loch. 2000. (Little House Ser.). (Illus.). (J). 11.00 (*0-606-18689-1*) Turtleback Bks.

—Little House Chapter Book, No. 26. 2001. (J). pap. (*0-06-442112-0*, Harper Trophy) HarperCollins Children's Bk. Group.

—Little House in the Highlands. 1999. (Little House Ser.). (Illus.). (J). 288p. (gr. 3-7). pap. 5.99 (*0-06-440712-8*, Harper Trophy); 271p. (gr. 4-7). lib. bdg. 15.89 (*0-06-028202-9*) HarperCollins Children's Bk. Group.

—Little House in the Highlands. 1999. (Little House Ser.). 11.00 (*0-606-15838-3*) Turtleback Bks.

—On Tide Mill Lane, No. 2. 2001. (Little House Ser.). (Illus.). 272p. (J). (gr. k-4). 16.95 (*0-06-027013-6*); (gr. 3-7). lib. bdg. 16.89 (*0-06-027014-4*) HarperCollins Children's Bk. Group.

—The Road from Roxbury. 2002. (Little House Ser.). (Illus.). 256p. (J). 16.99 (*0-06-027019-5*); lib. bdg. 18.89 (*0-06-027020-9*) HarperCollins Children's Bk. Group.

Wiley, Melissa, et al. Little House in the Highlands. 1999. (Little House Ser.). (Illus.). 288p. (J). (gr. 3-7). 16.95 (*0-06-027983-4*) HarperCollins Children's Bk. Group.

Wilkes, Maria D. Little Clearing in the Woods. adapted ed. 1998. (Little House Ser.). (Illus.). 336p. (J). (gr. 3-7). lib. bdg. 15.89 (*0-06-026998-7*) HarperCollins Children's Bk. Group.

—Little Clearing in the Woods. 1998. (Little House Ser.). (Illus.). 336p. (J). (gr. 3-7). 15.95 (*0-06-026997-9*); pap. 5.99 (*0-06-440652-0*) HarperCollins Pubs.

—Little House in Brookfield. 1996. (Little House Ser.). (Illus.). 320p. (J). (gr. 3-7). 16.95 (*0-06-026459-4*); pap. 5.99 (*0-06-440610-5*, Harper Trophy); lib. bdg. 14.89 o.p. (*0-06-026462-4*) HarperCollins Children's Bk. Group.

—Little House in Brookfield. 1996. (Little House Ser.). (Illus.). (J). (gr. 3-6). 11.00 (*0-606-09559-4*) Turtleback Bks.

—On Top of Concord Hill. 2000. (Little House Ser.). (Illus.). 288p. (J). (gr. 3-7). 15.95 (*0-06-026999-5*); pap. 5.99 (*0-06-440689-X*, Harper Trophy); lib. bdg. 15.89 (*0-06-027003-9*) HarperCollins Children's Bk. Group.

Willard, Barbara. The Eldest Son. 1989. 192p. (J). (gr. k-12). mass mkt. 3.25 o.s.i (*0-440-20412-7*, Laurel Leaf) Random Hse. Children's Bks.

—Storm from the West. 1964. (Illus.). 189p. (J). (gr. 7 up). 5.95 o.p. (*0-15-280480-3*) Harcourt Children's Bks.

Willhoite, Michael. Uncle What-Is-It Is Coming to Visit!!! 1993. (Illus.). 32p. (J). 12.95 o.p. (*1-55583-205-9*) Alyson Pubns.

William, Kate. The Wakefields of Sweet Valley. 1991. (Sweet Valley Saga Ser.). (YA). (gr. 7 up). 10.55 (*0-606-05028-0*) Turtleback Bks.

Williams, Barbara. Michi y Su Nueva Familia. 1998. (SPA.). 136p. (gr. 6-8). (*84-239-7127-9*) Espasa Calpe, S.A.

Williams, Betty. Kalabashee: And His Sisters. 2002. 145p. (J). text 30.99 (*0-7388-6328-9*); E-Book 8.00 (*0-7388-6330-0*) Xlibris Corp.

Williams, Carol Lynch. Adeline Street. 1996. (J). 18.95 (*0-385-30998-8*, Dell Books for Young Readers); 192p. (gr. 3-7). pap. 3.99 o.s.i (*0-440-41206-4*, Yearling) Random Hse. Children's Bks.

—Adeline Street. 1996. (J). 9.09 o.p. (*0-606-08969-1*) Turtleback Bks.

—Christmas in Heaven. 2000. 171p. (J). (gr. 5-9). 16.99 o.s.i (*0-399-23436-5*, G. P. Putnam's Sons) Penguin Group (USA) Inc.

—Esther's Celebration. 1996. (Latter-Day Daughters Ser.). (Illus.). 80p. (J). (gr. 3-9). pap. 4.95 (*1-56236-507-X*) Aspen Bks.

Williams-Garcia, Rita. Like Sisters on the Homefront. 1995. 176p. (J). (gr. 7 up). 15.99 (*0-525-67465-9*, Dutton Children's Bks.) Penguin Putnam Bks. for Young Readers.

—Like Sisters on the Homefront. 1998. (J). 12.04 (*0-606-12980-4*) Turtleback Bks.

Williams, Karen Lynn. One Thing I'm Good At. 1999. 137p. (J). (gr. 3-7). 14.95 (*0-688-16846-9*) Morrow/Avon.

Williams, Kathy B. The Can Family. Newton, Beulah & Hargrove, Fred, eds. 1998. (Illus.). iii, 15p. (J). (gr. 1-3). pap. text 6.95 (*0-9665043-0-5*) Can Family, The.

Williams, Laura E. Behind the Bedroom Wall. 1996. (Illus.). (J). 184p. (gr. 4-7). pap. 6.95 (*1-57131-606-X*); 200p. (gr. 7 up). 15.95 (*1-57131-607-8*) Milkweed Editions.

—Behind the Bedroom Wall. 1996. (J). 13.00 (*0-606-13079-9*) Turtleback Bks.

Williams, Lori Aurelia. Shayla's Double Brown Baby Blues. 304p. 2003. (Illus.). (YA). pap. 7.99 (*0-689-85670-9*, Simon Pulse); 2001. (J). (gr. 7 up). 17.00 (*0-689-82469-6*, Simon & Schuster Children's Publishing) Simon & Schuster Children's Publishing.

—When Kambia Elaine Flew in from Neptune. unabr. ed. 2001. 256p. (YA). (gr. 7 up). pap. 50.00 incl. audio (*0-8072-8851-9*, Listening Library) Random Hse. Audio Publishing Group.

—When Kambia Elaine Flew in from Neptune. (Illus.). 256p. 2001. (J). pap. 10.00 (*0-689-84593-6*, Simon Pulse); 2000. (YA). (gr. 8 up). 17.00 (*0-689-82468-8*, Simon & Schuster Children's Publishing) Simon & Schuster Children's Publishing.

—When Kambia Elaine Flew in from Neptune. 2002. 16.05 (*0-606-22109-3*) Turtleback Bks.

Williams, Marian. The Fame of Zeelotee. 1983. 37p. (J). 5.95 o.p. (*0-533-05523-7*) Vantage Pr., Inc.

Williams, Sherley Anne. Working Cotton. 2002. (Illus.). (J). 14.04 (*0-7587-0168-3*) Book Wholesalers, Inc.

—Working Cotton. (Illus.). 32p. (J). 1997. pap. 7.00 (*0-15-201482-9*, Harcourt Paperbacks); 1992. 17.00 (*0-15-299624-9*) Harcourt Children's Bks.

—Working Cotton. 1997. 13.15 (*0-606-12114-5*) Turtleback Bks.

Williams, Suzanne. My Dog Never Says Please. 1997. (Illus.). 32p. (J). 14.89 o.s.i (*0-8037-1681-8*); 15.99 o.p. (*0-8037-1679-6*) Penguin Putnam Bks. for Young Readers. (Dial Bks. for Young Readers).

Williams, Vera B. A Chair for My Mother. 1982. (Illus.). 32p. (J). (ps-3). 15.99 (*0-688-00914-X*); lib. bdg. 16.89 (*0-688-00915-8*) HarperCollins Children's Bk. Group. (Greenwillow Bks.).

—A Chair for My Mother. (J). (ps-6). 1988. pap. 9.95 incl. audio (*0-688-08400-1*); 1984. (Illus.). 32p. pap. 5.99 (*0-688-04074-8*) Morrow/Avon. (Morrow, William & Co.).

—A Chair for My Mother. unabr. ed. 1991. (Picture Book Read-Along Ser.). (Illus.). 29p. (J). (gr. k-3). pap. 17.00 incl. audio (*0-8072-6031-2*, MR 24SP, Listening Library) Random Hse. Audio Publishing Group.

—A Chair for My Mother. 1988. (Reading Rainbow Bks.). (J). 12.10 (*0-606-02484-0*) Turtleback Bks.

—Lucky Song. 1997. (Illus.). 24p. (J). (ps-3). 15.99 (*0-688-14459-4*); lib. bdg. 14.89 (*0-688-14460-8*) HarperCollins Children's Bk. Group. (Greenwillow Bks.).

—Music, Music for Everyone. 1984. Tr. of iMusica para todo el mundo!. (Illus.). 32p. (J). (gr. k-3). lib. bdg. 15.93 o.p. (*0-688-02604-4*); 17.95 (*0-688-02603-6*) HarperCollins Children's Bk. Group. (Greenwillow Bks.).

—Something Special for Me. 1983. (Illus.). 32p. (J). (gr. k-3). 16.99 (*0-688-01806-8*); 15.93 o.s.i (*0-688-01807-6*) HarperCollins Children's Bk. Group. (Greenwillow Bks.).

Willis, Jeanne. Relativity, As Explained by Professor Xargle. 1994. (Professor Xargle Ser.). (Illus.). 32p. (J). (gr. 5 up). 13.99 o.p. (*0-525-45245-1*, Dutton Children's Bks.) Penguin Putnam Bks. for Young Readers.

Wilmer, Diane. Daytime. 1988. (Step by Step Bks.). (Illus.). 10p. (J). (ps). pap. 3.95 o.s.i (*0-689-71240-5*, Simon & Schuster Children's Publishing) Simon & Schuster Children's Publishing.

Wilson. Lucky Lily. 2003. (Illus.). 80p. (J). pap. (*0-330-39818-0*) Macmillan Children's Bks.

Wilson, Henry. Do Goldfish Play the Violin? unabr. ed. 2000. (Read-Along Ser.). 136p. (J). pap. 24.95 incl. audio (*0-7540-6220-1*, RA021, Chivers Children's Audio Bks.) BBC Audiobooks America.

Wilson, Jacqueline. The Bed & Breakfast Star. l.t. ed. 2000. (J). (Illus.). pap. (*0-7540-6090-X*); 242p. pap. 29.95 incl. audio (*0-7540-6231-7*, RA032, Chivers Children's Audio Bks.) BBC Audiobooks America.

—The Bed & Breakfast Star. 2000. 32p. (J). pap. 6.95 (*0-440-86324-4*, Delacorte Pr.) Dell Publishing.

—Double Act. 2000. 32p. pap. 6.95 (*0-440-86334-1*, Delacorte Pr.) Dell Publishing.

—Double Act. 1999. 10.55 (*0-606-16442-1*) Turtleback Bks.

—Elsa, Star of the Shelter! 1996. (Illus.). 208p. (J). (gr. 4-7). lib. bdg. 14.95 o.p. (*0-8075-1981-2*) Whitman, Albert & Co.

—Girls in Tears. 2003. 176p. (J). lib. bdg. 11.99 (*0-385-90104-6*); (gr. 7). 9.95 (*0-385-73082-9*) Dell Publishing. (Delacorte Pr.).

Relationships

—Girls in Tears. 2004. 192p. (YA). (gr. 7). mass mkt. 4.99 (*0-440-23807-2*, Laurel Leaf) Random Hse. Children's Bks.
—Girls Out Late. 2003. 224p. (YA). (gr. 7). mass mkt. 4.99 (*0-440-22959-6*, Laurel Leaf) Random Hse. Children's Bks.
—Girls Out Late. 2002. 224p. (YA). (gr. 7). 9.95 (*0-385-72976-6*); lib. bdg. 11.99 (*0-385-90042-2*) Random Hse., Inc.
—Girls Out Late. 2003. (Illus.). 192p. (YA). mass mkt. (*0-552-54523-6*) Transworld Publishers Ltd. GBR. *Dist:* Random Hse. of Canada, Ltd.
—Lola Rose. 2004. 99p. (J). (gr. 5). pap. (*0-552-54712-3*, Corgi) Bantam Bks.
Wilson-Max, Ken. Max. 1998. (Jump at the Sun Ser.). (Illus.). 14p. (J). (ps-k). 12.95 (*0-7868-0412-2*) Disney Pr.
Wilson, Nancy Hope. Becoming Felix, RS. 1996. 192p. (J). (gr. 3-7). 16.00 o.p. (*0-374-30664-8*, Farrar, Straus & Giroux (BYR)) Farrar, Straus & Giroux.
—The Reason for Janey. 1994. 176p. (J). (gr. 5 up). 15.00 (*0-02-793127-7*, Atheneum) Simon & Schuster Children's Publishing.
Wilson, Sarah. Big Day on the River, ERS. 2003. (Illus.). 32p. (J). (gr. k-2). 16.95 (*0-8050-6787-6*, Holt, Henry & Co. Bks. For Young Readers) Holt, Henry & Co.
Wilson, Trevor. Let's Go Fishing. 1994. (Illus.). (J). 4.25 (*0-383-03758-1*) SRA/McGraw-Hill.
Wilton, Elizabeth. Riverboat Family, RS. 1969. 224p. (J). (gr. 7 up). 3.75 o.p. (*0-374-36336-6*, Farrar, Straus & Giroux (BYR)) Farrar, Straus & Giroux.
Winans, Ruthann & Lee, Linda. Dusty's Beary Tales: Building Character with Bible Virtues. 1996. 72p. (J). (ps-4). 16.99 o.p. (*1-56507-496-3*) Harvest Hse. Pubs.
Windsor, Patricia. Home Is Where Your Feet Are Standing. 1975. 256p. (J). (gr. 5 up). lib. bdg. 8.79 o.p. (*0-06-026522-1*) HarperCollins Pubs.
Winfrey, Elizabeth. Welcome to My World. 1997. (Party of Five: No. 1). 144p. (Orig.). (J). (gr. 3-6). pap. 3.99 (*0-671-00676-2*, Aladdin) Simon & Schuster Children's Publishing.
Winn, Christine M. & Walsh, David. Clover's Secret: Helping Kids Cope with Domestic Violence. 1996. (Illus.). 32p. (J). (gr. 1-4). 14.95 o.p. (*0-925190-89-6*) Fairview Pr.
Winter, Rick & Lester, Mike. Dirty Birdy Feet. 2000. (Illus.). 32p. (J). (ps-2). 15.95 o.p. (*0-87358-768-5*, Rising Moon Bks. for Young Readers) Northland Publishing.
Winthrop, Elizabeth. I'm the Boss! 1994. (Illus.). 32p. (J). (ps-3). tchr. ed. 15.95 (*0-8234-1113-3*) Holiday Hse., Inc.
Wishing Well Staff. Night Night, God Bless. 1996. 5.99 o.p. (*0-88705-966-X*) Reader's Digest Children's Publishing, Inc.
Wittlinger, Ellen. Gracie's Girl. l.t. ed. 2002. 224p. (J). 22.95 (*0-7862-3761-9*) Gale Group.
—Gracie's Girl. (Illus.). 192p. (J). 2002. (gr. 4-7). pap. 4.99 (*0-689-84960-5*, Aladdin); 2000. (gr. 3-7). 16.95 (*0-689-82249-9*, Simon & Schuster Children's Publishing) Simon & Schuster Children's Publishing.
—Heart on My Sleeve. 2004. (YA). (*0-689-84997-4*, Simon & Schuster Children's Publishing) Simon & Schuster Children's Publishing.
Wohl, Lauren L. Christopher Davis's Best Year Yet. 1995. (Hyperion Chapters Ser.). (Illus.). 64p. (J). (ps-3). pap. 3.95 (*0-7868-1083-1*) Disney Pr.
—Christopher Davis's Best Year Yet. 1995. (Hyperion Chapters Ser.). (Illus.). 64p. (J). (ps-3). 13.95 o.p. (*0-7868-0106-9*) Hyperion Bks. for Children.
—Christopher Davis's Best Year Yet. 1995. (Hyperion Chapters Ser.). 10.10 (*0-606-09147-5*) Turtleback Bks.
Wojciechowska, Maia. Hey, What's Wrong with This One? 1969. (Illus.). 90p. (J). (gr. 3-6). lib. bdg. 12.89 o.p. (*0-06-026579-5*) HarperCollins Children's Bk. Group.
—The Hollywood Kid. 1966. (YA). (gr. 7 up). lib. bdg. 11.89 o.p. (*0-06-026573-6*) HarperCollins Children's Bk. Group.
Wojciechowski, Susan. Don't Call Me Beanhead! (Illus.). 80p. (J). (ps-4). 1996. bds. 5.99 (*1-56402-587-X*); Set. 1994. 15.99 (*1-56402-319-2*) Candlewick Pr.
—Don't Call Me Beanhead! 1996. (J). 11.14 (*0-606-08727-3*) Turtleback Bks.
Wolf, Jake. Daddy, Could I Have an Elephant? 1998. (Picture Puffin Ser.). (J). 12.14 (*0-606-13303-8*) Turtleback Bks.
Wolfe, Mary L. Jocko Comes to Stay. 1995. (Illus.). 32p. (J). pap. 3.00 (*0-7880-0683-5*, Fairway Pr.) CSS Publishing Co.
Wolff, Barbara M. Mi Abuelito y Yo. 1992. (SPA., Illus.). 16p. (J). (ps-1). lib. bdg. 13.95 (*1-879567-12-1*, Valeria Bks.) Wonder Well Pubs.
—Pappa & Me. 1991. (Illus.). 16p. (J). (ps-1). lib. bdg. 13.95 (*1-879567-11-3*, Valeria Bks.) Wonder Well Pubs.
Wolitzer, Hilma. Toby Lived Here, RS. 1986. 160p. (J). (gr. 5-11). pap. 3.45 o.p. (*0-374-47924-0*, Sunburst) Farrar, Straus & Giroux.
Wong, Janet S. The Trip Back Home. 2000. (Illus.). 32p. (J). (ps-2). 16.00 (*0-15-200784-9*) Harcourt Children's Bks.
Wood, Douglas. What Dads Can't Do. ed. 2001. (J). (gr. 1). spiral bd. (*0-616-07247-3*) Canadian National Institute for the Blind/Institut National Canadien pour les Aveugles.
Wood, Frances M. Becoming Rosemary. 1998. 256p. (gr. 7-12). pap. text 3.99 o.s.i (*0-440-41238-2*) Dell Publishing.
—Becoming Rosemary. 1997. 192p. (gr. 5-9). text 14.95 o.s.i (*0-385-32248-8*, Dell Books for Young Readers) Random Hse. Children's Bks.
Wood, June Rae. When Pigs Fly. 1995. 224p. (J). (gr. 4-7). 16.95 o.s.i (*0-399-22911-6*, G. P. Putnam's Sons) Penguin Group (USA) Inc.
—When Pigs Fly. 1997. (Illus.). 272p. (J). (gr. 3-7). pap. 5.99 (*0-698-11570-8*, PaperStar) Penguin Putnam Bks. for Young Readers.
—When Pigs Fly. 1997. 12.04 (*0-606-10990-0*) Turtleback Bks.
Woodruff, Elvira. Magnificent Mummy Maker. 1994. (J). 10.55 (*0-606-07828-2*) Turtleback Bks.
—The Magnificent Mummy Maker. 1995. 160p. (J). (gr. 4-7). 4.50 (*0-590-45743-8*) Scholastic, Inc.
Woodson, Jacqueline. If You Come Softly. 192p. (YA). (gr. 5 up). 2000. pap. 5.99 (*0-698-11862-6*); 1998. 15.99 (*0-399-23112-9*) Putnam Publishing Group, The.
—If You Come Softly. 2000. 11.04 (*0-606-17863-5*) Turtleback Bks.
—Lena. 2000. 128p. (YA). (gr. 5-9). mass mkt. 4.99 o.s.i (*0-440-22669-4*, Laurel Leaf) Random Hse. Children's Bks.
—Miracle's Boys. 2002. (Illus.). 13.19 (*1-4046-0953-9*) Book Wholesalers, Inc.
—Miracle's Boys. 2001. (Illus.). 192p. (J). pap. 5.99 (*0-698-11916-9*, Puffin Bks.) Penguin Putnam Bks. for Young Readers.
—Miracle's Boys. abr. unabr. ed. 2001. (YA). (gr. 5 up). audio 18.00 (*0-8072-0437-4*); 2002. 192p. (J). (gr. 4-6). pap. 28.00 incl. audio (*0-8072-0789-6*, LYA 322 SP) Random Hse. Audio Publishing Group. (Listening Library).
—We Had a Picnic This Sunday Past. 1998. (Illus.). 32p. (J). (ps-3). 14.99 (*0-7868-0242-1*); lib. bdg. 15.49 (*0-7868-2192-2*) Hyperion Bks. for Children.
Woolley, Catherine. A Room for Cathy. 1956. (Illus.). (J). (gr. 3-7). lib. bdg. 12.88 o.p. (*0-688-31687-5*, Morrow, William & Co.) Morrow/Avon.
Wosmek, Frances. A Brown Bird Singing. 1993. (Illus.). 128p. (J). (gr. 5 up). pap. 4.95 o.p. (*0-688-04596-0*, Morrow, William & Co.) Morrow/Avon.
Wright, Betty R. I Like Being Alone. 1993. (Life & Living from a Child's Point of View Ser.). (J). pap. 4.95 o.p. (*0-8114-5208-5*) Raintree Pubs.
Wright, Betty Ren. Crandall's Castle. 2003. 192p. (J). tchr. ed. 16.95 (*0-8234-1726-3*) Holiday Hse., Inc.
Wynne-Jones, Tim. Stephen Fair. 1998. (Illus.). 256p. (J). (gr. 7-12). pap. 15.95 o.p. (*0-7894-2495-9*) Dorling Kindersley Publishing, Inc.
Wyss, Johann David. The Swiss Family Robinson. 2002. (Great Illustrated Classics). (Illus.). 240p. (J). (gr. 3-8). lib. bdg. 21.35 (*1-57765-801-9*, ABDO & Daughters) ABDO Publishing Co.
—The Swiss Family Robinson. 1964. (Airmont Classics Ser.). (YA). (gr. 5 up). mass mkt. 1.95 o.p. (*0-8049-0013-2*, CL-13) Airmont Publishing Co., Inc.
—The Swiss Family Robinson. unabr. ed. 2001. (Juvenile Classics). 336p. (J). 3.00 (*0-486-41660-7*) Dover Pubns., Inc.
—The Swiss Family Robinson. unabr. ed. 1999. (Wordsworth Classics Ser.). (YA). (gr. 6-12). pap. 15.32 (*0-89061-111-4*, R1114WW) Jamestown.
—The Swiss Family Robinson. 1994. (Everyman's Library Children's Classics Ser.). (Illus.). 304p. (gr. 2 up). 14.95 (*0-679-43640-5*, Everyman's Library) Knopf Publishing Group.
—The Swiss Family Robinson. 1990. 336p. (J). (ps up). mass mkt. 4.95 (*0-451-52481-0*, Signet Classics) NAL.
—The Swiss Family Robinson. 1986. (Classics for Young Readers Ser.). 384p. (J). (gr. 4-6). pap. 3.99 o.p. (*0-14-035044-6*, Puffin Bks.) Penguin Putnam Bks. for Young Readers.
—The Swiss Family Robinson. Vogel, Malvina, ed. 1990. (Great Illustrated Classics Ser.: Vol. 11). (Illus.). 240p. (J). (gr. 3-6). 9.95 (*0-86611-962-0*) Playmore, Inc., Pubs.
—The Swiss Family Robinson. 2001. 272p. (YA). (gr. 7). mass mkt. 5.50 (*0-440-22829-8*); 1999. 336p. (gr. 5-9). pap. text 4.99 (*0-440-41594-2*) Random Hse. Children's Bks. (Dell Books for Young Readers).
—The Swiss Family Robinson. 1993. (Children's Classics Ser.). (J). 12.99 o.s.i (*0-517-06022-1*) Random Hse. Value Publishing.
—The Swiss Family Robinson. 1996. (Tor Classic Ser.). 9.04 (*0-606-18657-3*) Turtleback Bks.
—Swiss Family Robinson: With a Discussion of Teamwork. 2003. (Values in Action Illustrated Classics Ser.). (Illus.). 191p. (J). (*1-59203-036-X*) Learning Challenge, Inc.
Yaccarino, Dan. Where the Four Winds Blow. 2003. (Illus.). 104p. (J). 16.99 (*0-06-623626-6*); lib. bdg. 17.89 (*0-06-623627-4*) HarperCollins Children's Bk. Group. (Cotler, Joanna Bks.).
Ye, Ting-Xing & Bell, William. Throwaway Daughter. 2003. (Illus.). 240p. (YA). (gr. 7 up). pap. 10.95 (*0-385-65952-0*) Doubleday Publishing.
Yee, Paul. Breakaway. 1997. (J). text (*0-88899-289-0*) Groundwood Bks.
—Breakaway. 2000. 144p. (YA). (gr. 4-7). pap. 5.95 (*0-88899-201-7*) Groundwood Bks. CAN. *Dist:* Publishers Group West.
—The Jade Necklace. 2002. (Illus.). 32p. (J). (ps-3). 15.95 (*1-56656-455-7*, Crocodile Bks.) Interlink Publishing Group, Inc.
Yektai, Niki. The Secret Room. 1992. 192p. (J). (gr. 4-7). 14.95 o.p. (*0-531-05456-X*); mass mkt. 14.99 o.p. (*0-531-08606-2*) Scholastic, Inc. (Orchard Bks.).
Yep, Laurence. Ribbons. 1996. 192p. (J). (gr. 5-9). 16.99 o.p. (*0-399-22906-X*, G. P. Putnam's Sons) Penguin Group (USA) Inc.
—Ribbons. 1997. 192p. (J). (gr. 5-9). pap. 5.99 (*0-698-11606-2*, PaperStar) Penguin Putnam Bks. for Young Readers.
—Ribbons. 1999. pap. 13.99 (*0-670-85929-X*) Viking Penguin.
—Spring Pearl: The Last Flower. 2002. (Girls of Many Lands Ser.). (Illus.). 224p. (J). (gr. 4-7). 12.95 (*1-58485-595-9*); pap. 7.95 (*1-58485-519-3*) Pleasant Co. Pubns. (American Girl).
—Thief of Hearts. 1997. (Golden Mountain Chronicles). 208p. (J). (gr. 5 up). pap. 6.95 (*0-06-440591-5*, Harper Trophy) HarperCollins Children's Bk. Group.
—Thief of Hearts. 1995. (Illus.). 208p. (J). (gr. 5-9). 14.95 o.p. (*0-06-025341-X*); lib. bdg. 15.89 o.p. (*0-06-025342-8*) HarperTrade.
—Thief of Hearts. 1997. 12.00 (*0-606-11978-7*) Turtleback Bks.
Yezerski, Thomas F. Queen of the World, RS. 2000. (Illus.). 32p. (J). (gr. k-3). 16.00 (*0-374-36165-7*, Farrar, Straus & Giroux (BYR)) Farrar, Straus & Giroux.
Ylvisaker, Anne. Dear Papa. 2002. 192p. (J). (gr. 5-8). 15.99 (*0-7636-1618-4*) Candlewick Pr.
Yolen, Jane. And Twelve Chinese Acrobats. 1995. (Illus.). 50p. (J). 15.95 o.p. (*0-399-22691-5*, Philomel) Penguin Putnam Bks. for Young Readers.
Young, Alida E. The Klutz Is Back. 1996. (J). (gr. 5-9). pap. 3.50 (*0-87406-766-9*) Darby Creek Publishing.
Young, Karen Romano. The Beetle & Me: A Love Story. 224p. (J). (gr. 7 up). 2001. pap. 5.95 (*0-380-73295-5*, Harper Trophy); 1999. (Illus.). 15.95 (*0-688-15922-2*, Greenwillow Bks.) HarperCollins Children's Bk. Group.
—The Beetle & Me: A Love Story. 2001. (Illus.). (J). 12.00 (*0-606-21054-7*) Turtleback Bks.
—Video. 1999. 192p. (J). (gr. 7 up). 16.00 (*0-688-16517-6*, Greenwillow Bks.) HarperCollins Children's Bk. Group.
Young, Ronder T. Learning by Heart. 1995. 176p. (J). pap. 3.99 o.s.i (*0-14-037252-0*, Puffin Bks.) Penguin Putnam Bks. for Young Readers.
—Moving Mama to Town. 1997. 224p. (J). (gr. 3-8). lib. bdg. 18.99 (*0-531-33025-7*, Orchard Bks.) Scholastic, Inc.
Young, Ronder Thomas. Learning by Heart. 1993. 176p. (J). (gr. 4-6). 14.95 (*0-395-65369-X*) Houghton Mifflin Co.
—Objects in Mirror. 2002. 176p. (YA). (gr. 6-9). 22.90 (*0-7613-2600-6*); (Single Titles Ser.: 9). 15.95 (*0-7613-1580-2*) Millbrook Pr., Inc. (Roaring Brook Pr.).
Zach, Cheryl. Dear Diary Vol. 3: Family Secrets. 1996. (Archive Ser.). 224p. (YA). mass mkt. 4.50 o.s.i (*0-425-15292-8*) Berkley Publishing Group.
Zafris, Nancy. The Metal Shredders: A Novel. 2003. 320p. reprint ed. pap. 13.00 (*0-425-19080-3*, BlueHen Bks.) Putnam Publishing Group, The.
Zamorano, Ana. Let's Eat! 1999. (Illus.). 32p. (J). (gr. k-1). mass mkt. 5.99 (*0-439-06758-8*, SO1095) Scholastic, Inc.
—Let's Eat! 1999. lib. bdg. 12.14 (*0-606-16652-1*) Turtleback Bks.
Zanimo & Perkes, Carolyn. My Day. 2000. (Maki's Words Ser.). (Illus.). 24p. (J). (ps-k). pap. (*1-894363-54-X*) Dominique & Friends.
Zarin, Cynthia. Wallace Hoskins, the Boy Who Grew Down. 1999. (Illus.). 32p. (J). (gr. k-3). pap. 16.95 o.p. (*0-7894-2523-8*) Dorling Kindersley Publishing, Inc.
Zeplin, Zeno. Secrets of Silver Valley. 2nd ed. 1987. (Illus.). 130p. (J). 16.95 (*0-9615760-4-9*); pap. 9.95 (*0-9615760-5-7*) Nel-Mar Publishing.
Ziefert, Harriet. Cousins Are for Holiday Visits. 2002. (Lift-the-Flap Book Ser.). (Illus.). 16p. (J). pap. 6.99 (*0-14-230106-X*) Penguin Putnam Bks. for Young Readers.
—Kisses for Baby. 2001. (Illus.). 8p. (J). 13.99 (*0-448-42605-6*, Grosset & Dunlap) Penguin Putnam Bks. for Young Readers.
Zolotow, Charlotte. A Father Like That. 1971. (Charlotte Zolotow Bk.). (Illus.). (J). (ps-3). lib. bdg. 12.89 o.p. (*0-06-026950-2*) HarperCollins Children's Bk. Group.
—May I Visit? 1976. (Ursula Nordstrom Bk.). (Illus.). 32p. (J). (gr. k-3). 13.00 (*0-06-026932-4*); lib. bdg. 13.89 o.p. (*0-06-026933-2*) HarperCollins Children's Bk. Group.
Zorzoli, Alicia. Pinafores & Pelotas. 1996. (Illus.). 24p. (J). (gr. 1-3). pap. text 3.99 (*1-56309-179-8*, N968104, New Hope) Woman's Missionary Union.
Zucker, David. Uncle Carmello. 1993. (Illus.). 32p. (J). (gr. k-4). lib. bdg. 14.95 (*0-02-793760-7*, Simon & Schuster Children's Publishing) Simon & Schuster Children's Publishing.
—Uncle Carmello. (Illus.). 32p. (J). 4.98 o.p. (*0-7651-0029-0*) Smithmark Pubs., Inc.

FATHERS—FICTION

Abbott, Deborah & Kisor, Henry. One TV Blasting & a Pig Outdoors. Tucker, Kathy, ed. 1994. (Illus.). 40p. (J). (gr. 4-7). lib. bdg. 14.95 (*0-8075-6075-8*) Whitman, Albert & Co.
Agell, Charlotte, illus. Welcome Home or Someplace Like It, ERS. 2003. 240p. (J). 16.95 (*0-8050-7083-4*, Holt, Henry & Co. Bks. For Young Readers) Holt, Henry & Co.
Aiken, Joan. Dido & Pa. 2002. (Illus.). 304p. (J). (gr. 5). pap. 5.95 (*0-618-19623-4*); 16.00 (*0-618-19624-2*) Houghton Mifflin Co.
—Dido & Pa. 1988. 256p. (J). (gr. k-6). pap. 3.25 o.s.i (*0-440-40052-X*, Yearling) Random Hse. Children's Bks.
Alcock, Vivien. A Kind of Thief. 1992. 192p. (J). (gr. 4-7). 14.00 o.s.i (*0-385-30564-8*, Delacorte Pr.) Dell Publishing.
Alda, Arlene. Matthew & His Dad. 1983. (Illus.). 48p. (J). 7.75 o.p. (*0-671-45158-8*, Atheneum) Simon & Schuster Children's Publishing.
Alden, Laura. Father's Day. 1994. (Circle the Year with Holidays Ser.). (Illus.). 32p. (J). (ps-2). pap. 3.95 o.p. (*0-516-40693-0*); lib. bdg. 18.30 o.p. (*0-516-00693-2*) Scholastic Library Publishing. (Children's Pr.).
Alexander, Earl, et al. My Dad Has HIV. 1996. (Illus.). 32p. (J). (gr. 1-4). 14.95 o.p. (*0-925190-99-3*) Fairview Pr.
Allen, Suzanne. Almost Starring Dad. 1990. (Scrambled Eggs Ser.: No. 2). (J). (gr. 4-7). mass mkt. 2.75 o.p. (*0-425-12218-2*) Berkley Publishing Group.
Ames, Adele Z. A Flower for My Papa. unabr. ed. 1999. (J). (gr. 1-6). audio 5.00 (*0-9677692-1-3*) Butterfly Pr.
Ames, Adele Z. & Brown, Blake Adele. A Flower for My Papa. 1999. (Illus.). 32p. (J). (gr. 1-6). pap. 7.50 (*0-9677692-0-5*) Butterfly Pr.
Anastasio, Dina. Kissyfur & His Dad. 1986. (Illus.). (J). (ps-2). pap. 1.95 o.p. (*0-590-40108-4*) Scholastic, Inc.
Anderson, Launi K. Janey's Own. 1997. (Latter-Day Daughters Ser.). (J). pap. o.p. (*1-57345-319-6*, Cinnamon Tree) Deseret Bk. Co.
Anderson, Laurie Halse. Catalyst. 2002. 240p. (J). (gr. 7 up). text 17.99 (*0-670-03566-1*, Viking) Viking Penguin.
Anfousse, Ginette. Arthur's Dad. 1991. (First Novels Ser.). (Illus.). 64p. (J). (gr. 1-4). (*0-88780-095-5*) Formac Publishing Co., Ltd.
—Arthur's Dad. 1991. (First Novel Ser.: Vol. 4). (Illus.). 64p. (J). (gr. 1-4). pap. 3.99 (*0-88780-094-7*) Formac Publishing Co., Ltd. CAN. *Dist:* Formac Distributing, Ltd., Orca Bk. Pubs.
—El Papa de Arturo. 1994. (Coleccion Rosa Ser.). (SPA., Illus.). 60p. (J). (gr. 4-7). pap. 5.95 (*958-07-0065-6*) Firefly Bks., Ltd.
—Le Pere d'Arthur. 1989. (Premier Roman Ser.). (FRE.). 64p. (J). (gr. 2-5). pap. 7.95 (*2-89021-112-6*) La Courte Echelle CAN. *Dist:* Firefly Bks., Ltd.
Apperley, Dawn. Dad Mine. 2003. (Illus.). 16p. (J). bds. 6.99 (*0-316-73839-5*, Tingley, Megan Bks.) Little Brown Children's Bks.
Arno, Iris H. I Love You, Dad. 1998. 9.65 (*0-606-13507-3*) Turtleback Bks.
Asch, Frank. Just Like Daddy. 1981. (J). (ps-3). 10.95 o.s.i (*0-13-514042-0*) Prentice Hall PTR.
—Just Like Daddy. (Illus.). 32p. (J). (ps-3). 1984. pap. 9.60 (*0-671-66457-3*, Aladdin); 1981. pap. 13.00 o.s.i (*0-671-66456-5*, Simon & Schuster Children's Publishing); 1984. reprint ed. 4.95 o.s.i (*0-13-514035-8*, Simon & Schuster Children's Publishing) Simon & Schuster Children's Publishing.
Auch, Mary Jane. The Road to Home, ERS. 2000. 224p. (YA). (gr. 5-8). 16.95 (*0-8050-4921-5*, Holt, Henry & Co. Bks. For Young Readers) Holt, Henry & Co.

—The Road to Home. 2002. 224p. (gr. 5). pap. text 4.99 (*0-440-41805-4*, Random Hse. Bks. for Young Readers) Random Hse. Children's Bks.

Avi. Poppy & Rye. (Illus.). (J). (gr. 3-7). 1999. 208p. pap. 5.99 (*0-380-79717-8*, Harper Trophy); 1998. 192p. 15.99 (*0-380-97638-2*) HarperCollins Children's Bk. Group.

—Poppy & Rye, 2000. (J). (gr. 8). pap., stu. ed. 50.24 incl. audio (*0-7887-3185-8*, 40920E5) Recorded Bks., LLC.

—Poppy & Rye. 1999. 11.00 (*0-606-16352-2*); 1997. (J). 11.00 (*0-606-10906-4*) Turtleback Bks.

Aylesworth, Jim. Through the Night. 1998. (Illus.). 32p. (J). (ps-2). 16.00 (*0-689-80642-6*, Atheneum) Simon & Schuster Children's Publishing.

Azean, Evon, Sr. Aataq Maktuq. l.t. ed. 1999. Tr. of Father Gets Up. (ESK., Illus.). 12p. (J). (gr. k-3). pap. text 6.00 (*1-58084-145-7*) Lower Kuskokwim Schl. District.

—At'a Maktur (Father Gets Up) l.t. ed. 1999. (ESK., Illus.). 12p. (J). (gr. k-3). pap. text 6.00 (*1-58084-146-5*) Lower Kuskokwim Schl. District.

—Father Gets Up. l.t. ed. 1999. (Illus.). 12p. (J). (gr. k-3). pap. text 6.00 (*1-58084-144-9*) Lower Kuskokwim Schl. District.

Bache, Ellyn. Daddy & the Pink Flash. 2003. (Illus.). 32p. (J). 14.95 (*1-889199-11-7*) Banks Channel Bks.

Bailey, Debbie. Mi Papa. 2003. (SPA., Illus.). 14p. (J). (ps). bds. 5.95 (*1-55037-265-3*) Annick Pr., Ltd. CAN. *Dist:* Firefly Bks., Ltd., Lectorum Pubns., Inc.

Bailey, Debbie & Huszar, Susan. Mon Papa. 1992. Tr. of My Dad. (FRE., Illus.). 14p. (J). (ps). bds. 4.95 (*1-55037-266-1*) Annick Pr., Ltd. CAN. *Dist:* Firefly Bks., Ltd.

Ballard, Robin. Gracie. 1993. (Illus.). 24p. (J). (ps up). lib. bdg. 13.93 o.p. (*0-688-11807-0*, Greenwillow Bks.) HarperCollins Children's Bk. Group.

Barrett, Judith. I'm Too Small, You're Too Big. 1981. (Illus.). 32p. (J). (ps-1). 12.95 o.s.i (*0-689-30800-0*, Atheneum) Simon & Schuster Children's Publishing.

Barrows, Allison. The Artist's Model. 1996. (Illus.). 32p. (J). (ps-3). lib. bdg. 15.95 o.s.i (*0-87614-948-4*, Carolrhoda Bks.) Lerner Publishing Group.

Bauer, Marion Dane. Face to Face. 1991. 192p. (J). (gr. 5-9). 14.95 o.s.i (*0-395-55440-3*, Clarion Bks.) Houghton Mifflin Co. Trade & Reference Div.

Bawden, Nina. The Robbers. 1979. (Illus.). 160p. (J). (gr. 4-7). reprint ed. 12.95 o.p. (*0-688-41902-X*); lib. bdg. 12.88 o.p. (*0-688-51902-4*) HarperCollins Children's Bk. Group.

Baynton, Martin. Why Do You Love Me? 1990. (Illus.). 32p. (J). (ps up). 16.00 o.p. (*0-688-09156-3*, Greenwillow Bks.) HarperCollins Children's Bk. Group.

—Why Do You Love Me. 1990. (Illus.). 32p. (J). (ps-3). 15.93 o.s.i (*0-688-09157-1*, Greenwillow Bks.) HarperCollins Children's Bk. Group.

Bea, Holly. Good Night, God. 2000. (Illus.). 32p. (J). (ps-k). 15.00 (*0-915811-84-7*, Starseed Pr.) Kramer, H.J. Inc.

Bell, Caroline. I Love My Dad. 1999. (Illus.). 28p. (J). (ps-1). (*0-88902-736-6*) Fitzhenry & Whiteside, Ltd.

Bennett, James W. Plunking Reggie Jackson. 2001. (Illus.). 208p. (J). (gr. 7-12). 16.00 (*0-689-83137-4*, Simon & Schuster Children's Publishing) Simon & Schuster Children's Publishing.

Berenstain, Stan. The Berenstain Bears & the Papa's Day Roast. 2003. (Illus.). 32p. (J). lib. bdg. 8.99 (*0-375-91129-4*); pap. 3.25 (*0-375-81129-X*) Random Hse. Children's Bks.

Berenstain, Stan & Berenstain, Jan. The Berenstain Bears Get Their Kicks. 1998. (Berenstain Bears First Time Bks.). 32p. (gr. k-2). (J). lib. bdg. 8.99 (*0-679-98955-2*); (Illus.). pap. 3.25 (*0-679-88955-8*) Random Hse. Children's Bks. (Random Hse. Bks. for Young Readers).

—The Berenstain Bears Get Their Kicks. 1998. (Berenstain Bears First Time Bks.). (J). (gr. k-2). 9.40 (*0-606-13955-9*) Turtleback Bks.

—The Berenstain Bears' That Stump Must Go! 2000. (I Can Read It All by Myself: Beginner Books). (Illus.). 48p. (J). (gr. k-3). lib. bdg. 11.99 o.s.i (*0-679-98963-3*, Random Hse. Bks. for Young Readers) Random Hse. Children's Bks.

—That Stump Must Go! 2000. (Berenstain Bears Bright & Early Bks.). (Illus.). 48p. (J). (ps-3). 7.99 o.s.i (*0-679-88963-9*, Random Hse. Bks. for Young Readers) Random Hse. Children's Bks.

Berry, Carmen Renee. Daddies & Daughters. 1999. 288p. pap. 11.00 (*0-684-84993-3*, Fireside) Simon & Schuster.

Berry, Carmen Renee & Barrington, Lynn. Daddies & Daughters. 1998. 288p. (YA). 20.00 (*0-684-84992-5*, Simon & Schuster) Simon & Schuster.

Best, Cari. Getting Used to Harry. 1996. (Illus.). 32p. (J). (ps-3). pap. 15.95 o.p. (*0-531-09494-4*); lib. bdg. 16.99 (*0-531-08794-8*) Scholastic, Inc. (Orchard Bks.).

Bishop, R. Christopher Sphere, Vol. 1. 1997. (Illus.). 128p. (YA). (gr. 3-12). pap. 4.95 (*0-87505-409-9*) Borden Publishing Co.

Black, Claudia. My Dad Loves Me, My Dad Has a Disease. 1982. (Illus.). 88p. (Orig.). (J). (gr. k-9). pap. 9.95 o.p. (*0-9607940-2-6*) MAC Publishing.

Blackwell, Donald A. Rounding Third. Rodriguez, Pamela S. & Rothkopf, Michelle, eds. 1997. (Illus.). 32p. (Orig.). pap. (*0-9650332-1-X*) Blackwell, Donald A.

Blair, L. E. Problem Dad. 1993. (Girl Talk Ser.: No. 22). (Illus.). 128p. (J). (ps-3). pap. 2.95 o.s.i (*0-307-22022-2*, 22022, Golden Bks.) Random Hse. Children's Bks.

Blake, Robert J. The Perfect Spot. (Illus.). 32p. (J). (ps-3). 1997. pap. 6.99 (*0-698-11431-0*, PaperStar); 1992. 16.99 (*0-399-22132-8*, Philomel) Penguin Putnam Bks. for Young Readers.

Blue, Rose. Bring Me a Memory. 1995. (Illus.). 93p. (Orig.). (J). (gr. 4-6). pap. 9.95 (*0-931625-28-9*) DIMI Pr.

Bograd, Larry. Travelers. 1986. 192p. (YA). (gr. 7 up). 11.95 (*0-397-32128-7*); lib. bdg. 11.89 (*0-397-32129-5*) HarperCollins Children's Bk. Group.

Bongiorno, Patti Lynn. My Dad's Footsteps. 2002. (J). spiral bd. 20.00 (*0-9715819-8-3*) Bongiorno Bks.

Bonsall, Crosby N. & Reed, E. Let Papa Sleep. 1989. (Easy Reader Ser.). (J). (gr. k-3). 1.25 o.s.i (*0-8431-4311-8*, Price Stern Sloan) Penguin Putnam Bks. for Young Readers.

Borger, Judy. Pop. 1995. (Illus.). 32p. (Orig.). (J). (gr. k-3). pap. 4.95 (*0-9642086-9-5*) Popular Pr., Inc.

Bostrom, Kathleen Long. Papa's Gift. 2002. 40p. 15.99 (*0-310-70274-7*) Zondervan.

—Peter's Dad. 2004. (Illus.). 32p. 9.99 (*0-310-70655-6*) Zondervan.

Bowler, Tim. Firmament. 2004. (Illus.). 320p. (YA). 16.95 (*0-689-86161-3*, McElderry, Margaret K.) Simon & Schuster Children's Publishing.

Boyd, Candy Dawson. Charlie Pippin. 1988. 192p. (J). (gr. 4-7). pap. 5.99 (*0-14-032587-5*, Puffin Bks.) Penguin Putnam Bks. for Young Readers.

—Charlie Pippin. 1987. 192p. (J). (gr. 3-7). lib. bdg. 14.95 o.s.i (*0-02-726350-9*, Simon & Schuster Children's Publishing) Simon & Schuster Children's Publishing.

—Charlie Pippin. 1987. (J). 11.04 (*0-606-03752-7*) Turtleback Bks.

Bradman, Tony. Not Like That, Like This. 1988. (Illus.). 32p. (J). (ps up). 13.95 o.p. (*0-19-520712-2*) Oxford Univ. Pr., Inc.

Brandon, Paul. Swim the Moon. 2001. 384p. 25.95 (*0-312-87794-3*, Tor Bks.) Doherty, Tom Assocs., LLC.

Braun, Sebastien. I Love My Daddy. 2004. 32p. (J). 12.99 (*0-06-054311-6*) HarperCollins Pubs.

Bray, Jeannine D. My Poppie. Kenyatta, Imani, ed. 1998. (Illus.). 80p. (J). (gr. k-6). 14.95 (*1-886580-62-6*) Pinnacle-Syatt Pubns.

Bridges, Margaret P. If I Were Your Father. 1999. (Illus.). 32p. (J). (ps-3). lib. bdg. 15.89 o.p. (*0-688-15193-0*, Morrow, William & Co.) Morrow/Avon.

Bridges, Margaret Park. If I Were Your Father. 1999. (Illus.). 32p. (J). (ps-3). 16.00 (*0-688-15192-2*, Morrow, William & Co.) Morrow/Avon.

Bridwell, Norman. Clifford's Day with Dad. 2003. (Clifford Ser.). 32p. (J). mass mkt. 3.50 (*0-439-41073-8*) Scholastic, Inc.

Brighton, Catherine. Five Secrets in a Box. 1987. (Illus.). 32p. (J). (ps-3). 11.95 o.p. (*0-525-44318-5*, 01160-350, Dutton Children's Bks.) Penguin Putnam Bks. for Young Readers.

Brillhart, Julie. When Daddy Came to School. 1995. (Illus.). 24p. (J). (ps-3). lib. bdg. 13.95 (*0-8075-8878-4*) Whitman, Albert & Co.

Britton, Susan. The Treekeepers. 2003. 256p. (J). 16.99 (*0-525-46944-3*, Dutton Children's Bks.) Penguin Putnam Bks. for Young Readers.

Brooks, Ben. Lemonade Parade. 1991. (Explorations in Science Ser.). (Illus.). 32p. (J). (ps-2). (*1-55074-009-1*) Kids Can Pr., Ltd.

Brown, Marc. Arthur & the 1,001 Dads. 2003. (Arthur Chapter Book Ser.: No. 28). (Illus.). 64p. (J). (gr. 2-4). 14.95 (*0-316-12516-4*); pap. 4.25 (*0-316-12280-7*) Little Brown Children's Bks.

Brown, Sandra. Coming in from the Rain. Ewen, David, ed. 1997. (Little Worthen Brown Ser.). (Illus.). 48p. (Orig.). (J). (gr. k-3). pap. 7.00 (*1-889436-01-1*) Ewen Prime Co.

Browne, Anthony. My Dad. 2001. (Illus.). 32p. (J). pap. (*0-552-54668-2*, Corgi) Bantam Bks.

—My Dad. 2000. (J). (ps-3). 16.00 (*0-7894-2681-1*) Dorling Kindersley Publishing, Inc.

—My Dad, RS. (Illus.). 2004. 5.95 (*0-374-35100-7*); 2001. 32p. (J). 16.00 (*0-374-35101-5*) Farrar, Straus & Giroux. (Farrar, Straus & Giroux (BYR)).

Bryant, Megan E. Just Like Daddy. 2003. (Illus.). 32p. (J). 6.99 (*0-448-43106-8*, Grosset & Dunlap) Penguin Putnam Bks. for Young Readers.

Buckley, Helen E. Someday with My Father. 1985. (Illus.). 32p. (J). (ps-3). lib. bdg. 12.89 o.p. (*0-06-020878-3*) HarperCollins Children's Bk. Group.

Bunting, Eve. A Perfect Father's Day. 2002. (Illus.). (J). 13.79 (*0-7587-3390-9*) Book Wholesalers, Inc.

—A Perfect Father's Day. (Illus.). 32p. (J). (ps-3). 2000. pap. 9.95 incl. audio (*0-618-04079-X*); 1993. pap. 5.95 (*0-395-66416-0*) Houghton Mifflin Co. Trade & Reference Div. (Clarion Bks.).

—A Perfect Father's Day. Giblin, James C., ed. 1991. (Illus.). 32p. (J). (ps-3). 13.95 o.p. (*0-395-52590-X*, Clarion Bks.) Houghton Mifflin Co. Trade & Reference Div.

—A Perfect Father's Day. 1991. 12.10 (*0-606-18045-1*) Turtleback Bks.

Burgess, Gelett. The Little Father, RS. (Sunburst Ser.). (Illus.). 32p. (J). (ps-3). 1987. pap. 3.95 o.p. (*0-374-44486-2*, Sunburst); 1985. 14.00 o.p. (*0-374-34596-1*, Farrar, Straus & Giroux (BYR)) Farrar, Straus & Giroux.

Burstein, Fred. Anna's Rain. 1990. (Illus.). 32p. (J). (ps-1). 14.95 o.p. (*0-531-05827-1*); mass mkt. 14.99 o.p. (*0-531-08427-2*) Scholastic, Inc. (Orchard Bks.).

Burton, Yvette M. A Twinkle in His Eye. l.t. ed. 2000. (Illus.). 28p. (J). 10.00 (*0-615-11477-6*) Shooting Star Publishing.

Busser, Marianne & Schroder, Ron. On the Road with Poppa Whopper. 1945. (Illus.). 64p. (J). (gr. 2-4). 13.95 o.p. (*1-55858-373-4*); 14.50 o.p. (*1-55858-374-2*) North-South Bks., Inc.

Butterworth, Nick. My Dad Is Awesome. (Illus.). 32p. (J). 2003. 5.99 (*0-7636-2056-4*); 1992. bds. 4.99 (*1-56402-033-9*) Candlewick Pr.

Butterworth, Oliver. Visiting the Big House. Cohn, Amy, ed. 1995. Orig. Title: A Visit to the Big House. (Illus.). 48p. (J). reprint ed. pap. 3.95 o.p. (*0-688-13303-7*, Morrow, William & Co.) Morrow/Avon.

Byalick, Marcia. It's a Matter of Trust. 1995. (YA). (gr. 7 up). 272p. 11.00 (*0-15-276660-X*); 192p. pap. 5.00 (*0-15-200240-5*) Harcourt Children's Bks.

—It's a Matter of Trust. 1995. 11.05 (*0-606-09480-6*) Turtleback Bks.

Caines, Jeannette F. Daddy. 1977. (Illus.). 32p. (J). (gr. k-3). lib. bdg. 12.89 o.p. (*0-06-020924-0*) HarperCollins Children's Bk. Group.

Caletti, Deb. The Queen of Everything. 2002. 384p. (YA). (gr. 9 up). pap. 6.99 (*0-7434-3684-9*, Simon Pulse) Simon & Schuster Children's Publishing.

Calvert, Patricia. Glennis, Before & After. 1996. 160p. (J). (gr. 4-7). 16.00 (*0-689-80641-8*, Atheneum) Simon & Schuster Children's Publishing.

—The Hour of the Wolf. 1983. 160p. (YA). (gr. 7 up). 12.95 o.p. (*0-684-17961-X*, Atheneum) Simon & Schuster Children's Publishing.

Campbell, Mike. Dandy the Chipbear's . . . Fun Day at Dad's. 1997. (Adventures of Dandy Ser.: No. 1). (Illus.). 28p. (J). (ps-1). pap. text (*0-9660574-0-6*) Dandy Creations.

Cannon, Bettie. A Bellsong for Sarah Raines. 1987. 192p. (YA). (gr. 7 up). text 14.95 o.s.i (*0-684-18839-2*, Atheneum) Simon & Schuster Children's Publishing.

Capucilli, Alyssa Satin. Only My Dad & Me. 2003. (Illus.). 16p. (J). (ps up). 6.99 (*0-694-52584-7*, Harper Festival) HarperCollins Children's Bk. Group.

Carle, Eric. Papa, Please Get the Moon for Me. 1999. (Classic Board Bks). (Illus.). 32p. (J). (ps-k). bds. 9.99 (*0-689-82959-0*, Little Simon) Simon & Schuster Children's Publishing.

Carmichael, Clay. Bear at the Beach. 1996. (Illus.). 48p. (J). (gr. 1-3). 13.95 o.p. (*1-55858-569-9*); (ps-3). 14.50 o.p. (*1-55858-570-2*) North-South Bks., Inc.

Carter, Alden R. Robodad. 1990. 144p. (YA). 14.95 o.s.i (*0-399-22191-3*, G. P. Putnam's Sons) Penguin Putnam Bks. for Young Readers.

Carter, Anne. From Poppa. Pavanel, Jane, ed. 1999. (Illus.). 32p. (J). (gr. 4-7). 16.95 (*1-894222-02-4*) Lobster Pr. CAN. *Dist:* Publishers Group West.

Cartwright, Pauline. Jimmy Parker's New Job. 1994. (Illus.). (J). pap. (*0-383-03679-8*) SRA/McGraw-Hill.

Catalanotto, Peter. Dad & Me. 1999. (Illus.). 40p. (J). (gr. k-3). pap. 16.95 (*0-7894-2584-X*, D K Ink) Dorling Kindersley Publishing, Inc.

—The Painter. (Illus.). 32p. (J). (ps-2). 1999. mass mkt. 5.95 (*0-531-07116-2*); 1996. pap. 15.95 (*0-531-09465-0*); 1996. lib. bdg. 16.99 (*0-531-08765-4*) Scholastic, Inc. (Orchard Bks.).

Cazet, Denys. Dancing. 1995. (Illus.). 32p. (J). (ps-3). pap. 15.95 (*0-531-09466-9*); lib. bdg. 16.99 (*0-531-08766-2*) Scholastic, Inc. (Orchard Bks.).

Chambers, Veronica. Marisol & Magdalena: The Sound of Our Sisterhood. 2001. 176p. (J). (gr. 3-7). pap. 5.99 (*0-7868-1304-0*) Hyperion Bks. for Children.

—Marisol & Magdalena: The Sound of Our Sisterhood. 1998. 141p. (gr. 3-7). (J). 14.95 (*0-7868-0437-8*); (YA). lib. bdg. 15.49 (*0-7868-2385-2*) Hyperion Pr.

Charles, Norma M. The Accomplice. 2001. (Illus.). 144p. (J). (gr. 3-7). pap. 6.95 (*1-55192-430-7*) Raincoast Bk. Distribution CAN. *Dist:* Publishers Group West.

Chase, Diana. Timeslip. 1997. 165p. pap. 10.95 (*1-86368-187-6*) Fremantle Arts Centre Pr. AUS. *Dist:* International Specialized Bk. Services.

Chethik, Neil. Fatherloss: How Sons of All Ages Come to Terms with the Deaths of Their Dads. 2001. (Illus.). 288p. pap. 14.00 (*0-7868-8449-5*) Hyperion Pr.

Chiappetta, Joe. Silly Daddy: A Death in the Family. unabr. ed. 1999. (Illus.). 96p. pap. 8.00 (*0-9644323-1-5*) Chiappetta, Joe.

—Silly Daddy: The Long Goodbye. 1994. (Silly Daddy Ser.). (Illus.). 98p. (Orig.). (YA). pap. text 7.95 (*0-9644323-0-7*) Chiappetta, Joe.

Cleary, Beverly. Ramona y Su Padre. 10th ed. (SPA., Illus.). 136p. (J). (gr. 3-5). 9.95 (*84-239-9020-6*, EC1443) Espasa Calpe, S.A. ESP. *Dist:* Lectorum Pubns., Inc., Planeta Publishing Corp.

—Ramona y Su Padre. 1987. (J). 14.05 o.p. (*0-606-10497-6*) Turtleback Bks.

Cleaver, Vera. Sugar Blue. 1986. (J). (gr. 3-6). pap. 2.95 o.s.i (*0-440-48422-7*, Yearling) Random Hse. Children's Bks.

Clifton, Lucille. Amifika. 1977. (Illus.). (J). (ps-1). 7.95 o.p. (*0-525-25548-6*, Dutton) Dutton/Plume.

Close, Jessie. The Warping of Al. 1990. (Charlotte Zolotow Bk.). 288p. (YA). (gr. 7 up). 15.95 (*0-06-021280-2*); lib. bdg. 15.89 o.p. (*0-06-021281-0*) HarperCollins Children's Bk. Group.

Cocca-Leffler, Maryann. Daddy Hugs. 1997. (Illus.). 14p. (J). (ps-k). 5.99 (*0-689-80982-4*, Little Simon) Simon & Schuster Children's Publishing.

Cohen, Cindy Klein & Heiney, John T. Daddy's Promise. l.t. ed. 1997. (Illus.). 32p. (J). (ps up). pap. 14.95 (*0-9656498-0-6*) Promise Pubns.

Cohlene, Terri. Ribbons for Mikele. 2003. (Illus.). 32p. (J). lib. bdg. 16.89 (*0-688-13094-1*, Morrow, William & Co.) Morrow/Avon.

—Won't Papa Be Surprised! 2003. (Illus.). 32p. (J). 15.99 (*0-688-13093-3*, Morrow, William & Co.) Morrow/Avon.

Colato Lainez, Rene. Waiting for Papa: Esperando a Papa. Accardo, Anthony, tr. & illus. by. 2003. (ENG & SPA.). (J). (*1-55885-403-7*, Piñata Books) Arte Publico Pr.

Cole, Babette. Babette Cole's Dad. 1997. (Illus.). 10p. (J). (*0-434-80100-3*) Heinemann, William Ltd.

—The Trouble with Dad. 1993. (J). (ps-3). 5.95 o.s.i (*0-399-22534-X*, Sandcastle Bks.) Penguin Group (USA) Inc.

Cole, Brock. Buttons, RS. 2004. pap. 6.95 (*0-374-41013-5*); 2000. (Illus.). 32p. (J). 16.00 (*0-374-31001-7*, Farrar, Straus & Giroux (BYR)) Farrar, Straus & Giroux.

—Buttons. 2001. (J). (ps-3). 26.90 incl. audio (*0-8045-6881-2*, 6881) Spoken Arts, Inc.

—Buttons. 2001. (J). (gr. k-4). 26.90 incl. audio Spoken Word.

Colfer, Eoin. The Arctic Incident. l.t. ed. 2003. (Artemis Fowl Ser.: Bk. 2). (J). (gr. 3-6). 16.95 (*0-7540-7839-6*, Galaxy Children's Large Print) BBC Audiobooks America.

—The Arctic Incident. 2002. (Artemis Fowl Ser.: Bk. 2). 288p. (J). (gr. 3-6). 16.99 (*0-7868-0855-1*) Hyperion Bks. for Children.

—The Arctic Incident. l.t. ed. 2003. (Artemis Fowl Ser.: Bk. 2). 313p. (J). (gr. 3-6). 25.95 (*0-7862-4825-4*) Thorndike Pr.

Collins, Judith G. Josh's Scary Dad. 1983. (Illus.). 32p. (Orig.). (J). (gr. 3-5). pap. text 1.95 o.p. (*0-687-20546-8*) Abingdon Pr.

Conly, Jane Leslie. While No One Was Watching. 2000. 240p. (J). (gr. 7 up). pap. 5.99 (*0-06-440787-X*, Harper Trophy) HarperCollins Children's Bk. Group.

—While No One Was Watching. 2000. 11.00 (*0-606-18728-6*) Turtleback Bks.

Cooley, Beth. Ostrich Eye. 2004. (Illus.). 192p. (YA). lib. bdg. 17.99 (*0-385-90132-1*); (gr. 7). 15.95 (*0-385-73106-X*) Random Hse. Children's Bks. (Delacorte Bks. for Young Readers).

Cooney, Doug. The Beloved Dearly. (Illus.). 192p. (J). 2003. pap. 4.99 (*0-689-86354-3*, Aladdin); 2002. 16.00 (*0-689-83127-7*, Simon & Schuster Children's Publishing) Simon & Schuster Children's Publishing.

Corbalis, Judy. Your Dad's a Monkey. 1990. (Illus.). 123p. (J). (gr. 2-4). pap. 15.95 o.p. (*0-233-98465-8*) Andre Deutsch GBR. *Dist:* Trafalgar Square, Trans-Atlantic Pubns., Inc.

Cosby, Bill. The Day I Saw My Father Cry. 2000. (Little Bill Books for Beginning Readers Ser.). (Illus.). 40p. (J). (gr. k-3). pap. 15.95 (*0-590-52197-7*); mass mkt. 3.99 (*0-590-52199-3*) Scholastic, Inc.

—The Day I Saw My Father Cry. 2000. (Little Bill Books for Beginning Readers Ser.). (Illus.). (J). 10.14 (*0-606-20470-9*) Turtleback Bks.

Courtin, Thierry. Daddy & Me. 1997. (Lift & Look Board Bks.). (Illus.). 12p. (J). (ps). 4.99 o.p. (*0-448-41617-4*, Grosset & Dunlap) Penguin Putnam Bks. for Young Readers.

Coy, John. Night Driving, ERS. 1996. (Illus.). 32p. (J). (ps-3). 14.95 (*0-8050-2931-1*, Holt, Henry & Co. Bks. For Young Readers) Holt, Henry & Co.

Crew, Gary. First Light. 1996. (Illus.). 32p. (J). (gr. 3 up). lib. bdg. 22.60 (*0-8368-1664-1*) Stevens, Gareth Inc.

Croteau, Marie-Danielle. Le Tresor de Mon Pere. 2003. (Premier Roman Ser.). (FRE., Illus.). 64p. (J). (gr. 2-5). pap. 8.95 (*2-89021-246-7*) La Courte Echelle CAN. *Dist:* Firefly Bks., Ltd.

Crutcher, Chris. Ironman: A Novel. 1996. (YA). 11.04 (*0-606-09477-6*) Turtleback Bks.

Curtis, Chara M. No One Walks on My Father's Moon. 1996. (Illus.). 32p. (J). (gr. 2 up). lib. bdg. 16.95 (*0-9649454-1-X*) Voyage Publishing.

Curwood, James Oliver. Kazan, Father of Baree. 1995. 256p. (YA). 18.95 o.p. (*1-55704-236-5*) Newmarket Pr.

Daly, Niki. My Dad. 1995. (Illus.). 32p. (J). (gr. k-3). 16.00 (*0-689-50620-1*, McElderry, Margaret K.) Simon & Schuster Children's Publishing.

—Papa Lucky's Shadow. 1999. (Illus.). 32p. (J). (gr. k-3). pap. 6.99 o.s.i (*0-689-82430-0*, Aladdin) Simon & Schuster Children's Publishing.

—Papa Lucky's Shadow. 1999. 12.14 (*0-606-16283-6*) Turtleback Bks.

Davies, Bettilu D. The Secret of the Hidden Cave. 1980. (Pathfinder Ser.). (Illus.). 144p. (J). pap. 2.95 o.p. (*0-310-37891-5*) Zondervan.

Dawson Boyd, Candy. Daddy, Daddy, Be There. 1998. (Illus.). 40p. (J). (ps-3). pap. 5.99 o.s.i (*0-698-11750-6*, PaperStar) Penguin Putnam Bks. for Young Readers.

de Paola, Tomie. The Days of the Blackbird: A Tale of Northern Italy. 1997. (Illus.). 32p. (J). (ps-3). 16.99 (*0-399-22929-9*, G. P. Putnam's Sons) Penguin Group (USA) Inc.

De Pressense, Domitille. Natalie: The Spanking. 1990. (Illus.). 28p. (J). (ps-1). pap. 0.30 o.p. (*0-8120-4506-8*) Barron's Educational Series, Inc.

Degen, Bruce. Daddy Is a Doodlebug. (J). (ps-1). 2002. (Illus.). 40p. pap. 5.95 (*0-06-443578-4*); 2000. (Illus.). 40p. 15.95 (*0-06-028415-3*); 2000. (Illus.). 40p. lib. bdg. 15.89 (*0-06-028416-1*); 1998. 32p. bds. 7.95 (*0-694-01352-8*) HarperCollins Children's Bk. Group.

DeJong, Meindert. The House of Sixty Fathers. 1987. (Trophy Bk.). (Illus.). 208p. (J). (gr. 4-7). pap. 5.99 (*0-06-440200-2*, Harper Trophy) HarperCollins Children's Bk. Group.

—The House of Sixty Fathers. 1987. (J). 12.00 (*0-606-02140-X*) Turtleback Bks.

Delton, Judy. All Dads on Deck. 1994. (Pee Wee Scouts Ser.: No. 23). 96p. (gr. 2-5). pap. 3.99 o.s.i (*0-440-40943-8*) Dell Publishing.

—All Dads on Deck. 1994. (Pee Wee Scouts Ser.: No. 23). (J). (gr. 2-5). 9.19 (*0-606-06173-8*) Turtleback Bks.

Deuker, Carl. High Heat. 2003. 288p. (J). (gr. 7-9). tchr. ed. 16.00 (*0-618-31117-3*) Houghton Mifflin Co.

DiCamillo, Kate. The Tiger Rising. 2002. (Illus.). 128p. (YA). (gr. 5-12). pap. 5.99 (*0-7636-1898-5*) Candlewick Pr.

Dickens, Charles. Dombey & Son. 1990. (J). (ps-8). reprint ed. lib. bdg. 29.95 o.p. (*0-89966-678-7*) Buccaneer Bks., Inc.

Dijs, Carla. Daddy, Would You Love Me If . . .? 1996. (Illus.). 14p. (J). (ps-k). 8.99 (*0-689-80812-7*, Little Simon) Simon & Schuster Children's Publishing.

Dillon, Barbara. My Stepfather Shrank! 1992. (Illus.). 128p. (J). (gr. 3-7). 13.00 (*0-06-021574-7*); lib. bdg. 12.89 o.p. (*0-06-021581-X*) HarperCollins Children's Bk. Group.

DiTerlizzi, Tony. Ted. 2001. (Illus.). 40p. (J). (ps-1). 16.00 (*0-689-83235-4*, Simon & Schuster Children's Publishing) Simon & Schuster Children's Publishing.

Dorsey, David. Fathers Day. 1997. 304p. (J). 23.95 o.s.i (*0-670-87471-X*) Viking Penguin.

Dr. Seuss Enterprises Staff. Hop on Pop. 2004. (Illus.). 24p. (J). bds. 4.99 (*0-375-82837-0*) Random Hse. Children's Bks.

Dragonwagon, Crescent. The Sun Begun. 1999. (J). 16.00 (*0-689-81159-4*, Atheneum) Simon & Schuster Children's Publishing.

Duey, Kathleen. Alexia Ellery Finsdale: San Francisco, 1905. 1997. (American Diaries Ser.: No. 7). 144p. (J). (gr. 3-7). pap. 4.50 (*0-689-81620-0*, Aladdin) Simon & Schuster Children's Publishing.

—Alexia Ellery Finsdale: San Francisco, 1905. 1997. (American Diaries Ser.: No. 7). (J). (gr. 3-7). 10.55 (*0-606-12614-7*) Turtleback Bks.

Dutton, Cheryl. Not in Here, Dad! 1993. (Illus.). (J). 3.99 o.p. (*0-517-09929-2*) Random Hse. Value Publishing.

—Not in Here, Dad! 1989. (J). 17.27 o.p. (*0-516-08699-5*, Children's Pr.) Scholastic Library Publishing.

Edwards, Frank B. A Dog Called Dad. 1994. (Illus.). 24p. (J). (gr. 1-4). pap. 4.95 (*0-921285-34-5*); lib. bdg. 14.95 (*0-921285-35-3*) Bungalo Bks. CAN. *Dist:* Firefly Bks., Ltd.

Edwards, Michelle. Papa's Latkes. 2001. (Illus.). (J). 15.99 (*0-7636-0779-7*) Candlewick Pr.

Eifrig, Kate. Scary Monster. 1998. (Illus.). 8p. (J). (gr. k-1). pap. 4.95 (*1-879835-29-0*, Kaeden Bks.) Kaeden Corp.

Eliot, George. Silas Marner, Level 4. Hedge, Tricia, ed. 2000. (Bookworms Ser.). (Illus.). 96p. (J). pap. text 5.95 (*0-19-423044-9*) Oxford Univ. Pr., Inc.

Elmer, Irene. Anthony's Father. 1972. (Illus.). (J). (gr. 3-5). 4.39 o.p. (*0-399-60741-2*) Putnam Publishing Group, The.

Emery, Clayton. Father-Daughter Disaster! 1997. (Secret World of Alex Mack Ser.: No. 16). 128p. (J). (gr. 4-7). pap. 3.99 (*0-671-01372-6*, Aladdin) Simon & Schuster Children's Publishing.

Ernst, Lisa Campbell. Squirrel Park. 1993. (Illus.). 40p. (J). (ps-2). lib. bdg. 15.95 o.s.i (*0-02-733562-3*, Simon & Schuster Children's Publishing) Simon & Schuster Children's Publishing.

Evans, Edie. I Love You Daddy! 2001. (Little Golden Bks.). (Illus.). 16p. (J). (ps-3). 2.99 (*0-307-99508-9*, Golden Bks.) Random Hse. Children's Bks.

Eyerly, Jeannette. He's My Baby Now. 1977. (J). o.p. (*0-397-31744-1*) HarperCollins Children's Bk. Group.

Farley, Carol. Twilight Waves. 1981. 144p. (J). (gr. 4-6). 8.95 o.p. (*0-689-30842-6*, Atheneum) Simon & Schuster Children's Publishing.

Farnes, Catherine. The Slide. 2003. 128p. (J). 6.49 (*1-57924-967-1*) Jones, Bob Univ. Pr.

Fassler, Joan. All Alone with Daddy: A Young Girl Plays the Role of Mother. 1975. (Illus.). 32p. (J). (ps-3). 16.95 (*0-87705-009-0*, Kluwer Academic/Human Science Pr.) Kluwer Academic Pubs.

Faucher, Elizabeth. Getting Even with Dad. 1994. 224p. (YA). mass mkt. 3.50 o.p. (*0-590-48263-7*) Scholastic, Inc.

Feiffer, Jules. The Daddy Mountain. 2004. (Illus.). (J). (ps). 15.95 (*0-7868-0912-4*) Hyperion Bks. for Children.

Ferris, Jean. All That Glitters, RS. 1996. 192p. (YA). (gr. 7 up). 16.00 (*0-374-30204-9*, Farrar, Straus & Giroux (BYR)) Farrar, Straus & Giroux.

—Relative Strangers, RS. 1993. 240p. (YA). 16.00 o.p. (*0-374-36243-2*, Farrar, Straus & Giroux (BYR)) Farrar, Straus & Giroux.

Feuer, Elizabeth. Lost Summer. 1997. (J). (gr. 3-7). pap. 3.99 o.p. (*0-380-72732-3*, Avon Bks.) Morrow/Avon.

Fine, Anne. Summer House Loon. 1979. (J). (gr. 6 up). o.p. (*0-690-03933-6*) HarperCollins Children's Bk. Group.

Fleischman, Paul. Rear-View Mirror. 1986. (Charlotte Zolotow Bk.). 128p. (YA). (gr. 7 up). 12.95 o.s.i (*0-06-021866-5*); lib. bdg. 12.89 o.p. (*0-06-021867-3*) HarperCollins Children's Bk. Group.

Foster, Kelli C. & Erickson, Gina Clegg. A Mop for Pop. 1996. (Get Ready...Get Set...Read! Ser.: Set 1). (Illus.). (J). lib. bdg. 11.95 (*1-56674-136-X*) Forest Hse. Publishing Co., Inc.

Fox, Mem. Zoo-Looking. (Illus.). (J). (ps-2). 2001. pap. 6.00 (*1-57255-011-2*); 1995. 32p. 15.95 (*1-57255-010-4*) Mondo Publishing.

—Zoo-Looking. 1996. 12.15 (*0-606-22652-4*) Turtleback Bks.

Fox, Paula. Blowfish Live in the Sea. 1986. 128p. (J). (gr. 6-8). reprint ed. pap. 3.95 o.p. (*0-689-71092-5*, Aladdin) Simon & Schuster Children's Publishing.

—Ivan. 2002. (SPA.). (YA). pap. 8.50 (*84-279-3245-6*, NG31202) Molino, Editorial ESP. *Dist:* Lectorum Pubns., Inc.

—Portrait of Ivan. 1985. (Illus.). 144p. (J). (gr. 5-7). lib. bdg. 15.00 o.p. (*0-02-735510-1*, Simon & Schuster Children's Publishing) Simon & Schuster Children's Publishing.

Francomano, Alfred. Dilemma: Story of a Father & Two Sons. 1998. 64p. pap. 8.00 (*0-8059-4431-1*) Dorrance Publishing Co., Inc.

Friend, David. Baseball, Football, Daddy & Me. 1990. (Illus.). 320p. (J). (ps-3). 12.95 o.p. (*0-670-82420-8*, Viking Children's Bks.) Penguin Putnam Bks. for Young Readers.

Fuqua, Jonathon Scott. The Reappearance of Sam Webber. 2001. 15.04 (*0-606-21397-X*) Turtleback Bks.

Gaiman, Neil. The Day I Swapped My Dad for Two Goldfish. (Illus.). 1997. 52p. 21.99 o.p. (*1-56504-944-6*, 13401, Borealis); 1998. 256p. (J). reprint ed. pap. 14.99 (*1-56504-199-2*, 12553) White Wolf Publishing, Inc.

Gakis, Nick. Mr. Executive's Heroic Adventures. 1998. (J). (gr. 3-5). pap. 7.95 o.p. (*0-533-12403-4*) Vantage Pr., Inc.

Galbraith, Kathryn O. Holding Onto Sunday. 1995. (Illus.). 48p. (J). (gr. 1-4). mass mkt. 14.00 o.s.i (*0-689-50623-6*, McElderry, Margaret K.) Simon & Schuster Children's Publishing.

Gardiner, Lindsey. Good Night, Poppy & Max: A Bedtime Counting Book. 2002. (Illus.). 11p. (J). (ps). bds. 6.95 (*0-316-60122-5*) Little Brown Children's Bks.

Gauthier, Bertrand. Zachary in I'm Zachary! 1993. Tr. of Zunik dans Je Suis Zunik. (Illus.). 24p. (J). (gr. 2 up). lib. bdg. 18.60 o.p. (*0-8368-1007-4*) Stevens, Gareth Inc.

—Zachary in the Championship. 1993. Tr. of Zunik dans le Championnat. (Illus.). 24p. (J). (gr. 2 up). lib. bdg. 19.93 o.p. (*0-8368-1008-2*) Stevens, Gareth Inc.

—Zachary in the Present. 1993. (Illus.). 24p. (J). (gr. 2 up). lib. bdg. 19.93 o.p. (*0-8368-1010-4*) Stevens, Gareth Inc.

—Zachary in the Wawabongbong. 1993. (Illus.). 24p. (J). (gr. 2 up). lib. bdg. 19.93 o.p. (*0-8368-1011-2*) Stevens, Gareth Inc.

Geller, Mark. What I Heard. 1987. (Charlotte Zolotow Bk.). 128p. (J). (gr. 5 up). 11.95 (*0-06-022160-7*); lib. bdg. 11.89 o.p. (*0-06-022161-5*) HarperCollins Children's Bk. Group.

Gellman, Ellie. Jeremy's Dreidel. 1992. (Illus.). 32p. (J). 13.95 o.p. (*0-929371-33-X*); pap. 6.95 o.p. (*0-929371-34-8*) Kar-Ben Publishing.

—Jeremy's Dreidel. 1992. (J). 11.15 (*0-606-05384-0*) Turtleback Bks.

Geringer, Laura. Silverpoint. 1991. (Charlotte Zolotow Bk.). 160p. (YA). (gr. 5 up). 13.95 o.p. (*0-06-023849-6*); (Illus.). lib. bdg. 13.89 (*0-06-023850-X*) HarperCollins Children's Bk. Group.

Gifaldi, David. One Thing for Sure. 1986. 160p. (J). (gr. 4-7). 13.95 o.p. (*0-89919-462-1*, Clarion Bks.) Houghton Mifflin Co. Trade & Reference Div.

—One Thing for Sure. 2001. 184p. (gr. 4-7). pap. 12.95 (*0-595-15326-7*, Backinprint.com) iUniverse, Inc.

Gilbert, Nan. The Strange New World Across the Street. 1979. (J). (gr. 5-9). pap. 1.50 o.p. (*0-380-45922-1*, 45922-1, Avon Bks.) Morrow/Avon.

Glassman, Peter. Dad's Job. 2003. (Illus.). 36p. (J). (gr. k-3). 15.95 (*0-689-82890-X*, Simon & Schuster Children's Publishing) Simon & Schuster Children's Publishing.

Gleason, Rachel. Daddy's in the Navy. 1994. (J). (ps-3). pap. text 8.95 o.p. (*1-881116-69-7*) Black Forest Pr.

Gleeson, Kate. I Love My Daddy. 1995. (Shaped Naptime Tales Bks.). (Illus.). 14p. (J). (ps-3). bds. 3.49 o.s.i (*0-307-12878-4*, Golden Bks.) Random Hse. Children's Bks.

Gleitzman, Morris. Blabber Mouth. 1995. 144p. (J). (gr. 3 up). 11.00 (*0-15-200369-X*) Harcourt Children's Bks.

—Sticky Beak. 1995. 144p. (J). (gr. 3 up). pap. 5.00 (*0-15-200367-3*, Harcourt Paperbacks) Harcourt Children's Bks.

Glenn, Mel. One Order to Go. 1984. 192p. (J). (gr. 7 up). 11.95 o.p. (*0-89919-257-2*, Clarion Bks.) Houghton Mifflin Co. Trade & Reference Div.

Golden Books Staff. Natasha's Daddy. 1993. (First Little Golden Bks.). (Illus.). 24p. (J). 1.29 o.s.i (*0-307-30134-6*, Golden Bks.) Random Hse. Children's Bks.

Gomi, Taro. I Lost My Dad! 2001. Orig. Title: Tousan Maigo. (Illus.). 32p. (J). (ps-2). 12.95 (*1-929132-04-2*, Cranky Nell Bks.) Kane/Miller Bk. Pubs.

Graham, Georgia. The Strongest Man This Side of Cremona. 1998. (Illus.). 32p. (J). (ps-3). 15.95 (*0-88995-182-9*) Red Deer Pr. CAN. *Dist:* General Distribution Services, Inc.

Graham, Michelle. But Daddy, Why? 1997. (Illus.). 96p. (J). (gr. k-5). pap. 5.00 (*0-9658766-1-6*) Rays of Hope.

—Mais Papa, Pourquoi. Pichot, Sylvie, tr. 1997. Tr. of But Daddy, Why?. (Illus.). 96p. (J). (gr. k-5). pap. 5.00 (*0-9658766-2-4*) Rays of Hope.

Grambling, Lois G. Daddy Will Be There. 1998. (Illus.). 24p. (J). (ps-3). 15.99 (*0-688-14983-9*, Greenwillow Bks.) HarperCollins Children's Bk. Group.

Grant, Cynthia D. Keep Laughing. 1991. 192p. (YA). (gr. 7 up). lib. bdg. 14.95 o.p. (*0-689-31514-7*, Atheneum) Simon & Schuster Children's Publishing.

—Mary Wolf. (gr. 7 up). 1997. 224p. (J). per. 4.99 (*0-689-81251-5*, Simon Pulse); 1995. 176p. (YA). 16.00 (*0-689-80007-X*, Atheneum) Simon & Schuster Children's Publishing.

—Mary Wolf. 1997. (YA). 11.04 (*0-606-11600-1*) Turtleback Bks.

Greene-Alexander, Alesia. Sunflowers & Rainbows for Tia: Saying Goodbye to Daddy. 1999. (Illus.). (J). 7.95 (*1-56123-128-2*) Centering Corp.

Greene, Shep. The Boy Who Drank Too Much. 1979. 160p. (YA). (gr. 7 up). 11.50 o.p. (*0-670-18381-4*, Viking Children's Bks.) Penguin Putnam Bks. for Young Readers.

—The Boy Who Drank Too Much. 1980. 160p. (YA). (gr. 7 up). mass mkt. 5.50 (*0-440-90493-5*, Laurel Leaf) Random Hse. Children's Bks.

—The Boy Who Drank Too Much. 1979. (J). 11.04 (*0-606-00651-6*) Turtleback Bks.

Greenfield, Eloise. Lisa's Daddy & Daughter Day, Big bk. 1993. (Illus.). (J). (gr. k-2). pap. 17.95 o.p. (*0-88741-918-6*, 04723) Sundance Publishing.

—My Daddy & I... 1991. (Illus.). 12p. (J). bds. 5.95 (*0-86316-206-1*) Writers & Readers Publishing, Inc.

Griffin, Peni R. Vikki Vanishes. 1995. 160p. (J). (gr. 7 up). pap. 15.00 (*0-689-80028-2*, McElderry, Margaret K.) Simon & Schuster Children's Publishing.

Guess How Much I Love You. 2000. (Illus.). 15.99 (*0-7636-1516-1*) Candlewick Pr.

Gutman, Anne. Daddy Kisses. 2003. (Illus.). 14p. (J). bds. 5.95 o.s.i (*0-8118-3914-1*) Chronicle Bks. LLC.

Halecroft, David. Breaking Loose. 1992. (Alden All Stars Ser.). 128p. (J). (gr. 3-7). 13.00 o.p. (*0-670-84697-X*, Viking Children's Bks.) Penguin Putnam Bks. for Young Readers.

Hall, Lynn. Denison's Daughter. 1983. 128p. (YA). (gr. 7 up). 10.95 o.s.i (*0-684-17955-5*, Macmillan Reference USA) Gale Group.

Hallinan, P. K. We're Very Good Friends, My Father & I. 24p. (J). 7.95 (*0-8249-5375-4*); pap. 5.95 (*0-8249-5376-2*) Ideals Pubns. (Ideals).

Hamilton, Virginia. A Little Love. 1985. 2.50 o.p. (*0-425-08424-8*) Berkley Publishing Group.

—A Little Love. 1984. 192p. (J). 12.95 o.s.i (*0-399-21046-6*, Philomel) Penguin Putnam Bks. for Young Readers.

Hamm, Diane J. Bunkhouse Journal. 1990. 96p. (YA). (gr. 7 up). 13.95 (*0-684-19206-3*, Atheneum) Simon & Schuster Children's Publishing.

Hampton, Janie. Come Home Soon, Baba. 1993. (Illus.). 32p. (J). (gr. 4 up). 12.95 o.p. (*0-87226-511-0*, Bedrick, Peter Bks.) McGraw-Hill Children's Publishing.

Haseley, Dennis. Kite Flier. 1986. (Illus.). 32p. (J). (gr. k-4). 13.95 o.s.i (*0-02-743110-X*, Simon & Schuster Children's Publishing) Simon & Schuster Children's Publishing.

—My Father Doesn't Know about the Woods & Me. 1988. (Illus.). 32p. (J). (gr. 1-3). lib. bdg. 13.95 o.s.i (*0-689-31365-9*, Atheneum) Simon & Schuster Children's Publishing.

Hawks, Robert. This Stranger, My Father. 1988. 228p. (J). (gr. 5-9). 13.95 o.p. (*0-395-44089-0*) Houghton Mifflin Co.

—This Stranger, My Father. 1990. 240p. (J). (gr. 4). mass mkt. 2.95 (*0-380-70739-X*, Avon Bks.) Morrow/Avon.

Hayes, Alan. Dad's Golf Story: Coloring Book. 2000. (Illus.). 24p. (J). (ps-2). pap. 4.95 (*0-615-11424-5*) A R T L U Publishing.

Haynes, Betsy. Great Dad Disaster. 1994. 8.60 o.p. (*0-606-06426-5*) Turtleback Bks.

—The Great Dad Disaster. 1994. 176p. (J). (gr. 4-7). pap. 3.50 o.s.i (*0-553-48169-X*) Bantam Bks.

Hearn, Diane Dawson. Dad's Dinosaur Day. (Illus.). 32p. (J). (ps-3). 1999. pap. 5.99 (*0-689-82611-7*, 076714005990, Aladdin); 1993. lib. bdg. 16.00 (*0-02-743485-0*, Simon & Schuster Children's Publishing) Simon & Schuster Children's Publishing.

—Dad's Dinosaur Day. 1999. 12.14 (*0-606-16309-3*) Turtleback Bks.

Hekkanen, Ernest. The Last Thing My Father Gave Me. 1998. 170p. pap. (*0-9682800-1-3*) New Orphic Publishers.

Helm, Lynn Z. Living with Dad. 1990. (J). (gr. 5-7). mass mkt. 2.75 o.p. (*0-590-43011-4*) Scholastic, Inc.

Henderson, Malcolm. Katie & Her Friends. 1998. (Illus.). 32p. (J). (ps-3). 15.95 (*0-9665198-0-9*, 0998001000) Moss Portfolio, The.

Henkes, Kevin. Protecting Marie. 1996. (Illus.). 208p. (YA). (gr. 5-9). pap. 5.99 (*0-14-038320-4*) Penguin Putnam Bks. for Young Readers.

Hermes, Patricia. Cheat the Moon: A Novel. 1998. (Illus.). 176p. (J). (gr. 3-7). 15.95 o.p. (*0-316-35929-7*) Little Brown & Co.

—Papa's Junky Music. 2015. (J). 15.95 (*0-399-23125-0*, Philomel) Penguin Putnam Bks. for Young Readers.

—When Snow Lay Soft on the Mountains. 1996. (Illus.). 32p. (J). (ps-3). 15.95 o.p. (*0-316-36005-8*) Little Brown & Co.

Heron, Ann & Maran, Meredith. How Would You Feel If Your Dad Was Gay? 1994. (Illus.). 32p. (J). (gr. 1-5). reprint ed. pap. 6.95 o.p. (*1-55583-243-1*) Alyson Pubns.

Hess, Donna L. Reading for Christian Schools, 6. 1987. (Illus.). 250p. (YA). (gr. 7 up). pap. 6.49 (*0-89084-379-1*, 031229) Jones, Bob Univ. Pr.

Hesse, Karen. Just Juice. 1998. (Illus.). iv, 138p. (*0-05-900332-4*) Scholastic, Inc.

—Sable. 1994. 96p. (YA). (gr. 2 up). 15.95 (*0-8050-2416-6*, Holt, Henry & Co. Bks. For Young Readers) Holt, Henry & Co.

Hickman, Martha W. When Can Daddy Come Home? 1983. (Illus.). 48p. (J). (gr. 1-3). pap. text 9.50 o.p. (*0-687-44969-3*) Abingdon Pr.

Hickman, Martha Whitmore. When Andy's Father Went to Prison. Levine, Abby, ed. rev. ed. 1990. (Albert Whitman Concept Bks.). Orig. Title: When Can Daddy Come Home?. (Illus.). 40p. (J). (gr. 4-7). lib. bdg. 13.95 (*0-8075-8874-1*) Whitman, Albert & Co.

High, Linda Oatman. Barn Savers. 2003. (Illus.). 32p. (J). (gr. k-3). 15.95 (*1-56397-403-7*) Boyds Mills Pr.

Hilbrecht, Kirk & Hilbrecht, Sharron. My Daddy Is a Soldier. 1996. (Illus.). 30p. (J). (ps-3). reprint ed. pap. 5.75 (*1-889658-01-4*) New Canaan Publishing Co., Inc.

Hill, Pamela Smith. A Voice from the Border. 1998. 320p. (YA). (gr. 7-12). tchr. ed. 16.95 (*0-8234-1356-X*) Holiday Hse., Inc.

Hines, Anna Grossnickle. Daddy Makes the Best Spaghetti. 2002. (Illus.). (J). 13.79 (*0-7587-2332-6*) Book Wholesalers, Inc.

—Daddy Makes the Best Spaghetti. 1999. (ps-3). pap. 13.35 (*0-8335-2786-X*) Econo-Clad Bks.

—Daddy Makes the Best Spaghetti. (Illus.). (J). (ps-ps). 1999. 28p. bds. 5.95 (*0-395-98036-4*); 1988. 32p. pap. 5.95 (*0-89919-794-9*); 1986. 40p. 15.00 o.p. (*0-89919-388-9*) Houghton Mifflin Co. Trade & Reference Div. (Clarion Bks.).

—Sky All Around. 1989. (Illus.). 32p. (J). (gr. 4-7). 13.95 o.p. (*0-89919-801-5*) Clarion IND. *Dist:* Houghton Mifflin Co.

Hiris, Monica. Just Like Dad. l.t. ed. 1996. (Illus.). 8p. (J). (gr. k-2). pap. 4.95 (*1-879835-76-2*) Kaeden Corp.

Hogan, Paula Z. Will Dad Ever Move Back Home? 1993. (Life & Living from a Child's Point of View Ser.). (J). (ps-3). pap. 4.95 o.p. (*0-8114-7160-8*) Raintree Pubs.

Holmes, Barbara Ware. Following Fake Man. 2001. (Illus.). 240p. (gr. 5-9). text 15.95 (*0-375-81266-0*); lib. bdg. 17.99 (*0-375-91266-5*) Random Hse. Children's Bks. (Knopf Bks. for Young Readers).

Holub, Josef. The Robber & Me. Crawford, Elizabeth D., tr. 1999. 224p. (gr. 5-9). pap. text 4.50 o.s.i (*0-440-41540-3*, Dell Books for Young Readers) Random Hse. Children's Bks.

—The Robber & Me. 1999. (gr. 4-7). 19.25 (*0-8446-7007-3*) Smith, Peter Pub., Inc.

—The Robber & Me. 1999. 10.55 (*0-606-15909-6*) Turtleback Bks.

Honig, Donald. Hurry Home. 1976. (Illus.). 32p. (J). (gr. 3-7). lib. bdg. 5.95 o.p. (*0-201-02975-8*) Addison-Wesley Longman, Inc.

Hoopes, Lyn Littlefield. Daddy's Coming Home. 1984. (Charlotte Zolotow Bk.). (Illus.). 32p. (J). (ps-2). 13.95 o.p. (*0-06-022568-8*); lib. bdg. 12.89 o.p. (*0-06-022569-6*) HarperCollins Children's Bk. Group.

Horlacher, Bill & Horlacher, Kathy. I'm Glad I'm Your Dad. 1985. (Happy Day Bks.). (Illus.). 24p. (J). (ps-2). 2.50 o.p. (*0-87239-875-7*, 3675) Standard Publishing.

Horn, Peter. The Best Father of All. James, J. Alison, tr. from GER. 2003. (Illus.). 32p. (J). (ps-1). 15.95 (*0-7358-1679-4*); lib. bdg. 16.50 (*0-7358-1680-8*) North-South Bks., Inc.

Horowitz, Jordan. Getting Even with Dad. 1994. 128p. (J). (gr. 4-7). mass mkt. 3.50 (*0-590-48262-9*) Scholastic, Inc.

Horowitz, Ruth. Bat Time. 1991. (Illus.). 32p. (J). (ps-2). lib. bdg. 13.95 o.p. (*0-02-744541-0*, Simon & Schuster Children's Publishing) Simon & Schuster Children's Publishing.

Howard, Elizabeth Fitzgerald. Papa Tells Chita a Story. (Illus.). 32p. (J). (ps-2). 1998. pap. 5.99 (*0-689-82220-0*, Aladdin); 1995. 15.00 (*0-02-744623-9*, Simon & Schuster Children's Publishing) Simon & Schuster Children's Publishing.

—Papa Tells Chita a Story. 1998. 12.14 (*0-606-15670-4*) Turtleback Bks.

Howe, Fanny. Radio City. 1984. 128p. (YA). (gr. 7 up). pap. 2.25 o.p. (*0-380-86025-2*, 86025, Avon Bks.) Morrow/Avon.

Howe, James. Pinky & Rex & the Double-Dad Weekend. 1999. (Pinky & Rex Ser.). (Illus.). (J). (gr. 1-4). pap. text 11.10 (*0-7857-9131-0*) Econo-Clad Bks.

—Pinky & Rex & the Double-Dad Weekend, unabr. ed. 1997. (Pinky & Rex Ser.). (Illus.). (J). (gr. 1-4). 22.24 incl. audio (*0-7887-1824-X*, 40604) Recorded Bks., LLC.

—Pinky & Rex & the Double-Dad Weekend. 1995. (Pinky & Rex Ser.). (Illus.). (J). (gr. 1-4). 10.14 (*0-606-09752-X*) Turtleback Bks.

Howker, Janni. The Nature of the Beast. 1987. (Novels Ser.). (J). (gr. 5-9). pap. 4.95 o.p. (*0-14-032254-X*, Puffin Bks.) Penguin Putnam Bks. for Young Readers.

Hughes, Dean. Lucky Comes Home. 1994. (Lucky Ladd Ser.: Bk. 10). 138p. (Orig.). (J). (gr. 4-6). pap. o.p. (*0-87579-941-8*, Cinnamon Tree) Deseret Bk. Co.

—Lucky's Cool Club. 1993. (Lucky Ladd Ser.: No. 8). 141p. (Orig.). (J). (gr. 3-7). pap. 4.95 o.p. (*0-87579-786-5*, Cinnamon Tree) Deseret Bk. Co.

Hughey, Roberta. The Question Box. 1984. (J). (gr. 7 up). 14.95 o.p. (*0-385-29358-5*, Delacorte Pr.) Dell Publishing.

—The Question Box. 1986. (J). mass mkt. 2.95 o.s.i (*0-440-97222-1*, Dell Books for Young Readers) Random Hse. Children's Bks.

Humphrey, Paul. In Dad's Day. 1995. (Read All about It Ser.). 32p. (J). (gr. k-3). pap. 4.95 (*0-8114-3718-3*); (Illus.). lib. bdg. 5.00 (*0-8114-5731-1*) Raintree Pubs.

Hunt, Irene. The Everlasting Hills. 1985. 192p. (J). (gr. 6-8). lib. bdg. 14.95 o.s.i (*0-684-18340-4*, Atheneum) Simon & Schuster Children's Publishing.

Hunter, Terri. One Starry Night. 2000. 32p. (J). 16.95 (*0-9705974-0-1*) Baby Star Productions, LLC.

Hurst, Carol Otis. In Plain Sight. 2002. 160p. (YA). (gr. 5-9). 15.00 (*0-618-19699-4*) Houghton Mifflin Co.

Hurwitz, Johanna. Ozzie on His Own. 1995. (Illus.). 128p. (J). (gr. 4-7). 15.99 (*0-688-13742-3*) HarperCollins Children's Bk. Group.

Hébert, Marie-Francine. A Monster in My Cereal. Cummins, Sarah, tr. from FRE. 1990. (Illus.). 54p. (J). (gr. 3-6). pap. 4.50 (*0-929005-12-0*) Second Story Pr. CAN. *Dist:* Orca Bk. Pubs.

Isadora, Rachel. At the Crossroads. 1991. (Illus.). 32p. (J). (ps up). 16.00 o.s.i (*0-688-05270-3*); lib. bdg. 15.93 o.p. (*0-688-05271-1*) HarperCollins Children's Bk. Group. (Greenwillow Bks.).

—At the Crossroads. 1994. (Illus.). 32p. (J). (ps-3). reprint ed. pap. 5.95 (*0-688-13103-4*, Morrow, William & Co.) Morrow/Avon.

—At the Crossroads. 1994. 11.10 (*0-606-06192-4*) Turtleback Bks.

Jacobson, Jennifer. Winnie Dancing on Her Own. 2003. (Illus.). 112p. (J). (gr. 4-6). pap. 5.95 (*0-618-36921-X*) Houghton Mifflin Co.

Jerman, Jerry. My Father the Horse Thief. 1995. (Journeys of Jessie Land Ser.). 132p. (Orig.). (J). (gr. 3-8). pap. 5.99 o.p. (*1-56476-347-1*, 6-3347) Cook Communications Ministries.

Johns, Michael-Anne, et al. What a Girl Wants. novel ed. 2003. 80p. (J). mass mkt. 4.99 (*0-439-53062-8*) Scholastic, Inc.

Johnson, Angela. Songs of Faith. 1999. 108p. (YA). (gr. 5-8). reprint ed. pap. 4.99 (*0-679-89488-8*, Knopf Bks. for Young Readers) Random Hse. Children's Bks.

—Songs of Faith. 1998. (Illus.). 112p. (J). (gr. 3-7). pap. 15.95 (*0-531-30023-4*); lib. bdg. 16.99 (*0-531-33023-0*) Scholastic, Inc. (Orchard Bks.).

Johnson, Dolores. Papa's Stories. 1994. (Illus.). 32p. (J). (gr. k-3). lib. bdg. 14.95 (*0-02-747847-5*, Atheneum) Simon & Schuster Children's Publishing.

—Your Dad Was Just Like You. 1993. (Illus.). 32p. (J). (gr. k-3). text 13.95 (*0-02-747838-6*, Atheneum) Simon & Schuster Children's Publishing.

Johnson, Pete. Rescuing Dad. (Read-Along Ser.). (J). 2003. pap. 29.95 incl. audio (*0-7540-6254-6*); 2002. (Illus.). 16.95 (*0-7540-7809-4*) BBC Audiobooks America. (Galaxy Children's Large Print).

Johnson, Scott K. I Can't Wait until I'm Old Enough to Hunt with Dad. 1995. 32p. (J). (gr. 1-3). 14.95 (*1-887251-56-1*) Deer Pond Pub.

Joyce, James. Eveline. 1990. (Short Story Library). (Illus.). 32p. (YA). (gr. 5 up). lib. bdg. 13.95 o.p. (*0-88682-308-0*, Creative Education) Creative Co., The.

Jukes, Mavis. Like Jake & Me. (Borzoi Sprinters Ser.). (Illus.). 32p. (ps-3). 1987. pap. 7.99 (*0-394-89263-1*); 1984. (J). 13.99 o.s.i (*0-394-95608-7*); 1984. (J). 12.95 o.s.i (*0-394-85608-2*) Random Hse. Children's Bks. (Knopf Bks. for Young Readers).

—Like Jake & Me. 1987. (J). 14.14 (*0-606-02359-3*) Turtleback Bks.

Kalifon, Mary. My Dad Lost His Job. 1995. (Illus.). 32p. (Orig.). (J). (ps-4). pap. 5.95 (*0-9641981-0-X*) Cedars Sinai Health System.

Kantenwein, Louise. A True Scotsman. 1996. (Illus.). (J). (gr. 2-4). 8.95 o.p. (*0-533-11643-0*) Vantage Pr., Inc.

Kaye, Marilyn. Like Father, Like Son. 2001. (Replica Ser.: No. 20). (Illus.). 144p. (gr. 3-7). pap. text 4.50 o.s.i (*0-553-48748-5*, Skylark) Random Hse. Children's Bks.

Keats, Ezra Jack. Louie's Search. 2002. (Illus.). (J). 13.19 (*0-7587-5737-9*) Book Wholesalers, Inc.

—Louie's Search. 2001. (Illus.). 40p. (J). (ps-3). 15.99 (*0-670-89224-6*, Viking Children's Bks.) Penguin Putnam Bks. for Young Readers.

Kennedy, Shannon. Daddy, Please Tell Me What's Wrong. 1988. (Lifelines Ser.). 144p. (Orig.). (J). (gr. 6-9). pap. 1.95 o.p. (*0-87406-239-X*) Darby Creek Publishing.

Kennemore, Tim. Wall of Words. 1983. 173p. (J). (gr. 5-8). o.p. (*0-571-11856-9*) Faber & Faber Ltd.

Ketteman, Helen. I Remember Papa. (Illus.). 32p. (J). (ps-3). 2001. pap. 6.99 (*0-14-056607-4*, Puffin Bks.); 1998. 16.99 o.s.i (*0-8037-1848-9*, Dial Bks. for Young Readers); 1998. 15.89 o.p. (*0-8037-1849-7*, Dial Bks. for Young Readers) Penguin Putnam Bks. for Young Readers.

—I Remember Papa. 2001. 13.14 (*0-606-21244-2*) Turtleback Bks.

Kidd, Nina. June Mountain Secret. 1991. (Illus.). 32p. (J). (gr. k-3). 15.00 o.p. (*0-06-023167-X*); lib. bdg. 14.89 o.p. (*0-06-023168-8*) HarperCollins Children's Bk. Group.

King, Stephen Michael. A Special Kind of Love. 1996. (Illus.). 32p. (J). (ps-3). pap. 15.95 (*0-590-67681-4*) Scholastic, Inc.

Koertge, Ronald. Harmony Arms. 1992. (YA). 15.95 o.p. (*0-316-50104-2*, Joy Street Bks.) Little Brown & Co.

—The Harmony Arms. 1994. 192p. (YA). (gr. 5 up). mass mkt. 3.99 (*0-380-72188-0*, Avon Bks.) Morrow/Avon.

—Mariposa Blues. 1991. (YA). 15.95 o.p. (*0-316-50103-4*) Little Brown & Co.

—Mariposa Blues. 1993. 176p. (J). mass mkt. 3.50 (*0-380-71761-1*, Avon Bks.) Morrow/Avon.

—Mariposa Blues. 1991. 8.60 o.p. (*0-606-02737-8*) Turtleback Bks.

Koralek, Jenny. Dad, Me & the Dinosaurs. (Illus.). 32p. (J). pap. 7.95 (*0-14-038700-5*) Penguin Bks., Ltd. GBR. *Dist:* Trafalgar Square.

Krensky, Stephen. My Dad Can Do Anything. 2004. (J). pap. 3.99 (*0-375-82627-0*) Random Hse. Children's Bks.

Krisher, Trudy B. Kinship. 1997. 304p. (YA). (gr. 7). 15.95 o.s.i (*0-385-32272-0*, Delacorte Pr.) Dell Publishing.

—Kinship. 1997. mass mkt. 15.95 (*0-385-44695-0*) Doubleday Publishing.

—Kinship. 1999. 304p. (YA). (gr. 7 up). mass mkt. 4.50 o.s.i (*0-440-22023-8*, Dell Books for Young Readers) Random Hse. Children's Bks.

—Kinship. 1999. 10.55 (*0-606-16170-8*) Turtleback Bks.

Kroll, Steven. Gone Fishing. 1991. (Illus.). (J). 1.99 o.p. (*0-517-07856-2*) Random Hse. Value Publishing.

—Happy Father's Day. 1988. (Illus.). 32p. (J). (ps-3). lib. bdg. 15.95 o.p. (*0-8234-0671-7*) Holiday Hse., Inc.

Kroll, Virginia L. Africa Brothers & Sisters. (Illus.). 32p. (J). (ps-2). 1998. pap. 5.99 o.s.i (*0-689-81816-5*, Aladdin); 1993. lib. bdg. 15.00 (*0-02-751166-9*, Simon & Schuster Children's Publishing) Simon & Schuster Children's Publishing.

—Africa Brothers & Sisters. 1998. 12.14 (*0-606-12870-0*) Turtleback Bks.

Krulik, Nancy E. Getting Even with Dad. 1994. 32p. (J). (ps-3). mass mkt. 2.95 (*0-590-48261-0*) Scholastic, Inc.

—Jungle to Jungle. 1997. 96p. (J). (gr. 3-7). pap. 4.95 o.p. (*0-7868-4119-2*) Disney Pr.

Kurtz, Jane. Faraway Home. 2000. (Illus.). 32p. (J). (gr. 1-5). 16.00 (*0-15-200036-4*, Gulliver Bks.) Harcourt Children's Bks.

LaFaye, A. Dad, in Spirit. 2001. (Illus.). 176p. (J). (gr. 3-6). 16.00 (*0-689-81514-X*, Simon & Schuster Children's Publishing) Simon & Schuster Children's Publishing.

Landalf, Helen & McConnell, Mary. Getting Used to Candy. 2000. (Illus.). (J). (gr. k-5). 6.95 (*1-56123-139-8*) Centering Corp.

Landis, J. D. Daddy's Girl. 1984. 208p. (J). (gr. 7 up). 11.95 o.p. (*0-688-02763-6*, Morrow, William & Co.) Morrow/Avon.

—Daddy's Girl. 1985. (YA). (gr. 8 up). pap. (*0-671-55823-4*, Simon Pulse) Simon & Schuster Children's Publishing.

Langley, Karen. Shine! 2002. (Illus.). 32p. (J). (gr. k-3). 15.95 (*0-7614-5127-7*) Cavendish, Marshall Corp.

Laufer, Judy E. Where Did Papa Go? Looking at Death from a Young Child's Perspective. 1991. (Illus.). 32p. (Orig.). (J). (ps-2). pap. 9.95 (*1-881669-00-9*) Little Egg Publishing Co.

Le Saux, Alain. Daddy Scratches, ERS. 1992. (Illus.). 28p. (J). (ps). pap. 6.95 o.p. (*0-8050-2195-7*, Holt, Henry & Co. Bks. For Young Readers) Holt, Henry & Co.

—Daddy Sleeps, ERS. 1992. (Illus.). 28p. (J). (ps). pap. 6.95 o.p. (*0-8050-2196-5*, Holt, Henry & Co. Bks. For Young Readers) Holt, Henry & Co.

Lee, Jeffrey. True Blue. 2003. 144p. (gr. 5). text 14.95 (*0-385-73093-4*, Delacorte Bks. for Young Readers) Random Hse. Children's Bks.

Leitch, Patricia. Show Jumper Wanted. 1997. (Horseshoes Ser.: Vol. 5). 112p. (J). (gr. 3-7). pap. 3.95 o.p. (*0-06-440638-5*, Harper Trophy) HarperCollins Children's Bk. Group.

Leonard, Marcia. My Camp-Out. 1999. (Real Kids Readers Ser.). (Illus.). 32p. (J). (ps-1). 18.90 (*0-7613-2052-0*); pap. 4.99 (*0-7613-2077-6*) Millbrook Pr., Inc.

—My Camp-Out. 1999. (J). 10.14 (*0-606-19165-8*) Turtleback Bks.

—My Camp-Out. 1999. E-Book (*1-58824-480-6*); E-Book (*1-58824-728-7*); E-Book (*1-58824-811-9*) ipicturebooks, LLC.

Levi, Adoff Jaime. Rock-n-Roll Dad. 1924. (*0-688-17550-3*); lib. bdg. (*0-688-17551-1*) HarperCollins Children's Bk. Group.

Levy, Elizabeth. My Life as a Fifth-Grade Comedian. 1999. (J). pap., stu. ed. 41.20 incl. audio (*0-7887-3180-7*, 40915) Recorded Bks., LLC.

—My Life as a Fifth Grade Comedian. 192p. (J). 1998. (gr. 3-7). pap. 5.99 (*0-06-440723-3*, Harper Trophy); 1997. (ps-2). 15.99 (*0-06-026602-3*) HarperCollins Children's Bk. Group.

—My Life as a Fifth Grade Comedian. 1998. 11.00 (*0-606-15647-X*) Turtleback Bks.

Lewis, Beverly. Pickle Pizza. 1996. (Cul-de-Sac Kids Ser.: Vol. 8). 80p. (J). (gr. 2-5). pap. 3.99 (*1-55661-728-3*) Bethany Hse. Pubs.

—Secret Summer Dreams. 1993. (Holly's Heart Ser.: Vol. 2). 160p. (J). (gr. 6-9). pap. 6.99 o.p. (*0-310-38061-8*) Zondervan.

—Secret Summer Dreams: Holly's Heart. 2001. (Hollys Heart Ser.). 144p. (J). (gr. 6-9). pap. 5.99 (*0-7642-2501-4*) Bethany Hse. Pubs.

L'Heureux, Christine. Caillou: Como Papa. 2004. (SPA.). (J). 3.95 (*1-58728-347-6*) Creative Publishing international, Inc.

—Caillou My Daddy. 2001. (Kite Ser.). (Illus.). 12p. (J). (ps-k). bds. 3.95 (*2-89450-225-7*) Editions Chouette, Inc. CAN. *Dist:* Client Distribution Services.

Light, John. Odd Jobs. 1991. (Light Reading Ser.). (J). (Illus.). 24p. (ps-1). 1.99 (*0-85953-339-5*); (ITA.). (gr. 4-7). pap. 3.99 (*0-85953-603-3*) Child's Play of England GBR. *Dist:* Child's Play-International.

Lindbergh, Reeve. If I'd Known Then What I Know Now. (Illus.). 32p. (J). (ps-3). 1996. pap. 4.99 o.s.i (*0-14-055772-5*, Puffin Bks.); 1994. 13.99 o.p. (*0-670-85351-8*, Viking Children's Bks.) Penguin Putnam Bks. for Young Readers.

—If I'd Known Then What I Know Now. 1996. 10.19 o.p. (*0-606-09458-X*) Turtleback Bks.

Lindenbaum, Pija. Else-Marie & Her Seven Little Daddies, ERS. 1991. (Illus.). 32p. (J). (ps-2). 14.95 o.p. (*0-8050-1752-6*, Holt, Henry & Co. Bks. For Young Readers) Holt, Henry & Co.

Locker, Thomas. Miranda's Smile. (J). 2000. (Illus.). pap. 4.99 (*0-14-055669-9*, Puffin Bks.); 1994. 32p. 15.99 o.s.i (*0-8037-1688-5*, Dial Bks. for Young Readers); 1994. 32p. 15.89 o.s.i (*0-8037-1689-3*, Dial Bks. for Young Readers) Penguin Putnam Bks. for Young Readers.

LoMonaco, Palmyra. Watch the Day Move. 2015. (J). 14.95 (*0-399-22162-X*) Penguin Putnam Bks. for Young Readers.

London, Jonathan. Giving Thanks. 2003. (Illus.). 32p. (J). 16.99 (*0-7636-1680-X*) Candlewick Pr.

—Old Salt, Young Salt. 1996. (Illus.). 32p. (J). (gr. 1 up). lib. bdg. 15.93 o.p. (*0-688-12976-5*) HarperCollins Children's Bk. Group.

Loomis, Christine. The 10 Best Things about My Dad. Urbanovic, Jackie, tr. & illus. by. 2004. (J). mass mkt. (*0-439-57769-1*, Cartwheel Bks.) Scholastic, Inc.

Lorelli, Michael K. Traveling Again, Dad? Struzan, Dylan, ed. 1995. (Illus.). 32p. (J). (ps-7). 17.95 (*0-9646302-0-6*) Awesome Bks., LLC.

Lotu, Denize. Father & Son. 1996. 11.15 o.p. (*0-606-09261-7*) Turtleback Bks.

Low, Joseph. Little Though I Be. 1976. (Illus.). 40p. (J). (ps-3). 5.95 o.p. (*0-07-038842-3*); lib. bdg. 8.95 o.p. (*0-07-038843-1*) McGraw-Hill Cos., The.

Lowery, Linda. Laurie Tells. 1994. (Illus.). (J). (gr. 3-6). lib. bdg. 19.95 (*0-87614-790-2*, Carolrhoda Bks.) Lerner Publishing Group.

Lyle, Letcher L. Dark but Full of Diamonds. 1981. (YA). (gr. 12 up). 10.95 o.s.i (*0-698-20517-0*, Coward-McCann) Putnam Publishing Group, The.

Lyon, George Ella. Gina, Jamie, Father, Bear. 2002. 144p. (J). (gr. 6-9). 15.95 (*0-689-84370-4*, Atheneum/Richard Jackson Bks.) Simon & Schuster Children's Publishing.

Maccarone, Grace. I Shop with My Daddy. 1998. (Hello Reader! Ser.). (J). 10.14 (*0-606-13510-3*) Turtleback Bks.

Malone, James H. No-Job Dad. 1992. (Illus.). 30p. (J). (gr. 1-2). pap. 13.95 (*1-878217-06-2*) Victory Pr.

Mandelbaum, Pili. You Be Me, I'll Be You. 1990. Tr. of Noire Comme le Cafe, Blanc Comme la Lune. (Illus.). 40p. (J). (ps-3). 13.95 o.p. (*0-916291-27-8*) Kane/Miller Bk. Pubs.

Mandrell, Louise & Collins, Ace. Best Man for the Job: A Story about the Meaning of Father's Day. 1993. (Illus.). 32p. (J). (gr. 1-4). 12.95 o.p. (*1-56530-039-4*) Summit Publishing Group - Legacy Bks.

Mann, Peggy. There Are Two Kinds of Terrible. 1979. (J). (gr. 5 up). pap. 1.50 o.p. (*0-380-45823-3*, 45823, Avon Bks.) Morrow/Avon.

Rojany, Lisa. Casper: Junior Novelization. 1995. (Illus.). (J). (gr. 2 up). 3.95 o.s.i (*0-8431-3854-8*, Price Stern Sloan) Penguin Putnam Bks. for Young Readers.

Roop, Peter & Roop, Connie. Ahyoka & the Talking Leaves. 1992. (Illus.). 48p. (J). (gr. 1 up). 15.00 o.p. (*0-688-10697-8*) HarperCollins Children's Bk. Group.

Rosen, David. Henry's Tower. 1984. (Illus.). 36p. (J). (gr. k-5). 10.95 (*0-930905-01-6*); pap. 4.95 (*0-930905-00-8*) Platypus Bks., Ltd.

Roy, Ronald. Breakfast with My Father, 001. 1980. (Illus.). 32p. (J). (ps-3). 7.95 o.p. (*0-395-29430-4*, Clarion Bks.) Houghton Mifflin Co. Trade & Reference Div.

Ruel, Francine. Mon Pere et Moi. (FRE.). (YA). 2001. 96p. pap. 12.95 (*2-89021-514-8*); 1993. (Illus.). 160p. (gr. 8 up). pap. 8.95 o.p. (*2-89021-192-4*) La Courte Echelle CAN. *Dist:* Firefly Bks., Ltd.

Ryder, Joanne. My Father's Hands. 1994. (Illus.). 32p. (J). (ps-3). 16.99 (*0-688-09189-X*) HarperCollins Children's Bk. Group.

—My Father's Hands. 1994. (Illus.). 32p. (YA). (ps up). lib. bdg. 15.93 (*0-688-09190-3*, Morrow, William & Co.) Morrow/Avon.

Sachar, Louis. Monkey Soup. 1992. (Illus.). 32p. (J). (ps-3). 12.00 o.s.i (*0-679-80297-5*); 13.99 o.s.i (*0-679-90297-X*) Random Hse. Children's Bks. (Knopf Bks. for Young Readers).

Salisbury, Graham. Shark Bait. 1999. 160p. (YA). (gr. 5-9). mass mkt. 4.50 (*0-440-22803-4*, Dell Books for Young Readers) Random Hse. Children's Bks.

—Shark Bait. 1999. 10.55 (*0-606-16449-9*) Turtleback Bks.

Salus, Naomi P. My Daddy's Mustache. 1979. (Illus.). 32p. (gr. 1-3). lib. bdg. 7.95 o.p. (*0-385-13189-5*) Doubleday Publishing.

Samuel, Lynette M. Daddy's T-Shirt. 1996. (Illus.). 32p. (J). (gr. 2-5). 21.95 (*0-9651270-1-X*); per. 15.95 (*0-9651270-0-1*) Bright Lamb Pubs., Inc.

Samuels, Gertrude. Adam's Daughter. 1977. (YA). (gr. 7 up). 12.95 (*0-690-01322-1*) HarperCollins Children's Bk. Group.

—Adam's Daughter. 1979. 192p. (YA). (gr. 6). mass mkt. 1.75 o.p. (*0-451-11486-8*, AE1486, Signet Bks.) NAL.

Schindel, John. Dear Daddy. 1995. (Illus.). 24p. (J). (ps-3). lib. bdg. 13.95 (*0-8075-1531-0*) Whitman, Albert & Co.

Schnur, Steven. Beyond Providence. 1996. 256p. (YA). (gr. 7 up). 12.00 (*0-15-200982-5*) Harcourt Children's Bks.

Schwandt, Stephen. Holding Steady. 1996. 184p. (J). (gr. 7-9). reprint ed. pap. 5.95 o.p. (*0-915793-94-6*) Free Spirit Publishing, Inc.

Scotellaro, Robert. Daddy Fixed the Vacuum Cleaner. 1993. 24p. (J). (gr. k-3). pap. 2.99 o.p. (*0-87406-630-1*) Darby Creek Publishing.

Scott, Stefanie. Everybody Say Moesha! 1997. (Moesha Ser.). 160p. (YA). (gr. 7 up). per. 3.99 (*0-671-01147-2*, Simon Pulse) Simon & Schuster Children's Publishing.

Shalev, Meir. My Father Always Embarrasses Me. Klein, Zanvel, ed. Herrmann, Dagmar, tr. from HEB. 1990. (Illus.). 30p. (J). (gr. k-3). 12.95 (*0-922984-02-6*) Wellington Publishing, Inc.

Shange, Ntozake. Daddy Says. 2003. 192p. (J). (gr. 5-9). 15.95 (*0-689-83081-5*, Simon & Schuster Children's Publishing) Simon & Schuster Children's Publishing.

Sharmat, Mitchell. Hello...This Is My Father Speaking. 1994. (Illus.). 128p. (J). (gr. 5-9). lib. bdg. 13.89 o.p. (*0-06-024472-0*); 14.00 o.p. (*0-06-024469-0*) HarperCollins Children's Bk. Group.

Sharratt, Nick. Robopop. 2000. (Illus.). 121p. (J). pap. 6.95 (*0-440-86352-X*) Transworld Publishers Ltd. GBR. *Dist:* Trafalgar Square.

Shaw, Richard C. My Dad Sells Insurance. 1988. (Illus.). 40p. (J). (ps-5). lib. bdg. (*0-944900-00-3*) Shaw & Co.

Shreve, Susan Richards. The Formerly Great Alexander Family. 1995. (Illus.). 128p. (J). (gr. 3 up). 13.00 o.s.i (*0-688-13551-X*, Morrow, William & Co.) Morrow/Avon.

—The Goalie. 1996. 96p. (J). (gr. 3 up). 15.00 o.p. (*0-688-14379-2*, Morrow, William & Co.) Morrow/Avon.

—Jonah, the Whale. (J). (gr. 3-7). 1999. 128p. mass mkt. 4.99 (*0-590-37134-7*, Scholastic Paperbacks); 1997. 115p. pap. 14.95 (*0-590-37133-9*) Scholastic, Inc.

Shusterman, Neal. Dissidents. 1989. 224p. (YA). (gr. 7 up). 13.95 (*0-316-78904-6*) Little Brown & Co.

—What Daddy Did. 1991. (YA). pap. 15.95 (*0-316-78906-2*) Little Brown & Co.

Simpson, Juwairiah J. The Four Daughters of Yusuf the Dairy Farmer. 1894. (Illus.). 40p. (Orig.). (J). (gr. 1-4). pap. 3.75 (*0-89259-056-4*) American Trust Pubns.

—A Wicked Wazir. 1990. (Illus.). 48p. (Orig.). (J). (gr. 3-6). pap. 6.50 (*0-89259-084-X*) American Trust Pubns.

Smith, Beatrice S. The Road to Galveston. 1973. (Books for Adults & Young Adults). (Illus.). 132p. (J). (gr. 4 up). lib. bdg. 10.95 o.p. (*0-8225-0755-2*, Lerner Pubns.) Lerner Publishing Group.

Smith, Eddie. A Lullaby for Daddy. 1994. (Illus.). 32p. (J). (gr. 4-7). pap. 8.95 (*0-86543-404-2*); (ps). 16.95 (*0-86543-403-4*) Africa World Pr.

Smith, Roland. Jaguar. 1997. (gr. 5 up). 256p. (J). 15.95 (*0-7868-0282-0*); 249p. (YA). 16.49 (*0-7868-2226-0*) Hyperion Bks. for Children.

Sollinger, Emily. Giggles for Daddy. 2002. (Illus.). 14p. (J). bds. 5.99 (*0-448-42548-3*, Grosset & Dunlap) Penguin Putnam Bks. for Young Readers.

Solomon, Joan. News for Dad. 1980. (Illus.). (J). (ps-3). text 8.50 o.p. (*0-241-10215-4*) Trafalgar Square.

Sonneborn, Ruth A. Friday Night Is Papa Night. 1987. (Picture Puffin Ser.). (Illus.). (J). 10.19 o.p. (*0-606-01810-7*) Turtleback Bks.

Spinelli, Eileen. Boy, Can He Dance! 1993. (Illus.). 32p. (J). (ps-2). lib. bdg. 14.95 o.p. (*0-02-786350-6*, Simon & Schuster Children's Publishing) Simon & Schuster Children's Publishing.

—Boy, Can He Dance. 1997. (Illus.). 32p. (J). (ps-3). pap. 5.99 (*0-689-81533-6*, Aladdin) Simon & Schuster Children's Publishing.

—Night Shift Daddy. 2000. (Illus.). 32p. (J). (ps-2). 14.99 (*0-7868-0495-5*); lib. bdg. 15.49 (*0-7868-2424-7*) Hyperion Pr.

Spohn, David. Home Field. 1993. (J). 10.00 o.p. (*0-688-11172-6*); lib. bdg. 9.93 o.p. (*0-688-11173-4*) HarperCollins Children's Bk. Group.

St. Aubin, Bruno. Daddy's a Busy Beaver. Perkes, Carolyn, tr. from FRE. 2001. (Little Wolf Bks.: Level 1). (Illus.). 32p. (J). (gr. 1 up). (*1-894363-74-4*) Dominique & Friends.

St. George, Judith S. The Shad Are Running. 1977. (Illus.). (J). (gr. 3-6). 5.29 o.p. (*0-399-61045-6*) Putnam Publishing Group, The.

Stafford, Kim R. We Got Here Together. 1994. (Illus.). 40p. (J). (ps-3). 13.95 o.s.i (*0-15-294891-0*) Harcourt Trade Pubs.

Stanley, Diane. A Time Apart. 2001. (J). 12.00 (*0-606-21490-9*) Turtleback Bks.

Steadman, Ralph. That's My Dad. 2001. (Illus.). 32p. pap. 8.95 (*1-84270-011-1*) Andersen Pr., Ltd. GBR. *Dist:* Trafalgar Square.

Stecher, Miriam B. Daddy & Ben Together. 1981. (Illus.). (J). (ps-2). 12.95 o.p. (*0-688-00735-X*); lib. bdg. 12.88 o.p. (*0-688-00736-8*) HarperCollins Children's Bk. Group.

Steel, Danielle. Martha's New Daddy. 1989. (Illus.). 32p. (J). (ps-2). 8.95 o.s.i (*0-385-29799-8*, Delacorte Pr.) Dell Publishing.

Steptoe, John L. Daddy Is a Monster... Sometimes. (Trophy Picture Bk.). (Illus.). 32p. (J). (gr. k-3). 1983. pap. 6.95 o.p. (*0-06-443042-1*, Harper Trophy); 1980. lib. bdg. 14.89 o.p. (*0-397-31893-6*) HarperCollins Children's Bk. Group.

—Daddy Is a Monster... Sometimes. 1980. (Illus.). (J). (gr. k-3). 12.95 (*0-397-31762-X*, 849228) Lippincott Williams & Wilkins.

Stevens, Florence & Lamont-Clarke, Ginette. What If Dad Gets Lost at the Zoo? 1991. (Illus.). 24p. (J). (ps-3). pap. 6.95 (*0-88776-272-7*) Tundra Bks. of Northern New York.

Stewart, Josie & Salem, Lynn. Notes to Dad. 1994. (Illus.). 12p. (J). (gr. k-2). pap. 3.75 (*1-880612-46-1*) Seedling Pubns., Inc.

Still, Wayne Anthony, illus. Desert Treasure. 1999. 30.00 (*0-8172-7296-8*) Raintree Pubs.

Stine, R. L. Stay Out of the Basement. (Goosebumps Ser.). (J). 2003. 144p. mass mkt. 4.99 (*0-439-56845-5*, 53657972); 1992. 160p. (gr. 3-7). mass mkt. 3.99 (*0-590-45366-1*) Scholastic, Inc. (Scholastic Paperbacks).

—Stay Out of the Basement. l.t. ed. 1997. (Goosebumps Ser.: No. 2). 144p. (J). (gr. 3-7). lib. bdg. 21.27 o.p. (*0-8368-1974-8*) Stevens, Gareth Inc.

—Stay Out of the Basement. 1992. (Goosebumps Ser.: No. 2). (J). (gr. 3-7). 10.04 (*0-606-01950-2*) Turtleback Bks.

Strasser, Todd. Hey Dad, Get a Life! 1996. 160p. (J). (gr. 4-7). tchr. ed. 15.95 (*0-8234-1278-4*) Holiday Hse., Inc.

Strohl, Roger R., Jr. Jake & Duke Camp Paw Mountain. 1989. (J). 6.95 o.p. (*0-533-08163-7*) Vantage Pr., Inc.

Strong, Jeremy. Pirate Pendemonium. 2002. (J). pap. 24.95 incl. audio (*0-7540-6252-X*) BBC Audiobooks America.

Swanson, Gary B. My Father Owns This Place. 1997. (Orig.). (YA). (gr. 8-11). pap. 8.99 o.p. (*0-8280-1252-0*) Review & Herald Publishing Assn.

Syme, Marguerite Hann. Chickpea. 1998. 64p. (*1-86388-642-7*) Scholastic Australia.

Take Me Out to the Ball Game. 1995. (Little Golden Sound Story Bks.). (Illus.). 24p. (J). bds. o.p. (*0-307-74831-6*, Golden Bks.) Random Hse. Children's Bks.

Talbert, Marc. The Purple Heart. 1992. (Willa Perlman Bks.). 144p. (J). (gr. 4-8). lib. bdg. 14.89 o.p. (*0-06-020429-X*); 14.95 (*0-06-020428-1*) HarperCollins Children's Bk. Group.

Taylor, Sydney. A Papa Like Everyone Else. 1988. 160p. (J). (gr. k-6). pap. 2.95 o.s.i (*0-440-40129-1*, Yearling) Random Hse. Children's Bks.

Tedrow, T. L. Days of Laura Ingalls Wilder, Vol. 4: Home to the Prairie. 1992. (J). pap. 4.99 o.p. (*0-8407-3401-8*) Nelson, Thomas Inc.

Thomas, Jane Resh. Daddy Doesn't Have to Be a Giant Anymore. 1996. 14.95 (*0-395-69419-1*) Houghton Mifflin Co.

Thomas, Joyce Carol. The Golden Pasture. 144p. (YA). (gr. 7 up). 1987. pap. 2.50 o.p. (*0-590-33638-X*); 1986. 11.95 o.p. (*0-590-33681-9*) Scholastic, Inc.

Thompson, Virginia N. Butch, the Man of the House. 1987. 25p. (J). (gr. 1-6). 5.95 o.p. (*0-533-07343-X*) Vantage Pr., Inc.

Todd, Leonard. Squaring Off. 1990. 192p. (YA). (gr. 7 up). 13.95 o.p. (*0-670-83377-0*, Viking Children's Bks.) Penguin Putnam Bks. for Young Readers.

Tolan, Stephanie S. The Liberation of Tansy Warner. 1982. 144p. (gr. 6-9). pap. 1.95 o.p. (*0-440-94636-0*) Dell Publishing.

Tretiak, Susie. Good-Bye Daddy. 1982. (Illus.). 52p. (J). (gr. k-6). pap. 5.95 o.p. (*0-938594-04-4*) Special Literature Pr.

Tyler, Amy J. Best Dad in the Sea. 2003. (Step into Reading Ser.). (Illus.). 32p. (J). (ps-1). pap. 3.99 (*0-7364-2131-9*); lib. bdg. 11.99 (*0-7364-8021-8*) Random Hse. Children's Bks. (RH/Disney).

Tyler, Linda W. When Daddy Comes Home. 1988. (Illus.). 320p. (J). (ps-1). pap. 3.95 o.p. (*0-14-050615-2*, Puffin Bks.) Penguin Putnam Bks. for Young Readers.

Uhlberg, Myron. The Printer. Sorensen, Henri, tr. & illus. by. 2003. (J). (gr. 1-5). 16.95 (*1-56145-221-1*, Peachtree Junior) Peachtree Pubs., Ltd.

Valentine, Johnny. The Daddy Machine. 1992. (Illus.). 48p. (Orig.). (J). (gr. k-4). pap. 6.95 o.p. (*1-55583-107-9*, Alyson Wonderland) Alyson Pubns.

—One Dad, Two Dads, Brown Dad, Blue Dads. 2004. (Illus.). 32p. (J). (ps-1). 10.95 (*1-55583-253-9*, Alyson Wonderland) Alyson Pubns.

Vestergaard, Hope. Driving Daddy. 2003. (Illus.). 24p. 6.99 (*0-525-47032-8*, Dutton Children's Bks.) Penguin Putnam Bks. for Young Readers.

Voigt, Cynthia. Sons from Afar. 1988. 3.95p. mass mkt. 4.50 o.s.i (*0-449-70293-6*, Fawcett) Ballantine Bks.

—Sons from Afar. (gr. 7 up). 1996. 256p. mass mkt. 5.50 (*0-689-80889-5*, Simon Pulse); 1987. 224p. (YA). lib. bdg. 15.95 (*0-689-31349-7*, Atheneum) Simon & Schuster Children's Publishing.

—Sons from Afar. 1996. 11.55 (*0-606-10935-8*) Turtleback Bks.

—Tree by Leaf. 1989. 176p. (J). (gr. 7 up). mass mkt. 4.50 o.s.i (*0-449-70334-7*, Fawcett) Ballantine Bks.

—Tree by Leaf. (J). (gr. 4-7). 2000. 240p. pap. 4.99 (*0-689-83527-2*, Aladdin); 1988. 208p. 15.95 (*0-689-31403-5*, Atheneum) Simon & Schuster Children's Publishing.

—Tree by Leaf. 1989. (J). 9.60 o.p. (*0-606-01223-0*) Turtleback Bks.

Warner, Sally. Some Friend. 1997. 160p. (J). (gr. 3-9). pap. 4.99 o.s.i (*0-679-87619-7*) Random Hse., Inc.

—Some Friend. 1997. 10.09 o.p. (*0-606-11857-8*) Turtleback Bks.

Warren, Donna. Daddy Loves Me. 1996. (Baby Flap Book Ser.). (Illus.). 20p. (J). (ps). bds. 2.99 (*1-56293-901-7*, McClanahan Bk.) Learning Horizons, Inc.

—Mommy Loves Me. 1996. (Baby Flap Book Ser.). (Illus.). 20p. (J). (ps). bds. 2.99 (*1-56293-900-9*, McClanahan Bk.) Learning Horizons, Inc.

Watanabe, Shigeo. Daddy, Play with Me. 1985. (Illus.). 32p. (J). (ps). 9.95 o.s.i (*0-399-21211-6*, Philomel) Penguin Putnam Bks. for Young Readers.

—Daddy, Play with Me! 1986. (Illus.). (J). (ps). 3.95 o.s.i (*0-399-21334-1*, Philomel) Penguin Putnam Bks. for Young Readers.

—Where Is My Daddy? 1985. (I Can Do It All by Myself Bks.). (Illus.). 32p. (J). 3.95 o.s.i (*0-399-21049-0*, Philomel) Penguin Putnam Bks. for Young Readers.

—Where's My Daddy? (J). (ps-3). 1996. 5.95 o.s.i (*0-399-22427-0*); 1982. (Illus.). 32p. 10.95 o.s.i (*0-399-20899-2*) Penguin Putnam Bks. for Young Readers. (Philomel).

Watson, Kim. Just Like Dad. 2001. (Little Bill Ser.). (Illus.). 32p. (J). (gr. k-3). pap. 5.99 (*0-689-83999-5*, Simon Spotlight/Nickelodeon) Simon & Schuster Children's Publishing.

—Just Like Dad. 2001. (Little Bill Books for Beginning Readers Ser.). (Illus.). (J). 12.14 (*0-606-21276-0*) Turtleback Bks.

Weaver, Will. Hard Ball. (gr. 6 up). 1999. 256p. (J). pap. 5.99 (*0-06-447208-6*, Harper Trophy); 1998. 240p. (YA). 15.95 (*0-06-027121-3*); 1998. 240p. (YA). lib. bdg. 15.89 (*0-06-027122-1*) HarperCollins Children's Bk. Group.

—Hard Ball. 1999. 11.00 (*0-606-16706-4*) Turtleback Bks.

Webster, Jean. Daddy-Long-Legs. 1999. (Chapter Book Charmers Ser.). (Illus.). 73p. (J). (gr. 2-5). 2.99 o.p. (*0-694-01282-3*) HarperCollins Children's Bk. Group.

Welch, Willy. Dancing with Daddy. (Illus.). (J). (ps-3). 2002. 32p. pap. 6.95 (*1-58089-078-4*); 1999. (*1-58089-020-2*, Whispering Coyote) Charlesbridge Publishing, Inc.

Weller, Frances Ward. Boat Song. 1987. 180p. (J). (gr. 3-7). 13.95 o.p. (*0-02-792611-7*, Simon & Schuster Children's Publishing) Simon & Schuster Children's Publishing.

Welty, Harry R. Visit to the Attic. 1992. (Illus.). 250p. (Orig.). (YA). (gr. 6-8). pap. 6.95 (*0-9632953-0-6*) Welty Pr.

Wersba, Barbara. Run Softly, Go Fast. 1972. 176p. (gr. 9-12). pap. 1.75 o.p. (*0-553-13429-9*) Bantam Bks.

Whitehouse, Melissa. The Care & Training of Parents. 1995. 64p. (J). pap. 6.00 (*1-56002-499-2*, University Editions) Aegina Pr., Inc.

Wigand, Molly. Major League Dads. 1999. (Ready-to-Read Ser.). (Illus.). 31p. (J). (ps-3). pap. 3.99 (*0-689-82630-3*, 076714003996, Simon Spotlight/Nickelodeon) Simon & Schuster Children's Publishing.

Wiggins, VeraLee. LeeAnne, the Disposable Kid. 1994. (J). (gr. 7-10). pap. 5.99 o.p. (*0-8280-0791-8*) Review & Herald Publishing Assn.

Wilder, Laura Ingalls. Laura's Pa. 1999. (Little House Ser.: No. 12). (Illus.). 80p. (J). (gr. 3-6). pap. 4.25 (*0-06-442082-5*, Harper Trophy) HarperCollins Children's Bk. Group.

—Laura's Pa. 1999. (Little House Chapter Bks.: No. 12). (J). (gr. 3-6). 10.40 (*0-606-15840-5*) Turtleback Bks.

Willson, Sarah. Brand New Daddy. 2001. (Rugrats Ser.). (Illus.). 32p. (J). (ps-2). pap. 5.99 (*0-689-83598-1*, Simon Spotlight/Nickelodeon) Simon & Schuster Children's Publishing.

Wolfgram, Barbara. I Know My Daddy Loves Me. 1998. (Illus.). 32p. (J). (ps-1). 6.99 (*0-570-05050-2*, 56-1874GJ) Concordia Publishing Hse.

Wood, Douglas. What Dads Can't Do. ed. 2001. (J). (gr. 1). spiral bd. (*0-616-07247-3*); (gr. 2). spiral bd. (*0-616-07248-1*) Canadian National Institute for the Blind/Institut National Canadien pour les Aveugles.

—What Dads Can't Do. 2000. (Illus.). 32p. (J). (ps-3). 14.00 (*0-689-82620-6*, Simon & Schuster Children's Publishing) Simon & Schuster Children's Publishing.

Wood, Phyllis A. Win Me & You Lose. 1977. (Hiway Book). 136p. (J). (gr. 7 up). 8.95 o.p. (*0-664-32605-6*) Westminster John Knox Pr.

Wooldridge, Frosty. Strike Three! Take Your Base. 2001. 160p. (YA). (gr. 6-12). pap. 6.95 (*1-930093-07-1*) Brookfield Reader, Inc., The.

Wright, Lynn F. Daddy, Tell Me a Story. 1997. (Illus.). (J). (ps-2). 13.95 (*1-881519-08-2*); pap. 6.95 (*1-881519-09-0*) WorryWart Publishing Co.

Wunderli, Steve. Heartbeat of Halftime, ERS. 1996. 128p. (J). (gr. 4-7). 14.95 o.s.i (*0-8050-4713-1*, Holt, Henry & Co. Bks. For Young Readers) Holt, Henry & Co.

Wyeth, Sharon Dennis. Always My Dad. (Illus.). (J). (gr. k-3). 1997. 32p. pap. 6.99 o.s.i (*0-679-88934-5*); 1994. 40p. 15.99 o.s.i (*0-679-93447-2*); 1994. 40p. 17.00 o.s.i (*0-679-83447-8*) Random Hse. Children's Bks. (Knopf Bks. for Young Readers).

—Always My Dad. 1997. 12.19 o.p. (*0-606-12873-5*) Turtleback Bks.

Wynne-Jones, Tim. The Maestro. 1996. 240p. (YA). (gr. 5 up). pap. 16.95 (*0-531-09544-4*); lib. bdg. 17.99 (*0-531-08894-4*) Scholastic, Inc. (Orchard Bks.).

Yolen, Jane. All Those Secrets of the World. 1991. (J). (ps-3). 14.95 o.p. (*0-316-96891-9*) Little Brown & Co.

—All Those Secrets of the World. 1991. 12.10 (*0-606-05113-9*) Turtleback Bks.

Young, Alida E. What's Wrong with Daddy? 1986. 176p. (J). (gr. 5-8). 2.25 o.p. (*0-87406-066-4*) Darby Creek Publishing.

Young, David C. A Father's Love. 1993. (Illus.). 24p. (J). 14.00 (*0-9638833-0-5*) Young & Young Productions.

Young, Eleanor R. Fathers, Fathers, Fathers. 1981. (Early Childhood Bk.). (Illus.). (ps-2). lib. bdg. 4.95 o.p. (*0-513-01108-0*) Denison, T. S. & Co., Inc.

Young, Ella. Wonder Smith & His Son. (J). pap. 14.95 (*0-86315-521-9*, 1622) Floris Bks. GBR. *Dist:* SteinerBooks, Inc.

Zalben, Jane Breskin. Papa's Latkes, ERS. 1996. (Illus.). 32p. (J). (ps-3). 13.95 o.s.i (*0-8050-4634-8*, Holt, Henry & Co. Bks. For Young Readers) Holt, Henry & Co.

Ziefert, Harriet. Daddies Are for Catching Fireflies. 1999. (Lift-the-Flap Bks.). (Illus.). 16p. (J). (ps-1). pap. 6.99 (*0-14-056553-1*, Puffin Bks.) Penguin Putnam Bks. for Young Readers.

—Keeping Daddy Awake on the Way Home from the Beach. 1986. (Illus.). 12p. (J). (ps-2). 5.95 o.p. (*0-694-00080-9*) HarperCollins Children's Bk. Group.

—When Daddy Had the Chicken Pox. 1991. (Illus.). 32p. (J). (ps-3). 13.95 (*0-06-026906-5*); lib. bdg. 13.89 o.p. (*0-06-026907-3*) HarperCollins Children's Bk. Group.

Zolotow, Charlotte. A Father Like That. 1971. (Charlotte Zolotow Bk.). (Illus.). (J). (ps-3). lib. bdg. 12.89 o.p. (*0-06-026950-2*) HarperCollins Children's Bk. Group.

—A Father Like That. 1999. (Illus.). 32p. (J). (ps-3). 14.95 (*0-06-027864-1*); lib. bdg. 14.89 (*0-06-027865-X*) HarperCollins Pubs.

FRIENDSHIP—FICTION

A un Insecto Tu Amigo. 2002. (How 2 Ser.).Tr. of Make a Bug Your Friend. (SPA., Illus.). 16p. (J). (ps-3). 6.95 (*968-5308-52-7*) Silver Dolphin Spanish Editions MEX. *Dist:* Publishers Group West.

Aardema, Verna. Bimwili & The Zimwi. 1992. (Illus.). 32p. (ps-3). pap. 5.99 o.s.i (*0-14-054608-1*) Penguin Putnam Bks. for Young Readers.

—Bimwili & the Zimwi. 1988. (Pied Piper Paperback Ser.). (Illus.). 32p. (J). (ps-3). pap. 4.95 o.p. (*0-8037-0553-0*) Penguin Putnam Bks. for Young Readers.

—Oh, Kojo! How Could You? 1988. (Pied Piper Bks.). (Illus.). 32p. (J). (ps-3). pap. 4.99 o.p. (*0-8037-0449-6*, Dial Bks. for Young Readers) Penguin Putnam Bks. for Young Readers.

—What's So Funny, Ketu? 32p. (J). (ps-3). 1992. pap. 5.99 o.s.i (*0-14-054722-3*, Puffin Bks.); 1989. (Illus.). pap. 4.95 o.p. (*0-8037-0646-4*) Penguin Putnam Bks. for Young Readers.

Aaron, Chester. Lackawanna. 1986. 224p. (YA). (gr. 7 up). lib. bdg. 11.89 (*0-397-32058-2*) HarperCollins Children's Bk. Group.

Abdo Publishing Staff, contrib. by. Flower Girl Friends. 2000. (Faithful Friends Ser.). (Illus.). 64p. (J). (gr. 4). lib. bdg. 21.35 (*1-57765-229-0*, ABDO & Daughters) ABDO Publishing Co.

Abramchik, Lois. Is Your Family Like Mine? 2nd ed. 2002. (Illus.). 36p. (Orig.). (J). pap. 9.95 (*0-9674468-9-9*) Two Lives Publishing.

Ackerman, Karen. Broken Boy. 1991. 160p. (YA). 14.95 o.s.i (*0-399-22254-5*, Philomel) Penguin Putnam Bks. for Young Readers.

—The Tin Heart. 1990. (Illus.). 32p. (J). (gr. 1-3). 13.95 (*0-689-31461-2*, Atheneum) Simon & Schuster Children's Publishing.

Ackerman, Tova. Group Soup. (Orig.). pap. 6.95 (*0-9720183-0-1*) Puppetry in Practice.

Ada, Alma Flor. Amigos: Big Book. (Superbooks Ser.).Tr. of Friends. (J). (gr. k-1). (ENG & SPA., Illus.). 26p. 21.95 (*0-88272-501-7*); 1989. (SPA.). 21.95 (*0-88272-569-6*) Santillana USA Publishing Co., Inc.

—Jordi's Star. 1996. (Illus.). 32p. (J). (ps-3). 15.95 o.s.i (*0-399-22832-2*, G. P. Putnam's Sons) Penguin Group (USA) Inc.

—Me Llamo Maria Isabel. 1996. (SPA.). 11.14 (*0-606-10485-2*) Turtleback Bks.

—Pio Peep! 2000. mass mkt. 8.95 (*0-06-443868-6*) HarperCollins Children's Bk. Group.

—Querido Pedrín. 1997. 12.19 o.p. (*0-606-11775-X*) Turtleback Bks.

—Sale el Oso: Small Book. 1992. (Rimas y Risas Ser.). (SPA., Illus.). 16p. (Orig.). (J). (gr. k-3). pap. text 6.00 (*1-56334-079-8*) Hampton-Brown Bks.

Adair, Peggy. Chance. 1990. 200p. (Orig.). (YA). (gr. 6-12). pap. 4.95 (*0-9626803-9-7*) Deep River Pr.

Adams, Jean Ekman. Clarence Returns to 831 Eggplant Avenue. 2003. (Illus.). 32p. (J). (ps-3). 15.95 (*0-87358-826-6*) Northland Publishing.

Adams, Pam. Playmates. 1991. (Baby Carriage Ser.). (Illus.). 8p. (J). (gr. 3 up). 6.99 (*0-85953-449-9*) Child's Play of England GBR. *Dist:* Child's Play-International.

—Six in a Bath. 1990. (Soap Opera Ser.). (Illus.). 8p. (J). (ps-1). 4.99 (*0-85953-443-X*) Child's Play of England GBR. *Dist:* Child's Play-International.

Adams, Pam, illus. Alf 'N Bet. 1992. 32p. (J). (ps-3). 4.99 (*0-85953-167-8*) Child's Play of England GBR. *Dist:* Child's Play-International.

Adler, C. S. Always & Forever Friends. 1990. 176p. (J). pap. 3.99 (*0-380-70687-3*, Avon Bks.) Morrow/Avon.

—Binding Ties. 1985. (Illus.). 192p. (gr. 7 up). 14.95 o.p. (*0-385-29293-7*, Delacorte Pr.) Dell Publishing.

—Binding Ties. 1989. (J). (gr. k-12). mass mkt. 2.95 o.s.i (*0-440-20413-5*, Laurel Leaf) Random Hse. Children's Bks.

—The Magic of the Glits. 2000. 112p. (gr. 4-7). pap. 9.95 (*0-595-09233-0*, Backinprint.com) iUniverse, Inc.

—Mismatched Summer. 1991. 144p. (YA). 14.95 o.p. (*0-399-21776-2*, G. P. Putnam's Sons) Penguin Group (USA) Inc.

—More Than a Horse. 1997. 192p. (J). (gr. 4-6). tchr. ed. 15.00 (*0-395-79769-1*, Clarion Bks.) Houghton Mifflin Co. Trade & Reference Div.

—One Unhappy Horse. l.t. ed. 2002. 184p. (J). 21.95 (*0-7862-3758-9*) Gale Group.

—One Unhappy Horse. 2001. (Illus.). 160p. (J). (gr. 4-6). tchr. ed. 15.00 (*0-618-04912-6*, Clarion Bks.) Houghton Mifflin Co. Trade & Reference Div.

—Some Other Summer. 1988. (J). (gr. 3-7). pap. 2.95 (*0-380-70515-X*, Avon Bks.) Morrow/Avon.

—What's to Be Scared of, Suki? 1996. 176p. (J). (gr. 3-7). tchr. ed. 13.95 o.s.i (*0-395-77600-7*, Clarion Bks.) Houghton Mifflin Co. Trade & Reference Div.

—Young He & Me. 1995. 192p. (J). (gr. 4-7). pap. 5.00 o.s.i (*0-15-200376-2*) Harcourt Trade Pubs.

Adler, Carole S. Always & Forever Friends. 1988. 192p. (J). (gr. 4-7). 12.95 o.p. (*0-89919-681-0*, Clarion Bks.) Houghton Mifflin Co. Trade & Reference Div.

—Kiss the Clown. 1986. (J). (gr. 7 up). 12.95 o.p. (*0-89919-419-2*, Clarion Bks.) Houghton Mifflin Co. Trade & Reference Div.

Adler, David A. Andy & Tamika. 1999. (Andy Russell Ser.). (Illus.). 144p. (YA). (gr. 2-5). pap. 4.95 (*0-15-201901-4*, Gulliver Bks.) Harcourt Children's Bks.

—Andy & Tamika. 1999. (Illus.). (J). 11.00 (*0-606-18166-0*) Turtleback Bks.

—The Many Troubles of Andy Russell. (Andy Russell Ser.). (Illus.). 144p. (YA). (gr. 2-5). 1999. pap. 4.95 (*0-15-201900-6*); 1998. 14.00 (*0-15-201295-8*) Harcourt Children's Bks. (Gulliver Bks.).

—The Many Troubles of Andy Russell. 1998. 11.00 (*0-606-18183-0*) Turtleback Bks.

Adler, Susan S. Meet Samantha: An American Girl. Thieme, Jeanne, ed. 1986. (American Girls Collection: Bk. 1). (Illus.). 72p. (YA). (gr. 2 up). pap. 5.95 (*0-937295-04-3*, American Girl); lib. bdg. 12.95 (*0-937295-80-9*, American Girl); 12.95 o.p. (*0-937295-03-5*) Pleasant Co. Pubns.

—Meet Samantha: An American Girl. 1986. (American Girls Collection: Bk. 1). (YA). (gr. 2 up). 12.10 (*0-606-02770-X*) Turtleback Bks.

Adler, Susan S, et al. Samantha's Boxed Set: Meet Samantha; Samantha Learns a Lesson; Samantha's Surprise; Happy Birthday, Samantha!; Samantha Saves the Day; Changes for Samantha, 6 bks. Thieme, Jeanne, ed. 1992. (American Girls Collection: Bks. 1-6). (Illus.). 388p. (YA). (gr. 2 up). 74.95 (*1-56247-050-7*, American Girl) Pleasant Co. Pubns.

—Samantha's Boxed Set: Meet Samantha; Samantha Learns a Lesson; Samantha's Surprise; Happy Birthday, Samantha!; Samantha Saves the Day; Changes for Samantha, 6 bks. 1991. (American Girls Collection: Bks. 1-6). (Illus.). 432p. (YA). pap. 34.95 (*0-937295-77-9*, American Girl); (gr. 2 up). 74.95 o.p. (*1-56247-013-2*) Pleasant Co. Pubns.

Adoff, Arnold. Flamboyan. 1988. (Illus.). 32p. (J). (ps-3). 14.95 o.p. (*0-15-228404-4*) Harcourt Children's Bks.

Adorjan, Carol. The Electric Man. 1981. (Prime Time Adventures Ser.). (Illus.). 64p. (J). (gr. 4 up). lib. bdg. 9.25 o.p. (*0-516-02104-4*, Children's Pr.) Scholastic Library Publishing.

—That's What Friends Are For. 1990. (J). pap. 2.75 o.p. (*0-590-42454-8*) Scholastic, Inc.

Adshead, Paul S. Trilby. 1990. (Child's Play Library). 72p. (J). (ps-3). 7.99 (*0-85953-513-4*) Child's Play of England GBR. *Dist:* Child's Play-International.

The Adventures of Tom Sawyer. 1987. mass mkt. 1.95 (*0-938819-01-1*, Aerie) Doherty, Tom Assocs., LLC.

The Adventures of Tom Sawyer. 2003. (Classic Retelling Ser.). (J). (*0-618-12053-X*) McDougal Littell Inc.

The Adventures of Tom Sawyer. 1998. 44p. (YA). stu. ed. 11.95 (*1-56137-528-4*, NU5284SP) Novel Units, Inc.

The Adventures of Tom Sawyer. 2004. (Literature Units Ser.). (J). 48p. 7.99 (*1-57690-637-X*) Teacher Created Materials, Inc.

Aertssen, Kristen. Count on Me, No. 4. 1994. (Count Me in Bks.: Bk. 4). (Illus.). 24p. (Orig.). (J). (ps-1). pap. 4.95 (*1-55037-362-5*) Annick Pr., Ltd. CAN. *Dist:* Firefly Bks., Ltd.

Aesop. The Lion & the Mouse. 1995. (Single Titles Ser.). (Illus.). 32p. (J). 14.95 o.p. (*1-56294-933-0*) Millbrook Pr., Inc.

—The Lion & the Mouse. 2000. (Illus.). 32p. (J). (gr. k-3). 15.95 (*0-7358-1220-9*) North-South Bks., Inc.

Agard, John & Paul, Korky. Brer Rabbit & the Great Tug-O-War. 1998. (Illus.). 32p. (J). (ps-2). 13.95 (*0-7641-5077-4*); pap. 6.95 o.p. (*0-7641-0513-2*) Barron's Educational Series, Inc.

Agee, Jon. Dmitri the Astronaut. 1996. (Michael di Capua Bks.). (Illus.). 32p. (J). (ps up). 14.95 o.s.i (*0-06-205074-5*); lib. bdg. 14.89 o.p. (*0-06-205075-3*) HarperCollins Children's Bk. Group.

—Ludlow Laughs, RS. (Illus.). 32p. (J). (ps-3). 1987. pap. 6.95 (*0-374-44663-6*, Sunburst); 1985. 12.95 o.s.i (*0-374-34666-6*, Farrar, Straus & Giroux (BYR)) Farrar, Straus & Giroux.

—Ludlow Laughs. 1985. E-Book (*1-58824-321-4*) ipicturebooks, LLC.

Agell, Charlotte, illus. Welcome Home or Someplace Like It, ERS. 2003. 240p. (J). 16.95 (*0-8050-7083-4*, Holt, Henry & Co. Bks. For Young Readers) Holt, Henry & Co.

Ahlberg, Allan. Ten in a Bed. 1989. (Illus.). 96p. (J). 12.95 o.p. (*0-670-82042-3*, Viking Children's Bks.) Penguin Putnam Bks. for Young Readers.

Ahlberg, Janet. Funnybones. 1990. (J). 10.15 o.p. (*0-606-04676-3*) Turtleback Bks.

Aiello, Barbara & Shulman, Jeffrey. Friends for Life: Featuring Amy Wilson. 1995. (Kids on the Block Bks.). (Illus.). (J). 48p. (gr. 3-6). lib. bdg. 13.95 o.s.i (*0-941477-03-7*); 88p. (gr. 5-8). lib. bdg. 14.98 o.p. (*0-8050-4137-0*) Millbrook Pr., Inc. (21st Century Bks., Inc.).

—Secrets Aren't (Always) for Keeps: Featuring Jennifer Hauser. 1997. (Kids on the Block Bks.). (Illus.). 89p. (J). (gr. 5-8). 16.90 (*0-8050-3069-7*, 21st Century Bks., Inc.) Millbrook Pr., Inc.

Ainsworth, Ruth. The Little Yellow Taxi & His Friends. 1997. (Illus.). 118p. (J). 16.95 (*0-7188-2554-3*) Lutherworth Pr., The GBR. *Dist:* Parkwest Pubns., Inc.

Akio, Terumasa. Me & Alves: A Japanese Journey. Matsui, Susan, tr. 1993. (Illus.). 24p. (J). pap. 4.95 (*1-55037-222-X*); lib. bdg. 14.95 (*1-55037-223-8*) Annick Pr., Ltd. CAN. *Dist:* Firefly Bks., Ltd.

Aks, Pat. Lisa's Choice. 1981. 192p. (J). 1.95 o.p. (*0-448-16997-5*) Ace Bks.

Alan Novell Studios Staff, illus. Doug Gets His Wish: Look Look Book. 1999. (Golden Book Ser.). 32p. (J). (gr. k-3). pap. text 3.99 o.p. (*0-307-13140-8*, Golden Bks.) Random Hse. Children's Bks.

Albee, Sarah. My Best Friend Is Out of This World. (Road to Reading Ser.). (J). 2003. lib. bdg. 11.99 (*0-375-99999-X*); 1998. (Illus.). 32p. 3.99 (*0-307-26202-2*, 26202) Random Hse. Children's Bks. (Golden Bks.).

—My Best Friend Is Out of This World. 1998. 10.14 (*0-606-16140-6*) Turtleback Bks.

Alcock, Vivien. The Stranger at the Window. 1998. 208p. (YA). (gr. 7-9). 16.00 (*0-395-81661-0*) Houghton Mifflin Co.

—The Stranger at the Window. 1999. 208p. (J). (gr. 5-9). pap. 4.95 (*0-395-94329-9*) Houghton Mifflin Co. Trade & Reference Div.

—The Trial of Anna Cotman. 1990. 160p. (J). (gr. 5-9). 13.95 o.s.i (*0-385-29981-8*, Delacorte Pr.) Dell Publishing.

—The Trial of Anna Cotman. 1997. 224p. (YA). (gr. 7-9). pap. 6.95 (*0-395-81649-1*) Houghton Mifflin Co.

Alcott, Louisa May. Jack & Jill. (J). E-Book 3.95 (*0-594-06550-X*) 1873 Pr.

—Jack & Jill. Date not set. 352p. (YA). 25.95 (*0-8488-2671-X*) Amereon, Ltd.

—Jack & Jill. 1880. (YA). reprint ed. pap. text 28.00 (*1-4047-1638-6*) Classic Textbooks.

—Jack & Jill. 2002. 248p. (gr. 4-7). 24.99 (*1-4043-1058-4*); per. 20.99 (*1-4043-1059-2*) IndyPublish.com.

—Jack & Jill. 1999. (Illus.). 304p. (J). (gr. 5-9). pap. 9.95 (*0-316-03084-8*); 1997. (YA). (*0-316-03778-8*); 1979. (YA). (gr. 5 up). 17.95 o.s.i (*0-316-03092-9*) Little Brown & Co.

—Jack & Jill. 1991. (Illus.). 352p. (YA). (gr. 5 up). pap. 3.50 o.s.i (*0-14-035128-0*, Puffin Bks.) Penguin Putnam Bks. for Young Readers.

—Jack & Jill. 1971. (Louisa May Alcott Library). (YA). (gr. 5-9). reprint ed. 5.95 o.p. (*0-448-02361-X*) Putnam Publishing Group, The.

—Jack & Jill. 1989. (Works of Louisa May Alcott). (YA). reprint ed. lib. bdg. 79.00 (*0-7812-1638-9*) Reprint Services Corp.

—Under the Lilacs. 1878. 302p. (YA). reprint ed. pap. text 28.00 (*1-4047-1637-8*) Classic Textbooks.

—Under the Lilacs. Exams Unlimited, Inc. Staff, ed. 2001. 256p. (C). reprint ed. cd-rom 5.45 (*1-59132-028-3*) Exams Unlimited, Inc.

—Under the Lilacs. 1996. (Illus.). 272p. (J). (gr. 4-7). pap. 9.99 (*0-316-03087-2*) Little Brown & Co.

—Under the Lilacs. 1989. (Works of Louisa May Alcott). reprint ed. lib. bdg. 79.00 (*0-7812-1637-0*) Reprint Services Corp.

Alexander, Liza. My Name Is Zoe. 1995. (Illus.). 24p. (J). (ps-3). pap. 1.79 o.s.i (*0-307-91614-6*, 11614, Golden Bks.) Random Hse. Children's Bks.

Alexander, Marsha. Popularity Plus. 1986. 160p. (YA). (gr. 7 up). 2.50 o.p. (*0-425-08439-6*, Berkley/Pacer) Berkley Publishing Group.

Alexander, Martha. My Outrageous Friend Charlie. 1989. (J). (ps-2). 11.95 o.p. (*0-8037-0587-5*); 11.89 o.p. (*0-8037-0588-3*) Penguin Putnam Bks. for Young Readers. (Dial Bks. for Young Readers).

Alexander, Nina. Playing for Keeps. 1999. (Love Stories Ser.). 192p. (gr. 7-12). mass mkt. 4.50 o.s.i (*0-553-49292-6*) Bantam Bks.

Alexander, Sue. Ellsworth & Millicent. 1993. (Illus.). 28p. (J). (gr. k up). 14.95 (*0-88708-247-5*, Simon & Schuster Children's Publishing) Simon & Schuster Children's Publishing.

Alice. Dinky & Sam: And the Long Way Home. 1981. (Illus.). 4.95 o.p. (*0-533-04711-0*) Vantage Pr., Inc.

Aliki. Best Friends Together Again. 1995. (Illus.). 32p. (J). (ps-3). 15.00 o.s.i (*0-688-13753-9*); lib. bdg. 14.89 o.s.i (*0-688-13754-7*) HarperCollins Children's Bk. Group. (Greenwillow Bks.).

—Feelings. 1986. (Illus.). 32p. (J). (ps-3). pap. 5.99 (*0-688-06518-X*, Harper Trophy) HarperCollins Children's Bk. Group.

—Overnight at Mary Bloom's. 1987. (Illus.). 32p. (J). lib. bdg. 15.93 o.p. (*0-688-06765-4*); 16.00 o.p. (*0-688-06764-6*) HarperCollins Children's Bk. Group. (Greenwillow Bks.).

—We Are Best Friends. (Illus.). 32p. (J). (gr. k-3). 1982. lib. bdg. 15.93 o.p. (*0-688-00823-2*, Greenwillow Bks.); 1982. 16.99 (*0-688-00822-4*, Greenwillow Bks.); 1987. reprint ed. pap. 5.99 (*0-688-07037-X*, Harper Trophy) HarperCollins Children's Bk. Group.

All That Jazz No. 2: Pink Parrots. 1990. (Sports Illustrated for Kids Bks.). (Illus.). (J). (gr. 3-7). pap. 3.50 o.p. (*0-316-12445-1*) Little Brown & Co.

Allan-Meyer, Kathleen. Little Bear's Crunch-a-Roo Cookies. 2000. (Little Bear Adventure Ser.: Vol. 5). (Illus.). 27p. (J). (ps-1). pap. 5.49 (*1-57924-438-6*) Jones, Bob Univ. Pr.

Allan, Nicholas. You're All Animals. 2001. (Illus.). 32p. pap. (*0-09-941125-3*) Random Hse. of Canada, Ltd. CAN. *Dist:* Random Hse., Inc.

Allard, Harry. I Will Not Go to Market Today. 1979. (Pied Piper Bks.). (Illus.). 32p. (J). (ps-2). 2.75 o.p. (*0-8037-4178-2*, Dial Bks. for Young Readers) Penguin Putnam Bks. for Young Readers.

—There's a Party at Mona's Tonight. 1997. pap. 5.99 (*0-440-91191-5*); (Illus.). 32p. pap. text 5.99 o.s.i (*0-440-41366-4*) Dell Publishing.

—There's a Party at Mona's Tonight. 1981. (Illus.). 32p. (gr. 3). 8.95 o.p. (*0-385-15186-1*); lib. bdg. o.p. (*0-385-15187-X*) Doubleday Publishing.

—There's a Party at Mona's Tonight. 1985. (Snuggle & Read Story Bks.). (Illus.). 32p. (J). (ps-3). pap. 2.50 o.p. (*0-380-69920-6*, Avon Bks.) Morrow/Avon.

—There's a Party at Mona's Tonight. 1997. 11.19 (*0-606-11976-0*) Turtleback Bks.

Allen, C. William. The African Interior Mission. 2001. (J). pap. (*0-9653308-5-0*) Africana Homestead Legacy Pubs.

Allen, Pamela. Mr. Archimedes' Bath. 2004. (Illus.). 81p. (J). (ps-1). pap. 7.95 (*0-207-17285-4*) Collins Australia AUS. *Dist:* Consortium Bk. Sales & Distribution.

—Mr. Archimedes' Bath. 1991. (Illus.). 26p. (J). (gr. k-3). pap. 7.95 o.p. (*0-7322-7236-X*) HarperCollins Pubs.

Allen, Richard E. Ozzy on the Outside. 1991. 208p. (YA). mass mkt. 3.50 o.s.i (*0-440-20767-3*) Dell Publishing.

Allen, Suzanne. Scrambled Eggs, No. 3. 1990. (J). (gr. 3 up). mass mkt. 2.75 o.p. (*0-425-12476-2*) Berkley Publishing Group.

—Totally Summer. 1991. (Scrambled Eggs Ser.: No. 9). (J). (gr. 4-7). mass mkt. 3.50 o.p. (*0-425-12613-7*) Berkley Publishing Group.

Allert, Kathy, illus. The Get along Gang on the Go. 1984. (Get along Gang Ser.). 12p. (Orig.). (J). (gr. 2-4). pap. 2.95 o.p. (*0-590-33198-1*) Scholastic, Inc.

Almon, Russell. Kid Can't Miss. 1992. 224p. (YA). pap. 3.50 (*0-380-76261-7*, Avon Bks.) Morrow/Avon.

Alonso, Fernando, et al. Amigos. 1998. (Superbooks Ser.).Tr. of Friends. (ENG & SPA.). (J). (gr. k-12). 21.95 o.p. (*0-88272-568-8*) Santillana USA Publishing Co., Inc.

Alpert, Sandra F. Horrible Howard: The Bully & Coward. Date not set. (Bully Busting Trilogy Ser.: Bk. 1). (Illus.). (Orig.). (J). (gr. k-5). pap. (*1-884931-02-2*) Global Commitment Publishing.

Alter, Judy. Katie & the Recluse. 1991. 176p. (J). (gr. 3-10). reprint ed. pap. 5.95 (*0-936650-13-3*) Temple, Ellen C. Publishing, Inc.

Althaus, Anne-Marie. A Touch of Sepia. 1994. (Illus.). (J). 4.25 (*0-383-03781-6*) SRA/McGraw-Hill.

Althoff, Victoria M. Watch Out! Here's Casey! 1988. (Impressions Ser.). 96p. (Orig.). (J). (gr. 5-8). pap. 2.50 o.p. (*0-87406-347-7*) Darby Creek Publishing.

Alton, Jennifer. Party With Bartok! 1998. (Anastasia Ser.). (J). pap. 5.99 o.p. (*0-06-107087-4*) HarperCollins Children's Bk. Group.

Amdur, Nikki. One of Us. 1981. (Illus.). (J). (gr. 3-6). 8.95 o.p. (*0-8037-6742-0*); 8.89 o.p. (*0-8037-6743-9*) Penguin Putnam Bks. for Young Readers. (Dial Bks. for Young Readers).

Amos, Janine. Friendly. 1994. (Feelings Ser.). (J). (gr. 4-7). lib. bdg. 21.40 o.p. (*0-8114-9230-3*) Raintree Pubs.

Ancona, George. Bananas: From Manolo to Margie. 1982. (J). 12.51 (*0-606-04612-7*) Turtleback Bks.

Anderson, Ho Che. The No-Boys Club. 1998. 160p. (J). (gr. 4-7). text 14.95 (*0-88899-322-6*) Groundwood Bks. CAN. *Dist:* Publishers Group West.

Anderson, Janet S. The Monkey Tree. 1998. (Illus.). 176p. (J). (gr. 7-12). 15.99 o.p. (*0-525-46032-2*, Dutton Children's Bks.) Penguin Putnam Bks. for Young Readers.

Anderson, Laurie Halse. The Big Cheese of Third Street. 2002. (Illus.). 32p. (J). (gr. k-3). 16.00 (*0-689-82464-5*, Simon & Schuster Children's Publishing) Simon & Schuster Children's Publishing.

Anderson, Marcie. Nothing to Cheer About. 1985. 96p. (J). (gr. 5-8). 2.25 o.p. (*0-87406-016-8*) Darby Creek Publishing.

Anderson, Marilyn D. Barkley Come Home. 1985. (Illus.). 96p. (J). (gr. 3-5). 2.25 o.p. (*0-87406-027-3*) Darby Creek Publishing.

—Bring Back Barkley. 1998. (Illus.). 112p. (J). (gr. 3-5). pap. 3.99 (*0-87406-890-8*, Willowisp Pr.) Darby Creek Publishing.

—Nobody Wants Barkley. 1996. (Illus.). 128p. (Orig.). (J). (gr. 3-6). pap. text 3.99 (*0-87406-808-8*) Darby Creek Publishing.

Anderson, Mary Elizabeth. That's Why God Made Friends. (J). pap. 6.99 o.p. (*0-7814-3901-9*) Cook Communications Ministries.

Anderson, Rachel. The Bus People, ERS. 1995. 112p. (YA). (gr. 4-7). pap. 5.95 o.s.i (*0-8050-4250-4*, Holt, Henry & Co. Bks. For Young Readers) Holt, Henry & Co.

Andreae, Giles. The Lion Who Wanted to Love. 1998. (Illus.). 32p. (J). (ps-2). 14.95 (*1-888444-25-8*, 21023) Little Tiger Pr.

Andrews, Jean F. The Flying Fingers Club. 1988. (Illus.). 100p. (Orig.). (YA). (gr. 3-5). pap. 3.95 o.p. (*0-930323-44-0*) Kendall Green Pubns.

Andrews, Kate. Cool It, Carrie. 1999. (Making Friends Ser.: No. 2). (Illus.). 128p. (J). (gr. 3-7). mass mkt. 3.99 (*0-380-80931-1*, Avon Bks.) Morrow/Avon.

—Grow up, Amy. 2003. (Illus.). 128p. (J). pap. (*0-330-35123-0*) Macmillan Children's Bks.

—Making Friends: Grow up, Amy. 1999. (Making Friends Ser.: No. 4). 128p. (J). (gr. 3-7). mass mkt. 3.99 (*0-380-80933-8*, Avon Bks.) Morrow/Avon.

—Wise up, Alex. 1999. (Making Friends Ser.: No. 1). (Illus.). 128p. (J). (gr. 3-7). mass mkt. 3.99 (*0-380-80930-3*, Avon Bks.) Morrow/Avon.

Anfousse, Ginette. Jiji et Pichou, Vol. 1. 1999. (Classiques Ser.). 96p. (J). pap. 24.95 (*2-89021-374-9*) La Courte Echelle CAN. *Dist:* Firefly Bks., Ltd.

Angelin. Date not set. (*0-517-80137-X*) Random Hse. Value Publishing.

Anglund, Joan Walsh. Be My Friend: Book & Locket. 2000. (Illus.). 32p. (J). (ps-3). 9.99 (*0-689-82638-9*, Little Simon) Simon & Schuster Children's Publishing.

—Cowboy & His Friend. 2002. (Illus.). 40p. (J). 6.95 (*0-7407-2211-5*) Andrews McMeel Publishing.

—Cowboy & His Friend. 1901. (Illus.). (J). (ps-2). 3.95 o.p. (*0-15-220369-9*) Harcourt Children's Bks.

—A Friend Is Someone Who Likes You: Silver Anniversary Edition. anniv. ed. 1983. (Illus.). 32p. (J). (gr. 2 up). 9.95 (*0-15-229678-6*) Harcourt Children's Bks.

Anholt, Laurence. Camille & the Sunflowers. 1994. (Illus.). 32p. (J). (ps-2). 14.95 (*0-8120-6409-7*) Barron's Educational Series, Inc.

—I Like Me, I Like You. 2001. (Share-a-Story Ser.). (Illus.). (J). (ps-1). 24p. pap. 5.95 o.p. (*0-7894-5617-6*); 32p. pap. 9.95 o.p. (*0-7894-6352-0*) Dorling Kindersley Publishing, Inc.

—Like Me, I Like You. 2001. (Illus.). (J). 12.10 (*0-606-21295-7*) Turtleback Bks.

Anzaldua, Gloria. Friends from the Other Side: Amigos del Otro Lado. 1993. 13.10 (*0-606-09303-6*) Turtleback Bks.

—Friends from the Other Side (Amigos del Otro Lado) (Illus.). 32p. (J). 1995. (ENG & SPA.). (gr. 1 up). pap. 7.95 (*0-89239-130-8*); 1993. (SPA., (ps-3). 17.50 (*0-89239-113-8*, CBP1138) Children's Bk. Pr.

Appelbaum, Stanley, ed. Platero & I/Platero y Yo: A Dual Language Book. 2004. 176p. pap. 8.95 (*0-486-43565-2*) Dover Pubns., Inc.

Appelt, Kathi A. The Alley Cat's Meow. 2002. (Illus.). 32p. (J). (gr. k-2). 16.00 (*0-15-201980-4*) Harcourt Children's Bks.

Apperley, Dawn. Blossom & Boo. 2001. (J). pap. 1.35 (*0-316-06370-3*); pap. 1.48 (*0-316-06514-5*) Little Brown & Co.

—Boo & Blossom: A Story about Best Friends. 2001. (Illus.). 32p. (J). (ps-k). 14.95 o.p. (*0-316-04963-8*) Little Brown & Co.

Applegate, Cathy. Red Sand, Blue Sky. 2004. (Girls First! Ser.). 142p. (J). (gr. 4-7). pap. 13.50 (*1-55861-278-5*) Feminist Pr. at The City Univ. of New York.

Applegate, K. A. Ben Takes a Chance. 1999. (Making Out Ser.: No. 11). 192p. (YA). (gr. 7-12). pap. 3.99 (*0-380-80867-6*, Avon Bks.) Morrow/Avon.

—Never Trust Lara. 2000. (Making Out Ser.: No. 20). 176p. (YA). (gr. 7-12). pap. 3.99 (*0-380-81309-2*, Avon Bks.) Morrow/Avon.

—Spring Break Special Edition: Special Edition. 1996. (Summer Ser.: Vol. SPEC). 240p. (YA). (gr. 7 up). per. 3.99 (*0-671-51041-X*, Simon Pulse) Simon & Schuster Children's Publishing.

Ardizzone, Edward. Tim & Charlotte. 2000. (Tim Bks.). (Illus.). 48p. (J). (ps-3). 15.95 (*0-688-17680-1*) HarperCollins Children's Bk. Group.

—Tim & Charlotte. 1987. (Illus.). 48p. (J). (gr. k-3). pap. 7.95 o.p. (*0-19-272118-6*) Oxford Univ. Pr., Inc.

—Tim & Ginger. 2000. (Tim Bks.). (Illus.). 48p. (J). (ps-3). 15.95 (*0-688-17676-3*) HarperCollins Children's Bk. Group.

—Tim & Ginger. 1987. (Illus.). 48p. (J). (gr. k-3). reprint ed. pap. 7.95 o.p. (*0-19-272113-5*) Oxford Univ. Pr., Inc.

—Tim's Friend Towser. 2000. (Tim Bks.). (Illus.). 48p. (J). (ps-3). 15.95 (*0-688-17677-1*) HarperCollins Children's Bk. Group.

—Tim's Friend Towser. 1987. (Illus.). 48p. (J). (gr. k-3). reprint ed. pap. 7.95 o.p. (*0-19-272112-7*) Oxford Univ. Pr., Inc.

Arensen, Sheldon. Kenyan Chronicles Bk. 1: The Secret Oath. 2000. 108p. (gr. 4-7). pap. 9.95 o.p. (*0-595-15844-7*) iUniverse, Inc.

Argent, Kerry. Wombat & Bandicoot: Best Friends. 1990. (Illus.). (J). (ps-2). 13.95 o.s.i (*0-316-05096-2*, Joy Street Bks.) Little Brown & Co.

Armistead, John. The Return of Gabriel. 2002. (Illus.). 240p. (J). (gr. 3-8). 17.95 (*1-57131-637-X*); pap. 6.95 (*1-57131-638-8*) Milkweed Editions.

Armstrong, Gene. Tanya's Desert Star. 1997. 128p. (J). (gr. 5-8). pap. 3.99 (*0-87406-867-3*, Willowisp Pr.) Darby Creek Publishing.

Armstrong, Luanne & Collective Books Staff. Arly & Spike. 1997. (Illus.). 48p. (J). (gr. 3-6). pap. 4.95 (*1-895836-37-9*) Tesseract Bks. CAN. *Dist:* Fitzhenry & Whiteside, Ltd.

Armstrong, Robb. Drew & the Filthy Rich Kid. 96p. (J). (gr. 2-5). Date not set. (Illus.). lib. bdg. 13.89 (*0-06-026660-0*); pap. 4.25 (*0-06-442070-1*); 1997. (Illus.). pap. 3.95 (*0-06-443434-6*, Harper Trophy) HarperCollins Children's Bk. Group.

—Got Game? 1998. (Patrick's Pals Ser.: No. 3). (Illus.). 96p. (J). (gr. 2-7). mass mkt. 3.99 (*0-06-107069-6*, HarperEntertainment) Morrow/Avon.

—Large & in Charge. 1999. (Patrick's Pals Ser.: No. 7). (Illus.). 96p. (J). (gr. 2-7). pap. 3.99 (*0-06-107073-4*) HarperCollins Pubs.

—Runnin' with the Big Dawgs. 1998. (Patrick's Pals Ser.: No. 1). (Illus.). 96p. (J). (gr. 2-7). mass mkt. 3.99 (*0-06-107067-X*, HarperEntertainment) Morrow/Avon.

—Schoolin' 1999. (Patrick's Pals Ser.: No. 5). (Illus.). 96p. (J). (gr. 2-7). mass mkt. 3.99 (*0-06-107071-8*, HarperEntertainment) Morrow/Avon.

—Trashmaster. 1999. (Patrick's Pals Ser.: No. 6). (Illus.). 96p. (J). (gr. 2-7). mass mkt. 3.99 (*0-06-107072-6*, HarperEntertainment) Morrow/Avon.

Arneson, D. J. Friend Indeed. 1981. (J). (gr. 4 up). lib. bdg. 11.90 o.p. (*0-531-04257-X*, Watts, Franklin) Scholastic Library Publishing.

Arnold, Diane Elizabeth. The Freckle Collection. 2000. 352p. E-Book 8.00 (*0-7388-8988-1*) Xlibris Corp.

Arnold, Tedd. Huggly & the Toy Monster. 1999. (Huggly Ser.). (Illus.). 32p. (J). (ps-3). mass mkt. 3.25 (*0-439-10270-7*) Scholastic, Inc.

—Ollie Forgot. 1991. (Illus.). 32p. (J). (ps-3). pap. 3.95 o.p. (*0-8037-0985-4*, Puffin Bks.) Penguin Putnam Bks. for Young Readers.

Arnosky, Jim. Wild & Swampy. 2000. (Illus.). 32p. (J). (gr. 1-5). lib. bdg. 16.89 (*0-688-17120-6*); 15.95 (*0-688-17119-2*) HarperCollins Children's Bk. Group.

Arrington, H. J. Friends Again? 2001. (Illus.). 32p. (J). 14.95 (*1-56554-834-5*) Pelican Publishing Co., Inc.

Arthur. 2001. (Illus.). (J). 7.95 (*0-7853-4852-2*) Publications International, Ltd.

Arundel, Honor. The Girl in the Opposite Bed. 1971. (J). (gr. 6-9). 6.95 o.p. (*0-8407-6128-7*, Dutton Children's Bks.) Penguin Putnam Bks. for Young Readers.

Arvella, Wendy. Pray for a Rainbow. 2002. pap. 8.99 (*0-89610-201-7*) Island Heritage Publishing.

Asare, Meshack. Cat in Search of a Friend. 1988. Tr. of Die Katze Sucht Sich Einen Freund. (Illus.). 32p. (J). (ps-3). reprint ed. pap. 6.95 (*0-86543-107-8*) Africa World Pr.

Asch, Frank. Moonbear's Pet. 2002. (Moonbear Ser.). (Illus.). (J). 14.47 (*1-4046-0167-8*) Book Wholesalers, Inc.

—Moonbear's Pet. (Moonbear Ser.). (Illus.). 32p. (J). (ps-k). 2000. pap. 4.99 o.s.i (*0-689-82094-1*, Aladdin); 2000. pap. 5.99 (*0-689-83580-9*, Aladdin); 1997. 15.00 o.s.i (*0-689-80794-5*, Simon & Schuster Children's Publishing) Simon & Schuster Children's Publishing.

—Moonbear's Pet. 1998. (Moonbear Ser.). (J). (ps-k). 12.14 (*0-606-15637-2*) Turtleback Bks.

Asher, Sandy. Ballet: Best Friends Get Better, No. 1. 1989. (J). pap. 2.50 o.p. (*0-590-41843-2*) Scholastic, Inc.

Ashford, Ann. If I Found a Wistful Unicorn: A Gift of Love. (Illus.). 2002. 32p. (J). 8.95 (*1-56145-271-8*); 1992. 40p. (YA). 6.95 (*1-56145-047-2*); 1978. 39p. (J). 18.95 (*0-931948-00-2*) Peachtree Pubs., Ltd.

Ashwill, Beverley B. Marlina & McGee. 1987. (Illus.). 32p. (J). (ps-3). pap. 5.95 (*0-941381-00-5*) BJO's Enterprises.

—The Runaways. 1988. (Illus.). 48p. (J). (gr. 4-8). 12.95 (*0-941381-02-1*); pap. 5.95 (*0-941381-01-3*) BJO's Enterprises.

Athkins, D. E. Mirror, Mirror. 1992. 160p. (J). (gr. 7-9). mass mkt. 3.50 o.p. (*0-590-45246-0*, Scholastic Paperbacks) Scholastic, Inc.

Atkinson, John. Bamboo & Friends. 1988. (Illus.). 104p. (J). (gr. 1-12). 13.95 (*0-929155-05-X*) Windward Bks. International.

Atlas, Yehuda. It's Me! Lacks, Roslyn, tr. 1985. (Illus.). 48p. (J). (gr. 4 up). 9.95 o.p. (*0-915361-20-5*) Lambda Pubs., Inc.

Atwater, Martha. Murphy & Myrtle: The First Day of School. 2002. (Illus.). 32p. (J). mass mkt. 3.50 (*0-439-38210-6*, Cartwheel Bks.) Scholastic, Inc.

Auch, Mary Jane. Angel & Me & the Bayside Bombers. 1991. (Illus.). (J). (gr. 2-4). pap. 2.95 (*0-316-05915-3*) Little Brown & Co.

—Bird Dogs Can't Fly. 1993. (Illus.). (J). (ps-3). tchr. ed. 15.95 (*0-8234-1050-1*) Holiday Hse., Inc.

—Seven Long Years until College. 1991. 176p. (J). (gr. 4-7). 13.95 (*0-8234-0901-5*) Holiday Hse., Inc.

—Seven Long Years until College. Clancy, Lisa, ed. 1994. 176p. (YA). (gr. 4-7). reprint ed. pap. 2.99 (*0-671-78140-5*, Aladdin) Simon & Schuster Children's Publishing.

Aust, Patricia H. Benni & Victoria: Friends Through Time. 1996. (Illus.). 117p. (J). (ps-5). pap. 5.95 (*0-87868-629-0*, Child & Family Pr.) Child Welfare League of America, Inc.

Avi. Encounter at Easton. 2000. 144p. (J). (gr. 3-7). pap. 5.99 (*0-380-73241-6*, Harper Trophy) HarperCollins Children's Bk. Group.

—Nothing but the Truth: A Documentary Novel. 2004. 192p. (J). pap. 9.95 (*0-439-32730-X*, Orchard Bks.) Scholastic, Inc.

—Ragweed: A Tale from Dimwood Forest. 1999. (Avon Camelot Bks.). (Illus.). 192p. (J). (gr. 3-7). 15.95 (*0-380-97690-0*) HarperCollins Children's Bk. Group.

Awdry, Wilbert V. Edward, Trevor, & the Really Useful Party. 1994. (Thomas the Tank Engine Photographic Board Bks.). (Illus.). 16p. (J). (ps-k). 3.99 o.s.i (*0-679-86186-6*, Random Hse. Bks. for Young Readers) Random Hse. Children's Bks.

—Gordon & the Famous Visitor. 1993. (Illus.). (J). o.s.i (*0-679-86205-6*) Random Hse. Children's Bks.

—James the Red Engine. 1999. (Thomas the Tank Engine & Friends Ser.). (Illus.). 12p. (J). (ps). bds. 6.99 (*0-679-89389-X*, Random Hse. Bks. for Young Readers) Random Hse. Children's Bks.

—Meet Thomas the Tank Engine & His Friends. 1989. (Illus.). 32p. (J). (ps-1). 6.95 o.s.i (*0-679-80102-2*, Random Hse. Bks. for Young Readers) Random Hse. Children's Bks.

—Thomas & Bertie. 1997. (Illus.). 16p. (ps-k). bds. 5.99 o.s.i (*0-679-88682-6*, Random Hse. Bks. for Young Readers) Random Hse. Children's Bks.

—Thomas & Trevor. 1993. o.s.i (*0-679-86211-0*) Random Hse., Inc.

—Tracking Thomas the Tank Engine & His Friends: A Book with Finger Tabs. 1992. (Illus.). 16p. (J). (ps-1). 8.99 o.s.i (*0-679-83458-3*, Random Hse. Bks. for Young Readers) Random Hse. Children's Bks.

Aylesworth, Jim. McGraw's Emporium, ERS. 1998. (Illus.). (J). (ps-2). pap. 7.95 (*0-8050-5797-8*, Holt, Henry & Co. Bks. For Young Readers) Holt, Henry & Co.

Babe & Ace. 1997. (Reading Group Guides Ser.). (J). pap. o.s.i (*0-676-76238-7*, Knopf Bks. for Young Readers) Random Hse. Children's Bks.

Bach, Alice. He Will Not Walk with Me. 1985. (Illus.). 192p. (J). (gr. 7 up). 15.95 o.p. (*0-385-29410-7*, Delacorte Pr.) Dell Publishing.

Bach, Richard. Jonathan Livingston Seagull. 1973. (J). 12.04 (*0-606-03682-2*) Turtleback Bks.

Baehr, Patricia G. Louisa Eclipsed. 1924. (J). lib. bdg. o.s.i (*0-688-07683-1*, Morrow, William & Co.) Morrow/Avon.

—Summer of the Dodo. 1990. 144p. (J). (gr. 3-6). 12.95 o.s.i (*0-02-708135-4*, Simon & Schuster Children's Publishing) Simon & Schuster Children's Publishing.

Baer, Judy. Camp Pinetree Pals. 1991. 128p. (J). (gr. 4-6). pap. 2.50 o.p. (*0-87406-469-4*) Darby Creek Publishing.

—New Girl in Town. 1988. (Cedar River Daydreams Ser.: No. 1). 144p. (Orig.). (YA). (gr. 7-10). mass mkt. 4.99 o.p. (*1-55661-022-X*) Bethany Hse. Pubs.

—Tomorrow's Promise. 1990. (Cedar River Daydreams Ser.: No. 10). 128p. (Orig.). (YA). (gr. 7-10). mass mkt. 4.99 o.p. (*1-55661-143-9*) Bethany Hse. Pubs.

—Trouble with a Capital "T" 1988. (Cedar River Daydreams Ser.: No. 2). 144p. (Orig.). (YA). (gr. 7-10). mass mkt. 4.99 o.p. (*1-55661-021-1*) Bethany Hse. Pubs.

—Yesterday's Dream. 1990. (Cedar River Daydreams Ser.: No. 9). 144p. (YA). (gr. 7-10). mass mkt. 4.99 o.p. (*1-55661-142-0*) Bethany Hse. Pubs.

Baglio, Ben M. Frog Friends. 2001. (Animal Ark Pets Ser.: Vol. 16). (Illus.). 128p. (J). (ps-3). mass mkt. 3.99 (*0-439-23025-X*) Scholastic, Inc.

Bahous, Sally. Sitti & the Cats: A Tale of Friendship. 1997. (Illus.). 48p. (gr. 1-5). pap. 7.95 (*1-57098-171-X*) Rinehart, Roberts Pubs.

Baker, Barbara. Digby & Kate Again. 1989. (Easy Reader Ser.). (Illus.). 48p. (J). (ps-2). 9.95 o.p. (*0-525-44477-7*, Dutton Children's Bks.) Penguin Putnam Bks. for Young Readers.

—Digby & Kate 1-2-3. 2004. (Illus.). 48p. 14.99 (*0-525-46854-4*, Dutton Children's Bks.) Penguin Putnam Bks. for Young Readers.

—N-O Spells No. 1991. (Speedster Ser.). (Illus.). 64p. (J). (gr. 2-5). 10.95 o.p. (*0-525-44639-7*, Dutton Children's Bks.) Penguin Putnam Bks. for Young Readers.

—The William Problem. 1994. (Illus.). 120p. (J). 13.99 o.p. (*0-525-45235-4*, Dutton Children's Bks.) Penguin Putnam Bks. for Young Readers.

—The William Problem. 1997. (Puffin Chapters Ser.). (J). 10.04 (*0-606-13069-1*) Turtleback Bks.

Baker, Barbara & Winborn, Martha. Digby & Kate Again. 1994. (Easy-to-Read Bks.: Level 2, Red). (Illus.). 4p. (J). (gr. k-3). pap. 3.50 o.p. (*0-14-036665-2*, Puffin Bks.) Penguin Putnam Bks. for Young Readers.

Baker, Barbara B. & Wysinger, Donna. Allie & the Pal. 1994. (Pre-Readers Ser.: Vol. 1). (Illus.). 12p. (J). (gr. k-1). pap. text 3.00 o.p. (*1-57812-013-6*) Learning Crew, The.

Baker, C. David. The Fencerow Tails. 1991. (Illus.). 48p. (J). (gr. k-5). 12.95 (*0-9630669-0-0*) Liberty Lines.

Baker, Camy. Camy Baker's Love You Like a Sister: Thirty Cool Rules for Making & Being a Better Best Friend! 1998. 176p. (gr. 2-7). pap. text 3.99 o.s.i (*0-553-48656-X*) Bantam Bks.

—Camy Baker's Love You Like a Sister: Thirty Cool Rules for Making & Being a Better Best Friend! 1998. 10.04 (*0-606-15475-2*) Turtleback Bks.

Baker, Jennifer. Eternally Yours. 1999. (Enchanted Hearts Ser.: No. 2). 176p. (YA). (gr. 7-12). pap. 4.50 (*0-380-80073-X*, Avon Bks.) Morrow/Avon.

Baker, Laura N. Go Away, Ruthie. 1966. (Illus.). (J). (gr. 6 up). lib. bdg. 5.39 o.s.i (*0-394-91212-8*, Knopf Bks. for Young Readers) Random Hse. Children's Bks.

Baker, Liza. Harold & the Purple Crayon: Harold Finds a Friend. 2002. (Festival Reader Ser.). (Illus.). 32p. (J). (ps-2). pap. 3.99 (*0-06-000176-3*) HarperCollins Children's Bk. Group.

Baker, Roberta. Lizard Walinsky. 2004. (Illus.). 32p. (J). 16.00 (*0-316-07331-8*) Little Brown & Co.

Baker, Thomas A. Second Chance in Centerville. 1991. (Illus.). 96p. (J). (gr. 3-9). pap. 11.00 (*0-87879-908-7*) High Noon Bks.

Baldwin, Jean S. More George. 2001. (Illus.). 34p. (J). (gr. 3-6). pap. 44.95 (*1-879418-58-4*) Biddle Publishing Co.

Balgassi, Haemi. Tae's Sonata. 1997. (Illus.). 128p. (J). (gr. 4-6). tchr. ed. 15.00 (*0-395-84314-6*, Clarion Bks.) Houghton Mifflin Co. Trade & Reference Div.

Balian, Lorna. Wilbur's Space Machine. 1990. (Illus.). 32p. (J). (gr. k-5). lib. bdg. 19.95 (*0-8234-0836-1*) Humbug Bks.

Balis, Andrea & Reiser, Robert. P. J., 001. 1984. 160p. (J). (gr. 3-6). 10.95 o.p. (*0-395-36006-4*, 5-81180) Houghton Mifflin Co.

Ballard, Carol L. & Ballard, Bryan L. Nikki's Adventures. 1999. (Illus.). 40p. (J). (gr. k-6). pap. 18.00 (*0-8059-4675-6*) Dorrance Publishing Co., Inc.

Balloon Books Staff. Me & My Friends. 2003. (Illus.). 64p. 5.95 (*1-4027-0419-4*) Sterling Publishing Co., Inc.

Banks, Marcus. The Soup Kitchen. 1993. 32p. (J). (gr. 9 up). pap. 5.95 o.p. (*0-8059-3322-0*) Dorrance Publishing Co., Inc.

Bantle, Lee F. Diving for the Moon. 1995. 176p. (J). (gr. 4-7). per. 14.00 (*0-689-80004-5*, Atheneum) Simon & Schuster Children's Publishing.

Barasch, Lynne. Old Friends, RS. 1998. (Illus.). 32p. (J). (gr. k-3). 16.00 o.p. (*0-374-35611-4*, Farrar, Straus & Giroux (BYR)) Farrar, Straus & Giroux.

—The Reluctant Flower Girl. 2001. (Illus.). 40p. (J). (gr. k-3). 14.95 (*0-06-028809-4*); lib. bdg. 14.89 (*0-06-028810-8*) HarperCollins Children's Bk. Group.

Barber, Antonia. Dancing Shoes Friends & Rivals. (Illus.). 96p. (J). pap. 5.95 (*0-14-038684-X*) Penguin Bks., Ltd. GBR. *Dist:* Trafalgar Square.

Relationships

Bargar, Gary W. Life Is Not Fair. 1984. 180p. (J). (gr. 4-7). 13.95 o.p. (*0-89919-218-1*, Clarion Bks.) Houghton Mifflin Co. Trade & Reference Div.

Barkan, Joanne. A Tale of Two Sitters. 1998. (Adventures of Wishbone Ser.: No. 9). (Illus.). 144p. (J). (gr. 2-5). mass mkt. 3.99 o.p. (*1-57064-277-X*, Big Red Chair Bks.) Lyrick Publishing.

—A Tale of Two Sitters. l.t. ed. 1999. (Adventures of Wishbone Ser.: No. 9). (Illus.). 144p. (J). (gr. 4 up). lib. bdg. 22.60 (*0-8368-2305-2*) Stevens, Gareth Inc.

Barker, Cicely Mary. Lavender Finds a Friend. 2003. (Illus.). 24p. 4.99 (*0-7232-4899-0*, Warne, Frederick) Penguin Putnam Bks. for Young Readers.

Barney's Friend Book & Toy. (J). pap. 12.95 o.p. (*1-57064-050-5*) Scholastic, Inc.

Baron, Alan. Little Pig's Bouncy Ball. 1997. (Giggle Club Ser.). (Illus.). 24p. (J). (ps-1). reprint ed. bds. 3.29 o.s.i (*0-7636-0126-8*) Candlewick Pr.

Barr, Linda. Best Friends Don't Tell Lies. 1989. 128p. (Orig.). (J). (gr. 5-8). pap. text 2.99 o.s.i (*0-87406-423-6*) Darby Creek Publishing.

—I Won't Let Them Hurt You. (Lifelines Ser.). 112p. (J). (gr. 6-9). 1996. pap. 3.99 (*0-87406-777-4*); 1988. pap. 2.95 o.p. (*0-87406-314-0*) Darby Creek Publishing.

Barrett, Anna Pearl. Neecie & the Swarming Germs. Carmical, Phillip, ed. 1998. (Illus.). 50p. (J). (gr. 2-4). pap. 9.95 (*0-9661330-0-5*) Over the Rainbow Productions.

Barrett, Joyce D. Willie's Not the Hugging Kind. 1989. (Illus.). 32p. (J). (gr. k-3). 16.00 o.s.i (*0-06-020416-8*); lib. bdg. 15.89 o.s.i (*0-06-020417-6*) HarperCollins Children's Bk. Group.

Barrett, Mary Brigid. Sing to the Stars. 1994. (Illus.). (J). 15.95 o.p. (*0-316-08224-4*) Little Brown & Co.

Barrie, J. M. Tommy & Grizel, Vol. 6. reprint ed. 57.50 (*0-404-08786-8*) AMS Pr., Inc.

—Tommy & Grizel. reprint ed. lib. bdg. 98.00 (*0-7426-2515-X*); 2001. pap. text 28.00 (*0-7426-7515-7*) Classic Bks.

—Tommy & Grizel. 2001. 540p. per. 29.95 (*1-58963-131-5*) International Law & Taxation Pubs.

Barron, David. The Adventures of Bob & Red. Thatch, Nancy R., ed. 1999. (Books for Students by Students). (Illus.). 29p. (J). (ps-3). lib. bdg. 15.95 (*0-933849-71-0*) Landmark Editions, Inc.

Barron, Kirk W. Johnny Tractor & Friends: A New Kind of Job. Torgerson, Dell & Reyner, Mark, eds. 1999. (John Deere Storybook for Little Folks Ser.). (Illus.). 14p. (J). (gr. 3 up). 6.95 (*1-887327-26-6*) Ertl Co., Inc.

—Johnny Tractor & Friends: Afraid of Nothing. Torgerson, Dell & Reyner, Mark, eds. 1999. (John Deere Storybook for Little Folks Ser.). (Illus.). 14p. (J). (gr. 3 up). 6.95 (*1-887327-25-3*) Ertl Co., Inc.

Barstow, Stan. Joby. l.t. ed. 1988. (Windrush Bks.). 163p. (YA). (gr. 9 up). reprint ed. lib. bdg. 18.95 o.p. (*1-85089-214-8*) ISIS Large Print Bks. GBR. *Dist:* Transaction Pubs.

Bartlett, Craig & Groening, Maggie. Hey Arnold! The Movie. novel ed. 2002. (Hey Arnold! Ser.). (Illus.). 144p. (J). (gr. 3-7). pap. 4.99 (*0-689-85136-7*, Simon Spotlight) Simon & Schuster Children's Publishing.

Baskin. The Invitation. 1993. 288p. (J). pap. (*0-920813-54-2*) Sister Vision Pr.

Baskin, Nora Raleigh. Almost Home. 2003. 192p. (J). (gr. 5-8). 16.95 (*0-316-09313-0*) Little Brown Children's Bks.

—What Every Girl (Except Me) Knows. 2001. 224p. (J). (gr. 4-7). 16.95 (*0-316-07021-1*) Little Brown & Co.

Bassede, Francine. A Day with the Bellyflops. 2000. (Illus.). 32p. (J). (ps-2). pap. 14.95 (*0-531-30242-3*, Orchard Bks.) Scholastic, Inc.

Bassett, Lisa. Beany & Scamp. 1987. (Illus.). (J). (gr. k-3). 12.95 o.p. (*0-399-21703-7*, G. P. Putnam's Sons) Penguin Group (USA) Inc.

Bastin, Marjolein. My Name Is Vera. 1985. (Illus.). 28p. (J). (ps-2). 2.95 o.p. (*0-8120-5690-6*) Barron's Educational Series, Inc.

—Vera & Her Friends. 1985. (Illus.). 28p. (J). (ps-2). 2.95 o.p. (*0-8120-5689-2*) Barron's Educational Series, Inc.

—Vera Dresses Up. 1985. 28p. (J). (ps-2). 2.95 o.p. (*0-8120-5691-4*) Barron's Educational Series, Inc.

Bateman, Teresa. The Ring of Truth. 1999. (Illus.). (J). (ps-3). pap. 6.95 (*0-8234-1518-X*) Holiday Hse., Inc.

Bates, A. Party Line. 1989. (J). (gr. 6). pap. 2.75 o.p. (*0-590-42439-4*); 176p. (gr. 7 up). mass mkt. 3.99 (*0-590-44238-4*) Scholastic, Inc.

—What's the Opposite of a Best Friend? 1993. 160p. (J). (gr. 4-7). pap. 2.95 (*0-590-44145-0*) Scholastic, Inc.

Bates, Betty. Herbert & Hortense. Tucker, Kathleen, ed. 1984. (Just for Fun Bks.). (Illus.). 32p. (J). (gr. 1-4). lib. bdg. 10.25 o.p. (*0-8075-3222-3*) Whitman, Albert & Co.

—Thatcher Payne-in-the-Neck. 1985. (Illus.). 144p. (J). (gr. 3-7). 12.95 o.p. (*0-8234-0584-2*) Holiday Hse., Inc.

—Thatcher Payne-in-the-Neck. 1986. 144p. (J). (gr. k-6). pap. 3.25 o.s.i (*0-440-48598-3*, Yearling) Random Hse. Children's Bks.

Bates, Ivan. All by Myself. 2000. (Illus.). 32p. (J). (ps-2). 14.95 (*0-06-028585-0*) HarperCollins Children's Bk. Group.

Battles, Edith. One to Teeter-Totter. 1973. (Self Starter Bks.). (Illus.). 32p. (J). (ps-1). 6.95 o.p. (*0-8075-6103-7*) Whitman, Albert & Co.

Bauer, Joan. Sticks. 192p. (gr. 3-7). 1997. (Illus.). pap. text 3.99 o.s.i (*0-440-41387-7*); 1996. (J). text 15.95 o.s.i (*0-385-32165-1*, Delacorte Pr.) Dell Publishing.

—Sticks. 2002. 192p. (J). 18.99 (*0-399-23752-6*) Penguin Group (USA) Inc.

—Sticks. 2002. 192p. pap. 5.99 (*0-698-11933-9*, Puffin Bks.) Penguin Putnam Bks. for Young Readers.

—Sticks. 1997. (J). 10.04 (*0-606-11912-4*) Turtleback Bks.

Bauer, Marion Dane. The Double Digit Club. 2004. (J). (*0-8234-1805-7*) Holiday Hse., Inc.

—A Frog's Best Friend: A Holiday House Reader. 2002. (Reader Level 2 Ser.). (Illus.). 32p. (J). (gr. k-3). tchr. ed. 14.95 (*0-8234-1501-5*) Holiday Hse., Inc.

—On My Honor. 1997. 96p. (J). (gr. 3-6). mass mkt. 2.69 o.p. (*0-440-22742-9*) Dell Publishing.

—On My Honor. 1986. 96p. (YA). (gr. 7-7). tchr. ed. 15.00 (*0-89919-439-7*, Clarion Bks.) Houghton Mifflin Co. Trade & Reference Div.

—On My Honor. 1987. (Yearling Newbery Ser.). 96p. (gr. 3-7). pap. text 4.99 (*0-440-46633-4*, Yearling) Random Hse. Children's Bks.

—On My Honor. 1986. (J). 11.04 (*0-606-03630-X*) Turtleback Bks.

Baum, Louis. One More Time. ALC Staff, ed. 1992. (Illus.). 32p. (J). (ps up). pap. 3.95 o.p. (*0-688-11698-1*, Morrow, William & Co.) Morrow/Avon.

—One More Time. 1986. (Illus.). 32p. (J). (ps). 11.95 o.p. (*0-688-06586-4*); lib. bdg. 11.93 o.p. (*0-688-06587-2*) Morrow/Avon. (Morrow, William & Co.).

Baumgart, Klaus. Laura's Star. 1997. (Illus.). 32p. (J). (ps-2). 16.95 (*1-888444-24-X*, 21022) Little Tiger Pr.

—Laura's Star. 2002. (Illus.). 32p. (J). pap. 7.95 (*1-58925-374-4*, Tiger Tales) ME Media LLC.

—Lenny & Tweek. 2002. (Illus.). (J). 31p. pap. (*1-59034-387-5*); 32p. 15.95 (*1-59034-197-X*) Mondo Publishing.

Baur, Deborah. Rosie the Talking Parrot Learns about Friendship & Love. 1996. (Illus.). 32p. (J). (gr. k-3). 8.00 o.p. (*0-8059-3862-1*) Dorrance Publishing Co., Inc.

Bawden, Nina. Rebel on a Rock. 1978. 160p. (J). (gr. 7 up). lib. bdg. 13.89 (*0-397-32140-6*) HarperCollins Children's Bk. Group.

—The Robbers. 1979. (Illus.). 160p. (J). (gr. 4-7). reprint ed. 12.95 o.p. (*0-688-41902-X*); lib. bdg. 12.88 o.p. (*0-688-51902-4*) HarperCollins Children's Bk. Group.

—The Witch's Daughter. 1991. 192p. (J). (gr. 3-7). 13.95 o.s.i (*0-395-58635-6*, Clarion Bks.) Houghton Mifflin Co. Trade & Reference Div.

Bayles, Miriam. Si Bantay, Si Puti, at Si Ngaw. 1988. (TAG., Illus.). (J). (gr. k-2). pap. 9.50 (*971-10-0359-7*) New Day Pubs., Philippines PHL. *Dist:* Book Bin - Pacifica, The.

—Si Wayt at Ang Kanyang Mga Kaibigan. 1990. (TAG., Illus.). 35p. (J). (gr. k-2). pap. 10.50 (*971-10-0416-X*) New Day Pubs., Philippines PHL. *Dist:* Book Bin - Pacifica, The.

Baylis-White, Mary. Sheltering Rebecca. 112p. (J). 1993. (gr. 5-9). pap. 3.99 o.p. (*0-14-036448-X*, Puffin Bks.); 1991. (gr. 3-7). 14.95 o.p. (*0-525-67349-0*, Dutton Children's Bks.) Penguin Putnam Bks. for Young Readers.

Baylor, Byrd. Amigo. 1963. (J). 12.14 (*0-606-03982-1*) Turtleback Bks.

—And It Is Still That Way. 1987. (Illus.). 96p. (J). (gr. k-8). reprint ed. pap. 7.95 o.p. (*0-939729-06-7*) Trails West Publishing.

—Guess Who My Favorite Person Is. (Illus.). 32p. (J). (gr. 1-5). 1985. pap. 4.95 o.s.i (*0-689-71052-6*, Aladdin); 2nd ed. 1992. text 14.95 (*0-684-19514-3*, Atheneum) Simon & Schuster Children's Publishing.

Bazaldua, Barbara. Fine-Feathered Friend: Disney's Aladdin. 1995. (Illus.). 24p. (J). (ps-3). pap. text 2.25 o.p. (*0-307-12883-0*, Golden Bks.) Random Hse. Children's Bks.

Be Nice to Your Friends: Super Paint with Water. 1999. (Disney Ser.). (Illus.). 64p. (J). (ps-4). pap. text 2.99 (*0-307-08362-4*, 08362, Golden Bks.) Random Hse. Children's Bks.

Beard, Darleen Bailey. The Flim-Flam Man, RS. (Illus.). 96p. (J). 2003. pap. 5.95 (*0-374-42345-8*, Sunburst); 1998. (gr. 2-6). 15.00 (*0-374-32346-1*, Farrar, Straus & Giroux (BYR)) Farrar, Straus & Giroux.

Beast Has Too Much to Do. 1987. (Illus.). 32p. (J). (gr. 5-8). pap. 4.95 o.p. (*0-8431-2653-1*, Price Stern Sloan) Penguin Putnam Bks. for Young Readers.

Beatty, Monica D. Blueberry Eyes. 1996. (Illus.). 32p. (J). (gr. k-6). pap. 8.95 (*0-929173-24-4*) Health Pr. NA, Inc.

Beatty, Patricia. Jonathan down Under. 1982. (J). (gr. 5-9). 11.95 o.p. (*0-688-01467-4*, Morrow, William & Co.) Morrow/Avon.

—Lupita Manana. 1992. 192p. (YA). (gr. 7 up). pap. 4.95 (*0-688-11497-0*, Morrow, William & Co.) Morrow/Avon.

—O the Red Rose Tree. 1994. 208p. (YA). (gr. 5 up). 17.00 o.p. (*0-688-21429-0*, Morrow, William & Co.) Morrow/Avon.

—O the Red Rose Tree. 1994. 10.05 o.p. (*0-606-06629-2*) Turtleback Bks.

—The Red Rose Tree. 1994. (Illus.). 208p. (YA). (gr. 5 up). mass mkt. 4.95 o.p. (*0-688-13627-3*, Morrow, William & Co.) Morrow/Avon.

—Sarah & Me & the Lady from the Sea. Cohn, Amy, ed. 1994. 208p. (YA). (gr. 5 up). reprint ed. pap. 5.95 (*0-688-13626-5*, Harper Trophy) HarperCollins Children's Bk. Group.

Beatty, Patricia & Robbins, Phillip. Eben Tyne, Powdermonkey. 1990. 240p. (YA). (gr. 5 up). 12.95 o.p. (*0-688-08884-8*, Morrow, William & Co.) Morrow/Avon.

Beaumont, Karen & Allen, Joy. Being Friends. 2002. (Illus.). 32p. (J). 15.99 (*0-8037-2529-9*, Dial Bks. for Young Readers) Penguin Putnam Bks. for Young Readers.

Beazley, William O. Apache, the Horse Who Needs a Friend. l.t. ed. 1995. (White Horse Ser.). (Illus.). 46p. (Orig.). (J). (gr. k-5). pap. 7.95 (*1-884758-09-6*) Beazley, William O.

Bechard, Margaret E. My Mom Married the Principal. 1998. 144p. (J). (gr. 5-9). 14.99 o.s.i (*0-670-87394-2*) Penguin Putnam Bks. for Young Readers.

—Really No Big Deal. 160p. (J). (gr. 3-7). 1996. (Illus.). pap. 3.99 o.s.i (*0-14-036912-0*, Puffin Bks.); 1994. 13.99 o.s.i (*0-670-85444-1*, Viking Children's Bks.) Penguin Putnam Bks. for Young Readers.

Beck, Amanda. The Pegasus Club & Me. 1992. (Publish-a-Book Ser.). (Illus.). 32p. (J). (gr. 1-6). lib. bdg. 22.83 o.p. (*0-8114-3577-6*) Raintree Pubs.

Beck, Jennifer & Belton, Robyn. The Choosing Day. 1989. (Illus.). 32p. (J). (gr. 1-4). pap. 13.95 o.p. (*0-09-173590-4*) Trafalgar Square.

Becker, Lois & Stratton, Mark. ABC & T for Teddy. Becker, Mary et al, eds. 1995. (Teddy Ruxpin Tell Me Again Ser.). (Illus.). 24p. (J). pap. 11.95 incl. audio (*0-934323-82-8*) Alchemy Communications Group, Ltd.

—All Around Town. Becker, Mary et al, eds. 1995. (Teddy Ruxpin Tell Me Again Ser.). (Illus.). 24p. (J). pap. 11.99 incl. audio (*0-934323-81-X*) Alchemy Communications Group, Ltd.

Becker, Mary, et al. Let's Play Today. 1995. (Teddy Ruxpin Tell Me Again Ser.). (Illus.). 24p. (J). pap. 11.95 incl. audio (*0-934323-83-6*) Alchemy Communications Group, Ltd.

Becker, Shirley. Buddy's Shadow. l.t. ed. (Turtle Bks.). (Illus.). 32p. (J). (ps-2). 1991. pap. 8.95 (*0-944727-08-5*); 1992. reprint ed. lib. bdg. 14.95 (*0-944727-19-0*) Jason & Nordic Pubs. (Turtle Bks.).

Becker, Suzy. Bud & Scooter. Date not set. (Illus.). 48p. (J). (gr. k-3). 15.99 (*0-06-028970-8*); lib. bdg. 16.89 (*0-06-028971-6*) HarperCollins Children's Bk. Group.

—Bud & Scooter. Date not set. 48p. (J). (gr. k-3). pap. 3.99 (*0-06-444286-1*) HarperCollins Pubs.

Bedard, Michael. Sitting Ducks. 1998. (Illus.). 40p. (J). (ps-3). 15.99 (*0-399-22847-0*) Penguin Putnam Bks. for Young Readers.

—Stained Glass. 312p. (gr. 6). 2002. pap. 8.95 (*0-88776-602-1*); 2001. (YA). 17.95 o.s.i (*0-88776-552-1*) Tundra Bks. of Northern New York.

Bedford, David. The Copy Crocs. Bolam, Emily, tr. & illus. by. 2004. 32p. (J). 15.95 (*1-56145-304-8*, Peachtree Junior) Peachtree Pubs., Ltd.

—It's My Turn! 2001. (Illus.). 32p. (J). (ps-k). pap. 5.95 (*1-58925-351-5*, Tiger Tales) ME Media LLC.

Beerbohm, Max. The Happy Hypocrite. 1991. (Illus.). 40p. (J). pap. 16.95 o.p. (*0-88138-038-5*, Simon & Schuster Children's Publishing) Simon & Schuster Children's Publishing.

Behrens, Michael. At the Edge. 1988. 208p. (YA). (gr. 7 up). pap. 2.95 (*0-380-75610-2*, Avon Bks.) Morrow/Avon.

Beidler, Michelle, illus. Rosita y Mateo Coloring Book. 1988. (ENG & SPA.). 40p. (J). (ps-4). pap. 1.90 (*0-7399-0181-8*, 29.35.1) Rod & Staff Pubs., Inc.

Beim, Lorraine & Beim, Jerrold. Two Is a Team. (Illus.). (J). (gr. k-3). 1945. 8.95 o.p. (*0-15-291948-1*); 1974. 58p. reprint ed. pap. 1.25 o.p. 5.95 (*1-58925-351-5*, Tiger Tales) ME Media LLC. (*0-15-692050-6*, Voyager Bks./Libros Viajeros) Harcourt Children's Bks.

Bell, William. Death Wind. rev. ed. 2002. (Soundings Ser.). 96p. (YA). pap. 7.95 (*1-55143-215-3*) Orca Bk. Pubs.

Bellafiore, Sharyn. Amos & Abraham. 1994. (Illus.). 32p. (J). (gr. k-5). lib. bdg. 14.95 (*1-56148-139-4*) Good Bks.

Bellingham, Brenda. Lilly's Good Deed. 1998. (First Novels Ser.). (Illus.). 64p. (J). (gr. 1-4). (*0-88780-461-6*) Formac Publishing Co., Ltd.

—Lilly's Good Deed. 1998. (First Novels Ser.: Vol. 7). (Illus.). 64p. (J). (gr. 1-4). pap. 3.99 (*0-88780-460-8*) Formac Publishing Co., Ltd. CAN. *Dist:* Formac Distributing, Ltd., Orca Bk. Pubs.

Belpré, Pura. Perez & Martina. 1991. (Illus.). 64p. (J). 15.95 o.p. (*0-670-84166-8*, Viking Children's Bks.) Penguin Putnam Bks. for Young Readers.

—Perez y Martina. 1991. (Illus.). (J). (ps-3). 15.95 o.p. (*0-670-84167-6*, Viking Children's Bks.) Penguin Putnam Bks. for Young Readers.

Belton, Sandra. Ernestine & Amanda. (Ernestine & Amanda Ser.: Vol. 1). 160p. (J). 1996. (gr. 4-7). 16.00 o.p. (*0-689-80848-8*, Simon & Schuster Children's Publishing); Bk. 1. 1998. (gr. 3-7). pap. 4.50 (*0-689-80847-X*, Aladdin) Simon & Schuster Children's Publishing.

—Ernestine & Amanda: Mysteries on Monroe Street. 1998. (Ernestine & Amanda Ser.). 176p. (J). (gr. 3-7). 16.00 (*0-689-81612-X*, Simon & Schuster Children's Publishing) Simon & Schuster Children's Publishing.

—Ernestine & Amanda: Summer Camp Ready or Not!, No. 2. (Ernestine & Amanda Ser.: Vol. 2). 176p. (J). (gr. 3-7). 1998. bds. 3.99 o.p. (*0-689-80845-3*, Aladdin); 1997. 16.00 o.p. (*0-689-80846-1*, Simon & Schuster Children's Publishing) Simon & Schuster Children's Publishing.

—Members of the C. L. U. B. (Ernestine & Amanda Ser.). 176p. (J). (gr. 3-7). 1998. pap. 4.50 (*0-689-81661-8*, Aladdin); 1997. lib. bdg. 16.00 o.p. (*0-689-81611-1*, Simon & Schuster Children's Publishing) Simon & Schuster Children's Publishing.

Belton, Sandra & Carpenter, Nancy. Ernestine & Amanda: Mysteries on Monroe Street. 1999. (Ernestine & Amanda Ser.: No. 4). 176p. (J). (gr. 4-7). mass mkt. 4.50 o.p. (*0-689-81662-6*, 076714004504, Aladdin) Simon & Schuster Children's Publishing.

Benard, Robert. Do You Like It Here? 1989. 256p. (YA). (gr. 10-12). mass mkt. 3.50 o.s.i (*0-440-20435-6*, Laurel Leaf) Random Hse. Children's Bks.

Benard, Robert, ed. All Problems Are Simple. 1988. 336p. (J). (gr. k-12). mass mkt. 3.95 o.s.i (*0-440-20164-0*, Laurel Leaf) Random Hse. Children's Bks.

Benchley, Nathaniel. Kilroy & the Gull. 1977. (I Can Read Bks.). (Illus.). 128p. (J). (ps-3). o.p. (*0-06-020502-4*); lib. bdg. 6.89 o.p. (*0-06-020503-2*) HarperCollins Pubs.

—Only Earth & Sky Last Forever. 1992. (YA). (gr. 7 up). 17.25 o.p. (*0-8446-6583-5*) Smith, Peter Pub., Inc.

Benduhn, Tea. Gravel Queen. 2003. (Illus.). 160p. (J). (gr. 7 up). 15.95 (*0-689-84994-X*, Simon & Schuster Children's Publishing) Simon & Schuster Children's Publishing.

Benes, Veronica. Lilaveles "A Little Tale" 1997. (Illus.). 30p. (J). (ps-4). 12.97 (*0-9662368-0-7*) Benes, Veronica.

Benfanti, Russell. Hide, Clyde! 2002. (Illus.). 32p. (J). (ps-3). 17.95 (*1-59019-047-5*) ipicturebooks, LLC.

Benjamin, A. H. The Mouse & Mole & the Falling Star. 2002. (Illus.). 32p. (J). (ps-1). 15.99 (*0-525-46880-3*, Dutton Children's Bks.) Penguin Putnam Bks. for Young Readers.

Benjamin, Alan. Buck. 1994. (Illus.). (J). 15.00 o.p. (*0-671-88718-1*, Simon & Schuster Children's Publishing) Simon & Schuster Children's Publishing.

Benjamin, Amanda. Two's Company. 1995. 32p. (J). (ps-2). 13.99 o.p. (*0-670-84876-X*, Viking) Penguin Putnam Bks. for Young Readers.

Bennett, Cherie. Good-Bye, Best Friend. 1993. 160p. (YA). mass mkt. 3.50 o.p. (*0-06-106739-3*, HarperTorch) Morrow/Avon.

—Heaven Help Us! 1996. (Teen Angels Ser.: No. 4). (Orig.). (J). mass mkt. 3.99 o.p. (*0-380-78577-3*, Avon Bks.) Morrow/Avon.

—Sunset Reunion. 1991. (Sunset Island Ser.: No. 5). (J). mass mkt. 3.99 o.s.i (*0-425-13318-4*, Splash) Berkley Publishing Group.

—Zink. 2001. (Illus.). (J). 11.04 (*0-606-21543-3*) Turtleback Bks.

Bennett, Cherie & Gottesfeld, J. A-List No. 2: Untitled Cherie Bennett. 2004. (Illus.). 256p. (J). pap. 8.99 (*0-316-73475-6*) Little Brown & Co.

Bennett, James W. Blue Star Rapture. 2001. (J). 11.04 (*0-606-20574-8*) Turtleback Bks.

Bennett, Jill. Teeny Tiny. 1998. 10.19 (*0-606-13050-0*) Turtleback Bks.

Benning, Elizabeth. Please Don't Go. 1993. 160p. (YA). (gr. 9-12). mass mkt. 3.50 o.p. (*0-06-106148-4*, HarperTorch) Morrow/Avon.

Relationships

Benton-Borghi, Beatrice Hope. Best Friends. 1996. (Illus.). 109p. (J). (gr. 3-8). 14.95 (*1-888927-00-3*, BFB); pap. 4.50 (*1-888927-78-X*, BFB) Open Minds, Inc.

—Whoa, Nellie! 1996. (Illus.). 102p. (J). (gr. 3-8). 14.95 (*1-888927-01-1*, WNB); pap. 4.50 (*1-888927-79-8*, WNB) Open Minds, Inc.

Berenstain, Michael. The Dwarks at the Mall. 1985. 48p. (J). (gr. 2 up). pap. 2.25 o.s.i (*0-553-15341-2*) Bantam Bks.

—The Dwarks at the Mall. 1983. (J). pap. 2.25 o.s.i (*0-553-15378-1*, Dell Books for Young Readers) Random Hse. Children's Bks.

Berenstain, Stan & Berenstain, Jan. The Berenstain Bears & the Goofy, Goony Guy. 2001. (Berenstain Bears First Time Chapter Bks.). (Illus.). 96p. (J). (gr. 1-3). pap. 3.99 (*0-375-81270-9*); lib. bdg. 11.99 o.s.i (*0-375-91270-3*) Random Hse. Children's Bks. (Random Hse. Bks. for Young Readers).

—The Berenstain Bears & the New Girl in Town. 1993. (Berenstain Bears Big Chapter Bks.). (Illus.). 112p. (gr. 4-6). pap. 3.99 (*0-679-83613-6*, Random Hse. Bks. for Young Readers) Random Hse. Children's Bks.

—Los Osos Berenstain y las Paleas Entre Amigos. Guibert, Rita, tr. from ENG. 1993. (Berenstain Bears First Time Bks.). (SPA., Illus.). 32p. (J). (gr. k-2). pap. 3.25 (*0-679-84006-0*, Random Hse. Bks. for Young Readers) Random Hse. Children's Bks.

Berenzy, Alix. What's the Matter Sammy? 1999. (J). 15.95 (*0-8050-4024-2*, Holt, Henry & Co. Bks. For Young Readers) Holt, Henry & Co.

Bergen, Lara Rice. Into the Woods. 2000. (Illus.). (J). 9.34 o.p. (*0-606-18779-0*) Turtleback Bks.

—Sleepover! For the Coolest Night of Your Life. 1996. (Books & Stuff Ser.). (Illus.). 32p. (J). (gr. 1 up). 9.95 o.p. (*0-448-40956-9*, Grosset & Dunlap) Penguin Putnam Bks. for Young Readers.

Berger, Kathy L. The Hailey & Max Stories. Wise, Noreen, ed. 2000. (Book-a-Day Collection). 48p. (YA). (ps up). pap. 6.95 (*1-58584-415-2*) Huckleberry Pr.

Bergstrom, Corinne. Losing Your Best Friend. 1980. (Illus.). 32p. (J). (ps-3). 16.95 (*0-87705-471-1*, Kluwer Academic/Human Science Pr.) Kluwer Academic Pubs.

Berk, Sheryl. Barney's Little Lessons: Be My Friend! 2002. (Barney Ser.). 8p. (J). (ps-1). bds. 5.99 (*1-58668-293-8*) Lyrick Publishing.

Bernard, Elizabeth. Starting Over. 1989. (Satin Slippers Ser.: No. 11). (J). (gr. 6 up). mass mkt. 3.50 o.s.i (*0-449-14547-6*, Fawcett) Ballantine Bks.

Bernardo, Anilu. Fitting In. 1996. 16.00 (*0-606-13390-9*) Turtleback Bks.

—Loves Me, Loves Me Not. 1998. 169p. (gr. 6-12). (J). pap. 9.95 (*1-55885-259-X*); (YA). 16.95 o.p. (*1-55885-258-1*) Arte Publico Pr. (Piñata Books).

Bernier-Grand, Carmen T. In the Shade of the Nispero Tree. 2001. 192p. (gr. 4-7). pap. text 4.50 o.s.i (*0-440-41660-4*, Dell Books for Young Readers) Random Hse. Children's Bks.

—In the Shade of the Nispero Tree. 1999. 192p. (J). (gr. 4-7). pap. 15.95 (*0-531-30154-0*); lib. bdg. 16.99 (*0-531-33154-7*) Scholastic, Inc. (Orchard Bks.).

—In the Shade of the Nispero Tree. 2001. 10.55 (*0-606-20722-8*) Turtleback Bks.

Bernthal, Mark S. Francesco's Friends. 1998. (Francesco's Friendly World Ser.). 24p. (J). pap. text 2.95 o.p. (*1-57064-265-6*) Scholastic, Inc.

Berrios, Frank. Share a Smile. 2004. (Illus.). 12p. (J). bds. 3.99 (*0-375-82911-3*, Golden Bks.) Random Hse. Children's Bks.

Bertoleio, Noah. I'm with You No Matter How Far Away. 1997. (Illus.). 52p. (J). (gr. k up). pap., spiral bd. 15.95 (*0-9658823-1-4*) Love Street Publishing.

Bertrand, Cecile. Let's Pretend. 1993. (Illus.). (J). (ps-3). 13.00 o.p. (*0-688-12377-5*) HarperCollins Children's Bk. Group.

Bertrand, Diane Gonzales. Sweet Fifteen. (YA). 1996. 296p. (gr. 6-12). pap. text 7.95 o.p. (*1-55885-184-4*); 1995. 224p. (gr. 6-12). 12.95 o.p. (*1-55885-122-4*); 2nd ed. 1995. 224p. (gr. 7 up). pap. 9.95 o.p. (*1-55885-133-X*) Arte Publico Pr.

Beskow, Elsa. Woody, Hazel & Little Pip. 1990. Orig. Title: Ocke, Nutta Och Pillerill. (Illus.). 32p. (J). (ps-2). 17.95 (*0-86315-109-4*, 24578) Floris Bks. GBR. *Dist:* Gryphon Hse., Inc., SteinerBooks, Inc.

Bess, Clayton. Big Man & the Burn-Out, 001. 1985. 208p. (J). (gr. 5 up). 12.95 o.p. (*0-395-36173-7*) Houghton Mifflin Co.

Besst, Nancy. Milton & Matilda. 1982. (Illus.). 48p. (J). (gr. 4-9). pap. 3.95 o.p. (*0-8351-0998-4*) China Bks. & Periodicals, Inc.

Best Friends. 2001. (First Readers Ser.: Vol. 4). (J). lib. bdg. (*1-59054-327-0*) Fitzgerald Bks.

Best Friends. 2001. (Bubblegum Ser.). (Illus.). 32p. (J). (gr. 3 up). 7.99 (*0-689-84429-8*, Little Simon) Simon & Schuster Children's Publishing.

Betancourt, Jeanne. Exposed. 2003. (Three Girls in the City Ser.). 160p. (J). mass mkt. 4.99 (*0-439-49840-6*, Scholastic Paperbacks) Scholastic, Inc.

—The Missing Pony Pal. 1997. (Pony Pals Ser.: No. 16). (Illus.). 96p. (J). (gr. 2-5). mass mkt. 3.99 (*0-590-37459-1*) Scholastic, Inc.

—The Missing Pony Pal. 1997. (Pony Pals Ser.: Vol. 16). (J). (gr. 2-5). 10.14 (*0-606-19594-7*) Turtleback Bks.

—More Than Meets the Eye. 1991. 176p. (YA). mass mkt. 3.50 o.s.i (*0-553-29351-6*) Bantam Bks.

—The Moving Pony. 1999. (Pony Pals Ser.: Vol. 19). 112p. (J). (gr. 2-5). mass mkt. 3.99 (*0-590-63397-X*) Scholastic, Inc.

—The Moving Pony. 1999. (Pony Pals Ser.: Vol. 19). (J). (gr. 2-5). 10.14 (*0-606-19597-1*) Turtleback Bks.

—My Name Is Brain Brian. 1993. 144p. (J). (gr. 3-7). pap. 14.95 (*0-590-44921-4*) Scholastic, Inc.

—Ponies on Parade. 2003. (Pony Pals Ser.). 112p. (J). mass mkt. 3.99 (*0-439-55988-X*, Scholastic Paperbacks) Scholastic, Inc.

—The Pony & the Lost Swan. 2002. (Pony Pals Ser.: No. 34). (Illus.). 96p. (J). mass mkt. 3.99 (*0-439-30644-2*, Scholastic Paperbacks) Scholastic, Inc.

—Pony Pals. 9999. (Pony Pals Ser.). (Illus.). (J). (gr. 2-5). pap. o.s.i (*0-590-06807-5*) Scholastic, Inc.

—Pony Problem. 2003. (Pony Pals Super Special Ser.: No. 5). (Illus.). 128p. (J). (gr. 2-7). pap. 3.99 (*0-439-42626-X*, Scholastic Paperbacks) Scholastic, Inc.

—Self-Portrait. 2003. (Three Girls in the City Ser.: No. 1). 176p. (J). (gr. 3-7). mass mkt. 4.99 (*0-439-49839-2*, 53517295, Scholastic Paperbacks) Scholastic, Inc.

—Too Many Ponies. 1995. (Pony Pals Ser.: No. 6). (Illus.). (J). (gr. 2-5). 10.04 (*0-606-08312-X*) Turtleback Bks.

Better Homes and Gardens Editors. A Tree Full of Friends. 1989. 32p. (J). 4.95 o.p. (*0-696-01910-8*) Meredith Bks.

Beveridge, Donna. Henry. 1999. (Books for Young Learners).Tr. of Henry. (Illus.). 12p. (J). (gr. k-2). pap. text 5.00 (*1-57274-263-1*) Owen, Richard C. Pubs., Inc.

Bial, Raymond. A Handful of Dirt. 2000. (Illus.). 32p. (J). (gr. 3-7). lib. bdg. 17.85 (*0-8027-8699-5*); 16.95 (*0-8027-8698-7*) Walker & Co.

Biddulph, Robert. Hello Kitty, Hello Love! 2003. (Illus.). 24p. (J). (gr. k-3). 12.95 (*0-8109-8538-1*) Abrams, Harry N., Inc.

Billin-Frye, Paige. Meet the Sweet-Hearts. 1997. (Sticker Stories Ser.). (Illus.). 16p. (J). (ps-1). 4.99 (*0-448-41715-4*, Grosset & Dunlap) Penguin Putnam Bks. for Young Readers.

Billingham, Brenda. Lilly to the Rescue. 1998. (First Novels Ser.). (Illus.). 64p. (J). (gr. 1-4). pap. 3.99 (*0-88780-386-5*) Formac Publishing Co., Ltd. CAN. *Dist:* Formac Distributing, Ltd.

Birch, Beverley & Gardner, Sally. Suzi, Sam, George & Alice. 1993. (Illus.). 32p. (J). (ps-1). o.p. (*0-370-31771-8*) Random Hse., Inc.

Birchman, David F. A Green Horn Blowing. 1997. (Illus.). 32p. (J). (ps up). 15.00 (*0-688-12388-0*) HarperCollins Children's Bk. Group.

Bird, Isobel. Merry Meet, 7 Vols., No. 2. 2001. (Circle of Three Ser.). 224p. (J). (gr. 7 up). pap. 4.99 (*0-06-447292-2*, Avon) HarperCollins Children's Bk. Group.

Birdseye, Tom. I'M Going to Be Famous. 1986. 144p. (J). (gr. 4-7). tchr. ed. 16.95 (*0-8234-0630-X*) Holiday Hse., Inc.

—I'M Going to Be Famous. (J). 1990. pap. o.s.i (*0-440-80193-1*, Dell Books for Young Readers); 1989. 176p. reprint ed. pap. 2.95 o.s.i (*0-440-40212-3*, Yearling) Random Hse. Children's Bks.

—Just Call Me Stupid. 1993. 192p. (J). (gr. 4-7). tchr. ed. 16.95 (*0-8234-1045-5*) Holiday Hse., Inc.

Birdseye, Tom & Birdseye, Debbie H. She'll Be Comin' Round the Mountain. 1994. (Illus.). 32p. (J). (ps-3). tchr. ed. 15.95 (*0-8234-1032-3*) Holiday Hse., Inc.

Birnhack, Sarah. Promise Me Tomorrow. 1990. (YA). (gr. 6 up). 12.95 o.p. (*1-56062-025-0*); pap. 9.95 o.p. (*1-56062-026-9*) CIS Communications, Inc.

Biro, Val. Gumdrop Forever. (Illus.). 26p. (J). text 22.95 (*0-340-71448-4*); pap. text 11.95 (*0-340-71449-2*) Hodder & Stoughton, Ltd. GBR. *Dist:* Lubrecht & Cramer, Ltd., Trafalgar Square.

Bishop, Claire Huchet. The Man Who Lost His Head. 1989. (Illus.). 64p. (J). (ps-3). pap. 3.95 o.p. (*0-14-050976-3*, Puffin Bks.) Penguin Putnam Bks. for Young Readers.

Bissett, Isabel. Here Comes Annette! 1993. (Voyages Ser.). (Illus.). (J). 3.75 (*0-383-03628-3*) SRA/McGraw-Hill.

BJ & Scooter. 2002. (Barney Ser.). (J). pap. text o.p. (*1-58668-282-2*) Lyrick Publishing.

Black, Sonia W. The Get along Gang & the New Neighbor. 1984. (Get along Gang Ser.). (Illus.). 32p. (Orig.). (J). (ps-2). pap. 1.95 o.p. (*0-590-40134-3*) Scholastic, Inc.

—The Get along Gang & the Tattletale. 1984. (Get along Gang Ser.). (Illus.). 32p. (Orig.). (J). (ps-2). pap. 1.95 o.p. (*0-590-40127-0*) Scholastic, Inc.

Blackburn. Waiting for Sunday. 1989. (J). (ps-2). 19.95 o.p. (*0-590-50158-5*) Scholastic, Inc.

Blackburn, Joyce K. Suki & the Invisible Peacock. rev. ed. 1996. (Suki Ser.). (Illus.). 64p. (J). (ps-3). 14.95 (*1-881576-69-8*) Providence Hse. Pubs.

—Suki & the Magic Sand Dollar. rev. ed. 1996. (Suki Ser.). (Illus.). 64p. (J). (ps-3). 14.95 (*1-881576-70-1*) Providence Hse. Pubs.

—Suki & the Old Umbrella. rev. ed. 1996. (Suki Ser.). (Illus.). 64p. (J). (ps-3). 14.95 (*1-881576-71-X*) Providence Hse. Pubs.

—Suki & the Wonder Star. rev. ed. 1996. (Suki Ser.). (Illus.). 64p. (J). (ps-3). 14.95 (*1-881576-72-8*) Providence Hse. Pubs.

Blacklock, Dyan. Crab Bait. 1997. 112p. (Orig.). (J). (gr. 4-8). pap. 6.95 o.p. (*1-86448-172-2*) Allen & Unwin Pty., Ltd. AUS. *Dist:* Independent Pubs. Group.

Blair, Cynthia. The Double-Dip Disguise. 1988. (J). (gr. 4 up). mass mkt. 3.50 o.s.i (*0-449-70256-1*, Fawcett) Ballantine Bks.

Blair, L. E. Falling in Like. 1990. (J). (gr. 4-8). pap. o.p. (*0-307-22010-9*, Golden Bks.) Random Hse. Children's Bks.

—Odd Couple. 1994. 48p. (J). (gr. 4-7). pap. 2.95 o.s.i (*0-307-22007-9*, Golden Bks.) Random Hse. Children's Bks.

—Stealing the Show. 1994. (Illus.). 48p. (J). (ps-3). pap. 2.95 o.s.i (*0-307-22008-7*, Golden Bks.) Random Hse. Children's Bks.

Blair, Shannon. Kiss & Tell. 1985. (Sweet Dreams Ser.: No. 92). 176p. (Orig.). (J). (gr. 5 up). mass mkt. 2.50 o.s.i (*0-553-26843-0*) Bantam Bks.

Blance, Ellen & Cook. Monster Looks for Friend. Date not set. pap. text 129.15 (*0-582-18591-2*) Addison-Wesley Longman, Ltd. GBR. *Dist:* Trans-Atlantic Pubns., Inc.

Blatchford, Claire. Por el Camino. Writer, C. C. & Nielsen, Lisa C., trs. 1992. (Hippy Ser.). (SPA., Illus.). 24p. (Orig.). (J). (ps). pap. text 3.00 o.s.i (*1-56134-152-5*, McGraw-Hill/Dushkin) McGraw-Hill Higher Education.

—A Surprise for Reggie. 2nd ed. 1992. (Hippy Ser.). (Illus.). 24p. (Orig.). (J). (ps). pap. text 3.00 o.s.i (*1-56134-141-X*, McGraw-Hill/Dushkin) McGraw-Hill Higher Education.

Blaustein, Muriel. Make Friends, Zachary! 1990. (Illus.). 32p. (J). (ps-2). 12.95 (*0-06-020545-8*); lib. bdg. 12.89 o.p. (*0-06-020546-6*) HarperCollins Children's Bk. Group.

—Make Friends, Zachary! 1992. (Illus.). (J). 3.99 o.p. (*0-517-08509-7*) Random Hse. Value Publishing.

Blegvad, Lenore. First Friends. 2000. (Growing Tree Ser.). (Illus.). 24p. (J). (ps up). 9.95 (*0-694-01273-4*, Harper Festival) HarperCollins Children's Bk. Group.

Bliss, Corinne Demas. Snow Day. 1998. (Step into Reading Ser.). (Illus.). 47p. (J). (gr. k-3). 11.99 o.s.i (*0-679-98222-1*) Random Hse., Inc.

Block, Francesca Lia. Violet & Claire. 176p. (J). 2000. (gr. 8-12). pap. 6.99 (*0-06-447253-1*, Harper Trophy); 1999. (Illus.). (ps-2). 14.95 (*0-06-027749-1*, Cotler, Joanna Bks.) HarperCollins Children's Bk. Group.

—Violet & Claire. 1999. (Illus.). 176p. (YA). (gr. 7-12). lib. bdg. 14.89 (*0-06-027750-5*) HarperCollins Pubs.

—Weetzie Bat. (Charlotte Zolotow Bk.). 1991. 96p. (J). (gr. 12 up). pap. 4.50 o.s.i (*0-06-447068-7*, Harper Trophy); 1989. 96p. (YA). (gr. 7 up). lib. bdg. 14.89 o.p. (*0-06-020536-9*); 10th anniv. ed. 1999. 128p. (J). (gr. 5 up). pap. 7.99 (*0-06-440818-3*, Harper Trophy) HarperCollins Children's Bk. Group.

—Weetzie Bat. 1991. (J). 14.00 (*0-606-05688-2*) Turtleback Bks.

—Weetzie Bat: 10th Anniversary Edition. 10th anniv. ed. 1999. (Charlotte Zolotow Book Ser.). 128p. (YA). (gr. 7-k). 14.95 (*0-06-020534-2*) HarperCollins Children's Bk. Group.

Bloom, Daniel. Bubbie & Zadie Come to My House. 1985. (Illus.). 32p. (J). (gr. k up). 9.95 o.p. (*0-917657-49-7*) Fine, Donald I. Bks.

Bloom, Hanya. Friendly Fangs. 1991. (Vic the Vampire Ser.: No. 4). 80p. (J). (gr. 4-7). mass mkt. 2.95 o.p. (*0-06-106032-1*, HarperTorch) Morrow/Avon.

Bloor, Edward. Tangerine. 2001. 304p. (gr. 6 up). mass mkt. 4.99 o.s.i (*0-439-28603-4*) Scholastic, Inc.

Blos, Joan W. A Gathering of Days: A New England Girl's Journal, 1830-1832. 2nd ed. 1990. 144p. (J). (gr. 4-7). reprint ed. pap. 4.99 (*0-689-71419-X*, Aladdin) Simon & Schuster Children's Publishing.

—Old Henry. 1990. (Illus.). 32p. (J). (ps-3). pap. 6.99 (*0-688-09935-1*, Harper Trophy) HarperCollins Children's Bk. Group.

—Old Henry. 1990. (J). 13.10 (*0-606-04761-1*) Turtleback Bks.

Bloss, Janet A. The Creep's at It Again. 1988. (Treetop Tales Ser.). (Illus.). 128p. (Orig.). (J). (gr. 3-6). pap. 1.00 o.p. (*0-87406-345-0*) Darby Creek Publishing.

Blum, Vicki. The Trouble with Spitt. 1996. 108p. (Orig.). (J). (gr. 4-8). pap. o.p. (*1-57345-147-9*) Deseret Bk. Co.

Blume, Judy. Are You There God? It's Me, Margaret. 2002. (J). 13.94 (*0-7587-9131-3*) Book Wholesalers, Inc.

—Are You There God? It's Me, Margaret. l.t. ed. 2002. (LRS Large Print Cornerstone Ser.). (J). lib. bdg. 28.95 (*1-58118-088-8*, 24873) LRS.

—Are You There God? It's Me, Margaret. unabr. ed. 2000. (YA). (gr. 4-7). audio 18.00 (*0-8072-7859-9*, 396013, Listening Library) Random Hse. Audio Publishing Group.

—The Best of Judy Blume, 4 vols., Set. 2004. (J). 23.47 (*0-440-42022-9*, Yearling) Random Hse. Children's Bks.

—Blubber. 153p. (J). (gr. 4-6). pap. 3.99 (*0-8072-1404-3*, Listening Library) Random Hse. Audio Publishing Group.

—Fudge-a-Mania, 3 vols., Set. 1992. (J). (gr. 4-7). 14.00 (*0-440-36051-X*) Dell Publishing.

—Judy Blume, 4 bks. 1992. (J). (gr. 4-7). 14.00 (*0-440-36053-6*) Dell Publishing.

—Judy Blume Collection, 5 bks. 1986. (J). (gr. 3-8). 16.25 (*0-440-44356-3*) Dell Publishing.

—Just as Long as We're Together. l.t. ed. 1986. (J). (gr. 1-8). 16.95 o.p. (*0-7451-0826-1*, Galaxy Children's Large Print) BBC Audiobooks America.

—Just as Long as We're Together. l.t. ed. 1988. 210p. (YA). (gr. 5 up). reprint ed. lib. bdg. 15.95 o.p. (*1-55736-046-4*) Bantam Doubleday Dell Large Print Group, Inc.

—Just as Long as We're Together. 1988. (J). pap. 3.50 o.s.i (*0-440-70013-2*) Dell Publishing.

—Just as Long as We're Together. 304p. (gr. 4-7). 1991. (YA). mass mkt. 5.99 (*0-440-21094-1*); 1988. pap. text 5.50 (*0-440-40075-9*) Random Hse. Children's Bks. (Yearling).

—Just as Long as We're Together. 1987. 304p. (gr. 5-8). (J). mass mkt. 17.99 o.p. (*0-531-08329-2*); (YA). pap. 16.95 o.p. (*0-531-05729-1*) Scholastic, Inc. (Orchard Bks.).

—Just as Long as We're Together. 1987. (J). 11.55 (*0-606-04063-3*) Turtleback Bks.

—The One in the Middle Is the Green Kangaroo. 1992. (Illus.). 32p. (J). (ps-3). pap. 5.99 (*0-440-40668-4*, Yearling) Random Hse. Children's Bks.

—Otherwise Known As Sheila the Great. 2003. 144p. pap. 5.99 (*0-14-240099-8*, Puffin Bks.); 2003. (Illus.). 144p. pap. 5.99 (*0-14-230228-7*, Puffin Bks.); 2002. (Illus.). 128p. (YA). 15.99 (*0-525-46928-1*, Dutton Children's Bks.); 1972. 128p. (J). (gr. 4-7). 15.99 o.s.i (*0-525-36455-2*, Dutton Children's Bks.) Penguin Putnam Bks. for Young Readers.

—Otherwise Known As Sheila the Great. unabr. ed. 1997. (Fudge Ser.). 166p. (J). (gr. 2-4). pap. 28.00 incl. audio (*0-8072-7646-4*, YA912CX, Listening Library) Random Hse. Audio Publishing Group.

—Otherwise Known As Sheila the Great. 128p. (gr. 3-7). 2000. (Illus.). mass mkt. 2.99 o.s.i (*0-375-80679-2*, Random Hse. Bks. for Young Readers); 1976. pap. text 4.99 o.s.i (*0-440-46701-2*, Yearling) Random Hse. Children's Bks.

—Quiza No lo Haga. 1992. Orig. Title: Then Again, Maybe I Won't. 16.05 o.p. (*0-606-10494-1*) Turtleback Bks.

—Superfudge. 2002. (Illus.). (J). 13.40 (*0-7587-6668-8*) Book Wholesalers, Inc.

—Superfudge. (J). 1993. 176p. (gr. 4-7). pap. 1.99 o.s.i (*0-440-21619-2*); 1923. pap. 2.95 o.s.i (*0-440-78433-6*) Dell Publishing.

—Superfudge. l.t. ed. 2000. (LRS Large Print Cornerstone Ser.). 216p. (YA). (gr. 5-10). lib. bdg. 28.95 (*1-58118-061-6*, 23475) LRS.

—Superfudge. 1999. 9.95 (*1-56137-175-0*) Novel Units, Inc.

—Superfudge. l.t. ed. 1987. 239p. (J). (gr. 2-6). reprint ed. lib. bdg. 16.95 o.s.i (*1-55736-014-6*, Cornerstone Bks.) Pages, Inc.

—Superfudge. 2003. 192p. pap. 5.99 (*0-14-240098-X*, Puffin Bks.); 2003. (Illus.). 192p. pap. 5.99 (*0-14-230229-5*, Puffin Bks.); 2002. (Illus.). 176p. (YA). 15.99 (*0-525-46930-3*, Dutton Children's Bks.); 1980. 176p. (J). (gr. 4-7). 15.99 o.s.i (*0-525-40522-4*, Dutton Children's Bks.) Penguin Putnam Bks. for Young Readers.

—Superfudge. 166p. (J). (gr. 2-4). pap. 4.99 (*0-8072-1457-4*); 1993. pap. 28.00 incl. audio (*0-8072-7407-0*, YA842SP) Random Hse. Audio Publishing Group. (Listening Library).

—Superfudge. 1994. (J). pap. 4.99 (*0-440-91028-5*, Dell Books for Young Readers); 1988. (J). pap. o.s.i (*0-440-80039-0*, Dell Books for Young Readers); 1988. (J). mass mkt. o.s.i (*0-440-*

Relationships

80007-2, Dell Books for Young Readers); 1986. 176p. (gr. 3-7). pap. text 4.99 o.s.i (*0-440-48433-2*, Yearling); 1981. (J). mass mkt. o.s.i (*0-440-70006-X*, Dell Books for Young Readers) Random Hse. Children's Bks.

—Superfudge. 1996. (SPA.). (YA). (gr. 5-8). pap. 11.95 (*1-56014-665-6*) Santillana USA Publishing Co., Inc.

—Superfudge. (J). 1996. 16.00 (*0-606-10512-3*); 1980. 11.04 (*0-606-02659-2*) Turtleback Bks.

—Tales of a Fourth Grade Nothing. 2004. 144p. mass mkt. 5.99 (*0-425-19379-9*) Berkley Publishing Group.

—Tales of a Fourth Grade Nothing. 2002. (Illus.). (J). 13.40 (*0-7587-6609-2*) Book Wholesalers, Inc.

—Tales of a Fourth Grade Nothing. 1999. 11.95 (*1-56137-709-0*) Novel Units, Inc.

—Tales of a Fourth Grade Nothing. 2003. 192p. pap. 5.99 (*0-14-240101-3*, Puffin Bks.) Penguin Putnam Bks. for Young Readers.

—Tales of a Fourth Grade Nothing. 1923. pap. 3.25 o.s.i (*0-440-78474-3*, Yearling) Random Hse. Children's Bks.

—Tiger Eyes. 2003. 256p. (J). 16.00 (*0-689-85872-8*, Atheneum/Richard Jackson Bks.) Simon & Schuster Children's Publishing.

Blume, Karin & Pokornik, Brigitte. My New Friends. 1996. (Funny Fingers Ser.). (Illus.). 16p. (J). (ps-1). 6.95 (*0-7892-0180-1*, Abbeville Kids) Abbeville Pr., Inc.

Blundell, Tony. Beware of Boys. 1996. (J). (ps-3). mass mkt. 4.95 (*0-688-14739-9*, Morrow, William & Co.) Morrow/Avon.

Bluth Brothers Staff. A Day for Knights. 1984. (Buddies Ser.). (Illus.). 48p. (J). (gr. k-6). 5.95 o.p. (*0-8249-8062-X*) Ideals Pubns.

—Somebody's Hero. 1984. (Buddies Ser.). (Illus.). 48p. (J). (gr. k-6). 5.95 o.p. (*0-8249-8063-8*) Ideals Pubns.

Bluthenthal, Diana Cain. I'm Not Invited. 2003. (Illus.). 32p. (J). (gr. k-2). 16.95 (*0-689-84141-8*, Atheneum/Richard Jackson Bks.) Simon & Schuster Children's Publishing.

—Matilda the Moocher. 1997. (Illus.). 32p. (J). (ps-2). pap. 15.95 (*0-531-30003-X*); lib. bdg. 16.99 (*0-531-33003-6*) Scholastic, Inc. (Orchard Bks.).

Blyton, Enid. Five Get into Trouble. l.t. ed. 1993. (J). (gr. 1-8). 16.95 o.p. (*0-7451-1910-7*, Galaxy Children's Large Print) BBC Audiobooks America.

—Five on a Hike Together. l.t. ed. 1995. (J). 16.95 o.p. (*0-7451-3145-X*, Galaxy Children's Large Print) BBC Audiobooks America.

—Mr. Pink-Whistle Has Some Fun. 2000. (Enid Blyton's Happy Days Ser.). (Illus.). 96p. (J). (gr. 1-4). pap. 6.95 (*0-7475-4345-3*) Bloomsbury Publishing, Ltd. GBR. *Dist:* Trafalgar Square.

Bock, Shelly V. Lonely Lyla. 1992. (YA). 7.95 o.p. (*0-533-09389-9*) Vantage Pr., Inc.

Boczkowski, Tricia. Bear Loves Visitors. 2003. (Bear in the Big Blue House Ser.). (Illus.). 22p. (J). bds. 4.99 (*0-689-85254-1*, Simon Spotlight) Simon & Schuster Children's Publishing.

Boegehold, Betty D. The Fight. 1991. 32p. (J). (ps-3). pap. 3.99 o.s.i (*0-553-35206-7*) Bantam Bks.

—The Fight. 1999. (Bank Street Reader Collection). (Illus.). (J). (gr. 1-3). lib. bdg. 21.26 (*0-8368-2420-2*) Stevens, Gareth Inc.

—The Fight. (J). E-Book 3.99 (*1-58824-156-4*); 1991. (Illus.). E-Book (*1-59019-325-3*); 1991. (Illus.). E-Book (*1-58824-072-X*) ipicturebooks, LLC.

Boelts, Maribeth. Grace & Joe. Tucker, Kathy, ed. 1994. (Illus.). 32p. (J). (ps-3). lib. bdg. 14.95 (*0-8075-3019-0*) Whitman, Albert & Co.

—Little Bunny's Cool Tool Set. 1997. (Concept Bks.). (Illus.). 32p. (J). (ps-1). lib. bdg. 14.95 (*0-8075-4584-8*) Whitman, Albert & Co.

Bogacki, Tomek. Cat & Mouse, RS. 1996. (Illus.). 32p. (J). (ps-3). 14.00 o.p. (*0-374-31225-7*, Farrar, Straus & Giroux (BYR)) Farrar, Straus & Giroux.

Bogart, JoEllen. Ten for Dinner. l.t. ed. 1989. (J). (ps-2). bds. 19.95 (*0-590-73173-4*) Scholastic, Inc.

Bograd, Larry. Bad Apple, RS. 1986. (Sunburst Ser.). 152p. (YA). (gr. 9 up). pap. 3.45 o.p. (*0-374-40476-3*, Sunburst) Farrar, Straus & Giroux.

—The Better Angel. 1985. 256p. (YA). (gr. 7 up). 12.95 (*0-397-32126-0*); lib. bdg. 12.89 (*0-397-32127-9*) HarperCollins Children's Bk. Group.

Bohlmeijer, Arno. Something Very Sorry. 1997. (Orig.). 11.05 (*0-606-13032-2*) Turtleback Bks.

Boland, Janice. Breakfast with John. 1997. (Books for Young Learners). (Illus.). 8p. (J). (gr. k-2). pap. text 5.00 (*1-57274-109-0*, A2130) Owen, Richard C. Pubs., Inc.

Boldizsar, Anneliese. How to Make Friends. 2000. (Illus.). 59p. pap. (*0-7541-0916-X*) Minerva Pr. GBR. *Dist:* Unity Distribution.

Boldt, Mark. CC & the Cool Rule! l.t. ed. 2000. (U-Do Book Ser.). (Illus.). 32p. (J). (gr. k-8). (*0-9662556-5-8*, U-Do, 06) Boldt.Entertainment.

Bolinger, Camille J. The Forever Wreath. 1993. (Illus.). 40p. (J). (ps-4). 17.95 (*0-9632777-6-6*) Dutch Run Publishing.

Bond, Michael. Paddington on Screen. 1992. (Paddington Ser.). (Illus.). 128p. (J). (ps-3). pap. 2.75 o.s.i (*0-440-40029-5*, Yearling) Random Hse. Children's Bks.

Bond, Nancy. The Love of Friends. 1997. 304p. (YA). (gr. 7 up). 17.00 (*0-689-81365-1*, McElderry, Margaret K.) Simon & Schuster Children's Publishing.

Bond, Rebecca. When Marcus Moore Moved In. 2003. (Illus.). 32p. (J). 15.95 (*0-316-10458-2*, Tingley, Megan Bks.) Little Brown Children's Bks.

Bonners, Susan. Above & Beyond, RS. 2001. 160p. (J). (gr. 5-7). 16.00 (*0-374-30018-6*, Farrar, Straus & Giroux (BYR)) Farrar, Straus & Giroux.

—The Silver Balloon, RS. 1997. (Illus.). 80p. (J). (gr. 2-4). 14.00 (*0-374-36913-5*, Farrar, Straus & Giroux (BYR)) Farrar, Straus & Giroux.

Bonnette, Jeanne. Three Friends. 1982. 23p. (J). (gr. k-4). pap. 4.95 (*0-89992-066-7*) Council for Indian Education.

Bonsall, Crosby N. Mine's the Best. (My First I Can Read Bks.). (Illus.). (J). (ps-k). 1984. 32p. pap. 3.50 o.p. (*0-06-444054-0*, Harper Trophy); 1973. 32p. 14.89 (*0-06-020578-4*); 1973. 14.89 (*0-06-020577-6*, 133480); 1997. 32p. reprint ed. pap. 3.99 (*0-06-444213-6*, Harper Trophy); 1996. 32p. lib. bdg. 16.89 (*0-06-027091-8*); 1996. 32p. 12.95 o.p. (*0-06-027090-X*) HarperCollins Children's Bk. Group.

—Mine's the Best. 1997. (My First I Can Read Bks.). (J). (ps-k). 10.10 (*0-606-11627-3*) Turtleback Bks.

—Piggle: A Homer Story. 2002. (I Can Read Book 2 Ser.). (Illus.). 64p. (J). (gr. 1-3). pap. 3.99 (*0-06-444320-5*) HarperCollins Pubs.

—Who's a Pest? 1992. (I Can Read Bks.). (Illus.). (J). (gr. 1-3). 6.93 (*0-06-020620-9*, 133597) HarperCollins Children's Bk. Group.

Bontemps, Arna & Hughes, Langston. The Pasteboard Bandit. 1997. (Iona & Peter Opie Library of Children's Literature). (Illus.). 96p. (J). (gr. 3-7). 16.95 o.p. (*0-19-511476-0*) Oxford Univ. Pr., Inc.

Boock, Paula. Dare Truth or Promise. 1999. 208p. (YA). (gr. 7-12). tchr. ed. 15.00 (*0-395-97117-9*) Houghton Mifflin Co.

—Dare Truth or Promise. 1999. (J). E-Book 15.00 (*0-585-36691-8*) netLibrary, Inc.

Booher, Dianna. Boyfriends & Boy Friends. 1988. (Orig.). (YA). (gr. 7 up). pap. 5.99 o.p. (*0-8007-5274-0*) Revell, Fleming H. Co.

Boom-Boom & His Friends. 1982. 16p. (J). pap. 2.50 o.p. (*0-8431-0287-X*, Price Stern Sloan) Penguin Putnam Bks. for Young Readers.

Booth, Zilpha M. Finding a Friend. (Illus.). (J). 1987. 54p. (gr. 1-5). pap. 3.95 o.p. (*0-932433-22-7*); 2nd ed. 1996. 40p. pap. 8.95 (*1-883650-32-1*) Windswept Hse. Pubs.

Borden, Louise. Albie the Lifeguard. 1999. (Illus.). 32p. (J). (ps-3). mass mkt. 5.99 (*0-590-44586-3*) Scholastic, Inc.

Borg, Veronique. The Next Balcony Down. 1992. (Child's World Library Ser.). (Illus.). 32p. (J). (gr. 1-5). lib. bdg. 8.50 (*0-89565-757-0*) Child's World, Inc.

Bornstein, Ruth Lercher. Butterflies & Lizards, Beryl & Me. 2002. (Illus.). 160p. (J). (gr. 3-7). lib. bdg. 14.95 (*0-7614-5118-8*, Cavendish Children's Bks.) Cavendish, Marshall Corp.

Borton, Lady. Junk Pile. 1997. (Illus.). 32p. (J). (ps-3). 15.95 o.s.i (*0-399-22728-8*, Philomel) Penguin Putnam Bks. for Young Readers.

Botner, Barbara. Wallace's Lists. 2004. (J). lib. bdg. (*0-06-000225-5*) HarperCollins Pubs.

Bottner, Barbara. The World's Greatest Expert on Absolutely Everything... Is Crying. 1986. (J). (gr. 3-7). pap. 2.95 o.s.i (*0-440-49739-6*, Yearling) Random Hse. Children's Bks.

Bottner, Barbara. Dumb Old Casey Is a Fat Tree. 1991. (Trophy Bk.). (Illus.). 64p. (J). (gr. 1-4). pap. 3.50 (*0-06-440346-7*, Harper Trophy) HarperCollins Children's Bk. Group.

—Nothing in Common. 1988. (J). (gr. 5 up). mass mkt. 2.95 o.s.i (*0-553-27060-5*, Starfire) Random Hse. Children's Bks.

—Rosa's Room. Spiegel, Beth, tr. & illus. by. 2004. 32p. (J). (gr. 1-2). 15.95 (*1-56145-302-1*, Peachtree Junior) Peachtree Pubs., Ltd.

—Two Messy Friends. 1999. (Hello Reader! Ser.). (Illus.). 32p. (gr. k-2). mass mkt. 3.99 (*0-590-63285-X*) Scholastic, Inc.

—Two Messy Friends. 1998. (Hello Reader! Ser.). 9.65 (*0-606-18611-5*) Turtleback Bks.

Bottner, Barbara & Kruglik, Gerald. Wallace's Lists. Landstrom, Olof, tr. & illus. by. 2004. (J). (*0-06-000224-7*) HarperCollins Pubs.

Boughton, Richard. Rent-a-Puppy, Inc. 1995. (J). pap. 3.95 o.s.i (*0-689-71836-5*, Aladdin) Simon & Schuster Children's Publishing.

Boulden, Jim. All Together: Blended Family Activity Book. 1991. (Illus.). 32p. (J). (gr. 1-7). 5.95 (*1-878076-10-8*, 108) Boulden Publishing.

—Alone Together: Single Parent Activity Book. 1991. (Illus.). 32p. (J). (gr. 1-6). 5.95 (*1-878076-09-4*, 094) Boulden Publishing.

—Feeling Good: Self Esteem Activity Book. 1991. (Illus.). 32p. (J). (gr. 1-7). pap. 5.95 (*1-878076-11-6*) Boulden Publishing.

—My Secret: Parental Substance Abuse Activity Book. 1991. (Illus.). 32p. (J). (gr. 1-7). pap. 5.95 (*1-878076-13-2*) Boulden Publishing.

Bourgeois, Paulette. Franklin's New Friend. ed. 1999. (gr. 1). spiral bd. (*0-616-01590-9*); (J). (gr. 2). spiral bd. (*0-616-01591-7*) Canadian National Institute for the Blind/Institut National Canadien pour les Aveugles.

—Franklin's New Friend. (Franklin Ser.). 96p. (J). (ps-3). pap. (*1-55074-363-5*) Kids Can Pr., Ltd.

—Franklin's New Friend. 1997. (Franklin Ser.). (Illus.). 260p. (J). (ps-3). 10.95 (*1-55074-352-X*); 10.95 (*1-55074-361-9*) Kids Can Pr., Ltd. CAN. *Dist:* General Distribution Services, Inc.

—Franklin's New Friend. 1997. (Franklin Ser.). (Illus.). 32p. (J). (ps-3). pap. 4.50 (*0-590-02592-9*) Scholastic, Inc.

—Franklin's New Friend. 1997. (Franklin Ser.). (J). (ps-3). 10.65 (*0-606-11352-5*) Turtleback Bks.

—Franklin's Valentines. 1998. (Franklin Ser.). (Illus.). 268p. (J). (ps-3). text 10.95 (*1-55074-480-1*) Kids Can Pr., Ltd. CAN. *Dist:* General Distribution Services, Inc.

Bourgeois, Paulette & Clark, Brenda. Franklin & His Friend. 2002. (Franklin TV-Tie In Ser.: No. 12). (Illus.). 32p. (J). pap. 4.50 (*0-439-33878-6*) Scholastic, Inc.

—Franklin & the Computer. 2003. (Franklin Ser.: Bk. 16). 32p. (J). pap. 4.50 (*0-439-43121-2*) Scholastic, Inc.

—Franklin's New Friend. 1999. (Franklin Ser.). (Illus.). 180p. (J). (ps-3). pap. incl. audio (*1-55074-797-5*) Kids Can Pr., Ltd.

Bourgeois, Paulette, et al. Franklin en la Oscuridad. López Varela, Alejandra, tr. from ENG. 1998. (Franklin Ser.). (SPA., Illus.). 32p. (J). (ps-3). pap. 5.95 (*1-880507-43-9*, LC7861) Lectorum Pubns., Inc.

Bourke, Linda. Signs of a Friend. 1982. (Illus.). (J). pap. 2.95 (*0-201-10094-0*) HarperCollins Children's Bk. Group.

Bowdish, Lynea. Downey & Buttercup. 1995. (Really Reading Ser.). (Illus.). 24p. (J). (gr. k-1). pap. 2.99 o.p. (*0-87406-778-2*) Darby Creek Publishing.

—A Friend for Caitlin. 1998. (Illus.). 48p. (J). (gr. 3-5). pap. 3.50 (*0-87406-894-0*, Willowisp Pr.) Darby Creek Publishing.

Bowen, Elizabeth. Friends & Relations. 1980. 192p. (YA). (gr. 7 up). pap. 2.25 (*0-380-49601-1*, 49601-1, Avon Bks.) Morrow/Avon.

Bowers, Tim. A New Home. (Green Light Readers Level 1 Ser.). (Illus.). (J). 2003. 24p. 11.95 (*0-15-204808-1*); 2003. 24p. pap. 3.95 (*0-15-204848-0*); 2002. 20p. 11.95 o.s.i (*0-15-216564-9*); 2002. 20p. pap. 3.95 o.s.i (*0-15-216570-3*) Harcourt Children's Bks. (Green Light Readers).

Boyce, Katie. Hector the Hermit Crab. 2003. (Illus.). 32p. (J). (ps-1). 15.95 (*1-58234-800-6*, Bloomsbury Children) Bloomsbury Publishing.

Boyd, Candy Dawson. Forever Friends. 1986. (Novels Ser.). 224p. (J). (gr. 7 up). pap. 4.99 o.s.i (*0-14-032077-6*, Puffin Bks.) Penguin Putnam Bks. for Young Readers.

—Forever Friends. 1992. (J). (gr. 4-8). 17.75 o.p. (*0-8446-6571-1*) Smith, Peter Pub., Inc.

Boykin, Edwina. To the Boy I Shared with the Crabapple Tree. Tinsley, Arnold, ed. 1999. 105p. (YA). pap. (*0-9669230-0-6*) Ebo Ink.

Bozza, Katherine-Kerry L. & Cherry, Jessica. A Very Special Day. 1997. (Illus.). o.p. (*0-7872-2889-3*) Kendall/Hunt Publishing Co.

Bradbury, Ray. Switch on the Night. 1993. (Umbrella Bks.). (Illus.). 40p. (J). (ps-2). 8.99 o.s.i (*0-394-80486-4*); 9.99 o.s.i (*0-394-90486-9*) Random Hse. Children's Bks. (Knopf Bks. for Young Readers).

Bradley, Virginia. Wait & See. 1994. 176p. (J). (gr. 5 up). 14.99 o.p. (*0-525-65158-6*, Dutton Children's Bks.) Penguin Putnam Bks. for Young Readers.

Brancato, Robin F. Something Left to Lose. 1976. (Illus.). 192p. (J). (gr. 7 up). 6.95 o.s.i (*0-394-83183-7*, Knopf Bks. for Young Readers) Random Hse. Children's Bks.

Brandenberg, Franz. The Hit of the Party. 1985. (Illus.). 32p. (J). (gr. k-3). 12.95 o.p. (*0-688-04240-6*); lib. bdg. 12.88 o.p. (*0-688-04241-4*) HarperCollins Children's Bk. Group. (Greenwillow Bks.).

—Leo & Emily. 1981. (Greenwillow Read-Alone Bks.). (Illus.). 56p. (J). (gr. 1-3). 15.00 o.p. (*0-688-80292-3*); lib. bdg. 8.88 o.p. (*0-688-84292-5*) HarperCollins Children's Bk. Group. (Greenwillow Bks.).

—Leo & Emily. 1990. 64p. (J). (gr. k-6). pap. 2.95 o.s.i (*0-440-40294-8*, Yearling) Random Hse. Children's Bks.

—Nice New Neighbors. 1977. (Greenwillow Read-Alone Bks.). (Illus.). 56p. (J). (gr. 1-4). 5.95 o.p. (*0-688-80105-6*); lib. bdg. 13.88 o.p. (*0-688-84105-8*) HarperCollins Children's Bk. Group. (Greenwillow Bks.).

Brandt, Betty. Special Delivery. 1988. (Carolrhoda On My Own Bks.). (Illus.). 48p. (J). (gr. k-4). lib. bdg. 14.95 o.s.i (*0-87614-312-5*, Carolrhoda Bks.) Lerner Publishing Group.

Branscum, Robbie. The Girl. 1986. 128p. (J). (gr. 5 up). lib. bdg. 10.89 o.p. (*0-06-020703-5*) HarperCollins Children's Bk. Group.

Brashares, Ann. The Second Summer of the Sisterhood. 2003. 384p. (YA). (gr. 7 up). 15.95 (*0-385-72934-0*, Delacorte Bks. for Young Readers) Random Hse. Children's Bks.

—The Second Summer of the Sisterhood. 2003. 384p. (YA). (gr. 7). lib. bdg. 17.99 (*0-385-90852-0*) Random Hse., Inc.

—The Sisterhood of the Traveling Pants. 2003. 294p. (YA). reprint ed. 15.00 (*0-7567-6771-7*) DIANE Publishing Co.

—The Sisterhood of the Traveling Pants. 2001. 304p. (J). 14.95 (*0-553-97041-0*, Delacorte Pr.) Dell Publishing.

—The Sisterhood of the Traveling Pants. l.t. ed. 2002. 344p. (YA). 24.95 (*0-7862-3966-2*) Gale Group.

—The Sisterhood of the Traveling Pants. unabr. ed. 2001. (YA). (gr. 7 up). audio 26.00 (*0-8072-0589-3*, Listening Library) Random Hse. Audio Publishing Group.

—The Sisterhood of the Traveling Pants. 320p. (YA). (gr. 7). 2004. mass mkt. 6.99 (*0-440-22970-7*, Laurel Leaf); 2003. pap. 8.95 (*0-385-73058-6*, Delacorte Bks. for Young Readers); 2001. (Illus.). 14.95 (*0-385-72933-2*, Delacorte Bks. for Young Readers) Random Hse. Children's Bks.

Braun, Nora M. Pickle in the Middle. 1997. 9.09 o.p. (*0-606-11746-6*) Turtleback Bks.

Bray, Jeannine D. Rabbie. Kenyatta, Imani, ed. 1998. (Illus.). 56p. (J). (gr. k-6). 14.95 (*1-886580-68-5*) Pinnacle-Syatt Pubns.

Bray, Marian F. Kayla's Secret. 1996. (Reba Novel Ser.: Vol. 3). 128p. (J). pap. 5.99 o.p. (*0-310-43351-7*) Zondervan.

Braybrooks, Ann. Just Be Nice... & Help a Friend! 2000. (Disney Ser.). (Illus.). 24p. (J). (ps-k). pap. 3.29 (*0-307-13312-5*, 13312, Golden Bks.) Random Hse. Children's Bks.

—Two Best Buddy Tales. 2000. (Disney Ser.: Vol. 2). (Illus.). 24p. (J). (ps-2). pap. 1.69 o.p. (*0-307-13269-2*, 13269, Golden Bks.) Random Hse. Children's Bks.

Brearley, Sue & Matthews, Jenny. Talk to Me. 1996. (Illus.). 25p. (J). pap. 6.95 (*0-7136-4410-9*) A & C Black GBR. *Dist:* Lubrecht & Cramer, Ltd.

Brennan, Joseph K. Gobo & the River, ERS. 1985. (Illus.). 48p. (J). (gr. 2-4). o.p. (*0-03-004552-5*, Holt, Henry & Co. Bks. For Young Readers) Holt, Henry & Co.

Brennan, Melissa. Careless Kisses. 1991. (Pizza Paradise Ser.: No. 2). 79p. (YA). mass mkt. 3.50 o.p. (*0-06-106052-6*, HarperTorch) Morrow/Avon.

—Could This Be Love? 1991. (Pizza Paradise Ser.: No. 3). 192p. (YA). mass mkt. 3.50 o.p. (*0-06-106067-4*, HarperTorch) Morrow/Avon.

—Paradise Lost? 1991. (Pizza Paradise Ser.: No. 4). 192p. (YA). mass mkt. 3.50 o.p. (*0-06-106068-2*, HarperTorch) Morrow/Avon.

—The Real Thing. 1992. (Pizza Paradise Ser.: No. 6). 192p. (YA). (gr. 7 up). mass mkt. 3.50 o.p. (*0-06-106070-4*, HarperTorch) Morrow/Avon.

—Whispers & Rumors. 1994. (Pizza Parade Ser.: No. 1). 208p. (YA). mass mkt. 1.99 o.p. (*0-06-106225-1*) HarperCollins Pubs.

—Whispers & Rumors. 1991. (Pizza Paradise Ser.: No. 1). 79p. (YA). mass mkt. 3.50 o.p. (*0-06-106049-6*, HarperTorch) Morrow/Avon.

Brenner, Barbara. Ups & Downs with Lion & Lamb. 1991. 48p. (J). (ps-3). 9.99 o.s.i (*0-553-07088-6*); pap. 3.99 o.s.i (*0-553-35207-5*) Bantam Bks.

—Ups & Downs with Lion & Lamb. 1991. E-Book (*1-58824-125-4*); (J). E-Book (*1-58824-202-1*) ipicturebooks, LLC.

Brenner, Barbara & Hooks, William H. Lion & Lamb Step Out. 1998. (Bank Street Reader Collection). (Illus.). 48p. (J). (gr. 2-4). lib. bdg. 21.26 (*0-8368-1772-9*) Stevens, Gareth Inc.

—Lion & Lamb Step Out. (Illus.). 2000. (J). E-Book (*1-58824-167-X*); 1990. E-Book (*1-59019-337-7*); 1990. E-Book (*1-58824-116-5*) ipicturebooks, LLC.

—Ups & Downs with Lion & Lamb. 1999. (Bank Street Reader Collection). (Illus.). 48p. (J). (gr. 2-4). lib. bdg. 21.26 (*0-8368-1783-4*) Stevens, Gareth Inc.

—Ups & Downs with Lion & Lamb. 1991. E-Book (*1-59019-341-5*) ipicturebooks, LLC.

Brewster, Patience. Two Bushy Badgers. 1995. (Illus.). 32p. (J). 14.95 o.p. (*0-316-10862-6*) Little Brown & Co.

Brian, Kate. The V Club. 2004. 288p. (J). 14.95 (*0-689-86764-6*, Simon & Schuster Children's Publishing) Simon & Schuster Children's Publishing.

Relationships

Brian, Sarah Jane. Let's Be Friends. 2001. (Girl Talk Ser.). (Illus.). 24p. (J). (gr. 1-3). pap. 3.99 (*0-307-10771-X*, Golden Bks.) Random Hse. Children's Bks.

Bridgers, Sue E. All Together Now. (YA). (gr. 7 up). 1990. 192p. mass mkt. 3.99 o.s.i (*0-553-24530-9*, Starfire); 1979. 256p. reprint ed. 13.99 o.s.i (*0-394-94098-9*, Knopf Bks. for Young Readers) Random Hse. Children's Bks.

—Keeping Christina. 1993. (YA). (gr. 7 up). 288p. 15.00 o.p. (*0-06-021504-6*); 80p. lib. bdg. 14.89 o.p. (*0-06-021505-4*) HarperCollins Children's Bk. Group.

—Keeping Christina. 1998. 290p. reprint ed. lib. bdg. 29.95 (*0-7351-0042-X*) Replica Bks.

—Notes for Another Life. 1989. 208p. (J). (gr. 7 up). mass mkt. 2.95 o.s.i (*0-553-27185-7*) Bantam Bks.

—Permanent Connections. rev. ed. 1999. 264p. (J). (gr. 9-10). pap. 12.00 (*1-889199-02-8*) Banks Channel Bks.

—Permanent Connections. 1987. 283p. (YA). (gr. 7 up). 14.00 o.p. (*0-06-020711-6*); lib. bdg. 13.89 o.p. (*0-06-020712-4*) HarperCollins Children's Bk. Group.

Bridgers, Sue Ellen. All Together Now. 2001. 244p. (YA). (gr. 4-7). per. 12.00 (*1-889199-06-0*) Banks Channel Bks.

Bridwell, Norman. The Big Egg Hunt. 2002. (Big Red Readers Ser.). (Illus.). (J). 11.91 (*0-7587-9315-4*) Book Wholesalers, Inc.

—Clifford Makes a Friend. 2002. (Clifford Bks.). (Illus.). (J). 11.91 (*0-7587-5017-X*) Book Wholesalers, Inc.

—Clifford Makes a Friend. 1998. (Clifford, the Big Red Dog Ser.). (Illus.). 32p. (J). (gr. k-2). mass mkt. 3.99 (*0-590-37930-5*) Scholastic, Inc.

—Clifford Makes a Friend. 1998. (Clifford, the Big Red Dog Ser.). (J). (gr. k-2). 10.14 (*0-606-15487-6*) Turtleback Bks.

—Take Me to School with You! 2002. (Clifford, the Big Red Dog Ser.). (Illus.). 16p. (J). mass mkt. 3.99 (*0-439-39454-6*) Scholastic, Inc.

Bridwell, Norman & Weyn, Suzanne. The Big Egg Hunt. 2002. (Clifford Big Red Readers Ser.). (Illus.). 32p. (J). (gr. k-2). mass mkt. 3.99 (*0-439-33246-X*) Scholastic, Inc.

Briggs-Bunting, Jane. Whoop for Joy: A Christmas Wish. 1995. (Barnyard Tales Ser.). (Illus.). 36p. (J). (gr. 1-5). 13.95 (*0-9649083-0-1*) Black River Trading Co.

Brimner, Larry Dane. Aggie & Will. (Rookie Readers Ser.). (Illus.). 32p. (J). (gr. 1-2). 1999. pap. 4.95 (*0-516-26409-5*); 1998. lib. bdg. 19.00 (*0-516-20754-7*) Scholastic Library Publishing. (Children's Pr.).

—Cory Coleman, Grade 2, ERS. 1990. (Redfeather Bks.). (Illus.). 80p. (J). (gr. 2-4). 12.95 o.s.i (*0-8050-1312-1*, Holt, Henry & Co. Bks. For Young Readers) Holt, Henry & Co.

—Here Comes Trouble. 2002. (Rookie Reader Level B Ser.). (Illus.). 32p. (J). (gr. 1-2). pap. 4.95 (*0-516-25968-7*, Children's Pr.) Scholastic Library Publishing.

—Here Comes Trouble Level B. 2001. (Rookie Readers Ser.). (Illus.). 32p. (J). (gr. 1-2). lib. bdg. 19.00 (*0-516-22220-1*, Children's Pr.) Scholastic Library Publishing.

—The New Kid. 2003. (Rookie Choices Ser.). (Illus.). pap. 5.95 (*0-516-27835-5*); 32p. (J). lib. bdg. 19.00 (*0-516-22546-4*) Scholastic Library Publishing. (Children's Pr.).

—The Promise. 2002. (Rookie Choices Ser.). (Illus.). 32p. (J). (gr. 1-2). lib. bdg. 19.00 (*0-516-22538-3*, Children's Pr.) Scholastic Library Publishing.

Brimner, Larry Dane & Tripp, Christine. The Promise. 2002. (Rookie Choices Ser.). (Illus.). 32p. (J). pap. 5.95 (*0-516-27388-4*, Children's Pr.) Scholastic Library Publishing.

Brinkerhoff, Shirley. Balancing Act. 1998. (Nikki Sheridan Ser.: Vol. 4). 208p. (J). (gr. 9-12). pap. 5.99 (*1-56179-559-3*) Bethany Hse. Pubs.

Briscoe, Jill. The Innkeeper's Daughter. 1984. (Illus.). (J). (gr. k-3). 11.93 o.p. (*0-516-09484-X*, Children's Pr.) Scholastic Library Publishing.

Brisley, Joyce Lakester. Milly-Molly-Mandy Storybook. 2001. (Milly-Molly-Mandy Ser.). (Illus.). 224p. (J). (gr. k-3). tchr. ed. 13.95 (*0-7534-5332-0*, Kingfisher) Houghton Mifflin Co. Trade & Reference Div.

—Milly-Molly-Mandy Storybook. 1998. (Milly-Molly-Mandy Ser.). (Illus.). 224p. (J). (gr. k-3). tchr. ed. 13.95 o.p. (*1-85697-493-6*) Larousse Kingfisher Chambers, Inc.

Brisson, Pat. Hot Fudge Hero, ERS. (J). (Illus.). o.p. (*0-8050-5328-X*); 1997. 80p. (gr. 1-4). 15.95 (*0-8050-4551-1*) Holt, Henry & Co. (Holt, Henry & Co. Bks. For Young Readers).

—Your Best Friend, Kate. 1989. (Illus.). 40p. (J). (gr. k-3). 15.00 o.p. (*0-02-714350-3*, Simon & Schuster Children's Publishing) Simon & Schuster Children's Publishing.

Broach, Elise. The Finding Place. 2004. (J). 16.95 (*0-8050-7387-6*, Holt, Henry & Co. Bks. For Young Readers) Holt, Henry & Co.

Brockmann, Carolee. Going for Great. 1999. (American Girls Collection Ser.). 128p. (J). (gr. 5-7). pap. 5.95 (*1-56247-752-8*); (Illus.). (gr. 4-6). 9.95 (*1-56247-847-8*) Pleasant Co. Pubns. (American Girl).

—Going for Great. 2000. (Illus.). (J). 12.00 (*0-606-18355-8*) Turtleback Bks.

Broger, Achim. The Day Chubby Became Charles. Cafiero, Renee V., tr. from GER. 1990. (Illus.). 96p. (J). (gr. 2-5). 12.95 (*0-397-32144-9*); lib. bdg. 12.89 (*0-397-32145-7*) HarperCollins Children's Bk. Group.

Brokaw, Nancy Steele. Leaving Emma. 1999. 144p. (J). (gr. 4-6). tchr. ed. 15.00 (*0-395-90699-7*, Clarion Bks.) Houghton Mifflin Co. Trade & Reference Div.

Bromberg, Brian. Meet Joe. 2002. (Blue's Clues Ser.). 12p. bds. 7.99 (*0-689-84839-0*, Simon Spotlight/Nickelodeon) Simon & Schuster Children's Publishing.

Bronin, Andrew. Gus & Buster Work Things Out. 1976. (Illus.). 64p. (J). (gr. k-4). pap. 0.95 o.s.i (*0-440-43318-5*, Yearling) Random Hse. Children's Bks.

Brooks, Bertha. Somewhere on the Rainbow. 2001. 32p. (J). (gr. 3-5). (*1-58374-032-5*) Chicago Spectrum Pr.

Brooks, Bruce. All That Remains. 2002. 176p. (YA). (gr. 7 up). pap. 6.99 (*0-689-83442-X*, Simon Pulse) Simon & Schuster Children's Publishing.

—Everywhere. 1990. 80p. (J). (gr. 4 up). 13.00 (*0-06-020728-0*); (Illus.). lib. bdg. 16.89 (*0-06-020729-9*) HarperCollins Children's Bk. Group.

—Midnight Hour Encores. 1986. 288p. (YA). (gr. 7 up). 14.00 (*0-06-020709-4*); lib. bdg. 14.89 o.p. (*0-06-020710-8*) HarperCollins Children's Bk. Group.

—The Moves Make the Man. (Trophy Bk.). (gr. 7 up). 1996. 288p. (J). pap. 5.99 (*0-06-440564-8*, Harper Trophy); 1987. 256p. (J). pap. 6.99 (*0-06-447022-9*, Harper Trophy); 1984. 320p. (YA). 15.00 o.s.i (*0-06-020679-9*) HarperCollins Children's Bk. Group.

—The Moves Make the Man. 3rd ed. (J). pap. text 3.95 (*0-13-800079-4*) Prentice Hall (Schl. Div.).

—The Moves Make the Man. 1987. 12.00 (*0-606-09638-8*) Turtleback Bks.

—No Kidding. 1991. (Trophy Keypoint Bks.). 224p. (YA). (gr. 7 up). mass mkt. 4.95 o.p. (*0-06-447051-2*, Harper Trophy) HarperCollins Children's Bk. Group.

—Zip. 1997. (Wolfbay Wings Ser.: No. 2). 128p. (J). (gr. 5 up). pap. 4.50 o.s.i (*0-06-440598-2*, Harper Trophy) HarperCollins Children's Bk. Group.

Brooks, Hindi. Computer Pals: A Short Comedy. 1998. (Illus.). 8p. pap. 3.50 (*0-88680-452-3*, C4523) Clark, I. E. Pubns.

Brooks, Kevin. Martyn Pig. 240p. (J). 2003. pap. 6.99 o.s.i (*0-439-50752-9*); 2002. (gr. 5 up). pap. 15.95 (*0-439-29595-5*, Chicken Hse., The) Scholastic, Inc.

Brooks, Martha. Being with Henry. 2000. (Melanie Kroupa Bks.). (Illus.). 224p. (J). (gr. 7-12). pap. 17.99 (*0-7894-2588-2*, D K Ink) Dorling Kindersley Publishing, Inc.

—Being with Henry. 1999. 192p. pap. (*0-88899-377-3*) Douglas & McIntyre, Ltd.

—Two Moons in August. 1990. (YA). (gr. 7-12). 14.95 (*0-88899-123-1*) Groundwood Bks. CAN. *Dist:* Publishers Group West.

—Two Moons in August. 1992. (YA). (gr. 7 up). 15.95 (*0-316-10979-7*) Little Brown & Co.

—Two Moons in August. 1993. 208p. (J). (gr. 7-9). pap. 3.25 o.p. (*0-590-45923-6*, Scholastic Paperbacks) Scholastic, Inc.

Brooks, Walter R. Freddy & the Popinjay. 2001. (Illus.). 244p. (J). (gr. 4-7). 23.95 (*1-58567-134-7*) Overlook Pr., The.

—The Wit & Wisdom of Freddy & His Friends. 2000. 256p. (J). (gr. 4-7). 23.95 (*0-87951-736-0*) Overlook Pr., The.

Broome, Errol. Dear Mr. Sprouts. (J). 1994. 132p. (gr. 3-7). pap. 3.99 o.s.i (*0-679-85394-4*, Random Hse. Bks. for Young Readers); 1993. 128p. (gr. 5-9). 15.00 o.s.i (*0-679-83714-0*, Knopf Bks. for Young Readers) Random Hse. Children's Bks.

—Missing Mem. 2003. (Illus.). 144p. (J). (gr. 1-5). pap. 4.99 (*0-7434-3797-7*, Aladdin) Simon & Schuster Children's Publishing.

Brouillet, Chrystine. Mon Amie Clementine. 2003. (Premier Roman Ser.). (FRE.). 64p. (J). (gr. 2-5). pap. 8.95 (*2-89021-313-7*) La Courte Echelle CAN. *Dist:* Firefly Bks., Ltd.

Brouillet, Chrystine & Gagnon, Nathalie. La Disparution de Baffuto. 2000. (Roman Jeunesse Ser.). 96p. (J). (gr. 4-7). pap. 8.95 (*2-89021-392-7*) La Courte Echelle CAN. *Dist:* Firefly Bks., Ltd.

Brouwer, Sigmund. The Disappearing Jewel of Madagascar. 2002. (Accidental Detectives). 144p. (J). pap. 5.99 (*0-7642-2565-0*) Bethany Hse. Pubs.

—The Disappearing Jewel of Madagascar. 1994. (Accidental Detective Ser.: Vol. 4). 132p. (J). (gr. 3-7). pap. 4.99 (*1-56476-373-0*, 6-3373) Cook Communications Ministries.

—The Disappearing Jewel of Madagascar. 1990. (Accidental Detective Ser.). 132p. (J). (gr. 3-7). pap. text 4.99 o.p. (*0-89693-014-9*) Scripture Pr. Pubs., Inc.

—Dr. Drabble's Remarkable Underwater Breathing Pills. rev. ed. 1994. (Doctor Drabble Ser.: Bk. 1). (Illus.). 32p. (J). (gr. 1-5). pap. text 3.99 o.p. (*0-8499-3659-4*) W Publishing Group.

—The Volcano of Doom. 2002. (Accidental Detectives). 144p. (J). pap. 5.99 (*0-7642-2564-2*) Bethany Hse. Pubs.

Brower, Jamie L. Do unto Others. 1992. (J). (gr. 4 up). 6.95 o.p. (*0-533-09665-0*) Vantage Pr., Inc.

Brown, Ann. The Portal & the Key. 2001. 128p. (gr. 4-7). pap. 9.95 (*0-595-15850-1*, Writer's Showcase Pr.) iUniverse, Inc.

Brown, Betsy. Rollo & the Wishee. 1995. 16p. (J). (gr. 1-3). (*1-888479-00-0*) Tarpley Publishing.

Brown, Irene Bennett. Skitterbrain. l.t. ed. 2002. 158p. (J). 21.95 (*0-7862-4646-4*) Thorndike Pr.

Brown, Kenneth. Mucky Pup. 1997. (Illus.). 32p. (J). (ps-4). 14.99 o.p. (*0-525-45886-7*) Penguin Putnam Bks. for Young Readers.

Brown, Laurene Krasny. Rex & Lilly Family Time. 1997. (Rex & Lilly Ser.). (Illus.). 32p. (J). (ps-1). 10.10 (*0-606-11793-8*) Turtleback Bks.

—Rex & Lilly Playtime. 1997. (Rex & Lilly Ser.). (Illus.). 32p. (J). (ps-1). 10.10 (*0-606-11794-6*) Turtleback Bks.

Brown, Marc. Arthur & His Best Friend. 2004. (Illus.). (J). mass mkt. 3.99 (*0-316-73387-3*) Little Brown Children's Bks.

—Arthur & the Double Dare. 2002. (Arthur Chapter Book Ser.: No. 25). (Illus.). 64p. (J). (gr. 2-4). pap. 4.25 (*0-316-12087-1*); (gr. 3-6). 13.95 (*0-316-12264-5*) Little Brown Children's Bks.

—Arthur & the Perfect Brother. 2000. (Arthur Chapter Book Ser.: No. 21). (Illus.). 64p. (J). (gr. 3-6). 13.95 (*0-316-12163-0*); pap. 3.95 (*0-316-12226-2*) Little Brown Children's Bks.

—Arthur & the Perfect Brother. 2000. (Arthur Chapter Book Ser.: No. 21). (Illus.). (J). (gr. 3-6). 10.10 (*0-606-18252-7*) Turtleback Bks.

—Arthur & the True Francine. 1981. (Arthur Adventure Ser.). (Illus.). 32p. (J). (gr. k-3). 15.95 o.p. (*0-316-11212-7*) Little Brown Children's Bks.

—Arthur Rocks with Binky. 1998. (Arthur Chapter Book Ser.: No. 11). (Illus.). 64p. (J). (gr. 3-6). 12.95 (*0-316-11542-8*); pap. 4.25 (*0-316-11543-6*) Little Brown Children's Bks.

—Arthur's Friendship Treasury, 3 bks. in 1. 2002. (Arthur Adventure Ser.). (Illus.). 112p. (J). (gr. k-3). 18.95 (*0-316-12588-1*) Little Brown Children's Bks.

—The Cloud Over Clarence. 1979. (Illus.). (J). (ps-3). 8.95 o.p. (*0-525-28013-8*, Dutton) Dutton/Plume.

—El Cumpleanos de Arturo. Sarfatti, Esther, tr. from ENG. 2000. (Arthur Adventure Ser.). (SPA., Illus.). (J). (ps-3). pap. 6.95 (*1-880507-78-1*, LC7609) Lectorum Pubns., Inc.

—Francine, Believe It or Not. unabr. ed. 2001. (Arthur Chapter Bks.: Vol. 14). 58p. (J). (gr. 1-3). pap. 17.00 incl. audio (*0-8072-0345-9*, Listening Library) Random Hse. Audio Publishing Group.

—Francine, Believe It or Not. 1999. (Arthur Chapter Book Ser.: No. 14). (J). (gr. 3-6). 10.10 (*0-606-17021-9*) Turtleback Bks.

Brown, Marc, illus. Arthur & the Double Dare. 2002. (Arthur Chapter Bks.). (J). 11.70 (*0-7587-9423-1*) Book Wholesalers, Inc.

Brown, Marc & Delton, Judy. Rabbit's New Rug. 1993. (Parents Magazine Read Aloud Original Ser.). (Illus.). (J). lib. bdg. 17.27 o.p. (*0-8368-0972-6*) Stevens, Gareth Inc.

Brown, Marc, et al. Arthur & the True Francine. 1996. (Arthur Adventure Ser.). (Illus.). 32p. (J). (gr. k-3). reprint ed. 15.95 (*0-316-11136-8*) Little Brown Children's Bks.

—Arthur's Birthday. 1989. (Arthur Adventure Ser.). (Illus.). 32p. (J). (gr. k-3). 15.95 (*0-316-11073-6*) Little Brown Children's Bks.

Brown, Mick, et al. Bantam. Gelsthorpe, Loraine & Rex, Sue, eds. 2002. 144p. (J). pap. 14.95 (*1-86368-373-9*) Fremantle Arts Centre Pr. AUS. *Dist:* International Specialized Bk. Services.

Brown, Palmer. Hickory. 1978. (Illus.). 48p. (J). (ps-3). lib. bdg. o.p. (*0-06-020887-2*); lib. bdg. 11.89 o.p. (*0-06-020888-0*) HarperCollins Children's Bk. Group.

Brown, Terry. Portrait of Lies. 2003. (Today's Girls Only Ser.: Bk. 2). 144p. (J). pap. 5.99 (*1-4003-0322-2*) Nelson, Tommy.

—Stranger Online. 2003. (Today's Girls Only Ser.: Bk. 1). 128p. (J). pap. 5.99 (*1-4003-0321-4*) Nelson, Tommy.

Browne, Anthony. Willy & Hugh. 2003. (Illus.). (J). bds. 5.99 (*0-7636-1977-9*) Candlewick Pr.

—Willy & Hugh. 1991. (Illus.). 32p. (J). (ps-3). 13.99 o.s.i (*0-679-91446-3*); 13.00 o.s.i (*0-679-81446-9*) Random Hse. Children's Bks. (Knopf Bks. for Young Readers).

—Willy & Hugh. 1996. (Illus.). 32p. (J). (gr. k-4). pap. 6.99 o.s.i (*0-679-87654-5*) Random Hse., Inc.

—Willy & Hugh. 1996. (J). 12.19 o.p. (*0-606-10073-3*) Turtleback Bks.

Brownrigg, Sheri. All Tutus Should Be Pink. 1992. (Hello Reader! Ser.). (Illus.). 32p. (J). (ps-3). mass mkt. 3.99 (*0-590-43904-9*, Cartwheel Bks.) Scholastic, Inc.

—All Tutus Should Be Pink. 1992. (Hello Reader! Ser.). (J). 10.14 (*0-606-01776-3*) Turtleback Bks.

—Best Friends Wear Pink Tutus. 1993. (Hello Reader! Ser.). (Illus.). 32p. (J). (ps-3). mass mkt. 3.99 (*0-590-46437-X*) Scholastic, Inc.

Bruce, Lisa. Fran's Friend. 2003. (Illus.). 32p. (J). (ps-1). 15.95 (*1-58234-777-8*, Bloomsbury Children) Bloomsbury Publishing.

Bruce, Robert D. Petey Putt-Putt & His Friends. Bruce, Britta, ed. 1999. (Illus.). 20p. 5.95 (*0-9664248-9-1*) Sloane Pubns.

Bruce, Sheilah. Everybody Wins! 2001. (Math Matters Ser.). (Illus.). 32p. (J). (gr. 1-3). pap. 4.95 (*1-57565-101-7*) Kane Pr., The.

Brugman, Alyssa. Walking Naked. 2004. (YA). 224p. lib. bdg. 17.99 (*0-385-90141-0*); 192p. (gr. 7). 15.95 (*0-385-73115-9*) Dell Publishing. (Delacorte Pr.).

Bruhn, John G. Angles to Grow By. 1981. (Illus.). 107p. pap. 6.00 (*0-9616570-1-4*) Bruhn, John G.

Bruna, Dick. Miffy & Melanie Storybook. 2000. (Miffy Ser.). (Illus.). 28p. (J). (ps-k). 4.95 (*1-56836-305-2*) Kodansha America, Inc.

Brutschy, Jennifer. Celeste & Crabapple Sam. 1994. (Illus.). 32p. (J). (gr. k-3). 14.99 o.p. (*0-525-67416-0*, Dutton Children's Bks.) Penguin Putnam Bks. for Young Readers.

Bruyninckx, John & Swanson, Susanne M. My Friend Emily: Library Set. (Enrichment Collection: No. 1). (Illus.). (Orig.). (J). (gr. k-5). pap. 29.95 o.p. (*1-885101-56-2*) Writers Pr., Inc.

Bruzzone, Catherine. A Friendship in French & English. 1998. (Pen Pals Ser.). (Illus.). 28p. (J). (gr. 4-7). 14.95 (*0-8442-1375-6*, 13756, Passport Bks.) McGraw-Hill Trade.

—A Spanish & English Friendship. 1998. (Pen Pals Ser.). (Illus.). 28p. (J). (gr. 4-7). 14.95 (*0-8442-7501-8*, 75018) McGraw-Hill/Contemporary.

Bryant, Bonnie. Best Friends. 2001. (Illus.). 160p. (gr. 4-7). pap. text 4.50 o.s.i (*0-553-48743-4*, Skylark) Random Hse. Children's Bks.

—Changing Leads. 1999. (Pine Hollow Ser.: No. 4). 240p. (gr. 7 up). mass mkt. 4.50 o.s.i (*0-553-49245-4*, Dell Books for Young Readers) Random Hse. Children's Bks.

—Conformation Faults. 1999. (Pine Hollow Ser.: No. 5). 272p. (gr. 7 up). mass mkt. 4.50 o.s.i (*0-553-49246-2*, Dell Books for Young Readers) Random Hse. Children's Bks.

—Conformation Faults. 1999. (Pine Hollow Ser.: No. 5). (YA). (gr. 7 up). 10.55 (*0-606-18958-0*) Turtleback Bks.

—Corey's Secret Friend. 1997. (Pony Tails Ser.: No. 12). (Illus.). 112p. (gr. 3-5). pap. text 3.99 o.s.i (*0-553-48482-6*, Skylark) Random Hse. Children's Bks.

—Course of Action. 1999. (Pine Hollow Ser.: No. 8). 224p. (gr. 7 up). mass mkt. 4.50 o.s.i (*0-553-49286-1*) Bantam Bks.

—Course of Action. 1999. (Pine Hollow Ser.: No. 8). (YA). (gr. 7 up). 10.55 (*0-606-18959-9*) Turtleback Bks.

—Dude Ranch. l.t. ed. 1995. (Saddle Club Ser.). 144p. (J). (gr. 4-6). lib. bdg. 19.93 o.p. (*0-8368-1285-9*) Stevens, Gareth Inc.

—Dude Ranch. 1989. (Saddle Club Ser.: No. 6). (J). (gr. 4-6). 9.09 o.p. (*0-606-08120-8*) Turtleback Bks.

—Hoof Beat. l.t. ed. 1996. (Saddle Club Ser.: No. 9). 144p. (J). (gr. 4-6). lib. bdg. 19.93 o.p. (*0-8368-1531-9*) Stevens, Gareth Inc.

—Hoof Beat. 1990. (Saddle Club Ser.: No. 9). (J). (gr. 4-6). 9.09 o.p. (*0-606-08123-2*) Turtleback Bks.

—Horse Crazy. l.t. ed. 1995. (Saddle Club Ser.: No. 1). 144p. (J). (gr. 4-6). lib. bdg. 19.93 o.p. (*0-8368-1280-8*) Stevens, Gareth Inc.

—Horse Play. 1989. (Saddle Club Ser.: No. 7). 144p. (J). (gr. 4-6). pap. 3.99 o.s.i (*0-553-15754-X*) Bantam Bks.

—Horse Play. l.t. ed. 1996. (Saddle Club Ser.: No. 7). 144p. (J). (gr. 4-6). lib. bdg. 21.27 o.p. (*0-8368-1529-7*) Stevens, Gareth Inc.

—Horse Play. 1989. (Saddle Club Ser.: No. 7). (J). (gr. 4-6). 9.09 o.p. (*0-606-08121-6*) Turtleback Bks.

—Horse Power. l.t. ed. 1995. (Saddle Club Ser.: No. 4). 144p. (J). (gr. 4-6). lib. bdg. 15.93 o.p. (*0-8368-1283-2*) Stevens, Gareth Inc.

—Horse Power. 1989. (Saddle Club Ser.: No. 4). (J). (gr. 4-6). 9.09 o.p. (*0-606-08112-7*) Turtleback Bks.

—Horse Sense. l.t. ed. 1995. (Saddle Club Ser.: No. 3). 144p. (J). (gr. 4-6). lib. bdg. 15.93 o.p. (*0-8368-1282-4*) Stevens, Gareth Inc.

—Horse Sense. 1989. (Saddle Club Ser.: No. 3). (J). (gr. 4-6). 9.09 o.p. (*0-606-08101-1*) Turtleback Bks.

—Horse Show. 1989. (Saddle Club Ser.: No. 8). 144p. (gr. 4-6). pap. text 3.99 o.s.i (*0-553-15769-8*) Bantam Bks.

—Horse Show. l.t. ed. 1996. (Saddle Club Ser.: No. 8). 144p. (J). (gr. 4-6). lib. bdg. 21.27 o.p. (*0-8368-1530-0*) Stevens, Gareth Inc.

—Horse Show. 1989. (Saddle Club Ser.: No. 8). (J). (gr. 4-6). 9.09 o.p. (*0-606-08122-4*) Turtleback Bks.

—Horse Shy. l.t. ed. 1995. (Saddle Club Ser.: No. 2). 144p. (J). (gr. 4-6). lib. bdg. 15.93 o.p. (*0-8368-1281-6*) Stevens, Gareth Inc.

—Horse Shy. 1996. (Saddle Club Ser.: No. 2). (J). (gr. 4-6). 9.09 o.p. (*0-606-08091-0*) Turtleback Bks.

—Horse Wise. 1990. (Saddle Club Ser.: No. 11). 144p. (J). (gr. 4-6). pap. 3.99 o.p. (*0-553-15805-8*) Bantam Bks.

—Horse Wise. l.t. ed. 1996. (Saddle Club Ser.: No. 11). 144p. (J). (gr. 4-6). lib. bdg. 21.27 o.p. (*0-8368-1533-5*) Stevens, Gareth Inc.

—Horse Wise. 1990. (Saddle Club Ser.: No. 11). (J). (gr. 4-6). 9.09 o.p. (*0-606-03650-4*) Turtleback Bks.

—New Rider. 2001. (Saddle Club Ser.: No. 96). 176p. (gr. 4-7). pap. text 4.50 o.s.i (*0-553-48700-0*, Skylark) Random Hse. Children's Bks.

—Penalty Points. 1999. (Pine Hollow Ser.: No. 7). 224p. (gr. 7 up). mass mkt. 4.50 o.s.i (*0-553-49285-3*) Bantam Bks.

—Penalty Points. 1999. (Pine Hollow Ser.: No. 7). (YA). (gr. 7 up). 10.55 (*0-606-18964-5*) Turtleback Bks.

—Riding to Win. 1999. (Pine Hollow Ser.: No. 9). 272p. (gr. 7 up). mass mkt. 4.50 o.s.i (*0-553-49287-X*) Bantam Bks.

—Riding to Win. 1999. (Pine Hollow Ser.: No. 9). (YA). (gr. 7 up). 10.55 (*0-606-19287-5*) Turtleback Bks.

—Shying at Trouble. 1999. (Pine Hollow Ser.: No. 6). 224p. (gr. 7 up). mass mkt. 4.50 o.s.i (*0-553-49247-0*) Bantam Bks.

—Shying at Trouble. 1999. (Pine Hollow Ser.: No. 6). (YA). (gr. 7 up). 10.55 (*0-606-18967-X*) Turtleback Bks.

—Stevie: The Inside Story. 1999. (Illus.). 304p. (gr. 4-6). pap. text 4.50 o.s.i (*0-553-48674-8*, Dell Books for Young Readers) Random Hse. Children's Bks.

—Stevie: The Inside Story. 1999. 10.55 (*0-606-17154-1*) Turtleback Bks.

—The Trail Home. 1998. (Pine Hollow Ser.: No. 2). 176p. (gr. 7 up). mass mkt. 4.50 o.s.i (*0-553-49243-8*) Bantam Bks.

—Trail Mates. l.t. ed. 1995. (Saddle Club Ser.: No. 5). 144p. (J). (gr. 4-6). lib. bdg. 15.93 o.p. (*0-8368-1284-0*) Stevens, Gareth Inc.

—Trail Mates. 1989. (Saddle Club Ser.: No. 5). (J). (gr. 4-6). 9.09 o.p. (*0-606-04563-5*) Turtleback Bks.

—The Yankee Swap. 1995. (Saddle Club Ser.: No. 50). 144p. (J). (gr. 4-6). pap. 3.99 o.s.i (*0-553-48268-8*, Skylark) Random Hse. Children's Bks.

Bryant, Bonnie & Hiller, B. B. Horse Sense. 1989. (Saddle Club Ser.: No. 3). 144p. (gr. 4-6). pap. text 3.99 o.s.i (*0-553-15626-8*, Skylark) Random Hse. Children's Bks.

Bryant, Megan E. Strawberry Shortcake at the Beach. 2003. (Strawberry Shortcake Ser.). (Illus.). 32p. (J). pap. 3.49 (*0-448-43187-4*, Grosset & Dunlap) Penguin Putnam Bks. for Young Readers.

Bryant-Mole, Karen. Rojo. 1996. (Imagenes Ser.).Tr. of Red. (J). 10.15 o.p. (*0-606-10498-4*) Turtleback Bks.

Buchan, Stuart. When We Lived with Pete. 1986. (J). (gr. 4-7). pap. 2.95 o.s.i (*0-440-49483-4*, Yearling) Random Hse. Children's Bks.

Buchanan, Jane. Goodbye Charlie, RS. 2004. (J). (*0-374-35020-5*, Farrar, Straus & Giroux (BYR)) Farrar, Straus & Giroux.

Buchanan, Paul & Randall, Rod. A House Divided. 2001. (Misadventures of Willie Plummett Ser.: Vol. 20). (Illus.). 124p. (J). (gr. 3-7). pap. 5.99 (*0-570-07131-3*) Concordia Publishing Hse.

Buchanan, Paul & Randall, Rod, contrib. by. Friend or Foe. 2000. (Misadventures of Willie Plummett Ser.: Vol. 16). 124p. (J). (gr. 3-7). pap. 5.99 (*0-570-07005-8*) Concordia Publishing Hse.

Buchwald, Emilie. Floramel & Esteban. 1982. (Illus.). 72p. (J). 9.95 o.p. (*0-15-228678-0*) Harcourt Children's Bks.

Buck, Nola. Sid & Sam. 1997. (My First I Can Read Bks.). (Illus.). 32p. (J). (ps up). reprint ed. pap. 3.99 (*0-06-444211-X*, Harper Trophy) HarperCollins Children's Bk. Group.

—Sid & Sam. 1997. (My First I Can Read Bks.). (J). (ps-k). 10.10 (*0-606-11841-1*) Turtleback Bks.

Buckman, Carole Duncan. Neighbors & Traitors. 2000. (StarMaker Bks.). 81p. (J). (gr. 6-9). pap. 5.50 (*0-88489-548-3*) St. Mary's Pr.

Budbill, David. Bones on Black Spruce Mountain. 1986. 128p. (J). pap. 2.75 o.s.i (*0-553-15596-2*) Bantam Bks.

—Bones on Black Spruce Mountain. 1994. 128p. (YA). (gr. 5 up). pap. 3.99 o.s.i (*0-14-036854-X*, Puffin Bks.); 1978. 7.89 o.p. (*0-8037-0699-5*, Dial Bks. for Young Readers); 1978. (J). 7.95 o.p. (*0-8037-0691-X*, Dial Bks. for Young Readers) Penguin Putnam Bks. for Young Readers.

—Bones on Black Spruce Mountain. 1994. (J). 9.09 o.p. (*0-606-05762-5*) Turtleback Bks.

Bulla, Clyde Robert. Last Look. 1979. (Illus.). 96p. (J). (gr. 3-5). lib. bdg. 12.89 o.p. (*0-690-03966-2*) HarperCollins Children's Bk. Group.

—Last Look. 1995. 80p. (J). pap. 3.99 o.s.i (*0-14-036733-0*, Puffin Bks.) Penguin Putnam Bks. for Young Readers.

Bullard, Lisa. My Day: Morning, Noon & Night. 2002. (All about Me Ser.). (Illus.). 24p. (J). (ps-1). lib. bdg. 19.90 (*1-4048-0045-X*) Picture Window Bks.

Bunnett, Rochelle. Amigos en la Escuela. 1997. Tr. of Friends at School. (SPA., Illus.). 32p. (J). (ps-3). 12.95 (*1-887734-15-5*) Star Bright Bks., Inc.

—Friends in the Park. 1993. (Illus.). 32p. (J). 7.95 (*1-56288-347-X*) Checkerboard Pr., Inc.

—Friends Together: More Alike Than Different. 1993. (Illus.). 12p. (J). (gr. k-4). tchr. ed. 24.95 (*1-56288-429-8*) Checkerboard Pr., Inc.

Bunting, Eve. The Big Find. 1979. (Challenge Bks.). (Illus.). (J). (gr. 4-8). lib. bdg. 7.95 o.p. (*0-87191-681-9*, Creative Education) Creative Co., The.

—The Blue & the Gray. (Illus.). 32p. (gr. k-2). 2001. pap. 5.99 (*0-590-60200-4*); 1996. (J). pap. 14.95 (*0-590-60197-0*) Scholastic, Inc.

—Clancy's Coat. (J). 1985. 12.95 o.p. (*0-670-80698-6*, Viking Children's Bks.); 1984. (Illus.). 48p. (gr. 1-5). 11.95 o.p. (*0-7232-6252-7*, Warne, Frederick) Penguin Putnam Bks. for Young Readers.

—The Empty Window. 1980. (Illus.). 48p. (J). (gr. 4-9). 7.95 o.p. (*0-7232-6186-5*, Warne, Frederick) Penguin Putnam Bks. for Young Readers.

—For Always. 1993. (Eve Bunting Collection Ser.). (Illus.). 48p. (J). (gr. 2-6). lib. bdg. 12.79 o.p. (*0-89565-969-7*) Child's World, Inc.

—For Always. 1984. (FastBack Romance Ser.). 11.27 o.p. (*0-606-00275-8*) Turtleback Bks.

—I Like the Way You Are. 2000. (Illus.). 48p. (J). (ps-3). tchr. ed. 15.00 (*0-395-89066-7*, Clarion Bks.) Houghton Mifflin Co. Trade & Reference Div.

—If I Asked You, Would You Stay? (Lippincott Page-Turner Ser.). 160p. (YA). (gr. 7 up). 1987. mass mkt. 3.95 o.s.i (*0-06-447023-7*, Harper Trophy); 1984. lib. bdg. 12.89 (*0-397-32066-3*) HarperCollins Children's Bk. Group.

—Maggie the Freak. 1992. (Eve Bunting Collection Ser.). (Illus.). 48p. (J). (gr. 2-6). lib. bdg. 12.79 o.p. (*0-89565-775-9*) Child's World, Inc.

—Maggie the Freak. 1984. (FastBack Romance Ser.). 11.27 o.p. (*0-606-00339-8*) Turtleback Bks.

—Nobody Knows but Me. 1993. (Eve Bunting Collection Ser.). (Illus.). 48p. (J). (gr. 2-6). lib. bdg. 12.79 o.p. (*0-89565-971-9*) Child's World, Inc.

—On Call Back Mountain. 1997. (Illus.). 32p. (J). pap. 15.95 (*0-590-25929-6*) Scholastic, Inc.

—Our Sixth-Grade Sugar Babies. 1992. (Trophy Bk.). (Illus.). 160p. (J). (gr. 4-6). pap. 5.99 (*0-06-440390-4*, Harper Trophy) HarperCollins Children's Bk. Group.

—Our Sixth-Grade Sugar Babies. 1992. (J). 11.00 (*0-606-06150-9*) Turtleback Bks.

—Snowboarding on Monster Mountain. 2003. (J). 15.95 (*0-8126-2704-0*) Cricket Bks.

—Such Nice Kids. 1990. 160p. (J). (gr. 4-9). 13.95 o.p. (*0-395-54998-1*, Clarion Bks.) Houghton Mifflin Co. Trade & Reference Div.

—Summer Wheels. (Illus.). 48p. (J). 1996. (ACE.). (gr. 4-7). pap. 7.00 (*0-15-200988-4*, Harcourt Paperbacks); 1992. (ps-3). 14.95 (*0-15-207000-1*) Harcourt Children's Bks.

—Summer Wheels. 1996. 12.15 (*0-606-09912-3*) Turtleback Bks.

Burch, Robert. Wilkin's Ghost. 1978. (Illus.). (J). (gr. 5-9). 9.95 o.p. (*0-670-76897-9*) Viking Penguin.

Burgess, Melvin. The Copper Treasure. 2002. (Illus.). 112p. (J). (gr. 4-7). pap. 4.95 (*0-380-73325-0*, Harper Trophy) HarperCollins Children's Bk. Group.

—The Copper Treasure, ERS. 2000. (Illus.). 104p. (J). (gr. 4-7). 15.95 (*0-8050-6381-1*, Holt, Henry & Co. Bks. For Young Readers) Holt, Henry & Co.

Burgess, Thornton W. The Adventures of Prickly Porky. unabr. ed. 1998. (Children's Thrift Classics Ser.). (Illus.). 80p. (J). (gr. 1). reprint ed. pap. 1.00 (*0-486-29170-7*) Dover Pubns., Inc.

Burke, Terrill M. I Love Gee Gees, Bk. 2. 1996. (Illus.). 96p. (J). (gr. 1-4). pap. 7.95 (*1-880485-53-2*) Alpha-Dolphin Pr.

Burke, Timothy. Cocoa Puppy. 1989. (Illus.). 32p. (Orig.). (J). (ps-3). 5.00 (*0-9623227-0-9*) Thunder & Ink.

Burke-Weiner, Kimberly. Penny Wishes. 1996. (Illus.). 32p. (J). (gr. 3-6). 15.95 (*0-9634637-3-X*); pap. 8.95 (*0-9634637-4-8*) Inquiring Voices Pr.

Burningham, John. Aldo. 1992. (Illus.). 32p. (J). (ps-2). 15.99 o.s.i (*0-517-58699-1*, Random Hse. Bks. for Young Readers) Random Hse. Children's Bks.

—Friend. 1966. (J). 3.95 (*0-690-01273-X*) HarperCollins Children's Bk. Group.

—The Friend. (Illus.). 24p. (J). (ps). 1996. reprint ed. bds. 2.99 o.p. (*1-56402-931-X*); 2nd ed. 1994. 6.95 o.p. (*1-56402-327-3*) Candlewick Pr.

Burris, Barbara. Callie & Zora. 1997. (Illus.). 136p. (Orig.). (YA). (gr. 3 up). lib. bdg. 13.95 o.p. (*0-9654197-0-3*) PennyRoyal Bks.

Burt, Denise. Meet My Friends. 1985. (Growing Up Bks.). (J). (Illus.). 32p. (gr. 2-3). lib. bdg. 10.95 o.p. (*0-918831-20-2*); 7.95 o.p. (*0-918831-43-1*) Stevens, Gareth Inc.

Burton, Margie, et al. Friends. Adams, Alison, ed. 1999. (Early Connections Ser.). 16p. (J). (gr. k-2). pap. 4.50 (*1-58344-062-3*) Benchmark Education Co.

Burton, Virginia L. La Casita. (SPA., Illus.). (J). (gr. 1-2). pap. 9.95 (*970-629-050-8*, SI6411) Sistemas Tecnicos de Edicion, S.A. de C.V. MEX. *Dist:* AIMS International Bks., Inc., Lectorum Pubns., Inc.

—La Casita. 1988. 17.10 (*0-606-10434-8*) Turtleback Bks.

—Mike Mulligan y Su Maquina Maravillosa. 1997. (SPA.). 12.10 (*0-606-12768-2*) Turtleback Bks.

Bush, Max. Thirteen Bells of Boglewood. 1987. (J). (gr. k-3). pap. 6.00 (*0-87602-272-7*) Anchorage Pr.

Butcher, Kristin. Cairo Kelly & the Mann. 2002. 176p. (J). (gr. 4-7). pap. 6.95 (*1-55143-211-0*) Orca Bk. Pubs.

Butcher, Samuel J. A Friend Is. 1992. (Precious Moments Ser.). (Illus.). 12p. (J). (ps). bds. 2.49 o.s.i (*0-307-06119-1*, 6119, Golden Bks.) Random Hse. Children's Bks.

Butler, Dori Hillestad. Trading Places with Tank Talbott. 2003. 136p. (J). lib. bdg. 14.95 (*0-8075-1708-9*) Whitman, Albert & Co.

Butler, Stephen. The Mouse & the Apple. 2000. (Illus.). 32p. (J). (ps-k). pap. 7.99 (*0-7112-0856-5*) Lincoln, Frances Ltd. GBR. *Dist:* Antique Collectors' Club.

—The Mouse & the Apple. 1994. (Illus.). 32p. (J). (ps up). 15.00 o.p. (*0-688-12810-6*); lib. bdg. 14.93 o.p. (*0-688-12811-4*) Morrow/Avon. (Morrow, William & Co.).

Buttenwieser, Paul. Their Pride & Joy. 1988. (J). (gr. 6 up). pap. 8.95 o.s.i (*0-440-50073-7*, Laurel) Dell Publishing.

Butterworth, Nick. Just Like Jasper. 1989. (Illus.). (J). (ps). 13.95 o.s.i (*0-316-11917-2*) Little Brown & Co.

—Making Faces. 1993. (Illus.). 32p. (J). (ps). 12.95 o.p. (*1-56402-212-9*) Candlewick Pr.

Butterworth, Nick & Inkpen, Mick. Nice or Nasty. 1987. (Illus.). (J). (ps-3). pap. 12.95 o.s.i (*0-316-11915-6*) Little Brown & Co.

Butterworth, W. E., pseud. Leroy & the Old Man. 1982. pap. 1.95 o.p. (*0-590-32635-X*) Scholastic, Inc.

—Leroy & the Old Man. 1980. (Point Ser.). (J). 10.55 (*0-606-01139-0*) Turtleback Bks.

Byalick, Marcia. Quit It. 2004. 176p. (gr. 3-7). pap. text 5.50 (*0-440-41865-8*, Yearling) Random Hse. Children's Bks.

—Quit It. 2002. 176p. (gr. 3-7). lib. bdg. 17.99 (*0-385-90061-9*); (gr. 4-8). text 15.95 (*0-385-72997-9*) Random Hse., Inc.

Byars, Betsy C. Beans on the Roof. 1988. 80p. (J). 14.95 o.s.i (*0-385-29855-2*); (Illus.). 13.95 o.s.i (*0-440-50055-9*) Dell Publishing. (Delacorte Pr.).

—Beans on the Roof. 1990. 80p. (gr. 4-7). pap. text 3.99 (*0-440-40314-6*, Yearling) Random Hse. Children's Bks.

—Beans on the Roof. 1990. (J). 10.14 (*0-606-03054-9*) Turtleback Bks.

—Bolas Locas. 1985. (SPA., Illus.). 14.55 (*0-606-10382-1*) Turtleback Bks.

—Coast to Coast. 1994. 176p. (gr. 4-7). pap. text 3.99 o.s.i (*0-440-40926-8*) Dell Publishing.

—The Cybil War. l.t. ed. 1991. (Lythway Ser.). 136p. (J). 14.95 o.p. (*0-7451-1403-2*, Galaxy Children's Large Print) BBC Audiobooks America.

—The Cybil War. (Illus.). 1990. 128p. (J). (gr. 3-7). pap. 4.99 (*0-14-034356-3*, Puffin Bks.); 1981. 14p. (YA). (gr. 8-12). 13.99 o.s.i (*0-670-25248-4*, Viking Children's Bks.) Penguin Putnam Bks. for Young Readers.

—The Cybil War. (J). 1988. pap. 2.75 o.p. (*0-590-42609-5*); 1982. pap. 1.95 o.p. (*0-590-32500-0*); 1982. pap. 2.25 o.p. (*0-590-33750-5*); 1987. pap. 2.50 o.p. (*0-590-40466-0*) Scholastic, Inc.

—The Cybil War. 1981. (J). 11.04 (*0-606-03178-2*) Turtleback Bks.

—The Joy Boys. 1996. (J). pap. 4.99 (*0-440-91102-8*, Dell Books for Young Readers) Random Hse. Children's Bks.

—The Joy Boys. 1996. 9.19 o.p. (*0-606-09496-2*) Turtleback Bks.

—The Pinballs. l.t. ed. 1988. 185p. (J). (gr. 3-8). reprint ed. 15.95 o.p. incl. audio (*1-55736-028-6*); 29.95 o.p. incl. audio (*1-55736-090-1*); 15.95 o.p. incl. audio (*1-55736-028-6*) Bantam Doubleday Dell Large Print Group, Inc.

—The Pinballs. (Trophy Bk.). (gr. 5 up). 1996. 80p. (YA). pap. 2.25 o.p. (*0-06-447150-0*); 1992. 144p. (J). pap. 5.99 (*0-06-440198-7*) HarperCollins Children's Bk. Group. (Harper Trophy).

—The Pinballs. (J). (gr. 4-6). 137p. pap. 4.95 (*0-8072-1356-X*); 137p. pap. 4.95 (*0-8072-1383-7*); 1999. pap. 15.98 incl. audio (*0-8072-1800-6*, JJRH100SP); 1989. 137p. pap. 28.00 incl. audio (*0-8072-8536-6*, LB2SP) Random Hse. Audio Publishing Group. (Listening Library).

—The Pinballs. 1982. (J). pap. 2.25 o.p. (*0-590-33785-8*); pap. 1.95 o.p. (*0-590-32427-6*) Scholastic, Inc.

—The Pinballs. 1987. (J). 11.00 (*0-606-03346-7*) Turtleback Bks.

—Wanted... Mud Blossom. 1993. (Illus.). 160p. (gr. 4-7). pap. text 4.99 (*0-440-40761-3*) Dell Publishing.

Byers, Carla Rae. Lucky Little Duck Lessons! The Adventures of Snowflake & Astar. l.t. ed. 2000. Vol. 8. 18p. (gr. 1 up). 7.95 (*1-930910-05-3*) Heyokah Publishing Co.

Byers, Carolyn. Forever Friends, 5 vols. 1994. (J). 49.95 o.p. (*0-00-504733-1*) Review & Herald Publishing Assn.

Byng, Georgia. Molly Moon's Incredible Book of Hypnotism. 2004. (Illus.). 400p. (J). pap. 6.99 (*0-06-051409-4*, Harper Trophy) HarperCollins Children's Bk. Group.

—Molly Moon's Incredible Book of Hypnotism. 2003. (Illus.). 384p. (J). (gr. 3-7). 16.99 (*0-06-051406-X*); (Illus.). 384p. (J). (gr. 3-7). lib. bdg. 17.89 (*0-06-051407-8*); 135.92 (*0-06-057217-5*) HarperCollins Pubs.

—Molly Moon's Incredible Book of Hypnotism. 2002. 330p. (J). (gr. 3-7). 24.95 (*0-333-98489-7*) Macmillan Children's Bks. GBR. *Dist:* Trans-Atlantic Pubns., Inc.

Bynum, Janie. Otis. (Illus.). (J). 2003. 40p. pap. 6.00 (*0-15-204604-6*, Voyager Bks./Libros Viajeros); 2000. 36p. 14.00 (*0-15-202153-1*) Harcourt Children's Bks.

Byrd, Lee Merrill. Treasure on Gold Street/El Tesoro de la Calle Oro. Castro, Antonio, tr. & illus. by. 2003. (ENG & SPA.). 40p. (J). 16.95 (*0-938317-75-X*) Cinco Puntos Pr.

Byrd, Sandra. Camp Cowgirl. 2000. (Secret Sisters Ser.: Vol. 10). 112p. (J). (gr. 3-7). pap. 4.95 o.s.i (*1-57856-065-9*) WaterBrook Pr.

—Change of Heart. 2002. (Hidden Diary Ser.: Bk. 6). 112p. (J). pap. 4.99 (*0-7642-2485-9*) Bethany Hse. Pubs.

—Cross My Heart. 2001. (Hidden Diary Ser.). 112p. (J). (gr. 3-7). pap. 4.99 (*0-7642-2480-8*) Bethany Hse. Pubs.

—Double Dare. 1998. (Secret Sisters Ser.: Vol. 5). 112p. (gr. 3-7). pap. 5.95 o.s.i (*1-57856-019-5*) WaterBrook Pr.

—First Place. 2000. (Secret Sisters Ser.: Vol. 9). 112p. (J). (gr. 4-7). pap. 4.95 o.s.i (*1-57856-066-7*) WaterBrook Pr.

—Indian Summer. 12th ed. 2000. (Secret Sisters Ser.: Vol. 12). 112p. (J). (gr. 3-7). pap. 4.95 (*1-57856-270-8*) WaterBrook Pr.

—Just Between Friends. 2001. (Hidden Diary Ser.). 112p. (J). (gr. 3-7). pap. 4.99 (*0-7642-2482-4*) Bethany Hse. Pubs.

—One Plus One. 2002. (Hidden Diary Ser.). 112p. (J). (gr. 3-7). pap. 4.99 (*0-7642-2487-5*) Bethany Hse. Pubs.

—Pass It On. 2002. (Hidden Diary Ser.: Bk. 5). 112p. (J). pap. 4.99 (*0-7642-2484-0*) Bethany Hse. Pubs.

—Petal Power. 1999. (Secret Sisters Ser.: Vol. 8). 112p. (J). (gr. 4-7). pap. 4.95 (*1-57856-115-9*) WaterBrook Pr.

—Take a Bow. 2001. (Hidden Diary Ser.). 112p. (J). (gr. 3-7). pap. 4.99 (*0-7642-2483-2*) Bethany Hse. Pubs.

Cabal, Graciela Beatriz. Miedo. 2002. (SPA.). 32p. pap. 8.95 (*1-4000-0014-9*) Random Hse., Inc.

Cabrera, Jane. The Lonesome Polar Bear. 2003. (Illus.). 32p. (J). 13.95 (*0-375-82410-3*) Random Hse. Children's Bks.

Cadnum, Michael. Breaking the Fall. (gr. 7 up). 1994. 144p. (YA). pap. 3.99 o.p. (*0-14-036004-2*, Puffin Bks.); 1992. 160p. (J). 15.00 o.s.i (*0-670-84687-2*, Viking Children's Bks.) Penguin Putnam Bks. for Young Readers.

Calaci, Iris. Matthew Mouse. Karper, Deborah, ed. 2002. (Illus.). 40p. (J). pap. (*1-928681-07-7*, MM077) Gladstone Publishing.

Calamari, Barbara. Green with Envy. 2002. (Angela Anaconda Ser.: Vol. 7). (Illus.). 64p. (J). pap. 3.99 (*0-689-84583-9*, Simon Spotlight) Simon & Schuster Children's Publishing.

Caldecott, Moyra. The Tower & the Emerald. (J). E-Book (*1-899142-59-2*) Mushroom Publishing.

Calder, Lyn. Blue-Ribbon Friends. 1991. (Minnie 'n Me Ser.). (Illus.). 32p. (J). (gr. k-3). 5.95 o.p. (*1-56282-034-6*) Disney Pr.

—That's What Friends Are For: Minnie 'n Me. 1992. (Golden Little Look-Look Bks.). (Illus.). 24p. (J). (ps-k). pap. o.p. (*0-307-11629-8*, 11629, Golden Bks.) Random Hse. Children's Bks.

Calhoun, B. B. Out of Place. 1994. (Dinosaur Detective Ser.: No. 4). (Illus.). 128p. (J). (gr. 3-7). pap. text 3.95 o.p. (*0-7167-6551-9*) Freeman, W. H. & Co.

Calmenson, Stephanie & Cole, Joanna. Rockin' Reptiles. (Illus.). 80p. (J). 1998. pap. 5.95 (*0-688-15633-9*); 1997. (ps-3). lib. bdg. 14.93 o.p. (*0-688-12740-1*, 707272); 1997. (Gator Girls Ser.: Vol. 2). (gr. 1-4). 15.00 (*0-688-12739-8*) Morrow/Avon. (Morrow, William & Co.).

Cameron, Ann. Gloria's Way. 2002. (Illus.). 12.34 (*1-4046-0952-0*) Book Wholesalers, Inc.

—Gloria's Way, RS. 2000. (Illus.). 96p. (J). (ps-3). 15.00 (*0-374-32670-3*, Farrar, Straus & Giroux (BYR)) Farrar, Straus & Giroux.

—Gloria's Way. 2001. (Chapter Ser.). (Illus.). 112p. (J). pap. 4.99 (*0-14-230023-3*, Puffin Bks.) Penguin Putnam Bks. for Young Readers.

—Gloria's Way. 2001. 11.04 (*0-606-22055-0*) Turtleback Bks.

—The Stories Julian Tells. 1995. (J). pap. text 15.40 (*0-15-305580-4*) Harcourt Trade Pubs.

—The Stories Julian Tells. 1999. (J). 9.95 (*1-56137-671-X*) Novel Units, Inc.

—The Stories Julian Tells. (J). 1996. pap. 3.99 o.p. (*0-679-88125-5*, Random Hse. Bks. for Young Readers); 1989. (Illus.). 80p. reprint ed. pap. 4.99 (*0-394-82892-5*, Knopf Bks. for Young Readers) Random Hse. Children's Bks.

—The Stories Julian Tells. 1981. (J). 11.14 (*0-606-03480-3*) Turtleback Bks.

Cameron, Ann & Strugnell, Ann. The Stories Julian Tells. 1981. (Illus.). 96p. (J). (gr. k-5). 15.99 o.s.i (*0-394-94301-5*, Pantheon) Knopf Publishing Group.

Camp, Lindsay. Keeping up with Cheetah. 1993. (Illus.). (J). (gr. k-4). 14.00 o.p. (*0-688-12655-3*) HarperCollins Children's Bk. Group.

Campbell, Eric. The Year of the Leopard Song. 1992. 224p. (YA). (gr. 5 up). 16.95 o.s.i (*0-15-299806-3*) Harcourt Children's Bks.

—The Year of the Leopard Song. 1995. 224p. (C). (gr. 5 up). pap. 5.00 o.s.i (*0-15-200873-X*) Harcourt Trade Pubs.

—The Year of the Leopard Song. 1995. (J). 10.10 o.p. (*0-606-08406-1*) Turtleback Bks.

Campbell, Joanna. The Prize. 2002. (Ashleigh Ser.: No. 13). 176p. (gr. 3-7). mass mkt. 4.99 (*0-06-009144-4*, HarperEntertainment) Morrow/Avon.

Canady, Pat. Boots the World's Best Kid-Sitter: Springtime Adventures. 2000. (Illus.). 6p. (J). (ps-4). pap. 10.00 (*1-929889-02-X*) Canady SW Publishing.

Canning, Shelagh. Friendship, No. 7. 1997. (Adventures from the Book of Virtues Ser.). (Illus.). 24p. (J). (ps-2). 3.25 (*0-689-81279-5*, Simon Spotlight) Simon & Schuster Children's Publishing.

Cannon, Elaine. Eight Is Great. 1987. (J). pap. 7.95 (*0-88494-612-6*, Bookcraft, Inc.) Deseret Bk. Co.

Cannon, Janell. Stelaluna. 1996. 15.10 (*0-606-13815-3*) Turtleback Bks.

Cantillon, Eli. The Mysterious Pen Pal. 1994. (J). (ps-5). 16.95 (*0-938971-83-2*) JTG of Nashville.

Cantillon, Eli A. The Mysterious Pen Pal. 1994. (Illus.). 34p. (J). (gr. k). 12.97 o.p. (*1-881445-40-2*) Sandvik Publishing.

Cantwell, Lee G. Finders Keepers. 1996. pap. o.p. (*1-57008-224-3*, Bookcraft, Inc.) Deseret Bk. Co.

Capalija, Marie A. Five Friends. 2004. (My Little Pony Ser.). (Illus.). 20p. (J). pap. 8.99 (*0-06-055406-1*, Harper Festival) HarperCollins Children's Bk. Group.

Caple, Kathy. Fox & Bear. 1992. (Illus.). 40p. (J). (gr. k-3). 13.95 o.p. (*0-395-55634-1*) Houghton Mifflin Co.

—The Friendship Tree. 2000. (House Readers Ser.). (Illus.). 48p. (J). (gr. k-3). tchr. ed. 14.95 (*0-8234-1376-4*) Holiday Hse., Inc.

Capote, Truman. A Christmas Memory. 1989. (Knopf Book & Cassette Classic Ser.). (Illus.). 48p. (J). (gr. 2 up). 19.00 (*0-679-80040-9*, Knopf Bks. for Young Readers) Random Hse. Children's Bks.

—A Christmas Memory, One Christmas, & the Thanksgiving Visitor. 1996. (Modern Library Ser.). 128p. 14.95 (*0-679-60237-2*) Random Hse., Inc.

—Miriam. 1982. (Short Story Library). (Illus.). 32p. (YA). (gr. 5 up). lib. bdg. 13.95 o.p. (*0-87191-829-3*, Creative Education) Creative Co., The.

Caproni, Deidre. Hallowell's Friends. 2000. (Illus.). 88p. (J). (gr. k-7). pap. 10.95 (*0-9678923-1-7*) AmityWorks.

Capucilli, Alyssa Satin. Biscuit Finds a Friend. (My First I Can Read Bks.). (Illus.). 32p. (J). (ps up). 1998. pap. 3.99 (*0-06-444243-8*, Harper Trophy); 2001. pap. 8.99 incl. audio (*0-06-029324-1*) HarperCollins Children's Bk. Group.

—Biscuit Finds a Friend. 1998. (My First I Can Read Bks.). (Illus.). (J). (ps-k). 10.10 (*0-606-13203-1*) Turtleback Bks.

—Biscuit's Big Friend. 2004. (My First I Can Read Ser.). (Illus.). 32p. (J). pap. 3.99 (*0-06-444288-8*, Harper Trophy) HarperCollins Children's Bk. Group.

—Biscuit's Big Friend. 2003. (My First I Can Read Ser.). (Illus.). 32p. (J). (ps up). 14.99 (*0-06-029167-2*); lib. bdg. 15.89 (*0-06-029168-0*) HarperCollins Pubs.

Carbone, Elisa. Sarah & the Naked Truth. 2000. 160p. (YA). (gr. 5-8). lib. bdg. 17.99 (*0-375-90264-3*) Knopf, Alfred A. Inc.

—Starting School with an Enemy. 112p. (J). 1999. (gr. 5-8). pap. 4.99 o.s.i (*0-679-88640-0*, Knopf Bks. for Young Readers); 1998. (gr. 3-8). 17.99 o.s.i (*0-679-98639-1*, Random Hse. Bks. for Young Readers) Random Hse. Children's Bks.

—Starting School with an Enemy. 1999. 11.04 (*0-606-16568-1*) Turtleback Bks.

Carkeet, David. The Silent Treatment. (Charlotte Zolotow Bk.). 288p. (YA). (gr. 7 up). 1990. mass mkt. 3.25 (*0-06-447014-8*, Harper Trophy); 1988. 13.95 o.p. (*0-06-020978-X*); 1988. lib. bdg. 13.89 o.p. (*0-06-020979-8*) HarperCollins Children's Bk. Group.

Carle, Eric & Iwamura, Kazuo. Where Are You Going? To See My Friend! 2003. (ENG & JPN., Illus.). 32p. (J). 19.95 (*0-439-41659-0*, Orchard Bks.) Scholastic, Inc.

Carlson, Lorentz. Here Come the Littles. 1984. (Illus.). 64p. (Orig.). (J). (gr. 1 up). pap. 5.95 o.p. (*0-590-33149-3*) Scholastic, Inc.

Carlson, Margaret. The Canning Season. 1999. (First Person Ser.). (Illus.). (J). (gr. 2-4). 32p. pap. 7.95 (*1-57505-283-0*, Carolrhoda Bks.); 40p. lib. bdg. 19.93 o.s.i (*1-57505-260-1*) Lerner Publishing Group.

Carlson, Melody. It's My Life. 2000. (Diary of a Teenage Girl Ser.). 252p. (J). (gr. 7 up). pap. 12.99 o.p. (*1-57673-772-1*) Multnomah Pubs., Inc.

Carlson, Nancy. Arnie & the New Kid. 1992. (Picture Puffin Ser.). (Illus.). (J). 11.14 (*0-606-01678-3*) Turtleback Bks.

—Harriet & Walt. 1994. (Nancy Carlson's Neighborhood Ser.). (Illus.). 32p. (J). (ps-1). pap. 4.95 (*0-87614-851-8*); lib. bdg. 15.95 (*0-87614-185-8*) Lerner Publishing Group. (Carolrhoda Bks.).

—Harriet & Walt. (Illus.). (J). (gr. k-3). pap., tchr. ed. 31.95 incl. audio (*0-941078-58-2*); 24.95 incl. audio (*0-941078-59-0*); 24.95 incl. audio (*0-941078-59-0*); pap. 15.95 incl. audio (*0-941078-57-4*) Live Oak Media.

—How to Lose All Your Friends. 32p. (J). (ps-3). 1997. pap. 5.99 (*0-14-055862-4*); 1994. text 15.99 (*0-670-84906-5*, Viking Children's Bks.) Penguin Putnam Bks. for Young Readers.

—My Best Friend Moved Away. (Illus.). 32p. 2003. pap. 5.99 (*0-14-250067-4*, Puffin Bks.); 2001. (J). 15.99 (*0-670-89498-2*, Viking Children's Bks.) Penguin Putnam Bks. for Young Readers.

—Snowden. 1998. (Illus.). 32p. (J). (ps-3). 15.99 o.s.i (*0-670-88078-7*, Viking Children's Bks.) Penguin Putnam Bks. for Young Readers.

Carlson, Natalie S. Ann Aurelia & Dorothy. 1968. (Illus.). (J). (gr. 4-8). lib. bdg. 13.89 o.p. (*0-06-020959-3*) HarperCollins Children's Bk. Group.

Carlson, Nathan, et al. The Great Train Set Robbery. 2001. (Little Dogs on the Prairie Ser.). (Illus.). 64p. (J). (gr. 1-4). 4.99 (*0-8499-7649-9*) Nelson, Tommy.

Carlson, Ron. Speed of Light. 2003. 288p. (J). lib. bdg. 16.89 (*0-06-029825-1*, HarperTempest) HarperCollins Children's Bk. Group.

—The Speed of Light. 288p. (J). 2004. pap. 6.99 (*0-380-81312-2*); 2003. 15.99 (*0-380-97837-7*) HarperCollins Children's Bk. Group. (HarperTempest).

Carlsruh, Dan K. The Cannibals of Sunset Drive. 1993. 143p. (J). (gr. 3-7). lib. bdg. 13.95 o.s.i (*0-02-717110-8*, Simon & Schuster Children's Publishing) Simon & Schuster Children's Publishing.

Carlstrom, Nancy White. Fish & Flamingo. 1993. (Illus.). (J). (ps-3). 14.95 o.p. (*0-316-12859-7*) Little Brown & Co.

—The Way to Wyatt's House. 2000. (Illus.). 32p. (J). (ps-3). 15.95 (*0-8027-8740-1*) Walker & Co.

Carpenter, Humphrey. Mr. Majeika. l.t. ed. 1992. (Children's Lythway Ser.). (Illus.). 96p. (J). (gr. 1-8). 13.95 o.p. (*0-7451-1582-9*, Galaxy Children's Large Print) BBC Audiobooks America.

Carpino, Nancy. The Leprechaun & His Bag of Gold. 2000. (Illus.). 50p. (J). (gr. k-4). 8.95 (*1-928675-03-4*) Carpino Bks.

Carr, Jan. Frozen Noses. 1999. (Illus.). 32p. (J). (ps-1). tchr. ed. 15.95 (*0-8234-1462-0*) Holiday Hse., Inc.

Carr, Jan, adapted by. Oliver & Company. 1988. 64p. (J). (gr. 2-7). pap. 2.50 o.p. (*0-590-42049-6*) Scholastic, Inc.

Carr, Jan & Martin, Ann M. The Baby-Sitters Club: The Movie Keepsake. 1995. (Baby-Sitters Club Ser.). 48p. (J). (gr. 2-5). pap. 12.95 (*0-590-60405-8*) Scholastic, Inc.

Carrick, Carol. Sleep Out. 1973. (J). 13.10 (*0-606-00576-5*) Turtleback Bks.

—Some Friend!, 001. 1979. (Illus.). 112p. (J). (gr. 3-6). 13.95 o.p. (*0-395-28966-1*, Clarion Bks.) Houghton Mifflin Co. Trade & Reference Div.

—Some Friend. 1987. (Illus.). 112p. (J). (gr. 4-7). pap. 5.95 o.p. (*0-89919-525-3*, Clarion Bks.) Houghton Mifflin Co. Trade & Reference Div.

Carson, Jo. You Hold Me & I'll Hold You. 1997. 13.10 (*0-606-12583-3*) Turtleback Bks.

Carter, Alden R. Bull Catcher. 1997. 288p. (J). (gr. 7-12). pap. 15.95 (*0-590-50958-6*) Scholastic, Inc.

Carter, Debby L. Clipper. 1981. (Illus.). 32p. (J). (ps-3). o.p. (*0-06-021127-X*); lib. bdg. 10.89 o.p. (*0-06-021128-8*) HarperCollins Children's Bk. Group.

Carter, Peter. Gates of Paradise. 1979. (Illus.). (J). (gr. 6-12). reprint ed. 8.95 o.p. (*0-19-271367-1*) Oxford Univ. Pr., Inc.

Casanova, Mary. Wolf Shadows. 144p. (J). (gr. 3-7). 1999. pap. 5.99 (*0-7868-1340-7*); 1997. (Illus.). 14.95 o.p. (*0-7868-0325-8*); 1997. (Illus.). lib. bdg. 15.49 (*0-7868-2269-4*) Hyperion Bks. for Children.

—Wolf Shadows. 1999. 144p. (J). pap. 5.99 (*0-7868-1415-2*) Little Brown & Co.

—Wolf Shadows. 1999. 12.04 (*0-606-16667-X*) Turtleback Bks.

Caseley, Judith. Harry & Willy & Carrothead. 1991. (Illus.). 24p. (J). (ps-3). 16.95 (*0-688-09492-9*); lib. bdg. 15.93 o.p. (*0-688-09493-7*) HarperCollins Children's Bk. Group. (Greenwillow Bks.).

—Starring Dorothy Kane. 1992. 154p. (J). (ps-3). 13.00 o.s.i (*0-688-10182-8*, Greenwillow Bks.) HarperCollins Children's Bk. Group.

—Starring Dorothy Kane. 1994. (Illus.). 160p. (J). (gr. 4-7). mass mkt. 4.95 o.p. (*0-688-12548-4*, Morrow, William & Co.) Morrow/Avon.

Cassedy, Sylvia. M. E. & Morton. 1987. 288p. (J). (gr. 4-7). lib. bdg. 13.89 o.p. (*0-690-04562-X*) HarperCollins Children's Bk. Group.

—Me & Morton. (Trophy Bk.). (J). (gr. 4-7). 1989. 320p. pap. 3.95 o.s.i (*0-06-440306-8*, Harper Trophy); 1987. 288p. 14.00 o.p. (*0-690-04560-3*) HarperCollins Children's Bk. Group.

Cassidy, Anne. Jasper & Jess. 2002. (Read-It! Readers Ser.). (Illus.). 32p. (J). (ps-3). lib. bdg. 18.60 (*1-4048-0061-1*) Picture Window Bks.

Castellarin, Loretta & Roberts, Ken. Spike. 1988. (Degrassi Book Ser.). 117p. (J). (gr. 7-9). mass mkt. (*1-55028-113-5*); bds. (*1-55028-115-1*) Formac Distributing, Ltd.

Casterline, Charlotte L. My Friend Has Asthma. 1985. (Illus.). 24p. (Orig.). (J). (ps-6). pap. 4.95 (*0-9617218-0-4*) Info-All Bk. Co.

—Sam the Allergen. 1985. (Illus.). 26p. (Orig.). (J). (ps-6). pap. 4.95 (*0-9617218-1-2*) Info-All Bk. Co.

Castilla, Julia Mercedes. Emilio. 1999. 105p. (J). (gr. 4-7). pap. 9.95 (*1-55885-271-9*, Piñata Books) Arte Publico Pr.

Castle, Caroline. Rosie Pugh & the Great Clothes War. 1995. (Illus.). 128p. (J). (gr. 4-7). pap. 3.50 o.p. (*0-8120-9181-7*) Barron's Educational Series, Inc.

Castor, Harriet. Fat Puss & Friends. 1985. 96p. (J). (gr. 3). pap. 7.95 o.p. (*0-14-031658-2*) Penguin Bks., Ltd. GBR. *Dist:* Trafalgar Square.

Caswell, Brian. Relax Max! 1997. (Storybridge Ser.). (Illus.). 86p. (J). pap. 10.95 (*0-7022-2897-4*) Univ. of Queensland Pr. AUS. *Dist:* International Specialized Bk. Services.

Cates, Karin, et al. The Secret Remedy Book: A Story of Comfort & Love. 2003. (My Great-Great-Grandmother's Secret Remedy Book Ser.). (Illus.). 40p. (J). pap. 16.95 (*0-439-35226-6*, Orchard Bks.) Scholastic, Inc.

Cavanna, Betty. Banner Year. 1924. (YA). lib. bdg. o.s.i (*0-688-05780-2*, Morrow, William & Co.) Morrow/Avon.

—Lasso Your Heart. 1952. (J). (gr. 6-9). 5.50 o.p. (*0-664-32089-9*) Westminster John Knox Pr.

Cave, Hugh B. Conquering Kilmarnie. 1989. 192p. (J). (gr. 3-7). lib. bdg. 14.95 o.s.i (*0-02-717781-5*, Simon & Schuster Children's Publishing) Simon & Schuster Children's Publishing.

Cave, Kathryn. Something Else. 1998. (Illus.). 32p. (J). (gr. 1-5). pap. 5.95 (*1-57255-563-7*) Mondo Publishing.

Cazet, Denys. Minnie & Moo Go Dancing. 1999. (Illus.). 48p. (J). pap. 15.95 (*0-7737-3105-9*) Dorling Kindersley Publishing, Inc.

—Minnie & Moo Go Dancing. 1998. 10.10 (*0-606-16461-8*) Turtleback Bks.

—Minnie & Moo Go to the Moon. (Illus.). 48p. (J). 2000. pap. 6.95 o.p. (*0-7737-5983-2*); 1999. pap. 15.95 o.p. (*0-7737-3104-0*); 1998. (Minnie & Moo Ser.: Vol. 1). (gr. 1-3). pap. 12.95 (*0-7894-2516-5*, D K Ink) Dorling Kindersley Publishing, Inc.

—Never Poke a Squid. 2000. (Illus.). 32p. (J). (ps-2). lib. bdg. 17.99 (*0-531-33279-9*, Watts, Franklin) Scholastic Library Publishing.

—Never Poke a Squid. 2000. (Illus.). 32p. (J). (ps-2). pap. 16.95 (*0-531-30279-2*, Orchard Bks.) Scholastic, Inc.

Center for Learning Network Staff. All the Pretty Horses: Curriculum Unit —Novel Series — Grades 9-12. 2001. (Novel Ser.). 60p. tchr. ed., spiral bd. 18.95 (*1-56077-667-6*) Ctr. for Learning, The.

Chaikin, Miriam. Getting Even. 1982. (Charlotte Zolotow Bk.). (Illus.). 128p. (J). (gr. 3-7). lib. bdg. 12.89 o.p. (*0-06-021165-2*) HarperCollins Children's Bk. Group.

—Lower! Higher! You're a Liar! 1984. (Charlotte Zolotow Bk.). (Illus.). 160p. (J). (gr. 3-7). 12.95 (*0-06-021186-5*); lib. bdg. 12.89 o.p. (*0-06-021187-3*) HarperCollins Children's Bk. Group.

Chall, Marsha W. Mattie. 1994. (J). pap. 3.50 o.p. (*0-380-72116-3*, Avon Bks.) Morrow/Avon.

Chambers, Aidan. NIK: Now I Know. 1988. (Charlotte Zolotow Bk.). 288p. (YA). (gr. 7 up). 13.95 (*0-06-021208-X*); lib. bdg. 13.89 o.p. (*0-06-021209-8*) HarperCollins Children's Bk. Group.

Chambers, Aiden. Toll Bridge. 1995. (Laura Geringer Bks.). (Illus.). 272p. (YA). (gr. 8 up). 14.95 o.p. (*0-06-023598-5*); lib. bdg. 14.89 o.p. (*0-06-023599-3*) HarperCollins Children's Bk. Group.

Chambers, Nancy. Patches of Time. 2001. 253p. pap. 21.95 (*1-58851-171-5*) PublishAmerica, Inc.

Chambers, Veronica. Double Dutch: A Celebration of Jump Rope, Rhyme, & Sisterhood. Date not set. pap. 8.99 (*0-7868-1363-6*) Hyperion Paperbacks for Children.

—Marisol & Magdalena: The Sound of Our Sisterhood. 2001. 176p. (J). (gr. 3-7). pap. 5.99 (*0-7868-1304-0*) Hyperion Bks. for Children.

—Marisol & Magdalena: The Sound of Our Sisterhood. 1998. 141p. (gr. 3-7). (J). 14.95 (*0-7868-0437-8*); (YA). lib. bdg. 15.49 (*0-7868-2385-2*) Hyperion Pr.

—Quinceanera Means Sweet Fifteen. 2001. 192p. (J). (gr. 3-7). 15.99 (*0-7868-0497-1*); (Illus.). (gr. 5-8). lib. bdg. 16.49 (*0-7868-2426-3*) Hyperion Bks. for Children.

Chambless, Jane. Tucker & the Bear. 1989. (J). (ps-2). pap. 13.95 o.s.i (*0-671-67357-2*, Simon & Schuster Children's Publishing) Simon & Schuster Children's Publishing.

Champion, Joyce. Emily & Alice. (Emily & Alice Ser.). (Illus.). 32p. (J). 1996. pap. 5.00 (*0-15-201347-4*, Voyager Bks./Libros Viajeros); 1993. (gr. 1-4). 13.95 (*0-15-200588-9*) Harcourt Children's Bks.

—Emily & Alice Again. 1995. (Emily & Alice Ser.). (Illus.). 32p. (J). (ps-3). 14.00 (*0-15-200439-4*, Gulliver Bks.) Harcourt Children's Bks.

—Emily & Alice, Best Friends. 2001. (Emily & Alice Ser.: Bk. 1). (Illus.). 32p. (J). (gr. 1-4). pap. 5.95 (*0-15-202198-1*, Gulliver Bks.) Harcourt Children's Bks.

—Emily & Alice Best Friends. 2001. (Illus.). (J). 12.10 (*0-606-21177-2*) Turtleback Bks.

—Emily & Alice Stick Together. 2001. (Emily & Alice Ser.: Bk. 2). (Illus.). 32p. (J). (gr. 1-4). pap. 5.95 (*0-15-202189-2*, Gulliver Bks.) Harcourt Children's Bks.

—Emily & Alice Stick Together. 2001. (Illus.). (J). 12.10 (*0-606-21178-0*) Turtleback Bks.

Chanda, J-P. Ah-Choo! 2003. (Oswald Pre-School Ready-to-Read Ser.: Vol. 2). (Illus.). 24p. (J). pap. 3.99 (*0-689-85853-1*, Simon Spotlight/ Nickelodeon) Simon & Schuster Children's Publishing.

Chang, Heidi. Elaine & the Flying Frog. 1991. (Stepping Stone Bks.). (Illus.). 64p. (J). (gr. 2-4). pap. 2.50 o.s.i (*0-679-80870-1*, Random Hse. Bks. for Young Readers) Random Hse. Children's Bks.

Chapian, Marie. Alula-Belle Blows into Town. 1995. (Alula-Belle Adventures Ser.: Vol. 1). (Illus.). 84p. (J). text 9.99 o.p. (*1-55661-649-X*) Bethany Hse. Pubs.

Chapman, Susan. The Get Along Gang & the Crybaby. 1984. (Get along Gang Ser.). (Illus.). 32p. (Orig.). (J). (ps-2). pap. 1.95 o.p. (*0-590-40219-6*) Scholastic, Inc.

Chapouton, Anne-Marie. Ben Finds a Friend. 1986. (Illus.). 32p. (J). (ps-2). 7.95 o.s.i (*0-399-21268-X*, G. P. Putnam's Sons) Penguin Putnam Bks. for Young Readers.

—Downy, Pistachio & Fanny. 1992. (I Love to Read Collections). (Illus.). 46p. (J). (gr. 1-5). lib. bdg. 8.50 o.p. (*0-89565-808-9*) Child's World, Inc.

—Krustnkrum! 1992. (Child's World Library Ser.). (Illus.). 32p. (J). (gr. 1-5). lib. bdg. 8.50 (*0-89565-744-9*) Child's World, Inc.

Charbonnet, Gabrielle. Adventure at Walt Disney World. 1999. (Disney Girls Ser.: Vol. 7). 120p. (J). (gr. 2-5). pap. 3.99 (*0-7868-4271-7*) Disney Pr.

—Attack of the Beast. 1998. (Disney Girls Ser.: Vol. 2). 96p. (J). (gr. 2-5). pap. 3.95 (*0-7868-4160-5*) Disney Pr.

—Beauty's Revenge. 1999. (Disney Girls Ser.: Vol. 8). 83p. (J). (gr. 2-5). pap. text 3.99 (*0-7868-4272-5*) Hyperion Pr.

—Cinderella's Castle. 1998. (Disney Girls Ser.: Vol. 5). 96p. (J). (gr. 2-5). pap. 3.95 (*0-7868-4165-6*) Disney Pr.

—Good-Bye, Jasmine. 1999. (Disney Girls Ser.: Vol. 9). 84p. (J). (gr. 2-5). pap. text 3.99 (*0-7868-4273-3*) Hyperion Pr.

—The Gum Race. 1999. (Disney Girls Ser.: 11). 83p. (J). (gr. 2-5). pap. text 3.99 (*0-7868-4275-X*) Disney Pr.

—One of Us. 1998. (Disney Girls Ser.: No. 1). 96p. (J). (gr. 2-5). pap. 3.95 (*0-7868-4156-7*) Disney Pr.

—One Pet Too Many. 1998. (Disney Girls Ser.: 6). 96p. (J). (gr. 2-5). pap. 3.95 (*0-7868-4166-4*) Disney Pr.

—Princess of Power. 1999. (Disney Girls Ser.: Vol. 10). 78p. (J). (gr. 2-5). pap. text 3.99 (*0-7868-4274-1*) Disney Pr.

Chardiet, Bernice & Maccarone, Grace. Merry Christmas, What's Your Name School Friends. 1991. (Illus.). 32p. (J). (ps-2). pap. text 2.50 (*0-590-43306-7*) Scholastic, Inc.

—The Snowball War. 1999. (*0-439-10803-9*) Scholastic, Inc.

Charlip, Remy & Rettenmund, Tamara, illus. Little Old Big Beard & Big Young Little Beard: A Short & Tall Tale. 2002. (J). (*1-58837-000-3*) Winslow Pr.

Charlotte's Web. 1998. 40p. (J). 11.95 (*1-56137-630-2*, NU6302SP) Novel Units, Inc.

Chase, Diana. Surf's Up. 1999. 200p. (J). 12.95 (*1-86368-250-3*) Fremantle Arts Centre Pr. AUS. *Dist:* International Specialized Bk. Services.

Chase, Emily. Three of a Kind. 1985. (J). pap. 1.95 (*0-590-33706-8*) Scholastic, Inc.

Chass, Vikentia. The Visiting Angels. 1999. 16p. (J). (gr. k-6). pap. 8.00 (*0-8059-4713-2*) Dorrance Publishing Co., Inc.

Chbosky, Stephen. The Perks of Being a Wallflower. 1999. 256p. (gr. 7-12). pap. 13.00 (*0-671-02734-4*, MTV) Simon & Schuster.

—The Perks of Being a Wallflower. 1999. 18.05 (*0-606-18378-7*) Turtleback Bks.

Chesanow, Neil. Where Do I Live? 1995. (J). 13.10 (*0-606-13910-9*) Turtleback Bks.

Chesworth, Michael D. Archibald Frisby, RS. 1996. 32p. (J). (ps-3). pap. 6.95 (*0-374-40436-4*, Sunburst) Farrar, Straus & Giroux.

Chetwin, Grace. The Crystal Stair: From Tales of Gom in the Legends of Ulm. 1988. 240p. (YA). (gr. 5 up). lib. bdg. 14.95 (*0-02-718311-4*, Simon & Schuster Children's Publishing) Simon & Schuster Children's Publishing.

Child, A. My Best Friend & Me. 1992. (Foundations Ser.). 19p. (J). (gr. 1). pap. text 4.50 (*1-56843-072-8*) EMG Networks.

—My Best Friend & Me: Big Book. 1992. (Foundations Ser.). 19p. (J). (gr. 1). pap. text 23.00 (*1-56843-022-1*) EMG Networks.

—Show Me a Face. 1992. (Cityscapes Ser.). 14p. (J). (ps). pap. text 4.50 (*1-56843-056-6*); pap. text 23.00 (*1-56843-006-X*) EMG Networks.

Child, Lauren. Clarice Bean, That's Me. 1999. (Illus.). 32p. (J). (gr. 1-5). 16.99 (*0-7636-0961-7*) Candlewick Pr.

Child Study Children's Book Committee. Friends Are Like That! Stories to Read to Yourself. 1979. (Illus.). (J). (gr. 3-6). 12.95 (*0-690-03979-4*); lib. bdg. 12.89 (*0-690-03980-8*) HarperCollins Children's Bk. Group.

Child, Vivian M. Puffy & Buttons. 1991. (J). 7.95 o.p. (*0-533-09365-1*) Vantage Pr., Inc.

Chin-Lee, Cynthia. Almond Cookies & Dragon Well Tea. 1993. (Illus.). 36p. (J). (gr. 1-4). 14.95 (*1-879965-03-8*) Polychrome Publishing Corp.

Chittum, Ida. The Hermit Boy. 1972. (Illus.). 160p. (J). (gr. 4-6). 4.95 o.p. (*0-440-03557-0*, Delacorte Pr.) Dell Publishing.

Choldenko, Gennifer. Tales of a Second-Grade Giant. 2004. (J). (*0-399-23779-8*) Putnam Publishing Group, The.

Chorao, Kay. George Told Kate. 1990. (Unicorn Paperbacks Ser.). (Illus.). 32p. (J). (ps up). pap. 3.95 o.p. (*0-525-44649-4*, Dutton Children's Bks.) Penguin Putnam Bks. for Young Readers.

—Ida & Betty & the Secret Eggs. Giblin, James C., ed. 1991. (Illus.). 32p. (J). (ps-2). 13.95 o.p. (*0-395-52591-8*, Clarion Bks.) Houghton Mifflin Co. Trade & Reference Div.

Chottin, Ariane. Little Mouse's Rescue. 1993. (Little Animal Adventures Ser.). 22p. (J). (ps-3). 5.98 o.p. (*0-89577-505-0*) Reader's Digest Assn., Inc., The.

Choyce, Lesley. Carrie's Crowd. 1998. (First Novels Ser.: Vol. 8). (Illus.). 64p. (J). (gr. 1-4). (*0-88780-465-9*) Formac Publishing Co., Ltd.

—Carrie's Crowd. 1999. (First Novels Ser.: Vol. 8). (Illus.). 64p. (J). (gr. 1-4). pap. 3.99 (*0-88780-464-0*) Formac Publishing Co., Ltd. CAN. *Dist:* Formac Distributing, Ltd., Orca Bk. Pubs.

—Wrong Time, Wrong Place. 1995. 116p. (YA). (gr. 6 up). pap. (*0-88780-098-X*) Formac Distributing, Ltd.

—Wrong Time, Wrong Place. 1995. 115p. (YA). (gr. 6 up). 16.95 (*0-88780-099-8*) Formac Publishing Co., Ltd. CAN. *Dist:* Formac Distributing, Ltd.

Christian, Cheryl. Matty & Patty. 1998. (Domino Readers Ser.). (Illus.). 24p. (J). (ps-1). pap. 5.95 (*1-887734-30-9*) Star Bright Bks., Inc.

Christian, Mary Blount. Penrod Again. 1990. (Ready-to-Read Ser.). (Illus.). 56p. (J). (gr. 1-4). reprint ed. pap. 3.95 o.s.i (*0-689-71432-7*, Aladdin) Simon & Schuster Children's Publishing.

—Penrod's Party. 1990. (Ready-to-Read Ser.). (Illus.). 48p. (J). (gr. 1-4). lib. bdg. 11.95 o.p. (*0-02-718525-7*, Simon & Schuster Children's Publishing) Simon & Schuster Children's Publishing.

—Penrod's Picture. 1991. (Ready-to-Read Ser.). (Illus.). 48p. (J). (gr. 1-4). lib. bdg. 11.95 o.p. (*0-02-718523-0*, Simon & Schuster Children's Publishing) Simon & Schuster Children's Publishing.

—Singin' Somebody Else's Song. 1990. 192p. (J). (gr. 5 up). pap. 3.95 o.p. (*0-14-034169-2*, Puffin Bks.) Penguin Putnam Bks. for Young Readers.

Christiansen, C. B. A Snowman on Sycamore Street. 1996. (Illus.). 48p. (J). (gr. 1-3). 15.00 (*0-689-31927-4*, Atheneum) Simon & Schuster Children's Publishing.

—Sycamore Street. 1993. (Illus.). 48p. (J). (gr. 1-3). 13.95 (*0-689-31784-0*, Atheneum) Simon & Schuster Children's Publishing.

Christopher, Matt. The Extreme Team, No. 2. 2004. (Extreme Team Ser.: Vol. 2). (Illus.). (J). pap. 4.99 (*0-316-73753-4*); (gr. 2-4). 15.95 (*0-316-73751-8*) Little Brown Children's Bks.

—Face-Off. 1989. (Matt Christopher Sports Classics Ser.). 131p. (J). (gr. 3-7). pap. 4.50 (*0-316-13994-7*) Little Brown Children's Bks.

—Mountain Bike Mania. 1998. 160p. (J). (gr. 2-7). 15.95 (*0-316-14355-3*); (gr. 3-7). pap. 4.50 (*0-316-14292-1*) Little Brown & Co.

—Mountain Bike Mania. 1998. 10.00 (*0-606-15983-5*) Turtleback Bks.

—One Smooth Move. 2004. (Extreme Team Ser.: Vol. 1). 64p. (J). 15.95 (*0-316-73746-1*); pap. 4.99 (*0-316-73749-6*) Little Brown & Co.

—Slam Dunk. 2004. (Illus.). (J). pap. 4.99 (*0-316-60762-2*) Little Brown & Co.

—Soccer Cats, Vol. 10. 2003. (Illus.). 64p. (J). 13.95 (*0-316-07660-0*) Little Brown Children's Bks.

—Stranger in Right Field. (Peach Street Mudders Story Ser.). (Illus.). 64p. (J). (gr. 2-4). 2000. pap. 4.50 (*0-316-10677-1*); 1997. 13.95 o.p. (*0-316-14111-9*) Little Brown & Co.

—Stranger in Right Field. 2000. 10.65 (*0-606-18266-7*) Turtleback Bks.

—Stranger in Right Field. 2002. (J). E-Book (*1-58824-674-4*); 2001. (J). E-Book (*1-58824-560-8*); 1997. E-Book (*1-58824-894-1*); 1997. E-Book (*1-58824-675-2*) ipicturebooks, LLC.

Christopher, Matt & Hirschfeld, Robert. Inline Skater. 2001. 160p. (J). (gr. 3-7). 15.95 o.p. (*0-316-12071-5*) Little Brown & Co.

Cisneros, Phil. Gabriela Gecko, the Story of Belonging. 1996. (Illus.). 22p. (J). (gr. 1-6). pap. 8.00 (*0-9651804-1-7*, 102) New Horizons, Unlimited.

Clar, David Austin, illus. Follow the Leader. 2003. (Rainbow Fish & Friends Ser.). 24p. (J). (ps-2). pap. 3.99 (*1-59014-106-7*); lib. bdg. 9.95 (*1-59014-115-6*) Night Sky Bks.

Clardy, Andrea F. Dusty Was My Friend. 1984. (Illus.). 32p. (J). (gr. 5 up). 16.95 (*0-89885-141-6*, Kluwer Academic/Human Science Pr.) Kluwer Academic Pubs.

Clark, Emma Chichester. What Shall We Do, Blue Kangaroo? 2003. (Illus.). (J). 15.95 (*0-385-74635-0*); lib. bdg. 17.99 (*0-385-90866-0*) Random Hse. Children's Bks. (Doubleday Bks. for Young Readers).

—Where Are You, Blue Kangaroo. 2002. 32p. (J). pap. 6.99 (*0-440-41760-0*, Dell Books for Young Readers) Random Hse. Children's Bks.

Clark, Johnnie M. Semper Fidelis. 1988. mass mkt. 4.95 o.s.i (*0-345-33529-5*) Ballantine Bks.

Clark, Kimberly. Three Is the Perfect Number. 1998. (Illus.). 16p. (J). (ps-k). pap. 5.95 (*1-891846-01-9*) Business Word, The.

Clarke, Beverly. Creek Watchers. 1998. 128p. (Orig.). (YA). (gr. 7-9). pap. 7.99 o.p. (*0-8280-1312-8*) Review & Herald Publishing Assn.

Clarke, J. Al Capsella Takes a Vacation, ERS. 1993. 144p. (YA). (gr. 7 up). 14.95 o.p. (*0-8050-2685-1*, Holt, Henry & Co. Bks. For Young Readers) Holt, Henry & Co.

—Riffraff, ERS. 1992. 112p. (YA). (gr. 9-12). 14.95 o.p. (*0-8050-1774-7*, Holt, Henry & Co. Bks. For Young Readers) Holt, Henry & Co.

Clarke, Pauline. The Return of the Twelve. 1986. 192p. (J). (gr. 3-7). pap. 4.95 o.s.i (*0-440-47536-8*) Dell Publishing.

Cleary, Beverly. Beezus & Ramona. 1988. (Ramona Ser.). (J). (gr. 3-5). mass mkt. o.s.i (*0-440-80009-9*) Doubleday Publishing.

—Beezus & Ramona. 1955. (Ramona Ser.). (Illus.). 160p. (J). (gr. 4-7). 15.95 (*0-688-21076-7*) HarperCollins Children's Bk. Group.

—Beezus & Ramona. 1979. (Ramona Ser.). (Illus.). 160p. (J). (gr. 3-5). pap. 1.75 o.s.i (*0-440-40665-X*, Yearling) Random Hse. Children's Bks.

—Beezus & Ramona. 9999. (Ramona Ser.). (J). (gr. 3-5). pap. 1.95 o.s.i (*0-590-11828-5*) Scholastic, Inc.

—The Beezus & Ramona Diary. 1986. (Ramona Ser.). (Illus.). 224p. (J). (gr. 3-5). pap. 11.95 (*0-688-06353-5*, Morrow, William & Co.) Morrow/Avon.

—Beverly Cleary, 4 vols. 1991. (J). (gr. 4-7). pap. 18.00 (*0-380-71719-0*, Avon Bks.) Morrow/Avon.

—Dear Mr. Henshaw. (J). 1992. pap. o.s.i (*0-440-80308-X*); 1988. pap. o.s.i (*0-440-80008-0*) Random Hse. Children's Bks. (Dell Books for Young Readers).

—Henry & Ribsy. 1954. (Henry Huggins Ser.). (J). (gr. 1-4). 11.04 (*0-606-03446-3*) Turtleback Bks.

—Jean & Johnny. 2003. (Cleary Reissue Ser.). (Illus.). 256p. (J). (gr. 5 up). pap. 5.99 (*0-06-053301-3*) HarperCollins Children's Bk. Group.

—Jean & Johnny. 1996. 11.04 (*0-606-10231-0*) Turtleback Bks.

—Mitch & Amy. 1991. (Illus.). 224p. (J). (gr. 4-7). 15.95 (*0-688-10806-7*); pap. 5.99 (*0-380-70925-2*, Harper Trophy) HarperCollins Children's Bk. Group.

—Mitch & Amy. 1991. (Illus.). 224p. (J). (gr. 2 up). lib. bdg. 13.88 o.p. (*0-688-10807-5*, Morrow, William & Co.) Morrow/Avon.

—Mitch & Amy. 1980. (Illus.). 224p. (J). (gr. k-6). pap. 1.75 o.s.i (*0-440-45411-5*, Yearling) Random Hse. Children's Bks.

—Mitch & Amy. 1991. (J). 11.00 (*0-606-04747-6*) Turtleback Bks.

—Otis Spofford. 2000. (J). pap., stu. ed. 34.24 incl. audio (*0-7887-4181-0*, 47089) Recorded Bks., LLC.

—Otis Spofford. 1953. (J). 11.04 (*0-606-04766-2*) Turtleback Bks.

—Pen Pals, 6 vols. 1990. (J). (gr. 4-7). 17.70 (*0-440-36028-5*) Dell Publishing.

—Querido Senor Henshaw. Bustelo, Gabriela, tr. 1997. (SPA., Illus.). 176p. (J). (gr. 2-6). pap. 6.99 (*0-688-15485-9*, MR8013, Morrow, William & Co.) Morrow/Avon.

—Ramona & Her Friends. 9999. (J). mass mkt. 9.00 o.s.i (*0-440-47222-9*) Dell Publishing.

—Ramona la Chinche. 1996. Tr. of Ramona the Pest. 12.00 (*0-606-10495-X*) Turtleback Bks.

—Ramona's World. 1999. (Ramona Ser.). (Illus.). 192p. (J). (gr. 3-5). 15.99 (*0-688-16816-7*, Morrow, William & Co.) Morrow/Avon.

Cleaver, Vera. Moon Lake Angel. 1989. (J). (gr. k-6). pap. 2.95 o.s.i (*0-440-40165-8*, Yearling) Random Hse. Children's Bks.

Cleaver, Vera & Cleaver, Bill. Me Too. 1985. (Trophy Bk.). 160p. (YA). (gr. 5-7). pap. 2.95 (*0-06-440161-8*, Harper Trophy) HarperCollins Children's Bk. Group.

—Mock Revolt. 1971. 160p. (J). (gr. 6 up). pap. 1.95 o.p. (*0-397-31237-7*); lib. bdg. 12.89 (*0-397-31238-5*) HarperCollins Children's Bk. Group.

Clegg, Helen. Yup Finds a Friend. 1998. (Illus.). (J). 19.95 (*1-56763-354-4*); pap. (*1-56763-355-2*) Ozark Publishing.

Clement, Claude. Little Squirrel's Special Nest. 1993. (Little Animal Adventures Ser.). (Illus.). 24p. (J). (ps-3). 6.99 o.p. (*0-89577-542-5*, Reader's Digest Young Families, Inc.) Reader's Digest Children's Publishing, Inc.

Clement, Frederic. The Merchant of Marvels & the Peddler of Dreams. 2001. (Illus.). 64p. (J). 16.95 (*0-8118-3294-5*) Chronicle Bks. LLC.

—The Merchant of Marvels & the Peddler of Dreams. Cole, Emma, tr. from FRE. 1997. (Illus.). 64p. (gr. 1-4). 17.95 o.p. (*0-8118-1664-8*) Chronicle Bks. LLC.

Clements, Andrew. Big Al & Shrimpy. 2002. (Illus.). 40p. (J). (gr. k-3). 16.95 (*0-689-84247-3*, Simon & Schuster Children's Publishing) Simon & Schuster Children's Publishing.

—Jake Drake, Know-It-All. l.t. ed. 2002. (Juvenile Ser.). (Illus.). 76p. (J). 21.95 (*0-7862-4139-X*) Gale Group.

—Jake Drake, Know-It-All. 2001. (Jake Drake Ser.: Bk. 2). (Illus.). 96p. (J). (gr. 2-5). 15.00 (*0-689-83918-9*, Simon & Schuster Children's Publishing); pap. 3.99 (*0-689-83881-6*, Aladdin) Simon & Schuster Children's Publishing.

—The Report Card. 2004. (Illus.). 176p. (J). 15.95 (*0-689-84515-4*, Simon & Schuster Children's Publishing) Simon & Schuster Children's Publishing.

Clements, Bruce. Coming About, RS. 1984. 180p. (J). (gr. 5 up). 14.00 o.p. (*0-374-31457-8*, Farrar, Straus & Giroux (BYR)) Farrar, Straus & Giroux.

—Two Against the Tide, RS. 1987. (Sunburst Ser.). 224p. (J). (gr. 4 up). pap. 3.50 o.p. (*0-374-48016-8*, Sunburst) Farrar, Straus & Giroux.

Clifford, Eth. I Hate Your Guts, Ben Brooster. 1989. 112p. (J). (gr. 3-7). 13.95 o.p. (*0-395-51079-1*) Houghton Mifflin Co.

—I Never Wanted to be Famous, 001. 1986. (J). (gr. 3-5). 12.95 o.p. (*0-395-40420-7*) Houghton Mifflin Co.

—Just Tell Me When We're Dead! 1985. 144p. (J). (gr. 5-7). mass mkt. 3.50 (*0-590-44010-1*, Scholastic Paperbacks) Scholastic, Inc.

Clifford, Laurie B. The Peppermint Gang & the Evergreen Castle. 1983. (Peppermint Gang Ser.: No. 1). (J). pap. o.p. (*0-8423-0776-1*) Tyndale Hse. Pubs.

Clifton, Lucille. Everett Anderson's Friend, ERS. (Illus.). 32p. (J). (gr. k-3). 1976. o.p. (*0-03-015161-9*); 1992. 16.95 (*0-8050-2246-5*) Holt, Henry & Co. (Holt, Henry & Co. Bks. For Young Readers).

—The Lucky Stone. 1986. (Illus.). 64p. (gr. 4-7). pap. text 3.99 (*0-440-45110-8*, Yearling) Random Hse. Children's Bks.

—Three Wishes. 1994. (Illus.). 32p. (J). (ps-3). pap. 4.99 o.s.i (*0-440-40921-7*) Dell Publishing.

—Three Wishes. 1992. 32p. (J). (ps-3). 15.00 o.s.i (*0-385-30497-8*) Doubleday Publishing.

—Three Wishes. (J). 1993. mass mkt. o.p. (*0-440-90064-6*); 1991. o.s.i (*0-385-30560-5*) Random Hse. Children's Bks. (Dell Books for Young Readers).

—Three Wishes. 1976. (Illus.). (J). (gr. k-3). 6.95 o.p. (*0-670-71063-6*) Viking Penguin.

Cline, Don. Antrim & Billy. 1990. (Early West Ser.). (Illus.). 170p. (YA). 19.95 (*0-932702-48-1*) Creative Publishing Co., Inc.

Clish, Marian L. Brice & Breezy: The Mall Adventure, Set. 2000. (Brice & Breezy Ser.). (J). (gr. k-3). (Illus.). 41p. pap. 7.95 (*1-928632-45-9*); (Illus.). 41p. per. 7.95 (*1-928632-46-7*); pap. 10.95 incl. audio (*1-928632-47-5*); (Illus.). pap. 14.95 incl. audio compact disk (*1-928632-48-3*) Writers Marketplace:Consulting, Critiquing & Publishing.

Clover, Peter. Sheltie Finds a Friend. 2000. (Sheltie! Ser.: Vol. 4). (Illus.). 96p. (J). (gr. 2-4). pap. 3.99 o.s.i (*0-689-83975-8*, Aladdin) Simon & Schuster Children's Publishing.

Clowes, Daniel. Ghost World. 1997. (YA). 19.95 o.p. (*1-56097-280-7*) Fantagraphics Bks.

Clymer, E. The Spider, the Cave & the Pottery Bowl. 1989. 80p. (J). (gr. k-6). pap. 2.75 o.s.i (*0-440-40166-6*, Yearling) Random Hse. Children's Bks.

Clymer, Eleanor. Luke Was There. 1992. (J). (gr. 4-6). 16.00 o.p. (*0-8446-6599-1*) Smith, Peter Pub., Inc.

Clymer, Susan. Four Month Friend. 1991. (J). (ps-3). pap. 2.75 o.p. (*0-590-42545-5*) Scholastic, Inc.

Clymer, Ted & Miles, Miska. Horse & The Bad Morning. 1982. (Illus.). 32p. (J). (ps-2). 8.95 o.p. (*0-525-45103-X*, Dutton) Dutton/Plume.

Cneut, Carll. The Amazing Love Story of Mr. Morf: An Astonishing Circus Romance. 2003. (Illus.). 32p. (J). (ps-3). tchr. ed. 15.00 (*0-618-33170-0*, Clarion Bks.) Houghton Mifflin Co. Trade & Reference Div.

Coady, Mary-Francis. Lucy Maud & Me. 121p. pap. 5.95 (*0-88878-398-1*) Beach Holme Pubs., Ltd. CAN. *Dist:* Strauss Consultants.

Coburn, John B. Anne & the Sand Dobbies. 1986. 121p. (J). (gr. 7-12). pap. 8.95 o.p. (*0-8192-1354-3*) Morehouse Publishing.

Coe-Hauskins, Carole. Eddy Ant & Friends: An Unexpected Journey. 1997. 36p. (J). (gr. k-3). 17.95 (*1-884187-49-8*) AMICA Publishing Hse.

Coffey, Maria. A Seal in the Family. 1999. (Illus.). 32p. (J). (gr. k-3). lib. bdg. 17.95 (*1-55037-581-4*) Annick Pr., Ltd. CAN. *Dist:* Firefly Bks., Ltd.

Cohen, Amanda. Two's Company. 1999. pap. 4.99 (*0-14-054901-3*) NAL.

Cohen, Barbara. Headless Roommate. 1984. (J). (gr. 7-12). mass mkt. 2.25 o.s.i (*0-553-26679-9*) Bantam Bks.

—The Long Way Home. 1992. (Illus.). 176p. (J). pap. 3.50 o.s.i (*0-553-15984-4*) Bantam Bks.

—Make a Wish, Molly. 1995. 48p. (gr. 4-7). pap. text 3.99 (*0-440-41058-4*); 1994. (Illus.). 40p. (J). 14.95 o.s.i (*0-385-31079-X*, Delacorte Pr.) Dell Publishing.

—Make a Wish, Molly. 1993. (J). o.s.i (*0-385-44599-7*) Doubleday Publishing.

—Make a Wish, Molly. 1994. (J). pap. 4.50 (*0-440-91018-8*, Dell Books for Young Readers) Random Hse. Children's Bks.

—Make a Wish, Molly. 1995. (J). 10.14 (*0-606-07831-2*) Turtleback Bks.

—Make a Wish Molly. 1995. (Illus.). (J). 10.55 (*0-7857-5404-0*) Econo-Clad Bks.

—Thank You, Jackie Robinson. annuals (Illus.). 128p. (J). 1997. (ps-3). pap. 4.99 (*0-688-15293-7*, Harper Trophy); 1988. (gr. 3-6). 15.00 o.p. (*0-688-07909-1*) HarperCollins Children's Bk. Group.

—Thank You, Jackie Robinson. 1997. 11.00 (*0-606-18309-4*) Turtleback Bks.

Cohen, Charles & Cohen, Miriam. See You Tomorrow, Charles. 1989. 32p. (J). (gr. k-6). pap. 2.95 o.s.i (*0-440-40162-3*) Dell Publishing.

Cohen, Miriam. It's George! 1989. (Welcome to First Grade! Ser.). 32p. (J). (gr. k-6). reprint ed. pap. 3.25 o.s.i (*0-440-40198-4*) Dell Publishing.

—Jim Meets the Thing. 1997. (Welcome to First Grade! Ser.). 10.19 (*0-606-13538-3*) Turtleback Bks.

—Liar, Liar, Pants on Fire! 1987. 32p. (J). (gr. k-6). pap. 3.25 o.s.i (*0-440-44755-0*, Yearling) Random Hse. Children's Bks.

—Second-Grade Friends. 1993. (J). pap. 3.99 (*0-590-47463-4*) Scholastic, Inc.

—Second-Grade Friends. 1993. (J). 8.19 o.p. (*0-606-05585-1*) Turtleback Bks.

—Second Grade-Friends Again! 1994. (J). (ps-3). pap. 3.99 (*0-590-45906-6*) Scholastic, Inc.

—Second Grade-Friends Again! 1994. (J). 8.70 o.p. (*0-606-06723-X*) Turtleback Bks.

—So What? 1988. 32p. (J). (gr. k-6). pap. 2.95 o.s.i (*0-440-40048-1*, Yearling) Random Hse. Children's Bks.

—Will I Have a Friend? 2002. (Illus.). (J). 13.40 (*0-7587-4028-X*) Book Wholesalers, Inc.

—Will I Have a Friend? 2nd ed. 1989. (Illus.). 32p. (J). (ps-3). reprint ed. pap. 4.99 (*0-689-71333-9*, Aladdin) Simon & Schuster Children's Publishing.

—Will I Have a Friend? 2nd ed. 1989. (J). 11.14 (*0-606-03955-4*) Turtleback Bks.

Colbert, Norman. Norman Okay, Not Today. 2001. 109p. pap. 10.95 (*0-7414-0674-8*) Buy Bks. on the Web.Com.

Cole, Babette. Prince Cinders. 1992. (Sandcastle Ser.). (Illus.). 32p. (J). (ps-3). 5.95 o.s.i (*0-399-21882-3*, Philomel) Penguin Group (USA) Inc.

—The Silly Book. 1990. 40p. (J). 12.95 o.s.i (*0-385-41237-1*); 13.99 o.s.i (*0-385-41238-X*) Doubleday Publishing.

—Winni Allfours. 1993. (J). 9.15 o.p. (*0-606-08389-8*) Turtleback Bks.

Cole, Brock. Celine, RS. 224p. (YA). (gr. 7-12). 2003. pap. 5.95 (*0-374-41082-8*, Sunburst); 1993. pap. 3.95 o.p. (*0-374-41083-6*, Aerial); 1989. 15.00 o.p. (*0-374-31234-6*, Farrar, Straus & Giroux (BYR)) Farrar, Straus & Giroux.

—Celine. Barbadillo, Pedro, tr. 1992. (SPA.). 176p. (YA). (gr. 7-12). 9.95 (*84-204-4711-0*) Santillana USA Publishing Co., Inc.

—Celine. 1991. (J). 10.00 (*0-606-00340-1*) Turtleback Bks.

—The Goats, RS. 192p. 1990. (J). (gr. 4-7). pap. 5.95 (*0-374-42575-2*, Sunburst); 1987. 15.00 o.p. (*0-374-32678-9*, Farrar, Straus & Giroux (BYR)); 1992. (YA). (gr. 7 up). reprint ed. pap. 3.95 o.p. (*0-374-42576-0*, Aerial) Farrar, Straus & Giroux.

—The Goats. l.t. ed. 1989. (Illus.). 208p. (J). lib. bdg. 16.95 o.s.i (*1-55736-113-4*, Cornerstone Bks.) Pages, Inc.

—The Goats. 2003. 20.75 (*0-8446-7238-6*) Smith, Peter Pub., Inc.

—The Goats. 1987. 11.00 (*0-606-03389-0*) Turtleback Bks.

Cole, Joanna. Anna Banana: 101 Jump-Rope Rhymes. 2002. (J). pap. (*0-590-44846-3*) Scholastic, Inc.

—El Autobus Magico Dentro de una Colmena. 1998. (Coleccion El Autobus Magico). (SPA., Illus.). 48p. (J). (gr. 4-7). pap. 4.99 (*0-590-25745-5*, SO7128, Scholastic en Espanola) Scholastic, Inc.

—Big Goof & Little Goof. (J). 1992. pap. 3.95 o.p. (*0-590-41592-1*); 1989. pap. 12.95 o.p. (*0-590-41591-3*) Scholastic, Inc.

—Bully Trouble. (Step into Reading Step 2 Bks.). (Illus.). 48p. 2004. (gr. 1-3). lib. bdg. 11.99 (*0-394-94949-8*); 1989. (ps-3). pap. 3.99 (*0-394-84949-3*) Random Hse. Children's Bks. (Random Hse. Bks. for Young Readers).

—Get Well, Gators! 2000. (gr. 1-4). pap. 4.95 (*0-688-17641-0*, Morrow, William & Co.) Morrow/Avon.

—The Missing Tooth. (Step into Reading Step 2 Bks.). (Illus.). 48p. (J). 2003. (gr. 1-3). lib. bdg. 11.99 (*0-394-99279-2*); 1988. (ps-3). pap. 3.99 (*0-394-89279-8*) Random Hse. Children's Bks. (Random Hse. Bks. for Young Readers).

Cole, Michelle. Lilla Belle the First Stages. 2003. (J). pap. 10.99 (*0-9722173-0-4*) Write World, Inc.

Cole, Sheila R. Meaning Well. 1975. 80p. (gr. 4-7). pap. 0.95 o.p. (*0-440-45556-1*) Dell Publishing.

Coleman, Gail S. Kevin & Ben. 1998. (Illus.). 16p. (J). (ps-k). pap. text 5.95 (*0-9655442-8-1*) Business Word, The.

Coleman, Michael. Hank the Clank. 1996. (Illus.). 32p. (J). (ps up). lib. bdg. 21.27 o.p. (*0-8368-1625-0*) Stevens, Gareth Inc.

—Weirdo's War. 1998. 192p. (J). (gr. 6-9). 17.99 o.p. (*0-531-33103-2*); (Illus.). (gr. 4-8). pap. 16.95 (*0-531-30103-6*) Scholastic, Inc. (Orchard Bks.).

Coles, William E., Jr. Another Kind of Monday. 1999. 256p. (J). (gr. 7-12). pap. 7.99 (*0-380-73133-9*, HarperTempest) HarperCollins Children's Bk. Group.

—Another Kind of Monday. 1996. 240p. (J). (gr. 7-12). 17.00 (*0-689-80254-4*, Atheneum) Simon & Schuster Children's Publishing.

—Another Kind of Monday. 1999. 13.04 (*0-606-16357-3*) Turtleback Bks.

Colfer, Eoin. Benny & Babe. 2001. 240p. (YA). pap. 7.95 (*0-86278-603-7*) O'Brien Pr., Ltd., The IRL. *Dist:* Independent Pubs. Group.

Collins, Pat L. My Friend Andrew. 1980. (Illus.). (J). (ps-2). o.p. (*0-13-608844-9*) Prentice-Hall.

Colman, Hila. Not for Love. 1983. 192p. (J). (gr. 5 up). 11.95 o.p. (*0-688-02419-X*, Morrow, William & Co.) Morrow/Avon.

Coman, Carolyn. Tell Me Everything, RS. 1995. 160p. (YA). pap. 3.95 o.p. (*0-374-47506-7*, Aerial) Farrar, Straus & Giroux.

—What Jamie Saw. 1997. (J). 11.04 (*0-606-12072-6*) Turtleback Bks.

Comfort, Louise. Daisy's Necklace. 2003. (Fairy Phones Ser.). (Illus.). 10p. (J). bds. 4.95 (*0-7641-5691-8*) Barron's Educational Series, Inc.

—Poppy's Party. 2003. (Fairy Phones Ser.). (Illus.). 10p. (J). bds. 4.95 (*0-7641-5694-2*) Barron's Educational Series, Inc.

—Rosie's Surprise. 2003. (Fairy Phones Ser.). (Illus.). 10p. (J). bds. 4.95 (*0-7641-5693-4*) Barron's Educational Series, Inc.

Compestine, Ying Chang. The Runaway Rice Cake. 2001. (Illus.). 40p. (J). (gr. k-4). 16.95 (*0-689-82972-8*, Simon & Schuster Children's Publishing) Simon & Schuster Children's Publishing.

Conford, Ellen. Anything for a Friend. 1992. 192p. (J). (gr. 4-7). pap. 3.50 o.s.i (*0-553-48081-2*) Bantam Bks.

—Anything for a Friend. 1979. (J). (gr. 3-7). 14.95 o.p. (*0-316-15308-7*) Little Brown & Co.

—Anything for a Friend. (J). (gr. 5-7). 1984. pap. (*0-671-54314-8*); 1981. pap. (*0-671-56069-7*) Simon & Schuster Children's Publishing. (Simon Pulse).

—Anything for Friend. 1987. (J). mass mkt. o.p. (*0-553-16762-6*, Dell Books for Young Readers) Random Hse. Children's Bks.

—Can Do, Jenny Archer. 1991. (Springboard Bks.). (Illus.). (J). (gr. 2-4). 11.95 o.p. (*0-316-15356-7*) Little Brown & Co.

—Can Do, Jenny Archer. 1993. 64p. (J). (ps-3). pap. 4.95 (*0-316-15372-9*, Tingley, Megan Bks.) Little Brown Children's Bks.

—Can Do, Jenny Archer. 1991. (Springboard Bks.). (J). 10.65 (*0-606-05778-1*) Turtleback Bks.

—Me & the Terrible Two. 1991. (J). (gr. 4-7). mass mkt. 4.95 o.p. (*0-316-15366-4*) Little Brown & Co.

—Me & the Terrible Two. 1987. (Illus.). (J). (gr. 3-6). pap. (*0-671-63666-9*, Aladdin) Simon & Schuster Children's Publishing.

—Why Me? 1985. 156p. (J). (gr. 5 up). 14.95 (*0-316-15326-5*) Little Brown & Co.

—Why Me? 1987. (YA). (gr. 7 up). pap. (*0-671-62841-0*, Simon Pulse) Simon & Schuster Children's Publishing.

—You Never Can Tell. 1988. 160p. (YA). (gr. 7 up). pap. (*0-671-66182-5*, Simon Pulse) Simon & Schuster Children's Publishing.

Conley, Lucy. Tattletale Sparkie & Other Stories. 1983. (Illus.). 197p. (J). (gr. 3-6). 9.40 (*0-7399-0078-1*, 2427) Rod & Staff Pubs., Inc.

Conly, Jane Leslie. What Happened on Planet Kid? 2002. (Illus.). 224p. (J). (gr. 5 up). pap. 5.95 (*0-06-441076-5*, Harper Trophy) HarperCollins Children's Bk. Group.

Conner, Ted. Friend vs. Friend in the Virtual World. 1994. (VR Troopers Ser.). 144p. (J). (gr. 2 up). 3.95 o.p. (*0-8431-3841-6*, Price Stern Sloan) Penguin Putnam Bks. for Young Readers.

Connors, Stompin' Tom. My Stompin' Grounds. 1992. 32p. pap. o.s.i (*0-385-25406-7*) Doubleday Canada, Ltd. CAN. *Dist:* Random Hse., Inc.

Connors, Tom. Bud the Spud. 1994. (Illus.). 74p. (J). (ps up). pap. 5.95 (*0-921556-43-8*) Ragweed Pr. CAN. *Dist:* Univ. of Toronto Pr.

Conrad, Pam. Holding Me Here. 192p. (YA). (gr. 7 up). 1997. pap. 4.95 (*0-06-447166-7*, Harper Trophy); 1986. 11.95 (*0-06-021338-8*); 1986. lib. bdg. 12.89 o.s.i (*0-06-021339-6*) HarperCollins Children's Bk. Group.

—What I Did for Roman. 1996. 9.60 o.p. (*0-606-10044-X*) Turtleback Bks.

Constance, Allen. Tickle Me: My Name Is Elmo. 1999. (Golden's Sesame Street Ser.). (J). 2.29 o.s.i (*0-307-98837-6*, Golden Bks.) Random Hse. Children's Bks.

Constantine. Kiquoti & the Coati. 2001. 40p. (J). (gr. k-3). 15.95 (*0-06-028309-2*) HarperCollins Children's Bk. Group.

Cook, Lyn. The Hiding Place. 148p. (J). mass mkt. 6.95 (*0-7737-5838-0*) Stoddart Kids CAN. *Dist:* Fitzhenry & Whiteside, Ltd.

Cooney, Caroline B. Among Friends. 1988. 176p. (YA). mass mkt. 3.99 o.p. (*0-553-27592-5*, Starfire); (gr. 8-12). mass mkt. 4.99 (*0-440-22692-9*, Dell Books for Young Readers) Random Hse. Children's Bks.

—Among Friends. 1987. (J). 10.55 (*0-606-04044-7*) Turtleback Bks.

—Fatality. 2001. 176p. mass mkt. 4.99 o.s.i (*0-439-13524-9*) Scholastic, Inc.

—Saturday Night. 1986. (J). pap. 2.95 o.p. (*0-590-44626-6*) Scholastic, Inc.

—Stranger. 1993. 176p. (YA). (gr. 7 up). mass mkt. 4.50 (*0-590-45680-6*) Scholastic, Inc.

Cooney, Doug. I Know Who Likes You. 2004. (Illus.). 224p. (J). 15.95 (*0-689-85419-6*, Simon & Schuster Children's Publishing) Simon & Schuster Children's Publishing.

Cooney, Ellen. Small Town Girl, 001. 1983. 208p. (J). (gr. 7 up). 9.95 o.p. (*0-395-33881-6*) Houghton Mifflin Co.

Cooney, Linda A. Breaking Away. 1991. (Totally Hot Ser.: No. 2). 224p. (J). mass mkt. 2.95 o.p. (*0-590-44561-8*) Scholastic, Inc.

—Playing Games. 1992. (Totally Hot Ser.: No. 6). (J). mass mkt. 2.95 o.p. (*0-590-44565-0*, Scholastic Paperbacks) Scholastic, Inc.

—Totally Hot, Staying Cool, No. 5. 1992. 176p. (J). mass mkt. 2.95 o.p. (*0-590-44564-2*, Scholastic Paperbacks) Scholastic, Inc.

Cooney, Linda A. & Cooney, Kevin. Making Changes. 1992. (Totally Hot Ser.: No. 4). 176p. (J). mass mkt. 2.95 o.p. (*0-590-44563-4*) Scholastic, Inc.

—Standing Alone. 1991. (Totally Hot Ser.: No. 3). 176p. (J). mass mkt. 2.95 o.p. (*0-590-44562-6*) Scholastic, Inc.

Coontz, Otto. Isle of the Shapeshifters, 001. 1983. 224p. (J). (gr. 5). 6.95 o.p. (*0-395-34552-9*) Houghton Mifflin Co.

Cooper, Ilene. Choosing Sides. 1990. 224p. (J). (gr. 4-7). 15.95 (*0-688-07934-2*) HarperCollins Children's Bk. Group.

—Frances Dances. 1991. (Frances in the Fourth Grade Ser.). (Illus.). 112p. (J). (gr. 3-6). pap. 2.95 o.s.i (*0-679-81111-7*, Knopf Bks. for Young Readers) Random Hse. Children's Bks.

—Mean Streak. 1992. (Kennedy School Kids Ser.: No. 3). 192p. (J). (gr. 3-7). pap. 3.99 o.p. (*0-14-034978-2*, Puffin Bks.) Penguin Putnam Bks. for Young Readers.

—No-Thanks Thanksgiving, Bk. 5. 1996. (Holiday Five Ser.). 128p. (J). (gr. 3-8). 14.99 o.s.i (*0-670-85657-6*, Viking) Penguin Putnam Bks. for Young Readers.

—Stupid Cupid. 1995. (Holiday Five Ser.). 144p. (J). (gr. 3-7). 14.99 o.s.i (*0-670-85059-4*, Viking Children's Bks.) Penguin Putnam Bks. for Young Readers.

—The Worst Noel. (Holiday 5 Ser.: Bk. 2). 160p. (J). (gr. 3-7). 1995. pap. 3.99 o.p. (*0-14-036518-4*, Puffin Bks.); 1994. 14.99 o.p. (*0-670-85058-6*, Viking Children's Bks.) Penguin Putnam Bks. for Young Readers.

Cooperman, Jeff & Salvadeo, Michele B. Waiting. 1994. (Under Twenty Writing Society Ser.). (Illus.). 48p. (J). (gr. 3-5). pap. 6.95 o.s.i (*1-56721-062-7*) 25th Century Pr.

Corcoran, Barbara. Rising Damp. 1980. (J). (gr. 5-9). 7.95 o.p. (*0-689-30736-5*, Atheneum) Simon & Schuster Children's Publishing.

—You Put up with Me, I'll Put up with You. 1989. 176p. (J). (gr. 3-7). pap. 2.50 (*0-380-70558-3*, Avon Bks.) Morrow/Avon.

—You Put up with Me, I'll Put up with You. 1987. 176p. (J). (gr. 5-9). lib. bdg. 12.95 o.s.i (*0-689-31305-5*, Atheneum) Simon & Schuster Children's Publishing.

Coret, Harriette. Better off Without Me: Reading Level 3. Billups, Annie, ed. 1993. (Sundown Fiction Collection). (Illus.). 80p. (J). pap. text 3.75 o.p. (*0-88336-762-9*); pap. text 21.00 o.p. incl. audio (*0-88336-222-8*); audio 18.50 o.p. (*0-88336-798-X*) New Readers Pr.

Corey, Deirdre. Best Wishes Whoever You Are. 1992. (Friends 4-Ever Ser.: No. 11). 144p. (J). mass mkt. 2.75 o.p. (*0-590-45111-1*, Scholastic Paperbacks) Scholastic, Inc.

—Friends 'til the Ocean Waves. 1990. (Friends 4-Ever Ser.: No. 6). 128p. (J). (gr. 3-7). pap. 2.75 o.p. (*0-590-44028-4*) Scholastic, Inc.

—Friends 'til the Thunder Claps. 1992. (Friends 4-Ever Ser.: No. 12). 144p. (J). mass mkt. 2.75 o.p. (*0-590-45112-X*, Scholastic Paperbacks) Scholastic, Inc.

—Friends 4-Ever: P.S. We'll Miss You, No. 1. 1990. (J). pap. 2.75 o.p. (*0-590-42627-3*) Scholastic, Inc.

—Mysteriously Yours. 1991. (Friends 4-Ever Ser.: No. 08). (J). (gr. 4-7). pap. 2.75 o.p. (*0-590-44030-6*, Scholastic Paperbacks) Scholastic, Inc.

—Remember Me When This You See. 1990. (Friends 4-Ever Ser.: No. 4). 144p. (J). (gr. 4-7). mass mkt. 2.75 (*0-590-42624-9*) Scholastic, Inc.

Cormier, Michael J. A Second Thought. 1992. (Publish-a-Book Ser.). (Illus.). 32p. (J). (gr. 1-6). lib. bdg. 22.83 (*0-8114-3578-4*) Raintree Pubs.

Cormier, Robert. Take Me Where the Good Times Are. 1991. 224p. (YA). mass mkt. 3.99 o.s.i (*0-440-21096-8*, Yearling) Random Hse. Children's Bks.

Cornish, Sam. Your Hand in Mine. 1970. (Curriculum Related Bks.). (Illus.). (J). (gr. 2-4). 5.50 o.p. (*0-15-299916-7*) Harcourt Children's Bks.

Cornwell, Don M. Horace the Pony & You. 1996. (Illus.). (Orig.). (J). (ps-4). pap. 4.95 (*0-9646734-1-X*) Cornwell, Don M. & Co., Inc.

Cosgrove, Stephen. Catundra. 2001. (Serendipity Bks.). (Illus.). 32p. (J). mass mkt. 4.99 (*0-8431-7684-9*, Price Stern Sloan) Penguin Putnam Bks. for Young Readers.

—Crickle Crack. 2001. (Serendipity Bks.). (Illus.). 32p. (J). (gr. k-4). pap. 4.99 (*0-8431-7648-2*, Price Stern Sloan) Penguin Putnam Bks. for Young Readers.

—Flutterby. 1995. (Serendipity Bks.). (Illus.). 32p. (J). (gr. 1-4). 4.99 (*0-8431-3821-1*, Price Stern Sloan) Penguin Putnam Bks. for Young Readers.

—Kartusch. 2001. (Serendipity Bks.). (Illus.). (J). pap. 4.99 (*0-8431-7650-4*, Price Stern Sloan) Penguin Putnam Bks. for Young Readers.

—Misty Morgan. 1987. (Serendipity Bks.: Set II). (Illus.). 32p. (J). (gr. k-4). lib. bdg. 12.66 o.p. (*0-86592-368-X*) Rourke Enterprises, Inc.

—Morgan & Me. 1985. (Serendipity Ser.). 9.15 o.p. (*0-606-02418-2*) Turtleback Bks.

—Morgan & Yew. (Serendipity Bks.). (Illus.). (J). 2001. pap. 4.99 (*0-8431-7651-2*); 1982. 32p. (gr. 1-4). 4.99 o.s.i (*0-8431-0589-5*) Penguin Putnam Bks. for Young Readers. (Price Stern Sloan).

—Morgan Mine. (Serendipity Bks.). (Illus.). 32p. (J). 1982. (gr. 1-6). 2.50 o.s.i (*0-8431-0590-9*); 2002. reprint ed. mass mkt. 4.99 (*0-8431-4873-X*) Penguin Putnam Bks. for Young Readers. (Price Stern Sloan).

—Morgan Morning. 1982. (Serendipity Bks.). (Illus.). 32p. (Orig.). (J). (gr. 1-4). 3.95 o.p. (*0-8431-0591-7*, Price Stern Sloan) Penguin Putnam Bks. for Young Readers.

—Rooty Tooty Snooty. 1988. (Snuffin Chronicles Ser.). (Illus.). 32p. (Orig.). (J). (ps-3). pap. 3.95 o.p. (*0-8249-8209-6*) Ideals Pubns.

—Sassafras. 1988. (Serendipity Bks.). (Illus.). 32p. (J). (gr. 1-4). 2.95 o.p. (*0-8431-2302-8*, Price Stern Sloan) Penguin Putnam Bks. for Young Readers.

—Tee Tee. 2003. (Serendipity Ser.). (Illus.). 32p. 4.99 (*0-8431-0488-0*, Price Stern Sloan) Penguin Putnam Bks. for Young Readers.

—Trafalgar True. 1987. (Serendipity Bks.). (Illus.). 32p. (J). (gr. k-4). 2.50 o.p. (*0-8431-0575-5*, Price Stern Sloan) Penguin Putnam Bks. for Young Readers.

Cosgrove, Stephen E. Hannah & Hickory: The Value of Honesty. 1990. (Stephen Cosgrove's Value Tales Ser.). (Illus.). 32p. (J). (gr. 1-5). lib. bdg. 21.36 o.p. (*0-89565-664-7*) Child's World, Inc.

—Persimmony: The Value of Friendship. 1990. (Stephen Cosgrove's Value Tales Ser.). (Illus.). 32p. (J). (gr. 1-5). lib. bdg. 21.36 o.p. (*0-89565-661-2*) Child's World, Inc.

Cosmic Debris Staff. Emily & Her Posse Journal. 2001. (Illus.). 128p. (YA). (gr. 8 up). 9.95 (*0-8118-3103-5*) Chronicle Bks. LLC.

—Emily I Want You to Leave Me Alone Journal. 2001. (Illus.). 128p. (YA). (gr. 8 up). 9.95 (*0-8118-3104-3*) Chronicle Bks. LLC.

Cossi, Olga. Adventure on the Graveyard of the Wrecks. 1991. 164p. (YA). (gr. 4-7). pap. 10.95 (*0-88289-808-6*) Pelican Publishing Co., Inc.

Costa, Nicoletta. A Friend Comes to Play. 1984. (Molly & Tom Bks.). (Illus.). 16p. (J). (gr. k-1). 3.50 o.p. (*0-448-23403-3*, Grosset & Dunlap) Penguin Putnam Bks. for Young Readers.

Costanza, Stephen. Mozart & Miss Bimbes. 2004. (J). 17.00 (*0-8050-6627-6*, Holt, Henry & Co. Bks. For Young Readers) Holt, Henry & Co.

Cote, Nancy. Palm Trees. 1993. (Illus.). 40p. (J). (ps-2). lib. bdg. 14.95 (*0-02-724760-0*, Simon & Schuster Children's Publishing) Simon & Schuster Children's Publishing.

Cotich, Felicia. Valda. 1983. 128p. (J). (gr. 7 up). 9.95 o.p. (*0-698-20574-X*) Putnam Publishing Group, The.

Cottonwood, Joe. Babcock. 1996. 240p. (YA). (gr. 4-7). pap. 15.95 (*0-590-22221-X*) Scholastic, Inc.

Cottringer, Anne. Bruna. 2003. (Illus.). 32p. (J). 16.95 (*1-58234-836-7*, Bloomsbury Children) Bloomsbury Publishing.

Couch, Donna E. The Photograph. 1992. (Illus.). 40p. (J). (gr. 1-6). 10.00 (*0-9634359-0-6*) Seabright Pr.

Coulton, Mia. Danny & Abby Are Friends. 2001. 16p. (J). 4.95 (*0-9713518-1-3*) Maryruth Bks., Inc.

Couric, Katie. The Brand New Kid. ed. 2001. (J). (gr. 1). spiral bd. (*0-616-07225-2*); (gr. 2). spiral bd. (*0-616-07226-0*) Canadian National Institute for the Blind/Institut National Canadien pour les Aveugles.

Relationships

Coursen, Valerie. Mordant's Wish, ERS. 1997. (Illus.). 40p. (J). (ps-3). 15.95 o.s.i (*0-8050-4374-8*, Holt, Henry & Co. Bks. For Young Readers) Holt, Henry & Co.

Cousins, Lucy. Maisy & Her Friends. 1999. (Maisy Bks.). (J). (ps). bds. 1.49 (*0-7636-0821-1*) Candlewick Pr.

—Maisy Cleans Up. 2002. (Illus.). 24p. (J). (ps-k). 9.99 o.s.i (*0-7636-1711-3*); bds. 3.29 (*0-7636-1712-1*) Candlewick Pr.

—Maisy's Best Friends. 2003. (Illus.). 10p. (J). bds. 5.99 (*0-7636-2128-5*) Candlewick Pr.

Coutant, Helen. The Gift. 1983. (Illus.). 48p. (J). (gr. 2-5). 9.95 o.s.i (*0-394-85499-3*, Knopf Bks. for Young Readers) Random Hse. Children's Bks.

Covault, Ruth M. Pablo & Pimienta (Pablo y Pimienta) 1998. (ENG & SPA., Illus.). 32p. (J). (ps-3). pap. 7.95 o.p. (*0-87358-708-1*, Rising Moon Bks. for Young Readers) Northland Publishing.

Covey, Stephen R. Walt Disney's Minnie Mouse & the Friendship Lockets. 1993. (Golden Book Ser.). (Illus.). 32p. (J). (ps-2). bds. o.p. (*0-307-16150-1*, Golden Bks.) Random Hse. Children's Bks.

Coville, Bruce. The Skull of Truth. 1997. (Magic Book Shop Ser.). (Illus.). 208p. (YA). (gr. 3-7). 17.00 (*0-15-275457-1*) Harcourt Children's Bks.

Cowan, Catherine. My Life with the Wave. ed. 2000. (J). (gr. 2). spiral bd. (*0-616-01621-2*) Canadian National Institute for the Blind/Institut National Canadien pour les Aveugles.

—My Life with the Wave. 2004. (Illus.). 32p. (J). pap. 6.99 (*0-06-056200-5*, Harper Trophy) HarperCollins Children's Bk. Group.

Cowan, Catherine & Paz, Octavio. My Life with the Wave. 1997. (Illus.). 32p. (J). (ps-3). 16.99 (*0-688-12660-X*); 16.89 (*0-688-12661-8*) HarperCollins Children's Bk. Group.

Cowan, Geoff. Hector Specter. 1996. (Little House of Horrors Ser.). (Illus.). (J). 3.50 o.p. (*0-8120-6605-7*) Barron's Educational Series, Inc.

Cowley, Joy. Agapanthus Hum & the Eyeglasses. 2001. (Easy-to-Read Ser.). (Illus.). 48p. (J). pap. 3.99 o.s.i (*0-698-11883-9*) Penguin Putnam Bks. for Young Readers.

Cox, Judy. Butterfly Buddies. 2001. (Illus.). 80p. (J). (gr. 1-4). tchr. ed. 15.95 (*0-8234-1654-2*) Holiday Hse., Inc.

—Butterfly Buddies. 2003. (Illus.). 96p. (gr. 2-5). pap. text 4.50 (*0-440-41885-2*, Yearling) Random Hse. Children's Bks.

Cox, Rhonda. Best Friends. (Illus.). 16p. (J). 2003. pap. text 20.00 net. (*1-57274-699-8*, BB2126); 1999. pap. text 5.00 (*1-57274-237-2*) Owen, Richard C. Pubs., Inc.

Coxe, Molly. Bookworm. 2000. (Road to Reading Ser.). (Illus.). 32p. (J). (ps-3). 11.99 (*0-307-46112-2*); pap. 3.99 (*0-307-26112-3*) Random Hse. Children's Bks. (Golden Bks.).

—Bookworm. 2000. (J). 10.14 (*0-606-18920-3*) Turtleback Bks.

Craig, Helen. Charlie & Tyler at the Seashore. 1996. 12.14 (*0-606-09136-X*) Turtleback Bks.

—A Welcome for Annie. 1994. (Illus.). 32p. (J). (ps up). bds. 4.99 o.p. (*1-56402-144-0*) Candlewick Pr.

Craig, Lynn. Friends Make the Difference. 1994. (Forever Friends Ser.: Bk. 2). (J). pap. 5.99 o.p. (*0-8407-9240-9*) Nelson, Thomas Inc.

—New Friends in New Places. 1994. (Forever Friends Ser.: Vol. 1). (J). pap. 5.99 o.p. (*0-8407-9239-5*) Nelson, Thomas Inc.

—Summer of Choices. 1994. (Forever Friends Ser.: Vol. 3). (J). pap. 5.99 o.p. (*0-8407-9241-7*) Nelson, Thomas Inc.

Crawford, Alice O. Please Say Yes. 1984. (Sweet Dreams Ser.: No. 59). 128p. (gr. 6-8). pap. text 2.25 o.p. (*0-553-24096-X*) Bantam Bks.

Crawford, Diane M. Comedy of Errors. 1992. (Sweet Dreams Ser.: No. 195). 144p. (J). (gr. 4-7). pap. 2.99 o.s.i (*0-553-29457-1*) Bantam Bks.

Creech, Sharon. Heartbeat. 2004. 192p. (J). 15.99 (*0-06-054022-2*); lib. bdg. 16.89 (*0-06-054023-0*) HarperCollins Pubs.

—Walk Two Moons. 2002. (Illus.). (J). 15.00 (*0-7587-0223-X*) Book Wholesalers, Inc.

—Walk Two Moons. (J). 2004. 304p. pap. 6.50 (*0-06-056013-4*, Harper Trophy); 1996. 288p. (gr. 7 up). pap. 6.50 (*0-06-440517-6*, Harper Trophy); 1994. 288p. (gr. 7 up). 16.99 (*0-06-023334-6*); 1994. 288p. (gr. 7 up). lib. bdg. 17.89 (*0-06-023337-0*) HarperCollins Children's Bk. Group.

—Walk Two Moons. 1999. (J). 9.95 (*1-56137-770-8*); 11.95 (*1-56137-771-6*) Novel Units, Inc.

—Walk Two Moons. (Assessment Packs Ser.). (J). 1998. 15p. pap. text, tchr.'s training gde. ed. 15.95 (*1-58303-067-0*); 1997. 32p. (gr. 5 up). pap. text, stu. ed., tchr.'s training gde. ed. 19.95 (*1-58303-030-1*) Pathways Publishing.

—Walk Two Moons. 280p. (J). (gr. 4-6). pap. 4.95 (*0-8072-1509-0*); 1997. pap. 37.00 incl. audio (*0-8072-7872-6*, YA 938 SP) Random Hse. Audio Publishing Group. (Listening Library).

—Walk Two Moons. l.t. ed. 2000. (Illus.). 287p. (J). 21.95 (*0-7862-2773-7*) Thorndike Pr.

—Walk Two Moons. 1996. (J). (gr. 5 up). 12.00 (*0-606-10018-0*) Turtleback Bks.

Cresswell, Helen. Bagthorpes Unlimited: Being the Third Part of the Bagthorpe Saga. 1978. 192p. (J). (gr. 5 up). lib. bdg. 14.95 o.p. (*0-02-725430-5*, Simon & Schuster Children's Publishing) Simon & Schuster Children's Publishing.

—Posy Bates & the Bag Lady. l.t. ed. 1994. (J). 16.95 o.p. (*0-7451-2669-3*) Chivers Large Print GBR. *Dist:* BBC Audiobooks America.

—The Watchers: A Mystery at Alton Towers. 1994. 160p. (J). (gr. 3-7). 15.95 o.s.i (*0-02-725371-6*, Simon & Schuster Children's Publishing) Simon & Schuster Children's Publishing.

Crew, Gary. The Watertower. 32p. (J). 2000. (gr. 2-9). pap. 7.95 (*1-56656-331-3*); 1998. (Illus.). (ps-6). 14.95 o.p. (*1-56656-233-3*) Interlink Publishing Group, Inc. (Crocodile Bks.).

Crimi, Carolyn. Don't Need Friends. 1999. (Illus.). 32p. (J). (ps-3). 15.95 o.s.i (*0-385-32643-2*) Doubleday Publishing.

—Don't Need Friends. 2001. 32p. (J). (ps-3). reprint ed. pap. 6.99 (*0-440-41532-2*, Dell Books for Young Readers) Random Hse. Children's Bks.

—Don't Need Friends. 2001. (Illus.). (J). 13.14 (*0-606-21156-X*) Turtleback Bks.

Crist, Darlene T. Losing Eubie. 1998. (Illus.). 40p. (J). (gr. 3-5). pap. 9.95 (*0-9665072-0-7*) Red Bird Publishing.

Cristaldi, Kathryn. Princess Lulu Goes to Camp. 1997. (All Aboard Reading Ser.: Level 2). (Illus.). 48p. (J). (gr. 1-3). 13.99 o.s.i (*0-448-41126-1*); 3.99 (*0-448-41125-3*) Penguin Putnam Bks. for Young Readers. (Grosset & Dunlap).

—Samantha the Snob. 1994. (Step into Reading Step 2 Bks.). (Illus.). 48p. (J). (ps-3). lib. bdg. 11.99 o.p. (*0-679-94640-3*); (gr. 1-3). pap. 3.99 (*0-679-84640-9*) Random Hse. Children's Bks. (Random Hse. Bks. for Young Readers).

Criswell, Millie. The Trials of Angela. 2002. 336p. mass mkt. 6.99 (*0-8041-1993-7*) Ballantine Bks.

—The Trials of Angela. l.t. ed. 2002. (Wheeler Softcover Ser.). 366p. pap. 23.95 (*1-58724-276-1*, Wheeler Publishing, Inc.) Gale Group.

Croll, Carolyn. Too Many Babas. 1994. (I Can Read Bks.). (Illus.). 80p. (J). (ps-1). pap. 3.50 o.p. (*0-06-444168-7*, Harper Trophy) HarperCollins Children's Bk. Group.

Cromwell, Patricia L. Marguerita & Sarabella's Glad Day. l.t. ed. 2001. (Illus.). 16p. (J). (ps-6). pap. 6.95 (*0-9664794-0-8*, 041998) Patty Cake Bks.

Cross, Gillian. Chartbreaker. 1989. (J). (gr. k-12). reprint ed. mass mkt. 2.95 o.s.i (*0-440-20312-0*, Laurel Leaf) Random Hse. Children's Bks.

—On the Edge. 1987. (J). (gr. 7 up). reprint ed. mass mkt. 2.75 o.s.i (*0-440-96666-3*, Laurel Leaf) Random Hse. Children's Bks.

Crossley, David, illus. Chitter Chatter! 2001. 12p. (ps-3). bds. 5.99 o.p. (*0-448-42454-1*) Penguin Putnam Bks. for Young Readers.

—Yakety Yak! 2001. 12p. (ps-3). bds. 5.99 o.p. (*0-448-42453-3*) Penguin Putnam Bks. for Young Readers.

Croteau-Fleury, Marie-Danielle. Des Citrouilles pour Cendrillon. 2003. (Premier Roman Ser.). (FRE., Illus.). 64p. (J). (gr. 2-5). pap. 8.95 (*2-89021-359-5*) La Courte Echelle CAN. *Dist:* Firefly Bks., Ltd.

Croteau-Fleury, Marie-Danielle & Back, Francis. De l'Or dans les Sabots. 1997. (Roman Jeunesse Ser.). (FRE.). 96p. (YA). (gr. 4-7). pap. 8.95 (*2-89021-297-1*) La Courte Echelle CAN. *Dist:* Firefly Bks., Ltd.

Croteau, Marie-Danielle. Un Pas dans L'Eternite. 1997. (Roman + Ser.). (FRE.). 160p. (YA). (gr. 8 up). pap. 8.95 (*2-89021-287-4*) La Courte Echelle CAN. *Dist:* Firefly Bks., Ltd.

Croteau, Marie-Danielle & Beauregard, Christiane. La Petite Fille Qui Voulait Etre Roi. 2001. (FRE., Illus.). 24p. (J). pap. 7.95 (*2-89021-541-5*) La Courte Echelle CAN. *Dist:* Firefly Bks., Ltd.

Croteau, Marie-Danielle & Cote, Genevieve. Et Si Quelqu'un Venait un Jour. 2002. (FRE.). 160p. (YA). pap. (*2-89021-560-1*) La Courte Echelle.

Crowther, Kitty. Jack & Jim. 2000. (Illus.). (J). lib. bdg. (*0-7868-1439-X*); 32p. 15.99 (*0-7868-0614-1*); 32p. lib. bdg. 16.49 (*0-7868-2527-8*) Hyperion Bks. for Children.

Cruise, Beth. Finders, Keepers. 1995. (Saved by the Bell: No. 9). 128p. (YA). (gr. 5-8). 3.95 (*0-689-80196-3*, Aladdin) Simon & Schuster Children's Publishing.

—Scene One, Take Two. 1995. (Saved by the Bell Ser.: No. 17). 144p. (YA). (gr. 5-8). 3.50 (*0-689-80091-6*, Simon Pulse) Simon & Schuster Children's Publishing.

Cruise, Robin & Cruise, Roberta Ann. Fiona's Private Pages. 200p. (J). (gr. 3-7). 2002. pap. 6.00 (*0-15-216572-X*, Harcourt Paperbacks); 2000. 15.00 o.s.i (*0-15-202210-4*) Harcourt Children's Bks.

Crum, Shutta. Spitting Image. 2003. 224p. (J). tchr. ed. 15.00 (*0-618-23477-2*, Clarion Bks.) Houghton Mifflin Co. Trade & Reference Div.

Crummel, Susan Stevens. Town Dog, Country Dog. Donohue, Dorothy, tr. & illus. by. 2004. (J). (*0-7614-5156-0*, Cavendish Children's Bks.) Cavendish, Marshall Corp.

Crummel, Susan Stevens & Stevens, Janet. Shoe Town. 2003. (Green Light Readers Level 2 Ser.). (Illus.). 32p. (J). 11.95 (*0-15-204882-0*); pap. 3.95 (*0-15-204842-1*, Green Light Readers) Harcourt Children's Bks.

Cullen, Lynn. The Backyard Ghost. 1993. 160p. (J). (gr. 4-7). 13.95 o.s.i (*0-395-64527-1*, Clarion Bks.) Houghton Mifflin Co. Trade & Reference Div.

—Ready, Set - Regina! 1996. (J). pap. 3.99 o.p. (*0-380-78427-0*, Avon Bks.) Morrow/Avon.

Cumings, Jean. Luna. 2001. (Illus.). 32p. (J). (ps-3). pap. 7.50 (*1-884083-24-2*) Maval Publishing, Inc.

Cummings, Carol. Sticks & Stones: Social Skill: Giving Compliments. 1992. (Get-Along Ser.). (Illus.). 24p. (J). (ps-3). pap. 4.99 (*0-9614574-8-1*) Teaching, Inc.

Cummings, Priscilla. Oswald & the Timberdoodles. 1990. (Illus.). 30p. (J). (gr. k-5). bds. 8.95 o.p. (*0-87033-411-5*, Tidewater Pubs.) Cornell Maritime Pr., Inc.

Cunliffe, John. Pat & the Puzzle Parcels. 1991. (Illus.). 32p. (J). (gr. k-2). pap. 11.95 o.p. (*0-233-98417-8*) Andre Deutsch GBR. *Dist:* Trafalgar Square, Trans-Atlantic Pubns., Inc.

Cunningham, Julia. Come to the Edge. 1977. (J). (gr. 7 up). 4.95 o.p. (*0-394-83432-1*); lib. bdg. 6.99 o.p. (*0-394-93432-6*) Knopf Publishing Group. (Pantheon).

—Oaf. 1986. (Illus.). 128p. (J). (gr. 2-6). 10.95 o.s.i (*0-394-87430-7*); 10.99 o.s.i (*0-394-97430-1*) Random Hse. Children's Bks. (Knopf Bks. for Young Readers).

Curtis, Christopher Paul. Bud, Not Buddy. unabr. ed. 2002. 256p. (J). (gr. 4-6). pap. 35.00 incl. audio (*0-8072-8210-3*, LYA 140 S(, Listening Library) Random Hse. Audio Publishing Group.

—Bud, Not Buddy. 2002. 256p. (gr. 4-7). pap. text 5.99 (*0-440-41328-1*, Random Hse. Bks. for Young Readers) Random Hse. Children's Bks.

Cusick, Richie Tankersley. Help Wanted. 1993. 224p. (YA). (gr. 7 up). mass mkt. 3.99 (*0-671-79403-5*, Simon Pulse) Simon & Schuster Children's Publishing.

—Teacher's Pet. 1990. 224p. (Orig.). (YA). (gr. 7-9). mass mkt. 3.50 (*0-590-43114-5*) Scholastic, Inc.

Cuthbert, Bob. Friends & More. 1999. (Illus.). 36p. (J). (gr. k-3). 14.95 (*0-9670394-0-1*) Billy B Enterprises.

Cuyler, Margery. The Trouble with Soap. 1982. 144p. (J). (gr. 5 up). 9.95 o.p. (*0-525-45111-0*, Dutton Children's Bks.) Penguin Putnam Bks. for Young Readers.

Dadey, Debbie & Jones, Marcia Thornton. Ghosts Don't Eat Potato Chips. 1992. (Adventures of the Bailey School Kids Ser.: No. 5). (Illus.). 96p. (J). (gr. 2-4). mass mkt. 3.99 (*0-590-45854-X*) Scholastic, Inc.

—Ghosts Don't Eat Potato Chips. 1992. (Adventures of the Bailey School Kids Ser.: No. 5). (J). (gr. 2-4). 10.14 (*0-606-01843-3*) Turtleback Bks.

Dafydd ab Hugh. The Pit. 1996. (Swept Away Ser.). 9.60 o.p. (*0-606-10339-2*) Turtleback Bks.

Dahan, Andre. My Friend the Moon. 1987. 32p. (J). (ps-3). 12.95 o.p. (*0-670-81569-1*, Viking Children's Bks.) Penguin Putnam Bks. for Young Readers.

Dahl, Roald. Matilda. 1989. (J). 16.00 (*0-606-10484-4*) Turtleback Bks.

—The Minpins. 1993. 12.14 (*0-606-07039-7*) Turtleback Bks.

Dahl, Roald & Blake, Quentin. Matilda. 1999. (J). 16.95 (*0-7540-6060-8*) BBC Audiobooks America.

Dahl, Tessa. Same but Different. 1993. (Illus.). 32p. (J). pap. 3.99 o.s.i (*0-14-054823-8*, Puffin Bks.) Penguin Putnam Bks. for Young Readers.

Dale. The Ivy. 1989. (J). (ps-2). 19.95 o.p. (*0-590-50128-3*) Scholastic, Inc.

Dale, Elizabeth. Scrumpy. 1996. (SPA.). 32p. (J). (gr. 1-3). 7.50 (*84-480-0150-8*) Lectorum Pubns., Inc.

Dale, Jack. A Sleep-Over Visit. 1986. (Big Little Golden Bks.). (Illus.). 24p. (J). (gr. k-3). o.p. (*0-307-10261-0*, Golden Bks.) Random Hse. Children's Bks.

Dalmatian Press Staff, adapted by. Anne of Green Gables. 2002. (Spot the Classics Ser.). (Illus.). 192p. (J). (gr. k-5). 4.99 (*1-57759-543-2*) Dalmatian Pr.

—Black Beauty. 2002. (Spot the Classics Ser.). (Illus.). 192p. (J). (gr. k-5). 4.99 (*1-57759-544-0*) Dalmatian Pr.

Dalton, Annie. The Real Tilly Beany. l.t. ed. 1993. (Illus.). (J). 16.95 o.p. (*0-7451-1807-0*, Galaxy Children's Large Print) BBC Audiobooks America.

Daly, Brian. Big & Hairy. Ashby, Ruth, ed. 1994. 144p. (Orig.). (J). (gr. 3-7). pap. 3.99 (*0-671-87111-0*, Aladdin) Simon & Schuster Children's Publishing.

Daly, Catherine. Best Friends, Vol. 7. 2000. (Bear in the Big Blue House Ser.: Vol. 7). (Illus.). 24p. (J). pap. 3.50 (*0-689-83453-5*, Simon Spotlight) Simon & Schuster Children's Publishing.

Daly, Niki. Bravo! Zan Angelo. 1924. (J). o.s.i (*0-688-15145-0*) HarperCollins Children's Bk. Group.

Daly, Niki, illus. & text. Once upon a Time, RS. 2003. 40p. (J). (gr. k-3). 16.00 (*0-374-35633-5*, Farrar, Straus & Giroux (BYR)) Farrar, Straus & Giroux.

Damon, Valerie H. Willo Mancifoot (and the Mugga Killa Whomps) Damon, Dave, ed. 1985. (Illus.). (J). (gr. 2-6). 14.95 (*0-932356-07-9*); 100.00 (*0-932356-08-7*) Star Pubns.

Dana, Barbara. Zucchini. 1984. 160p. (J). pap. 3.99 o.s.i (*0-553-15608-X*) Bantam Bks.

—Zucchini. 1982. (Charlotte Zolotow Bk.). (Illus.). 128p. (J). (gr. 3-6). 12.95 o.p. (*0-06-021394-9*); (gr. 4-7). lib. bdg. 15.89 (*0-06-021395-7*) HarperCollins Children's Bk. Group.

—Zucchini. 1984. 160p. pap. text 3.99 o.s.i (*0-440-41402-4*, Dell Books for Young Readers); (Illus.). (J). (gr. 3-6). pap. 2.50 o.s.i (*0-553-15437-0*, Skylark) Random Hse. Children's Bks.

—Zucchini. 1988. (Charlotte Zolotow Bks.). (J). 9.09 o.p. (*0-606-12588-4*) Turtleback Bks.

—Zucchini Out West. 1997. (Illus.). 160p. (J). (gr. 3-5). 14.95 o.p. (*0-06-024897-1*); lib. bdg. 14.89 o.s.i (*0-06-024898-X*) HarperCollins Children's Bk. Group.

Daniels, Lucy. Into the Blue. 2002. (J). pap. 29.95 incl. audio (*0-7540-6245-7*) BBC Audiobooks America.

Daniels, Teri. The Feet in the Gym. 1999. (Illus.). 40p. (J). (ps-3). 15.95 (*1-890817-12-0*) Winslow Pr.

Dank, Gloria R. The Forest of App. 1984. (J). (gr. 7 up). 2.25 (*0-399-21142-X*) Putnam Publishing Group, The.

Dann, Max. Adventures with My Worst Best Friend. 1987. (Illus.). 128p. (J). (gr. 2-6). 10.95 o.p. (*0-19-554361-0*) Oxford Univ. Pr., Inc.

—Bernice Knows Best. 1987. (Illus.). 32p. (J). (gr. k-3). 9.95 o.p. (*0-19-554414-5*) Oxford Univ. Pr., Inc.

—Going Bananas. 1987. (Illus.). 136p. (J). (ps up). 10.95 o.p. (*0-19-554460-9*) Oxford Univ. Pr., Inc.

—One Night at Lottie's House. 1987. (Illus.). 32p. (J). (gr. 1-4). 8.95 o.p. (*0-19-554637-7*) Oxford Univ. Pr., Inc.

Danziger, Paula. Amber Brown Goes Fourth. 1995. (Amber Brown Ser.: No. 3). (Illus.). 112p. (J). (gr. 3-6). 15.99 (*0-399-22849-7*, G. P. Putnam's Sons) Penguin Group (USA) Inc.

—Amber Brown Is Not a Crayon. 1994. (Amber Brown Ser.: No. 1). (Illus.). 80p. (J). (gr. 3-6). 15.99 (*0-399-22509-9*, G. P. Putnam's Sons) Penguin Group (USA) Inc.

—A Day No Pigs Would Fly. 1979. (J). mass mkt. 4.99 (*0-440-80173-7*) Dell Publishing.

—Forever Amber Brown. 1996. (Amber Brown Ser.: No.5). (Illus.). 112p. (J). (gr. 3-6). 14.99 (*0-399-22932-9*, G. P. Putnam's Sons) Penguin Group (USA) Inc.

—Forever Amber Brown. 1997. (Amber Brown Ser.: No.5). (J). (gr. 3-6). 10.04 (*0-606-11345-2*) Turtleback Bks.

—It's a Fair Day, Amber Brown. 2003. (Illus.). 48p. (J). pap. 3.99 (*0-698-11982-7*, PaperStar) Penguin Putnam Bks. for Young Readers.

—It's a Fair Day, Amber Brown. 2002. (Illus.). 48p. (J). (*0-399-23471-3*) Putnam Publishing Group, The.

—It's an Aardvark-Eat-Turtle World. 1985. 144p. (J). (gr. 7 up). 12.95 o.s.i (*0-385-29371-2*, Delacorte Pr.) Dell Publishing.

—It's an Aardvark-Eat-Turtle World. l.t. unabr. ed. 1989. 145p. (J). (gr. 4 up). 13.95 o.p. (*0-8161-4704-3*, Macmillan Reference USA) Gale Group.

—It's an Aardvark-Eat-Turtle World. 2000. 144p. (YA). (gr. 5-9). pap. 4.99 (*0-698-11691-7*, Puffin Bks.) Penguin Putnam Bks. for Young Readers.

—It's an Aardvark-Eat-Turtle World. 144p. 1996. (J). pap. 3.99 o.s.i (*0-440-41399-0*, Dell Books for Young Readers); 1986. (YA). (gr. 5 up). mass mkt. 3.99 o.p. (*0-440-94028-1*, Laurel Leaf) Random Hse. Children's Bks.

—It's an Aardvark-Eat-Turtle World. 2000. (Illus.). (J). 11.04 (*0-606-18469-4*); 1996. 9.09 o.p. (*0-606-00305-3*) Turtleback Bks.

—It's Justin Time, Amber Brown. 2002. (J). pap., tchr.'s planning gde. ed. 29.95 incl. audio (*0-87499-908-1*); pap., tchr.'s planning gde. ed. 29.95 incl. audio (*0-87499-908-1*); 25.95 incl. audio (*0-87499-907-3*); pap. 16.95 incl. audio (*0-87499-906-5*) Live Oak Media.

—It's Justin Time, Amber Brown. 2001. (Amber Brown Ser.: No. 10). (Illus.). 48p. (J). (gr. 3-6). 12.99 (*0-399-23470-5*, G. P. Putnam's Sons) Penguin Group (USA) Inc.

—It's Justin Time, Amber Brown. 2001. 10.14 (*0-606-22522-6*) Turtleback Bks.

—Not for a Billion Gazillion Dollars. 1998. (Matthew Martin Book Ser.). (Illus.). 126p. (J). (gr. 3-7). pap. 4.99 (*0-698-11693-3*, PaperStar) Penguin Putnam Bks. for Young Readers.

—Not for a Billion Gazillion Dollars. 1998. (Matthew Martin Book Ser.). 11.04 (*0-606-15956-8*) Turtleback Bks.

—Remember Me to Harold Square. 1987. 168p. (J). (gr. 7 up). 13.95 o.s.i (*0-385-29610-X*, Delacorte Pr.) Dell Publishing.

—Remember Me to Harold Square. 1999. (Illus.). 160p. (YA). (gr. 5-9). pap. 4.99 (*0-698-11694-1*, PaperStar) Penguin Putnam Bks. for Young Readers.

—Remember Me to Harold Square. 139p. (YA). (gr. 6 up). pap. 3.99 (*0-8072-1472-8*); 1995. (J). (gr. 7 up). pap. 23.00 incl. audio (*0-8072-7526-3*, YA874SP) Random Hse. Audio Publishing Group. (Listening Library).

—Remember Me to Harold Square. 1988. 144p. (J). (gr. k-12). mass mkt. 3.99 o.p. (*0-440-20153-5*, Laurel Leaf) Random Hse. Children's Bks.

—Remember Me to Harold Square. 1999. 10.04 (*0-606-16795-1*) Turtleback Bks.

—Seguiremos Siendo Amigos. 1994. (J). 16.00 (*0-606-10506-9*) Turtleback Bks.

—Seguiremos Siendo Amigos? 1997. (SPA., Illus.). 112p. (J). (gr. 3-5). 10.95 (*84-204-4857-5*, SAN8575) Alfaguara, Ediciones, S.A.- Grupo Santillana ESP. *Dist:* Santillana USA Publishing Co., Inc.

—Snail Mail No More. 2001. (Illus.). (J). 11.04 (*0-606-21436-4*) Turtleback Bks.

—United Tates of America. 2002. (J). (gr. 4). lib. bdg. 28.00 incl. audio compact disk (*1-932076-03-4*, 02003CA) Full Cast Audio.

—United Tates of America. 2002. (Illus.). 144p. (J). (gr. 3-7). pap. 15.95 (*0-590-69221-6*, Scholastic Pr.) Scholastic, Inc.

—What a Trip, Amber Brown. 2002. (J). pap., tchr.'s planning gde. ed. 29.95 incl. audio (*0-87499-912-X*); pap., tchr.'s planning gde. ed. 29.95 incl. audio (*0-87499-912-X*); 25.95 incl. audio (*0-87499-911-1*) Live Oak Media.

—What a Trip, Amber Brown. 2001. (Amber Brown Ser.: No. 9). (Illus.). 48p. (J). (gr. 3-6). 12.99 (*0-399-23469-1*, G. P. Putnam's Sons) Penguin Group (USA) Inc.

—What a Trip, Amber Brown. 2001. (Illus.). 48p. (J). pap. 3.99 (*0-698-11908-8*, Puffin Bks.) Penguin Putnam Bks. for Young Readers.

—What a Trip, Amber Brown. 2001. 10.14 (*0-606-22523-4*) Turtleback Bks.

Danziger, Paula & Martin, Ann M. P. S. Longer Letter Later: A Novel in Letters. 240p. (J). (gr. 3-5). pap. 4.99 (*0-8072-1537-6*, Listening Library) Random Hse. Audio Publishing Group.

—P. S. Longer Letter Later: A Novel in Letters. 234p. (J). 1999. (gr. 3-7). mass mkt. 4.99 o.s.i (*0-590-21311-3*); 1998. (gr. 5-8). pap. 15.95 (*0-590-21310-5*) Scholastic, Inc.

—Snail Mail No More. unabr. ed. 2000. (J). (gr. 3-6). audio 30.00 (*0-8072-8412-2*, YA194CX); 307p. (gr. 4-6). pap. 35.00 incl. audio (*0-8072-8413-0*) Random Hse. Audio Publishing Group. (Listening Library).

—Snail Mail No More. (Illus.). (J). 2001. 320p. (gr. 3-7). mass mkt. 4.99 (*0-439-06336-1*); 2000. 307p. (gr. 4-7). pap. 16.95 (*0-439-06335-3*, Scholastic Reference) Scholastic, Inc.

Darden, Hunter D. The Everlasting Snowman. 1996. (Illus.). 37p. (J). (gr. k-5). 16.95 (*0-9653729-0-1*) Sunfleur Pubns., Inc.

—The Reel Thing: A Story of Faith, Hope & Friendship. 2001. (Illus.). 44p. (J). (gr. k-5). 19.95 (*0-9653729-3-6*) Sunfleur Pubns., Inc.

Daugherty, George. Cat & Mouse. 2003. (Sagwa, the Chinese Siamese Cat Ser.). 24p. (J). mass mkt. 3.50 (*0-439-45598-7*) Scholastic, Inc.

David, Lawrence. The Terror of the Pink Dodo Balloons. 2003. (Illus.). 128p. (J). 14.99 (*0-525-46867-6*, Dutton Children's Bks.) Penguin Putnam Bks. for Young Readers.

David, Luke. Tommy's New Playmate. 1998. (Rugrats Ser.). (Illus.). 24p. (J). (ps-2). pap. 3.50 (*0-689-82141-7*, Simon Spotlight/Nickelodeon) Simon & Schuster Children's Publishing.

Davidson, Alice Joyce. Charlie Finds a Friend. 1996. (Charlie the Gentle Bear Ser.). (Illus.). (J). (ps-k). 5.95 (*0-88271-530-5*, 10117) Regina Pr., Malhame & Co.

Davidson, Betsy. Twyla Tulip & Her Talking Toes: A Friendship Story. 2000. (Illus.). 16p. (J). (gr. 1-3). pap. 6.95 (*1-57543-080-0*) MAR*CO Products, Inc.

Davidson, Doud P. Along the Endless Strip. 1992. 225p. (Orig.). (YA). pap. text 5.95 (*0-9630884-2-4*) Team Effort Publishing Co.

Davidson, Linda. Fast Forward, No. 6. 1989. (Endless Summer Ser.: No. 6). (YA). (gr. 10 up). mass mkt. 2.95 o.s.i (*0-8041-0246-5*, Ivy Bks.) Ballantine Bks.

Davidson, Neil. The Sweet Revenge of Melissa Chavez: A Novel. 1995. 178p. (YA). (gr. 9 up). lib. bdg. 18.95 o.p. (*0-936389-39-7*) Tudor Pubs., Inc.

Davies, Bettilu D. Tall Trouble. 1981. (Marty Ser.). 160p. (J). (gr. 6). pap. 2.95 o.p. (*0-8024-8112-4*) Moody Pr.

Davies, Sally J. K. When William Went Away. 1998. (Picture Bks.). (Illus.). 32p. (J). (ps-3). lib. bdg. 15.95 (*1-57505-303-9*, Carolrhoda Bks.) Lerner Publishing Group.

—Why Did We Have to Move Here? 1997. (Picture Bks.). (Illus.). 32p. (J). (ps-3). lib. bdg. 15.95 (*1-57505-046-3*, Carolrhoda Bks.) Lerner Publishing Group.

Davis, Allison. Rosita's New Friends. 1994. (Golden's Sesame Street Ser.). (Illus.). 24p. (J). o.p. (*0-307-13129-7*, Golden Bks.) Random Hse. Children's Bks.

Davis, Allison & Brannon, Tom. Imagine, a Wish for Grover: Sesame Street. 1999. (Illus.). 24p. (J). (ps-3). pap. 3.29 o.s.i (*0-307-13130-0*, Golden Bks.) Random Hse. Children's Bks.

Davis, Dawn S. Fishing Buddies. 1991. (Illus.). 52p. (Orig.). (J). (gr. 5-6). pap. 3.95 o.p. (*1-879318-03-2*) Country Lane Ltd.

Davis, Gibbs. Fishman & Charly, 001. 1983. 160p. (J). (gr. 5 up). 8.95 o.p. (*0-395-33882-4*) Houghton Mifflin Co.

—Swann Song. 1989. 176p. (YA). (gr. 7 up). mass mkt. 2.50 (*0-380-75609-9*, Avon Bks.) Morrow/Avon.

Davis, Jennie. Julie's New Home: A Story about Being a Friend. 1983. (Making Choices Ser). (Illus.). 30p. (J). (gr. k-3). 11.93 o.p. (*0-516-06384-7*, Children's Pr.) Scholastic Library Publishing.

Davis, Jenny. Good-Bye & Keep Cold. 1989. 224p. (J). mass mkt. 2.95 o.s.i (*0-440-20481-X*, Laurel Leaf) Random Hse. Children's Bks.

Davis, Maggie S. The Rinky-Dink Cafe. 1988. (Illus.). 32p. (J). (ps-3). pap. 12.95 o.p. (*0-671-66408-5*, Simon & Schuster Children's Publishing) Simon & Schuster Children's Publishing.

Davis, Rebecca. Jake Riley: Irreparably Damaged. 2003. 272p. (J). 15.99 (*0-06-051837-5*) HarperCollins Pubs.

Davis, Russell B. & Ashabranner, Brent K. The Choctaw Code. 1994. (Illus.). 152p. (J). (gr. 4-8). reprint ed. lib. bdg. 19.50 (*0-208-02377-1*, Linnet Bks.) Shoe String Pr., Inc.

Davoli, Barbara. Saved by the Bell. 1997. 24p. (J). (ps-2). pap. (*0-7814-3025-9*) Cook Communications Ministries.

Davoll, Barbara. Christopher & His Friends. 2003. (Christopher Churchmouse Ser.). (Illus.). 128p. (J). 14.99 (*0-8423-5734-3*) Tyndale Hse. Pubs.

—Flood of Friends. 1990. (Christopher Churchmouse Classics Ser.). (Illus.). (J). (ps-2). 8.99 (*0-89693-538-8*, 6-1538) Cook Communications Ministries.

—Saved by the Bell. 1988. (Christopher Churchmouse Classics Ser.). (Illus.). 24p. (J). (ps-2). 8.99 (*0-89693-403-9*, 6-1403) Cook Communications Ministries.

—Saved by the Bell. 1999. (Christopher Churchmouse Classics Ser.). (Illus.). 24p. (J). (ps-3). 7.99 (*0-8024-4934-4*) Moody Pr.

—A Visit from Rudy Beaver. 1996. (Tales from Schroon Lake Ser.: No. 2). (Illus.). (J). (ps-3). 7.99 (*0-8024-1034-0*, 672) Moody Pr.

Davoll, Barbara & Hockerman, Dennis. Saved by the Bell. 1988. (Christopher Churchmouse Ser.). (Illus.). 24p. (J). (ps-2). 11.99 incl. audio (*0-89693-614-7*, 3-1614) Cook Communications Ministries.

Dawson, Phoebe. Joshua Finds a Friend. 1998. (Child of Destiny Ser.). (Illus.). 24p. (J). (gr. k-5). 9.95 (*1-889018-47-3*) Micah Publishing.

Day, Alexandra. Children from the Golden Age. 1998. (J). pap. 14.95 (*0-671-75200-6*, Simon & Schuster Children's Publishing) Simon & Schuster Children's Publishing.

—Frank & Ernest. 1991. (Illus.). 48p. (J). (gr. k-3). mass mkt. 3.95 o.p. (*0-590-41556-5*, Scholastic Paperbacks) Scholastic, Inc.

Day, Lauren. Can You Keep a Secret? 2000. (Rockett's World Ser.: No. 4). 128p. (J). (gr. 4-7). mass mkt. 3.99 (*0-439-08210-2*, Scholastic Paperbacks) Scholastic, Inc.

—Can You Keep a Secret? 2000. (Rockett's World Ser.: No. 4). (J). (gr. 4-7). 10.04 (*0-606-18594-1*) Turtleback Bks.

—What Kind of Friend Are You? 1999. (Rockett's World Ser.: No. 2). (Illus.). 128p. (J). (gr. 4-7). mass mkt. 3.99 (*0-439-06312-4*) Scholastic, Inc.

—What Kind of Friend Are You? 1999. (Rockett's World Ser.: No. 2). (J). (gr. 4-7). 10.04 (*0-606-17050-2*) Turtleback Bks.

De Backker, Vera. En Cuerpo y Alma. 1993. (SPA., Illus.). 32p. (J). (ps-1). pap. 5.95 (*0-8120-1743-9*) Barron's Educational Series, Inc.

De Beer, Hans. Ahoy There, Little Polar Bear. (Illus.). (J). (ps). 1999. 14p. 6.95 o.p. (*0-7358-1079-6*); 1997. (JPN., 32p. 15.95 o.s.i (*4-924684-46-5*); 1995. 32p. pap. 6.95 (*1-55858-389-0*); 1988. 32p. 15.95 (*1-55858-028-X*); 1945. 32p. 13.88 o.p. (*1-55858-240-1*) North-South Bks., Inc.

—Ahoy There, Little Polar Bear. 1995. (J). 13.10 (*0-606-08683-8*) Turtleback Bks.

—Der Kleine Eisbar und der Angsthase.Tr. of Little Polar Bear & the Brave Little Hare. (GER., Illus.). (J). (gr. k-3). 1999. 15.95 (*3-314-00675-6*); 1995. 12.95 o.p. (*3-314-00000-6*) North-South Bks., Inc.

—Little Polar Bear Finds a Friend. 1996. (Illus.). 32p. (J). (gr. k-3). pap. 6.95 (*1-55858-607-5*) North-South Bks., Inc.

—Little Polar Bear, Take Me Home! 1996. (Illus.). 32p. (J). (gr. k-3). 15.95 (*1-55858-630-X*); 14.50 o.p. (*1-55858-631-8*) North-South Bks., Inc.

—Llevame a Casa, Osito Polar! Gambolini, Gerardo, tr. from GER. 2001. (ENG & SPA., Illus.). 32p. (J). (gr. k-3). pap. 6.95 (*0-7358-1500-3*, NS30711, Ediciones Norte-Sur) North-South Bks., Inc.

—El Osito Polar y el Conejito Valiente. Antresyan, Augustin, tr. from GER. 2000. (SPA., Illus.). 32p. (J). (gr. k-3). 15.95 (*0-7358-1004-4*, NS1830); pap. 6.95 (*0-7358-1005-2*, NS1539) North-South Bks., Inc.

—El Osito Polar y el Gran Globo. Gambolini, Gerardo, tr. from GER. 2002. (SPA., Illus.). 32p. (J). (gr. k-3). 15.95 (*0-7358-1738-3*, Ediciones Norte-Sur) North-South Bks., Inc.

—Piuma E il Coniglietto Fifone. 1998. Tr. of Little Polar Bear & the Brave Little Hare. (ITA., Illus.). (J). 15.95 (*88-8203-045-8*) North-South Bks., Inc.

—Piuma Nel Paese delle Tigri. 1997. Tr. of Little Polar Bear, Take Me Home!. (ITA., Illus.). 32p. (J). (ps-3). 15.95 (*88-8203-020-2*) North-South Bks., Inc.

De Beer, Hans & Gambolini, Gerardo. Llevame a Casa, Osito Polar! 2001. (ENG & SPA., Illus.). 32p. (J). (gr. k-3). 15.95 (*0-7358-1499-6*, NS30712, Ediciones Norte-Sur) North-South Bks., Inc.

de Brunhoff, Laurent. Babar's Little Girl Makes a Friend. 2002. (Babar Ser.). (Illus.). 32p. (J). (ps-3). 9.95 (*0-8109-0556-6*) Abrams, Harry N. , Inc.

De Graaf, Anne. Peter. 2001. (Illus.). 38p. (J). (ps-1). 5.99 (*0-8054-2189-0*) Broadman & Holman Pubs.

de la Mare, Walter. Visitors. 1993. (Creative Short Stories Ser.). 32p. (YA). (gr. 3-12). lib. bdg. 18.60 (*0-88682-070-7*, 1078-9, Creative Education) Creative Co., The.

de Paola, Tomie. Big Anthony: His Story. 1998. (Illus.). 32p. (J). (ps-3). 16.99 (*0-399-23189-7*) Penguin Group (USA) Inc.

—Bill & Pete. 1992. (Illus.). 32p. (J). (ps-1). 5.95 o.s.i (*0-399-22402-5*, Sandcastle Bks.) Penguin Group (USA) Inc.

—Four Friends at Christmas. 2002. (Illus.). 32p. (J). 14.95 (*0-689-85282-7*, Simon & Schuster Children's Publishing) Simon & Schuster Children's Publishing.

—Four Friends in Autumn. 2004. (J). 14.95 (*0-689-85980-5*, Simon & Schuster Children's Publishing) Simon & Schuster Children's Publishing.

—Four Friends in Summer. 2003. (Illus.). 32p. (J). reprint ed. 14.95 (*0-689-85693-8*, Simon & Schuster Children's Publishing) Simon & Schuster Children's Publishing.

—Four Stories for Four Seasons. 1987. (Illus.). 48p. (J). (gr. 5 up). 12.95 o.s.i (*0-13-330119-2*) Prentice Hall PTR.

—Four Stories for Four Seasons. 1980. (Illus.). (J). (ps-3). lib. bdg. 9.95 o.p. (*0-13-330175-3*, Simon & Schuster) Simon & Schuster.

—Four Stories for Four Seasons. (Illus.). (J). (ps-3). 1994. 48p. pap. 6.99 (*0-671-88633-9*, Aladdin); 1987. 48p. pap. 15.00 o.s.i (*0-671-66686-X*, Simon & Schuster Children's Publishing); 1980. 3.95 o.s.i (*0-13-330100-1*, Simon & Schuster Children's Publishing) Simon & Schuster Children's Publishing.

—Kit & Kat. 1994. (All Aboard Reading Ser.). (J). 10.14 (*0-606-07765-0*) Turtleback Bks.

—Memo y Leo, 1999. (SPA., Illus.). 32p. (J). (gr. 1-3). pap. text 6.99 (*980-257-223-3*) Ekare, Ediciones VEN. *Dist:* Kane/Miller Bk. Pubs., Lectorum Pubns., Inc.

—T-Rex Is Missing! 2002. (All Aboard Reading Ser.). (Illus.). 32p. (J). 3.99 (*0-448-42870-9*); 13.89 (*0-448-42882-2*) Penguin Putnam Bks. for Young Readers.

—26 Fairmount Avenue Flip-Over Book. 2002. pap. 5.99 (*0-698-11954-1*) Penguin Putnam Bks. for Young Readers.

De Regniers, Beatrice Schenk. Going for a Walk. 1993. (Illus.). 32p. (J). (ps-1). 15.00 o.p. (*0-06-022954-3*); lib. bdg. 14.89 o.p. (*0-06-022957-8*) HarperCollins Children's Bk. Group.

—How Joe the Bear & Sam the Mouse Got Together. 1990. (Illus.). 32p. (J). (ps-2). 12.95 o.p. (*0-688-09079-6*); lib. bdg. 12.88 o.p. (*0-688-09080-X*) HarperCollins Children's Bk. Group.

—May I Bring a Friend? 1999. pap. 13.40 (*0-88103-362-6*) Econo-Clad Bks.

—May I Bring a Friend? 1964. 12.14 (*0-606-01049-1*) Turtleback Bks.

—A Week in the Life of Best Friends. 1988. (Illus.). 48p. (J). (gr. 2-7). pap. 2.50 o.p. (*0-590-41461-5*) Scholastic, Inc.

—A Week in the Life of Best Friends: And Other Poems of Friendship. 1986. (Illus.). 48p. (J). (gr. 3-7). lib. bdg. 13.95 o.p. (*0-689-31179-6*, Atheneum) Simon & Schuster Children's Publishing.

de Trevino, Elizabeth Borton. I, Juan de Pareja. 1965. (J). 11.00 (*0-606-04126-5*) Turtleback Bks.

De Vries, Anke. Piggy's Birthday Dream. 1997. (Illus.). 32p. (J). (ps-k). 14.95 (*1-886910-21-9*, Front Street) Front Street, Inc.

Dean, Karen S. Cammy Takes a Bow. 1988. (J). (gr. 3-7). pap. 2.50 (*0-380-75400-2*, Avon Bks.) Morrow/Avon.

Dean, Theresa M. Pocket Full of Memories Journal. 1994. (Illus.). 24p. (J). (gr. 4-7). pap. 9.95 (*1-881511-03-0*) Pockets Pr.

Deaver, Julie Reece. First Wedding, Once Removed. (Charlotte Zolotow Bk.). 224p. (gr. 5-9). 1993. (YA). pap. 4.95 o.p. (*0-06-440402-1*, Harper Trophy); 1990. (J). 13.95 (*0-06-021426-0*); 1990. (J). lib. bdg. 13.89 o.p. (*0-06-021427-9*) HarperCollins Children's Bk. Group.

DeBear, Kirsten. Be Quiet Marina! 2001. (Illus.). 40p. (J). (ps-3). 16.95 (*1-887734-79-1*) Star Bright Bks., Inc.

DeBruyn, Monica. Lauren's Secret Ring. Fay, Ann, ed. 1980. (Albert Whitman Concept Bks.: Level 1). (Illus.). (J). (gr. 1-3). lib. bdg. 10.75 o.p. (*0-8075-4391-8*) Whitman, Albert & Co.

Decker, Marjorie Ainsborough. Bless My Little Friends! 2001. (Christian Mother Goose Ser.). (Illus.). 14p. (J). (ps-k). bds. 5.99 o.s.i (*0-448-42510-6*, Philomel) Penguin Putnam Bks. for Young Readers.

DeClements, Barthe. I Never Asked You to Understand Me. 1998. (Puffin Novel Ser.). 144p. (YA). (gr. 7-12). pap. 4.99 o.p. (*0-14-130059-0*) Penguin Putnam Bks. for Young Readers.

—Liar, Liar. 1998. (Accelerated Reader Bks.). 144p. (J). (gr. 3-7). lib. bdg. 14.95 (*0-7614-5021-1*, Cavendish Children's Bks.) Cavendish, Marshall Corp.

—Monkey See, Monkey Do. 1992. 160p. (J). (gr. 4-7). pap. 3.50 o.s.i (*0-440-40675-7*, Yearling) Random Hse. Children's Bks.

—No Place for Me. 1988. 144p. (J). (gr. 6-8). reprint ed. mass mkt. 2.50 o.p. (*0-590-41812-2*, Scholastic Paperbacks) Scholastic, Inc.

—Nothing's Fair in Fifth Grade. 1981. 144p. (J). (gr. 4-7). 15.99 (*0-670-51741-0*, Viking Children's Bks.) Penguin Putnam Bks. for Young Readers.

—Nothing's Fair in Fifth Grade. 1988. (J). pap. 2.75 o.p. (*0-590-42316-9*) Scholastic, Inc.

—The Pickle Song. (J). (gr. 3-7). 1995. (Illus.). 144p. pap. 3.99 o.p. (*0-14-036567-2*, Puffin Bks.); 1993. 160p. 13.99 o.s.i (*0-670-85101-9*, Viking Children's Bks.) Penguin Putnam Bks. for Young Readers.

—Spoiled Rotten. 1996. (Hyperion Chapters Ser.). (Illus.). 64p. (J). (gr. 2-3). pap. 3.95 o.s.i (*0-7868-1145-5*) Disney Pr.

—Spoiled Rotten. (J). (gr. 3-4). 1997. 64p. lib. bdg. 14.49 (*0-7868-2317-8*); 1996. (Illus.). 13.95 (*0-7868-0275-8*) Hyperion Bks. for Children.

Deem, James M. Three NBs of Julian Drew. 1994. 224p. (J). (gr. 7 up). tchr. ed. 16.00 o.s.i (*0-395-69453-1*) Houghton Mifflin Co.

—Three NBs of Julian Drew. 1996. 176p. (J). pap. 4.50 o.s.i (*0-380-72587-8*, Avon Bks.) Morrow/Avon.

—Three NBs of Julian Drew. 1996. 9.60 o.p. (*0-606-08959-4*) Turtleback Bks.

Deeter, Catherine. Seymour Bleu: A Space Odyssey. 1998. (Illus.). 40p. (J). (ps-3). 16.00 (*0-689-80137-8*, Simon & Schuster Children's Publishing) Simon & Schuster Children's Publishing.

Degens, T. Freya on the Wall. 1997. 288p. (J). 19.00 o.s.i (*0-15-200210-3*) Harcourt Trade Pubs.

—Friends. 1981. 160p. (J). (gr. 7 up). 9.95 o.p. (*0-670-33051-5*) Viking Penguin.

DeGroat, Diane. Happy Birthday to You, You Belong in a Zoo. 1999. (Illus.). 32p. (J). (ps-3). 15.00 (*0-688-16544-3*); lib. bdg. 15.89 (*0-688-16545-1*) HarperCollins Children's Bk. Group.

—Roses Are Pink, Your Feet Really Stink. 1997. 11.10 (*0-606-11812-8*) Turtleback Bks.

Delaney, Mark. The Vanishing Chip. 1998. (Misfits, Inc. Ser.: No. 1). 192p. (YA). (gr. 7-11). pap. 5.95 (*1-56145-176-2*, Peachtree Junior) Peachtree Pubs., Ltd.

—The Vanishing Chip. 1998. (Misfits, Inc. Ser.). 12.00 (*0-606-15752-2*) Turtleback Bks.

Delaney, Michael. Birdbrain Amos. 2004. (Illus.). 160p. 5.99 (*0-14-240031-9*, Puffin Bks.) Penguin Putnam Bks. for Young Readers.

—Deep Doo-Doo & the Mysterious E-mails. Monfried, Lucia, ed. 2001. 128p. (J). (gr. 3-7). 15.99 (*0-525-46530-8*, Dutton Children's Bks.) Penguin Putnam Bks. for Young Readers.

—Deep Doo-Doo & the Mysterious E-Mails. 2002. 160p. (J). (gr. 3-7). pap. 5.99 (*0-14-230205-8*, Puffin Bks.) Penguin Putnam Bks. for Young Readers.

Delaney, Ned. A Worm for Dinner, 001. 1977. (Illus.). (J). (gr. k-3). 6.95 o.p. (*0-395-25153-2*) Houghton Mifflin Co.

Dell, Pamela. Blood in the Water: A Story of Friendship During the Mexican War. 2003. (J). (*1-59187-042-9*) Tradition Publishing Co.

Delton, Jina. Two Blocks Down. 1981. 160p. (gr. 7 up). 8.95 o.p. (*0-06-021590-9*); lib. bdg. 8.79 o.p. (*0-06-021591-7*) HarperCollins Pubs.

Delton, Judy. Angel Bites the Bullet. 2000. (Illus.). 112p. (J). (gr. 4-6). tchr. ed. 15.00 (*0-618-04085-4*) Houghton Mifflin Co. Trade & Reference Div.

—Angel's Mother's Boyfriend. 1986. (Illus.). 176p. (J). (gr. 4-6). tchr. ed. 16.00 (*0-395-39968-8*) Houghton Mifflin Co.

—Blue Skies, French Fries. 1988. (Pee Wee Scouts Ser.: No. 4). 96p. (gr. 2-5). pap. text 3.99 (*0-440-40064-3*, Yearling) Random Hse. Children's Bks.

—Bookworm Buddies. 1996. (Pee Wee Scouts Ser.: No. 30). (Illus.). 112p. (gr. 2-5). pap. text 3.99 o.s.i (*0-440-40981-0*) Dell Publishing.

—Bookworm Buddies. 1996. (Pee Wee Scouts Ser.: No. 30). (J). (gr. 2-5). 10.04 (*0-606-10902-1*) Turtleback Bks.

—Lee Henry's Best Friend. Fay, Ann, ed. 1980. (Albert Whitman Concept Bks.: Level I). (Illus.). (J). (gr. k-3). lib. bdg. 10.25 o.p. (*0-8075-4417-5*) Whitman, Albert & Co.

—Merry Merry Huckleberry. 1990. (Condo Kids Ser.: No. 6). (Illus.). 128p. (J). pap. 2.95 o.s.i (*0-440-40365-0*) Dell Publishing.

—On a Picnic. 1979. (Illus.). 64p. (gr. k-3). lib. bdg. 6.95 o.p. (*0-385-12945-9*) Doubleday Publishing.

—The Pee Wee Jubilee. 1989. (Pee Wee Scouts Ser.: No. 11). 96p. (gr. 2-5). pap. text 3.99 o.s.i (*0-440-40226-3*, Yearling) Random Hse. Children's Bks.

—The Pee Wee Jubilee. 1989. (Pee Wee Scouts Ser.: No. 11). (J). (gr. 2-5). 10.14 (*0-606-04296-2*) Turtleback Bks.

—The Perfect Christmas Gift. 1992. (Illus.). 32p. (J). (gr. k-3). lib. bdg. 13.95 (*0-02-728471-9*, Simon & Schuster Children's Publishing) Simon & Schuster Children's Publishing.

—Scary, Scary Huckleberry. 1990. (Congo Kids Ser.: No. 5). (Illus.). 128p. (J). (gr. k-6). pap. 2.95 o.s.i (*0-440-40336-7*, Yearling) Random Hse. Children's Bks.

—Super Duper Pee Wee! 1995. (Pee Wee Scouts Ser.: No. 26). 144p. (gr. 2-5). pap. text 3.99 o.s.i (*0-440-40992-6*) Dell Publishing.

—Two Good Friends. 1988. (Illus.). 32p. (J). (gr. k-3). 5.50 o.s.i (*0-517-51401-X*, Crown) Crown Publishing Group.

—Two Good Friends. 1985. (Illus.). 32p. (J). (ps-3). 1.00 o.p. (*0-517-55949-8*) Random Hse. Value Publishing.

—Wild, Wild West. 1999. (Pee Wee Scouts Ser.: No. 37). (Illus.). 112p. (gr. 2-5). pap. text 3.99 o.s.i (*0-440-41342-7*, Dell Books for Young Readers) Random Hse. Children's Bks.

—Wild, Wild West. 1999. (Pee Wee Scouts Ser.: No. 37). (J). (gr. 2-5). 10.04 (*0-606-16585-1*) Turtleback Bks.

Demarest, Chris. Kitman & Willy at Sea. 1991. (J). (gr. k-3). pap. 13.95 o.p. (*0-671-65696-1*, Simon & Schuster Children's Publishing) Simon & Schuster Children's Publishing.

Demers, Jan. What Do You Do with a . . . ? 1990. (Predictable Reading Bks). (Illus.). 24p. (J). (gr. k-2). pap. text 1.95 o.p. (*0-87406-010-9*) Darby Creek Publishing.

DePaolo, Paula. Rosie & the Yellow Ribbon. 1992. (Illus.). 32p. (J). (ps-3). 14.95 o.p. (*0-316-18100-5*, Joy Street Bks.) Little Brown & Co.

DePrisco, Dorothea. Meet Gator: A Picture Clues Touch & Feel Book. 2002. (Illus.). 10p. (J). (ps up). 9.95 (*1-58117-123-4*, Piggy Toes Pr.) Intervisual Bks., Inc.

Derby, Janice. Are You My Friend? 1993. (Illus.). 40p. (J). (ps-3). 12.99 (*0-8361-3609-8*) Herald Pr.

Deriso, Christine Hurley. Dreams to Grow On. 2002. (Illus.). 32p. (YA). 15.95 (*0-9701907-2-7*) Illumination Arts Publishing Co., Inc.

Derman, Martha. The Friendstone. 1981. 160p. (J). (gr. 4-7). 8.95 o.p. (*0-8037-2472-1*); 8.44 o.p. (*0-8037-2480-2*) Penguin Putnam Bks. for Young Readers. (Dial Bks. for Young Readers).

DeRubertis, Barbara. Perky Otter. 1998. (Let's Read Together Ser.). (Illus.). 32p. (J). (ps-3). pap. 4.95 (*1-57565-045-2*) Kane Pr., The.

—Rooney 'Roo. 1998. (Let's Read Together Ser.). (Illus.). 32p. (J). (ps-3). pap. 4.95 (*1-57565-044-4*) Kane Pr., The.

—Rooney Roo. 1998. (Let's Read Together Ser.). (Illus.). 32p. (J). (ps-3). pap. 8.95 incl. audio (*1-57565-049-5*) Kane Pr., The.

Desai Hidier, Tanuja, et al. Born Confused. 2002. 432p. (J). pap. 16.95 (*0-439-35762-4*, Scholastic Pr.) Scholastic, Inc.

Desbarats, Peter. Gabrielle & Selena. 1974. (Illus.). 32p. (J). (gr. k-3). reprint ed. pap. 0.95 o.p. (*0-15-634080-1*, AVB87, Voyager Bks./Libros Viajeros) Harcourt Children's Bks.

Deschaine, Scott & Bonno, Chris. Head On. 1990. (Illus.). 36p. (J). pap. 2.00 (*1-878181-02-5*) Discovery Comics.

Desimini, Lisa. The Sun & Moon: A Giant Love Story. 1999. (Illus.). 40p. (YA). (ps-3). pap. 16.95 (*0-590-18720-1*, Blue Sky Pr., The) Scholastic, Inc.

Dessen, Sarah. Someone Like You. 272p. (gr. 7 up). 2000. (Illus.). (YA). pap. 5.99 (*0-14-130269-0*, Puffin Bks.); 1998. (J). 16.99 (*0-670-87778-6*) Penguin Putnam Bks. for Young Readers.

—Someone Like You. unabr. ed. 2003. (J). (gr. 7). audio 26.00 (*0-8072-1564-3*, Listening Library) Random Hse. Audio Publishing Group.

—Someone Like You. 2000. 11.04 (*0-606-18847-9*) Turtleback Bks.

—Someone Like You/Keeping the Moon Flip-Over Book. 2002. pap. 5.99 (*0-14-230165-5*) Penguin Putnam Bks. for Young Readers.

—That Summer. 2003. (J). audio 30.00 (*0-8072-1568-6*) Random Hse. Audio Publishing Group.

Deuker, Carl. Heart of a Champion. 1994. 176p. (J). (gr. 7-12). pap. 5.99 (*0-380-72269-0*, Harper Trophy) HarperCollins Children's Bk. Group.

—Heart of a Champion. 1993. (J). 15.95 o.p. (*0-316-18166-8*, Joy Street Bks.) Little Brown & Co.

—Heart of a Champion. 1993. (YA). 11.00 (*0-606-06454-0*) Turtleback Bks.

—Night Hoops. 2001. 256p. (J). (gr. 7 up). pap. 5.99 (*0-06-447275-2*, Harper Trophy) HarperCollins Children's Bk. Group.

—Night Hoops. 2000. (Illus.). 256p. (J). (gr. 7-12). tchr. ed. 15.00 (*0-395-97936-6*) Houghton Mifflin Co.

—Night Hoops. 2001. 12.00 (*0-606-22927-2*) Turtleback Bks.

—Night Hoops. 2000. E-Book 15.00 (*0-585-36795-7*) netLibrary, Inc.

Devlin, Harry & Devlin, Wende. Tales from Cranberryport: Cranberry Moving Day. 1994. (Tales from Cranberryport Ser.). (Illus.). 24p. (J). pap. 2.95 o.p. (*0-689-71777-6*, Little Simon) Simon & Schuster Children's Publishing.

Devlin, Wende & Devlin, Harry. Cranberry Valentine. 1986. (Illus.). 40p. (J). (gr. k-3). lib. bdg. 14.95 o.s.i (*0-02-729200-2*, Simon & Schuster Children's Publishing) Simon & Schuster Children's Publishing.

Diary. 1996. (Barbie Ser.). (J). 9.98 o.s.i (*1-57082-380-4*) Mouse Works.

DiCamillo, Kate. The Tiger Rising. (Illus.). 128p. (gr. 5-12). 2002. (YA). pap. 5.99 (*0-7636-1898-5*); 2001. (J). 14.99 (*0-7636-0911-0*) Candlewick Pr.

Dickens, Charles. A Tale of Two Cities. 2002. (Great Illustrated Classics). (Illus.). 240p. (J). (gr. 3-8). lib. bdg. 21.35 (*1-57765-802-7*, ABDO & Daughters) ABDO Publishing Co.

Dickerson, Karle. Best Friend Blues. 1988. (Impressions Ser.). 144p. (Orig.). (J). (gr. 6-9). pap. 2.75 o.p. (*0-87406-319-1*) Darby Creek Publishing.

—Now That Andi's Gone. 1994. 144p. (J). (gr. 5-8). pap. 2.99 (*0-87406-676-X*) Darby Creek Publishing.

Dickie, Julie S. & Hoffman, Catherine S. Bobcat Meets Pippy Gordon. 1996. (Series of Tuck Ins). (Illus.). (J). (gr. k-5). pap. 8.95 o.p. (*0-938985-17-5*) Quarrier Pr.

Dickinson, Peter. Heartsease. 1988. (Changes Trilogy Ser.). (J). (gr. k-10). mass mkt. 2.95 o.s.i (*0-440-20096-2*, Laurel Leaf) Random Hse. Children's Bks.

Didier, Stephen A. The Magic of Kindness. 1994. 64p. (Orig.). (J). pap. 8.00 (*1-56002-347-3*, University Editions) Aegina Pr., Inc.

Diggs, Lucy. Everyday Friends. 1986. 268p. (J). (gr. 4-8). 14.95 o.s.i (*0-689-31197-4*, Atheneum) Simon & Schuster Children's Publishing.

Dines, Carol. Best Friends Tell. 1990. (J). mass mkt. 12.95 (*0-440-80153-2*) Dell Publishing.

The Disappearing Airplane. 2001. 108p. pap. 9.95 (*0-595-18789-7*, Writers Club Pr.) iUniverse, Inc.

Disney Famous Friends. 1991. (J). (gr. 2 up). pap. 1.97 (*1-56297-122-0*) Lee Pubns.

Disney Staff. La Ballenita Perdida. 2002. (SPA., Illus.). 24p. (J). pap. 3.25 (*0-7364-2064-9*, RH/Disney) Random Hse. Children's Bks.

—Be Good, Stitch! 2002. (Illus.). 12p. (J). (ps-k). bds. 7.99 (*0-7364-1343-X*, RH/Disney) Random Hse. Children's Bks.

—Beauty & the Beast. ed. 1999. (J). (gr. 2). spiral bd. (*0-616-01631-X*) Canadian National Institute for the Blind/Institut National Canadien pour les Aveugles.

—Beauty & the Beast: The Perfect Party. 1997. (Disney's "Storytime Treasures" Library: Vol. 4). (Illus.). 44p. (J). (gr. 1-6). 3.49 o.p. (*1-57973-000-0*) Advance Pubs. LLC.

—La Bella y la Bestia: Un Cuento Contado. 2002. (SPA., Illus.). 72p. (J). 8.99 (*0-7364-2110-6*, RH/Disney) Random Hse. Children's Bks.

—Finding Nemo. 2003. (Illus.). (J). 24p. (ps-k). 2.99 (*0-7364-2139-4*); 72p. (ps-3). 8.99 (*0-7364-2126-2*); 128p. (gr. 4-7). pap. 4.99 (*0-7364-2130-0*) Random Hse. Children's Bks. (RH/Disney).

—Friendship Day. 2000. (Lessons from the Hundred-Acre Woods: Vol. 11). (Illus.). 32p. (J). (ps-4). 3.49 (*1-57973-087-6*) Advance Pubs. LLC.

—Hang Ten. 2002. (Illus.). 32p. (J). (ps-3). pap. 3.99 (*0-7364-1341-3*, RH/Disney) Random Hse. Children's Bks.

—Hello Friend. 2002. (Illus.). 16p. (J). pap. 2.99 (*0-7364-1282-4*) Mouse Works.

—The Jungle Book: A Friend for Life. 1997. (Disney's "Storytime Treasures" Library: Vol. 6). (Illus.). 44p. (J). (gr. 1-6). 3.49 o.p. (*1-57973-002-7*) Advance Pubs. LLC.

—Lady & the Tramp: A Trusty Old Pal. 1997. (Disney's "Storytime Treasures" Library: Vol. 15). (Illus.). 44p. (J). (gr. 1-6). 3.49 o.p. (*1-57973-011-6*) Advance Pubs. LLC.

—Lilo & Stitch. novel ed. 2002. (Illus.). 128p. (J). (gr. 4-7). pap. 4.99 (*0-7364-1342-1*, RH/Disney) Random Hse. Children's Bks.

—Lilo's Backpack. 2002. (Illus.). 14p. (J). bds. 7.99 (*0-7364-1340-5*, RH/Disney) Random Hse. Children's Bks.

—Monsters to Go. 2002. 12p. (J). bds. 9.99 (*0-7364-2058-4*, RH/Disney) Random Hse. Children's Bks.

—Pocahontas: An Unlikely Pair. 1997. (Disney's "Storytime Treasures" Library: Vol. 10). (Illus.). 44p. (J). (gr. 1-6). 3.49 o.p. (*1-57973-006-X*) Advance Pubs. LLC.

—Princess Collection. 2001. (Illus.). 48p. (J). (gr. k-3). bds. 9.99 (*0-7364-1138-0*, RH/Disney) Random Hse. Children's Bks.

—The Princess Collection. 2nd ed. 2002. 12p. (J). bds. 9.99 (*0-7364-2057-6*, RH/Disney) Random Hse. Children's Bks.

—Que Dulces Son Los Amigos. 2002. 24p. (J). pap. 3.25 (*0-7364-2061-4*, RH/Disney) Random Hse. Children's Bks.

—Trouble in Paradise. 2002. (Illus.). 80p. (J). (ps-3). pap. 2.99 (*0-7364-1344-8*, RH/Disney) Random Hse. Children's Bks.

Disney, Walter Elias. Friends to the End: A Friendship Bracelet Book. 1997. (Barbie Ser.). 24p. (J). 7.98 o.s.i (*1-57082-570-X*) Mouse Works.

Distad, Audree. Dakota Sons. 1972. (Illus.). (J). (gr. 3-7). 144p. lib. bdg. 6.89 o.p. (*0-06-024778-9*); pap. 1.25 o.p. (*0-06-440050-6*) HarperCollins Pubs.

DiTerlizzi, Tony. Ted. ed. 2001. (J). (gr. 2). spiral bd. (*0-616-07230-9*) Canadian National Institute for the Blind/Institut National Canadien pour les Aveugles.

—Ted. 2004. (Illus.). 40p. (J). pap. 6.99 (*0-689-86374-8*, Aladdin) Simon & Schuster Children's Publishing.

Dobkin, Bonnie. Collecting. 1993. (Rookie Readers Ser.). (Illus.). 32p. (J). (ps-2). pap. 3.50 o.p. (*0-516-42015-1*); (gr. 1-2). lib. bdg. 19.00 (*0-516-02015-3*) Scholastic Library Publishing. (Children's Pr.).

—Everybody Says. 1993. (Rookie Readers Ser.). (Illus.). 32p. (J). (ps-2). mass mkt. 4.95 (*0-516-42019-4*); (gr. 1-2). lib. bdg. 19.00 (*0-516-02019-6*) Scholastic Library Publishing. (Children's Pr.).

—Just a Little Different. 1994. (Rookie Readers Ser.). (Illus.). 32p. (J). (ps-2). pap. 3.50 o.p. (*0-516-42018-6*); (gr. 1-2). lib. bdg. 19.00 (*0-516-02018-8*) Scholastic Library Publishing. (Children's Pr.).

Dockray, Tracy. My Life Story. 2003. (Illus.). 40p. (J). lib. bdg. 15.95 (*1-58717-218-6*) SeaStar Bks.

Dodd, Lynley. Hairy Maclary's Bone. 1989. (Illus.). 28p. (J). (gr. 1 up). lib. bdg. 18.60 o.p. (*0-918831-06-7*) Stevens, Gareth Inc.

—Slinky Malinki. 1991. (Illus.). 32p. (J). lib. bdg. 19.93 o.p. (*0-8368-0197-0*) Stevens, Gareth Inc.

Dodds, Dayle Ann. Ghost & Pete. 1995. (Step into Reading Ser.). (Illus.). 48p. (J). (gr. 3-5). lib. bdg. 11.99 (*0-679-96199-2*) Random Hse., Inc.

Dodds, Siobhan. Ting-a-Ling! 1999. (DK Toddlers Ser.). (Illus.). 24p. (J). (ps). pap. 9.95 o.p. (*0-7894-4841-6*) Dorling Kindersley Publishing, Inc.

Dodson, Susan. Shadows Across the Sand. 1984. (J). (gr. 7 up). mass mkt. 2.25 o.s.i (*0-449-70114-X*, Fawcett) Ballantine Bks.

Doherty, Berlie. Willa & Old Miss Annie. 1994. (Illus.). 96p. (J). (gr. 3-6). 14.95 o.p. (*1-56402-331-1*) Candlewick Pr.

Donahue, Marilyn C. Violets Grow in Secret Places. 1901. (Pennypinchers Ser.). 128p. (J). (gr. 5-9). pap. 2.95 o.p. (*0-89191-885-X*, 58859) Cook Communications Ministries.

Donaldson, Julia. Follow the Swallow. 2001. (Blue Bananas Ser.). (Illus.). 48p. (J). (gr. 1-2). pap. 4.95 (*0-7787-0888-8*); lib. bdg. 19.96 (*0-7787-0842-X*) Crabtree Publishing Co.

Donovan, John. Remove Protective Coating a Little at a Time. 1973. 108p. (YA). (gr. 7 up). lib. bdg. 12.89 o.p. (*0-06-021720-0*) HarperCollins Children's Bk. Group.

Donovan, Kevin M. Billy & His Friends Tame the Wild Wolf. 1996. 28p. (YA). (gr. 3 up). 15.95 (*1-889279-03-X*) Best of Small Pr. Pubs.

Donovan, Mary Lee. Snuffles Makes a Friend. (Gund Children's Library). (Illus.). 32p. (J). (ps up). 1995. 8.95 o.p. (*1-56402-497-0*); 1997. reprint ed. bds. 3.99 (*0-7636-0096-2*) Candlewick Pr.

Dooley Makes Friends. 2002. (Illus.). 24p. (J). (gr. k-5). pap. 2.99 (*1-57759-472-X*) Dalmatian Pr.

Doray, Andrea. Friends. Gress, Jonna, ed. 1992. (Illus.). 12p. (J). (ps-2). pap. text 14.25 o.p. (*0-944943-13-6*, CODE 19723-6) Current, Inc.

Dorion, Betty F. Whose Side Are You On? 2001. (Illus.). 192p. (YA). (gr. 6 up). pap. 7.95 (*1-55050-179-8*) Coteau Bks. CAN. *Dist:* General Distribution Services, Inc.

Doughty, Rebecca, tr. & illus. You Are to Me. 2003. (J). 12.99 (*0-399-24176-0*) Putnam Publishing Group, The.

Douglas, Marjory S. Freedom River. 1994. (Illus.). 240p. (J). (gr. 4 up). 19.95 (*0-9633461-4-8*); pap. 14.95 (*0-9633461-5-6*) Valiant Pr., Inc.

Douglass, Barbara. Skateboard Scramble. 1979. (Illus.). 92p. (J). (gr. 3-6). 8.95 o.p. (*0-664-32641-2*) Westminster John Knox Pr.

Douthwaite, Wendy. The Orange Pony. 2003. (Illus.). 86p. (J). (gr. 2-7). mass mkt. 4.99 (*0-330-33631-2*) Macmillan Children's Bks. GBR. *Dist:* Trans-Atlantic Pubns., Inc.

Dower, Laura. From the Files of Madison Finn: Boy, Oh Boy!, Bk. 2. 2001. (Illus.). 144p. (J). (gr. 3-7). pap. 4.99 (*0-7868-1554-X*, Volo) Hyperion Bks. for Children.

—From the Files of Madison Finn Bk. 1: Only the Lonely. 2001. (Illus.). 144p. (J). (gr. 3-7). pap. 4.99 (*0-7868-1553-1*, Volo) Hyperion Bks. for Children.

Dragonwagon, Crescent. Brass Button. 1997. (Illus.). 40p. (J). (gr. k-4). 16.00 (*0-689-80582-9*, Atheneum) Simon & Schuster Children's Publishing.

Drake, David. Search for Rainbow's End: The Cricket of Dew Drop Dell. 2002. (Tree of Life Mini-Books Ser.). (Illus.). 32p. (J). 3.49 (*1-885631-65-0*, Family Of Man Pr., The) Hutchison, G.F. Pr.

Draper, Sharon M. Double Dutch. 192p. (J). 2004. pap. 4.99 (*0-689-84231-7*, Aladdin); 2002. (gr. 7 up). 16.00 (*0-689-84230-9*, Atheneum) Simon & Schuster Children's Publishing.

Draper, Tani, illus. Playmate Big Book: Black & White Nellie Edge I Can Read & Sing Big Book. 1994. (J). (ps-2). pap. text 20.00 (*0-922053-31-6*) Nellie Edge Resources, Inc.

Dubanevich, Arlene. Pig William. 1985. (Illus.). 32p. (J). (ps-2). lib. bdg. 14.95 (*0-02-733200-4*, Simon & Schuster Children's Publishing) Simon & Schuster Children's Publishing.

Dubowski, Cathy. My Best Friend Is a Movie Star. 1996. (Full House Michelle Ser.: No. 10). 144p. (J). (gr. 2-4). pap. 3.99 (*0-671-56835-3*, Simon Spotlight) Simon & Schuster Children's Publishing.

—My Two Best Friends. 1995. (Full House Michelle Ser.: No. 3). 96p. (Orig.). (J). (gr. 2-4). pap. 3.99 (*0-671-52271-X*, Simon Spotlight) Simon & Schuster Children's Publishing.

Duchesne, Christiane. Edmund & Amanda. 1999. (Illus.). 29p. (*1-894363-17-5*) Dominique & Friends.

—Nox & Archimusse in the Monsters' Feast. Perkes, Carolyn, tr. 2000. (Illus.). (ps-3). pap. (*1-894363-20-5*) Dominique & Friends.

Dudko, Mary Ann & Larsen, Margie. BJ & Scooter. 1995. (Illus.). 24p. (J). pap. 3.25 o.p. (*1-57064-043-2*) Scholastic, Inc.

—BJ's Fun Week. 1994. (Barney Ser.). (Illus.). 20p. (J). (ps-k). 3.95 o.p. (*1-57064-015-7*) Scholastic, Inc.

Duey, Kathleen. Patch: Time Soldiers Book #3, Vol. 3. 2003. (Time Soldiers Ser.: Vol. 3). (Illus.). 48p. (J). (ps-5). pap. 8.95 (*1-929945-28-0*); 15.95 (*1-929945-02-7*) Big Guy Bks., Inc.

Duey, Kathleen & Bale, Karen. Three of Hearts. 1998. (J). (gr. 3-7). pap. 3.99 (*0-380-78720-2*, Avon Bks.) Morrow/Avon.

—Three of Hearts. 1998. 10.04 (*0-606-16346-8*) Turtleback Bks.

Duffey, Betsy. Coaster. 1996. (J). 10.04 (*0-606-11217-0*) Turtleback Bks.

—Hey, New Kid! 1996. (Illus.). 96p. (J). (gr. 4-7). 13.99 o.s.i (*0-670-86760-8*, Viking Children's Bks.) Penguin Putnam Bks. for Young Readers.

—Utterly Yours, Booker Jones. 1997. (J). 11.04 (*0-606-13061-6*) Turtleback Bks.

Duffy, Daniel M., illus. Benny's New Friend. 1998. (Adventures of Benny & Watch: Vol. No. 3). 32p. (J). (gr. 1-3). pap. 3.95 (*0-8075-0649-4*) Whitman, Albert & Co.

Dugan, Barbara. Good-Bye, Hello. 1994. 160p. (J). (gr. 5 up). 13.00 (*0-688-12447-X*, Greenwillow Bks.) HarperCollins Children's Bk. Group.

—Loop the Loop. (Illus.). (J). (gr. k up). 1992. 32p. lib. bdg. 15.93 o.p. (*0-688-09648-4*); 1992. 32p. 16.95 (*0-688-09647-6*); 1924. o.s.i (*0-688-10186-0*); 1924. lib. bdg. o.s.i (*0-688-10187-9*) HarperCollins Children's Bk. Group. (Greenwillow Bks.).

—Loop the Loop. 1993. (Illus.). 32p. (J). (ps-3). pap. 4.99 o.s.i (*0-14-054904-8*, Puffin Bks.) Penguin Putnam Bks. for Young Readers.

—Loop the Loop. 1993. (Picture Puffin Ser.). (Illus.). (J). 10.19 o.p. (*0-606-05444-8*) Turtleback Bks.

Dunbar, Joyce. The Secret Friend. (Panda & Gander Stories Ser.). (Illus.). (J). (ps-2). 1999. 24p. 9.99 (*0-7636-0720-7*); 1998. pap. (*0-7636-0719-3*) Candlewick Pr.

—Seven Sillies. 1994. (Illus.). 32p. (J). (ps-3). o.p. (*0-307-17504-9*, Golden Bks.) Random Hse. Children's Bks.

Duncan, Alice F. Miss Viola & Uncle Ed Lee. 1999. (Illus.). 40p. (J). (gr. k-3). 16.00 (*0-689-80476-8*, Atheneum) Simon & Schuster Children's Publishing.

Duncan, Lois. The Third Eye. 2002. (Illus.). (J). 13.40 (*0-7587-4792-6*) Book Wholesalers, Inc.

—The Third Eye. 1991. (YA). mass mkt. o.p. (*0-440-80274-1*) Dell Publishing.

—The Third Eye. 1985. (YA). 11.04 (*0-606-00474-2*) Turtleback Bks.

Dunlop, Eileen. Finn's Search. 1994. 160p. (J). (gr. 4-7). 14.95 (*0-8234-1099-4*) Holiday Hse., Inc.

Dunmore, Helen. Zillah & Me. 2001. 160p. (gr. 3-7). mass mkt. 4.50 (*0-439-20669-3*) Scholastic, Inc.

Dunrea, Olivier. Essie & Myles, RS. 2005. (J). (*0-374-39991-3*, Farrar, Straus & Giroux (BYR)) Farrar, Straus & Giroux.

—Gossie & Gertie. 2002. (Illus.). 32p. (J). tchr. ed. 9.95 (*0-618-17676-4*) Houghton Mifflin Co.

—It's Snowing! 2002. 32p. (J). 16.00 (*0-374-39993-X*);RS. (Illus.). 16.00 (*0-374-39992-1*, Farrar, Straus & Giroux (BYR)) Farrar, Straus & Giroux.

—Mogwogs on the March. 1985. (Illus.). 32p. (J). (ps-1). pap. 5.95 o.p. (*0-8234-0845-0*); lib. bdg. 12.95 o.p. (*0-8234-0578-8*) Holiday Hse., Inc.

Dunster, Mark. Doricio. 1989. 11p. (Orig.). (J). pap. 4.00 (*0-89642-170-8*) Linden Pubs.

—Nutcrack. 1990. 11p. (Orig.). (J). (gr. 1-7). pap. 4.00 (*0-89642-190-2*) Linden Pubs.

Duplex, Mary H. Trouble with a Capital T. 1992. (Starburst Ser.). 96p. (J). pap. 2.97 o.p. (*0-8163-1057-2*) Pacific Pr. Publishing Assn.

Dussling, Jennifer. Anne of Green Gables. 2001. (All Aboard Reading Ser.). (Illus.). 48p. (J). (gr. 4-7). 13.89 o.s.i (*0-448-42460-6*); pap. 3.99 (*0-448-42459-2*) Penguin Putnam Bks. for Young Readers. (Philomel).

—Bug Off! 1997. (Eek! Stories to Make You Shriek Ser.). 9.15 o.p. (*0-606-11172-7*) Turtleback Bks.

—Gotcha! 2003. (Science Solves It! Ser.). (Illus.). 32p. (J). 4.99 (*1-57565-124-6*) Kane Pr., The.

—A Simple Wish 8 x 8. 1997. (Simple Wish Ser.). (Illus.). 24p. (Orig.). (J). (gr. k-3). 3.95 o.s.i (*0-448-41637-9*, Grosset & Dunlap) Penguin Putnam Bks. for Young Readers.

Duvoisin, Roger. Snowy & Woody. 1979. (Illus.). (J). (ps-2). lib. bdg. 6.99 o.s.i (*0-394-94241-8*, Knopf Bks. for Young Readers) Random Hse. Children's Bks.

—Snowy & Woody. 1979. 6.95 o.s.i (*0-394-84241-3*) Random Hse., Inc.

Dygard, Thomas J. Backfield Package. 1993. 208p. (J). (gr. 5 up). pap. 4.99 o.p. (*0-14-036348-3*, Puffin Bks.) Penguin Putnam Bks. for Young Readers.

—Infield Hit. 1995. (Illus.). 208p. (YA). (gr. 7 up). 16.00 (*0-688-14037-8*, Morrow, William & Co.) Morrow/Avon.

—Infield Hit. 1997. 160p. (gr. 5-9). pap. 5.99 (*0-14-037935-5*) Penguin Putnam Bks. for Young Readers.

—Infield Hit. 1997. 11.04 (*0-606-10999-4*) Turtleback Bks.

—Running Wild. 1998. (Illus.). 176p. (J). (gr. 5-9). pap. 4.99 o.s.i (*0-14-038687-4*, Puffin Bks.) Penguin Putnam Bks. for Young Readers.

Eager, Edward. Magic or Not? (Odyssey Classics). (Illus.). 1999. 208p. (YA). (gr. 3-7). pap. 6.00 (*0-15-202080-2*, Odyssey Classics); 1989. 208p. (J). (gr. 3-7). pap. 3.95 o.p. (*0-15-251160-1*, Odyssey Classics); 1959. (J). (gr. 4-6). 5.95 o.p. (*0-15-251157-1*); 1979. 192p. (J). (gr. 3-6). reprint ed. pap. 4.95 o.p. (*0-15-655121-7*, Voyager Bks./Libros Viajeros) Harcourt Children's Bks.

—Magic or Not? 1984. (Illus.). (J). (gr. 4-6). 17.55 o.p. (*0-8446-6154-6*) Smith, Peter Pub., Inc.

—Magic or Not? 1999. (J). 12.05 (*0-606-19001-5*) Turtleback Bks.

Eastman, P. D. Big Dog... Little Dog. 2003. (I Can Read It All by Myself Ser.). (Illus.). 48p. (J). (gr. k-3). 8.99 (*0-375-82297-6*); lib. bdg. 13.99 (*0-375-92297-0*, Golden Bks.) Random Hse. Children's Bks.

Easton, Kelly. Trouble at Betts' Pets. 2002. 144p. (J). (gr. 3-7). 14.99 (*0-7636-1580-3*) Candlewick Pr.

Easton, Richard. A Real American. 2002. 160p. (J). (gr. 4-6). 15.00 (*0-618-13339-9*, Clarion Bks.) Houghton Mifflin Co. Trade & Reference Div.

Ebert, Tom. My Name Is Blackie. 2000. pap. 6.95 (*0-533-13601-6*) Vantage Pr., Inc.

Echewa, O. T. The Ancestor Tree. 1994. (Illus.). 32p. (J). (gr. k-3). 13.99 o.p. (*0-525-67467-5*, Dutton Children's Bks.) Penguin Putnam Bks. for Young Readers.

Edens, Cooper. Hugh's Hues. 1991. (Illus.). 32p. (J). 11.95 o.p. (*0-88138-114-4*, Simon & Schuster Children's Publishing) Simon & Schuster Children's Publishing.

—With Secret Friends. (Illus.). 48p. (YA). (gr. 7-12). 1991. pap. 8.00 o.p. (*0-671-74970-6*, Aladdin); 1991. pap. 8.95 o.s.i (*0-914676-57-1*, Aladdin); 1992. pap. 20.00 o.p. (*0-671-75593-5*, Simon & Schuster Children's Publishing) Simon & Schuster Children's Publishing.

Edge, Nellie, adapted by. The More We Get Together Big Book: Black & White Nellie Edge I Can Read & Sing Big Book. 1994. (Illus.). (J). (ps-2). pap. text 20.00 (*0-922053-32-4*) Nellie Edge Resources, Inc.

Edwards, Byron. The Mystery of Melissa's First Date: Book One. 2001. 108p. pap. 9.95 (*0-595-18836-2*, Writers Club Pr.) iUniverse, Inc.

Edwards, Dorothy. My Naughty Little Sister & Bad Harry's Rabbit. 1981. (Illus.). (J). (ps-2). 8.95 o.p. (*0-13-608935-6*) Prentice Hall PTR.

Edwards, Michelle. Eve & Smithy. 1994. (J). (gr. 4 up). 15.00 o.p. (*0-688-11825-9*); (Illus.). 24p. lib. bdg. 14.93 o.p. (*0-688-11826-7*) HarperCollins Children's Bk. Group.

—Pa Lia's First Day. 1999. (Jackson Friends Bk.). (Illus.). 56p. (J). (gr. 1-4). 14.00 (*0-15-201974-X*) Harcourt Children's Bks.

—Pa Lia's First Day. 2001. (Jackson Friends Book Ser.). (Illus.). (J). 11.10 (*0-606-21377-5*) Turtleback Bks.

Edwards, Pamela. Annette & Nannette. 2004. (Illus.). (J). lib. bdg. (*0-06-050753-5*) HarperCollins Pubs.

Edwards, Pamela Duncan. Gigi & Lulu's Twin Day. Cole, Henry, tr. & illus. by. 2004. (J). (*0-06-050752-7*) HarperCollins Pubs.

—Warthogs in a Box, 3 bks. 2002. (Illus.). 32p. (J). (gr. k-3). 9.99 (*0-7868-0894-2*) Disney Pr.

Edwards, Pat. Little John & Plutie. 1988. 180p. (J). (gr. 3-7). 13.95 o.p. (*0-395-48223-2*) Houghton Mifflin Co.

Edwards, Roberta. Don't Cry, Leon. 1996. (Puzzle Place Ser.). (Illus.). 32p. (J). 13.99 o.s.i (*0-448-41331-0*); 4.95 o.s.i (*0-448-41288-8*) Penguin Putnam Bks. for Young Readers. (Grosset & Dunlap).

Egan, Tim. Metropolitan Cow. 1996. (Illus.). 32p. (J). (ps-3). tchr. ed. 15.00 o.p. (*0-395-73096-1*) Houghton Mifflin Co.

Eggleston, Edward. Mister Blake's Walking Stick. 1988. (Collected Works of Edward Eggleston). (YA). reprint ed. lib. bdg. 59.00 (*0-7812-1170-0*) Reprint Services Corp.

Egielski, Richard. Slim & Jim. 2002. (Illus.). 40p. (J). (ps-2). 15.95 (*0-06-028352-1*, Geringer, Laura Bk.) HarperCollins Children's Bk. Group.

—Spike & Mike. (J). (ps-2). Date not set. 32p. pap. 5.99 (*0-06-443564-4*); 2002. (Illus.). 48p. lib. bdg. 15.89 (*0-06-028353-X*, Geringer, Laura Bk.) HarperCollins Children's Bk. Group.

Ehrenhaft, Daniel. Tell It to Naomi. 2004. 208p. (YA). lib. bdg. 9.99 (*0-385-90155-0*); (J). (gr. 7). pap. 7.95 (*0-385-73129-9*) Random Hse. Children's Bks. (Delacorte Bks. for Young Readers).

Ehrlich, Amy. Leo, Zack & Emmie. (Puffin Easy-to-Read Ser.). (Illus.). 64p. (J). 1997. (gr. 1-4). pap. 3.99 o.p. (*0-14-036199-5*, Puffin Bks.); 1981. (ps-3). 9.89 o.s.i (*0-8037-4761-6*, Dial Bks. for Young Readers); 1981. (ps-3). pap. 4.95 o.p. (*0-8037-4760-8*, Puffin Bks.) Penguin Putnam Bks. for Young Readers.

—Leo, Zack & Emmie Together Again. (Easy-to-Read Ser.). (Illus.). 56p. (J). 1998. (gr. 1-4). pap. 3.99 o.p. (*0-14-037946-0*, Puffin Bks.); 1990. (gr. 1-4). pap. 3.95 o.p. (*0-8037-0837-8*, Dial Bks. for Young Readers); 1987. (ps-3). 9.95 o.p. (*0-8037-0381-3*, Dial Bks. for Young Readers); 1987. (ps-3). 9.89 o.p. (*0-8037-0382-1*, Dial Bks. for Young Readers) Penguin Putnam Bks. for Young Readers.

—Leo, Zack & Emmie Together Again. 1997. (Puffin Easy-to-Read Ser.). (Illus.). (J). 10.14 (*0-606-20463-6*) Turtleback Bks.

Eige, Lillian. Dangling. 176p. (J). 2003. (Illus.). pap. 4.99 (*0-689-86350-0*, Aladdin); 2001. (gr. 3-7). 16.00 (*0-689-83581-7*, Atheneum) Simon & Schuster Children's Publishing.

Eisenberg, Lisa & Hall, Katy. Quickie Comebacks. 1992. 96p. (YA). pap. 1.95 (*0-590-44998-2*) Scholastic, Inc.

Eisenberg, Phyllis Rose. You're My Nikki. 1995. (J). 11.19 o.p. (*0-606-08410-X*) Turtleback Bks.

Eitan, Ora. A Veces Grande, a Veces Pequeno. Writer, C. C. & Nielsen, Lisa C., trs. 1992. (Hippy Ser.). (SPA., Illus.). 24p. (Orig.). (J). (ps). pap. text 3.00 o.p. (*1-56134-149-5*, McGraw-Hill/Dushkin) McGraw-Hill Higher Education.

Elzbieta. Dikou & the Snively Snoak. 1985. (J). (gr. k-6). 0.50 o.p. (*0-8120-5622-1*) Barron's Educational Series, Inc.

—Dikou-Troon Who Walks at Night. 1985. (J). (gr. k-6). 0.50 o.p. (*0-8120-5621-3*) Barron's Educational Series, Inc.

Elkins, Stephen. Ebony & Ivory. 2003. (Illus.). 32p. (J). (gr. k up). 14.99 (*0-8054-2674-4*) Broadman & Holman Pubs.

Ellie the Elephant: Has an Earache. 1996. (Dr. Wellbook Collection). (Illus.). 20p. (J). (ps-3). reprint ed. pap. 7.95 (*1-879874-40-7*) Peters, Tim & Co., Inc.

Elliot, David. The Cool Crazy Crickets to the Rescue! 2001. (Illus.). (J). 10.65 (*0-606-21642-1*) Turtleback Bks.

Elliott, Ann. GypsyBridge Friends: The Vine. 2002. 40p. (J). per. 12.95 (*0-9721825-0-0*) Open Vision Entertainment Corp.

Elliott, David. The Cool Crazy Crickets. 2001. 64p. (J). (gr. 1-3). bds. 4.99 (*0-7636-1403-3*) Candlewick Pr.

—The Cool Crazy Crickets to the Rescue! 2001. (Illus.). 64p. (J). (gr. 1-3). bds. 4.50 o.s.i (*0-7636-1402-5*) Candlewick Pr.

Elliott, Laura. Hunter's Best Friend at School: A Hunter & Stripe Story. 2002. (Illus.). 32p. (J). (ps-2). 15.99 (*0-06-000230-1*); lib. bdg. 17.89 (*0-06-000231-X*) HarperCollins Children's Bk. Group.

Elliott, Paula. Fluffy & Sparky: A Story about True Buddies. 1991. (Illus.). 32p. (J). (ps up). 12.95 o.p. (*1-879052-00-8*) HeartMath LLC.

Ellis, Carol. Cry in the Night. 1990. (J). mass mkt. 2.75 o.p. (*0-590-42845-4*) Scholastic, Inc.

—There's a Troll in My Closet. 1994. 8.09 o.p. (*0-606-06055-3*) Turtleback Bks.

—There's a Troll in My Popcorn. 1994. 96p. (YA). (gr. 4-7). pap. 3.50 (*0-671-87162-5*, Aladdin) Simon & Schuster Children's Publishing.

—There's a Troll in My Popcorn. 1994. 8.60 o.p. (*0-606-06803-1*) Turtleback Bks.

Ellis, Deborah. A Company of Fools. 2002. 180p. (YA). (gr. 5-8). (*1-55041-719-3*) Fitzhenry & Whiteside, Ltd.

Ellis, Ella Thorp. The Year of My Indian Prince. 2002. 224p. (YA). (gr. 7). mass mkt. 5.50 (*0-440-22950-2*, Random Hse. Bks. for Young Readers) Random Hse. Children's Bks.

Ellis, Sarah. Next-Door Neighbors. 1992. 160p. (J). (gr. 4-7). pap. 3.25 o.s.i (*0-440-40620-X*) Dell Publishing.

—Next-Door Neighbors. 1990. 160p. (J). (gr. 4-7). 16.00 (*0-689-50495-0*, McElderry, Margaret K.) Simon & Schuster Children's Publishing.

Ellison, Suzanne Pierson. The Best of Enemies. 1998. (YA). 200p. (gr. 7 up). 12.95 o.p. (*0-87358-714-6*); pap. 8.95 o.p. (*0-87358-717-0*) Northland Publishing.

Ellwand, David. Alfred's Camera: A Collection of Picture Puzzles. 1999. (Illus.). 32p. (J). (ps-3). bds. 15.99 o.p. (*0-525-45978-2*, Dutton Children's Bks.) Penguin Putnam Bks. for Young Readers.

Elste, Joan & DiSalvo-Ryan, DyAnne. True Blue. 1996. (All Aboard Reading Ser.: Level 3). (Illus.). 48p. (Orig.). (J). (gr. 4-7). 3.99 (*0-448-41264-0*, Grosset & Dunlap) Penguin Putnam Bks. for Young Readers.

Elzbieta. Flon Flon & Annette, ERS. 1994. (J). 12.95 o.p. (*0-8050-3299-1*, Holt, Henry & Co. Bks. For Young Readers) Holt, Henry & Co.

Emberley, Rebecca. Three Cool Kids. 1998. (J). 12.10 (*0-606-13847-1*) Turtleback Bks.

Emerson, Charlotte. Meg's Dearest Wish. 1999. (Little Women Journals). 10.04 (*0-606-16350-6*) Turtleback Bks.

Emerson, Charlotte & Alcott, Louisa May. Meg's Dearest Wish. (Little Women Journals). (Illus.). (J). 1999. 128p. (gr. 3-7). pap. 3.99 (*0-380-79705-4*); 1998. 144p. mass mkt. 10.00 o.p. (*0-380-97633-1*) Morrow/Avon. (Avon Bks.).

Enderle, Dotti. Something's Glowing in Lightfoot Creek. 2004. 160p. (J). pap. 4.99 (*0-7387-0389-3*) Llewellyn Worldwide Ltd.

Enderle, Judith R. What's the Matter, Kelly Beans? 1998. (J). 11.04 (*0-606-13906-0*) Turtleback Bks.

Endersby, Frank. Let's Talk Together. 1992. (Duckling Ser.). (Illus.). 32p. (J). (ps). 15.95 (*0-460-88059-4*) Dent, J.M. & Sons GBR. *Dist:* Trafalgar Square.

Engel, Diana. The Shelf-Paper Jungle. 1994. (Illus.). 32p. (J). (gr. k-3). 14.95 o.p. (*0-02-733464-3*, Simon & Schuster Children's Publishing) Simon & Schuster Children's Publishing.

Engelbreit, Mary. All You Need Is a Friend. 1995. (Illus.). 48p. 5.99 (*0-8362-0795-5*) Andrews McMeel Publishing.

English, Karen. Francie. 2002. (Illus.). (J). 25.45 (*0-7587-0355-4*) Book Wholesalers, Inc.

—Francie, RS. 2002. 208p. (J). pap. 5.95 (*0-374-42459-4*, Sunburst) Farrar, Straus & Giroux.

—Francie. l.t. ed. 2002. 220p. (J). 21.95 (*0-7862-3717-1*) Gale Group.

—Hot Day on Abbott Avenue. 2004. (Illus.). 32p. (J). 15.00 (*0-395-98527-7*, Clarion Bks.) Houghton Mifflin Co. Trade & Reference Div.

—Neeny Coming, Neeny Going. 1998. 12.10 (*0-606-13656-8*) Turtleback Bks.

—Strawberry Moon, RS. 2001. 128p. (J). (gr. 4-6). 16.00 (*0-374-47122-3*, Farrar, Straus & Giroux (BYR)) Farrar, Straus & Giroux.

Enright, Elizabeth. Thimble Summer, ERS. 1938. (J). 11.95 o.p. (*0-03-015686-6*, Holt, Henry & Co. Bks. For Young Readers) Holt, Henry & Co.

—Thimble Summer. unabr. ed. 2001. 136p. pap. 35.00 incl. audio (*0-8072-0671-7*); (YA). audio 25.00 (*0-8072-0554-0*) Random Hse. Audio Publishing Group. (Listening Library).

Epstein, Anne M. Good Stones, 001. 1977. (Illus.). 274p. (J). (gr. 5-9). 6.95 o.p. (*0-395-25154-0*) Houghton Mifflin Co.

Erickson, Betty. Big Bad Rex. 1998. (Illus.). 12p. (J). (gr. k-2). pap. 3.75 (*1-880612-77-1*) Seedling Pubns., Inc.

Erickson, Gina Clegg. Pip & Kip. 1993. (Get Ready...Get Set...Read! Ser.). 9.65 (*0-606-13708-4*) Turtleback Bks.

Erickson, Russell E. A Toad for Tuesday. 1993. (Illus.). 64p. (J). (gr. 3 up). reprint ed. pap. 3.95 (*0-688-12276-0*, Morrow, William & Co.) Morrow/Avon.

Eriksson, Ake. Joel, Jesper, & Julia. 1990. (Illus.). 32p. (J). (ps-3). lib. bdg. 7.95 o.s.i (*0-87614-419-9*, Carolrhoda Bks.) Lerner Publishing Group.

Eriksson, Eva. Hocus Pocus. 1985. (Victor & Rosalie Bks.).Tr. of Hokus Pokus. (Illus.). 32p. (J). (ps-3). lib. bdg. 8.95 o.p. (*0-87614-235-8*, Carolrhoda Bks.) Lerner Publishing Group.

—Jealousy. 1985. (Victor & Rosalie Bks.).Tr. of Svartsjuka. (Illus.). 32p. (J). (ps-3). lib. bdg. 8.95 o.p. (*0-87614-237-4*, Carolrhoda Bks.) Lerner Publishing Group.

—One Short Week. 1985. (Victor & Rosalie Bks.).Tr. of OM in Liten Vecka. (Illus.). 32p. (J). (ps-3). lib. bdg. 8.95 o.p. (*0-87614-234-X*, Carolrhoda Bks.) Lerner Publishing Group.

—The Tooth Trip. 1985. (Victor & Rosalie Bks.).Tr. of Tandresan. (Illus.). 32p. (J). (ps-3). lib. bdg. 8.95 o.p. (*0-87614-236-6*, Carolrhoda Bks.) Lerner Publishing Group.

Ernst, Kathryn. Owl's New Cards. 1988. (Illus.). (J). (gr. k-2). 5.95 o.s.i (*0-517-53090-2*, Crown) Crown Publishing Group.

Ernst, Lisa Campbell. Bubba & Trixie. (Illus.). (J). (ps-3). 2000. 40p. pap. 5.99 o.s.i (*0-689-83851-4*, Aladdin); 1997. 32p. 17.00 (*0-689-81357-0*, Simon & Schuster Children's Publishing) Simon & Schuster Children's Publishing.

—Miss Penny & Mr. Grubbs. 1995. (Illus.). 40p. (J). (ps-2). mass mkt. 4.95 (*0-689-80035-5*, Aladdin) Simon & Schuster Children's Publishing.

—Zinnia & Dot. 1995. (J). 12.14 (*0-606-08415-0*) Turtleback Bks.

Ernst, Lisa Campbell, illus. Zinnia & Dot. 1995. 32p. (ps-3). pap. 5.99 o.s.i (*0-14-054199-3*, Puffin Bks.) Penguin Putnam Bks. for Young Readers.

Escudie, Rene. Paul & Sebastian. 1992. (I Love to Read Collections). (Illus.). 46p. (J). (gr. 1-5). lib. bdg. 8.50 o.p. (*0-89565-806-2*) Child's World, Inc.

—Paul & Sebastian. Townley, Roderick, tr. from FRE. 1988. (Illus.). 32p. (J). (ps-3). 11.95 o.p. (*0-916291-19-7*) Kane/Miller Bk. Pubs.

Esparza, Esther L. Humpty Dumpty & Friends in the Southwest, Books 1, 2, 3, 3 Books. 1997. Tr. of Coco Loco y Sus Amigos en el Suroeste, Libros 1, 2, 3. (SPA., Illus.). (Orig.). (J). (ps-9). 14.95 (*1-879817-08-X*, Bilingual) Star Light Pr.

—Humpty Dumpty & Friends in the Southwest, Coloring Book 1. 1991. Tr. of Coco Loco y Amigos en el Sur Este, Libro 1. (SPA., Illus.). 28p. (J). (ps-9). 5.95 (*1-879817-05-5*, Bilingual) Star Light Pr.

—Humpty Dumpty & Friends in the Southwest, Coloring Book 2. 1991. (SPA., Illus.). 28p. (J). (ps-9). 5.95 (*1-879817-06-3*, Bilingual) Star Light Pr.

—Humpty Dumpty & Friends in the Southwest, Coloring Book 3. 1997. (SPA., Illus.). 28p. (Orig.). (J). (ps-9). 5.95 (*1-879817-07-1*, Bilingual) Star Light Pr.

Esparza, Esther L., et al. Humpty Dumpty & Friends in the Southwest. unabr. ed. 1991. (Illus.). 28p. (J). (ps-9). Bk. I. pap., pap. text 12.95 incl. audio (*1-879817-15-2*); Bk. II. pap., pap. text 12.95 incl. audio (*1-879817-16-0*); Bk. III. pap., pap. text 12.95 incl. audio (*1-879817-17-9*) Star Light Pr.

—Humpty Dumpty & Friends in the Southwest Books 1, 2 & 3, 3 vols., unabr. ed. 1991. (Illus.). (J). (ps-9). pap. text 34.95 incl. audio (*1-879817-14-4*) Star Light Pr.

—Humpty Dumpty & Friends in the Southwest, Cassette 1. unabr. ed. 1991. Tr. of Coco Loco y Amigos en el Suroeste, Casete 1. (Illus.). 28p. (J). (ps-9). audio 5.95 (*1-879817-10-1*, Bilingual) Star Light Pr.

—Humpty Dumpty & Friends in the Southwest, Cassette 2. unabr. ed. 1991. Tr. of Coco Loco y Amigos en el Suroeste, Casete 2. (J). (ps-9). audio 5.95 (*1-879817-11-X*, Bilingual) Star Light Pr.
—Humpty Dumpty & Friends in the Southwest, Cassette 3. unabr. ed. 1990. Tr. of Coco Loco y Amigos en el Suroeste, Casete 2. (Illus.). 28p. (J). (ps-9). audio 5.95 (*1-879817-12-8*) Star Light Pr.
—Humpty Dumpty & Friends in the Southwest, Cassettes 1, 2, 3, 3 vols., unabr. ed. 1990. Tr. of Coco Loco y Amigos en el Suroeste, Casetes 1, 2, 3. (Illus.). (J). (ps-9). audio 14.95 (*1-879817-13-6*) Star Light Pr.
Estes, Allison. Friends to the Finish. 1996. (Short Stirrup Club Ser.: No. 6). 144p. (J). (gr. 3-7). mass mkt. 3.99 (*0-671-00100-0*, Aladdin) Simon & Schuster Children's Publishing.
Estes, Eleanor. The Alley. 2003. (Illus.). 288p. (J). 17.00 (*0-15-204917-7*, Harcourt Young Classics); pap. 5.95 (*0-15-204918-5*, Odyssey Classics) Harcourt Children's Bks.
—Los Cien Vestidos. Mlawer, Teresa, tr. (SPA., Illus.). (J). 1994. (gr. k-2). pap. 6.95 (*1-880507-15-3*, LC1571); 1993. 80p. (gr. 4-7). lib. bdg. 14.95 (*1-880507-06-4*, LC4677) Lectorum Pubns., Inc.
—The Hundred Dresses. 2002. (Illus.). (J). 13.19 (*0-7587-0272-8*) Book Wholesalers, Inc.
—The Hundred Dresses. (Illus.). 88p. (J). 1944. (gr. 4-7). 16.00 (*0-15-237374-8*); 1974. (gr. 1-5). reprint ed. pap. 6.00 (*0-15-642350-2*, Voyager Bks./Libros Viajeros) Harcourt Children's Bks.
—The Hundred Dresses. 1971. (J). (gr. 4-7). 12.15 (*0-606-03310-6*) Turtleback Bks.
—The Tunnel of Hugsy Goode. 2003. (Illus.). 256p. (J). 17.00 (*0-15-204914-2*, Harcourt Young Classics); pap. 5.95 (*0-15-204916-9*, Odyssey Classics) Harcourt Children's Bks.
Ethridge, Kenneth E. Toothpick. 1985. 128p. (YA). (gr. 7 up). 13.95 o.p. (*0-8234-0585-0*) Holiday Hse., Inc.
Eulo, Elena Yates. Mixed-up Doubles. 2003. 208p. (J). tchr. ed. 16.95 (*0-8234-1706-9*) Holiday Hse., Inc.
Evans, Karen & Urmston, Kathleen. Sammy Gets a Ride. l.t. ed. 1997. (Illus.). 12p. (J). (gr. k-2). pap. 4.95 (*1-879835-03-7*) Kaeden Corp.
Evans, Mari. Dear Corinne, Tell Somebody! Love, Annie: A Book about Secrets. 1999. 64p. (J). (gr. 3-7). 12.95 (*0-940975-81-5*) Just Us Bks., Inc.
Evans, Sanford. Naomi's Geese. 1993. (Illus.). (YA). (gr. 5 up). pap. 15.00 o.p. (*0-671-75623-0*, Simon & Schuster Children's Publishing) Simon & Schuster Children's Publishing.
Evans, Shane W. Down the Winding Road. 2000. (Richard Jackson Bks.). (Illus.). 32p. (J). (ps-1). pap. 15.95 (*0-7894-2596-3*, D K Ink) Dorling Kindersley Publishing, Inc.
Eversole, Robyn H. Red Berry Wool. 1999. (Illus.). 32p. (J). (ps-3). lib. bdg. 15.95 (*0-8075-0654-0*) Whitman, Albert & Co.
Everybody Needs a Friend Like You. 1984. 32p. (J). pap. 2.25 o.p. (*0-89542-453-3*) Ideals Pubns.
The Experiment. 1994. (YA). pap. 1.99 o.p. (*0-590-48833-3*) Scholastic, Inc.
Eyerly, Jeannette. Seth & Me & Rebel Make Three. 1983. 128p. (YA). (gr. 7 up). 12.95 (*0-397-32042-6*); lib. bdg. 12.89 (*0-397-32043-4*) HarperCollins Children's Bk. Group.
Ezra, Mark. The Hungry Otter. 1996. (Illus.). 32p. (J). 14.95 (*1-56656-216-3*, Crocodile Bks.) Interlink Publishing Group, Inc.
Faber, Adele & Mazlish, Elaine. Bobby & the Brockles Go to School. 1994. (Illus.). 64p. (Orig.). (J). pap. 15.00 o.p. (*0-380-77068-7*, Avon Bks.) Morrow/Avon.
Faber, Doris. Bing E. Roosevelt. 1924. (J). o.s.i (*0-688-05567-2*); lib. bdg. o.s.i (*0-688-05568-0*) Harper-Collins Children's Bk. Group.
Fabian, Margaret W. My Friend Luke, the Stenciller. 1987. (Illus.). 35p. (J). (gr. 3-4). pap., bds. 8.95 (*0-931474-25-6*) TBW Bks.
Fabian, Stella. The Opal Mystery. 1991. (Boomer Ser.). (Illus.). 192p. (Orig.). (J). (gr. 3-7). pap. 3.25 (*0-922434-39-5*) Brighton & Lloyd.
Fairchild, Elisabeth. A Game of Patience. 2002. (Signet Regency Romance Ser.). 240p. mass mkt. 4.99 o.s.i (*0-451-20606-1*, Signet Bks.) NAL.
Faithful Friends, Set. Incl. Best Friends under the Sun. Whalen, Sharla Scannell. 2000. lib. bdg. 21.35 (*1-57765-228-2*); Flower Girl Friends. Abdo Publishing Staff, contrib. by. 2000. lib. bdg. 21.35 (*1-57765-229-0*); Friends on Ice. Whalen, Sharla Scannell. 1998. lib. bdg. 21.35 (*1-57765-227-4*); Meet the Friends. Whalen, Sharla Scannell. 2000. lib. bdg. 21.35 (*1-57765-226-6*); 64p. (J). (gr. 4)., ABDO & Daughters (Illus.). 1998. Set lib. bdg. 91.12 (*1-57765-254-1*) ABDO Publishing Co.
Falda, Dominique. El Cofre Del Tesoro. Gambolini, Gerardo, tr. from GER. 2002. (SPA., Illus.). 32p. (J). (ps-2). 15.95 (*0-7358-1697-2*); pap. 6.95 (*0-7358-1698-0*) North-South Bks., Inc. (Ediciones Norte-Sur).
—The Treasure Chest. 2002. (Illus.). 32p. (J). (ps-2). pap. 6.95 (*0-7358-1696-4*) North-South Bks., Inc.
—The Treasure Chest. Lanning, Rosemary, tr. from GER. 1999. (Illus.). 32p. (J). (ps-2). 15.95 (*0-7358-1049-4*); 16.50 o.p. (*0-7358-1050-8*) North-South Bks., Inc.
Falkner, J. Meade. Moonfleet. 2002. (Twelve-Point Ser.). (YA). lib. bdg. 25.00 (*1-58287-175-2*) North Bks.
Falwell, Cathryn. David's Drawings. 2001. (Illus.). 32p. (J). (ps-3). 16.00 (*1-58430-031-0*) Lee & Low Bks., Inc.
Fanelli, Sara. Wolf. 1997. 40p. (J). 14.99 o.s.i (*0-8037-2093-9*, Dial Bks. for Young Readers) Penguin Putnam Bks. for Young Readers.
Farish, Terry. The Cat Who Liked Potato Soup. 2003. (Illus.). 40p. (J). (ps-3). 15.99 (*0-7636-0834-3*) Candlewick Pr.
—Talking in Animal. 1996. 160p. (YA). (gr. 5 up). 15.00 o.s.i (*0-688-14671-6*, Greenwillow Bks.) HarperCollins Children's Bk. Group.
Farmer, Lynne. Guess What I Eat? 1996. (Illus.). 20p. (J). (ps-k). bds. 3.99 (*0-689-80690-6*, Little Simon) Simon & Schuster Children's Publishing.
Farmer, Nancy. Do You Know Me ? 1994. 9.09 o.p. (*0-606-06968-2*) Turtleback Bks.
Fames, Catherine. The Rivers of Judah. 1996. 133p. (YA). (gr. 9 up). pap. 6.49 (*0-89084-864-5*, 094045) Jones, Bob Univ. Pr.
Farnette, Cherrie, et al. People Need Each Other. rev. ed. 1989. (Kids' Stuff Ser.). (Illus.). 80p. (J). (gr. 4-7). pap. text 9.95 (*0-86530-070-4*, IP 63-3) Incentive Pubns., Inc.
Farrar, Susan C. Samantha on Stage. 1990. (Illus.). 164p. (J). (gr. 3 up). pap. 3.95 o.p. (*0-14-034328-8*, Puffin Bks.) Penguin Putnam Bks. for Young Readers.
Farrell, Mame. And Sometimes Why, RS. 2001. 176p. (J). (gr. 4-7). 16.00 (*0-374-32289-9*, Farrar, Straus & Giroux (BYR)) Farrar, Straus & Giroux.
—Marrying Malcolm Murgatroyd, RS. 128p. (J). (gr. 4-7). 1998. pap. 4.95 (*0-374-44744-6*, Sunburst); 1995. 14.00 o.p. (*0-374-34838-3*, Farrar, Straus & Giroux (BYR)) Farrar, Straus & Giroux.
—Marrying Malcolm Murgatroyd. 1995. 11.00 (*0-606-18134-2*) Turtleback Bks.
Fassina, Marene P. The Invisible Friend, , 1991. (J). audio 3.95 (*1-892996-02-2*) Fassina, Marene P.
—The Invisible Friend: Book, No. 1, No. 1000. 1998. 36p. (J). mass mkt. 4.75 (*1-892996-09-X*) Fassina, Marene P.
Fassler, Joan. The Boy with a Problem: Johnny Learns to Share His Troubles. 1971. (Illus.). 32p. (J). (ps-3). 16.95 (*0-87705-054-6*, Kluwer Academic/Human Science Pr.) Kluwer Academic Pubs.
The Fastest One of All. 1991. (Illus.). (J). (ps-2). pap. 5.10 (*0-8136-5641-9*); lib. bdg. 7.95 (*0-8136-5141-7*) Modern Curriculum Pr.
Faulkner, Keith. Sharing & Caring. 1998. (Illus.). 4p. (J). bds. 7.99 (*1-58048-036-5*) Sandvik Publishing.
Fearnley, Jan. A Perfect Day for It. 2002. (Illus.). 32p. (J). (gr. k-2). 16.00 (*0-15-216634-3*) Harcourt Children's Bks.
Feelings, Tom. Daydreamers. 1993. 32p. (gr. 1-3). pap. 6.99 (*0-14-054624-3*) Penguin Putnam Bks. for Young Readers.
Feiffer, Jules. A Barrel of Laughs, a Vale of Tears. (Illus.). 192p. (J). 1998. (gr. 4-7). pap. 6.95 (*0-06-205926-2*); 1995. (gr. 3-7). lib. bdg. 14.89 o.p. (*0-06-205099-0*); 1995. (gr. 4-7). 14.95 (*0-06-205098-2*) HarperCollins Children's Bk. Group.
Feil, Hila. Between Friends. 1990. (Portraits Collection: No. 6). (YA). mass mkt. 3.50 o.s.i (*0-449-14609-X*, Fawcett) Ballantine Bks.
Feinberg, Anna. Wiggy & Boa. 1990. (Illus.). 112p. (J). (gr. 3-7). 13.95 o.p. (*0-395-53704-5*) Houghton Mifflin Co.
Feldman, Eve B. That Cat! 1994. (Illus.). 112p. (J). 14.00 (*0-688-13310-X*, Morrow, William & Co.) Morrow/Avon.
—We Are Friends. 1989. (Real Readers Ser.: Level Blue). (Illus.). 32p. (J). (ps-3). pap. 3.95 o.p. (*0-8114-6716-3*); lib. bdg. 21.40 (*0-8172-3517-5*) Raintree Pubs.
Feldman, Thea. Mummy with the Golden Mask. 2003. (Festival Reader Ser.). (Illus.). 32p. (J). (ps-2). pap. 3.99 (*0-06-054865-7*) HarperCollins Children's Bk. Group.
Fender, Kay. Odette: A Springtime in Paris. 1991. (Illus.). 32p. (J). (ps-3). 10.95 o.p. (*0-916291-33-2*) Kane/Miller Bk. Pubs.
Fenton, Anne. Tikun Olam: Fixing the World. 1997. (Illus.). 32p. (J). (gr. 1-4). 15.95 (*1-57129-049-4*, Lumen Editions) Brookline Bks., Inc.
Ferguson, Alane. Overkill. 1994. 176p. (J). (gr. 5 up). mass mkt. 3.99 (*0-380-72167-8*, Avon Bks.) Morrow/Avon.
—Stardust. 1995. (J). pap. 3.99 (*0-380-72321-2*, Avon Bks.) Morrow/Avon.
Ferraro, Bonita. Big Book: Wait for Me. l.t. ed. 1997. (Sadlier Phonics Reading Program). (Illus.). 8p. (J). (ps-1). (*0-8215-0862-8*, Sadlier-Oxford) Sadlier, William H. Inc.
Ferreira, Anton. Zulu Dog, RS. 2002. (Illus.). 208p. (J). (gr. 5 up). 16.00 (*0-374-39223-4*, Farrar, Straus & Giroux (BYR)) Farrar, Straus & Giroux.
Ferris, Amy Schor. A Greater Goode. 2002. 192p. (YA). (gr. 5-9). 15.00 (*0-618-13154-X*) Houghton Mifflin Co.
Ferris, Jean. Across the Grain, RS. 1990. 212p. (YA). (gr. 7 up). 15.00 o.p. (*0-374-30030-5*, Farrar, Straus & Giroux (BYR)) Farrar, Straus & Giroux.
—Of Sound Mind, RS. (YA). 2004. pap. 5.95 (*0-374-45584-8*); 2001. 224p. (gr. 8 up). 16.00 (*0-374-35580-0*, Farrar, Straus & Giroux (BYR)) Farrar, Straus & Giroux.
—The Stainless Steel Rule, RS. 1986. 192p. (J). (gr. 7 up). 15.00 o.p. (*0-374-37212-8*, Farrar, Straus & Giroux (BYR)) Farrar, Straus & Giroux.
Ferry, Charles. A Fresh Start. 1996. 76p. (Orig.). (YA). (gr. 7 up). pap. 8.95 (*1-882792-18-1*) Proctor Pubns.
—Raspberry 1, 001. 1983. 224p. (J). (gr. 7 up). 13.95 o.p. (*0-395-34069-1*) Houghton Mifflin Co.
Field, Eugene. Wynken, Blynken & Nod. 1980. (Illus.). (J). (gr. k-2). 6.95 o.s.i (*0-8038-8046-4*) Hastings Hse. Daytrips Pubs.
—Wynken, Blynken & Nod. unabr. ed. 1989. (Illus.). (J). (gr. k-3). pap. 15.95 incl. audio (*0-87499-142-0*) Live Oak Media.
—Wynken, Blynken & Nod. (Illus.). 32p. (ps-3). 1992. pap. 5.99 o.s.i (*0-14-054794-0*); 1985. (J). pap. 4.95 o.p. (*0-525-44199-9*, 0383-120, Dutton Children's Bks.); 1982. (J). 13.50 o.s.i (*0-525-44022-4*, Dutton Children's Bks.) Penguin Putnam Bks. for Young Readers.
Field, Rachel. Calico Bush. 1999. pap. 2.99 (*0-689-82968-X*, Aladdin) Simon & Schuster Children's Publishing.
—Calico Bush. 1999. (Illus.). (J). 8.34 o.p. (*0-606-17916-X*) Turtleback Bks.
Fielding, Daphne Vivian. The Rainbow Picnic: A Portrait of Iris Tree. 1974. 160 of plate.p. (*0-413-28520-0*) Heinemann.
Fielding, William H., Jr. Molly, Teddy & Friends. 2001. (J). spiral bd. (*0-945069-16-2*) Freedom Pr. Assocs.
Fienberg, Anna. The Hottest Boy Who Ever Lived. Grant, Christy, ed. 1994. (Illus.). 32p. (J). (ps-3). lib. bdg. 15.95 o.p. (*0-8075-3387-4*) Whitman, Albert & Co.
—Vico y Boa (Wiggy & Boa) Mills, Tedi L., tr. 1992. (SPA., Illus.). 116p. (J). (gr. 5-6). pap. 5.99 (*968-16-3747-X*) Fondo de Cultura Economica MEX. *Dist:* Continental Bk. Co., Inc.
Fienberg, Anna & Fienberg, Barbara. The Big Big Big Book of Tashi. 2002. (Illus.). 448p. (J). (gr. 1-5). pap. 11.95 (*1-86508-563-4*) Allen & Unwin Pty., Ltd. AUS. *Dist:* Independent Pubs. Group.
Finch, Margo. The Lunch Bunch. 1998. (Real Kids Readers Ser.). (Illus.). 32p. (gr. k-2). pap. 4.99 (*0-7613-2030-X*); lib. bdg. 18.90 (*0-7613-2005-9*) Millbrook Pr., Inc.
—The Lunch Bunch. 1998. (Real Kids Readers Ser.). lib. bdg. 10.14 (*0-606-15801-4*) Turtleback Bks.
—The Lunch Bunch. 1998. E-Book (*1-58824-476-8*); E-Book (*1-58824-724-4*); E-Book (*1-58824-806-2*) ipicturebooks, LLC.
Finch, Susan. The Intimacy of Indiana. 2000. (Illus.). 177p. (YA). pap. 5.95 (*0-936389-79-6*) Tudor Pubs., Inc.
Find Simba. 1994. (Pop-Up Pals Ser.). (Illus.). 10p. (J). (ps-1). 6.98 o.p. (*1-57082-143-7*) Mouse Works.
Findlay, Grace R. Pinto & Sprinto. 2000. (J). (ps-1). pap. 6.95 o.p. (*0-533-13487-0*) Vantage Pr., Inc.
Fine, Anne. Bad Dreams. 2000. (Illus.). 144p. (gr. 5-9). text 15.95 o.s.i (*0-385-32757-9*, Delacorte Pr.) Dell Publishing.
—Bad Dreams. 2001. (Illus.). 144p. pap. text 4.99 (*0-440-41690-6*, Yearling) Random Hse. Children's Bks.
—The Tulip Touch. l.t. ed. (J). 2000. (Illus.). pap. (*0-7540-6091-8*); 2003. 200p. pap. 29.95 incl. audio (*0-7540-6227-9*, RA028, Galaxy Children's Large Print) BBC Audiobooks America.
—The Tulip Touch. 1997. 160p. (J). (gr. 5-12). 15.95 o.p. (*0-316-28325-8*) Little Brown & Co.
—The Tulip Touch. 1999. 160p. (YA). (gr. 4-7). mass mkt. 4.99 (*0-440-22785-2*, Dell Books for Young Readers) Random Hse. Children's Bks.
—The Tulip Touch. 1999. 11.04 (*0-606-16711-0*) Turtleback Bks.
—Up on Cloud Nine. l.t. ed. 2003. (Illus.). (J). pap. 16.95 incl. audio (*0-7540-7878-7*, Galaxy Children's Large Print) BBC Audiobooks America.
—Up on Cloud Nine. 2003. 160p. (gr. 5). pap. text 4.99 (*0-440-41916-6*, Dell Books for Young Readers); 2003. 176p. pap. (*0-552-54840-5*, Yearling); 2002. 160p. (gr. 5-7). text 15.95 (*0-385-73009-8*, Delacorte Bks. for Young Readers); 2002. 160p. (gr. 5-7). lib. bdg. 17.99 (*0-385-90058-9*, Delacorte Bks. for Young Readers) Random Hse. Children's Bks.
Fink, Christopher. Leopold & Brink No. 1: Introductions. 1997. (Illus.). 24p. (YA). pap. 2.50 (*1-930281-00-5*) FINK, Inc.
—Leopold & Brink No. 2: Orbit. 32p. (YA). 1998. pap. 2.95 (*1-930281-02-1*); 1997. (Illus.). pap. 2.95 (*1-930281-01-3*) FINK, Inc.
Finley, Martha. Elsie & the Raymonds, Bk. 15. 2001. mass mkt. 5.99 (*1-931343-24-1*) Hibbard Pubns., Inc.
—Elsie & the Raymonds. 1997. (Elsie Dinsmore Ser.: Bk. 15). 332p. (gr. 4-7). 28.99 (*1-58960-277-3*) Sovereign Grace Pubs., Inc.
—Elsie's Friends at Woodburn, Bk. 13. 2001. mass mkt. 5.99 (*1-931343-22-5*) Hibbard Pubns., Inc.
—Elsie's Friends at Woodburn. 1996. (Elsie Dinsmore Ser.: Bk. 13). 344p. (gr. 4-7). 28.99 (*1-58960-275-7*) Sovereign Grace Pubs., Inc.
Finnegan, Evelyn M. My Little Friend Goes to a Baseball Game. 1995. (Illus.). 32p. (J). (ps-3). 14.95 (*0-9641285-0-0*) Little Friend Pr.
—My Little Friend Goes to School. 1996. (My Little Friend Ser.). (Illus.). 32p. (J). (ps-3). pap. 6.95 (*0-9641285-6-X*) Little Friend Pr.
—My Little Friend Goes to the Dentist. 1997. (My Little Friend Ser.). (Illus.). 32p. (J). (ps-3). pap. 6.95 (*1-890453-00-5*) Little Friend Pr.
First Graders at Clara Barton Elementary School Staff. I Need a Hug! 1992. (Kids Are Authors Picture Bks.). (Illus.). 32p. (J). (gr. k-3). pap. 3.50 (*0-87406-605-0*) Darby Creek Publishing.
First, Julia. Flat on My Face. 1984. (J). (gr. 4-6). pap. 1.25 o.p. (*0-380-00204-3*, 52324-8, Avon Bks.) Morrow/Avon.
Fishbein, Amy. Seventeen Girlfriends: Your Total Guide to Friendships. 2001. (Seventeen Ser.). 128p. (YA). (gr. 7 up). pap. 5.95 (*0-06-447243-4*, Harper Trophy) HarperCollins Children's Bk. Group.
Fisher-Price Staff & Hood, Susan. Firefighter Sam Finds a Friend. 1997. (Fisher-Price Take-Me-Out Playbook Ser.). (Illus.). 14p. (J). (ps-k). bds. 9.99 (*1-57584-182-7*) Reader's Digest Children's Publishing, Inc.
Fitch, Janet. Kicks. 1996. (J). (gr. 7). mass mkt. 4.50 o.s.i (*0-449-70452-1*, Fawcett) Ballantine Bks.
—Kicks. 1995. 192p. (J). (gr. 7 up). tchr. ed. 14.95 o.p. (*0-395-69624-0*, Clarion Bks.) Houghton Mifflin Co. Trade & Reference Div.
Fitch, Sheree. Little Toby & Big Hair. 1998. (Illus.). 32p. (J). pap. 8.95 (*0-385-25678-7*) Doubleday Publishing.
Fitts, J. Stuart. A Stranger in the Park. l.t. ed. 1999. (Caution Crew : Vol. I). (Illus.). 36p. (J). (ps-6). 16.95 o.p. (*1-888106-95-6*) Agreka Bks., LLC.
Fitzgerald, Matthew. Harvey's Wish. 1995. (Publish-a-Book Ser.). (Illus.). 32p. (J). (gr. 1-6). lib. bdg. 22.83 o.p. (*0-8114-7271-X*) Raintree Pubs.
Fitzhugh, Louise. Harriet the Spy. 2001. (Illus.). (J). 12.04 (*0-606-21226-4*) Turtleback Bks.
—The Long Secret: Harriet the Spy Adventure. 2001. (Illus.). 288p. (gr. 5 up). text 15.95 (*0-385-32784-6*, Delacorte Bks. for Young Readers) Random Hse. Children's Bks.
Fitzpatrick, Marie-Louise. I'm a Tiger, Too! 2002. 6.95 (*0-86327-871-X*) Interlink Publishing Group, Inc.
Fleischman, Sid. The Scarebird. 1994. (Illus.). 32p. (J). (ps-3). reprint ed. pap. 4.95 (*0-688-13105-0*, Harper Trophy) HarperCollins Children's Bk. Group.
Fletcher, Ralph J. Flying Solo. 2000. 144p. (gr. 5-9). pap. text 4.99 (*0-440-41601-9*, Yearling) Random Hse. Children's Bks.
Flinn, Alex. Breaking Point. 2002. (J). 224p. (gr. 7 up). 15.95 (*0-06-623847-1*); 256p. (ps-k). lib. bdg. 15.89 (*0-06-623848-X*) HarperCollins Pubs.
Flood, Pansie Hart. Secret Holes. 2003. (Illus.). 122p. (J). 15.95 (*0-87614-923-9*, Carolrhoda Bks.) Lerner Publishing Group.
Flora, James. My Friend Charlie. 1972. (Illus.). (J). (gr. 1-4). reprint ed. pap. 1.25 o.p. (*0-15-662330-7*, Voyager Bks./Libros Viajeros) Harcourt Children's Bks.
Foland, Constance M. Flying High, Pogo! 2002. (American Girls Collection Ser.). (Illus.). 144p. (J). (gr. 5 up). pap. 5.95 (*1-58485-535-5*); trans. 14.95 (*1-58485-624-6*) Pleasant Co. Pubns. (American Girl).
—A Song for Jeffrey. 1999. (American Girls Collection Ser.). (Illus.). 192p. (J). (gr. 4-7). pap. 5.95 (*1-56247-754-4*); (gr. 5 up). 9.95 (*1-56247-849-4*) Pleasant Co. Pubns. (American Girl).
—A Song for Jeffrey. 1999. 12.00 (*0-606-18357-4*) Turtleback Bks.
Foley, Pat. Seismo & Ellie. 2nd ed. 1990. (Illus.). 14p. (J). (gr. k-1). reprint ed. pap. 6.00 (*0-9624315-1-6*) Pajari Pr.
Foley, Patricia. John & the Fiddler. 1990. (Illus.). 64p. (J). (gr. 1-5). lib. bdg. 12.89 o.p. (*0-06-021842-8*); 12.95 (*0-06-021841-X*) HarperCollins Children's Bk. Group.
Folse, Pamela. A Sweet Surprise. 1995. (Illus.). 32p. (J). (ps-7). lib. bdg. 10.00 (*1-884725-11-2*) Blue Heron Pr.

Relationships

Fontenay, Charles L. Kipton & Gruff. 1995. (Kipton Chronicles Ser.: Bk. 1). (YA). (gr. 5 up). pap. 9.99 (0-88092-170-6); (J). (gr. 6-9). lib. bdg. o.p. (0-88092-171-4) Royal Fireworks Publishing Co.

—Kipton & the Ovoid. (Kipton Chronicles Ser.: Bk. 2). 1996. (YA). (gr. 5 up). pap. 9.99 (0-88092-283-4); 1995. (J). (gr. 6-9). lib. bdg. 19.99 o.p. (0-88092-284-2) Royal Fireworks Publishing Co.

Fontenot, Mary Alice. Clovis Crawfish & Silvie Sulphur. 2003. (Illus.). 32p. (J). 15.95 (1-56554-864-7) Pelican Publishing Co., Inc.

—Clovis Crawfish & the Curious Crapaud. 1986. (Clovis Crawfish Ser.). (Illus.). 32p. (J). (ps-3). 14.95 (0-88289-610-5) Pelican Publishing Co., Inc.

—Clovis Ecrevisse et Pailasse Poule D'Eau. Landry, Julie Fontenot, tr. & illus. by. 1997. (ENG & FRE.). 32p. (J). (gr. 1-4). 15.95 incl. audio (1-56554-278-9) Pelican Publishing Co., Inc.

—Clovis Ecrevisse et Sidonie Souris-De-Champ. Landry, Julie F., tr. 1998. (FRE., Illus.). 32p. (J). (ps-3). 15.95 (1-56554-345-9) Pelican Publishing Co., Inc.

Fontes, Justine. Friends in Need: Disney's The Lion King. 1994. (Illus.). 24p. (J). (ps-3). pap. text 2.25 o.p. (0-307-12848-2, Golden Bks.) Random Hse. Children's Bks.

—Toy Trouble. 2003. (Illus.). 24p. (J). pap. (1-59034-447-2); 14.95 (1-59034-446-4) Mondo Publishing.

Fontes, Justine & Fontes, Ron. George & Stuart. 1999. (Stuart Little Tie-In Ser.). (Illus.). 24p. (J). (ps-1). pap. 3.25 (0-694-01415-X, Harper Festival) HarperCollins Children's Bk. Group.

Ford, George Cephas, illus. A Camel Called Bump-Along. 1997. (0-7802-8030-X) Wright Group, The.

Foreman, Mary M., tr. from ENG. Encuentralo con Elena. 1992. (Gus Is Gone Ser.). (SPA., Illus.). 24p. (J). pap. 3.95 (1-56288-238-4) Checkerboard Pr., Inc.

—Paseate Con Paco. 1929. (Gus Is Gone Ser.). (SPA., Illus.). 24p. (J). pap. 3.95 (1-56288-240-6) Checkerboard Pr., Inc.

Forman. We'll Meet Again. 9999. 15.95 o.s.i (0-689-80536-5); 1995. (J). 15.95 (0-684-19737-5) Simon & Schuster Children's Publishing. (Atheneum).

Fornof, John. Tads Glad Sad Mad Glad Day. 2003. 12p. 6.99 (0-310-70647-5) Zondervan.

Forsse, Ken. Branson Bear & the Kite Contest: Springtime Stormbook. l.t. ed. 1997. (Illus.). 32p. (J). (ps-4). 15.95 (1-890315-00-1) Xploractive Concepts, Inc.

Forster, E. M. Where Angels Fear to Tread. 1996. 320p. (J). mass mkt. 4.50 o.s.i (0-553-21446-2, Bantam Classics) Bantam Bks.

Forward, Toby. Pie Magic. (Illus.). (J). (gr. 3 up). 1998. 112p. pap. 4.95 o.s.i (0-688-15856-0); 1996. 128p. 15.00 o.p. (0-688-14511-6) Morrow/Avon. (Morrow, William & Co.).

Fosburgh, Liza. Bella Arabella. 1987. 112p. (J). pap. 2.50 o.s.i (0-553-15484-2, Skylark) Random Hse. Children's Bks.

Foster, Kelli C. Bub & Chub. 1992. (Get Ready...Get Set...Read! Ser.). (J). 9.65 (0-606-01616-3) Turtleback Bks.

Foster, Kelli C. & Erickson, Gina Clegg. Bub & Chub. 1996. (Get Ready...Get Set...Read! Ser.: Set 2). (Illus.). 24p. (J). lib. bdg. 11.95 (1-56674-154-8) Forest Hse. Publishing Co., Inc.

Fowler, Susi Gregg. Albertina, the Animals & Me. 2000. (Illus.). 96p. (YA). (gr. 5 up). lib. bdg. 14.89 (0-06-029160-5, Greenwillow Bks.) HarperCollins Children's Bk. Group.

—Albertina the Practically Perfect. 1998. (Illus.). 80p. (J). (gr. 2 up). 15.95 (0-688-15829-3, Greenwillow Bks.) HarperCollins Children's Bk. Group.

—When Joel Comes Home. 1993. (Illus.). 24p. (J). (ps up). lib. bdg. 13.93 o.p. (0-688-11065-7, Greenwillow Bks.) HarperCollins Children's Bk. Group.

The Fox & the Hound. 1994. (Classics Ser.). (Illus.). 96p. (J). (ps-4). 7.98 o.p. (1-57082-038-4) Mouse Works.

The Fox & the Hound That's What Friends Are For. 1995. (Golden Look-Look Bks.). (Illus.). 24p. (J). (ps-3). bds. o.p. (0-307-11859-2, Golden Bks.) Random Hse. Children's Bks.

Fox, Mem. Guillermo Jorge Manuel Jose. 1992. (SPA., Illus.). 32p. (J). (gr. k-3). pap. 7.49 (980-257-051-6, EK2901) Ekare, Ediciones VEN. *Dist:* AIMS International Bks., Inc., Kane/Miller Bk. Pubs., Lectorum Pubns., Inc.

—Wilfrid Gordon McDonald Partridge. 2002. (Illus.). (J). 16.55 (0-7587-4024-7) Book Wholesalers, Inc.

—Wilfrid Gordon McDonald Partridge. 1985. (Illus.). 32p. (J). (ps-3). 13.95 (0-916291-04-9) Kane/Miller Bk. Pubs.

—Wilfrid Gordon McDonald Partridge. 1989. (J). 14.10 (0-606-04588-0) Turtleback Bks.

Fox, Paula. Lily & the Lost Boy. 1989. 160p. (J). (gr. k-6). pap. 3.99 o.s.i (0-440-40235-2, Yearling) Random Hse. Children's Bks.

France, Anthony. From Me to You. 2004. 32p. (J). 15.99 (0-7636-2255-9) Candlewick Pr.

Francia, Silvia. Roberta's Vacation. 1998. (Illus.). 32p. (J). (ps-3). 13.95 (0-916291-83-9) Kane/Miller Bk. Pubs.

Frank, E. R. Friction. 2003. (J). audio 30.00 (0-8072-1648-8) Random Hse. Audio Publishing Group.

Frank, Lucy. Oy, Joy! 1999. (Illus.). 288p. (J). (gr. 6-9). pap. 16.95 o.p. (0-7894-2538-6) Dorling Kindersley Publishing, Inc.

—Will You Be My Brussels Sprout? 1996. 160p. (YA). (gr. 7-12). tchr. ed. 15.95 (0-8234-1220-2) Holiday Hse., Inc.

—Will You Be My Brussels Sprout? 1998. (J). 10.04 (0-606-13918-4) Turtleback Bks.

Franklin, Kristine L. Eclipse. 160p. (J). 1998. (Illus.). (gr. 6-10). bds. 4.99 (0-7636-0241-8); 1995. (gr. 4-7). 14.99 (1-56402-544-6) Candlewick Pr.

—Eclipse. 1998. 11.04 (0-606-15515-5) Turtleback Bks.

—Lone Wolf. (J). 1998. 224p. (gr. 3-7). bds. 4.99 o.s.i (0-7636-0480-1); 1997. (gr. 4-8). 17.99 o.s.i (1-56402-935-2) Candlewick Pr.

—Lone Wolf. 1998. (J). 11.04 (0-606-13578-2) Turtleback Bks.

—Nerd No More. 1998. (Illus.). 144p. (YA). (gr. 4-7). bds. 4.99 o.s.i (0-7636-0487-9) Candlewick Pr.

—Nerd No More. 1999. 11.04 (0-606-15653-4) Turtleback Bks.

Fraser, Sylvia. Tom & Francine: A Love Story. 1998. (Illus.). 32p. (J). (ps-5). text 12.95 (1-55013-944-4) Key Porter Bks. CAN. *Dist:* Firefly Bks., Ltd.

Frazier, Bessie. Exciting Stories & Plays. 2001. (J). 15.95 o.p. (0-533-13392-0) Vantage Pr., Inc.

Frechette, Carole. In the Key of Do. Ouriou, Susan, tr. from FRE. 2002. 196p. (YA). (gr. 8 up). pap. 9.95 (0-88995-254-X) Red Deer Pr. CAN. *Dist:* General Distribution Services, Inc.

Fredericks, Mariah. The True Meaning of Cleavage. 2003. (Illus.). 224p. (YA). 15.95 (0-689-85092-1, Atheneum/Richard Jackson Bks.) Simon & Schuster Children's Publishing.

Freed, Shirley Ann & Moon, Louise. My Forever Friend. Morelan, Bill, ed. l.t. ed. 2002. (Illus.). 16p. (J). (gr. 1-2). pap. 3.99 (1-58938-034-7) Concerned Communications.

Freeman, Bill. Cedric & the North End Kids. 1985. (Illus.). 80p. (J). pap. 5.95 (0-88862-177-9); bds. 12.95 (0-88862-187-6) Lorimer, James & Co. CAN. *Dist:* Formac Distributing, Ltd.

Freeman, Don. Corduroy. (Corduroy Ser.). (Illus.). 1982. pap., tchr. ed. 33.95 incl. audio (0-941078-07-8); 1990. (SPA., (J). reprint ed. pap. 15.95 incl. audio (0-87499-213-3, LK3796); 1982. (J). 24.95 incl. audio (0-941078-08-6); 1982. (J). pap. 15.95 incl. audio (0-941078-06-X) Live Oak Media.

—Corduroy. (Corduroy Ser.). (gr. k-1). 1990. (SPA., Illus.). 32p. (J). pap. 6.99 (0-14-054252-3, VK3790, Puffin Bks.); 1970. pap. 0.95 o.p. (0-670-05046-6, Dutton Children's Bks.) Penguin Putnam Bks. for Young Readers.

—Corduroy. 1968. 3.37 o.p. (0-670-24134-2, Viking) Viking Penguin.

—Corduroy's Day. 1985. (Corduroy Ser.). (Illus.). 144p. (J). (gr. k-1). bds. 3.99 (0-670-80521-1, Viking Children's Bks.) Penguin Putnam Bks. for Young Readers.

—Mop Top. 1982. (Illus.). (J). (gr. k-3). 22.95 o.p. incl. audio (0-941078-14-0); pap. 15.95 incl. audio (0-941078-12-4) Live Oak Media.

—Mop Top. 1955. (J). 12.14 (0-606-02182-5) Turtleback Bks.

—Mop Top, Grades K-3. 1982. (Illus.). pap., tchr. ed. 33.95 incl. audio (0-941078-13-2) Live Oak Media.

—A Pocket for Corduroy. 1982. (Corduroy Ser.). (Illus.). (J). (gr. k-1). pap., stu. ed. 33.95 incl. audio (0-941078-16-7); 24.95 incl. audio (0-941078-17-5); pap. 15.95 incl. audio (0-941078-15-9) Live Oak Media.

—A Rainbow of My Own. 1982. (Illus.). (gr. k-3). (J). 22.95 o.p. incl. audio (0-941078-20-5); pap., tchr. ed. 33.95 incl. audio (0-941078-19-1); (J). pap. 15.95 incl. audio (0-941078-18-3) Live Oak Media.

—A Rainbow of My Own. 1974. pap. 1.25 o.p. (0-670-05086-5, Dutton Children's Bks.) Penguin Putnam Bks. for Young Readers.

—A Rainbow of My Own. 1966. (J). 12.14 (0-606-02236-8) Turtleback Bks.

—A Rainbow of My Own. 1966. 2.96 o.p. (0-670-58929-2, Viking) Viking Penguin.

Freeman, Martha. The Spy Wore Shades. 2001. (Illus.). 240p. (J). (gr. 3 up). 15.95 (0-06-029269-5); lib. bdg. 15.89 (0-06-029270-9) HarperCollins Children's Bk. Group.

—The Spy Wore Shades. Date not set. 160p. (YA). (gr. 3 up). pap. 4.99 (0-06-440957-0) HarperCollins Pubs.

—The Year My Parents Ruined My Life. 1997. 192p. (J). (gr. 5-9). tchr. ed. 15.95 (0-8234-1324-1) Holiday Hse., Inc.

—The Year My Parents Ruined My Life. 1999. (Illus.). 192p. (gr. 4-7). pap. text 4.99 (0-440-41533-0, Dell Books for Young Readers) Random Hse. Children's Bks.

—The Year My Parents Ruined My Life. 1999. 10.55 (0-606-16453-7) Turtleback Bks.

Fremlin, Robert. Three Friends. 1976. 64p. (gr. 1-3). pap. 0.95 o.p. (0-440-48699-8) Dell Publishing.

French, Michael. Us Against Them. 1988. 160p. (YA). (gr. 7-12). mass mkt. 2.95 o.s.i (0-553-27647-6, Starfire) Random Hse. Children's Bks.

Freschet, Gina. Winnie & Ernst, RS. 2003. (Illus.). 48p. 15.00 (0-374-38452-5, Farrar, Straus & Giroux (BYR)) Farrar, Straus & Giroux.

Fresh, Doug E. Think Again. 2002. (Hipkidhop Ser.). 32p. (J). (gr. 2-5). pap. 13.95 (0-439-31387-2, Cartwheel Bks.) Scholastic, Inc.

Freymann, Saxton & Elffers, Joost. One Lonely Sea Horse. 2000. (Illus.). 10p. (J). (ps-3). pap. 15.95 (0-439-11014-9, Levine, Arthur A. Bks.) Scholastic, Inc.

Friedman, Laurie B. Mallory on the Move. Schmitz, Tamara, tr. & illus. by. 2004. (Middle Grade Fiction Ser.). (J). lib. bdg. 15.95 (1-57505-538-4, Carolrhoda Bks.) Lerner Publishing Group.

Friedman, Melanie. Jennifer No. 5: Cool It! 1991. (YA). mass mkt. 3.50 o.p. (0-425-12773-7, Splash) Berkley Publishing Group.

Friedrich, Joachim. 4 1/2 Friends & the Secret Cave, Bk. 1. Crawford, Elizabeth D., tr. from GER. 2001. (Illus.). 154p. (J). (gr. 3-7). 14.99 (0-7868-0648-6) Hyperion Bks. for Children.

Friel, Maeve. Charlie's Story. 2004. 144p. (YA). (gr. 7-9). 7.95 (1-56145-315-3, Freestone) Peachtree Pubs., Ltd.

Friend in Need. 1996. (J). 9.98 o.p. (1-57082-341-3) Mouse Works.

A Friend Is Special. 1984. 80p. (J). pap. 3.95 o.p. (0-89542-051-1) Ideals Pubns.

Friends Forever. 1987. (Boxed-Apples Ser.: No. 4). (J). pap. 10.00 o.p. (0-590-63232-9) Scholastic, Inc.

Friends, Paz. Dos Amigos. 2001. Tr. of Two Friends. (SPA.). (J). (gr. 2-4). 16.76 (84-88342-17-9) S.A. Kokinos ESP. *Dist:* Lectorum Pubns., Inc.

Friendship Tales. 1996. (Disney Ser.). (Illus.). 70p. (J). (ps-3). pap. text 2.29 (0-307-08545-7, 08545, Golden Bks.) Random Hse. Children's Bks.

Fritz, Anna M. Fredi. 1997. (Illus.). 40p. (J). (gr. k-6). per. 7.95 (0-9660959-0-1) Star Image Studio.

Fritz, Jean. Early Thunder. 1987. (Illus.). 256p. (YA). (gr. 4-7). reprint ed. pap. 5.99 (0-14-032259-0, Puffin Bks.) Penguin Putnam Bks. for Young Readers.

—The Great Little Madison. 1998. (Illus.). 160p. (J). (gr. 5-9). pap. 5.99 (0-698-11621-6, PaperStar) Penguin Putnam Bks. for Young Readers.

Froggy World: Where All Your Dreams Come True. 2003. 14.99 (0-310-70577-0) Zonderkidz.

Fryar, Jane L. The Locked-In Friend. 1991. (Morris the Mouse Adventure Ser.). (Illus.). 32p. (J). (ps-2). 7.99 o.s.i (0-570-04195-3) Concordia Publishing Hse.

Fuchs, Menucha. Children's Stories about Friendship. 2000. (Children's Learning Ser.: Vol. 5). (Illus.). 48p. (J). (gr. 1-4). pap. 4.95 (1-880582-51-1) Judaica Pr., Inc., The.

Fujikawa, Gyo. Are You My Friend Today? 1999. 3.99 (0-375-80125-1) Random Hse., Inc.

—Faraway Friends. 1981. (Gyo Fujikawa Ser.). (Illus.). 14p. (J). 2.25 o.p. (0-448-15103-0) Putnam Publishing Group, The.

—Welcome Is a Wonderful Word. 1980. (Fujikawa Storybooks). (Illus.). 32p. (J). (ps-2). 4.19 o.p. (0-448-13650-3) Putnam Publishing Group, The.

Fujimoto, Michi. Celebrating Side by Side: Sticker Activity Storybook. 1998. (Puzzle Place Sticker Activity Bks.). (Illus.). 24p. (J). (ps-1). 4.99 o.s.i (0-8431-7935-X, Price Stern Sloan) Penguin Putnam Bks. for Young Readers.

—I See You, Can You See Me? 1998. (Puzzle Place Sticker Activity Bks.). (Illus.). 24p. (J). (ps-1). 4.99 o.s.i (0-8431-7932-5, Price Stern Sloan) Penguin Putnam Bks. for Young Readers.

Fun in the Park. 1999. (Tami & Moishy Ser.: Vol. 3). bds. 6.95 (1-58330-378-2) Feldheim, Philipp Inc.

Fuqua, Jonathon Scott. Catie & Josephine. 2003. (Illus.). 72p. (J). (gr. 2-5). 16.00 (0-618-39403-6) Houghton Mifflin Co.

Furlong, Monica. Colman. 2004. (Illus.). 288p. (J). (gr. 5). lib. bdg. 17.99 (0-375-91514-1) Random Hse. Children's Bks.

Futcher, Jane. Promise Not to Tell. 1991. 192p. (J). (gr. 4-5). pap. 2.95 (0-380-76037-1, Avon Bks.) Morrow/Avon.

Gabhart, Ann. Only in Sunshine. 1988. (YA). (gr. 7 up). pap. 2.95 (0-380-75395-2, Avon Bks.) Morrow/Avon.

—Two of a Kind. 1992. (J). (gr. 4-7). pap. 3.50 (0-380-76153-X, Avon Bks.) Morrow/Avon.

Gabriel, Nal. A Day with May, Level 1. 2000. (All-Star Readers Ser.). (Illus.). 32p. (J). (ps-1). mass mkt. 3.99 (1-57584-384-6, Reader's Digest Children's Bks.) Reader's Digest Children's Publishing, Inc.

Gabrielson, Christine & Carpenter, Anita. Alpha-Yabba-Zoo. 1995. (Illus.). 28p. (Orig.). (J). (ps-3). pap. 12.95 (0-9635580-0-5) PeriWrinkle Productions, Inc.

Gackenbach, Dick. McGoogan Moves the Mighty Rock. 1981. (Illus.). 48p. (J). (gr. 1-4). 8.95 o.p. (0-06-021967-X); lib. bdg. 10.89 o.p. (0-06-021968-8) HarperCollins Children's Bk. Group.

—More from Hound & Bear, 001. 1979. (Illus.). 48p. (J). (ps-3). 7.95 o.p. (0-395-28973-4, Clarion Bks.) Houghton Mifflin Co. Trade & Reference Div.

—What's Claude Doing? (Illus.). 32p. (J). (ps-3). 1986. pap. 5.95 o.p. (0-89919-464-8); 1984. 13.95 o.p. (0-89919-224-6) Houghton Mifflin Co. Trade & Reference Div. (Clarion Bks.).

—What's Claude Doing? 1984. (J). 12.10 (0-606-03316-5) Turtleback Bks.

Gaeddart, LouAnn. Your Former Friend, Matthew. 1985. 80p. (J). pap. 2.25 o.s.i (0-553-15345-5, Skylark) Random Hse. Children's Bks.

Gaeddert, LouAnn. Just Like Sisters. 1981. (Illus.). 96p. (J). (gr. 4-6). 9.95 o.p. (0-525-32959-5, Dutton) Dutton/Plume.

—Your Former Friend, Matthew. 1984. (Illus.). 80p. (J). (gr. 3-6). 11.95 o.p. (0-525-44086-0, Dutton Children's Bks.) Penguin Putnam Bks. for Young Readers.

Gaeddert, LouAnn Bigge. Friends & Enemies. 2000. (Illus.). 176p. (J). (gr. 5-9). 16.00 (0-689-82822-5, Atheneum) Simon & Schuster Children's Publishing.

Gago, Jenny & McKay, Sindy. The Perfect Gift. 2001. (We Both Read Ser.). (Illus.). 48p. (J). (gr. 1-2). 7.99 (1-891327-33-X); pap. 3.99 (1-891327-34-8) Treasure Bay, Inc.

Gaine-Winkelman, Barbara. Without Friends, You're Nothing: Tales of Friendship. 1999. (One Saturday Morning Ser.: Vol. 2). (Illus.). 105p. (J). (gr. 2-5). pap. text 3.99 o.p. (0-7868-4308-X) Hyperion Pr.

Gainer, Cindy. I'M Like You, You're Like Me: A Child's Book about Understanding & Celebrating Each Other. 1998. (Illus.). 48p. (J). (ps-3). pap. 10.95 (1-57542-039-2) Free Spirit Publishing, Inc.

Gaines, Isabel. Eeyore Finds Friends. (Illus.). (J). 2000. 40p. pap. o.s.i (0-7868-4475-2); 1999. (Winnie the Pooh First Readers Ser.: No. 11). 37p. pap. 3.99 (0-7868-4269-5) Disney Pr.

—Pooh's Best Friend. 1998. (Winnie the Pooh First Readers Ser.: No. 7). (Illus.). 40p. (J). (ps-3). pap. 3.95 (0-7868-4265-2) Disney Pr.

—Pooh's Christmas Gifts. 2001. (Winnie the Pooh First Readers Ser.). (Illus.). (J). 10.14 (0-606-21653-7) Turtleback Bks.

—Pooh's Graduation. 22nd ed. 2000. (Winnie the Pooh Ser.). (Illus.). 37p. (J). (gr. k-3). pap. 3.99 (0-7868-4369-1) Disney Pr.

—Pooh's Halloween Parade. 2001. (Winnie the Pooh First Readers Ser.). (Illus.). (J). 10.14 (0-606-21656-1) Turtleback Bks.

—Pooh's Surprise Basket. 1999. (Winnie the Pooh First Readers Ser.: No. 13). (Illus.). 37p. (J). (gr. k-3). pap. 3.99 (0-7868-4332-2) Disney Pr.

—Pooh's Surprise Basket. 1999. (Winnie the Pooh First Readers Ser.). 40p. (J). (gr. k-3). pap. 3.99 o.s.i (0-7364-1153-4, RH/Disney) Random Hse. Children's Bks.

—Tiggers Hate to Lose. 2001. (Winnie the Pooh First Readers Ser.). (Illus.). (J). 10.14 (0-606-21664-2) Turtleback Bks.

Gaines, Isabel & Milne, A. A. Pooh's Graduation. 2003. (Step into Reading Ser.). (Illus.). 32p. (J). pap. 3.99 (0-7364-1353-7); lib. bdg. 11.99 (0-7364-8011-0) Random Hse., Inc.

Gaiser, Conrad. Tad & Mr. Boom: Volume I. 1998. (Illus.). 24p. (J). (gr. k-3). pap. 7.00 o.p. (0-8059-4016-2) Dorrance Publishing Co., Inc.

Galbraith, Kathryn O. Roommates Again. 1994. (Illus.). 48p. (J). (gr. 1-4). 13.00 (0-689-50597-3, McElderry, Margaret K.) Simon & Schuster Children's Publishing.

Gantos, Jack. Fair-Weather Friends, 001. 1977. (Illus.). (J). (gr. k-3). 6.95 o.p. (0-395-25156-7) Houghton Mifflin Co.

—The Perfect Pal, 001. 1979. (Illus.). (J). (gr. k-3). lib. bdg. 7.95 o.p. (0-395-28380-9) Houghton Mifflin Co.

Gantschev, Ivan. Good Morning, Good Night. Clements, Andrew, tr. 1991. (Illus.). 28p. (J). (gr. k up). pap. 14.95 (0-88708-183-5, Simon & Schuster Children's Publishing) Simon & Schuster Children's Publishing.

Ganz, Yaffa. Sharing a Sunshine Umbrella: A Mimmy & Simmy Story. 1989. (Illus.). (J). 12.95 (0-87306-496-8) Feldheim, Philipp Inc.

Garcia, Maria. The Adventures of Connie & Diego. 1992. (J). mass mkt. 30.60 o.p. (0-516-80033-7, Children's Pr.) Scholastic Library Publishing.

—The Adventures of Connie & Diego. 1987. (Fifth World Tales Ser.). 13.10 (0-606-06162-2) Turtleback Bks.

—The Adventures of Connie & Diego Read-Along. 1988. (J). 22.95 incl. audio (0-89239-033-6) Children's Bk. Pr.

Garcia, Pelayo P. From Amigos to Friends. 1997. 180p. (YA). (gr. 6-12). pap. 7.95 (*1-55885-207-7*, Piñata Books) Arte Publico Pr.

Gardam, Jane. Un Poney en la Nieve. 2002. (SPA., Illus.). 64p. (J). (gr. 3-5). pap. 7.95 (*968-19-0315-3*) Aguilar Editorial MEX. *Dist:* Santillana USA Publishing Co., Inc.

—Un Poney en la Nieve. (SPA.). (J). (gr. k-4). pap. 6.95 o.s.i (*968-29-3165-7*) Direccion General de Publicaiones MEX. *Dist:* Univ. of Pittsburgh, Latin American Archaeology Pubns.

Garden, Nancy. Annie on My Mind, RS. 1984. 232p. (J). (gr. 7 up). pap. 3.95 o.p. (*0-374-40413-5*, Sunburst) Farrar, Straus & Giroux.

—Meeting Melanie, RS. 2002. 208p. (J). (gr. 5 up). 16.00 (*0-374-34943-6*, Farrar, Straus & Giroux (BYR)) Farrar, Straus & Giroux.

Gardiner, Lindsey. Not Fair, Won't Share! A Pinky & Blue Story. 2002. (Illus.). 32p. (J). (ps-1). pap. 5.95 (*0-7641-2262-2*) Barron's Educational Series, Inc.

Gardner, Theodore R., II. Something Nice to See. 1994. (Illus.). 32p. (J). (gr. k up). 15.95 (*0-9627297-6-0*) Knoll, Allen A. Pubs.

Garfield, Leon. The December Rose. l.t. ed. 1987. 344p. (J). (gr. 3-7). 16.95 o.p. (*0-7451-0588-2*, Galaxy Children's Large Print) BBC Audiobooks America.

Garland, Sarah. Billy & Belle. 1999. (Illus.). (J). pap. (*0-14-054824-6*) NAL.

—Billy & Belle. (Illus.). 32p. (J). pap. 9.95 (*0-14-054437-2*) Penguin Bks., Ltd. GBR. *Dist:* Trafalgar Square.

Garland, Sherry. I Never Knew Your Name. 1994. (Illus.). 32p. (J). (ps-3). tchr. ed. 14.95 o.p. (*0-395-69686-0*) Houghton Mifflin Co.

—Letters from the Mountain. 1996. 256p. (YA). (gr. 7 up). 12.00 (*0-15-200661-3*); pap. 6.00 (*0-15-200659-1*, Harcourt Paperbacks) Harcourt Children's Bks.

—Letters from the Mountain. 1996. 12.05 (*0-606-16166-X*) Turtleback Bks.

Garner, Helen. Children's Bach. 1986. 104p. (J). pap. 4.95 o.p. (*0-14-008371-5*, Penguin Bks.) Viking Penguin.

Garrigue, Sheila. Between Friends (R) 1986. (J). pap. 2.50 (*0-590-40773-2*) Scholastic, Inc.

Garrigus, Charles B. Chas & the Summer of '26. 1994. 322p. (J). 12.50 (*0-9638964-0-7*) Cypress Pr.

Gass, L. E. Mr. D. & His Little Friends. 2001. pap. 12.42 (*0-7596-2299-X*) 1stBooks Library.

Gates, Doris. A Morgan for Melinda. 1980. (J). (gr. 3-7). 11.95 o.p. (*0-670-48932-8*, Viking Children's Bks.) Penguin Putnam Bks. for Young Readers.

Gauch, Patricia L. Christina Katerina & Fats & the Great Neighborhood War. 1997. (Illus.). 32p. (J). (ps-3). 15.95 o.s.i (*0-399-22651-6*, G. P. Putnam's Sons) Penguin Group (USA) Inc.

—The Green of Me. 1984. 160p. (J). (gr. 7 up). reprint ed. 2.25 (*0-448-47763-7*) Putnam Publishing Group, The.

—Night Talks. 1983. 160p. (J). (gr. 5 up). 10.95 o.s.i (*0-399-20911-5*, G. P. Putnam's Sons) Penguin Putnam Bks. for Young Readers.

—Tanya & Emily in a Dance for Two. (Illus.). 40p. (J). (ps-3). 1998. pap. 5.99 (*0-698-11635-6*, PaperStar); 1994. 16.99 o.p. (*0-399-22688-5*, Philomel) Penguin Putnam Bks. for Young Readers.

Gauch, Patricia Lee. Tanya & Emily in a Dance for Two. 1998. 12.14 (*0-606-13838-2*) Turtleback Bks.

Gauthier, Bertrand. Pauvre Ani Croche! 1990. (Roman Jeunesse Ser.). (FRE.). 96p. (YA). (gr. 4-7). pap. 8.95 (*2-89021-133-9*) La Courte Echelle CAN. *Dist:* Firefly Bks., Ltd.

—The Swank Prank. 1995. (First Novels Ser.). (Illus.). 64p. (J). (gr. 1-4). pap. 3.99 (*0-88780-092-0*) Formac Publishing Co., Ltd. CAN. *Dist:* Formac Distributing, Ltd.

—The Swank Prank! 1991. (First Novels Ser.). (Illus.). 64p. (J). (gr. 1-4). (*0-88780-093-9*) Formac Publishing Co., Ltd.

—Swank Talk. Cummins, Sarah, tr. from FRE. 1992. (First Novels Ser.). (Illus.). 64p. (J). (gr. 1-4). (*0-88780-209-5*) Formac Publishing Co., Ltd.

—Swank Talk. 1992. (First Novel Ser.). (Illus.). 64p. (J). (gr. 1-4). pap. 3.99 (*0-88780-208-7*) Formac Publishing Co., Ltd. CAN. *Dist:* Formac Distributing, Ltd.

—Zachary in the Winner. 1993. (Just Me & My Dad Ser.). (Illus.). 24p. (J). (gr. 2 up). lib. bdg. 19.93 (*0-8368-1009-0*) Stevens, Gareth Inc.

Gauthier, Gilles. A Gift from Mooch. Cummins, Sarah, tr. from FRE. 2001. (First Novels Ser.: Vol. 39). (Illus.). 64p. (J). pap. (*0-88780-548-5*); bds. (*0-88780-549-3*) Formac Publishing Co., Ltd.

—Mooch & Me. 1995. (First Novels Ser.). (Illus.). 60p. (J). (gr. 1-4). bds. (*0-88780-097-1*) Formac Publishing Co., Ltd.

—Mooch & Me. 1991. (First Novel Ser.). (Illus.). 64p. (J). (gr. 1-4). pap. 3.99 (*0-88780-096-3*) Formac Publishing Co., Ltd. CAN. *Dist:* Formac Distributing, Ltd., Orca Bk. Pubs.

—Mooch Gets Jealous. 1995. (First Novels Ser.). (Illus.). 59p. (J). (gr. 1-4). bds. (*0-88780-218-4*) Formac Publishing Co., Ltd.

—Mooch Gets Jealous. 1995. (First Novels Ser.). (Illus.). 64p. (J). (gr. 1-4). pap. 3.99 (*0-88780-217-6*) Formac Publishing Co., Ltd. CAN. *Dist:* Formac Distributing, Ltd., Orca Bk. Pubs.

Gauthier, Gilles & Derome, Pierre-Andre. Le Grand Antonio a le Coeur Gros. 2002. (Premier Roman Ser.). (FRE., Illus.). 64p. pap. 8.95 (*2-89021-562-8*) La Courte Echelle CAN. *Dist:* Firefly Bks., Ltd.

Geary, Susan R. & Geary, Joe. Best Friends Forever. 1991. (Paws for Kids Ser.). (Illus.). 100p. (Orig.). (J). (gr. 2-4). pap. (*0-9629760-0-8*) Bear Paw Bks.

Gee, Genese. The Story of Jack, Sprat, & the Backpack. (Illus.). 20p. (J). (ps-1). 2002. 14.99 (*0-9719935-1-3*); 2001. pap. 10.49 (*0-9719935-0-5*) Gee, Genese Celeste.

Gelbart, Ofra. Sonidos Que Oigo. Writer, C. C. & Nielsen, Lisa C., trs. 1992. (Hippy Ser.). (SPA., Illus.). 24p. (Orig.). (J). (ps). pap. text 3.00 o.s.i (*1-56134-148-7*, McGraw-Hill/Dushkin) McGraw-Hill Higher Education.

Gelbert, Ofra. Otra Cosa. Writer, C. C. & Nielsen, Lisa C., trs. 1992. (Hippy Ser.). (SPA., Illus.). 24p. (Orig.). (J). (ps). pap. text 3.00 o.p. (*1-56134-175-4*, McGraw-Hill/Dushkin) McGraw-Hill Higher Education.

Geller, Mark. The Strange Case of the Reluctant Partners. 1990. (Charlotte Zolotow Bk.). 96p. (J). (gr. 5-9). 13.95 o.p. (*0-06-021972-6*); lib. bdg. 13.89 o.p. (*0-06-021973-4*) HarperCollins Children's Bk. Group.

George, Gail. The Popples' Pajama Party. 1986. (Pictureback Ser.). (Illus.). 32p. (J). (ps-3). pap. 1.95 o.p. (*0-394-88041-2*, Random Hse. Bks. for Young Readers) Random Hse. Children's Bks.

George, Lindsay B. William & Boomer. 1990. (Illus.). 24p. (J). (ps-3). 19.95 o.p. (*0-924483-23-7*) Soundprints.

Geras, Adele. Pictures of the Night. Stearns, Michael, ed. 1998. (Egerton Hall Trilogy Ser.: Vol. 3). (Illus.). 192p. (gr. 7-12). pap. 6.00 o.s.i (*0-15-201519-1*, Harcourt Paperbacks) Harcourt Children's Bks.

Gershon, Dann & Gershon, Gina. Hollyhive Hunnie. 2000. (Hangin' with the Hombeez Ser.: Vol. 5). (Illus.). 40p. (J). (gr. k-6). 9.95 (*0-9656985-7-2*) Noware Bks.

Gerson, Corinne. Passing Through. 1978. (J). (gr. 8 up). 7.95 o.p. (*0-8037-6842-7*, Dial Bks. for Young Readers) Penguin Putnam Bks. for Young Readers.

—Passing Through. 1980. 208p. (YA). (gr. 8 up). pap. 1.50 o.s.i (*0-440-96958-1*, Laurel Leaf) Random Hse. Children's Bks.

Gerstein, Mordicai. The Giant. 1995. (Illus.). 40p. (J). (ps-2). 13.95 (*0-7868-0131-X*); lib. bdg. 14.49 (*0-7868-2104-3*) Hyperion Bks. for Children.

—The Room. 1984. (Illus.). 32p. (J). (ps-3). 11.95 (*0-06-021998-X*); lib. bdg. 11.89 o.p. (*0-06-021999-8*) HarperCollins Children's Bk. Group.

Ghent, Natale. Piper. 2001. (J). 13.00 (*0-606-21772-X*) Turtleback Bks.

Gibbons, Gail. Paper, Paper Everywhere. 1997. 10.65 (*0-606-11720-2*) Turtleback Bks.

—The Quilting Bee. 1924. (J). 15.99 (*0-688-16397-1*); lib. bdg. (*0-688-16398-X*) Morrow/Avon. (Morrow, William & Co.).

Gibbs, Bridget. What's in the Bag? 1990. (J). 9.95 o.p. (*1-55782-333-2*) Little Brown & Co.

—What's in the Box? 1990. (J). 9.95 (*1-55782-334-0*) Little Brown & Co.

Gibbs, Lynne. Ping Won't Share. (Growing Pains (Columbus, Ohio) Ser.). (Illus.). 32p. (J). 2003. 12.95 (*1-57768-480-X*); 2002. pap. 4.95 (*1-57768-927-5*) McGraw-Hill Children's Publishing.

Giberga, Jane Sughrue. Friends to Die For. 1999. (J). pap. 14.89 (*0-8037-2095-5*, Dial Bks. for Young Readers); (Illus.). 176p. (YA). (gr. 7-12). pap. 5.99 (*0-14-038599-1*, Puffin Bks.) Penguin Putnam Bks. for Young Readers.

Gibson, Eva. Laina. 1986. (Springflower Ser.). 176p. (Orig.). (YA). (gr. 9-12). mass mkt. 3.99 o.p. (*0-87123-896-9*) Bethany Hse. Pubs.

Gibson, Kathleen. Zibber Bibber. 1996. (Illus.). 32p. (Orig.). (J). (ps-3). pap. 12.50 incl. audio (*1-888862-00-9*, RR6200) Rainbow Readers Publishing.

Gifaldi, David. Listening for Crickets. 2004. (J). 16.95 (*0-8050-7385-X*, Holt, Henry & Co. Bks. For Young Readers) Holt, Henry & Co.

Giff, Patricia Reilly. Adios, Anna. 1995. (Illus.). 80p. (J). pap. text 3.50 o.s.i (*0-440-41070-3*) Dell Publishing.

—Adios, Anna. 1998. (Friends & Amigos Ser.: No. 1). (ENG & SPA., Illus.). 86p. (J). (gr. 3 up). lib. bdg. 22.60 (*0-8368-2049-5*) Stevens, Gareth Inc.

—Adios, Anna. 1995. (Friends & Amigos Ser.). (ENG & SPA.). (J). 8.70 o.p. (*0-606-07543-7*) Turtleback Bks.

—All about Stacy. 1988. (New Kids at the Polk Street School Ser.: No. 3). (Illus.). 80p. (ps-3). pap. text 3.99 (*0-440-40088-0*, Yearling) Random Hse. Children's Bks.

—All the Way Home. 2001. 176p. (gr. 3-7). lib. bdg. 17.99 (*0-385-90021-X*, Delacorte Pr.) Dell Publishing.

—All the Way Home. 176p. (gr. 3-7). 2003. pap. text 5.99 (*0-440-41182-3*, Yearling); 2001. text 15.95 (*0-385-32209-7*, Dell Books for Young Readers) Random Hse. Children's Bks.

—B-E-S-T Friends. 1988. (New Kids at the Polk Street School Ser.: No. 4). 80p. (ps-3). pap. text 3.99 (*0-440-40090-2*, Yearling) Random Hse. Children's Bks.

—B-E-S-T Friends. 1988. (New Kids of the Polk Street School Ser.). (J). 10.14 (*0-606-03997-X*) Turtleback Bks.

—Best Friends. 73p. (J). (gr. 1-2). pap. 3.99 (*0-8072-1277-6*, Listening Library) Random Hse. Audio Publishing Group.

—Cara de Pez. 2000. (SPA.). (YA). (gr. 1). 3.95 (*0-922852-46-4*) AIMS International Bks., Inc.

—Cara de Pez. 1996. 10.10 (*0-606-10384-8*) Turtleback Bks.

—Concurso de Pastelillos. 2001. (Kids of Polk Street School Ser.). (SPA.). (YA). 4.50 (*0-922852-44-8*) AIMS International Bks., Inc.

—Concurso de Pastelillos. 1993. 10.10 (*0-606-10398-8*) Turtleback Bks.

—Dance with Rosie. 1996. (Ballet Slippers Ser.: Vol. 1). (Illus.). 64p. (J). (gr. 4-7). 13.99 o.s.i (*0-670-86864-7*, Viking) Penguin Putnam Bks. for Young Readers.

—December Secrets. 1986. (Kids of the Polk Street School Ser.). (Illus.). (J). (ps-3). 9.95 o.p. (*0-385-29495-6*, Delacorte Pr.) Dell Publishing.

—December Secrets. 1987. (Kids of the Polk Street School Ser.: Vol. 4). (Illus.). 80p. (gr. 1-4). pap. text 4.50 (*0-440-41795-3*, Yearling) Random Hse. Children's Bks.

—December Secrets. 1984. (Kids of the Polk Street School Ser.). (J). 10.14 (*0-606-03357-2*) Turtleback Bks.

—Fish Face. (J). 1988.; 1986. (Illus.). 9.95 o.s.i (*0-385-29493-X*, Delacorte Pr.) Dell Publishing.

—Fish Face. (J). (gr. 1-2). 75p. pap. 3.99 o.s.i (*0-8072-1251-2*); 1984. pap. 17.00 incl. audio (*0-8072-0092-1*, FTR101SP) Random Hse. Audio Publishing Group. (Listening Library).

—Fish Face. 1990. (J). pap. o.s.i (*0-440-80192-3*, Dell Books for Young Readers); 1984. (Kids of the Polk Street School Ser.: Vol. 2). (Illus.). 80p. (gr. 1-4). pap. text 4.50 (*0-440-42557-3*, Yearling) Random Hse. Children's Bks.

—Fish Face. 1987. (Illus.). (gr. 6-12). 12.50 o.p. (*0-8446-6236-4*) Smith, Peter Pub., Inc.

—Fish Face. 1984. (Kids of the Polk Street School Ser.). (J). 10.65 (*0-606-03358-0*) Turtleback Bks.

—Friends & Amigos, 6 bks. Incl. Adios, Anna. lib. bdg. 22.60 (*0-8368-2049-5*); Good Dog, Bonita. lib. bdg. 22.60 (*0-8368-2053-3*); Happy Birthday, Anna, Sorpresa! lib. bdg. 22.60 (*0-8368-2052-5*); Ho, Ho, Benjamin, Feliz Navidad. lib. bdg. 22.60 (*0-8368-2051-7*); It's a Fiesta, Benjamin. lib. bdg. 22.60 (*0-8368-2054-1*); Say Hola, Sarah. lib. bdg. 22.60 (*0-8368-2050-9*); 86p. (J). (gr. 3 up). (ENG & SPA., Illus.). 1998. Set lib. bdg. 135.60 (*0-8368-2048-7*) Stevens, Gareth Inc.

—Good Dog, Bonita! 1996. (Friends & Amigos Ser.). 9.19 o.p. (*0-606-09301-X*) Turtleback Bks.

—Good Luck, Ronald Morgan! 1999. (Ronald Morgan Ser.). (Illus.). 32p. (gr. k-4). pap. 5.99 o.s.i (*0-14-055648-6*, Puffin Bks.) Penguin Putnam Bks. for Young Readers.

—Good Luck, Ronald Morgan! unabr. ed. 2000. (YA). pap. 24.24 incl. audio (*0-7887-3796-1*, 41040X4) Recorded Bks., LLC.

—Happy Birthday, Anna, Sorpresa! 1998. (Friends & Amigos Ser.: No. 4). (ENG & SPA., Illus.). 86p. (J). (gr. 3 up). lib. bdg. 22.60 (*0-8368-2052-5*) Stevens, Gareth Inc.

—It's a Fiesta, Benjamin. 1996. (Friends & Amigos Ser.). (Illus.). 80p. (J). (gr. 1-3). pap. 3.99 o.s.i (*0-440-41089-4*, Yearling) Random Hse. Children's Bks.

—It's a Fiesta, Benjamin. 1996. (Friends & Amigos Ser.). 9.19 o.p. (*0-606-09302-8*) Turtleback Bks.

—Lily's Crossing. 2002. (Illus.). (J). 13.94 (*0-7587-0287-6*) Book Wholesalers, Inc.

—Lily's Crossing. 1997. 192p. (gr. 3-7). text 15.95 (*0-385-32142-2*, Delacorte Pr.) Dell Publishing.

—Lily's Crossing. 1999. (Yearling Newbery Ser.). 208p. (gr. 3-7). pap. text 5.50 (*0-440-41453-9*, Dell Books for Young Readers) Random Hse. Children's Bks.

—Lily's Crossing. l.t. ed. 2000. (Illus.). 200p. (J). (ps up). 22.95 (*0-7862-2771-0*) Thorndike Pr.

—Lily's Crossing. 1999. (Yearling Newbery Ser.). (Illus.). (J). 11.55 (*0-606-14423-4*) Turtleback Bks.

—Love, from the Fifth-Grade Celebrity. 1987. 128p. (gr. 3-7). pap. text 3.99 o.s.i (*0-440-44948-0*, Yearling) Random Hse. Children's Bks.

—Not-So Perfect Rosie. 1997. (Ballet Slippers Ser.: No. 4). (Illus.). 80p. (J). (gr. 2-6). 13.99 o.p. (*0-670-86968-6*) Penguin Putnam Bks. for Young Readers.

—Ronald Morgan Goes to Camp. 1995. (Ronald Morgan Ser.). (Illus.). 32p. (J). 13.99 o.s.i (*0-670-86195-2*) Penguin Putnam Bks. for Young Readers.

—Say Hola, Sarah. 1996. (J). pap. 4.75 (*0-440-91188-5*, Dell Books for Young Readers); 1996. (J). pap. 4.75 (*0-440-91117-6*, Dell Books for Young Readers); 1995. (Friends & Amigos Ser.: No. 2). (Illus.). 80p. (gr. 1-4). pap. text 3.50 o.s.i (*0-440-41077-0*, Yearling) Random Hse. Children's Bks.

—Say Hola, Sarah. 1998. (Friends & Amigos Ser.: No. 2). (ENG & SPA., Illus.). 86p. (J). (gr. 3 up). lib. bdg. 22.60 (*0-8368-2050-9*) Stevens, Gareth Inc.

—Say Hola, Sarah. 1995. (Friends & Amigos Ser.). (ENG & SPA.). (J). 8.95 o.p. (*0-606-07544-5*) Turtleback Bks.

—Tootsie Tanner, Why Don't You Talk? 1990. 192p. (J). (gr. k-6). pap. 2.95 o.s.i (*0-440-40239-5*, Yearling) Random Hse. Children's Bks.

Giff, Patricia Reilly & Natti, Susanna. Ronald Morgan Goes to Camp. 1997. (Ronald Morgan Ser.). (Illus.). 32p. (J). (gr. k-4). pap. 4.99 o.s.i (*0-14-055647-8*) Penguin Putnam Bks. for Young Readers.

Gifford, Kathie Lee. Best Friends, Vol. 4. 1997. pap. 2.75 (*0-679-88498-X*, Random Hse. Bks. for Young Readers) Random Hse. Children's Bks.

Gikow, Louise. Follow That Fraggle, ERS. 1985. (Illus.). 32p. (J). (gr. k-2). o.p. (*0-03-004558-4*, Holt, Henry & Co. Bks. For Young Readers) Holt, Henry & Co.

—The Last Days of Fraggle Rock, ERS. 1985. (Illus.). 48p. (J). (gr. 1-4). o.p. (*0-03-004548-7*, Holt, Henry & Co. Bks. For Young Readers) Holt, Henry & Co.

—Wembley & the Soggy Map, ERS. 1986. (Illus.). 32p. (J). (ps-2). pap. o.p. (*0-03-007242-5*, Holt, Henry & Co. Bks. For Young Readers) Holt, Henry & Co.

Gikow, Louise & Chauhan, Manhar. I'm Mad at You! 1991. (Golden Look-Look Bks.). (Illus.). 24p. (J). (ps-3). pap. 3.29 o.s.i (*0-307-12648-X*, 12648, Golden Bks.) Random Hse. Children's Bks.

Gilbert, Lisa W. & Weedn, Flavia M. The Little Snow Bear. l.t. ed. 1995. (Flavia's Dream Maker Stories Ser.). (Illus.). 48p. (J). (ps-3). 10.95 (*0-7868-0044-5*) Hyperion Bks. for Children.

Gilbert, Suzie. Hawk Hill. 1996. (Illus.). 40p. (J). (ps-3). 14.95 o.p. (*0-8118-0839-4*) Chronicle Bks. LLC.

Gilden, Mel. Beverly Hills, 90210: 'Tis the Season. 1992. 192p. (YA). mass mkt. 3.99 o.p. (*0-06-106786-5*, HarperTorch) Morrow/Avon.

—Born to Howl. 1987. (Illus.). 96p. (J). pap. 2.50 o.p. (*0-380-75425-8*, Avon Bks.) Morrow/Avon.

Gill, Janet E. Fly 'n Free. 1997. (Swim Team Ser.: No. 2). (J). (gr. 3-7). pap. 3.99 (*0-380-78673-7*, Avon Bks.) Morrow/Avon.

—Swimmers, Take Your Marks! 1997. (Swim Team Ser.: No. 1). (J). (gr. 3-7). pap. 3.99 (*0-380-78672-9*, Avon Bks.) Morrow/Avon.

Gill, Janie S. I Wish What I Could Do for You. 2001. (Predictable Readers Ser.). (Illus.). (J). (gr. k-2). lib. bdg. 11.95 (*0-89868-540-0*) ARO Publishing Co.

Gill, Janie Spaht. Just Like You. Date not set. (Illus.). 5.95 (*0-89868-430-7*) ARO Publishing Co.

Gilligan, Shannon. There's a Body in the Brontosaurus Room!, Vol. 6. 1992. 112p. (J). pap. 2.99 o.s.i (*0-553-15994-1*) Bantam Bks.

Gilmer, Chris & Milam, June M. Let's All Be Friends! Daley, Charlotte C., ed. Miranda, Carmen, tr. 1997. (Drugless Douglass Tales Ser.). (SPA., Illus.). 24p. (Orig.). (J). (ps). pap. 32.95 (*1-884307-28-0*); pap., stu. ed. 6.95 (*1-884307-29-9*) Developing Resources for Education in America, Inc. (DREAM).

—Let's All Be Friends! 1994. (Drugless Douglass Tales Ser.). (Illus.). 20p. (Orig.). (J). (ps). pap. text 32.95 (*1-884307-09-4*); stu. ed. 6.95 (*1-884307-10-8*) Developing Resources for Education in America, Inc. (DREAM).

Gilmore, Rachna. A Friend Like Zilla. 1995. (Illus.). 84p. (J). (gr. 3-8). pap. 4.50 (*0-929005-71-6*) Second Story Pr. CAN. *Dist:* Orca Bk. Pubs.

—Lights for Gita. (J). 2002. (ENG & TUR.). 15.95 (*1-85269-298-7*); 2000. (BEN & ENG.). 15.50 (*1-85269-283-9*); 2000. (ENG & GUJ.). 15.95 (*1-85269-288-X*) Mantra Publishing, Ltd. GBR. *Dist:* AIMS International Bks., Inc.

—Lights for Gita. 2000. (Illus.). 24p. (J). (ps-3). pap. 7.95 (*0-88448-151-4*) Tilbury Hse. Pubs.

—Lights for Gita. 2000. (CHI & ENG.). (J). 15.50 (*1-85269-284-7*) Yuan-liou Publishing Co., Ltd. TWN. *Dist:* AIMS International Bks., Inc.

—Roses for Gita. 1996. (Illus.). 24p. (J). (gr. k-3). 12.95 (*0-929005-86-4*); pap. 5.95 (*0-929005-85-6*) Second Story Pr. CAN. *Dist:* Univ. of Toronto Pr.

—Roses for Gita. 2001. (Illus.). 24p. (J). (gr. 1-5). pap. 7.95 (0-88448-224-3, Harpswell Pr.) Tilbury Hse. Pubs.

Gilmour, H. B. Cher & Cher Alike. 1997. (Clueless Ser.). 176p. (YA). (gr. 6 up). per. 4.99 (0-671-01161-8, Simon Pulse) Simon & Schuster Children's Publishing.

—Friend or Faux. 1996. (Clueless Ser.). 160p. (YA). (gr. 6 up). pap. 4.99 (0-671-00323-2, Simon Pulse) Simon & Schuster Children's Publishing.

Gilson, Jamie. Double Dog Dare. 1998. 144p. (J). (gr. 3-7). pap. 5.99 (0-688-16361-0, Harper Trophy) HarperCollins Children's Bk. Group.

—Hobie Hanson, You're Weird. (Illus.). (J). (gr. 4-7). 1996. 176p. pap. 5.99 (0-688-14747-X, Harper Trophy); 1987. 172p. 16.00 (0-688-06700-X) HarperCollins Children's Bk. Group.

—Hobie Hanson, You're Weird. MacDonald, Pat, ed. 1990. (Illus.). 176p. (J). (gr. 3-6). pap. 3.50 (0-671-73752-X, Aladdin) Simon & Schuster Children's Publishing.

—Hobie Hanson, You're Weird. 1996. 11.00 (0-606-09425-3) Turtleback Bks.

—It Goes Eeeeeeeeeeeee! 1994. (ITA., Illus.). 80p. (J). (ps-3). tchr. ed. 15.00 (0-395-67063-2, Clarion Bks.) Houghton Mifflin Co. Trade & Reference Div.

—Sticks & Stones & Skeleton Bones. 1991. (Illus.). (J). (gr. 3-6). 16.00 o.p. (0-688-10098-8) HarperCollins Children's Bk. Group.

Gipson, Morrell & Mayer, Lene. Let's Be Friends. Stefoff, Rebecca, ed. 1990. (Magic Mountain Fables Ser.). (Illus.). 24p. (J). (gr. k-3). lib. bdg. 14.60 (0-944483-92-5) Garrett Educational Corp.

Gire, Ken. Rhythm & Blues: A Story about Doing Right When You Feel Wronged. 1988. (Kids' Praise! Adventure Ser.). (Illus.). 30p. (J). 5.99 o.p. (0-929608-11-9) Focus on the Family Publishing.

Girion, Barbara. Portfolio to Fame. 1987. (Going Places Ser.: No. 3). (J). (gr. k-12). mass mkt. 2.50 o.s.i (0-440-97148-9, Laurel Leaf) Random Hse. Children's Bks.

—Prescription for Success. 1987. (Going Places Ser.: No. 1). (YA). (gr. 7 up). mass mkt. 2.50 o.s.i (0-440-97165-9) Dell Publishing.

Gitomer, Helaine D. & Weinstock, Harriett. The Magic Cow: A Gift. 2000. (Illus.). (J). (0-9676205-0-3) Orbin Publishing, Ltd.

Glassman, Jackie. The Berry Best Friends' Picnic. 2003. (All Aboard Reading Station Stop Ser.). (Illus.). 32p. 13.89 (0-448-43156-4); (J). mass mkt. 3.99 (0-448-43134-3) Penguin Putnam Bks. for Young Readers. (Grosset & Dunlap).

Glassman, Miriam. Box Top Dreams. 192p. 1999. (Illus.). (gr. 4-7). pap. text 3.99 (0-440-41417-2); 1998. (gr. 2-6). text 14.95 o.s.i (0-385-32532-0) Random Hse. Children's Bks. (Dell Books for Young Readers).

—Box Top Dreams. 1999. 10.04 (0-606-15910-X) Turtleback Bks.

Glassman, Peter. Princess & Curdie. 1924. (J). o.s.i (0-688-14696-1, Morrow, William & Co.) Morrow/Avon.

Glater, Sara D. A Wish for Wings & Other Things: A Magical Tale for Everyone of Every Age Ever Touched by Illness. 1995. (Illus.). 52p. (J). (gr. 3 up). 15.95 (0-9647799-1-9) Lemonade Sundays.

Gleeson, Kate. Best Friends. 1998. (Golden Shaped Board Book Ser.). 12p. (J). (ps). bds. 2.29 o.s.i (0-307-25600-6, Golden Bks.) Random Hse. Children's Bks.

Glover, Robert. Friends Forever. 1996. (Illus.). (J). 12.95 (1-56763-178-9); pap. 5.95 (1-56763-179-7) Ozark Publishing.

Glover, Sandra. Can You Keep a Secret? 2004. 369p. (J). pap. (0-552-54804-9, Corgi) Bantam Bks.

Go Ask Alice. 1998. 11.04 (0-606-13431-X) Turtleback Bks.

Godden, Rumer. The Story of Holly & Ivy. 1987. (Picture Puffin Ser.). (J). 11.19 o.p. (0-606-03657-1) Turtleback Bks.

Godfrey, Jane. Who Made the Morning? 1995. (Illus.). 32p. (J). 7.99 (1-56476-472-9, 6-3472) Cook Communications Ministries.

Godfrey, Martyn N. It Seemed Like a Good Idea at the Time. 1995. 128p. (Orig.). (J). mass mkt. 3.50 (0-380-77934-X, Avon Bks.) Morrow/Avon.

Godwin. Two by Two. 1998. (J). 13.00 (0-671-75354-1, Simon & Schuster Children's Publishing) Simon & Schuster Children's Publishing.

Goffin, Josse. Yes. 1993. (Illus.). (J). (ps-3). 13.00 o.p. (0-688-12375-9) HarperCollins Children's Bk. Group.

Goffstein, M. B. Neighbors. 1979. (Illus.). (J). (ps-3). 12.95 (0-06-022018-X) HarperCollins Children's Bk. Group.

Gold, Porter. Who's There? 1989. (Real Readers Ser.). (Illus.). 32p. (J). (gr. 1-4). pap. 4.95 (0-8114-6717-1); (ps-3). lib. bdg. 21.40 o.p. (0-8172-3514-0) Raintree Pubs.

Golden Books Staff. All Aboard! 2004. (Illus.). 32p. (J). pap. 4.99 (0-375-82652-1, Golden Bks.) Random Hse. Children's Bks.

—Always Friends. 2000. (Precious Moments Ser.). (Illus.). 56p. (J). (ps-3). pap. 3.99 (0-307-27620-1, 27620, Golden Bks.) Random Hse. Children's Bks.

—Baby's Bestest Friend/Matchmaker Mix-Up. 2003. 64p. (J). pap. 2.99 (0-307-10126-6, Golden Bks.) Random Hse. Children's Bks.

—Bambi & His Forest Adventures: A Book about Friendship. 1987. (Disney Ser.). (Illus.). 32p. (J). (ps-2). pap. 3.95 o.s.i (0-307-11675-1, Golden Bks.) Random Hse. Children's Bks.

—Best Buddies. 2002. (Illus.). 48p. (J). pap. 3.99 (0-307-10854-6, Golden Bks.) Random Hse. Children's Bks.

—Best Friends. 1998. (Precious Moments Ser.). (Illus.). 70p. (J). (ps-3). pap. 2.29 o.s.i (0-307-25705-3, 25705, Golden Bks.) Random Hse. Children's Bks.

—Best Friends 4-Ever. 2000. (Illus.). 16p. (J). (ps-3). pap. 2.99 (0-307-28330-5, 28330, Golden Bks.) Random Hse. Children's Bks.

—The Best of Barbie. 2003. (Illus.). (J). 17.99 (0-375-82676-9, Golden Bks.) Random Hse. Children's Bks.

—Blue's Friendship Day/What's Blue Building? 2003. 64p. (J). pap. 2.99 (0-307-10122-3, Golden Bks.) Random Hse. Children's Bks.

—Chill Out! 2002. (Illus.). 56p. (J). pap. 4.99 (0-307-10811-2, Golden Bks.) Random Hse. Children's Bks.

—Christmas with Friends: Easy Peel Sticker Book. 2000. (Illus.). 16p. (J). (ps-3). pap. o.p. (0-307-28325-9, 28325, Golden Bks.) Random Hse. Children's Bks.

—Ernie Gets Lost. 1999. (Golden's Sesame Street Ser.). 24p. (J). (ps-3). 6.98 incl. audio (0-307-47705-3, Golden Bks.) Random Hse. Children's Bks.

—Friends Forever? 2003. 32p. (J). pap. 4.99 (0-307-10304-8, Golden Bks.) Random Hse. Children's Bks.

—Friendship. 1998. (Adventures from the Book of Virtues Ser.). 70p. (J). (ps-4). pap. 2.29 o.s.i (0-307-28002-0, Golden Bks.) Random Hse. Children's Bks.

—The Golden Egg Book. 1996. 72p. pap. 4.69 o.s.i (0-307-13082-7, Golden Bks.) Random Hse. Children's Bks.

—The Golden Egg Book. 2001. 24p. 2.29 o.s.i (0-307-59503-X) Random Hse., Inc.

—The Greatest Treasure of All. 2003. 32p. (J). pap. 2.99 (0-307-10329-3, Golden Bks.) Random Hse. Children's Bks.

—If You Believe: My Coloring Book. 1997. 32p. (J). pap. 1.09 o.s.i (0-307-03807-6, 03807, Golden Bks.) Random Hse. Children's Bks.

—Just Between Friends. 2001. 16p. pap. 4.99 (0-307-21834-1, Golden Bks.) Random Hse. Children's Bks.

—Just for Friends. 2002. (Barbie Ser.). (Illus.). 48p. (J). (gr. 1-5). pap. 3.99 (0-307-21251-3, Golden Bks.) Random Hse. Children's Bks.

—Just Not Invited. 2002. (Illus.). 24p. (J). pap. 3.29 (0-307-13289-7, Golden Bks.) Random Hse. Children's Bks.

—Ordinary Amos & the Amazing Fish. 2001. 24p. pap. 3.29 o.s.i (0-307-12783-4, Golden Bks.) Random Hse. Children's Bks.

—Pajama Party, Large Frame ed. 1998. (Bananas in Pajamas Ser.). (ps-3). o.p. (0-307-08305-5, Golden Bks.) Random Hse. Children's Bks.

—Poky & Friends: Out & About. 2000. (Illus.). 70p. (J). (ps-3). pap. 2.99 (0-307-25738-X, Golden Bks.) Random Hse. Children's Bks.

—Royal & Loyal. 2004. (Illus.). (J). pap. 3.99 (0-375-82654-8, Golden Bks.) Random Hse. Children's Bks.

—Scoop's in Charge. 2003. 64p. (J). pap. 2.99 (0-307-10118-5, Golden Bks.) Random Hse. Children's Bks.

—Super Celebration. 2000. (Precious Moments Ser.). (Illus.). 16p. (J). (ps-3). pap. 2.99 (0-307-28326-7, 28326, Golden Bks.) Random Hse. Children's Bks.

—Tawny Scrawny Lion. (Little Golden Bks.). (J). (ps-2). 2001. (Illus.). 24p. 2.99 (0-307-02168-8, 98093); 1998. 2.22 o.s.i (0-307-34076-7) Random Hse. Children's Bks. (Golden Bks.).

—A True Boo Friend. 2003. (Illus.). 32p. (J). (ps-2). pap. 3.99 (0-375-82561-4) Random Hse. Children's Bks.

—Very Best Friends. 1999. (Disney Ser.). 24p. (J). (ps-3). pap. 3.29 (0-307-13142-4, Golden Bks.) Random Hse. Children's Bks.

—Who's Afraid of Elmo? 1999. (Golden's Sesame Street Ser.). 24p. (J). (ps-3). 6.98 incl. audio (0-307-47711-8, Golden Bks.) Random Hse. Children's Bks.

Golden Books Staff & Margulies, Teddy. Oscar's New Neighbor. 1994. (Little Golden Bks.). (Illus.). 24p. (J). (ps-2). 2.29 o.s.i (0-307-00128-8, Golden Bks.) Random Hse. Children's Bks.

Golden Western Staff. Bonkers. 9999. (J). pap. o.p. (0-307-08221-0, Golden Bks.) Random Hse. Children's Bks.

Golding, Leila P. Rachel. 1988. (Heartsong Ser.). 192p. (Orig.). (YA). (gr. 10-12). mass mkt. 3.99 o.p. (0-87123-963-9) Bethany Hse. Pubs.

—Shelly. 1986. (Heartsong Ser.). 176p. (Orig.). (YA). (gr. 9-12). mass mkt. 3.99 o.p. (0-87123-867-5) Bethany Hse. Pubs.

Goldman, E. Maureen. Money to Burn. 1994. 160p. (J). (gr. 5-9). 14.99 o.p. (0-670-85339-9, Viking Children's Bks.) Penguin Putnam Bks. for Young Readers.

Goldman, Katie. In the Wings. 1985. 176p. (gr. 5 up). pap. 2.25 o.p. (0-553-25068-X) Bantam Bks.

—Pay As You Exit. 1985. (J). (gr. 6). 13.95 o.p. (0-8037-0191-8, 01258-370, Dial Bks. for Young Readers) Penguin Putnam Bks. for Young Readers.

Goldman-Rubin, Susan. Emily in Love. 1997. 176p. (J). 14.00 o.s.i (0-15-200961-2) Harcourt Trade Pubs.

Goldsboro, Bobby. Better Together. 1998. (J). pap. 6.99 (1-58083-207-5); (Illus.). 24p. pap. 3.50 (1-58083-203-2) Animazing Entertainment, Inc.

Goldstein, Doris. Imagination Collaboration. 1998. (Illus.). 16p. (J). (ps-k). pap. 5.95 (0-9655442-6-5) Business Word, The.

Gomi, Taro. Coco Can't Wait. 1984. 32p. (J). (ps-1). 12.95 o.p. (0-688-02789-X); lib. bdg. 12.88 o.p. (0-688-02790-3) Morrow/Avon. (Morrow, William & Co.).

—First Comes Harry. 1924. (J). o.s.i (0-688-06825-1); lib. bdg. o.s.i (0-688-06826-X) Morrow/Avon. (Morrow, William & Co.).

Gondosch, Linda. Who's Afraid of Haggerty House? 1987. (Illus.). (J). (gr. 4-6). 11.95 o.p. (0-525-67198-6, Dutton Children's Bks.) Penguin Putnam Bks. for Young Readers.

—Who's Afraid of Haggerty House? 1989. (J). pap. 2.99 (0-671-67237-1, Aladdin) Simon & Schuster Children's Publishing.

Gonzalez, Gloria. The Glad Man. (J). 1979. mass mkt. 1.50 o.s.i (0-440-92927-X, Dell Books for Young Readers); 1975. 176p. (gr. 4 up). lib. bdg. 6.99 o.p. (0-394-93065-7, Knopf Bks. for Young Readers) Random Hse. Children's Bks.

Goobie, Beth. I'm Not Convinced. 1997. (Northern Lights Young Novels Ser.). 144p. (YA). (gr. 7 up). pap. 7.95 (0-88995-159-4) Red Deer Pr. CAN. *Dist:* General Distribution Services, Inc.

Goodman, Joan Elizabeth. Edward Hopper's Great Find. 1987. (Golden Friendly Bks.). (Illus.). 32p. (J). (ps-3). o.p. (0-307-10905-4, Golden Bks.) Random Hse. Children's Bks.

Goodman, Roger B. A Bed for the Wind. 1988. (Illus.). 32p. (J). (gr. 1-4). pap. 12.95 o.p. (0-671-66117-5, Simon & Schuster Children's Publishing) Simon & Schuster Children's Publishing.

Goodrich, Dawn. Eery. 1997. (Illus.). vi, 23p. (Orig.). pap. 7.00 (0-9657367-2-5) Less Pr.

Goofy & Friends Take a Trip. 1994. (Stamp & Book Box Set Ser.). (Illus.). 16p. (J). 9.98 o.p. (1-57082-151-8) Mouse Works.

Gorbachev, Valeri. The Big Trip. 2004. 32p. (J). 15.99 (0-399-23965-0, Philomel) Penguin Putnam Bks. for Young Readers.

—Chicken Chickens Go to School. 2003. (Illus.). 32p. (J). (ps-1). 15.95 (0-7358-1600-X); lib. bdg. 16.50 (0-7358-1767-7) North-South Bks., Inc. (Cheshire Studio Bks.).

Gordon, Amy. The Gorillas of Gill Park. 2003. 256p. (J). tchr. ed. 16.95 (0-8234-1751-4) Holiday Hse., Inc.

Gordon, Ethel E. Where Does the Summer Go? 1975. (J). (gr. 6-9). pap. (0-671-29768-6, Simon Pulse) Simon & Schuster Children's Publishing.

Gordon, Sheila. Waiting for the Rain. 1987. 224p. (YA). (gr. 7 up). 15.95 o.p. (0-531-05726-7); mass mkt. 15.99 o.p. (0-531-08326-8) Scholastic, Inc. (Orchard Bks.).

Gordon, Shirley. Crystal Is the New Girl. 1976. (Illus.). 32p. (J). (ps-3). lib. bdg. 9.89 o.p. (0-06-022025-2) HarperCollins Pubs.

—Happy Birthday, Crystal. 1981. (Illus.). 32p. (J). (gr. k-4). 7.95 o.p. (0-06-022006-6); lib. bdg. 9.89 o.p. (0-06-022007-4) HarperCollins Pubs.

Gorman, Carol. Chelsey & the Green-Haired Kid. 1992. (J). pap. 12.95 o.p. (0-395-44767-4) Houghton Mifflin Co.

—Dork in Disguise. (Harper Trophy Bks.). 176p. (J). 2000. (gr. 3-7). pap. 5.99 (0-06-440891-4, Harper Trophy); 1999. (gr. 7 up). lib. bdg. 16.89 (0-06-024867-X); 1999. (gr. 3-7). 15.95 (0-06-024866-1) HarperCollins Children's Bk. Group.

—Million Dollar Winner. 1994. (I Witness Ser.). (Illus.). 96p. (Orig.). (J). (gr. 4-7). pap. 4.99 o.p. (0-570-04630-0) Concordia Publishing Hse.

—Nobody's Friend. 1993. (Tree House Kids Ser.: Bk. 4). (Illus.). 64p. (Orig.). (J). (gr. 1-4). pap. 3.99 o.p. (0-570-04729-3, 56-1688) Concordia Publishing Hse.

Gormley, Beatrice. Best Friend Insurance. 1985. (Illus.). 160p. (J). (gr. 3-7). pap. 2.50 (0-380-69854-4, Avon Bks.) Morrow/Avon.

—Best Friend Insurance. 1983. (Illus.). 160p. (J). (gr. 3-6). 10.95 o.s.i (0-525-44066-6, Dutton Children's Bks.) Penguin Putnam Bks. for Young Readers.

Goscinny, René & Uderzo, M. Obelix et Compagnie. 1990. (FRE., Illus.). (J). 24.95 (0-8288-5479-3) French & European Pubns., Inc.

Goudge, Eileen. Don't Say Goodbye. 1985. (Senior Ser.: No. 12). 153p. (J). (gr. 6-12). mass mkt. 2.25 o.s.i (0-440-92108-2, Laurel Leaf) Random Hse. Children's Bks.

—Looking for Love. 1986. (Senior Ser.: No. 14). (J). mass mkt. 2.25 o.s.i (0-440-94730-8, Laurel Leaf) Random Hse. Children's Bks.

—Night after Night. 1986. (Senior Ser.: No. 18). (J). (gr. 6-12). mass mkt. 2.25 o.s.i (0-440-96369-9, Laurel Leaf) Random Hse. Children's Bks.

—Smart Enough to Know. 1984. (Senior Ser.: No. 2). (J). (gr. 7-12). mass mkt. 2.25 o.s.i (0-440-98168-9, Laurel Leaf) Random Hse. Children's Bks.

Gould, Deborah. Brendan's Best-Timed Birthday. 1988. (Illus.). 32p. (J). (ps-1). 13.95 o.s.i (0-02-737390-8, Simon & Schuster Children's Publishing) Simon & Schuster Children's Publishing.

Gould, Marilyn. Friends True & Periwinkle Blue. 1992. (J). pap. 2.99 (0-380-76484-9, Avon Bks.) Morrow/Avon.

—Friends True & Periwinkle True. 1992. 152p. (YA). (gr. 5 up). reprint ed. pap. 10.95 (0-9632305-5-7) Allied Crafts Pr.

—The Twelfth of June. 1994. 183p. (J). (gr. 4 up). lib. bdg. 12.95 (0-9632305-4-9) Allied Crafts Pr.

Graef, Renee, illus. Laura & Nellie. 1998. (Little House Chapter Bks.: No. 5). (J). (gr. 3-6). 10.40 (0-606-12979-0) Turtleback Bks.

—Little House Friends. 1998. (Little House Ser.: No. 9). 80p. (J). (gr. 3-6). pap. 4.25 (0-06-442080-9, Harper Trophy) HarperCollins Children's Bk. Group.

—Little House Friends. 1998. (Little House Chapter Bks.: No. 9). 80p. (J). (gr. 3-6). lib. bdg. 14.89 (0-06-027894-3) HarperCollins Pubs.

—The Magic Friend-Maker. 1991. (Step Ahead Ser.). 184p. (J). (gr. 4-8). reprint ed. pap. 1.99 o.s.i (0-307-03682-0, Golden Bks.) Random Hse. Children's Bks.

Graeme, Jocelyn & Fahlman, Ruth. Rainy Day Friends. 1990. (CHI, ENG, FRE & SPA., Illus.). (C). pap. o.s.i (0-201-54653-1) Addison-Wesley Longman, Inc.

Graf, Virginia L. Forever Friends. l.t. ed. 1997. (RCI Summer Ser.: No. 2). (Illus.). 64p. (J). (gr. 4-6). pap. 7.50 (1-882788-08-7) Vangar Pubs./Baltimore.

Graham, Ann M. Cody & Kyle: Big Heroes! 1998. (Illus.). 52p. (J). (gr. k-6). pap. 5.99 (0-9655719-1-2) KCDI Publishing.

Graham, Bob. The Adventures of Charlotte & Henry. 1987. 48p. (J). (ps-3). 10.95 o.p. (0-670-81660-4, Viking Children's Bks.) Penguin Putnam Bks. for Young Readers.

—Crusher Is Coming! 1990. (Illus.). 320p. (J). (ps-3). pap. 3.95 o.p. (0-14-050826-0, Puffin Bks.) Penguin Putnam Bks. for Young Readers.

—Rose Meets Mr. Wintergarten. 1994. (Illus.). 32p. (YA). (ps-3). bds. 4.99 (1-56402-395-8) Candlewick Pr.

Graham, Harriet & McElderry, Margaret K. A Boy & His Bear. 1996. 192p. (J). (gr. 4-7). 16.00 (0-689-80943-3, McElderry, Margaret K.) Simon & Schuster Children's Publishing.

Graham, Rosemary. My Not-So-Terrible Time at the Hippie Hotel. 2003. 224p. (J). (gr. 5-9). 16.99 (0-670-03611-0, Viking) Viking Penguin.

Graham, Steve. Dear Old Donegal. 2000. (Illus.). 32p. (J). reprint ed. text 16.00 (0-7881-6870-3) DIANE Publishing Co.

Grahame, Kenneth. Mr. Toad. Johnson, Joe, tr. from FRE. 1998. (Wind in the Willows Ser.: Vol. 2). (Illus.). 32p. (J). (gr. 4-7). 15.95 (1-56163-218-X) NBM Publishing Co.

—The Open Road. 1990. (Shaped Board Bks. Ser.). (Illus.). 10p. (J). 2.99 o.s.i (0-517-02028-9, Random Hse. Bks. for Young Readers) Random Hse. Children's Bks.

—The Open Road. (J). 1987. pap. 2.25 o.p. (0-671-63626-X, Little Simon); 1986. (Illus.). 48p. 9.95 o.s.i (0-671-61095-3, Simon & Schuster Children's Publishing) Simon & Schuster Children's Publishing.

—The River Bank. 1987. (J). pap. 2.25 o.p. (0-671-63627-8, Little Simon) Simon & Schuster Children's Publishing.

—El Viento en los Sauces. (SPA.). 192p. (J). I. 9.50 (84-372-1882-9); II. 9.50 (84-372-1883-7) Santillana USA Publishing Co., Inc.

—The Wild Wood. Johnson, Joe, tr. from FRE. 1997. (Wind in the Willows Ser.: Vol. 1). (Illus.). 32p. (J). (gr. 4-7). 15.95 (1-56163-196-5) NBM Publishing Co.

—The Wind in the Willows. 2002. (Great Illustrated Classics). (Illus.). 240p. (J). (gr. 3-8). lib. bdg. 21.35 (1-57765-808-6, ABDO & Daughters) ABDO Publishing Co.

—The Wind in the Willows. 1999. (Abbeville Classics Ser.). (Illus.). 192p. (J). 12.95 *(0-7892-0559-9)*; pap. 7.95 *(0-7892-0549-1)* Abbeville Pr., Inc. (Abbeville Kids).

—The Wind in the Willows. 1966. (Airmont Classics Ser.). (J). (gr. 4 up). mass mkt. 2.75 *(0-8049-0105-8,* CL-105) Airmont Publishing Co., Inc.

—The Wind in the Willows. 253p. (J). (gr. 5-6). reprint ed. lib. bdg. 22.95 *(0-88411-877-0)* Amereon, Ltd.

—The Wind in the Willows. 1983. (Illus.). 256p. (J). (gr. 4-12). mass mkt. 1.95 o.s.i *(0-553-21129-3)*; (gr. 7 up). mass mkt. 3.95 *(0-553-21368-7)* Bantam Bks. (Bantam Classics).

—The Wind in the Willows. (Longmeadow Press Children's Library). (Illus.). (J). 1995. 256p. 10.95 o.p. *(0-681-00768-0)*; 1987. 352p. (gr. 4 up). 11.95 o.p. *(0-681-40057-9)* Borders Pr.

—The Wind in the Willows. (Classics for Children 8 & Younger Ser.). (J). (ps-3). 1997. (Illus.). 48p. 6.98 *(1-85854-601-X)*; 1994. 64p. 5.98 o.p. *(0-86112-823-0)*; 1994. 160p. 9.98 o.p. *(0-86112-354-9)* Brimax Bks., Ltd.

—The Wind in the Willows. 1981. 234p. (J). reprint ed. lib. bdg. 17.95 *(0-89966-305-2)* Buccaneer Bks., Inc.

—The Wind in the Willows. 2000. (Illus.). 180p. 4.50 o.p. *(0-7445-7553-2)* Candlewick Pr.

—The Wind in the Willows. Moore, Inga, ed. & illus. by. 1999. (YA). (gr. 3-7). 39.99 o.p. *(0-7636-0980-3)* Candlewick Pr.

—The Wind in the Willows. 2003. 192p. (J). 4.99 *(1-57759-567-X)* Dalmatian Pr.

—The Wind in the Willows. 1990. (Illus.). 256p. (gr. 2 up). pap. text 4.99 *(0-440-40385-5)* Dell Publishing.

—The Wind in the Willows. 1989. mass mkt. 3.25 o.s.i *(0-8125-0511-5)*; (Illus.). 224p. (J). (gr. 4-7). mass mkt. 2.99 *(0-8125-0510-7)* Doherty, Tom Assocs., LLC. (Tor Classics).

—The Wind in the Willows. (Illus.). (J). 1999. 256p. pap. text 3.00 *(0-486-40785-3)*; 1998. 96p. pap. text 1.00 *(0-486-28600-2)* Dover Pubns., Inc.

—The Wind in the Willows. (J). E-Book 2.49 *(0-7574-0469-3)* Electric Umbrella Publishing.

—The Wind in the Willows. 1996. (Illus.). 185p. (J). (gr. 3-5). pap. 15.95 *(0-575-06209-6)* Gollancz, Victor GBR. *Dist:* Trafalgar Square.

—The Wind in the Willows. collector's ed. 2002. (Illus.). 240p. (YA). 24.00 *(0-15-216807-9)* Harcourt Children's Bks.

—The Wind in the Willows. (J). ERS. 2003. (Illus.). 224p. (gr. 1 up). 25.95 *(0-8050-7237-3)*; Vol. 1. 1980. 17.95 o.p. *(0-03-056294-5)* Holt, Henry & Co. (Holt, Henry & Co. Bks. For Young Readers).

—The Wind in the Willows. 1991. (J). pap. 12.95 o.p. *(0-395-60728-0)* Houghton Mifflin Co.

—The Wind in the Willows. l.t. ed. 211p. pap. 21.18 *(0-7583-3377-3)*; 830p. pap. 66.19 *(0-7583-3383-8)*; 715p. pap. 57.46 *(0-7583-3382-X)*; 581p. pap. 48.64 *(0-7583-3381-1)*; 473p. pap. 40.94 *(0-7583-3380-3)*; 369p. pap. 33.14 *(0-7583-3379-X)*; 162p. pap. 18.16 *(0-7583-3376-5)*; 289p. pap. 26.62 *(0-7583-3378-1)*; 369p. lib. bdg. 39.14 *(0-7583-3371-4)*; 715p. lib. bdg. 63.46 *(0-7583-3374-9)*; 289p. lib. bdg. 32.62 *(0-7583-3370-6)*; 830p. lib. bdg. 85.40 *(0-7583-3375-7)*; 581p. lib. bdg. 55.19 *(0-7583-3373-0)*; 473p. lib. bdg. 46.97 *(0-7583-3372-2)*; 162p. (J). lib. bdg. 24.16 *(0-7583-3368-4)*; 211p. (J). lib. bdg. 27.18 *(0-7583-3369-2)* Huge Print Pr.

—The Wind in the Willows. 1993. (Everyman's Library Children's Classics Ser.). (Illus.). 260p. (gr. 5 up). 13.95 *(0-679-41802-4)* Knopf, Alfred A. Inc.

—The Wind in the Willows. l.t. ed. 2000. (LRS Large Print Heritage Ser.). 271p. (J). (gr. 3-8). lib. bdg. 29.95 *(1-58118-066-7,* 23661) LRS.

—The Wind in the Willows. 1985. (Illus.). 224p. (J). (gr. 2 up). 12.95 o.p. *(0-915361-32-9)* Lambda Pubs., Inc.

—The Wind in the Willows. (YA). E-Book 2.95 *(1-57799-886-3)* Logos Research Systems, Inc.

—The Wind in the Willows. (Classics Ser.). (J). pap. 3.95 o.p. 1989. (Illus.). pap. text 7.87 *(0-582-54142-5,* TG7244) Longman Publishing Group.

—The Wind in the Willows. 1988. (Illus.). 196p. (YA). pap. 7.95 o.p. *(0-8092-4489-6)* McGraw-Hill/ Contemporary.

—The Wind in the Willows. 1924. (J). 22.99 o.s.i *(0-688-12422-4,* Morrow, William & Co.) Morrow/ Avon.

—The Wind in the Willows. 1969. (J). mass mkt. 1.95 o.p. *(0-451-51733-4)*; (Illus.). 224p. (YA). (gr. 2 up). mass mkt. 3.95 *(0-451-52462-4)*; (Illus.). 224p. (J). (gr. 4). mass mkt. 2.50 o.p. *(0-451-52164-1,* Signet Classics) NAL.

—The Wind in the Willows. l.t. ed. (Large Print Ser.). reprint ed. 1997. 284p. lib. bdg. 25.00 *(0-939495-18-X)*; 1998. 185p. lib. bdg. 24.00 *(1-58287-080-2)* North Bks.

—The Wind in the Willows. 2002. (Illus.). 208p. (J). 19.95 *(1-58717-204-6)* North-South Bks., Inc.

—The Wind in the Willows. 1999. (Oxford World's Classics Ser.). 192p. (J). pap. 9.95 *(0-19-283515-7)* Oxford Univ. Pr., Inc.

—The Wind in the Willows. Bassett, Jennifer, ed. 1995. (Illus.). 64p. (J). pap. text 5.95 o.p. *(0-19-422753-7)* Oxford Univ. Pr., Inc.

—The Wind in the Willows. 1983. (Oxford World's Classics Ser.). 224p. (YA). (gr. 5 up). pap. 4.95 o.p. *(0-19-281640-3)* Oxford Univ. Pr., Inc.

—The Wind in the Willows, Level 3. Hedge, Tricia, ed. 2000. (Bookworms Ser.). (Illus.). 74p. (J). pap. text 5.95 *(0-19-423022-8)* Oxford Univ. Pr., Inc.

—The Wind in the Willows. (Illus.). 192p. 2000. pap. 8.95 *(1-85793-914-X)*; 1992. (J). (gr. 3-6). 24.95 o.p. *(1-85145-603-1)* Pavilion Bks., Ltd. GBR. *Dist:* Trafalgar Square.

—The Wind in the Willows. (Illus.). (J). 9999. (Children's Classics Ser.: No. 740-13). (gr. 3-5). pap. 3.50 o.p. *(0-7214-0757-9)*; 1996. (Classic Ser.). 52p. (gr. 2-4). 2.99 o.s.i *(0-7214-5608-1)*; 1994. (Classics Ser.). 56p. text 3.50 *(0-7214-1653-5)* Penguin Group (USA) Inc. (Ladybird Bks.).

—The Wind in the Willows. (Puffin Classics Ser.). 1995. (Illus.). 220p. (YA). (gr. 4-7). 4.99 *(0-14-036685-7,* Puffin Bks.); 1988. 224p. (J). pap. 3.50 o.p. *(0-14-035087-X,* Puffin Bks.); 1985. (Illus.). 224p. (J). (gr. 3-9). 12.95 o.p. *(0-399-20944-1,* Grosset & Dunlap); 1984. (Illus.). 240p. (J). (gr. 4-6). pap. 2.95 o.p. *(0-14-031544-6,* Viking Children's Bks.); 1983. (Illus.). 240p. (J). (gr. 1 up). 15.75 o.p. *(0-670-77120-1,* Viking Children's Bks.); 1989. 128p. (J). (gr. 2-6). 2.95 o.p. *(0-448-11079-2,* Platt & Munk); 1981. (Illus.). (J). (gr. 3-9). reprint ed. 6.95 o.p. *(0-448-11028-8,* Grosset & Dunlap); 1967. (Illus.). 224p. (J). reprint ed. 15.99 *(0-448-06028-0,* Grosset & Dunlap) Penguin Putnam Bks. for Young Readers.

—The Wind in the Willows. Hanft, Joshua, ed. (Great Illustrated Classics Ser.: Vol. 39). (Illus.). 240p. (J). (gr. 3-6). 9.95 *(0-86611-990-6)* Playmore, Inc., Pubs.

—The Wind in the Willows. 1966. (Illus.). (J). 12.95 o.p. *(0-529-00119-5)* Putnam Publishing Group, The.

—The Wind in the Willows. 1969. (Illus.). 256p. (J). (gr. 1 up). pap. 3.25 o.s.i *(0-440-49555-5,* Yearling) Random Hse. Children's Bks.

—The Wind in the Willows. (J). 1996. 9.99 o.s.i *(0-517-16023-4)*; 1991. 2.99 o.s.i *(0-517-02026-2)*; 1991. 2.99 o.s.i *(0-517-02027-0)*; 1988. 12.99 o.s.i *(0-517-63230-6)*; 1988. 7.99 o.s.i *(0-517-49284-9)* Random Hse. Value Publishing.

—The Wind in the Willows. (J). 2000. 6.00 o.p. *(0-7624-0558-9)*; 1994. 176p. text 5.98 o.p. *(1-56138-455-0,* Courage Bks.) Running Pr. Bk. Pubs.

—The Wind in the Willows. 208p. (J). (gr. 4-7). 1988. pap. 2.75 o.p. *(0-590-43404-7)*; 1987. (Illus.). mass mkt. 4.50 *(0-590-44774-2,* Scholastic Paperbacks) Scholastic, Inc.

—The Wind in the Willows. 1987. (YA). 3.98 *(0-671-08895-5)* Simon & Schuster.

—The Wind in the Willows. 1991. (Illus.). 264p. (YA). (gr. 3 up). 25.00 o.s.i *(0-684-19345-0,* Atheneum); 1972. (Wind in the Willows Ser.: Vol. 1). (Illus.). 272p. (J). (gr. 2 up). 17.00 *(0-684-12819-5,* Atheneum); 1950. (J). pap. 7.95 o.s.i *(0-684-71788-3,* Simon & Schuster Children's Publishing); 1989. (Illus.). 272p. (J). (gr. 2 up). reprint ed. pap. 5.99 *(0-689-71310-X,* Aladdin); 75th anniv. ed. 1983. (Illus.). 256p. (J). (gr. 2 up). 19.95 *(0-684-17957-1,* Atheneum) Simon & Schuster Children's Publishing.

—The Wind in the Willows. 1991. (J). pap. 9.95 *(0-8045-1033-4)* Spoken Arts, Inc.

—The Wind in the Willows. (Illus.). 272p. 3rd ed. 1995. (J). (gr. 2 up). 19.95 *(0-312-13624-2)*; 5th ed. 1996. (gr. 4-7). pap. 11.95 *(0-312-14826-7,* Saint Martin's Griffin) St. Martin's Pr.

—The Wind in the Willows. l.t. ed. 1996. 248p. (J). lib. bdg. 21.95 *(0-7838-1874-2)* Thorndike Pr.

—The Wind in the Willows. l.t. ed. 1981. (Classics Ser.). 260p. (J). 13.95 o.p. *(0-7089-8007-4,* Charnwood) Thorpe, F. A. Pubs. GBR. *Dist:* Ulverscroft Large Print Bks., Ltd.

—The Wind in the Willows. 1969. (Signet Classics Ser.). (J). 10.00 *(0-606-01976-6)* Turtleback Bks.

—The Wind in the Willows. 1985. (J). 15.95 o.p. *(0-670-80764-8)* Viking Penguin.

—The Wind in the Willows. 1998. (Children's Classics). (Illus.). 192p. (YA). (ps up). pap. 3.95 *(1-85326-122-X,* 122XWW); 160p. (J). (gr. 4-7). pap. 3.95 *(1-85326-017-7,* 0177WW) Wordsworth Editions, Ltd. GBR. *Dist:* Advanced Global Distribution Services, Combined Publishing.

—The Wind in the Willows: A Young Reader's Edition of the Classic Story. abr. ed. 1993. (Children's Illustrated Classics Ser.). (Illus.). 56p. (J). (gr. 3-7). 9.98 *(1-56138-276-0,* Courage Bks.) Running Pr. Bk. Pubs.

—The Wind in the Willows: Anniversary Edition. 1960. (J). 16.95 o.s.i *(0-684-20838-5,* Atheneum) Simon & Schuster Children's Publishing.

—The Wind in the Willows: With Charm. 2003. (Charming Classics Ser.). (Illus.). 256p. (J). pap. 6.99 *(0-06-053723-X)* HarperCollins Children's Bk. Group.

—The Wind in the Willows Vol. 3: The Gates of Dawn. Johnson, Joe, tr. 1999. (Illus.). 31p. (J). (gr. 4-7). 15.95 *(1-56163-245-7)* NBM Publishing Co.

—A Wind in the Willows Christmas. 2000. (Illus.). 41p. (J). (ps-3). lib. bdg. 16.50 *(1-58717-007-8)* North-South Bks., Inc.

—A Wind in the Willows Christmas. 2000. (Illus.). 41p. (J). (ps-3). 15.95 o.p. *(1-58717-006-X)* SeaStar Bks.

—The Wind in the Willows Pop-up-Book, ERS. 1983. (Illus.). 12p. (J). (gr. k-4). o.p. *(0-03-063862-3,* Holt, Henry & Co. Bks. For Young Readers) Holt, Henry & Co.

Grahame, Kenneth & Cooper, intros. The Wind in the Willows. 1999. (Aladdin Classics Ser.). (Illus.). 304p. (J). (gr. 4-7). pap. 3.99 *(0-689-83140-4,* Aladdin) Simon & Schuster Children's Publishing.

Grahame, Kenneth & Golden Books Staff. The Wind in the Willows. 1987. (Golden Classics Ser.). (Illus.). 128p. (J). pap. 8.95 o.s.i *(0-307-17117-5,* Golden Bks.) Random Hse. Children's Bks.

Gralley, Jean. Hogula: Dread Pig of Night, ERS. (Illus.). (J). (ps-3). 2002. 32p. pap. 6.95 *(0-8050-7164-4)*; 1999. 40p. 15.95 *(0-8050-5700-5)* Holt, Henry & Co. (Holt, Henry & Co. Bks. For Young Readers).

—Hogula: Dread Pig of Night. 1999. E-Book *(1-58824-604-3)*; E-Book *(1-58824-618-3)*; E-Book *(1-58824-575-6)* ipicturebooks, LLC.

Granger, Michele. Fifth Grade Fever. 144p. (J). (gr. 3-7). 1998. pap. 4.99 o.p. *(0-14-037972-X)*; 1995. 14.99 o.s.i *(0-525-45279-6,* Dutton Children's Bks.) Penguin Putnam Bks. for Young Readers.

Graves, Ann P. Color Me Santa. (Illus.). l.t. ed. 2002. 108p. per. 4.99 *(0-9721653-0-4)*; 2nd rev. ed. 2003. (J). per. 14.99 *(0-9721653-1-2)* Stylewriter Pubns.

Graves, Bonnie. The Best, Worst Day. 1996. (Hyperion Chapters Ser.). (Illus.). 64p. (J). (gr. 2-4). pap. 3.95 *(0-7868-1090-4)* Disney Pr.

—The Best, Worst Day. 1996. (Illus.). 64p. (J). (gr. 2-4). 13.95 *(0-7868-0167-0)* Hyperion Bks. for Children.

—No Copycats Allowed! 1998. (Hyperion Chapters Ser.). (Illus.). 64p. (J). (gr. 2-4). pap. 3.95 *(0-7868-1166-8)* Disney Pr.

—No Copycats Allowed! 1998. (Hyperion Chapters Ser.). (Illus.). 64p. (J). (gr. 2-4). lib. bdg. 14.49 *(0-7868-2235-X)* Hyperion Paperbacks for Children.

—No Copycats Allowed! 1998. (J). 10.10 *(0-606-13664-9)* Turtleback Bks.

Graves, Bonnie B. The Best, Worst Day. 1996. (Illus.). (J). lib. bdg. o.p. *(0-7868-2139-6)* Hyperion Bks. for Children.

—Best Worst Day. 1996. (Hyperion Chapters Ser.). 9.15 o.p. *(0-606-09071-1)* Turtleback Bks.

—The Best Worst Day. 1997. (J). lib. bdg. 14.49 o.p. *(0-7868-2301-1)* Disney Pr.

Graves, Kassie. Brave Little Sailboat. 2003. (Illus.). 20p. (J). bds. 14.95 *(0-9728019-0-1)* Bright Eyes Pr.

Gray, Libba Moore. Is There Room on the Feather Bed? ed. 2000. (J). (gr. 1). spiral bd. *(0-616-03037-1)*; (gr. 2). spiral bd. *(0-616-04555-7)* Canadian National Institute for the Blind/Institut National Canadien pour les Aveugles.

—Is There Room on the Feather Bed? 1999. (Illus.). 32p. (J). (ps-1). mass mkt. 5.95 *(0-531-07137-5,* Orchard Bks.) Scholastic, Inc.

—Is There Room on the Feather Bed? 1999. (Illus.). (J). 12.10 *(0-606-18333-7)* Turtleback Bks.

Gray, Nigel. The Deserter. 1977. (Illus.). (J). (gr. 4-7). o.p. *(0-06-022061-9)*; lib. bdg. 7.40 o.p. *(0-06-022062-7)* HarperCollins Pubs.

Green, Jane. Bookends: A Novel. 2000. 393p. *(0-7181-4456-2,* Joseph, Michael) Viking Penguin.

Green, Kate. Between Friends: Setting Boundaries. 1991. (Fossil Family Tales Ser.). (Illus.). 32p. (J). (gr. 1-5). lib. bdg. 22.79 o.p. *(0-89565-780-5)* Child's World, Inc.

Green, Phyllis. Walkie-Walkie. 1978. (J). lib. bdg. 6.95 o.p. *(0-201-02630-9)* Addison-Wesley Longman, Inc.

Greenberg, Jan. The Iceberg & Its Shadow, RS. 1980. 132p. (J). (gr. 4-7). 10.95 o.p. *(0-374-33624-5,* Farrar, Straus & Giroux (BYR)) Farrar, Straus & Giroux.

—Just the Two of Us, RS. 128p. (J). (gr. 4-7). 1991. pap. 3.95 o.p. *(0-374-43982-6,* Sunburst); 1988. 14.00 o.p. *(0-374-36198-3,* Farrar, Straus & Giroux (BYR)) Farrar, Straus & Giroux.

Greenberg, Kenneth R. The Adventures of Tusky & His Friends, Bk. 1: A Jungle Adventure. 1991. (Snuggle-up Ser.). (Illus.). 51p. (J). (gr. k-3). 13.95 *(1-879100-00-2)* Tusky Pr., The.

Greene, Bette. Get on Out of Here, Philip Hall. 1981. 160p. (J). (gr. 3-6). 14.95 o.p. *(0-8037-2871-9)*; 14.89 o.p. *(0-8037-2872-7)* Penguin Putnam Bks. for Young Readers. (Dial Bks. for Young Readers).

—I've Already Forgotten Your Name. 2004. 176p. (J). lib. bdg. 16.89 *(0-06-051836-7)* HarperCollins Pubs.

Greene, Carol. Golden Locket. 1996. 10.20 o.p. *(0-606-09339-7)* Turtleback Bks.

Greene, Constance C. Ask Anybody. 1991. (Illus.). 160p. (YA). (gr. 5-9). pap. 3.95 o.p. *(0-14-034787-9,* Puffin Bks.); 1983. 156p. (J). (gr. 4-6). 11.95 o.p. *(0-670-13813-4,* Viking Children's Bks.) Penguin Putnam Bks. for Young Readers.

—A Girl Called Al. 1969. (Illus.). (J). (gr. 6-8). 15.00 o.p. *(0-670-34153-3,* Viking Children's Bks.) Penguin Putnam Bks. for Young Readers.

—I Know You, Al. 1991. 128p. (YA). (gr. 5-9). pap. 3.95 o.p. *(0-14-034884-0,* Puffin Bks.) Penguin Putnam Bks. for Young Readers.

—Isabelle & Little Orphan Frannie. 1988. 128p. (J). (gr. 8-12). 11.95 o.p. *(0-670-82266-3,* Viking Children's Bks.) Penguin Putnam Bks. for Young Readers.

—Isabelle the Itch. 1992. 128p. (J). (gr. 3-7). pap. 4.50 o.s.i *(0-14-036028-X,* Puffin Bks.) Penguin Putnam Bks. for Young Readers.

—Your Old Pal, Al. 1981. 160p. (J). (gr. k-6). pap. 2.95 o.s.i *(0-440-49862-7,* Yearling) Random Hse. Children's Bks.

Greene, Stephanie. Owen Foote, Frontiersman. 2002. (Illus.). 96p. (J). (ps-3). pap. 4.95 *(0-618-24620-7,* Clarion Bks.) Houghton Mifflin Co. Trade & Reference Div.

—Owen Foote, Soccer Star. 1998. (Illus.). 96p. (J). (ps-3). tchr. ed. 14.00 *(0-395-86143-8,* Clarion Bks.) Houghton Mifflin Co. Trade & Reference Div.

—Owen Foote, Super Spy. 2001. (Illus.). 96p. (J). (gr. 4-6). tchr. ed. 14.00 *(0-618-11752-0,* Clarion Bks.) Houghton Mifflin Co. Trade & Reference Div.

—Show & Tell. 1998. (Illus.). 84p. (J). (ps-3). tchr. ed. 15.00 *(0-395-88898-0,* Clarion Bks.) Houghton Mifflin Co. Trade & Reference Div.

Greenfield, Eloise. Big Friend, Little Friend. 1991. (Illus.). 12p. (J). (ps-1). bds. 5.95 *(0-86316-204-5)* Writers & Readers Publishing, Inc.

Greenspun, Adele Aron. Ariel & Emily. 2003. (Illus.). 32p. (J). 12.99 *(0-525-46861-7)* NAL.

Greenwald, Sheila. The Atrocious Two. 1989. 160p. (J). (gr. k-6). pap. 2.95 o.s.i *(0-440-40141-0,* Yearling) Random Hse. Children's Bks.

—Here's Hermione: A Rosy Cole Production. 1991. (Illus.). (J). (gr. 3-7). 13.95 o.p. *(0-316-32715-8)* Little Brown & Co.

—My Fabulous New Life. 1993. (Illus.). (gr. 3-7). 176p. (J). pap. 3.95 o.s.i *(0-15-276716-9)*; 128p. (YA). 10.95 o.s.i *(0-15-277693-1)* Harcourt Children's Bks.

—Rosy Cole: She Grows & Graduates. 1997. (Illus.). 96p. (J). (gr. 2-6). pap. 15.95 *(0-531-30022-6)*; mass mkt. 15.99 o.p. *(0-531-33022-2)* Scholastic, Inc. (Orchard Bks.).

Gregorich, Barbara. My Friend Goes Left, Level 1. Hoffman, Joan, ed. 1984. (Start to Read! Ser.). (Illus.). (J). (ps-2). 16p. 2.29 *(0-88743-008-2,* 06008); 32p. pap. 3.95 *(0-88743-406-1,* 06058) School Zone Publishing Co.

Gregory, Deborah. The Cheetah Girls No. 1: Livin Large. 2003. 544p. (J). pap. 9.99 *(0-7868-1789-5,* Jump at the Sun) Hyperion Bks. for Children.

—Woof, There It Is!, 2000. (Cheetah Girls Ser.: No. 5). 144p. (J). (gr. 3-7). pap. 3.99 *(0-7868-1424-1)* Disney Pr.

Gregory, Diana. I'm Boo... That's Who. 1979. (Illus.). (J). 9.95 *(0-201-02628-7)* HarperCollins Children's Bk. Group.

Gregory, Valiska. Happy Burpday, Maggie McDougal! 1992. (Illus.). 64p. (J). (gr. 2-4). 11.95 o.p. *(0-316-32777-8)* Little Brown & Co.

—Sunny Side Up. 1986. (Mr. Poggle & Scamp Bk.). (Illus.). 24p. (J). (ps). 8.95 o.s.i *(0-02-738050-5)*; bds. 3.95 o.s.i *(0-02-738060-2)* Simon & Schuster Children's Publishing. (Simon & Schuster Children's Publishing).

Grejniec, Michael. Bonjour, Bonsoir. 1945. Tr. of Good Morning, Good Night. (FRE., Illus.). (J). (ps-1). 15.95 o.p. *(3-314-20775-1)* North-South Bks., Inc.

—Qui Aime Quoi? 1945. (FRE.). (J). 14.95 o.p. *(3-314-20772-7)* North-South Bks., Inc.

Gretz, Susanna. Frog, Duck & Rabbit. 1992. (Illus.). 32p. (J). (ps-1). lib. bdg. 12.95 *(0-02-737327-4,* Simon & Schuster Children's Publishing) Simon & Schuster Children's Publishing.

—Rabbit Rambles On. 1992. (Illus.). 32p. (J). (ps-1). lib. bdg. 12.95 *(0-02-737325-8,* Simon & Schuster Children's Publishing) Simon & Schuster Children's Publishing.

Grifalconi, Ann. Not Home: Somehow, Somewhere, There Must Be Love: A Novel. 1995. (J). 15.95 o.p. *(0-316-32905-3)* Little Brown & Co.

Relationships

Griffin, Adele. Overnight. 2004. 160p. pap. 5.99 (*0-14-240143-9*, Puffin Bks.) Penguin Putnam Bks. for Young Readers.

Griffin, Hedley. Cyril's Bad Day & The Funny Little Creature. 1997. (Cyril & Friends Ser.). (Illus.). 32p. (J). bds. 8.95 (*0-7188-2865-8*) Lutherworth Pr., The GBR. *Dist:* Parkwest Pubns., Inc.

—Cyril's New Flower & The Green New Giant. 1997. (Cyril & Friends Ser.). (Illus.). 32p. (J). bds. 8.95 (*0-7188-2869-0*) Lutherworth Pr., The GBR. *Dist:* Parkwest Pubns., Inc.

Griffith, Clay S. The Tick. 1995. 195p. (J). (gr. 4-7). pap. 3.99 o.s.i (*0-553-48325-0*) Bantam Bks.

Grimes, Nikki. Growin' 6.95 o.p. (*0-8037-3272-4*, Dial Bks. for Young Readers); 6.46 o.p. (*0-8037-3273-2*, Dial Bks. for Young Readers); 1995. 112p. (J). pap. 5.99 o.p. (*0-14-037066-8*, Puffin Bks.) Penguin Putnam Bks. for Young Readers.

—Growin' 1995. 9.09 o.p. (*0-606-07603-4*) Turtleback Bks.

Grindley, Sally. The Big What Are Friends For? Storybook. 2002. (Illus.). 96p. (J). (ps up). tchr. ed. 16.95 (*0-7534-5556-0*, Kingfisher) Houghton Mifflin Co. Trade & Reference Div.

—The Giant Postman. 2000. (I Am Reading Bks.). (Illus.). 48p. (J). (gr. k up). pap. o.p. (*0-7534-5319-3*) Kingfisher Publications, plc.

—What Are Friends For? (Illus.). 32p. (J). (ps-3). 2000. pap. 6.95 (*0-7534-5285-5*); 1998. tchr. ed. 15.95 (*0-7534-5108-5*) Houghton Mifflin Co. Trade & Reference Div. (Kingfisher).

—What Are Friends For? 1998. (Illus.). 18p. (J). pap. 11.98 (*1-58048-053-5*) Sandvik Publishing.

Grindley, Sally & Dann, Penny. What Will I Do Without You? 2001. (Illus.). 32p. (J). (ps). pap. 6.95 (*0-7534-5411-4*, Kingfisher) Houghton Mifflin Co. Trade & Reference Div.

Gripe, Maria. Elvis & His Secret. La Farge, Sheila, tr. 1976. (Illus.). 208p. (J). 6.95 o.s.i (*0-440-02282-7*); lib. bdg. 6.46 o.s.i (*0-440-02283-5*) Dell Publishing. (Delacorte Pr.).

—Hugo & Josephine. Austin, Paul B., tr. 1970. (Illus.). (J). (gr. 4-6). 4.95 o.p. (*0-440-04283-6*, Delacorte Pr.) Dell Publishing.

Gritz-Gilbert, Ona. The Starfish Summer. 1998. (Illus.). 96p. (J). (gr. 2-5). 14.95 o.s.i (*0-06-027193-0*) HarperCollins Children's Bk. Group.

Grohskopf, Bernice. Children in the Wind. 1977. (J). (gr. 6-8). 2.49 o.p. (*0-689-30583-4*, Atheneum) Simon & Schuster Children's Publishing.

—End of Summer. 1982. 208p. (YA). (gr. 7 up). pap. 2.25 o.p. (*0-380-79293-1*, Avon Bks.) Morrow/Avon.

Gross, Bill. Poor Roger. 1998. (Doug Chronicles Ser.: No. 7). (Illus.). 64p. (J). (gr. 2-4). pap. 3.99 (*0-7868-4260-1*) Disney Pr.

Gross, Theodore F. Everyone Asked about You. 1990. (Illus.). 32p. (J). (ps-3). 14.95 o.p. (*0-399-21727-4*, Philomel) Penguin Putnam Bks. for Young Readers.

Gross, U. B. Fun Gus & Polly Pus. 1996. (Slimeballs Ser.: No. 1). (J). (gr. 4-7). pap. 3.99 o.s.i (*0-679-88234-0*, Random Hse. Bks. for Young Readers) Random Hse. Children's Bks.

Grove, Ella. This Is Mohan. (Illus.). 24p. (J). 1996. (SPA.). pap. 2.20 (*0-7399-0288-1*, 2437.1); 1989. pap. 2.70 (*0-7399-0034-X*, 2437) Rod & Staff Pubs., Inc.

Grove, Vicki. The Crystal Garden. 1995. 112p. (J). (gr. 4-7). 16.99 o.p. (*0-399-21813-0*, G. P. Putnam's Sons) Penguin Group (USA) Inc.

—The Crystal Garden. 1997. (Illus.). 224p. (J). (gr. 5-9). pap. 6.99 o.s.i (*0-698-11432-9*, PaperStar) Penguin Putnam Bks. for Young Readers.

—The Crystal Garden. 1997. 12.04 (*0-606-10988-9*) Turtleback Bks.

—The Fastest Friend in the West. 1990. 176p. (J). (gr. 4-8). 14.95 o.p. (*0-399-22184-0*, G. P. Putnam's Sons) Penguin Putnam Bks. for Young Readers.

—The Fastest Friend in the West. 1992. (J). (gr. 4-7). 176p. pap. 2.95 o.p. (*0-590-44338-0*, Scholastic Paperbacks); pap. 2.95 o.p. (*0-590-44339-9*) Scholastic, Inc.

—Reaching Dustin. 2000. (Illus.). 208p. (YA). (gr. 4-9). pap. 5.99 (*0-698-11839-1*, Puffin Bks.) Penguin Putnam Bks. for Young Readers.

—Reaching Dustin. 2000. 12.04 (*0-606-18844-4*) Turtleback Bks.

Groves, Sheila & Stowell, Gordon. Whisperings. 1981. (Tortoise Tales Ser.). (J). pap. 0.79 o.p. (*0-8010-3774-3*) Baker Bks.

Grovet, Heather. Prince Prances Again. 2001. (Julius & Friends Ser.: Bk. 9). (Illus.). 94p. (J). 6.99 (*0-8163-1807-7*) Pacific Pr. Publishing Assn.

Gruelle, Johnny. Raggedy Ann's Candy Heart Wisdom. 1999. (Raggedy Ann Ser.). (Illus.). 48p. (J). 8.95 (*0-689-82485-8*, Simon & Schuster Children's Publishing) Simon & Schuster Children's Publishing.

Gruenberg, Jeremiah. Ki'i & Li'i: A Story from the Stories. Salisbury, Graham, ed. 2001. 44p. (J). (ps-3). 15.95 (*0-9662945-3-X*) Goodale Publishing.

Gryspeerdt, Rebecca. Counting Friends. 1993. (Illus.). 24p. (J). (ps-1). o.p. (*1-85681-092-5*) Random Hse. of Canada, Ltd. CAN. *Dist:* Random Hse., Inc.

Guest, Elissa Haden. Iris & Walter. (Iris & Walter Ser.). (Illus.). 44p. (J). 2002. pap. 5.95 (*0-15-216442-1*); 2000. (gr. 1-3). 14.00 (*0-15-202122-1*) Harcourt Children's Bks. (Gulliver Bks.).

—Iris & Walter, True Friends. (Iris & Walter Ser.). (Illus.). 44p. (J). 2002. pap. 5.95 (*0-15-216448-0*); 2001. (gr. 1-4). 14.00 (*0-15-202121-3*) Harcourt Children's Bks. (Gulliver Bks.).

Guggenheim, Jaenet. Herman & Poppy Go Singing in the Hills. Eisenhardt, Gae, ed. l.t. ed. 1997. (Illus.). 38p. (J). (ps-k). 15.95 (*0-9660239-1-9*) Azro Pr., Inc.

Guiberson, Brenda Z. Instant Soup. 1991. 112p. (J). (gr. 3-7). text 12.95 o.p. (*0-689-31688-7*, Atheneum) Simon & Schuster Children's Publishing.

Gunn, Robin J. A Promise Is Forever. 1998. (Christy Miller Ser.: No. 12). 160p. (YA). (gr. 7-11). pap. 5.99 o.p. (*1-56179-284-5*) Focus on the Family Publishing.

—Sweet Dreams. 1998. (Christy Miller Ser.: Vol. 11). 162p. (YA). (gr. 7-11). pap. 5.99 o.p. (*1-56179-255-1*) Focus on the Family Publishing.

Gunn, Robin Jones. Island Dreamer. rev. ed. 1999. (Christy Miller Ser.: Vol. 5). 176p. (J). (gr. 7-12). pap. 6.99 (*1-56179-718-9*) Bethany Hse. Pubs.

—Island Dreamer. 1998. (Christy Miller Ser.: Vol. 5). 184p. (YA). (gr. 7-11). pap. 5.99 o.p. (*1-56179-072-9*) Focus on the Family Publishing.

—Time Will Tell. 1998. (Sierra Jensen Ser.: No. 8). 160p. (YA). (gr. 7-11). pap. 6.99 (*1-56179-568-2*) Focus on the Family Publishing.

—True Friends. rev. ed. 1999. (Christy Miller Ser.: Vol. 7). 160p. (J). (gr. 7-12). pap. 6.99 (*1-56179-720-0*) Bethany Hse. Pubs.

—True Friends. 1998. (Christy Miller Ser.: Vol. 7). 168p. (YA). (gr. 7-11). pap. 5.99 o.p. (*1-56179-131-8*) Focus on the Family Publishing.

Gunnison, Nina. Alex Makes New Friends. 1972. (Illus.). 32p. (J). (ps-2). 1.95 o.p. (*0-87397-019-5*, Strode Pubs.) Circle Bk. Service, Inc.

Gutelle, Andrew M. But Not Nate! A Book about Opposites. Crawford, Jean, ed. 1999. (Snugglebug Bks.). (Illus.). 32p. (J). (ps-1). 4.95 o.p. (*0-7835-4501-0*) Time-Life, Inc.

Gutman, Anne & Hallensleben, Georg. Gaspard & Lisa's Rainy Day. 2003. (Misadventures of Gaspard & Lisa Ser.). (Illus.). 32p. (J). 9.95 (*0-375-82252-6*) Knopf, Alfred A. Inc.

Gutman, Dan. Honus & Me. 1998. (J). 11.04 (*0-606-13487-5*) Turtleback Bks.

—Joe & Me. 2003. (Baseball Card Adventures Ser.). 176p. (J). pap. 5.99 (*0-06-447259-0*) HarperCollins Pubs.

—Shoeless Joe & Me. 2002. (Baseball Card Adventure Ser.). (Illus.). 176p. (J). (gr. 4-7). lib. bdg. 16.89 (*0-06-029254-7*) HarperCollins Children's Bk. Group.

—Shoeless Joe & Me: A Baseball Card Adventure. 2002. (Baseball Card Adventure Ser.). (Illus.). 176p. (J). (gr. 4-7). 15.95 (*0-06-029253-9*) HarperCollins Children's Bk. Group.

Gutsche, Brigitte. Asaley's Secret: The Holt's Freinds Series. Kemnitz, Myrna, ed. 2000. (Holt's Friends Ser.: Vol. 4). 126p. (J). (ps-2). pap. 9.99 (*0-88092-517-5*, 5175) Royal Fireworks Publishing Co.

—To Be a Friend. 2000. (Holt's Friends Ser.: No. 2). 115p. (J). (gr. k-3). pap. 9.99 (*0-88092-515-9*, 5159) Royal Fireworks Publishing Co.

Guy, Rosa. Billy the Great. 1994. (Illus.). 32p. (J). (ps-3). pap. 4.99 o.s.i (*0-440-40920-9*) Dell Publishing.

—The Friends. 1981. 192p. (J). mass mkt. 2.95 o.s.i (*0-553-27326-4*); (YA). (gr. 7-12). mass mkt. 2.50 o.s.i (*0-553-26519-9*) Bantam Bks.

—The Friends, ERS. 1973. 208p. (J). (gr. 4-6). 13.95 o.p. (*0-8050-1742-9*, Holt, Henry & Co. Bks. For Young Readers) Holt, Henry & Co.

—The Friends. 1995. 192p. (YA). (gr. 4-7). mass mkt. 5.99 (*0-440-22667-8*); 1991. (J). mass mkt. o.s.i (*0-553-54044-0*) Random Hse. Children's Bks. (Dell Books for Young Readers).

—The Ups & Downs of Carl Davis III. 1992. 128p. (J). (gr. 4-7). pap. 3.50 o.s.i (*0-440-40744-3*) Dell Publishing.

Gyenes, Betty Traylo. Buckaroo & the Angel. 1999. (Illus.). 208p. (gr. 3-7). text 14.95 o.s.i (*0-385-32637-8*, Dell Books for Young Readers) Random Hse. Children's Bks.

Gág, Wanda. Snippy & Snappy. 2003. (Illus.). 48p. (J). (gr. k-3). 14.95 (*0-8166-4245-1*) Univ. of Minnesota Pr.

Haalman, Perry. Mordechai. 1990. (Illus.). 36p. (J). (gr. 4 up). pap. 8.00 (*0-9624155-2-9*) Cottage Wordsmiths.

Haas, Dorothy. New Friends. 1988. (Peanut Butter & Jelly Ser.: No. 1). (J). (gr. 3-7). mass mkt. 2.75 o.p. (*0-590-41506-9*, Scholastic Paperbacks) Scholastic, Inc.

Haas, Jessie. A Blue for Beware. 1995. (Illus.). 64p. (J). (gr. 4-7). 14.00 (*0-688-13678-8*, Greenwillow Bks.) HarperCollins Children's Bk. Group.

Haberman, Lia. Friendship Forever. 2000. (All about You Ser.). (Illus.). 80p. (J). (gr. 4-7). mass mkt. 4.50 (*0-439-15530-4*) Scholastic, Inc.

Haddad, Charles. Captain Tweakerbeak's Revenge. 2002. 192p. (gr. 3-7). pap. text 4.99 (*0-440-41607-8*, Laurel Leaf) Random Hse. Children's Bks.

Haddix, Margaret Peterson. Don't You Dare Read This, Mrs. Dunphrey. unabr. ed. 1997. (J). (gr. 2). 39.75 incl. audio (*0-7887-1251-9*, 40497) Recorded Bks., LLC.

—Don't You Dare Read This, Mrs. Dunphrey. 1997. (J). 10.55 (*0-606-12680-5*) Turtleback Bks.

—The Girl with 500 Middle Names. l.t. ed. 2002. 102p. (J). 21.95 (*0-7862-4412-7*) Gale Group.

—The Girl with 500 Middle Names. 2001. (Illus.). 96p. (J). (gr. 2-4). 15.00 (*0-689-84135-3*, Simon & Schuster Children's Publishing); pap. 3.99 (*0-689-84136-1*, Aladdin) Simon & Schuster Children's Publishing.

—The Girl with 500 Middle Names. 2001. (Ready-for-Chapters Ser.). (Illus.). (J). 10.14 (*0-606-20672-8*) Turtleback Bks.

Hafner. The Adventures of Molly & Emmett. (J). 7.95 (*0-8126-0052-5*) Open Court Publishing Co.

Hafner, Marylin. A Year with Molly & Emmett. 1997. (Illus.). 32p. (J). (gr. k-2). 15.99 o.s.i (*1-56402-966-2*) Candlewick Pr.

—Year with Molly & Emmett. 1998. (Illus.). 32p. (J). (ps-2). bds. 5.99 (*0-7636-0573-5*) Candlewick Pr.

Haft, Erin. A Kiss Between Friends. 1997. (Love Stories Ser.). 192p. (YA). (gr. 7-12). mass mkt. 3.99 o.s.i (*0-553-57078-1*, Dell Books for Young Readers) Random Hse. Children's Bks.

Hager, Betty. Marcie & the Monster of the Bayou. 1994. (Tales from the Bayou Ser.: Bk. 4). 128p. (J). (gr. 3-7). pap. 5.99 o.p. (*0-310-38431-1*) Zondervan.

Haggerty, Mary Elizabeth. Una Grieta en la Pared. 1993. 13.10 (*0-606-10527-1*) Turtleback Bks.

Hague, Michael. The Wind in the Willows, ERS. 1980. (Illus.). 216p. (YA). (gr. 2 up). 25.95 o.s.i (*0-8050-0213-8*, Holt, Henry & Co. Bks. For Young Readers) Holt, Henry & Co.

Hahn, Mary. Anna on the Farm. 2003. (Illus.). 160p. (J). pap. 5.99 (*0-06-441100-1*, Harper Trophy) HarperCollins Children's Bk. Group.

Hahn, Mary Downing. As Ever, Gordy. 2000. (Illus.). 192p. (J). (gr. 3-7). pap. 5.99 (*0-380-73206-8*, Harper Trophy) HarperCollins Children's Bk. Group.

—As Ever, Gordy. 1998. 11.04 (*0-606-17878-3*) Turtleback Bks.

—The Sara Summer. 1985. 160p. (J). pap. 2.99 o.s.i (*0-553-15600-4*); (gr. 5 up). pap. 2.50 o.s.i (*0-553-15481-8*) Bantam Bks.

—The Sara Summer, 001. 1979. 160p. (J). (gr. 3-6). 7.95 o.p. (*0-395-28968-8*, Clarion Bks.) Houghton Mifflin Co. Trade & Reference Div.

—The Sara Summer. 1995. (J). (gr. 4-5). reprint ed. pap. 4.50 o.p. (*0-380-72354-9*, Avon Bks.) Morrow/Avon.

—The Sara Summer. 1995. (J). 9.60 o.p. (*0-606-08129-1*) Turtleback Bks.

—Tallahassee Higgins. 1988. 192p. (J). (gr. 4-7). pap. 4.99 (*0-380-70500-1*, Avon Bks.) Morrow/Avon.

Hale, Irina. How I Found a Friend. 1992. (Illus.). 320p. (J). (ps-1). 12.50 o.p. (*0-670-84286-9*, Viking Children's Bks.) Penguin Putnam Bks. for Young Readers.

Hale, Jane. Heartland. 1999. (Illus.). 288p. (J). (gr. 8-12). pap. 12.95 (*0-934426-91-0*) NAPSAC Reproductions.

Haley, Amanda, illus. Let Me Call You Sweetheart. 2001. (Sing-Along Storybks.). 10p. (J). (ps up). bds. 6.95 (*0-694-01556-3*, Harper Festival) HarperCollins Children's Bk. Group.

Haley, Lin. Knoll Knowls. 1996. 16p. (J). (gr. 4-7). 12.95 o.p. (*1-56763-255-6*); pap. text 2.95 o.p. (*1-56763-256-4*) Ozark Publishing.

Hall, Katy. We're in This Together, Patti!, No. 5. 1995. (Peabody Rebus Reading Program Ser.). 144p. (Orig.). (J). (gr. 3-6). pap. 3.50 (*0-671-52051-2*, Aladdin) Simon & Schuster Children's Publishing.

Hall, Kirsten. Double Trouble. 2004. (Beastieville-Pb Ser.). pap. 3.95 (*0-516-24653-4*, Children's Pr.) Scholastic Library Publishing.

—Double Trouble: All about Colors. 2003. (Beastieville Ser.). (Illus.). lib. bdg. 18.50 (*0-516-22892-7*, Children's Pr.) Scholastic Library Publishing.

—Help! All about Telling Time. 2003. (Beastieville Ser.). (Illus.). 31p. (J). lib. bdg. 18.50 (*0-516-22890-0*, Children's Pr.) Scholastic Library Publishing.

—Little Lies: All about Math. 2003. (Beastieville Ser.). (Illus.). 30p. (J). lib. bdg. 18.50 (*0-516-22896-X*, Children's Pr.) Scholastic Library Publishing.

—My Best Friend. 2001. (All-Star Readers Ser.). (Illus.). 31p. (J). 3.99 (*1-57584-913-5*, Reader's Digest Children's Bks.) Reader's Digest Children's Publishing, Inc.

—Princess Daisy Finds a Friend. 1999. (Illus.). 24p. (J). (ps-1). 12.95 o.p. (*0-8118-2361-X*) Chronicle Bks. LLC.

Hall, Patricia. Old Friends, New Friends. 2002. (Raggedy Ann Ser.). 32p. (J). pap. 3.99 (*0-689-85224-X*); (Illus.). lib. bdg. 11.89 (*0-689-85225-8*) Simon & Schuster Children's Publishing. (Little Simon).

Hall, Phoebe. Big Donkey, Wee Chicken & Ashley. 1996. (Illus.). 60p. (Orig.). (J). (gr. k-5). pap. 6.50 (*0-9637936-3-2*) Deerlick Enterprise.

Hallensleben, Georg. Pauline, RS. 1999. (Illus.). 32p. (J). (ps-1). 16.00 o.p. (*0-374-35758-7*, Farrar, Straus & Giroux (BYR)) Farrar, Straus & Giroux.

—Pauline. 1999. E-Book (*1-59019-388-1*) ipicturebooks, LLC.

Halliday, John. Predicktions. 2003. (Illus.). 192p. (J). (gr. 3-6). 16.95 (*0-689-84564-2*, McElderry, Margaret K.) Simon & Schuster Children's Publishing.

Hallinan, P. K. My Daddy & I! 2002. (Illus.). 26p. (J). 7.95 (*0-8249-4217-5*, Candy Cane Pr.) Ideals Pubns.

—My Grandma & I! 2002. (Illus.). 26p. (J). 7.95 (*0-8249-4220-5*, Candy Cane Pr.) Ideals Pubns.

—My Grandpa & I! 2002. (Illus.). 26p. (J). 7.95 (*0-8249-4219-1*, Candy Cane Pr.) Ideals Pubns.

—My Mommy & I! 2002. (Illus.). 26p. (J). 7.95 (*0-8249-4218-3*, Candy Cane Pr.) Ideals Pubns.

—A Rainbow of Friends. 2002. (Illus.). 24p. (J). (ps-3). pap. 5.95 (*0-8249-5395-9*, Ideals) Ideals Pubns.

—That's What a Friend Is. 2001. (Illus.). 24p. (J). 7.95 (*0-8249-5390-8*); pap. 5.95 (*0-8249-5391-6*) Ideals Pubns. (Ideals).

—That's What a Friend Is. 1977. (P. K. Books Values for Life). (Illus.). 32p. (J). (gr. k-3). pap. 3.95 o.p. (*0-516-43628-7*); lib. bdg. 13.27 o.p. (*0-516-03628-9*) Scholastic Library Publishing. (Children's Pr.).

—We're Very Good Friends, My Brother & I. 1973. (P. K. Books Values for Life). (Illus.). 32p. (J). (gr. k-3). lib. bdg. 13.27 o.p. (*0-516-03659-9*, Children's Pr.) Scholastic Library Publishing.

—We're Very Good Friends, My Uncle & I. 1989. (P. K. Books Values for Life). (Illus.). 32p. (J). (ps-3). lib. bdg. 13.27 o.p. (*0-516-03650-5*, Children's Pr.) Scholastic Library Publishing.

Hallinan, P. K., illus. A Rainbow of Friends. 2001. 24p. (J). (ps-3). 7.95 (*0-8249-5394-0*, Ideals) Ideals Pubns.

Hallinan, P. K., tr. & illus. Forever Friends! 2003. 26p. (J). 7.95 (*0-8249-5454-8*, Candy Cane Pr.) Ideals Pubns.

—My Brother & I. 2003. 26p. (J). 7.95 (*0-8249-5455-6*, Candy Cane Pr.) Ideals Pubns.

Halvorson, Marilyn. Let It Go. 1988. (YA). (gr. 5 up). mass mkt. 2.95 o.s.i (*0-440-20053-9*, Laurel Leaf) Random Hse. Children's Bks.

Ham, Karri, et al. All Booked Up! 1986. (Illus.). 64p. (Orig.). (J). (gr. 4-8). pap. 6.95 o.p. (*0-933606-43-5*, MS-642) Sussman, Ellen Educational Services.

Hambrick, Sharon. Arby Jenkins. 1996. 117p. (J). (gr. 4-7). pap. 6.49 (*0-89084-879-3*, 099622) Jones, Bob Univ. Pr.

—Booklinks, Level 1. 1997. 128p. (J). (gr. 6). pap. 6.49 (*0-89084-932-3*, 106138) Jones, Bob Univ. Pr.

Hamer, Irene. Booda's Story: A Cross-Cultural Story for Girls & Boys. 2001. (Illus.). 100p. (J). (gr. 3-7). 12.95 (*0-9700306-1-4*, Cosmic Aye) Hastings Ende Design Partners.

Hamilton, Dorothy. Bittersweet Days. 1978. (Illus.). 128p. (J). (gr. 4-8). 4.95 o.p. (*0-8361-1845-6*); pap. 3.95 o.p. (*0-8361-1846-4*) Herald Pr.

—The Castle. 1975. (Illus.). 112p. (J). (gr. 4-8). 4.95 o.p. (*0-8361-1775-1*); pap. 3.95 o.p. (*0-8361-1776-X*) Herald Pr.

—Holly's New Year. 1981. (Illus.). 112p. (J). (gr. 3-9). pap. 4.95 o.p. (*0-8361-1961-4*) Herald Pr.

Hamilton, Gail. May the Best Man Win. 1993. (Road to Avonlea Ser.: No. 17). 128p. (J). (gr. 4-6). pap. 3.99 o.s.i (*0-553-48043-X*) Bantam Bks.

—Nothing Endures but Change. 1993. (Road to Avonlea Ser.: No. 11). 128p. (J). (gr. 4-7). pap. 3.99 o.p. (*0-553-48037-5*) Bantam Bks.

Hamilton, Harriet E. The Sunbeam & the Wave. 2000. (Illus.). 33p. (J). (gr. 4-7). 17.95 (*0-87159-250-9*) Unity Schl. of Christianity.

Hamilton, Virginia. Bluish: A Novel. (gr. 4-6). 2002. 128p. (J). mass mkt. 4.99 (*0-439-36786-7*, Scholastic Paperbacks); 1999. 127p. (YA). pap. 15.95 (*0-590-28879-2*, Blue Sky Pr., The) Scholastic, Inc.

—The Planet of Junior Brown. 1998. (J). pap. 4.50 (*0-87628-347-4*) Ctr. for Applied Research in Education, The.

—The Planet of Junior Brown. 240p. 2002. (J). E-Book 6.99 (*0-689-84805-6*, Simon & Schuster Children's Publishing); 1971. (YA). (gr. 5-9). 18.00

(0-02-742510-X, Simon & Schuster Children's Publishing); 2nd ed. 1993. (YA). (gr. 5-9). reprint ed. mass mkt. 4.99 (0-689-71721-0, Simon Pulse); 3rd ed. 1986. (Illus.). (YA). (gr. 5-9). mass mkt. 4.99 (0-02-043540-1, Simon Pulse) Simon & Schuster Children's Publishing.

—The Planet of Junior Brown. 1993. (YA). 11.04 (0-606-05975-X) Turtleback Bks.

—A White Romance. 1989. 240p. (YA). (gr. 7 up). pap. 3.95 o.p. (0-15-295888-6, Odyssey Classics) Harcourt Children's Bks.

—A White Romance. 1987. 200p. (YA). (gr. 8 up). 14.95 o.s.i (0-399-21213-2, Philomel) Penguin Putnam Bks. for Young Readers.

—A White Romance. 1998. (Point Signature Ser.). 4.50p. (YA). (gr. 8-12). mass mkt. 4.50 (0-590-13005-6) Scholastic, Inc.

—A White Romance. 1998. 10.09 o.p. (0-606-13912-5); 1987. (J). 10.00 (0-606-04421-3) Turtleback Bks.

Hammerschlag, Carl A. The Go-Away Doll. Havill, Juanita, ed. l.t. ed. 1998. (Dr. H. Bks.). (Illus.). 32p. (J). (ps-12). 16.95 (1-889166-22-7, 299-5425, Dr. H Bks.) Turtle Island Pr., Inc.

Hammond, Pearle L. The Prize in the Packard. 1990. (Illus.). 100p. (Orig.). (J). (gr. 5-8). pap. 8.95 o.p. (0-9615161-6-X) Incline Pr.

Handley, Phyllis. First Day Out. 1992. (Illus.). 32p. (J). (gr. 2). 8.95 o.p. (0-8059-3228-3) Dorrance Publishing Co., Inc.

Hanna, Mary C. Cassie & Ike. 1973. 207p. 8.95 o.p. (0-910244-70-7) Blair, John F. Pub.

Hansen, Joyce. The Gift-Giver. 128p. (J). (gr. 4-6). 1989. pap. 6.95 (0-89919-852-X); 1980. 14.95 o.p. (0-395-29433-9) Houghton Mifflin Co. Trade & Reference Div. (Clarion Bks.).

—Yellow Bird & Me. (J). 1986. (gr. 3-7). 13.95 o.p. (0-89919-335-8); 1991. 168p. (gr. 4-6). reprint ed. pap. 6.95 (0-395-55388-1) Houghton Mifflin Co. Trade & Reference Div. (Clarion Bks.).

—Yellow Bird & Me. 1986. 13.00 (0-606-05050-7) Turtleback Bks.

Hantman, Clea. The Muses on the Move, Vol. 3. 2002. (Goddesses Ser.). 160p. (J). (gr. 5 up). pap. 4.99 (0-06-440804-3) HarperCollins Pubs.

Hao, K. T. One Pizza, One Penny. Feldman, Roxanne Hsu, tr. from CHI. 2003. (J). 15.95 (0-8126-2702-4) Cricket Bks.

Hapka, Catherine. Mucha Lucha Doggone It. 2004. (Mucha Lucha Ser.). 24p. (J). pap. 3.50 (0-06-054863-0, Harper Festival) HarperCollins Children's Bk. Group.

Hapka, Catherine, adapted by. Disney's Lilo & Stitch. 2002. (Read-Aloud Storybook Ser.). (Illus.). 72p. (J). (gr. k-3). 8.99 (0-7364-1321-9, RH/Disney) Random Hse. Children's Bks.

Happy Baby Friends. 2001. (Baby Grip Ser.). (Illus.). 12p. (J). bds. 4.95 (0-312-49002-X, Priddy Bks.) St. Martin's Pr.

The Happy Egg. 9999. (J). pap. 1.50 o.p. (0-590-01623-7) Scholastic, Inc.

Harbo, Gary. Bart Becomes a Friend. 1995. (If You Want to Succeed, You Need to Read! Ser.). (SPA., Illus.). 33p. (J). (gr. 1-5). 8.95 o.p. (1-884149-08-1) Kutie Kari Bks., Inc.

—Bart Becomes a Friend: Advanced Reader. 1992. (If You Want to Succeed, You Need to Read! Ser.: Vol. Book 3). (Illus.). 33p. (J). (gr. 1-4). per. 10.95 (1-884149-05-7) Kutie Kari Bks., Inc.

—My New Friend. 1995. (If You Want to Succeed, You Need to Read! Ser.). (SPA., Illus.). 33p. (J). (gr. 1-5). 8.95 o.p. (1-884149-02-2) Kutie Kari Bks., Inc.

—My New Friend: Advanced Reader. 1988. (If You Want to Succeed, You Need to Read! Ser.: Vol. Book 1). (Illus.). 33p. (J). (gr. 1-4). per. 10.95 (1-884149-01-4) Kutie Kari Bks., Inc.

Harcourt Brace Staff, ed. Carver. 93rd ed. 1993. pap. text 14.00 (0-15-300344-8) Harcourt Children's Bks.

Harder Tangvald, Christine. Leif Likes to Play. 1986. (My Friend Leif Ser.). (Illus.). (J). (ps). pap. 2.95 o.p. (0-89191-214-2) Cook Communications Ministries.

—Leif Takes a Bath. 1901. (My Friend Leif Ser.). (Illus.). (J). (ps). pap. 2.95 o.p. (0-89191-356-4) Cook Communications Ministries.

—My Friends Are Special. 1987. (God Made Me Special Bks.). 20p. (J). (ps). bds. 5.88 o.p. (1-55513-170-0) Cook Communications Ministries.

Harding, Donal. The Leaving Summer. 1996. 192p. (YA). (gr. 5 up). 15.00 (0-688-13893-4, Morrow, William & Co.) Morrow/Avon.

—The Leaving Summer. 1998. 9.09 o.p. (0-606-13566-9) Turtleback Bks.

Harding, Kitchener L. Clarence & Amous Become Famous. l.t. ed. 1999. (Illus.). 10p. (J). (gr. 1-5). spiral bd. 4.95 (1-930503-01-6) Office Max.

Harley, Bill. Nothing Happened. 2003. (Illus.). 32p. (J). (gr. 1 up). 14.95 (1-883672-09-0) Tricycle Pr.

Harley, Rex. Last Laugh. 1988. 160p. (J). (gr. 5-8). 17.95 o.p. (0-575-03920-5) Gollancz, Victor GBR. *Dist:* Trafalgar Square.

Harlow, Joan Hiatt. Shadows on the Sea. 2003. (Illus.). 256p. (J). (gr. 3-6). 16.95 (0-689-84926-5, McElderry, Margaret K.) Simon & Schuster Children's Publishing.

—Shadows on the Sea. 2004. (J). (0-7862-6145-5) Thorndike Pr.

Harman, Betty & Meador, Nancy. The Moon Rock Heist. 1988. 112p. (J). (gr. 6-7). 13.95 (0-89015-667-0) Eakin Pr.

Harman, Chuck. Artie Saves the Day. Payne, Sandra J., ed. 1998. (Adventures of Artie the Airplane & His Friends Ser.). (Illus.). 44p. (J). (ps-6). pap. 6.95 (1-891736-00-0) Studio Five/Fourteen.

—The Big Race. Payne, Sandra J., ed. 1998. (Adventures of Artie the Airplane & His Friends Ser.). (Illus.). 24p. (J). (ps-6). pap. 6.99 (1-891736-01-9) Studio Five/Fourteen.

—It's More Than Just a Scarf. Payne, Sandra J., ed. 1998. (Adventures of Artie the Airplane & His Friends Ser.). (Illus.). 28p. (J). (ps-6). pap. 6.99 (1-891736-03-5) Studio Five/Fourteen.

—The Year Artie Saved Christmas. Payne, Sandra J., ed. 1998. (Adventures of Artie the Airplane & His Friends Ser.). (Illus.). 24p. (J). (ps-6). pap. 6.99 (1-891736-05-1) Studio Five/Fourteen.

—You Can't Judge a Plane by Its Paint Job. Payne, Sandra J., ed. 1998. (Adventures of Artie the Airplane & His Friends Ser.). (Illus.). 28p. (J). (ps-6). pap. 6.99 (1-891736-02-7) Studio Five/Fourteen.

Harper, Anita. Just a Minute! 1987. (Illus.). (J). (ps-1). 9.95 o.p. (0-399-21461-5) Putnam Publishing Group, The.

Harper, Jo. Whistling Willie. Date not set. 32p. (J). (0-7868-0113-1); lib. bdg. (0-7868-2095-0) Hyperion Pr.

Harper, Jon. Blue Ridge. 1995. (Illus.). 160p. (J). pap. 8.95 (0-9611872-7-1) Our Child Pr.

Harrell, Janice. Betrayal. 1994. (Secret Diaries Ser.: No. 02). 304p. (J). (gr. 7-9). mass mkt. 3.95 o.p. (0-590-47712-9) Scholastic, Inc.

—Secret Diaries Vol. 1: Temptation. 1994. 304p. (YA). (gr. 7-9). mass mkt. 3.95 o.p. (0-590-47692-0) Scholastic, Inc.

—Tiffany, the Disaster. Ashby, Ruth, ed. 1992. 112p. (Orig.). (J). (gr. 3-6). pap. 2.99 (0-671-72860-1, Aladdin) Simon & Schuster Children's Publishing.

Harris, Carol Flynn. A Place for Joey. 2003. (Illus.). 96p. (J). (gr. 3-6). 15.95 (1-56397-108-9) Boyds Mills Pr.

Harris, Daniel. Billy's Bounce. 2001. (Illus.). 32p. (J). (ps-3). pap. 7.50 (1-884083-70-6) Maval Publishing, Inc.

Harris, Dorothy Joan. Goodnight, Jeffrey. 1983. (Illus.). 32p. (J). (gr. 1-4). 10.95 o.p. (0-7232-6224-1, Warne, Frederick) Penguin Putnam Bks. for Young Readers.

Harris, Geraldine. Prince of the Godborn. 1983. (Seven Citadels Ser.: Pt. 1). 196p. (J). (gr. 6 up). 11.95 o.p. (0-688-01792-4, Greenwillow Bks.) HarperCollins Children's Bk. Group.

Harris, Jennifer. My Cool Friends. 1996. (I-See-You Bks.). (Illus.). 8p. (J). bds. 3.50 (1-56293-829-0, McClanahan Bk.) Learning Horizons, Inc.

Harris, Mark. The Amazing Adventure in Tovia. 2001. pap. 12.95 (0-595-19230-0, Writers Club Pr.) iUniverse, Inc.

Harris, Mark J. Confessions of a Prime Time Kid. 1986. 144p. (J). (gr. 5 up). pap. 2.50 o.p. (0-380-70101-4, Avon Bks.) Morrow/Avon.

Harris, Peter & Weir, Doffy. Bottomley at the Cattery. 1998. (Illus.). 32p. (J). pap. 5.95 (0-7641-0667-8) Barron's Educational Series, Inc.

Harrison, Dorothy L. Gold in the Garden. 1997. (Chronicles of Courage Ser.). 128p. (YA). (gr. 5 up). pap. 4.99 (0-7814-0302-2) Cook Communications Ministries.

Harrison, Lisi. Untitled Clique, No. 1. 2004. (J). (gr. 5-8). pap. 8.99 (0-316-70129-7) Little Brown Children's Bks.

Hart, Alison & Leonhardt, Alice. Foxhunt! 1995. (Riding Academy Ser.: No. 11). 132p. (YA). (gr. 5-8). pap. 3.99 o.s.i (0-679-87143-8) Fodor's Travel Pubns.

—Trouble at Foxhall. 1995. (Riding Academy Ser.: No. 10). 132p. (YA). (gr. 5-8). pap. 3.99 o.s.i (0-679-87142-X) Random Hse., Inc.

Hart, Paul. Caleb Finds a Friend. 1994. (Illus.). 40p. (Orig.). (J). (ps-5). pap. 4.95 (1-885101-05-8) Writers Pr., Inc.

Hartley, Bernard & Viney, Peter, eds. The Visit. 1988. pap. text 3.50 o.p. (0-19-421906-2) Oxford Univ. Pr., Inc.

Harvey, Dean. The Secret Elephant of Harlan Kooter. 1992. (Illus.). 160p. (J). (gr. 2-5). 13.95 o.s.i (0-395-62523-8) Houghton Mifflin Co.

Harwood, Pearl A. Mrs. Moon & Her Friends. 1967. (Mrs. Moon Bks.). (Illus.). 32p. (J). (gr. k-3). lib. bdg. 5.95 o.p. (0-8225-0112-0, Lerner Pubns.) Lerner Publishing Group.

Haseley, Dennis. Ghost Catcher. 1991. (Laura Geringer Bks.). (Illus.). 40p. (J). (gr. 1-5). 15.95 (0-06-022244-1); lib. bdg. 15.89 o.p. (0-06-022247-6) HarperCollins Children's Bk. Group.

Haskins, Francine. I Remember "121" 1991. (Illus.). 32p. (J). (gr. 1 up). 14.95 (0-89239-100-6) Children's Bk. Pr.

Hassall, Angela. Nowhere to Hide. 1987. 140p. (YA). (gr. 7 up). 13.95 o.p. (0-19-271494-5) Oxford Univ. Pr., Inc.

Hassler, Jon. Four Miles to Pinecone. 1989. 128p. (gr. 7-12). mass mkt. 5.99 (0-449-70323-1, Fawcett) Ballantine Bks.

—Four Miles to Pinecone. 1977. (Illus.). (J). (gr. 5 up). 6.95 o.p. (0-7232-6143-1, Warne, Frederick) Penguin Putnam Bks. for Young Readers.

—Jemmy. 1988. 160p. (J). (gr. 7-12). mass mkt. 5.50 (0-449-70302-9, Fawcett) Ballantine Bks.

Hathorn, Libby. The Surprise Box. 1994. (Voyages Ser.). (Illus.). (J). 4.25 (0-383-03778-6) SRA/McGraw-Hill.

Hauff, Wilhelm. Der Zwerg Nase. 1945. (GER., Illus.). (J). 17.95 o.p. (3-85195-332-0) North-South Bks., Inc.

Hauser, Thomas. Martin Bear & Friends. 1998. (Illus.). 128p. (J). 22.95 o.p. (0-8038-9409-0) Hastings Hse. Daytrips Pubs.

Hausman, Gerald. Night Flight. 1996. 144p. (J). (gr. 5-9). 15.95 o.s.i (0-399-22758-X, Philomel) Penguin Putnam Bks. for Young Readers.

Hautman, Pete. Mr. Was. 1998. (J). 10.55 (0-606-13625-8) Turtleback Bks.

Havill, Juanita. Jamaica & Brianna. 1993. (Illus.). 32p. (J). (ps-3). lib. bdg., tchr. ed. 16.00 (0-395-64489-5) Houghton Mifflin Co.

—Jamaica & Brianna. 1996. (Illus.). 32p. (J). (ps-3). pap. 5.95 (0-395-77939-1) Houghton Mifflin Co. Trade & Reference Div.

—Jamaica & Brianna. unabr. ed. 2000. (J). (ps up). pap. 24.20 incl. audio (0-7887-3645-0, 41011X4) Recorded Bks., LLC.

—Jamaica & Brianna. 1993. 11.15 o.p. (0-606-08785-0) Turtleback Bks.

—Jamaica Tag-Along. (Carry-Along Book & Cassette Favorites Ser.). (J). 1996. (Illus.). 1p. (ps-3). pap. 9.95 incl. audio (0-395-77941-3, 4-95859); 1994. pap. 44.32 (0-395-70375-1); 1992. (gr. 1). pap. 8.72 (0-395-61768-5); 1990. (Illus.). 32p. (ps-3). pap. 6.95 (0-395-54949-3); 1989. (Illus.). 32p. (ps-3). lib. bdg., tchr. ed. 16.00 (0-395-49602-0) Houghton Mifflin Co.

—Jamaica Tag-Along. 1990. 12.10 (0-606-17136-3) Turtleback Bks.

—Leona & Ike. (Illus.). 128p. (J). (gr. 2-6). 1992. pap. 2.99 o.s.i (0-679-83278-5, Knopf Bks. for Young Readers); 1991. 14.99 o.s.i (0-517-57688-0, Random Hse. Bks. for Young Readers); 1991. 13.95 o.s.i (0-517-57687-2, Random Hse. Bks. for Young Readers) Random Hse. Children's Bks.

Hawes, Louise. Waiting for Christopher. 2002. 240p. (J). (gr. 7 up). 15.99 (0-7636-1371-1) Candlewick Pr.

Hawkins, Colin & Hawkins, Jacqui. Foxy & Friends Go Racing. (Illus.). 32p. 8.95 (0-00-664565-8) Collins Willow GBR. *Dist:* Trafalgar Square.

—When I Was One. 1990. (Illus.). 32p. (J). (ps). 11.95 o.p. (0-670-81154-8, Viking Children's Bks.) Penguin Putnam Bks. for Young Readers.

Hawkins, Laura. The Cat That Could Spell Mississippi. 1992. 160p. (J). (gr. 3-5). 13.95 o.p. (0-395-61627-1) Houghton Mifflin Co.

Hay, John M. Rover & Coo Coo. 1991. (Illus.). 32p. (J). (gr. 3-6). 12.95 o.s.i (0-88138-078-4, Simon & Schuster Children's Publishing) Simon & Schuster Children's Publishing.

Hayashi, Nancy. The Fantastic Stay-Home-from-School Day. 1992. (Illus.). 105p. (J). (gr. 2-5). 12.00 o.p. (0-525-44864-0, Dutton Children's Bks.) Penguin Putnam Bks. for Young Readers.

Hayden, Torey L. The Very Worst Thing. 2003. 176p. (J). (gr. 5 up). 15.99 (0-06-029792-1); lib. bdg. 16.89 (0-06-029812-X) HarperCollins Pubs.

Hayes, Daniel. Flyers. l.t. ed. 2002. (Young Adult Ser.). 263p. (J). 22.95 (0-7862-3897-6) Gale Group.

—Flyers. (gr. 7-12). 1998. 192p. (J). pap. 4.99 (0-689-80373-7, Simon Pulse); 1996. 208p. (YA). 16.00 (0-689-80372-9, Simon & Schuster Children's Publishing) Simon & Schuster Children's Publishing.

—Flyers. 1998. 10.55 (0-606-13392-5) Turtleback Bks.

Hayes, Geoffrey. Patrick & Ted. 1986. (Illus.). 32p. (J). (ps-3). reprint ed. pap. 2.95 o.p. (0-590-40436-9) Scholastic, Inc.

—Patrick & Ted. 1984. (Illus.). 32p. (J). (ps-2). 5.95 o.p. (0-02-743380-3, Simon & Schuster Children's Publishing) Simon & Schuster Children's Publishing.

Hayes, Sheila. The Carousel Horse. 1973. (J). 7.95 o.p. (0-525-66610-9, Dutton Children's Bks.) Penguin Putnam Bks. for Young Readers.

—The Gift Horse. 1988. 160p. (J). (gr. 4-8). pap. 2.50 o.p. (0-590-41581-6, Scholastic Paperbacks) Scholastic, Inc.

—Speaking of Snapdragons. 1982. 144p. (J). (gr. 5-9). 13.95 o.p. (0-525-66785-7, 01063-320, Dutton Children's Bks.) Penguin Putnam Bks. for Young Readers.

—The Tinker's Daughter. 1995. 160p. (J). (gr. 5-9). 14.99 o.p. (0-525-67497-7, Dutton Children's Bks.) Penguin Putnam Bks. for Young Readers.

—You've Been Away All Summer. 1986. 160p. (J). (gr. 4-7). 12.95 o.p. (0-525-67182-X, Dutton Children's Bks.) Penguin Putnam Bks. for Young Readers.

—Zoe's Gift. 1994. 160p. (J). 14.99 o.p. (0-525-67484-5, Dutton Children's Bks.) Penguin Putnam Bks. for Young Readers.

Haynes, Betsy. The Boys Only Club. 1990. (Fabulous Five Ser.: No. 19). 128p. (J). (gr. 4 up). pap. 2.95 o.s.i (0-553-15809-0) Bantam Bks.

—The Bragging War. 1989. (Fabulous Five Ser.). 120p. (J). (gr. 5-7). pap. 2.75 o.s.i (0-553-15651-9) Bantam Bks.

—Breaking Up. 1991. (Fabulous Five Ser.: No. 28). 128p. (J). (gr. 4-7). pap. 2.99 o.s.i (0-553-15873-2) Bantam Bks.

—Celebrity Auction. 1990. (Fabulous Five Ser.: No. 17). 144p. (J). (gr. 4 up). pap. 2.75 o.s.i (0-553-15784-1) Bantam Bks.

—Laura's Secret: Breaking Up. 1991. (Fabulous Five Ser.: No. 26). 128p. (J). (gr. 4-7). pap. 2.99 o.s.i (0-553-15871-6) Bantam Bks.

—Melanie Edwards, Super Kisser. 1992. (Fabulous Five Ser.: No. 29). 128p. (J). pap. 2.99 o.s.i (0-553-15874-0) Bantam Bks.

—Minus One. 1991. (Fabulous Five Ser.: No. 25). 128p. (J). (gr. 4-7). pap. 2.99 o.s.i (0-553-15867-8) Bantam Bks.

—Missing You No. 3. 1991. 192p. (J). pap. 2.99 o.s.i (0-553-15876-7) Bantam Bks.

—The Popularity Trap. 1988. (Fabulous Five Ser.: Vol. 3). 128p. (J). (gr. 4-7). pap. 2.95 o.s.i (0-553-15634-9, Skylark) Random Hse. Children's Bks.

—The Scapegoat. 1991. (Fabulous Five Ser.: No. 27). 128p. (J). (gr. 4-7). pap. 2.99 o.s.i (0-553-15872-4) Bantam Bks.

—A Seventh-Grade Menace. 1989. (Fabulous Five Ser.: No. 14). 128p. (J). (gr. 4 up). pap. 2.75 o.s.i (0-553-15763-9) Bantam Bks.

—Sibling Rivalry, Vol. 30. 1992. (Fabulous Five Ser.). 128p. (J). pap. 2.99 o.s.i (0-553-15875-9) Bantam Bks.

—Taffy Sinclair & the Melanie Makeover. 1988. (Taffy Sinclair Bks.). 128p. (J). (gr. 2-6). pap. 2.75 o.s.i (0-553-15604-7, Skylark) Random Hse. Children's Bks.

—Taffy Sinclair & the Secret Admirer Epidemic. 1988. 128p. (J). pap. 2.75 o.s.i (0-553-15714-0) Bantam Bks.

—Taffy Sinclair & the Secret Admirer Epidemic. 1988. (Taffy Sinclair Bks.). (J). (gr. 2-6). pap. 2.50 o.s.i (0-553-15582-2, Skylark) Random Hse. Children's Bks.

—Taffy Sinclair, Baby Ashley & Me. 1987. 128p. (J). pap. 2.75 o.s.i (0-553-15713-2) Bantam Bks.

—Taffy Sinclair, Baby Ashley & Me. 1987. 128p. (J). (gr. 4-7). pap. 2.50 o.s.i (0-553-15557-1, Skylark) Random Hse. Children's Bks.

Haynes, David. Right by My Side, a Novel. 1998. 17.00 (0-606-13740-8) Turtleback Bks.

Haynes, Max. Love & Kisses, Kitty. 1999. (Illus.). 18p. (J). (ps-k). 6.99 o.s.i (0-525-46150-7, Dutton Children's Bks.) Penguin Putnam Bks. for Young Readers.

Hays, Anna Jane. Silly Sara. 2002. (Step into Reading Ser.). (Illus.). 32p. (J). lib. bdg. 11.99 (0-375-91231-2, Random Hse. Bks. for Young Readers) Random Hse. Children's Bks.

—Silly Sara: A Phonics Reader. 2002. (Step into Reading Early Bks.). (Illus.). 32p. (J). (ps-1). pap. 3.99 (0-375-81231-8, Random Hse. Bks. for Young Readers) Random Hse. Children's Bks.

Hays, Bradley C. Dragonfly. 1997. (J). lib. bdg. 15.95 (1-56763-261-0); (Illus.). pap. 5.55 (1-56763-262-9) Ozark Publishing.

Haywood, Carolyn. Betsy & the Boys. 2004. (Illus.). 160p. (J). 16.00 (0-15-205106-6, Harcourt Young Classics); pap. 5.95 (0-15-205102-3, Odyssey Classics) Harcourt Children's Bks.

—Betsy & the Boys. 1978. (Voyager/HBJ Bks.). 12.05 (0-606-02041-1) Turtleback Bks.

—Eddie & His Big Deals. 1990. (Illus.). 192p. (J). (gr. 3 up). reprint ed. pap. 3.95 o.p. (0-688-10075-9, Morrow, William & Co.) Morrow/Avon.

—Eddie's Friend Boodles. 1924. (J). lib. bdg. o.s.i (0-688-09029-X, Morrow, William & Co.) Morrow/Avon.

—Little Eddie. 1990. (Illus.). 160p. (J). (gr. 3 up). reprint ed. pap. 3.95 o.p. (0-688-10074-0, Morrow, William & Co.) Morrow/Avon.

Hazen, Barbara Shook. Good Bye, Hello: Spanish. 1999. (SPA.). (J). pap. 4.95 (0-689-31953-3, Atheneum) Simon & Schuster Children's Publishing.

He Was My Best Friend. 1996. (Lucky the Cat Bk.). (YA). (gr. 8-10). pap. 9.95 (0-9647200-0-0) Gato Pr., The.

Heap, Sue. Four Friends in the Garden. 2004. 32p. (J). 15.99 (*0-7636-2371-7*) Candlewick Pr.

Hedderwick, Mairi. Katie Morag & the Big Boy Cousins. 1999. (Katie Morag Stories Ser.). (Illus.). 32p. (J). pap. (*0-09-911891-2*) Random Hse. of Canada, Ltd. CAN. *Dist:* Random Hse., Inc.

—Katie Morag & the Tiresome Ted. 1999. (Illus.). 32p. (J). (gr. 1-4). pap. (*0-09-911881-5*) Random Hse. of Canada, Ltd. CAN. *Dist:* Random Hse., Inc.

Hegg, Tom. Peef & His Best Friend. 2001. (Illus.). 48p. (J). (ps up). 15.95 (*0-931674-49-2*) Waldman Hse. Pr., Inc.

Heide, Florence Parry, et al. That's What Friends are For. 2003. (Illus.). 40p. (J). 15.99 (*0-7636-1397-5*) Candlewick Pr.

Heiligman, Deborah. Pockets. 1997. (Illus.). (J). o.p. (*0-7868-0169-7*) Hyperion Bks. for Children.

Hein, Lucille E. That Wonderful Summer. 1978. (J). pap. 1.95 o.p. (*0-8170-0772-5*) Judson Pr.

Heine, Helme. Mollywoop, RS. Manheim, Ralph, tr. 1991. (Illus.). 32p. (J). (ps-3). 14.95 o.p. (*0-374-35001-9*, Farrar, Straus & Giroux (BYR)) Farrar, Straus & Giroux.

Heiner, Garth Farr. Unwanted Muddy. l.t. unabr. ed. 2001. (Fun-with-the-Law Ser.: No. 5). (Illus.). 32p. (J). (gr. k-7). pap. 5.95 (*1-929905-05-X*) Fun With the Law, Inc.

Hempel, Marc. The 4-Fisted Misadventures of Tug & Buster. 1998. (Illus.). 176p. pap. 17.95 (*1-887279-85-7*) Image Comics.

Henderson, Angela. Jojo Meets Scrappy. 1992. (Illus.). (J). (ps-3). pap. 3.95 (*1-882185-07-2*) Cornerstone Publishing.

Henderson, Gordon. Kittrina's New Friend, Incl. doll. 1995. (Illus.). 32p. (J). pap. 24.00 (*1-890414-07-7*) Bow Tie Enterprises.

Henderson, Holly E. & Tigelaar, Liz. Mysterious Boarder. 2001. (Dawson's Creek Suspense Ser.: No. 3). (Illus.). 224p. (YA). (gr. 8 up). pap. 5.99 (*0-7434-1696-1*, Simon Pulse) Simon & Schuster Children's Publishing.

Henderson, Malcolm. Katie & Her Friends. 1998. (Illus.). 32p. (J). (ps-3). 15.95 (*0-9665198-0-9*, 0998001000) Moss Portfolio, The.

Hendry, Diana. Harvey Angell. 1995. (SPA.). (YA). 5.99 (*968-16-4718-1*) Fondo de Cultura Economica MEX. *Dist:* Continental Bk. Co., Inc.

Henkes, Kevin. Chester's Way. 1988. (Illus.). 32p. (J). (ps-3). 15.99 (*0-688-07607-6*); lib. bdg. 16.89 (*0-688-07608-4*) HarperCollins Children's Bk. Group. (Greenwillow Bks.).

—Jessica. (Illus.). (J). (ps-3). 1998. 24p. pap. 5.99 (*0-688-15847-1*, Harper Trophy); 1989. 32p. 15.99 (*0-688-07829-X*, Greenwillow Bks.); 1989. 32p. lib. bdg. 15.89 (*0-688-07830-3*, Greenwillow Bks.) HarperCollins Children's Bk. Group.

—Jessica. 1990. (Illus.). 32p. (J). (ps-3). pap. 5.99 o.s.i (*0-14-054194-2*, Puffin Bks.) Penguin Putnam Bks. for Young Readers.

—Jessica. 1998. 12.10 (*0-606-13536-7*); 1989. (Illus.). (J). 11.19 o.p. (*0-606-04445-0*) Turtleback Bks.

—A Weekend with Wendell. (Illus.). 32p. (J). 1986. (gr. 7 up). lib. bdg. 16.89 (*0-688-06326-8*, Greenwillow Bks.); 1986. (ps-3). 15.99 (*0-688-06325-X*, Greenwillow Bks.); 1995. (ps-3). reprint ed. pap. 5.99 (*0-688-14024-6*, Harper Trophy) HarperCollins Children's Bk. Group.

—A Weekend with Wendell. 1987. 32p. (J). (ps-3). reprint ed. pap. 3.99 o.p. (*0-14-050728-0*, Puffin Bks.) Penguin Putnam Bks. for Young Readers.

—A Weekend with Wendell. 1995. 12.10 (*0-606-08355-3*) Turtleback Bks.

—A Weekend with Wendell. 1989. (J). (ps-4). pap. text 12.95 incl. audio (*0-89719-987-1*, RAC329) Weston Woods Studios, Inc.

—Words of Stone. 1992. 160p. (J). (gr. 3 up). 15.95 (*0-688-11356-7*, Greenwillow Bks.) HarperCollins Children's Bk. Group.

—Words of Stone. 1993. (Illus.). 160p. (J). (gr. 3-7). reprint ed. pap. 5.99 (*0-14-036601-6*, Puffin Bks.) Penguin Putnam Bks. for Young Readers.

—Words of Stone. 1993. (J). 11.04 (*0-606-06106-1*) Turtleback Bks.

Henson, Heather. Making the Run. 2002. 240p. (J). (gr. k-4). lib. bdg. 15.89 (*0-06-029797-2*); (gr. 10 up). 15.95 (*0-06-029796-4*) HarperCollins Children's Bk. Group. (HarperTempest).

Heo, Yumi. Father's Rubber Shoes. 1996. (Illus.). 32p. (J). (ps-3). pap. 15.95 (*0-531-06873-0*); lib. bdg. 16.99 (*0-531-08723-9*) Scholastic, Inc. (Orchard Bks.).

Herlihy, Dirlie. Ludie's Song. 1990. 224p. (J). (gr. 4 up). pap. 4.99 o.p. (*0-14-034245-1*, Puffin Bks.) Penguin Putnam Bks. for Young Readers.

Herman, Charlotte. Millie Cooper & Friends. 1995. (Illus.). 96p. (J). (gr. 3-7). 13.99 o.s.i (*0-670-86043-3*, Viking Children's Bks.) Penguin Putnam Bks. for Young Readers.

Herman, Gail. Keep Away from Bunk 13: And Other Spooky Campfire Stories. 1996. (Illus.). 64p. (J). (gr. 2-5). 6.95 o.p. (*0-694-00802-8*, Harper Festival) HarperCollins Children's Bk. Group.

—Meet Spike. 2001. (First Friends Ser.). (Illus.). 32p. (J). mass mkt. 3.99 o.s.i (*0-448-42540-8*, Grosset & Dunlap) Penguin Putnam Bks. for Young Readers.

Herman, R. A. Pal & Sal. 1998. (All Aboard Reading Ser.). (Illus.). 32p. (YA). (ps-3). 3.99 (*0-448-41716-2*, Grosset & Dunlap) Penguin Putnam Bks. for Young Readers.

Hermes, Patricia. Friends Are Like That. (J). 1988. 160p. (gr. 7-9). pap. 2.50 o.p. (*0-590-40757-0*); 1985. 128p. (gr. 5-8). reprint ed. pap. 2.50 o.p. (*0-590-33558-8*, Scholastic Paperbacks) Scholastic, Inc.

—I Hate Being Gifted. 1990. 144p. (YA). 14.95 o.p. (*0-399-21687-1*, G. P. Putnam's Sons) Penguin Putnam Bks. for Young Readers.

—I Hate Being Gifted. MacDonald, Pat, ed. 1992. 128p. (J). reprint ed. pap. 3.50 (*0-671-74786-X*, Aladdin) Simon & Schuster Children's Publishing.

—I Hate Being Gifted. 1990. (J). 8.60 o.p. (*0-606-02079-9*) Turtleback Bks.

—In God's Novel. 2000. (Illus.). (J). 15.95 (*0-7614-5074-2*) Cavendish, Marshall Corp.

—A Solitary Secret. 1985. 135p. (J). (gr. 6 up). 11.95 o.p. (*0-15-277190-5*) Harcourt Children's Bks.

—What If They Knew? 1980. (J). (gr. 4-6). 10.95 o.p. (*0-15-295317-5*) Harcourt Children's Bks.

—What If They Knew? 1981. 128p. (J). (gr. k-6). pap. 2.95 o.s.i (*0-440-49515-6*, Yearling) Random Hse. Children's Bks.

—Zeus & Roxanne. 1997. 160p. (J). (gr. 3-7). pap. 3.99 (*0-671-00370-4*, Aladdin) Simon & Schuster Children's Publishing.

Hernandez, Irene B. Heartbeat - Drumbeat. 1992. 134p. (YA). (ps up). pap. text 9.50 (*1-55885-052-X*) Arte Publico Pr.

Hernandez, Mary L. How the Tornado Got It's Wind. 2001. (Illus.). 32p. (J). (ps-3). pap. 7.50 (*1-884083-69-2*) Maval Publishing, Inc.

Herrmann, Marjorie E. Perez y Martina (Perez & Martina) 1978. (Bilingual Ser.). (ENG & SPA.). (J). 13.10 (*0-606-01431-4*) Turtleback Bks.

Herzig, Alison C. The Big Deal. 1994. 80p. (J). (gr. 2-5). pap. 3.99 o.p. (*0-14-034959-6*, Puffin Bks.) Penguin Putnam Bks. for Young Readers.

—Mystery on October Road. 1991. 64p. (J). (gr. 4-7). 11.95 o.p. (*0-670-83635-4*, Viking Children's Bks.) Penguin Putnam Bks. for Young Readers.

—Mystery on October Road. 1993. (J). 11.14 (*0-606-05936-9*) Turtleback Bks.

Herzig, Alison C. & Mali, Jane L. Mystery on October Road. 1993. 64p. (J). (gr. 3-7). pap. 4.99 o.s.i (*0-14-034614-7*, Puffin Bks.) Penguin Putnam Bks. for Young Readers.

Hesse, Karen. Phoenix Rising, ERS. 1994. 192p. (YA). (gr. 6-8). 16.95 (*0-8050-3108-1*, Holt, Henry & Co. Bks. For Young Readers) Holt, Henry & Co.

—Phoenix Rising. 1995. 192p. (J). (gr. 4-7). pap. 5.99 (*0-14-037628-3*, Puffin Bks.) Penguin Putnam Bks. for Young Readers.

—Phoenix Rising. 1995. (YA). (gr. 6 up). 11.04 (*0-606-08012-0*) Turtleback Bks.

—Sable. 1998. (YA). (gr. 4 up). 13.10 (*0-606-13755-6*) Turtleback Bks.

Hesser, Terry Spencer. Kissing Doorknobs. 1998. 176p. (YA). (gr. 6 up). 15.95 (*0-385-32329-8*, Delacorte Pr.) Dell Publishing.

Hest, Amy. Best-Ever Good-Bye Party. 1989. (Illus.). 32p. (J). (gr. k up). 13.95 o.p. (*0-688-07325-5*); lib. bdg. 13.88 o.p. (*0-688-07326-3*) Morrow/Avon. (Morrow, William & Co.).

—Getting Rid of Krista. 1924. (J). lib. bdg. 99.98 o.p. (*0-688-07150-3*, Morrow, William & Co.) Morrow/Avon.

—The Go-Between. 1992. (Illus.). 32p. (J). (gr. k-3). lib. bdg. 14.95 o.s.i (*0-02-743632-2*, Simon & Schuster Children's Publishing) Simon & Schuster Children's Publishing.

—Mr. Joe Baker. 2003. (J). (*0-7636-1233-2*) Candlewick Pr.

—Nannies for Hire. 1994. (Illus.). 48p. (J). (gr. 2 up). 15.00 o.p. (*0-688-12527-1*); lib. bdg. 14.93 o.p. (*0-688-12528-X*) Morrow/Avon. (Morrow, William & Co.).

—Pajama Party. (Illus.). 48p. (J). 1992. lib. bdg. 13.93 o.p. (*0-688-07870-2*); 1992. (gr. 2 up). 14.00 o.p. (*0-688-07866-4*); 1994. (gr. 2 up). reprint ed. pap. 4.95 (*0-688-12949-8*) Morrow/Avon. (Morrow, William & Co.).

—Pajama Party. 1994. 10.15 o.p. (*0-606-06654-3*) Turtleback Bks.

—Party on Ice. 1995. (Illus.). 48p. (J). (gr. 2 up). lib. bdg. 14.93 o.p. (*0-688-14268-0*); (ps-3). 15.00 (*0-688-08394-3*) Morrow/Avon. (Morrow, William & Co.).

—Pete & Lily. 1993. 128p. (J). (gr. 6 up). pap. 4.95 o.p. (*0-688-12490-9*, Morrow, William & Co.) Morrow/Avon.

—Pete & Lily. 1989. (J). (gr. k-6). reprint ed. pap. 2.75 o.s.i (*0-440-40145-3*, Yearling) Random Hse. Children's Bks.

Hetherington, Sands. Night Buddies. 1999. (Illus.). 64p. (J). (gr. k-6). pap. 8.00 (*0-8059-4754-X*) Dorrance Publishing Co., Inc.

Heuck, Sigrid. Pony & Bear Are Friends. 1992. (Illus.). (J). 3.99 o.p. (*0-517-08306-X*) Random Hse. Value Publishing.

Heurtelou, Maude. Istwa Tipoul. 1999. Tr. of Four Friends. (CRP., Illus.). 20p. (J). (gr. 3-5). pap. 19.00 incl. audio (*1-881839-95-8*) Educa Vision.

—Twa Zanmi. 1999. Tr. of Three Friends. (CRP., Illus.). 23p. (J). (gr. 3-5). pap. 19.00 incl. audio (*1-881839-92-3*) Educa Vision.

—Twa Zanmi: Three Friends. Vilsaint, Fequiere, ed. 1993. (Illus.). 30p. (J). (gr. 1-3). pap. (*1-881839-35-4*) Educa Vision.

Hewes, Constance. Meeting New Friends from Meg Mel Planet. 1996. (Illus.). 16p. (Orig.). (J). (ps-2). mass mkt. (*1-889969-00-1*) Zuka Publishing Co.

Hewett, Lorri. Soulfire. 1996. 240p. (YA). (gr. 7 up). 15.99 o.p. (*0-525-45559-0*, Dutton Children's Bks.) Penguin Putnam Bks. for Young Readers.

Heynen, Jim. Being Youngest, ERS. 1997. 160p. (J). (gr. 5-9). 15.95 (*0-8050-5486-3*, Holt, Henry & Co. Bks. For Young Readers) Holt, Henry & Co.

Hickey, Tony. Flip 'n' Flop. 1996. 112p. (J). pap. 6.95 (*0-947962-56-5*) Dufour Editions, Inc.

Hickman, Janet. Susannah. 2001. (J). 11.00 (*0-606-20934-4*) Turtleback Bks.

Hickman, Martha W. My Friend William Moved Away. 1979. (Illus.). (J). (gr. k-3). 8.75 o.p. (*0-687-27540-7*) Abingdon Pr.

Hicyilmaz, Gaye. Against the Storm. 1993. 208p. (J). pap. 3.50 o.s.i (*0-440-40892-X*) Dell Publishing.

Highlights for Children Editorial Staff. The Joinables. 1991. (Illus.). (J). (ps-2). pap. 2.95 o.p. (*0-87534-339-2*) Highlights for Children.

Higman, Anita. The Living Darkness: Texas Caves. 2nd ed. 2003. (J). (*1-57168-783-1*, Eakin Pr.) Eakin Pr.

—Texas Twisters. 1999. (Illus.). viii, 47 p. (J). 13.95 (*1-57168-316-X*) Eakin Pr.

—Texas Twisters. 1999. E-Book 13.95 (*0-585-16342-1*) netLibrary, Inc.

Hill, David. See Ya, Simon. (Illus.). 160p. (J). 1996. pap. 3.99 o.p. (*0-14-037056-0*, Puffin Bks.); 1994. 14.99 o.p. (*0-525-45247-8*, Dutton Children's Bks.) Penguin Putnam Bks. for Young Readers.

Hill, Sandi. Best Friends, Vol. 4409. Kupperstein, Joel, ed. 1998. (Learn to Read Social Studies). (Illus.). 16p. (J). (ps-2). pap. 2.99 (*1-57471-332-9*, 4409) Creative Teaching Pr., Inc.

Hill, William. The Vampire Hunters. 1998. (YA). (gr. 7-11). 286p. pap. 12.95 (*1-890611-02-6*); 288p. 19.95 (*1-890611-05-0*) Otter Creek Pr., Inc.

Hillert, Margaret. Four Good Friends. 2001. (Margaret Hillerts Fabulous Firsts Ser.). lib. bdg. (*1-59054-140-5*) Fitzgerald Bks.

—Four Good Friends. 1981. (Illus.). (J). (ps-k). pap. 5.10 (*0-8136-5561-7*, TK2299); lib. bdg. 7.95 (*0-8136-5061-5*, TK2298) Modern Curriculum Pr.

—Four Good Friends. 1981. 12.20 (*0-606-14020-4*) Turtleback Bks.

—A Friend for Dear Dragon. 1985. (Illus.). (J). (ps-k). pap. 5.10 (*0-8136-5636-2*, TK2973); lib. bdg. 7.95 (*0-8136-5136-0*, TK2972) Modern Curriculum Pr.

—A Friend for Dear Dragon. 1985. 12.20 (*0-606-14021-2*) Turtleback Bks.

—Fun Days. 2002. (Illus.). (J). 15.00 (*0-7587-9470-3*) Book Wholesalers, Inc.

—Fun Days. 1982. (Illus.). (J). (ps-k). pap. 5.10 (*0-8136-5593-5*, TK2163); lib. bdg. 7.95 (*0-8136-5093-3*, TK2162) Modern Curriculum Pr.

—Fun Days. 1982. 12.20 (*0-606-14022-0*) Turtleback Bks.

Hilton, Nette. Andrew Jessup. 1993. (Illus.). 32p. (J). (ps-2). 13.95 (*0-395-66900-6*) Houghton Mifflin Co.

Hinds, P. Mignon & Golden Books Staff. My Best Friend. 1999. 24p. (J). 3.99 o.s.i (*0-307-16167-6*, Golden Bks.) Random Hse. Children's Bks.

Hinds, Patricia Mignon. My Best Friend. 1998. (Illus.). 36p. (J). pap. 5.49 o.s.i (*0-307-11441-4*, Golden Bks.) Random Hse. Children's Bks.

Hine, Ruth H. It Happened at the Pond. 1997. (Illus.). 16p. (J). (gr. k-3). pap. 6.00 o.p. (*0-8059-4108-8*) Dorrance Publishing Co., Inc.

Hines, Anna Grossnickle. Cassie Bowen Takes Witch Lessons. 1985. (Illus.). (J). (gr. 3-7). 11.95 o.p. (*0-525-44214-6*, Dutton Children's Bks.) Penguin Putnam Bks. for Young Readers.

—The Greatest Picnic in the World. Giblin, James C., ed. 1991. (Illus.). 32p. (J). 13.95 o.p. (*0-395-55266-4*, Clarion Bks.) Houghton Mifflin Co. Trade & Reference Div.

—Pieces: A Year in Poems & Quilts. 2003. (Illus.). 32p. (J). pap. 6.99 (*0-06-055960-8*) HarperCollins Children's Bk. Group.

—The Secret Keeper. 1990. (Illus.). 24p. (J). (ps up). 12.95 o.p. (*0-688-08945-3*); lib. bdg. 12.88 o.p. (*0-688-08946-1*) HarperCollins Children's Bk. Group. (Greenwillow Bks.).

Hines, Vicki. Paul & His Friends. 1997. (Great Big Bks.). 16p. (J). (gr. k-1). pap. text 8.00 o.p. (*0-687-06667-0*) Abingdon Pr.

Hinman, Bonnie. Earthquake in Cincinnati: Disaster Changes Life Forever, 1999. (American Adventure Ser.: No. 14). 144p. (J). (gr. 3-7). lib. bdg. 15.95 (*0-7910-5589-2*) Chelsea Hse. Pubs.

Hinojosa, Francisco. Amadis de Anis Amadis de Codorniz (Anise Amadis, Amadis of Quail) 1993. (SPA., Illus.). 48p. (J). (gr. 3-4). 5.99 (*968-16-4236-8*) Fondo de Cultura Economica MEX. *Dist:* Continental Bk. Co., Inc.

—Anibal y Melquiades (Anibal & Melquiades) 1991. (SPA.). 48p. (J). (gr. 3-4). pap. 5.99 (*968-16-3677-5*) Fondo de Cultura Economica MEX. *Dist:* Continental Bk. Co., Inc.

Hinton, S. E. The Outsiders. 1997. (J). 12.04 (*0-606-12150-1*) Turtleback Bks.

Hirsch, Karen. Becky. 1981. (Contemporary Concerns Ser.). (Illus.). 40p. (J). (gr. 1-4). lib. bdg. 13.50 o.p. (*0-87614-144-0*, Carolrhoda Bks.) Lerner Publishing Group.

—Ellen Anders on Her Own. 1994. 112p. (J). (gr. 3-7). 15.00 o.s.i (*0-02-743975-5*, Simon & Schuster Children's Publishing) Simon & Schuster Children's Publishing.

Hirsch, Odo. Hazel Green. 2003. (Illus.). 188p. (Orig.). (J). (gr. 2-6). 15.95 (*1-58234-820-0*, Bloomsbury Children) Bloomsbury Publishing.

Hiser, Constance. The Missing Doll. 1993. (Illus.). 72p. (J). (gr. 4-7). 13.95 o.p. (*0-8234-1046-3*) Holiday Hse., Inc.

Hissey, Jane. Best Friends: More Old Bear Tales. 1989. (Illus.). 80p. (J). (ps-3). 16.95 o.p. (*0-399-21674-X*, Philomel) Penguin Putnam Bks. for Young Readers.

—Old Bear Board Book. 1998. (Illus.). 28p. (J). (ps-1). 6.99 o.s.i (*0-399-23205-2*, Philomel) Penguin Putnam Bks. for Young Readers.

Hixson, Nancy E. Distorted Vision. 1999. (J). pap. 15.95 (*0-936389-62-1*) Tudor Pubs., Inc.

Hoban, Lillian. Arthur's Great Big Valentine. 1989. (I Can Read Bks.). (Illus.). 64p. (J). (gr. k-3). lib. bdg. 15.89 (*0-06-022407-X*) HarperCollins Children's Bk. Group.

—Arthur's Pen Pal. 2002. (Arthur the Chimpanzee Ser.). (Illus.). (J). 12.34 (*0-7587-5989-4*) Book Wholesalers, Inc.

—Arthur's Pen Pal. 1982. (gr. 1-3). pap. 11.05 (*0-8085-3054-2*) Econo-Clad Bks.

—Arthur's Pen Pal. (I Can Read Bks.). (Illus.). 64p. (J). (gr. k-3). 1982. pap. 3.99 (*0-06-444032-X*, Harper Trophy); 1976. lib. bdg. 15.89 (*0-06-022372-3*) HarperCollins Children's Bk. Group.

—Arthur's Pen Pal. 1990. (I Can Read Bks.). (Illus.). (J). 32p. (gr. 1-3). pap. 6.95 incl. audio (*0-00-004236-6*, Caedmon); 64p. (gr. k-3). pap. 8.99 incl. audio (*1-55994-238-X*, HarperAudio) HarperTrade.

—Arthur's Pen Pal. 1976. (I Can Read Bks.). (J). (gr. 1-3). 10.10 (*0-606-00380-0*) Turtleback Bks.

Hoban, Russell. A Bargain for Frances. (I Can Read Bks.). (Illus.). 64p. (J). (ps-3). 1999. 12.95 (*0-694-01295-5*, Harper Festival); 1970. 15.95 (*0-06-022329-4*); 1970. lib. bdg. 15.89 (*0-06-022330-8*); 1992. pap. 3.99 (*0-06-444001-X*, Harper Trophy) HarperCollins Children's Bk. Group.

—A Bargain for Frances. abr. ed. 1993. (I Can Read Bks.). (Illus.). 64p. (J). (gr. k-3). pap. 8.99 incl. audio (*1-55994-224-X*, TBC 224X, HarperAudio) HarperTrade.

—A Bargain for Frances. 9999. pap. 7.50 o.s.i (*0-590-20026-7*); (J). (gr. 1-3). pap. 3.95 o.s.i (*0-590-04357-9*) Scholastic, Inc.

—Best Friends for Frances. 1976. (Trophy Picture Book Ser.). (Illus.). 32p. (J). (ps-3). reprint ed. pap. 5.99 (*0-06-443008-1*, Harper Trophy) HarperCollins Children's Bk. Group.

—The Rain Door. 1987. (Illus.). 32p. (J). (ps-3). lib. bdg. 11.89 (*0-690-04577-8*); 11.95 o.p. (*0-690-04575-1*) HarperCollins Children's Bk. Group.

Hobbie, Holly. I'll Be Home for Christmas. 2001. (Toot & Puddle Ser.). (Illus.). 32p. (J). (ps-3). 15.95 (*0-316-36623-4*) Little Brown Children's Bks.

—Toot & Puddle. 1997. (Illus.). 32p. (J). (ps-3). 15.95 (*0-316-36552-1*) Little Brown & Co.

—Toot & Puddle. 1999. (J). pap. 2.54 (*0-316-36625-0*) Little Brown Children's Bks.

—Toot & Puddle. 1997. E-Book (*1-58824-277-3*); E-Book (*1-59019-274-5*); (J). E-Book 9.99 (*1-59019-275-3*) ipicturebooks, LLC.

—Toot & Puddle: Charming Opal. 2003. (Illus.). 32p. (J). (gr. k-3). 15.95 (*0-316-36633-1*) Little Brown & Co.

—Toot & Puddle: The New Friend. 2004. (J). (*0-316-36636-6*) Little Brown & Co.

—Toot & Puddle Bk. 3: You Are My Sunshine. 1999. (Illus.). 32p. (J). (ps-3). 14.95 (*0-316-36562-9*) Little Brown & Co.

—Travels with Toot & Puddle, 3 bks. 2003. (Illus.). 32p. (J). (ps-k). 11.99 (*0-316-14564-5*) Little Brown Children's Bks.

Hobbs, Valerie. Get It While It's Hot. or Not: A Novel. 1996. 192p. (YA). (gr. 7 up). pap. 16.95 (*0-531-09540-1*); lib. bdg. 17.99 (*0-531-08890-1*) Scholastic, Inc. (Orchard Bks.).

Relationships

—Stefan's Story, RS. 2003. 176p. (J). 16.00 (*0-374-37240-3*, Farrar, Straus & Giroux (BYR)) Farrar, Straus & Giroux.

Hoberman, Mary Ann. And to Think That We Thought That We'd Never Be Friends. 1999. (Illus.). 40p. (J). (gr. k-3). lib. bdg. 17.99 o.p. (*0-517-80070-5*) Crown Publishing Group.

—And to Think That We Thought That We'd Never Be Friends. 2003. (Illus.). 32p. pap. 6.99 (*0-440-41776-7*, Dragonfly Bks.) Random Hse. Children's Bks.

—One of Each. 1997. (Illus.). 32p. (J). (ps-3). 15.95 o.s.i (*0-316-36731-1*) Little Brown & Co.

—One of Each. 2000. (Illus.). 32p. (J). (ps-3). pap. 5.95 (*0-316-36644-7*) Little Brown Children's Bks.

Hockett, Betty M. Down a Winding Road: The Life-Story of Roscoe & Tina Knight. 1985. (Illus.). 80p. (J). (gr. 3-8). pap. 5.00 (*0-943701-11-2*) Barclay Pr., Inc.

—Eight of a Kind: Stories of Eight Friends (Quakers) Who Willingly Obeyed God, No Matter What the Consequences. 1988. 140p. (J). pap. 7.50 (*0-913342-64-5*) Barclay Pr., Inc.

—Eight of a Kind & More Than Empty Dreams, Set. 1988. (Illus.). (Orig.). (J). (gr. 3-8). pap. 13.95 (*0-913342-66-1*) Barclay Pr., Inc.

—From Here to There & Back Again: The Life Story of Charles Edward DeVol. 1984. (Illus.). 80p. (J). (gr. 3-8). pap. 5.00 (*0-943701-09-0*) Barclay Pr., Inc.

—Happiness under the Indian Trees: The Life-Story of Catherine Cattell. 1986. (Illus.). 80p. (J). (gr. 3-8). pap. 5.00 (*0-943701-12-0*) Barclay Pr., Inc.

—More Than Empty Dreams: Stories of Friends (Quakers) Who Did More Then Just Dream of Doing Good. 1988. (Illus.). 140p. (J). (gr. 3-8). pap. 7.50 (*0-913342-65-3*) Barclay Pr., Inc.

—What Will Tomorrow Bring? 1985. (Illus.). 80p. (J). (gr. 3-8). pap. 5.00 o.p. (*0-943701-10-4*) Barclay Pr., Inc.

Hodgman, Ann. There's a Bat Wing in My Lunchbox. 1988. (Illus.). 96p. (J). pap. 2.95 (*0-380-75426-6*, Avon Bks.) Morrow/Avon.

Hodgson, Mona Gansberg. I Wonder Who Hung the Moon in the Sky. 1999. (I Wonder Ser.). (Illus.). 32p. (J). (ps-2). pap. 6.99 (*0-570-05067-7*) Concordia Publishing Hse.

—Smelly Tales. 1998. (Desert Critter Friends Ser.: Vol. 4). (Illus.). 48p. (J). (ps-2). 4.99 (*0-570-05071-5*, 56-1895) Concordia Publishing Hse.

—Thorny Treasures. 1998. (Desert Critter Friends Ser.: Vol. 2). (Illus.). 48p. (J). (ps-2). pap. 4.99 (*0-570-05029-4*, 56-1853) Concordia Publishing Hse.

Hoehne, Marcia. The Fairy Tale Friend. 1994. (Adventures of Jenna V. Ser.). 160p. (J). (gr. 4-7). pap. 4.99 o.p. (*0-89107-813-4*) Crossway Bks.

—Paper Route Treasure. (J). (gr. 4-7). pap. 4.99 o.p. (*0-7459-2801-3*) Lion Publishing.

Hoestlandt, Jo. Star of Fear, Star of Hope. Polizzotti, Mark, tr. from FRE. Tr. of Grande Peur sous les Etoiles. (Illus.). 32p. (J). (gr. 2-5). 1995. lib. bdg. 16.85 (*0-8027-8374-0*); 2000. reprint ed. 16.95 (*0-8027-8373-2*); 2000. reprint ed. pap. 8.95 (*0-8027-7588-8*) Walker & Co.

Hoff, Syd. Irving & Me. 1972. (gr. 1-3). 1.25 o.p. (*0-440-44116-1*) Dell Publishing.

—Who Will Be My Friends? 2001. (First Readers Ser.: Vol. 1). (J). lib. bdg. (*1-59054-092-1*) Fitzgerald Bks.

—Who Will Be My Friends? 1960. (I Can Read Bks.). (Illus.). 32p. (J). (ps-2). lib. bdg. 16.89 (*0-06-022556-4*) HarperCollins Children's Bk. Group.

—Who Will Be My Friends? 1960. (I Can Read Bks.). (Illus.). (J). (ps-1). 17.02 (*0-06-022555-6*, 452049) HarperCollins Pubs.

—Who Will Be My Friends? 1985. (I Can Read Bks.). (J). (ps-1). 10.10 (*0-606-12574-4*) Turtleback Bks.

Hoffer, Alice. Gretchen's World. 1981. (Illus.). 48p. (J). (gr. k-3). lib. bdg. 11.85 o.p. (*0-448-13491-8*); 5.95 o.p. (*0-448-16560-0*) Penguin Putnam Bks. for Young Readers. (Grosset & Dunlap).

Hoffius, Stephen. Winners & Losers. (YA). 1996. 176p. (gr. 7 up). mass mkt. 3.99 (*0-689-80165-3*, Simon Pulse); 1993. 123p. (gr. 5-9). pap. 16.00 (*0-671-79194-X*, Simon & Schuster Children's Publishing) Simon & Schuster Children's Publishing.

—Winners & Losers. 1996. (J). 10.04 (*0-606-10075-X*) Turtleback Bks.

Hoffman, Alice. Aquamarine & Indigo. 2003. 128p. (J). (gr. 5 up). pap. 5.99 (*0-439-47414-0*, Scholastic Paperbacks) Scholastic, Inc.

—Indigo. (J). 2003. 96p. mass mkt. 4.99 (*0-439-25636-4*, Scholastic Paperbacks); 2002. (Illus.). 112p. (gr. 5 up). pap. 16.95 (*0-439-25635-6*, Scholastic Pr.) Scholastic, Inc.

Hoffman, Mary. Encore, Grace! 2003. (Illus.). 112p. (J). 14.99 (*0-8037-2951-0*) Penguin Putnam Bks. for Young Readers.

Hoffman, Phyllis. Meatballs. 1991. (Charlotte Zolotow Bk.). (Illus.). 32p. (J). (ps-2). lib. bdg. 14.89 (*0-06-022564-5*); 14.95 (*0-06-022563-7*) HarperCollins Children's Bk. Group.

Hofmann, Ginnie. The Bear Next Door: Story & Pictures. 1994. (Pictureback Ser.). (Illus.). (J). (ps-3). o.p. (*0-679-93957-1*); 32p. pap. 3.25 o.s.i (*0-679-83957-7*) Random Hse. Children's Bks. (Random Hse. Bks. for Young Readers).

—One Teddy Bear Is Enough! 1991. (Pictureback Ser.). (Illus.). 32p. (Orig.). (J). (ps-3). pap. 3.25 o.s.i (*0-394-89582-7*, Random Hse. Bks. for Young Readers) Random Hse. Children's Bks.

Hofmeister, Alan, et al. Ann & Nan. (Reading for All Learners Ser.). (Illus.). (J). pap. (*1-56861-085-8*) Swift Learning Resources.

—Mit & the Weed. (Reading for All Learners Ser.). (Illus.). (J). pap. (*1-56861-113-7*) Swift Learning Resources.

—Nell & Ed. (Reading for All Learners Ser.). (Illus.). (J). pap. (*1-56861-097-1*) Swift Learning Resources.

—The Pond. (Reading for All Learners Ser.). (Illus.). (J). pap. (*1-56861-131-5*) Swift Learning Resources.

Hogan, Paula Z. I Hate Boys-I Hate Girls. 1980. (Life & Living from a Child's Point of View Ser.). (Illus.). 32p. (J). (gr. k-6). lib. bdg. 21.40 o.p. (*0-8172-1358-9*) Raintree Pubs.

Hogg, Gary. Friendship in the Forest. 1994. (Happy Hawk Golden Thought Ser.). (Illus.). 24p. (J). pap. 4.95 (*0-930771-14-1*) Buckaroo Bks.

Hoh, Diane. Funhouse. 1990. 176p. (J). (gr. 7-9). mass mkt. 3.25 (*0-590-43050-5*) Scholastic, Inc.

—The Invitation. 1991. 176p. (YA). (gr. 7-9). mass mkt. 3.25 (*0-590-44904-4*, Scholastic Paperbacks) Scholastic, Inc.

Hol, Coby. Punch & His Friends. (J). pap. 14.95 (*0-86315-206-6*, 1823) Floris Bks. GBR. *Dist:* Gryphon Hse., Inc., SteinerBooks, Inc.

Holabird, Katharine. Angelina & Alice. 1988. (Angelina Ballerina Ser.). (Illus.). 24p. (J). (ps-3). 16.00 o.p. (*0-517-56074-7*, Clarkson Potter) Crown Publishing Group.

—Angelina & Alice. (Angelina Ballerina Ser.). (Illus.). 24p. (J). (ps-3). 2002. 12.95 (*1-58485-651-3*); 2001. 9.95 (*1-58485-130-9*) Pleasant Co. Pubns.

—Angelina & Alice: Includes Alice Doll. 2001. (Angelina Ballerina Ser.). (Illus.). (J). (ps-3). 27.95 (*1-58485-332-8*) Pleasant Co. Pubns.

—Angelina Loves: A Story of Love & Friendship. 2002. (Illus.). 24p. (J). pap. 6.95 (*1-58485-566-5*, American Girl) Pleasant Co. Pubns.

Hole, Dorothy. Real Friends. 144p. (Orig.). (J). (gr. 5-8). 1994. pap. 2.99 o.p. (*0-87406-678-6*); 1988. pap. 1.95 o.p. (*0-87406-341-8*) Darby Creek Publishing.

Holeman, Linda. Mercy's Birds. 1998. 208p. (YA). (gr. 6-9). pap. 6.95 (*0-88776-463-0*) Tundra Bks. of Northern New York.

—Mercy's Birds. 1998. 13.00 (*0-606-16647-5*) Turtleback Bks.

Holl, Kristi. Two of a Kind. 1990. (Julie McGregor Bks.). (Illus.). 128p. (Orig.). (J). (gr. 3-5). pap. 4.99 o.p. (*0-87403-748-4*, 24-03968) Standard Publishing.

Holl, Kristi D. Cast a Single Shadow. 1989. 144p. (J). (gr. k-6). pap. 2.95 o.s.i (*0-440-40222-0*, Yearling) Random Hse. Children's Bks.

—First Things First. 1989. (J). (gr. k-6). reprint ed. pap. 2.95 o.s.i (*0-440-40147-X*, Yearling) Random Hse. Children's Bks.

Holland, Isabelle. Henry & Grudge. 1986. (Illus.). 64p. (J). (gr. 3-6). 10.95 (*0-8027-6611-0*); lib. bdg. 10.85 (*0-8027-6612-9*) Walker & Co.

—Now Is Not Too Late. 1985. 160p. (J). (gr. 4 up). pap. 2.75 o.s.i (*0-553-15548-2*) Bantam Bks.

Holland, Margaret & Demers, Jan. Ticktock Around the Clock. 1987. (Predictable Reading Bks). (Illus.). 24p. (J). (gr. k-2). 1.95 o.p. (*0-87406-191-1*) Darby Creek Publishing.

Holland, Steve. He Said, He Said: Kenan & Kel. 2000. (Kenan & Kel Ser.: Vol. 9). 96p. (gr. 4-7). 4.50 (*0-7434-0603-6*, Simon Pulse) Simon & Schuster Children's Publishing.

Hollander, Cass. A New Friend for Me. 1992. (Storytime Bks.). (Illus.). 24p. (J). (ps-2). pap. 1.29 o.p. (*1-56293-108-3*, McClanahan Bk.) Learning Horizons, Inc.

Holly, Cate. BFF: Best Friends Forever. 2001. (Little Bks.). (Illus.). 80p. 4.95 (*0-7407-1447-3*) Andrews McMeel Publishing.

Holly, Kate. Disney's Jungle Cubs: Louie's Surprise. 1997. (Look-Look Bks.). (Illus.). 24p. (J). (ps). pap. text 2.79 o.p. (*0-307-10568-7*, 10568, Golden Bks.) Random Hse. Children's Bks.

—Disney's Jungle Cubs: The Jungle Race. 1997. (Look-Look Bks.). (Illus.). 24p. (J). (ps). pap. text 2.79 o.p. (*0-307-10565-2*, Golden Bks.) Random Hse. Children's Bks.

Holm, Todd. The Apple & the Worm. 1995. (Illus.). 22p. (J). text 12.50 (*0-930329-91-0*) Kabel Pubs.

Holman, Felice. Secret City, U. S. A. 1993. 208p. (J). (gr. 4-7). reprint ed. pap. 3.95 o.s.i (*0-689-71755-5*, Aladdin) Simon & Schuster Children's Publishing.

Holmes, Barbara W. Charlotte the Starlet. 1989. (Trophy Bk.). (Illus.). 128p. (J). (gr. 3-6). pap. 2.95 o.p. (*0-06-440292-4*, Harper Trophy) HarperCollins Children's Bk. Group.

Holmes, Barbara Ware. Letters to Julia. 1999. (Illus.). 320p. (YA). (gr. 7 up). pap. 5.95 (*0-06-447215-9*, Harper Trophy) HarperCollins Children's Bk. Group.

Holmes, Efner Tudor. Carrie's Gift. 1978. (Illus.). (J). (gr. 1-4). 7.95 o.p. (*0-529-05428-0*); 7.99 o.p. (*0-529-05429-9*) Putnam Publishing Group, The.

Holohan, Maureen. Ice Cold: By Molly. (Broadway Ballplayers Ser.: No. 6). (J). (gr. 3-7). E-Book (*0-7434-2727-0*); 2002. 176p. (YA). pap. 4.50 (*0-7434-0747-4*) Simon & Schuster Children's Publishing. (Aladdin).

—Left Out. 2001. (Broadway Ballplayers Ser.: No. 2). (J). (gr. 4-8). reprint ed. E-Book 4.50 (*0-7434-2724-6*); (Illus.). 176p. pap. 4.50 (*0-7434-0744-X*) Simon & Schuster Children's Publishing. (Aladdin).

—Sideline Blues. 2001. (Broadway Ballplayers Ser.: No. 5). (J). (gr. 4-8). reprint ed. E-Book 4.50 (*0-7434-2725-4*, Aladdin) Simon & Schuster Children's Publishing.

Holt, Kimberly Willis. Mister & Me. 1998. (Illus.). 80p. (J). (gr. 2-6). 13.99 (*0-399-23215-X*) Penguin Group (USA) Inc.

—Mister & Me. 2000. (Chapter Ser.). (Illus.). 80p. (J). (gr. 2-5). pap. 4.99 (*0-698-11869-3*, Puffin Bks.) Penguin Putnam Bks. for Young Readers.

—Mister & Me. 2000. (J). (gr. 2 up). pap., stu. ed. 39.99 incl. audio (*0-7887-4341-4*, 41135) Recorded Bks., LLC.

—Mister & Me. 1998. 11.14 (*0-606-20366-4*) Turtleback Bks.

—My Louisiana Sky, ERS. 1998. 176p. (J). (gr. 4-7). 16.95 (*0-8050-5251-8*, Holt, Henry & Co. Bks. For Young Readers) Holt, Henry & Co.

—My Louisiana Sky. 208p. (YA). (gr. 5 up). 4.99 (*0-8072-8291-X*, Listening Library) Random Hse. Audio Publishing Group.

—When Zachary Beaver Came to Town, ERS. 1999. 227p. (YA). (gr. 5-9). 16.95 (*0-8050-6116-9*, Holt, Henry & Co. Bks. For Young Readers) Holt, Henry & Co.

—When Zachary Beaver Came to Town. 2000. tchr. ed. 9.95 (*1-58130-674-1*); (YA). stu. ed. 11.95 (*1-58130-675-X*) Novel Units, Inc.

—When Zachary Beaver Came to Town. unabr. ed. 2000. 227p. pap. 35.00 incl. audio (*0-8072-8394-0*); (YA). (gr. 5-9). audio 22.00 (*0-8072-8247-2*, LL0202); (YA). (gr. 5 up). audio 30.00 (*0-8072-8393-2*, YA200CX) Random Hse. Audio Publishing Group. (Listening Library).

—When Zachary Beaver Came to Town. (YA). (gr. 5 up). 2003. (Illus.). 256p. pap. 5.99 (*0-440-23841-2*, Laurel Leaf); 2001. 240p. pap. 5.50 (*0-440-22904-9*, Yearling) Random Hse. Children's Bks.

—When Zachary Beaver Came to Town. l.t. ed. 2000. (Young Adult Ser.). 224p. (YA). 22.95 (*0-7862-2515-7*) Thorndike Pr.

—When Zachary Beaver Came to Town. 2000. 11.55 (*0-606-20113-0*); (J). 6.20 (*0-606-20114-9*) Turtleback Bks.

Holub, Joan. Abby Cadabra, Super Speller. 2000. (All Aboard Reading Ser.). (Illus.). 48p. (J). (gr. 1-3). 13.89 o.p. (*0-448-42281-6*); mass mkt. 3.99 (*0-448-42168-2*) Penguin Putnam Bks. for Young Readers. (Grosset & Dunlap).

—Abby Cadabra, Super Speller. 2000. (All Aboard Reading Ser.). 10.14 (*0-606-18849-5*) Turtleback Bks.

—Pen Pals. 1997. (All Aboard Reading Ser.: Level 2). (Illus.). (J). (gr. 1-3). 32p. 13.89 o.s.i (*0-448-41613-1*); 48p. 3.95 o.p. (*0-448-41612-3*) Penguin Putnam Bks. for Young Readers. (Grosset & Dunlap).

—Pen Pals. 1997. (All Aboard Reading Ser.). (J). 10.10 (*0-606-13016-0*) Turtleback Bks.

Holubitsky, Katherine. Last Summer in Agatha. 192p. (YA). 2002. pap. 7.95 (*1-55143-190-4*); 2001. (gr. 7 up). 16.95 (*1-55143-188-2*) Orca Bk. Pubs.

Honeycutt, Natalie. The All New Jonah Twist. 1987. (J). (gr. 3-5). pap. 3.50 (*0-380-70317-3*, Avon Bks.) Morrow/Avon.

—The All New Jonah Twist. 1986. 128p. (J). (gr. 3-5). text 13.95 o.p. (*0-02-744840-1*, Simon & Schuster Children's Publishing) Simon & Schuster Children's Publishing.

—Ask Me Something Easy. 1993. 160p. (YA). pap. 3.50 (*0-380-71723-9*, Avon Bks.) Morrow/Avon.

—Invisible Lissa. 1986. 128p. (J). (gr. 3-7). pap. 2.75 (*0-380-70120-0*, Avon Bks.) Morrow/Avon.

Hood, C. W. & Swanson, Maggie. Look at Me! 1999. (Golden Little Super Shape Bks.). (Illus.). 24p. (J). (ps). pap. 1.79 o.s.i (*0-307-10557-1*, Golden Bks.) Random Hse. Children's Bks.

Hood, Susan. Let's Jump In!, Level 1. 1999. (All-Star Readers Ser.). (Illus.). 32p. (J). (ps-3). mass mkt. 3.99 (*1-57584-320-X*, Reader's Digest Children's Bks.) Reader's Digest Children's Publishing, Inc.

—The New Kid. 1998. (Real Kids Readers Ser.). (Illus.). 32p. (ps-1). (J). 18.90 (*0-7613-2014-8*); pap. 4.99 (*0-7613-2039-3*) Millbrook Pr., Inc.

—The New Kid. Hood, Susan, ed. 1998. (Real Kids Readers Ser.). 10.14 (*0-606-15804-9*) Turtleback Bks.

—The New Kid. 1998. E-Book (*1-58824-484-9*); E-Book (*1-58824-732-5*); E-Book (*1-58824-815-1*) ipicturebooks, LLC.

—Too-Tall Paul, Too-Small Paul. 1998. (Real Kids Readers Ser.). (Illus.). 32p. (J). (gr. k-2). 18.90 (*0-7613-2021-0*); pap. 4.99 (*0-7613-2046-6*) Millbrook Pr., Inc.

—Too-Tall Paul, Too-Small Paul. 1998. (Real Kids Readers Ser.). 10.14 (*0-606-15813-8*) Turtleback Bks.

—Too-Tall Paul, Too-Small Paul. 1998. E-Book (*1-58824-500-4*); E-Book (*1-58824-748-1*); E-Book (*1-58824-831-3*) ipicturebooks, LLC.

—Tyler Is Shy. 2000. (Fisher-Price All-Star Readers Ser.: Level 2). (Illus.). 32p. (J). (gr. k-3). mass mkt. 3.99 (*1-57584-657-8*) Reader's Digest Children's Publishing, Inc.

Hooks, William H. Mr. Bubble Gum. 1989. (J). o.s.i (*0-553-17671-4*, Dell Books for Young Readers) Random Hse. Children's Bks.

—Where's Lulu? 1991. (J). E-Book (*1-58824-205-6*) ipicturebooks, LLC.

Hope. Punctuation Pals. Anders, Tim, ed. 2000. (Life Lessons Ser.). (Illus.). 38p. (J). (gr. k-4). 16.95 (*1-885624-56-5*) Alpine Publishing.

Hope, Christopher. The Dragon Wore Pink. 1985. (Illus.). 32p. (J). (gr. 2). 12.95 o.s.i (*0-689-31175-3*, Atheneum) Simon & Schuster Children's Publishing.

Hopkins, Cathy. Mates, Dates, & Sleepover Secrets. 2003. (Illus.). 208p. (YA). pap. 4.99 (*0-689-85991-0*, Simon Pulse) Simon & Schuster Children's Publishing.

Hopkins, Lee Bennett, ed. Best Friends. 1986. (Charlotte Zolotow Bk.). (Illus.). 48p. (J). (gr. k-4). lib. bdg. 14.89 o.p. (*0-06-022562-9*) HarperCollins Children's Bk. Group.

—Best Friends. 1986. (Illus.). (J). (gr. 1-5). 11.50 o.p. (*0-06-022561-0*, 463294) HarperCollins Pubs.

Hopper, Nancy J. The Queen of Put-Down. 1993. 112p. (J). (gr. 4-6). pap. 3.95 o.p. (*0-689-71670-2*, Aladdin) Simon & Schuster Children's Publishing.

Horn, Douglas C. Moves. 1995. (J). (gr. 3-6). 189p. pap. 9.99 (*0-88092-150-1*); lib. bdg. 15.00 o.p. (*0-88092-151-X*) Royal Fireworks Publishing Co.

Horse, Harry. A Friend for Little Bear. (Illus.). 32p. (J). (ps-3). 1996. 14.99 o.s.i (*1-56402-876-3*); 1997. reprint ed. bds. 5.99 o.p. (*0-7636-0342-2*) Candlewick Pr.

Horvath, Polly. When the Circus Comes to Town. 1969. (Americana Books Ser.). (Illus.). (J). 2.00 o.p. (*0-911410-23-6*) Applied Arts Pubs.

—When the Circus Comes to Town, RS. 1996. 112p. (J). (gr. 3-7). 15.00 o.p. (*0-374-38308-1*, Farrar, Straus & Giroux (BYR)) Farrar, Straus & Giroux.

Horwood, William. Toad Triumphant. 1996. 288p. (gr. 4-7). 19.95 (*0-312-14821-6*) St. Martin's Pr.

—The Willows at Christmas. 2001. (J). 21.95 (*0-312-28386-5*) St. Martin's Pr.

Hossack, Sylvie A. Flying Chickens of Paradise Lane. 1992. 144p. (J). (gr. 3-7). text 13.95 o.s.i (*0-02-744565-8*, Simon & Schuster Children's Publishing) Simon & Schuster Children's Publishing.

Hostetter, Joyce M. Best Friends Forever. 1995. (Illus.). 96p. (J). (gr. 3-5). pap. 5.95 (*0-377-00297-6*) Friendship Pr.

Hot Dog & Friends. 1986. (Illus.). (J). pap. 3.00 o.s.i (*0-440-85089-4*) Dell Publishing.

Hough, Libby. If Somebody Lived Next Door. 1997. (Illus.). 32p. (J). (ps). 10.99 o.s.i (*0-525-45497-7*) Penguin Putnam Bks. for Young Readers.

Houghton Mifflin Company Staff. The Glad Man. 1992. (Literature Experience 1993 Ser.). (J). (gr. 7). pap. 11.04 (*0-395-61851-7*) Houghton Mifflin Co.

—Good Friends. 1993. (Literature Experience 1993 Ser.). (J). pap. 4.48 (*0-395-62577-7*) Houghton Mifflin Co.

—Not Just Any Ring. 1992. (Literature Experience 1993 Ser.). (J). (gr. 2). pap. 9.48 (*0-395-61782-0*) Houghton Mifflin Co.

Howard, Arthur. When I Was Five. 1996. (Illus.). 40p. (J). (ps-3). 15.00 (*0-15-200261-8*) Harcourt Children's Bks.

Howard, Elizabeth Fitzgerald. Lulu's Birthday. 2001. (Illus.). 24p. (J). (ps-3). 15.95 (*0-688-15944-3*); lib. bdg. 15.89 (*0-688-15945-1*) HarperCollins Children's Bk. Group. (Greenwillow Bks.).

—Lulu's Birthday. 1999. (YA). (ps up). 17.00 (*0-689-81073-3*, Simon & Schuster Children's Publishing) Simon & Schuster Children's Publishing.

Howard, Jo Ann. The Little Boy Who Made a Difference. 2001. 41p. per. 8.95 (*0-7414-0575-X*) Infinity Publishing.com.

Howard, Megan. I've Lost My Best Friend, Bk. 1. 1994. (Diary S. O. S. Ser.: No. 1). 144p. (Orig.). (J). (gr. 3-9). pap. 3.99 o.s.i (*0-679-85701-X*, Random Hse. Bks. for Young Readers) Random Hse. Children's Bks.

Howard, Mildred T. On Yonder Mountain. 1989. 120p. (J). (gr. 2-4). pap. 6.49 (*0-89084-462-3*, 037358) Jones, Bob Univ. Pr.

Howard, Reginald. The Big, Big Wall. 2003. (Green Light Readers Level 1 Ser.). (Illus.). 24p. (J). 11.95 (*0-15-204813-8*); pap. 3.95 (*0-15-204853-7*) Harcourt Children's Bks. (Green Light Readers).

—The Big, Big Wall, Level 1. 2001. (Green Light Readers Ser.). (Illus.). 20p. (J). (gr. k-2). 10.95 o.s.i (*0-15-216504-5*); pap. 3.95 o.s.i (*0-15-216522-3*) Harcourt Children's Bks. (Green Light Readers).

Howe, D. H., adapted by. Pickwick Papers: Simplified Edition. 1995. (Illus.). 94p. pap. text 5.95 (*0-19-586308-9*) Oxford Univ. Pr., Inc.

Howe, Fanny. Yeah, But. 1982. 128p. (YA). (gr. 7 up). pap. 1.95 o.p. (*0-380-79186-2*, 79186-2, Avon Bks.) Morrow/Avon.

Howe, James. Horace & Morris but Mostly Dolores. 2002. (Illus.). (J). 25.11 (*0-7587-2749-6*) Book Wholesalers, Inc.

—Horace & Morris but Mostly Dolores. 1999. (Illus.). 32p. (J). (ps-3). 16.00 (*0-689-31874-X*, Atheneum) Simon & Schuster Children's Publishing.

—Houndsley & Catina. 2001. (J). text 16.00 (*0-689-82995-7*, Atheneum) Simon & Schuster Children's Publishing.

—The Misfits. 288p. (J). 2003. mass mkt. 5.99 (*0-689-83956-1*, Aladdin); 2001. (Illus.). (gr. 5-9). 16.00 (*0-689-83955-3*, Atheneum) Simon & Schuster Children's Publishing.

—A Night Without Stars. 1985. 192p. (YA). (gr. 7 up). pap. 2.95 (*0-380-69877-3*, Avon Bks.) Morrow/Avon.

—Pinky & Rex: Ready to Read Level 3. 1991. (Pinky & Rex Ser.). (Illus.). 48p. (J). (gr. 1-4). pap. 3.99 (*0-380-71190-7*, Avon Bks.) Morrow/Avon.

—Pinky & Rex: Ready to Read Level 3. (Pinky & Rex Ser.). (Illus.). 48p. (J). (gr. 1-4). 1998. pap. 3.99 (*0-689-82348-7*, Aladdin); 1990. 15.00 (*0-689-31454-X*, Atheneum) Simon & Schuster Children's Publishing.

—Pinky & Rex: Ready to Read Level 3. 1998. (Pinky & Rex Ser.). (J). (gr. 1-4). 10.14 (*0-606-16134-1*) Turtleback Bks.

—Pinky & Rex & the Bully. 1996. (Pinky & Rex Ser.). (Illus.). 48p. (J). (gr. 1-4). 15.00 (*0-689-80021-5*, Atheneum) Simon & Schuster Children's Publishing.

—Pinky & Rex & the Mean Old Witch. 1992. (Pinky & Rex Ser.). (Illus.). (J). (gr. 1-4). pap. 3.99 (*0-380-71644-5*, Avon Bks.) Morrow/Avon.

—Pinky & Rex & the New Baby. 1999. (Pinky & Rex Ser.). (Illus.). 48p. (J). (gr. 1-4). pap. 3.99 (*0-689-82548-X*, Aladdin) Simon & Schuster Children's Publishing.

—Pinky & Rex & the New Baby. 1999. (Pinky & Rex Ser.). (Illus.). (J). (gr. 1-4). 10.14 (*0-606-15941-X*) Turtleback Bks.

—Pinky & Rex & the New Neighbors. 1997. (Pinky & Rex Ser.). (Illus.). 48p. (J). (gr. 1-4). 15.00 (*0-689-80022-3*, Atheneum) Simon & Schuster Children's Publishing.

—Pinky & Rex & the Perfect Pumpkin. 1998. (Pinky & Rex Ser.). (Illus.). 48p. (J). (gr. 1-4). 15.00 o.s.i (*0-689-81782-7*, Atheneum); pap. 3.99 (*0-689-81777-0*, Aladdin) Simon & Schuster Children's Publishing.

—Pinky & Rex & the School Play. 1998. (Pinky & Rex Ser.). (Illus.). 48p. (J). (gr. 1-4). pap. 3.99 (*0-689-81704-5*, Aladdin);Vol. 2. 15.00 o.s.i (*0-689-31872-3*, Atheneum) Simon & Schuster Children's Publishing.

—Pinky & Rex & the Spelling Bee. 1991. (Pinky & Rex Ser.). (Illus.). 48p. (J). (gr. 1-4). 15.00 (*0-689-31618-6*, Atheneum) Simon & Schuster Children's Publishing.

—Pinky & Rex Get Married. 1991. (Pinky & Rex Ser.). (Illus.). 48p. (J). (gr. 1-4). pap. 3.99 (*0-380-71191-5*, Avon Bks.) Morrow/Avon.

—Pinky & Rex Get Married. (Pinky & Rex Ser.). (Illus.). 48p. (J). (gr. 1-4). 1999. pap. 3.99 (*0-689-82526-9*, 076714003996, Aladdin); 1990. text 12.95 o.s.i (*0-689-31453-1*, Atheneum) Simon & Schuster Children's Publishing.

—Pinky & Rex Get Married. 1999. (Pinky & Rex Ser.). (J). (gr. 1-4). 10.14 (*0-606-16307-7*) Turtleback Bks.

—Pinky & Rex Go to Camp. 1993. (Pinky & Rex Ser.). (Illus.). (J). (gr. 1-4). pap. 3.99 (*0-380-72082-5*, Avon Bks.) Morrow/Avon.

—Pinky & Rex Go to Camp. (Pinky & Rex Ser.). (Illus.). 48p. (gr. 1-4). 1999. pap. 3.99 (*0-689-82588-9*, 076714003996, Aladdin); 1992. (J). 15.00 (*0-689-31718-2*, Atheneum) Simon & Schuster Children's Publishing.

—Pinky & Rex Go to Camp. 1999. (Pinky & Rex Ser.). (J). (gr. 1-4). 10.14 (*0-606-16306-9*) Turtleback Bks.

—The Watcher. 2001. 192p. (YA). (gr. 8-12). mass mkt. 4.99 (*0-689-83533-7*, Simon Pulse) Simon & Schuster Children's Publishing.

Howe, Norma. In With the Out Crowd, 001. 1986. 208p. (YA). (gr. 7 up). 12.95 o.p. (*0-395-40490-8*) Houghton Mifflin Co.

Hubley, Faith & Hubley, John. The Hat. 1974. 48p. (J). (gr. 2-5). 5.95 o.p. (*0-15-233611-7*) Harcourt Children's Bks.

Huelin, Jodi. My Little Pony a Ponys Tale. 2003. (My Little Pony Ser.). (Illus.). 24p. (J). (ps-1). pap. 3.50 (*0-06-054948-3*) HarperCollins Children's Bk. Group.

Hughes, Dean. End of the Race. 1993. 160p. (YA). (gr. 5 up). 13.95 (*0-689-31779-4*, Atheneum) Simon & Schuster Children's Publishing.

—Lucky Breaks Loose. 1990. (Lucky Ladd Ser.: Bk. 2). 136p. (Orig.). (J). (gr. 3-6). pap. 4.95 o.p. (*0-87579-194-8*) Deseret Bk. Co.

—Lucky Fights Back. 1991. (Lucky Ladd Ser.: Bk. 4). 150p. (Orig.). (J). (gr. 3-6). pap. text 4.95 (*0-87579-559-5*, Cinnamon Tree) Deseret Bk. Co.

—Lucky's Crash Landing. 1990. (Lucky Ladd Ser.: Bk. 1). 160p. (Orig.). (J). (gr. 3-6). pap. 4.95 o.p. (*0-87579-193-X*) Deseret Bk. Co.

—Nutty Can't Miss, Vol. 18. 1988. 144p. (J). (gr. 2-5). pap. 2.50 o.s.i (*0-553-15584-9*, Skylark) Random Hse. Children's Bks.

—Nutty Can't Miss. 1987. (Nutty Ser.). 144p. (J). (gr. 3-7). lib. bdg. 13.95 o.s.i (*0-689-31319-5*, Atheneum) Simon & Schuster Children's Publishing.

—Team Player. 1999. (Scrappers Ser.: No. 3). (J). (gr. 3-7). 128p. 14.00 (*0-689-81926-9*, Atheneum); 96p. pap. 3.99 (*0-689-81936-6*, Aladdin) Simon & Schuster Children's Publishing.

—Team Player. 1999. (Scrappers Ser.: No. 3). (J). (gr. 3-7). 10.04 (*0-606-16290-9*) Turtleback Bks.

Hughes, Francine. A Simple Wish: The Junior Novelization. 1997. (Simple Wish Ser.). (Illus.). 64p. (Orig.). (J). (gr. 3-5). 4.95 o.s.i (*0-448-41636-0*, Grosset & Dunlap) Penguin Putnam Bks. for Young Readers.

Hughes, Monica. Jan on the Trail. 2000. (New First Novels Ser.). (Illus.). 64p. (J). pap. 3.99 (*0-88780-502-7*); (gr. 1-4). (*0-88780-503-5*) Formac Publishing Co., Ltd. CAN. *Dist:* Orca Bk. Pubs., Formac Distributing, Ltd.

Hughes, Shirley. The Alfie Collection: Alfie's Feet; an Evening at Alfie'S; Alfie Gives a Hand; Alfie Gets in First, 4 bks., Set. 1993. (Illus.). (J). (ps up). pap. 16.95 o.p. (*0-688-12750-9*, Morrow, William & Co.) Morrow/Avon.

—Alfie Gives a Hand. 1986. (Illus.). 32p. (J). (ps up). pap. 4.95 o.p. (*0-688-06521-X*, Morrow, William & Co.) Morrow/Avon.

—All about Alfie. 1998. (Illus.). 128p. (J). (ps-5). pap. 14.98 (*1-58048-042-X*) Sandvik Publishing.

—Being Together. 1997. (Illus.). 14p. (J). (ps). bds. 3.99 o.p. (*0-7636-0399-6*) Candlewick Pr.

—Chips & Jessie. 1986. (Illus.). 64p. (J). (gr. 2-4). 11.95 o.p. (*0-688-06402-7*); lib. bdg. 11.88 o.p. (*0-688-06631-3*) HarperCollins Children's Bk. Group.

—Dogger. 1993. (J). 10.15 o.p. (*0-606-05239-9*) Turtleback Bks.

—Lucy & Tom's Day. 1986. (Picture Puffin Ser.). (Illus.). 32p. (J). (ps-1). pap. 3.50 o.p. (*0-14-050068-5*, Puffin Bks.) Penguin Putnam Bks. for Young Readers.

—Moving Molly. 1988. (Illus.). 32p. (J). (ps-2). 11.95 o.p. (*0-688-07982-2*); lib. bdg. 11.88 o.p. (*0-688-07984-9*) HarperCollins Children's Bk. Group.

—Wheels. 1991. (Illus.). (J). (ps-3). 13.95 o.p. (*0-688-09880-0*) HarperCollins Children's Bk. Group.

Humphrey, L. Spencer. Noozles: New Friends. 1993. 32p. (J). (ps-3). mass mkt. 2.95 (*0-8125-2320-2*, Tor Bks.) Doherty, Tom Assocs., LLC.

Humphrey, Margo. The River That Gave Gifts: An Afro American Story. 1987. (J). 13.95 o.p. (*0-89239-019-0*); (Illus.). 24p. (gr. 1 up). 14.95 (*0-89239-027-1*); (Illus.). 24p. (gr. 1 up). pap. 6.95 (*0-89239-128-6*) Children's Bk. Pr.

—The River That Gave Gifts: An Afro American Story. 1987. (Fifth World Tales Ser.). 12.15 o.p. (*0-606-09792-9*) Turtleback Bks.

Humphreys, Martha M. Until Whatever. 1991. 176p. (YA). (gr. 9 up). 13.95 o.p. (*0-395-58022-6*, Clarion Bks.) Houghton Mifflin Co. Trade & Reference Div.

—Until Whatever. 1993. (J). pap. 3.25 o.p. (*0-590-46616-X*) Scholastic, Inc.

Hunt, Angela Elwell. A Forever Friend, Vol. 2. 1991. (Cassie Perkins Ser.). (J). (gr. 5-7). pap. 4.99 o.p. (*0-8423-0462-2*) Tyndale Hse. Pubs.

—A Forever Friend. 2000. (Cassie Perkins Ser.: Vol. 2). 164p. (gr. 4-7). pap. 11.95 (*0-595-09001-X*) iUniverse, Inc.

—The Much-Adored Sandy Shore. 2000. (Cassie Perkins Ser.: Vol. 5). 184p. (J). (gr. 4-7). pap. 12.95 (*0-595-09000-1*, Backinprint.com) iUniverse, Inc.

—Star Light, Star Bright. 1993. (Cassie Perkins Ser.: Vol. 7). (YA). pap. 4.99 o.p. (*0-8423-1117-3*) Tyndale Hse. Pubs.

—Star Light, Star Bright. 2000. (Cassie Perkins Ser.: Vol. 7). 180p. (gr. 4-7). pap. 11.95 (*0-595-08996-8*, Backinprint.com) iUniverse, Inc.

Hunt, Irene. No Promises in the Wind. 1983. 224p. (J). (gr. 5 up). 2.25 o.s.i (*0-441-58864-6*) Ace Bks.

—No Promises in the Wind. 1986. 224p. (YA). (gr. 7-12). mass mkt. 4.99 (*0-425-09969-5*) Berkley Publishing Group.

—No Promises in the Wind. 1986. 11.04 (*0-606-02210-4*) Turtleback Bks.

Hunt, Joyce. Four of Us & Victoria Chubb. 1990. (J). (gr. 4-7). pap. 2.75 o.p. (*0-590-42976-0*) Scholastic, Inc.

Hunter, Aileen. The Green Gang. 1994. (Kelpie Ser.). 108p. (J). (gr. 3-5). pap. 6.95 o.p. (*0-86241-364-8*) Trafalgar Square.

Hunter, Dawn & Hunter, Karen. Heads Up! 2001. 128p. (J). (gr. 3-8). mass mkt. 5.50 (*1-55028-718-4*) Lorimer, James & Co. CAN. *Dist:* Orca Bk. Pubs.

Hunter, Mollie. The Walking Stones. 1996. (Jackson Friends Bk.). 176p. (J). (gr. 3 up). pap. 5.00 (*0-15-200995-7*, Magic Carpet Bks.) Harcourt Children's Bks.

Hunter, Tom. Build It up & Knock It Down. 2002. (Growing Tree Ser.). (Illus.). 24p. (J). (ps up). 9.95 (*0-694-01568-7*, Harper Festival) HarperCollins Children's Bk. Group.

Hupp, Sarah M. Gatorboat Goof Up. 2003. 24p. (J). 9.99 (*0-310-70566-5*) Zondervan.

Hurt-Newton, Tania. Let's Go! 2001. (Illus.). 16p. (J). bds. 5.95 (*0-7641-5384-6*) Barron's Educational Series, Inc.

Hurwin, Davida Lewis. The Farther You Run. 2003. 256p. (YA). text 16.99 (*0-670-03627-7*, Viking) Viking Penguin.

Hurwin, Davida Wills. A Time for Dancing. 1995. 256p. (YA). 15.95 o.p. (*0-316-38351-1*) Little Brown & Co.

—A Time for Dancing. 1997. (Illus.). 272p. (YA). (gr. 5-9). pap. 5.99 (*0-14-038618-1*) Penguin Putnam Bks. for Young Readers.

Hurwitz, Johanna. Aldo Applesauce. 1979. (Illus.). 128p. (J). (gr. 3-7). lib. bdg. 15.89 (*0-688-32199-2*); (gr. 4-6). 15.00 (*0-688-22199-8*) Morrow/Avon. (Morrow, William & Co.).

—Even Stephen. 1998. (Illus.). 128p. (YA). (gr. 5-9). reprint ed. pap. 4.95 (*0-688-16362-9*, Morrow, William & Co.) Morrow/Avon.

—The Hot & Cold Summer. 1984. (Illus.). 176p. (J). (gr. 4-7). 15.99 (*0-688-02746-6*) HarperCollins Children's Bk. Group.

—The Hot & Cold Summer. 1985. 176p. (J). (gr. 4-7). pap. 4.50 (*0-590-42858-6*); (Illus.). reprint ed. pap. 2.50 o.p. (*0-590-33572-3*, Scholastic Paperbacks) Scholastic, Inc.

—The Hot & Cold Summer. 1984. 10.55 (*0-606-02531-6*) Turtleback Bks.

—The Just Desserts Club. 1999. (Illus.). 144p. (J). (gr. 2 up). 16.00 o.s.i (*0-688-16266-5*) HarperCollins Children's Bk. Group.

—Oh No, Noah! (J). (gr. 2-4). 2003. 144p. pap. 4.95 (*1-58717-231-3*); 2002. (Illus.). 128p. 14.95 (*1-58717-133-3*) North-South Bks., Inc.

—Roz & Ozzie. 1995. 128p. (J). (gr. 2 up). pap. 4.95 o.p. (*0-688-14424-1*, Morrow, William & Co.) Morrow/Avon.

—Roz & Ozzie. 1995. (J). 10.05 o.p. (*0-606-08085-6*) Turtleback Bks.

—Russell Rides Again. 1999. (Beech Tree Chapter Bks.). (Illus.). 96p. (J). (ps-3). pap. 4.99 (*0-688-16665-2*, Harper Trophy) HarperCollins Children's Bk. Group.

—Russell Rides Again. 1985. (Illus.). 96p. (J). (ps-2). 16.00 o.p. (*0-688-04628-2*); lib. bdg. 15.93 o.p. (*0-688-04629-0*) Morrow/Avon. (Morrow, William & Co.).

—Russell Rides Again. (Puffin Chapters Ser.). 96p. (J). 1998. (gr. k-3). pap. 3.99 o.s.i (*0-14-038842-7*); 1989. (Illus.). (gr. 2-5). pap. 3.99 o.p. (*0-14-032941-2*, Puffin Bks.) Penguin Putnam Bks. for Young Readers.

—Russell Rides Again. (Beech Tree Chapter Bks.). 1999. (Illus.). (J). 11.00 (*0-606-21760-6*); 1998. 9.09 o.p. (*0-606-13754-8*) Turtleback Bks.

—Spring Break. 1997. (Illus.). 144p. (J). (gr. 2 up). 15.95 (*0-688-14937-5*) HarperCollins Children's Bk. Group.

—Spring Break. 1999. (Illus.). 144p. (J). (gr. 2-7). mass mkt. 4.95 (*0-688-16672-5*, Morrow, William & Co.) Morrow/Avon.

—Teacher's Pet. 1988. (Illus.). 128p. (J). (gr. 2-5). 16.00 o.s.i (*0-688-07506-1*, Morrow, William & Co.) Morrow/Avon.

—Teacher's Pet. 1989. 128p. (J). (gr. 2-5). pap. 2.99 (*0-590-42031-3*, Scholastic Paperbacks) Scholastic, Inc.

—The Up & down Spring. 1993. (Illus.). 112p. (J). (gr. 3 up). 14.00 o.s.i (*0-688-11922-0*, Morrow, William & Co.) Morrow/Avon.

—Yellow Blue Jay. 1993. (Illus.). 128p. (J). (ps-3). reprint ed. pap. 4.95 (*0-688-12278-7*, Harper Trophy) HarperCollins Children's Bk. Group.

—Yellow Blue Jay. 1993. (Illus.). (J). 11.00 (*0-606-22072-0*) Turtleback Bks.

Huszar, Karen. Meet Matt & Roxy. 1996. (Illus.). 24p. (J). (ps-3). 12.95 (*1-55143-053-3*) Orca Bk. Pubs.

Hutchins, Hazel J. Robyn Looks for Bears. 2000. (New First Novels Ser.: Vol. 16). (Illus.). 64p. (J). (gr. 1-4). (*0-88780-497-7*); pap. 3.99 (*0-88780-496-9*) Formac Publishing Co., Ltd. CAN. *Dist:* Formac Distributing, Ltd., Orca Bk. Pubs.

—Within a Painted Past. 1994. (Illus.). 120p. (J). (gr. 5-7). pap. 5.95 (*1-55037-989-5*) Annick Pr., Ltd. CAN. *Dist:* Firefly Bks., Ltd.

Hutchins, Pat. My Best Friend. 1993. (Illus.). 32p. (J). (ps-3). 16.99 (*0-688-11485-7*); lib. bdg. 15.93 o.p. (*0-688-11486-5*) HarperCollins Children's Bk. Group. (Greenwillow Bks.).

—Titch & Daisy. 1996. (Illus.). 32p. (J). lib. bdg. 14.93 o.p. (*0-688-13960-4*); 15.00 (*0-688-13959-0*) HarperCollins Children's Bk. Group. (Greenwillow Bks.).

Hutchinson, Hanna. Caperucita Roja. rev. ed. 1995. (Interlingo Ser.). (SPA., Illus.). 24p. (J). (gr. 1-2). pap. 2.95 (*0-922852-00-6*, J063) AIMS International Bks., Inc.

—Caperucita Roja. 1989. (Aims Interlingo Ser.). (SPA.). (J). 9.10 (*0-606-01535-3*) Turtleback Bks.

Hutchinson, Uthman. Bismillah. 1995. (Children Stories Project Ser.). (Illus.). (Orig.). (J). (gr. 2 up). pap. 3.95 (*0-915957-37-X*) amana-pubns.

Hyde, Dayton O. Mr. Beans. 2003. (Illus.). 160p. (YA). (gr. 5-9). 14.95 (*1-56397-866-0*) Boyds Mills Pr.

Hyman, John H. The Relationship. 1995. (Illus.). 251p. (YA). (gr. 7 up). 16.95 (*1-880664-14-3*) E. M. Productions.

Hyppolite, Joanne. Seth & Samona. 1996. (Illus.). 128p. pap. text 3.99 o.s.i (*0-440-41272-2*) Dell Publishing.

—Seth & Samona. 1995. (J). 18.95 (*0-385-44630-6*, Dell Books for Young Readers) Random Hse. Children's Bks.

—Seth & Samona. 1997. 9.09 o.p. (*0-606-10928-5*) Turtleback Bks.

Ikeda, Daisaku. Over the Deep Blue Sea. 1993. (Illus.). 32p. (J). (ps-3). 15.00 o.s.i (*0-679-84184-9*); 15.99 o.s.i (*0-679-94184-3*) Random Hse. Children's Bks. (Knopf Bks. for Young Readers).

Illsley, Amber Jo. Biggledy Boo Knows What to Do. 1999. (J). (ps-5). E-Book 6.95 (*0-87714-465-6*) Denlingers Pubs., Ltd.

I'm Still Herbie: Coping with Leukemia. 1997. (Dr. Wellbook Collection). (Illus.). 24p. (J). (ps-3). pap. 7.95 (*1-879874-54-7*) Peters, Tim & Co., Inc.

In the Meadow Activity Book, Unit 4. 1991. (Networks Ser.). (J). (gr. 1). pap. 3.90 o.p. (*0-88106-729-6*); pap. 3.90 o.p. (*0-88106-730-X*, N144) Charlesbridge Publishing, Inc.

In the Meadow Anthology, Unit 4. 1991. (Networks Ser.). (J). (gr. 3-4). pap. 7.45 o.p. (*0-88106-728-8*, N141) Charlesbridge Publishing, Inc.

Inches, Alison. My Visit with Periwinkle. 2003. (Ready-to-Read Ser.). (Illus.). 24p. (J). pap. 3.99 (*0-689-85230-4*, Simon Spotlight/Nickelodeon) Simon & Schuster Children's Publishing.

—A Surprise for Wendy. 2002. (Bob the Builder Ready-to-Read Ser.: Vol. 4). (Illus.). 24p. (J). pap. 3.99 (*0-689-84754-8*, Simon Spotlight) Simon & Schuster Children's Publishing.

—Wendy Helps Out. 2001. (Bob the Builder Ready-to-Read Ser.: Vol. 2). (Illus.). 32p. (J). pap. 3.99 (*0-689-84391-7*, Simon Spotlight) Simon & Schuster Children's Publishing.

Inkpen, Mick. Kipper's Christmas Eve. 2000. (Kipper Ser.). (Illus.). 32p. (J). (ps-3). 13.95 (*0-15-202660-6*, Red Wagon Bks.) Harcourt Children's Bks.

—Swing. 2000. (Kipper Ser.). (Illus.). 24p. (J). (ps-3). pap. 4.95 (*0-15-202672-X*, Red Wagon Bks.) Harcourt Children's Bks.

Innes, Grant. The Flight of the Whirligigs. 1999. (Illus.). 24p. (J). lib. bdg. 17.95 (*1-55037-587-3*) Annick Pr., Ltd. CAN. *Dist:* Firefly Bks., Ltd.

Irwin, Hadley. Jim-Dandy. 1994. (J). 10.00 (*0-606-08556-4*) Turtleback Bks.

—Moon & Me. 1981. 168p. (J). (gr. 5-9). lib. bdg. 13.95 o.s.i (*0-689-50194-3*, McElderry, Margaret K.) Simon & Schuster Children's Publishing.

Isadora, Rachel. Friends. 1990. (Illus.). (J). (ps up). 13.95 o.p. (*0-688-08264-5*); lib. bdg. 13.88 o.p. (*0-688-08265-3*) HarperCollins Children's Bk. Group. (Greenwillow Bks.).

Isele, Elizabeth. Pooks. 1983. (Illus.). 32p. (J). (ps-3). 8.95 (*0-397-32044-2*); lib. bdg. 8.89 o.p. (*0-397-32045-0*) HarperCollins Children's Bk. Group.

Ismail, Suzy. The BFF Sisters: Jennah's New Friends. 2001. 64p. (J). (*1-59008-005-X*) amana-pubns.

It's Too Bad, Beast. 1987. (Illus.). 32p. (J). (ps-3). pap. 4.95 o.p. (*0-8431-2651-5*, Price Stern Sloan) Penguin Putnam Bks. for Young Readers.

Izcoa, Carmen R. & Montanez, Nivea O. Mediopollito. 1996. (SPA.). 46p. (J). (gr. 1-3). 10.50 (*0-929157-43-5*) Ediciones Huracan, Inc.

Jackson, Bobby L. Roberto, Berto y el Huerto. Garcia, Jose & Garcia, Diana, trs. l.t. ed. 2001. Orig. Title: Pops, Chops & Crops. (ENG & SPA., Illus.). 32p. (YA). (gr. k up). pap. 10.95 (*1-884242-71-5*) Multicultural Pubns.

—Roberto, Berto y el Huerto: First Translated Edition. Garcia, Jose & Garcia, Diana, trs. l.t. ed. 2001. Orig. Title: Pops, Chops & Crops. (ENG & SPA., Illus.). 32p. (YA). (gr. k up). lib. bdg. 19.95 (*1-884242-75-8*) Multicultural Pubns.

Jackson, Carla. Katie's Plight. Cowan, Cathy, ed. 1997. (Illus.). 28p. (J). (ps-7). pap. 8.95 incl. audio (*0-9669166-0-3*) Beajo Pub.

Jackson, Dave & Jackson, Neta. Drawn by a China Moon: Lottie Moon. 2000. (Trailblazer Bks.: Vol. 34). (Illus.). 160p. (J). (gr. 3-7). pap. 5.99 o.s.i (*0-7642-2267-8*) Bethany Hse. Pubs.

Jackson, Isaac. Somebody's New Pajamas. 1996. (Illus.). 32p. (J). (gr. 1-5). 14.89 o.s.i (*0-8037-1549-8*); (ps-3). 14.99 o.s.i (*0-8037-1570-6*) Penguin Putnam Bks. for Young Readers. (Dial Bks. for Young Readers).

Jackson, Jean. Thorndike & Nelson: A Monster Story. 1997. (Illus.). 32p. (J). (ps-k). pap. 15.95 o.p. (*0-7894-2452-5*) Dorling Kindersley Publishing, Inc.

Jackson, Kamichi. You're Too Much, Reggie Brown. l.t. ed. 2000. (Illus.). 110p. (J). (gr. 2-5). pap. 5.95 (*0-615-11287-0*) Shug' n Spice Pr.

Jackson, William. The First Step. Spruill, Shawn, ed. 1999. 190p. (YA). (gr. 9 up). pap. 10.00 (*0-9652528-7-6*) Neshui Publishing, Inc.

Jacob, Lucinda. Lily & Ted. 1998. (Illus.). 32p. (ps). pap. 7.95 (*1-85371-747-9*) Poolbeg Pr. IRL. *Dist:* Dufour Editions, Inc.

Jacobs, Linda. Everyone's Watching Tammy. 1974. (Really Me! Ser.). (J). (gr. 6-9). pap. 3.95 o.p. (*0-88436-153-5*, 35352); lib. bdg. 6.95 o.p. (*0-88436-152-7*, 35564) Paradigm Publishing, Inc.

Jacobson, Jennifer. Truly Winnie. 2003. (Illus.). 112p. (J). (gr. 3-5). tchr. ed. 15.00 (*0-618-28008-1*) Houghton Mifflin Co.

—Winnie Dancing on Her Own. 2003. (Illus.). 112p. (J). (gr. 4-6). pap. 5.95 (*0-618-36921-X*) Houghton Mifflin Co.

Jacobson, Jennifer, ed. Winnie Dancing on Her Own. 2001. (Illus.). 96p. (J). (gr. 4-6). tchr. ed. 15.00 (*0-618-13287-2*) Houghton Mifflin Co.

Jaeger, Peggy. The Kindness Tales: Billy & the Bear - The Story of Felina Catina - Peter's Pumpkin. 1994. (Illus.). 18p. (J). text 12.50 (*0-930329-87-2*) Kabel Pubs.

Jaffe, Nina. While Standing on One Foot: Puzzle Stories & Wisdom Tales from the Jewish Tradition, ERS. 1996. (Illus.). 128p. (YA). (gr. 4-7). pap. 8.95 (*0-8050-5073-6*, Holt, Henry & Co. Bks. For Young Readers) Holt, Henry & Co.

Jahn-Clough, Lisa. Alicia's Best Friends. 2003. (Illus.). 32p. (J). (ps-3). tchr. ed. 15.00 (*0-618-23951-0*) Houghton Mifflin Co.

—Missing Molly. 2000. (Illus.). 32p. (J). (ps-3). lib. bdg., tchr. ed. 15.00 (*0-618-00980-9*) Houghton Mifflin Co.

—My Friend & I. 1999. (Illus.). 32p. (J). (ps-3). tchr. ed. 15.00 (*0-395-93545-8*) Houghton Mifflin Co.

—My Friend & I. 2003. (Illus.). 32p. (J). (ps-3). pap. 5.95 (*0-618-39108-8*, Lorraine, A. Walter) Houghton Mifflin Co. Trade & Reference Div.

—Simon & Molly Plus Hester. 2001. (Illus.). 32p. (J). (ps-3). lib. bdg., tchr. ed. 15.00 (*0-618-08220-4*, Lorraine, A. Walter) Houghton Mifflin Co. Trade & Reference Div.

Jam, Teddy. Ttum. 1999. (Charlotte Stories). (Illus.). 112p. (gr. 2-4). text 14.95 (*0-88899-373-0*) Groundwood Bks. CAN. *Dist:* Publishers Group West.

James, Betsy. Mary Ann. 1994. (Illus.). 32p. (J). (ps-3). 14.99 o.s.i (*0-525-45077-7*, Dutton Children's Bks.) Penguin Putnam Bks. for Young Readers.

James, Brian. Pure Sunshine. 2002. (Illus.). 176p. (YA). (gr. 8 up). mass mkt. 6.99 (*0-439-27989-5*, PUSH) Scholastic, Inc.

—The Shark Who Was Afraid of Everything. 2002. (Illus.). (J). (*0-439-36865-0*) Scholastic, Inc.

James, Simon. Dear Mr. Blueberry. (Illus.). 32p. (J). (ps-3). 1996. pap. 5.99 (*0-689-80768-6*, Aladdin); 1991. 15.00 (*0-689-50529-9*, McElderry, Margaret K.) Simon & Schuster Children's Publishing.

—Dear Mr. Blueberry. 1996. 12.14 (*0-606-09186-6*) Turtleback Bks.

—Leon & Bob. 1997. (Illus.). 32p. (J). (gr. 1-4). 15.99 o.s.i (*1-56402-991-3*) Candlewick Pr.

Jane, Pamela. Noelle of the Nutcracker. 1988. 80p. (J). pap. 2.99 o.s.i (*0-553-15673-X*, Skylark) Random Hse. Children's Bks.

—Noelle of the Nutcracker. 2003. (Illus.). 64p. (J). (gr. 4-6). pap. 5.95 (*0-618-36922-8*) Houghton Mifflin Co.

Janover, Caroline. The Worst Speller in Jr. High. Wallner, Rosemary, ed. 1994. 208p. (YA). (gr. 5 up). pap. 4.95 o.p. (*0-915793-76-8*, FS301) Free Spirit Publishing, Inc.

Janover, Caroline D. The Worst Speller in Jr. High. 2000. 208p. (gr. 4-7). pap. 13.95 (*0-595-15328-3*, Backinprint.com) iUniverse, Inc.

Jaques, Florence Page. There Once Was a Puffin. 2003. 32p. (J). lib. bdg. 16.50 (*0-7358-1771-5*); (Illus.). 15.95 (*0-7358-1770-7*) North-South Bks., Inc.

Jareckie, Ellen. A House-Mouse Party. 2003. (House-Mouse Tales Ser.). (Illus.). 22p. (J). bds. 6.99 (*0-316-45150-9*, Tingley, Megan Bks.) Little Brown Children's Bks.

—House-Mouse Tales: Friends. 2004. (Illus.). 22p. (J). bds. 6.99 (*0-316-73812-3*) Little Brown & Co.

Jarrett, Clare. Dancing Maddy. (Illus.). 26p. pap. (*0-00-664670-0*) HarperCollins Pubs. Canada, Ltd.

Jason. Jason & Edeia. pap. 6.95 (*0-394-74096-3*) Random Hse., Inc.

Jaspersohn, William. Cranberries. 1991. (Illus.). 32p. (J). (gr. 2-6). 14.95 o.s.i (*0-395-52098-3*) Houghton Mifflin Co.

Jeans, Peter D. Bodger & Me. 2001. (Illus.). 320p. (YA). pap. 14.95 (*1-876268-65-4*) Univ. of Western Australia Pr. AUS. *Dist:* International Specialized Bk. Services.

Jeffs, Stephanie. Christopher Bear Makes Friends. 2004. (Christopher Bear Ser.). (Illus.). 32p. (J). 5.99 (*0-8066-4401-X*, Augsburg Bks.) Augsburg Fortress, Pubs.

Jenkins, A. M. Breaking Boxes. 192p. (YA). (gr. 9-12). 2000. mass mkt. 4.99 o.s.i (*0-440-22717-8*); 1997. 15.95 o.s.i (*0-385-32513-4*, Delacorte Pr.) Dell Publishing.

—Breaking Boxes. 2000. 11.04 (*0-606-17834-1*) Turtleback Bks.

Jenkins-Pearce, Susie. Percy Short & Cuthbert. 1991. 32p. (J). (ps-3). 12.95 o.p. (*0-670-82803-3*, Viking Children's Bks.) Penguin Putnam Bks. for Young Readers.

Jenkins, Steve. Actual Size. 2004. (Illus.). 32p. (J). (ps-3). 16.00 (*0-618-37594-5*) Houghton Mifflin Co.

Jennings, Linda. Buster. 1998. (J). (*1-85430-558-1*); (BEN, CHI, ENG, PAN & SOM., Illus.). 40p. (*1-85430-545-X*); (BEN, CHI, ENG, PAN & SOM., Illus.). 40p. (*1-85430-543-3*); (BEN, CHI, ENG, PAN & SOM., Illus.). 40p. (*1-85430-540-9*); (BEN, CHI, ENG, PAN & SOM., Illus.). 40p. (*1-85430-542-5*); (BEN, CHI, ENG, PAN & SOM., Illus.). 40p. (*1-85430-544-1*) Magi Pubns.

—Penny & Pup. 1997. (Illus.). 32p. (J). (ps-2). 14.95 o.p. (*1-888444-18-5*, 21018) Little Tiger Pr.

Jennings, Patrick. Putnam & Pennyroyal. 1999. (Illus.). 192p. (J). (gr. 2-5). pap. 15.95 (*0-439-07965-9*) Scholastic, Inc.

Jennings, Sharon. Jeremiah & Mrs. Ming. 1990. (Illus.). 24p. (J). (ps-k). text 15.95 (*1-55037-079-0*); pap. 5.95 (*1-55037-078-2*) Annick Pr., Ltd. CAN. *Dist:* Firefly Bks., Ltd.

—Jeremiah & Mrs. Ming: A Big Book. 1990. (Illus.). 24p. (J). (ps-k). 21.95 (*1-55037-124-X*) Annick Pr., Ltd. CAN. *Dist:* Firefly Bks., Ltd.

—Priscilla & Rosy. 2001. (Illus.). 32p. (J). (gr. k-2). (*1-55041-676-6*) Fitzhenry & Whiteside, Ltd.

Jiménez, Juan Ramón. Platero & I. 2003. (Illus.). 64p. (J). (gr. 4-6). pap. 5.95 (*0-618-37838-3*, Clarion Bks.) Houghton Mifflin Co. Trade & Reference Div.

—Platero & I. 1960. mass mkt. 0.50 o.p. (*0-451-50017-2*); mass mkt. 0.60 o.p. (*0-451-50302-3*); mass mkt. 0.75 o.p. (*0-451-50370-8*); mass mkt. 0.95 o.p. (*0-451-50849-1*, CQ849) NAL. (Signet Classics).

—Platero & I. Roach, Eloise, tr. from SPA. (Illus.). 1983. 218p. (C). pap. 14.95 (*0-292-76479-0*); 1957. 228p. pap. 12.95 o.p. (*0-292-73328-3*) Univ. of Texas Pr.

—Platero & I. 2000. (Illus.). 200p. pap. 12.95 (*0-595-00345-1*) iUniverse, Inc.

—Platero y Yo. (SPA.). 192p. 13.95 (*84-206-1851-9*, AZ1851); (Illus.). 159p. 9.95 (*84-206-3408-5*) Alianza Editorial, S. A. ESP. *Dist:* Continental Bk. Co., Inc., Distribooks, Inc., Distribooks, Inc.

—Platero y Yo. (SPA.). pap. 9.95 (*968-432-357-3*, PM223) Editorial Porrua MEX. *Dist:* Continental Bk. Co., Inc.

—Platero y Yo. Cardwell, Richard A., ed. 1991. (Nueva Austral Ser.: Vol. 58). (SPA.). 288p. 24.95 (*84-239-1858-0*) Elliot's Bks.

—Platero y Yo. annot. ed. (SPA., Illus.). 232p. 15.95 (*84-207-2636-2*, ANY010) Grupo Anaya, S.A. ESP. *Dist:* Continental Bk. Co., Inc.

—Platero y Yo. (SPA.). (YA). (gr. 5-8). pap. (*958-30-0744-7*, PV0560) Panamericana Editorial COL. *Dist:* Lectorum Pubns., Inc.

—Platero y Yo (Platero & I) (SPA.). pap. 9.95 (*968-416-022-4*, AOR01) Fernandez USA Publishing.

Jiménez, Juan Ramón & Dominguez, Joseph P. Platero & I. Livingston, Myra C., tr. 1994. (ENG & SPA., Illus.). 64p. (J). (gr. 4-6). tchr. ed. 15.00 (*0-395-62365-0*, BT3650, Clarion Bks.) Houghton Mifflin Co. Trade & Reference Div.

Jin, Sarunna. My First American Friend. 1990. (Young Publish-a-Book Ser.). (Illus.). 32p. (J). (gr. 1-6). lib. bdg. 22.83 o.p. (*0-8172-2785-7*); (gr. 2-4). pap. 4.95 o.p. (*0-8114-4310-8*) Raintree Pubs.

Jobling, Brenda. Pirate the Seal. 1998. (Animal Tales Ser.). (Illus.). 131p. (J). (gr. 3-7). pap. 3.95 o.p. (*0-7641-0601-5*) Barron's Educational Series, Inc.

Jocelyn, Marthe. The Invisible Harry. 1998. (Illus.). 144p. (J). (gr. 3-7). 14.99 o.s.i (*0-525-46078-0*, Dutton Children's Bks.) Penguin Putnam Bks. for Young Readers.

Johansson, Alice Nicole. The Best Friend Game. 1994. (Unicorn Club Ser.: No. 3). 144p. (J). (gr. 3-7). pap. 3.50 o.s.i (*0-553-48210-6*) Bantam Bks.

John, Laurie. College Girls. 1993. (Sweet Valley University Ser.: No. 1). (YA). (gr. 7 up). 9.09 o.p. (*0-606-05655-6*) Turtleback Bks.

John, Liza St. Abby's Wish. 1995. (Publish-a-Book Ser.). (Illus.). 32p. (J). (gr. 1-6). lib. bdg. 22.83 (*0-8114-7272-8*) Raintree Pubs.

Johns, Michael-Anne. Hangin' with Aaron Carter. 2001. (Illus.). 48p. (J). (gr. 3-7). pap. 5.99 (*0-439-32693-1*) Scholastic, Inc.

Johnson, Amy Crane. Lewis Cardinal's First Winter/El Primer Invierno de Luis, el Cardenal: A Solomon Raven Story/Un Cuento Del Cuervo Salomon, Vol. 2. Creative Marketing of Green Bay, tr. 2002. (Solomon Raven Ser.).Tr. of Primer Invierno de Luis, el Cardenal. (ENG & SPA., Illus.). 32p. (J). (gr. k-3). 16.95 o.s.i (*0-9701107-8-2*, 626999) Raven Tree Pr., LLC.

Johnson, Angela. One of Three. 1995. (J). 12.10 (*0-606-09716-3*) Turtleback Bks.

Johnson, B. J. & Aiello, Susan. My Blanket Burt. 1986. (Once upon a Time Bks.). (Illus.). 14p. (J). (ps-1). 4.95 o.p. (*0-312-55600-4*) St. Martin's Pr.

Johnson-Choong, Shelly. A Light to Come Home By. 1996. (YA). pap. 9.95 o.p. (*1-55503-816-6*, 01112120) Covenant Communications, Inc.

Johnson, Diana F. Princesa & Friskie. Castillo, Carlos E., tr. 1997. (ENG & SPA., Illus.). 32p. (Orig.). (J). (ps-6). pap. 9.95 (*0-9657928-0-3*) Interkids.

Johnson, Joli. Kimmy, Joey, & Robert the Goose. 1995. (Illus.). 12p. (J). pap. 3.95 (*0-937242-18-7*) Scandia Pubs.

Johnson, Kimberly P. Tag-Along Fred. 2002. (Illus.). 32p. (J). (ps-3). 14.95 (*1-57197-290-0*) Pentland Pr., Inc.

Johnson, Lissa Halls. Stuck in the Sky. 2001. (Brio Girls Ser.). 192p. (J). (gr. 7-11). pap. 6.99 (*1-56179-951-3*) Bethany Hse. Pubs.

Johnson, Nora. The World of Henry Orient. 2002. 224p. (YA). 12.95 (*0-9714612-0-1*, 01-GMP-001) Green Mansion Pr. LLC.

—The World of Henry Orient. 1998. lib. bdg. 18.95 (*1-56723-068-7*) Yestermorrow, Inc.

Johnson, Paul Brett. Bearhide & Crow. 2000. (Illus.). 32p. (J). (ps-3). tchr. ed. 16.95 (*0-8234-1470-1*) Holiday Hse., Inc.

Johnson, Pete. Catch You on the Flip Side. 1989. 135p. (YA). (gr. 7-9). pap. 9.95 o.p. (*0-233-98074-1*) Andre Deutsch GBR. *Dist:* Trafalgar Square, Trans-Atlantic Pubns., Inc.

—Traitor. 2002. (Illus.). 208p. (J). pap. (*0-440-86438-0*, Corgi) Bantam Bks.

Johnson, S. Kwames' Girl. 1994. (Eighteen Pine Street Ser.: No. 10). 160p. (YA). mass mkt. 3.50 o.s.i (*0-553-56313-0*) Bantam Bks.

—The Prince. 1992. (Eighteen Pine Street Ser.: No. 3). 160p. (YA). mass mkt. 3.50 o.s.i (*0-553-29721-X*) Bantam Bks.

Johnson, Scott. Hide & Seek. 1997. (Deer Tales Ser.: No. 1). (Illus.). 128p. (Orig.). (J). (gr. 5). pap. 3.95 (*1-887251-10-3*) Deer Pond Pub.

—One of the Boys. 1992. 256p. (YA). (gr. 7 up). text 16.00 o.s.i (*0-689-31520-1*, Atheneum) Simon & Schuster Children's Publishing.

Johnson, Sherrie. Abish. 1995. (Steppingstone Ser.). (Illus.). 32p. (Orig.). (J). (ps-4). pap. 5.95 (*1-57345-023-5*) Deseret Bk. Co.

Johnson-Simpson, Gwendolyn. Difference. 1998. (Illus.). 32p. (J). pap. 8.00 (*0-8059-4409-5*) Dorrance Publishing Co., Inc.

Johnson, Stacie. Sort of Sisters. 1992. (Eighteen Pine Street Ser.: No. 1). 160p. (YA). mass mkt. 3.50 o.s.i (*0-553-29719-8*) Bantam Bks.

Johnson, Ward. Ben's New Buddy. 1985. (Care Bear Ser.). (J). pap. 11.95 o.p. (*0-516-09008-9*, Children's Pr.) Scholastic Library Publishing.

Johnston, Norma. Over Jordan. 1999. 192p. (J). (gr. 4-7). 15.00 (*0-380-97635-8*) HarperCollins Children's Bk. Group.

Johnston, Tony. Alien & Possum: Friends No Matter What. (Ready-to-Reads Ser.). 48p. (J). 2002. pap. 3.99 (*0-689-85326-2*, Aladdin); 2001. (Illus.). 15.00 (*0-689-83835-2*, Simon & Schuster Children's Publishing) Simon & Schuster Children's Publishing.

—Alien & Possum Hanging Out. (Ready-to-Reads Ser.). (Illus.). 48p. (J). 2003. pap. 3.99 (*0-689-85771-3*, Aladdin); 2002. (gr. 1-3). 15.00 (*0-689-83836-0*, Simon & Schuster Children's Publishing) Simon & Schuster Children's Publishing.

—Amber on the Mountain. 1994. (Illus.). 32p. (J). (ps-3). 14.99 o.s.i (*0-8037-1219-7*); 14.89 o.s.i (*0-8037-1220-0*) Penguin Putnam Bks. for Young Readers. (Dial Bks. for Young Readers).

—Night Noises & Other Mole & Troll Stories. 1977. (See & Read Storybook Ser.). (Illus.). (J). (gr. k-4). 6.99 o.p. (*0-399-61016-2*) Putnam Publishing Group, The.

—Sparky & Eddie: The First Day of School. 1997. (Sparky & Eddie Ser.). (Illus.). 32p. (J). (gr. k-2). pap. 13.95 (*0-590-47978-4*); pap. 3.99 (*0-590-47979-2*) Scholastic, Inc.

—Sparky & Eddie: The Rodeo. 1997. (Sparky & Eddie Ser.). (Illus.). 40p. (J). (gr. 1-3). pap. 13.95 (*0-590-47984-9*) Scholastic, Inc.

—Sparky & Eddie: The Rodeo. 1997. (Illus.). (J). mass mkt. 3.99 (*0-590-47985-7*) Scholastic, Inc.

—Sparky & Eddie: Trouble with Rats. (Illus.). 32p. (J). 1999. pap. 4.95 (*0-590-47981-4*); 1998. 13.95 (*0-590-47980-6*) Scholastic, Inc.

Join In. 1993. (J). o.s.i (*0-385-30945-7*, Dell Books for Young Readers) Random Hse. Children's Bks.

Jolin, Dominique. Deecee Loves Sounds. Perkes, Carolyn, tr. from FRE. 2001. (Deecee Ser.). (Illus.). 14p. (J). bds. (*1-894363-65-5*) Dominique & Friends.

—Merry Christmas, Washington! Perkes, Carolyn, tr. from FRE. 2000. (Illus.). 16p. (ps-k). bds. (*1-894363-63-9*) Dominique & Friends.

—Peek-a-Boo, Deecee! Perkes, Carolyn, tr. from FRE. 2001. (Deecee Ser.). (Illus.). 14p. (J). bds. (*1-894363-53-1*) Dominique & Friends.

—Toupie Aime Toupie. braille ed. 2001. (J). (gr. 1). bds. (*0-616-07269-4*) Canadian National Institute for the Blind/Institut National Canadien pour les Aveugles.

—Washington Loves Washington. Perkes, Carolyn, tr. from FRE. 2000. (Illus.). 16p. (ps). bds. (*1-894363-62-0*) Dominique & Friends.

Joly, Fanny. Mr. Fine, Porcupine. 1997. (Illus.). 32p. (J). (ps-1). 12.95 o.p. (*0-8118-1842-X*) Chronicle Bks. LLC.

Jones, Brian. To Find a Friend. 1996. (Illus.). 64p. (Orig.). (J). (ps-4). pap. 4.95 (*1-57733-006-4*) Blue Dolphin Publishing, Inc.

Jones, Deirdre J. White. Something about That Smile. 2002. (Illus.). (J). 18.00 (*0-9709718-5-0*) Plainsong Publishing.

Jones, Diana Wynne. Cart & Cwidder. 2001. (Dalemark Quartet Ser.: Vol. 1). (Illus.). 240p. (J). (gr. 7 up). pap. 6.95 (*0-06-447313-9*, Harper Trophy) HarperCollins Children's Bk. Group.

Jones, Elisabeth. Sunshine & Storm. 2001. (Illus.). 36p. (J). (ps-3). 14.95 o.s.i (*1-929927-27-4*) Ragged Bears USA.

Jones, Elizabeth McDavid. Mystery on Skull Island. 2001. (American Girl Collection: Bk. 15). (Illus.). 192p. (J). 9.95 (*1-58485-342-5*); pap. 5.95 (*1-58485-341-7*) Pleasant Co. Pubns. (American Girl).

Jones, Janice. Secrets of a Summer Spy. 1990. 192p. (J). (gr. 5-9). lib. bdg. 14.95 o.s.i (*0-02-747861-0*, Simon & Schuster Children's Publishing) Simon & Schuster Children's Publishing.

Jones, Jennifer B. Dear Mrs. Ryan, You're Ruining My Life. 2000. 122p. (J). (gr. 5-9). 15.95 (*0-8027-8728-2*) Walker & Co.

Jones, Linda K. Fear Strikes at Midnight. 1990. 128p. (J). (gr. 4-7). pap. 5.99 (*0-8361-3507-5*) Herald Pr.

Jones, Martha R. Willow Finds a Friend. 1993. (Illus.). 32p. (J). (gr. 2-4). pap. 6.95 o.p. (*0-8059-3315-8*) Dorrance Publishing Co., Inc.

Jones, Rebecca C. Mateo y Mati. 1995. Tr. of Matthew & Tilly. (J). 10.19 o.p. (*0-606-08567-X*) Turtleback Bks.

—Matthew & Tilly. 1991. (Illus.). 32p. (J). (ps-3). 13.95 o.p. (*0-525-44684-2*, Dutton Children's Bks.) Penguin Putnam Bks. for Young Readers.

—Matthew & Tilly. 1995. 13.14 (*0-606-08568-8*) Turtleback Bks.

Jones, Rhodri. Different Friends. 1990. 122p. (YA). (gr. 6-9). pap. 9.95 o.p. (*0-233-98096-2*) Andre Deutsch GBR. *Dist:* Trafalgar Square, Trans-Atlantic Pubns., Inc.

Jones, Veda Boyd. Coming Home. 1999. (American Adventure Ser.: No. 48). (Illus.). 144p. (J). (gr. 3-7). pap. 3.97 (*1-57748-514-9*) Barbour Publishing, Inc.

Jones, Weynan. Edge of Two Worlds. 1968. (Illus.). 160p. (J). (gr. 4-6). 7.95 o.p. (*0-8037-2211-7*, Dial Bks. for Young Readers) Penguin Putnam Bks. for Young Readers.

Joosse, Barbara M. Alien Brain Fryout. 2000. (Wild Willie Mystery Ser.). (Illus.). 96p. (J). (gr. 4-6). tchr. ed. 15.00 (*0-395-68964-3*, Clarion Bks.) Houghton Mifflin Co. Trade & Reference Div.

—Ghost Trap: A Wild Willie Mystery. 1998. (Wild Willie Mystery Ser.). (Illus.). 80p. (J). (gr. 4-6). tchr. ed. 15.00 (*0-395-66587-6*, Clarion Bks.) Houghton Mifflin Co. Trade & Reference Div.

—The Losers Fight Back: A Wild Willie Mystery. 9999. pap. 4.99 o.s.i (*0-440-91140-0*) Bantam Bks.

—The Losers Fight Back: A Wild Willie Mystery. 1994. (Illus.). 112p. (J). (gr. 4-6). tchr. ed. 15.00 (*0-395-62335-9*, Clarion Bks.) Houghton Mifflin Co. Trade & Reference Div.

—The Losers Fight Back: A Wild Willie Mystery. 1996. (Illus.). 112p. (J). (gr. 2-6). pap. 3.99 o.s.i (*0-440-41110-6*, Yearling) Random Hse. Children's Bks.

—The Losers Fight Back: A Wild Willie Mystery. 1996. 9.09 o.p. (*0-606-09578-0*) Turtleback Bks.

Jordan, P. D. Cooper Street. 1989. 147p. (Orig.). (YA). (gr. 5-12). pap. 5.95 (*0-929885-21-X*) Haypenny Pr.

Jordan, Sherryl. Juniper Game. 240p. (YA). (gr. 7-9). 1994. mass mkt. 3.50 (*0-590-44729-7*); 1991. pap. 13.95 o.p. (*0-590-44728-9*) Scholastic, Inc.

Jordano, Kimberly. By Myself or with My Friends, Vol. 4411. Kupperstein, Joel, ed. 1998. (Learn to Read Social Studies). (Illus.). 16p. (J). (ps-2). pap. 2.99 (*1-57471-334-5*, 4411) Creative Teaching Pr., Inc.

Jorgensen, Dan. Dawn's Diamond Defense. 1988. 144p. (YA). pap. 4.99 o.p. (*1-55513-062-3*) Cook Communications Ministries.

—Sky Hook. 1985. (Pennypinchers Ser.). 128p. (J). (gr. 4-9). pap. 3.95 o.p. (*0-89191-682-2*, 56820) Cook Communications Ministries.

Joseph, Oreste R. Lakay. Theodat, J. et al, eds. 2nd ed. 1995. (CRP., Illus.). 13p. (J). pap. 3.00 (*1-885566-01-8*) Oresjozef Pubns.

Joyce, Bill. Olie. 2001. (Rolie Polie Olie Ser.). (Illus.). 10p. (J). (ps-k). bds. 3.99 (*0-7868-3322-X*) Disney Pr.

—Rolie Polie Olie & Friends. 2002. (Illus.). 10p. (J). (*0-7868-3391-2*); (*0-7868-3392-0*); (*0-7868-3393-9*); (*0-7868-3394-7*) Disney Pr.

Joyce, William. Buddy. 1997. (Laura Geringer Bks.). (Illus.). (ps up). 96p. (J). lib. bdg. 15.89 (*0-06-027661-4*); 48p. (YA). 14.95 (*0-06-027660-6*) HarperCollins Children's Bk. Group.

—Rolie Polie Olie & Friends: Friendship Box. 2002. (Illus.). 10p. (J). bds. 9.99 (*0-7868-3294-0*) Disney Pr.

Joyce, William, illus. Buddy. 1999. 48p. (J). (gr. 2-7). pap. 6.95 (*0-06-440710-1*) HarperCollins Children's Bk. Group.

Jukes, Mavis. Getting Even. 1988. 160p. (J). (gr. 4-7). 11.95 o.s.i (*0-394-89594-0*, Knopf Bks. for Young Readers) Random Hse. Children's Bks.

—Planning the Impossible. 176p. (gr. 5-7). 2000. (Illus.). pap. text 4.50 (*0-440-41230-7*, Yearling); 1999. text 14.95 o.s.i (*0-385-32243-7*, Dell Books for Young Readers) Random Hse. Children's Bks.

—Planning the Impossible. 2000. 10.55 (*0-606-20022-3*) Turtleback Bks.

Jussek, Nicole. Seymour & Opal. 1996. (J). (ps-3). 16.99 o.s.i (*0-679-96722-2*) Random Hse., Inc.

Justus, Adalu. The Storyteller House. 1999. 180p. (YA). (gr. 5-12). per. (*0-937109-11-8*) Ike, J. Bks.

Kaczman, James. A Bird & His Worm. 2002. (Illus.). 32p. (J). (ps-3). lib. bdg., tchr. ed. 15.00 (*0-618-09460-1*) Houghton Mifflin Co.

Kadish, Sharona. Discovering Friendship. 1994. (Publish-a-Book Ser.). (Illus.). 32p. (J). (gr. 1-6). lib. bdg. 22.83 o.p. (*0-8114-4458-9*) Raintree Pubs.

Kadohata, Cynthia. Kirakira. 2004. (Illus.). 256p. (J). 15.95 (*0-689-85639-3*, Atheneum) Simon & Schuster Children's Publishing.

Kafka, Sherry. I Need a Friend. 1971. (Illus.). (J). (gr. k-2). 4.29 o.p. (*0-399-60300-X*) Putnam Publishing Group, The.

Kako, Satoshi. Little Daruma & Little Tengu. Howlett, Peter & McNamara, Richard B., trs. 2003. 32p. (J). (ps-3). 10.95 (*0-8048-3347-8*) Tuttle Publishing.

Kalamvocas, Patty O. Another Underserved Lickin' Kindle, Judy & Variety Printing Staff, eds. ltd. ed. 1995. 280p. (Orig.). pap. 13.95 (*0-9648412-0-7*) Kalamvocas, Patricia Osborne.

Kalan, Robert. Salta, Ranita, Salta! unabr. ed. 1996. (SPA., Illus.). (J). (gr. k-3). pap. 15.95 incl. audio (*0-87499-367-9*, LK1626) Live Oak Media.

—Salta, Ranita, Salta!, Grades K-3. 1996. Tr. of Jump, Frog, Jump!. (SPA., Illus.). pap., tchr. ed. 31.95 incl. audio (*0-87499-369-5*) Live Oak Media.

—Salta, Ranita, Salta! (Jump, Frog, Jump!) unabr. ed. 1996. (SPA., Illus.). (J). (gr. k-3). 24.95 incl. audio (*0-87499-368-7*) Live Oak Media.

Kalbacken, Joan. The Menominee. 1994. (New True Books Ser.). (Illus.). 48p. (J). (gr. k-4). mass mkt. 5.50 o.p. (*0-516-41054-7*, Children's Pr.) Scholastic Library Publishing.

Kaldhol, Marit. Goodbye Rune. Crosby-Jones, Michael, tr. 1987. Tr. of Farvel, Rune. (NOR., Illus.). 32p. (J). (gr. k-5). 13.95 (*0-916291-11-1*) Kane/Miller Bk. Pubs.

Kamhi, Ralph. Hi Fives. 1990. (Illus.). 8p. (J). (gr. 4-5). stu. ed. (*0-9627292-1-3*) Extra.

—The Times of Your Life. 1989. 8p. (J). (gr. 6-12). (*0-9627292-0-5*) Extra.

Kaminsky, Jef. Poppy & Ella: 3 Stories about 2 Friends. 2000. (Illus.). 48p. (J). (ps-1). 14.99 (*0-7868-0511-0*) Disney Pr.

—Poppy & Ella: 3 Stories about 2 Friends. 2000. (Illus.). 48p. (J). (ps-3). 15.49 (*0-7868-2447-6*) Hyperion Bks. for Children.

Kantenwein, Louise. Jean Marie. 1993. (J). 7.95 o.p. (*0-533-10667-2*) Vantage Pr., Inc.

Kantor, Melissa. Confessions of a Not It Girl. 2004. (J). (gr. 7). 14.99 (*0-7868-1837-9*) Hyperion Bks. for Children.

Kapper, Jon. Super Duper Lucy. 2001. (Little Lucy & Friends Ser.). (Illus.). 24p. (J). (gr. k-3). 9.99 (*1-57151-703-0*) Playhouse Publishing.

Karen Poth. Three Pirates & Me. 2004. (Illus.). 32p. 7.99 (*0-310-70725-0*) Zondervan.

Karlin, Nurit. I See, You Saw. 1999. (My First I Can Read Bks.). (Illus.). 32p. (J). (ps up). pap. 3.99 (*0-06-444249-7*, Harper Trophy) HarperCollins Children's Bk. Group.

—I See, You Saw. 1999. (I Can Read Bks.). 10.10 (*0-606-16674-2*) Turtleback Bks.

Karr, Kathleen. It Ain't Always Easy, RS. 1990. (ITA., Illus.). 236p. (J). (gr. 4-7). 14.95 o.p. (*0-374-33645-8*, Farrar, Straus & Giroux (BYR)) Farrar, Straus & Giroux.

Kassem, Lou. Secret Wishes. 1989. 144p. (J). (gr. 3-7). pap. 2.95 (*0-380-75544-0*, Avon Bks.) Morrow/Avon.

Kastner, Erich. Lisa & Lottie. Books, Cyrus, tr. 1982. (Illus.). 136p. (J). (gr. 3-7). pap. 2.95 (*0-380-57117-X*, Avon Bks.) Morrow/Avon.

Kasza, Keiko. Dorotea y Miguel. Aparicio, Cristina, tr. 2001. (SPA.). (J). (ps-2). pap. 7.16 (*958-04-6033-7*) Norma S.A. COL. *Dist:* Lectorum Pubns., Inc.

—Dorothy & Mikey. 2000. (Illus.). 32p. (J). (ps-3). 12.99 (*0-399-23356-3*, G. P. Putnam's Sons) Penguin Group (USA) Inc.

—The Rat & the Tiger. 1993. (Illus.). 32p. (J). (ps-3). 14.95 o.s.i (*0-399-22404-1*, G. P. Putnam's Sons) Penguin Group (USA) Inc.

Katchen, Carole. Your Friend Annie. 1989. (J). pap. 2.75 o.p. (*0-590-42732-6*) Scholastic, Inc.

Kathan, Christine. Ashford's Prayer. 2001. (Illus.). 32p. (J). (ps-3). pap. 7.50 (*1-884083-68-4*) Maval Publishing, Inc.

—La Oracion de Ashford. 2001. Tr. of Ashford's Prayer. (SPA., Illus.). 32p. (J). (gr. k-3). pap. 7.50 (*1-59134-013-6*); pap. 7.50 (*1-884083-65-X*) Maval Publishing, Inc.

Katschke, Judy. Shore Thing. 2001. (Two of a Kind Ser.: No. 17). (Illus.). 112p. (gr. 3-7). mass mkt. 4.99 (*0-06-106657-5*, HarperEntertainment) Morrow/Avon.

Katz, Welwyn W. False Face. (J). 1991. mass mkt. o.s.i (*0-440-80242-3*, Dell Books for Young Readers); 1990. 208p. mass mkt. 3.50 o.s.i (*0-440-20676-6*, Laurel Leaf) Random Hse. Children's Bks.

Katz, Welwyn W., ed. Time Ghost. 1995. 144p. (J). (gr. 4-7). per. 16.00 (*0-689-80027-4*, McElderry, Margaret K.) Simon & Schuster Children's Publishing.

Kawai'ae'a, Keiki. Ke Nui A'e Au. 1995. (Illus.). (J). 14.95 o.p. (*0-9645646-1-0*) Aha Punana Leo.

Kay, Catherine. When I'm by Myself. 1998. (Sis & Beezie Ser.: Vol. 1). (Illus.). 32p. (J). (ps-6). 17.95 (*0-9663651-0-0*) Portos Publishing Co.

Kaye, Marilyn. Cabin Six Plays Cupid. 1989. (Camp Sunnyside Friends Ser.: No. 2). 128p. (Orig.). (J). (ps-8). pap. 2.95 (*0-380-75701-X*, Avon Bks.) Morrow/Avon.

—Camp Sunnyside Friends No. 16: Happily Ever After. 1992. 128p. (Orig.). (J). pap. 3.50 (*0-380-76555-1*, Avon Bks.) Morrow/Avon.

—No Boys Allowed. 1989. (Camp Sunnyside Friends Ser.: No. 1). 128p. (Orig.). (J). (ps-8). pap. 2.95 (*0-380-75700-1*, Avon Bks.) Morrow/Avon.

—Three of a Kind No. 1: With Friends Like These, Who Needs Enemies. 1994. 144p. (J). (gr. 4-7). mass mkt. 3.50 o.p. (*0-06-106001-1*, HarperTorch) Morrow/Avon.

—Three of a Kind No. 4: Two's Company, Four's a Crowd. 1991. 144p. (J). (gr. 4-7). mass mkt. 3.50 o.p. (*0-06-106058-5*, HarperTorch) Morrow/Avon.

—Three of a Kind No. 5: Cat Morgan, Working Girl. 1991. 144p. (J). (gr. 4-7). mass mkt. 3.50 o.p. (*0-06-106059-3*, HarperTorch) Morrow/Avon.

—Too Many Counselors. 1990. (Camp Sunnyside Friends Ser.: No. 8). 128p. (J). pap. 2.95 (*0-380-75913-6*, Avon Bks.) Morrow/Avon.

—Will You Cross Me? 1985. (I Can Read Bks.). (Illus.). 32p. (J). (ps-3). lib. bdg. 10.89 o.p. (*0-06-023103-3*) HarperCollins Children's Bk. Group.

Keaney, Brian. Don't Hang About. 1987. 114p. (YA). (gr. 7 up). 14.95 o.p. (*0-19-271532-1*) Oxford Univ. Pr., Inc.

Keats, Ezra Jack. Apt. 3. 2002. (Illus.). (J). 22.72 (*0-7587-1965-5*) Book Wholesalers, Inc.

—Apt. 3. 1999. (Illus.). 32p. (J). (ps-3). pap. 6.99 (*0-14-056507-8*) Penguin Putnam Bks. for Young Readers.

—Louie's Search. rev. ed. 1983. (Illus.). 40p. (J). (ps-3). lib. bdg. 16.89 (*0-688-02383-5*, Greenwillow Bks.) HarperCollins Children's Bk. Group.

—Over in the Meadow. 1999. (Illus.). 32p. (J). (ps-3). 16.99 (*0-670-88344-1*) Penguin Putnam Bks. for Young Readers.

Keehn, Sally M. I Am Regina. 2001. (Novels Ser.). 240p. (YA). (gr. 5-7). pap. 5.99 (*0-698-11920-7*, Puffin Bks.) Penguin Putnam Bks. for Young Readers.

Keene, Carolyn. Between the Lines. 1990. (River Heights Ser.: No. 5). 160p. (Orig.). (YA). (gr. 6 up). pap. 2.95 (*0-671-67763-2*, Simon Pulse) Simon & Schuster Children's Publishing.

—Hard to Handle. 1991. (River Heights Ser.: No. 12). 160p. (Orig.). (YA). (gr. 6 up). pap. 2.95 (*0-671-73116-5*, Simon Pulse) Simon & Schuster Children's Publishing.

—Love & Games. Greenberg, Anne, ed. 1992. (River Heights Ser.: No. 14). 160p. (Orig.). (YA). (gr. 6 up). pap. 2.99 (*0-671-73118-1*, Simon Pulse) Simon & Schuster Children's Publishing.

—A Mind of Her Own. Greenberg, Ann, ed. 1991. (River Heights Ser.: No. 14). 160p. (Orig.). (YA). (gr. 6 up). pap. 2.99 (*0-671-73117-3*, Simon Pulse) Simon & Schuster Children's Publishing.

—New Lives, New Loves. 1995. (Nancy Drew on Campus Ser.: No. 1). 192p. (YA). (gr. 8 up). pap. 3.99 (*0-671-52737-1*, Simon Pulse) Simon & Schuster Children's Publishing.

Keeshan, Robert. Hurry, Murray, Hurry! 1996. (Illus.). 32p. (J). (gr. 4-7). 14.95 o.p. (*0-925190-84-5*) Fairview Pr.

Keeton, Elizabeth B. Second-Best Friend. 1985. 180p. (J). (gr. 4-7). 12.95 o.s.i (*0-689-31096-X*, Atheneum) Simon & Schuster Children's Publishing.

Keffer, Lois. Think Slink! Think! (Pond Pals Ser.). (Illus.). 16p. (J). bds. 10.99 (*0-7814-3728-8*) Cook Communications Ministries.

—Twinkle's Book of Hope. (Pond Pals Ser.). (Illus.). 16p. (J). bds. 10.99 (*0-7814-3727-X*) Cook Communications Ministries.

Kehret, Peg. The Richest Kids in Town. 1994. 128p. (YA). (gr. 4 up). 13.99 o.p. (*0-525-65166-7*, Dutton Children's Bks.) Penguin Putnam Bks. for Young Readers.

—The Richest Kids in Town. 1997. (J). 10.04 (*0-606-11796-2*) Turtleback Bks.

—The Stranger Next Door. 2003. (Illus.). 176p. pap. 5.99 (*0-14-250178-6*, Puffin Bks.); 2002. 160p. (J). (gr. 4-8). 15.99 (*0-525-46829-3*, Dutton Children's Bks.) Penguin Putnam Bks. for Young Readers.

Keister, Douglas. El Regalo de Fernando. 1998. Tr. of Fernando's Gift. (SPA., Illus.). 32p. (J). (ps-3). pap. 6.95 (*0-87156-927-2*) Sierra Club Bks.

—El Regalo de Fernando. 1998. (Sierra Club Bks.).Tr. of Fernando's Gift. (J). 13.10 (*0-606-13382-8*) Turtleback Bks.

Keizer, Garret. God of Beer. 256p. (J). 2003. pap. 6.99 (*0-06-447276-0*); 2002. (gr. 8 up). 15.95 (*0-06-029456-6*); 2002. (gr. 8 up). lib. bdg. 15.89 (*0-06-029457-4*) HarperCollins Children's Bk. Group.

Keller, Beverly. Fiona's Bee. 1975. (Break-of-Day Bks.). (Illus.). 48p. (J). (gr. 1-4). 6.99 o.p. (*0-698-30595-7*) Putnam Publishing Group, The.

—The Genuine, Ingenious, Thrift Shop Genie, Clarissa Mae Bean & Me. 1977. (Illus.). (J). (gr. 3-6). 6.95 o.p. (*0-698-20433-6*) Putnam Publishing Group, The.

Keller, Charles. Norma Lee I Don't Knock on Doors: Knock Knock Jokes. 1983. (Illus.). 44p. (J). (gr. 3-7). 9.95 o.s.i (*0-13-623587-5*) Prentice Hall PTR.

Keller, Debra & McNeill, Shannon. The Trouble with Mister. 1999. (Endangered Species Ser.). (Illus.). 32p. (J). (ps-3). pap. 6.95 o.p. (*0-8118-2337-7*) Chronicle Bks. LLC.

Keller, Holly. Farfallina & Marcel. 2002. (Illus.). 32p. (J). 15.99 (*0-06-623932-X*); lib. bdg. 17.89 (*0-06-623933-8*) HarperCollins Children's Bk. Group. (Greenwillow Bks.).

—Harry & Tuck. 1993. (Illus.). 24p. (J). (ps up). 14.00 o.p. (*0-688-11462-8*, Greenwillow Bks.) HarperCollins Children's Bk. Group.

—Rosata. 1995. (Illus.). 32p. (J). (ps up). 15.00 o.p. (*0-688-05320-3*); lib. bdg. 14.93 o.p. (*0-688-05321-1*) HarperCollins Children's Bk. Group. (Greenwillow Bks.).

Kellogg, Steven. Best Friends. 1992. 32p. pap. 6.99 (*0-14-054607-3*) Penguin Putnam Bks. for Young Readers.

—Best Friends. Fogelman, Phyllis J., ed. 1990. (Illus.). 32p. (J). (ps-3). pap. 4.99 o.p. (*0-8037-0829-7*, Dial Bks. for Young Readers) Penguin Putnam Bks. for Young Readers.

—Best Friends. 1986. (Illus.). 32p. (J). (ps-3). 16.99 (*0-8037-0099-7*); 13.89 o.p. (*0-8037-0101-2*) Penguin Putnam Bks. for Young Readers. (Dial Bks. for Young Readers).

—Best Friends. 1986. (J). 12.14 (*0-606-03075-1*) Turtleback Bks.

—Can I Keep Him? 1976. (Pied Piper Bks.). (Illus.). 32p. (J). (gr. k-3). pap. 4.99 o.p. (*0-8037-1305-3*, Dial Bks. for Young Readers) Penguin Putnam Bks. for Young Readers.

—Ralph's Secret Weapon. 1986. (Pied Piper Bks.). (Illus.). 32p. (J). (ps-3). pap. 4.95 o.s.i (*0-8037-0024-5*, Dial Bks. for Young Readers) Penguin Putnam Bks. for Young Readers.

—Tallyho, Pinkerton! 1985. (Pied Piper Bks.). (Illus.). 32p. (J). (ps-3). pap. 4.95 o.p. (*0-8037-0166-7*, Dial Bks. for Young Readers) Penguin Putnam Bks. for Young Readers.

—Won't Somebody Play With Me? 1994. 32p. pap. 5.99 o.s.i (*0-14-054729-0*) Penguin Putnam Bks. for Young Readers.

Kelly, Theresa. Dream a Little Dream. 2000. (Aloha Cove Ser.: Vol. 7). (Illus.). 254p. (J). (gr. 7-11). 5.99 (*0-570-07072-4*) Concordia Publishing Hse.

Kemper, Kristen. What a Friend! Friendship Tips from 2 Grrrls. 2000. (Two Grrrls Ser.: Vol. 2). (Illus.). 64p. (J). (gr. 4-7). mass mkt. 3.99 (*0-439-20893-9*) Scholastic, Inc.

Kennedy, Elba H. Danny & Tommy Show & Tell. 1988. (Illus.). 89p. (J). 6.95 o.p. (*0-533-07489-4*) Vantage Pr., Inc.

Kennedy, M. L. Almost Like a Sister. 1986. 192p. (Orig.). (J). (gr. 6-8). pap. 2.50 o.p. (*0-590-33957-5*, Scholastic Paperbacks) Scholastic, Inc.

Kennedy, X. J. Brats. 1995. (Illus.). (J). (gr. 3 up). pap. 3.95 o.s.i (*0-689-71884-5*, Aladdin) Simon & Schuster Children's Publishing.

Kent, Deborah. Too Soon to Say Good-Bye. 1996. (J). mass mkt. 3.50 o.p. (*0-590-47798-6*) Scholastic, Inc.

—Too Soon to Say Good-Bye. 1996. 8.60 o.p. (*0-606-09982-4*) Turtleback Bks.

—Why Me? 1992. (J). (gr. 4-7). pap. 3.50 (*0-590-44179-5*) Scholastic, Inc.

—Why Me? 1992. (J). 8.60 o.p. (*0-606-02991-5*) Turtleback Bks.

Kent, Gordon. All Day Suckers. 1992. (Widgets Ser.). (J). (gr. 2). lib. bdg. 13.99 (*1-56239-155-0*); lib. bdg. 19.98 (*1-56239-156-9*) ABDO Publishing Co.

Kent, Jack. Socks for Supper. 1993. (Parents Magazine Read Aloud Original Ser.). (J). lib. bdg. 17.27 o.p. (*0-8368-0975-0*) Stevens, Gareth Inc.

Kent, Renee Holmes. Adventures in Misty Falls. 2001. (Adventures in Misty Falls Ser.: Vol. 8). (Illus.). 101p. (J). (gr. 4-7). pap. 4.99 (*1-56309-456-8*) Woman's Missionary Union.

—Best Friends Forever? 2000. (Adventures in Misty Falls Ser.: Bk. 2). (Illus.). v, 112p. (J). (gr. 4-7). 4.99 (*1-56309-734-6*) Woman's Missionary Union.

—Girl Talk. 2001. (Adventures in Misty Falls Ser.: Vol. 7). (Illus.). 106p. (J). (gr. 4-7). pap. 4.99 (*1-56309-455-X*, New Hope) Woman's Missionary Union.

Kent, Richard. The Mosquito Test. Weinberger, Jane, ed. 1994. 250p. (Orig.). (YA). (gr. 8-12). pap. 8.95 (*1-883650-03-8*) Windswept Hse. Pubs.

Kern, Jennifer A. & Elliott, Bill. Cindy Snake in the Adventure of Skull Mountain. l.t. ed. 1994. (Jimmy Roo Adventure Ser.: No. 2). (Illus.). 100p. (J). (gr. k-6). 14.95 (*1-888086-00-9*, 1-A) New Era Publishing Co.

—Golly Cricket in the Adventure of the Spider King. l.t. ed. 1994. (Jimmy Roo Adventure Ser.: No. 3). (Illus.). 110p. (J). (gr. k-6). 14.95 (*1-888086-01-7*, 1-B) New Era Publishing Co.

Kerr, Judith. Mog & Barnaby. (J). (*0-00-195978-6*) HarperCollins Pubs. Canada, Ltd.

—Mog & Me. 2002. (Illus.). 18p. (J). 4.50 (*0-00-138416-3*) HarperCollins Pubs. Ltd. GBR. *Dist:* Trafalgar Square.

Kerr, M. E. Fell Down. 1993. (Charlotte Zolotow Bk.). 208p. (YA). (gr. 7 up). pap. 3.95 o.p. (*0-06-447086-5*, Harper Trophy) HarperCollins Children's Bk. Group.

—I Stay Near You: 1 Story in 3. 1997. 208p. (YA). (gr. 7 up). pap. 6.00 (*0-15-201420-9*, Harcourt Paperbacks) Harcourt Children's Bks.

—Little Little. 1991. (Trophy Keypoint Bks.). 256p. (J). (gr. 7 up). mass mkt. 5.99 (*0-06-447061-X*, Harper Trophy) HarperCollins Children's Bk. Group.

—Night Kites. 1987. (Trophy Keypoint Bks.). 256p. (J). (gr. 7 up). mass mkt. 5.99 (*0-06-447035-0*, Harper Trophy) HarperCollins Children's Bk. Group.

—Night Kites. 1987. 11.00 (*0-606-03523-0*) Turtleback Bks.

Kessler, Christina. No Condition Is Permanent. 2000. (Illus.). 183p. (J). (gr. 5-9). 17.99 (*0-399-23486-1*, Philomel) Penguin Putnam Bks. for Young Readers.

Kessler, Leonard. Aqui Viene el Que Se Poncha! González, Tomás, tr. 1995. Tr. of Here Comes the Strikeout. (SPA., Illus.). 64p. (J). (gr. 1-3). 13.95 o.p. (*0-06-025437-8*); pap. 3.50 o.p. (*0-06-444189-X*, Harper Trophy) HarperCollins Children's Bk. Group.

—Last One in Is a Rotten Egg. 2002. (Illus.). (J). 11.91 (*0-7587-6178-3*) Book Wholesalers, Inc.

—Last One in Is a Rotten Egg. 1999. (I Can Read Bks.). (Illus.). 64p. (J). (gr. k-3). lib. bdg. 14.89 (*0-06-028485-4*) HarperCollins Children's Bk. Group.

—Last One in Is a Rotten Egg. abr. ed. 1969. (I Can Read Bks.). (Illus.). 64p. (J). (ps-3). 8.95 incl. audio (*1-55994-356-4*, 285382, HarperAudio) HarperTrade.

—Last One in Is a Rotten Egg. 1969. (I Can Read Bks.). (J). (gr. 1-3). 10.10 (*0-606-04263-6*) Turtleback Bks.

Keyes, Marian. Lucy Sullivan Is Getting Married. 2000. 624p. mass mkt. 6.99 (*0-380-79610-4*); 1999. 448p. 24.00 (*0-380-97618-8*) Morrow/Avon. (Avon Bks.).

Khan, Nahnatchka, ed. Old Best Friend. 1999. (Illus.). 24p. (J). (gr. k-3). pap. text 3.99 o.p. (*0-307-13147-5*, Golden Bks.) Random Hse. Children's Bks.

Khan, Rukhsana. Dahling, If You Luv Me, Would You Please, Please Smile. l.t. ed. 1999. 196p. (YA). (gr. 7-9). pap. 8.95 (*0-7737-6016-4*) Stoddart Kids CAN. *Dist:* Fitzhenry & Whiteside, Ltd.

Kidd, Ronald. Building Friends. (Illus.). 32p. (YA). text (*1-887921-26-5*) Habitat for Humanity International.

—Building Friends (Edificando Amistades) 1996. (SPA.). 32p. (YA). (gr. 1-4). 14.95 (*1-887921-28-1*) Habitat for Humanity International.

—Dunker. 1984. 176p. (YA). (gr. 5 up). mass mkt. 2.50 o.s.i (*0-553-26431-1*) Bantam Bks.

—That's What Friends Are For. 1978. (J). reprint ed. 6.95 o.p. (*0-525-66614-1*, Dutton Children's Bks.) Penguin Putnam Bks. for Young Readers.

—Trading Places. 1999. (Golden Book Ser.). (Illus.). 24p. (J). (gr. k-3). pap. 1.69 o.p. (*0-307-13258-7*, Golden Bks.) Random Hse. Children's Bks.

Kiesel, Stanley. Skinny Malinky Leads the War for Kidness. 1985. 176p. (J). (gr. 7 up). pap. 2.50 (*0-380-69875-7*, Avon Bks.) Morrow/Avon.

—Skinny Malinky Leads the War for Kidness. 1984. 176p. (J). (gr. 7 up). 12.95 o.p. (*0-525-66918-3*, 01258-370, Dutton Children's Bks.) Penguin Putnam Bks. for Young Readers.

Kieveach, Marshal. Counting on Cold Friends. 1992. (J). (ps-3). 3.99 o.p. (*0-8431-3426-7*, Price Stern Sloan) Penguin Putnam Bks. for Young Readers.

Kilborne, Sarah S. Peach & Blue. 1994. (Illus.). 40p. (J). (gr. k-3). 18.00 o.s.i (*0-679-83929-1*, Knopf Bks. for Young Readers) Random Hse. Children's Bks.

—Peach & Blue. 1998. 13.14 (*0-606-13697-5*) Turtleback Bks.

Kilborne, Sarah S., illus. Peach & Blue. 1998. 32p. (J). (gr. k-3). pap. 6.99 (*0-679-89095-5*) Knopf, Alfred A. Inc.

Killien, Christi. Putting on an Act. 1986. (YA). (gr. 5 up). 12.95 o.p. (*0-395-41027-4*) Houghton Mifflin Co.

Killilea, Marie. Newf. 1996. (J). 11.15 o.p. (*0-606-11680-X*) Turtleback Bks.

Kilphuis, Christine. Robbie & Ronnie. 2002. (Illus.). 48p. (J). (gr. 1-3). 13.95 (*0-7358-1626-3*); lib. bdg. 14.50 (*0-7358-1627-1*) North-South Bks., Inc.

Kimball, H. Maria & Mr. Feathers. 1983. (Beginning-To-Read Bks.). (Illus.). 32p. (J). (gr. k-2). 6.60 o.p. (*0-516-09690-7*, Children's Pr.) Scholastic Library Publishing.

Kimmel, Cody. Lily Pages. 2003. 256p. (J). 15.99 (*0-06-000586-6*) HarperCollins Pubs.

Kimmel, Elizabeth Cody. Lily Pages. 2003. 256p. (J). lib. bdg. 16.89 (*0-06-000587-4*) HarperCollins Pubs.

—Visiting Miss Caples. 176p. (YA). (gr. 5-9). 2001. pap. 5.99 o.s.i (*0-14-230029-2*, Puffin Bks.); 2000. 17.99 o.p. (*0-8037-2502-7*, Dial Bks. for Young Readers) Penguin Putnam Bks. for Young Readers.

Kimpel, Linda S. Charlie Chose a Champion; Shawn's Tiny Ship; Soldiers, Jeeps & Jelly Beans. l.t. ed. 1998. (Speech Creature Ser.). (Illus.). 24p. (J). (ps-3). pap. 24.95 (*1-893240-00-2*) Chestleigh's Bks. Publishing Co.

Kindig, Tess Eileen. March Mania. 2000. (Slam Dunk Ser.: Vol. 6). 95p. (J). (gr. 1-4). 4.99 (*0-570-07092-9*) Concordia Publishing Hse.

—Muggsy Makes an Assist. 2000. (Slam Dunk Ser.: Vol. 3). (J). (gr. 1-4). (Illus.). 94p. pap. 4.99 (*0-570-07018-X*);Vol. 4. 96p. pap. 4.99 (*0-570-07019-8*) Concordia Publishing Hse.

Kindred, Wendy. Hank & Fred. 1976. (J). (gr. 1-3). o.p. (*0-397-31672-0*) HarperCollins Children's Bk. Group.

King, Deborah. Custer: The Story of a Horse. 1992. (Illus.). 32p. (J). (ps-3). 14.95 o.p. (*0-399-22147-6*, Philomel) Penguin Putnam Bks. for Young Readers.

King, Larry L. Because of Lozo Brown. 1990. 320p. (J). (ps-3). pap. 3.95 o.s.i (*0-14-050593-8*, Puffin Bks.) Penguin Putnam Bks. for Young Readers.

King-Smith, Dick. Mr. Potter's Pet. 1996. (Illus.). (J). (gr. 2-5). 62p. 13.95 (*0-7868-0174-3*); 128p. lib. bdg. 14.49 o.p. (*0-7868-2146-9*) Hyperion Bks. for Children.

—Three Terrible Trins. 1997. (J). 11.04 (*0-606-11985-X*) Turtleback Bks.

King, Zachary X. & Tompkins-Brown, Barbara. Mizzy & Zizzy Learn to Share. 1996. (Mizzy & Zizzy Ser.). (Illus.). 32p. 14.99 (*1-886290-00-8*); pap. 6.99 (*1-886290-01-6*); (J). lib. bdg. 21.99 (*1-886290-13-X*) Brown, Jack Enterprises.

Kingston, George. Goldilocks Makes Friends. 1999. (Illus.). 52p. (J). 7.95 (*0-9669852-0-6*) G Sharp Productions.

Kinsey-Warnock, Natalie. Best of Friends. 2015. 64p. 15.99 (*0-525-65260-4*) Penguin Putnam Bks. for Young Readers.

Kirby, Susan E. Goodbye, Desert Rose. 1995. (Main Street Ser.: Vol. 4). 128p. (J). (gr. 3-6). pap. 3.50 (*0-380-77409-7*, Avon Bks.) Morrow/Avon.

Kiser, SuAnn. Hazel Saves the Day. 1994. (Easy-to-Read Bks.). (Illus.). 48p. (J). 12.99 o.s.i (*0-8037-1488-2*); 12.89 o.p. (*0-8037-1489-0*) Penguin Putnam Bks. for Young Readers. (Dial Bks. for Young Readers).

Kiss, Kathrin. Que Hace un Cocodrilo por la Noche? 2001. (SPA., Illus.). (J). (gr. k-3). (*84-88342-18-7*, KK8906) S.A. Kokinos ESP. *Dist:* Lectorum Pubns., Inc.

Kitchen, Bert. And So They Build. (Illus.). 32p. (J). (ps-3). 1995. bds. 5.99 (*1-56402-502-0*); 1993. 15.95 o.p. (*1-56402-217-X*) Candlewick Pr.

—And So They Build. 1995. 12.14 (*0-606-07194-6*) Turtleback Bks.

Kitten's New Friend. 2002. 10p. (J). bds. 2.50 (*1-56021-397-3*) W.J. Fantasy, Inc.

Kittinger, Jo S. Un Almuerzo con Ponche. 2003. (Rookie Reader Espanol Ser.). (SPA., Illus.). (J). lib. bdg. 15.00 (*0-516-25892-3*, Children's Pr.) Scholastic Library Publishing.

Klar, Elizabeth. Lily's Crossing. Robbins, Dawn Michelle, ed. 2000. (J). 9.95 (*1-58130-644-X*); 11.95 (*1-58130-645-8*) Novel Units, Inc.

Klas, Nell. McDurfee: Billy's Special Pal. 1991. (Illus.). 20p. (Orig.). (J). (gr. k-3). pap. 4.00 (*0-9628560-0-2*) Klas, Nell.

Klass, Sheila S. Alive & Starting Over. 1985. 128p. (YA). (gr. 7 up). mass mkt. 1.95 o.s.i (*0-449-70099-2*, Fawcett) Ballantine Bks.

—The Bennington Stitch. 1986. 144p. (YA). (gr. 7-12). mass mkt. 2.50 o.s.i (*0-553-26049-9*) Bantam Bks.

—Next Stop: Nowhere. 1995. (Illus.). 176p. (YA). (gr. 7-9). pap. 14.95 (*0-590-46686-0*) Scholastic, Inc.

—Page Four. 1987. 176p. (YA). mass mkt. 2.95 o.s.i (*0-553-26901-1*, Starfire) Random Hse. Children's Bks.

—The Uncivil War. 1999. 176p. (gr. 4-7). pap. text 4.50 (*0-440-41572-1*) Bantam Bks.

—The Uncivil War. 1997. 162p. (J). (gr. 3-7). tchr. ed. 15.95 (*0-8234-1329-2*) Holiday Hse., Inc.

—The Uncivil War. 1999. 10.55 (*0-606-17477-X*) Turtleback Bks.

Klaveness, Jan O. The Griffin Legacy. 1985. (J). (gr. 4-6). pap. 3.25 o.s.i (*0-440-43165-4*, Yearling) Random Hse. Children's Bks.

Klein, Norma. Give & Take: A Novel. 1985. 224p. (J). (gr. 7 up). 15.95 o.p. (*0-670-80651-X*) Viking Penguin.

—Just Friends. 1991. 160p. (YA). (gr. 7 up). mass mkt. 4.50 o.s.i (*0-449-70352-5*, Fawcett) Ballantine Bks.

—Just Friends. 1990. 192p. (YA). (gr. 7 up). 12.95 o.s.i (*0-679-80213-4*, Knopf Bks. for Young Readers) Random Hse. Children's Bks.

—Tomboy. 1982. (J). (gr. 3-5). pap. (*0-671-45533-8*, Simon Pulse) Simon & Schuster Children's Publishing.

Klein, Robin. Enemies. 1989. (Illus.). 8p. (J). (gr. 2-5). 11.95 o.p. (*0-525-44479-3*, Dutton Children's Bks.) Penguin Putnam Bks. for Young Readers.

—Enemies. 1991. (J). (gr. 4-7). pap. 2.50 o.p. (*0-590-43689-9*) Scholastic, Inc.

Klein, William H. My Friendship Cross. 1998. (Illus.). 48p. (J). pap. text 12.99 o.p. (*0-8054-1716-8*) Broadman & Holman Pubs.

Kleitsch, Christel & Stephens, Paul. Dancing Feathers. 1996. (Illus.). 96p. (J). (gr. 3-7). pap. 5.95 (*0-920303-25-0*) Annick Pr., Ltd. CAN. *Dist:* Firefly Bks., Ltd.

Kleven, Elisa. Ernst. 1993. (Illus.). 32p. (J). (ps-3). pap. 4.50 o.s.i (*0-14-054944-7*, Puffin Bks.) Penguin Putnam Bks. for Young Readers.

Klevin, Jill R. The Best of Friends. 1981. 176p. (Orig.). (J). (gr. 7 up). pap. 2.25 o.p. (*0-590-33782-3*) Scholastic, Inc.

Kline, Lisa Williams. The Princesses of Atlantis. 2002. (Illus.). 192p. (J). 16.95 (*0-8126-2855-1*) Cricket Bks.

Kline, Suzy. Herbie Jones & Hamburger Head. (Herbie Jones Ser.). 112p. (J). 2002. (Illus.). pap. 4.99 (*0-698-11940-1*, PaperStar); 1991. (gr. 4-7). pap. 3.99 o.s.i (*0-14-034583-3*, Puffin Bks.); 1989. (Illus.). (gr. 2-6). 13.95 o.s.i (*0-399-21748-7*, G. P. Putnam's Sons) Penguin Putnam Bks. for Young Readers.

—Herbie Jones & Hamburger Head. 1991. (J). 10.04 (*0-606-00498-X*) Turtleback Bks.

—Herbie Jones & the Birthday Showdown. 1993. 96p. (J). (gr. 2-6). 14.95 o.p. (*0-399-22600-1*, G. P. Putnam's Sons) Penguin Group (USA) Inc.

—Herbie Jones & the Birthday Showdown. 1995. (Herbie Jones Ser.). (Illus.). 96p. (J). pap. 3.99 o.s.i (*0-14-037500-7*, Puffin Bks.) Penguin Putnam Bks. for Young Readers.

—Herbie Jones & the Birthday Showdown. 1995. 9.09 o.p. (*0-606-07638-7*) Turtleback Bks.

—Herbie Jones Moves On. 2003. 80p. (J). 14.99 (*0-399-23635-X*, G. P. Putnam's Sons) Penguin Putnam Bks. for Young Readers.

—Horrible Harry & the Dragon War. 2002. (Illus.). 64p. (J). (gr. 1-3). text 13.99 (*0-670-03559-9*) Penguin Putnam Bks. for Young Readers.

—Horrible Harry & the Purple People. 1997. (Horrible Harry Ser.: No. 8). (Illus.). 64p. (J). (gr. 2-4). 13.99 (*0-670-87035-8*) Penguin Putnam Bks. for Young Readers.

—Horrible Harry in Room 2B. (Horrible Harry Ser.: No. 1). (Illus.). 64p. (J). (gr. 2-4). 1997. pap. 3.99 (*0-14-038552-5*); 1990. pap. 3.99 o.s.i (*0-14-032825-4*) Penguin Putnam Bks. for Young Readers. (Puffin Bks.).

—Marvin & the Meanest Girl. 2000. (Illus.). 70p. (J). (gr. 2-3). 14.99 (*0-399-23409-8*, G. P. Putnam's Sons) Penguin Group (USA) Inc.

—Marvin & the Meanest Girl. 2002. (Chapters Ser.). (Illus.). 80p. pap. 4.99 (*0-698-11967-3*, PaperStar) Penguin Putnam Bks. for Young Readers.

—Molly's in a Mess. 1999. (Illus.). 71p. (J). (gr. 1-4). 14.99 (*0-399-23131-5*) Penguin Group (USA) Inc.

—Molly's in a Mess. 2002. (Chapters Ser.). (Illus.). 80p. pap. 4.99 (*0-698-11928-2*, Puffin Bks.) Penguin Putnam Bks. for Young Readers.

—Orp & the FBI. 1995. 100p. (J). (gr. 4-7). 14.99 o.p. (*0-399-22664-8*, G. P. Putnam's Sons) Penguin Group (USA) Inc.

—Song Lee & the Leech Man. 1997. (Puffin Chapters Ser.). (J). 10.14 (*0-606-11862-4*) Turtleback Bks.

—Song Lee in Room 2B. (Song Lee Ser.). 64p. 1999. (J). (gr. 2-5). pap. 3.99 (*0-14-130408-1*, Puffin Bks.); 1995. pap. 3.99 o.s.i (*0-14-036316-5*, Puffin Bks.); 1993. (Illus.). (J). (gr. 2-5). 13.99 o.s.i (*0-670-84772-0*, Viking Children's Bks.) Penguin Putnam Bks. for Young Readers.

—Song Lee in Room 2B. 1995. (J). 10.14 (*0-606-08182-8*) Turtleback Bks.

—What's the Matter with Herbie Jones? 1986. (Illus.). 96p. (J). (gr. 2-6). 13.95 o.p. (*0-399-21315-5*, G. P. Putnam's Sons) Penguin Putnam Bks. for Young Readers.

—Who's Orp's Girlfriend? 1993. 112p. (J). (gr. 3-6). 13.95 o.s.i (*0-399-22431-9*, G. P. Putnam's Sons) Penguin Group (USA) Inc.

Kline, Suzy Remkiewicz, ed. Horrible Harry & the Dragon War. 2003. (Illus.). 64p. pap. 3.99 (*0-14-250166-2*, Puffin Bks.) Penguin Putnam Bks. for Young Readers.

Klingel/Noyed. The Amazing Letter Z. 2003. (Alphaphonics Ser.). (Illus.). 24p. (J). (ps-3). lib. bdg. 24.21 (*1-59296-116-9*) Child's World, Inc.

Klisiewicz, Jim. Who Is My Friend? 1977. (Illus.). (J). (gr. 5 up). 4.50 o.p. (*0-533-02884-1*) Vantage Pr., Inc.

Klopp, Barbara Murray. Alex & Zig. 1997. (Illus.). 52p. (J). (ps-7). spiral bd. 10.95 (*0-9659428-0-5*) Klopp, Barbara Murray.

Klugman, Miriam. Captain David. 1991. 100p. (J). 11.95 (*1-56062-095-1*, CJR129H); pap. 7.95 o.p. (*1-56062-096-X*) CIS Communications, Inc.

Klusmeyer, Joann. The Us 4 Ever Club. 1987. (Illus.). 96p. (J). (gr. 4-7). pap. 3.99 o.s.i (*0-570-03644-5*, 39-1128) Concordia Publishing Hse.

Knaff, Jean C. Manhattan. 1987. (Illus.). 32p. (J). (ps up). bds. o.p. (*0-571-14653-8*) Faber & Faber Ltd.

Knorr, Dandi D. A Super Friend. 1987. (Jenny & Josh Bks.). (Illus.). 32p. (J). (gr. 1-3). 4.99 o.p. (*0-87403-316-0*, 3546) Standard Publishing.

Know When to Stop. 1991. (Illus.). (J). (ps-2). pap. 5.10 (*0-8136-5583-8*); lib. bdg. 7.95 (*0-8136-5083-6*) Modern Curriculum Pr.

Knowles, Anne. Under the Shadow. 1983. 128p. (J). (gr. 5 up). 10.95 (*0-06-023221-8*) HarperCollins Children's Bk. Group.

Knowlton, Laurie Lazzaro, et al. Unpredictable. 2001. (TodaysGirls.com Ser.: Vol. 11). 144p. (J). (gr. 5-9). pap. 5.99 o.s.i (*0-8499-7714-2*) Nelson, Tommy.

Knox, Jeri A. Introducing Nikki & Kiana. 1993. 82p. (Orig.). (J). (gr. 6-10). pap. text 7.00 (*1-880679-03-5*) Mountaintop Bks., Inc.

Koda-Callan, Elizabeth. The Two Best Friends. 1994. (Magic Charm Book Ser.). (Illus.). 48p. (J). (ps-3). tchr. ed. 12.95 (*1-56305-730-1*, 3730) Workman Publishing Co., Inc.

Koehler-Pentacoff, Elizabeth. Too Hot Tofer. 1997. (J). 12.00 (*0-689-80542-X*, Simon & Schuster Children's Publishing) Simon & Schuster Children's Publishing.

Koehler, Phoebe. The Day We Met You. 1997. (J). 12.14 (*0-606-11242-1*) Turtleback Bks.

Koelsch, Michael, tr. & illus. Roller Hockey Rumble. 2004. (Extreme Team Ser.: Vol. 3). 64p. (J). 16.00 (*0-316-73754-2*); pap. 5.00 (*0-316-73755-0*) Little Brown & Co.

Koertge, Ronald. The Boy in the Moon. 1992. 176p. (J). pap. 3.99 o.p. (*0-380-71474-4*, Avon Bks.) Morrow/Avon.

—Boy in the Moon, Vol. 1. 1990. (J). (gr. 4-7). 15.95 o.p. (*0-316-50102-6*, Joy Street Bks.) Little Brown & Co.

—The Heart of the City. 1998. (J). (gr. 3-7). 144p. pap. 15.95 (*0-531-30078-1*); 128p. lib. bdg. 16.99 (*0-531-33078-8*) Scholastic, Inc. (Orchard Bks.).

—Mariposa Blues. 1991. (YA). 15.95 o.p. (*0-316-50103-4*) Little Brown & Co.

—Mariposa Blues. 1993. 176p. (J). mass mkt. 3.50 (*0-380-71761-1*, Avon Bks.) Morrow/Avon.

—Mariposa Blues. 1991. 8.60 o.p. (*0-606-02737-8*) Turtleback Bks.

Kohler, Christine. My Friend Is Moving. 1985. (Growing up Christian Ser.). 24p. (Orig.). (J). (ps-4). pap. 3.95 o.s.i (*0-570-04116-3*, 56-1527) Concordia Publishing Hse.

Kolar, Bob. Do You Want to Play? A Book about Being Friends. (Illus.). 32p. (ps-3). 2001. pap. 6.99 o.s.i (*0-14-056830-1*); 1999. (J). 16.99 o.p. (*0-525-45938-3*, Dutton Children's Bks.) Penguin Putnam Bks. for Young Readers.

—Do You Want to Play? A Book about Being Friends. 2001. (Illus.). (J). 13.14 (*0-606-21153-5*) Turtleback Bks.

Kollars, Helmut. The Lonely Wizard. 1998. Tr. of Es War Einmal Zauberer Ganz Allein. (Illus.). 32p. (J). (ps-3). pap. 16.95 (*1-56711-804-6*, Blackbirch Pr., Inc.) Gale Group.

Koller, Jackie French. Mole & Shrew All Year Through. Loehr, Mallory, ed. 1997. (Stepping Stone Book Ser.: Vol. 2). (Illus.). 80p. (J). (gr. 1-4). pap. 3.99 o.s.i (*0-679-88666-4*, Random Hse. Bks. for Young Readers) Random Hse. Children's Bks.

—Mole & Shrew All Year Through. 1997. (Stepping Stone Book Ser.). 10.14 (*0-606-12772-0*) Turtleback Bks.

—Mole & Shrew Are Two. Loehr, Mallory, ed. 2000. (Stepping Stone Book Ser.: No. 1). (Illus.). 64p. (J). (gr. 1-4). lib. bdg. 11.99 (*0-375-90690-8*); pap. 3.99 o.p. (*0-375-80690-3*) Random Hse. Children's Bks. (Random Hse. Bks. for Young Readers).

—Mole & Shrew Have Jobs to Do. 2001. (Stepping Stone Book Ser.: Vol. 3). (Illus.). 80p. (J). (gr. 1-4). lib. bdg. 11.99 (*0-375-90691-6*, Random Hse. Bks. for Young Readers) Random Hse. Children's Bks.

—Mole & Shrew Have Jobs to Do. 2001. (Stepping Stone Bks.). (Illus.). (J). 10.14 (*0-606-21335-X*) Turtleback Bks.

—Mole & Shrew Have Jobs to Do: Mole & Shrew. 2001. (Stepping Stone Book Ser.: Vol. 3). (Illus.). 80p. (J). (gr. k-3). pap. 3.99 o.p. (*0-375-80691-1*, Random Hse. Bks. for Young Readers) Random Hse. Children's Bks.

—Mole & Shrew Step Out. 1992. (Illus.). 32p. (J). (ps-3). 13.95 o.p. (*0-689-31713-1*, Atheneum) Simon & Schuster Children's Publishing.

—The Primrose Way. 1995. (Great Episodes Ser.). 352p. (YA). (gr. 7-12). pap. 6.00 (*0-15-200372-X*, Gulliver Bks.) Harcourt Children's Bks.

—Someday. 2002. 224p. (J). (gr. 5 up). pap. 16.95 (*0-439-29317-0*, Orchard Bks.) Scholastic, Inc.

Komaiko, Leah. Annie Bananie: Best Friends to the End. 1998. (Annie Bananie Ser.). (Illus.). 96p. (gr. 2-6). reprint ed. pap. text 3.99 o.s.i (*0-440-41036-3*, Yearling) Random Hse. Children's Bks.

—Annie Bananie & the Pain Sisters. 1998. (Annie Bananie Ser.). (Illus.). 80p. (gr. 2-6). text 14.95 o.s.i (*0-385-32118-X*, Delacorte Pr.) Dell Publishing.

—Annie Bananie & the People's Court. 1999. (Illus.). 96p. (gr. 2-6). pap. text 4.50 (*0-440-41037-1*) Dell Publishing.

—Annie Bananie & the People's Court, 10 vols. 1998. (Illus.). 96p. (gr. 2-6). text 14.95 o.s.i (*0-385-32115-5*, Dell Books for Young Readers) Random Hse. Children's Bks.

—Annie Bananie & the People's Court. 1998. (Illus.). (J). 10.04 (*0-606-18099-0*) Turtleback Bks.

—Annie Bananie, Best Friends to the End. 1997. (Illus.). 96p. text 14.95 o.s.i (*0-385-32112-0*, Dell Books for Young Readers) Random Hse. Children's Bks.

—Best Friends to the End. 1998. (Annie Bananie Ser.). (J). (gr. 2-6). 10.14 (*0-606-13143-4*) Turtleback Bks.

Konigsburg, E. L. George. 1985. 160p. (J). (gr. k-6). pap. 3.50 o.p. (*0-440-42847-5*, Yearling) Random Hse. Children's Bks.

—Jennifer, Hecate, MacBeth, William McKinley & Me, Elizabeth. 117p. (J). (gr. 3-6). pap. 4.99 (*0-8072-1417-5*, Listening Library) Random Hse. Audio Publishing Group.

—Jennifer, Hecate, Macbeth, William McKinley & Me, Elizabeth. 1999. 144p. mass mkt. 2.99 o.s.i (*0-440-22824-7*) Bantam Bks.

—Jennifer, Hecate, Macbeth, William McKinley & Me, Elizabeth. l.t. ed. 1989. (J). (gr. 3-7). reprint ed. lib. bdg. 16.95 o.s.i (*1-55736-143-6*, Cornerstone Bks.) Pages, Inc.

—Jennifer, Hecate, Macbeth, William McKinley & Me, Elizabeth. 1984. 128p. (gr. 4-7). pap. text 5.50 (*0-440-44162-5*, Yearling) Random Hse. Children's Bks.

—Jennifer, Hecate, Macbeth, William McKinley & Me, Elizabeth. 1971. (Illus.). 128p. (J). (gr. 3-5). 16.95 (*0-689-30007-7*, Atheneum) Simon & Schuster Children's Publishing.

—Jennifer, Hecate, Macbeth, William McKinley & Me, Elizabeth. 1985. (J). 11.55 (*0-606-03672-5*) Turtleback Bks.

—Jennifer, Hecate, MacBeth, William McKinley & Me, Elizabeth. unabr. ed. 1998. 177p. (J). (gr. 3-6). pap. 28.00 incl. audio (*0-8072-8001-1*, YA963SP, Listening Library) Random Hse. Audio Publishing Group.

—A Proud Taste for Scarlet & Miniver. 1985. 208p. (gr. 4-7). pap. text 4.99 (*0-440-47201-6*, Yearling) Random Hse. Children's Bks.

—Silent to the Bone. unabr. ed. 2002. 272p. (YA). (gr. 10 up). pap. 35.00 incl. audio (*0-8072-8741-5*, LYA 253 SP); 2000. (J). (ps up). audio 25.00 (*0-8072-6165-3*) Random Hse. Audio Publishing Group. (Listening Library).

—Silent to the Bone. 272p. 2004. (YA). mass mkt. 5.99 (*0-689-86715-8*, Simon Pulse); 2002. (Illus.). (J). (gr. 5-9). pap. 5.99 (*0-689-83602-3*, Aladdin); 2000. (Illus.). (J). (gr. 5-9). 16.00 (*0-689-83601-5*, Atheneum) Simon & Schuster Children's Publishing.

—Silent to the Bone. l.t. ed. 2001. (Young Adult Ser.). 271p. (J). (gr. 4-7). 23.95 (*0-7862-3169-6*) Thorndike Pr.

—The View from Saturday. 2002. (Illus.). (J). 25.11 (*0-7587-0221-3*) Book Wholesalers, Inc.

—The View from Saturday. 2000. (J). 11.95 (*1-56137-936-0*) Novel Units, Inc.

—The View from Saturday. (YA). (gr. 5 up). 280p. pap. 4.95 (*0-8072-1511-2*); 2001. audio 25.00 (*0-8072-0469-2*) Random Hse. Audio Publishing Group. (Listening Library).

—The View from Saturday. (J). 1999. pap. 2.99 (*0-689-82964-7*, Aladdin); 1998. 176p. (gr. 4-6). pap. 2.65 o.s.i (*0-689-82163-8*, Aladdin); 1998. 160p. (gr. 5-9). pap. 4.99 (*0-689-82120-4*, Aladdin); 1996. 128p. (gr. 3-7). 16.00 (*0-689-80993-X*, Atheneum); 1998. 176p. (gr. 3-7). reprint ed. pap. 4.99 (*0-689-81721-5*, Aladdin) Simon & Schuster Children's Publishing.

—The View from Saturday. l.t. ed. 2000. (Young Adult Ser.). 227p. (YA). (gr. 8-12). 20.95 (*0-7862-2691-9*) Thorndike Pr.

—The View from Saturday. 1998. (J). 11.04 (*0-606-13063-2*) Turtleback Bks.

Koontz, Robin M. Chicago & the Cat: The Family Reunion. 1999. 32p. (J). pap. 3.99 (*0-14-038650-5*, Puffin Bks.) Penguin Putnam Bks. for Young Readers.

Koontz, Robin M. Chicago & the Cat. 1993. (Illus.). 32p. (J). (gr. k-3). 12.00 o.p. (*0-525-65097-0*, Dutton Children's Bks.) Penguin Putnam Bks. for Young Readers.

—Chicago & the Cat. 2002. (J). E-Book (*1-59019-758-5*); 1993. E-Book (*1-59019-759-3*) ipicturebooks, LLC.

Koopmans, Loek. Any Room for Me? 1992. (Illus.). 28p. (J). (ps-k). 14.95 (*0-86315-160-4*, 1644) Floris Bks. GBR. *Dist:* Gryphon Hse., Inc., Steinerbooks, Inc.

Korman, Gordon. MacDonald Hall Goes Hollywood. 1991. 224p. (J). (gr. 3-7). pap. 13.95 o.p. (*0-590-43940-5*) Scholastic, Inc.

—Our Man Weston. 1986. (J). mass mkt. 2.95 o.p. (*0-590-43755-0*); 240p. (gr. 4-6). pap. 2.50 o.p. (*0-590-41848-3*, Scholastic Paperbacks) Scholastic, Inc.

—The War with Mr. Wizzle. 1990. 192p. (J). (gr. 3-7). mass mkt. 3.25 o.p. (*0-590-44206-6*); 1983. pap. 2.50 o.p. (*0-590-40378-8*); 1983. pap. 1.95 o.p. (*0-590-32643-0*) Scholastic, Inc.

Kornblatt, Marc. Understanding Buddy. l.t. ed. 2002. 100p. (J). 21.95 (*0-7862-3712-0*) Gale Group.

—Understanding Buddy. 2001. (Illus.). 128p. (J). (gr. 4-6). 16.00 (*0-689-83215-X*, McElderry, Margaret K.) Simon & Schuster Children's Publishing.

Kornfeld, Joanne. The Chocolate Train. 2002. (Illus.). 24p. (J). (ps-4). 12.95 (*0-9704629-3-X*) Earthkids Publishing.

Kornhauser, Barry. Lincoln's Log. 1999. 96p. (YA). (gr. 5-12). pap. 7.00 (*0-87602-369-3*) Anchorage Pr.

Kornreich, Leron. Ivory Towers. 2001. (YA). 7.99 (*0-9707509-0-0*) Banana Peel Bks.

Korth-Sander, Irmtraut. Will You Be My Friend? Lanning, Rosemary, tr. from GER. 1945. (Illus.). 32p. (J). (gr. k-2). 14.95 o.p. (*1-55858-071-9*) North-South Bks., Inc.

Koss, Amy Goldman. The Ashwater Experiment. November, S., ed. 2001. 160p. (J). (gr. 4-7). pap. 5.99 o.s.i (*0-14-131092-8*, Puffin Bks.) Penguin Putnam Bks. for Young Readers.

—The Ashwater Experiment. Kane, Cindy, ed. 1999. 128p. (J). (gr. 4-8). 16.99 (*0-8037-2391-1*, Dial Bks. for Young Readers) Penguin Putnam Bks. for Young Readers.

—The Ashwater Experiment. l.t. ed. 2000. (Young Adult Ser.). 188p. (YA). (gr. 8-12). 20.95 (*0-7862-2686-2*) Thorndike Pr.

—The Ashwater Experiment. 2001. (J). 12.04 (*0-606-21046-6*) Turtleback Bks.

—The Cheat. 2004. pap. 5.99 (*0-14-240128-5*, Puffin Bks.) Penguin Putnam Bks. for Young Readers.

—The Girls. 128p. 2002. pap. 4.99 (*0-14-230033-0*, Puffin Bks.); 2000. (Illus.). (J). (gr. 5-9). 16.99 (*0-8037-2494-2*, Dial Bks. for Young Readers) Penguin Putnam Bks. for Young Readers.

—The Girls. l.t. ed. 2000. (Young Adult Ser.). (Illus.). 136p. (J). (gr. 8-12). 20.95 (*0-7862-2911-X*) Thorndike Pr.

—Gossip Times Three. 2003. 176p. (J). 16.99 (*0-8037-2849-2*, Dial Bks. for Young Readers) Penguin Putnam Bks. for Young Readers.

—The Trouble with Zinny Weston. 1998. (Illus.). 112p. (J). (gr. 4-7). 15.99 o.s.i (*0-8037-2287-7*, Dial Bks. for Young Readers) Penguin Putnam Bks. for Young Readers.

Kraft, Erik P. Lenny & Mel. (Ready-for-Chapters Ser.). (Illus.). 64p. (J). 2003. pap. 3.99 (*0-689-85891-4*, Aladdin); 2002. (gr. 2-5). 15.00 (*0-689-84173-6*, Simon & Schuster Children's Publishing) Simon & Schuster Children's Publishing.

Krahn, Fernando. Bernardo y Canelo. 1999. (Jardin de los Ninos Ser.). (SPA., Illus.). 28p. (J). (ps-1). pap. text 6.99 (*980-257-207-1*) Ekare, Ediciones VEN. *Dist:* Kane/Miller Bk. Pubs., Lectorum Pubns., Inc.

Kramer, Kay. Danny's Angel. 1980. (Illus.). 64p. (J). (ps-2). pap. 1.95 o.p. (*0-87793-203-4*) Ave Maria Pr.

Kraus, Robert. Ladybug, Ladybug. 1957. (Illus.). 28p. (J). (gr. 1 up). pap. 1.95 o.p. (*0-671-96150-0*, Simon & Schuster Children's Publishing) Simon & Schuster Children's Publishing.

—Three Friends. 1975. (Illus.). (J). (gr. k-3). 6.95 o.s.i (*0-525-61528-8*); pap. 2.95 (*0-525-62346-9*) Dutton/Plume. (Dutton).

—Three Friends. 1980. (Illus.). 32p. (J). (ps-4). pap. 3.95 o.p. (*0-671-96061-X*, Simon & Schuster Children's Publishing) Simon & Schuster Children's Publishing.

Krauss, Ruth. Un Dia Feliz. Fiol, Maria A., tr. 1995. (SPA., Illus.). 80p. (J). (gr. k-2). 14.95 o.p. (*0-06-025450-5*, HC0810) HarperCollins Children's Bk. Group.

—I'll Be You & You Be Me. 1988. (Illus.). 48p. (J). (ps-3). reprint ed. mass mkt. 3.95 o.p. (*0-590-41094-6*, Scholastic Paperbacks) Scholastic, Inc.

Krauss, Ruth & Noonan, Julia. You're Just What I Need Board Book. 1999. (Growing Tree Ser.). (Illus.). 36p. (J). (ps-k). 7.95 (*0-694-01304-8*, Harper Festival) HarperCollins Children's Bk. Group.

Krementz, Jill. Sweet Pea. 1969. (J). 5.95 o.p. (*0-15-283536-9*) Harcourt Children's Bks.

Krensky, Stephan. Scoop after Scoop: A History of Ice Cream. 1986. (Illus.). 56p. (J). (gr. 4-7). 12.95 o.s.i (*0-689-31276-8*, Atheneum) Simon & Schuster Children's Publishing.

Krensky, Stephen. Lionel & His Friends. (Easy-to-Read Ser.). (Illus.). 48p. (J). 1999. (gr. 1-4). pap. 3.99 o.s.i (*0-14-038742-0*, Puffin Bks.); 1996. (gr. 1-4). 13.99 o.p. (*0-8037-1750-4*, Dial Bks. for Young Readers); 1996. (ps-3). 13.89 o.s.i (*0-8037-1751-2*, Dial Bks. for Young Readers) Penguin Putnam Bks. for Young Readers.

—Lionel & His Friends. 2001. (J). pap., stu. ed. 23.24 incl. audio Recorded Bks., LLC.

—Lionel & His Friends. 1999. (Illus.). (J). 10.14 (*0-606-18418-X*) Turtleback Bks.

—Lionel & Louise. 1997. (Puffin Easy-to-Read Ser.). (J). 9.65 (*0-606-11564-1*) Turtleback Bks.

Krischanitz, Raoul. Molto's Dream. James, J. Alison, tr. from GER. 2001. (Illus.). 36p. (J). (gr. k-3). 15.95 o.p. (*0-7358-1507-0*, Michael Neugebauer Bks.); 16.50 o.p. (*0-7358-1508-9*) North-South Bks., Inc.

—Nobody Likes Me! 1999. (Illus.). 32p. (J). (ps-2). 16.50 (*0-7358-1055-9*) North-South Bks., Inc.

—Nobody Likes Me! Lanning, Rosemary, tr. from GER. 1999. (Illus.). 32p. (J). (ps-2). 15.95 o.s.i (*0-7358-1054-0*) North-South Bks., Inc.

Kroll, Virginia L. New Friends, True Friends, Stuck-Like-Glue Friends. 1994. (Illus.). 32p. (J). (ps). 15.00 o.p. (*0-8028-5085-5*) Eerdmans, William B. Publishing Co.

Kropp, Paul. The Countess & Me. 2003. (Illus.). (YA). pap. (*1-55041-692-8*) Fitzhenry & Whiteside, Ltd.

—Getting Even. 1986. 192p. (J). pap. 3.50 o.s.i (*0-7704-2112-1*) Bantam Bks.

—Moonkid & Liberty. unabr. ed. 1996. (Gemini Bks.). 192p. (YA). (gr. 7-10). mass mkt. 4.95 (*0-7736-7442-X*) Stoddart Kids CAN. *Dist:* Fitzhenry & Whiteside, Ltd.

Krulik, Nancy E. Floppy Friends Go to School. 1999. (Illus.). 32p. (J). (*0-439-08767-8*) Scholastic, Inc.

—Heath Ledger: The Heath Is On! 2001. (YA). (gr. 5 up). reprint ed. E-Book 4.99 (*0-7434-2777-7*, Simon Pulse) Simon & Schuster Children's Publishing.

Krull, Kathleen. Alex Fitzgerald, TV Star. 1991. (J). (ps-3). 10.95 o.p. (*0-316-50479-3*) Little Brown & Co.

—Bridges to Change. 1999. (Illus.). 48p. pap. 5.99 (*0-14-036523-0*) Viking Penguin.

Krumgold, Joseph. Onion John. (Illus.). (J). (gr. 5 up). 1987. 256p. lib. bdg. 16.89 (*0-690-04698-7*); 1959. 248p. 13.95 o.p. (*0-690-59957-9*) HarperCollins Children's Bk. Group.

Krumgold, Joseph, et al. Newbery Award Library II: And Now Miguel - Bridge to Terabithia - Sarah, Plain & Tall - The Wheel on the School, 4 bks., Set. 1988. (Trophy Bk.). (Illus.). (J). (gr. 4-7). pap. 19.80 (*0-06-440277-0*, Harper Trophy) HarperCollins Children's Bk. Group.

Krupinski, Loretta. Best Friends. 1998. (Illus.). 32p. (J). (gr. k-4). 14.95 (*0-7868-0332-0*); lib. bdg. 15.49 (*0-7868-2356-9*) Hyperion Bks. for Children.

Kruusval, Catarina. Beach Day. 1997. (Illus.). 28p. (J). (ps). 7.95 (*91-29-63923-9*) R & S Bks. SWE. *Dist:* Farrar, Straus & Giroux, Holtzbrinck Pubs.

Kuhn, Betsy. Not Exactly Nashville. 1998. 144p. (gr. 3-7). text 14.95 o.s.i (*0-385-32589-4*, Delacorte Pr.) Dell Publishing.

—Not Exactly Nashville. 1999. 144p. (gr. 3-7). pap. text 3.99 o.s.i (*0-440-41478-4*, Dell Books for Young Readers) Random Hse. Children's Bks.

—Not Exactly Nashville. 1999. 10.04 (*0-606-16708-0*) Turtleback Bks.

Kuhn, Walter N., Jr. Un Amigo Especial. Kuhn, Jean M., ed. Rivera, Norberto, tr. unabr. ed. 1997. (Freddy el Grillo y la Ciudad de Corncob Ser.: Vol. 7S). (SPA., Illus.). 20p. (J). (ps-10). spiral bd. 6.95 (*1-891547-13-5*) Hoppa Productions, Inc.

—A Special Friend (Un Amigo Especial) Rivera, Norberto, tr. unabr. ed. 1997. (Freddy Cricket & the Town of Corncob Ser.: Vol. 7C). (ENG & SPA., Illus.). 20p. (J). (ps-10). spiral bd. 6.95 (*1-891547-26-7*) Hoppa Productions, Inc.

Kuhn, Walter N., Jr. & Putney, Erika K. A Special Friend. Kuhn, Jean M., ed. unabr. ed. 1997. (Freddy Cricket & the Town of Corncob Ser.: Vol. 7). (Illus.). 20p. (J). (ps-10). spiral bd. 6.95 (*1-891547-12-7*) Hoppa Productions, Inc.

Kulling, Monica. Edgar Badger's Butterfly Day. 1999. (Illus.). 48p. (J). (gr. 1-5). pap. 4.50 (*1-57255-604-8*) Mondo Publishing.

—Edgar Badger's Fishing Day. 1999. (Illus.). 48p. (J). (gr. 1-5). pap. 4.50 (*1-57255-603-X*) Mondo Publishing.

—Waiting for Amos. 1993. (Illus.). 32p. (J). (ps-2). text 13.95 (*0-02-751245-2*, Simon & Schuster Children's Publishing) Simon & Schuster Children's Publishing.

Kurtz, Jane. Bicycle Madness, ERS. 2003. (Illus.). 128p. (J). 15.95 (*0-8050-6981-X*, Holt, Henry & Co. Bks. For Young Readers) Holt, Henry & Co.

—Does a Spider Wear a Seatbelt. 2004. (Illus.). (J). 14.00 (*0-689-84482-4*, Aladdin) Simon & Schuster Children's Publishing.

—I'm Sorry Almira Ann. 2001. pap. 10.95 (*0-439-20645-6*) Scholastic, Inc.

—I'm Sorry, Almira Ann, ERS. 1999. (Illus.). 120p. (J). (gr. 4-7). 15.95 (*0-8050-6094-4*, Holt, Henry & Co. Bks. For Young Readers) Holt, Henry & Co.

Kuskin, Karla. Just Like Everyone Else. 1982. (Trophy Picture Bk.). (Illus.). 32p. (J). (ps-3). pap. 5.95 o.s.i (*0-06-443032-4*, Harper Trophy) HarperCollins Children's Bk. Group.

Kvasnosky, Laura McGee. One Lucky Summer. 2002. (Illus.). 96p. (J). (gr. 3-6). 15.99 (*0-525-46455-7*, Dutton Children's Bks.) Penguin Putnam Bks. for Young Readers.

—Zelda & Ivy & the Boy Next Door. 1999. (Illus.). 48p. (J). (gr. k-4). 15.99 o.s.i (*0-7636-0672-3*) Candlewick Pr.

Kwitz, Mary D. Little Chick's Friend, Duckling. 1992. (I Can Read Bks.). (Illus.). 32p. (J). (ps-1). 13.00 o.p. (*0-06-023638-8*); lib. bdg. 15.89 o.p. (*0-06-023639-6*) HarperCollins Children's Bk. Group.

Kwitz, Mary Deball. Little Chick's Friend, Duckling. 1995. (I Can Read Bks.). (Illus.). 32p. (J). (ps-2). pap. 3.99 (*0-06-444179-2*, Harper Trophy) HarperCollins Children's Bk. Group.

—Little Chick's Friend, Duckling. 1995. (I Can Read Bks.). (J). (ps-1). 8.95 o.p. (*0-606-07793-6*) Turtleback Bks.

Kyi, Tanya Lloyd. Truth. 2003. (Orca Soundings Ser.). 108p. (YA). (gr. 7 up). pap. 7.95 (*1-55143-265-X*) Orca Bk. Pubs.

La Borde, Roger. Hello Kitty, Hello Love! Secret Drawer Locked Diary. 2003. (J). (gr. 2-7). 12.95 (*0-8109-8559-4*) Abrams, Harry N., Inc.

Labaronne, Charlotte. Best Friends. 2003. (Illus.). 32p. (J). pap. 16.95 (*0-439-37252-6*) Scholastic, Inc.

LaBate, Jim. Let's Go, Gaels: A Novella by Jim LaBate. 1998. (Illus.). 60p. (YA). (gr. 7-12). pap. 5.95 (*0-9662100-4-2*) Mohawk River Pr.

Labatt, Mary & Sarrazin, Marisol. A Friend for Sam. 2003. (Kids Can Read Ser.). (Illus.). 32p. (J). 14.95 (*1-55337-374-X*); pap. 3.95 (*1-55337-375-8*) Kids Can Pr., Ltd.

Label, Arnold. Days with Frog & Toad. 9999. (I Can Read Bks.). (J). (gr. 1-3). pap. 1.95 o.s.i (*0-590-31778-4*) Scholastic, Inc.

Lachner, Dorothea. Look Out, Cinder! Lanning, Rosemary, tr. from GER. 1996. (Illus.). 32p. (J). (ps-3). 15.95 o.p. (*1-55858-520-6*); 15.88 o.p. (*1-55858-521-4*) North-South Bks., Inc.

Lachtman, Ofelia Dumas. Pepita Thinks Pink (Pepita y el Color Rosado) 1998. (ENG & SPA., Illus.). 32p. (J). (ps-2). 14.95 (*1-55885-222-0*, Piñata Books) Arte Publico Pr.

—Tina & the Scarecrow Skins / Tina y Las Pieles de Espantapajaros. Colin, Jose Juan, tr. 2002. (ENG & SPA., Illus.). 32p. (J). 14.95 (*1-55885-373-1*, Piñata Books) Arte Publico Pr.

Ladd, Louise. A Whole Summer of Weird Susan. 1987. (Skylark Ser.). 144p. (Orig.). (J). pap. 2.99 o.s.i (*0-553-15520-2*) Bantam Bks.

Lager, Claude. Jeanette & Josie. 1999. pap. (*0-14-050989-5*) NAL.

—Jeanette & Josie. 1989. (Illus.). 320p. (J). (ps-3). 12.95 o.p. (*0-670-82657-X*, Viking Children's Bks.) Penguin Putnam Bks. for Young Readers.

Lagonegro, Melissa. Friends for a Princess. 2004. (J). 3.99 (*0-7364-2208-0*); 11.99 (*0-7364-8027-7*) Random Hse., Inc.

Laird, Elizabeth. Secret Friends. (Illus.). 93p. (J). mass mkt. (*0-340-66473-8*) Hodder & Stoughton Canada.

—Secret Friends. 1999. 80p. (YA). (gr. 5-9). 14.99 o.s.i (*0-399-23334-2*) Penguin Group (USA) Inc.

Lake, Simon. He Told Me To! 1993. (Midnight Place Ser.: No. 4). 144p. (YA). mass mkt. 3.50 o.s.i (*0-553-56168-5*) Bantam Bks.

Lakin, Pat. Beach Day! 2004. (Illus.). 32p. (J). 15.99 (*0-8037-2894-8*, Dial Bks. for Young Readers) Penguin Putnam Bks. for Young Readers.

Lakin, Patricia. Stuart Finds a Friend. 2002. (Festival Reader Ser.). (Illus.). 32p. (J). (ps-2). pap. 3.99 (*0-06-000182-8*, Harper Festival) HarperCollins Children's Bk. Group.

Lamb, Nancy. The Great Mosquito, Bull, & Coffin Caper. 1992. (Illus.). 48p. (J). (gr. 3 up). 12.00 o.p. (*0-688-10933-0*) HarperCollins Children's Bk. Group.

—The Great Mosquito, Bull, & Coffin Caper. 1994. (Illus.). 128p. (YA). (gr. 4-7). reprint ed. mass mkt. 4.95 (*0-688-12944-7*, Morrow, William & Co.) Morrow/Avon.

Lambert, Derek. Blackstone's Fancy. 1973. 189p. (J). (*0-413-44950-5*) Heinemann.

Lambert, Marilyn. Franny & Roxxy. 1999. (J). (gr. k-3). pap. 6.95 (*0-533-12820-X*) Vantage Pr., Inc.

Lamirande, Carole A. Able & the Tree of Life. 1997. (Illus.). 128p. (J). (gr. 3-9). pap. 9.95 (*0-9661385-0-3*) Dream Catcher Bks.

Lamperti, Noelle. Brown Like Me. 2nd l.t. ed. 1999. (Illus.). 32p. (J). (gr. 4-7). 12.95 (*1-892281-03-1*) New Victoria Pubs., Inc.

Landis, James D. Joey & the Girls. 1987. 192p. (Orig.). (J). (gr. 7-12). mass mkt. 2.95 o.s.i (*0-553-26415-X*, Starfire) Random Hse. Children's Bks.

Landis, Mary. David & Susan at the Little Green House. 1975. (Illus.). 170p. (J). (gr. 3-6). 8.20 (*0-7399-0097-8*, 2185) Rod & Staff Pubs., Inc.

—David & Susan at Wild Rose Cottage. 1980. (Illus.). 231p. 9.60 (*0-7399-0099-4*, 2190) Rod & Staff Pubs., Inc.

Landuyt, Sylvia. The Cemetery Gang. 1996. (Illus.). (J). (gr. 5-8). 8.95 o.p. (*0-533-11779-8*) Vantage Pr., Inc.

Langeland, Deirdre. Mucha Lucha! 2003. (Mucha Lucha Ser.). (Illus.). 48p. (J). (ps-3). pap. 3.99 (*0-06-054535-6*) HarperCollins Children's Bk. Group.

Langley, Charles P. Catherine & Geku: The Adventure Begins. 1996. (Illus.). 25p. (Orig.). (J). (gr. k-2). pap. 6.95 (*1-884570-54-2*) Research Triangle Publishing.

Langreuter, Jutta. Little Bear & the Big Fight. 1998. (Little Bear Collection). (Illus.). 32p. (ps-k). 22.90 o.p. (*0-7613-0403-7*); pap. 6.95 o.p. (*0-7613-0375-8*) Millbrook Pr., Inc.

Lanham, Cheryl. Dear Diary No. 2: Remember Me. 1996. (Dear Diary Ser.). 208p. (Orig.). (J). (gr. 7 up). mass mkt. 4.50 o.s.i (*0-425-15194-8*) Berkley Publishing Group.

Lansing, Karen E. Time to Be a Friend. 1993. 96p. (J). (gr. 4-7). pap. 5.99 (*0-8361-3614-4*) Herald Pr.

Lantz, Francess L. Dear Celeste, My Life Is a Mess. 1991. 160p. (J). (gr. 4-7). pap. 3.25 o.s.i (*0-553-15961-5*) Bantam Bks.

—Making It on Our Own. 1986. (Overnight Sensation Ser.: No. 2). (J). (gr. 6-12). mass mkt. 2.75 o.s.i (*0-440-95202-6*, Laurel Leaf) Random Hse. Children's Bks.

—Sing Me a Love Song. 2000. (You're the One Ser.: Vol. 1). 128p. (J). (gr. 4-7). pap. 3.99 (*0-689-83420-9*, Aladdin) Simon & Schuster Children's Publishing.

Larry, Charles. Peboan & Seegwun, RS. 1995. 32p. (J). (ps-3). pap. 4.95 o.p. (*0-374-45750-6*, Sunburst) Farrar, Straus & Giroux.

—Peboan & Seegwun. 1993. (J). 10.15 o.p. (*0-606-09737-6*) Turtleback Bks.

Larson, Kirby. Cody & Quinn, Sitting in a Tree. 1996. (Illus.). 64p. (J). (gr. 4-7). tchr. ed. 14.95 (*0-8234-1227-X*) Holiday Hse., Inc.

—Cody & Quinn, Sitting in a Tree. 1997. (Illus.). 96p. (gr. 2-5). pap. text 3.99 o.s.i (*0-440-41378-8*, Dell Books for Young Readers) Random Hse. Children's Bks.

—Cody & Quinn, Sitting in a Tree. 1998. (Picture Puffin Ser.). (J). 10.14 (*0-606-13287-2*) Turtleback Bks.

—Second-Grade Pig Pals. 1994. (Illus.). 96p. (J). (ps-3). tchr. ed. 14.95 o.p. (*0-8234-1107-9*) Holiday Hse., Inc.

—Second-Grade Pig Pals. 1995. (Illus.). 96p. (gr. 4-7). pap. text 3.50 o.s.i (*0-440-41104-1*, Yearling) Random Hse. Children's Bks.

—Second-Grade Pig Pals. 1996. 8.70 o.p. (*0-606-09835-6*) Turtleback Bks.

Lasky, Kathryn. Pond Year. (Illus.). 32p. (J). (ps-3). 1995. 13.99 o.p. (*1-56402-187-4*); 1997. reprint ed. bds. 5.99 o.s.i (*0-7636-0112-8*) Candlewick Pr.

—Pond Year. 1997. 12.14 (*0-606-12794-1*) Turtleback Bks.

—The Solo. 1994. (Illus.). 32p. (J). (ps-2). lib. bdg. 14.95 o.p. (*0-02-751664-4*, Simon & Schuster Children's Publishing) Simon & Schuster Children's Publishing.

Lattimore, Eleanor F. Little Pear & His Friends. 1992. (J). (gr. 1-4). 18.00 o.p. (*0-8446-6575-4*) Smith, Peter Pub., Inc.

Lavelle, Sheila. Holiday with the Fiend. 1988. (Illus.). 112p. (J). (gr. 2-5). 14.95 o.p. (*0-241-11857-3*) Trafalgar Square.

Lavelle, Sheila. My Best Fiend. 1988. (Illus.). 112p. (J). (gr. 1-3). 13.95 o.p. (*0-241-10103-4*) Trafalgar Square.

Lavis, Steve. Little Mouse Has a Friend. 2000. (Ready Readers Ser.). (Illus.). 24p. (J). (ps). 6.95 (*1-929927-12-6*) Ragged Bears USA.

Lawlor, Laurie. Addie's Dakota Winter. MacDonald, Patricia, ed. 1991. (Illus.). 160p. (J). (gr. 4-7). reprint ed. pap. 4.99 (*0-671-70148-7*, Aladdin) Simon & Schuster Children's Publishing.

—Addie's Dakota Winter. 1991. 10.04 (*0-606-00254-5*) Turtleback Bks.

—Addie's Dakota Winter. Tucker, Kathy, ed. Gowing, Toby, tr. 1989. (Illus.). 160p. (J). (gr. 4-7). lib. bdg. 13.95 (*0-8075-0171-9*) Whitman, Albert & Co.

—Addie's Forever Friend. 1997. (Illus.). 128p. (J). (gr. 2-5). lib. bdg. 13.95 (*0-8075-0164-6*) Whitman, Albert & Co.

—Addie's Long Summer. 1995. (Illus.). 176p. (J). (gr. 3-7). reprint ed. pap. 3.50 (*0-671-52607-3*, Aladdin) Simon & Schuster Children's Publishing.

—Addie's Long Summer. 1995. (J). 9.55 (*0-606-07178-4*) Turtleback Bks.

—Addie's Long Summer. Tucker, Kathleen, ed. 1992. (Illus.). 176p. (J). (gr. 7 up). 13.95 o.p. (*0-8075-0167-0*) Whitman, Albert & Co.

—How to Survive Third Grade. Levine, Abby, ed. 1988. (Illus.). 80p. (J). (ps-3). lib. bdg. 9.95 o.p. (*0-8075-3433-1*) Whitman, Albert & Co.

—Take to the Sky. 1996. (Heartland Ser.: No. 2). 176p. (J). (gr. 3-6). per. 3.99 (*0-671-53717-2*, Aladdin) Simon & Schuster Children's Publishing.

Lawrence, S. J. Aquarius Ahoy! 1985. (Zodiac Club Ser.). 160p. (J). (gr. 7 up). 2.25 (*0-399-21222-1*) Putnam Publishing Group, The.

Le Clezio, J. M. Celui Qui N'Avait Jamais Vu la Mer. 1988. (Folio - Junior Ser.: No. 492). (FRE., Illus.). 107p. (J). (gr. 5-10). pap. 6.95 (*2-07-033492-9*) Schoenhof's Foreign Bks., Inc.

Le Guin, Ursula K. Tom Mouse. ed. 2003. (gr. 2). spiral bd. (*0-616-14584-5*) Canadian National Institute for the Blind/Institut National Canadien pour les Aveugles.

—Tom Mouse. 2002. (Illus.). 40p. (ps-3). 22.90 (*0-7613-2663-4*); (J). 15.95 (*0-7613-1599-3*) Millbrook Pr., Inc. (Roaring Brook Pr.).

Le Jars, David. Mis Amigos, los Animales: Hablemos, un Libro para los Que Comienzan a Leer. 2001. (Hablemos Ser.). (SPA., Illus.). 24p. (J). (ps-k). pap. 5.95 (*1-58728-950-4*, Two-Can) Creative Publishing international, Inc.

—Mis Amigos, los Animales: Hablemos, un Libro para los Que Comienzan a Leer. 2000. (SPA., Illus.). (J). 11.10 (*0-606-20801-1*) Turtleback Bks.

Leach, Bernadette. 4 Ever Friends. 1998. (Bright Sparks Ser.). 176p. (YA). (gr. 8 up). pap. 7.95 (*1-85594-189-9*) Attic Pr. IRL. *Dist:* International Specialized Bk. Services.

Leah's Song Apple. 2003. (J). mass mkt. 2.75 (*0-590-44567-7*) Scholastic, Inc.

LeBlanc, Anne. Benjamin Finds a Friend. 1999. (Adventures with Benjamin Bear Ser.). (Illus.). 20p. (J). (ps-k). 4.95 (*0-8069-1923-X*) Sterling Publishing Co., Inc.

Leblanc, Louise. Deux Amis Dans la Nuit. 1996. (Premier Roman Ser.). (FRE., Illus.). 64p. (J). (gr. 2-5). pap. 8.95 (*2-89021-247-5*) La Courte Echelle CAN. *Dist:* Firefly Bks., Ltd.

Leblanc, Louise. Leo & Julio. 2000. (First Novels Ser.: Vol. 32). (Illus.). 62p. (J). (gr. 1-6). (*0-88780-479-9*) Formac Publishing Co., Ltd.

Lebowitz, Fran. Mr. Chas & Lisa Sue Meet the Pandas. 1994. (Illus.). 72p. (J). (gr. 2-7). 15.00 o.s.i (*0-679-86052-5*, Knopf Bks. for Young Readers) Random Hse. Children's Bks.

Lee, Huy Voun. In the Leaves. 2004. (J). 17.00 (*0-8050-6764-7*, Holt, Henry & Co. Bks. For Young Readers) Holt, Henry & Co.

Lee, Jeanne M. Bitter Dumplings, RS. 2002. (Illus.). 32p. (J). (gr. 2-5). 16.00 (*0-374-39966-2*, Farrar, Straus & Giroux (BYR)) Farrar, Straus & Giroux.

—Silent Lotus, RS. 1994. (Illus.). 32p. (J). (ps-3). pap. 6.95 (*0-374-46646-7*, Sunburst) Farrar, Straus & Giroux.

—Silent Lotus. 1994. 12.10 (*0-606-08163-1*) Turtleback Bks.

Lee, Marie G. F Is for Fabuloso. 1999. 192p. (J). (gr. 5-9). 15.95 (*0-380-97648-X*) HarperCollins Children's Bk. Group.

—Saying Goodbye. 1994. 240p. (YA). (gr. 7 up). tchr. ed. 16.00 (*0-395-67066-7*) Houghton Mifflin Co.

Lee, Patrick. Little Buddy Meets Bobo. 1993. 24p. (J). (ps). 10.95 o.p. (*0-670-84803-4*, Viking Children's Bks.) Penguin Putnam Bks. for Young Readers.

Leeson, Christine. Molly & the Storm. 2003. (Illus.). 32p. (J). (gr. k-2). tchr. ed. 15.95 (*1-58925-027-3*, Tiger Tales) ME Media LLC.

Legault, Anne & Franson, Leanne. Une Fille Pas Comme les Autres. 2002. (Roman Jeunesse Ser.). (FRE.). 96p. (YA). (gr. 4-7). pap. 8.95 (*2-89021-299-8*) La Courte Echelle CAN. *Dist:* Firefly Bks., Ltd.

Lehman, Yvonne. Picture Perfect. 1997. (White Dove Romances Ser.: No. 4). 176p. (J). (gr. 7-12). mass mkt. 4.99 o.p. (*1-55661-708-9*) Bethany Hse. Pubs.

Leitch, Patricia. Cross-Country Gallop. 1996. (Horseshoes Ser.: Vol. 3). (Illus.). 128p. (J). (gr. 3-7). lib. bdg. 13.89 o.p. (*0-06-027287-2*); pap. 3.95 o.p. (*0-06-440636-9*, Harper Trophy) HarperCollins Children's Bk. Group.

—Show Jumper Wanted. 1997. (Horseshoes Ser.: Vol. 5). 112p. (J). (gr. 3-7). pap. 3.95 o.p. (*0-06-440638-5*, Harper Trophy) HarperCollins Children's Bk. Group.

Leland, Debbie. The Jalapeno Man. 2000. (Illus.). 24p. (J). (ps-5). 14.95 (*0-9667086-1-X*) Wildflower Run.

LeMieux, Anne. Fruit Flies, Fish & Fortune Cookies. 1994. (Illus.). (J). 15.00 o.p. (*0-688-13299-5*, Morrow, William & Co.) Morrow/Avon.

LeMieux, Anne Connelly. Dare to Be, M. E.! (J). 1998. (gr. 3-7). pap. 3.99 (*0-380-72889-3*); 1997. 224p. 14.00 o.p. (*0-380-97496-7*) Morrow/Avon. (Avon Bks.).

Lemieux, Jean & Casson, Sophie. Le Bonheur Est une Tempête Avec un Chien. 2002. (Premier Roman Ser.). (FRE., Illus.). 64p. pap. 8.95 (*2-89021-568-7*) La Courte Echelle CAN. *Dist:* Firefly Bks., Ltd.

L'Engle, Madeleine. And Both Were Young. 1983. 240p. (J). (gr. 7 up). 14.95 o.s.i (*0-385-29237-6*, Delacorte Pr.) Dell Publishing.

—And Both Were Young. 1983. (Young Love Romance Ser.). 256p. (YA). (gr. 7-12). mass mkt. 4.99 (*0-440-90229-0*, Laurel Leaf) Random Hse. Children's Bks.

—And Both Were Young. 1983. 11.04 (*0-606-01439-X*) Turtleback Bks.

Lenhard, Elizabeth. W.I.T.C.H. The Fire of Friendship, No. 4. 2004. (Illus.). 144p. (J). pap. 4.99 (*0-7868-1731-3*) Time Warner Bk. Group.

Lennon, John. Amor Verdadero: Dibujos para Sean (Real Love: The Drawings for Sean) 2001. (ENG & SPA.). 44p. (J). (gr. k-1). 10.36 (*84-233-3180-6*) Ediciones Destino ESP. *Dist:* Lectorum Pubns., Inc.

Leonard, Marcia. Best Friends. 1999. (Real Kids Readers Ser.). (Illus.). 32p. (ps-1). pap. 4.99 (*0-7613-2089-X*) Millbrook Pr., Inc.

—My Pal Al. 1998. (Real Kids Readers Ser.). (Illus.). 32p. (J). (ps-1). 18.90 (*0-7613-2001-6*); pap. 4.99 (*0-7613-2026-1*) Millbrook Pr., Inc.

—My Pal Al. 1998. (Real Kids Readers Ser.). 10.14 (*0-606-15802-2*) Turtleback Bks.

—My Pal Al. 1998. E-Book (*1-58824-482-2*); E-Book (*1-58824-730-9*); E-Book (*1-58824-813-5*) ipicturebooks, LLC.

—Take a Bow, Krissy! A Brownie Girl Scout Book. 1994. (Here Comes the Brownies Ser.: No. 7). (Illus.). 64p. (J). (gr. 1-4). 9.99 o.p. (*0-448-40838-4*); 3.95 o.p. (*0-448-40837-6*) Penguin Putnam Bks. for Young Readers. (Grosset & Dunlap).

Leppard, Lois Gladys. Mandie & the Charleston Phantom. 1986. (Mandie Bks.: No. 7). 144p. (J). (gr. 4-7). pap. 4.99 (*0-87123-650-8*) Bethany Hse. Pubs.

—Mandie & the Charleston Phantom. 1986. (Mandie Bks.: No. 7). (J). (gr. 4-7). 11.04 (*0-606-06125-8*) Turtleback Bks.

Leppard, Shannon M. The Ballet Class Mystery. 1997. (Adventures of Callie Ann Ser.: Vol. 2). 80p. (J). (gr. 2-5). pap. 3.99 (*1-55661-814-X*) Bethany Hse. Pubs.

Lerangis, Peter. Last Stop. 1998. (Watchers Ser.: No. 1). 176p. (J). (gr. 4-7). pap. 4.50 o.s.i (*0-590-10996-0*) Scholastic, Inc.

LeRoy, Gen. Emma's Dilemma. 1975. (Illus.). (J). (gr. 5 up). pap. 1.50 o.p. (*0-06-440078-6*) HarperCollins Pubs.

Les Becquets, Diane. The Stones of Mourning Creek. 2001. (Illus.). 320p. (J). (gr. 7 up). 16.95 (*1-58837-004-6*) Winslow Pr.

Leslie, Robyn. Rinny & the Trail of Clues. 2003. Orig. Title: Miss President & the Trail of Clues. (Illus.). 192p. (YA). pap. 7.95 (*0-9727388-8-6*) Sugar Ducky Bks., Inc.

LeSourd, Nancy. The Personal Correspondence of Catherine Clark & Meredith Lyons. 2004. 224p. 9.99 (*0-310-70353-0*) Zondervan.

—The Personal Correspondence of Emma Edmunds & Mollie Turner. 2004. 224p. 9.99 (*0-310-70352-2*) Zondervan.

Lester, Helen. Listen, Buddy. 2002. (Illus.). (J). 14.74 (*0-7587-2993-6*) Book Wholesalers, Inc.

—Listen, Buddy. 1997. (J). 12.10 (*0-606-11567-6*) Turtleback Bks.

—Three Cheers for Tacky. 1996. (Illus.). 32p. (J). (ps-3). pap. 5.95 (*0-395-82740-X*) Houghton Mifflin Co.

—The Wizard, the Fairy, & the Magic Chicken. 1988. (Illus.). 32p. (J). (ps-3). pap. 6.95 (*0-395-47945-2*) Houghton Mifflin Co.

Levene, Nancy S. Cherry Cola Champions. (Alex Ser.). (Illus.). (J). 1988. 120p. (gr. 3-7). pap. 4.99 (*1-55513-519-6*); 6. 128p. (gr. 2-5). pap. 5.99 (*0-7814-3372-X*) Cook Communications Ministries.

—French Fry Forgiveness. 1987. 120p. (J). (gr. 3-6). pap. 4.99 (*1-55513-302-9*) Cook Communications Ministries.

—Hot Chocolate Friendship. 1987. 128p. (J). (gr. 3-6). pap. 4.99 o.p. (*1-55513-304-5*) Cook Communications Ministries.

—Mint Cookie Miracles. 1988. (Alex Ser.). 120p. (J). (gr. 3-7). pap. 4.99 (*1-55513-514-5*) Cook Communications Ministries.

—Peach Pit Popularity. 1994. (Alex Ser.). (Illus.). 128p. (J). (gr. 2-5). pap. 4.99 (*1-55513-529-3*) Cook Communications Ministries.

Leverich, Kathleen. Best Enemies. (Best Enemies Ser.). (Illus.). (J). 1998. 80p. (gr. 2 up). pap. 4.99 (*0-688-15853-6*, Harper Trophy); 1989. (gr. 1 up). 15.00 o.p. (*0-688-08316-1*, Greenwillow Bks.) HarperCollins Children's Bk. Group.

—Best Enemies. 1998. 11.10 (*0-606-13195-7*) Turtleback Bks.

—Best Enemies Again. (Best Enemies Ser.). (Illus.). 96p. (J). (gr. 2-5). 1999. pap. 4.95 (*0-688-16197-9*, Harper Trophy); 1991. 15.00 o.p. (*0-688-09440-6*, Greenwillow Bks.) HarperCollins Children's Bk. Group.

—Best Enemies Forever. 1998. (Illus.). 144p. (J). (gr. 2 up). pap. 4.95 o.p. (*0-688-15854-4*, Morrow, William & Co.) Morrow/Avon.

Levin, Betty. Creature Crossing. 1999. (Illus.). 96p. (J). (gr. 3 up). 15.00 (*0-688-16220-7*, Greenwillow Bks.) HarperCollins Children's Bk. Group.

Levine, Gail Carson. Ella Enchanted. 2004. 288p. (J). pap. 6.99 (*0-06-055886-5*, Avon Bks.) Morrow/Avon.

—The Wish. 2000. (Illus.). 208p. (J). (gr. 3-7). 15.99 (*0-06-027900-1*); lib. bdg. 15.89 (*0-06-027901-X*) HarperCollins Children's Bk. Group.

Levinson, Marilyn. The Fourth-Grade Four, ERS. 1989. (Redfeather Bks.). (Illus.). 64p. (J). (gr. 2-4). 12.95 o.p. (*0-8050-1082-3*, Holt, Henry & Co. Bks. For Young Readers) Holt, Henry & Co.

Levinson, Nancy. Prairie Friends. 2003. (I Can Read Book Ser.). (Illus.). 64p. (J). (gr. 2-4). 15.99 (*0-06-028001-8*) HarperCollins Pubs.

Levitin, Sonia. Annie's Promise. 192p. 1996. (Illus.). (J). (gr. 4-7). pap. 4.99 (*0-689-80440-7*, Aladdin); 1993. (YA). (gr. 5 up). 15.00 (*0-689-31752-2*, Atheneum) Simon & Schuster Children's Publishing.

—Annie's Promise. 1996. 11.04 (*0-606-09007-X*) Turtleback Bks.

—A Season for Unicorns. 1986. 204p. (J). (gr. 5-9). 13.95 o.p. (*0-689-31113-3*, Atheneum) Simon & Schuster Children's Publishing.

—Yesterday's Child. (J). (gr. 7-12). 1998. 336p. mass mkt. 4.99 (*0-689-82073-9*, Simon Pulse); 1997. 256p. 17.00 (*0-689-80810-0*, Simon & Schuster Children's Publishing) Simon & Schuster Children's Publishing.

—Yesterday's Child. 1998. 11.04 (*0-606-15872-3*) Turtleback Bks.

Levoy, Myron. Alan & Naomi. (Trophy Bk.). (gr. 6 up). 1987. 192p. (J). pap. 5.99 (*0-06-440209-6*, Harper Trophy); 1977. 176p. (YA). lib. bdg. 12.89 o.p. (*0-06-023800-3*) HarperCollins Children's Bk. Group.

—A Shadow Like a Leopard. 1981. 192p. (YA). (gr. 7 up). lib. bdg. 12.89 o.p. (*0-06-023817-8*) HarperCollins Children's Bk. Group.

—Three Friends. 1984. (Charlotte Zolotow Bk.). 192p. (YA). (gr. 7 up). 12.95 o.p. (*0-06-023826-7*); lib. bdg. 12.89 o.p. (*0-06-023827-5*) HarperCollins Children's Bk. Group.

—Three Friends. 2000. 187p. (gr. 7-12). pap. 12.95 (*0-595-09352-3*) iUniverse, Inc.

Levy, Elizabeth. The Case of the Tattletale Heart. (J). 1992. (Illus.). 64p. (gr. 2-4). pap. 3.00 o.s.i (*0-671-74064-4*, Aladdin); 1990. pap. 10.95 o.p. (*0-671-63657-X*, Simon & Schuster Children's Publishing) Simon & Schuster Children's Publishing.

—Cheater, Cheater. 1993. 176p. (J). (gr. 4-7). pap. 13.95 o.p. (*0-590-45865-5*) Scholastic, Inc.

—Rude Rowdy Rumors, No. 2. 1994. (Illus.). (J). (gr. 2-5). 80p. 13.95 o.p. (*0-06-023462-8*); 96p. lib. bdg. 13.89 o.p. (*0-06-023463-6*) HarperCollins Children's Bk. Group.

—Seventh-Grade Tango. 2000. 153p. (J). (gr. 3-7). 15.99 (*0-7868-0498-X*) Disney Pr.

—Seventh-Grade Tango. 2000. 153p. (J). (gr. 3-7). 16.49 (*0-7868-2427-1*) Hyperion Bks. for Children.

—Seventh-Grade Tango. 2001. (J). 12.04 (*0-606-22571-4*) Turtleback Bks.

—Seventh Grade Tango. 2001. (Illus.). 160p. (J). (gr. 3-7). pap. 5.99 (*0-7868-1565-5*) Hyperion Bks. for Children.

—Seventh-Grade Tango. l.t. ed. 2001. (Illus.). 174p. (J). (gr. 3-7). 20.95 (*0-7862-3105-X*) Thorndike Pr.

—Something Queer at the Birthday Party. 1990. (Something Queer Ser.: No. 8). 48p. (J). (gr. 2-5). 12.95 o.s.i (*0-385-29973-7*) Doubleday Publishing.

Levy, Marilyn. No Way Home. 1990. 160p. (YA). mass mkt. 3.95 o.s.i (*0-449-70326-6*, Fawcett) Ballantine Bks.

—Remember to Remember Me. 1988. (J). (gr. 5 up). mass mkt. 2.95 o.s.i (*0-449-70278-2*, Fawcett) Ballantine Bks.

—Rumors & Whispers. 1990. 160p. (YA). (gr. 8 up). mass mkt. 3.95 o.s.i (*0-449-70327-4*, Fawcett) Ballantine Bks.

Lewis, Beverly. Best Friend, Worst Enemy: Holly's Heart. 2001. (Hollys Heart Ser.). 160p. (J). (gr. 6-9). pap. 2.99 (*0-7642-2500-6*) Bethany Hse. Pubs.

—Better Than Best. 2000. (Girls Only (Go!) Ser.: Vol. 6). (Illus.). 128p. (J). (gr. 3-8). pap. 5.99 (*1-55661-641-4*) Bethany Hse. Pubs.

—Freshman Frenzy. 2003. (Holly's Heart Ser.). (Illus.). 160p. (J). pap. 5.99 (*0-7642-2618-5*) Bethany Hse. Pubs.

—Freshmen Frenzy. 1996. (Holly's Heart Ser.: Bk. 11). 144p. (J). (gr. 6-9). pap. 6.99 (*0-310-20842-4*) Zondervan.

—Holly's First Love. 1993. (Holly's Heart Ser.: Vol. 1). 160p. (J). pap. 6.99 (*0-310-38051-0*) Zondervan.

—Little White Lies. 2002. (Hollys Heart Ser.). 160p. (J). (gr. 5-9). pap. 5.99 (*0-7642-2617-7*) Bethany Hse. Pubs.

—Little White Lies, Bk. 10. 1995. (Holly's Heart Ser.: Vol. 10). 160p. (J). (gr. 5-9). pap. 6.99 (*0-310-20194-2*) Zondervan.

—Mailbox Mania. 1996. (Cul-de-Sac Kids Ser.: Vol. 9). 80p. (J). (gr. 2-5). pap. 3.99 (*1-55661-729-1*) Bethany Hse. Pubs.

—Mystery at Midnight. 1995. (Ready, Set, Read!). (Illus.). 64p. (J). pap. 4.99 o.p. (*0-8066-2749-2*, 9-2749) Augsburg Fortress, Pubs.

—Mystery Letters. 2003. (Holly's Heart Ser.). (Illus.). 160p. (J). pap. 5.99 (*0-7642-2619-3*) Bethany Hse. Pubs.

—Mystery Letters. 1996. (Holly's Heart Ser.: Bk. 12). 144p. (J). (gr. 6-9). pap. 6.99 (*0-310-20843-2*) Zondervan.

—The "No-Guys" Pact, Bk. 9. 1995. (Holly's Heart Ser.: Vol. 9). 160p. (J). pap. 6.99 (*0-310-20193-4*) Zondervan.

—Second-Best Friend. 2002. (Hollys Heart Ser.). 160p. (J). pap. 5.99 (*0-7642-2505-7*) Bethany Hse. Pubs.

—Second-Best Friend. 1994. (Holly's Heart Ser.: Vol. 6). 160p. (J). (gr. 6-9). pap. 6.99 (*0-310-43331-2*) Zondervan.

—Star Status. 2002. (Girls Only Go Ser.: Vol. 8). 128p. (J). pap. 5.99 (*1-55661-643-0*) Bethany Hse. Pubs.

—Straight-A Teacher. 2002. (Hollys Heart Ser.). 160p. (J). pap. 5.99 (*0-7642-2615-0*) Bethany Hse. Pubs.

Lewis, Clarissa. Vay Kamo, Vay! Andonian, Aramais, tr. from ENG. 1995. (ARM., Illus.). 28p. (J). (ps-2). 14.00 (*1-886434-00-X*) Blue Crane Bks., Inc.

Lewis, Harriet. Pampoody & Max. 1977. 72p. (J). pap. 4.50 (*0-933294-01-8*) Backroads.

Lewis, Jean & Baker, Darrell. Shari Lewis' Lamb Chop & Friends Blue Ribbon Kitten. 1995. (Illus.). 24p. (J). (ps). pap. 1.79 o.s.i (*0-307-10564-4*, Golden Bks.) Random Hse. Children's Bks.

Lewis, Kim. Friends. 1998. o.p. (*0-7636-0324-4*); 32p. (J). 15.99 o.p. (*0-7636-0346-5*) Candlewick Pr.

—Good Night, Harry. 2004. 32p. (J). 15.99 (*0-7636-2206-0*) Candlewick Pr.

Lewis, Rob. Friends, ERS. 2001. (Illus.). 32p. (J). (ps-1). 15.95 (*0-8050-6691-8*, Holt, Henry & Co. Bks. For Young Readers) Holt, Henry & Co.

Lewison, Wendy Cheyette. Easter Bunny's Amazing Egg Machine. 2002. (Random House Pictureback Ser.). (Illus.). 24p. (J). (ps-1). pap. 3.25 (*0-375-81263-6*, Random Hse. Bks. for Young Readers) Random Hse. Children's Bks.

Liberts, Jennifer. Theodore's Friends. 2001. (Illus.). 12p. (J). bds. 4.99 (*0-375-81183-4*, Random Hse. Bks. for Young Readers) Random Hse. Children's Bks.

Lichtman, Wendy. Telling Secrets. 1986. 256p. (YA). (gr. 7 up). lib. bdg. 13.89 o.p. (*0-06-023885-2*) HarperCollins Children's Bk. Group.

Lieberman, Lillian. Comprehension. 1987. (Reading Superstar Ser.). 64p. (J). (gr. 2-5). pap. 6.95 o.p. (*0-912107-66-9*) Monday Morning Bks., Inc.

Lies, Brian. Hamlet & the Magnificent Sandcastle. (Illus.). 32p. (J). (gr. k-3). 2003. pap. 7.95 (*1-931659-03-6*); 2001. 15.95 (*0-9677929-2-4*) Moon Mountain Publishing, Inc.

Lies, Jalon E. Friends in My Neighborhood, Vol. 1, Bk. 2. Holland, David, ed. 1996. (Illus.). (J). (ps-2). 7.50 (*1-889994-01-4*) For His Kingdom.

—My Best Friend, Vol. 2, Bk. 2. Holland, David, ed. 1996. (Illus.). (J). (ps-2). 7.50 (*1-889994-03-0*) For His Kingdom.

Lifton, Betsy & Lifton, Karen. Five's a Crowd. 1992. (Not for Blondes Only Ser.). 176p. (J). (gr. 3-7). pap. 2.95 (*0-590-45526-5*, Scholastic Paperbacks) Scholastic, Inc.

—Show Time! 1992. (Not for Blondes Only Ser.). 176p. (J). (gr. 3-7). pap. 2.95 o.p. (*0-590-45683-0*, Scholastic Paperbacks) Scholastic, Inc.

Lillie, Patricia. Jake & Rosie. 1989. (Illus.). 24p. (J). (ps up). 11.95 o.p. (*0-688-07624-6*); lib. bdg. 11.88 o.p. (*0-688-07625-4*) HarperCollins Children's Bk. Group. (Greenwillow Bks.).

Lillington, Kenneth. Gabrielle. 1988. (Illus.). (J). (gr. 3-7). bds. o.p. (*0-571-15143-4*) Faber & Faber Ltd.

—Selkie. 1985. 145p. (YA). (gr. 7-10). o.p. (*0-571-13421-1*) Faber & Faber Ltd.

Lindberg, Becky T. Chelsea Martin Turns Green. Tucker, Kathy, ed. 1993. (Illus.). 144p. (J). (ps-3). lib. bdg. 13.95 o.p. (*0-8075-1134-X*) Whitman, Albert & Co.

Lindbergh, Anne M. The Worry Week. 2003. (J). pap. 12.95 (*1-56792-239-2*) Godine, David R. Pub.

—The Worry Week. 1985. (Illus.). 144p. (J). (gr. 3-7). 12.95 (*0-15-299675-3*) Harcourt Children's Bks.

—The Worry Week. 1988. (J). (gr. 3-7). pap. 2.95 (*0-380-70394-7*, Avon Bks.) Morrow/Avon.

Lindbergh, Anne M. & Hoguet, Susan R. Next Time, Take Care. 1988. (Illus.). 32p. (J). (ps-3). 13.95 o.s.i (*0-15-257200-7*) Harcourt Children's Bks.

Linders, Clara & Cate, Marijke. The Very Best Door of All. 2001. (Illus.). 28p. (J). (ps-1). 15.95 (*1-886910-64-2*) Front Street, Inc.

Lindgren, Astrid. Do You Know Pippi Longstocking? Dyssegaard, Elisabeth Kallick, tr. from SWE. 1999. (Pippi Longstocking Storybooks). (Illus.). 32p. (J). (gr. k-2). 9.95 (*91-29-64661-8*) R & S Bks. SWE. *Dist:* Holtzbrinck Pubs.

—Most Beloved Sister. Dyssegaard, Elizabeth Kallick, tr. from SWE. 2002. (Illus.). 28p. (J). (ps-2). 15.00 (*91-29-65502-1*) R & S Bks. SWE. *Dist:* Farrar, Straus & Giroux, Holtzbrinck Pubs.

Lindgren, Barbro. Benny & Binky. Dyssegaard, Elisabeth Kallick, tr. 2002. (Illus.). 28p. (J). (ps-1). 15.00 o.s.i (*91-29-65497-1*) R & S Bks. SWE. *Dist:* Farrar, Straus & Giroux, Holtzbrinck Pubs.

—Rosa Goes to Daycare. 2000. (Illus.). 32p. (J). (ps-1). 15.95 (*0-88899-391-9*) Groundwood Bks. CAN. *Dist:* Publishers Group West.

Lindley, Alice. The Story of the Little Round Man. 1979. (Illus.). (J). (ps-1). 6.95 o.p. (*0-7232-2185-5*, Warne, Frederick) Penguin Putnam Bks. for Young Readers.

Lindman, Maj. Flicka, Ricka, Dicka & Their New Friend. 1995. (Illus.). (J). (ps-3). pap. 6.95 (*0-8075-2498-0*) Whitman, Albert & Co.

Lindquist, Marie. Untamed Heart. 1987. (Texas Promises Ser.: No. 2). 160p. (Orig.). (YA). (gr. 7-12). mass mkt. 2.50 o.s.i (*0-553-26474-5*, Starfire) Random Hse. Children's Bks.

Lindquist, N. J. Friends in Need. 2001. (Circle of Friends Ser.: Vol. 3). 208p. (YA). (gr. 7 up). pap. 7.95 (*0-9685495-4-3*, 973-008) That's Life! Communications CAN. *Dist:* Spring Arbor Distributors, Inc.

Lindroos, Marianne. Engine People. 1989. (Illus.). 32p. (J). (gr. 3-5). 4.25 o.p. (*0-901269-54-9*) Grosvenor U.S.A.

Line, David. Screaming High. l.t. ed. 1987. (J). (gr. 4-8). 16.95 o.p. (*0-7451-0628-5*, Galaxy Children's Large Print) BBC Audiobooks America.

Lionni, Leo. An Extraordinary Egg. (Illus.). (J). (ps up). 1998. 32p. pap. 5.99 (*0-679-89385-7*, Random Hse. Bks. for Young Readers); 1994. 40p. 16.99 (*0-679-95840-1*, Knopf Bks. for Young Readers); 1994. 40p. 16.00 (*0-679-85840-7*, Knopf Bks. for Young Readers) Random Hse. Children's Bks.

—An Extraordinary Egg. 1998. 12.14 (*0-606-15526-0*) Turtleback Bks.

—It's Mine. 1986. (Illus.). 32p. (J). (ps-1). 15.00 o.s.i (*0-394-87000-X*); 15.99 o.s.i (*0-394-97000-4*) Random Hse. Children's Bks. (Knopf Bks. for Young Readers).

—Little Blue & Little Yellow. 1995. (Illus.). 48p. (J). (ps-3). reprint ed. pap. 6.99 (*0-688-13285-5*, Harper Trophy) HarperCollins Children's Bk. Group.

—Swimmy. 1973. (Children's Paperbacks Ser.). (Illus.). 32p. (ps-3). pap. 5.99 (*0-394-82620-5*, Knopf Bks. for Young Readers) Random Hse. Children's Bks.

Lipp, Frederick. Bread Song. Gaillard, Jason, tr. & illus. by. 2004. (J). (*1-59336-000-2*); pap. (*1-59336-001-0*) Mondo Publishing.

Lipp, Frederick J. Some Lose Their Way. 1980. 132p. (J). (gr. 5-9). 3.49 o.p. (*0-689-50178-1*, McElderry, Margaret K.) Simon & Schuster Children's Publishing.

Lisle, Janet Taylor. Angela's Aliens. 1996. 128p. (J). (gr. 4-7). pap. 14.95 (*0-531-09541-X*); (Investigators of the Unknown Ser.: Bk. 4). lib. bdg. 15.99 (*0-531-08891-X*) Scholastic, Inc. (Orchard Bks.).

—The Gold Dust Letters. 1994. (Investigators of the Unknown Ser.: Vol. 1). 128p. (J). (gr. 4-7). pap. 15.95 (*0-531-06830-7*); lib. bdg. 16.99 (*0-531-08680-1*) Scholastic, Inc. (Orchard Bks.).

—Looking for Juliette. 1994. (Investigators of the Unknown Ser.: Vol. 2). 128p. (J). (gr. 4-7). pap. 15.95 (*0-531-06870-6*); lib. bdg. 16.99 (*0-531-08720-4*) Scholastic, Inc. (Orchard Bks.).

—A Message from the Match Girl. 1997. pap. 3.99 (*0-380-72518-5*, Avon Bks.) Morrow/Avon.

—A Message from the Match Girl. 1996. (Investigators of the Unknown Ser.: Bk. 3). (Illus.). 128p. (J). (gr. 4-7). pap. 15.95 (*0-531-09487-1*); lib. bdg. 16.99 (*0-531-08787-5*) Scholastic, Inc. (Orchard Bks.).

Liston, B. & Choate, C. School & Friends. 1995. (Exploring Literature Theme Ser.: Bk. 2). (J). pap. text 44.28 (*0-201-59545-1*) Longman Publishing Group.

Litkowski, Mary Pelagia. Two Hearts, One Great Love: Frank Duff & Edel Quinn. 2000. (Illus.). 80p. (YA). (gr. 7 up). pap. 7.95 (*0-916927-24-5*) Growth Unlimited, Inc.

Litke, Lael J. Run, Ducky, Run. 1996. (Bee There Ser.: Bk. 6). 168p. (Orig.). (J). (gr. 3-7). pap. 6.95 (*1-57345-134-7*, Cinnamon Tree) Deseret Bk. Co.

Little, Jean. Emma's Magic Winter. (I Can Read Bks.). (Illus.). 64p. (J). (ps-3). 2000. pap. 3.99 (*0-06-443706-X*, Harper Trophy); 1998. 15.95 (*0-06-025389-4*); 1998. lib. bdg. 15.89 (*0-06-025390-8*) HarperCollins Children's Bk. Group.

—His Banner over Me. 1995. (Illus.). 224p. (J). (gr. 3-7). 13.99 o.s.i (*0-670-85664-9*, Viking Children's Bks.) Penguin Putnam Bks. for Young Readers.

—Kate. (Trophy Bk.). 174p. (J). (gr. 5-8). 1973. pap. 3.95 o.s.i (*0-06-440037-9*, Harper Trophy); 1971. (Illus.). lib. bdg. 12.89 o.p. (*0-06-023914-X*) HarperCollins Children's Bk. Group.

—Look Through My Window. 1970. (Illus.). 270p. (J). (gr. 4-7). lib. bdg. 14.89 o.p. (*0-06-023924-7*) HarperCollins Children's Bk. Group.

—Look Through My Window. 1970. (J). (gr. 4-7). pap. 2.95 o.p. (*0-06-440010-7*) HarperCollins Pubs.

Littlefield, Holly. Fire at the Triangle Factory. 1996. (On My Own History Ser.). (Illus.). 48p. (J). (gr. 1-3). pap. 6.95 (*0-87614-970-0*); lib. bdg. 21.27 (*0-87614-868-2*) Lerner Publishing Group. (Carolrhoda Bks.).

Littleton, Mark. Friends No Matter What. 1995. (Crista Chronicles Ser.: No. 6). (Orig.). (YA). mass mkt. 3.99 o.p. (*1-56507-256-1*) Harvest Hse. Pubs.

—Winter Thunder. 1993. (Crista Chronicles Ser.: Bk. 2). (J). mass mkt. 3.99 o.p. (*1-56507-008-9*) Harvest Hse. Pubs.

Littleton, Mark R. Adventure at Rocky Creek. Norton, LoraBeth, ed. 1993. (Rocky Creek Adventures Ser.). 208p. (J). (gr. 4-6). pap. 5.99 o.p. (*1-55513-761-X*) Cook Communications Ministries.

Llama on the Lam. 2001. (LLAMA ON THE LAM). 96p. (J). 22.00 (*0-9649083-4-4*) Black River Trading Co.

Lobe, Mira. Ben & the Child of the Forest. 1988. (Illus.). 96p. (J). (gr. 3-4). 4.95 o.p. (*0-8120-5831-3*); pap. 2.95 o.p. (*0-8120-3936-X*) Barron's Educational Series, Inc.

Lobel, Arnold. Days with Frog & Toad. 1979. (I Can Read Bks.). (Illus.). 64p. (J). (gr. k-3). 15.99 (*0-06-023963-8*); lib. bdg. 16.89 (*0-06-023964-6*) HarperCollins Children's Bk. Group.

—Dias con Sapo y Sepo. (SPA.). 72p. (J). (gr. 1-6). 8.95 (*84-204-3743-3*) Santillana USA Publishing Co., Inc.

—Dias con Sapo y Sepo (Days with Frog & Toad) 1995. 15.10 (*0-606-10401-1*) Turtleback Bks.

—Sapo y Sepo Inseparables. 1996. 15.10 (*0-606-10501-8*) Turtleback Bks.

—Sapo y Sepo Son Amigos. 2002. (SPA.). 66p. (J). (gr. k-3). pap. 12.95 (*968-19-0714-0*) Aguilar Editorial MEX. *Dist:* Santillana USA Publishing Co., Inc.

—Sapo y Sepo Son Amigos. 1995. 15.10 (*0-606-10502-6*) Turtleback Bks.

—Sapo y Sepo un Ano Entero. 1990. (Infantil Alfaguara Ser.). (SPA., Illus.). 72p. (J). (ps-3). 12.95 (*84-204-3052-8*) Alfaguara, Ediciones, S.A.-Grupo Santillana ESP. *Dist:* Lectorum Pubns., Inc., Santillana USA Publishing Co., Inc.

—Sapo y Sepo un Ano Entero. 1992. 15.10 (*0-606-10503-4*) Turtleback Bks.

Locke, Joseph. Petrified. 1992. 176p. (YA). (gr. 7 up). mass mkt. 3.50 o.s.i (*0-553-29657-4*, Starfire) Random Hse. Children's Bks.

Loggia, Wendy. Summer Love. 1999. (Love Stories Super Edition Ser.). 224p. (gr. 7-12). mass mkt. 4.50 o.s.i (*0-553-49276-4*, Dell Books for Young Readers) Random Hse. Children's Bks.

Lomasney, Eileen. What Do You Do with the Rest of the Day, Mary Ann? 1991. (J). pap. 3.95 o.p. (*0-8091-6601-1*) Paulist Pr.

Lonborg, Rosemary. Helpin' Bugs. 1995. (Illus.). 32p. (J). (ps-3). 14.95 (*0-9641285-2-7*) Little Friend Pr.

London, Jonathan. Shawn & Keeper: Show & Tell. 2000. (Easy-to-Read Ser.). (Illus.). 32p. (J). (ps-2). pap. 3.99 o.p. (*0-14-130367-0*, Puffin Bks.) Penguin Putnam Bks. for Young Readers.

—Shawn & Keeper: Show & Tell. 2000. (Puffin Easy-to-Read Ser.). 10.14 (*0-606-18450-3*) Turtleback Bks.

—The Sugaring-Off Party. ed. 1997. (J). (gr. 2). spiral bd. (*0-616-01705-7*) Canadian National Institute for the Blind/Institut National Canadien pour les Aveugles.

—What Newt Could Do for Turtle. 1996. (Illus.). 40p. (J). (ps-3). 16.99 o.p. (*1-56402-259-5*) Candlewick Pr.

The Lonely One. 2001. 32p. (YA). (gr. 6-12). pap. (*0-8224-3769-4*) Globe Fearon Educational Publishing.

Long, Kathy. A Surprise for Mrs. Dodds: A Little Boy's Friendship Changes a Lonely Woman's Life. 1989. (Illus.). 32p. (J). (gr. 3-5). pap. 5.99 o.p. (*0-8066-2437-X*, 9-2437) Augsburg Fortress, Pubs.

Long, Susan Hill. Hide & Seek. 2003. (Illus.). 16p. (J). (ps-2). pap. 3.99 (*1-59014-110-5*) Night Sky Bks.

—Sea of Riddles. 2003. (Illus.). 16p. (J). (ps-2). pap. 3.99 (*1-59014-111-3*) Night Sky Bks.

Lonsberry, Daniel. Mr. Tall Cactus & His Shorter, Prickly Neighbors. 1997. (Illus.). 32p. (J). (ps-4). pap. (*0-9658255-1-5*) Magic Carpet Rides Co.

Look, Lenore. Ruby Lu, Brave & True. Wilsdorf, Anne, tr. & illus. by. 2004. 112p. (J). 15.95 (*0-689-84907-9*, Atheneum/Anne Schwartz Bks.) Simon & Schuster Children's Publishing.

Loomis, Christine. In the Diner. 1994. (Illus.). 32p. (J). (ps-2). pap. 14.95 (*0-590-46716-6*) Scholastic, Inc.

Loomis, Debbie. Best of Friends. Hood, W. Edmund, ed. 1996. (Illus.). (J). pap. 3.00 (*0-9647539-4-4*) QDP Publishing.

Lopetegui, Leqnor. I Muy Bien! Very Good! La Casa de Ann Mary Big Book. 2001. (SPA., Illus.). 16p. (J). (gr. 1-3). pap. (*0-9713381-6-7*) Double R Publishing, LLC.

—I Muy Bien! (Very Good!) La Escuela de Maricela Big Book. 2001. (SPA., Illus.). 16p. (J). (gr. 1-3). pap. (*0-9713381-5-9*) Double R Publishing, LLC.

Lopetegui, Leqnor, et al. I Muy Bien! (Very Good!) Las Estaciones. 2001. (SPA., Illus.). 16p. (J). (gr. 1-3). pap. (*0-9713381-7-5*) Double R Publishing, LLC.

Lord, Athena V. Z. A. P., Zoe, & the Musketeers. 1992. 160p. (J). (gr. 3-7). text 13.95 o.p. (*0-02-759561-7*, Simon & Schuster Children's Publishing) Simon & Schuster Children's Publishing.

Lord, Wendy. Gorilla on the Midway. 1994. (Tabitha Sarah Bigbee Book). 96p. (J). pap. 4.99 (*0-7814-0892-X*) Cook Communications Ministries.

—Pickle Stew. 1994. (Tabitha Sarah Bigbee Book). 96p. (J). pap. 4.99 (*0-7814-0886-5*) Cook Communications Ministries.

Love, D. Anne. My Lone Star Summer. 1996. 192p. (J). (gr. 4-7). tchr. ed. 15.95 (*0-8234-1235-0*) Holiday Hse., Inc.

—My Lone Star Summer. 1998. 192p. (gr. 4-7). reprint ed. pap. text 3.99 o.s.i (*0-440-41375-3*, Yearling) Random Hse. Children's Bks.

Lovejoy, N. L. The DWEEBZ Bk. 1: JaneLee & Some DWEEBZ. 2000. (Illus.). 48p. (J). (ps-3). 8.95 (*0-9700943-0-2*) Small Secrets Unlimited, Inc.

Lovelace, Maud Hart. Betsy & Tacy Go Downtown. 1979. (Betsy-Tacy Ser.). (Illus.). 240p. (J). (gr. 3 up). pap. 5.99 (*0-06-440098-0*, Harper Trophy) HarperCollins Children's Bk. Group.

—Betsy & Tacy Go over the Big Hill. 1979. (Betsy-Tacy Ser.). (Illus.). 192p. (J). (gr. 5 up). pap. 5.99 (*0-06-440099-9*, Harper Trophy) HarperCollins Children's Bk. Group.

—Betsy-Tacy. 60th ed. 1979. (Betsy-Tacy Ser.). (Illus.). 144p. (J). (gr. 3 up). pap. 5.99 (*0-06-440096-4*, Harper Trophy) HarperCollins Children's Bk. Group.

—Betsy-Tacy & Tib. 1979. (Betsy-Tacy Ser.). (Illus.). 160p. (J). (gr. 3 up). pap. 5.95 (*0-06-440097-2*, Harper Trophy) HarperCollins Children's Bk. Group.

—Betsy-Tacy Books, 6 vols., Set. 1981. (Trophy Bk.). (J). (gr. 4-6). pap. 12.95 o.p. (*0-06-440127-8*, Harper Trophy) HarperCollins Children's Bk. Group.

—The Betsy-Tacy Treasury. 1995. (Illus.). (J). (gr. 1-8). 5.50 o.p. (*0-06-024919-6*) HarperCollins Pubs.

Lowell, Melissa. Ice Princess. l.t. ed. 1998. (Silver Blades Ser.: No. 7). 144p. (J). (gr. 4 up). lib. bdg. 22.60 (*0-8368-2096-7*) Stevens, Gareth Inc.

—The Perfect Pair. l.t. ed. 1998. (Silver Blades Ser.: No. 5). 96p. (J). (gr. 4 up). lib. bdg. 22.60 (*0-8368-2067-3*) Stevens, Gareth Inc.

—Rumors at the Rink. l.t. ed. 1998. (Silver Blades Ser.: No. 8). 144p. (J). (gr. 4 up). lib. bdg. 22.60 (*0-8368-2097-5*) Stevens, Gareth Inc.

—Skating Camp. l.t. ed. 1998. (Silver Blades Ser.: No. 6). 96p. (J). (gr. 4 up). lib. bdg. 22.60 (*0-8368-2068-1*) Stevens, Gareth Inc.

—Spring Break. l.t. ed. 1998. (Silver Blades Ser.: No. 9). 144p. (J). (gr. 4 up). lib. bdg. 22.60 (*0-8368-2098-3*) Stevens, Gareth Inc.

Lowry, Lois. Anastasia, Absolutely. 1995. 128p. (J). (gr. 4-6). 16.00 (*0-395-74521-7*) Houghton Mifflin Co.

—Anastasia, Absolutely. 1997. 128p. (gr. 4-7). pap. text 3.99 (*0-440-41222-6*, Yearling) Random Hse. Children's Bks.

—Anastasia, Absolutely. 1997. (J). 10.04 (*0-606-11041-0*) Turtleback Bks.

—Anastasia "Asusordenes"Tr. of Anastasia at Your Order. (SPA.). 120p. (J). 9.95 (*84-239-7073-6*) Espasa Calpe, S.A. ESP. *Dist:* Planeta Publishing Corp.

—Anastasia at Your Service. l.t. ed. 1988. 224p. (J). lib. bdg. 15.95 o.p. (*1-55736-101-0*) Bantam Doubleday Dell Large Print Group, Inc.

—Anastasia at Your Service. 1982. (Illus.). 160p. (J). (gr. 4-6). 16.00 (*0-395-32865-9*) Houghton Mifflin Co.

—Anastasia at Your Service. 149p. (J). (gr. 4-6). pap. 3.99 (*0-8072-1409-4*, Listening Library) Random Hse. Audio Publishing Group.

—Anastasia at Your Service. 1983. 160p. (gr. 4-7). pap. text 4.50 (*0-440-40290-5*, Yearling) Random Hse. Children's Bks.

—Anastasia at Your Service. 1984. (J). 10.55 (*0-606-02648-7*) Turtleback Bks.

—Anastasia Elige Profesion.Tr. of Anastasia's Chosen Career. (SPA.). (J). 188p. 9.95 (*84-239-9066-4*); 1996. 232p. 9.95 (*84-239-7133-3*) Espasa Calpe, S.A. ESP. *Dist:* Planeta Publishing Corp., Lectorum Pubns., Inc.

—Anastasia Elige Profesion. 1990. Tr. of Anastasia's Chosen Career. 16.00 (*0-606-16063-9*) Turtleback Bks.

—Anastasia's Chosen Career. l.t. ed. 1992. 216p. (J). lib. bdg. 12.95 o.p. (*0-7451-1468-7*, Macmillan Reference USA) Gale Group.

—Anastasia's Chosen Career. 1987. 160p. (J). (gr. 4-6). tchr. ed. 16.00 (*0-395-42506-9*) Houghton Mifflin Co.

—Anastasia's Chosen Career. 1990. (J). pap. o.s.i (*0-440-80199-0*, Dell Books for Young Readers); 1988. 160p. (gr. 4-7). pap. text 4.50 (*0-440-40100-3*, Yearling) Random Hse. Children's Bks.

—Anastasia's Chosen Career. 1987. (J). 10.55 (*0-606-04083-8*) Turtleback Bks.

—Find a Stranger, Say Good-Bye. 1990. 192p. (YA). (gr. 7 up). mass mkt. 5.50 (*0-440-20541-7*, Laurel Leaf) Random Hse. Children's Bks.

—Find a Stranger, Say Good-Bye. (J). (gr. 7-9). 1985. pap. (*0-671-62116-5*); 1980. reprint ed. pap. (*0-671-42062-3*) Simon & Schuster Children's Publishing. (Simon Pulse).

Marshall, Edward. Four on the Shore. 1987. (Easy-to-Read Bks.). (Illus.). 4p. (J). (ps-3). pap. 4.99 o.p. (*0-8037-0437-2*, Dial Bks. for Young Readers) Penguin Putnam Bks. for Young Readers.

—Fox All Week. 1984. (Easy-to-Read Bks.). (Illus.). 48p. (J). (ps-3). 10.95 o.s.i (*0-8037-0062-8*); 10.89 o.p. (*0-8037-0066-0*) Penguin Putnam Bks. for Young Readers. (Dial Bks. for Young Readers).

—Zorro y Sus Amigos. 1996. (Libro Puffin Facil-de-Leer Ser.).Tr. of Fox & His Friends. 8.70 o.p. (*0-606-10538-7*) Turtleback Bks.

Marshall, James. The Cut-Ups Cut Loose. (Illus.). 32p. (J). (ps-3). 1989. pap. 4.99 o.s.i (*0-14-050672-1*, Puffin Bks.); 1987. 15.99 o.p. (*0-670-80740-0*, Viking Children's Bks.) Penguin Putnam Bks. for Young Readers.

—The Cut-Ups Cut Loose. 1987. (J). 10.19 o.p. (*0-606-04189-3*) Turtleback Bks.

—George & Martha Back in Town. 2002. (George & Martha Ser.). (Illus.). (J). 14.74 (*0-7587-2569-8*) Book Wholesalers, Inc.

—George & Martha Back in Town. (Carry-Along Book & Cassette Favorites Ser.). 48p. (J). (ps-3). 2000. (Illus.). pap. 9.95 incl. audio (*0-618-04935-5*); 1988. pap. 6.95 (*0-395-47946-0*); 1984. (Illus.). lib. bdg., tchr. ed. 16.00 (*0-395-35386-6*, 5-90939) Houghton Mifflin Co.

—George & Martha Back in Town. 1984. 13.10 (*0-606-02800-5*) Turtleback Bks.

—Jorge y Marta. 2000. (SPA., Illus.). 32p. (J). (ps-3). pap. 6.95 (*0-618-05076-0*, HM0196); lib. bdg. 16.00 (*0-618-05075-2*, HM4632) Houghton Mifflin Co.

—Jorge y Marta en la Ciudad. 2001. (SPA., Illus.). 52p. (J). (ps-3). (*84-239-2829-2*, EC0827) Espasa Calpe, S.A. ESP. *Dist:* Lectorum Pubns., Inc.

—Jorge y Marta (George & Martha) 2000. (SPA., Illus.). (J). 13.10 (*0-606-18210-1*) Turtleback Bks.

—Tres en un Arbol (Three up a Tree) 1989. 15.15 o.p. (*0-606-10519-0*) Turtleback Bks.

—Willis. 2001. (Illus.). 48p. (J). (ps-3). tchr. ed. 15.00 (*0-618-12441-1*) Houghton Mifflin Co.

—Willis. 2001. (J). 11.10 (*0-606-21530-1*) Turtleback Bks.

—Wings: A Tale of Two Chickens. 2003. (Illus.). 32p. (J). (ps-3). tchr. ed. 15.00 (*0-618-22587-0*); pap. 4.95 (*0-618-31659-0*) Houghton Mifflin Co.

—Wings: A Tale of Two Chickens. 1988. 32p. (J). (ps up). pap. 5.99 o.s.i (*0-14-050579-2*, Puffin Bks.) Penguin Putnam Bks. for Young Readers.

Marsoli, Lisa Ann. Leap's Friends A-Z. (Illus.). 24p. (J). (gr. k-2). (*1-58605-008-7*) LeapFrog Enterprises, Inc.

Martin, Ann M. Abby & the Best Kid Ever. 1998. (Baby-Sitters Club Ser.: No. 116). (J). (gr. 3-7). 10.04 (*0-606-13160-4*) Turtleback Bks.

—The Baby-Sitters Club Boxed Set No. 1: Kristy's Great Idea; Claudia & the Phantom Phone Calls; The Truth about Stacey; Mary Anne Saves the Day. 1990. (Baby-Sitters Club Ser.: Nos. 1-4). (J). (gr. 3-7). pap. 14.95 (*0-590-63673-1*) Scholastic, Inc.

—Boy-Crazy Stacey. l.t. ed. 1988. (Baby-Sitters Club Ser.: No. 8). 138p. (J). (gr. 3-7). reprint ed. 9.50 o.p. (*0-942545-69-9*); lib. bdg. 10.50 o.p. (*0-942545-79-6*) Grey Castle Pr.

—Boy-Crazy Stacey. 1987. (Baby-Sitters Club Ser.: No. 8). (J). (gr. 3-7). 160p. pap. 2.50 o.p. (*0-590-41040-7*, Scholastic Paperbacks); 192p. mass mkt. 3.50 (*0-590-43509-4*) Scholastic, Inc.

—Boy-Crazy Stacey. l.t. ed. 1995. (Baby-Sitters Club Ser.: No. 8). 144p. (J). (gr. 3-7). lib. bdg. 21.27 o.p. (*0-8368-1321-9*) Stevens, Gareth Inc.

—Boy-Crazy Stacey. 1987. (Baby-Sitters Club Ser.: No. 8). (J). (gr. 3-7). 10.04 (*0-606-03548-6*) Turtleback Bks.

—Claudia & Mean Janine. l.t. ed. 1988. (Baby-Sitters Club Ser.: No. 7). 145p. (J). (gr. 3-7). reprint ed. 9.50 o.p. (*0-942545-68-0*); lib. bdg. 10.50 o.p. (*0-942545-78-8*) Grey Castle Pr.

—Claudia & Mean Janine. (Baby-Sitters Club Ser.: No. 7). (J). (gr. 3-7). 1995. mass mkt. 3.99 (*0-590-25162-7*); 1987. 160p. pap. 2.75 o.p. (*0-590-41041-5*, Scholastic Paperbacks); 1987. 192p. mass mkt. 3.50 (*0-590-43719-4*) Scholastic, Inc.

—Claudia & Mean Janine. 1995. (Baby-Sitters Club Ser.: No. 7). 176p. (J). (gr. 3-7). lib. bdg. 21.27 o.p. (*0-8368-1320-0*) Stevens, Gareth Inc.

—Claudia & Mean Janine. 1987. (Baby-Sitters Club Ser.: No. 7). (J). (gr. 3-7). 10.04 (*0-606-00551-X*) Turtleback Bks.

—Claudia & the Bad Joke. (Baby-Sitters Club Ser.: No. 19). (J). (gr. 3-7). 1996. mass mkt. 3.99 (*0-590-60671-9*); 1988. 192p. mass mkt. 3.50 (*0-590-43510-8*) Scholastic, Inc.

—Claudia & the Bad Joke. 1988. (Baby-Sitters Club Ser.: No. 19). (J). (gr. 3-7). 10.04 (*0-606-04084-6*) Turtleback Bks.

—Claudia & the Friendship Feud. 1999. (Baby-Sitters Club Friends Forever Ser.: No. 4). 130p. (J). (gr. 3-7). mass mkt. 4.50 (*0-590-52331-7*, Scholastic Paperbacks) Scholastic, Inc.

—Claudia & the New Girl. (Baby-Sitters Club Ser.: No. 12). (J). (gr. 3-7). 1988. 160p. pap. 2.75 o.p. (*0-590-41126-8*, Scholastic Paperbacks); 1988. 192p. mass mkt. 3.50 (*0-590-43721-6*); 1996. 160p. mass mkt. 3.99 (*0-590-25167-8*) Scholastic, Inc.

—Claudia & the New Girl. l.t. ed. 1993. (Baby-Sitters Club Ser.: No. 12). 176p. (J). (gr. 3-7). lib. bdg. 21.27 o.p. (*0-8368-1016-3*) Stevens, Gareth Inc.

—Claudia & the New Girl. 1989. (Baby-Sitters Club Ser.: No. 12). (J). (gr. 3-7). 10.04 (*0-606-03758-6*) Turtleback Bks.

—Claudia & the Perfect Boy. 1994. (Baby-Sitters Club Ser.: No. 71). 192p. (J). (gr. 3-7). mass mkt. 3.99 (*0-590-47009-4*) Scholastic, Inc.

—Claudia & the Perfect Boy. 1994. (Baby-Sitters Club Ser.: No. 71). (J). (gr. 3-7). 10.04 (*0-606-05736-6*) Turtleback Bks.

—Claudia & the Sad Good-Bye. 1997. (Baby-Sitters Club Ser.: No. 26). (J). (gr. 3-7). mass mkt. 3.99 (*0-590-67394-7*) Scholastic, Inc.

—Claudia Kishi, Live from WSTO! 1995. (Baby-Sitters Club Ser.: No. 85). (J). (gr. 3-7). pap. text 3.99 (*0-590-94784-2*) Scholastic, Inc.

—Claudia, Queen of the Seventh Grade. 1997. (Baby-Sitters Club Ser.: No. 106). (J). (gr. 3-7). 10.04 (*0-606-11066-6*) Turtleback Bks.

—Claudia's Freind Friend. 1993. (Baby-Sitters Club Ser.: No. 63). 192p. (J). (gr. 3-7). mass mkt. 3.50 (*0-590-45665-2*) Scholastic, Inc.

—A Corner of the Universe. 2004. 208p. (YA). pap. 5.99 (*0-439-38881-3*, Scholastic Paperbacks) Scholastic, Inc.

—Dawn & the Older Boy. l.t. ed. 1995. (Baby-Sitters Club Ser.: No. 37). 144p. (J). (gr. 3-7). lib. bdg. 21.27 o.p. (*0-8368-1417-7*) Stevens, Gareth Inc.

—Dawn & Whitney, Friends Forever. 1994. (Baby-Sitters Club Ser.: No. 77). 192p. (J). (gr. 3-7). mass mkt. 3.99 (*0-590-48221-1*) Scholastic, Inc.

—Everything Changes. 1999. (Baby-Sitters Club Friends Forever Special Ser.: No. 1). (J). (gr. 3-7). pap. 4.50 (*0-590-50391-X*); 5.50 (*0-439-08324-9*) Scholastic, Inc.

—Good-Bye Stacey, Good-Bye. (Baby-Sitters Club Ser.: No. 13). (J). (gr. 3-7). 1996. 176p. mass mkt. 3.99 (*0-590-25168-6*); 1988. 192p. mass mkt. 3.50 (*0-590-43386-5*) Scholastic, Inc.

—Good-Bye Stacey, Good-Bye. l.t. ed. 1993. (Baby-Sitters Club Ser.: No. 13). 176p. (J). (gr. 3-7). lib. bdg. 19.93 o.p. (*0-8368-1017-1*) Stevens, Gareth Inc.

—Hello, Mallory. (Baby-Sitters Club Ser.: No. 14). (J). (gr. 3-7). 1996. mass mkt. 3.99 (*0-590-25169-4*); 1988. 144p. pap. 2.75 o.p. (*0-590-41128-4*, Scholastic Paperbacks); 1988. 192p. mass mkt. 3.50 (*0-590-43385-7*) Scholastic, Inc.

—Hello, Mallory. l.t. ed. 1993. (Baby-Sitters Club Ser.: No. 14). 176p. (J). (gr. 3-7). lib. bdg. 21.27 o.p. (*0-8368-1018-X*) Stevens, Gareth Inc.

—Hello, Mallory. 1988. (Baby-Sitters Club Ser.: No. 14). (J). (gr. 3-7). 10.04 (*0-606-03809-4*) Turtleback Bks.

—Karen's New Friend. 1993. (Baby-Sitters Little Sister Ser.: No. 36). 112p. (J). (gr. 3-7). mass mkt. 3.50 (*0-590-45651-2*) Scholastic, Inc.

—Karen's Pen Pal. 1992. (Baby-Sitters Little Sister Ser.: No. 25). 112p. (J). (gr. 3-7). mass mkt. 3.50 (*0-590-44831-5*) Scholastic, Inc.

—Kristy & the Snobs. (Baby-Sitters Club Ser.: No. 11). (J). (gr. 3-7). 1996. 176p. mass mkt. 3.99 (*0-590-25166-X*); 1988. 160p. pap. 2.75 o.p. (*0-590-41125-X*, Scholastic Paperbacks); 1988. 192p. mass mkt. 3.50 (*0-590-43660-0*) Scholastic, Inc.

—Kristy & the Snobs. l.t. ed. 1993. (Baby-Sitters Club Ser.: No. 11). 176p. (J). (gr. 3-7). lib. bdg. 19.93 o.p. (*0-8368-1015-5*) Stevens, Gareth Inc.

—Kristy & the Snobs. 1988. (Baby-Sitters Club Ser.: No. 11). (J). (gr. 3-7). 10.55 (*0-606-03547-8*) Turtleback Bks.

—Mallory Hates Boys (and Gym) 1992. (Baby-Sitters Club Ser.: No. 59). 192p. (J). (gr. 3-7). mass mkt. 3.50 (*0-590-45660-1*) Scholastic, Inc.

—Mary Anne & the Little Princess. 1996. (Baby-Sitters Club Ser.: No. 102). 142p. (J). (gr. 3-7). mass mkt. 3.99 (*0-590-69208-9*) Scholastic, Inc.

—Mary Anne & the Little Princess. 1996. (Baby-Sitters Club Ser.: No. 102). (J). (gr. 3-7). 10.04 (*0-606-10132-2*) Turtleback Bks.

—Mary Anne & the Memory Garden. 1996. (Baby-Sitters Club Ser.: No. 93). (J). (gr. 3-7). mass mkt. 3.99 (*0-590-22877-3*) Scholastic, Inc.

—Mary Anne & the Memory Garden. 1996. (Baby-Sitters Club Ser.: No. 93). (J). (gr. 3-7). 9.09 o.p. (*0-606-08482-7*) Turtleback Bks.

—Mary Anne & Too Many Boys. 1990. (Baby-Sitters Club Ser.: No. 34). (J). (gr. 3-7). mass mkt. 3.99 (*0-590-73283-8*); 192p. mass mkt. 3.50 (*0-590-42494-7*) Scholastic, Inc.

—Mary Anne & Too Many Boys. l.t. ed. 1995. (Baby-Sitters Club Ser.: No. 34). 144p. (J). (gr. 3-7). lib. bdg. 21.27 o.p. (*0-8368-1414-2*) Stevens, Gareth Inc.

—Mary Anne & Too Many Boys. 1990. (Baby-Sitters Club Ser.: No. 34). (J). (gr. 3-7). 8.60 (*0-606-04475-2*) Turtleback Bks.

—Mary Anne Misses Logan. 1991. (Baby-Sitters Club Ser.: No. 46). 192p. (J). (gr. 3-7). mass mkt. 3.50 (*0-590-43569-8*) Scholastic, Inc.

—Mary Anne Misses Logan. 1996. (Baby-Sitters Club Ser.: No. 46). 144p. (J). (gr. 3-7). lib. bdg. 21.27 o.p. (*0-8368-1570-X*) Stevens, Gareth Inc.

—Mary Anne Saves the Day. l.t. ed. 1988. (Baby-Sitters Club Ser.: No. 4). 157p. (J). (gr. 3-7). reprint ed. 9.50 o.p. (*0-942545-65-6*); lib. bdg. 10.50 o.p. (*0-942545-75-3*) Grey Castle Pr.

—Mary Anne Saves the Day. (Baby-Sitters Club Ser.: No. 4). (J). (gr. 3-7). 1995. 192p. mass mkt. 3.99 (*0-590-25159-7*); 1987. 176p. pap. 2.75 o.p. (*0-590-42123-9*, Scholastic Paperbacks); 1987. pap. 2.75 o.p. (*0-590-33953-2*); 1987. mass mkt. 3.50 (*0-590-43512-4*) Scholastic, Inc.

—Mary Anne Saves the Day. l.t. ed. 1995. (Baby-Sitters Club Ser.: No. 4). 167p. (J). (gr. 3-7). lib. bdg. 19.93 o.p. (*0-8368-1317-0*) Stevens, Gareth Inc.

—Mary Anne Saves the Day. 1987. (Baby-Sitters Club Ser.: No. 4). (J). (gr. 3-7). 10.04 (*0-606-03085-9*) Turtleback Bks.

—Mary Anne to the Rescue. 1997. (Baby-Sitters Club Ser.: No. 109). (J). (gr. 3-7). mass mkt. 3.99 (*0-590-69215-1*, Scholastic Paperbacks) Scholastic, Inc.

—Rachel Parker, Kindergarten Show-Off. 1992. (Illus.). 40p. (J). (ps-3). tchr. ed. 16.95 o.p. (*0-8234-0935-X*); pap. 6.95 (*0-8234-1067-6*) Holiday Hse., Inc.

—Secret Santa. 1994. (Baby-Sitters Club Ser.). 40p. (J). (gr. 3-7). pap. 14.95 (*0-590-48295-5*) Scholastic, Inc.

—Stacey's Ex-Best Friend. 1992. (Baby-Sitters Club Ser.: No. 51). (J). (gr. 3-7). 8.60 o.p. (*0-606-00770-9*) Turtleback Bks.

—Stacey's Secret Friend. 1997. (Baby-Sitters Club Ser.: No. 111). (Illus.). 160p. (J). (gr. 3-7). mass mkt. 3.99 (*0-590-05989-0*) Scholastic, Inc.

—Stacey's Secret Friend. 1997. (Baby-Sitters Club Ser.: No. 111). (J). (gr. 3-7). 10.04 (*0-606-11071-2*) Turtleback Bks.

—Sunny: Diary Two. 1998. (California Diaries). (YA). (gr. 6-8). mass mkt. 3.99 (*0-590-29840-2*) Scholastic, Inc.

—With You & Without You. 1987. 192p. (J). (gr. 4-6). pap. 2.95 o.p. (*0-590-43625-2*) Scholastic, Inc.

Martin, Bill, Jr. Words. 1993. (Illus.). 14p. (J). (ps up). 4.95 (*0-671-87174-9*, Little Simon) Simon & Schuster Children's Publishing.

Martin, Bill, Jr. & Archambault, John. White Dynamite & Curly Kidd, ERS. 1989. (Illus.). 32p. (J). (ps-3). pap. 6.95 (*0-8050-1018-1*, Holt, Henry & Co. Bks. For Young Readers) Holt, Henry & Co.

Martin, David. Lizzie & Her Friend. 1995. (Illus.). (J). bds. 2.99 o.p. (*1-56402-448-2*) Candlewick Pr.

Martin, Dorothy. Chapter Closed. 1985. (Peggy Ser.: No. 8). (J). (gr. 7). pap. 3.50 o.p. (*0-8024-8308-9*) Moody Pr.

Martin, Jacqueline Briggs. Bizzy Bones & Moosemouse. 1986. (Illus.). 32p. (J). (ps-3). 12.95 o.p. (*0-688-05745-4*); lib. bdg. 12.88 o.p. (*0-688-05746-2*) HarperCollins Children's Bk. Group.

Martin Larraanaga, Ana. Pepo & Lolo Are Friends. 2004. 24p. (J). 8.99 (*0-7636-1982-5*) Candlewick Pr.

Martin, Linda. When Dinosaurs Go Visiting. 1993. (Illus.). 32p. (J). 11.95 o.p. (*0-8118-0122-5*) Chronicle Bks. LLC.

Martin, Marilyn. Friends Forever. 2000. (Illus.). (YA). (gr. 4-7). pap. 12.95 (*1-891929-58-5*) Four Seasons Pubs.

Martin, Marla. Birthday Friend. 1993. (Jewel Book Ser.: Set 4). (Illus.). 32p. (J). (ps-2). pap. 2.70 (*0-7399-0042-0*, 2136) Rod & Staff Pubs., Inc.

Martin, S. R. Talk to Me. 1999. (Insomniacs Ser.: No. 3). (Illus.). 80p. (YA). (gr. 7-12). mass mkt. 2.99 (*0-590-69142-2*) Scholastic, Inc.

Martin, Trude. Obee & Mungedeech. 1999. 107p. (J). (gr. 3-6). reprint ed. text 15.00 (*0-7881-6639-5*) DIANE Publishing Co.

—Obee & Mungedeech. 1996. (Illus.). 112p. (J). (gr. 4-7). 15.00 (*0-689-80644-2*, Simon & Schuster Children's Publishing); pap. 3.99 (*0-689-80725-2*, Aladdin) Simon & Schuster Children's Publishing.

—Obee & Mungedeech. 1996. (J). 9.09 o.p. (*0-606-09702-3*) Turtleback Bks.

Martini, Teri. All Because of Jill. 1976. 154p. (J). (gr. 7-9). 6.95 o.p. (*0-664-32589-0*) Westminster John Knox Pr.

Martin Larrañaga, Ana, illus. Whose Toes Are Those? 2001. 10p. (J). (ps-1). bds. 6.99 o.s.i (*0-689-84072-1*, Little Simon) Simon & Schuster Children's Publishing.

Martinez, Carol. Paco y Ana Aprenden Acerca de la Amistad: Frankie & Ann Learn about Friendship. 1988. (Paco y Ana Aprenden Ser.). (SPA., Illus.). (Orig.). (J). (gr. 2-4). pap. 2.50 (*0-311-38589-3*, Editorial Mundo Hispano) Casa Bautista de Publicaciones.

Marzollo, Jean. Best Friends Club. 1990. (Thirty-Nine Kids on the Block Ser.: No. 4). (J). pap. 2.50 o.p. (*0-590-42726-1*) Scholastic, Inc.

—Close Your Eyes. 1981. (Pied Piper Bks.). (Illus.). (J). (ps). pap. 4.95 o.p. (*0-8037-1617-6*, Dial Bks. for Young Readers) Penguin Putnam Bks. for Young Readers.

—Companeros en el Futbol. 1999. (Coleccion "Hola, Lector" Ser.). (SPA., Illus.). 48p. (J). (gr. 2-4). pap. 3.99 (*0-439-08056-8*, SO8904, Scholastic en Espanola) Scholastic, Inc.

Maselli, Christopher P. N. Dangerous Encounters: Fifty-Two Soul Gear Laptop Five Danger Enco. 2003. 128p. (J). pap. 4.99 (*0-310-70664-5*) Zondervan.

—Power Play. 2003. (2:52 Soul Gear Ser.). (Illus.). 128p. (J). pap. 4.99 (*0-310-70341-7*) Zondervan.

Mason, Adrienne & Cupples, Patricia. Lu & Clancy's Secret Codes. 1999. 144p. (J). (gr. 2-5). pap. (*1-55074-553-0*) Kids Can Pr., Ltd.

Mason, Margo C. Two Good Friends. 1990. 32p. (J). (ps-3). pap. 3.50 o.s.i (*0-553-34885-X*) Bantam Bks.

Mass, Wendy. Leap Day. 2004. (Illus.). 224p. (J). 16.95 (*0-316-53728-4*) Little Brown & Co.

—A Mango-Shaped Space. 2003. 224p. (J). (gr. 5-9). 16.95 (*0-316-52388-7*) Little Brown Children's Bks.

Massey, Ed. Milton. 1996. (Illus.). 48p. (J). (gr. 1-5). 19.95 (*1-57143-047-4*, Wetlands Pr.) RDR Bks.

Massi, Jeri. Abandoned. 1989. (Peabody Adventure Ser.). 136p. (J). (gr. 4-7). pap. 6.49 (*0-89084-467-4*, 044164) Jones, Bob Univ. Pr.

Masterson, Audrey. The Day the Gypsies Came to Town. 1983. (Heritage Bks.). (Illus.). 32p. (J). (gr. 3-6). lib. bdg. 14.65 o.p. (*0-940742-22-5*) Raintree Pubs.

Matas, Carol. Kris's War. 1992. 160p. (YA). (gr. 7-9). pap. 3.25 o.p. (*0-590-45034-4*, Scholastic Paperbacks) Scholastic, Inc.

—Sparks Fly Upward. 2002. 192p. (YA). (gr. 5-9). 15.00 (*0-618-15964-9*, Clarion Bks.) Houghton Mifflin Co. Trade & Reference Div.

Matchette, Katharine E. Oh, Suzannah. 1998. 158p. (YA). (gr. 6 up). pap. 8.75 (*0-9645045-2-9*) Deka Pr.

Mathers, Petra. Herbie's Secret Santa. 2002. (Illus.). 32p. (J). (gr. k-3). 15.95 (*0-689-83550-7*, Atheneum/Anne Schwartz Bks.) Simon & Schuster Children's Publishing.

—Lottie's New Friend. (Illus.). 32p. (J). (ps-3). 2002. pap. 5.99 (*0-689-84896-X*, Aladdin); 1999. 15.00 (*0-689-82014-3*, Atheneum/Anne Schwartz Bks.) Simon & Schuster Children's Publishing.

Mathias, B. J. Jeffrey William & The Little Prince. 2002. 10.00 (*0-9711320-9-7*) Electronic Publishing Services.

Mathis, Sharon Bell. Sidewalk Story. 1981. (J). (gr. 2-4). pap. 0.95 o.p. (*0-380-00851-3*, 31146, Avon Bks.) Morrow/Avon.

—Sidewalk Story. 1986. (Novels Ser.). 64p. (J). (gr. 4-7). pap. 4.99 (*0-14-032165-9*, Puffin Bks.) Penguin Putnam Bks. for Young Readers.

—Sidewalk Story. 1986. 10.14 (*0-606-12514-0*) Turtleback Bks.

Matlin, Marlee. Deaf Child Crossing. (Illus.). 208p. (J). 2004. pap. 4.99 (*0-689-86696-8*, Aladdin); 2002. (gr. 3-6). 15.95 (*0-689-82208-1*, Simon & Schuster Children's Publishing) Simon & Schuster Children's Publishing.

Matranga, Frances C. One Step at a Time. 1987. (Illus.). (J). (gr. 4-7). pap. 3.99 o.s.i (*0-570-03642-9*, 39-1126) Concordia Publishing Hse.

Matthews, Andrew. Crackling Brat, ERS. 1993. (Illus.). 32p. (J). (gr. k-3). 15.95 o.p. (*0-8050-2608-8*, Holt, Henry & Co. Bks. For Young Readers) Holt, Henry & Co.

—Mallory Cox & His Interstellar Socks. 1993. (Duckling Ser.). (Illus.). 96p. (J). (gr. 4-6). 18.95 o.p. (*0-460-88126-4*) Dent, J.M. & Sons GBR. *Dist:* Trafalgar Square.

Matthews, Kay. I'm Glad You Asked. 1994. (Illus.). 32p. (Orig.). (J). (ps-3). pap. 7.50 (*0-940875-03-9*) Acequia Madre.

Matthews, Phoebe. Switchstance. 1989. 176p. (Orig.). (YA). (gr. 7 up). pap. 2.95 (*0-380-75729-X*, Avon Bks.) Morrow/Avon.

Maugham, W. Somerset. Princess September & the Nightingale. 1998. (Iona & Peter Opie Library of Children's Literature). (Illus.). 48p. (YA). (gr. k-6). 16.95 o.p. (*0-19-512480-4*) Oxford Univ. Pr., Inc.

Maupassant, Guy de. Two Friends. Redpath, Ann A., ed. 1985. (Short Story Library). (Illus.). 32p. (YA). (gr. 4 up). lib. bdg. 13.95 o.p. (*0-88682-003-0*, 1076-K, Creative Education) Creative Co., The.

Maurer, Donna. Annie, Bea & Chi Chi Dolores. 1998. (J). 13.10 (*0-606-13144-2*) Turtleback Bks.

Mayer, Mercer. Appelard & Liverwurst. 1990. (Illus.). 40p. (J). (gr. k up). lib. bdg. 13.88 o.p. (*0-688-09660-3*); 13.95 (*0-688-09659-X*) Morrow/Avon. (Morrow, William & Co.).

—A Boy, a Dog, a Frog & a Friend. 2003. (Illus.). 32p. bds. 5.99 (*0-8037-2882-4*, Dial Bks. for Young Readers) Penguin Putnam Bks. for Young Readers.

—Frog on His Own. 2003. 32p. bds. 5.99 (*0-8037-2883-2*, Dial Bks. for Young Readers) Penguin Putnam Bks. for Young Readers.

—Just for You. 1982. (Little Critter Ser.). (J). (ps-3). 9.44 (*0-606-12373-3*) Turtleback Bks.

—Just My Friend & Me. 1988. (Little Critter Ser.). (J). (ps-3). 9.44 (*0-606-12381-4*) Turtleback Bks.

—New Kid in Town, Level 3. 2001. (First Readers, Skills & Practice Ser.). (Illus.). 24p. (J). (gr. 1-2). pap. 3.95 (*1-57768-829-5*) McGraw-Hill Children's Publishing.

—No One Can Play. 2000. (First Readers, Skills & Practice Ser.). (Illus.). 24p. (J). pap. 3.95 (*1-57768-804-X*) McGraw-Hill Children's Publishing.

—One Frog Too Many. 2003. 32p. bds. 5.99 (*0-8037-2885-9*, Dial Bks. for Young Readers) Penguin Putnam Bks. for Young Readers.

—Our Friend Sam. 2002. (Illus.). 24p. (J). (gr. 1-2). 10.95 (*1-57768-458-3*, Mercer Mayer First Readers) McGraw-Hill Children's Publishing.

—This Is My Friend. 1990. (Little Critter Ser.). (Illus.). 40p. (J). (ps-3). pap. 4.50 o.s.i (*0-307-11685-9*, Golden Bks.) Random Hse. Children's Bks.

—Yo Solito. 1997. (Spanish Golden Look-Look Bks.).Tr. of All by Myself. (SPA., Illus.). 24p. (J). (ps-3). pap. 3.29 o.s.i (*0-307-71938-3*, Golden Bks.) Random Hse. Children's Bks.

Mayer, Mercer & Mayer, Gina. Just Lost! 1999. (Little Critter Ser.). (Illus.). 24p. (J). (ps-3). pap. 3.29 (*0-307-12844-X*, 12844, Golden Bks.) Random Hse. Children's Bks.

Mayer, Mercer, et al. Backstage Pass. 1995. (Little Critter Ser.: No. 6). (Illus.). 48p. (J). (ps-3). pap. 3.99 o.s.i (*0-307-16031-9*, Golden Bks.) Random Hse. Children's Bks.

—The Pizza War. 1995. (Little Critter Ser.: No. 5). (Illus.). 72p. (J). (gr. 4-7). pap. 3.99 o.s.i (*0-307-15979-5*, 15979, Golden Bks.) Random Hse. Children's Bks.

Mayfield, Sue. Drowning Anna. 2002. 320p. (J). (gr. 5-9). 15.99 (*0-7868-0870-5*) Disney Pr.

—Drowning Anna. 2004. (J). (gr. 7). pap. 5.99 (*0-7868-0957-4*) Hyperion Bks. for Children.

Mayhew, James. Secret in the Garden. 2003. (Illus.). 32p. (J). pap. 15.95 (*0-439-40435-5*, Chicken Hse., The) Scholastic, Inc.

Mayne, William. The Blue Book of Hob Stories. 1984. (Illus.). 32p. (J). (ps). 7.95 o.s.i (*0-399-21037-7*, Philomel) Penguin Putnam Bks. for Young Readers.

—A House in Town. 1988. (Illus.). 32p. (J). (ps-3). 9.95 o.p. (*0-13-395880-9*, Simon & Schuster Children's Publishing) Simon & Schuster Children's Publishing.

Mazer, Anne. Good Things Come in Small Packages. 2003. (Amazing Days of Abby Hayes Ser.). 112p. (J). pap. 4.50 (*0-439-48280-1*, Scholastic Paperbacks) Scholastic, Inc.

—The Pen Is Mightier Than the Sword. 2001. (Amazing Days of Abby Hayes Ser.: No. 6). (Illus.). 144p. (J). (gr. 4-7). pap. 4.50 (*0-439-17882-7*) Scholastic, Inc.

—Too Close for Comfort. 2003. (Amazing Days of Abby Hayes Ser.: No. 11). 128p. (J). (gr. 3-6). pap. 4.50 (*0-439-48273-9*, Scholastic Paperbacks) Scholastic, Inc.

Mazer, Harry. When the Phone Rang. 1986. 192p. (YA). (gr. 7-9). mass mkt. 4.50 (*0-590-44773-4*) Scholastic, Inc.

Mazer, Norma Fox. A, My Name Is Ami. 1994. 160p. (Orig.). (J). (gr. 4-6). mass mkt. 3.25 o.p. (*0-590-43896-4*, Scholastic Paperbacks) Scholastic, Inc.

—Crazy Fish. 1999. 160p. (J). (gr. 4-7). pap. 4.50 (*0-380-73189-4*, Harper Trophy) HarperCollins Children's Bk. Group.

—Crazy Fish. 1998. 192p. (YA). (gr. 5-9). 15.00 (*0-688-16281-9*, Morrow, William & Co.) Morrow/Avon.

—Crazy Fish. 1999. 10.55 (*0-606-16339-5*) Turtleback Bks.

—E, My Name Is Emily. 1991. 176p. (J). pap. 13.95 o.p. (*0-590-43653-8*) Scholastic, Inc.

—Mrs. Fish, Ape, & Me, the Dump Queen. 1980. 144p. (J). (gr. 4-7). 10.95 o.p. (*0-525-35380-1*, Dutton) Dutton/Plume.

—Out of Control. (gr. 7 up). 1994. 272p. (J). pap. 5.99 (*0-380-71347-0*, Avon Bks.); 1993. 224p. (YA). 16.00 o.p. (*0-688-10208-5*, Morrow, William & Co.) Morrow/Avon.

—Out of Control. 1993. 12.00 (*0-606-06652-7*) Turtleback Bks.

—Silver. 1989. 208p. (J). (gr. 7 up). pap. 5.99 (*0-380-75026-0*, Harper Trophy) HarperCollins Children's Bk. Group.

—Silver. 1988. 272p. (YA). (gr. 7 up). 16.00 (*0-688-06865-0*, Morrow, William & Co.) Morrow/Avon.

—Silver. 1988. (J). 11.04 (*0-606-04325-X*) Turtleback Bks.

Mazzeo Zocchi, Judy. Circus or Not - Here We Come. 1998. (Adventures of Paulie & Sasha Ser.). (Illus.). 32p. (J). (gr. k-4). 15.95 (*1-891997-00-9*, THC 01, Treehouse Court) Dingles & Co.

McAllan, Marina, illus. Troublemaker. 1997. (*0-7608-0768-X*) Sundance Publishing.

McBratney, Sam. I'm Sorry. 1999. (Illus.). 24p. (J). (*0-7636-0981-1*) Candlewick Pr.

—Stranger from Somewhere in Time. (Yellow Bananas Ser.). (Illus.). 48p. (J). (gr. 3-4). 2003. lib. bdg. 19.96 (*0-7787-0937-X*); 2002. pap. 4.95 (*0-7787-0983-3*) Crabtree Publishing Co.

McBride, Earvin, Jr. The Joyous Adventures of Sam & Pam. unabr. ed. 2002. (Earvin MacBride's Fun Fun Lovable Cartoons Ser.). (Illus.). 123p. (J). (gr. 7-12). pap. 3.95 (*1-892511-03-7*) MacBride, E. J. Pubn., Inc.

—Neddy Buddy Basil. unabr. ed. 2002. (Illus.). 6p. (J). (gr. 7-12). pap. (*1-892511-13-4*) MacBride, E. J. Pubn., Inc.

McBride, Eve. Dandelions Help. 160p. pap. (*0-9698752-5-8*) Shoreline.

McBrier, Page. First Course: Trouble. 1990. (Treehouse Times Ser.: No. 4). 128p. (J). pap. 2.50 (*0-380-75783-4*, Avon Bks.) Morrow/Avon.

—The Great Rip-Off. 1990. (Treehouse Times Ser.: No. 8). 128p. (J). pap. 2.95 (*0-380-75902-0*, Avon Bks.) Morrow/Avon.

—Rats. 1990. (Treehouse Times Ser.: No. 7). 128p. (J). pap. 2.95 (*0-380-75901-2*, Avon Bks.) Morrow/Avon.

McCabe, Bernard. Bottle Rabbit & Friends. 1991. (Illus.). 136p. (J). (gr. 3-7). 14.95 o.p. (*0-571-15318-6*) Faber & Faber, Inc.

McCaffrey, Laura Williams. Alia Waking. 2003. 224p. (J). (gr. 4-9). tchr. ed. 15.00 (*0-618-19461-4*, Clarion Bks.) Houghton Mifflin Co. Trade & Reference Div.

McCann, Helen. What's French for Help, George? 1993. (Illus.). 460p. (J). (gr. 5-9). pap. 13.00 o.s.i (*0-671-74689-8*, Simon & Schuster Children's Publishing) Simon & Schuster Children's Publishing.

McCauley, Adam. My Friend Chicken. 1999. (Illus.). 28p. (J). (ps-k). 9.95 o.p. (*0-8118-2327-X*) Chronicle Bks. LLC.

McCaw, Mabel N. My Friend Next Door. 1968. (J). (ps-1). 0.75 o.p. (*0-8272-2308-0*) Chalice Pr.

McCloud, Susan Evans. Mormon Girls Bk. 4: New Friends. 1996. pap. 5.95 (*1-57008-282-0*, Bookcraft, Inc.) Deseret Bk. Co.

—Mormon Girls Bk. 6: The Little Stranger. 1996. pap. 5.95 (*1-57008-284-7*, Bookcraft, Inc.) Deseret Bk. Co.

McConnell, Christine. Don't Be Mad, Ivy. 1988. (Illus.). (J). (gr. 2-5). pap. 3.95 o.p. (*0-14-032329-5*, Puffin Bks.) Penguin Putnam Bks. for Young Readers.

McConnell, Robert. Davenport Dumpling. 1991. (Illus.). 48p. (J). (gr. 2-6). pap. 9.95 o.p. (*1-56523-018-3*) Fox Chapel Publishing Co., Inc.

McCord, Mark. Clodrow's Adventure: A Book about Friendship. 1996. (Illus.). 8p. (J). (ps). 8.99 (*0-7814-0292-1*) Cook Communications Ministries.

—Rattlebang: The Picture Book. 1996. (Illus.). 32p. (J). (ps-2). 14.99 (*0-7814-0290-5*) Cook Communications Ministries.

—Rattlebang Helps: A Book about Helpfulness. 1996. (Illus.). 8p. (J). (ps). 8.99 (*0-7814-0293-X*) Cook Communications Ministries.

McCormack, Erin. Disney's Princess Collection: Love & Friendship Stories. Heller, Sarah E., ed. 1999. (Disneys Ser.). (Illus.). 304p. (J). (gr. k-5). 15.99 (*0-7868-3247-9*) Disney Pr.

McCourt, Lisa. The Braids Girl. 1998. (Chicken Soup for Little Souls Ser.). (Illus.). 32p. (J). (ps-3). tchr. ed. 14.95 (*1-55874-554-8*) Health Communications, Inc.

—Chicken Soup for Little Souls: The Never-Forgotten Doll. 1997. (Chicken Soup for Little Souls Ser.). (Illus.). 32p. (J). (ps-3). tchr. ed. 14.95 (*1-55874-507-6*) Health Communications, Inc.

—The New Kid & the Cookie Thief. 2002. (Illus.). 32p. (J). (ps-3). 14.95 (*1-55874-588-2*) Health Communications, Inc.

McCoy, Sharon. The Best Friends Book. 1995. (Illus.). 64p. (J). (gr. 2 up). pap. 4.95 o.p. (*1-56565-204-5*) Lowell Hse. Juvenile.

McCue, Lisa, illus. Corduroy's Day & Corduroy's Party. 1987. (Corduroy Ser.). (J). (gr. k-1). bds. 15.95 incl. audio (*0-87499-041-6*) Live Oak Media.

McCully, Emily Arnold. Starring Mirette & Bellini. 2000. (Illus.). 32p. (J). (ps-3). pap. 6.99 o.s.i (*0-698-11822-7*) Penguin Putnam Bks. for Young Readers.

—Starring Mirette & Bellini. 1997. 13.14 (*0-606-20374-5*) Turtleback Bks.

McCusker, Paul. A Carnival of Secrets. 1997. (Adventures in Odyssey Ser.: Bk. 12). 120p. (J). (gr. 3-7). 4.99 (*1-56179-546-1*) Focus on the Family Publishing.

—Danger Lies Ahead. 1995. (Adventures in Odyssey Ser.: No. 7). 99p. (J). (gr. 3-7). pap. 4.99 (*1-56179-369-8*) Focus on the Family Publishing.

—The Point of No Return. 1995. (Adventures in Odyssey Ser.: No. 8). 125p. (J). (gr. 3-7). 4.99 (*1-56179-401-5*) Focus on the Family Publishing.

McDaniel, Lurlene. All the Days of Her Life. 1994. (One Last Wish Ser.: No. 10). 192p. (YA). (gr. 5-9). mass mkt. 4.99 (*0-553-56264-9*) Bantam Bks.

—Dawn Rochelle: Four Novels. 2000. 544p. (YA). (gr. 7 up). mass mkt. 6.99 o.s.i (*0-553-57095-1*, Starfire) Random Hse. Children's Bks.

—Dawn Rochelle: Four Novels. 2000. (Illus.). (J). 13.04 (*0-606-17994-1*) Turtleback Bks.

—Goodbye Doesn't Mean Forever. 1989. 208p. (YA). (gr. 5 up). mass mkt. 4.99 (*0-553-28007-4*, Starfire) Random Hse. Children's Bks.

—Head over Heels. 1987. (Impressions Ser.). 112p. (Orig.). (J). (gr. 6-8). pap. 2.25 o.p. (*0-87406-263-2*) Darby Creek Publishing.

—I Want to Live. 1996. 128p. (J). (gr. 5-8). pap. 3.99 (*0-87406-237-3*) Darby Creek Publishing.

—The Legacy: Making Wishes Come True. 1993. (One Last Wish Ser.: No. 7). 224p. (YA). (gr. 7 up). mass mkt. 4.99 (*0-553-56134-0*) Bantam Bks.

—Lifted up by Angels. 1997. 240p. (YA). (gr. 7-12). mass mkt. 4.99 (*0-553-57112-5*, Dell Books for Young Readers) Random Hse. Children's Bks.

—Please Don't Die. 1993. (One Last Wish Ser.: Vol. 8). 192p. (YA). (gr. 7 up). mass mkt. 4.99 (*0-553-56262-2*) Bantam Bks.

—Telling Christina Goodbye. 2002. 240p. (YA). (gr. 7 up). mass mkt. 4.99 (*0-553-57087-0*, Starfire) Random Hse. Children's Bks.

—Three's a Crowd. 1987. (Impressions Ser.). 128p. (Orig.). (J). (gr. 6-8). pap. 2.50 o.p. (*0-87406-274-8*) Darby Creek Publishing.

McDaniel, Whitt. Addie Fay & Old Yellow Streak. 2000. 220p. pap. 12.95 (*0-87714-666-7*) Denlingers Pubs., Ltd.

McDonald, Janet. Spellbound. 2003. 144p. pap. 5.99 (*0-14-250193-X*, Puffin Bks.) Penguin Putnam Bks. for Young Readers.

McDonald, Megan. Beezy. (Illus.). 48p. (J). (gr. 1-4). 2000. mass mkt. 4.95 (*0-531-07162-6*); 1997. pap. 13.95 (*0-531-30046-3*); 1997. lib. bdg. 14.99 o.p. (*0-531-33046-X*) Scholastic, Inc. (Orchard Bks.).

—Beezy & Funnybone. 2000. (Illus.). 48p. (J). (gr. 1-4). mass mkt. 4.95 (*0-531-07161-8*, Orchard Bks.) Scholastic, Inc.

—Beezy at Bat. (Illus.). 48p. (J). (gr. 1-4). 2000. mass mkt. 4.95 (*0-531-07164-2*); 1998. pap. 13.95 (*0-531-30085-4*); 1998. lib. bdg. 14.99 (*0-531-33085-0*) Scholastic, Inc. (Orchard Bks.).

—Beezy at Bat. 2000. (J). 11.10 (*0-606-20453-9*) Turtleback Bks.

—Beezy Magic. (Illus.). 48p. (J). (gr. 1-4). 2000. mass mkt. 4.95 (*0-531-07163-4*); 1998. pap. 13.95 (*0-531-30064-1*); 1998. lib. bdg. 14.99 (*0-531-33064-8*) Scholastic, Inc. (Orchard Bks.).

—Beezy Magic. 2000. (Illus.). (J). 11.10 (*0-606-18331-0*) Turtleback Bks.

—Lucky Star. 2000. (Road to Reading Ser.). (Illus.). 48p. (J). (gr. 1-3). 11.99 (*0-307-46329-X*, Golden Bks.) Random Hse. Children's Bks.

—Lucky Star. 2000. 10.14 (*0-606-18924-6*) Turtleback Bks.

—Mile 3. 2002. (Road to Writing Ser.). (Illus.). 48p. (J). (gr. 1-3). pap. 3.99 (*0-307-45607-2*, Golden Bks.) Random Hse. Children's Bks.

—Reptiles Are My Life. 2001. (Illus.). 32p. (J). (ps-2). pap. 15.95 (*0-439-29306-5*, Orchard Bks.) Scholastic, Inc.

—Shining Star. 2003. (Illus.). 48p. (J). (gr. 1-3). pap. 3.99 (*0-307-26340-1*); lib. bdg. 11.99 (*0-307-46340-0*) Random Hse., Inc.

McDonald, Megan & Wallace, Andrea, illus. Lucky Star. 2000. (Road to Reading Ser.). 48p. (J). (gr. 1-3). pap. 3.99 (*0-307-26329-0*, Golden Bks.) Random Hse. Children's Bks.

McDonnell, Christine. Los Amigos Primero (Friends First) Bracho, Coral & Uribe, Marcelo, trs. 1994. (SPA., Illus.). 216p. (J). (gr. 5-6). 5.99 (*968-16-4466-2*) Fondo de Cultura Economica MEX. *Dist:* Continental Bk. Co., Inc.

—Don't Be Mad, Ivy. 1981. (Illus.). 80p. (J). (gr. 1-5). 8.95 o.p. (*0-8037-2127-7*); 8.89 o.p. (*0-8037-2128-5*) Penguin Putnam Bks. for Young Readers. (Dial Bks. for Young Readers).

—Friends First. 1992. 176p. (J). (gr. 5 up). pap. 3.99 o.p. (*0-14-032477-1*, Puffin Bks.) Penguin Putnam Bks. for Young Readers.

—Just for the Summer. 1989. (Illus.). 128p. (J). (gr. 2-6). pap. 3.95 o.s.i (*0-14-032147-0*, Puffin Bks.) Penguin Putnam Bks. for Young Readers.

McDonnell, Janet. Two Special Valentines. 1994. (Circle the Year with Holidays Ser.). (Illus.). 32p. (J). lib. bdg. 19.00 o.p. (*0-516-00692-4*, Children's Pr.) Scholastic Library Publishing.

—An XYZ Adventure in Alphabet Town. 1992. (Read Around Alphabet Town Ser.). (Illus.). 32p. (J). mass mkt. 19.00 o.p. (*0-516-05424-4*, Children's Pr.) Scholastic Library Publishing.

McDonnell, Lois E. Stevie's Other Eyes. 1962. (J). (gr. 1-3). pap. 1.75 o.p. (*0-377-22701-3*) Friendship Pr.

McDonnell, Margot B. My Own Worst Enemy. 1984. (Pacer Bks.). 192p. (J). (gr. 7 up). 11.95 o.p. (*0-399-21102-0*, G. P. Putnam's Sons) Penguin Putnam Bks. for Young Readers.

McDougal, Scarlett. Popover. 2001. (Have a Nice Life Ser.: Vol. 3). 224p. (YA). (gr. 7-12). pap. 4.99 o.s.i (*0-14-131090-1*, Puffin-Alloy) Penguin Putnam Bks. for Young Readers.

McElligott, Matthew. Absolutely Not. 2004. (J). (*0-8027-8888-2*); (*0-8027-8889-0*) Walker & Co.

McGaw, Victoria. The Memory Box. Wise, Noreen, ed. 2001. (Lemonade Collection). (Illus.). 64p. (J). (gr. 2-8). pap. 7.50 (*1-58584-256-7*) Huckleberry Pr.

—Old Tree, Old Friend. Wise, Noreen, ed. 2001. (Lemonade Collection). (Illus.). 64p. (J). (gr. 1-5). pap. 7.50 (*1-58584-260-5*) Huckleberry Pr.

McGeorge, Constance W. Boomer's Big Day. 1996. (Illus.). 32p. (J). (ps-1). pap. 6.95 (*0-8118-1492-0*) Chronicle Bks. LLC.

McGhee, Alison. Snap: A Novel. 2004. 144p. (J). 15.99 (*0-7636-2002-5*) Candlewick Pr.

McGinnis, Diane. Bimbo: A Friend for Kindsay Lane. 1999. (Illus.). 28p. (J). 14.99 (*1-57921-190-9*) WinePress Publishing.

McGovern, Ann. Nicholas Bentley Stoningpot III. 1997. 11.19 o.p. (*0-606-12782-8*) Turtleback Bks.

McGugan, Jim. Josepha: A Prairie Boy's Story. ed. 1996. (J). (gr. 2). spiral bd. (*0-616-01722-7*) Canadian National Institute for the Blind/Institut National Canadien pour les Aveugles.

—Josepha: A Prairie Boy's Story. 1994. (Illus.). 32p. (J). (gr. 1-7). 11.95 o.p. (*0-8118-0802-5*) Chronicle Bks. LLC.

—Josepha: A Prairie Boy's Story. (Illus.). 32p. (J). pap. 8.95 (*0-88995-142-X*) Red Deer Pr. CAN. *Dist:* General Distribution Services, Inc.

McGuigan, Mary Ann. Where You Belong. (J). (gr. 5-9). 1998. 192p. per. 4.50 (*0-689-82318-5*, Simon Pulse); 1997. 176p. 16.95 (*0-689-81250-7*, Atheneum) Simon & Schuster Children's Publishing.

—Where You Belong. 1998. 10.55 (*0-606-15763-8*) Turtleback Bks.

McGuire, Leslie. Casper: The Movie Storybook. 1995. (Illus.). (J). (ps up). 8.95 o.p. (*0-8431-3856-4*, Price Stern Sloan) Penguin Putnam Bks. for Young Readers.

McHugh, Fiona, adapted by. The Anne of Green Gables Storybook. 2003. (Illus.). 80p. (J). (gr. 2-7). 19.95 (*0-920668-43-7*); pap. 9.95 (*0-920668-42-9*) Firefly Bks., Ltd.

McKay, Hilary. The Amber Cat. 1999. (YA). pap., stu. ed. 41.00 incl. audio (*0-7887-3635-3*, 41000) Recorded Bks., LLC.

—The Amber Cat. 1997. 144p. (J). 15.00 (*0-689-81360-0*, McElderry, Margaret K.) Simon & Schuster Children's Publishing.

—The Amber Cat. 1999. 'p. 10.55 (*0-606-16326-3*) Turtleback Bks.

—Dog Friday. 1995. (J). 16.95 o.p. (*0-7451-3021-6*, Galaxy Children's Large Print) BBC Audiobooks America.

—Happy & Glorious. 1999. 16.95 (*0-7540-6061-6*) BBC Audiobooks America.

—Indigo's Star. 2004. (J). 15.95 (*0-689-86563-5*, McElderry, Margaret K.) Simon & Schuster Children's Publishing.

McKay, Hilary & Piazza, Gail. The Amber Cat. 1999. 144p. (J). pap. 4.50 (*0-689-82557-9*, Aladdin) Simon & Schuster Children's Publishing.

McKay, Sharon E. What Are Friends For? 2001. (Hippo Tub Co. Ser.). (Illus.). 40p. (J). pap. 6.95 (*1-894454-00-6*) Balmur Entertainment, Ltd. CAN. *Dist:* General Distribution Services, Inc.

McKee, Craig B. & Holland, Margaret. A Peacock Ate My Lunch. 1985. (Predictable Reading Bks.). (Illus.). 24p. (J). (gr. k-4). 7.95 o.p. (*0-87406-036-2*) Darby Creek Publishing.

McKee, David. Elmer, Level 4.9. 3rd ed. 2001. (Picture Books Collection). (SPA., Illus.). 32p. (J). (gr. k-3). 12.95 (*84-372-2186-2*) Altea, Ediciones, S.A. - Grupo Santillana ESP. *Dist:* Santillana USA Publishing Co., Inc.

—Elmer's Friends. 1994. (Elmer Bks.).Tr. of Amigos de Elmer. (Illus.). 16p. (J). (ps up). bds. 5.99 (*0-688-13761-X*, Harper Festival) HarperCollins Children's Bk. Group.

—Elmer's Friends. 2004. (Elmers Ser.).Tr. of Amigos de Elmer. (BEN, CHI, ENG, GUJ & SPA., Illus.). 16p. (J). bds. 6.95 (*1-84059-071-8*); bds. 6.95 (*1-84059-069-6*); bds. 6.95 (*1-84059-070-X*); bds. 6.95 (*1-84059-073-4*); bds. 6.95 (*1-84059-075-0*); bds. 6.95 (*1-84059-077-7*) Milet Publishing, Ltd. GBR. *Dist:* Consortium Bk. Sales & Distribution.

—Elmer's Friends. Pullin, Beatriz, tr. 2004. Tr. of Amigos de Elmer. (BEN, CHI, ENG, GUJ & SPA., Illus.). 14p. (J). (ps-k). bds. 6.95 (*1-84059-072-6*) Milet Publishing, Ltd. GBR. *Dist:* Consortium Bk. Sales & Distribution.

McKenna, Colleen O'Shaughnessy. Doggone... Third Grade! 2002. (Illus.). 80p. (J). (gr. 2-5). tchr. ed. 15.95 (*0-8234-1696-8*) Holiday Hse., Inc.

—New Friends. 1995. (Dr. Quinn, Medicine Woman Ser.: No. 1). (J). mass mkt. 3.99 (*0-590-60372-8*) Scholastic, Inc.

McKissack, Patricia C. Nettie Jo's Friends. 1994. (J). 14.14 (*0-606-06612-8*) Turtleback Bks.

—Run Away Home. 1997. 128p. (J). (gr. 3-7). pap. 14.95 (*0-590-46751-4*) Scholastic, Inc.

McLerran, Alice. Secrets. 1990. 128p. (J). 12.95 o.p. (*0-688-09545-3*) HarperCollins Children's Bk. Group.

McMahon, Kara. Way to Go, Zoe! 2003. (Illus.). 24p. (J). (ps-k). pap. 3.25 (*0-375-82464-2*) Random Hse. Children's Bks.

McMahon, Maggie. The Problem with Pen Pals. 1998. (Full House Michelle Ser.: No. 22). 96p. (J). (gr. 2-4). pap. 3.99 (*0-671-01732-2*, Simon Spotlight) Simon & Schuster Children's Publishing.

McMorrow, Catherine. The Jellybean Principal. 1994. (Step into Reading Step 3 Bks.). (Illus.). 48p. (gr. 1-3). pap. 3.99 (*0-679-84743-X*, Random Hse. Bks. for Young Readers) Random Hse. Children's Bks.

McMullan, Kate. Great Advice from Lila Fenwick. 1989. (Illus.). 176p. (J). (gr. 5-9). pap. 3.95 o.p. (*0-14-034086-6*, Puffin Bks.) Penguin Putnam Bks. for Young Readers.

—The Great Ideas of Lila Fenwick. 1986. (Illus.). 128p. (J). (gr. 3-7). 11.95 o.p. (*0-8037-0316-3*); 11.89 o.p. (*0-8037-0317-1*) Penguin Putnam Bks. for Young Readers. (Dial Bks. for Young Readers).

—Hey, Pipsqueak! 1995. (Michael di Capua Bks.). (Illus.). 32p. (J). (ps up). 14.95 o.s.i (*0-06-205100-8*) HarperCollins Children's Bk. Group.

—Pearl & Wagner: Two Good Friends. 2003. (Easy-to-Read Ser.). (Illus.). 48p. (J). 13.99 (*0-8037-2573-6*, Dial Bks. for Young Readers) Penguin Putnam Bks. for Young Readers.

McMullen, Shawn A. That's What Friends Are For. 1992. (Timely Tales Ser.). (Illus.). 32p. (J). (gr. 4-8). 5.99 o.p. (*0-87403-975-4*, 24-03865) Standard Publishing.

McNamara, John. Revenge of the Nerd. 1985. 128p. (J). (gr. 5 up). mass mkt. 2.25 o.s.i (*0-440-97353-8*, Laurel Leaf) Random Hse. Children's Bks.

McNamee, Graham. Nothing Wrong with a Three-Legged Dog. 2000. (Illus.). 144p. (gr. 3-7). text 14.95 o.s.i (*0-385-32755-2*, Delacorte Pr.) Dell Publishing.

—Nothing Wrong with a Three-Legged Dog. 2001. 144p. (gr. 3-7). pap. text 4.50 (*0-440-41687-6*, Yearling) Random Hse. Children's Bks.

—Sparks. 128p. (gr. 2-5). 2003. pap. 4.99 (*0-440-41847-X*, Dell Books for Young Readers); 2002. (Illus.). text 15.95 (*0-385-72977-4*, Lamb, Wendy); 2002. (Illus.). lib. bdg. 17.99 (*0-385-90054-6*, Lamb, Wendy) Random Hse. Children's Bks.

McNaughton, Colin. The Great Zoo Escape. 1979. (Illus.). (J). (gr. k-3). 7.95 o.p. (*0-670-35145-8*) Viking Penguin.

McNeal, Laura & McNeal, Tom. Crooked. 1999. 352p. (YA). (gr. 9-11). 16.95 (*0-679-89300-8*) Knopf, Alfred A. Inc.

McNeal, Tom & McNeal, Laura. Crooked. 2002. 352p. (YA). (gr. 9-11). mass mkt. 5.50 (*0-440-22946-4*) Random Hse., Inc.

McNeil, Florence. Miss P & Me. 1984. 128p. (J). (gr. 5-7). 11.95 (*0-06-024136-5*); lib. bdg. 11.89 o.p. (*0-06-024137-3*) HarperCollins Children's Bk. Group.

McNichols, Ann. Falling from Grace. 2000. 164p. (J). (gr. 6-9). 16.95 (*0-8027-8750-9*) Walker & Co.

McOmber, Rachel B., ed. McOmber Phonics Storybooks: Hello Again. rev. ed. (Illus.). (J). (*0-944991-84-X*) Swift Learning Resources.

—McOmber Phonics Storybooks: Jud & Nell. rev. ed. (Illus.). (J). (*0-944991-33-5*) Swift Learning Resources.

—McOmber Phonics Storybooks: The Gal Pals. rev. ed. (Illus.). (J). (*0-944991-42-4*) Swift Learning Resources.

McPhail, David. Big Pig & Little Pig. 2002. (Illus.). (J). 11.45 (*0-7587-5345-4*) Book Wholesalers, Inc.

—Big Pig & Little Pig. 2003. (Green Light Readers Level 1 Ser.). (Illus.). 24p. (J). 11.95 (*0-15-204818-9*); pap. 3.95 (*0-15-204857-X*) Harcourt Children's Bks. (Green Light Readers).

—Jack & Rick. 2003. (Green Light Readers Level 1 Ser.). (Illus.). 24p. (J). 11.95 (*0-15-204819-7*); pap. 3.95 (*0-15-204859-6*) Harcourt Children's Bks. (Green Light Readers).

McPhail, David M. Big Pig & Little Pig. 2001. (Green Light Readers Ser.). (Illus.). 20p. (J). (gr. k-2). 10.95 o.s.i (*0-15-216516-9*); pap. 3.95 o.s.i (*0-15-216510-X*) Harcourt Children's Bks. (Green Light Readers).

—Big Pig & Little Pig. 2001. (Green Light Readers Ser.). (Illus.). (J). 10.10 (*0-606-21066-0*) Turtleback Bks.

—A Bug, a Bear & a Boy. 1998. (Hello Reader! Ser.). (Illus.). 32p. (J). (ps-1). mass mkt. 3.99 (*0-590-14904-0*) Scholastic, Inc.

—Ed & Me. 1990. (Illus.). 32p. (J). (ps-3). 13.95 o.s.i (*0-15-224888-9*) Harcourt Trade Pubs.

—Ed & Me. 1996. 11.15 (*0-606-09227-7*) Turtleback Bks.

—Fix It All. 1992. (Illus.). 24p. (J). (ps). pap. 4.99 (*0-14-054752-5*, Puffin Bks.) Penguin Putnam Bks. for Young Readers.

—A Girl, a Goat & a Goose. 2000. (Hello Reader! Ser.). (Illus.). (J). 10.14 (*0-606-18875-4*) Turtleback Bks.

—Jack & Rick. 2002. (Green Light Readers Ser.). (Illus.). 24p. (J). (ps-1). 11.95 o.s.i (*0-15-216552-5*); pap. 3.95 o.s.i (*0-15-216540-1*) Harcourt Children's Bks. (Green Light Readers).

—Something Special. 1992. (J). (ps-3). pap. 4.95 o.p. (*0-316-56333-1*, Joy Street Bks.) Little Brown & Co.

Mead, Alice. Billy & Emma, RS. 2000. (Illus.). 32p. (J). (ps-3). 16.00 o.p. (*0-374-30705-9*, Farrar, Straus & Giroux (BYR)) Farrar, Straus & Giroux.

—Girl of Kosovo, RS. 2001. 113p. (J). (gr. 4-7). 16.00 (*0-374-32620-7*, Farrar, Straus & Giroux (BYR)) Farrar, Straus & Giroux.

—Girl of Kosovo. 2003. (Illus.). 128p. (gr. 5). pap. text 4.99 (*0-440-41853-4*, Yearling) Random Hse. Children's Bks.

—Madame Squidley & Beanie, RS. 2004. (J). (*0-374-34688-7*, Farrar, Straus & Giroux (BYR)) Farrar, Straus & Giroux.

Mebs, Gudrun. Sunday's Child. 1986. 144p. (J). (gr. 3-6). 11.95 o.p. (*0-8037-0192-6*, 01063-320); 11.89 o.p. (*0-8037-0197-7*) Penguin Putnam Bks. for Young Readers. (Dial Bks. for Young Readers).

—Sunday's Child. 1989. (J). (gr. k-6). pap. 2.95 o.s.i (*0-440-40167-4*, Yearling) Random Hse. Children's Bks.

Medearis, Angela Shelf. The Adventures of Sugar & Junior. 1995. (Illus.). 32p. (J). (ps-3). 15.95 (*0-8234-1182-6*) Holiday Hse., Inc.

Medina, Jane. My Name Is Jorge: On Both Sides of the River. 2003. (ENG & SPA., Illus.). 48p. (YA). (gr. 4-7). pap. 8.95 (*1-56397-842-3*) Boyds Mills Pr.

—My Name Is Jorge: On Both Sides of the River. 1999. 14.10 (*0-606-18014-1*) Turtleback Bks.

Meeko's New Friend Little Play. 6.98 (*0-7853-1336-2*) Publications International, Ltd.

Mega-Books Staff. My Friend Fang. 1992. (Glow in the Dark Ser.: No. 2). 24p. (J). pap. 3.99 o.s.i (*0-553-37116-9*) Bantam Bks.

Meister, Cari. Skinny & Fats, Best Friends. 2002. (Reader Level 2 Ser.). (Illus.). 32p. (J). (gr. k-3). tchr. ed. 14.95 (*0-8234-1692-5*) Holiday Hse., Inc.

Mellor, Corinne. Bruce the Balding Moose: 3-D Picture Book. 1996. (Illus.). 20p. (J). (ps-2). 13.99 o.s.i (*0-8037-2064-5*, Dial Bks. for Young Readers) Penguin Putnam Bks. for Young Readers.

Melmed, Laura Krauss. A Hug Goes Around. 2002. (Illus.). 32p. (J). (ps-3). 15.95 (*0-688-14680-5*); lib. bdg. 15.89 (*0-688-14681-3*) HarperCollins Children's Bk. Group.

Meltabarger, P. J. Baaz. 1996. 94p. (J). (gr. 4-7). pap. text 3.50 o.p. (*1-56763-189-4*); (Illus.). 18.80 (*1-56763-188-6*) Ozark Publishing.

Melton, Holly. A Day at Moss Lake. (Illus.). 24p. (J). (gr. k-2). (*1-58605-010-9*) LeapFrog Enterprises, Inc.

Menschell, Mindy. Big Book: J My Name Is Jess. l.t. ed. 1997. (Sadlier Phonics Reading Program). (Illus.). 8p. (J). (ps-1). (*0-8215-0871-7*, Sadlier-Oxford) Sadlier, William H. Inc.

Meres, Jonathan. Somewhere Out There. 1998. (Illus.). 32p. (J). (gr. 1-4). o.p. (*0-09-176638-9*) Random Hse. of Canada, Ltd. CAN. *Dist:* Random Hse., Inc.

Mericle, Suzanne. Trippin with Mabel & Margaret. 1998. per. 14.95 (*1-889131-28-8*) CasAnanda Publishing.

Merriam, Eve. Blackberry Ink. 1985. (Illus.). 40p. (J). (ps-2). 16.00 o.p. (*0-688-04150-7*); lib. bdg. 13.93 o.p. (*0-688-04151-5*) Morrow/Avon. (Morrow, William & Co.).

—Jamboree. 1984. 96p. (J). (ps-6). pap. 2.50 o.s.i (*0-440-44199-4*, Yearling) Random Hse. Children's Bks.

Messer, Ronald K. Shumway. 1975. 192p. (J). (gr. 7 up). 6.95 o.p. (*0-8407-6419-7*, Dutton Children's Bks.) Penguin Putnam Bks. for Young Readers.

Metcalf, Paula, illus. Norma No Friends. 1999. 40p. (J). (ps-3). 15.95 (*1-902283-87-2*) Barefoot Bks., Inc.

Metz, Melinda. The Case of the Sundae Surprise. 2003. (New Adventures of Mary-Kate & Ashley Ser.: No. 34). (Illus.). 96p. (gr. 4-7). mass mkt. 4.50 (*0-06-009332-3*, HarperEntertainment) Morrow/Avon.

—Sunny & Matt. 2000. (Sweet Sixteen Ser.: No. 6). 224p. (YA). (gr. 12 up). pap. 5.95 (*0-06-440815-9*, Harper Trophy) HarperCollins Children's Bk. Group.

Metzger, Lois. Missing Girls. (YA). (gr. 5-9). 2001. 192p. pap. 5.99 o.p. (*0-14-131086-3*); 1999. 208p. 15.99 o.s.i (*0-670-87777-8*) Penguin Putnam Bks. for Young Readers.

—Missing Girls. 2001. (J). 12.04 (*0-606-21334-1*) Turtleback Bks.

Metzger, Steve. I'm Having a Bad Day! 1998. (Dinofours Ser.: No. 2). (Illus.). 32p. (J). (ps-1). mass mkt. 3.25 (*0-590-03551-7*) Scholastic, Inc.

—I'm Having a Bad Day! 1998. (Dinofours Ser.: No. 2). (J). (ps-1). 9.40 (*0-606-16628-9*) Turtleback Bks.

—I'm Not Your Friend! 1997. (Dinofours Ser.: No. 3). (Illus.). 32p. (J). (ps-1). mass mkt. 3.25 (*0-590-68991-6*) Scholastic, Inc.

—It's Snowing. 1998. (Dinofours Ser.: No. 14). (Illus.). (J). (ps-1). mass mkt. 3.25 (*0-590-03550-9*) Scholastic, Inc.

Meyer, Carolyn. Drummers of Jericho. 1995. 320p. (YA). (gr. 5-9). 11.00 (*0-15-200441-6*); pap. 6.00 (*0-15-200190-5*) Harcourt Children's Bks. (Gulliver Bks.).

—Drummers of Jericho. 1995. 11.05 (*0-606-10997-8*) Turtleback Bks.

—Elliott & Win. 1986. 204p. (YA). (gr. 9 up). 12.95 o.s.i (*0-689-50368-7*, McElderry, Margaret K.) Simon & Schuster Children's Publishing.

Meyer, Jane G. Hands Across the Moon. 2003. 224p. (J). pap. 10.99 (*0-8423-8286-0*) Tyndale Hse. Pubs.

Meyer, Kathleen A. I Have a New Friend. 1995. (Illus.). 32p. (J). (gr. 3-7). 10.95 o.p. (*0-8120-6532-8*); (ps-2). pap. 4.95 (*0-8120-9408-5*) Barron's Educational Series, Inc.

Meyers, Susan. Cricket Goes to the Dogs. 1995. (Always Friends Club Ser.). 8.05 o.p. (*0-606-07402-3*) Turtleback Bks.

—Meg & the Secret Scrapbook. 1995. (Always Friends Club Ser.). (J). 8.05 o.p. (*0-606-07857-6*) Turtleback Bks.

Michaels, Tina Marie. Mac & Tosh: The Search for Stolen Smiles. 2000. (Illus.). 28p. (J). (ps-5). E-Book 3.95 (*1-930677-02-2*) London Circle Publishing.

Michals, Duane. Upside down, Inside Out, & Backwards. 1994. 80p. (J). pap. 19.95 (*0-9638863-0-4*) Sonny Boy Bks.

Michels, Tilde. Who's That Knocking at My Door? 1992. (Illus.). 28p. (J). (ps-3). pap. 4.95 (*0-8120-1486-3*) Barron's Educational Series, Inc.

Micklish, Rita. Sugar Bee. 1972. (J). (gr. 3-7). 5.95 o.p. (*0-440-08358-3*); lib. bdg. 5.47 o.p. (*0-440-08350-8*) Dell Publishing. (Delacorte Pr.).

Middleton, Charlotte. Enrico Starts School. 2004. 32p. (J). 14.99 (*0-8037-3017-9*, Dial Bks. for Young Readers) Penguin Putnam Bks. for Young Readers.

Miles, Betty. I Would If I Could. 1983. 120p. (J). (gr. 3-6). pap. 2.95 o.p. (*0-380-63438-4*, Avon Bks.) Morrow/Avon.

—I Would If I Could. 2000. 128p. (gr. 4-7). pap. 9.95 (*0-595-00490-3*, Backinprint.com) iUniverse, Inc.

—Maudie & Me & the Dirty Book. 1981. 140p. (J). (gr. 4-7). pap. 2.95 o.p. (*0-380-55541-7*, Avon Bks.) Morrow/Avon.

—Maudie & Me & the Dirty Book. 1980. 7.95 o.s.i (*0-394-84343-6*) Random Hse., Inc.

—The Trouble with Thirteen. 1980. 116p. (J). (gr. 3-7). pap. 2.25 o.p. (*0-380-51136-3*, Avon Bks.) Morrow/Avon.

—The Trouble with Thirteen. 1979. (J). (gr. 4-7). 6.95 o.s.i (*0-394-83930-7*); 12.99 o.s.i (*0-394-93930-1*) Random Hse. Children's Bks. (Knopf Bks. for Young Readers).

Milgrim, David. My Friend Lucky: A Love Story. 2002. (Illus.). 32p. (J). (ps-k). 12.00 (*0-689-84253-8*, Atheneum/Anne Schwartz Bks.) Simon & Schuster Children's Publishing.

—See Pip Point. 2003. (Ready-to-Reads Ser.). (Illus.). 32p. (J). 14.95 (*0-689-85116-2*, Atheneum) Simon & Schuster Children's Publishing.

Milios, Rita. Sneaky Pete Big Book. 1990. (Rookie Readers Big Bks.). (Illus.). 32p. (J). (ps-2). pap. 33.70 o.p. (*0-516-49455-4*, Children's Pr.) Scholastic Library Publishing.

Millais, Raoul. Elijah & Pin-Pin. 1992. (Illus.). 48p. (J). (ps-1). pap. 14.00 (*0-671-75543-9*, Simon & Schuster Children's Publishing) Simon & Schuster Children's Publishing.

Miller, Frances A. The Truth Trap. 1986. 208p. (YA). (ps up). reprint ed. mass mkt. 4.50 o.s.i (*0-449-70247-2*, Fawcett) Ballantine Bks.

Miller, Judi. My Crazy Cousin Courtney Comes Back. MacDonald, Pat, ed. 1994. 128p. (J). pap. 3.50 o.p. (*0-671-88734-3*, Aladdin) Simon & Schuster Children's Publishing.

Miller, Lynda. Two Friends. 1999. (Illus.). 20p. (J). (gr. k-5). 10.00 (*0-9636140-3-7*, Neon Rose Productions) Smart Alternatives, Inc.

Miller-Marx, Kim. I Have a Friendly Smile. 1994. (Illus.). 33p. (J). (gr. k-3). pap. 9.99 (*0-9644265-0-1*) Miller-Marx, Kim.

Miller, Mary Beth. Aimee. 2002. (Illus.). 308p. (YA). (gr. 9 up). 16.99 (*0-525-46894-3*) Dutton/Plume.

—Aimee. 2004. (Illus.). 288p. pap. 6.99 (*0-14-240025-4*, Puffin Bks.) Penguin Putnam Bks. for Young Readers.

Miller, Mary J. Fast Forward. 1993. 224p. (J). (gr. 3-7). 14.99 o.s.i (*0-670-84339-3*, Viking Children's Bks.) Penguin Putnam Bks. for Young Readers.

—Fast Forward. 1999. pap. 3.95 (*0-14-034992-8*, Viking) Viking Penguin.

—Upside Down. 1994. 160p. (J). (gr. 3-7). pap. 3.99 o.s.i (*0-14-034624-4*, Puffin Bks.) Penguin Putnam Bks. for Young Readers.

Miller, Maryann. Friends Forever. 1999. 68p. (YA). E-Book 5.80 incl. disk (*1-58608-000-8*) New Concepts Publishing.

Miller, Sara. A Wedding to Remember. 2003. (Illus.). 32p. (J). (gr. 1-3). 5.99 (*0-307-10424-9*, Golden Bks.) Random Hse. Children's Bks.

Miller, Sara Swan. Better Than TV. 1998. (First Choice Chapter Book Ser.). (J). 10.14 (*0-606-13199-X*) Turtleback Bks.

Miller, Shirley J. My House, Your House. 1993. (Illus.). 60p. (Orig.). (J). (gr. 2-6). pap. 6.95 o.p. (*1-878580-91-4*) Asylum Arts.

—School Days. 1993. (Illus.). 80p. (Orig.). (J). (gr. 2-6). pap. 6.95 (*1-878580-90-6*) Asylum Arts.

Miller, Susan Martins. Changing Times. 1999. (American Adventure Ser.: No. 44). 144p. (J). (gr. 3-7). pap. 3.97 (*1-57748-510-6*) Barbour Publishing, Inc.

Miller, Wayne H. Making New Friends: People Who Look Different. Smith, Denise M., ed. 1995. (Sandy Dallas Series of Books for Children, Parents, & Teachers). (Illus.). 100p. (Orig.). (YA). (gr. 6-12). pap. text 4.95 (*0-9634735-8-1*) Hiram Charles Publishing.

Milliken, Linda. Native American: Arts, Crafts, Cooking, & Historical Aids. Rogers, Kathy, ed. abr. ed. 1980. (Illus.). 48p. (J). (gr. 2-6). pap., act. bk. ed. 6.95 (*1-56472-000-4*, EP000) Edupress, Inc.

Millman, Isaac. Moses Sees a Play, RS. 2004. (J). 16.00 (*0-374-35066-3*, Farrar, Straus & Giroux (BYR)) Farrar, Straus & Giroux.

Millman, Malka. Too Tough to Care. 1993. 150p. (J). (gr. 6). 11.95 (*1-56062-237-7*, CJR141H) CIS Communications, Inc.

Mills, Claudia. Dinah Forever, RS. 1995. 144p. (J). (gr. 4-7). 14.00 o.p. (*0-374-31788-7*, Farrar, Straus & Giroux (BYR)) Farrar, Straus & Giroux.

—Dynamite Dinah. 1992. 128p. (J). (gr. 3-7). reprint ed. pap. 3.95 o.s.i (*0-689-71591-9*, Aladdin) Simon & Schuster Children's Publishing.

—Hannah on Her Way. 1991. 160p. (J). (gr. 3-7). 15.00 o.s.i (*0-02-767011-2*, Simon & Schuster Children's Publishing) Simon & Schuster Children's Publishing.

—Losers, Inc., RS. 1997. 160p. (J). (gr. 3-7). 16.00 (*0-374-34661-5*, Farrar, Straus & Giroux (BYR)) Farrar, Straus & Giroux.

—Losers, Inc. 1998. 160p. (J). pap. 4.95 (*0-7868-1364-4*) Hyperion Paperbacks for Children.

—Losers, Inc. 1998. 96p. (J). (gr. 3-7). pap. 4.95 (*0-7868-1274-5*) Hyperion Pr.

—Losers, Inc. 1998. 11.00 (*0-606-14259-2*) Turtleback Bks.

Milne, A. A., pseud. Eeyore Has a Birthday. (Easy-to-Read Ser.). (Illus.). 2001. 48p. (J). pap. 3.99 (*0-14-230042-X*, Puffin Bks.); 1999. 12p. bds. 5.99 o.s.i (*0-525-46118-3*); 1996. 24p. (J). bds. 3.99 o.s.i (*0-525-45528-0*, Dutton Children's Bks.) Penguin Putnam Bks. for Young Readers.

—Eeyore Has a Birthday. 2001. (Illus.). 48p. (J). 13.99 o.s.i (*0-525-46764-5*, Dutton Children's Bks.) Penguin Putnam Bks. for Young Readers.

—Pooh Goes Visiting. 1993. (Winnie-the-Pooh Story Bks.). (Illus.). 32p. (J). 4.99 o.p. (*0-525-45040-8*, Dutton Children's Bks.) Penguin Putnam Bks. for Young Readers.

—Pooh Goes Visiting & Other Stories. 1998. (J). mass mkt. 7.95 incl. audio (*1-84032-047-8*) Hodder Headline Audiobooks GBR. *Dist:* Trafalgar Square.

—Pooh Goes Visiting Puzzle. 1999. (Illus.). 14p. (J). (ps-3). 7.99 o.s.i (*0-525-46272-4*, Dutton) Penguin Putnam Bks. for Young Readers.

—Pooh's Grand Adventure. 1997. (Illus.). 24p. (J). (ps-3). 6.98 o.s.i (*1-57082-671-4*) Mouse Works.

Minarik, Else Holmelund. Los Amigos de Osito. 1981. 15.15 o.p. (*0-606-10479-8*) Turtleback Bks.

—Little Bear's Friend. (I Can Read Bks.). (Illus.). 64p. (J). (gr. k-3). 1984. mass mkt. 3.99 (*0-06-444051-6*, Harper Trophy); 1960. lib. bdg. 15.89 (*0-06-024256-6*) HarperCollins Children's Bk. Group.

—Little Bear's Friend. 1984. (I Can Read Bks.). (J). (ps-1). 10.10 (*0-606-03384-X*) Turtleback Bks.

—Little Bear's Friend. unabr. ed. 1990. (I Can Read Bks.). (Illus.). 64p. (J). (gr. k-3). pap. 8.95 incl. audio (*1-55994-235-5*, HarperAudio) HarperTrade.

—Little Bear's Friend, Level 1. 1985. (I Can Read Bks.). (Illus.). 64p. (J). (ps-1). 5.98 o.p. incl. audio (*0-694-00031-0*, Harper Trophy) HarperCollins Children's Bk. Group.

—Little Bear's Friends - Los Amigos de Osito. (SPA.). 64p. (J). 7.95 (*84-204-3049-8*) Santillana USA Publishing Co., Inc.

—Little Bear's New Friend. 2002. (Maurice Sendak's Little Bear Ser.). (Illus.). 32p. (J). (ps-1). lib. bdg. 14.89 (*0-06-623688-6*) HarperCollins Children's Bk. Group.

—Maurice Sendak's Little Bear's New Friend. 2002. (Little Bear Ser.). (Illus.). 32p. (J). (ps-1). 14.99 (*0-06-623817-X*) HarperCollins Children's Bk. Group.

Miner, Jane C. What Will My Friends Say? 1986. (J). (gr. 7 up). pap. (*0-671-62512-8*, Simon Pulse) Simon & Schuster Children's Publishing.

Miyake, Yoshi, illus. Selena Who Speaks in Silence. 1997. (*0-7802-8032-6*) Wright Group, The.

Modarressi, Mitra. The Beastly Visits. 1996. (Illus.). 32p. (J). (ps-2). mass mkt. 16.99 o.p. (*0-531-08880-4*); mass mkt. 15.95 o.p. (*0-531-09530-4*) Scholastic, Inc. (Orchard Bks.).

—The Dream Pillow. 1994. (Illus.). 32p. (J). (ps-2). mass mkt. 15.95 o.p. (*0-531-06855-2*); mass mkt. 16.99 o.p. (*0-531-08705-0*) Scholastic, Inc. (Orchard Bks.).

Modell, Frank. Look Out, It's April Fools' Day. 1985. (Illus.). 24p. (ps up). (J). lib. bdg. 12.88 o.p. (*0-688-04017-9*); (YA). 16.00 o.p. (*0-688-04016-0*) HarperCollins Children's Bk. Group. (Greenwillow Bks.).

Modern Staff. Abby Makes New Friends. 1993. (Richard Scarry Collection Ser.). (J). o.p. incl. audio (*0-8136-4889-0*) Modern Curriculum Pr.

Modrell, Dolores. Tales of Tiddly. 1990. (Illus.). 48p. (J). (ps-1). pap. 13.95 o.p. (*0-671-69204-6*, Simon & Schuster Children's Publishing) Simon & Schuster Children's Publishing.

Moe. The Ghost Wore Knickers. 1975. (J). 6.95 o.p. (*0-525-66427-0*) NAL.

Moeri, Louise. The Forty-Third War. 1989. 208p. (J). (gr. 5-9). 13.95 o.p. (*0-395-50215-2*) Houghton Mifflin Co.

Moers, Hermann. Katie & the Big, Brave Bear. Martens, Marianne, tr. from GER. 1995. Tr. of Holpeltolpel Starker Freund. (Illus.). 32p. (J). (ps-3). 14.95 o.p. (*1-55858-397-1*); 15.50 o.p. (*1-55858-398-X*) North-South Bks., Inc.

Mogensen, Jan. Teddy's Christmas Gift. 1985. (Teddy Tales Ser.). (Illus.). 32p. (J). (gr. 3-4). lib. bdg. 13.95 o.p. (*1-55532-004-X*) Stevens, Gareth Inc.

—The Tiger's Breakfast. 1991. (Illus.). 32p. (J). (ps-3). 14.95 o.p. (*0-940793-83-0*, Crocodile Bks.) Interlink Publishing Group, Inc.

Moncure, Jane Belk. My Baby Brother Needs a Friend. 1979. (Understanding Myself Picture Books Ser.). (Illus.). 24p. (J). (ps-3). lib. bdg. 21.36 o.p. (*0-89565-019-3*) Child's World, Inc.

—Word Bird's New Friend. 2002. (New Word Bird Library). (Illus.). 32p. (J). (ps-3). lib. bdg. 22.79 (*1-56766-844-5*) Child's World, Inc.

Moncure, Jane Belk & Davis, Jennie. Julie's New Home. 1982. (Making Choices Ser.). (Illus.). 32p. (J). (gr. 3-4). lib. bdg. 19.93 o.p. (*0-89565-254-4*) Child's World, Inc.

Monsell, Mary E. Toohy & Wood. 1992. (Illus.). 80p. (J). (gr. 2-5). 12.95 (*0-689-31721-2*, Atheneum) Simon & Schuster Children's Publishing.

Monson, A. M. The Deer Stand. 1992. 160p. (J). (gr. 4 up). 14.00 o.p. (*0-688-11057-6*) HarperCollins Children's Bk. Group.

—Wanted: Best Friend. 1997. (Illus.). 32p. (J). (ps-3). 15.99 (*0-8037-1483-1*); 14.89 o.s.i (*0-8037-1485-8*) Penguin Putnam Bks. for Young Readers. (Dial Bks. for Young Readers).

Montes, Marisa & Cepeda, Joe. Who's That Girl. 2003. (Get Ready for Gabi Ser.). 96-112p. (J). mass mkt. 3.99 (*0-439-47521-X*, Scholastic Paperbacks) Scholastic, Inc.

Montgomery, Bobbie. Fruit Tramp Kids. 2000. (Pathfinder Junior Book Club Ser.). 143p. (J). (gr. 4-7). pap. 6.99 (*0-8280-1422-1*) Review & Herald Publishing Assn.

Montgomery, L. M. Anne of Green Gables. 2002. (Great Illustrated Classics). (Illus.). 240p. (J). (gr. 3-7). lib. bdg. 21.35 (*1-57765-816-7*, ABDO & Daughters) ABDO Publishing Co.

—Anne of Green Gables. 1984. (Avonlea Ser.: No. 1). (YA). (gr. 5-8). mass mkt. 1.95 o.p. (*0-8049-0218-6*, CL218) Airmont Publishing Co., Inc.

—Anne of Green Gables. 1976. (Avonlea Ser.: No. 1). 244p. (YA). (gr. 5-8). 23.95 (*0-8488-0584-4*) Amereon, Ltd.

—Anne of Green Gables, 3 vols. (Avonlea Ser.: No. 1). (YA). (gr. 5-8). 1997. mass mkt. 13.50 (*0-553-33307-0*); 1987. mass mkt. 8.85 o.s.i (*0-553-30838-6*); 1986. mass mkt. o.s.i (*0-553-16646-8*); 1983. 320p. pap. 3.95 (*0-7704-2205-5*); 1982. 320p. mass mkt. 2.95 o.s.i (*0-553-24295-4*); 1982. 336p. mass mkt. 4.50 (*0-553-21313-X*, Bantam Classics) Bantam Bks.

—Anne of Green Gables. 1998. (J). E-Book 5.00 (*0-7607-1341-3*) Barnes & Noble, Inc.

—Anne of Green Gables. 2001. (J). per. 12.50 (*1-891355-34-1*) Blue Unicorn Editions.

—Anne of Green Gables. 2002. pap. 4.50 (*1-59109-388-0*) Booksurge, LLC.

—Anne of Green Gables. (Avonlea Ser.: No. 1). (Illus.). (YA). (gr. 5-8). 1995. 352p. o.p. (*0-681-00770-2*); 1988. 240p. 11.95 o.p. (*0-681-40501-5*) Borders Pr.

—Anne of Green Gables. 2000. (Avonlea Ser.: No. 1). 280p. (YA). (gr. 5-8). pap. text 15.00 (*0-7881-9155-1*) DIANE Publishing Co.

—Anne of Green Gables. 1995. (Avonlea Ser.: No. 1). 307p. (YA). (gr. 5-8). pap. text 2.99 (*0-8125-5152-4*, Tor Classics); 1994. mass mkt. 2.50 (*1-55902-906-4*, Aerie) Doherty, Tom Assocs., LLC.

—Anne of Green Gables. (Avonlea Ser.: No. 1). (YA). (gr. 5-8). 2000. 320p. pap. 3.00 (*0-486-41025-0*); 1995. (Illus.). iv, 91p. pap. text 1.00 (*0-486-28366-6*) Dover Pubns., Inc.

—Anne of Green Gables. 1989. (Avonlea Ser.: No. 1). (YA). (gr. 5-8). pap. 5.60 (*0-87129-242-4*, A41) Dramatic Publishing Co.

—Anne of Green Gables. (J). E-Book 2.49 (*0-7574-3112-7*) Electric Umbrella Publishing.

—Anne of Green Gables. 1999. (Focus on the Family Great Stories Ser.). (Illus.). 368p. (J). (gr. 4-7). 15.99 o.p. (*1-56179-625-5*) Focus on the Family Publishing.

—Anne of Green Gables. 1999. (Avonlea Ser.: No. 1). (YA). (gr. 5-8). 23.95 (*0-8057-8090-4*, Macmillan Reference USA) Gale Group.

—Anne of Green Gables. 1989. (Avonlea Ser.: No. 1). (Illus.). 320p. (YA). (gr. 5-8). 19.95 o.s.i (*0-87923-783-X*) Godine, David R. Pub.

—Anne of Green Gables. (Avonlea Ser.: No. 1). (YA). (gr. 5-8). 2000. (*0-06-028227-4*); 1999. (Illus.). 80p. 2.99 o.s.i (*0-694-01284-X*, Harper Festival) HarperCollins Children's Bk. Group.

—Anne of Green Gables. (Avonlea Ser.: No. 1). (YA). (gr. 5-8). pap. 3.50 (*0-340-71500-6*) Hodder & Stoughton, Ltd. GBR. *Dist:* Lubrecht & Cramer, Ltd., Trafalgar Square.

—Anne of Green Gables. Greenwood, Barbara, ed. 2001. (Avonlea Ser.: No. 1). 94p. (YA). (gr. 5-8). pap. 9.95 (*1-55013-431-0*) Key Porter Bks. CAN. *Dist:* Firefly Bks., Ltd.

—Anne of Green Gables. 1995. (Avonlea Ser.: No. 1). (Illus.). 416p. (gr. 5-8). 14.95 (*0-679-44475-0*, Everyman's Library) Knopf Publishing Group.

—Anne of Green Gables. 1994. (Avonlea Ser.: No. 1). (Illus.). 256p. (YA). (gr. 5-8). 25.00 (*0-88363-994-7*) Levin, Hugh Lauter Assocs.

—Anne of Green Gables. (Avonlea Ser.: No. 1). (YA). (gr. 5-8). E-Book 1.95 (*1-57799-946-0*) Logos Research Systems, Inc.

—Anne of Green Gables. MQ Publications Staff, ed. 1998. (Little Brown Notebooks Ser.). (Illus.). 256p. 9.99 (*1-84072-063-8*) M Q Pubns. GBR. *Dist:* Watson-Guptill Pubns., Inc.

—Anne of Green Gables. 1992. (Avonlea Ser.: No. 1). 338p. (YA). (gr. 5-8). mass mkt. 4.95 (*0-7710-9883-9*) McClelland & Stewart/Tundra Bks.

—Anne of Green Gables. (Avonlea Ser.: No. 1). (YA). (gr. 5-8). E-Book 1.95 (*1-58515-198-X*) MesaView, Inc.

—Anne of Green Gables. 1987. (Avonlea Ser.: No. 1). 320p. (YA). (gr. 5-8). mass mkt. 4.95 o.p. (*0-451-52112-9*, Signet Classics) NAL.

—Anne of Green Gables. 1998. 354p. (J). pap. (*1-55109-249-2*) Nimbus Publishing, Ltd.

—Anne of Green Gables. Bassett, Jennifer, ed. 1995. (Avonlea Ser.: No. 1). (Illus.). 48p. (YA). (gr. 5-8). pap. text 5.95 o.p. (*0-19-422725-1*) Oxford Univ. Pr., Inc.

—Anne of Green Gables. 2002. (Cageworld Ser.). (Illus.). (J). pap. 9.99 (*0-14-250102-6*, Puffin Bks.); 1996. (Avonlea Ser.: No. 1). (Illus.). 384p. (YA). (gr. 5-8). 4.99 (*0-14-036741-1*, Puffin Bks.); 1994. (Avonlea Ser.: No. 1). 256p. (YA). (gr. 5-8). pap. 2.99 o.p. (*0-14-035148-5*, Puffin Bks.); 1993. (Avonlea Ser.: No. 1). (Illus.). 16p. (YA). (gr. 5-8). o.p. (*0-525-45173-0*); 1992. (Avonlea Ser.: No. 1). 256p. (YA). (gr. 5-8). pap. 2.99 o.p. (*0-14-032462-3*, Puffin Bks.); 1983. (Avonlea Ser.: No. 1). (Illus.). 384p. (YA). (gr. 5-8). 17.99 (*0-448-06030-2*, Grosset & Dunlap) Penguin Putnam Bks. for Young Readers.

—Anne of Green Gables. Hanft, Joshua, ed. 1995. (Great Illustrated Classics Ser.: Vol. 42). (Illus.). 240p. (J). (gr. 3-6). 9.95 (*0-86611-993-0*) Playmore, Inc., Pubs.

—Anne of Green Gables. 1999. (Avonlea Ser.: No. 1). (YA). (gr. 5-8). E-Book 8.99 o.p. incl. cd-rom (*1-57646-052-5*) Quiet Vision Publishing.

—Anne of Green Gables. 2002. (Illus.). 256p. (J). 16.99 (*0-517-22111-X*, Random Hse. Bks. for Young Readers); 1999. (Avonlea Ser.: No. 1). (Illus.). 112p. (gr. 5-8). pap. text 3.99 (*0-440-41356-7*, Dell Books for Young Readers); 1998. (Avonlea Ser.: No. 1). 352p. (gr. 5-8). mass mkt. 2.99 o.s.i (*0-440-22787-9*, Yearling); 1994. (Avonlea Ser.: No. 1). (YA). (gr. 5-8). mass mkt. o.s.i (*0-553-85018-0*, Dell Books for Young Readers); 1994. (Step into Classics Ser.). (Illus.). 112p. (J). (gr. 3-5). pap. 3.99 (*0-679-85467-3*, Random Hse. Bks. for Young Readers); 1993. (Avonlea Ser.: No. 1). (YA). (gr. 5-8). pap. o.s.i (*0-553-56712-8*, Dell Books for Young Readers) Random Hse. Children's Bks.

—Anne of Green Gables. (Children's Classics Ser.: No. 1). 1998. (Illus.). 256p. (J). (gr. 4-7). 5.99 (*0-517-18968-2*); 1995. (YA). (gr. 5-8). 1.10 o.s.i (*0-517-14154-X*); 1988. (Illus.). xvi, 240p. (YA). (gr. 5-8). 12.99 o.s.i (*0-517-65958-1*) Random Hse. Value Publishing.

—Anne of Green Gables. 1993. (Avonlea Ser.: No.1). 287p. (YA). (gr. 5-8). text 5.98 o.p. (*1-56138-324-4*, Courage Bks.) Running Pr. Bk. Pubs.

—Anne of Green Gables. 1989. (Avonlea Ser.: No. 1). 384p. (YA). (gr. 5-8). mass mkt. 4.50 (*0-590-42243-X*, Scholastic Paperbacks) Scholastic, Inc.

—Anne of Green Gables, 3 vol. set. 1997. (YA). (*0-7704-2218-7*) Seal Bks. CAN. *Dist:* Random Hse. of Canada, Ltd.

—Anne of Green Gables. 2001. (Aladdin Classics Ser.). (Illus.). 480p. (J). pap. 3.99 (*0-689-84622-3*, Aladdin) Simon & Schuster Children's Publishing.

—Anne of Green Gables. 1994. (Avonlea Ser.: No. 1). (Illus.). 256p. (YA). (gr. 5-8). 9.99 o.p. (*1-897954-26-3*) Sterling Publishing Co., Inc.

—Anne of Green Gables. 2000. (Avonlea Ser.: No. 1). (Illus.). 328p. (J). (gr. 5-8). 24.95 (*0-88776-515-7*) Tundra Bks. of Northern New York.

—Anne of Green Gables. Morgan, Sally, ed. 1994. (Avonlea Ser.: No. 1). (YA). (gr. 5-8). 9.09 o.p. (*0-606-09006-1*) Turtleback Bks.

—Anne of Green Gables. 1987. (Avonlea Ser.: No. 1). (YA). (gr. 5-8). 10.55 (*0-606-00282-0*) Turtleback Bks.

—Anne of Green Gables. 2001. (Children's Classics). 288p. (J). pap. 3.95 (*1-85326-139-4*) Wordsworth Editions, Ltd. GBR. *Dist:* Advanced Global Distribution Services.

—Anne of Green Gables. 2001. (Illus.). 40p. (J). (gr. k-3). 15.95 o.p. (*0-385-32715-3*, Doubleday Bks. for Young Readers) Random Hse. Children's Bks.

—Anne of Green Gables. abr. ed. 1986. (Avonlea Ser.: No. 1). (YA). (gr. 5-8). pap. 12.95 incl. audio (*1-882071-07-7*, 009) B&B Audio, Inc.

—Anne of Green Gables, Vol. 1. 1984. (Avonlea Ser.: Vol. 1). 320p. (gr. 5-8). pap. text 4.50 (*0-553-15327-7*) Bantam Bks.

—Anne of Green Gables. unabr. ed. 1992. (Avonlea Ser.: Bk. 1). (J). audio 49.95 (*1-55686-447-7*, 447) Books in Motion.

—Anne of Green Gables. 1977. (Avonlea Ser.: No. 1). 429p. (YA). (gr. 5-8). reprint ed. lib. bdg. 27.95 (*0-89966-262-5*) Buccaneer Bks., Inc.

—Anne of Green Gables, RS. 1950. (Avonlea Ser.: No. 1). (YA). (gr. 5-8). pap. o.p. (*0-374-40403-8*, Sunburst) Farrar, Straus & Giroux.

—Anne of Green Gables, ERS. 1994. (Avonlea Ser.: No. 1). (FRE., Illus.). xx, 486p. (YA). (gr. 5-8). 15.95 o.p. (*0-8050-3126-X*, Holt, Henry & Co. Bks. For Young Readers) Holt, Henry & Co.

—Anne of Green Gables. l.t. ed. (Avonlea Ser.: No. 1). (YA). (gr. 5-8). 614p. pap. 44.14 (*0-7583-0235-5*); 966p. pap. 72.70 (*0-7583-0237-1*); 1379p. pap. 93.47 (*0-7583-0239-8*); 280p. pap. 24.84 (*0-7583-0232-0*); 350p. pap. 28.82 (*0-7583-0233-9*); 480p. pap. 35.78 (*0-7583-0234-7*); 786p. pap. 62.17 (*0-7583-0236-3*); 480p. lib. bdg. 41.78 (*0-7583-0226-6*); 786p. lib. bdg. 74.17 (*0-7583-0228-2*); 966p. lib. bdg. 84.70 (*0-7583-0229-0*); 1189p. lib. bdg. 95.30 (*0-7583-0230-4*); 1379p. lib. bdg. 105.47 (*0-7583-0231-2*); 280p. lib. bdg. 30.84 (*0-7583-0224-X*); 350p. lib. bdg. 34.82 (*0-7583-0225-8*); 614p. lib. bdg. 50.14 (*0-7583-0227-4*) Huge Print Pr.

—Anne of Green Gables. l.t. ed. 1991. (Avonlea Ser.: No. 1). 376p. (YA). (gr. 5-8). 17.95 o.p. (*1-85089-895-2*) ISIS Large Print Bks. GBR. *Dist:* Transaction Pubs.

—Anne of Green Gables. l.t. ed. 1998. (Avonlea Ser.: No. 1). 472p. (YA). (gr. 5-8). lib. bdg. 35.95 (*1-58118-035-7*, 22019) LRS.

—Anne of Green Gables. 1998. (Avonlea Ser.). 352p. (YA). (gr. 5-8). reprint ed. (*1-55109-013-9*) Nimbus Publishing, Ltd.

—Anne of Green Gables. l.t. ed. (Avonlea Ser.: No. 1). (YA). (gr. 5-8). reprint ed. 1993. 494p. lib. bdg. 26.00 (*0-939495-25-2*); 1998. 310p. lib. bdg. 25.00 (*1-58287-014-4*) North Bks.

—Anne of Green Gables, Level 2. Hedge, Tricia, ed. 2000. (Bookworms Ser.). (Illus.). 64p. (J). pap. text 5.95 (*0-19-422965-3*) Oxford Univ. Pr., Inc.

—Anne of Green Gables. l.t. ed. 2000. (Anne of Green Gables Ser.: Vol. 1). 414p. (YA). (gr. 5-8). pap. 24.99 (*1-57646-302-8*); lib. bdg. 37.99 (*1-57646-303-6*) Quiet Vision Publishing.

—Anne of Green Gables, Set. 1992. (Avonlea Ser.: No. 1). (YA). (gr. 5-8). 16.24 o.p. (*0-553-62867-4*, Dell Books for Young Readers) Random Hse. Children's Bks.

—Anne of Green Gables. abr. ed. 1997. (Avonlea Ser.: No. 1). (YA). (gr. 5-8). mass mkt. 16.95 o.p. incl. audio (*1-85998-749-4*) Trafalgar Square.

—Anne of Green Gables. deluxe ed. 1997. (Avonlea Ser.: No. 1). (Illus.). 112p. (YA). (gr. 5-8). 22.95 o.p. (*0-670-87031-5*) Viking Penguin.

—Anne of Green Gables: Address & Birthday Book, 2 vols., Set. 2001. (Illus.). 238p. (J). 12.95 (*1-55263-180-X*) Key Porter Bks. CAN. *Dist:* Firefly Bks., Ltd.

—Anne of Green Gables: Anne of Avonlea. 1996. (Avonlea Ser.: No. 1). (YA). (gr. 5-8). 12.98 o.p. (*0-7651-9979-3*) Smithmark Pubs., Inc.

—Anne of Green Gables: Anne of Avonlea; Anne of the Island; Anne of Green Gables. 1997. (Avonlea Ser.: No. 1). (YA). (gr. 5-8). mass mkt. 13.50 (*0-553-33306-2*) Bantam Bks.

—Anne of Green Gables: Seal Edition. abr. ed. 1987. (Avonlea Ser.: No. 1). (YA). (gr. 5-8). audio 18.99 o.s.i (*0-7704-3998-5*, RH Audio) Random Hse. Audio Publishing Group.

—Anne of Green Gables Book & Charm. 1999. (Charming Classic Bks.). 400p. (J). (ps up). pap. 6.99 (*0-694-01251-3*, Harper Festival) HarperCollins Children's Bk. Group.

—The Anne of Green Gables Collection. 1999. (Workhorse Library Ser.). E-Book 19.99 incl. cd-rom (*1-891595-36-9*) Quiet Vision Publishing.

—Anne of Green Gables Promo. 384p. 2003. pap. 3.99 o.p. (*0-14-250092-5*); 2000. pap. 2.99 o.p. (*0-14-130935-0*) Penguin Putnam Bks. for Young Readers. (Puffin Bks.).

—Anne's House of Dreams. 1976. (Avonlea Ser.: No. 5). 192p. (YA). (gr. 5-8). 20.95 (*0-8488-0587-9*) Amereon, Ltd.

—Anne's House of Dreams, unabr. ed. 1999. (Avonlea Ser.: No. 5). (YA). (gr. 5-8). audio 35.95 (*1-55685-586-9*) Audio Bk. Contractors, Inc.

—Anne's House of Dreams. 1983. (Avonlea Ser.: No. 5). (YA). (gr. 5-8). 256p. mass mkt. 4.50 (*0-553-21318-0*, Bantam Classics); 5th ed. 256p. mass mkt. 3.95 (*0-7704-2210-1*);No. 5. 240p. mass mkt. 2.95 o.s.i (*0-553-24195-8*) Bantam Bks.

—Anne's House of Dreams, unabr. ed. 1997. (Avonlea Ser.: No. 5). (YA). (gr. 5-8). audio 44.95 (*0-7861-1230-1*, 1976) Blackstone Audio Bks., Inc.

—Anne's House of Dreams, unabr. ed. 1999. (Avonlea Ser.: No. 5). (YA). (gr. 5-8). audio 44.95 Highsmith Inc.

—Anne's House of Dreams. l.t. ed. 1999. (Avonlea Ser.: No. 5). 364p. (YA). (gr. 5-8). lib. bdg. 34.95 (*1-58118-048-9*, 22517) LRS.

—Anne's House of Dreams. (Avonlea Ser.: No. 5). (YA). (gr. 5-8). E-Book 1.95 (*1-57799-880-4*) Logos Research Systems, Inc.

—Anne's House of Dreams. 1989. (J). pap. o.p. (*0-7710-6161-7*) McClelland & Stewart/Tundra Bks.

—Anne's House of Dreams. 1989. (Avonlea Ser.: No. 5). (YA). (gr. 5-8). mass mkt. 2.95 o.p. (*0-451-52319-9*, Signet Classics) NAL.

—Anne's House of Dreams. 1992. (Avonlea Ser.: No. 5). 304p. (YA). (gr. 5-8). pap. 2.99 o.p. (*0-14-032569-7*, Puffin Bks.); 1970. (Avonlea Ser.: No. 5). (YA). (gr. 5-8). 6.95 o.p. (*0-448-02549-3*, Grosset & Dunlap); Vol. 5. 1999. 320p. (J). pap. 3.99 (*0-14-036799-3*, Puffin Bks.) Penguin Putnam Bks. for Young Readers.

—Anne's House of Dreams. (YA). (gr. 5-8). 2000. (Anne of Green Gables Ser.: Vol. No. 5). 182p. pap. 14.99 (*1-57646-312-5*); 2000. (Anne of Green Gables Ser.: Vol. No. 5). 182p. lib. bdg. 30.99 (*1-57646-313-3*); 1999. (Avonlea Ser.: No. 5). E-Book 8.99 o.p. incl. cd-rom (*1-57646-055-X*); 2000. (Anne of Green Gables Ser.: Vol. 5). 336p. pap. 24.99 (*1-57646-314-1*); 2000. (Anne of Green Gables Ser.: Vol. No. 5). 336p. lib. bdg. 33.99 (*1-57646-315-X*) Quiet Vision Publishing.

—Anne's House of Dreams. 1994. (Avonlea Ser.: No. 5). (YA). (gr. 5-8). o.s.i (*0-553-85030-X*, Dell Books for Young Readers) Random Hse. Children's Bks.

—Anne's House of Dreams. 1996. (Avonlea Ser.: No. 5). viii, 193p. (YA). (gr. 5-8). 8.99 o.s.i (*0-517-14820-X*) Random Hse. Value Publishing.

—Anne's House of Dreams. 1994. (Avonlea Ser.: No. 5). 238p. (YA). (gr. 5-8). text 5.98 o.p. (*1-56138-430-5*, Courage Bks.) Running Pr. Bk. Pubs.

—Anne's House of Dreams. 1972. (Avonlea Ser.: No. 5). (YA). (gr. 5-8). 10.55 (*0-606-00376-2*) Turtleback Bks.

—The Annotated Anne of Green Gables. Jones, Mary E. Doody et al, eds. annot. ed. 1997. (Illus.). 504p. (J). 39.95 (*0-19-510428-5*) Oxford Univ. Pr., Inc.

—Mistress Pat. 288p. (YA). 1997. mass mkt. 4.99 (*0-7704-2246-2*); 1989. mass mkt. 3.99 o.s.i (*0-553-28048-1*) Bantam Bks.

—Mistress Pat. 1989. (J). pap. o.p. (*0-7710-6163-3*) McClelland & Stewart/Tundra Bks.

—A Tangled Web. 1989. (YA). 288p. mass mkt. 4.99 (*0-7704-2245-4*); 272p. mass mkt. 3.99 o.s.i (*0-553-28050-3*) Bantam Bks.

—A Tangled Web. 1989. (J). pap. o.p. (*0-7710-6160-9*) McClelland & Stewart/Tundra Bks.

Relationships

Montgomery, L. M. & Tanaka, Shelley. Anne of Green Gables. 1998. (Avonlea Ser.: No. 1). 112p. (gr. 5-8). text 12.95 o.s.i (*0-385-32333-6*, Dell Books for Young Readers) Random Hse. Children's Bks.

Montgomery, Rutherford G. Kildee House. 1993. (Newbery Honor Roll Ser.). (J). 14.00 (*0-606-05899-0*) Turtleback Bks.

—Kildee House. 1993. (Newbery Honor Roll Ser.). (Illus.). 224p. (J). (gr. 4-7). reprint ed. pap. 7.95 (*0-8027-7388-5*) Walker & Co.

Moon, Nicola. I Am Reading: Alligator Tales. 2000. (I Am Reading Bks.). (Illus.). 45p. (J). (gr. k-3). pap. o.p. (*0-7534-5121-2*) Kingfisher Publications, plc.

Mooney, E. S. Bubbles & the Secret Admirer. 2004. (Powerpuff Girls Ser.). 48p. (J). mass mkt. 3.99 (*0-439-49177-0*, Scholastic Paperbacks) Scholastic, Inc.

Moore, David. Dynamic Duos, 3. 1998. (Fast Breaks Ser.). 10.14 (*0-606-13376-3*) Turtleback Bks.

Moore, Emerson. Old Dan. 1996. (Illus.). 32p. (J). (gr. 1-3). pap. 7.00 o.p. (*0-8059-3876-1*) Dorrance Publishing Co., Inc.

Moore, Emily. Just My Luck. 1991. 9.09 o.p. (*0-606-04952-5*) Turtleback Bks.

—Just My Luck! 1983. 112p. (J). (gr. 4-7). 10.95 o.p. (*0-525-44009-7*, Dutton) Dutton/Plume.

—Something to Count On. 1991. 112p. (J). (gr. 3-7). pap. 3.99 o.s.i (*0-14-034791-7*, Puffin Bks.) Penguin Putnam Bks. for Young Readers.

—Whose Side Are You On?, RS. 128p. (J). (gr. 4-7). 1990. pap. 5.95 (*0-374-48373-6*, Sunburst); 1988. 14.00 o.p. (*0-374-38409-6*, Farrar, Straus & Giroux (BYR)) Farrar, Straus & Giroux.

Moore, Inga. Little Dog Lost. 1991. (Illus.). 32p. (J). (ps-3). text 14.95 o.p. (*0-02-767648-X*, Simon & Schuster Children's Publishing) Simon & Schuster Children's Publishing.

Moore, Ishbel. Dolina's Decision. 2001. 132p. (YA). (gr. 9 up). pap. 6.95 (*1-896184-74-X*) Roussan Pubs., Inc./Roussan Editeur, Inc. CAN. *Dist:* Orca Bk. Pubs.

Moore, Lilian. Don't Be Afraid, Amanda. (Ready-for-Chapters Ser.). (Illus.). 2001. 64p. (gr. 2-5). pap. 3.99 (*0-689-84497-2*, Aladdin); 1992. 80p. (J). (ps-3). 12.95 (*0-689-31725-5*, Atheneum) Simon & Schuster Children's Publishing.

—I'll Meet You at the Cucumbers. 1989. (Illus.). 80p. (J). (gr. 1-4). pap. 3.99 o.s.i (*0-553-15705-1*, Skylark) Random Hse. Children's Bks.

—I'll Meet You at the Cucumbers. (Ready-for-Chapters Ser.). (Illus.). (J). (gr. 2-5). 2001. 64p. pap. 3.99 (*0-689-84496-4*, Aladdin); 1988. 72p. 15.00 (*0-689-31243-1*, Atheneum) Simon & Schuster Children's Publishing.

Moore, Margie, illus. Ruby Bakes a Cake. 2004. (My First I Can Read Book Ser.). (J). (*0-06-008975-X*); lib. bdg. (*0-06-008976-8*) HarperCollins Pubs.

Moore, Martha. Under the Mermaid Angel. 2001. (Illus.). 176p. (YA). pap. 12.00 (*0-375-89507-8*, Random Hse. Bks. for Young Readers) Random Hse. Children's Bks.

Moore, Martha A. Under the Mermaid Angel. (YA). (gr. 7 up). 1997. 176p. mass mkt. 3.99 o.s.i (*0-440-22682-1*, Laurel Leaf); 1995. 192p. 14.95 o.s.i (*0-385-32160-0*, Dell Books for Young Readers) Random Hse. Children's Bks.

Mooser, Stephen. The Mind Bandits. 1985. (Which Way Bks.: No. 20). (Illus.). (J). (gr. 3-6). pap. (*0-671-55829-3*, Simon Pulse) Simon & Schuster Children's Publishing.

Moran, Alex. Boots for Beth. 2003. (Green Light Readers Level 2 Ser.). (Illus.). 24p. (J). 11.95 (*0-15-204878-2*); pap. 3.95 (*0-15-204838-3*) Harcourt Children's Bks. (Green Light Readers).

—Sam & Jack: Three Stories. 2001. (Green Light Readers Ser.). (Illus.). 24p. (J). (gr. k-2). 10.95 o.s.i (*0-15-216240-2*); pap. 3.95 o.s.i (*0-15-216234-8*) Harcourt Children's Bks. (Green Light Readers).

—Sam & Jack: Three Stories. 2003. (Green Light Readers Level 1 Ser.). (Illus.). 24p. (J). 11.95 (*0-15-204822-7*); pap. 3.95 (*0-15-204862-6*) Harcourt Children's Bks. (Green Light Readers).

Moreau, Patricia. Suzanne Masterson: Dangerous Games. 1994. 412p. (YA). pap. 8.99 o.p. (*0-88070-648-1*, Multnomah Bks.) Multnomah Pubs., Inc.

Morgan, Geoffrey. Tea with Mr. Timothy. 2nd l.t. ed. 1993. (Illus.). 111p. (J). 18.95 (*1-85695-300-9*) ISIS Large Print Bks. GBR. *Dist:* Transaction Pubs.

Morgan, Pierr. The Turnip. 1996. (J). 11.15 o.p. (*0-606-12015-7*) Turtleback Bks.

Morganstern, Mimi. The House at Hemlock Farms. 2000. (Illus.). vi, 54p. (J). (gr. 3-6). pap. 6.95 (*0-9700522-3-5*) Morganstern, Mimi.

—The House at Hemlock Farms-"Read-Along with Mimi" A Cool Chapterbook-Package. 2000. (Illus.). vi, 54p. (J). (gr. 3-6). per. 9.99 incl. audio (*0-9700522-4-3*) Morganstern, Mimi.

Morgenroth, Barbara. Tramps Like Us. 1979. (J). (gr. 6 up). 6.95 o.p. (*0-689-30690-3*, Atheneum) Simon & Schuster Children's Publishing.

Morgenstern, Susie. Hallo Sarah! Hier Ist Salah. 2003. (GER.). 128p. pap. 15.00 (*1-4000-3976-2*) Random Hse. Information Group.

—Secret Letters from 0 to 10. 2000. (Illus.). 144p. (J). (gr. 3-7). pap. 4.99 (*0-14-130819-2*, Puffin Bks.) Penguin Putnam Bks. for Young Readers.

—Secret Letters from 0 to 10. Rosner, Gill, tr. 1998. 208p. (J). (gr. 4-7). 16.99 (*0-670-88007-8*, Viking) Penguin Putnam Bks. for Young Readers.

—Secret Letters from 0 to 10. 2000. 11.04 (*0-606-18846-0*) Turtleback Bks.

Morgenstern, Susie S. It's Not Fair, RS. 1983. (Illus.). 100p. (J). (gr. 4 up). 10.95 o.p. (*0-374-33649-0*, Farrar, Straus & Giroux (BYR)) Farrar, Straus & Giroux.

Moriarty, Jaclyn. The Year of Secret Assignments. 2004. (YA). 16.95 (*0-439-49881-3*) Scholastic, Inc.

Morozumi, Atsuko. My Friend Gorilla, RS. 1998. (Illus.). 32p. (J). (ps-k). 15.00 (*0-374-35458-8*, Farrar, Straus & Giroux (BYR)) Farrar, Straus & Giroux.

Morpurgo, Michael. The Dancing Bear. 1996. (Illus.). 64p. (J). (gr. 2-7). 13.95 o.p. (*0-395-77980-4*) Houghton Mifflin Co.

—Waiting for Anya. l.t. ed. 1992. 240p. (J). 13.95 o.p. (*0-7451-1527-6*, Galaxy Children's Large Print) BBC Audiobooks America.

—Waiting for Anya. 1997. 176p. (gr. 5-9). pap. 5.99 (*0-14-038431-6*); 1991. 174p. (J). 14.99 o.s.i (*0-670-83735-0*, Viking Children's Bks.) Penguin Putnam Bks. for Young Readers.

—Waiting for Anya. 1997. (J). 11.04 (*0-606-12044-0*) Turtleback Bks.

Morris, Carroll H. Saddle Shoe Blues. 1987. 167p. (J). 9.95 o.p. (*0-87579-077-1*) Deseret Bk. Co.

Morrison, Dorothy N. Whisper Goodbye. 1985. 192p. (J). (gr. 4-8). 12.95 o.s.i (*0-689-31109-5*, Atheneum) Simon & Schuster Children's Publishing.

Moser, Barry. Tucker Pfeffercorn. 1994. (J). 15.95 o.s.i (*0-316-58542-4*) Little Brown & Co.

Mosher, Richard. The Taxi Navigator. 1996. 144p. (J). (gr. 4-7). 15.95 o.s.i (*0-399-23104-8*, Philomel) Penguin Putnam Bks. for Young Readers.

Mosionier, Beatrice. Unusual Friendships: A Little Black Cat & a Little White Rat. 2002. (Illus.). 74p. (J). pap. 10.95 (*1-894778-04-9*) Theytus Bks., Ltd. CAN. *Dist:* Orca Bk. Pubs.

Moss, Marissa. The All-New Amelia. 1999. (Amelia Ser.). (Illus.). 40p. (YA). (gr. 3 up). 12.95 (*1-56247-840-0*); pap. 5.95 (*1-56247-822-2*) Pleasant Co. Pubns. (American Girl).

—The All-New Amelia: And Brighter Than Bright Amelia. 1999. (Amelia Ser.). (J). (gr. 3-5). 12.10 (*0-606-19866-0*) Turtleback Bks.

—Luv, Amelia Luv, Nadia. 1999. (Amelia Ser.). (Illus.). 32p. (YA). (gr. 3 up). 12.95 (*1-56247-839-7*); pap. 7.95 (*1-56247-823-0*) Pleasant Co. Pubns. (American Girl).

Moss, Miriam. I'll Be Your Friend, Smudge! 2002. (Illus.). 24p. (J). (ps-2). 12.95 (*1-86233-207-X*) Gullane Children's Bks. GBR. *Dist:* Sterling Publishing Co., Inc.

Most, Bernard. The Littlest Dinosaurs, Grades 1-6. 1993. (Illus.). pap., tchr. ed. 33.95 incl. audio (*0-87499-193-5*) Live Oak Media.

Most, Bernard & Freeman, Don. The Little Dinosaurs. unabr. ed. 1993. (Illus.). (J). (gr. k-1). 22.95 incl. audio (*0-87499-192-7*) Live Oak Media.

Mostacchi, Massimo. A Dog's Best Friend. 1995. (Illus.). 32p. (J). (gr. k-3). 15.88 o.p. (*1-55858-498-6*) North-South Bks., Inc.

Mostacchi, Massimo & Miceli, Monica. The Beast & the Boy. Clements, Andrew, tr. from GER. 1945. Orig. Title: Marcolino und das Monster. (Illus.). 32p. (J). (gr. k-3). 14.95 o.p. (*1-55858-443-9*); 14.88 o.p. (*1-55858-444-7*) North-South Bks., Inc.

Motter, Charlott L. Poca. 1988. (Illus.). 27p. (J). 5.95 o.p. (*0-533-07661-7*) Vantage Pr., Inc.

Moulton, Mark K. A Snowman Named Just Bob. 2003. 40p. (J). 14.95 (*0-8249-5860-8*, 53876801, Ideals Children's Bks.) Ideals Pubns.

Mouse Works Staff. Disney's The Jungle Book: Mowgli Makes a Friend. 1995. (Tiny Changing Pictures Bk.). (Illus.). 10p. (J). (ps-k). 4.95 o.p. (*0-7868-3068-9*) Disney Pr.

—Friends Forever: Friends Forever. 1995. (Illus.). (J). bds. 5.98 o.p. (*1-57082-275-1*) Mouse Works.

—Good Friends. 1997. (Roly Poly Lift-the-Flaps Bks.). 20p. (J). (ps-k). bds. 3.99 (*1-57082-566-1*) Mouse Works.

—Goofy. 1998. (Friendly Tales Ser.). (Illus.). 10p. (J). (ps). 6.99 (*1-57082-928-4*) Mouse Works.

—Heroes & Friends. 1997. (J). 31.92 (*1-57082-772-9*) Mouse Works.

—Mickey Mouse. 1998. (Friendly Tales Ser.). (Illus.). 10p. (J). (ps-k). 6.99 (*1-57082-929-2*) Mouse Works.

—Minnie Mouse. 1998. (Friendly Tales Ser.). (Illus.). 10p. (J). (ps). 6.99 (*1-57082-930-6*) Mouse Works.

—On the Go! 1997. (Giant Lift-the-Flap Ser.). (Illus.). 5p. (J). (ps). 7.98 o.p. (*1-57082-637-4*) Mouse Works.

—Simba. 1999. (Disney's Friendly Tales Ser.). (Illus.). 10p. (J). (ps-k). 6.99 (*0-7364-1011-2*) Mouse Works.

—Toy Story 2: Slheriff Woody & the Roundup Gant. 1999. (Toy Story 2 Ser.). (Illus.). 10p. (J). (ps up). 9.99 (*0-7364-0170-9*) Mouse Works.

—101 Dalmatians Follow the Leader. 1997. (Lift the Flaps Ser.). (Illus.). 18p. (J). (ps-3). 3.98 o.p. (*1-57082-628-5*) Mouse Works.

Mr. Rogers You're Growing. 1993. (J). audio 8.98 (*0-7935-2635-3*) Leonard, Hal Corp.

Mueller, Charles S. Almost Adult: Preteen Story Devotions. 1993. 160p. (Orig.). (J). (gr. 4-7). pap. 6.99 o.p. (*0-570-04598-3*, 12-3184) Concordia Publishing Hse.

Muggs. Lady & Me. 1995. (Illus.). 48p. (J). (gr. 1-3). pap. 8.00 o.p. (*0-8059-3671-8*) Dorrance Publishing Co., Inc.

Muldrow, Diane. Into the Mix, Vol. 4. 2002. (Dish Ser.). (Illus.). 160p. (J). mass mkt. 4.99 (*0-448-42829-6*, Grosset & Dunlap) Penguin Putnam Bks. for Young Readers.

—Lights, Camera, Cook!, No. 8. 2003. (Dish Ser.: Vol. 8). (Illus.). 160p. (J). mass mkt. 4.99 (*0-448-43175-0*) Penguin Putnam Bks. for Young Readers.

—A Measure of Thanks. 2003. (Dish! Ser.). (Illus.). 160p. (J). mass mkt. 4.99 (*0-448-43201-3*, Grosset & Dunlap) Penguin Putnam Bks. for Young Readers.

—On the Back Burner. 2003. (Dish Ser.: No. 6). (Illus.). 160p. (J). mass mkt. 4.99 (*0-448-42897-0*, Grosset & Dunlap) Penguin Putnam Bks. for Young Readers.

—Recipe for Trouble, Vol. 7. 2003. (Dish Ser.: No. 7). (Illus.). 160p. (J). mass mkt. 4.99 (*0-448-42898-9*, Grosset & Dunlap) Penguin Putnam Bks. for Young Readers.

—Stirring It Up: Friends Cooking, Eating, Talking Life. 2002. (Dish Ser.: No. 1). (Illus.). 160p. (J). (gr. 4-7). mass mkt. 4.99 (*0-448-42815-6*, Grosset & Dunlap) Penguin Putnam Bks. for Young Readers.

—Sweet & Sour Summer. 2003. (Dish Ser.: Vol. 9). (Illus.). 160p. (J). mass mkt. 4.99 (*0-448-43176-9*, Grosset & Dunlap) Penguin Putnam Bks. for Young Readers.

—Truth Without the Trimmings, Vol. 5. 2002. (Dish Ser.). (Illus.). 160p. (J). mass mkt. 4.99 (*0-448-42871-7*) Penguin Putnam Bks. for Young Readers.

—Turning up the Heat: Friends Cooking, Eating, Talking Life. 2002. (Dish Ser.: No. 2). (Illus.). 160p. (J). mass mkt. 4.99 (*0-448-42816-4*) Penguin Putnam Bks. for Young Readers.

Mulford, Philippa G. If It's Not Funny, Why Am I Laughing? 1982. 144p. (J). (gr. 7 up). 9.95 o.s.i (*0-440-03961-4*, Delacorte Pr.) Dell Publishing.

—The World Is My Eggshell. 1988. (J). (gr. k-12). mass mkt. 2.95 o.s.i (*0-440-20243-4*, Laurel Leaf) Random Hse. Children's Bks.

Mulford, Philippa Greene. Everything I Hoped For. 1990. 192p. (YA). (gr. 8-12). pap. 2.95 (*0-380-76074-6*, Avon Bks.) Morrow/Avon.

—If It's Not Funny, Why Am I Laughing? 1986. 144p. (gr. 7-12). pap. 2.50 o.p. (*0-440-93976-3*) Dell Publishing.

Muller, Norbert. Fuera de Juego. 2nd ed. 1988. (Punto Juvenil Ser.). (SPA.). (J). 10.05 o.p. (*0-606-05302-6*) Turtleback Bks.

Mullican, Judy. Going to Benny's. 1995. (Big Bks.). (Illus.). 8p. (Orig.). (J). (ps-k). pap. text 10.95 (*1-57332-054-4*) HighReach Learning, Inc.

—My Forest Friends. (Big Bks.). (Illus.). 8p. (J). (ps-k). 1994. pap. text 10.95 (*1-57332-003-X*); 2000. pap. text 10.95 (*1-57332-172-9*); 2000. pap. text 10.95 (*1-57332-180-X*) HighReach Learning, Inc.

—Who Am I? 1995. (Little Bks.). (Illus.). 8p. (J). (ps-k). pap. text 10.95 (*1-57332-017-X*); pap. text 10.95 (*1-57332-018-8*) HighReach Learning, Inc.

—Who Can? Loomis, Linda, tr. 1995. (Big Bks.).Tr. of Quien Puede?. (SPA., Illus.). 8p. (J). (ps-k). pap. text 10.95 (*1-57332-056-0*) HighReach Learning, Inc.

—Who Can? 1994. (Big Bks.).Tr. of Quien Puede?. (Illus.). 8p. (J). (ps-k). pap. text 10.95 (*1-57332-001-3*) HighReach Learning, Inc.

Munoz-Furlong, Anne. Alexander & His Pals Visit the Main Street School. 1999. (J). (gr. k-6). pap. (*1-882541-07-3*) Food Allergy & Anaphylaxis Network.

Munro, Roxie. Blimps. (Illus.). 32p. (J). (gr. 2-5). 1994. pap. 4.99 o.p. (*0-14-055292-8*, Puffin Bks.); 1988. 12.95 o.p. (*0-525-44441-6*, Dutton Children's Bks.) Penguin Putnam Bks. for Young Readers.

Munsch, Robert. Mortimer. 1985. (Illus.). 24p. (J). (ps). pap. 5.95 (*0-920303-11-0*); text 15.95 (*0-920303-12-9*) Annick Pr., Ltd. CAN. *Dist:* Firefly Bks., Ltd.

—Murmel, Murmel, Murmel. 2003. (Illus.). 32p. (J). (gr. k-2). lib. bdg. 15.95 (*0-920236-29-4*); pap. 5.95 (*0-920236-31-6*) Annick Pr., Ltd. CAN. *Dist:* Firefly Bks., Ltd.

—Something Good. (Illus.). 24p. (J). (ps-2). 2003. pap. 5.95 (*1-55037-100-2*); 2003. lib. bdg. 15.95 (*1-55037-099-5*); 2003. (Annikin Ser.: Vol. 14). pap. 1.25 (*1-55037-390-0*); 1993. (CHI., pap. 5.95 o.p. (*1-55037-305-6*) Annick Pr., Ltd. CAN. *Dist:* Firefly Bks., Ltd.

—Something Good. 1990. (Munsch for Kids Ser.). (J). 12.10 (*0-606-05612-2*) Turtleback Bks.

—Wait & See. 2003. (Illus.). 24p. (J). (ps-2). pap. 5.95 (*1-55037-334-X*); lib. bdg. 15.95 (*1-55037-335-8*) Annick Pr., Ltd. CAN. *Dist:* Firefly Bks., Ltd.

—Wait & See. ed. 1994. (J). (gr. 2). spiral bd. (*0-616-01747-2*) Canadian National Institute for the Blind/Institut National Canadien pour les Aveugles.

—Wait & See. 1993. (Munsch for Kids Ser.). (J). 12.10 (*0-606-06079-0*) Turtleback Bks.

—We Share Everything. ed. 2000. (J). (gr. 1). spiral bd. (*0-616-01749-9*); (gr. 2). spiral bd. (*0-616-01750-2*) Canadian National Institute for the Blind/Institut National Canadien pour les Aveugles.

—We Share Everything. 2000. (Illus.). 32p. (J). (ps-1). pap. text 4.99 (*0-590-89601-6*) Scholastic, Inc.

—We Share Everything. 2000. 11.14 (*0-606-18891-6*) Turtleback Bks.

Munsch, Robert & Kusugak, Michael Arvaarluk. A Promise Is a Promise. 1988. (Illus.). 32p. (J). (gr. k-3). pap. 5.95 (*1-55037-008-1*); text 15.95 (*1-55037-009-X*) Annick Pr., Ltd. CAN. *Dist:* Firefly Bks., Ltd.

Munsch, Robert & Martchenko, Michael. We Share Everything. 2002. 32p. (J). 3.99 (*0-439-38824-4*) Scholastic, Inc.

Munson, Derek. Enemy Pie: For My Best Enemy. 2000. (Illus.). 40p. (J). (gr. k-3). 14.95 (*0-8118-2778-X*) Chronicle Bks. LLC.

Murphy, Barbara B. Home Free. 1970. (Illus.). (J). (gr. 4-6). 4.95 o.p. (*0-440-03675-5*, Delacorte Pr.) Dell Publishing.

Murphy, Elspeth Campbell. Curtis Anderson. 1986. (Apple Street Church Ser.). (Illus.). 120p. (J). (gr. 3-7). pap. 4.49 o.p. (*1-55513-027-5*) Cook Communications Ministries.

—Danny Petrowski. 1985. (Kids from Apple Street Church Ser.). 120p. (Orig.). (J). (gr. 3-7). pap. 4.49 o.p. (*0-89191-730-6*) Cook Communications Ministries.

—The Littlest One. 1987. (Brenda Learns about God Ser.). (J). (ps). 3.95 o.p. (*1-55513-268-5*) Cook Communications Ministries.

—Mary Jo Bennett. 1985. (Kids from Apple Street Church Ser.). 107p. (Orig.). (J). (gr. 3-7). pap. 4.99 o.p. (*0-89191-711-X*, 57117) Cook Communications Ministries.

—Too Many Bunnies. 1987. (Brenda Learns about God Ser.). (J). (ps). pap. 2.99 o.p. (*1-55513-247-2*) Cook Communications Ministries.

Murphy, Frank. Lockie & Dadge. 1997. 192p. (YA). pap. 6.95 (*0-86278-424-7*) O'Brien Pr., Ltd., The IRL. *Dist:* Irish American Bk. Co.

Murphy, Jill. All for One. ed. 2003. (gr. 1). spiral bd. (*0-616-14591-8*); (gr. 2). spiral bd. (*0-616-14592-6*) Canadian National Institute for the Blind/Institut National Canadien pour les Aveugles.

—All for One. 2002. (Illus.). 32p. (J). (ps-1). 15.99 (*0-7636-0785-1*) Candlewick Pr.

—A Piece of Cake. 1997. 11.14 (*0-606-12791-7*) Turtleback Bks.

Murphy, Mary. Roxie & Bo Together. 1999. (Illus.). 24p. (J). (ps). 12.99 o.s.i (*0-7636-0870-X*) Candlewick Pr.

Murphy, Patricia J. I Need You. 2003. (Rookie Reader Ser.). (Illus.). pap. 4.95 (*0-516-26966-6*, Children's Pr.) Scholastic Library Publishing.

—Te Necesito. 2003. (Rookie Reader Espanol Ser.). (SPA., Illus.). (J). lib. bdg. 15.00 (*0-516-25890-7*, Children's Pr.) Scholastic Library Publishing.

Murphy, Patti Beling. Elinor & Violet: Two Naughty Chickens at the Beach. 2003. (Illus.). 32p. (J). (ps-3). 15.95 (*0-316-91034-1*) Little Brown Children's Bks.

Murphy, Stuart J. Give Me Half! 1996. (MathStart Ser.). (Illus.). 40p. (J). (gr. 1 up). pap. 4.99 (*0-06-446701-5*, Harper Trophy) HarperCollins Children's Bk. Group.

—Monster Musical Chairs. 2000. (MathStart Ser.). (Illus.). 40p. (J). (gr. 1 up). pap. 4.99 (*0-06-446730-9*, Harper Trophy) HarperCollins Children's Bk. Group.

Murray, Marguerite. Like Seabirds Flying Home. 1988. 192p. (YA). lib. bdg. 13.95 o.s.i (*0-689-31459-0*, Atheneum) Simon & Schuster Children's Publishing.

Murray, Mary & Vischer. Junior & Laura Share the Year Together. 2003. (Big Idea Bks.). 12p. (YA). 4.99 (*0-310-70541-X*) Zondervan.

Murrieta, Ed & Wakeman, Diana, illus. Minnie's Tea Party. 1999. 18p. (ps-1). reprint ed. text 10.00 (*0-7881-6632-8*) DIANE Publishing Co.

Muscat, Charles. Little Joe & the Alien. 1990. (J). 6.95 o.p. (*0-533-08799-6*) Vantage Pr., Inc.

My Best Friends. 2003. (Illus.). 64p. (J). (gr. 1-4). 5.95 (*0-8069-1950-7*) Sterling Publishing Co., Inc.

My Little Golden Book about God. 2000. (Little Golden Bks.). (Illus.). 24p. (J). (ps-2). 2.99 (0-307-02105-X, 98246, Golden Bks.) Random Hse. Children's Bks.

My Name Is Ariel! 2004. (Bath Books with Crayon Ser.). 6p. (J). 5.99 (0-7364-2194-7, RH/Disney) Random Hse. Children's Bks.

Myers, Anna. Rosie's Tiger. 1994. 128p. (J). (gr. 4-7). 14.95 (0-8027-8305-8) Walker & Co.

—Stolen by the Sea. 2001. 160p. (J). (gr. 3-7). 16.95 (0-8027-8787-8) Walker & Co.

Myers, Bill. The Blunder Years. 1993. (McGee & Me! Ser.: Vol. 11). (J). pap. 5.99 o.p. (0-8423-4123-4) Tyndale Hse. Pubs.

Myers, Bill & Johnson, Ken. The Big Lie. 1989. (McGee & Me! Ser.: Vol. 1). (J). pap. 5.99 o.p. (0-8423-4169-2) Tyndale Hse. Pubs.

—Skate Expectations. 1989. (McGee & Me! Ser.: Vol. 4). 92p. (J). (gr. 3-7). pap. 3.99 (0-8423-4165-X) Tyndale Hse. Pubs.

—A Star in the Breaking. 1989. (McGee & Me! Ser.: Vol. 2). (J). pap. 5.99 o.p. (0-8423-4168-4) Tyndale Hse. Pubs.

Myers, Bill & West, Robert E. Beauty in the Least. 1993. (McGee & Me! Ser.: Vol. 12). 85p. (J). pap. 3.99 o.p. (0-8423-4124-2) Tyndale Hse. Pubs.

Myers, Walter Dean. Dangerous Games. 1993. (Eighteen Pine Street Ser.: No. 8). 160p. (YA). mass mkt. 3.50 o.s.i (0-553-56269-X) Bantam Bks.

—Intensive Care. 1993. (Eighteen Pine Street Ser.: No. 7). 160p. (YA). mass mkt. 3.50 o.s.i (0-553-56268-1) Bantam Bks.

—Mojo & the Russians. 1977. (J). 12.95 o.p. (0-670-48437-7) Viking Penguin.

—Three Swords for Granada. 2002. (Illus.). 80p. (J). (gr. 2-5). tchr. ed. 15.95 (0-8234-1676-3) Holiday Hse., Inc.

Myracle, Lauren. Eleven. 2004. 160p. (J). 16.99 (0-525-47165-0, Dutton Children's Bks.) Penguin Putnam Bks. for Young Readers.

—Kissing Kate. 2003. 176p. (YA). 16.99 (0-525-46917-6, Dutton Children's Bks.) Penguin Putnam Bks. for Young Readers.

Bratz Model Friendship. 2004. (Bratz Ser.). (Illus.). 112p. 4.99 (0-448-43503-9, Grosset & Dunlap) Penguin Putnam Bks. for Young Readers.

—Dick & Jane Sidekick. 2003. mass mkt. 430.92 (0-448-43442-3, Grosset & Dunlap) Penguin Putnam Bks. for Young Readers.

—Dick & Jane Sidekick for Levy. 2003. mass mkt. 287.28 (0-448-43445-8, Grosset & Dunlap) Penguin Putnam Bks. for Young Readers.

Nabb, Magdalen. Josie Smith & Eileen. 1992. (Illus.). 96p. (J). (gr. 1-5). 12.95 o.p. (0-689-50534-5, McElderry, Margaret K.) Simon & Schuster Children's Publishing.

Nadler, Beth. Jack: Junior Novel. 1996. 96p. (J). (gr. 4-7). pap. 4.95 (0-7868-1155-2) Disney Pr.

Nagda, Ann Whitehead. Dear Whiskers. 2000. (Illus.). 75p. (J). (gr. 2-5). tchr. ed. 15.95 (0-8234-1495-7) Holiday Hse., Inc.

Nakagawa, Rieko. Guri & Gura Magical Friend. 2003. (Illus.). 32p. (J). 10.95 (0-8048-3356-7) Tuttle Publishing.

—Guri & Gura's Surprise Visitor. 2003. (Guri & Gura Ser.). (Illus.). 32p. (J). 10.95 (0-8048-3353-2) Tuttle Publishing.

Namey, Laura. In the Groove. 2001. (Gold Mixed Collection). (Illus.). 128p. (J). (gr. 1-6). pap. 9.95 (1-58584-270-2) Huckleberry Pr.

Namioka, Lensey. Yang the Third & Her Impossible Family. 1995. (Illus.). 160p. (J). 15.95 o.p. (0-316-59726-0) Little Brown & Co.

Namovicz, Gene I. The Joke War. 1988. (J). (gr. 3-6). pap. (0-671-66577-4, Aladdin) Simon & Schuster Children's Publishing.

Napoli, Donna Jo. Friends Everywhere. 1999. (Aladdin Angelwings Ser.: No. 1). (Illus.). 96p. (J). (gr. 2-5). pap. 3.99 (0-689-82694-X, Aladdin) Simon & Schuster Children's Publishing.

—Friends Everywhere. 1999. (Illus.). (J). 10.04 (0-606-17904-6) Turtleback Bks.

—Zel. 1998. (Puffin Novel Ser.). 240p. (YA). (gr. 5-9). pap. 5.99 (0-14-130116-3, Puffin Bks.) Penguin Putnam Bks. for Young Readers.

—Zel. 1996. 11.04 (0-606-14373-4) Turtleback Bks.

Napoli, Donna Jo & Kane, Marie. Rocky: The Cat Who Barks. 2002. (Illus.). 32p. (J). (ps-2). 15.99 (0-525-46544-8, Dutton Children's Bks.) Penguin Putnam Bks. for Young Readers.

Narahashi, Keiko. Two Girls Can! 2000. Orig. Title: Friends. (Illus.). 32p. (ps-3). 16.00 Simon & Schuster Children's Publishing.

Nash, Bruce. So You Think You Know Your Boyfriend-Girlfriend? Schneider, Meg F., ed. 1982. (Flip-Overs Ser.). 64p. (Orig.). (J). (gr. 3-7). pap. 2.85 o.p. (0-671-45548-6, Simon & Schuster Children's Publishing) Simon & Schuster Children's Publishing.

Naylor, Phyllis Reynolds. Alice Alone. (Alice Ser.). 240p. (J). 2002. mass mkt. 4.99 (0-689-85189-8, Simon Pulse); 2001. (Illus.). (gr. 5-9). 16.00 (0-689-82634-6, Atheneum) Simon & Schuster Children's Publishing.

—Alice in Blunderland. 2003. (Alice Ser.). (Illus.). 208p. (J). 15.95 (0-689-84397-6, Atheneum) Simon & Schuster Children's Publishing.

—Being Danny's Dog. 160p. (J). (gr. 4-7). 1997. (Illus.). pap. 4.50 (0-689-81472-0, Aladdin); 1995. 15.00 (0-689-31756-5, Atheneum) Simon & Schuster Children's Publishing.

—Being Danny's Dog. 1997. 10.04 (0-606-11105-0) Turtleback Bks.

—The Grooming of Alice. (Alice Ser.). (Illus.). 224p. (gr. 5-9). 2001. (YA). pap. 4.99 (0-689-84618-5, Aladdin); 2000. (J). 16.00 (0-689-82633-8, Atheneum) Simon & Schuster Children's Publishing.

—Josie's Troubles. 1992. (Illus.). 112p. (J). (gr. 3-7). lib. bdg. 13.95 (0-689-31659-3, Atheneum) Simon & Schuster Children's Publishing.

—One of the Third Grade Thonkers. 1991. 144p. (J). (gr. 4-7). pap. text 4.50 (0-440-40407-X) Dell Publishing.

—Patiently Alice. 2003. (Alice Ser.). (Illus.). 256p. (YA). 15.95 (0-689-82636-2, Atheneum) Simon & Schuster Children's Publishing.

—Saving Shiloh. unabr. ed. 2002. 137p. pap. 28.00 incl. audio (0-8072-0456-0, Listening Library) Random Hse. Audio Publishing Group.

—A Spy among the Girls. 2002. 144p. (gr. 4-7). pap. text 4.99 (0-440-41390-7, Random Hse. Bks. for Young Readers) Random Hse. Children's Bks.

—A Spy among the Girls. l.t. ed. 2003. (Boys=Girls Battle Ser.). 145p. (J). 23.95 (0-7862-5821-7) Thorndike Pr.

—Starting with Alice. (Alice Ser.). (J). 2004. (Illus.). 208p. pap. 4.99 (0-689-84396-8, Aladdin); 2002. 192p. 15.95 (0-689-84395-X, Atheneum) Simon & Schuster Children's Publishing.

—Starting with Alice. l.t. ed. 2003. 199p. (J). 22.95 (0-7862-5091-7) Thorndike Pr.

—A String of Chances. 1982. 252p. (YA). (gr. 6 up). lib. bdg. 13.95 o.s.i (0-689-30935-X, Atheneum) Simon & Schuster Children's Publishing.

Needham, Nancy. They Called Me Kite. 2000. 272p. pap. 21.99 (0-7388-2199-3); E-Book 8.00 (0-7388-8822-2) Xlibris Corp.

Neenan, Colin. Live a Little. 1996. 264p. (YA). (gr. 7 up). 12.00 (0-15-201242-7) Harcourt Children's Bks.

Neighborhood Friends. 1984. (Mickey's Kindergarten Workbooks Ser.). (Illus.). 64p. (J). (gr. k-1). 1.25 o.p. (0-448-16137-0, Grosset & Dunlap) Penguin Putnam Bks. for Young Readers.

Nelson, Nan F. My Day with Anka. 1996. (Illus.). 24p. (J). (ps up). 16.00 (0-688-11058-4) HarperCollins Children's Bk. Group.

Nelson, Theresa. And One for All. 1991. 192p. (J). (gr. 4-7). pap. text 4.50 (0-440-40456-8) Dell Publishing.

—The Empress of Elsewhere. 1998. (Illus.). 224p. (J). (gr. 5-9). pap. 17.95 o.p. (0-7894-2498-3) Dorling Kindersley Publishing, Inc.

—Empress of Elsewhere. 2000. (Illus.). 224p. (J). (gr. 5-9). pap. 5.99 o.s.i (0-14-130813-3, Puffin Bks.) Penguin Putnam Bks. for Young Readers.

—Empress of Elsewhere. 2000. (Illus.). (J). 12.04 (0-606-18836-3) Turtleback Bks.

Neri, Joseph. So I Said to the Little Old Man. Edwards, Kristen, ed. 1994. (Illus.). 96p. (Orig.). (J). (gr. k-6). pap. 12.95 (0-9639428-3-2); lib. bdg. 14.99 (0-9639428-1-6) Tympanon Productions.

Ness, Caroline. Let's Be Friends. 1995. (Illus.). 22p. (J). 5.95 o.p. (0-694-00725-0, Harper Festival) HarperCollins Children's Bk. Group.

Ness, Evaline. Sam, Bangs, & Moonshine. 1966. (J). 13.10 (0-606-01326-1) Turtleback Bks.

—Tom Tit Tot. 1997. (Illus.). 32p. (J). (ps-3). mass mkt. 5.99 (0-689-81398-8, Aladdin) Simon & Schuster Children's Publishing.

Nethery, Mary. Hannah & Jack: A Very Special Friendship. 1996. (Illus.). 32p. (J). (ps-3). 15.00 (0-689-80533-0, Atheneum) Simon & Schuster Children's Publishing.

Netzarel, Orly. Yellow, Yellow-Brown, Yellow-Brown & Black. 2001. 160p. pap. 11.95 (0-595-18742-0, Writers Club Pr.) iUniverse, Inc.

Neumann, Rainer. Masama: The Adventures of Twing & Twang. 2000. 128p. E-Book 8.00 (0-7388-7130-3) Xlibris Corp.

New Leaf Press Staff. Bombus Finds a Friend: The Bombus Creativity Book. 1999. (Illus.). (J). (gr. 1-7). pap. 15.99 o.p. (0-89051-260-4) Master Bks.

Newberry, Clare Turlay. Marshmallow. 1999. (Clare Newberry Classics Ser.). (Illus.). 32p. (J). (ps-3). 9.98 (0-7651-0951-4) Smithmark Pubs., Inc.

Newman. Yo-Ho-Ho. 2000. (Illus.). 62p. (J). pap. 6.95 (0-552-52843-9) Transworld Publishers Ltd. GBR. *Dist:* Trafalgar Square.

Newman, Jerry. Green Earrings & a Felt Hat, ERS. 1993. (Illus.). 48p. (J). (gr. 1-3). 14.95 o.p. (0-8050-2392-5, Holt, Henry & Co. Bks. For Young Readers) Holt, Henry & Co.

Newman, Leslea. Hachi-Ko Waits. 2004. (J). 15.95 (0-8050-7336-1, Holt, Henry & Co. Bks. For Young Readers) Holt, Henry & Co.

Newman, Marjorie. Is That What Friends Do? 2000. (Illus.). 32p. (J). (ps). pap. (0-09-922162-4) Random Hse. of Canada, Ltd. CAN. *Dist:* Random Hse., Inc.

—Knocked Out! 1984. 48p. (J). (gr. 6-9). text 3.95 o.p. (0-241-11072-6) Trafalgar Square.

Newsome, Jill. Shadow. 1999. (Illus.). 32p. (J). (ps-2). pap. 15.95 o.p. (0-7894-2631-5) Dorling Kindersley Publishing, Inc.

Newton, Suzanne. An End to Perfect. 1984. 192p. (J). (gr. 7 up). 12.95 o.p. (0-670-29487-X, Viking Children's Bks.) Penguin Putnam Bks. for Young Readers.

—Where Are You When I Need You? 208p. 1993. (YA). (gr. 7 up). pap. 3.99 o.s.i (0-14-034454-3, Puffin Bks.); 1991. (J). 14.00 o.p. (0-670-81702-3, Viking Children's Bks.) Penguin Putnam Bks. for Young Readers.

Nikly, Michelle. The Perfume of Memory. 1999. (Illus.). 40p. (J). (ps-3). pap. 16.95 (0-439-08206-4, Levine, Arthur A. Bks.) Scholastic, Inc.

Nilsen, Anna. My Best Friends. 2003. (Illus.). 24p. (J). 15.95 (0-7696-3159-2, Gingham Dog Pr.) McGraw-Hill Children's Publishing.

—Where Are Percy's Friends? 1996. (Illus.). 16p. (J). (ps-3). 7.99 o.p. (0-7636-0017-2) Candlewick Pr.

Nimeth, Albert J. I Like You, Just Because. 1971. (Illus.). 112p. (J). (gr. 5 up). pap. 3.50 (0-8199-0422-8, Franciscan Herald Pr.) Franciscan Pr.

Nimmo, Jenny. Esmeralda & the Children Next Door. 2000. (Illus.). 32p. (J). (ps-3). tchr. ed. 15.00 (0-618-02902-8, Lorraine, A. Walter) Houghton Mifflin Co. Trade & Reference Div.

Nister, Ernest. Special Days. 1989. (Illus.). 10p. (J). (gr. k up). 6.95 o.p. (0-399-21694-4, Philomel) Penguin Putnam Bks. for Young Readers.

Nitz, Kristin Wolden. Defending Irene. 2004. 224p. (J). (gr. 4-6). 14.95 (1-56145-309-9, Peachtree Junior) Peachtree Pubs., Ltd.

Nixon, Joan Lowery. A Family Apart. 1987. (Orphan Train Adventures Ser.). 176p. (YA). (gr. 7-12). 14.95 o.s.i (0-553-05432-5, Starfire) Random Hse. Children's Bks.

—The Honeycutt Street Celebrities. 1991. 112p. (J). (gr. 4-7). pap. 2.99 o.s.i (0-440-40464-9) Dell Publishing.

—Keeping Secrets. 1996. (Orphan Train Adventures Ser.: No. 6). 176p. (YA). (gr. 4-7). mass mkt. 4.99 o.s.i (0-440-21992-2) Dell Publishing.

—Maggie, Too. 1985. 101p. (J). (gr. 3-7). 11.95 (0-15-250350-1) Harcourt Children's Bks.

Noble, Kate. Bubble Gum. 1995. (Africa Stories Ser.). (Illus.). 32p. (J). (ps-4). 14.95 (0-9631798-0-2) Silver Seahorse Pr.

Nobody Listens. 1991. (Illus.). (J). (ps-2). pap. 5.10 (0-8136-5959-0) Modern Curriculum Pr.

Nodelman, Jeffrey. Power Trip. 1998. (Doug Chronicles: No. 5). (Illus.). 64p. (J). (gr. 2-4). pap. 3.99 (0-7868-4258-X) Disney Pr.

Nodset, Joan L. Go Away, Dog. (My First I Can Read Bks.). (Illus.). 32p. (J). (ps up). 1997. 14.95 (0-06-027502-2); 1997. lib. bdg. 14.89 (0-06-027503-0); 1963. lib. bdg. 9.89 o.p. (0-06-024556-5) HarperCollins Children's Bk. Group.

Nolen, Jerdine. Raising Dragons. 2002. (Illus.). (J). 21.70 (0-7587-3493-X) Book Wholesalers, Inc.

—Raising Dragons. (Illus.). 40p. (J). 2002. (gr. 1-4). pap. 6.00 (0-15-216536-3, Voyager Bks./Libros Viajeros); 1998. (ps-3). 16.00 (0-15-201288-5) Harcourt Children's Bks.

Nones, Eric J. Caleb's Friend, RS. 1993. 32p. (J). (ps-3). 15.00 o.p. (0-374-31017-3, Farrar, Straus & Giroux (BYR)) Farrar, Straus & Giroux.

—Wendell, RS. 1989. 32p. (J). (ps up). 13.95 o.p. (0-374-38266-2, Farrar, Straus & Giroux (BYR)) Farrar, Straus & Giroux.

Noonan, Julia. Friends Forever: Hare & Rabbit. 2000. (Hello Reader! Ser.: Level 3). (Illus.). 40p. (J). (gr. 1-2). mass mkt. 3.99 (0-439-08753-8) Scholastic, Inc.

—Hare & Rabbit: Friends Forever. 2000. (Illus.). (J). 10.14 (0-606-18556-9) Turtleback Bks.

Noonan, R. A. Don't Go into the Graveyard! 1995. (Monsterville USA Ser.: No. 2). 144p. (J). (gr. 4-5). pap. 3.95 o.p. (0-689-71864-0, Simon Pulse) Simon & Schuster Children's Publishing.

Norby, Lisa. Friendly Rivals, Vol. 7. 1986. (Heart to Heart Ser.: No. 9). 176p. (Orig.). (YA). (gr. 7-12). mass mkt. 2.25 o.s.i (0-345-32985-6) Ballantine Bks.

—The Holly Hudnut Admiration Society. 1989. (Fifth Grade S.T.A.R.S Ser.). 128p. (Orig.). (J). (gr. 3-7). lib. bdg. 5.99 o.s.i (0-394-99604-6, Knopf Bks. for Young Readers) Random Hse. Children's Bks.

Norris, Gunilla B. The Friendship Hedge. 1973. (Illus.). 48p. (J). (gr. 2-4). lib. bdg. 6.95 o.p. (0-525-30210-7, Dutton) Dutton/Plume.

North, Emily. Old Friends, New Friends. 1980. (Social Values Ser.). (Illus.). 32p. (J). (gr. k-3). pap. 3.95 o.p. (0-516-41479-8); lib. bdg. 13.27 o.p. (0-516-01479-X) Scholastic Library Publishing. (Children's Pr.).

Nostlinger, Christine. Luke & Angela. Bell, Anthea, tr. 1981. 144p. (J). (gr. 7 up). 8.95 o.p. (0-15-249902-4) Harcourt Children's Bks.

Novak, Matt. Little Wolf, Big Wolf. (I Can Read Bks.). (Illus.). 48p. (J). (gr. k-3). 2001. pap. 3.95 (0-06-444230-6); 2000. lib. bdg. 14.89 (0-06-027487-5) HarperCollins Children's Bk. Group.

—Little Wolf, Big Wolf. 2000. (I Can Read Bks.: 2). (Illus.). 48p. (J). (gr. k-3). 14.95 (0-06-027486-7) HarperCollins Pubs.

—Little Wolf, Big Wolf. 2001. (I Can Read Bks.). (Illus.). (J). 10.10 (0-606-20769-4) Turtleback Bks.

—Newt. 1996. (I Can Read Bks.). (Illus.). 48p. (J). (gr. k-3). lib. bdg. 15.89 (0-06-024502-6); (gr. 1-3). 14.95 o.p. (0-06-024501-8) HarperCollins Children's Bk. Group.

Novak, Matt, illus. It's about Time. 1993. (J). (ps-3). pap. 14.00 o.s.i (0-671-78512-5, Simon & Schuster Children's Publishing) Simon & Schuster Children's Publishing.

Nuebacher, R. Jeramie & Max. 1987. (Illus.). 32p. (J). (gr. 2-5). 9.95 o.p. (0-88625-204-0) Durkin Hayes Publishing Ltd.

Nunes, Lygia Bojunga. My Friend the Painter. Pontiero, Giovanni, tr. 1995. (Illus.). 96p. (J). (gr. 4-7). pap. 5.00 (0-15-200872-1, Harcourt Paperbacks) Harcourt Children's Bks.

—My Friend the Painter. Pontiero, Giovanni, tr. from POR. 1991. 96p. (J). (gr. 3-7). 13.95 (0-15-256340-7) Harcourt Trade Pubs.

Nunes, Susan. To Find the Way. 1992. (Kolowalu Bks.). (Illus.). 48p. (J). (gr. 7 up). 12.95 (0-8248-1376-6, Kolowalu Bk.) Univ. of Hawaii Pr.

Nye, Naomi Shihab. Come with Me: Poems for a Journey. 2000. (Illus.). 40p. (J). (gr. k-3). lib. bdg. 16.89 (0-688-15947-8, Greenwillow Bks.) HarperCollins Children's Bk. Group.

Oates, Joyce Carol. Big Mouth & Ugly Girl. 2002. 272p. (J). (gr. 8-12). 16.99 (0-06-623756-4); lib. bdg. 17.89 (0-06-623758-0) HarperCollins Pubs.

O'Bannon, Romonia G. Zora's House. 1994. (J). 7.95 o.p. (0-533-11056-4) Vantage Pr., Inc.

O'Brien, Anne Sibley. Don't Say No!, ERS. 1986. (Busy Day Board Bks.). (Illus.). 14p. (J). (ps-2). pap. 3.95 o.p. (0-8050-0049-6, Holt, Henry & Co. Bks. For Young Readers) Holt, Henry & Co.

O'Brien, Teresa. Memories. 1985. (Illus.). 5p. (J). (ps-3). 6.99 (0-85953-319-0) Child's Play of England GBR. *Dist:* Child's Play-International.

O'Brien, Walker. The Chu Chi Chronicles. 2001. 153p. (J). pap. 20.99 (0-7388-5384-4); E-Book 8.00 (1-4010-0704-X) Xlibris Corp.

O'Callahan, Jay. Herman & Marguerite: An Earth Story. (Illus.). 36p. (J). 2003. pap. 7.95 (1-56145-283-1); 1996. 15.95 (1-56145-103-7) Peachtree Pubs., Ltd.

O'Connell, Rebecca. Myrtle of Willendorf. 2000. 128p. (YA). (gr. 7-12). 15.95 (1-886910-52-9) Front Street, Inc.

O'Conner, Karen. Service with a Smile. 1994. (Action Readers Ser.: Vol. 4). 80p. (J). (ps-3). pap. 4.99 o.p. (0-570-04772-2, 56-1791) Concordia Publishing Hse.

O'Connor, Barbara. Beethoven in Paradise, RS. 160p. (gr. 5-8). 1999. (Illus.). (YA). pap. 4.95 (0-374-40588-3, Sunburst); 1997. (J). 16.00 o.p. (0-374-30666-4, Farrar, Straus & Giroux (BYR)) Farrar, Straus & Giroux.

—Beethoven in Paradise. 1997. (YA). Class Set. 97.30 incl. audio (0-7887-2777-X, 46097); Homework Set. (gr. 7). 40.20 incl. audio (0-7887-1845-2, 40625) Recorded Bks., LLC.

—Fame & Glory in Freedom, Georgia. l.t. ed. 2003. 126p. (J). 22.95 (0-7862-5994-9) Thorndike Pr.

—Me & Rupert Goody, RS. 2003. 112p. (J). pap. 4.95 (0-374-44804-3, Sunburst) Farrar, Straus & Giroux.

O'Connor, Carol M. Jackie's New Friend. 1998. (Illus.). 12p. (J). (ps-2). pap. 3.75 (1-880612-71-2) Seedling Pubns., Inc.

O'Connor, Jane. Amy's (Not So) Great Camp-Out: A Brownie Girl Scout Book. 1993. (Here Comes the Brownies Ser.: No. 4). (Illus.). 64p. (J). (gr. 1-3). 7.99 o.p. (0-448-40167-3); 5.99 (0-448-40166-5) Penguin Putnam Bks. for Young Readers. (Grosset & Dunlap).

—Corrie's Secret Pal: A Brownie Girl Scout Book. 1993. (Here Comes the Brownies Ser.: No. 1). (Illus.). 64p. (J). (gr. 1-4). 7.99 o.s.i (0-448-40161-4); 5.99 (0-448-40160-6) Penguin Putnam Bks. for Young Readers. (Grosset & Dunlap).

—Just Good Friends. 1983. 192p. (J). (gr. 6-9). lib. bdg. 12.89 o.p. (0-06-024591-3) HarperCollins Children's Bk. Group.

Relationships

—Molly the Brave & Me. 2003. (Step into Reading Step 2 Bks.). (Illus.). 48p. (J). (gr. 1-3). lib. bdg. 11.99 (*0-394-94175-6*, Random Hse. Bks. for Young Readers) Random Hse. Children's Bks.

—Molly the Brave & Me. 1990. (Step into Reading Step 2 Bks.). (J). (gr. 1-3). 10.14 (*0-606-12425-X*) Turtleback Bks.

—Nina, Nina, Star Ballerina. 1997. (All Aboard Reading Ser.). (Illus.). 32p. (J). (ps-1). 13.99 o.p. (*0-448-41611-5*); 3.99 (*0-448-41492-9*) Penguin Putnam Bks. for Young Readers. (Grosset & Dunlap).

—Think, Corrie, Think! A Brownie Girl Scout Book. 1994. (Here Comes the Brownies Ser.: No. 5). (Illus.). 64p. (J). (gr. 1-4). 7.99 o.p. (*0-448-40466-4*); 3.95 o.s.i (*0-448-40465-6*) Penguin Putnam Bks. for Young Readers. (Grosset & Dunlap).

—Yours till Niagara Falls, Abbey. 1997. (Illus.). 128p. (Orig.). (J). (gr. 3-7). pap. 5.95 o.s.i (*0-698-11597-X*, PaperStar) Penguin Putnam Bks. for Young Readers.

—Yours till Niagara Falls, Abby. 1982. pap. 1.95 o.p. (*0-590-31957-4*); pap. 2.25 o.p. (*0-590-40141-6*) Scholastic, Inc.

—Yours till Niagara Falls, Abby. 1997. (J). 11.05 o.p. (*0-606-12128-5*) Turtleback Bks.

O'Connor, Jane, et al. Molly the Brave & Me. 1990. (Step into Reading Ser.). (Illus.). 48p. (J). (ps-3). pap. 3.99 (*0-394-84175-1*, Random Hse. Bks. for Young Readers) Random Hse. Children's Bks.

O'Connor, Jim. Sticking It Out. 1996. (No Stars Ser.: Vol. 1). (Illus.). 176p. (J). (gr. 4-7). pap. 3.99 o.s.i (*0-679-87858-0*) McKay, David Co., Inc.

O'Dell, Kathleen. Agnes Parker... Girl in Progress. 2003. 160p. (J). 16.99 (*0-8037-2648-1*, Dial Bks. for Young Readers) Penguin Putnam Bks. for Young Readers.

Odenbach, Ginny & Osborn, Linda. Feather. Yarnaught, Paula, ed. 1995. (Illus.). 88p. (Orig.). (J). (gr. 3-8). pap. 4.50 (*1-885101-14-7*) Writers Pr., Inc.

Odenbach, Osborn. Feather: Class Set, 31 bks., Set. Bruyninckx, John, ed. (Feather, Resource Guide Ser.). (Illus.). (Orig.). (J). (gr. 3-6). pap. 142.99 o.p. (*1-885101-51-1*) Writers Pr., Inc.

—Sunblade: Classroom Set, 31 bks., Set. Bruyninckx, John, ed. (Resource Guide, Sunblade Ser.). (Illus.). (Orig.). (J). (gr. 3-7). pap., tchr. ed. 112.99 o.p. (*1-885101-50-3*) Writers Pr., Inc.

O'Donnell, Peter. Pinkie Leaves Home. 1992. 32p. (J). (ps-2). 13.95 o.p. (*0-590-45485-4*) Scholastic, Inc.

Odor, Ruth S. A Friend Is One Who Helps. rev. ed. 1979. (Values to Live By Ser.). (Illus.). (J). (ps-3). lib. bdg. 4.95 o.p. (*0-89565-074-6*) Child's World, Inc.

Offerman, Lynn. My Little School Friends. 1997. (Illus.). 10p. (J). (ps up). bds. 15.99 o.p. (*1-57584-063-4*, Reader's Digest Young Families, Inc.) Reader's Digest Children's Publishing, Inc.

Ogaz, Nancy. Buster & the Amazing Daisy. 2002. (Illus.). 128p. (J). pap. 12.95 (*1-84310-721-X*) Kingsley, Jessica Pubs. GBR. *Dist:* Taylor & Francis, Inc.

Oh, Jiwon. Cat & Mouse. 2003. (Illus.). 32p. (J). lib. bdg. 15.89 (*0-06-052744-7*) HarperCollins Pubs.

—Cat & Mouse: A Delicious Tale. 2003. (Illus.). 32p. (J). (gr. k-2). 14.99 (*0-06-050865-5*) HarperCollins Pubs.

O'Hanlon, Jacklyn. The Other Michael. (J). (gr. 5 up). 1985. 6.95 o.p. (*0-8037-6744-7*); 1977. 6.46 o.p. (*0-8037-6745-5*) Penguin Putnam Bks. for Young Readers. (Dial Bks. for Young Readers).

Oke, Janette. New Kid in Town. 2001. (J Okes Animal Friends Ser.: Vol. 5). (Illus.). 80p. (Orig.). (J). (ps-3). pap. 5.99 (*0-7642-2449-2*) Bethany Hse. Pubs.

Okimoto, Jean Davies. Dear Ichiro. 2002. (J). 16.95 (*1-57061-373-7*) Sasquatch Bks.

—Jason's Women. 2000. 220p. (gr. 4-7). pap. 12.95 (*0-595-00797-X*, Backinprint.com) iUniverse, Inc.

—Take a Chance, Gramps!, Vol. 1. 1990. (J). (gr. 4-7). 15.95 o.p. (*0-316-63812-9*, Joy Street Bks.) Little Brown & Co.

Older, Effin. My Worst Friend, Woody. 1997. (Silver Blades Figure Eights Ser.). (Illus.). 80p. (ps-3). pap. text 3.50 o.s.i (*0-553-48510-5*, Dell Books for Young Readers) Random Hse. Children's Bks.

Oldfield, J. Sugar & Spice, Bk. 14. (Illus.). 120p. (J). mass mkt. 7.95 (*0-340-69986-8*) Hodder & Stoughton, Ltd. GBR. *Dist:* Lubrecht & Cramer, Ltd., Trafalgar Square.

Olsen, Ashley & Olsen, Mary-Kate. The Facts about Flirting. 2003. (Two of a Kind Ser.: Vol. 27). (Illus.). 112p. mass mkt. 4.99 (*0-06-009323-4*, HarperEntertainment) Morrow/Avon.

—The Love Factor. 2003. (So Little Time Ser.: Vol. 8). (Illus.). 128p. mass mkt. 4.99 (*0-06-009312-9*, HarperEntertainment) Morrow/Avon.

—So Little Time: Girl Talk. 2003. (Mary-Kate & Ashley Ser.: Vol. 7). (Illus.). 128p. mass mkt. 4.99 (*0-06-009311-0*, HarperEntertainment) Morrow/Avon.

Olsen, Mary-Kate. Love Is in the Air. 2000. (Illus.). 32p. (J). (ps-3). pap. 3.99 (*0-307-29906-6*, Golden Bks.) Random Hse. Children's Bks.

Olsen, Mary-Kate & Olsen, Ashley. Best Friends Forever. 2003. (So Little Time Ser.: No. 12). 128p. mass mkt. 4.99 (*0-06-009316-1*, HarperEntertainment) Morrow/Avon.

—Closer Than Ever. 2002. (Two of a Kind Ser.: No. 25). 112p. mass mkt. 4.99 (*0-06-009321-8*) HarperCollins Children's Bk. Group.

—The Friendship Journal. 2001. (Mary-Kate & Ashley Sweet 16 Ser.). 32p. mass mkt. 4.25 (*0-06-621007-0*) HarperCollins Children's Bk. Group.

—Heart to Heart. 2004. (Two of a Kind Ser.: No. 33). 112p. mass mkt. 4.99 (*0-06-009329-3*, HarperEntertainment) Morrow/Avon.

—How to Train a Boy. 2002. (So Little Time Ser.: Vol. 1). (Illus.). 128p. mass mkt. 4.99 (*0-06-008368-9*) HarperCollins Pubs.

—Love-Set-Match. 2003. (Two of a Kind Ser.: No. 29). (Illus.). 112p. mass mkt. 4.99 (*0-06-009325-0*, HarperEntertainment) Morrow/Avon.

—Making a Splash. 2003. (Two of a Kind Ser.: No. 30). (Illus.). 112p. mass mkt. 4.99 (*0-06-009326-9*, HarperEntertainment) Morrow/Avon.

—Mary-Kate & Ashley Starring In, No. 5. 2002. 96p. mass mkt. 4.99 (*0-06-052053-1*, HarperEntertainment) Morrow/Avon.

—Mary-Kate & Ashley Sweet 16 No. 10: Telling Secrets. 2003. (Illus.). 144p. mass mkt. 4.99 (*0-06-055645-5*, HarperEntertainment) Morrow/Avon.

—Two for the Road. 2001. (Two of a Kind Ser.: No. 18). 112p. mass mkt. 4.99 (*0-06-106658-3*) HarperCollins Pubs.

Olsen, Mary-Kate Ashley. Spring Breakup. 2004. (So Little Time Ser.: No. 14). 128p. mass mkt. 4.99 (*0-06-059069-6*, HarperEntertainment) Morrow/Avon.

Olson, Gretchen. Joyride. 1998. 200p. (J). (gr. 6-9). pap. 14.95 o.s.i (*1-56397-687-0*) Boyds Mills Pr.

Olson, Kris Elingboe. Inside the Painted Box. Wise, Noreen, ed. 2001. (Lemonade Collection). (Illus.). 48p. (J). (gr. 1-5). pap. 6.95 (*1-58584-208-7*) Huckleberry Pr.

Olson, Kris Ellingboe. Crabby Abby. Wise, Noreen, ed. 2002. (Book-a-Day Collection). (Illus.). 32p. (J). (ps up). pap. 6.95 (*1-58584-375-X*) Huckleberry Pr.

O'Malley, Kevin. Bud. 2000. (Illus.). 32p. (J). (gr. k-3). 15.95 (*0-8027-8718-5*); lib. bdg. 16.85 (*0-8027-8719-3*) Walker & Co.

One Fine Day. 2001. (Early Readers Ser.: Vol. 1). (J). lib. bdg. (*1-59054-487-0*) Fitzgerald Bks.

One Fine Day. 1999. (J). 9.95 (*1-56137-249-8*) Novel Units, Inc.

Oneal, Zibby. Turtle & Snail. 1979. (Lippincott-I-Like-to-Read Bks.). (Illus.). (J). (gr. k-2). 11.95 (*0-397-31829-4*) HarperCollins Children's Bk. Group.

O'Neil, Catherine. Fine & Dandy. Wise, Noreen, ed. 2000. (Lemonade Collection). (YA). (gr. 4 up). pap. 6.95 (*1-58584-250-8*) Huckleberry Pr.

Oram, Hiawyn. Badger's Bad Mood. (Illus.). 32p. (J). (ps-3). 2002. mass mkt. 5.99 (*0-590-21693-7*); 1998. pap. 15.95 (*0-590-18920-4*) Scholastic, Inc.

Ordal, Stina Langlo. Princess Aasta. 2002. (Illus.). 32p. (J). (ps-3). 16.95 (*1-58234-783-2*, Bloomsbury Children) Bloomsbury Publishing.

Orenstein, Denise G. When the Wind Blows Hard. 1982. (Illus.). (J). 11.95 (*0-201-10740-6*) HarperCollins Children's Bk. Group.

Orgel, Doris. The Devil in Vienna. 1978. (YA). (gr. 7 up). 8.95 o.p. (*0-8037-1920-5*, Dial Bks. for Young Readers) Penguin Putnam Bks. for Young Readers.

—Don't Call Me Slob-O. 1996. (West Side Kids Ser.: No. 2). (Illus.). 80p. (J). (gr. 2-5). lib. bdg. 14.49 (*0-7868-2086-1*) Hyperion Bks. for Children.

—Don't Call Me Slob-O. 1996. (West Side Kids Ser.). 10.10 (*0-606-10038-5*) Turtleback Bks.

—Friends to the Rescue. 1996. (West Side Kids Ser.: No. 3). (Illus.). 80p. (J). (gr. 4-7). pap. 3.95 (*0-7868-1045-9*) Disney Pr.

—Friends to the Rescue. 1996. (West Side Kids Ser.). 9.15 o.p. (*0-606-10359-7*) Turtleback Bks.

—Nobodies & Somebodies. 1991. 160p. (J). (gr. 3-7). 13.95 o.p. (*0-670-82754-1*, Viking Children's Bks.) Penguin Putnam Bks. for Young Readers.

Orgel, Doris, et al. Don't Call Me Slob-O. 1996. (West Side Kids Ser.: No. 2). (Illus.). 80p. (J). (ps-3). pap. 3.95 (*0-7868-1044-0*) Disney Pr.

Orloff, Erica & Milo, Alexa. The Best Friends' Handbook: The Totally Cool One of a Kind Book about You & Your Best Friend. 2002. (Illus.). 96p. (J). (gr. 3-9). pap. 7.95 (*0-8027-7645-0*) Walker & Co.

Ormerod, Jan. Making Friends. 1987. (Illus.). 24p. (J). (ps). 5.95 o.p. (*0-688-07270-4*) HarperCollins Children's Bk. Group.

Ormondroyd, Edward. Time at the Top. 1986. 176p. (J). pap. 2.50 o.s.i (*0-553-15420-6*) Bantam Bks.

—Time at the Top. 40th anniv. ed. 2003. (Illus.). (J). 17.95 (*1-930900-19-8*) Purple Hse. Pr.

O'Rourke, Frank. Burton & Stanley. 1996. 11.10 (*0-606-11176-X*) Turtleback Bks.

Orr, Wendy. Nim's Island. 128p. (gr. 3-7). 2002. pap. text 4.99 (*0-440-41868-2*, Delacorte Bks. for Young Readers); 2001. (Illus.). text 14.95 (*0-375-81123-0*, Knopf Bks. for Young Readers); 2001. (Illus.). lib. bdg. 16.99 o.s.i (*0-375-91123-5*, Knopf Bks. for Young Readers) Random Hse. Children's Bks.

Orsini, Darlene. Slinky & His Friend, Peanut. 1996. (Illus.). 11p. (J). (gr. k-3). pap. 6.00 o.p. (*0-8059-3826-5*) Dorrance Publishing Co., Inc.

Osborne, Mary Pope. Mo & His Friends. 48p. (J). (ps-3). 1996. (Puffin Easy-to-Read Ser.: Level 2). (Illus.). pap. 3.99 o.s.i (*0-14-036202-9*, Puffin Bks.); 1991. (Easy-to-Read Ser.). pap. 3.95 o.p. (*0-8037-0924-2*, Puffin Bks.); 1989. (Easy-to-Read Bks.). (Illus.). 9.95 o.p. (*0-8037-0504-2*, Dial Bks. for Young Readers); 1989. (Easy-to-Read Bks.). (Illus.). 9.89 o.p. (*0-8037-0505-0*, Dial Bks. for Young Readers) Penguin Putnam Bks. for Young Readers.

—Mo & His Friends. 1996. (Puffin Easy-to-Read Ser.). 10.14 (*0-606-09623-X*) Turtleback Bks.

—Mo to the Rescue. 1985. (Easy-to-Read Bks.). (Illus.). 56p. (J). (ps-3). 8.95 o.p. (*0-8037-0180-2*); 8.89 o.p. (*0-8037-0182-9*) Penguin Putnam Bks. for Young Readers. (Dial Bks. for Young Readers).

Oscar's Grouch Jamboree. 1999. audio 6.98 (*0-307-47721-5*, Golden Bks.) Random Hse. Children's Bks.

O'Shaughnessy & McKenna, Colleen O'Shaughnessy. Eenie, Meenie, Murphy, No! 1992. 208p. (J). (gr. 4-6). pap. 3.25 o.p. (*0-590-42900-0*, Scholastic Paperbacks) Scholastic, Inc.

Osofsky, Audrey. My Buddy, ERS. 1992. (Illus.). 32p. (J). (ps-3). 16.95 o.s.i (*0-8050-1747-X*, Holt, Henry & Co. Bks. For Young Readers) Holt, Henry & Co.

—My Buddy. 1995. (Illus.). (J). (gr. 3). 8.60 (*0-395-73228-X*) Houghton Mifflin Co.

Osofsky, Audrey, et al. My Buddy, ERS. 1994. (Illus.). 32p. (J). (ps-3). pap. 6.95 (*0-8050-3546-X*, Holt, Henry & Co. Bks. For Young Readers) Holt, Henry & Co.

Ottley, Matt. What Faust Saw. (J). 2000. pap. (*0-14-056197-8*, Puffin Bks.); 1996. (Illus.). 32p. 13.99 o.s.i (*0-525-45650-3*, Dutton Children's Bks.) Penguin Putnam Bks. for Young Readers.

Oughton, Jerrie. Music from a Place Called Half Moon. 1995. 176p. (YA). (gr. 7-7). 16.00 (*0-395-70737-4*) Houghton Mifflin Co.

—Music from a Place Called Half Moon. 1997. 176p. (YA). (gr. 5-9). mass mkt. 3.99 o.s.i (*0-440-21999-X*, Yearling) Random Hse. Children's Bks.

—Music from a Place Called Half Moon. 1997. 10.04 (*0-606-11003-8*) Turtleback Bks.

Ouriou, Katie. Love You Like a Sister. E-Book 4.95 (*0-88776-530-0*) McClelland & Stewart/Tundra Bks.

Outlet Book Company Staff. Friends in Fern Hollow. 1984. 1.00 o.s.i (*0-517-45847-0*) Random Hse. Value Publishing.

—Mrs. Merryweather's Letter. 1985. (Tales from Fern Hollow Ser.). (Illus.). 22p. (J). (ps-1). 1.99 o.s.i (*0-517-45796-2*) Random Hse. Value Publishing.

—Muddles at the Manor. 1984. (Tales from Fern Hollow Ser.). (Illus.). 22p. (J). 1.99 o.s.i (*0-517-44573-5*) Crown Publishing Group.

—New Friends. 1988. 1.99 o.s.i (*0-517-64966-7*) Crown Publishing Group.

—Who's My Friend? Dial the Answer. 1992. (J). 3.99 o.s.i (*0-517-06618-1*) Random Hse. Value Publishing.

Owens, Gail, illus. The Down & up Fall. 1996. 128p. (J). (gr. 3-7). 15.00 o.s.i (*0-688-14568-X*, Morrow, William & Co.) Morrow/Avon.

Oxley, Dorothy. Summer Dreams. 1984. Orig. Title: Wheelchair Summer. 144p. (J). (gr. 6-10). reprint ed. pap. 3.95 o.p. (*0-89107-319-1*) Crossway Bks.

Packard, Mary. Chelli Can Share. 1996. (Big Bag Ser.). (Illus.). 14p. (J). (ps). bds. 3.99 o.s.i (*0-307-12706-0*, 12706, Golden Bks.) Random Hse. Children's Bks.

—Hands Off! They're Mine! A Book about Sharing. 12p. (J). (ps-k). bds. 4.99 o.p. (*0-7814-3557-9*) Cook Communications Ministries.

—Surprise! 2004. (My First Reader (Reissue) Ser.). (Illus.). 29p. (J). pap. 3.95 (*0-516-24639-9*, Children's Pr.) Scholastic Library Publishing.

—Where Is Jake? (My First Reader Ser.). (Illus.). (J). 2003. 30p. lib. bdg. 17.50 (*0-516-22957-5*); 1990. 28p. pap. 3.95 (*0-516-45361-0*); 1990. 28p. mass mkt. 16.00 o.p. (*0-516-05361-2*) Scholastic Library Publishing. (Children's Pr.).

Packard, Mary & Golden Books Staff. Best Friends. 1996. (Dear Barbie Ser.). 24p. (J). (ps-3). pap. 3.29 o.s.i (*0-307-12939-X*, 12939, Golden Bks.) Random Hse. Children's Bks.

Packard, Mary & Reader's Digest Editors. Hands Off! They're Mine! A Book about Sharing. 1999. (Refrigerator Bks.: Vol. 1). (Illus.). 12p. (J). (ps-k). bds. 3.50 o.p. (*1-57584-264-5*, Reader's Digest Children's Bks.) Reader's Digest Children's Publishing, Inc.

Padoan, Gianni. Follow My Leader. 1989. (Facing Up Ser.). (Illus.). 28p. (J). (gr. 3-7). 11.99 (*0-85953-313-1*) Child's Play-International.

Page, Bishpham. Tea at Miss Jean's. 2000. (Illus.). 32p. (Orig.). (gr. 2 up). pap. 8.95 (*0-9628129-1-9*) Rinehart, Roberts Pubs.

Page, Carole G. Never Ashamed: Based on the Screenplay by the Same Name. 1986. (Orig.). (J). (gr. 7). pap. text 5.95 o.p. (*0-8024-5925-0*) Moody Pr.

Page, David E. The Lemonade War. 1993. (Illus.). 64p. (J). (gr. 1-3). pap. 2.50 o.p. (*0-87406-648-4*) Darby Creek Publishing.

Paige, Rob. Some of My Best Friends Are Monsters. 1988. (Illus.). 32p. (J). (ps-2). 13.95 o.s.i (*0-02-769640-5*, Simon & Schuster Children's Publishing) Simon & Schuster Children's Publishing.

A Pal for Pat. 1998. (Fisher-Price Phonics Storybooks Ser.: Vol. 6). (Illus.). (J). pap. (*0-7666-0174-9*, Honey Bear Bks.) Modern Publishing.

Palatini, Margie. Capricorn & Co. 1984. (Zodiac Club Ser.: No. 5). 160p. (J). (gr. 7 up). 1.95 (*0-399-21186-1*) Putnam Publishing Group, The.

—Lab Coat Girl & the Amazing Benjamin Bone. 1999. (L.A.F. Ser.). (Illus.). 97p. (J). (gr. 2-5). lib. bdg. 13.49 (*0-7868-2440-9*) Disney Pr.

Palmer, Mary R. Sharing Secrets. 1991. (Illus.). 60p. (J). (ps-4). pap. 4.00 (*0-932433-82-0*) Windswept Hse. Pubs.

Palmer, Todd S. Rhino & Mouse. 1994. (Easy-to-Read Ser.). (Illus.). (J). (ps-3). 48p. 12.99 o.s.i (*0-8037-1322-3*); 40p. 12.89 o.s.i (*0-8037-1323-1*) Penguin Putnam Bks. for Young Readers. (Dial Bks. for Young Readers).

Pandell, Karen. By Day & by Night. Kramer, Linda, ed. 1991. (Illus.). 32p. (J). (gr. 2 up). 14.95 o.p. (*0-915811-26-X*, Starseed Pr.) Kramer, H.J. Inc.

Papademetriou, Lisa. My Pen Pal, Pat. 1998. (Real Kids Readers Ser.). (Illus.). 48p. (gr. 1-3). 18.90 (*0-7613-2023-7*); (J). pap. 4.99 (*0-7613-2048-2*) Millbrook Pr., Inc.

—My Pen Pal, Pat. 1998. (Real Kids Readers Ser.). 10.14 (*0-606-15803-0*) Turtleback Bks.

—My Pen Pal, Pat. 1998. E-Book (*1-58824-483-0*); E-Book (*1-58824-731-7*); E-Book (*1-58824-814-3*) ipicturebooks, LLC.

—Really? 1999. (Real Kids Readers Ser.). (Illus.). 48p. (gr. 1-3). 18.90 (*0-7613-2072-5*); (J). pap. 4.99 (*0-7613-2097-0*) Millbrook Pr., Inc.

—Really? 1999. (J). 10.14 (*0-606-19171-2*) Turtleback Bks.

—Really? 1999. E-Book (*1-58824-489-X*); E-Book (*1-58824-737-6*); E-Book (*1-58824-820-8*) ipicturebooks, LLC.

Pappas, Debra. Mom, Dad, Come Back Soon. 2001. (Illus.). 32p. (J). (ps-2). 14.95 (*1-55798-799-8*); pap. 8.95 (*1-55798-798-X*) American Psychological Assn. (Magination Pr.).

Paraskevas, Betty. Green Monkeys. 2001. lib. bdg. 16.00 (*0-689-82866-7*, Simon & Schuster Children's Publishing) Simon & Schuster Children's Publishing.

—Hoppy & Joe. (Illus.). 32p. (J). (ps-3). 1999. 16.00 (*0-689-82199-9*, Simon & Schuster Children's Publishing); 2002. reprint ed. pap. 6.99 (*0-689-85046-8*, Aladdin) Simon & Schuster Children's Publishing.

Pardy, Da. Coco & Motley: Based on a True Story. 2000. (Illus.). 32p. (J). (ps-4). 7.95 (*0-9705332-0-9*) Pardy Chick Pubns.

Pare, R. A Friend Like You. 1984. (Illus.). 24p. (J). (ps-8). 12.95 o.p. (*0-920303-04-8*) Annick Pr., Ltd. CAN. *Dist:* Firefly Bks., Ltd.

Pare, Roger. A Friend Like You. (Illus.). 24p. (J). (ps-2). 2003. (Annikins Ser.: Vol. 6). pap. 1.25 (*0-920303-80-3*); 1984. pap. 4.95 (*0-920303-05-6*) Annick Pr., Ltd. CAN. *Dist:* Firefly Bks., Ltd.

Parents Magazine Whole Language Library, 17 bks., Set. Incl. Bicycle Bear Rides Again. Muntean, Michaela. (Illus.). 1995. lib. bdg. 19.93 o.p. (*0-8368-0964-5*); Bread & Honey. Ash, Frank. (Illus.). 42p. (ps-3). 1992. lib. bdg. 18.60 o.p. (*0-8368-0880-0*); Buggly Bear's Hiccup Cure. Kelley, True. 48p. 1994. lib. bdg. 18.60 o.p. (*0-8368-0982-3*); Clown-Arounds. Cole, Joanna. (Illus.). 48p. (gr. 1 up). 1994. lib. bdg. 19.93 o.p. (*0-8368-0995-5*); Clown-Arounds Go on Vacation. Cole, Joanna. (Illus.). 48p. 1993. lib. bdg. 19.93 o.p. (*0-8368-0966-1*); Elephant Goes to School. Smath, Jerry. 48p. (gr. 1 up). 1993. lib. bdg. 19.93 o.p. (*0-8368-0967-X*); Fox with Cold Feet. Kendrick, Dennis. (Illus.). 42p. (ps-3). 1993. lib. bdg. 18.60 o.p. (*0-8368-0890-8*); Garden for Miss Mouse. Muntean, Michaela. (Illus.). 42p. (ps-3). 1993. lib. bdg. 17.27 o.p. (*0-8368-0891-6*); (J). (Illus.). Set pap. 338.87 o.p. (*0-8368-1168-2*) Stevens, Gareth Inc.

Park, Barbara. Beanpole. 1984. (J). (gr. 5 up). pap. 2.95 (*0-380-69840-4*, Avon Bks.) Morrow/Avon.

—Buddies. 1986. (YA). (gr. 7 up). pap. 2.95 (*0-380-69992-3*, Avon Bks.) Morrow/Avon.

Perkins, Lynne Rae. All Alone in the Universe. (Illus.). 160p. (J). (gr. 5 up). 1999. 15.95 (*0-688-16881-7*, Greenwillow Bks.); 2001. reprint ed. pap. 5.99 (*0-380-73302-1*, Harper Trophy) HarperCollins Children's Bk. Group.

—All Alone in the Universe. unabr. ed. 2001. 143p. (J). (gr. 3-5). pap. 28.00 incl. audio (*0-8072-0443-9*, Listening Library) Random Hse. Audio Publishing Group.

—All Alone in the Universe. 2001. (J). 11.00 (*0-606-21021-0*) Turtleback Bks.

Perkins, Mitali. The Sunita Experiment. 1994. (Illus.). 192p. (J). (gr. 5-9). pap. 4.50 o.p. (*1-56282-671-9*) Hyperion Bks. for Children.

—The Sunita Experiment. 1993. 144p. (J). (gr. 1-6). 15.95 o.p. (*0-316-69943-8*, Joy Street Bks.) Little Brown & Co.

Perkins, Myrna. Bored Betty's Wish. 1986. (Illus.). 32p. (Orig.). (J). (gr. 2-5). pap. 5.95 (*0-937729-02-7*) Markins Enterprises.

Perl, Lila. Me & Fat Glenda. 1985. 160p. (YA). (gr. 4-6). pap. (*0-671-60503-8*, Simon Pulse) Simon & Schuster Children's Publishing.

Perlman, Ruthie. Working It Out. 1990. (YA). (gr. 7 up). 15.95 (*1-56062-033-1*, BRE105H); pap. 12.95 (*1-56062-035-8*, BRE105S) CIS Communications, Inc.

Perrow, Angeli. Captain's Castaway. 1998. (Illus.). 32p. (J). (ps-3). 15.95 (*0-89272-419-6*) Down East Bks.

Perry, Carol J. Thirteen & Loving It. 1989. 156p. (J). (gr. 5-8). pap. 2.95 o.p. (*0-87406-371-X*) Darby Creek Publishing.

Pescetti, Luis Maria. Caperucita Roja: Tal Como Se lo Contaron a Jorge, 1. 5th ed. 1998. (SPA., Illus.). 30p. (ps-3). 9.95 (*84-204-4490-1*) Santillana USA Publishing Co., Inc.

Peters, Julie A. B. J.'s Billion Dollar Bet. 1994. (J). 12.95 o.p. (*0-316-70254-4*) Little Brown & Co.

—B. J.'s Billion Dollar Bet. 1995. 8.70 o.p. (*0-606-09027-4*) Turtleback Bks.

—Risky Friends. 1993. 144p. (J). (gr. 5-8). pap. 2.99 o.p. (*0-87406-646-8*) Darby Creek Publishing.

—The Stinky Sneakers Contest. 1992. (J). (ps-3). 13.95 o.p. (*0-316-70214-5*) Little Brown & Co.

—The Stinky Sneakers Contest. 1994. 64p. (J). pap. 3.99 o.p. (*0-380-72278-X*, Avon Bks.) Morrow/Avon.

Peters, Julie Anne. Define "Normal" 2000. 208p. (J). (gr. 7-10). 16.95 (*0-316-70631-0*) Little Brown & Co.

—Define "Normal" 2003. (Illus.). 208p. (J). (gr. 3-7). pap. 5.95 (*0-316-73489-6*) Little Brown Children's Bks.

—Define "Normal" l.t. ed. 2001. (Young Adult Ser.). 250p. 22.95 (*0-7862-3527-6*) Thorndike Pr.

—How Do You Spell G-E-E-K? 1997. 9.09 o.p. (*0-606-12727-5*) Turtleback Bks.

—How Do You Spell Geek? 1996. 144p. (J). (gr. 4-7). 12.95 o.p. (*0-316-70266-8*) Little Brown & Co.

—How Do You Spell Geek? 1999. (YA). pap. 40.24 incl. audio (*0-7887-2992-6*, 40874) Recorded Bks., LLC.

—Revenge of the Snob Squad. 2000. (Illus.). 144p. (J). (gr. 5-9). pap. 4.99 o.p. (*0-14-130818-4*, Puffin Bks.) Penguin Putnam Bks. for Young Readers.

Petersen, P. J. Corky & the Brothers Cool. 1986. (J). (gr. 6 up). reprint ed. mass mkt. 2.75 o.s.i (*0-440-91624-0*, Laurel Leaf) Random Hse. Children's Bks.

—I Hate Camping. (Puffin Chapters Ser.). (Illus.). 96p. (J). (gr. 2-5). 1998. pap. 3.99 o.s.i (*0-14-038968-7*); 1993. pap. 3.99 o.s.i (*0-14-036446-3*, Puffin Bks.) Penguin Putnam Bks. for Young Readers.

—I Hate Company. 1998. (Puffin Chapters Ser.). 9.09 o.p. (*0-606-13505-7*) Turtleback Bks.

—My Worst Friend. 1998. (Illus.). 144p. (J). (gr. 2-5). 15.99 (*0-525-46028-4*, Dutton Children's Bks.) Penguin Putnam Bks. for Young Readers.

—Nobody Else Can Walk It for You. 1984. 224p. (J). (gr. 6 up). mass mkt. 2.50 o.s.i (*0-440-96733-3*, Laurel Leaf) Random Hse. Children's Bks.

—The Sub. 96p. (J). 1995. pap. 4.99 o.s.i (*0-14-037442-6*); 1993. (Illus.). (gr. 2-5). 13.99 o.p. (*0-525-45059-9*, Dutton Children's Bks.) Penguin Putnam Bks. for Young Readers.

Peterson. Anne of Green Gables. 1999. (Avonlea Ser.: No. 1). 32p. (YA). (gr. 5-8). pap. 4.95 (*0-06-443535-0*) HarperCollins Children's Bk. Group.

Peterson, George C. Stuck in the Mud, Vol. 1. 1988. (Illus.). 208p. (Orig.). (YA). (gr. 9-12). pap. (*0-9621320-0-4*) Peterson, George.

Peterson, John. The Littles Make a Friend. 2000. (Littles Ser.). (Illus.). 32p. (J). (ps-3). mass mkt. 3.99 (*0-439-20301-5*) Scholastic, Inc.

—The Littles to the Rescue. 1986. (Littles Ser.). (Illus.). (J). (gr. 1-5). mass mkt. 2.75 o.p. (*0-590-44114-0*) Scholastic, Inc.

Peterson, Mike & Gadbois, Robert. The Biggest Giraffe. 1977. (Books by Children for Children Ser.). (Illus.). (J). (gr. 2-6). lib. bdg. 6.95 o.p. (*0-87191-609-6*, Creative Education) Creative Co., The.

Petty, Dini. The Queen, the Bear & the Bumblebee. 2000. (Illus.). 32p. (J). (ps-3). 15.95 (*1-58270-036-2*) Beyond Words Publishing, Inc.

Petty, Kate. Making Friends. 1991. (Playground Ser.). (Illus.). 24p. (J). (ps-2). pap. 5.95 (*0-8120-4660-9*) Barron's Educational Series, Inc.

Pevsner, Stella. I'll Always Remember You... Maybe. 1983. (J). (gr. 7-10). reprint ed. pap. (*0-671-49416-3*, Simon Pulse) Simon & Schuster Children's Publishing.

—The Night the Whole Class Slept Over. 1991. 176p. (J). (gr. 4-9). 14.95 o.p. (*0-89919-983-6*, Clarion Bks.) Houghton Mifflin Co. Trade & Reference Div.

Peyton, K. M. The Boy Who Wasn't There. 2000. pap. 5.95 (*0-552-52717-3*) Transworld Publishers Ltd. GBR. *Dist:* Trafalgar Square.

—Dear Fred. 1981. 9.95 o.p. (*0-399-20813-5*) Putnam Publishing Group, The.

Pfeffer, Susan Beth. Darcy Downstairs, ERS. 1990. 144p. (J). (gr. 4-6). 13.95 o.p. (*0-8050-1307-5*, Holt, Henry & Co. Bks. For Young Readers) Holt, Henry & Co.

—The Friendship Pact. 1986. 112p. (Orig.). (J). (gr. 3-7). pap. 2.75 o.p. (*0-590-42319-3*); (gr. 4-6). pap. 2.50 o.p. (*0-590-32143-9*, Scholastic Paperbacks) Scholastic, Inc.

—Getting Even. 1986. 192p. (J). (gr. 7 up). 13.95 o.p. (*0-448-47777-7*, Grosset & Dunlap) Penguin Putnam Bks. for Young Readers.

—Just Between Us. 1981. 128p. (J). (gr. k-6). pap. 2.25 o.s.i (*0-440-44194-3*, Yearling) Random Hse. Children's Bks.

—A Matter of Principle. 1983. 192p. (gr. 7 up). pap. 2.25 o.p. (*0-440-96091-6*) Dell Publishing.

—Most Precious Blood. 1993. 176p. (YA). mass mkt. 3.99 o.s.i (*0-553-56128-6*) Bantam Bks.

—Rewind to Yesterday. 1991. 144p. (J). (gr. 4-7). pap. 3.25 o.s.i (*0-440-40474-6*) Dell Publishing.

—Starring Peter & Leigh. 1978. (J). 7.95 o.s.i (*0-440-08226-9*, Delacorte Pr.) Dell Publishing.

—Twice Taken. 1996. (Laurel-Leaf Bks.). 208p. (YA). (gr. 7 up). mass mkt. 4.50 o.s.i (*0-440-22004-1*, Laurel Leaf) Random Hse. Children's Bks.

Pfeffer, Susan Beth & Alcott, Louisa May. Meg Makes a Friend. 1998. (Portraits of Little Women Ser.). (Illus.). 112p. (gr. 3-7). text 9.95 (*0-385-32580-0*, Delacorte Pr.) Dell Publishing.

Pfister, Marcus. Arcobaleno, Non Lasciarmi Solo! 1998. (Rainbow Fish Ser.). Orig. Title: Regenbogenfisch, Komm Hilf Mir!. (ITA.). (J). (ps-3). 18.95 (*88-8203-041-5*) North-South Bks., Inc.

—Chris & Croc. 1945. (Illus.). 32p. (J). (gr. k-3). 14.95 o.p. (*1-55858-273-8*); 14.88 o.p. (*1-55858-274-6*) North-South Bks., Inc.

—Une Etoile, Cette Nuit-La. 1995. (FRE., Illus.). (J). (gr. k-3). 18.95 (*3-314-20776-X*) North-South Bks., Inc.

—Fiocco Trova un Amico. 1998. Tr. of Hopper Hunts for Spring. (ITA., Illus.). 32p. (J). (ps-3). 15.95 (*88-8203-040-7*) North-South Bks., Inc.

—Flocon Trouve un Ami. 1995. Tr. of Hopper Hunts for Spring. (FRE., Illus.). 32p. (J). (gr. k-3). 15.95 o.s.i (*3-314-20754-9*) North-South Bks., Inc.

—Hoppel Weiss Sich Zu Helfen. 1998. Tr. of Hopper's Treetop Adventure. (GER.). (J). 15.95 (*3-314-00769-8*) North-South Bks., Inc.

—Milo y la Isla Misteriosa. Moreno, Carmen, tr. from GER. 2001. (SPA., Illus.). 32p. (J). (ps-3). 18.95 (*0-7358-1403-1*, NS30339, Michael Neugebauer Bks.) North-South Bks., Inc.

—Nuovi Amici Per Pit. 1998. Tr. of Penguin Pete's New Friends. (ITA., Illus.). (J). (gr. k-3). 15.95 (*88-8203-131-4*) North-South Bks., Inc.

—Penguin Pete's New Friends. (Illus.). (J). (ps). 1997. 12p. 6.95 o.p. (*1-55858-691-1*); 1995. 32p. pap. 6.95 (*1-55858-414-5*); 1988. 32p. 15.95 (*1-55858-025-5*); 1988. 32p. 16.50 o.p. (*1-55858-244-0*) North-South Bks., Inc.

—Penguin Pete's New Friends. 1995. 13.10 (*0-606-08843-1*) Turtleback Bks.

—El Pez Arco Iris. (Rainbow Fish Ser.). Orig. Title: Der Regenbogenfisch. (SPA., Illus.). (J). (ps-3). 1996. 12p. 9.95 (*1-55858-559-1*); 1994. 32p. 18.95 (*1-55858-361-0*); 1994. pap. 25.00 (*1-55858-440-4*); 1994. 32p. 18.88 o.p. (*1-55858-362-9*) North-South Bks., Inc. (Ediciones Norte-Sur).

—El Pez Arco Iris al Rescate! 1998. (Rainbow Fish Ser.). Orig. Title: Regenbogenfisch, Komm Hilf Mir!. (SPA., Illus.). 12p. (J). (ps-3). 9.95 (*1-55858-885-X*, Ediciones Norte-Sur) North-South Bks., Inc.

—El Pez Arco Iris al Rescate! Gutiérrez, Guillermo, tr. from GER. (Rainbow Fish Ser.). Orig. Title: Regenbogenfisch, Komm Hilf Mir!. (SPA., Illus.). 32p. (J). (ps-3). 1997. pap. 25.00 (*1-55858-815-9*); 1996. 18.95 (*1-55858-558-3*, NSB583) North-South Bks., Inc. (Ediciones Norte-Sur).

—El Pez Arco Iris y la Ballena Azul. 1998. (Rainbow Fish Ser.). Orig. Title: Regenbogenfisch und Grosser Blauer Wal. (SPA., Illus.). 32p. (J). (ps-3). 18.95 (*0-7358-1002-8*, NSB028, Ediciones Norte-Sur) North-South Bks., Inc.

—El Pez Arco Iris y la Ballena Azul Libro Grande. 1999. (Rainbow Fish Ser.). Orig. Title: Regenbogenfisch und Grosser Blauer Wal. (SPA., Illus.). 32p. (J). (ps-3). pap. 25.00 (*0-7358-1215-2*) North-South Bks., Inc.

—El Pinguino Pedro y Sus Nuevos Amigos. 1997. (SPA., Illus.). 12p. (J). (ps). 6.95 (*1-55858-740-3*, NS6637, Ediciones Norte-Sur) North-South Bks., Inc.

—The Rainbow Fish. James, J. Alison, tr. from GER. 1992. (Rainbow Fish Ser.).Tr. of Regenbogenfisch. (Illus.). 32p. (J). (ps-3). 18.95 (*1-55858-009-3*); (SPA., lib. bdg. 18.88 (*1-55858-010-7*, NSB107, Ediciones Norte-Sur) North-South Bks., Inc.

—The Rainbow Fish. (Rainbow Fish Ser.).Tr. of Regenbogenfisch. (Illus.). 32p. (J). (ps-3). 1997. (ENG & VIE.). 40.60 (*1-57227-028-4*); 1997. (CAM & ENG., 40.60 (*1-57227-031-4*); 1997. 18.95 (*1-57227-032-2*); 1997. (CHI & ENG., 40.60 (*1-57227-027-6*); 1992. (ENG & KOR., 18.95 (*1-57227-029-2*); 1992. (ENG & TAG., 18.95 (*1-57227-030-6*) Pan Asia Pubns. (USA), Inc.

—Rainbow Fish to the Rescue! 2000. (Rainbow Fish Ser.).Tr. of Regenbogenfisch, Komm Hilf Mir!. (Illus.). 25p. (J). (ps-3). 12.95 (*0-7358-1289-6*) North-South Bks., Inc.

—Rainbow Fish to the Rescue! James, J. Alison, tr. from GER. 1998. (Rainbow Fish Ser.).Tr. of Regenbogenfisch, Komm Hilf Mir!. (ENG & SPA., Illus.). 12p. (J). (ps-3). 9.95 (*1-55858-880-9*) North-South Bks., Inc.

—Rainbow Fish to the Rescue! 1997. (Rainbow Fish Ser.).Tr. of Regenbogenfisch, Komm Hilf Mir!. (JPN., Illus.). (J). (ps-3). 18.95 (*4-06-261969-5*) North-South Bks., Inc.

—Rainbow Fish to the Rescue! James, J. Alison, tr. from GER. 1995. (Rainbow Fish Ser.).Tr. of Regenbogenfisch, Komm Hilf Mir!. (Illus.). 32p. (J). (ps-3). 18.95 (*1-55858-486-2*); lib. bdg. 18.88 (*1-55858-487-0*) North-South Bks., Inc.

—Rainbow Fish to the Rescue! l.t. ed. 1997. (Rainbow Fish Ser.).Tr. of Regenbogenfisch, Komm Hilf Mir!. (Illus.). 32p. (J). (ps-3). pap. 25.00 (*1-55858-816-7*) North-South Bks., Inc.

—Rainbow Fish to the Rescue! 1992. (Rainbow Fish Ser.).Tr. of Regenbogenfisch, Komm Hilf Mir!. (Illus.). 32p. (J). (ps-3). (CHI & ENG.). 18.95 (*1-57227-037-3*); (ENG & VIE., 18.95 (*1-57227-038-1*); (ENG & KOR., 18.95 (*1-57227-041-1*); (ENG & TAG., 18.95 (*1-57227-042-X*) Pan Asia Pubns. (USA), Inc.

—Where Is My Friend? (Illus.). 12p. (ps-k). 2001. 4.95 (*0-7358-1365-5*); 1945. (J). 3.95 o.p. (*1-55858-043-3*) North-South Bks., Inc.

Phelan, Terry W. Best Friends, Hands Down. 1986. (Illus.). 48p. (Orig.). (J). (gr. 2-5). 9.95 o.p. (*0-936915-00-5*); pap. 3.95 o.p. (*0-936915-01-3*) Shoe Tree Pr.

Philbrick, Rodman. Freak the Mighty. 1993. 176p. (YA). (gr. 5-9). pap. 15.95 o.s.i (*0-590-47412-X*) Scholastic, Inc.

—Max the Mighty. 1998. (J). pap. text 47.88 (*0-590-65859-X*, Blue Sky Pr., The) Scholastic, Inc.

—Max the Mighty. 1998. 11.04 (*0-606-15632-1*) Turtleback Bks.

Philbrick, Rodman & Philbrick, W. R. Max the Mighty. 1998. 166p. (J). (gr. 7-12). pap. 16.95 (*0-590-18892-5*, Blue Sky Pr., The) Scholastic, Inc.

Phillips, Clifton J. Chupacabra, You Don't Scare Me! 1999. (Illus.). 32p. (J). (gr. 3-6). pap. 7.00 (*0-8059-4490-7*) Dorrance Publishing Co., Inc.

Phillips, Louise S. The First Snowflake of Winter. 1996. (Illus.). 40p. (J). (ps up). pap. 6.95 (*0-932433-37-5*) Windswept Hse. Pubs.

Phipson, Joan. Hit & Run. 1985. 132p. (YA). (gr. 7 up). 12.95 o.s.i (*0-689-50362-8*, McElderry, Margaret K.) Simon & Schuster Children's Publishing.

—Polly's Tiger. 1974. (Illus.). 48p. (J). (gr. 1-3). 5.95 o.p. (*0-525-37325-X*, Dutton) Dutton/Plume.

Pickering, Jimmy. It's Fall. 2003. (Illus.). 32p. (J). (ps-3). 16.95 (*1-931290-15-6*, Smallfellow Pr.) Tallfellow Pr.

—It's Winter. 2003. (Illus.). 32p. (J). (ps-3). 16.95 (*1-931290-16-4*, Smallfellow Pr.) Tallfellow Pr.

Pickford, Susan B. Zic-Zac & the Crocodile. 1997. (Illus.). 16p. (Orig.). (J). (gr. k-6). pap. 6.95 (*1-889664-04-9*) SBP Collaboratoin Works.

Pickford, Ted. Bobbie's Back, No. 2. 1993. 160p. (YA). mass mkt. 3.50 o.s.i (*0-553-56096-4*) Bantam Bks.

A Picture of Freedom: The Diary of Clotee, a Slave Girl. 2003. (J). lib. bdg. 12.95 (*0-439-55501-9*) Scholastic, Inc.

Pienkowski, Jan. Bel & Bub & the Black Hole. 2000. (Bel & Bub Stories Ser.). (Illus.). 32p. (J). (ps-k). pap. 9.95 o.p. (*0-7894-6528-0*) Dorling Kindersley Publishing, Inc.

Pierce, Tamora. Daja's Book. 1998. (Circle of Magic Ser.: Bk. 3). 224p. (YA). (gr. 6-12). pap. 15.95 o.s.i (*0-590-55358-5*) Scholastic, Inc.

—Sandry's Book. 1997. (Circle of Magic Ser.: No. 1). 256p. (J). (gr. 6-12). pap. 15.95 (*0-590-55356-9*) Scholastic, Inc.

Pierson, Jim. Just Like Everybody Else. 1993. (Illus.). 32p. (J). (ps-3). 5.99 o.p. (*0-87403-842-1*, 03661) Standard Publishing.

Pike, Christopher, pseud. The Dance. 1989. (Final Friends Ser.: No. 2). (YA). (gr. 9 up). pap. 2.95 (*0-671-70011-1*, Simon Pulse) Simon & Schuster Children's Publishing.

—Fall into Darkness. 1991. 224p. (YA). (gr. 8 up). pap. 3.99 (*0-671-73684-1*); 1990. (J). mass mkt. 2.95 (*0-671-67655-5*) Simon & Schuster Children's Publishing. (Simon Pulse).

—The Party. 1997. (Final Friends Ser.: Vol. 1). 224p. (J). (gr. 7-12). pap. 3.99 (*0-671-01926-0*, Simon Pulse) Simon & Schuster Children's Publishing.

—The Party. 1988. (Final Friends Ser.). (J). 10.04 (*0-606-04122-2*) Turtleback Bks.

—Weekend. 1986. pap. 2.25 o.p. (*0-590-33637-1*); (J). pap. 2.75 (*0-590-42968-X*); 230p. (J). (gr. 7 up). pap. 2.50 o.p. (*0-590-40753-8*, Scholastic Paperbacks) Scholastic, Inc.

—Weekend. 1986. (Point Ser.). 10.09 o.p. (*0-606-01207-9*) Turtleback Bks.

Pilgrim, Jane. Henry Goes Visiting Blackberry. 1988. (Blackberry Farm Books Ser.). 0.99 o.s.i (*0-517-64347-2*) Crown Publishing Group.

Pilkey, Dav. A Friend for Dragon. 1991. (Illus.). 48p. (J). (gr. 1-3). mass mkt. 15.99 o.p. (*0-531-08534-1*); (ps-3). pap. 14.95 (*0-531-05934-0*) Scholastic, Inc. (Orchard Bks.).

The Pinballs. 1999. (J). 9.95 (*1-56137-082-7*) Novel Units, Inc.

Pinkwater, Daniel M. The Big Orange Splot. 1993. 32p. (J). (ps-3). mass mkt. 4.99 o.s.i (*0-590-44510-3*) Scholastic, Inc.

—Doodle Flute. 1991. (Illus.). 32p. (J). (gr. k-3). lib. bdg. 13.95 o.p. (*0-02-774635-6*, Atheneum) Simon & Schuster Children's Publishing.

—The Muffin Fiend. 1988. (J). pap. o.p. (*0-553-16816-9*, Dell Books for Young Readers) Random Hse. Children's Bks.

—Spaceburger: A Kevin Spoon & Mason Mintz Story. 1993. (Illus.). 32p. (J). (gr. k-3). 13.95 o.p. (*0-02-774643-7*, Atheneum) Simon & Schuster Children's Publishing.

Pinsker, Judith. A Lot Like You. 1989. (J). (gr. 5 up). mass mkt. 2.95 o.s.i (*0-553-27852-5*, Starfire) Random Hse. Children's Bks.

Piper, Molly. Rosey & Amanda. Date not set. (Illus.). (J). (gr. k-6). pap. 7.95 (*1-891360-01-9*) Little Deer Pr.

Piper, Sophie. Little Kitten's Friendship Book. 2003. (Illus.). 64p. (J). 5.95 (*0-7459-4710-7*) Lion Publishing PLC GBR. *Dist:* Trafalgar Square.

Pittar, Gill. Milly, Molly & Oink. 2004. (J). 9.95 (*1-86972-002-4*) Milly Molly Bks. NZL. *Dist:* National Bk. Network.

Pittau, Francisco. Voyage under the Stars. 1992. (Illus.). 32p. (J). (ps-3). 13.00 o.p. (*0-688-11328-1*); lib. bdg. 12.93 o.p. (*0-688-11329-X*) HarperCollins Children's Bk. Group.

Pittman, Helena Clare. The Angel Tree. 1998. (Illus.). 32p. (J). (gr. k-3). 16.99 o.p. (*0-8037-1939-6*); 15.89 o.s.i (*0-8037-1941-8*) Penguin Putnam Bks. for Young Readers. (Dial Bks. for Young Readers).

—The Snowman's Path. 2000. (Illus.). 32p. (J). (ps-3). 15.99 o.s.i (*0-8037-2170-6*, Dial Bks. for Young Readers) Penguin Putnam Bks. for Young Readers.

Pitts, Paul. Crossroads. 1994. 160p. (J). (gr. 5). pap. 3.99 o.p. (*0-380-77606-5*, Avon Bks.) Morrow/Avon.

—Crossroads. 1994. 9.09 o.p. (*0-606-06297-1*) Turtleback Bks.

—For a Good Time, Don't Call Claudia. 1986. 128p. (J). (gr. 7 up). pap. 2.50 (*0-380-75117-8*, Avon Bks.) Morrow/Avon.

Pitts, Sadie T. The Tri Bros. 1994. (J). 7.95 o.p. (*0-533-10929-9*) Vantage Pr., Inc.

Pizer, Abigail. It's a Perfect Day. 1992. (Trophy Picture Bk.). (Illus.). 32p. (J). (ps-3). pap. 4.95 o.s.i (*0-06-443302-1*, Harper Trophy) HarperCollins Children's Bk. Group.

—It's a Perfect Day. 1990. (Illus.). 28p. (J). (ps). lib. bdg. 11.89 o.p. (*0-397-32421-9*) Lippincott Williams & Wilkins.

Planet Dexter Staff. Whaddaya Doin' in There: A Bathroom Companion for Kids. 1999. (Planet Dexter Ser.). (Illus.). 128p. (J). (gr. 3-7). 5.99 o.p. (*0-448-44082-2*, Grosset & Dunlap) Penguin Putnam Bks. for Young Readers.

Planeta Staff. Las Travesuras Ratitas Verdes. 1998. (SPA.). (J). (*84-395-5386-2*) GeoPlaneta, Editorial, S. A.

Plante, Raymond. Marilou Cries Wolf. 2003. (Illus.). 64p. pap. 3.99 (*0-88780-580-9*) Formac Publishing Co., Ltd. CAN. *Dist:* Orca Bk. Pubs.

Plemons, Marti. Georgie & the New Kid. 1992. (Grace Street Kids Ser.). (Illus.). 128p. (J). (gr. 3-6). pap. 4.99 o.p. (*0-87403-687-9*, 24-03727) Standard Publishing.

Plop! Plop! 1982. (J). 3.95 o.p. (*0-8351-1245-4*) China Bks. & Periodicals, Inc.

Pochocki, Ethel. Mushroom Man. 1993. (J). pap. 15.00 o.p. (*0-671-75951-5*, Simon & Schuster Children's Publishing) Simon & Schuster Children's Publishing.

—A Penny for a Hundred. 1996. (Illus.). 32p. (J). (gr. 3-6). 14.95 (*0-89272-392-0*) Down East Bks.

—Rosebud & Red Flannel. 1999. (Illus.). 32p. (YA). (gr. 2-4). 14.95 (*0-89272-474-9*) Down East Bks.

Polacco, Patricia. The Butterfly. 2002. (Illus.). (J). 23.64 (*0-7587-2166-8*) Book Wholesalers, Inc.

—The Butterfly. unabr. ed. 2001. (J). (gr. 1-6). 27.95 incl. audio (*0-8045-6875-8*, 6875) Spoken Arts, Inc.

—Chicken Sunday. 1992. (Illus.). 32p. (J). (ps-3). 16.99 (*0-399-22133-6*, Philomel) Penguin Putnam Bks. for Young Readers.

—Mrs. Katz & Tush. 1993. pap. 19.95 o.s.i incl. audio (*0-553-45913-9*) Bantam Bks.

—Mrs. Katz & Tush. 2002. (Illus.). (J). 14.79 (*0-7587-3191-4*) Book Wholesalers, Inc.

—Mrs. Katz & Tush. ed. 1994. (J). (gr. 2). spiral bd. (*0-616-01760-X*) Canadian National Institute for the Blind/Institut National Canadien pour les Aveugles.

—Mrs. Katz & Tush. 1994. (Picture Yearling Ser.). (Illus.). 32p. (ps-3). pap. text 6.99 (*0-440-40936-5*) Dell Publishing.

—Mrs. Katz & Tush. (J). 1993. mass mkt. o.p. (*0-440-90065-4*); 1992. (Illus.). 15.00 (*0-553-08122-5*); 1991. mass mkt. o.s.i (*0-553-53092-5*) Random Hse. Children's Bks. (Dell Books for Young Readers).

—Mrs. Katz & Tush. 1994. 13.14 (*0-606-05930-X*) Turtleback Bks.

—Pink & Say. 2002. (Illus.). (J). 23.64 (*0-7587-3418-2*) Book Wholesalers, Inc.

—Pink & Say. 1994. (Illus.). 48p. (J). (ps-5). 16.99 (*0-399-22671-0*, Philomel) Penguin Putnam Bks. for Young Readers.

—Pink & Say. 2001. (J). 27.95 incl. audio (*0-8045-6835-9*, 6835) Spoken Arts, Inc.

Polo & Cuddles. (J). text 14.64 (*0-8136-0618-7*) Modern Curriculum Pr.

Poltarness, Weller. Martin & Tommy. 1994. (Illus.). (J). (gr. 4 up). 14.00 o.p. (*0-671-88067-5*, Simon & Schuster Children's Publishing) Simon & Schuster Children's Publishing.

Pomerantz, Charlotte. You're Not My Best Friend Anymore. 1998. (Illus.). 32p. (J). (ps-3). 15.99 o.s.i (*0-8037-1559-5*); 15.89 o.s.i (*0-8037-1560-9*) Penguin Putnam Bks. for Young Readers. (Dial Bks. for Young Readers).

Ponti, Claude. DeZert Isle. Holliday, Mary Martin, tr. from FRE. 2003. (J). 16.95 (*1-56792-237-6*) Godine, David R. Pub.

Ponti, James. Friends in Need. 1999. (Mystery Files of Shelby Woo Ser.: No. 14). 144p. (J). (gr. 4-6). pap. 3.99 (*0-671-03465-0*, Aladdin) Simon & Schuster Children's Publishing.

Pontiflet, Ted. Poochie. 1978. (Illus.). (J). (gr. 1-4). 7.50 o.p. (*0-8037-7029-4*); 7.50 o.p. (*0-8037-7030-8*) Penguin Putnam Bks. for Young Readers. (Dial Bks. for Young Readers).

Pooh Christmas with Friends. (J). pap. 3.99 o.p. (*0-307-09193-7*, 09193, Golden Bks.) Random Hse. Children's Bks.

Pooh Hello Friend Book & Box. 2002. (Illus.). (J). pap. 9.98 (*0-7853-5251-1*) Publications International, Ltd.

Pooh's Word Book. 1995. (Wheel & Window Ser.). (Illus.). 14p. (J). (ps-1). 7.98 o.p. (*1-57082-216-6*) Mouse Works.

Poortvliet, Rien. Gnome Friends: Gnomes Are Friends with All Animals. 1997. (Illus.). 10p. (J). 4.95 (*1-57909-021-4*) Kabouter Products.

Pope, Gisele & Kern, Carla. Tailfeathers, Vol. 2. 1999. (Illus.). 84p. (J). pap. 10.50 (*1-56770-451-4*) Scheewe, Susan Pubns., Inc.

Porte, Barbara Ann. Harry's Visit. 1983. (Greenwillow Read-Alone Bks.). (Illus.). 48p. (J). (gr. 1-3). 9.00 o.p. (*0-688-01207-8*); lib. bdg. 8.88 o.p. (*0-688-01208-6*) HarperCollins Children's Bk. Group. (Greenwillow Bks.).

Porter, Cassyashton. Colin's Eagle. 2003. 134p. pap. 19.95 (*1-59286-517-8*) PublishAmerica, Inc.

Porter, Connie Rose. Addy Learns a Lesson: A School Story. Johnson, Roberta, ed. 1993. (American Girls Collection: Bk. 2). (Illus.). 80p. (J). (gr. 2 up). 12.95 (*1-56247-078-7*); pap. 5.95 (*1-56247-077-9*) Pleasant Co. Pubns. (American Girl).

—Addy Saves the Day: A Summer Story. Johnson, Roberta, ed. 1993. (American Girls Collection: Bk. 5). (Illus.). 80p. (YA). (gr. 2 up). 12.95 (*1-56247-084-1*); pap. 5.95 (*1-56247-083-3*) Pleasant Co. Pubns. (American Girl).

Porus, Marcus & Porus, Shirley. Who Is Gribich? 1995. (Gribich & Friends Ser.). (Illus.). 32p. (J). (ps). 14.95 (*0-9646125-0-X*) Doog Publishing Group.

Post, Douglas. The Wind in the Willows - Musical. 1987. 87p. (J). pap. 5.95 (*0-87129-172-X*, W05) Dramatic Publishing Co.

Post, T. K. & Anastasio, Dina. The Tiff. 1995. (Re Boot Ser.). 48p. (J). (gr. 1-4). 4.95 o.p. (*0-8431-3944-7*, Price Stern Sloan) Penguin Putnam Bks. for Young Readers.

Potter, Beatrix. Lavender Finds a Friend Giftset. 2004. (Illus.). 5.99 (*0-7232-8484-9*, Warne, Frederick) Penguin Putnam Bks. for Young Readers.

—Panache Petitgris. 1990. (FRE., Illus.). 60p. (J). 9.95 (*0-7859-3713-7*) French & European Pubns., Inc.

Potter, Keith R. & Fulk, Ken. Count Us In. 1999. (Doodlezoo Ser.). (Illus.). 26p. (J). (ps). bds. 6.95 (*0-8118-2064-5*) Chronicle Bks. LLC.

Powell, Opal N. Two Lives for Giant Jack Pumpkin: The Story of a Boy, a Jack O'Latern & a Pie. 2001. (Illus.). 24p. (J). (ps-4). pap. (*0-9710477-1-5*) Western Printers, Inc.

Powell, Randy. Three Clams & an Oyster, RS. 2002. 224p. (YA). (gr. 7-10). 16.00 (*0-374-37526-7*, Farrar, Straus & Giroux (BYR)) Farrar, Straus & Giroux.

Powers, Marshall K. Era Mi Major Amigo. Bernall, Carmen, tr. 1997. (Lucky the Cat Book Ser.). (SPA.). (YA). (gr. 8-10). 15.95 (*0-9647200-8-6*); pap. 9.95 (*0-9647200-9-4*) Gato Pr., The.

Pray, Ralph. Jingu: The Hidden Princess. 2002. (Illus.). 80p. (J). 14.95 (*1-885008-21-X*, 188500821x) Shen's Bks.

Preller, James. Wake Me in the Spring. 1994. (Hello Reader! Ser.). (Illus.). 32p. (J). (ps-3). pap. 3.99 (*0-590-47500-2*, Cartwheel Bks.) Scholastic, Inc.

Prentiss, Elizabeth. Urbane & His Friends. 1999. (J). (ps up). pap. 7.99 (*1-881545-68-7*) Angela's Bookshelf.

Presti, Joan Lo. Flump. 2001. (Illus.). 32p. (J). (ps-3). pap. 7.50 (*1-884083-23-4*) Maval Publishing, Inc.

Pretty Please. 1994. (YA). pap. 1.99 o.p. (*0-590-48832-5*) Scholastic, Inc.

Price, Joan. Truth Is a Bright Star. 2003. 156p. (J). (gr. 3-7). pap. 8.95 (*1-58246-055-8*) Tricycle Pr.

Price, Mathew. Amigos (Friends) 1993. (Levanta la Tapa Ser.). 10p. (J). (gr. 3 up). 4.99 o.s.i (*0-553-09561-7*) Bantam Bks.

—Friends. 2003. (Illus.). 10p. 4.99 (*0-7696-3165-7*) McGraw-Hill Children's Publishing.

—Patch Finds a Friend. 2000. (Illus.). 12p. (J). (ps-k). 5.95 (*0-531-30264-4*, Orchard Bks.) Scholastic, Inc.

Price, Reynolds. Michael Egerton. 1993. (J). (gr. 6 up). o.p. (*0-88682-591-1*, Creative Education) Creative Co., The.

Priceman, Marjorie. It's Me, Marva! A Story about Color & Optical Illusions. 2001. (Illus.). 40p. (J). (ps-3). 15.95 o.s.i (*0-679-88993-0*, Knopf Bks. for Young Readers) Random Hse. Children's Bks.

Priddy, Roger. Squishy Turtle & Friends. 2003. 14p. (J). 8.95 (*0-312-49184-0*, Priddy Bks.) St. Martin's Pr.

Prior, Natalie Jane. Lily Quench & the Dragon of Ashby. 2004. (Illus.). 160p. (J). pap. 4.99 (*0-14-240020-3*, Puffin Bks.) Penguin Putnam Bks. for Young Readers.

Provost, Gary & Levine-Provost, Gail. David & Max. 1991. 196p. (J). (gr. 5-9). pap. 9.95 (*0-8276-0392-4*) Jewish Pubn. Society.

Pryor, Bonnie. Amanda & April. 1986. (Illus.). 32p. (J). (ps-1). 17.00 o.p. (*0-688-05869-8*); lib. bdg. 16.93 o.p. (*0-688-05870-1*) Morrow/Avon. (Morrow, William & Co.).

—Louie & Dan Are Friends. 1997. (Illus.). 32p. (J). lib. bdg. 15.93 o.p. (*0-688-08561-X*); 16.00 (*0-688-08560-1*) Morrow/Avon. (Morrow, William & Co.).

—Vinegar Pancakes & Vanishing Cream. 1996. (Illus.). 128p. (J). (gr. 4-7). pap. 4.95 (*0-688-14744-5*, Morrow, William & Co.) Morrow/Avon.

—Vinegar Pancakes & Vanishing Cream. 1996. (J). 11.00 (*0-606-10016-4*) Turtleback Bks.

Publications International Staff. Puppy Dog Tales. 2001. (Illus.). 36p. (J). 14.98 (*0-7853-5849-8*) Publications International, Ltd.

Publishers Group Advantage Staff. My Little Book Friends: Hey Diddle Diddle, Sing a Song of Sixpence, This Little Piggy, Mary Had, 1. 1998. (My Little Book Friends Ser.). (Illus.). 5p. (ps-k). 19.95 o.p. (*1-57145-335-0*) Advantage Pubs. Group.

Pullein-Thompson, Christine. Come Home, Jessie. 1991. 112p. (J). (gr. 3-5). pap. 2.50 o.p. (*0-87406-561-5*) Darby Creek Publishing.

Pullman, Philip. Spring-Heeled Jack: A Story of Bravery & Evil. 2002. (Illus.). 112p. (J). (gr. 3-7). 9.95 (*0-375-81601-1*); lib. bdg. 11.99 (*0-375-91601-6*) Random Hse. Children's Bks. (Knopf Bks. for Young Readers).

Purdy, Carol. Least of All. 1987. (Illus.). 32p. (J). (gr. 1-4). lib. bdg. 12.95 (*0-689-50404-7*, McElderry, Margaret K.) Simon & Schuster Children's Publishing.

Putnam, Alice. That New Guy! 1987. 96p. (Orig.). (J). (gr. 6-8). pap. 2.25 o.p. (*0-87406-252-7*) Darby Creek Publishing.

Puttock, Simon. "Here I Am!" Said Smedley. 2001. (Blue Bananas Ser.). (Illus.). 48p. (J). (gr. 1-2). pap. 4.95 (*0-7787-0884-5*); lib. bdg. 19.96 (*0-7787-0838-1*) Crabtree Publishing Co.

—Squeaky Clean. 2002. (Illus.). 32p. (J). (ps-2). 13.95 (*0-316-78816-3*) Little Brown Children's Bks.

—A Story for Hippo: A Book about Loss. 2001. (Illus.). 32p. (J). (ps-2). 15.95 (*0-439-26219-4*) Scholastic, Inc.

Puzzle House Staff. Friends. 2001. (File-Online.Com). (Illus.). 128p. (J). (gr. 3-8). mass mkt. 7.95 (*0-439-22008-4*) Scholastic, Inc.

Quackenbush, Robert. Chuck Lends a Paw. 1986. (J). (ps-2). 12.95 o.p. (*0-89919-363-3*, Clarion Bks.) Houghton Mifflin Co. Trade & Reference Div.

Quattlebaum, Mary. Jackson Jones & the Puddle of Thorns. 1995. (Illus.). 128p. (J). (gr. 3-7). pap. 4.50 (*0-440-41066-5*) Dell Publishing.

—Jackson Jones & the Puddle of Thorns. 1995. (J). 10.55 (*0-606-07725-1*) Turtleback Bks.

—A Year on My Street. 1996. (Yearling First Choice Chapter Book Ser.). (Illus.). 48p. (J). (ps-3). pap. 3.99 o.s.i (*0-440-41106-8*) Dell Publishing.

Quimonsieur, Christopher. Perfect Harmony. 1997. 48p. (J). pap. 6.95 o.p. (*1-56167-319-6*) American Literary Pr., Inc.

Quin-Harkin, Janet. The Boy Next Door. 1995. (Love Stories Ser.). 192p. (gr. 7-12). mass mkt. 4.50 (*0-553-56663-6*) Bantam Bks.

—Forever Friday. 1995. (TGIF Ser.: No. 4). 128p. (J). (gr. 3-6). pap. 3.50 (*0-671-51020-7*, Aladdin) Simon & Schuster Children's Publishing.

—Ginger's First Kiss. 1994. (Boyfriend Club Ser.: Vol. 1). 176p. (J). (gr. 4-7). pap. 2.95 (*0-8167-3414-3*) Rainbow Bridge.

—The Graduates. 1986. (Sweet Dreams - On Our Own Ser.: No. 1). 176p. (Orig.). (YA). (gr. 7-12). mass mkt. 2.50 o.s.i (*0-553-25723-4*) Bantam Bks.

—Helpful Hattie. 1983. (Let Me Read Ser.). (Illus.). 64p. (J). (ps-3). 9.95 o.p. (*0-15-233756-3*) Harcourt Children's Bks.

—Make Me a Star. 1987. (Sugar & Spice Ser.: No. 10). (YA). (gr. 6 up). mass mkt. 2.95 o.s.i (*0-8041-0075-6*, Ivy Bks.) Ballantine Bks.

—Old Friends, New Friends. 1986. (On Our Own Ser.: No. 4). 224p. (Orig.). (YA). (gr. 6 up). mass mkt. 2.50 o.s.i (*0-553-26186-X*) Bantam Bks.

—One Step Too Far, No. 19. 1989. (Sugar & Spice Ser.). 192p. (YA). (gr. 9-11). mass mkt. 2.95 o.s.i (*0-8041-0337-2*, Ivy Bks.) Ballantine Bks.

—Roadtrip, No. 18. 1989. (Sugar & Spice Ser.: No. 18). (YA). (gr. 6 up). mass mkt. 2.95 o.s.i (*0-8041-0336-4*, Ivy Bks.) Ballantine Bks.

—Sleepover Madness. 1995. (TGIF Ser.: No. 1). 128p. (J). (gr. 4-7). pap. 3.50 (*0-671-51017-7*, Aladdin) Simon & Schuster Children's Publishing.

—Summer Heat. 1990. (Portraits Collection: No. 1). 95p. (Orig.). (YA). mass mkt. 3.50 o.s.i (*0-449-14604-9*, Fawcett) Ballantine Bks.

—Tess & Ali & the Teeny Bikini. 1991. (Friends Ser.: No. 02). 176p. (YA). mass mkt. 3.50 o.p. (*0-06-106064-X*, HarperTorch) Morrow/Avon.

Quinn, John. The Summer of Lily & Esme. 1992. 190p. (Orig.). (J). (gr. 6 up). pap. 8.95 (*1-85371-208-6*) Poolbeg Pr. IRL. *Dist:* Dufour Editions, Inc.

Rabe, Tish. Fine Feathered Friends: All about Birds. 1998. (Cat in the Hat's Learning Library). (Illus.). 48p. (gr. k-3). 11.99 o.s.i (*0-679-98362-7*); (J). 8.99 (*0-679-88362-2*) Random Hse. Children's Bks. (Random Hse. Bks. for Young Readers).

Rabinowitz, Ann. Bethie. 1989. 208p. (YA). (gr. 7 up). lib. bdg. 14.95 o.p. (*0-02-775661-0*, Simon & Schuster Children's Publishing) Simon & Schuster Children's Publishing.

Radin, Ruth Y. All Joseph Wanted. 1991. (Illus.). 80p. (J). (gr. 4-7). 15.00 o.s.i (*0-02-775641-6*, Simon & Schuster Children's Publishing) Simon & Schuster Children's Publishing.

—Carver. 1990. (Illus.). 80p. (J). (gr. 3-7). text 12.95 o.p. (*0-02-775651-3*, Simon & Schuster Children's Publishing) Simon & Schuster Children's Publishing.

—Tac's Island. 1986. (Illus.). 80p. (J). (gr. 3-6). 10.95 o.s.i (*0-02-775780-3*, Simon & Schuster Children's Publishing) Simon & Schuster Children's Publishing.

Radley, Gail. CF in His Corner. 1984. 128p. (J). (gr. 7 up). 11.95 o.p. (*0-02-777390-6*, Simon & Schuster Children's Publishing) Simon & Schuster Children's Publishing.

—Dear Gabby, Things Are Getting Out of Hand . . . 1998. 9.09 o.p. (*0-606-13325-9*) Turtleback Bks.

—The Golden Days. 1992. 160p. (J). (gr. 5 up). pap. 3.99 o.p. (*0-14-036002-6*, Puffin Bks.) Penguin Putnam Bks. for Young Readers.

—Nothing Stays the Same. (J). E-Book 4.50 (*1-931071-01-2*, Bookmice) McGraw Publishing, Inc.

Raffi. Down by the Bay. 1999. (Raffi Board Bks.). (Illus.). 32p. (J). (ps). bds. 6.99 (*0-517-80058-6*) Crown Publishing Group.

Raintree Steck-Vaughn Staff. The River That Gave Gifts. 1992. 24p. 5.00 (*0-8172-6727-1*) Raintree Pubs.

Ramirez, Michael Rose. Gingerbread Sleepover, 3. 1997. (Chana! Ser.). (J). 9.09 o.p. (*0-606-12652-X*) Turtleback Bks.

—Live from Cedar Hills! 1998. (Chana! Ser.: No. 4). 80p. (J). pap. 3.99 o.p. (*0-380-79021-1*, Avon Bks.) Morrow/Avon.

Ramos, Isabel. Aleph-Alfa-Alfa. 1998. (J). (gr. 3-5). pap. 7.95 o.p. (*0-533-12774-2*) Vantage Pr., Inc.

Rand, Suzanne. The Good Luck Girl. 1986. (Winners Ser.: No. 3). 192p. (Orig.). (YA). (gr. 7-12). mass mkt. 2.50 o.s.i (*0-553-25644-0*) Bantam Bks.

Randall, Florence E. All the Sky Together. 1983. 240p. (J). (gr. 5-9). 11.95 o.s.i (*0-689-30996-1*, Atheneum) Simon & Schuster Children's Publishing.

Randall, Ronne. A Hose of a Nose! 2002. (Little Friends Ser.). (Illus.). 14p. (J). (ps-1). 12.95 o.p. (*1-57145-773-9*, Silver Dolphin Bks.) Advantage Pubs. Group.

Randle, Kristen D. Breaking Rank. 1999. (Illus.). 208p. (J). (gr. 8 up). 15.95 (*0-688-16243-6*) HarperCollins Children's Bk. Group.

—Breaking Rank. 1999. (J). lib. bdg. (*0-688-16244-4*, Morrow, William & Co.) Morrow/Avon.

—The Only Alien on the Planet. 1995. 272p. (YA). (gr. 7 up). pap. 14.95 o.p. (*0-590-46309-8*) Scholastic, Inc.

Randle, Kristin. Slumming. 2003. 240p. (J). 15.99 (*0-06-001022-3*); lib. bdg. 16.89 (*0-06-001023-1*) HarperCollins Children's Bk. Group. (HarperTempest).

Random House Beginners Books Staff. All about Cassie. 2002. 48p. (J). pap. 2.99 (*0-375-81483-3*, Random Hse. Bks. for Young Readers) Random Hse. Children's Bks.

—Everybodee Loves. 2002. 80p. (J). pap. 2.99 (*0-375-81456-6*, Random Hse. Bks. for Young Readers) Random Hse. Children's Bks.

—Friends All Day. 2002. (Illus.). 14p. (J). (ps). bds. 4.99 (*0-375-81558-9*, Random Hse. Bks. for Young Readers) Random Hse. Children's Bks.

Random House Books for Young Readers Staff. Betty Spaghetty, Where Are You? 2003. (Illus.). 24p. (J). (ps-2). pap. 3.99 (*0-375-82370-0*) Random Hse. Children's Bks.

—Betty Spaghetty's Super Cool Dress-Up Book. 2003. (Illus.). 12p. (J). (ps-2). bds. 5.99 (*0-375-82471-5*) Random Hse. Children's Bks.

—Elmo's World: !Bailando! 2003. (Illus.). 10p. (J). (ps). bds. 4.99 (*0-375-82496-0*) Random Hse. Children's Bks.

—Elmo's World: !Muzsica! 2003. (Illus.). 10p. (J). (ps). bds. 4.99 (*0-375-82495-2*) Random Hse. Children's Bks.

—Meet Betty Spaghetty. 2003. (Illus.). 24p. (J). (ps-2). pap. 3.99 (*0-375-82371-9*) Random Hse. Children's Bks.

—Thomas & Friends: Shhh! It's a Surprise! 2002. (Illus.). 12p. (J). bds. 5.99 (*0-375-82165-1*, Random Hse. Bks. for Young Readers) Random Hse. Children's Bks.

Random House Disney Staff. Beauty & the Beast. 2002. (Illus.). 24p. (J). pap. 3.25 (*0-7364-2065-7*, RH/Disney) Random Hse. Children's Bks.

—Buzz Blows Bubbles & Other Tongue Twisters. 2003. 24p. (J). pap. 3.25 (*0-7364-2086-X*, RH/Disney) Random Hse. Children's Bks.

—A Friend Like You. 2003. 16p. (J). pap. 3.99 (*0-7364-2082-7*, RH/Disney) Random Hse. Children's Bks.

—Me Too, Woody! 2002. (Step into Reading Ser.). 32p. (J). (gr. k-2). pap. 3.99 (*0-7364-1266-2*); (Illus.). lib. bdg. 11.99 (*0-7364-8004-8*) Random Hse. Children's Bks. (RH/Disney).

—Treasure Planet SIR Step 3. 2002. (Step into Reading Ser.). 48p. (J). (gr. 1-3). pap. 3.99 (*0-7364-2021-5*, RH/Disney) Random Hse. Children's Bks.

—Treasure Planet Sir 3. 2002. (Step into Reading Ser.). 48p. (J). lib. bdg. 11.99 (*0-7364-8014-5*, RH/Disney) Random Hse. Children's Bks.

Random House Staff. Friends Forever. 2000. (Sticker Time Ser.). (Illus.). 16p. (J). (ps-3). pap. 2.99 (*0-375-80639-3*, Random Hse. Bks. for Young Readers) Random Hse. Children's Bks.

—Percy. 2001. (Illus.). 12p. (J). bds. 7.99 o.p. (*0-375-81305-5*, Random Hse. Bks. for Young Readers) Random Hse. Children's Bks.

—Singing Springs. 2002. 32p. (J). pap. 4.99 (*0-375-82170-8*) Random Hse. Children's Bks.

—Take It Easy, Zak & Wheezie! 2001. (Illus.). 12p. (J). (ps). bds. 7.99 (*0-375-81311-X*, Random Hse. Bks. for Young Readers) Random Hse. Children's Bks.

—Thomas. 2001. (Illus.). 12p. (J). bds. 7.99 o.s.i (*0-375-81304-7*, Random Hse. Bks. for Young Readers) Random Hse. Children's Bks.

—Tomas y Sus Amigos. 2003. Tr. of Thomas & Friends. (SPA., Illus.). 12p. (J). (ps). bds. 3.99 (*0-375-82421-9*, RH Para Ninos) Random Hse. Children's Bks.

Random House Staff & Schuett, Stacey. Best Friends. 1995. (Jewelry Bks.). (J). bds. 4.99 o.s.i (*0-679-87677-4*) Random Hse., Inc.

Random House Value Publishing Staff. Play with Me. 1995. 4.99 o.s.i (*0-517-14184-1*) Random Hse. Value Publishing.

Ransom, Candice F. Thirteen. 1990. 192p. (J). (gr. 4-6). pap. 2.95 (*0-590-43742-9*); 1986. 192p. (YA). (gr. 6 up). pap. 2.50 o.p. (*0-590-40192-0*, Scholastic Paperbacks); 1984. (J). mass mkt. 2.75 (*0-590-43459-4*) Scholastic, Inc.

Raphael, Taffy E. The View from Saturday. (Book Club Novel Guide Ser.). 48p. 2002. 17.95 (*1-931376-10-7*); 2001. E-Book 9.95 (*0-9656211-5-4*) Small Planet Communications, Inc.

Raschka, Chris. Ring! Yo? 2000. (Richard Jackson Bks.). (Illus.). 40p. (J). (ps-2). pap. 15.95 (*0-7894-2614-5*, D K Ink) Dorling Kindersley Publishing, Inc.

—Yo! Yes? (Illus.). 32p. (J). (ps-1). 1998. mass mkt. 6.95 (*0-531-07108-1*); 1993. pap. 15.95 (*0-531-05469-1*); 1993. lib. bdg. 16.99 (*0-531-08619-4*) Scholastic, Inc. (Orchard Bks.).

—Yo! Yes? 1998. 13.10 (*0-606-15776-X*) Turtleback Bks.

—Yo! Yes? 2000. (J). (ps-5). pap. 12.95 incl. audio (*1-55592-067-5*, QPRA566) Weston Woods Studios, Inc.

Raskin, Ellen. Figgs & Phantoms. 1989. (Puffin Newbery Library). (Illus.). 160p. (J). (gr. 4-7). pap. 5.99 (*0-14-032944-7*, Puffin Bks.) Penguin Putnam Bks. for Young Readers.

Ravilious, Robin. Two in a Pocket. 1991. (J). (ps-3). 14.95 o.p. (*0-316-73449-7*) Little Brown & Co.

Ray. Alvah & Arvilla. 1998. (J). pap. (*0-15-201547-7*) Harcourt Children's Bks.

Reader, Dennis. Butterfingers. 1991. (Illus.). 32p. (J). (gr. k-3). 13.95 o.p. (*0-395-57581-8*) Houghton Mifflin Co.

Ready Reader Staff. Friends Forever. (J). pap. text 25.99 (*0-8136-0988-7*) Modern Curriculum Pr.

Reardon, Ruth & Rodegast, Roland. Listen to My Feelings. 1992. (Illus.). (J). (ps up). 8.95 (*0-8378-2499-0*) Gibson, C. R. Co.

Reaver, Chap. Mote. 224p. 1992. (YA). mass mkt. 3.50 o.s.i (*0-440-21173-5*); 1990. (J). 14.95 o.s.i (*0-385-30163-4*, Delacorte Pr.) Dell Publishing.

Reber, Deborah. Magenta & Me. 2000. (Blues Clue's Ready to Read Ser.: No. 2). (Illus.). 24p. (J). (ps-1). pap. 3.99 (*0-689-83123-4*, Simon Spotlight/ Nickelodeon) Simon & Schuster Children's Publishing.

Recknagel, Friedrich. Meg's Wish. 1999. (Illus.). 32p. (J). (gr. k-3). 15.95 o.p. (*0-7358-1116-4*); 16.50 o.p. (*0-7358-1117-2*) North-South Bks., Inc.

Recorvits, Helen. Where Heroes Hide, RS. 2002. (Illus.). 144p. (J). (gr. 4-6). 16.00 (*0-374-33057-3*, Farrar, Straus & Giroux (BYR)) Farrar, Straus & Giroux.

Rector, Rebecca Kraft. Tria & the Great Star Rescue. 2002. 192p. (gr. 3-7). text 14.95 (*0-385-72941-3*, Delacorte Pr.) Dell Publishing.

Redmond, Patrick. Something Dangerous. l.t. ed. 2000. (J). 26.95 (*1-56895-832-3*, Wheeler Publishing, Inc.) Gale Group.

Reed, Don C. The Kraken. 2003. (Illus.). 224p. (YA). (gr. 5-9). pap. 7.95 (*1-56397-693-5*) Boyds Mills Pr.

—The Kraken. 1997. lib. bdg. 14.00 (*0-606-14348-3*) Turtleback Bks.

Reeves, Faye C. Howie Merton & the Magic Dust. 1991. (Stepping Stone Bks.). (Illus.). 64p. (Orig.). (J). (gr. 2-4). pap. 2.50 o.s.i (*0-679-81527-9*, Random Hse. Bks. for Young Readers) Random Hse. Children's Bks.

Regan, Dana. Be Mine. 1997. (J). 6.95 o.p. (*0-694-01157-6*) HarperCollins Children's Bk. Group.

Regan, Dian Curtis. The Friendship of Milly & Tug, ERS. 1999. (Illus.). 78p. (J). (gr. 1-3). 15.95 (*0-8050-5935-0*, Holt, Henry & Co. Bks. For Young Readers) Holt, Henry & Co.

—Game of Survival. 1989. (Orig.). (J). pap. 2.75 (*0-380-75585-8*, Avon Bks.) Morrow/Avon.

—The Peppermint Race, ERS. (J). 1996. (Illus.). 64p. (gr. 2-4). pap. 5.95 o.p. (*0-8050-4675-5*); 1994. 14.95 o.p. (*0-8050-2753-X*) Holt, Henry & Co. (Holt, Henry & Co. Bks. For Young Readers).

Regan, Dian Curtis & Dewdney, Anna. The Peppermint Race. 1994. E-Book (*1-59019-624-4*) ipicturebooks, LLC.

Reilly, Patricia G. Next Year I'll Be Special. 1996. (Illus.). 32p. (J). (gr. k-3). pap. 4.99 o.s.i (*0-440-41031-2*) Dell Publishing.

Reinsma, Carol. Friends Forever. 1993. (Really Reading! Bks.). (Illus.). 48p. (Orig.). (J). (gr. 1-3). pap. 4.49 o.p. (*0-7847-0096-6*, 03946) Standard Publishing.

Reiser, Lynn W. Best Friends Think Alike. 1997. (Illus.). 32p. (J). (ps-3). 16.00 (*0-688-15199-X*); lib. bdg. 15.93 o.p. (*0-688-15200-7*) HarperCollins Children's Bk. Group. (Greenwillow Bks.).

—Margaret & Margarita, Margarita y Margaret. 1993. (Illus.). 32p. (J). (ps-3). (SPA.). 15.99 (*0-688-12239-6*); (ENG & SPA., lib. bdg. 15.93 o.p. (*0-688-12240-X*, Greenwillow Bks.) HarperCollins Children's Bk. Group.

—Margaret & Margarita, Margarita y Margaret. 1996. 12.10 (*0-606-10482-8*) Turtleback Bks.

Reiss, Johanna. The Upstairs Room. 1984. (J). mass mkt. 2.50 o.s.i (*0-553-24784-0*) Bantam Bks.

—The Upstairs Room. (gr. 7 up). 1990. 208p. (J). pap. 5.99 (*0-06-440370-X*, Harper Trophy); 1987. 196p. (YA). lib. bdg. 14.89 o.p. (*0-690-04702-9*); 1972. 208p. (J). 16.99 (*0-690-85127-8*) HarperCollins Children's Bk. Group.

—The Upstairs Room. 1972. (J). 12.00 (*0-606-04132-X*) Turtleback Bks.

—Upstairs Room. 1987. (Trophy Keypoint Bks.). 192p. (J). (gr. 7 up). reprint ed. pap. 5.99 (*0-06-447043-1*, Harper Trophy) HarperCollins Children's Bk. Group.

Reiss, Kathryn. The Glass House People. 1992. (YA). (gr. 7 up). pap. 6.95 (*0-15-231041-X*) Harcourt Children's Bks.

Reit, Ann. I Thought You Were My Best Friend. 1988. 144p. (J). (gr. 6-8). pap. 2.50 o.p. (*0-590-40445-8*) Scholastic, Inc.

Reitz, Ric. The Journey of Sir Douglas Fir: A Reader's Musical. Bell, Suzanne, ed. 1999. (Illus.). 48p. (J). (gr. 2-6). per. 19.95 (*0-9670160-0-2*, Sir Fir Bks. & Music) Sir Fir Enterprises, LLC.

Renahan, Doug. Goldilocks & Little Bear's Birthday. 1988. pap. 3.75 o.p. (*0-89137-050-1*); (Illus.). 34p. (J). 8.34 (*0-89137-072-2*) Quality Pubns.

Renauld, Christiane. A Pal for Martin. 1992. (Child's World Library Ser.). (Illus.). 32p. (J). (gr. 1-5). lib. bdg. 8.50 (*0-89565-756-2*) Child's World, Inc.

Rennison, Louise. Knocked Out by My Nunga-Nungas: Further, Further Confessions of Georgia Nicolson. 3rd ed. 2003. 208p. (J). (gr. 5 up). pap. 6.99 (*0-06-447362-7*) HarperCollins Children's Bk. Group.

—On the Bright Side, I'm Now the Girlfriend of a Sex God: Further Confessions of Georgia Nicolson. 2001. 256p. (J). (gr. 7 up). 15.99 (*0-06-028813-2*) HarperCollins Children's Bk. Group.

—On the Bright Side, I'm Now the Girlfriend of a Sex God: Further Confessions of Georgia Nicolson. 2002. 272p. (J). pap. 6.99 (*0-06-447226-4*) HarperCollins Pubs.

—On the Bright Side, I'm Now the Girlfriend of a Sex God: Further Confessions of Georgia Nicolson. 2003. 256p. (J). mass mkt. 6.99 (*0-06-052185-6*, Avon Bks.) Morrow/Avon.

Repp, Gloria. Noodle Soup. 1994. (Illus.). 32p. (J). (ps-1). pap. 5.49 (*0-89084-582-4*, 055681) Jones, Bob Univ. Pr.

Resalt, Manfred Sommer. Naga, el Pequeno Sabio. 2001. (SPA.). (J). (gr. 1-3). (*84-241-7911-0*) Everest de Ediciones y Distribucion, S.L. ESP. *Dist:* Lectorum Pubns., Inc.

Resciniti, Angelo G. The Ketchup Kid. 1987. (Treetop Tales Ser.). (Illus.). 96p. (Orig.). (J). (gr. 3-5). pap. 2.25 o.p. (*0-87406-228-4*) Darby Creek Publishing.

Retino, Ernie & Kerner Rettino, Debbie. Choosing Good Friends. 1992. (Wisdom Ser.). 32p. (J). (ps-2). 7.99 o.p. (*0-8499-1017-X*) W Publishing Group.

Reuter, Elisabeth. Best Friends. 1993. Orig. Title: Judith & Lisa. 26p. (J). (gr. 3-7). 12.95 (*0-943706-18-1*) Pitspopany Pr.

Rex, Michael. Pals. 2003. (Word-by-Word First Reader Ser.). (Illus.). 32p. (J). mass mkt. 3.99 (*0-439-49310-2*, Cartwheel Bks.) Scholastic, Inc.

Reyes, Raquel, et al. I Muy Bien! Very Good!, Level B. 2001. (SPA., Illus.). 126p. (gr. 1-3). spiral bd., tchr.'s training gde. ed. (*0-9713381-2-4*) Double R Publishing, LLC.

Reynolds, Marilynn. A Dog for a Friend. 1994. (Illus.). 32p. (J). (ps-3). reprint ed. pap. 6.95 (*1-55143-020-7*) Orca Bk. Pubs.

—Love Rules. 2001. (True-to-Life Series from Hamilton High). 224p. (YA). (gr. 8 up). 18.95 (*1-885356-75-7*); pap. 9.95 (*1-885356-76-5*) Morning Glory Pr., Inc.

—A Present for Mrs. Kazinski. 2001. (Illus.). 32p. (J). (gr. k-3). lib. bdg. 15.95 (*1-55143-196-3*); pap. 7.95 (*1-55143-198-X*) Orca Bk. Pubs.

Reynolds, Peter. Sydney's Star. 2001. (Illus.). 32p. (J). (ps-3). 14.00 (*0-689-83184-6*, Simon & Schuster Children's Publishing) Simon & Schuster Children's Publishing.

Reynolds, Susan L. Strandia, RS. 1991. (Illus.). 240p. (YA). (gr. 9-12). 14.95 o.p. (*0-374-37274-8*, Farrar, Straus & Giroux (BYR)) Farrar, Straus & Giroux.

RH Disney Staff. Amigos en la Selva. 2003. Tr. of Jungle Friends. (SPA.). 32p. (J). (ps-1). pap. 3.99 (*0-7364-2142-4*, RH/Disney) Random Hse. Children's Bks.

—Piglet se Siente Pequeno. 2003. Tr. of Piglet Feels Small. (SPA.). 32p. (J). (ps-1). pap. 3.99 (*0-7364-2143-2*, RH/Disney) Random Hse. Children's Bks.

Ricchiuti, Paul B. Rocky & Me. 1990. (J). (ps-3). pap. 5.95 o.p. (*0-8163-0898-5*) Pacific Pr. Publishing Assn.

Richards, Arlene K. & Willis, Irene. Boy Friends, Girl Friends, Just Friends. 1979. 180p. (J). (gr. 7 up). 11.95 o.s.i (*0-689-30695-4*, Atheneum) Simon & Schuster Children's Publishing.

Richardson, Arleta. New Faces, New Friends. (Grandma's Attic Ser.). (J). 1995. 160p. (gr. 4-7). pap. 4.99 (*0-7814-0214-X*); 1989. 176p. (gr. 3-7). pap. 3.99 o.p. (*1-55513-985-X*) Cook Communications Ministries.

Richardson, Delores. Can You Dig It? (J). 2001. 25.00 (*0-9619482-0-5*); 1990. (Illus.). 20p. (gr. 3-7). (*0-9619482-9-9*) Little Spirit Publishing, Inc.

Richardson, Dorothea. Moose Girl. 2002. 108p. (YA). pap. 16.95 (*1-58851-797-7*) PublishAmerica, Inc.

Richardson, Gillian & Collective Books Staff. A Friend for Mr. Granville. 1997. (Illus.). 98p. (J). (gr. 3-6). pap. 5.95 (*1-895836-38-7*) Books Collective, The CAN. *Dist:* General Distribution Services, Inc.

Richardson, Kara. Simon & Barklee in France. 2000. (Another Country Calling Ser.: No. 1). (Illus.). 48p. (J). (gr. 2-5). 12.00 (*0-9704661-0-2*, Explorer Media) Simon & Barklee, Inc./ExplorerMedia.

Richemont, Enid. The Glass Bird. 1993. (Illus.). 112p. (J). (gr. 3-6). 14.95 o.p. (*1-56402-195-5*) Candlewick Pr.

—Jamie & the Whippersnapper. 2000. (Illus.). 64p. (J). mass mkt. o.s.i (*0-09-940098-7*) Random Hse. of Canada, Ltd. CAN. *Dist:* Random Hse., Inc.

—The Time Tree. 1990. (J). (gr. 3-7). 12.95 (*0-316-74452-2*) Little Brown & Co.

Richmond, Gary. The Forgotten Friend. 1991. (J). (gr. 1-5). text 6.99 o.s.i (*0-8499-0913-9*) W Publishing Group.

Ridings, Jim. Ashpile, No. 1. 1998. (Illus.). 142p. (YA). (gr. 6 up). pap. 7.95 (*0-9664974-2-2*, Side Show Comics) Ink & Feathers Comics.

Riggio, Anita. Gert & Frieda. 1990. (Illus.). 32p. (J). lib. bdg. 12.95 o.s.i (*0-689-31568-6*, Atheneum) Simon & Schuster Children's Publishing.

Riise, Torben. Emily & the Arabic Letter. 2001. 164p. pap. 11.95 (*0-595-17399-3*, Writers Club Pr.) iUniverse, Inc.

Ripper, Georgie. Brian & Bob: The Tale of Two Guinea Pigs. 2003. (Illus.). 32p. (J). 15.99 (*0-7868-1925-1*) Hyperion Bks. for Children.

Ripslinger, Jon. Triangle. 1994. 224p. (YA). (gr. 9 up). 10.95 o.s.i (*0-15-200048-8*); pap. 3.95 (*0-15-200049-6*, Harcourt Paperbacks) Harcourt Children's Bks.

Risk, Mary, et al. Puppy Finds a Friend. 2000. (I Can Read Bks.). (ENG, FRE & SPA., Illus.). 28p. (J). (gr. k-2). 6.95 (*0-7641-5283-1*) Barron's Educational Series, Inc.

Rispin, Karen. The Impossible Lisa Barnes. 1992. (Anika Scott Ser.: Vol. 1). 185p. (J). (gr. 3-7). pap. 4.99 o.p. (*0-8423-1614-0*) Tyndale Hse. Pubs.

—The Impossible Lisa Barnes. (J). E-Book 6.99 (*1-58586-524-9*) ereads.com.

—Sabrina the Schemer. 1994. (Anika Scott Ser.: Vol. 5). 130p. (J). (gr. 3-7). pap. 4.99 o.p. (*0-8423-1296-X*) Tyndale Hse. Pubs.

—Sabrina the Schemer. 74p. E-Book 6.99 (*1-58586-790-X*); 2002. pap. 6.99 (*1-58586-793-4*); 2002. E-Book 6.99 (*0-7592-0310-5*); 2001. E-Book 6.99 (*0-7592-1002-0*) ereads.com.

Rissik, Maureen. The Friendship Box. 2000. (Keepsakes! Ser.). (Illus.). 24p. (J). (gr. 1-5). pap. text 9.95 (*0-7624-0145-1*) Running Pr. Bk. Pubs.

Ritchie, Harry. Last Pink Bits: Travels Through the Remnants of the British Empire. 1999. (Illus.). 230p. (J). mass mkt. 13.95 (*0-340-66683-8*) Hodder & Stoughton, Ltd. GBR. *Dist:* Lubrecht & Cramer, Ltd., Trafalgar Square.

Ritter, John H. Choosing up Sides. 2000. 176p. (gr. 5-9). pap. 5.99 (*0-698-11840-5*, PaperStar) Penguin Putnam Bks. for Young Readers.

Rivera, Geraldo. Miguel Robles—So Far. 1973. 30 p. (J). o.s.i (*0-15-253900-X*) Harcourt Trade Pubs.

Roberts, Barbara A. Phoebe's Best Best Friend. 2000. (Phoebe Flower's Adventures Ser.). (Illus.). 70p. (J). 5.95 (*0-9660366-9-7*) Advantage Bks., LLC.

Roberts, Brenda C. Sticks & Stones, Bobbie Bones. 1993. 96p. (J). (gr. 4-6). mass mkt. 2.99 o.p. (*0-590-46518-X*) Scholastic, Inc.

Roberts, Laura Peyton. Ghost of a Chance. 1997. 192p. (YA). (gr. 7-12). 14.95 o.s.i (*0-385-32508-8*, Delacorte Pr.) Dell Publishing.

—Ghost of a Chance. 1999. 192p. (gr. 5 up). pap. text 3.99 o.s.i (*0-440-41534-9*, Dell Books for Young Readers) Random Hse. Children's Bks.

—Ghost of a Chance. 1999. 10.04 (*0-606-16448-0*) Turtleback Bks.

Roberts, Willo Davis. Don't Hurt Laurie! 1988. 11.04 (*0-606-12262-1*) Turtleback Bks.

—Elizabeth. 1984. 368p. (J). (gr. 7 up). pap. 2.95 o.p. (*0-590-33136-1*) Scholastic, Inc.

Robins, Joan. Addie Meets Max. 1985. (I Can Read Bks.). (Illus.). 32p. (J). (gr. k-3). lib. bdg. 15.89 (*0-06-025064-X*); (gr. 1-3). 9.95 (*0-06-025063-1*) HarperCollins Children's Bk. Group.

—Addie Meets Max. 1988. (I Can Read Bks.). (J). (gr. 1-3). 10.10 (*0-606-03540-0*) Turtleback Bks.

—Addie's Bad Day. 1993. (I Can Read Bks.). (Illus.). 32p. (J). (gr. 1-3). 14.00 o.p. (*0-06-021297-7*); lib. bdg. 14.89 o.p. (*0-06-021298-5*) HarperCollins Children's Bk. Group.

—Addie's Bad Day. 1994. (I Can Read Bks.). (J). (gr. 1-3). 10.10 (*0-606-06159-2*) Turtleback Bks.

Robinson, Barbara. The Best School Year Ever. (Trophy Bk.). 128p. (J). (gr. 3 up). 1997. pap. 4.99 (*0-06-440492-7*, Harper Trophy); 1994. 15.99 (*0-06-023039-8*); 1994. lib. bdg. 15.89 (*0-06-023043-6*) HarperCollins Children's Bk. Group.

Robinson, Charles. New Kid in Town. 1975. (Illus.). 32p. (J). (gr. 1-3). 6.95 o.p. (*0-689-30484-6*, Atheneum) Simon & Schuster Children's Publishing.

Robinson, Mary. Give It up, Mom. 1989. (J). (gr. 5-9). 13.95 o.p. (*0-395-49700-0*) Houghton Mifflin Co.

—Give It up, Mom. 1992. 144p. (J). (gr. 4). pap. 2.99 (*0-380-71126-5*, Avon Bks.) Morrow/Avon.

Roche, P. K. Goodbye, Arnold. 1981. (Pied Piper Bks.). (Illus.). 32p. (J). (ps-2). 2.75 o.p. (*0-8037-3033-0*, Dial Bks. for Young Readers) Penguin Putnam Bks. for Young Readers.

Rochman, Hazel. Who Do You Think You Are? Stories of Friends & Enemies. 1993. (YA). 16.95 o.p. (*0-316-75355-6*) Little Brown & Co.

—Who Do You Think You Are? Stories of Friends & Enemies. 1997. (J). 14.75 (*0-606-13913-3*) Turtleback Bks.

Rochman, Hazel & McCampbell, Darlene, selected by. Who Do You Think You Are? Stories of Friends & Enemies. 1997. 176p. (J). (gr. 7-12). reprint ed. pap. 9.99 (*0-316-75320-3*) Little Brown & Co.

Rock, Gail. A Dream for Addie. l.t. ed. 1977. (gr. 4-6). pap. 1.95 o.p. (*0-553-15089-8*, 15044-8) Bantam Bks.

Rocklin, Joanne. For Your Eyes Only! 2001. (Illus.). 144p. (J). (gr. 3-7). mass mkt. 3.99 (*0-590-67448-X*) Scholastic, Inc.

—For Your Eyes Only! 2001. (J). 10.04 (*0-606-20492-X*) Turtleback Bks.

—Sonia Begonia. 1986. (Illus.). 96p. (J). (gr. 3-7). lib. bdg. 12.95 o.p. (*0-02-777310-8*, Simon & Schuster Children's Publishing) Simon & Schuster Children's Publishing.

—Three Smart Pals. 1994. (Hello Reader! Ser.). (Illus.). 48p. (J). (ps-3). pap. 3.99 (*0-590-47431-6*, Cartwheel Bks.) Scholastic, Inc.

—Three Smart Pals. 1994. (Hello Reader! Ser.). 10.14 (*0-606-06811-2*) Turtleback Bks.

Rockwell, Anne F. Big Boss. 1996. 64p. (J). (ps-3). per. 14.00 (*0-689-80883-6*, Simon & Schuster Children's Publishing) Simon & Schuster Children's Publishing.

—Big Boss: Level 2. 1996. (Ready-to-Read Ser.). (Illus.). 64p. (J). (ps-3). pap. 3.99 (*0-689-80884-4*, Aladdin) Simon & Schuster Children's Publishing.

Rockwell, Thomas. How to Fight a Girl. l.t. ed. 1988. (J). (gr. 3-7). reprint ed. lib. bdg. 16.95 o.s.i (*1-55736-077-4*, Cornerstone Bks.) Pages, Inc.

—How to Fight a Girl. 1988. 112p. (gr. 4-7). pap. text 4.50 (*0-440-40111-9*, Yearling) Random Hse. Children's Bks.

—How to Fight a Girl. 1987. (J). 13.95 o.p. (*0-531-15082-8*); (Illus.). 128p. (gr. 4-6). lib. bdg. 13.90 o.p. (*0-531-10140-1*) Scholastic Library Publishing. (Watts, Franklin).

—How to Fight a Girl. 1987. (J). 10.04 (*0-606-04097-8*) Turtleback Bks.

Rodda, Emily. Something Special, ERS. 1991. (Redfeather Paperback Ser.). (Illus.). 80p. (J). (gr. 2-4). reprint ed. pap. 4.95 o.p. (*0-8050-1641-4*, Holt, Henry & Co. Bks. For Young Readers) Holt, Henry & Co.

Roddie, Shen. Sandbear. 2002. (Illus.). (J). (ps up). 15.95 (*1-58234-758-1*, Bloomsbury Children) Bloomsbury Publishing.

—Too Close Friends. 1998. (Illus.). 32p. (J). (ps-3). 14.99 o.s.i (*0-8037-2188-9*, Dial Bks. for Young Readers) Penguin Putnam Bks. for Young Readers.

Roddy, Lee. Road to Freedom. 1999. (Between Two Flags Ser.: Vol. 4). 160p. (J). (gr. 6-9). pap. 5.99 o.p. (*0-7642-2028-4*) Bethany Hse. Pubs.

Rodgers, Dorothy. Polka Dots & Friendship. 1988. (J). 5.95 o.p. (*0-533-07728-1*) Vantage Pr., Inc.

Rodman, Mary Ann. Yankee Girl, RS. 2004. (J). 16.00 (*0-374-38661-7*, Farrar, Straus & Giroux (BYR)) Farrar, Straus & Giroux.

Rodowsky, Colby. Gathering Room. 1995. 11.05 o.p. (*0-606-09311-7*) Turtleback Bks.

—P. S. Write Soon, RS. 1987. (Sunburst Ser.). 158p. (J). (gr. 5 up). reprint ed. pap. 3.50 o.p. (*0-374-46032-9*, Sunburst) Farrar, Straus & Giroux.

—Remembering Mog. 1998. 144p. (J). (gr. 7-12). pap. 3.99 o.s.i (*0-380-72922-9*, Avon Bks.) Morrow/ Avon.

—What about Me?, RS. 1989. 144p. (J). (gr. 3 up). pap. 3.50 o.p. (*0-374-48316-7*, Sunburst) Farrar, Straus & Giroux.

Rodriguez, K. S. Major Meltdown. 1999. (Dawson's Creek Ser.: No. 4). 176p. (YA). (gr. 8 up). pap. 4.99 (*0-671-02477-9*, Simon Pulse) Simon & Schuster Children's Publishing.

Roffey, Maureen. Bathtime. 1990. (Illus.). 32p. (J). (ps). reprint ed. pap. 4.95 o.p. (*0-689-70808-4*, Aladdin) Simon & Schuster Children's Publishing.

Rogers, Fred. Making Friends. 1987. (First Experience Bks.). (Illus.). (J). (ps-1). 12.95 o.s.i (*0-399-21382-1*); 32p. 6.95 o.s.i (*0-399-21385-6*) Penguin Putnam Bks. for Young Readers. (PaperStar).

Rogers, Jacqueline. Best Friends Sleep Over. 1993. (Best Friends Ser.). 32p. (J). (ps-1). pap. 14.95 (*0-590-44793-9*) Scholastic, Inc.

Rogers, Karen M. Max & Me. 1998. (Think-Kids Book Collection). (Illus.). 16p. (J). (gr. 1-4). pap. 2.95 (*1-58237-013-3*) Creative Thinkers, Inc.

—Yipes! Stripes! 1998. (Think-Kids Book Collection). (Illus.). 16p. (J). (gr. 1-4). pap. 2.95 (*1-58237-002-8*) Creative Thinkers, Inc.

Rogers, Paul & Rogers, Emma. What's Wrong, Tom? 1989. (Illus.). 32p. (J). (ps-1). 11.95 o.p. (*0-670-82394-5*, Viking Children's Bks.) Penguin Putnam Bks. for Young Readers.

Rohmann, Eric. My Friend Rabbit. 2002. (Illus.). 32p. (ps-3). 22.90 (*0-7613-2420-8*); (J). 15.95 (*0-7613-1535-7*) Millbrook Pr., Inc. (Roaring Brook Pr.).

Rohmer, Harriet, et al. Atariba & Niguayona. 1988. (J). 15.95 o.p. incl. audio (*0-89239-039-5*) Children's Bk. Pr.

Rojany, Lisa. Casper: Junior Novelization. 1995. (Illus.). (J). (gr. 2 up). 3.95 o.s.i (*0-8431-3854-8*, Price Stern Sloan) Penguin Putnam Bks. for Young Readers.

Romanelli, Serena. Little Bobo. 1999. (Illus.). 32p. (J). (gr. k-3). pap. 6.95 (*0-7358-1097-4*) North-South Bks., Inc.

—Little Bobo. 1999. 13.10 (*0-606-16194-5*) Turtleback Bks.

The Roommate. 1994. (YA). pap. 1.99 o.p. (*0-590-48827-9*) Scholastic, Inc.

Roop, Peter. Keep the Lights Burning, Abbie. 1987. (Carolrhoda on My Own Bks.). 12.10 (*0-606-12385-7*) Turtleback Bks.

Roos, Stephen. The Fair-Weather Friends. 1987. (Plymouth Island Chronicles Ser.: Bk. 1). (Illus.). 144p. (J). (gr. 3-6). lib. bdg. 13.95 o.p. (*0-689-31297-0*, Atheneum) Simon & Schuster Children's Publishing.

—Terrible Truth. 1984. (J). pap. 2.25 o.s.i (*0-440-78578-2*) Dell Publishing.

Rose, Anne. Hamid & the Sultan's Son. 1975. (Illus.). 48p. (J). (gr. 2-5). 6.25 o.p. (*0-15-270101-X*) Harcourt Children's Bks.

Rose Five Book Boxed Set: Cheyenne Rose; Rose Faces the Music; Rose's Magic Touch; Trapped Beyond the Magic Attic; The Secret of the Attic, 5 vols. Incl. Cheyenne Rose. Williams, Laura E. Korman, Susan, ed. 1997. pap. 5.95 (*1-57513-103-X*); Rose Faces the Music. Williams, Laura E. & Alexander, Nina. Korman, Susan, ed. 1997. pap. 5.95 (*1-57513-107-2*); Rose's Magic Touch. Alexander, Nina & Williams, Laura E. Korman, Susan, ed. 1997. pap. 5.95 (*1-57513-105-6*); Secret of the Attic. Sinykin, Sheri Cooper. 1995. pap. 5.95 (*1-57513-001-7*); Trapped Beyond the Magic Attic. Sinykin, Sheri Cooper. Bodnar, Judith, ed. 1997. pap. 5.95 (*1-57513-101-3*); (Illus.). 80p. (J). (gr. 2-6). (Magic Attic Club Ser.). 1997. Set pap. 22.95 (*1-57513-110-2*, Magic Attic Pr.) Millbrook Pr., Inc.

Rose, Gerald. Bad Boy Billy. 2004. (Cambridge Storybooks Ser.). (Illus.). 16p. pap. (*0-521-75209-4*) Cambridge Univ. Pr.

Rose, Karen & Halfyard, Lynda. Kristin & Boone, 001. 1983. 224p. (J). (gr. 5). 6.95 o.p. (*0-395-34560-X*) Houghton Mifflin Co.

Rose Ramirez, Michael. Live from Cedar Hills!, 4. 1998. (Chana! Ser.). (J). 9.09 o.p. (*0-606-13263-5*) Turtleback Bks.

Rosen, Michael. Mind Your Own Business. 1974. (Illus.). 96p. (J). (gr. 3 up). 26.95 (*0-87599-209-9*) Phillips, S.G. Inc.

Rosen, Michael J. Elijah's Angel: A Story for Chanukah & Christmas. (Illus.). 32p. (J). (gr. k up). 1992. 16.00 (*0-15-225394-7*); 1997. reprint ed. pap. 7.00 (*0-15-201558-2*, Harcourt Paperbacks) Harcourt Children's Bks.

Rosenbloom, Joseph. Maximillian, You're the Greatest. 1980. (J). (gr. 3-7). 8.95 o.p. (*0-525-66705-9*, Dutton Children's Bks.) Penguin Putnam Bks. for Young Readers.

Rosenbluth, Rolf & Edgar. 1998. (J). 11.95 (*0-671-75272-3*, Simon & Schuster Children's Publishing) Simon & Schuster Children's Publishing.

Rosenfeld, Dina. Labels for Laibel. 1990. (Illus.). 32p. (J). (ps-1). 9.95 (*0-922613-35-4*) Hachai Publishing.

Rosenstock, D. Misfits & Miracles. 1993. 128p. (YA). pap. 3.99 o.s.i (*0-553-48046-4*) Bantam Bks.

Roser, Wiltrud. Lena & Leopold. 1988. (Illus.). 320p. (J). (ps-3). pap. 3.95 o.p. (*0-14-050818-X*, Puffin Bks.) Penguin Putnam Bks. for Young Readers.

Rosie in the Way. 2002. (Illus.). 24p. (J). (gr. k-5). pap. 2.99 (*1-57759-367-7*) Dalmatian Pr.

Rosner, Ruth. I Hate My Best Friend. 1997. (Hyperion Chapters Ser.). (Illus.). 64p. (J). (gr. 2-4). pap. 3.95 (*0-7868-1169-2*) Disney Pr.

—I Hate My Best Friend. 1997. (Hyperion Chapters Ser.). (Illus.). 64p. (J). (gr. 2-4). lib. bdg. 14.49 (*0-7868-2079-9*) Hyperion Bks. for Children.

—My Super Best Friend. 1997. (Illus.). (J). pap. o.p. (*0-7868-1130-7*) Hyperion Paperbacks for Children.

Ross, Andrea. About the Ant. 1995. (Chester Earth Ant Ser.). 20p. (J). (gr. k-3). 7.95 (*1-887683-01-1*) Storybook Pr. & Productions.

—To Touch the Sun. Davenport, May, ed. l.t. ed. 2000. 195p. (YA). (gr. 9-12). pap. text 15.95 (*0-943864-99-2*) Davenport, May Pubs.

Ross, Anna. Be My Friend. 1991. (Sesame Street Toddler Bks.). (Illus.). 24p. (J). (ps). 5.99 o.s.i (*0-394-85496-9*, Random Hse. Bks. for Young Readers) Random Hse. Children's Bks.

Ross, Dave. A Book of Friends. 1999. (Illus.). 40p. (J). (ps-3). 13.95 (*0-06-028170-7*) HarperCollins Children's Bk. Group.

—A Book of Hugs. 1991. (Illus.). 32p. (J). (gr. 2 up). reprint ed. mass mkt. 3.95 (*0-06-107418-7*) HarperCollins Children's Bk. Group.

Ross, Katharine. Sweetie & Petie. (Jellybean Bks.). (Illus.). 24p. (J). (ps-1). 2000. 2.99 o.s.i (*0-375-80143-X*); 1999. lib. bdg. 7.99 (*0-375-90143-4*) Random Hse. Children's Bks. (Random Hse. Bks. for Young Readers).

Ross, Pat. M & M & the Santa Secrets. (Puffin Chapters for Readers on the Move Ser.). (J). 1998. 48p. (gr. 2-5). pap. 3.99 o.p. (*0-14-130094-9*, Puffin Bks.); 1987. (Illus.). pap. 3.99 o.s.i (*0-14-032222-1*, Puffin Bks.); 1985. (Illus.). 9.95 o.p. (*0-670-80624-2*, Viking Children's Bks.) Penguin Putnam Bks. for Young Readers.

—M & M & the Santa Secrets. 1987. 10.14 (*0-606-14062-X*) Turtleback Bks.

—M & M & the Super Child Afternoon. (M & M Ser.). (Illus.). (J). (gr. 1-4). 1989. 4p. pap. 3.99 o.s.i (*0-14-032145-4*, Puffin Bks.); 1987. 9.95 o.p. (*0-670-81208-0*, Viking Children's Bks.) Penguin Putnam Bks. for Young Readers.

—Meet M & M. 1982. 48p. (gr. k-6). pap. 1.75 o.p. (*0-440-45546-4*) Dell Publishing.

—Meet M & M. 1980. (I Am Reading Bks.). (Illus.). 48p. (J). (gr. 1-4). pap. 6.95 o.s.i (*0-394-84184-0*, Pantheon) Knopf Publishing Group.

—Meet M & M. (M & M Ser.). (Illus.). (J). 1988. 4p. (gr. 1-4). pap. 3.99 o.s.i (*0-14-032651-0*); 1997. 64p. (gr. 2-5). pap. 4.99 (*0-14-038731-5*) Penguin Putnam Bks. for Young Readers. (Puffin Bks.).

—Meet M & M. 1999. (J). (gr. 2 up). pap., stu. ed. 22.24 incl. audio (*0-7887-3178-5*, 40913X4) Recorded Bks., LLC.

—Meet M & M. 1997. (Puffin Chapters Ser.). 10.14 (*0-606-12766-6*) Turtleback Bks.

Ross, Ramon R. Harper & Moon. 1995. 192p. (J). (gr. 4 up). pap. 3.99 o.p. (*0-380-72356-5*, Avon Bks.) Morrow/Avon.

—Harper & Moon. 1993. (Illus.). 160p. (YA). (gr. 4 up). 15.00 (*0-689-31803-0*, Atheneum) Simon & Schuster Children's Publishing.

Ross, Tony. A Fairy Tale. 1992. (Illus.). 32p. (J). (ps-3). 13.95 o.p. (*0-316-75750-0*) Little Brown & Co.

Rossiter, Nan Parson. Rugby & Rosie. 1997. (Illus.). 32p. (J). (gr. k-4). 15.99 (*0-525-45484-5*) Penguin Putnam Bks. for Young Readers.

Rostkowski, Margaret I. The Best of Friends. 1989. 192p. (YA). (gr. 7 up). 12.95 (*0-06-025104-2*); lib. bdg. 12.89 o.p. (*0-06-025105-0*) HarperCollins Children's Bk. Group.

Roth, Carol. Little Bunny's Sleepless Night. 1999. (Illus.). 32p. (J). (ps-2). 15.95 (*0-7358-1069-9*) North-South Bks., Inc.

Roth, David. The Hermit of Fog Hollow Station. 1980. 160p. (gr. 7 up). 7.95 o.p. (*0-8253-0012-6*) Beaufort Bks., Inc.

Rothstein, Chaya L. Mentchkins Make Friends. 1988. (J). (gr. 4-8). pap. 7.95 (*0-87306-453-4*) Feldheim, Philipp Inc.

Rovetch, Lissa. Trigwater Did It. 1991. (Illus.). 32p. (J). (ps-3). pap. 3.95 o.p. (*0-14-054238-8*, Puffin Bks.) Penguin Putnam Bks. for Young Readers.

Rowlands, Avril. Milk & Honey. 1990. 152p. (J). (gr. 4 up). 15.00 o.p. (*0-19-271627-1*) Oxford Univ. Pr., Inc.

Roy, Ron. Frankie is Staying Back. 1981. (Illus.). 64p. (J). (gr. 2-5). 8.95 (*0-395-31025-3*, Clarion Bks.) Houghton Mifflin Co. Trade & Reference Div.

Rubel, William. The Stone Soup Book of Friendship Stories. 2003. (Illus.). 128p. (J). (gr. 3-8). pap. 8.95 (*1-883672-76-7*) Tricycle Pr.

Ruby, Lois. Skin Deep. (gr. 7). 1996. (J). mass mkt. 4.99 (*0-590-47700-5*); 1994. 224p. (YA). pap. 14.95 (*0-590-47699-8*) Scholastic, Inc.

—Skin Deep. 1994. 10.09 o.p. (*0-606-09864-X*) Turtleback Bks.

Ruckman, Ivy. In Care of Cassie Tucker. 2000. 176p. (gr. 4-7). pap. text 4.50 o.s.i (*0-440-41406-7*, Yearling) Random Hse. Children's Bks.

—In Care of Cassie Tucker. 2000. 10.55 (*0-606-17893-7*) Turtleback Bks.

—This Is Your Captain Speaking. 1987. (YA). (gr. 5 up). 14.95 o.p. (*0-8027-6734-6*) Walker & Co.

Rudisill, J. J., et al, illus. LouLou's Lemonade Stand. 1999. (Wimzie's House Bks.). 24p. (J). pap. 3.99 (*0-88724-541-2*, CD-4847) Carson-Dellosa Publishing Co., Inc.

Rudner, Barry. My Friends That Rhyme with Orange. 1995. 29p. (J). (ps). pap. 6.95 (*0-9642206-2-8*) Windword Pr.

Ruepp, Krista. Midnight Rider. James, J. Alison, tr. from GER. 1995. (Illus.). (J). (ps-3). 64p. 13.95 o.p. (*1-55858-494-3*); 61p. 13.88 o.p. (*1-55858-495-1*) North-South Bks., Inc.

—The Sea Pony. James, J. Alison, tr. from GER. 2001. (Illus.). 64p. (J). 13.95 (*0-7358-1534-8*); lib. bdg. 14.50 (*0-7358-1535-6*) North-South Bks., Inc.

Ruffell, Ann. Blood Brother. 1980. (Julia MacRae Blackbird Bks.). 160p. (J). (gr. 7 up). lib. bdg. 8.90 o.p. (*0-531-04177-8*, Watts, Franklin) Scholastic Library Publishing.

Rupert, Rona. Straw Sense. 1993. (Illus.). (J). pap. 14.00 (*0-671-77047-0*, Simon & Schuster Children's Publishing) Simon & Schuster Children's Publishing.

Russell, Stephanie. Light Through the Leaves. 1984. 256p. (Orig.). (J). (gr. 7 up). mass mkt. 2.25 o.s.i (*0-449-70045-3*, Fawcett) Ballantine Bks.

Russo, Marisabina. Alex Is My Friend. 1992. 32p. (J). 14.00 o.p. (*0-688-10418-5*); lib. bdg. 13.93 o.p. (*0-688-10419-3*) HarperCollins Children's Bk. Group. (Greenwillow Bks.).

—Alex Is My Friend. (Illus.). (J). 3.98 o.p. (*0-8317-3465-5*) Smithmark Pubs., Inc.

—Waiting for Hannah. 1989. (Illus.). 32p. (J). (ps up). 16.00 o.p. (*0-688-08015-4*); lib. bdg. 14.93 o.p. (*0-688-08016-2*) HarperCollins Children's Bk. Group. (Greenwillow Bks.).

Rutledge, Margie. The Busybody Buddha. 2002. (Illus.). 184p. (J). (gr. 4-7). pap. 8.95 (*0-929141-91-1*, Napoleon Publishing) Napoleon Publishing/Rendezvous Pr. CAN. *Dist:* Words Distributing Co.

Ruzzier, Sergio. Dwarf Giant. 2004. (Illus.). 32p. (J). (ps-2). 15.99 (*0-06-052951-2*); lib. bdg. 16.89 (*0-06-052952-0*) HarperCollins Children's Bk. Group. (Geringer, Laura Bk.).

Ryan, Cheryl. Sally Arnold. 1996. (Illus.). 32p. (J). (ps-4). 14.99 o.s.i (*0-525-65176-4*, Dutton Children's Bks.) Penguin Putnam Bks. for Young Readers.

Ryan, Margaret. Littlest Dragon. 2003. (Roaring Good Reads Ser.). (Illus.). 64p. (J). pap. 6.95 (*0-00-714163-7*) HarperCollins Pubs. Ltd. GBR. *Dist:* Trafalgar Square.

Ryan, Mary C. My Friend, O'Connell. 1991. (Orig.). (J). (gr. 3-4). pap. 2.95 (*0-380-76145-9*, Avon Bks.) Morrow/Avon.

Ryan, Mary E. Alias. 1998. 160p. (YA). (gr. 7-12). mass mkt. 4.99 (*0-689-82264-2*, Simon Pulse) Simon & Schuster Children's Publishing.

—Alias. 1998. 11.04 (*0-606-15429-9*) Turtleback Bks.

—Dance a Step Closer. 1984. 192p. (J). (gr. 7 up). 14.95 o.p. (*0-385-29350-X*, Delacorte Pr.) Dell Publishing.

Ryce, C. J. Napsha, the Miracle Dragon. 1997. (Illus.). 64p. (Orig.). (J). (gr. 1-5). per. 13.95 (*0-9653695-2-8*) Spellbound Pubns.

Ryden, Hope. Backyard Rescue. (Illus.). (J). 1997. 128p. (gr. 3-7). pap. 4.95 (*0-688-15496-4*); 1994. 15.00 (*0-688-12880-7*) Morrow/Avon. (Morrow, William & Co.).

—Backyard Rescue. 1997. (J). 11.00 (*0-606-11088-7*) Turtleback Bks.

Ryder. Won't You Be My Kissaroo. 2004. (Illus.). 32p. 16.00 (*0-15-202641-X*, Gulliver Books) Harcourt Children's Bks. CAN. *Dist:* Harcourt Trade Pubs.

Ryder, Joanne. The Goodbye Walk. 1993. (Illus.). 32p. (J). (gr. k-3). 13.99 o.p. (*0-525-67405-5*, Dutton Children's Bks.) Penguin Putnam Bks. for Young Readers.

—The Goodbye Walk. (Illus.). 32p. (J). 4.98 o.p. (*0-8317-4991-1*) Smithmark Pubs., Inc.

—Old Friends, New Friends. 1986. (Big Little Golden Bks.). (Illus.). 24p. (J). (gr. k-3). o.p. (*0-307-10257-2*, Golden Bks.) Random Hse. Children's Bks.

Ryder, Stephanie. New Christmas Friends. 1995. (Illus.). 18p. (J). (ps). bds. 3.98 o.p. (*1-85854-255-3*) Brimax Bks., Ltd.

Rylant, Cynthia. A Fine White Dust. 1987. 112p. (J). (gr. k-6). pap. 3.50 o.p. (*0-440-42499-2*, Yearling) Random Hse. Children's Bks.

—A Fine White Dust. 2002. (J). E-Book 6.99 (*0-689-84862-5*, Atheneum); 2000. (Illus.). (YA). (gr. 5-9). 16.00 (*0-689-84087-X*, Atheneum/Richard Jackson Bks.); 1998. (J). pap. 2.65 (*0-689-82166-2*, Aladdin); 1996. 120p. (YA). (gr. 5-9). pap. 4.99 (*0-689-80462-8*, Aladdin); 1986. 120p. (J). (gr. 6-8). lib. bdg. 16.00 (*0-02-777240-3*, Atheneum/Richard Jackson Bks.) Simon & Schuster Children's Publishing.

—A Fine White Dust. 1996. 11.04 (*0-606-09274-9*) Turtleback Bks.

—Henry & Mudge: The First Book of Their Adventures. 1992. (Henry & Mudge Ser.). (J). (gr. k-3). pap. 9.48 (*0-395-61769-3*) Houghton Mifflin Co.

—Henry & Mudge: The First Book of Their Adventures. 1987. (Henry & Mudge Ser.). (Illus.). 40p. (J). (gr. k-3). text 13.00 o.p. (*0-02-778001-5*, Atheneum/Richard Jackson Bks.) Simon & Schuster Children's Publishing.

—Henry y Mudge: El Primer Libro de Sus Aventuras. 1999. (Henry & Mudge Ser.). (SPA., Illus.). (J). (gr. k-3). 13.00 (*0-689-80685-X*, Atheneum) Simon & Schuster Children's Publishing.

—Henry y Mudge: El Primer Libro de Sus Aventuras. Ada, Alma Flor, tr. from ENG. 1996. (Henry & Mudge Ser.). (SPA., Illus.). 40p. (J). (gr. k-3). mass mkt. 3.99 (*0-689-80684-1*, Aladdin) Simon & Schuster Children's Publishing.

—Henry y Mudge con Barro Hasta el Rabo. (Henry & Mudge Ser.).Tr. of Henry & Mudge in Puddle Trouble. (SPA.). (J). (gr. k-3). 1998. 13.00 (*0-689-80686-8*, Atheneum); 1996. (Illus.). 48p. mass mkt. 5.99 (*0-689-80687-6*, Aladdin) Simon & Schuster Children's Publishing.

—Henry y Mudge y el Mejor Dia del Ano. 1997. (Henry & Mudge Ser.).Tr. of Henry & Mudge & the Best Day of All. (SPA.). (J). (gr. k-3). 12.14 (*0-606-12724-0*) Turtleback Bks.

—Mr. Putter & Tabby Books. 1994. (J). 47.60 (*0-15-201279-6*) Harcourt Trade Pubs.

—Mr. Putter & Tabby Pour the Tea. 2000. pap. 10.95 o.p. (*0-15-200282-0*); 1994. (J). 7.50 o.p. (*0-15-200752-0*); 1994. (J). pap. 3.00 o.p. (*0-15-200753-9*) Harcourt Trade Pubs.

—Mr. Putter & Tabby Pour the Tea. 1994. (J). 12.10 (*0-606-06584-9*) Turtleback Bks.

—Poppleton. ed. 1998. (J). (gr. 1). spiral bd. (*0-616-01776-6*); (gr. 2). spiral bd. (*0-616-01777-4*) Canadian National Institute for the Blind/Institut National Canadien pour les Aveugles.

—Poppleton. 1997. (Poppleton Ser.). (Illus.). (J). (gr. k-3). 56p. pap. 14.95 (*0-590-84782-1*); 72p. mass mkt. 3.99 (*0-590-84783-X*) Scholastic, Inc. (Blue Sky Pr., The).

—Poppleton. 1997. (Poppleton Ser.). (J). (gr. k-3). 10.14 (*0-606-11760-1*) Turtleback Bks.

—Poppleton & Friends. 1997. (Poppleton Ser.). (Illus.). (J). (ps-2). 56p. pap. 15.95 (*0-590-84786-4*); 48p. mass mkt. 3.99 (*0-590-84788-0*) Scholastic, Inc. (Blue Sky Pr., The).

—Poppleton & Friends. 1998. (Poppleton Ser.). (J). (gr. k-3). 10.14 (*0-606-13716-5*) Turtleback Bks.

—Poppleton Forever. 1998. (Poppleton Ser.). (Illus.). 56p. (J). (gr. k-3). pap. 15.95 (*0-590-84843-7*, Blue Sky Pr., The); mass mkt. 3.99 (*0-590-84844-5*) Scholastic, Inc.

—Poppleton Forever. 1998. (Poppleton Ser.). (J). (gr. k-3). 10.14 (*0-606-13718-1*) Turtleback Bks.

—Poppleton in Fall. 1999. (Poppleton Ser.). (Illus.). 56p. (J). (gr. k-3). pap. 15.95 (*0-590-84789-9*); mass mkt. 3.99 (*0-590-84794-5*) Scholastic, Inc. (Blue Sky Pr., The).

—Poppleton in Fall. 1999. (J). (gr. k-3). 10.14 (*0-606-17273-4*) Turtleback Bks.

—Poppleton in Winter. 2001. (Poppleton Ser.). (Illus.). 58p. (J). (ps-2). pap. 15.95 (*0-590-84837-2*, Blue Sky Pr., The) Scholastic, Inc.

Rylant, Cynthia & Teague, Mark, illus. Poppleton Through & Through. 2000. (Poppleton Ser.). 52p. (J). (gr. k-3). pap. 15.95 (*0-590-84839-9*) Scholastic, Inc.

Saal, Jocelyn. Running Mates. 1983. 199p. (gr. 6-10). pap. 2.25 o.p. (*0-553-17847-4*) Bantam Bks.

Sachar, Louis. The Boy Who Lost His Face. 1989. 192p. (J). (gr. 5-9). 12.99 o.s.i (*0-394-92863-6*, Knopf Bks. for Young Readers) Random Hse. Children's Bks.

—Holes, RS. 1998. 240p. (J). (gr. 4-7). 17.00 (*0-374-33265-7*, Farrar, Straus & Giroux (BYR)) Farrar, Straus & Giroux.

—Holes. 240p. (J). (gr. 4-6). pap. 5.99 (*0-8072-8073-9*, Listening Library) Random Hse. Audio Publishing Group.

—Holes. 2003. (Newbery Ser.). (Illus.). 240p. (gr. 5-6). reprint ed. pap. 6.50 (*0-440-41480-6*, Yearling) Random Hse. Children's Bks.

—Holes. l.t. ed. 1999. (Young Adult Ser.). 286p. (J). (gr. 7-12). 23.95 (*0-7862-2186-0*) Thorndike Pr.

—A Magic Crystal? Loehr, Mallory, ed. 2000. (Marvin Redpost Ser.: No. 8). (Illus.). 96p. (J). (ps-3). pap. 3.99 (*0-679-89002-5*, Random Hse. Bks. for Young Readers) Random Hse. Children's Bks.

—Marvin Redpost: Why Pick on Me? 1993. (First Stepping Stone Bks.). (J). 10.14 (*0-606-12417-9*) Turtleback Bks.

Sachar, Louis, et al. Best of Friends: Sixth Grade Can Really Kill You; Sixth Grade Sleepover; Sixth Grade Secrets; & A Really Popular Girl. 1989. (J). (gr. 2-6). 11.00 (*0-590-63454-2*) Scholastic, Inc.

Sachs, Elizabeth-Ann. I Love You, Janie Tannenbaum. 1990. Orig. Title: Where Are You, Cow Patty?. 160p. (J). (gr. 3-7). reprint ed. pap. 3.95 o.p. (*0-689-71390-8*, Aladdin) Simon & Schuster Children's Publishing.

—Kiss Me, Janie Tannenbaum. 1992. 144p. (J). (gr. 5-9). 13.95 o.s.i (*0-689-31664-X*, Atheneum) Simon & Schuster Children's Publishing.

—Where Are You, Cow Patty? 1984. 156p. (J). (gr. 5-8). 10.95 o.p. (*0-689-31057-9*, Atheneum) Simon & Schuster Children's Publishing.

Sachs, Marilyn. Amy & Laura. 1984. (Amy & Laura Bks.). (Illus.). 176p. (J). (gr. 4-6). pap. 2.50 o.p. (*0-590-40529-2*, Scholastic Paperbacks) Scholastic, Inc.

—Amy Moves In. 1984. pap. 1.95 o.p. (*0-590-33298-8*); 208p. (J). (gr. 4-6). pap. 2.50 o.p. (*0-590-41070-9*, Scholastic Paperbacks) Scholastic, Inc.

—Amy Moves In. 2002. 212p. (gr. 4-7). pap. 14.95 (*0-595-17589-9*, Backinprint.com) iUniverse, Inc.

—Beach Towels. 1982. (Skinny Bks.). (Illus.). 80p. (J). (gr. 7-11). 11.95 o.p. (*0-525-44003-8*, Dutton Children's Bks.) Penguin Putnam Bks. for Young Readers.

—Class Pictures. 1980. (J). (gr. 4-7). 13.95 o.p. (*0-525-27985-7*, Dutton Children's Bks.) Penguin Putnam Bks. for Young Readers.

—Fourteen. 1983. 128p. (J). (gr. 4-9). 10.95 o.p. (*0-525-44044-5*, Dutton Children's Bks.) Penguin Putnam Bks. for Young Readers.

—Hello Wrong Number. 1981. (Skinny Bks.). (Illus.). 112p. (J). (gr. 7-11). 10.95 o.p. (*0-525-31629-9*, Dutton) Dutton/Plume.

—Jojo & Winnie: Sister Stories. (Chapter Ser.). (Illus.). 80p. (J). 2001. (gr. 4-7). pap. 4.99 o.p. (*0-14-131113-4*, Puffin Bks.); 1999. (gr. 2-5). 14.99 (*0-525-46005-5*, Dutton Children's Bks.) Penguin Putnam Bks. for Young Readers.

—Jojo & Winnie: Sister Stories. 2001. (Illus.). (J). 11.14 (*0-606-21271-X*) Turtleback Bks.

—Laura's Luck. 1984. pap. 1.95 o.p. (*0-590-33299-6*); 224p. (J). (gr. 4-6). pap. 2.25 o.p. (*0-590-40375-3*, Scholastic Paperbacks); (J). (gr. 4-6). reprint ed. pap. 2.50 o.p. (*0-590-41073-3*) Scholastic, Inc.

—Laura's Luck. 2001. 224p. (gr. 4-7). per. 15.95 (*0-595-17590-2*, Backinprint.com) iUniverse, Inc.

—Matt's Mitt & Fleet-Footed Florence. 1989. (Illus.). 48p. (J). (gr. 2-5). 11.95 o.p. (*0-525-44450-5*, Dutton Children's Bks.) Penguin Putnam Bks. for Young Readers.

—Peter & Veronica. 1995. 160p. (J). (gr. 4-7). pap. 5.99 (*0-14-037082-X*, Puffin Bks.) Penguin Putnam Bks. for Young Readers.

—Peter & Veronica. 1995. (J). 11.04 (*0-606-08009-0*) Turtleback Bks.

—A Secret Friend. 1978. (gr. 4-7). 8.95 o.p. (*0-385-13569-6*); lib. bdg. 8.95 o.p. (*0-385-13570-X*) Doubleday Publishing.

—Thunderbird. 1985. (Skinny Bks.). (Illus.). 88p. (J). (gr. 7 up). 10.95 o.s.i (*0-525-44163-8*, 01063-320, Dutton Children's Bks.) Penguin Putnam Bks. for Young Readers.

Sadler, Marilyn. Bob 'n' John at Lake Kitty Paw-Paw. 1995. 7.45 o.p. (*0-606-07303-5*) Turtleback Bks.

—The Parakeet Girl. 1997. (Step into Reading Step 2 Bks.). (Illus.). 48p. (gr. 1-4). lib. bdg. 11.99 (*0-679-97289-7*); pap. 3.99 (*0-679-87289-2*) Random Hse. Children's Bks. (Random Hse. Bks. for Young Readers).

—P.J. The Spoiled Bunny. 1986. (Pictureback Ser.). (Illus.). 32p. (J). (ps-3). 6.99 o.s.i (*0-394-97245-7*); pap. 2.50 o.s.i (*0-394-87245-2*) Random Hse. Children's Bks. (Random Hse. Bks. for Young Readers).

Sage, Michael. One Good Friend. 2nd ed. 1999. iv, 126p. (YA). (gr. 7-12). reprint ed. pap. 10.00 (*0-9669813-0-8*) Sage, Joan.

Saint-Exupéry, Antoine de. Introducing The Little Prince: Gift Set. 2003. (Illus.). 12p. (J). bds. 12.95 (*0-15-204726-3*) Harcourt Trade Pubs.

Salassi, Otto R. Jimmy D. Sidewinder, & Me. 1987. (J). (gr. 5 up). 12.95 o.p. (*0-688-05237-1*, Greenwillow Bks.) HarperCollins Children's Bk. Group.

Salat, Cristina. Living in Secret. 3rd ed. 1999. 183p. (YA). (gr. 5-10). reprint ed. pap. 7.95 (*0-916020-02-9*) Books Marcus.

Salat, Cristina. Alias Diamond Jones. 1993. (Ghostwriter Ser.). (Illus.). 112p. (J). (gr. 4-6). pap. 3.50 o.s.i (*0-553-37216-5*) Bantam Bks.

—Living in Secret. 1994. 192p. (J). (gr. 4-7). pap. 3.99 o.s.i (*0-440-40950-0*) Dell Publishing.

Salem, Lynn & Stewart, Josie. Hope Not! 1993. (Illus.). 8p. (J). (gr. k-2). pap. 3.75 (*1-880612-04-6*) Seedling Pubns., Inc.

—Just Enough. 1992. (Illus.). 12p. (J). (gr. k-2). pap. 3.75 (*1-880612-12-7*) Seedling Pubns., Inc.

—Never Be. 1992. (Illus.). 8p. (J). (gr. k-2). pap. 3.75 (*1-880612-00-3*) Seedling Pubns., Inc.

Salisbury, Graham. Shark Bait. 1999. 160p. (YA). (gr. 5-9). mass mkt. 4.50 (*0-440-22803-4*, Dell Books for Young Readers) Random Hse. Children's Bks.

—Shark Bait. 1999. 10.55 (*0-606-16449-9*) Turtleback Bks.

Sallis, Susan. An Open Mind. 1978. (YA). (gr. 7 up). o.p. (*0-06-025162-X*); lib. bdg. 9.89 o.p. (*0-06-025163-8*) HarperCollins Children's Bk. Group.

Salmansohn, Karen. One Puppy, Three Tales Bk. 1: Alexandra Rambles On! 2002. (Alexandra Rambles on! Ser.: Bk. 1). (Illus.). 70p. (J). (gr. 4-6). 12.95 (*1-58246-044-2*) Tricycle Pr.

Salmansohn, Karen, et al. Crashed, Smashed & Mashed: One Puppy, Three Tales. 2003. (Alexandra Rambles on! Ser.). (Illus.). 32p. (J). (gr. 3-6). 14.95 (*1-58246-034-5*) Tricycle Pr.

Saltzberg, Barney. Hip, Hip, Hooray Day! 2002. (Hip & Hop Ser.). (Illus.). 40p. (J). (gr. k-3). 15.00 (*0-15-202495-6*, Gulliver Bks.) Harcourt Children's Bks.

Samton, Sheila White. Jenny's Journey. 1993. (Illus.). 32p. (J). (ps-3). pap. 4.99 o.s.i (*0-14-054308-2*, Puffin Bks.) Penguin Putnam Bks. for Young Readers.

—El Viaje de Jenny. 1993. Tr. of Jenny's Journey. (SPA., Illus.). 32p. (J). (ps-3). 14.99 o.s.i (*0-670-84843-3*, Viking Children's Bks.) Penguin Putnam Bks. for Young Readers.

Samuels, Barbara. Duncan & Dolores. (Illus.). 32p. (J). (ps-2). 1986. text 13.95 o.s.i (*0-02-778210-7*, Simon & Schuster Children's Publishing); 1989. reprint ed. pap. 4.99 (*0-689-71294-4*, Aladdin) Simon & Schuster Children's Publishing.

—Faye & Dolores. 1985. (Illus.). 40p. (J). (ps-2). lib. bdg. 13.95 o.s.i (*0-02-778120-8*, Simon & Schuster Children's Publishing) Simon & Schuster Children's Publishing.

Sanchez, Elaine K. & Hughes, Janee. How Francis Got His Wink. 2000. (Illus.). 40p. (J). 14.95 (*0-89802-737-3*) Beautiful America Publishing Co.

Sandburg, Carl. Rootabaga Stories, Pt. 1. 1988. (Illus.). 176p. (J). 19.95 (*0-15-269061-1*) Harcourt Trade Pubs.

Sander, Sonia. Tattle Tale. 2002. (Rainbow Fish Ser.). 32p. (J). (ps-2). pap. 3.99 (*0-694-52587-1*) HarperCollins Children's Bk. Group.

Sanders, Nancy I. My Book about Ben & Me. 1994. (J). pap. 3.99 o.s.i (*0-570-04773-0*, 56-1792) Concordia Publishing Hse.

—My Book about Sara & Me. 1994. 32p. pap. 3.99 o.s.i (*0-570-04774-9*, 56-1793) Concordia Publishing Hse.

Sanders, Nancy I. & Osborne, Susan Titus. The Super-Duper Seed Surprise. 2000. (Parables in Action Ser.: Vol. 6). (Illus.). 48p. (J). (ps-2). 4.99 (*0-570-07113-5*) Concordia Publishing Hse.

Sanschagrin, Joceline. Le Cercle des Magiciens. 2002. (Roman Jeunesse Ser.). (FRE., Illus.). 96p. (YA). (gr. 4-7). pap. 8.95 (*2-89021-334-X*) La Courte Echelle CAN. *Dist:* Firefly Bks., Ltd.

Santacruz, Daniel, tr. Mis Cinco Sentidos. 1995. (SPA., Illus.). 32p. (J). (ps-1). 14.95 o.p. (*0-06-025358-4*) HarperCollins Children's Bk. Group.

Santomero, Angela C. Blue's Felt Friends. 1998. (Blue's Clues Ser.). (Illus.). 20p. (J). (ps-k). bds. 4.99 (*0-689-81910-2*, Simon Spotlight/Nickelodeon) Simon & Schuster Children's Publishing.

Santomero, Angela C., et al. What to Do, Blue? 1999. (Blue's Clues Ser.). (Illus.). 24p. (J). (gr. k-3). pap. 3.50 (*0-689-83214-1*, Simon Spotlight/Nickelodeon) Simon & Schuster Children's Publishing.

Santucci, Barbara. Abby's Chairs. 2003. (Illus.). (J). (*0-8028-5205-X*, Eerdmans Bks For Young Readers) Eerdmans, William B. Publishing Co.

Sanvoisin, Eric. A Straw for Two. 2003. (Illus.). 48p. (gr. 3-7). pap. text 4.99 (*0-440-41665-5*) Bantam Dell Publishing Group.

Sara. The Rabbit, the Fox, & the Wolf. 1991. (Illus.). 32p. (J). (ps-2). 13.95 o.p. (*0-531-05953-7*); mass mkt. 13.99 o.p. (*0-531-08553-8*) Scholastic, Inc. (Orchard Bks.).

Sarfati, Sonia. Le Manuscrit Envole. 1999. (Roman Jeunesse Ser.). (Illus.). 96p. (YA). (gr. 4-7). pap. 8.95 (*2-89021-346-3*) La Courte Echelle CAN. *Dist:* Firefly Bks., Ltd.

Sargent, Dave. Best Friends. 1993. (Illus.). 40p. (J). pap. 6.00 (*1-56763-057-X*); lib. bdg. 17.25 (*1-56763-056-1*) Ozark Publishing.

—Me & Buck. Bowen, Debbie, ed. (Illus.). (J). (gr. k-8). pap. text 8.95 (*1-56763-070-7*); lib. bdg. 18.95 (*1-56763-069-3*) Ozark Publishing.

Sargent, Dave & Sargent, Pat. Ginny Giraffe, 60 vols. 2001. (Animal Pride Ser.: Vol. 46). 36p. (J). lib. bdg. 19.95 (*1-56763-533-4*) Ozark Publishing.

—Pal (palomino) Be Friendly #44. 2001. (Saddle Up Ser.). 36p. (J). pap. 6.95 (*1-56763-622-5*); lib. bdg. 22.60 (*1-56763-621-7*) Ozark Publishing.

Sargent, Dave, et al. Ginny Giraffe. 2000. (Illus.). (J). pap. 6.95 (*1-56763-534-2*) Ozark Publishing.

Sasso, Sandy Eisenberg. For Heaven's Sake. 1999. (Illus.). 32p. (J). (ps-3). 16.95 (*1-58023-054-7*) Jewish Lights Publishing.

Sateren, Shelley Swanson. Cat on a Hottie's Tin Roof. 2003. 208p. (gr. 3-7). text 14.95 (*0-385-73059-4*); lib. bdg. 16.99 (*0-385-90088-0*) Random Hse. Children's Bks. (Delacorte Bks. for Young Readers).

Sauer, I. Eve's Little Friends. 1981. (J). text 8.95 o.p. (*0-07-054830-7*) McGraw-Hill Cos., The.

Saul, Barbara. Jordy. 1992. (Illus.). 32p. (Orig.). (J). (gr. k-2). pap. 3.00 (*0-88092-026-2*) Royal Fireworks Publishing Co.

Saunders, Marshall. Beautiful Joe. 1999. (Illus.). 304p. (gr. 4-7). pap. 15.95 (*1-55709-307-5*) Applewood Bks.

Saunders, Susan. Great Kate. 1989. (Sleepover Friends Ser.: No. 19). (J). mass mkt. 2.50 o.p. (*0-590-42815-2*) Scholastic, Inc.

—Kate's Crush. 1989. (Sleepover Friends Ser.: No. 16). (J). mass mkt. 2.50 o.p. (*0-590-42366-5*) Scholastic, Inc.

—Kate's Sleepover Disaster. 1989. (Sleepover Friends Ser.: No. 12). (J). mass mkt. 2.50 o.p. (*0-590-41846-7*) Scholastic, Inc.

—Lauren I. 1990. (Sleepover Friends Ser.: No. 20). (J). mass mkt. 2.50 o.p. (*0-590-42816-0*) Scholastic, Inc.

—Lauren Takes Charge. 1989. (Sleepover Friends Ser.: No. 14). (J). mass mkt. 2.50 o.p. (*0-590-42300-2*) Scholastic, Inc.

—Lauren's Big Mix-Up. 1988. (Sleepover Friends Ser.: No. 5). 80p. (J). (gr. 3-7). mass mkt. 2.50 o.p. (*0-590-41336-8*, Scholastic Paperbacks) Scholastic, Inc.

—Lauren's New Friend. 1990. (Sleepover Friends Ser.: No. 24). (J). (gr. 5-7). mass mkt. 2.50 o.p. (*0-590-43194-3*) Scholastic, Inc.

—The New Kate, No. 26. 1990. (Sleepover Friends Ser.: 26). (J). mass mkt. 2.50 (*0-590-43192-7*) Scholastic, Inc.

—The New Stephanie. 1991. (Sleepover Friends Ser.: No. 35). (J). (gr. 4-7). mass mkt. 2.75 o.p. (*0-590-43924-3*) Scholastic, Inc.

—Patti's Last Sleepover?, No. 9. 1988. 96p. (J). (gr. 3-7). mass mkt. 2.50 o.p. (*0-590-41696-0*) Scholastic, Inc.

—Patti's Luck. 1987. (Sleepover Friends Ser.: No. 1). 96p. (J). (gr. 4-6). mass mkt. 2.50 o.p. (*0-590-40641-8*) Scholastic, Inc.

—The Sleepover Friends. 1989. (Sleepover Friends Ser.). (J). pap. 10.00 o.p. (*0-590-63339-2*) Scholastic, Inc.

—Starstruck Stephanie. 1990. (Sleepover Friends Ser.: No. 21). (J). mass mkt. 2.50 o.p. (*0-590-42817-9*) Scholastic, Inc.

—Stephanie. 1989. (Sleepover Friends Ser.: No. 18). (J). pap. 2.50 o.p. (*0-590-42814-4*) Scholastic, Inc.

—Stephanie's Big Story. 1989. (Sleepover Friends Ser.: No. 15). (J). mass mkt. 2.50 o.p. (*0-590-42299-5*) Scholastic, Inc.

—Stephanie's Family Secret. 1989. (Sleepover Friends Ser.: No. 11). (J). mass mkt. 2.50 o.p. (*0-590-41845-9*) Scholastic, Inc.

Savage, Cindy. Even Best Friends Say Goodbye. 1991. (Forever Friends Ser.: No. 8). 112p. (J). (gr. 4-6). pap. 2.75 o.p. (*0-87406-446-5*) Darby Creek Publishing.

—Friends Save the Day. 1989. (Forever Friends Ser.: No. 5). 125p. (Orig.). (J). (gr. 4-6). pap. text 2.75 o.p. (*0-87406-422-8*) Darby Creek Publishing.

—Friends to the Rescue. 1989. (Forever Friends Ser.). 111p. (J). (gr. 4-8). pap. 2.25 o.p. (*0-87406-380-9*) Darby Creek Publishing.

—Friendship Fever. 1991. (Forever Friends Ser.: No. 9). 128p. (J). (gr. 4-6). pap. 2.75 o.p. (*0-87406-587-9*) Darby Creek Publishing.

—Keeping Secrets, Keeping Friends. 1989. (Forever Friends Ser.: No. 3). 125p. (Orig.). (J). (gr. 4-6). pap. text 2.75 o.p. (*0-87406-413-9*) Darby Creek Publishing.

—Let's Be Friends Forever. 1989. 127p. (J). (gr. 3-8). pap. 2.25 o.p. (*0-87406-373-6*) Darby Creek Publishing.

—More Than Just a Friend. 1990. (Forever Friends Ser.). 112p. (Orig.). (J). (gr. 5-8). pap. 2.75 o.p. (*0-87406-447-3*) Darby Creek Publishing.

—New Friend Blues. 1989. (Forever Friends Ser.: No. 6). 128p. (J). (gr. 5-8). 2.75 o.p. (*0-87406-439-2*, 39-19334-2) Darby Creek Publishing.

Savitz, Harriet May. Girl's Best Friend. 1995. (J). mass mkt. 3.50 o.p. (*0-590-45708-X*) Scholastic, Inc.

Savoldi, Gloria R. Tennessee Boy. 1972. 160p. (J). (gr. 5 up). 4.75 o.p. (*0-664-32513-0*) Westminster John Knox Pr.

Sawyers, Anita M. The Two Friends. 1998. (J). pap. 6.95 o.p. (*0-533-12547-2*) Vantage Pr., Inc.

Saxon, Nancy. Panky & William. 1983. (Illus.). 104p. (J). (gr. 3-7). 10.95 o.s.i (*0-689-30997-X*, Atheneum) Simon & Schuster Children's Publishing.

Sayles, Rasheeda A. Rasheeda's Visitors. 1990. (J). 6.95 o.p. (*0-533-08920-4*) Vantage Pr., Inc.

Schaefer, Carole Lexa. Beeper's Friends. 2002. (Brand New Readers Ser.). (Illus.). 8p. (J). 12.99 (*0-7636-1243-X*); bds. 4.99 (*0-7636-1244-8*) Candlewick Pr.

Schaefer, Lola M. Where Once a Flower Bloomed. 2001. (J). lib. bdg. 15.89 (*0-688-17835-9*, Greenwillow Bks.) HarperCollins Children's Bk. Group.

Schami, Rafik. Alberto y Lila. Gambolini, Gerardo, tr. from GER. 2002. (SPA., Illus.). 32p. (J). (gr. k-3). 15.95 (*0-7358-1694-8*); pap. 6.95 (*0-7358-1695-6*) North-South Bks., Inc. (Ediciones Norte-Sur).

Schantz, Daniel D. Eddie Holds On. 1985. (Adventures with Eddie Ser.). 96p. (J). (gr. 4-7). 2.50 o.p. (*0-87239-922-2*, 2852) Standard Publishing.

—Eddie's Impossible Friend. 1985. (Adventures with Eddie Ser.). 96p. (J). (gr. 4-7). 2.50 o.p. (*0-87239-923-0*, 2853) Standard Publishing.

Schecter, Ellen. The Big Idea. 1996. (West Side Kids Ser.). 9.15 o.p. (*0-606-10037-7*) Turtleback Bks.

Scheer, Julian. By the Light of the Captured Moon. 2001. (Illus.). 32p. (J). (ps-3). tchr. ed. 16.95 (*0-8234-1624-0*) Holiday Hse., Inc.

Scheffler, Ursel. Who Has Time for Little Bear? 1998. (Illus.). 32p. (J). (ps-3). 13.95 (*0-385-32536-3*) Doubleday Publishing.

Schein, Jonah. Forget-Me-Not. 1988. (Illus.). 24p. (J). 12.95 o.p. (*1-55037-001-4*); pap. 4.95 o.p. (*1-55037-000-6*) Annick Pr., Ltd. CAN. *Dist:* Firefly Bks., Ltd.

Schenker, Dona. The Secret Circle. 1998. 176p. (J). (gr. 5-8). 16.00 o.s.i (*0-679-88989-2*, Knopf Bks. for Young Readers) Random Hse. Children's Bks.

Scherer, Catherine W. Simon & Barklee in England: Fun Book. Scherer, Catherine W., ed. 2001. (Another Country Calling Ser.). (Illus.). 32p. (J). (gr. 2-6). pap. 4.00 (*0-9704661-5-3*, Explorer Media) Simon & Barklee, Inc./ExplorerMedia.

—Simon & Barklee in France: Fun Book. 2001. (Another Country Calling Ser.). (Illus.). 32p. (J). (gr. 2-6). pap. 4.00 (*0-9704661-3-7*, Explorer Media) Simon & Barklee, Inc./ExplorerMedia.

Schiffer, Valerie. Instant Stationery. 1997. 64p. (J). mass mkt. 9.95 (*0-590-99624-X*) Scholastic, Inc.

Schipul, Martha. Philippa. 2000. 168p. E-Book 8.00 (*0-7388-7728-X*) Xlibris Corp.

Schneider, Meg F. The Practically Popular Crowd: Pretty Enough. 1992. 192p. (J). (gr. 4-6). mass mkt. 2.95 (*0-590-44804-8*, Scholastic Paperbacks) Scholastic, Inc.

—The Practically Popular Crowd: Wanting More. 1992. 176p. (J). (gr. 4-6). mass mkt. 2.95 o.p. (*0-590-44803-X*, Scholastic Paperbacks) Scholastic, Inc.

Schnur, Steven. Hannah & Cyclops. 2000. 108p. (gr. 4-7). pap. 9.95 (*0-595-00634-5*, Backinprint.com) iUniverse, Inc.

Scholastic, Inc. Staff. Jack & Jill. 2000. (Teletubbies Ser.). (Illus.). 22p. (J). (ps). bds. 3.99 (*0-439-06393-0*) Scholastic, Inc.

—Keroppi & Friends: The Best Friends Book. 1998. (Illus.). (J). (gr. 3-7). mass mkt. 3.50 (*0-590-55823-4*) Scholastic, Inc.

—Murphy & Myrtle Plush. 2002. pap. 27.99 (*0-439-30503-9*, Sidekicks) Scholastic, Inc.

—Pochacco & Friends: Silly Time Races. 1998. (Sanrio Ser.). (Illus.). 48p. (J). (gr. 2-5). 6.99 (*0-590-55825-0*, Cartwheel Bks.) Scholastic, Inc.

Schories, Pat. Dinner for One Is a Bore. 1993. (Illus.). 32p. (J). (ps-2). 7.95 o.p. (*1-56288-354-2*) Checkerboard Pr., Inc.

—Mouse Around, RS. 1993. (Illus.). 40p. (J). (ps-3). pap. 4.95 (*0-374-45414-0*, Sunburst) Farrar, Straus & Giroux.

Schorsch, Laurence. Mr. Boffin. 1993. (Illus.). 32p. (J). (gr. k-3). 6.95 (*1-56288-353-4*) Checkerboard Pr., Inc.

Schotter, Roni. Captain Snap & the Children of Vinegar Lane. 1989. (Illus.). 32p. (J). (ps-3). 15.95 o.p. (*0-531-05797-6*); mass mkt. 16.99 o.p. (*0-531-08397-7*) Scholastic, Inc. (Orchard Bks.).

—Captain Snap & the Children of Vinegar Lane. 1993. 12.10 (*0-606-05183-X*) Turtleback Bks.

—F Is for Freedom. 2000. (Illus.). 112p. (J). (gr. 2-5). pap. 15.99 (*0-7894-2641-2*, D K Ink) Dorling Kindersley Publishing, Inc.

—Northern Fried Chicken. 1983. (J). (gr. 6-9). 10.95 o.p. (*0-399-20920-4*, Philomel) Penguin Putnam Bks. for Young Readers.

—Rhoda, Straight & True. 1986. 192p. (J). (gr. 6 up). 11.95 o.p. (*0-688-06157-5*) HarperCollins Children's Bk. Group.

Schraff, Anne. Darkness. 2000. 119p. (J). (*0-7807-9367-6*); pap. (*0-7891-5183-9*) Perfection Learning Corp.

Schreiber, Anne. Brent's B-Day Party. 2000. (Scholastic At-Home Phonics Reading Program Ser.). (Illus.). 24p. (J). (*0-590-68837-5*) Scholastic, Inc.

Schroeder, Binette. Tuffa & Her Friends. 1983. (Very First Bks.). (Illus.). 12p. (J). (ps-2). 3.95 o.p. (*0-8037-9894-6*, 0383-120, Dial Bks. for Young Readers) Penguin Putnam Bks. for Young Readers.

Schubert, Ingrid & Schubert, Dieter. Beaver's Lodge. 2001. (Illus.). 40p. (J). (ps-3). 15.95 (*1-886910-68-5*) Front Street, Inc.

—Little Big Feet. 1990. (Illus.). 32p. (J). (ps-3). lib. bdg. 7.95 o.s.i (*0-87614-426-1*, Carolrhoda Bks.) Lerner Publishing Group.

—There's Always Room for One More. 2002. (Illus.). (J). (ps-1). 15.95 (*1-886910-77-4*, Front Street) Front Street, Inc.

Schulman, Janet. The Big Hello. 1976. (Greenwillow Read-Alone Bks.). (Illus.). (J). (gr. 1-4). 13.95 o.p. (*0-688-80036-X*, Greenwillow Bks.) HarperCollins Children's Bk. Group.

Schulte, Elaine L. Jess & the Fireplug. 1992. (Twelve Candles Club Ser.: Bk. 2). 128p. (Orig.). (J). (gr. 3-7). pap. 5.99 o.p. (*1-55661-251-6*) Bethany Hse. Pubs.

—Melanie & the Modeling Mess. 1994. (Twelve Candles Club Ser.: No. 5). 128p. (J). (gr. 3-7). pap. 5.99 o.p. (*1-55661-254-0*) Bethany Hse. Pubs.

Schultz, Betty K. Chooch. 1990. (Illus.). 64p. (J). (gr. k-3). 14.95 (*0-929568-00-1*) Raspberry Pr., Ltd.

—The Stairway from Here to There. 1995. (Illus.). 78p. (J). (gr. 5-6). 8.95 (*0-929568-03-6*) Raspberry Pr., Ltd.

Schulz, Charles M. Friends Forever, Snoopy. 2001. (Ready-to-Read Ser.). (Illus.). 32p. (J). pap. 3.99 (*0-689-84597-9*, Little Simon) Simon & Schuster Children's Publishing.

—It's Your First Kiss, Charlie Brown. 9999. (J). pap. 46.80 o.s.i (*0-590-09660-5*) Scholastic, Inc.

—Why, Charlie Brown, Why? A Story about What Happens When a Friend is Very Ill. 2002. (Illus.). 64p. 15.95 (*0-345-45531-2*) Random Hse., Inc.

—You're the Greatest, Charlie Brown: Selected Cartoons from "As You Like It, Charlie Brown" 9999. (J). pap. 1.95 o.s.i (*0-590-72029-5*) Scholastic, Inc.

—You're the Greatest, Charlie Brown: Selected Cartoons from "As You Like It, Charlie Brown" Scholastic, Inc. Staff, ed. 9999. (J). pap. 29.25 o.s.i (*0-590-39523-8*) Scholastic, Inc.

Schulz, Charles M. & Fontes, Justine. Snoopy's a Little Help from My Friend. 1987. (Golden Friendly Bks.). (Illus.). 32p. (J). (gr. 3-6). o.p. (*0-307-10911-9*, Golden Bks.) Random Hse. Children's Bks.

Schumacher, Claire. Alto & Tango. 1984. 32p. (J). (ps-1). lib. bdg. 11.88 o.p. (*0-688-02740-7*, Morrow, William & Co.) Morrow/Avon.

Schumacher, Julie. Grass Angel. 2004. 144p. lib. bdg. 17.99 (*0-385-90163-1*, Delacorte Pr.) Dell Publishing.

Schurr, Cathleen. The Shy Little Kitten. 1999. (Little Golden Bks.). (Illus.). 24p. (ps-2). 2.99 (*0-307-00145-8*, 98103, Golden Bks.) Random Hse. Children's Bks.

Schwandt, Stephen. Holding Steady. ERS. 1988. 160p. (YA). (gr. 6 up). 13.95 o.p. (*0-8050-0575-7*, Holt, Henry & Co. Bks. For Young Readers) Holt, Henry & Co.

—Holding Steady. 1990. 176p. (J). pap. 2.95 (*0-380-70754-3*, Avon Bks.) Morrow/Avon.

Schwartz, Amy. Camper of the Week. 1991. (Illus.). 32p. (J). (gr. k-2). 15.95 o.p. (*0-531-05942-1*); mass mkt. 16.99 o.p. (*0-531-08542-2*) Scholastic, Inc. (Orchard Bks.).

—Her Majesty, Aunt Bessie. 1986. (Picture Puffin Ser.). 32p. (J). (ps-3). pap. 3.95 o.p. (*0-14-050570-9*, Puffin Bks.) Penguin Putnam Bks. for Young Readers.

—Oma & Bobo. (Illus.). 32p. (J). (ps-2). 1998. pap. 5.99 (*0-689-82115-8*, Aladdin); 1987. text 14.95 o.s.i (*0-02-781500-5*, Atheneum/Richard Jackson Bks.) Simon & Schuster Children's Publishing.

Schwartz, Harriet B. Backstage with Clawdio. 1993. (Illus.). 40p. (J). (ps-4). 15.00 o.s.i (*0-679-81763-8*, Knopf Bks. for Young Readers) Random Hse. Children's Bks.

Schwartz, Joel L. Best Friends Don't Come in Threes. 1985. (Illus.). 126p. (J). (gr. 4-6). pap. 2.50 o.s.i (*0-440-40603-X*, Yearling) Random Hse. Children's Bks.

—Upchuck Summer. 9999. (Illus.). 144p. (J). (gr. 4-8). 9.95 o.s.i (*0-440-09264-7*); lib. bdg. 9.89 o.s.i (*0-440-09269-8*) Dell Publishing. (Delacorte Pr.).

—Upchuck Summer's Revenge. 1991. 176p. (J). (gr. 4-7). pap. 3.50 o.s.i (*0-440-40471-1*) Dell Publishing.

Schwartz, Linda. From Me to You. 1994. (Illus.). 32p. (J). (gr. 1-6). pap. 4.95 o.p. (*0-88160-237-X*, LW332) Creative Teaching Pr., Inc.

—How Can You Help? 1994. (Illus.). 184p. (J). (gr. 4-8). pap. 9.95 o.p. (*0-88160-213-2*, LW207) Creative Teaching Pr., Inc.

Schwartz, Sara. Head Trips. 1994. 8p. (J). (ps-3). 11.95 o.p. (*1-55550-884-7*) Universe Publishing.

Schwemm, Diane. Behind His Back. 1999. (Love Stories Ser.). 192p. (gr. 7-12). mass mkt. 3.99 o.s.i (*0-553-49291-8*, Dell Books for Young Readers) Random Hse. Children's Bks.

Schwiebert, Pat & DeKlyen, Chuck. Tear Soup: A Recipe for Healing after Loss. 2nd l.t. rev. ed. 1999. (Illus.). 56p. reprint ed. pap. 19.95 (*0-9615197-6-2*) Perinatal Loss.

Scieszka, Jon. El Cuento Verdadero de los Tres Cerditos! 1991. (SPA., Illus.). 32p. (J). (gr. k-3). 16.99 (*0-670-84162-5*, VK4318, Viking Children's Bks.) Penguin Putnam Bks. for Young Readers.

Scorcia, Yvonne. Joey's Big Adventure. 2001. 56p. pap. 9.00 (*0-8059-5485-6*) Dorrance Publishing Co., Inc.

Scott, Ann Herbert. Hi. 1997. (Illus.). 32p. (J). (ps-1). pap. 5.95 o.s.i (*0-698-11446-9*, PaperStar) Penguin Putnam Bks. for Young Readers.

Scott, C. Anne. Lizard Meets Ivana the Terrible, ERS. 1999. (Illus.). 128p. (J). (gr. 4-7). 15.95 o.s.i (*0-8050-6093-6*, Holt, Henry & Co. Bks. For Young Readers) Holt, Henry & Co.

Scott, C. Anne & Roth, Stephanie. Lizard Meets Ivana the Terrible. 2001. 128p. (J). mass mkt. 3.99 (*0-439-21999-X*, Scholastic Paperbacks) Scholastic, Inc.

Scott, Carlton T. Little Big Wolf. 1999. (Illus.). 32p. (J). (gr. k-5). 9.95 (*0-9636652-8-6*) Ends of the Earth Books.com.

Scott, Elaine. Friends. 2000. (Illus.). 40p. (J). (ps-3). 16.00 (*0-689-82105-0*, Atheneum) Simon & Schuster Children's Publishing.

Scott, Sally. The Three Wonderful Beggars. 1988. (Illus.). 30p. (J). (gr. k-3). reprint ed. 13.00 o.p. (*0-688-06656-9*); lib. bdg. 12.88 o.p. (*0-688-06657-7*) HarperCollins Children's Bk. Group. (Greenwillow Bks.).

Scribner, Virginia. Gopher Draws Conclusions. 1994. (Illus.). 160p. (J). (gr. 3-7). 13.99 o.p. (*0-670-85660-6*, Viking Children's Bks.) Penguin Putnam Bks. for Young Readers.

—Gopher Draws Conclusions. 1999. (J). pap. 3.99 (*0-14-037749-2*) Viking Penguin.

Seabrook, Elizabeth. Cabbages & Kings. 1997. (Illus.). 32p. (J). (ps-3). 16.99 o.s.i (*0-670-87462-0*) Penguin Putnam Bks. for Young Readers.

Seabrooke, Brenda. Jerry on the Line. 1992. 128p. (J). (gr. 3-7). pap. 3.99 o.p. (*0-14-034868-9*, Puffin Bks.) Penguin Putnam Bks. for Young Readers.

—Jerry on the Line. 1990. 128p. (J). (gr. 3-5). lib. bdg. 13.95 o.p. (*0-02-781432-7*, Simon & Schuster Children's Publishing) Simon & Schuster Children's Publishing.

Seagrove, John K. My Friend Josh. 1997. 54p. (YA). (gr. 12). per. 12.00 (*0-9647633-3-8*) Kendall Publishing.

SeaStar Publishing Staff. Friendship Stories You Can Share. 2001. (Reading Rainbow Readers Ser.). (Illus.). (J). 10.14 (*0-606-21202-7*) Turtleback Bks.

Sebestyen, Ouida. IOU's. 1982. 192p. (J). (gr. 7). 14.95 o.s.i (*0-316-77933-4*, Joy Street Bks.) Little Brown & Co.

—IOU's. 1986. (YA). (gr. 7 up). mass mkt. 2.75 o.s.i (*0-440-93986-0*, Laurel Leaf) Random Hse. Children's Bks.

Selway, Martina. Greedyguts. 1994. (Illus.). 32p. (J). (ps-2). o.p. (*0-09-174151-3*) Random Hse. of Canada, Ltd. CAN. *Dist:* Random Hse., Inc.

Selway, Martina, illus. Fred's Cold. 1999. (J). (*0-7608-3192-0*) Sundance Publishing.

Sempe, Goscinny. Joachim a des Ennuis. 1997. (FRE.). (gr. 4-7). pap. (*2-07-051341-6*) Gallimard, Editions.

Sendak, Maurice. Very Far Away. (Sendak Reissues Ser.). (J). 2004. 56p. 15.95 (*0-06-029723-9*); 2003. 64p. 17.89 (*0-06-029724-7*) HarperCollins Pubs.

—We Are All in the Dumps with Jack & Guy. 1998. (Illus.). 54p. (J). (gr. 4-7). pap. text 20.00 (*0-7881-5645-4*) DIANE Publishing Co.

Sendak, Maurice, illus. Little Bear's Friend. 2002. (Little Bear Ser.). (J). 12.34 (*0-7587-6185-6*) Book Wholesalers, Inc.

Sendak, Maurice & Minarik, Else Holmelund. Little Bear's Friend. 1960. (I Can Read Bks.). (Illus.). 64p. (J). (gr. k-3). 15.95 (*0-06-024255-8*) HarperCollins Children's Bk. Group.

Seredy, Kate. Good Master. 1986. (Puffin Newbery Library). 11.04 (*0-606-00884-5*) Turtleback Bks.

Sesame Street Side Kick. 1994. (J). 77.88 (*0-676-73298-4*) Random Hse., Inc.

Sesame Street Staff. Wait for Elmo. 1998. (J). (ps-3). 7.99 (*0-679-99190-5*, Random Hse. Bks. for Young Readers) Random Hse. Children's Bks.

Seuling, Barbara. Robert & the Great Escape. 2003. (Illus.). 120p. (J). 15.95 (*0-8126-2700-8*) Cricket Bks.

Seuss, Dr. Horton & Friends. 1998. 80p. (J). (ps-3). pap. 2.75 o.s.i (*0-679-89176-5*, Random Hse. Bks. for Young Readers) Random Hse. Children's Bks.

Sevela, Ephraim. Why There Is No Heaven on Earth. Lourie, Richard, tr. 1982. (RUS.). 224p. (YA). (gr. 7 up). o.p. (*0-06-025502-1*); lib. bdg. 10.89 o.p. (*0-06-025503-X*) HarperCollins Children's Bk. Group.

Seymour, Tres. The Revelation of Saint Bruce. 1998. 128p. (YA). (gr. 7 up). lib. bdg. 17.99 o.p. (*0-531-33109-1*); (Illus.). pap. 16.95 (*0-531-30109-5*) Scholastic, Inc. (Orchard Bks.).

Sfar, Joann. Little Vampire Goes to School. Siegel, Mark & Siegel, Alexis, trs. from FRE. 2003. (Illus.). 40p. (J). 12.95 (*0-689-85717-9*, Simon & Schuster Children's Publishing) Simon & Schuster Children's Publishing.

Sh... Sh... Sh... No Talking! 1999. (Tami & Moishy Ser.: Vol. 6). bds. 6.95 (*0-87306-967-6*) Feldheim, Philipp Inc.

Shahan, Sherry. Operation Dump the Boyfriend. 1988. (Treetop Tales Ser.). (Illus.). 96p. (J). (gr. 3-6). 1.00 o.p. (*0-87406-287-X*, 22-15397-9) Darby Creek Publishing.

Shalant, Phyllis. The Transformation of Faith Futterman. (J). 1992. 144p. (gr. 3-7). pap. 3.99 o.p. (*0-14-036026-3*, Puffin Bks.); 1990. 14p. (gr. 5 up). 13.95 o.p. (*0-525-44570-6*, Dutton Children's Bks.) Penguin Putnam Bks. for Young Readers.

—When Pirates Came to Brooklyn. 2002. 176p. (J). (gr. 4-7). 16.99 (*0-525-46920-6*, Dutton Children's Bks.) Penguin Putnam Bks. for Young Readers.

Shan, Darren. Cirque du Freak: A Living Nightmare. l.t. ed. 2001. 253p. (J). 24.95 (*0-7862-3733-3*) Thorndike Pr.

—A Living Nightmare. 2001. (Saga of Darren Shan Ser.: Bk. 1). (gr. 5 up). (Illus.). viii, 279p. (YA). pap. (*0-316-64852-3*);Bk. 1. 272p. (J). 15.95 (*0-316-60340-6*) Little Brown Children's Bks.

Shannon, George. Heart to Heart. 1995. (Illus.). 32p. (J). (ps-3). tchr. ed. 15.00 (*0-395-72773-1*) Houghton Mifflin Co.

—Seeds. 1994. (Illus.). 32p. (J). (ps-3). tchr. ed. 13.95 o.p. (*0-395-66990-1*) Houghton Mifflin Co.

Shannon, Jacqueline. I Hate My Hero. 1992. (J). (gr. 4-7). pap. 13.00 o.s.i (*0-671-75442-4*, Simon & Schuster Children's Publishing) Simon & Schuster Children's Publishing.

—It's in Your Hands, Daisy P. Duckwitz. 1998. (J). (gr. 4-6). pap. 3.99 (*0-380-78769-5*, Avon Bks.) Morrow/Avon.

—It's in Your Hands, Daisy P. Duckwitz. 1998. 10.04 (*0-606-13531-6*) Turtleback Bks.

—Too Much T. J. 1988. (J). (gr. k-12). mass mkt. 2.95 o.s.i (*0-440-20222-1*, Laurel Leaf) Random Hse. Children's Bks.

Shapshot Staff. Who's My Friend? Big Board. 1994. (Big Board Books Ser.). (Illus.). 10p. (J). (ps). bds. 4.95 o.p. (*1-56458-736-3*) Dorling Kindersley Publishing, Inc.

Sharing. 1983. 2.95 o.p. (*0-86112-041-8*) Brimax Bks., Ltd.

Sharmat, Marjorie Weinman. For Members Only. 1986. (Sorority Sisters Ser.: No. 1). (YA). (gr. 5 up). mass mkt. 2.50 o.s.i (*0-440-92654-8*, Laurel Leaf) Random Hse. Children's Bks.

—Getting Something on Maggie Marmelstein. 1971. (Illus.). (J). 110p. (gr. 4-6). 14.89 o.p. (*0-06-025551-X*); 112p. (ps-3). lib. bdg. 15.89 (*0-06-025552-8*) HarperCollins Children's Bk. Group.

—Getting Something on Maggie Marmelstein. 1973. (Trophy Bk.). (Illus.). (J). (gr. 3-7). pap. 3.50 o.p. (*0-06-440038-7*, Harper Trophy) HarperCollins Children's Bk. Group.

—Gladys Told Me to Meet Her Here. 1970. (Illus.). 32p. (J). (ps-3). lib. bdg. 13.89 o.p. (*0-06-025550-1*) HarperCollins Children's Bk. Group.

—How to Meet a Gorgeous Guy. 1983. 160p. (J). (gr. 7 up). mass mkt. 2.95 o.s.i (*0-440-93553-9*, Laurel Leaf) Random Hse. Children's Bks.

—I Saw Him First. 1983. (Young Love Romance Ser.). 192p. (YA). (gr. 7 up). mass mkt. 2.25 o.s.i (*0-440-94009-5*, Laurel Leaf) Random Hse. Children's Bks.

—I'm Not Oscar's Friend Anymore. 1975. (J). (gr. k-2). 9.95 o.p. (*0-525-32537-9*, 0966-290, Dutton) Dutton/Plume.

—Mooch the Messy Meets Prudence the Neat. 1979. (Break-of-Day Bks.). (Illus.). (J). (gr. 1-3). 6.99 o.p. (*0-698-30703-8*, Coward-McCann) Putnam Publishing Group, The.

—Richie & the Fritzes. 1997. (Trophy Chapter Bks.). Orig. Title: Chasing after Annie. (Illus.). 80p. (J). (gr. 3-6). pap. 3.95 o.p. (*0-06-442055-8*, Harper Trophy) HarperCollins Children's Bk. Group.

—Richie & the Fritzes. 1997. (Trophy Chapter Bks.). Orig. Title: Chasing after Annie. 9.15 o.p. (*0-606-11797-0*) Turtleback Bks.

—Say Hello, Vanessa. 1979. (Illus.). 32p. (J). (gr. k-3). 7.95 o.p. (*0-8234-0354-8*) Holiday Hse., Inc.

—The Three Hundred Twenty-Ninth Friend. 1984. (Illus.). 48p. (J). (gr. k-3). 9.95 o.p. (*0-02-782260-5*, Simon & Schuster Children's Publishing) Simon & Schuster Children's Publishing.

—Tiffany Dino Works Out. 1995. (Illus.). 32p. (J). (ps-4). per. 15.00 (*0-689-80309-5*, Simon & Schuster Children's Publishing) Simon & Schuster Children's Publishing.

Sharp, Donna. The Names Still Charlie. 1993. (Illus.). 320p. (YA). pap. 16.95 (*0-7022-2471-5*) Univ. of Queensland Pr. AUS. *Dist:* International Specialized Bk. Services.

Sharpe, Susan. Real Friends. 1994. 144p. (J). lib. bdg. 14.95 o.s.i (*0-02-782352-0*, Simon & Schuster Children's Publishing) Simon & Schuster Children's Publishing.

—Spirit Quest. 1993. 128p. (J). (gr. 4-7). pap. 4.99 o.s.i (*0-14-036282-7*, Puffin Bks.) Penguin Putnam Bks. for Young Readers.

—Spirit Quest. 1991. (Illus.). 128p. (J). (gr. 4-6). lib. bdg. 13.95 (*0-02-782355-5*, Simon & Schuster Children's Publishing) Simon & Schuster Children's Publishing.

—Spirit Quest. 1993. 11.04 (*0-606-02904-4*) Turtleback Bks.

Shaw, Janet Beeler. Kaya & Lone Dog: A Friendship Story. 2002. (American Girls Collection: Bk. 4). (Illus.). 96p. (J). (gr. 2-7). 12.95 (*1-58485-430-8*); pap. 5.95 (*1-58485-429-4*) Pleasant Co. Pubns. (American Girl).

—Kirsten & the New Girl. 2000. (American Girls Short Stories Ser.). (Illus.). 56p. (YA). (gr. 2 up). 3.95 (*1-58485-034-5*, American Girl) Pleasant Co. Pubns.

—Kirsten on the Trail. 1999. (American Girls Short Stories Ser.). (Illus.). 56p. (YA). (gr. 2 up). 3.95 (*1-56247-764-1*, American Girl) Pleasant Co. Pubns.

Shaw, Mary. Pierre & Sophia: A True Tale. 2000. (ENG & FRE., Illus.). 44p. (J). (ps-4). 18.50 (*0-9705404-0-X*) Criqueville Pr.

Shealy, Dennis R. Going Buggy. 2002. (Illus.). 24p. (J). pap. 3.25 (*0-7364-1173-9*, RH/Disney) Random Hse. Children's Bks.

Shearer, A. Wilmot & Chips. 167p. pap. 7.50 (*0-340-80557-9*); (J). mass mkt. 8.95 (*0-340-72740-3*) Hodder & Stoughton, Ltd. GBR. *Dist:* Trafalgar Square, Lubrecht & Cramer, Ltd., Trafalgar Square.

—Wilmot & the Pops. (Illus.). 184p. (J). mass mkt. 8.95 (*0-340-71641-X*) Hodder & Stoughton, Ltd. GBR. *Dist:* Lubrecht & Cramer, Ltd., Trafalgar Square.

Shecter, Ben. Molly Patch & Her Animal Friends. 1975. (Illus.). 64p. (J). (ps-3). lib. bdg. 8.89 o.p. (*0-06-025589-7*) HarperCollins Pubs.

—The Toughest & Meanest Kid on the Block. 1973. (Illus.). 32p. (J). (ps-3). 4.69 o.p. (*0-399-60797-8*) Putnam Publishing Group, The.

Shelton, Rick. Hoggle's Christmas. 1993. (Illus.). 80p. (J). (gr. 2-6). 12.99 o.p. (*0-525-65129-2*, Dutton Children's Bks.) Penguin Putnam Bks. for Young Readers.

Sherman, Eileen. Victor's Place. 1989. (Illus.). 598p. (Orig.). (YA). (gr. 10-12). pap. (*0-9604382-2-X*) Cornerstone Pr.

Sherman, Jane. Clean Clothes for Oliver. 2001. (Illus.). 14p. (J). (ps-3). 12.99 o.p. (*0-8431-7561-3*, Price Stern Sloan) Penguin Putnam Bks. for Young Readers.

Sherrow, Victoria. Wilbur Waits. 1990. (Illus.). 32p. (J). (ps-3). 13.95 (*0-06-025483-1*); lib. bdg. 13.89 o.p. (*0-06-025484-X*) HarperCollins Children's Bk. Group.

Sherwood, Barbara B. Jan & Ann & the Pet Rabbit. 1998. (Illus.). 16p. (J). (ps). pap. 5.95 (*1-891846-03-5*) Business Word, The.

Shi, Sharon. Girlfriends. rev. ed. 2000. (Illus.). 15p. (J). (ps-2). pap. 4.99 (*0-9678636-5-1*, B006, Tattootles Bks.) Tattoo Manufacturing.

—Wonderful Things. rev. ed. 2000. (Illus.). 23p. (J). (ps-2). pap. 4.99 (*0-9678636-1-9*, B002, Tattootles Bks.) Tattoo Manufacturing.

Shine, Deborah. The Race. 1992. (Whole-Language Big Bks.). 16p. (J). (ps-2). pap. 16.95 (*1-56784-051-5*) Newbridge Educational Publishing.

Shinhav, Chaya. Adios, Berry. Writer, C. C. & Nielsen, Lisa C., trs. 1992. (Hippy Ser.). (SPA., Illus.). 24p. (Orig.). (J). (ps). pap. text 3.00 o.s.i (*1-56134-154-1*, McGraw-Hill/Dushkin) McGraw-Hill Higher Education.

—Goodbye, Berry. Kriss, David, tr. from HEB. 2nd ed. 1992. (Hippy Ser.). (Illus.). 24p. (Orig.). (J). (ps). pap. text 3.00 o.s.i (*1-56134-144-4*, McGraw-Hill/Dushkin) McGraw-Hill Higher Education.

Shleifer, Mark. Mike & Nick. 1999. (J). pap. 7.95 o.p. (*0-533-12913-3*) Vantage Pr., Inc.

Shoup, Barbara. Stranded in Harmony. 2001. 194p. (YA). pap. 15.95 (*1-57860-094-4*) Emmis Bks.

—Stranded in Harmony. 1997. 192p. (YA). (gr. 7 up). 17.95 (*0-7868-0287-1*); lib. bdg. 18.49 (*0-7868-2284-8*) Hyperion Bks. for Children.

Shreve, Susan Richards. A Country of Strangers. 1990. 240p. (YA). pap. 9.95 o.s.i (*0-385-26775-4*) Doubleday Publishing.

—The Gift of the Girl Who Couldn't Hear. 1993. 80p. (J). (gr. 5 up). 4.95 (*0-688-11694-9*, Harper Trophy) HarperCollins Children's Bk. Group.

—The Gift of the Girl Who Couldn't Hear. 1991. 80p. (J). (gr. 3 up). 16.00 o.p. (*0-688-10318-9*, Morrow, William & Co.) Morrow/Avon.

—Gift of the Girl Who Couldn't Hear. 1993. (J). 11.10 (*0-606-05844-3*) Turtleback Bks.

—Goodbye, Amanda the Good. 144p. (gr. 5-9). 2002. pap. text 4.99 (*0-440-41646-9*, Yearling); 2000. (YA). lib. bdg. 18.99 (*0-679-99241-3*, Random Hse. Bks. for Young Readers) Random Hse. Children's Bks.

—Trout & Me. 2002. (Illus.). 144p. (J). (gr. 4-8). 15.95 (*0-375-81219-9*); lib. bdg. 17.99 (*0-375-91219-3*) Random Hse. Children's Bks. (Knopf Bks. for Young Readers).

—Wait for Me. Cohn, Amy, ed. 1994. (Illus.). 96p. (J). (gr. 4 up). reprint ed. pap. 4.95 o.p. (*0-688-13622-2*, Morrow, William & Co.) Morrow/Avon.

—Zoe & Columbo. 1995. (Illus.). 96p. (J). (gr. 3-4). 15.00 o.p. (*0-688-13552-8*, Morrow, William & Co.) Morrow/Avon.

Shriver, Maria. What's Wrong with Timmy? 2001. (Illus.). 48p. (J). (ps-3). 14.95 (*0-316-23337-4*) Little Brown Children's Bks.

Shua, Ana María. La Puerta para Salir del Mundo. 2002. (SPA.). 64p. pap. 6.95 (*1-4000-0059-9*) Random Hse., Inc.

Shub, Elizabeth. Seeing Is Believing. 1994. (Illus.). 64p. (J). 14.00 o.s.i (*0-688-13647-8*, Greenwillow Bks.) HarperCollins Children's Bk. Group.

Shulman, Dee. The Visit. 1992. (Illus.). 32p. (J). (ps-1). o.p. (*0-370-31584-7*) Random Hse., Inc.

Shura, Mary Francis. Don't Call Me Toad! 1988. 128p. (J). pap. 2.95 (*0-380-70496-X*, Avon Bks.) Morrow/Avon.

Shurfranz, Vivian. Different Kind of Friend. 1990. (J). mass mkt. 2.75 o.p. (*0-590-42878-0*) Scholastic, Inc.

Shusterman, Neal. Downsiders. l.t. ed. 2000. 336p. (YA). (gr. 6-12). lib. bdg. 29.95 (*1-58118-071-3*) LRS.

—Downsiders. 256p. 2001. (J). (gr. 8-12). mass mkt. 4.99 (*0-689-83969-3*, Simon Pulse); 1999. (Illus.). (YA). (gr. 5-9). 16.95 (*0-689-80375-3*, Simon & Schuster Children's Publishing) Simon & Schuster Children's Publishing.

Sibley, Brian. Great Food Fend. 1994. 40p. (J). (gr. 4-7). 12.95 (*0-7459-2461-1*) Lion Publishing.

Siconolfi, Theresa. Carlyle's Backyard Adventures No. I: Coloring Storybook. Williams, Susan, ed. & illus. by. l.t. ed. 1997. 32p. (J). (ps-2). spiral bd. 6.95 (*0-9660252-0-2*) Mi Tes Su, Inc.

Siebert, Diane. Heartland. 1999. (Trophy Picture Bk.). (Illus.). 32p. (J). (ps-3). pap. 6.95 (*0-06-443287-4*, Harper Trophy) HarperCollins Children's Bk. Group.

Siegel, Beatrice. The Basket Maker & the Spinner. 1987. 64p. (J). (gr. 3 up). 10.95 o.p. (*0-8027-6694-3*); lib. bdg. 11.85 o.p. (*0-8027-6695-1*) Walker & Co.

Siegenthaler, Rolf. Never Fear, Snake My Dear! James, J. Alison, tr. from GER. 1999. (Illus.). 32p. (J). (gr. k-3). 15.95 o.p. (*0-7358-1103-2*) North-South Bks., Inc.

—Seamos Valientes, Querida Serpiente! Secreto, Angel, tr. from GER. 2001. (SPA., Illus.). 32p. (J). (gr. k-3). pap. 6.95 (*0-7358-1495-3*, NS30717, Ediciones Norte-Sur) North-South Bks., Inc.

Siegenthaler, Rolf & Secreto, Angel. Seamos Valientes, Querida Serpiente! 2001. (SPA., Illus.). 32p. (J). (gr. k-3). 15.95 (*0-7358-1494-5*, NS30718, Ediciones Norte-Sur) North-South Bks., Inc.

Siegenthaler, Rolf, et al. Never Fear, Snake My Dear! James, J. Alison, tr. from GER. 1999. (Illus.). 32p. (J). (gr. k-3). 16.50 o.p. (*0-7358-1104-0*) North-South Bks., Inc.

Silbert, Linda P. & Silbert, Alvin J. Agnes' Cardboard Piano. 1978. (Little Twirps Understanding People Bks.). (Illus.). (J). (gr. k-4). pap. 4.98 (*0-89544-054-7*) Silbert & Bress Pubns.

—I'll Be Your Best Friend. 1978. (Little Twirps Understanding People Bks.). (Illus.). (J). (gr. k-4). pap. 4.98 (*0-89544-056-3*) Silbert & Bress Pubns.

—Lost in the Cave. 1978. (Little Twirps Understanding People Bks.). (Illus.). (J). (gr. k-4). pap. 4.98 (*0-89544-057-1*) Silbert & Bress Pubns.

—Penelope's Pen Pal. 1978. (Little Twirps Understanding People Bks.). (Illus.). (J). (gr. k-4). pap. 4.98 (*0-89544-053-9*) Silbert & Bress Pubns.

—Tiger, Take off Your Hat. 1978. (Little Twirps Understanding People Bks.). (Illus.). (J). (gr. k-4). pap. 4.98 (*0-89544-051-2*) Silbert & Bress Pubns.

—Tuffy's Bike Race. 1978. (Little Twirps Understanding People Bks.). (Illus.). (J). (gr. k-4). pap. 4.98 (*0-89544-058-X*) Silbert & Bress Pubns.

—Tyrone Goes Camping. 1978. (Little Twirps Understanding People Bks.). (Illus.). (J). (gr. k-4). pap. 4.98 (*0-89544-055-5*) Silbert & Bress Pubns.

—Whitney's New Glasses. 1978. (Little Twirps Understanding People Bks.). (Illus.). (J). (gr. k-4). pap. 4.98 (*0-89544-052-0*) Silbert & Bress Pubns.

Silk, Courtney. Best Buds. 2003. (Illus.). 32p. (J). (ps-3). pap. 3.99 (*0-307-10586-5*, Golden Bks.) Random Hse. Children's Bks.

—Letter Lookout. 2003. (Illus.). 32p. (J). (ps-3). pap. 3.99 (*0-7364-1184-4*, RH/Disney) Random Hse. Children's Bks.

Silver, Jody. Rupert, Polly & Daisy. 1994. (Illus.). 48p. (J). (gr. 1 up). lib. bdg. 19.93 o.p. (*0-8368-0994-7*) Stevens, Gareth Inc.

Silverman, Maida. The Get along Gang & the Bad Loser. 1984. (Get along Gang Ser.). (Illus.). 32p. (Orig.). (J). (ps-2). pap. 1.95 o.p. (*0-590-40196-3*) Scholastic, Inc.

Silverstein, Shel. Who Wants a Cheap Rhinoceros? (Illus.). (J). (ps-3). 2002. 64p. 17.95 (*0-689-85113-8*); 1983. 56p. 17.00 (*0-02-782690-2*) Simon & Schuster Children's Publishing. (Simon & Schuster Children's Publishing).

Silverthorne, Sandy. Marpel is Stuck! And Other Really Good Reasons to Forgive. (Kirkland Street Kids Ser.). (Illus.). 32p. (J). (ps-2). 10.99 o.p. (*0-7814-3241-3*) Cook Communications Ministries.

Simard, Remy. Monsieur Iletaitunefois. 1998. (Illus.). (J). (ps-3). pap. 6.95 (*1-55037-544-X*); lib. bdg. 16.95 (*1-55037-545-8*) Annick Pr., Ltd. CAN. *Dist:* Firefly Bks., Ltd.

—Monsieur Iletaitunefois. ed. 1999. (J). (gr. 1). spiral bd. (*0-616-01843-6*) Canadian National Institute for the Blind/Institut National Canadien pour les Aveugles.

—Mr. Once-upon-a-Time. Homel, David, tr. from FRE. 1998. (Illus.). 32p. (J). (ps-3). pap. 6.95 (*1-55037-538-5*); lib. bdg. 16.95 (*1-55037-539-3*) Annick Pr., Ltd. CAN. *Dist:* Firefly Bks., Ltd.

Simbal, Joanne. Long Shot. 1988. (Sweet Dreams Ser.). 134p. (YA). pap. 2.50 o.s.i (*0-553-27594-1*) Bantam Bks.

Simmons, Jane. Ebb & Flo & the New Friend. 1999. (Illus.). 32p. (J). (ps-2). 14.95 o.s.i (*0-689-82483-1*, McElderry, Margaret K.) Simon & Schuster Children's Publishing.

Simon & Barklee in England. 2001. (Another Country Calling Ser.). (Illus.). 64p. (J). (gr. 3-5). pap. text 12.00 (*0-9704661-1-0*, Explorer Media) Simon & Barklee, Inc./ExplorerMedia.

Simon & Barklee in Germany. 2001. (Another Country Calling Ser.). (Illus.). 64p. (J). (gr. 3-5). pap. text 12.00 (*0-9704661-2-9*, Explorer Media) Simon & Barklee, Inc./ExplorerMedia.

Simon, Charnan. Sam & Dasher. 1998. (Rookie Readers Ser.). (Illus.). 32p. (J). (gr. 1-2). pap. 4.95 (*0-516-26252-1*, Children's Pr.) Scholastic Library Publishing.

Simon, Mary Manz. Sientate! Maria y Marta, 1. 1999. (Hear Me Read Bible Stories Ser.). pap. text 2.75 (*0-570-09929-3*) Concordia Publishing Hse.

Simon, Shirley. Best Friend. 1981. (J). (gr. 4-6). pap. (*0-671-44380-1*, Simon Pulse) Simon & Schuster Children's Publishing.

Simone, Carisa. Best Friends Forever: The Story of a Friendship That Was Supposed to Last Forever. 2001. pap. 14.95 o.p. (*0-595-16987-2*, Writers Club Pr.) iUniverse, Inc.

Simonson, Louise. I Hate Superman! 1996. (Illus.). 32p. (J). (gr. 1-5). 13.95 o.p. (*0-316-17806-3*) Little Brown & Co.

Simpson, Louis. Wei Wei & Other Friends. 1990. (Illus.). 24p. (J). pap. 25.00 (*0-930126-30-0*) Typographeum.

Simpson, Nancy. French Fry Forgiveness. (Alex Ser.). (J). (gr. 2-5). pap. 5.99 (*0-7814-3243-X*) Cook Communications Ministries.

—Hot Chocolate Friendship. (Alex Ser.). (J). (gr. 2-5). pap. 5.99 (*0-7814-3257-X*) Cook Communications Ministries.

—Peanut Butter & Jelly Secrets. 2010. (Alex Ser.). (J). (gr. 2-5). pap. 5.99 (*0-7814-3256-1*) Cook Communications Ministries.

—Shoelaces & Brussels Sprouts. (Alex Ser.). (J). (gr. 2-5). pap. 5.99 (*0-7814-3258-8*) Cook Communications Ministries.

Singer, Marilyn. Block Party Today! 2004. (J). 16.95 (*0-375-82216-X*); lib. bdg. 18.99 (*0-375-92216-4*) Random Hse. Children's Bks. (Knopf Bks. for Young Readers).

—The First Few Friends. 1981. 320p. (YA). (gr. 7 up). 11.50 (*0-06-025728-8*); lib. bdg. 10.89 o.p. (*0-06-025729-6*) HarperCollins Children's Bk. Group.

—Lizzie Silver of Sherwood Forest. 1986. (Illus.). 192p. (J). (gr. 4-7). lib. bdg. 11.89 o.p. (*0-06-025622-2*) HarperCollins Children's Bk. Group.

—Several Kinds of Silence. 1988. 288p. (YA). (gr. 7 up). 13.95 (*0-06-025627-3*); lib. bdg. 13.89 o.p. (*0-06-025628-1*) HarperCollins Children's Bk. Group.

—Twenty Ways to Lose Your Best Friend. (Trophy Bk.). (Illus.). 128p. (J). (gr. 2-5). 1993. pap. 3.95 o.p. (*0-06-440353-X*, Harper Trophy); 1990. 12.95 (*0-06-025642-7*); 1990. lib. bdg. 14.89 o.p. (*0-06-025643-5*) HarperCollins Children's Bk. Group.

Singer, Melody. Rufus & the Nitwits, Vol. 1. l.t. ed. 1996. (Illus.). 67p. (J). (gr. 4-6). 16.00 (*0-9655349-0-1*) Rufus Pr.

Sinykin, Sheri Cooper. Next Thing to Strangers. 1991. (Illus.). 176p. (J). (gr. 5 up). 12.95 o.s.i (*0-688-10694-3*) HarperCollins Children's Bk. Group.

Sis, Peter. An Ocean World. 2002. (Illus.). (YA). 14.43 (*1-4046-0278-X*) Book Wholesalers, Inc.

Sis, Peter, illus. An Ocean World. 24p. (J). (ps-3). 2000. pap. 5.95 (*0-688-17518-X*, Harper Trophy); 1992. 16.00 o.p. (*0-688-09067-2*, Greenwillow Bks.); 1992. lib. bdg. 15.93 o.p. (*0-688-09068-0*, Greenwillow Bks.) HarperCollins Children's Bk. Group.

Sivers, Brenda. The Snailman. 1978. (Illus.). (J). (gr. 3-7). 6.95 o.p. (*0-316-79118-0*) Little Brown & Co.

Skogan, Joan. The Good Companion. 1998. (Illus.). (J). (ps-3). 32p. 15.95 (*1-55143-134-3*); 8.95 o.p. (*1-55143-136-X*) Orca Bk. Pubs.

Skolsky, Mindy Warshaw. Love from Your Friend, Hannah. 1998. (Illus.). 256p. (J). (gr. 3-7). pap. 17.95 o.p. (*0-7894-2492-4*) Dorling Kindersley Publishing, Inc.

—Love from Your Friend, Hannah. 256p. (J). (gr. 4-6). pap. 5.95 (*0-8072-1546-5*); 1999. pap. 37.00 incl. audio (*0-8072-8079-8*, YA996SP) Random Hse. Audio Publishing Group. (Listening Library).

—You're the Best, Hannah! 2000. (Illus.). 176p. (J). (gr. 3-7). pap. 5.95 (*0-06-440846-9*, Harper Trophy) HarperCollins Children's Bk. Group.

Skorpen, Liesel M. Plenty for 3. 1971. (Illus.). (J). (gr. k-3). 4.39 o.p. (*0-698-30284-2*, Coward-McCann) Putnam Publishing Group, The.

Skurzynski, Gloria. Good-Bye, Billy Radish. 1992. (Illus.). 160p. (YA). (gr. 5 up). lib. bdg. 15.00 (*0-02-782921-9*, Simon & Schuster Children's Publishing) Simon & Schuster Children's Publishing.

—The Tempering. 2000. (Golden Triangle Bks.). 192p. (J). (gr. 4-7). pap. 9.95 (*0-8229-5741-8*) Univ. of Pittsburgh Pr.

Slaaten, Evelyn. In the Captain's Shoes. 1978. (gr. 7 up). lib. bdg. 6.90 o.p. (*0-531-02215-3*, Watts, Franklin) Scholastic Library Publishing.

Slate, Joseph. Who Is Coming to Our House? 1991. (Sandcastle Ser.). (Illus.). 32p. (J). 5.95 o.s.i (*0-399-21790-8*, Philomel) Penguin Group (USA) Inc.

Slater, Teddy. Dana's Best Friend. 1996. (Junior Gymnasts Ser.: No. 4). (J). (gr. 4-7). mass mkt. 3.99 (*0-590-86003-8*) Scholastic, Inc.

—Dana's Best Friend. 1996. (Junior Gymnasts Ser.). 8.09 o.p. (*0-606-09503-9*) Turtleback Bks.

—Who's Afraid of the Big Bad Bully? 1995. (Hello Reader! Ser.). (J). 8.70 o.p. (*0-606-08380-4*) Turtleback Bks.

Slaughter, Hope. Buckley & Wilberta. 1996. (Illus.). 64p. (J). (gr. 1-3). lib. bdg. 14.95 (*0-931093-15-5*) Red Hen Pr.

—Buckley & Wilberta, Forever Friends. l.t. ed. 1998. (Illus.). 64p. (J). (gr. 1-3). lib. bdg. 14.95 (*0-931093-16-3*) Red Hen Pr.

—A Cozy Place. 1990. (Illus.). 32p. (J). (ps-2). lib. bdg. 15.95 (*0-931093-13-9*) Red Hen Pr.

Slawski, Wolfgang. The Friendship Trip. Lanning, Rosemary, tr. from GER. 1996. (Illus.). 32p. (J). (gr. k-3). 15.95 o.p. (*1-55858-554-0*); 15.88 o.p. (*1-55858-555-9*) North-South Bks., Inc.

Sleator, William. Dangerous Wishes. 1995. (Illus.). 192p. (J). (gr. 4-6). 14.99 o.s.i (*0-525-45283-4*, Dutton Children's Bks.) Penguin Putnam Bks. for Young Readers.

—The Duplicate. 1990. 160p. (YA). (gr. 5 up). mass mkt. 3.99 o.s.i (*0-553-28634-X*, Starfire) Random Hse. Children's Bks.

—Oddballs. 144p. (gr. 7 up). 1995. (YA). pap. 5.99 (*0-14-037438-8*, Puffin Bks.); 1993. (J). 14.99 o.p. (*0-525-45057-2*, Dutton Children's Bks.) Penguin Putnam Bks. for Young Readers.

Slepian, Jan. The Alfred Summer. 2001. (Illus.). 119p. (J). (gr. 5-9). 15.99 o.s.i (*0-399-23747-X*, Philomel) Penguin Putnam Bks. for Young Readers.

—The Alfred Summer. 1982. pap. 1.95 o.p. (*0-590-32333-4*); pap. 2.25 o.p. (*0-590-33822-6*); 128p. (J). (gr. 7 up). reprint ed. 1.25 o.p. (*0-590-40983-2*, Scholastic Paperbacks); 128p. (J). (gr. 7 up). reprint ed. pap. 2.50 o.p. (*0-590-40570-5*, Scholastic Paperbacks) Scholastic, Inc.

—The Alfred Summer. 1980. 132p. (YA). (gr. 6 up). text 15.00 o.p. (*0-02-782920-0*, Simon & Schuster Children's Publishing) Simon & Schuster Children's Publishing.

—The Alfred Summer. 2001. 12.04 (*0-606-22507-2*) Turtleback Bks.

—Getting on with It. 1985. 204p. (YA). (gr. 7 up). 11.95 o.s.i (*0-02-782930-8*, Simon & Schuster Children's Publishing) Simon & Schuster Children's Publishing.

—Risk 'n Roses. 1992. 176p. (J). (gr. 4-6). reprint ed. mass mkt. 2.95 o.p. (*0-590-45361-0*, Scholastic Paperbacks) Scholastic, Inc.

Sloan & Philamena. (J). audio HarperTrade.

Slote, Alfred. A Friend Like That. 160p. (J). (gr. 3-7). 1988. 11.95 (*0-397-32310-7*); 1988. lib. bdg. 12.89 (*0-397-32311-5*); 1990. reprint ed. pap. 3.50 o.p. (*0-06-440266-5*, Harper Trophy) HarperCollins Children's Bk. Group.

—A Friend Like That. 1994. (J). 18.05 o.p. (*0-8446-6775-7*) Smith, Peter Pub., Inc.

—Moving In. 1988. 128p. (J). (gr. 3-6). 15.00 (*0-397-32261-5*); lib. bdg. 14.89 (*0-397-32262-3*) HarperCollins Children's Bk. Group.

Small, David. Paper John, RS. 1989. (Illus.). 32p. (J). (ps-3). reprint ed. pap. 6.95 (*0-374-45725-5*, Sunburst) Farrar, Straus & Giroux.

Small, Hattie Thompson. Ms. Butterfly & Old Bumblebee. Slack, Una H., ed. 2002. 192p. (J). pap. 7.95 (*1-56167-362-5*) American Literary Pr., Inc.

Smallcomb, Pam. The Last Burp of Mac McGerp. 2003. (J). 150p. 15.95 (*1-58234-856-1*, Bloomsbury Children); (Illus.). 117p. (*1-58234-881-2*); (Illus.). 150p. pap. 6.95 (*1-58234-868-5*, Bloomsbury Children) Bloomsbury Publishing.

Smalls, Irene. Because You're Lucky. 1997. (Illus.). 32p. (J). (ps-3). 15.95 (*0-316-79867-3*) Little Brown & Co.

—Because You're Lucky. 2003. (Illus.). 32p. (J). (ps-1). pap. 5.99 (*0-316-76425-6*) Little Brown Children's Bks.

—Don't Say Ain't. (Illus.). 32p. (J). (gr. k-3). 2004. pap. 6.95 (*1-57091-382-X*); 2003. 15.95 (*1-57091-381-1*) Charlesbridge Publishing, Inc.

Smee, Nicola. Invitation, Vol. 1. 1990. (J). (ps-3). 12.95 o.s.i (*0-316-79894-0*, Joy Street Bks.) Little Brown & Co.

Smith. Changing Places. 1986. (Orig.). (J). pap. 2.95 o.p. (*0-590-44723-8*) Scholastic, Inc.

Smith, David J. The Red Bandanna. 1999. (Illus.). 151p. (J). (gr. 3-7). pap. 5.95 (*1-55143-138-6*) Orca Bk. Pubs.

Smith, Deborah V. With a Hop, Skip, & a Jump! 1987. (J). (ps). pap. 5.95 o.p. (*0-8224-9465-5*, Fearon Teacher Aids) McGraw-Hill Children's Publishing.

Smith, Doris B. The Pennywhistle Tree. 1991. (Illus.). 144p. (YA). (gr. 5-9). 14.95 o.p. (*0-399-21840-8*, G. P. Putnam's Sons) Penguin Group (USA) Inc.

Smith, Doris Buchanan. The Secret War. 1999. (J). pap. 14.99 (*0-670-84930-8*) Viking Penguin.

Smith, Geof. The Good, the Bad, & the Krabby. 2001. 32p. pap. 3.99 (*0-307-10498-2*, Golden Bks.) Random Hse. Children's Bks.

Smith, Jane D. Charlie Is a Chicken. 176p. (J). 2000. (Illus.). (gr. 3-7). pap. 4.95 (*0-06-440824-8*); 1998. (gr. 2 up). 14.95 (*0-06-027594-4*) HarperCollins Children's Bk. Group.

—Charlie Is a Chicken. 2000. (Illus.). (J). 11.00 (*0-606-18682-4*) Turtleback Bks.

Smith, Janice Lee. The Kid Next Door. 1995. (Trophy Chapter Bk.: No. 2). (Illus.). 112p. (J). (gr. 2-5). pap. 3.95 o.s.i (*0-06-442004-3*, Harper Trophy) HarperCollins Children's Bk. Group.

—Superkid! 1995. (Trophy Chapter Bks.: No. 3). (Illus.). 80p. (J). (gr. 2-5). pap. 3.95 o.s.i (*0-06-442005-1*, Harper Trophy) HarperCollins Children's Bk. Group.

Smith, Kay Jordan. Skeeter. 1992. 216p. (YA). (gr. 7-7). pap. 6.95 (*0-395-61621-2*) Houghton Mifflin Co.

Smith, Kay Jordan, ed. Skeeter. 1989. (J). (gr. 6 up). 14.95 o.p. (*0-395-49603-9*) Houghton Mifflin Co.

—Skeeter. 1989. (J). 12.00 (*0-606-01441-1*) Turtleback Bks.

Smith, Linda. Mrs. Biddlebox. Date not set. (Illus.). 32p. (J). (ps-3). pap. 5.99 (*0-06-443620-9*) HarperCollins Pubs.

Smith, Mavis. Crescents. 1991. (J). (ps-8). 3.95 o.p. (*1-55782-367-7*) Little Brown & Co.

—I'm Going to Get You! 1991. (J). (ps-3). pap. 5.95 o.s.i (*0-14-054435-6*, Puffin Bks.) Penguin Putnam Bks. for Young Readers.

Smith, Nancy C. & Beech, Tamara. Cloud House. 1997. (Orig.). (J). (gr. 3-7). pap. 3.99 (*0-380-72773-0*, Avon Bks.) Morrow/Avon.

Smith, Susan. Angela & the Greatest Guy in the World. 1989. (J). pap. 2.50 (*0-671-68161-3*, Aladdin) Simon & Schuster Children's Publishing.

—Angela & the King-Size Crusade. 1988. (Best Friends Ser.: No. 2). 96p. (J). (gr. 3-6). pap. (*0-671-64041-0*, Aladdin) Simon & Schuster Children's Publishing.

—Linda & the Little White Lies. MacDonald, Patricia, ed. 1990. (Best Friends Ser.: No. 9). 112p. (Orig.). (J). (gr. 4-7). pap. 2.75 (*0-671-69454-5*, Aladdin) Simon & Schuster Children's Publishing.

—One Hundred Thousand Dollar Dawn. 1990. (Best Friends Ser.: No. 7). 112p. (YA). pap. 2.75 (*0-671-69452-9*, Aladdin) Simon & Schuster Children's Publishing.

—Our Friend, Public Nuisance, No. 1. 1987. (Samantha Slade Ser.: No. 3). (J). (gr. 5 up). pap. (*0-671-63715-0*, Simon Pulse) Simon & Schuster Children's Publishing.

—The Sonya & Howard Wars. MacDonald, Patricia, ed. 1991. (Best Friends Ser.: No. 15). 112p. (Orig.). (J). pap. 2.95 (*0-671-72490-8*, Aladdin) Simon & Schuster Children's Publishing.

—Sonya & the Chain Letter Gang. 1990. (Best Friends Ser.: No. 5). (Orig.). (J). (gr. 3-6). pap. 2.75 (*0-671-73035-5*, Aladdin) Simon & Schuster Children's Publishing.

—Stevie. (Trophy Picture Bk.). (Illus.). 32p. (J). (ps-3). 1986. pap. 6.99 (*0-06-443122-3*, Harper Trophy); 1969. 12.95 (*0-06-025763-6*); 1969. lib. bdg. 14.89 o.p. (*0-06-025764-4*) HarperCollins Children's Bk. Group.

—Stevie. Mlawer, Teresa, tr. 1969. (SPA., Illus.). 32p. (J). (gr. k-3). 15.95 o.p. (*0-06-027038-1*) HarperCollins Children's Bk. Group.

—Stevie. unabr. ed. 1987. (Illus.). (J). (gr. 1-3). 24.95 incl. audio (*0-87499-050-5*); pap. 15.95 incl. audio (*0-87499-049-1*) Live Oak Media.

—Stevie, Grades 1-3. 1987. (Illus.). (J). pap., tchr. ed. 37.95 incl. audio (*0-87499-051-3*) Live Oak Media.

Steptoe, John L. Creativity. 1997. (Illus.). 32p. (J). (ps-3). lib. bdg., tchr. ed. 17.00 (*0-395-68706-3*) Houghton Mifflin Co.

Stern, Ricki. Beryl E. Bean. 2nd ed. 2002. (Beryl E. Bean Ser.). (Illus.). 64p. (J). lib. bdg. 14.89 (*0-06-028772-1*) HarperCollins Children's Bk. Group.

—Mighty Adventurer. 2002. (Beryl E. Bean Ser.: Vol. 1). (Illus.). 64p. (J). (ps-1). lib. bdg. 14.89 (*0-06-028771-3*) HarperCollins Children's Bk. Group.

—Mission Impossible. Date not set. (Beryl E. Bean Ser.: Vol. 3). (Illus.). (J). lib. bdg. 15.89 (*0-06-028773-X*, Harper Trophy) HarperCollins Children's Bk. Group.

Stern, Ricki & Worcester, Heidi P. Beryl E. Bean: Expedition Sleepaway Camp. 2nd ed. 2002. (Beryl E. Bean Ser.). (Illus.). 64p. (J). pap. 5.95 (*0-06-442121-X*) HarperCollins Pubs.

—Beryl E. Bean Book 1: Mighty Adventurer of the Planet. 2002. (Beryl E. Bean Ser.). (Illus.). 64p. (J). (gr. 2-4). pap. 5.95 (*0-06-442120-1*) HarperCollins Pubs.

Stern, Ricky & Worcester, Heidi P. Beryl E. Bean: Mission Impossible Friendship. 2002. (Illus.). (J). pap. 5.99 (*0-06-442122-8*, Harper Trophy) HarperCollins Children's Bk. Group.

Stevens, Bryna. Deborah Sampson Goes to War. 1984. (Carolrhoda On My Own Bks.). (Illus.). 48p. (J). (gr. k-4). lib. bdg. 9.95 o.p. (*0-87614-254-4*, Carolrhoda Bks.) Lerner Publishing Group.

Stevens, Diane. Liza's Blue Moon. 1995. 192p. (YA). (gr. 7 up). 15.00 o.s.i (*0-688-13542-0*, Greenwillow Bks.) HarperCollins Children's Bk. Group.

Stevens, Serita. An Unholy Alliance. 1988. (J). (gr. 5 up). mass mkt. 2.50 o.s.i (*0-449-70232-4*, Fawcett) Ballantine Bks.

Stevenson, James. Fast Friends. 1979. (Greenwillow Read-Alone Bks.). (Illus.). 64p. (J). (gr. 1-3). 8.50 o.p. (*0-688-80197-8*); lib. bdg. 11.88 o.p. (*0-688-84197-X*) HarperCollins Children's Bk. Group. (Greenwillow Bks.).

—Fast Friends. 9999. (J). pap. 1.95 o.s.i (*0-590-31986-8*) Scholastic, Inc.

—Monty. 1995. (SPA., Illus.). 32p. (J). (gr. k-3). 11.50 (*980-257-171-7*, EK6472) Ekare, Ediciones VEN. *Dist:* Kane/Miller Bk. Pubs., Lectorum Pubns., Inc.

—No Friends. 1986. (Illus.). 32p. (J). (gr. k-3). 12.95 o.p. (*0-688-06506-6*); lib. bdg. 12.88 o.p. (*0-688-06507-4*) HarperCollins Children's Bk. Group. (Greenwillow Bks.).

—Wilfred the Rat. 1977. (Illus.). 32p. (J). (ps-3). 7.25 o.p. (*0-688-80103-X*); lib. bdg. 12.88 o.p. (*0-688-84103-1*) HarperCollins Children's Bk. Group. (Greenwillow Bks.).

—The Worst Person in the World. 1978. (Illus.). 32p. (J). (gr. k-3). lib. bdg. 13.93 o.p. (*0-688-84127-9*, Greenwillow Bks.) HarperCollins Children's Bk. Group.

—The Worst Person in the World. 1995. (J). 10.15 o.p. (*0-606-08404-5*) Turtleback Bks.

—Worst Person in the World. 1978. (Illus.). 32p. (J). (gr. k-3). 12.95 o.p. (*0-688-80127-7*, Greenwillow Bks.) HarperCollins Children's Bk. Group.

Stevenson, Jocelyn. Best Friends, ERS. (Illus.). (J). (ps-2). 1985. pap. o.p. (*0-03-004562-2*); 1984. 5.95 o.p. (*0-03-000723-2*) Holt, Henry & Co. (Holt, Henry & Co. Bks. For Young Readers).

Stewart, Emily. Cinderella. 1998. (Disney Chapters Ser.). (Illus.). 48p. (J). (gr. 2-4). pap. 3.95 o.p. (*0-7868-4295-4*) Disney Pr.

Stewart, Josie & Salem, Lynn. No Luck! 1996. (Illus.). 12p. (J). (gr. k-2). pap. 3.75 (*1-880612-07-0*) Seedling Pubns., Inc.

Stewart, Melanie. Picture Perfect? 1999. (Generation Girl Ser.: Vol. 5). (Illus.). 128p. (gr. 2-5). pap. 3.99 o.s.i (*0-307-23454-1*, Golden Bks.) Random Hse. Children's Bks.

Stewart, Molly Mia. And the Winner Is...Jessica Wakefield! 1996. (Sweet Valley Kids Ser.: No. 66). (J). (gr. 1-3). 8.60 o.p. (*0-606-09930-1*) Turtleback Bks.

—Good-Bye, Eva? 1993. (Sweet Valley Kids Ser.: No. 38). (J). (gr. 1-3). 8.70 o.p. (*0-606-05641-6*) Turtleback Bks.

—Good-Bye, Mrs. Otis. 1997. (Sweet Valley Kids Ser.: No. 70). (J). (gr. 1-3). 9.55 (*0-606-11950-7*) Turtleback Bks.

—The Jessica & Elizabeth Show. 1995. (Sweet Valley Kids Ser.: No. 55). (J). (gr. 1-3). 8.19 o.p. (*0-606-08229-8*) Turtleback Bks.

—Jessica & the Jumbo Fish. 1991. (Sweet Valley Kids Ser.: No. 19). (J). (gr. 1-3). 8.19 o.p. (*0-606-04947-9*) Turtleback Bks.

—Lila's April Fool. 1994. (Sweet Valley Kids Ser.: No. 48). (J). (gr. 1-3). 8.70 o.p. (*0-606-06033-2*) Turtleback Bks.

—Lois & the Sleepover. 1994. (Sweet Valley Kids Ser.: No. 51). (J). (gr. 1-3). 8.70 o.p. (*0-606-06784-1*) Turtleback Bks.

—Robin in the Middle. 1993. (Sweet Valley Kids Ser.: No. 40). (J). (gr. 1-3). 8.70 o.p. (*0-606-05643-2*) Turtleback Bks.

—Sweet Valley Trick or Treat. 1990. (Sweet Valley Kids Ser.: No. 12). 80p. (J). (gr. 1-3). pap. 3.50 o.s.i (*0-553-15825-2*) Bantam Bks.

Stewart, Paul. A Little Bit of Winter. 1999. (Illus.). 32p. (J). (ps-2). 14.95 (*0-06-028278-9*) HarperCollins Children's Bk. Group.

—Rabbit's Wish. 2001. (Illus.). 32p. (J). (ps-2). 12.95 (*0-06-029518-X*) HarperCollins Children's Bk. Group.

—What Do You Remember? 2003. (Illus.). 32p. (J). 16.95 (*1-84270-080-4*); pap. (*1-84270-229-7*) Andersen Pr., Ltd. GBR. *Dist:* Trafalgar Square, Random Hse. of Canada, Ltd.

Stewart, Sarah. The Friends, RS. 2004. (*0-374-32463-8*) Farrar, Straus & Giroux.

Stewart, Toni D., illus. Jill & the Imp. 1999. 13p. (Orig.). (J). (gr. k-2). pap. 2.50 (*1-889658-04-9*) New Canaan Publishing Co., Inc.

Stimson, Joan. Oscar Needs a Friend. 1998. (Illus.). 32p. (J). (ps-1). pap. 5.95 (*0-7641-0746-1*) Barron's Educational Series, Inc.

Stine, R. L. Best Friend. McDonald, Patricia, ed. 1992. (Fear Street Ser.: No. 14). 160p. (YA). (gr. 7 up). pap. 4.99 (*0-671-73866-6*, Simon Pulse) Simon & Schuster Children's Publishing.

—Best Friend. 1992. (Fear Street Ser.: No. 14). (YA). (gr. 7 up). 10.04 (*0-606-02517-0*) Turtleback Bks.

—Bozos on Patrol. 1992. (Space Cadets Ser.: No. 3). 160p. (J). mass mkt. 2.75 o.p. (*0-590-44747-5*, Scholastic Paperbacks) Scholastic, Inc.

—My Best Friend Is Invisible. 1997. (Goosebumps Ser.: No. 57). (J). (gr. 3-7). 10.04 (*0-606-11649-4*) Turtleback Bks.

—La Noche del Muneco Viviente. 1997. (Escalofrios/Goosebumps Ser.: No. 7). Tr. of Night of the Living Dummy. (SPA.). 144p. (J). (gr. 3-7). mass mkt. 3.99 (*0-590-04141-X*) Scholastic, Inc.

—The Overnight. l.t. ed. 1994. (Fear Street Ser.: No. 16). (YA). (gr. 7 up). lib. bdg. 14.60 o.p. (*0-8368-1158-5*) Stevens, Gareth Inc.

—Panico en el Campamento. 1997. (Escalofrios/Goosebumps Ser.: No. 9). (SPA., Illus.). 72p. (J). (gr. 3-7). pap. text 3.99 (*0-590-29963-8*, SO6910) Scholastic, Inc.

Stoddart, Matthew. Bear in the Big Blue House: Bear Bakes a Cake. 2001. (Sticker Time Ser.). (Illus.). 16p. (J). (ps-3). pap. 2.99 o.s.i (*0-375-81139-7*, Random Hse. Bks. for Young Readers) Random Hse. Children's Bks.

Stoeke, Janet Morgan. A Friend for Minerva Louise. November, S., ed. 2001. (Illus.). 32p. (J). (ps-k). pap. 5.99 o.p. (*0-14-056526-4*) Penguin Putnam Bks. for Young Readers.

Stolz, Mary. Bully of Barkham Street. 1963. (Illus.). 224p. (J). (gr. 3-6). lib. bdg. 14.89 o.p. (*0-06-025821-7*) HarperCollins Children's Bk. Group.

—Bully of Barkham Street. 1985. 11.00 (*0-606-00261-8*) Turtleback Bks.

—Cider Days. 1980. 160p. (J). (gr. 3-7). pap. 1.95 o.p. (*0-06-990113-9*) HarperCollins Pubs.

—Ferris Wheel. 1980. 144p. (J). (gr. 3-7). pap. o.p. (*0-06-440112-X*, J 112) HarperCollins Pubs.

—The Noonday Friends. (Harper Trophy Bks.). (Illus.). 192p. (J). 1971. (gr. 3-7). pap. 5.99 (*0-06-440009-3*, Harper Trophy); 1965. (ps-2). lib. bdg. 16.89 (*0-06-025946-9*) HarperCollins Children's Bk. Group.

—The Noonday Friends. 1965. (J). 11.00 (*0-606-02852-8*) Turtleback Bks.

—Quentin Corn. 1985. (Illus.). 128p. (J). (gr. 1-7). 14.95 o.p. (*0-87923-553-5*) Godine, David R. Pub.

Stone, Chuck. Squizzy the Black Squirrel: A Fabulous Fable of Friendship. Jackson, Jeannie, tr. & illus. by. 2003. 30p. (J). 16.95 (*0-940880-71-7*) Open Hand Publishing, LLC.

Stone, Nancy. Whistle up the Bay. 1966. (J). (gr. 4-7). pap. 10.00 o.p. (*0-8028-4033-7*) Eerdmans, William B. Publishing Co.

Stone, Susheila. Where Is Batool? 1991. (Duets Ser.). (Illus.). 25p. (J). (gr. 2-4). 15.95 o.p. (*0-237-60157-5*) Evans Brothers, Ltd. GBR. *Dist:* Trafalgar Square.

Storace, Patricia. Sugar Cane. 2002. (Illus.). 32p. (J). (*0-7868-0791-1*) Disney Pr.

Storr, Catherine. Marianne & Mark. 1979. (Fanfares Ser.). (Illus.). (J). (gr. 6-9). pap. o.p. (*0-571-11336-2*) Faber & Faber Ltd.

Stortz, Diane M. Love One Another: With Skedaddle Skunk & Friends. 1995. (Coloring Bks.). (Illus.). 16p. (J). (ps-3). pap. 1.69 (*0-7847-0275-6*, 02565, Bean Sprouts) Standard Publishing.

Storybook Treasury of Dick & Jane & Friends. 2003. (Illus.). 200p. 10.99 (*0-448-43340-0*, Grosset & Dunlap) Penguin Putnam Bks. for Young Readers.

Stouffer, N. K. Larry Potter & His Best Friend Lilly. 2001. (Larry Potter Storybks.). (Illus.). 22p. (J). (ps-2). 7.95 (*1-58989-300-X*) Thurman Hse., LLC.

Stouse, Karla F. Diff'rent Is Kind of Nice. 1987. (Learn a Value Ser.). (Illus.). 16p. (J). (gr. 2 up). pap. 0.95 o.p. (*0-87029-208-0*) Abbey Pr.

—Nellie & the Nasty Nast. 1987. (Learn a Value Ser.). (Illus.). 16p. (Orig.). (J). (gr. 2 up). pap. 0.95 o.p. (*0-87029-205-6*) Abbey Pr.

Strand, Jeff. Elrod McBugle on the Loose. (J). E-Book 3.50 (*1-58495-717-4*); 2000. 7.50 (*1-58495-716-6*) DiskUs Publishing.

Strasser, Todd. The Complete Computer Popularity Program. 1984. 137p. (J). (gr. 4-6). 14.95 o.p. (*0-385-29352-6*, Delacorte Pr.) Dell Publishing.

—Con-fidence. 2002. 176p. (J). (gr. 5 up). tchr. ed. 16.95 (*0-8234-1394-2*) Holiday Hse., Inc.

—Friends till the End. 1982. 224p. (YA). (gr. 7 up). mass mkt. 3.25 o.s.i (*0-440-92625-4*, Laurel Leaf) Random Hse. Children's Bks.

—A Very Touchy Subject. 1986. (J). (gr. 6 up). mass mkt. 2.95 o.s.i (*0-440-98851-9*, Laurel Leaf) Random Hse. Children's Bks.

—Wordsworth & the Tasty Treat Trick. 1996. 8.60 o.p. (*0-606-10085-7*) Turtleback Bks.

Strauss, Gwen. The Night Shimmy. 1992. (Illus.). 32p. (J). (ps-2). 15.99 o.s.i (*0-679-92384-5*, Knopf Bks. for Young Readers) Random Hse. Children's Bks.

Strayer, Debbie. Jack & Stan, Winky, Blinky & Pinky: Bridge Blend Books, 2 bks., Set, Nos. 3 & 4. 1992. (Bridge Story Bks.). (Illus.). 16p. (J). (gr. 1). pap. 8.00 (*1-880892-12-X*) Common Sense Pr.

—Sally & Sam, Mike & Spike: Bridge Blend Books, 2 bks., Nos. 5 & 6. 1992. (Bridge Story Bks.). (Illus.). 16p. (J). (gr. 1). pap. 8.00 (*1-880892-13-8*) Common Sense Pr.

Streatfeild, Noel. Good-Bye Gemma. 1987. (Orig.). (J). (gr. k-6). pap. 3.25 o.s.i (*0-440-42871-8*, Yearling) Random Hse. Children's Bks.

Stren, Patti. Hug Me. (Illus.). (J). 2001. 32p. 14.95 (*0-06-029317-9*); 2001. 32p. 14.89 (*0-06-029318-7*); 1984. 32p. pap. 3.95 (*0-06-443062-6*, Harper Trophy); 1977. lib. bdg. 11.89 o.p. (*0-06-026081-5*) HarperCollins Children's Bk. Group.

—Sloan & Philamina. 1979. (J). (ps-2). 6.95 o.p. (*0-525-39485-0*, Dutton) Dutton/Plume.

Strete, Craig K. Big Thunder Magic. 1990. (Illus.). 32p. (J). (ps up). 12.95 o.p. (*0-688-08853-8*); lib. bdg. 12.88 o.p. (*0-688-08854-6*) HarperCollins Children's Bk. Group. (Greenwillow Bks.).

—The Boy Who Became a Rattlesnake. 2004. (Illus.). 32p. (J). 15.99 (*0-399-23572-8*, Putnam & Grosset) Putnam Publishing Group, The.

Strickland, Alison. Why Can't He Be Mine? 1983. 96p. (J). (gr. 4-8). 1.95 o.p. (*0-87406-182-2*) Darby Creek Publishing.

Stringham, Alene. Kate & Nate. 1986. (Illus.). 60p. (Orig.). (J). (gr. 1-2). pap. text 5.95 o.p. (*0-933606-45-1*, 645) Sussman, Ellen Educational Services.

Strom, Maria Diaz. Rainbow Joe & Me. ed. 2000. (J). (gr. 1). spiral bd. (*0-616-03097-5*) Canadian National Institute for the Blind/Institut National Canadien pour les Aveugles.

—Rainbow Joe & Me. (Illus.). 32p. (J). 2002. pap. 6.95 (*1-58430-050-7*); 1999. 15.95 (*1-880000-93-8*) Lee & Low Bks., Inc.

Strommen, Judith B. Grady the Great, ERS. 1990. 160p. (J). (gr. 4-6). 13.95 o.p. (*0-8050-1405-5*, Holt, Henry & Co. Bks. For Young Readers) Holt, Henry & Co.

Stroschin, Jane H. Fingertip Friends. rev. ed. 1997. (Illus.). 32p. (J). (gr. 3 up). 17.50 incl. audio (*1-883960-23-1*) Henry Quill Pr.

Stuart, Jesse H. Hie to the Hunters. Herndon, Jerry A., ed. 6th ed. 1996. (Illus.). 272p. (YA). reprint ed. 22.00 (*0-945084-58-7*); (gr. 9-12). pap. 12.00 (*0-945084-59-5*) Stuart, Jesse Foundation, The.

Su Chen Fang. Happy Birthday to You! 1997. (Illus.). 32p. (J). (gr. k-4). 12.95 (*0-7641-5030-8*); pap. 5.95 (*0-7641-0046-7*) Barron's Educational Series, Inc.

Su Chen Fang & Gui Fong Chang. Happy Birthday to You! l.t. ed. 1999. (Children's Stories Published in Other Lands Ser.). (Illus.). 32p. (J). (ps up). lib. bdg. 15.95 (*1-56674-241-2*) Forest Hse. Publishing Co., Inc.

Suen, Anastasia. The Clubhouse. 2003. (Easy-to-Read Ser.). (Illus.). 32p. pap. 3.99 (*0-14-250054-2*, Puffin Bks.) Penguin Putnam Bks. for Young Readers.

Sula, Sondra. Katie: Katie & the Ogre. 2000. (Illus.). 32p. (J). (gr. 1-3). pap. (*1-931179-01-8*) Long Hill Productions, Inc.

Sullivan, Arlene R. The Journey of Hanna Heart: You Never Know Where the Wind Will Blow. 1998. (Illus.). 16p. (J). (gr. k-5). pap. 12.95 (*0-9665793-0-5*) Changing Images Art Foundation, Inc.

Sullivan, Sarah. Root Beer & Banana. 2004. (J). (*0-7636-1748-2*) Candlewick Pr.

Sumpolec, Sarah Anne. The Masquerade. 2003. (YA). 12.99 (*0-8024-6451-3*) Moody Pr.

Sun, Chyng F. Cat & Cat-Face. 1996. (Illus.). 32p. (J). (ps-3). tchr. ed. 14.95 o.p. (*0-395-72038-9*) Houghton Mifflin Co.

Sundgaard, Arnold. Meet Jack Appleknocker. 1988. (Illus.). 32p. (J). (ps-2). 13.95 o.p. (*0-399-21472-0*, Philomel) Penguin Putnam Bks. for Young Readers.

Supplee, Audra. I Almost Love You Eddie Clegg. 2004. 192p. (J). (gr. 4-6). 14.95 (*1-56145-308-0*, Peachtree Junior) Peachtree Pubs., Ltd.

Surman, Susan. Max & Friends. 1999. (Illus.). 150p. (J). pap. 9.99 (*0-88092-388-1*) Royal Fireworks Publishing Co.

Sutcliff, Rosemary. The Shining Company, RS. 1992. (Illus.). 304p. (YA). (gr. 7 up). pap. 6.95 (*0-374-46616-5*, Sunburst) Farrar, Straus & Giroux.

Sutherland, Margaret. Hello, I'm Karen. 1976. (Illus.). 96p. (J). (gr. k-5). 4.95 o.p. (*0-698-20371-2*) Putnam Publishing Group, The.

Sutherland, Tui. Fun with Mo & Ella. 2002. (First Friends Ser.). (Illus.). 32p. (J). mass mkt. 3.99 (*0-448-42638-2*, Grosset & Dunlap) Penguin Putnam Bks. for Young Readers.

—Meet Mo & Ella. Anastas, Margaret, ed. 2001. (First Friends, First Readers Ser.). (Illus.). 32p. (J). (ps-1). mass mkt. 3.99 o.s.i (*0-448-42456-8*, Grosset & Dunlap) Penguin Putnam Bks. for Young Readers.

—Meet Mo & Ella. 2001. (First Friends, First Readers Ser.). (Illus.). (J). 10.14 (*0-606-21323-6*) Turtleback Bks.

Sutton, Elizabeth H. Racing for Keeneland. 1994. 96p. (J). (gr. 4-7). 14.95 o.p. (*1-56566-051-X*) Lickle Publishing, Inc.

Sutton, Jane. Me & the Weirdos. 1983. (J). (ps-7). pap. 2.25 o.s.i (*0-553-15395-1*, Skylark) Random Hse. Children's Bks.

Sutton, Laverne. Peacock Feathers. 1988. 23p. (J). 4.95 o.p. (*0-533-07722-2*) Vantage Pr., Inc.

Suzanne, Jamie. Against the Rules. l.t. ed. 1991. (Sweet Valley Twins Ser.: No. 9). 104p. (J). (gr. 3-7). reprint ed. 9.95 o.p. (*1-55905-072-1*) Grey Castle Pr.

—Amy's Secret Sister. 1994. (Sweet Valley Twins Ser.: No. 83). (J). (gr. 3-7). 8.60 o.p. (*0-606-07110-5*) Turtleback Bks.

—Best Friends. l.t. ed. 1990. (Sweet Valley Twins Ser.: No. 1). 104p. (J). (gr. 3-7). reprint ed. 9.95 o.p. (*1-55905-064-0*) Grey Castle Pr.

—Best Friends. 1986. (Sweet Valley Twins Ser.: No. 1). (J). (gr. 3-7). 8.60 (*0-606-01490-X*) Turtleback Bks.

—The Big Camp Secret. 1989. (Sweet Valley Twins Super Edition Ser.: No. 3). (J). (gr. 3-7). 9.09 o.p. (*0-606-04171-0*) Turtleback Bks.

—Breakfast of Enemies. 1997. (Sweet Valley Twins Ser.: No. 106). (J). (gr. 3-7). 9.55 (*0-606-11955-8*) Turtleback Bks.

—Choosing Sides. 1987. (Sweet Valley Twins Ser.: No. 4). (J). (gr. 3-7). pap. 1.25 o.s.i (*0-440-82085-5*) Dell Publishing.

—Choosing Sides. 1986. (Sweet Valley Twins Ser.: No. 4). (J). (gr. 3-7). pap. o.s.i (*0-553-16699-9*); pap. o.s.i (*0-553-16684-0*); pap. o.s.i (*0-553-16694-8*) Random Hse. Children's Bks. (Dell Books for Young Readers).

—Claim to Fame. 1988. (Sweet Valley Twins Ser.: No. 23). 112p. (J). (gr. 3-7). pap. 2.75 o.s.i (*0-553-15624-1*) Bantam Bks.

—Danny Means Trouble. 1990. (Sweet Valley Twins Ser.: No. 40). 144p. (J). (gr. 3-7). pap. 3.25 o.s.i (*0-553-15806-6*) Bantam Bks.

—Don't Talk to Brian. 1996. (Sweet Valley Twins Ser.: No. 94). 144p. (gr. 3-7). pap. text 3.50 o.s.i (*0-553-48197-5*) Bantam Bks.

—Don't Talk to Brian. 1996. (Sweet Valley Twins Ser.: No. 94). (J). (gr. 3-7). 8.60 o.p. (*0-606-09932-8*) Turtleback Bks.

—Elizabeth Solves It All. 1996. (Sweet Valley Twins Ser.: No. 103). 144p. (gr. 3-7). pap. text 3.50 o.s.i (*0-553-48434-6*, Sweet Valley) Random Hse. Children's Bks.

—The Gossip War. 1994. (Sweet Valley Twins Ser.: No. 80). (J). (gr. 3-7). 8.60 o.p. (*0-606-06787-6*) Turtleback Bks.

—If Looks Could Kill. 1997. (Sweet Valley Twins Ser.: No. 112). 144p. (gr. 3-7). pap. text 3.50 o.s.i (*0-553-48443-5*, Dell Books for Young Readers) Random Hse. Children's Bks.

—The Incredible Madame Jessica. 1995. (Sweet Valley Twins Ser.: No. 93). 144p. (J). (gr. 3-7). pap. 3.50 o.s.i (*0-553-48196-7*, Sweet Valley) Random Hse. Children's Bks.

—Jessica & the Earthquake. 1994. (Sweet Valley Twins Ser.: No. 75). (J). (gr. 3-7). 8.60 o.p. (*0-606-06036-7*) Turtleback Bks.

—Keeping Secrets. 1987. (Sweet Valley Twins Ser.: No. 12). (J). (gr. 3-7). pap. o.s.i (*0-553-16760-X*); pap. o.s.i (*0-553-16759-6*); pap. o.s.i (*0-553-16756-1*) Random Hse. Children's Bks. (Dell Books for Young Readers).

—Keeping Secrets. 1987. (Sweet Valley Twins Ser.: No. 12). (J). (gr. 3-7). 9.55 (*0-606-03594-X*) Turtleback Bks.

—Lila's Music Video. 1993. (Sweet Valley Twins Ser.: No. 73). 144p. (J). (gr. 3-7). pap. 3.50 o.s.i (*0-553-48059-6*) Bantam Bks.

—Lila's Music Video. 1993. (Sweet Valley Twins Ser.: No. 73). (J). (gr. 3-7). 8.60 o.p. (*0-606-05653-X*) Turtleback Bks.

—Las Mejores Amigas. Utrilla, Hortensia Martinez, tr. 1991. (Gemelas de Sweet Valley Ser.: No. 1). Tr. of Best Friends. (SPA.). (J). (gr. 3-7). 9.70 o.p. (*0-606-05411-1*) Turtleback Bks.

—One of the Gang, Vol. 10. 1987. (Sweet Valley Twins Ser.: No. 10). (J). (gr. 3-7). pap. 2.50 o.s.i (*0-553-15531-8*, Skylark) Random Hse. Children's Bks.

—Out of Place. 1988. (Sweet Valley Twins Ser.: No. 22). (J). (gr. 3-7). pap. o.s.i (*0-553-16830-4*, Dell Books for Young Readers) Random Hse. Children's Bks.

—Pumpkin Fever. 1997. (Sweet Valley Twins Ser.: No. 110). 144p. (Orig.). (J). (gr. 3-7). pap. text 3.50 o.s.i (*0-553-48441-9*, Dell Books for Young Readers) Random Hse. Children's Bks.

—Second Best. 1988. (Sweet Valley Twins Ser.: No. 16). (J). (gr. 3-7). pap. o.s.i (*0-553-16819-3*, Dell Books for Young Readers) Random Hse. Children's Bks.

—Steven the Zombie. 1994. (Sweet Valley Twins Ser.: No. 78). (J). (gr. 3-7). 8.60 o.p. (*0-606-06039-1*) Turtleback Bks.

—Three's a Crowd. 1987. (Sweet Valley Twins Ser.: No. 7). (J). (gr. 3-7). 8.60 o.p. (*0-606-03488-9*) Turtleback Bks.

Svend, Otto. Tim & Trisha. 1988. 9.95 o.p. (*0-7207-0930-X*, Pelham Bks.) Viking Penguin.

Swallow, Pamela C. No Promises. 1989. 176p. (J). (gr. 5 up). 14.95 o.s.i (*0-399-21561-1*, G. P. Putnam's Sons) Penguin Putnam Bks. for Young Readers.

—Wading Through Peanut Butter. 1993. 128p. (J). (gr. 4-6). pap. 2.95 o.p. (*0-590-45793-4*) Scholastic, Inc.

Swanson, Steve. Triumph. 1901. (Pennypinchers Ser.). 128p. (J). (gr. 5-9). pap. 2.95 o.p. (*0-89191-793-4*, 57935) Cook Communications Ministries.

Swanson, Susanne M. My Friend Emily. (Illus.). (Orig.). (J). (gr. k-5). 1994. 36p. pap. 6.99 (*1-885101-04-X*); Large Class Set. 1995. pap. 209.65 o.p. (*1-885101-23-6*); Resource Room Set. 1995. pap. 59.90 o.p. (*1-885101-21-X*); Small Class Set. 1995. pap. 149.75 o.p. (*1-885101-22-8*) Writers Pr., Inc.

—The Sandbox King. 1995. (Illus.). 28p. (Orig.). (J). (ps-5). pap. 6.99 (*1-885101-08-2*) Writers Pr., Inc.

Sweeney, Jacqueline. Meadow Magic. 2001. (We Can Read! Ser.). (Illus.). 32p. (J). (gr. 1-2). lib. bdg. 21.36 (*0-7614-1124-0*, Benchmark Bks.) Cavendish, Marshall Corp.

Sweeney, Joyce. Free Fall. 1996. 240p. (YA). 15.95 (*0-385-32211-9*, Delacorte Pr.) Dell Publishing.

—Waiting for June. 2003. 144p. (YA). 15.95 (*0-7614-5138-2*, Cavendish Children's Bks.) Cavendish, Marshall Corp.

Swerdfeger, Steven E. Thursday's Child. 1996. (Illus.). 312p. (J). (gr. 5-9). pap. 8.95 o.p. (*0-9651835-0-5*) Cloudbank Creations, Inc.

Swiftly Tilting. 1979. (J). mass mkt. 2.99 (*0-440-80267-9*) Dell Publishing.

Swimley, Alison. Dizzy & Terry. 2000. (Illus.). (J). pap. 15.95 (*0-7541-1080-X*) Minerva Pr. GBR. *Dist:* Unity Distribution.

Swindells, Robert. Rolf y Rosi (Rolf & Rosie) 1995. (SPA.). (J). (gr. 2). 5.99 (*968-16-4721-1*) Fondo de Cultura Economica MEX. *Dist:* Continental Bk. Co., Inc.

Swope, Sam. The Araboolies of Liberty Street. 2001. 12.10 (*0-606-21040-7*) Turtleback Bks.

Szekeres, Cyndy & Golden Books Staff. Giggles. 1996. (Illus.). 12p. (J). (ps). bds. 2.49 o.s.i (*0-307-06160-4*, Golden Bks.) Random Hse. Children's Bks.

T-Neck. 2nd rev. ed. 1993. 180p. (J). (gr. 5 up). pap. 7.95 (*0-9626608-5-X*) Magik Pubs.

Tada, Joni Eareckson. Meet My Friends. 1987. 96p. (J). (gr. 3-7). pap. 4.99 o.p. (*1-55513-808-X*) Cook Communications Ministries.

—You've Got a Friend. 1999. (Illus.). 31p. (J). (ps-3). 14.99 (*1-58134-060-5*) Crossway Bks.

Tada, Joni Eareckson & Carlson, Melody. Forever Friends. 2000. (Toy Shop on Periwinkle Lane Ser.). (Illus.). 32p. (J). (ps-3). 14.99 (*1-58134-216-0*) Crossway Bks.

Tafuri, Nancy. My Friends. 1987. (Illus.). 12p. (J). (ps). mass mkt. 4.95 o.s.i (*0-688-07187-2*, Greenwillow Bks.) HarperCollins Children's Bk. Group.

—Where Did Bunny Go? A Bunny & Bird Story. 2001. (Illus.). (J). pap. (*0-439-16960-7*); 32p. pap. 15.95 (*0-439-16959-3*, Levine, Arthur A. Bks.) Scholastic, Inc.

—Will You Be My Friend? A Bunny & Bird Story. 2000. (Illus.). 32p. (J). (ps-3). pap. 16.95 (*0-590-63782-7*, Scholastic Reference) Scholastic, Inc.

Taggart, Misty. Let's Be Friends. 1995. (Angel Academy Ser.: Vol. 5). (Illus.). (J). (ps-3). pap. 3.99 o.p. (*0-8499-5084-8*) W Publishing Group.

Talbert, Marc. The Purple Heart. 1993. 128p. (J). (gr. 6). pap. 3.50 (*0-380-71985-1*, Avon Bks.) Morrow/Avon.

—The Purple Heart. 2000. 148p. (gr. 4-7). pap. 10.95 (*0-595-09771-5*, Backinprint.com) iUniverse, Inc.

—Rabbit in the Rock. 1989. (YA). (gr. 7 up). 14.95 o.p. (*0-8037-0693-6*, Dial Bks. for Young Readers) Penguin Putnam Bks. for Young Readers.

Talley, Linda. Bastet. (Key Concepts in Personal Development Ser.). (Illus.). 2001. 32p. pap., tchr. ed. 79.95 incl. VHS (*1-55942-176-2*, 9390K3); 2000. 30p. (J). 79.95 incl. VHS (*1-55942-161-4*) Marsh Media.

Tamar, Erika. Out of Control. 1991. 208p. (YA). (gr. 7 up). lib. bdg. 14.95 o.p. (*0-689-31689-5*, Atheneum) Simon & Schuster Children's Publishing.

Tamar, Erika, et al. My Ex-Best Friend. 1998. (Party of Five: No. 8). 144p. (J). (gr. 3-6). pap. 3.99 (*0-671-01895-7*, Aladdin) Simon & Schuster Children's Publishing.

Tanaka, Shelley. Anne of Green Gables. 1998. (Avonlea Ser.: No. 1). 112p. (gr. 5-8). mass mkt. 5.99 (*0-7704-2744-8*) Bantam Bks.

Tania y Sus Amigos (Tanya Thinker & the Gizmo Gang) 1996. (SPA., Illus.). 64p. (J). (gr. k-2). 16.95 (*0-7835-3516-3*) Time-Life, Inc.

Tassies, Jose, illus. Carabola. 1997. Tr. of Roundface. (SPA.). 22p. (J). (gr. 1-3). 13.99 (*968-16-5342-4*, FC3424) Fondo de Cultura Economica MEX. *Dist:* Continental Bk. Co., Inc.

Tate, Joan. Tina & David. 1973. 96p. (J). (gr. 7 up). 6.95 o.p. (*0-8407-6350-6*, Dutton Children's Bks.) Penguin Putnam Bks. for Young Readers.

Tatler, Sarah. We Can Share It. 2nd ed. 1995. (Let Me Read Ser.). (Illus.). 16p. (J). (ps-3). pap. 2.95 (*0-673-36274-4*, Good Year Bks.) Celebration Pr.

Taulbert, Clifton L. Little Cliff & the Porch People. Kane, Cindy, ed. 1999. (Illus.). 32p. (J). (ps-3). 16.99 (*0-8037-2174-9*, Dial Bks. for Young Readers) Penguin Putnam Bks. for Young Readers.

Taylor, Courtney. Cape Cod Adventure. 1996. 72p. (Orig.). (J). (gr. 3-5). pap. 8.00 (*1-56002-573-5*) Aegina Pr., Inc.

Taylor, Judy. Sophie & Jack. 1983. (Illus.). 32p. (J). (ps-2). 9.95 o.p. (*0-399-20947-6*, Philomel) Penguin Putnam Bks. for Young Readers.

Taylor, Kim. Hidden Inside. 1990. 32p. (J). 10.99 o.s.i (*0-385-30183-9*) Doubleday Publishing.

—Hidden Inside. 1990. (J). o.s.i (*0-385-30208-8*, Dell Books for Young Readers) Random Hse. Children's Bks.

Taylor, Lisa. Beryl's Box. 1993. (Illus.). 32p. (J). (ps-2). 12.95 o.p. (*0-8120-6355-4*); pap. 5.95 o.p. (*0-8120-1673-4*) Barron's Educational Series, Inc.

Taylor, Marilyn. Call Yourself a Friend? 1997. 190p. (YA). pap. 6.95 (*0-86278-500-6*) O'Brien Pr., Ltd., The IRL. *Dist:* Irish American Bk. Co.

Taylor, Mark A. A Friend Is... 1987. (I'm Growing up Ser.). (Illus.). 32p. (J). (gr. 1-4). ring bd. 4.99 o.p. (*0-87403-324-1*, 3669) Standard Publishing.

Taylor, Maureen. Without Warning. 1991. 144p. (YA). pap. 4.99 o.p. (*0-8066-2538-4*, 9-2538) Augsburg Fortress, Pubs.

Taylor, Mildred D. The Friendship. (Illus.). 56p. 1998. (gr. 2-6). pap. 4.99 (*0-14-038964-4*, Puffin Bks.); 1987. (J). (gr. 4-7). 16.99 (*0-8037-0417-8*, Dial Bks. for Young Readers) Penguin Putnam Bks. for Young Readers.

Taylor, Theodore. The Cay. l.t. ed. 1990. 154p. (J). (gr. k-6). reprint ed. lib. bdg. 15.95 o.p. (*1-55736-163-0*) Bantam Doubleday Dell Large Print Group, Inc.

—The Cay. (YA). (gr. 5 up). 1977. 416p. pap. 4.95 (*0-380-00142-X*); 1976. 512p. reprint ed. pap. 4.95 (*0-380-01003-8*) HarperCollins Children's Bk. Group. (Harper Trophy).

—The Cay. 2000. 171p. (J). 15.60 (*0-03-054604-4*) Holt, Rinehart & Winston.

—The Cay. 144p. 2003. (Illus.). (YA). (gr. 5). mass mkt. 5.50 (*0-440-22912-X*, Laurel Leaf); 2002. (gr. 4-7). pap. text 5.50 (*0-440-41663-9*, Yearling); 1987. (gr. 4-7). text 16.95 (*0-385-07906-0*, Delacorte Bks. for Young Readers) Random Hse. Children's Bks.

—The Cay. 1970. (J). 11.00 (*0-606-04889-8*); 1969. 11.04 (*0-606-02584-7*) Turtleback Bks.

—Into the Wind: The Odyssey of Ben O'Neal, Bk. 3. 1991. 192p. (YA). pap. 3.99 (*0-380-71026-9*, Avon Bks.) Morrow/Avon.

—The Weirdo. 1991. 304p. (YA). (gr. 7 up). 17.00 (*0-15-294952-6*) Harcourt Children's Bks.

—The Weirdo. 1991. (J). 11.00 (*0-606-05704-8*) Turtleback Bks.

—Weirdo. 1993. (Avon Flare Book Ser.). 240p. (J). (gr. 7-12). pap. 5.99 (*0-380-72017-5*, Avon Bks.) Morrow/Avon.

Taylor, Tom & Reilly, Carol, eds. One Track. 1995. 244p. (Orig.). (YA). pap. 10.00 (*0-9648262-0-8*) Mozart Park Pr.

Teague, Mark. The Lost & Found. 32p. (J). (ps-2). 2001. mass mkt. 5.99 (*0-439-27869-4*); 1998. (Illus.). pap. 15.95 (*0-590-84619-1*) Scholastic, Inc.

Teaming Up. 2002. (Illus.). (J). pap. text 7.00 (*0-7398-5136-5*) Raintree Pubs.

Tegen, Katherine. Dracula & Frankenstein Are Friends. 2003. (Illus.). 32p. (J). (ps-3). 15.99 (*0-06-000115-1*); lib. bdg. 16.89 (*0-06-000116-X*) HarperCollins Pubs.

Teitelbaum, Michael. Web of Friendship. 2002. (Digimon Ser.: No. 3). 32p. (J). mass mkt. 3.99 (*0-439-32115-8*) Scholastic, Inc.

Telander, Rick. String Music. 2002. (Illus.). 144p. (J). (gr. 4-7). 15.95 (*0-8126-2657-5*) Cricket Bks.

Tenorio-Coscarelli, Jane. The Tamale Quilt. Coscarelli, Nichole, tr. 1998. (Illus.). 48p. (J). (gr. k-6). pap. 11.95 (*0-9653422-4-7*) Quarter-Inch Publishing.

Tenorio-Coscarelli, Jane & Coscarelli, Nicole. The Tamale Quilt. l.t. ed. 1998. (Illus.). 48p. (J). (gr. k-6). 15.95 (*0-9653422-3-9*) Quarter-Inch Publishing.

Terban, Marvin. It Figures! Fun Figures of Speech. 1993. (Illus.). 64p. (J). (gr. 4-6). pap. 7.95 (*0-395-66591-4*, Clarion Bks.) Houghton Mifflin Co. Trade & Reference Div.

Terris, Susan. Two P's in a Pod. 1977. 181p. (J). (gr. 5-9). 12.95 o.p. (*0-688-80107-2*); lib. bdg. 12.88 o.p. (*0-688-84107-4*) HarperCollins Children's Bk. Group. (Greenwillow Bks.).

Terry, Angela. A Carrot for Two: A Story about Being Different. 1990. (Illus.). (J). (ps up). 6.95 o.p. (*1-55782-092-9*) Warner Bks., Inc.

Testa, Fulvio. Never Satisfied. 1945. (Illus.). 32p. (J). (gr. k-3). 12.95 o.p. (*1-55858-051-4*); pap. 3.95 o.p. (*1-55858-052-2*) North-South Bks., Inc.

—The Visit. Martens, Marianne, tr. from GER. 2002. (Illus.). 32p. (J). 15.95 (*0-7358-1684-0*); lib. bdg. 16.50 (*0-7358-1685-9*) North-South Bks., Inc.

—Wolf's Flavor. 1990. (J). (ps-3). pap. 3.95 o.p. (*0-8037-0744-4*) Penguin Putnam Bks. for Young Readers.

Thaler, Mike. The Moon & the Balloon. 1982. (Illus.). 32p. (J). (ps-3). 8.95 o.s.i (*0-8038-4744-0*) Hastings Hse. Daytrips Pubs.

Tharlet, Eve, pseud. Little Pig, Big Trouble. Clements, Andrew, tr. 1992. (Pixies Ser.). (Illus.). 28p. (J). (gr. k up). reprint ed. pap. 4.95 o.s.i (*0-88708-227-0*, Simon & Schuster Children's Publishing) Simon & Schuster Children's Publishing.

Thavis, Richard. Letters to Sarah. 2000. 132p. E-Book 8.00 o.p. (*0-7388-7812-X*) Xlibris Corp.

Theo. Oscar & Hoo. 2003. (Illus.). 32p. pap. 8.95 (*0-00-710794-3*) Collins Willow GBR. *Dist:* Trafalgar Square.

—Oscar & Hoo. 2003. (Illus.). 32p. (J). 16.95 (*0-00-710793-5*) HarperCollins Pubs. Ltd. GBR. *Dist:* Trafalgar Square.

Thesman, Jean. Calling the Swan. l.t. ed. 2000. (Young Adult Ser.). 207p. (gr. 8-12). 20.95 o.p. (*0-7862-2910-1*) Thorndike Pr.

—In the House of Queen's Beasts. 2001. 32p. (J). (gr. 6-9). 15.99 o.s.i (*0-670-89285-8*, Viking Children's Bks.) Penguin Putnam Bks. for Young Readers.

—Was It Something I Said? 1988. 160p. (gr. 7-10). mass mkt. 2.75 (*0-380-75462-2*, Avon Bks.) Morrow/Avon.

Things We Like to Do. 1999. (Tami & Moishy Ser.: Vol. 5). bds. 6.95 (*0-87306-966-8*) Feldheim, Philipp Inc.

Thomas, Abigail. Pearl Paints, ERS. 1996. (Illus.). 32p. (J). pap. 5.95 o.p. (*0-8050-4071-4*, Holt, Henry & Co. Bks. For Young Readers) Holt, Henry & Co.

Thomas & Friends Picture Day. 2001. (Illus.). (J). 7.95 (*0-7853-4782-8*) Publications International, Ltd.

Thomas, Frances. Polly's Really Secret Diary. 2003. (Illus.). 96p. (gr. 1-4). pap. text 4.50 (*0-440-41704-X*, Yearling) Random Hse. Children's Bks.

Thomas, Janet. Newcomer. 1987. 33p. (J). (gr. k-3). pap. 6.00 (*0-87602-268-9*) Anchorage Pr.

Thomas, Jerry D. My Friend Fang & Other Great Stories for Kids: Learning How to Be Someone Who Has Good Friends. 2001. (Illus.). 95p. (J). (*0-8163-1822-0*) Pacific Pr. Publishing Assn.

Thomas, Karen. Changing of the Guard. 1986. 192p. (YA). (gr. 7 up). lib. bdg. 11.89 o.p. (*0-06-026164-1*) HarperCollins Children's Bk. Group.

Thomas, Marlo. Free to Be... You & Me. 2001. 144p. pap. text 12.95 (*0-7624-1306-9*) Running Pr. Bk. Pubs.

Thomas, Pat & Harker, Lesley. My Friends & Me: A First Look at Friendship. 2001. (First Look at Bks.). (Illus.). 32p. (J). (ps-2). pap. 5.95 (*0-7641-1763-7*) Barron's Educational Series, Inc.

Thomas, Peter. The Adventures of Billy Bee: Billy & Friends. 1995. (Illus.). 32p. (J). (gr. k-6). 14.95 (*1-886919-00-3*) Billy Bee Productions.

Thomasson, Clarissa. Who's a Friend? 2001. (Little Green Monkey Stories Ser.). (Illus.). 14p. (J). (gr. k-3). pap. 6.95 (*1-929202-16-4*) Salt Marsh Pubns.

Thompkins, Janet E. Cameron & Sammie Making Friends. 1999. (Illus.). 28p. (J). (gr. 1-5). pap. 6.95 (*1-890667-10-2*, Hand-In-Hand Bks.) Introspect Bks.

Thompson, Del. Putt-Putt & Pep. 1996. (Illus.). (J). (ps-1). 4.99 o.s.i (*0-679-87958-7*, Random Hse. Bks. for Young Readers) Random Hse. Children's Bks.

Thompson, Elizabeth M. Fat Cat Blue (And Friends) l.t. ed. 1987. (Illus.). 40p. (Orig.). (J). (gr. k-2). pap. 5.95 (*0-9619576-0-3*) Thompson, Elizabeth.

Thompson, Joan. The Mudpack & Me. MacDonald, Patricia, ed. 1993. 160p. (J). (gr. 3-6). per. 3.50 (*0-671-72862-8*, Aladdin) Simon & Schuster Children's Publishing.

Thompson, Julian F. The Fling, ERS. 1994. (J). 15.95 o.p. (*0-8050-2881-1*, Holt, Henry & Co. Bks. For Young Readers) Holt, Henry & Co.

—The Fling. 1996. 208p. (YA). (gr. 7 up). pap. 4.99 o.s.i (*0-14-037503-1*, Puffin Bks.) Penguin Putnam Bks. for Young Readers.

—Gypsyworld, ERS. 1992. 172p. (YA). (gr. 7 up). 15.95 o.p. (*0-8050-1907-3*, Holt, Henry & Co. Bks. For Young Readers) Holt, Henry & Co.

—Shepherd, ERS. 1993. 176p. (YA). (gr. 8 up). 15.95 o.p. (*0-8050-2106-X*, Holt, Henry & Co. Bks. For Young Readers) Holt, Henry & Co.

—Shepherd. 1996. 176p. (YA). (gr. 7 up). pap. 4.99 o.s.i (*0-14-037502-3*, Puffin Bks.) Penguin Putnam Bks. for Young Readers.

—Shepherd. 1996. 10.09 o.p. (*0-606-09853-4*) Turtleback Bks.

Thompson, Pat. My Friend Mr. Morris. 1988. (Share-a-Story Ser.: No. 6). (J). (gr. k-6). reprint ed. pap. 2.50 o.s.i (*0-440-40061-9*) Dell Publishing.

Thompson, Richard. The Last Story, the First Story. 1996. (Young Novels Ser.). (Illus.). 128p. (J). (gr. 4-6). 8.95 (*1-55037-025-1*); pap. 5.95 (*1-55037-024-3*) Annick Pr., Ltd. CAN. *Dist:* Firefly Bks., Ltd.

—Who. 1993. (Illus.). 32p. (J). (gr. 1-4). pap. 9.95 o.p. (*0-920501-98-2*) Orca Bk. Pubs.

Thomson, Emma. Felicity Wishes Little Book of Friendship. 2002. 20p. (J). 5.99 (*0-670-03590-4*) Penguin Putnam Bks. for Young Readers.

Thomson, Pat. Best Pest. 1990. (Illus.). 28p. (J). (gr. 1-4). 13.95 o.p. (*0-575-04573-6*) Gollancz, Victor GBR. *Dist:* Trafalgar Square.

—The Best Thing of All. 1995. (Illus.). 32p. (J). (ps-1). pap. 8.95 o.p. (*0-575-05997-4*) Gollancz, Victor GBR. *Dist:* Trafalgar Square.

—My Friend Mr. Morris. 1995. (Illus.). 32p. (J). (ps-2). pap. 8.95 o.p. (*0-575-05998-2*) Gollancz, Victor GBR. *Dist:* Trafalgar Square.

—No Trouble at All. (Illus.). (J). 1995. 32p. (gr. 2-4). pap. 8.95 o.p. (*0-575-05999-0*); 1990. 28p. (gr. 1-4). 13.95 o.p. (*0-575-04577-9*) Gollancz, Victor GBR. *Dist:* Trafalgar Square.

—Share a Story: No Trouble at All. (Illus.). 48p. (J). pap. 7.95 o.p. (*0-14-038883-4*) Penguin Bks., Ltd. GBR. *Dist:* Trafalgar Square.

Thornton, Terry & Thornton, Sandy. Recess. 1987. (Illus.). 32p. (J). (gr. 2-5). pap. 0.30 o.p. (*0-687-35660-1*) Abingdon Pr.

Thorpe, Kiki. Muck's Sleepover. 2002. (Bob the Builder Ser.: Bk. 3). (Illus.). 24p. (J). (ps-2). pap. 3.50 (*0-689-84755-6*, Simon Spotlight) Simon & Schuster Children's Publishing.

Thorpe, Kiki & Golden Books Staff. Smooch Is a Smoocher. 1999. (Golden Book Ser.). (Illus.). 24p. (J). (ps-2). bds. 4.99 o.s.i (*0-307-30428-0*, Golden Bks.) Random Hse. Children's Bks.

Thurston, Dorie. Thank-You for the Thistle. 2001. (Illus.). 36p. (J). (ps-3). pap. 9.95 (*0-9703326-0-2*) Dorie Bks.

Tibo, Gilles. Naomi & Mrs. Lumbago. Ouriou, Susan, tr. from FRE. 2001. (Illus.). 96p. (J). (gr. 1-4). pap. 6.95 (*0-88776-551-3*) Tundra Bks. of Northern New York.

Tibo, Gilles & Perkes, Carolyn. Alex & Sarah. 2001. (Little Wolf Bks.: Level 3). (Illus.). 32p. (J). (gr. 1 up). (*1-894363-76-0*) Dominique & Friends.

Tibo, Gilles & Vaillancourt, Francois. Mr. Patapoum's First Trip. 1993. (Illus.). 32p. (J). pap. 5.95 (*1-55037-294-7*); lib. bdg. 15.95 (*1-55037-293-9*) Annick Pr., Ltd. CAN. *Dist:* Firefly Bks., Ltd.

Time-Life Books Editors. Hello Molly! A Book about Friendship. 1999. (Big Comfy Couch Ser.). (Illus.). 32p. (J). (ps-1). 4.95 o.p. (*0-7835-4504-5*) Time-Life Education, Inc.

Timm, Stephen A. The Floor That Said "No More" 1986. (Illus.). 48p. (J). pap. 5.95 (*0-939728-12-5*); lib. bdg. 13.95 o.p. (*0-939728-13-3*) Steppingstone Enterprises, Inc.

Tingle, Dolli. Going to Be a Bride. 1987. (Illus.). 32p. (J). 5.95 o.p. (*0-8378-5080-0*) Gibson, C. R. Co.

Tingley, Janice R. Nolan's Dream. Gong, Janice, ed. 1.t. ed. 1997. (Illus.). 64p. (J). (gr. k-6). 12.95 (*0-9660985-0-1*) Tingley, J.R. Publishing, Inc.

Tippette, Giles. Warner & Laura. 1995. (Illus.). 320p. (J). mass mkt. 4.99 (*0-671-87160-9*, Pocket) Simon & Schuster.

Titlebaum, Ellen. I Love You, Winnie the Pooh. 1999. (Pooh Ser.). (Illus.). 32p. (J). (ps-2). 12.99 (*0-7868-3227-4*) Disney Pr.

Tobin Learns to Make Friends. 2001. mass mkt. 16.95 (*1-885477-79-1*) Future Horizons, Inc.

Tocher, Timothy. Long Shot. 2001. (J). 137p. (*0-88166-395-6*); 144p. mass mkt. 4.95 (*0-689-84331-3*) Meadowbrook Pr.

Todd, Pamela. Pig & the Shrink. Wojtyla, Karen, ed. 2000. (Illus.). 192p. (gr. 3-7). pap. text 4.50 (*0-440-41587-X*, Yearling) Random Hse. Children's Bks.

Together Is Best, Vol. 1. 1999. (Tami & Moishy Ser.: Vol. 1). bds. 6.95 (*0-87306-962-5*) Feldheim, Philipp Inc.

Tolan, Stephanie S. A Good Courage. 1989. (YA). (gr. 7 up). mass mkt. 1.50 o.s.i (*0-449-70329-0*, Fawcett) Ballantine Bks.

—A Good Courage. 1998. 256p. (YA). (gr. 7 up). reprint ed. pap. 4.95 (*0-688-16124-3*, Harper Trophy) HarperCollins Children's Bk. Group.

—A Good Courage. 1988. 240p. (YA). (gr. 7 up). 15.00 o.p. (*0-688-07446-4*, Morrow, William & Co.) Morrow/Avon.

—A Good Courage. 1998. 11.00 (*0-606-15553-8*) Turtleback Bks.

—Pride of the Peacock. 1987. 176p. (J). mass mkt. 1.50 o.s.i (*0-449-70207-3*, Fawcett) Ballantine Bks.

—Who's There? 1997. (J). 11.00 (*0-606-12091-2*) Turtleback Bks.

Tomalin, Ruth. Another Day. 1988. (J). (gr. 5-8). o.p. (*0-571-14976-6*) Faber & Faber Ltd.

Tomanio, Ronald. Lilly & Peggy. 1.t. ed. 1997. (Illus.). (J). (gr. 3). pap. 8.95 (*0-85398-420-4*) Ronald, George Pub., Ltd.

Tomes, Margaret & St. George, Judith S. By George, Bloomers. 9999. (J). pap. 1.75 o.s.i (*0-590-03318-2*) Scholastic, Inc.

Tomkins, Jasper. Nimby. 1991. (Illus.). 60p. (J). pap. 7.95 o.s.i (*0-671-74973-0*); 7.95 o.s.i (*0-914676-83-0*) Simon & Schuster Children's Publishing. (Aladdin).

—Nimby. 1987. pap. 6.95 (*0-310-57091-3*, 16109P) Zondervan.

Tomlinson, Theresa. Child of the May. 2000. 128p. (gr. 5-9). pap. text 4.99 o.s.i (*0-440-41577-2*, Yearling) Random Hse. Children's Bks.

—Child of the May. 2000. (Illus.). (J). 11.04 (*0-606-18782-0*) Turtleback Bks.

—Summer Witches. 1991. 96p. (J). (gr. 2-7). lib. bdg. 12.95 o.s.i (*0-02-789206-9*, Simon & Schuster Children's Publishing) Simon & Schuster Children's Publishing.

Town, Florida A. With a Silent Companion. 2000. 160p. (YA). (gr. 9 up). pap. 7.95 (*0-88995-211-6*) Red Deer Pr. CAN. *Dist:* General Distribution Services, Inc.

Townsend, John R. Tom Tiddler's Ground. 1.t. ed. 1987. 168p. (J). (gr. 3-7). 16.95 o.p. (*0-7451-0591-2*, Galaxy Children's Large Print) BBC Audiobooks America.

—Tom Tiddler's Ground. 1998. (Cambridge Reading Ser.). (Illus.). 160p. pap. text 10.25 (*0-521-46889-2*) Cambridge Univ. Pr.

Toye, Williama. Loon's Necklace. 1977. (J). 14.10 (*0-606-04470-1*) Turtleback Bks.

Tracey, Diane Eurich. Look Out for Virgil. Kuessner, Pat, ed. 2001. (Illus.). 24p. (J). (ps-7). pap. 12.00 (*0-9701441-4-8*, 628548) Bokmal Pr.

Trembath, Don. Lefty Carmichael Has a Fit. 2000. 215p. (J). (gr. 8 up). pap. 6.95 (*1-55143-166-1*) Orca Bk. Pubs.

—Lefty Carmichael Has a Fit. 2000. (Illus.). (J). 13.00 (*0-606-18328-0*) Turtleback Bks.

Trent, John T. The Two Trails: A Treasure Tree Adventure. 1997. (Illus.). 96p. (J). (gr. k-5). 14.99 (*0-8499-1450-7*) Nelson, Tommy.

Trevaskis, Ian. Periwinkle's Ride. 1994. (Illus.). (J). 19.30 (*0-383-03708-5*) SRA/McGraw-Hill.

Trimble, Irene. Max & Emmy's Flower Power. 2001. (Pictureback Shape Ser.). (Illus.). 24p. (J). (ps-k). pap. 3.25 (*0-375-81156-7*, Random Hse. Bks. for Young Readers) Random Hse. Children's Bks.

—Raining Cats & Dogs. 2003. 24p. (J). pap. 3.25 (*0-375-81427-2*, Random Hse. Bks. for Young Readers) Random Hse. Children's Bks.

—Taking Care of Quetzal. 2001. (Jellybean Books). (Illus.). 32p. (J). (ps-k). 3.99 o.s.i (*0-375-81284-9*, Random Hse. Bks. for Young Readers) Random Hse. Children's Bks.

Trimble, Marcia. Flower Green: A Flower for All Seasons. 2002. (Illus.). 32p. (J). (ps-2). 15.95 (*1-891577-67-0*) Images Pr.

Tripp, Valerie. Changes for Felicity: A Winter Story. 1992. (American Girls Collection: Bk. 6). (Illus.). 80p. (J). (gr. 2 up). 12.95 (*1-56247-038-8*, American Girl) Pleasant Co. Pubns.

—Changes for Felicity: A Winter Story. Johnson, Roberta, ed. 1992. (American Girls Collection: Bk. 6). (Illus.). 80p. (J). (gr. 2 up). pap. 5.95 (*1-56247-037-X*, American Girl) Pleasant Co. Pubns.

—Changes for Felicity: A Winter Story. 1992. (American Girls Collection: Bk. 6). (Illus.). (YA). (gr. 2 up). 12.10 (*0-606-01039-4*) Turtleback Bks.

—Changes for Samantha: A Winter Story. Thieme, Jeanne, ed. 1988. (American Girls Collection: Bk. 6). (Illus.). (YA). (gr. 2 up). 80p. pap. 5.95 (*0-937295-47-7*, American Girl); 80p. lib. bdg. 12.95 (*0-937295-95-7*, American Girl); 72p. 12.95 o.p. (*0-937295-46-9*) Pleasant Co. Pubns.

—Changes for Samantha: A Winter Story. 1988. (American Girls Collection: Bk. 6). (Illus.). (YA). (gr. 2 up). 12.10 (*0-606-03751-9*) Turtleback Bks.

—Good Sport Gwen. 2004. (Hopscotch Hill School Ser.: Vol. 5). (Illus.). (J). per. 3.99 (*1-58485-901-6*, American Girl) Pleasant Co. Pubns.

—Kit's Surprise: A Christmas Story. 2000. (American Girls Collection: Bk. 3). (Illus.). 80p. (J). (gr. 2 up). 12.95 (*1-58485-021-3*); pap. 5.95 (*1-58485-020-5*) Pleasant Co. Pubns. (American Girl).

—Kit's Surprise: A Christmas Story. 2000. (American Girls Collection: Bk. 3). (YA). (gr. 2 up). 12.10 (*0-606-18944-0*) Turtleback Bks.

—Kit's Tree House. 2003. (American Girls Collection). (Illus.). 40p. (J). pap. 4.95 (*1-58485-699-8*, American Girl) Pleasant Co. Pubns.

—Molly's A+ Partner. 2002. (American Girls Short Stories Ser.). (Illus.). 56p. (J). 4.95 (*1-58485-483-9*, American Girl) Pleasant Co. Pubns.

—Samantha's Winter Party. 1999. (American Girls Short Stories Ser.). (Illus.). 56p. (YA). 3.95 (*1-56247-766-8*, American Girl) Pleasant Co. Pubns.

Trivelpiece, Laurel. Just a Little Bit Lost. 1988. 192p. (J). (gr. 6-8). pap. 2.50 o.p. (*0-590-41465-8*, Scholastic Paperbacks) Scholastic, Inc.

Trivizas, Eugene. Los Tres Lobitos y el Cochino Feroz (The Three Little Wolves & the Big Bad Pig) 1995. (SPA., Illus.). 32p. (J). (gr. 1-4). 18.50 (*980-257-177-6*) Ekare, Ediciones VEN. *Dist:* AIMS International Bks., Inc., Kane/Miller Bk. Pubs.

The Trouble with Tuck. 1986. (J). pap. 1.25 o.s.i (*0-440-82064-2*) Dell Publishing.

Trudel, Sylvain. Une Saison au Paradis. 2002. (Premier Roman Ser.). (Illus.). 64p. (J). (gr. 2-5). pap. 8.95 (*2-89021-353-6*) La Courte Echelle CAN. *Dist:* Firefly Bks., Ltd.

Trudel, Sylvain & Langlois, Suzane. Le Grenier de Monsieur Basile. 1997. (Premier Roman Ser.). 64p. (J). (gr. 2-5). pap. 8.95 (*2-89021-294-7*) La Courte Echelle CAN. *Dist:* Firefly Bks., Ltd.

—Un Secret dans Mon Jardin. 2001. (Premier Roman Ser.). (FRE., Illus.). 64p. (J). pap. 8.95 (*2-89021-452-4*) La Courte Echelle CAN. *Dist:* Firefly Bks., Ltd.

—Le Voleur du Poisson D'or. 2001. (Premier Roman Ser.). (FRE., Illus.). 64p. (J). pap. 8.95 (*2-89021-542-3*) La Courte Echelle CAN. *Dist:* Firefly Bks., Ltd.

Truus. Kouka. 1924. (J). lib. bdg. o.p. (*0-688-12382-1*) HarperCollins Children's Bk. Group.

Tryon, Thomas. The Adventures of Opal & Cupid. 1992. (Illus.). 192p. (J). 14.00 o.p. (*0-670-82239-6*, Viking Children's Bks.) Penguin Putnam Bks. for Young Readers.

Tsutsui, Yoriko. Anna's Special Present. 1988. (Illus.). 32p. (J). (ps-3). 11.95 o.p. (*0-670-81671-X*, Viking Children's Bks.) Penguin Putnam Bks. for Young Readers.

Tung, Angela. Trane & Me. 2000. 160p. (J). (gr. 4-7). 12.95 o.p. (*0-7373-0397-2*, 03972W) Lowell Hse.

—Trane & Me. 2000. (Roxbury Park Bks.). (Illus.). 160p. (J). (gr. 3-7). pap. 4.95 (*0-7373-0180-5*, 01805W) McGraw-Hill/Contemporary.

Turin, Adela. Una Felize Catastrofe. 2002. (SPA.). 40p. 13.95 (*1-4000-0241-9*) Random Hse., Inc.

Turkle, Brinton. Thy Friend, Obadiah. 1982. (Picture Puffins Ser.). (Illus.). 400p. (J). (gr. 4-7). pap. 5.99 (*0-14-050393-5*, Puffin Bks.) Penguin Putnam Bks. for Young Readers.

—Thy Friend, Obadiah. 1985. (Picture Puffin Ser.). (J). 12.14 (*0-606-03489-7*) Turtleback Bks.

Turnbull, Ann. No Friend of Mine. 1995. (Illus.). 128p. (J). (gr. 5-9). 15.95 o.p. (*1-56402-565-9*) Candlewick Pr.

Turner, Ann Warren. One Brave Summer. 1995. (J). 13.95 o.p. (*0-06-023732-5*) HarperCollins Pubs.

—One Brave Summer. 1995. 80p. (J). lib. bdg. 13.89 o.p. (*0-06-023875-5*) HarperTrade.

Turner, Glennette Tilley. Take a Walk in Their Shoes. 1989. (Illus.). 176p. (J). (gr. 4-8). 15.99 o.s.i (*0-525-65006-7*, Dutton Children's Bks.) Penguin Putnam Bks. for Young Readers.

Tusa, Tricia. Maebelle's Suitcase. (Illus.). 32p. (J). (gr. k-3). 1987. lib. bdg. 15.00 o.s.i (*0-02-789250-6*, Simon & Schuster Children's Publishing); 1991. reprint ed. pap. 6.99 (*0-689-71444-0*, Aladdin) Simon & Schuster Children's Publishing.

—Maebelle's Suitcase. 1991. (Reading Rainbow Bks.). 12.14 (*0-606-12407-1*) Turtleback Bks.

—Miranda. 1985. (Illus.). 32p. (J). (ps up). lib. bdg. 13.95 o.p. (*0-02-789520-3*, Simon & Schuster Children's Publishing) Simon & Schuster Children's Publishing.

—Stay Away from the Junkyard! (Illus.). 32p. (J). (gr. k-3). 1988. lib. bdg. 14.95 (*0-02-789541-6*, Simon & Schuster Children's Publishing); 1992. reprint ed. pap. 6.99 (*0-689-71626-5*, Aladdin) Simon & Schuster Children's Publishing.

—Stay Away from the Junkyard! 1992. (Reading Rainbow Bks.). (J). 12.14 (*0-606-01997-9*) Turtleback Bks.

Tutela, Dawn. Jenny's First Friend. Newberger, Eli, ed. 1981. (Jenny Ser.). (Illus.). 48p. (J). (gr. 4-9). pap. 3.50 o.p. (*0-8326-2608-2*, 7610) Penguin Group (USA) Inc.

Twain, Mark. The Adventures of Huckleberry Finn. 2nd ed. 1998. (Illustrated Classic Book Ser.). (Illus.). 61p. (J). (gr. 3 up). reprint ed. pap. text 4.95 (*1-56767-255-8*) Educational Insights, Inc.

—The Adventures of Huckleberry Finn: With a Discussion of Friendship. Lauter, Richard, tr. & illus. by. 2003. (Values in Action Illustrated Classics Ser.). (J). (*1-59203-042-4*) Learning Challenge, Inc.

—The Adventures of Tom Sawyer. 1997. (J). 11.00 (*0-606-01797-6*) Turtleback Bks.

—The Adventures of Tom Sawyer. 2001. 184p. pap. 9.95 (*1-57002-169-4*) University Publishing Hse., Inc.

—Huckleberry Finn. 6th ed. 1997. (FRE., Illus.). (J). (gr. 4-7). pap. 13.95 (*2-07-051625-3*) Gallimard, Editions FRA. *Dist:* Distribooks, Inc.

—A Story Without an End. 1986. (Short Story Library). (Illus.). 32p. (YA). (gr. 5 up). lib. bdg. 13.95 o.p. (*0-88682-064-2*, 1078-A, Creative Education) Creative Co., The.

Twinn, Michael. Bully for You. 1996. (J). lib. bdg. 11.95 (*0-85953-849-4*) Child's Play of England GBR. *Dist:* Child's Play-International.

Two Coconuts Ask "Why"? A Story about Trust. 1998. (Excellence in Character Series Storybks.). (Illus.). 30p. (J). (gr. k-8). pap. 6.00 (*1-58259-028-1*) Global Classroom, The.

Two Leaf Friends: A Story about Tolerance. 1998. (Excellence in Character Series Storybks.). (Illus.). 30p. (J). (gr. k-8). pap. 6.00 (*1-58259-027-3*) Global Classroom, The.

Twohill, Maggie. Big Mouth. 1989. 128p. (J). (gr. k-6). pap. 2.95 o.s.i (*0-440-40223-9*, Yearling) Random Hse. Children's Bks.

—Valentine Frankenstein. 1991. 144p. (J). (gr. 3-6). text 13.95 o.s.i (*0-02-789692-7*, Simon & Schuster Children's Publishing) Simon & Schuster Children's Publishing.

Uchida, Yoshiko. The Bracelet. 1993. (Illus.). 32p. (J). (ps-3). 16.99 (*0-399-22503-X*, Philomel) Penguin Putnam Bks. for Young Readers.

—The Happiest Ending. 1985. 120p. (J). (gr. 3-7). 15.00 (*0-689-50326-1*, McElderry, Margaret K.) Simon & Schuster Children's Publishing.

Udry, Janice May. Let's Be Enemies. 1961. (J). 12.10 (*0-606-03844-2*) Turtleback Bks.

Ugly Beast. 1987. (Illus.). 32p. (J). (ps-3). pap. 4.95 o.p. (*0-8431-2652-3*, Price Stern Sloan) Penguin Putnam Bks. for Young Readers.

Uhlig, Susan. Lindsey & the Tree House Gang. (J). (gr. 3-6). pap. 3.75 o.p. (*1-889658-10-3*) New Canaan Publishing Co., Inc.

—Lindsey Hits the Club. 1999. (Illus.). 96p. (J). (gr. 3-6). pap. 6.75 (*1-889658-17-0*) New Canaan Publishing Co., Inc.

UIS Preschoolers Staff. The Bears & Dinosaurs Make Friends. (WeWrite Kids! Ser.: No. 3). (Illus.). 23p. (J). (ps-2). 1995. pap. 3.95 (*1-884987-13-3*); 1994. lib. bdg. 18.95 o.p. (*1-884987-12-5*); Big Bk. 1994. 32.95 o.p. (*1-884987-14-1*) WeWrite Corp.

Ullman, James Ramsey. Banner in the Sky. 1984. 256p. (J). (gr. 7-10). pap. (*0-671-54629-5*, Simon Pulse) Simon & Schuster Children's Publishing.

—Banner in the Sky. 1954. (J). 12.00 (*0-606-03550-8*) Turtleback Bks.

Unada, G. Andrews Amazing Boxes. 1971. (See & Read Storybook Ser.). (Illus.). (J). (gr. 1-3). 4.49 o.p. (*0-399-60025-6*) Putnam Publishing Group, The.

Underneath I'm Different. 1983. (J). pap. 13.95 o.s.i (*0-385-29234-1*) Doubleday Publishing.

Unger, Jim. Where's the Kids, Herman? 1984. mass mkt. 1.95 o.p. (*0-451-12922-9*); (Illus.). 96p. mass mkt. 2.25 o.p. (*0-451-15795-8*) NAL. (Signet Bks.).

Unk. Chester's Way. 93rd ed. 1993. pap. text 12.40 (*0-15-300319-7*) Harcourt Children's Bks.

Urbide, Fernando & Engler, Dan. Ben-Hur: A Race to Glory. 1992. (Illus.). 35p. (J). (ps-8). 14.99 incl. VHS (*1-56814-006-1*) CCC of America.

Ure, Jean. The Most Important Thing. 1986. (Illus.). 192p. (J). (gr. 5 up). 12.95 o.p. (*0-688-05859-0*, Morrow, William & Co.) Morrow/Avon.

—See You Thursday. 1985. 176p. (gr. k-12). pap. 2.50 o.p. (*0-440-97742-8*) Dell Publishing.

—Skinny Melon & Me, ERS. 2001. (Illus.). 202p. (J). (gr. 3-6). 16.00 (*0-8050-6359-5*, Holt, Henry & Co. Bks. For Young Readers) Holt, Henry & Co.

—The You-Two. 1984. (Illus.). (J). (gr. 4-7). 11.95 o.p. (*0-688-03857-3*, Morrow, William & Co.) Morrow/Avon.

Uttley, Alison. Wise Owl's Story. 1990. (Little Grey Rabbit Ser.). (J). 4.98 o.p. (*0-8317-5630-6*) Smithmark Pubs., Inc.

Vail, Rachel. Ever After. 1994. 176p. (J). (gr. 6-9). mass mkt. 15.95 o.p. (*0-531-06838-2*); (gr. 7 up). lib. bdg. 16.99 (*0-531-08688-7*) Scholastic, Inc. (Orchard Bks.).

—If You Only Knew: Zoe. (Friendship Ring Ser.: No. 1). 240p. (J). (gr. 4-8). 1999. mass mkt. 3.99 (*0-439-08761-9*); 1998. pap. 14.95 (*0-590-03370-0*); 1998. mass mkt. 4.99 (*0-590-37451-6*) Scholastic, Inc.

—Mama Rex & T: The Horrible Play Date. 2002. (Mama Rex & T Ser.). (Illus.). 32p. (J). pap. 14.95 (*0-439-40627-7*); pap. 4.99 (*0-439-28335-3*); mass mkt. 4.99 (*0-439-42617-0*) Scholastic, Inc. (Orchard Bks.).

—Not That I Care: Morgan. (Friendship Ring Ser.: No.3). (J). (gr. 4-8). 1999. pap.; 1998. 240p. pap. 14.95 (*0-590-03476-6*); 1998. 240p. mass mkt. 4.99 (*0-590-37453-2*); 1998. 59.88 (*0-590-95214-5*) Scholastic, Inc.

—Please, Please, Please: CJ. 1998. (Friendship Ring Ser.: No. 2). 240p. (J). (gr. 4-8). mass mkt. 4.99 (*0-590-37452-4*) Scholastic, Inc.

—Popularity Contest: Zoe. 2000. (Friendship Ring Ser.: No. 5). (J). (gr. 4-8). (Illus.). 240p. mass mkt. 3.99 (*0-590-68911-8*, Scholastic Paperbacks);Vol. 5. pap. 47.88 (*0-439-16067-7*) Scholastic, Inc.

—What Are Friends For? Olivia. (Friendship Ring Ser.: No. 4). (J). (gr. 4-8). 2000. pap. 59.88 (*0-439-05981-X*); 1999. 240p. mass mkt. 3.99 (*0-590-37454-0*) Scholastic, Inc.

—Wonder. 1993. 128p. (J). (gr. 5-9). pap. 4.99 o.s.i (*0-14-036167-7*, Puffin Bks.) Penguin Putnam Bks. for Young Readers.

—Wonder. 1991. 128p. (YA). (gr. 4-7). pap. 15.95 (*0-531-05964-2*, Orchard Bks.) Scholastic, Inc.

—Wonder. 1993. (J). 11.04 (*0-606-05710-2*) Turtleback Bks.

Vail, Rachel, illus. Wonder. 1991. 128p. (YA). (gr. 6 up). mass mkt. 16.99 o.p. (*0-531-08564-3*, Orchard Bks.) Scholastic, Inc.

Vainio, Pirkko. Don't Be Scared, Scarecrow. 1945. (Illus.). 32p. (J). (gr. k-3). 14.95 o.p. (*1-55858-275-4*); 15.50 o.p. (*1-55858-276-2*) North-South Bks., Inc.

—The Dream House. James, J. Alison, tr. from GER. 1997. (Illus.). 32p. (J). (gr. k-3). 15.95 (*1-55858-749-7*); 16.50 (*1-55858-750-0*) North-South Bks., Inc.

Valat, Pierre-Marie. Fun Faces. 1989. (Illus.). 32p. (J). pap. 13.99 o.p. (*0-525-44544-7*, Dutton Children's Bks.) Penguin Putnam Bks. for Young Readers.

Valdes, Leslie. Meet Diego! 2003. (Dora the Explorer Ser.). (Illus.). 24p. (J). pap. 3.50 (*0-689-85993-7*, Simon Spotlight/Nickelodeon) Simon & Schuster Children's Publishing.

Valencak, Hannelore. A Tangled Web. Crampton, Patricia, tr. from GER. 1978. (J). (gr. 7-9). 12.95 o.p. (*0-688-22169-6*, Morrow, William & Co.) Morrow/Avon.

Vallee, Brian. Life with Billy. 1986. 256p. (J). mass mkt. 8.99 o.p. (*0-7704-2239-X*) Bantam Bks.

Vallik, Malle. Andy & Andie. 2000. (Love Stories Super Edition Ser.). 224p. (gr. 7-12). mass mkt. 4.99 o.s.i (*0-553-49321-3*, Skylark) Random Hse. Children's Bks.

Van de Wetering, Janwillem. Hugh Pine & Something Else. 1989. (Illus.). 96p. (J). (gr. 3 up). 13.95 o.p. (*0-395-49216-5*) Houghton Mifflin Co.

—Hugh Pine & Something Else. ALC Staff, ed. 1992. (Illus.). 80p. (J). (gr. 2 up). pap. 3.95 o.p. (*0-688-11800-3*, Morrow, William & Co.) Morrow/Avon.

—Hugh Pine & the Good Place, 001. 1986. (Illus.). 80p. (J). (gr. 3 up). 13.95 o.p. (*0-395-40147-X*) Houghton Mifflin Co.

—Hugh Pine & the Good Place. ALC Staff, ed. 1992. (Illus.). 72p. (J). pap. 3.95 o.p. (*0-688-11801-1*, Morrow, William & Co.) Morrow/Avon.

—Hugh Pine & the Good Place. 1988. 64p. (J). pap. 2.50 o.s.i (*0-553-15572-5*, Skylark) Random Hse. Children's Bks.

van Genechten, Guido. Flop Ear. 2001. (Illus.). (J). 12.10 (*0-606-21191-8*) Turtleback Bks.

Ward, Geoffrey C. Closest Companion. 1995. 384p. (J). 24.95 o.p. (*0-395-66080-7*) Houghton Mifflin Co.

Ward, Heather P. I Promise I'll Find You. braille ed. 1996. (J). (gr. 2). spiral bd. (*0-616-01809-6*) Canadian National Institute for the Blind/Institut National Canadien pour les Aveugles.

—I Promise I'll Find You. 2003. (Illus.). 32p. (J). (ps-3). pap. 5.95 (*1-55209-094-9*) Firefly Bks., Ltd.

—I Promise I'll Find You. 1997. (J). 12.10 (*0-606-12732-1*) Turtleback Bks.

Ward, Nanda. Hi Tom. 1962. (J). 6.95 o.p. (*0-8038-2991-4*) Hastings Hse. Daytrips Pubs.

Ward, Sally G. Punky Spends the Day. 1989. (Illus.). 32p. (J). (ps-1). 11.95 o.p. (*0-525-44526-9*, Dutton Children's Bks.) Penguin Putnam Bks. for Young Readers.

Ware, Cheryl. Flea Circus Summer. 1997. 144p. (J). (gr. 4-6). pap. 15.95 (*0-531-30032-3*); lib. bdg. 16.99 (*0-531-33032-X*) Scholastic, Inc. (Orchard Bks.).

—Sea Monkey Summer. 1996. 144p. (J). (gr. 4-6). mass mkt. 15.99 o.p. (*0-531-08868-5*); mass mkt. 14.95 o.p. (*0-531-09518-5*) Scholastic, Inc. (Orchard Bks.).

Ware, Martin E. Carly's & Amy's, Friends & Fables. 1991. (Illus.). 40p. (J). (gr. 3-8). 7.50 o.p. (*0-8059-3194-5*) Dorrance Publishing Co., Inc.

Warner, Gertrude Chandler, creator. Benny's New Friend. 1998. (Adventures of Benny & Watch: No. 3). (J). (gr. 1-3). 10.10 (*0-606-13217-1*) Turtleback Bks.

—The Haunted Cabin Mystery. 1991. (Boxcar Children Ser.: No. 20). (Illus.). 121p. (J). (gr. 2-5). lib. bdg. 13.95 (*0-8075-3179-0*); mass mkt. 3.95 (*0-8075-3178-2*) Whitman, Albert & Co.

Warner, Sally. Bad Girl Blues. 2001. 224p. (J). (gr. 3-7). lib. bdg. 16.89 (*0-06-028275-4*); (YA). (gr. 5-9). 15.95 (*0-06-028274-6*) HarperCollins Children's Bk. Group.

—Leftover Lily. 2000. (Lily Ser.). (Illus.). 128p. (gr. k-3). pap. 3.99 o.s.i (*0-375-80347-5*) Knopf, Alfred A. Inc.

—Leftover Lily. 1999. (Illus.). 128p. (J). (gr. k-3). lib. bdg. 16.99 (*0-679-99139-5*, Knopf Bks. for Young Readers) Random Hse. Children's Bks.

—Leftover Lily. 2000. (Illus.). (J). 10.04 (*0-606-18238-1*) Turtleback Bks.

—A Long Time Ago Today. 2003. (Illus.). 208p. (J). (gr. 3-6). 15.99 (*0-670-03604-8*, Viking) Viking Penguin.

—Some Friend. 1997. 160p. (J). (gr. 3-9). pap. 4.99 o.s.i (*0-679-87619-7*) Random Hse., Inc.

—Some Friend. 1997. 10.09 o.p. (*0-606-11857-8*) Turtleback Bks.

—Sort of Forever. (J). 1999. 128p. (gr. 5-8). pap. 4.99 o.s.i (*0-375-80207-X*, Knopf Bks. for Young Readers); 1998. 128p. (gr. 3-6). 16.00 o.s.i (*0-679-88648-6*, Knopf Bks. for Young Readers); 1998. 128p. (gr. 5-8). 17.99 o.s.i (*0-679-98648-0*, Knopf Bks. for Young Readers); 1998. (gr. 3-6). pap. (*0-679-88649-4*, Random Hse. Bks. for Young Readers) Random Hse. Children's Bks.

—Sort of Forever. 1999. 11.04 (*0-606-17153-3*) Turtleback Bks.

Warnes, Tim. Can't You Sleep, Dotty? (J). 2003. 32p. pap. 5.95 (*1-58925-376-0*); 2001. (Illus.). tchr. ed. 14.95 (*1-58925-010-9*) ME Media LLC. (Tiger Tales).

Warren, Jean. The Bear & the Mountain: A Totline Teaching Tale. 1994. (Nature Ser.). (Illus.). 32p. (J). (ps-2). pap. 5.95 o.p. (*0-911019-98-7*, WPH 1905, Totline Pubns.) McGraw-Hill Children's Publishing.

—The Bear & the Mountain: Themes: Bears, Flowers, Friendship. 1994. (Nature Ser.). (Illus.). 32p. (J). (ps-2). pap. 12.95 o.p. (*0-911019-99-5*, WPH 1906, Totline Pubns.) McGraw-Hill Children's Publishing.

Warren, Sandra & Pfleger, Deborah Bel. Arlie the Alligator. 1992. (Illus.). 48p. (J). (ps-3). lib. bdg. 13.95 (*1-880175-13-4*); 19.90 incl. audio (*1-880175-11-8*) Arlie Enterprises.

Wartski, Maureen C. Belonging. 1993. 176p. (Orig.). (YA). (gr. 7 up). mass mkt. 3.99 o.s.i (*0-449-70419-X*, Fawcett) Ballantine Bks.

Washington, Donna. When Are You Gonna Be Here? 32p. (J). pap. 4.99 (*0-7868-1231-1*) Hyperion Pr.

Washington, Linda. Mel & Les More or Less. 2002. (Piece of My Mind Devotional Ser.). 96p. pap. 8.99 (*0-8423-5374-7*) Tyndale Hse. Pubs.

Watch Out for Big Bad Brad. 1991. (J). (gr. 2 up). pap. 1.97 (*1-56297-115-8*) Lee Pubns.

Watson, James, Jr. The Freedom Tree. 1986. 160p. (YA). (gr. 8-12). 17.95 o.p. (*0-575-03779-2*) Gollancz, Victor GBR. *Dist:* Trafalgar Square.

Watson, Pauline. My Turn, Your Turn. 1983. (Illus.). (J). (ps-2). o.p. (*0-13-608703-5*) Prentice-Hall.

Watson, Wendy. Holly's Christmas Eve. 2002. (Illus.). 32p. (J). (ps-3). lib. bdg. 17.89 (*0-688-17653-4*) HarperCollins Children's Bk. Group.

—Holly's Christmas Eve. 2002. (Illus.). 32p. (J). (ps-3). 15.99 (*0-688-17652-6*) HarperCollins Pubs.

Watts, Robert A. Who Are Billy's Friends. 1964. (Illus.). (J). bds. 0.60 o.p. (*0-8054-4134-4*) Broadman & Holman Pubs.

Weatherby, Mark Alan. My Dinosaur. 1997. (Illus.). 32p. (J). (ps-2). pap. 15.95 (*0-590-97203-0*) Scholastic, Inc.

Weathers, Anah D. Secrets of the Cave. unabr. ed. 2000. (Treasures from the Past Ser.). (Illus.). x, 104p. (J). (gr. 4-8). pap. 7.98 (*0-9702584-0-2*) Creative Services.

Weaver, Ann. A Wiggly Spider a Slug a Salamander & the Bug! 2000. (Illus.). 16p. (J). pap. 5.95 (*0-87012-649-0*) McClain Printing Co.

Weaver-Gelzer, Charlotte. In the Time of Trouble. 1993. 288p. (J). (gr. 7 up). 15.99 o.p. (*0-525-44973-6*, Dutton Children's Bks.) Penguin Putnam Bks. for Young Readers.

Webb, Angela. Reflections. Franklin Watts, Inc. Staff, ed. 1988. (Talk Abouts Ser.). (Illus.). 32p. (J). (ps-6). 10.90 o.p. (*0-531-10457-5*, Watts, Franklin) Scholastic Library Publishing.

Webb, Dave. Slinky Inkermann & the Crazy Contest. 1996. (Illus.). 100p. (Orig.). (J). (gr. 3-6). pap. 3.95 (*1-57502-290-7*, PO1000) Morris Publishing.

Weber, Lenora Mattingly. The More the Merrier. 1999. (Beany Malone Ser.). 246p. (J). reprint ed. pap. 12.95 (*1-930009-00-3*) Image Cascade Publishing.

—Welcome Stranger. 1999. (Beany Malone Ser.). 291p. (J). reprint ed. pap. 12.95 (*1-930009-02-X*) Image Cascade Publishing.

Webster, Jean. Dear Enemy. 1991. 320p. (J). (gr. 4-7). pap. 3.50 o.s.i (*0-440-40440-1*) Dell Publishing.

Weeks, Sarah. Guy Wire. 2002. 144p. (J). lib. bdg. 17.89 (*0-06-029493-0*); (gr. 3-7). 15.99 (*0-06-029492-2*) HarperCollins Children's Bk. Group. (Geringer, Laura Bk.).

Weigelt, Udo. All-Weather Friends. 1999. (Illus.). 32p. (J). (gr. k-3). 16.50 (*0-7358-1048-6*); 15.95 o.p. (*0-7358-1047-8*) North-South Bks., Inc.

—Fair-Weather Friend. James, J. Alison, tr. from GER. 2002. (Illus.). 32p. (J). (gr. k-3). 15.95 (*0-7358-1785-5*); lib. bdg. 16.50 (*0-7358-1786-3*) North-South Bks., Inc.

—The Sandman. 2003. (Illus.). 32p. (J). (gr. k-3). lib. bdg. 16.50 (*0-7358-1790-1*) North-South Bks., Inc.

—The Sandman. James, J. Alison, tr. from GER. 2003. (Illus.). 32p. (J). (gr. k-3). 15.95 (*0-7358-1789-8*) North-South Bks., Inc.

—Who Stole the Gold? James, J. Alison, tr. from GER. 2000. (Illus.). 32p. (J). (gr. k-3). 15.95 o.p. (*0-7358-1372-8*) North-South Bks., Inc.

Weigelt, Udo, et al. Who Stole the Gold? James, J. Alison, tr. from GER. 2000. (Illus.). 32p. (J). (gr. k-3). 16.50 o.p. (*0-7358-1373-6*) North-South Bks., Inc.

Weil, Jennifer C. And Peter Said Goodbye. 1993. (Illus.). 40p. (J). (gr. k-4). 14.95 (*1-56844-000-6*) Enchante Publishing.

—And Peter Said Goodbye. Hoy, Gudrun & Martin, Bobi, eds. 2nd rev. ed. 1996. (Emotional Literacy Ser.). (Illus.). 40p. (J). (gr. k-5). 14.95 (*1-56844-100-2*) Enchante Publishing.

Weimer, Tonja Evetts. Family & Friends, Vol. 2. 2nd ed. 1995. (Fingerplays & Action Chants). (Illus.). 64p. (J). (ps-1). pap. 14.95 incl. audio (*0-936823-14-3*) Pearce-Evetts Publishing.

Weinberg, Ben. Out to the Edge. Holmes, B., ed. 1993. 200p. (YA). (gr. 6-10). pap. 8.95 (*0-932433-47-2*) Windswept Hse. Pubs.

Weinberger, Kimberly. Be-a-Good-Friend Sticker Book. 2001. (Clifford, the Big Red Dog Ser.). (Illus.). 24p. (J). (gr. k-2). 5.99 (*0-439-22945-6*) Scholastic, Inc.

Weir, Liz. Boom Chicka Boom. 1997. (Illus.). (J). 80p. pap. 7.95 (*0-86278-417-4*); pap. 12.95 incl. audio compact disk (*0-86278-461-1*); audio compact disk 14.95 (*0-86278-469-7*) O'Brien Pr., Ltd., The IRL. *Dist:* Irish American Bk. Co.

Weiss, Anne E. Lies, Deception, & Truth, 001. 1988. 160p. (J). (gr. 5-9). 13.95 o.p. (*0-395-40486-X*) Houghton Mifflin Co.

Weiss, Ellen. Kitten Alert. 1995. (Animal Rescue Squad: No. 1). (J). pap. 3.99 o.s.i (*0-679-85865-2*) Random Hse., Inc.

—New Friend, Blue Friend. 1999. (Road to Reading Ser.). (Illus.). 32p. (J). (ps-3). pap. 3.99 (*0-307-26210-3*, Golden Bks.) Random Hse. Children's Bks.

—Nobody's Dog. 1996. (Animal Rescue Squad Ser.: No. 4). (J). pap. 3.99 o.s.i (*0-679-85868-7*, Random Hse. Bks. for Young Readers) Random Hse. Children's Bks.

—Scary, Scary Monsters. 1999. (Road to Reading Ser.). (Illus.). 32p. (J). (ps-3). 10.99 (*0-307-46210-2*, Golden Bks.) Random Hse. Children's Bks.

Weiss, M. Jerry & Weiss, Helen S., eds. Lost & Found. 2001. 224p. mass mkt. 5.99 (*0-8125-6866-4*, Forge Bks.) Doherty, Tom Assocs., LLC.

Weiss, Nicki. Hank & Oogie. 1991. 48p. (J). (ps-3). pap. 2.75 o.s.i (*0-553-15954-2*) Bantam Bks.

—Maude & Sally. 1983. (Illus.). 32p. (J). (gr. k-3). 15.00 o.p. (*0-688-01859-9*); lib. bdg. 14.93 o.p. (*0-688-01861-0*) HarperCollins Children's Bk. Group. (Greenwillow Bks.).

—Maude & Sally. 1988. (J). (ps-3). pap. 3.95 o.p. (*0-14-050760-4*, Puffin Bks.) Penguin Putnam Bks. for Young Readers.

Weissman, Bob. Katie the Square Shouldered Girl. 2001. 128p. pap. 7.95 (*0-87714-449-4*); (J). 6.95 (*0-87714-624-1*) Denlingers Pubs., Ltd.

Well, Rosemary. McDuff's New Friend with Plush Box Set. 2003. (Illus.). 112p. (J). 14.99 (*0-7868-1866-2*, Disney Editions) Disney Pr.

Wells, Rosemary. Bubble-Gum Radar. 2002. (Yoko & Friends School Days Ser.: No. 9). 32p. (J). pap. 3.99 (*0-7868-1528-0*, Volo); (Illus.). 9.99 (*0-7868-0722-9*) Hyperion Bks. for Children.

—Lucas y Virginia. 1999. Orig. Title: Benjamin & Tulip. (SPA., Illus.). (J). (ps-3). lib. bdg. 12.95 (*0-88272-321-9*) Santillana USA Publishing Co., Inc.

—McDuff Friendship Box. 2001. (Illus.). 96p. (J). (ps-k). 9.99 (*0-7868-0666-4*) Hyperion Bks. for Children.

—Only You/Solo Tu. 2004. 14.99 (*0-670-03692-7*, Viking) Viking Penguin.

—Stanley & Rhoda. (Illus.). (J). (ps-2). 1985. 9.89 o.p. (*0-8037-8249-7*); 1981. 4p. pap. 4.95 o.p. (*0-8037-7995-X*, 0383-120); 1978. 13.95 o.s.i (*0-8037-8248-9*) Penguin Putnam Bks. for Young Readers. (Dial Bks. for Young Readers).

—Yoko & Friends: School Days #11: Make New Friends. 2002. (Yoko & Friends School Days Ser.). (Illus.). 32p. (J). (gr. k-2). 9.95 (*0-7868-0730-X*); pap. 3.99 (*0-7868-1536-1*) Hyperion Bks. for Children. (Volo).

Weninger, Brigitte, pseud. Don't Fight, Davy. 2003. 16p. (J). bds. 6.95 (*0-7358-1753-7*) North-South Bks., Inc.

—Why Are You Fighting, Davy? Lanning, Rosemary, tr. from GER. 2002. (Illus.). 32p. (J). pap. 6.95 (*0-7358-1601-8*, Michael Neugebauer Bks.) North-South Bks., Inc.

—Why Are You Fighting, Davy? 1999. (Illus.). 32p. (J). (gr. k-3). 15.95 (*0-7358-1073-7*); 16.50 (*0-7358-1074-5*) North-South Bks., Inc.

Werner, Vivian. Petrouchka. 1999. pap. 3.95 (*0-14-054333-3*) NAL.

Wersba, Barbara. Crazy Vanilla. 1986. (Charlotte Zolotow Bk.). 192p. (YA). (gr. 7 up). 11.95 (*0-06-026368-7*); lib. bdg. 11.89 o.p. (*0-06-026369-5*) HarperCollins Children's Bk. Group.

Wesley, Mary. Speaking Terms. 1971. (Illus.). (J). (gr. 3-7). 6.95 o.p. (*0-87645-041-9*) Harvard Common Pr.

—Speaking Terms. 1994. 128p. (J). (gr. 7-12). 14.95 (*0-87951-524-4*) Overlook Pr., The.

West, Colin. Buzz, Buzz, Buzz, Went Bumblebee. 1996. (Illus.). (J). (ps up). 9.99 o.p. (*1-56402-681-7*) Candlewick Pr.

West, Jessamyn. Friendly Persuasion. 1991. 17.05 (*0-606-12299-0*) Turtleback Bks.

West, Tracey. Mr. Peale's Bones. 1994. (Stories of the States Ser.). (Illus.). 64p. (J). (gr. 4-6). lib. bdg. 14.95 (*1-881889-50-5*) Silver Moon Pr.

—The Power of Friendship. 2002. (Sailor Moon Junior Chapter Bks.: No. 3). (Illus.). 48p. (J). (ps-3). mass mkt. 3.99 (*0-439-22444-6*) Scholastic, Inc.

—Power Pals. 2002. (Powerpuff Girls Ser.: No. 13). (Illus.). 32p. (J). (gr. 4-6). mass mkt. 3.50 (*0-439-37229-1*) Scholastic, Inc.

Westermann, John. High Crimes. McCarthy, Paul, ed. 1989. 256p. mass mkt. 5.99 (*0-671-67968-6*, Pocket) Simon & Schuster.

Weston, Carol. The Diary of Melanie Martin: Or How I Survived Matt the Brat, Michelangelo & the Leaning Tower of Pizza. 2001. 11.04 (*0-606-21144-6*) Turtleback Bks.

—Melanie Martin Goes Dutch: The Private Diary of My Almost Bummer Summer with Cecily, Matt the Brat, & Vincent van Go Go Go. 2002. (Illus.). 240p. (J). (gr. 3-7). 15.95 (*0-375-82195-3*); lib. bdg. 17.99 (*0-375-92195-8*) Knopf, Alfred A. Inc.

—Melanie Martin Goes Dutch: The Private Diary of My Almost Bummer Summer with Cecily, Matt the Brat, & Vincent van Go Go Go. 2003. (Illus.). 240p. (J). (gr. 3-7). pap. 4.99 (*0-440-41899-2*, Yearling) Random Hse. Children's Bks.

Weyland, Jack. Ashley & Jen. 2000. (Illus.). 287p. (YA). 16.95 (*1-57345-803-1*) Deseret Bk. Co.

—Lean on Me. 1996. vii, 279p. (J). 14.95 (*1-57345-214-9*) Deseret Bk. Co.

Whalen, Sharla Scannell. Best Friends under the Sun. (Faithful Friends Ser.). (Illus.). 64p. (J). 2000. (gr. 4). lib. bdg. 21.35 (*1-57765-228-2*, ABDO & Daughters); 1997. pap. 5.95 o.p. (*1-56239-839-3*) ABDO Publishing Co.

—Flower Girl Friends. 1997. (Illus.). 64p. (J). pap. 5.95 o.p. (*1-56239-840-7*) ABDO Publishing Co.

—Friends on Ice. 1997. (Illus.). 64p. (J). pap. 5.95 o.p. (*1-56239-901-2*) ABDO Publishing Co.

—Meet the Friends. (Faithful Friends Ser.). (Illus.). 64p. (J). 2000. (gr. 4). lib. bdg. 21.35 (*1-57765-226-6*, ABDO & Daughters); 1997. pap. 5.95 o.p. (*1-56239-900-4*) ABDO Publishing Co.

What's the Big Idea? 1923. (J). pap. 1.50 o.s.i (*0-440-86177-2*) Dell Publishing.

Wheeler, Joe L. Heart to Heart: Stories of Friendship. 1999. 288p. 12.99 (*0-8423-0586-6*) Tyndale Hse. Pubs.

Wheeler, Kathryn. No Room for Neighbors: A Tale in Which Two Strangers Become Friends. 2000. (Stories to Grow By Ser.). (Illus.). (J). 3.95 (*1-56822-594-6*, Instructional Fair * T S Denison) McGraw-Hill Children's Publishing.

Wheeler, Lisa. Fitch & Chip. 2004. (Illus.). 48p. (J). 14.95 (*0-689-84950-8*, Atheneum/Richard Jackson Bks.) Simon & Schuster Children's Publishing.

Whelan, Gloria. Are There Bears in Starvation Lake? 2002. (Road to Reading Ser.). (Illus.). 80p. (J). (gr. 2-4). pap. 3.99 (*0-307-26515-3*); lib. bdg. 11.99 (*0-307-46515-2*) Random Hse. Children's Bks. (Golden Bks.).

—Friends. 1997. (Illus.). 73p. (YA). 16.95 (*1-882376-55-2*); pap. 6.95 (*1-882376-54-4*) Thunder Bay Pr.

—A Haunted House in Starvation Lake. 2003. (Illus.). 80p. (J). (gr. 2-5). pap. 3.99 (*0-307-26516-1*); lib. bdg. 11.99 (*0-307-46516-0*) Random Hse. Children's Bks.

—Rich & Famous in Starvation Lake. (Road to Reading Ser.). (Illus.). 80p. (J). (gr. 3-5). 2003. 11.99 (*0-307-46511-X*); 2001. pap. 3.99 (*0-307-26511-0*) Random Hse. Children's Bks. (Golden Bks.).

—That Wild Berries Should Grow. 1994. 122p. (J). (gr. 4-9). pap. 6.00 o.p. (*0-8028-5091-X*, Eerdmans Bks For Young Readers) Eerdmans, William B. Publishing Co.

—That Wild Berries Should Grow: The Story of a Summer. 1994. 122p. (J). (gr. 4-6). 13.99 o.p. (*0-8028-3754-9*) Eerdmans, William B. Publishing Co.

—A Time to Keep Silent. 1993. 124p. (J). (gr. 4-9). pap. 6.00 (*0-8028-0118-8*, Eerdmans Bks For Young Readers) Eerdmans, William B. Publishing Co.

Whinnem, Reade S. Utten & Plumley. 2003. 256p. (J). (gr. 3-7). pap. 11.95 (*1-57174-346-4*, Young Spirit Bks.) Hampton Roads Publishing Co., Inc.

Whisper's Rainbow Treasure. 1990. (J). (gr. 4-7). pap. 2.50 o.p. (*0-89954-965-9*) Antioch Publishing Co.

Whitcher, Susan. Something for Everyone, RS. 1995. (Illus.). 32p. (J). (ps-3). 15.00 o.p. (*0-374-37138-5*, Farrar, Straus & Giroux (BYR)) Farrar, Straus & Giroux.

White, B. E. Charlotte's Web: Book & Charm. 2003. (Charming Classics Ser.). (Illus.). 192p. (J). pap. 6.99 (*0-06-052779-X*) HarperCollins Children's Bk. Group.

White, Christopher M. Monkey Tricks. 1984. 48p. (J). (gr. 6-9). text 3.95 o.p. (*0-241-11071-8*) Trafalgar Square.

White, Dori. Sarah & Katie. 1984. (J). (gr. 4-7). pap. 1.95 o.p. (*0-06-440047-6*) HarperCollins Pubs.

White, Ellen E. Life Without Friends. 256p. (gr. 7 up). 1988. (J). pap. 2.75 o.p. (*0-590-33829-3*); 1988. (YA). mass mkt. 3.25 o.p. (*0-590-44628-2*); 1987. (Illus.). (YA). pap. 12.95 o.p. (*0-590-33781-5*) Scholastic, Inc.

White, Linda. Too Many Pumpkins. 1996. (Illus.). 32p. (J). (ps-3). tchr. ed. 16.95 (*0-8234-1245-8*) Holiday Hse., Inc.

White, Rosalyn, illus. The Best of Friends. 1989. (Jataka Tales Ser.). 32p. (Orig.). (J). (ps-3). pap. 7.95 (*0-89800-187-0*) Dharma Publishing.

White, Stephen. Just Like You. 1995. (Barney Ser.). (Illus.). 32p. (J). (ps-k). 6.95 o.p. (*1-57064-021-1*) Scholastic, Inc.

Whitley, Mary A. A Sheltering Tree. 1985. 90p. (J). 11.95 (*0-8027-6587-4*) Walker & Co.

Whitlock, Rosemary. Makin' Do. 1983. (Illus.). 131p. (Orig.). (J). (gr. 6-7). pap. 6.90 o.p. (*0-88100-032-9*) Makin' Do Enterprises.

Whitney, Phyllis A. Nobody Likes Trina. 1982. (J). (gr. 6). mass mkt. 1.75 o.p. (*0-451-11532-5*, AE1532, Signet Bks.) NAL.

Whittaker, Michael T. Mr. Don & Mr. Dimple. 1997. (Illus.). 44p. (Orig.). (J). (gr. k-4). pap. 5.95 (*1-889832-01-4*) Auburn Publishing Co.

Whitten, Wendy. The Adventures of Flumpa & Friends Bk. 1: Someday... Someday. 1995. (Illus.). 44p. (J). (ps-3). 24.95 incl. audio (*1-886184-00-3*) Ion Imagination Publishing.

Who Said That? 1991. (Illus.). (J). (ps-2). pap. 3.50 o.p. (*0-8136-5642-7*, TK3392); lib. bdg. 7.95 (*0-8136-5142-5*) Modern Curriculum Pr.

Whybrow, Ian. Wish, Change, Friend. 2002. (Illus.). 32p. (J). (ps-3). 16.00 (*0-689-84930-3*, McElderry, Margaret K.) Simon & Schuster Children's Publishing.

Widerberg, Siv. Suddenly One Day. Nunnally, Tiina, tr. 1993. (Illus.). 28p. (J). (ps-3). 13.00 o.p. (*91-29-62248-4*) R & S Bks. SWE. *Dist:* Farrar, Straus & Giroux, Holtzbrinck Pubs.

Wier, Ester. Loner. 1963. (Illus.). (J). (gr. 7-9). 5.95 o.p. (*0-679-20097-5*) McKay, David Co., Inc.
—Loner. 1992. 160p. (J). (gr. 4-7). pap. 4.50 (*0-590-44352-6*) Scholastic, Inc.
Wiesma, Debbie. Forever Friends: Precious Moments. 1992. (Golden Book Ser.). (Illus.). 48p. (J). (ps-2). pap. 8.95 o.s.i (*0-307-15605-2*, 15605, Golden Bks.) Random Hse. Children's Bks.
Wiesner, David. Tuesday. 2002. (Illus.). (J). 14.74 (*0-7587-0080-6*) Book Wholesalers, Inc.
—Tuesday. 1995. (Illus.). 32p. (J). (ps-3). 22.00 o.s.i (*0-395-73511-4*, Clarion Bks.) Houghton Mifflin Co. Trade & Reference Div.
—Tuesday. 1997. (J). 12.10 (*0-606-12832-8*) Turtleback Bks.
Wiethorn, Randall J. Rock Finds a Friend. (J). 1998. 5.95 (*0-671-75289-8*); 1991. (Illus.). 32p. pap. 5.95 (*0-88138-110-1*) Simon & Schuster Children's Publishing. (Simon & Schuster Children's Publishing).
Wilbourne, David. Summers Diary. 2002. (Illus.). 288p. (J). pap. 12.99 (*0-00-710007-8*) HarperCollins Pubs.
Wild, Margaret. Big Cat Dreaming. 1997. (Illus.). 32p. (J). (ps up). 16.95 (*1-55037-493-1*) Annick Pr., Ltd. CAN. *Dist:* Firefly Bks., Ltd.
—Fox. 2000. (Illus.). (J). 40p. (*1-86448-465-9*); 163p. pap. (*1-86448-933-2*) Allen & Unwin Pty., Ltd.
—Fox. 2001. (Illus.). 40p. (J). (gr. 1 up). 14.95 (*1-929132-16-6*, Creative Nell) Kane/Miller Bk. Pubs.
—Mr. Nick's Knitting. 1989. (Illus.). 32p. (J). (ps-3). 12.95 o.s.i (*0-15-200518-8*, Gulliver Bks.) Harcourt Children's Bks.
—The Very Best of Friends. 1994. (Illus.). 32p. (J). (ps-3). pap. 4.95 o.s.i (*0-15-200077-1*, Voyager Bks./Libros Viajeros) Harcourt Children's Bks.
—The Very Best of Friends. 1990. 11.10 (*0-606-06848-1*) Turtleback Bks.
Wild, Robyn. Benjamin's Basket. 1999. (Illus.). (J). (ps-4). 12.95 (*0-944576-17-6*) Rocky River Pubs., LLC.
Wilde, Nicholas. Into the Dark. 1992. (J). pap. 2.95 o.p. (*0-590-43423-3*, Scholastic Paperbacks) Scholastic, Inc.
Wilde, Oscar. The Devoted Friend. 1986. (Creative's Classic Short Stories Ser.). (Illus.). 31p. (J). (gr. 4 up). lib. bdg. 13.95 o.p. (*0-88682-067-7*, 1078-D, Creative Education) Creative Co., The.
—The Devoted Friend. Batmanglij, Najmieh Khalili, tr. from ENG. 1988. (Illus.). 28p. (J). (gr. 4 up). 15.00 o.p. (*0-934211-16-7*); 15.00 o.p. (*0-934211-10-8*) Mage Pubs., Inc.
—El Joven Rey y Otros Cuentos. 1998. (SPA.). 208p. (gr. 6-8). (*84-239-2781-4*) Espasa Calpe, S.A.
Wilder, Laura Ingalls. Little House Friends. 1998. (Little House Chapter Bks.: No. 9). (J). (gr. 3-6). 10.40 (*0-606-17698-5*) Turtleback Bks.
Wiley, Margaret. The Melinda Zone. 1994. (J). mass mkt. o.p. (*0-440-90098-0*) Dell Publishing.
Wilhelm, Doug. The Revealers, RS. 2003. 224p. (J). 16.00 (*0-374-36255-6*, Farrar, Straus & Giroux (BYR)) Farrar, Straus & Giroux.
Wilhelm, Hans. The Boy Who Wasn't There. 1993. 32p. (J). (gr. 1-5). pap. 14.95 (*0-590-46635-6*) Scholastic, Inc.
—Let's Be Friends Again! 1986. (Illus.). 32p. (J). (ps-3). 10.95 o.s.i (*0-517-56252-9*, Random Hse. Bks. for Young Readers) Random Hse. Children's Bks.
—Seamos Amigos Otra Vez. 13.95 (*84-261-2514-X*) Juventud, Editorial ESP. *Dist:* AIMS International Bks., Inc.
Wilkes, Maria D. Brookfield Friends. 2000. (Little House Chapter Bks.: No. 4). (Illus.). 80p. (J). (gr. 3-6). pap. 4.25 (*0-06-442107-4*, Harper Trophy); lib. bdg. 14.89 (*0-06-028552-4*) HarperCollins Children's Bk. Group.
Wilkins, Christopher. The Horizontal Instrument. 1999. 288p. (gr. 9). (*0-385-60031-3*, Corgi) Bantam Bks.
Wilkon, Piotr. Katzenausflug. 1945. (GER., Illus.). 32p. (J). (gr. k-3). 14.95 o.p. (*3-314-00536-9*) North-South Bks., Inc.
Willard, John A. Ember & His Friends of the Mountain. 1985. (Illus.). 20p. (Orig.). (J). (gr. 3-5). pap. 2.95 o.p. (*0-9612398-2-4*) Willard, John A.
Willard, Nancy. The Highest Hit. 1993. (Illus.). 127p. (J). (gr. 4-7). pap. 3.95 (*0-15-234279-6*, Harcourt Paperbacks) Harcourt Children's Bks.
Willey, Margaret. The Bigger Book of Lydia. 2001. 228p. pap. 16.95 (*0-595-17700-X*, Backinprint.com) iUniverse, Inc.
—Finding David Dolores. 1986. 192p. (YA). (gr. 7 up). lib. bdg. 11.89 o.p. (*0-06-026484-5*) HarperCollins Children's Bk. Group.
—Finding David Dolores. 2001. 164p. (gr. 7-12). per. 13.95 (*0-595-19641-1*) iUniverse, Inc.
—If Not for You. 1990. (Trophy Keypoint Bks.). 160p. (YA). (gr. 7 up). mass mkt. 3.25 (*0-06-447015-6*, Harper Trophy) HarperCollins Children's Bk. Group.
—Saving Lenny. 1991. 160p. (J). mass mkt. 2.99 o.s.i (*0-553-29204-8*, Starfire) Random Hse. Children's Bks.
William, Kate. Elizabeth's Rival. 1996. (Sweet Valley High Ser.: No. 123). (YA). (gr. 7 up). 9.09 o.p. (*0-606-09922-0*) Turtleback Bks.
—Friend Against Friend. 1990. (Sweet Valley High Ser.: No. 69). (YA). (gr. 7 up). 8.60 o.p. (*0-606-04549-X*) Turtleback Bks.
—Outcast. 1987. (Sweet Valley High Ser.: No. 41). (YA). (gr. 7 up). 8.05 o.p. (*0-606-03633-4*) Turtleback Bks.
—Playing with Fire. 1983. (Sweet Valley High Ser.: No. 3). (YA). (gr. 7 up). 9.09 o.p. (*0-606-01268-0*) Turtleback Bks.
Williams, Barbara. H-E-L-L-L-P! The Crazy Gang Is Back. 1995. (J). (gr. 3-7). 168p. 13.95 o.p. (*0-06-025887-X*); 80p. lib. bdg. 13.89 o.p. (*0-06-025888-8*) HarperCollins Children's Bk. Group.
Williams, Brenda. Silla, Silla Nosilla. 1997. (Illus.). 40p. (J). (gr. k-3). pap. 5.95 (*0-9659718-0-5*) Tartan Tabby Pr.
Williams, Carol. Kelly & Me. 1993. (J). o.s.i (*0-385-30957-0*, Dell Books for Young Readers) Random Hse. Children's Bks.
Williams, Carol Lynch. Christmas in Heaven. 2000. 171p. (J). (gr. 5-9). 16.99 o.s.i (*0-399-23436-5*, G. P. Putnam's Sons) Penguin Group (USA) Inc.
—Esther's Celebration. 1996. (Latter-Day Daughters Ser.). (Illus.). 80p. (J). (gr. 3-9). pap. 4.95 (*1-56236-507-X*) Aspen Bks.
—Kelly & Me. 1995. (J). 8.60 o.p. (*0-606-07759-6*) Turtleback Bks.
Williams, Connie. Right-Hand Man. 1992. 100p. (J). (gr. 4-7). pap. 6.49 (*0-89084-638-3*, 061614) Jones, Bob Univ. Pr.
Williams-Garcia, Rita. No Laughter Here. 2004. 144p. (J). 15.99 (*0-688-16247-9*); lib. bdg. 16.89 (*0-688-16248-7*) HarperCollins Pubs.
Williams, Judy B. Mrs. Magruder & the Purple Hat: A Story about Friendship & Grief. 1993. (Illus.). 28p. (Orig.). (J). (gr. 3-6). pap. 6.95 (*1-884063-53-5*) MAR*CO Products, Inc.
Williams, Karen L. Applebaum's Garage. 1993. (J). 13.95 o.p. (*0-395-65227-8*, Clarion Bks.) Houghton Mifflin Co. Trade & Reference Div.
Williams, Karen S. Best Friends Are for Keeps. 1992. (J). pap. 5.99 o.p. (*0-8280-0660-1*) Review & Herald Publishing Assn.
Williams, Laura. The Executioner's Daughter, ERS. 2000. 134p. (YA). (gr. 5-8). 16.95 (*0-8050-6234-3*, Holt, Henry & Co. Bks. For Young Readers) Holt, Henry & Co.
Williams, Laura E. Boo Who?, 5. 1997. (Let's Have a Party Ser.). 9.19 o.p. (*0-606-12754-2*) Turtleback Bks.
—School's Out! 1997. (Let's Have a Party Ser.: No. 1). (J). (gr. 1-4). pap. 3.99 o.p. (*0-380-78925-6*, Avon Bks.) Morrow/Avon.
—School's Out! 1997. (Let's Have a Party Ser.). (J). 9.19 (*0-606-11554-4*) Turtleback Bks.
—Sleepover. 1997. (Let's Have a Party Ser.). (J). 10.14 (*0-606-11556-0*) Turtleback Bks.
—Splash! 1997. (Let's Have a Party Ser.: No. 2). (J). (gr. 1-4). pap. 3.99 o.p. (*0-380-78922-1*, Avon Bks.) Morrow/Avon.
Williams, Margery. The Velveteen Rabbit. 1994. 40p. (J). (ps-3). mass mkt. 3.95 (*0-8125-3627-4*, Tor Bks.) Doherty, Tom Assocs., LLC.
Williams, Michael. The Genuine Half-Moon Kid. 1996. 208p. (YA). (gr. 7-12). pap. 4.99 o.p. (*0-14-037698-4*, Puffin Bks.) Penguin Putnam Bks. for Young Readers.
Williams, Sam. Angel's Christmas Cookies. 2002. (Angel & Elf Ser.). (Illus.). 32p. (J). (ps-3). 9.99 (*0-06-029651-8*, Harper Festival) HarperCollins Children's Bk. Group.
Williams, Sherley Anne. Girls Together. 1999. (Illus.). 32p. (J). (ps-3). 16.00 (*0-15-230982-9*) Harcourt Children's Bks.
Williams, Sue. Sali de Paseo. Ada, Alma Flor, tr. 1995. (SPA., Illus.). 32p. (J). (ps-3). pap. 7.00 (*0-15-200288-X*, HB0272, Voyager Bks./Libros Viajeros) Harcourt Children's Bks.
Williams, Vera B. Algo Especial Para Mi. Cohn, Amy, ed. Marcuse, Aida E., tr. 1994. (SPA., Illus.). 32p. (J). (gr. k-2). pap. 4.95 (*0-688-13802-0*, MR6339, Morrow, William & Co.) Morrow/Avon.
—Algo Especial Para Mi. 1994. 11.10 (*0-606-06169-X*) Turtleback Bks.
—Scooter. 1993. (Illus.). 160p. (J). (gr. 2 up). 17.95 (*0-688-09376-0*); (ps-3). 14.89 o.p. (*0-688-09377-9*) HarperCollins Children's Bk. Group. (Greenwillow Bks.).
Williamson, Greg. What's the Recipe for Friends? 1999. (Illus.). 24p. pap. 7.99 (*0-9666076-0-0*) Peerless Publishing, L.L.C.
Willis, Jeanne. When Stephanie Smiled. 2003. (Illus.). 32p. (*1-84270-075-8*) Andersen Pr., Ltd. GBR. *Dist:* Random Hse. of Canada, Ltd.
—The Wind in the Willows. 1998. (Illus.). 32p. (J). (ps-1). 15.95 (*0-86264-782-7*) Andersen Pr., Ltd. GBR. *Dist:* Trafalgar Square.
Willner-Pardo, Gina. Figuring Out Frances. 1999. (Illus.). 144p. (J). (gr. 4-6). tchr. ed. 14.00 (*0-395-91510-4*, Clarion Bks.) Houghton Mifflin Co. Trade & Reference Div.
—Jason & the Losers. 1995. 128p. (J). 14.95 o.p. (*0-395-70160-0*, Clarion Bks.) Houghton Mifflin Co. Trade & Reference Div.
—Jason & the Losers. 1997. (J). (gr. 3-7). pap. 3.99 (*0-380-72809-5*, Avon Bks.) Morrow/Avon.
—Jason & the Losers. 1997. 10.04 (*0-606-13534-0*) Turtleback Bks.
—Spider Storch, Rotten Runner. 2001. (Illus.). 88p. (J). (gr. 2-5). lib. bdg. 11.95 (*0-8075-7594-1*) Whitman, Albert & Co.
—Spider Storch's Carpool Catastrophe. 1997. 10.10 (*0-606-17182-7*) Turtleback Bks.
—Spider Storch's Carpool Catastrophe. 1997. (Illus.). (J). (gr. 3-5). 56p. pap. 3.95 (*0-8075-7576-3*); 64p. lib. bdg. 11.95 (*0-8075-7575-5*) Whitman, Albert & Co.
Willner-Pardo, Gina & Poydar, Nancy. When Jane-Marie Told My Secret. 1995. (Illus.). 48p. (J). (gr. 4-6). 14.95 (*0-395-66382-2*, Clarion Bks.) Houghton Mifflin Co. Trade & Reference Div.
Willson, Sarah. Be Nice, Nanette. 2001. (Angela Anaconda Ser.: Vol. 2). (Illus.). 64p. (J). (gr. 4-7). pap. 3.99 (*0-689-83997-9*, Simon Spotlight) Simon & Schuster Children's Publishing.
Wilmer, Diane. Big & Little. 1988. (Step by Step Bks.). (Illus.). 32p. (J). (ps). pap. 4.95 o.s.i (*0-689-71246-4*, Simon & Schuster Children's Publishing) Simon & Schuster Children's Publishing.
Wilson, Brad. The Winterland Friends. 2001. 32p. (J). 19.00 (*0-8059-5491-0*) Dorrance Publishing Co., Inc.
Wilson, Deborah & Slate, Barbara. Just Around the Corner: Sesame Street. 1994. (Golden Super Shape Book Ser.). (Illus.). 16p. (J). pap. 3.49 o.s.i (*0-307-10364-1*, Golden Bks.) Random Hse. Children's Bks.
Wilson, Gina. A Friendship of Equals. 1981. 160p. (J). (gr. 5 up). o.p. (*0-571-11632-9*) Faber & Faber Ltd.
Wilson, Jacqueline. Bad Girls. l.t. ed. 1997. (Illus.). (J). 16.95 o.p. (*0-7451-8923-7*, Galaxy Children's Large Print) BBC Audiobooks America.
—Bad Girls. 2002. (Illus.). 176p. (gr. 3-7). pap. text 4.99 (*0-440-41806-2*, Random Hse. Bks. for Young Readers) Random Hse. Children's Bks.
—Bad Girls. 2000. (Illus.). pap. 8.95 (*0-440-86356-2*); 177p. (J). (gr. 3-7). 16.95 (*0-385-40702-5*) Transworld Publishers Ltd. GBR. *Dist:* Trafalgar Square.
—Bad Girls: American Edition. 2001. (Illus.). 176p. (gr. 3-7). text 15.95 o.s.i (*0-385-72916-2*, Delacorte Pr.) Dell Publishing.
—Vicky Angel. 2001. (J). 16.95 (*0-7540-6165-5*) BBC Audiobooks America.
—Vicky Angel. 2002. 144p. (J). pap. (*0-440-86415-1*, Corgi) Bantam Bks.
—Vicky Angel. (Illus.). 176p. (gr. 3-7). 2003. pap. text 4.99 (*0-440-41808-9*, Yearling); 2001. text 15.95 (*0-385-72920-0*, Dell Books for Young Readers) Random Hse. Children's Bks.
Wilson, Karma. Mr. Murry & Thumbkin. Hoyt, Ard, tr. & illus. by. 2004. (J). (*0-316-07613-9*) Little Brown & Co.
Wilson, Linda Miller. A Few Days Journey. 1998. 124p. (J). (gr. 6-9). pap. 9.99 (*0-88092-402-0*, 4020) Royal Fireworks Publishing Co.
Wilson, Nancy Hope. Becoming Felix, RS. 1996. 192p. (J). (gr. 3-7). 16.00 o.p. (*0-374-30664-8*, Farrar, Straus & Giroux (BYR)) Farrar, Straus & Giroux.
Wilson, Orpha N. Twinky & Friends. 1995. (Illus.). (J). 7.95 o.p. (*0-533-11420-9*) Vantage Pr., Inc.
Windstrom, Charley. Are You a Pudin', Too? 1999. (Illus.). (J). (ps-k). E-Book 6.95 (*0-87714-404-4*) Denlingers Pubs., Ltd.
Winick, Judd. Pedro & Me: Friendship, Loss & What I Learned. 2001. (Illus.). (J). 21.05 (*0-606-20504-7*) Turtleback Bks.
Winkler, Allan M. Cassie's War. 1994. (J). (gr. 5-7). 94p. pap. 9.99 (*0-88092-106-4*); lib. bdg. 15.00 o.p. (*0-88092-107-2*) Royal Fireworks Publishing Co.
Winkler, David. Scotty & the Gypsy Bandit, RS. 2000. 208p. (J). (gr. 5 up). 16.00 o.p. (*0-374-36420-6*, Farrar, Straus & Giroux (BYR)) Farrar, Straus & Giroux.
Winn, Christine M. & Walsh, David. Clover's Secret: Helping Kids Cope with Domestic Violence. 1996. (Illus.). 32p. (J). (gr. 1-4). 14.95 o.p. (*0-925190-89-6*) Fairview Pr.
Winslow, Vicki. Follow the Leader. 1998. (Illus.). 224p. (gr. 2-6). pap. text 3.99 o.s.i (*0-440-41296-X*) Dell Publishing.
—Follow the Leader. 1998. 10.04 (*0-606-15531-7*) Turtleback Bks.
Winston, Helena. Pride & Joy. 2001. (Illus.). 32p. (J). pap. 3.99 (*0-7364-1194-1*, RH/Disney) Random Hse. Children's Bks.
Winthrop, Elizabeth. The Best Friends Club. 1989. (Illus.). 32p. (J). (ps-3). 12.95 o.p. (*0-688-07582-7*); lib. bdg. 12.88 o.p. (*0-688-07583-5*) HarperCollins Children's Bk. Group.
—Lizzie & Harold. 1986. (Illus.). 32p. (J). (gr. k-3). 12.95 o.p. (*0-688-02711-3*); lib. bdg. 12.88 o.p. (*0-688-02712-1*) HarperCollins Children's Bk. Group.
—Miranda in the Middle. 1990. 128p. (J). (gr. 4 up). pap. 3.95 o.s.i (*0-14-034392-X*, Puffin Bks.) Penguin Putnam Bks. for Young Readers.
Winton, Tim. Lockie Leonard, Scumbuster. 1999. 140p. (J). (gr. 5-9). 16.00 (*0-689-82247-2*, McElderry, Margaret K.) Simon & Schuster Children's Publishing.
Wishinsky, Frieda. Each One Special. ed. 2000. (J). (gr. 1). spiral bd. (*0-616-01814-2*); (gr. 2). spiral bd. (*0-616-01815-0*) Canadian National Institute for the Blind/Institut National Canadien pour les Aveugles.
—Each One Special. (Illus.). 32p. (J). (gr. k-2). 2001. pap. 7.95 (*1-55143-124-6*); 1999. 14.95 (*1-55143-122-X*) Orca Bk. Pubs.
—Jennifer Jones Won't Leave Me Alone. 2002. (Illus.). 32p. (J). (ps-3). 15.95 (*0-87614-921-2*, Carolrhoda Bks.) Lerner Publishing Group.
—Just Mabel. 2001. (I Am Reading Bks.). (Illus.). (J). (*0-7534-5353-3*) Kingfisher Publications, plc.
—Nothing Scares Us. (Carolrhoda Picture Books Ser.). (J). 2004. pap. 6.95 (*1-57505-669-0*, First Avenue Editions); 2000. (Illus.). 32p. lib. bdg. 15.95 (*1-57505-490-6*, Carolrhoda Bks.) Lerner Publishing Group.
Wisniewski, David. Tough Cookie. 1999. (Illus.). 32p. (J). (gr. 1-4). lib. bdg. 15.93 (*0-688-15338-0*); 16.99 (*0-688-15337-2*) HarperCollins Children's Bk. Group.
Withrow, Sarah. Box Girl. 184p. (J). 2002. pap. 5.95 (*0-88899-436-2*); 2001. (gr. 5-7). 15.95 (*0-88899-407-9*) Groundwood Bks. CAN. *Dist:* Publishers Group West.
Witmer, Edith. Miguel, the Shepherd Boy. De Mejia, Maria Juana, tr. 1995. (SPA., Illus.). 220p. (J). (gr. 3-6). 8.10 (*0-7399-0090-0*, 2237.1) Rod & Staff Pubs., Inc.
—Miguel, the Shepherd Boy. 1992. (Illus.). 189p. (J). (gr. 3-6). 8.55 (*0-7399-0089-7*, 2237) Rod & Staff Pubs., Inc.
Witter, Evelyn. The Locked Drawer. 1981. (J). (gr. 1-3). 5.95 o.p. (*0-8054-4272-3*, 4242-72) Broadman & Holman Pubs.
Wittlinger, Ellen. Razzle. 2001. (Illus.). 256p. (J). (gr. 7-10). 17.00 (*0-689-83565-5*, Simon & Schuster Children's Publishing) Simon & Schuster Children's Publishing.
—Razzle. Gould, Jason, ed. 2003. (Illus.). 256p. (YA). pap. 7.99 (*0-689-85600-8*, Simon Pulse) Simon & Schuster Children's Publishing.
—What's in a Name. 2000. 160p. (J). (gr. 7-12). 16.00 (*0-689-82551-X*, Simon & Schuster Children's Publishing) Simon & Schuster Children's Publishing.
—What's in a Name. l.t. ed. 2001. 199p. (J). 22.95 (*0-7862-3505-5*) Thorndike Pr.
Wittman, Sally. Jessie's Wishes. 1990. (J). (gr. 5-7). mass mkt. 2.50 o.p. (*0-590-42991-4*) Scholastic, Inc.
—A Special Trade. 1978. (Illus.). 32p. (J). (ps-3). lib. bdg. 11.89 o.p. (*0-06-026554-X*) HarperCollins Children's Bk. Group.
Witton, Dorothy. Crossroads for Chela. 1967. (J). (gr. 7-9). pap. (*0-671-29002-9*, Simon Pulse) Simon & Schuster Children's Publishing.
Rodman, Maia. Don't Play Dead Before You Have To. 1970. (YA). (gr. 7 up). lib. bdg. 11.89 o.p. (*0-06-026568-X*) HarperCollins Children's Bk. Group.
Wojciechowski, Susan. Beany & the Dreaded Wedding. 2003. (Illus.). 128p. (J). bds. 4.99 (*0-7636-2054-8*) Candlewick Pr.
—Beany Goes to Camp. (Illus.). 112p. (J). 2003. bds. 4.99 (*0-7636-2053-X*); 2002. (gr. 2-4). 15.99 (*0-7636-1615-X*) Candlewick Pr.
—The Christmas Miracle of Jonathan Toomey. (Illus.). 40p. (J). 2002. (gr. 1-6). 12.99 (*0-7636-1930-2*); 1995. (ps-3). 18.99 (*1-56402-320-6*) Candlewick Pr.
—The Christmas Miracle of Jonathan Toomey. 1998. (Illus.). 40p. (J). (ps-3). 18.99 incl. cd-rom (*0-8499-5905-5*) Nelson, Tommy.
Wojtowycz, David. Come on Dudley! Friends. 2002. (Illus.). bds. 3.95 (*1-58925-668-9*) ME Media LLC.
Wolf, Jill. Cheepers in Special Times to Share. 1984. (Antioch Little Shape Bks.). (Illus.). 22p. (J). (ps-3). 2.50 o.p. (*0-89954-277-8*) Antioch Publishing Co.
Wolf, Joyce. Between the Cracks. 1992. 176p. (J). (gr. 5 up). 14.95 o.p. (*0-8037-1270-7*, Dial Bks. for Young Readers) Penguin Putnam Bks. for Young Readers.

Wolf, Matt. Pipo y Filipo Son Amigos. 2001. (Pollito Con Tapitas Ser.).Tr. of Pippo & Filippa Are Friends. (SPA., Illus.). 10p. (J). 9.95 (968-5308-44-6) Silver Dolphin Spanish Editions MEX. *Dist:* Publishers Group West.

Wolfer, Dianne. Border Line. 1998. 190p. (J). pap. 11.95 (1-86368-208-2) Fremantle Arts Centre Pr. AUS. *Dist:* International Specialized Bk. Services.

Wolff, Ferida. Watch Out for Bears: The Adventures of Henry & Bruno. 1999. (Step into Reading Step 2 Bks.). (Illus.). 48p. (J). (gr. 1-3). pap. 3.99 o.s.i (0-679-88761-X, Random Hse. Bks. for Young Readers) Random Hse. Children's Bks.

—Watch Out for Bears: The Adventures of Henry & Bruno. 1999. (Step into Reading Ser.). 10.14 (0-606-16893-1) Turtleback Bks.

—Watch Out for Bears! The Adventures of Henry & Bruno. 1999. (Step into Reading Step 2 Bks.). (Illus.). 48p. (J). (gr. k-3). lib. bdg. 11.99 o.s.i (0-679-98761-4, Random Hse. Bks. for Young Readers) Random Hse. Children's Bks.

Wolff, Virginia Euwer. Make Lemonade, ERS. 1993. 208p. (YA). (gr. 5-9). 17.95 (0-8050-2228-7, Holt, Henry & Co. Bks. For Young Readers) Holt, Henry & Co.

—Make Lemonade. 2003. 208p. (J). (gr. 5 up). mass mkt. 5.99 (0-590-48141-X, Scholastic Paperbacks) Scholastic, Inc.

—Make Lemonade. l.t. ed. 1993. (Teen Scene Ser.). (YA). (gr. 9-12). 17.95 (0-7862-0056-1) Thorndike Pr.

—Make Lemonade. 1993. (Point Signature Ser.). (J). 11.04 (0-606-06555-5) Turtleback Bks.

—True Believer. unabr. ed. 2002. (YA). (gr. 5 up). audio 25.00 (0-8072-0691-1, Listening Library) Random Hse. Audio Publishing Group.

—True Believer. 272p. (J). 2002. (Illus.). pap. 7.99 (0-689-85288-6, Simon Pulse); 2001. (gr. 7 up). 17.00 (0-689-82827-6, Atheneum) Simon & Schuster Children's Publishing.

—True Believer. l.t. ed. 2001. (YA). 23.95 (0-7862-3371-0) Thorndike Pr.

Wolitzer, Meg. Operation: Save the Teacher: Saturday Night Toast. 1993. 128p. (Orig.). (J). pap. 3.50 (0-380-76462-8, Avon Bks.) Morrow/Avon.

Wolkoff, Judie. In a Pig's Eye. 1989. (J). (gr. k-6). reprint ed. pap. 2.95 o.s.i (0-440-40140-2, Yearling) Random Hse. Children's Bks.

—In a Pig's Eye. 1986. (Illus.). 144p. (J). (gr. 3-5). lib. bdg. 13.95 o.s.i (0-02-793370-9, Simon & Schuster Children's Publishing) Simon & Schuster Children's Publishing.

Wolkstein, Diane. Little Mouse's Painting. 1992. (Illus.). 32p. (J). (ps-3). 16.00 (0-688-07609-2); lib. bdg. 15.93 o.p. (0-688-07610-6) Morrow/Avon. (Morrow, William & Co.).

—Little Mouse's Painting. 2002. (Illus.). 32p. (J). (gr. k-3). 15.95 (1-58717-124-4); pap. 5.95 (1-58717-125-2) North-South Bks., Inc.

—Step by Step. 1994. (Illus.). 40p. (J). (ps-3). 15.00 (0-688-10315-4); lib. bdg. 14.93 o.p. (0-688-10316-2) Morrow/Avon. (Morrow, William & Co.).

Wollard, Kathy. How Come? 1993. (Illus.). 320p. (J). (gr. 4-7). pap. 12.95 (1-56305-324-1, 3324) Workman Publishing Co., Inc.

Woloson, Eliza. My Friend Isabelle. Gough, Bryan, tr. & illus. by. 2003. 28p. (J). 14.95 (1-890627-50-X) Woodbine Hse.

Wong, Janet S. Minn & Jake, RS. 2003. (Illus.). 160p. (J). (gr. 2-5). 16.00 (0-374-34987-8, Farrar, Straus & Giroux (BYR)) Farrar, Straus & Giroux.

Wood, A. J. Errata. 1992. (J). (ps-3). 15.00 o.s.i (0-671-77569-3, Simon & Schuster Children's Publishing) Simon & Schuster Children's Publishing.

Wood, Audrey. Orlando's Littlewhile Friends. (J). (ps-3). 1996. lib. bdg. 15.95 (0-85953-847-8); 1989. (Illus.). 32p. 13.99 (0-85953-111-2); 1989. (Illus.). 32p. pap. 6.99 (0-85953-106-6) Child's Play of England GBR. *Dist:* Child's Play-International.

Wood, June Rae. About Face. 1999. 272p. (YA). (gr. 5-9). 19.99 o.s.i (0-399-23419-5, G. P. Putnam's Sons) Penguin Group (USA) Inc.

—About Face. 2001. 272p. pap. 5.99 o.s.i (0-698-11891-X) Penguin Putnam Bks. for Young Readers.

—About Face. 2001. (J). 12.04 (0-606-21014-8) Turtleback Bks.

—When Pigs Fly. 1995. 224p. (J). (gr. 4-7). 16.95 o.s.i (0-399-22911-6, G. P. Putnam's Sons) Penguin Group (USA) Inc.

—When Pigs Fly. 1997. (Illus.). 272p. (J). (gr. 3-7). pap. 5.99 (0-698-11570-8, PaperStar) Penguin Putnam Bks. for Young Readers.

—When Pigs Fly. 1997. 12.04 (0-606-10990-0) Turtleback Bks.

Wood, Kim Marie, ed. Heart, Hoof & Soul. 1999. (Illus.). 64p. (YA). (gr. 4-9). pap. 7.95 (0-9671978-6-4) Syncopated Pr.

Wood, Phyllis A. This Time Count Me In. 1981. (J). (gr. 7-10). pap. (0-671-42689-3, Simon Pulse) Simon & Schuster Children's Publishing.

Woodruff, Elvira. Dear Levi: Letters from the Overland Trail. 1998. (Illus.). 128p. (J). (gr. 5-8). pap. 4.99 (0-679-88558-7, Knopf Bks. for Young Readers) Random Hse. Children's Bks.

Woodson, Jacqueline. Between Madison & Palmetto. 128p. (J). 1995. (gr. 5 up). pap. 3.50 o.s.i (0-440-41062-2); 1993. (gr. 1-6). 13.95 o.s.i (0-385-30906-6, Delacorte Pr.) Dell Publishing.

—Between Madison & Palmetto. 2002. 128p. (J). 16.99 (0-399-23757-7); (YA). pap. 5.99 (0-698-11958-4) Putnam Publishing Group, The.

—I Hadn't Meant to Tell You This. 1994. 128p. (YA). (gr. 7 up). 15.95 o.s.i (0-385-32031-0, Delacorte Pr.) Dell Publishing.

—I Hadn't Meant to Tell You This. 1995. 128p. (YA). (gr. 7 up). mass mkt. 4.99 (0-440-21960-4, Dell Books for Young Readers) Random Hse. Children's Bks.

—I Hadn't Meant to Tell You This. 1995. (YA). (gr. 7 up). 10.55 (0-606-08551-3) Turtleback Bks.

—I Hadn't Meant To Tell You This. 1995. (YA). (gr. 7 up). mass mkt. 4.99 (0-440-91087-0, Dell Books for Young Readers) Random Hse. Children's Bks.

—Last Summer with Maizon. 1991. 112p. (YA). pap. 3.99 o.s.i (0-440-40555-6) Dell Publishing.

—Last Summer with Maizon. 2002. 112p. (J). 16.99 (0-399-23755-0); (Illus.). 128p. (YA). (gr. 3-7). pap. 4.99 (0-698-11929-0) Putnam Publishing Group, The.

—The Other Side. 2001. (Illus.). 32p. (J). (gr. k up). 16.99 (0-399-23116-1) Penguin Group (USA) Inc.

Woolf, Paula. Old Ladies with Brooms Aren't Always Witches. 1998. 154p. (J). (gr. 3-6). pap. 9.99 (0-88092-395-4, 3954) Royal Fireworks Publishing Co.

Wordshop Editorial Staff. Twink 'n' Twinkle: The Beginning. 1999. (Illus.). 28p. (J). (ps-4). 19.95 (0-9668469-0-7) WordSHOP, Inc.

Wormell, Christopher. Blue Rabbit & Friends. 2000. (Illus.). 32p. (J). (ps-k). 15.99 o.p. (0-8037-2499-3, Fogelman, Phyllis Bks.) Penguin Putnam Bks. for Young Readers.

Wormell, Mary. Why Not?, RS. 2003. (Illus.). 32p. (J). (ps-1). pap. 5.95 (0-374-48384-1, Sunburst) Farrar, Straus & Giroux.

Worth, Bonnie. Way to Go, Chipmunk Cheeks. (Full House Ser.). 96p. (J). (gr. 4-6). pap. 3.25 (0-938753-57-6, PP1) Parachute Publishing, LLC.

—Way to Go, Chipmunk Cheeks. 1991. (Full House Ser.). 96p. (J). (gr. 4-6). pap. 3.25 o.s.i (0-440-40596-3, Yearling) Random Hse. Children's Bks.

Worth, Kathryn. They Loved to Laugh. 1996. (Young Adult Bookshelf Ser.). (Illus.). 254p. (J). (gr. 3 up). reprint ed. pap. 11.95 (1-883937-16-7, 16-7) Bethlehem Bks.

Wright, Alexandra. Will We Miss Them? 1991. (Illus.). 32p. (J). (gr. 4-7). 14.95 (0-88106-489-0); (ps-8). lib. bdg. 15.88 o.p. (0-88106-675-3) Charlesbridge Publishing, Inc.

—Will We Miss Them? 2001. (J). E-Book (1-59019-568-X); 1992. E-Book (1-59019-569-8) ipicturebooks, LLC.

—Will We Miss Them? Endangered Species. 1991. (Reading Rainbow Bks.). (Illus.). 30p. (J). (ps-3). pap. 7.95 (0-88106-488-2, CB4882) Charlesbridge Publishing, Inc.

Wright, Barbara. Harry Berry. 2001. 214p. E-Book 8.00 (0-7388-8333-6) Xlibris Corp.

Wright, Dare. Edith & Mr. Bear: A Lonely Doll Story. 2000. (Illus.). 64p. (J). (ps-3). tchr. ed. 16.00 (0-618-00332-0); pap. 6.95 (0-618-04253-9) Houghton Mifflin Co.

Wright, Randall. A Hundred Days from Home, ERS. 2002. 160p. (YA). (gr. 6 up). 15.95 (0-8050-6885-6, Holt, Henry & Co. Bks. For Young Readers) Holt, Henry & Co.

Wright, S. Myron & Wright, Chris M. The Story of Frankie Frown. 1994. (Illus.). 32p. (Orig.). (J). (gr. k-6). pap. 5.95 (0-9636377-1-1) Wright, Shirley L.

Wrightson, Patricia. The Sugar-Gum Tree. 1992. (Illus.). 64p. (J). (gr. 2-6). 11.95 o.p. (0-670-83910-8, Viking Children's Bks.) Penguin Putnam Bks. for Young Readers.

Wujing Well. 1981. (J). 1.95 o.p. (0-8351-0938-0) China Bks. & Periodicals, Inc.

Wunderli, Stephen. The Blue Between the Clouds, ERS. 1992. 80p. (YA). (gr. 5 up). 13.95 o.p. (0-8050-1772-0, Holt, Henry & Co. Bks. For Young Readers) Holt, Henry & Co.

Wurmfeld, Hope H. Baby Blues. 1992. 80p. (YA). (gr. 7 up). 14.00 o.p. (0-670-84151-X, Viking Children's Bks.) Penguin Putnam Bks. for Young Readers.

Wurtz, K. D. Digby Finds a Friend. 2001. (Digby in Disguise Ser.: Vol. 2). (J). (0-9712840-2-4, Bear & Co.) Bear & Co.

Wyeth, Sharon Dennis. Dream Holiday. 1990. 176p. (J). (gr. 4-7). pap. 3.50 o.s.i (0-440-40395-2) Dell Publishing.

—Ginger Brown, the Nobody Boy. 1997. (First Stepping Stone Bks.). 10.14 (0-606-11388-6) Turtleback Bks.

—Handle with Care. 1990. (Pen Pals Ser.: No. 7). 128p. (J). (gr. 4-7). pap. 2.95 o.s.i (0-440-40267-0, Yearling) Random Hse. Children's Bks.

—Lisa, We Miss You. 1990. (Pen Pals Ser.: No. 13). 144p. (J). pap. 2.95 o.s.i (0-440-40393-6) Dell Publishing.

—No Creeps Need Apply. 1989. (Pen Pals Ser.: No. 4). 144p. (J). (gr. k-6). pap. 2.95 o.s.i (0-440-40241-7, Yearling) Random Hse. Children's Bks.

—P. S. Forget It. 1989. (Pen Pals Ser.: No. 3). (J). (gr. k-6). pap. 2.95 o.s.i (0-440-40230-1, Yearling) Random Hse. Children's Bks.

—Palmer at Your Service. 1990. (Pen Pals Ser.). 128p. (J). (gr. 4 up). pap. 2.95 o.s.i (0-440-40343-X, Yearling) Random Hse. Children's Bks.

—Roommate Trouble. 1990. (Pen Pals Ser.: No. 11). 128p. (J). pap. 2.95 o.s.i (0-440-40345-6) Dell Publishing.

—Sam the Sham. 1989. (Pen Pals Ser.: No. 5). 128p. (J). (gr. k-6). reprint ed. pap. 2.95 o.s.i (0-440-40250-6, Yearling) Random Hse. Children's Bks.

—Stolen Pen Pals, Vol. 9. 1990. 128p. (J). (gr. 4-7). pap. 2.95 o.s.i (0-440-40342-1) Dell Publishing.

Wyllie, Stephen. Bear Buys a Car: A 3-D Picture Book. 1995. (Illus.). 22p. (J). (ps-2). 13.95 o.p. (0-8037-1840-3, Dial Bks. for Young Readers) Penguin Putnam Bks. for Young Readers.

Wynne, Carrie E. That Looks Like a Nice House. 1987. (Illus.). 42p. (Orig.). (YA). (gr. 8). pap. 6.95 (0-9613205-3-2) Launch Pr.

Yaccarino, Dan. Unlovable. 2004. (J). pap. 6.95 (0-8050-7532-1, Holt, Henry & Co. Bks. For Young Readers) Holt, Henry & Co.

Yaeger, Stephen S. Ian & the Woodins. 2001. 152p. (Orig.). pap. 11.95 (0-595-18366-2, Writers Club Pr.) iUniverse, Inc.

Yang, Dori Jones. The Secret Voice of Gina Zhang. 2000. (American Girls Collection Ser.). 232p. (J). (gr. 4-6). 12.95 (1-58485-204-6); pap. 5.95 (1-58485-203-8) Pleasant Co. Pubns. (American Girl).

—The Secret Voice of Gina Zhang. 2000. 12.00 (0-606-21790-8) Turtleback Bks.

Yarbro, Chelsea Quinn. Floating Illusions. 1986. 224p. (YA). (gr. 7 up). lib. bdg. 12.89 o.p. (0-06-026643-0) HarperCollins Children's Bk. Group.

Yates, Alma J. Ghosts in the Baker Mine. 1992. 197p. (Orig.). (J). (gr. 3-7). pap. 4.95 (0-87579-581-1) Deseret Bk. Co.

Yates, Elizabeth. Sound Friendships. 1992. 113p. (YA). (gr. 7 up). reprint ed. pap. 6.49 (0-89084-650-2, 063321) Jones, Bob Univ. Pr.

Yeatman, Linda. Buttons. 1988. (Illus.). 64p. (J). (gr. 2-5). pap. 2.95 o.p. (0-8120-3956-4) Barron's Educational Series, Inc.

Yee, Lisa. Millicent Min, Girl Genius. 2003. 240p. (J). pap. 16.95 (0-439-42519-0, Levine, Arthur A. Bks.) Scholastic, Inc.

Yee, Paul. The Boy in the Attic. 1998. (Illus.). 32p. (J). (gr. 2-5). 15.95 (0-88899-330-7) Groundwood Bks. CAN. *Dist:* Publishers Group West.

Yep, Laurence. Kind Hearts & Gentle Monsters. 1982. (Charlotte Zolotow Bk.). 192p. (YA). (gr. 7 up). lib. bdg. 12.89 o.p. (0-06-026733-X) HarperCollins Children's Bk. Group.

—Thief of Hearts. 1997. (Golden Mountain Chronicles). 208p. (J). (gr. 5 up). pap. 6.95 (0-06-440591-5, Harper Trophy) HarperCollins Children's Bk. Group.

—Thief of Hearts. 1995. (Illus.). 208p. (J). (gr. 5-9). 14.95 o.p. (0-06-025341-X); lib. bdg. 15.89 o.p. (0-06-025342-8) HarperTrade.

—Thief of Hearts. 1997. 12.00 (0-606-11978-7) Turtleback Bks.

—The Traitor. 2003. (Golden Mountain Chronicles Ser.). 320p. (J). 16.99 (0-06-027522-7); (Illus.). lib. bdg. 17.89 (0-06-027523-5) HarperCollins Children's Bk. Group.

Yingling, Phyllis S. The Adventures of Dan & Sam. 1997. (Success in Steps Ser.). (Illus.). 32p. (J). (gr. 2-5). spiral bd. 4.95 (1-882788-07-9) Vangar Pubs./Baltimore.

Yolen, Jane. Child of Faerie, Child of Earth. 1997. (Illus.). 32p. (J). (ps-3). 16.95 (0-316-96897-8) Little Brown & Co.

—Child of Faerie, Child of Earth. 2000. (Illus.). 32p. (J). (ps-3). pap. 5.95 (0-316-95720-8) Little Brown Children's Bks.

—Dove Isabeau. 1997. 12.15 (0-606-11275-8) Turtleback Bks.

—Encuentro. 1996. (J). 12.15 (0-606-10418-6) Turtleback Bks.

—Owl Moon. 2002. (Illus.). (J). 23.64 (0-7587-0064-4) Book Wholesalers, Inc.

—Owl Moon. 1987. (Illus.). 32p. (J). (ps-3). 16.99 (0-399-21457-7, Philomel) Penguin Putnam Bks. for Young Readers.

—The Rainbow Rider. 1974. (Illus.). 32p. (J). (ps-3). lib. bdg. 12.89 o.p. (0-690-00311-0) HarperCollins Children's Bk. Group.

—Tam Lin. 1998. 12.15 (0-606-13836-6) Turtleback Bks.

Yorgason, Blaine M. & Yorgason, Brenton. Pardners: Three Stories on Friendship. 1988. (Illus.). 64p. (Orig.). (YA). (gr. 9 up). pap. 3.95 o.p. (0-929985-05-2) Jackman Publishing.

Yorinks, Arthur. Sid & Sol, RS. 1991. 32p. (J). (gr. 4-8). pap. 3.95 o.p. (0-374-46634-3, Sunburst) Farrar, Straus & Giroux.

York, Carol B. Miss Know-It-All. 1985. 96p. (Orig.). (J). (gr. 4 up). pap. 2.25 o.s.i (0-553-15408-7, Skylark) Random Hse. Children's Bks.

—Miss Know-It-All & the Three Ring Circus. 1988. (Illus.). 96p. (Orig.). (J). pap. 2.75 o.s.i (0-553-15590-3, Skylark) Random Hse. Children's Bks.

—Nothing Ever Happens Here. 1987. (J). (gr. 7 up). pap. 2.25 o.p. (0-451-15025-2, Signet Bks.); 1975. (Illus.). 128p. (YA). (gr. 9-12). mass mkt. 2.25 o.p. (0-451-14665-4, Signet Vista) NAL.

You Are Special! 1985. (Wellinworld Tapes & Books for Children: 2-9). 36p. (J). (ps-4). 8.95 (0-88684-176-3) Listen U.S.A.

Young, Alida E. I Never Got to Say Good-Bye. 1988. (Lifelines Ser.). 128p. (Orig.). (J). (gr. 6-9). pap. 2.95 o.p. (0-87406-359-0) Darby Creek Publishing.

—Is Chelsea Going Blind? 1986. 160p. (J). (gr. 5-8). 2.50 o.p. (0-87406-134-2) Darby Creek Publishing.

—The Klutz Strikes Again. 1988. 160p. (Orig.). (J). (gr. 5-8). pap. 2.50 o.p. (0-87406-339-6) Darby Creek Publishing.

Young, Mahy. Good Fortunes Gang. 1993. (J). o.s.i (0-385-30940-6, Dell Books for Young Readers) Random Hse. Children's Bks.

Young, Ruth. Golden Bear. (Picture Puffins Ser.). (Illus.). 32p. (J). (ps-1). 1994. pap. 6.99 (0-14-050959-3, Puffin Bks.); 1992. 15.99 o.s.i (0-670-82577-8, Viking Children's Bks.) Penguin Putnam Bks. for Young Readers.

Younger, Barbara. Lewis Pixley & the Story Buddies. 2005. 128p. 14.99 (0-525-46732-7, Dutton Children's Bks.) Penguin Putnam Bks. for Young Readers.

Yumi & Her Best-Forever Friend. 2000. (J). mass mkt. 4.99 (0-89610-448-6) Island Heritage Publishing.

Yumoto, Kazumi. The Friends, RS. Hirano, Cathy, tr. from JPN. 1996. 176p. (J). (gr. 5-9). 15.00 (0-374-32460-3, Farrar, Straus & Giroux (BYR)) Farrar, Straus & Giroux.

—The Friends. Hirano, Cathy, tr. 1998. 176p. (gr. 5-9). pap. text 4.99 (0-440-41446-6, Yearling) Random Hse. Children's Bks.

—The Friends. unabr. ed. 1997. (J). (gr. 5 up). 55.50 incl. audio (0-7887-1134-2, 40483) Recorded Bks., LLC.

—The Friends. 1998. (J). 10.55 (0-606-13103-5) Turtleback Bks.

Zabar, Abbie. Fifty-Five Friends. 1994. (J). (ps-2). pap. o.p. (0-7868-2017-9); (Illus.). 13.95 (0-7868-0021-6) Hyperion Bks. for Children.

Zach, Cheryl. Benny & the No-Good Teacher. 1992. (Illus.). 80p. (J). (gr. 2-6). lib. bdg. 13.00 o.s.i (0-02-793706-2, Simon & Schuster Children's Publishing) Simon & Schuster Children's Publishing.

—The Winds of Betrayal. 1995. (Southern Angels Ser.: No. 2). 256p. (YA). mass mkt. 3.99 o.s.i (0-553-56218-5) Bantam Bks.

Zadra, Dan. Dare to Be Different. 1986. (Value of Self-Esteem Ser.). (Illus.). 32p. (J). (gr. 6 up). lib. bdg. 12.95 o.p. (0-88682-016-2, Creative Education) Creative Co., The.

—Mistakes Are Great! 1986. (Value of Self-Esteem Ser.). (Illus.). 32p. (J). (gr. 6 up). lib. bdg. 12.95 o.p. (0-88682-019-7, Creative Education) Creative Co., The.

—More Good Time for You. 1986. (Value of Self-Esteem Ser.). (Illus.). 32p. (J). (gr. 6 up). lib. bdg. 12.95 o.p. (0-88682-022-7, Creative Education) Creative Co., The.

Zalben, Jane Breskin. Here's Looking at You, Kid. 1987. (J). (gr. k-12). reprint ed. mass mkt. 2.50 o.s.i (0-440-93573-3, Laurel Leaf) Random Hse. Children's Bks.

—Oliver & Alison's Week, RS. 1980. (Illus.). 32p. (J). (gr. k-3). 9.95 o.p. (0-374-35618-1, Farrar, Straus & Giroux (BYR)) Farrar, Straus & Giroux.

—Porcupine's Christmas Blues. 1982. (Illus.). 32p. (J). 9.95 o.p. (0-399-20893-3, Philomel) Penguin Putnam Bks. for Young Readers.

Zehler, Antonia. Two Fine Ladies Have a Tiff. 2002. (Step into Reading Ser.). (Illus.). 32p. (J). lib. bdg. 11.99 (0-375-91105-7, Random Hse. Bks. for Young Readers) Random Hse. Children's Bks.

—Two Fine Ladies Have a Tiff. 2002. (Step into Reading Ser.). 32p. (J). 3.99 (0-375-81105-2) Random Hse., Inc.

Zeier, Joan T. Stick Boy. 1993. 144p. (J). (gr. 2-6). lib. bdg. 13.95 o.s.i (0-689-31835-9, Atheneum) Simon & Schuster Children's Publishing.

Zelonky, Joy. My Best Friend Moved Away. 1901. (Good Days-Bad Days Ser.). (Illus.). 32p. (J). (gr. 1-3). 4.95 o.p. (0-89191-600-8) Cook Communications Ministries.

—My Best Friend Moved Away. (Life & Living from a Child's Point of View Ser.). (J). (ps-3). 1993. pap. 3.95 o.p. (0-8114-7157-8); 1980. (Illus.). lib. bdg. 21.40 o.p. (0-8172-1353-8) Raintree Pubs.
Zemser, Amy Bronwen. Beyond the Mango Tree. (Illus.). (gr. 5 up). 2000. 176p. (J). pap. 5.99 (0-06-440786-1, Harper Trophy); 1998. 156p. (YA). 14.95 (0-688-16005-0, Greenwillow Bks.) HarperCollins Children's Bk. Group.
—Beyond the Mango Tree. 2000. 11.00 (0-606-17879-1) Turtleback Bks.
Ziebel, Peter. Look Closer. 1993. (J). (ps-3). pap. 5.95 o.p. (0-395-66509-4) Houghton Mifflin Co.
Ziefert, Harriet. Follow Me! 1990. (Hello Reading! Ser.). (Illus.). 32p. (J). (ps-3). pap. 3.50 o.p. (0-14-054220-5) Penguin Putnam Bks. for Young Readers.
—Friends Stick Together. 2001. (Illus.). 40p. (J). (gr. 3-7). pap. 5.95 (0-439-23226-0) Scholastic, Inc.
—Let's Trade. (Illus.). 32p. (J). (ps-2). 1996. (Easy-to-Read Bks.: Level 1). pap. 3.50 o.s.i (0-14-038109-0, Puffin Bks.); 1989. (Hello Reading! Ser.). 8.95 o.p. (0-670-82666-9, Viking Children's Bks.); 1989. (Hello Reading! Ser.). pap. 3.50 o.p. (0-14-050982-8) Penguin Putnam Bks. for Young Readers.
—Let's Trade. 1996. (Puffin Easy-to-Read Ser.). (J). 8.70 o.p. (0-606-09550-0) Turtleback Bks.
—Little Hippo's New Friend. 1998. (Little Hippo Board Books Ser.). (Illus.). 18p. (J). pap. 12.95 o.p. (0-7894-3409-1) Dorling Kindersley Publishing, Inc.
—Mike & Tony Level 1, Blue: Best Friends. (Easy-to-Read Bks.). (Illus.). (J). (ps-2). 1994. 32p. pap. 3.99 o.s.i (0-14-036853-1, Puffin Bks.); 1987. 8.95 o.p. (0-670-81719-8, Viking Children's Bks.); 1987. pap. 3.50 o.p. (0-14-050744-2, Puffin Bks.) Penguin Putnam Bks. for Young Readers.
—Move Over! 1991. (Stickerbook Reader). (Illus.). 24p. (J). (ps-3). mass mkt. 3.95 (0-06-107421-7) HarperCollins Children's Bk. Group.
—Nicky Upstairs & Down, Level. 1987. (Hello Reading! Ser.). (Illus.). (J). (ps-3). 8.95 o.p. (0-670-81717-1); pap. 3.50 o.p. (0-14-050742-6) Penguin Putnam Bks. for Young Readers.
—The Small Potatoes & the Sleep-over. 1985. (Illus.). 64p. (J). (gr. k-6). pap. 2.75 o.s.i (0-440-48036-1, Yearling) Random Hse. Children's Bks.
—Stitches. 1990. (Hello Reading! Ser.). (Illus.). 32p. (J). (ps-3). pap. 3.50 o.p. (0-14-054224-8) Penguin Putnam Bks. for Young Readers.
—39 Uses for a Friend. 2001. (Illus.). 32p. (J). (gr. k-4). 11.99 (0-399-23616-3) Putnam Publishing Group, The.
Ziegler, Jack. Mr. Knocky. 1993. (Illus.). 32p. (J). (gr. k-3). lib. bdg. 14.95 (0-02-793725-9, Simon & Schuster Children's Publishing) Simon & Schuster Children's Publishing.
Ziggy & His Friends. 1987. 64p. (J). (gr. k-5). pap. 3.95 o.p. (0-89542-939-X) Ideals Pubns.
Zindel, Bonnie. Hollywood Dream Machine. 1985. 192p. (YA). (gr. 7-12). mass mkt. 2.50 o.s.i (0-553-25240-2, Starfire) Random Hse. Children's Bks.
Zindel, Paul. A Begonia for Miss Applebaum. 1989. (Charlotte Zolotow Bk.). 192p. (YA). (gr. 7 up). 14.95 o.p. (0-06-026877-8); lib. bdg. 14.89 o.s.i (0-06-026878-6) HarperCollins Children's Bk. Group.
—A Begonia for Miss Applebaum. 1990. 192p. (YA). (gr. 7 up). mass mkt. 4.99 (0-553-28765-6, Starfire) Random Hse. Children's Bks.
—A Begonia for Miss Applebaum. 1989. (J). 11.04 (0-606-03065-4) Turtleback Bks.
—Fright Party. 1993. (Wacky Facts Lunch Bunch Ser.: No. 2). (Illus.). 144p. (J). (gr. 4-7). pap. 3.50 o.s.i (0-553-48082-0) Bantam Bks.
—Harry & Hortense at Hormone High. 1984. (Charlotte Zolotow Bk.). 160p. (YA). (gr. 7 up). lib. bdg. 14.89 o.p. (0-06-026869-7) HarperCollins Children's Bk. Group.
—Harry & Hortense at Hormone High. 1985. 160p. (YA). (gr. 7 up). mass mkt. 3.99 o.s.i (0-553-25175-9, Starfire) Random Hse. Children's Bks.
—The Pigman & Me. 1993. (Bantam Starfire Bks.). 176p. (YA). (gr. 7-12). mass mkt. 4.99 (0-553-56456-0) Bantam Bks.
Zinsser, Anne. Pirates on Our River. 1998. (Illus.). (J). (gr. 3-5). pap. 5.95 (0-933951-77-9) Locust Hill Pr.
Zoehfeld, Kathleen Weidner. Lessons from the Hundred-Acre Wood: Stories, Songs, & Wisdom from Winnie the Pooh. 1999. (Pooh Ser.). (Illus.). 208p. (J). (ps-3). 12.99 (0-7868-3243-6) Disney Pr.
—Pooh's Friends. 1998. (Chunky Roly-Poly Book Ser.). (Illus.). 18p. (J). (ps-3). bds. 3.99 (1-57082-991-8) Mouse Works.
Zollman, Pam. Don't Bug Me! 2001. (Illus.). 134p. (J). (gr. 2-6). tchr. ed. 15.95 (0-8234-1584-8) Holiday Hse., Inc.
Zolotow, Charlotte. The Hating Book. (Trophy Picture Bk.). (Illus.). (J). (ps-3). 1989. 32p. pap. 5.99 (0-06-443197-5, Harper Trophy); 1969. 80p. 14.95 o.p. (0-06-026923-5); 1969. 80p. lib. bdg. 14.89 o.p. (0-06-026924-3) HarperCollins Children's Bk. Group.
—The Hating Book. 9999. (J). pap. 1.50 o.s.i (0-590-03118-X) Scholastic, Inc.
—The Hating Book. 1989. (J). 12.10 (0-606-04242-3) Turtleback Bks.
—Hold My Hand. 1972. (Charlotte Zolotow Bk.). (Illus.). 32p. (J). (gr. k-3). 13.00 (0-06-026951-0); lib. bdg. 13.89 o.p. (0-06-026952-9) HarperCollins Children's Bk. Group.
—If It Weren't for You. 2002. 32p. (J). (ps-3). lib. bdg. 15.89 (0-06-027876-5) HarperCollins Children's Bk. Group.
—Janey. 1973. (Charlotte Zolotow Bk.). (Illus.). 80p. (J). (ps-3). lib. bdg. 13.89 o.p. (0-06-026928-6) HarperCollins Children's Bk. Group.
—My Friend John. 1968. (Illus.). (J). (gr. k-3). 12.95 o.p. (0-06-026947-2); 80p. lib. bdg. 14.89 o.p. (0-06-026948-0) HarperCollins Children's Bk. Group.
—My Friend John. 32p. (J). 2002. pap. 6.99 (0-440-41562-4, Dragonfly Bks.); 2000. (Illus.). 14.95 (0-385-32651-3, Dell Books for Young Readers) Random Hse. Children's Bks.
—The New Friend. 1981. (J). 11.95 o.p. (0-690-04086-5) HarperCollins Children's Bk. Group.
—Over & Over. 1987. (J). 12.10 (0-606-08431-2) Turtleback Bks.
—Three Funny Friends. 1982. (Trophy Picture Bk.). (Illus.). 32p. (J). (gr. k-3). pap. 1.95 o.p. (0-06-443035-9, Harper Trophy) HarperCollins Children's Bk. Group.
—The Three Funny Friends. 2003. (Illus.). 32p. (J). (gr. k-3). text 15.95 (0-7624-1553-3) Running Pr. Bk. Pubs.
—The Unfriendly Book. 1975. (Ursula Nordstrom Bk.). (Illus.). 32p. (J). (ps-3). lib. bdg. 12.89 o.p. (0-06-026931-6) HarperCollins Children's Bk. Group.

G

GRANDPARENTS—FICTION

Aaron, Chester. Catch Calico! 1979. (J). (gr. 4-8). 7.95 o.p. (0-525-27551-7, Dutton) Dutton/Plume.
Aber, Linda Williams. Carrie Measures Up! 2001. (Math Matters Ser.). (Illus.). 32p. (J). (gr. 1-3). pap. 4.95 (1-57565-100-9) Kane Pr., The.
—Carrie Measures Up! 2001. (Math Matters Ser.). (Illus.). (J). 11.10 (0-606-20593-4) Turtleback Bks.
Abercrombie, Barbara. Cat-Man's Daughter. 1981. 160p. (J). (gr. 6-9). 11.95 (0-06-020030-8); lib. bdg. 12.89 o.p. (0-06-020031-6) HarperCollins Children's Bk. Group.
Ackerman, Karen. By the Dawn's Early Light. 1999. (Illus.). 32p. (J). (ps-3). pap. 5.99 (0-689-82481-5, Aladdin) Simon & Schuster Children's Publishing.
—By the Dawn's Early Light. 1999. 12.14 (0-606-15924-X) Turtleback Bks.
—By the Dawn's Early Light: Al Amanecer. Ada, Alma Flor, tr. 1994. (ENG & SPA., Illus.). 32p. (J). (ps-3). 16.00 (0-689-31788-3); 14.95 (0-689-31917-7) Simon & Schuster Children's Publishing. (Atheneum).
—Song & Dance Man. 2002. (Illus.). (J). 14.79 (0-7587-4226-6) Book Wholesalers, Inc.
—Song & Dance Man. 1993. o.p. (0-679-84319-1); 1992. (Illus.). 32p. pap. 6.99 (0-679-81995-9, Dragonfly Bks.); 1988. (Illus.). 32p. (J). 15.95 (0-394-89330-1, Knopf Bks. for Young Readers); 1988. (Illus.). 32p. (J). lib. bdg. 17.99 (0-394-99330-6, Knopf Bks. for Young Readers) Random Hse. Children's Bks.
—Song & Dance Man. 1992. 13.14 (0-606-01543-4) Turtleback Bks.
Ada, Alma Flor. I Love Saturdays y Domingos. (gr. k-3). 2002. (Illus.). 32p. (J). 16.95 (0-689-31819-7, Atheneum); 1999. (SPA.). pap. 4.95 (0-689-80591-8, Aladdin) Simon & Schuster Children's Publishing.
Adams, H. J. The Song of the Blackbirds in the Reeds: In Which Great-Grandpa Nicholas Winslow Applewood Entertains Young Folk with Stories & Fables & Has Some Remarkable Betimes. 1998. 168p. lib. bdg. 20.00 (0-923687-48-3) Celo Valley Bks.
Adams, Ken. When I Was Your Age. (Illus.). 32p. (J). 1995. pap. 4.95 o.p. (0-8120-9269-4); 1991. 12.95 o.p. (0-8120-6249-3) Barron's Educational Series, Inc.
Adams, Pam. Mrs. Honey's Glasses. 1993. (Illus.). 32p. (J). (ps-3). 7.99 (0-85953-757-9) Child's Play of England GBR. *Dist:* Child's Play-International.
—Mrs. Honey's Glasses. 1993. (Early Reading Ser.). (Illus.). 32p. (J). (ps-3). pap. 3.99 (0-85953-758-7) Child's Play-International.
Adler, C. S. The Silver Coach. 1979. (J). (gr. 4-7). 8.95 o.p. (0-698-20504-9) Putnam Publishing Group, The.
Adler, David A. Cam Jansen & the Birthday Mystery. (Cam Jansen Ser.: Vol. 20). (Illus.). 64p. (J). 2000. (gr. 2-5). 13.99 (0-670-88877-X, Viking Children's Bks.); Vol. 20. 2002. pap. 3.99 (0-14-230203-1) Penguin Putnam Bks. for Young Readers.
—A Little at a Time. 1976. (Illus.). (J). (ps-2). 4.95 o.p. (0-394-82533-0); lib. bdg. 5.99 o.p. (0-394-92533-5) Random Hse. Children's Bks. (Random Hse. Bks. for Young Readers).
Agell, Charlotte, illus. Welcome Home or Someplace Like It, ERS. 2003. 240p. (J). 16.95 (0-8050-7083-4, Holt, Henry & Co. Bks. For Young Readers) Holt, Henry & Co.
Ahlberg, Allan. The Snail House. 2001. (Illus.). 32p. (J). (gr. k-3). 13.99 (0-7636-0711-8) Candlewick Pr.
Alberts, Nancy Markham. Elizabeth's Beauty. 1997. (Illus.). 32p. (J). (ps-5). 16.95 o.p. (0-8192-1677-1) Morehouse Publishing.
Alda, Arlene. Hurry Granny Annie. 2003. 32p. pap. 6.95 (1-58246-067-1); (Illus.). (J). 14.95 (1-883672-72-4) Tricycle Pr.
Alex, Marlee & Alex, Ben. Grandpa & Me: We Learn about Death. 1983. 44p. (Orig.). (J). (gr. k-2). text 8.95 o.p. (0-87123-257-X, 230257) Bethany Hse. Pubs.
Alexander Greene, Alesia. A Mural for Mamita. Lara, Susana, tr. 2001. Tr. of Mural Para Mamita. (ENG & SPA., Illus.). (J). 8.95 (1-56123-154-1, MFMC) Centering Corp.
Alexander, Marge. Adventures at the Grandparents' House. 2001. 96p. 9.95 (1-58169-064-9, Evergreen Pr.) Genesis Communications, Inc.
Alexander, Martha. Where Does the Sky End, Grandpa? 1992. (Illus.). 32p. (J). (ps-3). 12.95 (0-15-295603-4) Harcourt Children's Bks.
—Where Does the Sky End, Grandpa? 1993. (Illus.). (J). 5.99 o.p. (0-517-11180-2) Random Hse. Value Publishing.
Alice by Accident Bound Galley. 2000. (J). (0-06-029056-0) HarperCollins Children's Bk. Group.
Aliki. The Two of Them. (Illus.). 32p. (J). (ps-3). 1987. pap. 5.95 (0-688-07337-9, Harper Trophy); 1979. 16.00 o.p. (0-688-80225-7, Greenwillow Bks.); 1979. lib. bdg. 15.93 o.p. (0-688-84225-9, Greenwillow Bks.) HarperCollins Children's Bk. Group.
—The Two of Them. 1979. (J). 12.10 (0-606-04354-3) Turtleback Bks.
Allen, Linda. When Grandfather's. 1992. 80p. (J). pap. 2.99 o.s.i (0-553-15970-4) Bantam Bks.
Allende, Isabel. City of the Beasts. Peden, Margaret Sayers, tr. from SPA. 2002. Tr. of Ciudad de las Bestias. 416p. (J). (gr. 5 up). 19.99 (0-06-050918-X); lib. bdg. 21.89 (0-06-050917-1) HarperCollins Children's Bk. Group.
—City of the Beasts. l.t. ed. 2002. Tr. of Ciudad de las Bestias. 400p. (J). (gr. 5). pap. 19.99 (0-06-051195-8) HarperCollins Pubs.
—City of the Beasts. 2004. Tr. of Ciudad de las Bestias. 432p. (J). pap. 7.99 (0-06-053503-2, Rayo) HarperTrade.
Allred, Mary. Grandmother Poppy & the Children's Tea Party. 1984. (Illus.). (J). (gr. k-3). 5.95 o.p. (0-8054-4292-8, 4242-92) Broadman & Holman Pubs.
—Grandmother Poppy & the Funny-Looking Bird. 1981. (J). (gr. k-3). bds. 5.95 o.p. (0-8054-4269-3, 4242-69) Broadman & Holman Pubs.
Almond, David. Kit's Wilderness. l.t. ed. 2000. pap. 16.95 (0-7540-6115-9, Galaxy Children's Large Print) BBC Audiobooks America.
—Kit's Wilderness. 2000. (J). audio 24.00 (0-7366-9017-4) Books on Tape, Inc.
—Kit's Wilderness. unabr. ed. 2000. (J). (gr. 4-6). 240p. pap. 35.00 incl. audio (0-8072-8216-2); audio 30.00 (0-8072-8215-4, LL0166) Random Hse. Audio Publishing Group. (Listening Library).
—Kit's Wilderness. (YA). (gr. 7). 2001. (Illus.). 256p. mass mkt. 4.99 (0-440-41605-1, Laurel Leaf); 2000. 240p. 15.95 (0-385-32665-3, Dell Books for Young Readers) Random Hse. Children's Bks.
—Kit's Wilderness. l.t. ed. 2001. (Illus.). 272p. (J). (gr. 4-7). 22.95 (0-7862-2772-9) Thorndike Pr.
Altman, Linda Jacobs. Singin' with Momma Lou. 2002. (Illus.). 32p. (J). (gr. 1-5). 16.95 (1-58430-040-X) Lee & Low Bks., Inc.
Amato, Carol A. On the Trail of the Grizzly. 1997. (Young Readers' Ser.). (Illus.). 48p. (J). (gr. 2-4). pap. 4.95 (0-8120-9312-7) Barron's Educational Series, Inc.
—On the Trail of the Grizzly, Vol. 9. 1998. (Young Reader Ser.: No. 9). (Illus.). 48p. (J). (gr. 3-6). lib. bdg. 13.45 (1-56674-240-4) Forest Hse. Publishing Co., Inc.
—On the Trail of the Grizzly. 1997. (Young Readers' Series). 11.10 (0-606-11706-7) Turtleback Bks.
Anaya, Rudolfo A. Farolitos for Abuelo. 1999. (Illus.). 32p. (J). (gr. k-4). pap. 15.99 (0-7868-0237-5); lib. bdg. 16.49 (0-7868-2186-8) Hyperion Bks. for Children.
—The Farolitos of Christmas. 1995. (Illus.). 32p. (J). (gr. k-4). lib. bdg. 16.49 (0-7868-2047-0); 16.95 (0-7868-0060-7) Hyperion Bks. for Children.
Andersen, Honey & Reinholdt, Bill. Pop's Truck. 1994. (Illus.). (J). (0-383-03709-3) SRA/McGraw-Hill.
Anderson, Janet. The Key into Winter. 1993. (Illus.). (YA). lib. bdg. 15.95 o.p. (0-8075-4170-2) Whitman, Albert & Co.
Anderson, Laurie Halse. Time to Fly. 2003. (Wild at Heart Ser.). (Illus.). 113p. (J). (gr. 4 up). lib. bdg. 22.60 (0-8368-3262-0) Stevens, Gareth Inc.
—Turkey Pox. 1996. 13.10 (0-606-15748-4) Turtleback Bks.
—Turkey Pox. (Illus.). 32p. (J). (ps-2). 1998. pap. 6.95 (0-8075-8128-3); 1996. lib. bdg. 14.95 (0-8075-8127-5) Whitman, Albert & Co.
Anderson, Lena. Stina's Visit. 1991. (Illus.). 32p. (J). (ps up). 13.95 o.p. (0-688-09665-4); lib. bdg. 13.88 o.p. (0-688-09666-2) HarperCollins Children's Bk. Group. (Greenwillow Bks.).
Anderson, Mary Elizabeth. Good Medicine. (J). pap. 6.99 o.p. (0-7814-3904-3) Cook Communications Ministries.
Andreae, Giles. Heaven Is Having You. 2002. (Illus.). (J). tchr. ed. 14.95 (1-58925-016-8, Tiger Tales) ME Media LLC.
—My Grandson Is a Genius. 2003. (Illus.). 32p. (J). 15.95 (1-58234-815-4, Bloomsbury Children) Bloomsbury Publishing.
Anholt, Laurence. The Magpie Song. 1996. (Illus.). 40p. (J). (ps-3). 14.95 o.p. (0-395-75280-9) Houghton Mifflin Co.
—Summerhouse. 1999. (Illus.). 32p. (J). (ps-3). pap. 14.95 o.p. (0-7894-4377-5, D K Ink) Dorling Kindersley Publishing, Inc.
Anna, Jennifer. Grandma's Button Box. 2003. (Trutle's Back Bks.). (Illus.). 30p. (Orig.). (J). (gr. k-4). pap. 11.95 (1-886383-36-7, Little Blue Works) Windstorm Creative Ltd.
Antle, Nancy. Champions. 1997. (Illus.). 32p. (J). (gr. k up). 14.89 o.s.i (0-8037-1877-2, Dial Bks. for Young Readers) Penguin Putnam Bks. for Young Readers.
—Playing Solitaire. 2000. (Illus.). 112p. (YA). (gr. 7 up). 16.99 o.p. (0-8037-2406-3, Dial Bks. for Young Readers) Penguin Putnam Bks. for Young Readers.
—Staying Cool. 1997. (Illus.). 32p. (J). (gr. k-4). 14.99 o.s.i (0-8037-1876-4, Dial Bks. for Young Readers) Penguin Putnam Bks. for Young Readers.
Applegate, Stanley. Natchez under-the-Hill. 1999. (Illus.). 186p. (YA). (gr. 3-7). pap. 8.95 (1-56145-191-6, 51916) Peachtree Pubs., Ltd.
Appleton-Smith, Laura. It Is Halloween! 1999. (Book to Remember Ser.). (Illus.). (J). (ps-3). pap. 8.95 (0-9658246-4-0, Books To Remember) Flyleaf Publishing.
Arbuckle, Kathy. Grandma's House Coloring Book. 1994. (Illus.). 96p. (J). pap. 1.99 o.p. (1-55748-525-9) Barbour Publishing, Inc.
Archipowa, Anastassija & Outlet Book Company Staff. Little Red Riding Hood. 1990. (J). 5.99 o.s.i (0-517-05141-9) Random Hse. Value Publishing.
Arkin, Alan. One Present from Flekman's. 1999. (Illus.). 32p. (J). (gr. k-3). 15.95 (0-06-024530-1); lib. bdg. 14.89 o.p. (0-06-024531-X) HarperCollins Children's Bk. Group.
—Some Fine Grampa! 1995. (Illus.). 80p. (J). (gr. k-3). lib. bdg. 14.89 o.p. (0-06-021534-8); 14.95 o.p. (0-06-021533-X) HarperCollins Children's Bk. Group.
Armstrong, Jennifer. Steal Away. 224p. 1993. (J). (gr. 3-7). pap. 4.50 (0-590-46921-5, Scholastic Paperbacks); 1992. (YA). (gr. 6 up). mass mkt. 16.99 o.p. (0-531-08583-X, Orchard Bks.); 1992. (YA). (gr. 6 up). 15.95 o.p. (0-531-05983-9, Orchard Bks.) Scholastic, Inc.
—Steal Away. 1992. (J). 10.55 (0-606-05623-8) Turtleback Bks.
Arnold, Jeanne. Amy Asks a Question: Grandma, What's a Lesbian. 1997. (Illus.). 64p. (J). (gr. 4 up). 10.95 (0-941300-28-5) Mother Courage Pr.
Arnold, Marsha D. The Chicken Salad Club. 1998. (Illus.). 32p. (J). (ps-3). 15.99 o.s.i (0-8037-1915-9, Dial Bks. for Young Readers) Penguin Putnam Bks. for Young Readers.
Arnosky, Jim. Little Champ. 1995. (Illus.). 69p. (J). (ps-3). 13.95 o.s.i (0-399-22759-8, G. P. Putnam's Sons) Penguin Group (USA) Inc.
Arnosky, Jim, illus. Little Champ. 2001. (J). pap. 6.95 (0-9657144-5-4) Onion River Pr.
Aunt Eeebs. Let's Go to Grammy's. 1994. (Dino-Buddies Ser.). (Illus.). 160p. (Orig.). (J). (ps-2). pap. 3.95 (1-878908-06-5) Rivercrest Industries.
Aver, Kate. Joey's Way. 1992. (Illus.). 48p. (J). (gr. 1-4). 13.95 o.s.i (0-689-50552-3, McElderry, Margaret K.) Simon & Schuster Children's Publishing.
Avery, Najiyyah. My Grandmother's House Plant. 1999. 16p. (J). (gr. k-6). 7.00 (0-8059-4539-3) Dorrance Publishing Co., Inc.
Ayres, Katherine. A Long Way. 2003. (Illus.). 32p. (J). 15.99 (0-7636-1047-X) Candlewick Pr.

Babbitt, Ellen. Granny's Blackie. 1991. (Envelope Library Ser.). (Illus.). (YA). (gr. 7-9). pap. 2.50 o.p. (*0-88138-007-5*, Simon & Schuster Children's Publishing) Simon & Schuster Children's Publishing.

Bacon, Katharine J. Shadow & Light. 1987. 208p. (YA). (gr. 7 up). lib. bdg. 14.95 o.s.i (*0-689-50431-4*, McElderry, Margaret K.) Simon & Schuster Children's Publishing.

Badoe, Adwoa A. Nana's Cold Days. 2002. (Illus.). 32p. (J). 15.95 (*0-88899-479-6*) Groundwood Bks. CAN. *Dist:* Publishers Group West.

Baggette, Susan K. Jonathan & Papa. 1999. (Jonathan Adventures Ser.). (Illus.). 24p. (J). (ps-3). bds. 7.95 (*0-9660172-7-7*) Brookfield Reader, Inc., The.

—Jonathan Goes to the Grocery Store. 1998. (Jonathan Adventures Ser.). (Illus.). 16p. (J). (ps-k). bds. 5.95 (*0-9660172-2-6*) Brookfield Reader, Inc., The.

—Jonathan Goes to the Library. 1998. (Jonathan Adventures Ser.). (Illus.). 16p. (J). (ps-k). bds. 5.95 (*0-9660172-3-4*) Brookfield Reader, Inc., The.

Bagnall, Jill. Crayfishing with Grandmother. 1973. (Illus.). 32p. (J). (gr. 1-5). 6.90 o.p. (*0-8002-0081-0*) International Pubns. Service.

Bahr, Mary. The Memory Box. Tucker, Kathleen, ed. 1992. (Illus.). 32p. (J). (gr. 1-4). lib. bdg. 14.95 o.p. (*0-8075-5052-3*); (ps-3). pap. 5.95 (*0-8075-5053-1*) Whitman, Albert & Co.

Bailey, Linda. When Addie Was Scared. ed. 1999. (J). (gr. 1). spiral bd. (*0-616-01535-6*); (gr. 2). spiral bd. (*0-616-01537-2*) Canadian National Institute for the Blind/Institut National Canadien pour les Aveugles.

—When Addie Was Scared. unabr. ed. 2002. (Illus.). 138p. (J). (ps-3). pap. 5.95 (*1-55337-163-1*) Kids Can Pr., Ltd.

Baker, Barbara. Staying with Grandmother. 1994. (Illus.). 480p. (J). (gr. 1-4). 12.99 o.p. (*0-525-44603-6*, Dutton Children's Bks.) Penguin Putnam Bks. for Young Readers.

Baker, Sanna Anderson. Grandpa Is a Flyer. 1995. (Illus.). (J). (ps-3). lib. bdg. 15.95 o.p. (*0-8075-3033-6*) Whitman, Albert & Co.

Balgassi, Haemi. Peacebound Trains. (Illus.). 48p. (J). (gr. 4-6). 2000. pap. 6.95 (*0-618-04030-7*); 1996. tchr. ed. 15.00 (*0-395-72093-1*) Houghton Mifflin Co. Trade & Reference Div. (Clarion Bks.).

Ball, Duncan. Grandfather's Wheeliething. 1994. (Illus.). (J). pap. 15.00 o.p. (*0-671-79817-0*, Simon & Schuster Children's Publishing) Simon & Schuster Children's Publishing.

Ballard, Robin. Granny & Me. 1992. (Illus.). 24p. (J). (ps up). 14.00 o.p. (*0-688-10548-3*); lib. bdg. 13.93 o.p. (*0-688-10549-1*) HarperCollins Children's Bk. Group. (Greenwillow Bks.).

Banks, Lynne Reid. Alice-by-Accident. 2000. (Avon Camelot Bks.). 144p. (J). (gr. 4-7). 14.95 (*0-380-97865-2*) HarperCollins Children's Bk. Group.

Bannatyne-Cugnet, Jo. Grampa's Alkali. 1993. (Northern Lights Young Novels Ser.). (Illus.). 96p. (J). (gr. 3-7). pap. 7.95 (*0-88995-096-2*) Red Deer Pr. CAN. *Dist:* General Distribution Services, Inc.

Barasch, Lynne. A Country Schoolhouse, RS. 2004. (J). (*0-374-31577-9*, Farrar, Straus & Giroux (BYR)) Farrar, Straus & Giroux.

Barnwell, Ysaye M. No Mirrors in My Nana's House. 1998. (Illus.). 32p. (J). (gr. k-3). 18.00 incl. audio compact disk (*0-15-201825-5*) Harcourt Children's Bks.

Barrett, Elizabeth. Free Fall. 1994. 272p. (YA). (gr. 7 up). lib. bdg. 14.89 o.p. (*0-06-024466-6*); 15.00 o.p. (*0-06-024465-8*) HarperCollins Children's Bk. Group.

Barrett, Judith. Pickles to Pittsburgh. 1999. (Illus.). (J). (gr. 1-6). 24.95 incl. audio (*0-87499-538-8*) Live Oak Media.

—Pickles to Pittsburgh. 2000. (Illus.). 32p. (J). (ps-3). pap. 6.99 (*0-689-83929-4*, Aladdin) Simon & Schuster Children's Publishing.

—Pickles to Pittsburgh: The Sequel to Cloudy with a Chance of Meatballs. 1997. (Illus.). 32p. (J). (ps-3). 16.00 (*0-689-80104-1*, Atheneum) Simon & Schuster Children's Publishing.

Barron, T. A. Where Is Grandpa? 2001. (Illus.). 32p. (J). (ps-3). pap. 6.99 (*0-698-11904-5*, Puffin Bks.) Penguin Putnam Bks. for Young Readers.

Barron, T. A. Where is Grandpa? 2000. (Illus.). 32p. (J). (ps-3). 16.99 (*0-399-23037-8*, Philomel) Penguin Putnam Bks. for Young Readers.

Barsotti, Joan B. Christopher & Grandma on Safari. 1996. (Apple Hill Ser.). (Illus.). 32p. (J). (ps-3). per. 6.95 (*0-9642112-2-X*) Barsotti Bks.

Bartholomew, Carl. Granmax: The Saving of a Steam Train. 1997. (J). 25.25 (*1-56763-356-0*); pap. (*1-56763-357-9*) Ozark Publishing.

Bartlett, Craig. Parents Day. 2001. (Hey Arnold! Ser.: Bk. 4). (Illus.). 64p. (J). (gr. 4-7). pap. 3.99 (*0-689-83818-2*, Simon Spotlight) Simon & Schuster Children's Publishing.

Bartoletti, Susan Campbell. Dancing with Dziadziu. 1997. (Illus.). 40p. (J). (ps-3). 15.00 (*0-15-200675-3*) Harcourt Children's Bks.

Base, Graeme. My Grandma Lived in Gooligulch. (Illus.). 1995. 18p. (J). (gr. 2 up). 19.95 o.p. (*0-8109-4288-7*); 1990. 42p. (gr. 4-7). 16.95 (*0-8109-1547-2*) Abrams, Harry N., Inc.

—My Grandma Lived in Gooligulch. 1988. (Illus.). 44p. (J). (gr. k-5). reprint ed. 12.95 o.p. (*0-944176-01-1*) Terra Nova Pr.

Bauer, Joan. Sticks. 192p. (gr. 3-7). 1997. (Illus.). pap. text 3.99 o.s.i (*0-440-41387-7*); 1996. (J). text 15.95 o.s.i (*0-385-32165-1*, Delacorte Pr.) Dell Publishing.

—Sticks. 2002. 192p. (J). 18.99 (*0-399-23752-6*) Penguin Group (USA) Inc.

—Sticks. 1997. (J). 10.04 (*0-606-11912-4*) Turtleback Bks.

Bauer, Marion Dane. An Early Winter. 1999. (Illus.). 160p. (J). (gr. 5-9). tchr. ed. 15.00 (*0-395-90372-6*, Clarion Bks.) Houghton Mifflin Co. Trade & Reference Div.

—An Early Winter. 2001. 128p. (gr. 4-7). pap. text 4.50 (*0-440-41694-9*, Dell Books for Young Readers) Random Hse. Children's Bks.

—An Early Winter. 2000. (YA). pap. 42.00 incl. audio (*0-7887-4328-7*, 41123) Recorded Bks., LLC.

—Grandmother's Song. 2000. (Illus.). 32p. (J). (ps-3). 16.00 (*0-689-82272-3*, Simon & Schuster Children's Publishing) Simon & Schuster Children's Publishing.

—When I Go Camping with Grandma. 1996. 10.15 o.p. (*0-606-10057-1*) Turtleback Bks.

Bawden, Nina. Granny the Pag. l.t. ed. 1997. (J). 16.95 o.p. (*0-7451-6905-8*, Galaxy Children's Large Print) BBC Audiobooks America.

—Granny the Pag. 1996. 192p. (YA). (gr. 7-7). 15.00 (*0-395-77604-X*, Clarion Bks.) Houghton Mifflin Co. Trade & Reference Div.

—Granny the Pag. 1998. 192p. (J). (gr. 5-9). pap. 4.99 o.s.i (*0-14-038447-2*, Puffin Bks.) Penguin Putnam Bks. for Young Readers.

—Granny the Pag. 1998. (J). 10.09 (*0-606-12955-3*) Turtleback Bks.

—Off the Road. 1998. (Illus.). 190p. (J). (gr. 5-9). 16.00 (*0-395-91321-7*, Clarion Bks.) Houghton Mifflin Co. Trade & Reference Div.

—Off the Road. 2001. 192p. (J). (gr. 5-9). pap. 5.99 (*0-14-131100-2*, Puffin Bks.) Penguin Putnam Bks. for Young Readers.

—Off the Road. 2001. (J). 12.04 (*0-606-21364-3*) Turtleback Bks.

—The Real Plato Jones. 1993. 176p. (YA). (gr. 7-7). tchr. ed. 15.00 (*0-395-66972-3*, Clarion Bks.) Houghton Mifflin Co. Trade & Reference Div.

—The Real Plato Jones. 1996. 176p. (J). (gr. 5-9). pap. 4.99 o.s.i (*0-14-037947-9*, Puffin Bks.) Penguin Putnam Bks. for Young Readers.

—The Real Plato Jones. 1996. (J). 10.09 o.p. (*0-606-10907-2*) Turtleback Bks.

—The Robbers. 1979. (Illus.). 160p. (J). (gr. 4-7). reprint ed. 12.95 o.p. (*0-688-41902-X*); lib. bdg. 12.88 o.p. (*0-688-51902-4*) HarperCollins Children's Bk. Group.

Beardshaw, Rosalind. Grandma's Beach. 2004. (J). (*1-58234-935-5*) Bloomsbury Publishing.

—Grandpa's Surprise. 2004. (J). 15.95 (*1-58234-934-7*) Bloomsbury Publishing.

Beattie, Ann. Spectacles. 1985. (Goblin Tales Ser.). (Illus.). 48p. (J). (gr. 4-6). 10.95 o.p. (*0-89480-926-1*) Workman Publishing Co., Inc.

Beck, Ian. Peter & the Wolf. 2000. (Illus.). 25p. (J). pap. 9.95 (*0-552-52755-6*) Transworld Publishers Ltd. GBR. *Dist:* Trafalgar Square.

Becker, Bonny. The Quiet Way Home, ERS. 1995. (Illus.). 88p. (J). (gr. k-2). 15.95 o.p. (*0-8050-3530-3*, Holt, Henry & Co. Bks. For Young Readers) Holt, Henry & Co.

Beckhorn, Susan Williams. The Kingfisher's Gift. 2002. (Illus.). 208p. (J). 17.99 (*0-399-23712-7*) Putnam Publishing Group, The.

Beil, Karen M. Grandma According to Me. 1992. (Illus.). 32p. (J). (ps-3). 15.00 o.s.i (*0-385-41484-6*) Doubleday Publishing.

—Grandma According to Me. 1992. (J). o.s.i (*0-385-44554-7*, Dell Books for Young Readers) Random Hse. Children's Bks.

Beil, Karen Magnuson. Grandma According to Me. 1994. (Illus.). 32p. (gr. k-3). pap. text 4.99 o.s.i (*0-440-40995-0*) Dell Publishing.

—Grandma According to Me. 1994. 10.19 (*0-606-06992-5*) Turtleback Bks.

Bell, Mary Reeves. Sagebrush Rebellion. 1999. (Passport to Danger Ser.: Vol. 2). 208p. (J). (gr. 7-12). pap. 5.99 o.p. (*1-55661-550-7*) Bethany Hse. Pubs.

—Sagebrush Rebellion. 1999. (J). 12.04 (*0-606-18973-4*) Turtleback Bks.

Bellante, V. I Did It Myself. (Illus.). 29p. (*1-85863-502-0*) Minerva Pr. GBR. *Dist:* Unity Distribution.

Belton, Sandra. Beauty, Her Basket. 2004. 32p. (J). 15.99 (*0-688-17821-9*); lib. bdg. 16.89 (*0-688-17822-7*) HarperCollins Children's Bk. Group. (Greenwillow Bks.).

—May'naise Sandwiches & Sunshine Tea. 1994. (Illus.). 32p. (J). (ps-4). mass mkt. 14.95 o.p. (*0-02-709035-3*, Simon & Schuster Children's Publishing) Simon & Schuster Children's Publishing.

Bender, Esther. Search for a Fawn. 1998. (Illus.). 32p. (J). (gr. k-5). pap. 8.99 (*0-8361-9099-8*) Herald Pr.

Bennett-Brown, Irene. Before the Lark. l.t. ed. 2002. (Juvenile Ser.). 205p. (J). 21.95 (*0-7862-4127-6*) Gale Group.

Bentley, Dawn. My Make-Believe Purse. 1997. (Look-Inside Ser.). (Illus.). 7p. (J). (ps-2). 9.95 o.s.i (*0-525-45847-6*, Dutton Children's Bks.) Penguin Putnam Bks. for Young Readers.

Bercaw, Edna C. Halmoni's Day. 2000. (Illus.). 32p. (J). (gr. k-3). 16.99 (*0-8037-2444-6*, Dial Bks. for Young Readers) Penguin Putnam Bks. for Young Readers.

Berenstain, Stan & Berenstain, Jan. The Berenstain Bears & the Week at Grandma's. 1986. (Berenstain Bears First Time Bks.). (Illus.). 32p. (gr. k-2). (J). 6.99 o.s.i (*0-394-97335-6*); pap. 3.25 (*0-394-87335-1*) Random Hse. Children's Bks. (Random Hse. Bks. for Young Readers).

Berger, Barbara Helen. Grandfather Twilight. 1996. (Illus.). 32p. (J). (ps-3). pap. 6.99 (*0-698-11394-2*, PaperStar) Penguin Putnam Bks. for Young Readers.

—Grandfather Twilight. 1988. (Illus.). (J). (ps-3). 6.95 o.s.i (*0-399-21596-4*, Sandcastle Bks.) Putnam Publishing Group, The.

Berlitz Kids Editors Staff. A Visit to Grandma: French-English. 1997. (Adventures with Nicholas Ser.). (ENG & FRE., Illus.). 64p. (J). (ps-3). pap. 16.95 incl. audio (*2-8315-6249-X*, Berlitz Kids) Berlitz International, Inc.

—A Visit to Grandma: German-English. 1997. (Adventures with Nicholas Ser.). (ENG & GER., Illus.). 64p. (J). (ps-3). pap. 16.95 incl. audio (*2-8315-6250-3*) Berlitz International, Inc.

Bernstein, Susan H. N. E. Pominonous Epstein & Change. l.t. ed. 2003. (E. Pominonous Epstein Ser.: No. 3). (Illus.). 20p. (Orig.). (J). (gr. k-3). pap. 8.95 (*0-9706596-2-8*) Bernstein, Susan.

Best, Cari. Three Cheers for Catherine the Great. 2001. (J). (gr. k-4). audio 6.95 (*1-55592-984-2*) Weston Woods Studios, Inc.

—Three Cheers for Catherine the Great! 1999. (Illus.). 32p. (J). (ps-3). pap. 16.99 (*0-7894-2622-6*, D K Ink) Dorling Kindersley Publishing, Inc.

—Three Cheers for Catherine the Great!, RS. 2003. (Illus.). 32p. (J). pap. 6.95 (*0-374-47551-2*, Sunburst) Farrar, Straus & Giroux.

—When Catherine the Great & I Were Eight, RS. 2003. (Illus.). 32p. (gr. k-3). 16.00 (*0-374-39954-9*, Farrar, Straus & Giroux (BYR)) Farrar, Straus & Giroux.

Betancourt, Lin. Grandfathers & Demons. 1997. (Illus.). 88p. (J). pap. text 4.95 (*1-56002-336-8*, University Editions) Aegina Pr., Inc.

Bijan, Nancy N. Rolling Pumpkin. 2nd ed. 1998. (First Ser.). (PER., Illus.). 17p. (J). (ps-6). pap. 5.95 (*1-880710-10-2*) Monterey Pacific Pubs.

Birch, Barbara & Lewis, Beverly. Katie & Jake & the Haircut Mistake. 1995. (J). (gr. k-3). pap. 4.99 o.p. (*0-8066-2816-2*, 9-2816) Augsburg Fortress, Pubs.

Black, Frank M. Grandpa Knows Everyone. 1999. (J). pap. (*1-929157-07-X*) Inside-OUT Corp.

Blakeslee, Ann R. Summer Battles. 2000. (Illus.). 128p. (YA). (gr. 5-9). 14.95 (*0-7614-5064-5*, Cavendish Children's Bks.) Cavendish, Marshall Corp.

Bledsoe, Lucy Jane. The Big Bike Race. 1997. (Illus.). 96p. (J). (gr. 3). pap. 4.95 (*0-380-72830-3*, Harper Trophy) HarperCollins Children's Bk. Group.

—The Big Bike Race. 1995. (Illus.). 96p. (J). (gr. 4-5). 15.95 (*0-8234-1206-7*) Holiday Hse., Inc.

—The Big Bike Race. 1997. 11.10 (*0-606-10996-X*) Turtleback Bks.

Blegvad, Lenore. Once upon a Time & Grandma. 1993. (Illus.). 32p. (J). (ps-3). 14.95 (*0-689-50548-5*, McElderry, Margaret K.) Simon & Schuster Children's Publishing.

Blevins, Wade. And Then the Feather Fell. 1996. (Cherokee Indian Legend Ser.: No. 1). (Illus.). 35p. (J). pap. 2.95 o.p. (*1-56763-097-9*); 17.25 (*1-56763-096-0*) Ozark Publishing.

—Atagahi's Gift. 51p. (J). (gr. 4-7). 1996. (Cherokee Indian Legend Ser.: Vol. 6). (Illus.). lib. bdg. 17.25 (*1-56763-135-5*); 1995. pap. text 2.95 o.p. (*1-56763-136-3*) Ozark Publishing.

Bliss, Corinne Demas. The Disappearing Island. 2000. (Illus.). 32p. (J). (ps-3). 16.00 (*0-689-80539-X*, Simon & Schuster Children's Publishing) Simon & Schuster Children's Publishing.

Blomberg, Dianne L. Sam & Gram & the First Day of School. 1999. (Illus.). 32p. (J). (ps-1). (*1-55798-562-6*, 441-5626, Magination Pr.) American Psychological Assn.

Blos, Joan W. Bedtime! 1998. (Illus.). 32p. (J). (ps-4). 13.00 (*0-689-81031-8*, Simon & Schuster Children's Publishing) Simon & Schuster Children's Publishing.

—The Grandpa Days. 32p. (J). (ps-3). 1994. pap. 3.95 (*0-671-88244-9*, Aladdin); 1989. (Illus.). 8.95 o.s.i (*0-671-64640-0*, Simon & Schuster Children's Publishing) Simon & Schuster Children's Publishing.

—Hello, Shoes! 1999. (Illus.). 32p. (J). (ps). 13.95 (*0-689-81441-0*, Simon & Schuster Children's Publishing) Simon & Schuster Children's Publishing.

Blue, Rose. Grandma Didn't Wave Back. 1972. (Illus.). 64p. (gr. 3-5). lib. bdg. 9.90 o.p. (*0-531-02557-8*, Watts, Franklin) Scholastic Library Publishing.

Bobbi. Grandma's Teapot. 1992. (Illus.). 37p. (J). pap. 3.95 (*0-9626608-3-3*) Magik Pubs.

Boelts, Maribeth. Sarah's Grandma. 2004. (Illus.). 32p. 9.99 (*0-310-70656-4*) Zondervan.

Bogart, JoEllen. Gifts. ed. 1996. Tr. of Cadeaux. (J). (gr. 1). spiral bd. (*0-616-01559-3*); (gr. 2). spiral bd. (*0-616-01560-7*) Canadian National Institute for the Blind/Institut National Canadien pour les Aveugles.

—Gifts. 1996. Tr. of Cadeaux. (Illus.). 44p. (J). (ps-2). 15.95 (*0-590-55260-0*) Scholastic, Inc.

Bongiorno, Patti Lynn. Grandma, Does God Make Mistakes? 2nd ed. 2001. (J). spiral bd. 20.00 (*0-9715819-3-2*) Bongiorno Bks.

Bonners, Susan. The Wooden Doll. 1991. (Illus.). (J). (ps-3). 13.95 (*0-688-08280-7*) HarperCollins Children's Bk. Group.

Bonnici, Peter. Amber's Other Grandparents. 1986. (J). o.s.i (*0-370-30671-6*) Random Hse., Inc.

Bono. Peter & the Wolf. 2003. (Illus.). 64p. (J). 22.95 (*1-58234-388-8*) Bloomsbury Publishing.

Boon, Debbie. My Gran. 1997. E-Book (*1-58824-532-2*); E-Book (*1-58824-779-1*); E-Book (*1-58824-862-3*) ipicturebooks, LLC.

Boon, Debbie, illus. My Gran. 1998. 2. 32p. (ps-3). 20.90 o.p. (*0-7613-0312-X*) Millbrook Pr., Inc.

Boone, Debby. The Snow Angel. 1991. (Illus.). 32p. (J). (ps-1). 16.99 o.p. (*0-89081-871-1*) Harvest Hse. Pubs.

Boonstra, Jean Elizabeth. Song for Grandfather A: Sarah 1842-1844. 2002. 95p. (J). (*0-8163-1873-5*) Pacific Pr. Publishing Assn.

Booth, Barbara D. Mandy. 1991. (Illus.). 32p. (J). (gr. 1 up). lib. bdg. 15.93 o.p. (*0-688-10339-1*); (ps-3). 16.95 (*0-688-10338-3*) HarperCollins Children's Bk. Group.

Booth-Cartwright, Karan. A Grandma's Love. 1999. (Illus.). 30p. (J). (ps-6). 22.95 (*1-929819-00-5*) A+ Bk. Publishing.

Borden, Louise. Watching Game. 1991. (J). (ps-3). 12.95 o.p. (*0-590-43600-7*) Scholastic, Inc.

Borders, Christine Kareem. Gram Makes a House Call. 1999. (Illus.). 77p. (J). (gr. 2-4). pap. 5.95 (*0-9671160-0-7*) Greenhills Pr.

Bornstein, Ruth L. A Beautiful Seashell. 1990. (Charlotte Zolotow Bk.). (Illus.). 32p. (J). (gr. k-3). 12.95 o.p. (*0-06-020594-6*); lib. bdg. 12.89 o.p. (*0-06-020595-4*) HarperCollins Children's Bk. Group.

Bosak, Susan V. Something to Remember Me By: A Story about Love & Legacies. 2003. (Illus.). 32p. (gr. 1-6). (*1-896232-01-9*) Communication Project, The.

Bottner, Barbara. Nana Hannah's Piano. 1996. (Illus.). 32p. (J). (ps-3). 15.95 o.s.i (*0-399-22656-7*, G. P. Putnam's Sons) Penguin Group (USA) Inc.

Bouchard, Dave. The Song Within My Heart. 2003. (Illus.). 32p. (J). (gr. 2 up). 14.95 (*1-55192-559-1*) Raincoast Bk. Distribution CAN. *Dist:* Publishers Group West.

Bourgeois, Paulette. Grandma's Secret, Vol. 1. 1990. (J). 14.95 o.s.i (*0-316-10355-1*, Joy Street Bks.) Little Brown & Co.

—Oma's Quilt. (Illus.). 32p. (J). 2003. pap. 5.95 (*1-55337-625-0*); 2001. 15.95 (*1-55074-777-0*) Kids Can Pr., Ltd.

Bowdish, Lynea & Carpenter, Nancy, illus. Brooklyn, Bugsy & Me, RS. 2000. 96p. (J). (gr. 4-7). 15.00 (*0-374-30993-0*, Farrar, Straus & Giroux (BYR)) Farrar, Straus & Giroux.

Bowen, Anne M. I Loved You Even Before You Were Born. 2001. (Illus.). 32p. (J). (gr. 3 up). lib. bdg. 15.89 (*0-06-028721-7*); (ps-3). 15.99 (*0-06-028720-9*) HarperCollins Children's Bk. Group.

—I Loved You Even Before You Were Born. 2004. (Illus.). 32p. (J). (ps-3). pap. 5.99 (*0-06-443631-4*) HarperCollins Pubs.

Bower, Gary & Bower, Jan. Ivy's Icicle Bk. 3: Forgiving Others. 2002. (Thinking of Others Books Ser.). (Illus.). 32p. (J). (ps-3). 14.99 (*0-8423-7417-5*) Tyndale Hse. Pubs.

Bowler, Tim. River Boy. 2003. (Read-Along Ser.). (J). pap. 29.95 incl. audio (*0-7540-6214-7*, Galaxy Children's Large Print) BBC Audiobooks America.

—River Boy. (Illus.). 160p. (J). 2002. mass mkt. 4.99 (*0-689-84804-8*, Simon Pulse); 2000. (gr. 7 up). 16.00 (*0-689-82908-6*, McElderry, Margaret K.) Simon & Schuster Children's Publishing.

—River Boy. l.t. ed. 2001. 190p. (J). 22.95 (*0-7862-3507-1*) Thorndike Pr.

Bowman, Crystal. Jonathan James Says, "Let's Play Ball" 1995. (Jonathan James Ser.: Bk. 4). (Illus.). 48p. (J). (ps-3). pap. 4.99 (*0-310-49621-7*) Zondervan.
—Windmills & Woodenshoes. 1999. (Illus.). 40p. (J). (gr. 2-6). 15.00 (*0-9636050-2-X*) Cygnet Publishing Co.
Boyden, Linda. The Blue Roses. 2002. (Illus.). 32p. (J). (gr. 1-5). 16.95 (*1-58430-037-X*) Lee & Low Bks., Inc.
Brady, Kimberley S. Keeper for the Sea. 1995. (J). (gr. k-3). 16.00 (*0-02-711851-7*, Simon & Schuster Children's Publishing) Simon & Schuster Children's Publishing.
Brammer, Ethriam Cash. Alla en el Rancho Grande: The Rowdy, Rowdy Ranch. Cruz, D. Nina, tr. & illus. by. 2003. (ENG & SPA.). (J). (*1-55885-409-6*, Piñata Books) Arte Publico Pr.
Brandenberg, Franz. A Secret for Grandmother's Birthday. 1985. (Illus.). 32p. (J). (gr. k-3). lib. bdg. 11.88 o.p. (*0-688-05782-9*); 11.95 o.p. (*0-688-05781-0*) HarperCollins Children's Bk. Group. (Greenwillow Bks.).
Branscum, Robbie. Toby, Granny & George. 1976. 112p. (gr. 3-9). 7.95 o.p. (*0-385-11269-6*) Doubleday Publishing.
Bray, Jeannine D. How My Grandmother Sees. Kenyatta, Imani, ed. 1998. (Illus.). 64p. (J). (gr. k-6). 14.95 (*1-886580-39-1*) Pinnacle-Syatt Pubns.
Breckler, Rosemary. Sweet Dried Apples: A Vietnamese Wartime Childhood. 1996. (Illus.). 32p. (J). (gr. 1-4). tchr. ed. 15.95 o.p. (*0-395-73570-X*) Houghton Mifflin Co.
Breckler, Rosemary & Birney, Berry G. Pie's in the Oven. 1996. (Illus.). 32p. (J). (ps-3). 15.95 (*0-395-76501-3*) Houghton Mifflin Co.
Brennan, Herbie. Emily & the Werewolf. 1993. (Illus.). 96p. (J). (gr. 3-7). 16.95 o.p. (*0-689-50593-0*, McElderry, Margaret K.) Simon & Schuster Children's Publishing.
Brennan, Kevin. Jimmy Jammers/Jaimito Pijama/ Bilingual in English & Spanish. de la Vega, Eida, tr. 2003. Tr. of Jaimito Pijama. (ENG & SPA., Illus.). 32p. (J). (gr. k-3). 16.95 o.s.i (*0-9701107-9-0*, 626999) Raven Tree Pr., LLC.
Breslin, Paul. The Grandpa Stories. 1996. (Orig.). (J). (gr. 3-6). pap. 6.95 o.p. (*0-533-12048-9*) Vantage Pr., Inc.
Brett, Jan. On Noah's Ark. 2003. 32p. (J). 16.99 (*0-399-24028-4*, G. P. Putnam's Sons) Penguin Putnam Bks. for Young Readers.
Brighton, Catherine. Dearest Grandmama. 1991. (J). (ps-3). 14.99 o.s.i (*0-385-41844-2*) Doubleday Publishing.
Brimner, Larry Dane. Nana's Fiddle. (Rookie Readers Ser.). (Illus.). 32p. (J). (gr. 1-2). 2003. pap. 4.95 (*0-516-27820-7*); 2002. pap. 19.00 (*0-516-22373-9*) Scholastic Library Publishing. (Children's Pr.).
—The Promise. 2002. (Rookie Choices Ser.). (Illus.). 32p. (J). (gr. 1-2). lib. bdg. 19.00 (*0-516-22538-3*, Children's Pr.) Scholastic Library Publishing.
Brimner, Larry Dane & Tripp, Christine. The Promise. 2002. (Rookie Choices Ser.). (Illus.). 32p. (J). pap. 5.95 (*0-516-27388-4*, Children's Pr.) Scholastic Library Publishing.
Brooks, Bruce. Everywhere. 1992. (Trophy Bk.). 80p. (J). (gr. 4 up). pap. 3.95 o.p. (*0-06-440433-1*, Harper Trophy) HarperCollins Children's Bk. Group.
—Prince. 1998. (Wolfbay Wings Ser.: No. 5). (Illus.). (J). 144p. (gr. 4-7). pap. 4.50 (*0-06-440600-8*); 40p. (ps-k). lib. bdg. 14.89 o.s.i (*0-06-027542-1*) HarperCollins Pubs.
—Prince. 1998. (Wolfbay Wings Ser.: No. 5). (J). (gr. 4-7). 10.55 (*0-606-13925-7*) Turtleback Bks.
Brooks, Jennifer & Engstrom, Kim. How Sweet the Sound. 1997. (Illus.). 48p. (Orig.). (ps-3). 10.99 o.p. (*1-57673-056-5*) Zonderkidz.
Brown, Cathy. The World's Most Forgotten Grandmother, Granny Goose. 1998. (Illus.). (J). (ps-4). 10.95 (*1-892089-55-6*); pap. 5.95 (*1-892089-52-1*) Our Kids Pubn., Inc.
Brown, Irene Bennett. Before the Lark. 1992. (Sunflower Editions Ser.). (Illus.). 180p. (J). (gr. 4 up). reprint ed. pap. 7.95 o.p. (*0-936085-22-3*) Blue Heron Publishing.
Brown, Janet Mitsui. Thanksgiving at Obaachan's. 1994. (Illus.). 36p. (J). (ps-3). 15.95 (*1-879965-07-0*) Polychrome Publishing Corp.
Brown, Tehane. Saturn's Garden. 1993. (Illus.). 16p. (J). (gr. 2). (*0-9637099-0-9*) Brown, Tehane.
Brown, Terry. Tangled Web. 2003. (Today's Girls Only Ser.: Bk. 3). 128p. (J). pap. 5.99 (*1-4003-0323-0*) Nelson, Tommy.
Brown, Terry, creator. Tangled Web. 2000. (Todays-Girls.com Ser.: Vol. 3). 128p. (J). (gr. 5-9). pap. 5.99 o.s.i (*0-8499-7562-X*) Nelson, Tommy.
Browne, Frances. Granny's Wonderful Chair. 1975. (Dent's Illustrated Children's Classics Ser.). (Illus.). 158p. (J). reprint ed. 9.00 o.p. (*0-460-05055-9*) Biblio Distribution.
Bruchac, Joseph. Children of the Longhouse. 1996. (Illus.). 160p. (J). (gr. 3-6). 14.89 o.s.i (*0-8037-1794-6*); 14.99 o.p. (*0-8037-1793-8*) Penguin Putnam Bks. for Young Readers. (Dial Bks. for Young Readers).
Buchanan, Joan. The Nana Rescue. 1994. (Illus.). (J). 4.25 (*0-383-03740-9*) SRA/McGraw-Hill.
Buckley, Helen E. Grandfather & I. (Illus.). 24p. (J). (ps-3). 2000. pap. 5.95 (*0-688-17526-0*, Harper Trophy); 1994. 15.89 (*0-688-12534-4*); 1994. 15.95 (*0-688-12533-6*) HarperCollins Children's Bk. Group.
—Grandmother & I. (Illus.). 24p. (J). 2000. (ps-3). pap. 5.99 (*0-688-17525-2*, Harper Trophy); 1994. (ps-3). 16.99 (*0-688-12531-X*); 1994. (gr. 3 up). lib. bdg. 15.93 o.p. (*0-688-12532-8*) HarperCollins Children's Bk. Group.
Bunn, T. Davis. Tidings of Comfort & Joy: A Tender Story of Love, Loss & Reunion. 1997. (Illus.). 128p. 12.99 (*0-7852-7203-8*) Nelson, Thomas Pubs.
Bunting, Eve. The Butterfly House. 1998. (Illus.). 32p. (J). (gr. k-3). pap. 15.95 o.s.i (*0-590-84884-4*) Scholastic, Inc.
—Days of Summer. 2001. (Illus.). 40p. (J). (gr. k-3). 16.00 (*0-15-201840-9*) Harcourt Children's Bks.
—A Day's Work. 2002. (Illus.). (J). 13.79 (*0-7587-2361-X*) Book Wholesalers, Inc.
—A Day's Work. 1994. (Illus.). 32p. (J). (gr. k-3). lib. bdg., tchr. ed. 16.00 (*0-395-67321-6*) Houghton Mifflin Co.
—A Day's Work. 1997. (Illus.). 32p. (J). (gr. k-3). pap. 5.95 (*0-395-84518-1*, Clarion Bks.) Houghton Mifflin Co. Trade & Reference Div.
—A Day's Work. 1997. (J). 12.10 (*0-606-11243-X*) Turtleback Bks.
—Magic & the Night River. 1978. (Illus.). 48p. (J). (gr. 1-4). o.p. (*0-06-020912-7*); lib. bdg. 5.79 o.p. (*0-06-020913-5*) HarperCollins Pubs.
—So Far from the Sea. 1998. (Illus.). 32p. (J). (gr. 4-6). lib. bdg., tchr. ed. 16.00 (*0-395-72095-8*, Clarion Bks.) Houghton Mifflin Co. Trade & Reference Div.
—The Spook Birds. Tucker, Kathleen, ed. 1981. (Illus.). 40p. (J). (gr. 3-7). lib. bdg. 7.50 o.p. (*0-8075-7587-9*) Whitman, Albert & Co.
—Sunshine Home. 1994. (Illus.). 32p. (J). (gr. k-3). lib. bdg. 16.00 (*0-395-63309-5*, Clarion Bks.) Houghton Mifflin Co. Trade & Reference Div.
—The Wednesday Surprise. 1989. (Illus.). 32p. (J). (ps-3). lib. bdg., tchr. ed. 16.00 (*0-89919-721-3*, Clarion Bks.) Houghton Mifflin Co. Trade & Reference Div.
Burnett, Frances Hodgson. Little Lord Fauntleroy. 2002. (Evergreen Classics). (Illus.). 176p. (J). pap. 2.50 (*0-486-42368-9*) Dover Pubns., Inc.
—Little Lord Fauntleroy. 2002. 164p. 93.99 (*1-4043-1340-0*); per. 88.99 (*1-4043-1341-9*) IndyPublish.com.
—Little Lord Fauntleroy. E-Book 1.95 (*1-57799-840-5*) Logos Research Systems, Inc.
—Little Lord Fauntleroy. 1981. pap. 2.50 o.p. (*0-14-031411-3*, Puffin Bks.) Penguin Putnam Bks. for Young Readers.
—Little Lord Fauntleroy. E-Book 5.00 (*0-7410-0417-8*) SoftBook Pr.
Burrowes, Adjoa J. Grandma's Purple Flowers. ed. 2001. (J). (gr. 1). spiral bd. (*0-616-07252-X*) Canadian National Institute for the Blind/Institut National Canadien pour les Aveugles.
—Grandma's Purple Flowers. 2000. (Illus.). 32p. (J). (ps-3). 15.95 (*1-880000-73-3*) Lee & Low Bks., Inc.
Burt, Denise. I Love My Grandma. 1985. (Growing Up Bks.). (J). (Illus.). 32p. (gr. 2-3). lib. bdg. 10.95 o.p. (*0-918831-19-9*); lib. bdg. 7.95 o.p. (*0-918831-41-5*) Stevens, Gareth Inc.
Butterworth, Nick. My Grandma Is Wonderful. (Illus.). 32p. (J). 2003. 5.99 (*0-7636-2051-3*); 1992. bds. 4.99 (*1-56402-100-9*) Candlewick Pr.
—My Grandpa Is Amazing. (Illus.). 32p. (J). 2003. 5.99 (*0-7636-2057-2*); 1992. bds. 4.99 (*1-56402-099-1*) Candlewick Pr.
Butterworth, W. E., pseud. Leroy & the Old Man. 1982. 168p. (J). (gr. 7 up). pap. 2.50 o.p. (*0-590-40573-X*, Scholastic Paperbacks) Scholastic, Inc.
Byars, Betsy C. A Blossom Promise. 1987. (Illus.). 160p. (J). (gr. 4-6). 14.95 o.s.i (*0-385-29578-2*, Delacorte Pr.) Dell Publishing.
—A Blossom Promise. (Blossom Ser.). (J). (gr. 4-6). 145p. pap. 4.50 (*0-8072-1444-2*); 1990. pap. 24.00 incl. audio (*0-8072-7292-2*, YA826CX);Set. pap. 29.00 incl. audio (*0-8072-7322-8*, YA826SP) Random Hse. Audio Publishing Group. (Listening Library).
—A Blossom Promise. 1989. (Illus.). 160p. (gr. 4-7). reprint ed. pap. text 4.50 (*0-440-40137-2*, Yearling) Random Hse. Children's Bks.
—A Blossom Promise. 1987. (J). 10.55 (*0-606-04064-1*) Turtleback Bks.
—Coast to Coast. 1992. (Illus.). 76p. (J). (gr. 5-9). 14.00 o.s.i (*0-385-30787-X*, Delacorte Pr.) Dell Publishing.
Caldwell, V. M. The Ocean Within. 1999. (Illus.). (J). (gr. 3-8). 273p. 15.95 (*1-57131-623-X*); 275p. pap. 6.95 (*1-57131-624-8*) Milkweed Editions.
—The Ocean Within. 1999. (J). (gr. 3-9). 13.00 (*0-606-19035-X*) Turtleback Bks.
Calmenson, Stephanie. Hotter Than a Hot Dog! 1994. (Illus.). (J). (gr. 1-8). 14.95 o.p. (*0-316-12479-6*) Little Brown & Co.
—Marigold & Grandma on the Town. 1999. (I Can Read Bks.). (J). (gr. 1-3). pap., stu. ed. 22.00 incl. audio (*0-7887-3172-6*, 40907X4) Recorded Bks., LLC.
Campbell, Rod. From Gran. 1987. (Illus.). 16p. (J). (ps). 9.95 o.p. (*0-87226-035-6*, Bedrick, Peter Bks.) McGraw-Hill Children's Publishing.
Canales, Viola. Orange Candy Slices & Other Secret Tales. 2001. 176p. (J). pap. 9.95 (*1-55885-332-4*, Piñata Books) Arte Publico Pr.
Cannon, A. E. Great-Granny Rose & the Family Christmas Tree. 1996. (Illus.). 32p. (J). (ps-3). 13.95 (*1-57345-118-5*) Deseret Bk. Co.
Cappucceto Rosso. 1999. Tr. of Little Red Riding Hood. (ITA., Illus.). 24p. (J). (ps-5). pap. 7.95 (*88-8148-254-1*) European Language Institute ITA. *Dist:* Distribooks, Inc., Midwest European Pubns.
Carabine, Sue. Grandma's Night Before Christmas. 1998. (Night Before Christmas Ser.: Vol. 13). (Illus.). 60p. 5.95 (*0-87905-820-X*) Smith, Gibbs Pub.
Carlson, Nancy. Hooray for Grandparents' Day! 2002. (Illus.). (YA). 13.19 (*1-4046-0774-9*) Book Wholesalers, Inc.
—Hooray for Grandparents' Day! 32p. (J). 2002. pap. 5.99 (*0-14-230125-6*, Puffin Bks.); 2000. (Illus.). 15.99 (*0-670-88876-1*, Viking Children's Bks.) Penguin Putnam Bks. for Young Readers.
—A Visit to Grandma's. (J). (ps-3). 1993. (Illus.). 32p. pap. 4.99 o.s.i (*0-14-054243-4*, Puffin Bks.); 1991. 320p. 13.95 o.s.i (*0-670-83288-X*, Viking Children's Bks.) Penguin Putnam Bks. for Young Readers.
Carlson, Natalie S. A Grandmother for the Orphelines. 1980. (Illus.). 96p. (J). (gr. 3-6). lib. bdg. 13.89 o.p. (*0-06-020994-1*) HarperCollins Children's Bk. Group.
Carlson-Savage, Natalie. A Grandmother for the Orphelines. 1988. (J). (gr. k-6). pap. 2.75 o.s.i (*0-440-40016-3*, Yearling) Random Hse. Children's Bks.
Carlstrom, Nancy White. Grandpappy. 1990. (Illus.). (J). (ps-3). 14.95 o.p. (*0-316-12855-4*) Little Brown & Co.
—The Moon Came Too. 1987. (Illus.). 32p. (J). (ps-1). lib. bdg. 15.00 o.s.i (*0-02-717380-1*, Simon & Schuster Children's Publishing) Simon & Schuster Children's Publishing.
Carney, Margaret. The Biggest Fish in the Lake. 2003. (Illus.). 32p. (J). (gr. k-3). pap. 5.95 (*1-55337-528-9*); 15.95 (*1-55074-720-7*) Kids Can Pr., Ltd.
—Grandpa's Sugar Bush. unabr. ed. 2002. (Illus.). 32p. (J). (ps-3). pap. 5.95 (*1-55074-671-5*) Kids Can Pr., Ltd.
Carpenter, Mary E. A Summer on Choctaw Mountain. 1997. (Illus.). 36p. (J). (gr. 2-6). lib. bdg. 19.95 (*1-55618-162-0*) Brunswick Publishing Corp.
Carrick, Carol. Valentine. 1995. (Illus.). 40p. (J). (ps-3). lib. bdg., tchr. ed. 16.00 (*0-395-66554-X*, Clarion Bks.) Houghton Mifflin Co. Trade & Reference Div.
Carris, Joan D. Stolen Bones: A Novel. 1993. (J). 14.95 o.p. (*0-316-13018-4*) Little Brown & Co.
Carter, Don. Heaven's All-Star Jazz Band. 2002. (Illus.). 40p. (J). (gr. k-3). 15.95 (*0-375-81571-6*); lib. bdg. 17.99 (*0-375-91571-0*) Random Hse. Children's Bks. (Knopf Bks. for Young Readers).
Carter, Dorothy. Grandma's General Store: The Ark, RS. 2004. (J). (*0-374-32766-1*, Farrar, Straus & Giroux (BYR)) Farrar, Straus & Giroux.
Caseley, Judith. Apple Pie & Onions. 1987. (Illus.). 32p. (J). (gr. 1-4). 16.00 o.p. (*0-688-06762-X*); lib. bdg. 12.88 o.p. (*0-688-06763-8*) HarperCollins Children's Bk. Group. (Greenwillow Bks.).
—Dear Annie. 1991. (Illus.). 32p. (J). (ps-3). 16.00 o.s.i (*0-688-10010-4*); lib. bdg. 15.93 o.p. (*0-688-10011-2*) HarperCollins Children's Bk. Group. (Greenwillow Bks.).
—Dear Annie. Cohn, Amy, ed. 1994. (Illus.). 32p. (J). (ps-3). reprint ed. pap. 5.99 (*0-688-13575-7*, Harper Trophy) HarperCollins Children's Bk. Group.
—Dear Annie. 1994. 12.10 (*0-606-06314-5*) Turtleback Bks.
—Grandpa's Garden Lunch. 1990. (Illus.). 32p. (J). (ps up). 12.95 o.p. (*0-688-08816-3*); 12.89 o.s.i (*0-688-08817-1*) HarperCollins Children's Bk. Group. (Greenwillow Bks.).
—When Grandpa Came to Stay. 1986. (Illus.). 32p. (J). (gr. k-2). 12.95 o.p. (*0-688-06128-1*); lib. bdg. 12.93 o.p. (*0-688-06129-X*) HarperCollins Children's Bk. Group. (Greenwillow Bks.).
Cassidy, Anne. Cleo & Leo. 2002. (Read-It! Readers Ser.). (Illus.). 32p. (J). (ps-3). lib. bdg. 18.60 (*1-4048-0049-2*) Picture Window Bks.
Castañeda, Omar S. Abuela's Weave. (Illus.). 32p. (J). (ps up). 1995. pap. 6.95 (*1-880000-20-2*); 1993. (ENG & SPA., 15.95 (*1-880000-00-8*, LLB008) Lee & Low Bks., Inc.
—Abuela's Weave. 1993. 13.10 (*0-606-08912-8*) Turtleback Bks.
—El Tapiz de Abuela. ed. 2000. Tr. of Abuela's Weave. (J). (gr. 1). spiral bd. (*0-616-03088-6*) Canadian National Institute for the Blind/Institut National Canadien pour les Aveugles.
—El Tapiz de Abuela. Marcuse, Aida E., tr. from ENG. 1994. Tr. of Abuela's Weave. (SPA., Illus.). 32p. (J). (ps-4). pap. 6.95 (*1-880000-11-3*) Lee & Low Bks., Inc.
—El Tapiz de la Abuela. Marcuse, Aida E., tr. from ENG. 1994. Tr. of Abuela's Weave. (ENG & SPA., Illus.). 32p. (J). (ps-4). 15.95 (*1-880000-08-3*, LC083) Lee & Low Bks., Inc.
Castle, Caroline. Grandpa Baxter & the Photographs. 1993. (Illus.). 32p. (J). (ps-1). mass mkt. 14.95 o.p. (*0-531-05487-X*); mass mkt. 14.99 o.p. (*0-531-08637-2*) Scholastic, Inc. (Orchard Bks.).
Cates, Karin. The Far-Fetched Story Quilt. 2002. (Illus.). 32p. (J). 15.95 (*0-688-15938-9*); 15.95 (*0-688-15938-9*); (gr. 7 up). lib. bdg. 15.89 (*0-688-15939-7*) HarperCollins Children's Bk. Group. (Greenwillow Bks.).
Cazet, Denys. Christmas Moon. 1988. (Illus.). 32p. (J). (ps-2). pap. 4.95 (*0-689-71259-6*, Aladdin) Simon & Schuster Children's Publishing.
Cech, John. My Grandmother's Journey. (Illus.). 40p. (J). (ps-4). 1998. pap. 5.99 (*0-689-81890-4*, Aladdin); 1991. lib. bdg. 16.00 (*0-02-718135-9*, Simon & Schuster Children's Publishing) Simon & Schuster Children's Publishing.
—My Grandmother's Journey. 1998. 12.14 (*0-606-13633-9*) Turtleback Bks.
Chambers, Aidan. Postcards from No Man's Land. 2004. pap. 7.99 (*0-14-240145-5*, Puffin Bks.) Penguin Putnam Bks. for Young Readers.
Chambers, Veronica. Marisol & Magdalena: The Sound of Our Sisterhood. 2001. 176p. (J). (gr. 3-7). pap. 5.99 (*0-7868-1304-0*) Hyperion Bks. for Children.
—Marisol & Magdalena: The Sound of Our Sisterhood. 1998. 141p. (gr. 3-7). (J). 14.95 (*0-7868-0437-8*); (YA). lib. bdg. 15.49 (*0-7868-2385-2*) Hyperion Pr.
Chandler, Mitzi. I See Something Grand. 1995. (Illus.). 32p. (J). (ps-1). pap. 8.95 (*0-938216-50-3*) Grand Canyon Assn.
Charnas, Suzy McKee. The Silver Glove. 2001. 176p. pap. 14.95 (*1-58715-479-X*) Wildside Pr.
Chavarria-Chairez, Becky. Magda's Tortillas (Las Tortillas de Magda) Castilla, Julia Mercedes, tr. 2000. (ENG & SPA., Illus.). 32p. (J). (ps-2). 14.95 (*1-55885-286-7*, Piñata Books) Arte Publico Pr.
Cheng, Andrea. Goldfish & Chrysanthemums. 2003. (Illus.). 32p. (J). 16.95 (*1-58430-057-4*) Lee & Low Bks., Inc.
—Grandfather Counts. (Illus.). (J). 2003. pap. (*1-58430-158-9*); 2000. 32p. 15.95 (*1-58430-010-8*) Lee & Low Bks., Inc.
—The Key Collection, ERS. 2003. (Illus.). 128p. (J). (gr. 3-6). 15.95 (*0-8050-7153-9*, Holt, Henry & Co. Bks. For Young Readers) Holt, Henry & Co.
Chichester-Clark, Emma. Mimi's Book of Counting. 2003. (Illus.). 24p. (J). 9.95 (*1-57091-573-3*) Charlesbridge Publishing, Inc.
Child of the Owl. pap. text, stu. ed. (*0-13-053125-1*) Prentice Hall (Schl. Div.).
Child of the Owl. 8.97 (*0-13-437497-5*) Prentice Hall PTR.
Chin-Lee, Cynthia. Almond Cookies & Dragon Well Tea. 1993. (Illus.). 36p. (J). (gr. 1-4). 14.95 (*1-879965-03-8*) Polychrome Publishing Corp.
Chirinian, Helene. Visiting Grandma: An Activity Book That's Fun for You & Grandma! 1990. (Illus.). (J). (gr. k-3). pap. 2.50 o.s.i (*1-55782-114-3*) Warner Bks., Inc.
—Visiting Grandpa: An Activity Book That's Fun for You & Grandpa! 1990. (Illus.). (J). (gr. k-3). pap. 2.50 o.s.i (*1-55782-115-1*) Warner Bks., Inc.
Chiu, Esther. The Lobster & the Sea. 1998. (Illus.). 32p. (J). (gr. 2-5). 14.95 (*1-879965-14-3*) Polychrome Publishing Corp.
Chocolate, Deborah M. Newton. The Piano Man. 1998. (Illus.). 32p. (J). (gr. k-3). 15.95 (*0-8027-8646-4*); lib. bdg. 16.85 (*0-8027-8647-2*) Walker & Co.
—Piano Man. 2000. 13.10 (*0-606-17886-4*) Turtleback Bks.
—Piano Man. 2000. (Illus.). 32p. (J). (gr. k-3). pap. 6.95 (*0-8027-7578-0*) Walker & Co.
Choi, Sook-Nyul. The Best Older Sister. 1997. (First Choice Chapter Book Ser.). (Illus.). 48p. (J). (gr. k-3). 13.95 o.s.i (*0-385-32208-9*); pap. 3.99 o.s.i (*0-440-41149-1*) Random Hse. Children's Bks. (Dell Books for Young Readers).
—Halmoni & the Picnic. 1993. (Illus.). 32p. (J). (ps-3). lib. bdg., tchr. ed. 16.00 (*0-395-61626-3*) Houghton Mifflin Co.
—Yunmi & Halmoni's Trip. 1997. (Illus.). 32p. (J). (ps-3). tchr. ed. 15.00 o.s.i (*0-395-81180-5*) Houghton Mifflin Co.

Chorao, Kay. Up & down with Kate. 2002. (Dutton Easy Reader Ser.). (Illus.). 48p. (J). 13.99 (*0-525-46891-9*, Dutton Children's Bks.) Penguin Putnam Bks. for Young Readers.

Christie, Sally & Kavanaugh, Peter. Mean & Mighty Me. 1991. (Speedster Ser.). (Illus.). 64p. (J). (gr. 2-5). 10.95 o.p. (*0-525-44700-8*, Dutton Children's Bks.) Penguin Putnam Bks. for Young Readers.

Clary, Margie Willis. A Sweet, Sweet Basket. Stone, Barbara, ed. 1995. (Illus.). 40p. (J). (gr. k-7). 15.95 (*0-87844-127-1*) Sandlapper Publishing Co., Inc.

Clement, Rod. Grandpa's Teeth. 2002. (Illus.). (J). 14.43 (*0-7587-2647-3*) Book Wholesalers, Inc.

—Grandpa's Teeth. (Trophy Picture Book Ser.). (Illus.). 32p. (J). (ps-3). 1999. pap. 5.99 (*0-06-443557-1*, Harper Trophy); 1998. 16.99 (*0-06-027671-1*) HarperCollins Children's Bk. Group.

Cohen, Caron Lee. Everything Is Different at Nonna's House. 2003. (Illus.). 32p. (J). lib. bdg., tchr. ed. 16.00 (*0-618-07335-3*, Clarion Bks.) Houghton Mifflin Co. Trade & Reference Div.

Cole, Babette. Drop Dead. 1997. (Illus.). 30p. (J). (gr. 1-4). 2.99 o.s.i (*0-679-88358-4*) Knopf, Alfred A. Inc.

—The Trouble with Gran. 1991. (Sandcastle Ser.). 32p. (J). 5.95 o.s.i (*0-399-21791-6*, Philomel) Penguin Group (USA) Inc.

Cole, Norma. The Final Tide. 1990. 160p. (YA). (gr. 5 up). 14.95 (*0-689-50510-8*, McElderry, Margaret K.) Simon & Schuster Children's Publishing.

Coleman, Evelyn. The Glass Bottle Tree. 1996. (Illus.). 32p. (J). (ps-3). pap. 15.95 (*0-531-09467-7*); lib. bdg. 16.99 (*0-531-08767-0*) Scholastic, Inc. (Orchard Bks.).

Coleman, Paul. Where the Balloons Go: Saying Goodbye. 1995. (Illus.). 56p. (J). pap. 8.95 (*1-56123-089-8*) Centering Corp.

Collins, Pat Lowery. Signs & Wonders. 1999. 192p. (J). (gr. 5-9). tchr. ed. 15.00 (*0-395-97119-5*) Houghton Mifflin Co.

Collins, Ross. Alvie Eats Soup. 2002. (Illus.). (J). (ps-3). 32p. pap. 15.95 (*0-439-27260-2*); (*0-439-27265-3*) Scholastic, Inc. (Levine, Arthur A. Bks.).

Conrad, Pam. The Tub Grandfather. (Laura Geringer Bks.). (Illus.). 32p. (J). (gr. k-3). 1996. pap. 5.95 o.s.i (*0-06-443469-9*, Harper Trophy); 1993. 15.00 o.s.i (*0-06-022895-4*); 1993. lib. bdg. 14.89 o.s.i (*0-06-022896-2*) HarperCollins Children's Bk. Group.

—Tub Grandfather. 1993. (J). 11.15 o.p. (*0-606-09997-2*) Turtleback Bks.

Consky, Susan B. Mischief on the Farm. 1970. (Childrens Bks.). (Illus.). 128p. (J). (gr. 1-5). pap. 1.50 o.p. (*0-8024-1540-7*) Moody Pr.

Conteh-Morgan, Jane. I Love My Grandma! 1998. (First Blessings Flap Bks.). (Illus.). 20p. (J). bds. 4.99 o.p. (*0-8054-1264-6*) Broadman & Holman Pubs.

Cooke, Trish. Full, Full, Full of Love. 2003. (Illus.). 32p. (YA). 15.99 (*0-7636-1851-9*) Candlewick Pr.

—The Grandad Tree. 2000. (Illus.). 32p. (J). (ps-3). 15.99 (*0-7636-0815-7*) Candlewick Pr.

Cookson, Lorraine Marie. A Caution of a Boy. 2000. (J). pap. 5.95 o.p. (*0-533-13164-2*) Vantage Pr., Inc.

Corcoran, Barbara. The Faraway Island. 1977. (J). (gr. 5-9). lib. bdg. 6.95 o.p. (*0-689-30550-8*, Atheneum) Simon & Schuster Children's Publishing.

Cordova, Amy. Abuelita's Heart. 1997. (ENG & SPA., Illus.). 32p. (J). (ps-3). 16.00 (*0-689-80181-5*, Simon & Schuster Children's Publishing) Simon & Schuster Children's Publishing.

Cornish, Sam. Grandmother's Pictures. 1978. (Illus.). (J). pap. 0.95 o.p. (*0-380-01912-4*, 37416, Avon Bks.) Morrow/Avon.

Cosgrove, Stephen. Grampa-Lop. 1981. (Serendipity Bks.). (Illus.). 32p. (J). (ps-3). 2.95 o.p. (*0-8431-0586-0*, Price Stern Sloan) Penguin Putnam Bks. for Young Readers.

—Grampa-Lop. 1985. (Serendipity Ser.). (J). 11.14 (*0-606-02389-5*) Turtleback Bks.

Cotter, Noreen. Definitely Different. 1994. (Illus.). (J). (*0-383-03685-2*) SRA/McGraw-Hill.

Cottrell, Janet L. Train Ride to Grandma's. 2000. 27p. pap. 8.00 (*0-8059-5065-6*) Dorrance Publishing Co., Inc.

Countess, Mary Alice. Cowpath Days. Fallis, Janet M., ed. 2001. (Illus.). 128p. (J). (gr. 4-8). pap. 6.95 (*0-9662431-1-0*) Viewpoint Pr., Inc.

Coville, Bruce. I Lost My Grandfather's Brain. unabr. ed. 2000. (I Was a Sixth Grade Alien Ser.). 160p. (J). (gr. 3-5). pap. 28.00 incl. audio (*0-8072-8385-1*, YA180SP, Listening Library) Random Hse. Audio Publishing Group.

—I Lost My Grandfather's Brain. 1999. (I Was a Sixth Grade Alien Ser.: Vol. 3). 176p. (J). (gr. 3-7). pap. 3.99 (*0-671-02652-6*, Aladdin) Simon & Schuster Children's Publishing.

—I Lost My Grandfather's Brain. 1999. (I Was a Sixth Grade Alien Ser.). (Illus.). (J). 10.04 (*0-606-18306-X*) Turtleback Bks.

Cowley, Joy. The Rusty, Trusty Tractor. 2003. (Illus.). 32p. (J). (ps-3). 14.95 (*1-56397-565-3*); pap. 7.95 (*1-56397-873-3*) Boyds Mills Pr.

Crabberg, Edna Dookie. Time to Go Home. 2000. (Illus.). 6p. (J). pap. 8.00 (*0-9667830-5-0*) Early Learning Assessment 2000.

Crandall, Sharon Olexa. Sick Bay. 2001. 24p. (J). pap. 14.95 incl. audio compact disk (*0-9662378-5-4*) Astoria Productions.

Creech, Sharon. Granny Torrelli. 2003. (Illus.). 160p. (J). (gr. 4-7). lib. bdg. 16.89 (*0-06-029291-1*, Cotler, Joanna Bks.) HarperCollins Children's Bk. Group.

—Granny Torrelli Makes Soup. 2003. (Illus.). 160p. (J). (gr. 3-6). 15.99 (*0-06-029290-3*, HarperChildren's Audio) HarperCollins Children's Bk. Group.

—Heartbeat. 2004. 192p. (J). 15.99 (*0-06-054022-2*); lib. bdg. 16.89 (*0-06-054023-0*) HarperCollins Pubs.

—Walk Two Moons. 2002. (Illus.). (J). 15.00 (*0-7587-0223-X*) Book Wholesalers, Inc.

—Walk Two Moons. (J). 2004. 304p. pap. 6.50 (*0-06-056013-4*, Harper Trophy); 1996. 288p. (gr. 7 up). pap. 6.50 (*0-06-440517-6*, Harper Trophy); 1994. 288p. (gr. 7 up). 16.99 (*0-06-023334-6*); 1994. 288p. (gr. 7 up). lib. bdg. 17.89 (*0-06-023337-0*) HarperCollins Children's Bk. Group.

—Walk Two Moons. 1999. (J). 9.95 (*1-56137-770-8*); 11.95 (*1-56137-771-6*) Novel Units, Inc.

—Walk Two Moons. (Assessment Packs Ser.). (J). 1998. 15p. pap. text, tchr.'s training gde. ed. 15.95 (*1-58303-067-0*); 1997. 32p. (gr. 5 up). pap. text, stu. ed., tchr.'s training gde. ed. 19.95 (*1-58303-030-1*) Pathways Publishing.

—Walk Two Moons. 280p. (J). (gr. 4-6). pap. 4.95 (*0-8072-1509-0*); 1997. pap. 37.00 incl. audio (*0-8072-7872-6*, YA 938 SP) Random Hse. Audio Publishing Group. (Listening Library).

—Walk Two Moons. l.t. ed. 2000. (Illus.). 287p. (J). 21.95 (*0-7862-2773-7*) Thorndike Pr.

—Walk Two Moons. 1996. (J). (gr. 5 up). 12.00 (*0-606-10018-0*) Turtleback Bks.

—Walk Two Moons: Chasing Redbird. 1999. (J). (gr. 3-7). pap. text o.p. (*0-06-449366-0*) HarperCollins Pubs.

—The Wanderer. 2000. (Illus.). 320p. (J). (ps-3). 16.99 (*0-06-027730-0*); lib. bdg. 16.89 (*0-06-027731-9*) HarperCollins Children's Bk. Group. (Cotler, Joanna Bks.).

—The Wanderer. 2002. (Illus.). 320p. (J). (gr. 3-7). pap. 5.99 (*0-06-441032-3*) HarperCollins Pubs.

—The Wanderer. unabr. ed. 2000. (YA). (gr. 4-7). audio 22.00 (*0-8072-8243-X*, Listening Library) Random Hse. Audio Publishing Group.

—The Wanderer. l.t. ed. 2002. (Illus.). 263p. (J). 24.95 (*0-7862-4125-X*) Thorndike Pr.

Cross, Verda. Great-Grandma Tells of Threshing Day. Tucker, Kathleen, ed. 1992. (Illus.). 40p. (J). (gr. 1-6). lib. bdg. 16.95 o.p. (*0-8075-3042-5*) Whitman, Albert & Co.

Crowe, Chris. The Mississippi Trial, 1955. 240p. 2003. pap. 5.99 (*0-14-250192-1*, Puffin Bks.); 2002. (YA). (gr. 6-8). 17.99 (*0-8037-2745-3*, Dial Bks. for Young Readers) Penguin Putnam Bks. for Young Readers.

Crunk, Tony. Big Mama, RS. 2003. (Illus.). 32p. (J). pap. 5.95 (*0-374-40634-0*, Sunburst) Farrar, Straus & Giroux.

—Grandpa's Overalls. 2001. (Illus.). (J). (ps). 32p. pap. 15.95 (*0-531-30321-7*); lib. bdg. (*0-531-33321-3*) Scholastic, Inc. (Orchard Bks.).

Crunk, Tony & Apple, Margot. Big Mama, RS. 2000. (Illus.). 32p. (J). (ps-3). 16.00 (*0-374-30688-5*, Farrar, Straus & Giroux (BYR)) Farrar, Straus & Giroux.

Crystal, Billy. I Already Know I Love You. 2004. 40p. (J). 16.99 (*0-06-059391-1*); lib. bdg. 17.89 (*0-06-059392-X*) HarperCollins Pubs.

Cullen, Ruth V. My Letter from Grandma. 1993. (Illus.). 32p. (J). pap. 4.95 o.p. (*0-8091-6610-0*) Paulist Pr.

Curtis, Chara M. How Far to Heaven? 1993. (Illus.). 28p. (YA). (ps up). 15.95 (*0-935699-06-6*) Illumination Arts Publishing Co., Inc.

Curtis, Gavin. Grandma's Baseball. 1992. (Illus.). (J). 3.99 o.p. (*0-517-08302-7*) Random Hse. Value Publishing.

Cutler, Jane. Darcy & Gran Don't Like Babies, RS. rev. ed. 2002. (Illus.). 32p. (J). (ps-2). 16.50 (*0-374-31696-1*, Farrar, Straus & Giroux (BYR)); pap. 6.95 (*0-374-41686-9*, Sunburst) Farrar, Straus & Giroux.

—Darcy & Gran Don't Like Babies. (J). (ps-2). 1995. 32p. pap. 4.95 (*0-590-44588-X*, Cartwheel Bks.); 1995. mass mkt. 4.95 (*0-590-72126-7*, Cartwheel Bks.); 1993. (Illus.). 32p. pap. 14.95 (*0-590-44587-1*) Scholastic, Inc.

Cuyler, Margery. That's Good! That's Bad! In the Grand Canyon, ERS. 2002. (Illus.). 32p. (J). (ps-2). 16.95 (*0-8050-5975-X*, Holt, Henry & Co. Bks. For Young Readers) Holt, Henry & Co.

Czech, Jan. The Garden Angel: A Young Child Discovers a Grandparent's Love Grows Even after Death. Johnson, Joy, ed. 2000. (Illus.). 20p. (J). (gr. k-4). 7.95 (*1-56123-130-4*) Centering Corp.

Dagit, Rosi. Grandmother Oak. 2000. (Illus.). 40p. (ps-3). pap. 6.95 (*1-57098-114-0*) Rinehart, Roberts Pubs.

Dahl, Roald. The Witches. 2002. (J). pap. 29.95 incl. audio (*0-7540-6247-3*) BBC Audiobooks America.

—The Witches. 1999. (gr. 3-7). pap. 13.55 (*0-8085-7491-4*) Econo-Clad Bks.

—The Witches, RS. 1983. (Illus.). 208p. (J). (gr. 3-7). 17.00 (*0-374-38457-6*); 35.00 o.p. (*0-374-38458-4*) Farrar, Straus & Giroux. (Farrar, Straus & Giroux (BYR)).

—The Witches. (Illus.). (J). 1999. 200p. (gr. 3-7). pap. 3.95 (*0-14-031730-9*, Viking Children's Bks.); 1998. 208p. (gr. 3-7). pap. 5.99 (*0-14-130110-4*, Puffin Bks.); 1989. 208p. pap. 4.99 o.s.i (*0-14-034020-3*, Puffin Bks.) Penguin Putnam Bks. for Young Readers.

—The Witches. 1985. (J). 11.04 (*0-606-00540-4*) Turtleback Bks.

Daly, Niki. Bravo, Zan Angelo! A Comedia Dell'Arte Tale with Story & Pictures, RS. 1998. (Illus.). 36p. (J). (ps-3). 16.00 (*0-374-30953-1*, Farrar, Straus & Giroux (BYR)) Farrar, Straus & Giroux.

—Not So Fast, Songololo. 1998. (J). pap. 4.95 (*0-87628-975-8*) Ctr. for Applied Research in Education, The.

—Not So Fast, Songololo. 1987. 32p. (J). (ps-3). pap. 4.99 o.p. (*0-14-050715-9*, Puffin Bks.) Penguin Putnam Bks. for Young Readers.

—Not So Fast, Songololo. (Illus.). 32p. (J). (gr. k-3). 1996. pap. 6.99 (*0-689-80154-8*, Aladdin); 1986. 16.00 (*0-689-50367-9*, McElderry, Margaret K.) Simon & Schuster Children's Publishing.

—Not So Fast, Songololo. 1996. (J). 10.15 o.p. (*0-606-09700-7*) Turtleback Bks.

—Papa Lucky's Shadow. 1992. (Illus.). 32p. (J). (ps-3). lib. bdg. 16.00 o.s.i (*0-689-50541-8*, McElderry, Margaret K.) Simon & Schuster Children's Publishing.

D'Arc, Karen Scourby. My Grandmother Is a Singing Yaya. 2001. (Illus.). 32p. (J). (gr. k-2). pap. 15.95 (*0-439-29309-X*, Orchard Bks.) Scholastic, Inc.

D'Arc, Karen Scourby. My Grandmother Is a Singing Yaya. 2001. (Illus.). (J). lib. bdg. (*0-531-33323-X*, Orchard Bks.) Scholastic, Inc.

Darian, Shea. Grandpa's Garden. 1996. (Illus.). (J). (ps-5). 36p. 16.95 (*1-883220-42-4*); 32p. pap. 7.95 o.p. (*1-883220-41-6*) Dawn Pubns.

—Grandpa's Garden. 1996. 14.10 (*0-606-09350-8*) Turtleback Bks.

Darling, Benjamin. Valerie & the Silver Pear. 1992. (Illus.). 32p. (J). (gr. k-3). mass mkt. 14.95 (*0-02-726100-X*, Simon & Schuster Children's Publishing) Simon & Schuster Children's Publishing.

David, Lawrence. Full Moon. 2001. (Illus.). 32p. (J). (gr. k-2). 15.95 o.p. (*0-385-32792-7*, Doubleday Bks. for Young Readers) Random Hse. Children's Bks.

Davis, Ascher. My Grandma the Monster. 1990. (Illus.). 32p. (J). reprint ed. pap. 3.95 (*0-88961-099-1*) Women's Pr. CAN. *Dist:* Univ. of Toronto Pr.

Davis, Jenny. Checking on the Moon. 1993. 224p. (YA). mass mkt. 3.99 o.s.i (*0-440-21491-2*) Dell Publishing.

—Checking on the Moon. 1991. 224p. (J). (gr. 4-7). 16.95 (*0-531-05960-X*); (gr. 7 up). lib. bdg. 17.99 (*0-531-08560-0*) Scholastic, Inc. (Orchard Bks.).

—Checking on the Moon. 1991. 9.09 o.p. (*0-606-05199-6*) Turtleback Bks.

Davoll, Barbara. Grandpa's Secret. 1993. (Christopher Churchmouse Classics Ser.). (Illus.). 24p. (J). 8.99 (*1-56476-161-4*, 6-3161) Cook Communications Ministries.

Dawson, Brianog Brady. Granny's Teeth. 2002. (Panda Ser.). (Illus.). 64p. (YA). (gr. k up). pap. 4.95 o.p. (*0-86278-754-8*) O'Brien Pr., Ltd., The IRL. *Dist:* Independent Pubs. Group.

De Bode & Broere. Grandad I'll Always Remember. 1997. (Illus.). 33p. (J). 19.95 (*0-237-51755-8*) Evans Brothers, Ltd. GBR. *Dist:* Trafalgar Square.

De la Garza, Beatriz. Pillars of Gold & Silver. 1997. 260p. (YA). (gr. 6-12). pap. 9.95 (*1-55885-206-9*, Piñata Books) Arte Publico Pr.

—Pillars of Gold & Silver. 1997. 16.00 (*0-606-16042-6*) Turtleback Bks.

de Paola, Tomie. Nana Upstairs & Nana Downstairs. 1997. (Illus.). 32p. (J). (ps-3). 16.99 (*0-399-23108-0*, G. P. Putnam's Sons) Penguin Group (USA) Inc.

—Nana Upstairs & Nana Downstairs. (Illus.). 32p. (J). (ps-3). 2000. pap. 6.99 (*0-698-11836-7*, Puffin Bks.); 1987. 14.95 o.s.i (*0-399-21417-8*, G. P. Putnam's Sons); 1978. pap. 5.99 o.s.i (*0-14-050290-4*, Puffin Bks.) Penguin Putnam Bks. for Young Readers.

—Nana Upstairs & Nana Downstairs. 1975. (J). (ps-2). 8.99 o.s.i (*0-399-60787-0*) Putnam Publishing Group, The.

—Nana Upstairs & Nana Downstairs. 1973. (J). 12.14 (*0-606-02202-3*) Turtleback Bks.

—Now One Foot, Now the Other. 1981. (Illus.). 48p. (J). (ps-3). 15.99 (*0-399-20774-0*, G. P. Putnam's Sons) Penguin Group (USA) Inc.

—Now One Foot, Now the Other. 1981. (Illus.). 48p. (J). (gr. 3-7). 5.95 o.s.i (*0-399-20775-9*, G. P. Putnam's Sons) Penguin Putnam Bks. for Young Readers.

—Strega Nona: Her Story. 2002. (Illus.). (J). 23.64 (*0-7587-3720-3*) Book Wholesalers, Inc.

—Strega Nona: Her Story. 1996. (Illus.). 32p. (J). (ps-3). 16.99 (*0-399-22818-7*, G. P. Putnam's Sons) Penguin Group (USA) Inc.

—Strega Nona: Her Story. 2000. (Illus.). 32p. (J). (gr. k-4). pap. 5.99 (*0-698-11814-6*, Puffin Bks.) Penguin Putnam Bks. for Young Readers.

—Strega Nona: Her Story. 2000. 12.14 (*0-606-20375-3*); 1975. (J). 13.10 (*0-606-02282-1*) Turtleback Bks.

—Watch Out for the Chicken Feet in Your Soup. (Illus.). (J). (ps-3). 1985. pap. 5.95 o.p. (*0-13-945766-6*); 1974. 12.95 o.s.i (*0-13-945782-8*) Simon & Schuster Children's Publishing. (Simon & Schuster Children's Publishing).

DeFelice, Cynthia C. Old Granny & the Bean Thief, RS. 2003. (Illus.). 32p. (J). 16.00 (*0-374-35614-9*, Farrar, Straus & Giroux (BYR)) Farrar, Straus & Giroux.

—When Grampa Kissed His Elbow. 1992. (Illus.). 32p. (J). (gr. k-3). 16.00 (*0-02-726455-6*, Atheneum) Simon & Schuster Children's Publishing.

—Willy's Silly Grandma. 1997. (Illus.). 32p. (J). (ps-2). pap. 15.95 (*0-531-30012-9*); lib. bdg. 16.99 (*0-531-33012-5*) Scholastic, Inc. (Orchard Bks.).

DeGross, Monalisa. Grandaddy's Street Songs. (Jump at the Sun Bks.). (Illus.). 32p. (J). (ps-3). Date not set. 14.99 (*0-7868-0160-3*); 1999. 15.49 (*0-7868-2132-9*) Hyperion Bks. for Children.

DeKlyne, Betty. The Adventures of Alexander & His Ragtime Gran: The Scourge of the Sand (Spanish Vocabulary) unabr. ed. 1997. (Illus.). 40p. (Orig.). (J). (gr. 3-5). pap. 10.00 (*0-9651559-1-9*) Rising Eagle Pubs.

Demarest, Chris L. A Visit to Grandma: Italian-English. 1997. (Adventures with Nicholas Ser.). (ENG & ITA., Illus.). 64p. (J). (ps-3). pap. 16.95 incl. audio (*2-8315-6251-1*, Berlitz Kids) Berlitz International, Inc.

—A Visit to Grandma: Spanish-English. 1997. (Adventures with Nicholas Ser.). (ENG & SPA., Illus.). 64p. (J). (ps-3). pap. 16.95 o.s.i incl. audio (*2-8315-6252-X*, Berlitz Kids) Berlitz International, Inc.

—A Visit to Grandma: Una Visita a La Abuelita. 1997. (*2-8315-6558-8*) Berlitz International, Inc.

—A Visit to Grandma - Ingles. 1997. (Adventures with Nicholas Ser.). (ENG & SPA., Illus.). 64p. (J). (ps-3). pap. 16.95 incl. audio (*2-8315-6248-1*, Berlitz Kids) Berlitz International, Inc.

Demarest, Dorothy E. Mrs. Cooderberry's Nine Grandchildren. 1992. (J). text 8.95 o.p. (*0-533-10117-4*) Vantage Pr., Inc.

Dengler, Marianna. The Worry Stone. 1996. (Illus.). 40p. (J). (gr. 1-3). lib. bdg. 14.95 (*0-87358-642-5*, Rising Moon Bks. for Young Readers) Northland Publishing.

Denslow, Sharon Phillips. Georgie Lee. 2002. (Illus.). 96p. (J). (gr. 2 up). 15.95 (*0-688-17940-1*); lib. bdg. 16.89 (*0-688-17941-X*) HarperCollins Children's Bk. Group. (Greenwillow Bks.).

Denton, Kady MacDonald. Granny Is a Darling. (Illus.). 32p. (J). (ps-3). 1988. text 13.95 o.p. (*0-689-50452-7*, McElderry, Margaret K.); 1990. reprint ed. pap. 4.95 o.p. (*0-689-71207-3*, Aladdin) Simon & Schuster Children's Publishing.

Derby, Pat. Grams, Her Boyfriend, My Family & Me, RS. 256p. (YA). (gr. 5 up). 1997. pap. 7.95 (*0-374-42790-9*, Sunburst); 1994. 16.00 o.p. (*0-374-38131-3*, Farrar, Straus & Giroux (BYR)) Farrar, Straus & Giroux.

DeRubertis, Barbara. Count on Pablo. 1999. (Math Matters Ser.). (Illus.). 32p. (J). (gr. k-2). pap. 4.95 (*1-57565-090-8*) Kane Pr., The.

—Count on Pablo. 1999. (Math Matters Ser.). (Illus.). (J). 11.10 (*0-606-18217-9*) Turtleback Bks.

Devlin, Wende & Devlin, Harry. Cranberry Autumn. 1993. (Illus.). 40p. (J). (gr. k-3). lib. bdg. 13.95 o.s.i (*0-02-729936-8*, Simon & Schuster Children's Publishing) Simon & Schuster Children's Publishing.

—The Trouble with Henriette. 1995. (J). 15.00 o.s.i (*0-02-729937-6*, Simon & Schuster Children's Publishing) Simon & Schuster Children's Publishing.

Devries, Karen. Peekabo, Pearly Moon. 2003. (Illus.). 32p. (J). (ps). 12.99 (*0-8254-2448-8*) Kregel Pubns.

DeWitt, Dawn Davis. Searching for Blue Bears. Rolando, Cecilia, tr. & illus. by. 2003. (J). (*0-9677057-5-4*) Raven Productions, Inc..

Dexter, Alison. Grandma. 1993. (Willa Perlman Bks.). (Illus.). 32p. (J). (ps-2). 15.00 (*0-06-021143-1*); lib. bdg. 14.89 o.p. (*0-06-021144-X*) HarperCollins Children's Bk. Group.

Dickens, Charles. The Child's Story. 2000. (Illus.). 32p. (J). (ps-3). 17.00 (*0-689-83482-9*, Simon & Schuster Children's Publishing) Simon & Schuster Children's Publishing.

Dickerson, Julie G. Grandpa's Berries: A Story to Help Children Understand Grief & Loss. 1995. (Helping Children Understand Ser.). 32p. (J). (gr. k-6). pap. 11.95 (*0-9646576-9-4*) Cherubic Pr.

Dickins, Robert, illus. My Teacher Turns into a Tyrannosaurus. 1997. (*0-7608-0770-1*) Sundance Publishing.

Dickinson, Peter. Inside Grandad. 2004. 128p. (gr. 4-7). lib. bdg. 17.99 (*0-385-90873-3*, Lamb, Wendy) Random Hse. Children's Bks.

Dils, Tracey E. Grandpa's Magic. 1991. (Predictable Read-Together Bks.). (Illus.). 24p. (J). (gr. k-3). pap. 2.25 o.p. (*0-87406-493-7*) Darby Creek Publishing.

Dingles, Molly. Jinka, Jinka Jelly Bean. 1998. (Illus.). (J). (ps-6). 12.95 (*1-891997-03-3*) Dingles & Co.

Dionetti, Michelle V. Coal Mine Peaches. 1991. (Illus.). 32p. (J). (ps-2). 14.95 o.p. (*0-531-05948-0*); mass mkt. 14.99 o.p. (*0-531-08548-1*) Scholastic, Inc. (Orchard Bks.).

DiSalvo-Ryan, DyAnne. Going to Grandma's House. 1998. (All Aboard Bks.). 32p. (J). (ps-3). 2.99 o.s.i (*0-448-41744-8*, Grosset & Dunlap) Penguin Putnam Bks. for Young Readers.

—Grandpa's Corner Store. 2000. (Illus.). 40p. (J). (gr. k-3). 15.99 (*0-688-16716-0*); 15.99 (*0-688-16716-0*) HarperCollins Children's Bk. Group.

—Grandpa's Corner Store. 2000. (Illus.). 40p. (J). (gr. k-3). 15.89 (*0-688-16717-9*, Morrow, William & Co.) Morrow/Avon.

—Spaghetti Park. 2002. (Illus.). (J). (gr. 3). tchr. ed. 16.95 (*0-8234-1682-8*) Holiday Hse., Inc.

Dobson, Danae. Woof & the Midnight Prowler. 1989. (Woof Ser.). 29p. (J). 7.99 o.p. (*0-8499-8347-9*) W Publishing Group.

Dodd, Anne W. The Story of the Sea Glass. 1999. (Illus.). 32p. (J). (gr. k-3). 15.95 (*0-89272-416-1*) Down East Bks.

Dodds, Siobhan. Grandpa Bud. (J). 1995. bds. 5.99 o.p. (*1-56402-489-X*); 1993. (Illus.). 32p. 13.95 o.p. (*1-56402-175-0*) Candlewick Pr.

Doherty, Berlie. Granny Was a Buffer Girl. l.t. ed. 1986. (J). (gr. 1-8). 16.95 o.p. (*0-7451-0725-7*, Galaxy Children's Large Print) BBC Audiobooks America.

Doray, Malika. One More Wednesday. Freeman, Suzanne, tr. from FRE. 2001. (Illus.). (J). (ps-3). 48p. 15.95 (*0-06-029589-9*); 32p. lib. bdg. 15.89 (*0-06-029590-2*) HarperCollins Children's Bk. Group. (Greenwillow Bks.).

Dorros, Arthur. Abuela. 2002. (Illus.). (J). 14.04 (*0-7587-1901-9*) Book Wholesalers, Inc.

—Abuela. (Picture Puffin Bks.). (J). (ps-1). 1997. (SPA.). 40p. pap. 6.99 (*0-14-056226-5*); 1997. (Illus.). 40p. pap. 6.99 (*0-14-056225-7*, Puffin Bks.); 1995. (SPA., Illus.). 48p. 15.99 (*0-525-45438-1*, Dutton Children's Bks.); 1991. (Illus.). 40p. 16.99 (*0-525-44750-4*, Dutton Children's Bks.) Penguin Putnam Bks. for Young Readers.

—Abuela. 1997. (Picture Puffin Ser.). 13.14 (*0-606-11019-4*); (J). 13.14 (*0-606-11018-6*) Turtleback Bks.

—Isla. Orig. Title: The Island. (Illus.). (ps-1). 1999. 40p. pap. 5.99 (*0-14-056505-1*, Puffin Bks.); 1995. (SPA., 48p. (J). 16.99 (*0-525-45149-8*, Dutton Children's Bks.) Penguin Putnam Bks. for Young Readers.

—Isla. 1999. Orig. Title: The Island. 13.14 (*0-606-16811-7*); 12.14 (*0-606-16810-9*) Turtleback Bks.

—La Isla. 1999. (Picture Puffins Ser.). (SPA., Illus.). 32p. (J). (gr. k-3). pap. 6.99 (*0-14-056541-8*, DT8806, Puffin Bks.) Penguin Putnam Bks. for Young Readers.

Doyle, Malachy. Antonio on the Other Side of the World, Getting Smaller. 2003. 32p. (J). 15.99 (*0-7636-2173-0*) Candlewick Pr.

—Jody's Beans. (Read & Wonder Bks.). (Illus.). (J). (ps-1). 2002. 32p. bds. 5.99 (*0-7636-1713-X*); 1999. 29p. 15.99 o.p. (*0-7636-0687-1*) Candlewick Pr.

Dozier, Jennifer. Love, Grandpa. 2002. 27p. (J). 14.95 (*0-9713985-2-6*) CDA Publishing.

Drucker, Malka. Grandma's Latkes. (Illus.). 32p. (J). 1996. pap. 6.00 o.s.i (*0-15-201388-1*, Voyager Bks./Libros Viajeros); 1992. 13.95 o.s.i (*0-15-200468-8*, Gulliver Bks.) Harcourt Children's Bks.

—Grandma's Latkes. 1996. 12.15 (*0-606-10201-9*) Turtleback Bks.

Duble, Kathleen Benner. Bridging Beyond. 2002. 208p. (J). (gr. 7-9). 17.99 (*0-399-23637-6*) Putnam Publishing Group, The.

Duffey, Betsy. Fur-Ever Yours, Booker Jones. 128p. 2002. (YA). (gr. 5-9). pap. 4.99 (*0-14-230215-5*, Puffin Bks.); 2001. (J). (gr. 4-6). 15.99 (*0-670-89287-4*, Viking Children's Bks.) Penguin Putnam Bks. for Young Readers.

—Utterly Yours, Booker Jones. 1995. (Illus.). 128p. (YA). (gr. 3 up). 14.99 o.p. (*0-670-86007-7*, Viking Children's Bks.) Penguin Putnam Bks. for Young Readers.

Duffy, Daniel M., illus. A Present for Grandfather. 1998. (Adventures of Benny & Watch: Vol. No. 2). 32p. (J). (gr. 1-3). pap. 3.95 (*0-8075-6625-X*) Whitman, Albert & Co.

Dumas Lachtman, Ofelia. Call Me Consuelo. 1997. 152p. (YA). (gr. 3-7). 14.95 o.p. (*1-55885-188-7*); (Illus.). pap. 9.95 (*1-55885-187-9*) Arte Publico Pr. (Piñata Books).

Dunbar, James. When I Was Young. 1999. (Picture Bks.). (Illus.). 32p. (J). (ps-3). lib. bdg. 15.95 (*1-57505-359-4*, Carolrhoda Bks.) Lerner Publishing Group.

Dupasquier, Philippe. Sunday with Grandpa. (Illus.). 33p. pap. 8.95 (*0-86264-029-6*) Andersen Pr., Ltd. GBR. *Dist:* Trafalgar Square.

—Sunday with Grandpa. 1998. (Illus.). 33p. (J). text 19.95 (*0-86264-791-6*) Random Hse. UK, Ltd. GBR. *Dist:* Trafalgar Square.

Dupre, Rick. The Wishing Chair. 1993. (Illus.). 32p. (J). (ps-3). lib. bdg. 14.95 (*0-87614-774-0*, Carolrhoda Bks.) Lerner Publishing Group.

Dwyer, Mindy. Quilt of Dreams. 2000. (Illus.). 32p. (J). (gr. 2-4). 15.95 (*0-88240-522-5*); pap. 8.95 (*0-88240-521-7*) Graphic Arts Ctr. Publishing Co. (Alaska Northwest Bks.).

Dyjak, Elisabeth. I Should Have Listened to Moon. 1990. 130p. (J). (gr. 4-6). 13.95 o.p. (*0-395-52279-X*) Houghton Mifflin Co.

Eakle, Kit. In My Grandmother's Garden. l.t. ed. 2001. (Illus.). 32p. (J). (gr. k-5). 21.95 (*0-9713194-0-5*, MusicTales) MusicKit.COM.

Eastman, David. Peter & the Wolf. 1988. (J). 8.15 o.p. (*0-606-03636-9*) Turtleback Bks.

Easwaran, Eknath. The Monkey & the Mango: Stories of My Granny. 1996. (Illus.). 32p. (J). (ps-3). 15.95 (*0-915132-82-6*) Nilgiri Pr.

Edwards, Frank B. Abuelita Luna Perdio Su Voz. 1997. Tr. of Grandma Mooner Lost Her Voice. (SPA., Illus.). 24p. (Orig.). (J). (ps-3). pap. 5.95 (*0-921285-61-2*) Bungalo Bks. CAN. *Dist:* Firefly Bks., Ltd.

—Grandma Mooner Lost Her Voice. 1992. (Illus.). 24p. (J). (ps-2). pap. 5.95 (*0-921285-17-5*); lib. bdg. 14.95 o.p. (*0-921285-19-1*) Bungalo Bks. CAN. *Dist:* Firefly Bks., Ltd.

Edwards, Julie Andrews & Hamilton, Emma Walton. Dumpy the Dump Truck. 2000. (Dumpy Ser.). (Illus.). 32p. (J). (ps-2). 15.99 (*0-7868-0609-5*) Hyperion Bks. for Children.

Edwards, Michelle. The Talent Show. 2002. (Jackson Friends Bk.). (Illus.). 64p. (J). (gr. 1-4). 14.00 (*0-15-216403-0*) Harcourt Children's Bks.

—Zero Grandparents. (Jackson Friends Bk.). (Illus.). 64p. (J). (gr. 1-4). 2002. pap. 4.95 (*0-15-216309-3*, Harcourt Paperbacks); 2001. 14.00 (*0-15-202083-7*) Harcourt Children's Bks.

Egger, Bettina. Marianne's Grandmother. 1987. (Illus.). 32p. (J). (ps-3). 11.95 o.p. (*0-525-44335-5*, 01160-350, Dutton Children's Bks.) Penguin Putnam Bks. for Young Readers.

Eisenberg, Phyllis R. A Mitzvah Is Something Special. 1978. (Illus.). 32p. (J). (gr. k-4). 12.95 (*0-06-021807-X*); lib. bdg. 12.89 o.p. (*0-06-021808-8*) HarperCollins Children's Bk. Group.

Elliott, Dean. Grampa Dean's Hunting Adventures. 1999. (Grampa Dean Ser.: Vol. 1). (Illus.). 176p. pap. 12.95 (*0-9671996-0-3*) Rascal Publishing.

Elster, Jean Alicia. I'll Do the Right Thing. 2003. (Joe Joe in the City Ser.). (Illus.). 32p. (J). (gr. 1-5). 12.00 (*0-8170-1408-X*) Judson Pr.

Emard, Jeanne Gagne. Victoria & Gramma Discover a Secret in the Attic. 1999. (Illus.). (J). (gr. k-3). pap. 6.95 o.p. (*0-533-12884-6*) Vantage Pr., Inc.

Engel, Diana. Eleanor, Arthur, & Claire. 1992. (Illus.). 32p. (J). (gr. k-3). 14.95 o.p. (*0-02-733462-7*, Simon & Schuster Children's Publishing) Simon & Schuster Children's Publishing.

—Fishing. 1993. (Illus.). 32p. (J). (gr. k-3). 14.95 o.p. (*0-02-733463-5*, Simon & Schuster Children's Publishing) Simon & Schuster Children's Publishing.

—Fishing. (Illus.). 32p. (J). 4.98 o.p. (*0-7651-0068-1*) Smithmark Pubs., Inc.

English, Karen. Sweet Little Baby. 2005. (J). (*0-374-37361-2*, Farrar, Straus & Giroux (BYR)) Farrar, Straus & Giroux.

Erdrich, Louise. Grandmother's Pigeon. 1999. (Illus.). 32p. (J). (gr. k-4). pap. 5.99 (*0-7868-1204-4*) Disney Pr.

Erdrich, Louise. Grandmother's Pigeon. 1996. (Illus.). (J). (gr. k-3). 32p. 15.95 (*0-7868-0165-4*); lib. bdg. 16.49 o.s.i (*0-7868-2137-X*) Hyperion Bks. for Children.

—Grandmother's Pigeon. 1999. (J). 13.14 (*0-606-16663-7*) Turtleback Bks.

Erickson, John R. Moonshiner's Gold. 2001. 176p. (J). (gr. 5-9). 15.99 (*0-670-03502-5*, Viking) Penguin Putnam Bks. for Young Readers.

Ericsson, Jennifer A. The Most Beautiful Kid in the World. 1996. (Illus.). 32p. (J). (ps-3). 16.99 (*0-688-13941-8*) HarperCollins Children's Bk. Group.

—The Most Beautiful Kid in the World. 1996. (Illus.). 32p. (YA). (ps up). lib. bdg. 15.93 o.p. (*0-688-13942-6*, Morrow, William & Co.) Morrow/Avon.

Ernst, Lisa Campbell. The Luckiest Kid on the Planet. (Illus.). 40p. (J). (ps-2). 1999. per. 5.99 (*0-689-82426-2*, Aladdin); 1994. mass mkt. 14.95 o.s.i (*0-02-733566-6*, Simon & Schuster Children's Publishing) Simon & Schuster Children's Publishing.

—The Luckiest Kid on the Planet. 1999. 12.14 (*0-606-15923-1*) Turtleback Bks.

Esbaum, Jill. Stink Soup, RS. 2004. (J). 16.00 (*0-374-37252-7*, Farrar, Straus & Giroux (BYR)) Farrar, Straus & Giroux.

Esley, Joan. The Visit. 1980. (Illus.). 32p. (ps-1). 5.95 o.p. (*0-528-82286-1*) Rand McNally.

Everdenn, Margery. The Dream Keeper. 1985. (Illus.). 160p. (J). (gr. 6 up). 11.95 o.p. (*0-688-04638-X*) HarperCollins Children's Bk. Group.

Eversole, Robyn H. The Gift Stone. 1998. (Illus.). 32p. (J). (gr. k-3). 17.00 o.s.i (*0-679-88684-2*) Knopf, Alfred A. Inc.

Fakih, Kimberly O. Grandpa Putter & Granny Hoe, RS. 1992. (Illus.). 128p. (J). (gr. 2-5). 13.00 o.p. (*0-374-32762-9*, Farrar, Straus & Giroux (BYR)) Farrar, Straus & Giroux.

—High on the Hog, RS. 1994. 160p. (J). (gr. 5-7). 16.00 o.p. (*0-374-33209-6*, Farrar, Straus & Giroux (BYR)) Farrar, Straus & Giroux.

Fakih, Kimberly O. & Pearson, Tracey Campbell. Grandpa Putter & Granny Hoe. 1996. 128p. (J). (gr. 3-7). pap. 3.50 o.s.i (*0-440-41078-9*) Dell Publishing.

Fakih, Kimberly Olson. Grandpa Putter & Granny Hoe. 1996. 8.60 o.p. (*0-606-09348-6*) Turtleback Bks.

Falwell, Cathryn. Nicky & Grandpa. 1991. (Illus.). 32p. (J). (ps). 5.95 o.p. (*0-395-56917-6*, Clarion Bks.) Houghton Mifflin Co. Trade & Reference Div.

Farthing-Knight, Catherine. Days with Gran. (Illus.). 32p. pap. 12.95 (*0-7022-2708-0*); 1995. (J). 19.95 (*0-7022-2828-1*) Univ. of Queensland Pr. AUS. *Dist:* International Specialized Bk. Services.

Feder, Paula K. The Feather-Bed Journey. 1995. (Illus.). (J). (ps-3). lib. bdg. 15.95 (*0-8075-2330-5*) Whitman, Albert & Co.

Feldman, Annette & Leavitt, Nancy. To Grandma & Grandpa with Love. 1990. (Illus.). (J). 7.95 o.p. (*0-8378-2062-6*) Gibson, C. R. Co.

Fellows, Rebecca N. A Lei for Tutu. 1998. (Illus.). 32p. (J). (gr. 1-3). lib. bdg. 14.95 o.p. (*0-8075-4426-4*) Whitman, Albert & Co.

Fernandes, Kim. Visiting Granny. 1990. (Illus.). 24p. (J). (ps). 12.95 (*1-55037-077-4*); pap. 4.95 (*1-55037-084-7*) Annick Pr., Ltd. CAN. *Dist:* Firefly Bks., Ltd.

Fettig, Art. The Three Robots Find a Grandpa. 1984. (Illus.). 96p. (Orig.). (J). (gr. k-7). pap. 5.95 incl. audio (*0-9601334-8-8*) Growth Unlimited, Inc.

Fine, Anne. The Granny Project, RS. 1983. 167p. (J). (gr. 4 up). 11.95 o.p. (*0-374-32763-7*, Farrar, Straus & Giroux (BYR)) Farrar, Straus & Giroux.

Finkelstein, Ruth. We're So Lucky! A Book about Our Bubbies & Zaidies. 1996. (Illus.). 26p. (J). (ps-5). 12.95 (*0-9628157-3-X*) Finkelstein, Ruth.

Finley, Martha. Christmas with Grandma Elsie, Bk. 14. 2001. mass mkt. 5.99 (*1-931343-23-3*) Hibbard Pubns., Inc.

—Christmas with Grandma Elsie. 1997. (Elsie Dinsmore Ser.: Bk. 14). (Illus.). 332p. (gr. 4-7). 28.99 (*1-58960-276-5*) Sovereign Grace Pubs., Inc.

—Elsie at Home. 2001. (Elsie Bks.: Vol. 22). 320p. (J). (gr. 4-7). pap. 5.95 (*1-58182-175-1*) Cumberland Hse. Publishing.

—Elsie at Home. unabr. ed. 1998. (Elsie Dinsmore Collection: Vol. 22). 295p. reprint ed. 15.00 (*1-889128-22-8*) Mantle Ministries.

—Elsie at Home. 1998. (Elsie Dinsmore Ser.: Bk. 22). (Illus.). 308p. (gr. 4-7). 28.99 (*1-58960-284-6*) Sovereign Grace Pubs., Inc.

—Grandmother Elsie. 1998. (Elsie Bks.: Vol. 8). 200p. (J). (gr. 7-12). reprint ed. pap. 6.99 (*1-888306-41-6*, Full Quart Pr.) Holly Hall Pubns., Inc.

Fisher, Phyllis Mae Richardson. Twiglet the Little Christmas Tree. 2003. (Illus.). (J). 29.95 (*0-9745615-1-7*, Twiglet The Little Christmas Tree) PJs Corner.

Fleischman, Paul. Lost: A Story in String, ERS. 2000. (Illus.). 32p. (J). (ps-3). 16.95 (*0-8050-5583-5*, Holt, Henry & Co. Bks. For Young Readers) Holt, Henry & Co.

Flournoy, Valerie. The Patchwork Quilt. 1985. (Illus.). 32p. (J). (gr. 4-8). 14.89 o.p. (*0-8037-0098-9*); (ps-3). 16.99 (*0-8037-0097-0*) Penguin Putnam Bks. for Young Readers. (Dial Bks. for Young Readers).

—Tanya's Reunion. 1995. (Illus.). 40p. (J). 15.89 o.p. (*0-8037-1605-2*); 16.99 (*0-8037-1604-4*) Penguin Putnam Bks. for Young Readers. (Dial Bks. for Young Readers).

Foreman, Michael. Grandfather's Pencil & the Room of Stories. abr. ed. 1994. (Illus.). 32p. (J). (ps-3). 14.95 o.s.i (*0-15-200061-5*) Harcourt Trade Pubs.

—Jack's Fantastic Voyage. abr. ed. 1992. (Illus.). 32p. (J). (ps-3). 14.95 (*0-15-239496-6*) Harcourt Children's Bks.

—Seal Surfer. 1997. (Illus.). 36p. (J). (gr. 1-5). 16.00 (*0-15-201399-7*) Harcourt Children's Bks.

Forrest, Ellen. In a Child's House. 2001. 132p. pap. 10.95 (*0-595-18889-3*) iUniverse, Inc.

Forward, Toby. Traveling Backward. 1994. (Illus.). 128p. (J). 15.00 o.p. (*0-688-13076-3*, Morrow, William & Co.) Morrow/Avon.

—Traveling Backward. 1996. (Illus.). 128p. (J). (gr. 3-7). pap. 3.99 o.p. (*0-14-037875-8*, Puffin Bks.) Penguin Putnam Bks. for Young Readers.

Fowler, Zinita. Bubba Bailey & the Farkleberry Bush. 1998. 56p. (J). (gr. 3-4). 14.95 (*1-57168-187-6*) Eakin Pr.

Fox, Mem. Shoes from Grandpa. 1992. (Illus.). 32p. (J). (ps-3). mass mkt. 6.95 (*0-531-07031-X*, Orchard Bks.) Scholastic, Inc.

—Sophie. abr. ed. (Illus.). 32p. (J). (ps-3). 1994. 15.00 (*0-15-277160-3*); 1997. reprint ed. pap. 6.00 (*0-15-201598-1*, Harcourt Paperbacks) Harcourt Children's Bks.

Fox, Paula. Western Wind. 1993. 208p. (YA). (gr. 4-7). lib. bdg. 17.99 (*0-531-08652-6*); (gr. 5 up). pap. 16.95 (*0-531-06802-1*) Scholastic, Inc. (Orchard Bks.).

Franco, Betsy. Going to Grandma's Farm. (Rookie Reader Level a Ser.). (Illus.). 23p. (J). 2004. pap. 4.95 (*0-516-27787-1*); 2003. lib. bdg. 16.00 (*0-516-22875-7*) Scholastic Library Publishing. (Children's Pr.).

—Grandpa's Quilt. 1999. (Rookie Readers Ser.). (Illus.). 32p. (J). (gr. 1-2). lib. bdg. 19.00 (*0-516-21604-X*, Children's Pr.) Scholastic Library Publishing.

—Vamos a la Granja de la Abuela. 2003. (Rookie Reader Espanol Ser.). (SPA., Illus.). (J). lib. bdg. 15.00 (*0-516-25889-3*, Children's Pr.) Scholastic Library Publishing.

Franco, Betsy & Bild, Linda A. Grandpa's Quilt. 2000. (Rookie Readers Ser.). (Illus.). 32p. (J). (gr. 1-2). pap. 4.95 (*0-516-26551-2*, Children's Pr.) Scholastic Library Publishing.

Frankford, Marilyn. Going to Grandpa's House. Kaeden Corp. Staff, ed. 1993. (Illus.). 12p. (J). (gr. k-2). pap. text 4.50 (*1-879835-60-6*) Kaeden Corp.

Fraustino, Lisa Rowe. Grass & Sky. 1994. 160p. (J). (gr. 4-8). 15.95 o.p. (*0-531-06823-4*, Orchard Bks.) Scholastic, Inc.

—Grass & Sky: No Longer Ours. 1994. 160p. (J). (gr. 4-8). mass mkt. 16.99 o.p. (*0-531-08673-9*, Orchard Bks.) Scholastic, Inc.

—The Hickory Chair. 2001. (Illus.). 32p. (J). (ps-3). pap. 15.95 (*0-590-52248-5*, Levine, Arthur A. Bks.) Scholastic, Inc.

Freedman, Claire. Good Night, Sleep Tight. 2003. (J). 14.95 (*0-8109-4513-4*) Abrams, Harry N. , Inc.

Freeman, Martha. The Polyester Grandpa. 1998. 160p. (J). (gr. 4-7). tchr. ed. 15.95 (*0-8234-1398-5*) Holiday Hse., Inc.

Fremont, Eleanor. A Surprise in the Mailbox. 1999. (Bear in the Big Blue House Ser.). (Illus.). 24p. (J). (ps-2). pap. 3.50 (*0-689-82336-3*, 076714003507, Simon Spotlight) Simon & Schuster Children's Publishing.

French, Simon. Where in the World. 2003. 208p. (J). (gr. 3-6). 14.95 (*1-56145-292-0*) Peachtree Pubs., Ltd.

French, Vivian. Oliver's Vegetables. (Illus.). 32p. (J). (ps-1). 1998. mass mkt. 6.95 (*0-531-07104-9*); 1996. pap. 14.95 (*0-531-09462-6*) Scholastic, Inc. (Orchard Bks.).

French, Vivien. Oliver's Fruit Salad. 1998. (Illus.). 32p. (J). (ps-1). pap. 14.95 (*0-531-30087-0*, Orchard Bks.) Scholastic, Inc.

Friend, Catherine. The Sawfin Stickleback: A Very Fishy Story. 1994. (Illus.). 32p. (J). 13.95 o.p. (*1-56282-473-2*); lib. bdg. 14.49 (*1-56282-474-0*) Hyperion Bks. for Children.

Frienz, D. J. Where Will Nana Go Next: An Illustrated Tour of 19 Places to Go & Things to Do Across America & the World. 1999. (Illus.). 32p. (J). (ps-3). 15.95 (*0-9654333-0-7*) Howling at the Moon Pr.

Gackenbach, Dick. With Love from Gran. 32p. (J). (ps-3). 1990. pap. 6.95 o.s.i (*0-395-54775-X*); 1989. (Illus.). 13.95 o.p. (*0-89919-842-2*) Houghton Mifflin Co. Trade & Reference Div. (Clarion Bks.).

—With Love from Gran. 1988. 12.15 o.p. (0-606-04849-9) Turtleback Bks.

Gaeddert, LouAnn. A Summer Like Turnips, ERS. 1989. 80p. (J). (gr. 2-4). 13.95 o.s.i (0-8050-0839-X, Holt, Henry & Co. Bks. For Young Readers) Holt, Henry & Co.

Gaffney, Timothy R. Grandpa Takes Me to the Moon. 1996. (Illus.). 32p. (J). 16.00 (0-688-13937-X); lib. bdg. 15.93 o.p. (0-688-13938-8) Morrow/Avon. (Morrow, William & Co.).

Galindo, Mary Sue & Howard, Pauline Rodriguez. Icy Watermelon. 2000. Tr. of Sandia Fria. (ENG & SPA., Illus.). 32p. (J). (ps-2). 14.95 (1-55885-306-5, Piñata Books) Arte Publico Pr.

Gallacher, Marcie. Amaryllis Lilies. 1996. (Values for Young Women Ser.). pap. 7.95 o.p. (0-15-623645-1) Aspen Bks.

Gantos, Jack. What Would Joey Do?, RS. 2002. 240p. (J). (gr. 5-9). 16.00 (0-374-39986-7, Farrar, Straus & Giroux (BYR)) Farrar, Straus & Giroux.

—What Would Joey Do? 2004. (Illus.). 240p. (J). pap. 5.99 (0-06-054403-1, Harper Trophy) HarperCollins Children's Bk. Group.

—What Would Joey Do? 2002. (J). (gr. 4-8). 30.00 (0-8072-0949-X); audio 25.00 (0-8072-0948-1) Random Hse. Audio Publishing Group. (Listening Library).

—What Would Joey Do? 2003. (Juvenile Ser.). 264p. (J). 22.95 (0-7862-5468-8) Thorndike Pr.

Gantschev, Ivan. The Christmas Teddy Bear. 1994. (Illus.). 32p. (J). (gr. k-3). 14.88 o.p. (1-55858-348-3) North-South Bks., Inc.

—The Christmas Teddy Bear. 1993. (J). (gr. 4 up). (0-88708-333-1, Simon & Schuster Children's Publishing) Simon & Schuster Children's Publishing.

—The Train to Grandma's. 1991. (Illus.). 36p. (J). (ps up). pap. 16.95 o.p. (0-88708-053-7, Simon & Schuster Children's Publishing) Simon & Schuster Children's Publishing.

Gardella, Tricia. Casey's New Hat. 1997. (Illus.). 32p. (J). (ps-3). lib. bdg., tchr. ed. 15.00 (0-395-72035-4) Houghton Mifflin Co.

Garland, Sherry. The Silent Storm. 1995. 288p. (J). (gr. 4-7). pap. 6.00 (0-15-200016-X, Harcourt Paperbacks) Harcourt Children's Bks.

—The Silent Storm. 1993. 288p. (J). (gr. 4-7). 14.95 (0-15-274170-4) Harcourt Trade Pubs.

—The Silent Storm: Scholastic Edition. 1996. pap. 5.00 o.s.i (0-15-201336-9) Harcourt Trade Pubs.

Garrett, Ann. El Guardian del Pantano. 2001. (SPA., Illus.). 40p. (J). (gr. 3-5). pap. 8.95 (1-890515-28-0, TK30971) Turtle Bks.

—El Guardian del Pantano. Gutiérrez, Guillermo, tr. 1999. (SPA., Illus.). 40p. (J). (gr. 3-5). 16.95 (1-890515-13-2, TK2991) Turtle Bks.

—Keeper of the Swamp. (Illus.). 40p. 2001. (ps-3). pap. 8.95 (1-890515-27-2); 1999. (SPA., (J). (gr. 1-4). 16.95 (1-890515-12-4) Turtle Bks.

Gavalda, Anna. 95 Pounds of Hope. Rosner, Gill, tr. from FRE. 2003. (Illus.). 112p. (J). 14.99 (0-670-03672-2, Viking) Viking Penguin.

Gay, Marie-Louise. Fat Charlie's Circus. 1997. (Illus.). 32p. (J). (ps-3). 12.95 o.p. (0-916291-73-1) Kane/Miller Bk. Pubs.

Geisert, Arthur. The Etcher's Studio. 1997. (Illus.). 32p. (J). (ps-3). lib. bdg., tchr. ed. 15.95 (0-395-79754-3) Houghton Mifflin Co.

—Mystery. 2003. (Illus.). 32p. (J). (ps-3). 16.00 (0-618-27293-3, Lorraine, A. Walter) Houghton Mifflin Co. Trade & Reference Div.

Gelfand, Marilyn. My Great Grandpa Joe. 1986. (Illus.). 32p. (J). (gr. 1-3). 11.95 o.p. (0-02-736830-0, Simon & Schuster Children's Publishing) Simon & Schuster Children's Publishing.

Geller, Norman. I Don't Want to Visit Grandma Anymore. 1984. (Illus.). 28p. (J). (gr. 1-4). pap. 4.95 (0-915753-05-7) Geller, Norman Pubs.

George, Jean Craighead. Dear Katie, the Volcano Is a Girl. 32p. (J). pap. (0-7868-1178-1); 1998. (Illus.). (gr. 2-5). 14.95 (0-7868-0314-2); 1998. (Illus.). (gr. 2-5). lib. bdg. 15.49 (0-7868-2254-6) Hyperion Bks. for Children.

George, William T. & George, Lindsay B. Fishing at Long Pond. 1991. (Illus.). 24p. (J). (ps up). 15.00 o.p. (0-688-09401-5); lib. bdg. 14.93 o.p. (0-688-09402-3) HarperCollins Children's Bk. Group. (Greenwillow Bks.).

Geraghty, Paul. The Hunter. 1994. (Illus.). 32p. (J). (ps-3). 15.00 o.s.i (0-517-59692-X); 15.99 o.s.i (0-517-59693-8) Random Hse. Children's Bks. (Random Hse. Bks. for Young Readers).

Gershator, Phillis. Sambalena Show-Off. 1995. (Illus.). 32p. (J). (gr. k-3). 15.00 o.p. (0-689-80314-1, Simon & Schuster Children's Publishing) Simon & Schuster Children's Publishing.

Gerstein, Mordicai. Fox Eyes. 2001. (Road to Reading Ser.). (Illus.). 80p. (J). (gr. 3-5). lib. bdg. 11.99 (0-307-46509-8, Golden Bks.) Random Hse. Children's Bks.

Gibson, Andrew. Jemima, Grandma & the Great Lost Zone. 1992. (Illus.). 128p. (J). (gr. 3-7). pap. 6.95 o.p. (0-571-16737-3); 15.95 o.p. (0-571-16455-2) Faber & Faber, Inc.

Giff, Patricia Reilly. A Glass Slipper for Rosie. 1997. (Ballet Slippers Ser.: Vol. 5). (Illus.). 96p. (J). (gr. 2-5). 13.99 o.s.i (0-670-87469-8) Penguin Putnam Bks. for Young Readers.

Gilbert, Barbara Snow. Stone Water. 1996. 169p. (YA). (gr. 5-9). 15.95 (1-886910-11-1, Front Street) Front Street, Inc.

—Stone Water. 1998. 176p. (YA). (gr. 5-9). mass mkt. 4.50 o.s.i (0-440-22755-0, Dell Books for Young Readers) Random Hse. Children's Bks.

—Stone Water. 1998. 10.55 (0-606-15720-4) Turtleback Bks.

Giles, Gail. Breath of the Dragon. 1998. 10.04 (0-606-15465-5) Turtleback Bks.

—The Breath of the Dragon. 1997. (Illus.). 112p. (J). (gr. 4-6). tchr. ed. 14.95 (0-395-76476-9) Houghton Mifflin Co.

—Breath of the Dragon. 1998. (Illus.). 112p. (gr. 4-7). reprint ed. pap. text 3.99 o.s.i (0-440-41496-2) Dell Publishing.

Gill, Janie S. When Grandma Comes to Visit. 1997. pap. 4.95 (0-89868-408-0) ARO Publishing Co.

Gill, Janie S. When Grandma Visits Me. 1998. (Predictable Readers Ser.). (J). (ps-3). lib. bdg. 11.95 (0-89868-350-5) ARO Publishing Co.

Gillard, Denise. Music from the Sky. 2001. (Illus.). 32p. (J). (gr. k-2). 15.95 (0-88899-311-0) Groundwood Bks. CAN. *Dist:* Publishers Group West.

Gilman, Phoebe. Algo de Nada. Roehrich-Rubio, Esther, tr. from ENG. 1999. (SPA., Illus.). 40p. (J). (gr. k-3). lib. bdg. 15.95 (1-880507-53-6, LC8621) Lectorum Pubns., Inc.

—Grandma & the Pirates. ed. 1993. (J). (gr. 2). spiral bd. (0-616-01651-4) Canadian National Institute for the Blind/Institut National Canadien pour les Aveugles.

—Grandma & the Pirates. (J). (gr. k-3). 1992. 32p. pap. 4.99 (0-590-43425-X); 1990. 12.95 o.p. (0-590-43426-8) Scholastic, Inc.

—Grandma & the Pirates. 1990. (J). 10.19 o.p. (0-606-01846-8) Turtleback Bks.

Gilmore, Rachna. A Group of One. 2001. 192p. (YA). (gr. 6-9). 16.95 (0-8050-6475-3, Holt, Henry & Co. Bks. For Young Readers) Holt, Henry & Co.

—Mina's Spring of Colors. 2000. 150p. (J). (gr. 4-7). (1-55041-549-2); pap. (1-55041-534-4) Fitzhenry & Whiteside, Ltd.

Glass, Sue. Remember Me?/Te Acuerdas de Mi?/Bilingual in English & Spanish: Alzheimer's Through the Eyes of a Child/la Enfermedad de Alzheimer a Traves de Los Ojos de un Nino. de la Vega, Eida, tr. 2003. Tr. of Te Acuerdas de Mi?: la Enfermedad de Alzheimer a Traves de Los Ojos de un Nino. (ENG & SPA., Illus.). 32p. (J). (gr. 4-6). 16.95 o.s.i (0-9720192-5-1, 626999) Raven Tree Pr., LLC.

Godard, Alex. Mama, Across the Sea. Wen, George, tr. from FRE. 2000. (Illus.). 48p. (J). (ps-3). 16.95 (0-8050-6161-4, Holt, Henry & Co. Bks. For Young Readers) Holt, Henry & Co.

Godden, Rumer. The Doll's House. 126p. (J). (gr. 3-5). pap. 4.99 (0-8072-1408-6, Listening Library) Random Hse. Audio Publishing Group.

—The Doll's House. 1976. 11.04 (0-606-02086-1) Turtleback Bks.

—Great Grandfather's House. 1993. (Illus.). 80p. (J). (gr. 1 up). 18.00 o.p. (0-688-11319-2, Greenwillow Bks.) HarperCollins Children's Bk. Group.

Godfrey, Jan. The Cherry Blossom Tree: A Grandfather Talks about Life & Death. 1996. (Illus.). 32p. (J). (ps-3). 9.99 (0-8066-2843-X, 9-2843) Augsburg Fortress, Pubs.

Gold, Carolyn J. Dragonfly Secret. 1997. (Illus.). 144p. (J). (gr. 3-7). 15.00 (0-689-31938-X, Atheneum) Simon & Schuster Children's Publishing.

Goldman, Susan. Grandma Is Somebody Special. Rubin, Caroline, ed. 1976. (Self-Starter Bks.). (Illus.). 32p. (J). (ps-1). lib. bdg. 11.95 o.p. (0-8075-3034-4) Whitman, Albert & Co.

—Grandpa & Me Together. Tucker, Kathleen, ed. 1980. (Self-Starter Bks.). (Illus.). (ps-2). lib. bdg. 8.75 o.p. (0-8075-3036-0) Whitman, Albert & Co.

Gonzalez, Maya Christina, tr. & illus. Nana's Chicken Coop Surprise: Nana, Que Sorpresa! 2004. (ENG & SPA.). (J). (0-89239-190-1) Children's Bk. Pr.

Gordon, Shirley. Grandma Zoo. 1978. (Illus.). (J). (ps-2). 6.95 o.p. (0-06-022049-X); lib. bdg. 9.89 o.p. (0-06-022050-3) HarperCollins Pubs.

Gould, Deborah. Grandpa's Slide Show. 1987. (Illus.). 32p. (J). (ps-3). 13.95 o.p. (0-688-06972-X); lib. bdg. 13.88 o.p. (0-688-06973-8) HarperCollins Children's Bk. Group.

Graham, Bob. Grandad's Magic. 1989. (Illus.). (J). (gr. k-2). 13.95 o.p. (0-316-32321-7) Little Brown & Co.

Grambling, Lois G. Grandma Tells a Story. (Illus.). pap. 6.95 (1-58089-072-5); 2001. (J). 15.95 (1-58089-057-1) Charlesbridge Publishing, Inc. (Whispering Coyote).

Grandpa. Sir Reginald's Meeting. 1993. (J). pap. 10.95 o.p. (0-533-10487-4) Vantage Pr., Inc.

Grandpa & Me. 1999. (Toddlers' Storytime Ser.). (Illus.). 96p. (J). (ps). (1-85854-778-4) Brimax Bks., Ltd.

Grandpa's Back. 1998. (PNI Healing Stories for Children Ser.). 8p. (J). (gr. k-6). 6.95 (1-893351-03-3) Asclepian Pr.

Grandpa's Boat. 2001. (J). (1-58453-168-1) Pioneer Valley Educational Pr., Inc.

Grandpa's Secret. 1993. (J). Cook Communications Ministries.

Grandpa's Secret: Job 12:12. 1993. (J). 11.99 o.p. incl. audio (7-900882-13-8) Cook Communications Ministries.

Gray, Juliette, ed. Cherubic Children's New Classic Storybook Vol. 2: Teaching & Healing Stories to Help Children Learn, Understand & Cope. 1997. (Illus.). 384p. (J). (gr. k up). 24.95 (1-889590-24-X) Cherubic Pr.

Gray, Nigel. Little Bear's Grandad. 2001. (Illus.). 32p. (J). (ps-k). tchr. ed. 14.95 (1-58925-008-7, Tiger Tales) ME Media LLC.

Greaves, Margaret. The Serpent Shell. 1993. (Illus.). 32p. (J). (ps-3). 13.95 o.p. (0-8120-6350-3) Barron's Educational Series, Inc.

Green, Donna. My Little Artist. 1999. (Illus.). 32p. (J). (gr. 2-5). 11.98 (0-7651-1742-8) Smithmark Pubs., Inc.

—My Little Artist. 1999. (Illus.). 32p. (J). 12.95 (1-883746-20-5); 15.95 (1-883746-21-3) Vermilion.

Green, Michelle. Essence: That's My Grandpa! 1997. (Look-Look Bks.). (Illus.). 24p. (J). pap. text 2.99 o.p. (0-307-12915-2, Golden Bks.) Random Hse. Children's Bks.

Green, Phyllis. It's Me, Christy. (J). (gr. 4-6). 1983. 96p. pap. 2.50 o.p. (0-590-40651-5, Scholastic Paperbacks); 1979. reprint ed. pap. 1.75 o.p. (0-590-12097-2) Scholastic, Inc.

Green, Richard G. Skywoman's Granddaughter. 1998. (Darrin Captain Ser.). 128p. (J). (gr. 7 up). pap. 12.95 (0-911737-04-9) Ricara Features.

Greenburg, Dan. Great-Grandpa's in the Litter Box. 1996. (Zack Files Ser.: No. 1). (Illus.). 64p. (J). (gr. 2-5). 11.99 o.p. (0-448-41289-6); 4.99 (0-448-41260-8) Penguin Putnam Bks. for Young Readers. (Grosset & Dunlap).

—Great-Grandpa's in the Litter Box. 1996. (Zack Files Ser.: No. 1). (J). (gr. 2-5). 10.14 (0-606-10981-1) Turtleback Bks.

—My Grandma, Major League Slugger, Vol. 24. 2001. (Zack Files Ser.: No. 24). (Illus.). 64p. (J). (gr. 2-5). mass mkt. 4.99 (0-448-42550-5, Grosset & Dunlap) Penguin Putnam Bks. for Young Readers.

—Yikes! Grandma's a Teenager. (Zack Files Ser.: No. 17). (Illus.). (J). 2000. 2.66 o.p. (0-448-42574-2); 1999. 64p. (gr. 2-5). 3.99 (0-448-41999-8, Grosset & Dunlap) Penguin Putnam Bks. for Young Readers.

—Yikes! Grandma's a Teenager. 1999. (Zack Files Ser.: No. 17). (J). (gr. 2-5). 10.14 (0-606-17783-3) Turtleback Bks.

Greene, Michelle. That's My Grandpa. 1997. 24p. o.p. (0-307-16115-3, Golden Bks.) Random Hse. Children's Bks.

Greene, Rhonda Gowler. At Grandma's, ERS. 2003. (Illus.). 32p. (J). (ps-k). 15.95 (0-8050-6336-6, Holt, Henry & Co. Bks. For Young Readers) Holt, Henry & Co.

Greene, Stephanie. Falling into Place. 2002. (Illus.). 128p. (J). (gr. 4-7). tchr. ed. 15.00 (0-618-17744-2, Clarion Bks.) Houghton Mifflin Co. Trade & Reference Div.

Greenfield, Eloise. Grandmama's Joy. 1999. (Illus.). 32p. (ps-3). pap. 5.99 o.p. (0-698-11754-9, PaperStar); 1988. (Illus.). 32p. (J). (ps-3). 16.99 o.p. (0-399-21064-4, Philomel); 1980. (J). 8.95 o.p. (0-529-05536-8); 1980. (Illus.). 32p. (J). (gr. 2-5). 8.99 o.p. (0-529-05537-6, Philomel) Penguin Putnam Bks. for Young Readers.

—Grandmama's Joy. 1999. 12.14 (0-606-16847-8) Turtleback Bks.

—Grandpa's Face. 1992. (Illus.). (J). o.p. (0-09-174177-7) Hutchinson Children's Bks, Ltd. GBR. *Dist:* Random Hse. of Canada, Ltd.

—Grandpa's Face. (Illus.). 32p. (J). (ps-3). 1996. pap. 6.99 (0-698-11381-0, PaperStar); 1993. (SPA., 5.95 o.p. (0-399-22511-0, Philomel); 1991. 5.95 o.s.i (0-399-22106-9, Sandcastle Bks.); 1988. 16.99 (0-399-21525-5, Philomel) Penguin Putnam Bks. for Young Readers.

—Grandpa's Face. 1996. 13.14 (0-606-09349-4) Turtleback Bks.

—William & the Good Old Days. 1993. (Illus.). 32p. (J). (gr. k-3). 15.00 o.p. (0-06-021093-1); lib. bdg. 15.89 (0-06-021094-X) HarperCollins Children's Bk. Group.

—William & the Good Old Days. Date not set. (Illus.). 32p. (J). (gr. k-3). pap. 4.99 (0-06-443453-2) HarperCollins Pubs.

Greenspun, Adele Aron & Schwarz, Joanie. Grand Parents Are the Greatest Because... 2003. (Illus.). 32p. (J). 12.99 (0-525-47131-6, Dutton Children's Bks.) Penguin Putnam Bks. for Young Readers.

Gregory, Nan. Wild Girl & Gran. 2001. (Northern Lights Books for Children Ser.). (Illus.). 32p. (ps-3). (0-88995-221-3) Red Deer Pr.

Gregory, Valiska. Looking for Angels. 1996. (Illus.). (J). o.p. (0-671-50546-7, Simon & Schuster Children's Publishing) Simon & Schuster Children's Publishing.

Grender, Iris. Did I Ever Tell You about My Irish Great Grandmother? 1987. (Did I Ever Tell You? Ser.). (Illus.). 64p. (J). (gr. 1-3). 12.95 o.p. (0-09-146570-2) Hutchinson GBR. *Dist:* Trafalgar Square.

Greve, Andreas. The Good Night Story. 1993. (Illus.). 24p. (J). pap. 4.95 (1-55037-319-6); lib. bdg. 14.95 (1-55037-288-2) Annick Pr., Ltd. CAN. *Dist:* Firefly Bks., Ltd.

Griffin, Peni R. A Dig in Time. 1992. 160p. (J). (gr. 3-7). pap. 3.99 o.p. (0-14-036001-8, Puffin Bks.) Penguin Putnam Bks. for Young Readers.

—A Dig in Time. 1991. 192p. (J). (gr. 4-7). 14.95 (0-689-50525-6, McElderry, Margaret K.) Simon & Schuster Children's Publishing.

Griffith, Helen V. Grandaddy & Janetta. 1993. (Illus.). 32p. (J). (gr. k up). lib. bdg. 15.93 o.p. (0-688-11227-7); 16.00 (0-688-11226-9) HarperCollins Children's Bk. Group. (Greenwillow Bks.).

—Grandaddy & Janetta. 1999. (Illus.). 32p. (J). (ps-3). pap. 4.95 (0-688-17114-1, Morrow, William & Co.) Morrow/Avon.

—Grandaddy & Janetta Together: The Three Stories in One Book. 2001. (Illus.). 80p. (gr. 2 up). (YA). 15.95 (0-06-029148-6); (J). lib. bdg. 15.89 (0-06-029238-5) HarperCollins Children's Bk. Group. (Greenwillow Bks.).

—Grandaddy's Place. 1987. (Illus.). 40p. (J). (gr. 1-4). 15.00 o.p. (0-688-06253-9); (ps-3). 15.89 (0-688-06254-7) HarperCollins Children's Bk. Group. (Greenwillow Bks.).

—Grandaddy's Stars. 1995. (Illus.). 32p. (J). (gr. k up). 15.00 o.s.i (0-688-13654-0); lib. bdg. 14.93 o.p. (0-688-13655-9) HarperCollins Children's Bk. Group. (Greenwillow Bks.).

Grimm, Jacob W. & Grimm, Wilhelm K. Little Red Riding Hood/Caperucita Roja: A Bilingual Book. Surges, James, tr. from CAT. 1999. (ENG & SPA., Illus.). 32p. (J). (ps-3). 12.95 (0-8118-2561-2) Chronicle Bks. LLC.

Grimm-Richardson, Anne. Granny Grimm, Read Aloud Storybook. 2002. (Illus.). pap. 24.95 (0-937953-89-X) Tiptoe Literary Service.

Grimm. Caperucita Roja. 2001. Tr. of Little Red Ridinghood. (SPA.). (968-6347-35-6) Larousse, Ediciones, S. A. de C. V.

Grindley, Sally. A Flag for Grandma. 1998. (Illus.). 32p. (J). (ps-2). pap. 15.95 o.p. (0-7894-3490-3, D K Ink) Dorling Kindersley Publishing, Inc.

—No Trouble at All. 2002. (Illus.). 32p. (J). 15.95 (1-58234-757-3, Bloomsbury Children) Bloomsbury Publishing.

Grindley, Sally & Spyri, Johanna. Heidi. 2001. (Young Classics Ser.). (Illus.). 48p. (J). (gr. 1-3). pap. 9.95 o.p. (0-7894-3596-9) Dorling Kindersley Publishing, Inc.

Gryn, Goldie O. Grandma's Birthday Wish. 1993. (Illus.). 24p. (J). (gr. 1-4). pap. o.s.i (0-919591-51-5, Polestar Book Pubs.) Raincoast Bk. Distribution.

Guback, Georgia. Luka's Quilt. 1994. (Illus.). 32p. (J). (ps-3). 16.99 (0-688-12154-3); lib. bdg. 13.93 o.p. (0-688-12155-1) HarperCollins Children's Bk. Group. (Greenwillow Bks.).

Gudel, Helen. Dear Alexandra: A Story of Switzerland. 1999. Orig. Title: Leiber Alex. (Illus.). 32p. (J). (ps-3). 15.95 (1-56899-739-6); pap. 5.95 (1-56899-740-X) Soundprints.

Guernsey, JoAnn B. Journey to Almost There. 1985. 156p. (J). (gr. 5-8). 11.95 o.p. (0-89919-338-2, Clarion Bks.) Houghton Mifflin Co. Trade & Reference Div.

Guest, C. Z. Tiny Green Thumbs. 2000. (Illus.). 32p. (J). (ps-2). pap. 15.99 (0-7868-0516-1) Hyperion Bks. for Children.

Guest, Elissa Haden. Iris & Walter & Baby Rose. (Iris & Walter Ser.). (Illus.). 44p. (J). 2003. pap. 5.95 (0-15-216713-7); 2002. (gr. 1-4). 14.00 (0-15-202120-5) Harcourt Children's Bks. (Gulliver Bks.).

Guiffre, William. Gramma's Glasses. 1998. (Illus.). (J). pap. 6.95 (1-56763-347-1); lib. bdg. 19.95 (1-56763-346-3) Ozark Publishing.

Guo, Jing Jing. Grandpa's Mask. 2001. (Illus.). 32p. (J). (1-876615-05-2) Benchmark Pubns. Pty, Ltd.

Guthridge, Bettina, illus. The Mystery of the Talking Tail. 1997. (0-7608-0771-X) Sundance Publishing.

Guy, Rosa. The Ups & Downs of Carl Davis III. 1992. 128p. (J). (gr. 4-7). pap. 3.50 o.s.i (0-440-40744-3) Dell Publishing.

Relationships

Haas, Irene. A Summertime Song. (J). 1997. 16.00 (*0-689-81082-2*, McElderry, Margaret K.); 1997. (Illus.). 32p. 16.00 (*0-689-50549-3*, McElderry, Margaret K.); 2000. (Illus.). 32p. reprint ed. pap. 7.99 (*0-689-83528-0*, Aladdin) Simon & Schuster Children's Publishing.

Haas, Jessie. Beware the Mare. 1993. (Illus.). 64p. (J). (gr. 4-7). 15.00 o.p. (*0-688-11762-7*, Greenwillow Bks.) HarperCollins Children's Bk. Group.

—Hurry! 2000. (Illus.). 24p. (J). (gr. k up). 15.95 (*0-688-16889-2*, Greenwillow Bks.) HarperCollins Children's Bk. Group.

—Mowing. 1994. (Illus.). 32p. (J). (ps-3). 14.00 o.s.i (*0-688-11680-9*); lib. bdg. 13.93 o.p. (*0-688-11681-7*) HarperCollins Children's Bk. Group. (Greenwillow Bks.).

—Sugaring. 1996. (Illus.). 24p. (J). (ps-3). 15.99 (*0-688-14200-1*, Greenwillow Bks.) HarperCollins Children's Bk. Group.

—Will You, Won't You. 2000. 176p. (J). (gr. 5 up). 15.95 (*0-06-029196-6*, Greenwillow Bks.) HarperCollins Children's Bk. Group.

Hahn, Mary Downing. Following My Own Footsteps. 1996. 192p. (YA). (gr. 7-9). tchr. ed. 15.00 (*0-395-76477-7*, Clarion Bks.) Houghton Mifflin Co. Trade & Reference Div.

Halak, Glenn. A Grandmother's Story. 1992. (Illus.). 48p. (J). (ps). 14.00 o.s.i (*0-671-74953-6*, Simon & Schuster Children's Publishing) Simon & Schuster Children's Publishing.

Haley, Lin. Grandmother's Story. 1996. (J). (ps-3). 22p. 12.95 o.p. (*1-56763-257-2*); 22p. pap. text 2.95 o.p. (*1-56763-258-0*); (Illus.). (*1-56763-205-X*); (Illus.). pap. (*1-56763-206-8*) Ozark Publishing.

Hall, Donald. The Farm Summer 1942. 1994. (Illus.). 32p. (J). (gr. 1-5). 15.99 o.s.i (*0-8037-1501-3*); 15.89 o.p. (*0-8037-1502-1*) Penguin Putnam Bks. for Young Readers. (Dial Bks. for Young Readers).

Hallinan, P. K. My Grandma & I! 2002. (Illus.). 26p. (J). 7.95 (*0-8249-4220-5*, Candy Cane Pr.) Ideals Pubns.

—My Grandpa & I! 2002. (Illus.). 26p. (J). 7.95 (*0-8249-4219-1*, Candy Cane Pr.) Ideals Pubns.

—Three Freckles Past a Hair: A Grandfather's Legacy of Love. 1996. (P. K. Hallinan - Personal Values Ser.). (Illus.). 32p. (J). (ps-3). lib. bdg. 14.95 (*1-56674-105-X*) Forest Hse. Publishing Co., Inc.

—We're Very Good Friends, My Grandma & I. 24p. (J). 7.95 (*0-8249-5379-7*); pap. 5.95 (*0-8249-5380-0*) Ideals Pubns. (Ideals).

—We're Very Good Friends, My Grandma & I. 1989. (P. K. Books Values for Life). (Illus.). 32p. (J). (ps-3). lib. bdg. 13.27 o.p. (*0-516-03652-1*, Children's Pr.) Scholastic Library Publishing.

—We're Very Good Friends, My Grandpa & I. 24p. (J). 7.95 (*0-8249-5377-0*); pap. 5.95 (*0-8249-5378-9*) Ideals Pubns. (Ideals).

—We're Very Good Friends, My Grandpa & I. 1989. (P. K. Books Values for Life). (Illus.). 32p. (J). (ps-2). lib. bdg. 13.27 o.p. (*0-516-03653-X*, Children's Pr.) Scholastic Library Publishing.

Hamanaka, Sheila. Grandparent's Song. 2003. (Illus.). 32p. (J). 15.99 (*0-688-17852-9*) HarperCollins Children's Bk. Group.

—Grandparent's Story. 2003. (Illus.). 32p. (J). lib. bdg. 16.89 (*0-688-17853-7*, Morrow, William & Co.) Morrow/Avon.

Hambrick, Sharon. Arby Jenkins Meets His Match. 2000. (Illus.). 120p. (J). (gr. 4-7). 6.49 (*1-57924-461-0*) Jones, Bob Univ. Pr.

Hamilton, Dorothy. Tony Savala. 1972. (Illus.). 104p. (J). (gr. 4-9). 4.95 o.p. (*0-8361-1664-X*); pap. 3.95 o.p. (*0-8361-1674-7*) Herald Pr.

Hamilton, Virginia. Cousins. 1990. 128p. (J). (gr. 3-7). 17.99 (*0-399-22164-6*, Philomel) Penguin Putnam Bks. for Young Readers.

—Cousins. (J). 1997. mass mkt. 3.99 (*0-590-05377-9*); 1993. 128p. (gr. 4-7). mass mkt. 4.99 (*0-590-45436-6*) Scholastic, Inc.

—Cousins. l.t. ed. 2001. 129p. (J). 21.95 (*0-7862-3602-7*) Thorndike Pr.

—Cousins. 1990. (J). 10.55 (*0-606-02570-7*) Turtleback Bks.

Hanel, Wolfram. The Gold at the End of the Rainbow. Bell, Anthea, tr. from GER. 1997. (ENG & GEH., Illus.). 32p. (J). (gr. k-3). 15.95 o.p. (*1-55858-692-X*); 15.88 o.p. (*1-55858-693-8*) North-South Bks., Inc.

—Weekend with Grandma. Rasdeuschek-Simmons, Martina, tr. from GER. 2002. (Illus.). 64p. (J). 13.95 (*0-7358-1630-1*); lib. bdg. 14.50 (*0-7358-1631-X*) North-South Bks., Inc.

Hanson, P. H. My Granny's Purse. 2003. (Illus.). 14p. (J). (gr. k-3). bds. 15.95 (*0-7611-2978-2*, 12978) Workman Publishing Co., Inc.

Hardcastle, Michael. Soccer Star. 2002. (Yellow Bananas Ser.). (Illus.). 48p. (J). (gr. 3-4). pap. 4.95 (*0-7787-0979-5*); lib. bdg. 19.96 (*0-7787-0933-7*) Crabtree Publishing Co.

Harding, Sandy Bacon. A Stick, a Stone & a Bone. 1999. (Farm Adventures Ser.: Vol. 2). (Illus.). 79p. (J). (gr. 1-6). pap. 6.95 (*1-890609-08-0*, Lion's Paw Bks.) Coronet Bks. & Pubns.

Harlow, Joan Hiatt. Shadows on the Sea. 2003. (Illus.). 256p. (J). (gr. 3-6). 16.95 (*0-689-84926-5*, McElderry, Margaret K.) Simon & Schuster Children's Publishing.

—Shadows on the Sea. 2004. (J). (*0-7862-6145-5*) Thorndike Pr.

Harmeyer, Barbara E. Once upon a Time, I Used to Be Older. 1987. (Book Friends Ser.). (J). (ps). 4.95 o.p. (*0-312-00777-9*) St. Martin's Pr.

Harranth, Wolf. My Old Grandad. Carter, Peter, tr. 1987. (Illus.). 30p. (J). (ps-6). 11.95 o.p. (*0-19-279787-5*) Oxford Univ. Pr., Inc.

Harrar, George. Not as Crazy as I Seem. 2003. 224p. (J). tchr. ed. 15.00 (*0-618-26365-9*) Houghton Mifflin Co.

Harrison, Troon. Goodbye to Atlantis. 2002. 231p. (YA). (gr. 7 up). pap. 7.95 (*0-7737-6229-9*) Stoddart Kids CAN. *Dist:* Fitzhenry & Whiteside, Ltd.

—The Memory Horse. (Illus.). 32p. (J). (gr. 1-4). 2001. pap. 7.95 (*0-88776-570-X*); 1999. 15.95 (*0-88776-440-1*) Tundra Bks. of Northern New York.

Harshman, Marc. Roads. 2002. (Illus.). 32p. (J). (ps-2). 16.95 (*0-7614-5112-9*) Cavendish, Marshall Corp.

Hart, James W. Grandpa & the Computer. Kingsley, Steven, ed. l.t. ed. 2001. 84p. per. 12.95 (*1-893798-18-6*) AIL Newmedia Publishing.

Hartling, Peter. Old John. Crawford, Elizabeth D., tr. from GER. 1990. 128p. (J). (gr. 4-9). 11.95 o.p. (*0-688-08734-5*) HarperCollins Children's Bk. Group.

—Oma. Bell, Althea, tr. 1977. (ENG & GER., Illus.). (J). (gr. 2-5). o.p. (*0-06-022237-9*); lib. bdg. 6.79 o.p. (*0-06-022238-7*) HarperCollins Pubs.

Haseley, Dennis. Shadows. RS. 1991. (Illus.). 80p. (J). (gr. 2-6). 12.95 o.p. (*0-374-36761-2*, Farrar, Straus & Giroux (BYR)) Farrar, Straus & Giroux.

Haskins, Francine. Things I Like about Grandma. 32p. (gr. 1 up). 1994. (J). pap. 7.95 (*0-89239-123-5*); 1992. (Illus.). (YA). 14.95 o.p. (*0-89239-107-3*) Children's Bk. Pr.

—Things I Like About Grandma. 1992. 13.10 (*0-606-06806-6*) Turtleback Bks.

Hathaway, Trace. The Button Box. 2001. E-Book 4.75 incl. disk (*1-58749-069-2*); E-Book 4.75 (*1-58749-070-6*) Awe-Struck E-Bks.

Hathorn, Libby. Grandma's Shoes. 1994. (Illus.). (J). (ps-3). 14.95 o.p. (*0-316-35135-0*) Little Brown & Co.

Hautzig, Esther Rudomin. A Picture of Grandmother, RS. 2002. (Illus.). 80p. (J). (gr. 2-5). 15.00 (*0-374-35920-2*, Farrar, Straus & Giroux (BYR)) Farrar, Straus & Giroux.

Hawxhurst, Joan C. Bubbe & Gram: My Two Grandmothers. 1996. (Illus.). 32p. (J). (ps-2). 12.95 (*0-9651284-2-3*) Dovetail Publishing.

Hayashi, Akiko. Aki & the Fox. 1991. 48p. (J). (ps-3). 14.99 o.s.i (*0-385-41948-1*) Doubleday Publishing.

Hayes, Daniel. Flyers. 1998. 192p. (J). (gr. 7-12). pap. 4.99 (*0-689-80373-7*, Simon Pulse) Simon & Schuster Children's Publishing.

Hayes, Joe & Ortega, Josbe. Grandfather Horned Toad. 1997. 16p. 2.85 (*0-673-75724-2*, Good Year Bks.) Celebration Pr.

Haynes, Max. Grandma's Gone to Live in the Stars. 2000. (Concept Book Ser.). (Illus.). 32p. (J). (ps-3). lib. bdg. 15.95 (*0-8075-3026-3*) Whitman, Albert & Co.

Hazen, Lynn E. Mermaid Mary Margaret. 2003. (J). 15.95 (*1-58234-842-1*) Bloomsbury Publishing.

Heal, Gillian. Grandpa Bear's Fantastic Scarf. 1997. (Illus.). 32p. (J). (gr. k-5). 14.95 (*1-885223-41-2*) Beyond Words Publishing, Inc.

Hearson, Ruth. Knitted by Grandma. 2001. (Illus.). 16p. (J). 12.99 (*0-8037-2689-9*, Dial Bks. for Young Readers) Penguin Putnam Bks. for Young Readers.

Hedderwick, Mairi. Katie Morag & the Two Grandmothers. 1986. (Illus.). 32p. (J). (gr. k-3). 10.95 o.p. (*0-316-35400-7*) Little Brown & Co.

Hein, Lucille E. My Very Special Friend. 1974. (Illus.). 32p. (J). pap. 3.95 o.p. (*0-8170-0618-4*) Judson Pr.

Heineman, A. John. Grampa's Journal. 1995. (Illus.). 68p. (J). 15.00 (*1-887440-05-4*) Huckleberry Pr.

Helldorfer, M. C. Got to Dance. 2004. (Illus.). (J). (*0-385-32628-9*); 32p. lib. bdg. 17.99 (*0-385-90865-2*) Random Hse. Children's Bks. (Doubleday Bks. for Young Readers).

Heller, Marcy. Just You & Me, Grandpa. 1995. (Pop-Up Storybks Ser.). (Illus.). 12p. (J). (gr. k-3). pap. 9.95 o.p. (*0-89577-664-2*, Reader's Digest Young Families, Inc.) Reader's Digest Children's Publishing, Inc.

Heller, Nicholas. The Giant. 1997. (Illus.). 24p. (J). (gr. k-3). 15.00 o.s.i (*0-688-15224-4*); lib. bdg. 14.93 o.p. (*0-688-15225-2*) HarperCollins Children's Bk. Group. (Greenwillow Bks.).

—This Little Piggy. 1997. (Illus.). 24p. (J). (ps-3). 16.00 (*0-688-14049-1*, Greenwillow Bks.) HarperCollins Children's Bk. Group.

Hemery, Kathleen Maresh. The Healing Tree. 2001. (J). (*1-56123-153-3*, HTRC) Centering Corp.

Henderson, Aileen Kilgore. The Summer of the Bonepile Monster. (Illus.). 144p. (J). (gr. 3-7). 1995. 15.95 (*1-57131-603-5*); 1994. pap. 6.95 (*1-57131-602-7*) Milkweed Editions.

—The Summer of the Bonepile Monster. 1995. (J). 13.00 (*0-606-08932-2*) Turtleback Bks.

Henkes, Kevin. Grandpa & Bo. 2002. (Illus.). (J). 32p. 14.95 (*0-06-623837-4*); 323p. lib. bdg. 14.89 (*0-06-623838-2*, Greenwillow Bks.) HarperCollins Children's Bk. Group.

—Olive's Ocean. 2003. 224p. (J). (gr. 5 up). 15.99 (*0-06-053543-1*, 53396925); lib. bdg. 16.89 (*0-06-053544-X*) HarperCollins Children's Bk. Group. (Greenwillow Bks.).

—Sun & Spoon. 1997. 144p. (J). (gr. 3 up). 14.95 (*0-688-15232-5*, Greenwillow Bks.) HarperCollins Children's Bk. Group.

—Sun & Spoon. 1998. (Puffin Novel Ser.). 144p. (J). (gr. 3-7). pap. 4.99 (*0-14-130095-7*, Puffin Bks.) Penguin Putnam Bks. for Young Readers.

Hennessy, B. G. When You Were Just a Little Girl. 1994. (Illus.). 32p. (J). (ps-3). pap. 4.99 o.s.i (*0-14-054172-1*, Puffin Bks.) Penguin Putnam Bks. for Young Readers.

Henry, Gale. Grandpa's Garden. 1995. (Illus.). 24p. pap. 6.95 (*0-88961-213-7*) Woman's Pr., The.

Hering, Marianne. Mockingbird Mystery. (White House Adventures Ser.: Vol. 1). 64p. (J). (gr. 2-5). pap. 4.99 (*0-7814-3065-8*) Cook Communications Ministries.

Herman, Charlotte. The Memory Cupboard: A Thanksgiving Story. 2003. (Illus.). 32p. (J). (gr. 1-4). 15.95 (*0-8075-5055-8*) Whitman, Albert & Co.

—Our Snowman Had Olive Eyes. 1989. 112p. (J). pap. 3.95 o.p. (*0-14-034246-X*, Puffin Bks.) Penguin Putnam Bks. for Young Readers.

Hermes, Patricia. Someone to Count On. 1993. (J). (ps-6). 15.95 o.p. (*0-316-35925-4*) Little Brown & Co.

—Sweet by & By. 2002. 208p. (J). (gr. 3-6). 15.99 (*0-380-97452-5*) HarperCollins Pubs.

—Take Care of My Girl: A Novel. 1992. (J). 15.95 o.p. (*0-316-35913-0*) Little Brown & Co.

Herrera, Juan Felipe. Grandma & Me at the Flea / Los Meros Meros Remateros. Rohmer, Harriet & Cumpiano, Ina, eds. 2002. Tr. of Los Meros Meros Remateros. (ENG & SPA., Illus.). 32p. (J). (gr. 1 up). 15.95 (*0-89239-171-5*) Children's Bk. Pr.

Hershey, Kathleen. Cotton Mill Town. 1993. (Illus.). 32p. (J). (ps-2). 12.99 o.p. (*0-525-44966-3*, Dutton Children's Bks.) Penguin Putnam Bks. for Young Readers.

Hesse, Karen. Poppy's Chair. 2000. (Illus.). 32p. (J). (ps-3). mass mkt. 5.99 (*0-439-16130-4*) Scholastic, Inc.

—Poppy's Chair. 1993. (Illus.). 32p. (J). (gr. k-3). lib. bdg. 14.95 (*0-02-743705-1*, Simon & Schuster Children's Publishing) Simon & Schuster Children's Publishing.

—Poppy's Chair. 2000. 12.14 (*0-606-18884-3*) Turtleback Bks.

Hest, Amy. Baby Duck & the Bad Eyeglasses. 1996. (Illus.). 32p. (J). (ps-1). 16.99 o.s.i (*1-56402-680-9*) Candlewick Pr.

—The Crack-of-Dawn Walkers. 1988. (Illus.). 32p. (Orig.). (J). (ps-3). pap. 3.99 o.p. (*0-14-050829-5*, Puffin Bks.) Penguin Putnam Bks. for Young Readers.

—The Friday Nights of Nana. 2001. (Illus.). 32p. (J). (ps-2). 15.99 (*0-7636-0658-8*) Candlewick Pr.

—Gabby Growing Up. 1998. (Illus.). 32p. (J). (gr. k-3). 16.00 (*0-689-80573-X*, Simon & Schuster Children's Publishing) Simon & Schuster Children's Publishing.

—The Go-Between. 1992. (Illus.). 32p. (J). (gr. k-3). lib. bdg. 14.95 o.s.i (*0-02-743632-2*, Simon & Schuster Children's Publishing) Simon & Schuster Children's Publishing.

—In the Rain with Baby Duck. 1995. (Illus.). 32p. (J). (ps-3). 16.99 (*1-56402-532-2*) Candlewick Pr.

—Jamaica Louise James. (Illus.). 32p. (J). (ps-3). 1996. 15.99 o.s.i (*1-56402-348-6*); 1997. reprint ed. bds. 5.99 (*0-7636-0284-1*) Candlewick Pr.

—Jamaica Louise James. 1997. (J). 12.14 (*0-606-12745-3*) Turtleback Bks.

—Make the Team, Baby Duck! 2002. (Illus.). 32p. (J). (ps-1). 16.99 (*0-7636-1541-2*) Candlewick Pr.

—Nana's Birthday Party. 1993. (Illus.). 32p. (J). (ps-3). 15.95 (*0-688-07497-9*) HarperCollins Children's Bk. Group.

—Nana's Birthday Party. 1993. (Illus.). 32p. (J). (gr. k up). lib. bdg. 14.93 o.p. (*0-688-07498-7*, Morrow, William & Co.) Morrow/Avon.

—Off to School, Baby Duck! 2002. (Illus.). (J). 26.15 (*0-7587-3294-5*) Book Wholesalers, Inc.

—Off to School, Baby Duck! (Illus.). 32p. (J). (ps-1). 2001. bds. 5.99 (*0-7636-1054-2*); 1997. 16.99 (*0-7636-0244-2*) Candlewick Pr.

—The Purple Coat. (Illus.). 32p. (J). (gr. k-3). 1986. lib. bdg. 14.95 o.s.i (*0-02-743640-3*, Simon & Schuster Children's Publishing); 1992. reprint ed. pap. 6.99 (*0-689-71634-6*, Aladdin) Simon & Schuster Children's Publishing.

—Rosie's Fishing Trip. (Illus.). 32p. (J). (ps-3). 1994. 13.95 o.p. (*1-56402-296-X*); 1996. reprint ed. bds. 4.99 o.p. (*1-56402-849-6*) Candlewick Pr.

—Rosie's Fishing Trip. 1996. 10.19 o.p. (*0-606-09800-3*) Turtleback Bks.

—Ruby's Storm. 1994. (Illus.). 32p. (J). (ps-2). lib. bdg. 14.95 o.s.i (*0-02-743160-6*, Simon & Schuster Children's Publishing) Simon & Schuster Children's Publishing.

—Travel Tips from Harry: A Guide to Family Vacations in the Sun. 1989. (Illus.). 64p. (J). (gr. 2 up). 11.95 o.p. (*0-688-07972-5*); lib. bdg. 11.88 o.p. (*0-688-09291-8*) Morrow/Avon. (Morrow, William & Co.).

—Weekend Girl. 1993. (Illus.). 32p. (J). (gr. k up). lib. bdg. 14.93 o.p. (*0-688-09690-5*, Morrow, William & Co.) Morrow/Avon.

—You're the Boss, Baby Duck! 2001. (Illus.). 32p. (J). (ps-1). bds. 5.99 (*0-7636-0801-7*) Candlewick Pr.

Hickcox, Ruth. Great-Grandmother's Treasure. 1998. (Illus.). 32p. (J). (gr. k-3). 15.99 o.s.i (*0-8037-1513-7*); 15.89 o.p. (*0-8037-1514-5*) Penguin Putnam Bks. for Young Readers. (Dial Bks. for Young Readers).

Hickey, Tony. Granny & the American Witch. 1999. (Illus.). 112p. (YA). (gr. 1 up). pap. 7.95 (*1-901737-13-6*) Anvil Bks., Ltd. IRL. *Dist:* Dufour Editions, Inc.

—Granny Learns to Fly. 1997. 80p. (J). pap. 6.95 (*0-947962-96-4*) Dufour Editions, Inc.

Hickman, Janet. Jericho. 1994. 144p. (J). (gr. 3 up). 15.00 (*0-688-13398-3*, Greenwillow Bks.) HarperCollins Children's Bk. Group.

—Jericho. 1996. 144p. (YA). (gr. 4-7). pap. 3.99 (*0-380-72693-9*, Avon Bks.) Morrow/Avon.

—Jericho. 1996. 9.09 o.p. (*0-606-09488-1*) Turtleback Bks.

Hickman, Martha Whitmore. Robert Lives with His Grandparents. 1995. (Albert Whitman Concept Bks.). (Illus.). 32p. (J). (ps-3). lib. bdg. 14.95 (*0-8075-7084-2*) Whitman, Albert & Co.

—When James Allen Whitaker's Grandfather Came to Stay. 1985. (Illus.). 48p. (J). (gr. 2-4). pap. text 12.95 o.p. (*0-687-45016-0*) Abingdon Pr.

Hicks, Clifford B. Pop & Peter Potts, ERS. 1984. (Peter Potts Ser.). (Illus.). 144p. (J). (gr. 4-6). o.p. (*0-03-069627-5*, Holt, Henry & Co. Bks. For Young Readers) Holt, Henry & Co.

High, Linda O. Beekeepers. 2003. (Illus.). 32p. (J). (gr. k-3). 15.95 (*1-56397-486-X*) Boyds Mills Pr.

—Hound Heaven. 1995. 208p. (J). (gr. 4-7). 15.95 (*0-8234-1195-8*) Holiday Hse., Inc.

High, Linda Oatman. A Stone's Throw from Paradise. 1997. 143p. (YA). (gr. 5-9). pap. 5.00 (*0-8028-5142-8*, Eerdmans Bks For Young Readers) Eerdmans, William B. Publishing Co.

Hill, Elizabeth S. Curtain Going Up! 1995. 144p. (J). 14.99 o.p. (*0-670-85919-2*, Viking) Penguin Putnam Bks. for Young Readers.

—The Street Dancers. 1993. 192p. (J). (gr. 3-7). pap. 3.99 o.p. (*0-14-034491-8*, Puffin Bks.) Penguin Putnam Bks. for Young Readers.

Hill, Eric. Spot & His Grandparents. 1998. (Spot Ser.). (Illus.). 24p. (J). (ps). pap. 5.99 o.s.i (*0-14-056319-9*, Puffin Bks.) Penguin Putnam Bks. for Young Readers.

—Spot Visits His Grandparents. 1996. (Spot Ser.). (Illus.). 32p. (J). (ps). 12.99 (*0-399-23033-5*, G. P. Putnam's Sons) Penguin Group (USA) Inc.

Hill, Karen. A Grandmother's Book of Promises. 2000. (Illus.). 48p. (J). (ps-2). 12.99 (*1-57856-221-X*) WaterBrook Pr.

—Grandmother's Book of Promises. 2002. 48p. (J). 17.95 (*1-57856-579-0*) Random Hse., Inc.

Hilton, Nette. Web. 1998. (Illus.). 88p. (ps-3). pap. 5.95 (*0-207-17245-5*) HarperCollins Pubs.

Hines, Anna Grossnickle. Gramma's Walk. 1993. 32p. (J). (ps up). 14.00 o.s.i (*0-688-11480-6*); lib. bdg. 13.93 o.p. (*0-688-11481-4*) HarperCollins Children's Bk. Group. (Greenwillow Bks.).

—Grandma Gets Grumpy. (Illus.). (J). (ps-3). 1990. 32p. pap. 6.95 (*0-395-52595-0*); 1988. 13.95 o.p. (*0-89919-529-6*) Houghton Mifflin Co. Trade & Reference Div. (Clarion Bks.).

—Grandma Gets Grumpy. 1988. (J). 11.15 o.p. (*0-606-03404-8*) Turtleback Bks.

—My Grandma Is Coming to Town. 2003. (Illus.). 24p. (J). (ps). 13.99 (*0-7636-1237-5*) Candlewick Pr.

Hippely, Hilary Horder. September Song. 1995. (Illus.). (J). (gr. 5 up). 15.95 o.p. (*0-399-22646-X*, G. P. Putnam's Sons) Penguin Putnam Bks. for Young Readers.

—A Song for Lena. 1996. (Illus.). 40p. (J). (ps-3). 16.00 o.s.i (*0-689-80763-5*, Simon & Schuster Children's Publishing) Simon & Schuster Children's Publishing.

Hirschi, Ron. Harvest Song. 1991. (Illus.). 32p. (J). (ps-3). 13.95 o.p. (*0-525-65067-9*, Dutton Children's Bks.) Penguin Putnam Bks. for Young Readers.

Hodes, Loren. Too Big, Too Little. . . Just Right! 2002. (Illus.). (J). 9.95 (*1-880582-72-4*, TTTH) Judaica Pr., Inc., The.

Hodge, John. Finding Grandpa Everywhere: A Young Child Discovers Memories of a Grandparent. 1999. (Illus.). (J). 6.95 (*1-56123-125-8*) Centering Corp.

Hoffman, Alice. Horsefly. 2000. (Illus.). 48p. (J). 15.99 (*0-7868-0367-3*); lib. bdg. 16.49 (*0-7868-2318-6*) Disney Pr.

Hoffman, Mary. My Grandma Has Black Hair. 1988. (Illus.). 32p. (J). (ps-3). 9.95 o.p. (*0-8037-0510-7*, Dial Bks. for Young Readers) Penguin Putnam Bks. for Young Readers.

—Starring Grace. (Chapters Ser.). (Illus.). 96p. (J). 2001. (gr. 2-6). pap. 4.99 (*0-14-230022-5*, Puffin Bks.); 2000. (gr. k-4). 14.99 (*0-8037-2559-0*, Dial Bks. for Young Readers) Penguin Putnam Bks. for Young Readers.

Hogan, Bernice. My Grandmother Died-But I Won't Forget Her. Munger, Nancy, tr. 1983. 32p. (J). (gr. 1-3). pap. text 4.35 o.p. (*0-687-27548-2*) Abingdon Pr.

Hogeweg, Margriet & Forestell, Nancy. The God of Grandma Forever. 2001. (Illus.). 112p. (J). (gr. 5 up). 14.95 (*1-886910-69-3*) Front Street, Inc.

Holden, Dwight L. El Mejor Truco del Abuelo. Ramirez, Laureana, tr. 1993. (SPA., Illus.). 52p. (J). (gr. 1-3). 12.99 (*968-16-4032-2*, FC6404) Fondo de Cultura Economica MEX. *Dist:* Continental Bk. Co., Inc., Lectorum Pubns., Inc.

Holl, Kristi. 4Give & 4Get. 2001. (TodaysGirls.com Ser.: Vol. 9). (Illus.). 144p. (J). (gr. 5-9). pap. 5.99 o.s.i (*0-8499-7712-6*) Nelson, Tommy.

Holl, Kristi D. Just Like a Real Family. 1983. 132p. (J). (gr. 4-6). lib. bdg. 13.95 o.p. (*0-689-30970-8*, Atheneum) Simon & Schuster Children's Publishing.

—The Rose Beyond the Wall. 1985. 180p. (J). (gr. 5-9). lib. bdg. 13.95 o.p. (*0-689-31150-8*, Atheneum) Simon & Schuster Children's Publishing.

Holman, Sandy Lynne. Grandpa, Is Everything Black Bad? Holman, Sandy Lynne, ed. 1998. (Illus.). 32p. (J). (gr. 2-6). lib. bdg. 18.95 (*0-9644655-0-7*) Culture C.O.-O.P., The.

Holt, Kimberly Willis. Dancing in Cadillac Light. 2002. 176p. (YA). (gr. 5 up). pap. 5.99 (*0-698-11970-3*, PaperStar) Penguin Putnam Bks. for Young Readers.

—Dancing in Cadillac Light. unabr. ed. 2001. (J). (gr. 5-7). audio 25.00 (*0-8072-6194-7*, Listening Library) Random Hse. Audio Publishing Group.

—Dancing in Cadillac Light. l.t. ed. 2002. 195p. (J). 23.95 (*0-7862-4395-3*) Thorndike Pr.

—My Louisiana Sky, ERS. 1998. 176p. (J). (gr. 4-7). 16.95 (*0-8050-5251-8*, Holt, Henry & Co. Bks. For Young Readers) Holt, Henry & Co.

—My Louisiana Sky. 208p. (YA). (gr. 5 up). 4.99 (*0-8072-8291-X*, Listening Library) Random Hse. Audio Publishing Group.

Holt, Kimberly Willis & Colon, Raul. Dancing in Cadillac Light. 2001. 167p. (J). (gr. 5-8). 16.99 (*0-399-23402-0*, G. P. Putnam's Sons) Penguin Group (USA) Inc.

Holub, Joan. Goldie's Fortune: A Story of the Great Depression. 2002. (Doll Hospital Ser.: No. 2). 112p. (J). mass mkt. 3.99 o.s.i (*0-439-40179-8*, Scholastic Paperbacks) Scholastic, Inc.

Hooker, Ruth. At Grandma & Grandpa's House. 1986. (Illus.). 32p. (J). (gr. k-3). 11.95 o.p. (*0-8075-0477-7*) Whitman, Albert & Co.

Hooks, William H. The Mighty Santa Fe. 1993. (Illus.). 32p. (J). (gr. k-3). 14.95 (*0-02-744432-5*, Simon & Schuster Children's Publishing) Simon & Schuster Children's Publishing.

Hooper, Meredith. A Cow, a Bee, a Cookie & Me. 1997. (Illus.). 32p. (J). (ps-2). tchr. ed. o.p. (*0-7534-5067-4*) Kingfisher Publications, plc.

Hoopes, Lyn Littlefield. Half a Button. 1989. (Charlotte Zolotow Bk.). (Illus.). 32p. (J). (ps-2). 13.95 (*0-06-024017-2*); lib. bdg. 13.89 o.p. (*0-06-024018-0*) HarperCollins Children's Bk. Group.

Hopkinson, Deborah. Bluebird Summer. 2001. (Illus.). 32p. (J). (gr. 1 up). 15.95 (*0-688-17398-5*); 15.95 (*0-688-17398-5*); lib. bdg. 16.89 (*0-688-17399-3*) HarperCollins Children's Bk. Group. (Greenwillow Bks.).

Horlacher, Bill & Horlacher, Kathy. I'm Glad I'm Your Grandma. 1987. (Happy Day Bks.). (Illus.). 32p. (J). (gr. k-2). 2.50 o.p. (*0-87403-276-8*, 3776) Standard Publishing.

—I'm Glad I'm Your Grandpa. 1987. (Happy Day Bks.). (Illus.). 32p. (J). (gr. k-2). 1.89 o.p. (*0-87403-277-6*, 3777) Standard Publishing.

Horlacher, Bill, et al. I'm Glad I'm Your Grandma: African American. 1996. (Happy Day Bks.). (Illus.). 28p. (J). (ps-3). pap. 1.99 o.p. (*0-7847-0554-2*, 04244) Standard Publishing.

Houghton, Eric. The Backwards Watch. 1992. (Illus.). 32p. (J). (ps-2). 14.95 o.p. (*0-531-05968-5*); mass mkt. 15.99 o.p. (*0-531-08568-6*) Scholastic, Inc. (Orchard Bks.).

Houghton Mifflin Company Staff. Takao & Grandfather. 1992. (Literature Experience 1993 Ser.). (J). (gr. 5). pap. 10.24 (*0-395-61815-0*) Houghton Mifflin Co.

Houston, James R. Akavak: An Inuit-Eskimo Legend. 1990. (Illus.). 80p. (YA). (gr. 4-7). pap. 9.00 o.s.i (*0-15-201731-3*, Harcourt Paperbacks) Harcourt Children's Bks.

Howard, Ellen. The Log Cabin Quilt. 1996. (Illus.). 32p. (J). (ps-3). tchr. ed. 16.95 (*0-8234-1247-4*) Holiday Hse., Inc.

Howard, Kim. In Wintertime. 1994. (J). 16.00 o.p. (*0-688-11378-8*); lib. bdg. 15.93 o.p. (*0-688-11379-6*) HarperCollins Children's Bk. Group.

Howard, Mildred T. The Case of the Sassy Parrot. 2002. (Crimebusters, Inc Ser.: Bk. 2). (Illus.). 168p. (J). pap. 6.49 (*1-57924-721-0*) Jones, Bob Univ. Pr.

Howe, Quincy. StreetSmart. 1993. (Illus.). 106p. (YA). (gr. 7-12). pap. 6.95 o.p. (*0-932765-42-4*, 1325-93) Close Up Foundation.

Hubbard, Louise G. Grandfather's Gold Watch. 1997. (Illus.). 32p. (J). (ps-3). 11.95 (*1-57345-242-4*, Shadow Mountain) Deseret Bk. Co.

Hudson, Eleanor. A Valentine Bouquet. 2000. (Sparkle 'n' Twinkle Ser.). (Illus.). 12p. (J). (ps-k). bds. 4.99 (*0-689-83306-7*, Little Simon) Simon & Schuster Children's Publishing.

Hughes, Monica. A Handful of Seeds. 1996. (Illus.). 32p. (J). (ps-3). pap. 15.95 (*0-531-09498-7*, Orchard Bks.) Scholastic, Inc.

Humphrey, L. Spencer. Heidi. 1994. 32p. (J). (gr. 4-7). pap. text 2.95 (*0-8125-2323-7*, Tor Bks.) Doherty, Tom Assocs., LLC.

Humphrey, Paul. In Grandma's Day. 1995. (Read All about It Ser.). 32p. (J). (gr. k-3). pap. 4.95 (*0-8114-3717-5*); (Illus.). lib. bdg. 5.00 (*0-8114-5730-3*) Raintree Pubs.

The Hundred Penny Box. 1999. (J). 9.95 (*1-56137-386-9*) Novel Units, Inc.

Hunt, Angela Elwell. Gift for Grandpa. 1991. 32p. (J). (ps-3). 13.99 o.p. (*1-55513-425-4*) Cook Communications Ministries.

Hunter, Helen W. Turkey Hunting with Grandpa. 2000. (Young American Hunting & Fishing Ser.: Vol. 2). (Illus.). (J). (gr. 2-7). pap. 9.99 (*0-9662769-2-2*) Hunter Hse. Pubns.

Hurd, Edith Thacher. I Dance in My Red Pajamas. 1982. (Charlotte Zolotow Bk.). (Illus.). 32p. (J). (ps-3). lib. bdg. 15.89 o.s.i (*0-06-022700-1*) HarperCollins Children's Bk. Group.

Hutchins, Hazel J. One Dark Night. 2001. (Illus.). 32p. (J). (ps-2). 15.99 (*0-670-89246-7*, Viking Children's Bks.) Penguin Putnam Bks. for Young Readers.

Igus, Toyomi. Two Mrs. Gibsons. 1996. (Illus.). 32p. (YA). (gr. 4-7). 14.95 (*0-89239-135-9*) Children's Bk. Pr.

—When I Was Little. 1992. (Illus.). 32p. (J). (ps-3). 14.95 (*0-940975-32-7*); pap. 6.95 (*0-940975-33-5*) Just Us Bks., Inc.

—When I Was Little. 1992. (J). 12.15 o.p. (*0-606-08900-4*) Turtleback Bks.

—When I Was Little. 2001. (J). E-Book (*1-59019-149-8*); 1992. E-Book (*1-59019-150-1*) ipicturebooks, LLC.

Irwin, Hadley. What about Grandma? 1991. 176p. (YA). pap. 2.99 (*0-380-71138-9*, Avon Bks.) Morrow/Avon.

—What about Grandma?, 1. 1982. (J). 8.95 (*0-689-50224-9*, McElderry, Margaret K.) Simon & Schuster Children's Publishing.

Isabella's Rainbow & Grandma's Teapots. 2000. vi, 126p. (YA). (gr. 7-12). pap. 9.95 (*0-9707575-0-6*) Slator, Laraine.

Isadora, Rachel. Lili Backstage. 2002. (Illus.). (J). 13.19 (*0-7587-2987-1*) Book Wholesalers, Inc.

—Lili Backstage. 1997. (Illus.). 32p. (J). 16.99 o.s.i (*0-399-23025-4*, G. P. Putnam's Sons) Penguin Group (USA) Inc.

—Lili Backstage. 1999. (Illus.). 32p. (J). (ps-3). pap. 5.99 o.s.i (*0-698-11793-X*, Puffin Bks.) Penguin Putnam Bks. for Young Readers.

Ives, Penny. Granny's Quilt. (Illus.). 32p. (J). pap. 9.95 (*0-14-054560-3*) Penguin Bks., Ltd. GBR. *Dist:* Trafalgar Square.

Jacobek, Kristi. Bitty Bear Takes a Trip. 1999. (Illus.). (J). o.p. (*1-56247-221-6*) Pleasant Co. Pubns.

Jam, Teddy. The Year of Fire. 1992. (Illus.). (J). (gr. 2-5). (*0-88899-154-1*) Groundwood Bks.

—The Year of Fire. 1993. (Illus.). 48p. (J). (gr. 1-5). per. 14.95 (*0-689-50566-3*, McElderry, Margaret K.) Simon & Schuster Children's Publishing.

James, Betsy. Flashlight. 1997. (Illus.). 32p. (J). (ps-3). 18.99 o.s.i (*0-679-97970-0*); 17.00 o.s.i (*0-679-87970-6*) Knopf, Alfred A. Inc.

James, Sara. Boots Visits Grandma. 1993. (Boots Storybooks Ser.). (Illus.). 24p. (J). lib. bdg. 3.98 o.p. (*1-56156-134-7*) Kidsbooks, Inc.

—Boots Visits Grandma. 1993. (Boots Flat Bks.). (Illus.). 24p. (J). (ps). 3.98 o.p. (*0-8317-0603-1*) Smithmark Pubs., Inc.

James, Simon. The Birdwatchers. 2002. (Illus.). 32p. (J). (ps-3). 15.99 (*0-7636-1676-1*) Candlewick Pr.

—The Wild Woods. (Illus.). 32p. (J). (ps up). 1996. bds. 5.99 (*1-56402-637-X*); 1993. 13.95 o.p. (*1-56402-219-6*) Candlewick Pr.

—The Wild Woods. 1996. 11.19 o.p. (*0-606-08908-X*); 12.14 (*0-606-18019-2*) Turtleback Bks.

Jane & Kenilwood Occurrences. 1979. 128p. (J). (gr. 4-7). o.p. (*0-571-11359-1*) Faber & Faber Ltd.

Janover, Caroline. How Many Days until Tomorrow? 2000. (Illus.). 173p. (J). (gr. 4-8). pap. 11.95 (*1-890627-22-4*) Woodbine Hse.

Jenkins, Catherine. Monday Came. 1994. (Voyages Ser.). (Illus.). (J). 4.25 (*0-383-03762-X*) SRA/McGraw-Hill.

Jennings, Linda. The Best Christmas Present of All. (J). 1999. 32p. pap. 5.99 (*0-14-056646-5*, Puffin Bks.); 1996. (Illus.). 28p. 13.99 o.s.i (*0-525-45692-9*, Dutton Children's Bks.) Penguin Putnam Bks. for Young Readers.

Jennings, Patrick. The Ears of Corn: An Ike & Mem Story. 2003. (Illus.). 56p. (J). (gr. 1-3). tchr. ed. 15.95 (*0-8234-1770-0*) Holiday Hse., Inc.

—The Weeping Willow. 2002. (Ike & Mem Story Ser.: No. 3). (Illus.). 56p. (J). (gr. 1-4). tchr. ed. 15.95 (*0-8234-1671-2*) Holiday Hse., Inc.

Jennings, Sharon. The Bye-Bye Pie. 1999. (Illus.). 32p. (J). (gr. k-3). (*1-55041-405-4*) Fitzhenry & Whiteside, Ltd.

Jeschke, Susan. Mia, Grandma, & the Genie. 1977. (J). (gr. k-4). 6.95 o.p. (*0-03-028586-0*) Holt, Henry & Co.

Jessup, Harley. Grandma Summer. 32p. (J). (ps-3). 2001. (Illus.). pap. 6.99 (*0-14-056833-6*, Puffin Bks.); 1999. 15.99 o.p. (*0-670-88260-7*) Penguin Putnam Bks. for Young Readers.

Johnson, Angela. The Rolling Store. 1997. (Illus.). 32p. (J). (ps-2). pap. 15.95 (*0-531-30015-3*); lib. bdg. 16.99 (*0-531-33015-X*) Scholastic, Inc. (Orchard Bks.).

—Toning the Sweep. 2002. (J). 13.19 (*0-7587-0401-1*) Book Wholesalers, Inc.

—Toning the Sweep. 112p. 2003. (J). (gr. 7 up). mass mkt. 5.99 (*0-590-48142-8*, Scholastic Paperbacks); 1993. (YA). (gr. 6 up). mass mkt. 15.99 o.p. (*0-531-08626-7*, Orchard Bks.); 1993. (YA). (gr. 6 up). pap. 15.95 (*0-531-05476-4*, Orchard Bks.) Scholastic, Inc.

—Toning The Sweep. 1993. (Point Signature Ser.). 11.04 (*0-606-06817-1*) Turtleback Bks.

—When I Am Old with You. (Illus.). 32p. (J). (ps-3). 1993. mass mkt. 6.95 (*0-531-07035-2*); 1990. pap. 15.95 (*0-531-05884-0*); 1990. lib. bdg. 16.99 (*0-531-08484-1*) Scholastic, Inc. (Orchard Bks.).

—When I Am Old with You. 1993. (J). 13.10 (*0-606-05696-3*) Turtleback Bks.

Johnson, Dinah. Quinnie Blue, ERS. 2000. (Illus.). 32p. (J). (ps-2). 16.95 (*0-8050-4378-0*, Holt, Henry & Co. Bks. For Young Readers) Holt, Henry & Co.

Johnson, Dolores. Your Dad Was Just Like You. 1993. (Illus.). 32p. (J). (gr. k-3). text 13.95 (*0-02-747838-6*, Atheneum) Simon & Schuster Children's Publishing.

Johnson, Dolores, illus. Grandma's Hands. 1998. (Accelerated Reader Bks.). 32p. (J). (gr. 1-4). 15.95 (*0-7614-5025-4*, Cavendish Children's Bks.) Cavendish, Marshall Corp.

Johnson, Herschel. A Visit to the Country. 1989. (Illus.). 32p. (J). (ps-3). 13.95 (*0-06-022849-0*); lib. bdg. 13.89 o.p. (*0-06-022854-7*) HarperCollins Children's Bk. Group.

Johnson, Lindsay Lee. Soul Moon Soup. 2002. 134p. (J). (gr. 5 up). 15.95 (*1-886910-87-1*, Front Street) Front Street, Inc.

Johnston, Annie F. The Little Colonel. 2004. (Little Colonel Ser.). (Illus.). 192p. (J). (gr. 4-7). reprint ed. pap. 9.95 (*1-55709-315-6*) Applewood Bks.

—The Little Colonel. 1974. (Illus.). (J). 145p. (gr. 5-9). 8.95 o.p. (*0-88289-050-6*); 168p. (gr. 4-7). pap. 16.95 (*1-56554-542-7*) Pelican Publishing Co., Inc.

Johnston, Julie. The Only Outcast. (YA). (gr. 6-9). 1998. 232p. 14.95 (*0-88776-441-X*); 1999. 248p. reprint ed. pap. 6.95 (*0-88776-488-6*) Tundra Bks. of Northern New York.

—The Only Outcast. 1999. (J). 13.00 (*0-606-19122-4*) Turtleback Bks.

Johnston, Tony. Fishing Sunday. (Illus.). (J). (gr. k-3). 1996. 32p. 16.00 (*0-688-13458-0*); 1924. lib. bdg. o.p. (*0-688-13538-2*) Morrow/Avon. (Morrow, William & Co.).

—Fishing Sunday. 2001. (Illus.). (J). E-Book (*1-58824-234-X*); E-Book (*1-59019-213-3*) ipicturebooks, LLC.

—Grandpa's Song. (Illus.). (J). (ps-3). 1996. 32p. pap. 4.99 o.s.i (*0-14-055682-6*, Puffin Bks.); 1991. 32p. 15.99 o.s.i (*0-8037-0801-7*, Dial Bks. for Young Readers); 1991. 320p. 12.89 o.p. (*0-8037-0802-5*, Dial Bks. for Young Readers) Penguin Putnam Bks. for Young Readers.

—Grandpa's Song. 1996. (J). 10.19 o.p. (*0-606-08532-7*) Turtleback Bks.

—Little Rabbit Goes to Sleep. 1994. (Charlotte Zolotow Bk.). (Illus.). 32p. (J). (ps). 15.00 o.p. (*0-06-021239-X*); lib. bdg. 14.89 o.p. (*0-06-021241-1*) HarperCollins Children's Bk. Group.

Jones, Joy. Tambourine Moon. 1999. (Illus.). 32p. (J). (ps-3). 16.00 (*0-689-80648-5*, Simon & Schuster Children's Publishing) Simon & Schuster Children's Publishing.

Jones, Marcia Thornton & Dadey, Debbie. Happy Boo Day. 2000. (Bailey City Monsters Ser.: No. 9). (Illus.). (J). (gr. 2-4). 10.14 (*0-606-18515-1*) Turtleback Bks.

Joosse, Barbara M. Ghost Wings. 2001. (Illus.). 40p. (J). (ps-3). 15.95 (*0-8118-2164-1*) Chronicle Bks. LLC.

—A Houseful of Christmas, ERS. 2001. (Illus.). 32p. (J). (ps-3). 15.95 (*0-8050-6391-9*, Holt, Henry & Co. Bks. For Young Readers) Holt, Henry & Co.

Joyce, Jacqueline. Dust Devil Dan. 1997. (Illus.). 36p. (Orig.). (J). (ps-4). pap. 7.95 (*0-9652211-4-8*, 11129) Bear Path, The.

—Dust Devil Dan. DelMar Communication International Staff, tr. 1997. (SPA., Illus.). 36p. (Orig.). (J). (ps-4). pap. 7.95 (*0-9652211-5-6*, 11130) Bear Path, The.

—Grandma's Rocker. DelMar Communication International Staff, tr. 1998. (Illus.). 36p. (J). (ps-4). pap. 7.95 (*1-891317-02-4*, 11145); (ENG & SPA., pap. 7.95 (*1-891317-03-2*, 11146) Bear Path, The.

Jukes, Mavis. Blackberries in the Dark. 2002. (Illus.). 48p. (J). (gr. 2-6). 14.95 (*0-394-87599-0*, Knopf Bks. for Young Readers) Random Hse. Children's Bks.

Kaderli, Janet. Molasses Cookies. 1988. (Illus.). 64p. (J). (gr. 4 up). 16.95 (*1-885777-05-1*) Hendrick-Long Publishing Co.

Kadono, Eiko. Grandpa's Soup. 1999. (Illus.). 32p. (J). (ps-3). 16.00 (*0-8028-5195-9*, Eerdmans Bks For Young Readers) Eerdmans, William B. Publishing Co.

Kahn, Milne. Grandma's Hat. 1999. (Illus.). (J). pap. (*0-14-054402-X*) NAL.

Kahn, Rosemary. Grandma's Hat. 1991. (J). (ps-3). 13.95 o.p. (*0-670-84023-8*, Viking Children's Bks.) Penguin Putnam Bks. for Young Readers.

Karim, Roberta. Faraway Grandpa. 2004. (J). 15.95 (*0-8050-6785-X*, Holt, Henry & Co. Bks. For Young Readers) Holt, Henry & Co.

Karkowsky, Nancy. Grandma's Soup. 1989. (Illus.). 32p. (J). (gr. k-5). 8.95 o.p. (*0-930494-98-9*); pap. 5.95 (*0-930494-99-7*) Kar-Ben Publishing.

Kastner, Jill. Snake Hunt. 1993. (Illus.). 32p. (J). (ps-2). lib. bdg. 14.95 o.s.i (*0-02-749395-4*, Simon & Schuster Children's Publishing) Simon & Schuster Children's Publishing.

Kasza, Keiko. Grandpa Toad's Secrets. 2002. (Illus.). (J). 13.19 (*0-7587-2644-9*) Book Wholesalers, Inc.

—Grandpa Toad's Secrets. 1995. (Illus.). 32p. (J). (ps-3). 16.99 o.s.i (*0-399-22610-9*, G. P. Putnam's Sons) Penguin Group (USA) Inc.

—Grandpa Toad's Secrets. 1998. (Illus.). 32p. (J). (ps-3). pap. 5.99 o.s.i (*0-698-11617-8*, PaperStar) Penguin Putnam Bks. for Young Readers.

—Grandpa Toad's Secrets. 1998. (J). 12.14 (*0-606-12954-5*) Turtleback Bks.

Katz, Karen. Grandma & Me. 2002. (Illus.). 14p. (J). bds. 5.99 (*0-689-84905-2*, Little Simon) Simon & Schuster Children's Publishing.

Katz, Welwyn W., ed. Time Ghost. 1995. 144p. (J). (gr. 4-7). per. 16.00 (*0-689-80027-4*, McElderry, Margaret K.) Simon & Schuster Children's Publishing.

Kayne, Sheryl W. Queen of the Kisses Meets Sam under a Soup Pot. 1995. (Illus.). 32p. (J). (ps-3). 14.95 (*1-880851-18-0*) Greene Bark Pr., Inc.

Keens-Douglas, Richardo. Grandpa's Visit. 1996. (Illus.). 24p. (J). (ps-3). pap. 6.95 (*1-55037-488-5*); lib. bdg. 16.95 (*1-55037-489-3*) Annick Pr., Ltd. CAN. *Dist:* Firefly Bks., Ltd.

Keeshan, Robert. Alligator in the Basement. 1996. (Illus.). 32p. (J). (ps-3). 14.95 o.p. (*0-925190-90-X*) Fairview Pr.

Kehret, Peg. Night of Fear. 1994. 144p. (YA). (gr. 5 up). 14.99 o.s.i (*0-525-65136-5*, Dutton Children's Bks.) Penguin Putnam Bks. for Young Readers.

—Night of Fear. 1996. 144p. (J). (gr. 5-9). reprint ed. pap. 3.99 (*0-671-89217-7*, Aladdin) Simon & Schuster Children's Publishing.

—Night of Fear. 1996. 10.04 (*0-606-10895-5*) Turtleback Bks.

Keller, Holly. The Best Present. 1989. (Illus.). 32p. (J). (gr. k up). 11.95 o.p. (*0-688-07319-0*); lib. bdg. 11.88 o.p. (*0-688-07320-4*) HarperCollins Children's Bk. Group. (Greenwillow Bks.).

—Grandfather's Dream. 1994. (Illus.). 32p. (J). (ps-3). 16.99 (*0-688-12339-2*); lib. bdg. 15.93 o.p. (*0-688-12340-6*) HarperCollins Children's Bk. Group. (Greenwillow Bks.).

Kelley, Barbara. Harpo's Horrible Secret. 1993. (Illus.). 130p. (Orig.). (J). (gr. 3-7). pap. 8.80 (*1-56763-059-6*); lib. bdg. 25.25 (*1-56763-058-8*) Ozark Publishing.

Kemper, Bebe. Seeing Zach. 1999. (Illus.). 32p. (J). 14.95 (*0-9674363-0-3*, Rainy Day Bks.) Purple Chickie Pr.

Kern, Denise B. Rachel & Her Grandma: A Program on Grief & Loss. 1996. (Illus.). 25p. (Orig.). (J). (ps-5). pap. 9.95 (*1-884063-92-6*) MAR*CO Products, Inc.

Kerr, M. E. Gentlehands. 1982. 144p. (gr. 8 up). mass mkt. 2.75 o.s.i (*0-553-26677-2*) Bantam Bks.

—Gentlehands. (Ursula Nordstrom Bk.). (gr. 7 up). 1990. (Illus.). 208p. (J). pap. 5.99 (*0-06-447067-9*, Harper Trophy); 1978. (YA). lib. bdg. 16.89 o.p. (*0-06-023177-7*) HarperCollins Children's Bk. Group.

—Gentlehands. 1990. 11.00 (*0-606-04678-X*) Turtleback Bks.

Kesselman, Wendy Ann. Emma. 1993. (Picture Yearling Ser.). (Illus.). 32p. (ps-3). pap. text 6.99 (*0-440-40847-4*) Dell Publishing.

—Emma. 1980. (Illus.). 32p. (gr. k-3). 10.95 o.p. (*0-385-13461-4*); lib. bdg. o.p. (*0-385-13462-2*) Doubleday Publishing.

—Emma. 1985. (Trophy Picture Bk.). (Illus.). 32p. (J). (ps-3). reprint ed. pap. 4.95 o.p. (*0-06-443077-4*, Harper Trophy) HarperCollins Children's Bk. Group.

—Emma. 1980. (Dell Picture Yearling Ser.). (Illus.). (J). 13.14 (*0-606-05822-2*) Turtleback Bks.

Kessler, Cristina. My Great-Grandmother's Gourd. 2000. (Illus.). 32p. (J). (gr. k-4). pap. 16.95 (*0-531-30284-9*); lib. bdg. 17.99 (*0-531-33284-5*) Scholastic, Inc. (Orchard Bks.).

Ketteman, Helen. Grandma's Cat. 1996. (Illus.). 32p. (J). (ps-3). tchr. ed. 17.00 (*0-395-73094-5*) Houghton Mifflin Co.

Kezzeiz, Ediba. Grandma's Garden. 1991. (Illus.). 21p. (Orig.). (J). (ps-4). pap. 3.50 (*0-89259-113-7*) American Trust Pubns.

Khalsa, Dayal Kaur. Tales of a Gambling Grandma. (Dragonfly Bks.). (Illus.). 32p. (J). 1994. (ps-4). 5.99 o.s.i (*0-517-88262-0*); 1986. (gr. 1 up). 12.95 o.s.i (*0-517-56137-9*) Crown Publishing Group. (Clarkson Potter).

—Tales of a Gambling Grandma. 1994. (Illus.). 32p. (J). (gr. 1-3). pap. 9.95 (*0-88776-335-9*) Tundra Bks. of Northern New York.

Kibbey, Marsha. The Helping Place. 1991. (Contemporary Concerns Ser.). (Illus.). 40p. (J). (gr. 1-4). lib. bdg. 14.95 o.s.i (*0-87614-680-9*, Carolrhoda Bks.) Lerner Publishing Group.

—My Grammy: A Book about Alzheimer's Disease. (Illus.). (J). (ps-3). 1991. pap. 4.95 (*0-87614-544-6*, First Avenue Editions); 1988. 32p. lib. bdg. 14.95 o.p. (*0-87614-328-1*, Carolrhoda Bks.) Lerner Publishing Group.

Kilgore, Kathleen. The Ghost-Maker. 1986. 176p. (J). pap. 2.50 o.p. (*0-380-70057-3*, Avon Bks.) Morrow/Avon.

Kilroy, Sally. Grandpa's Garden. 1986. (Viking Kestrel Picture Bks.). (Illus.). 16p. (J). (gr. 1-3). 2.95 o.p. (*0-670-80338-3*, Viking Children's Bks.) Penguin Putnam Bks. for Young Readers.

Kimmelman, Leslie. Me & Nana. 1990. (Illus.). 32p. (J). (ps-3). 12.95 (*0-06-023166-1*); lib. bdg. 12.89 o.p. (*0-06-023163-7*) HarperCollins Children's Bk. Group.

King, Zachary X. & Tompkins-Brown, Barbara. Granny Takes a Flight. 1996. (Mizzy & Zizzy Ser.). (Illus.). 40p. (J). (gr. k-3). 15.99 (*1-886290-02-4*); pap. 7.99 (*1-886290-03-2*); lib. bdg. 22.99 (*1-886290-14-8*) Brown, Jack Enterprises.

Kinsey-Warnock, Natalie. The Canada Geese Quilt. 1992. (Illus.). 64p. (gr. 4-7). pap. text 3.99 o.s.i (*0-440-40719-2*, Yearling) Random Hse. Children's Bks.

—The Fiddler of the Northern Lights. 1994. (Illus.). (J). (ps-3). o.p. (*0-525-65143-8*, Dutton Children's Bks.) Penguin Putnam Bks. for Young Readers.

—In the Language of Loons. 1998. 112p. (J). (gr. 5-9). 15.99 o.s.i (*0-525-65237-X*, Dutton Children's Bks.) Penguin Putnam Bks. for Young Readers.

—Sweet Memories Still. 80p. (gr. 3-7). 1999. pap. 4.99 o.p. (*0-14-130168-6*, Puffin Bks.); 1997. (Illus.). (J). 14.99 o.s.i (*0-525-65230-2*) Penguin Putnam Bks. for Young Readers.

Kirkpatrick, Patricia. Plowie. abr. ed. 1994. (Illus.). 32p. (J). (ps-3). 14.95 o.s.i (*0-15-262802-9*) Harcourt Trade Pubs.

Kitchen, Margaret. Grandmother Goes up the Mountain. 1986. (Illus.). 156p. (J). (gr. 4-8). 10.95 o.p. (*0-233-97749-X*) Andre Deutsch GBR. *Dist:* Trafalgar Square, Trans-Atlantic Pubns., Inc.

Klaveness, Jan O. Beyond the Cellar Door. 1991. (J). (gr. 4-7). 13.95 o.p. (*0-590-43021-1*) Scholastic, Inc.

Klein, Norma. Going Backwards. 1986. 192p. (J). (gr. 7-9). pap. 12.95 (*0-590-40328-1*) Scholastic, Inc.

Kline, Suzy. Horrible Harry's Holiday Story. 2003. 64p. (J). 13.99 (*0-670-03642-0*, Viking) Viking Penguin.

Klingel, Cynthia Fitterer and Noyed, Robert B. The Amazing Letter G. 2003. (Alphaphonics Ser.). (Illus.). 24p. (J). (ps-3). lib. bdg. 24.21 (*1-59296-097-9*) Child's World, Inc.

Knipe, Floyd P. Forest & Grandpa Go Fishing. 2000. (Forest the Huggable Dog Ser.: Vol. 2). (Illus.). 23p. (J). (ps-3). pap. 4.95 (*1-930130-06-6*) Nature's Nest Bks.

—Forest & Grandpa Go Fishing Coloring Book. 2000. (Forest the Huggable Dog Ser.: Vol. 2). (Illus.). 23p. (J). (ps-3). pap. 2.00 (*1-930130-07-4*) Nature's Nest Bks.

Knowlton, Laurie Lazzaro. Nana's Rice Pie. 1997. (Illus.). 32p. (J). (ps-3). 14.95 (*1-56554-234-7*) Pelican Publishing Co., Inc.

Knox-Wagner, Elaine. My Grandpa Retired Today. Tucker, Kathleen, ed. 1982. (Albert Whitman Concept Bks.). (Illus.). 32p. (J). (gr. 1-3). lib. bdg. 12.95 o.p. (*0-8075-5334-4*) Whitman, Albert & Co.

—The Oldest Kid. Tucker, Kathleen, ed. 1981. (Albert Whitman Concept Bks.). (Illus.). 32p. (J). (gr. k-3). lib. bdg. 10.50 o.p. (*0-8075-5986-5*) Whitman, Albert & Co.

Koftan, Jenelle & Koftan, Kenneth. Long-Distance Grandparenting Series, 3. Incl. Long-Distance Grandparenting. pap. 12.95 (*0-945184-00-X*); Bk. II. Long-Distance Grandparenting. Mar, Carl, illus. (gr. k-2). pap. 12.95 (*0-945184-01-8*); Bk. III. Long-Distance Grandparenting. Mar, Carl, illus. (gr. 3-5). pap. 12.95 (*0-945184-02-6*); 96p. (J). 1988. 1990. 37.95 (*0-945184-06-9*) Spring Creek Pubns.

Kolanovic, Dubravka. A Special Day. Thatch, Nancy R., ed. 1993. (Books for Students by Students). (Illus.). 29p. (J). (gr. k-2). lib. bdg. 15.95 (*0-933849-45-1*) Landmark Editions, Inc.

Konigsburg, E. L. Amy Elizabeth Explores Bloomingdale's. 1992. (Illus.). 32p. (J). (ps-3). 14.95 (*0-689-31766-2*, Atheneum) Simon & Schuster Children's Publishing.

—Amy Elizabeth Explores Bloomingdale's. 1999. 12.14 (*0-606-17201-7*) Turtleback Bks.

Kopen, Pamela A. Grandpa's Magic Drawer. 1992. (Illus.). 32p. (J). (ps-3). 14.95 (*0-9628914-1-X*) Padakami Pr.

Koralek, Jenny. The Boy & the Cloth of Dreams. 1994. (Illus.). 32p. (J). (ps up). 14.95 o.p. (*1-56402-349-4*) Candlewick Pr.

—Night Ride to Nanna's. 2000. (Illus.). 32p. (J). (ps-3). 15.99 (*0-7636-1192-1*) Candlewick Pr.

Kornblatt, Marc. Izzy's Place. 2003. (Illus.). 128p. (J). 16.95 (*0-689-84639-8*, McElderry, Margaret K.) Simon & Schuster Children's Publishing.

Kosman, Miriam. Red Blue & Yellow Yarn: A Tale of Forgiveness. 1996. (Illus.). 32p. (J). (ps-1). 9.95 (*0-922613-78-8*) Hachai Publishing.

Koutsky, Jan Dale. My Grandma, My Pen Pal. 2003. (Illus.). 32p. (J). 15.95 (*1-56397-118-6*) Boyds Mills Pr.

Kranendonk, Anke. A Grandpa Cookie for Grandpa. Weikart, David P., ed. Van Deventer, Eric, tr. from DUT. 1998. (Illus.). (J). 10.95 (*1-57379-073-7*, K1010) High/Scope Pr.

Kranich, Jane. The Adventures of Froggie & Grandma: Froggie Visits Grandma's House. 2002. (Illus.). 50p. (J). (ps-3). pap. 7.50 (*0-9716515-0-7*) Crane & Rogers Pubs.

Krensky, Stephen. The Monster Trap. 2004. (J). 15.99 (*0-06-052498-7*); 16.89 (*0-06-052499-5*) HarperCollins Pubs.

Kroll, Steven. Annabelle's Un-Birthday. 1991. (Illus.). 40p. (J). (gr. 1-5). lib. bdg. 13.95 o.p. (*0-02-751171-5*, Simon & Schuster Children's Publishing) Simon & Schuster Children's Publishing.

—Annie's Four Grannies. 1986. (Illus.). 32p. (J). (ps-3). 12.95 o.p. (*0-8234-0605-9*) Holiday Hse., Inc.

—If I Could Be My Grandmother. 1977. (Illus.). (J). (ps-2). 5.95 o.p. (*0-394-83554-9*); lib. bdg. 5.99 o.p. (*0-394-93554-3*) Knopf Publishing Group. (Pantheon).

—Patrick's Tree House. 1994. (Illus.). 64p. (J). (gr. 2-5). mass mkt. 13.95 o.p. (*0-02-751005-0*, Simon & Schuster Children's Publishing) Simon & Schuster Children's Publishing.

—Toot! Toot! 1983. (Illus.). 32p. (J). (ps-3). 12.95 o.p. (*0-8234-0471-4*) Holiday Hse., Inc.

Kroll, Virginia L. Butterfly Boy. (Illus.). 32p. (J). 2003. (gr. k-3). pap. 7.95 (*1-59078-055-8*); 1997. (gr. 1-4). 15.95 o.s.i (*1-56397-371-5*) Boyds Mills Pr.

Krupinski, Loretta & Spyri, Johanna. Heidi. 1996. (Illus.). 32p. (J). (gr. k-4). lib. bdg. 14.89 o.p. (*0-06-023439-3*); 14.95 o.p. (*0-06-023438-5*) HarperCollins Children's Bk. Group.

Kuklin, Susan & Byrd, Donald. Harlem Nutcracker. 2001. (Illus.). 48p. (J). 19.99 (*0-7868-0633-8*) Disney Pr.

Kurtz, Jane. Pulling the Lion's Tail. 1995. (Illus.). (J). pap. 14.00 (*0-671-88183-3*, Simon & Schuster Children's Publishing) Simon & Schuster Children's Publishing.

La Fevers, Robin. The Falconmaster. 2003. 176p. (J). 16.99 (*0-525-46993-1*, Dutton Children's Bks.) Penguin Putnam Bks. for Young Readers.

La Mers, Joyce. Grandma Rationalizes an Enthusiasm for Skydiving. 1996. 40p. (Orig.). pap. 6.00 (*0-9638843-7-9*) Mille Grazie Pr.

Lachtman, Ofelia Dumas. A Good Place for Maggie. 2002. 144p. (J). pap. 9.95 (*1-55885-372-3*, Piñata Books) Arte Publico Pr.

Laieule Qui Venait de Dworitz. 1969. (J). (ps-7). 7.95 o.p. (*0-88776-010-4*) Tundra Bks. of Northern New York.

Lake, Julie. Galveston's Summer of the Storm. 2003. (Chaparral Book for Young Readers Ser.). 210p. (J). 16.95 (*0-87565-272-7*) Texas Christian Univ. Pr.

LaMarche, Jim. The Raft. (Illus.). 40p. (J). (gr. 1 up). 2000. 15.99 (*0-688-13977-9*); 2000. 15.99 (*0-688-13977-9*); 2000. lib. bdg. 16.89 (*0-688-13978-7*); 2002. reprint ed. pap. 6.99 (*0-06-443856-2*, Harper Trophy) HarperCollins Children's Bk. Group.

Laminack, Lester. Saturdays & Tea Cakes. 2004. 32p. (J). (gr. 1-2). 16.95 (*1-56145-303-X*) Peachtree Pubs., Ltd.

Laminack, Lester L. The Sunsets of Miss Olivia Wiggins. 1998. (Illus.). 32p. (J). (gr. 1-5). 15.95 (*1-56145-139-8*) Peachtree Pubs., Ltd.

Lansky, Bruce. When Grandma Was a Girl. 2002. (Illus.). 22p. (J). 9.95 (*0-7432-3694-7*) Meadowbrook Pr.

Lasky, Kathryn. I Have Four Names for My Grandfather. 1976. (Illus.). (J). (gr. k-3). lib. bdg. 14.95 o.s.i (*0-316-51520-5*) Little Brown & Co.

—My Island Grandma. 1993. (Illus.). 32p. (J). (ps up). 15.00 o.p. (*0-688-07946-6*); lib. bdg. 14.93 o.p. (*0-688-07948-2*) Morrow/Avon. (Morrow, William & Co.).

—My Island Grandma. 1979. (Illus.). (J). (ps-3). 7.95 o.p. (*0-7232-6159-8*, Warne, Frederick) Penguin Putnam Bks. for Young Readers.

—My Island Grandma. (Illus.). (J). 3.98 o.p. (*0-8317-1207-4*) Smithmark Pubs., Inc.

—True North: A Novel of the Underground Railroad. 208p. 1998. (J). (gr. 5-9). mass mkt. 4.99 (*0-590-20524-2*); 1996. (YA). (gr. 7 up). pap. 15.95 (*0-590-20523-4*) Scholastic, Inc. (Blue Sky Pr., The).

—True North: A Novel of the Underground Railroad. 1998. (J). 11.04 (*0-606-13874-9*) Turtleback Bks.

Le Tord, Bijou. My Grandma Leonie. 1987. (Illus.). 32p. (J). (ps-2). 12.95 o.p. (*0-02-756490-8*, Simon & Schuster Children's Publishing) Simon & Schuster Children's Publishing.

Leavey, Peggy Dymond. Help Wanted: Wednesdays Only. 1994. 120p. (J). pap. 5.95 (*0-929141-23-7*, Napoleon Publishing) Napoleon Publishing/ Rendezvous Pr. CAN. *Dist:* Words Distributing Co.

Leavy, Una. Good-Bye, Papa. 1996. (Illus.). 32p. (J). (ps-2). mass mkt. 14.95 o.p. (*0-531-09545-2*, Orchard Bks.) Scholastic, Inc.

Lebentritt, Julia & Ploetz, Richard. The Kooken, ERS. 1992. (Illus.). 32p. (J). (gr. 1-3). 14.95 o.p. (*0-8050-1749-6*, Holt, Henry & Co. Bks. For Young Readers) Holt, Henry & Co.

Lee, Milly. Nim & the War Effort. (Illus.). (J). 1997. o.p. (*0-374-22262-2*); RS. 2002. 40p. pap. 5.95 (*0-374-45506-6*, Sunburst); RS. 1997. 40p. (gr. 1 up). 16.00 (*0-374-35523-1*, Farrar, Straus & Giroux (BYR)) Farrar, Straus & Giroux.

Lee, Uk-Bae. Sori's Harvest Moon Day: A Story of Korea. 1999. Orig. Title: Sori's Chu-Suk. (Illus.). 32p. (J). (ps-3). 15.95 (*1-56899-687-X*); pap. 5.95 (*1-56899-688-8*) Soundprints.

Legge, David. Bamboozled. 1995. (Illus.). 32p. (J). (ps-2). pap. 14.95 (*0-590-47989-X*) Scholastic, Inc.

Lehr, Norma. The Secret of the Floating Phantom. 1994. 1p. (J). (gr. 4-7). lib. bdg. 14.95 o.s.i (*0-8225-0736-6*, Lerner Pubns.) Lerner Publishing Group.

Leighton, Audrey O. A Window of Time. 1995. (Illus.). 32p. (J). (ps-3). 15.95 (*0-9636335-1-1*) Nadja Publishing.

Leiviska, Karen. The War with Grandpa. 1999. (Literature Units Ser.). (Illus.). 48p. (gr. 3-5). pap., tchr. ed. 7.99 (*1-57690-334-6*, TCA2334) Teacher Created Materials, Inc.

Leonard, Marcia. Dan & Dan. 1998. (Real Kids Readers Ser.). (Illus.). 32p. (ps-1). (J). pap. 4.99 (*0-7613-2028-8*); lib. bdg. 18.90 (*0-7613-2003-2*) Millbrook Pr., Inc.

—Dan & Dan. 1998. (Real Kids Readers Ser.). 10.14 (*0-606-15794-8*) Turtleback Bks.

—Dan & Dan. (Illus.). E-Book (*1-58824-709-0*); 1998. E-Book (*1-58824-461-X*); 1998. E-Book (*1-58824-791-0*) ipicturebooks, LLC.

—The Giant Baby & Other Giant Tales. 1994. (Hello Reader! Ser.: Level 4). (Illus.). 48p. (J). (ps-3). pap. 3.99 (*0-590-46892-8*) Scholastic, Inc.

Leppard, Lois Gladys. Mandie & the Unwanted Gift, 29. 1997. (Mandie Bks.: No. 29). 176p. (J). (gr. 4-7). pap. 4.99 (*1-55661-556-6*) Bethany Hse. Pubs.

—Mandie & the Unwanted Gift. 1998. (Mandie Bks.: No. 29). (J). (gr. 4-7). 11.04 (*0-606-18916-5*) Turtleback Bks.

LeShan, Eda J. Grandparents: A Special Kind of Love. 1984. (Illus.). 128p. (J). (gr. 3-7). text 15.00 o.s.i (*0-02-756380-4*, Simon & Schuster Children's Publishing) Simon & Schuster Children's Publishing.

Lester, Alison. Isabella's Bed. 1993. (Illus.). 32p. (J). (ps-3). reprint ed. tchr. ed. 14.95 o.p. (*0-395-65565-X*) Houghton Mifflin Co.

Leverich, Kathleen. Daisy. 1997. (Flower Girls Ser.: Vol. 2). (Illus.). 96p. (J). (gr. 1-4). pap. 4.25 (*0-06-442019-1*, Harper Trophy) HarperCollins Children's Bk. Group.

Levine, Arthur A. Bono & Nonno. (Illus.). (J). (ps up). 1995. 32p. 15.00 o.p. (*0-688-13233-2*); 1924. lib. bdg. o.p. (*0-688-13234-0*) Morrow/Avon. (Morrow, William & Co.).

Levine, Evan. Not the Piano, Mrs. Medley! 1991. (Illus.). 32p. (J). (ps-2). pap. 15.95 (*0-531-05956-1*); lib. bdg. 16.99 (*0-531-08556-2*) Scholastic, Inc. (Orchard Bks.).

Levinson, Riki. Grandpa's Hotel. 1995. (Illus.). 32p. (J). (gr. k-3). mass mkt. 15.95 o.p. (*0-531-09475-8*); mass mkt. 16.99 o.p. (*0-531-08775-1*) Scholastic, Inc. (Orchard Bks.).

—I Go with My Family to Grandma's. 1992. 32p. (J). (ps-3). pap. 4.99 o.s.i (*0-14-054762-2*, Puffin Bks.) Penguin Putnam Bks. for Young Readers.

—Watch the Stars Come Out. 1985. (Illus.). 32p. (J). (ps-3). 15.00 o.s.i (*0-525-44205-7*, Dutton Children's Bks.) Penguin Putnam Bks. for Young Readers.

Levy, Janice. Abuelito Eats with His Fingers. 1998. (Illus.). 32p. (J). 14.95 (*1-57168-177-9*) Eakin Pr.

Lewin, Ted. The Storytellers. 1998. (Illus.). 40p. (J). (gr. k-3). 16.00 (*0-688-15178-7*) HarperCollins Children's Bk. Group.

Lewis, Beverly. Follow the Dream. 2000. (Girls Only (Go!) Ser.: Vol. 5). 128p. (J). (gr. 3-8). pap. 5.99 (*1-55661-640-6*) Bethany Hse. Pubs.

—No Grown-Ups Allowed. 1995. (Cul-de-Sac Kids Ser.: Vol. 4). (Illus.). 80p. (J). (gr. 2-5). pap. 3.99 (*1-55661-644-9*) Bethany Hse. Pubs.

—Pickle Pizza. 1996. (Cul-de-Sac Kids Ser.: Vol. 8). 80p. (J). (gr. 2-5). pap. 3.99 (*1-55661-728-3*) Bethany Hse. Pubs.

Lewis, Rob. Grandpa at the Beach. 1998. (Mondo Ser.). (Illus.). 48p. (J). (gr. 1-5). pap. 4.50 (*1-57255-552-1*) Mondo Publishing.

—Grandpa Comes to Stay. 1996. (Mondo Ser.). (Illus.). 48p. (J). (gr. 1-5). pap. 4.50 (*1-57255-212-3*) Mondo Publishing.

—Hide & Seek with Grandpa. 1997. (Mondo Ser.). (Illus.). 48p. (J). (gr. 1-5). pap. 4.50 (*1-57255-226-3*) Mondo Publishing.

—Too Much Trouble for Grandpa. 1998. (Mondo Ser.). (Illus.). 48p. (J). (gr. 1-5). pap. 4.50 (*1-57255-551-3*) Mondo Publishing.

Life, Kay, illus. The Secret under the Tree. 2001. (Adventures of Benny & Watch: Vol. No. 7). 32p. (J). (gr. 1-3). pap. 3.95 (*0-8075-0643-5*) Whitman, Albert & Co.

Lightburn, Ron & Lightburn, Sandra. Driftwood Cove. 1998. (Illus.). 32p. (J). 19.95 o.s.i (*0-385-25626-4*) Doubleday Publishing.

Lindbergh, Reeve. Grandfather's Lovesong. (Illus.). 32p. (J). 1995. pap. 4.99 o.s.i (*0-14-055481-5*, Puffin Bks.); 1993. 15.99 o.s.i (*0-670-84842-5*, Viking Children's Bks.) Penguin Putnam Bks. for Young Readers.

—Grandfather's Lovesong. 1995. 10.19 o.p. (*0-606-07591-7*) Turtleback Bks.

—My Hippie Grandmother. 2003. (Illus.). 24p. (YA). 15.99 (*0-7636-0671-5*) Candlewick Pr.

Linden, Ann M. One Smiling Grandma. 1995. (Illus.). 32p. (J). pap. 4.99 o.s.i (*0-14-055341-X*, Puffin Bks.) Penguin Putnam Bks. for Young Readers.

Linden, Anne Marie. Emerald Blue. 1994. (Illus.). 32p. (J). 15.95 o.s.i (*0-689-31946-0*, Atheneum) Simon & Schuster Children's Publishing.

Linko, Gina. Tess's Touchstone. 2004. (Seekers Ser.: No. 5). 108p. (J). pap. 5.99 (*0-8066-4189-4*, Augsburg Bks.) Augsburg Fortress, Pubs.

Lipp, Frederick. Bread Song. Gaillard, Jason, tr. & illus. by. 2004. (J). (*1-59336-000-2*); pap. (*1-59336-001-0*) Mondo Publishing.

Lisle, Janet Taylor. The Art of Keeping Cool. (Illus.). (J). (gr. 5-9). 2002. 256p. pap. 4.99 (*0-689-83788-7*, Aladdin); 2000. 216p. 17.00 (*0-689-83787-9*, Atheneum/Richard Jackson Bks.) Simon & Schuster Children's Publishing.

—The Art of Keeping Cool. l.t. ed. 2001. 207p. (J). 21.95 (*0-7862-3427-X*) Thorndike Pr.

Littke, Lael J. Blue Skye. 1991. 192p. (J). 13.95 o.p. (*0-590-43448-9*) Scholastic, Inc.

Little, Jean. Bats about Baseball. ed. 1996. (J). (gr. 2). spiral bd. (*0-616-01702-2*) Canadian National Institute for the Blind/Institut National Canadien pour les Aveugles.

Relationships

—Gruntle Piggle Takes Off. 1997. (Illus.). 32p. (J). (ps-3). 13.99 o.s.i (*0-670-86340-8*) Penguin Putnam Bks. for Young Readers.

Littman, Jennifer. Matzo Ball Soup: The Balls That Bobbed in the Broth That Bubbe Brewed. 1997. (Illus.). 32p. (Orig.). (J). (ps-2). pap. 7.95 (*0-9656431-0-7*) Brickford Lane Pubs.

Lobel, Gillian. Does Anybody Love Me? 2002. (Illus.). 28p. (J). (gr. k-3). 16.00 (*1-56148-368-0*) Good Bks.

Lohans, Alison. Sundog Rescue. 1999. (Illus.). 24p. (J). (ps-2). per. 5.95 (*1-55037-570-9*) Annick Pr., Ltd. CAN. *Dist:* Firefly Bks., Ltd.

Lomask, Milton. Secret of Grandfather's Diary. 1976. (Illus.). (J). (gr. 4-6). pap. (*0-671-29797-X*, Simon Pulse) Simon & Schuster Children's Publishing.

London, Jonathan. Liplap's Wish. (Illus.). 32p. (J). (ps-3). 1997. pap. 6.95 (*0-8118-1810-1*); 1994. 13.95 o.p. (*0-8118-0505-0*) Chronicle Bks. LLC.

—Liplap's Wish. 1994. 13.10 (*0-606-15615-1*) Turtleback Bks.

—The Sugaring-Off Party. 1995. (Illus.). 32p. (J). 15.99 o.s.i (*0-525-45187-0*, Dutton Children's Bks.) Penguin Putnam Bks. for Young Readers.

—The Sugaring-Off Party. 1999. (J). pap. 5.99 (*0-14-056360-1*) Viking Penguin.

—The Village Basket Weaver. 1996. (Illus.). 32p. (J). (ps-3). 14.99 o.p. (*0-525-45314-8*, Dutton Children's Bks.) Penguin Putnam Bks. for Young Readers.

London, Sara. Firehorse Max. 1997. (Michael di Capua Bks.). (Illus.). 32p. (J). (ps up). lib. bdg. 14.89 (*0-06-205095-8*); 14.95 o.s.i (*0-06-205094-X*) HarperCollins Children's Bk. Group.

Long, Kathy. Fix It, Grandma, Fix It. 1995. (Ready, Set, Read!). (Illus.). 32p. (J). (ps-3). pap. 5.99 (*0-8066-2815-4*, 9-2815) Augsburg Fortress, Pubs.

Long, Melinda. When Papa Snores. 2000. (Illus.). 32p. (J). (gr. 3). 16.00 (*0-689-81943-9*, Simon & Schuster Children's Publishing) Simon & Schuster Children's Publishing.

Look, Lenore. Henry's First-Moon Birthday. 2001. (Illus.). 40p. (J). (ps-2). 16.00 (*0-689-82294-4*, Atheneum/Anne Schwartz Bks.) Simon & Schuster Children's Publishing.

—Love As Strong As Ginger. 1999. (Illus.). 32p. (J). (gr. 1-4). 15.95 (*0-689-81248-5*, Atheneum/Anne Schwartz Bks.) Simon & Schuster Children's Publishing.

Lorenzo, Carol L. Mama's Ghosts. (Illus.). 176p. (gr. 5 up). 1989. (J). 6.95 o.p. (*0-06-024007-5*); 1974. (YA). lib. bdg. 12.89 o.p. (*0-06-024008-3*) HarperCollins Children's Bk. Group.

Love, D. Anne. Dakota Spring. 1995. (Illus.). 96p. (J). (gr. 4-7). 14.95 o.p. (*0-8234-1189-3*) Holiday Hse., Inc.

—Dakota Spring. 1997. (J). pap. 3.99 (*0-440-91306-3*, Dell Books for Young Readers) Random Hse. Children's Bks.

Lovell, Patty. Stand Tall, Molly Lou Melon. 2001. (Illus.). 32p. (J). (ps-3). 15.99 (*0-399-23416-0*) Putnam Publishing Group, The.

—Stand Tall, Molly Lou Melon. 2002. (J). (gr. k-3). 25.95 incl. audio (*0-8045-6891-X*); 25.95 incl. audio (*0-8045-6891-X*) Spoken Arts, Inc.

Low, William. Chinatown, ERS. 1997. (Illus.). 32p. (J). (ps-3). 16.95 (*0-8050-4214-8*, Holt, Henry & Co. Bks. For Young Readers) Holt, Henry & Co.

Luenn, Nancy. A Gift for Abuelita: Celebrating the Day of the Dead. 1998. Tr. of Un Regalo para Abuelita: En Celebration del Dia de los Muertos. (ENG & SPA., Illus.). 32p. (J). (gr. k-3). 15.95 (*0-87358-688-3*, Rising Moon Bks. for Young Readers) Northland Publishing.

Lum, Kate. What! Cried Granny: An Almost Bedtime Story. 2002. (Illus.). 14.04 (*1-4046-0859-1*) Book Wholesalers, Inc.

—What! Cried Granny: An Almost Bedtime Story. 2002. (Illus.). 32p. (J). (ps-2). pap. 6.99 (*0-14-230092-6*) Penguin Putnam Bks. for Young Readers.

—What! Cried Granny: An Almost Bedtime Story. Skwarek, Skip, ed. 1999. (Illus.). 32p. (J). (ps-2). 16.99 (*0-8037-2382-2*, Dial Bks. for Young Readers) Penguin Putnam Bks. for Young Readers.

Lum, Kate & Johnson, Adrian. What! Cried Granny. 1999. (Illus.). 32p. (J). (*0-7475-4178-7*) Bloomsbury Publishing, Ltd.

Lum, Kate & Johnson, Adrian, eds. What! 1998. (Illus.). 25p. (*0-7475-3054-8*) Bloomsbury Publishing, Ltd.

Lundberg, Betty. Grandmas Are Special. 1991. (Happy Day Bks.). (Illus.). 32p. (J). (gr. k-2). 2.50 o.s.i (*0-87403-816-2*, 24-03916) Standard Publishing.

Lynch, Chris. Freewill. 2001. 160p. (J). (gr. k-3). 15.95 (*0-06-028176-6*); (Illus.). (gr. 8 up). lib. bdg. 15.89 (*0-06-028177-4*) HarperCollins Children's Bk. Group.

—Freewill. 2002. 160p. (J). (gr. 8 up). pap. 6.99 (*0-06-447202-7*) HarperCollins Pubs.

Lyon, George Ella. Basket. 1990. (Illus.). 32p. (J). (ps-2). lib. bdg. 16.99 o.p. (*0-531-08486-8*); mass mkt. 15.95 o.p. (*0-531-05886-7*) Scholastic, Inc. (Orchard Bks.).

—Come a Tide. (Illus.). 32p. (J). (ps-3). 1993. mass mkt. 6.95 (*0-531-07036-0*); 1990. lib. bdg. 16.99 (*0-531-08454-X*); 1990. mass mkt. 15.95 o.p. (*0-531-05854-9*) Scholastic, Inc. (Orchard Bks.).

—Come a Tide. 1993. 13.10 (*0-606-05212-7*) Turtleback Bks.

Mac Laverty, Bernard. Andrew McAndrew. 1993. (Illus.). 80p. (J). (gr. k-3). 13.95 o.p. (*1-56402-173-4*) Candlewick Pr.

MacDonald, Caroline. Secret Lives. 1995. 133p. (J). (gr. 7-10). 15.00 o.s.i (*0-671-51081-9*, Simon & Schuster Children's Publishing) Simon & Schuster Children's Publishing.

Machado, Ana Maria. Me in the Middle. Unger, David, tr. from POR. (Illus.). (J). 2003. 112p. (gr. 3-6). pap. 5.95 (*0-88899-467-2*, Libros Tigrillo); 2002. 96p. (gr. 2-6). 14.95 (*0-88899-463-X*) Groundwood Bks. CAN. *Dist:* Publishers Group West.

Mackall, Dandi Daley. Horse Whispers in the Air. 2000. (Horsefeathers Ser.: Vol. 3). 191p. (J). (gr. 7-11). pap. 5.99 (*0-570-07008-2*) Concordia Publishing Hse.

MacLachlan, Patricia. Caleb's Story. 2001. (Sarah, Plain & Tall Ser.). 128p. (J). (gr. 3-5). 14.95 (*0-06-023605-1*); (gr. 7 up). lib. bdg. 15.89 (*0-06-023606-X*) HarperCollins Children's Bk. Group. (Cotler, Joanna Bks.).

—Journey. 1993. (Illus.). 96p. (gr. 4-7). pap. text 4.99 (*0-440-40809-1*) Dell Publishing.

—Journey. 1991. 96p. (gr. 2 up). text 14.95 o.s.i (*0-385-30427-7*) Doubleday Publishing.

—Journey. 1990. (J). o.s.i (*0-385-30368-8*, Dell Books for Young Readers) Random Hse. Children's Bks.

—Journey. 1991. (J). 11.14 (*0-606-05387-5*) Turtleback Bks.

—Three Names. 1991. (Charlotte Zolotow Bk.). (Illus.). 32p. (J). (gr. k-4). 14.95 o.p. (*0-06-024035-0*); lib. bdg. 16.89 (*0-06-024036-9*) HarperCollins Children's Bk. Group.

—Through Grandpa's Eyes. (Reading Rainbow Bks.). (Illus.). (J). 1983. 40p. (ps-3). pap. 5.99 (*0-06-443041-3*, Harper Trophy); 1983. (gr. 2-5). 13.89 (*0-06-024044-X*, 595015); 1980. 40p. (ps-3). lib. bdg. 16.89 (*0-06-024043-1*) HarperCollins Children's Bk. Group.

—Through Grandpa's Eyes. 1983. (Reading Rainbow Bks.). (J). 12.10 (*0-606-01956-1*) Turtleback Bks.

Maguire, Gregory. Lucas Fishbone. 1990. (Illus.). 48p. (J). (gr. k-3). 14.95 (*0-06-024089-X*); lib. bdg. 14.89 o.p. (*0-06-024090-3*) HarperCollins Children's Bk. Group.

Mahy, Margaret. A Busy Day for a Good Grandmother. 1993. (Illus.). 32p. (J). (gr. k-3). 14.95 (*0-689-50595-7*, McElderry, Margaret K.) Simon & Schuster Children's Publishing.

Malanga, Tara & Okeefe, Susan Heyboer. Sleepy Angel's First Bedtime Story. 2000. (Illus.). 32p. (J). (ps-2). 9.95 (*0-8091-6670-4*) Paulist Pr.

Malanga, Tara, et al. Sleepy Angel's First Bedtime Story. 1999. (Illus.). (J). pap. o.p. (*0-8091-6671-2*) Paulist Pr.

Malyon, Carol. Mixed-Up Grandmas. 1998. (Illus.). 32p. (J). (ps-1). pap. 12.95 (*0-88984-194-2*) Porcupine's Quill, Inc. CAN. *Dist:* Univ. of Toronto Pr.

Manes, Stephen. An Almost Perfect Game. 1995. 176p. (J). (gr. 4-7). pap. 14.95 (*0-590-44432-8*) Scholastic, Inc.

Mann, Kenny. I Can Ride a Bike. 1999. (Bank Street Ready-to-Read Ser.). (J). pap. o.s.i (*0-553-37589-X*) Bantam Bks.

—I Can Ride a Bike. 1999. (Illus.). E-Book (*1-58824-970-0*); E-Book (*1-58824-971-9*); E-Book (*1-58824-969-7*) ipicturebooks, LLC.

Manuel, Lynn. The Christmas Thingamajig. 2002. (Illus.). 32p. (J). 15.99 (*0-525-46120-5*, Dutton Children's Bks.) Penguin Putnam Bks. for Young Readers.

—Fifty-Five Grandmas & a Llama. 1997. (Illus.). 32p. (J). (ps-3). 15.95 (*0-87905-785-8*) Smith, Gibbs Pub.

—The Night the Moon Blew Kisses. 1996. (Illus.). 32p. (J). (ps-3). tchr. ed. 14.95 o.p. (*0-395-73979-9*) Houghton Mifflin Co.

Mariconda, Barbara. Turn the Cup Around. 1997. 160p. (J). (gr. 3-7). text 15.95 o.s.i (*0-385-32292-5*, Delacorte Pr.) Dell Publishing.

—Turn the Cup Around. 1998. 160p. (gr. 3-7). reprint ed. pap. text 3.99 o.s.i (*0-440-41311-7*, Yearling) Random Hse. Children's Bks.

—Turn the Cup Around. 1998. 10.04 (*0-606-13878-1*) Turtleback Bks.

Marie, Evelyn. Grandma from Manhattan or Danger I Carry a "Meshok" 2001. (Illus.). (YA). (gr. 5 up). pap. 10.50 (*1-890579-02-5*) Berry Bks.

—Oatmeal. 1997. (Illus.). 24p. (J). (gr. k-3). pap. 3.50 (*1-890579-00-9*) Berry Bks.

Marie, Sharon. Granny's Crooked Teeth. 1993. (J). 7.95 o.p. (*0-533-10602-8*) Vantage Pr., Inc.

Marino, Jan. The Mona Lisa of Salem Street: A Novel. 1995. 176p. (J). 14.95 o.p. (*0-316-54614-3*) Little Brown & Co.

Markle, Sandra. Fledglings. 2003. 144p. (J). (gr. 5 up). pap. 9.95 (*1-56397-696-X*) Boyds Mills Pr.

Marlow, Herb. Twisters, Bronc Riders & Cherry Pie. 1996. (Illus.). 118p. (J). pap. 8.95 (*0-9666858-9-X*, TW100); lib. bdg. 18.95 (*0-9666858-8-1*, TW100) Four Seasons Bks., Inc.

—Twisters, Bronc Riders & Cherry Pie. 1997. (Illus.). (J). 25.25 (*1-56763-273-4*); pap. (*1-56763-274-2*) Ozark Publishing.

Marshall, Bridget. Animal Crackers: A Tender Book about Death & Funerals & Love. 1997. (Illus.). (J). 6.95 (*1-56123-101-0*) Centering Corp.

Marshall, Val & Tester, Bronwyn. And Grandpa Sat on Friday. 1993. (Voyages Ser.). (Illus.). (J). 4.25 (*0-383-03610-0*) SRA/McGraw-Hill.

Marshall, William. Adam's Island. 1993. (I Love to Read Collections). (Illus.). 46p. (J). (gr. 1-5). lib. bdg. 8.50 o.p. (*0-89565-889-5*) Child's World, Inc.

Martin, Ann M. Claudia & the Sad Good-Bye. 1989. (Baby-Sitters Club Ser.: No. 26). 192p. (J). (gr. 3-7). mass mkt. 3.50 (*0-590-42503-X*) Scholastic, Inc.

—Claudia & the Sad Good-Bye. l.t. ed. 1994. (Baby-Sitters Club Ser.: No. 26). 176p. (J). (gr. 3-7). lib. bdg. 21.27 o.p. (*0-8368-1247-6*) Stevens, Gareth Inc.

—Claudia & the Sad Good-Bye. 1989. (Baby-Sitters Club Ser.: No. 26). (J). (gr. 3-7). 10.04 (*0-606-04187-7*) Turtleback Bks.

—Karen's Grandmothers. 1990. (Baby-Sitters Little Sister Ser.: No. 10). 112p. (J). (gr. 3-7). mass mkt. 3.50 (*0-590-43651-1*) Scholastic, Inc.

—Karen's Grandmothers. 1990. (Baby-Sitters Little Sister Ser.: No. 10). (J). (gr. 3-7). 9.55 (*0-606-04457-4*) Turtleback Bks.

Martin, Bill, Jr. Knots on a Counting Rope. ed. 1989. (gr. 2). spiral bd. (*0-616-01713-8*) Canadian National Institute for the Blind/Institut National Canadien pour les Aveugles.

—Knots on a Counting Rope, ERS. 1993. (Illus.). 32p. (J). (ps-3). pap. 19.95 (*0-8050-2955-9*, Holt, Henry & Co. Bks. For Young Readers) Holt, Henry & Co.

Martin, Bill, Jr. & Archambault, John. Knots on a Counting Rope, ERS. 1987. (Illus.). 32p. (J). (ps-3). 16.95 (*0-8050-0571-4*, Holt, Henry & Co. Bks. For Young Readers) Holt, Henry & Co.

—Knots on a Counting Rope. unabr. ed. 1992. (J). (gr. k-5). pap. 17.90 incl. audio (*0-8045-6559-7*, 6559) Spoken Arts, Inc.

Martin, Bill, Jr., et al. Knots on a Counting Rope, ERS. 1997. (Illus.). 32p. (J). (ps-2). reprint ed. pap. 6.95 (*0-8050-5479-0*, Holt, Henry & Co. Bks. For Young Readers) Holt, Henry & Co.

Martin, C. L. Down Dairy Farm Road. 1994. (Illus.). 32p. (J). (ps-3). 14.95 (*0-02-762450-1*, Atheneum) Simon & Schuster Children's Publishing.

Martin, Jacqueline Briggs. Good Times on Grandfather Mountain. 1992. (Illus.). 32p. (J). (ps-1). mass mkt. 15.99 o.p. (*0-531-08577-5*); pap. 15.95 (*0-531-05977-4*) Scholastic, Inc. (Orchard Bks.).

—Grandmother Bryant's Pocket. (Illus.). 48p. (J). (ps-3). 2000. pap. 5.95 (*0-618-03309-2*); 1996. tchr. ed. 14.95 (*0-395-68984-8*) Houghton Mifflin Co.

—Grandmother Bryant's Pocket. 2000. (Illus.). (J). 12.10 (*0-606-18209-8*) Turtleback Bks.

—The Water Gift & the Pig of the Pig. 2003. (Illus.). 32p. (J). (ps-3). lib. bdg., tchr. ed. 15.00 (*0-618-07436-8*) Houghton Mifflin Co.

Martin, Rebecca. The House with Two Grandmothers. unabr. ed. 1997. 125p. (J). (gr. 4-8). pap. 5.95 (*0-87813-569-3*) Christian Light Pubns., Inc.

Martin, Terri L. A Family Trait. 1999. 192p. (J). (gr. 3-7). tchr. ed. 15.95 (*0-8234-1467-1*) Holiday Hse., Inc.

Marzollo, Jean. Soccer Cousins. 1997. (Hello Reader! Ser.). (Illus.). (J). (gr. 2-4). mass mkt. 3.99 (*0-590-74254-X*) Scholastic, Inc.

Mason, Ann M. The Weird Things in Nanna's House. 1992. (Illus.). 32p. (J). (ps-1). 13.95 o.p. (*0-531-05970-7*); mass mkt. 13.99 o.p. (*0-531-08570-8*) Scholastic, Inc. (Orchard Bks.).

Mason, Jane. River Day. 1994. (Illus.). 32p. (J). (gr. k-3). lib. bdg. 14.95 o.s.i (*0-02-762869-8*, Simon & Schuster Children's Publishing) Simon & Schuster Children's Publishing.

Massey, Barbara & DeLoach, Sylvia. Darby down Under. 2000. (Child Like Me Ser.: Vol. 4). (Illus.). (J). (gr. 2-5). 6.99 (*1-56309-766-4*, New Hope) Woman's Missionary Union.

Masters, Susan Rowan. Summer Song. 1995. 137p. (J). (gr. 4-7). 14.95 o.p. (*0-395-71127-4*, Clarion Bks.) Houghton Mifflin Co. Trade & Reference Div.

—Summer Song. 2000. 137p. (gr. 4-7). pap. 9.95 (*0-595-14407-1*) iUniverse, Inc.

Masurel, Claire. Emily's First Sleepover. 2003. (Reading Railroad Bks.). (Illus.). 32p. (J). mass mkt. 3.49 (*0-448-43128-9*, Grosset & Dunlap) Penguin Putnam Bks. for Young Readers.

Mathis, Sharon Bell. The Hundred Penny Box. 1995. (Illus.). (J). (gr. 5). 9.32 (*0-395-73254-9*) Houghton Mifflin Co.

—The Hundred Penny Box. 1986. (Puffin Newbery Library). (Illus.). 48p. (J). (gr. 1-4). pap. 5.99 (*0-14-032169-1*, Puffin Bks.) Penguin Putnam Bks. for Young Readers.

—The Hundred Penny Box. Dillon, Leo, ed. 1975. (Illus.). 48p. (J). (gr. k-3). 16.99 o.s.i (*0-670-38787-8*, Viking Children's Bks.) Penguin Putnam Bks. for Young Readers.

—The Hundred Penny Box. 1986. (J). 12.14 (*0-606-01280-X*) Turtleback Bks.

Matott, Justin. When Did I Meet You Grandpa? 2000. (Illus.). 32p. (J). (gr. 1-7). 16.95 (*1-889191-14-0*) Clove Pubns.

Matthis, Nina. The Grandma Hunt. 2002. (Illus.). 28p. (J). 16.00 (*91-29-65656-7*) R & S Bks. SWE. *Dist:* Holtzbrinck Pubs.

Matze, Claire Sidhom. The Stars in My Geddoh's Sky. 32p. (J). 2002. pap. 6.95 (*0-8075-7610-7*, Prairie Paperbacks); 1999. (Illus.). pap. 14.95 (*0-8075-5332-8*) Whitman, Albert & Co.

May, Kathy L. Molasses Man. 2000. (Illus.). 32p. (J). (ps-3). tchr. ed. 16.95 (*0-8234-1438-8*) Holiday Hse., Inc.

May, Scott. Outer Space Earl: The Trees Have the Blues. 2000. (Illus.). 32p. (J). (gr. 1-3). pap. (*0-9701450-1-2*) Long Hill Productions, Inc.

Mayer, Mercer. Grandma's Garden. 2001. (First Readers, Skills & Practice Ser.). (Illus.). 24p. (J). (gr. k-1). 3.95 (*1-57768-846-5*) McGraw-Hill Children's Publishing.

—Just Grandma & Me. (Little Critter Ser.). (J). (ps-3). Date not set. 79.95 (*1-57135-003-9*); 1995. lib. bdg. 119.95 o.s.i (*1-57135-004-7*) Broderbund Software, Inc.

—Just Grandma & Me. 2001. (Little Critter Ser.). (Illus.). 24p. (J). (ps-3). reprint ed. pap. 3.29 (*0-307-11893-2*, 11893, Golden Bks.) Random Hse. Children's Bks.

—Just Grandma & Me. 1983. (Little Critter Ser.). (J). (ps-3). 9.44 (*0-606-19803-2*) Turtleback Bks.

—Just Grandpa & Me. 1985. (Little Critter Ser.). (J). (ps-3). 9.44 (*0-606-12375-X*) Turtleback Bks.

—Mi Abuela y Yo. 1997. (Spanish Golden Look-Look Bks.).Tr. of Just Grandma & Me. (SPA., Illus.). 24p. (J). (ps-3). pap. 3.29 o.s.i (*0-307-71893-X*, Golden Bks.) Random Hse. Children's Bks.

—My Trip to the Farm. 2000. (First Readers, Skills & Practice Ser.). (Illus.). 24p. (J). (gr. 1-2). pap. 3.95 (*1-57768-817-1*) McGraw-Hill Children's Publishing.

Mayer, Pamela S. The Scariest Monster in the Whole Wide World. 2001. (Illus.). 32p. (J). (ps-3). 15.99 (*0-399-23459-4*, Philomel) Penguin Group (USA) Inc.

—The Scariest Monster in the Whole Wide World. 2003. (Illus.). 32p. pap. 6.99 (*0-14-250072-0*, Puffin Bks.) Penguin Putnam Bks. for Young Readers.

Mazer, Norma. A Figure of Speech. 1973. 192p. (J). (gr. 7 up). 8.95 o.s.i (*0-440-02638-5*, Delacorte Pr.) Dell Publishing.

Mazer, Norma Fox. After the Rain. 1987. 304p. (J). (gr. 7 up). 17.99 (*0-688-06867-7*) HarperCollins Children's Bk. Group.

McAllister, Angela. The Wind Garden. 1995. (Illus.). 32p. (J). (gr. k up). 15.00 o.p. (*0-688-13280-4*) HarperCollins Children's Bk. Group.

McCain, Becky R. Grandmother's Dreamcatcher. (Illus.). 32p. (J). (gr. k-3). 2001. pap. 6.95 (*0-8075-3032-8*); 1998. 15.95 (*0-8075-3031-X*) Whitman, Albert & Co.

McCartney, Jenny. Grandma's Hospital. 1993. (Voyages Ser.). (Illus.). (J). 4.25 (*0-383-03570-8*) SRA/McGraw-Hill.

McClintock, Barbara, illus. Goldilocks & the Three Bears. 2003. 32p. (J). pap. 15.95 (*0-439-39545-3*, Scholastic Pr.) Scholastic, Inc.

McCormick, Maxine. Pretty As You Please. 1999. (J). 15.95 o.s.i (*0-399-22536-6*, Philomel) Penguin Putnam Bks. for Young Readers.

McCully, Emily Arnold. First Snow. (Illus.). 32p. (J). (ps-1). 1988. pap. 4.95 o.p. (*0-06-443181-9*, Harper Trophy); 1985. 12.95 (*0-06-024128-4*); 1985. lib. bdg. 15.89 o.p. (*0-06-024129-2*) HarperCollins Children's Bk. Group.

—First Snow. 2004. 32p. (J). lib. bdg. 16.89 (*0-06-623853-6*); (Illus.). 15.99 (*0-06-623852-8*) HarperCollins Pubs.

—The Grandma Mix-Up. (I Can Read Bks.). (Illus.). 64p. (J). 1991. (gr. k-3). pap. 3.99 (*0-06-444150-4*, Harper Trophy); 1988. (gr. k-3). lib. bdg. 15.89 (*0-06-024202-7*); 1988. (gr. 1-3). 11.95 (*0-06-024201-9*) HarperCollins Children's Bk. Group.

—Grandmas at Bat. (I Can Read Bks.). (Illus.). 64p. (J). 1995. (gr. k-3). pap. 3.99 (*0-06-444193-8*, Harper Trophy); 1993. (gr. 1-3). 14.00 o.p. (*0-06-021031-1*); 1993. (gr. 1-3). lib. bdg. 13.89 o.p. (*0-06-021032-X*) HarperCollins Children's Bk. Group.

—Grandmas at Bat. 1995. (I Can Read Bks.). (J). (gr. 1-3). 10.10 (*0-606-09346-X*) Turtleback Bks.

—Grandmas at the Lake. (I Can Read Bks.). (Illus.). 64p. (J). 1994. (gr. k-3). pap. 4.95 (*0-06-444177-6*, Harper Trophy); 1990. (gr. 1-3). 10.95 (*0-06-024126-8*); 1990. (gr. 1-3). lib. bdg. 15.89 o.p. (*0-06-024127-6*) HarperCollins Children's Bk. Group.

—Grandmas at the Lake. 1994. (I Can Read Bks.). (J). (gr. 1-3). 8.95 o.p. (*0-606-06423-0*) Turtleback Bks.

—Grandma's Trick-or-Treat. 2001. (I Can Read Bks.). (Illus.). 48p. (J). (gr. k-3). 14.95 (*0-06-028730-6*); lib. bdg. 14.89 (*0-06-028731-4*) HarperCollins Children's Bk. Group.

—Grandma's Trick-or-Treat. 2002. (I Can Read Bks.). (Illus.). 48p. (J). (ps-1). pap. 3.99 (*0-06-444277-2*) HarperCollins Pubs.

McCutcheon, Marc. Grandfather's Christmas Camp. (Illus.). 32p. (J). (gr. k-3). 1997. pap. 5.95 o.p. (*0-395-86629-4*); 1995. 15.95 (*0-395-69626-7*) Houghton Mifflin Co. Trade & Reference Div. (Clarion Bks.).

McDermott, Beverly B. The Golem: A Jewish Legend. 1975. (Illus.). 48p. (J). (gr. 1-5). o.p. (*0-397-31674-7*) HarperCollins Children's Bk. Group.

McDonald, Diane. Treasure Chest. 2002. (Illus.). 34p. (J). spiral bd. 12.95 (*0-9721681-0-9*) McDonald, Diane.

McDonald, Megan. Beezy at Bat. (Illus.). 48p. (J). (gr. 1-4). 2000. mass mkt. 4.95 (*0-531-07164-2*); 1998. pap. 13.95 (*0-531-30085-4*); 1998. lib. bdg. 14.99 (*0-531-33085-0*) Scholastic, Inc. (Orchard Bks.).

—Beezy at Bat. 2000. (J). 11.10 (*0-606-20453-9*) Turtleback Bks.

McFarlane, Sheryl. Waiting for the Whales. ed. 1993. (J). (gr. 2). spiral bd. (*0-616-01720-0*) Canadian National Institute for the Blind/Institut National Canadien pour les Aveugles.

—Waiting for the Whales. rev. ed. 1992. (Illus.). 32p. (J). (gr. k-3). pap. 7.95 (*0-920501-96-6*) Orca Bk. Pubs.

—Waiting for the Whales. 1993. (Illus.). 32p. (J). (ps-3). 14.95 o.p. (*0-399-22515-3*, Philomel) Penguin Putnam Bks. for Young Readers.

—Waiting for the Whales. 1991. 13.10 (*0-606-14142-1*) Turtleback Bks.

McGill, Alice. Here We Go Round. 2002. (Illus.). 122p. (J). (gr. 2-5). 15.00 (*0-618-16064-7*) Houghton Mifflin Co.

McKay, Hilary. The Exiles. 1992. (Illus.). 208p. (J). (gr. 3-7). 17.99 o.s.i (*0-689-50555-8*, McElderry, Margaret K.) Simon & Schuster Children's Publishing.

—The Exiles at Home. 208p. (J). (gr. 4-8). 1997. (Illus.). pap. 3.99 (*0-689-81403-8*, Aladdin); 1994. 15.95 (*0-689-50610-4*, McElderry, Margaret K.) Simon & Schuster Children's Publishing.

—The Exiles at Home. 1997. 10.04 (*0-606-14202-9*) Turtleback Bks.

—The Exiles in Love. 176p. (J). (gr. 3-7). 1999. pap. 4.50 (*0-689-82013-5*, Aladdin); 1998. (Illus.). 16.00 o.s.i (*0-689-81752-5*, McElderry, Margaret K.) Simon & Schuster Children's Publishing.

—The Exiles in Love. 1999. 10.55 (*0-606-17315-3*) Turtleback Bks.

McKee, David. Who's a Clever Baby? Briley, D., ed. 1989. (Illus.). 32p. (J). (gr. 1-3). 12.95 o.p. (*0-688-08595-4*); lib. bdg. 12.88 o.p. (*0-688-08596-2*) HarperCollins Children's Bk. Group.

McKinley, Maura E. The Secret of the Eagle Feathers. 1997. (Publish-a-Book Ser.). (Illus.). 32p. (J). (gr. 1-6). lib. bdg. 22.83 (*0-8172-4436-0*) Raintree Pubs.

McLaughlin, Kirsten. The Memory Box. 2000. (Illus.). (J). 5.95 (*1-56123-136-3*, MEBC) Centering Corp.

McLeod, Elaine. Lessons from Mother Earth. 2002. (Illus.). 24p. (J). (ps-1). 15.95 (*0-88899-312-9*) Groundwood Bks. CAN. *Dist:* Publishers Group West.

McMillan, Bruce. Grandfather's Trolley. 1995. (Illus.). 32p. (J). (ps-3). 15.95 o.p. (*1-56402-633-7*) Candlewick Pr.

McQuade, Susan. Great-Grandpa. 1993. (Voyages Ser.). (Illus.). (J). 3.75 (*0-383-03622-4*) SRA/McGraw-Hill.

Melmed, Laura Krauss. The Marvelous Market on Mermaid. 1996. (Illus.). 24p. (J). (ps-3). 15.00 (*0-688-13053-4*); lib. bdg. 14.93 o.p. (*0-688-13054-2*) HarperCollins Children's Bk. Group.

Mendes, Valerie. Look at Me, Grandma! 2001. (Illus.). 32p. (J). (ps-1). pap. 15.95 (*0-439-29654-4*, Chicken Hse., The) Scholastic, Inc.

Menken, John. Grandpa's Gizmos. 1992. (Illus.). 32p. (J). (ps-1). pap. 5.49 (*0-89084-663-4*, 063693) Jones, Bob Univ. Pr.

Metzger, Lois. Missing Girls. (YA). (gr. 5-9). 2001. 192p. pap. 5.99 o.p. (*0-14-131086-3*); 1999. 208p. 15.99 o.s.i (*0-670-87777-8*) Penguin Putnam Bks. for Young Readers.

Meyer, Carolyn. Jubilee Journey. 1997. 288p. (YA). (gr. 5-9). 13.00 (*0-15-201377-6*); pap. 6.00 (*0-15-201591-4*) Harcourt Children's Bks. (Gulliver Bks.).

—Jubilee Journey. 1997. 12.05 (*0-606-14244-4*) Turtleback Bks.

Michelson, Richard. Too Young for Yiddish. 2002. (Illus.). 32p. (J). (gr. k-4). 15.95 (*0-88106-118-2*) Charlesbridge Publishing, Inc.

Miller, Joyce. A Home for Grandma. 1983. (Illus.). 280p. (YA). (gr. 7-10). 10.35 (*0-7399-0105-2*, 2282) Rod & Staff Pubs., Inc.

Miller, Rose. The Old Barn. 1992. (Publish-a-Book Ser.). (Illus.). 32p. (J). (gr. 1-6). lib. bdg. 22.83 (*0-8114-3581-4*) Raintree Pubs.

Miller, Wayne H. Granny "E" Smith, Denise M., ed. 1995. (Sandy Dallas Series of Books for Children, Parents, & Teachers). (Illus.). 100p. (Orig.). (YA). (gr. 6-12). pap. text 4.95 (*0-9634735-3-0*) Hiram Charles Publishing.

Mills, Claudia. Gus & Grandpa, RS. (Gus & Grandpa Ser.). (Illus.). 48p. (J). (gr. 1-3). 1999. pap. 4.95 (*0-374-42847-6*, Sunburst); 1997. 13.00 (*0-374-32824-2*, Farrar, Straus & Giroux (BYR)) Farrar, Straus & Giroux.

—Gus & Grandpa. 1999. 11.10 (*0-606-16474-X*) Turtleback Bks.

—Gus & Grandpa & Show & Tell, RS. 2000. (Gus & Grandpa Ser.). (Illus.). 48p. (J). (gr. 1-3). 13.00 (*0-374-32819-6*, Farrar, Straus & Giroux (BYR)) Farrar, Straus & Giroux.

—Gus & Grandpa & the Christmas Cookies, RS. 1997. (Gus & Grandpa Ser.). (Illus.). 48p. (J). (gr. 1-3). 13.00 o.p. (*0-374-32823-4*, Farrar, Straus & Giroux (BYR)) Farrar, Straus & Giroux.

—Gus & Grandpa & the Halloween Costume, RS. 2002. (Gus & Grandpa Ser.). (Illus.). 48p. (J). (gr. 1-3). 15.00 (*0-374-32816-1*, Farrar, Straus & Giroux (BYR)) Farrar, Straus & Giroux.

—Gus & Grandpa & the Piano Lesson, RS. 2004. (J). (*0-374-32814-5*, Farrar, Straus & Giroux (BYR)) Farrar, Straus & Giroux.

—Gus & Grandpa & the Two-Wheeled Bike, RS. 1999. (Gus & Grandpa Ser.). (Illus.). 48p. (J). (gr. 1-3). 15.00 (*0-374-32821-8*, Farrar, Straus & Giroux (BYR)) Farrar, Straus & Giroux.

—Gus & Grandpa & the Two Wheeled Bike, RS. 2001. pap. 4.95 (*0-374-42816-6*, Sunburst) Farrar, Straus & Giroux.

—Gus & Grandpa at Basketball, RS. 2001. (Illus.). 48p. (J). (gr. 1-3). 14.00 (*0-374-32818-8*, Farrar, Straus & Giroux (BYR)) Farrar, Straus & Giroux.

—Gus & Grandpa at the Hospital, RS. (Sunburst Bks.). (Illus.). 48p. (J). 2001. (gr. 1-3). pap. 4.95 (*0-374-42812-3*, Sunburst); 1998. (ps-3). 13.00 (*0-374-32827-7*, Farrar, Straus & Giroux (BYR)) Farrar, Straus & Giroux.

—Gus & Grandpa at the Hospital. 2001. (Illus.). (J). 11.10 (*0-606-20686-8*) Turtleback Bks.

—Gus & Grandpa Go Fishing, RS. 2003. (Gus & Grandpa Ser.). (Illus.). 48p. (J). 15.00 (*0-374-32815-3*, Farrar, Straus & Giroux (BYR)) Farrar, Straus & Giroux.

—Gus & Grandpa Ride the Train, RS. (Gus & Grandpa Ser.). (Illus.). (J). (ps-3). 2000. 48p. pap. 4.95 (*0-374-42813-1*, Sunburst); 1998. 47p. 13.00 o.p. (*0-374-32826-9*, Farrar, Straus & Giroux (BYR)) Farrar, Straus & Giroux.

—Gus & Grandpa Ride the Train. 2000. (Illus.). (J). 11.10 (*0-606-18133-4*) Turtleback Bks.

—Gus & Grandpa Show & Tell, RS. 2002. (Gus & Grandpa Ser.). (Illus.). 48p. (J). pap. 5.95 (*0-374-42848-4*, Sunburst) Farrar, Straus & Giroux.

Milstein, Linda B. Miami-Nanny Stories. 1994. (Illus.). (J). 16.00 o.p. (*0-688-11151-3*); lib. bdg. 15.93 o.p. (*0-688-11152-1*) Morrow/Avon. (Morrow, William & Co.).

Minchella, Nancy. Mama Will Be Home Soon. 2003. (Illus.). 32p. (J). pap. 15.95 (*0-439-38491-5*) Scholastic, Inc.

Mitchell, Lori. Different Just Like Me. (Illus.). 32p. (J). (ps-3). 2001. pap. 6.95 (*1-57091-490-7*); 1999. 15.95 (*0-88106-975-2*) Charlesbridge Publishing, Inc. (Talewinds).

Mitchell, Margaree King. Granddaddy's Gift. 1998. 12.10 (*0-606-13449-2*) Turtleback Bks.

Mochizuki, Chiemi. The Promise. Randle, Walt R., ed. 2003. (Illus.). 38p. (J). (gr. 3-6). 16.99 (*0-9720691-0-0*) Berkeley Major Publishing.

Mock, Dorothy K. Springtime Special: The Good News Kids Learn about Patience. 1993. (Good News Kids Ser.). (Illus.). 32p. (Orig.). (J). (ps-2). pap. 4.99 o.s.i (*0-570-04736-6*, 56-1693) Concordia Publishing Hse.

Moffatt, Frank. Grandma Ollie. 1995. (Jam Roll Picture Bks.). (Illus.). 32p. (J). pap. 10.95 (*0-7022-2850-8*) Univ. of Queensland Pr. AUS. *Dist:* International Specialized Bk. Services.

Mollel, Tololwa M. Kele's Secret. 1997. (Illus.). 32p. (J). 14.99 o.s.i (*0-525-67500-0*, Dutton) Dutton/Plume.

—Kele's Secret. 2000. (Illus.). (J). pap. 5.99 (*0-14-055649-4*, Puffin Bks.) Penguin Putnam Bks. for Young Readers.

Momaday, N. Scott. Circle of Wonder: A Native American Christmas Story. 1993. (Illus.). 42p. (J). (gr. 4-7). 17.95 o.p. (*0-940666-32-4*) Clear Light Pubs.

—Circle of Wonder: A Native American Christmas Story. 1999. (Illus.). 44p. (gr. 4-7). 19.95 (*0-8263-2149-6*) Univ. of New Mexico Pr.

Monjo, F. N. Grand Papa & Ellen Aroon. 1976. 64p. (J). (gr. k-6). reprint ed. pap. 0.95 o.s.i (*0-440-43004-6*, Yearling) Random Hse. Children's Bks.

Montaufier, Poupa. One Summer at Grandmother's House. 1985. Tr. of Ete chez grand-mere. (Illus.). 32p. (J). (gr. 2-5). lib. bdg. 12.95 o.p. (*0-87614-238-2*, Carolrhoda Bks.) Lerner Publishing Group.

Moon, Nicola. Lucy's Picture. (Illus.). 32p. 1997. pap. 5.99 o.s.i (*0-14-055769-5*); 1995. (J). 15.99 o.s.i (*0-8037-1833-0*, Dial Bks. for Young Readers) Penguin Putnam Bks. for Young Readers.

—My Most Favorite Thing. 2001. (Illus.). 32p. (J). 15.99 o.s.i (*0-525-46780-7*, Dutton Children's Bks.) Penguin Putnam Bks. for Young Readers.

Moore, Brenda M. Together on the Mountain. 1998. (Illus.). 32p. (J). (ps-3). 14.95 (*1-890326-14-3*) First Story Pr.

Moore, Elaine. Deep River. 1994. (Illus.). (J). pap. 15.00 o.s.i (*0-671-87278-8*, Simon & Schuster Children's Publishing) Simon & Schuster Children's Publishing.

—Grammy, Do You Love Me? 1995. (J). (ps-2). 7.95 o.p. (*0-681-00442-8*) Borders Pr.

—Grandma's Garden. 1994. (J). (ps-3). 15.00 (*0-688-08693-4*); (Illus.). 32p. lib. bdg. 14.93 o.p. (*0-688-08694-2*) HarperCollins Children's Bk. Group.

—Grandma's House. 1985. (Illus.). 32p. (J). (gr. k up). 16.00 o.p. (*0-688-04115-9*); lib. bdg. 15.93 o.p. (*0-688-04116-7*) HarperCollins Children's Bk. Group.

—Grandma's Promise. 1988. (Illus.). (J). (gr. k-3). 16.00 o.p. (*0-688-06740-9*); lib. bdg. 15.93 o.p. (*0-688-06741-7*) HarperCollins Children's Bk. Group.

—Grandma's Smile. 1995. (Illus.). 32p. (J). (ps up). 16.00 (*0-688-11075-4*); lib. bdg. 15.93 o.p. (*0-688-11076-2*) HarperCollins Children's Bk. Group.

Mora, Pat. Pablo's Tree. 1994. (Illus.). 32p. (J). (ps-1). 16.95 (*0-02-767401-0*, Simon & Schuster Children's Publishing) Simon & Schuster Children's Publishing.

Moranville, Sharelle Byars. Over the River, ERS. 2002. 192p. (YA). (gr. 4-9). 16.95 (*0-8050-7049-4*, Holt, Henry & Co. Bks. For Young Readers) Holt, Henry & Co.

Morgan, Mary. Night Ride. (J). 1999. (Illus.). 16.00 (*0-689-80545-4*); 1997. 14.95 (*0-02-767460-6*) Simon & Schuster Children's Publishing. (Atheneum).

Morning, Barbara. Grandfather's Shirt. Johnson, Joy, ed. 1996. (Illus.). 16p. (J). (ps-2). pap. 4.95 (*1-56123-074-X*) Centering Corp.

Morpurgo, Michael. Colly's Barn. 2002. (Yellow Bananas Ser.). (Illus.). 48p. (J). (gr. 3-4). pap. 4.95 (*0-7787-0978-7*); lib. bdg. 19.96 (*0-7787-0932-9*) Crabtree Publishing Co.

—Escape from Shangri-La. 1998. 192p. (J). (gr. 5-8). 16.99 o.s.i (*0-399-23311-3*, Philomel) Penguin Putnam Bks. for Young Readers.

—Farm Boy. 1999. (Illus.). 74p. (YA). pap. 16.95 (*1-86205-192-5*) Pavilion Bks., Ltd. GBR. *Dist:* Trafalgar Square.

Moses, Antoinette. Happy Granny. 2000. (Penguin Young Reader Ser.). (C). pap. 5.33 (*0-582-34413-1*) Longman Publishing Group.

Moses, Shelia P. The Legend of Buddy Bush. 2004. (Illus.). 224p. (YA). 15.95 (*0-689-85839-6*, McElderry, Margaret K.) Simon & Schuster Children's Publishing.

Mosher, Eunice D. Olympics, 2004? Ask Yia Yia & Pa Pou. Caso, Adolph, ed. 1st ed. 1998. (Illus.). 32p. (J). (ps-3). pap. 9.95 (*0-8283-2033-0*) Branden Bks.

Mosher, Richard. Zazoo. 2001. 224p. (YA). (gr. 7 up). tchr. ed. 16.00 (*0-618-13534-0*, Clarion Bks.) Houghton Mifflin Co. Trade & Reference Div.

Moss, Marissa. In America. 1994. (Illus.). 32p. (J). 14.99 o.s.i (*0-525-45152-8*, Dutton Children's Bks.) Penguin Putnam Bks. for Young Readers.

—The Ugly Menorah, RS. (Illus.). 32p. (J). (ps-3). 2000. pap. 5.95 (*0-374-48047-8*, Sunburst); 1996. 14.00 o.p. (*0-374-38027-9*, Farrar, Straus & Giroux (BYR)) Farrar, Straus & Giroux.

Most, Bernard. Catch Me If You Can! 1999. (Green Light Readers Ser.). (Illus.). 20p. (J). (gr. 1-3). pap. 3.95 o.s.i (*0-15-202001-2*, Green Light Readers) Harcourt Children's Bks.

Mower, Nancy A. I Visit My Tutu & Grandma. 1984. (Treasury of Children's Hawaiian Stories Ser.). (Illus.). (J). (ps). 8.95 (*0-916630-41-2*) Press Pacifica, Ltd.

Mundt, Brian. Jacob's Collection. 1997. (Publish-a-Book Ser.). (Illus.). 32p. (J). (gr. 1-6). lib. bdg. 22.83 (*0-8172-4433-6*) Raintree Pubs.

Munsch, Robert. Lighthouse: A Story of Remembrance. (J). 2004. pap. 5.95 (*0-439-49032-4*); 2003. (Illus.). 13.95 (*0-439-49031-6*) Scholastic, Inc.

Murphy, Claire Rudolf. Gold Star Sister. 176p. (J). (gr. 5-9). 1996. pap. 4.99 o.s.i (*0-14-037744-1*, Puffin Bks.); 1994. 14.99 o.p. (*0-525-67492-6*, Dutton Children's Bks.) Penguin Putnam Bks. for Young Readers.

Murphy, Jill. The Last Noo-Noo. 1995. (Illus.). 32p. (J). (ps up). 14.95 o.p. (*1-56402-581-0*) Candlewick Pr.

Murrow, Liza K. Dancing on the Table. 1990. (Illus.). 128p. (J). (gr. 3-7). 13.95 o.p. (*0-8234-0808-6*) Holiday Hse., Inc.

Myers, Bernice. Off to Grandpa's. 1994. (Whole-Language Big Bks.). (Illus.). 16p. (Orig.). (J). (ps-2). pap. 16.95 (*1-56784-068-X*) Newbridge Educational Publishing.

Nagda, Ann Whitehead. Meow Means Mischief. 2003. (Illus.). 92p. (J). (gr. 2-5). tchr. ed. 15.95 (*0-8234-1786-7*) Holiday Hse., Inc.

Nagy, David. Fear (Grandpa's Story) 1996. (Illus.). 24p. (J). (gr. 1-3). pap. 7.00 o.p. (*0-8059-3941-5*) Dorrance Publishing Co., Inc.

Namioka, Lensey. April & the Dragon Lady. 1994. 224p. (YA). (gr. 7 up). 10.95 (*0-15-276644-8*) Harcourt Children's Bks.

—April & the Dragon Lady. 1994. 12.05 (*0-606-06182-7*) Turtleback Bks.

Nanushkid, Fran. Grandma Beatrice Brings Spring to Minsk. Date not set. (J). lib. bdg. (*0-7868-2147-7*) Hyperion Bks. for Children.

—Grandma Beatrice Brings Spring to Minsk. 1999. (J). (*0-7868-0175-1*) Hyperion Pr.

Napoli, Donna Jo. April Flowers. 2000. (Aladdin Angelwings Ser.: No. 7). (Illus.). 80p. (J). (gr. 2-5). pap. 3.99 (*0-689-83207-9*, Aladdin) Simon & Schuster Children's Publishing.

—April Flowers. 2000. (Illus.). (J). 10.14 (*0-606-17910-0*) Turtleback Bks.

Naylor, Phyllis Reynolds. Ice. 256p. 1998. (J). (gr. 7-12). pap. 4.99 (*0-689-81872-6*, Simon Pulse); 1995. (YA). (gr. 4-7). 16.00 (*0-689-80005-3*, Atheneum) Simon & Schuster Children's Publishing.

—Ice. 1998. (J). 11.04 (*0-606-12970-7*) Turtleback Bks.

Neasi, Barbara J. Escucheme. 2002. (Spanish Rookie Readers Ser.). (Illus.). (J). (gr. k-2). pap. 4.95 (*0-516-26314-5*, Children's Pr.) Scholastic Library Publishing.

—Escucheme. 2001. (Rookie Espanol Ser.). (SPA., Illus.). 32p. (J). (gr. k-2). lib. bdg. 15.00 (*0-516-22358-5*, Children's Pr.) Scholastic Library Publishing.

—Listen to Me. (Rookie Readers Ser.). (Illus.). 32p. (J). 1986. (ps-3). mass mkt. 4.95 (*0-516-42072-0*); rev. ed. 1986. (gr. 1-2). lib. bdg. 19.00 (*0-516-02072-2*); 2nd rev. ed. 2001. (gr. 1-2). pap. 4.95 (*0-516-25970-9*) Scholastic Library Publishing. (Children's Pr.).

—Listen to Me Level C. rev. ed. 2001. (Rookie Readers Ser.). (Illus.). 32p. (J). (gr. 1-2). lib. bdg. 19.00 (*0-516-22154-X*, Children's Pr.) Scholastic Library Publishing.

Neitzel, Shirley. The Bag I'm Taking to Grandma's. 1998. (Illus.). 32p. (J). (ps-3). pap. 5.99 (*0-688-15840-4*, Harper Trophy) HarperCollins Children's Bk. Group.

—The Bag I'm Taking to Grandma's. 1998. (J). 11.10 (*0-606-13176-0*) Turtleback Bks.

Nelson, Lynda M. The Little Red Buckets: A Story of Family & Giving. 1997. 128p. (J). pap. 13.00 (*0-399-52357-X*, Perigee Bks.) Berkley Publishing Group.

Nelson, S. D. The Star People. 2003. (Illus.). 40p. (J). (gr. k-3). 14.95 (*0-8109-4584-3*) Abrams, Harry N., Inc.

Nelson, Vaunda M. Always Gramma. 1988. (Illus.). 32p. (J). (ps-3). 14.95 o.p. (*0-399-21542-5*, G. P. Putnam's Sons) Penguin Putnam Bks. for Young Readers.

Nethery, Mary. Hannah & Jack. 1995. (Illus.). (J). text 16.00 (*0-02-768125-4*, Simon & Schuster Children's Publishing) Simon & Schuster Children's Publishing.

Newbery, Linda. Sisterland. 2004. 384p. (J). (gr. 7). 15.95 (*0-385-75026-9*); lib. bdg. 17.99 (*0-385-75035-8*) Random Hse. Children's Bks. (Fickling, David Bks.).

Newman, Dolores A. Papa, How Do You Know? 2000. (Illus.). 32p. (J). pap. 9.95 (*0-9676438-0-5*) Sanctuary Pr.

Newman, Leslea. Matzo Ball Moon. 1998. 15.00 (*0-395-71519-9*) Houghton Mifflin Co.

—Matzo Ball Moon. 1998. (Illus.). 32p. (J). (ps-3). lib. bdg., tchr. ed. 15.00 (*0-395-71530-X*, Clarion Bks.) Houghton Mifflin Co. Trade & Reference Div.

—Remember That. 1996. (Illus.). 32p. (J). (ps-3). tchr. ed. 14.95 o.s.i (*0-395-66156-0*, Clarion Bks.) Houghton Mifflin Co. Trade & Reference Div.

Nicholas, Evangeline. These Old Rags. 1997. (Illus.). (J). (*0-7802-8021-0*) Wright Group, The.

Nicholetti, Terry & Campbell, Annie. Noralee's Adventures on Planet Ifwee. 2002. pap. 10.95 (*0-9716488-0-8*) Goldstar Magic.

Nickle, John. TV Rex. 2001. (Illus.). 40p. (J). (gr. k-2). pap. 15.95 (*0-439-12043-8*) Scholastic, Inc.

Nicolai, Margaret. Kitaq Goes Ice Fishing. (Illus.). 32p. (gr. k up). 2002. (YA). pap. 8.95 (*0-88240-569-1*); 1998. (J). 15.95 o.p. (*0-88240-504-7*) Graphic Arts Ctr. Publishing Co. (Alaska Northwest Bks.).

Nightingale, Sandy. Cider Apples. 1996. (Illus.). 32p. (J). (ps-3). 15.00 (*0-15-201244-3*) Harcourt Trade Pubs.

Nister, Ernest. Visiting Grandma: A Miniature Pop-Up & Pull-the-Tab Book. 1989. (Illus.). 10p. (J). (ps-3). 6.95 o.s.i (*0-399-21695-2*, Philomel) Penguin Putnam Bks. for Young Readers.

Nixon, Joan Lowery. The Gift. 1983. (Illus.). 96p. (J). (gr. 4-7). lib. bdg. 13.95 o.s.i (*0-02-768160-2*, Simon & Schuster Children's Publishing) Simon & Schuster Children's Publishing.

Nobisso, Josephine. Grandma's Scrapbook. 1991. (J). (Illus.). 12.95 (*0-671-74976-5*); pap. 12.95 o.s.i (*0-88138-137-3*) Simon & Schuster Children's Publishing. (Simon & Schuster Children's Publishing).

—Grandpa Loved. 2nd rev. ed. 2000. (Illus.). 32p. (J). (gr. 2 up). reprint ed. 16.95 (*0-940112-01-9*); pap. 8.95 (*0-940112-04-3*) Gingerbread Hse.

—Grandpa Loved. 1991. (J). pap. 14.00 o.p. (*0-671-75265-0*); (Illus.). 32p. 12.95 o.s.i (*0-88138-119-5*) Simon & Schuster Children's Publishing. (Simon & Schuster Children's Publishing).

—Grandpa Loved. 1989. (Illus.). E-Book (*1-59019-008-4*); E-Book (*1-59019-010-6*); E-Book (*1-59019-009-2*) ipicturebooks, LLC.

Nodar, Carmen M. Abuelita's Paradise. Mathews, Judith, ed. 1992. (Illus.). 32p. (J). (ps-3). lib. bdg. 14.95 o.p. (*0-8075-0129-8*) Whitman, Albert & Co.

Nodar, Carmen S. El Paraiso de Abuelita. Mathews, Judith, ed. Mlawer, Teresa, tr. 1992. (SPA., Illus.). 32p. (J). (gr. k-3). lib. bdg. 14.95 o.p. (*0-8075-6346-3*, WT4618) Whitman, Albert & Co.

Noll, Sally. Lucky Morning. 1994. (Illus.). 32p. (J). (ps up). 14.00 o.p. (*0-688-12474-7*); lib. bdg. 13.93 o.p. (*0-688-12475-5*) HarperCollins Children's Bk. Group. (Greenwillow Bks.).

Nomura, Takaaki. Grandpa's Town. Stinchecum, Amanda M., tr. from JPN. (Illus.). 32p. (J). (ps-3). 1995. pap. 7.95 (*0-916291-57-X*); 1991. 13.95 o.p. (*0-916291-36-7*) Kane/Miller Bk. Pubs.

Nozick, Betsy. Grandma & Me & Her Secret Recipe. 2000. (Illus.). 32p. (J). 16.95 (*1-57168-473-5*, Eakin Pr.) Eakin Pr.

Numeroff, Laura Joffe. What Grandmas Do Best. 2001. (Illus.). 24p. (J). 6.95 (*0-689-84700-9*, Simon & Schuster Children's Publishing) Simon & Schuster Children's Publishing.

—What Grandmas Do Best, What Grandpas Do Best. 2000. (Illus.). (gr. k-3). 36p. per. 14.00 (*0-689-83491-8*); 40p. (J). 14.00 (*0-689-80552-7*) Simon & Schuster Children's Publishing. (Simon & Schuster Children's Publishing).

—What Grandpas Do Best. 2001. (Illus.). 24p. (J). 6.95 (*0-689-84701-7*, Simon & Schuster Children's Publishing) Simon & Schuster Children's Publishing.

Nye, Naomi S. Benito's Dream Bottle. 1995. (Illus.). 32p. (J). (ps-3). text 15.00 (*0-02-768467-9*, Simon & Schuster Children's Publishing) Simon & Schuster Children's Publishing.

—Sitti's Secrets. 1994. (Illus.). 32p. (J). (ps-3). mass mkt. 16.95 (*0-02-768460-1*, Simon & Schuster Children's Publishing) Simon & Schuster Children's Publishing.

Oberman, Sheldon. Always Prayer Shawl. 1997. (Picture Puffin Ser.). (Illus.). 40p. (J). (ps-3). pap. 6.99 (*0-14-056157-9*) Penguin Putnam Bks. for Young Readers.

—Always Prayer Shawl. 1997. (Picture Puffin Ser.). (J). 13.14 (*0-606-11034-8*) Turtleback Bks.

—Always Prayer Shawl. 1999. 40p. (J). pap. 5.99 (*0-14-038214-3*) Viking Penguin.

O'Callahan, Jay. Tulips. 1996. (Illus.). 28p. (J). (gr. 1-5). 15.95 (*1-56145-134-7*) Peachtree Pubs., Ltd.

—Tulips. 1992. (Illus.). 28p. (J). (gr. k up). pap. 14.95 o.p. (*0-88708-223-8*, Simon & Schuster Children's Publishing) Simon & Schuster Children's Publishing.

Ogburn, Jacqueline K. The Jukebox Man. 1998. (Illus.). 32p. (J). 15.89 o.s.i (*0-8037-1430-0*); 15.99 o.s.i (*0-8037-1429-7*) Penguin Putnam Bks. for Young Readers. (Dial Bks. for Young Readers).

Ogden, David. Dreambirds. 1997. (Illus.). 32p. (YA). (ps up). 16.95 (*0-935699-09-0*) Illumination Arts Publishing Co., Inc.

Oke, Janette. Making Memories. 1999. (Illus.). 32p. (J). (ps-3). 14.99 (*0-7642-2190-6*) Bethany Hse. Pubs.

Okimoto, Jean Davies. Take a Chance, Gramps! 1996. 188p. (J). (gr. 4-7). mass mkt. 3.99 (*0-8125-4323-8*, Tor Bks.) Doherty, Tom Assocs., LLC.

—Take a Chance, Gramps!, Vol. 1. 1990. (J). (gr. 4-7). 15.95 o.p. (*0-316-63812-9*, Joy Street Bks.) Little Brown & Co.

—Take a Chance, Gramps! 1996. (J). 10.04 (*0-606-12531-0*) Turtleback Bks.

Older, Effin. My Two Grandmothers. 2000. (Illus.). 32p. (J). (ps-2). 16.00 (*0-15-200785-7*) Harcourt Children's Bks.

Oldfield, Pamela. Simon's Extra Gran. 1976. (Stepping Stones Ser.). (Illus.). 24p. (J). (gr. k-3). 7.00 o.p. (*0-516-03591-6*, Children's Pr.) Scholastic Library Publishing.

Olshan, Matthew. Finn. 2001. 245p. (YA). (gr. 8-12). 19.95 (*1-890862-13-4*) Bancroft Pr.

—Finn: Novel. 2001. 245p. (YA). (gr. 8-12). pap. 14.95 (*1-890862-14-2*) Bancroft Pr.

Olson, Arielle N. Hurry Home Grandma. 1992. (J). pap. 4.99 o.s.i (*0-14-054760-6*, Dutton Children's Bks.) Penguin Putnam Bks. for Young Readers.

—Hurry Home, Grandma! 1990. (Unicorn Paperbacks Ser.). (Illus.). 32p. (J). (ps-1). pap. 3.95 o.p. (*0-525-44650-8*, Dutton Children's Bks.) Penguin Putnam Bks. for Young Readers.

Onyefulu, Ifeoma. Grandfather's Work: A Traditional Healer in Nigeria. 1998. (Around the World Ser.). (Illus.). 32p. (gr. 2-4). lib. bdg. 22.90 o.p. (*0-7613-0412-6*) Millbrook Pr., Inc.

Oppenheim, Shulamith Levey. Fireflies for Nathan. 1994. (Illus.). (J). 16.00 (*0-688-12147-0*); lib. bdg. 15.93 o.p. (*0-688-12148-9*) Morrow/Avon. (Morrow, William & Co.).

—Fireflies for Nathan. 1996. (Picture Puffin Bks.). (Illus.). 32p. (J). (ps-3). pap. 4.99 o.p. (*0-14-055782-2*, Puffin Bks.) Penguin Putnam Bks. for Young Readers.

—Waiting for Noah. 1990. (Charlotte Zolotow Bk.). (Illus.). 32p. (J). (ps-2). 12.95 (*0-06-024633-2*); lib. bdg. 12.89 o.p. (*0-06-024634-0*) HarperCollins Children's Bk. Group.

—What Is the Moon Full Of? 2003. (Illus.). 32p. (J). (ps-3). 14.95 (*1-56397-479-7*) Boyds Mills Pr.

—What Is the Moon Full Of? 2000. 13.14 (*0-606-18793-6*) Turtleback Bks.

Orgel, Doris. Bunny & Grandma. 1999. (Illus.). (J). pap. (*0-14-054293-0*) NAL.

—The Mulberry Music. 1979. (Illus.). 144p. (J). (gr. 4-7). pap. 1.95 o.p. (*0-06-440104-9*) HarperCollins Pubs.

Orlev, Uri. La Abuela Tejedora. 1997. (SPA., Illus.). (YA). 7.95 (*968-16-5442-0*, FC4142) Fondo de Cultura Economica MEX. *Dist:* Continental Bk. Co., Inc., Lectorum Pubns., Inc.

Orr, Katherine S. My Grandpa & the Sea. (Picture Bks.). (Illus.). 32p. (J). (ps-3). 1991. pap. 5.95 (*0-87614-525-X*); 1990. lib. bdg. 19.95 (*0-87614-409-1*) Lerner Publishing Group. (Carolrhoda Bks.).

Orr, Wendy. Ark in the Park, ERS. 2000. (Redfeather Book Ser.). (Illus.). 78p. (J). (gr. k-5). 15.95 (*0-8050-6221-1*, Holt, Henry & Co. Bks. For Young Readers) Holt, Henry & Co.

Ortega, Cristina. Los Ojos del Tejedor: Through the Eyes of the Weaver. 1997. (Illus.). 64p. (YA). (gr. 4-7). pap. 14.95 (*0-940666-81-2*) Clear Light Pubs.

Ortiz, Mamie. My Grandfather & the Boys. 1982. (Illus.). 14p. (Orig.). (J). (ps-7). pap. 3.75 o.p. (*0-915347-03-2*) Pueblo of Acoma Pr.

Orzak, Carol. Grandpa & the Boys. 2000. (Illus.). 24p. (J). spiral bd. (*0-9679747-0-4*) Details Creative.

Ossorio, Nelson A., et al. Through Grandpa's Eyes. 1994. (We Are All Whole Ser.). (Illus.). 60p. (J). (gr. 4-6). pap. 6.95 o.s.i (*1-56721-051-1*) 25th Century Pr.

Outlet Book Company Staff. Granny Bouncer's Rescue. 1984. (Tales from Fern Hollow Ser.). (Illus.). 22p. (J). (ps-1). 1.99 o.s.i (*0-517-45798-9*) Random Hse. Value Publishing.

—Trip to Granny Rumbletummy. 1987. 1.99 o.s.i (*0-517-64963-2*) Crown Publishing Group.

Overstreet, Marcia Cate. A Day at Gramma's. 2001. (Illus.). 64p. 13.99 (*0-8254-3471-8*) Kregel Pubns.

Owens, Vivian W. The Rosebush Witch. 1996. (Illus.). 96p. (J). (gr. 3-9). pap. 8.95 (*0-9623839-4-5*) Eschar Pubns.

Oxenbury, Helen. En Casa de los Abuelos (At Grandparents' House) (SPA.). 24p. 7.50 (*84-261-2066-0*) Juventud, Editorial ESP. *Dist:* AIMS International Bks., Inc.

—Grandma & Grandpa. (Out & About Bks.). (Illus.). (J). (ps-1). 1993. 240p. pap. 3.99 o.s.i (*0-14-054978-1*, Puffin Bks.); 1984. 3.95 o.p. (*0-8037-0128-4*, 0383-120, Dial Bks. for Young Readers) Penguin Putnam Bks. for Young Readers.

—Grandma & Grandpa. 1993. (Out-and-About Bks.). (J). 9.19 o.p. (*0-606-05849-4*) Turtleback Bks.

Oxford, Mariesa. Going to Grandma's. 1992. (Publish-a-Book Contest Ser.). (Illus.). (J). lib. bdg. 22.83 o.p. (*0-8114-3575-X*) Raintree Pubs.

Padoan, Gianni. Remembering Grandad. 1989. (Facing Up Ser.). (Illus.). 28p. (J). (ps-3). 11.99 (*0-85953-311-5*) Child's Play of England GBR. *Dist:* Child's Play-International.

Pak, Soyung. Dear Juno. (Illus.). 32p. (J). (ps-2). 2001. pap. 5.99 (*0-14-230017-9*); 1999. 15.99 (*0-670-88252-6*) Penguin Putnam Bks. for Young Readers.

Palacios, Argentina. A Christmas Surprise for Chabelita. 1993. 10.10 (*0-606-06278-5*) Turtleback Bks.

Pallotta, Jerry. The Hershey's Milk Chocolate Multiplication Book. 2002. (Illus.). 32p. (J). (gr. 1-4). pap. 14.95 (*0-439-23623-1*) Scholastic, Inc.

Papademetriou, Lisa. Lucky Me! 1999. (Real Kids Readers Ser.). (Illus.). 48p. (gr. 1-3). (J). pap. 4.99 (*0-7613-2096-2*); 18.90 (*0-7613-2071-7*) Millbrook Pr., Inc.

—Lucky Me! 1999. (J). 10.14 (*0-606-19160-7*) Turtleback Bks.

—Lucky Me! 1999. (*1-58824-805-4*); E-Book (*1-58824-475-X*); E-Book (*1-58824-723-6*) ipicturebooks, LLC.

Paraskevas, Betty. Monster Beach. 1995. (Illus.). 32p. (J). (ps-3). 15.00 o.s.i (*0-15-292882-0*) Harcourt Trade Pubs.

Parish, Peggy. Granny & the Desperadoes. 1996. (Ready-to-Read Ser.: Level 2). (Illus.). 48p. (J). (ps-3). mass mkt. 3.99 (*0-689-80877-1*, Aladdin); mass mkt. 14.00 (*0-689-80878-X*, Simon & Schuster Children's Publishing) Simon & Schuster Children's Publishing.

—Granny & the Desperadoes. 1996. (Ready-to-Read Ser.). (J). 10.14 (*0-606-09351-6*) Turtleback Bks.

Park, Barbara. The Graduation of Jake Moon. unabr. ed. (gr. 4-6). 2001. 115p. (J). pap. 28.00 incl. audio (*0-8072-8722-9*); 2000. audio 18.00 (*0-8072-6160-2*, YA247CX); 2000. audio 18.00 (*0-8072-6160-2*, YA247CX) Random Hse. Audio Publishing Group. (Listening Library).

—The Graduation of Jake Moon. 128p. (J). (gr. 4-6). 2000. (Illus.). 15.00 (*0-689-83912-X*, Atheneum/Anne Schwartz Bks.); 2002. reprint ed. pap. 4.99 (*0-689-83985-5*, Aladdin) Simon & Schuster Children's Publishing.

Parrish, Shelley Berlin. Sharing Grandma's Gift. 2000. (Illus.). 40p. (J). 18.00 (*0-89716-936-0*) Peanut Butter Publishing.

Paterson, Diane. Hey, Cowboy! 1983. (Illus.). 48p. (J). (gr. 4-7). 9.95 o.p. (*0-394-85341-5*); lib. bdg. 9.99 o.p. (*0-394-95341-X*) Random Hse. Children's Bks. (Knopf Bks. for Young Readers).

Paterson, Katherine. The Same Stuff as Stars. 2004. 288p. (J). pap. 5.99 (*0-06-055712-5*, Harper Trophy) HarperCollins Children's Bk. Group.

Paton Walsh, Jill. Goldengrove, RS. 1985. (Sunburst Ser.). 130p. (YA). (gr. 7 up). pap. 3.50 o.p. (*0-374-42587-6*, Sunburst) Farrar, Straus & Giroux.

—Goldengrove. l.t. ed. 1973. (J). lib. bdg. 6.50 o.p. (*0-8161-6104-6*, Macmillan Reference USA) Gale Group.

—When Grandma Came. (Illus.). 32p. (J). (ps-3). 1994. pap. 4.99 o.s.i (*0-14-054327-9*, Puffin Bks.); 1992. 13.00 o.p. (*0-670-83581-1*, Viking Children's Bks.) Penguin Putnam Bks. for Young Readers.

—When I Was Little Like You. 1997. (Illus.). 32p. (J). (ps-3). 13.99 o.p. (*0-670-87608-9*, Viking Children's Bks.) Penguin Putnam Bks. for Young Readers.

Patterson, Nancy R. The Christmas Cup. 1989. (Illus.). 80p. (J). (gr. 3-5). mass mkt. 15.99 o.p. (*0-531-08421-3*); 15.95 o.p. (*0-531-05821-2*) Scholastic, Inc. (Orchard Bks.).

Paul, Ann Whitford. Everything to Spend the Night from A to Z. 1999. (Illus.). 40p. (J). (ps-2). pap. 15.95 o.p. (*0-7894-2511-4*, D K Ink) Dorling Kindersley Publishing, Inc.

Paulsen, Gary. Alida's Song. 1999. 96p. (gr. 5-9). text 15.95 (*0-385-32586-X*, Delacorte Pr.) Dell Publishing.

—Alida's Song. 2001. 96p. (gr. 5 up). pap. text 5.50 (*0-440-41474-1*, Yearling) Random Hse. Children's Bks.

—Alida's Song. 2001. (J). 11.65 (*0-606-21019-9*) Turtleback Bks.

—The Cookcamp. 1992. 128p. (gr. 5-6). pap. text 4.50 o.s.i (*0-440-40704-4*, Yearling); (J). pap. o.s.i (*0-440-80301-2*, Dell Books for Young Readers) Random Hse. Children's Bks.

—The Cookcamp. 128p. (J). 2003. pap. 4.99 (*0-439-52357-5*, Scholastic Paperbacks); 1991. (gr. 2-6). pap. 15.95 (*0-531-05927-8*, Orchard Bks.); 1991. (gr. 5-7). mass mkt. 16.99 o.p. (*0-531-08527-9*, Orchard Bks.) Scholastic, Inc.

—The Cookcamp. 1991. 10.55 (*0-606-00894-2*) Turtleback Bks.

—The Quilt. 2004. 96p. (YA). (gr. 3-7). 15.95 (*0-385-72950-2*); lib. bdg. 17.99 (*0-385-90886-5*) Random Hse. Children's Bks. (Lamb, Wendy).

Pearson, Susan. Happy Birthday Grampie. Dillon, Leo, ed. 1987. (Illus.). 32p. (J). (ps-3). 10.95 o.p. (*0-8037-3457-3*, Dial Bks. for Young Readers) Penguin Putnam Bks. for Young Readers.

—Happy Birthday, Grampie. 1997. (Illus.). 32p. (J). pap. 5.99 o.s.i (*0-14-054637-5*) Penguin Putnam Bks. for Young Readers.

—Happy Birthday, Grampie! Dillon, Leo, ed. 1987. (Illus.). 32p. (J). (ps-3). 10.89 o.p. (*0-8037-3458-1*, Dial Bks. for Young Readers) Penguin Putnam Bks. for Young Readers.

Peck, Richard. A Long Way from Chicago. 2002. (Illus.). (J). 13.19 (*0-7587-6520-7*) Book Wholesalers, Inc.

—A Long Way from Chicago. 2004. (Illus.). 160p. pap. 5.99 (*0-14-240110-2*, Puffin Bks.); 2000. (Illus.). 176p. (YA). (gr. 5-9). pap. 5.99 (*0-14-130352-2*, Puffin Bks.); 1998. 192p. (J). (gr. 4-7). 15.99 (*0-8037-2290-7*, Dial Bks. for Young Readers) Penguin Putnam Bks. for Young Readers.

—A Long Way from Chicago. unabr. ed. 2000. (ps up). audio 25.00 (*0-8072-6162-9*, LL0153, Listening Library) Random Hse. Audio Publishing Group.

—A Long Way from Chicago. 2000. 11.04 (*0-606-19769-9*) Turtleback Bks.

—Monster Night at Grandma's House. 2003. (Illus.). 32p. (J). (gr. k-3). reprint ed. 12.99 (*0-8037-2904-9*, Dial Bks. for Young Readers) Penguin Putnam Bks. for Young Readers.

—Monster Night at Grandma's House. (Picture Puffin Ser.). (J). (gr. k-3). 1979. (Illus.). pap. 2.95 o.p. (*0-14-050330-7*, Penguin Bks.); 1977. 11.50 o.p. (*0-670-48680-9*) Viking Penguin.

—Those Summer Girls I Never Met. 1988. 224p. (J). (gr. 7 up). 14.95 o.s.i (*0-440-50054-0*, Delacorte Pr.) Dell Publishing.

—A Year down Yonder. 2002. (Illus.). (YA). 13.19 (*1-4046-1795-7*) Book Wholesalers, Inc.

—A Year down Yonder. 144p. (gr. 5-8). 2002. (YA). pap. 5.99 (*0-14-230070-5*, Puffin Bks.); 2000. (J). 16.99 (*0-8037-2518-3*, Dial Bks. for Young Readers) Penguin Putnam Bks. for Young Readers.

—A Year down Yonder. unabr. ed. 2000. (J). (gr. 4-6). audio 23.00 (*0-8072-8750-4*, LL0222); (ps up). audio 18.00 (*0-8072-6167-X*, LL0222) Random Hse. Audio Publishing Group. (Listening Library).

—A Year down Yonder. l.t. ed. 2001. 160p. (J). 24.95 (*0-7862-3282-X*) Thorndike Pr.

Peck, Robert. Bro. 2004. (J). (*0-06-052974-1*); lib. bdg. (*0-06-052975-X*) HarperCollins Pubs.

Pegram, Laura. Daughter's Day Blues. (Illus.). 32p. 2002. pap. 6.99 (*0-14-056187-0*); 2000. (J). 15.99 o.s.i (*0-8037-1557-9*, Dial Bks. for Young Readers) Penguin Putnam Bks. for Young Readers.

Pellegrino, Marjorie White. My Grandma's the Mayor. 1999. (Illus.). 32p. (J). (gr. 1-7). (*1-55798-608-8*, 441-6088, Magination Pr.) American Psychological Assn.

Pellegrino, Marjorie White, ed. Too Nice. 2002. (Illus.). 48p. (J). (gr. 4-7). 14.95 (*1-55798-917-6*); pap. 8.95 (*1-55798-918-4*) American Psychological Assn. (Magination Pr.).

Pellowski, Anne. Willow Wind Farm: Betsy's Story. 1981. (Illus.). 176p. (J). (gr. 9-12). 8.95 o.s.i (*0-399-20781-3*, Philomel) Penguin Putnam Bks. for Young Readers.

Percy, Graham. Max & the Orange Door. 1994. (Meg & Max Bks.). (Illus.). 32p. (J). (ps-4). lib. bdg. 22.79 o.p. (*1-56766-076-2*) Child's World, Inc.

Perkins, Mitali. The Sunita Experiment. 1994. (Illus.). 192p. (J). (gr. 5-9). pap. 4.50 o.p. (*1-56282-671-9*) Hyperion Bks. for Children.

—The Sunita Experiment. 1993. 144p. (J). (gr. 1-6). 15.95 o.p. (*0-316-69943-8*, Joy Street Bks.) Little Brown & Co.

Perron, Donna W. Flowers for Grampa. 1997. (Illus.). 24p. (J). (ps-6). 17.95 (*0-9657986-7-4*) Just Good Vermont Products.

Perry, Katy. My Grandmother Wears Crazy Hats. Minor, Mary E., ed. 1993. (Illus.). 16p. (J). (gr. k-5). pap. 4.95 (*0-9626823-4-9*) Perry Publishing.

Petersen, Patricia. Magali/Magali: An Aztec Legend about Good Fortune (Una leyenja Azteca Sobre La Buena Fortuna) 1998. (Cuentos en Dos Idiomas Ser.). (Illus.). 32p. (J). (gr. 3-6). 16.95 (*1-56492-250-2*) Laredo Publishing Co., Inc.

Peterson, John. The Littles Give a Party. (Littles Ser.). (Illus.). (J). (gr. 1-5). 1993. 96p. mass mkt. 3.99 (*0-590-46597-X*); 1986. pap. 2.25 o.p. (*0-590-40138-6*); 1978. pap. 1.95 o.p. (*0-590-32004-1*); 1974. pap. 2.50 o.p. (*0-590-41988-9*) Scholastic, Inc.

—The Littles Give a Party. 1972. (Littles Ser.). (Illus.). (J). (gr. 1-5). 10.14 (*0-606-05435-9*) Turtleback Bks.

Pfister, Marcus. The Happy Hedgehog. (Illus.). 32p. (J). 2003. pap. 6.95 (*0-7358-1816-9*); 2000. 15.95 (*0-7358-1164-4*); 2000. 16.50 o.p. (*0-7358-1165-2*) North-South Bks., Inc.

Pitt, L. Toddler Gran. 2002. (Illus.). 105p. pap. (*1-84270-027-8*) Trafalgar Square.

Pittman, Helena Clare. One Quiet Morning: Story & Pictures. 1995. (Illus.). 32p. (J). (ps-3). 14.95 o.p. (*0-87614-838-0*, Carolrhoda Bks.) Lerner Publishing Group.

Pitzer, Susanna & Teis, Kyra. Grandfather Hurant Lives Forever. 2001. (Illus.). (J). 9.95 (*1-56123-159-2*) Centering Corp.

Placide, Jaira. Fresh Girl. 2002. 224p. (YA). (gr. 7 up). 15.95 (*0-385-32753-6*, Delacorte Pr.) Dell Publishing.

—Fresh Girl. 224p. (YA). (gr. 7). 2004. mass mkt. 5.50 (*0-440-23764-5*, Laurel Leaf); 2002. lib. bdg. 17.99 o.s.i (*0-385-90035-X*, Lamb, Wendy) Random Hse. Children's Bks.

Platt, Randall Beth. Honor Bright. 1997. 240p. (YA). (gr. 7 up). 14.95 o.s.i (*0-385-32216-X*, Dell Books for Young Readers) Random Hse. Children's Bks.

—Honor Bright. 1998. 10.55 (*0-606-13486-7*) Turtleback Bks.

Ploetz, Craig T. Milo's Trip to the Museum with Grandpa. 1994. (J). (ps-3). 11.95 (*1-882172-01-9*) Milo Productions.

Plourde, Lynn. Thank You & Good-Bye. 2001. (Illus.). (J). per. 16.00 (*0-689-81853-X*, Simon & Schuster Children's Publishing) Simon & Schuster Children's Publishing.

—Thank You Grandpa. 2003. (Illus.). 32p. 15.99 (*0-525-46992-3*, Dutton Children's Bks.) Penguin Putnam Bks. for Young Readers.

Pochocki, Ethel. Grandma Bagley to the Rescue: Adventures with the Brooksville Bunch. 1989. 112p. (Orig.). (J). (gr. 3-7). pap. 6.95 o.p. (*0-8066-2414-0*, 9-2414) Augsburg Fortress, Pubs.

Podoshen, Lois. Grandpa's Candy Store. 1997. (Books for Young Learners). (Illus.). 12p. (J). (gr. k-2). pap. text 5.00 (*1-57274-113-9*, A2160) Owen, Richard C. Pubs., Inc.

Polacco, Patricia. Babushka Baba Yaga. (Illus.). 32p. (ps-3). 1999. pap. 6.99 (*0-698-11633-X*); 1993. (J). 16.99 (*0-399-22531-5*, Philomel) Penguin Putnam Bks. for Young Readers.

—Babushka Baba Yaga. 1999. lib. bdg. 13.14 (*0-606-16844-3*) Turtleback Bks.

—Meteor! 2001. (J). (gr. k-4). pap. 17.95 incl. audio (*0-8045-6857-X*, 6857) Spoken Arts, Inc.

—The Trees of the Dancing Goats. 2002. (Illus.). (J). 25.11 (*0-7587-3858-7*) Book Wholesalers, Inc.

—The Trees of the Dancing Goats. 32p. (J). 2000. (Illus.). (gr. k-3). pap. 6.99 (*0-689-83857-3*, Aladdin); 1997. (gr. k-5). pap. 22.00 incl. audio compact disk (*0-689-81193-4*, Simon & Schuster Children's Publishing); 1997. (gr. k-5). pap. 22.00 incl. audio compact disk (*0-689-81193-4*, Simon & Schuster Children's Publishing); 1996. (Illus.). (gr. 4-7). 16.00 (*0-689-80862-3*, Simon & Schuster Children's Publishing) Simon & Schuster Children's Publishing.

—The Trees of the Dancing Goats. 2000. 13.14 (*0-606-20094-0*) Turtleback Bks.

—When Lightning Comes in a Jar: Come to a Family Reunion. 2002. (Illus.). 40p. (J). 16.99 (*0-399-23164-1*, Philomel) Penguin Putnam Bks. for Young Readers.

Polikoff, Barbara G. Life's a Funny Proposition, Horatio. 1992. 112p. (YA). (gr. 4-7). 14.95 o.s.i (*0-8050-1972-3*, Holt, Henry & Co. Bks. For Young Readers) Holt, Henry & Co.

—Life's a Funny Proposition, Horatio. 1994. (Illus.). 112p. (J). (gr. 5 up). pap. 4.99 o.s.i (*0-14-036644-X*, Puffin Bks.) Penguin Putnam Bks. for Young Readers.

—Life's a Funny Proposition, Horatio. 1994. (J). 11.04 (*0-606-05906-7*) Turtleback Bks.

Polland, Barbara K. Grandma & Grandpa Are Special People. 1984. (Illus.). 80p. (J). (gr. k-3). text 7.95 o.p. (*0-89087-343-7*) Celestial Arts Publishing Co.

Pollowitz, Melinda. Cinnamon Cane. 1977. (J). (gr. 5-8). 6.95 o.p. (*0-06-024762-2*); lib. bdg. 9.89 o.p. (*0-06-024763-0*) HarperCollins Pubs.

Pomerantz, Charlotte. The Outside Dog. (I Can Read Bks.). (Illus.). 64p. (J). 1995. (gr. k-3). pap. 3.99 (*0-06-444187-3*, Harper Trophy); 1993. (gr. k-3). lib. bdg. 15.89 (*0-06-024783-5*); 1993. (gr. 2-4). 14.95 o.p. (*0-06-024782-7*) HarperCollins Children's Bk. Group.

—The Outside Dog. 1995. (I Can Read Bks.). (J). (gr. 2-4). 10.10 (*0-606-07983-1*) Turtleback Bks.

Pope, Geraldine. The Empty Creel. 1995. (Illus.). 56p. (J). (ps-3). 17.95 (*1-56792-044-6*) Godine, David R. Pub.

Porte, Barbara Ann. Surprise! Surprise! It's Grandfather's Birthday! 1997. (Illus.). 32p. (J). (gr. k up). lib. bdg. 14.93 o.p. (*0-688-14158-7*); 15.00 (*0-688-14157-9*) HarperCollins Children's Bk. Group. (Greenwillow Bks.).

—When Grandma Almost Fell off the Mountain & Other Stories. 1993. (Illus.). 32p. (J). (ps-2). 15.95 o.p. (*0-531-05965-0*); mass mkt. 16.99 o.p. (*0-531-08565-1*) Scholastic, Inc. (Orchard Bks.).

Potaracke, Rochelle. Nanny's Special Gift. 1994. (Illus.). 32p. (Orig.). (J). (ps-3). pap. 4.95 o.p. (*0-8091-6615-1*) Paulist Pr.

Poulsen, Kathleen Phillips. Apple Doll. 2002. 32p. (J). 9.95 (*1-57072-222-6*) Overmountain Pr.

Powell, Richard. Grandma's Cottage. 1995. (Illus.). (J). 7.99 (*1-884628-01-X*, Flying Frog Publishing) Allied Publishing.

Poydar, Nancy. Busy Bea. 1994. (Illus.). 32p. (J). (ps-2). 14.95 (*0-689-50592-2*, McElderry, Margaret K.) Simon & Schuster Children's Publishing.

Poynter, Margaret. Crazy Minnie. 1979. (Challenge Bks.). (Illus.). 56p. (J). (gr. 4 up). lib. bdg. 8.95 o.p. (*0-87191-680-0*, Creative Education) Creative Co., The.

Prater, John. Again! A Baby Bear Book. 2000. (Illus.). 32p. (J). (ps-1). 12.95 o.p. (*0-7641-5279-3*) Barron's Educational Series, Inc.

Prechtel, Martin. Grandmother Sweat Bath: A Story of the Tzutujil Mana. Rodney, Janet, ed. 1990. (Illus.). 39p. (Orig.). (YA). (gr. 6 up). (*1-878460-00-5*) Weaselsleeves Pr.

Probasco, Teri. Simple Things. 1994. 36p. (J). (ps-6). pap. 5.90 (*0-932970-98-2*) Prinit Pr.

Proimos, James. Joe's Wish. 1998. (Illus.). 32p. (J). (ps-3). 13.00 (*0-15-201831-X*) Harcourt Children's Bks.

Prokofiev, Sergei. Peter & the Wolf. 1994. (Illus.). 24p. (ps-3). 22.95 o.s.i incl. audio (*0-679-86156-4*) Random Hse. Children's Bks.

Provost, Gary. Good If It Goes. 1990. 160p. (J). (gr. 4-7). pap. 3.95 o.s.i (*0-689-71381-9*, Aladdin) Simon & Schuster Children's Publishing.

Pryor, Bonnie. Grandpa Bear. 1985. (Illus.). 32p. (J). (ps-1). 16.00 o.p. (*0-688-04551-0*); lib. bdg. 12.88 o.p. (*0-688-04552-9*) Morrow/Avon. (Morrow, William & Co.).

Pulver, Robin. Alicia's Tutu. (Illus.). (J). 2004. pap. 5.99 (*0-14-056525-6*, Puffin Bks.); 1997. 32p. 14.89 o.s.i (*0-8037-1933-7*, Dial Bks. for Young Readers); 1997. 32p. 14.99 o.s.i (*0-8037-1932-9*, Dial Bks. for Young Readers) Penguin Putnam Bks. for Young Readers.

Raczek, Linda T. The Night the Grandfathers Danced. 1998. (Illus.). 32p. (J). (gr. k-3). pap. 7.95 o.p. (*0-87358-720-0*, Rising Moon Bks. for Young Readers) Northland Publishing.

Rael, Elsa Okon. When Zaydeh Danced on Eldridge Street. 1997. (Illus.). 40p. (J). (gr. k-4). 16.00 o.s.i (*0-689-80451-2*, Simon & Schuster Children's Publishing) Simon & Schuster Children's Publishing.

Rahaman, Vashanti. A Little Salmon for Witness. 1997. (Illus.). 32p. (J). 15.99 o.s.i (*0-525-67521-3*, Dutton Children's Bks.) Penguin Putnam Bks. for Young Readers.

Rahmlow, Lavina. Granny Glee & the Bear-Off Bear. 1998. (Illus.). 61p. (J). 13.95 o.p. (*0-533-12535-9*) Vantage Pr., Inc.

Ramos, Violet M. Sara & Grandmother Rose. 1997. (Illus.). 32p. (Orig.). (J). (ps-6). mass mkt. 3.95 (*0-9658334-0-2*) VR Pubns.

Random House Books for Young Readers Staff. Birthday Bear. 1999. (Bear in the Big Blue House Ser.). (Illus.). 80p. (J). (ps). pap. 2.99 (*0-375-80060-3*, Random Hse. Bks. for Young Readers) Random Hse. Children's Bks.

Ransom, Candice F. Little Red Riding Hood. 2001. (Brighter Child Keepsake Stories Ser.). (Illus.). 32p. (J). (ps-3). 3.99 (*1-57768-198-3*) McGraw-Hill Children's Publishing.

Ransom, Jeanie Franz. Grandma U. 2002. (Illus.). 32p. (J). 15.95 (*1-56145-214-9*) Peachtree Pubs., Ltd.

Rappaport, Doreen. Friday Night with Grandpa. 1995. (J). o.p. (*0-399-22639-7*, G. P. Putnam's Sons) Penguin Putnam Bks. for Young Readers.

Rau, Dana Meachen. Yahoo for You, Level B. 2002. (Compass Point Early Reader Ser.). (Illus.). 32p. (J). (gr. 1). lib. bdg. 18.60 (*0-7565-0177-6*) Compass Point Bks.

Raven, Margot T. Circle Unbroken: The Story of the Sweetgrass Basket, RS. 2004. 16.00 (*0-374-31289-3*, Farrar, Straus & Giroux (BYR)) Farrar, Straus & Giroux.

Raynor, Dorka. Grandparents Around the World. Rubin, Caroline, ed. 1977. (Albert Whitman Concept Bks.). (Illus.). (J). (ps-2). lib. bdg. 9.75 o.p. (*0-8075-3037-9*) Whitman, Albert & Co.

Reader's Digest Editors. I Love My Grandma! l.t. ed. 1998. (First Blessings Flap Bks.: Vol. 3). (Illus.). 18p. (J). (ps-k). bds. 3.99 (*1-57584-081-2*, Reader's Digest Children's Bks.) Reader's Digest Children's Publishing, Inc.

Reddix, Valerie. Dragon Kite of the Autumn Moon. 1992. (Illus.). (J). (ps-3). 14.00 o.p. (*0-688-11030-4*); lib. bdg. 13.93 (*0-688-11031-2*) HarperCollins Children's Bk. Group.

Redmond, Shirley-Raye. Grampa & the Ghost. 1994. 96p. (Orig.). (J). (gr. 3 up). pap. 3.50 (*0-380-77382-1*, Avon Bks.) Morrow/Avon.

Reeder, Carolyn. Grandpa's Mountain. 1993. 176p. (J). (gr. 4-7). reprint ed. pap. 4.95 (*0-380-71914-2*, Avon Bks.) Morrow/Avon.

—Grandpa's Mountain. 176p. (J). 2002. (Illus.). pap. 4.99 (*0-689-84867-6*, Aladdin); 1991. (gr. 3-7). text 14.95 o.p. (*0-02-775811-7*, Simon & Schuster Children's Publishing) Simon & Schuster Children's Publishing.

—Grandpa's Mountain. 1991. (J). 11.04 (*0-606-05321-2*) Turtleback Bks.

Reid, Mary C. Phantom Gardener, Vol. 3. 1997. (Backpack Mystery Ser.: Vol. 3). 80p. (J). (gr. 2-5). pap. 3.99 o.p. (*1-55661-717-8*) Bethany Hse. Pubs.

Reiser, Lynn W. Cherry Pies & Lullabies. 1998. (Illus.). 40p. (J). (ps-3). 16.99 (*0-688-13391-6*); 16.89 (*0-688-13392-4*) HarperCollins Children's Bk. Group. (Greenwillow Bks.).

Renken, Aleda. Grandma Haley. 1981. (Haley Adventure Bks.). (J). (gr. 3-9). pap. 1.75 o.s.i (*0-570-07234-4*, 39-1069) Concordia Publishing Hse.

Renner, Zainabu. My Grandma & I. 1998. 16p. pap. (*1-57579-107-2*) Pine Hill Pr., Inc.

Repp, Gloria. Booklinks, Level 2. 1998. 149p. (J). (gr. 6). pap. 6.49 (*1-57924-000-3*, 106484) Jones, Bob Univ. Pr.

Reynolds, Adrian. Pete & Polo's Farmyard Adventure. 2002. (Illus.). 32p. (J). (ps-1). pap. 16.95 (*0-439-30913-1*, Orchard Bks.) Scholastic, Inc.

Rhodes, Judy C. The King Boy. 1991. 160p. (J). (gr. 5-9). text 14.95 o.s.i (*0-02-776115-0*, Simon & Schuster Children's Publishing) Simon & Schuster Children's Publishing.

Rice, Eve. At Grammy's House. 1990. (Illus.). 32p. (J). (ps up). 12.95 o.p. (*0-688-08874-0*); lib. bdg. 12.88 o.p. (*0-688-08875-9*) HarperCollins Children's Bk. Group. (Greenwillow Bks.).

Rice, Joy. Grandad Doesn't Live Here Anymore. 1986. (Contemporary Literature for Children Ser.: Vol. 2). (Illus.). 28p. (Orig.). (J). (ps-5). pap. 5.95 o.p. (*0-916843-09-2*, 104, Writers Hse. Pr.) Order of the Legion of St. Michael.

Richardson, Arleta. Away from Home. (Grandma's Attic Ser.). 159p. (J). (gr. 3-7). pap. 6.99 (*0-7814-3290-1*) Cook Communications Ministries.

—The Grandma's Attic Storybook. 1993. 256p. (J). pap. 10.99 (*0-7814-0070-8*) Cook Communications Ministries.

—More Stories from Grandma's Attic. 1994. (Illus.). 128p. (J). (gr. 3-7). pap. 4.99 o.p. (*0-7814-0086-4*) Cook Communications Ministries.

Ridyard, David. Grandpa Loves Us. 1985. (Growing Up Bks.). (J). (Illus.). 32p. (gr. 2-3). lib. bdg. 10.95 o.p. (*0-918831-17-2*); lib. bdg. 7.95 o.p. (*0-918831-40-7*) Stevens, Gareth Inc.

Riefe, Barbara. Amelia Dale Archer Story. 1998. 304p. (YA). (gr. 8 up). 22.95 o.p. (*0-312-86077-3*, Forge Bks.) Doherty, Tom Assocs., LLC.

Riley, Janeway. Us & . . . Good Stuff. 1993. (Illus.). 176p. (J). 19.95 (*0-9637378-1-3*) Riley, Janeway.

Riley, Jocelyn. Crazy Quilt. 1986. (Starfire Ser.). 176p. (J). (gr. 7-12). mass mkt. 2.50 o.s.i (*0-553-25640-8*) Bantam Bks.

Riley, Kathryn. The Big Sale. 1999. (Real Kids Readers Ser.). (Illus.). 32p. (J). (gr. k-2). 18.90 (*0-7613-2057-1*); pap. 4.99 (*0-7613-2082-2*) Millbrook Pr., Inc.

—The Big Sale. 1999. (J). 10.14 (*0-606-19147-X*) Turtleback Bks.

—The Big Sale. 1999. E-Book (*1-58824-460-1*); E-Book (*1-58824-708-2*); (Illus.). E-Book (*1-58824-909-3*) ipicturebooks, LLC.

Rinaldi, Ann. The Blue Door: The Quilt Trilogy III. 1996. (Quilt Trilogy Ser.: No. 3). 272p. (YA). (gr. 7 up). pap. 15.95 (*0-590-46051-X*) Scholastic, Inc.

Rivera-Ashford, Roni Capin. My Nana's Remedies: Los Remedios de Mi Nana. 2002. (SPA.). 32p. (J). (ps-4). 15.95 (*1-886679-19-3*) Arizona-Sonora Desert Museum Pr.

Robb, Brian. My Grandmother's Djinn. 1978. (Illus.). 40p. (J). (gr. k-4). lib. bdg. 5.41 o.p. (*0-8193-0918-4*) Scholastic, Inc.

Roberts, Barbara A. Phoebe's Lost Treasure. 1999. (Phoebe Flower's Adventures Ser.). (Illus.). 68p. (J). (gr. 2-4). 5.95 (*0-9660366-6-2*) Advantage Bks., LLC.

Roberts, Bethany. Gramps & the Fire Dragon. 2000. (Illus.). 32p. (J). (ps-3). lib. bdg., tchr. ed. 15.00 (*0-395-69849-9*, Clarion Bks.) Houghton Mifflin Co. Trade & Reference Div.

Roberts, Elisabeth. Jumping Jackdaws! Here Comes Simon. 1975. (Illus.). 192p. (ps-2). lib. bdg. 5.79 o.p. (*0-528-80198-8*) Rand McNally.

Roberts, Sarah. I Want to Go Home. 1985. (Sesame Street Start-to-Read Bks.). (Illus.). 40p. (J). (ps-3). 4.95 o.s.i (*0-394-87027-1*); 6.99 o.s.i (*0-394-97027-6*) Random Hse. Children's Bks. (Random Hse. Bks. for Young Readers).

Roberts, Willo Davis. Rebel. 2003. (Illus.). 160p. (J). 15.95 (*0-689-85073-5*, Atheneum) Simon & Schuster Children's Publishing.

—Secrets at Hidden Valley. 1997. 160p. (J). (gr. 4-8). 16.00 (*0-689-81166-7*, Atheneum) Simon & Schuster Children's Publishing.

—To Grandmother's House We Go. 192p. (J). 1994. pap. 3.95 (*0-689-71838-1*, Aladdin); 1990. (gr. 3-7). lib. bdg. 16.00 o.s.i (*0-689-31594-5*, Atheneum) Simon & Schuster Children's Publishing.

Robertson, Barbara. Rosemary & the Island Treasure: Back to 1947. 2001. (Hourglass Adventures Ser.: Bk. 4). (Illus.). 128p. (J). (gr. 3-5). pap. 4.95 (*1-890817-58-9*) Winslow Pr.

—Rosemary in Paris: Back to 1889. 2001. (Hourglass Adventures Ser.: Bk. 2). (Illus.). 121p. (J). (gr. 4-7). pap. 4.95 (*1-890817-56-2*) Winslow Pr.

—Rosemary Meets Rosemarie Book #1: Berlin in 1870. 2001. (Hourglass Adventures Ser.: Bk. 1). (Illus.). 128p. (J). (gr. 4-6). pap. 5.95 (*1-890817-55-4*) Winslow Pr.

Robins, Kay C. Come with Me to Grandma's House. 1996. (Illus.). 16p. (Orig.). (J). (ps-2). pap. 4.65 (*0-9652177-0-1*) Whispering Oaks Pr.

Rochelle, Belinda. Jewels. 1998. (Illus.). 32p. (J). (gr. k-3). 15.99 o.s.i (*0-525-67502-7*, Dutton Children's Bks.) Penguin Putnam Bks. for Young Readers.

—When Jo Louis Won the Title. (Illus.). 32p. (J). (ps-3). 1996. pap. 6.95 (*0-395-81657-2*); 1994. tchr. ed. 14.95 o.p. (*0-395-66614-7*) Houghton Mifflin Co.

—When Jo Louis Won the Title. 1994. 12.10 (*0-606-10968-4*) Turtleback Bks.

Rodda, Emily. Fairy Realm. 2003. (Fairy Realm Ser.). (Illus.). 128p. (J). No. 1. (gr. 2-5). 8.99 (*0-06-009583-0*); No. 3. lib. bdg. 14.89 (*0-06-009590-3*); No. 4. 8.99 (*0-06-009592-X*); No. 4. lib. bdg. 14.89 (*0-06-009593-8*) HarperCollins Pubs.

—Fairy Realm: The Charm Bracelet, No. 1. 2003. (Fairy Realm Ser.). (Illus.). 128p. (J). (gr. 2-5). lib. bdg. 14.89 (*0-06-009584-9*) HarperCollins Pubs.

Rodowsky, Colby. Evy-Ivy-Over. 1978. (gr. 5 up). lib. bdg. 8.90 o.p. (*0-531-02245-5*, Watts, Franklin) Scholastic Library Publishing.

Rogers, Paul. A Letter to Grandma. 1994. (Illus.). 32p. (J). 14.95 o.p. (*0-689-31947-9*, Atheneum) Simon & Schuster Children's Publishing.

Rogers, Sherbrooke. Grandfather Webster's Strange Will. 1995. 90p. (J). (gr. 6-7). pap. 9.99 (*0-88092-066-1*); (Illus.). lib. bdg. 15.00 o.p. (*0-88092-067-X*) Royal Fireworks Publishing Co.

Roller, Rebecca T. Guess What, Gram! 1996. (Illus.). (J). (ps-3). 6.95 (*0-913515-91-4*, Elliott & Clark) River City Publishing.

Romain, Trevor. Under the Big Sky. 1994. (Illus.). 64p. (YA). (gr. 5-12). 13.95 (*1-880092-13-1*) Bright Bks., Inc.

—Under the Big Sky. 2001. (Illus.). 48p. (J). 14.95 (*0-06-029494-9*); (gr. 2 up). lib. bdg. 14.89 (*0-06-029495-7*) HarperCollins Children's Bk. Group.

Root, Phyllis. The Name Quilt, RS. 2003. (Illus.). 32p. (J). (gr. k-3). 16.00 (*0-374-35484-7*, Farrar, Straus & Giroux (BYR)) Farrar, Straus & Giroux.

Root, Phyllis & Marron, Carol A. Gretchen's Grandma. 1983. (Family Bks.). (Illus.). 32p. (J). (gr. k-3). lib. bdg. 14.65 o.p. (*0-940742-16-0*) Raintree Pubs.

Rosa-Casanova, Sylvia. Mama Provi & the Pot of Rice. (Illus.). 32p. (ps-3). 2001. pap. 5.99 (*0-689-84249-X*, Aladdin); 1997. (J). 16.00 o.s.i (*0-689-31932-0*, Atheneum) Simon & Schuster Children's Publishing.

Rosen, Michael J. Fishing with Dad. 2003. (Illus.). 32p. (J). tchr. ed. 14.95 (*1-885183-38-0*) Artisan.

—A Thanksgiving Wish. 1998. (Illus.). 32p. (YA). (ps-3). pap. 16.95 (*0-590-25563-0*, Blue Sky Pr., The) Scholastic, Inc.

Rosenberg, Liz. Grandmother & the Runaway Shadow. 1996. (Illus.). 32p. (J). (gr. 1-4). 15.00 o.s.i (*0-15-200948-5*) Harcourt Trade Pubs.

—Grandmother & the Runaway Shadow. 2015. (Illus.). (J). 14.95 (*0-399-22545-5*, Philomel) Penguin Putnam Bks. for Young Readers.

—The Silence in the Mountains. (Illus.). 32p. (J). (gr. k-4). 1999. lib. bdg. 16.99 (*0-531-33084-2*); 1998. pap. 15.95 (*0-531-30084-6*) Scholastic, Inc. (Orchard Bks.).

Ross, Kent & Ross, Alice. Cemetery Quilt. 1995. (Illus.). 32p. (J). (ps-3). 14.95 o.p. (*0-395-70948-2*) Houghton Mifflin Co.

Ross, Ramon R. The Dancing Tree. 1995. 64p. (J). (gr. 4-7). 14.00 (*0-689-80072-X*, Atheneum) Simon & Schuster Children's Publishing.

Rosselson, Leon. Rosa & Her Singing Grandfather. 1996. (Illus.). 96p. (J). (gr. k-3). 12.95 o.s.i (*0-399-22733-4*, Philomel) Penguin Putnam Bks. for Young Readers.

Rossi, Joyce. The Gullywasher. 1995. (Illus.). 32p. (J). (gr. k-3). lib. bdg. 14.95 o.p. (*0-87358-607-7*, Rising Moon Bks. for Young Readers) Northland Publishing.

—The Gullywasher (El Chaparron Torrencial) 1998. (ENG & SPA., Illus.). 32p. (J). (gr. k-3). pap. 7.95 (*0-87358-728-6*, Rising Moon Bks. for Young Readers) Northland Publishing.

Roth, Susan L. Grandpa Blows His Penny Whistle until the Angels Sing. 2001. (Illus.). 40p. (J). (gr. 3-5). 16.99 (*1-84148-247-1*) Barefoot Bks., Inc.

—Happy Birthday, Mr. Kang. 2001. (Illus.). 32p. (J). (gr. 2-5). pap. 16.95 (*0-7922-7723-6*) National Geographic Society.

Rothenberg, Joan. Inside-Out Grandma: A Hanukkah Story. 1997. (Illus.). 32p. (J). (ps-3). reprint ed. pap. 5.95 (*0-7868-1200-1*) Disney Pr.

—Inside-Out Grandma: A Hanukkah Story. 1995. (Illus.). 32p. (J). (ps-3). 14.95 (*0-7868-0107-7*); lib. bdg. 15.49 (*0-7868-2092-6*) Hyperion Bks. for Children.

—Inside-Out Grandma: A Hanukkah Story. 1997. (J). 12.10 (*0-606-13520-0*) Turtleback Bks.

Rubinstein, Gillian. Foxspell. 1996. 224p. (YA). (gr. 7 up). 16.00 (*0-689-80602-7*, Simon & Schuster Children's Publishing) Simon & Schuster Children's Publishing.

Ruelle, Karen Gray. Easy As Apple Pie. 2002. (Holiday House Reader Ser.). (Illus.). 32p. (J). (gr. k-3). 14.95 (*0-8234-1759-X*) Holiday Hse., Inc.

Rukeyser, Muriel. More Night. 1981. (Illus.). 32p. (J). (gr. k-3). o.p. (*0-06-025127-1*); lib. bdg. 9.89 o.p. (*0-06-025128-X*) HarperCollins Pubs.

Rumford, James. The Cloudmakers. 1996. (Illus.). 32p. (J). (ps-3). tchr. ed. 17.00 (*0-395-76505-6*) Houghton Mifflin Co.

—When Silver Needles Swam: The Story of Tutu's Quilt. 1998. (ENG & HAW., Illus.). 30p. (J). (gr. 1-6). 10.95 (*1-891839-00-4*) Manoa Pr.

Rusk, Irene J. A Letter to Grandmother. 1994. (Illus.). 64p. (Orig.). (J). pap. 8.00 (*1-56002-223-X*, University Editions) Aegina Pr., Inc.

Russell, Ching Yeung. Child Bride. 136p. (J). (gr. 3-7). 2003. pap. 9.95 (*1-59078-024-8*); 1999. (Illus.). 15.95 (*1-56397-748-6*) Boyds Mills Pr.

Russo, Marisabina. Grandpa Abe. 1996. (Illus.). 32p. (J). (ps-3). 15.00 o.s.i (*0-688-14097-1*); 14.93 o.s.i (*0-688-14098-X*) HarperCollins Children's Bk. Group. (Greenwillow Bks.).

—House of Sports. 2002. 192p. (J). (gr. 3 up). 15.95 (*0-06-623803-X*); lib. bdg. 16.89 (*0-06-623804-8*) HarperCollins Children's Bk. Group. (Greenwillow Bks.).

—A Visit to Oma. 1991. (Illus.). 32p. (J). (ps up). 13.95 o.p. (*0-688-09623-9*); lib. bdg. 13.88 o.s.i (*0-688-09624-7*) HarperCollins Children's Bk. Group. (Greenwillow Bks.).

Ryan, Pam Muñoz. Arroz con Frijoles y unos Amables Ratones. 2002. (SPA., Illus.). 32p. (J). (gr. k-2). pap. 5.99 (*0-439-31737-1*, SO30909, Scholastic en Espanola) Scholastic, Inc.

—Mice & Beans. 2001. (Illus.). 32p. (J). (ps-2). pap. 15.95 (*0-439-18303-0*, Levine, Arthur A. Bks.) Scholastic, Inc.

Rylant, Cynthia. The Islander. 1999. 112p. (gr. 5-12). reprint ed. pap. text 4.99 (*0-440-41542-X*) Bantam Bks.

—The Ticky-Tacky Doll. 2002. (Illus.). 32p. (J). (gr. k-2). 16.00 (*0-15-201078-5*) Harcourt Children's Bks.

Rylant, Cynthia & Jackson, Richard. The Islander. 1998. (Illus.). 112p. (J). (gr. 6-12). pap. 14.95 (*0-7894-2490-8*, D K Ink) Dorling Kindersley Publishing, Inc.

Sachs, Marilyn. Another Day. 1997. 176p. (J). (gr. 5-9). 15.99 o.p. (*0-525-45787-9*) Penguin Putnam Bks. for Young Readers.

Sackett, Mike. When Grandfather Sailed Away. (Orig.). (J). (gr. 3-5). 1996. (Illus.). 27p. pap. 3.00 (*0-88092-077-7*, 0777); 1995. lib. bdg. 15.00 o.p. (*0-88092-078-5*) Royal Fireworks Publishing Co.

Sadasivan, Lathika. My First Millennium. 2000. (Illus.). 20p. (J). (ps-3). 14.99 (*0-9700318-1-5*); pap. 7.99 (*0-9700318-0-7*) Peek-A-Bks.

Sadler, Marilyn. Zenon: Girl of the 21st Century. 1996. (Illus.). 48p. (J). (ps-3). 14.00 (*0-689-80514-4*, Simon & Schuster Children's Publishing) Simon & Schuster Children's Publishing.

Saenz, Benjamin Alire. A Gift from Papa Diego (Un Regalo de Papa Diego) 2004. (ENG & SPA., Illus.). 40p. (J). (gr. k-7). pap. 10.95 (*0-938317-33-4*) Cinco Puntos Pr.

—Grandma Fina & Her Wonderful Umbrellas: La Abuelita Fina y Sus Sombrillas Maravillosas. 2004. (Illus.). 32p. pap. 7.95 (*0-938317-61-X*) Cinco Puntos Pr.

—Grandma Fina & Her Wonderful Umbrellas: La Abuelita Fina y Sus Sombrillas Maravillosas. Herrera, Pilar, tr. 1999. (ENG & SPA., Illus.). 32p. (J). (ps-3). 15.95 (*0-938317-46-6*, CPP7466) Cinco Puntos Pr.

Sagel, Jim. Always the Heart. 1998. (Red Crane Literature Ser.).Tr. of Siempre el Corazon. (ENG & SPA., Illus.). 168p. (YA). (gr. 8-12). pap. 12.95 (*1-878610-68-6*) Red Crane Bks., Inc.

Sakai, Kimiko. Sachiko Means Happiness. (ENG & KOR., Illus.). 24p. (J). (gr. 1 up). 1994. pap. 6.95 (*0-89239-122-7*); 1990. 14.95 o.p. (*0-89239-065-4*) Children's Bk. Pr.

—Sachiko Means Happiness. 1990. 13.10 (*0-606-06707-8*) Turtleback Bks.

Salem, Lynn & Stewart, Josie. Staying with Grandma Norma. 1993. (Illus.). 16p. (J). (gr. k-2). pap. 3.75 (*1-880612-08-9*) Seedling Pubns., Inc.

Sarkar, Shelly. My Grandma & Me. 1999. (Illus.). 8p. (J). E-Book (*1-929981-08-2*) kahani.com, Inc.

Sathre, Vivian & Hunter, Anne. On Grandpa's Farm. 1997. (Illus.). 32p. (J). (ps-3). lib. bdg., tchr. ed. 17.00 (*0-395-76506-4*) Houghton Mifflin Co.

Satterfield, Barbara. The Story Dance. 1997. (Illus.). 32p. (J). (gr. 1-4). 14.95 o.p. (*1-57749-022-3*) Fairview Pr.

Saull, D. L. The Sunchildren. 1992. (J). 7.95 o.p. (*0-533-09619-7*) Vantage Pr., Inc.

Saulsman, Helen L. From Grandma... With Love. 1998. (Illus.). (J). (ps-6). pap. 10.00 (*0-9663051-0-8*) Saulsman, Helen L.

Saunders, Susan. Lucky Lady. 128p. (J). 2002. pap. 4.95 (*0-380-80756-4*, Harper Trophy); 2000. (gr. 4-7). 14.95 (*0-380-97784-2*) HarperCollins Children's Bk. Group.

Savageau, Cheryl. Muskrat Will Be Swimming. 1996. (Illus.). 32p. (J). (gr. 1-3). lib. bdg. 14.95 o.p. (*0-87358-604-2*, Rising Moon Bks. for Young Readers) Northland Publishing.

Say, Allen. Grandfather's Journey. 2002. (Illus.). (J). 26.83 (*0-7587-0050-4*) Book Wholesalers, Inc.

—Grandfather's Journey. (Illus.). (J). 9999. lib. bdg. 16.95 o.p. (*0-395-57136-7*); 1993. 32p. lib. bdg., tchr. ed. 16.95 (*0-395-57035-2*) Houghton Mifflin Co.

Scaglione, Joseph. My Lucky Penny. deluxe l.t. ed. 1999. (Illus.). 64p. (J). (ps-4). pap. 24.95 incl. cd-rom (*0-9675011-0-5*) New Day Enterprises, Ltd.

Scarffe, Bronwen. Walter Hottle Bottle. 1993. (Voyages Ser.). (Illus.). (J). 14.00 (*0-383-03664-X*) SRA/McGraw-Hill.

Schaap, Martine. Mop's Treasure Hunt. 2000. (Mop & Family Ser.). (Illus.). 32p. (J). (ps-1). 12.95 (*1-57768-891-0*, Cricket) McGraw-Hill Children's Publishing.

Schachner, Judith Byron. The Grannyman. (Illus.). 32p. 2003. pap. 6.99 (*0-14-250062-3*, Puffin Bks.); 1999. (J). 15.99 (*0-525-46122-1*, Dutton Children's Bks.) Penguin Putnam Bks. for Young Readers.

—The Grannyman. unabr. ed. 2000. (YA). pap. 32.99 incl. audio (*0-7887-3640-X*, 41005X4) Recorded Bks., LLC.

Scheer, Julian. A Thanksgiving Turkey. 2001. (Illus.). 32p. (J). (ps-2). tchr. ed. 16.95 (*0-8234-1674-7*) Holiday Hse., Inc.

Scheffler, Ursel. Grandpa's Amazing Computer. Lanning, Rosemary, tr. from GER. (Illus.). 48p. (J). (gr. 2-4). 1999. pap. 5.95 o.p. (*0-7358-1100-8*); 1997. 13.95 o.p. (*1-55858-795-0*); 1997. 14.50 o.p. (*1-55858-796-9*) North-South Bks., Inc.

Scheller, Melanie. My Grandfather's Hat. 1992. (Illus.). 32p. (J). (ps-3). lib. bdg. 13.95 o.p. (*0-689-50540-X*, McElderry, Margaret K.) Simon & Schuster Children's Publishing.

Schertle, Alice. William & Grandpa. Stevenson, D., ed. 1989. (Illus.). 32p. (J). (gr. k-3). 12.95 o.p. (*0-688-07580-0*); lib. bdg. 12.88 o.p. (*0-688-07581-9*) HarperCollins Children's Bk. Group.

Schlessinger, Laura. Dr. Laura Schlessinger's Where's God? 2003. (Illus.). 40p. (J). (ps-2). lib. bdg. 16.89 (*0-06-051910-X*) HarperCollins Pubs.

—Where's God? l.t. ed. 2003. (Illus.). 40p. (J). (ps-2). 15.99 (*0-06-051909-6*) HarperCollins Pubs.

Schneider, Antonie. The Birthday Bear. 1996. (Illus.). 48p. (J). (ps-3). 13.95 o.p. (*1-55858-655-5*); 14.50 o.p. (*1-55858-656-3*) North-South Bks., Inc.

—Good-Bye, Vivi! 1998. (Illus.). 32p. (J). (gr. k-3). 15.95 (*1-55858-985-6*, Michael Neugebauer Bks.); 16.50 (*1-55858-986-4*) North-South Bks., Inc.

Schotter, Roni. In the Piney Woods, RS. 2003. (Illus.). 32p. (J). (gr. k up). 16.00 (*0-374-33623-7*, Farrar, Straus & Giroux (BYR)) Farrar, Straus & Giroux.

Schwartz, Amy. Oma & Bobo. 1990. (Trophy Picture Bk.). (Illus.). 32p. (J). (gr. k-3). reprint ed. pap. 4.95 o.p. (*0-06-443225-4*, Harper Trophy) HarperCollins Children's Bk. Group.

Schwartz, David M. Super Grandpa. 1998. (Illus.). 32p. (J). (gr. k-3). pap. 5.95 (*0-688-16296-7*, Morrow, William & Co.) Morrow/Avon.

—Supergrandpa. 1991. (Illus.). (J). (ps-3). 17.00 o.p. (*0-688-09898-3*); lib. bdg. 16.93 o.p. (*0-688-09899-1*) HarperCollins Children's Bk. Group.

—Supergrandpa. 1998. 11.10 (*0-606-15728-X*) Turtleback Bks.

Scott, Ann Herbert. Grandmother's Chair. 1990. (Illus.). 32p. (J). (ps-1). 13.95 o.p. (*0-395-52001-0*, Clarion Bks.) Houghton Mifflin Co. Trade & Reference Div.

Scott, Blackie. It's Fun at Grandmother's House. 1992. (Illus.). 48p. (J). (ps-3). 8.95 (*0-934219-01-X*) Peachtree Pubs., Ltd.

Scott, C. Anne. Lizard Meets Ivana the Terrible, ERS. 1999. (Illus.). 128p. (J). (gr. 4-7). 15.95 o.s.i (*0-8050-6093-6*, Holt, Henry & Co. Bks. For Young Readers) Holt, Henry & Co.

Scott, C. Anne & Roth, Stephanie. Lizard Meets Ivana the Terrible. 2001. 128p. (J). mass mkt. 3.99 (*0-439-21999-X*, Scholastic Paperbacks) Scholastic, Inc.

Scrimger, Richard. Of Mice & Nutcrackers: A Peeler Christmas. 2001. (Illus.). 232p. (J). (gr. 3-7). pap. 7.95 (*0-88776-498-3*) Tundra Bks. of Northern New York.

Scripture Union Staff & Watson, Jean. Dan & Gramps. 1994. (Illus.). 32p. (J). 6.50 (*1-56476-364-1*, 6-3364) Cook Communications Ministries.

Seabrooke, Brenda. The Bridges of Summer. 1992. 160p. (J). (gr. 5 up). 14.99 o.p. (*0-525-65094-6*, Dutton Children's Bks.) Penguin Putnam Bks. for Young Readers.

—Looking for Diamonds. 1995. (Illus.). 32p. (J). (ps-3). 14.99 o.p. (*0-525-65173-X*, Dutton Children's Bks.) Penguin Putnam Bks. for Young Readers.

Segal, Lore. Why Mole Shouted & Other Stories, RS. 2004. (J). 16.00 (*0-374-38417-7*, Farrar, Straus & Giroux (BYR)) Farrar, Straus & Giroux.

Seidler, Tor. The Silent Spillbills. 1998. 224p. (J). (gr. 3-7). 14.95 (*0-06-205180-6*); lib. bdg. 14.89 (*0-06-205181-4*) HarperCollins Children's Bk. Group.

Seltzer, Eric. Granny Doodle Day. 2005. (J). (*0-689-85914-7*, Aladdin Library); (*0-689-85911-2*, Aladdin) Simon & Schuster Children's Publishing.

Sendak, Philip. In Grandpa's House. 2003. (Sendak Reissues Ser.). (Illus.). 48p. (J). 12.89 (*0-06-028788-8*) HarperCollins Children's Bk. Group.

—In Grandpa's House. Barofsky, Semour, tr. from YID. 1985. (Illus.). 48p. (J). (ps up). 13.00 o.s.i (*0-06-025462-9*); lib. bdg. 9.89 o.s.i (*0-06-025463-7*) HarperCollins Children's Bk. Group.

—In Grandpa's House. 2003. (Sendak Reissues Ser.). (Illus.). 48p. (J). reprint ed. 12.95 (*0-06-028787-X*) HarperCollins Children's Bk. Group.

Seymour, Tres. Too Quiet for These Old Bones. 1997. (Illus.). 32p. (J). (ps-2). pap. 15.95 (*0-531-30052-8*); lib. bdg. 16.99 (*0-531-33052-4*) Scholastic, Inc. (Orchard Bks.).

Shankar, Alaka. Life with Grandfather. 9th ed. 1980. (Illus.). 54p. (Orig.). (J). (gr. k-3). pap. 3.50 o.p. (*0-89744-212-1*) Children's Bk. Trust IND. *Dist:* Random Hse. of Canada, Ltd.

Shannon, Bob. Grandpap Remembers from the Book of Life. 1994. (Illus.). 40p. (J). pap. 7.95 o.p. (*0-8059-3476-6*) Dorrance Publishing Co., Inc.

Shannon, George. Unlived Affections. 1989. (Charlotte Zolotow Bk.). 144p. (YA). (gr. 7 up). 12.95 (*0-06-025304-5*); lib. bdg. 12.89 o.p. (*0-06-025305-3*) HarperCollins Children's Bk. Group.

Shapiro, Jody Fickes. Up, Up, Up! It's Apple-Picking Time. 2003. (Illus.). (J). (gr. k-3). tchr. ed. 16.95 (*0-8234-1610-0*) Holiday Hse., Inc.

Shasha, Mark. Hall of Beasts. 1994. (Illus.). 40p. (J). (ps-3). pap. 15.00 o.s.i (*0-671-79893-6*, Simon & Schuster Children's Publishing) Simon & Schuster Children's Publishing.

Shaw, Eve. Grandmother's Alphabet: Grandma Can Be Anything from A to Z. 1996. (Illus.). 32p. (J). (ps-3). 14.95 o.p. (*1-57025-127-4*) Scholastic, Inc.

Shawver, Margaret. What's Wrong with Grandma? A Family's Experience with Alzheimer's. 1996. (Young Readers Ser.). (Illus.). 62p. (YA). (gr. 2 up). 17.00 (*1-57392-107-6*) Prometheus Bks., Pubs.

Shea, Pegi Deitz. Tangled Threads: A Hmong Girl's Story. 2003. 240p. (J). (gr. 5-9). tchr. ed. 15.00 (*0-618-24748-3*, Clarion Bks.) Houghton Mifflin Co. Trade & Reference Div.

Shecter, Ben. Grandma Remembers. 1989. (Charlotte Zolotow Bk.). (Illus.). 32p. (J). (gr. k-3). 13.95 (*0-06-025617-6*); lib. bdg. 13.89 o.p. (*0-06-025618-4*) HarperCollins Children's Bk. Group.

Sheldon, Dyan. The Whales' Song. 1991. (Illus.). 32p. (J). (ps-3). 16.99 o.p. (*0-8037-0972-2*, Dial Bks. for Young Readers) Penguin Putnam Bks. for Young Readers.

Shelton, Jayne C. In Grandmother's Arms. 2001. (Illus.). 32p. (J). mass mkt. 3.25 (*0-439-21314-2*) Scholastic, Inc.

Sherlock, Patti. Four of a Kind. 1991. 196p. (J). (gr. 4-7). 13.95 (*0-8234-0913-9*) Holiday Hse., Inc.

Shetterly, Susan Hand. Shelterwood. 40p. (J). 2003. pap. 7.95 (*0-88448-256-1*); 1999. (Illus.). 16.95 (*0-88448-210-3*) Tilbury Hse. Pubs.

Shields, Carol Diggory. Lucky Pennies & Hot Chocolate. 2002. (Illus.). 32p. (J). pap. 5.99 (*0-14-230190-6*) Penguin Putnam Bks. for Young Readers.

—Lucky Pennies & Hot Chocolate with Grandpa. 2000. (Illus.). 32p. (J). (ps-2). 14.99 (*0-525-46450-6*, Dutton Children's Bks.) Penguin Putnam Bks. for Young Readers.

Shigekawa, Marlene. Blue Jay in the Desert. 1993. (Illus.). 36p. (J). (gr. 1-5). 14.95 (*1-879965-04-6*) Polychrome Publishing Corp.

Shriver, Maria. What's Heaven? ed. 2000. (J). (gr. 2). spiral bd. (*0-616-03056-8*) Canadian National Institute for the Blind/Institut National Canadien pour les Aveugles.

—What's Heaven? 1999. (J). 15.00 (*1-58238-100-3*); 10th ed. (Illus.). 32p. reprint ed. 15.00 (*0-307-44043-5*, NHC 0190) St. Martin's Pr. (Golden Bks. Adult Publishing Group).

Shub, Elizabeth. Cutlass in the Snow. 1986. (Illus.). 48p. (J). (gr. 1-4). 12.95 o.p. (*0-688-05927-9*); lib. bdg. 14.93 o.p. (*0-688-05928-7*) HarperCollins Children's Bk. Group. (Greenwillow Bks.).

Shuster, Bud. Double Buckeyes: A Story of the Way America Used to Be. (Illus.). vi, 149p. (J). (gr. 4-7). 2000. pap. 7.95 (*1-57249-177-9*, WM Kids); 1999. 19.95 (*1-57249-176-0*, White Mane Bks.) White Mane Publishing Co., Inc.

Siegel, Bruce H. Champion & Jewboy. 1995. (Illus.). 144p. (J). (gr. 8 up). 6.95 (*1-881283-11-9*) Alef Design Group.

Siegelson, Kim L. In the Time of the Drums. 1999. (Jump at the Sun Bks.). (Illus.). 32p. (J). (gr. 1-4). 15.99 (*0-7868-0436-X*); lib. bdg. 16.49 (*0-7868-2386-0*) Hyperion Bks. for Children.

—In the Time of the Drums. 1999. (J). 17.00 (*0-689-81084-9*); 17.00 (*0-689-80570-5*) Simon & Schuster Children's Publishing. (Simon & Schuster Children's Publishing).

—The Terrible, Wonderful Tellin' at Hog Hammock. 1996. (Illus.). 96p. (J). (gr. 2-5). 15.99 (*0-06-024877-7*); lib. bdg. 13.89 o.p. (*0-06-024878-5*) HarperCollins Children's Bk. Group.

Silverman, Erica. On Grandma's Roof. 1990. (Illus.). 32p. (J). (ps-2). 13.95 o.s.i (*0-02-782681-3*, Simon & Schuster Children's Publishing) Simon & Schuster Children's Publishing.

Silverstein, Ruth. Kirby Koala Visits Grandma. 1984. (Kirby Koala Ser.). (Illus.). 22p. (J). (ps-3). 2.50 o.p. (*0-89954-275-1*) Antioch Publishing Co.

Sinykin, Sheri Cooper. A Matter of Time. 1998. (Accelerated Reader Bks.). 208p. (J). (gr. 5-9). lib. bdg. 14.95 (*0-7614-5019-X*, Cavendish Children's Bks.) Cavendish, Marshall Corp.

Sisnett, Ana. Grannie Jus' Come! 1997. (Illus.). 32p. (YA). (gr. 1-3). 15.95 (*0-89239-150-2*) Children's Bk. Pr.

—Grannie Jus' Come! 1997. (Habitats Ser.). (Illus.). (J). (gr. 2-4). lib. bdg. 21.27 o.p. (*0-516-20937-X*, Children's Pr.) Scholastic Library Publishing.

Skolsky, Mindy Warshaw. Carnival & Kopeck & More about Hannah. 1979. (Illus.). 80p. (J). (gr. 2-5). lib. bdg. 12.89 o.p. (*0-06-025692-3*) HarperCollins Children's Bk. Group.

—Hannah & the Whistling Tea Kettle. 2000. (Richard Jackson Bks.). (Illus.). 40p. (J). (gr. k-3). pap. 15.95 o.p. (*0-7894-2602-1*) Dorling Kindersley Publishing, Inc.

Skorpen, Liesel M. Mandy's Grandmother. 1985. (Illus.). 32p. (J). (ps-3). 4.95 o.p. (*0-8037-4962-7*); 4.58 o.p. (*0-8037-4963-5*) Penguin Putnam Bks. for Young Readers. (Dial Bks. for Young Readers).

Slaaten, Evelyn. In the Captain's Shoes. 1978. (gr. 7 up). lib. bdg. 6.90 o.p. (*0-531-02215-3*, Watts, Franklin) Scholastic Library Publishing.

Slipian, Jan. Emily Just in Time. 1998. (Illus.). 32p. (J). (ps-2). 15.99 o.p. (*0-399-23043-2*, Philomel) Penguin Putnam Bks. for Young Readers.

Slipperjack, Ruby. Little Voice. 2001. (In the Same Boat Ser.: No. 4). (Illus.). 250p. (J). (gr. 4-6). pap. text 8.95 (*1-55050-182-8*) Coteau Bks. CAN. *Dist:* General Distribution Services, Inc.

Sloss, Lesley. Anthony & the Aardvark. 1991. (Illus.). 32p. (J). (ps up). 13.95 o.p. (*0-688-10302-2*); lib. bdg. 13.88 o.p. (*0-688-10303-0*) HarperCollins Children's Bk. Group.

Slote, Alfred. The Trading Game. 1990. 208p. (J). (gr. 3-7). lib. bdg. 15.89 o.p. (*0-397-32398-0*); 15.00 (*0-397-32397-2*) HarperCollins Children's Bk. Group.

Smalls, Irene. My Nana & Me. 2004. (Illus.). (J). 15.95 (*0-316-16821-1*) Little Brown & Co.

Smith, Barbara A. Somewhere Just Beyond. 1993. 96p. (J). (gr. 3-7). 12.95 o.s.i (*0-689-31877-4*, Atheneum) Simon & Schuster Children's Publishing.

Smith, Barry. Grandma Rabitty's Visit. 1999. (DK Toddlers Ser.). (Illus.). 24p. (J). (ps). pap. 9.95 o.p. (*0-7894-4839-4*) Dorling Kindersley Publishing, Inc.

Smith, Cynthia. Indian Shoes. 2002. (Illus.). 80p. (J). (gr. 2-5). 15.95 (*0-06-029531-7*); lib. bdg. 15.89 (*0-06-029532-5*) HarperCollins Children's Bk. Group.

Smith, Doris B. Remember the Red-Shouldered Hawk. 1994. 160p. (YA). (gr. 5-9). 14.95 o.p. (*0-399-22443-2*, G. P. Putnam's Sons) Penguin Group (USA) Inc.

Smith, Dorothy N. Gran, Please Tell Us a Story. 1986. (Illus.). 53p. (J). (gr. k-12). pap. 5.95 o.p. (*0-931494-87-7*) Brunswick Publishing Corp.

Smith, Joan. Grandmother's Donkey. 1983. (Julia MacRae Blackbird Bks.). (Illus.). 48p. (gr. k-3). lib. bdg. 5.95 o.p. (*0-531-04604-4*, Watts, Franklin) Scholastic Library Publishing.

Smith, Maggie. My Grandma's Chair. 1992. (J). (ps-3). 14.00 o.p. (*0-688-10663-3*); lib. bdg. 13.93 o.p. (*0-688-10664-1*) HarperCollins Children's Bk. Group.

Smith, MaryLou M. La Abuelita y Su Casa de Munecas. 1997. (SPA.). (J). pap. text 3.99 (*0-590-29197-1*) Scholastic, Inc.

Smith, Patricia. Janna & the Kings. 2003. (Illus.). (J). 16.95 (*1-58430-088-4*) Lee & Low Bks., Inc.

Smith, Peaches. Marcy's Granny. 1996. (Illus.). 62p. (J). 17.25 (*1-56763-184-3*); pap. 2.95 (*1-56763-185-1*) Ozark Publishing.

Smith, Robert Kimmel. The War with Grandpa. 2002. 13.40 (*0-7587-9609-9*) Book Wholesalers, Inc.

—The War with Grandpa. (J). (gr. 4-7). 1995. 160p. pap. 1.99 o.s.i (*0-440-21952-3*); 1984. (Illus.). 128p. pap. 12.95 o.s.i (*0-385-29314-3*, Delacorte Pr.); 1984. (Illus.). 128p. 12.95 o.p. (*0-385-29312-7*, Delacorte Pr.) Dell Publishing.

—The War with Grandpa. 128p. (J). (gr. 4-6). pap. 4.99 (*0-8072-1407-8*, Listening Library) Random Hse. Audio Publishing Group.

—The War with Grandpa. 1984. (Yearling Ser.). (Illus.). 160p. (gr. 5-9). pap. text 5.50 (*0-440-49276-9*, Yearling) Random Hse. Children's Bks.

—The War with Grandpa. 1984. (J). 11.04 (*0-606-03362-9*) Turtleback Bks.

Smothers, Ethel Footman. Moriah's Pond. 2003. 96p. (J). 7.00 (*0-8028-5249-1*, Eerdmans Bks For Young Readers) Eerdmans, William B. Publishing Co.

—Moriah's Pond. 1994. (J). lib. bdg. o.p. (*0-679-94504-0*) Knopf, Alfred A. Inc.

—Moriah's Pond. 1994. (Illus.). 128p. (J). 16.00 o.s.i (*0-679-84504-6*, Knopf Bks. for Young Readers) Random Hse. Children's Bks.

Smucker, Barbara. Selina & the Bear Paw Quilt. 1996. (Illus.). 32p. (J). (gr. 1-5). 16.00 o.s.i (*0-517-70904-X*, Crown) Crown Publishing Group.

—Selina & the Shoo-Fly Pie. 1999. (Illus.). 32p. (J). (ps-3). 15.95 (*0-7737-3018-4*) Stoddart Kids CAN. *Dist:* Fitzhenry & Whiteside, Ltd.

Snow, Jonathan. The Most Beautiful Gift. 1996. 96p. (J). 12.45 o.p. (*0-446-52082-9*) Warner Bks., Inc.

Snyder, Carol. God Must Like Cookies, Too. 1993. (Illus.). 32p. (J). (ps-3). 16.95 (*0-8276-0423-8*) Jewish Pubn. Society.

Snyder, Midori. Hannah's Garden. 2002. 208p. (J). text 16.99 (*0-670-03577-7*) Penguin Putnam Bks. for Young Readers.

Sobel, Barbara. Great-Grandma, Heroine! 1987. (J). (gr. 3-6). 7.59 o.p. (*0-87386-049-7*); pap. 2.95 (*0-87386-048-9*) January Productions, Inc.

Sonneborn, Ruth A. I Love Gram. 1971. (Illus.). (J). (gr. k-3). 5.95 o.p. (*0-670-39064-X*) Viking Penguin.

Soros, Barbara. Grandmother's Song. (Illus.). 32p. (J). (gr. 3-7). 2000. pap. 6.99 (*1-902283-09-0*); 1998. 15.95 (*1-902283-02-3*) Barefoot Bks., Inc.

Soto, Gary. My Little Car. 2015. Tr. of Mi Carrito. (J). 15.95 (*0-399-23220-6*) Penguin Group (USA) Inc.

Spalding, Andrea. Phoebe & the Gypsy. 1999. (Young Reader Ser.). (Illus.). 96p. (J). (gr. 3-6). pap. 4.99 (*1-55143-135-1*) Orca Bk. Pubs.

—Phoebe & the Gypsy. 1999. (Young Reader Ser.). 10.04 (*0-606-19478-9*) Turtleback Bks.

Spinelli, Eileen. Naptime, Laptime. 1995. (Illus.). 24p. (J). pap. 6.95 (*0-590-48510-5*, Cartwheel Bks.) Scholastic, Inc.

—Something to Tell the Grandcows. Slavin, Bill, tr. & illus. by. 2004. (J). (*0-8028-5236-X*, Eerdmans Bks For Young Readers) Eerdmans, William B. Publishing Co.

—Wanda's Monster. 2002. (Illus.). 32p. (J). (gr. k-3). lib. bdg. 15.95 (*0-8075-8656-0*) Whitman, Albert & Co.

Spinner, Stephanie. It's a Miracle! A Hanukkah Storybook. 2003. (Illus.). 48p. (J). (gr. k-3). 16.95 (*0-689-84493-X*, Atheneum/Anne Schwartz Bks.) Simon & Schuster Children's Publishing.

Springer, Nancy. Looking for Jamie Bridger. (J). 1999. pap. 14.89 (*0-8037-1774-1*); 1995. 160p. (gr. 7 up). 14.99 o.s.i (*0-8037-1773-3*) Penguin Putnam Bks. for Young Readers. (Dial Bks. for Young Readers).

Spyri, Johanna. Heidi. 2002. (Great Illustrated Classics). (Illus.). 240p. (J). (gr. 3-8). lib. bdg. 21.35 (*1-57765-688-1*, ABDO & Daughters) ABDO Publishing Co.

—Heidi. 2002. (SPA., Illus.). 96p. (YA). (gr. 5-8). 9.95 (*84-204-5788-4*) Alfaguara, Ediciones, S.A.- Grupo Santillana ESP. *Dist:* Santillana USA Publishing Co., Inc.

—Heidi. unabr. ed. 2000. (Juvenile Classics). (Illus.). 304p. (J). pap. 2.50 (*0-486-41235-0*) Dover Pubns., Inc.

—Heidi. 2nd ed. (Coleccion Clasicos en Accion). (SPA., Illus.). 80p. (YA). (gr. 5-8). 15.95 (*84-241-5784-2*, EV0790) Everest de Ediciones y Distribucion, S.L. ESP. *Dist:* Lectorum Pubns., Inc.

—Heidi. 2002. (Kingfisher Classics Ser.). (Illus.). 352p. (J). tchr. ed. 15.95 (*0-7534-5494-7*, Kingfisher) Houghton Mifflin Co. Trade & Reference Div.

—Heidi. 2002. (Twelve-Point Ser.). lib. bdg. 25.00 (*1-58287-183-3*) North Bks.

—Heidi. 2000. (Aladdin Classics Ser.). (Illus.). 304p. (J). (gr. 4-7). pap. 3.99 (*0-689-83962-6*, Aladdin) Simon & Schuster Children's Publishing.

—Heidi. abr. ed. 1974. (J). pap. 5.95 o.p. incl. audio (*0-88142-324-6*) Soundelux Audio Publishing.

—Heidi. 1998. (Children's Classics). 240p. (J). pap. 3.95 (*1-85326-125-4*, 1254WW) Wordsworth Editions, Ltd. GBR. *Dist:* Advanced Global Distribution Services.

—Heidi: With a Discussion of Optimism. 2003. (Values in Action Illustrated Classics Ser.). (J). (*1-59203-030-0*) Learning Challenge, Inc.

Spyri, Johanna & Blaisdell, Robert. Heidi. 1998. (Illus.). (J). 1.00 (*0-486-40166-9*) Dover Pubns., Inc.

Stahl, Hilda. Big Trouble for Roxie. 1992. (Best Friends Ser.: No. 2). 160p. (J). (gr. 4-7). pap. 4.99 o.p. (*0-89107-658-1*) Crossway Bks.

Stallone, Linda. The Flood That Came to Grandma's House. 1992. (Illus.). 21p. (J). (ps-3). 9.95 (*0-912975-02-4*) Upshur Pr.

Stanley, George Edward. The Battle of the Bakers. Corey, Shana, ed. 2000. (Stepping Stone Book Ser.: Vol. 3). (Illus.). 80p. (J). (gr. 1-4). pap. 3.99 o.s.i (*0-679-89222-2*); lib. bdg. 11.99 (*0-679-99222-7*) Random Hse. Children's Bks. (Random Hse. Bks. for Young Readers).

—The Battle of the Bakers. 2000. (Katie Lynn Cookie Company Ser. : Vol. 3). 10.14 (*0-606-19900-4*) Turtleback Bks.

—The Secret Ingredient. 1999. (Katie Lynn Cookie Company Ser.: Vol. 1). (Illus.). 80p. (J). (gr. 2-4). lib. bdg. 11.99 (*0-679-99220-0*, Random Hse. Bks. for Young Readers) Random Hse. Children's Bks.

—The Secret Ingredient. 1999. (Katie Lynn Cookie Company Ser.: Vol. 1). (Illus.). 80p. (J). (gr. 2-4). pap. 3.99 o.s.i (*0-679-89220-6*) Random Hse., Inc.

—The Secret Ingredient. 1999. (Katie Lynn Cookie Company Ser.). (Illus.). (J). 10.14 (*0-606-18500-3*) Turtleback Bks.

—Wedding Cookies: Katie Lynn Cookie Company. 2001. (Stepping Stone Book Ser.: Vol. 4). (Illus.). 54p. (J). (gr. k-3). lib. bdg. 11.99 (*0-679-99223-5*, Random Hse. Bks. for Young Readers) Random Hse. Children's Bks.

Starnes, Gigi. Grandmother's Tales: Discovering Archaeology. 1996. (Discovering Archaeology Ser.). (Illus.). 64p. (J). (gr. 3-5). 14.95 (*0-89015-979-3*) Eakin Pr.

Steel, Danielle. Max & Grandma & Grampa Winky. 1990. (J). o.s.i (*0-385-30362-9*, Dell Books for Young Readers) Random Hse. Children's Bks.

Steiner, Lili. Grandparents Around the World. 1998. (My Jewish Family Series with a Bissel Yiddish). (Illus.). 24p. (J). pap. 14.95 (*1-891397-03-6*) Steiner, Lili Pubns.

—My Bubbe - My Grandmother. 1998. (Illus.). 24p. (J). pap. 14.95 (*1-891397-02-8*) Steiner, Lili Pubns.

—My Zaidah - My Grandfather. 1998. (My Jewish Family Series with a Bissel Yiddish). (Illus.). 24p. (J). pap. 14.95 (*1-891397-01-X*) Steiner, Lili Pubns.

Stephenson, Jean. Dogwood Stew & Catnip Tea. 1993. (Granny Green-Gloves Adventure Ser.). 160p. (J). (gr. 4-7). pap. 4.99 o.p. (*0-89107-717-0*) Crossway Bks.

Steptoe, John L. Grandpa & Baby. 9999. lib. bdg. 24.95 o.s.i (*0-688-07426-X*); 1924. (J). o.s.i (*0-688-07425-1*) HarperCollins Children's Bk. Group.

Sterling Publishing Staff. Benjamin Visits Grandpa & Grandma. 1999. 16p. (ps-3). pap. text 4.95 (*0-8069-3132-9*) Sterling Publishing Co., Inc.

Stevens, Carla. Anna, Grandpa & the Big Storm. 1982. (Illus.). 48p. (J). (gr. 6-9). 13.95 o.p. (*0-89919-066-9*, Clarion Bks.) Houghton Mifflin Co. Trade & Reference Div.

—Anna, Grandpa & the Big Storm. 1982. (Young Puffin Read Alone Ser). (J). 9.19 o.p. (*0-606-02802-1*) Turtleback Bks.

—Anna, Grandpa, & the Big Storm. (Puffin Chapters for Readers on the Move Ser.). (Illus.). 64p. (J). 1998. (gr. 2-5). pap. 4.99 (*0-14-130083-3*); 1988. (gr. 2-5). pap. 3.99 o.s.i (*0-14-031705-8*); 1986. (gr. 1-4). pap. 3.50 o.p. (*0-14-032119-5*) Penguin Putnam Bks. for Young Readers. (Puffin Bks.).

—Anna, Grandpa, & the Big Storm. 1998. (Illus.). (J). 11.14 (*0-606-21777-0*) Turtleback Bks.

Stevens, Kathleen. Eddie's Luck. 1992. 176p. (J). (gr. 3-7). text 13.95 (*0-689-31682-8*, Atheneum) Simon & Schuster Children's Publishing.

Stevens, Margaret. When Grandpa Died. 1979. (Social Values Ser.). (Illus.). 32p. (J). (gr. k-3). pap. 3.95 o.p. (*0-516-42025-9*); lib. bdg. 13.27 o.p. (*0-516-02025-0*) Scholastic Library Publishing. (Children's Pr.).

Stevenson, Harvey. Grandpa's House. 1994. (Illus.). 32p. (J). (ps-3). 14.95 (*1-56282-588-7*); lib. bdg. 15.49 (*1-56282-589-5*) Hyperion Bks. for Children.

Stevenson, James. Brrr! 1991. (Illus.). 32p. (J). (ps up). 13.95 o.p. (*0-688-09210-1*); lib. bdg. 13.88 o.p. (*0-688-09211-X*) HarperCollins Children's Bk. Group. (Greenwillow Bks.).

—Could Be Worse! 1977. (Illus.). 32p. (J). (gr. k-3). 15.00 o.p. (*0-688-80075-0*); lib. bdg. 14.93 o.p. (*0-688-84075-2*) HarperCollins Children's Bk. Group. (Greenwillow Bks.).

—Sam the Zamboni Man. 1998. (Illus.). 32p. (J). (ps-3). 14.89 o.s.i (*0-688-14485-3*); 15.00 o.p. (*0-688-14484-5*) HarperCollins Children's Bk. Group. (Greenwillow Bks.).

—That's Exactly the Way It Wasn't. 1991. (Illus.). 30p. (J). (ps up). 13.95 o.p. (*0-688-09868-1*); lib. bdg. 13.88 o.p. (*0-688-09869-X*) HarperCollins Children's Bk. Group. (Greenwillow Bks.).

—There's Nothing to Do! 1986. (Illus.). 32p. (J). (gr. k-3). 12.95 o.p. (*0-688-04698-3*); lib. bdg. 12.88 o.p. (*0-688-04699-1*) HarperCollins Children's Bk. Group. (Greenwillow Bks.).

—What's under My Bed? 1983. (Illus.). 32p. (J). (gr. k-3). 15.89 (*0-688-02327-4*); 16.00 (*0-688-02325-8*) HarperCollins Children's Bk. Group. (Greenwillow Bks.).

—What's under My Bed? 1984. (Illus.). (J). pap. 3.95 o.p. (*0-14-050485-0*, Puffin Bks.) Penguin Putnam Bks. for Young Readers.

Stewart, Dianne. The Dove. 1993. (Illus.). 32p. (J). (ps up). 14.00 o.p. (*0-688-11264-1*); lib. bdg. 13.93 o.p. (*0-688-11265-X*) HarperCollins Children's Bk. Group. (Greenwillow Bks.).

Stiles, Martha Bennett & San Souci, Daniel. Island Magic. 1999. Orig. Title: The Island. (Illus.). 32p. (J). (gr. k-3). 16.00 (*0-689-80588-8*, Atheneum) Simon & Schuster Children's Publishing.

Stilz, Carol C. Grandma Buffalo, May & Me. 1995. (Illus.). 32p. (J). (gr. 4-7). 14.95 (*1-57061-015-0*) Sasquatch Bks.

Stine, R. L. Don't Ever Get Sick at Granny's. 1997. (Ghosts of Fear Street Ser.: No. 16). 144p. (J). (gr. 4-7). pap. 3.99 (*0-671-00188-4*, Aladdin) Simon & Schuster Children's Publishing.

—Don't Ever Get Sick at Granny's. 1997. (Ghosts of Fear Street Ser.: No. 16). (J). (gr. 4-7). 10.04 (*0-606-11378-9*) Turtleback Bks.

—Secret Agent Grandma. 1997. (Give Yourself Goosebumps Ser.: No. 16). (J). (gr. 3-7). 10.04 (*0-606-11825-X*) Turtleback Bks.

Stock, Catherine. Emma's Dragon Hunt. 1984. (Illus.). 32p. (J). (gr. k up). 16.00 o.p. (*0-688-02696-6*); lib. bdg. 15.93 o.p. (*0-688-02698-2*) HarperCollins Children's Bk. Group.

—Gugu's House. 2001. (Illus.). 32p. (J). (ps-3). lib. bdg., tchr. ed. 14.00 (*0-618-00389-4*, Clarion Bks.) Houghton Mifflin Co. Trade & Reference Div.

Stojic, Manya. Wet Pebbles under Our Feet. 2002. (Illus.). 32p. (J). (gr. k-3). 15.95 (*0-375-81519-8*); lib. bdg. 17.99 (*0-375-91519-2*) Random Hse. Children's Bks. (Knopf Bks. for Young Readers).

Stolz, Mary. Coco Grimes. (Trophy Bk.). (J). 1995. 96p. (gr. 4-7). pap. 4.50 o.p. (*0-06-440512-5*, Harper Trophy); 1994. 128p. (gr. 3-6). lib. bdg. 13.89 o.p. (*0-06-024233-7*); 1994. 128p. (gr. 3-6). 14.00 o.p. (*0-06-024232-9*) HarperCollins Children's Bk. Group.

—Coco Grimes. 1996. (J). 9.70 o.p. (*0-606-08507-6*) Turtleback Bks.

—Go Fish. (Trophy Chapter Bks.). (Illus.). 80p. (J). 1993. (gr. 4-7). pap. 4.50 (*0-06-440466-8*, Harper Trophy); 1991. (gr. 2-6). 13.95 o.p. (*0-06-025820-9*); 1991. (gr. 2-6). lib. bdg. 14.89 (*0-06-025822-5*) HarperCollins Children's Bk. Group.

—Go Fish. 1993. (Trophy Chapter Bks.). (J). 10.65 (*0-606-02653-3*) Turtleback Bks.

—Stealing Home. 160p. (J). (gr. 3-6). 1994. (Illus.). pap. 5.99 (*0-06-440528-1*, Harper Trophy); 1992. lib. bdg. 14.89 o.p. (*0-06-021157-1*); 1992. 15.95 (*0-06-021154-7*) HarperCollins Children's Bk. Group.

—Stealing Home. 1994. 11.00 (*0-606-06767-1*) Turtleback Bks.

—Storm in the Night. (Trophy Picture Bk.). (Illus.). 32p. (J). (gr. k-3). 1990. pap. 5.99 (*0-06-443256-4*, Harper Trophy); 1988. 15.00 o.p. (*0-06-025912-4*); 1988. lib. bdg. 16.89 (*0-06-025913-2*) HarperCollins Children's Bk. Group.

—Storm in the Night. 1990. 12.10 (*0-606-04814-6*) Turtleback Bks.

Strangis, Joel. Grandfather's Rock. 1993. (Illus.). (J). 14.95 o.p. (*0-395-65367-3*) Houghton Mifflin Co.

Streich, Corrine, ed. Grandparents' Houses: Poems about Grandparents. 1984. (Illus.). 32p. (J). (gr. 1 up). 12.50 o.p. (*0-688-03894-8*); lib. bdg. 11.47 o.p. (*0-688-03895-6*) HarperCollins Children's Bk. Group. (Greenwillow Bks.).

Strong, Jeremy. My Granny's Great Escape. l.t. ed. 1998. (Illus.). (J). pap. 16.95 (*0-7540-6031-4*, Galaxy Children's Large Print) BBC Audiobooks America.

—My Granny's Great Escape. (Illus.). 96p. (J). pap. 7.95 (*0-14-038390-5*) Penguin Bks., Ltd. GBR. *Dist:* Trafalgar Square.

Stroud, Virginia A. Doesn't Fall off His Horse. 1994. (Illus.). 32p. (J). 14.89 o.p. (*0-8037-1635-4*); (gr. 1-4). 15.99 o.p. (*0-8037-1634-6*) Penguin Putnam Bks. for Young Readers. (Dial Bks. for Young Readers).

—A Walk to the Great Mystery. 1995. (Illus.). 32p. (J). 14.99 o.s.i (*0-8037-1636-2*); 14.89 o.s.i (*0-8037-1637-0*) Penguin Putnam Bks. for Young Readers. (Dial Bks. for Young Readers).

Stuart, Jesse H. The Beatinest Boy. Herndon, Jerry A. et al, eds. 1989. (Illus.). 80p. (J). (gr. 3-6). reprint ed. 10.00 (*0-945084-12-9*); pap. 5.00 (*0-945084-13-7*) Stuart, Jesse Foundation, The.

Stump, Marjorie. Grandpa's New Home. 1994. (J). pap. 7.50 (*1-55673-928-1*, Fairway Pr.) CSS Publishing Co.

Stuve-Bodeen, Stephanie. Babu's Song. 2003. (Illus.). 32p. (J). 16.95 (*1-58430-058-2*) Lee & Low Bks., Inc.

Suhay, Lisa. Dream Catchers. 2001. 40p. (J). pap. 16.95 (*1-55942-181-9*) Marsh Media.

Sullivan, Silky. Grandpa Was a Cowboy. 1996. (Illus.). 32p. (J). (ps-3). pap. 15.95 (*0-531-09511-8*); lib. bdg. 16.99 (*0-531-08861-8*) Scholastic, Inc. (Orchard Bks.).

Sundvall, Viveca L. Mimi Gets a Grandpa. Fisher, Richard E., tr. 1991. (Illus.). 32p. (J). (ps up). bds. 13.95 o.p. (*91-29-59864-8*) R & S Bks. SWE. *Dist:* Farrar, Straus & Giroux, Holtzbrinck Pubs.

Sutherland, Ann. My Grandpa Has No Garbage. 1996. (Illus.). 24p. (Orig.). (J). (gr. 2-6). pap. 7.95 (*1-56550-027-X*) Vision Bks. International.

Swayne, Sam & Swayne, Zoa L. Great-Grandfather in the Honey Tree. 1982. (Illus.). 53p. (J). (gr. 3-5). reprint ed. per. 14.95 (*0-9608008-0-8*) Legacy Hse., Inc.

Sweeney, Joyce. The Spirit Window. 1998. 256p. (YA). 15.95 o.s.i (*0-385-32510-X*, Delacorte Pr.) Dell Publishing.

—The Spirit Window. 1999. (Laurel-Leaf Bks.). 256p. (YA). (gr. 7 up). mass mkt. 4.50 o.s.i (*0-440-22711-9*, Dell Books for Young Readers) Random Hse. Children's Bks.

Szaj, Kathleen C. Elizabeth, Who Is Not a Saint. 1997. (Illus.). 32p. (Orig.). (J). (ps-3). pap. 7.95 (*0-8091-6638-0*) Paulist Pr.

Tadjo, Veronique. Grandma Nana. 2004. (Illus.). 24p. (Orig.). (J). (ALB, BEN, CHI, ENG & FRE.). pap. 9.95 (*1-84059-289-3*); (ALB, BEN, CHI, ENG & FRE., pap. 9.95 (*1-84059-291-5*); (ALB, BEN, CHI, ENG & FRE., pap. 9.95 (*1-84059-293-1*); (ALB, BEN, CHI, ENG & FRE., pap. 9.95 (*1-84059-292-3*); (ALB, BEN, CHI, ENG & FRE., pap. 9.95 (*1-84059-290-7*); (ALB, BEN, CHI, ENG & FRE., pap. 9.95 (*1-84059-287-7*); pap. 7.95 (*1-84059-285-0*); (ALB, BEN, CHI, ENG & FRE., pap. 9.95 (*1-84059-295-8*); (ALB, BEN, CHI, ENG & FRE., pap. 9.95 (*1-84059-294-X*); (ALB, BEN, CHI, ENG & FRE., pap. 9.95 (*1-84059-288-5*); (ALB, BEN, CHI, ENG & FRE., pap. 9.95 (*1-84059-286-9*) Milet Publishing, Ltd. GBR. *Dist:* Consortium Bk. Sales & Distribution.

Talbert, Marc. A Sunburned Prayer. 112p. (J). 1997. (gr. 5-9). pap. 4.50 (*0-689-81326-0*, Aladdin); 1995. (gr. 4-7). mass mkt. 14.00 o.s.i (*0-689-80125-4*, Simon & Schuster Children's Publishing) Simon & Schuster Children's Publishing.

—A Sunburned Prayer. 1997. 10.55 (*0-606-11938-8*) Turtleback Bks.

Tamboise, Pierre. A Trip by Torpedo. 1993. (I Love to Read Collections). (Illus.). 46p. (J). (gr. 1-5). lib. bdg. 8.50 o.p. (*0-89565-894-1*) Child's World, Inc.

Tan, Amy. The Moon Lady. (Illus.). 32p. (J). 1995. (ps-3). pap. 6.99 (*0-689-80616-7*, Aladdin); 1992. (gr. 1 up). lib. bdg. 16.95 (*0-02-788830-4*, Simon & Schuster Children's Publishing) Simon & Schuster Children's Publishing.

—The Moon Lady. 1995. 11.15 o.p. (*0-606-07886-X*) Turtleback Bks.

Tang, Charles, illus. The Mystery in the Cave. 1996. (Boxcar Children Ser.: No. 50). (J). (gr. 2-5). mass mkt. 3.95 (*0-8075-5412-X*) Whitman, Albert & Co.

Tarlton. Going to Grandma's. 1989. (J). pap. 19.95 o.p. (*0-590-50159-3*) Scholastic, Inc.

Tate, Joan. Grandpa & My Sister Bee. 1976. (Stepping Stones Ser.). (Illus.). 24p. (J). (gr. k-3). 7.00 o.p. (*0-516-03581-9*, Children's Pr.) Scholastic Library Publishing.

—Luke's Garden & Gramp: Two Short Novels. 1981. 144p. (J). (gr. 5-7). lib. bdg. 11.89 o.p. (*0-06-026144-7*) HarperCollins Children's Bk. Group.

Taulbert, Clifton L. Little Cliff's First Day of School. (Illus.). 32p. 2003. pap. 6.99 (*0-14-250082-8*, Puffin Bks.); 2001. (J). 16.99 (*0-8037-2557-4*, Dial Bks. for Young Readers) Penguin Putnam Bks. for Young Readers.

Tavares, Matt. Olivers Game. 2004. 32p. (J). 15.99 (*0-7636-1852-7*) Candlewick Pr.

Taylor, Theodore. A Sailor Returns. 2002. 160p. (J). (gr. 3-7). mass mkt. 4.99 (*0-439-24880-9*, Scholastic Paperbacks) Scholastic, Inc.

Tchana, Katrin H. & Pami, Louise T. Oh, No, Toto! 1997. (Illus.). 32p. (J). (ps-2). pap. 15.95 (*0-590-46585-6*) Scholastic, Inc.

Tello, Jerry. Abuelo y los Tres Osos. 1997. Tr. of Grandfather & the Three Bears. (SPA.). (J). (ps-3). pap. 3.99 (*0-590-04320-X*, 691722Q) Scholastic, Inc.

—Abuelo y los Tres Osos. 1997. (Mariposa Scholastica en Espanol Ser.).Tr. of Grandfather & the Three Bears. (SPA.). 10.14 (*0-606-11020-8*) Turtleback Bks.

Temple, Charles. Cadillac. 1995. (Illus.). 32p. (J). (gr. k-2). 15.95 o.p. (*0-399-22654-0*) Penguin Group (USA) Inc.

Tews, Susan. Nettie's Gift. 1993. (Illus.). 32p. (J). (gr. k-3). 14.95 o.p. (*0-395-59027-2*, Clarion Bks.) Houghton Mifflin Co. Trade & Reference Div.

Theroux, Phyllis. Serefina under the Circumstances. 1999. (Illus.). 32p. (J). (gr. k-3). 16.00 (*0-688-15942-7*, Greenwillow Bks.) HarperCollins Children's Bk. Group.

—Serefina under the Circumstances. 2000. (J). 16.00 (*0-689-80450-4*, Simon & Schuster Children's Publishing) Simon & Schuster Children's Publishing.

Thomas, Abigail. Wake up, Wilson Street, ERS. 1993. (Illus.). 32p. (YA). (gr. 5 up). 15.95 o.p. (*0-8050-2006-3*, Holt, Henry & Co. Bks. For Young Readers) Holt, Henry & Co.

Thomas, Jane Resh. Saying Good-Bye to Grandma. (Illus.). (J). 1990. 48p. (ps-3). pap. 7.95 (*0-395-54779-2*); 1988. 40p. (gr. 1-4). 15.95 o.p. (*0-89919-645-4*) Houghton Mifflin Co. Trade & Reference Div. (Clarion Bks.).

—The Snoop. 1999. (Illus.). 64p. (J). (gr. 4-6). tchr. ed. 15.00 (*0-395-85821-6*, Clarion Bks.) Houghton Mifflin Co. Trade & Reference Div.

Thomas, Joyce Carol. The Golden Pasture. 144p. (YA). (gr. 7 up). 1987. pap. 2.50 o.p. (*0-590-33638-X*); 1986. 11.95 o.p. (*0-590-33681-9*) Scholastic, Inc.

Thomas, Karen. Changing of the Guard. 1986. 192p. (YA). (gr. 7 up). lib. bdg. 11.89 o.p. (*0-06-026164-1*) HarperCollins Children's Bk. Group.

Thomasma, Kenneth. Kunu: Winnebago Boy Escapes. 1989. (J). 12.99 (*1-880114-04-6*); pap. 7.99 (*1-880114-03-8*) Grandview Publishing Co.

—Pathki Nana: Kootenai Girl Solves a Mystery. 1991. (J). (gr. 3-8). 12.99 (*1-880114-10-0*) Grandview Publishing Co.

Thompson, Colin. Looking for Atlantis. (J). 1997. 30p. (gr. 1-4). pap. 6.99 o.s.i (*0-679-88547-1*, Random Hse. Bks. for Young Readers); 1994. (Illus.). 16.00 o.s.i (*0-679-85648-X*, Knopf Bks. for Young Readers) Random Hse. Children's Bks.

Thompson, Mary. Gran's Bees. 1996. (Single Titles Ser.: 4). (Illus.). 32p. (J). (gr. 2-4). 21.90 o.p. (*1-56294-652-8*) Millbrook Pr., Inc.

Thomson, Pat. Can You Hear Me, Grandad? 1995. (Illus.). 32p. (J). (gr. 2-4). pap. 8.95 o.s.i (*0-575-05760-2*) Gollancz, Victor GBR. *Dist:* Trafalgar Square.

—Can You Hear Me, Grandad? 1987. (Share-a-Story Ser.). (J). (gr. k-2). pap. 2.50 o.s.i (*0-440-40025-2*, Yearling) Random Hse. Children's Bks.

—Good Girl Granny. 1995. (Illus.). 32p. (J). (ps-2). pap. 8.95 o.p. (*0-575-05996-6*) Gollancz, Victor GBR. *Dist:* Trafalgar Square.

—Good Girl Granny. 1988. (J). (gr. k-6). pap. 2.50 o.s.i (*0-440-40026-0*, Yearling) Random Hse. Children's Bks.

—The Squeaky, Creaky Bed. 2003. (Illus.). 32p. (J). (-1). lib. bdg. 17.99 (*0-385-90856-3*); 15.95 (*0-385-74630-X*) Random Hse. Children's Bks. (Doubleday Bks. for Young Readers).

Thornton, Terence. Grandpa's Chair. Brown, Jane, ed. 1987. (Illus.). (gr. 1-3). pap. 10.99 o.p. (*0-88070-190-0*) Zonderkidz.

Thorson, Kristine & Thorson, Robert. Stone Wall Secrets. 2001. (Illus.). 40p. (J). (gr. 3-7). pap. 7.95 (*0-88448-229-4*, Harpswell Pr.) Tilbury Hse. Pubs.

Thorson, Robert & Thorson, Kristine. Stone Wall Secrets. 1998. (Illus.). 40p. (J). (gr. 3-6). 16.95 (*0-88448-195-6*) Tilbury Hse. Pubs.

Tiller, Ruth. Cinnamon, Mint, & Mothballs: A Visit to Grandmother's House. 1993. (Illus.). 32p. (J). (ps-2). 13.95 o.s.i (*0-15-276617-0*) Harcourt Children's Bks.

Time-Life Books Editors. Roberto's Magical Clocks: A Book about Telling Time. Kagan, Neil & Ward, Elizabeth, eds. 1992. (Early Learning Program Ser.). (Illus.). 30p. (J). (ps-2). o.s.i (*0-8094-9303-9*); lib. bdg. o.p. (*0-8094-9304-7*) Time-Life, Inc.

Tobias, Tobi. Pot Luck. 1993. (Illus.). (J). (ps-3). lib. bdg. 14.93 o.p. (*0-688-09825-8*) HarperCollins Children's Bk. Group.

—Wishes for You. Date not set. 32p. (J). (ps-2). pap. 5.99 (*0-06-443730-2*) HarperCollins Pubs.

—Wishes for You. 2003. (Illus.). 40p. (J). 15.99 (*0-688-10838-5*); lib. bdg. 16.89 (*0-688-10839-3*) Morrow/Avon.

Tolstoy, Leo. Philipok. 2000. (Illus.). 32p. (J). (gr. k-2). 16.99 (*0-399-23482-9*, Philomel) Penguin Putnam Bks. for Young Readers.

—Philipok. 2002. (Illus.). 32p. (J). pap. 6.99 (*0-698-11966-5*, PaperStar) Penguin Putnam Bks. for Young Readers.

Tomey, Ingrid. Grandfather's Day. 2003. (Illus.). 64p. (J). (gr. 3-7). pap. 9.95 (*1-56397-947-0*) Boyds Mills Pr.

—Grandfather's Day. 2001. (J). 16.10 (*0-606-20682-5*) Turtleback Bks.

—Nobody Else Has to Know. 2000. 240p. (YA). (gr. 7-12). mass mkt. 4.99 (*0-440-22782-8*, Laurel Leaf) Random Hse. Children's Bks.

—Nobody Else Has to Know. 1999. 240p. (YA). (gr. 7-12). 15.95 o.s.i (*0-385-32624-6*) Random Hse., Inc.

Tompert, Ann. Grandfather Tang's Story: A Tale Told with Tangrams. 1997. (Illus.). 32p. (J). (ps-2). reprint ed. pap. 6.99 (*0-517-88558-1*, Random Hse. Bks. for Young Readers) Random Hse. Children's Bks.

—Grandfather Tang's Story: A Tale Told with Tangrams. 1997. (J). 13.14 (*0-606-12953-7*) Turtleback Bks.

Torres, Leyla. Liliana's Grandmothers, RS. 1998. (Illus.). 32p. (J). (ps-5). 16.00 (*0-374-35105-8*, Farrar, Straus & Giroux (BYR)) Farrar, Straus & Giroux.

—Saturday Sancocho, RS. 1995. 32p. (J). (ps-3). 16.00 o.p. (*0-374-36418-4*, Farrar, Straus & Giroux (BYR)) Farrar, Straus & Giroux.

Townzen, L. Carl. Peter Slade. 1996. (Orig.). (J). pap. 8.95 o.p. (*0-533-11959-6*) Vantage Pr., Inc.

Tran, Truong. Going Home, Coming Home / Ve Nha Tham Que Hu'O'Ng. 2003. Tr. of Ve Nha Tham Que Hu'O'Ng. (ENG & VIE., Illus.). 32p. (J). 16.95 (*0-89239-179-0*) Children's Bk. Pr.

Tripp, Valerie. Just Josefina. 2002. (American Girls Short Stories Ser.). (Illus.). 64p. (J). 4.95 (*1-58485-478-2*, American Girl) Pleasant Co. Pubns.

—Samantha's Blue Bicycle. 2002. (American Girls Short Stories Ser.). (Illus.). 56p. (J). 4.95 (*1-58485-481-2*, American Girl) Pleasant Co. Pubns.

Tsubakiyama, Margaret. Mei-Mei Loves the Morning. 1999. (Illus.). 32p. (J). (ps-3). lib. bdg. 15.95 (*0-8075-5039-6*) Whitman, Albert & Co.

Tudor, Andrew, illus. Heidi. 1996. 64p. (J). (gr. 2-4). 5.98 (*1-85854-285-5*) Brimax Bks., Ltd.

Tung, Angela. Song of the Stranger. Artenstein, Michael, ed. 1999. (Roxbury Park Bks.). (J). 192p. (gr. 3-7). pap. 4.95 (*1-56565-948-1*, 09481W); 96p. (gr. 5-8). 12.95 (*1-56565-774-8*, 07748W) Lowell Hse. (Roxbury Park).

Tunnell, Michael O. Mailing May. 1997. (Illus.). 32p. (J). (ps-3). 15.95 (*0-688-12878-5*); lib. bdg. 15.89 (*0-688-12879-3*) HarperCollins Children's Bk. Group. (Greenwillow Bks.).

Turner, Ann Warren. Elfsong. abr. ed. 1995. 156p. (J). (gr. 4-7). 16.00 (*0-15-200826-8*) Harcourt Children's Bks.

Uhlig, Elizabeth. Grandmother Mary. 2000. (Illus.). 32p. (J). (gr. 4-6). 17.95 (*0-9677047-0-7*) Marble House Editions.

Seymour, Peter S. & Allert, Kathy. What Time Is Grandma Coming? 1984. (Surprise Bks.). (Illus.). 24p. (J). (ps-2). 7.95 o.s.i (*0-8431-0645-X*, Price Stern Sloan) Penguin Putnam Bks. for Young Readers.

Uslander, Arlene. That's What Grandparents Are For. 2001. (Illus.). 32p. (J). (ps-3). 15.95 (*0-939217-60-0*) Peel Productions, Inc.

Vainio, Pirkko. The Christmas Angel. Bell, Anthea, tr. from GER. 1997. (Illus.). 32p. (J). (gr. k-3). pap. 6.95 o.p. (*1-55858-774-8*) North-South Bks., Inc.

Valgardson, W. D. Winter Rescue. 1995. (Illus.). 48p. (J). (ps-3). per. 15.00 (*0-689-80094-0*, McElderry, Margaret K.) Simon & Schuster Children's Publishing.

Van Hook, Beverly. The Case of the Riverboat Riverbelle. 1986. (Supergranny Ser.: No. 2). (Illus.). 112p. (J). (gr. 3-6). pap. 2.95 (*0-916761-08-8*); lib. bdg. 7.95 (*0-916761-09-6*) Holderby & Bierce.

—The Character Who Came to Life. Nelken, Andrea, ed. 1989. (Supergranny Ser.: No. 5). (Illus.). 112p. (J). (gr. 3-6). pap. 2.95 (*0-916761-12-6*); lib. bdg. 7.95 (*0-916761-13-4*) Holderby & Bierce.

—The Ghost of Heidelberg Castle. 1987. (Supergranny Ser.: No. 3). (Illus.). 112p. (J). (gr. 3-6). pap. 2.95 (*0-916761-06-1*); lib. bdg. 7.95 (*0-916761-07-X*) Holderby & Bierce.

—The Great College Caper. Nelken, Andrea, ed. 1991. (Supergranny Ser.: No. 6). (Illus.). 112p. (J). (gr. 3-6). pap. 3.25 (*0-916761-14-2*); lib. bdg. 9.95 (*0-916761-15-0*) Holderby & Bierce.

—The Mystery of the Shrunken Heads. 1985. (Supergranny Ser.: No. 1). (Illus.). 96p. (J). (gr. 3-6). pap. 2.95 (*0-916761-10-X*); lib. bdg. 7.95 (*0-916761-11-8*) Holderby & Bierce.

—The Secret of Devil Mountain. Nelken, Andrea, ed. 1988. (Supergranny Ser.: No. 4). (Illus.). 112p. (J). (gr. 3-6). pap. 3.25 (*0-916761-04-5*); lib. bdg. 9.95 (*0-916761-05-3*) Holderby & Bierce.

Van Leeuwen, Jean. Touch the Sky Summer. 1997. (Illus.). 32p. (J). (ps-3). 14.99 o.s.i (*0-8037-1819-5*, Dial Bks. for Young Readers) Penguin Putnam Bks. for Young Readers.

—What I Did on My Summer Vacation. 1997. (Illus.). 32p. (J). 14.89 o.s.i (*0-8037-1820-9*, Dial Bks. for Young Readers) Penguin Putnam Bks. for Young Readers.

Vance, Joel M. Grandma & the Buck Deer. 3rd ed. 1988. (Illus.). 173p. (YA). reprint ed. pap. 11.95 (*0-87691-322-2*) Cedar Glade Pr.

Vaughan, Paula. Granny Bloomers. 2000. (Illus.). 28p. (J). 15.95 (*1-57486-222-7*) Leisure Arts, Inc.

Vaughan, Sherry T. Grandpa's Eyes. 1996. (Illus.). 64p. (Orig.). (YA). (gr. 5-7). pap. 5.95 (*1-57072-047-9*) Overmountain Pr.

Velasquez, Eric. Grandma's Records. 2001. (Illus.). 32p. (J). (gr. k-3). 17.85 (*0-8027-8761-4*); 16.95 (*0-8027-8760-6*) Walker & Co.

Velasquez, Eric & de la Vega, Eida. Los Discos de Mi Abuela. 2002. (SPA., Illus.). (J). (gr. 1-3). 16.95 (*1-930332-21-1*, LC7246) Lectorum Pubns., Inc.

Viglucci, Patricia C. Sun Dance at Turtle Rock. 1996. (Illus.). 128p. (Orig.). (J). (gr. 4-7). pap. 4.95 (*0-9645914-9-9*, Stone Pine Bks.) Patri Pubns.

Vigna, Judith. Grandma Without Me. Tucker, Kathleen, ed. 1984. (Albert Whitman Concept Bks.). (Illus.). 32p. (J). (ps-3). lib. bdg. 13.95 o.p. (*0-8075-3030-1*) Whitman, Albert & Co.

—My Two Uncles. 1995. (Albert Whitman Concept Bks.). (Illus.). 32p. (J). (gr. 7 up). lib. bdg. 14.95 (*0-8075-5507-X*) Whitman, Albert & Co.

Vogel, Ilse-Margret. Dodo Every Day. 1977. (Illus.). (J). (gr. k-4). 5.95 o.p. (*0-06-026315-6*); lib. bdg. 6.89 o.p. (*0-06-026316-4*) HarperCollins Pubs.

Vulliamy, Clara. Small. 2002. (Illus.). 32p. (J). (ps-1). 15.00 (*0-618-19459-2*, Clarion Bks.) Houghton Mifflin Co. Trade & Reference Div.

Waboose, Jan Bourdeau. Firedancers. 2000. (Illus.). 32p. (J). (ps-3). 14.95 (*0-7737-3138-5*) Stoddart Kids CAN. *Dist:* Fitzhenry & Whiteside, Ltd.

—Morning on the Lake. (J). (gr. k-4). 2002. 32p. pap. 5.95 (*1-55074-588-3*); 1998. (Illus.). 400p. (*1-55074-373-2*) Kids Can Pr., Ltd.

Waddell, Martin. Grandma's Bill. 1991. (Illus.). 32p. (J). (ps-2). 12.95 o.p. (*0-531-05923-5*); mass mkt. 12.99 o.p. (*0-531-08523-6*) Scholastic, Inc. (Orchard Bks.).

—My Great Grandpa. 1990. (Illus.). 32p. (J). (ps-3). 14.95 o.p. (*0-399-22155-7*, G. P. Putnam's Sons) Penguin Putnam Bks. for Young Readers.

Wahl, Jan. Grandmother Told Me. 1972. (Illus.). 32p. (J). (gr. k-3). 6.95 o.p. (*0-316-91744-3*) Little Brown & Co.

—Grandpa Gus's Birthday Cake. 1981. (Illus.). (J). (ps-3). o.p. (*0-13-363325-X*) Prentice-Hall.

—"I Remember!" Cried Grandma Pinky. 1994. 10.15 o.p. (*0-606-07687-5*) Turtleback Bks.

Wahl, Mats. Grandfather's Laika. 1990. (Illus.). 32p. (J). (ps-3). lib. bdg. 7.95 o.s.i (*0-87614-434-2*, Carolrhoda Bks.) Lerner Publishing Group.

Wainwright, Richard M. Nana, Grampa & Tecumseh. 1997. (Illus.). 64p. (J). 19.00 (*0-9619566-7-4*) Family Life Publishing/Richard Wainright Bks.

Waite, Michael P. Gilly Greenweed's Gift for Granny. 1992. 32p. (J). (ps-3). 9.99 o.p. (*0-7814-0035-X*) Cook Communications Ministries.

Walden, Joseph. Grandpa's Smile. 2000. (Illus.). 32p. (J). (ps-2). per. (*1-59093-058-4*, Eager Minds Pr.) Warehousing & Fulfillment Specialists, LLC (WFS, LLC).

Wallace, Barbara Brooks. Ghosts in the Gallery. 144p. (J). 2001. pap. 4.99 (*0-689-83915-4*, Aladdin); 2000. (Illus.). (gr. 4-7). 16.00 (*0-689-83175-7*, Atheneum) Simon & Schuster Children's Publishing.

—Ghosts in the Gallery. 2000. (Illus.). (J). 11.04 (*0-606-21612-X*) Turtleback Bks.

Wallace, Ian. Chin Chiang & the Dragon's Dance. ed. 1991. (J). (gr. 2). spiral bd. (*0-616-01806-1*) Canadian National Institute for the Blind/Institut National Canadien pour les Aveugles.

—Chin Chiang & the Dragon's Dance. 1998. (Illus.). 32p. (J). (ps-2). 19.95 (*0-88899-020-0*); pap. 5.95 (*0-88899-167-3*) Groundwood Bks. CAN. *Dist:* Publishers Group West.

—Chin Chiang & the Dragon's Dance. 1984. (Illus.). 32p. (J). (gr. k-4). lib. bdg. 13.95 o.p. (*0-689-50299-0*, McElderry, Margaret K.) Simon & Schuster Children's Publishing.

Wallace, Nancy Elizabeth, tr. & illus. Seeds! Seeds! Seeds! 2004. (J). (*0-7614-5159-5*, Cavendish Children's Bks.) Cavendish, Marshall Corp.

Walter, Mildred Pitts. Justin & the Best Biscuits in the World. 2002. (Illus.). (J). 13.40 (*0-7587-0371-6*) Book Wholesalers, Inc.

—Justin & the Best Biscuits in the World. 1986. (Illus.). 128p. (J). (gr. 4-7). 15.95 (*0-688-06645-3*) HarperCollins Children's Bk. Group.

—Justin & the Best Biscuits in the World. 1995. (Illus.). (J). (gr. 4). 9.00 (*0-395-73245-X*) Houghton Mifflin Co.

—Justin & the Best Biscuits in the World. 1999. (Illus.). 128p. (J). (gr. 3-5). pap. 4.99 (*0-679-89448-9*) Knopf, Alfred A. Inc.

—Justin & the Best Biscuits in the World. 1986. (J). 11.04 (*0-606-04714-X*) Turtleback Bks.

—Ray & the Best Family Reunion Ever. (Amistad Ser.). (Illus.). 128p. (J). 2002. lib. bdg. 15.89 (*0-06-623625-8*); 2001. 15.95 (*0-06-623624-X*) HarperTrade. (Amistad Pr.).

—Trouble's Child. 1985. 128p. (J). (gr. 4 up). 11.95 o.p. (*0-688-04214-7*) HarperCollins Children's Bk. Group.

Ward, Nick. Don't Worry, Grandpa. 1995. (Illus.). 32p. (J). (ps-3). pap. 4.95 (*0-8120-9425-5*); 12.95 o.p. (*0-8120-6533-6*) Barron's Educational Series, Inc.

Wardlaw, Lee. The Tales of Grandpa Cat. 1994. (Illus.). 32p. (J). 14.99 o.p. (*0-8037-1511-0*); 14.89 o.p. (*0-8037-1512-9*) Penguin Putnam Bks. for Young Readers. (Dial Bks. for Young Readers).

Ware, Cheryl. Catty-Cornered. 1998. (Illus.). 112p. (J). (gr. 4-8). pap. 15.95 (*0-531-30067-6*); lib. bdg. 16.99 (*0-531-33067-2*) Scholastic, Inc. (Orchard Bks.).

Wargin, Kathy-Jo. The Legend of the Loon. (Illus.). 48p. (J). (gr. k-5). 2003. pap. 7.95 (*1-58536-167-4*); 2000. 17.95 (*1-886947-97-X*) Sleeping Bear Pr.

Warmuth, Donna Akers & Gobble, DeAnna Akers, illus. Plumb Full of History: A Story of Abingdon, Virginia. 2003. 64p. (J). 9.95 (*1-932158-78-2*) High Country Pubs., Ltd.

Warner, Gertrude Chandler, creator. A Present for Grandfather. 1998. (Adventures of Benny & Watch: No. 2). (J). (gr. 1-3). 10.10 (*0-606-13216-3*) Turtleback Bks.

Warriner, Holly. Full Moon Magic. 1998. (Spell Casters Ser.: No. 2). 144p. (J). (gr. 3-7). 3.99 (*0-689-81900-5*, Aladdin) Simon & Schuster Children's Publishing.

Watkins, Dawn L. Chickadee Winter. 1999. (Illus.). (J). (ps-1). pap. 5.49 (*1-57924-273-1*, 120170) Jones, Bob Univ. Pr.

Watkins, Sherrin. Green Snake Ceremony. 1995. (Greyfeather Ser.). (Illus.). 408p. (J). (ps-5). 17.95 (*0-933031-89-0*) Council Oak Bks.

Watson. Grandpa's Slippers. 1990. (J). (ps-2). 19.95 o.p. (*0-590-75483-1*) Scholastic, Inc.

Watson, Joy & Hodder, Wendy. Le Gilet de Grand Papa. 9999. (FRE.). (J). pap. 6.99 o.p. (*0-590-24132-X*) Scholastic, Inc.

Watson, Mary. The Butterfly Seeds. 1995. (Illus.). 32p. (J). (ps-3). 16.00 (*0-688-14132-3*); lib. bdg. 15.89 (*0-688-14133-1*) Morrow/Avon. (Morrow, William & Co.).

Wayland, April Halprin. It's Not My Turn to Look for Grandma. 1995. (Illus.). 132p. (J). 15.00 o.s.i (*0-679-84491-0*) Knopf, Alfred A. Inc.

—It's Not My Turn to Look for Grandma. 1995. (Illus.). (J). 15.99 o.s.i (*0-679-94491-5*) Knopf, Alfred A. Inc.

Weatherford, Carole Boston. Grandma & Me. 1996. (Illus.). 12p. (J). (ps-k). bds. 5.95 (*0-86316-252-5*) Writers & Readers Publishing, Inc.

Wehmeyer, Betty J. Jesus Goes to Grandma's House. 1998. vi, 8p. (J). (ps-6). pap. 14.95 (*1-892611-00-7*) Wehmeyer, Betty Jean.

Wells, Rosemary. Bunny Money. 1997. (Max & Ruby Ser.). (Illus.). 32p. (J). (gr. k-2). 14.99 o.s.i (*0-8037-2146-3*); 14.89 o.p. (*0-8037-2147-1*) Penguin Putnam Bks. for Young Readers. (Dial Bks. for Young Readers).

—The Language of Doves. 1996. (Illus.). 32p. (J). (ps-3). 14.99 o.p. (*0-8037-1471-8*); 14.89 o.p. (*0-8037-1472-6*) Penguin Putnam Bks. for Young Readers. (Dial Bks. for Young Readers).

—Yoko's Paper Cranes. 2001. (Illus.). 32p. (J). (ps-2). 15.99 (*0-7868-0737-7*); lib. bdg. 16.49 (*0-7868-2602-9*) Hyperion Bks. for Children.

Wendelbo, Lynn. Looking Through Grandmother's Glasses: A Journey into a Child's Heart. 1999. (Illus.). 114p. (J). (ps-4). pap. 16.95 (*1-885473-97-4*, Preproduction Pr.) Wood 'N Barnes.

Weninger, Brigitte, pseud. Happy Birthday, Davy! 2000. (Illus.). 32p. (J). (ps-2). 15.95 (*0-7358-1345-0*) North-South Bks., Inc.

—Happy Birthday, Davy! Lanning, Rosemary, tr. from GER. 2000. (Illus.). 32p. (J). (ps-2). lib. bdg. 16.50 (*0-7358-1346-9*) North-South Bks., Inc.

Westheimer, Ruth Karola & Lehu, Pierre A. Dr. Ruth: Grandma on Wheels. 2001. (Illus.). 24p. (J). 2.99 o.s.i (*0-307-98239-4*, Golden Bks.) Random Hse. Children's Bks.

Weston, Martha. Apple Juice Tea. 1994. (Illus.). 32p. (J). (ps-3). tchr. ed. 14.95 (*0-395-65480-7*, Clarion Bks.) Houghton Mifflin Co. Trade & Reference Div.

Wheeler, Lisa. Who's Afraid of Granny Wolf? Ansley, Frank, tr. & illus. by. 2004. (J). (*0-689-84952-4*, Atheneum/Richard Jackson Bks.) Simon & Schuster Children's Publishing.

When Grandma Comes to Visit. Date not set. 5.95 (*0-89868-351-3*) ARO Publishing Co.

Whitelaw, Nancy. A Beautiful Pearl. Tucker, Kathleen, ed. 1991. (Albert Whitman Concept Bks.). (Illus.). 32p. (J). 14.95 o.p. (*0-8075-0599-4*) Whitman, Albert & Co.

Whitethorne, Baje, Sr. Father's Boots: Azhe'e bikenidoots'osii. Marvin, Yellowhair & Jerrold, Johnson, eds. Darlene, Redhair, tr. 2001. (ENG & NAV., Illus.). 42p. (J). (gr. 1-6). text 17.95 (*1-893354-29-6*) Salina Bookshelf.

Whitethorne, Baje, Sr., illus. Sunpainters: Eclipse of the Navajo Sun. 2002. (J). (*1-893354-33-4*) Salina Bookshelf.

WHO Staff. Grandma's off Her Rocker. 2001. 120p. pap. 10.95 (*0-595-18922-9*) iUniverse, Inc.

Whybrow, Ian. Sammy & the Robots. 2001. (Illus.). 32p. (J). (ps-1). pap. 15.95 (*0-531-30327-6*, Orchard Bks.) Scholastic, Inc.

Wigand, Molly. Junk, Sweet Junk. 1997. (Ready-to-Read Ser.). (Illus.). 32p. (J). (ps-3). pap. 3.99 (*0-689-81260-4*, Simon Spotlight/Nickelodeon) Simon & Schuster Children's Publishing.

Wiggin, Eric. Maggie: Life at the Elms. 1994. (Maggie Ser.). (J). mass mkt. 3.99 o.p. (*1-56507-133-6*) Harvest Hse. Pubs.

Wild, Margaret. Big Cat Dreaming. 1997. (Illus.). 32p. (J). (ps up). 16.95 (*1-55037-493-1*) Annick Pr., Ltd. CAN. *Dist:* Firefly Bks., Ltd.

—But Granny Did! 1993. (Voyages Ser.). (Illus.). (J). 3.75 (*0-383-03559-7*) SRA/McGraw-Hill.

—Our Granny. 2002. (Illus.). (J). 13.79 (*0-7587-3344-5*) Book Wholesalers, Inc.

—Our Granny. (Illus.). 32p. (J). (ps-3). 1998. pap. 5.95 (*0-395-88395-4*); 1994. lib. bdg. 16.00 (*0-395-67023-3*) Houghton Mifflin Co.

—Remember Me. 1995. (Albert Whitman Concept Bks.). (Illus.). 32p. (J). (ps-3). lib. bdg. 14.95 (*0-8075-6934-8*) Whitman, Albert & Co.

Wilder, Laura Ingalls. Dance at Grandpa's. 1995. (My First Little House Bks.). (Illus.). 40p. (J). (ps-3). pap. 5.99 (*0-06-443372-2*, Harper Trophy) HarperCollins Children's Bk. Group.

Wiles, Deborah. Love, Ruby Lavender. (YA). (gr. 3-7). 2002. 216p. pap. 5.95 (*0-15-204568-6*); 2001. (Illus.). 200p. 16.00 (*0-15-202314-3*) Harcourt Children's Bks. (Gulliver Bks.).

—Love, Ruby Lavender. unabr. ed. 2002. (gr. 3-7). audio 25.00 (*0-8072-0717-9*, Listening Library) Random Hse. Audio Publishing Group.

Wilkins, Verna A. Dave & the Tooth Fairy. 1996. (Illus.). 24p. (J). lib. bdg. 12.95 (*1-56674-120-3*) Forest Hse. Publishing Co., Inc.

Wilkins, Verna Allette. Dave & the Tooth Fairy. 1998. (Illus.). 24p. (J). (gr. 2 up). lib. bdg. 22.60 (*0-8368-2089-4*) Stevens, Gareth Inc.

Willard, Nancy. The Mountains of Quilt. 1987. (Illus.). 40p. (J). (ps-3). 12.95 (*0-15-256010-6*) Harcourt Children's Bks.

—The Mountains of Quilt. 1997. (Illus.). 32p. (J). pap. 6.00 (*0-15-201480-2*) Harcourt Trade Pubs.

—The Mouse, the Cat, & Grandmother's Hat. 2003. (Illus.). 32p. (J). (ps-3). 14.95 (*0-316-94006-2*) Little Brown Children's Bks.

Williams, Annie Morris. Gwyneth's Secret Grandpa. 2001. (Family History Adventures for Young Readers Ser.: Vol. 1). (Illus.). 168p. (J). (gr. 4-7). per. 10.95 (*0-9645272-7-8*) Field Stone Pubs.

Williams, Barbara. Guess Who's Coming to My Tea Party, ERS. 1978. (ps-1). o.p. (*0-03-021541-2*, Holt, Henry & Co. Bks. For Young Readers) Holt, Henry & Co.

—Kevin's Grandma. (Unicorn Paperbacks Ser.). (Illus.). 32p. (J). (ps-1). 1991. pap. 3.95 o.p. (*0-525-44785-7*, Puffin Bks.); 1978. pap. 3.95 o.p. (*0-525-45039-4*, Dutton Children's Bks.); 1975. 11.95 o.p. (*0-525-33115-8*, Dutton Children's Bks.) Penguin Putnam Bks. for Young Readers.

—Mitzi's Honeymoon with Nana Potts. 1985. 112p. (gr. k-6). pap. 2.50 o.p. (*0-440-45674-6*) Dell Publishing.

Williams, Carol Lynch. If I Forget, You Remember. 1998. 208p. text 15.95 o.s.i (*0-385-32534-7*, Delacorte Pr.) Dell Publishing.

Williams, Effie M. Daniel & Juanita at Grandpa's House. 1982. Tr. of Daniel y Juanita en la Casa de Abuelo. (SPA., Illus.). 52p. (J). (gr. 3-6). pap. 2.95 (*0-7399-0296-2*, 2181.1) Rod & Staff Pubs., Inc.

Williams, Laura E. The Long Silk Strand: A Grandmother's Legacy to Her Granddaughter. 2003. (Illus.). 32p. (J). (ps-3). pap. 7.95 (*1-56397-856-3*) Boyds Mills Pr.

—The Long Silk Strand: A Grandmother's Legacy to Her Granddaughter. 2000. (Illus.). (J). 14.10 (*0-606-18013-3*) Turtleback Bks.

—Torch Fishing with the Sun. 2003. (Illus.). 32p. (J). (gr. k-3). 15.95 (*1-56397-685-4*) Boyds Mills Pr.

Williams, Mardo. Great-Grandpa Fussy & the Little Puckerdoodles. 2000. (Illus.). 64p. (J). (ps-4). 17.95 (*0-9649241-3-7*) Calliope Pr.

Williams, Michael. The Genuine Half-Moon Kid. 1994. 208p. (J). (gr. 7 up). 15.99 o.p. (*0-525-67470-5*, Dutton Children's Bks.) Penguin Putnam Bks. for Young Readers.

Williams, Sophy. Nana's Garden. 1994. (Illus.). 32p. (J). (ps-1). 14.99 o.p. (*0-670-85287-2*, Viking Children's Bks.) Penguin Putnam Bks. for Young Readers.

Willner-Pardo, Gina. Figuring Out Frances. 1999. (Illus.). 144p. (J). (gr. 4-6). tchr. ed. 14.00 (*0-395-91510-4*, Clarion Bks.) Houghton Mifflin Co. Trade & Reference Div.

—Hunting Grandma's Treasures. 1996. (Illus.). 48p. (J). (ps-4). tchr. ed. 14.95 o.p. (*0-395-68190-1*, Clarion Bks.) Houghton Mifflin Co. Trade & Reference Div.

Willson, Sarah. The Perfect Formula. 1999. (Rugrats Chapter Bks.: No. 1). (Illus.). 64p. (J). (gr. 1-4). pap. 3.99 (*0-689-82677-X*, 076714003996, Simon Spotlight) Simon & Schuster Children's Publishing.

—The Rugrats Book of Chanukah. 1997. (Rugrats Ser.). (Illus.). 32p. (J). (ps-2). pap. 5.99 (*0-689-81676-6*, Simon Spotlight/Nickelodeon) Simon & Schuster Children's Publishing.

Wilson, Forrest. Super Gran. 1987. (Illus.). 160p. (J). (gr. 3-7). pap. 2.95 o.p. (*0-14-031266-8*, Puffin Bks.) Penguin Putnam Bks. for Young Readers.

—Super Gran Rules OK! 1987. (Illus.). (J). (gr. 3-7). pap. 3.95 o.p. (*0-14-031427-X*, Puffin Bks.) Penguin Putnam Bks. for Young Readers.

Wilson, Jane & Haas, Michaele. Meema's Memory Quilt: Treasured Stories of Watauga County History. 1999. (Illus.). 27p. (J). 16.95 (*1-887905-18-9*) Parkway Pubs., Inc.

Wilson, Nancy Hope. Mountain Pose, RS. 2001. 240p. (J). (gr. 5 up). 17.00 (*0-374-35078-7*, Farrar, Straus & Giroux (BYR)) Farrar, Straus & Giroux.

—Mountain Pose. 2003. 240p. (J). mass mkt. 4.50 (*0-439-44153-6*, Scholastic Paperbacks) Scholastic, Inc.

Winch, John. Keeping up with Grandma. 2000. (Illus.). 32p. (J). (ps-3). tchr. ed. 16.95 (*0-8234-1563-5*) Holiday Hse., Inc.

Windsor, Patricia. Mad Martin. 1976. (gr. 5 up). (J). 7.95 o.p. (*0-06-026517-5*); (YA). lib. bdg. 10.89 o.p. (*0-06-026518-3*) HarperCollins Pubs.

Winslow, Audrey H. My Grandma Says... 1997. (Illus.). 28p. (J). (ps-3). pap. 6.95 (*1-880218-28-3*) Marketing Directions, Inc.

—My Grandpa Says . . . 1996. (Illus.). 24p. (Orig.). (J). (ps-3). pap. 6.95 (*1-880218-23-2*) Marketing Directions, Inc.

Winters, Kay. How Will the Bunny Know? 1999. (Illus.). 48p. (J). (gr. k-3). 13.95 o.s.i (*0-385-32596-7*, Dell Books for Young Readers) Random Hse. Children's Bks.

—How Will the Easter Bunny Know? 1999. (Illus.). 48p. (J). (gr. k-3). pap. 4.50 (*0-440-41499-7*) Dell Publishing.

—How Will the Easter Bunny Know? 1999. 10.65 (*0-606-17670-5*) Turtleback Bks.

Winthrop, Elizabeth. Dancing Granny. 2003. (Illus.). (J). 16.95 (*0-7614-5141-2*, Cavendish Children's Bks.) Cavendish, Marshall Corp.

Wolf, Winfried. Christmas with Grandfather. James, J. Alison, tr. 1994. (Illus.). 32p. (J). (ps-3). 14.88 o.p. (*1-55858-297-5*) North-South Bks., Inc.

Wolff, Barbara M. Pappa & Me. 1991. (Illus.). 16p. (J). (ps-1). lib. bdg. 13.95 (*1-879567-11-3*, Valeria Bks.) Wonder Well Pubs.

Wood, Doug. Grandad's Prayers of the Earth. 1999. (Illus.). 32p. (J). (gr. 1-4). 16.99 (*0-7636-0660-X*) Candlewick Pr.

Wood, June Rae. About Face. 1999. 272p. (YA). (gr. 5-9). 19.99 o.s.i (*0-399-23419-5*, G. P. Putnam's Sons) Penguin Group (USA) Inc.

—About Face. 2001. 272p. pap. 5.99 o.s.i (*0-698-11891-X*) Penguin Putnam Bks. for Young Readers.

—About Face. 2001. (J). 12.04 (*0-606-21014-8*) Turtleback Bks.

Wood, Phyllis A. Then I'll Be Home Free. 1988. (YA). (gr. 6 up). mass mkt. 2.75 o.p. (*0-451-15373-1*, Signet Bks.) NAL.

—Then I'll Be Home Free. 1986. (YA). (gr. 7-11). 12.95 o.p. (*0-396-08766-3*, G. P. Putnam's Sons) Penguin Putnam Bks. for Young Readers.

Woodbury, Mary. Jess & the Runaway Grandpa. 1997. 208p. (J). (gr. 4-7). pap. 5.95 (*1-55050-113-5*) Coteau Bks. CAN. *Dist:* General Distribution Services, Inc.

Woodruff, Elvira. Can You Guess Where We're Going? 1998. (Illus.). 32p. (J). (ps-3). tchr. ed. 15.95 (*0-8234-1387-X*) Holiday Hse., Inc.

—Dear Napoleon, I Know You're Dead, But... 1994. 224p. (gr. 4-7). pap. text 4.99 (*0-440-40907-1*) Dell Publishing.

—Dear Napoleon, I Know You're Dead, But... 1992. (J). 10.04 (*0-606-06965-8*) Turtleback Bks.

—The Summer I Shrank My Grandmother. 1990. (Illus.). 160p. (J). (gr. 3-7). 15.95 o.p. (*0-8234-0832-9*) Holiday Hse., Inc.

—The Summer I Shrank My Grandmother. 1992. 160p. (gr. 4-7). pap. text 3.99 o.s.i (*0-440-40640-4*, Yearling) Random Hse. Children's Bks.

Woods, Lee Ann. Grandpa Whitt's Grocery. 1999. (J). (gr. 4-5). E-Book (*1-929776-06-3*) Chapter & Verse Publishing for Children.

Woodson, Jacqueline. Sweet, Sweet Memory. 2000. (Illus.). 32p. (J). lib. bdg. 15.49 (*0-7868-2191-4*) Disney Pr.

—Sweet, Sweet Memory. 2000. (Illus.). 32p. (J). (gr. 1-4). 14.99 (*0-7868-0241-3*, Jump at the Sun) Hyperion Bks. for Children.

—Visiting Day. 2002. (Illus.). 32p. (J). (ps-3). pap. 15.95 (*0-590-40005-3*, Scholastic Pr.) Scholastic, Inc.

Woodson, Jacqueline & Ransome, James. Visiting Day. 2001. (Illus.). (J). pap. (*0-590-55262-7*) Scholastic, Inc.

Woody, Marilyn J. Basil Bear Learns to Tell Time. 1999. 20p. (J). (ps-2). 12.99 o.p. (*1-57673-447-1*, Harmony) Crown Publishing Group.

Wrenn, Elizabeth. The Christmas Cactus. 2001. (Illus.). (J). (*1-56123-158-4*) Centering Corp.

Wright, Betty Ren. Out of the Dark. 1995. 128p. (J). (gr. 4-7). pap. 14.95 (*0-590-43598-1*) Scholastic, Inc.

—The Wish Master. 2000. (Illus.). 104p. (J). (gr. 3-7). tchr. ed. 15.95 (*0-8234-1611-9*) Holiday Hse., Inc.

Wright, Lynn F. Grandma, Tell Me a Story. 1999. (Illus.). (J). 13.95 (*1-881519-10-4*); pap. 6.95 (*1-881519-11-2*) WorryWart Publishing Co.

Wyeth, Sharon Dennis. Ginger Brown: Too Many Houses. 1996. (Illus.). 80p. (J). (ps-3). 11.99 o.s.i (*0-679-95437-6*); (gr. 1-4). pap. 3.99 o.s.i (*0-679-85437-1*) Random Hse. Children's Bks. (Random Hse. Bks. for Young Readers).

—Ginger Brown: Too Many Houses. 1996. 9.19 o.p. (*0-606-09327-3*) Turtleback Bks.

Wyman, Andrea. Red Sky at Morning. 1991. 240p. (J). (gr. 4-7). 15.95 o.p. (*0-8234-0903-1*) Holiday Hse., Inc.

—Red Sky at Morning. 1997. pap. 3.99 o.p. (*0-380-72877-X*, Avon Bks.) Morrow/Avon.

—Red Sky at Morning. 1997. 9.09 o.p. (*0-606-10908-0*) Turtleback Bks.

Wyse, Lois & Goldman, Molly Rose. How to Take Your Grandmother to the Museum. 1998. (Illus.). 48p. (J). (gr. k-3). bds. 12.95 (*0-7611-0990-0*) Workman Publishing Co., Inc.

Yamada, Debbie Leung. Striking It Rich: Treasures from Gold Mountain. l.t. ed. 2001. (Illus.). 128p. (J). (gr. 4-8). 13.95 (*1-879965-21-6*) Polychrome Publishing Corp.

Ye, Ting-Xing. Share the Sky. 1999. (Illus.). 32p. (J). (gr. k-3). lib. bdg. 17.95 (*1-55037-579-2*) Annick Pr., Ltd. CAN. *Dist:* Firefly Bks., Ltd.

Yep, Laurence. Angelfish. 2001. 216p. (J). (gr. 5 up). 16.99 (*0-399-23041-6*, G. P. Putnam's Sons) Penguin Group (USA) Inc.

—Child of the Owl. (Golden Mountain Chronicles). (J). (gr. 7 up). 1990. 288p. pap. 6.99 (*0-06-440336-X*, Harper Trophy); 1977. 224p. lib. bdg. 16.89 (*0-06-026743-7*) HarperCollins Children's Bk. Group.

—Child of the Owl. 1977. (J). 11.00 (*0-606-04634-8*) Turtleback Bks.

—The Cook's Family. 1998. (J). (*0-03-992907-8*) Holt, Rinehart & Winston.

—The Cook's Family. 1998. 186p. (J). (gr. 5-9). 15.99 o.p. (*0-399-22907-8*, G. P. Putnam's Sons) Penguin Group (USA) Inc.

—The Cook's Family. 1999. (Illus.). 192p. (J). (gr. 5-9). pap. 5.99 o.s.i (*0-698-11804-9*, PaperStar) Penguin Putnam Bks. for Young Readers.

—The Cook's Family. 1999. (J). 11.04 (*0-606-18932-7*) Turtleback Bks.

—The Cook's Family. 1999. (J). pap. 3.99 (*0-14-037472-8*, Viking) Viking Penguin.

—The Imp That Ate My Homework. (Illus.). 96p. (J). (gr. 3-7). 2000. pap. 4.99 (*0-06-440840-X*, Harper Trophy); 1998. lib. bdg. 14.89 (*0-06-027689-4*) HarperCollins Children's Bk. Group.

—The Imp That Ate My Homework. 1998. (Illus.). 96p. (J). (gr. 3-7). 14.95 (*0-06-027688-6*) HarperCollins Pubs.

—The Imp That Ate My Homework. 2000. 11.10 (*0-606-17671-3*) Turtleback Bks.

—The Magic Paintbrush. 2000. (Illus.). 96p. (J). (gr. 7 up). 14.95 (*0-06-028199-5*); lib. bdg. 13.89 (*0-06-028200-2*) HarperCollins Children's Bk. Group.

—The Magic Paintbrush. 2003. (Illus.). 96p. (J). (gr. 3-7). pap. 4.99 (*0-06-440852-3*) HarperCollins Pubs.

—Ribbons. 1996. 192p. (J). (gr. 5-9). 16.99 o.p. (*0-399-22906-X*, G. P. Putnam's Sons) Penguin Group (USA) Inc.

—Ribbons. 1999. pap. 13.99 (*0-670-85929-X*) Viking Penguin.

—Thief of Hearts. 1997. (Golden Mountain Chronicles). 208p. (J). (gr. 5 up). pap. 6.95 (*0-06-440591-5*, Harper Trophy) HarperCollins Children's Bk. Group.

—Thief of Hearts. 1995. (Illus.). 208p. (J). (gr. 5-9). 14.95 o.p. (*0-06-025341-X*); lib. bdg. 15.89 o.p. (*0-06-025342-8*) HarperTrade.

—Thief of Hearts. 1997. 12.00 (*0-606-11978-7*) Turtleback Bks.

Yolen, Jane. Grandad Bill's Song. (Illus.). 32p. (J). (ps-3). 1998. pap. 5.99 o.p. (*0-698-11614-3*, PaperStar); 1994. 16.99 o.p. (*0-399-21802-5*, Philomel) Penguin Putnam Bks. for Young Readers.

—Grandad Bill's Song. 1998. (J). 12.14 (*0-606-12952-9*) Turtleback Bks.

—The Hurrying Child. 2002. (Illus.). (J). 16.00 (*0-15-201813-1*, Silver Whistle) Harcourt Children's Bks. CAN. *Dist:* Harcourt Trade Pubs.

—No Bath Tonight. 1978. (Illus.). (J). (gr. k-3). 12.95 (*0-690-03881-X*) HarperCollins Children's Bk. Group.

—Off We Go! 2002. (Illus.). (J). 18.89 (*0-7587-3295-3*) Book Wholesalers, Inc.

—Off We Go! (J). (ps-3). 2000. (Illus.). 32p. 12.95 (*0-316-90228-4*); 1999. 12.95 (*0-316-90111-3*) Little Brown & Co.

—Off We Go! 2002. (Illus.). 8p. (J). bds. 5.95 (*0-316-90972-6*) Little Brown Children's Bks.

Yumoto, Kazumi. The Spring Tone, RS. 1999. (JPN.). 176p. (J). (gr. 7-12). 16.00 o.p. (*0-374-37153-9*, Farrar, Straus & Giroux (BYR)) Farrar, Straus & Giroux.

—The Spring Tone. Hirano, Cathy, tr. 2001. 176p. (YA). (gr. 7 up). mass mkt. 4.99 (*0-440-22855-7*, Laurel Leaf) Random Hse. Children's Bks.

—The Spring Tone. Hirano, Cathy, tr. 2000. (YA). pap., stu. ed. 52.00 incl. audio (*0-7887-4189-6*, 41112) Recorded Bks., LLC.

Zagwyn, Deborah Turney. The Winter Gift. 2003. (Illus.). 32p. (J). (gr. k-3). 15.95 (*1-883672-93-7*) Tricycle Pr.

Zakarin, Debra Mostow. Countdown to Grandma's House. 2002. (Reading Railroad Bks.). (Illus.). 32p. (J). mass mkt. 3.49 (*0-448-42813-X*, Grosset & Dunlap) Penguin Putnam Bks. for Young Readers.

—Grandpa Lets Me Be Me. 2002. (Reading Railroad Bks.). (Illus.). 32p. (J). mass mkt. 3.49 (*0-448-42814-8*, Grosset & Dunlap) Penguin Putnam Bks. for Young Readers.

Zalben, Jane Breskin. Pearl Plants a Tree. 1995. (Illus.). 32p. (J). (ps-3). per. 14.00 (*0-689-80034-7*, Simon & Schuster Children's Publishing) Simon & Schuster Children's Publishing.

—Pearl's Marigolds for Grandpa. 1997. (Illus.). 32p. (J). (ps-3). per. 15.00 (*0-689-80448-2*, Simon & Schuster Children's Publishing) Simon & Schuster Children's Publishing.

Zaugg, Sandra L. The Rock Slide Rescue. 1998. (Shoebox Kids Ser.: Vol. 8). (Illus.). 91p. (J). (gr. 2-5). pap. 6.99 (*0-8163-1387-3*) Pacific Pr. Publishing Assn.

Ziefert, Harriet. Grandmas Are for Giving Tickles. 2000. (Lift-the-Flap Ser.). (Illus.). 16p. (J). (ps-1). pap. 6.99 (*0-14-056718-6*, Puffin Bks.) Penguin Putnam Bks. for Young Readers.

—Grandpas Are for Finding Worms. 2000. (Lift-the-Flap Ser.). (Illus.). 16p. (J). (ps-1). pap. 6.99 (*0-14-056719-4*, Puffin Bks.) Penguin Putnam Bks. for Young Readers.

—Happy Birthday, Grandpa! 1988. (Illus.). 32p. (J). (ps). 4.95 o.p. (*0-694-00242-9*) HarperCollins Children's Bk. Group.

—Happy Easter, Grandma! 1988. (Illus.). 32p. (J). (ps). 4.95 o.p. (*0-694-00225-9*) HarperCollins Children's Bk. Group.

—Lunchtime for a Purple Snake. 2003. (Illus.). 32p. (J). (ps-3). tchr. ed. 15.00 (*0-618-31133-5*) Houghton Mifflin Co.

—No Kiss for Grandpa! 2001. (Illus.). 32p. (J). (ps-k). pap. 12.95 (*0-531-30328-4*, Orchard Bks.) Scholastic, Inc.

—With Love from Grandma. 1989. (Illus.). 40p. (J). (ps-3). 13.95 o.p. (*0-670-83004-6*, Viking Children's Bks.) Penguin Putnam Bks. for Young Readers.

Zolotow, Charlotte. My Grandson Lew. (Ursula Nordstrom Bk.). 32p. (J). (gr. k-3). 1974. (Illus.). 14.00 o.p. (*0-06-026961-8*); 1974. (Illus.). lib. bdg. 15.89 (*0-06-026962-6*); 1999. pap. 5.95 (*0-06-443549-0*); 1999. lib. bdg. 14.89 (*0-06-028300-9*); 1999. 14.95 (*0-06-028299-1*) HarperCollins Children's Bk. Group.

H

HOMOSEXUALITY—FICTION

Abel, Kathleen. Smile So Big. 2005. (J). (*0-15-200671-0*) Harcourt Trade Pubs.

Adams, Marc. The Preacher's Son. 1996. 224p. 22.95 (*1-889829-00-5*) Window Bks.

Arnold, Jeanne. Amy Asks a Question: Grandma, What's a Lesbian. 1997. (Illus.). 64p. (J). (gr. 4 up). 10.95 (*0-941300-28-5*) Mother Courage Pr.

Bargar, Gary W. What Happened to Mr. Forster?, 001. 1981. 192p. (J). (gr. 3-6). 8.95 o.p. (*0-395-31021-0*, Clarion Bks.) Houghton Mifflin Co. Trade & Reference Div.

Bauer, Marion Dane. Am I Blue? Coming Out from the Silence. 1995. 12.00 (*0-606-07184-9*) Turtleback Bks.

Bauer, Marion Dane, ed. Am I Blue? Coming Out from the Silence. (Trophy Bk.). (gr. 7 up). 1995. (Illus.). 288p. (J). pap. 6.99 (*0-06-440587-7*, Harper Trophy); 1994. 224p. (YA). 15.00 o.p. (*0-06-024253-1*); 1994. 224p. (YA). lib. bdg. 14.89 o.p. (*0-06-024254-X*) HarperCollins Children's Bk. Group.

Bechard, Margaret E. If It Doesn't Kill You. 1999. 160p. (YA). (gr. 7-12). 15.99 (*0-670-88547-9*) Penguin Putnam Bks. for Young Readers.

Benduhn, Tea. Gravel Queen. 2003. (Illus.). 160p. (J). (gr. 7 up). 15.95 (*0-689-84994-X*, Simon & Schuster Children's Publishing) Simon & Schuster Children's Publishing.

Cart, Michael. My Father's Scar. 1996. 208p. (YA). (gr. 7 up). mass mkt. 16.00 o.s.i (*0-689-80749-X*, Simon & Schuster Children's Publishing) Simon & Schuster Children's Publishing.

Chambers, Aidan. Dance on My Grave. 1983. (Charlotte Zolotow Bk.). 256p. (YA). (gr. 7 up). lib. bdg. 13.89 o.p. (*0-06-021254-3*) HarperCollins Children's Bk. Group.

—Postcards from No Man's Land. 2004. pap. 7.99 (*0-14-240145-5*, Puffin Bks.) Penguin Putnam Bks. for Young Readers.

Childress, Alice. Those Other People. 1989. 144p. (YA). (gr. 8 up). 14.95 o.s.i (*0-399-21510-7*, G. P. Putnam's Sons) Penguin Putnam Bks. for Young Readers.

Cohen, Richard A. Alfie's Home. 1993. (Illus.). 30p. (J). (gr. 3-12). 14.95 (*0-9637058-0-6*) International Healing Foundation, Inc.

De Haan, Linda & Nijland, Stern. King & King. 2003. (Illus.). 32p. (J). 14.95 (*1-58246-061-2*) Tricycle Pr.

Dhondy, Farrukh. Black Swan. 1993. 208p. (YA). (gr. 6 up). 14.95 o.p. (*0-395-66076-9*) Houghton Mifflin Co.

Donovan, John. I'll Get There: It Better Be Worth the Trip. 1969. (YA). (gr. 7 up). lib. bdg. 12.89 o.p. (*0-06-021718-9*) HarperCollins Children's Bk. Group.

Donovan, Stacey. Who I Am Keeps Happening. 2004. (YA). (*0-7636-1988-4*) Candlewick Pr.

Ecker, Beverly A. Independence Day. 1983. 208p. (YA). (gr. 7 up). pap. 2.25 o.p. (*0-380-82990-8*, 82990-8, Avon Bks.) Morrow/Avon.

Ferris, Jean. Eight Seconds. 2000. 192p. (YA). (gr. 7-12). 17.00 (*0-15-202367-4*) Harcourt Children's Bks.

—Eight Seconds. 2002. 192p. (J). pap. 5.99 (*0-14-230121-3*, Puffin Bks.) Penguin Putnam Bks. for Young Readers.

Fox, Paula. The Eagle Kite. 1996. 144p. (YA). (gr. 7-12). mass mkt. 4.50 o.s.i (*0-440-21972-8*) Dell Publishing.

—The Eagle Kite. 1995. 144p. (J). (gr. 7 up). pap. 15.95 (*0-531-06892-7*); lib. bdg. 16.99 (*0-531-08742-5*) Scholastic, Inc. (Orchard Bks.).

—The Eagle Kite. 1996. 10.55 (*0-606-10795-9*) Turtleback Bks.

Freymann-Weyr, Garret. My Heartbeat. 2002. 160p. (J). (gr. 7-12). 15.00 (*0-618-14181-2*) Houghton Mifflin Co.

—My Heartbeat. unabr. ed. 2003. (J). (gr. 7). audio 25.00 (*0-8072-1199-0*, Listening Library) Random Hse. Audio Publishing Group.

Galloway, Priscilla. Jennifer Has Two Daddies. 1990. (Illus.). 32p. (J). (gr. k-3). reprint ed. pap. 6.95 (*0-88961-095-9*) Women's Pr. CAN. *Dist:* Univ. of Toronto Pr.

Gantos, Jack. Desire Lines, RS. 1997. 144p. (YA). (gr. 7 up). 16.00 (*0-374-31772-0*, Farrar, Straus & Giroux (BYR)) Farrar, Straus & Giroux.

Garden, Nancy. Good Moon Rising, RS. 1996. 240p. (YA). (gr. 7 up). 16.00 o.p. (*0-374-32746-7*, Farrar, Straus & Giroux (BYR)) Farrar, Straus & Giroux.

—Holly's Secret, RS. 2000. 144p. (YA). (gr. 3-7). 16.00 (*0-374-33273-8*, Farrar, Straus & Giroux (BYR)) Farrar, Straus & Giroux.

—The Year They Burned the Books, RS. 1999. 256p. (YA). (gr. 7-12). 17.00 (*0-374-38667-6*, Farrar, Straus & Giroux (BYR)) Farrar, Straus & Giroux.

Greene, Bette. The Drowning of Stephan Jones. 1997. 224p. (YA). (gr. 7-12). mass mkt. 4.99 o.s.i (*0-440-22695-3*, Dell Books for Young Readers) Random Hse. Children's Bks.

—The Drowning of Stephan Jones. 1996. (J). 11.04 (*0-606-00734-2*) Turtleback Bks.

—The Drowning Of Stephan Jones. 1991. 224p. (YA). 16.00 o.s.i (*0-553-07437-7*) Bantam Bks.

Grima, Tony, ed. Not the Only One: Lesbian & Gay Fiction for Teens. 1995. 200p. (Orig.). (YA). (gr. 8-13). pap. 7.95 o.p. (*1-55583-275-X*) Alyson Pubns.

Guy, Rosa. Ruby. 1979. pap. 2.25 o.p. (*0-553-23367-X*) Bantam Bks.

—Ruby. 1991. 192p. (YA). mass mkt. 3.99 o.s.i (*0-440-21130-1*) Dell Publishing.

—Ruby. 1976. 192p. (YA). 8.95 o.p. (*0-670-61023-2*) Viking Penguin.

Hartinger, Brent. Geography Club. 2004. 240p. (J). pap. 6.99 (*0-06-001223-4*, HarperTempest) HarperCollins Children's Bk. Group.

—Geography Club. 2003. 240p. (J). 15.99 (*0-06-001221-8*); (Illus.). lib. bdg. 16.89 (*0-06-001222-6*) HarperCollins Pubs.

Heron, Ann & Maran, Meredith. How Would You Feel If Your Dad Was Gay? (Illus.). 32p. (J). 1991. text 9.95 o.p. (*1-55583-188-5*); 1994. (gr. 1-5). reprint ed. pap. 6.95 o.p. (*1-55583-243-1*) Alyson Pubns.

Hoffman, Eric. Best Colors (Los Mejores Colores) de la Vega, Eida, tr. 2004. (Anti-Bias Books for Kids). (ENG & SPA., Illus.). 32p. (J). (ps-3). pap. 11.95 (*1-884834-69-8*, 709201) Redleaf Pr.

Holland, Isabelle. The Man Without a Face. (gr. 7 up). reprint ed. 1988. 144p. (YA). lib. bdg. 12.89 o.p. (*0-397-32264-X*); 1987. 160p. (J). pap. 5.99 (*0-06-447028-8*, Harper Trophy) HarperCollins Children's Bk. Group.

—The Man without a Face. 1972. 144p. (YA). (gr. 7 up). reprint ed. 13.00 o.p. (*0-397-31211-3*) HarperCollins Children's Bk. Group.

Jenkins, A. M. Breaking Boxes. 192p. (YA). (gr. 9-12). 2000. mass mkt. 4.99 o.s.i (*0-440-22717-8*); 1997. 15.95 o.s.i (*0-385-32513-4*, Delacorte Pr.) Dell Publishing.

—Breaking Boxes. 2000. 11.04 (*0-606-17834-1*) Turtleback Bks.

Johnson-Calvo, Sarita. A Beach Party with Alexis. 1993. (Illus.). 32p. (Orig.). (J). pap., stu. ed. 2.95 o.p. (*1-55583-230-X*) Alyson Pubns.

Kerr, M. E. "Hello," I Lied. 1997. 176p. (YA). (gr. 7 up). lib. bdg. 15.89 (*0-06-027530-8*); 15.95 o.p. (*0-06-027529-4*) HarperCollins Children's Bk. Group.

Larson, Rodger. What I Know Now, ERS. 1997. 272p. (J). (gr. 7-12). 15.95 o.s.i (*0-8050-4869-3*, Holt, Henry & Co. Bks. For Young Readers) Holt, Henry & Co.

Lyon, George Ella. Sonny's House of Spies. 2004. (YA). (*0-689-85168-5*, Atheneum/Richard Jackson Bks.) Simon & Schuster Children's Publishing.

McClain, Ellen J. No Big Deal. 192p. 1997. pap. 4.99 o.s.i (*0-14-038046-9*); 1994. (J). (gr. 5-9). 14.99 o.p. (*0-525-67483-7*, Dutton Children's Bks.) Penguin Putnam Bks. for Young Readers.

Mosca, Frank. All American Boys. 1983. 116p. (Orig.). (J). (gr. 7-12). pap. 5.95 o.p. (*0-932870-44-9*) Alyson Pubns.

Murrow, Liza K., et al. Twelve Days in August: A Novel. 1993. 160p. (J). (gr. 7 up). tchr. ed. 16.95 o.p. (*0-8234-1012-9*) Holiday Hse., Inc.

Myracle, Lauren. Kissing Kate. 2003. 176p. (YA). 16.99 (*0-525-46917-6*, Dutton Children's Bks.) Penguin Putnam Bks. for Young Readers.

Newbery, Linda. The Shell House. 2002. 352p. (J). (gr. 7-11). 15.95 (*0-385-75011-0*) Doubleday Publishing.

—The Shell House. 2004. 352p. (YA). (gr. 7-11). mass mkt. 6.50 (*0-440-23786-6*, Laurel Leaf) Random Hse. Children's Bks.

Newman, Leslea. Gloria Goes to Gay Pride. 1991. (Illus.). 48p. (Orig.). (J). (ps-2). pap. 7.95 o.p. (*1-55583-185-0*) Alyson Pubns.

—Saturday Is Pattyday. 1993. (Illus.). 24p. (J). (gr. 1-3). lib. bdg. 14.95 (*0-934678-52-9*); (ps-5). pap. 6.95 (*0-934678-51-0*) New Victoria Pubs., Inc.

—Saturday Is Pattyday. 1993. (Illus.). 24p. (J). pap. 5.95 (*0-88961-181-5*) Women's Pr. CAN. *Dist:* Univ. of Toronto Pr.

Plum-Ucci, Carol. What Happened to Lani Garver. (YA). 2004. 336p. pap. (*0-15-205088-4*, Harcourt Paperbacks); 2002. 328p. (gr. 9 up). 17.00 (*0-15-216813-3*) Harcourt Children's Bks.

Reading, J. P. Bouquets for Brimbal. 1980. 224p. (J). (gr. 7 up). o.p. (*0-06-024843-2*); lib. bdg. 8.79 o.p. (*0-06-024844-0*) HarperCollins Pubs.

Reynolds, Marilynn. Love Rules. 2001. (True-to-Life Series from Hamilton High). 224p. (YA). (gr. 8 up). 18.95 (*1-885356-75-7*); pap. 9.95 (*1-885356-76-5*) Morning Glory Pr., Inc.

Rinaldi, Ann. The Good Side of My Heart. 1987. 288p. (YA). (gr. 7 up). 13.95 o.p. (*0-8234-0648-2*) Holiday Hse., Inc.

Ryan, Sara. Empress of the World. 2001. 196p. (YA). (gr. 7 up). 15.99 (*0-670-89688-8*) Penguin Putnam Bks. for Young Readers.

—The Empress of the World. 2003. 224p. (YA). pap. 7.99 (*0-14-250059-3*, Speak) Penguin Putnam Bks. for Young Readers.

Salat, Christina. Living in Secret. 3rd ed. 1999. 183p. (YA). (gr. 5-10). reprint ed. pap. 7.95 (*0-916020-02-9*) Books Marcus.

Salat, Cristina. Living in Secret. 1994. 192p. (J). (gr. 4-7). pap. 3.99 o.s.i (*0-440-40950-0*) Dell Publishing.

Sanchez, Alex. Rainbow Boys. 2001. 256p. (YA). (gr. 9 up). 17.00 (*0-689-84100-0*, Simon & Schuster Children's Publishing) Simon & Schuster Children's Publishing.

—The Rainbow Boys. 2003. (Illus.). 272p. (YA). pap. 7.99 (*0-689-85770-5*, Simon Pulse) Simon & Schuster Children's Publishing.

—Rainbow High. 2003. (Illus.). 272p. (YA). 16.95 (*0-689-85477-3*, Simon & Schuster Children's Publishing) Simon & Schuster Children's Publishing.

Scoppettone, Sandra. Happy Endings Are All Alike. 2004. 210p. (gr. 8-12). reprint ed. pap. 10.00 (*1-55583-511-2*) Alyson Pubns.

—Trying Hard to Hear You. 2nd ed. 1996. 256p. (YA). (gr. 7 up). reprint ed. pap. 9.95 o.p. (*1-55583-367-5*) Alyson Pubns.

—Trying Hard to Hear You. 1974. 272p. (YA). (gr. 7). lib. bdg. 13.89 o.p. (*0-06-025247-2*) HarperCollins Children's Bk. Group.

Shannon, George. Unlived Affections. 1995. 144p. (YA). (gr. 7 up). reprint ed. pap. 8.95 (*1-55583-299-7*) Alyson Pubns.

Shyer, Marlene Fanta. The Rainbow Kite. 2002. 208p. (J). (gr. 7-10). 14.95 (*0-7614-5122-6*) Cavendish, Marshall Corp.

Sones, Sonya. Miserably Yours, Ruby. 2004. (J). (*0-689-85820-5*, Simon & Schuster Children's Publishing) Simon & Schuster Children's Publishing.

Springer, Nancy. Looking for Jamie Bridger. (J). 1999. pap. 14.89 (*0-8037-1774-1*); 1995. 160p. (gr. 7 up). 14.99 o.s.i (*0-8037-1773-3*) Penguin Putnam Bks. for Young Readers. (Dial Bks. for Young Readers).

Steinhofel, Andreas. The Middle of the World. Skofield, James, tr. 2002. (YA). 16.95 (*0-385-72943-X*, Delacorte Pr.) Dell Publishing.

Stevens, Tracey. Chalice of the Goddess. Snowden, Susan, ed. 2003. 313p. (YA). per. 19.99 (*0-9719628-4-7*) Amazing Dreams Publishing.

Stoehr, Shelley. Tomorrow Wendy. 1998. 176p. (YA). (gr. 9-12). 15.95 o.s.i (*0-385-32339-5*, Delacorte Pr.) Dell Publishing.

Taylor, William. The Blue Lawn. 2004. 120p. (YA). (gr. 7-12). pap. 10.95 (*1-55583-493-0*) Alyson Pubns.

—The Blue Lawn. 1999. 16.00 (*0-606-19431-2*) Turtleback Bks.

Valentine, Johnny. Two Moms, the Zark, & Me. 1993. (Illus.). 48p. (J). 12.95 o.p. (*1-55583-236-9*) Alyson Pubns.

Velasquez, Gloria. Tommy Stands Alone. 1995. (Roosevelt High School Series Bks.). 135p. (YA). (gr. 7 up). pap. 9.95 (*1-55885-147-X*); 14.95 (*1-55885-146-1*) Arte Publico Pr. (Piñata Books).

—Tommy Stands Alone. 1995. (Roosevelt High School Ser.). 16.00 (*0-606-16337-9*) Turtleback Bks.

Vigna, Judith. My Two Uncles. 1995. (Albert Whitman Concept Bks.). (Illus.). 32p. (J). (gr. 7 up). lib. bdg. 14.95 (*0-8075-5507-X*) Whitman, Albert & Co.

Walker, Kate. Peter. (YA). 2001. 240p. (gr. 7). pap. 5.95 (*0-618-11130-1*); 1993. 176p. (gr. 8 up). 13.95 o.p. (*0-395-64722-3*) Houghton Mifflin Co.

—Peter. 2001. (Illus.). (J). 12.00 (*0-606-21380-5*) Turtleback Bks.

Wallens, Scott. Exposed, No. 2. 2002. (Sevens Ser.). (Illus.). 192p. (J). pap. 4.99 (*0-14-230099-3*, Puffin Bks.) Penguin Putnam Bks. for Young Readers.

Wersba, Barbara. Whistle Me Home, ERS. 1997. 160p. (YA). (gr. 7 up). 15.95 (*0-8050-4850-2*, Holt, Henry & Co. Bks. For Young Readers) Holt, Henry & Co.

Willhoite, Michael. Daddy's Roommate. 1990. (Illus.). 32p. (J). (ps). 15.95 o.p. (*1-55583-178-8*) Alyson Pubns.

—Daddy's Wedding. 1996. (Illus.). 32p. (J). (ps-2). reprint ed. 15.95 o.p. (*1-55583-350-0*, Alyson Wonderland) Alyson Pubns.

Winick, Judd. Pedro & Me: Friendship, Loss & What I Learned. 2001. (Illus.). (J). 21.05 (*0-606-20504-7*) Turtleback Bks.

Woodson, Jacqueline. Dear One. 1991. (Laurel-Leaf Contemporary Fiction Ser.). 10.04 (*0-606-02589-8*) Turtleback Bks.

—The Dear One. 1992. 160p. (YA). mass mkt. 3.99 o.s.i (*0-440-21420-3*) Dell Publishing.

—The Dear One. 2004. 160p. pap. 6.99 (*0-14-250190-5*, Puffin Bks.) Penguin Putnam Bks. for Young Readers.

—From the Notebooks of Melanin Sun. 160p. (gr. 7 up). 2003. (J). mass mkt. 5.99 (*0-590-45881-7*, Scholastic Paperbacks); 1995. (YA). pap. 14.95 o.p. (*0-590-45880-9*, Blue Sky Pr., The) Scholastic, Inc.

—From the Notebooks of Melanin Sun. 1997. (Point Signature Ser.). (J). 10.04 (*0-606-11357-6*) Turtleback Bks.

—The House You Pass on the Way. 2003. 128p. pap. 5.99 (*0-14-250191-3*, Puffin Bks.); 160p. (J). 16.99 (*0-399-23969-3*, G. P. Putnam's Sons) Penguin Putnam Bks. for Young Readers.

—The House You Pass on the Way. 1999. 128p. (YA). (gr. 7-12). mass mkt. 4.50 o.s.i (*0-440-22797-6*, Dell Books for Young Readers) Random Hse. Children's Bks.

—The House You Pass on the Way. 1999. 10.55 (*0-606-16085-X*) Turtleback Bks.

I

INTERRACIAL MARRIAGE—FICTION

Igus, Toyomi. Two Mrs. Gibsons. 1996. (Illus.). 32p. (YA). (gr. 4-7). 14.95 (*0-89239-135-9*) Children's Bk. Pr.

Otey-Little, Mimi. Yoshiko & the Foreigner, RS. 1996. 40p. (J). (ps-3). 16.00 (*0-374-32448-4*, Farrar, Straus & Giroux (BYR)) Farrar, Straus & Giroux.

Sharp, Priscilla Stone. Langhorn & Mary: A Nineteenth Century American Love Story. Rose, Tony & Rose, Yvonne, eds. 2003. 528p. 25.99 (*0-9727519-0-4*) Amber Bks.

Woodson, Jacqueline. The House You Pass on the Way. 2003. 128p. pap. 5.99 (*0-14-250191-3*, Puffin Bks.) Penguin Putnam Bks. for Young Readers.

Wyeth, Sharon Dennis. Ginger Brown: Too Many Houses. 1996. (Illus.). 80p. (J). (ps-3). 11.99 o.s.i (*0-679-95437-6*); (gr. 1-4). pap. 3.99 o.s.i (*0-679-85437-1*) Random Hse. Children's Bks. (Random Hse. Bks. for Young Readers).

—Ginger Brown: Too Many Houses. 1996. 9.19 o.p. (*0-606-09327-3*) Turtleback Bks.

—The World of Daughter McGuire. (J). 1996. pap. 4.99 (*0-440-91105-2*, Dell Books for Young Readers); 1995. 176p. (gr. 3-7). pap. 3.99 o.s.i (*0-440-41114-9*, Yearling) Random Hse. Children's Bks.

—The World of Daughter McGuire. 2001. 176p. (gr. 3-7). pap. text 12.00 (*0-375-89502-7*) Random Hse., Inc.

—The World of Daughter McGuire. 1995. (J). 9.09 o.p. (*0-606-08664-1*) Turtleback Bks.

Yep, Laurence. The Cook's Family. 1998. (J). (*0-03-992907-8*) Holt, Rinehart & Winston.

—The Cook's Family. 1998. 186p. (J). (gr. 5-9). 15.99 o.p. (*0-399-22907-8*, G. P. Putnam's Sons) Penguin Group (USA) Inc.

—The Cook's Family. 1999. (Illus.). 192p. (J). (gr. 5-9). pap. 5.99 o.s.i (*0-698-11804-9*, PaperStar) Penguin Putnam Bks. for Young Readers.

—The Cook's Family. 1999. (J). 11.04 (*0-606-18932-7*) Turtleback Bks.

—The Cook's Family. 1999. (J). pap. 3.99 (*0-14-037472-8*, Viking) Viking Penguin.

L

LOVE—FICTION

A. B. Publishing Staff. Nobody Loves Me. 1998. (J). (gr. 4-7). pap. text 6.95 (*1-881545-83-0*) Angela's Bookshelf.

Abels, Harriette S. A Special Love. 1987. 192p. 2.50 o.p. (*0-425-10036-7*, Berkley/Pacer) Berkley Publishing Group.

Abrams, Liesa. His Other Girlfriend. 1999. (Love Stories Ser.). 192p. (gr. 7-12). mass mkt. 4.50 o.s.i (*0-553-49295-0*) Bantam Bks.

Adams, K. J. Crazy in Love. 1993. 240p. (YA). mass mkt. 3.50 o.p. (*0-06-106161-1*, HarperTorch) Morrow/Avon.

Adler, C. S. Roadside Valentine. 1984. 2.25 (*0-399-21146-2*, G. P. Putnam's Sons) Penguin Putnam Bks. for Young Readers.

—Roadside Valentine. 1983. 180p. (YA). (gr. 7 up). 13.95 o.s.i (*0-02-700350-7*, Simon & Schuster Children's Publishing) Simon & Schuster Children's Publishing.

AG Publishers Editors. American Girl Backpack Books Little 5-Pack of Love, 5 vols. 2000. (J). (gr. 4-7). pap. 9.75 (*1-58485-283-6*) Pleasant Co. Pubns.

Aks, Patricia. Impossible Love. 1991. 144p. (Orig.). (YA). (gr. 9-12). mass mkt. 3.50 o.s.i (*0-449-70297-9*, Fawcett) Ballantine Bks.

—Love Knots. 1992. 144p. (Orig.). (YA). mass mkt. 3.99 o.s.i (*0-449-70357-6*, Fawcett) Ballantine Bks.

Albee, Sarah. Elmo Loves You. 2002. (Big Bird's Favorites Board Bks.). (Illus.). 24p. (J). (ps). bds. 4.99 (*0-375-81208-3*, Random Hse. Bks. for Young Readers) Random Hse. Children's Bks.

Alborough, Jez. The Grass Is Always Greener. 1987. (Illus.). 32p. (J). (ps-3). 9.95 o.p. (*0-8037-0468-2*, Dial Bks. for Young Readers) Penguin Putnam Bks. for Young Readers.

Alcock, Vivien. A Kind of Thief. l.t. ed. 1992. (Children's Lythway Ser.). 260p. (YA). 13.95 o.p. (*0-7451-1608-6*, Galaxy Children's Large Print) BBC Audiobooks America.

Alcott, Louisa May. The Inheritance. l.t. ed. 1997. 26.95 o.p. (*1-56895-505-7*, Wheeler Publishing, Inc.) Gale Group.

—The Inheritance. 1998. 192p. mass mkt. 5.99 o.s.i (*0-14-027729-3*) Penguin Group (USA) Inc.

—The Inheritance. Myerson, Joel & Shealy, Daniel, eds. 1997. 160p. (YA). 18.00 o.s.i (*0-525-45756-9*) Penguin Putnam Bks. for Young Readers.

—The Inheritance. 1998. (Illus.). (J). 12.04 (*0-606-18412-0*) Turtleback Bks.

—The Inheritance. Myerson, Joel & Shealy, Daniel, eds. 1998. (Classics Ser.). 192p. 13.00 (*0-14-043666-9*, Penguin Classics) Viking Penguin.

Alexander, Liza. Winnie the Pooh & Valentines, Too. 1998. (Pooh Ser.). (Illus.). 32p. (J). (ps-3). 12.95 (*0-7868-3217-7*) Disney Pr.

Alexander, Nina. He's the One. 1998. (Love Stories Ser.). 192p. (gr. 7-12). mass mkt. 3.99 o.s.i (*0-553-49250-0*, Dell Books for Young Readers) Random Hse. Children's Bks.

Alexander, Nina & Scott, Kieran. Kiss & Tell. 1998. (Love Stories Ser.). 192p. (gr. 7-12). mass mkt. 3.99 o.s.i (*0-553-49251-9*, Dell Books for Young Readers) Random Hse. Children's Bks.

Althoff, Victoria M. Key to My Heart. 176p. (J). (gr. 5-8). 1994. pap. 2.99 (*0-87406-677-8*); 1989. pap. 1.25 o.p. (*0-87406-384-1*) Darby Creek Publishing.

Ames, Diane. Never Say Good-Bye. 1992. (Camp Counselors Ser.: No. 4). 208p. (YA). mass mkt. 3.50 o.p. (*0-06-106077-1*, HarperTorch) Morrow/Avon.

Ames, Evelyn. Glimpse of Eden. 1981. (Keith Jennison Large Type Bks.). (gr. 7 up). lib. bdg. 7.95 o.p. (*0-531-00190-3*, Watts, Franklin) Scholastic Library Publishing.

Anderson, Mary. Catch Me, I'm Falling in Love. 1985. (Illus.). 144p. (J). (gr. 7 up). 14.95 o.p. (*0-385-29409-3*, Delacorte Pr.) Dell Publishing.

—Catch Me, I'm Falling in Love. 1987. (J). (gr. k-12). mass mkt. 2.50 o.s.i (*0-440-91122-2*, Laurel Leaf) Random Hse. Children's Bks.

—Do You Call That a Dream Date? 1987. 176p. (J). (gr. 7 up). 14.95 o.s.i (*0-385-29488-3*, Delacorte Pr.) Dell Publishing.

Andreae, Giles. Heaven Is Having You. 2002. (Illus.). (J). tchr. ed. 14.95 (*1-58925-016-8*, Tiger Tales) ME Media LLC.

—Love Is a Handful of Honey. 1999. (Illus.). 32p. (J). (ps-2). 14.95 (*1-888444-58-4*) Little Tiger Pr.

—Love Is a Handful of Honey. 2001. (Illus.). 32p. (ps-k). pap. 5.95 (*1-58925-353-1*, Tiger Tales) ME Media LLC.

Andrews, Kristi. All That Glitters: Upstaged, Vol. 7. 1988. (All That Glitters Ser.). 176p. (Orig.). (YA). (gr. 6 up). mass mkt. 2.50 o.s.i (*0-553-26704-3*) Bantam Bks.

Andrews, Stephanie. Fearless Love. 1985. (Dawn of Love Ser.: No. 4). (YA). (gr. 7 up). pap. 2.25 (*0-671-55158-2*, Simon Pulse) Simon & Schuster Children's Publishing.

Anglund, Joan Walsh. Do You Love Someone? 1971. (Illus.). 32p. (J). (ps up). 4.95 o.p. (*0-15-224190-6*) Harcourt Children's Bks.

—Love Is a Special Way of Feeling. 1999. (Illus.). 32p. (J). (ps-3). 9.95 (*0-15-202358-5*) Harcourt Children's Bks.

—Love Is Forever. 1998. 10.00 net. o.s.i (*0-15-202191-4*) Harcourt Trade Pubs.

Anson, Mandy. Focus on Love. 1991. (Sweet Dreams Ser.: No. 185). 144p. (YA). pap. 2.99 o.s.i (*0-553-29290-0*) Bantam Bks.

Applegate, K. A. Beaches, Boys & Betrayal. 1996. (Summer Ser.: No. 6). 224p. (YA). (gr. 7 up). mass mkt. 3.99 (*0-671-51040-1*, Simon Pulse) Simon & Schuster Children's Publishing.

—Ben's in Love. (Making Out Ser.: No. 4). (YA). (gr. 7-12). 1998. 208p. pap. 3.99 (*0-380-80214-7*, Avon Bks.); 1994. 240p. mass mkt. 3.99 o.p. (*0-06-106183-2*, HarperTorch) Morrow/Avon.

—Bonfire. 1993. (Ocean City Ser.: No. 1). 320p. (J). mass mkt. 3.50 o.p. (*0-06-106748-2*, HarperTorch) Morrow/Avon.

—Heat. 2001. (Making Waves Ser.: No. 5). 272p. mass mkt. 4.99 (*1-931497-16-8*) 17th Street Productions, An Alloy Online Inc. Co.

—Heat Wave. 1994. (Ocean City Ser.: No. 8). 240p. (YA). mass mkt. 3.99 o.p. (*0-06-106234-0*) Harper-Collins Pubs.

—Kate Finds Love. 1999. (Making Out Ser.: No. 19). 176p. (YA). (gr. 7-12). pap. 3.99 (*0-380-81121-9*, Avon Bks.) Morrow/Avon.

—Lara Gets Lucky. 2000. (Making Out Ser.: No. 23). 176p. (YA). (gr. 7-12). pap. 3.99 (*0-380-81527-3*, Avon Bks.) Morrow/Avon.

—Love Shack. 1993. (Ocean City Ser.: No. 2). 256p. (J). mass mkt. 3.50 o.p. (*0-06-106793-8*, Harper-Torch) Morrow/Avon.

—Making Waves. 2001. (Making Waves Ser.: No. 1). 320p. (YA). mass mkt. 4.99 (*1-931497-12-5*) 17th Street Productions, An Alloy Online Inc. Co.

—My Sister's Boyfriend. 1992. (Changes Romance Ser.: No. 9). 240p. (YA). mass mkt. 3.50 o.p. (*0-06-106717-2*, HarperTorch) Morrow/Avon.

—Never Trust Lara. 2000. (Making Out Ser.: No. 20). 176p. (YA). (gr. 7-12). pap. 3.99 (*0-380-81309-2*, Avon Bks.) Morrow/Avon.

—Sharing Sam. 1995. (Love Stories Ser.). 192p. (gr. 7-12). mass mkt. 4.50 o.s.i (*0-553-56660-1*) Bantam Bks.

—Sharing Sam. 2004. (YA). lib. bdg. 10.99 (*0-385-90173-9*); 160p. (gr. 7). pap. 8.95 (*0-385-73135-3*) Random Hse. Children's Bks. (Delacorte Bks. for Young Readers).

—Summer: Christmas Special Edition. 1996. (Summer Ser.). 208p. (YA). (gr. 8 up). pap. 3.99 (*0-671-51042-8*, Simon Pulse) Simon & Schuster Children's Publishing.

—Tease. 2001. (Making Waves Ser.: No. 2). 288p. (YA). mass mkt. 4.99 (*1-931497-13-3*) 17th Street Productions, An Alloy Online Inc. Co.

—Two-Timing Aisha. 1999. (Making Out Ser.: No. 17). 176p. (YA). (gr. 7-12). pap. 3.99 (*0-380-81119-7*, Avon Bks.) Morrow/Avon.

—The Unbelievable Truth. 1992. (Changes Romance Ser.: No. 3). 240p. (YA). (gr. 7 up). mass mkt. 3.50 o.p. (*0-06-106774-1*, HarperTorch) Morrow/Avon.

—Zoey's Broken Heart. 2000. (Making Out Ser.: No. 26). 176p. (YA). (gr. 7 up). pap. 3.99 (*0-380-81530-3*, Avon Bks.) Morrow/Avon.

Archipowa, Anastassija & Outlet Book Company Staff. Cinderella. 1990. (Illus.). (J). 5.99 o.s.i (*0-517-05142-7*) Random Hse. Value Publishing.

Archway Press, Inc. Staff, ed. Hunks & Kisses. 1999. (Most Wanted Ser.: Vol. 2). (Illus.). 32p. (YA). (gr. 8-12). pap. 7.99 (*0-671-02807-3*, Simon Pulse) Simon & Schuster Children's Publishing.

—Most Wanted Holiday Hunks, Vol. 1. 1998. (Illus.). 32p. (J). (gr. 7-12). pap. 7.99 (*0-671-02665-8*, Simon Pulse) Simon & Schuster Children's Publishing.

Arengo, Sue. Sleeping Beauty Level 4: 300-Word Vocabulary. 1996. (Illus.). 24p. (J). pap. text 4.95 (*0-19-422011-7*) Oxford Univ. Pr., Inc.

Ariel Books Staff. Love Love Love. 1997. 12p. 4.95 o.p. (*0-8362-2945-2*) Andrews McMeel Publishing.

Arno, Iris H. I Love You, Dad. 1998. 9.65 (*0-606-13507-3*) Turtleback Bks.

—I Love You, Mom. 1998. 10.10 (*0-606-13508-1*) Turtleback Bks.

Asher, Sandy. Everything Is Not Enough. 1988. (J). (gr. k-12). mass mkt. 2.75 o.s.i (*0-440-20002-4*, Laurel Leaf) Random Hse. Children's Bks.

Ausbun, Nellie M. Skip & Meow. 2001. 22p. per. 8.95 (*0-7414-0613-6*) Infinity Publishing.com.

Aven, Del. Anna's Tree Swing. 1981. (J). (gr. k-3). bds. 5.95 o.p. (*0-8054-4268-5*, 4242-68) Broadman & Holman Pubs.

Avi. Romeo & Juliet Together (And Alive!) at Last. 1987. 128p. (J). (gr. 4-7). lib. bdg. 16.99 (*0-531-08321-7*); (YA). (gr. 7 up). pap. 15.95 (*0-531-05721-6*) Scholastic, Inc. (Orchard Bks.).

—Romeo & Juliet Together (And Alive!) at Last. 1988. 10.55 (*0-606-11808-X*) Turtleback Bks.

—Sometimes I Think I Hear My Name. 1995. 144p. (J). (gr. 7 up). reprint ed. pap. 5.99 (*0-380-72424-3*, Harper Trophy) HarperCollins Children's Bk. Group.

—The True Confessions of Charlotte Doyle. 1997. (Illus.). 240p. (J). (gr. 5-7). pap. 5.99 (*0-380-72885-0*, Avon Bks.) Morrow/Avon.

—The True Confessions of Charlotte Doyle. 1997. (J). 11.04 (*0-606-12013-0*) Turtleback Bks.

Aydt, Deborah. Love Games. 1984. (J). pap. 2.25 (*0-590-32431-4*) Scholastic, Inc.

Bacher, June M. With All My Heart. 1989. 192p. (YA). (gr. 9 up). pap. 5.99 o.p. (*0-89081-707-3*); pap. 2.95 o.p. (*0-89081-410-4*) Harvest Hse. Pubs.

Baer, Judy. The Discovery. 1993. (Cedar River Daydreams Ser.: No. 20). 128p. (YA). (gr. 7-10). mass mkt. 4.99 o.p. (*1-55661-330-X*) Bethany Hse. Pubs.

—Fill My Empty Heart. 1990. (Cedar River Daydreams Ser.: No. 8). 128p. (Orig.). (YA). (gr. 7-10). mass mkt. 4.99 o.p. (*1-55661-128-5*) Bethany Hse. Pubs.

—The Girl Inside. 1984. (First Love Ser.). 155p. (YA). (gr. 7 up). pap. (*0-671-53411-4*, Silhouette) Harlequin Enterprises, Ltd.

—Riddles of Love-Sweet Dreams No. 63: Kiss Me Creep. 1991. (Sweet Dreams Ser.: Vol. 1, No. 148). (YA). pap. 2.50 o.s.i (*0-553-30233-7*) Bantam Bks.

Bailey, Erroll J. Mr. Dream Merchant. 2000. 288p. (YA). (gr. 7-12). 15.95 (*1-902618-30-0*) Element Children's Bks.

Baker, Camy. Camy Baker's It Must Be Love: 15 Cool Rules for Choosing a Better Boyfriend. 1999. (Camy Baker Ser.). 144p. (gr. 4-7). pap. text 3.99 o.s.i (*0-553-48657-8*, Dell Books for Young Readers) Random Hse. Children's Bks.

Baker, Jennifer. At Midnight a Novel Based on Cinderella. 1995. (Once Upon a Dream Ser.). (J). 9.09 o.p. (*0-606-07968-8*) Turtleback Bks.

—Eternally Yours. 1999. (Enchanted Hearts Ser.: No. 2). 176p. (YA). (gr. 7-12). pap. 4.50 (*0-380-80073-X*, Avon Bks.) Morrow/Avon.

—For Better, for Worse. 1993. (First Comes Love Ser.). 308p. (YA). (gr. 7-9). mass mkt. 3.50 o.p. (*0-590-46314-4*) Scholastic, Inc.

—Good-Bye to Love, Bk. 2. 1994. 240p. (J). (gr. 7-9). pap. 3.95 (*0-590-48324-2*) Scholastic, Inc.

—Her Secret He Said She Said. 1997. 176p. (YA). per. 3.99 (*0-671-00222-8*, Simon Pulse) Simon & Schuster Children's Publishing.

—His Secret. 1997. (He Said-She Said Ser.: Vol. 2). (Illus.). 176p. (YA). per. 3.99 (*0-671-00223-6*, Simon Pulse) Simon & Schuster Children's Publishing.

—In Sickness & in Health. 1993. (First Comes Love Ser.). 308p. (YA). (gr. 7-9). mass mkt. 3.50 (*0-590-46315-2*) Scholastic, Inc.

—Till Death Do Us Part. 1993. (First Comes Love Ser.). 308p. (YA). (gr. 7-9). mass mkt. 3.50 o.p. (*0-590-46316-0*) Scholastic, Inc.

—A Time to Love, Bk. 1. 1994. 240p. (J). (gr. 7-9). pap. 3.95 o.p. (*0-590-48323-4*) Scholastic, Inc.

—To Have & to Hold. 1993. (First Comes Love Ser.). 308p. (YA). (gr. 7-9). mass mkt. 3.50 o.p. (*0-590-46313-6*) Scholastic, Inc.

Baker, Liza. I Love You Because You're You. 2001. (Illus.). 32p. (J). (ps-k). pap. 9.95 (*0-439-20638-3*, Cartwheel Bks.) Scholastic, Inc.

Baldwin, Alicia. Secrets in the Sand. 1996. (YA). pap. 3.99 o.s.i (*0-679-88230-8*, Random Hse. Bks. for Young Readers) Random Hse. Children's Bks.

Balian, Lorna. I Love You, Mary Jane. 1994. (Illus.). 32p. (J). (ps-3). reprint ed. 12.95 o.p. (*0-687-37100-7*) Abingdon Pr.

Banks, Lynne Reid. Lynne Reid Banks, 3 vols. 1991. (J). (gr. 4-7). pap. 11.97 (*0-380-71680-1*, Avon Bks.) Morrow/Avon.

Barbie: I Love My Family. 2000. (Illus.). 64p. (ps-3). pap. 2.99 (*0-307-33766-9*, Golden Bks.) Random Hse. Children's Bks.

Barbieri, Elaine. Miranda & the Warrior. 2002. (Avon True Romance Ser.). (Illus.). 224p. (J). pap. 4.99 (*0-06-001134-3*, Avon) HarperCollins Children's Bk. Group.

Bardi, Carol A. & Bates, Georgia. Who Loves You. 1997. (Illus.). 34p. (J). (ps-k). pap. 9.95 (*0-9660498-0-2*, Bardi Pr.) Bardi Consulting.

Barkin, Carol & James, Elizabeth. Summer Love, No. 1. 1983. (Dream Your Own Romance Ser.). 128p. (J). (gr. 3-7). pap. 2.85 o.p. (*0-671-46449-3*, Simon & Schuster Children's Publishing) Simon & Schuster Children's Publishing.

Baronian, Jean-Baptiste. Forever. 2001. (Illus.). 32p. (J). 15.95 (*0-8118-3319-4*) Chronicle Bks. LLC.

—I Love You with All My Heart. 1998. (Illus.). 32p. (J). (ps-1). 14.95 (*0-8118-2031-9*) Chronicle Bks. LLC.

Baronian, Jean-Baptiste & Kern, Noris. I Love You with All My Heart. 2002. (Illus.). (J). bds. 6.95 (*0-8118-3622-3*) Chronicle Bks. LLC.

Barr, Linda. Nothing Hurts but My Heart. 1995. 112p. (Orig.). (J). (gr. 5-8). pap. 2.99 (*0-87406-722-7*) Darby Creek Publishing.

Bartlett, Craig. Summer Love. 2001. (Hey Arnold! Ser.: Bk. 5). (Illus.). 64p. (J). (gr. 2-5). pap. 3.99 (*0-689-83937-5*, Simon Spotlight) Simon & Schuster Children's Publishing.

Baskerville, Elizabeth. David's Kiss. 1999. (Illus.). 24p. (J). (ps-3). 14.95 (*1-890493-75-9*, Binnacle Kids) Binnacle Publishing Group.

Bates, A. Krazy 4 U. 1996. (J). mass mkt. 3.99 (*0-590-50951-9*) Scholastic, Inc.

Bates, Betty. The Great Male Conspiracy. 1986. 176p. (J). (gr. 3-7). 12.95 o.p. (*0-8234-0629-6*) Holiday Hse., Inc.

Bauer, Joan. Thwonk. 1995. 224p. (J). 14.95 o.p. (*0-385-32092-2*, Delacorte Pr.) Dell Publishing.

—Thwonk. 2001. 208p. (J). 16.99 (*0-399-23751-8*) Penguin Group (USA) Inc.

—Thwonk! 2001. (Illus.). 192p. (YA). (gr. 7 up). pap. 5.99 (*0-698-11914-2*, Puffin Bks.) Penguin Putnam Bks. for Young Readers.

—Thwonk, Set. unabr. ed. 1997. (J). (gr. 6). pap. 46.24 incl. audio (*0-7887-1552-6*, 40424) Recorded Bks., LLC.

Beaman, Joyce P. All for the Love of Cassie. 3rd ed. 1973. (Illus.). 102p. (gr. 4-12). 13.95 (*0-87716-046-5*) Beaman, Joyce Proctor.

Beauty & the Beast: Adaptation of Tale by Madame Le Prince de Beaumont. 1991. (Silver Elm Classic Ser.). (Illus.). 32p. (J). (gr. 1-3). pap. 2.99 o.p. (*0-87406-612-3*) Darby Creek Publishing.

Beauty & the Beast: Be Our Guest. 1994. (Bath Bk.). 4p. (J). 5.98 o.p. (*1-57082-000-7*) Mouse Works.

Becker, Eve. The Love Potion. 1989. (Abracadabra Ser.: No. 2). (J). (gr. 4-7). pap. 2.75 o.s.i (*0-553-15731-0*, Skylark) Random Hse. Children's Bks.

Beckman, Delores. Who Loves Sam Grant? 1986. 176p. (gr. 7-12). pap. 2.25 o.p. (*0-440-99478-0*) Dell Publishing.

Beecham, Jahnna. Dance with Me. 1987. (Sweet Dreams Ser.: No. 130). 192p. (Orig.). pap. 2.50 o.s.i (*0-553-26701-9*) Bantam Bks.

—The Right Combination, Vol. 139. 1988. 192p. (Orig.). (J). (gr. 5 up). pap. 2.50 o.s.i (*0-553-27005-2*, Dell Books for Young Readers) Random Hse. Children's Bks.

Behm, Barbara J. Tears of Joy. unabr. ed. 1999. (Illus.). 32p. (J). (gr. 1 up). lib. bdg. 16.95 (*0-9669647-0-5*) WayWord Publishing.

Bell, Margaret E. Watch for a Tall White Sail. 1973. 160p. (J). (gr. 7-9). 0.95 o.s.i (*0-448-05421-3*) Ace Bks.

La Bella y la Bestia. 1994. (Spanish Classics Ser.). (SPA., Illus.). 96p. (J). (ps-4). 7.98 o.p. (*1-57082-054-6*) Mouse Works.

Benchley, Nathaniel. Only Earth & Sky Last Forever. 1974. (Trophy Bk.). 204p. (YA). (gr. 7 up). pap. 4.95 o.s.i (*0-06-440049-2*, Harper Trophy) Harper-Collins Children's Bk. Group.

—Only Earth & Sky Last Forever. 1972. 196p. (J). (gr. 7 up). 10.95 o.p. (*0-06-020493-1*); lib. bdg. 8.79 o.p. (*0-06-020494-X*) HarperCollins Pubs.

—Only Earth & Sky Last Forever. 1992. (YA). (gr. 7 up). 17.25 o.p. (*0-8446-6583-5*) Smith, Peter Pub., Inc.

—Only Earth & Sky Last Forever. 1972. (J). 10.05 o.p. (*0-606-02346-1*) Turtleback Bks.

Benduhn, Tea. Gravel Queen. 2003. (Illus.). 160p. (J). (gr. 7 up). 15.95 (*0-689-84994-X*, Simon & Schuster Children's Publishing) Simon & Schuster Children's Publishing.

Benjamin, Alan. Little Love Notes. 1997. (Golden Book Ser.). 12p. (J). bds. 2.29 o.s.i (*0-307-25601-4*, Golden Bks.) Random Hse. Children's Bks.

Bennett, Cherie. The Accident: Love Hospital. 1996. (Hope Hospital Ser.). (J). 9.05 o.p. (*0-606-08965-9*) Turtleback Bks.

—Girls in Love. 1996. (J). (gr. 7 up). mass mkt. 4.99 (*0-590-88030-6*) Scholastic, Inc.

—The Haunted Heart. 1999. (Enchanted Hearts Ser.: No. 1). 192p. (YA). (gr. 7 up). pap. 4.50 (*0-380-80123-X*, Avon Bks.) Morrow/Avon.

—The Haunted Heart. 1999. 10.55 (*0-606-16362-X*) Turtleback Bks.

—Heaven Can Wait. 1996. (Teen Angels Ser.: No. 1). (J). (gr. 7). mass mkt. 3.99 (*0-380-78247-2*, Avon Bks.) Morrow/Avon.

—Hot Winter Nights. MacDonald, Pat, ed. 1994. (Wild Hearts Ser.). 192p. (Orig.). (J). (gr. 3-6). mass mkt. 3.50 (*0-671-88783-1*, Simon Pulse) Simon & Schuster Children's Publishing.

—Love Him Forever. 1999. (Enchanted Hearts Ser.: Vol. 6). 176p. (J). (gr. 7-12). pap. 4.50 (*0-380-80124-8*, Avon Bks.) Morrow/Avon.

—Love Him Forever. 1999. (Illus.). (YA). 10.55 (*0-606-17968-2*) Turtleback Bks.

—Love Never Dies. 1996. (Teen Angels Ser.: No. 2). (J). mass mkt. 3.99 (*0-380-78248-0*, Avon Bks.) Morrow/Avon.

—On the Edge. 1994. (Wild Hearts Ser.). 208p. (J). (gr. 3-6). pap. 3.50 (*0-671-88781-5*, Simon Pulse) Simon & Schuster Children's Publishing.

—Only Love Can Break Your Heart, No. 3. 1994. (Surviving Sixteen Ser.). 224p. (YA). (gr. 7 up). pap. 3.50 o.p. (*0-14-036320-3*, Puffin Bks.) Penguin Putnam Bks. for Young Readers.

—Passionate Kisses. MacDonald, Pat, ed. 1994. (Wild Hearts Ser.). 192p. (Orig.). (J). (gr. 7-12). mass mkt. 3.50 (*0-671-88782-3*, Simon Pulse) Simon & Schuster Children's Publishing.

—Searching for David's Heart. 1998. 176p. (gr. 3-7). mass mkt. 4.50 (*0-590-30673-1*) Scholastic, Inc.

—Sunset Fantasy. 1994. 224p. (YA). mass mkt. 3.99 o.s.i (*0-425-14458-5*) Berkley Publishing Group.

—Sunset Heart. 1994. 224p. (Orig.). (J). (ps-3). mass mkt. 3.99 o.s.i (*0-425-14183-7*, Splash) Berkley Publishing Group.

—Sunset Revenge. 1994. 224p. (Orig.). (YA). mass mkt. 3.99 o.s.i (*0-425-14228-0*) Berkley Publishing Group.

—Sunset Tears. 1995. 224p. (Orig.). (YA). mass mkt. 3.99 o.s.i (*0-425-15027-5*) Berkley Publishing Group.

—Sunset Touch. 1993. (YA). mass mkt. 3.99 o.s.i (*0-425-13708-2*) Berkley Publishing Group.

—Tori's Crush No. 3. 1994. 128p. (Orig.). (J). (gr. 4-7). mass mkt. 3.50 o.s.i (*0-425-14337-6*) Berkley Publishing Group.

—Wild Hearts on Fire. 1994. 208p. (J). (gr. 3-6). pap. 3.50 (*0-671-86514-5*, Simon Pulse) Simon & Schuster Children's Publishing.

Bennett, Jay. Masks: A Love Story. 1971. 121 p. (J). (*0-531-01979-9*, Watts, Franklin) Scholastic Library Publishing.

Bennett, Paul. Follow the River. 1987. 192p. (J). (gr. 6 up). 12.95 o.p. (*0-531-05714-3*); mass mkt. 12.99 o.p. (*0-531-08314-4*) Scholastic, Inc. (Orchard Bks.).

Benning, Elizabeth. The Dying of the Light. 1993. 160p. (J). mass mkt. 3.50 o.p. (*0-06-106796-2*, HarperTorch) Morrow/Avon.

—Losing David. 1994. 160p. (YA). mass mkt. 3.50 o.p. (*0-06-106147-6*, HarperTorch) Morrow/Avon.

Berenson, Laurien. Come As You Are. 1985. (Loveswept Ser.: No. 109). 208p. pap. 2.25 o.p. (*0-553-21718-6*) Bantam Bks.

Berenstain, Stan & Berenstain, Jan. The Berenstain Bears & the Love Match. 1998. (Berenstain Bears Big Chapter Bks.). (J). (gr. 2-6). 11.99 o.s.i (*0-679-98942-0*, Random Hse. Bks. for Young Readers) Random Hse. Children's Bks.

—The Berenstain Bears & the Love Match. 1998. (Berenstain Bears Big Chapter Bks.). (J). (gr. 2-6). 10.04 (*0-606-13952-4*) Turtleback Bks.

Bergstrom, Gunilla. You Have a Girlfriend, Alfie Atkins? Sandin, Joan, tr. from SWE. 1988. (Illus.). 28p. (J). (ps up). 6.95 o.p. (*91-29-59062-0*) R & S Bks. SWE. *Dist:* Farrar, Straus & Giroux, Holtzbrinck Pubs.

Bernard, Elizabeth. Changing Partners. 1988. (Satin Slippers Ser.: No. 4). (J). (gr. 6 up). mass mkt. 2.95 o.s.i (*0-449-13303-6*, Fawcett) Ballantine Bks.

—How to Kiss a Guy. 1995. (Love Stories Ser.). 192p. (YA). (gr. 7-12). mass mkt. 4.50 o.s.i (*0-553-56662-8*) Bantam Bks.

—Second Best. 1988. (Satin Slippers Ser.). (J). (gr. 6 up). mass mkt. 2.95 o.s.i (*0-449-13308-7*, Fawcett) Ballantine Bks.

Bernet, Elizabeth. Wings of Love. 1998. (J). 11.95 (*0-671-75203-0*); pap. 8.00 (*0-671-76959-6*) Simon & Schuster Children's Publishing. (Simon & Schuster Children's Publishing).

Berrios, Frank. Some Bunny Loves You. 2004. (Illus.). pap. 3.99 (*0-375-82734-X*, Golden Bks.) Random Hse. Children's Bks.

Betty Miles, 5 vols. 1983. (J). pap. 13.20 o.s.i (*0-380-84913-5*, Avon Bks.) Morrow/Avon.

Bischoff, David. Some Kind of Wonderful: Movie Tie-in. 1987. (YA). (gr. 9 up). mass mkt. 2.50 o.s.i (*0-440-98042-9*) Dell Publishing.

Bjorkman, Steve. Good Night, Little One. 1999. (Illus.). 40p. (J). (ps-3). 9.95 (*1-57856-275-9*) WaterBrook Pr.

Blackmore, Richard D. Lorna Doone, Level 4. Hedge, Tricia, ed. 2000. (Bookworms Ser.). (Illus.). 96p. (J). pap. text 5.95 (*0-19-423038-4*) Oxford Univ. Pr., Inc.

Blair, Alison. Love by the Book. 1989. (Roommates Ser.: No. 19). (YA). (gr. 10 up). mass mkt. 2.95 o.s.i (*0-8041-0331-3*, Ivy Bks.) Ballantine Bks.

Blair, Shannon. Star Struck. 1985. (Sweet Dreams Ser.: No. 79). 176p. (gr. 6 up). pap. 2.25 o.p. (*0-553-24971-1*) Bantam Bks.

Blake, Susan. A Change of Heart. 1986. (Sweet Dreams Special Ser.: No. 2). 224p. (Orig.). (YA). (gr. 7-12). pap. 2.95 o.s.i (*0-553-26168-1*) Bantam Bks.

—The Last Word. 1985. (Sweet Dreams Ser.: No. 84). 176p. (gr. 6). pap. 2.25 o.p. (*0-553-24718-2*) Bantam Bks.

Block, Francesca Lia. Echo. 2001. 224p. (J). (gr. 7 up). 14.95 (*0-06-028127-8*, Cotler, Joanna Bks.) HarperCollins Children's Bk. Group.

Bloss, Janet. If Only Love Could Last. 1985. 144p. (J). (gr. 6-8). 2.50 o.p. (*0-87406-014-1*) Darby Creek Publishing.

Blume, Judy. Forever. 1989. 224p. (gr. 7-12). mass mkt. 6.99 (*0-671-69530-4*, Pocket) Simon & Schuster.

—Forever. 1982. 216p. (YA). (gr. 7-12). 16.00 o.s.i (*0-02-711030-3*, Atheneum/Richard Jackson Bks.) Simon & Schuster Children's Publishing.

—Fudge-a-Mania. 1991. 160p. (gr. 3-7). pap. text 4.99 o.s.i (*0-440-40490-8*, Yearling) Random Hse. Children's Bks.

—The Judy Blume Memory Book. 1988. 160p. (J). (gr. k-6). pap. 8.95 o.s.i (*0-440-40120-8*, Yearling) Random Hse. Children's Bks.

—Just as Long as We're Together. 1988. mass mkt. o.s.i (*0-440-80023-4*) Doubleday Publishing.

—Just as Long as We're Together. 1991. (J). pap. o.s.i (*0-440-80240-7*, Dell Books for Young Readers) Random Hse. Children's Bks.

—The Pain & the Great One. 2002. (Illus.). (J). 14.79 (*0-7587-3361-5*) Book Wholesalers, Inc.

—The Pain & the Great One. 28p. (J). (gr. k-3). pap. 5.99 o.s.i (*0-8072-1265-2*); 1988. pap. 17.00 incl. audio (*0-8072-0122-7*, FTR118SP) Random Hse. Audio Publishing Group. (Listening Library).

—The Pain & the Great One. 1984. 13.14 (*0-606-00365-7*) Turtleback Bks.

—Then Again, Maybe I Won't. l.t. ed. 1988. (Children's Ser.). (J). (gr. 5-7). 13.95 o.p. (*0-8161-4417-6*, Macmillan Reference USA) Gale Group.

—Tiger Eyes. l.t. ed. 1987. 275p. (J). reprint ed. lib. bdg. 16.95 o.s.i (*1-55736-067-7*, Cornerstone Bks.) Pages, Inc.

—Tiger Eyes. 1981. (J). 11.04 (*0-606-00712-1*) Turtleback Bks.

Bode, Janet. Trust & Betrayal. 1996. (J). 20.95 (*0-385-30990-2*, Dell Books for Young Readers) Random Hse. Children's Bks.

Boies, Janice. Heart & Soul. 1987. (Sweet Dreams Ser.: No. 138). 192p. (YA). (gr. 7 up). pap. 2.50 o.s.i (*0-553-26949-6*) Bantam Bks.

—Just the Way You Are. 1986. (Sweet Dreams Ser.: No. 114). 176p. (Orig.). (YA). (gr. 7-12). mass mkt. 2.50 o.s.i (*0-553-25815-X*) Bantam Bks.

—Love on Strike. 1990. (Sweet Dreams Ser.: No. 174). 176p. (YA). (gr. 9-12). pap. 2.75 o.s.i (*0-553-28633-1*) Bantam Bks.

—Right Boy, Wrong Girl, No. 5. 1988. (First Kiss Ser.). 186p. (YA). (gr. 6 up). mass mkt. 2.95 o.s.i (*0-8041-0239-2*, Ivy Bks.) Ballantine Bks.

Boje, Shirley. Cry Softly Thule Rene. 1992. (Junior African Writers Ser.). (Illus.). (J). (gr. 7-8). pap. o.p. (*0-7910-2926-3*) Chelsea Hse. Pubs.

Bongiorno, Patti Lynn. Where Does a Mom's Love Go? 2nd ed. 2001. (J). spiral bd. 20.00 (*0-9715819-0-8*) Bongiorno Bks.

Boock, Paula. Dare Truth or Promise. 1999. 208p. (YA). (gr. 7-12). tchr. ed. 15.00 (*0-395-97117-9*) Houghton Mifflin Co.

—Dare Truth or Promise. 1999. (J). E-Book 15.00 (*0-585-36691-8*) netLibrary, Inc.

Boritzer, Etan. What Is Love? (Illus.). 32p. (J). (ps-4). 1996. 14.95 (*0-9637597-2-8*); 1994. pap. 6.95 (*0-9637597-3-6*) Lane, Veronica Bks.

Bottner, Barbara. Let Me Tell You Everything: Memoirs of a Lovesick Intellectual. 1989. 160p. (YA). (gr. 7 up). 12.95 (*0-06-020596-2*) HarperCollins Children's Bk. Group.

—Let Me Tell You Everything: Memoirs of a Lovesick Intellectual. MacDonald, Patricia, ed. 1991. 160p. (YA). reprint ed. pap. 2.95 (*0-671-72323-5*, Simon Pulse) Simon & Schuster Children's Publishing.

Bourgeois, Paulette. Un Nouvel Ami pour Benjamin. ed. 1999. Tr. of Franklin's New Friend. (J). (gr. 1). spiral bd. (*0-616-01828-2*) Canadian National Institute for the Blind/Institut National Canadien pour les Aveugles.

Boynton, Sandra. Consider Love: Its Moods & Many Ways. 2003. (Illus.). 32p. 12.95 (*0-689-85908-2*, Little Simon) Simon & Schuster Children's Publishing.

—Snuggle Puppy: A Love Song. 2003. (Boynton on Board Ser.). (Illus.). 24p. (J). bds. 6.95 (*0-7611-3067-5*, 13067) Workman Publishing Co., Inc.

Bracale, Carla. Fair-Weather Love. 1989. (First Kiss Ser.: No. 6). (YA). (gr. 5 up). mass mkt. 2.95 o.s.i (*0-8041-0240-6*, Ivy Bks.) Ballantine Bks.

—Fair-Weather Love. 1991. (Sweet Dreams Ser.: No. 187). 144p. (YA). pap. 2.99 o.s.i (*0-553-29449-0*) Bantam Bks.

—Puppy Love. 1990. (Sweet Dreams Ser.: No. 175). 144p. (YA). (gr. 9-12). pap. 2.95 o.s.i (*0-553-28830-X*) Bantam Bks.

Brady, Casey. Beach Invaders, 5. 1996. (J). (gr. 4-7). pap. 3.99 o.p. (*0-679-88232-4*, Random Hse. Bks. for Young Readers) Random Hse. Children's Bks.

Bramsch, Joan. A Kiss to Make It Better. 1984. (Loveswept Ser.: No. 64). 208p. pap. 2.25 o.p. (*0-553-21670-8*) Bantam Bks.

Brand, Debra. Green Eyes. 1982. (Sweet Dreams Ser.). (gr. 11 up). pap. 2.25 o.p. (*0-553-24321-7*) Bantam Bks.

Branscum, Robbie. Johnny May Grows Up. 1987. (Illus.). 128p. (J). (gr. 4-8). 11.95 (*0-06-020606-3*); lib. bdg. 12.89 o.p. (*0-06-020607-1*) HarperCollins Children's Bk. Group.

—Toby Alone. 1979. (gr. 5). lib. bdg. o.p. (*0-385-14018-5*) Doubleday Publishing.

—Toby & Johnny Joe. 1979. (gr. 5). lib. bdg. o.p. (*0-385-13036-8*) Doubleday Publishing.

Brennan, Melissa. Careless Kisses. 1991. (Pizza Paradise Ser.: No. 2). 79p. (YA). mass mkt. 3.50 o.p. (*0-06-106052-6*, HarperTorch) Morrow/Avon.

—Could This Be Love? 1991. (Pizza Paradise Ser.: No. 3). 192p. (YA). mass mkt. 3.50 o.p. (*0-06-106067-4*, HarperTorch) Morrow/Avon.

—Paradise Lost? 1991. (Pizza Paradise Ser.: No. 4). 192p. (YA). mass mkt. 3.50 o.p. (*0-06-106068-2*, HarperTorch) Morrow/Avon.

—Whispers & Rumors. 1994. (Pizza Parade Ser.: No. 1). 208p. (YA). mass mkt. 1.99 o.p. (*0-06-106225-1*) HarperCollins Pubs.

—Whispers & Rumors. 1991. (Pizza Paradise Ser.: No. 1). 79p. (YA). mass mkt. 3.50 o.p. (*0-06-106049-6*, HarperTorch) Morrow/Avon.

Bridgers, Sue E. Permanent Connections. 1988. (Trophy Keypoint Bks.). 80p. (YA). (gr. 7 up). mass mkt. 4.50 o.p. (*0-06-447020-2*, Harper Trophy) HarperCollins Children's Bk. Group.

Bridwell, Norman. Clifford I Love You. 2002. (Clifford, the Big Red Dog Ser.). (Illus.). 5p. (J). (ps-k). pap. 7.99 (*0-439-36774-3*) Scholastic, Inc.

Bright, J. E. A Song for Caitlin. 1998. (Love Stories Super Edition Ser.). 224p. (YA). (gr. 7-12). mass mkt. 4.50 o.s.i (*0-553-49248-9*, Dell Books for Young Readers) Random Hse. Children's Bks.

Brodsky, Richard M. Jodi the Greatest Love Story Ever Told. Garbo, Irene, ed. 2002. (Illus.). 254p. (YA). 21.95 (*0-9715423-0-9*) Trebloon Pubns.

Bronte, Charlotte. Jane Eyre. 1997. (Classics Illustrated Study Guides). (Illus.). 64p. (YA). (gr. 7 up). mass mkt., stu. ed. 4.99 o.p. (*1-57840-005-8*) Acclaim Bks.

—Jane Eyre. Farr, Naunerle C., ed. 1977. (Illus.). (J). (gr. 4-12). stu. ed. 1.25 (*0-88301-290-1*); text 7.50 o.p. (*0-88301-278-2*); pap. text 2.95 (*0-88301-266-9*) Pendulum Pr., Inc.

—Jane Eyre. 1999. (gr. 4-7). pap. 2.99 o.s.i (*0-14-130537-1*, Puffin Bks.); 1995. (Illus.). 656p. (YA). (gr. 4-7). pap. 4.99 (*0-14-036678-4*, Puffin Bks.); 1992. 448p. (J). (gr. 5 up). pap. 3.50 o.p. (*0-14-035131-0*, Puffin Bks.); 1983. (Illus.). 576p. (J). (gr. 4-7). 19.99 (*0-448-06031-0*, Grosset & Dunlap) Penguin Putnam Bks. for Young Readers.

—Jane Eyre. 1983. (Illus.). 48p. (J). (gr. 4 up). pap. 9.27 o.p. (*0-8172-2012-7*) Raintree Pubs.

—Jane Eyre. 1997. (Step into Classics Ser.). 112p. (J). (gr. 3-5). pap. 3.99 (*0-679-88618-4*) Random Hse., Inc.

—Jane Eyre. (Saddleback Classics). 1999. (Illus.). (J). 13.10 (*0-606-21557-3*); 1997. 10.04 (*0-606-11517-X*) Turtleback Bks.

—Jane Eyre. 1981. (Illus.). 48p. (J). (gr. 4 up). lib. bdg. 24.26 o.p. (*0-8172-1661-8*) Raintree Pubs.

—Jane Eyre. 2003. (Illus.). 48p. 16.95 (*0-7502-3668-X*) Hodder Wayland GBR. *Dist:* Trafalgar Square.

—Jane Eyre. 2nd ed. 1998. (Illustrated Classic Book Ser.). (Illus.). 61p. (J). (gr. 3 up). reprint ed. pap. text 4.95 (*1-56767-267-1*) Educational Insights, Inc.

—Jane Eyre. adapted ed. (YA). (gr. 5-12). pap. text 9.95 (*0-8359-0215-3*) Globe Fearon Educational Publishing.

—Jane Eyre. unabr. ed. 1998. (Wordsworth Classics Ser.). (YA). (gr. 6-12). 5.27 (*0-89061-020-7*, R0207WW) Jamestown.

—Jane Eyre, Level 6. Hedge, Tricia, ed. 2000. (Bookworms Ser.). (Illus.). 128p. pap. text 5.95 (*0-19-423088-0*) Oxford Univ. Pr., Inc.

—Jane Eyre Readalong. 1994. (Illustrated Classics Collection). 64p. pap. 14.95 incl. audio (*0-7854-0739-1*, 40458); (J). pap. 13.50 o.p. incl. audio (*1-56103-536-X*) American Guidance Service, Inc.

Brooke, Lauren. Love Is a Gift. 2004. (Heartland Ser.). 160p. (J). mass mkt. 4.99 (*0-439-42510-7*, Scholastic Paperbacks) Scholastic, Inc.

Brouwer, Aafke, illus. Love Stories. 1995. (Story Library). 260p. (J). (gr. 1 up). pap. 6.95 o.p. (*0-7534-5117-4*) Larousse Kingfisher Chambers, Inc.

Brown, Fern. Rodeo Love. 1988. 128p. (YA). (gr. 7 up). mass mkt. 2.75 o.s.i (*0-449-70249-9*, Fawcett) Ballantine Bks.

Brown, Irene Bennett. I Loved You, Logan McGee. 1987. 144p. (J). (gr. 5-8). 11.95 o.p. (*0-689-31295-4*, Atheneum) Simon & Schuster Children's Publishing.

—I Loved You, Logan McGee! 1988. 144p. (J). (gr. 5-9). pap. 3.95 o.p. (*0-14-032701-0*, Puffin Bks.) Penguin Putnam Bks. for Young Readers.

—Just Another Gorgeous Guy. 1985. 192p. (J). mass mkt. 2.25 o.s.i (*0-449-70121-2*, Fawcett) Ballantine Bks.

Brown, Joan W. Another Love. 1989. 192p. (YA). (gr. 9 up). reprint ed. pap. 5.99 o.p. (*0-89081-708-1*) Harvest Hse. Pubs.

Brown, Marc. Arthur's Valentine Countdown. 1999. (Arthur Ser.). (Illus.). 12p. (J). (ps-3). bds. 7.99 (*0-679-88475-0*, Random Hse. Bks. for Young Readers) Random Hse. Children's Bks.

—Who's in Love with Arthur? 1998. (Arthur Chapter Book Ser.: No. 10). (Illus.). 64p. (J). (gr. 3-6). 12.95 (*0-316-11539-8*); pap. 4.25 (*0-316-11540-1*) Little Brown Children's Bks.

—Who's in Love with Arthur? unabr. ed. 2001. (Arthur Chapter Bks.: Vol. 10). (Illus.). 57p. (J). (gr. 1-3). pap. 17.00 incl. audio (*0-8072-0407-2*, Listening Library) Random Hse. Audio Publishing Group.

—Who's in Love with Arthur? 1998. (Arthur Chapter Book Ser.: No. 10). (J). (gr. 3-6). 10.10 (*0-606-15917-7*) Turtleback Bks.

Brown, Marc, et al. Arthur & the Lost Diary. 1998. (Arthur Chapter Book Ser.: No. 9). (Illus.). 64p. (J). (gr. 3-6). 12.95 (*0-316-11573-8*) Little Brown Children's Bks.

Bryan, Ashley. Sh-Ko & His Eight Wicked Brothers. 1988. (Illus.). 32p. (J). (ps-3). lib. bdg. 13.95 o.s.i (*0-689-31446-9*, Atheneum) Simon & Schuster Children's Publishing.

Bryant, Bonnie. Stable Hearts. 1997. (Saddle Club Ser.: No. 63). 160p. (gr. 4-6). pap. text 3.99 o.s.i (*0-553-48418-4*, Skylark) Random Hse. Children's Bks.

—Starting Gate. 2000. (Saddle Club Ser.: No. 91). 160p. (gr. 4-7). pap. text 4.50 o.s.i (*0-553-48695-0*, Dell Books for Young Readers) Random Hse. Children's Bks.

Buchan, Stuart. All Our Yesterdays. 1987. (J). (gr. 6 up). pap. (*0-373-98006-X*, Harlequin Bks.) Harlequin Enterprises, Ltd.

—Flames from the Ashes. 1986. (Roots of Love Ser.: No. 5). 172p. (gr. 6-12). pap. 2.50 o.p. (*0-440-92602-5*) Dell Publishing.

—The Roots of Love. 1985. (Roots of Love Ser.: No. 1). 224p. (gr. k-12). pap. 2.25 o.p. (*0-440-97484-4*) Dell Publishing.

Buckley, Kate. Love Notes. Levine, Abby, ed. 1989. (Illus.). 32p. (J). (gr. k-3). lib. bdg. 13.95 o.p. (*0-8075-4780-8*) Whitman, Albert & Co.

Buffet, Pam & Buffet, Guy. Kahala: Where the Rainbow Ends. Tabrah, Ruth, ed. 1973. (Illus.). (J). (gr. 1-7). pap. 5.95 o.p. (*0-89610-006-5*) Island Heritage Publishing.

Buller, Jon & Schade, Susan. Sweet Dreams. 1999. (All by Myself Bks.). (Illus.). 16p. (J). 6.95 (*1-58260-010-4*) Infinity Plus One, LLC.

Bunin, Ivan A. Velga. Daniels, Guy, tr. 1970. (ENG & RUS., Illus.). (gr. 7 up). 7.95 o.p. (*0-87599-177-7*) Phillips, S.G. Inc.

Bunting, Eve. I Love You Too. 2004. 32p. (J). 8.95 (*0-439-45086-1*, Cartwheel Bks.) Scholastic, Inc.

—Karen Kepplewhite Is the World's Best Kisser. 1986. (J). (gr. 5-7). reprint ed. pap. (*0-671-63327-9*, Simon Pulse) Simon & Schuster Children's Publishing.

—Oh, Rick! 1992. (Eve Bunting Collection Ser.). (Illus.). 48p. (J). (gr. 2-6). lib. bdg. 12.79 o.p. (*0-89565-774-0*) Child's World, Inc.

—Survival Camp. 1978. (Young Romance Ser.). (Illus.). (J). (gr. 3-9). pap. 3.25 o.p. (*0-89812-063-2*); lib. bdg. 7.95 o.p. (*0-87191-631-2*) Creative Co., The. (Creative Education).

—Two Different Girls. 1992. (Eve Bunting Collection Ser.). (Illus.). 48p. (J). (gr. 2-6). lib. bdg. 12.79 o.p. (*0-89565-772-4*) Child's World, Inc.

—Two Different Girls. 1978. (Young Romance Ser.). (Illus.). (J). (gr. 3-9). pap. 3.25 o.p. (*0-89812-067-5*); lib. bdg. 7.95 o.p. (*0-87191-637-1*) Creative Co., The. (Creative Education).

—Two Different Girls. 2001. 32p. (YA). (gr. 6-12). pap. (*0-8224-3535-7*) Globe Fearon Educational Publishing.

—Will You Be My POSSLQ. 1987. 160p. (YA). (gr. 7 up). 12.95 (*0-15-297399-0*) Harcourt Children's Bks.

Burchard, Monica. First Affair. 1983. pap. 1.95 o.p. (*0-553-23634-2*) Bantam Bks.

Burchard, Peter. First Affair, RS. 1981. 128p. (J). (gr. 7 up). 10.95 o.p. (*0-374-32336-4*, Farrar, Straus & Giroux (BYR)) Farrar, Straus & Giroux.

—A Quiet Place. 1972. 96p. (J). (gr. 4-8). 5.95 o.p. (*0-698-20191-4*) Putnam Publishing Group, The.

Burdett, Lois & Coburn, Christine. Twelfth Night for Kids. 1995. (Shakespeare Can Be Fun Ser.). (Illus.). 40p. (YA). (gr. 2 up). pap. 8.95 (*0-88753-233-0*) Black Moss Pr. CAN. *Dist:* Firefly Bks., Ltd.

Burdick, John. Beauty & the Beast. 1994. (Little Library). 8p. (J). (ps-1). 4.98 o.p. (*0-8317-5525-3*) Smithmark Pubs., Inc.

Burman, Margaret. Dream Prom. 1983. (Sweet Dreams Ser.: No. 45). 182p. pap. 2.25 o.p. (*0-553-24341-1*) Bantam Bks.

Burton, Margie, et al. Life in the City. Adams, Alison, ed. 1999. (Early Connections Ser.). 16p. (J). (gr. k-2). pap. 4.50 (*1-58344-069-0*) Benchmark Education Co.

Bush, Nancy. Bittersweet Sixteen. 1984. (First Love Ser.). 186p. (YA). (gr. 7 up). pap. 1.95 o.s.i (*0-671-53378-9*, Pocket) Simon & Schuster.

Butcher, Samuel J. Love Is. 1990. (Golden Board Bks.). (Illus.). 12p. (J). (ps). bds. 2.49 o.s.i (*0-307-06111-6*, Golden Bks.) Random Hse. Children's Bks.

Byars, Betsy C. Bingo Brown & the Language of Love. l.t. ed. 1989. 152p. (J). lib. bdg. 16.95 o.s.i (*1-55736-146-0*, Cornerstone Bks.) Pages, Inc.

—Bingo Brown, Gypsy Lover. (Bingo Brown Ser.). (J). 1992. (Illus.). 128p. (gr. 4-7). pap. 4.99 (*0-14-034518-3*, Puffin Bks.); 1990. 160p. (gr. 3 up). 12.95 o.s.i (*0-670-83322-3*, Viking Children's Bks.) Penguin Putnam Bks. for Young Readers.

—Bingo Brown's Guide to Romance. l.t. ed. 1994. (J). 16.95 o.p. (*0-7451-2037-7*, Galaxy Children's Large Print) BBC Audiobooks America.

—Bingo Brown's Guide to Romance. (Bingo Brown Ser.). 128p. (J). 1994. (Illus.). (gr. 3-7). pap. 5.99 (*0-14-036080-8*, Puffin Bks.); 1992. (gr. 4-7). 14.99 o.s.i (*0-670-84491-8*, Viking Children's Bks.) Penguin Putnam Bks. for Young Readers.

—Bingo Brown's Guide to Romance. 1992. 11.04 (*0-606-06936-4*) Turtleback Bks.

—A Blossom Promise. 1987. (Illus.). 160p. (J). (gr. 4-6). 14.95 o.s.i (*0-385-29578-2*, Delacorte Pr.) Dell Publishing.

—A Blossom Promise. (Blossom Ser.). (J). (gr. 4-6). 145p. pap. 4.50 (*0-8072-1444-2*); 1990. pap. 24.00 incl. audio (*0-8072-7292-2*, YA826CX);Set. pap. 29.00 incl. audio (*0-8072-7322-8*, YA826SP) Random Hse. Audio Publishing Group. (Listening Library).

—A Blossom Promise. 1989. (Illus.). 160p. (gr. 4-7). reprint ed. pap. text 4.50 (*0-440-40137-2*, Yearling) Random Hse. Children's Bks.

—A Blossom Promise. 1987. (J). 10.55 (*0-606-04064-1*) Turtleback Bks.

Bywaters, Lynn, illus. Cinderella. 1992. (Children's Classics Ser.). 32p. (J). (ps-3). 6.95 (*0-8362-4905-4*) Andrews McMeel Publishing.

Cabot, Meg. Princess in Love. (Princess Diaries: Vol. III). 2003. (Illus.). 288p. (J). (gr. 6 up). pap. 6.99 (*0-06-447280-9*); 2002. 272p. (YA). (gr. 7 up). mass mkt. 5.99 (*0-06-052568-1*); 2002. 240p. (J). (gr. 7 up). 15.99 (*0-06-029467-1*); 2002. 240p. (J). (gr. 7 up). lib. bdg. 16.89 (*0-06-029468-X*) HarperCollins Children's Bk. Group.

—Princess in Love. 2002. (Princess Diaries: Vol. III). (YA). E-Book 5.95 (*0-06-051991-6*) HarperCollins Pubs.

—Princess in Love. unabr. ed. 2002. (Princess Diaries: Vol. III). (YA). (gr. 3 up). audio 25.00 (*0-8072-0711-X*, Listening Library) Random Hse. Audio Publishing Group.

—Princess in Love. 2003. (YA). 24.95 (*0-7862-4844-0*) Thorndike Pr.

Cadwallader, Sharon. Star-Crossed Love. 1987. (Sweet Dreams Ser.: No. 119). 176p. (Orig.). (YA). (gr. 7-12). mass mkt. 2.50 o.s.i (*0-553-26339-0*) Bantam Bks.

Cahn, Julie. Spotlight on Love. 1984. (Dream Your Own Romance Ser.: No. 3). (J). (gr. 2-7). pap. 2.95 (*0-671-52625-1*, Simon & Schuster Children's Publishing) Simon & Schuster Children's Publishing.

Calderone-Stewart, Lisa-Marie & Kunzman, Ed. Straight from the Heart & Other Stories. 1999. (Stories for Teens Ser.: Vol. 4). 72p. (YA). (gr. 7-12). pap. 4.95 (*0-88489-592-0*) St. Mary's Pr.

—That First Kiss & Other Stories. 1999. (Catechism Connection for Teens Ser.). 96p. (YA). (gr. 7-12). pap. 4.95 (*0-88489-589-0*) St. Mary's Pr.

Calhoun, B. B. New in Town. 1997. (His & Hers Ser.). (Orig.). (YA). pap. 3.99 (*0-380-78470-X*, Avon Bks.) Morrow/Avon.

Calhoun, Mary. Katie John & Heathcliff. 1981. (I Can Read Bks.). 160p. (J). (ps-3). pap. 3.50 (*0-06-440120-0*, Harper Trophy) HarperCollins Children's Bk. Group.

Cameron, Ann. The Most Beautiful Place in the World. (Illus.). 64p. (ps-3). 1993. pap. 4.50 (*0-394-80424-4*); 1988. (J). 13.00 o.s.i (*0-394-89463-4*); 1988. (J). 12.99 o.s.i (*0-394-99463-9*) Random Hse. Children's Bks. (Knopf Bks. for Young Readers).

Cann, Kate. Diving In. 1997. (Livewire Ser.). 238p. (YA). (gr. 7-11). pap. 9.95 (*0-7043-4937-X*) Women's Pr., Ltd., The GBR. *Dist:* Trafalgar Square.

—Go! 2001. (Love Trilogy). 240p. (gr. 7 up). (YA). pap. 6.95 (*0-06-440868-X*, HarperTempest);Vol. 3. (J). lib. bdg. 15.89 (*0-06-028939-2*) HarperCollins Children's Bk. Group.

—Ready? 2001. (Love Trilogy). 256p. (YA). (gr. 9 up). pap. 6.95 (*0-06-440869-8*, HarperTempest);Vol. 1. (J). (gr. 7 up). lib. bdg. 15.89 (*0-06-028938-4*) HarperCollins Children's Bk. Group.

—Sex. 2001. 240p. (gr. 7 up). (Love Trilogy Ser.: Vol. 2). (J). lib. bdg. 15.89 (*0-06-028937-6*); (Love Trilogy). (YA). pap. 6.95 (*0-06-440870-1*, HarperTempest) HarperCollins Children's Bk. Group.

—Too Hot to Handle. 1997. 144p. (J). pap. o.p. (*0-09-925122-1*) Random Hse. of Canada, Ltd. CAN. *Dist:* Random Hse., Inc.

Cantwell, Lee G. Finders Keepers. 1996. pap. o.p. (*1-57008-224-3*, Bookcraft, Inc.) Deseret Bk. Co.

Card, Orson Scott, ed. Future on Ice. 1998. 432p. (YA). (gr. 7 up). 24.95 (*0-312-86694-1*, Tor Bks.) Doherty, Tom Assocs., LLC.

Carlson, Melody. My Happy Heart. 2001. (Illus.). 32p. (J). (ps-5). 12.99 (*0-8054-2382-6*) Broadman & Holman Pubs.

Carson, Jo. You Hold Me & I'll Hold You. 1997. (Illus.). 32p. (J). (ps-2). mass mkt. 6.95 (*0-531-07088-3*, Orchard Bks.) Scholastic, Inc.

Carter, David A., creator. Finger Bugs Love Bug. 1997. (Finger Bugs Ser.). (Illus.). (J). (ps-3). 5.99 (*0-689-81738-X*, Little Simon) Simon & Schuster Children's Publishing.

Cash, Angela. Rich in Romance. 1995. (Sweet Dreams Ser.: No. 229). 160p. (YA). pap. 3.50 o.s.i (*0-553-56683-0*) Bantam Bks.

Casper, Dorothy. Come Fly with Me. 1997. (Magic of Love Ser.). (Illus.). 16p. (J). (gr. k-6). pap. 12.95 (*0-9662488-0-5*) Bee & Cee Enterprises.

Caswell, Brian & Chiem, David P. Only the Heart. 1997. 198p. (YA). pap. 12.95 (*0-7022-2927-X*) Univ. of Queensland Pr. AUS. *Dist:* International Specialized Bk. Services.

Caudell, Marian. Listen to Your Heart. 1986. (Sweet Dreams Ser.: No. 112). 176p. (Orig.). (YA). (gr. 7-12). mass mkt. 2.50 o.s.i (*0-553-25727-7*) Bantam Bks.

—One Boy Too Many. 1985. (Sweet Dreams Ser.: No. 100). 137p. (Orig.). (YA). mass mkt. 2.25 o.s.i (*0-553-25297-6*) Bantam Bks.

Caudill, Rebecca. Did You Carry the Flag Today, Charley? 1988. 96p. (J). (gr. 4-7). reprint ed. pap. text 4.50 (*0-440-40092-9*) Dell Publishing.

Cavanna, Betty. Catchpenny Street. 1975. (Illus.). 222p. (J). (gr. 6 up). 7.50 o.p. (*0-664-32574-2*) Westminster John Knox Pr.

—Romance on Trial. 1984. 96p. (J). (gr. 6-9). 10.95 o.p. (*0-664-32715-X*) Westminster John Knox Pr.

—Spring Comes Riding. 1950. (Illus.). (J). (gr. 5-9). 5.50 o.p. (*0-664-32069-4*) Westminster John Knox Pr.

—Storm in Her Heart. 1983. (Hiway Book). 94p. (J). (gr. 7-10). 9.95 o.p. (*0-664-32700-1*) Westminster John Knox Pr.

Cebulash, Mel. The Love Bug. 1970. (Illus.). (J). pap. 1.50 o.p. (*0-590-08780-0*) Scholastic, Inc.

Centeio, Tara Jaye. Mommy Loves Her Baby. Date not set. 32p. (ps-1). pap. 5.99 (*0-06-443715-9*) HarperCollins Pubs.

—Mommy Loves Her Baby, Daddy Loves His Baby. 2003. (Illus.). 32p. (J). (ps-1). 15.99 (*0-06-029077-3*) HarperCollins Pubs.

Chandler, Elizabeth. At First Sight. 1998. (Love Stories Ser.). 208p. (gr. 7-12). mass mkt. 4.50 o.s.i (*0-553-49254-3*, Dell Books for Young Readers) Random Hse. Children's Bks.

—Kissed by an Angel: Power of Love. 1995. (Little Nature Pops Ser.: Vol. 2). 240p. (YA). (gr. 7 up). pap. 4.50 (*0-671-89146-4*, Simon Pulse) Simon & Schuster Children's Publishing.

—Love Happens. 1997. (Love Stories Super Edition Ser.). 208p. (Orig.). (YA). (gr. 7-12). mass mkt. 4.50 o.s.i (*0-553-49217-9*, Dell Books for Young Readers) Random Hse. Children's Bks.

—Soulmates No. 3: Kissed by an Angel. 1995. 240p. (YA). (gr. 7 up). mass mkt. 3.99 (*0-671-89147-2*, Simon Pulse) Simon & Schuster Children's Publishing.

Chandler, Elizabeth & Mason, Lynn. I Do. 1999. (Love Stories Ser.). 208p. (gr. 7-12). mass mkt. 4.50 o.s.i (*0-553-49275-6*, Dell Books for Young Readers) Random Hse. Children's Bks.

Charbonnet, Gabrielle. Molly's Heart. 1995. (Princess Ser.). (J). 8.60 o.p. (*0-606-07878-9*) Turtleback Bks.

Chetwin, Grace. Beauty & the Beast: A Personalized Modern Retelling. 1998. (Illus.). 71p. (J). pap. text 25.00 (*0-9649349-6-5*, Rivet Bks.) Feral Pr., Inc.

Chick, Sandra. I Never Told Her I Loved Her. 1998. (Livewire Ser.). 128p. (Orig.). (J). (gr. 6-9). pap. 8.95 (*0-7043-4947-7*) Women's Pr., Ltd., The GBR. *Dist:* Trafalgar Square.

Chief Little Summer & Warm Night Rain. The Misfit, 2 vols., Vol. 1. unabr. ed. 1991. (Illus.). 300p. (YA). (gr. 8-12). 14.95 (*1-880440-03-2*) Piqua Pr., Inc.

—Reflections on a Rainy April Day. unabr. ed. 1991. (Reflections on a Rainy April Day). (Illus.). 23p. (J). (gr. 1-5). 8.95 (*1-880440-02-4*) Piqua Pr., Inc.

Chisholm, Gloria. Andrea. (Springsong Ser.). (Orig.). 1995. 192p. (J). (gr. 7-10). mass mkt. 4.99 o.p. (*1-55661-622-8*); 1983. 160p. (YA). (gr. 9 up). mass mkt. 3.99 o.p. (*0-87123-297-9*) Bethany Hse. Pubs.

Choi, Sook-Nyul. Year of Impossible Goodbyes. 1993. 176p. (J). (gr. 4-7). pap. text 5.50 (*0-440-40759-1*) Dell Publishing.

—Year of Impossible Goodbyes. 1991. 11.55 (*0-606-03001-8*) Turtleback Bks.

Christopher, Matt. Shadow over My Heart. 1998. (Peach Street Mudders Story Ser.). (Illus.). 64p. (J). (gr. 2-4). pap. 4.50 (*0-316-14204-2*) Little Brown & Co.

Churchill & Fuge. Butterfly Kiss. (Illus.). 28p. (J). pap. text 11.95 (*0-340-68614-6*) Hodder & Stoughton, Ltd. GBR. *Dist:* Lubrecht & Cramer, Ltd., Trafalgar Square.

Clark, Catherine. The Day I Met Him. 1995. (Love Stories Ser.). 192p. (gr. 7-12). mass mkt. 4.50 o.s.i (*0-553-56664-4*) Bantam Bks.

Clark, Clara. Nellie Bishop. 2003. (Illus.). 128p. (gr. 7-12). pap. 12.95 o.s.i (*1-56397-642-0*) Boyds Mills Pr.

Clark, Emma Chichester. Te Quiero Mucho Canguro Azul! 2002. Tr. of I Love You Blue Kangaroo!. (SPA.). 108p. (J). 14.95 (*84-488-1211-5*, BS31491) Beascoa, Ediciones S.A. ESP. *Dist:* Lectorum Pubns., Inc.

Clark, Marnie, et al, eds. Lighting Candles in the Dark: Stories of Courage & Love in Action. 1992. (Illus.). 215p. (Orig.). (YA). reprint ed. per. 13.00 (*0-9620912-3-5*) Quaker Press of Friends General Conference.

Classic Tales Elementary 1: Beauty & the Beast. 1996. (Illus.). 32p. (J). pap. text 4.95 (*0-19-422006-0*) Oxford Univ. Pr., Inc.

Claypool, Jane. Jasmine Finds Love. 1982. (Hiway Book). 80p. (J). (gr. 7-10). 8.95 o.p. (*0-664-32699-4*) Westminster John Knox Pr.

—A Love for Violet. 1982. (Hiway Book). 76p. (J). (gr. 7-10). 8.95 o.p. (*0-664-32697-8*) Westminster John Knox Pr.

Cleary, Beverly. Jean & Johnny. 1991. 240p. (YA). pap. 4.50 (*0-380-70927-9*, Avon Bks.) Morrow/Avon.

—The Luckiest Girl. 1996. (Illus.). 272p. (J). (gr. 5 up). pap. 5.99 (*0-380-72806-0*, Harper Trophy) HarperCollins Children's Bk. Group.

—The Luckiest Girl. 1991. 224p. (J). (gr. 5-6). reprint ed. pap. 4.50 (*0-380-70922-8*, Avon Bks.) Morrow/Avon.

Clements, Bruce. Tom Loves Anna Loves Tom, RS. 1992. 176p. (YA). (gr. 7 up). reprint ed. pap. 3.95 o.p. (*0-374-47939-9*, Aerial) Farrar, Straus & Giroux.

Clifford, Eth. The Remembering Box. ALC Staff, ed. 1992. (Illus.). 64p. (J). (gr. 4-7). pap. 4.95 (*0-688-11777-5*, Harper Trophy) HarperCollins Children's Bk. Group.

Cloverdale Press Staff. Almost Perfect: Sweet Dreams. 1992. (Sweet Dreams Ser.: No. 190). 144p. (Orig.). (YA). pap. 2.99 o.s.i (*0-553-29452-0*) Bantam Bks.

—Backstage Romance: Love on the Upbeat. 1992. (Sweet Dreams Ser.: No. 191). 112p. (YA). pap. 2.99 o.s.i (*0-553-29453-9*) Bantam Bks.

—Cheating Heart. 1992. (Sweet Dreams Ser.: No. 189). 144p. (YA). pap. 2.99 o.s.i (*0-553-29451-2*) Bantam Bks.

—Down with Love! 1991. (Sweet Dreams Ser.: No. 182). 144p. (J). pap. 2.99 o.s.i (*0-553-29144-0*) Bantam Bks.

—Lucky in Love. 1992. (Sweet Dreams Ser.: No. 194). 144p. (YA). pap. 2.99 o.s.i (*0-553-29456-3*) Bantam Bks.

—Play Me a Love Song. 1992. 144p. (YA). pap. 2.99 o.s.i (*0-553-29450-4*) Bantam Bks.

—Trust in Love, Vol. 147. 1988. (Sweet Dreams Ser.: No. 147). 176p. (Orig.). (J). pap. 2.50 o.s.i (*0-553-27229-2*, Dell Books for Young Readers) Random Hse. Children's Bks.

Cohen, Barbara. Lovers' Games. 1983. 252p. (J). (gr. 5-9). 12.95 o.s.i (*0-689-30981-3*, Atheneum) Simon & Schuster Children's Publishing.

Cohen, Daniel. Hollywood Dinosaur. 1987. (Illus.). (YA). (gr. 7 up). pap. (*0-671-64598-6*, Simon Pulse) Simon & Schuster Children's Publishing.

Cole, Babette. Truelove. 2001. (Illus.). 40p. (J). (gr. k-3). 15.99 (*0-8037-2717-8*, Dial Bks. for Young Readers) Penguin Putnam Bks. for Young Readers.

Cole, Joanna. The One & Only. 1924. (J). o.s.i (*0-688-15569-3*, Morrow, William & Co.) Morrow/Avon.

Coleman, Hila. Remind Me Not to Fall in Love. 1987. (YA). (gr. 7 up). pap. (*0-671-60123-7*, Simon Pulse) Simon & Schuster Children's Publishing.

Coleman, Michael. George & Sylvia: A Love Story. 2000. (Illus.). 32p. (J). (ps-3). 14.95 o.p. (*1-58431-021-9*) Little Tiger Pr.

Colman, Hila. A Fragile Love. 1985. (J). (gr. 7-10). pap. (*0-671-55655-X*, Simon Pulse) Simon & Schuster Children's Publishing.

Colquett, Mary S. Some Sweet Chance. 1997. 284p. 20.00 (*0-9648890-2-1*) Southern Ink Publishing.

—The Uninvited Tenant. 1997. 286p. 18.00 (*0-9648890-1-3*) Southern Ink Publishing.

Conford, Ellen. Crush. 1999. (Harper Trophy Bks.). 144p. (J). (gr. 5 up). pap. 4.95 (*0-06-440778-0*, Harper Trophy) HarperCollins Children's Bk. Group.

—Crush. 1999. 11.00 (*0-606-15853-7*) Turtleback Bks.

—Dear Lovey Hart, I Am Desperate. 1990. (J). pap. 2.95 o.p. (*0-590-43820-4*) Scholastic, Inc.

—If This Is Love, I'll Take Spaghetti. (gr. 7-9). 1990. 176p. (J). mass mkt. 3.50 o.p. (*0-590-43819-0*); 1984. (YA). pap. 2.25 o.p. (*0-590-32338-5*); 1984. 166p. (YA). mass mkt. 2.75 o.p. (*0-590-42754-7*) Scholastic, Inc.

—Loving Someone Else. 1992. 160p. (YA). mass mkt. 3.50 o.s.i (*0-553-29787-2*) Bantam Bks.

—The Things I Did for Love. 1988. 144p. (YA). mass mkt. 2.95 o.s.i (*0-553-27374-4*, Starfire) Random Hse. Children's Bks.

Conford, Ellen, et al. A Night to Remember. 1995. 160p. (Orig.). (YA). (gr. 7 up). mass mkt. 3.99 (*0-380-78038-0*, Avon Bks.) Morrow/Avon.

Conkie, Heather. Old Quarrels, Old Love. 1993. (Road to Avonlea Ser.: No. 15). 128p. (J). (gr. 4-6). pap. 3.99 o.s.i (*0-553-48041-3*) Bantam Bks.

Conklin, Barbara. Goodbye, Forever. 1984. (Sweet Dreams Ser.: No. 72). 144p. (gr. 7-12). pap. 2.25 o.p. (*0-553-24356-X*) Bantam Bks.

—P. S. I Love You. 1988. (J). mass mkt. 3.95 (*0-553-19550-6*, Dell Books for Young Readers) Random Hse. Children's Bks.

—The Summer Jenny Fell in Love. 1982. (Sweet Dreams Ser.). (gr. 7-12). pap. 2.25 o.p. (*0-553-24333-0*) Bantam Bks.

Conklin, Barbara P. P. S. I Love You, No. 1. 1984. 192p. (Orig.). (YA). pap. 3.50 o.s.i (*0-553-26976-3*) Bantam Bks.

Connell, Evan S. Double Honeymoon. 1976. 7.95 o.p. (*0-399-11663-X*) Putnam Publishing Group, The.

Conrad, Barnaby. Time Is All We Have. 1989. (YA). reprint ed. mass mkt. 4.95 o.s.i (*0-440-20245-0*) Dell Publishing.

Conrad, Pam. Holding Me Here. 1987. 160p. (YA). (gr. 7 up). mass mkt. 2.95 o.s.i (*0-553-26525-3*, Starfire) Random Hse. Children's Bks.

Cooney, Caroline B. Forbidden. 1993. 320p. (J). (gr. 7-9). mass mkt. 3.50 o.p. (*0-590-46574-0*) Scholastic, Inc.

—He Loves Me Not. 1982. 160p. (Orig.). (J). (gr. 7 up). pap. 2.25 o.p. (*0-590-40346-X*) Scholastic, Inc.

—Last Dance. 1992. (Point Romance Ser.). 256p. (Orig.). (J). (gr. 7-9). mass mkt. 3.25 o.p. (*0-590-45785-3*, Scholastic Paperbacks) Scholastic, Inc.

—The Party's Over. 1991. (J). pap. 13.95 o.p. (*0-590-42552-8*); 1992. 192p. (YA). (gr. 7-9). reprint ed. mass mkt. 3.25 (*0-590-42553-6*, Scholastic Paperbacks) Scholastic, Inc.

—The Party's Over. 1991. (J). 8.35 o.p. (*0-606-01919-7*) Turtleback Bks.

—The Perfume. 1992. 176p. (YA). (gr. 7-9). mass mkt. 3.50 (*0-590-45402-1*, Scholastic Paperbacks) Scholastic, Inc.

—Saturday Night. 1992. (Point Romance Ser.). 240p. (J). (gr. 7-9). mass mkt. 3.25 (*0-590-45784-5*, Scholastic Paperbacks) Scholastic, Inc.

—A Stage Set for Love. 1983. (Follow Your Heart Romance Ser.). (Orig.). (J). (gr. 5 up). pap. (*0-671-47396-4*, Simon Pulse) Simon & Schuster Children's Publishing.

—Summer Nights. (Point Romance Ser.). (gr. 7-9). 1992. 176p. (J). mass mkt. 3.25 (*0-590-45786-1*); 1988. 76p. (YA). pap. 2.50 o.p. (*0-590-41548-4*) Scholastic, Inc. (Scholastic Paperbacks).

—Sun, Sea, & Boys. 1984. (Follow Your Heart Romance Ser.: No. 4). (Orig.). (J). (gr. 5 up). pap. (*0-671-47580-0*, Simon Pulse) Simon & Schuster Children's Publishing.

Cooney, Linda A. Change of Hearts. 1985. (Couples Ser.: No. 1). 288p. (Orig.). (J). (gr. 7 up). pap. 2.50 o.p. (*0-590-33390-9*) Scholastic, Inc.

—Freshman Feud. 1992. (Freshman Dorm Ser.: No. 16). 224p. (YA). mass mkt. 3.50 o.p. (*0-06-106141-7*, HarperTorch) Morrow/Avon.

—Freshman Follies. 1992. (Freshman Dorm Ser.: No. 17). 240p. (YA). mass mkt. 3.50 o.p. (*0-06-106142-5*, HarperTorch) Morrow/Avon.

—Freshman Promises. 1992. (Freshman Dorm Ser.: No. 19). 240p. (YA). mass mkt. 3.99 o.p. (*0-06-106134-4*, HarperTorch) Morrow/Avon.

—Freshman Summer. 1992. (Freshman Dorm Super Ser.). 320p. (YA). mass mkt. 3.99 o.p. (*0-06-106780-6*, HarperTorch) Morrow/Avon.

—Freshman Wedding. 1992. (Freshman Dorm Ser.: No. 18). 240p. (YA). mass mkt. 3.50 o.p. (*0-06-106135-2*, HarperTorch) Morrow/Avon.

—Sworn Enemies, No. 7. 1985. (Couples Ser.). (YA). (gr. 7-12). pap. 2.50 o.p. (*0-590-33970-2*) Scholastic, Inc.

Cooper, Ilene. I'll See You in My Dreams. 2000. 160p. (J). pap. 4.99 (*0-14-037716-6*, Puffin Bks.) Penguin Putnam Bks. for Young Readers.

—Stupid Cupid. 1996. (Holiday 5 Ser.). 144p. (J). (gr. 3-7). pap. 3.99 o.p. (*0-14-036519-2*, Puffin Bks.) Penguin Putnam Bks. for Young Readers.

Cooper, J. B. Picture Perfect Romance. 1993. (Sweet Dreams Ser.: No. 204). 144p. (YA). pap. 2.99 o.s.i (*0-553-29983-2*) Bantam Bks.

Cooper, M. E. Bad Love. 1986. (Couples Ser.: No. 12). 208p. (Orig.). (J). (gr. 7 up). pap. 2.50 o.p. (*0-590-40162-9*) Scholastic, Inc.

—Break Away. 1988. (Couples Ser.: No. 35). 192p. (YA). (gr. 7 up). pap. 2.50 o.p. (*0-590-41688-X*) Scholastic, Inc.

—Don't Get Close. 1988. (Couples Ser.: No. 34). 192p. (Orig.). (YA). (gr. 7 up). pap. 2.50 o.p. (*0-590-41687-1*) Scholastic, Inc.

—Lovestruck. 1987. (Couples Ser.: No. 28). 176p. (Orig.). (J). (gr. 7 up). pap. 2.50 o.p. (*0-590-41262-0*) Scholastic, Inc.

—Made for Each Other. 1985. (Couples Ser.: No. 4). 192p. (Orig.). (YA). (gr. 7 up). pap. 2.50 o.p. (*0-590-33393-3*) Scholastic, Inc.

—Mean to Me. 1988. (Couples Ser.: No. 33). 192p. (Orig.). (YA). (gr. 7 up). pap. 2.50 o.p. (*0-590-41686-3*) Scholastic, Inc.

—Playing Dirty. 1988. (Couples Ser.: No. 32). 192p. (YA). (gr. 7 up). pap. 2.50 o.p. (*0-590-41267-1*) Scholastic, Inc.

—Prom Date. 1988. (Couples Ser.: No. 31). 192p. (YA). (gr. 12 up). pap. 2.50 o.p. (*0-590-41266-3*) Scholastic, Inc.

—Sealed with a Kiss: Couples Special Edition. 1988. 288p. (Orig.). (J). (gr. 7 up). pap. 2.95 o.p. (*0-590-41263-9*) Scholastic, Inc.

Cooper, Susan. Seaward. 1983. 180p. (YA). (gr. 5 up). lib. bdg. 16.00 (*0-689-50275-3*, McElderry, Margaret K.) Simon & Schuster Children's Publishing.

—Seaward. 1987. 11.04 (*0-606-03459-5*) Turtleback Bks.

Cooper, Zoe. Brides: Sherri's Perfect Day. 1997. (YA). (gr. 7 up). pap. 3.99 (*0-380-78699-0*, Avon Bks.) Morrow/Avon.

Corcoran, Barbara. The Sky Is Falling. 1988. 192p. (J). (gr. 3-7). lib. bdg. 14.95 o.s.i (*0-689-31388-8*, Atheneum) Simon & Schuster Children's Publishing.

Cormier, Robert. Tenderness. 1998. 240p. (YA). (gr. 9-12). mass mkt. 5.50 (*0-440-22034-3*, Dell Books for Young Readers) Random Hse. Children's Bks.

—Tenderness. 1998. 11.55 (*0-606-15733-6*) Turtleback Bks.

Costello, Emily. Tournament Trouble. 1998. (Soccer Stars Ser.: No. 6). 144p. (gr. 3-7). pap. text 3.99 o.s.i (*0-553-48649-7*, Dell Books for Young Readers) Random Hse. Children's Bks.

Cottonwood, Joe. Babcock. 1996. 240p. (YA). (gr. 4-7). pap. 15.95 (*0-590-22221-X*) Scholastic, Inc.

Coville, Bruce. Juliet Dove, Queen of Love. 2003. (Magic Shop Bks.). (Illus.). 208p. (J). (gr. 3-6). 17.00 (*0-15-204561-9*) Harcourt Children's Bks.

Cowan, Dale. Campfire Nights. 1984. (Sweet Dreams Ser.: No. 56). pap. text 2.25 o.p. (*0-553-23965-1*) Bantam Bks.

Craft, Elizabeth. Jake & Christy. 2000. (Love Stories). 192p. (gr. 7-12). mass mkt. 4.50 o.s.i (*0-553-49320-5*, Skylark) Random Hse. Children's Bks.

—Justin & Nicole. 2000. (Love Stories). 192p. (gr. 7-12). mass mkt. 4.50 (*0-553-49319-1*, Dell Books for Young Readers) Random Hse. Children's Bks.

—Max & Jane. 2000. (Love Stories). 192p. (gr. 7-12). mass mkt. 4.50 o.s.i (*0-553-49318-3*, Dell Books for Young Readers) Random Hse. Children's Bks.

—Show Me Love. 2000. (Turning Seventeen Ser.: No. 4). 208p. (YA). (gr. 7 up). pap. 4.95 (*0-06-447240-X*, Harper Trophy) HarperCollins Children's Bk. Group.

Craft, Marie. Cupid & Psyche. 1996. (Illus.). 40p. (J). (ps-3). 16.99 (*0-688-13163-8*) HarperCollins Children's Bk. Group.

—Cupid & Psyche. 1996. (Illus.). 40p. (J). lib. bdg. 15.93 o.p. (*0-688-13164-6*, Morrow, William & Co.) Morrow/Avon.

Crawford, Diane M. Comedy of Errors. 1992. (Sweet Dreams Ser.: No. 195). 144p. (J). (gr. 4-7). pap. 2.99 o.s.i (*0-553-29457-1*) Bantam Bks.

Cruise, Beth. Screech in Love. 1995. (Saved by the Bell Ser.: No. 21). 144p. (YA). (gr. 5-8). pap. 3.95 (*0-689-80210-2*, Simon Pulse) Simon & Schuster Children's Publishing.

Crystal, Billy. I Already Know I Love You. 2004. 40p. (J). 16.99 (*0-06-059391-1*); lib. bdg. 17.89 (*0-06-059392-X*) HarperCollins Pubs.

Curry, Jane Louise. The Lotus Cup. 1986. 164p. (YA). (gr. 7 up). text 13.95 o.s.i (*0-689-50384-9*, McElderry, Margaret K.) Simon & Schuster Children's Publishing.

Curtis, Jamie Lee. Tell Me Again about the Night I Was Born. ed. 1999. (J). (gr. 1). spiral bd. (*0-616-01623-9*) Canadian National Institute for the Blind/Institut National Canadien pour les Aveugles.

—Tell Me Again about the Night I Was Born. ed. 1999. (J). (gr. 2). spiral bd. (*0-616-01624-7*) Canadian National Institute for the Blind/Institut National Canadien pour les Aveugles.

—Tell Me Again about the Night I Was Born. 2000. (Illus.). 40p. (J). (gr. k-3). pap. 5.99 (*0-06-443581-4*, Harper Trophy) HarperCollins Children's Bk. Group.

Curtis, Stefanie. Heart to Heart. 1987. (Sweet Dreams Ser.: No. 118). 176p. (YA). (gr. 7-12). mass mkt. 2.50 o.s.i (*0-553-26293-9*) Bantam Bks.

Cutburth, Ronald W. Love from the Sea. Naumann, Cynthia E., ed. 1990. (Illus.). 27p. (J). (gr. 4-7). pap. 3.50 (*1-878291-01-7*) Love From the Sea.

—Love from the Sea. Naumann, Cynthia E., ed. West, Bobbie, tr. 1990. (CHI., Illus.). 27p. (J). (gr. 5-8). pap. (*1-878291-11-4*) Love From the Sea.

—Love from the Sea. Naumann, Cynthia E., ed. Tostado, Rocio G., tr. 1990. (SPA., Illus.). 27p. (J). (gr. 5-8). pap. (*1-878291-09-2*) Love From the Sea.

—Love from the Sea. Naumann, Cynthia E., ed. Witt, Hannelore, tr. 1989. (FRE., Illus.). 27p. (J). (gr. 5-8). pap. (*1-878291-07-6*) Love From the Sea.

—Love from the Sea. Naumann, Cynthia E., ed. Lander, Kerstin, tr. 1989. (SWE., Illus.). 27p. (J). (gr. 5-8). pap. (*1-878291-06-8*) Love From the Sea.

—Love from the Sea. Naumann, Cynthia E., ed. Witt, Hannelore, tr. 1989. (GER., Illus.). 27p. (J). (gr. 5-8). pap. (*1-878291-03-3*) Love From the Sea.

D'Abreo, Brendan. Heads & Hearts. 1994. 56p. (J). (gr. 3-6). pap. 11.00 o.p. (*0-8059-3522-3*) Dorrance Publishing Co., Inc.

Dager, Deborah. Heartaches. 1983. 224p. (Orig.). (YA). (gr. 9 up). mass mkt. 1.95 o.p. (*0-449-70042-9*, Fawcett) Ballantine Bks.

Dale, Elizabeth. How Long? 1998. (Illus.). 32p. (J). (ps-1). pap. 14.95 (*0-531-30101-X*, Orchard Bks.) Scholastic, Inc.

Daley, Dan. Stars In Her Eyes: A Song for Linda, Vol. 122. 1987. (Sweet Dreams Ser.). 144p. (Orig.). (YA). (gr. 7-12). mass mkt. 2.50 o.s.i (*0-553-26419-2*) Bantam Bks.

Daly, Maureen. Acts of Love. (gr. 7-9). 1987. 176p. (YA). pap. 2.75 o.p. (*0-590-43631-7*); 1986. 176p. (J). pap. 12.95 o.p. (*0-590-33873-0*); 1987. 192p. (J). reprint ed. pap. 2.95 o.p. (*0-590-40708-2*, Scholastic Paperbacks) Scholastic, Inc.

—Seventeenth Summer. 1981. 288p. (YA). (gr. 7 up). reprint ed. lib. bdg. 19.95 (*0-89967-029-6*, Harmony Raine & Co.) Buccaneer Bks., Inc.

—Seventeenth Summer. (YA). 2003. mass mkt. 5.99 (*0-689-85444-7*, Simon Pulse); 2002. 320p. 17.95 (*0-689-85383-1*, Simon & Schuster Children's Publishing); 1985. 306p. (gr. 7 up). mass mkt. 5.99 (*0-671-61931-4*, Simon Pulse); 1981. (gr. 7 up). pap. (*0-671-44386-0*, Simon Pulse) Simon & Schuster Children's Publishing.

—Seventeenth Summer. 1968. 11.04 (*0-606-04805-7*) Turtleback Bks.

D'Anard, Elizabeth. Cinderella Summer. 1992. (Changes Romance Ser.: No. 5). 240p. (YA). (gr. 7 up). mass mkt. 3.50 o.p. (*0-06-106776-8*, HarperTorch) Morrow/Avon.

Daniel, Kate. Sweet Dreams. 1992. 224p. (YA). mass mkt. 3.50 o.p. (*0-06-106720-2*, HarperTorch) Morrow/Avon.

—Sweetheart. 1993. 240p. (YA). mass mkt. 3.50 o.p. (*0-06-106735-0*, HarperTorch) Morrow/Avon.

—Teen Idol. 1992. 224p. (YA). mass mkt. 3.50 o.p. (*0-06-106779-2*, HarperTorch) Morrow/Avon.

Danner, Nikki. Face up to Love. 1994. (Sweet Dreams Ser.: No. 218). 160p. (YA). pap. 3.50 o.p. (*0-553-56483-8*) Bantam Bks.

Davenier, Christine. Leon & Albertine. Barth, Dominic, tr. 1998. (Illus.). 32p. (J). (ps-1). pap. 15.95 (*0-531-30072-2*, Orchard Bks.) Scholastic, Inc.

Davidson, Nicole. Final Cruise: Farewell Kiss. 1995. 208p. (Orig.). (YA). (gr. 7 up). pap. 3.99 (*0-380-72246-1*, Avon Bks.) Morrow/Avon.

—Final Cruise: First Kiss. 1995. 208p. (Orig.). (YA). (gr. 5 up). mass mkt. 3.99 o.p. (*0-380-72244-5*, Avon Bks.) Morrow/Avon.

Davis-Pack, Denise. Foolish Things. 1997. 256p. pap. 10.99 (*0-9660637-1-6*) Pack, Denise Davis.

Davol, Marguerite W. The Paper Dragon. 1997. (Illus.). 60p. (J). (gr. k-3). 19.95 (*0-689-31992-4*, Atheneum) Simon & Schuster Children's Publishing.

De Gale, Ann. Island Encounter. 1986. (Heartlines Ser.: No. 5). (Orig.). (J). (gr. 6 up). mass mkt. 2.50 o.s.i (*0-440-94026-5*, Laurel Leaf) Random Hse. Children's Bks.

De Montano, Marty K. Coyote in Love with a Star. 1998. (Tales of the People Ser.). (Illus.). 30p. (J). (ps up). 14.95 (*0-7892-0162-3*, Abbeville Kids) Abbeville Pr., Inc.

Decary, Marie. Amour Reglisse et Chocolat. 2002. (Roman Jeunesse Ser.). (FRE.). 96p. (YA). (gr. 4-7). pap. 8.95 (*2-89021-051-0*) La Courte Echelle CAN. *Dist:* Firefly Bks., Ltd.

Decker, Marjorie Ainsborough. My Little Book of Love. 2002. (Christian Mother Goose Ser.). (Illus.). 12p. (J). bds. 5.99 (*0-448-42680-3*) Penguin Putnam Bks. for Young Readers.

DeClements, Barthe. How Do You Lose Ninth Grade Blues? 1993. 144p. (J). (gr. 5 up). pap. 3.99 o.s.i (*0-14-036333-5*, Puffin Bks.) Penguin Putnam Bks. for Young Readers.

—How Do You Lose Those Ninth Grade Blues? 1984. 144p. (J). (gr. 7 up). pap. 2.50 o.p. (*0-590-40969-7*, Scholastic Paperbacks) Scholastic, Inc.

Deevoy, Jacqui. Love Games. 1997. 144p. (J). pap. o.p. (*0-09-925142-6*) Random Hse. of Canada, Ltd. CAN. *Dist:* Random Hse., Inc.

Delton, Judy. That Mushy Stuff. 1990. (Pee Wee Scouts Ser.: No. 8). (J). (gr. 2-5). pap. 4.99 (*0-440-80206-7*) Dell Publishing.

—That Mushy Stuff. 1989. (Pee Wee Scouts Ser.: No. 8). (Illus.). 80p. (gr. 2-5). pap. text 3.99 o.s.i (*0-440-40176-3*, Yearling) Random Hse. Children's Bks.

—That Mushy Stuff. 1989. (Pee Wee Scouts Ser.: No. 8). (J). (gr. 2-5). 10.14 (*0-606-04056-0*) Turtleback Bks.

Demers, Dominique. Un Hiver de Tourmente. 1996. (FRE.). 160p. (YA). (gr. 8 up). pap. 7.95 (*2-89021-171-1*) La Courte Echelle CAN. *Dist:* Firefly Bks., Ltd.

Demou, Doris B. A Part of Myself: I Give to You. Meredith, Mary, ed. 1990. (More to Give Ser.). (Illus.). (YA). (gr. 6 up). rev. ed. tchr. ed. 8.00 o.p. (*0-9604794-1-4*); 2nd rev. ed. pap. text 6.00 (*0-9604794-0-6*) Demou, Doris Beck.

Desrosiers, Sylvie. Qui Veut Entrer dans la Legende? 2003. (Roman Jeunesse Ser.). (FRE., Illus.). 96p. (YA). (gr. 4-7). pap. 8.95 (*2-89021-269-6*) La Courte Echelle CAN. *Dist:* Firefly Bks., Ltd.

Devore, Cynthia D. Do Rainbows Last Forever? 1993. (Children of Courage Ser.). (YA). (gr. 5 up). lib. bdg. 21.95 o.p. (*1-56239-248-4*) ABDO Publishing Co.

Dial L for Love. 1983. (Sweet Dreams Ser.: No. 48). pap. 1.95 o.p. (*0-553-23744-6*) Bantam Bks.

Dickens, Charles. Great Expectations. Hegarty, Carol, ed. 1998. (Classics Ser.: Set II). (Illus.). 77p. (YA). (gr. 5-12). pap. text 6.95 (*1-56254-266-4*, SP2664) Saddleback Publishing, Inc.

Dines, Carol. Talk to Me: Stories & a Novella. 1999. (Laurel-Leaf Bks.). 240p. (YA). (gr. 7 up). mass mkt. 4.50 o.s.i (*0-440-22026-2*, Dell Books for Young Readers) Random Hse. Children's Bks.

—Talk to Me: Stories & a Novella. 1999. 10.55 (*0-606-16451-0*) Turtleback Bks.

Dippold, Jane, illus. I Love My Baby. 1999. (Leap Frog Lift-a-Flap Ser.). (J). (*0-7853-3367-3*) Publications International, Ltd.

Disney Staff. Beauty & the Beast Bath Book. 1991. (J). 5.98 o.p. (*0-8317-2436-6*) Smithmark Pubs., Inc.

—Beauty & the Beast Little Library. 1991. (J). 5.98 o.p. (*0-8317-2446-3*) Smithmark Pubs., Inc.

—Everlasting Love. 2002. (Illus.). 32p. (J). pap. 4.99 (*0-7364-1278-6*) Mouse Works.

—Hugs & Kisses. 2002. (Illus.). 14p. (J). (ps). bds. 4.99 (*0-7364-1300-6*, RH/Disney) Random Hse. Children's Bks.

—Princess Collection. 2001. (Illus.). 48p. (J). (gr. k-3). bds. 9.99 (*0-7364-1138-0*, RH/Disney) Random Hse. Children's Bks.

Disney, Walter Elias. La Bella y la Bestia. 1996. (Spanish Classics Ser.). Orig. Title: Sp-la Bella y la Bestia. (SPA.). (J). 7.98 o.p. (*1-57082-372-3*) Mouse Works.

Dobkin, Kaye. A Valentine for Betsy. 1984. (Turning Points Ser.: No. 3). (J). (gr. 5-9). mass mkt. 2.50 o.p. (*0-451-14075-3*, Signet Vista) NAL.

Dokey, Cameron. Charlotte: Heart of Hope. 1997. (Hearts & Dreams Ser.: No. 2). (YA). (gr. 5 up). pap. 3.99 (*0-380-78566-8*, Avon Bks.) Morrow/Avon.

—Lost & Found. 1999. (Enchanted Hearts Ser.: No. 3). 208p. (YA). (gr. 7-12). pap. 4.50 (*0-380-80083-7*, Avon Bks.) Morrow/Avon.

—Lost & Found. 1999. (Enchanted Hearts Ser.). (Illus.). (YA). 10.55 (*0-606-17965-8*) Turtleback Bks.

Dokey, Cameron, et al. Be Mine: A Romantic Quartet of Special Valentines to Capture Your Heart. 1997. (gr. 8 up). pap. 3.99 (*0-380-78704-0*, Avon Bks.) Morrow/Avon.

—New Year, New Love. 1996. (Orig.). (YA). pap. 3.99 (*0-380-78663-X*, Avon Bks.) Morrow/Avon.

Donahue, Marilyn. Somebody Special to Love. 1988. (Quick Fox Line Ser.). 176p. (YA). pap. 4.49 o.p. (*0-89191-360-2*) Cook Communications Ministries.

Doyon, Stephanie. It Had to Be You. 1996. (Love Stories Ser.). 192p. (gr. 7-12). mass mkt. 4.50 o.s.i (*0-553-56669-5*, Dell Books for Young Readers) Random Hse. Children's Bks.

—Taking Chances. 1999. (On the Road Ser.: No. 3). 10.55 (*0-606-18899-1*) Turtleback Bks.

Doyon, Stephanie & Nielsen, Cliff. Taking Chances. 1999. (On the Road Ser.: No. 3). 224p. (J). (gr. 6-10). pap. 4.50 (*0-689-82109-3*, 076714004504, Simon Pulse) Simon & Schuster Children's Publishing.

Dragonwagon, Crescent. Brass Button. 1997. (Illus.). 40p. (J). (gr. k-4). 16.00 (*0-689-80582-9*, Atheneum) Simon & Schuster Children's Publishing.

—If You Call My Name. 1981. (Illus.). 32p. (J). (gr. k-4). 11.95 (*0-06-021743-X*); lib. bdg. 11.89 o.p. (*0-06-021744-8*) HarperCollins Children's Bk. Group.

Draper, Sharon M. Romiette & Julio. 2001. (Illus.). (J). 11.04 (*0-606-20415-6*) Turtleback Bks.

Du Jardin, Rosamond. Real Thing. 1956. (J). (gr. 4-9). 7.95 o.p. (*0-397-30344-0*) HarperCollins Children's Bk. Group.

Dube, Hope. Love Is a Challenge. 1992. (Junior African Writers Ser.). (Illus.). 80p. (J). (gr. 4-7). pap. 5.00 (*0-7910-2923-9*) Chelsea Hse. Pubs.

DuKore, Jesse. Long Distance Love. 1983. (Sweet Dreams Ser.: No. 44). (YA). (gr. 7-12). pap. 2.25 o.s.i (*0-553-17853-9*) Bantam Bks.

Dunbar, Joyce. The Love-Me Bird. 2004. 32p. (J). pap. 15.95 (*0-439-47431-0*, Orchard Bks.) Scholastic, Inc.

Dussling, Jennifer. A Heart for the Queen of Hearts. 1998. (Jewel Sticker Stories Ser.). (Illus.). 24p. (J). (ps-2). 3.99 o.s.i (*0-448-41864-9*, Grosset & Dunlap) Penguin Putnam Bks. for Young Readers.

Duvivier-Dodds, Eleanora. Apollo's Lover. 1997. 96p. (YA). (gr. 10-12). pap. 8.00 (*0-8059-4121-5*) Dorrance Publishing Co., Inc.

Edwards, Cassie. Heart Strings, No. 3. 1982. (Leisure First Romance Ser.). 192p. (J). (gr. 6-12). pap. 1.95 o.p. (*0-8439-1153-0*) Dorchester Publishing Co., Inc.

Eires, Anita. Summer Awakening. 1986. (Heartlines Ser.: No. 1). (J). (gr. 6 up). mass mkt. 2.50 o.s.i (*0-440-98369-X*, Laurel Leaf) Random Hse. Children's Bks.

Ekberg, Susan. The Trust Walk. 1995. (Illus.). 32p. (J). (gr. k-5). 17.95 (*0-9630419-6-7*) Spiritseeker Publishing, Inc.

Elkins, Stephen. Stories That End with a Hug. 1993. (Illus.). 32p. (J). (gr. k-8). 12.98 (*1-56919-002-X*) Wonder Workshop.

Ellis, Albert. My Secret Admirer. 1989. 192p. (J). (gr. 7-9). mass mkt. 3.25 (*0-590-44768-8*) Scholastic, Inc.

Ellis, Carol. See You in September. 1984. (Turning Points Ser.: No. 4). 160p. (J). (gr. 5-9). mass mkt. 1.95 o.p. (*0-451-13121-5*, Signet Vista) NAL.

Ellis, Lucy. Pink Parrots No. 3: Mixed Signals. 1991. (J). (gr. 4-7). pap. 3.50 o.p. (*0-316-18566-3*) Little Brown & Co.

Emberg, Kate. Recipe for Love. 1995. (Sweet Dreams Ser.: No. 225). 160p. (YA). pap. 3.50 o.s.i (*0-553-56679-2*) Bantam Bks.

Emberg, Kate & Page, Alexis. The Language of Love. 1996. (Love Stories Ser.). 192p. (gr. 7-12). mass mkt. 3.99 o.s.i (*0-553-56667-9*) Bantam Bks.

Enderele, Judith. S. W. A. K. Sealed with a Kiss. 1986. 100p. 2.50 o.p. (*0-425-09570-3*, Berkley/Pacer) Berkley Publishing Group.

Enderle, Judith. Secrets. 1984. (First Love Ser.). 154p. (YA). (gr. 7 up). pap. (*0-671-53415-7*, Silhouette) Harlequin Enterprises, Ltd.

Engelbreit, Mary. Baby Booky: Honey Bunny. 2004. (Illus.). 14p. (J). bds. 6.99 (*0-06-008135-X*, Harper Festival) HarperCollins Children's Bk. Group.

Erlbach, Arlene. A Little More to Love. 1994. (Sweet Dreams Ser.: No. 221). 160p. (YA). (gr. 7 up). pap. 3.50 o.s.i (*0-553-56486-2*) Bantam Bks.

Evans, Edie. I Love You Daddy! 2001. (Little Golden Bks.). (Illus.). 16p. (J). (ps-3). 2.99 (*0-307-99508-9*, Golden Bks.) Random Hse. Children's Bks.

—I Love You Mommy! 1999. (Little Golden Bks.). (Illus.). 16p. (J). (ps-3). 2.99 (*0-307-99507-0*, Golden Bks.) Random Hse. Children's Bks.

Everett, Percival. The One That Got Away. 1992. (J). (ps-3). 14.95 (*0-395-56427-1*, Clarion Bks.) Houghton Mifflin Co. Trade & Reference Div.

Eyerly, Jeannette. If I Loved You Wednesday. 1985. (J). (gr. 7-10). reprint ed. pap. (*0-671-61353-7*, Simon Pulse) Simon & Schuster Children's Publishing.

—More Than a Summer's Love. 1983. 176p. (J). (gr. 12 up). reprint ed. pap. (*0-671-45660-1*, Simon Pulse) Simon & Schuster Children's Publishing.

Faith, Susan. Purple Love. 2001. (Illus.). 32p. (J). (ps-7). 17.95 (*0-9707793-5-6*) Purple People, Inc.

Falda, Dominique. Night Flight. James, J. Alison, tr. from GER. 1945. Tr. of Julian's Reise ins Gluck. (Illus.). 32p. (J). 14.95 o.p. (*1-55858-306-8*); 14.88 o.p. (*1-55858-307-6*) North-South Bks., Inc.

Falk, Bonnie H. Forget-Me-Not. 1984. (Illus.). 192p. (J). (gr. 4-8). pap. 7.95 (*0-9614108-0-9*) BHF Memories Unlimited.

Favors, Jean. Tough Choices. 1992. (Fifteen - Nickelodeon Bks.: No. 3). 112p. (Orig.). (J). (gr. 4-9). 2.95 o.p. (*0-448-40492-3*, Grosset & Dunlap) Penguin Putnam Bks. for Young Readers.

Fields, Terri. The Other Me. 1986. (Sweet Dreams Ser.: No. 117). 160p. (Orig.). (YA). (gr. 7-12). pap. 2.50 o.s.i (*0-553-26196-7*) Bantam Bks.

—Recipe for Romance. 1986. 192p. (Orig.). (J). (gr. 7 up). pap. 2.25 o.p. (*0-590-33872-2*) Scholastic, Inc.

Finney, Shan. Geared for Romance. 1987. (Sweet Dreams Ser.: No. 135). 192p. (Orig.). (YA). (gr. 7-12). pap. 2.50 o.s.i (*0-553-26902-X*) Bantam Bks.

Fisher, Dorothy Canfield. Understood Betsy. 1973. (Illus.). 220p. (J). (gr. 5-9). pap. 1.50 o.p. (*0-380-01595-1*, 49692-5, Avon Bks.) Morrow/Avon.

Flare Young Love, 5 vols. 1984. (J). pap. 11.25 o.p. (*0-380-88435-6*, Avon Bks.) Morrow/Avon.

Foley, June. Falling in Love Is No Snap. 1986. 144p. (J). (gr. 7 up). 14.95 o.s.i (*0-385-29490-5*, Delacorte Pr.) Dell Publishing.

—Falling in Love Is No Snap. 1989. 144p. (J). (gr. 6 up). mass mkt. 2.95 o.s.i (*0-440-20349-X*, Laurel Leaf) Random Hse. Children's Bks.

—It's No Crush, I'm in Love. 1982. 224p. (J). (gr. 7 up). 13.95 o.s.i (*0-385-28465-9*, Delacorte Pr.) Dell Publishing.

—Love by Any Other Name. (Young Love Romance Ser.). 224p. (gr. 7-12). 1986. pap. 2.50 o.p. (*0-440-94738-3*); 1983. (J). pap. 13.95 o.s.i (*0-385-29245-7*, Delacorte Pr.) Dell Publishing.

Foster, Sharon. Stormy Leigh. 1988. 368p. (Orig.). (YA). (gr. 9 up). pap. 6.95 o.p. (*1-56292-535-0*) Honor Bks.

Foster, Stephanie. A Chance at Love No. 6. 1988. 192p. (YA). (gr. 5 up). pap. 2.95 o.s.i (*0-553-27017-6*, Dell Books for Young Readers) Random Hse. Children's Bks.

—Love Times Two: International Edition. 1994. (YA). pap. 3.50 (*0-553-24153-2*) Bantam Bks.

Fowler, Ruth. Lights! Camera! Love in Action! 1989. (Illus.). 64p. (Orig.). (J). (gr. 4-6). pap. text 3.95 (*0-936625-68-6*, W897109) Woman's Missionary Union.

Franco, Marjorie. Love in a Different Key. 1986. (gr. 7-12). pap. 2.50 o.p. (*0-440-95065-1*) Dell Publishing.

—Love in a Different Key, 001. 1983. 160p. (J). (gr. 7). 9.95 o.p. (*0-395-34827-7*) Houghton Mifflin Co.

Frank, Lucy. Will You Be My Brussels Sprout? 1998. 160p. (YA). (gr. 7-12). mass mkt. 3.99 o.s.i (*0-440-22734-8*, Dell Books for Young Readers) Random Hse. Children's Bks.

—Will You Be My Brussels Sprout? 1998. (J). 10.04 (*0-606-13918-4*) Turtleback Bks.

Freeman, Lory. Loving Touches. 1986. (Illus.). 32p. (J). (ps-3). pap. 5.95 (*0-943990-20-3*); lib. bdg. 15.95 (*0-943990-21-1*) Parenting Pr., Inc.

Futcher, Jane. Crush. 3rd ed. 2004. 280p. (YA). (gr. 7 up). mass mkt. 6.95 (*1-55583-602-X*) Alyson Pubns.

Gantschev, Ivan. La Pietra di Luna. 1998. (ITA., Illus.). (J). (ps-3). 18.95 (*88-8203-054-7*) North-South Bks., Inc.

Hart, Nicole. Courting Trouble. 1984. (First Love Ser.). 154p. (YA). (gr. 7 up). pap. (*0-671-53414-9*, Silhouette) Harlequin Enterprises, Ltd.

Hartling, Peter. Ben Loves Anna. 1990. (J). 11.95 (*0-87951-407-8*) Overlook Pr., The.

—Ben Loves Anna. Auerbach, J. H., tr. from GER. 1990. (YA). (gr. 4-7). 12.95 (*0-87951-401-9*) Overlook Pr., The.

Hasse, John. I Love You When... 2001. (Pictureback Shape Ser.). (Illus.). 24p. (J). (gr. k-3). pap. 3.25 (*0-375-81063-3*, Random Hse. Bks. for Young Readers) Random Hse. Children's Bks.

Hastings, Catt. Romance on the Run. 1993. (Sweet Dreams Ser.: No. 208). 144p. (YA). pap. 3.50 o.s.i (*0-553-29987-5*) Bantam Bks.

Hatonn, Gyeorgos C. & L-L Research Staff. What Is Love? A Coloring Book for Kids. 1984. (Illus.). 34p. (J). (ps-2). pap. 6.95 (*0-945007-05-1*) L/L Research.

Hawthorne, Rachel. Nick & the Nerd. 2001. (Love Stories Ser.). 192p. (YA). (gr. 7-12). mass mkt. 4.50 o.s.i (*0-553-49372-8*, Dell Books for Young Readers) Random Hse. Children's Bks.

Hayes, Daniel. No Effect. 1995. (YA). pap. 3.99 (*0-380-72392-1*, Avon Bks.) Morrow/Avon.

Hayes, Sheila. You've Been Away All Summer. 1988. 160p. (J). (gr. 4-8). pap. 2.50 o.p. (*0-590-40791-0*, Scholastic Paperbacks) Scholastic, Inc.

Haynes, Betsy. Taffy Sinclair & the Romance Machine. 1987. 128p. (YA). pap. 2.50 o.s.i (*0-553-15494-X*) Bantam Bks.

Hays, Richard. Stretch's Treasure Hunt. (Noah's Park Ser.). (Illus.). (J). (ps). 16p. bds. 8.99 o.p. (*0-7814-3539-0*); 28p. 8.99 o.p. (*0-7814-3367-3*) Cook Communications Ministries.

Hazen, Barbara Shook. Even If I Did Something Awful? 1992. (Illus.). 32p. (J). (ps-3). reprint ed. mass mkt. 4.99 (*0-689-71600-1*, Aladdin) Simon & Schuster Children's Publishing.

Headapohl, Betty R. Follow Your Heart. 1995. (Sweet Dreams Ser.: Vol. 233). 160p. (Orig.). (YA). (gr. 6 up). pap. 3.50 o.s.i (*0-553-56687-3*, Dell Books for Young Readers) Random Hse. Children's Bks.

Hearst, Particia & Biddle, Cordelia F. Murder at San Simeon: A Novel of the Roaring Twenties. 1997. 186p. pap. 6.99 (*0-671-53402-5*, Pocket) Simon & Schuster.

Heath, Lorraine. Samantha & the Cowboy. 2002. (True Romance Ser.). 256p. (J). pap. 4.99 (*0-06-447341-4*, Avon Bks.) Morrow/Avon.

Hehl, Eileen. Happily Ever After. 1995. (Sweet Dreams Ser.: Vol. 230). 160p. (Orig.). (YA). (gr. 6 up). pap. 3.50 o.s.i (*0-553-56684-9*, Dell Books for Young Readers) Random Hse. Children's Bks.

—No Strings Attached. 1995. (Sweet Dreams Ser.: No. 95). 176p. (Orig.). (YA). mass mkt. 3.50 o.s.i (*0-553-25178-3*) Bantam Bks.

—Playing Games. 1986. (Sweet Dreams Ser.: No. 110). 176p. (J). (gr. 5-6). mass mkt. 2.25 o.s.i (*0-553-25642-4*) Bantam Bks.

—Playing the Field, Vol. 133. 1987. (Sweet Dreams Ser.). 192p. (J). pap. 2.50 o.s.i (*0-553-26864-3*, Dell Books for Young Readers) Random Hse. Children's Bks.

Heitritter, Laura. I Love You Just Because. Date not set. (Illus.). 16p. (Orig.). (J). (ps up). pap. 6.95 (*1-885964-01-3*) P2 Educational Services, Inc.

Hemmeter, Karla. Heart Petals on the Hearth: A Collection of Children's Stories. 2003. (Illus.). 64p. (J). (ps-6). 20.00 (*1-891452-00-2*); pap. 16.00 (*1-891452-01-0*) Heart Arbor Bks.

—Heart Petals on the Hearth II: A Collection of Children's Stories. 1997. (Illus.). 80p. (J). (ps-6). 25.00 (*1-891452-04-5*); pap. 20.00 (*1-891452-05-3*) Heart Arbor Bks.

Henry, Emma. The Nine-Hour Date. 2001. (Love Stories Ser.). 192p. (YA). (gr. 7-12). mass mkt. 4.50 (*0-553-49370-1*, Dell Books for Young Readers) Random Hse. Children's Bks.

Henry, O. The Gift of the Magi. Pauk, Walter & Harris, Raymond, eds. 1980. (Classics Ser.). (Illus.). 35p. (YA). (gr. 6-12). pap. 17.96 incl. audio (*0-89061-187-4*, 402); pap. text 5.99 (*0-89061-186-6*, 401) Jamestown.

—The Gift of the Magi, Grades 6-12. Pauk, Walter & Harris, Raymond, eds. 1980. (Classics Ser.). (Illus.). 35p. tchr. ed. 7.32 (*0-89061-188-2*, 403) Jamestown.

Henson, Heather. Making the Run. 2002. 240p. (J). (gr. k-4). lib. bdg. 15.89 (*0-06-029797-2*); (gr. 10 up). 15.95 (*0-06-029796-4*) HarperCollins Children's Bk. Group. (HarperTempest).

Herman, Gail. Sweet Sixteen. 1996. (YA). (gr. 6 up). mass mkt. 3.99 (*0-590-67449-8*) Scholastic, Inc.

Hermes, Patricia. Be Still My Heart. MacDonald, Patricia, ed. 1991. 160p. (YA). reprint ed. pap. 2.99 (*0-671-70645-4*, Simon Pulse) Simon & Schuster Children's Publishing.

—You Shouldn't Have to Say Good-Bye. 1982. 117p. (J). (gr. 3-7). 11.95 o.p. (*0-15-299944-2*) Harcourt Children's Bks.

—You Shouldn't Have to Say Good-Bye. 9999. 128p. (J). (gr. 4-6). pap. 2.50 o.p. (*0-590-41355-4*, Scholastic Paperbacks) Scholastic, Inc.

Hermstad, Melanie. Bird, I Love You. Date not set. (*0-517-58561-8*) Random Hse. Value Publishing.

Herrick, Ann. The Perfect Guy. 1989. 160p. (J). (gr. 5 up). mass mkt. 2.95 o.s.i (*0-553-27927-0*) Bantam Bks.

Hershenburgh, Anne. Animal Designs, No. 3 Coloring Book. 1984. 48p. (J). pap. 2.95 o.p. (*0-8431-1014-7*, Price Stern Sloan) Penguin Putnam Bks. for Young Readers.

Herzig, Alison C. Shadows on the Pond. 1985. 200p. (J). (gr. 7 up). 14.95 o.p. (*0-316-35895-9*) Little Brown & Co.

Hesser, Terry Spencer. Kissing Doorknobs. 1999. 160p. (YA). (gr. 7-12). reprint ed. mass mkt. 5.50 (*0-440-41314-1*) Bantam Bks.

Hickey, Elizabeth & Cohen, James. I Love You More Than... 1998. (Illus.). 32p. (J). 16.95 (*1-884862-04-7*) Family Connections Publishing Co.

Hill, Carol. Let's Fall in Love. 1996. (Norton Paperback Fiction Ser.). 288p. pap. 11.00 o.p. (*0-393-31408-1*, Norton Paperbacks) Norton, W. W. & Co., Inc.

—Let's Fall in Love. 1974. 268p. (J). o.p. (*0-394-48926-8*, Random Hse. Bks. for Young Readers) Random Hse. Children's Bks.

Hill, Eric. Puppy Love. 1982. (Illus.). 36p. (J). (ps-3). 4.99 (*0-399-20935-2*, G. P. Putnam's Sons) Penguin Putnam Bks. for Young Readers.

Hill, Meredith. The Silent Witness. 1983. 192p. (J). pap. 1.95 o.p. (*0-590-32552-3*) Scholastic, Inc.

Hillman, Craig, et al. The Dance. 1999. (Love Stories Super Edition Ser.). 224p. (gr. 7-12). mass mkt. 4.99 o.s.i (*0-553-49294-2*, Dell Books for Young Readers) Random Hse. Children's Bks.

Hinton, Pat C. In Friendship's Garden. 1996. (Enchanted Hearts Ser.). (Illus.). 48p. pap. 3.95 (*1-879127-69-5*) Lighten Up Enterprises.

Hinton, Pat C. & Adventure Publications Staff. Cherished Friend. 1996. (Enchanted Hearts Ser.). (Illus.). 48p. (J). pap. 3.95 (*1-879127-66-0*) Lighten Up Enterprises.

—From the Heart. 1996. (Enchanted Hearts Ser.). (Illus.). 48p. pap. 3.95 (*1-879127-68-7*) Lighten Up Enterprises.

—Thinking of You. 1996. (Enchanted Hearts Ser.). (Illus.). 48p. pap. 3.95 (*1-879127-67-9*) Lighten Up Enterprises.

Hodges, Lynn & Buchanan. I Love You This Much. 2001. (Illus.). 36p. (J). 14.99 (*0-310-23268-6*) Zondervan.

Hoggarth, Janet. The Princess Party Book: Favorite Happy Ever after Stories... & More. 2002. (Illus.). 96p. (J). (gr. 2-4). pap. 17.95 (*0-439-40434-7*, Chicken Hse., The) Scholastic, Inc.

Hoh, Diane. Cheerleaders No. 7: Flirting. 1985. (YA). pap. 2.50 o.p. (*0-590-40838-0*) Scholastic, Inc.

—The Fever. 1992. 192p. (YA). (gr. 7 up). mass mkt. 4.50 (*0-590-45401-3*, Scholastic Paperbacks) Scholastic, Inc.

Holabird, Katharine. Angelina Loves: A Story of Love & Friendship. 2002. (Illus.). 24p. (J). pap. 6.95 (*1-58485-566-5*, American Girl) Pleasant Co. Pubns.

Hold Me Tight, No. 36. 1988. (Couples Ser.). (J). (gr. 7-12). pap. 2.50 o.p. (*0-590-41689-8*) Scholastic, Inc.

Holeman, Linda. Saying Good-Bye. unabr. ed. 1996. 176p. (YA). (gr. 7-9). (*1-895555-47-7*) Turnerbks.

—Toxic Love. 2003. 184p. (YA). (gr. 6-9). pap. 8.95 (*0-88776-647-1*) Tundra Bks. of Northern New York.

Holland, Isabelle. After the First Love. 1983. (YA). (gr. 7 up). mass mkt. 2.25 o.s.i (*0-449-70064-X*, Fawcett) Ballantine Bks.

—The Search. 1991. (YA). mass mkt. 3.95 o.s.i (*0-449-70342-8*, Fawcett) Ballantine Bks.

—Summer of My First Love. 1983. (Orig.). (YA). (gr. 7 up). mass mkt. 2.95 o.s.i (*0-449-70079-8*, Fawcett) Ballantine Bks.

Holly, Cate. You + Me = Love. 2001. (Illus.). 80p. 5.99 (*0-7407-1450-3*) Andrews McMeel Publishing.

Holt, Victoria. The House of a Thousand Lanterns. 1974. 336p. 9.95 o.s.i (*0-385-00817-1*) Doubleday Publishing.

Honeycutt, Natalie. Josie's Beau. 1987. 160p. (J). (gr. 6-8). 11.95 o.p. (*0-531-05718-6*); mass mkt. 11.99 o.p. (*0-531-08318-7*) Scholastic, Inc. (Orchard Bks.).

Hooper, Mary. Follow That Dream. 1986. (Heartlines Ser.: No. 6). (Orig.). (J). (gr. 6 up). mass mkt. 2.50 o.s.i (*0-440-92644-0*, Laurel Leaf) Random Hse. Children's Bks.

—Friends & Rivals. 1986. (Heartlines Ser.: No. 4). (Orig.). (J). (gr. 6 up). mass mkt. 2.50 o.s.i (*0-440-92660-2*, Laurel Leaf) Random Hse. Children's Bks.

Hope in Darkness. 1988. (J). 7.95 o.p. (*0-89954-775-3*) Antioch Publishing Co.

Hopkins, Lee Bennett. I Loved Rose Ann. 1976. (Illus.). 48p. (J). (gr. 1-4). 4.95 o.p. (*0-394-83100-4*, Knopf Bks. for Young Readers) Random Hse. Children's Bks.

Howard, Elizabeth J. Winter on Her Own. 1968. (J). (gr. 7 up). 12.95 o.p. (*0-688-21710-9*, Morrow, William & Co.) Morrow/Avon.

Howes, Joan. That's How Love Is. 1991. (Illus.). 32p. (J). (ps-3). pap. 6.95 (*0-938349-63-5*); 12.95 (*0-938349-62-7*) State Hse. Pr.

Hudson, Anne & Daniels, Neil. Ozzie: An Odyssey of Love. 1983. (Illus.). 72p. (Orig.). (J). (gr. 1-6). pap. 3.95 (*0-940258-10-2*) Kripalu Pubns.

Hudson, Wade. How Sweet the Sound. 1997. (J). 9.95 (*0-590-96911-0*) Scholastic, Inc.

Hughes, Monica. Beckoning Lights. unabr. ed. 1990. (Panda Bks.). 112p. (J). (gr. 3-6). pap. 4.95 (*0-7736-7280-X*) Stoddart Kids CAN. *Dist:* Fitzhenry & Whiteside, Ltd.

Hunter, Mollie. The Three-Day Enchantment. 1985. (Charlotte Zolotow Bk.). (Illus.). 64p. (J). (gr. k-4). lib. bdg. 12.89 o.p. (*0-06-022693-5*) HarperCollins Children's Bk. Group.

Huss, Sally. I Love You with All My Hearts: The Many Ways a Mother Loves Her Daughter. 1998. (Illus.). 32p. (J). (ps-2). pap. 7.99 (*0-8499-5923-3*) Nelson, Tommy.

—I Love You with All My Hearts: The Many Ways a Mother Loves Her Son. 1998. (Illus.). 32p. (J). (ps-2). 7.99 (*0-8499-5886-5*) Nelson, Tommy.

Hébert, Marie-Francine. Le Coeur en Bataille. (FRE.). 160p. (YA). 2001. pap. 12.95 (*2-89021-448-6*); 1990. (gr. 8 up). pap. 8.95 o.p. (*2-89021-122-3*) La Courte Echelle CAN. *Dist:* Firefly Bks., Ltd.

—Je T'Aime, Je Te Hais... (FRE.). 160p. (YA). 2001. pap. 12.95 (*2-89021-449-4*); 1991. (gr. 8 up). pap. 8.95 o.p. (*2-89021-147-9*) La Courte Echelle CAN. *Dist:* Firefly Bks., Ltd.

—Sauve Qui Peut l'Amour. (FRE.). 160p. (YA). 2001. pap. 12.95 (*2-89021-450-8*); 1992. (gr. 8 up). pap. 8.95 o.p. (*2-89021-168-1*) La Courte Echelle CAN. *Dist:* Firefly Bks., Ltd.

Island, John. World of the Heart. (Illus.). 48p. (J). (ps-6). text 14.95 (*0-9637712-0-5*) Island Flowers, Inc.

Jacobs, Barbara. Stolen Kisses. 1986. (Heartlines Ser.: No. 3). (Orig.). (J). (gr. 6 up). mass mkt. 2.50 o.s.i (*0-440-97734-7*, Laurel Leaf) Random Hse. Children's Bks.

James, Emily. Hillside Live! 1993. (Nickelodeon Fifteen Ser.: No. 6). 128p. (Orig.). (J). (gr. 3-9). 2.95 o.p. (*0-448-40495-8*, Grosset & Dunlap) Penguin Putnam Bks. for Young Readers.

James, Robin. Sadie. 1994. (Serendipity Bks.). (Illus.). 32p. (Orig.). (J). (gr. 1-4). 3.95 o.p. (*0-8431-3611-1*, Price Stern Sloan) Penguin Putnam Bks. for Young Readers.

Jane Eyre. 1988. (Short Classics Learning Files Ser.). (J). (gr. 4 up). 22.00 o.p. (*0-8172-2182-4*) Raintree Pubs.

Jarnow, Jill. Lifeguard Summer, Vol. 142. 1988. 192p. (Orig.). (YA). (gr. 7-9). pap. 2.50 o.s.i (*0-553-27124-5*, Dell Books for Young Readers) Random Hse. Children's Bks.

Jeffs, Stephanie. A Bad Day for Christopher Bear. 2004. (Christopher Bear Ser.). (Illus.). 30p. (J). 5.99 (*0-8066-4367-6*, Augsburg Bks.) Augsburg Fortress, Pubs.

—I Love You, Christopher Bear. 2004. (Christopher Bear Ser.). (Illus.). 32p. (J). 5.99 (*0-8066-4366-8*, Augsburg Bks.) Augsburg Fortress, Pubs.

Jenner, Caryn. Clashing Hearts. 1992. (Sweet Dreams Ser.: No. 196). 144p. (YA). pap. 2.99 o.s.i (*0-553-29458-X*) Bantam Bks.

Johansen, Iris. And the Desert Blooms. 1986. (Loveswept Ser.: No. 126). 192p. pap. 2.50 o.p. (*0-553-21696-1*) Bantam Bks.

John, Laurie. Anything for Love. 1994. (Sweet Valley University Ser.: No. 4). (YA). (gr. 7 up). 9.09 o.p. (*0-606-06042-1*) Turtleback Bks.

—Elizabeth's Summer Love. 1996. (Sweet Valley University Ser.: No. 22). (YA). (gr. 7 up). 9.09 o.p. (*0-606-09944-1*) Turtleback Bks.

—For the Love of Ryan. 1996. (Sweet Valley University Ser.: No. 21). (YA). (gr. 7 up). 9.09 o.p. (*0-606-09943-3*) Turtleback Bks.

—Good-Bye to Love. 1994. (Sweet Valley University Ser.: No. 7). (YA). (gr. 7 up). 9.09 o.p. (*0-606-07113-X*) Turtleback Bks.

—The Love of Her Life. 1994. (Sweet Valley University Ser.: No. 6). (YA). (gr. 7 up). 8.60 o.p. (*0-606-06791-4*) Turtleback Bks.

—Sweet Kiss of Summer. 1996. (Sweet Valley University Ser.: No. 23). (YA). (gr. 7 up). 9.09 o.p. (*0-606-09945-X*) Turtleback Bks.

Johnson, Audrey. Little Lies. 1984. 160p. (Orig.). (J). (gr. 7 up). pap. 2.25 o.p. (*0-590-33492-1*) Scholastic, Inc.

Johnson, Dolores, illus. Grandma's Hands. 1998. (Accelerated Reader Bks.). 32p. (J). (gr. 1-4). 15.95 (*0-7614-5025-4*, Cavendish Children's Bks.) Cavendish, Marshall Corp.

Johnson, Maud. The World of Christy, 4 bks. Incl. Christy's Choice. Christy's Love. Christy's Senior Year. (YA). I'm Christy. (Orig.). 1984. Set pap. 9.00 o.p. (*0-590-00661-4*) Scholastic, Inc.

Johnston, Norma. If You Love Me, Let Me Go. 1978. 168p. (J). (gr. 7 up). 8.95 o.p. (*0-689-30655-5*, Atheneum) Simon & Schuster Children's Publishing.

Jones, Adrienne. Long Time Passing. 1993. (Charlotte Zolotow Bk.). 256p. (YA). (gr. 7 up). mass mkt. 3.95 o.p. (*0-06-447070-9*, Harper Trophy) HarperCollins Children's Bk. Group.

Jones, Lara. I Love Hugs. 2002. (Illus.). 16p. (J). bds. 6.95 (*0-439-36767-0*, Cartwheel Bks.) Scholastic, Inc.

Jones, McClure. Lucky Signs for Teens. 1984. (J). (gr. 5-9). mass mkt. 1.95 o.p. (*0-451-13173-8*, Signet Bks.) NAL.

Jones, Sandy. Fool for Love. 1994. (Sweet Dreams Ser.: No. 222). 160p. (YA). (gr. 6 up). pap. 3.50 o.s.i (*0-553-56676-8*) Bantam Bks.

—Love on Wheels. 1993. (Sweet Dreams Ser.: No. 202). 144p. (YA). pap. 2.99 o.s.i (*0-553-29981-6*) Bantam Bks.

Jones, Terry. The Lady & the Squire. 2001. (Illus.). 304p. (J). (gr. 4-7). 22.95 (*1-86205-417-7*) Pavilion Bks., Ltd. GBR. *Dist:* Trafalgar Square.

Joosse, Barbara M. Mama, Do You Love Me? (Illus.). (ps). 1998. 24p. bds. 6.95 (*0-8118-2131-5*); 1991. 32p. (J). 14.95 (*0-87701-759-X*) Chronicle Bks. LLC.

—Me Quieres, Mama? Lasconi, Diego, tr. 1998. (SPA., Illus.). 32p. (J). (ps-1). 14.95 (*0-8118-2076-9*, CB0769) Chronicle Bks. LLC.

Jordan, Deloris & Jordan, Roslyn. Did I Tell You I Love You Today? Evans, Shane, tr. & illus. by. 2004. (J). (*0-689-85271-1*, Simon & Schuster/Paula Wiseman Bks.) Simon & Schuster Children's Publishing.

Jordan, June. His Own Where. 1971. (J). 11.95 o.p. (*0-690-38133-6*) HarperCollins Children's Bk. Group.

Kalman, Maira. Ooh-la-La! Max in Love. 1991. (Illus.). 32p. (J). (gr. 2 up). 17.99 (*0-670-84163-3*, Viking Children's Bks.) Penguin Putnam Bks. for Young Readers.

Kaplow, Robert. Alessandra in Love. 1989. 160p. (YA). (gr. 7 up). 11.95 o.p. (*0-397-32281-X*); lib. bdg. 12.89 (*0-397-32282-8*) HarperCollins Children's Bk. Group.

—Alex Icicle: A Romance in Ten Torrid Chapters, 001. 1984. 192p. (J). (gr. 5-9). 11.95 o.p. (*0-395-36230-X*) Houghton Mifflin Co.

Karas, Phyllis. Spellbound. 1999. (Enchanted Hearts Ser.: Vol. 5). 192p. (J). (gr. 7-12). pap. 4.50 (*0-380-78990-6*, Avon Bks.) Morrow/Avon.

—Spellbound. 1999. (Enchanted Hearts Ser.). (Illus.). (J). 10.55 (*0-606-17967-4*) Turtleback Bks.

Karst, Patrice. The Invisible String. 2003. (Illus.). 36p. (J). 15.95 (*0-87516-734-9*) DeVorss & Co.

Kasza, Keiko. A Mother for Choco. 1992. (Illus.). 32p. (J). (ps-3). 15.99 (*0-399-21841-6*, G. P. Putnam's Sons) Penguin Group (USA) Inc.

—A Mother for Choco. 2003. 32p. bds. 6.99 (*0-399-24191-4*) Penguin Putnam Bks. for Young Readers.

Katchke, Judy. Who Will Be My Valentine? 2004. (Full House Ser.: No. 3). 96p. mass mkt. 4.99 (*0-06-054085-0*, HarperEntertainment) Morrow/Avon.

Kaye, Marilyn. Choose Me. 1992. (Changes Romance Ser.: No. 8). 240p. (YA). mass mkt. 3.50 o.p. (*0-06-106714-8*, HarperTorch) Morrow/Avon.

—Runaway. 1992. (Changes Romance Ser.: No. 4). 240p. (YA). (gr. 7 up). mass mkt. 3.50 o.p. (*0-06-106782-2*, HarperTorch) Morrow/Avon.

Kayne, Sheryl W. Queen of the Kisses. 1994. (Illus.). 32p. (J). (ps-2). 14.95 (*1-880851-13-X*) Greene Bark Pr., Inc.

Keaney, Brian. Los Muchachos No Escriben Historias de Amor. Diez-Canedo, Joaquin, tr. 1997. Tr. of Boys Don't Write Love Stories. (SPA., Illus.). 194p. (YA). 7.95 (*968-16-5377-7*, FC3777) Fondo de Cultura Economica MEX. *Dist:* Continental Bk. Co., Inc.

Keene, Carolyn. Broken Hearts. Greenberg, Anne, ed. 1991. (River Heights Ser.: No. 11). 160p. (Orig.). (YA). (gr. 6 up). pap. 2.95 (*0-671-73115-7*, Simon Pulse) Simon & Schuster Children's Publishing.

—Captive Heart. 1995. (Nancy Drew Files: No. 108). (Illus.). 160p. (YA). (gr. 6 up). per. 3.99 (*0-671-88199-X*, Simon Pulse) Simon & Schuster Children's Publishing.

—Going Too Far. 1990. (River Heights Ser.: No. 3). 160p. (YA). (gr. 6 up). pap. 2.95 (*0-671-67761-6*, Simon Pulse) Simon & Schuster Children's Publishing.

—Greek Odyssey: Passport to Romance #3. Greenberg, Anne, ed. 1992. (Nancy Drew Files: No. 74). 160p. (Orig.). (YA). (gr. 6 up). pap. 3.75 (*0-671-73078-9*, Simon Pulse) Simon & Schuster Children's Publishing.

—Hard to Handle. 1991. (River Heights Ser.: No. 12). 160p. (Orig.). (YA). (gr. 6 up). pap. 2.95 (*0-671-73116-5*, Simon Pulse) Simon & Schuster Children's Publishing.

—Heart of Danger. 1991. (Nancy Drew Files: No. 11). (YA). (gr. 6 up). per. 3.50 (*0-671-73665-5*, Simon Pulse) Simon & Schuster Children's Publishing.

—Lies & Whispers. Greenberg, Ann, ed. 1991. (River Heights Ser.: No. 9). 160p. (Orig.). (YA). (gr. 6 up). pap. 2.95 (*0-671-73113-0*, Simon Pulse) Simon & Schuster Children's Publishing.

—Love & Games. Greenberg, Anne, ed. 1992. (River Heights Ser.: No. 14). 160p. (Orig.). (YA). (gr. 6 up). pap. 2.99 (*0-671-73118-1*, Simon Pulse) Simon & Schuster Children's Publishing.

—Love Notes. 1995. (Nancy Drew Files: No. 109). 160p. (YA). (gr. 6 up). pap. 3.99 (*0-671-88200-7*, Simon Pulse) Simon & Schuster Children's Publishing.

—Love Times Three. 1991. (River Heights Ser.: No. 1). (Orig.). (YA). (gr. 6 up). pap. 3.50 (*0-671-96703-7*, Simon Pulse) Simon & Schuster Children's Publishing.

—A Mind of Her Own. Greenberg, Ann, ed. 1991. (River Heights Ser.: No. 14). 160p. (Orig.). (YA). (gr. 6 up). pap. 2.99 (*0-671-73117-3*, Simon Pulse) Simon & Schuster Children's Publishing.

—Rehearsing for Romance. 1996. (Nancy Drew Files: No. 114). 160p. (YA). (gr. 6 up). mass mkt. 3.99 (*0-671-50355-3*, Simon Pulse) Simon & Schuster Children's Publishing.

—Rendezvous in Rome: Passport to Romance #2. Greenberg, Anne, ed. 1992. (Nancy Drew Files: No. 73). 160p. (Orig.). (YA). (gr. 6 up). pap. 3.75 (*0-671-73077-0*, Simon Pulse) Simon & Schuster Children's Publishing.

—Stolen Kisses. 1990. (River Heights Ser.: No. 4). 160p. (YA). (gr. 6 up). pap. 2.95 (*0-671-67762-4*, Simon Pulse) Simon & Schuster Children's Publishing.

—Swiss Secrets: Passport to Romance. Greenberg, Anne, ed. 1992. (Nancy Drew Files: No. 72). 160p. (YA). (gr. 6 up). mass mkt. 3.99 (*0-671-73076-2*, Simon Pulse) Simon & Schuster Children's Publishing.

—The Trouble with Love. Greenberg, Ann, ed. 1990. (River Heights Ser.: No. 8). 160p. (Orig.). (YA). (gr. 6 up). pap. 2.95 (*0-671-67766-7*, Simon Pulse) Simon & Schuster Children's Publishing.

Keeshan, Robert. She Loves Me, She Loves Me Not... 2003. (Sendak Reissues Ser.). (Illus.). 32p. (J). 12.95 (*0-06-028791-8*); 12.89 (*0-06-028792-6*) HarperCollins Children's Bk. Group.

Kehl, Richard. Lovers. 1984. (Star & Elephant Ser.). (Illus.). 48p. (J). pap. 6.95 o.s.i (*0-88138-025-3*) Simon & Schuster.

Kehret, Peg. Wally Amos Presents Chip & Cookie - The First Adventure: No More Chocolate Chips. 2002. (Illus.). 40p. (J). (ps-3). 14.95 (*1-58497-018-9*) Addax Publishing Group, Inc.

Kellogg, Marjorie B. Tell Me That You Love Me, Junie Moon, RS. 1993. 224p. (YA). (gr. 7 up). pap. 3.95 o.p. (*0-374-47510-5*, Aerial) Farrar, Straus & Giroux.

Kemp, Kristen. How to Create the Boy of Your Dreams. 2002. (Genny in a Bottle Ser.: Vol. 4). (Illus.). 128p. (J). (gr. 4-6). mass mkt. 4.50 (*0-439-21181-6*) Scholastic, Inc.

Kennedy, M. L. Ten Cupcake Romance. 1986. 176p. (Orig.). (YA). (gr. 7 up). pap. 2.25 o.p. (*0-590-33932-X*) Scholastic, Inc.

Kennedy, Richard. Crazy in Love. 1980. (Illus.). (J). (gr. 3-7). 7.95 o.p. (*0-525-28364-1*, Dutton) Dutton/Plume.

—Crazy in Love. Date not set. 48p. (J). (ps-3). 14.99 (*0-06-027213-9*); lib. bdg. 15.89 (*0-06-027214-7*) HarperCollins Children's Bk. Group. (Geringer, Laura Bk.).

Kent, Deborah. Jody. (J). 1996. pap. 1.95 o.p. (*0-590-30971-4*); 1983. 192p. pap. 1.95 o.p. (*0-590-32442-X*) Scholastic, Inc.

—Love to the Rescue. 1985. 176p. (Orig.). (J). (gr. 7 up). pap. 2.25 o.p. (*0-590-33264-3*) Scholastic, Inc.

—Talk to Me, My Love. 1987. (J). (gr. k-12). mass mkt. 2.75 o.s.i (*0-440-97810-6*, Laurel Leaf) Random Hse. Children's Bks.

Kenyon, Kate. Who's the Junior High Hunk? 1988. (Junior High Ser.: No. 9). 160p. (J). (gr. 5-9). pap. 2.50 o.p. (*0-590-41388-0*) Scholastic, Inc.

Kerr, M. E. Him She Loves? 1984. (Charlotte Zolotow Bk.). 224p. (YA). (gr. 7 up). lib. bdg. 12.89 o.p. (*0-06-023239-0*) HarperCollins Children's Bk. Group.

—I Stay Near You. 1986. 192p. (YA). 2.50 o.s.i (*0-425-08870-7*, Berkley/Pacer) Berkley Publishing Group.

—If I Love You, Am I Trapped Forever? (Trophy Keypoint Bks.). (YA). (gr. 7 up). 1988. 192p. mass mkt. 4.95 o.p. (*0-06-447032-6*, Harper Trophy); 1973. 176p. lib. bdg. 12.89 o.p. (*0-06-023149-1*) HarperCollins Children's Bk. Group.

—If I Love You, Am I Trapped Forever? 1988. (YA). 2.95 o.p. (*0-694-05635-9*, HarperTorch) Morrow/Avon.

—If I Love You, am I Trapped Forever? 1974. 192p. (YA). (gr. 7 up). mass mkt. 2.75 o.s.i (*0-440-94320-5*, Laurel Leaf) Random Hse. Children's Bks.

—Love Is a Missing Person. 1988. (Ursula Nordstrom Bk.). 176p. (YA). (gr. 7 up). mass mkt. 2.95 o.p. (*0-06-447034-2*, Harper Trophy) HarperCollins Children's Bk. Group.

Khan, Rukhsana. Dahling, If You Luv Me, Would You Please, Please Smile. l.t. ed. 1999. 196p. (YA). (gr. 7-9). pap. 8.95 (*0-7737-6016-4*) Stoddart Kids CAN. *Dist:* Fitzhenry & Whiteside, Ltd.

Khurram, Murad. The Longing Heart. 1980. 28p. (J). pap. 3.50 (*0-86037-138-7*) New Era Pubns., Inc.

Kidd, Diana. I Love You, Jason Delaney. 1998. 128p. (gr. 8-12). pap. 6.95 o.p. (*0-207-18987-0*) HarperCollins Pubs.

Kidd, Ronald. Sammy Carducci's Guide to Women. 112p. (J). (gr. 3-7). 1994. pap. 3.99 o.p. (*0-14-036481-1*, Puffin Bks.); 1991. 14.95 o.p. (*0-525-67363-6*, Dutton Children's Bks.) Penguin Putnam Bks. for Young Readers.

Killien, Christi. All of the Above. 1987. (J). (gr. 5-9). 13.95 o.p. (*0-395-43023-2*) Houghton Mifflin Co.

Kirby. My Secret Heart. 1993. 160p. (YA). pap. 3.50 o.s.i (*0-553-29986-7*) Bantam Bks.

Kirby, Susan. Partners in Love. 1992. (Sweet Dreams Ser.: No. 198). 144p. (YA). pap. 2.99 o.s.i (*0-553-29460-1*) Bantam Bks.

Kiss Me Creep. 1985. (J). pap. 1.75 o.s.i (*0-440-82009-X*) Dell Publishing.

Klein, Norma. Going Backwards. 1987. (Illus.). 192p. (YA). (gr. 7 up). pap. 2.50 o.p. (*0-590-40329-X*, Scholastic Paperbacks) Scholastic, Inc.

—It's Okay If You Don't Love Me. 1985. (J). (gr. 7 up). 10.95 o.p. (*0-8037-4053-0*, Dial Bks. for Young Readers) Penguin Putnam Bks. for Young Readers.

—Love Is One of the Choices. 1978. (J). 10.95 o.p. (*0-8037-5019-6*, Dial Bks. for Young Readers) Penguin Putnam Bks. for Young Readers.

—Older Men. 1988. 192p. (YA). mass mkt. 3.50 o.s.i (*0-449-70261-8*, Fawcett) Ballantine Bks.

—Older Men. 1987. 240p. (YA). (gr. 7 up). 15.95 o.p. (*0-8037-0178-0*, Dial Bks. for Young Readers) Penguin Putnam Bks. for Young Readers.

Klein, Robin. Laurie Loved Me Best. 1988. 208p. (J). (gr. 5-9). 11.95 o.p. (*0-670-82211-6*, Viking Children's Bks.) Penguin Putnam Bks. for Young Readers.

Klevin, Jill R. Miss Perfect. 1984. 176p. (J). (gr. 7 up). pap. 2.25 o.p. (*0-590-40882-8*) Scholastic, Inc.

Kline, Suzy. Horrible Harry's Secret. (Horrible Harry Ser.: No. 4). 64p. (J). (gr. 2-4). 1998. (Illus.). pap. 3.99 (*0-14-130093-0*, Puffin Bks.); 1992. (Illus.). pap. 3.99 o.s.i (*0-14-032915-3*, Puffin Bks.); 1990. 11.99 o.s.i (*0-670-82470-4*, Viking Children's Bks.) Penguin Putnam Bks. for Young Readers.

—Horrible Harry's Secret. 1992. (Horrible Harry Ser.: No. 4). (J). (gr. 2-4). 10.14 (*0-606-02674-6*) Turtleback Bks.

Knecht, Tracy L. The Magic of Love. 1995. (Illus.). 32p. (Orig.). (J). (gr. 3-5). pap. 7.95 (*1-884242-97-9*) Multicultural Pubns.

Knudson, R. R. Just Another Love Story, RS. 1983. 201p. (J). (gr. 7 up). 12.95 o.p. (*0-374-33967-8*, Farrar, Straus & Giroux (BYR)) Farrar, Straus & Giroux.

—Just Another Love Story. 1984. (YA). (gr. 7 up). pap. 2.50 (*0-380-65532-2*, 60172-9, Avon Bks.) Morrow/Avon.

Koechlin, Lionel. The Love Affair of Mr. Ding & Mrs. Dong. 1992. (Child's World Library Ser.). (Illus.). 32p. (J). (gr. 1-5). lib. bdg. 8.50 (*0-89565-817-8*) Child's World, Inc.

Koertge, Ronald. Where the Kissing Never Stops. 1988. (J). (gr. k-12). reprint ed. mass mkt. 2.95 o.s.i (*0-440-20167-5*) Dell Publishing.

Kolaczyk, Anne & Kolaczyk, Ed. The Butler & His Lady. 1986. (Loveswept Ser.: No. 131). 192p. (Orig.). pap. 2.50 o.p. (*0-553-21745-3*) Bantam Bks.

Koosak, Tara. Boy Girl Daze Craze. 1992. (School-Biz Kids Ser.: No. 2). (Illus.). 60p. (Orig.). (J). (gr. 4-8). pap. 3.50 o.p. (*0-934426-44-9*) NAPSAC Reproductions.

Kortepeter, Paul. The Hugs & Kisses Contest. 2001. (Illus.). 28p. (J). 14.99 (*0-525-46531-6*, Dutton Children's Bks.) Penguin Putnam Bks. for Young Readers.

Kosinski, Dahlia. Some Girls Do. 1991. (Love Stories Ser.). 192p. (YA). (gr. 7-12). mass mkt. 4.50 o.s.i (*0-553-56670-9*, Dell Books for Young Readers) Random Hse. Children's Bks.

Kosinsky, Dahlia. Never Fall in Love. 1995. (Reality 101 Ser.: No. 1). 192p. (YA). mass mkt. 3.50 o.p. (*0-06-106323-1*, HarperTorch) Morrow/Avon.

Kovacs, Deborah. Moonlight on the River. 1996. (Illus.). 32p. (J). (ps-3). pap. 5.99 o.s.i (*0-14-054513-1*, Puffin Bks.) Penguin Putnam Bks. for Young Readers.

Kovacs, Deborah & Golden Books Staff. The Evening Song Moondreamers. 1987. (Golden Super Fashion Bks.). (Illus.). 24p. (J). (gr. 5-9). pap. 3.29 o.s.i (*0-307-10197-5*, Golden Bks.) Random Hse. Children's Bks.

Kremer, Marcia. Aloha Love. 1995. (Sweet Dreams Ser.: No. 226). 160p. (YA). pap. 3.50 o.s.i (*0-553-56680-6*) Bantam Bks.

Kroeger, Kelly. The Love Line. 1995. (Sweet Dreams Ser.: Vol. 232). 160p. (Orig.). (YA). (gr. 6 up). pap. 3.50 o.s.i (*0-553-56686-5*, Dell Books for Young Readers) Random Hse. Children's Bks.

Kroll, Steven. Giant Journey. 1981. (Illus.). 32p. (J). (ps-3). 7.95 o.p. (*0-8234-0381-5*) Holiday Hse., Inc.

Krulik, Nancy E. Who Do You Love? Your Complete Guide to Romance. 2001. 112p. (gr. 7-12). pap. 3.99 (*0-689-84301-1*, Aladdin) Simon & Schuster Children's Publishing.

Laiken, Deidre S. What Is Love? 1924. (J). o.s.i (*0-688-05556-7*); lib. bdg. o.s.i (*0-688-05557-5*) HarperCollins Children's Bk. Group.

Lamb, Jane M. & Dodge, Nancy C. Sharing with Thumpy: My Story of Love & Grief. 1985. (Illus.). 48p. (J). (gr. k-12). pap. text, stu. ed. 9.95 (*0-918533-10-4*) SHARE-Pregnancy & Infant Loss Support, Inc.

Lamirande, Carole A. Able & the Tree of Life. 1997. (Illus.). 128p. (J). (gr. 3-9). pap. 9.95 (*0-9661385-0-3*) Dream Catcher Bks.

Landis, James D. Looks Aren't Everything. 1991. 192p. (YA). mass mkt. 3.50 o.s.i (*0-553-28860-1*) Bantam Bks.

Lane, Dakota. Johnny Voodoo. 1996. 224p. (J). (gr. 7 up). 15.95 o.s.i (*0-385-32230-5*, Delacorte Pr.) Dell Publishing.

—Johnny Voodoo. 1997. 208p. (YA). (gr. 7-12). mass mkt. 4.50 o.s.i (*0-440-21998-1*, Dell Books for Young Readers) Random Hse. Children's Bks.

Lantz, Francess L. Letters to Cupid. 2001. (American Girls Collection Ser.). 192p. (J). 14.95 (*1-58485-375-1*); (YA). pap. 5.95 (*1-58485-374-3*) Pleasant Co. Pubns. (American Girl).

—Lights, Camera, Love, Vol. 2. 2000. (You're the One Ser.: Vol. 3). 144p. (J). (gr. 4-7). pap. 3.99 (*0-689-83421-7*, Aladdin) Simon & Schuster Children's Publishing.

—A Love Song for Becky. 1983. (Caprice Romance Ser.). (gr. 7 up). 1.95 o.s.i (*0-448-15718-7*) Ace Bks.

—A Royal Kiss. 2000. (You're the One Ser.: Vol. 2). 144p. (J). (gr. 4-7). pap. 3.99 (*0-689-83422-5*, Aladdin) Simon & Schuster Children's Publishing.

—Someone to Love. 1998. (gr. 8-12). pap. 3.99 (*0-380-77590-5*, Avon Bks.) Morrow/Avon.

—Someone to Love. 1998. 10.04 (*0-606-13787-4*) Turtleback Bks.

—The Truth about Making Out. 1990. 160p. (J). (gr. 4 up). pap. 3.50 o.s.i (*0-553-15813-9*) Bantam Bks.

Larrison, Roxann. A Garden of Bitter Herbs: Two Young Slaves - Brother & Sister - Make Their Escape. 1993. 304p. (YA). (ps up). mass mkt. 3.95 (*0-87067-389-0*) Holloway Hse. Publishing Co.

Lawler, Janet. If Kisses Were Colors. 2003. (Illus.). 32p. (J). 15.99 (*0-8037-2617-1*, Dial Bks. for Young Readers) Penguin Putnam Bks. for Young Readers.

Lawlor, Laurie. Come Away with Me. 1996. (Heartland Ser.: ser. 1). 192p. (J). mass mkt. 3.99 (*0-671-53716-4*, Aladdin) Simon & Schuster Children's Publishing.

Lawrence, Amy. Color It Love. 1983. (Caprice Romance Ser.). (J). 1.95 o.s.i (*0-448-13576-0*) Ace Bks.

Lawrence, D. H. You Touched Me. 1982. (Short Story Library). (Illus.). 32p. (YA). (gr. 5 up). lib. bdg. 13.95 o.p. (*0-87191-894-3*, 1072-3, Creative Education) Creative Co., The.

Leach, Sheryl & Leach, Patrick. Barney's Book of Hugs. Larsen, Margie, ed. 1996. (Barney Ser.). (Illus.). 24p. (J). (ps-k). mass mkt. 3.25 (*1-57064-120-X*) Scholastic, Inc.

Lee, Chinlun. Good Dog, Paw. 2004. 40p. (J). 15.99 (*0-7636-2178-1*) Candlewick Pr.

Lehman, Yvonne. A Fighting Chance. 1997. (White Dove Romances Ser.: Bk. 5). 176p. (J). (gr. 7-12). mass mkt. 4.99 o.p. (*1-55661-709-7*) Bethany Hse. Pubs.

Leighton, Stephanie. It's Different for Guys. 1997. (Love Stories Super Edition Ser.). 224p. (YA). (gr. 7-12). mass mkt. 4.50 o.s.i (*0-553-57048-X*, Dell Books for Young Readers) Random Hse. Children's Bks.

Leroe, Ellen. Have a Heart, Cupid. 1987. (J). mass mkt. 3.95 (*0-553-16800-2*, Dell Books for Young Readers) Random Hse. Children's Bks.

—Have a Heart, Cupid Delaney. 1986. 160p. (YA). (gr. 7 up). 13.95 o.p. (*0-525-67188-9*, Dutton Children's Bks.) Penguin Putnam Bks. for Young Readers.

—Have a Heart, Cupid Delaney. 1988. 160p. (J). (gr. 5 up). mass mkt. 2.95 o.s.i (*0-553-27002-8*, Starfire) Random Hse. Children's Bks.

—Personal Business. 1987. 144p. (YA). (gr. 6 up). mass mkt. 2.95 o.s.i (*0-553-26652-7*, Starfire) Random Hse. Children's Bks.

Lester, Julius. This Strange New Feeling. 1982. 16p. (J). (gr. 7 up). 14.95 o.p. (*0-8037-8491-0*, Dial Bks. for Young Readers) Penguin Putnam Bks. for Young Readers.

—This Strange New Feeling. 1985. (gr. 7 up). 172p. (YA). pap. 4.50 (*0-590-44047-0*); 164p. (J). reprint ed. 1.25 o.p. (*0-590-40681-7*, Scholastic Paperbacks); 164p. (J). reprint ed. pap. 2.50 o.p. (*0-590-41061-X*, Scholastic Paperbacks) Scholastic, Inc.

—Two Love Stories. 1972. 224p. (J). (gr. 7 up). 4.95 o.p. (*0-8037-9145-3*, Dial Bks. for Young Readers) Penguin Putnam Bks. for Young Readers.

Levitin, Sonia. The Man Who Kept His Heart in a Bucket. (Illus.). (J). (ps-3). 1995. 40p. pap. 5.99 o.s.i (*0-14-055461-0*, Puffin Bks.); 1991. 32p. 14.95 o.s.i (*0-8037-1029-1*, Dial Bks. for Young Readers); 1991. 32p. 14.89 o.s.i (*0-8037-1030-5*, Dial Bks. for Young Readers) Penguin Putnam Bks. for Young Readers.

Levy, Elizabeth. First Date. 1990. (Gymnasts Ser.: No. 13). 112p. (J). (gr. 3-7). mass mkt. 2.75 (*0-590-42825-X*) Scholastic, Inc.

Levy, Marc. If Only It Were True. 2000. 224p. mass mkt. 6.99 (*0-7434-1717-8*, Pocket) Simon & Schuster.

—If Only It Were True. Leggatt, Jeremy, tr. from FRE. 2000. 224p. 22.95 o.s.i (*0-7434-0617-6*, Atria) Simon & Schuster.

—If Only It Were True. 2001. 256p. reprint ed. mass mkt. 6.99 (*0-7434-0618-4*, Pocket) Simon & Schuster.

—If Only It Were True. abr. ed. 2000. audio 26.00 (*0-7435-0545-X*); audio compact disk 32.00 (*0-7435-0546-8*) Simon & Schuster Audio. (Simon & Schuster Audioworks).

Levy, Marilyn. Touching. 1988. (J). (gr. 6 up). mass mkt. 3.50 o.s.i (*0-449-70267-7*, Fawcett) Ballantine Bks.

Lewis, Anthony, illus. So Much to Love. 1999. (Leap Frog Lift-a-Flap Ser.). (J). (*0-7853-3368-1*) Publications International, Ltd.

Lewis, Beverly. Straight - A Teacher. 1994. (Holly's Heart Ser.: Vol. 8). 160p. (J). pap. 6.99 (*0-310-46111-1*) Zondervan.

Lewis, Carrie. Call of the Wild. 1984. (First Love Ser.). 153p. (YA). pap. 1.95 o.s.i (*0-671-52648-0*, Pocket) Simon & Schuster.

Lewis, Linda. All for the Love of That Boy. 1989. 224p. (J). (gr. 7 up). pap. 2.95 (*0-671-68243-1*, Simon Pulse) Simon & Schuster Children's Publishing.

—Dedicated to That Boy I Love. 1990. (Linda Story Ser.). 168p. (J). (gr. 7 up). mass mkt. 2.75 (*0-671-68244-X*, Simon Pulse) Simon & Schuster Children's Publishing.

—My Heart Belongs to That Boy. 1990. (Orig.). (YA). (gr. 7 up). pap. 2.95 (*0-671-70353-6*, Simon Pulse) Simon & Schuster Children's Publishing.

—We Love Only Older Boys. 1990. 176p. (Orig.). (YA). (gr. 7 up). pap. 2.95 (*0-671-69558-4*, Simon Pulse) Simon & Schuster Children's Publishing.

Lexau, Joan M. Don't Be My Valentine: A Classroom Mystery. 1985. (I Can Read Bks.). (Illus.). 64p. (J). (gr. 1-3). 11.95 (*0-06-023872-0*); 15.89 (*0-06-023873-9*) HarperCollins Children's Bk. Group.

Lights, Camera, Love. 1983. (Sweet Dreams Ser.: No. 50). 150p. (gr. 6 up). pap. 2.25 o.p. (*0-553-24464-7*) Bantam Bks.

Linden, Jenni. The Red-Hot Love Hunt. 1997. 144p. (J). pap. o.p. (*0-09-925112-4*) Random Hse. of Canada, Ltd. CAN. *Dist:* Random Hse., Inc.

Lindquist, Marie. Dreams at Dawn. 1987. (Texas Promises Ser.). 160p. (Orig.). mass mkt. 2.50 o.s.i (*0-553-26289-0*, Starfire) Random Hse. Children's Bks.

Line, David. Screaming High. 1985. 176p. (J). (gr. 6 up). 12.95 o.p. (*0-316-52682-7*) Little Brown & Co.

Lipsyte, Robert. Jock & Jill. 1982. (Charlotte Zolotow Bk.). 160p. (YA). (gr. 7 up). lib. bdg. 13.89 o.p. (*0-06-023900-X*) HarperCollins Children's Bk. Group.

Littke, Lael J. Loydene in Love. 1986. 160p. (YA). (gr. 7 up). 13.95 (*0-15-249888-5*) Harcourt Children's Bks.

Little Golden Books Staff. Cinderella. 1999. (J). (ps-2). bds. 2.99 (*0-307-01035-X*, Golden Bks.) Random Hse. Children's Bks.

—Yes, I Love You. 1995. (First Little Golden Bks.). (Illus.). 24p. (J). (ps). 1.29 o.s.i (*0-307-10177-0*, Golden Bks.) Random Hse. Children's Bks.

Loggia, Wendy. Crushing on You. 1998. (Love Stories Ser.). 192p. (YA). (gr. 7-12). mass mkt. 3.99 o.s.i (*0-553-48591-1*, Dell Books for Young Readers) Random Hse. Children's Bks.

—Hard to Resist. 1998. (Love Stories Ser.). 208p. (gr. 7-12). mass mkt. 4.50 o.s.i (*0-553-49253-5*, Dell Books for Young Readers) Random Hse. Children's Bks.

—Summer Love. 1999. (Love Stories Super Edition Ser.). 224p. (gr. 7-12). mass mkt. 4.50 o.s.i (*0-553-49276-4*, Dell Books for Young Readers) Random Hse. Children's Bks.

Loomans, Diane. The Lovables. 1996. (Illus.). 10p. (J). (ps-k). bds. 4.95 (*0-915811-71-5*, Starseed Pr.) Kramer, H.J. Inc.

—The Lovables in the Kingdom of Self-Esteem. Carleton, Nancy, ed. 1991. (Illus.). 32p. (J). (ps-5). 15.95 (*0-915811-25-1*, Starseed Pr.) Kramer, H.J. Inc.

The Love Library, 3 vols., Set. Incl. Guess How Much I Love You. McBratney, Sam. 32p. 1996. reprint ed. bds. 6.99 (*0-7636-0013-X*); Hug. Alborough, Jez. 32p. 2001. bds. 6.99 (*0-7636-1576-5*); Love & Kisses. Wilson, Sarah. 22p. 2001. bds. 6.99 (*0-7636-1049-6*); (J). (ps). (Illus.). 96p. 2002. Set bds. 15.99 (*0-7636-1670-2*) Candlewick Pr.

Love, Loss, & Algebra Questions. 2001. 244p. pap. 14.95 (*0-595-17973-8*, Writers Club Pr.) iUniverse, Inc.

Love Notes. 1983. (Sweet Dreams Ser.: No. 52). pap. 1.95 o.p. (*0-553-17076-7*) Bantam Bks.

Lowell, Melissa. More Than Friends. 1996. (Silver Blades Ser.: No. 18). 128p. (J). (gr. 3-7). pap. 3.50 o.s.i (*0-553-48499-0*) Bantam Bks.

—More Than Friends. 1996. (Silver Blades Ser.: No. 18). (J). (gr. 3-7). pap. 4.75 (*0-553-54277-X*, Dell Books for Young Readers) Random Hse. Children's Bks.

—Rinkside Romance. 1996. (Silver Blades Super Ser.: No. 1). 176p. (J). (gr. 3-7). pap. 3.99 o.s.i (*0-553-48369-2*) Bantam Bks.

Lowry, Lois. Autumn Street. 1982. mass mkt. 1.95 o.s.i (*0-440-90344-0*) Dell Publishing.

—Autumn Street. 1986. 192p. (gr. 4-7). pap. text 5.50 (*0-440-40344-8*, Yearling) Random Hse. Children's Bks.

—A Summer to Die. 1983. 128p. (YA). mass mkt. 3.50 o.s.i (*0-553-27395-7*) Bantam Bks.

Lundell, Margo. The Enchanted Christmas. 1997. (Golden Look-Look Bks.). (Illus.). 24p. (J). (ps-3). pap. text 1.99 o.p. (*0-307-12974-8*, 12974, Golden Bks.) Random Hse. Children's Bks.

Lyback-Dahl, Susui M. Klara's Beautiful Isle of Love. 1996. (Illus.). 81p. (Orig.). (J). pap. (*1-57579-027-0*) Pine Hill Pr., Inc.

Lykken. Sweet Dreams: Oh, Promise Me. 1993. 160p. (YA). pap. 3.50 o.s.i (*0-553-29989-1*) Bantam Bks.

Lykken, Laurie. Priceless Love, Vol. 144. 1988. (Sweet Dreams Ser.: No. 144). 192p. (Orig.). (YA). (gr. 7 up). pap. 2.50 o.s.i (*0-553-27174-1*) Bantam Bks.

—The Truth about Love. 1991. (Sweet Dreams Ser.: No. 177). 176p. (YA). pap. 2.95 o.s.i (*0-553-28862-8*) Bantam Bks.

Lyons, Dorothy. Pedigree Unknown. 1973. (J). (gr. 7 up). 5.95 o.p. (*0-15-260170-8*) Harcourt Children's Bks.

Lyons, Pam. Danny's Girl. 1986. (Heartlines Ser.: No. 8). (Orig.). (J). (gr. 6 up). pap. 2.50 o.s.i (*0-440-91830-8*, Laurel Leaf) Random Hse. Children's Bks.

—Love Around the Corner. 1987. (Heartlines Ser.: No. 10). (Orig.). (J). (gr. k-12). mass mkt. 2.50 o.s.i (*0-440-94726-X*, Laurel Leaf) Random Hse. Children's Bks.

—Tug of Love. 1986. (Heartlines Ser.: No. 7). (Orig.). (J). (gr. 6 up). mass mkt. 2.50 o.s.i (*0-440-98818-7*, Laurel Leaf) Random Hse. Children's Bks.

MacBain, Carol. Heartbreak Hill. 1986. (Sweet Dreams Ser.: No. 116). 192p. (Orig.). (YA). (gr. 7-12). mass mkt. 2.50 o.s.i (*0-553-26195-9*) Bantam Bks.

—Stand by for Love. 1987. (Sweet Dreams Ser.: No. 136). 192p. (Orig.). (YA). (gr. 7-12). pap. 2.50 o.s.i (*0-553-26903-8*) Bantam Bks.

MacBride, Roger Lea. Bachelor Girl. 1999. (Little House Ser.). (Illus.). 256p. (J). (gr. 3-6). 15.95 (*0-06-027755-6*); (gr. 3-6). lib. bdg. 15.89 (*0-06-028434-X*); (gr. 5 up). pap. 5.99 (*0-06-440691-1*, Harper Trophy) HarperCollins Children's Bk. Group.

—Bachelor Girl. 1999. (Little House Ser.). (Illus.). (J). (gr. 3-6). 11.00 (*0-606-18676-X*) Turtleback Bks.

MacDonald, George. At the Back of the North Wind. (Young Reader's Christian Library). 1991. (Illus.). 224p. (J). (gr. 3-7). pap. 1.39 o.p. (*1-55748-188-1*); 1988. 384p. 8.97 o.p. (*1-55748-024-9*) Barbour Publishing, Inc.

—At the Back of the North Wind. 1987. (Illus.). (YA). (gr. 5 up). reprint ed. pap. 8.95 o.s.i (*0-8052-0595-0*, Schocken) Knopf Publishing Group.

—At the Back of the North Wind. 1985. (Classics for Young Readers Ser.). 336p. (J). (gr. 4-6). pap. 3.50 o.p. (*0-14-035030-6*, Puffin Bks.) Penguin Putnam Bks. for Young Readers.

—At the Back of the North Wind. 1990. 352p. (J). 12.99 o.s.i (*0-517-69120-5*) Random Hse. Value Publishing.

—At the Back of the North Wind. Watson, Jean, ed. 1981. (Illus.). 128p. (J). (gr. 3-7). reprint ed. 7.95 o.p. (*0-310-42340-6*, 9065P) Zondervan.

—The Landlady's Master. Phillips, Michael R., ed. 1989. 208p. (Orig.). (J). pap. 7.99 o.p. (*0-87123-904-3*) Bethany Hse. Pubs.

MacLachlan, Patricia. Seven Kisses in a Row. 1988. (Charlotte Zolotow Bk.). (Illus.). 64p. (J). (gr. 2-5). pap. 4.95 (*0-06-440231-2*, Harper Trophy) HarperCollins Children's Bk. Group.

Madison, Arnold. But This Girl Is Different. 1982. 176p. (Orig.). (J). (gr. 7 up). pap. 1.95 o.p. (*0-590-31998-1*) Scholastic, Inc.

Magic Moments. 1983. (Sweet Dreams Ser.: No. 51). (gr. 6 up). pap. 1.95 o.p. (*0-553-17075-9*) Bantam Bks.

Maguire, Gregory. Four Stupid Cupids. 2001. (Hamlet Chronicles Ser.). 192p. (J). (gr. 5 up). pap. 4.95 (*0-06-441072-2*, Harper Trophy) HarperCollins Children's Bk. Group.

—Four Stupid Cupids. 2001. (Illus.). 160p. (J). (gr. 4-6). tchr. ed. 15.00 (*0-395-83895-9*, Clarion Bks.) Houghton Mifflin Co. Trade & Reference Div.

—Four Stupid Cupids. l.t. ed. 2001. 225p. (J). 21.95 (*0-7862-3547-0*) Thorndike Pr.

Mahon, K. L. Just One Tear. 1994. (YA). (gr. 5 up). 14.00 (*0-688-13519-6*) HarperCollins Children's Bk. Group.

Mahy, Margaret. A Fortunate Name. 1993. (J). o.s.i (*0-385-30949-X*, Dell Books for Young Readers) Random Hse. Children's Bks.

—Memory. 288p. (YA). 1999. (Illus.). (gr. 7-12). pap. 8.00 (*0-689-82911-6*, Simon Pulse); 1988. (gr. 9 up). lib. bdg. 16.00 o.s.i (*0-689-50446-2*, McElderry, Margaret K.) Simon & Schuster Children's Publishing.

—The Tricksters. 272p. 1999. (Illus.). (J). (gr. 7-12). per. 8.00 (*0-689-82910-8*, Simon Pulse); 1987. (YA). (gr. 9 up). text 16.00 o.s.i (*0-689-50400-4*, McElderry, Margaret K.) Simon & Schuster Children's Publishing.

Malcolm, Jahnna N. Signed, Sealed & Delivered. 1991. (Hart & Soul Ser.). 160p. (YA). (gr. 7 up). mass mkt. 2.99 o.s.i (*0-553-28314-6*) Bantam Bks.

—Too Hot to Handle. 1991. (Hart to Hart Ser.: No. 5). 176p. (J). mass mkt. 2.99 o.s.i (*0-553-28262-X*) Bantam Bks.

Malek, Doreen O. Seasons of Mist. 1984. (First Love Ser.). 154p. (gr. 7 up). pap. (*0-671-53413-0*, Silhouette) Harlequin Enterprises, Ltd.

Mandelstein, Paul. Nightingale & the Wind. 1994. (Illus.). 32p. (YA). (gr. 4-7). 16.95 o.p. (*0-8478-1787-3*) Rizzoli International Pubns., Inc.

Manning, Sarra. Guitar Girl. 2004. 224p. 15.99 (*0-525-47234-7*, Dutton Children's Bks.) Penguin Putnam Bks. for Young Readers.

Marigold Beach. 1986. (First Love Ser.). 155p. (J). (*0-373-06183-8*, Silhouette) Harlequin Enterprises, Ltd.

Mark, Jan. Handles. 1987. 160p. (YA). (gr. 5-9). pap. 3.95 o.p. (*0-14-031587-X*, Puffin Bks.) Penguin Putnam Bks. for Young Readers.

Markas, Jenny. Crossroads Movie Novelization. movie tie-in ed. 2002. (Illus.). 128p. (J). (gr. 4-7). mass mkt. 4.99 (*0-439-39744-8*) Scholastic, Inc.

Marshall, Mollie. Ready for Romance. 1982. (Leisure First Romance Ser.: No. 2). 192p. (Orig.). (J). (gr. 6-12). pap. text, mass mkt. 1.95 o.p. (*0-8439-1129-8*) Dorchester Publishing Co., Inc.

Martin, Ann M. Claudia Gets Her Guy. 2000. (Baby-Sitters Club Friends Forever Ser.: No. 7). 144p. (J). (gr. 3-7). mass mkt. 4.50 (*0-590-52338-4*) Scholastic, Inc.

—Dawn & the Older Boy. 1990. (Baby-Sitters Club Ser.: No. 37). 192p. (J). (gr. 3-7). mass mkt. 3.25 (*0-590-43566-3*) Scholastic, Inc.

—Just a Summer Romance. 1987. 170p. (YA). (gr. 7 up). tchr. ed. 13.95 (*0-8234-0649-0*) Holiday Hse., Inc.

—Just a Summer Romance. 1988. 176p. (YA). (gr. 7-9). mass mkt. 3.50 (*0-590-43999-5*); (J). 2.50 o.p. (*0-590-41432-1*, Scholastic Paperbacks) Scholastic, Inc.

—Karen's in Love. 1991. (Baby-Sitters Little Sister Ser.: No. 15). (J). (gr. 3-7). 10.04 (*0-606-04716-6*) Turtleback Bks.

—Stacey & the Boyfriend Trap. 2000. (Baby-Sitters Club Friends Forever Ser.: No. 6). 144p. (J). (gr. 3-7). mass mkt. 4.50 (*0-590-52337-6*, Scholastic Paperbacks) Scholastic, Inc.

—Stacey's Big Crush. 1993. (Baby-Sitters Club Ser.: No. 65). 192p. (J). (gr. 3-7). mass mkt. 3.50 (*0-590-45667-9*) Scholastic, Inc.

—Stacey's Big Crush. 1993. (Baby-Sitters Club Ser.: No. 65). (J). (gr. 3-7). 9.55 (*0-606-05137-6*) Turtleback Bks.

—Stacey's Broken Heart. 1996. (Baby-Sitters Club Ser.: No. 99). (J). (gr. 3-7). mass mkt. 3.99 (*0-590-69205-4*) Scholastic, Inc.

—Stacey's Broken Heart. 1996. (Baby-Sitters Club Ser.: No. 99). (J). (gr. 3-7). 9.09 o.p. (*0-606-09035-5*) Turtleback Bks.

Martin, Dorothy. Heart's Surrender for Peggy. 1963. (Peggy Ser.). (J). (gr. 8 up). pap. 2.95 o.p. (*0-8024-7606-6*) Moody Pr.

—Hopes Fulfilled for Peggy. 1963. (Peggy Ser.). (J). (gr. 8 up). pap. 2.95 o.p. (*0-8024-7605-8*) Moody Pr.

Martin, LaJoyce. Heart-Shaped Pieces. 1991. (Illus.). 160p. (Orig.). (YA). (gr. 9 up). pap. 8.99 o.p. (*0-932581-78-1*) Word Aflame Pr.

Marzollo, Jean. Do You Love Me, Harvey Burns? 1984. 202p. (J). (gr. 7 up). pap. 2.25 o.p. (*0-590-33192-2*, Scholastic Paperbacks) Scholastic, Inc.

Mason, Lynn. As I Am. 1999. (Love Stories Ser.). 192p. (gr. 7-12). mass mkt. 3.99 o.s.i (*0-553-49274-8*, Dell Books for Young Readers) Random Hse. Children's Bks.

Masters, William. Love & Sex. Cart, Michael, ed. 2003. 240p. (YA). pap. 7.99 (*0-689-85668-7*, Simon Pulse) Simon & Schuster Children's Publishing.

Masterson, Linda. A Special Love. 2001. (Illus.). 32p. pap. 4.99 (*0-307-16445-4*, Golden Bks.) Random Hse. Children's Bks.

Masuda, Akiko. Neil Tofu Luvs Tee-dah Tuna. 1995. (Illus.). 32p. (J). (gr. k-8). pap. (*0-9629842-2-1*) Stew & Rice Productions.

Maxwell, Janet. Love Notes. 1995. (Sweet Dreams Ser.: Vol. 231). 160p. (Orig.). (YA). (gr. 6 up). pap. 3.50 o.s.i (*0-553-56685-7*, Dell Books for Young Readers) Random Hse. Children's Bks.

Mazer, Harry. The Girl of His Dreams. 1987. 192p. (YA). (gr. 7 up). 12.95 o.p. (*0-690-04640-5*); lib. bdg. 12.89 o.p. (*0-690-04642-1*) HarperCollins Children's Bk. Group.

—I Love You, Stupid! 1981. 192p. (YA). (gr. 7 up). lib. bdg. 12.89 o.p. (*0-690-04121-7*) HarperCollins Children's Bk. Group.

—I Love You, Stupid! 1983. 192p. (J). pap. 3.50 (*0-380-61432-4*, Avon Bks.) Morrow/Avon.

Mazer, Harry & Mazer, Norma Fox. Heartbeat. 1990. 176p. (YA). (gr. 7 up). mass mkt. 3.99 o.s.i (*0-553-28779-6*, Starfire) Random Hse. Children's Bks.

Mazer, Norma Fox. Girlhearts. (J). (gr. 5 up). 2002. 320p. pap. 6.99 (*0-380-72290-9*); 2001. 224p. lib. bdg. 16.89 (*0-688-06866-9*) HarperCollins Children's Bk. Group.

—Someone to Love. 1985. 256p. (J). (gr. k-12). mass mkt. 3.25 o.s.i (*0-440-98062-3*, Laurel Leaf) Random Hse. Children's Bks.

—Summer Girls, Love Boys & Other Short Stories. 1982. 192p. (J). (gr. 7 up). pap. 11.95 o.s.i (*0-385-28930-8*, Delacorte Pr.) Dell Publishing.

—When We First Met. 1991. (YA). pap. 2.95 o.p. (*0-590-43823-9*); 1984. (J). pap. 2.25 o.p. (*0-590-31987-6*); 1984. 192p. (J). (gr. 7 up). pap. 2.50 o.p. (*0-590-40359-1*, Scholastic Paperbacks) Scholastic, Inc.

McArthur, Nancy. The Plant That Ate Dirty Socks Gets a Girlfriend. 1997. (Plant That Ate Dirty Socks Ser.: Bk. 8). (J). (gr. k-3). pap. 3.99 o.s.i (*0-380-78319-3*, Avon Bks.) Morrow/Avon.

McAvoy, Elaine A. Irresistible Love. 1985. (Serenade Serenata Ser.: No. 12). 192p. (Orig.). (J). (gr. 10-12). pap. 2.50 o.p. (*0-310-46612-1*, 15520P) Zondervan.

McBratney, Sam. Guess How Much I Love You. 2002. (Illus.). (J). 23.40 (*0-7587-2668-6*) Book Wholesalers, Inc.

—Guess How Much I Love You. 1996. (Illus.). 32p. (J). reprint ed. bds. 6.99 (*0-7636-0013-X*) Candlewick Pr.

—Guess How Much I Love You. (BEN, CHI, ENG, FRE & PAN., Illus.). 40p. (J). o.p. (*1-85430-385-6*) Magi Pubns.

—Guess How Much I Love You. (ps). 1999. (Illus.). 24p. (J). bds. 6.99 (*0-8499-5971-3*); 1998. 32p. 15.99 o.s.i (*0-8499-5904-7*) Nelson, Tommy.

—Guess How Much I Love You: Book & Toy Gift Set. gif. ed. 2002. (Illus.). 32p. bds. 12.99 (*0-7636-1942-6*) Candlewick Pr.

—Guess How Much I Love You: My Baby Book. (Illus.). (J). (ps-k). 1998. 16p. 17.99 (*0-7636-0675-8*); 1998. 15.99 o.s.i (*0-7636-0599-9*); 1995. 32p. 15.99 (*1-56402-473-3*); 1996. 40p. reprint ed. 15.99 o.p. (*0-7636-0164-0*) Candlewick Pr.

—Guess How Much I Love You: My Baby Book. 1996. (BEN, CHI, ENG, FRE & PAN., Illus.). 40p. (J). (ps-3). (*1-85430-384-8*); (*1-85430-383-X*) Magi Pubns.

—Guess How Much I Love You: My Baby Book. 1997. (BEN, CHI, ENG, FRE & PAN., Illus.). 40p. (J). (ps-1). 36.40 (*1-85430-387-2*) Magi Pubns. GBR. *Dist:* Midpoint Trade Bks., Inc.

—Guess How Much I Love You: Sweetheart Edition. 2003. (Illus.). 32p. 12.00 (*0-7636-2240-0*) Candlewick Pr.

McCormack, Erin. Disney's Princess Collection: Love & Friendship Stories. Heller, Sarah E., ed. 1999. (Disneys Ser.). (Illus.). 304p. (J). (gr. k-5). 15.99 (*0-7868-3247-9*) Disney Pr.

McCourt, Lisa. Love You Until... 1999. (Illus.). 32p. (J). (ps-3). 16.95 (*0-8091-6658-5*) Paulist Pr.

McCullers, Carson. A Tree, a Rock, a Cloud. 1993. (Creative Short Stories Ser.). 32p. (YA). (gr. 3-12). lib. bdg. 18.60 (*0-88682-349-8*, 97225-098, Creative Education) Creative Co., The.

McDaniel, Lurlene. Angels Watching over Me. 1996. 192p. (YA). (gr. 7-12). mass mkt. 4.99 (*0-553-56724-1*) Bantam Bks.

—Angels Watching over Me. 1996. (J). 11.04 (*0-606-11044-5*) Turtleback Bks.

—As Long as We Both Shall Live: Two Novels. 2003. 416p. (YA). mass mkt. 6.99 (*0-553-57108-7*) Bantam Doubleday Dell Bks. for Young Readers CAN. *Dist:* Random Hse. of Canada, Ltd.

—How Do I Love Thee: Three Stories. 2001. 272p. (YA). (gr. 7-9). 9.95 (*0-553-57154-0*) Bantam Bks.

—How Do I Love Thee: Three Stories. 2002. 272p. (gr. 7). mass mkt. 5.50 (*0-553-57107-9*, Dell Books for Young Readers) Random Hse. Children's Bks.

—I'll Be Seeing You. 1996. 208p. (YA). (gr. 7 up). mass mkt. 4.99 (*0-553-56718-7*, Starfire) Random Hse. Children's Bks.

—I'll Be Seeing You. 1996. 11.04 (*0-606-09451-2*) Turtleback Bks.

—My Secret Boyfriend. 4th ed. 1997. 128p. (J). (gr. 5-8). reprint ed. pap. 3.99 (*0-87406-835-5*, Willowisp Pr.) Darby Creek Publishing.

—No Time to Cry. 1996. 160p. (YA). (gr. 5 up). mass mkt. 4.99 (*0-553-57079-X*, Starfire) Random Hse. Children's Bks.

—Til Death Do Us Part. 1997. 224p. (YA). (gr. 7-12). mass mkt. 4.99 (*0-553-57085-4*, Dell Books for Young Readers) Random Hse. Children's Bks.

—Until Angels Close My Eyes. 1998. 256p. (YA). (gr. 7-12). mass mkt. 4.99 (*0-553-57115-X*, Starfire) Random Hse. Children's Bks.

—When Happily Ever after Ends. 1992. (Bantam Starfire Bks.). 176p. (YA). (gr. 7 up). mass mkt. 4.99 (*0-553-29056-8*) Bantam Bks.

McDonagh, Barbara S. Makana Aloha: Gift of Love. 1994. 24p. (J). (gr. k-8). 12.95 (*0-9643781-0-8*) Liko Publishing.

McDonnell, Christine. Just for the Summer. 1987. (Illus.). (J). (gr. 2-5). 11.95 o.p. (*0-670-80059-7*, Viking Children's Bks.) Penguin Putnam Bks. for Young Readers.

McElderry, Mona. Beneath Her Gentle Wings. 1995. (Illus.). 20p. (Orig.). (J). (ps-4). pap. 8.95 (*0-9641573-2-2*) Sisu Pr.

McFann, Jane. Be Mine. 1994. 208p. (J). (gr. 7 up). mass mkt. 3.25 (*0-590-46690-9*) Scholastic, Inc.

McGill, Joyce. Here We Go Again. 1986. (First Love Ser.). 155p. (J). (*0-373-06184-6*, Silhouette) Harlequin Enterprises, Ltd.

McGoldrick, May. Tess & the Highlander. 2002. (Avon True Romance Ser.). 272p. (J). pap. 4.99 (*0-06-000486-X*, Avon) HarperCollins Children's Bk. Group.

McHugh, Elisabet. The Real Thing. 1991. (Sweet Dreams Ser.: No. 183). 144p. (YA). pap. 2.99 o.s.i (*0-553-29186-6*) Bantam Bks.

McHugh, Fiona. Of Corsets & Secrets & True, True Love. 1993. (Road to Avonlea Ser.: No. 14). 128p. (J). (gr. 4-7). pap. 3.99 o.p. (*0-553-48040-5*) Bantam Bks.

McKay, Robert. Canary Red. 9999. pap. 1.95 o.p. (*0-590-04435-4*) Scholastic, Inc.

McKillip, Patricia A. The Night Gift. 1976. (Illus.). 192p. (J). (gr. 5-9). 6.95 o.p. (*0-689-30508-7*, Atheneum) Simon & Schuster Children's Publishing.

McLerran, Alice. The Mountain That Loved a Bird. 2000. (Illus.). 28p. (J). (ps-3). pap. 6.99 (*0-689-83319-9*, Aladdin) Simon & Schuster Children's Publishing.

Mercuri, Carmela. Beauty & the Beast: Story with Music. 1976. (Illus.). 24p. (Orig.). (YA). (gr. 8-12). pap. 4.95 (*0-935474-24-2*) Carousel Pubns., Ltd.

Merrium, Eve. Boys & Girls, Girls & Boys, ERS. 1973. (J). pap. o.p. (*0-03-005716-7*, Holt, Henry & Co. Bks. For Young Readers) Holt, Henry & Co.

Meyer, Carolyn. Where the Broken Heart Still Beats: The Story of Cynthia Ann Parker. 1992. (Great Episodes Ser.). 208p. (J). (gr. 7 up). pap. 7.00 (*0-15-295602-6*, Gulliver Bks.) Harcourt Children's Bks.

—Where the Broken Heart Still Beats: The Story of Cynthia Ann Parker. 1992. 13.05 (*0-606-06148-7*) Turtleback Bks.

Michaels, Cheri. Defiant Dreams. 1985. (Dawn of Love Ser.: No. 5). (YA). (gr. 7 up). mass mkt. 2.95 o.s.i (*0-671-54430-6*, Pocket) Simon & Schuster.

—Wild Prairie Sky. 1985. (Dawn of Love Ser.: No. 2). (J). (gr. 7 up). pap. (*0-671-55154-X*, Simon Pulse) Simon & Schuster Children's Publishing.

Michaels, Fran. Mr. Wonderful. 1987. (Sweet Dreams Ser.: No. 120). 192p. (Orig.). (YA). (gr. 7-12). mass mkt. 2.50 o.s.i (*0-553-26340-4*) Bantam Bks.

—Past Perfect. 1987. (Sweet Dreams Ser.: No. 131). 192p. (Orig.). (YA). (gr. 7-12). pap. 2.50 o.s.i (*0-553-26789-2*) Bantam Bks.

Michot, Fabienne. Maki, I Love to Kiss You. braille ed. 2001. (J). (gr. 1). bds. (*0-616-07268-6*) Canadian National Institute for the Blind/Institut National Canadien pour les Aveugles.

Miglis, Jenny. Hugs Hugs Hugs Kisses Kisses Kisses. 2003. (Illus.). 40p. (J). 7.99 (*0-8431-0296-9*, Price Stern Sloan) Penguin Putnam Bks. for Young Readers.

Miklowitz, Gloria D. Goodbye Tomorrow. 1987. 192p. (J). (gr. 7 up). 13.95 o.s.i (*0-385-29562-6*, Delacorte Pr.) Dell Publishing.

—Goodbye Tomorrow. 1988. 160p. (J). (gr. k-12). mass mkt. 3.25 o.s.i (*0-440-20081-4*, Laurel Leaf) Random Hse. Children's Bks.

Mildred & Elsie. 2001. (Mildred Classics Ser.: Vol. 3). 288p. pap. 5.95 (*1-58182-229-4*) Cumberland Hse. Publishing.

Mildred at Roselands. 2001. (Mildred Classics Ser.: Vol. 2). 288p. pap. 5.95 (*1-58182-228-6*) Cumberland Hse. Publishing.

Miles, Betty. The Trouble with Thirteen. 1984. 112p. (YA). (gr. 7 up). pap. 2.50 o.p. (*0-380-67470-X*, Avon Bks.) Morrow/Avon.

Miller, Jessel. Mustard Bk. I: Soft Love & Strong Values. Gamble, Carolynne, ed. 1998. (Illus.). 48p. (J). (ps-6). 24.00 (*0-9660381-7-7*) Jessel Gallery.

Miller, Susan Martins. Starting Over. 1999. (American Adventure Ser.: No. 43). 144p. (J). (gr. 3-7). pap. 3.97 (*1-57748-509-2*) Barbour Publishing, Inc.

Mills, Claudia. Dinah in Love. 1993. 128p. (J). (gr. 3-7). lib. bdg. 14.00 (*0-02-766998-X*, Simon & Schuster Children's Publishing) Simon & Schuster Children's Publishing.

—Dinah in Love. 1996. (J). 9.05 o.p. (*0-606-09191-2*) Turtleback Bks.

Miner, Jane C. Roxanne, Vol. 15. 1985. 368p. (Orig.). (YA). (gr. 11 up). pap. 2.95 o.p. (*0-590-33686-X*) Scholastic, Inc.

—Senior Dreams Can Come True. 1985. 176p. (Orig.). (J). (gr. 7 up). pap. 2.25 o.p. (*0-590-33180-9*) Scholastic, Inc.

—Veronica, No. 18. 1986. 224p. (Orig.). (J). (gr. 7 up). pap. 2.25 o.p. (*0-590-33933-8*) Scholastic, Inc.

—Winter Love Story. 1993. 256p. (J). (gr. 7-9). mass mkt. 3.50 o.p. (*0-590-47610-6*) Scholastic, Inc.

Minters, Frances. Sleepless Beauty. 1999. (Illus.). 32p. (J). (ps-3). pap. 5.99 o.s.i (*0-14-056619-8*, Puffin Bks.) Penguin Putnam Bks. for Young Readers.

—Sleepless Beauty. 1999. 12.14 (*0-606-17431-1*) Turtleback Bks.

Mitchell, Jane. When the Stars Stop Spinning. 1996. 160p. pap. 8.95 (*1-85371-639-1*) Poolbeg Pr. IRL. *Dist:* Dufour Editions, Inc.

Mittermeyer, Helen. Vortex. 1984. (Loveswept Ser.: No. 67). 208p. pap. 2.25 o.p. (*0-553-21669-4*) Bantam Bks.

Moeyaert, Bart. It's Love We Don't Understand. Boeke, Wanda, tr. from DUT. 2001. 160p. (YA). (gr. 7 up). 15.95 (*1-886910-71-5*) Front Street, Inc.

Montgomery, L. M. The Blue Castle. Date not set. (J). 22.95 (*0-8488-2370-2*) Amereon, Ltd.

—The Blue Castle. 1988. 224p. (J). mass mkt. 4.50 o.s.i (*0-7704-2315-9*) Bantam Bks.

—The Blue Castle. 1989. (Illus.). 260p. (J). pap. 4.98 o.p. (*0-7710-6166-8*) McClelland & Stewart/ Tundra Bks.

—The Blue Castle. 1989. 224p. (YA). (gr. 4-7). mass mkt. 4.99 (*0-553-28051-1*, Starfire) Random Hse. Children's Bks.

—Emily's Quest. 1976. 236p. (J). 21.95 (*0-8488-0590-9*) Amereon, Ltd.

—Emily's Quest. 1984. 240p. (YA). mass mkt. 4.99 (*0-7704-2060-5*); 1983. (J). mass mkt. 2.95 o.s.i (*0-553-23323-8*); 1983. 240p. (YA). (gr. 4-7). mass mkt. 4.99 (*0-553-26493-1*) Bantam Bks.

—Emily's Quest. 1982. reprint ed. lib. bdg. 16.95 o.p. (*0-89966-418-0*) Buccaneer Bks., Inc.

—Emily's Quest. 1996. 248p. (J). (gr. 7 up). mass mkt. 4.95 (*0-7710-9981-9*) McClelland & Stewart/ Tundra Bks.

Moody, Rick & Steinke, Darcey, eds. Joyful Noise: The New Testament Revisited. 1999. 256p. pap. 13.00 (*0-316-57995-5*) Little Brown & Co.

Moore, Alan. Alan Moore's Another Suburban Romance. 2003. (Illus.). 64p. (YA). 17.95 (*1-59291-008-4*); (gr. 12 up). pap. 7.95 (*1-59291-007-6*) Avatar Pr., Inc.

Moore, Elaine. Grammy, Do You Love Me? 1995. (J). (ps-2). 7.95 o.p. (*0-681-00442-8*) Borders Pr.

Moreau, Patricia. Suzanne Masterson: Dangerous Games. 1994. 412p. (YA). pap. 8.99 o.p. (*0-88070-648-1*, Multnomah Bks.) Multnomah Pubs., Inc.

Morgan, Mary, illus. Guess Who I Love? 1992. (Pudgy Board Bks.). 18p. (J). (ps). 3.50 o.s.i (*0-448-40313-7*, Grosset & Dunlap) Penguin Putnam Bks. for Young Readers.

Morris, Ann. Kiss Time. 1986. (Illus.). 16p. (J). (ps). 3.50 o.p. (*0-694-00073-6*) HarperCollins Children's Bk. Group.

Morris, Kimberly. Wild Hearts. 1992. (Changes Romance Ser.: No. 6). 240p. (YA). mass mkt. 3.50 o.p. (*0-06-106781-4*, HarperTorch) Morrow/Avon.

Morrow, Tara Jaye. Mommy Loves Her Baby. 2003. (Illus.). 32p. (J). (ps-1). lib. bdg. 16.89 (*0-06-029078-1*) HarperCollins Pubs.

Mosher, Richard. Zazoo. 2001. 224p. (YA). (gr. 7 up). tchr. ed. 16.00 (*0-618-13534-0*, Clarion Bks.) Houghton Mifflin Co. Trade & Reference Div.

Mount, Guy. Lady Ocean: A Love Story for Children. 1986. (Illus.). (J). (gr. k-6). pap. 3.00 (*0-9604462-2-2*) Sweetlight Bks.

Mouse Works Staff. Beauty & the Beast & The Aristocats, 2 vols. 75th anniv. ed. 1998. (Illus.). (ps-3). (*0-7364-0092-3*) Mouse Works.

—La Bella y la Bestia: Read Aloud Storybook Classic. 1999. (SPA., Illus.). 64p. (J). 6.99 (*0-7364-0141-5*) Disney Pr.

—Romance Slip. 1997. (J). 31.92 (*1-57082-708-7*) Mouse Works.

—Sleeping Beauty/The Little Mermaid, 2 vols. 75th anniv. ed. 1998. (Illus.). (ps-3). 9.99 (*0-7364-0091-5*) Mouse Works.

Muldrow, Diane. Disney's Beauty & the Beast: Enchanted Christmas. 1997. (J). o.p. (*0-307-98828-7*, Golden Bks.) Random Hse. Children's Bks.

Munsch, Robert. Love You Forever. ed. 1987. (J). (gr. 2). spiral bd. (*0-616-01736-7*) Canadian National Institute for the Blind/Institut National Canadien pour les Aveugles.

—Love You Forever. 2003. (Illus.). 32p. (J). (ps-3). 12.95 (*0-920668-36-4*); pap. 4.95 (*0-920668-37-2*); 19.95 (*1-895565-66-9*); 17.95 (*1-55209-109-0*) Firefly Bks., Ltd.

—Love You Forever: A Big Book. 2003. (Illus.). 32p. (J). pap. 19.95 (*1-895565-37-5*) Firefly Bks., Ltd.

—Siempre Te Querre. ed. 2003. (gr. 1). spiral bd. (*0-616-14608-6*) Canadian National Institute for the Blind/Institut National Canadien pour les Aveugles.

—Siempre Te Querre. 2003. (SPA., Illus.). 32p. (J). (ps-3). pap. 4.95 (*1-895565-01-4*, AP4469) Firefly Bks., Ltd.

Munsil, Janet. Il N'y a Pas de Fumee (Where There's Smoke) 1996. (FRE., Illus.). 24p. (J). (ps-2). pap. 4.95 (*1-55037-311-0*) Annick Pr., Ltd. CAN. *Dist:* Firefly Bks., Ltd.

—Where There's Smoke. 1993. (ENG & FRE., Illus.). 24p. (J). (ps-2). pap. 4.95 o.p. (*1-55037-290-4*); lib. bdg. 14.95 (*1-55037-291-2*) Annick Pr., Ltd. CAN. *Dist:* Firefly Bks., Ltd.

Murakami, Maki. Gravitation, 12 vols. (Illus.). (YA). 208p. pap. 9.99 (*1-59182-338-2*); 208p. pap. 9.99 (*1-59182-339-0*);Vol. 1. 2003. 192p. (gr. 11 up). pap. 9.99 (*1-59182-333-1*);Vol. 2. 2003. 192p. (gr. 11 up). pap. 9.99 (*1-59182-334-X*);Vol. 3. 2003. 192p. (gr. 8 up). pap. 9.99 (*1-59182-335-8*);Vol. 4. 2004. 192p. (gr. 8 up). pap. 9.99 (*1-59182-336-6*);Vol. 5. 2004. 208p. (gr. 8 up). pap. 9.99 (*1-59182-337-4*) TOKYOPOP, Inc.

Murphy, Barbara B. One Another. 1986. 160p. (gr. 9 up). pap. 2.25 o.p. (*0-440-96724-4*) Dell Publishing.

Murphy, Chuck. I Love You. 1999. (Razzle Dazzle Book Ser.). (Illus.). 12p. (J). (ps-k). bds. 4.99 (*0-689-82258-8*, Little Simon) Simon & Schuster Children's Publishing.

Murphy, Lorraine M. The Prize. 1993. 192p. (J). (gr. 8). pap. text 7.95 (*1-883511-02-X*) Veritas Pr.

Musgrave, Florence. Like a Red, Red Rose. 1958. (Illus.). (J). (gr. 6-9). 4.95 o.p. (*0-8038-4236-8*) Hastings Hse. Daytrips Pubs.

My Antonia. 1999. (YA). 11.95 (*1-56137-759-7*) Novel Units, Inc.

My Bodyguard. 9999. (J). pap. 1.25 o.s.i (*0-590-72130-5*) Scholastic, Inc.

My Honey Valentine. 1997. (Pooh Ser.). (J). 5.98 o.s.i (*1-57082-441-X*) Mouse Works.

Namm, Diane. Never Tell Ben. 1996. (Love Stories Ser.). 192p. (YA). (gr. 7-12). mass mkt. 3.99 o.s.i (*0-553-57045-5*) Bantam Bks.

Napoli, Donna Jo. For the Love of Venice. 1998. 256p. (YA). (gr. 8 up). 15.95 o.s.i (*0-385-32531-2*, Delacorte Pr.) Dell Publishing.

—For the Love of Venice. 2000. 256p. (YA). (gr. 7-12). mass mkt. 4.99 (*0-440-41411-3*, Laurel Leaf) Random Hse. Children's Bks.

—For the Love of Venice. 2000. (Illus.). (J). 10.55 (*0-606-17998-4*) Turtleback Bks.

Naylor, Phyllis Reynolds. Achingly Alice. 2003. (Alice Ser.). (Illus.). 160p. (YA). mass mkt. 4.99 (*0-689-86396-9*, Simon Pulse) Simon & Schuster Children's Publishing.

Naylor, Phyllis Reynolds & Naylor, Magdelena R. Achingly Alice. 1999. (Alice Ser.). 128p. (YA). (gr. 5-9). pap. 4.99 (*0-689-80595-0*, 076714004504, Aladdin) Simon & Schuster Children's Publishing.

—Achingly Alice. 1999. (Alice Ser.). (YA). (gr. 5-9). 11.04 (*0-606-16332-8*) Turtleback Bks.

Nesbit, Edith. Long Ago When I Was Young. 1988. (Illus.). 136p. (J). (ps up). 14.95 o.p. (*0-8037-0476-3*, Dial Bks. for Young Readers) Penguin Putnam Bks. for Young Readers.

Neufeld, John. Freddy's Book. 1976. (J). (gr. 2-7). pap. 1.75 o.p. (*0-380-00203-5*, 53298-0, Avon Bks.) Morrow/Avon.

Newman, Marjorie. Mole & the Baby Bird. 2002. (Illus.). 32p. (J). (gr. k-3). 16.95 (*1-58234-784-0*, Bloomsbury Children) Bloomsbury Publishing.

Nielsen, Virginia. La Sauvage. 1988. (Orig.). (J). mass mkt. 3.95 o.s.i (*0-440-20190-X*) Dell Publishing.

Nighswander, Ada. The Little Martins Learn to Love. 1982. (Illus.). 187p. (J). (gr. 3-6). 8.50 (*0-7399-0085-4*, 2310) Rod & Staff Pubs., Inc.

Nikola-Lisa, W. La Alegria de Ser Tu y Yo. Canetti, Yanitzia, tr. from ENG. 1996. (SPA., Illus.). 32p. (J). (ps-3). 14.95 (*1-880000-35-0*, LW1926); pap. 6.95 (*1-880000-36-9*, LW1927) Lee & Low Bks., Inc.

—La Alegria de Ser Tu y Yo. 1996. (SPA.). (J). 13.10 (*0-606-09520-9*) Turtleback Bks.

Nilsson, Per. Heart's Delight. Chace, Tara, tr. from SWE. 2003. 160p. (YA). 16.95 (*1-886910-92-8*, Front Street) Front Street, Inc.

Nixon, Joan Lowery. Circle of Love. 1998. (Orphan Train Adventures Ser.: Vol. 7). 176p. (YA). (gr. 5-9). mass mkt. 4.50 o.s.i (*0-440-22731-3*, Dell Books for Young Readers) Random Hse. Children's Bks.

—A Family Apart. 1988. (Orphan Train Adventures Ser.: Bk. 1). 176p. (YA). (gr. 5 up). mass mkt. 4.50 o.s.i (*0-553-27478-3*, Starfire) Random Hse. Children's Bks.

Nobile, Jeanett. Portrait of Love. 1983. (Sweet Dreams Ser.). 166p. (J). (gr. 6-8). pap. 2.25 o.s.i (*0-553-17846-6*) Bantam Bks.

Noonan, Rosalind. Sarah: Don't Say You Love Me. 1998. (Party of Five: No. 5). 160p. (J). (gr. 3-6). pap. 4.50 (*0-671-02452-3*, Simon Pulse) Simon & Schuster Children's Publishing.

Norac, Carl. I Love You So Much. (J). 2003. 20p. bds. 5.99 (*0-385-74627-X*, Dell Books for Young Readers); 2002. 32p. pap. 5.99 (*0-440-41744-9*, Random Hse. Bks. for Young Readers); 1998. (Illus.). 32p. 9.95 (*0-385-32512-6*, Doubleday Bks. for Young Readers) Random Hse. Children's Bks.

Novak, Barbara. Down with Love. 2003. 288p. pap. 14.95 (*0-06-054162-8*, HarperEntertainment) Morrow/Avon.

Nyson, Violet W. The Sad Little Cottage. 1996. (Illus.). 32p. (Orig.). (J). (ps-4). pap. 5.95 (*1-888828-05-6*) Anchor Publishing.

O'Banyon, Constance. Song of the Nightingale. 1992. 336p. (J). mass mkt. 8.99 o.p. (*0-06-104122-X*, HarperTorch) Morrow/Avon.

O'Connell, June. His & Hers. 1993. (Sweet Dreams Ser.: No. 201). 144p. (YA). pap. 2.99 o.s.i (*0-553-29980-8*) Bantam Bks.

—Love on the Beat. 1992. (Sweet Dreams Ser.: No. 193). 144p. (YA). pap. 2.99 o.s.i (*0-553-29455-5*) Bantam Bks.

O'Connor, Jane. Just Good Friends. 1986. (gr. 7-12). pap. 2.75 o.p. (*0-440-94329-9*) Dell Publishing.

—Yours till Niagara Falls, Abby. 1991. 128p. (J). (gr. 3-7). mass mkt. 2.75 o.p. (*0-590-42854-3*) Scholastic, Inc.

O'Donnell, Thomas. The Journal of Malt Witty. 1989. (J). 10.00 o.p. (*0-533-08038-X*) Vantage Pr., Inc.

Offit, Sidney. What Kind of Guy Do You Think I Am? 1977. (J). (gr. 3-8). o.p. (*0-397-47372-9*) HarperCollins Children's Bk. Group.

Ogilvie, Elisabeth. My Summer Love. 1985. 192p. (Orig.). (J). (gr. 7 up). pap. 2.25 o.p. (*0-590-33266-X*) Scholastic, Inc.

—A Steady Kind of Love. 1979. (J). pap. 1.25 o.p. (*0-590-04599-7*) Scholastic, Inc.

Oke, Janette. What Does Love Look Like? 2001. (Illus.). 32p. (J). 14.99 (*0-7642-2509-X*) Bethany Hse. Pubs.

Okimoto, Jean Davies. Jason's Women. 1986. 210p. (YA). (gr. 7 up). 14.95 (*0-316-63809-9*, 638099, Joy Street Bks.) Little Brown & Co.

Older, Jules. Hank Prank in Love. 1991. (J). (gr. 4-7). pap. 2.50 o.p. (*0-590-43872-7*) Scholastic, Inc.

Oldham, June. Grow up, Cupid. 1989. (J). (gr. k-12). reprint ed. mass mkt. 2.95 o.s.i (*0-440-20256-6*, Laurel Leaf) Random Hse. Children's Bks.

Olkowski, Mary. From the Garden of My Soul. unabr. ed. 1998. (Illus.). 50p. 12.99 (*0-9668781-0-8*, 1001) Limpid Butterfly Productions, The.

Olsen, Mary-Kate. Love Is in the Air. 2000. (Illus.). 32p. (J). (ps-3). pap. 3.99 (*0-307-29906-6*, Golden Bks.) Random Hse. Children's Bks.

Olsen, Mary-Kate & Olsen, Ashley. Secret Crush. 2002. (So Little Time Ser.: No. 6). 128p. mass mkt. 4.99 (*0-06-008808-7*, HarperEntertainment) Morrow/Avon.

Oneal, Zibby. In Summer Light. 1985. 16p. (J). (gr. 7 up). 12.95 o.p. (*0-670-80784-2*, Viking Children's Bks.) Penguin Putnam Bks. for Young Readers.

Oniell, Laura. The Ski Trip. 1993. (Nickelodeon Fifteen Ser.: No. 5). 128p. (Orig.). (J). (gr. 3-9). 2.95 o.p. (*0-448-40494-X*, Grosset & Dunlap) Penguin Putnam Bks. for Young Readers.

Orgel, Doris. Crack in the Heart. 1989. (YA). (gr. 7 up). mass mkt. 2.95 o.s.i (*0-449-70204-9*, Fawcett) Ballantine Bks.

—The Princess & the God. 1997. 128p. (YA). (gr. 9-12). mass mkt. 4.50 o.s.i (*0-440-22691-0*, Dell Books for Young Readers) Random Hse. Children's Bks.

—The Princess & the God. 1996. (YA). 116p. (gr. 6 up). 15.95 o.p. (*0-531-09516-9*); 128p. (gr. 7 up). lib. bdg. 16.99 (*0-531-08866-9*) Scholastic, Inc. (Orchard Bks.).

Ormondroyd, Edward. Theodore's Rival. 1986. (Illus.). (J). (gr. 4-8). pap. 3.95 o.p. (*0-395-41669-8*) Houghton Mifflin Co. Trade & Reference Div.

Orwig, Sara. Dear Mit. 1985. (Loveswept Ser.: No. 111). 208p. pap. 2.25 o.p. (*0-553-21726-7*) Bantam Bks.

Osborne, Mary Pope. Love Always, Blue. 1983. 192p. (J). (gr. 6 up). 12.95 o.p. (*0-8037-0031-8*, 01258-370, Dial Bks. for Young Readers) Penguin Putnam Bks. for Young Readers.

Overend, Jenni. Welcome with Love. 2000. (Illus.). 32p. (J). (ps-4). 15.95 (*0-916291-96-0*, Cranky Nell Bks.) Kane/Miller Bk. Pubs.

Overton, Jenny. The Ship from Simnel Street. 1986. 224p. (YA). (gr. 5 up). 11.95 o.p. (*0-688-06182-6*, Greenwillow Bks.) HarperCollins Children's Bk. Group.

Owens, Everett. Out of My League. 1998. (Love Stories Super Edition Ser.). 224p. (YA). (gr. 7-12). mass mkt. 4.50 o.s.i (*0-553-48594-6*, Dell Books for Young Readers) Random Hse. Children's Bks.

Oxenbury, Helen. All Fall Down. (Oxenbury Board Bks.). (Illus.). 10p. (J). (ps-k). 1999. bds. 6.99 (*0-689-81985-4*); 1987. pap. 6.95 o.s.i (*0-02-769040-7*) Simon & Schuster Children's Publishing. (Little Simon).

Oz, Amos. Soumchi. Farmer, Penelope, tr. from HEB. 1981. (Illus.). 96p. (J). (gr. 4-7). 8.95 o.p. (*0-06-024621-9*); lib. bdg. 8.79 o.p. (*0-06-024622-7*) HarperCollins Children's Bk. Group.

Page, Alexis. Three-Guy Weekend. 1996. (Love Stories Ser.). 192p. (YA). (gr. 7-12). mass mkt. 3.99 o.s.i (*0-553-57044-7*) Bantam Bks.

Page, Peggy S. Little Boat Disappear. 2000. 40p. (YA). pap. 8.00 (*0-8059-4901-1*) Dorrance Publishing Co., Inc.

Pandell, Karen. I Love You Sun, I Love You Moon. 1994. (Illus.). 18p. (J). (ps). 6.99 (*0-399-22628-1*, G. P. Putnam's Sons) Penguin Group (USA) Inc.

—Te Amo Sol, Te Amo Luna/I Love You Sun, I Love You Moon. 2003. (ENG & SPA., Illus.). 18p. bds. 6.99 (*0-399-24165-5*) Penguin Putnam Bks. for Young Readers.

Park, Ruth. Playing Beatie Bow. 1982. 208p. (J). (gr. 5-9). lib. bdg. 16.00 o.s.i (*0-689-30889-2*, Atheneum) Simon & Schuster Children's Publishing.

Parker, Daniel. Dark Hearts Vol. 3: Dance of Death. 1996. 208p. (YA). mass mkt. 3.99 o.p. (*0-06-106318-5*, HarperTorch) Morrow/Avon.

Parry, Glyn. Scooter Boy. 1998. pap. 12.95 (*0-7022-2990-3*) Univ. of Queensland Pr. AUS. *Dist:* International Specialized Bk. Services.

Parsons, Jill. Curtain Going Up. 1995. (Voices Romance Ser.: No. 6). 224p. (J). (gr. 4-7). mass mkt. 3.99 o.s.i (*0-8217-4819-X*) Kensington Publishing Corp.

Pascal, Francine. All Night Long. 1984. (Sweet Valley High Ser.: No. 5). 144p. (YA). (gr. 7 up). mass mkt. 3.99 o.s.i (*0-553-27568-2*) Bantam Bks.

—Be Mine. 2002. (Illus.). 176p. (YA). (gr. 7). mass mkt. 4.50 (*0-553-49386-8*, Sweet Valley) Random Hse. Children's Bks.

—Close to You. 2001. (Sweet Valley High Senior Year Ser.: Vol. 30). 192p. (YA). (gr. 7 up). mass mkt. 4.50 o.s.i (*0-553-49346-9*, Dell Books for Young Readers) Random Hse. Children's Bks.

—Dangerous Love. 1984. (Sweet Valley High Ser.: No. 6). 144p. (YA). (gr. 7 up). mass mkt. 3.99 o.s.i (*0-553-27741-3*) Bantam Bks.

—Dear Sister. 1984. (Sweet Valley High Ser.: No. 7). 160p. (YA). (gr. 7 up). mass mkt. 3.99 o.s.i (*0-553-27672-7*) Bantam Bks.

—Double Love. 1984. (Sweet Valley High Ser.: No. 1). 192p. (J). (gr. 7 up). mass mkt. 3.99 o.s.i (*0-553-27567-4*) Bantam Bks.

—Elizabeth's Summer Love. 1996. (Sweet Valley University Ser.: No. 22). 240p. (gr. 7 up). mass mkt. 3.99 o.s.i (*0-553-56705-5*, Sweet Valley) Random Hse. Children's Bks.

—For the Love of Ryan. 1996. (Sweet Valley University Ser.: No. 21). 240p. (gr. 7 up). mass mkt. 3.99 o.s.i (*0-553-56704-7*, Sweet Valley) Random Hse. Children's Bks.

—Heartbreaker. 1984. (Sweet Valley High Ser.: No. 8). 144p. (YA). (gr. 7 up). mass mkt. 3.99 o.s.i (*0-553-27569-0*, Sweet Valley) Random Hse. Children's Bks.

Relationships

—In Love with the Enemy. 1995. (Sweet Valley High Ser.: No. 120). 208p. (YA). (gr. 7 up). mass mkt. 3.99 o.s.i (*0-553-56638-5*, Sweet Valley) Random Hse. Children's Bks.

—Jessica's Older Guy. 1995. (Sweet Valley High Ser.: No. 119). 208p. (YA). (gr. 7 up). mass mkt. 3.99 o.s.i (*0-553-56637-7*, Sweet Valley) Random Hse. Children's Bks.

—A Kiss Before Dying. 1996. (Sweet Valley High Ser.: No. 122). 208p. (YA). (gr. 7 up). mass mkt. 3.99 o.s.i (*0-553-56640-7*) Bantam Bks.

—Love & Betrayal & Hold the Mayo! 1986. 224p. (J). (gr. 5-9). mass mkt. 2.95 o.s.i (*0-440-94735-9*, Laurel Leaf) Random Hse. Children's Bks.

—Love & Betrayal & Hold the Mayo! 2003. (Illus.). 256p. (YA). mass mkt. 4.99 (*0-689-85990-2*, Simon Pulse) Simon & Schuster Children's Publishing.

—Max's Choice. 2001. (Elizabeth Ser.: Vol. 5). 240p. (YA). (gr. 9 up). mass mkt. 4.50 (*0-553-49357-4*, Sweet Valley) Random Hse. Children's Bks.

—Meet Me at Midnight. 1996. (Sweet Valley High Ser.: No. 124). 208p. (YA). (gr. 7 up). mass mkt. 3.99 o.s.i (*0-553-56761-6*, Sweet Valley) Random Hse. Children's Bks.

—My First Love & Other Disasters. (J). 1991. 192p. (gr. 4-7). pap. 3.95 o.s.i (*0-14-034886-7*, Puffin Bks.); 1979. (gr. 7 up). 14.95 o.p. (*0-670-49952-8*, Viking Children's Bks.) Penguin Putnam Bks. for Young Readers.

—My First Love & Other Disasters. 1986. 176p. (J). (gr. 7 up). mass mkt. 2.95 o.s.i (*0-440-95447-9*, Laurel Leaf) Random Hse. Children's Bks.

—My First Love & Other Disasters. 2003. (Illus.). 240p. (YA). mass mkt. 4.99 (*0-689-85989-9*, Simon Pulse) Simon & Schuster Children's Publishing.

—The Other Woman. 1995. (Sweet Valley University Ser.: No. 16). 240p. (YA). (gr. 7 up). mass mkt. 3.99 o.s.i (*0-553-56696-2*, Sweet Valley) Random Hse. Children's Bks.

—A Royal Pain. 2001. (Elizabeth Ser.: Vol. 3). 240p. (YA). (gr. 9-12). mass mkt. 4.50 o.s.i (*0-553-49355-8*, Sweet Valley) Random Hse. Children's Bks.

—Secret Love Diaries: Chloe. 2000. 240p. (YA). (gr. 9-12). mass mkt. 4.50 o.s.i (*0-553-49352-3*, Sweet Valley) Random Hse. Children's Bks.

—Secret Love Diaries: Sam. 2000. 240p. (YA). (gr. 9-12). mass mkt. 4.50 o.s.i (*0-553-49351-5*, Sweet Valley) Random Hse. Children's Bks.

—Tearing Me Apart. 2001. (Francine Pascal's SVH Senior Year Ser.: Vol. 36). (Illus.). 192p. (YA). (gr. 7). mass mkt. 4.50 (*0-553-49385-X*, Sweet Valley) Random Hse. Children's Bks.

Pascal, Francine, creator. All about Love. 2000. (Sweet Valley High Senior Year Ser.: No. 13). 192p. (gr. 7 up). mass mkt. 4.50 o.s.i (*0-553-49312-4*, Dell Books for Young Readers) Random Hse. Children's Bks.

—All Night Long. l.t. ed. 1989. (Sweet Valley High Ser.: No. 5). 134p. (YA). (gr. 7 up). reprint ed. 9.50 o.p. (*1-55905-004-7*); lib. bdg. 10.50 o.p. (*1-55905-014-4*) Grey Castle Pr.

—Amy's True Love. 1991. (Sweet Valley High Ser.: No. 75). 144p. (YA). (gr. 7 up). mass mkt. 2.99 o.s.i (*0-553-28963-2*) Bantam Bks.

—Anything for Love. 1994. (Sweet Valley University Ser.: No. 4). 240p. (YA). (gr. 7 up). mass mkt. 4.50 o.s.i (*0-553-56311-4*) Bantam Bks.

—Are We in Love. 1993. (Sweet Valley High Ser.: No. 94). 160p. (YA). (gr. 7 up). mass mkt. 3.25 o.s.i (*0-553-29851-8*) Bantam Bks.

—Boy Meets Girl. 1999. (Sweet Valley High Senior Year Ser.: No. 7). 192p. (gr. 7 up). mass mkt. 3.99 (*0-553-48613-6*) Bantam Bks.

—The Broken Angel. 1999. (Sweet Valley High Senior Year Ser.: No. 10). 192p. (gr. 7 up). mass mkt. 4.50 o.s.i (*0-553-49282-9*) Bantam Bks.

—Busted! 1996. (Sweet Valley University Ser.: No. 25). 240p. (YA). (gr. 7 up). mass mkt. 3.99 o.s.i (*0-553-57006-4*) Bantam Bks.

—California Love. 1995. (Sweet Valley High TV Ser.: No. 1). 144p. (YA). (gr. 7 up). mass mkt. 4.50 o.s.i (*0-553-57011-0*, Sweet Valley) Random Hse. Children's Bks.

—California Love. 1995. (Sweet Valley High TV Ser.: No. 1). (YA). (gr. 7 up). 9.60 o.p. (*0-606-08228-X*) Turtleback Bks.

—The Dating Game. 1991. (Sweet Valley High Ser.: No. 78). 160p. (YA). (gr. 7 up). mass mkt. 2.99 o.s.i (*0-553-29187-4*) Bantam Bks.

—Don't Go Home with John. 1992. (Sweet Valley High Ser.: No. 90). 160p. (YA). (gr. 7 up). mass mkt. 3.50 o.s.i (*0-553-29236-6*) Bantam Bks.

—Don't Let Go. 1999. (Sweet Valley University Ser.: No. 45). 240p. (gr. 7 up). mass mkt. 3.99 o.s.i (*0-553-49265-9*, Dell Books for Young Readers) Random Hse. Children's Bks.

—Elizabeth & Todd Forever. 1997. (University Ser.: No. 27). 240p. (gr. 7 up). mass mkt. 3.99 o.s.i (*0-553-57051-X*, Sweet Valley) Random Hse. Children's Bks.

—Elizabeth in Love. 2000. (Sweet Valley University Ser.: No. 59). 240p. (YA). (gr. 9 up). mass mkt. 4.50 o.s.i (*0-553-49347-7*, Sweet Valley) Random Hse. Children's Bks.

—Falling for Lucas. 1996. (Sweet Valley High Super Ser.). 240p. (YA). (gr. 7 up). mass mkt. 4.50 o.s.i (*0-553-57022-6*) Bantam Bks.

—The First Time. 2000. (Sweet Valley University Ser.: No. 55). 240p. (gr. 9 up). mass mkt. 4.50 o.s.i (*0-553-49307-8*, Sweet Valley) Random Hse. Children's Bks.

—Fooling Around. 1999. (Sweet Valley University Ser.: No. 52). 240p. (gr. 9 up). mass mkt. 4.50 o.s.i (*0-553-49272-1*) Bantam Bks.

—Forbidden Love. 1987. (Sweet Valley High Ser.: No. 34). 144p. (YA). (gr. 7 up). mass mkt. 3.99 o.s.i (*0-553-27521-6*) Bantam Bks.

—The Fowlers of Sweet Valley. 1996. (Sweet Valley Saga Ser.). 352p. (gr. 7 up). mass mkt. 4.50 o.s.i (*0-553-57003-X*) Bantam Bks.

—The Girl They Both Loved. 1991. (Sweet Valley High Ser.: No. 80). 160p. (YA). (gr. 7 up). mass mkt. 3.25 o.s.i (*0-553-29226-9*) Bantam Bks.

—Good-Bye to Love. 1994. (Sweet Valley University Ser.: No. 7). 240p. (gr. 7 up). mass mkt. 4.50 o.s.i (*0-553-56652-0*) Bantam Bks.

—Hands Off! 2000. (Sweet Valley Junior High Ser.: No. 15). 160p. (gr. 3-7). pap. text 4.50 (*0-553-48703-5*, Sweet Valley) Random Hse. Children's Bks.

—Head over Heels. 1985. (Sweet Valley High Ser.: No. 18). 176p. (Orig.). (YA). (gr. 7 up). mass mkt. 3.25 o.s.i (*0-553-27444-9*) Bantam Bks.

—He's Watching You. 1995. (Sweet Valley University Thriller Edition Ser.: No. 2). 288p. (YA). (gr. 7 up). mass mkt. 4.50 o.s.i (*0-553-56689-X*) Bantam Bks.

—I'll Never Love Again. 1999. (Sweet Valley University Ser.: No. 46). 240p. (gr. 7 up). mass mkt. 3.99 o.s.i (*0-553-49266-7*, Dell Books for Young Readers) Random Hse. Children's Bks.

—In Love Again. 1989. (Sweet Valley High Ser.: No. 59). 160p. (YA). (gr. 7 up). mass mkt. 2.99 o.s.i (*0-553-28193-3*) Bantam Bks.

—In Love with a Prince. 1993. (Sweet Valley High Ser.: No. 91). 160p. (YA). (gr. 7 up). mass mkt. 3.25 o.s.i (*0-553-29237-4*) Bantam Bks.

—Invisible Me. 2000. (Sweet Valley Junior High Ser.: No. 23). (Illus.). 160p. (gr. 3-7). pap. text 4.50 (*0-553-48725-6*, Sweet Valley) Random Hse. Children's Bks.

—Jessica's First Kiss. 1997. (Sweet Valley Twins Super Edition Ser.: No. 8). 192p. (gr. 3-7). (J). pap. 3.99 (*0-553-54290-7*); pap. text 3.99 o.s.i (*0-553-48392-7*) Random Hse. Children's Bks. (Sweet Valley).

—Jessica's Secret Friend. 1997. (Sweet Valley Kids Ser.: No. 71). 96p. (gr. 1-3). pap. text 3.50 o.s.i (*0-553-48338-2*, Sweet Valley) Random Hse. Children's Bks.

—Jessica's Secret Love. 1994. (Sweet Valley High Ser.: No. 107). 208p. (YA). (gr. 7 up). mass mkt. 3.50 o.s.i (*0-553-56229-0*) Bantam Bks.

—Keepin' It Real. 2000. (Sweet Valley Junior High Ser.: No. 16). 160p. (gr. 3-7). pap. text 4.50 o.s.i (*0-553-48704-3*, Sweet Valley) Random Hse. Children's Bks.

—Living Together. 1999. (Sweet Valley University Ser.: No. 51). 240p. (gr. 9 up). mass mkt. 4.50 o.s.i (*0-553-49271-3*) Bantam Bks.

—Love & Murder. 1998. (Sweet Valley University Thriller Edition Ser.: No. 11). 288p. (gr. 7 up). mass mkt. 4.50 o.s.i (*0-553-49225-X*, Sweet Valley) Random Hse. Children's Bks.

—Love Letters. 1985. (Sweet Valley High Ser.: No. 17). (YA). (gr. 7 up). mass mkt. 2.50 o.s.i (*0-553-24723-9*);Vol. 17. 160p. mass mkt. 2.75 o.s.i (*0-553-26883-X*) Bantam Bks.

—Love Letters for Sale. 1992. (Sweet Valley High Ser.: No. 88). 160p. (YA). (gr. 7 up). mass mkt. 3.25 o.s.i (*0-553-29234-X*) Bantam Bks.

—Love, Lies & Jessica Wakefield. 1993. (Sweet Valley University Ser.: No. 2). 240p. (YA). (gr. 7 up). mass mkt. 4.50 o.s.i (*0-553-56306-8*) Bantam Bks.

—The Love of Her Life. 1994. (Sweet Valley University Ser.: No. 6). 240p. (gr. 7 up). mass mkt. 3.99 o.s.i (*0-553-56310-6*) Bantam Bks.

—Loving. 1985. (Caitlin Ser.: No. 1). 208p. (Orig.). (YA). (gr. 7-12). mass mkt. 2.95 o.s.i (*0-553-24716-6*) Bantam Bks.

—Memories. 1985. (Sweet Valley High Ser.: No. 24). 160p. (YA). (gr. 7 up). mass mkt. 3.99 o.s.i (*0-553-27492-9*) Bantam Bks.

—My Best Friend's Boyfriend. 1992. (Sweet Valley High Ser.: No. 87). 160p. (YA). (gr. 7 up). mass mkt. 3.25 o.s.i (*0-553-29233-1*) Bantam Bks.

—My Perfect Guy. 2000. (Sweet Valley Junior High Ser.: No. 14). 176p. (gr. 3-7). pap. text 4.50 (*0-553-48702-7*, Sweet Valley) Random Hse. Children's Bks.

—A Night to Remember. 1993. (Sweet Valley High Magna Edition Ser.). 352p. (YA). (gr. 7 up). mass mkt. 4.99 o.s.i (*0-553-29309-5*) Bantam Bks.

—On My Own. 2000. (Sweet Valley High Senior Year Ser.: No. 15). 192p. (gr. 7 up). mass mkt. 4.50 o.s.i (*0-553-49314-0*, Dell Books for Young Readers) Random Hse. Children's Bks.

—The One that Got Away. 1999. (Sweet Valley High Senior Year Ser.: No. 9). 192p. (gr. 7 up). mass mkt. 4.50 o.s.i (*0-553-49281-0*) Bantam Bks.

—One 2 Many. 1999. (Sweet Valley Junior High Ser.: No. 2). 144p. (gr. 3-7). pap. text 4.50 (*0-553-48604-7*, Dell Books for Young Readers) Random Hse. Children's Bks.

—Operation Love Match. 1994. (Sweet Valley High Ser.: No. 103). 208p. (gr. 7 up). mass mkt. 3.99 o.s.i (*0-553-29860-7*) Bantam Bks.

—The Perfect Girl. 1991. (Sweet Valley High Ser.: No. 74). 144p. (YA). (gr. 7 up). mass mkt. 3.25 o.s.i (*0-553-28901-2*) Bantam Bks.

—Perfect Summer. 1985. (Sweet Valley High Super Edition Ser.). 256p. (YA). (gr. 7 up). mass mkt. 4.50 o.s.i (*0-553-25072-8*) Bantam Bks.

—Playing with Fire. 1984. (Sweet Valley High Ser.: No. 3). 160p. (YA). (gr. 7 up). mass mkt. 3.99 o.s.i (*0-553-27669-7*) Bantam Bks.

—Regina's Legacy. 1991. (Sweet Valley High Ser.: No. 73). 160p. (YA). (gr. 7 up). mass mkt. 3.25 o.s.i (*0-553-28863-6*) Bantam Bks.

—S. S. Heartbreak. 1995. (Sweet Valley University Ser.: No. 13). 240p. (gr. 7 up). mass mkt. 4.50 o.s.i (*0-553-56692-X*) Bantam Bks.

—Secret Admirer. 1987. (Sweet Valley High Ser.: No. 39). (Illus.). (YA). (gr. 7 up). mass mkt. 3.95 (*0-553-16777-4*, Dell Books for Young Readers) Random Hse. Children's Bks.

—Secrets. 1984. (Sweet Valley High Ser.: No. 2). 128p. (gr. 7 up). mass mkt. 3.99 o.s.i (*0-553-27578-X*) Bantam Bks.

—She Loves Me... Not. 2000. (Sweet Valley Junior High Ser.: No. 19). 160p. (gr. 3-7). pap. text 4.50 o.s.i (*0-553-48721-3*, Sweet Valley) Random Hse. Children's Bks.

—Shipboard Wedding. 1995. (Sweet Valley University Ser.: No. 14). 240p. (YA). (gr. 7 up). mass mkt. 4.50 o.s.i (*0-553-56693-8*) Bantam Bks.

—Showdown. 1985. (Sweet Valley High Ser.: No. 19). 160p. (YA). (gr. 7 up). mass mkt. 2.95 o.s.i (*0-553-27589-5*) Bantam Bks.

—Soulmates. 1999. (Sweet Valley Junior High Ser.: No. 3). 160p. (gr. 3-7). pap. text 4.50 (*0-553-48605-5*, Dell Books for Young Readers) Random Hse. Children's Bks.

—Split Decision. 2000. (Sweet Valley High Senior Year Ser.: No. 14). 192p. (gr. 7 up). mass mkt. 4.50 o.s.i (*0-553-49313-2*, Sweet Valley) Random Hse. Children's Bks.

—Starting Over. 1986. (Sweet Valley High Ser.: No. 33). 160p. (Orig.). (YA). (gr. 7 up). mass mkt. 2.95 o.s.i (*0-553-27491-0*) Bantam Bks.

—Steven's Big Crush. 1996. (Sweet Valley Kids Ser.: No. 65). 96p. (gr. 1-3). pap. text 3.50 o.s.i (*0-553-48219-X*) Bantam Bks.

—Taking Sides. 1986. (Sweet Valley High Ser.: No. 31). 144p. (YA). (gr. 7 up). mass mkt. 3.25 o.s.i (*0-553-27490-2*) Bantam Bks.

—Three Days, Two Nights. 2000. (Sweet Valley Junior High Ser.: No. 13). 176p. (gr. 3-7). pap. text 4.50 o.s.i (*0-553-48701-9*, Sweet Valley) Random Hse. Children's Bks.

—Three Girls & a Guy. 2000. (Sweet Valley High Senior Year Ser.: No. 16). 192p. (gr. 7 up). mass mkt. 4.50 o.s.i (*0-553-49315-9*, Sweet Valley) Random Hse. Children's Bks.

—Too Good to Be True, Vol. 11. 1984. (Sweet Valley High Ser.: No. 11). 592p. (YA). (gr. 7 up). mass mkt. 2.75 o.s.i (*0-553-26824-4*) Bantam Bks.

—Truth or Dare. 1999. (Sweet Valley University Ser.: No. 53). 240p. (gr. 9 up). mass mkt. 4.50 (*0-553-49273-X*) Bantam Bks.

—Very Bad Things. 2000. (Sweet Valley University Thriller Edition Ser.: No. 17). 288p. (gr. 9 up). mass mkt. 4.99 o.s.i (*0-553-49311-6*, Sweet Valley) Random Hse. Children's Bks.

—The Wakefield Legacy: The Untold Story. 1992. (Sweet Valley Saga Ser.). 352p. (YA). (gr. 7 up). mass mkt. 4.50 o.s.i (*0-553-29794-5*, Starfire) Random Hse. Children's Bks.

—What You Don't Know. 2000. (Sweet Valley Junior High Ser.: No. 22). (Illus.). 160p. (gr. 3-7). pap. text 4.50 (*0-553-48724-8*, Sweet Valley) Random Hse. Children's Bks.

—Wrong Kind of Girl. 1984. (Sweet Valley High Ser.: No. 10). 144p. (YA). (gr. 7 up). mass mkt. 3.99 o.s.i (*0-553-27668-9*) Bantam Bks.

—Your Basic Nightmare. 1999. (Sweet Valley High Senior Year Ser.: No. 6). 192p. (gr. 7 up). mass mkt. 4.50 (*0-553-48612-8*, Dell Books for Young Readers) Random Hse. Children's Bks.

Pascal, Francine & John, Laurie. Sweet Kiss of Summer. 1996. (Sweet Valley University Ser.: No. 23). 240p. (gr. 7 up). mass mkt. 3.99 o.s.i (*0-553-56707-1*, Sweet Valley) Random Hse. Children's Bks.

Paton Walsh, Jill. Torch, RS. 1988. 176p. (YA). (gr. 7 up). 15.00 o.p. (*0-374-37684-0*, Farrar, Straus & Giroux (BYR)) Farrar, Straus & Giroux.

Patterson, Sarah. The Distant Summer. 1976. 6.95 o.s.i (*0-671-22257-0*, Simon & Schuster) Simon & Schuster.

—The Distant Summer. l.t. ed. 1978. (Ulverscroft Large Print Ser.). 29.99 o.p. (*0-7089-0134-4*, Ulverscroft) Thorpe, F. A. Pubs. GBR. *Dist:* Ulverscroft Large Print Bks., Ltd., Ulverscroft Large Print Canada, Ltd.

Paulsen, Gary. The Night the White Deer Died. 1978. (J). 6.95 o.p. (*0-525-66616-8*, Dutton Children's Bks.) Penguin Putnam Bks. for Young Readers.

Payne, Marvin. Love & Oranges. 1988. (Keepsake Paperbacks Ser.). 62p. reprint ed. pap. 3.95 o.p. (*0-88494-402-6*, Bookcraft, Inc.) Deseret Bk. Co.

—Love & Oranges. 2nd ed. 1988. 64p. (YA). (gr. 9 up). reprint ed. pap. 3.95 o.p. (*0-929985-08-7*) Jackman Publishing.

Pearson, Mary E. Scribbler of Dreams. 240p. (YA). (gr. 7 up). 2002. pap. 5.95 (*0-15-204569-4*, Harcourt Paperbacks); 2001. (Illus.). 17.00 (*0-15-202320-8*) Harcourt Children's Bks.

Peart, Jane. Quest for Lasting Love. 1990. (Orphan Train West Ser.). 192p. (gr. 10 up). pap. 7.99 o.p. (*0-8007-5372-0*) Revell, Fleming H. Co.

Peck, Robert Newton. Soup in Love. 1993. 128p. (J). (gr. 4-7). pap. 3.50 o.s.i (*0-440-40755-9*) Dell Publishing.

—Soup in Love. 1992. (J). 17.95 (*0-385-30703-9*) Doubleday Publishing.

Pellowski, Michael. Double Trouble Dream Date. 2nd ed. 1997. (Illus.). 64p. (J). (gr. 4-6). reprint ed. pap. 3.99 (*0-87406-829-0*, Willowisp Pr.) Darby Creek Publishing.

Pellowski, Michael J. Bad News Boyfriend, No. 2. 1991. (Riverdale High Ser.). (Illus.). 128p. (YA). (gr. 4-8). pap. 2.99 (*1-56282-108-3*) Hyperion Bks. for Children.

—The Big Breakup, No. 5. 1992. (Riverdale High Ser.). (Illus.). 128p. (J). (gr. 4-8). pap. 2.99 o.p. (*1-56282-147-4*) Hyperion Bks. for Children.

—It's First Love, Jughead Jones, No. 4. 1991. (Riverdale High Ser.). (Illus.). 128p. (J). (gr. 4-8). pap. 2.99 o.p. (*1-56282-110-5*) Hyperion Bks. for Children.

Perl, Lila. Fat Glenda's Summer Romance. 1988. 176p. (J). (gr. 5-8). pap. (*0-671-64857-8*, Simon Pulse) Simon & Schuster Children's Publishing.

Perry Moore, Stephanie. Surrendered Heart: Living for God Is Challenging. 2002. (Payton Skky Ser.: Vol. 5). 176p. (J). pap. 8.99 (*0-8024-4240-4*) Moody Pr.

Petersen, P. J. The Boll Weevil Express. 1984. (Young Love Romance Ser.). 92p. (J). (gr. 6 up). mass mkt. 2.50 o.s.i (*0-440-91040-4*, Laurel Leaf) Random Hse. Children's Bks.

Pevsner, Stella. I'll Always Remember You . . . Maybe. 001. 1981. 192p. (J). (gr. 6 up). 12.95 o.p. (*0-395-31024-5*, Clarion Bks.) Houghton Mifflin Co. Trade & Reference Div.

Peyton, K. M. The Edge of the Cloud. 1989. (Illus.). 192p. (YA). (gr. 7 up). pap. 3.99 o.p. (*0-14-030905-5*, Puffin Bks.) Penguin Putnam Bks. for Young Readers.

—Flambards. 1989. (ALA Notable Bk.). (Illus.). 224p. (YA). (gr. 7 up). pap. 3.95 o.p. (*0-14-034153-6*, Puffin Bks.) Penguin Putnam Bks. for Young Readers.

—Flambards in Summer. 1989. (Flambards Ser.). (Illus.). 208p. (YA). (gr. 7 up). pap. 3.95 o.p. (*0-14-034154-4*, Puffin Bks.) Penguin Putnam Bks. for Young Readers.

Pfeffer, Susan Beth. The Year Without Michael. 2003. 176p. (YA). (gr. 7). 9.95 (*0-385-73120-5*, Delacorte Bks. for Young Readers); lib. bdg. 11.99 (*0-385-90150-X*) Random Hse. Children's Bks.

—The Year Without Michael. 1988. (Bantam Starfire Bks.). (J). 10.55 (*0-606-03959-7*) Turtleback Bks.

Phelps, Lauren M. Boyfriend Blues. 1995. (Sweet Dreams Ser.: No. 224). 160p. (YA). pap. 3.50 o.s.i (*0-553-56678-4*) Bantam Bks.

—The News Is Love. 1992. (Sweet Dreams Ser.: No. 197). 144p. (YA). pap. 2.99 o.s.i (*0-553-29459-8*) Bantam Bks.

Pierce, David. Forever Yours. 1994. 240p. (YA). mass mkt. 3.50 o.p. (*0-06-106174-3*, HarperTorch) Morrow/Avon.

Pike, Christopher, pseud. Gimme a Kiss. 1988. (J). 10.55 (*0-606-03792-6*) Turtleback Bks.

—See You Later. (J). 1998. 240p. (gr. 7-12). pap. 4.50 (*0-671-02025-0*); 1990. mass mkt. 2.95 (*0-671-67657-1*) Simon & Schuster Children's Publishing. (Simon Pulse).

—See You Later. MacDonald, Patricia, ed. 1991. 240p. (YA). (gr. 8 up). reprint ed. pap. 3.99 (*0-671-74390-2*, Simon Pulse) Simon & Schuster Children's Publishing.

—See You Later. 1990. (J). 10.55 (*0-606-04535-X*) Turtleback Bks.

Pines, Nancy. Spotlight on Love. 1984. (Sweet Dreams Ser.: No. 55). 151p. (gr. 6 up). pap. text 2.25 o.p. (*0-553-23964-3*) Bantam Bks.

Pitt, Jane. Secret Hearts. 1986. (Heartlines Ser.: No. 2). (Orig.). (J). (gr. 6 up). mass mkt. 2.50 o.s.i (*0-440-97722-3*, Laurel Leaf) Random Hse. Children's Bks.

Plummer, Louise. Unlikely Romance. 1995. (J). 21.95 (*0-385-31002-1*, Dell Books for Young Readers) Random Hse. Children's Bks.

—The Unlikely Romance of Kate Bjorkman. 1997. 192p. (YA). pap. 15.00 (*0-375-89521-3*, Laurel Leaf); (gr. 7-12). mass mkt. 4.50 o.s.i (*0-440-22704-6*, Dell Books for Young Readers) Random Hse. Children's Bks.

—The Unlikely Romance of Kate Bjorkman. 1997. (J). 10.55 (*0-606-12838-7*) Turtleback Bks.

Pohlmann, Lillian. The Unsuitable Behavior of America Martin. 1976. (J). 6.95 o.p. (*0-664-32603-X*) Westminster John Knox Pr.

Polcovar, Jane. Hey, Good Looking! 1985. (Sweet Dreams Ser.: No. 82). 144p. (J). (gr. 6 up). pap. 2.25 o.s.i (*0-553-24383-7*) Bantam Bks.

Pollowitz, Melinda. Princess Amy. 1981. (Sweet Dreams Ser.). (gr. 11 up). pap. 1.95 o.p. (*0-553-14020-5*) Bantam Bks.

Porter-Gaylord, Laurel. I Love My Mommy Because. 2004. (Illus.). 20p. bds. 6.99 (*0-525-47247-9*, Dutton Children's Bks.) Penguin Putnam Bks. for Young Readers.

Powers, Christine. Love Is a Rainbow. 1999. (Leap Frog Lift-A-Flap Ser.). (Illus.). (J). (*0-7853-3370-3*) Publications International, Ltd.

Powers, Eileen E. Love on the Range. 1986. (Swept Away Ser.: No. 3). 208p. (Orig.). (YA). (gr. 6-9). pap. 2.50 o.p. (*0-380-75130-5*, Avon Bks.) Morrow/Avon.

Presser, Arlynn. Love Changes Everything. 1995. (Love Stories Ser.). 176p. (Orig.). (YA). (gr. 7-12). mass mkt. 3.99 o.s.i (*0-553-56665-2*, Dell Books for Young Readers) Random Hse. Children's Bks.

Prestine, Joan S. Love Me Anyway. 1988. (My Special Feelings Ser.). (Illus.). 24p. (J). (gr. 5-8). 2.50 o.p. (*0-8431-4232-4*, Price Stern Sloan) Penguin Putnam Bks. for Young Readers.

Pryor, Bonnie. Rats, Spiders & Love. 1988. pap. o.p. (*0-440-80080-3*) Dell Publishing.

—Rats, Spiders & Love. 1986. (Illus.). 128p. (J). (gr. 4-6). 16.00 o.p. (*0-688-05867-1*, Morrow, William & Co.) Morrow/Avon.

Quin-Harkin, Janet. Best Friends Forever. 1986. (Sweet Dreams Ser.: No. 6). 176p. (Orig.). (YA). (gr. 7-12). mass mkt. 2.50 o.s.i (*0-553-26111-8*) Bantam Bks.

—Dream Come True, No. 16. 1988. (Sugar & Spice Ser.: No. 16). (YA). (gr. 6 up). mass mkt. 2.95 o.s.i (*0-8041-0334-8*, Ivy Bks.) Ballantine Bks.

—Exchange of Hearts. 1984. (Sweet Dreams Ser.: No. 61). 192p. pap. 2.25 o.p. (*0-553-24056-0*) Bantam Bks.

—Graduation Day. 1992. (Senior Year Ser.: No. 4). 192p. (YA). mass mkt. 3.50 o.p. (*0-06-106096-8*, HarperTorch) Morrow/Avon.

—Great Boy Chase. 1985. (J). mass mkt. 2.25 o.s.i (*0-553-25071-X*, Dell Books for Young Readers) Random Hse. Children's Bks.

—Growing Pains. 1986. (On Our Own Ser.: No. 5). 176p. (Orig.). (YA). (gr. 6 up). mass mkt. 2.50 o.s.i (*0-553-26034-0*) Bantam Bks.

—Home Sweet Home, 1988. (Sugar & Spice Ser.: No. 15). (YA). (gr. 6 up). mass mkt. 2.95 o.s.i (*0-8041-0333-X*, Ivy Bks.) Ballantine Bks.

—Love Potion. 1999. (Enchanted Hearts Ser.: No. 4). (Illus.). 192p. (YA). (gr. 7 up). pap. 4.50 (*0-380-80122-1*, Avon Bks.) Morrow/Avon.

—Love Potion. 1999. (Enchanted Hearts Ser.). (Illus.). (J). 10.55 (*0-606-17966-6*) Turtleback Bks.

—Lovebirds: International Edition. 1994. (YA). pap. 3.50 (*0-553-24181-8*) Bantam Bks.

—My Phantom Love. 1992. (Changes Romance Ser.: No. 1). 224p. (YA). (gr. 7 up). mass mkt. 3.50 o.p. (*0-06-106770-9*, HarperTorch) Morrow/Avon.

—My Secret Love. 1986. (Sweet Dreams Ser.: No. 1). 224p. (Orig.). (YA). (gr. 7-12). mass mkt. 2.95 o.s.i (*0-553-25884-2*) Bantam Bks.

—Never Say Good-Bye. 1987. (Sweet Dreams Special Ser.: No. 5). 240p. (Orig.). pap. 2.95 o.s.i (*0-553-26702-7*) Bantam Bks.

—On My Own. 1992. (Changes Romance Ser.: No. 10). 240p. (YA). mass mkt. 3.50 o.p. (*0-06-106722-9*, HarperTorch) Morrow/Avon.

—One Hundred One Ways to Meet Mr. Right. 1985. (Sweet Dreams Ser.: No. 89). 176p. (Orig.). (J). (gr. 6 up). mass mkt. 2.25 o.s.i (*0-553-24946-0*) Bantam Bks.

—Out of Love. 1986. (On Our Own Ser.: No. 3). 208p. (Orig.). (YA). (gr. 6 up). mass mkt. 2.50 o.s.i (*0-553-25937-7*) Bantam Bks.

—The Trouble with Toni. 1986. (Sweet Dreams Ser.: No. 2). 192p. (Orig.). (YA). (gr. 6 up). mass mkt. 2.50 o.s.i (*0-553-25724-2*) Bantam Bks.

—Wanted: Date for Saturday Night. 1986. 160p. (YA). 2.50 o.p. (*0-425-08448-5*, Berkley/Pacer) Berkley Publishing Group.

—Who Do You Love? 1996. (Love Stories Ser.). 192p. (gr. 7-12). mass mkt. 4.50 o.s.i (*0-553-57043-9*) Bantam Bks.

Rabinowich, Ellen. Underneath I'm Different. 1984. (Young Love Romance Ser.). 192p. (gr. 5 up). pap. 2.50 o.p. (*0-440-98850-0*) Dell Publishing.

Raine, Allison. Sweet Sixteen. 2000. (Love Stories Super Edition Ser.). 224p. (YA). (gr. 7-12). mass mkt. 4.99 o.s.i (*0-553-49325-6*, Dell Books for Young Readers) Random Hse. Children's Bks.

Raintree Steck-Vaughn Staff. Jane Eyre, 5 vols., Set. 1991. (Short Classics Ser.). (Illus.). (J). pap. 32.69 (*0-8114-6966-2*) Raintree Pubs.

Rand, Suzanne. The Boy She Left Behind. 1985. (Sweet Dreams Ser.: No. 85). 192p. (Orig.). (J). (gr. 6). mass mkt. 2.25 o.s.i (*0-553-24890-1*) Bantam Bks.

—Laurie's Song. 1981. (Sweet Dreams Ser.). (gr. 11 up). pap. 2.25 o.p. (*0-553-24318-7*) Bantam Bks.

Random House Staff. The Little Book of Hugs. 2002. 12p. (J). bds. 4.99 (*0-375-82396-4*, Random Hse. Bks. for Young Readers) Random Hse. Children's Bks.

—The Little Book of Kisses. 2002. 12p. (J). bds. 4.99 (*0-375-82395-6*, Random Hse. Bks. for Young Readers) Random Hse. Children's Bks.

Raney, Gail T. Another to Love. 1983. (Illus.). 48p. (J). 12.95 o.p. (*0-938934-06-6*); pap. 7.95 o.p. (*0-938934-05-8*) LCN, Inc.

Ransom, Candice F. Amanda, No. 1. 1984. 368p. (J). (gr. 7 up). pap. 2.95 o.p. (*0-590-32774-7*) Scholastic, Inc.

—Kathleen, No. 8. 1985. 368p. (Orig.). (J). (gr. 7 up). pap. 2.95 o.p. (*0-590-33240-6*) Scholastic, Inc.

—The Love Charm. 1990. 128p. (Orig.). (J). (gr. 4-8). pap. 2.95 o.p. (*0-87406-522-4*) Darby Creek Publishing.

Rathbun, Carolyn R. Sara Bear's Surprise. 1993. (Land of Pleasant Dreams Ser.). (Illus.). (Orig.). (J). (ps). 12.95 (*0-9634808-0-4*); pap. 4.50 (*0-9634808-1-2*) Endless Love Productions, Inc.

Raymond, Patrick. Daniel & Esther. 1990. 176p. (YA). (gr. 7 up). lib. bdg. 13.95 o.s.i (*0-689-50504-3*, McElderry, Margaret K.) Simon & Schuster Children's Publishing.

Reber, Deborah. Blue's Valentine's Day. 2000. (Blue's Clues Ser.). (Illus.). 16p. (J). (ps-k). pap. 3.99 (*0-689-83062-9*, Simon Spotlight/Nickelodeon) Simon & Schuster Children's Publishing.

Redish, Jane. Promise Me Love. 1986. (Sweet Dreams Ser.: No. 115). 176p. (Orig.). (YA). (gr. 7-12). mass mkt. 2.50 o.s.i (*0-553-26158-4*) Bantam Bks.

Rees, David. Quintin's Man. 1979. (J). 6.95 o.p. (*0-525-66593-5*, Dutton Children's Bks.) Penguin Putnam Bks. for Young Readers.

Rees, Elizabeth M. Last Dance. 1999. (Heart Beats Ser.: No. 6). 224p. (J). (gr. 4-8). pap. 3.99 (*0-689-81953-6*, Simon Pulse) Simon & Schuster Children's Publishing.

Reisfeld, Randi. All You Need Is a Love Spell. 1998. (Sabrina, the Teenage Witch Ser.: No. 7). 176p. (YA). (gr. 5 up). pap. 4.99 (*0-671-01695-4*, Simon Pulse) Simon & Schuster Children's Publishing.

Reit, Ann. The Bet. 1986. 148p. (Orig.). (J). (gr. 7 up). pap. 2.50 o.p. (*0-590-41862-9*, Scholastic Paperbacks) Scholastic, Inc.

—The First Time. 1986. (J). (gr. 5 up). mass mkt. 2.50 o.s.i (*0-440-92560-6*, Laurel Leaf) Random Hse. Children's Bks.

—Love at First Sight. 1987. 192p. (Orig.). (YA). (gr. 7 up). pap. 2.50 o.p. (*0-590-40051-7*, Scholastic Paperbacks) Scholastic, Inc.

Resciniti, Angelo G. Vanessa's First Love. 1987. (Impressions Ser.). 96p. (Orig.). (J). (gr. 5-8). pap. 2.25 o.p. (*0-87406-248-9*) Darby Creek Publishing.

Reynolds, Anne. Jeff's New Girl. 1984. (Magic Moments Ser.). 160p. (J). (gr. 7 up). mass mkt. 2.25 o.p. (*0-451-13290-4*, Signet Bks.) NAL.

Reynolds, Elizabeth. The Perfect Boy. 1986. (Sweet Dreams Ser.: No. 105). 176p. (Orig.). (YA). (gr. 7-12). mass mkt. 2.25 o.s.i (*0-553-25469-3*) Bantam Bks.

—The Perfect Boy. 1986. (Orig.). (J). mass mkt. 2.50 o.s.i (*0-553-27052-4*, Dell Books for Young Readers) Random Hse. Children's Bks.

—Stolen Kisses. 1986. (Sweet Dreams Ser.: No. 111). 144p. (Orig.). (YA). (gr. 7-12). mass mkt. 2.50 o.s.i (*0-553-25726-9*) Bantam Bks.

Rice, Bebe Faas. Love You to Death. 1994. 224p. (J). mass mkt. 3.50 o.p. (*0-06-106184-0*, HarperTorch) Morrow/Avon.

Richardson, Arleta. Grandma's Attic: Wedding Bells Ahead. (Grandma's Attic Ser.). 156p. (J). (gr. 3-7). pap. 6.99 (*0-7814-3292-8*) Cook Communications Ministries.

Ridley, Philip. Dreamboat Zing. 1997. (Illus.). 64p. (J). (ps-3). pap. 7.95 (*0-14-037282-2*) Penguin Bks., Ltd. GBR. *Dist:* Trafalgar Square.

Riley, Eugenia. Remember Me, Love? 1985. (Loveswept Ser.: No. 102). 208p. pap. 2.25 o.p. (*0-553-21713-5*) Bantam Bks.

Roberts, Laura Peyton. Dream On. 2000. (Clearwater Crossing Ser.: No. 13). 224p. (gr. 7-8). mass mkt. 3.99 o.s.i (*0-553-49298-5*, Dell Books for Young Readers) Random Hse. Children's Bks.

—Heart & Soul. 1998. (Clearwater Crossing Ser.: No. 3). (YA). (gr. 5-8). 10.04 (*0-606-13280-5*) Turtleback Bks.

—Just Friends. 1998. (Clearwater Crossing Ser.: No. 5). 224p. (gr. 5-8). mass mkt. 3.99 o.s.i (*0-553-49258-6*, Dell Books for Young Readers) Random Hse. Children's Bks.

—Just Friends. 1998. (Clearwater Crossing Ser.: 5). 10.04 (*0-606-16378-6*) Turtleback Bks.

—Keep the Faith. 1998. (Clearwater Crossing Ser.: No. 6). 240p. (gr. 5-8). mass mkt. 3.99 o.s.i (*0-553-49259-4*, Dell Books for Young Readers) Random Hse. Children's Bks.

—Love Hurts. 2000. (Clearwater Crossing Ser.: No. 14). 224p. (gr. 7-8). mass mkt. 3.99 o.s.i (*0-553-49299-3*, Dell Books for Young Readers) Random Hse. Children's Bks.

—More Than This. 1999. (Clearwater Crossing Ser.: No. 11). 224p. (gr. 7-8). mass mkt. 3.99 o.s.i (*0-553-49296-9*) Bantam Bks.

—Promises, Promises. 1998. (Clearwater Crossing Ser.: No. 4). 224p. (gr. 5-8). mass mkt. 4.50 o.s.i (*0-553-57127-3*, Dell Books for Young Readers) Random Hse. Children's Bks.

—Promises, Promises. 1998. (Clearwater Crossing Ser.: No. 4). (YA). (gr. 5-8). 10.04 (*0-606-13281-3*) Turtleback Bks.

Robertson, C. Letters of a Lovestruck Teen. 1999. 184p. pap. (*0-09-940252-1*) Random Hse. of Canada, Ltd. CAN. *Dist:* Random Hse., Inc.

—Letters of a Lovestruck Teenager. 1992. (J). pap. o.p. (*0-09-971320-9*) Random Hse. of Canada, Ltd. CAN. *Dist:* Random Hse., Inc.

Robinson, Barbara. Temporary Times, Temporary Places. 1982. (Charlotte Zolotow Bk.). 128p. (YA). (gr. 7 up). 9.95 (*0-06-025039-9*); lib. bdg. 11.89 o.p. (*0-06-025042-9*) HarperCollins Children's Bk. Group.

Rock, Gail. Addie & the King of Hearts. 1977. (gr. 4-6). pap. 1.75 o.p. (*0-553-15063-4*, 15063-4) Bantam Bks.

—Addie & the King of Hearts. 1976. (Illus.). 96p. (J). (gr. 4-6). 4.95 o.p. (*0-394-83228-0*); 5.99 o.s.i (*0-394-93228-5*) Random Hse. Children's Bks. (Knopf Bks. for Young Readers).

Rogers, Kayron Upton. Oh Little Speck of Love, So Deep in My Heart. 2000. 36p. (J). pap. 7.95 (*1-57921-321-9*) WinePress Publishing.

Roos, Stephen. Confessions of a Wayward Preppie. 1986. 144p. (J). (gr. 7 up). 13.95 o.s.i (*0-385-29454-9*, Delacorte Pr.) Dell Publishing.

—Love Me, Love My. 1991. (J). o.s.i (*0-385-30551-6*, Dell Books for Young Readers) Random Hse. Children's Bks.

—My Secret Admirer. 1985. (Illus.). 128p. (J). (gr. k-12). pap. 2.75 o.s.i (*0-440-45950-8*, Yearling) Random Hse. Children's Bks.

Rosen, Winifred. Three Romances: Love Stories from Camelot Retold. 1981. (Illus.). 128p. (YA). (gr. 7 up). lib. bdg. 8.95 o.p. (*0-394-84509-9*); lib. bdg. 8.99 o.p. (*0-394-94509-3*) Random Hse. Children's Bks. (Knopf Bks. for Young Readers).

Rosenberg, Liz. Carousel. 1998. 12.15 (*0-606-13244-9*) Turtleback Bks.

Ross, Dave. A Book of Hugs. (Illus.). (J). 2001. 30p. pap. 6.95 (*0-06-000273-5*, Harper Festival); 1991. 32p. (gr. 2 up). reprint ed. mass mkt. 3.95 (*0-06-107418-7*) HarperCollins Children's Bk. Group.

—A Book of Kisses. (J). 2001. (Illus.). 16p. pap. 6.95 (*0-06-000274-3*, Harper Festival); 2000. 40p. pap. 4.95 (*0-06-443524-5*); 2000. (Illus.). 40p. 13.95 (*0-06-028169-3*) HarperCollins Children's Bk. Group.

Ross, Diana. I Love My Love with an A. 1972. (Illus.). 32p. (J). (ps-5). o.p. (*0-571-09340-X*) Faber & Faber Ltd.

Rostand, Edmond. Cyrano de Bergerac. 8.97 (*0-673-58340-6*) Addison-Wesley Longman, Inc.

—Cyrano de Bergerac. 1999. 11.95 (*1-56137-622-1*) Novel Units, Inc.

Roth, Susan L. Mi Amor Por Ti/My Love for You. 2003. (ENG & SPA.). 24p. (J). bds. 5.99 (*0-8037-2944-8*, Dial Bks. for Young Readers) Penguin Putnam Bks. for Young Readers.

—My Love for You. Serlin, Andra, ed. 1999. (Illus.). 24p. (J). (ps). bds. 5.99 (*0-8037-2352-0*, Dial Bks. for Young Readers) Penguin Putnam Bks. for Young Readers.

Roth, Susan L., illus. & text. My Love for You All Year Round. 2003. 32p. (J). 14.99 (*0-8037-2796-8*, Dial Bks. for Young Readers) Penguin Putnam Bks. for Young Readers.

Rotsler, William. Joanie Loves Chachi: A Test of Hearts, No. 2. Schneider, Meg F., ed. 1982. 160p. (Orig.). (J). (gr. 3-7). pap. 2.85 o.s.i (*0-671-46011-0*, Simon & Schuster Children's Publishing) Simon & Schuster Children's Publishing.

—Joanie Loves Chachi: Secrets, No. 1. Barish, Wendy, ed. 1982. 160p. (J). (gr. 3-7). pap. 2.85 o.s.i (*0-671-46010-2*, Simon & Schuster Children's Publishing) Simon & Schuster Children's Publishing.

Rue, Nancy. Friends Don't Let Friends Date Jason. 1999. (Raise the Flag Ser.: Bk. 5). 224p. (YA). (gr. 7-12). pap. 6.95 o.s.i (*1-57856-087-X*) WaterBrook Pr.

Rue, Nancy N. Stop in the Name of Love. Rosen, Roger, ed. 1988. (Flipside Fiction Ser.). (YA). (gr. 7-12). lib. bdg. 12.95 o.p. (*0-8239-0794-5*) Rosen Publishing Group, Inc., The.

Rusackas, Francesca. Daddy All Day Long. Burris, Priscilla, tr. & illus. by. 2004. 32p. (J). 12.99 (*0-06-050284-3*); lib. bdg. 13.89 (*0-06-050285-1*) HarperCollins Pubs.

Rushton, Rosie. What a Week to Fall in Love. (Illus.). 144p. (J). pap. 7.95 (*0-14-038760-9*) Penguin Bks., Ltd. GBR. *Dist:* Trafalgar Square.

Ryan, Mary E. Dance a Step Closer. 1988. (J). mass mkt. 2.95 o.s.i (*0-440-20127-6*, Laurel Leaf) Random Hse. Children's Bks.

Ryce, C. J. Napsha, the Miracle Dragon. 1997. (Illus.). 64p. (Orig.). (J). (gr. 1-5). per. 13.95 (*0-9653695-2-8*) Spellbound Pubns.

Ryder. Won't You Be My Kissaroo. 2004. (Illus.). 32p. 16.00 (*0-15-202641-X*, Gulliver Books) Harcourt Children's Bks. CAN. *Dist:* Harcourt Trade Pubs.

Ryland, Cynthia. Couple of Kooks: And Other Stories about Love. 1992. 112p. (YA). mass mkt. 3.50 o.s.i (*0-440-21210-3*) Dell Publishing.

Rylant, Cynthia. A Couple of Kooks: And Other Stories about Love. 1990. 112p. (gr. 7 up). (J). mass mkt. 17.99 o.p. (*0-531-08500-7*); (YA). pap. 16.95 (*0-531-05900-6*) Scholastic, Inc. (Orchard Bks.).

—A Kindness. 1988. 128p. (YA). (gr. 7 up). 15.95 o.p. (*0-531-05767-4*); mass mkt. 15.99 o.p. (*0-531-08367-5*) Scholastic, Inc. (Orchard Bks.).

Saal, Jocelyn & Burman, Margaret. On Thin Ice. 1983. (Sweet Dreams Ser.). 181p. (J). (gr. 6 up). pap. 1.95 o.s.i (*0-553-17070-8*) Bantam Bks.

Sachs, Marilyn. Baby Sister. 1986. (J). (gr. 7-11). 13.95 o.p. (*0-525-44213-8*, Dutton Children's Bks.) Penguin Putnam Bks. for Young Readers.

—Fourteen. 1985. 128p. (J). (gr. 7 up). pap. 2.95 (*0-380-69842-0*, Avon Bks.) Morrow/Avon.

—Hello... Wrong Number. 1984. 96p. (J). (gr. 7 up). pap. 2.50 o.p. (*0-590-41570-0*, Scholastic Paperbacks) Scholastic, Inc.

Sadler, Mike. The Lonely Stranger. 1992. (Junior African Writers Ser.). (Illus.). 80p. (J). (gr. 4-7). pap. 4.99 (*0-7910-2922-0*) Chelsea Hse. Pubs.

Sage, Sheryl. Passionate Surrender. 1993. 384p. (Orig.). mass mkt. 4.50 (*0-380-76684-1*, Avon Bks.) Morrow/Avon.

Sainz, Frances. Carino. 1992. (Foundations Ser.). 23p. (J). (ps-1). pap. text 4.50 (*1-56843-094-9*) EMG Networks.

—Carino: Big Book. 1992. (Foundations Ser.). 23p. (J). (ps-1). pap. text 23.00 (*1-56843-047-7*) EMG Networks.

Sallis, Susan. Only Love. 1980. 256p. (YA). (gr. 7 up). lib. bdg. 12.89 o.p. (*0-06-025175-1*) HarperCollins Children's Bk. Group.

Sampson, Emma S. Miss Minerva & William Green Hill. 1992. 275p. (YA). reprint ed. lib. bdg. 21.95 (*0-89966-922-0*) Buccaneer Bks., Inc.

Sandberg, Rasemary. Great Boy Girl Stories. 2000. (*5-550-03094-2*) Chambers Harrap Pubs., Ltd.

Sanders, Louise. Knave of Hearts. 1993. (J). 12.95 o.p. (*0-89815-520-7*) Ten Speed Pr.

Sarasin, Jennifer. Spring Love. 1984. 240p. (Orig.). (J). (gr. 7 up). pap. 2.25 o.p. (*0-590-40345-1*) Scholastic, Inc.

Sargent, Dave. Say You Love Me. Bowen, Debbie, ed. 1998. (Illus.). 31p. (J). (gr. k-6). pap. 6.00 (*1-56763-130-4*); lib. bdg. 17.25 o.p. (*1-56763-129-0*) Ozark Publishing.

Savage, Deborah. Under a Different Sky. 1997. 288p. (YA). (gr. 7 up). tchr. ed. 16.00 (*0-395-77395-4*) Houghton Mifflin Co.

—Under a Different Sky. 1998. 288p. (J). (gr. 7 up). pap. 6.99 o.p. (*0-698-11697-6*, PaperStar) Penguin Putnam Bks. for Young Readers.

—Under a Different Sky. 1998. 12.04 (*0-606-16164-3*) Turtleback Bks.

Savitz, Harriet May. Summer's End. 1984. 160p. (J). (gr. 5-9). mass mkt. 2.25 o.p. (*0-451-13291-2*, Signet Bks.) NAL.

Saxon, Nancy & Saxon, Peter. Panky in Love. 1985. (Illus.). 168p. (J). (gr. 4-7). 12.95 o.p. (*0-689-31101-X*, Atheneum) Simon & Schuster Children's Publishing.

Scannell, Vernon. Love Shouts & Whispers. 1992. (Illus.). 64p. (J). (gr. k-3). 15.95 o.p. (*0-09-174365-6*) Hutchinson GBR. *Dist:* Trafalgar Square.

Scarbrough, Joyce. True Blue Forever. 2003. 310p. pap. 24.95 (*1-59129-993-4*) PublishAmerica, Inc.

Schertle, Alice. I Love You. 1924. (J). o.s.i (*0-688-15184-1*); lib. bdg. o.s.i (*0-688-15185-X*) HarperCollins Children's Bk. Group.

—When the Moon Is High. 2003. (Illus.). 32p. (J). lib. bdg. 16.89 (*0-688-15144-2*) HarperCollins Children's Bk. Group.

Schimel, Lawrence. Camelot Fantastic. 1998. 12.04 (*0-606-13242-2*) Turtleback Bks.

Schlessinger, Laura & Lambert, Martha L. Why Do You Love Me? 1999. (Illus.). 40p. (J). (ps-2). 15.95 (*0-06-027866-8*) HarperCollins Children's Bk. Group.

Schlessinger, Laura, et al. Why Do You Love Me? 2001. (Illus.). 40p. (J). (ps-2). pap. 5.99 (*0-06-443654-3*, Harper Trophy) HarperCollins Children's Bk. Group.

Schneider, Meg F. The Broken Heart. 1994. 128p. (YA). o.p. (*0-307-22603-4*) Whitman Publishing LLC.

—The Great Party Switch. 1994. (You Choose the Romance Ser.: Bk. 1). (Illus.). 128p. (J). (ps-3). o.p. (*0-307-22600-X*, Golden Bks.) Random Hse. Children's Bks.

—The New Girl. 1994. (You Choose the Romance Ser.: Bk. 3). (Illus.). 128p. (J). (ps-3). o.p. (*0-307-22602-6*, Golden Bks.) Random Hse. Children's Bks.

—Star Struck. 1994. (You Choose the Romance Ser.: Bk. 2). 128p. (YA). (*0-307-22601-8*) Whitman Publishing LLC.

Scholastic, Inc. Staff. 10 Things I Hate about You. 1999. (gr. 6-11). mass mkt. 4.99 (*0-439-08730-9*) Scholastic, Inc.

Schreiber, Ellen. Teenage Mermaid. 2003. 160p. (J). (gr. 4 up). 15.99 (*0-06-008204-6*); lib. bdg. 16.89 (*0-06-008205-4*) HarperCollins Pubs.

Schuler, Betty J. Heartthrob. 1995. (Sweet Dreams Ser.: No. 223). 160p. (YA). (gr. 6 up). pap. 3.50 o.p. (*0-553-56677-6*) Bantam Bks.

Schultz, Mary. Hand-Me-Down Heart, Vol. 134. 1987. (Sweet Dreams Ser.). 192p. (Orig.). (J). pap. 2.50 o.s.i (*0-553-26865-1*, Dell Books for Young Readers) Random Hse. Children's Bks.

Schulz, Charles M. You're in Love, Charlie Brown. 1974. (Illus.). (J). (ps up). 1.95 o.p. (*0-394-83044-X*); lib. bdg. 3.69 o.p. (*0-394-93044-4*) Random Hse. Children's Bks. (Random Hse. Bks. for Young Readers).

Schulze, Hertha. Before & After. 1985. (Loveswept Ser.: No. 120). 192p. pap. 2.50 o.p. (*0-553-21731-3*) Bantam Bks.

Schurfranz, Vivian. Cassie, No. 14. 1985. 368p. (Orig.). (J). (gr. 7 up). pap. 2.95 o.p. (*0-590-33688-6*) Scholastic, Inc.

—Danielle, No. 4. 1984. 368p. (J). (gr. 7 up). pap. 2.95 o.p. (*0-590-33156-6*) Scholastic, Inc.

—Megan, No. 16. 1986. 224p. (Orig.). (J). (gr. 7 up). pap. 2.75 o.p. (*0-590-41468-2*) Scholastic, Inc.

Schwemm, Diane. Don't Say Good-Bye. 1997. (Love Stories Ser.). 192p. (YA). (gr. 7-12). mass mkt. 3.99 o.s.i (*0-553-49219-5*, Dell Books for Young Readers) Random Hse. Children's Bks.

—Summer Love. 1995. (Silver Beach Ser.: No. 1). 224p. (YA). (gr. 9-12). mass mkt. 3.99 o.s.i (*0-553-56719-5*) Bantam Bks.

Scoppettone, Sandra. Long Time Between Kisses. 1984. 192p. (J). (gr. 3 up). pap. 2.50 o.s.i (*0-553-23982-1*) Bantam Bks.

—Long Time Between Kisses. 1982. 224p. (YA). (gr. 7 up). 12.95 (*0-06-025229-4*); lib. bdg. 10.89 o.p. (*0-06-025230-8*) HarperCollins Children's Bk. Group.

Scott, James. My Antonia: Reproducible Teaching Unit. 1999. 54p. (YA). (gr. 7-12). ring bd. 29.50 (*1-58049-144-8*, TU65) Prestwick Hse., Inc.

Scott, Kieran. How Do I Tell? 1999. (Love Stories Ser.). 192p. (gr. 7-12). mass mkt. 4.50 (*0-553-49293-4*) Bantam Bks.

—Trust Me. 1998. (Love Stories Ser.). 192p. (gr. 7-12). mass mkt. 3.99 o.s.i (*0-553-48593-8*, Dell Books for Young Readers) Random Hse. Children's Bks.

—While You Were Gone. 1999. (Love Stories Ser.). 192p. (gr. 7-12). mass mkt. 3.99 o.s.i (*0-553-49277-2*, Dell Books for Young Readers) Random Hse. Children's Bks.

Scott, Michael, photos by. Skidamarink! I Love You. 2004. (Illus.). 12p. (J). 5.99 (*0-7868-1915-4*, Disney Editions) Disney Pr.

Seavy, Marguita & Seary, Susan. The Kindling of the Flame. 1980. (gr. 6 up). lib. bdg. 9.90 o.p. (*0-531-04161-1*, E32, Watts, Franklin) Scholastic Library Publishing.

Service, Pamela F. Tomorrow's Magic. 1988. (J). (gr. 5 up). mass mkt. 3.95 o.s.i (*0-449-70305-3*, Fawcett) Ballantine Bks.

Shahan, Sherry. Fifth-Grade Crush. 1993. (Illus.). 128p. (J). (gr. 3-5). 2.50 o.p. (*0-87406-618-2*) Darby Creek Publishing.

—Sixth-Grade Crush. 1993. 144p. (J). (gr. 3-5). pap. 2.50 o.p. (*0-87406-647-6*) Darby Creek Publishing.

Shalant, Phyllis. Beware of Kissing Lizard Lips. 1997. (Illus.). 192p. (J). pap. 5.99 o.s.i (*0-14-038422-7*) Penguin Putnam Bks. for Young Readers.

—Beware of Kissing Lizard Lips. 1997. 9.09 o.p. (*0-606-11118-2*) Turtleback Bks.

Shannon, Jacqueline. Big Guy, Little Women. 1989. (J). (gr. 6-8). pap. 2.75 o.p. (*0-590-41685-5*, Scholastic Paperbacks) Scholastic, Inc.

—Class Crush. 1987. (Junior High Ser.: No. 2). 176p. (Orig.). (J). (gr. 5-9). pap. 2.25 o.p. (*0-590-40407-5*) Scholastic, Inc.

Sharmat, Marjorie Weinman. Fighting over Me. 1986. (Sorority Sisters Ser.: No. 4). (YA). (gr. 6 up). mass mkt. 2.50 o.s.i (*0-440-92530-4*, Laurel Leaf) Random Hse. Children's Bks.

—He Noticed I'm Alive & Other Hopeful Signs. 1985. 160p. (J). (gr. k-12). mass mkt. 2.25 o.s.i (*0-440-93809-0*, Laurel Leaf) Random Hse. Children's Bks.

—Here Comes Mr. Right. 1987. (Sorority Sisters Ser.: No. 6). (J). (gr. 5 up). mass mkt. 2.50 o.s.i (*0-440-93841-4*) Dell Publishing.

—How to Meet a Gorgeous Guy. 1983. 160p. (J). (gr. 7 up). 13.95 o.p. (*0-385-29302-X*, Delacorte Pr.) Dell Publishing.

—I Think I'm Falling in Love. 1986. (Sorority Sisters Ser.: No. 3). (J). (gr. 6 up). mass mkt. 2.50 o.s.i (*0-440-94011-7*, Laurel Leaf) Random Hse. Children's Bks.

—I'm Going to Get Your Boyfriend. 1987. (Sorority Sisters Ser.: No. 8). (J). (gr. k-12). mass mkt. 2.50 o.s.i (*0-440-94004-4*, Laurel Leaf) Random Hse. Children's Bks.

—Snobs Beware. 1986. (Sorority Sisters Ser.: No. 2). (J). (gr. 6 up). mass mkt. 2.50 o.s.i (*0-440-98092-5*, Laurel Leaf) Random Hse. Children's Bks.

—Two Guys Noticed Me... & Other Miracles. 1986. 160p. (J). (gr. k up). mass mkt. 2.50 o.s.i (*0-440-98846-2*, Laurel Leaf) Random Hse. Children's Bks.

Shay, Kathryn. Promises to Keep. 1999. 140p. (J). (gr. 5-8). pap. 5.99 (*0-9673794-1-5*) Small Miracles Pr.

Sheldon, Dyan. The Boy of My Dreams. 1997. (Illus.). 204p. (J). (gr. 6-10). 16.99 o.s.i (*0-7636-0004-0*) Candlewick Pr.

—Save the Last Dance for Me. 1993. (J). 9.05 (*0-606-08133-X*) Turtleback Bks.

—Tall, Thin, & Blonde. 1993. 176p. (YA). (gr. 6-10). 15.95 o.p. (*1-56402-139-4*) Candlewick Pr.

Sherburne, Zoa. Almost April. 1956. (J). (gr. 7 up). lib. bdg. 12.88 o.p. (*0-688-31013-3*, Morrow, William & Co.) Morrow/Avon.

Shipton, Jonathan. Busy! Busy! Busy! 1991. 32p. (J). (ps-3). 14.99 o.s.i (*0-385-30306-8*, Delacorte Pr.) Dell Publishing.

Shulman, Irving. West Side Story. (Orig.). 1990. 160p. mass mkt. 5.99 (*0-671-72566-1*); 1983. (J). (gr. 8 up). mass mkt. 2.95 (*0-671-50448-7*); 1981. pap. 2.50 o.s.i (*0-671-44142-6*) Simon & Schuster. (Pocket).

Shulman, Neil B. & Fleming, Sibley. Under the Backyard Sky. 1995. (Illus.). 32p. (J). (gr. 1-4). 13.95 o.p. (*1-56145-093-6*) Peachtree Pubs., Ltd.

Shura, Mary Francis. Diana. 1988. (Sunfire Ser.: No. 29). 224p. (J). (gr. 6-10). pap. 2.75 o.p. (*0-590-41416-X*) Scholastic, Inc.

—Marilee, No. 9. 1985. 368p. (Orig.). (J). (gr. 7 up). pap. 2.95 o.p. (*0-590-33433-6*) Scholastic, Inc.

—Winter Dreams, Christmas Love. 1992. 352p. (YA). (gr. 7-9). mass mkt. 3.50 o.p. (*0-590-44672-X*, Scholastic Paperbacks) Scholastic, Inc.

Shurfranz, Vivian. Another Time, Another Love. 1995. (J). mass mkt. 3.99 (*0-590-50966-7*) Scholastic, Inc.

—Another Time, Another Love. 1995. 9.09 o.p. (*0-606-09008-8*) Turtleback Bks.

Sierra, Patricia. One-Way Romance. 1986. 128p. (J). (gr. 6-10). pap. 2.50 (*0-380-75107-0*, Avon Bks.) Morrow/Avon.

Silkman, Anne. Say "Love" for Me. Doghouse Publishing, Inc. Staff, ed. & illus. by. 1994. (Togetherness Ser.). 192p. (Orig.). (YA). pap. 6.95 (*1-885531-00-1*) Mess Hall Writers.

Simbal, Joanne. Gifts from the Heart. 1988. (Sweet Dreams Ser.: No. 146). 176p. (Orig.). (J). pap. 2.50 o.s.i (*0-553-27228-4*, Dell Books for Young Readers) Random Hse. Children's Bks.

Simmons, Jane. Come Along, Daisy! 2003. (Illus.). 32p. (J). (ps-3). pap. 6.99 (*0-316-16878-5*) Little Brown Children's Bks.

Simons, Scott & Simons, Evelyn. Opening a Can of Words. 1994. (Orig.). (YA). pap. 3.50 (*0-8125-2948-0*, Tor Bks.) Doherty, Tom Assocs., LLC.

Sinclair, Stephanie. The Rumor about Julia. 1997. (Love Stories Ser.). 192p. (Orig.). (YA). (gr. 7-12). mass mkt. 3.99 o.s.i (*0-553-49218-7*, Dell Books for Young Readers) Random Hse. Children's Bks.

Singer, Marilyn. The Course of True Love Never Did Run Smooth. 1983. 256p. (YA). (gr. 7 up). 12.95 (*0-06-025753-9*); lib. bdg. 12.89 o.p. (*0-06-025754-7*) HarperCollins Children's Bk. Group.

—Haunted Heart. 1996. (J). (*0-7868-0182-4*) Hyperion Pr.

—Storm Rising. 1989. 224p. (J). (gr. 7-9). pap. 12.95 (*0-590-42173-5*) Scholastic, Inc.

Singleton, Joy. Deep in My Heart. 1994. (Sweet Dreams Ser.: No. 215). 176p. (YA). pap. 3.50 o.s.i (*0-553-56480-3*) Bantam Bks.

Singleton, Linda Joy. Camp Confessions, No. 6. 1997. (Cheer Squad Ser.: No. 6). (YA). (gr. 6-8). pap. 3.99 (*0-380-78510-2*, Avon Bks.) Morrow/Avon.

—The Love Boat. 1995. (Sweet Dreams Ser.: No. 227). 160p. (YA). pap. 3.50 o.s.i (*0-553-56681-4*) Bantam Bks.

—Love to Spare. 1993. (Sweet Dreams Ser.: No. 200). 144p. (YA). pap. 2.99 o.s.i (*0-553-29979-4*) Bantam Bks.

Skolnick, Evan. Torch for Meg. 1997. (Disney's Enchanting Stories Ser.). pap. text 4.50 (*1-57840-075-9*) Acclaim Bks.

Skurnick, Elizabeth. The Popular One. 2001. 192p. (YA). (gr. 7). mass mkt. 4.50 o.s.i (*0-553-49374-4*, Dell Books for Young Readers) Random Hse. Children's Bks.

Sleeping Beauty. (Classic Storybook Ser.). (J). 1996. 7.98 o.p. (*1-57082-329-4*); 1994. (Illus.). 96p. 7.98 o.p. (*1-57082-018-X*) Mouse Works.

Sloate, Susan. Head over Heels. 1994. (Sweet Dreams Ser.: No. 217). 144p. (YA). pap. 3.50 o.s.i (*0-553-56482-X*) Bantam Bks.

—Racing Hearts. 1991. (Sweet Dreams Ser.: No. 179). 144p. (J). (gr. 7 up). pap. 2.99 o.s.i (*0-553-28962-4*) Bantam Bks.

Smith, Barry. Minnie & Ginger: A Twentieth Century Romance. 1995. (Illus.). 32p. (J). (ps-2). pap. 9.95 o.p. (*1-85793-457-1*) Pavilion Bks., Ltd. GBR. *Dist:* Trafalgar Square.

Smith, Janice Lee. Nelson in Love. 1995. (Trophy Chapter Bk.: Vol. 9). (Illus.). 80p. (J). (gr. 2-5). pap. 3.95 o.p. (*0-06-442009-4*, Harper Trophy) HarperCollins Children's Bk. Group.

—Nelson in Love. 1996. (Adam Joshua Capers Ser.). (J). 9.15 o.p. (*0-606-08470-3*) Turtleback Bks.

Smith, K. T. Beverly Hills, 90210: Fantasies. 1992. 192p. (YA). mass mkt. 3.99 o.p. (*0-06-106727-X*, HarperTorch) Morrow/Avon.

Smith, Kathryn. Anna & the Duke. 2002. (True Romance Ser.). 304p. (J). pap. 4.99 (*0-06-447338-4*, Avon Bks.) Morrow/Avon.

—Emily & the Scot. 2002. (Avon True Romance Ser.). 288p. (J). pap. 4.99 (*0-06-000619-6*, Avon) HarperCollins Children's Bk. Group.

Smith, Nancy C. Apple Valley: Destiny. 1995. (Apple Valley Ser.: Vol. 4). (Orig.). (J). (gr. 6). pap. 3.50 (*0-380-78091-7*, Avon Bks.) Morrow/Avon.

—Apple Valley: The Proposal, Bk. 2. 1994. (Apple Valley Ser.). (Orig.). (YA). (gr. 6 up). pap. 3.50 (*0-380-77391-0*, Avon Bks.) Morrow/Avon.

Smith, Sherri C. Wrong-Way Romance. 1991. (Sweet Dreams Ser.: No. 176). 144p. (YA). (gr. 9-12). pap. 2.95 o.s.i (*0-553-28840-7*) Bantam Bks.

Smith, Wanda V. Love Knots. 1987. 144p. (J). (gr. 6-8). 2.25 o.p. (*0-87406-144-X*) Darby Creek Publishing.

Snelling, Lauraine. Out of the Mist. 1993. (Golden Filly Ser.: No. 7). 160p. (J). (gr. 4-7). pap. 5.99 (*1-55661-338-5*) Bethany Hse. Pubs.

Soliven, Marivi. Pillow Tales. 1991. (YA). 6.95 o.p. (*0-533-09188-8*) Vantage Pr., Inc.

Sommer-Bodenburg, Angela. The Vampire in Love. 1991. (Illus.). (J). (gr. 2-6). 128p. 13.00 o.p. (*0-8037-0905-6*); 144p. 12.89 o.p. (*0-8037-0906-4*) Penguin Putnam Bks. for Young Readers. (Dial Bks. for Young Readers).

—The Vampire in Love. 1993. 144p. (J). (gr. 3-6). pap. 2.99 (*0-671-75877-2*, Aladdin) Simon & Schuster Children's Publishing.

—The Vampire in Love. 1986. (J). 8.09 o.p. (*0-606-05681-5*) Turtleback Bks.

Sommers, Beverly. The Uncertainty Principle. 1990. (YA). (gr. 6-11). mass mkt. 3.50 o.s.i (*0-449-14608-1*, Fawcett) Ballantine Bks.

Sones, Sonya. What My Mother Doesn't Know. (Illus.). 272p. (YA). 2003. pap. 6.99 (*0-689-85553-2*, Simon Pulse); 2001. (gr. 6-8). 17.00 (*0-689-84114-0*, Simon & Schuster Children's Publishing) Simon & Schuster Children's Publishing.

Sonnenmark, Laura A. The Lie. 1994. 176p. (J). (gr. 7-9). mass mkt. 3.50 (*0-590-44741-6*) Scholastic, Inc.

South, Sheri C. Blame It on Love. 1995. (Sweet Dreams Ser.: No. 228). 160p. (YA). pap. 3.50 o.s.i (*0-553-56682-2*) Bantam Bks.

—The Cinderella Game. 1992. (Sweet Dreams Ser.: No. 192). 144p. (YA). pap. 2.99 o.s.i (*0-553-29454-7*) Bantam Bks.

—Don't Bet on Love. 1994. (Sweet Dreams Ser.: No. 214). 144p. (YA). pap. 3.50 o.s.i (*0-553-56479-X*) Bantam Bks.

—That Certain Feeling. 1991. (Sweet Dreams Ser.: No. 186). 144p. (YA). pap. 2.99 o.s.i (*0-553-29354-0*) Bantam Bks.

Sparks, Beatrice. Treacherous Love: The Diary of an Anonymous Teenager. 2000. 176p. (J). (gr. 7 up). pap. 5.99 (*0-380-80862-5*, Avon Bks.) Morrow/Avon.

—Treacherous Love: The Diary of an Anonymous Teenager. 2000. 11.04 (*0-606-17982-8*) Turtleback Bks.

Spector, Debra. Secret Admirer. 1985. (Sweet Dreams Ser.: No. 81). 160p. (J). (gr. 6 up). mass mkt. 3.50 o.s.i (*0-553-24688-7*) Bantam Bks.

Speed, Toby. One Leaf Fell. 1993. (Illus.). 32p. (YA). (ps up). 7.50 o.p. (*1-55670-271-X*) Stewart, Tabori & Chang.

Sperry, Armstrong. All Sail Set: A Romance of the Flying Cloud. 1984. (Nonpareil Books Ser.: Vol. 35). (Illus.). 192p. (J). (gr. 4 up). reprint ed. pap. 12.95 (*0-87923-523-3*) Godine, David R. Pub.

St. Pierre, Stephanie. Project Boyfriend. 1991. (Sweet Dreams Ser.: No. 178). 144p. (YA). pap. 2.95 o.s.i (*0-553-28900-4*) Bantam Bks.

—Sun Kissed. 1990. (Sweet Dreams Ser.: No. 173). 144p. (YA). pap. 2.75 o.s.i (*0-553-28517-3*) Bantam Bks.

Stacy, Lori Moore. Beautiful You. 2000. (All about You Ser.). (Illus.). 112p. (J). (gr. 4-7). mass mkt. 4.50 (*0-439-15531-2*) Scholastic, Inc.

Staff, Adrienne & Goldenbaum, Sally. Banjo Man. 1986. (Loveswept Ser.: No. 124). 192p. pap. 2.50 o.p. (*0-553-21741-0*) Bantam Bks.

Stahl, Hilda. Elizabeth Gail & the Missing Love Letters, Vol. 13. 1989. (Elizabeth Gail Ser.). 128p. (J). pap. 5.99 o.p. (*0-8423-0807-5*) Tyndale Hse. Pubs.

—Elizabeth Gail & the Music Camp Romance. 1983. (Windrider Ser.: No. 14). 128p. (J). (gr. 3-7). pap. 2.95 o.p. (*0-8423-0708-7*) Tyndale Hse. Pubs.

—Elizabeth Gail & the Secret Love. 1983. (Windrider Ser.: No. 16). 120p. (J). (gr. 3 up). pap. 2.95 o.p. (*0-8423-0706-0*) Tyndale Hse. Pubs.

—Elizabeth Gail & the Time for Love. 1983. (Windrider Ser.: No. 18). 120p. (J). (gr. 3 up). pap. 2.95 o.p. (*0-8423-0732-X*) Tyndale Hse. Pubs.

—Sadie Rose & the Secret Romance. 1992. (Sadie Rose Adventure Ser.: Vol. 8). 128p. (J). (gr. 4-7). pap. 4.99 o.p. (*0-89107-661-1*) Crossway Bks.

Stamaty, Mark Alan. Who Needs Donuts? 1985. (Illus.). 1.75 o.p. (*0-8037-9535-1*, Dial Bks. for Young Readers) Penguin Putnam Bks. for Young Readers.

—Who Needs Donuts? 2003. (Illus.). 40p. (J). 15.95 (*0-375-82550-9*); lib. bdg. 17.99 (*0-375-92550-3*) Random Hse. Children's Bks. (Knopf Bks. for Young Readers).

Stanek, Lou W. Gleanings. 1985. 192p. (YA). (gr. 6 up). lib. bdg. 12.89 o.p. (*0-06-025809-8*) HarperCollins Children's Bk. Group.

Stanley, Carol. In Love. 1986. (Cheerleaders Ser.: No. 16). 176p. (Orig.). (J). (gr. 7 up). pap. 2.25 o.p. (*0-590-40048-7*) Scholastic, Inc.

Steig, William. Made for Each Other. 2000. (Illus.). 48p. (J). (gr. 9 up). 13.95 (*0-06-028512-5*, Cotler, Joanna Bks.) HarperCollins Children's Bk. Group.

Steiner, Barbara. Puppy Love. 1990. 112p. (Orig.). (J). (gr. 4-6). pap. text 2.75 o.p. (*0-87406-463-5*) Darby Creek Publishing.

—The Searching Heart. 1982. 144p. (J). pap. 1.95 o.p. (*0-590-32361-X*) Scholastic, Inc.

—Secret Love. 1982. 158p. (Orig.). (J). (gr. 7 up). pap. 2.25 o.p. (*0-590-40774-0*) Scholastic, Inc.

Steinke, Ann. Your Cheating Heart. 1993. 240p. (YA). mass mkt. 3.50 o.p. (*0-06-106733-4*, HarperTorch) Morrow/Avon.

Stevens, Mallory. Can't Buy Me Love. 1992. (Changes Romance Ser.: No. 7). 240p. (YA). mass mkt. 3.50 o.p. (*0-06-106710-5*, HarperTorch) Morrow/Avon.

Stewart, A. C. Elizabeth's Tower. 1972. 220p. (J). (gr. 6-9). 25.95 o.p. (*0-87599-193-9*) Phillips, S.G. Inc.

Stewart, Molly Mia. Elizabeth's Valentine. 1990. (Sweet Valley Kids Ser.: No. 4). (J). (gr. 1-3). 8.70 o.p. (*0-606-00932-9*) Turtleback Bks.

—Steven's Big Crush. 1996. (Sweet Valley Kids Ser.: No. 65). (J). (gr. 1-3). 8.60 o.p. (*0-606-09929-8*) Turtleback Bks.

Stine, Megan. Dylan's Secret. 1992. (Fifteen - Nickelodeon Bks.: No. 4). 112p. (Orig.). (J). (gr. 4-9). 2.95 o.p. (*0-448-40493-1*, Grosset & Dunlap) Penguin Putnam Bks. for Young Readers.

Stine, R. L. Blind Date. 1986. 208p. (YA). (gr. 7 up). pap. 2.25 o.p. (*0-590-40326-5*); mass mkt. 3.99 (*0-590-43125-0*) Scholastic, Inc. (Scholastic Paperbacks).

—The Boyfriend. 1990. (Point Ser.). 176p. (YA). (gr. 7 up). mass mkt. 4.99 (*0-590-43279-6*, Scholastic Paperbacks) Scholastic, Inc.

—The Boyfriend. 1990. (Point Ser.). (J). 10.04 (*0-606-04620-8*) Turtleback Bks.

—First Date. 1992. (Fear Street Ser.: No. 12). (YA). (gr. 7 up). 10.04 (*0-606-02007-1*) Turtleback Bks.

Stockton, Anne. Honey-Bun: An Enchanting Memoir about an Exceptional Cat. Haas, Megan, ed. 2000. (Illus.). 40p. (J). 14.95 (*0-944638-15-5*) Educare Pr.

Stolz, Mary. Love, or a Season. 1964. (J). (gr. 9 up). lib. bdg. 8.79 o.p. (*0-06-025926-4*) HarperCollins Pubs.

—Pray Love, Remember. 1954. (J). (gr. 8 up). lib. bdg. 10.89 o.p. (*0-06-025981-7*) HarperCollins Pubs.

—To Tell Your Love. 1950. (J). (gr. 8 up). lib. bdg. 9.89 o.p. (*0-06-026046-7*) HarperCollins Pubs.

—Wait for Me, Michael. 1961. (J). (gr. 7 up). lib. bdg. 8.79 o.p. (*0-06-026056-4*) HarperCollins Pubs.

Storr, Catherine. Ruth's Story. 1988. (People of the Bible Ser.). (Illus.). 24p. (J). (gr. k-4). pap. 7.95 o.p. (*0-8249-7257-0*) Ideals Pubns.

Stowe, Aurelia. Love Will Come: Stories of Romance. 1963. (J). 4.99 o.s.i (*0-394-91363-9*, Random Hse. Bks. for Young Readers) Random Hse. Children's Bks.

Strachan, Linda. What Color Is Love? 2004. (Illus.). 32p. (J). pap. 6.95 (*1-58234-941-X*, Bloomsbury Children) Bloomsbury Publishing.

Strasser, Todd. Workin' for Peanuts. 1983. 192p. (J). (gr. 7 up). pap. 12.95 o.s.i (*0-385-29236-8*, Delacorte Pr.) Dell Publishing.

Stuart, Anne. Shadow Dance. 1993. (Orig.). pap. 4.50 (*0-380-76741-4*, Avon Bks.) Morrow/Avon.

Stuart, Becky. Once in California. 1984. (First Love Ser.). 155p. (YA). (gr. 7 up). pap. (*0-671-53412-2*, Silhouette) Harlequin Enterprises, Ltd.

Stuart, Jesse H. Daughter of the Legend. Spurlock, John H., ed. 1994. (Illus.). 256p. (YA). (gr. 8 up). reprint ed. 22.00 (*0-945084-42-0*) Stuart, Jesse Foundation, The.

Summers, Kate & Kneen, Maggie. Milly's Wedding. 1999. (Illus.). 32p. (J). 15.99 (*1-85881-360-3*) NAL.

Sunshine, Tina. An X-Rated Romance. 1982. 142p. (YA). (gr. 7 up). mass mkt. 2.50 (*0-380-79905-7*, Avon Bks.) Morrow/Avon.

Suntanned Days. 1985. (Follow Your Heart Romance Ser.: No. 9). (YA). (gr. 7 up). pap. (*0-671-55824-2*, Simon Pulse) Simon & Schuster Children's Publishing.

Sutcliff, Rosemary. Tristan & Iseult. 1991. (J). 12.00 (*0-606-21598-0*) Turtleback Bks.

Suzanne, Jamie. Big Brother's in Love. 1992. (Sweet Valley Twins Ser.: No. 57). (J). (gr. 3-7). pap. o.s.i (*0-553-54051-3*, Dell Books for Young Readers) Random Hse. Children's Bks.

—Big Brother's in Love Again. 1997. (Sweet Valley Twins Ser.: No. 104). 144p. (gr. 3-7). pap. text 3.50 o.s.i (*0-553-48435-4*, Sweet Valley) Random Hse. Children's Bks.

—Big Brother's in Love Again. 1997. (Sweet Valley Twins Ser.: No. 104). (J). (gr. 3-7). 9.55 (*0-606-11953-1*) Turtleback Bks.

—Elizabeth's First Kiss. 1990. (Sweet Valley Twins Ser.: No. 43). (J). (gr. 3-7). 8.60 o.p. (*0-606-04663-1*) Turtleback Bks.

—The Great Boyfriend Switch. 1993. (Sweet Valley Twins Ser.: No. 66). 144p. (gr. 3-7). pap. text 3.50 o.s.i (*0-553-48053-7*) Bantam Bks.

—The Great Boyfriend Switch. 1992. (Sweet Valley Twins Ser.: No. 66). (J). (gr. 3-7). pap. o.s.i (*0-553-54096-3*, Dell Books for Young Readers) Random Hse. Children's Bks.

—The Great Boyfriend Switch. 1993. (Sweet Valley Twins Ser.: No. 66). (J). (gr. 3-7). 8.60 o.p. (*0-606-02940-0*) Turtleback Bks.

—Jessica the Rock Star. 1989. (Sweet Valley Twins Ser.: No. 34). 112p. (J). (gr. 3-7). pap. 3.25 o.s.i (*0-553-15766-3*) Bantam Bks.

—Jessica's First Kiss. 1997. (Sweet Valley Twins Super Edition Ser.: No. 8). (J). (gr. 3-7). 9.34 (*0-606-11959-0*) Turtleback Bks.

—The Love Potion. 1993. (Sweet Valley Twins Ser.: No. 72). 144p. (J). (gr. 3-7). pap. 3.50 o.s.i (*0-553-48058-8*) Bantam Bks.

—The Love Potion. 1993. (Sweet Valley Twins Ser.: No. 72). (J). (gr. 3-7). 8.60 o.p. (*0-606-05652-1*) Turtleback Bks.

—The Older Boy. 1987. (Sweet Valley Twins Ser.: No. 15). 112p. (J). (gr. 3-7). pap. 3.25 o.s.i (*0-553-15664-0*, Skylark) Random Hse. Children's Bks.

—Three's a Crowd. 1987. (Sweet Valley Twins Ser.: No. 7). (J). (gr. 3-7). pap. 1.25 o.s.i (*0-440-82193-2*) Dell Publishing.

—Twins in Love. 1996. (Sweet Valley Twins Ser.: No. 101). 144p. (gr. 3-7). pap. text 3.50 o.s.i (*0-553-48346-3*, Dell Books for Young Readers) Random Hse. Children's Bks.

—Twins in Love. 1996. (Sweet Valley Twins Ser.: No. 101). (J). (gr. 3-7). 8.60 o.p. (*0-606-10333-3*) Turtleback Bks.

Swaby, Barbara. Love Is . . . 1995. (Illus.). 14p. (J). (ps). pap. 5.40 o.p. (*0-944943-60-8*) Current, Inc.

Sweeney, Joyce. The Dream Collector. 1991. 224p. (YA). mass mkt. 3.50 o.s.i (*0-440-21131-X*, Yearling) Random Hse. Children's Bks.

Sweet Dreams Diary. 1983. (Sweet Dreams Ser.). mass mkt. 5.95 o.p. (*0-553-01456-0*) Bantam Bks.

Szekeres, Cyndy. Toby: Do You Love Me? 2001. (Illus.). 14p. (ps-k). bds. 4.99 (*0-689-82653-2*, Little Simon) Simon & Schuster Children's Publishing.

Take a Hike, Romeo. (Full House Ser.). 96p. (J). (gr. 4-6). pap. 3.95 (*0-938753-75-4*, PP4) Parachute Publishing, LLC.

Tamar, Erika. Fair Game. abr. ed. 1993. 272p. (YA). pap. 3.95 o.s.i (*0-15-227065-5*, Harcourt Paperbacks) Harcourt Children's Bks.

—The Things I Did Last Summer. abr. ed. 1994. 256p. (YA). (gr. 7 up). pap. 3.95 (*0-15-200020-8*, Harcourt Paperbacks) Harcourt Children's Bks.

—The Things I Did Last Summer. abr. ed. 1994. 256p. (YA). (gr. 7 up). 10.95 (*0-15-282490-1*) Harcourt Trade Pubs.

Tarkington, Booth. Monsieur Beaucaire & the Beautiful Lady. 1968. (YA). (gr. 6 up). mass mkt. 0.95 (*0-8049-0158-9*) Airmont Publishing Co., Inc.

Taylor, Julie. Falling for Ryan. 1998. (Love Stories Ser.). 192p. (gr. 7-12). mass mkt. 4.50 o.s.i (*0-553-49252-7*, Dell Books for Young Readers) Random Hse. Children's Bks.

Taylor, Marilyn. Could I Love a Stranger? 1997. 174p. (YA). pap. 6.95 (*0-86278-442-5*) O'Brien Pr., Ltd., The IRL. *Dist:* Irish American Bk. Co.

—Could This be Love? 1997. 160p. (YA). pap. 6.95 (*0-86278-377-1*) O'Brien Pr., Ltd., The IRL. *Dist:* Irish American Bk. Co.

Taylor, Mildred D. Let the Circle Be Unbroken. 1983. 352p. (YA). (gr. 7-12). mass mkt. 3.50 o.s.i (*0-553-23436-6*) Bantam Bks.

Taylor, William. Paradise Lane. 176p. (gr. 7-9). 1989. (J). pap. 2.75 o.p. (*0-590-41014-8*); 1987. (YA). reprint ed. pap. 12.95 o.p. (*0-590-41013-X*) Scholastic, Inc.

Te Amo Means I Love You. 1983. (Sweet Dreams Ser.: No. 47). pap. 1.95 o.p. (*0-553-23743-8*) Bantam Bks.

Tedesco, Donna. Do You Know How Much I Love You? 1994. (Illus.). 32p. (J). (ps-1). lib. bdg. 14.00 o.s.i (*0-02-789120-8*, Simon & Schuster Children's Publishing) Simon & Schuster Children's Publishing.

Teeters. Romance on the Run: Weekend Romance. 1993. (Sweet Dreams Ser.). 176p. (YA). pap. 3.50 o.s.i (*0-553-29988-3*) Bantam Bks.

Tender Loving Care. 1983. (Sweet Dreams Ser.: No. 43). pap. 2.25 o.p. (*0-553-17852-0*) Bantam Bks.

Terris, Susan. Nell's Quilt, RS. 1996. 176p. (YA). (gr. 7 up). pap. 5.95 (*0-374-45497-3*, Sunburst) Farrar, Straus & Giroux.

—Nell's Quilt. 1988. 192p. (J). (gr. 7-9). pap. 2.50 o.p. (*0-590-41914-5*) Scholastic, Inc.

—Nell's Quilt. 1996. 12.00 (*0-606-10892-0*) Turtleback Bks.

Thesman, Jean. Couldn't I Start Over? 1989. 176p. (YA). (gr. 7 up). pap. 2.95 (*0-380-75717-6*, Avon Bks.) Morrow/Avon.

Thomas, Jean Monrad. How Many Kisses Good Night. 1997. (Classic Board Book Ser.). 8p. (J). (ps). bds. 5.99 o.s.i (*0-679-88226-X*, Random Hse. Bks. for Young Readers) Random Hse. Children's Bks.

Thompson, Julian F. Facing It. 1983. 240p. (YA). (gr. 7 up). pap. 2.95 (*0-380-84491-5*, Avon Bks.) Morrow/Avon.

—Philo Fortune's Awesome Journey to His Comfort Zone. 1995. 208p. (J). (gr. 7 up). 16.95 (*0-7868-0067-4*) Hyperion Bks. for Children.

—Shepherd, ERS. 1993. 176p. (YA). (gr. 8 up). 15.95 o.p. (*0-8050-2106-X*, Holt, Henry & Co. Bks. For Young Readers) Holt, Henry & Co.

Thompson, Mae. Janet of Olde Mill Farm. 1994. 300p. (Orig.). (YA). (gr. 8-12). pap. (*0-9641583-0-2*) Zionhouse Publishing.

Thrash, Jacquelyn R. A Piece of Heaven. 1996. (YA). pap. 24.95 (*0-9635247-4-7*) Three Pines Pr.

—Secret Hearts. 1994. (YA). 22.00 (*0-9635247-2-0*) Three Pines Pr.

Tolles, Martha. Katie & Those Boys. 1988. 112p. (J). (gr. 3-7). pap. 2.50 o.p. (*0-590-41794-0*) Scholastic, Inc.

Too Much to Lose. 1983. (Sweet Dreams Ser.: No. 49). 164p. (gr. 6 up). pap. 2.25 o.p. (*0-553-24463-9*) Bantam Bks.

Townsend, John R. The Summer People. 1972. 224p. (J). (gr. 9 up). 12.27 (*0-397-31421-3*) HarperCollins Children's Bk. Group.

—Top of the World. 1986. (Illus.). 96p. (gr. 3-7). pap. 1.25 o.p. (*0-440-48326-3*) Dell Publishing.

Tremblay, Carole. Romeo, le Rat Romantique. ed. 2001. (J). (gr. 1). spiral bd. (*0-616-07266-X*) Canadian National Institute for the Blind/Institut National Canadien pour les Aveugles.

Trimble, Irene. The Sweetest of Hearts. 2002. (Illus.). 12p. (J). 9.99 (*0-7364-2015-0*, RH/Disney) Random Hse. Children's Bks.

Trivelpiece, Laurel. In Love & in Trouble. 1983. (J). (gr. 7 up). pap. (*0-671-50443-6*, Simon Pulse) Simon & Schuster Children's Publishing.

Trying Not to Love You. 1985. (J). (gr. 7-9). pap. (*0-671-54394-6*, Simon Pulse) Simon & Schuster Children's Publishing.

Tudor, Tasha. All for Love. 2000. (Illus.). 96p. (YA). 18.95 (*0-689-82842-X*, Simon & Schuster Children's Publishing) Simon & Schuster Children's Publishing.

Turner, Ann Warren. In the Heart. 2001. (Illus.). 32p. (J). (ps-3). 14.95 (*0-06-023730-9*); lib. bdg. 14.89 (*0-06-023731-7*) HarperCollins Children's Bk. Group.

Twomey, Cathleen. Beachmont Letters. 2003. 224p. (J). (gr. 3-6). 16.95 (*1-59078-050-7*) Boyds Mills Pr.

Tyrrell, Melissa. Beauty & the Beast. 2001. (Fairytale Friends Ser.). (Illus.). 12p. (J). bds. 5.95 (*1-58117-153-6*, Piggy Toes Pr.) Intervisual Bks., Inc.

Ueda, Miwa. Peach Girl: Change of Heart, 7 vols. (Illus.). (YA). 2003. 184p. pap. 9.99 (*1-59182-198-3*); 2003. 184p. pap. 9.99 (*1-59182-197-5*); Bk. 7. 2004. 192p. pap. 9.99 (*1-59182-496-6*) TOKYOPOP, Inc.

Ullman, James Ramsey. Banner in the Sky. 1988. 288p. (J). (gr. 7 up). reprint ed. mass mkt. 5.99 (*0-06-447048-2*, Harper Trophy) HarperCollins Children's Bk. Group.

Umansky, Diane. My Secret Secret Admirer. 1997. (Full House Stephanie Ser.: No. 22). 160p. (J). (gr. 4-6). pap. 3.99 (*0-671-00363-1*, Simon Spotlight) Simon & Schuster Children's Publishing.

Underwood, Betty. The Forge & the Forest, 001. 1975. (Illus.). 240p. (YA). (gr. 6 up). 6.95 o.p. (*0-395-20492-5*) Houghton Mifflin Co.

Ure, Jean. See You Thursday. 1983. 224p. (J). (gr. 7 up). pap. 12.95 o.s.i (*0-385-29303-8*, Delacorte Pr.) Dell Publishing.

Vail, Linda. My Wicked Valentine. 1989. (Orig.). (YA). mass mkt. 3.95 o.s.i (*0-440-20233-7*) Dell Publishing.

Vail, Rachel. Ever After. 1995. 144p. (YA). (gr. 7 up). reprint ed. pap. 3.99 (*0-380-72465-0*, Avon Bks.) Morrow/Avon.

Valencak, Hannelore. When Half-Gods Go. Crampton, Patricia, tr. from GER. 1976. 192p. (Orig.). (J). (gr. 7 up). 9.50 o.p. (*0-688-22077-0*); lib. bdg. 12.88 o.p. (*0-688-32077-5*) Morrow/Avon. (Morrow, William & Co.).

Van der Meer, Ron. Give Me a Kiss. 1999. (Illus.). 6p. 12.95 (*90-76048-21-5*) Van Der Meer Tennis Univ.

Van Gool Studio Staff, illus. Sleeping Beauty. 1994. (Classic Ser.). 64p. (J). (ps-1). 4.98 o.p. (*0-8317-1666-5*) Smithmark Pubs., Inc.

Vande Velde, Vivian. Once upon a Test: Three Light Tales of Love. Fay, Ann, ed. 1984. (Illus.). 32p. (J). (gr. 4). lib. bdg. 8.25 o.p. (*0-8075-6070-7*) Whitman, Albert & Co.

Vilott, Rhondi. Runesword! 1984. (Dragontales Ser.: No. 2). (J). (gr. 7 up). mass mkt. 1.95 o.p. (*0-451-13083-9*, Signet Bks.) NAL.

Voeller, Sydell I. Careless Whispers. 1994. (Sweet Dreams Ser.: No. 216). 160p. (YA). pap. 3.50 o.s.i (*0-553-56481-1*) Bantam Bks.

Voigt, Cynthia. The Runner. 1986. (J). mass mkt. 2.50 o.s.i (*0-449-70154-9*, Fawcett) Ballantine Bks.

von Konigslow, Andrea Wayne. Would You Love Me? 2003. (Annikins Ser.). (Illus.). (J). 24p. pap. 1.25 (*1-55037-639-X*); 32p. pap. 5.95 (*1-55037-430-3*); 32p. lib. bdg. 15.95 (*1-55037-431-1*) Annick Pr., Ltd. CAN. *Dist:* Firefly Bks., Ltd.

Voyer, Kelly. For Love of Rock. 2003. (Annikins Ser.: Vol. 13). (Illus.). 11p. (Orig.). (J). (ps-1). pap. 1.25 (*1-55037-349-8*) Annick Pr., Ltd. CAN. *Dist:* Firefly Bks., Ltd.

Waddell, Martin. Who Do You Love? 1999. (Illus.). 32p. (J). (ps-1). 12.99 o.p. (*0-7636-0586-7*) Candlewick Pr.

Wahl, Jan. A Gift for Miss Milo. 1990. (Illus.). 46p. (J). 13.95 o.p. (*0-89815-329-8*) Ten Speed Pr.

Walker, Glenda & Adriana, Leah. Lovelet Kingdom. 1999. (Illus.). 45p. (J). (gr. 5-7). pap. 7.95 (*0-7392-0039-9*, PO2808) Morris Publishing.

Wallace, Bill. Beauty. 1989. 128p. (J). (gr. 4-7). pap. 2.95 (*0-671-68272-5*, Aladdin) Simon & Schuster Children's Publishing.

Walton, Rick. Will You Still Love Me? 1992. (Illus.). 32p. (J). (ps-3). 12.95 (*0-87579-582-X*) Deseret Bk. Co.

Warburton, Carol. Edge of Night: A Novel. 2002. (Illus.). 278p. (YA). (*1-59156-013-6*) Covenant Communications.

Ward, Heather P. I Promise I'll Find You. braille ed. 1996. (J). (gr. 1). spiral bd. (*0-616-01808-8*); (gr. 2). spiral bd. (*0-616-01809-6*) Canadian National Institute for the Blind/Institut National Canadien pour les Aveugles.

—I Promise I'll Find You. 2003. (Illus.). 32p. (J). (ps-3). pap. 5.95 (*1-55209-094-9*) Firefly Bks., Ltd.

—I Promise I'll Find You. 1997. (J). 12.10 (*0-606-12732-1*) Turtleback Bks.

Warner, Anne. Second Love. 1963. 172p. (J). (gr. 7-10). 3.25 o.p. (*0-664-32300-6*) Westminster John Knox Pr.

Warren, Andrea. Searching for Love. 1987. (Sweet Dreams Special Ser.: No. 3). 240p. (Orig.). (YA). (gr. 7-12). mass mkt. 2.95 o.s.i (*0-553-26292-0*) Bantam Bks.

Warren, Peggy. Where Love Goes. 1992. (Illus.). 36p. (J). (gr. k-3). 5.95 (*0-9628710-3-6*) Art After Five.

—Where Love Is. 1992. (Illus.). (J). (gr. k-3). 5.95 (*0-9628710-2-8*) Art After Five.

Watson, Clyde. Love's Sweet. 1999. pap. 4.99 (*0-14-054291-4*) Penguin Putnam Bks. for Young Readers.

Watts, Alycyn. Moonlight Melody. 1993. (Sweet Dreams Ser.: No. 206). 144p. (YA). pap. 2.99 o.s.i (*0-553-29985-9*) Bantam Bks.

Watts, Bernadette. Brigitte & Ferdinand: A Love Story. 1976. (Illus.). (J). (gr. 1-4). lib. bdg. o.p. (*0-13-081919-0*) Prentice-Hall.

Webb, Peggy. Birds of a Feather. 1985. (Loveswept Ser.: No. 112). 208p. pap. 2.25 o.p. (*0-553-21729-1*) Bantam Bks.

Weber, Judith. Changing Loves. 1987. (Cheerleaders Ser.: No. 36). 176p. (Orig.). (J). (gr. 7 up). pap. 2.50 o.p. (*0-590-41162-4*) Scholastic, Inc.

Weir, Joan. Sixteen Is Spelled O-U-C-H. unabr. ed. 1996. (Gemini Bks.). 144p. (YA). (gr. 7-9). pap. 4.95 (*0-7736-7290-7*) Stoddart Kids CAN. *Dist:* Fitzhenry & Whiteside, Ltd.

Weisinger, Steve. The Little Book of Hugs. 1990. (Chunky Book Ser.). (Illus.). 28p. (J). (ps). bds. 3.99 o.s.i (*0-679-80755-1*, Random Hse. Bks. for Young Readers) Random Hse. Children's Bks.

—The Little Book of Kisses. 1990. (Chunky Book Ser.). (Illus.). 28p. (J). (ps). bds. 3.99 o.s.i (*0-679-80754-3*, Random Hse. Bks. for Young Readers) Random Hse. Children's Bks.

Weiss, Dan. Language of Love. 1996. (J). mass mkt. 4.99 (*0-553-54264-8*, Dell Books for Young Readers) Random Hse. Children's Bks.

Wellman, Alice. The White Sorceress. 1976. 160p. (J). (gr. 6 up). 6.95 o.p. (*0-399-20505-5*) Putnam Publishing Group, The.

Wersba, Barbara. Beautiful Losers. 1988. (Charlotte Zolotow Bk.). 192p. (YA). (gr. 7 up). 11.95 (*0-06-026363-6*); lib. bdg. 11.89 o.p. (*0-06-026364-4*) HarperCollins Children's Bk. Group.

—Fat: A Love Story. 1987. (Charlotte Zolotow Bk.). 128p. (YA). (gr. 7 up). 11.95 (*0-06-026400-4*); lib. bdg. 11.89 o.p. (*0-06-026415-2*) HarperCollins Children's Bk. Group.

—Fat: A Love Story. 1989. 160p. (J). (gr. k-8). mass mkt. 3.50 o.s.i (*0-440-20537-9*, Laurel Leaf) Random Hse. Children's Bks.

—Just Be Gorgeous. 1991. 160p. (YA). mass mkt. 3.25 o.s.i (*0-440-20810-6*) Dell Publishing.

—Love Is the Crooked Thing. 1987. (Charlotte Zolotow Bk.). 160p. (YA). (gr. 7 up). 11.95 (*0-06-026366-0*); lib. bdg. 11.89 o.p. (*0-06-026367-9*) HarperCollins Children's Bk. Group.

—Love Is the Crooked Thing. 1990. 176p. (J). mass mkt. 3.50 o.s.i (*0-440-20542-5*, Laurel Leaf) Random Hse. Children's Bks.

—Tunes for a Small Harmonica. 1976. 192p. (YA). (gr. 7 up). 12.95 (*0-06-026372-5*); lib. bdg. 8.79 o.p. (*0-06-026373-3*) HarperCollins Children's Bk. Group.

—Whistle Me Home, ERS. 1997. 160p. (YA). (gr. 7 up). 15.95 (*0-8050-4850-2*, Holt, Henry & Co. Bks. For Young Readers) Holt, Henry & Co.

Wesker, Arnold. Fatlips. 1978. (Illus.). (J). (gr. 6 up). 6.95 o.p. (*0-06-026388-1*); lib. bdg. 7.49 o.p. (*0-06-026389-X*) HarperCollins Pubs.

West, Callie. My First Love. 1995. (Love Stories Ser.). 192p. (gr. 7-12). mass mkt. 4.50 (*0-553-56661-X*) Bantam Bks.

Westall, Robert. Falling into Glory, RS. 1995. 304p. (J). (gr. 7 up). 18.00 o.p. (*0-374-32256-2*, Farrar, Straus & Giroux (BYR)) Farrar, Straus & Giroux.

—The Promise. 1991. (Illus.). 176p. (J). (gr. 7-9). 13.95 (*0-590-43760-7*) Scholastic, Inc.

Weston, Carol. With Love from Spain, Melanie Martin. 2004. (Illus.). 256p. (J). (gr. 3-7). 15.95 (*0-375-82646-7*); lib. bdg. 17.99 (*0-375-92646-1*) Random Hse. Children's Bks. (Knopf Bks. for Young Readers).

White, Charlotte. No More Boys. 1986. (Sweet Dreams Ser.: No. 109). 176p. (J). (gr. 5-6). mass mkt. 2.25 o.s.i (*0-553-25643-2*) Bantam Bks.

White, Joe. Looking for Love in All The Wrong Places. rev. ed. 1991. 192p. (YA). pap. 3.95 o.p. (*0-8423-3829-2*) Tyndale Hse. Pubs.

Whitney, Phyllis A. The Highest Dream. 1981. 224p. mass mkt. 1.75 o.p. (*0-451-11218-0*, AE1218, Signet Bks.) NAL.

—Song of the Shaggy Canary. 1976. mass mkt. 1.50 o.p. (*0-451-09793-9*, W9793, Signet Bks.) NAL.

Wilde, Oscar. The Nightingale & the Rose. 1981. (Illus.). 32p. (J). (gr. 4 up). 14.95 o.p. (*0-19-520231-7*) Oxford Univ. Pr., Inc.

Wildfire Bestsellers, 4 Bks. Incl. Class Ring. Wunsch, Josephine. Homecoming Queen. Madison, Winifred. No Boys. Jones, McClure. Phone Calls. Reit, Ann. (Orig.). 1984. Set pap. 9.00 o.p. (*0-590-00660-6*) Scholastic, Inc.

Wildsmith, Brian. Carousel. 1998. (Illus.). 32p. (J). (ps). pap. 10.95 o.p. (*0-19-272318-9*) Oxford Univ. Pr., Inc.

Wilhelm, Hans. Yo Siempre te Quierre (I'll Always Love You) (SPA.). 296p. 13.95 (*84-261-2404-6*) Juventud, Editorial ESP. *Dist:* AIMS International Bks., Inc.

Willard. Beauty & the Beast. 1999. (J). pap. 7.00 (0-15-201549-3) Harcourt Children's Bks.

Willard, Barbara. The Iron Lily. 1989. (Mantlemass Ser.: No. 5). 192p. (J). (gr. k-12). mass mkt. 3.25 o.s.i (0-440-20434-8, Laurel Leaf) Random Hse. Children's Bks.

Willett, Edward. The Dark Unicorn. 18th ed. 1998. 158p. (J). pap. 9.99 (0-88092-414-4, 4144) Royal Fireworks Publishing Co.

Willey, Margaret. If Not for You. 1990. (Trophy Keypoint Bks.). 160p. (YA). (gr. 7 up). mass mkt. 3.25 (0-06-447015-6, Harper Trophy) HarperCollins Children's Bk. Group.

William, Kate. Are We in Love. 1993. (Sweet Valley High Ser.: No. 94). (YA). (gr. 7 up). 8.35 o.p. (0-606-05635-1) Turtleback Bks.

—Dangerous Love. 1984. (Sweet Valley High Ser.: No. 6). (YA). (gr. 7 up). 9.09 o.p. (0-606-01159-5) Turtleback Bks.

—The Dating Game. 1991. (Sweet Valley High Ser.: No. 78). (YA). (gr. 7 up). 8.09 o.p. (0-606-00379-7) Turtleback Bks.

—Double Love. 1983. (Sweet Valley High Ser.: No. 1). (YA). (gr. 7 up). 8.60 o.p. (0-606-03142-1) Turtleback Bks.

—Elizabeth Betrayed. 1992. (Sweet Valley High Ser.: No. 89). (YA). (gr. 7 up). 8.35 o.p. (0-606-02921-4) Turtleback Bks.

—Falling for Lucas. 1996. (Sweet Valley High Super Edition Ser.). (YA). (gr. 7 up). 9.60 o.p. (0-606-09928-X) Turtleback Bks.

—Forbidden Love. 1987. (Sweet Valley High Ser.: No. 34). (YA). (gr. 7 up). 9.09 o.p. (0-606-03097-2) Turtleback Bks.

—In Love with the Enemy. 1996. (Sweet Valley High Ser.: No. 120). (YA). (gr. 7 up). 10.04 (0-606-08627-7) Turtleback Bks.

—Jessica's Secret Love. 1994. (Sweet Valley High Ser.: No. 107). (YA). (gr. 7 up). 8.60 (0-606-06780-9) Turtleback Bks.

—A Kiss Before Dying. 1996. (Sweet Valley High Ser.: No. 122). (YA). (gr. 7 up). 10.04 (0-606-09921-2) Turtleback Bks.

—Left at the Altar! 1994. (Sweet Valley High Ser.: No. 108). (YA). (gr. 7 up). 8.60 o.p. (0-606-06781-7) Turtleback Bks.

—Love Letters for Sale. 1992. (Sweet Valley High Ser.: No. 88). (YA). (gr. 7 up). 8.35 o.p. (0-606-00685-0) Turtleback Bks.

—Lovestruck. 1986. (Sweet Valley High Ser.: No. 27). (YA). (gr. 7 up). 9.09 o.p. (0-606-01636-8) Turtleback Bks.

—Meet Me at Midnight. 1996. (Sweet Valley High Ser.: No. 124). (YA). (gr. 7 up). 9.09 o.p. (0-606-09923-9) Turtleback Bks.

—My Best Friend's Boyfriend. 1992. (Sweet Valley High Ser.: No. 87). (YA). (gr. 7 up). 8.60 o.p. (0-606-00684-2) Turtleback Bks.

—A Night to Remember. 1993. (Sweet Valley High Magna Edition Ser.). (YA). (gr. 7 up). 11.04 (0-606-05640-8) Turtleback Bks.

—Operation Love Match. 1994. (Sweet Valley High Ser.: No. 103). (YA). (gr. 7 up). 9.09 o.p. (0-606-06026-X) Turtleback Bks.

—Perfect Summer. 1985. (Sweet Valley High Super Edition Ser.). (YA). (gr. 7 up). 8.60 o.p. (0-606-00742-3) Turtleback Bks.

—Power Play. 1984. (Sweet Valley High Ser.: No. 4). (YA). (gr. 7 up). 9.09 o.p. (0-606-01264-8) Turtleback Bks.

—Promises. 1985. (Sweet Valley High Ser.: No. 15). (YA). (gr. 7 up). 8.35 o.p. (0-606-01263-X) Turtleback Bks.

—Say Goodbye. 1985. (Sweet Valley High Ser.: No. 23). (YA). (gr. 7 up). 9.09 o.p. (0-606-00758-X) Turtleback Bks.

—Too Much in Love. 1985. (Sweet Valley High Ser.: No. 22). (YA). (gr. 7 up). 9.09 o.p. (0-606-00798-9) Turtleback Bks.

Williams, Jeanne. To Buy a Dream. 2001. 164p. pap. 11.95 (0-595-16527-3, Backinprint.com) iUniverse, Inc.

Williams, Karen L. Galimoto. 1991. (Reading Rainbow Bks.). (J). 12.10 (0-606-00456-4) Turtleback Bks.

Wilson, Budge. The Courtship. unabr. ed. 1997. 156p. (YA). (gr. 7 up). mass mkt. (0-7736-7456-X) Stoddart Kids.

Wilson, Jacqueline. Girls in Love. 2002. 192p. (YA). (gr. 6-9). 9.95 (0-385-72974-X); (gr. 7-9). lib. bdg. 11.99 (0-385-90040-6) Dell Publishing. (Delacorte Pr.).

—Girls in Love. l.t. ed. 2000. 192p. pap. 18.99 (0-7089-9503-9) Harlequin Mills & Boon, Ltd. GBR. *Dist:* Ulverscroft Large Print Bks., Ltd., Ulverscroft Large Print Canada, Ltd.

—Girls in Love. 2002. 192p. (YA). (gr. 7). mass mkt. 4.99 (0-440-22957-X) Random Hse., Inc.

—Girls in Love. (Illus.). (J). 2003. 160p. mass mkt. (0-552-54521-X); 2000. 156p. 17.95 (0-385-40804-8) Transworld Publishers Ltd. GBR. *Dist:* Random Hse. of Canada, Ltd., Trafalgar Square.

Wilson, Sarah. Love & Kisses. (Illus.). (J). (ps). 2001. 22p. bds. 6.99 (0-7636-1049-6); 1999. 32p. 9.99 o.s.i (1-56402-792-9) Candlewick Pr.

Wine, Jeanine. Mrs. Tibbles & the Special Someone. 1987. (Illus.). 32p. (J). (ps-3). 12.95 (0-934672-54-7) Good Bks.

Winfield, Julia. Only Make-Believe. 1987. (Sweet Dreams Ser.: No. 121). 176p. (Orig.). (YA). (gr. 7-12). pap. 2.50 o.s.i (0-553-26418-4) Bantam Bks.

—Private Eyes. 1986. (Sweet Dreams Ser.: No. 113). 160p. (Orig.). (YA). (gr. 7-12). pap. 2.50 o.s.i (0-553-25814-1) Bantam Bks.

Winslow, Joan. Romance Is a Riot. 1985. 160p. (gr. k-12). pap. 2.25 o.p. (0-440-97479-8) Dell Publishing.

—Romance Is a Riot. 1983. (Lippincott Page-Turner Ser.). 160p. (YA). (gr. 7 up). 11.50 (0-397-32063-9); lib. bdg. 11.89 (0-397-32064-7) HarperCollins Children's Bk. Group.

Winters, Catherine. How to Talk to Boys & Other Important People. 1983. (Sweet Dreams Ser.). pap. 2.25 o.p. (0-553-17077-5) Bantam Bks.

Winthrop, Elizabeth. Sloppy Kisses. 1990. (Illus.). 32p. (J). (gr. k-3). reprint ed. pap. 4.95 o.p. (0-689-71410-6, Aladdin) Simon & Schuster Children's Publishing.

Wittbold, Maureen. Mending Peter's Heart. Anderson, David & Tronslin, Andrea, eds. 1995. (Illus.). 32p. (J). (gr. k-6). pap. 8.95 (0-9641330-2-4) Portunus Publishing Co.

Wittlinger, Ellen. Lombardo's Law. 144p. (YA). 2003. (gr. 5-9). pap. 5.95 (0-618-31108-4); 1993. (gr. 7-7). 16.00 (0-395-65969-8) Houghton Mifflin Co.

—Lombardo's Law. 1995. (Illus.). 144p. (YA). (gr. 5 up). reprint ed. pap. 4.95 (0-688-05294-0, Morrow, William & Co.) Morrow/Avon.

—Lombardo's Law. 1995. 10.05 o.p. (0-606-07802-9) Turtleback Bks.

—Razzle. Gould, Jason, ed. 2003. (Illus.). 256p. (YA). pap. 7.99 (0-689-85600-8, Simon Pulse) Simon & Schuster Children's Publishing.

Wittman, Kimberly. Stallions of Love. 1994. 200p. (Orig.). (YA). pap. 9.95 (1-885351-88-7) Cheval International.

Wittman, Sally. The Wonderful Mrs. Trumbly. 1982. (Illus.). 40p. (J). (gr. k-3). lib. bdg. 9.89 o.p. (0-06-026512-4) HarperCollins Children's Bk. Group.

Wojciechowska, Maia. Single Light. 1968. (J). (gr. 7 up). lib. bdg. 7.89 o.p. (0-06-026575-2) Harper-Collins Pubs.

Wolf, Erica. I Still Love You Just the Same, ERS. 2003. (Illus.). 32p. (J). 16.95 (0-8050-7128-8, Holt, Henry & Co. Bks. For Young Readers) Holt, Henry & Co.

Wolf, Jill. Puppy Love. 1986. (Illus.). 24p. (J). (gr. 3-7). pap. 1.95 o.p. (0-89954-730-3) Antioch Publishing Co.

Wolfe, Anne H. Wings of Love. 1993. (Sweet Dreams Ser.: No. 199). 128p. (J). (gr. 4-7). pap. 2.99 o.s.i (0-553-29978-6) Bantam Bks.

Wolitzer, Hilma. Out of Love, RS. (Illus.). 160p. (J). (gr. 5 up). 1984. pap. 3.50 o.p. (0-374-45685-2, Sunburst); 1976. 14.00 o.p. (0-374-35675-0, Farrar, Straus & Giroux (BYR)) Farrar, Straus & Giroux.

—Wish You Were Here, RS. 1984. 180p. (J). (gr. 5 up). 11.95 o.p. (0-374-38456-8, Farrar, Straus & Giroux (BYR)) Farrar, Straus & Giroux.

Wolitzer, Hilmer. Wish You Were Here, RS. 1986. 180p. (J). (gr. 4-7). pap. 3.45 o.p. (0-374-48412-0, Sunburst) Farrar, Straus & Giroux.

Wood, Phyllis A. Andy. 1971. (Hiway Book). (J). (gr. 9 up). 4.95 o.p. (0-664-32485-1) Westminster John Knox Pr.

Woodford, Peggy. Please Don't Go. 1973. 192p. (J). (gr. 6 up). 8.50 o.p. (0-525-37140-0, Dutton) Dutton/Plume.

Woodruff, Marian. Kiss Me, Creep. 1993. (J). pap. 3.50 (0-553-26931-3, Dell Books for Young Readers) Random Hse. Children's Bks.

Woodson, Jacqueline. The Dear One. 1990. (J). o.s.i (0-385-30372-6, Dell Books for Young Readers) Random Hse. Children's Bks.

Would You Love Me? I Feel Orange Today, Foo, 100 bks., Set. 2000. (Annikins Ser.: No. 16). (Illus.). (J). pap. 125.00 (1-55037-642-X) Annick Pr., Ltd. CAN. *Dist:* Firefly Bks., Ltd.

Wunsch, Josephine. The Perfect Ten. 1986. (First Love Ser.). 156p. (J). (0-373-06182-X, Silhouette) Harlequin Enterprises, Ltd.

Wyeth, Sharon Dennis. Boy Crazy. 1991. (Pen Pals Ser.: No. 16). 128p. (J). (gr. 4-7). pap. 2.95 o.s.i (0-440-40426-6, Yearling) Random Hse. Children's Bks.

—The Boy Project. 1991. 128p. (J). (gr. 4-7). pap. 2.95 o.s.i (0-440-40493-2) Dell Publishing.

—The Heartbreak Guy. 1991. 128p. (J). (gr. 4-7). pap. 2.95 o.s.i (0-440-40412-6) Dell Publishing.

—Rocky Romance, Vol. 137. 1987. (Sweet Dreams Ser.). 192p. (Orig.). (YA). (gr. 7-12). pap. 2.50 o.s.i (0-553-26948-8, Dell Books for Young Readers) Random Hse. Children's Bks.

—Sealed with a Kiss. 1990. (Pen Pals Ser.: No. 8). 144p. (J). (gr. k-6). pap. 2.95 o.s.i (0-440-40272-7, Yearling) Random Hse. Children's Bks.

Yates, Elizabeth. The Lighted Heart. 1974. (Illus.). (YA). (gr. 7 up). pap. 8.95 o.p. (0-87233-027-3) Bauhan, William L. Inc.

Yep, Laurence. Thief of Hearts. 1997. (Golden Mountain Chronicles). 208p. (J). (gr. 5 up). pap. 6.95 (0-06-440591-5, Harper Trophy) HarperCollins Children's Bk. Group.

—Thief of Hearts. 1995. (Illus.). 208p. (J). (gr. 5-9). lib. bdg. 15.89 o.p. (0-06-025342-8) HarperTrade.

—Thief of Hearts. 1997. 12.00 (0-606-11978-7) Turtleback Bks.

Yezerski, Thomas F. Together in Pinecone Patch. (J). Date not set. pap. (0-374-47579-2); RS. 1998. (Illus.). 32p. 16.00 (0-374-37647-6) Farrar, Straus & Giroux. (Farrar, Straus & Giroux (BYR)).

Young, Alida E. Summer Cruise, Summer Love. 1990. 144p. (Orig.). (J). (gr. 4-6). pap. text 2.95 o.p. (0-87406-451-1) Darby Creek Publishing.

Young, Cathy. One Hot Second: Stories about Desire. 2002. (Illus.). 224p. (YA). (gr. 7). 10.95 (0-375-81203-2); lib. bdg. 12.99 (0-375-91203-7) Random Hse. Children's Bks. (Knopf Bks. for Young Readers).

Youngblood, Marilyn. After Midnight. 1984. (First Love Ser.). 186p. (J). pap. 1.95 o.s.i (0-671-53403-3, Pocket) Simon & Schuster.

—Snap Judgement. 1984. (First Love Ser.). 155p. (YA). pap. (0-671-53409-2, Silhouette) Harlequin Enterprises, Ltd.

Zable, Rona S. Love at Laundromat. 1993. (J). mass mkt. o.s.i (0-553-54116-1, Dell Books for Young Readers) Random Hse. Children's Bks.

—Love at the Laundromat. 1988. 160p. (YA). (gr. 7 up). mass mkt. 2.95 o.s.i (0-553-27225-X, Starfire) Random Hse. Children's Bks.

Zach, Cheryl. The Frog Princess. 1995. (First Love Ser.). 320p. (J). mass mkt. (0-671-53404-1, Silhouette) Harlequin Enterprises, Ltd.

—Kissing Caroline. 1996. (Love Stories Super Edition Ser.). 224p. (YA). (gr. 7-12). mass mkt. 4.50 o.s.i (0-553-57014-5) Bantam Bks.

—Looking Out for Lacy. 1992. (Changes Romance Ser.: No. 2). 224p. (YA). mass mkt. 3.50 o.p. (0-06-106772-5, HarperTorch) Morrow/Avon.

Zadra, Dan. Talk Like an Eagle. 1986. (Value of Self-Esteem Ser.). (Illus.). 32p. (J). (gr. 6 up). lib. bdg. 12.95 o.p. (0-88682-021-9, Creative Education) Creative Co., The.

—There Will Never Be Another You. 1986. (Value of Self-Esteem Ser.). (Illus.). 32p. (J). (gr. 6 up). lib. bdg. 12.95 o.p. (0-88682-015-4, Creative Education) Creative Co., The.

Zalben, Jane Breskin. Here's Looking at You, Kid, RS. 1984. 124p. (J). (gr. 7 up). 11.95 o.p. (0-374-33055-7, Farrar, Straus & Giroux (BYR)) Farrar, Straus & Giroux.

Ziegler, J. F. & Blackwood, P. L., illus. Fables from the Hollow: The Great Sing: a Story for All Ages Based on the Teachings of Bhagavan Sri Sathya Sai Baba. 1995. (J). (0-9621235-1-X) Hallelujah Pr. Publishing Co.

Zimmerman, Zoe. Danny. 2000. (Love Stories). (Illus.). 192p. (YA). (gr. 7-12). mass mkt. 4.50 o.s.i (0-553-49322-1, Skylark) Random Hse. Children's Bks.

—Johnny. 2000. (Love Stories). 192p. (YA). (gr. 7-12). mass mkt. 4.50 (0-553-49324-8, Dell Books for Young Readers) Random Hse. Children's Bks.

—Kevin. 2000. (Love Stories). 192p. (YA). (gr. 7-12). mass mkt. 4.50 o.s.i (0-553-49323-X, Dell Books for Young Readers) Random Hse. Children's Bks.

Zindel, Paul. The Girl Who Wanted a Boy. 1985. 128p. (YA). mass mkt. 4.99 o.s.i (0-553-26486-9) Bantam Bks.

—The Girl Who Wanted a Boy. 1981. 160p. (YA). (gr. 7 up). lib. bdg. 12.89 o.p. (0-06-026868-9) Harper-Collins Children's Bk. Group.

—My Darling, My Hamburger. 1984. 160p. (YA). (gr. 7 up). mass mkt. 4.99 (0-553-27324-8) Bantam Bks.

—My Darling, My Hamburger. 1969. 176p. (YA). (gr. 7 up). lib. bdg. 14.89 o.p. (0-06-026824-7) Harper-Collins Children's Bk. Group.

—My Darling, My Hamburger. 1999. mass mkt. (0-553-24396-9); (YA). mass mkt. (0-553-20759-8) Random Hse., Inc.

—My Darling, My Hamburger. 1969. (J). 10.55 (0-606-04074-9) Turtleback Bks.

Zolotow, Charlotte. If You Listen. 1980. (Illus.). 32p. (J). (gr. k-3). 14.00 o.p. (0-06-027049-7); lib. bdg. 13.89 o.p. (0-06-027050-0) HarperCollins Children's Bk. Group.

—If You Listen. 2002. (Illus.). 32p. (J). (ps-3). reprint ed. text 15.95 (0-7624-1335-2) Running Pr. Bk. Pubs.

M

MARRIAGE—FICTION

Ada, Alma Flor. El Gallo Que Fue a la Boda de Su Tio. 1998. Tr. of Rooster Who Went to his Uncles Wedding. (SPA., Illus.). 32p. (J). (ps-3). pap. 6.99 o.s.i (0-698-11683-6, PaperStar) Penguin Putnam Bks. for Young Readers.

—The Rooster Who Went to His Uncle's Wedding. 1998. (Illus.). 32p. (J). (ps-3). pap. 5.99 o.s.i (0-698-11682-8, PaperStar) Penguin Putnam Bks. for Young Readers.

Adee, Donna J. Miriam & Timothy Face Life, Vol. 3. 2000. (Illus.). 384p. (J). pap. 12.95 (0-9654272-3-4) Harvest Pubns.

Alison, Marielle. How to Be a Bride & a Flower Girl, Too. 1999. (Illus.). 20p. (J). (ps-3). 14.95 (0-689-82354-1, 076714823549, Little Simon) Simon & Schuster Children's Publishing.

Anderson, Marilyn D. The Bridesmaid Wears Track Shoes. 1985. 96p. (J). (gr. 5-8). 2.25 o.p. (0-87406-008-7) Darby Creek Publishing.

Artigas de Sierra, Ione M. Las Bodas del Gallo Perico. (Superbks./Superlibros). (J). (gr. k-1). (SPA.). 21.95 (0-88272-488-6); (SPA.). pap. 6.95 (0-88272-489-4); 1989. pap. 6.95 (0-88272-491-6);Big Book. 1989. 21.95 (0-88272-490-8) Santillana USA Publishing Co., Inc.

Balter, Lawrence. The Wedding: Adjusting to a Parent's Remarriage. 1989. (Stepping Stone Stories Ser.). (Illus.). 40p. (J). (ps-2). 5.95 o.p. (0-8120-6118-7) Barron's Educational Series, Inc.

Barasch, Lynne. The Reluctant Flower Girl. 2001. (Illus.). 40p. (J). (gr. k-3). 14.95 (0-06-028809-4) HarperCollins Children's Bk. Group.

Barnes, Frances. Figaro. 1994. (Voyages Ser.). (Illus.). (J). (0-383-03686-0) SRA/McGraw-Hill.

Bennett, Cherie. Bridesmaids. 1996. (J). (gr. 6-10). mass mkt. 3.99 (0-590-54335-0) Scholastic, Inc.

—The Wedding That Almost Wasn't. 1998. (J). (gr. 3-7). mass mkt. 4.50 (0-590-05959-9, Scholastic Paperbacks) Scholastic, Inc.

Bennett, Olivia. A Sikh Wedding. 1986. (Way We Live Ser.). (Illus.). 32p. (J). (gr. 1-3). text 8.95 o.p. (0-241-11572-8) Trafalgar Square.

Benton-Borghi, Beatrice Hope. Down the Aisle. 1996. (Illus.). (J). (gr. 3-8). 14.95 (1-888927-02-X, DTAB); pap. 14.95 (1-888927-80-1, DTAB) Open Minds, Inc.

Bosley, Judith A. Bride in Pink: Reading Level 3. Billups, Annie, ed. 1993. (Sundown Fiction Collection). (Illus.). 95p. (J). pap. text 3.95 o.p. (0-88336-761-0); pap. text 21.00 o.p. incl. audio (0-88336-224-4); audio 17.95 o.p. (0-88336-799-8) New Readers Pr.

Bothwell, Jean. Defiant Bride. 1969. (J). (gr. 7 up). 5.95 o.p. (0-15-223090-4) Harcourt Children's Bks.

Branscum, Robbie. The Saving of P.S. 1979. 128p. (gr. 6 up). pap. 1.25 o.p. (0-440-49099-5) Dell Publishing.

Buehner, Caralyn. Fanny's Dream. (Illus.). 32p. 2003. pap. 6.99 (0-14-250060-7, Puffin Bks.); 1996. (J). 15.99 (0-8037-1496-3, Dial Bks. for Young Readers); 1996. (J). 14.89 o.p. (0-8037-1497-1, Dial Bks. for Young Readers) Penguin Putnam Bks. for Young Readers.

Burge, Constance M., creator. Soul of the Bride. 2001. (Charmed Ser.). (YA). (gr. 7 up). reprint ed. E-Book 5.99 (0-7434-2955-9, Simon Pulse) Simon & Schuster Children's Publishing.

Byrd, Sandra. Petal Power. 1999. (Secret Sisters Ser.: Vol. 8). 112p. (J). (gr. 4-7). pap. 4.95 (1-57856-115-9) WaterBrook Pr.

Campbell, Joanna. Bridal Dreams. 2004. (Thoroughbred Ser.: No. 65). mass mkt. (0-06-059524-8, HarperEntertainment) Morrow/Avon.

Christie, Amanda. Wedding Memories. 2004. 176p. (YA). (gr. 4-7). mass mkt. 4.99 (0-375-82754-4, Random Hse. Bks. for Young Readers) Random Hse. Children's Bks.

Cleary, Beverly. Sister of the Bride. (Illus.). (J). (gr. 5 up). 1996. 272p. pap. 5.99 (0-380-72807-9, Harper Trophy); 1963. 288p. 19.89 (0-688-31742-1) HarperCollins Children's Bk. Group.

—Sister of the Bride. 1992. 240p. (J). (gr. 6). pap. 4.50 (0-380-70928-7, Avon Bks.) Morrow/Avon.

—Sister of the Bride. 1992. 11.04 (0-606-14317-3) Turtleback Bks.

Clifton, Lucille. Everett Anderson's 1-2-3, ERS. (Illus.). (J). (gr. k-3). 1977. o.p. (0-03-017441-4); 1992. 32p. 16.95 (0-8050-2310-0) Holt, Henry & Co. (Holt, Henry & Co. Bks. For Young Readers).

Cone, Molly. Paul David Silverman Is a Father. 1983. (Skinny Bks.). (Illus.). 64p. (J). (gr. 2 up). 8.95 o.p. (0-525-44050-X, Dutton) Dutton/Plume.

Cooper, Ilene. Mean Streak. 1992. (Kennedy School Kids Ser.: No. 3). 192p. (J). (gr. 3-7). pap. 3.99 o.p. (0-14-034978-2, Puffin Bks.) Penguin Putnam Bks. for Young Readers.

Cooper, Zoe. Brides: Sherri's Perfect Day. 1997. (YA). (gr. 7 up). pap. 3.99 (*0-380-78699-0*, Avon Bks.) Morrow/Avon.

—Heather's Change of Heart. 1997. (Brides Ser.: No. 3). (YA). (gr. 5 up). pap. 3.99 (*0-380-78701-6*, Avon Bks.) Morrow/Avon.

Corrin, Sarah & Corrin, Stephen. Mrs. Fox's Wedding. 1983. (Illus.). 32p. (J). (ps-3). pap. 2.95 o.p. (*0-14-050375-7*, Penguin Bks.) Viking Penguin.

Crane, Stephen. The Bride Comes to Yellow Sky. 1993. (Short Stories Ser.). 40p. (YA). (gr. 3 up). lib. bdg. 13.95 o.p. (*0-87191-827-7*, Creative Education) Creative Co., The.

Crook, Carol. The Prophetic Wedding of the Bride. 2001. (Illus.). 61p. (YA). (gr. 10 up). pap. 5.95 (*0-939399-44-X*) Books of Truth.

Delton, Judy. Angel's Mother's Wedding. 176p. (J). (gr. 4-6). 2001. (Illus.). pap. 4.95 (*0-618-11118-2*); 1987. tchr. ed. 16.00 (*0-395-44470-5*) Houghton Mifflin Co.

—Angel's Mother's Wedding. 2001. (J). 11.00 (*0-606-21032-6*) Turtleback Bks.

Derby, Pat. Grams, Her Boyfriend, My Family & Me, RS. 1994. 256p. (YA). (gr. 5 up). 16.00 o.p. (*0-374-38131-3*, Farrar, Straus & Giroux (BYR)) Farrar, Straus & Giroux.

Dessen, Sarah. That Summer. 1998. (Illus.). 208p. (J). (gr. 5-9). pap. 5.99 (*0-14-038688-2*, Puffin Bks.) Penguin Putnam Bks. for Young Readers.

—That Summer. unabr. ed. 2003. (J). (gr. 7). audio 25.00 (*0-8072-1567-8*, Listening Library) Random Hse. Audio Publishing Group.

—That Summer. 1996. 208p. (YA). (gr. 7 up). pap. 16.95 (*0-531-09538-X*); lib. bdg. 17.99 (*0-531-08888-X*) Scholastic, Inc. (Orchard Bks.).

—That Summer. 1998. (J). 12.04 (*0-606-13842-0*) Turtleback Bks.

Disney Staff. Here Comes the Bride. 2001. (Illus.). 10p. (J). bds. 10.99 (*0-7364-1198-4*, RH/Disney) Random Hse. Children's Bks.

Dower, Laura. Sink or Swim. 2003. (From the Files of Madison Finn Ser.: No. 13). 176p. (J). pap. 4.99 (*0-7868-1735-6*, Volo) Hyperion Bks. for Children.

Drescher, Joan. My Mother's Getting Married. 1993. 32p. (J). (ps-3). pap. 5.99 o.s.i (*0-14-054667-7*, Puffin Bks.) Penguin Putnam Bks. for Young Readers.

Du Jardin, Rosamond. Double Wedding. 1959. (J). (gr. 4-9). 14.95 (*0-397-30446-3*) HarperCollins Children's Bk. Group.

Ellis, Ella Thorp. The Year of My Indian Prince. 2002. 224p. (YA). (gr. 7). mass mkt. 5.50 (*0-440-22950-2*, Random Hse. Bks. for Young Readers) Random Hse. Children's Bks.

Emecheta, Buchi. The Bride Price. 2000. (Illus.). 106p. pap. text 5.95 (*0-19-423059-7*) Oxford Univ. Pr., Inc.

—The Moonlight Bride. 1983. 77p. (gr. 6-10). (J). 7.95 (*0-8076-1062-3*); (YA). pap. 8.95 (*0-8076-1063-1*) Braziller, George Inc.

Emery, Anne. Stepfamily. 1980. 140p. (J). (gr. 5-7). 9.50 o.p. (*0-664-32660-9*) Westminster John Knox Pr.

Ewing, Kathryn. Things Won't Be the Same. 1980. (J). (gr. 4-6). 8.95 o.p. (*0-15-285663-3*) Harcourt Children's Bks.

Farber, Norma. There Once Was a Woman Who Married a Man. 1978. (Illus.). (J). lib. bdg. 6.95 o.p. (*0-201-01947-7*) Addison-Wesley Longman, Inc.

First, Julia. I, Rebekah Take You Lawrence. 1981. (gr. 6 up). lib. bdg. 9.90 o.p. (*0-531-04256-1*, Watts, Franklin) Scholastic Library Publishing.

Freeman, Mary E. Wilkins. The Revolt of Mother. 1993. (Short Stories Ser.). 32p. (YA). (gr. 5 up). lib. bdg. 18.60 (*0-88682-495-8*, Creative Education) Creative Co., The.

Gallagher, Diana G. Bridal Bedlam. 1999. (Sabrina, the Teenage Witch Ser.: No. 23). 176p. (YA). (gr. 5 up). mass mkt. 4.50 (*0-671-02818-9*, Simon Pulse) Simon & Schuster Children's Publishing.

Gauthier, Bertrand. La Princesse Qui Voulait Choisir Son Prince. 1996. (FRE., Illus.). 24p. (J). pap. 7.95 (*2-89021-270-X*) La Courte Echelle CAN. *Dist:* Firefly Bks., Ltd.

Godwin, Laura. The Flower Girl. 2000. (Illus.). 24p. (J). 12.99 (*0-7868-0408-4*) Hyperion Bks. for Children.

Green, Wendy. The Wedding. 1989. (Little Lions Ser.). 24p. (J). (ps-3). pap. 1.99 o.p. (*0-7459-1736-4*) Lion Publishing.

Hall, Amanda, illus. & adapted by. The Foolish Husbands. 1987. 26p. (J). (gr. k-3). lib. bdg. 12.95 o.p. (*0-87226-154-9*, Bedrick, Peter Bks.) McGraw-Hill Children's Publishing.

Hall, Monica. Doodlebugs. 1999. (Touched by an Angel Ser.: Vol. 4). 86p. (J). (gr. 5-9). pap. 4.99 (*0-8499-5805-9*) Nelson, Tommy.

Hamilton, Elizabeth L. Date with Responsibility. 2003. (Character-in-Action Ser.: Bk. 2). 384p. (YA). per. 19.95 (*0-9713749-0-2*) Quiet Impact, Inc.

Head, Ann. Mr. & Mrs. Bo Jo Jones. 1985. mass mkt. 0.95 o.p. (*0-451-05230-7*); 1968. mass mkt. 2.25 o.p. (*0-451-14140-7*); 1968. mass mkt. 1.95 o.p. (*0-451-12375-1*); 1968. mass mkt. 1.25 o.p. (*0-451-06440-2*); 1968. mass mkt. 1.50 o.p. (*0-451-07869-1*); 1968. mass mkt. 1.75 o.p. (*0-451-11255-5*); 1968. 192p. (YA). (gr. 9). mass mkt. 2.75 o.p. (*0-451-15734-6*) NAL. (Signet Bks.).

—Mr. & Mrs. Bo Jo Jones. 1967. 9.95 o.p. (*0-399-10562-X*, G. P. Putnam's Sons) Penguin Putnam Bks. for Young Readers.

—Mr. & Mrs. Bo Jo Jones. 9999. (J). pap. 1.95 o.s.i (*0-590-03201-1*) Scholastic, Inc.

—Mr. & Mrs. Bo Jo Jones. 1968. (J). 11.04 (*0-606-01102-1*) Turtleback Bks.

Henkes, Kevin. Two under Par. 1997. (Illus.). 128p. (gr. 3-7). pap. 4.99 (*0-14-038426-X*) Penguin Putnam Bks. for Young Readers.

Hennessy, B. G. Jake Baked the Cake. 1992. (Picture Puffins Ser.). (Illus.). 32p. (J). (ps-3). pap. 5.99 (*0-14-050882-1*, Puffin Bks.) Penguin Putnam Bks. for Young Readers.

Hillcrest, Dayne. Letena, Forever A-Flutter. 1999. (J). (gr. k-4). pap. 6.95 (*0-533-12757-2*) Vantage Pr., Inc.

Howard, Pearl A. A Special Guest for Mr. & Mrs. Bumba. 1983. (Mr. Bumba Bks.). 32p. (J). (gr. k-3). reprint ed. 5.95 o.p. (*0-8225-0123-6*, Lerner Pubns.) Lerner Publishing Group.

Howe, James. Pinky & Rex Get Married. 1999. (Pinky & Rex Ser.). (Illus.). 48p. (J). (gr. 1-4). pap. 3.99 (*0-689-82526-9*, 076714003996, Aladdin) Simon & Schuster Children's Publishing.

—Pinky & Rex Get Married. 1999. (Pinky & Rex Ser.). (J). (gr. 1-4). 10.14 (*0-606-16307-7*) Turtleback Bks.

Huggins, Alice M. The Red Chair Waits. 1948. (Illus.). (J). (gr. 4-6). 3.95 o.p. (*0-664-32047-3*) Westminster John Knox Pr.

Joha & His Wife. 1997. (Scheherezade Children's Stories Ser.). (Illus.). 16p. (J). (*1-85964-002-8*, Ithaca Pr.) Garnet Publishing, Ltd.

Johnson, Angela. The Wedding. 1999. (Illus.). 32p. (J). (ps-2). pap. 16.95 (*0-531-30139-7*); lib. bdg. 17.99 (*0-531-33139-3*) Scholastic, Inc. (Orchard Bks.).

Johnson, Annabel & Johnson, Edgar. Wilderness Bride. 2003. 232p. (YA). 12.95 (*0-9714612-7-9*) Green Mansion Pr. LLC.

Jordan, Penny. Research into Marriage. 1999. mass mkt. o.s.i (*0-373-83419-5*, 1-83419-1); 1987. mass mkt. (*0-373-10994-6*) Harlequin Enterprises, Ltd. (Harlequin Bks.).

Kanefield, Teri. Rivka's Way. 2001. (Illus.). 137p. (J). (gr. 5-9). 15.95 (*0-8126-2870-5*) Cricket Bks.

Kirk, David. Miss Spider's Wedding. White, Antoinette, ed. 1995. (Miss Spider Ser.). (Illus.). 32p. (J). (ps-2). pap. 16.95 o.s.i (*0-590-56866-3*) Scholastic, Inc.

LaFaye, A. The Year of the Sawdust Man. 224p. (J). (gr. 3-7). 1999. (Illus.). pap. 4.99 (*0-689-83106-4*, Aladdin); 1998. 16.00 (*0-689-81513-1*, Simon & Schuster Children's Publishing) Simon & Schuster Children's Publishing.

—The Year of the Sawdust Man. 1999. 11.04 (*0-606-17947-X*) Turtleback Bks.

Lantz, Francess L. Letters to Cupid. 2001. (American Girls Collection Ser.). 192p. (J). 14.95 (*1-58485-375-1*); (YA). pap. 5.95 (*1-58485-374-3*) Pleasant Co. Pubns. (American Girl).

Laurin, Anne. Little Things. 1978. (Illus.). (J). (ps-3). 1.79 o.p. (*0-689-30623-7*, Atheneum) Simon & Schuster Children's Publishing.

Leonard, Laura. Saving Damaris. 1989. 192p. (J). (gr. 3-7). lib. bdg. 14.95 o.p. (*0-689-31553-8*, Atheneum) Simon & Schuster Children's Publishing.

Leverich, Kathleen. Heather. 1997. (Flower Girls Ser.: Vol. 3). (Illus.). 96p. (J). (gr. 1-4). pap. 3.95 (*0-06-442021-3*, Harper Trophy) HarperCollins Children's Bk. Group.

—Rose. 1997. (Flower Girls Ser.: Vol. 4). (Illus.). 96p. (J). (gr. 1-4). pap. 3.95 (*0-06-442020-5*, Harper Trophy) HarperCollins Children's Bk. Group.

Levine, Gail Carson. The Princess Test. 1999. (Princess Tales Ser.). (Illus.). 96p. (J). (ps-k). lib. bdg. 14.89 (*0-06-028063-8*); (gr. 2-7). 9.99 (*0-06-028062-X*) HarperCollins Children's Bk. Group.

Lewis, Beverly. The Trouble with Weddings. 2001. (Hollys Heart Ser.). 160p. (J). pap. 5.99 (*0-7642-2503-0*) Bethany Hse. Pubs.

—The Trouble with Weddings. 1993. (Holly's Heart Ser.: Vol. 4). 160p. (J). (gr. 6-9). 6.99 (*0-310-38081-2*) Zondervan.

Lewison, Wendy Cheyette. I Am a Flower Girl. 1999. (Grossett & Dunlap All Aboard Books & Cassettes Ser.). (Illus.). 32p. (J). (ps-3). 2.99 o.p. (*0-448-41956-4*, Grosset & Dunlap) Penguin Putnam Bks. for Young Readers.

Liberts, Jennifer. Wishes Come True - Wedding Bells. 2001. 80p. (J). pap. 2.99 (*0-7364-1196-8*, RH/Disney) Random Hse. Children's Bks.

Lovelace, Maud Hart. Betsy's Wedding. 1996. (Betsy-Tacy Ser.). (Illus.). 320p. (J). (gr. 3-7). pap. 6.95 (*0-06-440544-3*, Harper Trophy) HarperCollins Children's Bk. Group.

—Betsy's Wedding. 1996. 13.00 (*0-606-14163-4*) Turtleback Bks.

Lowell, Melissa. Wedding Secrets. 1996. (Silver Blades Super Ser.: No. 2). 144p. (gr. 3-7). pap. text 3.99 o.s.i (*0-553-48523-7*) Bantam Bks.

Lyle, Letcher L. Dark but Full of Diamonds. 1981. (YA). (gr. 12 up). 10.95 o.s.i (*0-698-20517-0*, Coward-McCann) Putnam Publishing Group, The.

Martin, Ann M. Here Come the Bridesmaids! 1994. (Baby-Sitters Club Super Special Ser.: No. 12). 256p. (J). (gr. 3-7). mass mkt. 3.95 (*0-590-48308-0*) Scholastic, Inc.

—Here Come the Bridesmaids! 1994. (Baby-Sitters Club Super Special Ser.: No. 12). (J). (gr. 3-7). 9.05 o.p. (*0-606-06923-2*) Turtleback Bks.

—Kristy's Big Day. l.t. ed. 1995. (Baby-Sitters Club Ser.: No. 6). 144p. (J). (gr. 3-7). lib. bdg. 21.27 o.p. (*0-8368-1319-7*) Stevens, Gareth Inc.

Mathers, Petra. Dodo Gets Married. 2001. (Illus.). 32p. (J). (ps-3). 16.00 (*0-689-83018-1*, Atheneum/Anne Schwartz Bks.) Simon & Schuster Children's Publishing.

McDaniel, Lurlene. Til Death Do Us Part. 1997. 224p. (YA). (gr. 7-12). mass mkt. 4.99 (*0-553-57085-4*, Dell Books for Young Readers) Random Hse. Children's Bks.

McNeill, Janet. Ever After. 1975. 160p. (J). (gr. 7 up). 5.95 o.p. (*0-316-56302-1*) Little Brown & Co.

Miklowitz, Gloria D. The Day the Senior Class Got Married. 1985. 160p. (J). (gr. 6 up). mass mkt. 2.75 o.s.i (*0-440-92096-5*, Laurel Leaf) Random Hse. Children's Bks.

Mildred & Elsie. 2001. (Mildred Classics Ser.: Vol. 3). 288p. pap. 5.95 (*1-58182-229-4*) Cumberland Hse. Publishing.

Minarik, Else Holmelund. The Toys' Wedding. 2004. (Maurice Sendak's Little Bear Ser.). 24p. (J). pap. 3.99 (*0-06-053417-6*, Harper Festival) HarperCollins Children's Bk. Group.

Montgomery, L. M. At the Altar: Matrimonial Tales. 1995. 240p. (YA). (gr. 4-7). mass mkt. 5.50 o.s.i (*0-553-56748-9*) Bantam Bks.

Mouse That Wanted to Marry. 1993. (J). mass mkt. o.s.i (*0-553-54106-4*, Dell Books for Young Readers) Random Hse. Children's Bks.

Muchmore, Jo Ann. Johnny Rides Again. 1995. 128p. (J). (gr. 4-7). tchr. ed. 14.95 o.p. (*0-8234-1156-7*) Holiday Hse., Inc.

Munsch, Robert. Ribbon Rescue. ed. 1999. (J). (gr. 1). spiral bd. (*0-616-01742-1*); (gr. 2). spiral bd. (*0-616-01743-X*) Canadian National Institute for the Blind/Institut National Canadien pour les Aveugles.

—Ribbon Rescue. 1999. (Illus.). 32p. (J). (ps-1). pap. 11.95 (*0-590-89012-3*) Scholastic, Inc.

Munsch, Robert & Fernandes, Eugenie. Ribbon Rescue. 2002. 32p. (J). pap. 3.99 (*0-590-89597-4*) Scholastic, Inc.

Murphy, Elspeth Campbell. The Mystery of the Wedding Cake. 1998. (Three Cousins Detective Club Ser.: No. 19). (Illus.). 64p. (J). (gr. 2-5). pap. 3.99 o.s.i (*1-55661-857-3*) Bethany Hse. Pubs.

Naylor, Phyllis Reynolds. Patiently Alice. 2003. (Alice Ser.). (Illus.). 256p. (YA). 15.95 (*0-689-82636-2*, Atheneum) Simon & Schuster Children's Publishing.

Newman, Daisy. I Take Thee, Serenity, 001. 1975. 320p. (J). 8.95 o.p. (*0-395-20551-4*) Houghton Mifflin Co.

Otey-Little, Mimi. Yoshiko & the Foreigner, RS. 1996. 40p. (J). (ps-3). 16.00 (*0-374-32448-4*, Farrar, Straus & Giroux (BYR)) Farrar, Straus & Giroux.

Park, Barbara. Junie B. Jones Is (Almost) a Flower Girl. 1999. (Junie B. Jones Ser.: No. 13). (Illus.). 80p. (gr. 1-4). lib. bdg. 11.99 (*0-375-90038-1*, Random Hse. Bks. for Young Readers) Random Hse. Children's Bks.

—Junie B. Jones Is (Almost) a Flower Girl, 1999. (Junie B. Jones Ser.: No. 13). (Illus.). 80p. (J). (gr. k-2). pap. 3.99 (*0-375-80038-7*) Random Hse., Inc.

Pascal, Francine, creator. Left at the Altar! 1994. (Sweet Valley High Ser.: No. 108). 208p. (YA). (gr. 7 up). mass mkt. 3.99 o.s.i (*0-553-56230-4*) Bantam Bks.

—A Married Woman. 1994. (Sweet Valley University Ser.: No. 5). 240p. (gr. 7 up). mass mkt. 4.50 (*0-553-56309-2*) Bantam Bks.

Peterson, John. The Littles Have a Happy Valentine's Day. 2003. (Littles First Readers Ser.: No. 11). (Illus.). 32p. (J). (gr. k-2). mass mkt. 3.99 (*0-439-42499-2*, Scholastic Paperbacks) Scholastic, Inc.

—The Littles Have a Wedding. 1971. (Littles Ser.). (Illus.). (J). (gr. 1-5). 10.14 (*0-606-05437-5*) Turtleback Bks.

Pevsner, Stella. Me, My Goat, & My Sister's Wedding. 1985. 192p. (J). (gr. 4-7). 13.95 o.p. (*0-89919-305-6*, Clarion Bks.) Houghton Mifflin Co. Trade & Reference Div.

Picard, Barbara Leonie. The Midsummer Bride. 1999. (Illus.). 32p. (J). pap. (*0-19-272354-5*) Oxford Univ. Pr., Inc.

Pickford, Ted. The Bridesmaids, No. 3. 1993. 176p. (YA). mass mkt. 3.50 o.s.i (*0-553-56097-2*) Bantam Bks.

Pilkey, Dav & Denim, Sue. Ready, Set, Go! 1998. 40p. (J). (ps-3). pap. 8.95 o.s.i (*0-590-94733-8*) HarperCollins Children's Bk. Group.

Pittman, Rachel N. The Wedding of G. Washington Bear. 1986. (Illus.). 42p. (Orig.). (J). (ps-5). pap. 6.95 (*0-9615382-1-X*) Pittman Pub.

Playskool Staff. Our Wedding. 1999. (J). pap. 9.99 (*0-525-45782-8*) NAL.

Pokriefke, Jana. Barbie Loves Weddings. 1998. (Golden Book Ser.). (Illus.). 16p. (J). (ps-1). pap. 3.99 o.s.i (*0-307-21102-9*, 21102, Golden Bks.) Random Hse. Children's Bks.

Porte, Barbara Ann. Harry Gets An Uncle. 1991. (Illus.). 48p. (J). (gr. k up). 13.95 o.p. (*0-688-09389-2*); lib. bdg. 13.88 o.p. (*0-688-09390-6*) HarperCollins Children's Bk. Group. (Greenwillow Bks.).

—Harry Gets An Uncle. (Illus.). 48p. (J). 3.98 o.p. (*0-8317-3353-5*) Smithmark Pubs., Inc.

—Harry Gets an Uncle. 2002. (I Can Read Bks.). (Illus.). 48p. (J). pap. 3.99 (*0-06-001152-1*, Harper Trophy); 15.95 (*0-06-001150-5*); lib. bdg. 15.89 (*0-06-001151-3*) HarperCollins Children's Bk. Group.

Porter, Connie Rose & McAliley, Susan. Addy's Wedding Quilt. 2001. (American Girls Short Stories Ser.). (Illus.). 64p. (J). (gr. 2 up). 3.95 (*1-58485-274-7*, American Girl) Pleasant Co. Pubns.

Raphael, Elaine & Bolognese, Don. Turnabout. 1980. (Illus.). 32p. (J). (gr. 1-3). 8.95 o.p. (*0-670-73281-8*) Viking Penguin.

Redmond, Diane. Naughty Bridesmaid. 2001. (Illus.). 63p. pap. 5.50 o.p. (*0-00-710479-0*) HarperCollins Pubs. Ltd. GBR. *Dist:* Trafalgar Square.

—Snowy Bridesmaid. 2000. (Illus.). 63p. pap. 5.50 (*0-00-710480-4*) HarperCollins Pubs. Ltd. GBR. *Dist:* Trafalgar Square.

—Sporty Bridesmaid. 2000. (Illus.). 63p. pap. o.p. (*0-00-710478-2*, HarperCollins) HarperTrade.

RH Disney Staff. Make Believe Bride. 2004. (Illus.). (J). pap. 3.99 (*0-7364-2220-X*, RH/Disney) Random Hse. Children's Bks.

—My Perfect Wedding. 2004. (Illus.). (J). pap. 3.99 (*0-7364-2219-6*, RH/Disney) Random Hse. Children's Bks.

Richardson, Arleta. Wedding Bells Ahead. 1995. (Grandma's Attic Ser.). (Illus.). 156p. (J). (gr. 3-7). pap. 4.99 (*1-55513-668-0*) Cook Communications Ministries.

Rubel, Nicole. A Cowboy Named Ernestine. 2001. (Illus.). 32p. (J). (ps-3). 15.99 (*0-8037-2152-8*, Dial Bks. for Young Readers) Penguin Putnam Bks. for Young Readers.

—Uncle Henry & Aunt Henrietta's Honeymoon. 1988. (Pied Piper Bks.). (Illus.). 32p. (J). (ps-2). pap. 3.95 o.p. (*0-8037-0498-4*, Dial Bks. for Young Readers) Penguin Putnam Bks. for Young Readers.

Rylant, Cynthia. Wedding Flowers. 2002. (Cobble Street Cousins Ser.: Bk. 6). (Illus.). 80p. (J). (gr. 2-5). 15.00 (*0-689-83242-7*, Simon & Schuster Children's Publishing) Simon & Schuster Children's Publishing.

—The Wedding Flowers. 2003. (Cobble Street Cousins Ser.). 80p. (J). pap. 3.99 (*0-689-83418-7*, Aladdin) Simon & Schuster Children's Publishing.

Sharmat, Marjorie Weinman. How to Have a Gorgeous Wedding. 1985. 144p. (J). (gr. k-12). mass mkt. 2.95 o.s.i (*0-440-93794-9*, Laurel Leaf) Random Hse. Children's Bks.

Small, David. Hoover's Bride. 1995. (Illus.). 32p. (J). (ps-4). 16.00 o.s.i (*0-517-59707-1*); 17.99 o.s.i (*0-517-59708-X*) Random Hse. Children's Bks. (Random Hse. Bks. for Young Readers).

Snelling, Lauraine. Setting the Pace. 1996. (High Hurdles Ser.: No. 3). 176p. (Orig.). (YA). (gr. 6-9). pap. 5.99 (*1-55661-507-8*, Bethany Backyard) Bethany Hse. Pubs.

Solomon, Joan. Wedding Day. 1981. (Illus.). (J). (ps-3). 9.95 o.p. (*0-241-10552-8*) Trafalgar Square.

Soto, Gary. Snapshots from the Wedding. 1998. (Illus.). 32p. (J). (ps-3). pap. 5.99 (*0-698-11752-2*, PaperStar) Penguin Putnam Bks. for Young Readers.

—Snapshots from the Wedding. 1998. 12.14 (*0-606-15961-4*) Turtleback Bks.

Spinelli, Eileen. Lizzie Logan Gets Married. 96p. (J). (gr. 2-5). 1998. pap. 3.99 (*0-689-82071-2*, Aladdin); 1997. 15.00 (*0-689-81066-0*, Simon & Schuster Children's Publishing) Simon & Schuster Children's Publishing.

Thomas, Charlotte E. Our Little Flower Girl: A Child Has Her First Experience Participating in a Wedding. 1992. (Illus.). 32p. (J). (ps-5). lib. bdg. 19.95 (*0-9633607-0-1*) Golden Rings Publishing Co.

Thomas, Terry. At Least We Were Married. 1973. 156p. (gr. 10 up). reprint ed. pap. 2.95 o.p. (0-310-36932-0) Zondervan.

Tolles, Martha. Marrying off Mom. 1990. (J). pap. 2.75 o.p. (0-590-42843-8) Scholastic, Inc.

Tripp, Valerie. Samantha Saves the Wedding. 2000. (American Girls Short Stories Ser.). (Illus.). 56p. (YA). (gr. 2 up). 3.95 (1-58485-035-3, American Girl) Pleasant Co. Pubns.

Turner, Ann Warren. Third Girl from the Left. 1986. 180p. (YA). (gr. 7 up). 13.95 o.p. (0-02-789510-6, Simon & Schuster Children's Publishing) Simon & Schuster Children's Publishing.

Waricha, Jean. The Wonderful Wedding. 1996. (Golden Book Ser.). (Illus.). 24p. (J). (ps-3). pap. 3.29 o.s.i (0-307-12841-5, 12841, Golden Bks.) Random Hse. Children's Bks.

Watson, Jude. Dangerous: Savannah's Story. 1996. (Brides of Wildcat County Ser.). 196p. (J). (gr. 7). pap. 3.50 (0-689-80626-4, Simon Pulse) Simon & Schuster Children's Publishing.

Weber, Lenora Mattingly. Something Borrowed, Something Blue. 1999. (Beany Malone Ser.). 273p. (J). pap. 12.95 (1-930009-05-4) Image Cascade Publishing.

—Tarry Awhile. 1999. (Beany Malone Ser.). 292p. (J). reprint ed. pap. 12.95 (1-930009-04-6) Image Cascade Publishing.

Wharton, Edith. Ethan Frome, Level 3. Hedge, Tricia, ed. 2000. (Bookworms Ser.). (Illus.). 80p. (YA). pap. text 5.95 (0-19-423002-3) Oxford Univ. Pr., Inc.

Whelan, Gloria. Homeless Bird. Lt. ed. 2002. 147p. (J). 23.95 (0-7862-4060-1) Gale Group.

—Homeless Bird. (J). (gr. 5 up). 2001. 192p. pap. 5.99 (0-06-440819-1); 2000. 240p. 15.95 (0-06-028454-4); 2000. 240p. lib. bdg. 16.89 (0-06-028452-8) HarperCollins Children's Bk. Group.

—Homeless Bird. unabr. ed. 2001. (J). audio 18.00 (0-8072-6181-5, RH Audio) Random Hse. Audio Publishing Group.

Wierenga, Kathy. Double Exposure. 2002. (Brio Girls Ser.). 192p. (J). pap. 6.99 (1-56179-954-8) Bethany Hse. Pubs.

Wiggins, VeraLee. Julius Again: More Adventures with the Perfectly Pesky Pet Parrot. 1995. (Julius & Friends Ser.: No. 2). 94p. (J). (gr. 2 up). pap. 6.99 o.p. (0-8163-1239-7) Pacific Pr. Publishing Assn.

William, Kate. Almost Married. 1994. (Sweet Valley High Ser.: No. 102). (YA). (gr. 7 up). 10.04 (0-606-06025-1) Turtleback Bks.

Williams, Barbara. Mitzi & the Terrible Tyrannosaurus Rex. 1982. (Illus.). 112p. (J). (gr. 2-4). 10.95 o.p. (0-525-45105-6, 0966-290, Dutton) Dutton/Plume.

—Mitzi's Honeymoon with Nana Potts. 1983. (Illus.). 128p. (J). (gr. 2-4). 9.95 o.p. (0-525-44078-X, Dutton) Dutton/Plume.

Williams, David P. & Williams, Helen C. A Mouse Wedding Dance: A Read-with-Me Story for Grown-Ups & Others, Vol. 2. 1993. (Read-with-Me Mouse Stories Ser.). (Illus.). 12p. (J). pap. 3.00 (1-886058-02-4) Williams, David Park.

Wolkoff, Judie. Happily Ever after... Almost. 1984. 224p. (J). (gr. 5-9). pap. 2.50 o.s.i (0-440-43366-5, Yearling) Random Hse. Children's Bks.

Wood, Phyllis A. Meet Me in the Park, Angie. 1983. 118p. (YA). (gr. 7-10). 11.95 o.p. (0-664-32710-9) Westminster John Knox Pr.

Zelver, Patricia. The Wedding of Don Octavio. 1993. (Illus.). 32p. (J). (gr. k up). 14.00 o.p. (0-688-11334-6); lib. bdg. 13.93 o.p. (0-688-11335-4) Morrow/Avon. (Morrow, William & Co.).

10 Cool Things about Being a Ring Bearer. 2002. 24p. (J). per. 8.95 (0-9707944-2-8) Paper Posie.

10 Neat Things about Being a Flower Girl. 2002. (Illus.). 24p. (J). per. 8.95 (0-9707944-1-X) Paper Posie.

MARRIAGE CUSTOMS AND RITES—FICTION

Ambrus, Victor G. Country Wedding. 1975. (Illus.). 32p. (J). (gr. k-3). lib. bdg. 7.95 o.p. (0-201-00197-7) Addison-Wesley Longman, Inc.

Brandon, Linda T. The Little Flower Girl. 1997. (Please Read to Me Ser.). (Illus.). 24p. (ps-1). pap. 3.25 (0-679-87695-2) Random Hse., Inc.

Connor, Catherine. Alison Saves the Wedding. (Magic Attic Club Ser.). (Illus.). 80p. (gr. 2-6). 1998. 13.95 (1-57513-018-1); 1996. (J). pap. 5.95 (1-57513-019-X) Millbrook Pr., Inc. (Magic Attic Pr.).

Cox, Judy. Now We Can Have a Wedding! 1998. (Illus.). 32p. (J). (ps-k). tchr. ed. 15.95 (0-8234-1342-X) Holiday Hse., Inc.

English, Karen. Nadia's Hands. 2003. (Illus.). 32p. (J). (gr. k-3). 15.95 (1-56397-667-6) Boyds Mills Pr.

Fagan, Cary. The Market Wedding. 2000. (Illus.). 32p. (J). (gr. 2-5). 16.95 (0-88776-492-4) Tundra Bks. of Northern New York.

Gantos, Jack. Wedding Bells for Rotten Ralph. 1999. (Rotten Ralph Ser.: Vol. 2). (Illus.). (J). (ps-3). 40p. 15.99 (0-06-027533-2);Bk. 2. 32p. lib. bdg. 14.89 (0-06-027534-0) HarperCollins Children's Bk. Group.

Gonzalaz, Lucia. El Gallo de Bodas. 1995. (SPA., Illus.). 32p. (J). (ps-2). pap. 4.95 (0-590-53842-X, SO1447) Scholastic, Inc.

Gunn, Robin Jones. With This Ring. 1998. (Sierra Jensen Ser.: No. 6). 160p. (J). (gr. 7-11). pap. 6.99 (1-56179-540-2) Focus on the Family Publishing.

HB Staff. Rooster & Uncle's Wedding. 95th ed. 1995. (J). (gr. 2). lib. bdg. 9.50 (0-15-305201-5) Harcourt College Pubs.

Herman, Gail. Flower Girl. 1996. (All Aboard Reading Ser.: Level 2). (Illus.). 48p. (J). (gr. 1-3). 13.99 o.s.i (0-448-41107-5); (ps-3). 3.99 (0-448-41108-3) Penguin Putnam Bks. for Young Readers. (Grosset & Dunlap).

Keene, Carolyn. The Wedding Gift Goof. 1996. (Nancy Drew Notebooks Ser.: No. 13). (Illus.). 80p. (J). (gr. k-3). pap. 3.99 (0-671-53552-8, Aladdin) Simon & Schuster Children's Publishing.

—The Wedding Gift Goof. 1996. (Nancy Drew Notebooks Ser.: No. 13). (J). (gr. k-3). 10.04 (0-606-10267-1) Turtleback Bks.

Leverich, Kathleen. Violet. 1997. (Flower Girls Ser.: Vol. 1). (Illus.). 96p. (J). (gr. 1-4). pap. 3.95 (0-06-442018-3, Harper Trophy) HarperCollins Children's Bk. Group.

Lewin, Hugh. Jafta & the Wedding. 1983. (Jafta Collection). (Illus.). 24p. (J). (gr. 1-3). pap. 4.95 o.s.i (0-87614-497-0); lib. bdg. 15.95 (0-87614-210-2) Lerner Publishing Group. (Carolrhoda Bks.).

—Jafta's Father. 1989. (Jafta Collection). (Illus.). 24p. (J). (gr. 1-3). reprint ed. pap. 4.95 (0-87614-496-2, Carolrhoda Bks.) Lerner Publishing Group.

Martin, Ann M. Karen's Wedding. 1993. (Baby-Sitters Little Sister Ser.: No. 39). 112p. (J). (gr. 3-7). mass mkt. 3.50 (0-590-45654-7) Scholastic, Inc.

Morris, Gilbert. Barney Buck & the World's Wackiest Wedding. 1986. (Barney Buck Ser.). 160p. (Orig.). (J). (gr. 6-8). pap. 3.95 o.p. (0-8423-0339-1) Tyndale Hse. Pubs.

Orr, Wendy. The Wedding. 1993. (Illus.). 32p. (J). pap. 4.95 (1-55037-281-5); lib. bdg. 14.95 (1-55037-280-7) Annick Pr., Ltd. CAN. *Dist:* Firefly Bks., Ltd.

Pascal, Francine, creator. The Wedding. 1993. (Sweet Valley High Ser.: No. 98). 224p. (YA). (gr. 7 up). mass mkt. 3.99 o.s.i (0-553-29855-0) Bantam Bks.

Peterson, John. The Littles Have a Wedding. (Littles Ser.). (Illus.). (J). (gr. 1-5). 1993. 96p. mass mkt. 3.99 (0-590-46224-5); 1986. 96p. pap. 2.25 o.p. (0-590-40135-1); 1972. reprint ed. pap. 2.25 o.p. (0-590-32009-2) Scholastic, Inc.

—The Littles Have a Wedding. 1971. (Littles Ser.). (Illus.). (J). (gr. 1-5). 10.14 (0-606-05437-5) Turtleback Bks.

Reid, Alexandra. April Blossom's Wedding. 1996. (Sky Dancers Ser.). (Illus.). 80p. (J). (ps up). pap. 2.50 o.p. (0-694-00944-X, Harper Festival) HarperCollins Children's Bk. Group.

Russell, Ching Yeung. Child Bride. 136p. (J). (gr. 3-7). 2003. pap. 9.95 (1-59078-024-8); 1999. (Illus.). 15.95 (1-56397-748-6) Boyds Mills Pr.

Slightly Off-Center Writers Group Staff. Maid of Honor. 1994. 120p. (YA). pap. 6.95 o.p. (1-56721-067-8) 25th Century Pr.

Soto, Gary. Snapshots from the Wedding. 1997. (Illus.). 32p. (J). (ps-3). 15.99 o.p. (0-399-22808-X) Penguin Group (USA) Inc.

Staples, Suzanne Fisher. Shabanu: Daughter of the Wind. 3rd ed. (J). pap. text 3.99 (0-13-800053-0) Prentice Hall (Schl. Div.).

—Shabanu: Daughter of the Wind. 2003. 288p. pap. 6.50 (0-440-23856-0, Dell Books for Young Readers) Random Hse. Children's Bks.

Stoffle, Eric D. The Wedding Dress Disaster. 1997. (Shoebox Kids Ser.: No. 6). (J). pap. 6.99 (0-8163-1355-5) Pacific Pr. Publishing Assn.

Thomas, Charlotte E. Our Little Flower Girl: A Child Has Her First Experience Participating in a Wedding. 1992. (Illus.). 32p. (J). (ps-5). lib. bdg. 19.95 (0-9633607-0-1) Golden Rings Publishing Co.

—The Ring Bearer's Big Day: A Child Has His First Experience Participating in a Wedding. 1994. (Illus.). 32p. (J). (ps-5). lib. bdg. 19.95 (0-9633607-1-X) Golden Rings Publishing Co.

Van Laan, Nancy. La Boda: A Mexican Wedding Celebration. 1996. (ENG & SPA., Illus.). 32p. (J). (ps-3). 15.95 o.p. (0-316-89626-8) Little Brown & Co.

Willhoite, Michael. Daddy's Wedding. 1996. (Illus.). 32p. (J). (ps-2). reprint ed. 15.95 o.p. (1-55583-350-0, Alyson Wonderland) Alyson Pubns.

William, Kate. The Wedding. 1993. (Sweet Valley High Ser.: No. 98). (YA). (gr. 7 up). 8.60 o.p. (0-606-05639-4) Turtleback Bks.

Zalben, Jane Breskin. Beni's First Wedding, ERS. 1998. (Illus.). 32p. (J). (ps-2). 14.95 (0-8050-4846-4, Holt, Henry & Co. Bks. For Young Readers) Holt, Henry & Co.

MOTHERS—FICTION

A. B. Publishing Staff. Come Home Mother. 1998. (J). (gr. 4-7). pap. text 6.95 (1-881545-92-X) Angela's Bookshelf.

Abramson, Ruth. The Cresta Adventure. 1989. (J). (gr. 4-7). 8.95 o.p. (0-87306-493-3) Feldheim, Philipp Inc.

Ackerman, Karen. By the Dawn's Early Light: Al Amanecer. Ada, Alma Flor, tr. 1994. (ENG & SPA., Illus.). 32p. (J). (ps-3). 16.00 (0-689-31788-3); 14.95 (0-689-31917-7) Simon & Schuster Children's Publishing. (Atheneum).

Ada, Alma Flor. The Kite. 1992. (Stories the Year 'Round Ser.). (Illus.). 23p. (J). (gr. k-12). pap. 7.95 o.p. (1-56014-228-6) Santillana USA Publishing Co., Inc.

—No Fui Yo. . . 1997. (Cuentos para Todo el Ano Ser.). (SPA.). (J). (ps-3). pap. 7.95 o.p. (1-56014-218-9) Santillana USA Publishing Co., Inc.

—El Papalote. 1997. (Cuentos para Todo el Ano Ser.). (SPA., Illus.). 23p. (J). (ps-3). pap. 12.00 o.p. (1-56014-227-8) Santillana USA Publishing Co., Inc.

Adler, C. S. The Shell Lady's Daughter. 1984. 144p. (J). mass mkt. 1.95 o.s.i (0-449-70095-X, Fawcett) Ballantine Bks.

Albury, Gale. The Moonlight Unicorn. Albury, Gale, ed. 1994. (Illus.). 14p. (Orig.). (J). (ps-8). pap. 4.00 (0-9642344-0-8) TEA Printers & Pubs.

Alda, Arlene. Sonya's Mommy Works. Klimo, Kate, ed. 1982. (Illus.). 48p. (J). (ps-3). 7.75 o.p. (0-671-45157-X, Atheneum) Simon & Schuster Children's Publishing.

Alden, Laura. Something for Mother. 1994. (Circle the Year with Holidays Ser.). (Illus.). 32p. (J). lib. bdg. 17.50 o.p. (0-516-00690-8, Children's Pr.) Scholastic Library Publishing.

Alexander, Sue. One More Time, Mama. 1999. (Accelerated Reader Bks.). (Illus.). 32p. (J). (ps-k). 15.95 (0-7614-5051-3, Cavendish Children's Bks.) Cavendish, Marshall Corp.

Alfonsi, Alice. The Orchids & Gumbo Poker Club. Date not set. (Lizzie McGuire Ser.). (Illus.). (J). pap. 4.99 (0-7868-4646-1) Disney Pr.

Anderson, Laurie Halse. No Time for Mother's Day. 2001. 13.10 (0-606-21356-2) Turtleback Bks.

Anderson, Susan. Flowers for Mommy. 1995. (Illus.). (J). (ps-3). 16.95 (0-86543-452-2) Africa World Pr.

Andreae, Giles. Mama Tiene una Casa en la Barriga. 2002. (SPA., Illus.). 102p. (J). (gr. k-2). 14.95 (84-488-1101-1, BS30460) Beascoa, Ediciones S.A. ESP. *Dist:* Lectorum Pubns., Inc.

Andrews, Jan. Pumpkin Time. 1991. (Illus.). 32p. (J). (ps-3). text 12.95 (0-88899-112-6) Publishers Group West.

Apperley, Dawn. Mom Mine. 2003. (Illus.). 16p. (J). bds. 6.99 (0-316-73838-7, Tingley, Megan Bks.) Little Brown Children's Bks.

Arno, Iris H. I Love You, Mom. 1998. 10.10 (0-606-13508-1) Turtleback Bks.

Asch, Frank. Oats & Wild Apples. 1988. (Illus.). 32p. (J). (ps-3). 14.95 o.p. (0-8234-0677-6); pap. 5.95 o.p. (0-8234-0763-2) Holiday Hse., Inc.

Ashman, Linda. Mama's Day. 2002. (Illus.). (J). (gr. k-3). per. 16.00 (0-689-83475-6, Simon & Schuster Children's Publishing) Simon & Schuster Children's Publishing.

Auch, Mary Jane. Kidnapping Kevin Kowalski. 1990. 128p. (J). (gr. 4-6). 15.95 o.p. (0-8234-0815-9) Holiday Hse., Inc.

—Mom Is Dating Weird Wayne. 1991. 160p. (J). (gr. 4-7). pap. 2.99 o.s.i (0-553-15916-X) Bantam Bks.

Axworthy, Anni. Guess Who My Mommy Is. 1999. (Peephole Bks.). (Illus.). 28p. (J). (ps-k). 7.99 o.p. (0-7636-0734-7) Candlewick Pr.

Bailey, Debbie. Mi Mama. 2003. (SPA., Illus.). 14p. (J). (ps). bds. 5.95 (1-55037-264-5) Annick Pr., Ltd. CAN. *Dist:* Firefly Bks., Ltd., Lectorum Pubns., Inc.

Bailey, Debbie & Huszar, Susan. Ma Maman. 1992. Tr. of My Mom. (FRE., Illus.). 14p. (J). (ps). bds. 4.95 (1-55037-267-X) Annick Pr., Ltd. CAN. *Dist:* Firefly Bks., Ltd.

Balian, Lorna. Mother's Mothers' Day. 1994. (Illus.). 32p. (J). (ps-3). reprint ed. 12.95 o.p. (0-687-37097-3) Abingdon Pr.

Ballard, Robin. Gracie. 1993. (Illus.). 24p. (J). (ps up). lib. bdg. 13.93 o.p. (0-688-11807-0, Greenwillow Bks.) HarperCollins Children's Bk. Group.

Balter, Lawrence. A. J.'s Mom Gets a New Job. 1990. (Stepping Stone Stories Ser.). (Illus.). 40p. (J). (ps-3). 5.95 o.p. (0-8120-6151-9) Barron's Educational Series, Inc.

Banks, Kate. Close Your Eyes, RS. 2002. (Illus.). 40p. (J). (ps-1). 16.00 (0-374-31382-2, Farrar, Straus & Giroux (BYR)) Farrar, Straus & Giroux.

—Mama's Coming Home, RS. 2003. (Illus.). 32p. (J). (ps-1). 16.00 (0-374-34747-6, Farrar, Straus & Giroux (BYR)) Farrar, Straus & Giroux.

Barber, Barbara E. Saturday at the New You. 2002. (Illus.). (J). 14.66 (0-7587-3566-9) Book Wholesalers, Inc.

—Saturday at the New You. (Illus.). 32p. (J). (ps up). 1994. 14.95 (1-880000-06-7); 1996. reprint ed. pap. 6.95 (1-880000-43-1) Lee & Low Bks., Inc.

—Saturday at the New You. 1994. (J). 13.10 (0-606-09819-4) Turtleback Bks.

Baskin, Nora Raleigh. What Every Girl (Except Me) Knows. 2001. 224p. (J). (gr. 4-7). 16.95 (0-316-07021-1) Little Brown & Co.

Bat-Ami, Miriam. When the Frost Is Gone. 1994. (Illus.). 80p. (YA). (gr. 5 up). lib. bdg. 13.95 o.s.i (0-02-708497-3, Simon & Schuster Children's Publishing) Simon & Schuster Children's Publishing.

Bates, A. Mother's Helper. 1991. 176p. (YA). (gr. 7-9). mass mkt. 3.25 (0-590-44582-0, Scholastic Paperbacks) Scholastic, Inc.

Bates, Betty. It Must've Been the Fishsticks. 1983. 144p. (J). (gr. 5-7). pap. (0-671-46540-6, Simon Pulse) Simon & Schuster Children's Publishing.

—My Mom, the Money Nut. 1981. (Columbia University, Teachers College, Contributions to Education Ser.). (J). (gr. 4-6). pap. (0-671-56065-4, Simon Pulse) Simon & Schuster Children's Publishing.

Bauer, Caroline Feller. My Mom Travels a Lot. (Illus.). (J). (gr. k-3). 1983. flmstrp 32.95 (0-941078-24-8); 1983. pap. 14.95 o.p. incl. audio (0-941078-21-3); 1983. pap. 31.95 o.p. incl. audio (0-941078-22-1); 1983. pap. 31.95 o.p. incl. audio (0-941078-22-1); 1982. 22.95 o.p. incl. audio (0-941078-23-X) Live Oak Media.

—My Mom Travels a Lot. 1981. (Illus.). 48p. (J). (gr. k-3). 11.95 o.p. (0-7232-6203-9); pap. 4.95 o.p. (0-7232-6249-7) Penguin Putnam Bks. for Young Readers. (Warne, Frederick).

Bauer, Marion Dane. Grandmother's Song. 2000. (Illus.). 32p. (J). (ps-3). 16.00 (0-689-82272-3, Simon & Schuster Children's Publishing) Simon & Schuster Children's Publishing.

—Like Mother, Like Daughter. 1985. 156p. (J). (gr. 5-9). 12.95 o.p. (0-89919-356-0, Clarion Bks.) Houghton Mifflin Co. Trade & Reference Div.

—My Mother Is Mine. (Illus.). 40p. (J). 2004. pap. 5.99 (0-689-86695-X, Aladdin); 2001. 13.00 (0-689-82267-7, Simon & Schuster Children's Publishing) Simon & Schuster Children's Publishing.

—A Question of Trust. (YA). (gr. 4 up). 1995. mass mkt. 2.99 o.p. (0-590-47923-7); 1994. 128p. pap. 14.95 o.p. (0-590-47915-6) Scholastic, Inc.

—A Question of Trust. 1994. (YA). (gr. 4 up). 8.09 o.p. (0-606-08591-2) Turtleback Bks.

Baum, Louis. After Dark. 1990. (Illus.). 320p. (J). (ps-3). 11.95 o.p. (0-87951-382-9) Overlook Pr., The.

Beall, Pamela Conn. Wee Sing Mother Goose. 2003. (Wee Sing Ser.). (Illus.). 64p. pap. 9.99 incl. audio (0-8431-0299-3, Price Stern Sloan) Penguin Putnam Bks. for Young Readers.

—Wee Sing Mother Goose. 2003. (Illus.). 64p. pap. 2.99 incl. audio (0-8431-0301-9, Wee Sing Bks.) Putnam Publishing Group, The.

Beck, Scott & Kalidasa. Mud Pie for Mother. Ryder, Arthur W., tr. 2003. 32p. (J). (ps-1). 14.99 (0-525-47040-9, Dutton) Dutton/Plume.

Bell, Caroline. I Love My Mom. 2000. (J). (0-88902-292-5) Fitzhenry & Whiteside, Ltd.

Belle Prater's Boy. 1999. (Pathways to Critical Thinking Ser.). 32p. (YA). pap. text, stu. ed., tchr.'s training gde. ed. 19.95 (1-58303-081-6) Pathways Publishing.

Berenstain, Stan & Berenstain, Jan. The Berenstain Bears & the Mixed-Up Mama's Day. 2004. (J). 3.99 (0-375-81132-X); lib. bdg. (0-375-91132-4) Random Hse., Inc.

Bergman, Tamar. Where Is? 2002. (Illus.). 24p. (J). (ps-3). tchr. ed. 15.00 (0-618-09539-X, Lorraine, A. Walter) Houghton Mifflin Co. Trade & Reference Div.

Berridge, Celia. Hannah's Temper. 1993. (Illus.). 24p. (J). (ps-1). pap. 10.95 o.p. (0-590-45887-6) Scholastic, Inc.

Berry, Christine. Mama Went Walking, ERS. 1990. (Illus.). 32p. (J). (ps-2). 14.95 o.p. (0-8050-1261-3, Holt, Henry & Co. Bks. For Young Readers) Holt, Henry & Co.

Blackman, Malorie. Girl Wonder & the Terrific Twins. 1993. (Illus.). 80p. (J). (gr. 2-5). 12.99 o.s.i (0-525-45065-3, Dutton Children's Bks.) Penguin Putnam Bks. for Young Readers.

Blaine, Mary. Terrible Thing That Happened at Our House. 1983. (Illus.). 32p. (J). (gr. k-3). pap. 2.95 o.p. (0-590-40355-9) Scholastic, Inc.

Bliss, Corinne Demas. Electra & the Charlotte Russe. 1997. (Illus.). 32p. (J). (ps-3). 14.95 (1-56397-436-3) Boyds Mills Pr.

Bongiorno, Patti Lynn. Where Does a Mom's Love Go? 2nd ed. 2001. (J). spiral bd. 20.00 (0-9715819-0-8) Bongiorno Bks.

Book, Rita. My Soccer Mom from Mars. 2001. (All Aboard Reading Ser.). (Illus.). 48p. (J). 13.89 o.p. (0-448-42615-3); mass mkt. 3.99 (0-448-42599-8) Penguin Putnam Bks. for Young Readers. (Grosset & Dunlap).

Boulden, Jim & Boulden, Joan. Mom & Me: Single Parent Activity Book. 1993. (Illus.). 32p. (J). (gr. 3-6). pap. 5.95 (*1-878076-25-6*) Boulden Publishing.

Brabham, Barbara T. My Mom Is Handicapped: A "Grownup" Children's Book. 1996. (Illus.). 20p. (J). (gr. k-6). pap. 17.95 (*1-882185-22-6*) Cornerstone Publishing.

Bradbury, Judy. A Rip-Roaring High-Flying Mother's Day Fair! 1997. (Christopher Counts). (Illus.). 48p. (J). (gr. k-2). 10.95 (*0-07-007041-5*) McGraw-Hill Trade.

Bradby, Marie. Momma, Where Are You From? 2000. (Illus.). 32p. (J). lib. bdg. 17.99 (*0-531-33105-9*); pap. 16.95 (*0-531-30105-2*) Scholastic, Inc. (Orchard Bks.).

Brami, Elisabeth. Mommy Time. 2002. (Illus.). 48p. (YA). (gr. k up). 9.95 (*1-929132-22-0*) Kane/Miller Bk. Pubs.

Brandt, Amy. Benjamin Comes Back. de la Vega, Eida, tr. 2004. (Child Care Bks. for Kids).Tr. of Benjamin Regresa. (ENG & SPA., Illus.). 32p. (J). (ps-3). pap. 11.95 (*1-884834-79-5*, 709801) Redleaf Pr.

Braun, Sebastien. I Love My Mommy. 2004. 32p. (J). 12.99 (*0-06-054310-8*) HarperCollins Pubs.

Brelis, Nancy. The Mother Market. 1975. (Illus.). 160p. (J). pap. 1.50 o.p. (*0-06-440062-X*) HarperCollins Pubs.

Bridges, Margaret Park. If I Were Your Mother. 1950. (Illus.). 32p. (J). (ps-3). 15.89 (*0-688-15191-4*) HarperCollins Children's Bk. Group.

—If I Were Your Mother. 1999. (Illus.). 32p. (J). (ps-3). 15.95 (*0-688-15190-6*, Morrow, William & Co.) Morrow/Avon.

Bridwell, Norman. Clifford's Happy Mother's Day. 2000. (Clifford, the Big Red Dog Ser.). (Illus.). (J). 9.65 (*0-606-21114-4*) Turtleback Bks.

Brinkerhoff, Shirley. Tangled Web, 2000. (Nikki Sheridan Ser.: Vol. 5). 176p. (J). (gr. 9-12). pap. 5.99 (*1-56179-737-5*) Bethany Hse. Pubs.

Browne, Anthony. Piggybook. 1986. (Illus.). 32p. (J). (ps-3). 14.99 o.s.i (*0-394-98416-1*, Knopf Bks. for Young Readers) Random Hse. Children's Bks.

—Piggybook. 1986. (J). 14.14 (*0-606-04771-9*) Turtleback Bks.

Bryant, Megan E. Just Like Mommy. 2003. (Illus.). 32p. (J). 6.99 (*0-448-43107-6*, Grosset & Dunlap) Penguin Putnam Bks. for Young Readers.

Buehner, Caralyn. I Want to Say I Love You. 2001. (Illus.). 32p. (J). 16.99 (*0-8037-2547-7*, Fogelman, Phyllis Bks.) Penguin Putnam Bks. for Young Readers.

Buller, Jon & Schade, Susan. I Love You, Good Night. 1988. (J). pap. 5.95 o.s.i (*0-671-66561-8*, Simon & Schuster Children's Publishing) Simon & Schuster Children's Publishing.

Bunting, Eve. Mother, How Could You! 1986. (YA). (gr. 7 up). pap. (*0-671-60699-9*, Simon Pulse) Simon & Schuster Children's Publishing.

Butterworth, Nick. My Mom Is Excellent. (Illus.). 32p. (J). 2003. 5.99 (*0-7636-2050-5*); 1994. bds. 4.99 (*1-56402-289-7*) Candlewick Pr.

Cachiaras, Dot. I'm Glad God Thought of Mothers. 1979. (Happy Day Bks.). (Illus.). 24p. (J). (gr. k-3). 1.59 o.p. (*0-87239-360-7*, 3630) Standard Publishing.

Calvert, Patricia. Yesterday's Daughter. 1986. 144p. (YA). (gr. 7 up). 13.95 o.p. (*0-684-18746-9*, Atheneum) Simon & Schuster Children's Publishing.

Cannon, Ann E. I Know What You Do When I Go to School. 1996. (Illus.). 32p. (J). (gr. 1-4). 14.95 o.s.i (*0-87905-743-2*) Smith, Gibbs Pub.

Capucilli, Alyssa Satin. Only My Mom & Me. 2003. (Illus.). 16p. (J). (ps up). 6.99 (*0-694-52585-5*, Harper Festival) HarperCollins Children's Bk. Group.

Carlin, Joi. Mommy's Bed Is Best. 1995. (Illus.). (J). o.p. (*1-884244-08-4*) Volcano Pr.

Carlstrom, Nancy White. I'm Not Moving, Mama! (Illus.). 32p. (J). (ps-3). 1999. pap. 5.99 (*0-689-82881-0*, Aladdin); 1990. lib. bdg. 13.95 (*0-02-717286-4*, Simon & Schuster Children's Publishing) Simon & Schuster Children's Publishing.

—I'm Not Moving, Mama! 1990. (Illus.). (J). 12.14 (*0-606-17924-0*) Turtleback Bks.

Carrick, Carol. Mothers Are Like That. 2000. (Illus.). 32p. (J). (ps-ps). tchr. ed. 15.00 (*0-395-88351-2*, Clarion Bks.) Houghton Mifflin Co. Trade & Reference Div.

Caseley, Judith. Mama, Coming & Going. 1994. (Illus.). 32p. (J). (ps-3). 15.95 (*0-688-11441-5*); lib. bdg. 13.93 o.p. (*0-688-11442-3*) HarperCollins Children's Bk. Group. (Greenwillow Bks.).

Chaffin, Lillie D. Tommy's Big Problem. 1977. (Illus.). (J). (ps-2). lib. bdg. 7.19 o.p. (*0-8313-0016-7*) Lantern Pr., Inc., Pubs.

Chang, Cindy. Are You My Baby? Mini Peek Book. 1996. (J). bds. 3.99 o.s.i (*0-679-88275-8*, Random Hse. Bks. for Young Readers) Random Hse. Children's Bks.

Chapman, Christina. Treasure in the Attic. 1992. (Publish-a-Book Contest Ser.). (Illus.). 32p. (J). (gr. 1-6). lib. bdg. 22.83 o.p. (*0-8114-3582-2*) Raintree Pubs.

Charnley, Nathaniel & Charney, Betty J. Martha Ann & the Mother Store. 1973. (Illus.). 32p. (J). (gr. k-3). 5.50 o.p. (*0-15-252150-X*) Harcourt Children's Bks.

Chartier, Normand. Gertie's Not Alone. 1996. (Illus.). 40p. (ps-3). 8.99 o.p. (*0-88070-920-0*) Zonderkidz.

Chevalier, Christa. Spence Isn't Spence Anymore. Levine, Abby, ed. 1985. (Illus.). 32p. (J). (ps-1). 13.95 o.p. (*0-8075-7565-8*) Whitman, Albert & Co.

Chick, Sandra. On the Rocks. 1997. (Livewire Ser.). 148p. (YA). (gr. 7-11). pap. 8.95 (*0-7043-4938-8*) Women's Pr., Ltd., The GBR. *Dist:* Trafalgar Square.

Childress, Alice. Rainbow Jordan. 1982. 128p. (J). (gr. 7-12). pap. 4.99 (*0-380-58974-5*, Avon Bks.) Morrow/Avon.

—Rainbow Jordan. 1981. (Illus.). 182p. (J). (gr. 7 up). 14.99 o.s.i (*0-698-32500-1*, Coward-McCann) Penguin Group (USA) Inc.

—Rainbow Jordan. 1981. (J). 13.95 o.s.i (*0-698-20531-6*) Putnam Publishing Group, The.

—Rainbow Jordan. 1998. (YA). 20.25 (*0-8446-6966-0*) Smith, Peter Pub., Inc.

—Rainbow Jordan. 1981. 10.04 (*0-606-00560-9*) Turtleback Bks.

Christelow, Eileen. Don't Wake up Mama! 1996. (Illus.). 32p. (J). (ps-ps). pap. 5.95 (*0-395-76479-3*, Clarion Bks.) Houghton Mifflin Co. Trade & Reference Div.

—Don't Wake up Mama! 1992. 12.10 (*0-606-08728-1*) Turtleback Bks.

Chwast, Seymour. Traffic Jam. 1999. (Illus.). 32p. (J). (ps-3). tchr. ed. 15.00 o.s.i (*0-395-97495-X*) Houghton Mifflin Co.

Clark, Ann Nolan. In My Mother's House. 1992. (Picture Puffin Ser.). (Illus.). (J). 10.19 o.p. (*0-606-00517-X*) Turtleback Bks.

Clayton, Laura E. Molly Helps Mother. 1994. (Illus.). 24p. (J). (ps-2). pap. 2.70 (*0-7399-0049-8*, 2538) Rod & Staff Pubs., Inc.

Cleary, Beverly. Emily's Runaway Imagination. 2002. (J). 13.83 (*0-7587-9141-0*) Book Wholesalers, Inc.

—Emily's Runaway Imagination. 1988. mass mkt. o.s.i (*0-440-80049-8*) Dell Publishing.

—Emily's Runaway Imagination. (Cleary Reissue Ser.). (Illus.). (J). (gr. 4-7). 1990. 240p. pap. 5.99 (*0-380-70923-6*, Harper Trophy); 1961. 224p. lib. bdg. 16.89 (*0-688-31267-5*) HarperCollins Children's Bk. Group.

—Emily's Runaway Imagination. 1961. (Illus.). 224p. (J). (gr. 3-7). 16.00 o.p. (*0-688-21267-0*, Morrow, William & Co.) Morrow/Avon.

—Emily's Runaway Imagination. (J). (gr. 2-4). 221p. pap. 4.95 (*0-8072-1416-7*); 1986. audio 15.98 (*0-8072-1140-0*, SWR48SP) Random Hse. Audio Publishing Group. (Listening Library).

—Emily's Runaway Imagination, unabr. ed. 1992. (J). (gr. 4). audio 35.00 (*1-55690-609-9*, 92302E7) Recorded Bks., LLC.

—Emily's Runaway Imagination. 1990. (J). 11.00 (*0-606-04665-8*) Turtleback Bks.

Clifton, Lucille. Everett Anderson's 1-2-3, ERS. (Illus.). (J). (gr. k-3). 1977. o.p. (*0-03-017441-4*); 1992. 32p. 16.95 (*0-8050-2310-0*) Holt, Henry & Co. (Holt, Henry & Co. Bks. For Young Readers).

Clymer, Eleanor. My Mother Is the Smartest Woman in the World. 1982. (Illus.). 96p. (J). (gr. 4-6). 13.95 (*0-689-30916-3*, Atheneum) Simon & Schuster Children's Publishing.

Cohen, Caron Lee. Happy to You! 2001. (Illus.). 32p. (J). (ps-ps). tchr. ed. 15.00 (*0-618-04229-6*, Clarion Bks.) Houghton Mifflin Co. Trade & Reference Div.

Cohen, Caron Lee & Litzinger, Rosanne, illus. Happy to You! 2001. (J). (*0-689-82421-1*, Simon & Schuster Children's Publishing) Simon & Schuster Children's Publishing.

Cole, Babette. Babette Cole's Mum. 1997. (Illus.). 10p. (*0-434-80099-6*) Heinemann, William Ltd.

—The Trouble with Mom. 1984. (Illus.). 32p. (J). (gr. 5-8). pap. 5.95 o.s.i (*0-698-20681-9*, G. P. Putnam's Sons) Penguin Group (USA) Inc.

—The Trouble with Mom. (Illus.). 32p. (J). 1997. (ps-1). pap. 5.95 o.p. (*0-698-11593-7*, PaperStar); 1984. (gr. 5-8). 13.95 o.p. (*0-698-20597-9*, G. P. Putnam's Sons) Penguin Putnam Bks. for Young Readers.

—The Trouble with Mom. 1986. (J). (ps-3). 5.95 o.s.i (*0-698-20624-X*) Putnam Publishing Group, The.

Cole, Brock. The Facts Speak for Themselves. 1997. 192p. (YA). (gr. 7 up). 16.95 (*1-886910-14-6*) Front Street, Inc.

—The Facts Speak for Themselves. 2000. (Illus.). 192p. (J). (gr. 9-12). pap. 5.99 o.s.i (*0-14-130696-3*) Penguin Putnam Bks. for Young Readers.

—The Facts Speak for Themselves. 2000. (Illus.). (J). 12.04 (*0-606-18403-1*) Turtleback Bks.

Colfer, Eoin. The Arctic Incident. 2003. (Artemis Fowl Ser.: Bk. 1). 304p. (J). (gr. 3-6). pap. 7.99 (*0-7868-1708-9*) Hyperion Bks. for Children.

—Artemis Fowl. 2002. (Artemis Fowl Ser.: Bk. 1). 288p. (J). (gr. 4-7). pap. 7.99 (*0-7868-1707-0*) Disney Pr.

—Artemis Fowl. l.t. ed. 2001. (Artemis Fowl Ser.: Bk. 1). 312p. (J). (gr. 3-6). 27.95 (*1-58724-092-0*, Wheeler Publishing, Inc.) Gale Group.

—Artemis Fowl. 2003. (Artemis Fowl Ser.: Bk. 1). (Illus.). 304p. (J). (gr. 3-6). mass mkt. 5.99 (*0-7868-1787-9*) Hyperion Bks. for Children.

—Artemis Fowl. 2001. (Artemis Fowl Ser.: Bk. 1). 288p. (gr. 4-7). 16.95 (*0-7868-0801-2*) Talk Miramax Bks.

Colman, Hila. Sometimes I Don't Love My Mother. 1979. 188p. (J). (gr. 7 up). reprint ed. pap. 2.25 o.p. (*0-590-33736-X*) Scholastic, Inc.

Coman, Carolyn. Tell Me Everything, RS. 1993. 160p. (YA). (gr. 5-9). 15.00 o.p. (*0-374-37390-6*, Farrar, Straus & Giroux (BYR)) Farrar, Straus & Giroux.

Conford, Ellen. A Job for Jenny Archer. 1988. (Illus.). 76p. (J). (gr. 3-5). 9.95 o.p. (*0-316-15262-5*) Little Brown & Co.

—A Job for Jenny Archer. 1990. (Springboard Bks.). 80p. (J). (gr. 4-7). pap. 4.95 (*0-316-15349-4*, Tingley, Megan Bks.) Little Brown Children's Bks.

—A Job for Jenny Archer. 1988. (Springboard Bks.). (J). 10.65 (*0-606-04452-3*) Turtleback Bks.

Cooney, Caroline B. Operation: Homefront. 1992. 224p. (J). mass mkt. 3.99 o.s.i (*0-440-22689-9*, Dell Books for Young Readers) Random Hse. Children's Bks.

Cooper, Ilene. Stupid Cupid. 1995. (Holiday Five Ser.). 144p. (J). (gr. 3-7). 14.99 o.s.i (*0-670-85059-4*, Viking Children's Bks.) Penguin Putnam Bks. for Young Readers.

Corcoran, Barbara. Face the Music. 1985. 204p. (YA). (gr. 7 up). 12.95 o.p. (*0-689-31139-7*, Atheneum) Simon & Schuster Children's Publishing.

Cordes, Jayne A. The Hope Star. 1999. (Illus.). 32p. (YA). (ps up). 16.95 (*0-9662670-1-X*) J. Kid Productions, Ltd.

Corey, Dorothy. Will There Be a Lap for Me? Levine, Abby, ed. 1992. (Illus.). 24p. (J). (gr. k-2). lib. bdg. 13.95 (*0-8075-9109-2*); pap. 5.95 (*0-8075-9110-6*) Whitman, Albert & Co.

Cowell, Cressida. Don't Do That, Kitty Kilroy. 2000. (Illus.). 32p. (J). (ps-2). pap. 15.95 (*0-531-30209-1*, Orchard Bks.) Scholastic, Inc.

Cowen-Fletcher, Jane. Mama Zooms. (J). (ps-3). 1994. 32p. pap. 4.99 (*0-590-45775-6*); 1993. 19.95 (*0-590-72848-2*) Scholastic, Inc.

—Mama Zooms. 1995. 11.14 (*0-606-11593-5*) Turtleback Bks.

Crawford, Joy. Mom Come Quick. 1997. (Illus.). 8p. (Orig.). (J). (ps up). pap. 4.50 (*0-9652368-3-8*) Wright Publishing, Inc.

Curtis, Jamie Lee. My Mommy Hung the Moon. Date not set. 32p. (ps-3). lib. bdg. 17.89 (*0-06-029017-X*); (J). 16.99 (*0-06-029016-1*); (J). pap. 6.99 (*0-06-443696-9*) HarperCollins Pubs.

Dagon, Janet. Don't Tell Mom. 144p. (J). (gr. 5-8). 1991. pap. 2.99 o.p. (*0-87406-537-2*); 5th ed. 1997. reprint ed. pap. 3.99 (*0-87406-874-6*, Willowisp Pr.) Darby Creek Publishing.

Dale, Elizabeth. How Long? 1998. (Illus.). 32p. (J). (ps-1). pap. 14.95 (*0-531-30101-X*, Orchard Bks.) Scholastic, Inc.

Daly, Niki. Ben's Gingerbread Man. 1985. (Illus.). 24p. (J). (ps-1). 4.95 o.p. (*0-670-80806-7*, Viking Children's Bks.) Penguin Putnam Bks. for Young Readers.

Danis, Naomi. Walk with Me. 1995. (Story Corner Ser.). (Illus.). 24p. (J). (ps-3). bds. 6.95 (*0-590-45855-8*, Cartwheel Bks.) Scholastic, Inc.

Dannhauss, Dianne. The Day My Mom Almost Enrolled in Preschool. Bowen, Debbie, ed. 1998. (Professional Mom Ser.). (Illus.). 15p. (J). (gr. 1-4). pap. text 2.95 o.p. (*1-56763-150-9*); lib. bdg. 19.95 (*1-56763-149-5*) Ozark Publishing.

—My Mom, the Professional. 1994. (Illus.). 24p. (J). (gr. k-4). pap. 7.95 (*0-89896-104-1*) Larksdale.

—My Mom, the Professional. Bowen, Debbie, ed. 1998. (Professional Mom Ser.). (Illus.). 23p. (J). (gr. 1-4). pap. 6.95 o.p. (*1-56763-148-7*); lib. bdg. 19.95 (*1-56763-147-9*) Ozark Publishing.

De Regniers, Beatrice Schenk. Laura's Story. 1979. (Illus.). (J). (ps-1). 9.95 o.s.i (*0-689-30677-6*, Atheneum) Simon & Schuster Children's Publishing.

—Waiting for Mama. 1984. (Illus.). 32p. (J). (ps-2). 9.95 o.p. (*0-89919-222-X*, Clarion Bks.) Houghton Mifflin Co. Trade & Reference Div.

Delton, Judy. Angel's Mother's Boyfriend. 1986. (Illus.). 176p. (J). (gr. 4-6). tchr. ed. 16.00 (*0-395-39968-8*) Houghton Mifflin Co.

—Angel's Mother's Boyfriend. 1999. (Illus.). 176p. (J). (gr. 4-6). pap. 4.95 (*0-395-97913-7*) Houghton Mifflin Co. Trade & Reference Div.

—Angel's Mother's Boyfriend. 1990. 176p. (J). (gr. k-6). reprint ed. pap. 2.95 o.s.i (*0-440-40275-1*, Yearling) Random Hse. Children's Bks.

—Angel's Mother's Boyfriend. 1999. 11.00 (*0-606-17363-3*) Turtleback Bks.

—Angel's Mother's Wedding. 1990. 176p. (J). (gr. k-6). pap. 2.95 o.s.i (*0-440-40281-6*, Yearling) Random Hse. Children's Bks.

—Bad, Bad Bunnies. 1990. (Pee Wee Scouts Ser.: No. 12). 80p. (gr. 2-5). pap. text 3.99 o.s.i (*0-440-40278-6*, Yearling) Random Hse. Children's Bks.

—Bad, Bad Bunnies. 1990. (Pee Wee Scouts Ser.: No. 12). (J). (gr. 2-5). 10.14 (*0-606-03042-5*) Turtleback Bks.

Desrosiers, Sylvie. Ma Mere Est une Extraterrestre. 2002. (Premier Roman Ser.). (FRE., Illus.). 64p. (J). pap. 8.95 (*2-89021-561-X*) La Courte Echelle CAN. *Dist:* Firefly Bks., Ltd.

Dickinson, Peter. The Kin: Mana's Story. 1999. (Kin Ser.). (Illus.). (gr. 5-9). 160p. (J). 14.99 o.s.i (*0-399-23350-4*); 211p. (YA). 3.99 o.s.i (*0-448-41712-X*) Penguin Putnam Bks. for Young Readers. (Grosset & Dunlap).

—The Kin: Mana's Story. 1999. 10.04 (*0-606-17678-0*) Turtleback Bks.

Dijs, Carla. Are You My Mommy? 1990. (Illus.). 20p. (J). (ps). 6.95 (*0-671-70226-2*, Little Simon) Simon & Schuster Children's Publishing.

—Mommy, Would You Love Me If . . .? 1996. (Illus.). 14p. (J). (ps-k). 8.99 (*0-689-80813-5*, Little Simon) Simon & Schuster Children's Publishing.

Doman, Bruce K. Goodbye, Mommy. 1982. (Gentle Revolution Ser.). (Illus.). 86p. (J). (ps-2). 8.95 o.p. (*0-936676-00-0*) Institute for the Achievement of Human Potential.

Dorer, Ann. Mother Makes a Mistake. 1991. (People Who Have Helped the World Ser.). 32p. (J). (gr. 1-2). lib. bdg. 18.60 o.p. (*0-8368-0109-1*) Stevens, Gareth Inc.

Dorflinger, Carolyn. Tomorrow Is Mom's Birthday. 1996. (Illus.). 32p. (J). (ps-3). pap. 5.95 (*1-879085-67-4*, Whispering Coyote) Charlesbridge Publishing, Inc.

Dorn, Charlotte & Becker, Peter. Mother Holle. 1993. (Illus.). 24p. (J). per. 8.95 (*1-55082-043-5*) Quarry Pr. CAN. *Dist:* LPC/InBook.

Doty, Ruth. Elizabeth, the Real Mother Goose. Stollman, Carolyn, ed. 1997. (Illus.). 32p. (Orig.). (J). (gr. 4-6). 14.95 (*0-9658089-0-4*); pap. 8.95 (*0-9658089-1-2*) Howell Publishing Co.

Downing, Julie. Where Is My Mommy? 2003. (Illus.). 32p. (J). 15.99 (*0-688-17824-3*); lib. bdg. 16.89 (*0-688-17825-1*) Morrow/Avon. (Morrow, William & Co.).

Drescher, Joan. My Mother's Getting Married. 32p. (J). (ps-3). 1993. pap. 5.99 o.s.i (*0-14-054667-7*, Puffin Bks.); 1989. (Illus.). pap. 4.95 o.p. (*0-8037-0642-1*) Penguin Putnam Bks. for Young Readers.

Duncan. Just Like a Mama. 1997. (J). 14.95 (*0-689-80584-5*, Atheneum) Simon & Schuster Children's Publishing.

Eastman, P. D. Are You My Mother? l.t. ed. (Illus.). 72p. (ps-3). 1966. lib. bdg. 11.99 (*0-394-90018-9*); 1960. 8.99 (*0-394-80018-4*) Beginner Bks.

—Are You My Mother? 2000. (Storybook Blocks Ser.). (Illus.). (J). (ps-k). 19.95 (*1-58260-013-9*) Infinity Plus One, LLC.

—Are You My Mother? 1986. (J). (ps-1). pap. 8.95 o.s.i incl. audio (*0-394-88325-X*, Random Hse. Bks. for Young Readers) Random Hse. Children's Bks.

—Are You My Mother? Vallier, Jean, tr. 1967. (French Beginner Bks.). (ENG & FRE., Illus.). (J). (gr. k-3). 2.95 o.s.i (*0-394-80174-1*); lib. bdg. 6.99 o.s.i (*0-394-90174-6*) Random Hse. Children's Bks. (Random Hse. Bks. for Young Readers).

—Are You My Mother? Rivera, C., tr. l.t. ed. 1998. (Bright & Early Board Bks.). (ENG & SPA., Illus.). 24p. (J). (ps). bds. 4.99 (*0-679-89047-5*, Random Hse. Bks. for Young Readers) Random Hse. Children's Bks.

—Are You My Mother? - Eres Tu Mi Mama? 1993. (Bilingual Beginner Books & Cassettes Ser.). (ENG & SPA., Illus.). 64p. (J). (ps-3). 6.95 o.s.i incl. audio (*0-679-84330-2*, Random Hse. Bks. for Young Readers) Random Hse. Children's Bks.

Eastman, P. D. & Saunders, Paola Bedarida. Eres Tu Mi Mama? Includes Go, Dog Go! & Best Nest. Rivera, Carlos, tr. 1994. (Beginner Book Video Ser.). (ENG & SPA.). (J). 9.98 o.s.i (*0-679-85620-X*) Random Hse. Video.

Edwards, Michelle. Meera's Blanket. (Illus.). 40p. (J). (ps up). 1995. 15.00 o.p. (*0-688-09710-3*); 1924. lib. bdg. 14.93 o.s.i (*0-688-09711-1*) HarperCollins Children's Bk. Group.

Edwards, Richard. Copy Me, Copycub. 1999. (Illus.). 32p. (J). (ps-2). 14.95 (*0-06-028570-2*) HarperCollins Children's Bk. Group.

Ehrlich, Amy. Where It Stops, Nobody Knows. 1990. 224p. (YA). (gr. 6 up). pap. 4.99 o.s.i (*0-14-034266-4*, Puffin Bks.) Penguin Putnam Bks. for Young Readers.

Ehrlich, H. M. Gotcha, Louie! 2002. (Illus.). 32p. (J). (ps-3). 15.00 (*0-618-19549-1*) Houghton Mifflin Co.

Eisenberg, Phyllis R. You're My Nikki. (Illus.). 32p. (J). (ps-3). 1995. pap. 5.99 o.s.i (*0-14-055463-7*, Puffin Bks.); 1992. 13.89 o.s.i (*0-8037-1129-8*, Dial Bks. for Young Readers); 1992. 14.00 o.s.i (*0-8037-1127-1*, Dial Bks. for Young Readers) Penguin Putnam Bks. for Young Readers.

Esterl, Arnica. Okino & the Whales. abr. ed. 1995. Tr. of Okino und die Wale. (Illus.). 32p. (J). (ps-3). 16.00 (*0-15-200377-0*) Harcourt Trade Pubs.

ETR Associates Staff. The Day Mama Got Her Bonus, Set. 1993. (J). (gr. 4 up). 235.00 (*1-56071-081-0*) ETR Assocs.

Evans, Edie. I Love You Mommy! 1999. (Little Golden Bks.). (Illus.). 16p. (J). (ps-3). 2.99 (*0-307-99507-0*, Golden Bks.) Random Hse. Children's Bks.

Evans, Lezlie. If I Were the Wind. 1997. (Illus.). 32p. (J). (ps-2). (*1-59093-066-5*); per. (*1-59093-065-7*) Warehousing & Fulfillment Specialists, LLC (WFS, LLC). (Eager Minds Pr.).

Falwell, Cathryn. Where's Mommy? 1924. (J). o.s.i (*0-688-09277-2*); lib. bdg. o.s.i (*0-688-09278-0*) HarperCollins Children's Bk. Group.

Farber, Norma. Without Wings, Mother, How Can I Fly?, ERS. 1998. (Illus.). 32p. (J). (ps-1). 15.95 o.s.i (*0-8050-3380-7*, Holt, Henry & Co. Bks. For Young Readers) Holt, Henry & Co.

Farrell, Sue. To the Pool with Mama. 2000. (Illus.). 24p. (J). (ps). pap. 4.95 (*1-55037-620-9*); lib. bdg. 15.95 (*1-55037-621-7*) Annick Pr., Ltd. CAN. *Dist:* Firefly Bks., Ltd.

—To the Post Office with Mama. 1994. (Illus.). 24p. (J). (ps-k). pap. 4.95 (*1-55037-358-7*); lib. bdg. 15.95 (*1-55037-359-5*) Annick Pr., Ltd. CAN. *Dist:* Firefly Bks., Ltd.

—To the Post Office with Mama. ed. 1994. (J). (gr. 2). spiral bd. (*0-616-01636-0*) Canadian National Institute for the Blind/Institut National Canadien pour les Aveugles.

Ferguson, Alane. Secrets. 1997. 160p. (J). (gr. 3-7). 16.00 (*0-689-80313-3*, Simon & Schuster Children's Publishing) Simon & Schuster Children's Publishing.

Fernandes, Eugenie. Just You & Me. 1993. (Illus.). 32p. (J). (ps-k). pap. 4.95 (*1-55037-327-7*); lib. bdg. 14.95 (*1-55037-324-2*) Annick Pr., Ltd. CAN. *Dist:* Firefly Bks., Ltd.

Filichia, Peter. The Most Embarrassing Mother in the World. 1991. 192p. (J). pap. 3.50 (*0-380-76084-3*, Avon Bks.) Morrow/Avon.

Fine, Anne. Goggle-Eyes. 2003. (Read-Along Ser.). (J). pap. 29.95 incl. audio (*0-7540-6211-2*, Galaxy Children's Large Print) BBC Audiobooks America.

Finley, Martha. Elsie's Motherhood. 1981. 243p. (J). (ps up). reprint ed. lib. bdg. 6.95 (*0-89966-335-4*) Buccaneer Bks., Inc.

—Elsie's Motherhood. 2000. (Elsie Bks.: Bk. 5). 320p. (J). (gr. 7-12). pap. 5.95 (*1-58182-068-2*, Cumberland Hearthside) Cumberland Hse. Publishing.

—Elsie's Motherhood. 1998. (Elsie Books: Vol. 5). 256p. (J). mass mkt. 5.99 (*1-931343-09-8*) Hibbard Pubns., Inc.

—Elsie's Motherhood. 1998. (Elsie Bks.: Vol. 5). 256p. (J). (gr. 7-12). pap. 6.99 (*1-888306-38-6*, Full Quart Pr.) Holly Hall Pubns., Inc.

Fletcher, Susan. The Stuttgart Nanny Mafia. 1991. 160p. (J). (gr. 3-7). 14.95 (*0-689-31709-3*, Atheneum) Simon & Schuster Children's Publishing.

Ford, Ellen. The Day Mom Stopped the Bus! 1994. (Illus.). 16p. (Orig.). (J). (gr. 5-8). pap. 5.95 (*0-9615961-3-9*) Raven Rocks Pr.

Ford, Miela. Mom & Me. 1998. (Illus.). 24p. (J). (ps-3). 15.00 (*0-688-15889-7*); 14.89 o.p. (*0-688-15890-0*) HarperCollins Children's Bk. Group. (Greenwillow Bks.).

Foster, Barbara Spencer. Pecos Queen: A Novel. 2003. 192p. pap. 18.95 (*0-86534-391-8*) Sunstone Pr.

Foster, Karen S. Goodnight My Little Chicks. 1997. Tr. of Buenas Noches Mis Pollitos. (ENG & SPA., Illus.). 32p. (J). (ps-3). 14.95 (*1-890326-12-7*) First Story Pr.

Fox, Mem. Koala Lou. 1989. (Illus.). 32p. (J). (ps-3). 15.00 (*0-15-200502-1*, Gulliver Bks.) Harcourt Children's Bks.

Fran, Renee. What Happened to Mommy? 1994. (Illus.). 32p. (Orig.). (J). (ps-6). pap. 7.95 (*0-9640250-0-0*) D. R. Eastman.

Frankel, Alona. I Want My Mother. 2000. (Joshua & Prudence Bks.). (Illus.). 40p. (J). (ps-k). 6.95 (*0-694-01379-X*, Harper Festival) HarperCollins Children's Bk. Group.

Freeman, Becky & Archambault, Matthew. The Worm Surprise. (Gabe & Critters Ser.). (Illus.). 32p. (J). (ps-2). 8.99 o.p. (*0-7814-3339-8*) Cook Communications Ministries.

French, Susan M. Dressing up Like Mommy. 1992. (Storytime Bks.). (Illus.). 24p. (Orig.). (J). (ps-2). pap. 1.29 o.p. (*1-878624-35-0*, McClanahan Bk.) Learning Horizons, Inc.

Friedrich, Molly. You're Not My Real Mother! Hale, Christy, tr. & illus. by. 2004. (J). (*0-316-60553-0*) Little Brown & Co.

Fruisen, Catherine Myler. My Mother's Pearls. 2000. (Illus.). 32p. (J). (ps-3). 12.95 (*0-7683-2177-8*) CEDCO Publishing.

Fuchshuber, Annegert. Two Peas in a Pod. 1998. (Single Titles Ser.: 2). (Illus.). 32p. (J). (ps-2). 14.95 o.p. (*0-7613-0339-1*); 21.40 o.p. (*0-7613-0410-X*) Millbrook Pr., Inc.

Gabriel, Andrea. My Favorite Bear. 2003. (Illus.). 32p. (J). 15.95 (*1-58089-038-5*) Charlesbridge Publishing, Inc.

Gabriel, Andrea, illus. My Favorite Bear. 2003. (J). pap. 6.95 (*1-58089-039-3*) Charlesbridge Publishing, Inc.

Gaeddert, LouAnn. The Kid with the Red Suspenders. 1983. (Illus.). 80p. (J). (gr. 2-4). 9.95 o.p. (*0-525-44046-1*, Dutton) Dutton/Plume.

Gaines, Ernest J. The Sky Is Gray. 1993. (J). (gr. 4 up). o.p. (*0-88682-582-2*, Creative Education) Creative Co., The.

Gaines, Isabel. World's Best Mama. 2000. (Winnie the Pooh Ser.). (Illus.). 37p. (J). (ps-3). pap. 3.99 (*0-7868-4368-3*) Disney Pr.

Galbraith, Kathryn O. Laura Charlotte. (Illus.). 32p. (J). (ps-3). 1997. pap. 6.99 (*0-698-11437-X*, PaperStar); 1993. 5.95 o.s.i (*0-399-22514-5*, Philomel); 1990. 16.99 o.s.i (*0-399-21613-8*, Philomel) Penguin Putnam Bks. for Young Readers.

—Laura Charlotte. 1997. (J). 12.14 (*0-606-05419-7*) Turtleback Bks.

Galloway, Priscilla. Good Times, Bad Times - Mummy & Me. 1990. (Illus.). 32p. (J). reprint ed. pap. 6.95 (*0-88961-066-5*) Women's Pr. CAN. *Dist:* Univ. of Toronto Pr.

Garland, Sherry. The Last Rainmaker. 1997. 336p. (YA). (gr. 5-11). 12.00 (*0-15-200649-4*) Harcourt Children's Bks.

—Rainmaker's Dream. 1997. 336p. (J). (gr. 8 up). pap. 6.00 o.s.i (*0-15-200652-4*, Harcourt Paperbacks) Harcourt Children's Bks.

Garvey, Linda K. A Picture for Patti. 1998. (Doug Chronicles Ser.: No. 3). (Illus.). 64p. (J). (gr. 2-4). pap. 3.99 (*0-7868-4236-9*) Disney Pr.

Geisert, Arthur. Oink, Oink. 1993. (Illus.). 32p. (J). (ps-3). tchr. ed. 14.95 o.s.i (*0-395-64048-2*) Houghton Mifflin Co.

Geller, Nancy Jewell. Sailor Song. 1999. (Illus.). 32p. (J). (ps-3). tchr. ed. 13.00 (*0-395-82511-3*, Clarion Bks.) Houghton Mifflin Co. Trade & Reference Div.

Gibbons, Faye. Mama & Me & the Model T. 1999. (Illus.). 40p. (J). (ps-3). 16.95 (*0-688-15298-8*); lib. bdg. 15.89 (*0-688-15299-6*) HarperCollins Children's Bk. Group.

Giff, Patricia Reilly. Wake up, Emily, It's Mother's Day. 1991. (Kids of the Polk Street School Ser.). (J). 10.14 (*0-606-05042-6*) Turtleback Bks.

—Wake up, Emily, It's Mothers Day. 1991. (Kids of the Polk Street School Ser.: No. 16). 80p. (ps-3). pap. text 3.99 o.s.i (*0-440-40455-X*) Dell Publishing.

Gilchrist, Jan Spivey. Indigo & Moonlight Gold. (Illus.). 32p. 2000. (YA). pap. 6.95 (*0-86316-293-2*); 1992. (J). 15.95 (*0-86316-210-X*) Writers & Readers Publishing, Inc.

Gilden, Mel. Harry Newberry & the Raiders of the Red Drink, ERS. 1989. 144p. (J). (gr. 4-6). 14.95 o.p. (*0-8050-0698-2*, Holt, Henry & Co. Bks. For Young Readers) Holt, Henry & Co.

Glassman, Peter. My Working Mom. 1994. (Illus.). 32p. (J). (ps-3). 16.95 (*0-688-12259-0*) HarperCollins Children's Bk. Group.

—My Working Mom. 1994. (Illus.). (J). (ps-3). 15.89 (*0-688-12260-4*, Morrow, William & Co.) Morrow/Avon.

Gleeson, Kate. I Love My Mommy. 1995. (Shaped Naptime Tales Bks.). (Illus.). 14p. (J). (ps-3). bds. 3.49 o.s.i (*0-307-12877-6*, Golden Bks.) Random Hse. Children's Bks.

Gleeson, Libby. Mom Goes to Work. 1995. (J). pap. 4.95 (*0-590-46288-1*) Scholastic, Inc.

—Mom Goes to Work. 1995. 10.15 o.p. (*0-606-09624-8*) Turtleback Bks.

—Where's Mom? 1996. (Illus.). (J). pap. 4.99 o.p. (*0-590-46961-4*) Scholastic, Inc.

—Where's Mom? 1996. 10.19 o.p. (*0-606-10060-1*) Turtleback Bks.

Goffe, Toni. Ma, You're Driving Me Crazy! 1993. 32p. (J). 4.99 (*0-85953-401-4*) Child's Play of England GBR. *Dist:* Child's Play-International.

Golden Books Staff. I Love You, Mommy. 2001. 16p. 3.99 o.s.i (*0-307-16047-5*, Golden Bks.) Random Hse. Children's Bks.

—Shopping with (Aagh!) Mom. 1999. 12p. (ps-3). pap. text 3.29 o.p. (*0-307-20275-5*, Golden Bks.) Random Hse. Children's Bks.

Goode, Diane. Where's Our Mama? (Illus.). 32p. (J). (ps-2). 1995. pap. 4.99 o.s.i (*0-14-055555-2*, Puffin Bks.); 1991. 13.95 o.s.i (*0-525-44770-9*, Dutton Children's Bks.) Penguin Putnam Bks. for Young Readers.

—Where's Our Mama? 1995. 10.19 o.p. (*0-606-08661-7*) Turtleback Bks.

Gorbachev, Valeri. Nicky & the Fantastic Birthday Gift. 2000. (Illus.). 32p. (J). (ps-2). 15.95 o.p. (*0-7358-1378-7*); 16.50 (*0-7358-1379-5*) North-South Bks., Inc.

Gorog, Judith. Zilla Sasparilla & the Mud Baby. 1996. (Illus.). 32p. (J). (gr. 1-4). 14.99 o.p. (*1-56402-295-1*) Candlewick Pr.

Grancell-Frank, Barbara. The Oldest Mommy in the Park. 1993. (Illus.). 64p. (Orig.). (YA). (gr. 6-12). pap. 8.95 (*1-56883-022-X*) Colonial Pr.

Grassli, Michaelene, et al. All I Really Need Is My Mom. 1993. (J). pap. 1.50 o.p. (*0-88494-877-3*, Bookcraft, Inc.) Deseret Bk. Co.

Graves, Kimberlee. Mom Can Fix Anything, Vol. 3580. 1995. (Emergent Reader Big Bks.). (Illus.). 16p. (J). (gr. k-2). pap. 12.98 (*1-57471-020-6*) Creative Teaching Pr., Inc.

Gray, Libba Moore. My Mama Had a Dancing Heart. abr. ed. 2001. (J). (ps-2). pap. 16.95 incl. audio (*0-87499-739-9*); pap. 16.95 incl. audio (*0-87499-739-9*); 25.95 incl. audio (*0-87499-740-2*); 25.95 incl. audio (*0-87499-740-2*); pap. 33.95 incl. audio (*0-87499-741-0*) Live Oak Media.

—My Mama Had a Dancing Heart. (Illus.). 32p. (J). (ps-3). 1999. mass mkt. 5.95 o.s.i (*0-531-07142-1*); 1996. pap. 15.95 (*0-531-09470-7*); 1996. lib. bdg. 16.99 (*0-531-08770-0*) Scholastic, Inc. (Orchard Bks.).

—My Mama Had a Dancing Heart. 1999. 12.10 (*0-606-18334-5*) Turtleback Bks.

Greene, Stephanie. Owen Foote, Frontiersman. 2002. (Illus.). 96p. (J). (ps-3). pap. 4.95 (*0-618-24620-7*, Clarion Bks.) Houghton Mifflin Co. Trade & Reference Div.

Griffin, Sandra Ure. Earth Circles. 1989. (Illus.). 32p. (J). (ps-3). 14.95 (*0-8027-6843-1*); lib. bdg. 13.85 (*0-8027-6845-8*) Walker & Co.

Grove, Vicki. The Crystal Garden. 1995. 112p. (J). (gr. 4-7). 16.99 o.p. (*0-399-21813-0*, G. P. Putnam's Sons) Penguin Group (USA) Inc.

—The Crystal Garden. 1997. (Illus.). 224p. (J). (gr. 5-9). pap. 6.99 o.s.i (*0-698-11432-9*, PaperStar) Penguin Putnam Bks. for Young Readers.

—The Crystal Garden. 1997. 12.04 (*0-606-10988-9*) Turtleback Bks.

Gunson, Christopher. Over on the Farm: A Counting Picture Book Rhyme. 1997. (Illus.). 32p. (J). pap. 15.95 o.p. (*0-590-13445-0*) Scholastic, Inc.

Gutman, Anne. Mommy Hugs. 2003. (Illus.). 14p. (J). bds. 5.95 (*0-8118-3916-8*) Chronicle Bks. LLC.

Guy, Ginger F. Black Crow, Black Crow. 1991. (Illus.). 24p. (J). (ps up). 13.95 o.s.i (*0-688-08956-9*, Greenwillow Bks.) HarperCollins Children's Bk. Group.

Guy, Rosa. And I Heard a Bird Sing. 1988. 240p. (J). reprint ed. mass mkt. 3.25 o.s.i (*0-440-20152-7*) Dell Publishing.

Haas, Jessie. Clean House. 1996. (Illus.). 56p. (J). (ps-3). 15.00 (*0-688-14079-3*, Greenwillow Bks.) HarperCollins Children's Bk. Group.

Haddix, Margaret Peterson. Escape from Memory. 2003. (Illus.). 224p. (J). 16.95 (*0-689-85421-8*, Simon & Schuster Children's Publishing) Simon & Schuster Children's Publishing.

Hafner, Marylin. Mommies Don't Get Sick! (Illus.). 32p. (J). (gr. k-3). 1995. 14.95 o.p. (*1-56402-287-0*); 1997. reprint ed. bds. 5.99 (*0-7636-0154-3*) Candlewick Pr.

Hagy, Jeannie. And Then Mom Joined the Army. 1976. (Illus.). (J). (gr. 3-7). 4.75 o.p. (*0-687-01379-8*) Abingdon Pr.

Hale, Chaika P. Mama Is Hapai. l.t. ed. 1998. (Illus.). 32p. (J). (gr. 1-6). 14.00 (*0-9653971-2-2*) Anoai Pr.

Hall, Lynn. Letting Go. 1987. 112p. (YA). (gr. 6-9). 12.95 o.s.i (*0-684-18781-7*, Atheneum) Simon & Schuster Children's Publishing.

Hall, Monica. How Do You Spell Faith? 1999. (Touched by an Angel Ser.: Vol. 3). 96p. (J). (gr. 5-9). pap. 4.99 (*0-8499-5804-0*) Nelson, Tommy.

Hallinan, P. K. We're Very Good Friends, My Mother & I. 24p. (J). 7.95 (*0-8249-5373-8*); pap. 5.95 (*0-8249-5374-6*) Ideals Pubns. (Ideals).

—We're Very Good Friends, My Mother & I. 1989. (P. K. Books Values for Life). (Illus.). 32p. (J). (ps-3). lib. bdg. 13.27 o.p. (*0-516-03654-8*, Children's Pr.) Scholastic Library Publishing.

Hamilton, Dorothy. Joel's Other Mother. 1984. (Illus.). 120p. (J). (gr. 3-7). pap. 3.95 o.p. (*0-8361-3355-2*) Herald Pr.

Hamlin, Gwen. Changing Keys. 1984. 160p. (J). (gr. 7 up). mass mkt. 1.95 o.p. (*0-451-12828-1*, Signet Vista) NAL.

Hamm, Diane J. Laney's Lost Momma. Mathews, Judith, ed. 1991. (Illus.). 32p. (J). (ps-1). lib. bdg. 14.95 (*0-8075-4340-3*) Whitman, Albert & Co.

Hancock, Greg. My Hugger Is Empty. l.t. ed. 1999. (Illus.). 24p. (J). (ps-3). pap. (*1-894303-14-8*) Raven Rock Publishing.

Hanson, Mary Elizabeth. Snug. 1998. (Illus.). 32p. (J). (ps-2). 15.00 (*0-689-81164-0*, Simon & Schuster Children's Publishing) Simon & Schuster Children's Publishing.

Harris, Lois J. Big Mama. 1994. (Illus.). 16p. (J). 5.95 o.p. (*0-8059-3483-9*) Dorrance Publishing Co., Inc.

Harris, Robie H. Happy Birth Day! 2002. (Illus.). (J). 24.94 (*0-7587-2684-8*) Book Wholesalers, Inc.

—Happy Birth Day! 1996. (Illus.). 32p. (J). (ps-3). 17.99 (*1-56402-424-5*) Candlewick Pr.

Harrison, Claire. In a Mothers Heart. 1995. (Illus.). 384p. (J). mass mkt. 5.99 (*0-671-75898-5*, Pocket) Simon & Schuster.

Harrison, Joanna. When Mom Turned into a Monster. 1996. (Picture Bks.). (Illus.). 32p. (J). (ps-3). lib. bdg. 15.95 o.p. (*1-57505-013-7*, Carolrhoda Bks.) Lerner Publishing Group.

Haseley, Dennis. A Trick of the Eye. 2004. 208p. (YA). 16.99 (*0-8037-2856-5*, Dial Bks. for Young Readers) Penguin Putnam Bks. for Young Readers.

Hathorn, Libby. The Surprise Box. 1994. (Voyages Ser.). (Illus.). (J). 4.25 (*0-383-03778-6*) SRA/McGraw-Hill.

Hautzig, Deborah. Happy Mother's Day. 1989. (Step into Reading Step 1 Bks.). (J). (ps-1). 9.19 o.p. (*0-606-12325-3*) Turtleback Bks.

Hautzig, Esther. A Gift for Mama. 1997. (Puffin Chapters Ser.). (Illus.). 64p. (J). (gr. 2-5). pap. 4.99 (*0-14-038551-7*) Penguin Putnam Bks. for Young Readers.

—A Gift for Mama. 1992. (J). (gr. 1-4). 19.00 (*0-8446-6570-3*) Smith, Peter Pub., Inc.

—A Gift for Mama. 1997. (Puffin Chapters Ser.). (J). 11.14 (*0-606-11386-X*) Turtleback Bks.

—A Gift for Mama. 1981. (Illus.). 64p. (J). (gr. 3-7). 8.95 o.p. (*0-670-33976-8*) Viking Penguin.

Hawkins, Colin & Hawkins, Jacqui. Where's My Mommy? 1985. (It's Great to Read Ser.). (Illus.). 32p. (J). (ps-1). 1.99 o.p. (*0-517-55974-9*) Random Hse. Value Publishing.

Hay, John M. Mama, Were You Ever Young? 1991. (Illus.). 32p. (J). (gr. k-4). 13.95 (*0-88138-134-9*, Simon & Schuster Children's Publishing) Simon & Schuster Children's Publishing.

Hayes, Sheila. The Tinker's Daughter. 1995. 160p. (J). (gr. 5-9). 14.99 o.p. (*0-525-67497-7*, Dutton Children's Bks.) Penguin Putnam Bks. for Young Readers.

Haynes, Betsy. The Great Mom Swap. 1986. 160p. (gr. 4-7). pap. text 4.50 o.s.i (*0-553-15675-6*) Bantam Bks.

—The Great Mom Swap. (J). 1990. pap. o.s.i (*0-553-54003-3*, Dell Books for Young Readers); 1986. 160p. pap. 2.50 o.s.i (*0-553-15398-6*, Skylark) Random Hse. Children's Bks.

—The Great Mom Swap. 1994. 10.04 (*0-606-01585-X*) Turtleback Bks.

Hazen, Barbara Shook. Even If I Did Something Awful? 1981. (Illus.). 32p. (J). (ps-2). lib. bdg. 13.95 (*0-689-30843-4*, Atheneum) Simon & Schuster Children's Publishing.

—Mommy's Office. 1992. (Illus.). 32p. (J). (ps-1). 13.95 (*0-689-31601-1*, Atheneum) Simon & Schuster Children's Publishing.

—Why Can't You Stay Home with Me? A Book about Working Mothers. 1986. (Golden Learn About Living Bks.). (Illus.). 32p. (J). (gr. k-3). o.p. (*0-307-12487-8*, Golden Bks.) Random Hse. Children's Bks.

Heath, Kristina. Mama's Little One. 1996. (Illus.). 23p. (J). (ps-1). pap. 15.00 o.p. (*0-935790-03-9*) Muh-He-Con-Neew Pr.

Help for Mom. 1989. (Big & Easy Learn to Read Bks.). (Illus.). 24p. (J). (ps-2). pap. 1.29 o.p. (*0-02-898249-5*) Checkerboard Pr., Inc.

Henkes, Kevin. Words of Stone. 1992. 160p. (J). (gr. 3 up). 15.95 (*0-688-11356-7*, Greenwillow Bks.) HarperCollins Children's Bk. Group.

—Words of Stone. 1993. (Illus.). 160p. (J). (gr. 3-7). reprint ed. pap. 5.99 (*0-14-036601-6*, Puffin Bks.) Penguin Putnam Bks. for Young Readers.

—Words of Stone. 1993. (J). 11.04 (*0-606-06106-1*) Turtleback Bks.

Hennessy, B. G. A, B, C, D, Tummy, Toes, Hands, Knees. (Illus.). (J). (ps-1). 1991. 32p. pap. 4.99 o.s.i (*0-14-050739-6*, Puffin Bks.); 1989. 320p. 13.95 o.p. (*0-670-81703-1*, Viking Children's Bks.) Penguin Putnam Bks. for Young Readers.

Herman, Charlotte. My Mother Didn't Kiss Me Goodnight. 1980. (Illus.). 32p. (J). (ps-3). 7.95 o.p. (*0-525-35495-6*, Dutton Children's Bks.) Penguin Putnam Bks. for Young Readers.

Hernandez, Mary L. Mama Me Dio. 2001. Tr. of Mommy Gave Me. (SPA.). 32p. (J). (gr. k-3). pap. 7.50 (*1-59134-005-5*); (Illus.). pap. 7.50 (*1-884083-03-X*) Maval Publishing, Inc.

Hesse, Karen. Come on, Rain! 1999. (J). (ps up). (*0-439-06015-X*) Scholastic, Inc.

—Lavender. 1995. (Redfeather Bks.). 14.10 (*0-606-09530-6*) Turtleback Bks.

Hest, Amy. The Mommy Exchange. (Illus.). 32p. (J). (ps-2). 1988. lib. bdg. 13.95 (*0-02-743650-0*, Simon & Schuster Children's Publishing); 1991. reprint ed. pap. 3.95 (*0-689-71450-5*, Aladdin) Simon & Schuster Children's Publishing.

—You Can Do It, Sam! 2003. (Illus.). 32p. (J). 15.99 (*0-7636-1934-5*) Candlewick Pr.

Relationships

Hill, Susan. Beware Beware. 1993. (Illus.). 32p. (J). (ps up). 14.95 o.p. (*1-56402-245-5*) Candlewick Pr.

—Mother's Magic. 1988. (Illus.). 32p. (J). (gr. k-2). 13.95 o.p. (*0-241-11884-0*) Trafalgar Square.

Himmel, Roger J. Mother's Day Surprise. Manoni, Mary H., ed. 1978. (Holiday Adventures of the Lollipop Dragon Ser.). (Illus.). (J). (gr. k-3). pap. text 29.95 o.p. (*0-89290-042-3*) S V E & Churchill Media.

Hines, Anna Grossnickle. It's Just Me, Emily. 1987. (Illus.). (J). (ps-1). 12.95 o.p. (*0-89919-487-7*, Clarion Bks.) Houghton Mifflin Co. Trade & Reference Div.

Hoestlandt, Jo. Back to School with Mom. 1992. (I Love to Read Collections). (Illus.). 46p. (J). (gr. 1-5). lib. bdg. 8.50 o.p. (*0-89565-815-1*) Child's World, Inc.

Hood, Susan. The Bestest Mom. 1998. (Rugrats Ser.). (Illus.). 32p. (J). (ps-2). pap. 5.99 (*0-689-82047-X*, Simon Spotlight/Nickelodeon) Simon & Schuster Children's Publishing.

Horenstein, Henry. My Mom's a Vet. 1996. 14.14 (*0-606-10263-9*) Turtleback Bks.

Howard, Megan. I'm Going to Meet My Mother, Bk. 2. 1994. (Diary S. O. S. Ser.: No. 2). 144p. (Orig.). (J). (gr. 3-9). pap. 3.99 o.s.i (*0-679-85702-8*, Random Hse. Bks. for Young Readers) Random Hse. Children's Bks.

Howe, Quincy. StreetSmart. 1993. (Illus.). 106p. (YA). (gr. 7-12). pap. 6.95 o.p. (*0-932765-42-4*, 1325-93) Close Up Foundation.

Howitz, Jeannine O. Mama Moon. 1995. (Illus.). 32p. (J). (ps-1). mass mkt. 15.95 o.p. (*0-531-09472-3*); mass mkt. 16.99 o.p. (*0-531-08772-7*) Scholastic, Inc. (Orchard Bks.).

Humphries, Tudor. Hiding. 1997. (Illus.). 32p. (J). (ps-k). pap. 14.95 (*0-531-30056-0*, Orchard Bks.) Scholastic, Inc.

Hundal, Nancy. I Heard My Mother Call My Name. 1998. (Illus.). 24p. (J). (ps-3). pap. 6.95 (*0-00-647496-9*) HarperSanFrancisco.

Hunter, Sally M. Humphrey's Corner, ERS. (Illus.). 32p. (J). 2003. pap. 5.95 (*0-8050-7397-3*); 2001. 14.95 (*0-8050-6786-8*) Holt, Henry & Co. (Holt, Henry & Co. Bks. For Young Readers).

Hutchinson, Charlotte. My Mom's Purse. 1996. (Illus.). 36p. (J). (ps-3). pap. 7.95 (*0-88753-199-7*) Black Moss Pr.

Igus, Toyomi. Two Mrs. Gibsons. 1996. (Illus.). 32p. (YA). (gr. 4-7). 14.95 (*0-89239-135-9*) Children's Bk. Pr.

—Two Mrs. Gibsons. 1996. (Illus.). 32p. (J). (gr. 2-4). lib. bdg. 19.90 (*0-516-20001-1*, Children's Pr.) Scholastic Library Publishing.

Jacobson, Jennifer Richard. Moon Sandwich Mom. (Illus.). 24p. (J). (ps-1). 2001. pap. 6.95 (*0-8075-4072-2*); 1999. lib. bdg. 14.95 (*0-8075-4071-4*) Whitman, Albert & Co.

Jacoby, Alice. My Mother's Boyfriend & Me. 1988. (YA). (gr. 9 up). mass mkt. 2.95 o.s.i (*0-449-70311-8*, Fawcett) Ballantine Bks.

—My Mother's Boyfriend & Me. 1987. (J). (gr. 7 up). 14.95 o.p. (*0-8037-0200-0*, Dial Bks. for Young Readers) Penguin Putnam Bks. for Young Readers.

Jarrell, Pamela R. A Gift for Mother. l.t. ed. 1998. (Cuddle Bks.). (Illus.). 7p. (J). (ps-k). pap. text 10.95 (*1-57332-130-3*) HighReach Learning, Inc.

Jenks, Graham. Every Mom Is Special. 1994. (Illus.). (J). 4.99 o.p. (*0-7852-8215-7*) Nelson, Thomas Inc.

Jennings, Sharon. Into My Mother's Arms. 2000. (Illus.). 32p. (J). (ps-k). (*1-55041-533-6*) Fitzhenry & Whiteside, Ltd.

—Into My Mother's Arms: With Sticker & Card. 2001. (Illus.). 32p. (J). (ps-k). (*1-55041-669-3*) Fitzhenry & Whiteside, Ltd.

Joerg, Donna. When Dawn Stole the Dark. deluxe l.t. ed. 1997. (Illus.). iii, 29p. (J). (gr. k-5). lib. bdg. 18.95 (*0-9653018-0-X*); 17.95 (*0-9653018-1-8*) Cadence Pr.

Johnson, Angela. Mama Bird, Baby Birds. 1994. (Illus.). 12p. (J). (ps). mass mkt. 4.95 o.p. (*0-531-06848-X*, Orchard Bks.) Scholastic, Inc.

—Tell Me a Story, Mama. (Illus.). 32p. (J). (ps-3). 1992. mass mkt. 6.95 (*0-531-07032-8*); 1989. pap. 15.95 (*0-531-05794-1*); 1989. mass mkt. 16.99 o.p. (*0-531-08394-2*) Scholastic, Inc. (Orchard Bks.).

—Tell Me a Story, Mama. 1992. (J). 11.15 o.p. (*0-606-02944-3*) Turtleback Bks.

Johnson, Dolores. My Mom Is My Show-and-Tell. 1999. (Accelerated Reader Bks.). (Illus.). 32p. (J). (gr. k-3). 15.95 (*0-7614-5041-6*, Cavendish Children's Bks.) Cavendish, Marshall Corp.

—What Will Mommy Do When I'm at School? 1990. (Illus.). 32p. (J). (ps-1). lib. bdg. 15.00 (*0-02-747845-9*, Atheneum) Simon & Schuster Children's Publishing.

—What Will Mommy Do When I'm at School. 1998. (Illus.). 32p. (J). (ps-1). per. 5.99 (*0-689-82133-6*, Aladdin) Simon & Schuster Children's Publishing.

—What Will Mommy Do When I'm at School. 1998. 12.14 (*0-606-16132-5*) Turtleback Bks.

Johnson, Dorothy T. One Day, Mother/Un Dia, Madre. 1996. (ENG & SPA.). (Orig.). (J). (gr. 1-6). pap. 6.95 o.p. (*0-533-11716-X*) Vantage Pr., Inc.

Johnson, Paul Brett. The Goose Who Went off in a Huff. 2001. (Illus.). 40p. (J). (ps-1). pap. 15.95 (*0-531-30317-9*, Orchard Bks.) Scholastic, Inc.

Jonell, Lynne. Mom Pie. 2001. (Illus.). 28p. (J). (ps-3). 12.99 (*0-399-23422-5*, G. P. Putnam's Sons) Penguin Group (USA) Inc.

—Mommy Go Away! 2000. (Illus.). 32p. (ps-1). pap. 5.99 (*0-698-11810-3*) Penguin Putnam Bks. for Young Readers.

—Mommy Go Away! 2000. (Illus.). (J). 12.14 (*0-606-22033-X*) Turtleback Bks.

Joosse, Barbara M. Dinah's Mad, Bad Wishes. 1989. (Illus.). 32p. (J). (gr. k-3). 13.00 (*0-06-023098-3*); lib. bdg. 13.89 o.p. (*0-06-023099-1*) HarperCollins Children's Bk. Group.

—Mama, Do You Love Me? 2002. (Illus.). (J). 23.98 (*0-7587-3082-9*) Book Wholesalers, Inc.

—Mama, Do You Love Me? 2001. (Illus.). 19.95 (*0-8118-3259-7*); 10th anniv. l.t. ed. 36p. (J). 17.95 (*0-8118-3212-0*) Chronicle Bks. LLC.

—Pieces of the Picture. 1989. 144p. (J). (gr. 5-7). 12.95 (*0-397-32342-5*); lib. bdg. 12.89 (*0-397-32343-3*) HarperCollins Children's Bk. Group.

Jordan, Deloris & Jordan, Roslyn. Did I Tell You I Love You Today? Evans, Shane, tr. & illus. by. 2004. (J). (*0-689-85271-1*, Simon & Schuster/ Paula Wiseman Bks.) Simon & Schuster Children's Publishing.

Kari, James. Allegra's Window. 1997. (Allegra's Window Ser.: Vol. 9). (Illus.). 24p. (J). (ps-1). mass mkt. 3.25 (*0-689-81244-2*, Simon Spotlight/ Nickelodeon) Simon & Schuster Children's Publishing.

Kasza, Keiko. A Mother for Choco. 2002. (Illus.). (J). 13.19 (*0-7587-3173-6*) Book Wholesalers, Inc.

—A Mother for Choco. 1992. (Illus.). 32p. (J). (ps-3). 15.99 (*0-399-21841-6*, G. P. Putnam's Sons) Penguin Group (USA) Inc.

—A Mother for Choco. 2003. 32p. bds. 6.99 (*0-399-24191-4*) Penguin Putnam Bks. for Young Readers.

—A Mother for Choco. 1996. (J). 12.14 (*0-606-09632-9*) Turtleback Bks.

—A Mother for Chocolate. 1996. (Illus.) 32p. (J). (ps-3). pap. 5.99 (*0-698-11364-0*, PaperStar) Penguin Putnam Bks. for Young Readers.

Kehret, Peg. I'm Not Who You Think I Am. (gr. 5-9). 2001. 160p. (YA). pap. 4.99 (*0-14-131237-8*); 1999. 144p. (J). 15.99 (*0-525-46153-1*, Dutton Children's Bks.) Penguin Putnam Bks. for Young Readers.

—I'm Not Who You Think I Am. 2001. (J). 11.04 (*0-606-20717-1*) Turtleback Bks.

Kennaley, Lucinda H. My Mom Is Pregnant! 1990. (Illus.). 60p. (Orig.). (J). (ps). pap. text 9.95 (*0-9628067-0-6*) Thoth Publishing Co.

Kennemuth, Caroline & Gleeson, Kate. Wonderful You. 1993. (Golden Little Super Shape Bks.). (Illus.). 24p. (J). (ps). pap. 1.79 o.s.i (*0-307-10550-4*, Golden Bks.) Random Hse. Children's Bks.

Kerley, Barbara Kelly. Songs of Papa's Island. 1995. (Illus.). 64p. (J). (gr. 4-6). 14.95 o.p. (*0-395-71548-2*) Houghton Mifflin Co.

Ketteman, Helen. Mama's Way. (J). (ps-3). 2001. (Illus.). 32p. 15.99 (*0-8037-2413-6*); 2000. lib. bdg. 13.01 (*0-8037-2423-3*) Penguin Putnam Bks. for Young Readers. (Dial Bks. for Young Readers).

Killion, Bette. Think of It. 1993. (Laura Geringer Bks.). (Illus.). 32p. (J). (ps-1). 12.00 (*0-06-023257-9*); lib. bdg. 11.89 o.p. (*0-06-023258-7*) HarperCollins Children's Bk. Group.

Kjelle, Marylou M. Sometimes I Wish My Mom Was Two People. 1996. (Illus.). 14p. (J). (ps-4). pap. text 7.95 (*0-9648855-5-7*) MoranoCo, Inc.

Klevin, Jill R. Turtles Together Forever! 1982. (Illus.). 160p. (J). (gr. 4-6). pap. 9.95 o.s.i (*0-385-29045-4*); pap. 9.89 o.s.i (*0-385-29046-2*) Dell Publishing. (Delacorte Pr.).

Koechlin, Lionel. Los Ojos de Mama. 1999. (Jardin de los Ninos Ser.). (SPA., Illus.). 32p. (J). (ps-3). pap. 6.99 (*980-257-213-6*) Ekare, Ediciones VEN. *Dist:* Kane/Miller Bk. Pubs., Lectorum Pubns., Inc.

—Los Ojos de Mama. 1998. lib. bdg. 13.10 (*0-606-16015-9*) Turtleback Bks.

Koertge, Ronald. Confess-O-Rama. 1996. 176p. (YA). (gr. 7-12). pap. 16.95 (*0-531-09515-0*); lib. bdg. 17.99 (*0-531-08865-0*) Scholastic, Inc. (Orchard Bks.).

—Confess-O-Rama. 1998. 10.55 (*0-606-13291-0*) Turtleback Bks.

Kohlenberg, Sherry. Sammy's Mommy Has Cancer. 1993. (Illus.). 32p. (J). (ps-3). 16.95 (*0-945354-56-8*); pap. 8.95 (*0-945354-55-X*) American Psychological Assn.

Koller, Jackie French. A Place to Call Home. 208p. (YA). (gr. 7-12). 1997. mass mkt. 4.99 (*0-689-81395-3*, Simon Pulse); 1995. 16.00 (*0-689-80024-X*, Atheneum) Simon & Schuster Children's Publishing.

—A Place to Call Home. 1997. (YA). 11.04 (*0-606-11754-7*) Turtleback Bks.

Koss, Amy Goldman. Smoke Screen. 2000. (American Girls Collection Ser.). 152p. (J). (gr. 5-8). 12.95 o.p. (*1-58485-202-X*); pap. 5.95 (*1-58485-201-1*) Pleasant Co. Pubns. (American Girl).

—Smoke Screen. 2000. 12.00 (*0-606-21791-6*) Turtleback Bks.

Krauss, Ruth. You're Just What I Need. 1998. (Illus.). 40p. (J). (ps-2). 15.95 (*0-06-027514-6*) HarperCollins Children's Bk. Group.

Krisher, Trudy B. Kinship. 1997. 304p. (YA). (gr. 7). 15.95 o.s.i (*0-385-32272-0*, Delacorte Pr.) Dell Publishing.

—Kinship. 1997. mass mkt. 15.95 (*0-385-44695-0*) Doubleday Publishing.

—Kinship. 1999. 304p. (YA). (gr. 7 up). mass mkt. 4.50 o.s.i (*0-440-22023-8*, Dell Books for Young Readers) Random Hse. Children's Bks.

—Kinship. 1999. 10.55 (*0-606-16170-8*) Turtleback Bks.

Kroll, Virginia L. Motherlove. 1998. (Illus.). (J). (ps-3). 36p. 16.95 (*1-883220-81-5*); 32p. pap. 7.95 (*1-883220-80-7*) Dawn Pubns.

Kroninger, Stephen. If I Crossed the Road. 1997. (Illus.). 32p. (J). (ps-3). 16.00 (*0-689-81190-X*, Atheneum/Anne Schwartz Bks.) Simon & Schuster Children's Publishing.

Lachtman, Ofelia Dumas. Tina & the Scarecrow Skins / Tina y Las Pieles de Espantapajaros. Colin, Jose Juan, tr. 2002. (ENG & SPA., Illus.). 32p. (J). 14.95 (*1-55885-373-1*, Piñata Books) Arte Publico Pr.

Larrondo, Valerie & Desmarteau, Claudine. When Mommy Was Little. 2003. 48p. (J). 9.95 (*2-02-059693-8*) Editions du Seuil FRA. *Dist:* Continental Bk. Co., Inc.

Larson, R. D. Mama Stories. E-Book 7.95 (*1-930364-83-0*, Bookmice) McGraw Publishing, Inc.

Lasky, Kathryn. Before I Was Your Mother. 2003. (Illus.). 40p. (J). 16.00 (*0-15-201464-0*) Harcourt Children's Bks.

—Lucille Camps In. 2003. (Illus.). 32p. (J). (ps-2). 14.95 (*0-517-80041-1*); lib. bdg. 16.99 (*0-517-80042-X*) Random Hse. Children's Bks. (Knopf Bks. for Young Readers).

—Mommy, I Love Your Hands. 2002. (Illus.). (J). lib. bdg. 15.49 (*0-7868-2225-2*) Hyperion Pr.

—Mommy's Hands. 32p. (J). (ps-k). 2002. (Illus.). 15.99 (*0-7868-0280-4*); 2001. pap. 4.99 (*0-7868-1437-3*) Hyperion Bks. for Children.

Lawrence, Ingrid. The Day Mama Played. 1997. (Illus.). 32p. (J). (ps-2). pap. 5.99 (*1-56476-525-3*) Cook Communications Ministries.

Lee, Huy-Voun. In the Snow, ERS. 1995. (Illus.). (J). (ps-3). 15.95 o.s.i (*0-8050-3172-3*, Holt, Henry & Co. Bks. For Young Readers) Holt, Henry & Co.

Leffler, Maryann. Mommy Love Hugs. 1997. (Illus.). 14p. (J). (ps-k). 5.99 (*0-689-80981-6*, Little Simon) Simon & Schuster Children's Publishing.

Lehne, Judith Logan. When the Ragman Sings. 1993. 128p. (J). (gr. 3-7). 14.00 (*0-06-023316-8*); lib. bdg. 13.89 (*0-06-023317-6*) HarperCollins Children's Bk. Group.

Leuck, Laura. My Monster Mama Loves Me So. (Illus.). 24p. (J). (ps-3). 2002. pap. 5.99 (*0-06-008860-5*, Harper Trophy); 1999. 15.99 (*0-688-16866-3*); 1999. lib. bdg. 15.89 (*0-688-16867-1*) HarperCollins Children's Bk. Group.

—Sun is Falling, Night Is Calling. 1994. (Illus.). 32p. (J). (ps-k). mass mkt. 15.00 (*0-671-86940-X*, Simon & Schuster Children's Publishing) Simon & Schuster Children's Publishing.

Levine, Abby. What Did Mommy Do Before You? 1990. 320p. (J). (ps-3). pap. 3.95 o.s.i (*0-14-054215-9*, Puffin Bks.) Penguin Putnam Bks. for Young Readers.

Levitin, Sonia. Yesterday's Child. (J). (gr. 7-12). 1998. 336p. mass mkt. 4.99 (*0-689-82073-9*, Simon Pulse); 1997. 256p. 17.00 (*0-689-80810-0*, Simon & Schuster Children's Publishing) Simon & Schuster Children's Publishing.

—Yesterday's Child. 1998. 11.04 (*0-606-15872-3*) Turtleback Bks.

Levy, Elizabeth. The Case of the Mind-Reading Mommies. 1990. (Illus.). (J). pap. 2.95 o.s.i (*0-671-69435-9*, Aladdin) Simon & Schuster Children's Publishing.

Lewin, Hugh. Jafta's Mother. 24p. (J). (gr. 1-3). 1983. lib. bdg. 15.95 (*0-87614-208-0*); 1989. (Illus.). reprint ed. pap. 4.95 (*0-87614-495-4*) Lerner Publishing Group. (Carolrhoda Bks.).

Lichtman, Wendy. Blew & the Death of the Mag. 1975. (Illus.). 74p. (J). (gr. 3-9). 5.00 o.p. (*0-913512-53-2*) Freestone Publishing Co.

Liddle, Elizabeth. Pip & the Edge of Heaven. 2003. (Illus.). 48p. (J). 8.00 (*0-8028-5257-2*, Eerdmans Bks For Young Readers) Eerdmans, William B. Publishing Co.

Littke, Lael J. Blue Skye. 1991. 192p. (J). 13.95 o.p. (*0-590-43448-9*) Scholastic, Inc.

Loh, Morag. Tucking Mommy In. 1991. (Illus.). 40p. (J). (ps-3). mass mkt. 5.95 (*0-531-07025-5*, Orchard Bks.) Scholastic, Inc.

Loh, Morag Jeanette. Tucking Mommy In. 1991. (J). 11.15 o.p. (*0-606-09998-0*) Turtleback Bks.

Long, Susan Hill. Where Is Mother? 2003. (Little Polar Bear Story Ser.). (Illus.). 16p. (J). (ps-1). pap. 3.99 (*1-59014-109-1*) Night Sky Bks.

Love, Sandra. But What about Me? 1976. (Illus.). (J). (gr. 3-7). 8.95 o.p. (*0-15-249900-8*) Harcourt Children's Bks.

Lyon, George Ella. Mama Is a Miner. 1994. (Illus.). 32p. (J). (gr. k-3). pap. 15.95 (*0-531-06853-6*); lib. bdg. 16.99 o.p. (*0-531-08703-4*) Scholastic, Inc. (Orchard Bks.).

—Who Came Down That Road? 1992. (Illus.). 32p. (J). (ps-2). mass mkt. 17.99 o.p. (*0-531-08587-2*); mass mkt. 16.95 o.p. (*0-531-05987-1*) Scholastic, Inc. (Orchard Bks.).

—Who Came down That Road? 1996. (Illus.). 32p. (J). (ps-3). mass mkt. 5.95 (*0-531-07073-5*, Orchard Bks.) Scholastic, Inc.

MacDonald, Caroline. Speaking to Miranda. 1992. (Willa Perlman Bks.). 256p. (YA). (gr. 7 up). 14.00 (*0-06-021102-4*); lib. bdg. 13.89 (*0-06-021103-2*) HarperCollins Children's Bk. Group.

Mackall, Dandi Daley. Home Is Where Your Horse Is. 2000. (Horsefeathers Ser.: Vol. 6). (Illus.). 190p. (J). (gr. 7-11). pap. 5.99 (*0-570-07087-2*) Concordia Publishing Hse.

Mahy, Margaret. Boom, Baby, Boom, Boom! 1997. (Illus.). 32p. (J). (ps). 15.99 o.p. (*0-670-87314-4*, Viking) Penguin Putnam Bks. for Young Readers.

Major, Kevin. The Story of the House of Wooden Santas: An Advent Read-Along in 24 Chapters. rev. ed. 1998. (Illus.). 96p. (gr. 4-7). 12.98 (*0-7651-0829-1*) Smithmark Pubs., Inc.

Mandrell, Louise. All in a Day's Work: A Story about the Meaning of Mother's Day. 1993. (Louise Mandrell & Ace Collins Holiday Adventure Ser.). 32p. (J). 12.95 o.p. (*1-56530-036-X*) Summit Publishing Group - Legacy Bks.

Mann, Peggy. There Are Two Kinds of Terrible. 1977. (gr. 3-7). o.p. (*0-385-09588-0*); lib. bdg. 7.95 o.p. (*0-385-08185-5*) Doubleday Publishing.

Marron, Carol A. Mother Told Me So. 1983. (Family Bks.). (Illus.). 32p. (J). (gr. k-3). lib. bdg. 14.65 o.p. (*0-940742-26-8*) Raintree Pubs.

Marsh, Carole. If My Mama Ran the World. (J). 1997. pap. 14.95 (*0-7933-4437-9*); 1994. 29.95 (*1-55609-287-3*) Gallopade International.

Martin, Ann M. Karen's Stepmother. 1994. (Baby-Sitters Little Sister Ser.: No. 49). 112p. (J). (gr. 3-7). mass mkt. 3.50 (*0-590-47047-7*) Scholastic, Inc.

—Kristy & the Mother's Day Surprise. (Baby-Sitters Club Ser.: No. 24). (J). (gr. 3-7). 1997. 160p. mass mkt. 3.99 (*0-590-67392-0*); 1989. 192p. pap. 3.50 (*0-590-43506-X*); 1989. mass mkt. 2.75 o.p. (*0-590-42002-X*) Scholastic, Inc.

—Kristy & the Mother's Day Surprise. l.t. ed. 1994. (Baby-Sitters Club Ser.: No. 24). 176p. (J). (gr. 3-7). lib. bdg. 21.27 o.p. (*0-8368-1245-X*) Stevens, Gareth Inc.

—Kristy & the Mother's Day Surprise. 1989. (Baby-Sitters Club Ser.: No. 24). (J). (gr. 3-7). 10.04 (*0-606-04260-1*) Turtleback Bks.

Martin, David. Monkey Trouble. 2000. (Brand New Readers Ser.). (Illus.). 8p. (J). (ps-2). bds. 5.99 (*0-7636-0771-1*) Candlewick Pr.

Martin, Patricia. Travels with Rainie Marie. 1997. 192p. (J). (gr. 4-8). 15.95 (*0-7868-0257-X*) Hyperion Bks. for Children.

Marton, Jirina. Flores para Mama. 1994. Tr. of Flowers for Mom. (SPA., Illus.). 24p. (J). (ps-2). pap. 6.95 (*1-55037-970-4*) Annick Pr., Ltd. CAN. *Dist:* Firefly Bks., Ltd.

—Flowers for Mom. 1991. (Illus.). (J). (ps-3). 32p. 15.95 (*1-55037-155-X*); 24p. pap. 5.95 (*1-55037-158-4*) Annick Pr., Ltd. CAN. *Dist:* Firefly Bks., Ltd.

Marzollo, Jean. Mama, Mama. 1999. (Growing Tree Ser.). (Illus.). 16p. (J). (ps up). 5.99 (*0-694-01245-9*, Harper Festival) HarperCollins Children's Bk. Group.

Matthiessen, Peter. The Not-So-Wicked Stepmother. 1990. (Illus.). (J). pap. (*0-14-054080-6*) NAL.

May, Robert E. Poppa & Elizabeth: A Bobtail Romance. 1988. (Bobtail Chronicles). (Illus.). 32p. (Orig.). (J). (ps-3). pap. 5.95 (*0-87397-313-5*); lib. bdg. 15.89 (*0-87397-314-3*) Circle Bk. Service, Inc. (Strode Pubs.).

Mayer, Mercer. De Compras Con Mama - Just Shopping with Mom. 1997. (Spanish Golden Look-Look Bks.). (SPA., Illus.). 24p. (J). (ps-3). pap. 3.29 o.s.i (*0-307-71972-3*, Golden Bks.) Random Hse. Children's Bks.

—Just for You. 1998. (Little Critter Ser.). (Illus.). 24p. (J). (ps-3). pap. 3.29 (*0-307-11838-X*, 11838, Golden Bks.) Random Hse. Children's Bks.

—Just Me & My Mom. 2001. (Little Critter Ser.). (Illus.). 24p. (J). (ps-3). pap. 3.29 (*0-307-12584-X*, 12584, Golden Bks.) Random Hse. Children's Bks.

—Just Me & My Mom. 1990. (Little Critter Ser.). (Illus.). (J). 9.44 (*0-606-20441-5*) Turtleback Bks.

Relationships

—Just Shopping with Mom. 1989. (Little Critter Ser.). (J). (ps-3). 9.44 (*0-606-12382-2*) Turtleback Bks.

Mayer, Mercer, et al. Taking Care of Mom. 1998. (Little Critter Ser.). (Illus.). 24p. (J). (ps-3). 2.29 o.s.i (*0-307-98880-5*, 98880, Golden Bks.) Random Hse. Children's Bks.

Mazer, Harry. Someone's Mother. 1990. o.s.i (*0-385-30199-5*, Dell Books for Young Readers) Random Hse. Children's Bks.

—Someone's Mother Is Missing. 1990. 176p. (J). 14.95 o.s.i (*0-385-30161-8*, Delacorte Pr.) Dell Publishing.

—Someone's Mother Is Missing. 1991. 176p. (YA). mass mkt. 3.50 o.s.i (*0-440-21097-6*, Yearling) Random Hse. Children's Bks.

McCourt, Lisa. I Love You, Stinky Face. (J). 2004. pap. 15.95 (*0-439-63571-3*); 2004. bds. 6.99 (*0-439-63572-1*); 2003. 32p. mass mkt. 5.99 (*0-439-63469-5*) Scholastic, Inc.

—I Love You, Stinky Face. 1998. 12.10 (*0-606-15901-0*) Turtleback Bks.

—It's Time for School, Stinky Face. 2004. (J). pap. 15.95 (*0-439-63574-8*); mass mkt. 5.99 (*0-439-63575-6*) Scholastic, Inc.

McCue, Lisa. Mama Loves. 1999. (Bright & Early Bks.). (Illus.). 48p. (J). (ps-3). 7.99 (*0-679-89462-4*) Random Hse., Inc.

McCue, Lisa & Goode, Molly. Mama Loves. 1999. (Bright & Early Bks.). (Illus.). 48p. (J). (ps-3). lib. bdg. 11.99 o.s.i (*0-679-99462-9*) Random Hse., Inc.

McDaniel, Lurlene. Mother, Help Me Live. 1992. (One Last Wish Ser.: Vol. 3). 176p. (YA). (gr. 7 up). mass mkt. 4.99 (*0-553-29811-9*) Bantam Bks.

—Mother, Help Me Live. 1997. (One Last Wish Ser.: No. 3). (J). mass mkt. 4.99 (*0-553-54280-X*, Dell Books for Young Readers) Random Hse. Children's Bks.

—Mother, Please Don't Die. 1988. (Lifelines Ser.). 144p. (Orig.). (J). (gr. 6-8). pap. 2.95 o.p. (*0-87406-288-8*) Darby Creek Publishing.

McKenna, Colleen O'Shaughnessy. Mother Murphy. 160p. (J). (gr. 4-6). 1993. mass mkt. 2.95 (*0-590-44856-0*); 1992. 13.95 o.p. (*0-590-44820-X*) Scholastic, Inc.

McLellan, Stephanie Simpson. The Chicken Cat. 2001. (Illus.). 40p. (J). (gr. k-3). (*1-55041-531-X*); pap. (*1-55041-673-1*); pap. (*1-55041-677-4*) Fitzhenry & Whiteside, Ltd.

McMullan, Kate. If You Were My Bunny. 2002. (Illus.). 15.70 (*0-7587-2831-X*) Book Wholesalers, Inc.

—If You Were My Bunny. (J). 1996. pap. 4.95 (*0-590-73591-8*); 1996. (Illus.). 24p. pap. 7.95 (*0-590-52749-5*, Cartwheel Bks.); 1998. (Illus.). 26p. reprint ed. bds. 6.99 (*0-590-34126-X*) Scholastic, Inc.

Mead, Alice. Soldier Mom, RS. 1999. 160p. (J). (gr. 3-7). 16.00 (*0-374-37124-5*, Farrar, Straus & Giroux (BYR)) Farrar, Straus & Giroux.

—Soldier Mom. 2001. 160p. (YA). pap. 4.99 (*0-440-22900-6*, Dell Books for Young Readers) Random Hse. Children's Bks.

Meckley, Stephanie R., et al. Just Like Mom. 1998. (Illus.). 24p. (J). (gr. k-2). pap. 3.00 (*1-892464-03-9*) Meckley Publishing Co.

Melmed, Laura Krauss. I Love You As Much... (Illus.). (J). (ps-2). 2003. 22p. 12.99 (*0-06-008659-9*, Harper Festival); 2001. 22p. 12.95 (*0-06-001011-8*, Harper Festival); 2001. 32p. pap. 6.95 (*0-688-16806-X*); 1993. 24p. lib. bdg. 15.89 o.p. (*0-688-11719-8*); 1993. 24p. 15.95 (*0-688-11718-X*) HarperCollins Children's Bk. Group.

—I Love You As Much... 1998. (Illus.). 11p. (J). (ps up). bds. 7.99 (*0-688-15978-8*); bds. 7.99 (*0-688-15978-8*) Morrow/Avon. (Morrow, William & Co.).

Meresh-Hemery, Kathleen. The Brightest Star. 1998. (Illus.). (J). 6.95 (*1-56123-102-9*) Centering Corp.

Merriam, Eve. Mommies at Work. 1991. (J). (ps-3). pap. 3.25 o.s.i (*0-671-73275-7*, Little Simon) Simon & Schuster Children's Publishing.

Merritt, Kate. My Family: My Mom. 2002. (Illus.). 10p. (J). bds. 3.95 (*0-8069-8573-9*) Sterling Publishing Co., Inc.

Metzger, Steve. Where's Mommy? 1997. (Dinofours Ser.: No. 20). (Illus.). 32p. (J). (ps-1). mass mkt. 3.25 (*0-590-37456-7*) Scholastic, Inc.

Miller, Kathryn M. Did My First Mother Love Me? A Story for an Adopted Child. 1994. (Illus.). 48p. (J). (ps-3). 12.95 (*0-930934-85-7*); pap. 5.95 (*0-930934-84-9*) Morning Glory Pr., Inc.

Miller, Mary J. Upside Down. 1992. 128p. (J). (gr. 3-7). 13.00 o.p. (*0-670-83648-6*, Viking Children's Bks.) Penguin Putnam Bks. for Young Readers.

Miller, William. A House by the River. 1997. (Illus.). 32p. (J). (ps up). 15.95 (*1-880000-48-2*) Lee & Low Bks., Inc.

Minarik, Else Holmelund. Happy Mother's Day. 2003. (Festival Reader Ser.). (Illus.). 32p. (J). (ps-2). pap. 3.99 (*0-694-01692-6*, Harper Festival) HarperCollins Children's Bk. Group.

Minsky, Terri, creator. Lizzie McGuire Vol. 3: When Moms Attack & Misadventures in Babysitting. 2003. (Illus.). 192p. (J). pap. 7.99 (*1-59182-245-9*) TOKYOPOP, Inc.

Mire, Betty. It's Funny How Things Change. 1985. (Illus.). 160p. (YA). (gr. 5-10). 12.95 o.s.i (*0-88289-431-5*) Pelican Publishing Co., Inc.

Modesitt, Jeanne. Mama, If You Had a Wish. (Illus.). 40p. (J). (ps-1). 1999. pap. 5.99 (*0-689-82412-2*, Aladdin); 1993. 16.00 (*0-671-75437-8*, Simon & Schuster Children's Publishing) Simon & Schuster Children's Publishing.

—Mama, If You Had a Wish. 1999. 12.14 (*0-606-16286-0*) Turtleback Bks.

Mohr, Nichilasa. Jenny's Story. 1924. (J). o.s.i (*0-688-09314-0*) HarperCollins Children's Bk. Group.

Molk, Laurel. Good Job, Oliver! 2001. (Illus.). (J). 13.14 (*0-606-20679-5*) Turtleback Bks.

Moms Are Special. 1988. (Sparklers Ser.). 32p. (J). (ps-1). bds. 3.99 o.p. (*1-55513-999-X*) Cook Communications Ministries.

Moppets. Mommy, I Love You Just Because . . . gif. ed. 1997. (Illus.). 48p. (J). 8.99 (*0-310-97320-1*) Zondervan.

Mori, Kyoko. Shizuko's Daughter. 1994. 224p. (gr. 7-12). mass mkt. 6.99 (*0-449-70433-5*, Fawcett) Ballantine Bks.

—Shizuko's Daughter, ERS. 1993. 240p. (YA). (gr. 7-12). 15.95 o.s.i (*0-8050-2557-X*, Holt, Henry & Co. Bks. For Young Readers) Holt, Henry & Co.

—Shizuko's Daughter. 1994. (J). 11.55 (*0-606-07153-9*) Turtleback Bks.

Morozumi, Atsuko. Mummy, Is that You? 1996. 320p. o.s.i (*0-385-25582-9*) Doubleday Canada, Ltd. CAN. *Dist:* Random Hse., Inc.

Morris, Clarine. Mommie Star. 2000. (Illus.). (J). (ps-10). pap. 3.00 (*0-9650312-3-3*) Cosmo Starr Bks.

Morse-Travis, Heidi. And Mommy's On Her Side. 2000. (Illus.). 28p. (J). 14.95 (*0-9650848-3-3*, A Place to Remember) deRuyter-Nelson Pubns., Inc.

Moss, Miriam. Don't Forget I Love You. 2003. (Illus.). 32p. (J). 15.99 (*0-8037-2920-0*, Dial Bks. for Young Readers) Penguin Putnam Bks. for Young Readers.

Moulton, Deborah. Summer Girl. 1992. 128p. (J). (gr. 5-9). 15.00 o.p. (*0-8037-1153-0*, Dial Bks. for Young Readers) Penguin Putnam Bks. for Young Readers.

Mouse Works Staff. I Love You, Mama! 1999. (Disney's Pooh Ser.). (Illus.). 10p. (J). (ps). bds. 6.99 (*1-57082-985-3*) Mouse Works.

Mummy Long Arms. 1995. (Young Dragon Readers 1 Ser.). (J). pap. text (*962-359-530-1*) Addison-Wesley Longman, Inc.

Munsch, Robert. Love You Forever. 2003. (Illus.). 32p. (J). (ps-3). 12.95 (*0-920668-36-4*); pap. 4.95 (*0-920668-37-2*); 19.95 (*1-895565-66-9*); 17.95 (*1-55209-109-0*) Firefly Bks., Ltd.

—Love You Forever: A Big Book. 2003. (Illus.). 32p. (J). pap. 19.95 (*1-895565-37-5*) Firefly Bks., Ltd.

Murphy, Jill. The Last Noo-Noo. 1995. (Illus.). 32p. (J). (ps up). 14.95 o.p. (*1-56402-581-0*) Candlewick Pr.

My Mommy Works. 2001. 16p. 6.99 (*0-9716113-0-0*) Achievers Technology Resource, Inc.

My Mother's Cup. (J). (*0-02-538388-4*, Scribner) Simon & Schuster.

Nahum-Valensi, Maya. Mom's Sore Throat. 1992. (I Love to Read Collections). (Illus.). 46p. (J). (gr. 1-5). lib. bdg. 8.50 o.p. (*0-89565-807-0*) Child's World, Inc.

Neville, Emily C. Garden of Broken Glass. 1975. 228p. (J). (gr. 5-9). 6.95 o.s.i (*0-440-04839-7*); lib. bdg. 6.46 o.s.i (*0-440-04842-7*) Dell Publishing. (Delacorte Pr.).

Newman, Leslea. Heather Has Two Mommies. 2004. (Illus.). 33p. (J). reprint ed. pap. 8.95 (*1-55583-180-X*) Alyson Pubns.

Newman, Shirlee. Tell Me Grandma, Tell Me Grandpa, 001. 1979. (Illus.). (J). (ps-2). lib. bdg. 6.95 o.p. (*0-395-27815-5*) Houghton Mifflin Co.

Nixon, Joan Lowery. Star Baby. 1989. (Hollywood Daughters Ser.: Bk. 1). 192p. (YA). (gr. 7 up). 14.95 o.s.i (*0-553-05838-X*) Bantam Bks.

Nolen-Harold, Jerdine. In My Momma's Kitchen. 2001. (Amistad Ser.). (Illus.). 32p. (J). (gr. k up). reprint ed. pap. 5.95 (*0-06-443786-8*, Amistad Pr.) HarperTrade.

Nostlinger, Christine. Marrying off Mother. Bell, Anthea, tr. 1982. 132p. (J). (gr. 4-6). 10.95 o.p. (*0-15-252138-0*) Harcourt Children's Bks.

Numeroff, Laura Joffe. What Mommies Do Best/What Daddies Do Best. 1998. (Illus.). 40p. (J). (ps-3). 13.95 (*0-689-80577-2*, Simon & Schuster Children's Publishing) Simon & Schuster Children's Publishing.

O'Connor, Frank. My Oedipus Complex. 1986. (Creative's Classic Short Stories Ser.). (Illus.). 40p. (J). (gr. 4 up). lib. bdg. 13.95 o.p. (*0-88682-062-6*, 1078-2, Creative Education) Creative Co., The.

Oke, Janette. Pordy's Prickly Problem. 2001. (Animal Friends Ser.). (Illus.). 80p. (J). (gr. 1-5). pap. 5.99 (*0-7642-2458-1*) Bethany Hse. Pubs.

—Pordy's Prickly Problem. Pettifor, Grace, ed. 1998. (Oke Childrens Classics Ser.). (Illus.). 144p. (J). pap. 5.99 o.p. (*0-934998-50-7*) Bethany Hse. Pubs.

Olshan, Matthew. Finn. 2001. 245p. (YA). (gr. 8-12). 19.95 (*1-890862-13-4*) Bancroft Pr.

—Finn: Novel. 2001. 245p. (YA). (gr. 8-12). pap. 14.95 (*1-890862-14-2*) Bancroft Pr.

Ormerod, Jan. Bend & Stretch. 1987. (Illus.). 24p. (J). (ps). 5.95 o.p. (*0-688-07272-0*) HarperCollins Children's Bk. Group.

—Mom's Home. 1987. (Illus.). 24p. (J). (ps). pap. 5.95 o.p. (*0-688-07274-7*) HarperCollins Children's Bk. Group.

Ostrow, Kim. Gem of a Mom. 2002. (Wild Thornberrys Ser.). (Illus.). 64p. (J). pap. 3.99 (*0-689-84696-7*, Simon Spotlight/Nickelodeon) Simon & Schuster Children's Publishing.

Otterman, Lynn. Cuddly Chick. 2003. (Animal Snuggles Ser.). (Illus.). 8p. (J). bds. 7.95 (*0-8069-8413-9*) Sterling Publishing Co., Inc.

—Fluffy Bunny. 2003. (Animal Snuggles Ser.). (Illus.). 8p. (J). bds. 7.95 (*0-8069-8403-1*) Sterling Publishing Co., Inc.

Oxenbury, Helen. Mother's Helper. (J). (ps). 1991. (Illus.). 144p. 3.95 o.p. (*0-8037-0995-1*); 1982. 14p. 3.50 o.p. (*0-8037-5425-6*) Penguin Putnam Bks. for Young Readers. (Dial Bks. for Young Readers).

Paris, Lena. Mom Is Single. 1980. (Social Values Ser.). (Illus.). 32p. (J). (gr. k-3). pap. 3.95 o.p. (*0-516-41477-1*); lib. bdg. 13.27 o.p. (*0-516-01477-3*) Scholastic Library Publishing. (Children's Pr.).

Parr, Todd. The Mommy Book. 2002. (Illus.). 32p. (J). (gr. k-3). 14.95 (*0-316-60827-0*) Little Brown Children's Bks.

Pascal, Francine. Hangin' Out with Cici. 1981. (J). (gr. 7-9). pap. (*0-671-43879-4*, Simon Pulse) Simon & Schuster Children's Publishing.

Pearson, Susan. That's Enough for One Day, J.P.! 1985. (Illus.). (J). (gr. k-3). 7.95 o.p. (*0-8037-8566-6*); 7.89 o.p. (*0-8037-8567-4*) Penguin Putnam Bks. for Young Readers. (Dial Bks. for Young Readers).

Pennebaker, Ruth. Both Sides Now, ERS. 2000. 208p. (YA). (gr. 6-9). 16.95 (*0-8050-6105-3*, Holt, Henry & Co. Bks. For Young Readers) Holt, Henry & Co.

Peterson, Jeanne W. My Mama Sings. 1994. (Illus.). 32p. (J). (ps-3). lib. bdg. 15.89 o.p. (*0-06-023859-3*); 15.00 o.p. (*0-06-023854-2*) HarperCollins Children's Bk. Group.

Pfister, Marcus. Hopper. (Illus.). (J). (ps). 1998. 12p. 6.95 (*1-55858-888-4*); 1994. 32p. pap. 6.95 (*1-55858-352-1*); 1991. 32p. 15.95 (*1-55858-106-5*) North-South Bks., Inc.

—Saltarin. (SPA., Illus.). 32p. (J). (ps). 1998. 6.95 (*1-55858-890-6*, NS8959); 1996. 16.95 o.p. (*1-55858-563-X*, NS2103); 1996. pap. 6.95 (*1-55858-548-6*, NS2110) North-South Bks., Inc. (Ediciones Norte-Sur).

Phillips, Wanda C. My Mother Doesn't Like to Cook. 1935. (Illus.). 28p. (Orig.). (J). (gr. 1-5). pap. 6.95 (*0-936981-20-2*) Isha Enterprises, Inc.

Pinkney, Andrea Davis. Shake Shake Shake. 1997. (Illus.). 16p. (J). (ps). bds. 5.95 (*0-15-200632-X*, Red Wagon Bks.) Harcourt Children's Bks.

Pirotta, Saviour. Little Bird. 1992. (Illus.). 32p. (J). (ps-3). 14.00 o.p. (*0-688-11289-7*); lib. bdg. 13.93 o.p. (*0-688-11290-0*) Morrow/Avon. (Morrow, William & Co.).

Pitcher, Caroline. Run with the Wind. 1998. (Illus.). 32p. (J). (ps-3). 14.95 o.p. (*1-888444-29-0*, 21027) Little Tiger Pr.

Plourde, Lynn. Mother, May I? 2004. (Illus.). 32p. (J). 12.99 (*0-525-46988-5*, Dutton Children's Bks.) Penguin Putnam Bks. for Young Readers.

Polushkin, Maria. Mama's Secret. 1984. (Illus.). 32p. (J). (ps-2). 10.95 o.p. (*0-02-774750-6*, Simon & Schuster Children's Publishing) Simon & Schuster Children's Publishing.

Porte, Barbara Ann. Harry's Mom. 1985. (Greenwillow Read-Alone Bks.). (Illus.). 48p. (J). (gr. 1-4). 13.95 o.p. (*0-688-04817-X*); lib. bdg. 15.93 o.p. (*0-688-04818-8*) HarperCollins Children's Bk. Group. (Greenwillow Bks.).

Porter, Connie Rose. Addy's Surprise: A Christmas Story. Johnson, Roberta, ed. 1993. (American Girls Collection: Bk. 3). (Illus.). 80p. (J). (gr. 2 up). pap. 5.95 (*1-56247-079-5*, American Girl) Pleasant Co. Pubns.

—Addy's Surprise: A Christmas Story. 1993. (American Girls Collection: Bk. 3). (Illus.). (YA). (gr. 2 up). 12.10 (*0-606-05104-X*) Turtleback Bks.

Porter-Gaylord, Laurel. I Love My Mommy Because... 1991. (Illus.). 24p. (J). (ps-3). 7.99 (*0-525-44625-7*, Dutton Children's Bks.) Penguin Putnam Bks. for Young Readers.

Porter, Gene Stratton. A Girl of the Limberlost. 1992. (Illus.). 496p. (YA). 9.99 o.s.i (*0-517-07235-1*) Random Hse. Value Publishing.

Potts, Sandra. There's a Blue Bear in the Bathtub & My Mother Is Mad. 1994. (Illus.). 64p. (Orig.). (J). pap. 5.00 (*1-56002-327-9*, University Editions) Aegina Pr., Inc.

Poulin, Stephane. My Mother's Loves. 1990. (Illus.). 32p. (J). (gr. 4-7). pap. 5.95 (*1-55037-148-7*); (ps-3). lib. bdg. 15.95 (*1-55037-149-5*) Annick Pr., Ltd. CAN. *Dist:* Firefly Bks., Ltd.

Power, Barbara. I Wish Laura's Mommy Was My Mommy. 1979. (Harper I-Like-to-Read-Bks.). (Illus.). (J). (ps-2). 11.95 o.p. (*0-397-31838-3*); lib. bdg. 11.89 (*0-397-31859-6*) Lippincott Williams & Wilkins. (Lippincott).

Price, Mathew. My Mommy. 2003. (Illus.). 10p. (J). 4.99 (*0-7696-3155-X*, Gingham Dog Pr.) McGraw-Hill Children's Publishing.

—My Mommy. 1986. (Surprise Board Bks.). (Illus.). 12p. (J). (ps). 3.95 o.s.i (*0-394-88180-X*, Knopf Bks. for Young Readers) Random Hse. Children's Bks.

Pulver, Robin. Nobody's Mother Is in Second Grade. 1992. (Illus.). 320p. (J). (gr. k-3). 13.89 o.s.i (*0-8037-1211-1*); 15.99 o.p. (*0-8037-1210-3*) Penguin Putnam Bks. for Young Readers. (Dial Bks. for Young Readers).

Quarles, Heather. A Door Near Here. 1998. 240p. (YA). (gr. 7-10). 13.95 o.s.i (*0-385-32595-9*) Doubleday Publishing.

—A Door Near Here. 2000. (Illus.). 240p. (YA). (gr. 7 up). mass mkt. 4.99 (*0-440-22761-5*, Laurel Leaf) Random Hse. Children's Bks.

—A Door Near Here. l.t. ed. 2000. (Young Adult Ser.). 323p. (J). (gr. 8-12). 21.95 (*0-7862-2884-9*) Thorndike Pr.

—A Door Near Here. 2000. 10.55 (*0-606-17796-5*) Turtleback Bks.

Rach, Nikki. Dear Mommy. 1999. (Illus.). 64p. (J). 10.99 (*0-570-05364-1*, 12-3415GJ) Concordia Publishing Hse.

Rahaman, Vashanti. Read for Me, Mama. 2003. (Illus.). 32p. (J). (gr. 1). 15.95 (*1-56397-313-8*) Boyds Mills Pr.

Ray, Deborah Kogan. Fog Drift Morning. 1983. (Illus.). 32p. (J). (ps-3). lib. bdg. 12.89 o.p. (*0-06-023198-X*) HarperCollins Children's Bk. Group.

Regan, Dian Curtis. Mommies. 1996. (Illus.). 32p. (J). (ps-k). pap. 5.95 o.s.i (*0-590-47972-5*, Cartwheel Bks.) Scholastic, Inc.

Reiser, Lynn W. Cherry Pies & Lullabies. 1998. (Illus.). 40p. (J). (ps-3). 16.99 (*0-688-13391-6*); 16.89 (*0-688-13392-4*) HarperCollins Children's Bk. Group. (Greenwillow Bks.).

Reuter, Margaret. My Mother Is Blind. 1979. (Social Values Ser.). (Illus.). 32p. (J). (gr. k-3). pap. 3.95 o.p. (*0-516-42021-6*); lib. bdg. 13.27 o.p. (*0-516-02021-8*) Scholastic Library Publishing. (Children's Pr.).

Rich, Scharlotte. I Love My Mommy. 1995. (Love Ser.). (Illus.). 120p. (ps-k). 9.99 o.p. (*0-88070-748-8*) Zonderkidz.

Rich, Scharlotte. I Love My Mommy. 2001. 96p. (J). 7.99 (*0-310-70103-1*) Zondervan.

Ricks, Charlotte. Look at Me, 001. 1979. (J). (ps-2). 7.95 o.p. (*0-395-28480-5*) Houghton Mifflin Co.

Rinaldi, Ann. But in the Fall I'm Leaving. 1985. 224p. (YA). (gr. 7 up). 12.95 o.p. (*0-8234-0560-5*) Holiday Hse., Inc.

—Keep Smiling Through. 1996. 208p. (J). (gr. 4-7). pap. 6.00 (*0-15-201072-6*, Harcourt Paperbacks) Harcourt Children's Bks.

Ripa, Kelly. Thanks Mom! 2004. pap. 13.00 (*0-7868-8852-0*) Hyperion Pr.

Riskind, Mary. Follow That Mom. 1987. (J). (gr. 4-6). 13.95 o.p. (*0-395-41553-5*) Houghton Mifflin Co.

Robbins, Ina. From My Heart to Your Heart. 1994. (J). pap. o.p. (*0-8091-6619-4*) Paulist Pr.

Roberts, Laura Peyton. One Real Thing. 1999. (Clearwater Crossing Ser.: No. 8). 208p. (gr. 7-8). mass mkt. 3.99 o.s.i (*0-553-49257-8*, Dell Books for Young Readers) Random Hse. Children's Bks.

Robinson, Nancy K. Mom, You're Fired! (Orig.). 9999. 144p. (J). (gr. 4-6). pap. 2.50 o.p. (*0-590-41058-X*, Scholastic Paperbacks); 1992. 112p. (J). (gr. 4-6). pap. 3.50 (*0-590-44903-6*, Scholastic Paperbacks); 1991. 112p. (J). (gr. 3-7). pap. 2.75 o.p. (*0-590-42335-5*); 1983. (Illus.). 112p. (J). (gr. 4-6). pap. 2.50 o.p. (*0-590-40294-3*, Scholastic Paperbacks); 1983. pap. 1.95 o.p. (*0-590-32951-0*) Scholastic, Inc.

Roche, Hannah. My Mom Is Magic! 1996. (Science Made Simple Ser.). (Illus.). 24p. (J). (ps up). 6.95 o.p. (*1-899883-60-6*) Stewart, Tabori & Chang.

Roddie, Shen. Not Now, Mrs. Wolf. 2000. (Share-a-Story Ser.). (Illus.). 32p. (J). (ps-3). pap. 5.95 o.p. (*0-7894-5613-3*, D K Ink); pap. 9.95 o.p. (*0-7894-6355-5*) Dorling Kindersley Publishing, Inc.

Rodowsky, Colby. Sydney, Invincible, RS. 1995. 160p. (YA). (gr. 7 up). 14.00 o.p. (*0-374-37365-5*, Farrar, Straus & Giroux (BYR)) Farrar, Straus & Giroux.

Rogers, Paul & Rogers, Emma. Cat's Kittens. 1997. (Illus.). 32p. (J). 13.99 o.s.i (*0-670-86255-X*) Penguin Putnam Bks. for Young Readers.

Roper, Gayle G. Mom, My Tummy's Nervous. 1977. 3.95 o.p. (*0-8010-7650-1*) Baker Bks.
Rose, Deborah L. Meredith's Mother Takes the Train. Levine, Abby, ed. 1991. (Illus.). 24p. (J). (ps). 11.95 o.p. (*0-8075-5061-2*) Whitman, Albert & Co.
Rosenberg, Liz. Monster Mama. (Illus.). 32p. (J). (ps-3). 1997. pap. 6.99 (*0-698-11429-5*, PaperStar); 1993. 16.99 (*0-399-21989-7*, Philomel) Penguin Putnam Bks. for Young Readers.
Rosselson, Leon. Where's My Mom? 1996. (Illus.). 32p. (J). (ps-k). bds. 5.99 o.p. (*1-56402-835-6*) Candlewick Pr.
—Where's My Mom? 1996. 11.09 o.p. (*0-606-10061-X*) Turtleback Bks.
Rubalcaba, Jill. Saint Vitus' Dance. 1996. 112p. (J). (gr. 4-9). tchr. ed. 13.95 o.p. (*0-395-72768-5*, Clarion Bks.) Houghton Mifflin Co. Trade & Reference Div.
Ruckman, Ivy. Who Invited the Undertaker? 1989. 192p. (J). (gr. 3-7). 14.00 o.p. (*0-690-04832-7*); lib. bdg. 13.89 o.p. (*0-690-04834-3*) HarperCollins Children's Bk. Group.
Rushton, Rosie. Just Don't Make a Scene, Mum! 1999. (Fab Five Ser.). 231p. (J). (gr. 5-9). pap. text 3.99 (*0-7868-1370-9*) Hyperion Pr.
Russell, Barbara T. Remembering Stone. 1999. (Illus.). (J). (*0-7894-2583-1*) Dorling Kindersley Publishing, Inc.
Russo, Marisabina. Mama Talks Too Much. 1999. (Illus.). (J). lib. bdg. (*0-688-16412-9*); 288p. 16.00 (*0-688-16411-0*) HarperCollins Children's Bk. Group. (Greenwillow Bks.).
—Time to Wake Up! 1994. (Illus.). 24p. (J). (ps up). 14.00 o.p. (*0-688-04599-5*); lib. bdg. 13.93 o.p. (*0-688-04600-2*) HarperCollins Children's Bk. Group. (Greenwillow Bks.).
—Trade-In Mother. 1993. (Illus.). 32p. (J). (ps up). 14.00 o.s.i (*0-688-11416-4*, Greenwillow Bks.) HarperCollins Children's Bk. Group.
—When Mama Gets Home. 1998. (Illus.). (J). (gr. k-2). 32p. lib. bdg. 14.93 o.p. (*0-688-14986-3*); 2p. 15.99 (*0-688-14985-5*) HarperCollins Children's Bk. Group. (Greenwillow Bks.).
Rymill, Linda. Good Knight, ERS. 1998. (Illus.). 32p. (J). (ps-1). 15.95 o.s.i (*0-8050-4129-X*, Holt, Henry & Co. Bks. For Young Readers) Holt, Henry & Co.
Sachs, Marilyn. Fourteen. 1983. 128p. (J). (gr. 4-9). 10.95 o.p. (*0-525-44044-5*, Dutton Children's Bks.) Penguin Putnam Bks. for Young Readers.
Salem, Lynn & Stewart, Josie. Recados de Mama. Robles, Mariana, tr. 1994. (SPA., Illus.). 16p. (J). pap. 3.75 (*1-880612-22-4*) Seedling Pubns., Inc.
Samuel, Lynette M. Mommy's Hat. 1997. (Illus.). 32p. (J). (gr. 2-5). per. 15.95 (*0-9651270-4-4*) Bright Lamb Pubs., Inc.
Sauer, I. Eve's Little Friends. 1981. (J). text 8.95 o.p. (*0-07-054830-7*) McGraw-Hill Cos., The.
Sawicki, Norma J. Something for Mom. 1987. (Illus.). 32p. (J). (ps-1). 12.95 o.p. (*0-688-05589-3*); lib. bdg. 12.93 o.p. (*0-688-05590-7*) HarperCollins Children's Bk. Group.
Say, Allen. Tree of Cranes. 2002. (Illus.). 25.28 (*0-7587-3857-9*) Book Wholesalers, Inc.
—Tree of Cranes. 1991. (Illus.). 32p. (J). (ps-3). tchr. ed. 17.95 (*0-395-52024-X*) Houghton Mifflin Co. Trade & Reference Div.
Schlein, Miriam. Big Talk. 2nd rev. ed. 1990. (Illus.). 32p. (J). (ps-1). lib. bdg. 13.95 o.p. (*0-02-781231-6*, Simon & Schuster Children's Publishing) Simon & Schuster Children's Publishing.
—The Way Mothers Are. 2000. 13.10 (*0-606-18777-4*) Turtleback Bks.
—The Way Mothers Are. (Concept Book Ser.). (Illus.). (J). (ps-3). 2000. 32p. pap. 6.95 (*0-8075-8690-0*); 1963. lib. bdg. 13.95 o.p. (*0-8075-8692-7*) Whitman, Albert & Co.
—The Way Mothers Are: 13th Anniversary Edition. Tucker, Kathy, ed. 2nd rev. ed. 1993. (Illus.). 32p. (J). (ps-3). text 14.95 (*0-8075-8691-9*) Whitman, Albert & Co.
Schlessinger, Laura, et al. Why Do You Love Me? 2001. (Illus.). 40p. (J). (ps-2). pap. 5.99 (*0-06-443654-3*, Harper Trophy) HarperCollins Children's Bk. Group.
Schwartz, Sheila. Like Mother, Like Me. 1978. (YA). 6.95 o.p. (*0-394-83755-X*); lib. bdg. 6.99 o.p. (*0-394-93755-4*) Knopf Publishing Group. (Pantheon).
Scott, Ann Herbert. On Mother's Lap. 2002. (Illus.). (J). 14.74 (*0-7587-3318-6*) Book Wholesalers, Inc.
—On Mother's Lap. 1994. 1p. (J). (-ps). pap. 9.95 incl. audio (*0-395-69173-7*, 111692); pap. 9.95 incl. audio (*0-395-69173-7*, 111692) Houghton Mifflin Co.
—On Mother's Lap. (Illus.). 32p. (J). (ps-ps). 2000. bds. 4.95 (*0-618-05159-7*); 1992. pap. 6.95 (*0-395-62976-4*); 1992. lib. bdg., tchr. ed. 16.00 (*0-395-58920-7*) Houghton Mifflin Co. Trade & Reference Div. (Clarion Bks.).
—On Mother's Lap. 1972. (Illus.). 39p. (J). (ps). pap. 6.95 o.p. (*0-07-055896-5*); text 12.95 o.p. (*0-07-055897-3*) McGraw-Hill Cos., The.
—On Mother's Lap. 1992. 13.10 (*0-606-06633-0*) Turtleback Bks.
Seymour, Tres. I Love My Buzzard. 1994. (Illus.). 32p. (J). (ps-3). pap. 15.95 (*0-531-06819-6*); lib. bdg. 16.99 (*0-531-08669-0*) Scholastic, Inc. (Orchard Bks.).
Shahan, Sherry. Operation Dump the Boyfriend. 1988. (Treetop Tales Ser.). (Illus.). 96p. (J). (gr. 3-6). 1.00 o.p. (*0-87406-287-X*, 22-15397-9) Darby Creek Publishing.
Shannon. My Mother the Witch Lady. 1995. (J). 13.00 (*0-671-75440-8*, Simon & Schuster Children's Publishing) Simon & Schuster Children's Publishing.
Shannon, George. The Surprise. 1983. (Illus.). 32p. (J). (gr. k-3). 16.00 o.p. (*0-688-02313-4*); lib. bdg. 12.88 o.p. (*0-688-02314-2*) HarperCollins Children's Bk. Group. (Greenwillow Bks.).
—This Is the Bird. 1997. (Illus.). 32p. (J). (ps-3). tchr. ed. 15.95 o.p. (*0-395-72037-0*) Houghton Mifflin Co.
Sharmat, Marjorie Weinman. Hooray for Mother's Day! 1986. (Illus.). 32p. (J). (ps-3). 14.95 o.p. (*0-8234-0588-5*) Holiday Hse., Inc.
—Two Guys Noticed Me...& Other Miracles. 1985. 160p. (J). (gr. 7 up). 13.95 o.p. (*0-385-29394-1*, Delacorte Pr.) Dell Publishing.
Sheppherd, Joseph. Mama Buzurg Is Coming. 1986. (Illus.). 32p. (J). pap. 4.50 o.p. (*0-85398-219-8*) Ronald, George Pub., Ltd.
Sherkin-Langer, Ferne. When Mommy Is Sick. 1995. (J). (ps-3). lib. bdg. 13.95 (*0-8075-8894-6*) Whitman, Albert & Co.
Shine, Michael. Mama Llama's Pajamas. 1990. (Illus.). 45p. (Orig.). (J). (ps-3). pap. 8.95 o.p. (*0-945265-32-8*) Evergreen Pacific Publishing, Ltd.
Shipton, Jonathan. Busy! Busy! Busy! 1991. 32p. (J). (ps-3). 14.99 o.s.i (*0-385-30306-8*, Delacorte Pr.) Dell Publishing.
Simmons, Jane. Come on, Daisy! (ALB, ARA, BEN, CHI & ENG., Illus.). 36p. (Orig.). (J). 2004. pap. 11.95 (*1-84059-177-3*); 2004. pap. 11.95 (*1-84059-178-1*); 2004. pap. 11.95 (*1-84059-179-X*); 2004. pap. 11.95 (*1-84059-217-6*); 2004. pap. 11.95 (*1-84059-180-3*); 2004. pap. 11.95 (*1-84059-183-8*); 2004. pap. 11.95 (*1-84059-181-1*); 2002. pap. 11.95 (*1-84059-182-X*) Milet Publishing, Ltd. GBR. *Dist:* Consortium Bk. Sales & Distribution.
Simon, Norma. Mama Cat's Year. Tucker, Kathleen, ed. 1991. (Illus.). 32p. (J). (ps-2). 15.95 o.p. (*0-8075-4958-4*) Whitman, Albert & Co.
Smalls, Irene. Jonathan & His Mommy. (Illus.). 32p. (J). (ps-3). 1994. pap. 5.95 (*0-316-79880-0*); 1992. 15.95 o.p. (*0-316-79870-3*) Little Brown & Co.
—Jonathan & His Mommy. 1992. 11.10 (*0-606-06509-1*) Turtleback Bks.
Smee, Nicola. Freddie Learns to Swim. 1999. (Little Barron's Toddler Bks.). (Illus.). 20p. (J). (ps). pap. 4.95 o.p. (*0-7641-0864-6*) Barron's Educational Series, Inc.
Smith, Lucia B. My Mom Got a Job, ERS. 1979. (Illus.). (J). (gr. k-3). o.p. (*0-03-048321-2*, Holt, Henry & Co. Bks. For Young Readers) Holt, Henry & Co.
Smith, Marya. Across the Creek. 1989. 164p. (J). (gr. 5 up). lib. bdg. 13.95 o.p. (*1-55970-041-6*) Arcade Publishing, Inc.
Smollin, Michael J. The Sesame Street Mother Grouch Nursery Rhymes. 1995. (Illus.). (J). 4.99 o.s.i (*0-679-85459-2*) Random Hse., Inc.
Snyder, Carol. Ike & Mama & the Once-a-Year Suit. 1992. (Illus.). 48p. (J). (gr. 2-5). reprint ed. pap. 5.95 (*0-8276-0418-1*) Jewish Pubn. Society.
Snyder, Zilpha Keatley. The Birds of Summer. 1983. 204p. (J). (gr. 7 up). 10.95 o.s.i (*0-689-30967-8*, Atheneum) Simon & Schuster Children's Publishing.
Sollinger, Emily. Kisses for Mommy. 2002. (Illus.). 14p. (J). bds. 5.99 (*0-448-42547-5*, Grosset & Dunlap) Penguin Putnam Bks. for Young Readers.
Sondheimer, Ilse. The Boy Who Could Make His Mother Stop Yelling. 1982. (Illus.). 32p. (J). (ps-6). pap. 2.95 (*0-943156-01-7*); lib. bdg. 9.95 (*0-943156-00-9*) Rainbow Pr.
Spinelle, Nancy Louise. Mother & Me. l.t. ed. 1998. (Illus.). 12p. (J). (gr. k-1). text 4.95 (*1-57874-000-2*, Kaeden Bks.) Kaeden Corp.
Spinelli, Eileen. When Mama Comes Home Tonight. 1998. (Illus.). 32p. (J). (ps-k). 14.00 (*0-689-81065-2*, Simon & Schuster Children's Publishing) Simon & Schuster Children's Publishing.
Spinner, Stephanie, ed. Motherlove: Stories by Women About Motherhood. 1978. 2.25 o.p. (*0-440-35693-8*) Dell Publishing.
Srivastava, Sigrun, illus. My Mother. 1980. 22p. (J). (gr. k-3). pap. 3.00 o.p. (*0-89744-215-6*) Children's Bk. Trust IND. *Dist:* Random Hse. of Canada, Ltd.
Stanek, Muriel. I Speak English for My Mom. Tucker, Kathleen, ed. 1989. (Albert Whitman Concept Bks.). (Illus.). 32p. (J). (ps-3). lib. bdg. 13.95 (*0-8075-3659-8*) Whitman, Albert & Co.
Stanley, Diane. Elena. 1996. 64p. (J). (gr. 3-7). 13.95 (*0-7868-0256-1*); lib. bdg. 14.49 (*0-7868-2211-2*) Hyperion Bks. for Children.
Staples, Suzanne Fisher. Haveli. 1995. 336p. (gr. 7 up). mass mkt. 5.50 (*0-679-86569-1*) Random Hse., Inc.
Stehr, Frederic. Quack-Quack, RS. (Sunburst Ser.). (Illus.). (J). (ps up). 1988. 28p. pap. 3.95 o.p. (*0-374-46141-4*, Sunburst); 1987. 32p. 9.95 o.p. (*0-374-36161-4*, Farrar, Straus & Giroux (BYR)) Farrar, Straus & Giroux.
Sternberg, Kate. Mama's Morning. 1997. (Illus.). 32p. (J). (ps-3). pap. 9.95 (*0-9660366-0-3*) Advantage Bks., LLC.
Stewart, Josie & Salem, Lynn. Notes from Mom. 1992. (Seedlings Ser.). (Illus.). 16p. (J). (gr. k-2). pap. 3.75 (*1-880612-01-1*) Seedling Pubns., Inc.
Stewart, Maddie. Peg. 2001. (Blue Bananas Ser.). (Illus.). 48p. (J). (gr. 1-2). pap. 4.95 (*0-7787-0887-X*); lib. bdg. 19.96 (*0-7787-0841-1*) Crabtree Publishing Co.
Stimson, Joan. Big Panda, Little Panda. 1994. (Illus.). 32p. (J). (ps-2). 12.95 o.p. (*0-8120-6404-6*); pap. 5.95 o.p. (*0-8120-1691-2*) Barron's Educational Series, Inc.
Stratton-Porter, Gene. A Girl of the Limberlost. 1992. 432p. (J). (gr. 5 up). pap. 3.99 o.s.i (*0-14-035143-4*, Puffin Bks.) Penguin Putnam Bks. for Young Readers.
Stynes, Barbara White. Walking with Mama. Hovemann, Glenn J., ed. 1997. (Illus.). (J). (ps-2). 28p. 14.95 (*1-883220-56-4*); 24p. pap. 6.95 (*1-883220-57-2*) Dawn Pubns.
Suzanne, Jamie. Brooke & Her Rock Star Mom. 1992. (Sweet Valley Twins Ser.: No. 55). (J). (gr. 3-7). 8.35 o.p. (*0-606-00330-4*) Turtleback Bks.
—Jessica Takes Charge. 1998. (Sweet Valley Twins Ser.: No. 116). 144p. (gr. 3-7). pap. text 3.50 o.s.i (*0-553-48600-4*, Dell Books for Young Readers) Random Hse. Children's Bks.
Symes, Ruth. The Mum Trap. 2000. 128p. (J). pap. 8.95 (*0-86264-933-1*) Andersen Pr., Ltd. GBR. *Dist:* Trafalgar Square.
Tafuri, Nancy. I Love You, Little One. (ps-k). 2000. (Illus.). 15p. (J). bds. 7.99 o.s.i (*0-439-13746-2*, Scholastic Reference); 1998. 95.70 o.p. (*0-590-61689-7*); 1997. (J). pap. (*0-590-92208-4*); 1997. (Illus.). 32p. (J). pap. 15.95 (*0-590-92159-2*) Scholastic, Inc.
Tan, Amy H. My Mommy's an Angel! l.t. ed. 2002. (Angel Ser.). 20p. (J). text 18.95 incl. audio compact disk (*0-9717299-0-5*) JeaMei Publishing.
Testa, Maria. Nine Candles. 1996. (Illus.). 32p. (J). (gr. 2-4). lib. bdg. 19.93 (*0-87614-940-9*, Carolrhoda Bks.) Lerner Publishing Group.
Thompson, Jill. Scary Godmother, Vol. 1. 2003. (Illus.). 48p. 19.95 (*1-57989-015-6*) Sirius Entertainment, Inc.
Tobias, Tobi. The Dawdlewalk. 1983. (Illus.). 32p. (J). (ps-2). lib. bdg. 13.50 o.p. (*0-87614-190-4*, Carolrhoda Bks.) Lerner Publishing Group.
Tolan, Stephanie S. The Great Skinner Strike. 1983. 120p. (YA). (gr. 7 up). 12.95 o.p. (*0-02-789360-X*, Simon & Schuster Children's Publishing) Simon & Schuster Children's Publishing.
—The Liberation of Tansy Warner. 1982. 144p. (gr. 6-9). pap. 1.95 o.p. (*0-440-94636-0*) Dell Publishing.
Tolles, Martha. Marrying off Mom. 1990. (J). pap. 2.75 o.p. (*0-590-42843-8*) Scholastic, Inc.
Tomlinson, Theresa. Dancing Through the Shadows. 1997. (Illus.). 128p. (J). (gr. 4 up). pap. 14.95 o.p. (*0-7894-2459-2*) Dorling Kindersley Publishing, Inc.
Tonner, Leslie. The Mommie Chronicles. 2000. E-Book 6.99 (*1-58586-298-3*) ereads.com.
—The Mommy Chronicles. 2000. E-Book 9.99 (*1-58586-041-7*) ereads.com.
Turner, Ann Warren. Stars for Sarah. 1991. (Charlotte Zolotow Bk.). (Illus.). 32p. (J). (ps-3). 13.95 (*0-06-026186-2*); lib. bdg. 13.89 o.p. (*0-06-026187-0*) HarperCollins Children's Bk. Group.
Ungerer, Tomi. No Kiss for Mother. 1993. 40p. (J). pap. 4.99 o.s.i (*0-440-40886-5*) Dell Publishing.
—No Kiss for Mother. 1973. (Illus.). 48p. (J). (gr. 1-7). o.p. (*0-06-026236-2*); lib. bdg. 11.89 o.p. (*0-06-026237-0*) HarperCollins Pubs.
Urmston, Kathleen & Evans, Karen. A Surprise for Mom. Kaeden Corp. Staff, ed. 1991. (Illus.). 16p. (J). (gr. k-2). pap. text 4.50 (*1-879835-12-6*) Kaeden Corp.
Valdes, Leslie. Happy Mother's Day, Mami! 2003. (Dora the Explorer Ser.). (Illus.). 24p. (J). pap. 3.99 (*0-689-85233-9*, Simon Spotlight/ Nickelodeon) Simon & Schuster Children's Publishing.
Van Laan, Nancy. Sleep, Sleep, Sleep: A Lullaby for Little Ones Around the World. 1994. (Illus.). 32p. (J). (ps). 15.95 o.p. (*0-316-89732-9*) Little Brown & Co.
Van Leeuwen, Jean. Dear Mom You're Ruining My Life. 1990. 160p. (J). (gr. 4-7). pap. 4.99 (*0-14-034386-5*, Puffin Bks.) Penguin Putnam Bks. for Young Readers.
Vestergaard, Hope. Wake up Mama. 2003. (Illus.). 24p. 6.99 (*0-525-47030-1*, Dutton Children's Bks.) Penguin Putnam Bks. for Young Readers.
Viorst, Judith. My Mama Says There Aren't Any Zombies, Ghosts, Vampires, Creatures, Demons, Monsters, Fiends, Goblins, or Things. (Illus.). 48p. (J). (ps-3). 1973. (My Mama Says There Arent Any CL Ser.: Vol. 1). 16.00 (*0-689-30102-2*, Atheneum); 2nd ed. 1987. reprint ed. pap. 6.99 (*0-689-71204-9*, Aladdin) Simon & Schuster Children's Publishing.
—My Mama Says There Aren't Any Zombies, Ghosts, Vampires, Creatures, Demons, Monsters, Fiends, Goblins, or Things. 1988. 12.14 (*0-606-00534-X*) Turtleback Bks.
Voake, Charlotte. Mrs. Goose's Baby. 1997. (Illus.). 24p. (J). (ps-1). bds. 4.99 (*0-7636-0092-X*) Candlewick Pr.
—Mrs. Goose's Baby. 1992. 32p. (J). (ps). pap. 3.99 o.s.i (*0-440-40615-3*) Dell Publishing.
—Mrs. Goose's Baby. 1989. (Illus.). 24p. (J). (ps-1). 12.95 o.p. (*0-316-90511-9*, Joy Street Bks.) Little Brown & Co.
Vogel, Ilse-Margret. The Rainbow Dress & Other Tollush Tales. 1975. (Illus.). 64p. (J). (gr. k-4). 5.95 o.p. (*0-06-026313-X*); lib. bdg. 6.89 o.p. (*0-06-026314-8*) HarperCollins Pubs.
Voigt, Cynthia. Tree by Leaf. 1989. 176p. (J). (gr. 7 up). mass mkt. 4.50 o.s.i (*0-449-70334-7*, Fawcett) Ballantine Bks.
—Tree by Leaf. (J). (gr. 4-7). 2000. 240p. pap. 4.99 (*0-689-83527-2*, Aladdin); 1988. 208p. 15.95 (*0-689-31403-5*, Atheneum) Simon & Schuster Children's Publishing.
—Tree by Leaf. 1989. (J). 9.60 o.p. (*0-606-01223-0*) Turtleback Bks.
Waber, Bernard. Funny, Funny Lyle. 2002. (Lyle the Crocodile Ser.). (Illus.). (J). 14.74 (*0-7587-2559-0*) Book Wholesalers, Inc.
—Funny, Funny Lyle. 1987. (Lyle Ser.). (Illus.). 40p. (J). (ps-3). lib. bdg., tchr. ed. 16.00 (*0-395-43619-2*) Houghton Mifflin Co.
—Funny, Funny Lyle. 1991. (Lyle Ser.). (Illus.). 40p. (J). (ps-3). pap. 6.95 (*0-395-60287-4*) Houghton Mifflin Co. Trade & Reference Div.
—Funny, Funny Lyle. 1987. (Lyle Ser.). (J). (ps-3). 12.10 (*0-606-16122-8*) Turtleback Bks.
—Lyle Finds His Mother. 2002. (Lyle the Crocodile Ser.). (Illus.). (J). 14.74 (*0-7587-3060-8*) Book Wholesalers, Inc.
—Lyle Finds His Mother. (Lyle Ser.). (Illus.). 48p. (J). (ps-3). 1978. pap. 6.95 (*0-395-27398-6*); 1974. lib. bdg., tchr. ed. 16.00 (*0-395-19489-X*) Houghton Mifflin Co.
—Lyle Finds His Mother. 1974. (Lyle Ser.). (J). (ps-3). 12.10 (*0-606-01533-7*) Turtleback Bks.
Waddell, Martin. Owl Babies. 2002. (Illus.). (J). 13.83 (*1-4046-3008-2*) Book Wholesalers, Inc.
—Owl Babies. (Illus.). 2003. 22p. 12.99 (*0-7636-2157-9*); 2002. 32p. (J). pap. 5.99 (*0-7636-1710-5*); 2000. 32p. (J). bds. 19.99 (*0-7636-1283-9*); 1992. 32p. (J). 15.99 (*1-56402-101-7*); 1996. 32p. (J). reprint ed. bds. 6.99 (*1-56402-965-4*) Candlewick Pr.
—Owl Babies. (BEN, CHI, ENG, GUJ & PAN., Illus.). 25p. (J). 1995. (*1-85430-345-7*); 1995. (*1-85430-346-5*); 1995. (*1-85430-344-9*); 1995. (*1-85430-342-2*); 1995. (*1-85430-347-3*); (*1-85430-348-1*, 93442); (*1-85430-343-0*, 93441) Magi Pubns.
—Webster J. Duck. 2001. (Illus.). 32p. (J). (ps). 13.99 (*0-7636-1506-4*) Candlewick Pr.
—Yum Yum Yummy. 1998. (Giggle Club Ser.). (Illus.). 24p. (J). (ps-1). 9.99 o.p. (*0-7636-0477-1*); bds. 3.29 o.s.i (*0-7636-0479-8*) Candlewick Pr.
Wallace, Bill. Buffalo Gal. MacDonald, Patricia, ed. 1993. 192p. (J). (gr. 4-7). reprint ed. pap. 3.99 (*0-671-79899-5*, Aladdin) Simon & Schuster Children's Publishing.
—Buffalo Gal. 1992. (J). 10.04 (*0-606-05175-9*) Turtleback Bks.
Wallace, John. Anything for You. Horse, Harry, tr. & illus. by. 2004. 32p. (J). 15.99 (*0-06-058129-8*) HarperCollins Pubs.
Walton, Rick. That's What You Get... ! 2000. (Illus.). 32p. (J). (ps-3). 15.95 (*0-87905-964-8*) Smith, Gibbs Pub.
Wardlaw, Lee. Operation Rhinoceros. 1992. (Illus.). 120p. (Orig.). (J). (gr. 3-6). pap. 3.50 (*0-931093-14-7*) Red Hen Pr.
Warner, Sally. A Long Time Ago Today. 2003. (Illus.). 208p. (J). (gr. 3-6). 15.99 (*0-670-03604-8*, Viking) Viking Penguin.
Waterton, Betty. Plain Noodles. 1997. (Illus.). 32p. (J). (ps-1). pap. 5.95 (*0-88899-132-0*) Groundwood Bks. CAN. *Dist:* Publishers Group West.
Watson, Pauline. Surprise for Mother. 1976. (Illus.). (J). (ps-2). o.p. (*0-13-877902-3*) Prentice-Hall.

Weeks, Sarah. Mama. 2001. 32p. (J). (ps-2). 15.95 (0-06-027507-3) HarperCollins Children's Bk. Group.

Weiss, Ellen. Babar: A Gift for Mother. 2004. (Illus.). (J). 9.95 (0-8109-4837-0) Abrams, Harry N. , Inc.

Welber, Robert. Goodbye, Hello. 1974. (Illus.). 32p. (J). (ps-1). 2.50 o.p. (0-394-82770-8); lib. bdg. 5.99 o.p. (0-394-92770-2) Knopf Publishing Group. (Pantheon).

Wells, Rosemary. La Estupenda Mama de Roberta. 2001. (Picture Books Collection). (SPA., Illus.). 32p. (J). (gr. k-5). 12.95 (84-372-2187-0) Altea, Ediciones, S.A. - Grupo Santillana ESP. *Dist:* Santillana USA Publishing Co., Inc.

—La Estupenda Mama de Roberta. (SPA.). (J). 16.95 (84-372-1612-5); 1995. 32p. 12.95 (84-372-6612-2) Santillana USA Publishing Co., Inc.

—Hazel's Amazing Mother. (Picture Puffins Ser.). (Illus.). 32p. (J). (ps-3). 1992. pap. 5.99 (0-14-054911-0, Puffin Bks.); 1992. pap. 17.99 o.s.i (0-14-054538-7, Puffin Bks.); 1989. pap. 3.95 o.p. (0-8037-0703-7, Dial Bks. for Young Readers); 1985. 14.99 o.s.i (0-8037-0209-4, Dial Bks. for Young Readers); 1985. 13.89 o.s.i (0-8037-0210-8, Dial Bks. for Young Readers) Penguin Putnam Bks. for Young Readers.

—Hazel's Amazing Mother. 1985. (Picture Puffin Ser.). (Illus.). (J). 12.14 (0-606-01660-0) Turtleback Bks.

Weyland, Jack. Sara, Whenever I Hear Your Name. 1987. 152p. (J). 9.95 o.p. (0-87579-070-4) Deseret Bk. Co.

White, Ruth. Belle Prater's Boy, RS. 1996. 208p. (J). (gr. 5-9). 17.00 (0-374-30668-0, Farrar, Straus & Giroux (BYR)) Farrar, Straus & Giroux.

—Belle Prater's Boy. unabr. ed. 2000. 196p. (J). (gr. 4-6). pap. 37.00 incl. audio (0-8072-8682-6, YA234SP, Listening Library) Random Hse. Audio Publishing Group.

—Belle Prater's Boy. 1997. (YA). pap., tchr. ed. o.s.i (0-440-41497-0, Dell Books for Young Readers); 1998. 224p. (gr. 5-9). reprint ed. pap. text 5.50 (0-440-41372-9, Yearling) Random Hse. Children's Bks.

—Belle Prater's Boy. l.t. ed. 2000. (Illus.). 221p. (YA). (gr. 4-7). 21.95 (0-7862-2885-7) Thorndike Pr.

—Belle Prater's Boy. 1998. (YA). 11.04 (0-606-12610-4) Turtleback Bks.

Wilder, Alice. Mrs. Pepper's Mother's Day. 2001. (Blue's Clues Ser.). (Illus.). 24p. (J). (ps-k). pap. 3.50 (0-689-83934-0, Simon Spotlight/ Nickelodeon) Simon & Schuster Children's Publishing.

Williams. Heeey Ma. Date not set. (Illus.). 40p. (J). (ps-1). pap. 5.95 (0-06-443601-2) HarperCollins Pubs.

Williams, Linda. Horse in the Pigpen. 2002. (Illus.). 32p. (J). (ps-1). 15.95 (0-06-028547-8); lib. bdg. 15.89 (0-06-028548-6) HarperCollins Children's Bk. Group.

Williams, Suzanne. Mommy Doesn't Know My Name. 1990. (Illus.). 48p. (J). (ps). 14.95 o.s.i (0-395-54228-6) Houghton Mifflin Co.

—Mommy Doesn't Know My Name. 1996. (Illus.). 48p. (J). (ps-3). pap. 5.95 (0-395-77979-0) Houghton Mifflin Co. Trade & Reference Div.

—Mommy Doesn't Know My Name. 1990. 12.10 (0-606-08823-7) Turtleback Bks.

Williams, Vera B. A Chair for My Mother. 1984. (Reading Rainbow Bks.). (Illus.). 32p. (J). (ps-3). pap. 5.99 (0-688-04074-8, Morrow, William & Co.) Morrow/Avon.

—A Chair for My Mother Big Book. 1993. (Illus.). 32p. (J). (ps-3). reprint ed. pap. 21.95 (0-688-12612-X, Morrow, William & Co.) Morrow/Avon.

—Un Sillon Para Mama (A Chair for My Mother) 1994. (SPA., Illus.). 32p. (J). lib. bdg. 15.93 o.s.i (0-688-13616-8, Morrow, William & Co.) Morrow/ Avon.

—Un Sillon Para Mi Mama. 1994. Tr. of Chair for My Mother. 13.10 (0-606-06836-8) Turtleback Bks.

—Un Sillon para Mi Mama. Marcuse, Aida E., tr. from ENG. 1994. (un/Libro Mulberry en Espanol Ser.). (SPA., Illus.). 32p. (J). (gr. k-1). reprint ed. pap. 6.99 (0-688-13200-6, MR5678, Rayo) Harper-Trade.

—Un Sillon para Mi Mama. unabr. ed. (SPA., Illus.). (J). (gr. k-2). pap. 15.95 incl. audio (0-87499-335-0, LK6260) Live Oak Media.

—Un Sillon para Mi Mama, Grades 1-6.Tr. of Chair for My Mother. (SPA., Illus.). (J). pap., tchr. ed. 31.95 incl. audio (0-87499-337-7) Live Oak Media.

Wilson. The Mum-Minder. 2000. 32p. (J). pap. 6.95 (0-440-86302-3) Transworld Publishers Ltd. GBR. *Dist:* Trafalgar Square.

Wilson, Gina. All Ends Up. 1984. 160p. (J). (gr. 6 up). o.p. (0-571-13196-4) Faber & Faber Ltd.

Wilson, Johnniece M. Robin on His Own. (J). (gr. 4-6). 1992. 160p. mass mkt. 2.95 (0-590-41809-2, Scholastic Paperbacks); 1990. 12.95 o.p. (0-590-41813-0) Scholastic, Inc.

Winthrop, Elizabeth. Are You Sad, Mama? 1979. (Illus.). (J). (ps-1). o.p. (0-06-026539-6); lib. bdg. 8.89 o.p. (0-06-026544-2) HarperCollins Pubs.

—A Very Noisy Girl. 1991. (Illus.). 32p. (J). (ps-3). tchr. ed. 14.95 (0-8234-0858-2) Holiday Hse., Inc.

Wolf, Matt. Donde Esta Mi Mama. 2001. (Little Chick Ser.).Tr. of Where Is My Mother?. (SPA., Illus.). 10'p. (J). 9.95 (968-5308-43-8) Silver Dolphin Spanish Editions MEX. *Dist:* Publishers Group West.

Wolfgram, Barbara. I Know My Mommy Loves Me. 1998. (Illus.). 32p. (J). (ps-1). 6.99 (0-570-05049-9, 56-1873GJ) Concordia Publishing Hse.

Wood, Douglas. What Moms Can't Do. 2001. (Illus.). 32p. (J). (ps-3). 14.00 (0-689-83358-X, Simon & Schuster Children's Publishing) Simon & Schuster Children's Publishing.

Wright, Betty R. My New Mom & Me. 1993. (Life & Living from a Child's Point of View Ser.). (J). pap. 4.95 o.p. (0-8114-7154-3) Raintree Pubs.

Wright, Lynn F. Momma Tell Me a Story. 1995. (Illus.). 40p. (J). (ps-2). 13.95 (1-881519-04-X); pap. 6.95 (1-881519-05-8) WorryWart Publishing Co.

Wynot, Jillian. The Mother's Day Sandwich. 1990. (Illus.). 32p. (J). (ps-2). 14.95 o.p. (0-531-05857-3); mass mkt. 15.99 o.p. (0-531-08457-4) Scholastic, Inc. (Orchard Bks.).

Yates, Sharon Murphy. The Busy Mom. 2000. (J). 8.95 (0-87868-789-0, Child & Family Pr.) Child Welfare League of America, Inc.

Young, Ronder Thomas. Moving Mama to Town. 1998. 224p. (gr. 5-9). reprint ed. pap. text 4.50 o.s.i (0-440-41455-5, Dell Books for Young Readers) Random Hse. Children's Bks.

—Moving Mama to Town. 1998. 10.04 (0-606-15644-5) Turtleback Bks.

Zeder, Suzan L. Mother Hicks: Playscript. 1986. 68p. (J). (gr. k-3). pap. 7.00 (0-87602-263-8) Anchorage Pr.

Ziefert, Harriet. Mommies Are for Counting Stars. 1999. (Lift-the-Flap Bks.). (Illus.). 16p. (J). (ps-1). pap. 6.99 (0-14-056552-3, Puffin Bks.) Penguin Putnam Bks. for Young Readers.

—Mommy, Where Are You? 1999. pap. 4.95 (0-14-050899-6) NAL.

—Surprise! 1988. (Illus.). (Orig.). (J). (ps-3). pap. 3.50 o.p. (0-14-050814-7, Puffin Bks.) Penguin Putnam Bks. for Young Readers.

—Where's Mommy's Truck? 1992. (Illus.). 16p. (J). (ps). 5.95 (0-694-00377-8) HarperCollins Children's Bk. Group.

—31 Uses for a Mom. 2003. (Illus.). 32p. (J). 12.99 (0-399-23862-X, Putnam & Grosset) Putnam Publishing Group, The.

Zindel, Bonnie & Zindel, Paul. A Star for the Latecomer. 1980. 192p. (YA). (gr. 7 up). 12.95 (0-06-026847-6) HarperCollins Children's Bk. Group.

Zindel, Paul. I Love My Mother. 1975. (Illus.). 32p. (J). (gr. k-3). lib. bdg. 13.89 o.p. (0-06-026836-0) HarperCollins Children's Bk. Group.

Zindel, Paul & Zindel, Bonnie. A Star for the Latecomer. 1985. 160p. (J). (gr. 6 up). mass mkt. 2.50 o.s.i (0-553-25578-9) Bantam Bks.

Zolotow, Charlotte. But Not Billy. 1983. (Charlotte Zolotow Bk.). (Illus.). 32p. (J). (ps-k). 12.95 o.p. (0-06-026963-4) HarperCollins Children's Bk. Group.

—The Moon Was the Best. 1993. (Illus.). 32p. (J). (ps up). lib. bdg. 14.93 o.p. (0-688-09941-6, Greenwillow Bks.) HarperCollins Children's Bk. Group.

—One Step, Two ... rev. ed. 1981. (Illus.). 32p. (J). (gr. k-1). 12.95 o.p. (0-688-41971-2) HarperCollins Children's Bk. Group.

—Say It! 1980. (Illus.). 24p. (J). (gr. k-3). 12.95 o.p. (0-688-80276-1); lib. bdg. 14.93 o.p. (0-688-84276-3) HarperCollins Children's Bk. Group. (Greenwillow Bks.).

—This Quiet Lady. (Illus.). 24p. (ps-3). 2000. (J). pap. 5.95 (0-688-17527-9, Harper Trophy); 1992. (J). 15.95 (0-688-09305-1, Greenwillow Bks.); 1992. (YA). lib. bdg. 13.93 o.p. (0-688-09306-X, Greenwillow Bks.) HarperCollins Children's Bk. Group.

P

PARENT AND CHILD—FICTION

Abegg, Rainbow G. Peaches & Prayers. 2002. (Illus.). (J). 17.95 (1-59156-049-7) Covenant Communications.

Abel, Kathleen. Smile So Big. 2005. (J). (0-15-200671-0) Harcourt Trade Pubs.

Acker, Rick. The Case of the Autumn Rose. 2003. (Davis Detective Mysteries Ser.). 204p. (J). pap. 6.99 (0-8254-2004-0) Kregel Pubns.

Adler, C. S. Daddy's Climbing Tree. 1993. 144p. (J). (gr. 4-6). tchr. ed. 15.00 (0-395-63032-0, Clarion Bks.) Houghton Mifflin Co. Trade & Reference Div.

Adler, David A. The Babe & I. 1999. (Illus.). 32p. (J). (gr. k-4). 16.00 (0-15-201378-4, Gulliver Bks.) Harcourt Children's Bks.

Adshead, Paul S. The Secret Hedgehog. 1991. (Child's Play Library). 72p. (J). (ps-3). 7.99 (0-85953-510-X) Child's Play of England GBR. *Dist:* Child's Play-International.

Agell, Charlotte. I Wear Long Green Hair in Summer. 1994. (Illus.). 32p. (J). (ps-4). 7.95 (0-88448-113-1) Tilbury Hse. Pubs.

Ahlberg, Allan. Treasure Hunt. 2002. (Illus.). 24p. (J). (ps-1). 14.99 (0-7636-1542-0) Candlewick Pr.

Albert, Louise. Less Than Perfect. 2003. (J). tchr. ed. 17.95 (0-8234-1688-7) Holiday Hse., Inc.

Alborough, Jez. Hug. (Illus.). 32p. 2003. bds. 12.99 (0-7636-2105-6); 2001. (J). bds. 6.99 (0-7636-1576-5); 2000. (J). 15.99 (0-7636-1287-1) Candlewick Pr.

—Some Dogs Do. 2003. (Illus.). 40p. (J). 15.99 (0-7636-2201-X) Candlewick Pr.

Alcock, Vivien. The Sylvia Game. 1997. 224p. (YA). (gr. 7-7). pap. 4.95 o.s.i (0-395-81650-5) Houghton Mifflin Co.

Aldis, Dorothy. Hiding. 1993. (Illus.). 110p. (J). pap. (1-55074-342-2) Kids Can Pr., Ltd.

—Hiding. 1994. (Illus.). 32p. (J). (ps). 11.99 o.p. (0-670-85410-7, Viking Children's Bks.) Penguin Putnam Bks. for Young Readers.

Aldis, Dorothy & Collins, Heather. Hiding. (FRE.). (J). pap. 7.99 (0-590-24195-8) Scholastic, Inc.

Alexander, Anne. To Live a Lie. 1975. (Illus.). 176p. (J). (gr. 3-7). 8.95 o.p. (0-689-30470-6, Atheneum) Simon & Schuster Children's Publishing.

Alexander, Liza & Butler, Nate. Me & My Dad: The Story of Sylvester & Son. 1993. (Illus.). (J). 9.95 o.p. (0-681-41829-X) Borders Pr.

Alexander, Martha. When the New Baby Comes, I'm Moving Out! 1979. (Pied Piper Bks.). (Illus.). (J). (ps-2). 9.95 o.p. (0-8037-9557-2); 9.89 o.p. (0-8037-9558-0) Penguin Putnam Bks. for Young Readers. (Dial Bks. for Young Readers).

Aliki. Welcome, Little Baby. 1987. (Illus.). (J). (ps up). 32p. 15.95 (0-688-06810-3); 24p. 15.93 o.p. (0-688-06811-1) HarperCollins Children's Bk. Group. (Greenwillow Bks.).

Amaral, Gayla. Hooray for Daddies. 2001. (Barney Ser.). (Illus.). 22p. (J). (ps-k). bds. 5.95 (1-58668-053-6) Scholastic, Inc.

—Hooray for Mommies! Babies & Barney. 2002. (Barney Ser.). (Illus.). 22p. (J). (ps-k). bds. 5.99 o.p. (1-58668-220-2) Lyrick Publishing.

Ambrosio, Michael. I Don't Want to Take a Nap! 2002. 36p. (J). 16.95 (0-9716085-1-2) LionX Publishing.

Anastas, Margaret. Mommy's Best Kisses. 2003. (Illus.). 32p. (J). (ps-1). 15.99 (0-06-623601-0) HarperCollins Children's Bk. Group.

—Mommy's Best Kisses. 2003. (Illus.). 32p. (J). (ps-1). lib. bdg. 16.89 (0-06-623606-1) HarperCollins Pubs.

Anderson, Joan. Sally's Submarine. 1995. (Illus.). 32p. (J). (gr. k up). 15.00 o.p. (0-688-12690-1); lib. bdg. 14.93 o.p. (0-688-12691-X) Morrow/Avon. (Morrow, William & Co.).

Anderson, Laurie Halse. Catalyst. 2003. 240p. (YA). pap. 6.99 (0-14-240001-7, Puffin Bks.) Penguin Putnam Bks. for Young Readers.

—Time to Fly. 2002. (American Girl Wild at Heart Ser.: Bk. 10). 128p. (J). pap. 4.95 (1-58485-061-2, American Girl) Pleasant Co. Pubns.

—Time to Fly. 2003. (Wild at Heart Ser.). (Illus.). 113p. (J). (gr. 4 up). lib. bdg. 22.60 (0-8368-3262-0) Stevens, Gareth Inc.

Anderson, Peggy Perry. To the Tub. 1996. (Illus.). 32p. (J). (ps-ps). lib. bdg., tchr. ed. 13.95 (0-395-77614-7) Houghton Mifflin Co.

Anderson, Rachel. Black Water, ERS. 1995. 88p. (J). (gr. 5-8). 14.95 o.p. (0-8050-3847-7, Holt, Henry & Co. Bks. For Young Readers) Holt, Henry & Co.

—Black Water. 1996. 180p. (J). (gr. 5-9). pap. 5.95 o.s.i (0-698-11421-3, PaperStar) Penguin Putnam Bks. for Young Readers.

—Black Water. 1996. 10.05 o.p. (0-606-11141-7) Turtleback Bks.

—Paper Faces. l.t. ed. 1993. 216p. (J). 13.95 o.p. (0-7451-1683-3, Galaxy Children's Large Print) BBC Audiobooks America.

—Paper Faces, ERS. 1993. 88p. (J). (gr. 4-7). 14.95 o.p. (0-8050-2527-8, Holt, Henry & Co. Bks. For Young Readers) Holt, Henry & Co.

Andreasen, Dan. A Special Day for Mommy. 2002. (Illus.). 40p. (J). 15.95 (0-689-84977-X, McElderry, Margaret K.) Simon & Schuster Children's Publishing.

Angell, Judie. Yours Truly: A Novel. 1993. 192p. (YA). (gr. 7 up). mass mkt. 15.95 o.p. (0-531-05472-1); mass mkt. 15.99 o.p. (0-531-08622-4) Scholastic, Inc. (Orchard Bks.).

Annunziata, Jane & Nemiroff, Marc A. Why Am I an Only Child? 1998. (Illus.). 36p. (J). (ps-3). 19.95 (1-55798-506-5, 441-5065) American Psychological Assn.

Apperley, Dawn. Dad Mine. 2003. (Illus.). 16p. (J). bds. 6.99 (0-316-73839-5, Tingley, Megan Bks.) Little Brown Children's Bks.

—Mom Mine. 2003. (Illus.). 16p. (J). bds. 6.99 (0-316-73838-7, Tingley, Megan Bks.) Little Brown Children's Bks.

Arensen, Shel. The Test of the Tribal Challenge. 2000. 132p. (gr. 4-7). pap. 9.95 o.p. (0-595-15779-3) iUniverse, Inc.

Armstrong, Jennifer. Black-Eyed Susan. 1995. (Illus.). 128p. (J). (gr. 4-7). 15.00 o.s.i (0-517-70107-3) Random Hse., Inc.

Asch, Frank. Good Night, Baby Bear. (Illus.). 32p. (J). (ps-k). 2001. pap. 6.00 (0-15-216368-9, Voyager Bks./Libros Viajeros); 1998. 14.00 (0-15-200836-5, Gulliver Bks.) Harcourt Children's Bks.

Ash, Frank. Bread & Honey. 1992. (Illus.). 42p. (J). (ps-3). lib. bdg. 18.60 o.p. (0-8368-0880-0) Stevens, Gareth Inc.

Aston, Dianna Hutts. When You Were Born. 2004. (J). (0-7636-1438-6) Candlewick Pr.

Auch, Mary Jane. Out of Step. 1995. 128p. (J). (gr. 4-7). tchr. ed. 13.95 (0-8234-0985-6) Holiday Hse., Inc.

Austen, Jane. Persuasion. 1966. (Classics Ser.). (YA). (gr. 10 up). mass mkt. 2.50 o.p. (0-8049-0107-4, CL-107) Airmont Publishing Co., Inc.

Avi. Abigail Takes the Wheel. (I Can Read Chapter Bks.). (Illus.). 64p. (J). (gr. 3 up). 2000. pap. 3.95 (0-06-444281-0, Harper Trophy); 1999. 14.95 (0-06-027662-2); 1999. 15.89 (0-06-027663-0) HarperCollins Children's Bk. Group.

—Abigail Takes the Wheel. 2000. (Illus.). (J). 10.10 (0-606-18672-7) Turtleback Bks.

—The Barn. 1996. 128p. (J). (gr. 4-7). pap. 4.99 (0-380-72562-2, Harper Trophy) HarperCollins Children's Bk. Group.

—The Barn. 1994. 112p. (J). (gr. 4-7). pap. 14.95 (0-531-06861-7); mass mkt. 15.99 (0-531-08711-5) Scholastic, Inc. (Orchard Bks.).

—The Barn. 1996. (J). 11.04 (0-606-09056-8) Turtleback Bks.

—Ereth's Birthday. 2000. (Tales from Dimwood Forest Ser.). (Illus.). 192p. (J). (gr. 4-7). 15.95 (0-380-97734-6) HarperCollins Children's Bk. Group.

Ayres, Katherine. Family Tree. 1996. 144p. (J). (gr. 3-7). 15.95 o.s.i (0-385-32227-5, Delacorte Pr.) Dell Publishing.

—Family Tree. 1997. (Yearling Ser.). 176p. (gr. 3-7). pap. text 4.50 (0-440-41193-9, Dell Books for Young Readers) Random Hse. Children's Bks.

Baggette, Susan K. Jonathan Goes to the Doctor. 1998. (Jonathan Adventures Ser.). (Illus.). 16p. (J). (ps-k). bds. 5.95 (0-9660172-1-8) Brookfield Reader, Inc., The.

Baillie, Allan. Adrift. 128p. (J). (gr. 3-7). 1994. pap. 3.99 o.s.i (0-14-037010-2, Puffin Bks.); 1992. 14.00 o.s.i (0-670-84474-8, Viking Children's Bks.) Penguin Putnam Bks. for Young Readers.

—Adrift. 1994. 9.09 o.p. (0-606-06161-4) Turtleback Bks.

Bajaj, Varsha. How Many Kisses Do You Want Tonight? 2004. (J). (0-316-82381-3) Little Brown & Co.

Baker, Alan. Where's Mouse? 1992. (Illus.). 16p. (J). (ps-k). o.p. (1-85697-821-4) Kingfisher Publications, plc.

Baker, Liza. I Love You Because You're You. 2001. (Illus.). 32p. (J). (ps-k). pap. 9.95 (0-439-20638-3, Cartwheel Bks.) Scholastic, Inc.

Baker, Roberta. No Ordinary Olive. 2002. (Illus.). 32p. (J). (gr. k-3). 14.95 (0-316-07336-9) Little Brown Children's Bks.

Ballard, Robin. Gracie. 1993. (Illus.). 24p. (J). (ps up). lib. bdg. 13.93 o.p. (0-688-11807-0, Greenwillow Bks.) HarperCollins Children's Bk. Group.

—My Day, Your Day. 2001. (Illus.). 24p. (J). (ps-3). 14.95 (0-688-17796-4); lib. bdg. 14.89 (0-06-029187-7) HarperCollins Children's Bk. Group. (Greenwillow Bks.).

—My Father Is Far Away. 1992. (Illus.). 32p. (J). (ps-6). 14.00 o.p. (0-688-10953-5); lib. bdg. 13.93 o.p. (0-688-10954-3) HarperCollins Children's Bk. Group. (Greenwillow Bks.).

Balzac, Honoré de. Le Pere Goriot. 1965. (YA). (gr. 10 up). mass mkt. 1.50 o.p. (0-8049-0084-1, CL-84) Airmont Publishing Co., Inc.

—Le Pere Goriot: Level D. (FRE.). (YA). (gr. 7-12). text 8.95 (0-88436-043-1, 40280) EMC/Paradigm Publishing.

Banks, Kate. Mama's Little Baby. 2001. (Illus.). 32p. (J). pap. 15.95 (0-7894-7904-4, D K Ink) Dorling Kindersley Publishing, Inc.

—The Night Worker, RS. 2000. (Illus.). 40p. (J). (ps-1). 16.00 (0-374-35520-7, Farrar, Straus & Giroux (BYR)) Farrar, Straus & Giroux.

—Spider, Spider, RS. 1996. (Illus.). 32p. (J). (ps-3). 14.00 o.p. (0-374-37151-2, Farrar, Straus & Giroux (BYR)) Farrar, Straus & Giroux.

Banks, Lynne Reid. Alice-by-Accident. 2000. (Avon Camelot Bks.). 144p. (J). (gr. 4-7). 14.95 (0-380-97865-2) HarperCollins Children's Bk. Group.

Barber, Barbara E. Saturday at the New You. 2002. (Illus.). (J). 14.66 (*0-7587-3566-9*) Book Wholesalers, Inc.
—Saturday at the New You. (Illus.). 32p. (J). (ps up). 1994. 14.95 (*1-880000-06-7*); 1996. reprint ed. pap. 6.95 (*1-880000-43-1*) Lee & Low Bks., Inc.
—Saturday at the New You. 1994. (J). 13.10 (*0-606-09819-4*) Turtleback Bks.
Barnes, Joyce Annette. Promise Me the Moon. 1999. (YA). pap. 14.89 (*0-8037-1799-7*, Dial Bks. for Young Readers); 1999. 176p. (J). (gr. 3-7). pap. 4.99 o.p. (*0-14-038040-X*); 1997. 176p. (YA). (gr. 5-9). 15.99 o.s.i (*0-8037-1798-9*, Dial Bks. for Young Readers) Penguin Putnam Bks. for Young Readers.
—Promise Me the Moon. 1999. 11.04 (*0-606-14297-5*) Turtleback Bks.
Baronian, Jean-Baptiste. Forever. 2001. (Illus.). 32p. (J). 15.95 (*0-8118-3319-4*) Chronicle Bks. LLC.
—I Love You with All My Heart. 1998. (Illus.). 32p. (J). (ps-1). 14.95 (*0-8118-2031-9*) Chronicle Bks. LLC.
Baronian, Jean-Baptiste & Kern, Noris. I Love You with All My Heart. 2002. (Illus.). (J). bds. 6.95 (*0-8118-3622-3*) Chronicle Bks. LLC.
Barrett, John. Daniel Discovers Daniel. 1980. (Illus.). 32p. (J). (gr. k-5). 16.95 (*0-87705-423-1*, Kluwer Academic/Human Science Pr.) Kluwer Academic Pubs.
Bartlett, Craig. Parents Day. 2001. (Hey Arnold! Ser.: Bk. 4). (Illus.). 64p. (J). (gr. 4-7). pap. 3.99 (*0-689-83818-2*, Simon Spotlight) Simon & Schuster Children's Publishing.
Bartone, Elisa. Peppe the Lamplighter. 1993. (Illus.). 32p. (J). (ps-3). 16.95 (*0-688-10268-9*); lib. bdg. 16.89 (*0-688-10269-7*) HarperCollins Children's Bk. Group.
—Peppe the Lamplighter. 1997. (Illus.). 32p. (J). (gr. k-3). pap. 5.99 (*0-688-15469-7*, Morrow, William & Co.) Morrow/Avon.
Baskin, Nora Raleigh. What Every Girl (Except Me) Knows. 2002. 224p. (gr. 5 up). pap. text 4.99 (*0-440-41852-6*) Random Hse., Inc.
Bateman, Teresa. Hunting the Daddyosaurus. 2002. (Illus.). 32p. (J). (ps-1). 15.95 (*0-8075-1433-0*) Whitman, Albert & Co.
Bates, Betty. My Mom, the Money Nut. 1979. 160p. (J). (gr. 4-6). tchr. ed. 12.95 o.p. (*0-8234-0347-5*) Holiday Hse., Inc.
Battle-Lavert, Gwendolyn. Off to School. 1995. (Illus.). 32p. (J). (ps-3). 15.95 (*0-8234-1185-0*) Holiday Hse., Inc.
—Papa's Mark. 2003. (Illus.). (J). (gr. k-3). tchr. ed. 16.95 (*0-8234-1650-X*) Holiday Hse., Inc.
Bau, Gerald. Dee-Dee's Mushrooms. 1978. (J). 4.50 o.p. (*0-533-03719-0*) Vantage Pr., Inc.
Bauer, Cat. Harley, Like a Person. 2003. (J). (*0-7614-5179-X*) Cavendish, Marshall Corp.
—Harley, Like a Person. 2000. (Illus.). (J). 13.00 (*0-606-20690-6*) Turtleback Bks.
—Harley, Like a Person. 2000. (Illus.). 248p. (J). (gr. 7 up). pap. 5.95 (*1-58837-005-4*) Winslow Pr.
Bauer, Joan. Sticks. 192p. (gr. 3-7). 1997. (Illus.). pap. text 3.99 o.s.i (*0-440-41387-7*); 1996. (J). text 15.95 o.s.i (*0-385-32165-1*, Delacorte Pr.) Dell Publishing.
—Sticks. 2002. 192p. (J). 18.99 (*0-399-23752-6*) Penguin Group (USA) Inc.
—Sticks. 1997. (J). 10.04 (*0-606-11912-4*) Turtleback Bks.
Bawden, Nina. Granny the Pag. l.t. ed. 1997. (J). 16.95 o.p. (*0-7451-6905-8*, Galaxy Children's Large Print) BBC Audiobooks America.
—Granny the Pag. 1996. 192p. (YA). (gr. 7-7). 15.00 (*0-395-77604-X*, Clarion Bks.) Houghton Mifflin Co. Trade & Reference Div.
—Granny the Pag. 1998. 192p. (J). (gr. 5-9). pap. 4.99 o.s.i (*0-14-038447-2*, Puffin Bks.) Penguin Putnam Bks. for Young Readers.
—Humbug. 1992. 144p. (J). (gr. 4-7). 15.00 (*0-395-62149-6*, Clarion Bks.) Houghton Mifflin Co. Trade & Reference Div.
Beale, Fleur. I Am Not Esther. 2002. 256p. (J). (gr. 7-10). trans. 15.99 (*0-7868-0845-4*) Disney Pr.
—I Am Not Esther. 2004. (J). pap. 6.99 (*0-7868-1673-2*) Hyperion Bks. for Children.
Bechard, Margaret. Hanging on to Max. 2002. 160p. (gr. 6 up). lib. bdg. 22.90 (*0-7613-2574-3*, Roaring Brook Pr.) Millbrook Pr., Inc.
Bechard, Margaret E. Hanging on to Max. 2002. (Single Titles Ser.: 12). 160p. (gr. 7 up). 15.95 (*0-7613-1579-9*, Roaring Brook Pr.) Millbrook Pr., Inc.
—Hanging on to Max. 2003. (Illus.). 208p. (YA). pap. 6.99 (*0-689-86268-7*, Simon Pulse) Simon & Schuster Children's Publishing.
Becker, Bonny. My Brother, the Robot. l.t. ed. 2002. (Juvenile Ser.). 143p. (J). 21.95 (*0-7862-4134-9*) Gale Group.
—My Brother, the Robot. 2001. 144p. (J). (gr. 3-6). 15.99 (*0-525-46792-0*, Dutton Children's Bks.) Penguin Putnam Bks. for Young Readers.
Beckhorn, Susan Williams. The Kingfisher's Gift. 2002. (Illus.). 208p. (J). 17.99 (*0-399-23712-7*) Putnam Publishing Group, The.
Bedford, David. Touch the Sky, My Little Bear. 2001. (Illus.). 32p. (J). (ps-k). 15.95 (*1-929766-20-3*) Handprint Bks.
Bell, Clare. Ratha's Challenge. 1994. 256p. (J). (gr. 7 up). pap. 16.95 (*0-689-50586-8*, McElderry, Margaret K.) Simon & Schuster Children's Publishing.
Benkowski, Paul Vos. Mama's Home. Herbert, Jennifer, tr. & illus. by. (J). 5.95 (*0-8118-4214-2*) Chronicle Bks. LLC.
Bennett, Cherie. The Fall of the the Perfect Girl. 1993. (Surviving Sixteen Ser.: No. 2). 224p. (J). (gr. 7 up). pap. 3.50 o.p. (*0-14-036319-X*, Puffin Bks.) Penguin Putnam Bks. for Young Readers.
Berenstain, Stan & Berenstain, Jan. The Berenstain Bears & the Trouble with Grownups. 1992. (Berenstain Bears First Time Bks.). (Illus.). 32p. (J). (gr. k-2). pap. 3.25 (*0-679-83000-6*, Random Hse. Bks. for Young Readers) Random Hse. Children's Bks.
—The Berenstain Bears Play Ball. l.t. ed. 1998. (Berenstain Bears Ser.). (Illus.). 48p. (J). (ps-3). pap. 10.95 (*0-590-94732-X*) Scholastic, Inc.
Bergel, Colin. Mail by the Pail. 2000. (Great Lakes Bks.). (Illus.). (J). pap. 16.95 (*0-8143-2891-1*); 32p. (gr. 1-4). 16.95 (*0-8143-2890-3*, Great Lakes Bks.) Wayne State Univ. Pr.
Berry, Liz. The China Garden, RS. 1996. 288p. (YA). (gr. 7 up). 18.00 o.p. (*0-374-31248-6*, Farrar, Straus & Giroux (BYR)) Farrar, Straus & Giroux.
—Mel. 224p. (J). (gr. 7 up). 1991. 13.95 o.p. (*0-670-83925-6*, Viking Children's Bks.); 1993. reprint ed. pap. 3.99 o.p. (*0-14-036534-6*, Puffin Bks.) Penguin Putnam Bks. for Young Readers.
Bertram, Debbie & Bloom, Susan. The Best Place to Read. 2003. (Illus.). 32p. (J). lib. bdg. 16.99 (*0-375-92293-8*); 14.95 (*0-375-82293-3*) Random Hse. Children's Bks.
Bertrand, Cecile. Mr. & Mrs. Smith Have Only One Child, but What a Child! 1992. (Illus.). (J). (ps-3). lib. bdg. 12.93 o.p. (*0-688-11331-1*) HarperCollins Children's Bk. Group.
Bess, Stacey. Planting More Than Pansies: A Fable about Love. 2003. (Illus.). (J). 14.95 (*1-57008-893-4*, Shadow Mountain) Deseret Bk. Co.
Best, Cari. Red Light, Green Light, Mama & Me. 1995. (Illus.). 32p. (J). (ps-3). pap. 15.95 (*0-531-09452-9*); lib. bdg. 16.99 (*0-531-08752-2*) Scholastic, Inc. (Orchard Bks.).
—Taxi! Taxi! 1994. (Illus.). (J). 14.95 o.p. (*0-316-09259-2*) Little Brown & Co.
—Taxi! Taxi! 1997. (Illus.). 32p. (J). (ps-3). mass mkt. 6.95 o.p. (*0-531-07084-0*, Orchard Bks.) Scholastic, Inc.
Binch, Caroline. Since Dad Left. 1998. 4. (Illus.). 32p. (ps-3). (J). 22.40 (*0-7613-0357-X*); 15.95 o.p. (*0-7613-0290-5*) Millbrook Pr., Inc.
Bishop, Roma. Mommy & Baby. 1992. (Nursery Board Mini Pop Bks.). (J). (ps). pap. 2.95 o.s.i (*0-671-79119-2*, Little Simon) Simon & Schuster Children's Publishing.
Bittner, Wolfgang. Wake up, Grizzly! James, J. Alison, tr. from GER. 1996. (Illus.). 32p. (J). (gr. k-3). 15.95 o.p. (*1-55858-518-4*); 16.50 o.p. (*1-55858-519-2*) North-South Bks., Inc.
Black, Sonia W. Hanging Out with Mom. 2000. (Hello Reader! Ser.). (Illus.). 32p. (J). (ps-3). pap. 3.99 (*0-590-86636-2*) Scholastic, Inc.
—Hanging Out with Mom. 2000. (Hello Reader! Ser.). (Illus.). (J). 10.14 (*0-606-18554-2*) Turtleback Bks.
Blackwood, Gary L. Wild Timothy. 2002. 160p. (J). pap. 5.99 (*0-14-230214-7*, Puffin Bks.) Penguin Putnam Bks. for Young Readers.
Blatchford, Claire H. Nick's Mission. 1995. (Lerner Mysteries Ser.). 156p. (J). (gr. 4-7). lib. bdg. 14.95 (*0-8225-0740-4*, Lerner Pubns.) Lerner Publishing Group.
Block, Francesca Lia. The Hanged Man. 1994. (YA). 144p. (ps-2). lib. bdg. 15.89 (*0-06-024537-9*, Cotler, Joanna Bks.); 128p. (gr. 7 up). 14.00 o.p. (*0-06-024536-0*) HarperCollins Children's Bk. Group.
Blue, Rose. Wishful Lying. 1980. (Illus.). 32p. (J). (ps-3). 16.95 (*0-87705-473-8*, Kluwer Academic/Human Science Pr.) Kluwer Academic Pubs.
Boelts, Meribeth. With My Mom - With My Dad. 1992. (Sunshine Ser.). 32p. (J). pap. 0.97 o.p. (*0-8163-1060-2*) Pacific Pr. Publishing Assn.
Bogan, Paulette. Goodnight Lulu. 2003. (Illus.). 32p. (J). (ps-1). 15.95 (*1-58234-803-0*, Bloomsbury Children) Bloomsbury Publishing.
Bohlmeijer, Arno. Something Very Sorry. Bohlmeijer, Arno, tr. 1996. 192p. (Orig.). (YA). (gr. 7-7). 15.00 (*0-395-74679-5*) Houghton Mifflin Co.
—Something Very Sorry. 1997. (Illus.). 192p. (Orig.). (J). (gr. 3-7). pap. 5.95 o.s.i (*0-698-11610-0*, PaperStar) Penguin Putnam Bks. for Young Readers.
Bond, Katherine Grace. Sleepy-Time Dance. 2002. 12p. 5.99 (*0-310-70252-6*) Zondervan.
Bond, Nancy. Truth to Tell. 1994. 336p. (YA). (gr. 7 up). 17.95 (*0-689-50601-5*, McElderry, Margaret K.) Simon & Schuster Children's Publishing.
Bongiorno, Patti Lynn. Daddy, Look at Me! 2002. (Illus.). (J). spiral bd. (*0-9715819-6-7*) Bongiorno Bks.
Bonham, Frank. Vagabundos. 1969. (J). (gr. 7 up). 7.95 o.p. (*0-525-41925-X*, Dutton) Dutton/Plume.
Bopp, Joseph B. Herbie Capleenies. 1978. (Illus.). (J). lib. bdg. 7.95 o.p. (*0-201-04721-7*) Addison-Wesley Longman, Inc.
Borden, Louise. The Little Ships: The Heroic Rescue at Dunkirk in World War II. 2003. (Illus.). 32p. (J). (gr. 4 up). pap. 6.99 (*0-689-85396-3*, Aladdin) Simon & Schuster Children's Publishing.
Borntrager, Mary Christner. Polly. l.t. ed. 2002. 165p. (J). 25.95 (*0-7862-4030-X*) Gale Group.
—Polly. 1994. (Ellie's People Ser.: Vol. 7). 144p. (J). (gr. 4-7). pap. 8.99 (*0-8361-3670-5*) Herald Pr.
Bottner, Barbara. Marsha Makes Me Sick. (Road to Reading Ser.). 48p. (J). (gr. 1-3). 2003. 11.99 (*0-375-99993-0*); 1998. (Illus.). pap. 3.99 (*0-307-26302-9*, 26302) Random Hse. Children's Bks. (Golden Bks.).
—Marsha Makes Me Sick. 1999. (J). 10.14 (*0-606-16139-2*) Turtleback Bks.
Boulden, Jim & Boulden, Joan. Life with One Parent: Single Parent Activity Book. Ward, Evelyn M., ed. 1994. (Illus.). 16p. (Orig.). (J). (gr. k-2). pap. 5.95 (*1-878076-35-3*) Boulden Publishing.
Bowen, Fred. The Golden Glove. 1996. (All-Star Sport Story Ser.: Vol. 2). (Illus.). 112p. (J). (gr. 3-7). pap. 4.95 (*1-56145-133-9*, Peachtree Junior) Peachtree Pubs., Ltd.
—The Golden Glove. 1996. 11.00 (*0-606-14377-7*) Turtleback Bks.
Bowering, George. Parents from Space. 1994. (Out of This World Ser.). 200p. (YA). (gr. 6 up). pap. 5.95 (*1-896184-00-6*) Roussan Pubs., Inc./Roussan Editeur, Inc. CAN. *Dist:* Orca Bk. Pubs.
Boyd, Candy Dawson. Charlie Pippin. 1988. 192p. (J). (gr. 4-7). pap. 5.99 (*0-14-032587-5*, Puffin Bks.) Penguin Putnam Bks. for Young Readers.
—Charlie Pippin. 1987. 192p. (J). (gr. 3-7). lib. bdg. 14.95 o.s.i (*0-02-726350-9*, Simon & Schuster Children's Publishing) Simon & Schuster Children's Publishing.
—Charlie Pippin. 1987. (J). 11.04 (*0-606-03752-7*) Turtleback Bks.
—A Different Beat. 1996. 192p. (J). (gr. 3-7). pap. 4.99 o.s.i (*0-14-036582-6*, Puffin Bks.) Penguin Putnam Bks. for Young Readers.
Boynton, Sandra. Snuggle Puppy: A Love Song. 2003. (Boynton on Board Ser.). (Illus.). 24p. (J). bds. 6.95 (*0-7611-3067-5*, 13067) Workman Publishing Co., Inc.
Bradley, Kimberly Brubaker. Halfway to the Sky. 2002. 176p. (gr. 3-7). text 15.95 (*0-385-72960-X*, Delacorte Pr.) Dell Publishing.
—Halfway to the Sky: The Story of a French Spy. 2002. 176p. (gr. 3-7). lib. bdg. 17.99 (*0-385-90029-5*, Delacorte Pr.) Dell Publishing.
Bradman, Tony. Daddy's Lullaby. 2002. (Illus.). 32p. (J). (ps). 16.95 (*0-689-84295-3*, McElderry, Margaret K.) Simon & Schuster Children's Publishing.
Bridges, Margaret P. If I Were Your Father. 1999. (Illus.). 32p. (J). (ps-3). lib. bdg. 15.89 o.p. (*0-688-15193-0*, Morrow, William & Co.) Morrow/Avon.
Bridges, Margaret Park. Am I Big or Little? (Illus.). 32p. (J). (ps-2). 2002. pap. 5.95 (*1-58717-147-3*); 2000. 15.95 (*1-58717-019-1*); 2000. lib. bdg. 16.50 (*1-58717-020-5*) North-South Bks., Inc.
—If I Were Your Father. 1999. (Illus.). 32p. (J). (ps-3). 16.00 (*0-688-15192-2*, Morrow, William & Co.) Morrow/Avon.
—If I Were Your Mother. 1950. (Illus.). 32p. (J). (ps-3). 15.89 (*0-688-15191-4*) HarperCollins Children's Bk. Group.
—If I Were Your Mother. 1999. (Illus.). 32p. (J). (ps-3). 15.95 (*0-688-15190-6*, Morrow, William & Co.) Morrow/Avon.
—Now What Can I Do? 2003. (Illus.). 32p. (J). pap. 5.95 (*1-58717-242-9*) North-South Bks., Inc.
—Now What Can I Do? 2001. (Illus.). 32p. (J). 15.95 (*1-58717-046-9*); lib. bdg. 16.50 (*1-58717-047-7*) SeaStar Bks.
—Will You Take Care of Me? 1998. (Illus.). 32p. (J). (ps-k). 16.95 (*0-688-15194-9*); 16.95 (*0-688-15194-9*); lib. bdg. 15.89 (*0-688-15195-7*) HarperCollins Children's Bk. Group.
Brighton, Catherine. Galileo's Treasure Box. 2001. (Illus.). 32p. (J). (gr. k-3). 16.95 (*0-8027-8768-1*); lib. bdg. 17.85 (*0-8027-8770-3*) Walker & Co.
Brillhart, Julie. When Daddy Took Us Camping. 1997. (Illus.). 24p. (J). (gr. 1-4). lib. bdg. 13.95 (*0-8075-8879-2*) Whitman, Albert & Co.
Brinkerhoff, Shirley. Mysterious Love. 1998. (Nikki Sheridan Ser.: Bk. 2). 192p. (J). (gr. 4-7). pap. 5.99 (*1-56179-485-6*) Focus on the Family Publishing.
Brooks, Martha. Bone Dance. Date not set. 192p. (YA). (gr. 7 up). pap. (*0-88899-336-6*) Groundwood-Douglas & McIntyre CAN. *Dist:* Publishers Group West.
—Bone Dance. 1997. (Illus.). 192p. (YA). (gr. 7-12). 16.95 (*0-531-30021-8*); lib. bdg. 17.99 (*0-531-33021-4*) Scholastic, Inc. (Orchard Bks.).
Brouwer, Sigmund. Titan Clash. 1998. (Sigmund Brouwer's Sports Mystery Ser.: Vol. 4). 128p. (J). (gr. 5-9). pap. text 5.99 (*0-8499-5816-4*) Nelson, Tommy.
Brown, Alan. I Am a Dog. 2002. 28p. (J). pap. 7.95 (*1-929132-37-9*) Kane/Miller Bk. Pubs.
Brown, Jo. Where's My Mommy? 2002. (Illus.). (J). tchr. ed. 14.95 (*1-58925-019-2*, Tiger Tales) ME Media LLC.
Brown, Marc. Arthur's Computer Disaster. (Arthur Adventure Ser.). (J). (gr. k-3). 1999. pap. 5.95 (*0-316-12373-0*); 1999. (Illus.). 32p. pap. 5.95 (*0-316-10534-1*); 1997. (Illus.). 32p. 15.95 (*0-316-11016-7*) Little Brown Children's Bks.
—Arthur's Computer Disaster. 1997. (Arthur Adventure Ser.). (J). (gr. k-3). 12.10 (*0-606-17382-X*) Turtleback Bks.
—Kiss Hello, Kiss Good-Bye. 1997. (Arthur Ser.). 12p. (J). (ps-k). bds. 4.99 o.s.i (*0-679-86739-2*, Random Hse. Bks. for Young Readers) Random Hse. Children's Bks.
Brown, Margaret Wise. The Little Scarecrow Boy. 1998. (Illus.). 40p. (J). (ps-2). 15.99 (*0-06-026284-2*); lib. bdg. 16.89 (*0-06-026290-7*) HarperCollins Children's Bk. Group. (Cotler, Joanna Bks.).
—The Runaway Bunny. (Illus.). (J). (ps up). 2001. 36p. bds. 12.95 (*0-694-01671-3*); 1991. 34p. bds. 7.99 (*0-06-107429-2*) HarperCollins Children's Bk. Group.
—The Runaway Bunny. 2000. (Illus.). 40p. (J). (ps-3). pap. 6.95 (*0-9629298-8-3*, MHC-8-3) Minnesota Humanities Commission.
Browne, Anthony. Changes, RS. 2002. (Illus.). 32p. (J). (ps-1). reprint ed. pap. 6.95 (*0-374-41177-8*, Sunburst) Farrar, Straus & Giroux.
—Gorilla. 2002. 40p. (J). (gr. k-3). 14.99 (*0-7636-1813-6*) Candlewick Pr.
—Gorilla. (Illus.). 32p. (J). (ps-3). 1985. 13.99 o.s.i (*0-394-97525-1*); 1985. 8.95 o.s.i (*0-394-87525-7*); 1989. reprint ed. pap. 6.99 o.s.i (*0-394-82225-0*) Random Hse. Children's Bks. (Knopf Bks. for Young Readers).
—Gorilla. 1986. (Julia MacRae Blackbird Bks.). (Illus.). 32p. (J). (gr. 4-8). lib. bdg. 8.95 o.p. (*0-531-04609-5*, Watts, Franklin) Scholastic Library Publishing.
Brun-Cosme, Nadine & Backes, Michel. No, I Want Daddy! 2004. (J). (*0-618-38157-0*, Clarion Bks.) Houghton Mifflin Co. Trade & Reference Div.
Bryant, Sally S. Here's Juggins. 1996. (Illus.). 176p. (J). (gr. 4-7). 19.95 (*0-945980-62-0*) North Country Pr.
Buffie, Margaret. Someone Else's Ghost. 1995. 256p. (YA). 14.95 o.p. (*0-590-46922-3*) Scholastic, Inc.
Bullard, Lisa. My Home: Walls, Floors, Ceilings & Doors. 2002. (All about Me Ser.). (Illus.). 24p. (J). (ps-1). lib. bdg. 19.90 (*1-4048-0046-8*) Picture Window Bks.
Bunn, Scott. Just Hold On. 1982. 160p. (J). (gr. 7 up). pap. 9.95 o.s.i (*0-385-28490-X*, Delacorte Pr.) Dell Publishing.
Bunting, Eve. Flower Garden. 2002. (Illus.). (J). 13.19 (*0-7587-2519-1*) Book Wholesalers, Inc.
—Flower Garden. (Illus.). 32p. (J). (ps-3). 2000. pap. 6.00 (*0-15-202372-0*); 1994. 16.00 (*0-15-228776-0*) Harcourt Children's Bks.
—Flower Garden. 1999. (Illus.). 32p. (J). (ps-3). pap. 25.95 (*0-15-201968-5*) Harcourt Trade Pubs.
—Flower Garden. 2000. 12.15 (*0-606-17842-2*) Turtleback Bks.
—A Part of the Dream. 1992. (Eve Bunting Collection). (Illus.). 48p. (J). (gr. 2-6). lib. bdg. 12.79 o.p. (*0-89565-771-6*) Child's World, Inc.
—Sharing Susan. 1991. 128p. (J). (gr. 4-7). 14.95 o.p. (*0-06-021693-X*); lib. bdg. 14.89 o.p. (*0-06-021694-8*) HarperCollins Children's Bk. Group.
—Some Frog! 1998. (Illus.). 48p. (J). (gr. 1). 15.00 o.s.i (*0-15-277082-8*) Harcourt Children's Bks.
—Spying on Miss Muller. 1996. 160p. (gr. 4-7). mass mkt. 6.99 (*0-449-70455-6*, Fawcett) Ballantine Bks.
—Spying on Miss Muller. 1995. 192p. (J). (gr. 4-6). 15.00 (*0-395-69172-9*, Clarion Bks.) Houghton Mifflin Co. Trade & Reference Div.
—Spying on Miss Muller. 1996. 10.55 (*0-606-14320-3*) Turtleback Bks.
Burnett, Frances Hodgson. Editha's Burglar. 1994. (Illus.). 54p. (J). (gr. 4-7). 14.95 (*1-55709-244-3*) Applewood Bks.
Burnett, Karen Gedig. Katie's Rose: A Tale of Two Late Bloomers. (Grandma Rose Story). 32p. (J). 2001. pap. 8.50 (*0-9668530-3-2*); 2000. 14.50 (*0-9668530-2-4*) GR Publishing.

Burningham, John. Come Away from the Water, Shirley. 1977. (Illus.). (J). 160p. (gr. 5 up). 14.89 o.p. (*0-690-01361-2*); 32p. (gr. 1-2). 14.00 o.p. (*0-690-01360-4*) HarperCollins Children's Bk. Group.

Burstein, Fred. The Dancer. 1993. (Illus.). 40p. (J). (ps-3). lib. bdg. 14.95 o.s.i (*0-02-715625-7*, Simon & Schuster Children's Publishing) Simon & Schuster Children's Publishing.

Bussard, Paula. The Glad I Gotcha Day. 1985. (Critter County Ser.). (Illus.). 28p. (J). (gr. k-3). 1.39 o.p. (*0-87239-963-X*, 3383) Standard Publishing.

Butler, Charles. The Darkling. 1998. 176p. (YA). (gr. 7-12). 16.00 (*0-689-81796-7*, 870383, McElderry, Margaret K.) Simon & Schuster Children's Publishing.

Buzzeo, Toni. Dawdle Duckling. 2003. (Illus.). 32p. (J). 15.99 (*0-8037-2731-3*, Dial Bks. for Young Readers) Penguin Putnam Bks. for Young Readers.

Cadnum, Michael. Heat. 1998. 176p. (J). (gr. 7-12). 15.99 (*0-670-87886-3*) Penguin Putnam Bks. for Young Readers.

—Rundown. Moore, Lisa, ed. 2001. 176p. (YA). pap. 6.99 (*0-14-131087-1*) Penguin Putnam Bks. for Young Readers.

—Rundown. 1999. 160p. (YA). (gr. 7-12). 15.99 o.p. (*0-670-88377-8*) Penguin Putnam Bks. for Young Readers.

—Rundown. 2001. (J). 12.04 (*0-606-20894-1*) Turtleback Bks.

Cain, Sheridan. Why So Sad, Brown Rabbit? 1998. (Illus.). 32p. (J). (ps-2). 14.99 o.s.i (*0-525-45963-4*, Dutton Children's Bks.) Penguin Putnam Bks. for Young Readers.

Caisley, Raewyn. Hannah & Her Dad. 1994. (Voyages Ser.). (Illus.). (J). 4.25 (*0-383-03787-5*) SRA/McGraw-Hill.

Calvert, Patricia. Bigger. 144p. (J). 2003. pap. 4.99 (*0-689-86003-X*, Aladdin); 1994. (gr. 4-6). 16.00 (*0-684-19685-9*, Atheneum) Simon & Schuster Children's Publishing.

—Bigger. 1994. 10.00 (*0-606-07287-X*) Turtleback Bks.

Cameron, Ann. Gloria's Way. 2002. (Illus.). 12.34 (*1-4046-0952-0*) Book Wholesalers, Inc.

—Gloria's Way, RS. 2000. (Illus.). 96p. (J). (ps-3). 15.00 (*0-374-32670-3*, Farrar, Straus & Giroux (BYR)) Farrar, Straus & Giroux.

—Gloria's Way. 2001. (Chapter Ser.). (Illus.). 112p. (J). pap. 4.99 (*0-14-230023-3*, Puffin Bks.) Penguin Putnam Bks. for Young Readers.

Cameron, Eleanor. To the Green Mountains. 1975. 224p. (J). (gr. 5 up). 9.95 o.p. (*0-525-41355-3*, Dutton) Dutton/Plume.

Campbell, Ann. Queenie Farmer Had Fifteen Daughters. 2002. (Illus.). 32p. (J). (ps-2). 16.00 (*0-15-201933-2*, Silver Whistle) Harcourt Children's Bks.

Campbell, Ann-Jeanette. Dora's Box. 1998. (Illus.). 32p. (J). (gr. k-3). 18.99 o.s.i (*0-679-97642-6*) Knopf, Alfred A. Inc.

—Dora's Box. 1998. (Illus.). 32p. (J). (gr. k-3). 17.00 o.s.i (*0-679-87642-1*) Random Hse., Inc.

Campbell, Bebe Moore. Sometimes My Mommy Gets Angry. 2003. (Illus.). 32p. (J). 16.99 (*0-399-23972-3*, G. P. Putnam's Sons) Penguin Putnam Bks. for Young Readers.

Campbell, Joanna. The Bad Luck Filly. 2000. (Thoroughbred Ser.: No. 42). 176p. (gr. 4-7). mass mkt. 4.99 (*0-06-105873-4*, HarperEntertainment) Morrow/Avon.

Campbell, Louisa & Taylor, Bridget S. Phoebe's Fabulous Father. 1996. (Illus.). 32p. (J). (ps-3). 14.00 (*0-15-200996-5*) Harcourt Trade Pubs.

Campos, Tito. Muffler Man. Vigil-Pion, Evangelina, tr. 2001. Tr. of Hombre Mofle. (ENG & SPA., Illus.). 32p. (J). (ps-3). 14.95 (*1-55885-318-9*, Piñata Books) Arte Publico Pr.

Cannon, Ann. I Know What You Do When I Go to School. 2nd ed. 2001. 32p. (J). (ps-3). pap. 5.95 (*1-58685-107-1*) Smith, Gibbs Pub.

Cannon, Bettie. Begin the World Again. 1991. 192p. (YA). (gr. 7 up). text 14.95 o.p. (*0-684-19292-6*, Atheneum) Simon & Schuster Children's Publishing.

Carbone, Elisa. The Surfmen of Pea Island. 2001. 176p. (gr. 5-8). lib. bdg. 18.99 (*0-375-90664-9*) Random Hse., Inc.

Carey, Peter. The Big Bazoohley, ERS. 1995. (Illus.). 96p. (J). (gr. 4-7). 14.95 o.s.i (*0-8050-3855-8*, Holt, Henry & Co. Bks. For Young Readers) Holt, Henry & Co.

—The Big Bazoohley. 1996. (Illus.). 144p. (J). (gr. 4-7). pap. 4.99 o.s.i (*0-698-11420-5*, PaperStar) Penguin Putnam Bks. for Young Readers.

—The Big Bazoohley. 1995. (Storybridge Ser.). 96p. (J). (gr. 3-7). pap. 9.95 (*0-7022-2832-X*) Univ. of Queensland Pr. AUS. *Dist:* International Specialized Bk. Services.

Carlson, Melody. Cherished Wish. 1998. (Allison Chronicles Ser.: Vol. 2). 160p. (J). (gr. 6-9). pap. 5.99 o.p. (*1-55661-958-8*) Bethany Hse. Pubs.

Carlstrom, Nancy White. Goodbye Geese. 1991. (Illus.). 32p. (J). (ps-3). 14.95 o.p. (*0-399-21832-7*, Philomel) Penguin Putnam Bks. for Young Readers.

Carlstrom, Nancy White & Saport, Linda. Before You Were Born. 2001. (Illus.). 32p. (J). (ps-k). 17.00 (*0-8028-5185-1*, Eerdmans Bks For Young Readers) Eerdmans, William B. Publishing Co.

Carrick, Carol. Valentine. 1995. (Illus.). 40p. (J). (ps-3). lib. bdg., tchr. ed. 16.00 (*0-395-66554-X*, Clarion Bks.) Houghton Mifflin Co. Trade & Reference Div.

Carter, Ron. Me & the Geezer: A True Story about Growing up in Little League Style. 1996. 176p. (Orig.). (J). pap. 11.95 (*0-9643672-2-X*) Harbour Bks.

Casanova, Mary. When Eagles Fall. 2002. 144p. (J). 15.99 (*0-7868-0665-6*); lib. bdg. 16.49 (*0-7868-2557-X*) Hyperion Bks. for Children.

Caseley, Judith. Mama, Coming & Going. 1994. (Illus.). 32p. (J). (ps-3). 15.95 (*0-688-11441-5*); lib. bdg. 13.93 o.p. (*0-688-11442-3*) HarperCollins Children's Bk. Group. (Greenwillow Bks.).

—Witch Mama. 1996. (Illus.). 32p. (J). (ps-3). 15.00 (*0-688-14457-8*); lib. bdg. 14.93 (*0-688-14458-6*) HarperCollins Children's Bk. Group. (Greenwillow Bks.).

Castronovo, Michelle. My Daddy Likes to Be with Me. 1995. (Kids Comfort Inc. Ser.: No. 2). (Illus.). 16p. (Orig.). (J). pap. 9.95 (*1-887453-17-2*) Kids Comfort, Inc.

—My Daddy's Going Working. 1995. (Kids Comfort Inc. Ser.: No. 1). (Illus.). 16p. (Orig.). (J). pap. 9.95 (*1-887453-09-1*) Kids Comfort, Inc.

—My Mommy Likes to Be with Me. 1995. (Kids Comfort Inc. Ser.: No. 3). (Illus.). 16p. (Orig.). (J). pap. 9.95 (*1-887453-08-3*) Kids Comfort, Inc.

—My Mommy's Going Working. 1995. (Kids Comfort Inc. Ser.: No. 4). 16p. (Orig.). (J). pap. 9.95 (*1-887453-02-4*) Kids Comfort, Inc.

Catalano, Dominic. Hush. 2003. (Illus.). 32p. (J). 14.95 (*1-57768-679-9*, Gingham Dog Pr.) McGraw-Hill Children's Publishing.

Cazet, Denys. Are There Any Questions? 1992. (Illus.). 32p. (J). (ps-2). 15.95 o.p. (*0-531-05451-9*); mass mkt. 16.99 o.p. (*0-531-08601-1*) Scholastic, Inc. (Orchard Bks.).

—Born in the Gravy. 1993. (Illus.). 32p. (J). (ps-1). mass mkt. 15.99 o.p. (*0-531-08638-0*); pap. 15.95 (*0-531-05488-8*) Scholastic, Inc. (Orchard Bks.).

Centeio, Tara Jaye. Just Mommy & Me. 2004. (Illus.). 32p. (J). 12.99 (*0-06-000724-9*); lib. bdg. 13.89 (*0-06-000725-7*) HarperCollins Pubs.

—Mommy Loves Her Baby. Date not set. 32p. (ps-1). pap. 5.99 (*0-06-443715-9*) HarperCollins Pubs.

—Mommy Loves Her Baby, Daddy Loves His Baby. 2003. (Illus.). 32p. (J). (ps-1). 15.99 (*0-06-029077-3*) HarperCollins Pubs.

Chaconas, Dori. Goodnight, Dewberry Bear. 2003. (Illus.). 32p. (J). 17.00 (*0-687-02691-1*) Abingdon Pr.

Chang, Cindy. Are You My Baby? Mini Peek Book. 1996. (J). bds. 3.99 o.s.i (*0-679-88275-8*, Random Hse. Bks. for Young Readers) Random Hse. Children's Bks.

Chapman, Carol. Ig Lives in a Cave. 1979. (Smart Cat Bks.). (Illus.). (J). (ps-3). 7.95 o.p. (*0-525-32534-4*, Dutton) Dutton/Plume.

Charbonnet, Gabrielle. Good-Bye, Jasmine. 1999. (Disney Girls Ser.: Vol. 9). 84p. (J). (gr. 2-5). pap. text 3.99 (*0-7868-4273-3*) Hyperion Pr.

Chesnut, Sheryl Daane. I'll Be There. 2002. (Illus.). 32p. (J). 14.95 (*0-689-84181-7*, Simon & Schuster Children's Publishing) Simon & Schuster Children's Publishing.

Chetwin, Grace. Jason's Seven Magical Night Rides. 1994. (Illus.). 128p. (J). (gr. 2-6). lib. bdg. 14.95 o.s.i (*0-02-718221-5*, Simon & Schuster Children's Publishing) Simon & Schuster Children's Publishing.

Chorao, Kay. Lester's Overnight. 1977. (Illus.). (J). (ps-1). 6.95 o.p. (*0-525-33480-7*, Dutton) Dutton/Plume.

—Molly's Moe. 1979. (Illus.). 32p. (J). (ps-3). 7.50 o.p. (*0-395-28784-7*, Clarion Bks.) Houghton Mifflin Co. Trade & Reference Div.

Christiana, David. A Tooth Fairy's Tale, RS. 1996. 32p. (J). (ps-3). pap. 6.95 o.p. (*0-374-47942-9*, Sunburst) Farrar, Straus & Giroux.

Christopher, Matt. Centerfield Ballhawk. (Peach Street Mudders Story Ser.). (Illus.). (J). 1994. 59p. (ps-3). pap. 4.50 (*0-316-14272-7*); 1992. 64p. (gr. 2-4). 13.95 o.p. (*0-316-14079-1*) Little Brown & Co.

—Centerfield Ballhawk. 1992. (Springboard Bks.). 10.65 (*0-606-06270-X*) Turtleback Bks.

—Tennis Ace. 2000. 128p. (J). (gr. 3-7). pap. 4.50 (*0-316-13491-0*); (Illus.). 15.95 o.p. (*0-316-13519-4*) Little Brown & Co.

—Tennis Ace. 2000. 10.00 (*0-606-18267-5*) Turtleback Bks.

—Windmill Windup. 2002. (J). (gr. 3-7). 140p. 15.95 (*0-316-14531-9*); 144p. pap. 4.50 (*0-316-14432-0*) Little Brown Children's Bks.

Clark, Catherine. Gilmore Girls No. 1: Like Mother, Like Daughter. 2002. 160p. (YA). mass mkt. 5.99 (*0-06-009212-2*) HarperCollins Pubs.

Clark, Clara Gillow. Hill Hawk Hattie. 2003. 176p. (J). 15.99 (*0-7636-1963-9*) Candlewick Pr.

Clarke, J. The Heroic Life of Al Capsella, ERS. 160p. 1990. (YA). (gr. 6 up). 14.95 o.p. (*0-8050-1310-5*); 1997. (J). (gr. 7-12). reprint ed. pap. 6.95 o.s.i (*0-8050-5541-X*) Holt, Henry & Co. (Holt, Henry & Co. Bks. For Young Readers).

Clavel, Bernard. Castle of Books. 2002. (Illus.). 40p. (J). (gr. k-5). 14.95 (*0-8118-3501-4*) Chronicle Bks. LLC.

Cleary, Beverly. Dear Mr. Henshaw. l.t. ed. 1987. (Illus.). 141p. (J). (gr. 2-6). reprint ed. lib. bdg. 14.95 o.s.i (*1-55736-001-4*) Bantam Doubleday Dell Large Print Group, Inc.

—Dear Mr. Henshaw. 2002. (Illus.). (J). 13.83 (*0-7587-9140-2*) Book Wholesalers, Inc.

—Dear Mr. Henshaw. 1994. 128p. (J). (gr. 4-7). pap. 1.99 o.s.i (*0-440-21934-5*) Dell Publishing.

—Dear Mr. Henshaw. 2000. (Cleary Reissue Ser.). (Illus.). 160p. (J). (gr. 5 up). pap. 5.99 (*0-380-70958-9*, Harper Trophy) HarperCollins Children's Bk. Group.

—Dear Mr. Henshaw. 1995. (Illus.). (J). 9.32 (*0-395-73255-7*) Houghton Mifflin Co.

—Dear Mr. Henshaw. (J). 1996. pap. 4.99 (*0-380-72798-6*, Avon Bks.); 1983. (Illus.). 144p. (gr. 4-7). 15.99 (*0-688-02405-X*, Morrow, William & Co.); 1983. (Illus.). 144p. (gr. 4-7). lib. bdg. 16.89 (*0-688-02406-8*, Morrow, William & Co.) Morrow/Avon.

—Dear Mr. Henshaw. (J). 1992. pap. o.s.i (*0-440-80308-X*, Dell Books for Young Readers); 1984. (Illus.). 144p. pap. 4.50 o.s.i (*0-440-41794-5*, Yearling) Random Hse. Children's Bks.

—Dear Mr. Henshaw. (J). 1996. 9.60 o.p. (*0-606-09187-4*); 1983. 11.00 (*0-606-06315-3*) Turtleback Bks.

—Petey's Bedtime Story. 1993. (Illus.). 32p. (J). (ps-3). 14.89 (*0-688-10661-7*) HarperCollins Children's Bk. Group.

—Petey's Bedtime Story. 1993. (Illus.). 32p. (J). (gr. k up). 15.00 (*0-688-10660-9*, Morrow, William & Co.) Morrow/Avon.

—Querido Senor Henshaw. 1996. (SPA.). 144p. (J). (gr. 4-7). 9.50 (*84-239-2766-0*) Espasa Calpe, S.A. ESP. *Dist:* AIMS International Bks., Inc.

—Ramona & Her Father. 2002. (Illus.). (J). 13.83 (*0-7587-5636-4*) Book Wholesalers, Inc.

—Ramona & Her Father. (Ramona Ser.). (J). (gr. 3-5). 1983. pap.; 1923. pap. 2.95 o.s.i (*0-440-77241-9*) Dell Publishing.

—Ramona & Her Father. 1977. (Ramona Ser.). (Illus.). 192p. (J). (gr. 3-5). 15.95 (*0-688-22114-9*); lib. bdg. 16.89 (*0-688-32114-3*) HarperCollins Children's Bk. Group.

—Ramona & Her Father. 1990. (Ramona Ser.). (Illus.). 208p. (J). (gr. 3-5). pap. 5.99 (*0-380-70916-3*, Avon Bks.) Morrow/Avon.

—Ramona & Her Father. l.t. ed. 1988. (Ramona Ser.). 155p. (J). (gr. 3-5). reprint ed. lib. bdg. 16.95 o.s.i (*1-55736-076-6*, Cornerstone Bks.) Pages, Inc.

—Ramona & Her Father. (Ramona Ser.). (J). 186p. (gr. 3-5). pap. 4.99 (*0-8072-1439-6*); 2003. (gr. 2). audio 18.00 (*0-8072-1032-3*) Random Hse. Audio Publishing Group. (Listening Library).

—Ramona & Her Father. 1979. (Ramona Ser.). (Illus.). 196p. (J). (gr. 3-5). pap. 1.75 o.s.i (*0-440-47241-5*, Yearling) Random Hse. Children's Bks.

—Ramona & Her Father. 1977. (Ramona Ser.). (J). (gr. 3-5). 11.00 (*0-606-04522-8*) Turtleback Bks.

—Ramona & Her Mother. (Ramona Ser.). (J). (gr. 3-5). 1988. pap. o.p. (*0-440-80004-8*); 1980. 208p. pap. 3.25 o.s.i (*0-440-47243-1*); 1923. pap. 3.25 o.s.i (*0-440-77243-5*) Dell Publishing.

—Ramona & Her Mother. 1979. (Ramona Ser.). (Illus.). 208p. (J). (gr. 3-5). 16.99 (*0-688-22195-5*); (ps-3). lib. bdg. 17.89 (*0-688-32195-X*) HarperCollins Children's Bk. Group.

—Ramona & Her Mother. 1990. (Ramona Ser.). (Illus.). 224p. (J). (gr. 3-5). reprint ed. pap. 5.99 (*0-380-70952-X*) Morrow/Avon.

—Ramona & Her Mother. (Ramona Ser.). (J). 208p. (gr. 3-5). pap. 4.99 (*0-8072-1435-3*); 2003. (gr. 2). audio 18.00 (*0-8072-1030-7*); 1990. 186p. (gr. 3-5). pap. 28.00 incl. audio (*0-8072-7314-7*, YA 820 SP) Random Hse. Audio Publishing Group. (Listening Library).

—Ramona & Her Mother. 1980. (Ramona Ser.). (J). (gr. 3-5). pap. 4.50 (*0-440-70007-8*, Dell Books for Young Readers) Random Hse. Children's Bks.

—Ramona & Her Mother. 1979. (Ramona Ser.). (J). (gr. 3-5). 11.00 (*0-606-04781-6*) Turtleback Bks.

—Ramona y Su Madre. 1996. (Ramona Ser.). (SPA.). 184p. (J). (gr. 4-7). 9.95 (*84-239-2803-9*) Espasa Calpe, S.A. ESP. *Dist:* AIMS International Bks., Inc.

—Ramona y Su Madre. 1997. (Ramona Ser.). (SPA., Illus.). 208p. (J). (gr. 3-7). 15.00 (*0-688-15466-2*, MR7556, Morrow, William & Co.) Morrow/Avon.

—Ramona y su Madre. 1997. Orig. Title: Ramona & Her Mother. (SPA., Illus.). 184p. (J). (gr. 2-6). pap. 5.95 (*0-688-15486-7*, Morrow, William & Co.) Morrow/Avon.

Clements, Andrew. The Janitor's Boy. (J). 2001. (Illus.). 160p. pap. 4.99 (*0-689-83585-X*, Aladdin); 2000. 144p. (gr. 3-7). 15.00 (*0-689-81818-1*, Simon & Schuster Children's Publishing) Simon & Schuster Children's Publishing.

—The Janitor's Boy. l.t. ed. 2000. 152p. (J). (gr. 4-7). 21.95 (*0-7862-2903-9*) Thorndike Pr.

Clewes, Dorothy. The End of Summer. 1971. (J). (gr. 7-11). 5.95 o.p. (*0-698-20041-1*) Putnam Publishing Group, The.

Clifton, Lucille. Everett Anderson's 1-2-3, ERS. (Illus.). (J). (ps-3). 2002. 32p. pap. 6.95 (*0-8050-7048-6*); 1977. o.p. (*0-03-017441-4*); 1992. 32p. 16.95 (*0-8050-2310-0*) Holt, Henry & Co. (Holt, Henry & Co. Bks. For Young Readers).

Cohen, Barbara. Make a Wish, Molly. 1995. 48p. (gr. 4-7). pap. text 3.99 (*0-440-41058-4*); 1994. (Illus.). 40p. (J). 14.95 o.s.i (*0-385-31079-X*, Delacorte Pr.) Dell Publishing.

—Make a Wish, Molly. 1993. (J). o.s.i (*0-385-44599-7*) Doubleday Publishing.

—Make a Wish, Molly. 1994. (J). pap. 4.50 (*0-440-91018-8*, Dell Books for Young Readers) Random Hse. Children's Bks.

—Make a Wish, Molly. 1995. (J). 10.14 (*0-606-07831-2*) Turtleback Bks.

—Make a Wish Molly. 1995. (Illus.). (J). 10.55 (*0-7857-5404-0*) Econo-Clad Bks.

Cohen, Ron. My Dad's Baseball. 1994. (Illus.). 32p. (J). (gr. k up). 15.00 o.p. (*0-688-12390-2*); lib. bdg. 14.93 o.p. (*0-688-12391-0*) HarperCollins Children's Bk. Group.

Cole, Brock. The Facts Speak for Themselves. 1997. 192p. (YA). (gr. 7 up). 16.95 (*1-886910-14-6*) Front Street, Inc.

—The Facts Speak for Themselves. 2000. (Illus.). 192p. (J). (gr. 9-12). pap. 5.99 o.s.i (*0-14-130696-3*) Penguin Putnam Bks. for Young Readers.

—The Facts Speak for Themselves. 2000. (Illus.). (J). 12.04 (*0-606-18403-1*) Turtleback Bks.

Cole, Joanna. When Mommy & Daddy Go to Work. 2001. (Illus.). 32p. (J). (ps up). 5.95 (*0-688-17044-7*) HarperCollins Children's Bk. Group.

—When Mommy & Daddy Go to Work. 2001. (J). lib. bdg. (*0-06-029603-8*) HarperCollins Pubs.

Coleman, Evelyn. Mystery of the Dark Tower. 2000. (American Girl Collection: Bk. 6). (Illus.). 160p. (J). (gr. 5-9). pap. 5.95 (*1-58485-084-1*); 9.95 (*1-58485-085-X*) Pleasant Co. Pubns. (American Girl).

—Mystery of the Dark Tower. 2000. (History Mysteries Ser.). 12.00 (*0-606-18356-6*) Turtleback Bks.

Colfer, Eoin. The Arctic Incident. l.t. ed. 2003. (Artemis Fowl Ser.: Bk. 2). (J). (gr. 3-6). 16.95 (*0-7540-7839-6*, Galaxy Children's Large Print) BBC Audiobooks America.

—The Arctic Incident. (Artemis Fowl Ser.: Bk. 1). (J). (gr. 3-6). 2003. 304p. pap. 7.99 (*0-7868-1708-9*); 2002. 288p. 16.99 (*0-7868-0855-1*) Hyperion Bks. for Children.

—The Arctic Incident. l.t. ed. 2003. (Artemis Fowl Ser.: Bk. 2). 313p. (J). (gr. 3-6). 25.95 (*0-7862-4825-4*) Thorndike Pr.

—Artemis Fowl. 2002. (Artemis Fowl Ser.: Bk. 1). 288p. (J). (gr. 4-7). pap. 7.99 (*0-7868-1707-0*) Disney Pr.

—Artemis Fowl. l.t. ed. 2001. (Artemis Fowl Ser.: Bk. 1). 312p. (J). (gr. 3-6). 27.95 (*1-58724-092-0*, Wheeler Publishing, Inc.) Gale Group.

—Artemis Fowl. 2003. (Artemis Fowl Ser.: Bk. 1). (Illus.). 304p. (J). (gr. 3-6). mass mkt. 5.99 (*0-7868-1787-9*) Hyperion Bks. for Children.

—Artemis Fowl. 2001. (Artemis Fowl Ser.: Bk. 1). 288p. (gr. 4-7). 16.95 (*0-7868-0801-2*) Talk Miramax Bks.

Collier, James Lincoln. The Jazz Kid. 1996. 224p. (YA). (gr. 6 up). pap. 4.99 o.s.i (*0-14-037778-6*, Puffin Bks.) Penguin Putnam Bks. for Young Readers.

—The Jazz Kid. 1996. (YA). (gr. 6 up). 10.09 o.p. (*0-606-09485-7*) Turtleback Bks.

—Rich & Famous. 2001. (Lost Treasures Ser.: No. 6). (Illus.). 240p. (J). pap. 4.99 (*0-7868-1520-5*); (gr. 3-7). pap. 1.99 (*0-7868-1519-1*) Hyperion Bks. for Children. (Volo).

—The Teddy Bear Habit or How I Became a Winner. 2001. (Lost Treasures Ser.: No. 3). (Illus.). 240p. (J). pap. 4.99 (*0-7868-1544-2*); (gr. 3-7). reprint ed. pap. 1.99 (*0-7868-1543-4*) Hyperion Bks. for Children. (Volo).

Collins, H. When You Were Little & I Was Big. 1984. (Illus.). 32p. (J). (ps-8). pap. 4.95 (*0-920236-71-5*); 12.95 o.p. (*0-920236-84-7*) Annick Pr., Ltd. CAN. *Dist:* Firefly Bks., Ltd.

Collins, Pat Lowery. Signs & Wonders. 1999. 192p. (J). (gr. 5-9). tchr. ed. 15.00 (*0-395-97119-5*) Houghton Mifflin Co.

Colman, Hila. Claudia, Where Are You? 1969. (J). (gr. 7 up). lib. bdg. 6.96 o.p. (*0-688-31174-1*, Morrow, William & Co.) Morrow/Avon.

Coman, Carolyn. Tell Me Everything, RS. 160p. (YA). 1995. pap. 3.95 o.p. (*0-374-47506-7*, Aerial); 1993. (gr. 5-9). 15.00 o.p. (*0-374-37390-6*, Farrar, Straus & Giroux (BYR)) Farrar, Straus & Giroux.

—Tell Me Everything. 1998. 160p. (J). (gr. 5-9). pap. 4.99 o.p. (*0-14-038791-9*, Puffin Bks.) Penguin Putnam Bks. for Young Readers.

—Tell Me Everything. 1995. 9.05 o.p. (*0-606-09955-7*) Turtleback Bks.

Conlon-McKenna, Marita. Under the Hawthorn Tree. 2001. (Illus.). 160p. pap. 5.95 (*0-86278-206-6*) O'Brien Pr., Ltd., The IRL. *Dist:* Independent Pubs. Group.

Conly, Jane Leslie. What Happened on Planet Kid? 2002. (Illus.). 224p. (J). (gr. 5 up). pap. 5.95 (*0-06-441076-5*, Harper Trophy) HarperCollins Children's Bk. Group.

—What Happened on Planet Kid, ERS. 2000. 216p. (J). (gr. 5-9). 16.95 (*0-8050-6065-0*, Holt, Henry & Co. Bks. For Young Readers) Holt, Henry & Co.

Conrad, Pam. Blue Willow. 1999. (Illus.). 32p. (J). (ps-3). 16.99 (*0-399-22904-3*) Penguin Putnam Bks. for Young Readers.

—Zoe Rising. 144p. (J). (gr. 4 up). 1996. 13.95 o.p. (*0-06-027217-1*); 1996. (Illus.). lib. bdg. 14.89 o.s.i (*0-06-027218-X*); 1997. (Illus.). reprint ed. pap. 4.95 (*0-06-440687-3*, Harper Trophy) HarperCollins Children's Bk. Group.

—Zoe Rising. 1997. 11.00 (*0-606-12137-4*) Turtleback Bks.

Cook, Jean T. Room for a Stepdaddy. 1995. (Albert Whitman Concept Bks.). (Illus.). 32p. (J). (ps-3). lib. bdg. 14.95 (*0-8075-7106-7*) Whitman, Albert & Co.

Cooney, Caroline B. Tune in Anytime. 192p. (YA). (gr. 7). 2001. (Illus.). mass mkt. 4.99 (*0-440-22798-4*, Laurel Leaf); 1999. 8.95 o.s.i (*0-385-32649-1*, Dell Books for Young Readers) Random Hse. Children's Bks.

—Whatever Happened to Janie? (YA). 1994. 224p. (gr. 5-9). mass mkt. 5.50 (*0-440-21924-8*, Dell Bks.); 1993. 208p. (gr. 7 up). 16.95 (*0-385-31035-8*, Delacorte Pr.) Dell Publishing.

Corcoran, Barbara. Strike! 1983. 168p. (YA). (gr. 6-9). 12.95 o.p. (*0-689-30952-X*, Atheneum) Simon & Schuster Children's Publishing.

Corentin, Philipe. Papa! 1997. (Illus.). 32p. (J). (ps-1). 11.16 o.p. (*0-8118-1640-0*) Chronicle Bks. LLC.

Corey, Dorothy. Will There Be a Lap for Me? Levine, Abby, ed. 1992. (Illus.). 24p. (J). (gr. k-2). lib. bdg. 13.95 (*0-8075-9109-2*); pap. 5.95 (*0-8075-9110-6*) Whitman, Albert & Co.

Cottonwood, Joe. Danny Ain't. 1992. 304p. (YA). (gr. 4-7). pap. 13.95 (*0-590-45067-0*, 026) Scholastic, Inc.

Cousins, Lucy. Jazzy in the Jungle. 2002. (Illus.). 32p. (J). (ps-k). 14.99 (*0-7636-1903-5*) Candlewick Pr.

Covington, Dennis. Lasso the Moon. 1996. 208p. (YA). (gr. 7 up). mass mkt. 4.50 o.s.i (*0-440-22013-0*, Laurel Leaf); (J). 20.95 (*0-385-30991-0*, Dell Books for Young Readers) Random Hse. Children's Bks.

—Lasso the Moon. 1996. 9.60 o.p. (*0-606-09526-8*) Turtleback Bks.

Cowan, Catherine. My Friend the Piano. 1998. (Illus.). 32p. (J). (gr. k-3). 16.00 (*0-688-13239-1*) HarperCollins Children's Bk. Group.

Coy, John. Two Old Potatoes & Me. 2003. (Illus.). 40p. (J). (gr. k-3). 15.95 (*0-375-82180-5*, Knopf Bks. for Young Readers) Random Hse. Children's Bks.

Coyle, Carmela LaVigna. Do Princesses Wear Hiking Boots? 2003. (Illus.). 32p. (J). 15.95 (*0-87358-828-2*) Northland Publishing.

Cray, Jordan. Most Wanted. 1998. (Danger.com Ser.: No. 7). 240p. (YA). (gr. 6 up). pap. 3.99 (*0-689-82040-2*, Simon Pulse) Simon & Schuster Children's Publishing.

Creech, Sharon. Absolutely Normal Chaos. 240p. (J). (gr. 4 up). 1997. (Illus.). pap. 5.99 (*0-06-440632-6*, Harper Trophy); 1995. 16.99 (*0-06-026989-8*); 1995. lib. bdg. 16.89 (*0-06-026992-8*, Harper Trophy) HarperCollins Children's Bk. Group.

—Absolutely Normal Chaos. 1997. 12.00 (*0-606-10734-7*) Turtleback Bks.

—Fishing in the Air. (Illus.). 32p. (J). (ps-3). 2003. pap. 6.99 (*0-06-051606-2*, Harper Trophy); 2000. 15.95 (*0-06-028111-1*, Cotler, Joanna Bks.); 2000. lib. bdg. 15.89 (*0-06-028112-X*, Cotler, Joanna Bks.) HarperCollins Children's Bk. Group.

Crew, Gary. Mama's Babies. 2002. 160p. (J). (gr. 5-9). pap. 6.95 (*1-55037-724-8*); lib. bdg. 18.95 (*1-55037-725-6*) Annick Pr., Ltd. CAN. *Dist:* Firefly Bks., Ltd.

Crist-Evans, Craig. Amaryllis. 2003. 208p. (YA). 15.99 (*0-7636-1863-2*) Candlewick Pr.

—Moon over Tennessee: A Boy's Civil War Journal. (Illus.). (J). 2003. 64p. pap. 6.95 (*0-618-31107-6*); 1999. 62p. (gr. 4-6). tchr. ed. 15.00 (*0-395-91208-3*) Houghton Mifflin Co.

Crowe, Chris. The Mississippi Trial, 1955. 2002. 240p. (YA). (gr. 6-8). 17.99 (*0-8037-2745-3*, Dial Bks. for Young Readers) Penguin Putnam Bks. for Young Readers.

Cruise, Robin. The Top-Secret Journal of Fiona Claire Jardin. 1998. 160p. (J). (gr. 4-7). 13.00 (*0-15-201383-0*) Harcourt Children's Bks.

Crum, Shutta. Fox & Fluff. 2002. (Illus.). 32p. (J). (ps). lib. bdg. 15.95 (*0-8075-2544-8*) Whitman, Albert & Co.

Crutcher, Chris. Ironman. 1995. (Illus.). 192p. (J). (gr. 7 up). 16.99 (*0-688-13503-X*, Greenwillow Bks.) HarperCollins Children's Bk. Group.

Cummings, Pat. Carousel. 1994. (Illus.). 32p. (J). (ps-3). 14.95 (*0-02-725512-3*, Simon & Schuster Children's Publishing) Simon & Schuster Children's Publishing.

Cunningham, Bill. Flames in the Wind. 1984. (Illus.). 113p. (YA). (gr. 7-12). reprint ed. pap. 9.95 o.p. (*0-913383-01-5*) McClanahan Publishing Hse., Inc.

Curtis, Munzee. When the Big Dog Barks. 1997. (Illus.). 24p. (J). lib. bdg. 14.93 o.p. (*0-688-09540-2*); 15.00 o.s.i (*0-688-09539-9*) HarperCollins Children's Bk. Group. (Greenwillow Bks.).

Cusimano, Maryann K. You Are My I Love You. 2001. (Illus.). 32p. (J). (ps-2). 15.99 (*0-399-23392-X*, Philomel) Penguin Putnam Bks. for Young Readers.

Dahl, Roald. Danny the Champion of the World. 1999. (J). (gr. 5-9). 20.25 (*0-8446-7025-1*) Smith, Peter Pub., Inc.

Dahlberg, Maurine E. Play to the Angel. 2002. 192p. (J). pap. 5.99 (*0-14-230145-0*, Puffin Bks.) Penguin Putnam Bks. for Young Readers.

Dahlberg, Maurine F. Play to the Angel, RS. 2000. 192p. (J). (gr. 3-7). 16.00 (*0-374-35994-6*, Farrar, Straus & Giroux (BYR)) Farrar, Straus & Giroux.

Dale, Elizabeth. How Long? 1998. (Illus.). 32p. (J). (ps-1). pap. 14.95 (*0-531-30101-X*, Orchard Bks.) Scholastic, Inc.

Daly-Weir, Catherine. Daddy & Me. 1999. (Grossett & Dunlap All Aboard Books & Cassettes Ser.). (Illus.). 32p. (ps-3). 3.49 (*0-448-41964-5*) Penguin Putnam Bks. for Young Readers.

Danis, Naomi. Walk with Me. 1995. (Story Corner Ser.). (Illus.). 24p. (J). (ps-3). bds. 6.95 (*0-590-45855-8*, Cartwheel Bks.) Scholastic, Inc.

Danziger, Paula. Amber Brown Is Feeling Blue. 1998. (Amber Brown Ser.: No. 7). (Illus.). 128p. (J). (gr. 3-6). 14.99 (*0-399-23179-X*, G. P. Putnam's Sons) Penguin Putnam Bks. for Young Readers.

—Can You Sue Your Parents for Malpractice? 1998. 160p. (J). (gr. 5-9). pap. 4.99 (*0-698-11688-7*, PaperStar) Penguin Putnam Bks. for Young Readers.

—Can You Sue Your Parents for Malpractice? (gr. 5-6). 144p. (J). pap. 3.99 (*0-8072-1375-6*); 152p. (YA). pap. 3.99 (*0-8072-1540-6*); 1999. 152p. (YA). pap. 28.00 incl. audio (*0-8072-7991-9*, YA960SP) Random Hse. Audio Publishing Group. (Listening Library).

—Can You Sue Your Parents for Malpractice? 1998. 11.04 (*0-606-15476-0*) Turtleback Bks.

—The Divorce Express. 1983. 160p. (YA). (gr. 7 up). mass mkt. 3.99 o.p. (*0-440-92062-0*, Laurel Leaf) Random Hse. Children's Bks.

—Everyone Else's Parents Said Yes. l.t. ed. 1992. (Children's Lythway Ser.). 160p. (J). lib. bdg. 13.95 o.p. (*0-7451-1550-0*, Macmillan Reference USA) Gale Group.

—Everyone Else's Parents Said Yes. 1998. 126p. (J). (gr. 4-7). pap. 4.99 (*0-698-11687-9*, PaperStar) Penguin Putnam Bks. for Young Readers.

—Everyone Else's Parents Said Yes. 1990. 128p. (YA). (gr. k-6). pap. 3.99 o.s.i (*0-440-40333-2*, Yearling) Random Hse. Children's Bks.

—Everyone Else's Parents Said Yes. 1998. lib. bdg. 11.04 (*0-606-17100-2*); 1989. (J). 9.09 o.p. (*0-606-03267-3*) Turtleback Bks.

—I, Amber Brown. 1999. (Amber Brown Ser.: No. 8). (Illus.). 144p. (J). (gr. 3-6). 14.99 (*0-399-23180-3*, Ace/Putnam) Penguin Group (USA) Inc.

—It's a Fair Day, Amber Brown. (Illus.). 48p. (J). 2003. pap. 3.99 (*0-698-11982-7*, PaperStar); 2002. 12.99 (*0-399-23606-6*, G. P. Putnam's Sons) Penguin Putnam Bks. for Young Readers.

—It's a Fair Day, Amber Brown. 2002. (Illus.). 48p. (J). (*0-399-23471-3*) Putnam Publishing Group, The.

Davis, Jennifer. Before You Were Big. 2003. (Illus.). (J). 11.95 (*0-7611-2732-1*) Workman Publishing Co., Inc.

Davis, Katie. I Hate to Go to Bed! (Illus.). 40p. (J). (ps-2). 2002. pap. 6.00 (*0-15-216802-8*, Voyager Bks./Libros Viajeros); 1999. 14.00 (*0-15-201920-0*) Harcourt Children's Bks.

Davis, Ossie. Just Like Martin. 2001. (J). pap. (*0-7868-1642-2*); 176p. lib. bdg. 16.49 (*0-7868-2632-0*) Hyperion Bks. for Children. (Jump at the Sun).

—Just Like Martin. 1992. 208p. (YA). (gr. 5-9). pap. 15.00 (*0-671-73202-1*, Simon & Schuster Children's Publishing) Simon & Schuster Children's Publishing.

—Just Like Martin. 1996. (J). (gr. 5-9). 19.50 o.p. (*0-8446-6897-4*) Smith, Peter Pub., Inc.

Davol, Marguerite. Black, White, Just Right! 1993. (Albert Whitman Concept Bks.). (Illus.). 32p. (J). (gr. k-3). lib. bdg. 14.95 (*0-8075-0785-7*) Whitman, Albert & Co.

De Anda, Diane. Dancing Miranda. Castilla, Julia Mercedes, tr. from ENG. 2001. Tr. of Baila, Miranda, Baila. (ENG & SPA., Illus.). 32p. (J). (ps-3). 14.95 (*1-55885-323-5*, Piñata Books) Arte Publico Pr.

de Brunhoff, Jean. Babar & His Children. 1989. (Babar Ser.).Tr. of Babar en Famille. (Illus.). 48p. (J). (ps-3). 16.95 o.s.i (*0-679-80165-0*, Random Hse. Bks. for Young Readers) Random Hse. Children's Bks.

—Babar & His Children. Haas, Merle, tr. from FRE. (Babar Ser.).Tr. of Babar en Famille. (Illus.). 48p. (J). (ps-3). 1969. lib. bdg. 17.99 (*0-394-90577-6*); 1954. 15.95 (*0-394-80577-1*) Random Hse. Children's Bks. (Random Hse. Bks. for Young Readers).

de Graff, Anne. Please Wonderful Mommy. 1997. (Tiny Triumphs Ser.). (Illus.). 22p. (J). (ps-2). pap. text 1.88 o.p. (*0-687-07099-6*) Abingdon Pr.

De Smet, Marian. Anna's Tight Squeeze. 2003. Orig. Title: Op Slot. (Illus.). (J). pap. 5.95 (*1-58925-378-7*, Tiger Tales) ME Media LLC.

Deans, Sis B. Racing the Past, ERS. 2001. (Illus.). 160p. (YA). (gr. 5-10). 15.95 (*0-8050-6635-7*, Holt, Henry & Co. Bks. For Young Readers) Holt, Henry & Co.

Deaver, Julie Reece. You Bet Your Life. 1993. (Charlotte Zolotow Bk.). 224p. (YA). (gr. 7 up). 15.00 o.p. (*0-06-021516-X*); lib. bdg. 14.89 o.p. (*0-06-021517-8*) HarperCollins Children's Bk. Group.

Deem, James M. Three NBs of Julian Drew. 1996. 176p. (J). pap. 4.50 o.s.i (*0-380-72587-8*, Avon Bks.) Morrow/Avon.

—Three NBs of Julian Drew. 1996. 9.60 o.p. (*0-606-08959-4*) Turtleback Bks.

DeFelice, Cynthia C. Under the Same Sky, RS. 2003. 224p. (J). 16.00 (*0-374-38032-5*, Farrar, Straus & Giroux (BYR)) Farrar, Straus & Giroux.

del Castillo, Richard Griswold. Cesar Chavez: a Struggle for Justice / Cesar Chavez: La Lucha Por la Justicia. Colin, Jose Juan, tr. from ENG. 2002. (Hispanic Civil Rights Ser.). (ENG & SPA., Illus.). 32p. (J). (ps-3). 14.95 (*1-55885-324-3*, Piñata Books) Arte Publico Pr.

DenBoer, Helen. Please Don't Cry, Mom. 1993. (Illus.). (J). (gr. 1-4). lib. bdg. 14.95 o.p. (*0-87614-805-4*, Carolrhoda Bks.) Lerner Publishing Group.

Denchfield, Nick. Charlie the Chicken. 1997. (Illus.). 20p. (J). (ps). pap. 12.95 (*0-15-201451-9*) Harcourt Trade Pubs.

Desimini, Lisa. My Beautiful Child. Mahurin, Matt, tr. & illus. by. 2004. (J). (*0-439-45893-5*, Blue Sky Pr., The) Scholastic, Inc.

Dessen, Sarah. This Lullaby. 352p. 2004. pap. 7.99 (*0-14-250155-7*, Puffin Bks.); 2002. (YA). text 16.99 (*0-670-03530-0*) Penguin Putnam Bks. for Young Readers.

Devore, Cynthia D. Breakfast for Dinner. 1993. (Children of Courage Ser.). 32p. (J). (gr. 5 up). lib. bdg. 21.95 o.p. (*1-56239-245-X*) ABDO Publishing Co.

DeWitt, Dawn Davis. Searching for Blue Bears. Rolando, Cecilia, tr. & illus. by. 2003. (J). (*0-9677057-5-4*) Raven Productions, Inc..

Dexter, Catherine. A Is for Apple. 1997. (Illus.). 160p. (J). (gr. 3-7). reprint ed. bds. 4.99 (*0-7636-0385-6*) Candlewick Pr.

Dixon, Sylvia W. Sug Learns How to Cook. Angaza, Mai T., ed. 1991. (Illus.). 28p. (Orig.). (J). (gr. 3-10). pap. 5.00 (*0-9652951-0-9*) Dixon, S. W.

Dobson, Danae. The Pet-Sitting Service. 1996. (Sunny Street Kids' Club Ser.: Vol. 2). (Illus.). 32p. (J). (ps-3). pap. 4.99 o.p. (*0-8499-5113-5*) Nelson, Tommy.

Doherty, Berlie. Dear Nobody. 1994. 240p. (J). (gr. 7 up). pap. 5.95 (*0-688-12764-9*, Harper Trophy) HarperCollins Children's Bk. Group.

—Dear Nobody. 1992. 192p. (YA). (gr. 6 up). 16.95 (*0-531-05461-6*); mass mkt. 16.99 o.p. (*0-531-08611-9*) Scholastic, Inc. (Orchard Bks.).

—Dear Nobody. 1994. (J). 12.00 (*0-606-05805-2*) Turtleback Bks.

—Holly Starcross. 2002. 192p. (J). (gr. 7 up). 15.99 (*0-06-001341-9*); 17.89 (*0-06-001342-7*) HarperCollins Children's Bk. Group. (Greenwillow Bks.).

Dorrie, Doris. Lottie's Princess Dress. Skwarek, Skip, ed. 1999. (Illus.). 32p. (J). (ps-3). 15.99 (*0-8037-2388-1*, Dial Bks. for Young Readers) Penguin Putnam Bks. for Young Readers.

Dorris, Michael. The Window. 1999. 112p. (J). (gr. 4 up). pap. 4.99 (*0-7868-1317-2*) Disney Pr.

—The Window. 1997. (Illus.). 112p. (J). (gr. 4 up). 16.95 (*0-7868-0301-0*); lib. bdg. 17.49 (*0-7868-2240-6*) Hyperion Bks. for Children.

—The Window. 1999. 112p. (J). (gr. 4 up). pap. 4.99 (*0-7868-1373-3*) Hyperion Pr.

Dotlich, Rebecca Kai. Mama Loves. 2004. (Illus.). 32p. (J). 14.99 (*0-06-029407-8*); lib. bdg. 15.89 (*0-06-029408-6*) HarperCollins Pubs.

—Papa Love. Date not set. (J). 15.99 (*0-06-029405-1*); lib. bdg. 16.89 (*0-06-029406-X*) HarperCollins Pubs.

Dow, Unity. Far & Beyon' 2002. 208p. (YA). (gr. 7 up). pap. 11.95 (*1-879960-64-8*) Aunt Lute Bks.

Downey, Lynn. Papa's Birthday Gift. Schuett, Stacey, tr. & illus. by. 2003. (J). 16.99 (*0-8066-4557-1*, Augsburg Bks.) Augsburg Fortress, Pubs.

—Which Monster Do You Love Most? 2004. (Illus.). 32p. (J). 16.99 (*0-8037-2728-3*, Dial Bks. for Young Readers) Penguin Putnam Bks. for Young Readers.

Doyle, Brian. Hey, Dad! 1996. (J). (gr. 4-6). pap. 4.95 (*0-88899-148-7*) Groundwood Bks. CAN. *Dist:* Publishers Group West.

Doyle, Charlotte. It's Twins! 2003. (Illus.). 32p. (J). 10.99 (*0-399-23718-6*, G. P. Putnam's Sons) Penguin Putnam Bks. for Young Readers.

—Where's Bunny's Mommy? 1999. (Illus.). 29p. (J). (ps-k). reprint ed. text 14.00 (*0-7881-6653-0*) DIANE Publishing Co.

—Where's Bunny's Mommy? 1995. (Illus.). (J). (ps). 14.00 o.s.i (*0-671-89984-8*, Simon & Schuster Children's Publishing) Simon & Schuster Children's Publishing.

Doyle, Eugenie. Stray Voltage. 2002. 136p. (J). (gr. 5-7). 16.95 (*1-886910-86-3*, Front Street) Front Street, Inc.

—Stray Voltage. 2004. pap. 5.99 (*0-14-240153-6*, Puffin Bks.) Penguin Putnam Bks. for Young Readers.

Doyle, Malachy. Antonio on the Other Side of the World, Getting Smaller. 2003. 32p. (J). 15.99 (*0-7636-2173-0*) Candlewick Pr.

Dragonwagon, Crescent. Is This a Sack of Potatoes? 2001. (Illus.). 32p. (J). (ps-k). 16.95 (*0-7614-5089-0*) Cavendish, Marshall Corp.

Duble, Kathi Benner. Pilot Mom. 2003. (Illus.). 32p. (J). (gr. k-3). 15.95 (*1-57091-555-5*) Charlesbridge Publishing, Inc.

Dubowski, Cathy. Pigs, Pies & Plenty of Problems. 1999. (Full House Michelle Ser.: No. 28). 96p. (J). (gr. 2-4). pap. 3.99 (*0-671-02152-4*, Simon Spotlight) Simon & Schuster Children's Publishing.

—Take a Hike! 1996. (Secret World of Alex Mack Ser.: No. 7). 144p. (J). (gr. 4-7). pap. 3.99 (*0-671-56309-2*, Aladdin) Simon & Schuster Children's Publishing.

Dumbleton, Mike. Mr. Knuckles. (Illus.). 32p. (J). (ps-3). 14.95 o.p. (*1-86373-584-4*) Allen & Unwin Pty., Ltd. AUS. *Dist:* Independent Pubs. Group.

—Mr. Knuckles. 1994. (Illus.). 32p. (J). (ps-3). pap. 6.95 o.p. (*1-86373-595-X*) Independent Pubs. Group.

Dumond, Michael. Dad Is Leaving Home. 1987. (Flipside Fiction Ser.). 196p. (YA). (gr. 7-12). lib. bdg. 12.95 o.p. (*0-8239-0699-X*) Rosen Publishing Group, Inc., The.

Dunlop, Eileen. Finn's Island. 1992. 128p. (YA). (gr. 4-7). 13.95 (*0-8234-0910-4*) Holiday Hse., Inc.

Dupasquier, Philippe. Dear Daddy. 2003. (Illus.). 23p. (J). pap. 8.95 (*1-84270-165-7*) Andersen Pr., Ltd. GBR. *Dist:* Trafalgar Square.

—Dear Daddy. 1988. 24p. (J). (ps-3). pap. 3.95 o.s.i (*0-14-050822-8*, Puffin Bks.) Penguin Putnam Bks. for Young Readers.

Durbin, William. The Broken Blade. 176p. (gr. 5-9). 1997. text 14.95 o.s.i (*0-385-32224-0*, Dell Books for Young Readers); 1998. (Illus.). reprint ed. pap. text 4.99 (*0-440-41184-X*, Yearling) Random Hse. Children's Bks.

—The Broken Blade. 1998. (J). 10.55 (*0-606-13228-7*) Turtleback Bks.

Dwyer, Mindy. Quilt of Dreams. 2000. (Illus.). 32p. (J). (gr. 2-4). 15.95 (*0-88240-522-5*); pap. 8.95 (*0-88240-521-7*) Graphic Arts Ctr. Publishing Co. (Alaska Northwest Bks.).

Eber, Christine E. Just Momma & Me. 1975. (Illus.). 39p. (J). (ps-3). pap. 3.75 o.p. (*0-914996-09-6*) Lollipop Power Bks.

Edwards, Michelle. Meera's Blanket. (Illus.). 40p. (J). (ps up). 1995. 15.00 o.p. (*0-688-09710-3*); 1924. lib. bdg. 14.93 o.s.i (*0-688-09711-1*) HarperCollins Children's Bk. Group.

Egielski, Richard. Jazper. 1998. (Illus.). 32p. (J). (ps-2). 14.95 (*0-06-027817-X*) HarperCollins Children's Bk. Group.

Ehlert, Lois. Pie in the Sky. 2004. (Illus.). 40p. (J). (*0-15-216584-3*) Harcourt Trade Pubs.

Eisenberg, Phyllis R. You're My Nikki. (Illus.). 32p. (J). (ps-3). 1995. pap. 5.99 (*0-14-055463-7*, Puffin Bks.); 1992. 13.89 o.s.i (*0-8037-1129-8*, Dial Bks. for Young Readers); 1992. 14.00 o.s.i (*0-8037-1127-1*, Dial Bks. for Young Readers) Penguin Putnam Bks. for Young Readers.

Elias, Miriam L. Shimmy the Youngest. 1994. (Illus.). 32p. (J). pap. text 6.95 (*0-922613-72-9*) Hachai Publishing.

Eliot, George. Silas Marner, Level 4. Hedge, Tricia, ed. 2000. (Bookworms Ser.). (Illus.). 96p. (J). pap. text 5.95 (*0-19-423044-9*) Oxford Univ. Pr., Inc.

Elliott, Laura. Flying South. 2003. 160p. (J). (gr. 4 up). 15.99 (*0-06-001214-5*); lib. bdg. 16.89 (*0-06-001215-3*) HarperCollins Pubs.

Ellis, Sarah. Out of the Blue. 2001. 120p. (YA). (gr. 5-9). pap. 5.95 (*0-88899-236-X*) Groundwood Bks. CAN. *Dist:* Publishers Group West.

—Out of the Blue. 1996. 128p. (J). (gr. 5-9). pap. 3.99 o.s.i (*0-14-038066-3*) Penguin Putnam Bks. for Young Readers.

—Out of the Blue. 1995. 144p. (YA). (gr. 5-9). pap. 15.00 (*0-689-80025-8*, McElderry, Margaret K.) Simon & Schuster Children's Publishing.

—Out of the Blue. 1996. (J). 9.09 o.p. (*0-606-10278-7*) Turtleback Bks.

Elmore, Barbara. Breathing Room. 128p. (YA). (gr. 7-12). 1995. lib. bdg. 15.00 (*0-88092-109-9*); 1994. pap. 9.99 (*0-88092-108-0*) Royal Fireworks Publishing Co.

Emberley, Ed E. Thanks, Mom. 2003. (Illus.). 32p. (J). (ps-1). 15.95 (*0-316-24022-2*) Little Brown Children's Bks.

Emberley, Rebecca. My Mother's Secret Life. 1998. (Illus.). 32p. (J). (ps-3). 15.95 o.p. (*0-316-23496-6*) Little Brown & Co.

Emery, Clayton. Father-Daughter Disaster! 1997. (Secret World of Alex Mack Ser.: No. 16). 128p. (J). (gr. 4-7). pap. 3.99 (*0-671-01372-6*, Aladdin) Simon & Schuster Children's Publishing.

Emmons, Chip. Sammy Wakes His Dad. 2002. (Illus.). 32p. (J). (ps-3). 13.95 (*1-887734-87-2*) Star Bright Bks., Inc.

Encinas, Carlos. The New Engine: La Maquina Nueva. 2001. (Illus.). (J). 15.95 (*1-885772-24-6*) Kiva Publishing, Inc.

Ernst, Kathleen. Whistler in the Dark. 2002. (American Girl Collection: Bk. 16). (Illus.). 176p. (J). 10.95 (*1-58485-486-3*); pap. 6.95 (*1-58485-485-5*) Pleasant Co. Pubns. (American Girl).

Esterl, Arnica. Okino & the Whales. abr. ed. 1995. Tr. of Okino und die Wale. (Illus.). 32p. (J). (ps-3). 16.00 (*0-15-200377-0*) Harcourt Trade Pubs.

Evans, Lezlie. If I Were the Wind. 1997. (Illus.). 32p. (J). (ps-2). (*1-59093-066-5*); per. (*1-59093-065-7*) Warehousing & Fulfillment Specialists, LLC (WFS, LLC). (Eager Minds Pr.).

Evetts-Secker, Josephine. Father & Daughter Tales. 1997. (For the Family Ser.). (Illus.). 80p. (J). (gr. 4-7). 19.95 (*0-7892-0392-8*, Abbeville Kids) Abbeville Pr., Inc.

Ewart, Claire. The Giant. 2003. (Illus.). 32p. (J). (ps-3). 16.95 (*0-8027-8835-1*); 17.85 (*0-8027-8837-8*) Walker & Co.

Eyles, Heather. Well, I Never! 1990. (Illus.). 320p. (J). (ps-3). 11.95 (*0-87951-383-7*) Overlook Pr., The.

Facklam, Margery. The Trouble with Mothers. 1989. (J). 13.95 o.p. (*0-89919-773-6*) Houghton Mifflin Co.

—The Trouble with Mothers. 1991. 144p. (J). (gr. 5). reprint ed. pap. 2.95 (*0-380-71139-7*, Avon Bks.) Morrow/Avon.

Falwell, Cathryn. Nicky Loves Daddy. 1992. (Illus.). 32p. (J). (ps). 5.95 o.p. (*0-395-60820-1*, Clarion Bks.) Houghton Mifflin Co. Trade & Reference Div.

Farber, Norma. The Boy Who Longed for a Lift. 1997. (Laura Geringer Bks.). (Illus.). 32p. (J). (ps-1). lib. bdg. 15.89 o.p. (*0-06-027109-4*); 15.95 o.p. (*0-06-027108-6*) HarperCollins Children's Bk. Group.

—Without Wings, Mother, How Can I Fly?, ERS. 1998. (Illus.). 32p. (J). (ps-1). 15.95 o.s.i (*0-8050-3380-7*, Holt, Henry & Co. Bks. For Young Readers) Holt, Henry & Co.

Farmer, Patti. Bartholomew's Dream. 1994. (Illus.). 32p. (J). (ps-2). 12.95 o.p. (*0-8120-6403-8*); pap. 4.95 o.p. (*0-8120-1991-1*) Barron's Educational Series, Inc.

Fearnley, Jan. Colin & the Curly Claw. 2001. (Blue Bananas Ser.). (Illus.). 48p. (J). (gr. 1-2). pap. 4.95 (*0-7787-0886-1*); lib. bdg. 19.96 (*0-7787-0840-3*) Crabtree Publishing Co.

—Just Like You. (Illus.). 32p. (J). 2003. bds. 6.99 (*0-7636-2207-9*); 2001. 15.99 (*0-7636-1322-3*) Candlewick Pr.

Fehlner, Paul. No Way! 1996. (My First Hello Reader! Ser.). (Illus.). 32p. (J). (ps-3). pap. 3.99 (*0-590-48514-8*, Cartwheel Bks.) Scholastic, Inc.

Fenner, Carol. The King of Dragons. (J). (gr. 4-7). 2000. (Illus.). 160p. pap. 4.99 (*0-689-83540-X*, Aladdin); 1998. 224p. 17.00 (*0-689-82217-0*, McElderry, Margaret K.) Simon & Schuster Children's Publishing.

—A Summer of Horses. 1989. 160p. (Orig.). (J). (gr. 3-6). pap. 3.99 o.s.i (*0-394-80480-5*, Knopf Bks. for Young Readers) Random Hse. Children's Bks.

Ferguson, Virginia & Durkin, Peter. Tell Me a Story, Dad. 1994. (Illus.). (J). (*0-383-03717-4*) SRA/McGraw-Hill.

Ferris, Amy Schor. A Greater Goode. 2002. 192p. (YA). (gr. 5-9). 15.00 (*0-618-13154-X*) Houghton Mifflin Co.

Ferry, Charles. O Zebron Falls! 1994. 212p. (YA). (gr. 7 up). reprint ed. pap. 11.95 (*1-882792-04-1*) Proctor Pubns.

Feuer, Elizabeth. Lost Summer, RS. 1995. 192p. (J). (gr. 7 up). 16.00 o.p. (*0-374-31020-3*, Farrar, Straus & Giroux (BYR)) Farrar, Straus & Giroux.

Filichia, Peter. The Most Embarrassing Mother in the World. 1991. 192p. (J). pap. 3.50 (*0-380-76084-3*, Avon Bks.) Morrow/Avon.

Fine, Anne. Alias Madame Doubtfire. 1989. (Young Adults Ser.). 208p. (YA). mass mkt. 3.99 o.p. (*0-553-56615-6*) Bantam Bks.

—Alias Madame Doubtfire. 1988. (YA). (gr. 7 up). 12.95 o.p. (*0-316-28313-4*, Joy Street Bks.) Little Brown & Co.

—Flour Babies. l.t. ed. 2000. pap. 16.95 (*0-7540-6110-8*, Galaxy Children's Large Print) BBC Audiobooks America.

—Flour Babies. 1995. 192p. (YA). (gr. 4-7). mass mkt. 4.99 (*0-440-21941-8*, Laurel Leaf); (J). mass mkt. o.s.i (*0-440-91079-X*, Dell Books for Young Readers) Random Hse. Children's Bks.

—Flour Babies. 1995. (J). 10.55 (*0-606-07523-2*) Turtleback Bks.

—Flour Babies & the Boys of Room 8. 1994. (YA). (gr. 5 up). reprint ed. 15.95 o.p. (*0-316-28319-3*) Little Brown & Co.

—Senora Doubtfire. Pena, Flora, tr. 1992. Tr. of Mrs. Doubtfire. (SPA.). 165p. (J). (gr. 7 up). pap. 12.95 (*84-204-4680-7*) Santillana USA Publishing Co., Inc.

—Senora Doubtfire. 1992. Tr. of Mrs. Doubtfire. 19.00 (*0-606-17745-0*) Turtleback Bks.

Finley, Martha. Elsie's Impossible Choice. 1999. (Elsie Dinsmore: Bk. 2). (Illus.). 238p. (J). (gr. 5-9). 9.99 (*1-928749-02-X*) Mission City Pr., Inc.

—Elsie's New Life. 1999. (Elsie Dinsmore: Bk. 3). (Illus.). 232p. (J). (gr. 5-9). 9.99 (*1-928749-03-8*) Mission City Pr., Inc.

First, Julia. Move Over, Beethoven. 1978. (gr. 5 up). lib. bdg. 7.90 o.p. (*0-531-01472-X*, Watts, Franklin) Scholastic Library Publishing.

Fischer, Jackie. An Egg on Three Sticks. 2004. 272p. pap. 23.95 (*0-312-31774-3*) St. Martin's Pr.

Fishman, Cathy Goldberg. Car Wash Kid. 2003. (Rookie Reader Ser.). (Illus.). 24p. (J). lib. bdg. 16.00 (*0-516-22858-7*, Children's Pr.) Scholastic Library Publishing.

Fitzhugh, Louise. The Long Secret: Harriet the Spy Adventure. 2001. (Illus.). 288p. (gr. 5 up). text 15.95 (*0-385-32784-6*, Delacorte Bks. for Young Readers) Random Hse. Children's Bks.

—Nobody's Family Is Going to Change, RS. 1974. 222p. (J). (gr. 3 up). 15.00 o.p. (*0-374-35539-8*, Farrar, Straus & Giroux (BYR)) Farrar, Straus & Giroux.

Fitzpatrick, Marie-Louise. You & Me & the Big Blue Sea. 2002. (Illus.). 32p. (J). (ps-1). 15.95 (*0-7613-1691-4*, Roaring Brook Pr.) Millbrook Pr., Inc.

—You, Me & the Big Blue Sea. 2002. (Illus.). 32p. (J). (ps-3). 22.90 (*0-7613-2806-8*, Roaring Brook Pr.) Millbrook Pr., Inc.

Flake, Sharon G. Begging for Change. 2003. 240p. (J). 15.99 (*0-7868-0601-X*, Jump at the Sun) Hyperion Bks. for Children.

—Money Hungry. (J). 2003. 208p. pap. 5.99 (*0-7868-1503-5*); 2001. 192p. (gr. 3-7). 15.99 (*0-7868-0548-X*); 2001. 192p. (gr. 3-7). lib. bdg. 16.49 (*0-7868-2476-X*) Hyperion Bks. for Children. (Jump at the Sun).

Fleischman, Paul. Seek. braille ed. 2003. (gr. 2). spiral bd. (*0-616-15870-X*) Canadian National Institute for the Blind/Institut National Canadien pour les Aveugles.

—Seek. 2001. 176p. (J). (gr. 7-12). 16.95 (*0-8126-4900-1*) Cricket Bks.

—Seek. l.t. ed. 2002. 202p. (J). 22.95 (*0-7862-4140-3*) Gale Group.

—Seek. unabr. ed. 2002. (J). audio 18.00 (*0-8072-0820-5*, Listening Library) Random Hse. Audio Publishing Group.

—Seek. 2003. (Illus.). 176p. (YA). pap. 6.99 (*0-689-85402-1*, Simon Pulse) Simon & Schuster Children's Publishing.

Fleming, Sibley. How to Rock Your Baby. 1997. (Illus.). 32p. (J). (ps-k). 14.95 (*1-56145-142-8*) Peachtree Pubs., Ltd.

Fletcher, Ralph J. Uncle Daddy, ERS. 2001. (Illus.). 133p. (J). (gr. 4-6). 15.95 (*0-8050-6663-2*, Holt, Henry & Co. Bks. For Young Readers) Holt, Henry & Co.

Flinn, Alex. Breathing Underwater. 2001. (J). (gr. 8 up). 224p. lib. bdg. 16.89 (*0-06-029199-0*); (Illus.). 272p. 15.99 (*0-06-029198-2*) HarperCollins Children's Bk. Group.

—Breathing Underwater. 2002. 272p. (J). (gr. 5 up). pap. 7.99 (*0-06-447257-4*) HarperCollins Pubs.

Ford, Barbara. The Eagles' Child. 1990. 160p. (J). (gr. 3-7). lib. bdg. 13.95 o.p. (*0-02-735405-9*, Simon & Schuster Children's Publishing) Simon & Schuster Children's Publishing.

Ford, Miela. On My Own. 1999. (Illus.). 16p. (J). (ps-k). bds. 5.95 (*0-688-16452-8*, Greenwillow Bks.) HarperCollins Children's Bk. Group.

Foreman, Michael. Hello, World. 2003. 48p. (J). 16.99 (*0-7636-2112-9*) Candlewick Pr.

Fowler, Susi Gregg. I'll See You When the Moon Is Full. 1994. (Illus.). 24p. (J). (ps-3). 14.00 o.s.i (*0-688-10830-X*); lib. bdg. 13.93 o.p. (*0-688-10831-8*) HarperCollins Children's Bk. Group. (Greenwillow Bks.).

Fox, Mem. Harriet, You'll Drive Me Wild! 2000. (Illus.). 32p. (J). (ps-2). 16.00 (*0-15-201977-4*) Harcourt Children's Bks.

—Koala Lou. 2002. (Illus.). (J). 13.19 (*0-7587-2941-3*) Book Wholesalers, Inc.

—Koala Lou. (Illus.). 32p. (J). (ps-3). 1989. 15.00 (*0-15-200502-1*, Gulliver Bks.); 1994. pap. 6.00 (*0-15-200076-3*, Voyager Bks./Libros Viajeros) Harcourt Children's Bks.

—Koala Lou. 1989. 13.95 o.s.i (*0-15-201761-5*); 9999. (J). o.s.i (*0-15-201677-5*) Harcourt Trade Pubs.

Fox, Mem & Frazee, Marla. Harriet, You'll Drive Me Wild! 2003. (Illus.). 32p. (J). pap. 6.00 (*0-15-204598-8*) Harcourt Children's Bks.

Fox, Paula. The Eagle Kite. 1996. 144p. (YA). (gr. 7-12). mass mkt. 4.50 o.s.i (*0-440-21972-8*) Dell Publishing.

—The Eagle Kite. 1995. 144p. (J). (gr. 7 up). pap. 15.95 (*0-531-06892-7*); lib. bdg. 16.99 (*0-531-08742-5*) Scholastic, Inc. (Orchard Bks.).

—The Eagle Kite. 1996. 10.55 (*0-606-10795-9*) Turtleback Bks.

Frances, Ellen. Looking for Dad. 1999. (Supa Doopers Ser.). (Illus.). 64p. (J). (*0-7608-3292-7*) Sundance Publishing.

Franklin, Kristine L. Nerd No More. 1996. (Illus.). 144p. (J). (gr. 4-7). 16.99 (*1-56402-674-4*) Candlewick Pr.

Frederick, Heather Vogel. The Voyage of Patience Goodspeed. 224p. (J). 2004. (Illus.). pap. 4.99 (*0-689-84869-2*, Aladdin); 2002. (gr. 4-6). 16.00 (*0-689-84851-X*, Simon & Schuster Children's Publishing) Simon & Schuster Children's Publishing.

Freeman, Marcia S. Catfish & Spaghetti. 1997. (Illus.). 64p. (J). (gr. 2-6). pap. 4.50 (*0-929895-21-5*, Hoot Owl Bks.) Maupin Hse. Publishing.

Freeman, Martha. Stink Bomb Mom. 1996. (Illus.). 128p. (J). (gr. 3-7). 15.95 o.s.i (*0-385-32219-4*, Delacorte Pr.) Dell Publishing.

—Stink Bomb Mom. 1997. (Illus.). 160p. (gr. 3-7). pap. text 3.99 o.s.i (*0-440-41189-0*, Dell Books for Young Readers) Random Hse. Children's Bks.

—Stink Bomb Mom. 1997. 9.09 o.p. (*0-606-13817-X*) Turtleback Bks.

Freeman, Suzanne. The Cuckoo's Child. 1997. (Illus.). 256p. (J). (gr. 3-7). reprint ed. pap. 5.95 (*0-7868-1243-5*) Disney Pr.

—The Cuckoo's Child. 1996. 256p. (J). (gr. 3 up). 16.95 (*0-688-14290-7*, Greenwillow Bks.) HarperCollins Children's Bk. Group.

—The Cuckoo's Child. 1924. (J). pap. o.s.i (*0-688-15484-0*, Morrow, William & Co.) Morrow/Avon.

—The Cuckoo's Child. 249p. (YA). (gr. 5-8). pap. 5.95 (*0-8072-1510-4*, Listening Library) Random Hse. Audio Publishing Group.

—The Cuckoo's Child. 1997. (J). 12.00 (*0-606-12666-X*) Turtleback Bks.

Freeman, Tor. Roar! 2002. (Illus.). 32p. (J). 14.99 (*0-7636-1773-3*) Candlewick Pr.

French, Simon. Change the Locks. 1993. 112p. (J). (gr. 3-7). pap. 13.95 (*0-590-45593-1*) Scholastic, Inc.

—Change the Locks. 1991. (J). 8.05 o.p. (*0-606-06955-0*) Turtleback Bks.

Friedman, Aileen. A Cloak for the Dreamer. 1995. (Brainy Day Bks.). (Illus.). 36p. (J). (ps-3). pap. (*0-590-48987-9*) Scholastic, Inc.

Friend, David. Baseball, Football, Daddy & Me. 1992. (Illus.). 320p. (J). (ps-3). pap. 4.50 o.s.i (*0-14-050914-3*, Puffin Bks.) Penguin Putnam Bks. for Young Readers.

Fritz, April Young. Waiting to Disappear. 2004. (J). pap. 5.99 (*0-7868-1608-2*) Hyperion Bks. for Children.

—Waiting to Disappear. 2002. (Illus.). 192p. (J). (gr. 6-9). 15.99 (*0-7868-0790-3*) Hyperion Pr.

Gaines, Ernest J. The Sky Is Gray. 1993. (J). (gr. 4 up). o.p. (*0-88682-582-2*, Creative Education) Creative Co., The.

Gantos, Jack. Joey Pigza Loses Control. 2002. 208p. (J). (gr. 5 up). pap. 5.99 (*0-06-441022-6*, Harper Trophy) HarperCollins Children's Bk. Group.

—Joey Pigza Loses Control. l.t. ed. 2001. 196p. (J). 22.95 (*0-7862-3425-3*) Thorndike Pr.

Gardella, Tricia. Just Like My Dad. (Trophy Picture Bk.). (Illus.). 32p. (J). (ps-1). 1996. pap. 4.95 o.p. (*0-06-443463-X*, Harper Trophy); 1993. 15.00 o.p. (*0-06-021937-8*); 1993. lib. bdg. 14.89 (*0-06-021938-6*) HarperCollins Children's Bk. Group.

—Just Like My Dad. 1993. 10.15 o.p. (*0-606-09506-3*) Turtleback Bks.

Gardner, Sally. Mama, Don't Go Out Tonight. 2002. (Illus.). 32p. (J). (ps-k). 16.95 (*1-58234-790-5*, Bloomsbury Children) Bloomsbury Publishing.

Garfield, Leon. Footsteps, RS. 2001. (gr. 7 up). 192p. (J). 18.00 (*0-374-32450-6*, Farrar, Straus & Giroux (BYR)); 208p. pap. 6.95 (*0-374-42441-1*, Sunburst) Farrar, Straus & Giroux.

—Footsteps. 1988. (J). (gr. k-6). pap. 3.25 o.s.i (*0-440-40102-X*, Yearling) Random Hse. Children's Bks.

Gay, Michel. Zee. 2003. (Illus.). 32p. (J). 15.00 (*0-618-38148-1*, Clarion Bks.) Houghton Mifflin Co. Trade & Reference Div.

Geeslin, Campbell. Elena's Serenade. 2004. (Illus.). 40p. (J). 16.95 (*0-689-84908-7*, Atheneum/Anne Schwartz Bks.) Simon & Schuster Children's Publishing.

Geisert, Arthur. Oink, Oink. 1993. (Illus.). 32p. (J). (ps-3). tchr. ed. 14.95 o.s.i (*0-395-64048-2*) Houghton Mifflin Co.

Geller, Mark. What I Heard. 1987. (Charlotte Zolotow Bk.). 128p. (J). (gr. 5 up). 11.95 (*0-06-022160-7*); lib. bdg. 11.89 o.p. (*0-06-022161-5*) HarperCollins Children's Bk. Group.

George, Jean Craighead. Cliff Hanger. 2002. (Outdoor Adventures Ser.). (Illus.). 32p. (J). (ps-4). 15.95 (*0-06-000260-3*); lib. bdg. 15.89 (*0-06-000261-1*) HarperCollins Children's Bk. Group.

—There's an Owl in the Shower. 1995. (Illus.). 144p. (J). (gr. 2-5). lib. bdg. 14.89 (*0-06-024892-0*); (gr. 3-5). 14.95 (*0-06-024891-2*) HarperCollins Children's Bk. Group.

George, William T. Christmas at Long Pond. 1992. (Illus.). 32p. (J). (ps-8). 16.00 o.p. (*0-688-09214-4*); lib. bdg. 15.93 o.p. (*0-688-09215-2*) HarperCollins Children's Bk. Group. (Greenwillow Bks.).

Geras, Adele. My Wishes for You. 2002. 32p. (J). (ps-2). 15.95 (*0-689-85333-5*, Simon & Schuster Children's Publishing) Simon & Schuster Children's Publishing.

Gerver, Jane E. I Will Always Love You. 2002. 28p. (J). 12.99 (*0-7944-0011-6*, Reader's Digest Children's Bks.) Reader's Digest Children's Publishing, Inc.

Gettinger, Shifrah. A Very Special Gift. 1993. (Illus.). 32p. (J). (ps-3). 9.95 (*0-922613-52-4*); pap. text 6.95 (*0-922613-53-2*) Hachai Publishing.

Gilchrist, Guy. Bronty & the Birdosaur: A Tiny Dinos Story about Love. 1988. (Tiny Dinos Ser.). (Illus.). 24p. (J). (ps-2). bds. 4.95 o.p. (*1-55782-072-4*) Warner Bks., Inc.

Gilchrist, Jan Spivey. Madelia. 1997. (Illus.). 32p. (J). (ps-3). 14.99 o.s.i (*0-8037-2052-1*); 14.89 o.s.i (*0-8037-2054-8*) Penguin Putnam Bks. for Young Readers. (Dial Bks. for Young Readers).

Gilles, Almira Astudillo. Willie Wins. 2001. (Illus.). 32p. (J). (ps-3). 16.00 (*1-58430-023-X*) Lee & Low Bks., Inc.

Gilmore, Rachna. My Mother Is Weird. (FRE., Illus.). 24p. (J). (ps-3). pap. 6.95 o.p. (*0-921556-20-9*) Ragweed Pr. CAN. *Dist:* LPC/InBook.

Girl Who Didn't Mind. 2002. Tr. of Caileag a Bha Coma. 64p. (J). lib. bdg. 17.95 (*0-9703632-6-5*) Wakefield Connection, The.

Glaser, Linda. Rosie's Birthday Rat. 1996. (Illus.). 48p. (J). (gr. k-4). pap. 3.99 o.s.i (*0-440-41113-0*, Yearling) Random Hse. Children's Bks.

—Rosie's Birthday Rat. 1996. 9.19 o.p. (*0-606-09799-6*) Turtleback Bks.

Glassman, Peter. My Working Mom. 1994. (Illus.). 32p. (J). (ps-3). 16.95 (*0-688-12259-0*) HarperCollins Children's Bk. Group.

—My Working Mom. 1994. (Illus.). (J). (ps-3). 15.89 (*0-688-12260-4*, Morrow, William & Co.) Morrow/Avon.

Gleitzman, Morris. Blabber Mouth. 1995. 160p. (J). (gr. 3 up). pap. 5.00 o.s.i (*0-15-200370-3*) Harcourt Trade Pubs.

Gleitzman, Morris & Levers, John, illus. Misery Guts: And, Worry Warts. 2003. 121p. (J). mass mkt. (*0-330-39103-8*) Macmillan Children's Bks.

Gliori, Debi. Mr. Bear Says I Love You. 1997. (Mr. Bear Says Board Bks.). (Illus.). 10p. (J). (ps up). 4.99 (*0-689-81517-4*, Little Simon) Simon & Schuster Children's Publishing.

—No Matter What. 1999. (Illus.). 32p. (J). (ps-1). 16.00 (*0-15-202061-6*) Harcourt Children's Bks.

—No Matter What. 1999. (J). stu. ed. 16.00 o.s.i (*0-15-202459-X*) Harcourt Trade Pubs.

Godwin, Laura. What a Baby Hears. 2002. (Illus.). 32p. (J). lib. bdg. 16.49 (*0-7868-2484-0*) Hyperion Bks. for Children.

—What the Baby Hears. 2002. (Illus.). 32p. (J). (ps-k). trans. 15.99 (*0-7868-0560-9*) Hyperion Bks. for Children.

Gold, Sharlya. Time to Take Sides, 001. 1979. 176p. (J). (gr. 6 up). 6.95 o.p. (*0-395-28905-X*, Clarion Bks.) Houghton Mifflin Co. Trade & Reference Div.

Goldowsky, Jill. Dad's Big Idea. 2003. (All-Star Readers Ser.). (Illus.). 32p. (J). pap. 3.99 (*0-7944-0225-9*) Reader's Digest Assn., Inc., The.

Hoban, Julia. Amy Loves the Rain. 1989. (Illus.). 32p. (J). (ps). 9.95 (*0-06-022357-X*); lib. bdg. 9.89 o.p. (*0-06-022358-8*) HarperCollins Children's Bk. Group.

—Amy Loves the Snow. 1989. (Illus.). 24p. (J). 9.95 (*0-06-022361-8*); lib. bdg. 11.89 o.p. (*0-06-022395-2*) HarperCollins Children's Bk. Group.

Hobbs, Valerie. Tender, RS. 2001. 256p. (J). (gr. 7 up). 18.00 (*0-374-37397-3*, Farrar, Straus & Giroux (BYR)) Farrar, Straus & Giroux.

—Tender. 2004. 256p. (J). pap. 6.99 (*0-14-240075-0*, Puffin Bks.) Penguin Putnam Bks. for Young Readers.

Hoffius, Stephen. Winners & Losers. (YA). 1996. 176p. (gr. 7 up). mass mkt. 3.99 (*0-689-80165-3*, Simon Pulse); 1993. 123p. (gr. 5-9). pap. 16.00 (*0-671-79194-X*, Simon & Schuster Children's Publishing) Simon & Schuster Children's Publishing.

—Winners & Losers. 1996. (J). 10.04 (*0-606-10075-X*) Turtleback Bks.

Holeman, Linda. Raspberry House Blues. 2000. 248p. (J). (gr. 6-9). pap. 6.95 (*0-88776-493-2*) Tundra Bks. of Northern New York.

Holl, Kristi. 4Give & 4Get. 2001. (TodaysGirls.com Ser.: Vol. 9). (Illus.). 144p. (J). (gr. 5-9). pap. 5.99 o.s.i (*0-8499-7712-6*) Nelson, Tommy.

Holland, Isabelle. Of Love & Death & Other Journeys. 1977. 144p. (gr. 7 up). 1.50 o.p. (*0-440-96547-0*) Dell Publishing.

—Of Love & Death & Other Journeys. 1975. (YA). (gr. 7 up). 12.95 (*0-397-31566-X*) HarperCollins Children's Bk. Group.

Holt, Kimberly Willis. My Louisiana Sky, ERS. 1998. 176p. (J). (gr. 4-7). 16.95 (*0-8050-5251-8*, Holt, Henry & Co. Bks. For Young Readers) Holt, Henry & Co.

—My Louisiana Sky. 208p. (YA). (gr. 5 up). 4.99 (*0-8072-8291-X*, Listening Library) Random Hse. Audio Publishing Group.

Hooks, William H. Little Poss & Horrible Hound. 1998. (Bank Street Reader Collection). (Illus.). 48p. (J). (gr. 2-4). lib. bdg. 21.26 (*0-8368-1773-7*) Stevens, Gareth Inc.

—Little Poss & Horrible Hound. 1992. (Illus.). E-Book (*1-58824-119-X*) ipicturebooks, LLC.

Hopkins, Lee Bennett. Mama. (J). 1978. 112p. (gr. 4-6). pap. 1.25 o.s.i (*0-440-96174-2*, Laurel Leaf); 1977. (gr. 3 up). 4.95 o.p. (*0-394-83525-5*, Knopf Bks. for Young Readers); 1977. (gr. 3 up). lib. bdg. 5.99 o.p. (*0-394-93525-X*, Knopf Bks. for Young Readers) Random Hse. Children's Bks.

—Mama. 1992. (Illus.). 112p. (J). (gr. 2-8). pap. 14.00 o.p. (*0-671-74985-4*, Simon & Schuster Children's Publishing) Simon & Schuster Children's Publishing.

—Mama & Her Boys. 2003. 80p. (J). (gr. 4-7). pap. 8.95 (*1-56397-813-X*); pap. 8.95 (*1-56397-814-8*) Boyds Mills Pr.

—Mama & Her Boys. 1981. 192p. (J). (gr. 4-7). 12.95 (*0-06-022578-5*); lib. bdg. 12.89 o.p. (*0-06-022579-3*) HarperCollins Children's Bk. Group.

—Mama & Her Boys. 1993. (Illus.). 176p. (J). (gr. 5 up). pap. 13.00 o.s.i (*0-671-74986-2*, Simon & Schuster Children's Publishing) Simon & Schuster Children's Publishing.

Horn, Peter. When I Grow Up... 1999. (Illus.). 32p. (J). (gr. k-3). 15.95 (*0-7358-1148-2*); 16.50 (*0-7358-1149-0*) North-South Bks., Inc.

—When I Grow Up... 1999. (Illus.). (J). 13.10 (*0-606-20987-5*) Turtleback Bks.

Horton, Barbara S. What Comes in Spring? 1992. (Illus.). 40p. (J). (ps-1). 14.99 o.s.i (*0-679-90268-6*, Knopf Bks. for Young Readers) Random Hse. Children's Bks.

Horvath, Polly. Everything on a Waffle, RS. 2001. 160p. (J). (gr. 5 up). 16.00 (*0-374-32236-8*, Farrar, Straus & Giroux (BYR)) Farrar, Straus & Giroux.

—Everything on a Waffle. unabr. ed. 2002. (gr. 3-7). audio 18.00 (*0-8072-0714-4*, Listening Library) Random Hse. Audio Publishing Group.

—Everything on a Waffle. 2002. (Juvenile Ser.). (Illus.). (J). 22.95 (*0-7862-4832-7*) Thorndike Pr.

Hossack, Sylvie A. Green Mango Magic. (Avon Camelot Bks.). 128p. (J). (gr. 3-7). 1998. 14.00 (*0-380-97613-7*); Vol. 1. 1999. pap. 4.95 (*0-380-79601-5*, Harper Trophy) HarperCollins Children's Bk. Group.

—Green Mango Magic. 1998. 10.04 (*0-606-17328-5*) Turtleback Bks.

Houston, Gloria M. Littlejim. 1993. (Illus.). 176p. (J). (gr. 5 up). pap. 4.95 (*0-688-12112-8*, Harper Trophy) HarperCollins Children's Bk. Group.

—Littlejim's Dream. 1997. (Illus.). 240p. (J). (gr. 3-7). 16.00 (*0-15-201509-4*) Harcourt Children's Bks.

—Littlejim's Gift: An Appalachian Christmas Story. 1994. (Illus.). 32p. (J). (gr. 1-5). 16.99 o.s.i (*0-399-22696-6*, Philomel) Penguin Putnam Bks. for Young Readers.

Howard, Elizabeth Fitzgerald. Papa Tells Chita a Story. (Illus.). 32p. (J). (ps-2). 1998. pap. 5.99 (*0-689-82220-0*, Aladdin); 1995. 15.00 (*0-02-744623-9*, Simon & Schuster Children's Publishing) Simon & Schuster Children's Publishing.

—Papa Tells Chita a Story. 1998. 12.14 (*0-606-15670-4*) Turtleback Bks.

Howard, Ellen. Gilly's Secret. 1993. Orig. Title: Gillyflower. 128p. (J). (gr. 3-7). reprint ed. pap. 3.95 o.s.i (*0-689-71746-6*, Aladdin) Simon & Schuster Children's Publishing.

—The Tower Room. 1993. 144p. (J). (gr. 3-7). 13.95 o.p. (*0-689-31856-1*, Atheneum) Simon & Schuster Children's Publishing.

Howe, Fanny. Radio City. 1984. 128p. (YA). (gr. 7 up). pap. 2.25 o.p. (*0-380-86025-2*, 86025, Avon Bks.) Morrow/Avon.

Howe, James. Pinky & Rex & the Double-Dad Weekend. 1995. (Pinky & Rex Ser.). (Illus.). 48p. (J). (gr. 1-4). 14.00 (*0-689-31871-5*, Atheneum) Simon & Schuster Children's Publishing.

Howker, Janni. Isaac Campion. Pacheco, Laura E., tr. 1992. (SPA., Illus.). 128p. (YA). pap. 6.99 (*968-16-3783-6*) Fondo de Cultura Economica MEX. *Dist:* Continental Bk. Co., Inc.

—Isaac Campion. 1990. 96p. (J). (gr. k-6). pap. 2.95 o.s.i (*0-440-40280-8*, Yearling) Random Hse. Children's Bks.

Hru, Dakari. Tickle, Tickle. 2002. (Illus.). 32p. (ps-2). (J). 22.90 (*0-7613-2468-2*); 14.95 (*0-7613-1537-3*) Millbrook Pr., Inc. (Roaring Brook Pr.).

Hubbell, Patricia. Bouncing Time. 2000. (Illus.). 32p. (ps up). (J). lib. bdg. 15.89 (*0-688-17377-2*); (YA). 15.95 (*0-688-17376-4*) HarperCollins Children's Bk. Group.

Hughes, Shirley. Abel's Moon. 1999. (Illus.). 32p. (J). (ps-3). pap. 15.95 (*0-7894-4601-4*, D K Ink) Dorling Kindersley Publishing, Inc.

Hughes, Vi. Aziz the Story Teller. 2002. (Illus.). 32p. (J). (ps-3). 15.95 (*1-56656-456-5*, Crocodile Bks.) Interlink Publishing Group, Inc.

Humphries, Tudor. Hiding. 1997. (Illus.). 32p. (J). (ps-k). pap. 14.95 (*0-531-30056-0*, Orchard Bks.) Scholastic, Inc.

Hunter, Jana Novotny. Little Ones Do. 2001. (Illus.). 32p. (J). (ps-k). 14.99 o.s.i (*0-525-46690-8*, Dutton Children's Bks.) Penguin Putnam Bks. for Young Readers.

Hunter, Terri. One Starry Night. 2000. 32p. (J). 16.95 (*0-9705974-0-1*) Baby Star Productions, LLC.

Hurst, Carol Otis & Otis, Rebecca. A Killing in Plymouth Colony. 2003. 160p. (J). (gr. 5-9). tchr. ed. 15.00 (*0-618-27597-5*) Houghton Mifflin Co.

Huss, Sally. I Love You with All My Hearts: The Many Ways a Mother Loves Her Daughter. 1998. (Illus.). 32p. (J). (ps-2). pap. 7.99 (*0-8499-5923-3*) Nelson, Tommy.

—I Love You with All My Hearts: The Many Ways a Mother Loves Her Son. 1998. (Illus.). 32p. (J). (ps-2). 7.99 (*0-8499-5886-5*) Nelson, Tommy.

Hwa-I Publishing Co., Staff. Filial Piety Vols. 51-55: Chinese Children's Stories. Ching, Emily et al, eds. Wonder Kids Publications Staff, tr. from CHI. 1991. (Filial Piety Ser.). (Illus.). 28p. (J). (gr. 3-6). reprint ed. 39.75 (*1-56162-051-3*) Wonder Kids Pubns.

I'll Never Find Anything in Here: Coloring Book. 2001. 48p. 4.99 (*1-893108-15-5*) Neighborhood Pr. Publishing.

Ingman, Bruce. Bad News! I'm in Charge! 2003. (Illus.). 32p. (J). 15.99 (*0-7636-2072-6*) Candlewick Pr.

Ingold, Jeanette. Mountain Solo. 2003. 320p. (J). 17.00 (*0-15-202670-3*) Harcourt Children's Bks.

Jam, Teddy. The Kid Line. 2001. (Illus.). 32p. (J). (gr. k-3). 16.95 (*0-88899-432-X*) Groundwood Bks. CAN. *Dist:* Publishers Group West.

James, Mary. Frankenlouse. 1994. 176p. (J). (gr. 6). pap. 13.95 (*0-590-46528-7*) Scholastic, Inc.

Janovitz, Marilyn. Can I Help? (Illus.). 32p. (J). (ps-3). 1998. pap. 5.95 (*1-55858-904-X*); 1996. 13.95 o.p. (*1-55858-575-3*); 1996. 14.50 o.p. (*1-55858-576-1*) North-South Bks., Inc.

—Good Morning, Little Fox. 2001. (Illus.). 32p. (J). (ps). 15.95 (*0-7358-1440-6*); 16.50 o.p. (*0-7358-1441-4*) North-South Bks., Inc.

—Little Fox. (Illus.). (J). 2002. 40p. pap. 6.95 (*0-7358-1570-4*); 1999. 32p. 15.95 o.p. (*0-7358-1160-1*); 1999. 32p. 16.50 o.p. (*0-7358-1161-X*) North-South Bks., Inc.

—Maybe, My Baby. 2003. (Illus.). 32p. (J). (ps). 15.95 (*0-7358-1762-6*); lib. bdg. 16.50 (*0-7358-1763-4*) North-South Bks., Inc. (Cheshire Studio Bks.).

Janowitz, Tama. Hear That? 2001. (Illus.). 40p. (J). (ps). 15.95 o.p. (*1-58717-074-4*); lib. bdg. 16.50 o.p. (*1-58717-075-2*) SeaStar Bks.

Javernick, Ellen. Gifted & Talented Beginning Readers: Double the Trouble. 1994. (Illus.). 32p. (J). 7.95 o.p. (*1-56565-162-6*); (gr. 3 up). 7.95 o.p. (*1-56565-163-4*) Lowell Hse. Juvenile.

—Where's Brooke? 1992. (Rookie Readers Ser.). (Illus.). 32p. (J). (ps-2). mass mkt. 14.60 o.p. (*0-516-02012-9*, Children's Pr.) Scholastic Library Publishing.

Jennings, Dana A. Me, Dad & Number Six. 1997. (Illus.). 32p. (J). (ps-2). 15.00 o.s.i (*0-15-200085-2*, Gulliver Bks.) Harcourt Children's Bks.

Jeram, Anita. Bunny, My Honey. (Illus.). 40p. (J). (ps). 2001. bds. 6.99 (*0-7636-1201-4*); 1999. 13.99 (*0-7636-0710-X*) Candlewick Pr.

Jobling, Brenda. A Foxcub Named Freedom. 1998. (Animal Tales Ser.). (Illus.). 131p. (J). (gr. 3-7). pap. 3.95 (*0-7641-0600-7*) Barron's Educational Series, Inc.

Johns, Linda. I Can Bowl! (Rookie Readers Ser.). (J). 2003. (Illus.). 32p. (gr. 1-2). pap. 4.95 (*0-516-27496-1*); 2002. lib. bdg. 19.00 (*0-516-22565-0*); 2002. (Illus.). 32p. (gr. 1-2). pap. 19.00 (*0-516-22374-7*) Scholastic Library Publishing. (Children's Pr.).

Johnson, Angela. The First Part Last. 2003. (Illus.). 144p. (YA). (gr. 6 up). 15.95 (*0-689-84922-2*, Simon & Schuster Children's Publishing) Simon & Schuster Children's Publishing.

—Heaven. 2002. (Illus.). 13.40 (*0-7587-0359-7*) Book Wholesalers, Inc.

—Heaven. 2001. (YA). pap., stu. ed. 40.24 incl. audio. (gr. 7). audio 26.00 (*0-7887-4563-8*, 96334E7) Recorded Bks., LLC.

—Heaven. 144p. (YA). 2000. (Illus.). (gr. 8-12). mass mkt. 4.99 (*0-689-82290-1*, Simon Pulse); 1998. (gr. 7-12). 16.00 (*0-689-82229-4*, Simon & Schuster Children's Publishing) Simon & Schuster Children's Publishing.

—Heaven. l.t. ed. 2000. (Young Adult Ser.). 157p. (J). (gr. 7-12). 20.95 (*0-7862-2463-0*) Thorndike Pr.

—Heaven. 2000. (Illus.). (YA). 11.04 (*0-606-18799-5*) Turtleback Bks.

—Joshua's Night Whispers. 1994. (Illus.). 12p. (J). (ps). mass mkt. 4.95 o.p. (*0-531-06847-1*, Orchard Bks.) Scholastic, Inc.

—Tell Me a Story, Mama. (Illus.). 32p. (J). (ps-3). 1992. mass mkt. 6.95 (*0-531-07032-8*); 1989. pap. 15.95 (*0-531-05794-1*); 1989. mass mkt. 16.99 o.p. (*0-531-08394-2*) Scholastic, Inc. (Orchard Bks.).

—Tell Me a Story, Mama. 1992. (J). 11.15 o.p. (*0-606-02944-3*) Turtleback Bks.

Johnson, Dolores. Papa's Stories. 1994. (Illus.). 32p. (J). (gr. k-3). lib. bdg. 14.95 (*0-02-747847-5*, Atheneum) Simon & Schuster Children's Publishing.

—What Will Mommy Do When I'm at School? 1990. (Illus.). 32p. (J). (ps-1). lib. bdg. 15.00 (*0-02-747845-9*, Atheneum) Simon & Schuster Children's Publishing.

—Your Dad Was Just Like You. 1993. (Illus.). 32p. (J). (gr. k-3). text 13.95 (*0-02-747838-6*, Atheneum) Simon & Schuster Children's Publishing.

Johnson, Dorothy T. One Day, Mother/Un Dia, Madre. 1996. (ENG & SPA.). (Orig.). (J). (gr. 1-6). pap. 6.95 o.p. (*0-533-11716-X*) Vantage Pr., Inc.

Johnson, Lindsay Lee. Soul Moon Soup. 2002. 134p. (J). (gr. 5 up). 15.95 (*1-886910-87-1*, Front Street) Front Street, Inc.

Johnston, Tony. Angel City. 2002. (Illus.). (J). (*0-399-23405-5*, Philomel) Penguin Putnam Bks. for Young Readers.

—Go Track a Yak! 2003. (Illus.). 40p. (J). (gr. k-2). 15.95 (*0-689-83789-5*, Simon & Schuster Children's Publishing) Simon & Schuster Children's Publishing.

Jolin, Dominique. It's Not Fair! 1996. (Illus.). 24p. (J). (ps-3). 14.95 (*0-89594-780-3*) Crossing Pr., Inc., The.

Jonell, Lynne. When Mommy Was Mad. 2002. (Illus.). 32p. (J). (ps-3). 13.99 (*0-399-23433-0*) Putnam Publishing Group, The.

Jones, Elizabeth McDavid. Mystery on Skull Island. 2001. (American Girl Collection: Bk. 15). (Illus.). 192p. (J). 9.95 (*1-58485-342-5*); pap. 5.95 (*1-58485-341-7*) Pleasant Co. Pubns. (American Girl).

Joosse, Barbara M. I Love You the Purplest. 1996. (Illus.). 32p. (J). (ps-3). 15.95 (*0-8118-0718-5*) Chronicle Bks. LLC.

—Mama, Do You Love Me? (Illus.). (ps). 1998. 24p. bds. 6.95 (*0-8118-2131-5*); 1991. 32p. (J). 14.95 (*0-87701-759-X*) Chronicle Bks. LLC.

—Me Quieres, Mama? Lasconi, Diego, tr. 1998. (SPA., Illus.). 32p. (J). (ps-1). 14.95 (*0-8118-2076-9*, CB0769) Chronicle Bks. LLC.

—Stars in the Darkness. 2001. (Illus.). 36p. (J). (gr. k-3). 14.95 (*0-8118-2168-4*) Chronicle Bks. LLC.

Kalechofsky, Roberta. A Boy, a Chicken & the Lion of Judah: How Ari Became a Vegetarian. 1995. (Illus.). 45p. (J). (gr. 2-5). pap. 8.00 (*0-916288-39-0*) Micah Pubns.

Kalifon, Mary. Mom Doesn't Work There Anymore. 1995. (Illus.). 32p. (Orig.). (J). (ps-4). pap. 5.95 (*0-9641981-1-8*) Cedars Sinai Health System.

Kari, James. Allegra's Window. 1997. (Allegra's Window Ser.: Vol. 9). (Illus.). 24p. (J). (ps-1). mass mkt. 3.25 (*0-689-81244-2*, Simon Spotlight/Nickelodeon) Simon & Schuster Children's Publishing.

Karr, Kathleen. Gideon & the Mummy Professor, RS. 1993. 144p. (YA). (gr. 5 up). 16.00 o.p. (*0-374-32563-4*, Farrar, Straus & Giroux (BYR)) Farrar, Straus & Giroux.

Kassirer, Sue. What Daddy Loves. 2003. (Illus.). 24p. (J). 12.99 (*0-7944-0121-X*, Reader's Digest Children's Bks.) Reader's Digest Children's Publishing, Inc.

Kasza, Keiko. Don't Laugh, Joe. 1997. (Illus.). 32p. (J). (ps-3). 15.99 (*0-399-23036-X*, G. P. Putnam's Sons) Penguin Group (USA) Inc.

Katz, Karen. Daddy & Me. 2003. (Illus.). 14p. (J). bds. 5.99 (*0-689-84906-0*, Little Simon) Simon & Schuster Children's Publishing.

Katz, Welwyn W. Out of the Dark. 1996. 192p. (J). (gr. 6-9). 16.00 (*0-689-80947-6*, McElderry, Margaret K.) Simon & Schuster Children's Publishing.

Kavanagh, Peter. I Love My Mama. 2003. (Illus.). 32p. (J). (ps-1). 12.95 (*0-689-85691-1*, Simon & Schuster Children's Publishing) Simon & Schuster Children's Publishing.

—I Love My Mama. Chapman, Jane, tr. & illus. by. 2003. (J). (*1-85430-806-8*, Simon & Schuster Children's Publishing) Simon & Schuster Children's Publishing.

Kay, Alan N. On the Trail of John Brown's Body. 2001. (Young Heroes of History Ser.: Vol. 2). (Illus.). 175p. (J). (gr. 4-7). pap. 5.95 (*1-57249-239-2*, 1572492406, Burd Street Pr.) White Mane Publishing Co., Inc.

Kaye, Marilyn. Camp Sunnyside Friends No. 11: The Problem with Parents. 1991. 128p. (J). pap. 2.95 (*0-380-76183-1*, Avon Bks.) Morrow/Avon.

Keenan, Christopher. Toys Will Be Toys. 1993. (Illus.). (J). (gr. 3 up). 4.95 o.p. (*0-681-41722-6*) Borders Pr.

Kehret, Peg. I'm Not Who You Think I Am. (gr. 5-9). 2001. 160p. (YA). pap. 4.99 (*0-14-131237-8*); 1999. 144p. (J). 15.99 (*0-525-46153-1*, Dutton Children's Bks.) Penguin Putnam Bks. for Young Readers.

—I'm Not Who You Think I Am. 2001. (J). 11.04 (*0-606-20717-1*) Turtleback Bks.

—Searching for Candlestick Park. 1997. 160p. (J). (gr. 3-7). 14.99 (*0-525-65256-6*, Dutton Children's Bks.) Penguin Putnam Bks. for Young Readers.

Keller, Beverly. No Beasts! No Children! 1983. 128p. (J). (gr. 3-6). 11.95 o.p. (*0-688-01678-2*) HarperCollins Children's Bk. Group.

Kellerhals-Stewart, Heather. Brave Highland Heart. ed. 2000. (J). (gr. 2). spiral bd. (*0-616-01688-3*) Canadian National Institute for the Blind/Institut National Canadien pour les Aveugles.

—Brave Highland Heart. 1998. (Illus.). 32p. (J). (gr. k-3). 15.95 (*0-7737-3099-0*) Stoddart Kids CAN. *Dist:* Fitzhenry & Whiteside, Ltd., Stoddart Publishing.

Kerley, Barbara Kelly. Songs of Papa's Island. 1995. (Illus.). 64p. (J). (gr. 4-6). 14.95 o.p. (*0-395-71548-2*) Houghton Mifflin Co.

Kidd, Ronald. Who Is Felix the Great? 1983. 160p. (J). (gr. 7 up). 10.95 o.p. (*0-525-66778-4*, 01063-320, Dutton Children's Bks.) Penguin Putnam Bks. for Young Readers.

Killion, Bette. Think of It. 1993. (Laura Geringer Bks.). (Illus.). 32p. (J). (ps-1). 12.00 (*0-06-023257-9*); lib. bdg. 11.89 o.p. (*0-06-023258-7*) HarperCollins Children's Bk. Group.

Kimmel, Eric A. One Good Turn Deserves Another. 1994. 160p. (J). (gr. 4-7). tchr. ed. 14.95 o.p. (*0-8234-1138-9*) Holiday Hse., Inc.

Kinsey-Warnock, Natalie. In the Language of Loons. 1998. 112p. (J). (gr. 5-9). 15.99 o.s.i (*0-525-65237-X*, Dutton Children's Bks.) Penguin Putnam Bks. for Young Readers.

—On a Starry Night. 1994. (Illus.). 32p. (J). (ps-3). lib. bdg. 16.99 (*0-531-08670-4*); mass mkt. 15.95 (*0-531-06820-X*) Scholastic, Inc. (Orchard Bks.).

Kirk, Daniel. Moondogs. 1999. (Illus.). 32p. (J). (ps-3). 15.99 (*0-399-23128-5*) Penguin Group (USA) Inc.

—Snow Family. (Illus.). 32p. (J). (ps-2). 2002. pap. 5.99 (*0-7868-1605-8*); 2000. 14.99 (*0-7868-0304-5*); 2000. lib. bdg. 15.49 (*0-7868-2244-9*) Hyperion Bks. for Children.

Kirk, David. Miss Spider's Sunny Patch Kids. 2004. (Illus.). 40p. (J). 14.95 (*0-439-40870-9*) Scholastic, Inc.

Klass, Sheila S. The Uncivil War. 1999. 176p. (gr. 4-7). pap. text 4.50 (*0-440-41572-1*) Bantam Bks.

—The Uncivil War. 1997. 162p. (J). (gr. 3-7). tchr. ed. 15.95 (*0-8234-1329-2*) Holiday Hse., Inc.

—The Uncivil War. 1999. 10.55 (*0-606-17477-X*) Turtleback Bks.

Klein, Lee. The Best Gift for Mom. 1995. (Illus.). 32p. (Orig.). (J). (gr. k-6). pap. 5.95 o.p. (*0-8091-6627-5*) Paulist Pr.

Klein, Norma. If I Had My Way. 1974. (Illus.). 40p. (J). (gr. k-3). 6.99 o.s.i (*0-394-92654-4*, Pantheon) Knopf Publishing Group.

—Older Men. 1988. 192p. (YA). mass mkt. 3.50 o.s.i (*0-449-70261-8*, Fawcett) Ballantine Bks.

—Older Men. 1987. 240p. (YA). (gr. 7 up). 15.95 o.p. (*0-8037-0178-0*, Dial Bks. for Young Readers) Penguin Putnam Bks. for Young Readers.

Klingel, Cynthia Fitterer and Noyed, Roberts B. The Amazing Letter D. 2003. (Alphaphonics Ser.). (Illus.). 24p. (J). (ps-3). lib. bdg. 24.21 (*1-59296-094-4*) Child's World, Inc.

—The Amazing Letter M. 2003. (Alphaphonics Ser.). (Illus.). 24p. (J). (ps-3). lib. bdg. 24.21 (*1-59296-103-7*) Child's World, Inc.

—The Amazing Letter P. 2003. (Alphaphonics Ser.). (Illus.). 24p. (J). (ps-3). lib. bdg. 24.21 (*1-59296-106-1*) Child's World, Inc.

Koertge, Ronald. Confess-O-Rama. 1996. 176p. (YA). (gr. 7 up). lib. bdg. 17.99 (*0-531-08865-0*, Orchard Bks.) Scholastic, Inc.

—Confess-O-Rama. 1998. 10.55 (*0-606-13291-0*) Turtleback Bks.

—The Harmony Arms. 1994. 192p. (YA). (gr. 5 up). mass mkt. 3.99 (*0-380-72188-0*, Avon Bks.) Morrow/Avon.

Kolar, Bob. Stomp, Stomp! 1997. (Illus.). 32p. (J). (ps-1). 15.95 o.p. (*1-55858-632-6*); 16.50 o.p. (*1-55858-633-4*) North-South Bks., Inc.

Koller, Jackie French. A Place to Call Home. 1995. 208p. (YA). (gr. 7-12). 16.00 (*0-689-80024-X*, Atheneum) Simon & Schuster Children's Publishing.

—A Place to Call Home. 1997. (YA). 11.04 (*0-606-11754-7*) Turtleback Bks.

—The Promise. 1999. 80p. (YA). (gr. 5-8). lib. bdg. 17.99 (*0-679-99484-X*) Knopf, Alfred A. Inc.

—The Promise. 80p. (gr. 5-8). 2001. pap. text 4.99 (*0-440-41658-2*, Yearling); 1999. (Illus.). (YA). 15.95 (*0-679-89484-5*, Knopf Bks. for Young Readers) Random Hse. Children's Bks.

Komaiko, Leah. Just My Dad & Me. 1995. (Illus.). 32p. (J). lib. bdg. 15.89 (*0-06-024574-3*); 15.95 o.p. (*0-06-024573-5*) HarperCollins Children's Bk. Group. (Harper Festival).

Krauser, Susan A. Lilith A. Wilith. 2002. (J). lib. bdg. 16.95 (*0-9717860-0-3*) Lilith & Co.

Krauss, Ruth. You're Just What I Need. 1998. (Illus.). 40p. (J). (ps-2). 15.95 (*0-06-027514-6*) HarperCollins Children's Bk. Group.

Krisher, Trudy B. Spite Fences. 1994. 288p. (J). (gr. 6 up). 15.95 o.p. (*0-385-32088-4*, Delacorte Pr.) Dell Publishing.

—Spite Fences. 1995. 18.95 (*0-385-30978-3*) Doubleday Publishing.

—Spite Fences. 1996. 10.55 (*0-606-09882-8*) Turtleback Bks.

Kroll, Steven. That Makes Me Mad! 2002. (Illus.). 32p. (J). (ps-1). lib. bdg. 16.50 (*1-58717-184-8*); 15.95 (*1-58717-183-X*) North-South Bks., Inc.

Kroll, Virginia L. Motherlove. 1998. (Illus.). (J). (ps-3). 36p. 16.95 (*1-883220-81-5*); 32p. pap. 7.95 (*1-883220-80-7*) Dawn Pubns.

Krosoczka, Jarrett J. Good Night, Monkey Boy! 2001. (Illus.). 40p. (J). (ps). lib. bdg. 16.99 o.s.i (*0-375-91121-9*, Random Hse. Bks. for Young Readers) Random Hse. Children's Bks.

Kubler, Annie. Man's Work. 1999. (All in a Day Boardbooks Ser.). (Illus.). 14p. (ps-k). 2.99 (*0-85953-587-8*) Child's Play of England GBR. *Dist:* Child's Play-International.

Kuiper, Nannie. Bailey the Bear Cub. 2002. (Illus.). 32p. (J). lib. bdg. 16.50 (*0-7358-1625-5*) North-South Bks., Inc.

—Bailey the Bear Cub. James, J. Alison, tr. from DUT. 2002. (Illus.). 32p. (J). (gr. k-3). 15.95 (*0-7358-1624-7*) North-South Bks., Inc.

Kurtz, Jane. Rain Romp: Stomping Away a Grouchy Day. 2002. (Illus.). 32p. (J). lib. bdg. 17.89 (*0-06-029806-5*); 15.99 (*0-06-029805-7*, Greenwillow Bks.) HarperCollins Children's Bk. Group.

La Mann, Angela. Mom Is Going to Stop It. 1992. (Foundations Ser.). 27p. (J). pap. text 4.50 (*1-56843-064-7*) EMG Networks.

—Mom Is Going to Stop It: Big Book. 1992. (Foundations Ser.). 27p. (J). pap. text 23.00 (*1-56843-014-0*) EMG Networks.

Lachtman, Ofelia Dumas. Big Enough (Bastante Grande) Canetti, Yanitzia, tr. 1998. (ENG & SPA., Illus.). 32p. (J). (ps-2). 14.95 (*1-55885-221-2*, Piñata Books) Arte Publico Pr.

LaFaye, A. Nissa's Place. 256p. (gr. 3-7). 2001. pap. 4.99 (*0-689-84250-3*, Aladdin); 1999. (Illus.). (J). 16.00 (*0-689-82610-9*, Simon & Schuster Children's Publishing) Simon & Schuster Children's Publishing.

—The Strength of Saints. 2002. 192p. (J). (gr. 4-9). 16.95 (*0-689-83200-1*, Simon & Schuster Children's Publishing) Simon & Schuster Children's Publishing.

Laird, Elizabeth. A Book of Promises. 2000. (Illus.). 32p. (J). (gr. k-3). pap. 15.95 o.p. (*0-7894-2547-5*, D K Ink) Dorling Kindersley Publishing, Inc.

Lakin, Patricia. Dad & Me in the Morning. 1994. (Illus.). 32p. (J). (gr. 1-3). lib. bdg. 14.95 (*0-8075-1419-5*) Whitman, Albert & Co.

Lambert, Marilyn. Franny & Roxxy. 1999. (J). (gr. k-3). pap. 6.95 (*0-533-12820-X*) Vantage Pr., Inc.

Lane, Lindsey. Snuggle Mountain. 2003. (Illus.). 32p. (J). (-ps). lib. bdg., tchr. ed. 15.00 (*0-618-04328-4*, Clarion Bks.) Houghton Mifflin Co. Trade & Reference Div.

Langreuter, Jutta. Little Bear Brushes His Teeth. 1997. (Little Bear Collection). (Illus.). 32p. (J). (ps-k). 22.90 (*0-7613-0190-9*); pap. 7.95 (*0-7613-0230-1*) Millbrook Pr., Inc.

Lantz, Francess L. Stepsister from the Planet Weird. (J). (gr. 3-7). 1997. 11.99 o.s.i (*0-679-97330-3*); 1996. 176p. pap. 3.99 o.s.i (*0-679-87330-9*) Random Hse. Children's Bks. (Random Hse. Bks. for Young Readers).

—Stepsister from the Planet Weird. 1997. 10.04 (*0-606-13040-3*) Turtleback Bks.

Lasky, Kathryn. Before I Was Your Mother. 2003. (Illus.). 40p. (J). 16.00 (*0-15-201464-0*) Harcourt Children's Bks.

Lavallee, Barbara, illus. Mama, Do You Love Me? Doll & Book Set. 1993. (J). 14.95 o.s.i (*0-8118-0521-2*) Chronicle Bks. LLC.

Lawler, Janet. If Kisses Were Colors. 2003. (Illus.). 32p. (J). 15.99 (*0-8037-2617-1*, Dial Bks. for Young Readers) Penguin Putnam Bks. for Young Readers.

Lawrence, David. Good Little Girl. 2000. (Illus.). (J). 13.14 (*0-606-18784-7*) Turtleback Bks.

Lawrence, Iain. The Wreckers. 1998. 208p. (gr. 8-12). text 15.95 (*0-385-32535-5*, Delacorte Pr.) Dell Publishing.

—The Wreckers. 1999. (Dell Yearling Book Ser.). 224p. (gr. 5-9). reprint ed. pap. 5.50 (*0-440-41545-4*, Dell Books for Young Readers) Random Hse. Children's Bks.

—The Wreckers. 2000. (YA). (gr. 7). pap., stu. ed. 59.95 incl. audio (*0-7887-4195-0*, 41097) Recorded Bks., LLC.

—The Wreckers. l.t. ed. 1999. (Young Adult Ser.). (Illus.). 232p. (YA). (gr. 7-12). 22.95 (*0-7862-2189-5*) Thorndike Pr.

—The Wreckers. 1999. 11.04 (*0-606-17565-2*) Turtleback Bks.

Lawrence, Michael. Baby Loves. (Toddlers Storybook Ser.). (Illus.). 32p. (J). (ps). 2000. pap. 5.95 (*0-7894-5744-X*, D K Ink); 1999. pap. 9.95 o.p. (*0-7894-3410-5*) Dorling Kindersley Publishing, Inc.

Lawrence, Mildred. No Slipper for Cinderella. 1965. (J). (gr. 7 up). 5.25 o.p. (*0-15-257575-8*) Harcourt Children's Bks.

Layefsky, Virginia. Impossible Things. 1998. (Accelerated Reader Bks.). 208p. (J). (gr. 5-9). 14.95 (*0-7614-5038-6*, Cavendish Children's Bks.) Cavendish, Marshall Corp.

Le Saux, Alain. Daddy Shaves, ERS. 1992. (King Daddy Bks.). (Illus.). 28p. (J). (ps). pap. 6.95 o.p. (*0-8050-2194-9*, Holt, Henry & Co. Bks. For Young Readers) Holt, Henry & Co.

—King Daddy, ERS. 1992. (Illus.). 28p. (J). (ps). pap. 6.95 o.p. (*0-8050-2193-0*, Holt, Henry & Co. Bks. For Young Readers) Holt, Henry & Co.

Leavitt, Caroline. Girls in Trouble: A Novel. 2003. 368p. (YA). 24.95 (*0-312-27122-0*) St. Martin's Pr.

Lebrun, Claude. Good Morning, Little Brown Bear! (Little Brown Bear Ser.). (Illus.). 1997. 16p. mass mkt. 3.95 o.p. (*0-516-17849-0*); 1996. mass mkt. 12.00 o.p. (*0-516-07849-6*) Scholastic Library Publishing. (Children's Pr.).

Lee, Joanna. I Want to Keep My Baby! 1977. 176p. (Orig.). (YA). (gr. 9-12). mass mkt. 3.50 o.p. (*0-451-15733-8*, Signet Bks.) NAL.

Lee, Marie G. Finding My Voice. 1994. 176p. (J). mass mkt. 3.99 o.s.i (*0-440-21896-9*) Dell Publishing.

—Finding My Voice. 2001. 224p. (J). (gr. 7 up). pap. 5.99 (*0-06-447245-0*, Harper Trophy) HarperCollins Children's Bk. Group.

—Finding My Voice. 1992. 176p. (YA). (gr. 6 up). 13.95 o.p. (*0-395-62134-8*) Houghton Mifflin Co.

—Finding My Voice. 1994. 9.09 o.p. (*0-606-06979-8*) Turtleback Bks.

Leeka, M. C. Just Like Mommy, Just Like Daddy. 1993. (Storytime Bks.). (Illus.). 24p. (J). (ps-2). pap. 1.29 o.p. (*1-56293-345-0*, McClanahan Bk.) Learning Horizons, Inc.

Lehne, Judith Logan. When the Ragman Sings. 1993. 128p. (J). (gr. 3-7). 14.00 (*0-06-023316-8*); lib. bdg. 13.89 (*0-06-023317-6*) HarperCollins Children's Bk. Group.

Leigh, Peter. A Different Kind of Hero. 1998. (Livewire Kaleidoscope Ser.). 44 p. (J). (*0-89061-620-5*) McGraw-Hill/Contemporary.

—A Different Kind of Hero: Livewire Fiction. 2003. (Illus.). 48p. (J). pap. text (*0-340-69697-4*) Hodder Arnold GBR. *Dist:* Oxford Univ. Pr., Inc.

Leonard, Marcia. The Tin Can Man. 1998. (Real Kids Readers Ser.). (Illus.). 32p. (J). (ps-1). 18.90 (*0-7613-2012-1*); pap. 4.99 (*0-7613-2037-7*) Millbrook Pr., Inc.

—The Tin Can Man. 1998. E-Book (*1-58824-499-7*); E-Book (*1-58824-747-3*); E-Book (*1-58824-830-5*) ipicturebooks, LLC.

Lester, Jim. Fallout. 1997. 224p. (J). (gr. 7 up). mass mkt. 3.99 o.s.i (*0-440-22683-X*) Dell Publishing.

—Fallout. 1996. 224p. (YA). (gr. 7 up). 15.95 o.s.i (*0-385-32168-6*, Dell Books for Young Readers) Random Hse. Children's Bks.

—Fallout. 1997. 9.09 o.p. (*0-606-11312-6*) Turtleback Bks.

Lester, Julius. Pharaoh's Daughter: A Novel of Ancient Egypt. 2000. (Illus.). 192p. (YA). (gr. 7-12). 17.00 (*0-15-201826-3*, Silver Whistle) Harcourt Children's Bks.

—Pharaoh's Daughter: A Novel of Ancient Egypt. 2002. 192p. (J). (gr. 5 up). pap. 5.99 (*0-06-440969-4*, Harper Trophy) HarperCollins Children's Bk. Group.

—When Dad Killed Mom. (YA). 2003. 216p. pap. 6.95 (*0-15-204698-4*); 2003. (gr. 7-12). mass mkt. 6.95 (*0-15-524698-4*); 2001. (Illus.). 192p. (gr. 7-12). 17.00 (*0-15-216305-0*) Harcourt Children's Bks. (Silver Whistle).

Leuck, Laura. Sun is Falling, Night Is Calling. 1994. (Illus.). 32p. (J). (ps-k). mass mkt. 15.00 (*0-671-86940-X*, Simon & Schuster Children's Publishing) Simon & Schuster Children's Publishing.

Levert, Mireille. An Island in the Soup. 2002. (Illus.). 24p. (J). (ps-k). pap. 5.95 (*0-88899-505-9*) Groundwood Bks. CAN. *Dist:* Publishers Group West.

Levitin, Sonia. Evil Encounter: A Compelling Timely Novel about a Charismatic Leader's Hypnotic Power. 1996. 256p. (YA). (gr. 7 up). 17.00 (*0-689-80216-1*, Simon & Schuster Children's Publishing) Simon & Schuster Children's Publishing.

Levy, Elizabeth. My Life as a Fifth-Grade Comedian. 1999. (J). pap., stu. ed. 41.20 incl. audio (*0-7887-3180-7*, 40915) Recorded Bks., LLC.

—My Life as a Fifth Grade Comedian. 192p. (J). 1998. (gr. 3-7). pap. 5.99 (*0-06-440723-3*, Harper Trophy); 1997. (ps-2). 15.99 (*0-06-026602-3*) HarperCollins Children's Bk. Group.

—My Life as a Fifth Grade Comedian. 1998. 11.00 (*0-606-15647-X*) Turtleback Bks.

—Parents' Night Fright, 6. 1998. (Invisible Ink Ser.). 10.14 (*0-606-13526-X*) Turtleback Bks.

Levy, Janice. Totally Uncool. 1999. (Picture Bks.). (Illus.). 32p. (J). (ps-3). lib. bdg. 15.95 (*1-57505-306-3*, Carolrhoda Bks.) Lerner Publishing Group.

Lewin, Hugh. Jafta's Father. 1983. (Jafta Collection). (Illus.). 24p. (J). (gr. 1-3). lib. bdg. 15.95 (*0-87614-209-9*, Carolrhoda Bks.) Lerner Publishing Group.

Lewis, Beverly. Just Like Mama. 2002. (Illus.). 32p. (J). 14.99 (*0-7642-2507-3*) Bethany Hse. Pubs.

—Secret Summer Dreams. 1993. (Holly's Heart Ser.: Vol. 2). 160p. (J). (gr. 6-9). pap. 6.99 o.p. (*0-310-38061-8*) Zondervan.

Lewis, J. Patrick. Isabella Abnormella & the Very, Very Finicky Queen of Trouble. 2000. (Illus.). 32p. (J). (ps-3). pap. 15.95 o.p. (*0-7894-2605-6*) Dorling Kindersley Publishing, Inc.

Lewis, Kim. A Quilt for Baby. 2002. (Illus.). 32p. (J). 15.99 (*0-7636-1925-6*) Candlewick Pr.

Lewis, Paeony. I'll Always Love You. 2002. (Illus.). (J). pap. 5.95 (*1-58925-360-4*, Tiger Tales) ME Media LLC.

L'Heureux, Christine. Caillou, Just Like Daddy. 2001. (Illus.). 24p. (J). (*2-89450-256-7*) Editions Chouette, Inc. CAN. *Dist:* Client Distribution Services.

—Caillou My Mommy. 2001. (Kite Ser.). (Illus.). 12p. (J). (ps-k). bds. 3.95 (*2-89450-226-5*) Editions Chouette, Inc. CAN. *Dist:* Client Distribution Services.

—Caillou Play with Me. 2001. (Illus.). 24p. (J). (*2-89450-255-9*) Editions Chouette, Inc. CAN. *Dist:* Client Distribution Services.

Limmer, Milly J. Where Do Little Girls Grow? Levine, Abby, ed. 1993. (Illus.). 32p. (J). (ps-3). lib. bdg. 15.95 (*0-8075-8924-1*) Whitman, Albert & Co.

Lindgren, Astrid. Mio, My Son. 2003. Tr. of Mio, Min Mio. (Illus.). 179p. (J). 17.95 (*1-930900-23-6*) Purple Hse. Pr.

Lindquist, Susan H. Summer Soldiers. 1999. (Illus.). 192p. (gr. 5-9). text 14.95 o.s.i (*0-385-32641-6*, Dell Books for Young Readers) Random Hse. Children's Bks.

—Wander. 1998. 144p. (gr. 3-7). text 14.95 o.s.i (*0-385-32563-0*) Doubleday Publishing.

Lindquist, Susan Hart. Summer Soldiers. 2000. 192p. (gr. 5-9). pap. text 4.50 o.s.i (*0-440-41537-3*, Yearling) Random Hse. Children's Bks.

—Summer Soldiers. 2000. 10.55 (*0-606-19132-1*) Turtleback Bks.

Lisle, Janet Taylor. Angela's Aliens. 1996. 128p. (J). (gr. 4-7). pap. 14.95 (*0-531-09541-X*); (Investigators of the Unknown Ser.: Bk. 4). lib. bdg. 15.99 (*0-531-08891-X*) Scholastic, Inc. (Orchard Bks.).

—Angela's Aliens. 1997. (Investigators of the Unknown Ser.). 10.04 (*0-606-11043-7*) Turtleback Bks.

—The Crying Rocks. 2003. (Illus.). 208p. (YA). 16.95 (*0-689-85319-X*, Atheneum/Richard Jackson Bks.) Simon & Schuster Children's Publishing.

—The Gold Dust Letters. 1994. (Investigators of the Unknown Ser.: Vol. 1). 128p. (J). (gr. 4-7). pap. 15.95 (*0-531-06830-7*); lib. bdg. 16.99 (*0-531-08680-1*) Scholastic, Inc. (Orchard Bks.).

—A Message from the Match Girl. 1997. pap. 3.99 (*0-380-72518-5*, Avon Bks.) Morrow/Avon.

—A Message from the Match Girl. 1996. (Investigators of the Unknown Ser.: Bk. 3). (Illus.). 128p. (J). (gr. 4-7). pap. 15.95 (*0-531-09487-1*); lib. bdg. 16.99 (*0-531-08787-5*) Scholastic, Inc. (Orchard Bks.).

Little Golden Books Staff. Grover's Mommy. 1999. (Sesame Street Ser.). (Illus.). 24p. (J). (ps-3). 1.29 o.s.i (*0-307-30203-2*, Golden Bks.) Random Hse. Children's Bks.

Little, Kimberley G. Breakaway. 1997. 160p. (J). (gr. 5-7). 14.00 o.p. (*0-380-97488-6*, Avon Bks.) Morrow/Avon.

Littleton, Mark. Secrets of Moonlight Mountain. 1993. (J). mass mkt. 3.99 o.p. (*0-89081-960-2*) Harvest Hse. Pubs.

LoMonaco, Palmyra. Watch the Day Move. 2015. (J). 14.95 (*0-399-22162-X*) Penguin Putnam Bks. for Young Readers.

London, Jonathan. Froggy Learns to Swim. (Illus.). 32p. (J). (ps-1). 1997. pap. 5.99 (*0-14-055312-6*); 1995. 15.99 (*0-670-85551-0*, Viking) Penguin Putnam Bks. for Young Readers.

—A Koala for Katie: An Adoption Story. 1993. (Illus.). (J). (ps-1). lib. bdg. 13.95 o.p. (*0-8075-4209-1*) Whitman, Albert & Co.

—What Do You Love? (Illus.). (J). 2004. 30p. bds. (*0-15-205054-X*, Red Wagon Bks.); 2000. 32p. 14.00 (*0-15-201919-7*, Silver Whistle) Harcourt Children's Bks.

—Where's Home? 1997. 96p. pap. 3.99 o.s.i (*0-14-037513-9*); 1995. 128p. (J). 13.99 o.s.i (*0-670-86028-X*, Viking) Penguin Putnam Bks. for Young Readers.

—Where's Home? 1997. (J). 9.19 o.p. (*0-606-12087-4*) Turtleback Bks.

London, Jonathan & Ford, Susan. Loon Lake. 2002. (Illus.). 36p. (J). (ps-3). 15.95 (*0-8118-2003-3*) Chronicle Bks. LLC.

Loomis, Christine. Across America, I Love You. 2000. (Illus.). 32p. (J). (ps-3). lib. bdg. 16.49 (*0-7868-2314-3*);Vol. 1. 15.99 (*0-7868-0366-5*) Hyperion Bks. for Children.

Losier, Dave. Fred's Prayer Machine. 2002. (Illus.). 152p. (J). pap. 11.95 (*1-929039-07-7*) Ambassador Bks., Inc.

Loupy, Christophe. Hugs & Kisses. 2001. (Illus.). 36p. (J). (ps-k). 16.50 (*0-7358-1485-6*, Michael Neugebauer Bks.) North-South Bks., Inc.

—Hugs & Kisses. James, J. Alison, tr. from GER. 2001. (Illus.). 36p. (J). (ps-k). 15.95 (*0-7358-1484-8*, Michael Neugebauer Bks.) North-South Bks., Inc.

Love, Angelica. Words Can Break a Heart. Stancil, Mary H., ed. & illus. by. 1998. 20p. (J). (gr. k-2). pap. 4.95 (*1-892212-07-2*) Love Publishing Co.

Lowell, Melissa. Center Ice, l.t. ed. 1998. (Silver Blades Ser.: No. 10). 144p. (J). (gr. 4 up). lib. bdg. 22.60 (*0-8368-2099-1*) Stevens, Gareth Inc.

—The Competition. l.t. ed. 1998. (Silver Blades Ser.: No. 3). (J). (gr. 4 up). lib. bdg. 22.60 (*0-8368-2065-7*) Stevens, Gareth Inc.

Lowry, Brigid. Guitar Highway Rose. 2003. (YA). tchr. ed. 16.95 (*0-8234-1790-5*) Holiday Hse., Inc.

Lowry, Danielle. What Can I Do? A Book for Children of Divorce. 2001. (Illus.). 46p. (J). (gr. 3-7). 14.95 (*1-55798-769-6*); pap. 8.95 (*1-55798-770-X*) American Psychological Assn. (Magination Pr.).

Lucado, Max. Just in Case You Ever Wonder. (J). (ps-3). 2001. (Illus.). 32p. 15.99 (*0-8499-7612-X*); 9999. 7.97 o.p. (*0-8499-1451-5*) Nelson, Tommy.

Lucashenko, Melissa. Killing Darcy. 1998. 230p. (YA). (gr. 8-12). pap. 13.95 (*0-7022-3041-3*) Univ. of Queensland Pr. AUS. *Dist:* International Specialized Bk. Services.

Lutzeier, Elizabeth. The Wall. 1992. 160p. (J). (gr. 5-9). 14.95 o.p. (*0-8234-0987-2*) Holiday Hse., Inc.

Lynch, Chris. Gypsy Davey. 1994. 160p. (YA). (gr. 12 up). 14.00 o.s.i (*0-06-023586-1*); (gr. 7 up). lib. bdg. 13.89 o.p. (*0-06-023587-X*) HarperCollins Children's Bk. Group.

—Iceman. (Trophy Bk.). 1995. 192p. (J). (gr. 7 up). pap. 5.99 (*0-06-447114-4*, Harper Trophy); 1994. 160p. (YA). (gr. 12 up). 15.00 o.s.i (*0-06-023340-0*); 1994. 80p. (YA). (gr. 7 up). lib. bdg. 14.89 o.p. (*0-06-023341-9*) HarperCollins Children's Bk. Group.

—Iceman. 1995. (J). 11.00 (*0-606-08461-4*) Turtleback Bks.

—Shadow Boxer. (Trophy Bk.). 224p. (J). (gr. 5 up). 1995. pap. 5.95 (*0-06-447112-8*, Harper Trophy); 1993. 14.95 o.p. (*0-06-023027-4*); 1993. lib. bdg. 14.89 o.s.i (*0-06-023028-2*) HarperCollins Children's Bk. Group.

—Shadow Boxer. 1996. (YA). (gr. 9-12). 20.75 (*0-8446-6886-9*) Smith, Peter Pub., Inc.

Relationships

—Shadow Boxer. 1995. 11.00 (*0-606-08147-X*) Turtleback Bks.

Lyon, George Ella. Who Came Down That Road? 1992. (Illus.). 32p. (J). (ps-2). mass mkt. 17.99 o.p. (*0-531-08587-2*); mass mkt. 16.95 o.p. (*0-531-05987-1*) Scholastic, Inc. (Orchard Bks.).

—Who Came down That Road? 1996. (Illus.). 32p. (J). (ps-3). mass mkt. 5.95 (*0-531-07073-5*, Orchard Bks.) Scholastic, Inc.

Macaulay, David. Black & White. 1990. (Illus.). 32p. (J). (ps-3). lib. bdg., tchr. ed. 17.00 (*0-395-52151-3*) Houghton Mifflin Co.

Mack, Todd. Princess Penelope. 2003. (Illus.). 32p. (J). (ps-k). pap. 15.95 (*0-439-22436-5*, Scholastic Pr.) Scholastic, Inc.

Mackel, Kathy. A Season of Comebacks. 1997. 112p. (J). (gr. 3-7). 15.99 o.s.i (*0-399-23026-2*, G. P. Putnam's Sons) Penguin Group (USA) Inc.

—A Season of Comebacks. 1998. 126p. (J). (gr. 4-7). pap. 4.99 o.p. (*0-698-11637-2*, PaperStar) Penguin Putnam Bks. for Young Readers.

—A Season of Comebacks. 1998. (J). 11.04 (*0-606-13767-X*) Turtleback Bks.

MacLean, Christine Kole. Even Firefighters Hug Their Moms. 2002. (Illus.). 32p. (J). 15.99 (*0-525-46996-6*, Dutton Children's Bks.) Penguin Putnam Bks. for Young Readers.

Madenski, Melissa. In My Mother's Garden. 1995. (Illus.). 32p. (J). 15.95 o.p. (*0-316-54326-8*) Little Brown & Co.

Madrigal, Antonio H. Erandi's Braids. Peskin, Joy, ed. 2001. (Illus.). 32p. (J). (ps-3). pap. 6.99 (*0-698-11885-5*, PaperStar) Penguin Putnam Bks. for Young Readers.

Madrigal, Antonio Hernandez. Erandi's Braids. 1999. (Illus.). 32p. (J). (ps-3). 15.99 (*0-399-23212-5*) Penguin Group (USA) Inc.

Maguire, Gregory. Oasis. 1998. 170p. (J). (gr. 4-7). pap. 4.95 (*0-7868-1293-1*) Disney Pr.

—Oasis. 1996. 176p. (YA). (gr. 7-9). tchr. ed. 14.95 (*0-395-67019-5*, Clarion Bks.) Houghton Mifflin Co. Trade & Reference Div.

—Oasis. 1998. 11.00 (*0-606-15655-0*) Turtleback Bks.

Mahr, Juli. Mama Tiger, Baba Tiger. 2001. (Share-a-Story Ser.). (Illus.). (J). (ps-3). 32p. pap. 9.95 o.p. (*0-7894-6353-9*); 24p. pap. 5.95 o.p. (*0-7894-5615-X*) Dorling Kindersley Publishing, Inc.

—Mama Tiger, Baba Tiger. 2001. (Illus.). (J). 12.10 (*0-606-21314-7*) Turtleback Bks.

Mahy, Margaret. The Catalogue of the Universe. 1986. 192p. (YA). (gr. 9 up). 15.95 (*0-689-50391-1*, McElderry, Margaret K.) Simon & Schuster Children's Publishing.

—Catalogue of the Universe. 1987. (J). mass mkt. 2.75 (*0-590-42318-5*) Scholastic, Inc.

—Catalogue of the Universe. 2002. (Illus.). 192p. (J). pap. 7.99 (*0-689-85353-X*, Simon Pulse) Simon & Schuster Children's Publishing.

Major, Kevin. The Story of the House of Wooden Santas: An Advent Read-Along in 24 Chapters. rev. ed. 1998. (Illus.). 96p. (gr. 4-7). 12.98 (*0-7651-0829-1*) Smithmark Pubs., Inc.

Manushkin, Fran. The Best Toy of All. 1992. (Illus.). 240p. (J). (ps-1). 11.00 o.p. (*0-525-44897-7*, Dutton Children's Bks.) Penguin Putnam Bks. for Young Readers.

—Peeping & Sleeping. 1994. (Illus.). 31p. (J). (ps-3). 14.95 o.s.i (*0-395-64339-2*, Clarion Bks.) Houghton Mifflin Co. Trade & Reference Div.

Many, Paul. These Are the Rules. 1998. 160p. (J). mass mkt. 4.99 o.s.i (*0-679-88978-7*) Knopf, Alfred A. Inc.

—These Are the Rules. 1997. 192p. (YA). (gr. 7 up). 15.95 (*0-8027-8619-7*) Walker & Co.

Marcus, Irene W. & Marcus, Paul. Into the Great Forest: A Story for Children Away from Parents for the First Time. 1992. (Illus.). 32p. (J). (ps-3). 11.95 o.p. (*0-945354-39-8*); pap. 8.95 (*0-945354-40-1*) American Psychological Assn.

—Into the Great Forest: A Story for Children Away from Parents for the First Time. 1993. (Books to Help Children Ser.). (Illus.). 32p. (J). (ps up). lib. bdg. 18.60 o.p. (*0-8368-0932-7*) Stevens, Gareth Inc.

Marino, Jan. For the Love of Pete: A Novel. 1993. (J). 14.95 o.p. (*0-316-54627-5*) Little Brown & Co.

Marshall, Linda D. What Is a Step? 1992. (Illus.). 48p. (Orig.). (J). (ps-5). pap. 10.00 (*1-879289-00-8*) Native Sun Pubs., Inc.

Martin, C. L. The Blueberry Train. 1995. (Illus.). (J). (ps-3). 32p. 15.00 (*0-689-80304-4*, Atheneum); text 13.95 o.s.i (*0-02-762441-2*, Simon & Schuster Children's Publishing) Simon & Schuster Children's Publishing.

Martin, David. Piggy & Dad. 2001. (Brand New Readers Ser.). (Illus.). 40p. (J). (ps-2). 10.99 (*0-7636-1326-6*) Candlewick Pr.

—Piggy & Dad Play. 2002. (Brand New Readers Ser.). (Illus.). (J). (ps-2). 40p. 12.99 (*0-7636-1332-0*); 8p. bds. 5.99 (*0-7636-1333-9*) Candlewick Pr.

Martin, Gilbert. A New Baby at Our House. 1979. 48p. (J). 1.25 o.p. (*0-448-15883-3*) Ace Bks.

Marzollo, Jean. Mama Mama, Papa Papa. 2003. (Flip Boardbks.). (Illus.). 32p. (J). (ps up). 6.99 (*0-06-051915-0*, Harper Festival) HarperCollins Children's Bk. Group.

Maslac, Evelyn. Finding a Job for Daddy. 1996. (Illus.). 24p. (J). (ps-3). lib. bdg. 13.95 (*0-8075-2437-9*) Whitman, Albert & Co.

Masters, Susan Rowan. Summer Song. 1995. 137p. (J). (gr. 4-7). 14.95 o.p. (*0-395-71127-4*, Clarion Bks.) Houghton Mifflin Co. Trade & Reference Div.

—Summer Song. 2000. 137p. (gr. 4-7). pap. 9.95 (*0-595-14407-1*) iUniverse, Inc.

Matthews, Cecily. Why Not? 1994. (Voyages Ser.). (Illus.). (J). (*0-383-03727-1*) SRA/McGraw-Hill.

Mayer, Mercer. Beach Day. 2001. (First Readers, Skills & Practice Ser.). (Illus.). 24p. (J). (ps-k). pap. 3.95 (*1-57768-844-9*) McGraw-Hill Children's Publishing.

—Just Me & My Dad. 1982. (Little Critter Ser.). (J). (ps-3). 9.44 (*0-606-12377-6*) Turtleback Bks.

Maynard, Bill. Pondfire. 2000. 96p. (J). (gr. 3-7). 14.99 o.p. (*0-399-23439-X*, G. P. Putnam's Sons) Penguin Group (USA) Inc.

Mazer, Anne. The No-Nothings & Their Baby. 2000. (Illus.). (J). (gr. k-3). 40p. pap. 15.95 (*0-590-68049-8*, Scholastic Paperbacks); (*0-590-68051-X*) Scholastic, Inc.

Mazer, Harry. The Dollar Man. 1975. 190p. (J). (gr. k-12). mass mkt. 2.95 o.s.i (*0-440-94484-8*, Laurel Leaf) Random Hse. Children's Bks.

—The Dollar Man. 1990. (J). (gr. 6-12). 16.30 o.p. (*0-8446-6415-4*) Smith, Peter Pub., Inc.

—Dollar Man. 1974. 160p. (J). (gr. 7 up). 5.95 o.p. (*0-440-03210-5*, Delacorte Pr.) Dell Publishing.

—The War on Villa Street. 1978. (J). (gr. 7 up). 7.95 o.s.i (*0-440-09349-X*, Delacorte Pr.) Dell Publishing.

Mazer, Norma Fox. Up in Seth's Room. 1979. 208p. (J). (gr. 7 up). pap. 7.95 o.s.i (*0-385-29058-6*, Delacorte Pr.) Dell Publishing.

McAllister, Angela. Night Night, Little One. 2003. (Illus.). 32p. (J). (gr. 3-6). lib. bdg. 17.99 (*0-385-90861-X*); (ps-1). 15.95 (*0-385-32732-3*) Random Hse. Children's Bks. (Doubleday Bks. for Young Readers).

McCaughrean, Geraldine. Casting the Gods Adrift: A Tale of Ancient Egypt. 2003. (Illus.). 112p. (J). (gr. 4-7). 15.95 (*0-8126-2684-2*) Cricket Bks.

McCloskey, Robert. Blueberries for Sal. 2002. (Illus.). (J). 14.04 (*0-7587-0097-0*) Book Wholesalers, Inc.

—Blueberries for Sal. 2000. (J). pap. 19.97 incl. audio (*0-7366-9193-6*) Books on Tape, Inc.

—Blueberries for Sal. ed. 1980. (J). (gr. 2). spiral bd. (*0-616-01715-4*) Canadian National Institute for the Blind/Institut National Canadien pour les Aveugles.

—Blueberries for Sal. (StoryTape Ser.). (Illus.). (J). 1993. 9.99 (*0-14-095110-5*, Puffin Bks.); 1989. 6.95 o.p. (*0-14-095032-X*, Puffin Bks.); 1976. 64p. pap. 6.99 (*0-14-050169-X*, Puffin Bks.); 1948. 56p. 16.99 (*0-670-17591-9*, Viking Children's Bks.) Penguin Putnam Bks. for Young Readers.

—Blueberries for Sal. 1976. (Picture Puffin Ser.). (Illus.). (J). 12.14 (*0-606-01675-9*) Turtleback Bks.

—Blueberries for Sal. (J). (ps-k). pap. text 12.95 incl. audio Weston Woods Studios, Inc.

McConnaughhay, JoDee. Be Brave, Anna! God Helps Me When I'm Afraid. Caldwell, Lise, ed. 1999. (Happy Day Bks.). (Illus.). 24p. (J). (ps-2). pap. 2.49 (*0-7847-0895-9*, 04268, Bean Sprouts) Standard Publishing.

McCourt, Lisa. Good Night, Princess Pruney Toes. 2004. (J). mass mkt. 5.99 (*0-439-63593-4*) Scholastic, Inc.

—I Love You, Stinky Face. (J). 2004. pap. 15.95 (*0-439-63571-3*); 2004. bds. 6.99 (*0-439-63572-1*); 2003. 32p. mass mkt. 5.99 (*0-439-63469-5*) Scholastic, Inc.

—I Love You, Stinky Face. 1998. 12.10 (*0-606-15901-0*) Turtleback Bks.

—I Miss You, Stinky Face. (J). 2004. pap. 15.95 (*0-439-63573-X*); 2003. 32p. mass mkt. 5.99 (*0-439-63470-9*) Scholastic, Inc.

—I Miss You, Stinky Face. 2000. 12.10 (*0-606-18667-0*) Turtleback Bks.

McCully, Emily Arnold. Monk Camps Out. 2000. (Illus.). (J). (ps-4). 32p. pap. 15.95 (*0-439-09976-5*, Levine, Arthur A. Bks.); (*0-439-09977-3*) Scholastic, Inc.

—My Real Family. 1994. (Illus.). 32p. (J). (gr. k-3). 14.00 o.s.i (*0-15-277698-2*) Harcourt Children's Bks.

McDonald, Janet. Chill Wind, RS. 2002. 144p. (YA). (gr. 7 up). 16.00 (*0-374-39958-1*, Farrar, Straus & Giroux (BYR)) Farrar, Straus & Giroux.

—Chill Wind. 2003. 165p. (J). 24.95 (*0-7862-5502-1*) Thorndike Pr.

McDonald, Joyce. Comfort Creek. 1998. 208p. (gr. 3-7). reprint ed. pap. text 3.99 o.s.i (*0-440-41198-X*, Yearling) Random Hse. Children's Bks.

McDonald, Megan. Baya, Baya, Lulla-by-A. 2003. (Illus.). 32p. (J). 16.95 (*0-689-84932-X*, Atheneum/ Richard Jackson Bks.) Simon & Schuster Children's Publishing.

—The Bridge to Nowhere. 1993. 160p. (YA). (gr. 7 up). pap. 15.95 (*0-531-05478-0*); (J). (ps-3). lib. bdg. 16.99 (*0-531-08628-3*) Scholastic, Inc. (Orchard Bks.).

McDonough, Alison. Do the Hokey Pokey. 2001. (Illus.). 112p. (J). (gr. 3-7). 14.95 (*0-8126-2699-0*) Cricket Bks.

McGrath, Bob. I'm a Good Mommy. 1989. (Mommy, Daddy & Me Bks.). (Illus.). 48p. (J). (ps-2). 4.95 o.p. (*0-8431-2399-0*, Price Stern Sloan) Penguin Putnam Bks. for Young Readers.

—You're a Good Daddy. 1989. (Mommy, Daddy & Me Bks.). (Illus.). 48p. (J). (ps-2). 4.95 o.p. (*0-8431-2401-6*, Price Stern Sloan) Penguin Putnam Bks. for Young Readers.

McGuire, Leslie. Nightmares in the Mist. 1994. (Illus.). 40p. (J). (gr. k-4). 14.95 (*1-56844-003-0*) Enchante Publishing.

—Nightmares in the Mist. Hoy, Gudrun & Martin, Bobi, eds. 2nd rev. ed. 1996. (Emotional Literacy Ser.). (Illus.). 40p. (J). (gr. k-5). 14.95 (*1-56844-103-7*) Enchante Publishing.

McKendrick, Lisa. On a Whim. 2001. 156p. (J). (*1-57734-896-6*) Covenant Communications.

McKenzie, Ellen K. The King, the Princess, & the Tinker, ERS. 1993. (Illus.). 64p. (J). (gr. 2-4). 14.95 o.p. (*0-8050-1773-9*, Holt, Henry & Co. Bks. For Young Readers) Holt, Henry & Co.

McLean, Jacqueline. Grace from China. 2003. (J). (*0-9638472-8-7*) Yeong & Yeong Bk. Co.

McMullan, Kate. Papa's Song, RS. 2000. (Illus.). 32p. (J). (ps-3). 15.00 (*0-374-35732-3*, Farrar, Straus & Giroux (BYR)) Farrar, Straus & Giroux.

McNamee, Graham. Hate You. 1999. 128p. (YA). (gr. 7-12). 14.95 o.s.i (*0-385-32593-2*, Dell Books for Young Readers) Random Hse. Children's Bks.

McNeal, Laura & McNeal, Tom. Crooked. 1999. 352p. (YA). (gr. 9-11). lib. bdg. 18.99 o.s.i (*0-679-99300-2*) Knopf, Alfred A. Inc.

McOmber, Rachel B., ed. McOmber Phonics Storybooks: Mom & Dad Hop-Jig. rev. ed. (Illus.). (J). (*0-944991-16-5*) Swift Learning Resources.

McVeity, Jen. On Different Shores. 1998. (Illus.). 167p. (YA). (gr. 5-9). pap. 16.95 (*0-531-30115-X*); lib. bdg. 17.99 (*0-531-33115-6*) Scholastic, Inc. (Orchard Bks.).

Meadows, Michelle. The Way the Storm Stops, ERS. 2003. (Illus.). 32p. (J). 16.95 (*0-8050-6595-4*, Holt, Henry & Co. Bks. For Young Readers) Holt, Henry & Co.

Melmed, Laura Krauss. I Love You As Much... 2002. 24p. (J). (ps-2). pap. 5.99 (*0-06-000202-6*, Harper Festival) HarperCollins Children's Bk. Group.

Mennen, Ingrid. One Round Moon & a Star for Me. 1994. (Illus.). 32p. (J). (ps-2). pap. 15.95 (*0-531-06804-8*); lib. bdg. 16.99 (*0-531-08654-2*) Scholastic, Inc. (Orchard Bks.).

Metzger, Steve. Where's Mommy? 1997. (Dinofours Ser.: No. 20). (Illus.). 32p. (J). (ps-1). mass mkt. 3.25 (*0-590-37456-7*) Scholastic, Inc.

Miller, Alice Ann. Treasures of the Heart. 2003. (Illus.). 16p. (J). 15.95 (*1-58536-115-1*) Sleeping Bear Pr.

Miller, Kathryn M. Did My First Mother Love Me? A Story for an Adopted Child. 1994. (Illus.). 48p. (J). (ps-3). 12.95 (*0-930934-85-7*); pap. 5.95 (*0-930934-84-9*) Morning Glory Pr., Inc.

Miller, Virginia. Bartholomew Bear: Five Toddler Tales. 2002. (Illus.). 144p. (J). 14.99 (*0-7636-1941-8*) Candlewick Pr.

Miller, William. A House by the River. 1997. (Illus.). 32p. (J). (ps up). 15.95 (*1-880000-48-2*) Lee & Low Bks., Inc.

Mills, Charles. Stranger in the Shadows. 1998. (Shadow Creek Ranch Ser.: Vol. 11). 151p. (Orig.). (J). (gr. 4-7). pap. 5.99 (*0-8280-1316-0*) Review & Herald Publishing Assn.

Mills, Claudia. Alex Ryan, Stop That!, RS. 2003. 160p. (J). 16.00 (*0-374-34655-0*, Farrar, Straus & Giroux (BYR)) Farrar, Straus & Giroux.

—Boardwalk with Hotel. 1986. 144p. (YA). (gr. 7-12). reprint ed. pap. 2.50 o.s.i (*0-553-15397-8*, Skylark) Random Hse. Children's Bks.

—You're a Brave Man, Julius Zimmerman, RS. 1999. 160p. (J). (gr. 3-7). 16.00 (*0-374-38708-7*, Farrar, Straus & Giroux (BYR)) Farrar, Straus & Giroux.

—You're a Brave Man, Julius Zimmerman. 2001. 160p. (J). (gr. 4-7). pap. 5.99 (*0-7868-1448-9*) Hyperion Bks. for Children.

Minarik, Else Holmelund. Am I Beautiful? 1992. (Illus.). 24p. (J). (ps-3). 16.00 (*0-688-09911-4*); lib. bdg. 14.93 o.p. (*0-688-09912-2*) HarperCollins Children's Bk. Group. (Greenwillow Bks.).

—Little Bear's Valentine. 2002. (Maurice Sendak's Little Bear Ser.). (Illus.). 32p. (J). (ps-3). 14.99 (*0-694-01712-4*); lib. bdg. 15.89 (*0-06-052244-5*) HarperCollins Children's Bk. Group.

Minchella, Nancy. Mama Will Be Home Soon. 2003. (Illus.). 32p. (J). pap. 15.95 (*0-439-38491-5*) Scholastic, Inc.

Mister Smithster and His Sister Staff. But Mom, There's an Alligator in the Elevator! 1996. (Johnny Joe & the Magical Elevator Ser.). (Illus.). 36p. (Orig.). (J). (ps-4). 16.95 (*1-889637-01-7*); pap. 12.95 (*1-889637-00-9*) Butterfly Bks.

Miyamoto, Tadao. Papa & Me. 1994. (J). (ps-3). lib. bdg. 19.95 (*0-87614-843-7*, Carolrhoda Bks.) Lerner Publishing Group.

Modesitt, Jeanne. Mama, If You Had a Wish. 1993. (Illus.). 40p. (J). (ps-3). 16.00 (*0-671-75437-8*, Simon & Schuster Children's Publishing) Simon & Schuster Children's Publishing.

Moerbeek, Kees. Hi Mom, I'm Home. 1992. (Illus.). 20p. (J). 9.95 o.p. (*0-8431-3393-7*, Price Stern Sloan) Penguin Putnam Bks. for Young Readers.

Moeri, Louise. The Devil in Ol' Rosie. l.t. ed. 2002. (Juvenile Ser.). 161p. (J). 21.95 (*0-7862-3808-9*) Gale Group.

—The Devil in Ol' Rosie. 2001. 208p. (J). (gr. 3-7). 16.00 o.s.i (*0-689-82614-1*, Atheneum) Simon & Schuster Children's Publishing.

Moessinger, Pierre. Socrates. 1993. (Illus.). (J). 14.95 o.p. (*0-88682-606-3*, Creative Education) Creative Co., The.

Monnier, Miriam. Just Right! James, J. Alison, tr. from GER. 2001. (Illus.). 32p. (J). (ps-1). 15.95 (*0-7358-1521-6*); lib. bdg. 16.50 (*0-7358-1522-4*) North-South Bks., Inc. (Michael Neugebauer Bks.).

Moon, Pat. The Spying Game. 1999. 200p. (J). (gr. 5-9). 16.99 o.p. (*0-399-23354-7*) Penguin Group (USA) Inc.

Moore, Martha. Matchit. 2002. 208p. (gr. 3-7). text 15.95 (*0-385-72906-5*); lib. bdg. 17.99 (*0-385-90023-6*) Dell Publishing. (Delacorte Pr.).

—Matchit. 2003. (Illus.). 208p. (gr. 3-7). pap. text 4.99 (*0-440-41716-3*, Dell Books for Young Readers) Random Hse. Children's Bks.

Mora, Pat. Maria Paints the Hills. 2002. (J). 19.95 o.p. (*0-89013-401-4*); pap. 9.95 (*0-89013-410-3*) Museum of New Mexico Pr.

Mori, Kyoko. One Bird. 1996. 256p. (gr. 8 up). mass mkt. 6.50 (*0-449-70453-X*, Fawcett) Ballantine Bks.

—One Bird, ERS. 1995. (Edge Bks.). 242p. (YA). (gr. 7 up). 15.95 o.p. (*0-8050-2983-4*, Holt, Henry & Co. Bks. For Young Readers) Holt, Henry & Co.

—One Bird. 1996. 10.55 (*0-606-16246-1*) Turtleback Bks.

Moroney, Trace, illus. Mommy Always Loves You. 2004. (J). 6.99 (*0-7944-0381-6*, Reader's Digest Children's Bks.) Reader's Digest Children's Publishing, Inc.

Morris, Winifred. Liar. 1996. 176p. (YA). (gr. 7 up). 15.95 (*0-8027-8461-5*) Walker & Co.

Morrow, Tara Jaye. Mommy Loves Her Baby. 2003. (Illus.). 32p. (J). (ps-1). lib. bdg. 16.89 (*0-06-029078-1*) HarperCollins Pubs.

Mouse Works Staff. Dumbo. 2000. (Read-Aloud Storybook Ser.). 64p. (J). 6.99 (*0-7364-1052-X*) Hyperion Bks. for Children.

—Dumbo. 1999. (Disney's Friendly Tales Ser.). (Illus.). 10p. (J). (ps-k). 6.99 (*0-7364-1012-0*) Mouse Works.

—Me & Dad. 1995. (J). 6.98 o.p. (*1-57082-191-7*) Mouse Works.

Muhammad, Bilaal A. A Day with My Daddy. 1996. (Illus.). (Orig.). (J). (gr. 1-4). pap. 6.95 o.p. (*0-533-11679-1*) Vantage Pr., Inc.

Munsch, Robert. Lighthouse: A Story of Remembrance. (J). 2004. pap. 5.95 (*0-439-49032-4*); 2003. (Illus.). 13.95 (*0-439-49031-6*) Scholastic, Inc.

—Mais, Ou Est Donc Gah-Ning? 1994. (FRE., Illus.). 32p. (Orig.). (J). (ps-1). pap. 4.95 (*1-55037-984-4*) Annick Pr., Ltd. CAN. *Dist:* Firefly Bks., Ltd.

Munsil, Janet. Where There's Smoke. 1993. (ENG & FRE., Illus.). 24p. (J). (ps-2). pap. 4.95 o.p. (*1-55037-290-4*); lib. bdg. 14.95 (*1-55037-291-2*) Annick Pr., Ltd. CAN. *Dist:* Firefly Bks., Ltd.

Munson, Derek. Enemy Pie: For My Best Enemy. 2000. (Illus.). 40p. (J). (gr. k-3). 14.95 (*0-8118-2778-X*) Chronicle Bks. LLC.

Murphy, Barbara B. Eagles in Their Flight. 1994. 192p. (J). (gr. 6 up). 14.95 o.s.i (*0-385-32035-3*, Delacorte Pr.) Dell Publishing.

Murphy, Mary. I Kissed the Baby! 2003. (Illus.). 24p. (J). 12.99 (*0-7636-2122-6*) Candlewick Pr.

—I Like It When... 1997. (Illus.). 32p. (J). (ps). 11.95 (*0-15-200039-9*, Red Wagon Bks.) Harcourt Children's Bks.

—Please Be Quiet! 1999. (Illus.). 32p. (J). (ps-ps). 9.95 (*0-395-97113-6*) Houghton Mifflin Co.

Murphy, Rita. Night Flying. l.t. ed. 2001. (Young Adult Ser.). 148p. (YA). 22.95 (*0-7862-3521-7*) Thorndike Pr.

Myers, Anna. The Keeping Room. 1999. (Illus.). 128p. (J). (gr. 3-7). pap. 5.99 (*0-14-130468-5*) Penguin Putnam Bks. for Young Readers.

—The Keeping Room. 1999. 11.04 (*0-606-16786-2*) Turtleback Bks.

Quattlebaum, Mary. Grover G. Graham & Me. 192p. (gr. 3-7). 2003. pap. text 4.99 (*0-440-41918-2*, Yearling); 2001. text 14.95 (*0-385-32277-1*, Dell Books for Young Readers) Random Hse. Children's Bks.

Quentin, Brad. Attack of the Evil Cyber-God. (J). 1997. (Real Adventures of Jonny Quest Ser.: No. 8). (Illus.). 112p. (gr. 3-7). mass mkt. 3.99 o.p. (*0-06-105722-3*); No. 11. 1998. 128p. mass mkt. 3.99 o.p. (*0-06-105725-8*) Morrow/Avon. (Eos).

—Journey into Q-Space. 1997. (Real Adventures of Jonny Quest Ser.: No. 7). 128p. (J). (gr. 3-7). mass mkt. 3.99 o.p. (*0-06-105721-5*, Eos) Morrow/Avon.

—The Lake of Terror. 1998. (Adventures of Johnny Quest Ser.: No. 10). (Illus.). 144p. (J). (gr. 3-7). mass mkt. 3.99 o.p. (*0-06-105724-X*, Eos) Morrow/Avon.

—The Monsters from Beyond Time. 1997. (Real Adventures of Jonny Quest Ser.: No. 6). 128p. (J). (gr. 3-7). mass mkt. 3.99 o.p. (*0-06-105720-7*, Eos) Morrow/Avon.

—Trouble on Planet Q. 1997. (Real Adventures of Jonny Quest Ser.: No. 9). (Illus.). 144p. (J). (gr. 3-7). mass mkt. 3.99 o.p. (*0-06-105723-1*, Eos) Morrow/Avon.

Ramirez, Michael Rose. Hoppin' Halloween! 1997. (Chana! Ser.: No. 2). (J). pap. 3.99 (*0-380-79018-1*, Avon Bks.) Morrow/Avon.

Ransom, Candice F. The Big Green Pocketbook. (Illus.). 32p. (J). (ps-2). 1995. pap. 6.99 (*0-06-443395-1*, Harper Trophy); 1993. 14.95 o.s.i (*0-06-020848-1*); 1993. lib. bdg. 16.89 (*0-06-020849-X*, Geringer, Laura Bk.) HarperCollins Children's Bk. Group.

—The Big Green Pocketbook. 1993. 10.15 o.p. (*0-606-07285-3*) Turtleback Bks.

—The Christmas Dolls. 1998. (Illus.). 32p. (J). (gr. k-3). 15.95 (*0-8027-8659-6*); lib. bdg. 16.85 (*0-8027-8661-8*) Walker & Co.

—The Man on Stilts. 2015. (Illus.). (J). 15.95 (*0-399-22537-4*, Philomel) Penguin Putnam Bks. for Young Readers.

Ransom, Jeanie Franz. I Don't Want to Talk about It. 2000. (Illus.). 28p. (J). (ps-3). (*1-55798-664-9*, 441-6649); pap. (*1-55798-703-3*, 441-7033) American Psychological Assn. (Magination Pr.).

Rapson, Linda B. Kipper. 1981. 128p. (J). (gr. 3-7). pap. 3.50 o.p. (*0-8024-4558-6*) Moody Pr.

—Kipper Plays Cupid. 1981. 128p. (J). (gr. 3-7). pap. 3.50 o.p. (*0-8024-4559-4*) Moody Pr.

Rau, Dana Meachen. In the Yard, Level A. 2001. (Early Reader Ser.). (Illus.). 24p. (J). (gr. k-2). lib. bdg. 18.60 (*0-7565-0116-4*) Compass Point Bks.

—My Red Rowboat, Level A. 2002. (Compass Point Early Reader Ser.). (Illus.). 24p. (J). (gr. k-2). lib. bdg. 18.60 (*0-7565-0174-1*) Compass Point Bks.

Rawlings, Marjorie Kinnan. The Yearling. abr. ed. 1995. (J). (gr. 7-12). audio 16.95 (*1-55927-358-5*, 393213) Audio Renaissance.

—The Yearling. 1991. 250p. (YA). reprint ed. lib. bdg. 27.95 (*0-89966-841-0*) Buccaneer Bks., Inc.

—The Yearling. abr. ed. 1984. (J). audio 15.95 (*1-55994-076-X*, CPN 2057, Caedmon) HarperTrade.

—The Yearling. 1999. (Illus.). 444p. (J). (*0-03-054778-4*) Holt, Rinehart & Winston.

—The Yearling, Level 3. 2001. pap. 7.66 (*0-582-34439-5*) Longman Publishing Group.

—The Yearling. unabr. ed. (YA). 2000. pap. 104.20 incl. audio (*0-7887-3661-2*, 41027X4); 2000. (gr. 7). audio 90.00 (*0-7887-3530-6*, 95919E7); Class Set. 1999. audio 170.30 (*0-7887-3690-6*, 46994) Recorded Bks., LLC.

—The Yearling. 2002. 480p. pap. 14.00 (*0-7432-2525-2*, Scribner) Simon & Schuster.

—The Yearling. (Aladdin Classics Ser.). 2001. (Illus.). 528p. (J). pap. 5.99 (*0-689-84623-1*, Aladdin); 1985. (Illus.). 416p. (YA). (gr. 7-12). 28.00 (*0-684-18461-3*, Atheneum); 1982. 428p. (YA). pap. 4.95 o.s.i (*0-684-17617-3*, Simon & Schuster Children's Publishing); 1930. (YA). 20.00 o.s.i (*0-684-20922-5*, Atheneum); 1930. 428p. (YA). pap. 9.95 o.s.i (*0-684-71878-2*, Simon & Schuster Children's Publishing); deluxe ltd. ed. 1985. (Illus.). 416p. (J). 75.00 o.s.i (*0-684-18508-3*, Atheneum); 50th annot. ed. 1988. (Illus.). 416p. (YA). (gr. 7-12). mass mkt. 5.95 (*0-02-044931-3*, Simon Pulse) Simon & Schuster Children's Publishing.

—The Yearling. l.t. ed. 1994. 559p. (YA). lib. bdg. 23.95 (*0-8161-5992-0*) Thorndike Pr.

—The Yearling. 1988. (YA). 12.00 (*0-606-00109-3*) Turtleback Bks.

Ray, Mary Lyn. Basket Moon. 1999. (Illus.). 32p. (J). (ps-3). 15.95 (*0-316-73521-3*) Little Brown & Co.

Reid, Paul Carey. Swimming in the Starry River. 1995. 384p. (J). pap. 11.95 (*0-312-14136-X*, Saint Martin's Griffin) St. Martin's Pr.

Rendal, Justine. The Girl Who Listened to Sinks. 1993. (J). (ps-6). pap. 14.00 (*0-671-77745-9*, Simon & Schuster Children's Publishing) Simon & Schuster Children's Publishing.

Reynolds, Marilynn. The Magnificent Piano Recital. 2001. (Illus.). 32p. (J). (ps-3). 15.95 (*1-55143-180-7*) Orca Bk. Pubs.

—Too Soon for Jeff. 1994. 192p. (YA). (gr. 7-12). pap. 8.95 (*0-930934-91-1*); 15.95 o.p. (*0-930934-90-3*) Morning Glory Pr., Inc.

Rice, Eve. Swim! 1996. (Illus.). 24p. (J). (ps-3). 15.00 o.s.i (*0-688-14274-5*); lib. bdg. 14.93 o.p. (*0-688-14275-3*) HarperCollins Children's Bk. Group. (Greenwillow Bks.).

Riecken, Nancy. Today Is the Day. 1996. (Illus.). 32p. (J). (ps-3). 14.95 o.p. (*0-395-73917-9*) Houghton Mifflin Co.

Rinaldi, Ann. Keep Smiling Through. 1996. 208p. (YA). (gr. 3-7). 13.00 o.s.i (*0-15-200768-7*) Harcourt Children's Bks.

—Mine Eyes Have Seen. 1997. (Illus.). 288p. (J). (gr. 7-12). pap. 16.95 (*0-590-54318-0*) Scholastic, Inc.

—Rime of Mary Christian. 2004. 224p. (J). 15.99 (*0-06-029638-0*); lib. bdg. 16.89 (*0-06-029639-9*) HarperCollins Pubs.

—The Secret of Sarah Revere. (Great Episodes Ser.). 336p. (YA). 2003. pap. 6.95 (*0-15-204684-4*); 1995. (gr. 7 up). 13.00 (*0-15-200393-2*, Gulliver Bks.); 1995. (gr. 7 up). pap. 6.00 o.s.i (*0-15-200392-4*, Gulliver Bks.) Harcourt Children's Bks.

Robbins, Ina. From My Heart to Your Heart. 1994. (J). pap. o.p. (*0-8091-6619-4*) Paulist Pr.

Roberts, Willo Davis. Don't Hurt Laurie! 1977. (Illus.). 176p. (J). (gr. 4-6). 16.00 (*0-689-30571-0*, Atheneum) Simon & Schuster Children's Publishing.

Robinson, Fay. Pizza Soup. 1993. (Bear & Alligator Tales Ser.). (Illus.). 32p. (J). (ps-2). lib. bdg. 17.70 o.p. (*0-516-02373-X*); mass mkt. 3.95 o.p. (*0-516-42373-8*) Scholastic Library Publishing. (Children's Pr.).

Robinson, Hilary. Freddie's Fears. 2002. (Read-It! Readers Ser.). (Illus.). 32p. (J). (ps-3). lib. bdg. 18.60 (*1-4048-0056-5*) Picture Window Bks.

Roche, Denis. Little Pig Is Capable. 2002. (Illus.). 32p. (J). (ps-3). lib. bdg. 15.00 (*0-395-91368-3*) Houghton Mifflin Co.

Rockwell, Anne F. Ducklings & Pollywogs. 1994. (Illus.). 32p. (J). (ps-2). pap. 14.95 (*0-02-777452-X*, Simon & Schuster Children's Publishing) Simon & Schuster Children's Publishing.

Rockwell, Anne F. & Rockwell, Harlow. Can I Help? 1982. (My World Ser.). (Illus.). 24p. (J). (ps-k). lib. bdg. 9.95 o.s.i (*0-02-777720-0*, Simon & Schuster Children's Publishing) Simon & Schuster Children's Publishing.

Rodgers, Mary. Freaky Friday. 1972. (J). (gr. 5 up). 160p. 15.95 (*0-06-025048-8*); 160p. lib. bdg. 16.89 (*0-06-025049-6*); (Illus.). 144p. reprint ed. pap. 5.99 (*0-06-440046-8*, Harper Trophy) HarperCollins Children's Bk. Group.

—Freaky Friday. 1977. (J). (gr. 7 up). pap. 2.95 o.p. (*0-06-080392-4*, P392, Perennial) HarperTrade.

—Freaky Friday. l.t. ed. 1988. 184p. (J). (gr. 3-7). reprint ed. lib. bdg. 16.95 o.s.i (*1-55736-027-8*, Cornerstone Bks.) Pages, Inc.

—Freaky Friday. 1972. (J). 11.00 (*0-606-04374-8*) Turtleback Bks.

Rodowsky, Colby. Hannah in Between, RS. 1994. 160p. (YA). (gr. 7 up). 15.00 o.p. (*0-374-32837-4*, Farrar, Straus & Giroux (BYR)) Farrar, Straus & Giroux.

—The Turnabout Shop, RS. 1998. 144p. (J). (gr. 4-7). 16.00 (*0-374-37889-4*, Farrar, Straus & Giroux (BYR)) Farrar, Straus & Giroux.

—The Turnabout Shop. 2000. (Illus.). 144p. (J). (gr. 3-7). pap. 4.95 (*0-380-73192-4*, Harper Trophy) HarperCollins Children's Bk. Group.

—The Turnabout Shop. 2000. 11.00 (*0-606-17885-6*) Turtleback Bks.

Rosen, Michael J. Fishing with Dad. 2003. (Illus.). 32p. (J). tchr. ed. 14.95 (*1-885183-38-0*) Artisan.

Rosenberg, Liz. Heart & Soul. 1996. 224p. (YA). (gr. 7 up). pap. 5.00 o.s.i (*0-15-201270-2*, Harcourt Paperbacks) Harcourt Children's Bks.

—Heart & Soul. 1996. 224p. (YA). (gr. 7 up). 11.00 (*0-15-200942-6*) Harcourt Trade Pubs.

—We Wanted You. 1999. (J). (*0-7894-2600-5*) Dorling Kindersley Publishing, Inc.

—We Wanted You. 2002. (Illus.). 32p. (J). (gr. k-4). 23.90 (*0-7613-2661-8*); 16.95 (*0-7613-1597-7*) Millbrook Pr., Inc. (Roaring Brook Pr.).

Ross, Kent & Ross, Alice. Jezebel's Spooky Spot. 1999. (Illus.). 32p. (J). (gr. 1-4). 15.99 o.p. (*0-525-45448-9*, Dutton Children's Bks.) Penguin Putnam Bks. for Young Readers.

Ross, Ramon R. The Dancing Tree. 1995. 64p. (J). (gr. 4-7). 14.00 (*0-689-80072-X*, Atheneum) Simon & Schuster Children's Publishing.

Ross, Rhea B. Hillbilly Choir. 1991. 186p. (YA). (gr. 7 up). 13.95 o.p. (*0-395-53356-2*) Houghton Mifflin Co.

Ross-Rodgers, Martha J. Awakenings. rev. ed. 1998. 120p. (YA). pap. 9.95 (*0-9653197-0-9*) Jireh Pubs.

Rosselson, Leon. Where's My Mom? 1994. (Illus.). 32p. (J). (ps up). 13.95 o.p. (*1-56402-392-3*) Candlewick Pr.

Roy, J. Soul Daddy. 1992. 224p. (YA). (gr. 7 up). 16.95 o.s.i (*0-15-277193-X*, Gulliver Bks.) Harcourt Children's Bks.

Roybal, Laura. Billy. 240p. (YA). (gr. 7 up). 1999. pap. 5.95 o.p. (*0-395-96062-2*); 1994. tchr. ed. 16.00 o.p. (*0-395-67649-5*) Houghton Mifflin Co.

Rubalcaba, Jill. A Place in the Sun. 1997. 96p. (J). (gr. 4-6). tchr. ed. 15.00 (*0-395-82645-4*) Houghton Mifflin Co.

—A Place in the Sun. 1998. 11.14 (*0-606-17147-9*) Turtleback Bks.

—Place in the Sun. 1998. (Puffin Novel Ser.). 96p. (J). (gr. 3-7). pap. 4.99 (*0-14-130123-6*) Penguin Putnam Bks. for Young Readers.

Rue, Nancy. The Invasion. 1998. (Christian Heritage Ser.). 192p. (J). (gr. 3-7). pap. 5.99 (*1-56179-541-0*) Focus on the Family Publishing.

—The Rebel. 1998. (Christian Heritage Ser.). 192p. (J). (gr. 3-7). pap. 5.99 (*1-56179-478-3*) Focus on the Family Publishing.

Ruhmann, Karl. But I Want To! James, J. Alison, tr. from GER. 2002. (Illus.). 32p. (J). 15.95 (*0-7358-1604-2*); lib. bdg. 16.50 (*0-7358-1605-0*) North-South Bks., Inc. (Michael Neugebauer Bks.).

Ruiz-Flores, Lupe. Lupita's Papalote / el Papalote de Lupita. Ventura, Gabriela Baeza, tr. from ENG. 2002. (ENG & SPA., Illus.). 32p. (J). (gr. k-2). 14.95 (*1-55885-359-6*, Piñata Books) Arte Publico Pr.

Rusackas, Francesca. I Love You All Day Long. 2002. (Illus.). 32p. (J). (ps-k). 12.99 (*0-06-050276-2*); lib. bdg. 14.89 (*0-06-050277-0*) HarperCollins Children's Bk. Group.

Rush, Ken. Friday's Journey. 1994. (Illus.). 32p. (J). (ps-1). 15.95 o.p. (*0-531-06821-8*); mass mkt. 16.99 o.p. (*0-531-08671-2*) Scholastic, Inc. (Orchard Bks.).

Rushton, Rosie. What a Week to Break Free. (Illus.). 144p. (J). pap. 7.95 (*0-14-038762-5*) Penguin Bks., Ltd. GBR. *Dist:* Trafalgar Square.

Russell, Barbara T. The Remembering Stone, RS. 2004. (J). 16.00 (*0-374-36242-4*, Farrar, Straus & Giroux (BYR)) Farrar, Straus & Giroux.

Russo, Marisabina. Time to Wake Up! 1994. (Illus.). 24p. (J). (ps up). 14.00 o.p. (*0-688-04599-5*); lib. bdg. 13.93 o.p. (*0-688-04600-2*) HarperCollins Children's Bk. Group. (Greenwillow Bks.).

—Trade-in Mother. 1993. (Illus.). 32p. (J). (ps up). lib. bdg. 13.93 o.p. (*0-688-11417-2*, Greenwillow Bks.) HarperCollins Children's Bk. Group.

—Under the Table. 1997. (Illus.). 32p. (J). (ps up). 15.00 o.s.i (*0-688-14602-3*); lib. bdg. 14.93 o.p. (*0-688-14603-1*) HarperCollins Children's Bk. Group. (Greenwillow Bks.).

—When Mama Gets Home. 1998. (Illus.). (J). (gr. k-2). 32p. lib. bdg. 14.93 o.p. (*0-688-14986-3*); 2p. 15.99 (*0-688-14985-5*) HarperCollins Children's Bk. Group. (Greenwillow Bks.).

Ryan, Susan Jane. Esmeralda & the Enchanted Pond. 2001. (Illus.). (J). (gr. 2-5). 14.95 (*1-56164-236-3*) Pineapple Pr., Inc.

Ryan, Susan Jane & Cook, Sandra G. Esmeralda & the Enchanted Pond. 2001. 40p. (J). (gr. 4-7). pap. 5.00 (*1-56164-247-9*) Pineapple Pr., Inc.

Rylant, Cynthia. Birthday Presents. (Illus.). 32p. (J). (ps-1). 1991. mass mkt. 6.95 (*0-531-07026-3*); 1987. 14.95 o.p. (*0-531-05705-4*); 1987. mass mkt. 15.99 o.p. (*0-531-08305-5*) Scholastic, Inc. (Orchard Bks.).

—Birthday Presents. 1987. 12.10 (*0-606-09079-7*) Turtleback Bks.

Sachs, Marilyn. Call Me Ruth. 1995. 224p. (J). (gr. 4-7). pap. 4.95 (*0-688-13737-7*, Harper Trophy) HarperCollins Children's Bk. Group.

—Call Me Ruth. 1996. (J). (gr. 3 up). 18.75 o.p. (*0-8446-6905-9*) Smith, Peter Pub., Inc.

—Call Me Ruth. 1995. 11.00 (*0-606-07333-7*) Turtleback Bks.

—Ghosts in the Family. 1995. 176p. (J). (gr. 3-6). 15.99 o.s.i (*0-525-45421-7*, Dutton Children's Bks.) Penguin Putnam Bks. for Young Readers.

Sacks, Margaret. Themba. 1992. (Illus.). 48p. (J). (gr. 2-5). 12.00 o.p. (*0-525-67414-4*, Dutton Children's Bks.) Penguin Putnam Bks. for Young Readers.

Saldana, Rene, Jr. The Jumping Tree. 2002. (Illus.). 192p. (YA). (gr. 5). mass mkt. 5.50 (*0-440-22881-6*, Laurel Leaf) Random Hse. Children's Bks.

—The Jumping Tree: A Novel. 2001. (Illus.). 192p. (YA). (gr. 5-9). 14.95 (*0-385-32725-0*, Delacorte Bks. for Young Readers) Random Hse. Children's Bks.

Salisbury, Graham. Blue Skin of the Sea. 1997. 224p. pap. text 3.99 o.s.i (*0-440-41359-1*, Yearling); 1994. (J). mass mkt. o.s.i (*0-440-90121-9*, Dell Books for Young Readers) Random Hse. Children's Bks.

—Blue Skin of the Sea: A Novel in Stories. 1994. 224p. (gr. 5 up). mass mkt. 4.99 (*0-440-21905-1*) Dell Publishing.

—Blue Skin of the Sea: A Novel in Stories. 1992. 224p. (J). (gr. 4-7). 15.95 (*0-385-30596-6*) Doubleday Publishing.

—Blue Skin of the Sea: A Novel in Stories. 1997. (J). 10.04 (*0-606-11144-1*) Turtleback Bks.

Salmansohn, Karen, et al. Crashed, Smashed & Mashed: One Puppy, Three Tales. 2003. (Alexandra Rambles on! Ser.). (Illus.). 32p. (J). (gr. 3-6). 14.95 (*1-58246-034-5*) Tricycle Pr.

Saltzberg, Barney. The Soccer Mom from Outer Space. (Illus.). 40p. (J). (gr. k-3). 2002. pap. 6.99 (*0-440-41758-9*, Delacorte Bks. for Young Readers); 2000. 15.95 (*0-517-80063-2*, Random Hse. Bks. for Young Readers); 2000. lib. bdg. 17.99 o.s.i (*0-517-80064-0*, Random Hse. Bks. for Young Readers) Random Hse. Children's Bks.

Saltzburg, Barney. Show & Tell. 1994. (Illus.). 32p. (J). (gr. k-3). 14.95 (*0-7868-0020-8*); lib. bdg. 15.49 (*0-7868-2016-0*) Hyperion Bks. for Children.

Santucci, Barbara. Loon Summer. 2001. (Illus.). 16p. (J). (gr. k-3). 16.00 (*0-8028-5182-7*, Eerdmans Bks For Young Readers) Eerdmans, William B. Publishing Co.

Schecter, Ellen. Swim Like a Fish. 1997. (J). pap. 4.50 (*0-553-53133-6*); (Illus.). 32p. pap. 4.50 o.s.i (*0-553-37583-0*) Random Hse. Children's Bks. (Dell Books for Young Readers).

—Swim Like a Fish. 1998. (Bank Street Reader Collection). (Illus.). 48p. (J). (ps-2). lib. bdg. 21.26 (*0-8368-1767-2*) Stevens, Gareth Inc.

—Swim Like a Fish. 2000. (J). E-Book (*1-58824-195-5*); 1997. E-Book (*1-58824-107-6*); 1997. E-Book (*1-59019-336-9*) ipicturebooks, LLC.

Scheffler, Ursel. Who Has Time for Little Bear? 1998. (Illus.). 32p. (J). (ps-3). 13.95 (*0-385-32536-3*) Doubleday Publishing.

Schertle, Alice. Down the Road. (Illus.). 40p. (J). (gr. k-3). 2000. pap. 6.00 (*0-15-202471-9*, Harcourt Paperbacks); 1995. 16.00 (*0-15-276622-7*) Harcourt Children's Bks.

—Down the Road. 2000. 12.15 (*0-606-20324-9*) Turtleback Bks.

—That's What I Thought. 1990. (Illus.). 32p. (J). (gr. k-3). 13.95 (*0-06-025204-9*); lib. bdg. 13.89 o.p. (*0-06-025205-7*) HarperCollins Children's Bk. Group.

Schick, Eleanor. Mama. 2000. (Accelerated Reader Bks.). (Illus.). 32p. (J). (gr. k-3). 15.95 (*0-7614-5060-2*, Cavendish Children's Bks.) Cavendish, Marshall Corp.

Schlee, Ann. The Consul's Daughter. 1972. (J). (gr. 5-8). 1.29 o.p. (*0-689-30065-4*, Atheneum) Simon & Schuster Children's Publishing.

Schlein, Miriam. Big Talk. 2nd rev. ed. 1990. (Illus.). 32p. (J). (ps-1). lib. bdg. 13.95 o.p. (*0-02-781231-6*, Simon & Schuster Children's Publishing) Simon & Schuster Children's Publishing.

—Just Like Me. 1993. (Illus.). 32p. (J). (ps-2). 12.95 o.s.i (*1-56282-233-0*); lib. bdg. 13.49 o.s.i (*1-56282-234-9*) Hyperion Bks. for Children.

—Just Like Me. 1995. (Illus.). 32p. (J). (gr. 4-7). pap. 4.95 (*0-7868-1037-8*) Hyperion Paperbacks for Children.

—Just Like Me. 1998. (Illus.). 24p. (J). (ps). 5.95 (*0-7868-0401-7*) Hyperion Pr.

Schlessinger, Laura. Growing up Is Hard. 2003. (Illus.). 40p. (J). (ps-2). pap. 5.99 (*0-06-052623-8*, Harper Trophy) HarperCollins Children's Bk. Group.

—I Hate My Life! 2001. (Illus.). 40p. (J). (ps-2). 15.95 (*0-06-029200-8*) HarperCollins Children's Bk. Group.

Schlessinger, Laura & Lambert, Martha L. Why Do You Love Me? 1999. (Illus.). 40p. (J). (ps-2). 15.95 (*0-06-027866-8*) HarperCollins Children's Bk. Group.

Schlessinger, Laura & McFeeley, Daniel. Growing up Is Hard. 2001. (Illus.). 40p. (J). (ps-2). lib. bdg. 15.89 (*0-06-029201-6*) HarperCollins Children's Bk. Group.

Schlessinger, Laura, et al. Why Do You Love Me? 2001. (Illus.). 40p. (J). (ps-2). pap. 5.99 (*0-06-443654-3*, Harper Trophy) HarperCollins Children's Bk. Group.

Schnur, Steven. Beyond Providence. 1996. 256p. (YA). (gr. 7 up). 12.00 (*0-15-200982-5*) Harcourt Children's Bks.

Schotter, Roni. Missing Rabbit. 2002. (Illus.). 32p. (J). (gr. k-ps). lib. bdg. 15.00 (*0-618-03432-3*, Clarion Bks.) Houghton Mifflin Co. Trade & Reference Div.

Schraff, Anne. The Greatest Heroes. 2000. 143p. (J). (*0-7807-9271-8*); pap. (*0-7891-5133-2*) Perfection Learning Corp.

Schreier, Joshua. Hank's Work. 1993. 320p. (J). (ps-2). 13.50 o.p. (*0-525-44970-1*, Dutton Children's Bks.) Penguin Putnam Bks. for Young Readers.

Schroder, Jack. Looking for Sean's Father. 1995. 248p. (Orig.). (YA). pap. text 7.95 (*1-56002-486-0*, University Editions) Aegina Pr., Inc.

—Looking for Sean's Father. 1990. (Orig.). (YA). per. 7.95 net. (*0-9745665-4-3*) Catalpa Pr.

Schwartz, Amy. Some Babies. 2000. (Illus.). 32p. (J). (ps-k). pap. 15.95 (*0-531-30287-3*); lib. bdg. 16.99 (*0-531-33287-X*, Orchard Bks.) Scholastic, Inc.

—What's That Mom? What's That? 1998. (Think-Kids Book Collection). (Illus.). 16p. (J). (gr. 1-4). pap. 2.95 (*1-58237-010-9*) Creative Thinkers, Inc.

Tocher, Timothy. Long Shot. 2001. 137p. (J). (*0-88166-395-6*) Meadowbrook Pr.

Trent, John T. I'd Choose You: Giving the Blessing to Your Child. 1994. (Illus.). 32p. (J). (ps-2). 12.99 (*0-8499-1165-6*) Nelson, Tommy.

Turner, Ann. Through Moon & Stars & Night Skys. 2001. (First Readers Ser.: Vol. 2). (J). lib. bdg. (*1-59054-264-9*) Fitzgerald Bks.

Turner, Ann Warren. One Brave Summer. 1995. (J). 13.95 o.p. (*0-06-023732-5*) HarperCollins Pubs.

—One Brave Summer. 1995. 80p. (J). lib. bdg. 13.89 o.p. (*0-06-023875-5*) HarperTrade.

Udry, Janice May. Is Susan Here? 1993. (Illus.). 24p. (J). (gr. k-3). 14.00 (*0-06-026142-0*); lib. bdg. 13.89 o.p. (*0-06-026143-9*) HarperCollins Children's Bk. Group.

Ungerer, Tomi. The Mellops Go Spelunking. 1998. (Illus.). 32p. (J). (gr. k-4). pap. 5.95 (*1-57098-228-7*) Rinehart, Roberts Pubs.

—No Kiss for Mother. 1998. (Illus.). 40p. (J). (ps-3). pap. text 5.95 (*1-57098-208-2*) Rinehart, Roberts Pubs.

Vail, Rachel. The (Almost) Perfect Mother's Day. 2003. (Mama Rex & T Ser.). (Illus.). 32p. (J). pap. 14.95 (*0-439-40718-4*, Orchard Bks.) Scholastic, Inc.

—Do-Over. 1994. (YA). (gr. 7 up). pap. 3.99 (*0-380-72180-5*, Avon Bks.) Morrow/Avon.

—Do-Over. 1992. 160p. (YA). (gr. 6 up). mass mkt. 16.99 o.p. (*0-531-08610-0*); (gr. 7 up). pap. 15.95 (*0-531-05460-8*) Scholastic, Inc. (Orchard Bks.).

—Do-Over. 1994. 10.04 (*0-606-15505-8*); 1992. 9.09 o.p. (*0-606-06329-3*) Turtleback Bks.

—Mama Rex & T: Homework Trouble. 2002. (Mama Rex & T Ser.). (Illus.). 32p. (J). (gr. k-2). pap. 14.95 (*0-439-40628-5*); mass mkt. 4.99 (*0-439-42616-2*); pap. 4.99 (*0-439-33281-8*) Scholastic, Inc. (Orchard Bks.).

—Mama Rex & T: Lose a Waffle. 2000. (Mama Rex & T Ser.). (Illus.). (J). (*0-439-19918-2*) Scholastic, Inc.

—Mama Rex & T: Run Out of Tape. 2001. (Mama Rex & T Ser.). (Illus.). (J). (*0-439-19920-4*) Scholastic, Inc.

—Mama Rex & T: The (Almost) Perfect Mother's Day. 2003. (Mama Rex & T Ser.). (Illus.). 32p. (J). mass mkt. 4.99 (*0-439-46684-9*, Orchard Bks.) Scholastic, Inc.

—Mama Rex & T: The Horrible Play Date. 2002. (Mama Rex & T Ser.). (Illus.). 32p. (J). pap. 14.95 (*0-439-40627-7*); pap. 4.99 (*0-439-28335-3*); mass mkt. 4.99 (*0-439-42617-0*) Scholastic, Inc. (Orchard Bks.).

—Mama Rex & T: Turn off the TV. 2003. (Mama Rex & T Ser.). (Illus.). 32p. (J). mass mkt. 4.99 (*0-439-46681-4*, Orchard Bks.) Scholastic, Inc.

—Please, Please, Please: CJ. (Friendship Ring Ser.: No. 2). 240p. (J). (gr. 4-8). 1999. mass mkt. 3.99 (*0-439-08762-7*); 1998. pap. 14.95 (*0-590-00327-5*); 1998. mass mkt. 4.99 (*0-590-37452-4*) Scholastic, Inc.

—Stay up Late. 2003. (Mama Rex & T Ser.). 32p. (J). mass mkt. 4.99 (*0-439-46682-2*, Orchard Bks.) Scholastic, Inc.

—Turn off the TV. 2003. (Mama Rex & T Ser.). (Illus.). 32p. (J). pap. 14.95 (*0-439-40717-6*, Orchard Bks.) Scholastic, Inc.

Valens, Amy. Jesse's Day Care. 1990. (Illus.). 32p. (J). (ps-2). 13.95 o.p. (*0-395-53357-0*) Houghton Mifflin Co.

Valriu, Caterina. Thumbelina. (ENG & SPA.). (J). 13.95 (*0-8118-3927-3*); pap. 6.95 (*0-8118-3928-1*) Chronicle Bks. LLC.

Van Laan, Nancy. Little Fish, Lost. 1998. (Illus.). 32p. (J). (ps-2). 15.00 (*0-689-81331-7*, Atheneum/Anne Schwartz Bks.) Simon & Schuster Children's Publishing.

—Scrubba Dub. 2003. (Illus.). 32p. (J). 15.95 (*0-689-84459-X*, Atheneum/Anne Schwartz Bks.) Simon & Schuster Children's Publishing.

Van Laan, Nancy & Fudym, Bernadette Pons, illus. Tickle Tum. 2001. 32p. (J). (ps). 14.95 (*0-689-83143-9*, Atheneum/Anne Schwartz Bks.) Simon & Schuster Children's Publishing.

Vanasse, Debra. Out of the Wilderness. 1999. 176p. (J). (gr. 5-9). tchr. ed. 15.00 (*0-395-91421-3*, Clarion Bks.) Houghton Mifflin Co. Trade & Reference Div.

Vander Zee, Ruth. Mississippi Morning. 2003. (J). (*0-8028-5211-4*, Eerdmans Bks For Young Readers) Eerdmans, William B. Publishing Co.

Vendrell, Carmesole. Jon's Moon. 1999. Orig. Title: La Luna de Juan. (Illus.). 36p. (J). (gr. 4-7). 13.95 o.p. (*0-916291-87-1*) Kane/Miller Bk. Pubs.

Vertreace, Martha. Kelly in the Mirror. 1993. (Illus.). 32p. (J). (gr. 1-3). lib. bdg. 14.95 o.p. (*0-8075-4152-4*) Whitman, Albert & Co.

Vigna, Judith. I Live with Daddy. 1997. 32p. (J). (gr. 1-4). lib. bdg. 14.95 (*0-8075-3512-5*) Whitman, Albert & Co.

—When Eric's Mom Fought Cancer. ed. 2000. (gr. 2). spiral bd. (*0-616-03063-0*) Canadian National Institute for the Blind/Institut National Canadien pour les Aveugles.

—When Eric's Mom Fought Cancer. 1993. (J). (Illus.). lib. bdg. 14.95 o.p. (*0-8075-2133-7*); 32p. lib. bdg. 14.95 o.p. (*0-8075-8883-0*) Whitman, Albert & Co.

Viorst, Judith. The Good-Bye Book. (Illus.). 32p. (J). (ps-3). 1988. 16.00 (*0-689-31308-X*, Atheneum); 1992. reprint ed. pap. 5.99 (*0-689-71581-1*, Aladdin) Simon & Schuster Children's Publishing.

—The Good-Bye Book. 1992. 12.14 (*0-606-01572-8*) Turtleback Bks.

Voake, Charlotte. Mrs. Goose's Baby. 1997. (Illus.). 24p. (J). (ps-1). bds. 4.99 (*0-7636-0092-X*) Candlewick Pr.

—Mrs. Goose's Baby. 1992. 32p. (J). (ps). pap. 3.99 o.s.i (*0-440-40615-3*) Dell Publishing.

—Mrs. Goose's Baby. 1989. (Illus.). 24p. (J). (ps-1). 12.95 o.p. (*0-316-90511-9*, Joy Street Bks.) Little Brown & Co.

Voigt, Cynthia. Building Blocks. 1985. 128p. mass mkt. 3.99 o.s.i (*0-449-70130-1*, Fawcett) Ballantine Bks.

—Building Blocks. 1994. 128p. (YA). (gr. 7-9). mass mkt. 3.95 (*0-590-47732-3*) Scholastic, Inc.

—Building Blocks. (J). (gr. 3-7). 2002. 176p. pap. 4.99 (*0-689-85105-7*, Aladdin); 1984. 132p. lib. bdg. 14.95 o.s.i (*0-689-31035-8*, Atheneum) Simon & Schuster Children's Publishing.

—Building Blocks. 1984. (Point Ser.). 9.05 o.p. (*0-606-06256-4*) Turtleback Bks.

—A Solitary Blue. 1987. (YA). (gr. 6 up). mass mkt. 3.95 o.s.i (*0-449-70268-5*, Fawcett) Ballantine Bks.

—A Solitary Blue. l.t. ed. 2001. 369p. (J). lib. bdg. 33.95 net. (*1-58118-085-3*) LRS.

—A Solitary Blue. 1993. (Point Ser.). 320p. (J). (gr. 7 up). mass mkt. 4.99 (*0-590-47157-0*) Scholastic, Inc.

—A Solitary Blue. (Tillerman Ser.). 2003. 256p. (J). pap. 5.99 (*0-689-86360-8*, Aladdin); 2003. (Illus.). 256p. (YA). mass mkt. 5.99 (*0-689-86434-5*, Simon Pulse); 2001. 204p. (J). E-Book 6.99 (*0-689-84799-8*, Atheneum); 1983. 204p. (YA). (gr. 7 up). 18.00 (*0-689-31008-0*, Atheneum) Simon & Schuster Children's Publishing.

—A Solitary Blue. 1983. (Point Ser.). (J). 11.04 (*0-606-05611-4*) Turtleback Bks.

—Sons from Afar. 1988. 3.95p. mass mkt. 4.50 o.s.i (*0-449-70293-6*, Fawcett) Ballantine Bks.

—Sons from Afar. (gr. 7 up). 1996. 256p. mass mkt. 5.50 (*0-689-80889-5*, Simon Pulse); 1987. 224p. (YA). lib. bdg. 15.95 (*0-689-31349-7*, Atheneum) Simon & Schuster Children's Publishing.

—Sons from Afar. 1996. 11.55 (*0-606-10935-8*) Turtleback Bks.

—When She Hollers. 192p. (gr. 7 up). 2003. (J). pap. 5.99 (*0-590-46715-8*, Scholastic Paperbacks); 1994. (YA). pap. 13.95 o.p. (*0-590-46714-X*) Scholastic, Inc.

—When She Hollers. 1994. 9.09 o.p. (*0-606-08901-2*) Turtleback Bks.

Vulliamy, Clara. Wide Awake! 1996. (Illus.). (J). (ps). bds. 4.99 o.p. (*1-56402-816-X*) Candlewick Pr.

Waddell, Martin. The Big Big Sea. (Illus.). 32p. (J). (ps-3). 1998. bds. 5.99 o.s.i (*0-7636-0282-5*); 1994. 15.95 o.s.i (*1-56402-066-5*) Candlewick Pr.

—The Big Big Sea. 1998. 12.14 (*0-606-13201-5*) Turtleback Bks.

—Las Lechucitas. 1995. (SPA., Illus.). 14p. (J). (gr. k-3). 16.95 (*0-88272-137-2*) Santillana USA Publishing Co., Inc.

—Owl Babies. 2002. (Illus.). (J). 13.83 (*1-4046-3008-2*) Book Wholesalers, Inc.

—Owl Babies. (Illus.). 2003. 22p. 12.99 (*0-7636-2157-9*); 2002. 32p. (J). pap. 5.99 (*0-7636-1710-5*); 2000. 32p. (J). bds. 19.99 (*0-7636-1283-9*); 1992. 32p. (J). 15.99 (*1-56402-101-7*); 1996. 32p. (J). reprint ed. bds. 6.99 (*1-56402-965-4*) Candlewick Pr.

—Owl Babies. (BEN, CHI, ENG, GUJ & PAN., Illus.). 25p. (J). 1995. (*1-85430-344-9*); 1995. (*1-85430-345-7*); 1995. (*1-85430-346-5*); 1995. (*1-85430-342-2*); 1995. (*1-85430-347-3*); (*1-85430-343-0*, 93441); (*1-85430-348-1*, 93442) Magi Pubns.

—Snow Bears. 2002. (Illus.). 32p. (J). (ps-1). 14.99 (*0-7636-1906-X*) Candlewick Pr.

—Yum Yum Yummy. 1998. (Giggle Club Ser.). (Illus.). 24p. (J). (ps-1). 9.99 o.p. (*0-7636-0477-1*); bds. 3.29 o.s.i (*0-7636-0479-8*) Candlewick Pr.

Wahl, Jan. Christmas Present. 1999. (Illus.). 64p. (J). (gr. 5-9). 18.00 (*1-56846-165-8*, Creative Editions) Creative Co., The.

Wallace, Bill. Buffalo Gal. 1992. 192p. (J). (gr. 7 up). tchr. ed. 15.95 (*0-8234-0943-0*) Holiday Hse., Inc.

—Buffalo Gal. MacDonald, Patricia, ed. 1993. 192p. (J). (gr. 4-7). reprint ed. pap. 3.99 (*0-671-79899-5*, Aladdin) Simon & Schuster Children's Publishing.

—Buffalo Gal. 1992. (J). 10.04 (*0-606-05175-9*) Turtleback Bks.

—Skinny-Dipping at Monster Lake. 2003. (Illus.). 224p. (J). 16.95 (*0-689-85150-2*, Simon & Schuster Children's Publishing) Simon & Schuster Children's Publishing.

Wallace, Ian. Boy of the Deeps. 1999. (Illus.). 40p. (J). (gr. 3-6). pap. 16.95 o.p. (*0-7894-2569-6*, D K Ink) Dorling Kindersley Publishing, Inc.

Walter, Mildred Pitts. My Mama Needs Me. 1983. (Illus.). 32p. (J). lib. bdg. 15.93 o.p. (*0-688-01671-5*); 16.00 o.p. (*0-688-01670-7*) HarperCollins Children's Bk. Group.

—Ray & the Best Family Reunion Ever. (Amistad Ser.). (Illus.). 128p. (J). 2002. lib. bdg. 15.89 (*0-06-623625-8*); 2001. 15.95 (*0-06-623624-X*) HarperTrade. (Amistad Pr.).

Walters, Catherine. Play Gently, Alfie Bear. 2002. (Illus.). 32p. (J). (ps-k). 15.99 (*0-525-46885-4*, Dutton Children's Bks.) Penguin Putnam Bks. for Young Readers.

Walters, Virginia. Are We There Yet, Daddy? 1999. (Illus.). 32p. (J). (ps-3). 15.99 (*0-670-87402-7*, Viking Children's Bks.) Penguin Putnam Bks. for Young Readers.

Walton, Darwin M. Dance, Kayla! 1998. 160p. (J). (gr. 4-6). lib. bdg. 14.95 o.p. (*0-8075-1453-5*) Whitman, Albert & Co.

Walton, Rick. Will You Still Love Me? 1992. (Illus.). 32p. (J). (ps-3). 12.95 (*0-87579-582-X*) Deseret Bk. Co.

Walvoord, Linda. Razzamadaddy. Yoshikawa, Sachiko, tr. & illus. by. 2004. (J). (*0-7614-5158-7*, Cavendish Children's Bks.) Cavendish, Marshall Corp.

Wardlaw, Lee. 101 Ways to Bug Your Parents. 2002. 160p. pap. (*0-14-038739-0*); 1999. (J). (gr. 4-7). pap. 14.89 (*0-8037-1902-7*, Dial Bks. for Young Readers); 1996. 208p. (YA). (gr. 4-7). 16.99 (*0-8037-1901-9*, Dial Bks. for Young Readers) Penguin Putnam Bks. for Young Readers.

—101 Ways to Bug Your Parents. 1998. (J). 10.55 (*0-606-13076-4*) Turtleback Bks.

Ware, Jim. Crazy Jacob. 2000. (Kidwitness Tales Ser.). (Illus.). 128p. (J). (gr. 3-7). pap. 5.99 (*1-56179-885-1*) Bethany Hse. Pubs.

Waring, Shirley B. What Happened to Benjamin: A True Story. 1993. (Illus.). 38p. (J). (gr. k-6). pap. 13.95 (*0-9622808-2-8*); pap. 9.98 incl. audio (*0-9622808-3-6*) Waring, Shirley & Thomas Pubs.

Watson, Nancy D. Tommy's Mommy's Fish. 1971. (J). (ps-2). 4.50 o.p. (*0-670-71926-9*) Viking Penguin.

Watts, Leander. Wild Ride to Heaven. 2003. 176p. (J). (gr. 5-9). tchr. ed. 16.00 (*0-618-26805-7*) Houghton Mifflin Co.

Waugh, Sylvia. Space Race. 256p. (gr. 5 up). 2001. pap. text 4.99 (*0-440-41714-7*, Yearling); 2000. (Illus.). text 15.95 o.s.i (*0-385-32766-8*, Dell Books for Young Readers) Random Hse. Children's Bks.

—Space Race. l.t. ed. 2001. 300p. (J). 20.95 (*0-7862-3606-X*) Thorndike Pr.

Weaver, Will. Hard Ball: A Billy Baggs Novel. l.t. ed. 2000. (Illus.). 270p. (YA). (gr. 8-12). 20.95 (*0-7862-2752-4*) Thorndike Pr.

—Striking Out. (J). 1995. (Illus.). 304p. (gr. 6 up). pap. 6.99 (*0-06-447113-6*, Harper Trophy); 1993. 288p. (gr. 5 up). 15.00 o.p. (*0-06-023346-X*); 1993. 288p. (gr. 5 up). lib. bdg. 14.89 o.p. (*0-06-023347-8*) HarperCollins Children's Bk. Group.

—Striking Out. 1995. (J). 11.00 (*0-606-08211-5*) Turtleback Bks.

Weeks, Sarah. Guy Time. 176p. (J). (gr. 3-7). 2001. pap. 5.99 (*0-06-440783-7*, Harper Trophy); 2000. (Illus.). 14.95 (*0-06-028365-3*, Geringer, Laura Bk.); 2000. (Illus.). lib. bdg. 15.89 (*0-06-028366-1*, Geringer, Laura Bk.) HarperCollins Children's Bk. Group.

—Guy Wire. 2002. 144p. (J). lib. bdg. 17.89 (*0-06-029493-0*); (gr. 3-7). 15.99 (*0-06-029492-2*) HarperCollins Children's Bk. Group. (Geringer, Laura Bk.).

—My Guy. 2001. (Illus.). 192p. (J). (gr. 3-7). 14.95 (*0-06-028369-6*); lib. bdg. 14.89 (*0-06-028370-X*) HarperCollins Children's Bk. Group. (Geringer, Laura Bk.).

—My Guy. 2003. 192p. (J). (gr. 3-7). pap. 5.99 (*0-06-440781-0*) HarperCollins Pubs.

—My Somebody Special. 2002. (Illus.). 40p. (J). (ps-k). 16.00 (*0-15-202561-8*, Gulliver Bks.) Harcourt Children's Bks.

—Regular Guy. 1999. (Illus.). 128p. (J). (gr. 3-7). 14.95 (*0-06-028367-X*, Geringer, Laura Bk.) HarperCollins Children's Bk. Group.

—Without You. 2003. 40p. (J). (ps-2). lib. bdg. 17.89 (*0-06-000733-8*); (Illus.). 16.99 (*0-06-027816-1*) HarperCollins Children's Bk. Group.

Weiss, E. & Friedman, M. The Poof Point. 1992. (J). (gr. 3-7). 14.00 o.s.i (*0-679-83257-2*); 14.99 o.s.i (*0-679-93257-7*) Random Hse. Children's Bks. (Knopf Bks. for Young Readers).

Weiss, Ellen & de Brunhoff, Laurent. Babar Goes to School. 2003. (Illus.). 32p. (J). 9.95 (*0-8109-4582-7*) Abrams, Harry N. , Inc.

Weiss, Nicki. On a Hot, Hot Day. 1992. (Illus.). 32p. (J). (ps-1). 13.95 o.p. (*0-399-22119-0*, G. P. Putnam's Sons) Penguin Group (USA) Inc.

Wells, Rosemary. The Bear Went over the Mountain. 1998. (Bruno & Boots Book Ser.). (Illus.). 16p. (J). (ps). bds. 5.99 (*0-590-02910-X*) Scholastic, Inc.

—Only You. 2003. (Illus.). 24p. (J). 14.99 (*0-670-03634-X*, Viking) Viking Penguin.

Weninger, Brigitte, pseud. Good-Bye, Daddy! (Illus.). 32p. (J). (gr. k-3). 1997. pap. 6.95 (*1-55858-770-5*); 1995. 14.95 (*1-55858-383-1*); 1995. 15.50 o.p. (*1-55858-384-X*) North-South Bks., Inc.

Weninger, Brigitte, pseud, et al. Special Delivery. James, J. Alison, tr. from GER. 2000. (Illus.). 32p. (J). (ps-2). 15.95 o.p. (*0-7358-1318-3*) North-South Bks., Inc.

Westall, Robert. A Place to Hide. 1994. 208p. (YA). (gr. 5 up). 13.95 (*0-590-47748-X*) Scholastic, Inc.

Westerhout, Lynn. Business in Bangkok. 2001. (Illus.). 24p. (J). (ps-3). 10.95 (*1-896764-48-7*) Second Story Pr. CAN. *Dist:* Univ. of Toronto Pr.

Whelan, Gloria. Jam & Jelly by Holly & Nellie. 2002. (Illus.). 48p. (J). (ps-5). 17.95 (*1-58536-109-7*) Sleeping Bear Pr.

—A Time to Keep Silent. 1993. 124p. (J). (gr. 4-9). pap. 6.00 (*0-8028-0118-8*, Eerdmans Bks For Young Readers) Eerdmans, William B. Publishing Co.

—A Time to Keep Silent. 1979. (J). (gr. 7-12). 7.95 o.p. (*0-399-20693-0*) Putnam Publishing Group, The.

White, Ruth. Belle Prater's Boy. l.t. ed. 2000. (Illus.). 221p. (YA). (gr. 4-7). 21.95 (*0-7862-2885-7*) Thorndike Pr.

Whitman, John. The Mask of Zorro. 1998. (Mighty Chronicles Ser.). (Illus.). 320p. (J). (gr. 3-7). 9.95 o.p. (*0-8118-2036-X*) Chronicle Bks. LLC.

Wild, Margaret. Kiss Kiss. 2004. (Illus.). 24p. (J). 12.95 (*0-689-86279-2*, Simon & Schuster Children's Publishing) Simon & Schuster Children's Publishing.

Wilder, Laura Ingalls. Laura's Garden. 1996. (My First Little House Bks.). (Illus.). 10p. (J). (ps). 3.95 o.p. (*0-694-00778-1*, Harper Festival) HarperCollins Children's Bk. Group.

Wilhelm, Doug. Raising the Shades, RS. 2001. 192p. (J). (gr. 5 up). 16.00 (*0-374-36178-9*, Farrar, Straus & Giroux (BYR)) Farrar, Straus & Giroux.

Willey, Margaret. Finding David Dolores. 1986. 192p. (YA). (gr. 7 up). lib. bdg. 11.89 o.p. (*0-06-026484-5*) HarperCollins Children's Bk. Group.

—Finding David Dolores. 2001. 164p. (gr. 7-12). per. 13.95 (*0-595-19641-1*) iUniverse, Inc.

William, Kate. The Parent Plot. 1990. (Sweet Valley High Ser.: No. 67). (YA). (gr. 7 up). 8.60 o.p. (*0-606-04501-5*) Turtleback Bks.

Williams, Carol Lynch. Catherine's Remembrance. 1997. (Latter-Day Daughters Ser.). (J). pap. 4.95 (*1-57345-296-3*, Cinnamon Tree) Deseret Bk. Co.

—Christmas in Heaven. 2000. 171p. (J). (gr. 5-9). 16.99 o.s.i (*0-399-23436-5*, G. P. Putnam's Sons) Penguin Group (USA) Inc.

—A Mother to Embarrass Me. 2002. 144p. lib. bdg. 17.99 (*0-385-90028-7*); (gr. 3-7). text 15.95 o.p. (*0-385-72922-7*) Dell Publishing. (Delacorte Pr.).

—A Mother to Embarrass Me. 2003. 144p. (gr. 3-7). pap. text 4.99 (*0-440-41810-0*, Yearling) Random Hse. Children's Bks.

—Sarah's Quest. 1995. (Latter-Day Daughters Ser.). (J). pap. 4.95 (*1-56236-504-5*) Aspen Bks.

—The True Colors of Caitlynne Jackson. 1998. 176p. (gr. 5-9). pap. text 4.50 o.s.i (*0-440-41235-8*, Yearling) Random Hse. Children's Bks.

—The True Colors of Caitlynne Jackson. 1998. (J). 10.55 (*0-606-13873-0*) Turtleback Bks.

Williams, Laura. The Executioner's Daughter, ERS. 2000. 134p. (YA). (gr. 5-8). 16.95 (*0-8050-6234-3*, Holt, Henry & Co. Bks. For Young Readers) Holt, Henry & Co.

Williams, Laura E. Up a Creek, ERS. 2001. 144p. (YA). (gr. 5-10). 15.95 (*0-8050-6453-2*, Holt, Henry & Co. Bks. For Young Readers) Holt, Henry & Co.

—Up a Creek. l.t. ed. 2001. 121p. (J). 22.95 (*0-7862-3728-7*) Thorndike Pr.

Williams, Vera B. Scooter. 1993. (Illus.). 160p. (J). (gr. 2 up). 17.95 (*0-688-09376-0*); (ps-3). 14.89 o.p. (*0-688-09377-9*) HarperCollins Children's Bk. Group. (Greenwillow Bks.).

Willis, Jeanne. Don't Let Go! 2003. (Illus.). 32p. (J). 16.99 (*0-399-24008-X*, Putnam & Grosset) Putnam Publishing Group, The.

Wilson, Jacqueline. The Story of Tracy Beaker. l.t. ed. 1998. (Illus.). (J). pap. 16.95 (*0-7540-6021-7*, Galaxy Children's Large Print) BBC Audiobooks America.

—The Story of Tracy Beaker. 2001. (Illus.). 144p. (gr. 3-7). text 15.95 o.s.i (*0-385-72919-7*, Delacorte Pr.) Dell Publishing.

—The Story of Tracy Beaker. 2000. (J). pap. 8.95 (*0-440-86279-5*) Transworld Publishers Ltd. GBR. *Dist:* Trafalgar Square.

S

SIBLING RIVALRY—FICTION

SINGLE-PARENT FAMILIES—FICTION

—Joey Pigza Swallowed the Key. unabr. ed. 2000. 154p. (J). (gr. 4-6). pap. 28.00 incl. audio (0-8072-8166-2, YA120SP, Listening Library) Random Hse. Audio Publishing Group.

—Joey Pigza Swallowed the Key. l.t. ed. 2000. 174p. (J). 21.95 (0-7862-2912-8) Thorndike Pr.

—Joey Pigza Swallowed the Key. 2000. (Illus.). (J). 11.00 (0-606-18904-1) Turtleback Bks.

Gauthier, Gilles. Life Without Mooch. 2000. (First Novels Ser.: Vol. 35). (Illus.). 63p. (J). (gr. 1-4). (0-88780-525-6) Formac Publishing Co., Ltd.

—Life Without Mooch. 2001. (First Novels Ser.). (Illus.). 64p. (J). (gr. 1-4). pap. 3.99 (0-88780-524-8) Formac Publishing Co., Ltd. CAN. *Dist:* Orca Bk. Pubs.

Goodman, Joan Elizabeth. Songs from Home. 1994. (Illus.). 224p. (YA). (gr. 5 up). 10.95 o.s.i (0-15-203590-7) Harcourt Trade Pubs.

Grifalconi, Ann. Not Home: Somehow, Somewhere, There Must Be Love: A Novel. 1995. (J). 15.95 o.p. (0-316-32905-3) Little Brown & Co.

Griffin, Adele. Split Just Right. 1999. 208p. (J). (gr. 5-9). pap. 5.99 (0-7868-1295-8) Disney Pr.

—Split Just Right. 1997. 176p. (gr. 5-9). (J). 14.95 (0-7868-0347-9); (YA). lib. bdg. 15.49 (0-7868-2288-0) Hyperion Bks. for Children.

—Split Just Right. 1998. 11.04 (0-606-16662-9) Turtleback Bks.

Hamilton, Virginia. Sweet Whispers, Brother Rush. 1999. (gr. 4-7). pap. 12.25 (0-88103-610-2) Econo-Clad Bks.

—Sweet Whispers, Brother Rush. 1983. (Amistad Ser.). 224p. (J). (gr. 7 up). pap. 5.99 (0-380-65193-9, Amistad Pr.) HarperTrade.

—Sweet Whispers, Brother Rush. 1983. 220p. (J). (gr. 5 up). pap. 2.25 o.p. (0-380-64824-5, Avon Bks.) Morrow/Avon.

—Sweet Whispers, Brother Rush. 1982. 224p. (J). (gr. 7 up). 21.99 (0-399-20894-1, Philomel) Penguin Putnam Bks. for Young Readers.

—Sweet Whispers, Brother Rush. 1983. 12.00 (0-606-02885-4) Turtleback Bks.

High, Linda O. Maizie. 1995. 192p. (J). (gr. 4-7). tchr. ed. 14.95 (0-8234-1161-3) Holiday Hse., Inc.

Hixson, Nancy E. Distorted Vision. 1999. (J). pap. 15.95 (0-936389-62-1) Tudor Pubs., Inc.

Hopkins, Lee Bennett. Mama. (J). 1978. 112p. (gr. 4-6). pap. 1.25 o.s.i (0-440-96174-2, Laurel Leaf); 1977. (gr. 3 up). 4.95 o.p. (0-394-83525-5, Knopf Bks. for Young Readers); 1977. (gr. 3 up). lib. bdg. 5.99 o.p. (0-394-93525-X, Knopf Bks. for Young Readers) Random Hse. Children's Bks.

—Mama. 1992. (Illus.). 112p. (J). (gr. 2-8). pap. 14.00 o.p. (0-671-74985-4, Simon & Schuster Children's Publishing) Simon & Schuster Children's Publishing.

—Mama & Her Boys. 2003. 80p. (J). (gr. 4-7). pap. 8.95 (1-56397-813-X); pap. 8.95 (1-56397-814-8) Boyds Mills Pr.

—Mama & Her Boys. 1981. 192p. (J). (gr. 4-7). 12.95 (0-06-022578-5); lib. bdg. 12.89 o.p. (0-06-022579-3) HarperCollins Children's Bk. Group.

—Mama & Her Boys. 1993. (Illus.). 176p. (J). (gr. 5 up). pap. 13.00 o.s.i (0-671-74986-2, Simon & Schuster Children's Publishing) Simon & Schuster Children's Publishing.

Howland, Ethan. The Lobster War. 2001. (Illus.). 146p. (J). (gr. 7 up). 15.95 (0-8126-2800-4) Cricket Bks.

Kalifon, Mary. Mom Doesn't Work There Anymore. 1995. (Illus.). 32p. (Orig.). (J). (ps-4). pap. 5.95 (0-9641981-1-8) Cedars Sinai Health System.

Karr, Kathleen. In the Kaiser's Clutch, RS. 1995. 182p. (J). (gr. 4-7). 16.00 o.p. (0-374-33638-5, Farrar, Straus & Giroux (BYR)) Farrar, Straus & Giroux.

Ketteman, Helen. Mama's Way. 2000. (J). lib. bdg. 13.01 (0-8037-2423-3, Dial Bks. for Young Readers) Penguin Putnam Bks. for Young Readers.

Kinsey-Warnock, Natalie. Lumber Camp Library. 2002. (Illus.). 96p. (J). (gr. 2-5). 14.99 (0-06-029321-7); lib. bdg. 15.89 (0-06-029322-5) HarperCollins Children's Bk. Group.

—Lumber Camp Library. 2003. 96p. (J). pap. 4.99 (0-06-444292-6) HarperCollins Pubs.

Klein, Lee. The Best Gift for Mom. 1995. (Illus.). 32p. (Orig.). (J). (gr. k-6). pap. 5.95 o.p. (0-8091-6627-5) Paulist Pr.

Kurzweil, Allen. Leon & the Spitting Image. 2003. 320p. (J). 15.99 (0-06-053930-5); lib. bdg. 16.89 (0-06-053931-3) HarperCollins Children's Bk. Group. (Greenwillow Bks.).

Lachtman, Ofelia Dumas. The Summer of El Pintor. 2001. (Illus.). 234p. (J). (gr. 11 up). pap. 9.95 (1-55885-327-8) Arte Publico Pr.

Levy, Janice. Totally Uncool. (Picture Bks.). (Illus.). 32p. (J). (ps-3). 1999. lib. bdg. 15.95 (1-57505-306-3); 2001. reprint ed. pap. 6.95 (1-57505-555-4) Lerner Publishing Group. (Carolrhoda Bks.).

Lewis, Beverly. Star Status. 2002. (Girls Only Go Ser.: Vol. 8). 128p. (J). pap. 5.99 (1-55661-643-0) Bethany Hse. Pubs.

Lynch, Chris. Gypsy Davey. 1994. 160p. (YA). (gr. 12 up). 14.00 o.s.i (0-06-023586-1); (gr. 7 up). lib. bdg. 13.89 o.p. (0-06-023587-X) HarperCollins Children's Bk. Group.

Lyon, George Ella. Gina, Jamie, Father, Bear. 2002. 144p. (J). (gr. 6-9). 15.95 (0-689-84370-4, Atheneum/Richard Jackson Bks.) Simon & Schuster Children's Publishing.

Mead, Alice. Junebug, RS. 1995. 112p. (J). (gr. 3-7). 16.00 (0-374-33964-3, Farrar, Straus & Giroux (BYR)) Farrar, Straus & Giroux.

—Junebug. 1997. 112p. (gr. 3-7). pap. text 4.50 (0-440-41245-5, Yearling); 1996. (J). pap. 4.99 (0-440-91275-X, Dell Books for Young Readers) Random Hse. Children's Bks.

—Junebug. 1997. (J). 10.55 (0-606-11528-5) Turtleback Bks.

—Junebug & the Reverend. 2002. (Illus.). (J). 13.40 (0-7587-6518-5) Book Wholesalers, Inc.

—Junebug & the Reverend, RS. 1998. 192p. (J). (gr. 3-7). 16.00 (0-374-33965-1, Farrar, Straus & Giroux (BYR)) Farrar, Straus & Giroux.

—Junebug & the Reverend. 2000. (Illus.). 192p. (gr. 4-7). pap. text 4.99 (0-440-41571-3, Yearling) Random Hse. Children's Bks.

—Junebug & the Reverend. 2000. (Illus.). (J). 10.55 (0-606-18785-5) Turtleback Bks.

—Junebug in Trouble, RS. 2002. 144p. (J). (gr. 4-7). 16.00 (0-374-33969-4, Farrar, Straus & Giroux (BYR)) Farrar, Straus & Giroux.

—Junebug in Trouble. 2003. (Illus.). 144p. (gr. 4-7). pap. text 4.99 (0-440-41937-9, Dell Books for Young Readers) Random Hse. Children's Bks.

—Soldier Mom, RS. 1999. 160p. (J). (gr. 3-7). 16.00 (0-374-37124-5, Farrar, Straus & Giroux (BYR)) Farrar, Straus & Giroux.

Morris, Gilbert. Buckingham Palace & the Crown Jewels - Travels in England Vol. 2: Adventures of the Kerrigan Kids. 2001. (Illus.). 128p. (J). (gr. 3-7). pap. 5.99 (0-8024-1579-2) Moody Pr.

—Kangaroos & the Outback - Travels in Australia No. 3: Adventures of the Kerrigan Kids. 2001. (Illus.). 144p. (J). (gr. 3-7). pap. 5.99 (0-8024-1580-6) Moody Pr.

—Nine-Story Pagodas & Double Decker Buses - Travels in Hong Kong No. 4: Adventures of the Kerrigan Kids. 2001. (Illus.). 121p. (J). (gr. 3-7). pap. 5.99 (0-8024-1581-4) Moody Pr.

Naylor, Phyllis Reynolds. Alice In-Between. 1996. (Alice Ser.). 160p. (YA). (gr. 5-9). pap. text 4.50 (0-440-41064-9) Dell Publishing.

—Alice In-Between. 1994. (Alice Ser.). 160p. (YA). (gr. 5-9). 16.95 (0-689-31890-1, Atheneum) Simon & Schuster Children's Publishing.

—Alice In-Between. 1996. (Alice Ser.). (YA). (gr. 5-9). 10.55 (0-606-08976-4) Turtleback Bks.

—Alice in Blunderland. 2003. (Alice Ser.). (Illus.). 208p. (J). 15.95 (0-689-84397-6, Atheneum) Simon & Schuster Children's Publishing.

—Alice in Lace. (Alice Ser.). 144p. (YA). (gr. 5-9). 1997. pap. 4.99 (0-689-80597-5, Aladdin); 1996. 17.00 (0-689-80358-3, Atheneum) Simon & Schuster Children's Publishing.

—Alice in Lace. 1997. (Alice Ser.). (YA). (gr. 5-9). 11.04 (0-606-13114-0) Turtleback Bks.

—Alice on the Outside. (Alice Ser.). 176p. (gr. 5-9). 2000. (YA). mass mkt. 4.99 (0-689-80594-2, Simon Pulse); 1999. (J). 16.00 (0-689-80359-1, Atheneum) Simon & Schuster Children's Publishing.

—Alice on the Outside. 2000. (Alice Ser.). (YA). (gr. 5-9). 11.04 (0-606-19706-0) Turtleback Bks.

—Alice the Brave. (Alice Ser.). 144p. (YA). (gr. 5-9). 1996. pap. 4.99 (0-689-80598-5, Aladdin); 1995. 15.95 (0-689-80095-9, Atheneum) Simon & Schuster Children's Publishing.

—Alice the Brave. 1995. (Alice Ser.). (YA). (gr. 5-9). 10.55 (0-606-10737-1) Turtleback Bks.

—Outrageously Alice. (Alice Ser.). 144p. (gr. 5-9). 1998. (YA). pap. 4.99 (0-689-80596-9, Aladdin); 1997. (J). 15.95 (0-689-80354-0, Atheneum) Simon & Schuster Children's Publishing.

—Outrageously Alice. 1998. (Alice Ser.). (YA). (gr. 5-9). 11.04 (0-606-14288-6) Turtleback Bks.

—Patiently Alice. 2003. (Alice Ser.). (Illus.). 256p. (YA). 15.95 (0-689-82636-2, Atheneum) Simon & Schuster Children's Publishing.

—Starting with Alice. (Alice Ser.). (J). 2004. (Illus.). 208p. pap. 4.99 (0-689-84396-8, Aladdin); 2002. 192p. 15.95 (0-689-84395-X, Atheneum) Simon & Schuster Children's Publishing.

—Starting with Alice. l.t. ed. 2003. 199p. (J). 22.95 (0-7862-5091-7) Thorndike Pr.

Nelson, Theresa. Ruby Electric. 2003. (Illus.). 272p. (J). 16.95 (0-689-83852-2, Atheneum/Richard Jackson Bks.) Simon & Schuster Children's Publishing.

Newman, Leslea. Fat Chance. 1994. 224p. (J). (gr. 3-7). 15.95 o.p. (0-399-22760-1, G. P. Putnam's Sons) Penguin Group (USA) Inc.

—Fat Chance. 1996. 224p. (YA). (gr. 7 up). pap. 5.99 (0-698-11406-X, PaperStar) Penguin Putnam Bks. for Young Readers.

—Fat Chance. 1996. 11.04 (0-606-10806-8) Turtleback Bks.

North, Elizabeth. Ancient Enemies. 1986. 240p. reprint ed. 15.95 o.p. (0-89733-215-6); (J). pap. 14.00 (0-89733-214-8) Academy Chicago Pubs., Ltd.

Quattlebaum, Mary. Jackson Jones & the Puddle of Thorns. 1995. (Illus.). 128p. (J). (gr. 3-7). pap. 4.50 (0-440-41066-5) Dell Publishing.

—Jackson Jones & the Puddle of Thorns. 1995. (J). 10.55 (0-606-07725-1) Turtleback Bks.

Quinlan, Patricia M. My Dad Takes Care of Me. 1987. (Illus.). 24p. (J). (ps-2). pap. 4.95 (0-920303-76-5); text 15.95 (0-920303-79-X) Annick Pr., Ltd. CAN. *Dist:* Firefly Bks., Ltd.

Russo, Marisabina. When Mama Gets Home. 1998. (Illus.). (J). (gr. k-2). 32p. lib. bdg. 14.93 o.p. (0-688-14986-3); 2p. 15.99 (0-688-14985-5); 2p. 15.99 (0-688-14985-5) HarperCollins Children's Bk. Group. (Greenwillow Bks.).

Schotter, Roni. The World. 2003. (Illus.). (J). 16.95 (0-689-84485-9, Atheneum/Anne Schwartz Bks.) Simon & Schuster Children's Publishing.

Schwartz, Virginia Frances. Messenger. 2002. vii, 277p. (J). tchr. ed. 17.95 (0-8234-1716-6) Holiday Hse., Inc.

Shands, Linda I. Blind Fury. 2001. (Wakara of Eagle Lodge Ser.: Vol. 2). (Illus.). 176p. (YA). (gr. 7-9). pap. 5.99 (0-8007-5747-5) Revell, Fleming H. Co.

—White Water. 2001. (Wakara of Eagle Lodge Ser.).Tr. of Juv033010. (Illus.). 176p. (YA). (gr. 7-9). pap. 5.99 (0-8007-5772-6, Spire) Revell, Fleming H. Co.

—Wild Fire. 2001. (Wakara of Eagle Lodge Ser.: Vol. 1). (Illus.). 176p. (YA). (gr. 7-9). pap. 5.99 (0-8007-5746-7) Revell, Fleming H. Co.

Simons, Jay. In Search of the Messiah. 1994. 96p. pap. 8.99 o.p. (0-8280-0814-0) Review & Herald Publishing Assn.

Slate, Joseph. Crossing the Trestle. 1999. (Accelerated Reader Bks.). 144p. (J). (gr. 3-7). 14.95 (0-7614-5053-X, Cavendish Children's Bks.) Cavendish, Marshall Corp.

Smalls, Irene. Father's Day Blues: What Do You Do about Father's Day When All You Have Are Mothers? 1995. (Illus.). 32p. (J). 10.95 o.p. (0-681-00543-2) Borders Pr.

Stark, Ken, illus. Oh, Brother! 2003. 32p. (J). 15.99 (0-399-23766-6) Putnam Publishing Group, The.

Thomas, Eliza. The Red Blanket. Cepeda, Joe, tr. & illus. by. 2004. (J). (0-439-32253-7) Scholastic, Inc.

Thomas Young, Ronder. Moving Mama to Town. 1997. 224p. (J). (gr. 3-8). pap. 17.95 (0-531-30025-0, Orchard Bks.) Scholastic, Inc.

Thompson, Lauren. A Christmas Gift for Mama. 2003. (J). 48p. 16.95 (0-590-30725-8); pap. (0-590-30726-6) Scholastic, Inc.

Tocher, Timothy. Long Shot. 2001. (J). 137p. (0-88166-395-6); 144p. mass mkt. 4.95 (0-689-84331-3) Meadowbrook Pr.

Willard, Nancy. The Tortilla Cat. 1998. (Illus.). 48p. (J). (gr. 1-7). 16.00 o.s.i (0-15-289587-6) Harcourt Children's Bks.

Williams, Laura E. Up a Creek, ERS. 2001. 144p. (YA). (gr. 5-10). 15.95 (0-8050-6453-2, Holt, Henry & Co. Bks. For Young Readers) Holt, Henry & Co.

—Up a Creek. l.t. ed. 2001. 121p. (J). 22.95 (0-7862-3728-7) Thorndike Pr.

Wilson, Jacqueline. Double Act. 1998. (Illus.). 192p. (gr. 4-7). reprint ed. text 14.95 o.s.i (0-385-32312-3, Delacorte Pr.) Dell Publishing.

—Double Act. 1999. (Illus.). 192p. (gr. 3-7). pap. text 4.99 (0-440-41374-5) Random Hse. Children's Bks.

—The Lottie Project. 2001. (Illus.). 32p. pap. (0-440-86366-X, Corgi) Bantam Bks.

—The Lottie Project. 1999. (Illus.). 224p. (gr. 3-7). text 15.95 (0-385-32718-8, Delacorte Pr.) Dell Publishing.

—The Lottie Project. 2001. (Illus.). 224p. (gr. 3-7). pap. text 4.99 (0-440-41617-5, Dell Books for Young Readers) Random Hse. Children's Bks.

—The Lottie Project. 2000. (Illus.). 203p. 17.95 (0-385-40703-3) Transworld Publishers Ltd. GBR. *Dist:* Trafalgar Square.

Wolff, Virginia Euwer. Make Lemonade, ERS. 1993. 208p. (YA). (gr. 5-9). 17.95 (0-8050-2228-7, Holt, Henry & Co. Bks. For Young Readers) Holt, Henry & Co.

—Make Lemonade. 2003. 208p. (J). (gr. 5 up). mass mkt. 5.99 (0-590-48141-X, Scholastic Paperbacks) Scholastic, Inc.

—Make Lemonade. l.t. ed. 1993. (Teen Scene Ser.). (YA). (gr. 9-12). 17.95 (0-7862-0056-1) Thorndike Pr.

—Make Lemonade. 1993. (Point Signature Ser.). (J). 11.04 (0-606-06555-5) Turtleback Bks.

—True Believer. unabr. ed. 2002. (YA). (gr. 5 up). audio 25.00 (0-8072-0691-1, Listening Library) Random Hse. Audio Publishing Group.

—True Believer. 272p. (J). 2002. (Illus.). pap. 7.99 (0-689-85288-6, Simon Pulse); 2001. (gr. 7 up). 17.00 (0-689-82827-6, Atheneum) Simon & Schuster Children's Publishing.

—True Believer. l.t. ed. 2001. (YA). 23.95 (0-7862-3371-0) Thorndike Pr.

Wright, Betty Ren. The Moonlight Man. 2000. (Illus.). 181p. (J). (gr. 3-7). pap. 15.95 (0-590-25237-2, Scholastic Reference) Scholastic, Inc.

Young, Ronder T. Moving Mama to Town. 1997. 224p. (J). (gr. 3-8). lib. bdg. 18.99 (0-531-33025-7, Orchard Bks.) Scholastic, Inc.

Zisk, Mary. The Best Single Mom in the World: How I Was Adopted. 2001. (Illus.). 32p. (J). (ps-3). lib. bdg. 14.95 (0-8075-0666-4) Whitman, Albert & Co.

SISTERS—FICTION

Adler, C. S. The Lump in the Middle. 1991. 160p. (YA). pap. 3.50 (0-380-71176-1, Avon Bks.) Morrow/Avon.

—Split Sisters. 1990. 176p. (J). (gr. 4-7). pap. 3.95 o.s.i (0-689-71369-X, Aladdin) Simon & Schuster Children's Publishing.

Adorjan, Carol. I Can! Can You? Levine, Abby, ed. rev. ed. 1990. Orig. Title: Someone I Know. (Illus.). 24p. (J). (ps). lib. bdg. 13.95 (0-8075-3491-9) Whitman, Albert & Co.

Ahrens, Robin Isabel. Dee & Bee. 2000. (Illus.). 40p. (J). (ps-1). 14.95 (1-890817-26-0) Winslow Pr.

Aitken, Susan. Anna's Scrapbook: Journal of a Sister's Love. 2000. (Illus.). (J). (1-56123-134-7) Centering Corp.

Alcott, Louisa May. Good Wives. l.t. ed. 1987. (Classics Ser.). 432p. 29.99 o.p. (0-7089-8414-2, Charnwood) Thorpe, F. A. Pubs. GBR. *Dist:* Ulverscroft Large Print Bks., Ltd., Ulverscroft Large Print Canada, Ltd.

—Little Men: Life at Plumfield with Jo's Boys. 1995. (Illus.). 816p. (J). (gr. 3-5). 12.98 o.p. (0-8317-1212-0) Smithmark Pubs., Inc.

—Little Women. 2002. (Great Illustrated Classics). (Illus.). 240p. (J). (gr. 3-8). lib. bdg. 21.35 (1-57765-693-8, ABDO & Daughters) ABDO Publishing Co.

—Little Women. 1998. (Keepsake Collection Bks.). (J). 3.99 o.p. (1-57145-101-3, Thunder Bay Pr.) Advantage Pubs. Group.

—Little Women. 1966. (Airmont Classics Ser.). (Illus.). (YA). (gr. 6 up). pap. 2.95 o.p. (0-8049-0106-6, CL-106) Airmont Publishing Co., Inc.

—Little Women. 1996. (Andre Deutsch Classics). 264p. (J). (gr. 5-8). 11.95 (0-233-99040-2) Andre Deutsch GBR. *Dist:* Trafalgar Square, Trans-Atlantic Pubns., Inc.

—Little Women. 1983. 480p. (ps up). mass mkt. 3.95 (0-553-21275-3, Bantam Classics) Bantam Bks.

—Little Women. 1998. (Young Reader's Christian Library). (Illus.). 192p. (J). (gr. 3-7). pap. 1.39 o.p. (1-57748-229-8) Barbour Publishing, Inc.

—Little Women. (Paperback Classics Ser.). (J). 1995. 294p. pap. 2.95 o.p. (0-681-10333-7); 1994. (Illus.). 10.95 o.p. (0-681-00767-2); 1986. (Illus.). 388p. (gr. 4 up). 12.95 o.p. (0-681-40055-2) Borders Pr.

—Little Women. 1995. (Illus.). 93p. (J). 7.98 o.p. (1-85854-176-X) Brimax Bks., Ltd.

—Little Women. 1987. 608p. (gr. k-6). pap. text 4.99 o.s.i (0-440-44768-2) Dell Publishing.

—Little Women. Gerver, Jane E., ed. 1999. (Eyewitness Classics Ser.). (Illus.). 64p. (J). (gr. 2 up). pap. 14.95 (0-7894-4767-3, D K Ink) Dorling Kindersley Publishing, Inc.

—Little Women. 2000. (Juvenile Classics). (Illus.). 608p. (J). pap. 3.00 (0-486-41023-4) Dover Pubns., Inc.

—Little Women. 1999. (Focus on the Family Great Stories Ser.). (Illus.). 576p. (J). pap. 9.99 o.p. (1-56179-744-8) Focus on the Family Publishing.

—Little Women. 2001. (Young Reader's Classics Ser.). 94p. (J). pap. 9.95 (1-55013-783-2, Key Porter kids) Key Porter Bks. CAN. *Dist:* Firefly Bks., Ltd.

—Little Women. (Illus.). 192p. (J). 9.95 (1-56156-371-4) Kidsbooks, Inc.

—Little Women. 1994. (Everyman's Library Children's Classics Ser.). 530p. (gr. 4 up). 14.95 (0-679-43642-1, Everyman's Library) Knopf Publishing Group.

—Little Women. 1988. (Knopf Book & Cassette Classics Ser.). (Illus.). 512p. (J). 18.95 o.s.i (0-394-56279-8) Knopf, Alfred A. Inc.

—Little Women. 1994. 512p. (J). (gr. 4-7). 19.95 (0-316-03107-0); 1994. 512p. (J). (gr. 4-7). pap. 9.99 (0-316-03105-4); 1968. (Illus.). 524p. (YA). (gr. 7 up). 19.95 (0-316-03095-3) Little Brown & Co.

—Little Women. (J). E-Book 1.95 (1-58515-196-3) MesaView, Inc.

—Little Women. 1924. (Books of Wonder). (J). 22.99 o.s.i (0-688-14090-4, Morrow, William & Co.) Morrow/Avon.

—Little Women. 1983. 480p. (J). (gr. 3 up). mass mkt. 3.95 (0-451-52341-5, Signet Classics) NAL.

Relationships

Carlstrom, Nancy White. Kiss Your Sister, Rose Marie! 1992. (Illus.). 32p. (J). (ps-1). lib. bdg. 13.95 o.p. (*0-02-717271-6*, Simon & Schuster Children's Publishing) Simon & Schuster Children's Publishing.

Caseley, Judith. Sisters. 2004. 32p. (J). 15.99 (*0-06-051046-3*, Greenwillow Bks.) HarperCollins Children's Bk. Group.

Cerasini, Marc A., et al. Sisters Through the Seasons. 2002. 256p. (YA). (gr. 5). mass mkt. 4.99 (*0-375-82290-9*) Random Hse., Inc.

Cleary, Beverly. Beezus & Ramona. 1989. (Ramona Ser.). (J). (gr. 3-5). mass mkt. o.p. (*0-440-80144-3*) Dell Publishing.

—Beezus & Ramona. 1988. (Ramona Ser.). (J). (gr. 3-5). mass mkt. o.s.i (*0-440-80009-9*) Doubleday Publishing.

—Beezus & Ramona. 1955. (Ramona Ser.). (Illus.). 160p. (J). (gr. 4-7). 15.95 (*0-688-21076-7*); lib. bdg. 16.89 (*0-688-31076-1*) HarperCollins Children's Bk. Group.

—Beezus & Ramona. 1990. (Ramona Ser.). (Illus.). 176p. (J). (gr. 3-7). pap. 5.99 (*0-380-70918-X*, Avon Bks.) Morrow/Avon.

—Beezus & Ramona. (Ramona Ser.). 142p. (J). (gr. 3-5). pap. 4.99 (*0-8072-1441-8*); 1990. pap. 28.00 incl. audio (*0-8072-7317-1*, YA 822 SP) Random Hse. Audio Publishing Group. (Listening Library).

—Beezus & Ramona. 1979. (Ramona Ser.). (J). (gr. 3-5). pap. 3.25 o.s.i (*0-440-70665-3*, Dell Books for Young Readers); (Illus.). 160p. pap. 1.75 o.s.i (*0-440-40665-X*, Yearling) Random Hse. Children's Bks.

—Beezus & Ramona. 9999. (Ramona Ser.). (J). (gr. 3-5). pap. 1.95 o.s.i (*0-590-11828-5*) Scholastic, Inc.

—Beezus & Ramona. 1955. (Ramona Ser.). (J). (gr. 3-5). 11.04 (*0-606-03061-1*) Turtleback Bks.

—The Beezus & Ramona Diary. 1986. (Ramona Ser.). (Illus.). 224p. (J). (gr. 3-5). pap. 11.95 (*0-688-06353-5*, Morrow, William & Co.) Morrow/Avon.

—Ramona the Pest. 1988. (Ramona Ser.). (J). (gr. 3-5). pap. o.p. (*0-440-80051-X*) Dell Publishing.

—Sister of the Bride. (Cleary Reissue Ser.). (Illus.). (J). (gr. 5 up). 2003. 304p. pap. 5.99 (*0-06-053298-X*); 1996. 272p. pap. 5.99 (*0-380-72807-9*, Harper Trophy) HarperCollins Children's Bk. Group.

—Sister of the Bride. 1992. 240p. (J). (gr. 6). pap. 4.50 (*0-380-70928-7*, Avon Bks.) Morrow/Avon.

—Sister of the Bride. 1992. 11.04 (*0-606-14317-3*) Turtleback Bks.

Clifford, Eth. Will Somebody Please Marry My Sister? 1992. (Illus.). 128p. (J). (gr. 3-6). 13.95 o.p. (*0-395-58037-4*) Houghton Mifflin Co.

Cocca-Leffler, Maryann. What a Pest! 1994. (All Aboard Reading Ser.). (Illus.). 32p. (J). (ps-1). 7.99 o.p. (*0-448-40399-4*); 3.95 o.s.i (*0-448-40393-5*) Penguin Putnam Bks. for Young Readers. (Grosset & Dunlap).

Cohen, Miriam. Mimmy & Sophie, RS. 1999. (Illus.). 40p. (J). (gr. k up). 16.00 (*0-374-34988-6*, Farrar, Straus & Giroux (BYR)) Farrar, Straus & Giroux.

—Mimmy & Sophie: Six Stories, RS. 2004. (J). 15.00 (*0-374-34989-4*, Farrar, Straus & Giroux (BYR)) Farrar, Straus & Giroux.

Cole, Joanna. I'm a Big Sister. 1997. (Illus.). 32p. (J). (ps up). 6.99 (*0-688-14509-4*, Morrow, William & Co.) Morrow/Avon.

Colli, Monica. Twins. 1992. (Illus.). 24p. (J). (ps-3). 4.99 (*0-85953-394-8*) Child's Play of England GBR. *Dist:* Child's Play-International.

Cooney, Barbara. The Kellyhorns. 2001. (Lost Treasures Ser.: No. 1). 352p. (J). (Illus.). (gr. 3-7). reprint ed. pap. 1.99 (*0-7868-1522-1*);Bk. 3. pap. 4.99 (*0-7868-1523-X*) Hyperion Bks. for Children. (Volo).

Corcoran, Barbara. Wolf at the Door. 1993. 192p. (J). (gr. 3-7). 17.00 (*0-689-31870-7*, Atheneum) Simon & Schuster Children's Publishing.

Cossi, Olga. The Great Getaway. 1991. (People Who Have Helped the World Ser.). 32p. (J). (gr. 1-2). lib. bdg. 18.60 o.p. (*0-8368-0107-5*); (Illus.). o.p. (*0-8368-0833-9*) Stevens, Gareth Inc.

—The Great Getaway. (Illus.). 2002. (J). E-Book (*1-59019-741-0*); 1991. E-Book (*1-59019-742-9*) ipicturebooks, LLC.

Couloumbis, Audrey. Getting near to Baby. 1999. 224p. (J). (gr. 5-9). 17.99 (*0-399-23389-X*, G. P. Putnam's Sons) Penguin Group (USA) Inc.

—Getting near to Baby. 2001. 224p. (YA). (gr. 5-9). pap. 5.99 (*0-698-11892-8*, Puffin Bks.) Penguin Putnam Bks. for Young Readers.

—Getting near to Baby. unabr. ed. (J). (gr. 4-6). 2002. 211p. pap. 35.00 incl. audio (*0-8072-8876-4*, LYA 287 SP); 2001. audio 22.00 (*0-8072-6195-5*); 2001. audio 22.00 (*0-8072-6195-5*) Random Hse. Audio Publishing Group. (Listening Library).

—Getting near to Baby. l.t. ed. 2000. (Juvenile Ser.). (Illus.). 215p. (J). (gr. 4-7). 22.95 (*0-7862-2705-2*) Thorndike Pr.

—Getting near to Baby. 2001. (J). 12.04 (*0-606-21210-8*) Turtleback Bks.

Crabtree, Sally & Mathieson, Roberta. My Sister's Hair. 2001. (Illus.). 16p. (J). (-1). 12.95 (*0-375-81401-9*, Random Hse. Bks. for Young Readers) Random Hse. Children's Bks.

Curtis, Marcia. Big Sister, Little Sister. 2000. (Illus.). 32p. (J). (ps-3). 12.99 (*0-8037-2482-9*, Dial Bks. for Young Readers) Penguin Putnam Bks. for Young Readers.

Czernecki, Stefan. Don't Forget Winona. 2004. 32p. (J). (ps-2). 14.99 (*0-06-027197-3*) HarperCollins Children's Bk. Group.

Dahlback, Helena. My Sister Lotta & Me, ERS. Lesser, Rika, tr. from SWE. 1993. (Illus.). 32p. (J). (gr. k-3). 15.95 o.p. (*0-8050-2558-8*, Holt, Henry & Co. Bks. For Young Readers) Holt, Henry & Co.

Dalkey, Kara. Little Sister. 1996. (Jane Yolen Bks.). 208p. (J). (gr. 7-12). 17.00 o.s.i (*0-15-201392-X*) Harcourt Trade Pubs.

—Little Sister. 1998. 208p. (J). (gr. 5-9). pap. 4.99 o.s.i (*0-14-038631-9*) Penguin Putnam Bks. for Young Readers.

de Brunhoff, Laurent. Babar et Sa Petite Fille Isabelle. 1988. (Babar Ser.). (FRE., Illus.). (J). (ps-3). 24.95 (*0-7859-8787-8*) French & European Pubns., Inc.

Dean, Pamela. Juniper, Gentian & Rosemary. 352p. 1999. (J). pap. 14.95 (*0-312-85970-8*); 1998. (YA). (gr. 10 up). 24.95 o.p. (*0-312-86004-8*) Doherty, Tom Assocs., LLC. (Tor Bks.).

Deaver, Julie Reece. Chicago Blues. 1995. 192p. (J). (gr. 6-9). 15.95 (*0-06-024675-8*) HarperCollins Children's Bk. Group.

—Chicago Blues. 1995. 192p. (J). (gr. 6-9). lib. bdg. 14.89 o.p. (*0-06-024676-6*) HarperCollins Pubs.

DeMott, Mary. The Adventure of Lisa & the Drainpipe Prayer. 1998. (Illus.). 123p. (Orig.). (J). (ps-k). pap. 7.99 o.p. (*0-8280-1266-0*) Review & Herald Publishing Assn.

Dennee, JoAnne. In the Three Sisters Garden. 1994. 376p. (J). (gr. 1-2). pap. 24.95 (*1-884430-01-5*) Food Works.

Dessen, Sarah. Dreamland. 2000. (Illus.). 280p. (J). (gr. 7-12). 15.99 (*0-670-89122-3*, Viking Children's Bks.) Penguin Putnam Bks. for Young Readers.

—That Summer. 1998. (Illus.). 208p. (J). (gr. 5-9). pap. 5.99 (*0-14-038688-2*, Puffin Bks.) Penguin Putnam Bks. for Young Readers.

—That Summer. unabr. ed. 2003. (J). (gr. 7). audio 25.00 (*0-8072-1567-8*, Listening Library) Random Hse. Audio Publishing Group.

—That Summer. 1996. 208p. (YA). (gr. 7 up). pap. 16.95 (*0-531-09538-X*); lib. bdg. 17.99 (*0-531-08888-X*) Scholastic, Inc. (Orchard Bks.).

—That Summer. 1998. (J). 12.04 (*0-606-13842-0*) Turtleback Bks.

Dreyer, Ann L. After Elaine. 2002. 136p. (J). (gr. 4-7). 16.95 (*0-8126-2651-6*) Cricket Bks.

Dunkle, Clare B. The Hollow Kingdom, ERS. 2003. (Illus.). 240p. (YA). 16.95 (*0-8050-7390-6*, Holt, Henry & Co. Bks. For Young Readers) Holt, Henry & Co.

Dunrea, Olivier. Eppie M. Says... 1990. (Illus.). 32p. (J). (ps-2). lib. bdg. 14.95 (*0-02-733205-5*, Simon & Schuster Children's Publishing) Simon & Schuster Children's Publishing.

Edwards, Dorothy. My Naughty Little Sister. 2003. (Illus.). (J). 16.95 (*0-7540-7843-4*) BBC Audiobooks America.

—My Naughty Little Sister Storybook. 1991. (Illus.). 96p. (J). (ps-1). 16.95 o.p. (*0-89919-857-0*, Clarion Bks.) Houghton Mifflin Co. Trade & Reference Div.

—My Naughty Little Sister Storybook. 1992. (Illus.). (J). 4.99 o.p. (*0-517-07945-3*) Random Hse. Value Publishing.

Emerson, Charlotte. Amy's True Prize. 1999. (Little Women Journals Ser.). 10.04 (*0-606-16348-4*) Turtleback Bks.

—Beth's Snow Dancer. 1999. (Little Women Journals Ser.). 10.04 (*0-606-16347-6*) Turtleback Bks.

—Meg's Dearest Wish. 1999. (Little Women Journals). 10.04 (*0-606-16350-6*) Turtleback Bks.

Emerson, Charlotte & Alcott, Louisa May. Amy's True Prize. (Little Women Journals). (Illus.). (J). 1999. 128p. (gr. 3-7). mass mkt. 3.99 (*0-380-79706-2*); 1998. 144p. 10.00 o.p. (*0-380-97634-X*) Morrow/Avon. (Avon Bks.).

—Beth's Snow Dancer. (Little Women Journals). (J). 1999. (Illus.). 128p. (gr. 3-7). mass mkt. 3.99 (*0-380-79704-6*); 1998. 144p. 10.00 o.p. (*0-380-97632-3*) Morrow/Avon. (Avon Bks.).

—Jo's Troubled Heart. (Little Women Journals). (J). 1999. (Illus.). 128p. (gr. 3-7). pap. 3.99 (*0-380-79669-4*); 1998. 119p. (gr. 4-7). 10.00 o.p. (*0-380-97629-3*) Morrow/Avon. (Avon Bks.).

—Meg's Dearest Wish. (Little Women Journals). (Illus.). (J). 1999. 128p. (gr. 3-7). pap. 3.99 (*0-380-79705-4*); 1998. 144p. mass mkt. 10.00 o.p. (*0-380-97633-1*) Morrow/Avon. (Avon Bks.).

Ericsson, Jennifer A. She Did It!, RS. 2002. (Illus.). 32p. (J). (ps-3). 16.00 (*0-374-36776-0*, Farrar, Straus & Giroux (BYR)) Farrar, Straus & Giroux.

Eversole, Robyn H. The Magic House. 1992. (Illus.). 32p. (J). (ps-2). 15.95 o.p. (*0-531-05924-3*); mass mkt. 16.99 o.p. (*0-531-08524-4*) Scholastic, Inc. (Orchard Bks.).

Figley, Marty Rhodes. The Schoolchildren's Blizzard. 2004. (On My Own History Ser.). (J). pap. 5.95 (*1-57505-619-4*); lib. bdg. 22.60 (*1-57505-586-4*) Lerner Publishing Group. (Carolrhoda Bks.).

Fisher, Valorie. My Big Sister. 2003. (Illus.). 40p. (J). 14.95 (*0-689-85479-X*, Atheneum/Anne Schwartz Bks.) Simon & Schuster Children's Publishing.

Foggo, Cheryl. I Have Been in Danger. 2001. (In the Same Boat Ser.: No. 3). (Illus.). 176p. (J). (gr. 4-6). pap. 7.95 (*1-55050-185-2*) Coteau Bks. CAN. *Dist:* General Distribution Services, Inc.

Foxworth, Nilene O. Little Sia & the Sacred Cloud. l.t. ed. 1997. (Illus.). 21p. (J). (gr. 1-6). pap. text 12.95 (*0-9644137-5-2*) NOA International.

Freeman, Peggy P. The Coldest Day in Texas. 1997. (Chaparral Books for Young Readers). 126p. (J). (gr. 4-7). pap. 12.95 (*0-87565-169-0*) Texas Christian Univ. Pr.

Gabriel, Nat. Bubble Trouble. Nez, John, tr. & illus. by. 2004. (Science Solves It! Ser.). (J). pap. (*1-57565-133-5*) Kane Pr., The.

Galbraith, Kathryn O. Roommates. 1991. (J). (gr. 1-4). pap. 2.99 (*0-380-71357-8*, Avon Bks.) Morrow/Avon.

—Roommates. 1990. (Illus.). 48p. (J). (gr. 1-4). lib. bdg. 14.00 (*0-689-50487-X*, McElderry, Margaret K.) Simon & Schuster Children's Publishing.

—Roommates Again. 1994. (Illus.). 48p. (J). (gr. 1-4). 13.00 (*0-689-50597-3*, McElderry, Margaret K.) Simon & Schuster Children's Publishing.

—Roommates & Rachel. 1993. (J). (gr. 1). reprint ed. pap. 3.50 (*0-380-71762-X*, Avon Bks.) Morrow/Avon.

Gauch, Patricia Lee. Tanya & the Red Shoes. 2002. (Illus.). 40p. (J). 16.99 (*0-399-23314-8*, Philomel) Penguin Putnam Bks. for Young Readers.

Geisert, Bonnie. Prairie Summer. 2002. (Illus.). 96p. (YA). (gr. 3-7). 15.00 (*0-618-21293-0*, Lorraine, A. Walter) Houghton Mifflin Co. Trade & Reference Div.

Gerber, Merrill J. Handsome As Anything. 1990. (J). 13.95 (*0-590-43019-X*) Scholastic, Inc.

Gibbs, Lynne. Quiet As a Mouse. (Growing Pains (Columbus, Ohio) Ser.). (Illus.). 32p. (J). 2003. 12.95 (*1-57768-481-8*); 2002. pap. 4.95 (*1-57768-928-3*) McGraw-Hill Children's Publishing.

Giff, Patricia Reilly. Turkey Trouble. 1994. (Polk Street Special Ser.: Vol. 4). 112p. (gr. 1-4). pap. text 3.99 o.s.i (*0-440-40955-1*) Dell Publishing.

—Turkey Trouble. 1994. (Polk Street Special Ser.). 10.04 (*0-606-07125-3*) Turtleback Bks.

Giles, Gail. Dead Girls Don't Write Letters. 2003. 144p. (J). (gr. 7 up). 15.95 (*0-7613-1727-9*); lib. bdg. 22.90 (*0-7613-2813-0*) Millbrook Pr., Inc. (Roaring Brook Pr.).

Gill, Thomas. Kai: A Mission for Her Village. 1996. (Girlhood Journeys Ser.: No. 4). (Illus.). 72p. (J). (gr. 2-6). mass mkt. 5.99 (*0-689-80986-7*, Aladdin) Simon & Schuster Children's Publishing.

Glassman, Miriam. Box Top Dreams. 1998. 192p. (gr. 2-6). text 14.95 o.s.i (*0-385-32532-0*, Dell Books for Young Readers) Random Hse. Children's Bks.

Glencoe McGraw-Hill Staff. Topics from the Restless, Bk. 1. unabr. ed. 1999. (Wordsworth Classics Ser.). (YA). (gr. 10 up). pap. 21.00 (*0-89061-116-5*, R1165WW) Jamestown.

Golden Books Staff. Sisters Are the Best. 2000. (Illus.). 32p. (J). (ps-3). pap. 3.99 (*0-307-29900-7*, 29900, Golden Bks.) Random Hse. Children's Bks.

Good, Merle. Reuben & the Fire. 2003. 32p. (J). pap. 7.95 (*1-56148-388-5*) Good Bks.

Grant, Cynthia D. Phoenix Rising: Or, How to Survive Your Life. 1989. 160p. (YA). (gr. 8-10). lib. bdg. 15.00 o.p. (*0-689-31458-2*, Atheneum) Simon & Schuster Children's Publishing.

Greenwald, Sheila. Rosy's Romance. 1989. (Illus.). 96p. (J). (gr. 3-6). 12.95 o.p. (*0-316-32704-2*, Joy Street Bks.) Little Brown & Co.

—Rosy's Romance. 1990. (Illus.). 112p. (J). (gr. 3-6). pap. 2.75 (*0-671-70292-0*, Aladdin) Simon & Schuster Children's Publishing.

Gregory, Deborah. Oops, Doggy Dog! 2002. (Cheetah Girls Ser.: Bk. 13). 160p. (J). (gr. 3-7). pap. 3.99 (*0-7868-1484-5*) Disney Pr.

Griffin, Adele. The Other Shepards. (J). 2000. 224p. pap. o.s.i (*0-7868-1600-7*); 1998. 224p. (gr. 4-9). 14.95 (*0-7868-0423-8*); 1998. 218p. (gr. 4-9). lib. bdg. 15.49 (*0-7868-2370-4*) Disney Pr.

—The Other Shepards. 1999. 224p. (J). (gr. 5-9). pap. 5.99 (*0-7868-1333-4*) Hyperion Bks. for Children.

—The Other Shepards. l.t. ed. 2000. (Illus.). 209p. (J). (gr. 4-7). 20.95 (*0-7862-2914-4*) Thorndike Pr.

—The Other Shepards. 1999. 12.04 (*0-606-17144-4*) Turtleback Bks.

—Witch Twins. 2001. (Illus.). 160p. (J). (gr. 2-5). 14.99 (*0-7868-0739-3*, Volo) Hyperion Bks. for Children.

—Witch Twins. 2002. 160p. (J). (gr. 3-6). pap. 5.99 (*0-7868-1563-9*) Hyperion Paperbacks for Children.

—Witch Twins. l.t. ed. 2002. 174p. (J). 21.95 (*0-7862-4397-X*) Thorndike Pr.

—Witch Twins at Camp Bliss. (J). 2003. 144p. pap. 5.99 (*0-7868-1583-3*); 2002. (Illus.). 128p. (gr. 2-5). 15.99 (*0-7868-0763-6*) Hyperion Bks. for Children.

Griffin, Peni R. Hobkin. 1993. 192p. (J). (gr. 3-7). pap. 3.99 o.p. (*0-14-036356-4*, Puffin Bks.) Penguin Putnam Bks. for Young Readers.

—Hobkin. 1992. 208p. (J). (gr. 4-7). text 14.95 o.s.i (*0-689-50539-6*, McElderry, Margaret K.) Simon & Schuster Children's Publishing.

Grimes, Nikki. Jazmin's Notebook. 2002. (Illus.). (J). 12.34 (*0-7587-0368-6*) Book Wholesalers, Inc.

—Jazmin's Notebook. 112p. (YA). 1998. (gr. 8-12). 15.99 (*0-8037-2224-9*, Dial Bks. for Young Readers); 2000. (gr. 5-9). reprint ed. pap. 5.99 (*0-14-130702-1*, Puffin Bks.) Penguin Putnam Bks. for Young Readers.

—Jazmin's Notebook. 2000. (Illus.). (J). 11.04 (*0-606-18414-7*) Turtleback Bks.

Grove, Vicki. Rim Walkers. 1993. 224p. (YA). (gr. 7 up). 14.95 o.s.i (*0-399-22430-0*, G. P. Putnam's Sons) Penguin Group (USA) Inc.

Grunwald, Lisa. New Year's Eve. 1998. 384p. pap. 13.99 (*0-446-67403-6*) Warner Bks., Inc.

Guest, Elissa Haden. Iris & Walter: Lost & Found. 2004. (Iris & Walter Ser.). (Illus.). 44p. (J). 15.00 (*0-15-216701-3*) Harcourt Trade Pubs.

—Iris & Walter & Baby Rose. (Iris & Walter Ser.). (Illus.). 44p. (J). 2003. pap. 5.95 (*0-15-216713-7*); 2002. (gr. 1-4). 14.00 (*0-15-202120-5*) Harcourt Children's Bks. (Gulliver Bks.).

Gunn, Robin Jones. Don't You Wish. 1998. (Sierra Jensen Ser.: No. 3). (Illus.). 144p. (YA). (gr. 7-11). pap. 6.99 (*1-56179-486-4*) Focus on the Family Publishing.

Gutman, Anne & Hallensleben, Georg. Lisa's Baby Sister. 2003. (Misadventures of Gaspard & Lisa Ser.). (Illus.). 32p. (J). 9.95 (*0-375-82251-8*) Knopf, Alfred A. Inc.

Haas, Jessie. Horse Show Colors. 2004. 32p. (J). 14.99 (*0-06-001338-9*); lib. bdg. 15.89 (*0-06-001339-7*) HarperCollins Children's Bk. Group. (Greenwillow Bks.).

—Westminster West. 1997. (Illus.). 176p. (J). (gr. 5 up). 15.00 (*0-688-14883-2*, Greenwillow Bks.) HarperCollins Children's Bk. Group.

Hallinan, P. K. We're Very Good Friends, My Sister & I. 2001. (Illus.). 24p. (J). (ps-3). pap. 5.95 (*0-8249-5386-X*, Ideals) Ideals Pubns.

—We're Very Good Friends, My Sister & I. 1989. (P. K. Books Values for Life). (Illus.). 32p. (J). (ps-3). lib. bdg. 13.27 o.p. (*0-516-03656-4*, Children's Pr.) Scholastic Library Publishing.

Hallinan, P. K., tr. & illus. My Sister & I. 2003. 26p. (J). 7.95 (*0-8249-5456-4*, Candy Cane Pr.) Ideals Pubns.

Hamilton, Morse. Little Sister for Sale! 1992. (Illus.). 320p. (J). (ps-3). 13.00 o.p. (*0-525-65078-4*, Dutton Children's Bks.) Penguin Putnam Bks. for Young Readers.

Hanson, Mary. The Difference Between Babies & Cookies. 2002. (Illus.). 32p. (J). (ps-2). 16.00 (*0-15-202406-9*, Silver Whistle) Harcourt Children's Bks.

Harper, Jamie. Me Too! 2004. (J). (*0-316-60552-2*) Little Brown & Co.

Harris, Ruth Elwin. Sarah's Story. 2002. 304p. (YA). (gr. 7 up). bds. 5.99 (*0-7636-1707-5*) Candlewick Pr.

Harrison, Emma. Never Been Kissed. 2002. (Mary-Kate & Ashley Sweet 16 Ser.: Vol. 1). 144p. mass mkt. 4.99 (*0-06-009209-2*) HarperCollins Children's Bk. Group.

Hart, Alison & Leonhardt, Alice. Lauren Rides to the Rescue. 1995. (Riding Academy Ser.: No. 12). 132p. (YA). (gr. 5-8). pap. 3.99 o.s.i (*0-679-87144-6*, Random Hse. Bks. for Young Readers) Random Hse. Children's Bks.

Havill, Juanita. Briana, Jamaica, & the Dance of Spring. 2002. (Illus.). 32p. (J). (gr. 4-6). lib. bdg. 16.00 (*0-618-07700-6*) Houghton Mifflin Co.

Hazel, Beth & Harste, Jerome C. My Icky Picky Sister. 1984. (Predictable Read Together Bks.). (Illus.). 24p. (J). (gr. k-2). 1.95 o.p. (*0-87406-127-X*, 23-14389-7) Darby Creek Publishing.

Hazzard, Shirley. The Transit of Venus. 1980. 11.95 o.p. (*0-670-72426-2*) Viking Penguin.

Heinrich, Peggy. Forty-Four Freckles. 1995. (Illus.). 32p. (J). 9.95 o.p. (*0-681-00696-X*) Borders Pr.

Hendry, Diana. Double Vision. (gr. 7-11). 1995. (YA). bds. 6.99 o.p. (*1-56402-436-9*); 1993. 272p. (J). 14.95 o.p. (*1-56402-125-4*) Candlewick Pr.

—Double Vision. 1995. 12.09 o.p. (*0-606-08729-X*) Turtleback Bks.

Henkes, Kevin. Sheila Rae, the Brave. 1996. (J). 99.95 (*1-57135-154-X*) Broderbund Software, Inc.

—Sheila Rae, the Brave. 2002. (J). pap., tchr.'s planning gde. ed. 33.95 incl. audio (*0-87499-954-5*); 25.95 incl. audio (*0-87499-953-7*) Live Oak Media.

—Sheila Rae, the Brave: School Edition. 1996. (J). 49.95 (*1-57135-153-1*) Broderbund Software, Inc.

Herman, Gail. Flower Girl. 1996. (All Aboard Reading Ser.: Level 2). (Illus.). 48p. (J). (gr. 1-3). 13.99 o.s.i (*0-448-41107-5*); (ps-3). 3.99 (*0-448-41108-3*) Penguin Putnam Bks. for Young Readers. (Grosset & Dunlap).

—Keep Your Distance! 2001. (Math Matters Ser.). 32p. (J). (gr. 2-3). pap. 4.95 (*1-57565-107-6*) Kane Pr., The.

Hesse, Karen. A Time of Angels. 1997. (Illus.). 256p. (J). (gr. 5-9). reprint ed. pap. 5.95 (*0-7868-1209-5*) Disney Pr.

—A Time of Angels. 256p. 1997. pap. 5.95 o.s.i (*0-7868-1303-2*); 1995. (J). (gr. 5-9). 15.95 (*0-7868-0087-9*); 1995. (J). (gr. 5-9). lib. bdg. 16.49 (*0-7868-2072-1*) Hyperion Bks. for Children.

—A Time of Angels. 1997. 12.00 (*0-606-13088-8*) Turtleback Bks.

—Wish on a Unicorn. 1993. 112p. (J). (gr. 3-7). pap. 4.99 (*0-14-034935-9*, Puffin Bks.) Penguin Putnam Bks. for Young Readers.

—Wish on a Unicorn. 1993. 11.04 (*0-606-16843-5*) Turtleback Bks.

Hesse, Karen & Hesse, Hermann. Time of Angels. rev. ed. 2000. (J). 240p. (gr. 4-7). lib. bdg. 17.49 (*0-7868-2534-0*); 277p. (gr. 5-9). 16.99 (*0-7868-0621-4*) Hyperion Pr.

High, Linda O. Maizie. 1995. 192p. (J). (gr. 4-7). tchr. ed. 14.95 (*0-8234-1161-3*) Holiday Hse., Inc.

Hill, Eric. Spot's Baby Sister. 1995. (Spot Ser.). (Illus.). 20p. (J). (ps). pap. 6.99 (*0-14-055298-7*, Puffin Bks.) Penguin Putnam Bks. for Young Readers.

Hines, Anna Grossnickle. Jackie's Lunch Box. 1991. (Illus.). 24p. (J). (ps up). 13.95 o.p. (*0-688-09693-X*); lib. bdg. 13.88 o.p. (*0-688-09694-8*) Harper-Collins Children's Bk. Group. (Greenwillow Bks.).

Hiser, Constance. Sixth-Grade Star. 1992. 96p. (J). 13.95 o.p. (*0-8234-0967-8*) Holiday Hse., Inc.

Ho, Minfong. Gathering the Dew. 2003. (First Person Fiction Ser.). 208p. (J). (gr. 4-7). 16.95 (*0-439-38197-5*, Orchard Bks.) Scholastic, Inc.

Hoban, Russell. A Baby Sister for Frances. (Illus.). 32p. (J). (ps-3). 1964. 15.95 (*0-06-022335-9*); 1964. lib. bdg. 16.89 (*0-06-022336-7*); 1976. reprint ed. pap. 6.99 (*0-06-443006-5*, Harper Trophy) HarperCollins Children's Bk. Group.

—A Baby Sister for Frances. unabr. ed. 1995. (Tell Me a Story Ser.). (Illus.). 32p. (J). (ps-3). pap. 8.95 (*0-694-70018-5*, HarperAudio) HarperTrade.

—A Baby Sister for Frances. 1964. (J). 13.10 (*0-606-00665-6*) Turtleback Bks.

Hofmeister, Alan, et al. Sis in a Mess. (Reading for All Learners Ser.). (Illus.). (J). pap. (*1-56861-091-2*) Swift Learning Resources.

—Sis in the Well. (Reading for All Learners Ser.). (Illus.). (J). pap. (*1-56861-098-X*) Swift Learning Resources.

Holland, Isabelle. Friendly Sisters. Date not set. (J). 13.95 (*0-399-21128-4*) Penguin Group (USA) Inc.

—The Journey Home. 1924. (J). o.s.i (*0-688-01576-X*) HarperCollins Children's Bk. Group.

—The Journey Home. 224p. (J). 1993. (gr. 3-7). pap. 2.95 (*0-590-43111-0*, Scholastic Paperbacks); 1990. (gr. 4-7). 13.95 (*0-590-43110-2*) Scholastic, Inc.

—The Promised Land. 1996. 176p. (J). (gr. 3-7). pap. 15.95 (*0-590-47176-7*) Scholastic, Inc.

Holub, Joan. Goldie's Fortune: A Story of the Great Depression. 2002. (Doll Hospital Ser.: No. 2). 112p. (J). mass mkt. 3.99 o.s.i (*0-439-40179-8*, Scholastic Paperbacks) Scholastic, Inc.

Hood, Susan. I Am Mad! 1999. (Real Kids Readers Ser.). (Illus.). 32p. (J). (ps-1). 18.90 (*0-7613-2061-X*); pap. 4.99 (*0-7613-2086-5*) Millbrook Pr., Inc.

Hooks, William H. The Rainbow Ribbon. 1991. (J). 11.95 o.p. (*0-670-82866-1*, Viking Children's Bks.) Penguin Putnam Bks. for Young Readers.

Hooks, William H. & Boegehold, Betty D. The Rainbow Ribbon. 1999. (Illus.). 32p. (J). pap. 3.99 (*0-14-054092-X*, Puffin Bks.) Penguin Putnam Bks. for Young Readers.

Horrocks, Anita. What They Don't Know. braille ed. 2003. (gr. 2). spiral bd. (*0-616-15267-1*) Canadian National Institute for the Blind/Institut National Canadien pour les Aveugles.

—What They Don't Know. 1999. (Illus.). 192p. (YA). (gr. 7-10). pap. 8.95 (*0-7737-6001-6*) Stoddart Kids CAN. *Dist:* Fitzhenry & Whiteside, Ltd.

—What They Don't Know. 1999. (J). 15.00 (*0-606-19101-1*) Turtleback Bks.

Howard, Elizabeth Fitzgerald. The Train to Lulu's. 1998. (J). pap. 4.95 (*0-87628-336-9*) Simon & Schuster.

—The Train to Lulu's. (Illus.). 32p. (J). (ps-2). 1988. lib. bdg. 14.95 o.s.i (*0-02-744620-4*, Atheneum/Richard Jackson Bks.); 1994. reprint ed. pap. 4.95 (*0-689-71797-0*, Aladdin) Simon & Schuster Children's Publishing.

—The Train to Lulu's. 1994. 10.40 o.p. (*0-606-18946-7*); (J). 10.15 o.p. (*0-606-06064-2*) Turtleback Bks.

—What's in Aunt Mary's Room? 2002. (Illus.). 32p. (J). (ps-3). pap. 5.95 (*0-618-24621-5*, Clarion Bks.) Houghton Mifflin Co. Trade & Reference Div.

Howard, Elizabeth Fitzgerald & Lucas, Cedric. What's in Aunt Mary's Room? 1996. (Illus.). 32p. (J). (ps-3). lib. bdg., tchr. ed. 16.00 (*0-395-69845-6*, Clarion Bks.) Houghton Mifflin Co. Trade & Reference Div.

Jackson, Chris. The Gaggle Sisters River Tour. Pavanel, Jane, ed. 2002. (Illus.). 32p. (J). (ps-1). 16.95 (*1-894222-58-X*) Lobster Pr. CAN. *Dist:* Publishers Group West.

—The Gaggle Sisters Sing Again. 2003. (Illus.). 32p. (J). 15.95 (*1-894222-56-3*) Lobster Pr. CAN. *Dist:* Publishers Group West.

James, Breggie. Sister Secrets. 1997. 432p. (Orig.). pap. 12.95 (*0-9659042-0-2*) BeeJay Enterprises.

Jenkins, Emily. Daffodil, RS. 2004. (J). 16.00 (*0-374-31676-7*, Farrar, Straus & Giroux (BYR)) Farrar, Straus & Giroux.

Jocelyn, Marthe. Mable Riley: A Reliable Record of Humdrum, Peril, & Romance. 2004. 288p. (J). 1.00 (*0-7636-2120-X*) Candlewick Pr.

Johnson, Angela. A Cool Moonlight. 2003. 144p. (J). 14.99 (*0-8037-2846-8*, Dial Bks. for Young Readers) Penguin Putnam Bks. for Young Readers.

—Do Like Kyla. (Illus.). 32p. (J). (ps-3). 1993. mass mkt. 6.95 (*0-531-07040-9*); 1990. mass mkt. 16.99 o.p. (*0-531-08452-3*); 1990. pap. 15.95 (*0-531-05852-2*) Scholastic, Inc. (Orchard Bks.).

—Do Like Kyla. 1993. (J). 13.10 (*0-606-05810-9*) Turtleback Bks.

—Humming Whispers. 1996. pap. (*0-590-92617-9*); 1995. 128p. (YA). (gr. 4-7). pap. 15.95 o.p. (*0-531-06898-6*, Orchard Bks.); 1995. 128p. (YA). (gr. 4-7). lib. bdg. 16.99 (*0-531-08748-4*, Orchard Bks.) Scholastic, Inc.

—Humming Whispers. 1996. (J). 11.14 (*0-606-11488-2*) Turtleback Bks.

Johnston, Julie. In Spite of Killer Bees. 264p. (YA). (gr. 6 up). 2002. pap. 9.95 (*0-88776-601-3*); 2001. 17.95 o.s.i (*0-88776-537-8*) Tundra Bks. of Northern New York.

Jones, Diana Wynne. The Time of the Ghost. 2002. 304p. (J). (gr. 7 up). 16.99 (*0-06-029887-1*); 1997. 256p. (J). (gr. 5-9). pap. 5.95 (*0-688-15492-1*, Harper Trophy); 1996. 256p. (YA). (gr. 7 up). 15.00 (*0-688-14598-1*, Greenwillow Bks.) Harper-Collins Children's Bk. Group.

Joseph, Lynn & Keller, Laurie. Jump-Up Time: A Trinidad Carnival Story. 1998. (Illus.). 32p. (J). (gr. k-3). tchr. ed. 16.00 o.p. (*0-395-65012-7*, Clarion Bks.) Houghton Mifflin Co. Trade & Reference Div.

Jukes, Mavis. Expecting the Unexpected. 1999. 160p. (gr. 5-9). pap. text 3.99 (*0-440-41227-7*, Dell Books for Young Readers) Random Hse. Children's Bks.

—Expecting the Unexpected. 1999. 10.04 (*0-606-15911-8*) Turtleback Bks.

Kadohata, Cynthia. Kirakira. 2004. (Illus.). 256p. (J). 15.95 (*0-689-85639-3*, Atheneum) Simon & Schuster Children's Publishing.

Kakinouchi, Marumi. Shaolin Sisters. 2003. (Illus.). 208p. (YA). (gr. 8 up). Vol. 1. pap. 9.99 (*1-59182-024-3*); Vol. 2. pap. 9.99 (*1-59182-025-1*); Vol. 3. pap. 9.99 (*1-59182-026-X*); Vol. 4. pap. 9.99 (*1-59182-027-8*) TOKYOPOP, Inc.

Kantor, Susan. Tiny Tilda's Pumpkin Pie. 2002. (Reading Railroad Bks.). (Illus.). 32p. (J). mass mkt. 3.49 (*0-448-42681-1*, Grosset & Dunlap) Penguin Putnam Bks. for Young Readers.

Kassirer, Sue. What's Next, Nina? 2001. (Math Matters Ser.). (Illus.). 32p. (J). (gr. 1-3). pap. 4.29 (*1-57565-106-8*) Kane Pr., The.

Kaye, Marilyn. Camp Sunnyside Friends No. 13: Big Sister Blues. 1991. 128p. (Orig.). (YA). pap. 2.95 (*0-380-76551-9*, Avon Bks.) Morrow/Avon.

Kear, Cynthia. Searching for Grace. 1998. 24.95 (*0-947993-75-4*) Malvern Publishing Co., Ltd. GBR. *Dist:* British Bk. Co., Inc.

Keefer, Janice Kulyk. Anna's Goat. 2001. (Illus.). 32p. (J). (ps-3). 15.95 (*1-55143-153-X*) Orca Bk. Pubs.

Kehret, Peg. Sisters, Long Ago. 1990. (Illus.). 160p. (J). (gr. 5 up). 14.95 o.p. (*0-525-65021-0*, Dutton Children's Bks.) Penguin Putnam Bks. for Young Readers.

Kinsey-Warnock, Natalie. If Wishes Were Horses. (J). 2002. 144p. pap. 5.99 (*0-14-230143-4*, Puffin Bks.); 2000. (Illus.). (gr. 6-12). 15.99 o.s.i (*0-525-46448-4*, Dutton Children's Bks.) Penguin Putnam Bks. for Young Readers.

Knapp, Amy. Caps & Crowns. 1998. (Illus.). 72p. (J). (ps-3). 19.95 o.p. (*0-9658498-0-5*) Sandpiper Pr.

Knudson, Michelle. The Case of Vampire Vivian. 2003. (Science Solves It! Ser.). (Illus.). 32p. (J). 4.99 (*1-57565-127-0*) Kane Pr., The.

Koda-Callan, Elizabeth. The Secret Diary. 1997. (Magic Charm Book Ser.). (Illus.). 192p. (J). (gr. k-4). pap. 13.95 (*0-7611-0108-X*) Workman Publishing Co., Inc.

Krakauer, Hoong Y. Rabbit Mooncakes. 1994. (J). 15.95 o.p. (*0-316-50327-4*, Joy Street Bks.) Little Brown & Co.

Kroll, Virginia K. Faraway Drums. 1998. (Illus.). 32p. (J). (ps-3). 14.95 o.p. (*0-316-50449-1*) Little Brown & Co.

Kuhn, Betsy. Not Exactly Nashville. 1998. 144p. (gr. 3-7). text 14.95 o.s.i (*0-385-32589-4*, Delacorte Pr.) Dell Publishing.

—Not Exactly Nashville. 1999. 144p. (gr. 3-7). pap. text 3.99 o.s.i (*0-440-41478-4*, Dell Books for Young Readers) Random Hse. Children's Bks.

—Not Exactly Nashville. 1999. 10.04 (*0-606-16708-0*) Turtleback Bks.

Kurtz, Jane. Jakarta Missing. 2001. 272p. (J). (gr. 5 up). 15.99 (*0-06-029401-9*); lib. bdg. 16.89 (*0-06-029402-7*) HarperCollins Children's Bk. Group. (Greenwillow Bks.).

Kvasnosky, Laura McGee. Zelda & Ivy. 1998. (Illus.). 48p. (J). (gr. k-4). 15.99 (*0-7636-0469-0*) Candlewick Pr.

—Zelda & Ivy. 2001. (J). (gr. k-4). 26.95 incl. audio (*0-8045-6868-5*, 6868) Spoken Arts, Inc.

—Zelda & Ivy & the Boy Next Door. 1999. (Illus.). 48p. (J). (gr. k-4). 15.99 o.s.i (*0-7636-0672-3*) Candlewick Pr.

—Zelda & Ivy & the Boy Next Door: Three Stories about the Fabulous Fox Sisters. 2003. (Illus.). 48p. (J). (gr. k-4). bds. 6.99 (*0-7636-1053-4*) Candlewick Pr.

—Zelda & Ivy One Christmas. 2000. (Illus.). 48p. (J). (gr. 1-5). 15.99 (*0-7636-1000-3*) Candlewick Pr.

—Zelda & Ivy One Christmas: A Story about the Fabulous Fox Sisters. 2002. (Illus.). 48p. bds. 6.99 (*0-7636-1344-4*) Candlewick Pr.

Lasser, Bonnie. Let's Have a Sleepover. 2000. (Barbie Ser.). (Illus.). 24p. (J). (ps-3). pap. 3.29 (*0-307-12963-2*, 12963, Golden Bks.) Random Hse. Children's Bks.

Lattimore, Deborah Nourse. Punga: The Goddess of Ugly. 1993. (Illus.). 32p. (J). (ps-3). 14.95 o.s.i (*0-15-292862-6*) Harcourt Trade Pubs.

Lawlor, Laurie. Exploring the Chicago World's Fair, 1893. (American Sisters Ser.: Vol. 8). 2002. (Illus.). 240p. (YA). pap. 4.99 (*0-7434-3630-X*, Aladdin); 2001. 224p. (J). (gr. 4-7). 9.00 (*0-671-03924-5*, Simon & Schuster Children's Publishing) Simon & Schuster Children's Publishing.

—Saturn Coupes/Sedans Wagons 1630. 1998. (American Sisters Ser.: 03). 192p. (J). (gr. 3-7). 9.00 (*0-671-01552-4*, Aladdin) Simon & Schuster Children's Publishing.

—Voyage to a Free Land 1630. 2001. (American Sisters Ser.: Vol. 3). 192p. (J). (gr. 3-6). reprint ed. pap. 4.50 (*0-671-77562-6*, Aladdin) Simon & Schuster Children's Publishing.

—West along the Wagon Road 1852. 1998. (American Sisters Ser.: Vol. 1). 192p. (J). (gr. 4-7). pap. 9.00 (*0-671-01551-6*, Aladdin) Simon & Schuster Children's Publishing.

Lears, Laurie. Becky the Brave: A Story about Epilepsy. 2002. (Illus.). 32p. (J). (gr. 1-4). 14.95 (*0-8075-0601-X*) Whitman, Albert & Co.

Lerner, Harriet & Goldhor, Susan H. What's So Terrible about Swallowing an Apple Seed. 1996. (Illus.). 40p. (J). (ps-1). 15.95 (*0-06-024523-9*) HarperCollins Children's Bk. Group.

Lerner, Harriet G. & Goldhor, Susan H. What's So Terrible about Swallowing an Apple Seed? 1996. (Illus.). 40p. (J). (ps-1). lib. bdg. 14.89 o.p. (*0-06-024524-7*) HarperCollins Children's Bk. Group.

Levine, Gail Carson. The Two Princesses of Bamarre. 2001. 256p. (J). (gr. 5 up). 15.99 (*0-06-029315-2*); lib. bdg. 16.89 (*0-06-029316-0*) HarperCollins Children's Bk. Group.

—The Two Princesses of Bamarre. 2003. 256p. (J). (gr. 5 up). pap. 5.99 (*0-06-440966-X*) HarperCollins Pubs.

—The Two Princesses of Bamarre. 2004. (Illus.). 304p. (J). pap. 6.99 (*0-06-057580-8*, Eos) Morrow/Avon.

Levy, Elizabeth. Big Trouble in Little Twinsville. 2001. (Illus.). 96p. (J). (gr. 2-5). 14.95 (*0-06-028590-7*); lib. bdg. 15.89 (*0-06-028591-5*) HarperCollins Children's Bk. Group.

—Big Trouble in Little Twinsville. 2002. (Illus.). 96p. (J). pap. 4.25 (*0-06-442116-3*) HarperCollins Pubs.

Lewis, Beverly. A Cry in the Dark. 1996. (Summerhill Secrets Ser.: Vol. 5). 144p. (J). (gr. 6-9). pap. 5.99 (*1-55661-480-2*) Bethany Hse. Pubs.

Lieberg, Carolyn. West with Hopeless. 2004. 176p. (J). 16.99 (*0-525-47194-4*, Dutton Children's Bks.) Penguin Putnam Bks. for Young Readers.

Lillie, Patricia. Floppy Teddy Bear. (Illus.). 32p. (J). (ps up). 1995. 15.00 o.p. (*0-688-12570-0*); 1924. lib. bdg. 15.00 o.p. (*0-688-12571-9*) HarperCollins Children's Bk. Group. (Greenwillow Bks.).

Lindbergh, Reeve. Visit. 2015. (Illus.). 32p. (J). 14.95 (*0-8037-1189-1*, Dial Bks. for Young Readers) Penguin Putnam Bks. for Young Readers.

Lindman, Maj. Flicka, Ricka, Dicka & a Little Dog. 1995. (J). (ps-2). 6.95 o.p. (*0-8075-2486-7*) Whitman, Albert & Co.

—Flicka, Ricka, Dicka & the Big Red Hen. 1995. (J). (ps-3). pap. 6.95 (*0-8075-2493-X*) Whitman, Albert & Co.

—Flicka, Ricka, Dicka & the Strawberries. (Illus.). (gr. k-2). 1944. lib. bdg. 6.50 o.p. (*0-8075-2489-1*); 1996. 32p. (J). reprint ed. pap. 6.95 (*0-8075-2499-9*) Whitman, Albert & Co.

—Flicka, Ricka, Dicka & Their New Friend. 1995. (Illus.). (J). (ps-3). pap. 6.95 (*0-8075-2498-0*) Whitman, Albert & Co.

—Flicka, Ricka, Dicka Bake a Cake. 1995. (J). (ps-2). 6.95 o.p. (*0-8075-2480-8*); pap. 6.95 (*0-8075-2492-1*) Whitman, Albert & Co.

Lisle, Janet Taylor. The Lost Flower Children. (Illus.). (J). (gr. 3-7). 2001. 128p. pap. 4.99 (*0-698-11880-4*, PaperStar); 1999. 122p. 16.99 (*0-399-23393-8*, Philomel) Penguin Putnam Bks. for Young Readers.

—The Lost Flower Children. l.t. ed. 2000. (Illus.). 188p. (J). 21.95 (*0-7862-2890-3*) Thorndike Pr.

Littke, Lael. Haunted Sister, ERS. 1998. 160p. (J). (gr. 6-9). 16.95 (*0-8050-5729-3*, Holt, Henry & Co. Bks. For Young Readers) Holt, Henry & Co.

Little, Jean. Jess Was the Brave One. (Illus.). (J). 1995. 32p. pap. 4.99 o.s.i (*0-14-054309-0*, Puffin Bks.); 1992. 320p. 13.95 o.p. (*0-670-83495-5*, Viking Children's Bks.) Penguin Putnam Bks. for Young Readers.

—Jess Was the Brave One. 1994. 10.19 o.p. (*0-606-07738-3*) Turtleback Bks.

Littlefield, William. The Circus in the Woods. 2001. 240p. (J). (gr. 4-6). tchr. ed. 15.00 (*0-618-06642-X*) Houghton Mifflin Co.

Lopez, Loretta. The Birthday Swap. (Illus.). 32p. (J). (gr. k-3). 1999. pap. 6.95 (*1-880000-89-X*); 1997. 15.95 (*1-880000-47-4*) Lee & Low Bks., Inc.

—The Birthday Swap. 1997. 13.10 (*0-606-17378-1*) Turtleback Bks.

—Que Sorpresa de Cumpleanos. 1997. Tr. of Birthday Swap. 13.10 (*0-606-12795-X*) Turtleback Bks.

—Que Sorpresa de Cumpleanos! 1997. (SPA., Illus.). 32p. (J). (ps-3). 15.95 (*1-880000-55-5*, LW6614) Lee & Low Bks., Inc.

Lopez, Loretta & Lee, Hector Viveros. Que Sorpresa de Cumpleanos! 1997. (SPA., Illus.). 32p. (J). (ps-3). pap. 6.95 (*1-880000-56-3*, LW6611) Lee & Low Bks., Inc.

Lynch, L. M. How I Wonder What You Are. 2001. 208p. (gr. 4-8). text 15.95 o.s.i (*0-375-80663-6*); lib. bdg. 17.99 (*0-375-90663-0*) Random Hse. Children's Bks. (Knopf Bks. for Young Readers).

Mackel, Kathy. A Season of Comebacks. 1997. 112p. (J). (gr. 3-7). 15.99 o.s.i (*0-399-23026-2*, G. P. Putnam's Sons) Penguin Group (USA) Inc.

—A Season of Comebacks. 1998. 126p. (J). (gr. 4-7). pap. 4.99 o.p. (*0-698-11637-2*, PaperStar) Penguin Putnam Bks. for Young Readers.

—A Season of Comebacks. 1998. (J). 11.04 (*0-606-13767-X*) Turtleback Bks.

Mahy, Margaret. Five Sisters. 1999. (Puffin Chapters Ser.). (Illus.). 80p. (gr. 2-5). pap. 3.99 o.p. (*0-14-130334-4*, Puffin Bks.) Penguin Putnam Bks. for Young Readers.

Maifair, Linda L. Use Your Head, Molly Malone! 1997. (Winners! Ser.). 64p. (Orig.). (J). (gr. 2-5). pap. 3.99 (*0-310-20704-5*) Zondervan.

Man-Kong, Mary. Fashion Show Fun. 2004. (Illus.). (J). pap. 3.99 (*0-375-82746-3*, Golden Bks.) Random Hse. Children's Bks.

Martin, Ann M. Claudia & the Great Search. 1990. (Baby-Sitters Club Ser.: No. 33). 192p. (J). (gr. 3-7). mass mkt. 3.25 (*0-590-42495-5*); mass mkt. 3.99 (*0-590-73190-4*) Scholastic, Inc.

—Claudia & the Great Search. l.t. ed. 1995. (Baby-Sitters Club Ser.: No. 33). 147p. (J). (gr. 3-7). lib. bdg. 21.27 o.p. (*0-8368-1413-4*) Stevens, Gareth Inc.

—Claudia & the Great Search. 1990. (Baby-Sitters Club Ser.: No. 33). (J). (gr. 3-7). 10.04 (*0-606-03158-8*) Turtleback Bks.

—Dawn's Wicked Stepsister. 1990. (Baby-Sitters Club Ser.: No. 31). 192p. (J). (gr. 3-7). mass mkt. 3.50 (*0-590-42497-1*) Scholastic, Inc.

—Karen's Big Job. 1997. (Baby-Sitters Little Sister Ser.: No. 84). (J). (gr. 3-7). mass mkt. 3.50 (*0-590-69192-9*, 691553) Scholastic, Inc.

—Kristy & the Sister War. 1997. (Baby-Sitters Club Ser.: No. 112). 160p. (J). (gr. 3-7). mass mkt. 3.99 (*0-590-05990-4*) Scholastic, Inc.

—Kristy & the Sister War. 1997. (Baby-Sitters Club Ser.: No. 112). (J). (gr. 3-7). 10.04 (*0-606-11072-0*) Turtleback Bks.

Martin, Jane Read & Marx, Patricia. Now I Will Never Leave the Dinner Table. 1996. (Illus.). 32p. (J). (ps-3). lib. bdg. 14.89 o.p. (*0-06-024795-9*); 80th ed. 14.95 (*0-06-024794-0*) HarperCollins Children's Bk. Group.

Martin, Patricia M. Memory Jug. 1998. 236p. (J). (gr. 3-7). lib. bdg. 16.49 (*0-7868-2368-2*) Disney Pr.

—Memory Jug. 1998. 276p. (J). (gr. 3-7). 15.95 (*0-7868-0357-6*) Hyperion Pr.

Marzollo, Jean. My Sister, the Blabbermouth. 1990. (Thirty-Nine Kids on the Block Ser.). (J). (gr. 4-7). pap. 2.50 o.p. (*0-590-42728-8*) Scholastic, Inc.

Masters, Susan Rowan. Libby Bloom, ERS. 1995. (Redfeather Bks.). (Illus.). 86p. (J). (gr. 4-7). 14.95 o.p. (*0-8050-3374-2*, Holt, Henry & Co. Bks. For Young Readers) Holt, Henry & Co.

Mayne, William. A Year & a Day. 2000. (Candlewick Treasures Ser.). (Illus.). 125p. (J). (gr. 3-7). 11.99 o.p. (*0-7636-0850-5*) Candlewick Pr.

—A Year & a Day. 1976. 112p. (J). (gr. 4-6). lib. bdg. 6.95 o.p. (*0-525-43450-X*, Dutton) Dutton/Plume.

—A Year & a Day. 1990. (J). (gr. 4-7). 19.25 (*0-8446-6431-6*) Smith, Peter Pub., Inc.

Mazer, Anne. Every Cloud Has a Silver Lining. 2000. (Amazing Days of Abby Hayes Ser.: No. 1). (Illus.). 144p. (J). (gr. 4-7). pap. 4.50 (*0-439-14977-0*) Scholastic, Inc.

Mazer, Norma Fox. When She Was Good. 240p. (J). (gr. 7 up). 2003. (Illus.). mass mkt. 5.99 (*0-590-31990-6*, Scholastic Paperbacks); 2000. pap. 16.95 (*0-590-13506-6*) Scholastic, Inc.

—When She Was Good. 2000. 11.04 (*0-606-18615-8*) Turtleback Bks.

McDaniel, Lurlene. Angel of Hope. 2000. (Mercy Trilogy Ser.). 240p. (YA). (gr. 7-12). mass mkt. 4.99 (*0-553-57148-6*, Starfire) Random Hse. Children's Bks.

—Angel of Hope. 2000. (Illus.). (J). 11.04 (*0-606-17991-7*) Turtleback Bks.

McDonald, Janet. Twists & Turns, RS. 2003. 144p. (YA). 16.00 (*0-374-39955-7*, Farrar, Straus & Giroux (BYR)) Farrar, Straus & Giroux.

McDonald, Megan. Shining Star. 2003. (Illus.). 48p. (J). (gr. 1-3). pap. 3.99 (*0-307-26340-1*); lib. bdg. 11.99 (*0-307-46340-0*) Random Hse., Inc.

—The Sisters Club. 2003. (Pleasant Company Publications). (Illus.). (J). pap. 15.95 (*1-58485-782-X*, American Girl) Pleasant Co. Pubns.

McDonough, Yona Zeldis. The Dollhouse Magic: How to Make & Find Simple Dollhouse Furniture, ERS. 2000. (Illus.). 96p. (J). (gr. 2-4). 15.00 (*0-8050-6464-8*, Holt, Henry & Co. Bks. For Young Readers) Holt, Henry & Co.

McElmurry, Jill. Mess Pets. 2002. (Illus.). 40p. (J). (gr. k-3). 15.95 (*1-58717-174-0*); lib. bdg. 16.50 (*1-58717-175-9*) North-South Bks., Inc.

McElroy-Ansa, Tina. Ugly Ways. unabr. ed. 1994. audio 48.00 (*0-7366-2800-2*, 3515) Books on Tape, Inc.

McKay, Hilary. The Exiles at Home. 208p. (J). (gr. 4-8). 1997. (Illus.). pap. 3.99 (*0-689-81403-8*, Aladdin); 1994. 15.95 (*0-689-50610-4*, McElderry, Margaret K.) Simon & Schuster Children's Publishing.

—The Exiles in Love. 176p. (J). (gr. 3-7). 1999. pap. 4.50 (*0-689-82013-5*, Aladdin); 1998. (Illus.). 16.00 o.s.i (*0-689-81752-5*, McElderry, Margaret K.) Simon & Schuster Children's Publishing.

—The Exiles in Love. 1999. 10.55 (*0-606-17315-3*) Turtleback Bks.

McKissack, Patricia C. Color Me Dark: The Diary of Nellie Lee Love, the Great Migration North, Chicago, Illinois, 1919. 2000. (Dear America Ser.). (Illus.). 218p. (J). (gr. 4-9). pap. 10.95 (*0-590-51159-9*, Scholastic Pr.) Scholastic, Inc.

McVeity, Jen. On Different Shores. 1998. (Illus.). 167p. (YA). (gr. 5-9). pap. 16.95 (*0-531-30115-X*); lib. bdg. 17.99 (*0-531-33115-6*) Scholastic, Inc. (Orchard Bks.).

Messer, Celeste M. The Ghost of Piper's Landing. 2002. (Illus.). (J). 4.95 (*0-9702171-7-X*) Ashley-Alan Enterprises.

Meyer, Carolyn. Beware, Princess Elizabeth. (Young Royals Ser.). 2002. (Illus.). 224p. (YA). pap. 5.95 (*0-15-204556-2*); 2001. (J). 17.00 (*0-15-202639-8*); 2001. (Illus.). 224p. (YA). (gr. 7 up). 17.00 (*0-15-202659-2*) Harcourt Children's Bks. (Gulliver Bks.).

Michels-Gualtieri, Akaela S. I Was Born to Be a Sister. 2001. (Illus.). 32p. (J). (ps-1). 16.95 (*1-930775-03-2*) Platypus Media, L.L.C.

Mooney, E. S. & Thompson Brothers. Ms. Meane. 2002. (Powerpuff Girls Chapter Bks.: Vol. 12). 64p. (J). mass mkt. 3.99 (*0-439-33213-3*) Scholastic, Inc.

Moore, Liz. Zizi & Tish. 2003. (Illus.). 32p. (J). (ps-3). pap. 7.95 (*1-55143-254-4*) Orca Bk. Pubs.

Morgan, Stacy Towle. The Belgium Book Mystery. 1996. (Ruby Slippers School Ser.: Vol. 2). (Illus.). 80p. (Orig.). (J). (gr. 2-5). pap. 3.99 o.p. (*1-55661-601-5*, Bethany Backyard) Bethany Hse. Pubs.

Morris, Kim. Molly in the Middle. 1999. (Real Kids Readers Ser.). (Illus.). 48p. (J). (gr. 1-3). 18.90 (*0-7613-2059-8*); pap. 4.99 (*0-7613-2084-9*) Millbrook Pr., Inc.

—Molly in the Middle. 1999. (J). 10.14 (*0-606-19161-5*) Turtleback Bks.

Moss, Marissa. Amelia Hits the Road. 1999. (Amelia Ser.). (Illus.). 40p. (YA). (gr. 3 up). 12.95 (*1-56247-791-9*); pap. 5.95 (*1-56247-790-0*) Pleasant Co. Pubns. (American Girl).

—Amelia Hits the Road. 1997. (Amelia Ser.). (Illus.). 40p. (J). (gr. 3-5). 14.95 o.p. (*1-883672-57-0*) Tricycle Pr.

—Amelia Hits the Road. 1999. (Amelia Ser.). (J). (gr. 3-5). 12.10 (*0-606-19867-9*) Turtleback Bks.

—Amelia Lends a Hand. 2002. (Amelia Ser.). (Illus.). 32p. (J). 14.95 (*1-58485-539-8*); pap. 7.95 (*1-58485-508-8*) Pleasant Co. Pubns. (American Girl).

—Amelia's Notebook. 1999. (Amelia Ser.). 32p. (YA). (gr. 3 up). 12.95 (*1-56247-785-4*); (Illus.). pap. 5.95 (*1-56247-784-6*) Pleasant Co. Pubns. (American Girl).

—Amelia's Notebook. 1995. (Amelia Ser.). (Illus.). 32p. (J). (gr. 3-5). 14.00 o.p. (*1-883672-18-X*) Tricycle Pr.

—Amelia's Notebook. 1999. (Amelia Ser.). (Illus.). (J). (gr. 3-5). 12.10 (*0-606-18353-1*) Turtleback Bks.

—Oh Boy, Amelia! 2001. (Amelia Ser.). (Illus.). 38p. (J). (gr. 3 up). 12.95 (*1-58485-344-1*); pap. 5.95 (*1-58485-330-1*) Pleasant Co. Pubns. (American Girl).

—Oh Boy, Amelia! 2001. (American Girl Collection Ser.). (Illus.). (J). 12.10 (*0-606-21365-1*) Turtleback Bks.

Muldrow, Diane. Barbie Loves Her Sisters. 1997. (Golden Book Ser.). 16p. (J). (ps-3). pap. 3.99 o.s.i (*0-307-21100-2*, 21100, Golden Bks.) Random Hse. Children's Bks.

Mulford, Philippa Greene. The Holly Sisters on Their Own. 1998. (Accelerated Reader Bks.). 160p. (J). (gr. 5-9). lib. bdg. 14.95 (*0-7614-5022-X*, Cavendish Children's Bks.) Cavendish, Marshall Corp.

Murphy, Claire Rudolf. Gold Star Sister. 2000. 176p. (YA). (gr. 5-11). pap. 6.99 (*0-9704437-0-6*) North Star Publishing.

Murphy, Jim. West to a Land of Plenty: The Diary of Teresa Angelino Viscardi, New York to Idaho Territory, 1883. 1998. (Dear America Ser.). (Illus.). 204p. (YA). (gr. 4-9). pap. 10.95 (*0-590-73888-7*) Scholastic, Inc.

Murphy, Rita. Night Flying. 144p. (YA). (gr. 7 up). 2002. mass mkt. 4.99 (*0-440-22837-9*, Laurel Leaf); 2000. (Illus.). 14.95 o.s.i (*0-385-32748-X*, Delacorte Bks. for Young Readers) Random Hse. Children's Bks.

—Night Flying. l.t. ed. 2001. (Young Adult Ser.). 148p. (YA). 22.95 (*0-7862-3521-7*) Thorndike Pr.

Naylor, Phyllis Reynolds. The Boys Start the War. 1993. 144p. (J). (gr. 4-7). 15.95 o.s.i (*0-385-30814-0*) Doubleday Publishing.

—The Girls Take Over. 2002. 160p. (gr. 4-7). text 15.95 (*0-385-32738-2*, Delacorte Bks. for Young Readers) Random Hse. Children's Bks.

—The Girls Take Over. 2002. 160p. lib. bdg. 17.99 (*0-385-90059-7*) Random Hse., Inc.

—The Girls Take Over. 2004. (J). (*0-7862-5823-3*) Thorndike Pr.

—A Spy among the Girls. Poploff, Michelle, ed. 2000. (Illus.). 144p. (gr. 4-7). text 15.95 (*0-385-32336-0*, Delacorte Bks. for Young Readers) Random Hse. Children's Bks.

—A Traitor among the Boys. 1999. 144p. (gr. 4-7). text 15.95 o.s.i (*0-385-32335-2*) Bantam Bks.

—A Traitor among the Boys. 2001. 144p. (gr. 4-7). pap. text 4.99 (*0-440-41386-9*, Dell Books for Young Readers) Random Hse. Children's Bks.

—Witch's Sister. 2002. 160p. (J). pap. 4.99 (*0-689-85315-7*, Aladdin) Simon & Schuster Children's Publishing.

Neasi, Barbara J. Just Like Me. (Rookie Readers Ser.). (J). 1984. (Illus.). 32p. (ps-3). pap. 4.95 o.p. (*0-516-42047-X*); 1984. (Illus.). 32p. (gr. 1-2). lib. bdg. 19.00 (*0-516-02047-1*); 2003. (Illus.). 32p. (gr. 1-2). pap. 4.95 (*0-516-27495-3*); 2002. lib. bdg. 19.00 (*0-516-22564-2*); 2002. (Illus.). 31p. (gr. 1-2). pap. 19.00 (*0-516-22669-X*) Scholastic Library Publishing. (Children's Pr.).

Noll, Sally. That Bothered Kate. 1991. (Illus.). 32p. (J). (ps up). 13.95 o.p. (*0-688-10095-3*); lib. bdg. 13.88 o.p. (*0-688-10096-1*) HarperCollins Children's Bk. Group. (Greenwillow Bks.).

—That Bothered Kate. 1993. (Picture Puffins Ser.). (Illus.). 32p. (J). (ps-3). pap. 4.99 o.p. (*0-14-054885-8*, Puffin Bks.) Penguin Putnam Bks. for Young Readers.

Norling, Beth. Sister Night & Sister Day. 2001. (Illus.). 32p. (J). (ps). 14.95 (*1-86448-863-8*) Allen & Unwin Pty., Ltd. AUS. *Dist:* Independent Pubs. Group.

Northway, Jennifer. Get Lost, Laura! 1995. (Illus.). 32p. (J). (ps-2). pap. 10.95 o.s.i (*0-307-17520-0*, Golden Bks.) Random Hse. Children's Bks.

Numeroff, Laura Joffe. The Chicken Sisters. 1997. (Laura Geringer Bks.). (Illus.). 32p. (J). (ps-2). 15.99 (*0-06-026679-1*); lib. bdg. 14.89 (*0-06-026680-5*) HarperCollins Children's Bk. Group. (Geringer, Laura Bk.).

—What Sisters Do Best: What Brothers Do Best. 2003. (J). 15.00 (*0-689-82937-X*, Simon & Schuster Children's Publishing) Simon & Schuster Children's Publishing.

O'Connor, Jane. Kate Skates. (All Aboard Reading Ser.: Level 1). (Illus.). 32p. (J). (ps-1). 2015. 9.99 (*0-448-40936-4*); 1995. 3.99 (*0-448-40935-6*) Penguin Putnam Bks. for Young Readers. (Grosset & Dunlap).

Olsen, Ashley & Olsen, Mary-Kate. Santa Girls. 2003. (Two of a Kind Ser.: No. 32). 112p. mass mkt. 4.99 (*0-06-009328-5*, HarperEntertainment) Morrow/Avon.

Olsen, Mary-Kate & Olsen, Ashley. April Fools' Rules! 2002. (Two of a Kind Ser.: Vol. 22). (Illus.). 112p. mass mkt. 4.99 (*0-06-106662-1*) HarperCollins Pubs.

—The Case of Camp Crooked Lake. 2002. (New Adventures of Mary-Kate & Ashley Ser.: 30). 96p. (gr. 1-5). mass mkt. 4.50 (*0-06-106652-4*) HarperCollins Pubs.

—The Case of Clue's Circus Caper, No. 35. 2003. (New Adventures of Mary-Kate & Ashley Ser.). (Illus.). 96p. mass mkt. 4.50 (*0-06-009333-1*, HarperEntertainment) Morrow/Avon.

—The Case of the Weird Science Mystery. 2002. (New Adventures of Mary-Kate & Ashley Ser.: 29). 96p. (gr. 1-5). mass mkt. 4.50 (*0-06-106651-6*) HarperCollins Pubs.

—How to Flunk Your First Date. 1999. (Two of a Kind Ser.: No. 2). (Illus.). 112p. (gr. 3-7). mass mkt. 4.99 (*0-06-106572-2*, HarperEntertainment) Morrow/Avon.

—Mary-Kate & Ashley Starring In: The Challenge, No. 6. 2003. 96p. mass mkt. 4.99 (*0-06-056702-3*, HarperEntertainment) Morrow/Avon.

—Mary-Kate & Ashley Sweet 16. 2002. (J). (Sweet Sixteen Ser.: No. 6). (Illus.). mass mkt. 4.99 (*0-06-052812-5*); mass mkt. 19.96 (*0-06-052112-0*); No. 5. (Sweet Sixteen Ser.: No. 5). (Illus.). mass mkt. 4.99 (*0-06-052811-7*) Morrow/Avon. (HarperEntertainment).

—New Adventures of Mary-Kate & Ashley. 2001. pap. text 17.00 (*0-06-009013-8*) HarperCollins Children's Bk. Group.

—New Adventures of Mary-Kate & Ashley. 2002. (Illus.). (J). mass mkt. 18.00 (*0-06-052114-7*, HarperEntertainment) Morrow/Avon.

—Too Good to be True. 2002. (So Little Time Ser.: Vol. 3). 128p. mass mkt. 4.99 (*0-06-008805-2*) HarperCollins Pubs.

—Wish Come True. 2002. (Mary-Kate & Ashley Sweet 16 Ser.: Vol. 2). 144p. mass mkt. 4.99 (*0-06-009210-6*) HarperCollins Children's Bk. Group.

Outlet Book Company Staff. Little Women. 1988. o.s.i (*0-517-62442-7*) Crown Publishing Group.

Owens, Vivian. I Met a Great Lady: Ivy Meets Mary McLeod Bethune. Maxwell, Carolyn, ed. unabr. ed. 1998. (Illus.). 80p. (J). (gr. 4-11). pap. 8.95 (*0-9623839-5-3*) Eschar Pubns.

Palatini, Margie. Broom Mates. 2003. (J). 15.99 (*0-7868-0418-1*) Hyperion Bks. for Children.

Partridge, Elizabeth. Clara & the Hoodoo Man. 176p. (gr. 3-7). 1998. pap. 4.99 o.s.i (*0-14-038348-4*); 1996. (J). 14.99 o.s.i (*0-525-45403-9*, Dutton Children's Bks.) Penguin Putnam Bks. for Young Readers.

Pascal, Francine, creator. I'll Never Love Again. 1999. (Sweet Valley University Ser.: No. 46). 240p. (gr. 7 up). mass mkt. 3.99 o.s.i (*0-553-49266-7*, Dell Books for Young Readers) Random Hse. Children's Bks.

—Lila's Little Sister. 1994. (Unicorn Club Ser.: No. 4). 144p. (J). (gr. 3-7). pap. 3.50 o.s.i (*0-553-48214-9*) Bantam Bks.

—One 2 Many. 1999. (Sweet Valley Junior High Ser.: No. 2). 144p. (gr. 3-7). pap. text 4.50 (*0-553-48604-7*, Dell Books for Young Readers) Random Hse. Children's Bks.

—Stepsisters. 1993. (Sweet Valley High Ser.: No. 93). 160p. (YA). (gr. 7 up). mass mkt. 3.25 o.s.i (*0-553-29850-X*) Bantam Bks.

—You're Not My Sister. 1999. (Sweet Valley University Ser.: No. 47). 240p. (gr. 7 up). mass mkt. 3.99 o.s.i (*0-553-49267-5*, Dell Books for Young Readers) Random Hse. Children's Bks.

Paterson, Katherine. Ame a Jacob: Jacob Have I Loved. 1995. (SPA.). 216p. (J). 11.50 o.p. (*84-204-3649-6*) Santillana USA Publishing Co., Inc.

—Jacob Have I Loved. (Trophy Bk.). (J). (gr. 7 up). 1990. 272p. pap. 6.50 (*0-06-440368-8*, Harper Trophy); 1990. 256p. pap. 6.50 (*0-06-447059-8*, Harper Trophy); 1980. 224p. lib. bdg. 16.89 (*0-690-04079-2*); 1980. 224p. 15.99 (*0-690-04078-4*) HarperCollins Children's Bk. Group.

—Jacob Have I Loved. l.t. ed. 2000. (LRS Large Print Cornerstone Ser.). 266p. (J). (gr. 5-12). lib. bdg. 29.95 (*1-58118-073-X*, 23658) LRS.

—Jacob Have I Loved. 1981. (YA). (gr. 7 up). pap. 2.95 (*0-380-56499-8*, Avon Bks.) Morrow/Avon.

—Jacob Have I Loved. l.t. ed. 1990. 251p. (J). (gr. k-6). reprint ed. lib. bdg. 16.95 o.s.i (*1-55736-167-3*, Cornerstone Bks.) Pages, Inc.

—Jacob Have I Loved. 1980. (J). 12.00 (*0-606-04379-9*) Turtleback Bks.

Patron, Susan. Maybe Yes, Maybe No, Maybe Maybe. 1993. (Richard Jackson Bks.). (Illus.). 96p. (J). (gr. 3-5). pap. 15.95 (*0-531-05482-9*); lib. bdg. 16.99 o.p. (*0-531-08632-1*) Scholastic, Inc. (Orchard Bks.).

Paz, Senel. Las Hermanas. 1997. (Encuento/Literary Encounters Ser.).Tr. of Sisters. (SPA.). pap. text (*968-494-058-0*, CI2001) Centro de Informacion y Desarrollo de la Comunicacion y la Literatura MEX. *Dist:* Lectorum Pubns., Inc.

—Las Hermanas. 1990. Tr. of Sisters. 19.02 (*0-606-17691-8*) Turtleback Bks.

Pearson, Gayle. The Fog Doggies & Me. 1993. 128p. (J). (gr. 4-8). lib. bdg. 13.95 o.s.i (*0-689-31845-6*, Atheneum) Simon & Schuster Children's Publishing.

Pearson, Mary E. Generous Me. (Rookie Readers Ser.). (Illus.). (J). (gr. 1-2). 2003. 32p. pap. 4.95 (*0-516-27819-3*); 2002. 31p. pap. 19.00 (*0-516-22253-8*) Scholastic Library Publishing. (Children's Pr.).

Peck, Richard. Don't Look & It Won't Hurt, ERS. 1999. 176p. (J). (gr. 7-12). 16.95 (*0-8050-6316-1*, Holt, Henry & Co. Bks. For Young Readers) Holt, Henry & Co.

Perry, Carol. One Sister Too Many. 1998. 144p. (J). (gr. 5-8). reprint ed. pap. 3.99 (*0-87406-903-3*, Willowisp Pr.) Darby Creek Publishing.

Peters, Lisa Westberg. Hayloft. 1998. (Easy-to-Read Ser.). (Illus.). 32p. (J). (gr. 1-4). pap. 3.99 o.p. (*0-14-038643-2*) Penguin Putnam Bks. for Young Readers.

—The Hayloft. 1995. (Easy-to-Read Ser.). (Illus.). 48p. (J). 12.99 o.s.i (*0-8037-1490-4*); 12.89 o.s.i (*0-8037-1491-2*) Penguin Putnam Bks. for Young Readers. (Dial Bks. for Young Readers).

Peterson, Jeanne Whitehouse. Don't Forget Winona. 2004. 32p. (J). (ps-2). lib. bdg. 15.89 (*0-06-027198-1*) HarperCollins Children's Bk. Group.

Pevsner, Stella. Is Everyone Moonburned but Me? 2000. (Illus.). 208p. (J). (gr. 5-9). tchr. ed. 15.00 (*0-395-95770-2*, Clarion Bks.) Houghton Mifflin Co. Trade & Reference Div.

—Sister of the Quints. 1988. 192p. (YA). (gr. 7 up). pap. (*0-671-65973-1*, Simon Pulse) Simon & Schuster Children's Publishing.

Pfeffer, Susan Beth. A Gift for Jo. 1999. (Portraits of Little Women Ser.: No. 10). (Illus.). 112p. (gr. 3-7). text 9.95 o.s.i (*0-385-32668-8*, Dell Books for Young Readers) Random Hse. Children's Bks.

—Twin Surprises, ERS. 1991. (Redfeather Fiction Ser.). (Illus.). 64p. (J). (gr. 2-4). 13.95 o.p. (*0-8050-1850-6*, Holt, Henry & Co. Bks. For Young Readers) Holt, Henry & Co.

—Twin Troubles, ERS. 1992. (Illus.). (J). 14.95 o.p. (*0-8050-2146-9*, Holt, Henry & Co. Bks. For Young Readers) Holt, Henry & Co.

Pfeffer, Susan Beth & Alcott, Louisa May. Amy Makes a Friend. 1998. (Portraits of Little Women Ser.). (Illus.). 112p. (gr. 3-7). text 9.95 o.s.i (*0-385-32584-3*, Dell Books for Young Readers) Random Hse. Children's Bks.

—Amy's Story. 1997. (Portraits of Little Women Ser.). 112p. (gr. 3-7). text 9.95 o.s.i (*0-385-32529-0*, Delacorte Pr.) Dell Publishing.

—Beth's Story. 1997. (Portraits of Little Women Ser.). 112p. (gr. 3-7). text 9.95 o.s.i (*0-385-32526-6*, Delacorte Pr.) Dell Publishing.

—A Gift for Beth. 1999. (Portraits of Little Women Ser.: No. 11). (Illus.). 112p. (gr. 3-7). text 9.95 o.s.i (*0-385-32667-X*, Dell Books for Young Readers) Random Hse. Children's Bks.

—Jo Makes a Friend. 1998. (Portraits of Little Women Ser.). (Illus.). 112p. (gr. 3-7). text 9.95 (*0-385-32581-9*, Dell Books for Young Readers) Random Hse. Children's Bks.

—Jo's Story. 1997. (Portraits of Little Women Ser.). 112p. (gr. 3-7). text 9.95 o.s.i (*0-385-32523-1*, Dell Books for Young Readers) Random Hse. Children's Bks.

Pfeffer, Susan Beth & Ramsey, Marcy Dunn. Ghostly Tales. Bui, Francoise, ed. 2000. (Portraits of Little Women Ser.). (Illus.). 192p. (gr. 3-7). text 9.95 (*0-385-32741-2*, Delacorte Bks. for Young Readers) Random Hse. Children's Bks.

Pleasant Company Staff. Meet the American Girls, 6 bks., Set. 1997. (American Girls Collection Ser.). (YA). (gr. 2 up). pap. 34.95 o.p. (*1-56247-542-8*) Pleasant Co. Pubns.

Plourde, Lynn. Spring's Sprung. 2002. (Illus.). 32p. (J). (ps-3). 16.00 (*0-689-84229-5*, Simon & Schuster Children's Publishing) Simon & Schuster Children's Publishing.

Pohl, Peter & Gieth, Kinna. I Miss You, I Miss You! Greenwald, Roger, tr. from ENG. 1999. 256p. (YA). (gr. 7-12). 17.00 (*91-29-63935-2*) R & S Bks. SWE. *Dist:* Farrar, Straus & Giroux, Holtzbrinck Pubs.

Porte, Barbara Ann. When Aunt Lucy Rode a Mule & Other Stories. 1994. (Illus.). 32p. (J). (gr. k-2). 15.95 o.p. (*0-531-06816-1*); mass mkt. 16.99 o.p. (*0-531-08666-6*) Scholastic, Inc. (Orchard Bks.).

Potter, Giselle. Chloe's Birthday— & Me. 2005. (J). 16.95 (*0-689-86230-X*, Atheneum/Anne Schwartz Bks.) Simon & Schuster Children's Publishing.

Powell, Pamela. The Turtle Watchers. 1992. 160p. (J). (gr. 3-7). 13.00 o.s.i (*0-670-84294-X*, Viking Children's Bks.) Penguin Putnam Bks. for Young Readers.

Qing, Xia. Seven Clam Sisters. 1982. (Illus.). 18p. (Orig.). (J). (gr. 5-7). pap. 1.95 o.p. (*0-8351-1143-1*) China Bks. & Periodicals, Inc.

Quin-Harkin, Janet. One Crazy Christmas. 1996. (Sister Sister Ser.). 144p. (J). (gr. 4-7). pap. 3.99 (*0-671-00283-X*, Aladdin) Simon & Schuster Children's Publishing.

Reid, Barbara. The Party. braille ed. 1998. (J). (gr. 1). spiral bd. (*0-616-01766-9*); (gr. 2). spiral bd. (*0-616-01767-7*) Canadian National Institute for the Blind/Institut National Canadien pour les Aveugles.

—The Party. 1999. (Illus.). 32p. (J). (ps-2). 15.95 (*0-590-97801-2*) Scholastic, Inc.

Rice, Bebe Faas. My Sister, My Sorrow. 1991. (Day by Day Ser.: No. 2). (YA). mass mkt. 3.50 o.s.i (*0-440-21296-0*) Dell Publishing.

Richardson, Jean. Out of Step: The Twins Were So Alike . . . but So Different. 1993. (Illus.). 28p. (J). (ps-3). pap. 5.95 o.p. (*0-8120-1553-3*) Barron's Educational Series, Inc.

—Out of Step: The Twins Were So Alike... but So Different. 1993. (Illus.). 28p. (J). (ps-3). 12.95 o.p. (*0-8120-5790-2*) Barron's Educational Series, Inc.

Rinaldi, Ann. In My Father's House. (Point Ser.). 336p. (YA). 1994. (gr. 8-12). mass mkt. 4.99 (*0-590-44731-9*); 1993. (Illus.). (gr. 7-9). pap. 14.95 (*0-590-44730-0*) Scholastic, Inc.

—In My Father's House. 1993. 11.04 (*0-606-07012-5*) Turtleback Bks.

Rivers, Camilla Reghelini. Off the Wall. 2002. (Sport Stories Ser.). 128p. (J). (gr. 3-8). pap. 5.95 (*1-55028-750-8*) Lorimer, James & Co. CAN. *Dist:* Orca Bk. Pubs.

Rocklin, Joanne & Burns, Marilyn. Not Enough Room! 1998. (Hello Reader! Math Ser.). (Illus.). 32p. (J). (gr. k-2). pap. 3.99 (*0-590-39962-4*) Scholastic, Inc.

Roe, Jill. Angels Flying Slowly. l.t. ed. 1996. 270p. pap. 20.95 o.p. (*0-7838-1820-3*, Macmillan Reference USA) Gale Group.

—Angels Flying Slowly. 1995. 224p. 20.95 o.p. (*0-312-13427-4*) St. Martin's Pr.

Ross, Pat. Hannah's Fancy Notions: A Story of Industrial New England. 1992. (Once upon America Ser.). (Illus.). 64p. (J). (gr. 2-6). pap. 4.99 o.s.i (*0-14-032389-9*, Puffin Bks.) Penguin Putnam Bks. for Young Readers.

—Hannah's Fancy Notions: A Story of Industrial New England. 1992. (Once upon America Ser.). (J). (gr. 2-6). 11.14 (*0-606-02662-2*) Turtleback Bks.

Rue, Nancy. When Is Perfect, Perfect Enough? 1999. (Raise the Flag Ser.: Bk. 6). 224p. (YA). (gr. 7-12). pap. 6.95 (*1-57856-088-8*) WaterBrook Pr.

Rushton, Rosie. Poppy. 2000. (J). 224p. pap. o.s.i (*0-7868-1595-7*); 272p. (gr. 5-9). pap. 4.99 (*0-7868-1391-1*) Disney Pr.

Russo, Marisabina. Hannah's Baby Sister. 1998. (Illus.). 32p. (J). (ps-3). 15.00 (*0-688-15831-5*); lib. bdg. 14.89 o.p. (*0-688-15832-3*) HarperCollins Children's Bk. Group. (Greenwillow Bks.).

Sachs, Marilyn. What My Sister Remembered. 1994. 128p. (J). (gr. 5 up). pap. 3.99 o.s.i (*0-14-036944-9*, Puffin Bks.) Penguin Putnam Bks. for Young Readers.

Sacks, Margaret. Beyond Safe Boundaries. 1990. 160p. (J). (gr. 4-7). pap. 4.99 o.s.i (*0-14-034407-1*, Puffin Bks.); 1989. 16p. (YA). (gr. 7 up). 13.95 o.p. (*0-525-67281-8*, Dutton Children's Bks.) Penguin Putnam Bks. for Young Readers.

—Beyond Safe Boundaries. 1990. 11.04 (*0-606-04616-X*) Turtleback Bks.

Saller, Carol. Bridge Dancers. 1991. (Middle Grade Fiction Ser.). (J). lib. bdg. 19.95 o.p. (*0-87614-653-1*) Lerner Publishing Group.

Samuels, Barbara. Dolores on Her Toes, RS. 2003. (Illus.). 40p. (J). 16.50 (*0-374-31818-2*, Farrar, Straus & Giroux (BYR)) Farrar, Straus & Giroux.

—What's So Great about Cindy Snappleby? 1992. (Illus.). 32p. (J). (ps-1). 14.95 o.p. (*0-531-05979-0*); mass mkt. 14.99 o.p. (*0-531-08579-1*) Scholastic, Inc. (Orchard Bks.).

Sappey, Maureen S. A Rose at Bull Run: Romance & Realities at First Bull Run. 1999. (Young American Ser.: Vol. 1). (Illus.). 100p. (YA). (gr. 4-7). 5.99 (*1-57249-133-7*) White Mane Publishing Co., Inc.

Scarboro, Elizabeth, et al. Phoenix Upside Down. 1996. 160p. (J). (gr. 3-7). 14.99 o.s.i (*0-670-86335-1*, Viking Children's Bks.) Penguin Putnam Bks. for Young Readers.

Schindel, John. Frog Face: My Little Sister & Me, ERS. 1998. (Illus.). 32p. (J). (ps-2). 14.95 (*0-8050-5546-0*, Holt, Henry & Co. Bks. For Young Readers) Holt, Henry & Co.

Scholastic, Inc. Staff. Princess Sheegwa. 2002. (Sagwa, the Chinese Siamese Cat Ser.: No. 2). (Illus.). 32p. (J). mass mkt. 3.99 (*0-439-42880-7*) Scholastic, Inc.

Schwartz, Amy. Annabelle Swift, Kindergartner. 2000. (J). pap. 19.97 incl. audio (*0-7366-9198-7*) Books on Tape, Inc.

—Annabelle Swift, Kindergartner. 1996. (Illus.). (J). (gr. k-3). pap. 15.95 incl. audio (*0-87499-355-5*); pap. 37.95 incl. audio (*0-87499-357-1*); 22.95 o.p. incl. audio (*0-87499-356-3*) Live Oak Media.

—Annabelle Swift, Kindergartner. (Illus.). 32p. (J). (ps-3). 1991. mass mkt. 6.95 (*0-531-07027-1*); 1988. 15.95 o.p. (*0-531-05737-2*); 1988. mass mkt. 15.99 o.p. (*0-531-08337-3*) Scholastic, Inc. (Orchard Bks.).

—Annabelle Swift, Kindergartner. 1988. 13.10 (*0-606-09005-3*) Turtleback Bks.

Schwartz, Roslyn. The Mole Sisters & the Rainy Day. 1999. (Mole Sisters Ser.). (Illus.). 32p. (J). (ps-k). lib. bdg. 14.95 (*1-55037-611-X*) Annick Pr., Ltd. CAN. *Dist:* Firefly Bks., Ltd.

Schwarz, Christina. Drowning Ruth: A Novel. 2001. 20.05 (*0-606-21165-9*) Turtleback Bks.

Sendak, Maurice. Outside over There. 1989. (Caldecott Collection). (Illus.). 40p. (J). (ps-3). pap. 9.95 (*0-06-443185-1*, Harper Trophy) HarperCollins Children's Bk. Group.

Shaik, Fatima. Melitte. 160p. (J). (gr. 5-9). 1999. (Illus.). pap. 4.99 o.s.i (*0-14-130420-0*, Puffin Bks.); 1997. 15.99 o.s.i (*0-8037-2106-4*, Dial Bks. for Young Readers) Penguin Putnam Bks. for Young Readers.

—Melitte. 2000. 11.04 (*0-606-18432-5*) Turtleback Bks.

Shaw, Janet Beeler. Kaya Shows the Way: A Sister Story. 2002. (American Girls Collection: Bk. 5). (Illus.). 88p. (J). (gr. 2-7). 12.95 (*1-58485-432-4*, American Girl) Pleasant Co. Pubns.

Simon, Charnan. Come! Sit! Speak! 1997. (Rookie Readers Ser.). (Illus.). 32p. (J). (gr. 1-2). lib. bdg. 19.00 (*0-516-20397-5*, Children's Pr.) Scholastic Library Publishing.

Sister Trap Stepsisters, No. 2. 2003. (J). mass mkt. 2.50 (*0-590-40903-4*) Scholastic, Inc.

Smith, Jane D. Mary by Myself. 1994. (J). (gr. 3 up). 160p. 14.00 o.p. (*0-06-024517-4*); 80p. lib. bdg. 13.89 o.p. (*0-06-024518-2*) HarperCollins Children's Bk. Group.

Smothers, Ethel Footman. Moriah's Pond. 2003. 96p. (J). 7.00 (*0-8028-5249-1*, Eerdmans Bks For Young Readers) Eerdmans, William B. Publishing Co.

—Moriah's Pond. 1994. (J). lib. bdg. o.p. (*0-679-94504-0*) Knopf, Alfred A. Inc.

—Moriah's Pond. 1994. (Illus.). 128p. (J). 16.00 o.s.i (*0-679-84504-6*, Knopf Bks. for Young Readers) Random Hse. Children's Bks.

Sommerdorf, Norma. An Elm Tree & Three Sisters. 2001. (Illus.). 32p. (J). 15.99 o.s.i (*0-670-89308-0*, Viking Children's Bks.) Penguin Putnam Bks. for Young Readers.

Spirn, Michele Sobel. The Bridges in Paris. 2000. (Going to Ser.). (Illus.). 121p. (J). (gr. 4-8). pap. 5.99 (*1-893577-04-X*) Four Corners Publishing Co., Inc.

Springer, Nancy. The Great Pony Hassle. 1993. (Illus.). 80p. (J). (gr. 3-7). 13.99 o.p. (*0-8037-1306-1*); 13.89 o.p. (*0-8037-1308-8*) Penguin Putnam Bks. for Young Readers. (Dial Bks. for Young Readers).

—Separate Sisters. 2001. 160p. (J). (gr. 5-7). tchr. ed. 16.95 (*0-8234-1544-9*) Holiday Hse., Inc.

Stevens, Diane. Liza's Blue Moon. 1995. 192p. (YA). (gr. 7 up). 15.00 o.s.i (*0-688-13542-0*, Greenwillow Bks.) HarperCollins Children's Bk. Group.

Stewart, Molly Mia. Ellen is Home Alone. 1993. (Sweet Valley Kids Ser.: No. 39). (J). (gr. 1-3). 8.19 o.p. (*0-606-05642-4*) Turtleback Bks.

Stine, R. L. Dangerous Girls. 2003. 256p. (J). 111.92 (*0-06-056909-3*); 111.92 (*0-06-056910-7*); (Illus.). (gr. 7 up). 13.99 (*0-06-053080-4*) HarperCollins Children's Bk. Group.

—The Stepsister, Vol. 2. 1995. (Fear Street Ser.: No. 34). 160p. (J). (gr. 7 up). pap. 4.99 (*0-671-89426-9*, Simon Pulse) Simon & Schuster Children's Publishing.

Suzanne, Jamie. Amy's Secret Sister. 1994. (Sweet Valley Twins Ser.: No. 83). 144p. (J). (gr. 3-7). pap. 3.50 o.s.i (*0-553-48101-0*) Bantam Bks.

—Psychic Sisters. 1993. (Sweet Valley Twins Ser.: No. 70). 144p. (J). (gr. 3-7). pap. 3.50 o.s.i (*0-553-48057-X*) Bantam Bks.

—Psychic Sisters. 1993. (Sweet Valley Twins Ser.: No. 70). (J). (gr. 3-7). 8.60 o.p. (*0-606-05650-5*) Turtleback Bks.

Swicord, Robin. Little Women: The Children's Picture Book. 2004. (Illus.). 96p. (gr. 2 up). 15.95 (*1-55704-216-0*) Newmarket Pr.

Tada, Joni Eareckson & Jensen, Steve. The Mission Adventure. 2001. 143p. (J). (gr. 3-6). pap. 5.99 (*1-58134-257-8*) Crossway Bks.

Thesman, Jean. Calling the Swan. 2000. (Illus.). 176p. (J). (gr. 5-9). 15.99 o.s.i (*0-670-88874-5*, Viking Children's Bks.) Penguin Putnam Bks. for Young Readers.

Tolles, Martha. Secret Sister. 1992. (J). (gr. 4-7). mass mkt. 2.95 o.p. (*0-590-45245-2*) Scholastic, Inc.

Tripp, Valerie. Asi es Josefina: Una Nina Americana. 1998. (American Girls Collection: Bk. 1). (SPA.). 432p. (J). (gr. 2 up). pap. 34.95 (*1-56247-706-4*) Pleasant Co. Pubns.

—Asi es Josefina: Una Nina Americana. Moreno, Jose, tr. 1997. (American Girls Collection: Bk. 1). (SPA., Illus.). 96p. (J). (gr. 2 up). pap. 5.95 (*1-56247-496-0*, PE6901, American Girl) Pleasant Co. Pubns.

—Asi es Josefina: Una Nina Americana. 1997. (American Girls Collection: Bk. 1). (SPA., Illus.). (YA). (gr. 2 up). 12.10 (*0-606-11060-7*) Turtleback Bks.

—Changes for Josefina: A Winter Story. 1998. (American Girls Collection: Bk. 6). (Illus.). 80p. (J). (gr. 2 up). 12.95 (*1-56247-592-4*); pap. 5.95 (*1-56247-591-6*) Pleasant Co. Pubns. (American Girl).

—Changes for Josefina: A Winter Story. 1998. (American Girls Collection: Bk. 6). (Illus.). (YA). (gr. 2 up). 12.10 (*0-606-13264-3*) Turtleback Bks.

—Felicity's New Sister. 1999. (American Girls Short Stories Ser.). (Illus.). 56p. (YA). (gr. 2 up). 3.95 (*1-56247-762-5*, American Girl) Pleasant Co. Pubns.

—Josefina Aprende une Leccion: Un Cuento de la Escuela. Moreno, Jose, tr. 1997. (American Girls Collection: Bk. 2). (SPA., Illus.). 80p. (J). (gr. 2 up). pap. 5.95 (*1-56247-497-9*, BT4979, American Girl) Pleasant Co. Pubns.

—Josefina Learns a Lesson: A School Story. 1997. (American Girls Collection: Bk. 2). (Illus.). 80p. (J). (gr. 2 up). pap. 5.95 (*1-56247-517-7*); lib. bdg. 12.95 (*1-56247-518-5*) Pleasant Co. Pubns. (American Girl).

—Josefina Learns a Lesson: A School Story. 1997. (American Girls Collection: Bk. 2). (Illus.). (YA). (gr. 2 up). 12.10 (*0-606-11524-2*) Turtleback Bks.

—Josefina's Surprise: A Christmas Story. 1997. (American Girls Collection: Bk. 3). (Illus.). 80p. (J). (gr. 2 up). pap. 5.95 (*1-56247-519-3*); lib. bdg. 12.95 (*1-56247-520-7*) Pleasant Co. Pubns. (American Girl).

—Josefina's Surprise: A Christmas Story. 1997. (American Girls Collection: Bk. 3). (Illus.). (YA). (gr. 2 up). 12.10 (*0-606-11525-0*) Turtleback Bks.

—Meet Josefina: An American Girl. 1997. (American Girls Collection: Bk. 1). (Illus.). 96p. (J). (gr. 2 up). pap. 5.95 (*1-56247-515-0*); lib. bdg. 12.95 (*1-56247-516-9*) Pleasant Co. Pubns. (American Girl).

—Meet Josefina: An American Girl. 1997. (American Girls Collection: Bk. 1). (Illus.). (YA). (gr. 2 up). 12.10 (*0-606-11614-1*) Turtleback Bks.

—Una Sorpresa para Josefina: Un Cuento de Navidad. Moreno, Jose, tr. 1997. (American Girls Collection: Bk. 3). (SPA., Illus.). 80p. (J). (gr. 2 up). pap. 5.95 (*1-56247-498-7*, BT4987, American Girl) Pleasant Co. Pubns.

—Una Sorpresa para Josefina: Un Cuento de Navidad. 1997. (American Girls Collection: Bk. 3). (SPA.). (YA). (gr. 2 up). 12.10 (*0-606-12025-4*) Turtleback Bks.

—Thanks to Josefina. 2003. (American Girls Collection). (Illus.). 39p. (J). pap. 4.95 (*1-58485-698-X*, American Girl) Pleasant Co. Pubns.

Tucker, Kathy. The Seven Chinese Sisters. 2003. (Illus.). 32p. (J). (gr. k-3). 15.95 (*0-8075-7309-4*) Whitman, Albert & Co.

Turner, Ann. Finding Walter. 1997. 176p. (J). (gr. 3-7). 16.00 (*0-15-200212-X*) Harcourt Children's Bks.

Umansky, Kaye. Wilma's Wicked Revenge. l.t. unabr. ed. 2003. (Read-Along Ser.). 256p. (J). 29.95 incl. audio (*0-7540-6235-X*, RAO36, Galaxy Children's Large Print) BBC Audiobooks America.

Ungermann-Marshall, Yana. Gilda Gets Wise. 1996. (Illus.). 34p. (J). (gr. k-6). pap. 14.00 (*0-9670982-0-3*) Yana's Kitchen.

Van Leeuwen, Jean. Two Girls in Sister Dresses. 1994. (Illus.). 56p. (J). (gr. 1-5). 12.99 o.s.i (*0-8037-1230-8*); 12.89 o.p. (*0-8037-1231-6*) Penguin Putnam Bks. for Young Readers. (Dial Bks. for Young Readers).

—Two Girls in Sister Dresses. 1997. (Puffin Chapters Ser.). (J). 9.19 o.p. (*0-606-12021-1*) Turtleback Bks.

Velde, Vivian Vande. Alison, Who Went Away. 2001. (Illus.). 208p. (J). (gr. 5-9). tchr. ed. 15.00 (*0-618-04585-6*) Houghton Mifflin Co.

Waboose, Jan Bourdeau. Sky Sisters. 2000. (Illus.). 32p. (J). (ps-2). text 15.95 (*1-55074-697-9*) Kids Can Pr., Ltd.

—Skysisters. 2002. (Illus.). 32p. (J). (gr. k-3). pap. 5.95 (*1-55074-699-5*) Kids Can Pr., Ltd.

Wallace, John. The Twins. 2001. (Golden Books Family Storytime). (Illus.). 32p. (J). (ps). 9.95 (*0-307-10211-4*, Golden Bks.) Random Hse. Children's Bks.

Walter, Mildred Pitts. Mariah Keeps Cool. 1990. 144p. (J). (gr. 3-7). lib. bdg. 15.00 (*0-02-792295-2*, Simon & Schuster Children's Publishing) Simon & Schuster Children's Publishing.

—Mariah Loves Rock. 1988. 128p. (J). (gr. 3-7). lib. bdg. 13.95 o.p. (*0-02-792511-0*, Simon & Schuster Children's Publishing) Simon & Schuster Children's Publishing.

Warner, Sally. Sister Split. 2001. (American Girls Collection Ser.). 156p. (J). 14.95 (*1-58485-373-5*); pap. 5.95 (*1-58485-372-7*) Pleasant Co. Pubns. (American Girl).

Werner, Jane. Cinderella. 2002. (Illus.). 24p. (J). 2.99 (*0-7364-2151-3*, RH/Disney) Random Hse. Children's Bks.

Wesley, Valerie Wilson. Cookie Caper. 2000. 124p. (J). (gr. 2-5). 15.99 (*0-7868-0465-3*) Disney Pr.

—Willimena. (J). Bk. 2. 2002. 12.99 (*0-7868-0466-1*); Bk. 3. Date not set. 12.99 (*0-7868-0523-4*); Bk. 4. Date not set. 12.99 (*0-7868-0524-2*) Hyperion Bks. for Children.

—Willimena & Mrs. Sweetly's Guinea Pig. Date not set. (J). pap. 3.99 (*0-7868-1322-9*, Jump at the Sun) Hyperion Bks. for Children.

West, Tracey. Bad News Bike. 2002. (Powerpuff Girls Readers: No. 5). 32p. (J). mass mkt. 3.99 (*0-439-34435-2*) Scholastic, Inc.

White, Ruth. Memories of Summer, RS. 2000. 144p. (J). (gr. 7-10). 16.00 (*0-374-34945-2*, Farrar, Straus & Giroux (BYR)) Farrar, Straus & Giroux.

—Memories of Summer. 2002. 160p. (YA). (gr. 7 up). mass mkt. 5.99 (*0-440-22921-9*, Dell Books for Young Readers) Random Hse. Children's Bks.

—Memories of Summer. l.t. ed. 2001. (Illus.). 144p. (J). (gr. 5-9). 21.95 (*0-7862-3084-3*) Thorndike Pr.

Whybrow, Ian. A Baby for Grace. 1998. (Illus.). 32p. (J). (ps-k). tchr. ed. 15.95 (*0-7534-5142-5*, Kingfisher) Houghton Mifflin Co. Trade & Reference Div.

Widerberg, Siv. The Big Sister. Sjogren, Birgitta, tr. from SWE. 1989. (Illus.). 36p. (J). 9.95 o.p. (*91-29-59186-4*) R & S Bks. SWE. *Dist:* Holtzbrinck Pubs.

Wiebe, Trina. Ants Don't Catch Flying Saucers. 2001. (Abby & Tess Pet-Sitters Ser.: Vol. 5). (Illus.). 95p. (J). pap. 5.95 (*1-894222-31-8*) Lobster Pr. CAN. *Dist:* Publishers Group West.

—Goats Don't Brush Their Teeth. Pavanel, Jane, ed. 2002. (Abby & Tess Pet-Sitters Ser.). (Illus.). 96p. (J). (gr. 2-4). pap. (*1-894222-59-8*) Lobster Pr.

Wilder, Laura Ingalls. Little House Sisters: Collected Stories from the Little House Books. 1997. (Little House Ser.). (Illus.). 96p. (J). (gr. 3-7). 19.95 (*0-06-027587-1*) HarperCollins Children's Bk. Group.

Wiley, Melissa. Beyond the Heather Hills. 2003. (Little House Ser.). (Illus.). 208p. (J). pap. 5.99 (*0-06-440715-2*) HarperCollins Pubs.

Wilkes, Maria D. Caroline & Her Sister. 2000. (Little House Chapter Bks.: No. 2). (Illus.). 80p. (J). (gr. 3-6). pap. 4.25 (*0-06-442092-2*, Harper Trophy); lib. bdg. 14.89 (*0-06-028155-3*) HarperCollins Children's Bk. Group.

—Caroline & Her Sister. 2000. (Little House Chapter Bks.: No. 2). (J). (gr. 3-6). 10.40 (*0-606-20285-4*) Turtleback Bks.

William, Kate. Dear Sister. 1984. (Sweet Valley High Ser.: No. 7). (YA). (gr. 7 up). 9.09 o.p. (*0-606-01158-7*) Turtleback Bks.

Williams, Carol Lynch. Carolina Autumn. 2001. 160p. (YA). (gr. 5). mass mkt. 4.99 (*0-440-22878-6*, Laurel Leaf) Random Hse. Children's Bks.

Williams, Vera B. Amber Was Brave, Essie Was Smart: The Story of Amber & Essie Told Here in Poems & Pictures. 2001. (Illus.). 72p. (J). (gr. 2 up). 15.99 (*0-06-029460-4*); lib. bdg. 16.89 (*0-06-029461-2*) HarperCollins Children's Bk. Group. (Greenwillow Bks.).

Wilson, Jacqueline. Double Act. 1998. (Illus.). 192p. (gr. 4-7). reprint ed. text 14.95 o.s.i (*0-385-32312-3*, Delacorte Pr.) Dell Publishing.

—Double Act. 1999. (Illus.). 192p. (gr. 3-7). pap. text 4.99 (*0-440-41374-5*) Random Hse. Children's Bks.

Winer, Yvonne. Ssh, Don't Wake the Baby! 1993. (Voyages Ser.). (Illus.). (J). 3.75 (*0-383-03655-0*) SRA/McGraw-Hill.

Winfrey, Elizabeth. Lets Put on a Show! 2000. (Full House Sisters Ser.: No. 7). 160p. (J). (gr. 4-6). pap. 3.99 (*0-671-04088-X*, Simon Spotlight) Simon & Schuster Children's Publishing.

Winter, Susan. A Baby Just Like Me. 1994. (Illus.). 32p. (J). (ps-1). pap. 13.95 o.p. (*1-56458-668-5*) Dorling Kindersley Publishing, Inc.

—A Baby Just Like Me. (J). 2002. (ENG & TUR.). 13.95 (*1-85269-295-2*); 2000. (ARA & ENG.). 13.99 (*1-85269-297-9*); 2000. (BEN & ENG.). 13.95 (*1-85269-248-0*); 2000. (CHI.). 13.99 (*1-85269-259-6*); 2000. (ENG & GUJ.). 13.95 (*1-85269-290-1*); 2000. (ENG & SOM.). 19.95 (*1-85269-292-8*); 2000. (ENG & URD.). 13.95 (*1-85269-296-0*) Mantra Publishing, Ltd. GBR. *Dist:* AIMS International Bks., Inc.

Wood, Audrey. Three Sisters. 1989. (Easy-to-Read Bks.). (Illus.). 4p. (J). (ps-3). pap. 4.95 o.p. *(0-8037-0597-2*, Dial Bks. for Young Readers) Penguin Putnam Bks. for Young Readers.

Wood, Marcia. Always, Julia. 1993. 128p. (J). (gr. 5-9). lib. bdg. 13.95 o.s.i *(0-689-31728-X*, Atheneum) Simon & Schuster Children's Publishing.

Woods, Brenda. The Red Rose. 2003. 144p. pap. 5.99 *(0-14-250151-4*, Puffin Bks.) Penguin Putnam Bks. for Young Readers.

—The Red Rose Box. 2002. 160p. (J). (gr. 4-6). 16.99 *(0-399-23702-X)* Putnam Publishing Group, The.

Woodson, Jacqueline. Lena. 1999. (YA). pap., stu. ed. 42.95 incl. audio *(0-7887-3646-9*, 41012X4) Recorded Bks., LLC.

—Lena. 2000. 11.04 *(0-606-17832-5)* Turtleback Bks.

Wooley, Catherine. Cathy's Little Sister. 1988. 176p. (J). (gr. 5 up). pap. 3.95 o.p. *(0-14-032552-2*, Puffin Bks.) Penguin Putnam Bks. for Young Readers.

Wright, Betty R. My Sister Is Different. 1993. (Life & Living from a Child's Point of View Ser.). (J). (ps-3). pap. 4.95 o.p. *(0-8114-7158-6)* Raintree Pubs.

Wright, Betty Ren. The Dollhouse Murders. 1983. 160p. (J). (gr. 5-7). tchr. ed. 16.95 *(0-8234-0497-8)* Holiday Hse., Inc.

—The Dollhouse Murders. unabr. ed. 1999. (J). (gr. 4-6). 39.95 incl. audio *(0-87499-521-3)*; pap. 27.95 incl. audio *(0-87499-520-5)* Live Oak Media.

—The Dollhouse Murders. 1985. 160p. (J). (gr. 3-7). mass mkt. 4.50 *(0-590-43461-6)*; (gr. 4-6). reprint ed. 1.25 o.p. *(0-590-40929-8*, Scholastic Paperbacks); (gr. 4-6). reprint ed. pap. 2.50 o.p. *(0-590-33245-7*, Scholastic Paperbacks) Scholastic, Inc.

—The Dollhouse Murders. 1983. (J). 10.55 *(0-606-03400-5)* Turtleback Bks.

—The Dollhouse Murders, Grades 4-6. 1999. pap., tchr. ed. 41.95 incl. audio *(0-87499-522-1)* Live Oak Media.

—The Moonlight Man. 2000. (Illus.). 181p. (J). (gr. 3-7). pap. 15.95 *(0-590-25237-2*, Scholastic Reference) Scholastic, Inc.

Yates, Dan. Angels to the Rescue. 1997. (J). pap. 11.95 *(1-57734-210-0*, 01113267) Covenant Communications, Inc.

Yektai, Niki. Triplets! 1998. 3. (Illus.). 32p. (J). (gr. 1-3). 22.40 *(0-7613-0351-0)*; pap. 6.95 *(0-7613-0348-0)* Millbrook Pr., Inc.

Yezerski, Thomas F. Queen of the World, RS. 2000. (Illus.). 32p. (J). (gr. k-3). 16.00 *(0-374-36165-7*, Farrar, Straus & Giroux (BYR)) Farrar, Straus & Giroux.

Yglesias, Helen. The Girls. 2000. 240p. pap. 12.95 *(0-345-44112-5*, Ballantine Bks.) Ballantine Bks.

Yoemans, Ellen. Lost & Found: Remembering a Sister. Johnson, Joy, ed. 2000. (Illus.). 32p. (J). (gr. k-4). pap. 8.95 *(1-56123-129-0*, LAFC) Centering Corp.

STEPFAMILIES—FICTION

Adler, C. S. Her Blue Straw Hat. 1997. 112p. (YA). (gr. 3-7). 16.00 o.s.i *(0-15-201466-7)* Harcourt Children's Bks.

—Her Blue Straw Hat. 1997. pap. 5.00 *(0-15-201469-1)* Harcourt Trade Pubs.

—The No Place Cat. 2002. 160p. (YA). (gr. 5-9). 15.00 *(0-618-09644-2*, Clarion Bks.) Houghton Mifflin Co. Trade & Reference Div.

Altman, Adam. Liliana's Fan. 2001. 116p. (gr. 4-7). pap. 9.95 *(0-595-15873-0)* iUniverse, Inc.

Auch, Mary Jane. Out of Step. 1995. 128p. (J). (gr. 4-7). tchr. ed. 13.95 *(0-8234-0985-6)* Holiday Hse., Inc.

Baker, Jennifer. At Midnight: Once upon a Dream. 1995. 192p. (gr. 7-9). mass mkt. 3.99 *(0-590-25947-4)* Scholastic, Inc.

Ballard, Robin. When I Am a Sister. 1998. (Illus.). 24p. (J). (ps-3). 15.00 *(0-688-15397-6)*; 14.89 o.p. *(0-688-15398-4)* HarperCollins Children's Bk. Group. (Greenwillow Bks.).

Bechard, Margaret E. My Mom Married the Principal. 1998. 144p. (J). (gr. 5-9). 14.99 o.s.i *(0-670-87394-2)* Penguin Putnam Bks. for Young Readers.

Bender, Esther. Search for a Fawn. 1998. (Illus.). 32p. (J). (gr. k-5). pap. 8.99 *(0-8361-9099-8)* Herald Pr.

Bennerson, Denise. Daniel Gets a New Daddy. 2001. (Illus.). 12p. (J). 4.00 *(0-9646279-4-9)* Bennerson, Denise.

Biggar, Joan R. Missing on Castaway Island. 1997. (Megan Parnell Mysteries Ser.: Vol. 1). 160p. (J). (gr. 5-9). pap. text 5.99 *(0-570-05015-4*, 56-1842) Concordia Publishing Hse.

Bryant, Ann. You Can't Fall for Your Step-Sister. 2003. (Step-Chain Ser.). (J). (gr. 3-8). pap. 3.95 *(1-894222-77-6)* Lobster Pr. CAN. *Dist:* Publishers Group West.

Bullard, Lisa. Trick-or-Treat on Milton Street. 2001. (Picture Bks.). (Illus.). 32p. (J). (ps-3). lib. bdg. 15.95 *(1-57505-158-3*, Carolrhoda Bks.) Lerner Publishing Group.

Butler, Beverly. Witch's Fire. 144p. (J). (gr. 5-9). 1995. pap. 3.99 o.p. *(0-14-037614-3*, Puffin Bks.); 1993. 14.99 o.p. *(0-525-65132-2*, Dutton Children's Bks.) Penguin Putnam Bks. for Young Readers.

Butler, Charles. Timon's Tide. 2000. (Illus.). 192p. (YA). (gr. 7-12). 16.00 *(0-689-82593-5*, McElderry, Margaret K.) Simon & Schuster Children's Publishing.

Caso, A., ed. Cinderfella & the Slam Dunk Contest. 1994. (Illus.). 32p. (J). (gr. 2-6). pap. 13.95 *(0-8283-1966-9)* Branden Bks.

Christopher, Matt. Spike It! 1999. 144p. (J). (gr. 3-7). 15.95 *(0-316-13451-1)*; pap. 4.50 o.p. *(0-316-13401-5)* Little Brown & Co.

—Spike It! 1998. 10.00 *(0-606-16724-2)* Turtleback Bks.

Cinderella. 1990. (Puppet Fairy Tales Ser.). (Illus.). 20p. (J). (ps-2). 0.60 o.p. *(0-8120-6168-3)* Barron's Educational Series, Inc.

Cinderella. 1995. (J). (ps-1). 3.98 *(1-85854-278-2)* Brimax Bks., Ltd.

Cinderella. 2003. (My Side of the Story Ser.: Bk. 1). (Illus.). 72p. (J). 14.99 *(0-7868-3448-X*, Disney Editions) Disney Pr.

Cinderella. 2002. (Illus.). 48p. (J). pap. 12.95 incl. audio compact disk *(2-89558-089-8)* Editions Alexandre Stanke CAN. *Dist:* Penton Overseas, Inc.

Cinderella. 1987. (Ladybird Bks.). (ARA., Illus.). 52p. (J). (gr. 2-5). 4.95 *(0-86685-193-3*, LDL187) International Bk. Ctr., Inc.

Cinderella. (Illus.). (J). 1994. (Paint with Water Fairy Tales Ser.: No. II). 32p. (gr. k-2). pap. 1.95 o.s.i *(1-56144-487-1*, Honey Bear Bks.); 1993. (Treasury of Fairy Tales Ser.). 24p. (gr. 2-5). pap. 3.95 o.s.i *(1-56144-359-X*, Honey Bear Bks.); 1992. (Fun-to-Read Fairy Tales Ser.). 24p. pap. 2.50 *(1-56144-088-4)* Modern Publishing.

Cinderella. 1994. (Classics Ser.). (Illus.). 96p. (J). 7.98 o.p. *(1-57082-017-1)* Mouse Works.

Cinderella. 9999. (Illus.). (J). (Well-Loved Tales Ser.: Level 3, No. 606D-1). (gr. 2-4). 3.50 o.p. *(0-7214-0647-5)*; (Read It Yourself Ser.: Level 4, No. 777-3). (ps-2). 3.50 o.p. *(0-7214-5125-X)* Penguin Group (USA) Inc. (Ladybird Bks.).

Cinderella. 1993. (Favorite Fairy Tales Ser.). (Illus.). 24p. (J). 4.98 *(1-56173-913-8)* Publications International, Ltd.

Cinderella. 1974. (Puppet Pop-up Books). (Illus.). 6p. (J). (gr. k-2). 2.50 o.p. *(0-448-11804-1)* Putnam Publishing Group, The.

Cinderella. (Little Golden Bks.). (J). 1999. pap. 4.99 *(0-307-98064-2*, 98064); 1995. (Illus.). 24p. o.p. *(0-307-74034-X)* Random Hse. Children's Bks. (Golden Bks.).

Cinderella. 1986. (J). mass mkt. 13.27 o.p. *(0-516-09179-4*, Children's Pr.) Scholastic Library Publishing.

Cinderella. 1990. (Golden Fairy Tales Ser.). (J). 5.98 o.p. *(0-8317-3877-4)* Smithmark Pubs., Inc.

Cinderella. 2002. (Classic Tales Mini Bks.). (Illus.). 32p. (J). *(1-59069-034-6*, T1003); incl. audio compact disk *(1-59069-101-6*, T1103) Studio Mouse LLC.

Cinderella. unabr. ed. (Read-Along Ser.). (J). 7.99 incl. audio *(1-55723-007-2)* Walt Disney Records.

Cohn, Rachel. Gingerbread. 2002. (Illus.). 176p. (J). (gr. 9 up). 15.95 *(0-689-84337-2*, Simon & Schuster Children's Publishing) Simon & Schuster Children's Publishing.

—The Steps. unabr. ed. 2003. (J). (gr. 3-7). audio 18.00 *(0-8072-1558-9*, Listening Library) Random Hse. Audio Publishing Group.

—The Steps. 2003. (Illus.). 137p. (J). (gr. 3-7). 16.95 *(0-689-84549-9*, Simon & Schuster Children's Publishing) Simon & Schuster Children's Publishing.

Cohn, Rachel & Wattenberg, Jane. Gingerbread. 2003. (Illus.). 176p. (YA). pap. 6.99 *(0-689-86020-X*, Simon Pulse) Simon & Schuster Children's Publishing.

Colman, Hila. Weekend Sisters. 1985. 176p. (J). (gr. 7 up). 11.95 o.p. *(0-688-05785-3*, Morrow, William & Co.) Morrow/Avon.

Cooley, Beth. Ostrich Eye. 2004. (Illus.). 192p. (YA). lib. bdg. 17.99 *(0-385-90132-1)*; (gr. 7). 15.95 *(0-385-73106-X)* Random Hse. Children's Bks. (Delacorte Bks. for Young Readers).

Cooper, Ilene. The Worst Noel. (Holiday 5 Ser.: Bk. 2). 160p. (J). (gr. 3-7). 1995. pap. 3.99 o.p. *(0-14-036518-4*, Puffin Bks.); 1994. 14.99 o.p. *(0-670-85058-6*, Viking Children's Bks.) Penguin Putnam Bks. for Young Readers.

Cray, Jordan. Dead Man's Hand. 1998. (Danger.com Ser.: No. 8). 224p. (YA). (gr. 6 up). mass mkt. 3.99 *(0-689-82383-5*, Simon Pulse) Simon & Schuster Children's Publishing.

Danziger, Paula. It's an Aardvark-Eat-Turtle World. 1985. 144p. (J). (gr. 7 up). 12.95 o.s.i *(0-385-29371-2*, Delacorte Pr.) Dell Publishing.

—It's an Aardvark-Eat-Turtle World. l.t. unabr. ed. 1989. 145p. (J). (gr. 4 up). 13.95 o.p. *(0-8161-4704-3*, Macmillan Reference USA) Gale Group.

—It's an Aardvark-Eat-Turtle World. 2000. 144p. (YA). (gr. 5-9). pap. 4.99 *(0-698-11691-7*, Puffin Bks.) Penguin Putnam Bks. for Young Readers.

—It's an Aardvark-Eat-Turtle World. 144p. 1996. (J). pap. 3.99 o.s.i *(0-440-41399-0*, Dell Books for Young Readers); 1986. (YA). (gr. 5 up). mass mkt. 3.99 o.p. *(0-440-94028-1*, Laurel Leaf) Random Hse. Children's Bks.

—It's an Aardvark-Eat-Turtle World. 2000. (Illus.). (J). 11.04 *(0-606-18469-4)*; 1996. 9.09 o.p. *(0-606-00305-3)* Turtleback Bks.

Deem, James M. Three NBs of Julian Drew. 1994. 224p. (J). (gr. 7 up). tchr. ed. 16.00 o.s.i *(0-395-69453-1)* Houghton Mifflin Co.

Delton, Judy. Angel Spreads Her Wings. (Illus.). (J). 2002. 160p. (gr. 2-5). pap. 4.95 *(0-618-21617-0)*; 1999. 144p. (gr. 4-6). tchr. ed. 15.00 *(0-395-91006-4)* Houghton Mifflin Co.

Dessen, Sarah. This Lullaby. 2004. 352p. pap. 7.99 *(0-14-250155-7*, Puffin Bks.) Penguin Putnam Bks. for Young Readers.

Draper, Sharon M. Forged by Fire. 2002. (Illus.). (J). 13.40 *(0-7587-0354-6)* Book Wholesalers, Inc.

—Forged by Fire. (Hazelwood High Trilogy: Bk. 2). 160p. (YA). (gr. 7 up). 1998. mass mkt. 4.99 *(0-689-81851-3*, Simon Pulse); 1997. 16.95 *(0-689-80699-X*, Atheneum) Simon & Schuster Children's Publishing.

—Forged by Fire. 1998. 11.04 *(0-606-13397-6)* Turtleback Bks.

Fine, Anne. Step by Wicked Step: A Novel. 1997. 144p. (gr. 4-7). pap. text 3.99 o.s.i *(0-440-41329-X)* Dell Publishing.

—Step by Wicked Step: A Novel. 1996. 144p. (J). (gr. 4-7). 15.95 o.p. *(0-316-28345-2)* Little Brown & Co.

—Step by Wicked Step: A Novel. 1997. 10.04 *(0-606-11910-8)* Turtleback Bks.

Frances, Ellen. Looking for Dad. 1999. (Supa Doopers Ser.). (Illus.). 64p. (J). *(0-7608-3292-7)* Sundance Publishing.

Fransoy, Monse, illus. Cinderella. 2001. (ENG & SPA.). 32p. (J). (ps-3). 12.95 o.s.i *(0-8118-3084-5)* Chronicle Bks. LLC.

Friesen, Gayle. Losing Forever. (Illus.). (YA). (gr. 5-9). 2003. 247p. pap. 6.95 *(1-55337-032-5)*; 2002. 248p. 16.95 *(1-55337-031-7)* Kids Can Pr., Ltd.

Gondosch, Linda. Camp Kickapoo. 1993. (Illus.). 128p. (J). (gr. 4-6). 13.99 o.p. *(0-525-67373-3*, Dutton Children's Bks.) Penguin Putnam Bks. for Young Readers.

—Camp Kickapoo. 1995. (Illus.). 128p. (J). (gr. 3-6). reprint ed. pap. 3.50 *(0-671-75371-1*, Aladdin) Simon & Schuster Children's Publishing.

Greene, Stephanie. Falling into Place. 2002. (Illus.). 128p. (J). (gr. 4-7). tchr. ed. 15.00 *(0-618-17744-2*, Clarion Bks.) Houghton Mifflin Co. Trade & Reference Div.

Griffin, Adele. Dive. 1999. (gr. 5-9). 155p. (J). 14.99 *(0-7868-0440-8)*; 160p. (YA). lib. bdg. 15.49 *(0-7868-2389-5)* Hyperion Bks. for Children.

—Dive. 2001. 176p. (J). (gr. 5-9). pap. 5.99 *(0-7868-1567-1)* Hyperion Pr.

—Dive. 2001. (J). 12.04 *(0-606-21151-9)* Turtleback Bks.

Grimm. 630 - Cenicienta. 2001. Tr. of Cinderella. (SPA.). *(968-6347-30-5)* Larousse, Ediciones, S. A. de C. V.

Hahn, Mary Downing. Look for Me by Moonlight. 1997. 192p. (J). (gr. 7 up). pap. 5.99 *(0-380-72703-X*, Harper Trophy) HarperCollins Children's Bk. Group.

—Look for Me by Moonlight. 1995. (YA). 208p. (gr. 7 up). tchr. ed. 16.00 *(0-395-69843-X)*; E-Book 16.00 *(0-618-15205-9)* Houghton Mifflin Co.

—Look for Me by Moonlight. 1997. (J). 10.55 *(0-606-11573-0)* Turtleback Bks.

—The Spanish Kidnapping Disaster. Giblin, James C., ed. 1991. 144p. (J). (gr. 5-9). tchr. ed. 16.00 *(0-395-55696-1*, Clarion Bks.) Houghton Mifflin Co. Trade & Reference Div.

—The Spanish Kidnapping Disaster. 1993. 144p. (YA). (gr. 4-7). pap. 4.50 *(0-380-71712-3*, Avon Bks.) Morrow/Avon.

—The Spanish Kidnapping Disaster. 1991. (J). 10.55 *(0-606-02901-X)* Turtleback Bks.

Hinton, S. E. Esto Ya Es Otra Historia. (SPA.). (J). 6.95 *(84-204-4121-X)* Santillana USA Publishing Co., Inc.

—That Was Then, This Is Now. 1996. 160p. (J). pap. 2.49 o.s.i *(0-440-22012-2)* Dell Publishing.

—That Was Then, This Is Now. 160p. (YA). (gr. 7-12). 1998. pap. 6.99 *(0-14-038966-0)*; 1971. (Illus.). 15.99 *(0-670-69798-2*, Viking Children's Bks.) Penguin Putnam Bks. for Young Readers.

—That Was Then, This Is Now. (J). 1990. mass mkt. o.s.i *(0-440-80198-2*, Dell Books for Young Readers); 1989. 224p. mass mkt. 4.99 o.p. *(0-440-98652-4*, Laurel Leaf) Random Hse. Children's Bks.

—That Was Then, This Is Now. 1971. (YA). (gr. 7 up). 18.50 o.p. *(0-8446-6371-9)* Smith, Peter Pub., Inc.

—That Was Then, This Is Now. 1998. (Puffin Book Ser.). (YA). 12.04 *(0-606-12861-1)* Turtleback Bks.

Hoffman, Mary. Boundless Grace. 2002. (Illus.). (J). 25.45 *(0-7587-2139-0)* Book Wholesalers, Inc.

—Boundless Grace. (Illus.). 32p. (J). (ps-3). 2000. pap. 5.99 *(0-14-055667-2*, Puffin Bks.); 1995. 16.99 *(0-8037-1715-6*, Dial Bks. for Young Readers) Penguin Putnam Bks. for Young Readers.

—Boundless Grace. 2000. 12.14 *(0-606-20350-8)*; 12.14 *(0-606-20224-2)* Turtleback Bks.

Hunt, Angela Elwell. The Glory of Love. 1993. (Cassie Perkins Ser.: Vol. 9). (J). (gr. 5-7). pap. 4.99 o.p. *(0-8423-1119-X)* Tyndale Hse. Pubs.

—The Glory of Love. 2000. (Cassie Perkins Ser.: Vol. 9). 176p. (gr. 5-9). pap. 11.95 *(0-595-08994-1)* iUniverse, Inc.

Johnson, Tim. Never So Green, RS. 2002. 240p. (YA). 18.00 *(0-374-35509-6*, Farrar, Straus & Giroux (BYR)) Farrar, Straus & Giroux.

Jukes, Mavis. Cinderella 2000. 2001. (Illus.). (J). 11.04 *(0-606-20605-1)* Turtleback Bks.

Kelly, Theresa. Living on Nothing Atoll. 1999. (Aloha Cove Ser.: Vol. 1). (Illus.). 160p. (J). (gr. 8-12). pap. 5.99 *(0-570-05483-4)* Concordia Publishing Hse.

—Seaside High. 1999. (Aloha Cove Ser.: Vol. 2). (Illus.). 160p. (J). (gr. 8-12). pap. 5.99 *(0-570-05484-2)* Concordia Publishing Hse.

—Tomorrow I'll Miss You. 1999. (Aloha Cove Ser.: Vol. 3). (Illus.). 160p. (J). (gr. 8-12). pap. 6.00 *(0-570-05485-0)* Concordia Publishing Hse.

Lantz, Francess L. Stepbaby from Planet Weird. 2001. (Illus.). (J). 3.99 *(0-375-81259-8*, Random Hse. Bks. for Young Readers) Random Hse. Children's Bks.

—Stepsister from the Planet Weird. (J). (gr. 3-7). 1997. 11.99 o.s.i *(0-679-97330-3)*; 1996. 176p. pap. 3.99 o.s.i *(0-679-87330-9)* Random Hse. Children's Bks. (Random Hse. Bks. for Young Readers).

—Stepsister from the Planet Weird. 1997. 10.04 *(0-606-13040-3)* Turtleback Bks.

Leach, Norman. My Wicked Stepmother. 1993. (Illus.). 32p. (J). (ps-3). lib. bdg. 13.95 *(0-02-754700-0*, Simon & Schuster Children's Publishing) Simon & Schuster Children's Publishing.

Lewis, Beverly. California Christmas. 1994. (Holly's Heart Ser.: Vol. 5). 144p. (J). (gr. 6-9). pap. 6.99 *(0-310-43321-5)* Zondervan.

—California Crazy. 2002. (Hollys Heart Ser.). 160p. (J). pap. 5.99 *(0-7642-2504-9)* Bethany Hse. Pubs.

—Eight Is Enough. 2003. (Holly's Heart Ser.). 160p. (Orig.). (J). pap. 5.99 *(0-7642-2620-7)* Bethany Hse. Pubs.

—Eight Is Enough, Bk. 13. 1997. (Holly's Heart Ser.: Vol. 13). 144p. (Orig.). (J). (gr. 6-9). pap. 6.99 *(0-310-20844-0)* Zondervan.

—It's a Girl Thing. 2003. (Holly's Heart Ser.). 160p. (Orig.). (J). pap. 5.99 *(0-7642-2621-5)* Bethany Hse. Pubs.

—It's a Girl Thing, Bk. 14. 1997. (Holly's Heart Ser.: Vol. 14). 144p. (Orig.). (J). (gr. 6-9). pap. 6.99 *(0-310-20845-9)* Zondervan.

—Little White Lies. 2002. (Hollys Heart Ser.). 160p. (J). (gr. 5-9). pap. 5.99 *(0-7642-2617-7)* Bethany Hse. Pubs.

—Little White Lies, Bk. 10. 1995. (Holly's Heart Ser.: Vol. 10). 160p. (J). (gr. 5-9). pap. 6.99 *(0-310-20194-2)* Zondervan.

—Second-Best Friend. 2002. (Hollys Heart Ser.). 160p. (J). pap. 5.99 *(0-7642-2505-7)* Bethany Hse. Pubs.

—Second-Best Friend. 1994. (Holly's Heart Ser.: Vol. 6). 160p. (J). (gr. 6-9). pap. 6.99 *(0-310-43331-2)* Zondervan.

Love, D. Anne. A Year Without Rain. 2000. (Illus.). vii, 118p. (J). (gr. 3-7). tchr. ed. 15.95 *(0-8234-1488-4)* Holiday Hse., Inc.

Martin, Ann M. Dawn's Wicked Stepsister. l.t. ed. 1995. (Baby-Sitters Club Ser.: No. 31). 144p. (J). (gr. 3-7). lib. bdg. 21.27 o.p. *(0-8368-1411-8)* Stevens, Gareth Inc.

McClintock, Norah E. The Stepfather Game. 1991. 192p. (YA). pap. 2.95 o.p. *(0-590-43971-5*, Scholastic Paperbacks) Scholastic, Inc.

McGraw, Eloise Jarvis. Tangled Webb. 1993. 160p. (YA). (gr. 5 up). 13.95 *(0-689-50573-6*, McElderry, Margaret K.) Simon & Schuster Children's Publishing.

McNeal, Laura. Zipped. 2003. 288p. (J). (gr. 7-12). lib. bdg. 17.99 *(0-375-91491-9*, Knopf Bks. for Young Readers) Random Hse. Children's Bks.

McNeal, Laura & McNeal, Tom. Zipped. 2003. 288p. (J). (gr. 7). 15.95 *(0-375-81491-4*, Knopf Bks. for Young Readers) Random Hse. Children's Bks.

McVeity, Jen. On Different Shores. 1998. (Illus.). 167p. (YA). (gr. 5-9). pap. 16.95 *(0-531-30115-X)*; lib. bdg. 17.99 *(0-531-33115-6)* Scholastic, Inc. (Orchard Bks.).

Meyer, Carolyn. Denny's Tapes. 1987. 224p. (YA). (gr. 9 up). lib. bdg. 14.95 o.s.i *(0-689-50413-6*, McElderry, Margaret K.) Simon & Schuster Children's Publishing.

STEPPARENTS—FICTION

—Nancy's Story 1765. 2000. (Young Americans). (Illus.). 160p. (gr. 2-6). text 9.95 o.s.i (*0-385-32679-3*, Delacorte Bks. for Young Readers) Random Hse. Children's Bks.

Oneal, Zibby. A Formal Feeling. (J). 1990. pap. 3.95 o.p. (*0-14-034539-6*, Puffin Bks.); 1982. (Illus.). 168p. (gr. 7 up). 12.95 o.p. (*0-670-32488-4*, Viking Children's Bks.) Penguin Putnam Bks. for Young Readers.

Paterson, Katherine. The Field of the Dogs. 2001. (Illus.). 96p. (J). (gr. 4-7). 14.95 (*0-06-029474-4*); lib. bdg. 14.89 (*0-06-029475-2*) HarperCollins Children's Bk. Group.

—The Field of the Dogs. 2002. (Illus.). 112p. (J). pap. 4.99 (*0-06-442147-3*) HarperCollins Pubs.

Patneaude, David. Framed in Fire. 224p. (YA). (gr. 6-9). 2001. pap. 5.95 (*0-8075-9096-7*); 1999. (Illus.). lib. bdg. 14.95 (*0-8075-9098-3*) Whitman, Albert & Co.

Pevsner, Stella. Sister of the Quints. 1987. 192p. (J). (gr. 5-9). 13.95 o.p. (*0-89919-498-2*, Clarion Bks.) Houghton Mifflin Co. Trade & Reference Div.

Pfeffer, Susan Beth. Devil's Den. 1998. 115p. (J). (gr. 3-7). 15.95 (*0-8027-8650-2*) Walker & Co.

Platt, Randall Beth. Honor Bright. 1998. 240p. (YA). (gr. 7-12). mass mkt. 4.50 o.s.i (*0-440-21987-6*, Laurel Leaf) Random Hse. Children's Bks.

—Honor Bright. 1998. 10.55 (*0-606-13486-7*) Turtleback Bks.

Ransom, Candice F. We're Growing Together. 1993. (Illus.). 32p. (J). (ps-2). lib. bdg. 14.95 (*0-02-775666-1*, Simon & Schuster Children's Publishing) Simon & Schuster Children's Publishing.

—We're Growing Together. (Illus.). 32p. (J). 3.98 o.p. (*0-7651-0033-9*) Smithmark Pubs., Inc.

Rinaldi, Ann. Keep Smiling Through. 1996. 208p. (YA). (gr. 3-7). 13.00 o.s.i (*0-15-200768-7*) Harcourt Children's Bks.

Rinn, Miriam. The Saturday Secret. 1999. (Illus.). 144p. (J). (gr. 4-7). pap. 7.95 (*1-881283-26-7*) Alef Design Group.

Sherman, Charlotte W. Eli & the Swamp Man. 1996. (Illus.). 96p. (J). (gr. 2-5). 13.95 o.p. (*0-06-024722-3*) HarperCollins Children's Bk. Group.

Silver, Norman. Python Dance. 1993. 240p. (YA). 14.99 o.p. (*0-525-45161-7*) Penguin Putnam Bks. for Young Readers.

Spinelli, Eileen. Lizzie Logan, Second Banana. 96p. (gr. 2-5). 2000. per. 3.99 (*0-689-83048-3*, Aladdin); 1998. (J). per. 15.00 o.s.i (*0-689-81510-7*, Simon & Schuster Children's Publishing) Simon & Schuster Children's Publishing.

—Lizzie Logan, Second Banana. 2000. 10.04 (*0-606-17827-9*) Turtleback Bks.

Springer, Nancy. Secret Star. 1997. 144p. (YA). (gr. 5-9). 15.95 o.s.i (*0-399-23028-9*, Philomel) Penguin Putnam Bks. for Young Readers.

Spykman, E. C. The Wild Angel. 1981. (J). lib. bdg. 9.95 o.p. (*0-8398-2624-9*, Macmillan Reference USA) Gale Group.

Stewart, Jennifer J. The Bean King's Daughter. 2002. 176p. (J). (gr. 3-7). tchr. ed. 16.95 (*0-8234-1644-5*) Holiday Hse., Inc.

Sturtevant, Katherine. At the Sign of the Star, RS. 2000. 144p. (YA). (gr. 5 up). 16.00 (*0-374-30449-1*, Farrar, Straus & Giroux (BYR)) Farrar, Straus & Giroux.

Tamar, Erika. Junkyard Dog. 1997. (J). 11.04 (*0-606-12972-3*) Turtleback Bks.

Venable, Leslie Allgood. The Not So Wicked Stepmother. 1999. (Illus.). 24p. (J). (gr. 1-7). per. 9.95 (*0-9666817-0-3*) Venable, L.A. Publishing Co.

Vigna, Judith. She's Not My Real Mother. Fay, Ann, ed. 1980. (Albert Whitman Concept Bks.). (Illus.). 32p. (J). (gr. 1-3). lib. bdg. 14.95 o.p. (*0-8075-7340-X*) Whitman, Albert & Co.

Voigt, Cynthia. When She Hollers. 192p. (gr. 7 up). 2003. (J). pap. 5.99 (*0-590-46715-8*, Scholastic Paperbacks); 1994. (YA). pap. 13.95 o.p. (*0-590-46714-X*) Scholastic, Inc.

—When She Hollers. 1994. 9.09 o.p. (*0-606-08901-2*) Turtleback Bks.

Weber, Lenora Mattingly. Beany Has a Secret Life. 1955. (J). (gr. 5 up). 10.95 o.p. (*0-690-12384-1*) HarperCollins Children's Bk. Group.

—Beany Has a Secret Life. 1999. (Beany Malone Ser.). 296p. (J). pap. 12.95 (*0-9639607-7-6*) Image Cascade Publishing.

Wilkes, Maria D. On Top of Concord Hill. 2000. (Little House Ser.). (Illus.). 288p. (J). (gr. 3-7). 15.95 (*0-06-026999-5*); pap. 5.99 (*0-06-440689-X*, Harper Trophy); lib. bdg. 15.89 (*0-06-027003-9*) HarperCollins Children's Bk. Group.

Wilson, Jacqueline. Double Act. 2000. 32p. pap. 6.95 (*0-440-86334-1*, Delacorte Pr.) Dell Publishing.

—Double Act. 1999. 10.55 (*0-606-16442-1*) Turtleback Bks.

Zakhoder, Boris. The Good Stepmother. 1992. (Illus.). 40p. (J). (ps-2). pap. 14.00 o.s.i (*0-671-68270-9*, Simon & Schuster Children's Publishing) Simon & Schuster Children's Publishing.

T

TEACHER-STUDENT RELATIONSHIPS—FICTION

Anderson, Laurie Halse. Teacher's Pet. 2003. (Wild at Heart Ser.). (Illus.). 132p. (J). (gr. 4 up). lib. bdg. 22.60 (*0-8368-3261-2*) Stevens, Gareth Inc.

Codell, Esme Raji. Sahara Special. 2003. (Illus.). 177p. (J). 15.99 (*0-7868-0793-8*) Hyperion Bks. for Children.

Matthews, Andrew. A Winter Night's Dream. 2004. 160p. (J). (*0-385-73097-7*); lib. bdg. (*0-385-90127-5*) Dell Publishing. (Delacorte Pr.).

Tripp, Valerie. Hallie's Horrible Handwriting. 2003. (Hopscotch Hill Ser.). (Illus.). (J). pap. 3.99 (*1-58485-764-1*, American Girl) Pleasant Co. Pubns.

TWINS—FICTION

Aaron, Chester. Out of Sight, Out of Mind. 1986. 192p. pap. 2.95 o.p. (*0-553-26027-8*) Bantam Bks.

—Out of Sight, Out of Mind. 1985. 192p. (J). (gr. 6-9). lib. bdg. 11.89 (*0-397-32101-5*) HarperCollins Children's Bk. Group.

Adler, David A. The Fourth Floor Twins & the Disappearing Parrot Trick. (Fourth Floor Twins Ser.: No. 3). (Illus.). 64p. (J). (gr. 2-5). 1987. pap. 3.95 o.p. (*0-14-032214-0*, Puffin Bks.); 1986. 10.95 o.p. (*0-670-80926-8*, Viking Children's Bks.) Penguin Putnam Bks. for Young Readers.

—The Fourth Floor Twins & the Fish Snitch Mystery. (Young Puffins-The Fourth Floor Twins Ser.: No. 1). (Illus.). 64p. (J). 1986. (gr. 1-4). pap. 3.99 o.p. (*0-14-032082-2*, Puffin Bks.); 1985. 10.95 o.p. (*0-670-80087-2*, Viking Children's Bks.) Penguin Putnam Bks. for Young Readers.

—The Fourth Floor Twins & the Fortune Cookie Chase. (Young Puffins-The Fourth Floor Twins Ser.: No. 2). 64p. (J). 1986. (Illus.). (gr. 1-4). pap. 3.95 o.p. (*0-14-032083-0*, Puffin Bks.); 1985. 10.95 o.p. (*0-670-80641-2*, Viking Children's Bks.) Penguin Putnam Bks. for Young Readers.

—The Fourth Floor Twins & the Silver Ghost Express. 1986. (Fourth Floor Twins Ser.). (Illus.). 64p. (J). (gr. 2-5). 10.95 o.p. (*0-670-81236-6*, Viking Children's Bks.) Penguin Putnam Bks. for Young Readers.

—The Fourth Floor Twins & the Skyscraper Parade. (Fourth Floor Twins Ser.). (J). 1988. pap. 3.95 o.p. (*0-14-032298-1*, Puffin Bks.); 1987. (Illus.). (gr. 2-5). 10.95 o.p. (*0-670-81603-5*, Viking Children's Bks.) Penguin Putnam Bks. for Young Readers.

Ahrens, Robin Isabel. Dee & Bee. 2000. (Illus.). 40p. (J). (ps-1). 14.95 (*1-890817-26-0*) Winslow Pr.

Albee, Sarah. Double Trouble: A Story about Twins. (Jellybean Bks.). 24p. (J). (ps). 2000. (Illus.). 2.99 o.s.i (*0-375-80448-X*, Random Hse. Bks. for Young Readers); 1998. 2.29 o.s.i (*0-307-96001-3*, Golden Bks.) Random Hse. Children's Bks.

Alexander, Nina. The Case of the Haunted Camp. 1998. (New Adventures of Mary-Kate & Ashley Ser.). (Illus.). 85p. (J). (gr. 2-7). mass mkt. 3.99 (*0-590-29397-4*) Scholastic, Inc.

—The Case of the 202 Clues. 1998. (New Adventures of Mary-Kate & Ashley Ser.). (Illus.). 87p. (J). (gr. 2-7). mass mkt. 3.99 (*0-590-29307-9*) Scholastic, Inc.

—The Case of Thorn Mansion. 1997. (Adventures of Mary-Kate & Ashley Ser.). (J). (gr. 2-7). mass mkt. 3.99 (*0-590-88016-0*) Scholastic, Inc.

Anholt, Catherine & Anholt, Laurence. Twins: Two by Two. 1992. (Illus.). 32p. (J). (ps). 13.95 o.p. (*1-56402-041-X*) Candlewick Pr.

—Twins, Two by Two. 1994. (Illus.). 32p. (J). (ps-3). bds. 4.99 o.p. (*1-56402-397-4*) Candlewick Pr.

Armer, Alberta. Screwball. 1981. (Illus.). (J). (gr. 4-7). 4.95 o.p. (*0-399-20837-2*) Putnam Publishing Group, The.

Arnold, Tedd. More Parts. 32p. 2003. pap. 5.99 (*0-14-250149-2*, Puffin Bks.); 2001. (Illus.). (J). 15.99 (*0-8037-1417-3*, Dial Bks. for Young Readers) Penguin Putnam Bks. for Young Readers.

Bach, Alice. Grouchy Uncle Otto. 1977. (Illus.). 48p. (J). (gr. k-4). 8.89 o.p. (*0-06-020344-7*); lib. bdg. 12.89 o.p. (*0-06-020345-5*) HarperCollins Children's Bk. Group.

Bailey, Linda. Adventures with the Vikings. 2001. (Good Times Travel Agency Ser.). (Illus.). 48p. (J). (gr. 3-7). pap. 7.95 (*1-55074-544-1*);No. 3. 14.95 (*1-55074-542-5*) Kids Can Pr., Ltd.

Banim, Lisa, et al. Winner Take All. 2000. (Two of a Kind Ser.: No. 10). (Illus.). 112p. (gr. 3-7). mass mkt. 4.99 (*0-06-106580-3*, HarperEntertainment) Morrow/Avon.

Banks, Jacqueline Turner. Egg-Drop Blues. 128p. (J). 2003. pap. 4.95 (*0-618-25080-8*); 2003. (gr. 4-6). 15.00 (*0-618-34885-9*); 1995. (gr. 4-6). tchr. ed. 15.00 o.s.i (*0-395-70931-8*) Houghton Mifflin Co.

Banks, Lynne Reid. Angela & Diabola. 176p. (J). (gr. 3-7). 1998. pap. 4.95 (*0-380-79409-8*, Harper Trophy); 1997. 15.95 (*0-380-97562-9*) HarperCollins Children's Bk. Group.

—Angela & Diabola. 163p. (J). (gr. 4-6). pap. 4.50 (*0-8072-1515-5*, Listening Library) Random Hse. Audio Publishing Group.

—Angela & Diabola. 1998. (J). 10.55 (*0-606-13124-8*) Turtleback Bks.

Benjamin, Cynthia. I Am an Astronaut. 1996. (I Am a . . . Ser.). (Illus.). (J). (ps-k). 24p. 7.95 (*0-8120-6539-5*); 11.95 o.p. (*0-8120-6939-0*) Barron's Educational Series, Inc.

Birdseye, Tom. Tarantula Shoes. 1995. 144p. (J). (gr. 4-6). tchr. ed. 15.95 (*0-8234-1179-6*) Holiday Hse., Inc.

—Tarantula Shoes. 1996. 142p. (J). (gr. 3-7). pap. 4.99 (*0-14-037955-X*, Puffin Bks.) Penguin Putnam Bks. for Young Readers.

—Tarantula Shoes. 1996. (J). 11.04 (*0-606-09951-4*) Turtleback Bks.

Blackman, Malorie. Girl Wonder & the Terrific Twins. 1993. (Illus.). 80p. (J). (gr. 2-5). 12.99 o.s.i (*0-525-45065-3*, Dutton Children's Bks.) Penguin Putnam Bks. for Young Readers.

Bo, Ben. Skullcrack. 2003. pap. 6.95 (*0-8225-3311-1*, Carolrhoda Bks.); 2000. 168p. (YA). (gr. 9-12). lib. bdg. 14.95 (*0-8225-3308-1*, LernerSports) Lerner Publishing Group.

Boettcher, Cindy K. Whoop! An Aggie Football Weekend. 1997. (Illus.). 24p. (J). (ps-4). 17.99 (*0-9652751-1-6*) Beraam Publishing Co.

Bradman, Tony. Nicky & the Twins' Lost Rabbit. 1998. (Illus.). 32p. (J). pap. 9.95 (*0-00-664511-9*) HarperCollins Pubs. Ltd. GBR. *Dist:* Trafalgar Square.

Brandreth, Gyles. Myrtle Mouse & the Naughty Twins. 2000. (Tales from Mouse Village Ser.). 8.95 (*0-233-99576-5*) Andre Deutsch GBR. *Dist:* Trafalgar Square, Trans-Atlantic Pubns., Inc.

Bruchac, Joseph. Children of the Longhouse. 1996. (Illus.). 160p. (J). (gr. 3-6). 14.89 o.s.i (*0-8037-1794-6*); 14.99 o.p. (*0-8037-1793-8*) Penguin Putnam Bks. for Young Readers. (Dial Bks. for Young Readers).

Bryant, Bonnie. Star Rider. 1991. (Saddle Club Ser.: No. 19). 144p. (gr. 4-6). pap. text 3.99 o.s.i (*0-553-15938-0*) Bantam Bks.

—Star Rider. 1991. (Saddle Club Ser.: No. 19). (J). (gr. 4-6). 9.09 o.p. (*0-606-00772-5*) Turtleback Bks.

Bull, Angela. The Accidental Twins. 1983. (Illus.). 63p. (J). (gr. 2-4). o.p. (*0-571-11761-9*) Faber & Faber Ltd.

Bulla, Clyde Robert. Marco Moonlight. 1976. (Illus.). (J). (gr. 3-7). o.p. (*0-690-01011-7*) HarperCollins Children's Bk. Group.

Bunting, Eve. Twinnies. (Illus.). 32p. (J). (gr. 1-4). 2001. pap. 6.00 (*0-15-202401-8*, Voyager Bks./Libros Viajeros); 1997. 15.00 (*0-15-291592-3*) Harcourt Children's Bks.

—Twinnies. 2001. (Illus.). (J). 12.15 (*0-606-21497-6*) Turtleback Bks.

Burgess, Barbara H. Oren Bell. 192p. (J). (ps-3). 1992. pap. 3.50 o.s.i (*0-440-40747-8*); 1991. 15.00 o.s.i (*0-385-30325-4*, Delacorte Pr.) Dell Publishing.

Burgess, Thornton W. Buster Bear's Twins. 1992. (J). reprint ed. lib. bdg. 17.95 (*0-89966-981-6*) Buccaneer Bks., Inc.

Bush, Elizabeth. The Twins Who Quarrelled. 1982. (Illus.). 4.95 o.p. (*0-533-05275-0*) Vantage Pr., Inc.

Butcher, Nancy. It's Snow Problem. 2001. (Two of a Kind Ser.: No. 15). (Illus.). 128p. (gr. 3-7). mass mkt. 4.99 (*0-06-106655-9*, HarperEntertainment) Morrow/Avon.

Carr, Jan. Ballet Party! 1998. (You're Invited to Mary-Kate & Ashley's Ser.). (Illus.). 48p. (J). (gr. 2-4). pap. 12.95 (*0-590-29399-0*) Scholastic, Inc.

Caswell, Brian. Dreamslip. 1994. (Illus.). 197p. (J). pap. 12.95 (*0-7022-2641-6*) Univ. of Queensland Pr. AUS. *Dist:* International Specialized Bk. Services.

Christopher, Matt. Double Play at Short. 1995. (Illus.). 160p. (J). 15.95 o.p. (*0-316-14267-0*) Little Brown & Co.

—Soccer Cats, Vol. 9. 2003. (Illus.). 64p. (J). 13.95 (*0-316-07650-3*) Little Brown & Co.

Cleary, Beverly. The Growing up Feet. 1997. (Illus.). 32p. (J). (ps-3). pap. 5.95 (*0-688-15470-0*, Harper Trophy) HarperCollins Children's Bk. Group.

—The Growing up Feet. 1987. (Illus.). 32p. (J). (ps-1). lib. bdg. 11.88 o.p. (*0-688-06620-8*, Morrow, William & Co.) Morrow/Avon.

—The Growing-Up Feet. 1987. (Illus.). 32p. (J). (ps-3). 16.00 (*0-688-06619-4*) HarperCollins Children's Bk. Group.

—Janet's Thingamajigs. (Illus.). 32p. (J). (ps-3). 1997. pap. 6.99 (*0-688-15278-3*, Harper Trophy); 1987. 14.95 (*0-688-06617-8*) HarperCollins Children's Bk. Group.

—Janet's Thingamajigs. 1987. (Illus.). 32p. (J). (ps-1). lib. bdg. 12.88 o.p. (*0-688-06618-6*, Morrow, William & Co.) Morrow/Avon.

—Janet's Thingamajigs. 1988. (Illus.). 32p. (J). (gr. k-6). pap. 4.95 o.s.i (*0-440-40108-9*, Yearling) Random Hse. Children's Bks.

—Mitch & Amy. 1967. (Illus.). 224p. (J). (gr. 3-7). 16.00 o.p. (*0-688-21688-9*); lib. bdg. 15.93 o.p. (*0-688-31688-3*) Morrow/Avon. (Morrow, William & Co.).

—Mitch & Amy. 1991. (J). 11.00 (*0-606-04747-6*) Turtleback Bks.

—The Real Hole. 1996. (Illus.). 32p. (J). (ps-3). pap. 4.95 (*0-688-14741-0*, Harper Trophy) HarperCollins Children's Bk. Group.

—The Real Hole. rev. ed. 1986. (Illus.). 32p. (J). (ps-1). 11.95 o.p. (*0-688-05850-7*); lib. bdg. 11.88 o.p. (*0-688-05851-5*) Morrow/Avon. (Morrow, William & Co.).

—The Real Hole. 1990. (J). pap. o.s.i (*0-440-80185-0*, Dell Books for Young Readers) Random Hse. Children's Bks.

—The Real Hole. 1996. 11.10 (*0-606-09780-5*) Turtleback Bks.

Cohen, Barbara. The Long Way Home. 1990. 176p. (J). 12.95 o.p. (*0-688-09674-3*) HarperCollins Children's Bk. Group.

—The Orphan Game. 1988. (Illus.). (J). (gr. 3-6). 12.95 o.p. (*0-688-07615-7*) HarperCollins Children's Bk. Group.

Cohen, Dan. The Case of the Long Lost Twin. 1979. (Carolrhoda Mini-Mysteries Ser.). (Illus.). 32p. (J). (gr. 1-4). lib. bdg. 5.95 o.p. (*0-87614-094-0*, Carolrhoda Bks.) Lerner Publishing Group.

Cohen, Lane. Down Time. 2003. (YA). pap. 15.95 (*1-932133-67-4*) Writers' Collective, The.

Colli, Monica. Twins. 1992. (Illus.). 24p. (J). (ps-3). 4.99 (*0-85953-394-8*) Child's Play of England GBR. *Dist:* Child's Play-International.

—Twins' Party. 1993. (Illus.). 16p. (J). (ps-3). 6.99 o.p. (*0-85953-404-9*) Child's Play of England GBR. *Dist:* Child's Play-International.

Cooney, Barbara. The Kellyhorns. 2001. (Lost Treasures Ser.: No. 1). 352p. (J). (Illus.). (gr. 3-7). reprint ed. pap. 1.99 (*0-7868-1522-1*);Bk. 3. pap. 4.99 (*0-7868-1523-X*) Hyperion Bks. for Children. (Volo).

Cooney, Caroline B. Twins. 1994. 176p. (YA). (gr. 7-12). mass mkt. 4.50 (*0-590-47478-2*) Scholastic, Inc.

—Twins. 1994. 10.55 (*0-606-06832-5*) Turtleback Bks.

Courtney, Dayle. The Great UFO Chase. 1984. (Thorne Twins Adventure Bks.). (Illus.). 192p. (Orig.). (J). (gr. 6-10). pap. 2.98 o.p. (*0-87239-755-6*, 2905) Standard Publishing.

—The House That Ate People. 1983. (Thorne Twins Adventure Bks.). (Illus.). 192p. (Orig.). (J). (gr. 7-12). pap. 2.98 o.p. (*0-87239-683-5*, 2903) Standard Publishing.

—Mysterious Strangers. 1982. (Thorne Twins Adventure Bks.). (Illus.). 224p. (Orig.). (J). (gr. 5 up). pap. 2.98 o.p. (*0-87239-552-9*, 2893) Standard Publishing.

—The Olympic Plot. 1984. (Thorne Twins Adventure Bks.). (Illus.). 192p. (Orig.). (J). (gr. 6-10). pap. 2.98 o.p. (*0-87239-756-4*, 2906) Standard Publishing.

—Secret of Pirates' Cave. 1984. (Thorne Twins Adventure Bks.). (Illus.). 192p. (Orig.). (J). (gr. 6-10). pap. 2.98 o.p. (*0-87239-758-0*, 2908) Standard Publishing.

—Shadow of Fear. 1983. (Thorne Twins Adventure Bks.). (Illus.). 192p. (J). (gr. 7-12). pap. 2.98 o.p. (*0-87239-682-7*, 2902) Standard Publishing.

—The Sinister Circle. 1983. (Thorne Twins Adventure Bks.). (Illus.). 192p. (Orig.). (J). (gr. 7-12). pap. 2.98 o.p. (*0-87239-684-3*, 2904) Standard Publishing.

—The Trail of Bigfoot. 1983. (Thorne Twins Adventure Bks.). (Illus.). 192p. (Orig.). (J). (gr. 7-12). pap. 2.98 o.p. (*0-87239-681-9*, 2901) Standard Publishing.

Creech, Sharon. Ruby Holler. 320p. (J). 2004. pap. 5.99 (*0-06-056015-0*, Harper Trophy); 2002. (gr. 3-7). lib. bdg. 16.89 (*0-06-027733-5*, Cotler, Joanna Bks.); 2002. (gr. 4-7). 16.99 (*0-06-027732-7*, Cotler, Joanna Bks.) HarperCollins Children's Bk. Group.

—Ruby Holler. 2003. (Juvenile Ser.). 250p. (J). 22.95 (*0-7862-5429-7*) Thorndike Pr.

Cross, Gillian. Twin & Super-Twin. 1990. (Illus.). 176p. (J). (gr. 3-7). 13.95 o.p. (*0-8234-0840-X*) Holiday Hse., Inc.

Curry, Jane Louise. What the Dickens! 1993. 160p. (J). (gr. 5 up). pap. 3.99 o.p. (*0-14-036284-3*, Puffin Bks.) Penguin Putnam Bks. for Young Readers.

—What the Dickens! 1991. 160p. (J). (gr. 4-7). lib. bdg. 13.95 (*0-689-50524-8*, McElderry, Margaret K.) Simon & Schuster Children's Publishing.

David, Luke. Twin Trouble. 1999. (Rugrats Ser.). (Illus.). 24p. (J). (ps-2). pap. 3.50 (*0-689-82624-9*, 076714003507, Simon Spotlight/Nickelodeon) Simon & Schuster Children's Publishing.

De Armond, Elizabeth. Tiny Tired Twins. 1998. (Illus.). 16p. (J). (ps). pap. 5.95 (*0-9655442-5-7*) Business Word, The.

—The Bobbsey Twins & the Ghost in the Computer. 1984. (Bobbsey Twins Ser.: No. 10). (J). (gr. 3-5). pap. 3.50 (0-671-43591-4, Aladdin) Simon & Schuster Children's Publishing.

—The Bobbsey Twins & the Ghost in the Computer. Barish, Wendy, ed. 1984. (Bobbsey Twins Ser.: No. 10). (Illus.). 128p. (J). (gr. 3-5). pap. 3.50 o.p. (0-671-43590-6, Aladdin) Simon & Schuster Children's Publishing.

—The Bobbsey Twins & the Goldfish Mystery. 1962. (Bobbsey Twins Ser.). (Illus.). (J). (gr. 3-5). 4.50 o.s.i (0-448-08055-9, Grosset & Dunlap) Penguin Putnam Bks. for Young Readers.

—The Bobbsey Twins & the Greek Hat Mystery. 1964. (Bobbsey Twins Ser.). (J). (gr. 3-5). 4.50 o.s.i (0-448-08057-5, Grosset & Dunlap) Penguin Putnam Bks. for Young Readers.

—The Bobbsey Twins & the Haunted House Mystery. Arico, Diane, ed. 1985. (Bobbsey Twins Ser.: No. 12). (Illus.). 128p. (J). (gr. 3-5). pap. 3.50 (0-671-54996-0, Aladdin) Simon & Schuster Children's Publishing.

—The Bobbsey Twins & the Missing Pony Mystery. 1981. (Bobbsey Twins Ser.: No. 4). (Illus.). 112p. (J). (gr. 3-5). pap. 3.50 (0-671-42296-0, Aladdin); 7.95 (0-671-42295-2, Simon & Schuster Children's Publishing) Simon & Schuster Children's Publishing.

—The Bobbsey Twins & the Monster Mouse Mystery. Greenberg, Ann, ed. 1991. (New Bobbsey Twins Ser.: No. 23). (Illus.). 96p. (J). (gr. 3-5). pap. 2.95 (0-671-69295-X, Aladdin) Simon & Schuster Children's Publishing.

—The Bobbsey Twins & the Music Box Mystery. Barish, Wendy, ed. 1983. (Bobbsey Twins Ser.: No. 9). (Illus.). 128p. (J). (gr. 3-5). pap. 3.50 (0-671-43589-2); (0-671-43588-4) Simon & Schuster Children's Publishing. (Aladdin).

—The Bobbsey Twins & the Mystery at Cherry Corner. rev. ed. 1971. (Bobbsey Twins Ser.). (Illus.). (J). (gr. 3-5). 4.50 o.s.i (0-448-08020-6, Grosset & Dunlap) Penguin Putnam Bks. for Young Readers.

—The Bobbsey Twins & the Mystery at Meadowbrook. 1990. (Bobbsey Twins Ser.). (Illus.). 180p. (J). (gr. 3-5). 4.50 o.s.i (0-448-09100-3, Grosset & Dunlap) Penguin Putnam Bks. for Young Readers.

—The Bobbsey Twins & the Mystery at School. 1989. (Bobbsey Twins Ser.). (Illus.). 180p. (J). (gr. 3-5). 4.95 o.p. (0-448-09074-0, Grosset & Dunlap) Penguin Putnam Bks. for Young Readers.

—The Bobbsey Twins & the Mystery at Snow Lodge. (Bobbsey Twins Ser.). (J). (gr. 3-5). 1990. (Illus.). 180p. 4.95 o.s.i (0-448-09098-8); 1930. 4.50 o.s.i (0-448-08005-2) Penguin Putnam Bks. for Young Readers. (Grosset & Dunlap).

—The Bobbsey Twins & the Mystery of the Hindu Temple. Barish, Wendy, ed. 1985. (Bobbsey Twins Ser.: No. 13). (Illus.). 128p. (Orig.). (J). (gr. 3-5). pap. 3.50 (0-671-55499-9, Aladdin) Simon & Schuster Children's Publishing.

—The Bobbsey Twins & the Mystery of the King's Puppet. 1967. (Bobbsey Twins Ser.). (J). (gr. 3-5). 4.50 o.s.i (0-448-08060-5, Grosset & Dunlap) Penguin Putnam Bks. for Young Readers.

—The Bobbsey Twins & the Mystery of the Laughing Dinosaur. Barish, Wendy, ed. 1983. (Bobbsey Twins Ser.: No. 8). (Illus.). 128p. (J). (gr. 3-5). pap. (0-671-43586-8); pap. 3.50 (0-671-43587-6) Simon & Schuster Children's Publishing. (Aladdin).

—The Bobbsey Twins & the Mystery of the Mixed-Up Mail. MacDonald, Pat, ed. 1992. (New Bobbsey Twins Ser.: No. 30). (Illus.). 96p. (Orig.). (J). (gr. 3-5). pap. 2.99 (0-671-73042-8, Aladdin) Simon & Schuster Children's Publishing.

—The Bobbsey Twins & the Play House Secret. rev. ed. 1968. (Bobbsey Twins Ser.). (Illus.). (J). (gr. 3-5). 4.50 o.s.i (0-448-08018-4, Grosset & Dunlap) Penguin Putnam Bks. for Young Readers.

—The Bobbsey Twins & the Rose Parade Mystery. 1981. (Bobbsey Twins Ser.: No. 5). (Illus.). 112p. (Orig.). (J). (gr. 3-5). pap. (0-671-43372-5); pap. 3.50 (0-671-43371-7) Simon & Schuster Children's Publishing. (Aladdin).

—The Bobbsey Twins & the Secret at the Seashore. 1989. (Bobbsey Twins Ser.). (Illus.). 180p. (J). (gr. 3-5). 4.95 o.p. (0-448-09073-2, Grosset & Dunlap) Penguin Putnam Bks. for Young Readers.

—The Bobbsey Twins & the Secret in the Pirate's Cave. 1980. (Bobbsey Twins Ser.: No. 2). (Illus.). 128p. (J). (gr. 3-5). pap. (0-671-41118-7); pap. 3.50 (0-671-41113-6) Simon & Schuster Children's Publishing. (Aladdin).

—The Bobbsey Twins & the Secret of Candy Castle. 1968. (Bobbsey Twins Ser.). (Illus.). (J). (gr. 3-5). 4.50 o.p. (0-448-08061-3, Grosset & Dunlap) Penguin Putnam Bks. for Young Readers.

—The Bobbsey Twins & the Smokey Mountain Mystery. 1976. (Bobbsey Twins Ser.). (Illus.). (J). (gr. 3-5). 4.50 o.s.i (0-448-08070-2, Grosset & Dunlap) Penguin Putnam Bks. for Young Readers.

—The Bobbsey Twins & the Tagalong Giraffe. 1973. (Bobbsey Twins Ser.). (J). (gr. 3-5). 4.50 o.s.i (0-448-08066-4, Grosset & Dunlap) Penguin Putnam Bks. for Young Readers.

—The Bobbsey Twins & the Talking Fox Mystery. 1970. (Bobbsey Twins Ser.). (Illus.). (J). (gr. 3-5). 4.50 o.s.i (0-448-08063-X, Grosset & Dunlap) Penguin Putnam Bks. for Young Readers.

—The Bobbsey Twins & the TV Mystery Show. 1978. (Bobbsey Twins Ser.). (Illus.). (J). (gr. 3-5). 4.50 o.s.i (0-448-08071-0, Grosset & Dunlap) Penguin Putnam Bks. for Young Readers.

—The Bobbsey Twins & the Weird Science Mystery. 1990. (New Bobbsey Twins Ser.: No. 20). (Illus.). 96p. (Orig.). (J). (gr. 3-5). pap. 2.95 (0-671-69292-5, Aladdin) Simon & Schuster Children's Publishing.

—The Bobbsey Twins & Their Camel Adventure. 1978. (Bobbsey Twins Ser.). (J). (gr. 3-5). 3.29 o.p. (0-448-18059-6, Grosset & Dunlap) Penguin Putnam Bks. for Young Readers.

—The Bobbsey Twins at Big Bear Pond. 1954. (Bobbsey Twins Ser.). (J). (gr. 3-5). 4.50 o.p. (0-448-08047-8, Grosset & Dunlap) Penguin Putnam Bks. for Young Readers.

—The Bobbsey Twins at London Tower. 1959. (Bobbsey Twins Ser.). (Illus.). (J). (gr. 3-5). 4.50 o.s.i (0-448-08052-4, Grosset & Dunlap) Penguin Putnam Bks. for Young Readers.

—The Bobbsey Twins at Pilgrim Rock. 1957. (Bobbsey Twins Ser.). (J). (gr. 3-5). 4.50 o.s.i (0-448-08050-8, Grosset & Dunlap) Penguin Putnam Bks. for Young Readers.

—The Bobbsey Twins at School. (Bobbsey Twins Ser.). (J). (gr. 3-5). E-Book 2.49 (0-7574-0331-X) Electric Umbrella Publishing.

—The Bobbsey Twins at School. 2002. 136p. (gr. 4-7). per. 12.99 (1-4043-0023-6); 16.99 (1-4043-0022-8) IndyPublish.com.

—The Bobbsey Twins Camping Out. 1923. (Bobbsey Twins Ser.). (J). (gr. 3-5). 4.50 o.s.i (0-448-08016-8, Grosset & Dunlap) Penguin Putnam Bks. for Young Readers.

—The Bobbsey Twins' Forest Adventure. 1958. (Bobbsey Twins Ser.). (J). (gr. 3-5). 4.50 o.s.i (0-448-08051-6, Grosset & Dunlap) Penguin Putnam Bks. for Young Readers.

—The Bobbsey Twins in the Country. (Bobbsey Twins Ser.). (J). (gr. 3-5). E-Book 2.49 (0-7574-0332-8) Electric Umbrella Publishing.

—The Bobbsey Twins in the Country. 156p. (gr. 4-7). 2002. 17.99 (1-4043-0024-4); 2001. per. 12.99 (1-4043-0025-2) IndyPublish.com.

—The Bobbsey Twins in the Mystery Cave. 1960. (Bobbsey Twins Ser.). (Illus.). (J). (gr. 3-5). 4.50 o.s.i (0-448-08053-2, Grosset & Dunlap) Penguin Putnam Bks. for Young Readers.

—The Bobbsey Twins in Volcano Land. 1961. (Bobbsey Twins Ser.). (Illus.). (J). (gr. 3-5). 4.50 o.s.i (0-448-08054-0, Grosset & Dunlap) Penguin Putnam Bks. for Young Readers.

—The Bobbsey Twins of Lakeport. (Bobbsey Twins Ser.). (J). (gr. 3-5). 1989. (Illus.). 180p. 5.99 (0-448-09071-6); 1936. 4.50 o.s.i (0-448-08001-X) Penguin Putnam Bks. for Young Readers. (Grosset & Dunlap).

—The Bobbsey Twins on a Bicycle Trip. 1955. (Bobbsey Twins Ser.). (J). (gr. 3-5). 4.50 o.s.i (0-448-08048-6, Grosset & Dunlap) Penguin Putnam Bks. for Young Readers.

—The Bobbsey Twins on a Houseboat. (Bobbsey Twins Ser.). (J). (gr. 3-5). 1990. (Illus.). 180p. 4.95 o.s.i (0-448-09099-6); 1930. 4.50 o.s.i (0-448-08006-0) Penguin Putnam Bks. for Young Readers. (Grosset & Dunlap).

—The Bobbsey Twins on Blueberry Island. (Bobbsey Twins Ser.). (J). (gr. 3-5). 1991. (Illus.). 4.50 o.s.i (0-448-40110-X); 1930. 4.50 o.s.i (0-448-08010-9) Penguin Putnam Bks. for Young Readers. (Grosset & Dunlap).

—The Bobbsey Twins on the Deep Blue Sea. 1991. (Bobbsey Twins Ser.). (Illus.). (J). (gr. 3-5). 4.50 o.s.i (0-448-40113-4, Grosset & Dunlap) Penguin Putnam Bks. for Young Readers.

—The Bobbsey Twins on the Sun-Moon Cruise. 1975. (Bobbsey Twins Ser.). (Illus.). 196p. (J). (gr. 3-5). 4.50 o.s.i (0-448-08068-0, Grosset & Dunlap) Penguin Putnam Bks. for Young Readers.

—The Bobbsey Twins' Red, White, & Blue Mystery. 1971. (Bobbsey Twins Ser.). (Illus.). (J). (gr. 3-5). 4.50 o.s.i (0-448-08064-8, Grosset & Dunlap) Penguin Putnam Bks. for Young Readers.

—The Bobbsey Twins' Scarecrow Mystery. Barish, Wendy, ed. 1984. (Bobbsey Twins Ser.: No. 11). (Illus.). 128p. (J). (gr. 3-5). pap. 3.50 (0-671-53238-3, Aladdin) Simon & Schuster Children's Publishing.

—The Bobbsey Twins' Search for the Green Rooster. 1964. (Bobbsey Twins Ser.). (J). (gr. 3-5). 4.50 o.s.i (0-448-08058-3, Grosset & Dunlap) Penguin Putnam Bks. for Young Readers.

—The Bobbsey Twins' Search in the Great City. 1930. (Bobbsey Twins Ser.). (J). (gr. 3-6). 4.50 o.s.i (0-448-08009-5, Grosset & Dunlap) Penguin Putnam Bks. for Young Readers.

—The Bobbsey Twins Solve a Mystery. 1934. (Bobbsey Twins Ser.). (J). (gr. 3-5). 4.50 o.s.i (0-448-08027-3, Grosset & Dunlap) Penguin Putnam Bks. for Young Readers.

—The Bobbsey Twins' Visit to the Great West. (Bobbsey Twins Ser.). (J). (gr. 3-5). 1991. (Illus.). 4.50 o.s.i (0-448-40112-6); 1966. 4.50 o.s.i (0-448-08013-3) Penguin Putnam Bks. for Young Readers. (Grosset & Dunlap).

—The Bobbsey Twins' Wonderful Winter Secret. 1931. (Bobbsey Twins Ser.). (J). (gr. 3-5). 4.50 o.s.i (0-448-08024-9, Grosset & Dunlap) Penguin Putnam Bks. for Young Readers.

—The New Bobbsey Twins Series Boxed Set, 4 vols. 1988. (New Bobbsey Twins Ser.). (J). (gr. 3-5). 11.80 (0-671-91946-6, Aladdin) Simon & Schuster Children's Publishing.

Hrdlitschka, Shelley. Tangled Web. 2000. 240p. (YA). (gr. 7-12). pap. 6.95 (1-55143-178-5) Orca Bk. Pubs.

Hughes, Laura. Second Twins. 1998. (J). pap. 14.95 (0-8464-4914-5) Beekman Pubs., Inc.

James, B. J., et al. Supertwins Meet the Dangerous Dinobots. 2003. (Scholastic Reader Ser.). 32p. (J). mass mkt. 3.99 (0-439-46625-3, Cartwheel Bks.) Scholastic, Inc.

James, Brian. Bad Dogs from Outer Space. 2003. (Supertwins Ser.: No. 1). (Illus.). 32p. (J). mass mkt. 3.99 (0-439-46623-7, Cartwheel Bks.) Scholastic, Inc.

—Supertwins & the Sneaky, Slimy Book Worms. Demarest, Chris L., tr. & illus. by. 2004. (Scholastic Readers Ser.). (J). mass mkt. 3.99 (0-439-46626-1) Scholastic, Inc.

—Supertwins & Tooth Trouble. 2003. (Supertwins Ser.: Vol. 2). (Illus.). 32p. (J). mass mkt. 3.99 (0-439-46624-5, Cartwheel Bks.) Scholastic, Inc.

Javernick, Ellen. Gifted & Talented Beginning Readers: Double the Trouble. 1994. (Illus.). 32p. (J). 7.95 o.p. (1-56565-162-6); (gr. 3 up). 7.95 o.p. (1-56565-163-4) Lowell Hse. Juvenile.

Johnson, Lindsay L. & Kowitt, Holly. A Week with Zeke & Zach. 1993. (Speedster Ser.). (Illus.). 64p. (J). (gr. 2-5). 11.99 o.p. (0-525-45097-1, Dutton Children's Bks.) Penguin Putnam Bks. for Young Readers.

Johnson, Ruth I. Joy Sparton & Her Problem Twin. 1963. (Joy Sparton Ser. No. 4). (J). (gr. 5-8). pap. 3.50 o.p. (0-8024-4404-0) Moody Pr.

Karr, Kathleen. In the Kaiser's Clutch, RS. 1995. 182p. (J). (gr. 4-7). 16.00 o.p. (0-374-33638-5, Farrar, Straus & Giroux (BYR)) Farrar, Straus & Giroux.

Katschke, Judy. The Case of the Creepy Castle. 2000. (New Adventures of Mary-Kate & Ashley Ser.). 96p. (gr. 2-7). mass mkt. 4.50 (0-06-106592-7, HarperEntertainment) Morrow/Avon.

—The Case of the Summer Camp Caper. 1999. (New Adventures of Mary-Kate & Ashley Ser.). (Illus.). 96p. (gr. 2-7). mass mkt. 4.50 (0-06-106584-6, HarperEntertainment) Morrow/Avon.

—The Case of the Wild Wolf River. 1998. (New Adventures of Mary-Kate & Ashley Ser.). 87p. (J). (gr. 2-7). mass mkt. 3.99 (0-590-29401-6) Scholastic, Inc.

—It's a Twin Thing. 1999. (Two of a Kind Ser.: No. 1). (Illus.). 112p. (gr. 3-7). mass mkt. 4.99 (0-06-106571-4) HarperCollins Pubs.

—Let's Party! 8th ed. 1999. (Two of a Kind Ser.: No. 8). 112p. (gr. 3-7). mass mkt. 4.99 (0-06-106578-1, HarperEntertainment) Morrow/Avon.

—The Sleepover Secret. 1999. (Two of a Kind Ser.: No. 3). (Illus.). 112p. (gr. 3-7). mass mkt. 4.99 (0-06-106573-0, HarperEntertainment) Morrow/Avon.

—To Snoop or Not to Snoop. 1999. (Two of a Kind Ser.: No. 5). 112p. (gr. 3-7). mass mkt. 4.99 (0-06-106575-7, HarperEntertainment) Morrow/Avon.

—Two's a Crowd. 7th ed. 1999. (Two of a Kind Ser.: No. 7). (Illus.). 112p. (Orig.). (gr. 3-7). mass mkt. 4.25 (0-06-106577-3, HarperEntertainment) Morrow/Avon.

Katschke, Judy, et al. Calling All Boys. 2000. (Two of a Kind Ser.: No. 9). (Illus.). 112p. (gr. 2-7). mass mkt. 4.99 (0-06-106579-X, HarperEntertainment) Morrow/Avon.

Keller, Holly. Harry & Tuck. 1993. (Illus.). 24p. (J). (ps up). lib. bdg. 13.93 o.s.i (0-688-11463-6, Greenwillow Bks.) HarperCollins Children's Bk. Group.

Kingman, Lee. Head over Wheels, 001. 1978. 224p. (J). (gr. 5 up). 8.95 o.p. (0-395-27202-5) Houghton Mifflin Co.

Klein, Alan. Carousel Horses. 1991. (J). 6.95 o.p. (0-533-09160-8) Vantage Pr., Inc.

Kraft, Erik P. Lenny & Mel. (Ready-for-Chapters Ser.). (Illus.). 64p. (J). 2003. pap. 3.99 (0-689-85891-4, Aladdin); 2002. (gr. 2-5). 15.00 (0-689-84173-6, Simon & Schuster Children's Publishing) Simon & Schuster Children's Publishing.

—Lenny & Mel's Summer Vacation. 2003. (Illus.). 64p. (J). 14.95 (0-689-85108-1, Simon & Schuster Children's Publishing) Simon & Schuster Children's Publishing.

Krulik, Nancy E. The Case of the Fun House Mystery. 1996. (Adventures of Mary-Kate & Ashley Ser.). (Illus.). 80p. (J). (gr. 2-7). mass mkt. 3.99 (0-590-86231-6) Scholastic, Inc.

—The Case of the Shark Encounter. 1997. (Adventures of Mary-Kate & Ashley Ser.). 64p. (J). (gr. 2-7). mass mkt. 3.99 (0-590-88010-1) Scholastic, Inc.

Krulik, Nancy E., et al. Hawaiian Beach Party. 1997. (You're Invited to Mary-Kate & Ashley's Ser.). 48p. (J). (gr. 2-4). pap. 12.95 (0-590-88012-8) Scholastic, Inc.

Landis, Mary. The Twins Picnic. 1994. (Jewel Book Ser.: Set 5). (Illus.). 24p. (J). pap. 2.70 (0-7399-0047-1, 2528) Rod & Staff Pubs., Inc.

Laney, Shelby C. Two. 1993. 96p. (J). pap. 8.00 (1-56002-188-8, University Editions) Aegina Pr., Inc.

Lantz, Francess L. The Case of the Missing Mummy. 1998. (New Adventures of Mary-Kate & Ashley Ser.). (Illus.). 82p. (J). (gr. 2-7). mass mkt. 3.99 (0-590-29404-0) Scholastic, Inc.

Lasky, Kathryn. Shadows in the Water. 1992. (Starbuck Family Adventure Ser.: Vol. 2). 224p. (J). (gr. 4-7). pap. 8.00 (0-15-273534-8, Harcourt Paperbacks) Harcourt Children's Bks.

—Shadows in the Water: A Starbuck Family Adventure, Vol. 2. 1992. 224p. (J). (gr. 3-7). 16.95 o.s.i (0-15-273533-X) Harcourt Children's Bks.

—Voice in the Wind: A Starbuck Family Adventure. 1993. (Illus.). 224p. (J). (gr. 3-7). 10.95 (0-15-294102-9); pap. 3.95 o.s.i (0-15-294103-7) Harcourt Children's Bks.

Lattimore, Deborah Nourse. Punga: The Goddess of Ugly. 1993. (Illus.). 32p. (J). (ps-3). 14.95 o.s.i (0-15-292862-6) Harcourt Trade Pubs.

Lawrence, James. Binky Brothers, Detectives. 1968. (I Can Read Bks.). (Illus.). 64p. (J). (ps-3). lib. bdg. 13.89 o.p. (0-06-023759-7) HarperCollins Children's Bk. Group.

Leaf, Munro. The Story of Simpson & Sampson. 1989. (Illus.). 64p. (J). (gr. 1-3). reprint ed. lib. bdg. 16.50 o.p. (0-208-02244-9, Linnet Bks.) Shoe String Pr., Inc.

L'Engle, Madeleine. Many Waters. 2002. (Illus.). (J). 15.00 (0-7587-9605-6) Book Wholesalers, Inc.

—Many Waters. (J). 1991. mass mkt. 4.99 (0-440-80265-2); 1987. 336p. (gr. 5-9). pap. text 6.50 (0-440-40548-3) Dell Publishing.

—Many Waters, RS. (J). 1987. 310p. (gr. 4 up). 50.00 o.p. (0-374-34797-2); 1986. 320p. (gr. 8-12). 18.00 (0-374-34796-4) Farrar, Straus & Giroux. (Farrar, Straus & Giroux (BYR)).

—Many Waters. 1987. 320p. (J). (gr. k-12). mass mkt. 3.50 o.s.i (0-440-95252-2, Laurel Leaf); 1998. (Illus.). 336p. (YA). (gr. 5-8). mass mkt. 5.99 (0-440-22770-4, Dell Books for Young Readers) Random Hse. Children's Bks.

—Many Waters. (J). 1998. 12.04 (0-606-13596-0); 1986. 12.04 (0-606-05091-4) Turtleback Bks.

Leonard, Marcia. Get the Ball, Slim. 1998. (Real Kids Readers Ser.). (Illus.). 32p. (ps-1). (J). 18.90 (0-7613-2000-8); pap. 4.99 (0-7613-2025-3) Millbrook Pr., Inc.

—Get the Ball, Slim. 1998. 10.14 (0-606-15795-6) Turtleback Bks.

—Get the Ball, Slim. 1998. (Illus.). E-Book (1-58824-464-4); E-Book (1-58824-794-5); E-Book (1-58824-712-0) ipicturebooks, LLC.

—Spots. 1998. (Real Kids Readers Ser.). (Illus.). 32p. (J). (ps-1). 18.90 (0-7613-2016-4); pap. 4.99 (0-7613-2041-5) Millbrook Pr., Inc.

—Spots. 1998. (Real Kids Readers Ser.). 10.14 (0-606-15808-1) Turtleback Bks.

—Spots. 1998. E-Book (1-58824-823-2); E-Book (1-58824-740-6); E-Book (1-58824-492-X) ipicturebooks, LLC.

Levy, Elizabeth. Big Trouble in Little Twinsville. 2001. (Illus.). 96p. (J). (gr. 2-5). 14.95 (0-06-028590-7); lib. bdg. 15.89 (0-06-028591-5) HarperCollins Children's Bk. Group.

—Big Trouble in Little Twinsville. 2002. (Illus.). 96p. (J). pap. 4.25 (0-06-442116-3) HarperCollins Pubs.

Lewis, Beverly. Shadows Beyond the Gate. 2000. (Summerhill Secrets Ser.: 10). 144p. (J). (gr. 6-9). pap. 5.99 (1-55661-876-X) Bethany Hse. Pubs.

Lillington, Kenneth. Full Moon. 1986. 175p. o.p. (0-571-13792-X) Faber & Faber Ltd.

—Isabel's Double. 1984. 128p. (J). (gr. 6 up). o.p. (0-571-13197-2) Faber & Faber Ltd.

Lindbergh, Anne M. Three Lives to Live. 1992. 192p. (J). (gr. 3-7). 14.95 o.p. (0-316-52628-2) Little Brown & Co.

—Three Lives to Live. 1995. 192p. (J). (gr. 3-6). reprint ed. per. 3.50 (0-671-86732-6, Aladdin) Simon & Schuster Children's Publishing.

Lingard, Joan. The Same Only Different. 2001. (Illus.). 32p. (J). (ps-1). pap. (1-871512-64-6) Glowworm Bks., Ltd.

Relationships

Lipman, Ken. Bad News Babysitting! 1995. (Secret World of Alex Mack Ser.: No. 3). 144p. (J). (gr. 4-7). pap. 3.99 (*0-671-53446-7*, Aladdin) Simon & Schuster Children's Publishing.

Littke, Lael. Haunted Sister, ERS. 1998. 160p. (J). (gr. 6-9). 16.95 (*0-8050-5729-3*, Holt, Henry & Co. Bks. For Young Readers) Holt, Henry & Co.

Lochner, David. Twice As Funny. . . Twins: A Book of Cartoons. 1998. (Illus.). 104p. (Orig.). spiral bd. 10.95 (*1-891846-04-3*) Business Word, The.

Long, Linda A. Dragon Dinwitties Kingdom. 1988. (J). 6.95 o.p. (*0-533-07819-9*) Vantage Pr., Inc.

Lunel, Augusto. The Polka Dot Twins. 1964. (ENG & FRE., Illus.). (J). (gr. 4-6). 2.50 o.s.i (*0-8076-0271-X*) Braziller, George Inc.

Lunn, Janet. Twin Spell. 1971. (gr. 4-7). pap. 0.95 o.p. (*0-440-49177-0*) Dell Publishing.

Lynx Twins Together. 2002. (Wild Heritage Collection Mini Bks.). (Illus.). 32p. (J). (*1-59069-240-3*, H3011) Studio Mouse LLC.

Macguire, Gregory. Missing Sisters. 1998. 164p. (J). (gr. 5-9). pap. 4.95 (*0-7868-1273-7*) Hyperion Pr.

—Missing Sisters. 1998. (J). 11.00 (*0-606-13612-6*) Turtleback Bks.

Mackall, Dandi Daley. Kyra's Story. 2003. (Degrees of Guilt Ser.). 225p. (YA). pap. 12.99 (*0-8423-8284-4*) Tyndale Hse. Pubs.

Mackinnon, Debbie. Tom's Train. 1997. (Surprise Board Book Ser.). 8p. (J). (ps-k). 4.99 o.s.i (*0-8037-2105-6*, Dial Bks. for Young Readers) Penguin Putnam Bks. for Young Readers.

MacNeil, Joan & MacNeil, Robin. Twin Babies, Twin Babies. 2000. (Illus.). 16p. (J). pap. 5.95 (*1-891846-17-5*) Business Word, The.

Maguire, Gregory. Missing Sisters. 1994. 160p. (J). (gr. 5-9). lib. bdg. 15.00 o.s.i (*0-689-50590-6*, McElderry, Margaret K.) Simon & Schuster Children's Publishing.

Markham, Marion M. The St. Patrick's Day Shamrock Mystery. 1995. (Illus.). 48p. (J). (gr. 4-6). lib. bdg. 15.00 (*0-395-72137-7*) Houghton Mifflin Co.

Marshall, Hallie. Parent Trap Jr. 1998. 96p. (J). pap. 4.95 o.p. (*0-7868-4234-2*) Little Brown & Co.

Martin, Ann M. Abby's Twin. 1997. (Baby-Sitters Club Ser.: No. 104). 127p. (J). (gr. 3-7). mass mkt. 3.99 (*0-590-69210-0*) Scholastic, Inc.

—Abby's Twin. 1997. (Baby-Sitters Club Ser.: No. 104). (J). (gr. 3-7). 10.04 (*0-606-10744-4*) Turtleback Bks.

—Karen's Twin. 1994. (Baby-Sitters Little Sister Ser.: No. 45). 112p. (J). (gr. 3-7). mass mkt. 3.50 (*0-590-47044-2*) Scholastic, Inc.

—Mallory & the Trouble with Twins. (Baby-Sitters Club Ser.: No. 21). (J). (gr. 3-7). 1997. mass mkt. 3.99 (*0-590-67389-0*); 1989. 160p. pap. 2.75 o.p. (*0-590-42005-4*, Scholastic Paperbacks); 1989. mass mkt. 3.50 (*0-590-43507-8*) Scholastic, Inc.

—Mallory & the Trouble with Twins. l.t. ed. 1994. (Baby-Sitters Club Ser.: No. 21). 176p. (J). (gr. 3-7). lib. bdg. 19.93 o.p. (*0-8368-1242-5*) Stevens, Gareth Inc.

—Mallory & the Trouble with Twins. 1989. (Baby-Sitters Club Ser.: No. 21). (J). (gr. 3-7). 10.04 (*0-606-04089-7*) Turtleback Bks.

—Twin Trouble. 1997. (Kids in Ms. Colman's Class Ser.: No. 6). (J). (gr. 1-4). mass mkt. 3.50 o.p. (*0-590-69202-X*, Scholastic Paperbacks) Scholastic, Inc.

Matthew, Marlene. Double Trouble. 1994. (Road to Avonlea Ser.: No. 24). 128p. (J). (gr. 3-7). pap. 3.99 o.s.i (*0-553-48123-1*) Bantam Bks.

Mayfield, Julie. The Magical First Day. 1998. (Illus.). (J). 17.25 (*1-56763-336-6*); pap. (*1-56763-337-4*) Ozark Publishing.

McDaniel, Lurlene. The Time Capsule. 2003. 224p. (YA). (gr. 7). 9.95 (*0-553-57096-X*, Bantam Bks. for Young Readers) Random Hse. Children's Bks.

—The Time Capsule. 2003. 224p. (YA). (gr. 7). lib. bdg. 11.99 (*0-553-13051-X*) Random Hse., Inc.

McHenry, Janet Holm. Trick 'n Trouble. Reck, Sue, ed. 1994. (Golden Rule Duo Ser.). 48p. (J). (gr. 2-4). pap. 3.99 (*0-7814-0171-2*) Cook Communications Ministries.

McKean, Thomas. My Evil Twin. 1997. 160p. (J). (gr. 5-7). 14.00 o.p. (*0-380-97445-2*, Avon Bks.) Morrow/Avon.

McKissack, Patricia C. Who Is Who? 1983. (Rookie Readers Ser.). (Illus.). 32p. (J). (gr. k-2). mass mkt. 16.00 o.p. (*0-516-02042-0*); mass mkt. 4.95 (*0-516-42042-9*) Scholastic Library Publishing. (Children's Pr.).

Me & the Terrible Twins. 1986. (J). pap. 1.25 o.s.i (*0-440-82080-4*) Dell Publishing.

Menning, Lori. One Was Not Enough. 2000. (Illus.). 16p. (J). pap. 5.95 (*1-891846-18-3*) Business Word, The.

Messer, Celeste M. The Ghost of Piper's Landing. 2002. (Illus.). (J). 4.95 (*0-9702171-7-X*) Ashley-Alan Enterprises.

Metz, Melinda. The Case of the Flying Phantom. 2000. (New Adventures of Mary-Kate & Ashley Ser.). (Illus.). 96p. (gr. 2-7). mass mkt. 4.25 (*0-06-106591-9*) HarperCollins Children's Bk. Group.

—The Case of the Golden Slipper. 20th ed. 2000. (New Adventures of Mary-Kate & Ashley Ser.). 96p. (gr. 2-7). mass mkt. 4.50 (*0-06-106593-5*, HarperEntertainment) Morrow/Avon.

—The Case of the Golden Slipper. 2000. (New Adventures of Mary Kate & Ashley Ser.). (Illus.). (J). 10.30 (*0-606-21918-8*) Turtleback Bks.

—The Case of the Rock Star's Secret. 2000. (New Adventures of Mary-Kate & Ashley Ser.). (Illus.). 96p. (gr. 2-7). mass mkt. 4.50 (*0-06-106589-7*, HarperEntertainment) Morrow/Avon.

—The Case of the Surprise Call. 1999. (New Adventures of Mary-Kate & Ashley Ser.). 86p. (J). (gr. 2-7). mass mkt. 3.99 (*0-590-29403-2*) Scholastic, Inc.

Mills, Adam. Cold Chills. 1989. (Twin Connection Ser.: No. 10). (J). (gr. 4 up). mass mkt. 2.95 o.s.i (*0-345-35929-1*) Ballantine Bks.

—The Secret Ballot, No. 6. 1989. (Twin Connection Ser.: No. 6). (J). (gr. 4 up). mass mkt. 2.95 o.s.i (*0-345-35133-9*) Ballantine Bks.

Morris, Gilbert. The Dangerous Voyage. 1995. (Time Navigators Ser.: Vol. 1). 160p. (J). (gr. 6-9). pap. 5.99 o.p. (*1-55661-395-4*) Bethany Hse. Pubs.

—Vanishing Clues. 1996. (Time Navigators Ser.: Vol. 2). 144p. (J). (gr. 4-7). pap. 5.99 o.p. (*1-55661-396-2*) Bethany Hse. Pubs.

Muldrow, Diane. Boiling Point! Friends Cooking Eating Talking Life. 2002. (Dish Ser.: No. 3). (Illus.). 160p. (YA). mass mkt. 4.99 (*0-448-42828-8*, Grosset & Dunlap) Penguin Putnam Bks. for Young Readers.

—Lights, Camera, Cook!, No. 8. 2003. (Dish Ser.: Vol. 8). (Illus.). 160p. (J). mass mkt. 4.99 (*0-448-43175-0*) Penguin Putnam Bks. for Young Readers.

—A Measure of Thanks. 2003. (Dish! Ser.). (Illus.). 160p. (J). mass mkt. 4.99 (*0-448-43201-3*, Grosset & Dunlap) Penguin Putnam Bks. for Young Readers.

—Recipe for Trouble, Vol. 7. 2003. (Dish Ser.: No. 7). (Illus.). 160p. (J). mass mkt. 4.99 (*0-448-42898-9*, Grosset & Dunlap) Penguin Putnam Bks. for Young Readers.

—Stirring It Up: Friends Cooking, Eating, Talking Life. 2002. (Dish Ser.: No. 1). (Illus.). 160p. (J). (gr. 4-7). mass mkt. 4.99 (*0-448-42815-6*, Grosset & Dunlap) Penguin Putnam Bks. for Young Readers.

—Sweet & Sour Summer. 2003. (Dish Ser.: Vol. 9). (Illus.). 160p. (J). mass mkt. 4.99 (*0-448-43176-9*, Grosset & Dunlap) Penguin Putnam Bks. for Young Readers.

—Turning up the Heat: Friends Cooking, Eating, Talking Life. 2002. (Dish Ser.: No. 2). (Illus.). 160p. (J). mass mkt. 4.99 (*0-448-42816-4*) Penguin Putnam Bks. for Young Readers.

Mulford, Philippa G. The World Is My Eggshell. 1986. (J). (gr. 7 up). pap. 14.95 o.s.i (*0-385-29432-8*, Delacorte Pr.) Dell Publishing.

Neasi, Barbara J. Just Like Me. (Rookie Readers Ser.). (J). 1984. (Illus.). 32p. (ps-3). pap. 4.95 o.p. (*0-516-42047-X*); 1984. (Illus.). 32p. (gr. 1-2). lib. bdg. 19.00 (*0-516-02047-1*); 2003. (Illus.). 32p. (gr. 1-2). pap. 4.95 (*0-516-27495-3*); 2002. lib. bdg. 19.00 (*0-516-22564-2*); 2002. (Illus.). 31p. (gr. 1-2). pap. 19.00 (*0-516-22669-X*) Scholastic Library Publishing. (Children's Pr.).

Nicholson, William. Firesong. 2002. (Wind on Fire Trilogy: Bk. 3). 384p. (J). (gr. 5-9). 17.99 (*0-7868-0571-4*) Hyperion Bks. for Children.

—Slaves of the Mastery. 2001. (Wind on Fire Trilogy: Bk. 2). (Illus.). 434p. (J). (gr. 5-9). 17.99 (*0-7868-0570-6*) Hyperion Bks. for Children.

—Slaves of the Mastery. 2003. 256p. (J). mass mkt. 7.99 (*0-7868-1418-7*) Hyperion Pr.

—The Wind Singer. (gr. 5). 2004. (J). mass mkt. 7.99 (*0-7868-1826-3*); 2000. ix, 358p. (YA). lib. bdg. 17.99 (*0-7868-2494-8*); 2000. (Wind on Fire Trilogy: Vol. 1). (Illus.). ix, 358p. (J). 17.99 (*0-7868-0569-2*) Hyperion Bks. for Children.

—The Wind Singer. 2002. (Wind on Fire Trilogy: No. 1). 368p. (J). pap. 7.99 (*0-7868-1417-9*) Hyperion Paperbacks for Children.

—The Wind Singer. 2003. 368p. (J). pap. 7.99 (*0-7868-1799-2*) Hyperion Pr.

Nicholson, William & Sis, Peter. Firesong. 2002. (Wind on Fire Trilogy: Bk. 3). (Illus.). 384p. (J). (gr. 5-9). lib. bdg. 18.49 (*0-7868-2496-4*) Hyperion Pr.

Nolen, Jerdine. Max & Jax in Second Grade. 2002. (Max & Jax Ser.). (Illus.). 44p. (J). (gr. 1-4). 14.00 (*0-15-201668-6*, Silver Whistle) Harcourt Children's Bks.

Norling, Beth. Sister Night & Sister Day. 2001. (Illus.). 32p. (J). (ps). 14.95 (*1-86448-863-8*) Allen & Unwin Pty., Ltd. AUS. *Dist:* Independent Pubs. Group.

Nunes, Shiho S. The Power of the Stone. 2002. mass mkt. 4.99 (*0-89610-283-1*) Island Heritage Publishing.

Ogden, Charles. Rare Beasts. 2003. (Edgar & Ellen Ser.: Vol. 1). (Illus.). 120p. (J). 12.95 (*1-58246-110-4*) Tricycle Pr.

O'Hair, Margaret. Twin to Twin. 2003. (Illus.). 32p. (J). 15.95 (*0-689-84494-8*, McElderry, Margaret K.) Simon & Schuster Children's Publishing.

Older, Effin. Birthday Party. 1998. (You're Invited to Mary-Kate & Ashley's Ser.). (Illus.). 48p. (J). (gr. 2-4). pap. 12.95 (*0-590-22593-6*) Scholastic, Inc.

Oldfield, J. Homeless. 1996. (Home Farm Twins Ser.: No. 3). (Illus.). 117p. (J). mass mkt. 7.95 (*0-340-66129-1*) Hodder & Stoughton, Ltd. GBR. *Dist:* Lubrecht & Cramer, Ltd., Trafalgar Square.

—Skye Champion, Bk. 13. (Illus.). 122p. (J). mass mkt. 7.95 (*0-340-69985-X*) Hodder & Stoughton, Ltd. GBR. *Dist:* Lubrecht & Cramer, Ltd., Trafalgar Square.

—Sorrel Substitute, Bk. 12. (Illus.). 120p. (J). mass mkt. 7.95 (*0-340-69984-1*) Hodder & Stoughton, Ltd. GBR. *Dist:* Lubrecht & Cramer, Ltd., Trafalgar Square.

—Spike the Tramp. 1996. (Home Farm Twins Ser.: No. 5). (Illus.). 120p. (J). mass mkt. 8.95 (*0-340-66131-3*) Hodder & Stoughton, Ltd. GBR. *Dist:* Lubrecht & Cramer, Ltd., Trafalgar Square.

—Stanley Troublemaker. (Illus.). 120p. (J). mass mkt. 8.95 (*0-340-72675-X*) Hodder & Stoughton, Ltd. GBR. *Dist:* Lubrecht & Cramer, Ltd., Trafalgar Square.

—Sultan Patient, Vol. 2. (Illus.). 119p. (J). mass mkt. 7.95 (*0-340-69983-3*) Hodder & Stoughton, Ltd. GBR. *Dist:* Lubrecht & Cramer, Ltd., Trafalgar Square.

—X-Mas Special. 1997. (Home Farm Twins Ser.). (Illus.). 120p. (J). mass mkt. 7.95 (*0-340-70399-7*) Hodder & Stoughton, Ltd. GBR. *Dist:* Lubrecht & Cramer, Ltd., Trafalgar Square.

Oldfield, Jenny. Snip & Snap: The Truants. 1996. (Home Farm Twins Ser.: No. 6). (Illus.). 122p. (J). mass mkt. 7.95 (*0-340-66132-1*) Hodder & Stoughton, Ltd. GBR. *Dist:* Lubrecht & Cramer, Ltd., Trafalgar Square.

—Socks Survivor. 1997. (Home Farm Twins Ser.: Vol. 8). (Illus.). 120p. (J). mass mkt. 7.95 (*0-340-68991-9*) Hodder & Stoughton, Ltd. GBR. *Dist:* Lubrecht & Cramer, Ltd., Trafalgar Square.

—Stevie the Rebel. (Home Farm Twins Ser.: Vol. 9). (Illus.). 128p. (J). mass mkt. 7.95 (*0-340-68992-7*) Hodder & Stoughton, Ltd. GBR. *Dist:* Lubrecht & Cramer, Ltd., Trafalgar Square.

Olsen, Mary-Kate & Olsen, Ashley. April Fools' Rules! 2002. (Two of a Kind Ser.: Vol. 22). (Illus.). 112p. mass mkt. 4.99 (*0-06-106662-1*) HarperCollins Pubs.

—The Case of Camp Crooked Lake. 2002. (New Adventures of Mary-Kate & Ashley Ser.: 30). 96p. (gr. 1-5). mass mkt. 4.50 (*0-06-106652-4*) HarperCollins Pubs.

—The Case of Clue's Circus Caper, No. 35. 2003. (New Adventures of Mary-Kate & Ashley Ser.). (Illus.). 96p. mass mkt. 4.50 (*0-06-009333-1*, HarperEntertainment) Morrow/Avon.

—The Case of the Weird Science Mystery. 2002. (New Adventures of Mary-Kate & Ashley Ser.: 29). 96p. (gr. 1-5). mass mkt. 4.50 (*0-06-106651-6*) HarperCollins Pubs.

—The Cool Club. 2000. (Two of a Kind Ser.: No. 12). (Illus.). 112p. (gr. 3-7). mass mkt. 4.99 (*0-06-106582-X*, HarperEntertainment) Morrow/Avon.

—Dating Game, No. 9. 2003. (So Little Time Ser.). 128p. mass mkt. 4.99 (*0-06-009313-7*, HarperEntertainment) Morrow/Avon.

—A Girls Guide to Guys. 2003. (So Little Time Ser.: No. 10). (Illus.). 128p. mass mkt. 4.99 (*0-06-009314-5*, HarperEntertainment) Morrow/Avon.

—How to Flunk Your First Date. 1999. (Two of a Kind Ser.: No. 2). (Illus.). 112p. (gr. 3-7). mass mkt. 4.99 (*0-06-106572-2*, HarperEntertainment) Morrow/Avon.

—Island Girls. 2002. (Two of a Kind Ser.: 23). 112p. (gr. 3-7). mass mkt. 4.99 (*0-06-106663-X*) HarperCollins Pubs.

—Mary-Kate & Ashley Starring in... 2002. (Illus.). (J). mass mkt. 19.96 (*0-06-052110-4*, HarperEntertainment) Morrow/Avon.

—Mary-Kate & Ashley Starring In: The Challenge, No. 6. 2003. 96p. mass mkt. 4.99 (*0-06-056702-3*, HarperEntertainment) Morrow/Avon.

—Mary-Kate & Ashley Sweet 16. 2002. (J). (Sweet Sixteen Ser.: No. 6). (Illus.). mass mkt. 4.99 (*0-06-052812-5*); mass mkt. 19.96 (*0-06-052112-0*); No. 5. (Sweet Sixteen Ser.: No. 5). (Illus.). mass mkt. 4.99 (*0-06-052811-7*) Morrow/Avon. (HarperEntertainment).

—Mary-Kate & Ashley Sweet 16: Getting There, No. 4. 2002. 144p. mass mkt. 4.99 (*0-06-051595-3*, HarperEntertainment) Morrow/Avon.

—New Adventures of Mary-Kate & Ashley. 2001. pap. text 17.00 (*0-06-009013-8*) HarperCollins Children's Bk. Group.

—New Adventures of Mary-Kate & Ashley. 2002. (Illus.). (J). mass mkt. 18.00 (*0-06-052114-7*, HarperEntertainment) Morrow/Avon.

—P. S. Wish You Were Here. 2000. (Two of a Kind Ser.: No. 11). (Illus.). 112p. (gr. 3-7). mass mkt. 4.25 (*0-06-106581-1*, HarperEntertainment) Morrow/Avon.

—School Dance Party. 2001. (Mary-Kate & Ashley Starring In Ser.: No. 3). (Illus.). 96p. mass mkt. 4.99 (*0-06-106667-2*) HarperCollins Pubs.

—So Little Time. 2002. (Illus.). (J). mass mkt. 19.96 (*0-06-052095-7*, HarperEntertainment) Morrow/Avon.

—Switching Goals. 2000. (Mary-Kate & Ashley Ser.). 128p. (gr. 2-4). mass mkt. 4.99 (*0-06-107603-1*, HarperEntertainment) Morrow/Avon.

—Tell Me about It. 2002. (So Little Time Ser.: No. 5). 128p. mass mkt. 4.99 (*0-06-008807-9*, HarperEntertainment) Morrow/Avon.

—Too Good to Be True. 2002. (So Little Time Ser.: Vol. 3). 128p. mass mkt. 4.99 (*0-06-008805-2*) HarperCollins Pubs.

—Wish Come True. 2002. (Mary-Kate & Ashley Sweet 16 Ser.: Vol. 2). 144p. mass mkt. 4.99 (*0-06-009210-6*) HarperCollins Children's Bk. Group.

Olum, Adhiambo. Twins a Step Behind. 1999. (Illus.). 44p. (J). (gr. 1-4). pap. 7.95 (*1-881524-56-6*) Milligan Bks.

O'Neil, Laura. The Case of the Ballet Bandit. 1998. (New Adventures of Mary-Kate & Ashley Ser.). (Illus.). 87p. (J). (gr. 2-7). mass mkt. 3.99 (*0-590-29542-X*) Scholastic, Inc.

—The Case of the Hotel Who-Done-It. 1997. (Adventures of Mary-Kate & Ashley Ser.). 88p. (J). (gr. 2-7). mass mkt. 3.99 (*0-590-88013-6*) Scholastic, Inc.

Pallas, Jim, illus. Twins Together. 1995. 32p. (J). (ps-1). 13.95 (*1-887403-23-X*) Good Growing Bks.

Palmer, Bernard. Ted & Terri & the Broken Arrow. 1982. (J). (gr. 3-7). pap. 1.50 o.p. (*0-8024-4902-6*) Moody Pr.

—Ted & Terri & the Secret Captive. 1980. (J). (gr. 3-7). pap. 1.50 o.p. (*0-8024-4901-8*) Moody Pr.

Pascal, Francine. Ajuste de Cuentas. 2001. (Sweet Valley Twins Ser.).Tr. of Lois Strikes Back. (SPA.). 128p. (YA). 6.95 (*84-272-3599-2*) Molino, Editorial ESP. *Dist:* AIMS International Bks., Inc.

—El Autentico Ganador. 2001. (Gemelas de Sweet Valley Ser.: No. 16). Tr. of Second Best. (SPA.). 128p. (J). (gr. 3-7). 6.95 (*84-272-3786-3*) Molino, Editorial ESP. *Dist:* AIMS International Bks., Inc.

—Centro de Atencion. (Gemelas de Sweet Valley Ser.: No. 18). Tr. of Center of Attention. (SPA.). (J). (gr. 3-7). 6.95 (*84-272-3788-X*) Molino, Editorial ESP. *Dist:* AIMS International Bks., Inc.

—Chicos Contra Chicas. 2000. (Gemelas de Sweet Valley Ser.: No. 17). Tr. of Boys Against Girls. (SPA.). 136p. (J). (gr. 3-7). 7.50 (*84-272-3787-1*) Molino, Editorial ESP. *Dist:* AIMS International Bks., Inc.

—Contra Las Normas. 2002. (Sweet Valley Twins Ser.).Tr. of Against the Rules. (SPA.). 128p. (YA). 6.95 (*84-272-3779-0*) Molino, Editorial ESP. *Dist:* AIMS International Bks., Inc.

—Desaparecida. Orig. Title: Mary Is Missing. (SPA.). 128p. (YA). 6.95 (*84-272-3597-6*) Molino, Editorial ESP. *Dist:* AIMS International Bks., Inc.

—Estrella del Rock. Orig. Title: Jessica the Rock Star. (SPA.). (J). 6.95 (*84-272-3595-X*) Molino, Editorial ESP. *Dist:* AIMS International Bks., Inc.

—Gran Actuacion. 2001. (Sweet Valley Twins Ser.).Tr. of Jessica on Stage. (SPA.). 120p. (YA). 6.95 (*84-272-3592-5*) Molino, Editorial ESP. *Dist:* AIMS International Bks., Inc.

—Una Gran Luchadora. (Gemelas de Sweet Valley Ser.: No. 10). Tr. of One of the Gang. (SPA.). 128p. (J). (gr. 3-7). 6.95 (*84-272-3780-4*) Molino, Editorial ESP. *Dist:* AIMS International Bks., Inc.

—El Gran Secreto. 2002. (Sweet Valley Twins Ser.).Tr. of Keeping Secrets. (SPA.). 128p. (YA). 6.95 (*84-272-3782-0*) Molino, Editorial ESP. *Dist:* AIMS International Bks., Inc.

—Grandes Ideas.Tr. of Jessica's Bad Idea. (SPA.). 112p. 6.95 (*84-272-3593-3*) Molino, Editorial ESP. *Dist:* AIMS International Bks., Inc.

—Lo Que los Padres Ignoran.Tr. of What Your Parents Don't Know.... (SPA.). 224p. (J). 10.50 (*84-272-3163-6*) Molino, Editorial ESP. *Dist:* AIMS International Bks., Inc.

—Steven's Twin. 1994. (Sweet Valley Kids Ser.: No. 50). 80p. (J). (gr. 1-3). pap. 2.99 o.s.i (*0-553-48095-2*) Bantam Bks.

—Sweet Valley Twins. 1987. (Orig.). (J). pap. 1.25 o.s.i (*0-440-82187-8*) Dell Publishing.

—Sweet Valley Twins First. 1987. (J). pap. 1.25 o.s.i (*0-440-82138-X*) Dell Publishing.

—Un Tesoro Enterrado. 2001. (Gemelas de Sweet Valley Ser.: No. 11). Tr. of Buried Treasure. (SPA.). 128p. (J). (gr. 3-7). 6.95 (*84-272-3781-2*) Molino, Editorial ESP. *Dist:* AIMS International Bks., Inc.

—Tres Es Multitud. 2000. (Gemelas de Sweet Valley Ser.: No. 7). Tr. of Three's a Crowd. (SPA.). 144p. (J). (gr. 3-7). 7.50 (*84-272-3777-4*) Molino, Editorial ESP. *Dist:* AIMS International Bks., Inc.

—Twins, 2 vols. 1992. (J). 3.50 o.s.i (*0-553-62855-0*, Dell Books for Young Readers) Random Hse. Children's Bks.

—Twins. 2002. (Fearless Ser.: Bk. 19). 240p. (YA). (gr. 7-12). pap. 5.99 (*0-7434-4397-7*, Simon Pulse) Simon & Schuster Children's Publishing.

—Visita Inesperada. Orig. Title: Amy's Pen Pal. (SPA.). 144p. (YA). 6.95 (*84-272-3596-8*) Molino, Editorial ESP. *Dist:* AIMS International Bks., Inc.

Pascal, Francine, creator. The Arrest. 1993. (Sweet Valley High Ser.: No. 96). 224p. (gr. 7 up). mass mkt. 3.99 o.s.i (*0-553-29853-4*) Bantam Bks.

—Cammi's Crush. 1997. (Sweet Valley Twins Ser.: No. 108). (J). (gr. 3-7). 9.55 (*0-606-11957-4*) Turtleback Bks.

—Evil Elizabeth. 1995. (Sweet Valley Twins Super Chiller Ser.: No. 9). 192p. (gr. 3-7). pap. text 3.99 (*0-553-48283-1*, Sweet Valley) Random Hse. Children's Bks.

—The Evil Twin. 1993. (Sweet Valley High Ser.: No. 100). 352p. (gr. 7 up). mass mkt. 4.50 o.s.i (*0-553-29857-7*) Bantam Bks.

—The Evil Twin. 1993. (Sweet Valley High Ser.: No. 100). (YA). (gr. 7 up). mass mkt. o.s.i (*0-553-54130-7*, Dell Books for Young Readers) Random Hse. Children's Bks.

—Get Real! 1999. (Sweet Valley Junior High Ser.: No. 1). 160p. (gr. 3-7). pap. text 4.50 (*0-553-48603-9*, Dell Books for Young Readers) Random Hse. Children's Bks.

—Good-Bye, Mrs. Otis. 1997. (Sweet Valley Kids Ser.: No. 70). 96p. (gr. 1-3). pap. text 3.50 o.s.i (*0-553-48336-6*, Sweet Valley) Random Hse. Children's Bks.

—Holiday Mischief. 1988. (Sweet Valley Twins Super Edition Ser.: No. 2). 144p. (J). (gr. 3-7). pap. 3.99 o.s.i (*0-553-15641-1*, Skylark) Random Hse. Children's Bks.

—I'll Never Love Again. 1999. (Sweet Valley University Ser.: No. 46). 240p. (gr. 7 up). mass mkt. 3.99 o.s.i (*0-553-49266-7*, Dell Books for Young Readers) Random Hse. Children's Bks.

—Jessica's First Kiss. 1997. (Sweet Valley Twins Super Edition Ser.: No. 8). 192p. (J). (gr. 3-7). pap. 3.99 (*0-553-54290-7*, Sweet Valley) Random Hse. Children's Bks.

—Jessica's No Angel. 1998. (Sweet Valley Twins Super Edition Ser.: No. 11). 192p. (gr. 3-7). pap. text 3.99 o.s.i (*0-553-48350-1*, Sweet Valley) Random Hse. Children's Bks.

—Jessica's Secret. 1990. (Sweet Valley Twins Ser.: No. 42). 144p. (J). (gr. 3-7). pap. 3.50 o.s.i (*0-553-15824-4*) Bantam Bks.

—One 2 Many. 1999. (Sweet Valley Junior High Ser.: No. 2). 144p. (gr. 3-7). pap. text 4.50 (*0-553-48604-7*, Dell Books for Young Readers) Random Hse. Children's Bks.

—Return of the Evil Twin. 1995. (Sweet Valley High Magna Ser.). 352p. (gr. 7 up). mass mkt. 4.50 o.s.i (*0-553-57002-1*) Bantam Bks.

—Return of the Evil Twin. 1995. (Sweet Valley High Magna Edition Ser.). (YA). (gr. 7 up). pap. 5.99 (*0-553-54216-8*, Dell Books for Young Readers) Random Hse. Children's Bks.

—A Roller Coaster for the Twins! 1996. (Sweet Valley Kids Ser.: No. 68). 96p. (J). (gr. 1-3). pap. 3.50 o.s.i (*0-553-48334-X*) Bantam Bks.

—The Secret of the Magic Pen. 1995. (Sweet Valley Twins Super Chiller Ser.: No. 8). 192p. (gr. 3-7). pap. text 3.99 o.s.i (*0-553-48282-3*) Bantam Bks.

—Twin Switch. 1999. (Sweet Valley Junior High Ser.: No. 10). 160p. (gr. 3-7). pap. text 4.50 o.s.i (*0-553-48668-3*, Sweet Valley) Random Hse. Children's Bks.

—The Twins & the Wild West. 1990. (Sweet Valley Kids Ser.: No. 10). 80p. (J). (gr. 1-3). pap. 3.50 o.s.i (*0-553-15811-2*) Bantam Bks.

—The Twin's Big Pow-Wow. 1993. (Sweet Valley Kids Ser.: No. 44). 80p. (J). (gr. 1-3). pap. 2.99 o.s.i (*0-553-48098-7*) Bantam Bks.

—The Twins Go to College. 1997. (Sweet Valley Twins Super Edition Ser.: No. 9). 192p. (gr. 3-7). pap. text 3.99 o.s.i (*0-553-48347-1*, Sweet Valley) Random Hse. Children's Bks.

—The Twins Go to the Hospital. 1991. (Sweet Valley Kids Ser.: No. 20). 80p. (J). (gr. 1-3). pap. 3.50 o.p. (*0-553-15912-7*) Bantam Bks.

—The Year Without Christmas. 1997. (Sweet Valley Twins Super Edition Ser.: No. 10). 192p. (Orig.). (gr. 3-7). pap. text 3.99 o.s.i (*0-553-48348-X*, Dell Books for Young Readers) Random Hse. Children's Bks.

—You're Not My Sister. 1999. (Sweet Valley University Ser.: No. 47). 240p. (gr. 7 up). mass mkt. 3.99 o.s.i (*0-553-49267-5*, Dell Books for Young Readers) Random Hse. Children's Bks.

Pascal, Francine & Suzanne, Jamie. Mademoiselle Jessica. (Sweet Valley Twins Ser.: No. 46). (SPA.). 160p. (J). (gr. 3-7). 6.95 (*84-272-4646-3*) Molino, Editorial ESP. *Dist:* AIMS International Bks., Inc.

Paterson, Katherine. Jacob Have I Loved. (Trophy Bk.). (J). (gr. 7 up). 1990. 272p. pap. 6.50 (*0-06-440368-8*, Harper Trophy); 1990. 256p. pap. 6.50 (*0-06-447059-8*, Harper Trophy); 1980. 224p. lib. bdg. 16.89 (*0-690-04079-2*); 1980. 224p. 15.99 (*0-690-04078-4*) HarperCollins Children's Bk. Group.

—Jacob Have I Loved. l.t. ed. 2000. (LRS Large Print Cornerstone Ser.). 266p. (J). (gr. 5-12). lib. bdg. 29.95 (*1-58118-073-X*, 23658) LRS.

—Jacob Have I Loved. 1981. (YA). (gr. 7 up). pap. 2.95 (*0-380-56499-8*, Avon Bks.) Morrow/Avon.

—Jacob Have I Loved. l.t. ed. 1990. 251p. (J). (gr. k-6). reprint ed. lib. bdg. 16.95 o.s.i (*1-55736-167-3*, Cornerstone Bks.) Pages, Inc.

—Jacob Have I Loved. 1980. (J). 12.00 (*0-606-04379-9*) Turtleback Bks.

Payson, Dale. Almost Twins. 1999. 196p. (J). (ps-3). 5.95 (*0-13-022780-3*) Prentice Hall PTR.

Peel, John. Suddenly Twins! 2001. (Magical States Ser.: Vol. 1). (Illus.). 176p. (J). (gr. 4-6). pap. 4.99 (*0-7434-1762-3*, Aladdin) Simon & Schuster Children's Publishing.

Perkins, Lucy F. Spartan Twins. 1969. (Walker's Twins Ser.). (Illus.). (J). (gr. 2-5). reprint ed. lib. bdg. 4.85 o.s.i (*0-8027-6071-6*) Walker & Co.

—Swiss Twins. 1969. (Walker's Twins Ser.). (Illus.). (J). (gr. 3-6). reprint ed. 4.85 o.s.i (*0-8027-6072-4*) Walker & Co.

Perlberg, Deborah. The Case of the U. S. Navy Adventure. 1997. (Adventures of Mary-Kate & Ashley Ser.). (J). (gr. 2-7). mass mkt. 3.99 (*0-590-88015-2*) Scholastic, Inc.

Pfeffer, Susan Beth. Twin Surprises, ERS. (Redfeather Fiction Ser.). (Illus.). 64p. (J). (gr. 2-4). 1993. pap. 4.95 o.p. (*0-8050-2626-6*); 1991. 13.95 o.p. (*0-8050-1850-6*) Holt, Henry & Co. (Holt, Henry & Co. Bks. For Young Readers).

—Twin Troubles, ERS. 1994. 64p. (J). (ps-3). pap. 4.95 o.s.i (*0-8050-3272-X*, Holt, Henry & Co. Bks. For Young Readers) Holt, Henry & Co.

Platt, Randall Beth. Honor Bright. 240p. (YA). (gr. 7-12). 1998. mass mkt. 4.50 o.s.i (*0-440-21987-6*, Laurel Leaf); 1997. 14.95 o.s.i (*0-385-32216-X*, Dell Books for Young Readers) Random Hse. Children's Bks.

—Honor Bright. 1998. 10.55 (*0-606-13486-7*) Turtleback Bks.

Pohl, Peter & Gieth, Kinna. I Miss You, I Miss You! Greenwald, Roger, tr. from ENG. 1999. 256p. (YA). (gr. 7-12). 17.00 (*91-29-63935-2*) R & S Bks. SWE. *Dist:* Farrar, Straus & Giroux, Holtzbrinck Pubs.

Quagliano, Nancy E. The Morgan Twins in the Mystery of the Missing Toys. 1987. (J). (gr. 3-5). 6.95 o.p. (*0-533-07020-1*) Vantage Pr., Inc.

Radley, Gail. Old Man Out. 1995. 144p. (J). (gr. 4-7). 14.00 (*0-02-775792-7*, Atheneum) Simon & Schuster Children's Publishing.

Rae, John. The Third Twin: A Ghost Story. 1981. 128p. (J). (gr. 5-9). 8.95 o.p. (*0-7232-6192-X*, Warne, Frederick) Penguin Putnam Bks. for Young Readers.

Ramsey, Marcy Dunn, illus. Danger: Twins at Work! 1998. (Sweet Valley Kids Ser.: No. 76). 96p. (gr. 1-3). pap. text 3.50 o.s.i (*0-553-48615-2*, Sweet Valley) Random Hse. Children's Bks.

Reich, Ali. The Care Bear & the Terrible Twos. 1983. (Pictureback Ser.). (Illus.). 32p. (J). (gr. k-3). 1.95 o.s.i (*0-394-85918-9*); lib. bdg. 5.99 o.s.i (*0-394-95918-3*) Random Hse. Children's Bks. (Random Hse. Bks. for Young Readers).

Reisfeld, R. & Gilmour, H. B. Split Decision. 2003. (T*Witches Ser.). 288p. (J). (gr. 3-8). mass mkt. 5.50 (*0-439-49230-0*, Scholastic Paperbacks) Scholastic, Inc.

Reymes, Ellen. Christmas Party. 1997. (You're Invited to Mary-Kate & Ashley's Ser.). 48p. (J). (gr. 2-4). pap. 12.95 (*0-590-76958-8*) Scholastic, Inc.

Richardson, Jean. Out of Step: The Twins Were So Alike . . . but So Different. 1993. (Illus.). 28p. (J). (ps-3). pap. 5.95 o.p. (*0-8120-1553-3*) Barron's Educational Series, Inc.

—Out of Step: The Twins Were So Alike... but So Different. 1993. (Illus.). 28p. (J). (ps-3). 12.95 o.p. (*0-8120-5790-2*) Barron's Educational Series, Inc.

Roberts, Mark. The 12 Day Jinx. 2003. (Illus.). 128p. (J). pap. 8.95 (*1-84270-074-X*) Andersen Pr., Ltd. GBR. *Dist:* Trafalgar Square.

Robinet, Harriette Gillem. The Twins, the Pirates & the Battle of New Orleans. 144p. (J). 2001. (Illus.). pap. 4.99 (*0-689-84531-6*, Aladdin); 1997. (gr. 3-7). 15.00 o.s.i (*0-689-81208-6*, Atheneum) Simon & Schuster Children's Publishing.

Rogers, George L. Mac & Zach from Hackensack. 1992. (Illus.). 32p. (J). (gr. k-6). pap. 4.95 (*0-938399-06-3*); lib. bdg. 12.95 (*0-938399-07-1*) ChoiceSkills, Inc.

Rogers, Mary. The Twins' First Bike. 1992. (Foundations Ser.). 34p. (J). (gr. 1). pap. text 4.50 (*1-56843-069-8*) EMG Networks.

—The Twins' First Bike: Big Book. 1992. (Foundations Ser.). 34p. (J). (gr. 1). pap. text 23.00 (*1-56843-019-1*) EMG Networks.

Ross, Pat. M & M & the Bad News Babies. 1999. (Illus.). (J). pap. 12.40 (*0-8085-3696-6*) Econo-Clad Bks.

—M & M & the Bad News Babies. 1985. (Picture Puffin Bks.). (Illus.). 48p. (J). (ps-3). pap. 4.99 (*0-14-031851-8*, Puffin Bks.) Penguin Putnam Bks. for Young Readers.

—M & M & the Bad News Babies. 1983. (I Am Reading Bks.). (Illus.). 48p. (J). (gr. 6-9). pap. 6.95 o.p. (*0-394-84532-3*); 7.99 o.s.i (*0-394-94532-8*) Random Hse. Children's Bks. (Knopf Bks. for Young Readers).

—M & M & the Bad News Babies. 1985. (Picture Puffin Ser.). (Illus.). (J). 11.14 (*0-606-01684-8*) Turtleback Bks.

Roy, J. Soul Daddy. 1992. 224p. (YA). (gr. 7 up). 16.95 o.s.i (*0-15-277193-X*, Gulliver Bks.) Harcourt Children's Bks.

Rubel, Nicole. Sam & Violet Are Twins. 1981. (Illus.). 32p. (J). (gr. 1-3). pap. 1.95 o.p. (*0-380-76919-0*, 76919-0, Avon Bks.) Morrow/Avon.

—Sam & Violet Go Camping. 1981. (Illus.). 32p. (J). (gr. 1-3). pap. 1.95 o.p. (*0-380-76927-1*, 76927-1, Avon Bks.) Morrow/Avon.

Ryan, Mary E. Me, My Sister, & I. 1992. 160p. (YA). (gr. 5-9). pap. 15.00 (*0-671-73851-8*, Simon & Schuster Children's Publishing) Simon & Schuster Children's Publishing.

—My Sister Is Driving Me Crazy. 1991. 224p. (J). (gr. 5-9). pap. 15.00 o.p. (*0-671-73203-X*, Simon & Schuster Children's Publishing) Simon & Schuster Children's Publishing.

Sawicki, Norma J. The Little Red House. 1989. (Illus.). 24p. (J). (ps). 9.95 o.p. (*0-688-07891-5*); lib. bdg. 9.88 o.p. (*0-688-07892-3*) HarperCollins Children's Bk. Group.

Scholastic, Inc. Staff. The Case of the Missing Mummy. 1998. pap. text 71.82 (*0-590-63041-5*) Scholastic, Inc.

Schraff, Anne. The Twin. rev. ed. 1999. (Standing Tall Mysteries Ser.). 49p. (YA). (gr. 4-12). pap. 3.95 (*1-58659-081-2*) Artesian Pr.

—The Twin. 1995. (Standing Tall Mystery Ser.). 11.10 (*0-606-12018-1*) Turtleback Bks.

Scott, Elaine. Twins. 1998. (Illus.). 40p. (J). (ps-3). 16.00 (*0-689-80347-8*, Atheneum) Simon & Schuster Children's Publishing.

Scott, Michael. Gemini Game. 1994. 160p. (J). (gr. 7 up). 14.95 o.p. (*0-8234-1092-7*) Holiday Hse., Inc.

—Gemini Game. 1996. 10.00 (*0-606-14213-4*) Turtleback Bks.

Sescoe, Vincent E. Double Time. 2001. (Illus.). (gr. 6-12). 191p. (J). 17.95 (*1-930093-00-4*); 192p. (YA). pap. 6.95 (*1-930093-06-3*) Brookfield Reader, Inc., The.

Seymour, Jane & Keach, James. Yum! A Tale of Two Cookies. 1998. (This One & That One Ser.). (Illus.). 32p. (J). (ps-1). 12.99 o.s.i (*0-399-23310-5*) Penguin Group (USA) Inc.

Shatner, William. Beyond the Stars. 2001. (Quest for Tomorrow Ser.). 272p. mass mkt. 6.50 (*0-06-105996-X*, Eos) Morrow/Avon.

Shaw, Denis J. Pakistani Twins. 1965. (Twins Ser.). (Illus.). (J). (gr. 6-9). 12.95 (*0-8023-1094-X*) Dufour Editions, Inc.

Sherwood, Barbara B. Jan & Ann Are Twins. 1998. (Illus.). 16p. (J). (ps). pap. 5.95 (*1-891846-02-7*) Business Word, The.

Silverberg, Robert. Project Pendulum. 1987. 118p. (YA). (gr. 7 up). 15.95 o.p. (*0-8027-6712-5*) Walker & Co.

Singleton, Linda Joy. Twin Again. 1995. (My Sister, the Ghost Ser.: No. 1). (J). (gr. 3-5). 8.60 o.p. (*0-606-07910-6*) Turtleback Bks.

Skurnick, Elizabeth. The Popular One. 2001. 192p. (YA). (gr. 7). mass mkt. 4.50 o.s.i (*0-553-49374-4*, Dell Books for Young Readers) Random Hse. Children's Bks.

Snyder, Carol. One up, One down. 1995. (Illus.). 32p. (J). (ps-3). 15.00 (*0-689-31828-6*, Atheneum) Simon & Schuster Children's Publishing.

Spinner, Stephanie. Be First in the Universe. 2001. (J). 10.55 (*0-606-21051-2*) Turtleback Bks.

Spinner, Stephanie & Bisson, Terry. Expiration Date: Never. 2002. 128p. (gr. 3-7). pap. text 4.99 (*0-440-41560-8*, Delacorte Bks. for Young Readers) Random Hse. Children's Bks.

Springer, Nancy. The Great Pony Hassle. 1993. (Illus.). 80p. (J). (gr. 3-7). 13.99 o.p. (*0-8037-1306-1*); 13.89 o.p. (*0-8037-1308-8*) Penguin Putnam Bks. for Young Readers. (Dial Bks. for Young Readers).

St. James, Synthia. Sunday. 1996. (Illus.). 32p. (J). (ps-3). lib. bdg. 15.95 o.p. (*0-8075-7658-1*) Whitman, Albert & Co.

Stahl, Hilda. The Tyler Twins: Pet Show Panic. 1986. (Windrider Ser.). 112p. (Orig.). (J). (gr. 6-8). 3.50 o.p. (*0-8423-7627-5*) Tyndale Hse. Pubs.

—The Tyler Twins: Tree House Hideaway, No. 5. 1988. (Windrider Ser.). 128p. (J). (gr. 3-5). pap. 3.50 o.p. (*0-8423-7629-1*) Tyndale Hse. Pubs.

—The Tyler Twins No. 1: Surprise at Big Key Ranch. 1990. 128p. (J). (gr. 4-7). pap. 3.95 o.p. (*0-8423-7631-3*) Tyndale Hse. Pubs.

—The Tyler Twins No. 3: Pet Show Panic. 1990. 144p. (J). (gr. 4-7). pap. 4.99 o.p. (*0-8423-7633-X*) Tyndale Hse. Pubs.

—The Tyler Twins No. 5: Tree House Hideaway. 1990. 128p. (J). (gr. 4-7). pap. 4.99 o.p. (*0-8423-7635-6*) Tyndale Hse. Pubs.

Stamper, Judith Bauer. Breakfast at Danny's Diner. 2003. (All Aboard Math Reader Ser.). (Illus.). 48p. (J). 13.89 (*0-448-43266-8*, Grosset & Dunlap) Penguin Putnam Bks. for Young Readers.

Stanely, Carol. Twin Switch. 1989. (J). pap. 2.50 o.p. (*0-590-41665-0*) Scholastic, Inc.

Stanley, Diane. Joining the Boston Tea Party. 2001. (Time-Traveling Twins Ser.: No. 2). (Illus.). 48p. (J). (gr. k-5). 15.99 (*0-06-027067-5*); lib. bdg. 15.89 (*0-06-027068-3*) HarperCollins Children's Bk. Group. (Cotler, Joanna Bks.).

Stewart, Molly Mia. The Case of the Million-Dollar Diamonds. 1993. (Sweet Valley Kids Super Snooper Ser.: No. 6). (J). (gr. 1-3). 8.45 o.p. (*0-606-06034-0*) Turtleback Bks.

—Jessica's Snobby Club. 1992. (Sweet Valley Kids Ser.: No. 26). (J). (gr. 1-3). 8.19 o.p. (*0-606-00526-9*) Turtleback Bks.

—A Roller Coaster for the Twins! 1996. (Sweet Valley Kids Ser.: No. 68). (J). (gr. 1-3). 8.70 (*0-606-10331-7*) Turtleback Bks.

—Steven's Twin. 1994. (Sweet Valley Kids Ser.: No. 50). (J). (gr. 1-3). 8.19 o.p. (*0-606-06783-3*) Turtleback Bks.

—The Twins & the Wild West. 1990. (Sweet Valley Kids Ser.: No. 10). (J). (gr. 1-3). 8.70 o.p. (*0-606-04568-6*) Turtleback Bks.

Stillerman, Robbie. Twin Sisters Sticker Paper Dolls. 2003. (Dover Little Activity Bks.). (Illus.). (J). pap. 1.50 (*0-486-43018-9*) Dover Pubns., Inc.

Stine, Megan. My Sister the Supermodel. 1999. (Two of a Kind Ser.: No. 6). (Illus.). 112p. (gr. 3-7). mass mkt. 4.99 (*0-06-106576-5*, HarperEntertainment) Morrow/Avon.

—One Twin Too Many. 1999. (Two of a Kind Ser.: No. 4). (Illus.). 112p. (gr. 3-7). mass mkt. 4.99 (*0-06-106574-9*, HarperEntertainment) Morrow/Avon.

Stine, R. L. Dangerous Girls. 2003. 256p. (J). 111.92 (*0-06-056910-7*); 111.92 (*0-06-056909-3*); (Illus.). (gr. 7 up). 13.99 (*0-06-053080-4*) HarperCollins Children's Bk. Group.

—I Am Your Evil Twin. 1998. (Goosebumps Series 2000: No. 6). (J). (gr. 3-7). 9.09 o.p. (*0-606-13439-5*) Turtleback Bks.

—Night of the Living Dummy. l.t. ed. 1997. (Goosebumps Ser.: No. 7). 144p. (J). (gr. 3-7). lib. bdg. 21.27 o.p. (*0-8368-1979-9*) Stevens, Gareth Inc.

Stoddard, Michael Eugene. The Porthole to Time. 1999. 176p. (YA). pap. 9.95 (*0-9675924-0-2*) Stoddard, Michael Eugene.

Stolz, Mary. A Ballad of the Civil War. 1997. (Illus.). (J). 64p. (gr. 3-5). 14.95 (*0-06-027362-3*); 80p. (gr. 2-6). lib. bdg. 13.89 (*0-06-027363-1*) HarperCollins Children's Bk. Group.

Struble, Maegann M. Where Are the Twins? 2000. (Illus.). 16p. (J). pap. 5.95 (*1-891846-19-1*) Business Word, The.

Suzanne, Jamie. Against the Rules. 1987. (Sweet Valley Twins Ser.: No. 9). 112p. (J). (gr. 3-7). pap. 3.50 o.s.i (*0-553-15676-4*) Bantam Bks.

—Against the Rules. l.t. ed. 1991. (Sweet Valley Twins Ser.: No. 9). 104p. (J). (gr. 3-7). reprint ed. 9.95 o.p. (*1-55905-072-1*) Grey Castle Pr.

—Amy Moves In. 1990. (Sweet Valley Twins Ser.: No. 44). 144p. (J). (gr. 3-7). pap. 3.50 o.s.i (*0-553-15837-6*) Bantam Bks.

—Amy Moves In. 1990. (Sweet Valley Twins Ser.: No. 44). (J). (gr. 3-7). 8.60 o.p. (*0-606-04605-4*) Turtleback Bks.

—Amy's Pen Pal. 1990. (Sweet Valley Twins Ser.: No. 35). (J). (gr. 3-7). 8.60 o.p. (*0-606-00322-3*) Turtleback Bks.

—April Fool! 1989. (Sweet Valley Twins Ser.: No. 28). 112p. (J). (gr. 3-7). pap. 3.50 o.s.i (*0-553-15688-8*) Bantam Bks.

—El Autentico Ganador. 1991. (Gemelas de Sweet Valley Ser.: No. 16). Tr. of Second Best. (J). (gr. 3-7). 13.00 (*0-606-10454-2*) Turtleback Bks.

—The Beast is Watching You. 1996. (Sweet Valley Twins Ser.: No. 98). 144p. (gr. 3-7). pap. text 3.50 o.s.i (*0-553-48203-3*, Sweet Valley) Random Hse. Children's Bks.

—The Beast is Watching You. 1996. (Sweet Valley Twins Ser.: No. 98). (J). (gr. 3-7). 8.60 o.p. (*0-606-09936-0*) Turtleback Bks.

—The Beast Must Die. 1996. (Sweet Valley Twins Ser.: No. 99). 144p. (J). (gr. 3-7). pap. 3.50 (*0-553-48204-1*, Sweet Valley) Random Hse. Children's Bks.

—The Beast Must Die. 1996. (Sweet Valley Twins Ser.: No. 99). (J). (gr. 3-7). 8.60 o.p. (*0-606-09937-9*) Turtleback Bks.

—Big Brother's in Love. 1992. (Sweet Valley Twins Ser.: No. 57). (J). (gr. 3-7). 8.60 o.p. (*0-606-00465-3*) Turtleback Bks.

—Big Brother's in Love Again. 1997. (Sweet Valley Twins Ser.: No. 104). (J). (gr. 3-7). 9.55 (*0-606-11953-1*) Turtleback Bks.
—The Big Party Weekend. 1991. (Sweet Valley Twins Ser.: No. 54). 144p. (J). (gr. 3-7). pap. 3.50 o.s.i (*0-553-15952-6*) Bantam Bks.
—The Big Party Weekend. 1991. (Sweet Valley Twins Ser.: No. 54). (J). (gr. 3-7). 8.35 o.p. (*0-606-00313-4*) Turtleback Bks.
—The Boyfriend Game. 1998. (Sweet Valley Twins Ser.: No. 113). 144p. (gr. 3-7). pap. text 3.50 o.s.i (*0-553-48597-0*, Sweet Valley) Random Hse. Children's Bks.
—The Boyfriend Mess. 1998. (Sweet Valley Twins Ser.: No. 114). 144p. (gr. 3-7). pap. text 3.50 o.s.i (*0-553-48598-9*, Sweet Valley) Random Hse. Children's Bks.
—Boys Against Girls. 1988. (Sweet Valley Twins Ser.: No. 17). 112p. (J). (gr. 3-7). pap. 3.50 o.s.i (*0-553-15666-7*) Bantam Bks.
—Breakfast of Enemies. 1997. (Sweet Valley Twins Ser.: No. 106). (J). (gr. 3-7). 9.55 (*0-606-11955-8*) Turtleback Bks.
—Brooke & Her Rock Star Mom. 1991. (Sweet Valley Twins Ser.: No. 55). 144p. (J). (gr. 4-7). pap. 3.25 o.s.i (*0-553-15965-8*) Bantam Bks.
—Buried Treasure. 1987. (Sweet Valley Twins Ser.: No. 11). 112p. (J). (gr. 3-7). pap. 3.25 o.s.i (*0-553-15692-6*) Bantam Bks.
—The Carnival Ghost. 1990. (Sweet Valley Twins Super Chiller Ser.: No. 3). (J). (gr. 3-7). 9.09 o.p. (*0-606-04627-5*) Turtleback Bks.
—Center of Attention. 1988. (Sweet Valley Twins Ser.: No. 18). (J). (gr. 3-7). 112p. pap. 3.25 o.s.i (*0-553-15668-3*); pap. 3.25 (*0-553-16823-1*) Bantam Bks.
—Center of Attention. 1988. (Sweet Valley Twins Ser.: No. 18). (J). (gr. 3-7). pap. 2.50 o.s.i (*0-553-15581-4*, Skylark) Random Hse. Children's Bks.
—Centro de Atencion. Grau Aznar, Elena de, tr. 1992. (Gemelas de Sweet Valley Ser.: No. 18). Tr. of Center of Attention. (J). (gr. 3-7). 12.05 o.p. (*0-606-10456-9*) Turtleback Bks.
—Un Chico Para Jessica. Del Pozo, Maruja, tr. 1991. (Gemelas de Sweet Valley Ser.: No. 15). Tr. of Older Boy. (J). (gr. 3-7). 12.05 o.p. (*0-606-10453-4*) Turtleback Bks.
—Chicos Contra Chicas. Grau Aznar, Elena de, tr. 1992. (Gemelas de Sweet Valley Ser.: No. 17). Tr. of Boys Against Girls. (J). (gr. 3-7). 12.05 o.p. (*0-606-10455-0*) Turtleback Bks.
—Choosing Sides. 1986. (Sweet Valley Twins Ser.: No. 4). 112p. (gr. 4-7). pap. text 3.50 o.s.i (*0-553-15658-6*) Bantam Bks.
—Choosing Sides. l.t. ed. 1990. (Sweet Valley Twins Ser.: No. 4). 104p. (J). (gr. 3-7). reprint ed. 9.95 o.p. (*1-55905-067-5*) Grey Castle Pr.
—Choosing Sides. 1986. (Sweet Valley Twins Ser.: No. 4). (J). (gr. 3-7). 8.60 o.p. (*0-606-03093-X*) Turtleback Bks.
—Ciao, Sweet Valley! 1992. (Sweet Valley Twins Ser.: No. 60). (J). (gr. 3-7). 8.60 o.p. (*0-606-00654-0*) Turtleback Bks.
—The Class Trip. 1988. (Sweet Valley Twins Super Edition Ser.: No. 1). (J). (gr. 3-7). 8.60 o.p. (*0-606-03757-8*) Turtleback Bks.
—La Consentida de la Maestra. Utrilla, Hortensia Martinez, tr. 1991. (Gemelas de Sweet Valley Ser.: No. 2). Tr. of Teacher's Pet. (SPA.). (J). (gr. 3-7). 9.60 o.p. (*0-606-05412-X*) Turtleback Bks.
—Contra Las Normas. Bueno Bueno, Carmen, tr. 1990. (Gemelas de Sweet Valley Ser.: No. 9). Tr. of Against the Rules. (J). (gr. 3-7). 13.60 o.p. (*0-606-10459-3*) Turtleback Bks.
—The Curse of the Golden Heart. 1994. (Sweet Valley Twins Super Chiller Ser.: No. 6). (J). (gr. 3-7). 9.09 o.p. (*0-606-06789-2*) Turtleback Bks.
—The Curse of the Ruby Necklace. 1993. (Sweet Valley Twins Super Chiller Ser.: No. 5). (J). (gr. 3-7). 9.09 o.p. (*0-606-05654-8*) Turtleback Bks.
—Don't Go in the Basement. 1997. (Sweet Valley Twins Ser.: No. 109). (J). (gr. 3-7). 9.55 (*0-606-11958-2*) Turtleback Bks.
—Elizabeth the Hero. 1993. (Sweet Valley Twins Ser.: No. 74). (J). (gr. 3-7). 8.60 o.p. (*0-606-06035-9*) Turtleback Bks.
—Elizabeth's First Kiss. 1990. (Sweet Valley Twins Ser.: No. 43). 144p. (J). (gr. 3-7). pap. 3.50 o.s.i (*0-553-15835-X*) Bantam Bks.
—Elizabeth's First Kiss. 1990. (Sweet Valley Twins Ser.: No. 43). (J). (gr. 3-7). 8.60 o.p. (*0-606-04663-1*) Turtleback Bks.
—Escape from Terror Island. 1995. (Sweet Valley Twins Ser.: No. 92). (J). (gr. 3-7). 8.60 o.p. (*0-606-08634-X*) Turtleback Bks.
—Escogiendo Partido. Utrilla, Hortensia Martinez, tr. 1991. (Gemelas de Sweet Valley Ser.: No. 4). Tr. of Choosing Sides. (SPA.). (J). (gr. 3-7). 9.70 o.p. (*0-606-05414-6*) Turtleback Bks.
—First Place. l.t. ed. 1991. (Sweet Valley Twins Ser.: No. 8). 106p. (J). (gr. 3-7). reprint ed. 9.95 o.p. (*1-55905-071-3*) Grey Castle Pr.
—First Place. 1987. (Sweet Valley Twins Ser.: No. 8). (J). (gr. 3-7). 9.55 (*0-606-01709-7*) Turtleback Bks.
—The Gossip War. 1994. (Sweet Valley Twins Ser.: No. 80). 144p. (gr. 3-7). pap. text 3.50 o.s.i (*0-553-48112-6*) Bantam Bks.
—The Gossip War. 1994. (Sweet Valley Twins Ser.: No. 80). (J). (gr. 3-7). 8.60 o.p. (*0-606-06787-6*) Turtleback Bks.
—Una Gran Luchadora. del Molino, Conchita Peraire, tr. 1990. (Gemelas de Sweet Valley Ser.: No. 10). Tr. of One of the Gang. (J). (gr. 3-7). 12.05 o.p. (*0-606-10448-8*) Turtleback Bks.
—El Gran Secreto. Bueno Bueno, Carmen, tr. 1990. (Gemelas de Sweet Valley Ser.: No. 12). Tr. of Keeping Secrets. (J). (gr. 3-7). 12.05 o.p. (*0-606-10450-X*) Turtleback Bks.
—Happy Mother's Day, Lila. 1998. (Sweet Valley Twins Ser.: No. 115). 144p. (gr. 3-7). pap. text 3.50 o.s.i (*0-553-48599-7*, Sweet Valley) Random Hse. Children's Bks.
—The Haunted House. 1986. (Sweet Valley Twins Ser.: No. 3). 112p. (gr. 4-7). pap. text 3.99 o.s.i (*0-553-15657-8*) Bantam Bks.
—The Haunted House. 1986. (Sweet Valley Twins Ser.: No. 3). (J). (gr. 3-7). 10.04 (*0-606-02111-6*) Turtleback Bks.
—Holiday Mischief. 1988. (Sweet Valley Twins Super Edition Ser.: No. 2). (J). (gr. 3-7). 9.09 o.p. (*0-606-04094-3*) Turtleback Bks.
—If I Die Before I Wake. 1996. (Sweet Valley Twins Ser.: No. 100). (J). (gr. 3-7). 9.60 o.p. (*0-606-10332-5*) Turtleback Bks.
—If Looks Could Kill. 1997. (Sweet Valley Twins Ser.: No. 112). 144p. (gr. 3-7). pap. text 3.50 o.s.i (*0-553-48443-5*, Dell Books for Young Readers) Random Hse. Children's Bks.
—The Incredible Madame Jessica. 1996. (Sweet Valley Twins Ser.: No. 93). (J). (gr. 3-7). 8.60 o.p. (*0-606-08635-8*) Turtleback Bks.
—It Can't Happen Here. 1995. (Sweet Valley Twins Ser.: No. 86). 144p. (gr. 3-7). pap. text 3.50 o.s.i (*0-553-48113-4*) Bantam Bks.
—It Can't Happen Here. 1995. (Sweet Valley Twins Ser.: No. 86). (J). (gr. 3-7). 8.60 o.p. (*0-606-08241-7*) Turtleback Bks.
—Jessica & the Brat Attack. 1989. (Sweet Valley Twins Ser.: No. 29). 112p. (J). (gr. 3-7). pap. 2.75 o.s.i (*0-553-15695-0*) Bantam Bks.
—Jessica the Nerd. 1992. (Sweet Valley Twins Ser.: No. 61). (J). (gr. 3-7). 8.60 o.p. (*0-606-00656-7*) Turtleback Bks.
—Jessica's Cookie Disaster. 1995. (Sweet Valley Twins Ser.: No. 89). 144p. (gr. 3-7). pap. text 3.50 o.s.i (*0-553-48191-6*) Bantam Bks.
—Jessica's First Kiss. 1997. (Sweet Valley Twins Super Edition Ser.: No. 8). (J). (gr. 3-7). 9.34 (*0-606-11959-0*) Turtleback Bks.
—Jessica's Lucky Millions. 1997. (Sweet Valley Twins Ser.: No. 105). (J). (gr. 3-7). 9.55 (*0-606-11954-X*) Turtleback Bks.
—Left Behind. 1988. (Sweet Valley Twins Ser.: No. 21). 112p. (Orig.). (J). (gr. 3-7). pap. 3.25 o.s.i (*0-553-15609-8*, Skylark) Random Hse. Children's Bks.
—Lila's Music Video. 1993. (Sweet Valley Twins Ser.: No. 73). 144p. (J). (gr. 3-7). pap. 3.50 o.s.i (*0-553-48059-6*) Bantam Bks.
—Lila's Music Video. 1993. (Sweet Valley Twins Ser.: No. 73). (J). (gr. 3-7). 8.60 o.p. (*0-606-05653-X*) Turtleback Bks.
—Lucy Takes the Reins. 1991. (Sweet Valley Twins Ser.: No. 45). 144p. (J). (gr. 3-7). pap. 3.25 o.s.i (*0-553-15843-0*) Bantam Bks.
—Mentirijillas. 1991. (Gemelas de Sweet Valley Ser.: No. 13). Tr. of Streching the Truth. (J). (gr. 3-7). 12.05 o.p. (*0-606-10451-8*) Turtleback Bks.
—The Mysterious Dr. Q. 1996. (Sweet Valley Twins Ser.: No. 102). (J). (gr. 3-7). 8.60 o.p. (*0-606-10334-1*) Turtleback Bks.
—The New Girl. 1987. (Sweet Valley Twins Ser.: No. 6). 96p. (J). (gr. 3-7). pap. 2.50 o.s.i (*0-553-15475-3*, Skylark) Random Hse. Children's Bks.
—One of the Gang. 1987. (Sweet Valley Twins Ser.: No. 10). 112p. (J). (gr. 3-7). pap. 3.50 o.s.i (*0-553-15677-2*) Bantam Bks.
—One of the Gang. l.t. ed. 1991. (Sweet Valley Twins Ser.: No. 10). 104p. (J). (gr. 3-7). reprint ed. 9.95 o.p. (*1-55905-073-X*) Grey Castle Pr.
—One of the Gang. 1987. (Sweet Valley Twins Ser.: No. 10). (J). (gr. 3-7). 8.60 o.p. (*0-606-03167-7*) Turtleback Bks.
—Poor Lila! 1992. (Sweet Valley Twins Ser.: No. 63). 144p. (J). (gr. 3-7). pap. 3.50 o.s.i (*0-553-15962-3*) Bantam Bks.
—Poor Lila! 1992. (Sweet Valley Twins Ser.: No. 63). (J). (gr. 3-7). 8.60 o.p. (*0-606-00662-1*) Turtleback Bks.
—El Primer Puesto. del Molino, Conchita Peraire, tr. 1989. (Gemelas de Sweet Valley Ser.: No. 8). Tr. of First Place. (J). (gr. 3-7). 12.05 o.p. (*0-606-10458-5*) Turtleback Bks.
—La Recien Llegada. Romero, Javiedes, tr. 1991. (Gemelas de Sweet Valley Ser.: No. 6). Tr. of New Girl. (SPA.). (J). (gr. 3-7). 9.70 o.p. (*0-606-05416-2*) Turtleback Bks.
—Robbery at the Mall. 1994. (Sweet Valley Twins Ser.: No. 81). (J). (gr. 3-7). 8.60 o.p. (*0-606-06788-4*) Turtleback Bks.
—Romeo & 2 Juliets. 1994. (Sweet Valley Twins Ser.: No. 84). 144p. (gr. 3-7). pap. text 3.50 o.s.i (*0-553-48105-3*) Bantam Bks.
—Romeo & 2 Juliets. 1995. (Sweet Valley Twins Ser.: No. 84). (J). (gr. 3-7). 8.60 o.p. (*0-606-08239-5*) Turtleback Bks.
—Salida a Hurtadillas. Utrilla, Hortensia Martinez, tr. 1991. (Sweet Valley Twins Ser.: No. 5). Tr. of Sneaking Out. (SPA.). (J). (gr. 3-7). 12.10 (*0-606-05415-4*) Turtleback Bks.
—Sarah's Dad & Sophia's Mom. 1992. (Sweet Valley Twins Ser.: No. 62). (J). (gr. 3-7). 8.35 o.p. (*0-606-00657-5*) Turtleback Bks.
—Sneaking Out. 1986. (Sweet Valley Twins Ser.: No. 5). 112p. (J). (gr. 3-7). pap. 3.50 o.s.i (*0-553-15659-4*) Bantam Bks.
—Sneaking Out. l.t. ed. 1990. (Sweet Valley Twins Ser.: No. 5). 106p. (J). (gr. 3-7). reprint ed. 9.95 o.p. (*1-55905-068-3*) Grey Castle Pr.
—Steven Gets Even. 1995. (Sweet Valley Twins Ser.: No. 88). 144p. (J). (gr. 3-7). pap. 3.50 o.s.i (*0-553-48189-4*) Bantam Bks.
—Sweet Valley Twins Boxed Set, 10 bks., Set. l.t. ed. 1990. (Sweet Valley Twins Ser.). (J). (gr. 3-7). reprint ed. 99.50 o.p. (*1-55905-074-8*) Grey Castle Pr.
—Teacher's Pet. l.t. ed. 1990. (Sweet Valley Twins Ser.: No. 2). 103p. (J). (gr. 3-7). reprint ed. 9.95 o.p. (*1-55905-065-9*) Grey Castle Pr.
—Teacher's Pet. 1986. (Sweet Valley Twins Ser.: No. 2). (J). (gr. 3-7). 8.60 (*0-606-03145-6*) Turtleback Bks.
—Un Tesoro Enterrado. Bueno Bueno, Carmen, tr. 1990. (Gemelas de Sweet Valley Ser.: No. 11). Tr. of Buried Treasure. (J). (gr. 3-7). 12.05 o.p. (*0-606-10449-6*) Turtleback Bks.
—Three's a Crowd. l.t. ed. 1990. (Sweet Valley Twins Ser.: No. 7). 105p. (J). (gr. 3-7). reprint ed. 9.95 o.p. (*1-55905-070-5*) Grey Castle Pr.
—Too Scared to Sleep. 1996. (Sweet Valley Twins Ser.: No. 97). 144p. (gr. 3-7). pap. text 3.50 o.s.i (*0-553-48201-7*, Sweet Valley) Random Hse. Children's Bks.
—Too Scared to Sleep. 1996. (Sweet Valley Twins Ser.: No. 97). (J). (gr. 3-7). 8.60 o.p. (*0-606-09935-2*) Turtleback Bks.
—Tres Es Multitud. del Molino, Conchita Peraire, tr. 1989. (Gemelas de Sweet Valley Ser.: No. 7). Tr. of Three's a Crowd. (J). (gr. 3-7). 12.05 o.p. (*0-606-10457-7*) Turtleback Bks.
—Tug of War. 1987. (Sweet Valley Twins Ser.: No. 14). (J). (gr. 3-7). 112p. pap. 3.50 o.s.i (*0-553-15663-2*, Skylark); pap. 2.50 (*0-553-16799-5*, Dell Books for Young Readers) Random Hse. Children's Bks.
—The Twins Get Caught. 1990. (Sweet Valley Twins Ser.: No. 41). 144p. (J). (gr. 3-7). pap. 3.50 o.s.i (*0-553-15810-4*) Bantam Bks.
—The Twins Get Caught. 1990. (Sweet Valley Twins Ser.: No. 41). (J). (gr. 3-7). 8.60 o.p. (*0-606-04569-4*) Turtleback Bks.
—The Twins Go to College. 1997. (Sweet Valley Twins Super Edition Ser.: No. 9). (J). (gr. 3-7). 9.09 (*0-606-11960-4*) Turtleback Bks.
—The Twins Hit Hollywood. 1997. (Sweet Valley Twins Ser.: No. 107). (Illus.). 144p. (gr. 3-7). pap. text 3.50 o.s.i (*0-553-48438-9*, Sweet Valley) Random Hse. Children's Bks.
—The Twins Hit Hollywood. 1997. (Sweet Valley Twins Ser.: No. 107). (J). (gr. 3-7). 8.60 o.p. (*0-606-11956-6*) Turtleback Bks.
—Twins in Love. 1996. (Sweet Valley Twins Ser.: No. 101). 144p. (gr. 3-7). pap. text 3.50 o.s.i (*0-553-48346-3*, Dell Books for Young Readers) Random Hse. Children's Bks.
—Twins in Love. 1996. (Sweet Valley Twins Ser.: No. 101). (J). (gr. 3-7). 8.60 o.p. (*0-606-10333-3*) Turtleback Bks.
—The Unicorns Go Hawaiian. 1991. (Sweet Valley Twins Super Edition Ser.: No. 4). (J). (gr. 3-7). 9.09 o.p. (*0-606-00813-6*) Turtleback Bks.
—The War Between the Twins. 1990. (Sweet Valley Twins Ser.: No. 37). 144p. (J). (gr. 4-7). pap. 3.50 o.s.i (*0-553-15779-5*) Bantam Bks.
—The War Between the Twins. 1990. (Sweet Valley Twins Ser.: No. 37). (J). (gr. 3-7). 8.60 o.p. (*0-606-04573-2*) Turtleback Bks.
—Yours for a Day. 1994. (Sweet Valley Twins Ser.: No. 76). 144p. (J). (gr. 3-7). pap. 3.50 o.s.i (*0-553-48096-0*) Bantam Bks.
—Yours for a Day. 1994. (Sweet Valley Twins Ser.: No. 76). (J). (gr. 3-7). 8.60 o.p. (*0-606-06037-5*) Turtleback Bks.

Sweeney, Jacqueline. Just Call Me J. P. 2000. (We Can Read! Ser.). (Illus.). 32p. (J). (gr. 1-2). lib. bdg. 21.36 (*0-7614-0922-X*, Benchmark Bks.) Cavendish, Marshall Corp.

Swobud, I. K. The Case of the Blue-Ribbon-Horse. 1998. (New Adventures of Mary-Kate & Ashley Ser.). 86p. (J). (gr. 2-7). mass mkt. 3.99 (*0-590-29309-5*) Scholastic, Inc.

Tashjian, Janet. Tru Confessions. ERS. 1997. 161p. (J). (gr. 4-7). 15.95 (*0-8050-5254-2*, Holt, Henry & Co. Bks. For Young Readers) Holt, Henry & Co.
—Tru Confessions. 1999. (J). mass mkt. 4.99 (*0-590-96047-4*) Scholastic, Inc.
—Tru Confessions. 1999. 11.04 (*0-606-16611-4*) Turtleback Bks.

Tester, Sylvia R. The Loud-Noisy, Dirty-Grimy, Bad & Naughty Twins. 1977. (Using Words Ser.). (Illus.). 32p. (J). (gr. k-3). 6.95 o.p. (*0-516-06132-1*, Children's Pr.) Scholastic Library Publishing.

Thomasma, Kenneth. Om-Kas-Toe: Blackfeet Twin Captures an Elkdog. 1986. (Amazing Indian Children Ser.). 13.00 (*0-606-10272-8*) Turtleback Bks.

Thompson, Carol. The Case of the Mystery Cruise, 1996. (Adventures of Mary-Kate & Ashley Ser.). 64p. (J). (gr. 2-7). mass mkt. 3.99 (*0-590-86370-3*) Scholastic, Inc.
—The Case of the U. S. Space Camp Mission. 1996. (Adventures of Mary-Kate & Ashley Ser.). (J). (gr. 2-7). mass mkt. 3.99 (*0-590-88008-X*) Scholastic, Inc.
—The Case of the Volcano Mystery. 1997. (Adventures of Mary-Kate & Ashley Ser.). 64p. (J). (gr. 2-7). mass mkt. 3.99 (*0-590-88014-4*, Scholastic Paperbacks) Scholastic, Inc.

Trottier, Maxine. A Circle of Silver. 2000. (Circle of Silver Chronicles Ser.). 220p. (J). (gr. 7-12). pap. 7.95 (*0-7737-6055-5*) Stoddart Kids CAN. *Dist:* Fitzhenry & Whiteside, Ltd.

Upton, Joe. Runaways on the Inside Passage. 2002. (Illus.). 304p. (YA). (gr. 5 up). 17.95 (*0-88240-564-0*); pap. 9.95 (*0-88240-565-9*) Graphic Arts Ctr. Publishing Co. (Alaska Northwest Bks.).

Ure, Jean. Shrinking Violet. l.t. ed. 2002. (J). 16.95 (*0-7540-7833-7*, Galaxy Children's Large Print) BBC Audiobooks America.

Van Sickle, Lisa. Twin Stories: Shhhh... It's Bertha. McLaughlin, Wanda, ed. l.t. ed. 1998. (Illus.). 48p. (J). (gr. k-3). 16.95 (*0-9659001-5-0*) Write Team, The.
—Twin Stories - Kaos . . . Bad Dog! McLaughlin, Wanda J., ed. 1998. (Illus.). 48p. (J). (ps-3). 16.95 (*0-9659001-6-9*) Write Team, The.

VanOosting, James. The Last Payback. (J). (gr. 4-7). 1998. 160p. pap. 4.95 o.p. (*0-06-440722-5*, Harper Trophy); 1997. 160p. 14.95 o.s.i (*0-06-027491-3*); 1997. 144p. lib. bdg. 14.89 o.p. (*0-06-027492-1*) HarperCollins Children's Bk. Group.
—The Last Payback. 1998. 10.15 o.p. (*0-606-13565-0*) Turtleback Bks.

Vogel, Ilse-Margret. My Twin Sister Erika. 1976. (Illus.). 64p. (J). (gr. 5 up). lib. bdg. 12.89 o.p. (*0-06-026309-1*) HarperCollins Children's Bk. Group.

Vogiel, Eva. Facing the Music. 2003. 284p. 19.95 (*1-880582-94-5*) Judaica Pr., Inc., The.

Wallace, Barbara Brooks. The Twin in the Tavern. 192p. (J). (gr. 3-7). 1995. pap. 4.99 (*0-689-80167-X*, Aladdin); 1993. 15.00 (*0-689-31846-4*, Atheneum) Simon & Schuster Children's Publishing.
—The Twin in the Tavern. 1995. (Illus.). 11.04 (*0-606-08327-8*) Turtleback Bks.

Wallace, John. The Twins. 2001. (Golden Books Family Storytime). (Illus.). 32p. (J). (ps). 9.95 (*0-307-10211-4*, Golden Bks.) Random Hse. Children's Bks.

Waricha, Jean. The Case of the Christmas Caper. 1996. (Adventures of Mary-Kate & Ashley Ser.). (Illus.). (J). (gr. 2-7). mass mkt. 3.99 (*0-590-88009-8*) Scholastic, Inc.

Weis, Margaret, et al. War of the Twins. 1986. (Dragonlance Legends Ser.). 387p. (*0-394-74578-7*) Beginner Bks.

Weiss, Ellen. Twins Go to Bed. Williams, Sam, tr. & illus. by. 2004. (Ready-to-Read Ser.). (J). (*0-689-86518-X*, Aladdin Library); pap. (*0-689-86517-1*, Aladdin) Simon & Schuster Children's Publishing.
—Twins Have a Fight. Williams, Sam, tr. & illus. by. 2004. (Ready-to-Read Ser.). (J). (*0-689-86516-3*, Aladdin Library); pap. (*0-689-86515-5*, Aladdin) Simon & Schuster Children's Publishing.
—Twins in the Bath. 2003. (Ready-to-Read Ser.). (Illus.). 24p. (J). pap. 3.99 (*0-689-85740-3*, Aladdin); lib. bdg. 11.89 (*0-689-85741-1*, Aladdin Library) Simon & Schuster Children's Publishing.
—Twins in the Park. 2003. (Ready-to-Read Ser.). (Illus.). 24p. (J). pap. 3.99 (*0-689-85742-X*, Aladdin); lib. bdg. 11.89 (*0-689-85743-8*, Aladdin Library) Simon & Schuster Children's Publishing.

Welch, Sheila Kelly. The Shadowed Unicorn. 2000. 192p. (J). (gr. 5-9). 15.95 (*0-8126-2895-0*) Cricket Bks.

Werlin, Nancy. Are You Alone on Purpose? 1995. (J). (gr. 7 up). mass mkt. 4.50 o.s.i (*0-449-70445-9*, Fawcett) Ballantine Bks.

—Are You Alone on Purpose? 1994. 208p. (YA). (gr. 7-7). tchr. ed. 16.00 (*0-395-67350-X*) Houghton Mifflin Co.

Westwood, Chris. Brother of Mine. 1994. 192p. (YA). (gr. 9 up). tchr. ed. 13.95 o.p. (*0-395-66137-4*, Clarion Bks.) Houghton Mifflin Co. Trade & Reference Div.

Willard, Eliza. Holiday in the Sun. 2001. (Mary-Kate & Ashley Starring in Ser.: Vol. 4). (Illus.). 96p. (gr. 3-6). mass mkt. 4.99 (*0-06-106668-0*, HarperEntertainment) Morrow/Avon.

William, Kate. Are We in Love. 1993. (Sweet Valley High Ser.: No. 94). (YA). (gr. 7 up). 8.35 o.p. (*0-606-05635-1*) Turtleback Bks.

—The Arrest. 1993. (Sweet Valley High Ser.: No. 96). (YA). (gr. 7 up). 8.60 o.p. (*0-606-05637-8*) Turtleback Bks.

—Beware the Babysitter. 1993. (Sweet Valley High Ser.: No. 99). (YA). (gr. 7 up). 8.60 o.p. (*0-606-06028-6*) Turtleback Bks.

—El Campeon Asediado. Del Pozo, Maruja, tr. 1993. Tr. of Heartbreaker. (YA). (gr. 7 up). 13.05 o.p. (*0-606-10470-4*) Turtleback Bks.

—Demasiado Perfecta. Del Pozo, Maruja, tr. 1993. Tr. of Too Good to be True. (YA). (gr. 7 up). 13.05 o.p. (*0-606-10462-3*) Turtleback Bks.

—Don't Go Home with John. 1993. (Sweet Valley High Ser.: No. 90). (YA). (gr. 7 up). 8.60 o.p. (*0-606-02928-1*) Turtleback Bks.

—Esa Clase de Chica. Del Pozo, Maruja, tr. 1993. Tr. of Wrong Kind of Girl. (YA). (gr. 7 up). 13.05 o.p. (*0-606-10461-5*) Turtleback Bks.

—The Evil Twin. 1993. (Sweet Valley High Ser.: No. 100). (YA). (gr. 7 up). 10.55 (*0-606-06023-5*) Turtleback Bks.

—La Gran Carrera. 1993. Tr. of Racing Hearts. (YA). (gr. 7 up). 13.05 o.p. (*0-606-10471-2*) Turtleback Bks.

—Jugando con Fuego. Del Pozo, Maruja, tr. 1992. Tr. of Playing with Fire. (YA). (gr. 7 up). 13.05 o.p. (*0-606-10465-8*) Turtleback Bks.

—Una Larga Noche. 1993. (Gemelas de Sweet Valley Ser.).Tr. of All Night Long. (YA). (gr. 7 up). 13.05 o.p. (*0-606-10467-4*) Turtleback Bks.

—Olivia's Story. 1991. (Sweet Valley High Super Star Ser.: No. 4). (YA). (gr. 7 up). 8.60 o.p. (*0-606-00667-2*) Turtleback Bks.

—Peligrosa Tentacion. 1993. Tr. of Dangerous Love. (YA). (gr. 7 up). 13.05 o.p. (*0-606-10468-2*) Turtleback Bks.

—Promesa Rota. Del Pozo, Maruja, tr. 1993. Tr. of When Love Dies. (YA). (gr. 7 up). 13.05 o.p. (*0-606-10463-1*) Turtleback Bks.

—Prueba de Fuerza. 1992. Tr. of Power Play. (YA). (gr. 7 up). 13.05 o.p. (*0-606-10466-6*) Turtleback Bks.

—Querida Hermana. Del Pozo, Maruja, tr. 1993. Tr. of Dear Sister. (YA). (gr. 7 up). 13.05 o.p. (*0-606-10469-0*) Turtleback Bks.

—Return of the Evil Twin. 1995. (Sweet Valley High Magna Edition Ser.). (YA). (gr. 7 up). 10.55 (*0-606-08628-5*) Turtleback Bks.

—Secretos del Pasado. Del Pozo, Maruja, tr. 1992. (Sweet Valley Twins Ser.: No. 2). Tr. of Secrets. (YA). (gr. 7 up). 13.05 o.p. (*0-606-10464-X*) Turtleback Bks.

Williams, Laura E. The Mystery of the Bad Luck Curse. 2002. (Mystic Lighthouse Mysteries Ser.). (Illus.). 128p. (J). (gr. 2-7). mass mkt. 4.50 (*0-439-21727-X*) Scholastic, Inc.

—The Mystery of the Missing Tiger. 2002. (Mystic Lighthouse Mysteries Ser.). 112p. (J). mass mkt. 4.50 (*0-439-21728-8*) Scholastic, Inc.

—Mystery of the Phantom Ship. 2002. (Mystic Lighthouse Mysteries Ser.). (Illus.). 128p. (J). mass mkt. 4.50 (*0-439-21729-6*, Scholastic Paperbacks) Scholastic, Inc.

Wilson. Double Act. 2000. (Illus.). 187p. 16.95 (*0-385-40537-5*) Transworld Publishers Ltd. GBR. *Dist:* Trafalgar Square.

Wilson, Jacqueline. Double Act. 2000. 32p. pap. 6.95 (*0-440-86334-1*); 1998. (Illus.). 192p. (gr. 4-7). reprint ed. text 14.95 o.s.i (*0-385-32312-3*) Dell Publishing. (Delacorte Pr.).

—Double Act. 1999. (Illus.). 192p. (gr. 3-7). pap. text 4.99 (*0-440-41374-5*) Random Hse. Children's Bks.

—Double Act. 1999. 10.55 (*0-606-16442-1*) Turtleback Bks.

Windle, Jeanette. Captured in Colombia. 2002. (Parker Twins Ser.: No. 3). 176p. (J). (gr. 3-8). pap. 5.99 (*0-8254-4147-1*) Kregel Pubns.

—Escape to Deer Island. 1996. (Twin Pursuits Ser.). 128p. pap. 4.99 o.p. (*0-88070-906-5*, Multnomah Bks.) Multnomah Pubs., Inc.

—Secret of the Dragon Mark. 2002. (Parker Twins Ser.: No. 5). 160p. (J). (gr. 3-8). 5.99 (*0-8254-4149-8*) Kregel Pubns.

—Secret of the Dragon Mark. 1996. (Twin Pursuits Ser.: No. 2). 128p. pap. 4.99 o.p. (*0-88070-905-7*, Multnomah Bks.) Multnomah Pubs., Inc.

Wolf, Joan. How the Selves Became Elves. 2001. (J). (ps-2). 19.95 (*0-9711445-1-6*) Cruzane Mountain Publishing.

Wood, Brian. The Cramp Twins. 2001. (J). pap. 9.95 (*0-385-32714-5*, Random Hse. Bks. for Young Readers) Random Hse. Children's Bks.

—Opposites Attack: Swamp Fever. 2002. (Cramp Twins Ser.: Bk. 1). (Illus.). 96p. (J). (gr. 2-7). pap. 7.95 (*1-58234-765-4*, Bloomsbury Children) Bloomsbury Publishing.

—Swamp Fever. 2001. (Cramp Twins Ser.). (J). pap. (*0-385-32717-X*, Dell Books for Young Readers) Random Hse. Children's Bks.

Wood, Brian, creator. Swamp Fever. 2002. (Cramp Twins Ser.: Bk. 2). (Illus.). (J). (gr. 4-9). pap. 7.95 (*1-58234-766-2*, Bloomsbury Children) Bloomsbury Publishing.

Wyatt. Amazing Investigations Twins. 1998. (J). 12.95 (*0-13-023649-7*, Simon & Schuster Children's Publishing) Simon & Schuster Children's Publishing.

Yolen, Jane. The Bagpiper's Ghost. (Tartan Magic Ser.: Bk. 3). 144p. 2003. (Illus.). (J). pap. 5.95 (*0-15-204913-4*, Magic Carpet Bks.); 2002. (YA). (gr. 4-7). 16.00 (*0-15-202310-0*) Harcourt Children's Bks.

—The Wizard's Map. 1999. (Tartan Magic Ser.: Bk. 1). 144p. (YA). (gr. 3-7). 16.00 (*0-15-202067-5*) Harcourt Children's Bks.

Yorinks, Arthur. Oh, Brother, RS. 1989. (Illus.). 40p. (J). (ps-3). 15.95 o.p. (*0-374-35599-1*, Farrar, Straus & Giroux (BYR)) Farrar, Straus & Giroux.

U

UNMARRIED MOTHERS—FICTION

Cleaver, Vera & Cleaver, Bill. I Would Rather Be a Turnip. 1976. 160p. mass mkt. 2.25 o.p. (*0-451-12353-0*, Signet Bks.) NAL.

Dessen, Sarah. Someone Like You. 272p. (gr. 7 up). 2000. (Illus.). (YA). pap. 5.99 (*0-14-130269-0*, Puffin Bks.); 1998. (J). 16.99 (*0-670-87778-6*) Penguin Putnam Bks. for Young Readers.

—Someone Like You. unabr. ed. 2003. (J). (gr. 7). audio 26.00 (*0-8072-1564-3*, Listening Library) Random Hse. Audio Publishing Group.

—Someone Like You. 2000. 11.04 (*0-606-18847-9*) Turtleback Bks.

Doherty, Berlie. Dear Nobody. 1994. 240p. (J). (gr. 7 up). pap. 5.95 (*0-688-12764-9*, Harper Trophy) HarperCollins Children's Bk. Group.

—Dear Nobody. 1992. 192p. (YA). (gr. 6 up). 16.95 (*0-531-05461-6*); mass mkt. 16.99 o.p. (*0-531-08611-9*) Scholastic, Inc. (Orchard Bks.).

—Dear Nobody. 1994. (J). 12.00 (*0-606-05805-2*) Turtleback Bks.

Evans, Shirlee. A Life in Her Hands. 1987. 192p. (Orig.). (J). pap. 6.99 o.p. (*0-8361-3441-9*) Herald Pr.

Eyerly, Jeannette. Someone to Love Me. 1987. 160p. (YA). (gr. 7 up). lib. bdg. 11.89 (*0-397-32206-2*) HarperCollins Children's Bk. Group.

Ferris, Amy Schor. A Greater Goode. 2002. 192p. (YA). (gr. 5-9). 15.00 (*0-618-13154-X*) Houghton Mifflin Co.

Ferris, Jean. Looking for Home, RS. 176p. (YA). 1993. pap. 3.95 o.p. (*0-374-44566-4*, Aerial); 1989. (gr. 8 up). 15.00 o.p. (*0-374-34649-6*, Farrar, Straus & Giroux (BYR)) Farrar, Straus & Giroux.

—Looking for Home. 1993. (Aerial Fiction Ser.). (J). 9.05 o.p. (*0-606-05913-X*) Turtleback Bks.

Klein, Norma. Mom, the Wolf Man & Me. 1977. 160p. (J). (gr. 5-9). pap. 1.95 o.p. (*0-380-01725-3*, 60458-2, Avon Bks.) Morrow/Avon.

Lee, Mildred. Sycamore Year. 1974. 160p. (J). (gr. 6 up). 12.95 o.p. (*0-688-41643-8*); lib. bdg. 12.88 o.p. (*0-688-51643-2*) HarperCollins Children's Bk. Group.

Lowry, Lois. The Silent Boy. 2003. (Illus.). 192p. (YA). (gr. 5-12). tchr. ed. 15.00 (*0-618-28231-9*) Houghton Mifflin Co.

Minshull, Evelyn W. But I Thought You Really Loved Me. 1976. 150p. (YA). (gr. 7 up). 8.00 o.p. (*0-664-32600-5*) Westminster John Knox Pr.

Neufeld, John. Sharelle. 240p. (YA). 1984. (gr. 9-12). mass mkt. 3.50 o.p. (*0-451-14467-8*, Signet Vista); 1983. (gr. 7 up). 12.95 o.p. (*0-453-00440-7*) NAL.

Oughton, Jerrie. Perfect Family. 2000. 208p. (J). (gr. 5-9). tchr. ed. 15.00 (*0-395-98668-0*) Houghton Mifflin Co.

Pennebaker, Ruth. Don't Think Twice, ERS. 1996. 272p. (YA). (gr. 7 up). 15.95 o.s.i (*0-8050-4407-8*); (Illus.). (J). 15.95 o.p. (*0-8050-4601-1*) Holt, Henry & Co. (Holt, Henry & Co. Bks. For Young Readers).

—Don't Think Twice. 1998. 272p. (YA). (gr. 7-12). reprint ed. mass mkt. 3.99 o.s.i (*0-440-22697-X*, Laurel Leaf) Random Hse. Children's Bks.

—Don't Think Twice. 2001. (YA). 13.00 (*0-606-21159-4*); 1998. 10.04 (*0-606-13341-0*) Turtleback Bks.

Powers, Bill. A Test of Love. 1979. (Triumph Bks.). (Illus.). lib. bdg. 8.90 o.p. (*0-531-02888-7*, Watts, Franklin) Scholastic Library Publishing.

Shreve, Susan Richards. Loveletters. 1981. 160p. pap. 1.75 o.p. (*0-553-13998-3*) Bantam Bks.

—Loveletters. 1978. (YA). 6.95 o.p. (*0-394-83707-X*); lib. bdg. 6.99 o.p. (*0-394-93707-4*) Random Hse. Children's Bks. (Knopf Bks. for Young Readers).

Windsor, Patricia. Diving for Roses. 1976. (J). (gr. 7 up). o.p. (*0-06-026519-1*) HarperCollins Pubs.

Wood, June Rae. A Share of Freedom. 1994. 256p. (YA). 15.95 o.s.i (*0-399-22767-9*, G. P. Putnam's Sons) Penguin Group (USA) Inc.

Woodson, Jacqueline. Dear One. 1991. (Laurel-Leaf Contemporary Fiction Ser.). 10.04 (*0-606-02589-8*) Turtleback Bks.

—The Dear One. 160p. 1992. (YA). mass mkt. 3.99 o.s.i (*0-440-21420-3*); 1991. (J). (gr. 4-7). 14.00 o.s.i (*0-385-30416-1*, Delacorte Pr.) Dell Publishing.

—The Dear One. 2004. 160p. pap. 6.99 (*0-14-250190-5*, Puffin Bks.) Penguin Putnam Bks. for Young Readers.

—The Dear One. 2004. 128p. (J). 17.99 (*0-399-23968-5*, Putnam & Grosset) Putnam Publishing Group, The.

SETTINGS

A

ADIRONDACK MOUNTAINS (N.Y.)—FICTION

Clark, N. Laurie. It's Wesley! The Adirondack Guide. 1998. (Illus.). 32p. (J). (gr. k up). per. 14.95 (*0-9641197-1-4*) Clark Pubs.

Donnelly, Jennifer. A Northern Light. 2003. (Illus.). 400p. (YA). (gr. 7-12). 17.00 (*0-15-216705-6*) Harcourt Children's Bks.

—A Northern Light. unabr. ed. 2003. (J). (gr. 7). audio 30.00 (*0-8072-0895-7*, Listening Library) Random Hse. Audio Publishing Group.

The Elves of Loch Fada, Vol. 1. l.t. ed. 2001. Vol. 1. 243p. (YA). per. incl. 3.5 hd (*0-9712867-0-1*) Cold River Pubns.

Frenette, Liza. Dangerous Falls Ahead: An Adirondack Canoeing Adventure. 2001. (J). pap. 11.95 (*0-925168-79-3*) North Country Bks., Inc.

—Soft Shoulders: An Adirondack Story. 1998. (J). 9.95 (*0-925168-70-X*) North Country Bks., Inc.

Martin, Patricia M. Memory Jug. 1998. 236p. (J). (gr. 3-7). lib. bdg. 16.49 (*0-7868-2368-2*) Disney Pr.

—Memory Jug. 1998. 276p. (J). (gr. 3-7). 15.95 (*0-7868-0357-6*) Hyperion Pr.

Pearce, J. C. Tug of War. 1993. (Foul Play Ser.: No. 5). 128p. (J). (gr. 3-7). pap. 3.25 o.p. (*0-14-036663-6*, Puffin Bks.) Penguin Putnam Bks. for Young Readers.

Petrie, Lettie A. Let Me Tell You About "Minnie the Mule & the Erie Canal" 2001. (Erie Canal Ser.). (Illus.). (YA). (gr. 5-10). pap. 9.95 (*0-9711638-0-4*) Petrie Pr.

Vanriper, Justin & Vanriper, Gary. The Adirondack Kids. 2001. 86p. (J). (ps-3). pap. 8.95 (*0-9707044-0-2*) Adirondack Kids Pr.

AFGHANISTAN—FICTION

Ellis, Deborah. The Breadwinner. 170p. (J). 2001. (Illus.). (gr. 5-7). 15.95 (*0-88899-419-2*); 2000. (gr. 4-7). pap. 5.95 (*0-88899-416-8*) Groundwood Bks. CAN. *Dist:* Publishers Group West.

—The Breadwinner. unabr. ed. 2002. (J). (gr. 4-7). audio 18.00 (*0-8072-0973-2*, Listening Library) Random Hse. Audio Publishing Group.

—Mud City. 2003. 176p. (YA). (gr. 5-9). 15.95 (*0-88899-518-0*) Groundwood Bks. CAN. *Dist:* Publishers Group West.

—Parvana's Journey. 176p. (YA). (gr. 5-9). 2003. pap. 5.95 (*0-88899-519-9*); 2002. (Illus.). 15.95 (*0-88899-514-8*) Groundwood Bks. CAN. *Dist:* Publishers Group West.

Gill, Thomas. Kai: A Mission for Her Village. 1996. (Girlhood Journeys Ser.: No. 4). (Illus.). 72p. (J). (gr. 2-6). mass mkt. 5.99 (*0-689-80986-7*, Aladdin) Simon & Schuster Children's Publishing.

Khan, Rukhsana. The Roses in My Carpets. 1998. (Illus.). 32p. (J). (ps-3). 15.95 (*0-8234-1399-3*) Holiday Hse., Inc.

—The Roses in My Carpets. (Illus.). 29p. 16.95 (*0-7737-3092-3*) Stoddart Kids CAN. *Dist:* Fitzhenry & Whiteside, Ltd.

McKay, Lawrence, Jr. Caravan. 1995. (Illus.). 32p. (J). (ps-6). 14.95 (*1-880000-23-7*) Lee & Low Bks., Inc.

Wolbers, Marian T. Burundi. 1989. (Let's Visit Places & Peoples of the World Ser.). (Illus.). 120p. (J). (gr. 5 up). lib. bdg. 14.95 o.p. (*1-55546-785-7*) Chelsea Hse. Pubs.

AFRICA, CENTRAL—FICTION

Elting, Mary & McKown, Robin. A Mongo Homecoming. 1969. (Two Worlds Bks.). (Illus.). 64p. (J). (gr. 4-6). 3.95 o.p. (*0-87131-099-6*) Holt, Henry & Co.

Stirling, Emma, contrib. by. A Dangerous Gift. (*0-7540-3469-0*) BBC Audiobooks America.

AFRICA, EAST—FICTION

Andersen, Laurie H. Ndito Runs, ERS. 1996. (Illus.). 32p. (J). (ps-2). 15.95 o.s.i (*0-8050-3265-7*, Holt, Henry & Co. Bks. For Young Readers) Holt, Henry & Co.

Bulion, Leslie. Fatuma's New Cloth. (Illus.). 32p. 2003. pap. 7.95 (*1-931659-05-2*); 2002. (J). 15.95 (*0-9677929-7-5*) Moon Mountain Publishing, Inc.

Chase, Alyssa. Jomo & Mata. 1993. (Key Concepts in Personal Development Ser.). (Illus.). 32p. (J). (gr. k-4). pap., tchr. ed. 79.95 incl. VHS (*1-55942-054-5*, 9375); (gr. 1-4). 16.95 (*1-55942-051-0*, 7656) Marsh Media.

Gehman, Mary W. Abdi & the Elephants. 1995. (Illus.). 104p. (Orig.). (J). (gr. 6-8). pap. 5.99 (*0-8361-3699-3*) Herald Pr.

Pitcher, Caroline. The Time of the Lion. 1998. (Illus.). 32p. (J). (gr. k-6). 15.95 (*1-885223-83-8*) Beyond Words Publishing, Inc.

Stevenson, William. The Bushbabies, 001. 1965. (Illus.). (J). (gr. 4-6). 8.95 o.p. (*0-395-07116-X*) Houghton Mifflin Co.

Windham, Jeannette P. On the Horn of Africa: Let's Travel to Somalia Together. 1995. (Windows on the World Ser.: No. 1). (Illus.). 64p. (Orig.). (J). (gr. 3-10). pap. 5.95 (*1-887176-02-0*) Global Age Publishing/Global Academy Pr.

AFRICA—FICTION

Aardema, Verna. Bringing the Rain to Kapiti Plain. 1981. (Pied Piper Bks.). (Illus.). 32p. (J). (ps). 15.89 o.p. (*0-8037-0807-6*); 16.99 (*0-8037-0809-2*) Penguin Putnam Bks. for Young Readers. (Dial Bks. for Young Readers).

—Misoso: Once upon a Time Tales from Africa. 1994. (Illus.). 96p. (J). (gr. k-5). 19.95 o.s.i (*0-679-83430-3*, Knopf Bks. for Young Readers) Random Hse. Children's Bks.

Adlerman, Daniel. Africa Calling, Nighttime Falling. 2001. (Illus.). 32p. (J). (ps-2). pap. 6.95 (*1-58089-025-3*, Whispering Coyote) Charlesbridge Publishing, Inc.

Adlerman, Daniel, ed. Africa Calling, Nighttime Falling. 1996. (Illus.). 32p. (J). (ps-2). 15.95 (*1-879085-98-4*, Whispering Coyote) Charlesbridge Publishing, Inc.

—Africa Calling, Nighttime Falling. 2001. (J). 13.10 (*0-606-20533-0*) Turtleback Bks.

Aesop. Aesop: Tales of Aethiop the African, Vol. 1. 1991. (Illus.). 64p. (J). (gr. 2-9). 6.95 (*1-877610-03-8*) Sea Island Information Group.

African Adventures. 1979. (Animal Picture Bks.). (Illus.). 10p. (J). 1.95 o.p. (*0-89346-173-3*, A49) Heian International Publishing, Inc.

Akpan, Michael E. & Akpan, Ememobong M. The Power of Positive Thinking: From Poverty to Fame. 1992. (Illus.). 182p. (J). (gr. 7-12). pap. text 15.00 (*0-9634998-0-7*) Ebewo's African-American Publishing & Distribution Co.

Alakija, Polly. Catch That Goat! 2002. (Illus.). 32p. (J). (gr. k-2). 16.99 (*1-84148-908-5*) Barefoot Bks., Inc.

Alcock, Gudrun. Dooley's Lion: A Junior Novel. 1985. (Illus.). 112p. (J). (gr. 4 up). 11.95 o.p. (*0-88045-066-5*) Stemmer Hse. Pubs., Inc.

Alexander, Lloyd. The Fortune-Tellers. 1992. (Illus.). 32p. (J). (ps-3). 15.99 (*0-525-44849-7*, Dutton Children's Bks.) Penguin Putnam Bks. for Young Readers.

Allen, Christina G. Hippos in the Night: Autobiographical Adventures in Africa. 2003. (Illus.). 144p. (J). lib. bdg. 17.89 (*0-688-17827-8*, Morrow, William & Co.) Morrow/Avon.

Allen, Hubert A., Jr. Shadows on the Wall: A Story of Malawi Africa. 1988. (Illus.). 56p. (YA). (gr. 4-12). mass mkt. (*0-9641694-3-6*) Allen, Hubert & Assocs.

Alvin, John & Alvin, Andrea, illus. Simba's Pride. 1998. (Classic Storybook Ser.). 96p. (J). (ps-3). 7.99 (*1-57082-876-8*) Mouse Works.

Anderson, Bob. Obo. 1999. (Illus.). 48p. (J). (ps-5). bds. 16.00 (*1-57174-124-0*) Hampton Roads Publishing Co., Inc.

Angelou, Maya. Kofi & His Magic. 2003. 48p. (J). (gr. 1-4). pap. 7.99 (*0-375-82566-5*) Random Hse. Children's Bks.

Appiah, Peggy. Tales of an Ashanti Father. 1981. (Illus.). 160p. (J). 8.95 o.p. (*0-233-95927-0*) Blackwell Publishing.

Asare, Meshack. Sosu's Call. 2002. (Illus.). 40p. (J). (gr. k-4). 15.95 (*1-929132-21-2*) Kane/Miller Bk. Pubs.

Ashley, Bernard. Little Soldier: A Novel. 240p. (J). 2003. mass mkt. 5.99 (*0-439-28502-X*); 2002. (Illus.). (gr. 9 up). pap. 16.95 (*0-439-22424-1*, Scholastic Pr.) Scholastic, Inc.

Bandele, Ramla. Nzinga. 1992. (J). pap. 6.95 (*0-88378-023-2*) Third World Press.

Barker, Carol. An Oba of Benin. 1977. (J). lib. bdg. 6.95 o.p. (*0-201-00423-2*, 0423) Addison-Wesley Longman, Inc.

Barnes, Joyce Annette. Amistad. 1997. (Illus.). 144p. (J). (gr. 5-9). pap. 4.99 o.s.i (*0-14-039063-4*, Puffin Bks.) Penguin Putnam Bks. for Young Readers.

Beake, Lesley. The Song of Be. 1995. 112p. (J). pap. 3.99 o.s.i (*0-14-037498-1*, Puffin Bks.) Penguin Putnam Bks. for Young Readers.

Bell, Anthea, tr. Youpala, Queen of the Jungle. 1995. (Illus.). 32p. (J). (ps-3). tchr. ed. (*1-85697-625-4*) Kingfisher Publications, plc.

Bell, Sally. Young Indiana Jones: Safari in Africa. 1993. (Young Indiana Jones Chronicles: No. 2). (Illus.). 48p. (J). (gr. 2-4). pap. 3.25 o.s.i (*0-307-11470-8*, 11470, Golden Bks.) Random Hse. Children's Bks.

Bess, Clayton. Story for a Black Night, 001. 1982. (J). (gr. 7 up). 13.95 o.p. (*0-395-31857-2*) Houghton Mifflin Co.

—Story for a Black Night. 2nd rev. ed. 2002. (J). (*1-882405-03-X*) Lookout Pr.

Bianchi, John. The Bungalo Boys: Bushmen Brouhaha, Vol. II. 1987. (Illus.). 24p. (J). (ps-8). 16.95 (*0-921285-10-8*); pap. 5.95 (*0-921285-08-6*) Bungalo Bks. CAN. *Dist:* Firefly Bks., Ltd.

Boateng, Yaw A. The Young Detectives. 1992. (Junior African Writers Ser.). (Illus.). 61p. (YA). (gr. 6-10). pap. text 3.00 o.p. (*0-435-89234-7*) Heinemann.

Bofane, In Koli. The Lion Is No Longer King. 1997. (Illus.). 32p. (J). (ps-2). 16.95 o.p. (*1-55037-418-4*) Annick Pr., Ltd. CAN. *Dist:* Firefly Bks., Ltd.

Bognmo, Joe Eoueme. Madoulina. 2003. (Illus.). 32p. (J). (ps-3). 14.95 (*1-56397-769-9*) Boyds Mills Pr.

Boje, Shirley. Cry Softly, Thule Nene. 1992. (Junior African Writers Ser.). (Illus.). 123p. (YA). (gr. 12). pap. text 5.00 o.p. (*0-435-89358-0*) Heinemann.

Bothwell, Jean. African Herdboy: A Story of the Masai. 1970. (Illus.). (J). (gr. 4-6). 5.25 o.p. (*0-15-201630-9*) Harcourt Children's Bks.

Brightfield, Richard. African Safari. 1993. (Young Indiana Jones Chronicles Choose Your Own Adventure Ser.: No. 5). (YA). (gr. 5-8). 8.35 o.p. (*0-606-03004-2*) Turtleback Bks.

Brouillet, Chrystine. Secrets D'Afrique. 2002. (Roman Jeunesse Ser.). (FRE., Illus.). 96p. (YA). (gr. 4-7). pap. 8.95 (*2-89021-248-3*) La Courte Echelle CAN. *Dist:* Firefly Bks., Ltd.

Browne, Eileen. La Sorpresa de Nandi. 1997. (SPA., Illus.). 28p. (J). (ps-1). pap. 6.99 (*980-257-196-2*) Ekare, Ediciones VEN. *Dist:* Kane/Miller Bk. Pubs., Lectorum Pubns., Inc.

Bull, Schuyler. Through Tsavo: A Story of an East African Savanna. 1998. (Habitat Ser.). (Illus.). 36p. (J). (ps-3). 15.95 (*1-56899-552-0*) Soundprints.

Burroughs, Edgar Rice. Tarzan. 1999. (Illus.). 31p. (J). (gr. k-4). 15.99 (*0-7868-0384-3*) Disney Pr.

—Tarzan. 1998. (Children's Thrift Classics Ser.). (Illus.). 96p. (J). reprint ed. pap. text 1.00 (*0-486-29530-3*) Dover Pubns., Inc.

—Tarzan: Tarzan at the Earth's Core/Tarzan the Invincible. 1997. (Tarzan Ser.: Nos. 13 & 14). 432p. mass mkt. 6.99 o.s.i (*0-345-41349-0*, Del Rey) Ballantine Bks.

—Tarzan of the Apes. 1991. (J). 10.04 (*0-606-12823-9*) Turtleback Bks.

—Tarzan of the Apes. 1982. (Step into Classics Ser.). (Illus.). 96p. (J). (gr. 2-7). pap. 3.99 o.s.i (*0-394-85089-0*, Random Hse. Bks. for Young Readers) Random Hse. Children's Bks.

—Tarzan of the Apes: Adapted by Robin Moore from Edgar Rice Burrough's Tarzan of the Apes. abr. ed. 1999. (Illus.). 88p. (J). (gr. 2-5). pap. 3.99 (*0-689-82413-0*, 076714003886, Aladdin) Simon & Schuster Children's Publishing.

Catherall, Arthur M. Camel Caravan. 1968. (Illus.). (J). (gr. 3-7). 5.95 o.p. (*0-8164-3009-8*) Houghton Mifflin Co.

—Zebra Came to Drink. 1967. (J). (gr. 3-7). 6.25 o.p. (*0-525-43635-9*, Dutton) Dutton/Plume.

Chambers, Veronica. Amistad Rising: A Story of Freedom. Bowen, Shelly & Johnston, Allyn M., eds. 1998. (Illus.). 40p. (J). (gr. 3-7). 16.00 o.s.i (*0-15-201803-4*) Harcourt Children's Bks.

—Amistad Rising: A Story of Freedom. 1998. (Illus.). 40p. (J). (gr. 4-7). lib. bdg. 16.98 (*0-8172-5510-9*) Raintree Pubs.

Claire, Elizabeth. The Sun, the Wind & Tashira: A Hottentot Tale from Africa. 1994. (Mondo Folktales Ser.). (Illus.). 24p. (J). (gr. k-4). pap. 4.95 (*1-879531-20-8*); lib. bdg. 9.95 (*1-879531-41-0*) Mondo Publishing.

Clarke, Judith, et al, illus. Tarzan. 1999. (Disney Ser.). 24p. (J). (ps-3). 3.99 o.p. (*0-307-16230-3*, Golden Bks.) Random Hse. Children's Bks.

Cole, Babette. Nungu & the Hippopotamus. 1979. (Illus.). (J). (gr. k-2). text 7.95 o.p. (*0-07-011695-4*) McGraw-Hill Cos., The.

Conrad, Joseph. Heart of Darkness. 1990. (Thrift Editions Ser.). 80p. (J). pap. 1.00 (*0-486-26464-5*) Dover Pubns., Inc.

Courtney, Dayle. Flight to Terror. 1981. (Thorne Twins Adventure Bks.). (Illus.). 192p. (Orig.). (J). (gr. 5 up). pap. 2.98 o.p. (*0-87239-468-9*, 2713) Standard Publishing.

Davol, Marguerite W. How Snake Got His Hiss: An Original Tale. 1996. (Illus.). 32p. (J). (ps-3). pap. 14.95 (*0-531-09468-5*, Orchard Bks.) Scholastic, Inc.

Deetlefs, Rene. The Song of Six Birds. 1999. (Illus.). 32p. (J). (ps-4). 15.99 o.s.i (*0-525-46314-3*, Dutton Children's Bks.) Penguin Putnam Bks. for Young Readers.

Dent, Jenny. Peter Parrot Visits Africa. 2001. (Peter Parrot Ser.). (Illus.). (J). (gr. k-3). pap. 9.95 (*0-85487-120-9*) White Eagle Publishing Trust GBR. *Dist:* DeVorss & Co.

Dickinson, Peter. AK. 240p. (YA). 1993. mass mkt. 3.99 o.s.i (*0-440-21897-7*); 1992. 15.00 o.s.i (*0-385-30608-3*) Dell Publishing.

—AK. 1992. (J). 9.09 o.p. (*0-606-05727-7*) Turtleback Bks.

Disney Staff. The Lion King. 1999. (Disney's Read-Aloud Storybooks Ser.). (SPA., Illus.). 64p. (J). (ps-2). 4.99 o.p. (*0-7364-0130-X*) Mouse Works.

—Tarzan Flip Book. 1999. 96p. (J). (ps-3). pap. (*0-7364-0143-1*) Mouse Works.

—Tarzan, Me & You. 1999. (Illus.). 10p. (J). (ps). 3.99 (*0-7364-0132-6*) Mouse Works.

—Tarzan's Jungle Adventure. 1999. (Giant Lift-the-Flap Ser.). (Illus.). 10p. (J). (ps). 8.99 (*0-7364-0066-4*) Mouse Works.

Djoleto, Amu. The Frightened Thief. 1992. (Junior African Writers Ser.). (Illus.). 30p. (J). (gr. 2-6). pap. text 2.50 o.p. (*0-435-89105-7*) Heinemann.

—Twins in Trouble. 1992. (Junior African Writers Ser.). (Illus.). 29p. (J). (gr. 2-6). pap. text 2.50 o.p. (*0-435-89104-9*) Heinemann.

Dube, Hope. Love Is a Challenge. 1992. (Junior African Writers Ser.). (Illus.). 92p. (YA). (gr. 8-12). pap. text 4.00 o.p. (*0-435-89297-5*) Heinemann.

Echewa, T. Obinkaram. How Tables Came to Umu Madu. (Young Reader's Ser.). (Illus.). 90p. (J). (gr. 5 up). 19.95 (*0-86543-127-2*); 1993. (gr. 2 up). pap. 7.95 (*0-86543-128-0*) Africa World Pr.

Ekwensi, Cyprian O. King Forever! 1992. (Junior African Writers Ser.). (Illus.). 93p. (YA). (gr. 8-12). pap. text 4.00 o.p. (*0-435-89295-9*) Heinemann.

—Masquerade Time. 1992. (Junior African Writers Ser.). (Illus.). 80p. (J). (gr. 3 up). pap. 3.88 (*0-7910-2911-5*) Chelsea Hse. Pubs.

—Masquerade Time. 1992. (Junior African Writers Ser.). (Illus.). 29p. (J). (gr. 4-8). pap. text 2.50 o.p. (*0-435-89165-0*) Heinemann.

Ernst, B. J. Song of the Kalahari: Why the Giraffe Is Silent. 1997. 27p. (J). pap. 4.45 (*1-56763-284-X*); lib. bdg. 19.95 (*1-56763-283-1*) Ozark Publishing.

Farnham, Arthur L. & Farnham, Lorraine J. Teddy's Trip to Africa. 1982. (Illus.). (J). (gr. 3-5). 5.95 o.p. (*0-533-05288-2*) Vantage Pr., Inc.

Feelings, Muriel L. Zamani Goes to Market. 1989. (Young Reader's Ser.). (Illus.). 50p. (J). (gr. 2 up). reprint ed. pap. 8.95 (*0-86543-095-0*) Africa World Pr.

—Zamani Goes to Market, 001. 1979. (Illus.). 48p. (J). (ps-3). 6.95 o.p. (*0-395-28791-X*, Clarion Bks.) Houghton Mifflin Co. Trade & Reference Div.

Ferguson, Dwayne J. Captain Africa: The Battle for Egyptica. 1992. (Young Reader's Ser.). (Illus.). 156p. (YA). reprint ed. (gr. 7-10). 24.95 (*0-86543-335-6*); (ps up). pap. 12.95 (*0-86543-336-4*) Africa World Pr.

—Captain Africa & the Fury of Anubis: The Graphic Novel. 1994. (Illus.). 96p. (J). (gr. 4-11). 29.95 (*0-86543-397-6*); pap. 12.95 (*0-86543-398-4*) Africa World Pr.

Ferrone, John M. Margo Goes on Safari. Date not set. (Illus.). 36p. (J). (ps-5). pap. 16.95 (*1-928811-04-3*) Story Stuff, Inc.

Flegg, Aubrey. The Cinnamon Tree: A Novel Set in Africa. 2001. 208p. (YA). pap. 7.95 (*0-86278-657-6*) O'Brien Pr., Ltd., The IRL. *Dist:* Independent Pubs. Group.

Fourie, Corlia. Ganekwane & the Green Dragon: Four Stories from Africa. Grant, Christy, ed. 1994. (Illus.). 40p. (J). (gr. 3-6). lib. bdg. 14.95 o.p. (*0-8075-2744-0*) Whitman, Albert & Co.

Fox, Mem. Because of the Bloomers. 2000. (Illus.). (J). 15.00 (*0-15-200250-2*) Harcourt Trade Pubs.

Frost, T. Olly on Safari. 1987. (Illus.). 32p. (YA). (ps-3). pap. 4.95 o.p. (*0-88625-187-7*); lib. bdg. 14.65 o.p. (*0-88625-189-3*) Durkin Hayes Publishing Ltd.

Gelman, Rita Golden. Professor Coconut & the Thief, ERS. 1977. (J). (gr. 1-5). o.p. (*0-03-016931-3*, Holt, Henry & Co. Bks. For Young Readers) Holt, Henry & Co.

Geraghty, Paul. The Hunter. 1994. (Illus.). 32p. (J). (ps-3). 15.00 o.s.i (*0-517-59692-X*); 15.99 o.s.i (*0-517-59693-8*) Random Hse. Children's Bks. (Random Hse. Bks. for Young Readers).

Going Home - Lion King. 1995. (Sturdy Tab Book). (Illus.). 12p. (YA). (ps up). 6.98 o.p. (*1-57082-246-8*) Mouse Works.

Golden Books Staff. Always in My Heart. 1999. (Disney Ser.). (Illus.). 16p. (J). (ps-3). pap. text 1.99 o.p. (*0-307-28306-2*, Golden Bks.) Random Hse. Children's Bks.

—Amazing Adventures. 1999. (Disney Ser.). (Illus.). 48p. (J). (ps-3). pap. text 1.95 o.p. (*0-307-25276-0*, Golden Bks.) Random Hse. Children's Bks.

—Best Ape Ever. 1999. (Disney Ser.). (Illus.). 192p. (ps-3). pap. text 1.95 o.p. (*0-307-25250-7*, Golden Bks.) Random Hse. Children's Bks.

—Deep in the Jungle. 1999. (Disney Ser.). (Illus.). 72p. (J). (ps-3). pap. text 6.99 o.p. (*0-307-25720-7*, Golden Bks.) Random Hse. Children's Bks.

—Growing up in the Jungle: Paint Box Book. 1999. (Disney Ser.). (Illus.). 32p. (J). (ps-3). pap. 0.99 o.p. (*0-307-09229-1*, Golden Bks.) Random Hse. Children's Bks.

—Jungle Friends. 1999. (Disney Ser.). (Illus.). 56p. (J). (ps-3). pap. text 3.99 o.p. (*0-307-27614-7*, Golden Bks.) Random Hse. Children's Bks.

—Swing Time. 1999. (Disney Ser.). (Illus.). 84p. (J). (ps-3). pap. text 2.99 o.p. (*0-307-25721-5*, Golden Bks.) Random Hse. Children's Bks.

Greenfield, Eloise. Africa Dream. (Trophy Picture Bk.). (Illus.). 32p. (J). (ps-3). 1992. pap. 5.95 (*0-06-443277-7*, Harper Trophy); 1989. lib. bdg. 15.89 o.s.i (*0-690-04776-2*) HarperCollins Children's Bk. Group.

—Africa Dream. 1992. 12.10 (*0-606-00257-X*) Turtleback Bks.

Grifalcon, Ann. Flyaway Girl. 1992. (J). (ps-3). 15.95 o.p. (*0-316-32866-9*) Little Brown & Co.

Grifalconi, Ann. Osa's Pride, Vol. 1. 1990. (Illus.). (J). (ps-3). 15.95 o.p. (*0-316-32865-0*) Little Brown & Co.

—The Village That Vanished. 2002. (Illus.). 40p. (J). (gr. k up). 16.99 (*0-8037-2623-6*, Dial Bks. for Young Readers) Penguin Putnam Bks. for Young Readers.

Grimsdell, Jeremy. Kalinzu. 1993. (Illus.). 32p. (J). (ps-3). tchr. ed. o.p. (*1-85697-886-9*) Kingfisher Publications, plc.

Guy, Rosa. Mother Crocodile: An Uncle Amadou Tale from Senegal. 1982. (Illus.). 32p. (J). (ps-3). 8.89 o.s.i (*0-385-28455-1*); pap. 8.95 o.s.i (*0-385-28454-3*) Dell Publishing. (Delacorte Pr.).

Hadithi, Mwenye. Baby Baboon. 1993. (Illus.). (J). 15.95 o.p. (*0-316-33729-3*) Little Brown & Co.

Hagen, Michael. The African Term. Kemnitz, Myrna, ed. 1998. 81p. (YA). (gr. 7 up). pap. 9.99 (*0-88092-368-7*) Royal Fireworks Publishing Co.

Hampton, Janie. Come Home Soon, Baba. 1993. (Illus.). 32p. (J). (gr. 4 up). 12.95 o.p. (*0-87226-511-0*, Bedrick, Peter Bks.) McGraw-Hill Children's Publishing.

Hanel, Wolfram. Little Elephant Runs Away. James, J. Alison, tr. from GER. 2001. (Illus.). 32p. (J). (ps-2). 15.95 (*0-7358-1444-9*); lib. bdg. 16.50 (*0-7358-1445-7*) North-South Bks., Inc.

Hansen, Joyce. The Captive. 192p. (YA). 1995. (gr. 5 up). pap. 4.50 (*0-590-41624-3*); 1994. (Illus.). (gr. 7 up). pap. 13.95 (*0-590-41625-1*) Scholastic, Inc.

—The Captive. 1994. 8.60 o.p. (*0-606-07339-6*) Turtleback Bks.

Hillenbrand, Will, illus. Traveling to Tondo: A Tale of the Nkundo of Zaire. 1993. (Dragonfly Bks.). 40p. (J). (ps-3). pap. 5.99 o.s.i (*0-679-85309-X*, Knopf Bks. for Young Readers) Random Hse. Children's Bks.

Hoffman, Mary. Boundless Grace. 2002. (Illus.). (J). 25.45 (*0-7587-2139-0*) Book Wholesalers, Inc.

—Boundless Grace. (Illus.). 32p. (J). (ps-3). 2000. pap. 5.99 (*0-14-055667-2*, Puffin Bks.); 1995. 16.99 (*0-8037-1715-6*, Dial Bks. for Young Readers) Penguin Putnam Bks. for Young Readers.

—Boundless Grace. 2000. 12.14 (*0-606-20224-2*); 12.14 (*0-606-20350-8*) Turtleback Bks.

Hoosier, Wanda M. Princess Mandisa. 1999. (Illus.). 34p. (J). 15.00 (*1-56469-070-9*) Harmony Hse. Pubs.

Horn, Sandra. Kofi & the Butterflies. 1996. (Illus.). (J). (gr. 1-12). pap. 8.95 (*0-86543-519-7*); 16.95 (*0-86543-518-9*) Africa World Pr.

Hostetler, Marian. Aventura en A'frica. 1976. Tr. of African Adventure. (Illus.). 128p. (J). (gr. 3-8). pap. 4.95 o.p. (*0-8361-1329-2*) Herald Pr.

House, Janie. Mthunzi's Reed Mats. McClain, Cindy, ed. 1995. (Illus.). 24p. (J). (gr. 1-4). pap. text 3.99 (*1-56309-132-1*, N958101, New Hope) Woman's Missionary Union.

Hunter, Bobbie D. The Legend of the African Bao-Bab Tree. 1994. (Illus.). 32p. (J). (gr. 3-6). 16.95 (*0-86543-421-2*) Africa World Pr.

Ichikawa, Satomi. The First Bear in Africa! 2001. (Illus.). 32p. (J). (ps-1). 14.99 o.s.i (*0-399-23485-3*, Philomel) Penguin Putnam Bks. for Young Readers.

Ingoglia, Gina. The Lion King: Illustrated Classic (Mini Edition) 1996. (Disney Press Miniature Classics Ser.). (Illus.). 96p. (J). 5.95 o.p. (*0-7868-3074-3*) Disney Pr.

Innovative Kids Staff. Rescue Flight! A Sky Track Adventure. 2000. (Motor Books). (Illus.). 10 and 2 page fp. (J). (ps-3). 14.99 o.p. (*1-58476-013-3*, IKIDS) Innovative Kids.

Jackson, Dave & Jackson, Neta. Assassins in the Cathedral: Festo Kivengere. 1999. (Trailblazer Bks.: Vol. 27). 144p. (J). (gr. 3-7). pap. 5.99 (*0-7642-2012-8*) Bethany Hse. Pubs.

Jacobs, Shannon K. Song of the Giraffe. 1991. (Springboard Bks.). (Illus.). (J). (gr. 2-4). 11.95 o.p. (*0-316-45555-5*) Little Brown & Co.

Katschke, Judy. Tarzan Goes Bananas: Disney First Reader Ser. 1999. (Disney's Tarzan Ser.). (Illus.). 32p. (J). (gr. k-2). pap. text 2.99 (*0-7868-4281-4*) Hyperion Pr.

Kelleher, Victor. Rescue! 1992. 224p. (J). (gr. 5 up). 15.00 o.p. (*0-8037-0900-5*, Dial Bks. for Young Readers) Penguin Putnam Bks. for Young Readers.

Kennaway, Adrienne. Little Elephant's Walk. 1992. (Willa Perlman Bks.). (Illus.). 32p. (J). (ps-2). lib. bdg. 13.89 (*0-06-020378-1*); 13.95 (*0-06-020377-3*) HarperCollins Children's Bk. Group.

Kessler, Cristina. No Condition Is Permanent. 2000. (Illus.). 183p. (J). (gr. 5-9). 17.99 (*0-399-23486-1*, Philomel) Penguin Putnam Bks. for Young Readers.

Kessler, Cristina. Jubela. 2001. (Illus.). 32p. (J). 16.00 (*0-689-81895-5*, Simon & Schuster Children's Publishing) Simon & Schuster Children's Publishing.

Kessler, Cristina & Stammen, JoEllen McAllister. Jubela. 2004. 32p. (J). pap. 6.99 (*0-689-86690-9*, Aladdin) Simon & Schuster Children's Publishing.

Khoza, Valanga. Gezani & the Tricky Baboon. 2003. (Illus.). 32p. (J). text 14.95 (*1-86508-720-3*) Allen & Unwin Pty., Ltd. AUS. *Dist:* Independent Pubs. Group.

Kimenye, Barbara. The Money Game. 1992. (Junior African Writers Ser.). (Illus.). 124p. (YA). (gr. 12). pap. text 5.00 o.p. (*0-435-89360-2*) Heinemann.

Koranteng, Kwasi. The Gold Diggers. 1992. (Junior African Writers Ser.). (Illus.). 124p. (YA). (gr. 12). pap. text 5.00 o.p. (*0-435-89359-9*) Heinemann.

—The Innocent Prisoner. 1992. (Junior African Writers Ser.). (Illus.). 91p. (YA). (gr. 8-12). pap. text 4.00 o.p. (*0-435-89293-2*) Heinemann.

Kotzwinkle, William. The Leopard's Tooth, 001. 1979. (Illus.). 96p. (J). (gr. 3-6). 6.95 o.p. (*0-395-28862-2*, Clarion Bks.) Houghton Mifflin Co. Trade & Reference Div.

Kroll, Virginia K. Faraway Drums. 1998. (Illus.). 32p. (J). (ps-3). 14.95 o.p. (*0-316-50449-1*) Little Brown & Co.

Kroll, Virginia L. Africa Brothers & Sisters. (Illus.). 32p. (J). (ps-2). 1998. pap. 5.99 o.s.i (*0-689-81816-5*, Aladdin); 1993. lib. bdg. 15.00 (*0-02-751166-9*, Simon & Schuster Children's Publishing) Simon & Schuster Children's Publishing.

—Africa Brothers & Sisters. 1998. 12.14 (*0-606-12870-0*) Turtleback Bks.

Langner, Nolan. Rafiki. 1977. (Illus.). (J). (gr. k-3). 6.95 o.p. (*0-670-58907-1*) Viking Penguin.

Lee, Evelyn. Mountain Mists: A Story of the Virungas. 1999. (Habitat Ser.: No. 14). (Illus.). 36p. (J). (gr. 1-4). 26.95 (*1-56899-789-2*); (gr. 1-4). pap. 16.95 (*1-56899-790-6*); (ps-3). 15.95 (*1-56899-785-X*); (ps-3). pap. 5.95 (*1-56899-786-8*); (ps-3). 19.95 incl. audio (*1-56899-787-6*, BC7014) Soundprints.

Leggat, Gillian. The Artist & the Bully. 1992. (Junior African Writers Ser.). (Illus.). 59p. (YA). (gr. 6-10). pap. text 3.00 o.p. (*0-435-89233-9*) Heinemann.

Leonard, Marie. Tibili: The Little Boy Who Didn't Want to Go to School. 2002. (Illus.). 36p. (J). (ps-2). 15.95 (*1-929132-20-4*) Kane/Miller Bk. Pubs.

Lester, Julius. Shining. 2003. (Illus.). 32p. (J). 17.00 (*0-15-200773-3*) Harcourt Children's Bks.

Lewin, Hugh. Jafta. 2000. (Picture Bks.). (Illus.). 24p. (J). (ps-3). lib. bdg. 15.95 (*0-87614-207-2*, Carolrhoda Bks.) Lerner Publishing Group.

—Jafta & the Wedding. 1983. (Jafta Collection). (Illus.). 24p. (J). (gr. 1-3). pap. 4.95 o.s.i (*0-87614-497-0*); lib. bdg. 15.95 (*0-87614-210-2*) Lerner Publishing Group. (Carolrhoda Bks.).

—The Picture That Came Alive. 1992. (Junior African Writers Ser.). (Illus.). 30p. (J). (gr. 4-8). pap. text 2.50 o.p. (*0-435-89167-7*) Heinemann.

Lichtveld, Noni. I Lost My Arrow in a Kankan Tree. 1994. (J). 15.00 o.p. (*0-688-12748-7*) HarperCollins Children's Bk. Group.

Settings

Lindblad, Lisa. The Serengeti Migration. 1994. (Illus.). 40p. (J). (gr. 3-7). 15.95 (*1-56282-668-9*); lib. bdg. 16.49 (*1-56282-669-7*) Hyperion Bks. for Children.

Linfield, Esther. The Secret of the Mountain. 1986. 144p. (J). (gr. 5 up). 11.95 o.p. (*0-688-05992-9*, Greenwillow Bks.) HarperCollins Children's Bk. Group.

Lion King: Read Along - The Brightest Star. 1994. (J). pap. 6.98 incl. audio (*1-55723-618-6*) Walt Disney Records.

Lloyd, Tracey. The Old Man & the Rabbit. 1992. (Junior African Writers Ser.). (Illus.). 59p. (YA). (gr. 6-10). pap. text 3.00 o.p. (*0-435-89230-4*) Heinemann.

Lochmandy, Paula. What Come Out Dah Bottle. Miller, Jeffrey A., ed. 1998. (Illus.). (J). (gr. 2-6). ltd. ed. 30p. ring bd. 12.00 (*0-9639890-5-7*); 2nd ed. 35p. pap. text 13.50 (*0-9639890-9-X*) Tattersall Pr.

Mabalani, Kazi. Journey to Ahkabah: The Map & the Riddle. 2001. 236p. pap. 11.95 (*0-9709160-0-0*) Land's End Publishing.

MacDonald, Susan. Nanta's Lion. 1924. (J). lib. bdg. o.s.i (*0-688-13999-X*, Morrow, William & Co.) Morrow/Avon.

—Nanta's Lion: A Search - & - Find Adventure. 1995. (Illus.). 24p. (J). (ps-3). 15.00 (*0-688-13125-5*, Morrow, William & Co.) Morrow/Avon.

Manning, Russ & Burroughs, Edgar Rice. Tarzan: The Land That Time Forgot. unabr. ed. 1996. (Illus.). 112p. (YA). (gr. 9 up). pap. 12.95 (*1-56971-151-8*) Dark Horse Comics.

Margolies, Barbara A. Rehema's Journey, a Visit in Tanzania. 1997. (J). 10.19 o.p. (*0-606-11785-7*) Turtleback Bks.

Markman, Michael. The Path: An Adventure in African History. Gift, Wendy, ed. 1997. (Illus.). 32p. (J). (gr. 1-5). 7.95 (*1-881316-19-X*); (gr. 2-9). pap. 8.95 (*1-881316-35-1*) A & B Distributors & Pubs. Group.

Masilela, Johnny. We Shall Not Weep. 2003. 132p. pap. 9.95 (*0-7957-0147-0*) Kwela Bks. ZAF. *Dist:* Independent Pubs. Group.

McAllister, Angela. The Honey Festival. 1999. (Illus.). (J). (gr. 1-8). pap. 13.99 (*0-8037-1240-5*, Dial Bks. for Young Readers) Penguin Putnam Bks. for Young Readers.

McCormick, Wendy. Daddy, Will You Miss Me? (Illus.). 32p. (J). (ps-1). 2002. pap. 6.99 (*0-689-85063-8*, Aladdin); 1999. 16.00 (*0-689-81898-X*, Simon & Schuster Children's Publishing) Simon & Schuster Children's Publishing.

McDaniel, Lurlene. Angel of Hope. 2000. (Mercy Trilogy Ser.). 240p. (YA). (gr. 7-12). mass mkt. 4.99 (*0-553-57148-6*, Starfire) Random Hse. Children's Bks.

—Angel of Hope. 2000. (Illus.). (J). 11.04 (*0-606-17991-7*) Turtleback Bks.

—Angel of Mercy. 1999. (Mercy Trilogy Ser.). 224p. (YA). (gr. 7-12). 8.95 (*0-553-57145-1*, Dell Books for Young Readers) Random Hse. Children's Bks.

—Angel of Mercy. 1999. (Illus.). (J). 14.30 o.p. (*0-606-17992-5*) Turtleback Bks.

McDowell, Robert E. & Lavitt, Edward, eds. Third World Voices for Children. 1981. (Odarkai Book Ser.). (Illus.). 156p. (J). (gr. 5-9). 7.95 (*0-89388-020-5*, Odakai Books) Okpaku Communications Corp.

McKissack, Patricia C. Nzingha: Warrior Queen of Matamba, Angola, Africa, 1595. 2000. (Royal Diaries Ser.). (Illus.). 144p. (J). (gr. 4-8). 10.95 (*0-439-11210-9*) Scholastic, Inc.

Mead, Alice. Year of No Rain, RS. 2003. 144p. (J). 16.00 (*0-374-37288-8*, Farrar, Straus & Giroux (BYR)) Farrar, Straus & Giroux.

Medlicott, Mary. Tales from Africa. 2000. (Story Collections). (Illus.). 96p. (J). (gr. 3-5). pap. 11.95 (*0-7534-5290-1*, Kingfisher) Houghton Mifflin Co. Trade & Reference Div.

Meyer, Rosemary. Wendy's World. 1982. (J). 5.95 o.p. (*0-533-05146-0*) Vantage Pr., Inc.

Miller, David L. Baby the Lost Legend. 1985. (J). (gr. 3 up). pap. 6.95 o.p. (*0-671-54091-2*, Simon & Schuster Children's Publishing) Simon & Schuster Children's Publishing.

Milnes, Ellen. Tarzan Jungle Jam. 1999. (Chunky Roly-Poly Book Ser.). (Illus.). 16p. (J). 3.50 (*0-7364-0048-6*) Mouse Works.

Mitchison, Naomi. Sunrise Tomorrow: A Story of Botswana, RS. 1973. (J). (gr. 7 up). 4.50 o.p. (*0-374-37298-5*, Farrar, Straus & Giroux (BYR)) Farrar, Straus & Giroux.

Mogwe, Gaele. The Magic Pool. 1992. (Junior African Writers Ser.). (Illus.). 29p. (J). (gr. 4-8). pap. text 2.50 o.p. (*0-435-89166-9*) Heinemann.

Mollel, Tololwa M. Big Boy. 1997. (Illus.). 32p. (J). (ps-3). pap. 6.95 (*0-395-84515-7*, Clarion Bks.) Houghton Mifflin Co. Trade & Reference Div.

—Big Boy. 1997. (J). 12.10 (*0-606-11122-0*) Turtleback Bks.

—Big Boy. 1994. (Illus.). 32p. (J). (ps-ps). 14.95 (*0-395-67403-4*, Clarion Bks.) Houghton Mifflin Co. Trade & Reference Div.

—A Promise to the Sun: A Story of Africa. 1992. (Illus.). 32p. (J). (ps-3). 15.95 o.p. (*0-316-57813-4*, Joy Street Bks.) Little Brown & Co.

Molver, Eileen. Lindiwi Finds a Way. 1992. (Junior African Writers Ser.). (Illus.). 58p. (YA). (gr. 6-10). pap. text 3.00 o.p. (*0-435-89235-5*) Heinemann.

Moore, Robin & Dempsey, Al. Phase of Darkness. 1974. (J). 30.00 (*0-89388-136-8*) Okpaku Communications Corp.

Moskin, Marietta. Toto. 1972. (Illus.). (J). (gr. 1-3). 4.69 o.p. (*0-698-30372-5*) Putnam Publishing Group, The.

Mouse Works Staff. Tarzan. 1999. (Spanish Read-Aloud Storybook Classics). (Illus.). 64p. (J). (ps-2). (SPA.). 6.99 (*0-7364-0057-5*); 8.99 (*0-7364-0047-8*) Mouse Works.

Mrs. Moose. Raymond Floyd Goes to Africa: or There Are No Bears in Africa. 1993. (Illus.). 32p. (J). (gr. 1-4). 14.95 (*0-86543-375-5*) Africa World Pr.

Muchene, Barbara S. & Muchene, Munene. Suzanne's African Adventure: A Visit to Cucu's Land. Wagner, Shirley L., ed. 1993. (Illus.). 90p. (Orig.). (J). (gr. 3-6). pap. 9.95 (*1-878398-18-0*) Blue Note Pubns.

Mugo, Phoebe, ed. Lodu's Escape: And Other Stories from Africa. 1994. (Illus.). 64p. (Orig.). (J). (gr. 3-5). pap. 6.95 (*0-377-00269-0*) Friendship Pr.

Murdock, Babs M. Raymond Floyd Goes to Africa: or There Are No Bears in Africa. 1993. (Illus.). 32p. (J). (ps-3). pap. 6.95 (*0-86543-376-3*) Africa World Pr.

Niles, Douglas. Tarzan & the Well of Slaves. 1985. (Endless Quest Bks.). (Illus.). 160p. (J). (gr. 4-7). pap. 2.25 o.p. (*0-394-73968-X*, Random Hse. Bks. for Young Readers) Random Hse. Children's Bks.

Njeng, Pierre Yves. Vacation in the Village. 2003. (Illus.). 32p. (J). (ps-3). pap. 6.95 (*1-56397-823-7*) Boyds Mills Pr.

Njoku, Scholastica I. Dog What? 1989. (Ngozi of Africa Ser.: No. 2). (Illus.). 49p. (J). (gr. k up). per. 6.95 (*0-9617833-1-1*) Njoku, Scholastica Ibari.

Noble, Kate. Bubble Gum. 1995. (Africa Stories Ser.). (Illus.). 32p. (J). (ps-4). 14.95 (*0-9631798-0-2*) Silver Seahorse Pr.

—Oh Look, It's a Nosserus. 1995. (Africa Stories Ser.). (Illus.). 32p. (J). (ps-4). 14.95 (*0-9631798-2-9*) Silver Seahorse Pr.

Okri, Ben. Songs of Enchantment. 1994. 304p. pap. 12.00 o.s.i (*0-385-47157-2*) Doubleday Publishing.

Olaleye, Isaac. Bitter Bananas. 1996. (Illus.). 32p. (J). pap. 5.99 o.s.i (*0-14-055710-5*, Puffin Bks.) Penguin Putnam Bks. for Young Readers.

—Bitter Bananas. 1996. (J). 11.19 (*0-606-09080-0*) Turtleback Bks.

Oliver, Vickie. Kalyn's Life Adventures: Not Even in a Book. 1991. 32p. (J). (gr. 4-10). 4.95 (*1-877610-07-0*) Sea Island Information Group.

O'Neal, Katherine Pebley. The African Sniffari. 2003. (Ready-for-Chapters Ser.). (Illus.). 80p. (J). pap. 3.99 (*0-689-85701-2*, Aladdin) Simon & Schuster Children's Publishing.

O'Rourke, Frank. Burton & Stanley, RS. 1996. (Illus.). 64p. (J). (gr. 4-7). pap. 4.95 (*0-374-40989-7*, Sunburst) Farrar, Straus & Giroux.

Orr, Ryan. Beyond the Oasis. 2002. 216p. (YA). per. 18.95 (*0-9641861-1-X*) Redhawk Publishing.

Osborne, Mary Pope. Lions at Lunchtime. 1998. (Magic Tree House Ser.: No. 11). (Illus.). 96p. (J). (gr. k-3). pap. 3.99 (*0-679-88340-1*, Random Hse. Bks. for Young Readers) Random Hse. Children's Bks.

Packard, Edward. Africa: Where Do Elephants Live Underground. 1989. (Earth Inspectors Ser.: Bk. 6). 112p. (J). (gr. 4-6). pap. text 3.95 o.p. (*0-07-047998-4*) McGraw-Hill Cos., The.

Padt, Maartje. Shanti. 1998. (Illus.). 32p. (J). (ps-2). pap. 14.95 o.p. (*0-7894-2520-3*) Dorling Kindersley Publishing, Inc.

Parenteau, Shirley. Blue Hands, Blue Cloth. 1978. (Illus.). 32p. (J). (gr. 2-5). lib. bdg. 9.25 o.p. (*0-516-03414-6*, Children's Pr.) Scholastic Library Publishing.

Paton, Alan. Cry, the Beloved Country. 1985. (Barron's Book Notes Ser.). (J). (gr. 10-12). pap. 2.95 (*0-8120-3507-0*) Barron's Educational Series, Inc.

—Cry, the Beloved Country. abr. ed. 1991. (Bridge Ser.). (Illus.). 115p. (YA). pap. text 7.35 o.p. (*0-582-53009-1*, 79129) Longman Publishing Group.

Peretti, Frank E. The Secret of the Desert Stone. 1996. (Cooper Kids Adventures Ser.: Vol. 5). (Illus.). 160p. (J). (gr. 4-7). 5.99 (*0-8499-3643-8*) Nelson, Tommy.

Petruccio, Steven James. Tarzan. 1999. (Little Activity Bks.). (Illus.). (J). pap. 1.00 (*0-486-40933-3*) Dover Pubns., Inc.

Pickford, Susan B. Antonio's la Amistad. 1997. (Illus.). 100p. (Orig.). (J). (gr. 7-9). pap. 6.95 (*1-889664-08-1*) SBP Collaboratioin Works.

Pinkney, Andrea Davis. Shake Shake Shake. 1997. (Illus.). 16p. (J). (ps). bds. 5.95 (*0-15-200632-X*, Red Wagon Bks.) Harcourt Children's Bks.

Poland, Marguerite. The Mantis & the Moon: Stories for the Children of Africa. 1983. (Illus.). 120p. (J). (gr. 6-7). pap. 9.95 o.p. (*0-86975-102-6*) Ravan Pr. ZMB. *Dist:* Ohio Univ. Pr.

—Once at Kwafubesi. 1981. (Illus.). 1981p. (J). (gr. 6-7). pap. 9.95 o.p. (*0-86975-201-4*) Ravan Pr. ZMB. *Dist:* Ohio Univ. Pr.

Porter, Wesley. About Monkeys in Trees. 1979. (Illus.). (gr. k-3). 2.95 o.p. (*0-531-02506-3*); lib. bdg. 6.90 o.p. (*0-531-04085-2*) Scholastic Library Publishing. (Watts, Franklin).

Quintana, Anton. The Baboon King. 2001. 192p. (YA). (gr. 7 up). mass mkt. 4.99 (*0-440-22907-3*, Laurel Leaf) Random Hse. Children's Bks.

—The Baboon King. Nieuwenhuizen, John, tr. 1999. (DUT.). 192p. (YA). (gr. 7-12). 16.95 (*0-8027-8711-8*) Walker & Co.

Radcliffe, Theresa. Bashi Elephant Baby. 1998. (Illus.). 32p. (J). (ps-3). 15.99 o.s.i (*0-670-87054-4*) Penguin Putnam Bks. for Young Readers.

Reno, Dawn E. The Candace: Warrior Queens of the Kingdom of Kush. 1999. (Illus.). 120p. pap. text 8.95 (*1-58521-009-9*) Books for Black Children, Inc.

RH Disney Staff. Bug Stew! 2003. (Illus.). 32p. (J). pap. 3.99 (*0-7364-2168-8*, RH/Disney) Random Hse. Children's Bks.

—Bug Stew. 2003. (Illus.). 32p. (J). lib. bdg. 11.99 (*0-7364-8025-0*, RH/Disney) Random Hse. Children's Bks.

—The Little Lion King. 2003. (Illus.). 16p. (J). 3.99 (*0-7364-2184-X*, RH/Disney) Random Hse. Children's Bks.

Robinson, Adjai. Three African Tales. 1979. (Illus.). (J). (gr. 3-7). 6.95 o.p. (*0-399-20656-6*) Putnam Publishing Group, The.

Rockwood, Roy. Bomba, the Jungle Boy. 1977. (Bomba Books Ser.: Vol. 1). (Illus.). (J). (gr. 4-9). 2.95 o.p. (*0-448-14701-7*) Putnam Publishing Group, The.

—Bomba, the Jungle Boy: At the Moving Mountain. 1978. (Bomba Books Ser.: Vol. 2). (Illus.). (J). (gr. 4-9). 2.95 o.p. (*0-448-14702-5*) Putnam Publishing Group, The.

Rodanas, Kristina, illus. The Blind Hunter. 2003. (J). 16.95 (*0-7614-5132-3*) Cavendish, Marshall Corp.

Rodrigues, Ann & Winch, John. What Little Rhino Sees. 2002. (J). 15.99 (*0-7636-1396-7*) Candlewick Pr.

Rumford, James. Calabash Cat. 2003. (ARA & ENG., Illus.). 32p. (J). 16.00 (*0-618-22423-8*) Houghton Mifflin Co.

Sackett, Elisabeth. Danger on the African Grassland. 1991. (J). (ps-3). 12.95 o.p. (*0-316-76596-1*) Little Brown & Co.

Sadler, Mike. The Lonely Stranger. 1992. (Junior African Writers Ser.). (Illus.). 91p. (YA). (gr. 8-12). pap. text 4.00 o.p. (*0-435-89292-4*) Heinemann.

—The Mystery of Mister E. 1992. (Junior African Writers Ser.). (Illus.). 92p. (YA). (gr. 8-12). pap. text 4.00 o.p. (*0-435-89296-7*) Heinemann.

Sayre, April Pulley. Crocodile Listens. 2001. (Illus.). 24p. (J). (gr. 1 up). 15.99 (*0-688-16504-4*); lib. bdg. 16.89 (*0-688-16505-2*) HarperCollins Children's Bk. Group. (Greenwillow Bks.).

—If You Should Hear a Honey Guide. 2000. (Illus.). 32p. (J). (ps-3). pap. 5.95 (*0-618-07031-1*) Houghton Mifflin Co. Trade & Reference Div.

Schade, Susan & Buller, Jon. Bungee Baboon Rescue. 2002. (Danger Joe Show Ser.: No. 2). (Illus.). 112p. (J). mass mkt. 3.99 (*0-439-40976-4*, Scholastic Paperbacks) Scholastic, Inc.

Schroeder, Russell & Saxon, Victoria. Disney's Tarzan: Special Collector's Edition. 1999. (Illus.). 72p. (J). 17.99 (*0-7868-3221-5*) Disney Pr.

—Tarzan: Special Collector's Edition. 1999. (Illus.). 72p. (J). lib. bdg. 18.49 (*0-7868-5093-0*) Disney Pr.

Sealey, Patricia. Caught in the Act. 1992. (Junior African Writers Ser.). (Illus.). 30p. (J). (gr. 2-6). pap. text 2.50 o.p. (*0-435-89107-3*) Heinemann.

—Nothing Ever Happens Here. 1992. (Junior African Writers Ser.). (Illus.). 29p. (J). (gr. 2-6). pap. text 2.50 o.p. (*0-435-89103-0*) Heinemann.

Seyki, Kofi. The Haunted Taxi Driver. 1992. (Junior African Writers Ser.). (Illus.). 60p. (YA). (gr. 6-10). pap. text 3.00 o.p. (*0-435-89231-2*) Heinemann.

Shepard, Eva & Lehman, Celia. Nzuzi & the Spell. 1992. (Illus.). 160p. (J). (gr. 2-8). pap. 6.95 o.p. (*1-878893-22-X*) Telcraft Bks.

Silver, Norman. No Tigers in Africa. 1992. (Illus.). 100p. (J). (gr. 7 up). 15.00 o.p. (*0-525-44733-4*, Dutton Children's Bks.) Penguin Putnam Bks. for Young Readers.

Simba & the Lost Waterfall. 1995. (Creative Classic Ser.). (Illus.). 16p. (J). (ps-1). 7.98 o.p. (*1-57082-221-2*) Mouse Works.

Simba's Journey. 1995. (Giant Carousel Book). (Illus.). 12p. (J). (ps-1). 6.98 o.p. (*1-57082-244-1*) Mouse Works.

Stanley, Sanna. Monkey Sunday: Story from a Village in Zaire, RS. 1998. (Illus.). 32p. (J). (gr. k-3). 16.00 o.p. (*0-374-35018-3*, Farrar, Straus & Giroux (BYR)) Farrar, Straus & Giroux.

—The Rains Are Coming. 1993. (Illus.). 24p. (J). (ps up). lib. bdg. 13.93 o.p. (*0-688-10949-7*, Greenwillow Bks.) HarperCollins Children's Bk. Group.

Starks, Virginia L. The Spirit of Ancient Africa. 1997. (Illus.). 40p. (J). (gr. 1-5). 16.95 (*0-9656859-1-8*) Black Pyramid Pr.

Steig, William. Doctor De Soto Goes to Africa. 1992. (Michael di Capua Bks.). (Illus.). (J). (ps up). 32p. lib. bdg. 14.89 (*0-06-205003-6*); 80p. 15.00 o.p. (*0-06-205002-8*) HarperCollins Children's Bk. Group.

—Doctor De Soto Goes to Africa. 1992. (Trophy Picture Bks.). 12.10 (*0-606-06330-7*) Turtleback Bks.

—Doctor de Soto Goes to Africa. 1994. (Trophy Picture Book Ser.). (Illus.). 32p. (J). (gr. 2 up). pap. 5.99 (*0-06-205901-7*, Harper Trophy) HarperCollins Children's Bk. Group.

—Doctor De Soto Goes to Africa. unabr. ed. 1995. (Tell Me a Story Ser.). (Illus.). 32p. (J). (ps up). 8.95 incl. audio (*0-694-70003-7*, HarperAudio) HarperTrade.

Steptoe, John L. Mufaro's Beautiful Daughters: An African Tale. 1987. (Amistad Ser.). (Illus.). 32p. (J). (ps-3). lib. bdg. 16.89 (*0-688-04046-2*) HarperCollins Children's Bk. Group.

—Mufaro's Beautiful Daughters: An African Tale. Kohen, Clarita, tr. 1987. (Amistad Ser.). (Illus.). 32p. (J). (ps-3). 16.99 (*0-688-04045-4*) HarperCollins Children's Bk. Group.

—Mufaro's Beautiful Daughters: An African Tale. enl. ed. 1993. (Illus.). 32p. (J). (ps-3). pap. 22.99 (*0-688-12935-8*, Harper Trophy) HarperCollins Children's Bk. Group.

Stevenson, William. The Bushbabies. 1984. (Illus.). (J). (gr. 5-9). 16.00 o.p. (*0-8446-6167-8*) Smith, Peter Pub., Inc.

Stewart, Dianne. The Paper Chase. 1992. (Junior African Writers Ser.). (Illus.). 29p. (J). (gr. 2-6). pap. text 2.50 o.p. (*0-435-89102-2*) Heinemann.

Stojic, Manya. Rain. 2000. (Illus.). 32p. (J). (gr. k-3). 15.95 (*0-517-80085-3*); lib. bdg. 17.99 (*0-517-80086-1*) Random Hse. Children's Bks. (Random Hse. Bks. for Young Readers).

Strickland, Brad & Fuller, Thomas. Terrier of the Lost Mines. Ryan, Kevin, ed. 1999. (Adventures of Wishbone Ser.: No. 19). (Illus.). 144p. (J). (gr. 2-5). pap. 3.99 o.p. (*1-57064-278-8*, Big Red Chair Bks.) Lyrick Publishing.

Suben, Eric. Terk's Tale, SUPSB. 1999. (Disney Ser.). (Illus.). 24p. (J). (ps-k). pap. 3.29 o.p. (*0-307-13324-9*, Golden Bks.) Random Hse. Children's Bks.

Suben, Eric, et al, illus. Tarzan. 1999. (Disney Ser.). 24p. (ps-3). pap. 3.29 (*0-307-13194-7*, Golden Bks.) Random Hse. Children's Bks.

Tchana, Katrin H. & Pami, Louise T. Oh, No, Toto! 1997. (Illus.). 32p. (J). (ps-2). pap. 15.95 (*0-590-46585-6*) Scholastic, Inc.

Tembo, John. Dead Men Don't Talk. 1992. (Junior African Writers Ser.). (Illus.). 91p. (YA). (gr. 8-12). pap. text 4.00 o.p. (*0-435-89294-0*) Heinemann.

Thomas, Jim. Jungle Jumbles. 1995. (Ace Ventura Ser.). (J). lib. bdg. 3.99 o.p. (*0-679-87868-8*, Random Hse. Bks. for Young Readers) Random Hse. Children's Bks.

Tullock, Shirley. Who Made Me? 2000. (Illus.). 32p. (J). (ps-3). 16.99 (*0-8066-4045-6*) Augsburg Fortress, Pubs.

Van Laan, Nancy. Little Fish, Lost. 1998. (Illus.). 32p. (J). (ps-2). 15.00 (*0-689-81331-7*, Atheneum/Anne Schwartz Bks.) Simon & Schuster Children's Publishing.

Vega, Elizabeth H. The Laughing River: A Folktale for Peace. 1995. (Illus.). 32p. (J). 23.95 incl. audio (*1-877810-37-1*, LAFC); 16.95 (*1-877810-35-5*, LAFB) Rayve Productions, Inc.

Wallace, Joseph. Big & Noisy Simon. 2001. (Illus.). 32p. (J). (gr. 1-4). 15.99 (*0-7868-0515-3*) Hyperion Bks. for Children.

Walter, Mildred Pitts. Brother to the Wind. 1985. (Illus.). 32p. (J). (ps-2). 13.00 o.p. (*0-688-03811-5*) HarperCollins Children's Bk. Group.

—Brothers to the Wind. 1985. (Illus.). 32p. (J). (ps-3). 15.89 (*0-688-03812-3*) HarperCollins Children's Bk. Group.

Ward. I Am Eyes: Ni Macho. 1993. 32p. (J). (gr. k-2). 19.95 o.p. (*0-590-71935-1*) Scholastic, Inc.

Ward, Leila. I Am Eyes: Ni Macho. (Blue Ribbon Book Ser.). (J). 1991. (SPA.). (gr. 4-7). pap. 3.95 (*0-590-44854-4*); 1987. (Illus.). 32p. (gr. k-3). reprint ed. mass mkt. 3.95 (*0-590-40990-5*) Scholastic, Inc. (Scholastic Paperbacks).

Watson, Pete. The Market Lady & the Mango Tree. 1994. (Illus.). 32p. (J). 14.00 (*0-688-12970-6*); lib. bdg. 13.93 o.p. (*0-688-12971-4*) Morrow/Avon. (Morrow, William & Co.).

Weir, Bob & Weir, Wendy. Panther Dream: A Story of the African Rainforest. (Illus.). 40p. (J). (gr. k-5). 1993. pap. 4.95 o.p. (*1-56282-525-9*); 1993. pap. 8.95 o.s.i (*1-56282-591-7*); 1991. 21.95 o.s.i incl. audio (*1-56282-076-1*); 1991. lib. bdg. 16.49 o.s.i (*1-56282-075-3*) Hyperion Bks. for Children.

—Panther Dream: A Story of the African Rainforest, 12 bks., Set. 1993. (Illus.). 40p. (J). pap., tchr. ed. 33.95 o.p. incl. audio (*1-56282-548-8*) Hyperion Paperbacks for Children.

—Panther Dream: A Story of the African Rainforest. 1993. (J). 10.15 o.p. (*0-606-05969-5*) Turtleback Bks.

Welch, Leona N. Kai: Lost Statue: Girlhood Journey. 1997. (Girlhood Journeys Ser.: No. 3). (Illus.). 71p. (J). (gr. 2-6). per. 5.99 (*0-689-81571-9*, Simon Pulse) Simon & Schuster Children's Publishing.

Wellman, Alice. The White Sorceress. 1976. 160p. (J). (gr. 6 up). 6.95 o.p. (*0-399-20505-5*) Putnam Publishing Group, The.

—The Wilderness Has Ears. 1975. 160p. (J). (gr. 5 up). 6.95 o.p. (*0-15-297285-4*) Harcourt Children's Bks.

White, Paul. Maasai. 1993. (Jungle Doctor Novels Ser.). 156p. (J). 5.99 (*0-85892-280-0*) Gabriel Publishing.

Whiteley, Keith. Kagiso's Mad Uncle. 1992. (Junior African Writers Ser.). (Illus.). 29p. (J). (gr. 4-8). pap. text 2.50 o.p. (*0-435-89164-2*) Heinemann.

Williams, Karen L. When Africa Was Home. (Illus.). 32p. (J). (ps-3). 1998. mass mkt. 11.40 (*0-531-07043-3*); 1991. pap. 15.95 (*0-531-05925-1*); 1991. lib. bdg. 16.99 (*0-531-08525-2*) Scholastic, Inc. (Orchard Bks.).

Winter, Jeanette. Elsina's Clouds, RS. 2004. (J). 16.00 (*0-374-32118-3*, Farrar, Straus & Giroux (BYR)) Farrar, Straus & Giroux.

Zimelman, Nathan. Treed by a Pride of Irate Lions. 1990. (Illus.). (J). (gr. k-3). 14.95 o.p. (*0-316-98802-2*) Little Brown & Co.

Zoehfeld, Kathleen Weidner, adapted by. Tarzan. 1999. (Illus.). 48p. (J). (ps-3). 10.99 o.p. (*0-7868-3220-7*) Disney Pr.

AFRICA, SOUTHWEST—FICTION

Wellman, Alice. The Wilderness Has Ears. 1975. 160p. (J). (gr. 5 up). 6.95 o.p. (*0-15-297285-4*) Harcourt Children's Bks.

AFRICA, WEST—FICTION

Burns, Khephra. Mansa Musa: The Lion of Mali. 2001. (Illus.). 56p. (J). (gr. 3-5). 18.00 (*0-15-200375-4*, Gulliver Bks.) Harcourt Children's Bks.

Diouf, Sylviane. Bintou's Braids. 2001. (Illus.). 40p. (J). (ps-2). 14.95 (*0-8118-2514-0*) Chronicle Bks. LLC.

Gilroy, Tom. In Bikole: Modern Stories of Life in a West African Village. 1978. (Illus.). (gr. 7 up). lib. bdg. 5.95 o.p. (*0-394-83722-3*, Knopf Bks. for Young Readers) Random Hse. Children's Bks.

Graham, Lorenz. David He No Fear. 1971. (Illus.). (J). (gr. 2-5). lib. bdg. 6.89 o.p. (*0-690-23265-9*) HarperCollins Children's Bk. Group.

Hergé. Tintin au Congo. 1999. (Tintin Ser.). (FRE.). (gr. 4-7). 19.95 (*2-203-00101-1*) Casterman, Editions FRA. *Dist:* Distribooks, Inc.

—Tintin im Kongo. (GER., Illus.). 62p. (J). pap. 24.95 (*0-8288-4998-6*) French & European Pubns., Inc.

Mokosso, Henry E. My First Pair of Shoes & the Little Altar Boy: Two Childhood Memories. 1992. 90p. (YA). (gr. 6-12). 7.95 o.p. (*0-944957-08-0*) River-cross Publishing, Inc.

Robinson, Sandra C. The Rainstick: A Fable. 1994. (Illus.). 40p. (gr. 2 up). pap. 9.95 (*1-56044-284-0*, Falcon) Globe Pequot Pr., The.

ALABAMA—FICTION

Banks, Sarah Harrell. Under the Shadow of Wings. 1997. 160p. (J). (gr. 4-8). 16.00 o.s.i (*0-689-81207-8*, Atheneum/Anne Schwartz Bks.) Simon & Schuster Children's Publishing.

Barwick, Mary. The Alabama Angels. 1993. (Illus.). 64p. 15.00 o.s.i (*0-345-38574-8*) Ballantine Bks.

—The Alabama Angels. 3rd ed. 1989. (Illus.). 28p. (J). pap. 8.95 o.p. (*0-9622815-1-4*, Black Belt Pr.) River City Publishing.

Blackshear, Helen F. The Creek Captives: And Other Alabama Stories. 1990. (Illus.). 112p. (Orig.). (J). (ps up). pap. 9.95 o.p. (*0-9622815-2-2*, Black Belt Pr.) River City Publishing.

Capote, Truman. The Thanksgiving Visitor. 1996. (Illus.). 40p. (J). (gr. 4-7). 19.00 o.s.i (*0-679-83898-8*) Knopf, Alfred A. Inc.

Cole, Brenda. Alabama Night. 1988. (Keepsake Bks.). 157p. (YA). (gr. 9-12). pap. (*0-373-88037-5*, Harlequin Bks.) Harlequin Enterprises, Ltd.

Curtis, Christopher Paul. The Watsons Go to Birmingham. 1995. (J). 20.95 (*0-385-31004-8*, Dell Books for Young Readers) Random Hse. Children's Bks.

—The Watsons Go to Birmingham - 1963. 1999. 240p. (gr. 5-8). mass mkt. 2.99 o.s.i (*0-440-22836-0*) Bantam Bks.

—The Watsons Go to Birmingham - 1963. 1998. 15p. pap., stu. ed., tchr.'s training gde. ed. 15.95 (*1-58303-068-9*) Pathways Publishing.

—The Watsons Go to Birmingham - 1963. 210p. (YA). (gr. 5 up). pap. 5.50 (*0-8072-8336-3*); 2000. (J). pap. 37.00 incl. audio (*0-8072-8335-5*, YA166SP) Random Hse. Audio Publishing Group. (Listening Library).

—The Watsons Go to Birmingham - 1963. 2000. 224p. (YA). (gr. 5-7). mass mkt. 5.99 (*0-440-22800-X*, Laurel Leaf); 1997. 224p. (gr. 4-10). pap. text 6.50 (*0-440-41412-1*, Dell Books for Young Readers); 1997. (YA). pap. o.s.i (*0-440-41431-8*, Dell Books for Young Readers) Random Hse. Children's Bks.

—The Watsons Go to Birmingham - 1963. l.t. ed. 2000. (Illus.). 260p. (J). (ps up). 22.95 (*0-7862-2741-9*) Thorndike Pr.

—The Watsons Go to Birmingham - 1963. 1997. (YA). 12.04 (*0-606-10993-5*) Turtleback Bks.

—The Watsons Go to Birmingham—1963. 1995. 224p. (gr. 4-7). text 16.95 (*0-385-32175-9*, Dell Books for Young Readers) Random Hse. Children's Bks.

Davis, Ossie. Just Like Martin. 2001. (J). pap. (*0-7868-1642-2*); 176p. lib. bdg. 16.49 (*0-7868-2632-0*) Hyperion Bks. for Children. (Jump at the Sun).

—Just Like Martin. 1992. 208p. (YA). (gr. 5-9). pap. 15.00 (*0-671-73202-1*, Simon & Schuster Children's Publishing) Simon & Schuster Children's Publishing.

—Just Like Martin. 1996. (J). (gr. 5-9). 19.50 o.p. (*0-8446-6897-4*) Smith, Peter Pub., Inc.

—Just Like Martin. 1995. (YA). 12.04 (*0-606-07756-1*) Turtleback Bks.

Hager, Betty. Marcie & the Monster of the Bayou. 1994. (Tales from the Bayou Ser.: Bk. 4). 128p. (J). (gr. 3-7). pap. 5.99 o.p. (*0-310-38431-1*) Zondervan.

—Miss Tilly & the Haunted Mansion. 1994. (Tales from the Bayou Ser.: Bk. 2). 112p. (J). (gr. 3-7). 5.99 o.p. (*0-310-38411-7*) Zondervan.

—Old Jake & the Pirate's Treasure. 1994. (Tales from the Bayou Ser.: Bk. 1). (Illus.). 112p. (J). (gr. 3-7). 5.99 o.p. (*0-310-38401-X*) Zondervan.

Harrison, Henry F. Jimbo on Board the Nettie Quill: An Alabama Riverboat Adventure. 1995. (Illus.). 40p. (Orig.). (J). (ps-3). pap. 16.00 (*1-881320-19-7*, Black Belt Pr.) River City Publishing.

Hermes, Patricia. In God's Novel. 2000. (Illus.). (J). 15.95 (*0-7614-5074-2*) Cavendish, Marshall Corp.

Holmes, Mary Z. See You in Heaven. 1992. (History's Children Ser.). (Illus.). 48p. (J). (gr. 4-5). pap. o.p. (*0-8114-6427-X*); lib. bdg. 21.36 o.p. (*0-8114-3502-4*) Raintree Pubs.

Jackson, Dave & Jackson, Neta. The Forty-Acre Swindle: George Washington Carver. 2000. (Trail-blazer Bks.: Vol. 31). (Illus.). 144p. (J). (gr. 3-7). pap. 5.99 (*0-7642-2264-3*) Bethany Hse. Pubs.

Johnson, Allen, Jr. Picker McClikker. 1996. (Illus.). 48p. (J). (gr. 1-4). pap. text 6.95 (*1-887654-14-3*) Premium Pr. America.

—Picker McClikker. 1993. (Illus.). (J). (gr. k-3). 16.95 o.s.i (*1-878561-20-0*) Seacoast Publishing, Inc.

Les Becquets, Diane. The Stones of Mourning Creek. 2001. (Illus.). 320p. (J). (gr. 7 up). 16.95 (*1-58837-004-6*) Winslow Pr.

Lyon, George Ella. Sonny's House of Spies. 2004. (YA). (*0-689-85168-5*, Atheneum/Richard Jackson Bks.) Simon & Schuster Children's Publishing.

McKissack, Patricia C. Ma Dear's Aprons. 1997. (Illus.). (J). lib. bdg. 16.99 (*0-679-95099-0*, Knopf Bks. for Young Readers) Random Hse. Children's Bks.

—Ma Dear's Aprons. (Illus.). 32p. (J). (ps-3). 1997. 16.00 (*0-689-81051-2*, Atheneum/Anne Schwartz Bks.); 2000. reprint ed. pap. 5.99 (*0-689-83262-1*, Aladdin) Simon & Schuster Children's Publishing.

—Ma Dear's Aprons. 2000. (Illus.). (J). 12.14 (*0-606-17928-3*) Turtleback Bks.

—Run Away Home. 1997. 128p. (J). (gr. 3-7). pap. 14.95 (*0-590-46751-4*) Scholastic, Inc.

Nolan, Han. Send Me down a Miracle. 1996. 256p. (YA). (gr. 7-12). pap. 6.00 o.s.i (*0-15-200978-7*, Harcourt Paperbacks) Harcourt Children's Bks.

—Send Me Down a Miracle. 2003. 276p. (YA). pap. 6.95 (*0-15-204680-1*) Harcourt Children's Bks.

Robinet, Harriette Gillem. Walking to the Bus Rider Blues. 2000. (Illus.). 146p. (J). (gr. 4-7). 16.00 (*0-689-83191-9*, Atheneum) Simon & Schuster Children's Publishing.

St. George, Judith S. In the Shadow of the Bear. 1983. 144p. (J). (gr. 7-9). 10.95 o.s.i (*0-399-21015-6*, G. P. Putnam's Sons) Penguin Putnam Bks. for Young Readers.

Staples, Alfred. Mobile Carnival: Mardi Gras History, 1947, Vol. 1 No. 1. Plummer, Cameron M., ed. 1947. (Illus.). (YA). (gr. 7 up). pap. o.p. (*0-940882-04-3*) HB Pubns.

Warner, Gertrude Chandler. The Mystery of the Midnight Dog. 2001. (Boxcar Children Ser.: No. 81). (Illus.). 122p. (J). (gr. 2-7). pap. 3.95 (*0-8075-5476-6*); lib. bdg. 13.95 (*0-8075-5475-8*) Whitman, Albert & Co.

ALASKA—FICTION

Amato, Carol A. On the Trail of the Grizzly. 1997. (Young Readers' Ser.). (Illus.). 48p. (J). (gr. 2-4). pap. 4.95 (*0-8120-9312-7*) Barron's Educational Series, Inc.

—On the Trail of the Grizzly, Vol. 9. 1998. (Young Reader Ser.: No. 9). (Illus.). 48p. (J). (gr. 3-6). lib. bdg. 13.45 (*1-56674-240-4*) Forest Hse. Publishing Co., Inc.

—On the Trail of the Grizzly. 1997. (Young Readers' Series). 11.10 (*0-606-11706-7*) Turtleback Bks.

Andrew, Tommy. Neqsulartukut. 1998. Tr. of We Fish. (ESK., Illus.). 8p. (J). (gr. k-3). pap. text 6.00 (*1-58084-032-9*) Lower Kuskokwim Schl. District.

Arnold, Marti. Alaska, Uncle Jim & Me. Lesko, Marian, ed. 1983. (Illus.). 146p. (Orig.). (J). (gr. 6 up). pap. 5.95 (*0-912683-00-7*) Fireweed Pr.

Bell, Margaret E. Watch for a Tall White Sail. 1973. 160p. (J). (gr. 7-9). 0.95 o.s.i (*0-448-05421-3*) Ace Bks.

Blake, Robert J. Akiak: A Tale from the Iditarod. 1997. (Illus.). 32p. (J). (gr. k-3). 16.99 (*0-399-22798-9*, Philomel) Penguin Putnam Bks. for Young Readers.

—Togo. 2002. (Illus.). 48p. (J). 16.99 (*0-399-23381-4*, Philomel) Penguin Putnam Bks. for Young Readers.

Bodett, Tom. Williwaw! 2000. (Illus.). 208p. (gr. 5-8). pap. text 5.50 (*0-375-80687-3*, Knopf Bks. for Young Readers) Random Hse. Children's Bks.

Burnham, Saranne D. Three River Junction: A Story of an Alaskan Bald Eagle Preserve. 1997. (Habitat Ser.). (J). (gr. 1-4). audio 5.00 (*1-56899-448-6*, C7003); (Illus.). 36p. 19.95 incl. audio (*1-56899-443-5*, BC7003); (Illus.). 32p. 15.95 (*1-56899-441-9*); (Illus.). 36p. pap. 5.95 (*1-56899-442-7*);Incl. plush toy. (Illus.). 36p. 26.95 (*1-56899-444-3*);Incl. plush toy. (Illus.). 36p. 31.95 incl. audio (*1-56899-445-1*);Incl. toy. (Illus.). 36p. pap. 16.95 (*1-56899-446-X*) Soundprints.

Carey, Mary. Texas Brat in Alaska: The Cat Train Kid. 1991. (Illus.). 96p. (J). (gr. 5-7). 10.95 o.p. (*0-89015-831-2*) Eakin Pr.

Carlstrom, Nancy White. Raven & River. 1997. (Illus.). 32p. (J). (ps-3). 15.95 o.p. (*0-316-12894-5*) Little Brown & Co.

Chang, Cindy. Balto: Junior Novelization. 1995. 64p. (J). (gr. k-4). 3.95 o.p. (*0-448-41112-1*, Grosset & Dunlap) Penguin Putnam Bks. for Young Readers.

Cosgrove, Stephen. Gnome from Nome. (Serendipity Bks.). (Illus.). 32p. 2003. 4.99 (*0-8431-0585-2*); 1978. (J). (gr. 1-4). 3.95 o.p. (*0-8431-0555-0*) Penguin Putnam Bks. for Young Readers. (Price Stern Sloan).

—Gnome from Nome. 1986. (Serendipity Ser.). (J). 11.14 (*0-606-02388-7*) Turtleback Bks.

Dalmatian Press Staff, adapted by. The Call of the Wild. 2002. (Spot the Classics Ser.). (Illus.). 192p. (J). (gr. k-5). 4.99 (*1-57759-545-9*) Dalmatian Pr.

DeArmond, Dale, illus. & retold by. The Seal Oil Lamp: An Adaptation of an Eskimo Folktale. 1996. (Books for Children). 48p. (J). (ps-3). reprint ed. pap. 7.95 (*0-87156-858-6*) Sierra Club Bks.

DeClements, Barthe. The Bite of the Gold Bug: A Story of the Alaskan Gold Rush. (Once upon America Ser.). (Illus.). 64p. (J). (gr. 2-6). 1994. pap. 4.99 (*0-14-036081-6*, Puffin Bks.); 1992. 13.00 o.p. (*0-670-84495-0*, Viking Children's Bks.) Penguin Putnam Bks. for Young Readers.

—The Bite of the Gold Bug: A Story of the Alaskan Gold Rush. 1994. (Once upon America Ser.). (J). (gr. 2-6). 11.14 (*0-606-06938-0*) Turtleback Bks.

Dixon, Ann. The Sleeping Lady. 1994. (Illus.). 32p. (J). (gr. 7 up). 15.95 o.p. (*0-88240-444-X*, Alaska Northwest Bks.) Graphic Arts Ctr. Publishing Co.

Dussling, Jennifer. Balto Beware! 1995. (Illus.). 24p. (J). (ps-3). 2.95 (*0-448-41114-8*, Grosset & Dunlap) Penguin Putnam Bks. for Young Readers.

Dwyer, Mindy. The Salmon Princess: An Alaska Cinderella Story. 2004. (Illus.). 32p. (J). pap. (*1-57061-355-9*) Sasquatch Bks.

Fowler, Susi Gregg. Circle of Thanks. 1998. (Illus.). 32p. (J). (ps-3). pap. 15.95 o.s.i (*0-590-10066-1*) Scholastic, Inc.

Frisinger, Nellie. Jeff & Jenny Winter in Alaska. 1977. (Jeff & Jenny Adventure Ser.). (Illus.). (J). (gr. 2-6). pap. 2.95 o.p. (*0-916406-82-2*) Accent Pubns.

George, Jean Craighead. The Julie Trilogy. 1999. (Illus.). (YA). (gr. 5 up). pap. 17.97 (*0-06-449350-4*) HarperCollins Children's Bk. Group.

Gill, Shelley R. Kiana's Iditarod. 1984. (Illus.). 64p. (J). (gr. 4-7). 15.95 (*0-934007-07-1*) Paws IV Publishing.

Golden Books Staff. Gold Rush Winter. 2002. (Road to Reading Ser.). (Illus.). 48p. (J). (gr. 2-4). pap. 3.99 (*0-307-26413-0*, Golden Bks.) Random Hse. Children's Bks.

—Gold Rush Winter. 2002. (Road to Reading Ser.). (Illus.). 48p. (J). (gr. 2-4). lib. bdg. 11.99 (*0-307-46413-X*) Random Hse., Inc.

Gray, Genevieve. Alaska Woman. 1977. (Time of Danger, Time for Courage Ser.). (Illus.). (J). (gr. 3-9). pap. 3.95 o.p. (*0-88436-387-2*, 35300); lib. bdg. 6.95 o.p. (*0-88436-386-4*, 35482) Paradigm Publishing, Inc.

Guy, Glen E. The Trail to Wrangell: The Adventures of Dusty Sourdough, Vol. 2. 1995. (Illus.). 105p. (Orig.). (J). pap. 7.95 (*0-9644491-3-7*) Old Alaska Today.

Hamilton, Sue. Exxon Valdez Oil Spill. Hamilton, John, ed. 1990. (Day of Disaster Ser.). (Illus.). 32p. (J). (gr. 4). lib. bdg. 12.98 o.p. (*0-939179-84-9*) ABDO Publishing Co.

Herndon, Ernest. Smugglers on Grizzly Mountain. 1994. (Eric Sterling, Secret Agent Ser.: Vol. 4). 128p. (J). pap. 5.99 (*0-310-38281-5*) Zondervan.

Herreid, I. Jennie-m Inugugnina Fairbanks-mi. 1981. Tr. of Jennie Grows up in Fairbanks. (ESK.). 25p. (J). 3.00 (*0-933769-51-2*) Alaska Native Language Ctr.

Hill, Kirkpatrick. Minuk: Ashes in the Pathway. 2002. (Girls of Many Lands Ser.). (Illus.). 196p. (J). (gr. 4-7). 12.95 (*1-58485-596-7*); pap. 7.95 (*1-58485-520-7*) Pleasant Co. Pubns. (American Girl).

—The Year of Miss Agnes. 128p. (J). (gr. 3-7). 2002. pap. 4.99 (*0-689-85124-3*, Aladdin); 2000. 16.00 (*0-689-82933-7*, McElderry, Margaret K.) Simon & Schuster Children's Publishing.

Hobbs, William. Down the Yukon. 2001. (Illus.). 208p. (J). (gr. 5 up). 16.99 (*0-688-17472-8*); lib. bdg. 16.89 (*0-06-029540-6*) HarperCollins Children's Bk. Group.

—Jason's Gold. 240p. (J). 2000. (gr. 6 up). pap. 5.99 (*0-380-72914-8*); 1999. (Illus.). (gr. 5-9). 16.99 (*0-688-15093-4*, Morrow, William & Co.) Morrow/Avon.

—Jason's Gold. unabr. ed. 2000. (YA). (gr. 5-7). audio 32.00 (*0-8072-8228-6*, LL0168, Listening Library) Random Hse. Audio Publishing Group.

—Wild Man Island. 192p. (J). (gr. 5 up). 2003. pap. 5.99 (*0-380-73310-2*, Harper Trophy); 2002. (Illus.). lib. bdg. 15.89 (*0-06-029810-3*) Harper-Collins Children's Bk. Group.

Jordan, James L. Ricky's Adventure in Alaska. 1995. (Ricky Shafer Ser.). (Illus.). 176p. (J). (gr. 4-6). pap. 4.95 (*0-9630534-1-8*) Living Water Pubns.

Kittredge, Frances. Neeluk: An Eskimo Boy in the Days of the Whaling Ships. 2001. (Illus.). 88p. (J). (gr. 3-7). 18.95 (*0-88240-545-4*, Alaska Northwest Bks.) Graphic Arts Ctr. Publishing Co.

Kondak, Margarida. The Wild Horses of Summer Bay. l.t. ed. 2002. (Illus.). 32p. (J). pap. 9.95 (*1-890692-06-9*) Wizard Works.

Lipkind, William. Boy with a Harpoon. 1952. (Illus.). (J). (gr. 2-5). 4.50 o.p. (*0-15-210703-7*); lib. bdg. 3.56 o.p. (*0-15-210704-5*) Harcourt Children's Bks.

London, Jack. The Call of the Wild. unabr. ed. 1964. (Classics Ser.). (YA). (gr. 6 up). mass mkt. 2.95 o.p. (*0-8049-0030-2*, CL-30) Airmont Publishing Co., Inc.

—The Call of the Wild. 1994. (Illustrated Classics Collection). 64p. (gr. 6-12). (J). pap. 3.60 o.p. (*1-56103-417-7*); (YA). pap. 4.95 (*0-7854-0663-8*, 40334) American Guidance Service, Inc.

—The Call of the Wild. 1974. (Dent's Illustrated Children's Classics Ser.). (Illus.). 119p. (J). reprint ed. 9.00 o.p. (*0-460-05077-X*) Biblio Distribution.

—The Call of the Wild. 2002. 11.49 (*0-7587-7808-2*) Book Wholesalers, Inc.

—The Call of the Wild. 1990. 114p. (YA). (gr. 4-7). mass mkt. 2.99 (*0-8125-0432-1*, Tor Classics); 1987. mass mkt. 1.95 (*0-938819-02-X*, Aerie) Doherty, Tom Assocs., LLC.

—The Call of the Wild. 64p. 1999. (Illus.). pap. 1.00 (*0-486-40551-6*); 1990. (YA). pap. 1.00 (*0-486-26472-6*) Dover Pubns., Inc.

—The Call of the Wild. adapted ed. (YA). (gr. 5-12). pap. text 9.95 (*0-8359-0040-1*) Globe Fearon Educational Publishing.

—The Call of the Wild. 1997. (gr. 4-7). text 8.25 (*0-03-051498-3*) Holt, Rinehart & Winston.

—The Call of the Wild. 1992. (Illustrated Classics Ser.). (J). pap. 33.50 o.p. (*1-56156-094-4*) Kidsbooks, Inc.

—The Call of the Wild, Level 3. Hedge, Tricia, ed. 2000. (Bookworms Ser.). (Illus.). 80p. (J). pap. text 5.95 (*0-19-422997-1*) Oxford Univ. Pr., Inc.

—The Call of the Wild. Platt, Kin, ed. 1973. (Now Age Illustrated Ser.). (Illus.). 64p. (J). (gr. 5-10). 7.50 o.p. (*0-88301-201-4*); pap. 2.95 (*0-88301-095-X*) Pendulum Pr., Inc.

—The Call of the Wild. 1999. (gr. 4-7). pap. 2.99 o.p. (*0-14-130538-X*, Puffin Bks.); 1996. (Illus.). 128p. (YA). (gr. 7 up). 21.99 o.s.i (*0-670-86918-X*, Viking Children's Bks.); 1994. (Illus.). 144p. (J). (gr. 4-7). pap. 4.99 (*0-14-036669-5*, Puffin Bks.); 1983. 128p. (J). (gr. 3-7). pap. 2.99 o.p. (*0-14-035000-4*, Puffin Bks.); 1996. (Illus.). 128p. (J). (gr. 4-7). 18.99 (*0-670-86796-9*, Viking Children's Bks.) Penguin Putnam Bks. for Young Readers.

—The Call of the Wild. Vogel, Malvina, ed. 1989. (Great Illustrated Classics Ser.: Vol. 3). (Illus.). 240p. (J). (gr. 4-7). 9.95 (*0-86611-954-X*) Playmore, Inc., Pubs.

—The Call of the Wild. (Short Classics Ser.). (Illus.). 48p. (J). (gr. 4 up). 9999. pap. 9.27 o.p. (*0-8172-2006-2*); 1980. lib. bdg. 24.26 o.p. (*0-8172-1656-1*) Raintree Pubs.

—The Call of the Wild. 1991. (Children's Classics Ser.). 254p. (J). (gr. 4-7). 12.99 o.s.i (*0-517-06003-5*) Random Hse. Value Publishing.

—The Call of the Wild. 1987. (Apple Classics Ser.). 172p. (YA). (gr. 4-7). pap. 4.50 (*0-590-44001-2*); 176p. (J). (gr. 6 up). mass mkt. 2.50 o.p. (*0-590-40594-2*, Scholastic Paperbacks) Scholastic, Inc.

—The Call of the Wild. (Scribner Illustrated Classics Ser.). (Illus.). 1999. 128p. (YA). (gr. 4-7). 24.00 (*0-689-81836-X*, Atheneum); 1994. 144p. (J). (gr. 3-7). 19.95 (*0-02-759455-6*, Simon & Schuster Children's Publishing); 1970. 144p. (YA). (gr. 6 up). 13.95 o.s.i (*0-02-759510-2*, Simon & Schuster Children's Publishing) Simon & Schuster Children's Publishing.

—The Call of the Wild. 1996. 11.00 (*0-606-14383-1*); 1993. (Illus.). (J). 10.04 (*0-606-21594-8*); 1964. (J). 8.05 o.p. (*0-606-02504-9*) Turtleback Bks.

—The Call of the Wild. Dyer, Daniel, ed. annot. ed. 1997. (Illus.). 134p. (YA). (gr. 4-7). pap. 12.95 (*0-8061-2920-4*) Univ. of Oklahoma Pr.

—The Call of the Wild. abr. unabr. ed. 1997. (Children's Classics Ser.). (J). pap. 10.95 o.s.i incl. audio (*0-14-086238-2*, Penguin AudioBooks) Viking Penguin.

—The Call of the Wild & Other Stories. deluxe ed. 1965. (Illustrated Junior Library). (Illus.). 192p. (J). (gr. 4-7). 14.99 (*0-448-06027-2*, Grosset & Dunlap) Penguin Putnam Bks. for Young Readers.

—The Call of the Wild & White Fang. 1991. (Bantam Classics Ser.). 320p. (gr. 7-12). reprint ed. mass mkt. 4.99 (*0-553-21233-8*) Bantam Dell Publishing Group.

—Jack London's Stories of the North. 1989. 256p. (J). (gr. 4 up). pap. 4.50 (*0-590-44229-5*) Scholastic, Inc.

—White Fang. 1964. (Airmont Classics Ser.). (YA). (gr. 6 up). mass mkt. 2.50 (*0-8049-0036-1*, CL-36) Airmont Publishing Co., Inc.

—White Fang. (J). 9.95 (*1-56156-306-4*) Kidsbooks, Inc.

Luenn, Nancy. Arctic Unicorn. 1986. 180p. (J). (gr. 5 up). 14.95 o.s.i (*0-689-31278-4*, Atheneum) Simon & Schuster Children's Publishing.

Lynne, Janice. Courtney's Alaska Cruise. 1996. (Courtney Travel Adventure Ser.: Bk. 2). (Illus.). 32p. (J). pap. 6.95 (*0-9649522-1-1*) Destiny Pubns., Inc.

Magdanz, James. Go Home, River. (Illus.). 32p. 2002. (YA). (ps up). pap. 8.95 (*0-88240-568-3*); 1996. (J). (gr. 4-7). 15.95 o.p. (*0-88240-476-8*) Graphic Arts Ctr. Publishing Co. (Alaska Northwest Bks.).

Martin, Nora. The Eagle's Shadow. 1997. 176p. (YA). (gr. 5-9). pap. 15.95 (*0-590-36087-6*) Scholastic, Inc.

Mason, Jane B. Balto: The Movie Storybook. 1995. 32p. (J). (ps-3). 10.95 o.p. (*0-448-41111-3*, Grosset & Dunlap) Penguin Putnam Bks. for Young Readers.

Massi, Jeri. Treasure in the Yukon. 1986. (Peabody Adventure Ser.). 128p. (J). (gr. 4-7). pap. 6.49 (*0-89084-365-1*, 031070) Jones, Bob Univ. Pr.

Meyerhoff, Paul, 2nd. Sabotage Flight. 1995. (Illus.). 200p. (Orig.). (J). (gr. 5-9). pap. 9.95 (*0-931625-24-6*) DIMI Pr.

Mikaelsen, Ben. Touching Spirit Bear. 2001. 256p. (J). (gr. 5 up). 15.99 (*0-380-97744-3*) HarperCollins Children's Bk. Group.

Morey, Walt. Gentle Ben. 1965. (Illus.). 192p. (J). (gr. 4-7). 15.99 o.p. (*0-525-30429-0*, Dutton Children's Bks.) Penguin Putnam Bks. for Young Readers.

—Gloomy Gus. 1989. (Walt Morey Adventure Library). (Illus.). 192p. (YA). (gr. 4-8). reprint ed. pap. 7.95 o.p. (*0-936085-17-7*) Blue Heron Publishing.

—Kavik, the Wolf Dog. (Illus.). (J). (gr. 5-9). 1977. 1.95 o.p. (*0-525-45018-1*); 1968. 192p. 15.99 o.s.i (*0-525-33093-3*) Penguin Putnam Bks. for Young Readers. (Dutton Children's Bks.).

—Kavik, the Wolf Dog. 1989. (J). pap. 2.75 o.p. (*0-590-40937-9*) Scholastic, Inc.

Murphy, Claire Rudolf. Caribou Girl. 1955. (Illus.). 208p. (ps-3). pap. 16.95 (*1-57098-145-0*) Rinehart, Roberts Pubs.

—Free Radical. 2002. 192p. (YA). (gr. 7). 15.00 (*0-618-11134-4*, Clarion Bks.) Houghton Mifflin Co. Trade & Reference Div.

—To the Summit. 1998. 208p. pap. 3.99 (*0-380-79537-X*, Avon Bks.) Morrow/Avon.

—To the Summit. 1992. 160p. (YA). (gr. 7 up). 15.00 o.p. (*0-525-67383-0*, Dutton Children's Bks.) Penguin Putnam Bks. for Young Readers.

—To the Summit. 1998. (J). 9.09 o.p. (*0-606-13853-6*) Turtleback Bks.

Nelson, Marg. One Summer in Alaska, RS. 1971. (J). (gr. 7 up). 4.50 o.p. (*0-374-35650-5*, Farrar, Straus & Giroux (BYR)) Farrar, Straus & Giroux.

Norton, Browning. Wreck of the Blue Plane. 1978. (J). (gr. 5-9). 6.95 o.p. (*0-698-20448-4*) Putnam Publishing Group, The.

O'Dell, Scott. Black Star, Bright Dawn. 1989. 112p. (gr. 7-12). mass mkt. 6.50 (*0-449-70340-1*, Fawcett) Ballantine Bks.

—Black Star, Bright Dawn. 1988. 144p. (YA). (gr. 7-7). tchr. ed. 17.00 (*0-395-47778-6*) Houghton Mifflin Co.

—Black Star, Bright Dawn. 1990. 10.55 (*0-606-01201-X*) Turtleback Bks.

Orenstein, Denise G. Unseen Companions. 2003. 368p. (J). 15.99 (*0-06-052056-6*); lib. bdg. 16.89 (*0-06-052057-4*) HarperCollins Children's Bk. Group. (Tegen, Katherine Bks.).

Osborne, Chester G. The Memory String. 1984. 168p. (J). (gr. 4-8). 11.95 o.s.i (*0-689-31020-X*, Atheneum) Simon & Schuster Children's Publishing.

Paul, Gaither. Stories for My Grandchildren. Scollon, Ronald, ed. 1980. (ENG.). iv, 45p. (J). (gr. 1-6). pap. 4.00 o.p. (*0-933769-05-9*) Alaska Native Language Ctr.

Paulsen, Gary. Dogteam. 1995. (J). (Illus.). 32p. (gr. 4-7). pap. 6.99 (*0-440-41130-0*, Yearling); mass mkt. 7.99 (*0-440-91061-7*, Dell Books for Young Readers) Random Hse. Children's Bks.

—Dogteam. 1995. 13.14 (*0-606-07438-4*) Turtleback Bks.

Paulsen, Gary & Paulsen, Ruth Wright. Dogteam. 1993. (Illus.). 32p. (J). 15.95 o.s.i (*0-385-30550-8*, Delacorte Pr.) Dell Publishing.

Pennington, Bonnie. Tommy's Train Ride: On the Alaska Railroad. 1999. (Illus.). 16p. (J). (gr. k-3). per. 8.95 (*1-888125-51-9*) Publication Consultants.

Pinkerton, Kathrene S. Hidden Harbor. 1966. (Illus.). (J). (gr. 9 up). pap. 0.75 o.p. (*0-15-640185-1*, Voyager Bks./Libros Viajeros) Harcourt Children's Bks.

—Steer North. 1962. (J). (gr. 7 up). 4.95 o.p. (*0-15-280210-X*) Harcourt Children's Bks.

Pockets Learning Staff. Samantha's Alaska Adventure. 1998. (Illus.). 2p. (J). (ps-1). 15.00 (*1-888074-90-6*) Pockets of Learning.

Prince, Michael. The Totems of Seldovia. 1994. 160p. (J). (gr. 5-6). pap. 8.95 (*0-9642662-1-0*) Sundog Publishing.

Radcliffe, Theresa. Nanu, Penguin Chick. 2001. (Illus.). 32p. (J). (ps-3). 15.99 o.s.i (*0-670-88638-6*, Viking Children's Bks.) Penguin Putnam Bks. for Young Readers.

Rand, Gloria. Baby in a Basket. 1997. (Illus.). 32p. (J). (ps-3). 14.99 o.p. (*0-525-65233-7*, Dutton Children's Bks.) Penguin Putnam Bks. for Young Readers.

—Prince William, ERS. 32p. (J). 1994. (ps-3). pap. 7.95 (*0-8050-3384-X*); 1992. (Illus.). (gr. 1-3). 14.95 o.s.i (*0-8050-1841-7*) Holt, Henry & Co. (Holt, Henry & Co. Bks. For Young Readers).

—Salty Takes Off, ERS. 1991. (Salty Ser.). (Illus.). 32p. (J). (ps-3). 14.95 o.p. (*0-8050-1159-5*, Holt, Henry & Co. Bks. For Young Readers) Holt, Henry & Co.

Reiser, Joanne. Hannah's Alaska. 1983. (Heritage Bks.). (Illus.). 32p. (J). (gr. 3-6). lib. bdg. 14.65 o.p. (*0-940742-23-3*) Raintree Pubs.

Repp, Gloria. Charlie. 2002. (Illus.). 147p. (J). (*1-57924-817-9*) Jones, Bob Univ. Pr.

—Mik-Shrok. 1998. 133p. (J). (gr. 4-7). pap. 6.49 (*1-57924-069-0*, 113902) Jones, Bob Univ. Pr.

—Zebra 77. 2002. (Adventures of an Arctic Missionary Ser.). (Illus.). 156p. (J). (gr. 4-6). 6.49 (*1-57924-930-2*) Jones, Bob Univ. Pr.

Ritchie, Jo-An. Jonie in Alaska. Wheeler, Gerald, ed. 1985. 128p. (YA). (gr. 8 up). pap. 5.50 o.p. (*0-8280-0250-9*) Review & Herald Publishing Assn.

Roddy, Lee. Hunted in the Alaskan Wilderness. 1996. (Ladd Family Adventures Ser.: Vol. 13). (Orig.). (J). (gr. 3-7). pap. 5.99 o.p. (*1-56179-445-7*) Focus on the Family Publishing.

—Tracked by the Wolf Pack. 1997. (Ladd Family Adventure Ser.: Bk. 15). (J). (gr. 3-7). pap. 6.00 o.p. (*1-56179-548-8*) Focus on the Family Publishing.

Roe, JoAnn. Alaska Cat. 1990. (Illus.). 64p. (J). (gr. k-5). pap. 6.95 (*0-931551-04-8*); lib. bdg. 11.95 (*0-931551-05-6*) Montevista Pr.

—Castaway Cat. 1997. (Illus.). 56p. (Orig.). (J). (gr. k-5). reprint ed. pap. 6.95 o.p. (*0-931551-03-X*) Montevista Pr.

—Fisherman Cat, 3 bks. (Illus.). (J). (gr. k-5). 1988. 56p. pap. 6.95 o.p. (*0-931551-01-3*); 1994. 64p. reprint ed. lib. bdg. 11.95 (*0-931551-02-1*) Montevista Pr.

Rogers, Jean. Goodbye, My Island. 2001. (Illus.). 96p. (YA). (gr. 2 up). pap. 9.95 (*0-88240-538-1*, Alaska Northwest Bks.) Graphic Arts Ctr. Publishing Co.

—Goodbye, My Island. 1983. (Illus.). 96p. (J). (gr. 5-7). 15.00 o.p. (*0-688-01964-1*, Greenwillow Bks.) HarperCollins Children's Bk. Group.

—King Island Christmas. (Illus.). 32p. (J). (ps-3). 1998. pap. 5.95 (*0-688-16449-8*, Harper Trophy); 1985. 16.00 o.p. (*0-688-04236-8*, Greenwillow Bks.); 1985. lib. bdg. 15.93 o.p. (*0-688-04237-6*, Greenwillow Bks.) HarperCollins Children's Bk. Group.

—King Island Christmas. 1998. (J). 11.10 (*0-606-19040-6*) Turtleback Bks.

Schurfranz, Vivian. Megan, No. 16. 1986. 224p. (Orig.). (J). (gr. 7 up). pap. 2.75 o.p. (*0-590-41468-2*) Scholastic, Inc.

Shahan, Sherry. Frozen Stiff. 1998. 160p. (gr. 4-7). text 14.95 o.s.i (*0-385-32303-4*, Delacorte Pr.) Dell Publishing.

Shields, Mary. The Alaskan Happy Dog Trilogy: Can Dogs Talk?, Loving a Happy Dog, Secret Messages-Training a Happy Dog, 3 vols., Set. 1993. (Illus.). 32p. (J). (ps-3). pap. 34.00 (*0-9618348-2-X*) Pyrola Publishing.

Sloat, Teri. Eye of the Needle. 1993. (Picture Puffin Ser.). (Illus.). (J). 10.19 o.p. (*0-606-05828-1*) Turtleback Bks.

Smith, Sherri L. Lucy the Giant. 2002. 224p. (YA). (gr. 9 up). 15.95 (*0-385-72940-5*); lib. bdg. 17.99 (*0-385-90031-7*) Dell Publishing. (Delacorte Pr.).

—Lucy the Giant. l.t. ed. 2002. (Young Adult Ser.). 236p. 23.95 (*0-7862-4751-7*) Thorndike Pr.

Stern, Cecily. A Different Kind of Gold. 1981. (I Can Read Bks.). (Illus.). 128p. (J). (ps-3). pap. 1.95 (*0-06-440126-X*, Harper Trophy); o.p. (*0-06-025770-9*); lib. bdg. 11.89 o.p. (*0-06-025771-7*) HarperCollins Children's Bk. Group.

Thorpe, Kiki. Follow the Lemming. 2001. (Ready-to-Read Ser.: Vol. 5). (Illus.). 32p. (J). (ps-3). pap. 3.99 (*0-689-83599-X*, Simon Spotlight/ Nickelodeon) Simon & Schuster Children's Publishing.

Tjepkema, Edith R. Alaskan Paradise. 1989. (Northwest Paradise Ser.: Vol. 2). 115p. (Orig.). (YA). (gr. 8-12). pap. 4.50 (*0-9620280-1-0*) Northland Pr.

—Yukon Paradise. 1990. (Northwest Paradise Ser.: Vol. 3). 126p. (Orig.). (YA). (gr. 8-12). pap. 4.50 (*0-9620280-2-9*) Northland Pr.

Tung, Angela. Balto the Hero. 1995. 24p. (J). (ps-3). 3.25 o.p. (*0-448-41113-X*, Grosset & Dunlap) Penguin Putnam Bks. for Young Readers.

Upton, Deborah. Alaska Adventure. 2001. (Play-A-Sound Ser.). (Illus.). (J). (*0-7853-4806-9*) Publications International, Ltd.

Upton, Joe. Runaways on the Inside Passage. 2002. (Illus.). 304p. (YA). (gr. 5 up). 17.95 (*0-88240-564-0*); pap. 9.95 (*0-88240-565-9*) Graphic Arts Ctr. Publishing Co. (Alaska Northwest Bks.).

Van Gorden, Charles L. Olive, Char, Lizzie & Izzie: A Sea Otter Story. 1991. (Illus.). 24p. (Orig.). (J). (gr. 1-4). pap. 4.95 o.p. (*1-56167-050-2*) American Literary Pr., Inc.

Vanasse, Debra. Distant Enemy. 1997. 192p. (J). (gr. 5-9). 16.99 o.p. (*0-525-67549-3*) NAL.

—Out of the Wilderness. 1999. 176p. (J). (gr. 5-9). tchr. ed. 15.00 (*0-395-91421-3*, Clarion Bks.) Houghton Mifflin Co. Trade & Reference Div.

Wakeland, Marcia A. The Big Fish: An Alaskan Fairy Tale. 1993. (Illus.). 32p. (J). (ps-4). 14.95 (*0-9635083-1-8*) Misty Mountain Publishing Co.

Warbelow, Willy Lou & Warbelow-Tack, Cyndie, illus. The Guffinys Too. 1999. 104p. (J). (gr. 2-6). 19.95 (*0-9618314-4-8*) Warbelow, Willy Lou.

Warner, Gertrude Chandler. The Mystery of the Black Raven. 1999. (Boxcar Children Special Ser.: No. 12). (Illus.). (J). (gr. 2-5). 10.00 (*0-606-18770-7*) Turtleback Bks.

Warner, Gertrude Chandler, creator. The Mystery of the Black Raven. 1999. (Boxcar Children Special Ser.: No. 12). (Illus.). 144p. (J). (gr. 2-5). lib. bdg. 13.95 (*0-8075-2988-5*); mass mkt. 3.95 (*0-8075-2989-3*) Whitman, Albert & Co.

Watson, Jane Werner. The Case of the Vanishing Spaceship. 1982. 120p. (J). 9.95 o.p. (*0-698-20547-2*) Putnam Publishing Group, The.

Weaver, Jenny. Following the Raven. 2003. 113p. (YA). (gr. 5-8). pap. 14.95 (*1-878044-91-5*) Mayhaven Publishing.

Whelan, Gloria. Silver. (Stepping Stone Bks.). (Illus.). 64p. (J). (gr. 2-4). 2004. pap. 3.99 (*0-394-89611-4*); 1988. lib. bdg. 5.99 o.s.i (*0-394-99611-9*) Random Hse. Children's Bks. (Random Hse. Bks. for Young Readers).

Wittanen, Etolin. Auke Lake Tales. 1986. (Illus.). 53p. (Orig.). (J). (gr. 3-6). pap. 5.00 (*0-911523-05-7*) Synaxis Pr.

Wold, Jo A. Gold City Girl. 1971. (Illus.). (gr. 5-8). 5.95 o.p. (*0-8075-2986-9*) Whitman, Albert & Co.

Work, Virginia. Jodi: The Secret of the Alaskan Gift. 1983. (Jodi Mystery Ser.: No. 5). 128p. (J). (gr. 7-9). pap. 2.95 o.p. (*0-8024-0274-7*) Moody Pr.

ALBERTA—FICTION

Cook, Gerri. Christmas in the Badlands. 2002. (Dinosaur Soup Ser.). (Illus.). 120p. (J). pap. (*1-895836-94-8*) Books Collective, The.

—A Penny for Albert. 2001. (Illus.). 64p. pap. (*1-895836-93-X*) Books Collective, The.

Guest, Jacqueline. Team Rivals. 2002. 104p. (J). (gr. 3-8). pap. 5.50 (*1-55028-744-3*) Lorimer, James & Co. CAN. *Dist:* Orca Bk. Pubs.

Lippincott, Joseph W. Wolf King. 1949. (Illus.). (J). (gr. 7-9). 10.00 o.p. (*0-397-30156-1*) HarperCollins Children's Bk. Group.

Lottridge, Celia Barker. Wings to Fly. 1999. (Illus.). 216p. (J). (gr. 3-7). pap. 5.95 (*0-88899-346-3*) Groundwood-Douglas & McIntyre CAN. *Dist:* Publishers Group West.

—Wings to Fly. 1997. (J). (gr. 3-7). 15.95 o.p. (*0-88899-293-9*) Publishers Group West.

Oke, Janette. Drums of Change. 2003. (Classics for Girls Ser.). (Illus.). 176 p. (J). 9.99 (*0-7642-2714-9*) Bethany Hse. Pubs.

Saunders, Susan. Kate's Secret Plan. 1998. (Treasured Horses Ser.: Vol. 6). (J). (gr. 3-7). mass mkt. 3.99 (*0-590-31658-3*) Scholastic, Inc.

—Kate's Secret Plan. l.t. ed. 1999. (Treasured Horses Collection). (Illus.). 128p. (J). (gr. 4 up). lib. bdg. 22.60 (*0-8368-2278-1*) Stevens, Gareth Inc.

—Kate's Secret Plan, 6. 1998. (Treasured Horses Ser.). (J). 10.04 (*0-606-13866-8*) Turtleback Bks.

Sohl, Marcia & Dackerman, Gerald. The Call of the Wild Student Activity Book. 1976. (Now Age Illustrated Ser.). (Illus.). 16p. (J). (gr. 4-10). pap. 1.25 (*0-88301-182-4*) Pendulum Pr., Inc.

ALGERIA—FICTION

Camus, Albert. The Guest. 1993. (Short Stories Ser.). 32p. (YA). (gr. 5-8). lib. bdg. 18.60 (*0-88682-356-0*, Creative Education) Creative Co., The.

Schlee, Ann. The Consul's Daughter. 1972. (J). (gr. 5-8). 1.29 o.p. (*0-689-30065-4*, Atheneum) Simon & Schuster Children's Publishing.

ALPS—FICTION

Bishop, Claire Huchet. All Alone. 1953. (Illus.). 96p. (J). (gr. 2-5). 15.00 o.p. (*0-670-11336-0*, Viking Children's Bks.) Penguin Putnam Bks. for Young Readers.

Brogger, Fred & Brogger, Mark. Courage Mountain: The Further Adventures of Heidi. 1989. 160p. (J). pap. 3.95 o.p. (*0-14-034354-7*, Puffin Bks.) Penguin Putnam Bks. for Young Readers.

Loredo, Betsy. Avalanche in the Alps. 2000. (Explorers Club Ser.). (Illus.). 80p. (J). (gr. 4-7). 13.95 o.p. (*1-881889-12-2*) Silver Moon Pr.

Outlet Book Company Staff. Heidi. 1988. o.s.i (*0-517-62434-6*) Crown Publishing Group.

Scalora, Suza. The Witches & Wizards of Oberin. 2001. (Ageless Bks.). (Illus.). 48p. (J). 19.95 (*0-06-029535-X*, Cotler, Joanna Bks.) HarperCollins Children's Bk. Group.

Spyri, Johanna. Heidi. 1974. (Dent's Illustrated Children's Classics Ser.). (Illus.). 327p. (J). reprint ed. 9.00 o.p. (*0-460-05013-3*) Biblio Distribution.

—Heidi Book & Charm. 2000. (Charming Classics Ser.). 432p. (J). (gr. 3-7). 6.99 (*0-694-01453-2*, Harper Festival) HarperCollins Children's Bk. Group.

Spyri, Johanna, intro. Heidi. 1978. (Nancy Drew's Favorite Classics). (Illus.). (J). (gr. 6-9). 2.95 o.p. (*0-448-14941-9*) Penguin Putnam Bks. for Young Readers.

Tudor, Andrew, illus. Heidi. 1996. 64p. (J). (gr. 2-4). 5.98 (*1-85854-285-5*) Brimax Bks., Ltd.

Ullman, James Ramsey. Banner in the Sky. 256p. (YA). (gr. 7 up). 1988. 12.95 (*0-397-32141-4*); 1954. lib. bdg. 12.89 (*0-397-30264-9*) HarperCollins Children's Bk. Group.

ALSACE (FRANCE)—FICTION

Montaufier, Poupa. One Summer at Grandmother's House. 1985. Tr. of Ete chez grand-mere. (Illus.). 32p. (J). (gr. 2-5). lib. bdg. 12.95 o.p. (*0-87614-238-2*, Carolrhoda Bks.) Lerner Publishing Group.

Roth-Hano, Renee. Touch Wood: A Girlhood in Occupied France. 1988. 304p. (J). (gr. 5-9). 16.95 o.p. (*0-02-777340-X*, Simon & Schuster Children's Publishing) Simon & Schuster Children's Publishing.

AMAZON RIVER—FICTION

Abelove, Joan. Go & Come Back. 1998. (Illus.). 192p. (J). (gr. 6-12). pap. 16.95 o.p. (*0-7894-2476-2*) Dorling Kindersley Publishing, Inc.

—Go & Come Back. 2000. (Illus.). 192p. (YA). (gr. 7-12). pap. 5.99 (*0-14-130694-7*, Puffin Bks.) Penguin Putnam Bks. for Young Readers.

—Go & Come Back. 2000. (Illus.). (J). 12.04 (*0-606-18406-6*) Turtleback Bks.

Alexander, Nina. Megan & the Borealis Butterfly. 1999. (Magic Attic Club Ser.). (Illus.). 80p. (J). (gr. 2-6). 13.95 (*1-57513-153-6*); 18.90 (*1-57513-154-4*); pap. 5.95 (*1-57513-152-8*) Millbrook Pr., Inc. (Magic Attic Pr.).

Allende, Isabel. City of the Beasts. Peden, Margaret Sayers, tr. from SPA. 2002. Tr. of Ciudad de las Bestias. 416p. (J). (gr. 5 up). 19.99 (*0-06-050918-X*); lib. bdg. 21.89 (*0-06-050917-1*) HarperCollins Children's Bk. Group.

—City of the Beasts. l.t. ed. 2002. Tr. of Ciudad de las Bestias. 400p. (J). (gr. 5). pap. 19.99 (*0-06-051195-8*) HarperCollins Pubs.

—City of the Beasts. 2004. Tr. of Ciudad de las Bestias. 432p. (J). pap. 7.99 (*0-06-053503-2*, Rayo) HarperTrade.

—La Ciudad de las Bestias. 2002. (SPA., Illus.). 416p. 19.95 (*0-06-051031-5*, Rayo) HarperTrade.

Bischof, Larry & Lowry, William B. Amazon Adventure. 1992. (Widgets Ser.). (J). (gr. 2). lib. bdg. 19.98 (*1-56239-150-X*) ABDO Publishing Co.

Blake, Richard R. A Dolphin's Tale. 2001. per. 9.95 (*0-9670242-3-4*) Thornton Publishing.

Cherry, Lynne. The Great Kapok Tree: A Tale of the Amazon Rain Forest. 2002. (Illus.). (J). 14.04 (*0-7587-2651-1*) Book Wholesalers, Inc.

—The Great Kapok Tree: A Tale of the Amazon Rain Forest. (Illus.). 40p. (J). (ps-3). 2000. pap. 7.00 (*0-15-202614-2*, Voyager Bks./Libros Viajeros); 1990. 16.00 (*0-15-200520-X*, Gulliver Bks.) Harcourt Children's Bks.

Cherry, Lynne & Plotkin, Mark J. The Shaman's Apprentice: A Tale of the Amazon Rain Forest. 1998. (Illus.). 40p. (YA). 16.00 (*0-15-201281-8*) Harcourt Children's Bks.

Gates, Phil. Terror on the Amazon. 2000. (Readers Ser.). (Illus.). 48p. (J). (gr. 2-3). pap. 3.95 (*0-7894-6638-4*); pap. 12.95 (*0-7894-6639-2*) Dorling Kindersley Publishing, Inc. (D K Ink).

Gustaveson, Dave. Amazon Stranger. 1995. (Reel Kids Adventures Ser.: Bk. 5). 160p. (J). (gr. 5-7). pap. 5.99 (*0-927545-83-7*) YWAM Publishing.

Ibbotson, Eva. Journey to the River Sea. 2002. (Illus.). 336p. (J). (gr. 4-8). 17.99 (*0-525-46739-4*, Dutton Children's Bks.) Penguin Putnam Bks. for Young Readers.

Kendall, Sarita H. Ransom for a River Dolphin. 1993. 128p. (J). (gr. 3-6). lib. bdg. 19.95 o.p. (*0-8225-0735-8*, Lerner Pubns.) Lerner Publishing Group.

Lewin, Ted. Amazon Boy. 1993. (Illus.). 32p. (J). (gr. k-3). lib. bdg. 14.95 o.s.i (*0-02-757383-4*, Simon & Schuster Children's Publishing) Simon & Schuster Children's Publishing.

Osborne, Mary Pope. Afternoon on the Amazon. 1995. (Magic Tree House Ser.: No. 6). (Illus.). 80p. (gr. k-3). (J). lib. bdg. 11.99 (*0-679-96372-3*); pap. 3.99 (*0-679-86372-9*) Random Hse., Inc.

—Afternoon on the Amazon. 1995. (Magic Tree House Ser.: No. 6). (Illus.). (J). (gr. k-3). 10.14 (*0-606-08472-X*) Turtleback Bks.

Place, Francois. A Voyage of Discovery Vol. 1: From the Land of the Amazons to the Indigo Isles. 2001. (Illus.). 144p. (YA). (gr. 3 up). 22.95 (*1-86205-213-1*) Pavilion Bks., Ltd. GBR. *Dist:* Trafalgar Square.

Russo, Robert. Miaya's Amazon Adventure. 2000. 100p. (YA). (gr. 5-12). E-Book 4.95 (*0-9667911-4-2*) London Circle Publishing.

Wilhelm, Doug. Search the Amazon! 1994. (Choose Your Own Adventure Ser.: No. 149). (Illus.). 128p. (J). (gr. 4-8). pap. 3.50 o.s.i (*0-553-56392-0*) Bantam Bks.

—Search the Amazon! 1994. (Choose Your Own Adventure Ser.: No. 149). (J). (gr. 4-8). 8.60 o.p. (*0-606-06721-3*) Turtleback Bks.

Woodson, Marion. The Amazon Influence. 1994. 176p. (YA). (gr. 3-6). pap. 5.95 o.s.i (*1-55143-011-8*) Orca Bk. Pubs.

Zindel, Paul. Night of the Bat. 144p. (J). 2003. pap. 5.99 (*0-7868-1226-5*); 2001. (gr. 5-9). lib. bdg. 16.49 (*0-7868-2554-5*); 2001. (gr. 6-10). trans. 15.99 (*0-7868-0340-1*) Hyperion Bks. for Children.

Zoehfeld, Kathleen Weidner. Amazon Fever. 2001. (Road to Reading Ser.). (Illus.). 48p. (J). 11.99 (*0-307-46407-5*); pap. 3.99 (*0-307-26407-6*) Random Hse. Children's Bks. (Golden Bks.).

ANTARCTIC REGIONS—FICTION

L'Engle, Madeleine. Troubling a Star, RS. 1994. 304p. (J). (gr. 4-7). 19.00 (*0-374-37783-9*, Farrar, Straus & Giroux (BYR)) Farrar, Straus & Giroux.

Lerangis, Peter. Journey to the North Pole. 2000. (Antarctica Ser. : Vol. 1). (Illus.). 160p. (J). (gr. 4-7). mass mkt. 4.50 o.p. (*0-439-16387-0*) Scholastic, Inc.

—Journey to the North Pole. 2000. (Illus.). (J). 10.55 (*0-606-18864-9*) Turtleback Bks.

Williams, Geoffrey T. Antarctica: The Last Frontier. 1992. (Illus.). 32p. (J). (gr. 1-6). 14.95 o.p. (*0-8431-2995-6*, Price Stern Sloan) Penguin Putnam Bks. for Young Readers.

Young, Louise O. Ice Continent: A Story of Antarctica. 1997. (Habitat Ser.). (Illus.). 36p. (J). (gr. 1-4). 15.95 (*1-56899-499-0*); 19.95 incl. audio (*1-56899-502-4*, BC7005); pap. 5.95 (*1-56899-500-8*);Incl. toy. 26.95 (*1-56899-501-6*);Incl. toy. 35.95 incl. audio (*1-56899-503-2*);Incl. toy. pap. 16.95 (*1-56899-504-0*);Incl. toy. pap. 19.95 incl. audio (*1-56899-505-9*) Soundprints.

ANTWERP (BELGIUM)—FICTION

Jackson, Dave & Jackson, Neta. The Betrayer's Fortune: Menno Simons. 1994. (Trailblazer Bks.: Vol. 14). 144p. (J). (gr. 3-7). pap. 5.99 (*1-55661-467-5*) Bethany Hse. Pubs.

APPALACHIAN MOUNTAINS—FICTION

Bates, Artie A. Ragsale. 1995. (Illus.). 32p. (J). (gr. k-3). 14.95 o.p. (*0-395-70030-2*) Houghton Mifflin Co.

Borton, Lady. Junk Pile. 1997. (Illus.). 32p. (J). (ps-3). 15.95 o.s.i (*0-399-22728-8*, Philomel) Penguin Putnam Bks. for Young Readers.

Bradfield, Carl. Tecumseh's Trail: The Appalachian Trail, Then & Now. (Illus.). 137p. (Orig.). (YA). (gr. 8-12). pap. (*0-9632319-3-6*) ASDA Publishing, Inc.

Bradley, Kimberly Brubaker. Halfway to the Sky. 2003. 176p. (YA). pap. text 4.99 (*0-440-41830-5*, Yearling) Dell Bks. for Young Readers CAN. *Dist:* Random Hse. of Canada, Ltd.

Breeding, Robert L. From London to Appalachia. 1991. (Illus.). 200p. (J). (gr. 4-7). pap. 9.95 (*1-880258-03-X*) Thriftecon Publications.

Caudill, Rebecca. A Certain Small Shepherd, ERS. 1965. 9.95 o.s.i (*0-03-089755-6*, Holt, Henry & Co. Bks. For Young Readers) Holt, Henry & Co.

—Did You Carry the Flag Today?, ERS. 1995. (J). 16.95 o.p. (*0-8050-4400-0*); 1966. 9.95 o.s.i (*0-03-089753-X*) Holt, Henry & Co. (Holt, Henry & Co. Bks. For Young Readers).

Cleaver, Vera. Where the Lilies Bloom. 1986. pap. 1.25 o.s.i (*0-440-82197-5*) Dell Publishing.

Cleaver, Vera & Cleaver, Bill. Where the Lilies Bloom. (Illus.). (J). (gr. 7 up). 1991. 176p. lib. bdg. 14.89 o.p. (*0-397-32500-2*); 1989. 224p. pap. 5.99 (*0-06-447005-9*, Harper Trophy); 1969. 176p. 15.95 (*0-397-31111-7*) HarperCollins Children's Bk. Group.

—Where the Lilies Bloom. 1982. 175p. (J). mass mkt. 2.25 o.p. (*0-451-15203-4*, Signet Bks.) NAL.

—Where the Lilies Bloom. 1989. (J). 11.00 (*0-606-04364-0*) Turtleback Bks.

Dreibrodt, Stacie Champlin. Where the Lilies Bloom. 2000. (YA). 9.95 (*1-58130-634-2*); 11.95 (*1-58130-635-0*) Novel Units, Inc.

Gibbons, Faye. Emma Jo's Song. 2003. (Illus.). 32p. (J). (gr. k-3). 15.95 (*1-56397-935-7*) Boyds Mills Pr.

Houston, Gloria M. Littlejim's Gift: An Appalachian Christmas Story. 1998. (Illus.). 32p. (J). (ps-3). pap. 6.99 (*0-698-11656-9*, PaperStar) Penguin Putnam Bks. for Young Readers.

Lawrence, Mildred. Walk a Rocky Road. 1971. 187p. (J). (gr. 7 up). 6.50 o.p. (*0-15-294505-9*) Harcourt Children's Bks.

Lawson, John. You Better Come Home with Me. 1966. (Illus.). (J). (gr. 4 up). 7.95 o.p. (*0-690-90913-6*) HarperCollins Children's Bk. Group.

Lee, Mildred. The People Therein, 001. 1980. 320p. (J). (gr. 7 up). 10.95 o.p. (*0-395-29434-7*, Clarion Bks.) Houghton Mifflin Co. Trade & Reference Div.

Martin, Ann M. Belle Teal. 2004. 224p. (J). pap. 4.99 (*0-439-09824-6*, Scholastic Paperbacks); 2001. 256p. (YA). (gr. 5-9). pap. 15.95 (*0-439-09823-8*) Scholastic, Inc.

Miller, Jim W. Newfound. 1989. 256p. (J). (gr. 7 up). 14.95 o.p. (*0-531-05845-X*); mass mkt. 14.99 o.p. (*0-531-08445-0*) Scholastic, Inc. (Orchard Bks.).

Mills, Lauren A. The Rag Coat. 1991. (Illus.). 32p. (J). (ps-3). 16.95 (*0-316-57407-4*) Little Brown & Co.

Naylor, Phyllis Reynolds. Sang Spell. 224p. (YA). (gr. 5 up). pap. 4.99 (*0-8072-8294-4*); 2000. pap. 35.00 incl. audio (*0-8072-8293-6*, YYA153SP) Random Hse. Audio Publishing Group. (Listening Library).

—Sang Spell. (YA). (gr. 6-12). 2000. (Illus.). 224p. mass mkt. 4.99 (*0-689-82006-2*, Simon Pulse); 1998. 192p. 16.00 (*0-689-82007-0*, Atheneum) Simon & Schuster Children's Publishing.

—Sang Spell. 2000. 11.04 (*0-606-17828-7*) Turtleback Bks.

Rinaldi, Ann. The Coffin Quilt: The Feud Between the Hatfields & the McCoys. 1999. (Great Episodes Ser.). 240p. (YA). (gr. 5-9). 16.00 (*0-15-202015-2*, Magic Carpet Bks.) Harcourt Children's Bks.

Rylant, Cynthia. Silver Packages: An Appalachian Christmas Story. 1997. (Illus.). 32p. (J). (gr. k-3). pap. 16.95 (*0-531-30051-X*); lib. bdg. 17.99 (*0-531-33051-6*) Scholastic, Inc. (Orchard Bks.).

Samples, Mack. Doodle Bug Doodle Bug Your House Is on Fire. 1994. (J). pap. 10.00 o.p. (*0-87012-521-4*) McClain Printing Co.

—Dust on the Fiddle. 1995. 254p. (J). pap. 12.00 o.p. (*0-87012-537-0*) McClain Printing Co.

Showell, Ellen Harvey. The Ghost of Tillie Jean Cassaway. 2000. (Illus.). 128p. (gr. 4-7). pap. 9.95 (*0-595-14292-3*, Backinprint.com) iUniverse, Inc.

Smith, Doris Buchanan. Return to Bitter Creek. 2002. (J). (gr. 3-7). 19.75 (*0-8446-7212-2*) Smith, Peter Pub., Inc.

Still, James. Sporty Creek: A Novel About an Appalachian Boyhood. 1977. (Illus.). (J). (gr. 6-8). 5.95 o.p. (*0-399-20577-2*) Putnam Publishing Group, The.

Vaughn, Margaret Britton, et al. The Birthday Dolly. 2000. (Illus.). 47p. (J). pap. (*1-882845-09-9*) Bell Buckle Pr.

ARABIA—FICTION

Abu-Khalil, Shawqi. Uhibbu an Akun: Silsilat Qisas Il-Atfal, 20 vols. 1991. Set. 640p. pap. 35.90 (*1-57547-120-5*); Vol. 1. (J). pap. (*1-57547-121-3*); Vol. 2. (J). pap. (*1-57547-122-1*); Vol. 3. (J). pap. (*1-57547-123-X*); Vol. 4. (J). pap. (*1-57547-124-8*); Vol. 5. (J). pap. (*1-57547-125-6*); Vol. 6. pap. (*1-57547-126-4*); Vol. 7. pap. (*1-57547-127-2*); Vol. 8. pap. (*1-57547-128-0*); Vol. 9. pap. (*1-57547-129-9*); Vol. 10. pap. (*1-57547-130-2*); Vol. 11. pap. (*1-57547-131-0*); Vol. 12. pap. (*1-57547-132-9*); Vol. 13. pap. (*1-57547-133-7*); Vol. 14. pap. (*1-57547-134-5*); Vol. 15. pap. (*1-57547-135-3*); Vol. 16. pap. (*1-57547-136-1*); Vol. 17. pap. (*1-57547-137-X*); Vol. 18. pap. (*1-57547-138-8*); Vol. 19. pap. (*1-57547-139-6*); Vol. 20. pap. (*1-57547-140-X*) Dar Al-Fikr Al-Mouaser.

Abu Kir & Abu Sir. 1989. (J). (gr. 2-5). 8.95 o.p. (*0-86685-480-0*) International Bk. Ctr., Inc.

Applegate, K. A. Tales from Agrabah: Seven Original Stories of Aladdin & Jasmine. 1995. (Illus.). 96p. (J). (gr. 1-4). 14.95 (*0-7868-3023-9*); 14.89 (*0-7868-5038-8*) Disney Pr.

Arabian Nights. (Children's Storytime Treasury Ser.). (Illus.). 64p. (J). 4.98 o.p. (*0-7651-9672-7*) Smithmark Pubs., Inc.

Disney Staff. Aladdin: Wishful Thinking. 1997. (Disney's "Storytime Treasures" Library: Vol. 3). (Illus.). 44p. (J). (gr. 1-6). 3.49 o.p. (*1-885222-99-8*) Advance Pubs. LLC.

Disney's Aladdin. 1995. (Play Lights Bks.). (Illus.). (J). 5p. bds. o.p. (*0-307-75303-4*); 14p. bds. o.p. (*0-307-74102-8*) Random Hse. Children's Bks. (Golden Bks.).

Dixey, Kay. Judar & His Two Brothers. 1990. (Butterfly Collection). (J). (gr. 2-8). 8.95 (*0-86685-483-5*) Librairie du Liban Pubns. FRA. *Dist:* International Bk. Ctr., Inc.

Fontes, Justine. Aladdin: The Genie's Wish. 1997. (Golden Book Ser.). (Illus.). (J). pap. text o.p. (*0-307-13043-6*, Golden Bks.) Random Hse. Children's Bks.

Golden Books Staff. Thief among Us. 1997. (Golden Book Ser.). 70p. (J). (ps-4). pap. text o.p. (*0-307-03445-3*, Golden Bks.) Random Hse. Children's Bks.

Ladybird Books Staff. Aladdin & Ali Baba. 1997. (Classic Ser.). 56p. (J). 2.99 o.s.i (*0-7214-5615-4*, Ladybird Bks.) Penguin Group (USA) Inc.

Mouse Works Staff. Aladdin. 1997. (Illus.). (J). (SPA.). (*1-57082-809-1*); 7.98 (*1-57082-794-X*) Mouse Works.

Prince Jamil & Fair Leila. 1990. (J). (gr. 1-6). 9.95 (*0-86685-487-8*) International Bk. Ctr., Inc.

Riordan, James. Tales from the Arabian Nights. 1985. (Illus.). 128p. (J). (gr. 4 up). 14.95 (*1-56288-258-9*) Checkerboard Pr., Inc.

Singer, A. L., adapted by. Disney's Aladdin. 1992. (Junior Novelization Ser.). (Illus.). 64p. (J). (gr. 1-4). pap. 3.50 o.p. (*1-56282-241-1*) Disney Pr.

Thompkins, Kenny & Gallego, James, illus. Disney's Aladdin. 1992. (Illustrated Classics Ser.). 96p. (J). 14.95 o.p. (*1-56282-240-3*) Disney Pr.

Turpin, Lorna. The Sultan's Snakes. 1996. (J). lib. bdg. 11.95 (*0-85953-892-3*) Child's Play of England GBR. *Dist:* Child's Play-International.

Ulwani, Abd-al-Wahid. Uhibbu al-Madrasah, 12 vols. 1992. Set. 192p. pap. 13.95 (*1-57547-148-5*); Vol. 1. pap. (*1-57547-149-3*) Dar Al-Fikr Al-Mouaser.

ARCTIC REGIONS—FICTION

Aspen, Jean. Arctic Son: Fulfilling the Dream. 1995. (Illus.). 250p. (J). 19.95 o.p. (*0-89732-173-1*) Menasha Ridge Pr., Inc.

Baxter, Nicola. Mission to the Arctic. 2000. (Dorling Kindersley Readers). (Illus.). 48p. (J). (gr. 2-3). pap. 3.95 (*0-7894-5459-9*); pap. 12.95 (*0-7894-6095-5*) Dorling Kindersley Publishing, Inc. (D K Ink).

Bilgrami, Shaheen. Icy Antics. 2003. (Curious Creatures Bks.). (Illus.). 12p. (J). bds. 12.95 (*1-4027-0820-3*, Sterling/Pinwheel) Sterling Publishing Co., Inc.

Colfer, Eoin. The Arctic Incident. 2004. (Artemis Fowl Ser.). (Illus.). (J). mass mkt. 5.99 (*0-7868-5147-3*) Hyperion Bks. for Children.

Dwyer, Mindy. Aurora: A Tale of the Northern Lights. (Illus.). 32p. (ps up). 2000. (YA). pap. 8.95 (*0-88240-549-7*); 1997. (J). 15.95 o.p. (*0-88240-494-6*) Graphic Arts Ctr. Publishing Co. (Alaska Northwest Bks.).

Ekoomiak, Normee. Arctic Memories, ERS. 1992. (Illus.). 32p. (YA). (gr. 4-7). pap. 6.95 (*0-8050-2347-X*, Holt, Henry & Co. Bks. For Young Readers) Holt, Henry & Co.

Fuge, Charles & Hayles, Karen. Whale Is Stuck. 1993. (J). (ps-1). 14.00 (*0-671-86587-0*, Simon & Schuster Children's Publishing) Simon & Schuster Children's Publishing.

Geiger, John & Beattie, Owen. Buried in Ice: The Mystery of a Lost Arctic Expedition. 1993. (Time Quest Bks.). 64p. (YA). (gr. 8-12). pap. 6.95 (*0-590-43849-2*) Scholastic, Inc.

George, Jean Craighead. Arctic Son. (Illus.). 32p. (J). (gr. k-4). 1999. pap. 5.99 (*0-7868-1179-X*); 1997. 14.95 (*0-7868-0315-0*); 1997. lib. bdg. 15.49 (*0-7868-2255-4*) Hyperion Bks. for Children.

—Arctic Son. 1999. (J). 12.14 (*0-606-17381-1*) Turtleback Bks.

—Nutik & Amaroq Play Ball. (J). (gr. k-3). 2001. (Illus.). 40p. 15.95 (*0-06-028166-9*); 2000. 32p. pap. 5.95 (*0-06-443523-7*) HarperCollins Children's Bk. Group.

—Snow Bear. 1999. (Illus.). 32p. (J). (ps-3). lib. bdg. 16.49 (*0-7868-2398-4*) Disney Pr.

—Snow Bear. 2003. (Illus.). 32p. (J). (ps-3). pap. 5.99 (*0-7868-1733-X*) Hyperion Bks. for Children.

—The Wolf Pup Named Nutik. (J). (gr. k-3). 2001. (Illus.). 40p. 15.99 (*0-06-028164-2*); 2001. (Illus.). 40p. lib. bdg. 16.89 (*0-06-028165-0*); 2000. 32p. pap. 5.95 (*0-06-443522-9*) HarperCollins Children's Bk. Group.

George, Jean Craighead, et al. Snow Bear. 1999. (Illus.). 32p. (J). (ps-3). 15.99 (*0-7868-0456-4*) Disney Pr.

Gerber, Carole. Arctic Dreams. 1999. (Illus.). (J). (ps-2). 15.95 (*1-58089-021-0*, Whispering Coyote) Charlesbridge Publishing, Inc.

Grigg, Carol. The Singing Snowbear. 1999. (Illus.). 32p. (J). (ps-3). lib. bdg., tchr. ed. 15.00 (*0-395-94223-3*) Houghton Mifflin Co.

Heinz, Brian J. Kayuktuk: An Arctic Quest. 1996. (Illus.). 40p. (J). (ps-3). 14.95 o.p. (*0-8118-0411-9*) Chronicle Bks. LLC.

Himmelman, John. Pipaluk & the Whales. 2002. (Illus.). 32p. (J). 16.95 (*0-7922-8217-5*) National Geographic Society.

Houston, James. Frozen Fire: A Tale of Courage. (Illus.). 160p. (YA). 1977. (gr. 5-9). 16.99 (*0-689-50083-1*, McElderry, Margaret K.); 2nd ed. 1992. (gr. 4-7). reprint ed. mass mkt. 4.95 (*0-689-71612-5*, Simon Pulse) Simon & Schuster Children's Publishing.

—River Runners: A Tale of Hardship & Bravery. 1979. (Illus.). 160p. (J). (gr. 7 up). 11.95 o.s.i (*0-689-50151-X*, McElderry, Margaret K.) Simon & Schuster Children's Publishing.

—River Runners: A Tale of Hardship & Bravery. 1994. (J). 18.00 o.p. (*0-8446-6763-3*) Smith, Peter Pub., Inc.

Houston, James A. Long Claws: An Arctic Adventure. 1992. (Picture Puffin Ser.). (Illus.). (J). 10.19 o.p. (*0-606-01717-8*) Turtleback Bks.

Hoyt-Goldsmith, Diane. Angela from the Arctic. Evento, Susan, ed. 1996. (Newbridge Big America Ser.). (Illus.). 16p. (Orig.). (J). (gr. 1-3). pap. 17.95 (*1-56784-196-1*) Newbridge Educational Publishing.

—Angela from the Arctic: Mini Book. Evento, Susan, ed. 1996. (Newbridge Big America Ser.). (Illus.). 16p. (Orig.). (J). (gr. 1-3). pap. 3.95 (*1-56784-197-X*) Newbridge Educational Publishing.

Joosse, Barbara M. Mama, Do You Love Me? (Illus.). (ps). 1998. 24p. bds. 6.95 (*0-8118-2131-5*); 1991. 32p. (J). 14.95 (*0-87701-759-X*); 10th anniv. l.t. ed. 2001. 36p. (J). 17.95 (*0-8118-3212-0*) Chronicle Bks. LLC.

Kusugak, Michael Arvaarluk. Arctic Stories. 1998. (Illus.). 40p. (J). (gr. k-6). pap. 6.95 (*1-55037-452-4*); lib. bdg. 18.95 (*1-55037-453-2*) Firefly Bks., Ltd.

—Arctic Stories. 1999. 13.10 (*0-606-16482-0*) Turtleback Bks.

Lavallee, Barbara, illus. Mama, Do You Love Me? Doll & Book Set. 1993. (J). 14.95 o.s.i (*0-8118-0521-2*) Chronicle Bks. LLC.

London, Jonathan. Ice Bear & Little Fox. 1998. (Illus.). 40p. (J). (ps-2). 15.99 (*0-525-45907-3*, Dutton Children's Bks.) Penguin Putnam Bks. for Young Readers.

Luenn, Nancy. Nessa's Fish. (Aladdin Picture Bks.). 32p. (J). (gr. k-3). 1997. pap. 5.99 (*0-689-81465-8*, Aladdin); 1990. (Illus.). 15.00 (*0-689-31477-9*, Atheneum) Simon & Schuster Children's Publishing.

—Nessa's Fish. unabr. ed. 2001. (J). (gr. k-3). pap. 16.95 incl. audio (*0-8045-6844-8*, 6844) Spoken Arts, Inc.

—La Pesca de Nessa. Ada, Alma Flor, tr. 1997. (SPA., Illus.). 32p. (J). (gr. k-3). pap. 6.99 o.s.i (*0-689-81467-4*, SS7475, Aladdin) Simon & Schuster Children's Publishing.

MacGregor, Ellen. Miss Pickerell Goes to the Arctic. 1964. (Illus.). (J). (gr. 4-6). lib. bdg. o.p. (*0-07-044564-8*) McGraw-Hill Cos., The.

Settings

Matthews, Downs. Arctic Summer. 1993. (Illus.). 40p. (J). (gr. 2-5). 14.00 o.p. (*0-671-79539-2*, Simon & Schuster Children's Publishing) Simon & Schuster Children's Publishing.

Miller, Sherry C. Snowharry Takes a Vacation (with Arctic Friends) 1985. (Molly Character - Color Me Ser.: No. 4). (Illus.). 32p. (J). (gr. k-5). pap. (*0-913379-03-4*) Double M Publishing Co.

Mowat, Farley. The Snow Walker. 1976. (J). 10.95 o.p. (*0-316-58693-5*) Little Brown & Co.

Munsch, Robert. 50 below Zero. (Illus.). 24p. (J). (gr. k-3). 2003. pap. 5.95 (*0-920236-91-X*); 2003. lib. bdg. 16.95 (*0-920236-86-3*); 1993. (CHI., pap. 5.95 o.p. (*1-55037-298-X*) Annick Pr., Ltd. CAN. *Dist:* Firefly Bks., Ltd.

—50 below Zero. ed. 1993. (J). (gr. 1). spiral bd. (*0-616-01728-6*); (gr. 2). spiral bd. (*0-616-01729-4*) Canadian National Institute for the Blind/Institut National Canadien pour les Aveugles.

—50 below Zero. 1986. (Munsch for Kids Ser.). (J). 12.10 (*0-606-05098-1*) Turtleback Bks.

Oberman, Sheldon. The Shaman's Nephew: A Life in the Far North. 2001. (Illus.). 56p. (J). (gr. 4 up). pap. 13.95 (*0-7737-6189-6*) Stoddart Kids CAN. *Dist:* Fitzhenry & Whiteside, Ltd.

Rau, Dana Meachen. Arctic Adventure: Inuit Life in the 1800s. 1997. (Smithsonian Odyssey Ser.). (Illus.). (J). 32p. (gr. 1-4). pap. 5.95 (*1-56899-417-6*); 32p. (gr. 2-5). 14.95 (*1-56899-416-8*); 32p. (gr. 2-5). 19.95 incl. audio (*1-56899-423-0*, BC6005);Incl. toy. (gr. 2-5). 29.95 (*1-56899-418-4*);Incl. toy. 32p. (gr. 2-5). 35.95 incl. audio (*1-56899-421-4*);Incl. toy. 32p. (gr. 2-5). pap. 17.95 (*1-56899-419-2*);Incl. toy. 32p. (gr. 2-5). pap. 25.95 incl. audio (*1-56899-420-6*) Soundprints.

Roffey, Maureen. Polar Rescue. 1996. (Duplo Playbooks Ser.). (Illus.). 12p. (J). (ps). bds. 11.95 o.p. (*0-316-72380-0*) Little Brown & Co.

Roth, Arthur. Iceberg Hermit. 1976. 224p. (J). (gr. 7-12). reprint ed. pap. 2.25 o.p. (*0-590-01582-6*) Scholastic, Inc.

Sabuda, Robert. The Blizzard's Robe. 1999. (J). (gr. k-3). 16.00 (*0-689-81161-6*); (Illus.). 32p. 16.00 (*0-689-31988-6*) Simon & Schuster Children's Publishing. (Atheneum).

Sage, James. Where the Great Bear Watches. 1993. (Illus.). 32p. (J). (ps-3). 13.99 o.p. (*0-670-84933-2*, Viking Children's Bks.) Penguin Putnam Bks. for Young Readers.

Sis, Peter. A Small Tall Tale from Far Far North, RS. 2001. (Illus.). 40p. (J). (gr. 1-4). pap. 6.95 (*0-374-46725-0*, Sunburst) Farrar, Straus & Giroux.

—A Small, Tall Tale from the Far, Far North. 1993. (Illus.). 40p. (J). (gr. k-5). 15.99 o.s.i (*0-679-94345-5*, Knopf Bks. for Young Readers) Random Hse. Children's Bks.

—A Small Tall Tale from the Far Far North, RS. 2001. (Illus.). 40p. (J). (gr. 1-4). 17.00 (*0-374-37075-3*, Farrar, Straus & Giroux (BYR)) Farrar, Straus & Giroux.

—A Small Tall Tale from the Far Far North. 1993. (Illus.). 40p. (J). (gr. k-5). 15.00 o.s.i (*0-679-84345-0*, Knopf Bks. for Young Readers) Random Hse. Children's Bks.

Tapley, Caroline. John Come Down the Backstay. 1974. (Illus.). 192p. (J). (gr. 4-6). 1.49 o.p. (*0-689-30149-9*, Atheneum) Simon & Schuster Children's Publishing.

Taulbert, Clifton L. Little Cliff & the Cold Place. 2002. (Illus.). 32p. (J). (gr. k-3). 16.99 (*0-8037-2558-2*, Dial Bks. for Young Readers) Penguin Putnam Bks. for Young Readers.

Taylor, Theodore. Hello, Arctic! 2002. (Illus.). 40p. (J). (gr. k-2). 16.00 (*0-15-201577-9*) Harcourt Children's Bks.

Thompson, Kate. Switchers. 1999. 224p. (J). (gr. 7-12). pap. 5.99 (*0-7868-1396-2*) Disney Pr.

—Switchers. 1998. 224p. (gr. 7-12). (J). 14.95 (*0-7868-0380-0*); (YA). lib. bdg. 15.49 (*0-7868-2328-3*) Hyperion Bks. for Children.

—Switchers. 220p. (J). (gr. 4-7). pap. 5.99 (*0-8072-1553-8*); 1999. (Switchers Ser.: Vol. 1). pap. 37.00 incl. audio (*0-8072-8138-7*, YA115SP) Random Hse. Audio Publishing Group. (Listening Library).

—Switchers. 1999. 12.04 (*0-606-17387-0*) Turtleback Bks.

Turner, Bonnie. Haunted Igloo. 1991. 160p. (J). (gr. 3-7). 13.95 o.p. (*0-395-57037-9*) Houghton Mifflin Co. Trade & Reference Div.

Vyner, Sue. Arctic Spring. 1993. (Illus.). 32p. (J). (ps-3). 13.99 o.p. (*0-670-84934-0*, Viking Children's Bks.) Penguin Putnam Bks. for Young Readers.

Wiebe, Rudy. The Mad Trapper. rev. ed. 2003. (Illus.). 186p. (YA). (gr. 9 up). pap. (*0-88995-268-X*) Red Deer Pr.

Wilkinson, Stephan. Journey to the North Pole. Dupuy, Ernest, ed. 1989. (Captain Atlas & the Globe Riders Ser.). (Illus.). 48p. (Orig.). (J). (gr. 3-7). pap. 6.95 o.p. (*0-8437-3554-6*) Hammond World Atlas Corp.

Wojtowycz, David. Claude's Big Surprise. 2002. 32p. (J). 14.99 (*0-525-46844-7*) Penguin Putnam Bks. for Young Readers.

ARGENTINA—FICTION

Kalnay, Francis. Chicaro: Wild Pony of the Pampa. 1993. (Illus.). (J). 13.00 (*0-606-20598-5*) Turtleback Bks.

—Chucaro: Wild Pony of the Pampa. 1993. (Newbery Honor Roll Ser.). (J). 12.05 o.p. (*0-606-02560-X*) Turtleback Bks.

—Chucaro: Wild Pony of the Pampa. 1993. (Newbery Honor Roll Ser.). (Illus.). 115p. (J). (gr. 4-7). pap. 6.95 (*0-8027-7387-7*) Walker & Co.

—Chucaro, Wild Pony of the Pampa. 1958. (Illus.). (J). (gr. 4-6). 5.50 o.p. (*0-15-218042-7*) Harcourt Children's Bks.

Lamm, C. Drew. Gauchada. 2002. (Illus.). 40p. (J). (gr. k-3). 15.95 (*0-375-81267-9*); lib. bdg. 17.99 (*0-375-91267-3*) Random Hse. Children's Bks. (Knopf Bks. for Young Readers).

Zorzoli, Alicia. Pinafores & Pelotas. 1996. (Illus.). 24p. (J). (gr. 1-3). pap. text 3.99 (*1-56309-179-8*, N968104, New Hope) Woman's Missionary Union.

ARIZONA—FICTION

Adler, C. S. More Than a Horse. 1997. 192p. (J). (gr. 4-6). tchr. ed. 15.00 (*0-395-79769-1*, Clarion Bks.) Houghton Mifflin Co. Trade & Reference Div.

—The No Place Cat. 2002. 160p. (YA). (gr. 5-9). 15.00 (*0-618-09644-2*, Clarion Bks.) Houghton Mifflin Co. Trade & Reference Div.

Armer, Laura A. Waterless Mountain. 1980. (Illus.). (J). (gr. 5-8). 16.00 o.s.i (*0-679-20233-1*, Random Hse. Bks. for Young Readers) Random Hse. Children's Bks.

Benedict, Rex. Good Luck Arizona Man. 1972. (J). (gr. 5 up). 4.50 o.p. (*0-394-82441-5*); lib. bdg. 5.99 o.p. (*0-394-92441-X*) Knopf Publishing Group. (Pantheon).

Bly, Stephen. Daring Rescue at Sonora Pass. 2003. 144p. (J). pap. 6.99 (*1-58134-471-6*) Crossway Bks.

Bock, Shelly V. Lonely Lyla. 1992. (YA). 7.95 o.p. (*0-533-09389-9*) Vantage Pr., Inc.

Bury, Laurie D. The Adventures of Dalbert Juan: Dalbert Goes to Arizona. 2000. (Illus.). (J). (ps-2). 12.95 (*0-9702319-2-X*) Rhette Enterprises, Inc.

Campbell, Julie. The Mystery in Arizona. 2004. (Trixie Belden Ser.: No. 6). 272p. (gr. 3-7). lib. bdg. 9.99 (*0-375-92741-7*, Random Hse. Bks. for Young Readers) Random Hse. Children's Bks.

Charlie Moves to Arizona Vol. 2: Charlie's Great Adventure. 2001. 88p. (J). per. 5.95 (*0-9702546-9-5*) GoodyGoody Bks.

Dixon, Franklin W. Hot Wheels. Ashby, Ruth, ed. 1994. (Hardy Boys Casefiles Ser.: No. 91). 160p. (YA). (gr. 6 up). pap. 3.99 (*0-671-79475-2*, Simon Pulse) Simon & Schuster Children's Publishing.

—Hot Wheels. 1994. (Hardy Boys Casefiles Ser.: No. 91). (YA). (gr. 6 up). 10.04 (*0-606-06448-6*) Turtleback Bks.

Ellison, Suzanne P. The Last Warrior. 1997. (J). (gr. 7-10). 140p. pap. 6.95 (*0-87358-679-4*); 240p. lib. bdg. 12.95 o.p. (*0-87358-678-6*) Northland Publishing. (Rising Moon Bks. for Young Readers).

Golio, Janet & Golio, Mike. A Present from the Past. Anderson, David & Tronslin, Andrea, eds. 1995. (Environmental Adventure Ser.). 159p. (J). (gr. 4-6). pap. 8.95 (*0-9641330-5-9*) Portunus Publishing Co.

Golio, Janet, et al. A Present from the Past: Multimedia Edition. 2000. (Illus.). III, 157p. (J). (gr. 4-7). cd-rom 14.95 (*0-9704202-0-X*) GAGA.

Harris, Marian. Tuesday in Arizona. 1998. (Illus.). 32p. (J). (ps-3). 15.95 (*1-56554-233-9*) Pelican Publishing Co., Inc.

Henry, Marguerite. Brighty of the Grand Canyon. 2002. (Illus.). (YA). 13.40 (*1-4046-1351-X*) Book Wholesalers, Inc.

—Brighty of the Grand Canyon. Scholastic, Inc. Staff, ed. 1992. (J). pap. 2.25 (*0-590-02354-3*) Scholastic, Inc.

—Brighty of the Grand Canyon. 224p. (J). 2001. (Kids' Picks Ser.). pap. 2.99 o.s.i (*0-689-84522-7*, Aladdin); 1991. (Illus.). (gr. 3-7). lib. bdg. 15.00 o.s.i (*0-02-743664-0*, Simon & Schuster Children's Publishing); 2nd ed. 1991. (Marguerite Henry Horseshoe Library: Vol. 5). (Illus.). (gr. 3-7). reprint ed. pap. 4.99 (*0-689-71485-8*, Aladdin) Simon & Schuster Children's Publishing.

—Brighty of the Grand Canyon. 2001. (J). (gr. 3-6). 20.25 (*0-8446-7176-2*) Smith, Peter Pub., Inc.

—Brighty of the Grand Canyon. 1987. (Marguerite Henry Horseshoe Library). (J). 11.04 (*0-606-02444-1*) Turtleback Bks.

Hobbs, William. Downriver. (Complete Book of Food Counts Cookbook Ser.). (YA). (gr. 7-12). 1995. 224p. mass mkt. 5.50 (*0-440-22673-2*, Dell Books for Young Readers); 1992. 208p. mass mkt. 3.50 o.s.i (*0-553-29717-1*, Starfire) Random Hse. Children's Bks.

—River Thunder. 1997. 208p. (YA). (gr. 7-12). 15.95 o.s.i (*0-385-32316-6*, Dell Books for Young Readers) Random Hse. Children's Bks.

—River Thunder. 1999. 11.04 (*0-606-15817-0*) Turtleback Bks.

Hopkins, Suzette. Little Wolf's Christmas. 2003. (Illus.). 21p. (J). bds. 7.95 (*1-932133-72-0*) Writers' Collective, The.

Johnston, Annie F. The Little Colonel in Arizona. 1982. (YA). (gr. 5 up). 16.95 (*0-89201-033-9*) Zenger Publishing Co., Inc.

McLerran, Alice. The Year of the Ranch. 1996. (Illus.). 32p. (J). (ps-3). 14.99 o.p. (*0-670-85131-0*, Viking Children's Bks.) Penguin Putnam Bks. for Young Readers.

Mosier, Elizabeth. My Life As a Girl. (gr. 7). 2000. 204p. pap. text 12.00 (*0-375-89522-1*); 2000. 208p. mass mkt. 4.99 o.s.i (*0-375-80194-4*); 1999. 193p. (YA). 18.99 o.s.i (*0-679-99035-6*); 1999. 212p. (YA). 17.00 o.s.i (*0-679-89035-1*) Random Hse. Children's Bks. (Random Hse. Bks. for Young Readers).

—My Life As a Girl. 2000. (J). 11.04 (*0-606-19082-1*) Turtleback Bks.

Munch, Theodore W. & Winthrop, Robert D. Thunder on Forbidden Mountain. 1976. (J). (gr. 5-9). 6.95 o.p. (*0-664-32588-2*) Westminster John Knox Pr.

Papagapitos, Karen. Jose's Basket. Kleinman, Estelle, ed. 2nd ed. 1993. (JB Ser.). (Illus.). 32p. (J). (gr. 1-3). 6.95 (*0-9637328-1-1*) Kapa Hse. Pr.

Rallison, Janette. Dakota's Revenge. 1998. (J). o.p. (*1-57345-379-X*) Deseret Bk. Co.

Samantha's Arizona Adventure. 1998. (Illus.). 2p. (J). (ps-1). 15.00 (*1-888074-84-1*) Pockets of Learning.

Sandin, Joan. Coyote School News, ERS. 2003. (Illus.). 48p. (J). 17.95 (*0-8050-6558-X*, Holt, Henry & Co. Bks. For Young Readers) Holt, Henry & Co.

Sargent, Dave & Sargent, Pat. Buttons (Muddy Dun) Have Courage. 2003. (Saddle Up Ser.: Vol. 9). (Illus.). 42p. (J). lib. bdg. 22.60 (*1-56763-687-X*); mass mkt. 6.95 (*1-56763-688-8*) Ozark Publishing.

Sheafer, Silvia Anne. Tombstone Adventures for Kids. unabr. ed. 1996. (Illus.). 64p. (Orig.). (J). (gr. 4-12). pap. text 8.95 (*1-889971-01-4*) Journal Pubns.

Skurzynski, Gloria & Ferguson, Alane. Over the Edge. 2002. (Mysteries in Our National Parks Ser.: Vol. 7). 160p. (J). (gr. 3-7). pap. 5.95 (*0-7922-6686-2*);No. 7. 15.95 (*0-7922-6677-3*) National Geographic Society.

Spinelli, Jerry. Stargirl. 2003. 208p. (YA). mass mkt. 5.99 (*0-440-41677-9*, Laurel) Dell Publishing.

—Stargirl. 2002. (EMC Masterpiece Series Access Editions). xiv, 199p. (YA). 10.95 (*0-8219-2504-0*, 35378) EMC/Paradigm Publishing.

—Stargirl. unabr. ed. 2002. 192p. (YA). (gr. 5 up). pap. 40.00 incl. audio (*0-8072-0855-8*, LYA 323 SP); 2001. audio 25.00 (*0-8072-0571-0*); 2001. (YA). (gr. 5 up). audio compact disk 30.00 (*0-8072-0572-9*) Random Hse. Audio Publishing Group. (Listening Library).

—Stargirl. (YA). 2000. 192p. (gr. 5-8). 15.95 (*0-679-88637-0*, Knopf Bks. for Young Readers); 2000. 192p. (gr. 5-8). lib. bdg. 17.99 (*0-679-98637-5*, Knopf Bks. for Young Readers); 2002. 208p. (gr. 7 up). reprint ed. pap. 8.95 (*0-375-82233-X*) Random Hse. Children's Bks.

—Stargirl. l.t. ed. 2001. (Young Adult Ser.). 240p. (J). (gr. 8-12). 24.95 (*0-7862-3218-8*) Thorndike Pr.

Stewart, Jennifer J. The Bean King's Daughter. 2002. 176p. (J). (gr. 3-7). tchr. ed. 16.95 (*0-8234-1644-5*) Holiday Hse., Inc.

—If That Breathes Fire, We're Toast! 1999. 117p. (J). (gr. 2-6). tchr. ed. 15.95 (*0-8234-1430-2*) Holiday Hse., Inc.

Thoene, Jake & Thoene, Luke. Legend of the Desert Bigfoot. 1996. (Last Chance Detectives Ser.: No. 2). 131p. (J). (gr. 7 up). pap. 3.99 o.p. (*0-8423-2084-9*, Tyndale Kids) Tyndale Hse. Pubs.

—Mystery Lights of Navajo Mesa. 1994. (Last Chance Detectives Ser.: No. 1). 126p. (J). (gr. 3-7). pap. 3.99 o.p. (*0-8423-2082-2*, Tyndale Kids) Tyndale Hse. Pubs.

Vernon, Robert. Escape from Fire Lake. 1996. (Last Chance Detectives Ser.: No. 3). (Illus.). 141p. (J). (gr. 3-7). pap. 3.99 o.p. (*0-8423-2062-8*, Tyndale Kids) Tyndale Hse. Pubs.

Vick, Helen H. Tag Against Time. (Illus.). 1996. 100p. (ps up). tchr. ed. 9.95 (*1-57140-014-1*); 1955. 188p. (gr. 7 up). pap. 15.95 (*1-57140-006-0*); 1955. 128p. (gr. 7 up). pap. 9.95 (*1-57140-007-9*) Rinehart, Roberts Pubs.

Weiss, Ellen. Color Me Criminal. 1997. (Carmen Sandiego Mystery Ser.). (J). (gr. 4-6). 10.55 (*0-606-11188-3*) Turtleback Bks.

Weiss, Ellen & Friedman, Mel. Color Me Criminal. 1997. (Carmen Sandiego Mystery Ser.). (Illus.). 144p. (J). (gr. 4-6). pap. 4.50 o.s.i (*0-06-440663-6*, Harper Trophy) HarperCollins Children's Bk. Group.

Wilson, Pauline Hutchens & Dengler, Sandy. The Case of the Dinosaur in the Desert. 2001. (New Sugar Creek Gang Ser.: Vol. #4). (Illus.). 136p. (J). mass mkt. 5.99 (*0-8024-8664-9*) Moody Pr.

ARKANSAS—FICTION

Bowman, Eddie. Gravy on a Bucket Lid. 1998. (Silly Songs Ser.). (Illus.). (J). pap. 6.95 (*1-56763-430-3*); lib. bdg. 19.95 (*1-56763-429-X*) Ozark Publishing.

Branscum, Robbie. Cheater & Flitter Dick. 1983. 112p. (J). (gr. 3-7). 10.95 o.p. (*0-670-21350-0*, Viking Children's Bks.) Penguin Putnam Bks. for Young Readers.

—Johnny May. 1984. (YA). (gr. 7 up). pap. 1.25 o.p. (*0-380-00624-3*, 28951-2, Avon Bks.) Morrow/Avon.

—The Murder of Hound Dog Bates. 1982. 96p. (J). (gr. 3-7). 11.95 o.p. (*0-670-49521-2*, Viking Children's Bks.) Penguin Putnam Bks. for Young Readers.

—The Saving of P.S. 1977. (gr. 5-7). o.p. (*0-385-11270-X*); lib. bdg. 5.95 o.p. (*0-385-11271-8*) Doubleday Publishing.

—Toby, Granny & George. 1976. 112p. (gr. 3-9). 7.95 o.p. (*0-385-11269-6*) Doubleday Publishing.

Crofford, Emily. A Matter of Pride. 1991. (Illus.). 48p. (J). (gr. 2-5). reprint ed. lib. bdg. 17.50 o.s.i (*0-87614-171-8*, AACR2, Carolrhoda Bks.) Lerner Publishing Group.

—A Place to Belong. 1993. (J). (gr. 4-7). lib. bdg. 19.95 o.p. (*0-87614-808-9*, Carolrhoda Bks.) Lerner Publishing Group.

Darrow, Sharon. The Painters of Lexieville. 2003. 192p. (YA). 16.99 (*0-7636-1437-8*) Candlewick Pr.

Greene, Bette. Philip Hall Likes Me. I Reckon Maybe. 1974. (Illus.). 160p. (J). (gr. 3-6). 13.95 o.p. (*0-8037-6098-1*); 13.89 o.p. (*0-8037-6096-5*) Penguin Putnam Bks. for Young Readers. (Dial Bks. for Young Readers).

—Summer of My German Soldier. 1984. 208p. (YA). (gr. 7-12). mass mkt. 2.95 o.s.i (*0-553-27247-0*) Bantam Bks.

—Summer of My German Soldier. l.t. ed. 2000. (LRS Large Print Cornerstone Ser.). 305p. (YA). (gr. 6-12). lib. bdg. 29.95 (*1-58118-059-4*, 23473) LRS.

—Summer of My German Soldier. l.t. ed. 1989. 272p. (YA). reprint ed. lib. bdg. 16.95 o.s.i (*1-55736-134-7*, Cornerstone Bks.) Pages, Inc.

—Summer of My German Soldier. 2003. (Illus.). 256p. (J). 16.99 (*0-8037-2869-7*, Dial Bks. for Young Readers); 1999. (Illus.). 208p. (J). (gr. 5-9). pap. 6.99 (*0-14-130636-X*, Puffin Bks.); 1973. 240p. (YA). (gr. 7 up). 14.99 o.s.i (*0-8037-8321-3*, Dial Bks. for Young Readers) Penguin Putnam Bks. for Young Readers.

—Summer of My German Soldier. 1993. (YA). mass mkt. o.p. (*0-440-90056-5*, Dell Books for Young Readers) Random Hse. Children's Bks.

—Summer of My German Soldier. 2000. (YA). (gr. 6 up). 20.50 (*0-8446-7144-4*) Smith, Peter Pub., Inc.

—Summer of My German Soldier. 1999. 11.04 (*0-606-17432-X*); 1975. (YA). 10.09 o.p. (*0-606-05063-9*) Turtleback Bks.

Gyenes, Betty Traylo. Buckaroo & the Angel. 1999. (Illus.). 208p. (gr. 3-7). text 14.95 o.s.i (*0-385-32637-8*, Dell Books for Young Readers) Random Hse. Children's Bks.

Harris, Kathleen M. The Wonderful Hay Tumble. 1988. (Illus.). 32p. (J). (ps-2). 12.95 o.p. (*0-688-07151-1*); lib. bdg. 12.88 o.p. (*0-688-07152-X*) Morrow/Avon. (Morrow, William & Co.).

McNichols, Ann. Falling from Grace. 2000. 164p. (J). (gr. 6-9). 16.95 (*0-8027-8750-9*) Walker & Co.

Medearis, Mary. Big Doc's Girl. 1985. 142p. (YA). (gr. 7-12). reprint ed. pap. 9.95 o.p. (*0-87483-105-9*) August Hse. Pubs., Inc.

Rhodes, Judy C. The Hunter's Heart. 1993. 192p. (J). (gr. 5 up). lib. bdg. 14.95 (*0-02-773935-X*, Simon & Schuster Children's Publishing) Simon & Schuster Children's Publishing.

—The King Boy. 1991. 160p. (J). (gr. 5-9). text 14.95 o.s.i (*0-02-776115-0*, Simon & Schuster Children's Publishing) Simon & Schuster Children's Publishing.

Ross, Rhea B. Hillbilly Choir. 1991. 186p. (YA). (gr. 7 up). 13.95 o.p. (*0-395-53356-2*) Houghton Mifflin Co.

Sargent, Dave & Sargent, Pat. Kenny Kangaroo, 60 vols. 2001. (Animal Pride Ser.: Vol. 49). 36p. (J). lib. bdg. 19.95 (*1-56763-539-3*) Ozark Publishing.

Sargent, Dave, et al. Kenny Kangaroo. 2000. (Animal Pride Ser.). (Illus.). (J). pap. 6.95 (*1-56763-540-7*) Ozark Publishing.

Simon, Charlie M. The Arkansas Stories of Charlie May Simon. Hagen, Lyman B., ed. 1981. (Illus.). 83p. (J). (gr. 1-7). 7.95 o.s.i (*0-935304-22-3*); pap. 3.50 o.s.i (*0-935304-47-9*) August Hse. Pubs., Inc.

Summer of My German Soldier. 1999. (YA). 9.95 (*1-56137-113-0*) Novel Units, Inc.

ASIA—FICTION

Baker, Barrie. The Village of a Hundred Smiles. 2003. (Illus.). 48p. (J). (gr. 3-5). pap. 7.95 (*1-55037-535-0*) Annick Pr., Ltd. CAN. *Dist:* Firefly Bks., Ltd.

—The Village of a Hundred Smiles. 2003. (Illus.). 48p. (J). (gr. 1-5). lib. bdg. 18.95 (*1-55037-522-9*) Firefly Bks., Ltd.

Chen, Chih-Yuan. On My Way to Buy Eggs. 2003. (Illus.). 15.95 (*1-929132-49-2*) Kane/Miller Bk. Pubs.

Kilborne, Sarah S. Leaving Vietnam: The Journey of Tuan Ngo, a Boat Boy. 1999. (Ready-to-Read Ser.). (Illus.). 48p. (J). (gr. 1-4). 15.00 (*0-689-80798-8*, Simon & Schuster Children's Publishing) Simon & Schuster Children's Publishing.

—Leaving Vietnam: The Journey of Tuan Ngo, a Boat Boy. 1999. (Ready-to-Read Ser.). 10.14 (*0-606-15940-1*) Turtleback Bks.

Mason, David V. Get a Clue Hell High. 1996. (Orig.). (YA). (gr. 9 up). pap. 9.99 (*0-88092-401-2*, 4012) Royal Fireworks Publishing Co.

Place, Francois. The Last Giants. Rodarmor, William, tr. from FRE. 1993. (Illus.). 78p. (J). 15.95 (*0-87923-990-5*) Godine, David R. Pub.

—The Last Giants. 2001. (Illus.). 74p. (J). pap. 11.00 (*1-86205-289-1*) Pavilion Bks., Ltd. GBR. *Dist:* Trafalgar Square.

—Los Ultimos Gigantes. 1999. (SPA., Illus.). 78p. (J). (gr. 3 up). 16.95 (*980-257-235-7*, EK2575) Ekare, Ediciones VEN. *Dist:* Kane/Miller Bk. Pubs., Lectorum Pubns., Inc.

Pullman, Philip. The Firework-Maker's Daughter. 1999. 16.95 (*0-7540-6055-1*) BBC Audiobooks America.

—The Firework-Maker's Daughter. 1999. (Illus.). 97p. (J). (gr. 3-7). pap. 15.95 (*0-590-18719-8*, Levine, Arthur A. Bks.) Scholastic, Inc.

Stoberock, Johanna. City of Ghosts: A Novel. 2003. 256p. 23.95 (*0-393-05172-2*) Norton, W. W. & Co., Inc.

Weerusinghe, Christabel. Happy New Year in Sri Lanka. 1986. (Round the World Tales Ser.). (Illus.). 52p. (Orig.). (J). (gr. 2 up). pap. 6.50 (*0-941402-05-3*) Devon Publishing Co., Inc., The.

Welch, Sheila Kelly. Land of Another Sun. 1995. (Illus.). 138p. (J). (gr. 3-8). 16.95 (*0-9638819-2-2*); pap. 10.95 (*0-9638819-3-0*) ShadowPlay Pr.

Zhang, Song Nan. Balada de Mulan (Ballad of Mulan) 1998. (SPA., Illus.). 32p. (J). (gr. 2-4). 16.95 (*1-57227-056-X*) Pan Asia Pubns. (USA), Inc.

—The Ballad of Mulan. 1998. (Illus.). 32p. (J). (gr. 2-4). (ENG & VIE.). 16.95 (*1-57227-057-8*); (CHI & ENG., 16.95 (*1-57227-054-3*) Pan Asia Pubns. (USA), Inc.

—The Ballad of Mulan: English/Hmong. Moua, Xe S., tr. from SIT. 1998. (Illus.). 32p. (J). (gr. 2-4). 16.95 (*1-57227-058-6*) Pan Asia Pubns. (USA), Inc.

—The Legend of Hua Mu Lan. Kobylinski, Paulina & Ngan, Nguyen N., trs. 1998. (ENG & SPA., Illus.). 32p. (J). (gr. 2-4). 16.95 (*1-57227-055-1*) Pan Asia Pubns. (USA), Inc.

ASIA, SOUTHEASTERN—FICTION

Ho, Minfong. The Clay Marble, RS. 1991. 176p. (YA). (gr. 7 up). 14.95 o.p. (*0-374-31340-7*, Farrar, Straus & Giroux (BYR)) Farrar, Straus & Giroux.

—The Clay Marble. 1995. (J). 4.50 (*0-663-58510-4*) Silver, Burdett & Ginn, Inc.

Luangpraseut, Khamchong. Cambodia & Cambodians. 1995. (CAM., Illus.). 96p. (Orig.). (J). (gr. 2-5). pap. 13.95 (*1-879600-40-4*) Pacific Asia Pr.

Shusterman, Neal. Piggyback Ninja. 1994. (Illus.). 32p. (J). (ps up). 14.95 o.p. (*1-56565-105-7*) Lowell Hse. Juvenile.

Strasser, Todd & De Souza, Steven E. Street Fighter. 1994. (Illus.). 160p. (J). (gr. 4-7). pap. 4.50 o.p. (*1-55704-224-1*) Newmarket Pr.

ATHENS (GREECE)—FICTION

Ross, Stewart. Athens Is Saved! The First Marathon. 1998. (Coming Alive Ser.). (Illus.). 62p. (J). (gr. 3-5). 17.95 (*0-237-51747-7*); pap. 8.95 (*0-237-51748-5*) Evans Brothers, Ltd. GBR. *Dist:* Trafalgar Square.

Sorenson, Margo. Death of Lies: Socrates. 1998. (Cover-to-Cover Bks.). (J). 11.95 (*0-7807-6791-8*, Covercraft); pap. (*0-7891-2156-5*) Perfection Learning Corp.

AUSTRALIA—FICTION

Adams, Jeanie. Going for Oysters. 1993. (J). (gr. 2-6). lib. bdg. 15.95 (*0-8075-2978-8*) Whitman, Albert & Co.

Aldous, Allan. Bushfire. 1968. (Illus.). (J). (gr. 5-9). 4.50 o.p. (*0-200-00115-9*, 311620) HarperCollins Pubs.

Aldridge, James. The Broken Saddle. 1983. (Julia MacRae Blackbird Bks.). 128p. (gr. 5 up). 8.95 o.p. (*0-531-04579-X*, Watts, Franklin) Scholastic Library Publishing.

Andersen, Honey & Reinholdt, Bill. Don't Cut down This Tree. 1993. (Voyages Ser.). (Illus.). (J). 3.75 (*0-383-03621-6*) SRA/McGraw-Hill.

Applegate, Cathy. Red Sand, Blue Sky. 2004. (Girls First! Ser.). 142p. (J). (gr. 4-7). pap. 13.50 (*1-55861-278-5*) Feminist Pr. at The City Univ. of New York.

Arnold, Marsha D. The Pumpkin Runner. 1998. (Illus.). 32p. (J). (ps-3). 16.99 (*0-8037-2124-2*); 15.89 o.s.i (*0-8037-2125-0*) Penguin Putnam Bks. for Young Readers. (Dial Bks. for Young Readers).

Bailey, Nancy. Bound for Australia, Vol. 20. 1987. (Time Machine Ser.). 144p. (Orig.). (YA). (gr. 7-12). mass mkt. 2.50 o.s.i (*0-553-26793-0*) Bantam Bks.

—Bound for Australia. (Time Machine Ser.: Vol. 20). (Orig.). E-Book (*1-58824-450-4*); E-Book (*1-59019-085-8*) ipicturebooks, LLC.

Baillie, Allan. The Secrets of Walden Rising. 1997. 176p. (J). (gr. 5 up). 13.99 o.s.i (*0-670-87351-9*, Viking Children's Bks.) Penguin Putnam Bks. for Young Readers.

Baisley, Frederick R. The Legend of Roly Poly Peter. 1979. 7.95 o.p. (*0-533-03968-1*) Vantage Pr., Inc.

Baker, Jeannie. Window. 1991. (Illus.). 32p. (J). (ps-3). lib. bdg. 16.89 (*0-688-08918-6*); 16.00 o.p. (*0-688-08917-8*) HarperCollins Children's Bk. Group. (Greenwillow Bks.).

Balsam, Pearl. Kangaroo Girl. 1983. 45p. (J). 5.95 o.p. (*0-533-05733-7*) Vantage Pr., Inc.

Base, Graeme. My Grandma Lived in Gooligulch. (Illus.). 1995. 18p. (J). (gr. 2 up). 19.95 o.p. (*0-8109-4288-7*); 1990. 42p. (gr. 4-7). 16.95 (*0-8109-1547-2*) Abrams, Harry N., Inc.

—My Grandma Lived in Gooligulch. 1988. (Illus.). 44p. (J). (gr. k-5). reprint ed. 12.95 o.p. (*0-944176-01-1*) Terra Nova Pr.

Bernard, Virginia. Eliza down Under. 2000. (Going to Ser.). (Illus.). 96p. (J). (gr. 4-8). pap. 7.95 (*1-893577-02-3*) Four Corners Publishing Co., Inc.

Bodsworth, Nan. A Nice Walk in the Jungle. 1992. (Illus.). pap. o.p. (*0-14-054127-6*) NAL.

—A Nice Walk in the Jungle. (Illus.). (J). 1992. pap. 4.99 o.p. (*0-14-054573-5*, Puffin Bks.); 1990. 320p. 12.95 o.p. (*0-670-82476-3*, Viking Children's Bks.) Penguin Putnam Bks. for Young Readers.

Bunney, Ron. Eye of the Eagle. 1995. 156p. (YA). pap. 9.95 (*1-86368-126-4*) Fremantle Arts Centre Pr. AUS. *Dist:* International Specialized Bk. Services.

—Sink or Swim. 1999. 200p. (J). pap. 12.95 (*1-86368-238-4*) Fremantle Arts Centre Pr. AUS. *Dist:* International Specialized Bk. Services.

Calley, Karin & Pearson, Noel. Caden Walaa! 1995. (Jam Roll Picture Bks.). (Illus.). 32p. (J). 19.95 (*0-7022-2704-8*) Univ. of Queensland Pr. AUS. *Dist:* International Specialized Bk. Services.

Caswell, Brian & Chien, David Phu An. The Full Story. 2002. 216p. pap. 17.50 o.s.i (*0-7022-3299-8*) Univ. of Queensland Pr. AUS. *Dist:* International Specialized Bk. Services.

Chase, Diana. Surf's Up. 1999. 200p. (J). 12.95 (*1-86368-250-3*) Fremantle Arts Centre Pr. AUS. *Dist:* International Specialized Bk. Services.

Clark, Mavis T. If the Earth Falls In, 001. 1979. 176p. (J). (gr. 6 up). 6.95 o.p. (*0-395-28900-9*, Clarion Bks.) Houghton Mifflin Co. Trade & Reference Div.

Clarke, J. Al Capsella & the Watchdogs, ERS. 1991. 160p. (YA). (gr. 7 up). 14.95 o.s.i (*0-8050-1598-1*, Holt, Henry & Co. Bks. For Young Readers) Holt, Henry & Co.

—Al Capsella Takes a Vacation, ERS. 1993. 144p. (YA). (gr. 7 up). 14.95 o.p. (*0-8050-2685-1*, Holt, Henry & Co. Bks. For Young Readers) Holt, Henry & Co.

—The Heroic Life of Al Capsella, ERS. 160p. 1990. (YA). (gr. 6 up). 14.95 o.p. (*0-8050-1310-5*); 1997. (J). (gr. 7-12). reprint ed. pap. 6.95 o.s.i (*0-8050-5541-X*) Holt, Henry & Co. (Holt, Henry & Co. Bks. For Young Readers).

Clarke, Judith. The Lost Day, ERS. 1999. 154p. (YA). (gr. 7-12). 16.95 o.s.i (*0-8050-6152-5*, Holt, Henry & Co. Bks. For Young Readers) Holt, Henry & Co.

—Night Train, ERS. 2000. 200p. (YA). (gr. 7-12). 16.95 o.s.i (*0-8050-6151-7*, Holt, Henry & Co. Bks. For Young Readers) Holt, Henry & Co.

—Nighttrain. 2003. 180p. pap. 6.99 (*0-14-038772-2*) Penguin Group (USA) Inc.

Cleary, Jon. The Sundowners. 25.95 (*0-88411-467-8*) Amereon, Ltd.

—The Sundowners. 1973. 382p. pap. 7.95 o.p. (*0-684-13364-4*, Scribner Paper Fiction) Simon & Schuster.

Cohn, Rachel. The Steps. unabr. ed. 2003. (J). (gr. 3-7). audio 18.00 (*0-8072-1558-9*, Listening Library) Random Hse. Audio Publishing Group.

—The Steps. 2003. (Illus.). 137p. (J). (gr. 3-7). 16.95 (*0-689-84549-9*, Simon & Schuster Children's Publishing) Simon & Schuster Children's Publishing.

Collins, Alan. Joshua. 1995. 130p. (YA). pap. 14.95 (*0-7022-2809-5*) Univ. of Queensland Pr. AUS. *Dist:* International Specialized Bk. Services.

Concon, Ranulfo. Nirvana's Children. 2003. 224p. (J). 15.99 (*0-06-054155-5*, HarperTempest) HarperCollins Children's Bk. Group.

Corbet, Robert. Fifteen Love. 2003. 192p. (J). (gr. 7 up). 16.95 (*0-8027-8851-3*) Walker & Co.

Crew, Gary. Angel's Gate. 1995. 256p. (YA). (gr. 4-7). pap. 16.00 (*0-689-80166-1*, Simon & Schuster Children's Publishing) Simon & Schuster Children's Publishing.

—Mama's Babies. 2002. 160p. (J). (gr. 5-9). pap. 6.95 (*1-55037-724-8*); lib. bdg. 18.95 (*1-55037-725-6*) Annick Pr., Ltd. CAN. *Dist:* Firefly Bks., Ltd.

—No Such Country. 1994. 192p. (J). (gr. 5-9). pap. 15.00 (*0-671-79760-3*, Simon & Schuster Children's Publishing) Simon & Schuster Children's Publishing.

—The Watertower. 32p. (J). 2000. (gr. 2-9). pap. 7.95 (*1-56656-331-3*); 1998. (Illus.). (ps-6). 14.95 o.p. (*1-56656-233-3*) Interlink Publishing Group, Inc. (Crocodile Bks.).

Culton, Wilma. Down at the Billabong. 1993. (Voyages Ser.). (Illus.). (J). 3.75 (*0-383-03565-1*) SRA/McGraw-Hill.

Disher, Garry. The Bamboo Flute. 1993. 96p. (J). (gr. 4-6). tchr. ed. 15.00 (*0-395-66595-7*) Houghton Mifflin Co.

—The Divine Wind: A Love Story. (YA). 2003. 160p. pap. 5.95 (*0-439-36916-9*); 2002. 176p. (gr. 9 up). pap. 15.95 (*0-439-36915-0*) Scholastic, Inc. (Levine, Arthur A. Bks.).

Dumbleton, Mike. Dial-a-Croc. (Illus.). 32p. (J). (ps-2). 1995. mass mkt. 5.95 o.p. (*0-531-07059-X*); 1991. mass mkt. 15.95 o.p. (*0-531-05945-6*) Scholastic, Inc. (Orchard Bks.).

—Dial-a-Croc. 1995. 11.15 o.p. (*0-606-08725-7*) Turtleback Bks.

Durack, Mary & Durack, Elizabeth. Kookanoo & the Kangaroo. 1966. (Foreign Lands Bks.). (J). (gr. 2-7). lib. bdg. 3.95 o.p. (*0-8225-0356-5*) Lerner Publishing Group.

Earls, Nick. 48 Shades of Brown. 1999. 288p. (YA). (*0-14-028769-8*) Penguin Group (USA) Inc.

Elliott, Louise. Lone Bandits. 1995. 156p. (YA). 13.95 (*0-7022-2706-4*) Univ. of Queensland Pr. AUS. *Dist:* International Specialized Bk. Services.

Elmer, Robert. Captive at Kangaroo Springs. 1997. (Adventures down under Ser.: No. 2). 176p. (J). (gr. 3-8). pap. 5.99 (*1-55661-924-3*) Bethany Hse. Pubs.

—Dingo Creek Challenge. 1998. (Adventures down under Ser.: Vol. 4). 176p. (J). (gr. 3-8). pap. 5.99 (*1-55661-926-X*) Bethany Hse. Pubs.

—Escape to Murray River. 1997. (Adventures down under Ser.: No. 1). 192p. (J). (gr. 3-8). pap. 5.99 (*1-55661-923-5*) Bethany Hse. Pubs.

—Koala Beach Outbreak. 1999. (Adventures down under Ser.: Vol. 7). 176p. (J). (gr. 3-8). pap. 5.99 (*0-7642-2105-1*) Bethany Hse. Pubs.

Eversole, Robyn H. The Gift Stone. 1998. (Illus.). 32p. (J). (gr. k-3). 17.00 o.s.i (*0-679-88684-2*) Knopf, Alfred A. Inc.

—The Gift Stone. 1998. (Illus.). 32p. (J). (gr. k-3). 18.99 o.s.i (*0-679-98684-7*, Knopf Bks. for Young Readers) Random Hse. Children's Bks.

Fairbairn, John. Bindi. 1996. 96p. (J). pap. 10.95 (*0-7022-2805-2*) Univ. of Queensland Pr. AUS. *Dist:* International Specialized Bk. Services.

Farthing-Knight, Catherine. Days with Gran. (Illus.). 32p. pap. 12.95 (*0-7022-2708-0*); 1995. (J). 19.95 (*0-7022-2828-1*) Univ. of Queensland Pr. AUS. *Dist:* International Specialized Bk. Services.

Fienberg, Anna & Fienberg, Barbara. Tashi & the Big Stinker. 2001. (Illus.). 64p. (J). (gr. 2-4). pap. 5.95 (*1-86508-350-X*) Allen & Unwin Pty., Ltd. AUS. *Dist:* Independent Pubs. Group.

Foley, Louise. Australia: Find the Flying Foxes. 1989. (Earth Inspectors Ser.). 112p. (J). pap. text 3.95 o.p. (*0-07-047996-8*) McGraw-Hill Cos., The.

Fox, Mem. Possum Magic. 1987. (Illus.). 32p. (J). (ps-3). 11.95 o.p. (*0-687-31732-0*) Abingdon Pr.

French, Jackie. Somewhere Around the Corner, ERS. 11th ed. 1995. (J). (gr. 3-6). 14.95 o.p. (*0-8050-3889-2*, Holt, Henry & Co. Bks. For Young Readers) Holt, Henry & Co.

French, Simon. Where in the World. 2003. 208p. (J). (gr. 3-6). 14.95 (*1-56145-292-0*) Peachtree Pubs., Ltd.

Gascoigne, Toss, et al, eds. Dream Time. 1991. (Illus.). 192p. (YA). 13.95 o.p. (*0-395-57434-X*) Houghton Mifflin Co. Trade & Reference Div.

Germein, Katrina. Big Rain Coming. 2000. (Illus.). 32p. (J). (ps-3). tchr. ed. 15.00 (*0-618-08344-8*, Clarion Bks.) Houghton Mifflin Co. Trade & Reference Div.

Gleitzman, Morris. Blabber Mouth. 1995. 144p. (J). (gr. 3 up). 11.00 (*0-15-200369-X*) Harcourt Children's Bks.

—Blabber Mouth. 1995. 160p. (J). (gr. 3 up). pap. 5.00 o.s.i (*0-15-200370-3*) Harcourt Trade Pubs.

—Misery Guts. l.t. ed. 2003. (Illus.). (J). pap. 16.95 incl. audio (*0-7540-7867-1*, Galaxy Children's Large Print) BBC Audiobooks America.

—Misery Guts. 1995. 160p. (YA). (gr. 4-7). pap. 5.00 o.s.i (*0-15-200026-7*, Harcourt Paperbacks) Harcourt Children's Bks.

—Misery Guts. (J). 1993. 160p. (gr. 3-7). 12.95 o.s.i (*0-15-254768-1*); 94th ed. 1994. text 20.30 (*0-15-302254-X*) Harcourt Trade Pubs.

—Misery Guts. 1995. (J). (gr. 3-7). 11.05 (*0-606-07874-6*) Turtleback Bks.

—Toad Rage. l.t. ed. 2003. (J). 16.95 (*0-7540-7844-2*) BBC Audiobooks America.

—Toad Rage. 2004. 176p. (J). (gr. 3-7). 14.95 (*0-375-82762-5*); lib. bdg. 16.99 (*0-375-92762-X*) Random Hse., Inc.

—Worry Warts. 1993. 176p. (J). (gr. 4-7). 12.95 o.s.i (*0-15-299666-4*) Harcourt Trade Pubs.

Gleitzman, Morris & Levers, John, illus. Misery Guts: And, Worry Warts. 2003. 121p. (J). mass mkt. (*0-330-39103-8*) Macmillan Children's Bks.

Gray, Luli. Falcon & the Charles Street Witch. 2002. 144p. (J). (gr. 5-9). 15.00 (*0-618-16410-3*) Houghton Mifflin Co.

Gray, Nigel & Mackintosh, David. The Grocer's Daughter. 1994. (Illus.). 32p. (J). pap. 14.95 (*0-7022-2703-X*) Univ. of Queensland Pr. AUS. *Dist:* International Specialized Bk. Services.

Green, Olwyn. Winning Streak. 1993. 176p. (Orig.). pap. 11.95 (*0-7022-2500-2*) Univ. of Queensland Pr. AUS. *Dist:* International Specialized Bk. Services.

Guo, Jing Jing. Grandpa's Mask. 2001. (Illus.). 32p. (J). (*1-876615-05-2*) Benchmark Pubns. Pty, Ltd.

Hartnett, Sonya. All My Dangerous Friends. 1998. 186p. (*0-670-88027-2*, Viking) Viking Penguin.

Hausman, Gerald & Hausman, Loretta. Escape from Botany Bay: The True Story of Mary Bryant. 2003. 224p. (J). pap. 16.95 (*0-439-40327-8*, Orchard Bks.) Scholastic, Inc.

Henry, Lenny. Charlie, Queen of the Desert. 1997. (Illus.). 32p. (J). (gr. 1-3). 15.95 o.p. (*0-575-05939-7*) Gollancz, Victor GBR. *Dist:* Trafalgar Square.

Hill, Anthony. The Burnt Stick. 1995. (Illus.). 64p. (J). (gr. 4-7). 12.95 o.p. (*0-395-73974-8*) Houghton Mifflin Co.

Hirsch, Odo. Hazel Green. 2003. (Illus.). 188p. (Orig.). (J). (gr. 2-6). 15.95 (*1-58234-820-0*, Bloomsbury Children) Bloomsbury Publishing.

Honey, Elizabeth. Don't Pat the Wombat! (Illus.). 144p. 2001. (gr. 5-9). pap. text 4.99 (*0-440-41652-3*, Yearling); 2000. (YA). (gr. 4-9). lib. bdg. 16.99 (*0-375-90578-2*, Knopf Bks. for Young Readers) Random Hse. Children's Bks.

—Don't Pat the Wombat! 2001. (Illus.). (J). 10.55 (*0-606-21157-8*) Turtleback Bks.

Hulme, Joy N. Counting by Kangaroos: A Multiplication Concept Book. 1995. (Illus.). 32p. (J). (gr. k-4). text 15.95 o.p. (*0-7167-6602-7*) Freeman, W. H. & Co.

Jenkins, Wendy. Big Game. 1998. 178p. (J). pap. 12.95 (*1-86368-183-3*) Fremantle Arts Centre Pr. AUS. *Dist:* International Specialized Bk. Services.

Jennings, Paul. Undone! More Mad Endings. 128p. 1997. (J). (gr. 3-6). pap. 3.99 o.p. (*0-14-038398-0*); 1995. (YA). (gr. 5 up). 14.99 o.p. (*0-670-86005-0*, Viking Children's Bks.) Penguin Putnam Bks. for Young Readers.

—Undone! More Mad Endings. 1997. (J). 9.09 o.p. (*0-606-12028-9*) Turtleback Bks.

Kelleher, Victor. Del-Del. 1992. (YA). (gr. 7-10). 17.95 (*0-8027-8154-3*) Walker & Co.

—Micky Darlin' 1995. 276p. (YA). 14.95 (*0-7022-2801-X*) Univ. of Queensland Pr. AUS. *Dist:* International Specialized Bk. Services.

Kjelgaard, Jim. Boomerang Hunter. 1960. (Illus.). 172p. (J). (gr. 7 up). 5.95 o.p. (*0-8234-0012-3*) Holiday Hse., Inc.

Klein, Robin. The Listmaker. 1997. 218p. (J). (*0-670-87175-3*) Viking Penguin.

—The Sky in Silver Lace. 1996. 184p. (J). 13.99 o.s.i (*0-670-86692-X*) Penguin Putnam Bks. for Young Readers.

Kroll, Virginia L. & Jones, Dawn L. Kingston's Flowering Forest. 2001. (Illus.). (J). (*0-9712840-5-9*) Boyds Collection Ltd., The.

Kuchling, Guundie & Kuchling, Gerald. Yakkinn the Swamp Tortoise. 1997. (Illus.). 32p. (*1-86374-272-7*); (*1-86374-274-3*) Era Pubns.

Lang, Maud. Summer Station. 1976. 288p. 8.95 o.p. (*0-698-10732-2*) Putnam Publishing Group, The.

Lee, Julia Elizabeth. Seahorses Down Under. Weiser, Robert, ed. (Defenders of Wildlife Ser.). (Illus.). 50+p. (J). (gr. k-3). lib. bdg. 9.95 (*0-9666857-0-9*) Dawn of Day Childrens Publishing Co., Inc.

Lester, Alison. Ernie Dances to the Didgeridoo. 2001. (Illus.). 32p. (J). (ps-3). lib. bdg. 15.00 (*0-618-10442-9*, Lorraine, A. Walter) Houghton Mifflin Co. Trade & Reference Div.

—The Quicksand Pony. 1998. (Illus.). 162p. (J). (gr. 5-9). tchr. ed. 15.00 (*0-395-93749-3*) Houghton Mifflin Co.

—The Snow Pony. 2003. (Illus.). 208p. (J). (gr. 5-9). tchr. ed. 15.00 (*0-618-25404-8*) Houghton Mifflin Co.

Loder, Ann. The Wet Hat: And Other Stories from Beyond the Black Stump. 2nd ed. 1993. (Illus.). 100p. (J). (gr. 4-8). pap. 6.95 (*0-9636643-0-1*) Loder, Ann L.

Lowry, Brigid. Guitar Highway Rose. 2003. (YA). tchr. ed. 16.95 (*0-8234-1790-5*) Holiday Hse., Inc.

Lucashenko, Melissa. Killing Darcy. 1998. 230p. (YA). (gr. 8-12). pap. 13.95 (*0-7022-3041-3*) Univ. of Queensland Pr. AUS. *Dist:* International Specialized Bk. Services.

Malone, Geoffrey. Crocodile River. 2nd ed. 2002. 224p. pap. 8.95 (*0-340-86060-X*) Hodder & Stoughton, Ltd. GBR. *Dist:* Trafalgar Square.

Marchetta, Melina. Looking for Alibrandi. 1999. 256p. (YA). (gr. 7-12). pap. 16.95 (*0-531-30142-7*); lib. bdg. 17.99 (*0-531-33142-3*) Scholastic, Inc. (Orchard Bks.).

Marsden, John. Burning for Revenge. 2000. audio (*1-876584-93-9*, 591011) Bolinda Publishing Pty, Ltd.

—Burning for Revenge. 2000. 272p. (YA). (gr. 7-12). 16.00 (*0-395-96054-1*) Houghton Mifflin Co. Trade & Reference Div.

—Burning for Revenge. 2003. 274p. (J). pap. o.p. (*0-330-39070-8*) Pan Macmillan.

—Checkers. 1998. 122p. (YA). (gr. 7-12). 15.00 o.s.i (*0-395-85754-6*) Houghton Mifflin Co.

—Darkness, Be My Friend. 1999. 266p. (YA). (gr. 7-12). 16.00 (*0-395-92274-7*) Houghton Mifflin Co.

—The Dead of Night. 1997. 288p. (YA). (gr. 7-12). 16.00 (*0-395-83734-0*) Houghton Mifflin Co.

—The Dead of Night. 1999. (Laurel-Leaf Bks.). 304p. (YA). (gr. 7 up). mass mkt. 4.99 o.s.i (*0-440-22771-2*, Dell Books for Young Readers) Random Hse. Children's Bks.

—The Dead of Night. 1999. 10.55 (*0-606-16450-2*) Turtleback Bks.

—A Killing Frost. 1999. 320p. (YA). (gr. 7-12). mass mkt. 4.99 o.s.i (*0-440-22832-8*) Bantam Bks.

—A Killing Frost. 1998. 288p. (YA). (gr. 7-12). 16.00 (*0-395-83735-9*) Houghton Mifflin Co.

—Letters from the Inside. 1996. 160p. (YA). (gr. 7 up). mass mkt. 4.99 (*0-440-21951-5*) Dell Publishing.

—Letters from the Inside. 1994. 160p. (YA). (gr. 7 up). 16.00 (*0-395-68985-6*) Houghton Mifflin Co.

—Letters from the Inside. 1996. 9.09 o.p. (*0-606-09552-7*) Turtleback Bks.

—The Night Is for Hunting. 2000. audio (*1-876584-63-7*, 591113) Bolinda Publishing Pty, Ltd.

—The Night Is for Hunting. 2001. (Tomorrow Ser.). (Illus.). 278p. (YA). (gr. 7 up). 16.00 (*0-618-07026-5*) Houghton Mifflin Co.

—The Other Side of Dawn. 2002. (Tomorrow Ser.). (Illus.). 344p. (YA). (gr. 7 up). 16.00 (*0-618-07028-1*) Houghton Mifflin Co.

—Tomorrow, When the War Began. 1996. 304p. (YA). (gr. 7 up). mass mkt. 5.50 (*0-440-21985-X*) Dell Publishing.

—Tomorrow, When the War Began. 1995. 288p. (YA). (gr. 7 up). tchr. ed. 16.00 (*0-395-70673-4*) Houghton Mifflin Co.

—Tomorrow, When the War Began. 1996. 10.55 (*0-606-10954-4*) Turtleback Bks.

—Winter. (J). 2004. 160p. pap. 5.99 (*0-439-36850-2*, Scholastic Paperbacks); 2002. 144p. (gr. 7 up). pap. 16.95 (*0-439-36849-9*, Scholastic Pr.) Scholastic, Inc.

Marshall, Alan. Four Sunday Suits & Other Stories. 1975. (J). (gr. 7 up). 7.95 o.p. (*0-8407-6467-7*, Dutton Children's Bks.) Penguin Putnam Bks. for Young Readers.

Marshall, James V. Walkabout. 1992. pap. 5.75 (*0-435-27247-0*) Heinemann.

—Walkabout. 1984. 158p. (J). pap. 3.95 (*0-88741-099-5*, 6050) Sundance Publishing.

—Walkabout. 1959. 10.00 (*0-606-02369-0*) Turtleback Bks.

Massey, Barbara & DeLoach, Sylvia. Darby down Under. 2000. (Child Like Me Ser.: Vol. 4). (Illus.). (J). (gr. 2-5). 6.99 (*1-56309-766-4*, New Hope) Woman's Missionary Union.

Masson, Sophie. The Sun Is Rising. 1996. 114p. (YA). pap. 12.95 (*0-7022-2789-7*) Univ. of Queensland Pr. AUS. *Dist:* International Specialized Bk. Services.

Mathur-Kamat, Ambika. Miss Panda in Australia. 1998. (Illus.). 16p. (J). (gr. k-2). pap. 8.00 (*0-8059-4316-1*) Dorrance Publishing Co., Inc.

McVeity, Jen. On Different Shores. 1998. (Illus.). 167p. (YA). (gr. 5-9). pap. 16.95 (*0-531-30115-X*); lib. bdg. 17.99 (*0-531-33115-6*) Scholastic, Inc. (Orchard Bks.).

Metzenthen, David. Gilbert's Ghost Train. 1998. 170 p. (J). o.p. (*1-86388-852-7*) Scholastic, Inc.

Moloney, James. Touch Me. 2000. 243p. (YA). pap. 14.95 (*0-7022-3151-7*) Univ. of Queensland Pr. AUS. *Dist:* International Specialized Bk. Services.

Monson, J. Bruce. A Roo Rat's Tale. 1997. (Illus.). 64p. (Orig.). (J). pap. 16.95 (*1-56002-638-3*, University Editions) Aegina Pr., Inc.

Moriarty, Jaclyn. The Year of Secret Assignments. 2004. (YA). 16.95 (*0-439-49881-3*) Scholastic, Inc.

Morpurgo, Michael. Wombat Goes Walkabout. 2000. (Illus.). 32p. (J). (ps-3). 16.99 o.s.i (*0-7636-1168-9*) Candlewick Pr.

Morris, Gilbert. Kangaroos & the Outback - Travels in Australia No. 3: Adventures of the Kerrigan Kids. 2001. (Illus.). 144p. (J). (gr. 3-7). pap. 5.99 (*0-8024-1580-6*) Moody Pr.

Murray, Martine. The Slightly True Story of Cedar B. Hartley: (Who Planned to Live an Unusual Life) 2003. (Illus.). 240p. (J). (gr. 3-9). 15.95 (*0-439-48622-X*, Levine, Arthur A. Bks.) Scholastic, Inc.

Napoli, Donna Jo. Trouble on the Tracks. (J). 1997. 160p. (gr. 4-7). pap. 14.95 (*0-590-13447-7*); 1996. pap. (*0-590-13472-8*) Scholastic, Inc.

Olawsky, Lynn Ainsworth. Colors of Australia. 1997. (Colors of the World Ser.). (Illus.). 24p. (J). (gr. 1-4). pap. 5.95 (*1-57505-213-X*); lib. bdg. 19.93 (*0-87614-884-4*) Lerner Publishing Group. (Carolrhoda Bks.).

—Colors of Australia. 1997. (Colors of the World Ser.). (Illus.). (J). 12.10 (*0-606-21923-4*) Turtleback Bks.

Oliver, Narelle. The Best Beak in Boonaroo Bay. 1995. (Illus.). 32p. (J). (ps-3). 8.00 (*1-55591-227-3*) Fulcrum Publishing.

Orr, Wendy. Peeling the Onion. 1999. (Laurel-Leaf Bks.). 176p. (YA). (gr. 7-12). mass mkt. 4.99 (*0-440-22773-9*, Laurel Leaf) Random Hse. Children's Bks.

—Peeling the Onion. 1999. 11.04 (*0-606-15918-5*) Turtleback Bks.

Osborne, Mary Pope. Dingoes at Dinnertime. 2000. (Magic Tree House Ser.: No. 20). (Illus.). 96p. (J). (gr. k-3). pap. 3.99 (*0-679-89066-1*, Random Hse. Bks. for Young Readers) Random Hse. Children's Bks.

—Dingoes at Dinnertime, Vol. 20. 2000. (Magic Tree House Ser.: No. 20). (Illus.). 96p. (J). (gr. k-3). lib. bdg. 11.99 (*0-679-99066-6*) Random Hse., Inc.

—Dingoes at Dinnertime. 2000. (Magic Tree House Ser.: No. 20). (Illus.). (J). (gr. k-3). 10.04 (*0-606-18491-0*) Turtleback Bks.

Ottley, Reginald. Bates Family. 1969. (J). (gr. 4-6). 4.50 o.p. (*0-15-205726-9*) Harcourt Children's Bks.

—Boy Alone. 1966. (Illus.). (J). (gr. 4-7). 6.95 o.p. (*0-15-210682-0*) Harcourt Children's Bks.

—No More Tomorrow. 1971. (Illus.). 107p. (J). (gr. 7 up). 5.25 o.p. (*0-15-257495-6*) Harcourt Children's Bks.

—Roan Colt. 1967. (Illus.). (J). (gr. 5-7). 5.50 o.p. (*0-15-267700-3*) Harcourt Children's Bks.

Packham, Meg. Jake's Luck. 1995. 112p. (YA). (gr. 8-10). pap. 6.95 o.p. (*1-86373-710-3*) Allen & Unwin Pty., Ltd. AUS. *Dist:* Independent Pubs. Group.

Parry, Glyn. Monster Man. 1995. mass mkt. 4.50 o.s.i (*0-449-70444-0*, Fawcett) Ballantine Bks.

Paterson, A. B. Waltzing Matilda. 1991. (Illus.). 81p. (J). (ps-1). pap. 7.95 o.p. (*0-207-17098-3*) Collins Australia AUS. *Dist:* Consortium Bk. Sales & Distribution.

Pershall, Mary K. Hello, Barney! 1989. (Illus.). 320p. (J). (ps-3). 11.95 o.p. (*0-670-82406-2*, Viking Children's Bks.) Penguin Putnam Bks. for Young Readers.

Phipson, Joan. The Family Conspiracy. (Illus.). (J). (gr. 4-6). 1966. pap. 4.95 o.p. (*0-15-630150-4*, Voyager Bks./Libros Viajeros); 1964. 5.95 o.p. (*0-15-227110-4*) Harcourt Children's Bks.

—Six & Silver. 1971. (Illus.). 190p. (J). (gr. 4-6). 5.95 o.p. (*0-15-275330-3*) Harcourt Children's Bks.

—Threat to the Barkers. 1965. (Illus.). (J). (gr. 4-6). 4.95 o.p. (*0-15-286310-9*) Harcourt Children's Bks.

Platt, Pamela. Pig with a View. 1995. (Illus.). 80p. (J). (gr. 2-6). pap. 11.95 (*0-7022-2589-4*) Univ. of Queensland Pr. AUS. *Dist:* International Specialized Bk. Services.

—Rock & Roll Rainforest. 1996. 110p. (J). pap. 10.95 (*0-7022-2773-0*) Univ. of Queensland Pr. AUS. *Dist:* International Specialized Bk. Services.

Plourde, Josee. Un Colis pour l'Australie. 1999. (Premier Roman Ser.). (FRE., Illus.). 64p. (J). (gr. 2-5). pap. 8.95 (*2-89021-345-5*) La Courte Echelle CAN. *Dist:* Firefly Bks., Ltd.

Pople, Maureen. A Nugget of Gold, ERS. 1989. 192p. (YA). (gr. 9 up). 13.95 o.p. (*0-8050-0984-1*, Holt, Henry & Co. Bks. For Young Readers) Holt, Henry & Co.

Robinson, David. The Australian Cowboy & the Big Storm. 2002. (Illus.). 20p. (J). pap. 7.95 (*0-9718091-0-0*) Robinson Pubs.

Roth, Susan L. The Biggest Frog in Australia. (Illus.). (J). (ps-3). 2000. 32p. pap. 5.99 (*0-689-83314-8*, Aladdin); 1996. 32p. per. 15.00 (*0-689-80490-3*, Simon & Schuster Children's Publishing); 1996. mass mkt. 15.00 o.s.i (*0-671-50134-8*, Simon & Schuster Children's Publishing) Simon & Schuster Children's Publishing.

Roy, Thomas. The Curse of the Turtle. 1977. (J). (gr. 5 up). 6.95 o.p. (*0-529-05502-3*) Putnam Publishing Group, The.

Rubinstein, Gillian. Foxspell. 1996. 224p. (YA). (gr. 7 up). 16.00 (*0-689-80602-7*, Simon & Schuster Children's Publishing) Simon & Schuster Children's Publishing.

Saunders, G. K., et al, contrib. by. Maggie Jackson's Kid. 1998. 207p. pap. 14.50 (*0-85575-318-8*) Aboriginal Studies Pr. AUS. *Dist:* International Specialized Bk. Services.

Savage, Cindy. Danger down Under. 1992. 128p. (J). (gr. 5-8). pap. 2.99 o.p. (*0-87406-589-5*) Darby Creek Publishing.

Scott, Bill. Darkness under the Hills. 1981. (Illus.). (J). (gr. 7 up). 9.95 o.p. (*0-19-554274-6*) Oxford Univ. Pr., Inc.

Scott, Mark. Nell of the Seas. 2002. (Illus.). 160p. (YA). 32.50 (*1-85776-680-6*) Book Guild, Ltd. GBR. *Dist:* Trans-Atlantic Pubns., Inc.

Sharp, Donna. Holding On. 1994. 137p. (J). pap. 12.95 (*0-7022-2682-3*) Univ. of Queensland Pr. AUS. *Dist:* International Specialized Bk. Services.

Sheehan, Patty. Kylie's Concert. 1993. (Key Concepts in Personal Development Ser.). (Illus.). 32p. (J). 16.95 (*1-55942-046-4*, 7655); 79.95 incl. VHS (*1-55942-049-9*, 9374) Marsh Media.

Singer, Marilyn. The Company of Crows: A Book of Poems. 2002. (Illus.). 48p. (J). (gr. k-4). lib. bdg., tchr. ed. 16.00 (*0-618-08340-5*, Clarion Bks.) Houghton Mifflin Co. Trade & Reference Div.

Smith, Gordon. The Galleon of Fickle Bay. 1984. (Illus.). (J). 8.95 o.p. (*0-533-05780-9*) Vantage Pr., Inc.

Smith, Roland. Walkabout. 2001. 224p. (J). lib. bdg. 16.49 (*0-7868-2506-5*) Hyperion Pr.

Spillman, David. Yellow-Eye. 2001. (Illus.). 32p. (J). (gr. 2-4). 15.95 (*1-56656-410-7*, Crocodile Bks.) Interlink Publishing Group, Inc.

Stafford, Liliana. Chiko: Through the Starting Flags. 2001. (Illus.). 180p. pap. 12.95 (*1-876268-51-4*) Univ. of Western Australia Pr. AUS. *Dist:* International Specialized Bk. Services.

—Chiko Bk. 2: A Race Is Run. 2001. (Illus.). 128p. pap. 12.95 (*1-876268-52-2*) Univ. of Western Australia Pr. AUS. *Dist:* International Specialized Bk. Services.

Syme, Marguerite Hann. Chickpea. 1998. 64p. (*1-86388-642-7*) Scholastic Australia.

Thiele, Colin. February Dragon. 1976. 160p. (J). (gr. 5 up). lib. bdg. 10.89 o.p. (*0-06-026093-9*) Harper-Collins Pubs.

—The Hammerhead Light. 1977. (gr. 5 up). (J). lib. bdg. 6.89 o.p. (*0-06-026117-X*); (YA). 12.95 (*0-06-026116-1*) HarperCollins Children's Bk. Group.

—Rotten Egg Paterson to the Rescue. 1991. (Illus.). 144p. (J). (gr. 4-7). 13.95 (*0-06-026104-8*); lib. bdg. 13.89 o.p. (*0-06-026105-6*) HarperCollins Children's Bk. Group.

—The Shadow on the Hills. 1978. (YA). (gr. 7-9). 13.95 (*0-06-026126-9*) HarperCollins Children's Bk. Group.

Walker, Kate. Peter. 1993. 176p. (YA). (gr. 8 up). 13.95 o.p. (*0-395-64722-3*) Houghton Mifflin Co.

Walters, Celeste. The Killing of Mud-Eye. 1997. 200p. (YA). pap. 12.95 (*0-7022-2930-X*) Univ. of Queensland Pr. AUS. *Dist:* International Specialized Bk. Services.

Ward, Helen. Old Shell, New Shell: A Coral Reef Tale. 2002. (Illus.). 40p. (J). (gr. k-2). 24.90 (*0-7613-2708-8*); 17.95 (*0-7613-1635-3*) Millbrook Pr., Inc.

Weir, Bob & Weir, Wendy. Baru Bay: Australia. l.t. ed. 1995. (Illus.). 40p. (J). (ps-3). 19.95 incl. audio (*1-56282-622-0*); lib. bdg. 15.49 (*1-56282-623-9*) Hyperion Bks. for Children.

Wilton, Elizabeth. Riverboat Family, RS. 1969. 224p. (J). (gr. 7 up). 3.75 o.p. (*0-374-36336-6*, Farrar, Straus & Giroux (BYR)) Farrar, Straus & Giroux.

Winch, John. The Old Man Who Loved to Sing. 1996. (Illus.). 40p. (J). (ps-2). pap. 14.95 (*0-590-22640-1*) Scholastic, Inc.

—The Old Woman Who Loved to Read. 1997. (Illus.). 32p. (J). (ps-3). tchr. ed. 16.95 (*0-8234-1281-4*) Holiday Hse., Inc.

Winton, Tim. Lockie Leonard, Scumbuster. 1999. 140p. (J). (gr. 5-9). 16.00 (*0-689-82247-2*, McElderry, Margaret K.) Simon & Schuster Children's Publishing.

Woodhouse, Jena. Metis: The Octopus & the Olive Tree. 1994. (Illus.). 96p. (J). pap. 10.95 (*0-7022-2740-4*) Univ. of Queensland Pr. AUS. *Dist:* International Specialized Bk. Services.

Wrightson, Patricia. Balyet. 1990. 128p. (J). pap. 3.95 o.s.i (*0-14-034339-3*, Puffin Bks.) Penguin Putnam Bks. for Young Readers.

—Balyet. 1989. 144p. (YA). (gr. 7 up). lib. bdg. 13.95 o.s.i (*0-689-50468-3*, McElderry, Margaret K.) Simon & Schuster Children's Publishing.

—The Dark Bright Water. 1979. 240p. (J). (gr. 7 up). 7.95 o.p. (*0-689-50122-6*, McElderry, Margaret K.) Simon & Schuster Children's Publishing.

—Feather Star. 1963. (Illus.). (J). (gr. 7 up). 4.95 o.p. (*0-15-227501-0*) Harcourt Children's Bks.

—A Little Fear. 1987. 112p. (J). (gr. 5-7). pap. 3.95 o.p. (*0-14-031847-X*, Puffin Bks.) Penguin Putnam Bks. for Young Readers.

Yasas, Kathleen. Australian Fly. 1998. (Illus.). 48p. (J). (gr. k-5). pap. 12.95 (*0-9667146-0-1*, FLY001) Ivy Editorial Services, Inc.

Zindel, Paul. Reef of Death. 1999. 192p. (J). pap. 5.99 (*0-7868-1408-X*) Disney Pr.

—Reef of Death. 1998. (Illus.). 192p. (J). (gr. 3 up). 15.95 (*0-06-024728-2*); (gr. 6-10). lib. bdg. 15.89 (*0-06-024733-9*) HarperCollins Children's Bk. Group.

—Reef of Death. 1999. 12.04 (*0-606-16669-6*) Turtleback Bks.

AUSTRIA—FICTION

Bell, Mary Reeves. Secret of Mezuzah. 1999. (Passport to Danger Ser.: Vol. 1). 208p. (J). (gr. 7-12). pap. 5.99 o.p. (*1-55661-549-3*) Bethany Hse. Pubs.

—Secret of Mezuzah. 1999. (J). 12.04 (*0-606-18974-2*) Turtleback Bks.

Dahlberg, Maurine E. Play to the Angel. 2002. 192p. (J). pap. 5.99 (*0-14-230145-0*, Puffin Bks.) Penguin Putnam Bks. for Young Readers.

Denenberg, Barry. Elisabeth of Austria. 2003. (Royal Diaries Ser.). (Illus.). 144p. (J). 10.95 (*0-439-26644-0*, Scholastic Pr.) Scholastic, Inc.

—One Eye Laughing, the Other Weeping: The Diary of Julie Weiss, Vienna, Austria to New York, 1938. (Dear America Ser.). 2002. (YA). E-Book 4.50 (*0-439-42545-X*); 2000. (Illus.). 250p. (J). (gr. 4-9). pap. 12.95 (*0-439-09518-2*) Scholastic, Inc.

Duncan, Kathleen M. Sally & the Shepherdess. 1979. (Pathfinder Ser.). (Illus.). (J). (gr. 2-6). reprint ed. pap. 2.95 o.p. (*0-310-37801-X*) Zondervan.

Hartling, Peter. Crutches. Crawford, Elizabeth D., tr. from GER. 1988. 160p. (J). (gr. 4-7). 12.95 (*0-688-07991-1*) HarperCollins Children's Bk. Group.

Koss, Amy Goldman. Stolen Words. 2001. (American Girls Collection Ser.). (Illus.). 156p. (J). 14.95 (*1-58485-377-8*); pap. 5.95 (*1-58485-376-X*) Pleasant Co. Pubns. (American Girl).

—Stolen Words. 2001. 12.00 (*0-606-22775-X*) Turtleback Bks.

Nostlinger, Christine. Girl Missing. Bell, Anthea, tr. 1976. (ENG & GER.). 144p. (gr. 6 up). lib. bdg. 5.90 o.p. (*0-531-00346-9*, Watts, Franklin) Scholastic Library Publishing.

Orgel, Doris. The Devil in Vienna. 1978. (YA). (gr. 7 up). 8.95 o.p. (*0-8037-1920-5*, Dial Bks. for Young Readers) Penguin Putnam Bks. for Young Readers.

Walters, Celeste. The Last Race. 2000. (UQP Young Adult Fiction Ser.). 208p. (J). pap. 16.95 (*0-7022-3172-X*) Univ. of Queensland Pr. AUS. *Dist:* International Specialized Bk. Services.

B

BABYLONIA—FICTION

Lattimore, Deborah Nourse. Winged Cat: And Other Tales of Ancient Civilization. 2002. (Illus.). 80p. (J). pap. 4.25 (*0-06-442154-6*, Harper Trophy) HarperCollins Children's Bk. Group.

BAFFIN ISLAND (N.W.T.)—FICTION

Keep, Linda Lowery. Trouble on Ice. 1999. (Hannah & the Angels Ser.: No. 7). (Illus.). 144p. (YA). (gr. 5-8). pap. 3.99 o.s.i (*0-375-80112-X*, Random Hse. Bks. for Young Readers) Random Hse. Children's Bks.

BAHAMAS—FICTION

Baglio, Ben M. Riding the Storm. 2002. (Dolphin Diaries: No. 3). 176p. (J). mass mkt. 4.99 (*0-439-31949-8*) Scholastic, Inc.

Bothwell, Jean. Secret in the Wall. 1971. (J). (gr. 5-9). 7.95 o.p. (*0-200-00044-6*, B74240) Criterion Bks., Inc.

Cooper, Susan. Green Boy. 2002. (Illus.). 208p. (J). (gr. 4-6). 16.00 (*0-689-84751-3*, McElderry, Margaret K.) Simon & Schuster Children's Publishing.

—Green Boy. 2003. (Illus.). 208p. (J). pap. 4.99 (*0-689-84760-2*, Aladdin) Simon & Schuster Children's Publishing.

Dorris, Michael. Morning Girl. 80p. 1994. (YA). (gr. 4-7). pap. 4.95 (*1-56282-661-1*); 1992. (J). 12.95 o.p. (*1-56282-284-5*); 1992. (YA). (gr. 3 up). lib. bdg. 13.49 o.s.i (*1-56282-285-3*) Hyperion Bks. for Children.

—Morning Girl. 1999. 80p. (J). (gr. 4 up). pap. text 4.99 (*0-7868-1372-5*); mass mkt. 4.99 (*0-7868-1358-X*) Hyperion Pr.

—Morning Girl. 1994. (J). 11.14 (*0-606-06583-0*) Turtleback Bks.

Grover, Wayne. Dolphin Freedom. (Illus.). 112p. (J). 2000. (gr. 5 up). pap. 4.95 (*0-380-73305-6*, Harper Trophy); 1999. (gr. 3-7). 15.00 (*0-688-16010-7*, Greenwillow Bks.) HarperCollins Children's Bk. Group.

—Dolphin Freedom. 2000. (Illus.). (J). 11.10 (*0-606-18900-9*) Turtleback Bks.

Noronha, Francis P. The Magic Tree House. 1986. 42p. (J). (gr. 3-5). 4.95 o.p. (*0-533-06888-6*) Vantage Pr., Inc.

Oleksy, Walter. The Pirates of Deadman's Cay. 1982. (Hiway Book). (Illus.). 112p. (J). (gr. 7-9). 9.95 o.p. (*0-664-32693-5*) Westminster John Knox Pr.

Robertson, Barbara. Rosemary & the Island Treasure: Back to 1947. 2001. (Hourglass Adventures Ser.: Bk. 4). (Illus.). 128p. (J). (gr. 3-5). pap. 4.95 (*1-890817-58-9*) Winslow Pr.

Shaw, Cynthia. Grouper Moon. 1999. (Illus.). ix, 151p. (J). pap. 9.95 (*0-9670595-2-6*) Aurelia Pr.

BAJA CALIFORNIA (MEXICO)—FICTION

Barron, T. A. The Merlin Effect. 1996. (Lost Years of Merlin Ser.). 256p. (YA). mass mkt. 5.99 (*0-8125-5169-9*, Tor Bks.) Doherty, Tom Assocs., LLC.

—The Merlin Effect. 1994. 280p. (J). (gr. 5-9). 19.99 (*0-399-22689-3*, Philomel) Penguin Putnam Bks. for Young Readers.

—The Merlin Effect. 1996. 12.04 (*0-606-11618-4*) Turtleback Bks.

Bonham, Frank. Vagabundos. 1969. (J). (gr. 7 up). 7.95 o.p. (*0-525-41925-X*, Dutton) Dutton/Plume.

de Trevino, Elizabeth Borton. El Guero: A True Adventure Story, RS. 1989. (Illus.). 112p. (J). (gr. 3 up). 14.00 o.p. (*0-374-31995-2*, Farrar, Straus & Giroux (BYR)) Farrar, Straus & Giroux.

Gill, Shelley. Big Blue. 2003. (Illus.). 32p. (J). 15.95 (*1-57091-352-8*) Charlesbridge Publishing, Inc.

Taylor, Theodore. Sweet Friday Island. 1994. 192p. (YA). (gr. 7 up). 10.95 (*0-15-200009-7*); pap. 6.00 (*0-15-200012-7*, Harcourt Paperbacks) Harcourt Children's Bks.

—Sweet Friday Island. 1994. 10.10 o.p. (*0-606-06777-9*) Turtleback Bks.

BALINOR (IMAGINARY PLACE)—FICTION

Stanton, Mary. By Moonlight, by Fire. 1999. (Unicorns of Balinor Ser.: No. 4). 144p. (J). (gr. 3-7). mass mkt. 4.50 (*0-439-06283-7*) Scholastic, Inc.

—Night of the Shifter's Moon. 2000. (Unicorns of Balinor Ser.: Vol. 7). (Illus.). 144p. (J). (gr. 3-7). mass mkt. 4.50 (*0-439-16786-8*) Scholastic, Inc.

—The Road to Balinor. 1999. (Unicorns of Balinor Ser.: No. 1). 160p. (J). (gr. 3-7). mass mkt. 4.50 (*0-439-06280-2*) Scholastic, Inc.

—The Road to Balinor. 1999. (Unicorns of Balinor Ser.: No. 1). 10.55 (*0-606-17550-4*) Turtleback Bks.

—Shadows Over Balinor. 2000. (Unicorns of Balinor Ser.: Bk. 8). (Illus.). 144p. (J). (gr. 4-7). mass mkt. 4.50 (*0-439-16787-6*) Scholastic, Inc.

—Sunchaser's Quest. 1999. (Unicorns of Balinor Ser.: No. 2). 160p. (J). (gr. 3-7). mass mkt. 4.50 (*0-439-06281-0*) Scholastic, Inc.

—Sunchaser's Quest. 1999. (Unicorns of Balinor Ser.: No. 2). 10.55 (*0-606-17551-2*) Turtleback Bks.

—Valley of Fear. 1999. (Unicorns of Balinor Ser.: No. 3). (J). (gr. 3-7). mass mkt. 4.50 (*0-439-06282-9*) Scholastic, Inc.

—Valley of Fear. 1999. (Unicorns of Balinor Ser.: No. 3). 10.55 (*0-606-17552-0*) Turtleback Bks.

BALTIMORE (MD.)—FICTION

Agle, Nan H. Maple Street, 001. 1979. (Illus.). (J). (gr. 3-7). 6.95 o.p. (*0-395-28838-X*, Clarion Bks.) Houghton Mifflin Co. Trade & Reference Div.

Eichelberger, Rosa K. Big Fire in Baltimore. 1979. (Illus.). (J). (gr. 3 up). 11.95 o.p. (*0-916144-36-4*); pap. 7.95 o.p. (*0-916144-37-2*) Stemmer Hse. Pubs., Inc.

Fuqua, Jonathon Scott. The Reappearance of Sam Webber. 1999. (Illus.). 232p. (YA). 23.95 (*1-890862-03-7*) Bancroft Pr.

—The Reappearance of Sam Webber. 2001. (Illus.). 288p. (J). reprint ed. bds. 9.99 (*0-7636-1424-6*) Candlewick Pr.

Gurganus, Allan. Breathing Lessons. 1981. 16p. (Orig.). pap. 3.00 o.p. (*0-933598-01-7*) North Carolina Wesleyan College Pr.

Hahn, Mary Downing. Anna All Year Round. 2001. (Illus.). 144p. (J). (gr. 4-7). pap. 4.95 (*0-380-73317-X*, Harper Trophy) HarperCollins Children's Bk. Group.

—Anna All Year Round. 2001. (Illus.). (J). 11.00 (*0-606-21037-7*) Turtleback Bks.

—Anna All Year Round. 1999. (Illus.). 144p. (J). (gr. 4-6). tchr. ed. 15.00 (*0-395-86975-7*, Clarion Bks.) Houghton Mifflin Co. Trade & Reference Div.

Howard, Elizabeth Fitzgerald. Aunt Flossie's Hats (& Crab Cakes Later) 1991. (Illus.). 32p. (J). (ps-1). tchr. ed. 16.00 o.s.i (*0-395-54682-6*) Houghton Mifflin Co.

—Aunt Flossie's Hats (& Crab Cakes Later) 1991. 13.10 (*0-606-07214-4*) Turtleback Bks.

—Aunt Flossie's Hats (And Crab Cakes Later) 1995. (Illus.). 32p. (J). (ps-3). pap. 6.95 (*0-395-72077-X*, Clarion Bks.) Houghton Mifflin Co. Trade & Reference Div.

—Aunt Flossie's Hats (and Crab Cakes Later) 10th anniv. ed. 2001. (Illus.). 40p. (J). (ps-3). lib. bdg., tchr. ed. 16.00 (*0-618-12038-6*, Clarion Bks.) Houghton Mifflin Co. Trade & Reference Div.

—Chita's Christmas Tree. (Illus.). 32p. (J). (ps-2). 1989. lib. bdg. 14.95 (*0-02-744621-2*, Simon & Schuster Children's Publishing); 1993. reprint ed. pap. 5.99 (*0-689-71739-3*, Aladdin) Simon & Schuster Children's Publishing.

Howard, Elizabeth Fitzgerald & Lucas, Cedric. What's in Aunt Mary's Room? 1996. (Illus.). 32p. (J). (ps-3). lib. bdg., tchr. ed. 16.00 (*0-395-69845-6*, Clarion Bks.) Houghton Mifflin Co. Trade & Reference Div.

Jackson, Kamichi. You're Too Much, Reggie Brown. l.t. ed. 2000. (Illus.). 110p. (J). (gr. 2-5). pap. 5.95 (*0-615-11287-0*) Shug' n Spice Pr.

Lehne, Judith Logan. When the Ragman Sings. 1993. 128p. (J). (gr. 3-7). 14.00 (*0-06-023316-8*); lib. bdg. 13.89 (*0-06-023317-6*) HarperCollins Children's Bk. Group.

Reeder, Carolyn. Before the Creeks Ran Red. 2003. 384p. (J). (gr. 5 up). 16.99 (*0-06-623615-0*); lib. bdg. 17.89 (*0-06-623616-9*) HarperCollins Pubs.

Tyler, Anne. Breathing Lessons. 1998. 336p. pap. 14.00 (*0-425-16313-X*); 1989. 352p. mass mkt. 7.99 (*0-425-11774-X*) Berkley Publishing Group.

—Breathing Lessons. 1990. 4.99 o.p. (*0-517-05699-2*) Random Hse. Value Publishing.

—Breathing Lessons. 1998. 19.05 (*0-606-21885-8*) Turtleback Bks.

Williams, Barbara. Making Waves. 2000. (Illus.). 215p. (J). (gr. 4-8). 17.99 o.s.i (*0-8037-2515-9*, Dial Bks. for Young Readers) Penguin Putnam Bks. for Young Readers.

BARBADOS—FICTION

Chastain, Madye L. Magic Island. 1964. (Illus.). (J). (gr. 3-7). 4.50 o.p. (*0-15-250871-6*) Harcourt Children's Bks.

Gantos, Jack. Jack's New Power: Stories from a Caribbean Year, RS. (J). 1997. 224p. (gr. 5-9). pap. 5.95 (*0-374-43715-7*, Sunburst); 1995. E-Book 4.95 (*0-374-70052-4*, Farrar, Straus & Giroux (BYR)); 1995. E-Book 4.95 (*0-374-70053-2*, Farrar, Straus & Giroux (BYR)); 1995. 224p. (gr. 5-9). 16.00 (*0-374-33657-1*, Farrar, Straus & Giroux (BYR)) Farrar, Straus & Giroux.

—Jack's New Power: Stories from a Caribbean Year. 1997. 11.00 (*0-606-13532-4*) Turtleback Bks.

Jackson, Carl. Nor the Battle to the Strong. 1997. 352p. pap. 16.95 (*0-948833-97-1*) Peepal Tree Pr., Ltd. GBR. *Dist:* Independent Pubs. Group, Paul & Co. Pubs. Consortium, Inc.

Thomas, Dawn C. A Bicycle from Bridgetown. 1975. (Illus.). 64p. (J). (gr. 4-6). lib. bdg. o.p. (*0-07-064255-9*) McGraw-Hill Cos., The.

BELGIUM—FICTION

Breslin, Theresa. Remembrance. 304p. (YA). 2004. (gr. 7). mass mkt. 6.50 (*0-440-23778-5*, Laurel Leaf); 2002. lib. bdg. 18.99 (*0-385-90067-8*, Delacorte Bks. for Young Readers); 2002. (gr. 7 up). 16.95 (*0-385-73015-2*, Delacorte Bks. for Young Readers) Random Hse. Children's Bks.

Moeyaert, Bart. Bare Hands. Colmer, David, tr. 1998. 112p. (J). (gr. 5-9). 14.95 (*1-886910-32-4*) Front Street, Inc.

Ouida. A Dog of Flanders. 1992. (Illus.). 80p. (J). reprint ed. pap. 1.00 (*0-486-27087-4*) Dover Pubns., Inc.

Simoen, Jan. What about Anna? Nieuwenhuizen, John, tr. from DUT. 2002. (Illus.). 264p. (J). (gr. 7 up). 16.95 (*0-8027-8808-4*) Walker & Co.

Van Heerde, Gerrit. The Man with the Red Beard. 2002. (J). (*0-9579517-0-1*) Inheritance Pubns.

BERLIN (GERMANY)—FICTION

Hoobler, Dorothy & Hoobler, Thomas. The 1930s: Directions. 2000. (Century Kids Ser.). (Illus.). 160p. (YA). (gr. 5-8). 22.90 (*0-7613-1603-5*) Millbrook Pr., Inc.

—The 1930s: Directions. 2000. E-Book 21.90 (*0-585-34213-X*) netLibrary, Inc.

Kastner, Erich. Emil & the Detectives. 1930. (gr. 2-6). 5.95 o.p. (*0-385-07289-9*) Doubleday Publishing.

Lutzeier, Elizabeth. The Wall. 1992. 160p. (J). (gr. 5-9). 14.95 o.p. (*0-8234-0987-2*) Holiday Hse., Inc.

BERMUDA ISLANDS—FICTION

Weise, Selene H. C. Gold for a Boat. 2001. (Illus.). 68p. (J). (gr. 1-6). 5.95 (*1-57249-270-8*, Burd Street Pr.) White Mane Publishing Co., Inc.

BOLIVIA—FICTION

Holzwarth, Werner. I'm Jose & I'm Okay: Three Stories from Bolivia. McKenna, Laura, tr. from GER. 1999. Orig. Title: Ich Heibe Jose und Bin Ziemlich Okay!. (Illus.). 38p. (J). (gr. 3-7). 13.95 o.p. (*0-916291-90-1*) Kane/Miller Bk. Pubs.

BORNEO—FICTION

Bosse, Malcolm. Deep Dream of the Rain Forest, RS. 1994. 192p. (YA). (gr. 4-7). pap. 5.95 (*0-374-41702-4*, Sunburst) Farrar, Straus & Giroux.

Cushman, Doug. The Mystery of the Monkey's Maze. 1999. (From the Casebook of Seymour Sleuth Ser.). (Illus.). 32p. (J). (gr. k-3). 15.95 (*0-06-027719-X*); lib. bdg. 15.89 (*0-06-027720-3*) HarperCollins Children's Bk. Group.

Halam, Ann. Taylor Five. 2004. 120892p. (YA). (gr. 5). lib. bdg. 17.99 (*0-385-90114-3*, Lamb, Wendy) Random Hse. Children's Bks.

Myers, Christopher A. & Myers, Lynne B. Forest of the Clouded Leopard. 1994. 128p. (J). (gr. 4 up). 13.95 o.p. (*0-395-67408-5*) Houghton Mifflin Co.

Smith, Dale. What the Orangutan Told Alice: A Rain Forest Adventure. 2001. (Illus.). 192p. (YA). (gr. 6-12). pap. 14.95 (*0-9651452-8-X*) Deer Creek Publishing.

Wheeler, W. H. Wet Fire. 1978. (Pacesetters Ser.). (Illus.). 64p. (J). (gr. 4 up). lib. bdg. 9.25 o.p. (*0-516-02174-5*, Children's Pr.) Scholastic Library Publishing.

Youngberg, Norma R. Jungle Thorn. 2000. (Illus.). 128p. (J). reprint ed. pap. 8.95 (*1-57258-157-3*) TEACH Services, Inc.

BOSNIA AND HERCEGOVINA—FICTION

Graham, Franklin. Miracle in a Shoe Box: A Christmas Gift of Wonder. 1995. (Illus.). 32p. (J). (ps-4). 14.99 o.p. (*0-7852-7728-5*) Nelson, Thomas Inc.

—Miracle in a Shoe Box: A Christmas Gift of Wonder. 1998. (Illus.). 32p. (J). (ps-4). pap. 7.97 o.p. (*0-7852-6034-X*) Nelson, Tommy.

Kubert, Joe. Fax from Sarajevo: A Story of Survival. (Illus.). (YA). 1998. 224p. (gr. 9 up). pap. 16.95 (*1-56971-346-4*); 1996. 208p. (gr. 7 up). 24.95 o.p. (*1-56971-143-7*) Dark Horse Comics.

Lorbiecki, Marybeth. My Palace of Leaves in Sarajevo. 1997. (Illus.). 48p. (J). 14.99 o.s.i (*0-8037-2033-5*); 14.89 o.s.i (*0-8037-2034-3*) Penguin Putnam Bks. for Young Readers. (Dial Bks. for Young Readers).

BOSTON (MASS.)—FICTION

Ayres, Katherine. Under Copp's Hill. 2000. (American Girl Collection: Bk. 8). (Illus.). 176p. (gr. 5 up). (J). 9.95 (*1-58485-089-2*); (YA). pap. 5.95 (*1-58485-088-4*) Pleasant Co. Pubns. (American Girl).

—Under Copp's Hill. 2000. (American Girl Collection). (Illus.). (J). 12.00 (*0-606-20963-8*) Turtleback Bks.

Bolin, J. J. Yankee Doodle & the Secret Society. 1997. (Cover-to-Cover Bks.). (Illus.). 54p. (J). (*0-7807-6715-2*, Covercraft) Perfection Learning Corp.

Borden, Louise. Sleds on Boston Common: A Story from the American Revolution. 2000. (Illus.). 40p. (J). (gr. 3-7). 17.00 (*0-689-82812-8*, McElderry, Margaret K.) Simon & Schuster Children's Publishing.

Cocca-Leffler, Maryann. Bus Route to Boston. 2003. (Illus.). 32p. (J). (gr. k-3). 15.95 (*1-56397-723-0*) Boyds Mills Pr.

Denenberg, Barry. The Journal of William Thomas Emerson: A Revolutionary War Patriot: Boston, Massachusetts, 1774. 1998. (My Name Is America Ser.). (Illus.). 156p. (J). (gr. 4-8). pap. 10.95 o.s.i (*0-590-31350-9*, Scholastic Pr.) Scholastic, Inc.

Farber, Norma. As I Was Crossing Boston Common. 1991. (Unicorn Paperbacks Ser.). (Illus.). 32p. (J). (ps-2). pap. 3.95 o.s.i (*0-525-44781-4*, Puffin Bks.) Penguin Putnam Bks. for Young Readers.

Finlayson, Ann. Redcoat in Boston. 1971. (J). (gr. 7-12). 5.95 o.p. (*0-7232-6089-3*, Warne, Frederick) Penguin Putnam Bks. for Young Readers.

Forbes, Esther. Johnny Tremain. 2002. (Illus.). (J). 15.00 (*0-7587-0196-9*) Book Wholesalers, Inc.

—Johnny Tremain. 2002. (EMC Masterpiece Series Access Editions). (Illus.). xvi, 308p. (J). 10.95 (*0-8219-2408-7*) EMC/Paradigm Publishing.

Forbes, Esther Hoskins. Johnny Tremain. 1943. (Illus.). 288p. (YA). (gr. 7-7). tchr. ed. 16.00 (*0-395-06766-9*) Houghton Mifflin Co.

—Johnny Tremain: Illustrated American Classics. 1981. 305p. (J). reprint ed. lib. bdg. 27.95 (*0-89966-306-0*) Buccaneer Bks., Inc.

—Johnny Tremain: Illustrated American Classics. 1987. (Laurel-Leaf Bks.). (Illus.). 272p. (YA). (gr. 4-7). mass mkt. 6.50 (*0-440-94250-0*, Yearling) Random Hse. Children's Bks.

Giff, Patricia Reilly. Oh Boy, Boston! 1997. (Polk Street Special Ser.). 10.04 (*0-606-12785-2*) Turtleback Bks.

Glasser, Robin Preiss, illus. You Can't Take a Balloon into the Museum of Fine Arts. 2002. 40p. (J). (gr. k-4). 17.99 (*0-8037-2570-1*, Dial Bks. for Young Readers) Penguin Putnam Bks. for Young Readers.

Golden, Christopher. Body Bags. 1999. (Body of Evidence Ser.: Vol. 1). 272p. (YA). (gr. 7-12). mass mkt. 4.99 (*0-671-03492-8*, Simon Pulse) Simon & Schuster Children's Publishing.

—Head Games. 2000. (Body of Evidence Ser.: No. 5). (Illus.). 256p. (YA). (gr. 7-12). mass mkt. 4.99 (*0-671-77582-0*, Simon Pulse) Simon & Schuster Children's Publishing.

—Meets the Eye. 2000. (Body of Evidence Ser.: No. 4). 256p. (YA). (gr. 7 up). mass mkt. 4.99 (*0-671-03495-2*, Simon Pulse) Simon & Schuster Children's Publishing.

—Skin Deep. 2000. (Body of Evidence Ser.: Vol. 6). (Illus.). 288p. (YA). mass mkt. 5.99 o.s.i (*0-671-77583-9*, Simon Pulse) Simon & Schuster Children's Publishing.

—Soul Survivor. 1999. (Body of Evidence Ser.: Vol. 3). 256p. (YA). (gr. 7-12). pap. 4.99 (*0-671-03494-4*, Simon Pulse) Simon & Schuster Children's Publishing.

—Thief of Hearts. 1999. (Body of Evidence Ser.: Vol. 2). (Illus.). 272p. (YA). (gr. 8-12). pap. 4.99 (*0-671-03493-6*, Simon Pulse) Simon & Schuster Children's Publishing.

Grote, JoAnn A. The American Revolution. 1999. (American Adventure Ser.: No. 11). (J). (gr. 3-7). (*0-7910-5591-4*) Chelsea Hse. Pubs.

—Danger in the Harbor: Grain Riots Threaten Boston. 1999. (American Adventure Ser.: No. 6). (Illus.). 144p. (J). (gr. 3-7). lib. bdg. 15.95 (*0-7910-5046-7*) Chelsea Hse. Pubs.

—Queen Anne's War. 1999. (American Adventure Ser.: No. 5). 144p. (J). (gr. 3-7). lib. bdg. 15.95 (*0-7910-5045-9*) Chelsea Hse. Pubs.

Harlow, Joan Hiatt. Joshua's Song. (Illus.). (J). 2003. 160p. pap. 4.99 (*0-689-85542-7*, Aladdin); 2001. 192p. (gr. 3-7). 16.00 (*0-689-84119-1*, McElderry, Margaret K.) Simon & Schuster Children's Publishing.

—Joshua's Song. 2003. (Young Adult Ser.). 173p. (J). 22.95 (*0-7862-5558-7*) Thorndike Pr.

Hawthorne, Nathaniel. The Scarlet Letter. unabr. ed. 1962. (Classics Ser.). (YA). (gr. 9 up). mass mkt. 3.95 (*0-8049-0007-8*, CL-7) Airmont Publishing Co., Inc.

—The Scarlet Letter. 1965. (Bantam Classics Ser.). 256p. reprint ed. mass mkt. 3.95 (*0-553-21009-2*, Bantam Classics) Bantam Bks.

—The Scarlet Letter. Cockcroft, Susan, ed. 1997. (Cambridge Literature Ser.). (Illus.). 320p. pap. text 11.95 (*0-521-56783-1*) Cambridge Univ. Pr.

—The Scarlet Letter. 1989. 277p. (YA). (gr. 8-12). mass mkt. 3.99 (*0-8125-0483-6*, Tor Classics) Doherty, Tom Assocs., LLC.

—The Scarlet Letter. 1972. 106p. (YA). (gr. 10 up). pap. 5.60 (*0-87129-921-6*, SB6) Dramatic Publishing Co.

—The Scarlet Letter. adapted ed. (YA). (gr. 5-12). pap. text 9.95 (*0-8359-0262-5*) Globe Fearon Educational Publishing.

—The Scarlet Letter. Levin, Harry T., ed. 1960. (YA). (gr. 9 up). pap. 16.36 (*0-395-05142-8*, Riverside Editions) Houghton Mifflin Co.

—The Scarlet Letter. 1995. (Illus.). 288p. (YA). pap. 12.95 (*0-7868-8093-7*) Hyperion Pr.

—The Scarlet Letter. l.t. ed. 2000. (LRS Large Print Heritage Ser.). 379p. (YA). (gr. 7-12). lib. bdg. 34.95 (*1-58118-065-9*, 23660) LRS.

—The Scarlet Letter. 1981. 256p. (YA). mass mkt. 4.95 o.p. (*0-451-51908-6*, Signet Classics) NAL.

—The Scarlet Letter. 1998. (YA). 32p. 9.95 (*1-56137-338-9*, NU3389); 40p. 11.95 (*1-56137-339-7*, NU3397SP) Novel Units, Inc.

—The Scarlet Letter. 1987. (Portland House Illustrated Classics Ser.). (Illus.). 312p. (YA). 9.99 o.s.i (*0-517-64302-2*) Random Hse. Value Publishing.

—The Scarlet Letter. 1999. (Courage Unabridged Classics Ser.). 208p. (YA). pap. 6.00 o.p. (*0-7624-0552-X*, Courage Bks.) Running Pr. Bk. Pubs.

—The Scarlet Letter. (YA). 1994. 11.04 (*0-606-13027-6*); 1981. 10.00 (*0-606-13760-2*) Turtleback Bks.

Hemphill, Kris. A Secret Party in Boston Harbor. 1998. (Mysteries in Time Ser.: Vol. 6). (Illus.). 96p. (J). (gr. 4-7). text 14.95 (*1-881889-88-2*) Silver Moon Pr.

Hewes, Agnes D. Glory of the Seas. 1966. (J). (gr. 7-11). lib. bdg. 5.39 o.p. (*0-394-91187-3*, Knopf Bks. for Young Readers) Random Hse. Children's Bks.

Holm, Jennifer L. Boston Jane No. 3: The Claim. 2004. (Boston Jane Ser.). 240p. (J). lib. bdg. 16.89 (*0-06-029046-3*) HarperCollins Pubs.

—Boston Jane No. 3: The Claim. 2004. (Boston Jane Ser.: No. 3). 240p. (J). 15.99 (*0-06-029045-5*) HarperCollins Children's Bk. Group.

Holt, Rinehart and Winston Staff. The Fifth of March: A Story of the Boston Massacre. 2nd ed. 2002. (J). text 4.80 (*0-03-073524-6*) Holt, Rinehart & Winston.

Howells, William Dean. The Rise of Silas Lapham. 1968. (Airmont Classics Ser.). (J). (gr. 11 up). mass mkt. 2.95 o.p. (*0-8049-0165-1*, CL-165) Airmont Publishing Co., Inc.

—The Rise of Silas Lapham. Cady, Edwin H., ed. 1957. (YA). (gr. 9 up). pap. 13.56 o.p. (*0-395-05126-6*, Riverside Editions) Houghton Mifflin Co.

—The Rise of Silas Lapham. 1963. (YA). (gr. 9). 352p. mass mkt. 7.95 o.s.i (*0-451-52496-9*, CE1850); mass mkt. 3.50 o.p. (*0-451-52198-6*) NAL. (Signet Classics).

—The Rise of Silas Lapham. (J). E-Book 5.00 (*0-7410-0533-6*) SoftBook Pr.

Hughes, Dean. Lucky Fights Back. 1991. (Lucky Ladd Ser.: Bk. 4). 150p. (Orig.). (J). (gr. 3-6). pap. text 4.95 (*0-87579-559-5*, Cinnamon Tree) Deseret Bk. Co.

Hyppolite, Joanne. Seth & Samona. 1996. (Illus.). 128p. pap. text 3.99 o.s.i (*0-440-41272-2*) Dell Publishing.

—Seth & Samona. 1995. (J). 18.95 (*0-385-44630-6*, Dell Books for Young Readers) Random Hse. Children's Bks.

—Seth & Samona. 1997. 9.09 o.p. (*0-606-10928-5*) Turtleback Bks.

Kelley, Nancy J. The Whispering Rod: A Tale of Old Massachusetts. 2002. 160p. (J). lib. bdg. 17.95 (*1-57249-248-1*, WM Kids) White Mane Publishing Co., Inc.

Lasky, Kathryn. Home at Last. 2003. (My America Ser.). 112p. (J). mass mkt. 4.99 (*0-439-20644-8*) Scholastic, Inc.

—Home at Last: Sofia's Immigrant Diary, Bk. 2. 2003. (My America Ser.). 112p. (J). pap. 12.95 (*0-439-44963-4*) Scholastic, Inc.

—I Have an Aunt on Marlborough Street. 1992. (Illus.). 32p. (J). (gr. k-3). lib. bdg. 13.95 o.p. (*0-02-751701-2*, Simon & Schuster Children's Publishing) Simon & Schuster Children's Publishing.

—Prank. 1986. (J). (gr. 6 up). mass mkt. 2.75 o.s.i (*0-440-97144-6*, Laurel Leaf) Random Hse. Children's Bks.

Lent, Blair. Molasses Flood. 1992. (Illus.). 32p. (J). (ps-3). 14.95 o.p. (*0-395-45314-3*) Houghton Mifflin Co.

Lough, Loree. Fire by Night: The Great Fire Devastates Boston. 1999. (American Adventure Ser.: No. 4). 144p. (J). (gr. 3-7). lib. bdg. 15.95 (*0-7910-5044-0*) Chelsea Hse. Pubs.

Lowry, Lois. Anastasia Elige Profesion.Tr. of Anastasia's Chosen Career. (SPA.). (J). 188p. 9.95 (*84-239-9066-4*); 1996. 232p. 9.95 (*84-239-7133-3*) Espasa Calpe, S.A. ESP. *Dist:* Planeta Publishing Corp., Lectorum Pubns., Inc.

—Anastasia Elige Profesion. 1990. Tr. of Anastasia's Chosen Career. 16.00 (*0-606-16063-9*) Turtleback Bks.

—Anastasia's Chosen Career. l.t. ed. 1992. 216p. (J). lib. bdg. 12.95 o.p. (*0-7451-1468-7*, Macmillan Reference USA) Gale Group.

—Anastasia's Chosen Career. 1987. 160p. (J). (gr. 4-6). tchr. ed. 16.00 (*0-395-42506-9*) Houghton Mifflin Co.

—Anastasia's Chosen Career. 1990. (J). pap. o.s.i (*0-440-80199-0*, Dell Books for Young Readers); 1988. 160p. (gr. 4-7). pap. text 4.50 (*0-440-40100-3*, Yearling) Random Hse. Children's Bks.

—Anastasia's Chosen Career. 1987. (J). 10.55 (*0-606-04083-8*) Turtleback Bks.

—Taking Care of Terrific, 001. 1983. 176p. (J). (gr. 4-6). 16.00 (*0-395-34070-5*) Houghton Mifflin Co.

—Taking Care of Terrific. 1983. (J). 10.55 (*0-606-03177-4*) Turtleback Bks.

Lutz, Norma Jean. Maggie's Choice: Jonathan Edwards & the Great Awakening. 1999. (American Adventure Ser.: No. 8). (Illus.). 144p. (J). (gr. 3-7). lib. bdg. 15.95 (*0-7910-5048-3*) Chelsea Hse. Pubs.

—Smallpox Strikes! Cotton Mather's Bold Experiment. 1999. (American Adventure Ser.: No. 7). (Illus.). 144p. (J). (gr. 3-7). lib. bdg. 15.95 (*0-7910-5047-5*) Chelsea Hse. Pubs.

Lynch, Chris. Blood Relations. 1996. (Blue Eyed Son Ser.: No. 2). (Illus.). (YA). 224p. (gr. 12 up). lib. bdg. 13.89 o.s.i (*0-06-025399-1*); 192p. (gr. 7 up). pap. 4.50 o.s.i (*0-06-447122-5*) HarperCollins Children's Bk. Group. (Harper Trophy).

—Blood Relations. 1996. (Blue-Eyed Son Ser.: 2). (J). 9.60 o.p. (*0-606-09090-8*) Turtleback Bks.

—Gold Dust. l.t. ed. 2002. 238p. (J). 22.95 (*0-7862-4061-X*) Gale Group.

—Gold Dust. 2000. 208p. (J). (gr. 5 up). lib. bdg. 16.89 (*0-06-028175-8*); (Illus.). 15.95 (*0-06-028174-X*) HarperCollins Children's Bk. Group.

—Gold Dust. 2002. 208p. (J). (gr. 5 up). pap. 7.99 (*0-06-447201-9*) HarperCollins Pubs.

—Mick. 1996. (Blue Eyed Son Ser.: Bk. 1). (Illus.). 160p. (YA). (gr. 12 up). mass mkt. 4.50 o.s.i (*0-06-447121-7*, Harper Trophy) HarperCollins Children's Bk. Group.

—Mick. 1996. (Blue-Eyed Son Ser.). (YA). 9.60 o.p. (*0-606-09089-4*) Turtleback Bks.

Lynn, Jodi. The Blue Girl: Glory, Vol. 3. 2003. (Illus.). 176p. (J). bds. 9.99 (*0-14-250045-3*, Puffin Bks.) Penguin Putnam Bks. for Young Readers.

—Forget-Me-Not. 2003. 176p. (J). bds. 9.99 (*0-14-250046-1*, Puffin Bks.) Penguin Putnam Bks. for Young Readers.

—Glory Number. Winter. 2nd ed. 2003. (Gabe Wager Mystery Ser.). (Illus.). 176p. (J). bds. 9.99 (*0-14-250039-9*, Puffin Bks.) Penguin Putnam Bks. for Young Readers.

Margolin, H. Ellen. Goin' to Boston: An Exuberant Journey in Song. 2002. (Illus.). 40p. (J). (ps-2). 15.95 (*1-929766-45-9*) Handprint Bks.

Marino, Jan. The Mona Lisa of Salem Street: A Novel. 1995. 176p. (J). 14.95 o.p. (*0-316-54614-3*) Little Brown & Co.

McCloskey, Robert. Make Way for Ducklings. 2002. (Illus.). (J). 13.60 (*0-7587-0056-3*) Book Wholesalers, Inc.

—Make Way for Ducklings. 2000. (J). pap. 19.97 incl. audio (*0-7366-9196-0*) Books on Tape, Inc.

—Make Way for Ducklings. 2001. (Early Readers Ser.: Vol. 2). (J). lib. bdg. (*1-59054-038-7*) Fitzgerald Bks.

—Make Way for Ducklings. (J). 1999. (Illus.). 72p. (ps-3). pap. 7.99 (*0-14-056434-9*, Puffin Bks.); 1993. (Illus.). 1p. (ps-3). pap. 9.99 incl. audio (*0-14-095118-0*, Puffin Bks.); 1991. 72p. (ps-3). pap. 20.99 o.s.i (*0-14-054434-8*, Puffin Bks.); 1988. (Illus.). (ps-3). 6.95 o.p. (*0-14-095069-9*, Puffin Bks.); 1976. (Illus.). 64p. (gr. 1-3). pap. 4.99 (*0-14-050171-1*, Puffin Bks.); 1941. (Illus.). 68p. (ps-3). 17.99 (*0-670-45149-5*, Viking Children's Bks.) Penguin Putnam Bks. for Young Readers.

—Make Way for Ducklings. 1976. (Picture Puffin Ser.). (J). 13.14 (*0-606-03886-8*) Turtleback Bks.

—Make Way for Ducklings. 2000. (J). (ps-k). pap. text 12.95 incl. audio Weston Woods Studios, Inc.

Miller, Susan Martins. Lydia the Patriot: The Boston Massacre. 2004. 144p. (J). pap. 3.97 (*1-59310-204-6*) Barbour Publishing, Inc.

Moss, Marissa. Emma's Journal: The Story of a Colonial Girl. (Young American Voices Ser.: Bk. 2). (Illus.). 56p. (J). (gr. 3-7). 2001. pap. 7.00 (*0-15-216325-5*); 1999. 15.00 (*0-15-202025-X*) Harcourt Children's Bks. (Silver Whistle).

—Emma's Journal: The Story of a Colonial Girl. 2001. (Illus.). (J). 13.15 (*0-606-21179-9*) Turtleback Bks.

Ponti, James. History Mystery. 1998. (Mystery Files of Shelby Woo Ser.: No. 9). 144p. (J). (gr. 4-6). pap. 3.99 (*0-671-02009-9*, Aladdin) Simon & Schuster Children's Publishing.

Reilly Giff, Patricia. Oh Boy, Boston! 1997. (Polk Street Special Ser.: No. 10). (Illus.). 128p. (gr. 1-4). pap. text 3.99 o.s.i (*0-440-41365-6*, Dell Books for Young Readers) Random Hse. Children's Bks.

Richards, Laura E. Jiggle Joggle Jee! 2001. (Illus.). 32p. (J). (ps). 15.95 (*0-688-17832-4*, Greenwillow Bks.) HarperCollins Children's Bk. Group.

Rinaldi, Ann. The Fifth of March: A Story of the Boston Massacre. (Great Episodes Ser.). 352p. (YA). 2004. pap. (*0-15-205078-7*); 1993. (Illus.). (gr. 5 up). 13.00 (*0-15-200343-6*); 1993. (Illus.). (gr. 7 up). pap. 6.00 (*0-15-227517-7*) Harcourt Children's Bks. (Gulliver Bks.).

Schneider, Rex, illus. Yankee Doodle & the Secret Society. 1997. (Cover-to-Cover Bks.). (J). (*0-7891-2006-2*) Perfection Learning Corp.

Smith, L. J. The Chosen. 1997. (Night World Ser.). 224p. (YA). per. 3.99 (*0-671-55137-X*, Simon Pulse) Simon & Schuster Children's Publishing.

Speck, Nancy. The Freedom Trail Mystery. Barstow, Susannah Driver, ed. 2001. (Going to Ser.). 126p. (J). (gr. 4-8). pap. 7.95 (*1-893577-07-4*) Four Corners Publishing Co., Inc.

Staffier, Jane Sarah. Casey & the Boston Freedom Trail. l.t. ed. 1999. (Beacon Hill Ser.: No. 2). (Illus.). 28p. (J). (gr. k-7). spiral bd. 9.95 (*1-928895-01-8*) B.A.B., Ltd.

—Casey the Beacon Hill Cat Coloring Book Adventures, 4 vols., Set. l.t. ed. 2001. 130p. (J). (ps-7). pap. 32.95 (*1-928895-04-2*) B.A.B., Ltd.

Stone, Phoebe. Sonata #1 for Riley Red. 2003. 208p. (J). (gr. 3-6). 15.95 (*0-316-99041-8*) Little Brown & Co.

Thomas, Carroll. Ring Out Wild Bells: A Matty Trescott Novel. 2001. (Illus.). viii, 169p. (J). 9.95 (*1-57525-291-0*) Smith & Kraus Pubs., Inc.

White, Ellen Emerson. Where Have All the Flowers Gone? The Diary of Molly Mackenzie Flaherty, Boston, Massachusetts, 1968. 2002. (Dear America Ser.). (Illus.). 176p. (J). (gr. 4-9). pap. 10.95 (*0-439-14889-8*, Scholastic Pr.) Scholastic, Inc.

Wibberley, Leonard. John Treegate's Musket, RS. 1959. (Sunburst Ser.). 224p. (J). (gr. 5 up). 9.95 o.p. (*0-374-33762-4*, Farrar, Straus & Giroux (BYR)) Farrar, Straus & Giroux.

Wiley, Melissa. Charlotte Novel, No. 4. 2004. (J). pap. (*0-06-440740-3*) HarperCollins Pubs.

BOTSWANA—FICTION

Dow, Unity. Far & Beyon' 2002. 208p. (YA). (gr. 7 up). pap. 11.95 (*1-879960-64-8*) Aunt Lute Bks.

Mitchison, Naomi. Family at Ditlabeng, RS. 1970. (Illus.). 136p. (J). (gr. 4 up). 3.95 o.p. (*0-374-32265-1*, Farrar, Straus & Giroux (BYR)) Farrar, Straus & Giroux.

BRAMBLY HEDGE (IMAGINARY PLACE)—FICTION

Barklem, Jill. Autumn Story. 1980. (Brambly Hedge Bks.). (Illus.). 32p. (J). (gr. 1 up). 10.95 o.p. (*0-399-20745-7*); 6.99 o.p. (*0-399-61155-X*) Penguin Putnam Bks. for Young Readers. (Philomel).

—Autumn Story. 1999. (Brambly Hedge Ser.). (Illus.). 32p. (J). (ps-3). 9.95 (*0-689-83054-8*, Atheneum) Simon & Schuster Children's Publishing.

—The Brambly Hedge Birthday Book. 1994. (Brambly Hedge Bks.). (Illus.). 128p. (J). (gr. k up). 12.95 o.p. (*0-399-22669-9*, Philomel) Penguin Putnam Bks. for Young Readers.

—The Four Seasons of Brambly Hedge. 1990. (Illus.). 144p. (J). (gr. 3 up). 27.95 o.p. (*0-399-21869-6*, Philomel) Penguin Putnam Bks. for Young Readers.

—The High Hills. 1999. (Brambly Hedge Ser.). (Illus.). 32p. (J). (ps-3). 9.95 (*0-689-83091-2*, Atheneum) Simon & Schuster Children's Publishing.

—Poppy's Babies. 1995. (Brambly Hedge Ser.). (Illus.). 32p. (J). (ps-3). 11.95 o.s.i (*0-399-22743-1*, Philomel) Penguin Putnam Bks. for Young Readers.

—Poppy's Babies. 2000. (Brambly Hedge Ser.). (Illus.). 32p. (J). (ps-1). 9.95 o.s.i (*0-689-83172-2*, Atheneum) Simon & Schuster Children's Publishing.

—The Secret Staircase. 1983. (Brambly Hedge Ser.). (Illus.). (J). (ps-3). 13.95 o.p. (*0-399-20994-8*, Philomel) Penguin Putnam Bks. for Young Readers.

—The Secret Staircase. 1999. (Brambly Hedge Ser.). (Illus.). 32p. (J). (ps-3). 9.95 (*0-689-83090-4*, Atheneum) Simon & Schuster Children's Publishing.

—Spring Story. 1980. (Brambly Hedge Bks.). (Illus.). 32p. (J). (gr. 1 up). 10.95 o.p. (*0-399-20746-5*); 6.99 o.p. (*0-399-61156-8*) Penguin Putnam Bks. for Young Readers. (Philomel).

—Summer Story. 1980. (Brambly Hedge Bks.). (Illus.). 32p. (J). (gr. 1 up). 10.95 o.p. (*0-399-20747-3*); 6.99 o.p. (*0-399-61157-6*) Penguin Putnam Bks. for Young Readers. (Philomel).

—Winter Story. 1980. (Brambly Hedge Bks.). (Illus.). 32p. (J). (gr. 1 up). 10.95 o.p. (*0-399-20748-1*); 6.99 o.p. (*0-399-61158-4*) Penguin Putnam Bks. for Young Readers. (Philomel).

—Winter Story. 1999. (Brambly Hedge Ser.). (Illus.). 32p. (J). (ps-3). 9.95 (*0-689-83057-2*, Atheneum) Simon & Schuster Children's Publishing.

—The World of Brambly Hedge. 1993. (Pop-Up Bks.). (Illus.). 24p. (J). (ps up). 17.95 o.p. (*0-399-22012-7*, Philomel) Penguin Putnam Bks. for Young Readers.

BRAZIL—FICTION

Cohen, Miriam. Born to Dance Samba. 1984. (Illus.). 160p. (J). (gr. 4-7). lib. bdg. 12.89 o.p. (*0-06-021359-0*) HarperCollins Children's Bk. Group.

Cowen, Eve. Jungle Jenny. 1979. (Pacesetters Ser.). (Illus.). (J). (gr. 4 up). lib. bdg. 9.25 o.p. (*0-516-02185-0*, Children's Pr.) Scholastic Library Publishing.

Golembe, Carla, illus. How Night Came from the Sea: A Story from Brazil. 1994. (J). 15.95 o.p. (*0-316-30855-2*, Joy Street Bks.) Little Brown & Co.

Holtwijk, Ineke. Asphalt Angels. Boeke, Wanda, tr. 2000. 192p. (YA). (gr. 7-12). 15.95 (*1-886910-24-3*) Front Street, Inc.

Ibbotson, Eva. Journey to the River Sea. 2002. (Illus.). 336p. (J). (gr. 4-8). 17.99 (*0-525-46739-4*, Dutton Children's Bks.) Penguin Putnam Bks. for Young Readers.

Lewin, Ted. Amazon Boy. 1993. (Illus.). 32p. (J). (gr. k-3). lib. bdg. 14.95 o.s.i (*0-02-757383-4*, Simon & Schuster Children's Publishing) Simon & Schuster Children's Publishing.

Machado, Ana Maria. Me in the Middle. Unger, David, tr. from POR. (Illus.). (J). 2003. 112p. (gr. 3-6). pap. 5.95 (*0-88899-467-2*, Libros Tigrillo); 2002. 96p. (gr. 2-6). 14.95 (*0-88899-463-X*) Groundwood Bks. CAN. *Dist:* Publishers Group West.

—Nina Bonita. 1995. (SPA., Illus.). 24p. (J). (ps-3). pap. 6.99 (*980-257-165-2*, EK6355) Ekare, Ediciones VEN. *Dist:* AIMS International Bks., Inc., Kane/Miller Bk. Pubs., Lectorum Pubns., Inc.

—Nina Bonita. Iribarren, Elena, tr. from POR. (Illus.). 24p. (J). (ps-3). 1996. 9.95 o.p. (*0-916291-63-4*); 2001. reprint ed. pap. 6.95 (*1-929132-11-5*) Kane/Miller Bk. Pubs.

—Nina Bonita. 2001. (J). 13.10 (*0-606-20824-0*) Turtleback Bks.

Mezek, Karen. Katie & the Amazon Mystery. 1991. (Illus.). (J). pap. 4.99 o.p. (*0-89081-899-1*) Harvest Hse. Pubs.

Nunes, Lygia Bojunga. My Friend the Painter. Pontiero, Giovanni, tr. from POR. 1991. 96p. (J). (gr. 3-7). 13.95 (*0-15-256340-7*) Harcourt Trade Pubs.

Smith, Roland. Jaguar. 1998. 256p. (J). (gr. 4-7). pap. 5.95 (*0-7868-1312-1*) Disney Pr.

—Jaguar. 1997. (gr. 5 up). 256p. (J). 15.95 (*0-7868-0282-0*); 249p. (YA). 16.49 (*0-7868-2226-0*) Hyperion Bks. for Children.

—Jaguar. 1997. 12.00 (*0-606-15989-4*) Turtleback Bks.

Thomas, Rob. Green Thumb. unabr. ed. 2000. (YA). pap. 59.00 incl. audio (*0-7887-3641-8*, 41007) Recorded Bks., LLC.

—Green Thumb. (gr. 5-9). 2000. 192p. pap. 4.99 (*0-689-82886-1*, Aladdin); 1999. (Illus.). 186p. (YA). 16.00 o.s.i (*0-689-81780-0*, Simon & Schuster Children's Publishing) Simon & Schuster Children's Publishing.

—Green Thumb. 2000. 11.04 (*0-606-20048-7*) Turtleback Bks.

Williams, Anita. The Captain's Hat. 2000. (Illus.). 104p. (J). (gr. 1-5). pap. 7.95 (*1-57924-330-4*, 119743) Jones, Bob Univ. Pr.

—The Treasure Keeper. 1995. (Pennant Ser.). (Illus.). 90p. (J). (gr. 1-5). pap. 7.95 (*0-89084-835-1*, 091710) Jones, Bob Univ. Pr.

Zindel, Paul. Night of the Bat. 144p. (J). 2003. pap. 5.99 (*0-7868-1226-5*); 2001. (gr. 5-9). lib. bdg. 16.49 (*0-7868-2554-5*); 2001. (gr. 6-10). trans. 15.99 (*0-7868-0340-1*) Hyperion Bks. for Children.

Zoehfeld, Kathleen Weidner. Amazon Fever. 2001. (Road to Reading Ser.). (Illus.). 48p. (J). 11.99 (*0-307-46407-5*); pap. 3.99 (*0-307-26407-6*) Random Hse. Children's Bks. (Golden Bks.).

BRITISH COLUMBIA—FICTION

Alma, Ann. Summer of Adventures. 2003. (Summer Ser.). 144p. pap. 5.95 (*1-55039-122-4*) Sono Nis Pr. CAN. *Dist:* Orca Bk. Pubs.

Blades, Ann. A Boy of Tache. 1973. (Illus.). (J). (gr. 1-5). pap. 5.95 o.p. (*0-88776-034-1*) Tundra Bks. of Northern New York.

Cameron, Anne. Dreamspeaker. 2000. 128p. (YA). (gr. 7-9). mass mkt. 5.95 (*0-7736-7482-9*) Stoddart Kids CAN. *Dist:* Fitzhenry & Whiteside, Ltd.

Chamberlain, Penny. The Olden Days Locket. 2003. 200p. pap. 6.95 (*1-55039-128-3*) Sono Nis Pr. CAN. *Dist:* Orca Bk. Pubs.

Craven, Margaret. I Heard the Owl Call My Name. 1991. 250p. (J). (ps up). reprint ed. lib. bdg. 25.95 (*0-89966-854-2*) Buccaneer Bks., Inc.

—I Heard the Owl Call My Name. 1980. 160p. (gr. 7-12). mass mkt. 6.99 (*0-440-34369-0*, Laurel) Dell Publishing.

—I Heard the Owl Call My Name. 1973. (Illus.). 144p. 11.95 o.p. (*0-385-02586-6*) Doubleday Publishing.

—I Heard the Owl Call My Name. 1978. (Inspirational Ser.). 225p. reprint ed. lib. bdg. 9.95 o.p. (*0-8161-6203-4*, Macmillan Reference USA) Gale Group.

—I Heard the Owl Call My Name. 1973. 12.55 (*0-606-03572-9*) Turtleback Bks.

Foley, Louise Munro. Ghost Train. l.t. ed. 1995. (Choose Your Own Adventure Ser.: No. 120). (Illus.). 128p. (J). (gr. 4-8). lib. bdg. 21.27 o.p. (*0-8368-1307-3*) Stevens, Gareth Inc.

Friesen, Gayle. Janey's Girl. (YA). (gr. 6 up). 2001. 224p. pap. 6.95 (*1-55074-463-1*); 1998. (Illus.). 316p. text (*1-55074-461-5*) Kids Can Pr., Ltd.

Horne, Constance. The Tenth Pupil. 2001. 160p. (J). (gr. 3-9). pap. 8.95 (*0-921870-86-8*) Ronsdale Pr. CAN. *Dist:* General Distribution Services, Inc.

Horvath, Polly. Everything on a Waffle, RS. 2001. 160p. (J). (gr. 5 up). 16.00 (*0-374-32236-8*, Farrar, Straus & Giroux (BYR)) Farrar, Straus & Giroux.

Juby, Susan. Alice, I Think. 2003. (Illus.). 304p. (YA). 15.99 (*0-06-051543-0*); lib. bdg. 16.89 (*0-06-051544-9*) HarperCollins Children's Bk. Group. (HarperTempest).

—Miss Smithers. 2004. (YA). (*0-06-051546-5*); lib. bdg. (*0-06-051547-3*) HarperCollins Children's Bk. Group. (HarperTempest).

Lawrence, Iain. The Lightkeeper's Daughter. 256p. (YA). 2004. (gr. 9). pap. 7.95 (*0-385-73127-2*, Delacorte Bks. for Young Readers); 2002. lib. bdg. 18.99 (*0-385-90062-7*); 2002. (gr. 9-12). 16.95 (*0-385-72925-1*, Delacorte Bks. for Young Readers) Random Hse. Children's Bks.

Lawson, Julie. The Ghost of Avalanche Mountain. 2000. (Goldstone Trilogy Ser.). (Illus.). 176p. (YA). (gr. 5-9). pap. 7.95 (*0-7737-6091-1*) Stoddart Kids CAN. *Dist:* Fitzhenry & Whiteside, Ltd.

—Goldstone. unabr. ed. 1998. 176p. (J). (gr. 5-9). pap. 7.95 (*0-7737-5891-7*) Stoddart Kids CAN. *Dist:* Fitzhenry & Whiteside, Ltd.

Olsen, Sylvia. No Time to Say Goodbye. 2002. (Illus.). 194p. 6.95 (*1-55039-121-6*) Sono Nis Pr. CAN. *Dist:* Orca Bk. Pubs.

Reece, Colleen L. Friday Flight. 1998. (Juli Scott, Super Sleuth Ser.: Bk. 5). 176p. (J). pap. 2.97 o.p. (*1-57748-216-6*) Barbour Publishing, Inc.

—Friday Flight. l.t. ed. 2001. (Juli Scott, Super Sleuth Ser.). (Illus.). 204p. (J). 23.95 (*0-7862-3187-4*) Thorndike Pr.

Reekie, Jocelyn. Tess. 2003. 296p. (YA). (gr. 5-8). pap. 7.95 (*1-55192-471-4*) Raincoast Bk. Distribution CAN. *Dist:* Publishers Group West.

Repp, Gloria. The Mystery of the Indian Carvings. 2002. (Illus.). 118p. (J). pap. (*1-57924-726-1*) Jones, Bob Univ. Pr.

Roberts, Ken. The Thumb in the Box. (Illus.). 96p. (J). 2002. (gr. 2-4). pap. 5.95 (*0-88899-422-2*); 2001. (gr. 4-7). 14.95 (*0-88899-421-4*) Groundwood Bks. CAN. *Dist:* Publishers Group West.

Shull, Megan Elisabeth. The Skye's the Limit. 2003. (Pleasant Company Publications). (J). pap. 6.95 (*1-58485-769-2*, American Girl) Pleasant Co. Pubns.

Walsh, Ann. The Ghost of Soda Creek. 1990. 170p. (J). (gr. 3-8). reprint ed. pap. 5.95 (*0-88878-292-6*, Sandcastle Bks.) Beach Holme Pubs., Ltd. CAN. *Dist:* Strauss Consultants.

Walters, Eric. War of the Eagles. 1998. 160p. (YA). (gr. 7-11). pap. 7.95 (*1-55143-099-1*); 14.00 (*1-55143-118-1*) Orca Bk. Pubs.

—War of the Eagles. 1998. 14.00 (*0-606-16742-0*) Turtleback Bks.

Woodson, Marion. Charlotte's Vow. 2001. 144p. (YA). pap. 5.95 (*0-88878-413-9*) Beach Holme Pubs., Ltd. CAN. *Dist:* Strauss Consultants.

BRITISH—UNITED STATES—FICTION

Weisberg, Valerie H. Three Jolly Stories Include - Three Jollys, Jollys Visit L. A., Jolly Gets Mugged: An ESL Adult-Child Reader. 1985. (Jolly Ser.). (Illus.). 76p. (Orig.). (J). (gr. 4 up). pap. text 6.95 (*0-9610912-4-X*) VHW Publishing.

BRITTANY (FRANCE)—FICTION

Haugaard, Erik Christian. Slave's Tale, 001. 1965. (Illus.). (J). (gr. 7 up). 7.95 o.p. (*0-395-06804-5*) Houghton Mifflin Co.

BROOKLYN (NEW YORK, N.Y.)—FICTION

Avi. Don't You Know There's a War On? 2001. 208p. (J). (gr. 3 up). lib. bdg. 16.89 (*0-06-029214-8*) HarperCollins Children's Bk. Group.

—Don't You Know There's a War On? 2001. 208p. (J). (gr. 4-6). 15.95 (*0-380-97863-6*) Morrow/Avon.

Blos, Joan W. Brooklyn Doesn't Rhyme. (Illus.). 96p. (gr. 3-7). 2000. pap. 4.50 (*0-689-83557-4*, Aladdin); 1994. (J). 16.00 o.s.i (*0-684-19694-8*, Atheneum) Simon & Schuster Children's Publishing.

Bowdish, Lynea & Carpenter, Nancy, illus. Brooklyn, Bugsy & Me, RS. 2000. 96p. (J). (gr. 4-7). 15.00 (*0-374-30993-0*, Farrar, Straus & Giroux (BYR)) Farrar, Straus & Giroux.

Brown, Kay. Willy's Summer Dream. 1989. 144p. (YA). (gr. 7 up). 13.95 (*0-15-200645-1*, Gulliver Bks.) Harcourt Children's Bks.

Chaikin, Miriam. I Should Worry, I Should Care. 1979. (Illus.). (J). (gr. 3-6). 12.89 o.p. (*0-06-021174-1*); lib. bdg. 11.89 o.p. (*0-06-021175-X*) HarperCollins Children's Bk. Group.

—I Should Worry, I Should Care. 2000. (Illus.). 116p. (gr. 4-7). pap. 9.95 (*0-595-09011-7*, Backinprint.com) iUniverse, Inc.

Chambers, Veronica. Quinceanera Means Sweet Fifteen. 2001. 192p. (J). (gr. 3-7). 15.99 (*0-7868-0497-1*); (Illus.). (gr. 5-8). lib. bdg. 16.49 (*0-7868-2426-3*) Hyperion Bks. for Children.

Cohen, Miriam. Mimmy & Sophie, RS. 1999. (Illus.). 40p. (J). (gr. k up). 16.00 (*0-374-34988-6*, Farrar, Straus & Giroux (BYR)) Farrar, Straus & Giroux.

—Mimmy & Sophie: Six Stories, RS. 2004. (J). 15.00 (*0-374-34989-4*, Farrar, Straus & Giroux (BYR)) Farrar, Straus & Giroux.

—Robert & Dawn Marie Forever. 1986. 160p. (YA). (gr. 7 up). 11.95 (*0-06-021396-5*) HarperCollins Children's Bk. Group.

Crocitto, Frank. A Child's Christmas in Brooklyn. Horrigan, Jeremiah, ed. 2001. (Illus.). 96p. (YA). (gr. 4 up). 10.95 (*0-9677558-2-4*, CHBO1) Candlepower, Inc.

Estes, Eleanor. The Alley. 2003. (Illus.). 288p. (J). 17.00 (*0-15-204917-7*, Harcourt Young Classics); pap. 5.95 (*0-15-204918-5*, Odyssey Classics) Harcourt Children's Bks.

—The Tunnel of Hugsy Goode. 2003. (Illus.). 256p. (J). 17.00 (*0-15-204914-2*, Harcourt Young Classics); pap. 5.95 (*0-15-204916-9*, Odyssey Classics) Harcourt Children's Bks.

Fisher, Leonard Everett. The Jetty Chronicles. 1997. (Accelerated Reader Bks.). 96p. (J). (gr. 4-8). 15.95 (*0-7614-5017-3*, Cavendish Children's Bks.) Cavendish, Marshall Corp.

Frost, Jonathan. Gowanus Dogs, RS. 1999. (Illus.). 48p. (YA). (gr. k-3). 15.00 o.p. (*0-374-31058-0*, Farrar, Straus & Giroux (BYR)) Farrar, Straus & Giroux.

Giff, Patricia Reilly. All the Way Home. 2001. 176p. (gr. 3-7). lib. bdg. 17.99 (*0-385-90021-X*, Delacorte Pr.) Dell Publishing.

—All the Way Home. 176p. (gr. 3-7). 2003. pap. text 5.99 (*0-440-41182-3*, Yearling); 2001. text 15.95 (*0-385-32209-7*, Dell Books for Young Readers) Random Hse. Children's Bks.

Lancaster, Clay. Michiko: Or Mrs. Belmont's Brownstone on Brooklyn Heights. 1966. (Illus.). (J). (gr. k-4). 3.85 o.p. (*0-8048-0402-8*) Tuttle Publishing.

Laskin, Pamela L. Getting to Know You. 2003. (YA). (*0-936389-92-3*) Tudor Pubs., Inc.

Lurie, April. Dancing in the Streets of Brooklyn. 2002. 208p. lib. bdg. 17.99 (*0-385-90066-X*) Random Hse., Inc.

Mango, Karin N. Somewhere Green. 1987. 208p. (J). (gr. 5-9). 13.95 o.s.i (*0-02-762270-3*, Simon & Schuster Children's Publishing) Simon & Schuster Children's Publishing.

McCloskey, Kevin. Mrs. Fitz's Flamingos. 1992. (Illus.). (J). (ps-3). 14.00 o.p. (*0-688-10474-6*); lib. bdg. 13.93 (*0-688-10475-4*) HarperCollins Children's Bk. Group.

McDonald, Janet. Twists & Turns, RS. 2003. 144p. (YA). 16.00 (*0-374-39955-7*, Farrar, Straus & Giroux (BYR)) Farrar, Straus & Giroux.

Muldrow, Diane. Boiling Point! Friends Cooking Eating Talking Life. 2002. (Dish Ser.: No. 3). (Illus.). 160p. (YA). mass mkt. 4.99 (*0-448-42828-8*, Grosset & Dunlap) Penguin Putnam Bks. for Young Readers.

—Stirring It Up: Friends Cooking, Eating, Talking Life. 2002. (Dish Ser.: No. 1). (Illus.). 160p. (J). (gr. 4-7). mass mkt. 4.99 (*0-448-42815-6*, Grosset & Dunlap) Penguin Putnam Bks. for Young Readers.

—Turning up the Heat: Friends Cooking, Eating, Talking Life. 2002. (Dish Ser.: No. 2). (Illus.). 160p. (J). mass mkt. 4.99 (*0-448-42816-4*) Penguin Putnam Bks. for Young Readers.

Nelson, Carol Ann. Sammy Knows What to Do. 2000. (J). (gr. 1-3). 11.95 (*1-893886-02-6*) How I Learn & Grow.

Orden, J. Hannah. In Real Life. 1993. 192p. (YA). (gr. 7 up). pap. 3.99 o.s.i (*0-14-034039-4*, Puffin Bks.) Penguin Putnam Bks. for Young Readers.

Rosenblum, Richard. My Block. 1988. (Illus.). 32p. (J). (gr. k-2). 12.95 o.s.i (*0-689-31283-0*, Atheneum) Simon & Schuster Children's Publishing.

Rush, Ken. The Seltzer Man. 1993. (Illus.). 32p. (J). (ps-3). lib. bdg. 14.95 (*0-02-777917-3*, Simon & Schuster Children's Publishing) Simon & Schuster Children's Publishing.

Shotwell, Louisa R. Adam Bookout. 1967. (Illus.). (J). (gr. 4 up). 3.95 o.p. (*0-670-10401-9*) Viking Penguin.

Shura, Mary Francis. The Search for Grissi. 1986. (J). (gr. 3-7). 12.95 o.p. (*0-399-21705-3*, G. P. Putnam's Sons) Penguin Group (USA) Inc.

Singer, Marilyn. Didi & Daddy on the Promenade. 2001. (Illus.). 32p. (J). (ps-3). tchr. ed. 14.00 (*0-618-04640-2*, Clarion Bks.) Houghton Mifflin Co. Trade & Reference Div.

Uhlberg, Myron. Flying over Brooklyn. 1999. (Illus.). 32p. (J). (ps-3). 15.95 (*1-56145-194-0*) Peachtree Pubs., Ltd.

Woodson, Jacqueline. Between Madison & Palmetto. 128p. (J). 1995. (gr. 5 up). pap. 3.50 o.s.i (*0-440-41062-2*); 1993. (gr. 1-6). 13.95 o.s.i (*0-385-30906-6*, Delacorte Pr.) Dell Publishing.

—Between Madison & Palmetto. 2002. 128p. (J). 16.99 (*0-399-23757-7*); (YA). pap. 5.99 (*0-698-11958-4*) Putnam Publishing Group, The.

—Last Summer with Maizon. 1991. 112p. (YA). pap. 3.99 o.s.i (*0-440-40555-6*) Dell Publishing.

—Last Summer with Maizon. 2002. 112p. (J). 16.99 (*0-399-23755-0*); (Illus.). 128p. (YA). (gr. 3-7). pap. 4.99 (*0-698-11929-0*) Putnam Publishing Group, The.

Young, Karen. Cobwebs from the Sky. Date not set. (J). 15.99 (*0-06-029761-1*, Greenwillow Bks.) HarperCollins Children's Bk. Group.

BROOKLYN BRIDGE (NEW YORK, N.Y.)—FICTION

Lurie, April. Dancing in the Streets of Brooklyn. 2002. 208p. (gr. 3-7). text 15.95 (*0-385-72942-1*) Random Hse., Inc.

Placide, Jaira. Fresh Girl. 2002. 224p. (YA). (gr. 7 up). 15.95 (*0-385-32753-6*, Delacorte Pr.) Dell Publishing.

—Fresh Girl. 224p. (YA). (gr. 7). 2004. mass mkt. 5.50 (*0-440-23764-5*, Laurel Leaf); 2002. lib. bdg. 17.99 o.s.i (*0-385-90035-X*, Lamb, Wendy) Random Hse. Children's Bks.

Simpson, Louise M. The Quinns. 1996. 80p. (YA). pap. 5.00 (*1-56002-230-2*, University Editions) Aegina Pr., Inc.

Uhlberg, Myron. Flying over Brooklyn. (Illus.). (J). (gr. k-3). 2003. pap. 7.95 (*1-56145-294-7*); 1999. 32p. 15.95 (*1-56145-194-0*) Peachtree Pubs., Ltd.

BULGARIA—FICTION

Shannon, Monica. Dobry. 1993. (Newbery Library). (Illus.). 192p. (J). (gr. 5 up). pap. 4.99 o.s.i (*0-14-036334-3*, Puffin Bks.) Penguin Putnam Bks. for Young Readers.

BURMA—FICTION

Lindquist, Willis. Haji of the Elephants. 1976. (Illus.). (J). (gr. 5-8). lib. bdg. o.p. (*0-07-037892-4*) McGraw-Hill Cos., The.

C

CALIFORNIA—FICTION

Alef, Daniel. Centennial Stories: A Living History of San Francisco. 2nd ed. 2000. (Illus.). 227p. (J). pap. 15.95 (*0-9700174-2-1*) Maxit Publishing, Inc.

Allen, Steve. Die Laughing. 1999. 288p. mass mkt. 5.99 o.s.i (*1-57566-380-5*) Kensington Publishing Corp.

Alphin, Elaine Marie. Picture Perfect. 2003. (Illus.). 244p. (J). 15.95 (*0-8225-0535-5*, Carolrhoda Bks.) Lerner Publishing Group.

Altman, Linda Jacobs. The Legend of Freedom Hill. (Illus.). (J). 2003. pap. (*1-58430-169-4*); 2000. 32p. 15.95 (*1-58430-003-5*) Lee & Low Bks., Inc.

Atkins, Elizabeth H. Treasures of the Medranos, 001. 1957. (Illus.). (J). (gr. 3-7). 4.25 o.p. (*0-395-27666-7*) Houghton Mifflin Co.

Austin, Mary H. Basket Woman: A Book of Indian Tales for Children. 1904. (J). 10.00 o.p. (*0-403-00001-7*) Scholarly Pr., Inc.

Axelrod, Amy. The News Hounds Catch a Wave: A Geography Adventure. 2001. (Illus.). (J). (*0-689-82410-6*, Simon & Schuster Children's Publishing) Simon & Schuster Children's Publishing.

Bader, Bonnie. Golden Quest. 1993. (Stories of the States Ser.). (Illus.). 64p. (J). (gr. 4-7). lib. bdg. 14.95 (*1-881889-30-0*) Silver Moon Pr.

Balmes, Kathy. Thunder on the Sierra. 2001. (Adventures in America Ser.). (Illus.). 96p. (J). (gr. 3-7). lib. bdg. 14.95 (*1-893110-10-9*) Silver Moon Pr.

Beatty, Patricia. Nickle Plated Beauty. 1993. 272p. (YA). (gr. 5 up). reprint ed. mass mkt. 4.95 o.p. (*0-688-12279-5*, Morrow, William & Co.) Morrow/Avon.

Block, Francesca Lia. I Was a Teenage Fairy. 192p. (J). (gr. 7 up). 1998. lib. bdg. 14.89 (*0-06-027748-3*); 2000. reprint ed. pap. 7.99 (*0-06-440862-0*, Harper Trophy) HarperCollins Children's Bk. Group.

—I Was a Teenage Fairy. 2000. (Illus.). (J). 14.00 (*0-606-18903-3*) Turtleback Bks.

Boone, Sheila. Free As a Butterfly. 2003. (Illus.). 32p. (J). (ps-3). pap. 7.95 (*1-891577-80-8*) Image Pr., Inc.

—Free As a Butterfly. 2003. (Illus.). 32p. (J). (ps-8). 12.95 (*1-891577-79-4*) Images Pr.

Boyd, Candy Dawson. Fall Secrets. 1994. (Seasons Ser.). 224p. (J). (gr. 3-7). pap. 3.99 o.s.i (*0-14-036583-4*, Puffin Bks.) Penguin Putnam Bks. for Young Readers.

Bray, Marian. The Bounty Hunter. 1992. (Reba Novel Ser.: Vol. 1). 144p. (YA). pap. 5.99 o.p. (*0-310-54351-7*) Zondervan.

Brinkerhoff, Shirley. Narrow Walk. 1998. (Nikki Sheridan Ser.: Bk. 3). 192p. (J). (gr. 9-13). pap. 5.99 (*1-56179-539-9*) Focus on the Family Publishing.

Brooks, Chelsea. California Dreams, Vol 13. 1995. (J). pap. 2.95 (*0-689-80090-8*, Aladdin) Simon & Schuster Children's Publishing.

Bryant, Bonnie. The Long Ride. 1998. (Pine Hollow Ser.: No. 1). 192p. (gr. 7 up). mass mkt. 4.50 o.s.i (*0-553-49242-X*, Dell Books for Young Readers) Random Hse. Children's Bks.

—Reining In. 1998. (Pine Hollow Ser.: No. 3). 240p. (gr. 7 up). mass mkt. 4.50 o.s.i (*0-553-49244-6*) Bantam Bks.

Bulla, Clyde Robert. Secret Valley. (Trophy Bk.). (Illus.). (J). (gr. 2-5). 1993. 112p. pap. 4.50 (*0-06-440456-0*, Harper Trophy); 1949. lib. bdg. 7.95 o.p. (*0-690-72383-0*) HarperCollins Children's Bk. Group.

Bunting, Eve. Jumping the Nail. (YA). (gr. 7 up). 1993. (Illus.). 182p. pap. 6.00 (*0-15-241358-8*, Harcourt Paperbacks); 1991. 160p. 15.95 o.s.i (*0-15-241357-X*) Harcourt Children's Bks.

Burton, Virginia Lee. Maybelle the Cable Car. 1997. (Illus.). 48p. (J). (ps-3). pap. 5.95 (*0-395-84003-1*) Houghton Mifflin Co.

Burton, Virginia Lee, ed. Maybelle the Cable Car. 1996. 12.10 (*0-606-11607-9*) Turtleback Bks.

—Maybelle, the Cable Car. (Illus.). (J). (ps-3). 1997. 56p. lib. bdg., tchr. ed. 16.00 (*0-395-82847-3*); 1976. 7.95 o.p. (*0-395-24905-8*); 1976. 4.23 o.p. (*0-395-06679-4*) Houghton Mifflin Co.

Bush, Elsie R. Jungletown Lane. 1997. (Illus.). 96p. (J). (gr. 5-6). pap. 7.95 (*0-9609440-1-X*) E&R Publishing.

Byrd, Sandra. Change of Heart. 2002. (Hidden Diary Ser.: Bk. 6). 112p. (J). pap. 4.99 (*0-7642-2485-9*) Bethany Hse. Pubs.

—Cross My Heart. 2001. (Hidden Diary Ser.). 112p. (J). (gr. 3-7). pap. 4.99 (*0-7642-2480-8*) Bethany Hse. Pubs.

—Just Between Friends. 2001. (Hidden Diary Ser.). 112p. (J). (gr. 3-7). pap. 4.99 (*0-7642-2482-4*) Bethany Hse. Pubs.

—One Plus One. 2002. (Hidden Diary Ser.). 112p. (J). (gr. 3-7). pap. 4.99 (*0-7642-2487-5*) Bethany Hse. Pubs.

—Pass It On. 2002. (Hidden Diary Ser.: Bk. 5). 112p. (J). pap. 4.99 (*0-7642-2484-0*) Bethany Hse. Pubs.

—Take a Bow. 2001. (Hidden Diary Ser.). 112p. (J). (gr. 3-7). pap. 4.99 (*0-7642-2483-2*) Bethany Hse. Pubs.

—Take a Chance. 2002. (Hidden Diary Ser.). 112p. (J). (gr. 3-7). pap. 4.99 (*0-7642-2486-7*) Bethany Hse. Pubs.

Cadnum, Michael. Edge. (J). (gr. 7-12). 1999. (Illus.). 144p. 5.99 (*0-14-038714-5*); 1997. 256p. 15.99 o.p. (*0-670-87335-7*) Penguin Putnam Bks. for Young Readers.

Cameron, Eleanor. The Terrible Churnadryne. 1959. (Illus.). (J). (gr. 4-6). 14.45 o.p. (*0-316-12535-0*) Little Brown & Co.

Campbell Hale, Janet. Owl's Song. 1998. 153p. (J). pap. 12.95 (*0-8263-1861-4*) Univ. of New Mexico Pr.

Carroll, Jenny. The Ninth Key. 2001. (Mediator Ser.: Vol. 2). (YA). E-Book 4.99 (*0-7434-2675-4*, Simon Pulse) Simon & Schuster Children's Publishing.

—Ninth Key. 2001. (Mediator Ser.: Vol. 2). (Illus.). 240p. (YA). (gr. 7 up). mass mkt. 4.99 (*0-671-78798-5*, Simon Pulse) Simon & Schuster Children's Publishing.

—Shadowland. 2000. (Mediator Ser.: Vol. 1). 256p. (YA). mass mkt. 4.99 (*0-671-78791-8*, Simon Pulse) Simon & Schuster Children's Publishing.

Chambers, Vickie. In the Silence of the Hills. Taylor, LaVonne, ed. (Illus.). (YA). (gr. 9-12). (*0-9627735-1-4*) Excellence Enterprises.

Chase, Alyssa. Tessa on Her Own. 1994. (Key Concepts in Personal Development Ser.). (Illus.). 32p. (J). (gr. 1-4). 16.95 (*1-55942-064-2*, 7659) Marsh Media.

Choldenko, Gennifer. Al Capone Does My Shirts. 2004. (J). 16.99 (*0-399-23861-1*, Putnam & Grosset) Putnam Publishing Group, The.

Cleary, Beverly. The Luckiest Girl. 1970. (Illus.). 272p. (J). (gr. 5 up). 17.89 (*0-688-31741-3*) HarperCollins Children's Bk. Group.

Cochrane, Patricia A. Purely Rosie Pearl. 1996. 136p. (J). (gr. 4-7). 14.95 o.s.i (*0-385-32193-7*, Dell Books for Young Readers) Random Hse. Children's Bks.

Cole, Sheila. The Canyon. 2002. 160p. (J). (gr. 3-7). lib. bdg. 15.89 (*0-06-029496-5*) HarperCollins Children's Bk. Group.

Cooney, Caroline B. Flash Fire. (YA). (gr. 7 up). 1996. mass mkt. 4.50 (*0-590-48496-6*); 1995. 176p. pap. 14.95 (*0-590-25253-4*) Scholastic, Inc.

—Flash Fire. 1995. 10.55 (*0-606-09284-6*) Turtleback Bks.

Courtney, Vincent. Die Laughing. 1994. (Nightmare Club Ser.: No. 10). 224p. mass mkt. 3.50 o.s.i (*0-8217-4511-5*, Zebra Bks.) Kensington Publishing Corp.

Cushman, Karen. The Ballad of Lucy Whipple. 1996. 208p. (YA). (gr. 7-9). tchr. ed. 15.00 (*0-395-72806-1*, Clarion Bks.) Houghton Mifflin Co. Trade & Reference Div.

Duey, Kathleen. Anisett Lundberg: California, 1851. 1996. (American Diaries Ser.: No. 3). 144p. (J). (gr. 3-7). pap. 4.99 (*0-689-80386-9*, Aladdin) Simon & Schuster Children's Publishing.

—Anisett Lundberg: California, 1851. 1996. (American Diaries Ser.: No. 3). (J). (gr. 3-7). 10.55 (*0-606-08987-X*) Turtleback Bks.

Duey, Kathleen & Bale, Karen. Three of Hearts. 1998. (J). (gr. 3-7). pap. 3.99 (*0-380-78720-2*, Avon Bks.) Morrow/Avon.

—Three of Hearts. 1998. 10.04 (*0-606-16346-8*) Turtleback Bks.

Durbin, William. The Journal of C. J. Jackson: A Dust Bowl Migrant, Oklahoma to California, 1935. 2002. (My Name Is America Ser.). (Illus.). 144p. (J). (gr. 4-9). pap. 10.95 (*0-439-15306-9*, Scholastic Pr.) Scholastic, Inc.

Easton. Blood & Money. 1998. 20.00 (*0-7862-1103-2*, Macmillan Reference USA) Gale Group.

Easton, Kelly. The Life History of a Star. 208p. (YA). 2002. pap. 6.99 (*0-689-85270-3*, Simon Pulse); 2001. (Illus.). (gr. 7 up). 16.00 (*0-689-83134-X*, McElderry, Margaret K.) Simon & Schuster Children's Publishing.

—The Life History of a Star. l.t. ed. 2002. (Young Adult Ser.). 200p. 22.95 (*0-7862-4786-X*) Thorndike Pr.

Easton, Robert. Blood & Money. 1998. (Western Ser.). 372p. 19.95 (*0-7862-1154-7*, Five Star) Gale Group.

Ellis, Ella Thorp. The Year of My Indian Prince. 2002. 224p. (YA). (gr. 7). mass mkt. 5.50 (*0-440-22950-2*, Random Hse. Bks. for Young Readers) Random Hse. Children's Bks.

Ewing, Lynne. The Choice. 2003. (Daughters of the Moon Ser.: No. 9). 192p. (J). 9.99 (*0-7868-0851-9*, Volo) Hyperion Bks. for Children.

—Daughters of the Moon. 2000. 160p. (YA). pap. 4.99 (*0-7868-1409-8*);Vol. 2. pap. 4.99 (*0-7868-1410-1*) Disney Pr.

—Moon Demon. 2002. (Daughters of the Moon Ser.: No. 7). 288p. (J). 9.99 (*0-7868-0849-7*, Volo) Hyperion Bks. for Children.

Faber, Gail & Lasagna, Michele. Clara Rides the Rancho. (Whispers Ser.). (Illus.). (J). (gr. 3-7). 2002. 52p. pap., tchr.'s training gde. ed. 10.95 (*0-936480-17-3*); 2001. 185p. 12.95 (*0-936480-16-5*); 2001. 185p. pap. 9.95 (*0-936480-15-7*) Magpie Pubns.

Fleischman, Sid. By the Great Horn Spoon! (Illus.). 193p. (J). (gr. 4-7). 1988. pap. 6.99 (*0-316-28612-5*); 1963. 17.95 (*0-316-28577-3*) Little Brown & Co. (Joy Street Bks.).

Fletcher, Susan. Walk Across the Sea. 2001. (Illus.). 224p. (J). (gr. 5-9). 16.00 (*0-689-84133-7*, Atheneum) Simon & Schuster Children's Publishing.

—Walk Across the Sea. l.t. ed. 2002. (Young Adult Ser.). 218p. (J). 22.95 (*0-7862-4439-9*) Thorndike Pr.

Freeman, Martha. The Spy Wore Shades. 2001. (Illus.). 240p. (J). (gr. 3 up). 15.95 (*0-06-029269-5*); lib. bdg. 15.89 (*0-06-029270-9*) HarperCollins Children's Bk. Group.

—The Spy Wore Shades. Date not set. 160p. (YA). (gr. 3 up). pap. 4.99 (*0-06-440957-0*) HarperCollins Pubs.

—The Trouble with Babies. 2002. (Illus.). 80p. (J). (gr. 1-4). tchr. ed. 15.95 (*0-8234-1698-4*) Holiday Hse., Inc.

—The Year My Parents Ruined My Life. 1997. 192p. (J). (gr. 5-9). tchr. ed. 15.95 (*0-8234-1324-1*) Holiday Hse., Inc.

—The Year My Parents Ruined My Life. 1999. (Illus.). 192p. (gr. 4-7). pap. text 4.99 (*0-440-41533-0*, Dell Books for Young Readers) Random Hse. Children's Bks.

—The Year My Parents Ruined My Life. 1999. 10.55 (*0-606-16453-7*) Turtleback Bks.

Frieders, Robert. American Elves - The Yankoos Vol. 1: The Yankoos & Life in the Sonoran Desert. 1998. (Illus.). 152p. (J). (gr. 4 up). 16.00 (*0-9639284-6-5*) Yankoo Publishing Co.

Gallagher, Diana G. Gold Rush Fever! 1998. (Secret World of Alex Mack Ser.: No. 30). 144p. (J). (gr. 4-7). pap. 3.99 (*0-671-00703-3*, Aladdin) Simon & Schuster Children's Publishing.

Garfield, Henry. Moondog. 2001. 288p. (gr. 8-12). pap. 5.99 (*0-689-84152-3*, Simon Pulse) Simon & Schuster Children's Publishing.

—Moondog. 1995. 258p. (YA). (gr. 7 up). 21.00 o.p. (*0-312-11857-0*, Saint Martin's Minotaur) St. Martin's Pr.

Garland, Sherry. Valley of the Moon: The Diary of Maria Rosalia de Milagros, Sonoma Valley, Alta California, 1846. 2001. (Dear America Ser.). (Illus.). 224p. (J). (gr. 4-9). pap. 10.95 (*0-439-08820-8*) Scholastic, Inc.

Gates, Doris. Blue Willow. (Puffin Newbery Library). (Illus.). 176p. (J). (gr. 4-7). 1976. pap. 5.99 (*0-14-030924-1*, VS30, Puffin Bks.); 1940. 14.99 o.s.i (*0-670-17557-9*, Viking Children's Bks.) Penguin Putnam Bks. for Young Readers.

—Blue Willow. 2000. (J). (gr. 3-7). 20.75 (*0-8446-7143-6*) Smith, Peter Pub., Inc.

—Blue Willow. 1976. (Puffin Newbery Library). (J). 12.04 (*0-606-02396-8*) Turtleback Bks.

Gorog, Judith. Caught in the Turtle. 1983. (Illus.). (J). (gr. 5-8). 10.95 o.p. (*0-399-20981-6*, Philomel) Penguin Putnam Bks. for Young Readers.

Gray, Genevieve. How Far, Felipe? 1978. (I Can Read Bks.). (Illus.). 64p. (J). (ps-3). lib. bdg. 11.89 o.p. (*0-06-022108-9*) HarperCollins Children's Bk. Group.

Gregory, Kristiana. Seeds of Hope: The Gold Rush Diary of Susanna Fairchild, 1849. (Dear America Ser.). 2002. E-Book 9.95 (*0-439-42546-8*); 2002. E-Book 9.95 (*0-439-42547-6*); 2001. (Illus.). 176p. (YA). (gr. 5-8). pap. 10.95 (*0-590-51157-2*) Scholastic, Inc.

Grilley, Kate. Death Dances to a Reggae Beat. 2000. 272p. mass mkt. 5.99 o.s.i (*0-425-17506-5*, Prime Crime) Berkley Publishing Group.

Gunn, Robin J. Summer Promise. 1998. (Christy Miller Ser.: Vol. 1). 176p. (Orig.). (YA). (gr. 7-11). pap. 5.99 o.p. (*0-929608-13-5*) Focus on the Family Publishing.

Gunn, Robin Jones. Hold on Tight. 1998. (Sierra Jensen Ser.: No. 10). 160p. (YA). (gr. 7-11). pap. 6.99 (*1-56179-637-9*) Focus on the Family Publishing.

—Take My Hand. 1999. (Sierra Jensen Ser.: No. 12). 144p. (YA). (gr. 7-11). pap. 6.99 (*1-56179-736-7*) Bethany Hse. Pubs.

Hamilton, Elizabeth L. Secret of Cachuma Lake: Travel Adventure for Young Adults #1. 2001. (Illus.). 144p. (YA). per. 9.95 (*0-9713749-7-X*) Quiet Impact, Inc.

Handford, Martin. Where's Waldo in Hollywood. 2002. (Illus.). 32p. (J). (gr. 1-5). 5.99 (*0-7636-1919-1*) Candlewick Pr.

Harford, Martin. Wheres Waldo. 2003. (Big Bks.). (Illus.). 32p. 19.99 (*0-7636-2237-0*) Candlewick Pr.

Harrison, Harry. The California Iceberg. 1975. (Illus.). 128p. (J). (gr. 3-7). 5.95 o.s.i (*0-8027-6194-1*) Walker & Co.

Harte, Bret. The Outcasts of Poker Flat & Other Stories. 1964. (J). (gr. 8 up). mass mkt. 1.95 o.p. (*0-8049-0051-5*, CL51) Airmont Publishing Co., Inc.

Haskins, Lori. Butterfly Fever. Smath, Jerry, tr. & illus. by. 2004. (Science Solves It! Ser.). (J). pap. (*1-57565-134-3*) Kane Pr., The.

Henty, G. A. Captain Bayley's Heir: A Tale of the Gold Fields of California. 2000. 252p. (J). E-Book 9.95 (*0-594-02379-3*) 1873 Pr.

Hernandez, Natalie A. Las Aventuras con Padre Serra. Hernandez, Tony Y., tr. 1999. (ENG & SPA., Illus.). 112p. (Orig.). (J). (gr. 3-8). pap. 9.95 (*0-9644386-1-5*) Santa Ines Pubns.

Hernandez, Natalie N. Captain Sutter's Fort: Adventures with John A. Sutter. 1999. (Illus.). 107p. (Orig.). (J). (gr. 4-6). pap. 9.95 (*0-9644386-3-1*) Santa Ines Pubns.

Herndon, Ernest. Little People of the Lost Coast. 1997. (Eric Sterling, Secret Agent Ser.: Bk. 8). 128p. (J). (gr. 3-7). pap. 5.99 (*0-310-20733-9*) Zondervan.

Herrera, Juan Felipe. Grandma & Me at the Flea / Los Meros Meros Remateros. Rohmer, Harriet & Cumpiano, Ina, eds. 2002. Tr. of Los Meros Meros Remateros. (ENG & SPA., Illus.). 32p. (J). (gr. 1 up). 15.95 (*0-89239-171-5*) Children's Bk. Pr.

Hinman, Bonnie. San Francisco Earthquake. 32nd ed. 1998. (American Adventure Ser.: No. 32). (Illus.). (J). (gr. 3-7). pap. 3.97 (*1-57748-393-6*) Barbour Publishing, Inc.

Hobbs, Valerie. Charlie's Run, RS. 2000. (Illus.). 176p. (J). (gr. 4-7). 16.00 (*0-374-34994-0*, Farrar, Straus & Giroux (BYR)) Farrar, Straus & Giroux.

—Charlie's Run. 2002. 176p. (J). (gr. 3-7). pap. 5.99 (*0-14-230204-X*) Penguin Putnam Bks. for Young Readers.

—Charlie's Run. l.t. ed. 2001. (Illus.). 166p. (J). (gr. 4-7). 21.95 (*0-7862-3104-1*) Thorndike Pr.

—How Far Would You Have Gotten If I Hadn't Called You Back? 320p. 2003. (J). mass mkt. 5.99 (*0-439-58396-9*, Scholastic Paperbacks); 1995. (YA). (gr. 7 up). pap. 19.95 (*0-531-09480-4*, Orchard Bks.); 1995. (Illus.). (YA). (gr. 7 up). mass mkt. 20.99 o.p. (*0-531-08780-8*, Orchard Bks.) Scholastic, Inc.

—How Far Would You Have Gotten If I Hadn't Called You Back? 1997. 10.09 o.p. (*0-606-11483-1*) Turtleback Bks.

—How Far Would You Have Gotten If I Hadn't Called You Back? A Novel. 1997. 320p. (J). pap. 4.99 o.s.i (*0-14-038254-2*) Penguin Putnam Bks. for Young Readers.

—Tender, RS. 2001. 256p. (J). (gr. 7 up). 18.00 (*0-374-37397-3*, Farrar, Straus & Giroux (BYR)) Farrar, Straus & Giroux.

—Tender. 2004. 256p. (J). pap. 6.99 (*0-14-240075-0*, Puffin Bks.) Penguin Putnam Bks. for Young Readers.

Holder, Nancy. City of Angel. 1999. (Angel Ser.: No. 1). 192p. (YA). (gr. 7 up). pap. 4.99 (*0-671-04144-4*, Simon Pulse) Simon & Schuster Children's Publishing.

—Not Forgotten. 2000. (Angel Ser.: No. 2). 256p. (YA). (gr. 7 up). mass mkt. 5.99 (*0-671-04145-2*, Simon Pulse) Simon & Schuster Children's Publishing.

Jackson, Helen H. Ramona: Wyeth Edition. 1939. (Illus.). (YA). (gr. 6 up). reprint ed. 17.95 o.s.i (*0-316-45467-2*) Little Brown & Co.

Jiménez, Francisco. Breaking Through: A Migrant Child's Journey from the Fields. 2001. (Illus.). 208p. (YA). (gr. 7 up). tchr. ed. 15.00 (*0-618-01173-0*) Houghton Mifflin Co.

Johnson, Lissa Halls & Wierenga, Kathy. No Lifeguard on Duty. 2003. (Brio Girls Ser.). 192p. (J). (gr. 6-11). pap. 6.99 (*1-58997-081-0*) Bethany Hse. Pubs.

Johnston, Tony. Angel City. 2002. (Illus.). (J). (*0-399-23405-5*, Philomel) Penguin Putnam Bks. for Young Readers.

Jukes, Mavis. Expecting the Unexpected. 1999. 160p. (gr. 5-9). pap. text 3.99 (*0-440-41227-7*, Dell Books for Young Readers) Random Hse. Children's Bks.

—Expecting the Unexpected. 1999. 10.04 (*0-606-15911-8*) Turtleback Bks.

Kalpakian, Laura. Graced Land. 2nd ed. 1997. 304p. reprint ed. pap. 14.95 (*0-936085-39-8*) Blue Heron Publishing.

Katschke, Judy. The Case of the Summer Camp Caper. 1999. (New Adventures of Mary-Kate & Ashley Ser.). (Illus.). 96p. (gr. 2-7). mass mkt. 4.50 (*0-06-106584-6*, HarperEntertainment) Morrow/Avon.

Katz, Welwyn W. Whalesinger. 2002. 212p. (J). pap. 6.95 (*0-88899-191-6*) Groundwood Bks. CAN. *Dist:* Publishers Group West.

—Whalesinger. 1991. 224p. (YA). (gr. 7 up). mass mkt. 14.95 o.s.i (*0-689-50511-6*, McElderry, Margaret K.) Simon & Schuster Children's Publishing.

Kehret, Peg. Searching for Candlestick Park. 1999. (Illus.). 160p. (J). (gr. 3-7). pap. 5.99 (*0-14-130366-2*, Puffin Bks.) Penguin Putnam Bks. for Young Readers.

—Searching for Candlestick Park. 1999. 11.04 (*0-606-17427-3*) Turtleback Bks.

Kelso, Mary J. Goodbye, Bodie. 1989. (Illus.). 120p. (Orig.). (YA). (gr. 6 up). pap. 6.95 (*0-9621406-1-9*) MarKel Pr.

Kent, Peter. Quest for the West in Search of Gold. 1997. 6. (Illus.). 32p. (J). (gr. 3-6). 22.40 (*0-7613-0302-2*) Millbrook Pr., Inc.

Ketchum, Liza. The Gold Rush: The West. 1996. (Illus.). 128p. (J). (ps-3). pap. 12.95 o.p. (*0-316-49047-4*) Little Brown & Co.

Koss, Amy Goldman. How I Saved Hanukkah. 1998. (Illus.). 96p. (J). (gr. 2-5). 15.99 (*0-8037-2241-9*, Dial Bks. for Young Readers) Penguin Putnam Bks. for Young Readers.

—Kailey. 2003. (American Girl of Today Ser.). (J). pap. 6.95 (*1-58485-591-6*, American Girl) Pleasant Co. Pubns.

—A Stranger in Dadland. Hornik, Lauri, ed. 2001. (Illus.). 128p. (J). (gr. 5 up). 16.99 (*0-8037-2563-9*, Dial Bks. for Young Readers) Penguin Putnam Bks. for Young Readers.

Krensky, Stephen. Striking It Rich: The Story of the California Gold Rush. 1996. (Ready-to-Read Ser.). 64p. (J). (ps-3). mass mkt. 3.99 (*0-689-80803-8*, Aladdin) Simon & Schuster Children's Publishing.

Kresko, Robert G. Napa Jack's First Flight. 1995. 28p. (J). (gr. k-4). text 14.95 (*1-887534-00-8*) Napa Valley Mustard Celebration.

Krupowicz, Thomas E. Death Danced at the Boulevard Ballroom. 1992. 213p. (Orig.). (C). pap. 12.95 (*1-881690-00-8*) Terk Bks. & Pubs.

Kudlinski, Kathleen V. Shannon: A Chinatown Adventure, San Francisco, 1880. unabr. ed. 1996. (Girlhood Journeys Ser.). (Illus.). 71p. (J). (gr. 6-8). pap. 32.99 (*1-887327-06-1*) Aladdin Paperbacks.

—Shannon: A Chinatown Adventure, San Francisco, 1880. (Girlhood Journeys Ser.: Bk. 2). (J). 1997. 12.95 (*0-689-81204-3*, Simon & Schuster Children's Publishing); 1996. (Illus.). 72p. mass mkt. 5.99 (*0-689-80984-0*, Aladdin) Simon & Schuster Children's Publishing.

—Shannon: A Chinatown Adventure, San Francisco, 1880. 1996. (Girlhood Journeys Ser.: 2). (J). 11.19 o.p. (*0-606-10824-6*) Turtleback Bks.

—Shannon: Lost & Found, San Francisco, 1880. 1997. (Girlhood Journeys Ser.: Bk. 2). (Illus.). 72p. (J). (gr. 2-6). per. 5.99 (*0-689-80988-3*, Simon Pulse) Simon & Schuster Children's Publishing.

—Shannon: The Schoolmarm Mysteries, San Francisco, 1880. 1997. (Girlhood Journeys Ser.: No. 3). (Illus.). 72p. (J). (gr. 2-6). mass mkt. 5.99 (*0-689-81561-1*, Simon Pulse) Simon & Schuster Children's Publishing.

Kudlinski, Kathleen V. & Farnsworth, Bill. Shannon: A Chinatown Adventure, San Francisco, 1880. 1996. (Girlhood Journeys Ser.: 2). (Illus.). 72p. (J). (gr. 4-7). 13.00 o.s.i (*0-689-81138-1*, Simon & Schuster Children's Publishing) Simon & Schuster Children's Publishing.

Lachtman, Ofelia Dumas. A Good Place for Maggie. 2002. 144p. (J). pap. 9.95 (*1-55885-372-3*, Piñata Books) Arte Publico Pr.

Lantz, Francess L. Luna Bay: Oh, Buoy!, No. 4. 2003. 176p. mass mkt. 4.99 (*0-06-057373-2*, HarperEntertainment) Morrow/Avon.

Lee, Rebecca L. Concha: My Dancing Saint. 1997. (Illus.). 240p. (YA). (gr. 7-12). pap. 12.95 (*1-56474-215-6*) Fithian Pr.

Lehr, Norma. Haunting at Black Water Cove. 2000. (Illus.). 119p. (J). (gr. 3-7). pap. 6.95 o.p. (*0-87358-750-2*, Rising Moon Bks. for Young Readers) Northland Publishing.

—Haunting at Black Water Cove. 2000. (Illus.). (J). 13.00 (*0-606-18311-6*) Turtleback Bks.

Levitin, Sonia. Boom Town. 1997. (Illus.). 32p. (J). (gr. k-4). pap. 16.95 (*0-531-30043-9*); lib. bdg. 17.99 (*0-531-33043-5*) Scholastic, Inc. (Orchard Bks.).

—The Singing Mountain. (YA). (gr. 7-12). 1998. 272p. 17.00 (*0-689-80809-7*, Simon & Schuster Children's Publishing); 2000. 304p. reprint ed. mass mkt. 4.99 (*0-689-83523-X*, Simon Pulse) Simon & Schuster Children's Publishing.

Lowell, Susan. I Am Lavina Cumming. (Seeing Double Ser.). (Illus.). 200p. (J). (gr. 3-7). 1993. 14.95 (*0-915943-39-5*); 1992. pap. 6.95 (*0-915943-77-8*) Milkweed Editions.

—I Am Lavina Cumming. 1993. 12.05 o.p. (*0-606-07158-X*) Turtleback Bks.

Martin, Ann M. Amalia. 1997. (California Diaries). (YA). (gr. 6-8). mass mkt. 3.99 (*0-590-29838-0*, Scholastic Paperbacks) Scholastic, Inc.

—Amalia. 1997. (California Diaries). (YA). (gr. 6-8). 10.04 (*0-606-12640-6*) Turtleback Bks.

—Amalia: Diary Three. 2000. (California Diaries). (Illus.). 144p. (YA). (gr. 6-8). mass mkt. 4.99 (*0-439-09548-4*) Scholastic, Inc.

—Amalia: Diary Three. 1999. (California Diaries). (Illus.). (YA). (gr. 6-8). 11.04 (*0-606-18525-9*) Turtleback Bks.

—Amalia: Diary Two. 1998. (California Diaries). (YA). (gr. 6-8). mass mkt. 4.50 (*0-590-02385-3*) Scholastic, Inc.

—Amalia: Diary Two. 1998. (California Diaries). (YA). (gr. 6-8). 10.55 (*0-606-15472-8*) Turtleback Bks.

—Dawn. 1997. (California Diaries). 176p. (YA). (gr. 6-8). mass mkt. 3.99 (*0-590-29835-6*) Scholastic, Inc.

—Dawn. 1997. (California Diaries). (YA). (gr. 6-8). 10.04 (*0-606-11179-4*) Turtleback Bks.

—Dawn: Diary Three. 1999. (California Diaries). 144p. (YA). (gr. 6-8). mass mkt. 3.99 (*0-590-02389-6*) Scholastic, Inc.

—Dawn: Diary Three. 1999. (California Diaries: No. 11). 10.04 (*0-606-16609-2*) Turtleback Bks.

—Dawn: Diary Two. 1998. (California Diaries: No. 7). (YA). (gr. 6-8). mass mkt. 4.99 (*0-590-01846-9*) Scholastic, Inc.

—Dawn: Diary Two. 1998. (California Diaries). (YA). (gr. 6-8). 10.14 (*0-606-13238-4*) Turtleback Bks.

—Dawn on the Coast. (Baby-Sitters Club Ser.: No. 23). (J). (gr. 3-7). mass mkt. 3.95 (*0-590-42007-0*); 1997. 160p. mass mkt. 3.99 (*0-590-67391-2*); 1989. 192p. pap. 3.50 (*0-590-43900-6*) Scholastic, Inc.

—Dawn on the Coast. l.t. ed. 1994. (Baby-Sitters Club Ser.: No. 23). 176p. (J). (gr. 3-7). lib. bdg. 21.27 o.p. (*0-8368-1244-1*) Stevens, Gareth Inc.

—Dawn on the Coast. 1989. (Baby-Sitters Club Ser.: No. 23). (J). (gr. 3-7). 10.04 (*0-606-04085-4*) Turtleback Bks.

—Ducky. 1998. (California Diaries). (YA). (gr. 6-8). mass mkt. 4.50 (*0-590-29839-9*) Scholastic, Inc.

—Ducky. 1998. (California Diaries). (YA). (gr. 6-8). lib. bdg. 10.55 (*0-606-12901-4*) Turtleback Bks.

—Ducky: Diary Three. 15th ed. 2000. (California Diaries). 144p. (YA). (gr. 6-8). mass mkt. 4.99 (*0-439-09549-2*, Scholastic Paperbacks) Scholastic, Inc.

—Ducky: Diary Three. 2000. (California Diaries). (Illus.). (YA). (gr. 6-8). 11.04 (*0-606-18866-5*) Turtleback Bks.

—Ducky: Diary Two. 1998. (California Diaries). (YA). (gr. 6-8). pap. text 71.82 (*0-590-63083-0*);No. 10. 144p. mass mkt. 3.99 (*0-590-02387-X*) Scholastic, Inc.

—Ducky: Diary Two. 1998. (California Diaries). (YA). (gr. 6-8). 10.04 (*0-606-15471-X*) Turtleback Bks.

—Maggie. 1997. (California Diaries). (YA). (gr. 6-8). 10.04 (*0-606-11181-6*) Turtleback Bks.

—Maggie: Diary Three. (California Diaries). (YA). (gr. 6-8). 1999. 144p. mass mkt. 4.99 (*0-439-09547-6*); 1997. 160p. mass mkt. 3.99 (*0-590-29837-2*) Scholastic, Inc.

—Maggie: Diary Three. 1999. (California Diaries). (Illus.). (YA). (gr. 6-8). 11.04 (*0-606-18524-0*) Turtleback Bks.

—Maggie: Diary Two. 1998. (California Diaries). (YA). (gr. 6-8). mass mkt. 3.99 (*0-590-02383-7*) Scholastic, Inc.

—Maggie: Diary Two. 1998. (California Diaries). (YA). (gr. 6-8). 10.04 (*0-606-13239-2*) Turtleback Bks.

—Sunny. (California Diaries). (YA). (gr. 6-8). 1999. pap. text 54.00 (*0-439-09614-6*); 1997. 176p. mass mkt. 3.99 (*0-590-29836-4*) Scholastic, Inc.

—Sunny. 1997. (California Diaries). (YA). (gr. 6-8). 10.04 (*0-606-11180-8*) Turtleback Bks.

—Sunny: Diary Three, 1999. (California Diaries). 160p. (YA). (gr. 6-8). mass mkt. 4.50 (*0-590-02390-X*) Scholastic, Inc.

—Sunny: Diary Three. 1999. (California Diaries). (Illus.). (YA). (gr. 6-8). 10.55 (*0-606-18523-2*) Turtleback Bks.

—Sunny: Diary Two. 1998. (California Diaries). (YA). (gr. 6-8). pap. 71.82 (*0-590-65607-4*); mass mkt. 3.99 (*0-590-29840-2*) Scholastic, Inc.

—Sunny: Diary Two. 1998. (California Diaries). (YA). (gr. 6-8). 10.04 (*0-606-13237-6*) Turtleback Bks.

Marvin, John & Abbott, Raymond. Death Dances: Two Novellas on North American Indians. 1979. 8.95 o.p. (*0-918222-07-9*); pap. 3.95 o.p. (*0-918222-08-7*) Applewood Bks.

McCants, William D. Much Ado about Prom Night. 1995. 240p. (YA). (gr. 7 up). 11.00 o.p. (*0-15-200083-6*); pap. 5.00 o.p. (*0-15-200081-X*) Harcourt Children's Bks.

—Much Ado about Prom Night. 1995. 11.05 (*0-606-14276-2*) Turtleback Bks.

McCurtin, Peter. Death Dance. (Sundance Ser.). 1984. 224p. pap. text 2.50 o.s.i (*0-8439-2159-5*); 1979. pap. 1.75 o.p. (*0-8439-0669-3*) Dorchester Publishing Co., Inc.

—Death Dance. l.t. ed. 1983. (Ulverscroft Large Print Ser.). 416p. 29.99 o.p. (*0-7089-1055-6*, Ulverscroft) Thorpe, F. A. Pubs. GBR. *Dist:* Ulverscroft Large Print Bks., Ltd., Ulverscroft Large Print Canada, Ltd.

McGarrahan, Margaret. Nessie's California Adventures. 2002. (Illus.). 55p. (J). (gr. k-4). pap. 12.50 (*0-9672639-2-1*) Smith Lane Pubs.

McGinley, Jerry. Joaquin Strikes Back. 1998. 158p. (YA). (gr. 5-10). 18.95 (*0-936389-58-3*) Tudor Pubs., Inc.

McKinney, Jack. Death Dance. 1988. (Sentinels Ser.). 224p. (YA). (gr. 10 up). mass mkt. 4.95 o.s.i (*0-345-35302-1*, Del Rey) Ballantine Bks.

McMorrow, Catherine. Gold Fever! 1996. (Step into Reading Ser.). (Illus.). (J). (ps-3). 11.99 o.s.i (*0-679-96432-0*) Random Hse., Inc.

Moeri, Louise. Downwind. 1984. 144p. (J). (gr. 4-7). 13.95 o.p. (*0-525-44096-8*, Dutton Children's Bks.) Penguin Putnam Bks. for Young Readers.

Montes, Marisa. A Crazy Mixed-Up Spanglish Day. 2003. (Get Ready for Gabi Ser.). (Illus.). 96p. (J). pap. 12.95 (*0-439-51710-9*, Scholastic Paperbacks) Scholastic, Inc.

—Something Wicked's in Those Woods. 2000. 224p. (YA). (gr. 7-12). 17.00 (*0-15-202391-7*) Harcourt Children's Bks.

Montgomery, Rutherford G. Kildee House. 1993. (Newbery Honor Roll Ser.). (J). 14.00 (*0-606-05899-0*) Turtleback Bks.

—Kildee House. 1993. (Newbery Honor Roll Ser.). (Illus.). 224p. (J). (gr. 4-7). reprint ed. pap. 7.95 (*0-8027-7388-5*) Walker & Co.

Nasaw, Jonathan. Shakedown Street. 1995. 208p. (J). mass mkt. 3.99 o.s.i (*0-440-21930-2*) Dell Publishing.

—Shakedown Street. 1993. (J). o.s.i (*0-385-30951-1*, Dell Books for Young Readers) Random Hse. Children's Bks.

Nascimbene, Yan. Day in September. 2002. (J). (*0-89812-328-3*, Creative Paperbacks) Creative Co., The.

Nelson-Hernandez, Natalie. Stowaway to California: Adventures with Father Serra. 1994. (Illus.). 136p. (Orig.). (J). (gr. 3-8). pap. 9.95 (*0-9644386-0-7*) Santa Ines Pubns.

Nelson, Theresa. Ruby Electric. 2003. (Illus.). 272p. (J). 16.95 (*0-689-83852-2*, Atheneum/Richard Jackson Bks.) Simon & Schuster Children's Publishing.

Olsen, Mary-Kate & Olsen, Ashley. Love Is in the Air. 2004. (So Little Time Ser.: No. 13). 128p. mass mkt. 4.99 (*0-06-059068-8*, HarperEntertainment) Morrow/Avon.

Pascal, Francine, creator. Can't Stay Away. 1999. (Sweet Valley High Senior Year Ser.: No. 1). 192p. (gr. 7 up). mass mkt. 4.50 (*0-553-49234-9*, Dell Books for Young Readers) Random Hse. Children's Bks.

—Get Real! 1999. (Sweet Valley Junior High Ser.: No. 1). 160p. (gr. 3-7). pap. text 4.50 (*0-553-48603-9*, Dell Books for Young Readers) Random Hse. Children's Bks.

—I've Got a Secret. 1999. (Sweet Valley High Senior Year Ser.: No. 4). 192p. (gr. 7 up). mass mkt. 4.50 (*0-553-49278-0*, Dell Books for Young Readers) Random Hse. Children's Bks.

—So Cool. 1999. (Sweet Valley High Senior Year Ser.: No. 3). 192p. (gr. 7 up). mass mkt. 4.50 (*0-553-57028-5*, Sweet Valley) Random Hse. Children's Bks.

Pearce, Jonathan. The Far Side of the Moon: A California Story. 2nd ed. 2003. viii, 130p. (J). per. 15.95 (*1-59411-011-5*) Writers' Collective, The.

Peck, Richard. Bel Air Bambi. 1994. (J). mass mkt. 4.99 (*0-440-91031-5*, Dell Books for Young Readers) Random Hse. Children's Bks.

Pellowski, Michael J. Triple Trouble in Hollywood. (J). (gr. 3-5). 1996. pap. 3.50 o.p. (*0-87406-753-7*); 1989. (Illus.). 125p. pap. 2.75 o.p. (*0-87406-383-3*) Darby Creek Publishing.

Perez, L. King. First Day in Grapes. 2002. (Illus.). 32p. (J). (gr. 1-3). 16.95 (*1-58430-045-0*) Lee & Low Bks., Inc.

Perrin, Randy, et al. Time Like a River. 1999. 144p. (YA). (gr. 5 up). 14.95 (*1-57143-061-X*) RDR Bks.

Petersen, P. J. Liars. 1992. 176p. (YA). (gr. 7 up). 15.00 (*0-671-75035-6*, Simon & Schuster Children's Publishing) Simon & Schuster Children's Publishing.

Pfitsch, Patricia C. Riding the Flume. 2002. (Illus.). 240p. (J). (gr. 5-8). 16.95 (*0-689-83823-9*, Simon & Schuster Children's Publishing) Simon & Schuster Children's Publishing.

Phelan, Regina V. They Came Around the Horn, Vol. 5. l.t. ed. 1999. (History of California for the Young Reader Ser.). (Illus.). 64p. (J). lib. bdg. 15.00 (*0-87062-292-7*, Prosperity Pr.) Clark, Arthur H. Co.

Pike, Christopher, pseud. Chain Letter. 1986. 192p. (J). (gr. 7 up). pap. 4.99 (*0-380-89968-X*) HarperCollins Children's Bk. Group.

—Chain Letter. 1986. (J). 10.04 (*0-606-02005-5*) Turtleback Bks.

Pockets Learning Staff. Samantha's California Adventure. 1998. (Illus.). 2p. (ps-1). 15.00 (*1-888074-91-4*) Pockets of Learning.

Politi, Leo. Song of the Swallows. 1987. (Illus.). 32p. (J). (gr. 1-4). 16.95 (*0-684-18831-7*, Atheneum); 2nd ed. (ps-3). reprint ed. pap. 5.99 (*0-689-71140-9*, Aladdin) Simon & Schuster Children's Publishing.

—Song of the Swallows. 2nd ed. 1987. 12.14 (*0-606-02268-6*) Turtleback Bks.

Rafferty, S. S. Die Laughing. 1992. 200p. pap. 4.95 o.p. (*0-930330-16-1*) International Polygonics, Ltd.

Ramirez, Michael Rose. Hola, California! 1997. (Chana! Ser.: No. 1). (J). (gr. 3-5). pap. 3.99 (*0-380-79017-3*, Avon Bks.) Morrow/Avon.

—Hola, California! 1997. (Chana! Ser.). 9.09 o.p. (*0-606-11199-9*) Turtleback Bks.

Reiss, Kathryn. The Strange Case of Baby H. 2002. (American Girl Collection: Bk. 18). (Illus.). 176p. (J). (gr. 4-7). 10.95 (*1-58485-534-7*); pap. 6.95 (*1-58485-533-9*) Pleasant Co. Pubns. (American Girl).

Riefe, Barbara. Amelia Dale Archer Story. 1998. 304p. (YA). (gr. 8 up). 22.95 o.p. (*0-312-86077-3*, Forge Bks.) Doherty, Tom Assocs., LLC.

Ritter, John H. The Boy Who Saved Baseball. 2003. (Illus.). 224p. (J). (gr. 3-7). 17.99 (*0-399-23622-8*, Philomel) Penguin Putnam Bks. for Young Readers.

Roberts, Laura Peyton. Ghost of a Chance. 1997. 192p. (YA). (gr. 7-12). 14.95 o.s.i (*0-385-32508-8*, Delacorte Pr.) Dell Publishing.

—Ghost of a Chance. 1999. 192p. (gr. 5 up). pap. text 3.99 o.s.i (*0-440-41534-9*, Dell Books for Young Readers) Random Hse. Children's Bks.

—Ghost of a Chance. 1999. 10.04 (*0-606-16448-0*) Turtleback Bks.

Roberts, Willo Davis. Undercurrents. (Illus.). 240p. (J). 2003. pap. 4.99 (*0-689-85994-5*, Aladdin); 2002. (gr. 5-8). 16.00 (*0-689-81671-5*, Atheneum) Simon & Schuster Children's Publishing.

Romeyn, Debra. Juan & Mariano #1: Passage to Monterey. May, Dan, tr. & illus. by. 2003. 39p. (J). pap. 9.95 (*0-9729016-0-4*) Gossamer Bks.

Ryan, Pam Muñoz. California Aqui Vamos! 1997. Tr. of Along the California Trail. (SPA., Illus.). 32p. (J). (ps-3). pap. 6.95 (*0-88106-883-7*) Charlesbridge Publishing, Inc.

—California Aqui Vamos! 1997. Tr. of Along the California Trail. 13.10 (*0-606-13236-8*) Turtleback Bks.

—California, Here We Come! 1997. 13.10 (*0-606-13240-6*) Turtleback Bks.

—Esperanza Renace. 2002. (SPA., Illus.). 272p. (YA). (gr. 4-9). pap. 4.99 (*0-439-39885-1*, Scholastic en Espanola) Scholastic, Inc.

—Esperanza Rising. unabr. ed. 2001. (J). (gr. 4-6). audio 30.00 (*0-8072-8862-4*); (gr. 5-8). audio 25.00 (*0-8072-6207-2*) Random Hse. Audio Publishing Group. (Listening Library).

—Esperanza Rising. (Illus.). (gr. 4-9). 2002. 272p. (YA). mass mkt. 4.99 (*0-439-12042-X*); 2000. 262p. (J). pap. 15.95 (*0-439-12041-1*, Scholastic Pr.) Scholastic, Inc.

—Riding Freedom. 1999. (Illus.). 144p. (J). (gr. 3-7). pap. 4.99 (*0-439-08796-1*, Scholastic Paperbacks) Scholastic, Inc.

—Riding Freedom. 1999. 11.04 (*0-606-17445-1*) Turtleback Bks.

Sandoval, Victor. Roll over, Big Toben. 2003. 160p. (J). pap. 9.95 (*1-55885-401-0*, Piñata Books) Arte Publico Pr.

Santana, Patricia. Motorcycle Ride on the Sea of Tranquillity. 2002. 276p. (YA). 19.95 (*0-8263-2435-5*) Univ. of New Mexico Pr.

Santiago, Chiori. Home to Medicine Mountain. 1998. (Illus.). 32p. (J). (gr. 1 up). 15.95 o.p. (*0-89239-155-3*) Children's Bk. Pr.

Schaefer, Jack. Old Ramon. 1975. (Illus.). (J). (gr. 6-10). 7.95 o.p. (*0-395-07087-2*) Houghton Mifflin Co.

—Old Ramon. 1973. (Sandpipers Ser.). (Illus.). 102p. (J). (gr. 6 up). reprint ed. pap. 2.95 o.p. (*0-395-15056-6*) Houghton Mifflin Co. Trade & Reference Div.

—Old Ramon. 1993. (Newbery Honor Roll Ser.). 13.00 (*0-606-05959-8*) Turtleback Bks.

Schaeffer, Jack. Old Ramon. 1993. (Newbery Honor Roll Ser.). (Illus.). 112p. (J). (gr. 4-7). reprint ed. pap. 6.95 (*0-8027-7403-2*) Walker & Co.

Schraff, Anne. The Greatest Heroes. 2000. 143p. (J). (*0-7807-9271-8*); pap. (*0-7891-5133-2*) Perfection Learning Corp.

Schulte, Elaine L. Daniel Colton Kidnapped. 2002. (Colton Cousins Adventure Ser.: Bk. 4). (Illus.). 138p. (J). 6.49 (*1-57924-566-8*) Jones, Bob Univ. Pr.

—Daniel Colton Kidnapped. 1993. (Colton Cousins Adventure Ser.: Vol. 4). (Illus.). 144p. (J). (gr. 3-7). pap. 5.99 o.p. (*0-310-57261-4*) Zondervan.

—Melanie & the Modeling Mess. 1994. (Twelve Candles Club Ser.: No. 5). 128p. (J). (gr. 3-7). pap. 5.99 o.p. (*1-55661-254-0*) Bethany Hse. Pubs.

—Suzannah Strikes Gold. 2001. (Illus.). 144p. (J). pap. 6.49 (*1-57924-565-X*) Jones, Bob Univ. Pr.

—Suzannah Strikes Gold. 1992. (Colton Cousins Adventure Ser.: Vol. 3). 144p. (J). pap. 5.99 o.p. (*0-310-54611-7*) Zondervan.

Scott, Stefanie. Hollywood Hook-Up. 1998. (Moesha Ser.). 176p. (YA). (gr. 7 up). per. 3.99 (*0-671-01151-0*, Simon Pulse) Simon & Schuster Children's Publishing.

Simmons, Michael. Pool Boy. 2003. 176p. (gr. 7 up). 15.95 (*0-7613-1885-2*); lib. bdg. 22.90 (*0-7613-2924-2*) Millbrook Pr., Inc. (Roaring Brook Pr.).

Singer, Marilyn. California Demon. 1994. 160p. (J). (gr. 4-8). pap. 3.95 (*0-7868-1012-2*) Disney Pr.

—California Demon. 1992. 160p. (J). (gr. 5-9). 14.95 o.s.i (*1-56282-298-5*); lib. bdg. 15.49 o.s.i (*1-56282-299-3*) Hyperion Bks. for Children.

—California Demon. 1994. 10.00 (*0-606-06261-0*) Turtleback Bks.

Singleton, Linda Joy. Spring Break. 1994. (Pick Your Own Dream Date Ser.). 128p. (YA). (gr. 7 up). 3.95 o.p. (*1-56565-144-8*) Lowell Hse. Juvenile.

Snyder, Zilpha Keatley. Cat Running. 176p. 1996. (gr. 4-7). pap. text 4.99 (*0-440-41152-1*); 1994. (gr. 5 up). text 15.95 o.s.i (*0-385-31056-0*, Delacorte Pr.) Dell Publishing.

—Cat Running. 1995. (YA). (gr. 5 up). 18.95 (*0-385-30987-2*, Dell Books for Young Readers) Random Hse. Children's Bks.

—Cat Running. 1996. (YA). (gr. 5 up). 11.04 (*0-606-08710-9*) Turtleback Bks.

—Velvet Room. 1972. (Illus.). 224p. (J). (gr. 3-7). 7.95 o.p. (*0-689-30040-9*, Atheneum) Simon & Schuster Children's Publishing.

Soto, Gary. The Afterlife: A Novel. 2003. 176p. (J). (gr. 6 up). 16.00 (*0-15-204774-3*, 53597422) Harcourt Children's Bks.

—Chato y Su Cena. Ada, Alma Flor, tr. 1998. (SPA., Illus.). (gr. k-3). pap., tchr. ed. 37.95 incl. audio (*0-87499-439-X*) Live Oak Media.

—Chato's Kitchen. 1995. (Illus.). 32p. (J). (ps-3). 16.99 (*0-399-22658-3*, G. P. Putnam's Sons) Penguin Group (USA) Inc.

—Crazy Weekend. 1994. 160p. (J). (gr. 4-6). pap. 13.95 (*0-590-47814-1*) Scholastic, Inc.

—The Pool Party. 1993. (Illus.). 112p. (J). 13.95 (*0-385-30890-6*, Delacorte Pr.) Dell Publishing.

Spurr, Elizabeth. The Surfer Dog. 2002. 128p. (J). 15.99 (*0-525-46898-6*, Dutton Children's Bks.) Penguin Putnam Bks. for Young Readers.

Staples, Donna. Arena Beach. 1993. (YA). tchr. ed. 14.95 o.p. (*0-395-65366-5*) Houghton Mifflin Co.

Steinbeck, John. Of Mice & Men: The Play. 1983. (YA). (gr. 9-12). mass mkt. 2.75 o.s.i (*0-553-26675-6*) Bantam Bks.

Stites, Clara. Katya of Fort Ross. 2001. (Illus.). 80p. (J). pap. 8.95 (*1-56474-379-9*) Fithian Pr.

—Lixia of Gold Mountain: A Story of Early California. 2003. (Illus.). 64p. (J). pap. 8.95 (*1-56474-421-3*) Fithian Pr.

—Rosalba of Santa Juanita: A California Story. 2002. (Illus.). 80p. (J). pap. 8.95 (*1-56474-394-2*) Fithian Pr.

Stuckey, Ken. Conflict in California. 2001. (Orly Mann Racing Team Ser.). 208p. (YA). (gr. 9-12). pap. 6.99 o.p. (*0-8010-4478-2*) Baker Bks.

Taiz, Lincoln. Libra: The Cat Who Saved Silicon Valley. 2002. (Illus.). 326p. (J). pap. 14.95 incl. audio compact disk (*0-9723044-0-1*, AGP-1) Amsea Group, Inc.

Taylor, Theodore. Lord of the Kill. 2002. (Illus.). 256p. (J). (gr. 5-11). pap. 16.95 (*0-439-33725-9*, Blue Sky Pr., The) Scholastic, Inc.

—Maria. 1993. 80p. (J). (gr. 4-7). pap. 3.99 o.s.i (*0-380-72120-1*, Avon Bks.) Morrow/Avon.

—Maria: A Christmas Story. abr. ed. 1992. (Illus.). 96p. (J). (gr. 4-7). 15.00 o.s.i (*0-15-217763-9*) Harcourt Children's Bks.

—Maria: A Christmas Story. 1993. (J). 10.14 (*0-606-05452-9*) Turtleback Bks.

Thoene, Brock & Thoene, Bodie. Cannons of the Comstock. 1992. (Saga of the Sierras Ser.: Vol. 5). 208p. (J). (ps up). pap. 8.99 o.p. (*1-55661-166-8*) Bethany Hse. Pubs.

Uchida, Yoshiko. A Jar of Dreams. 1998. (J). pap. 3.95 (*0-87628-469-1*) Ctr. for Applied Research in Education, The.

—A Jar of Dreams. 1995. (J). (gr. 6). 9.28 (*0-395-73263-8*) Houghton Mifflin Co.

—A Jar of Dreams. (gr. 5-9). 1985. 131p. (J). pap. 3.95 o.s.i (*0-689-71041-0*, Aladdin); 1981. 144p. (YA). 16.00 (*0-689-50210-9*, McElderry, Margaret K.); 2nd ed. 1993. 144p. (YA). reprint ed. pap. 4.99 (*0-689-71672-9*, Aladdin) Simon & Schuster Children's Publishing.

—A Jar of Dreams. 1981. (J). 11.04 (*0-606-03337-8*) Turtleback Bks.

Van Draanen, Wendelin. Sammy Keyes & the Hollywood Mummy. unabr. ed. 2001. (Sammy Keyes Ser.). (J). audio 23.95 (*0-87499-799-2*, OAK011) Live Oak Media.

—Sammy Keyes & the Hollywood Mummy. 2001. (Sammy Keyes Ser.). 272p. (gr. 5-8). text 15.95 (*0-375-80266-5*, Knopf Bks. for Young Readers); lib. bdg. 17.99 (*0-375-90266-X*, Random Hse. Bks. for Young Readers) Random Hse. Children's Bks.

Walls, Pamela June. California Gold. 2001. (Abby Ser.: No. 3). (Illus.). 208p. (J). (gr. 3-7). mass mkt. 5.99 (*0-8423-3628-1*, Tyndale Kids) Tyndale Hse. Pubs.

—Lost at Sea. 2000. (Abby Ser.: No. 1). (Illus.). 224p. (J). (gr. 3-7). mass mkt. 2.99 (*0-8423-3626-5*, Tyndale Kids) Tyndale Hse. Pubs.

Warner, Penny. Mystery of the Haunted Caves: A Troop 13 Mystery. 2001. 102p. (J). (*0-88166-390-5*) Meadowbrook Pr.

Warner, Sally. This Isn't about the Money. 2002. 224p. (J). (gr. 3-6). 15.99 (*0-670-03574-2*, Viking Children's Bks.) Penguin Putnam Bks. for Young Readers.

Watson, Jude. Audacious: Ivy's Story. 1995. (Brides of Wildcat County Ser.: No. 3). 192p. (YA). (gr. 7 up). per. 3.95 (*0-689-80328-1*, Simon Pulse) Simon & Schuster Children's Publishing.

—Dangerous: Savannah's Story. 1996. (Brides of Wildcat County Ser.). 196p. (J). (gr. 7). pap. 3.50 (*0-689-80626-4*, Simon Pulse) Simon & Schuster Children's Publishing.

—Dangerous No. 1: Savannah's Story. 1995. (Brides of Wildcat County Ser.). 192p. (J). (gr. 7 up). pap. 3.95 (*0-689-80326-5*, Simon Pulse) Simon & Schuster Children's Publishing.

—Scandalous No. 2: Eden's Story. 1995. (Brides of Wildcat County Ser.). 192p. (J). (gr. 7 up). mass mkt. 3.95 (*0-689-80327-3*, Simon Pulse) Simon & Schuster Children's Publishing.

—Tempestuous: Opal's Story. 1996. (Brides of Wildcat County Ser.). 192p. (J). (gr. 7 up). mass mkt. 5.99 (*0-689-81023-7*, Simon Pulse) Simon & Schuster Children's Publishing.

Weir, Joan W. The Witcher. 1998. 157p. (YA). (gr. 3-7). pap. 5.95 (*1-896095-44-5*, Polestar Book Pubs.) Raincoast Bk. Distribution CAN. *Dist:* Publishers Group West.

Weiss, Ellen. Gold Rush Days. 2001. (Hitty's Travels Ser.: no. 2). (Illus.). 64p. (J). pap. 3.99 (*0-689-84677-0*, Aladdin) Simon & Schuster Children's Publishing.

Weitzman, David L. Pouring Iron: A Foundry Ghost Story. 1998. (Illus.). 32p. (J). (gr. 4-6). tchr. ed. 15.00 o.s.i (*0-395-84170-4*) Houghton Mifflin Co.

West, Tracey. Fire in the Valley. 1993. (Stories of the States Ser.). 80p. (J). (gr. 4-7). lib. bdg. 14.95 (*1-881889-32-7*) Silver Moon Pr.

Wilson, Eric G. Disneyland Hostage. 2000. (Illus.). 144p. (J). (gr. 6-8). pap. 4.99 (*1-55143-174-2*) Orca Bk. Pubs.

Windle, Jeanette. Jana's Journal. 2002. 256p. (J). 12.99 (*0-8254-4117-X*) Kregel Pubns.

Yamada, Debbie Leung. Striking It Rich: Treasures from Gold Mountain. l.t. ed. 2001. (Illus.). 128p. (J). (gr. 4-8). 13.95 (*1-879965-21-6*) Polychrome Publishing Corp.

Yep, Laurence. The Journal of Wong Ming-Chung: A Chinese Miner: California, 1852. 2000. (My Name Is America Ser.). (Illus.). 219p. (J). (gr. 4-8). pap. 10.95 (*0-590-38607-7*) Scholastic, Inc.

Yin. Coolies. (Illus.). 40p. 2003. pap. 7.99 (*0-14-250055-0*, Puffin Bks.); 2001. (J). 16.99 (*0-399-23227-3*, Philomel) Penguin Putnam Bks. for Young Readers.

Zach, Cheryl. Carrie's Gold. 1997. (YA). pap. 3.99 (*0-380-78952-3*, Avon Bks.) Morrow/Avon.

—Carrie's Gold. 1997. (American Dreams Ser.). 9.09 o.p. (*0-606-11194-8*) Turtleback Bks.

CAMBODIA—FICTION

Baillie, Allan. Little Brother. 144p. (J). 1994. (gr. 5 up). pap. 3.99 o.s.i (*0-14-036862-0*, Puffin Bks.); 1992. (gr. 3-7). 14.00 o.s.i (*0-670-84381-4*, Viking Children's Bks.) Penguin Putnam Bks. for Young Readers.

—Little Brother. 1994. 9.09 o.p. (*0-606-06535-0*) Turtleback Bks.

Bunting, Eve. Smoky Night. 1994. (Illus.). 40p. (J). (ps-3). 16.00 (*0-15-269954-6*) Harcourt Children's Bks.

Ho, Minfong. Gathering the Dew. 2003. (First Person Fiction Ser.). 208p. (J). (gr. 4-7). 16.95 (*0-439-38197-5*, Orchard Bks.) Scholastic, Inc.

Lee, Jeanne M. Silent Lotus, RS. 1994. (Illus.). 32p. (J). (ps-3). pap. 6.95 (*0-374-46646-7*, Sunburst) Farrar, Straus & Giroux.

—Silent Lotus. 1994. 12.10 (*0-606-08163-1*) Turtleback Bks.

Lipp, Frederick J. The Caged Birds of Phnom Penh. 2001. (Illus.). 32p. (J). (ps-3). tchr. ed. 16.95 (*0-8234-1534-1*) Holiday Hse., Inc.

CANADA—FICTION

Allen, Norman. Lies My Father Told Me. 1975. (J). (gr. 7). mass mkt. 1.95 o.p. (*0-451-09830-7*, J9830, Signet Bks.) NAL.

Allison, Rosemary. The Pillow. 1979. (Kids of Canada Ser.). (Illus.). 32p. (J). 5.95 (*0-88862-245-7*) Lorimer, James & Co. CAN. *Dist:* Formac Distributing, Ltd.

Andersen, Maria. Howlin' Marie. Elgaard, Elin, tr. 1985. 140p. (YA). (gr. 9-12). 7.95 (*0-920806-71-6*) Penumbra Pr. CAN. *Dist:* Univ. of Toronto Pr.

Arkin, Alan. Cassie Loves Beethoven. 2000. (Illus.). (J). (gr. 3-7). 176p. 16.99 (*0-7868-0564-1*); 170p. lib. bdg. 17.49 (*0-7868-2489-1*) Hyperion Bks. for Children.

—Cassie Loves Beethoven. l.t. ed. 2003. (Children's Large Print Ser.). 28.95 (*1-58118-108-6*) LRS.

Barber-Starkey, Joe. Jason & the Sea Otter. 1997. (Illus.). 32p. (J). reprint ed. pap. (*1-55017-162-3*) Harbour Publishing Co., Ltd.

Baskin. The Invitation. 1993. 288p. (J). pap. (*0-920813-54-2*) Sister Vision Pr.

Bastedo, Jaya. A Winter Walk with Haley. l.t. ed. 1999. (Illus.). 24p. (J). (ps-5). pap. (*1-894303-06-7*) Raven Rock Publishing.

Bayle, B. J. Battle Cry at Batoche. 2001. (Illus.). 144p. pap. 5.95 (*0-88878-414-7*) Beach Holme Pubs., Ltd. CAN. *Dist:* Strauss Consultants.

Bell, William. Absolutely Invincible. 2nd unabr. ed. 1993. 208p. (YA). (gr. 7 up). pap. 5.95 (*0-7736-7411-X*) Stoddart Kids CAN. *Dist:* Fitzhenry & Whiteside, Ltd.

—Zack. 1998. 176p. (YA). (gr. 5). pap. o.s.i (*0-385-25711-2*) Doubleday Canada, Ltd. CAN. *Dist:* Random Hse., Inc.

—Zack. l.t. ed. 2000. (LRS Large Print Cornerstone Ser.). 256p. (YA). (gr. 5-12). lib. bdg. 28.95 (*1-58118-072-1*, 23656) LRS.

—Zack. (Illus.). 192p. (YA). (gr. 7 up). 2000. mass mkt. 4.99 (*0-689-82529-3*, Simon Pulse); 1999. per. 16.95 (*0-689-82248-0*, Simon & Schuster Children's Publishing) Simon & Schuster Children's Publishing.

—Zack. 2000. (J). 11.04 (*0-606-20095-9*) Turtleback Bks.

Bilson, Geoffrey. Death over Montreal. 1982. 100p. (J). pap. (*0-919964-45-1*) Kids Can Pr., Ltd.

—Goodbye Sarah. 1981. 60p. (J). pap. (*0-919964-38-9*) Kids Can Pr., Ltd.

Blades, Ann. Mary of Mile 18. ed. 1980. (J). (gr. 2). spiral bd. (*0-616-01558-5*) Canadian National Institute for the Blind/Institut National Canadien pour les Aveugles.

—Mary of Mile 18. (Illus.). 40p. (J). (gr. 1-4). 1969. 11.95 o.s.i (*0-88776-015-5*); 1975. reprint ed. pap. 8.95 o.s.i (*0-88776-059-7*); 30th ed. 2001. 16.95 (*0-88776-581-5*) Tundra Bks. of Northern New York.

—Too Small. 2000. (Illus.). 32p. (J). (ps-3). 15.95 (*0-88899-400-1*) Groundwood Bks. CAN. *Dist:* Publishers Group West.

Bo, Ben. The Edge. 1999. (Young Adult Fiction Ser.). 144p. (YA). (gr. 9-12). lib. bdg. 14.95 (*0-8225-3307-3*, LernerSports) Lerner Publishing Group.

Book, Rick. Necking with Louise. 2001. 208p. (J). (gr. 7 up). pap. 6.95 (*0-06-447254-X*, HarperTempest) HarperCollins Children's Bk. Group.

—Necking with Louise. 1999. 168p. (YA). (gr. 9 up). pap. 7.95 (*0-88995-194-2*) Red Deer Pr. CAN. *Dist:* General Distribution Services, Inc.

Booth, David. The Dust Bowl. unabr. ed. 1997. (Illus.). 400p. (J). (gr. k-4). text (*1-55074-295-7*) Kids Can Pr., Ltd.

Boraks-Nemetz, Lillian. The Old Brown Suitcase: A Teenager's Story of War & Peace. 1994. 210p. (Orig.). (YA). (gr. 8-12). pap. 9.50 (*0-914539-10-8*) Ben-Simon Pubns.

Bouchard, Dave. Prairie Born. 1998. (Illus.). 32p. (J). (ps-3). 14.95 o.p. (*1-55143-092-4*) Orca Bk. Pubs.

Brandis, Marianne. Fire Ship. 1992. 120p. pap. (*0-88984-140-3*) Porcupine's Quill, Inc.

Brooks, Martha. Bone Dance. Date not set. 192p. (YA). (gr. 7 up). pap. (*0-88899-336-6*) Groundwood-Douglas & McIntyre CAN. *Dist:* Publishers Group West.

—Bone Dance. 1999. 192p. (YA). (gr. 7-12). mass mkt. 4.50 o.s.i (*0-440-22791-7*, Dell Books for Young Readers) Random Hse. Children's Bks.

—Bone Dance. 1997. (Illus.). 192p. (YA). (gr. 7-12). 16.95 (*0-531-30021-8*); lib. bdg. 17.99 (*0-531-33021-4*) Scholastic, Inc. (Orchard Bks.).

—True Confessions of Heartless Girl, RS. 2003. 192p. (J). 16.00 (*0-374-37806-1*, Farrar, Straus & Giroux (BYR)) Farrar, Straus & Giroux.

Brownridge, William Roy. The Moccasin Goalie. (Illus.). 32p. (J). (ps-3). 1996. 14.95 o.s.i (*1-55143-042-8*); 2001. reprint ed. pap. 7.95 (*1-55143-054-1*) Orca Bk. Pubs.

Buchanan, Dawna L. The Falcon's Wing. 1992. 144p. (YA). (gr. 4-7). pap. 15.95 (*0-531-05986-3*); pap. 16.99 (*0-531-08586-4*) Scholastic, Inc. (Orchard Bks.).

Burkett, Larry. Last Chance for Camp. 2000. (Great Smoky Mountain Storybook Ser.). (Illus.). 32p. (J). (ps-3). 7.99 (*0-8024-0985-7*) Moody Pr.

Carbone, Elisa. Stealing Freedom. 272p. (gr. 5-8). 2001. (Illus.). (YA). pap. 5.50 (*0-440-41707-4*, Dell Books for Young Readers); 1998. lib. bdg. 18.99 o.s.i (*0-679-99307-X*, Random Hse. Bks. for Young Readers); 1998. (Illus.). (YA). 17.00 o.s.i (*0-679-89307-5*, Random Hse. Bks. for Young Readers) Random Hse. Children's Bks.

Carey, Peter. The Big Bazoohley, ERS. 1995. (Illus.). 96p. (J). (gr. 4-7). 14.95 o.s.i (*0-8050-3855-8*, Holt, Henry & Co. Bks. For Young Readers) Holt, Henry & Co.

—The Big Bazoohley. 1996. (Illus.). 144p. (J). (gr. 4-7). pap. 4.99 o.s.i (*0-698-11420-5*, PaperStar) Penguin Putnam Bks. for Young Readers.

—The Big Bazoohley. 1995. (Storybridge Ser.). 96p. (J). (gr. 3-7). pap. 9.95 (*0-7022-2832-X*) Univ. of Queensland Pr. AUS. *Dist:* International Specialized Bk. Services.

Carlson, Natalie S. Alphonse, That Bearded One. 1954. (Illus.). (J). (gr. k-3). 7.95 o.p. (*0-15-202648-7*) Harcourt Children's Bks.

Carrier, Roch. The Boxing Champion. ed. 1995. Tr. of Champion. (J). (gr. 2). spiral bd. (*0-616-01612-3*) Canadian National Institute for the Blind/Institut National Canadien pour les Aveugles.

—The Boxing Champion.Tr. of Champion. (Illus.). 24p. (J). (gr. 3-7). 1993. pap. 7.95 (*0-88776-257-3*); 1991. 15.95 (*0-88776-249-2*) Tundra Bks. of Northern New York.

—The Hockey Sweater. Fischman, Sheila, tr. from FRE. 1985. Orig. Title: Le Chandail de Hockey. (Illus.). 24p. (J). (gr. 3-7). pap. 7.95 (*0-88776-174-7*) Tundra Bks. of Northern New York.

—The Hockey Sweater & Other Stories. Fischman, Sheila, tr. from FRE. 1979. Orig. Title: Le Chandail de Hockey. (Illus.). 160p. pap. (*0-88784-078-7*) House of Anansi Pr. CAN. *Dist:* Independent Pubs. Group.

Carter, Anne. Under a Prairie Sky. 2001. (Illus.). 30p. (J). (ps-3). trans. 16.95 (*1-55143-226-9*) Orca Bk. Pubs.

Cather, Willa. Shadows on the Rock. 1931. (YA). (gr. 7 up). 13.95 o.s.i (*0-394-44506-6*, Knopf Bks. for Young Readers) Random Hse. Children's Bks.

Chan, Gillian. The Carved Box. 2001. (Illus.). 232p. (YA). (gr. 5-9). 16.95 (*1-55074-895-5*) Kids Can Pr., Ltd.

Charles, Norma. Sophie Sea to Sea: Star Girl's Cross-Canada Adventures! 2000. 130p. (J). (gr. 3-8). pap. 5.95 (*0-88878-404-X*, Sandcastle Bks.) Beach Holme Pubs., Ltd. CAN. *Dist:* Strauss Consultants.

Cherry, Frances. Legs & Bizou. 1986. (Illus.). 36p. (J). (ps-8). 7.95 (*0-920806-60-0*) Penumbra Pr. CAN. *Dist:* Univ. of Toronto Pr.

Citra, Becky. Danger at the Landings. 2002. (Illus.). 96p. (J). (gr. 2-6). pap. 4.99 (*1-55143-232-3*) Orca Bk. Pubs.

—The Freezing Moon. 2001. (Young Reader Ser.). (Illus.). 96p. (J). (gr. 2-6). pap. 4.99 (*1-55143-181-5*) Orca Bk. Pubs.

Cleaver, Elizabeth, photos by. How Summer Came to Canada. 1988. (Illus.). 32p. (J). (ps up). pap. 5.95 o.p. (*0-19-540290-1*) Oxford Univ. Pr., Inc.

Cooper, Susan. The Boggart. 1995. (J). 11.04 (*0-606-07305-1*) Turtleback Bks.

Crook, Connie Brummel. The Hungry Year. 2001. 201p. (YA). (gr. 5 up). pap. 7.95 (*0-7737-6206-X*) Stoddart Kids CAN. *Dist:* Fitzhenry & Whiteside, Ltd.

—The Perilous Year. 2003. 197p. (YA). (*1-55041-816-5*) Fitzhenry & Whiteside, Ltd.

Curwood, James Oliver. Kazan: Father of Baree. 2004. 240p. (YA). (gr. 4-7). pap. 4.95 (*1-55704-225-X*) Newmarket Pr.

Czuchna-Curl, Ardyce. Days of Gold. 2002. (Illus.). 128p. (J). pap. text 12.95 (*0-88196-012-8*) Oak Woods Media.

Danakas, John. Hockey Night in Transcona. 1995. (Sports Novels Ser.). 115p. (J). (gr. 5-8). pap. 5.50 (*1-55028-504-1*) Lorimer, James & Co. CAN. *Dist:* Orca Bk. Pubs.

De Thomasis, Antonio. Le Montreal de Mon Enfance. 1994. (FRE., Illus.). 40p. (J). (gr. 1 up). 15.99 (*0-88776-343-X*) Tundra Bks. of Northern New York.

Dell, Pamela. Half-Breed: The Story of Two Boys During the Klondike Gold Rush. 2003. (J). (*1-59187-044-5*) Tradition Publishing Co.

Dorion, Betty F. Melanie Bluelake's Dream. 1995. 156p. (J). (gr. 4-7). pap. 4.95 (*1-55050-081-3*) Coteau Bks. CAN. *Dist:* General Distribution Services, Inc.

Downes, P. G. The Story of Chakapas. 1987. 32p. (J). (ps-8). 7.95 (*0-920806-91-0*) Penumbra Pr. CAN. *Dist:* Univ. of Toronto Pr.

Downie, Mary Alice & Rawlyk, George. A Proper Acadian. 1980. 60p. (J). pap. (*0-919964-29-X*) Kids Can Pr., Ltd.

Doyle, Brian. Easy Avenue. 1998. 128p. (YA). (gr. 6). text 14.95 (*0-88899-338-2*) Groundwood Bks. CAN. *Dist:* Publishers Group West.

—Mary Ann Alice. braille ed. 2003. (gr. 2). spiral bd. (*0-616-15266-3*) Canadian National Institute for the Blind/Institut National Canadien pour les Aveugles.

—Mary Ann Alice. (J). 2002. 144p. (gr. 4-8). pap. 12.95 (*0-88899-454-0*); 2001. 144p. (gr. 4-8). 15.95 (*0-88899-453-2*); 2nd ed. 2003. 168p. (gr. 9-13). pap. 5.95 (*0-88899-551-2*, Libros Tigrillo) Groundwood Bks. CAN. *Dist:* Publishers Group West.

—Uncle Ronald. 1997. (J). text 16.95 (*0-88899-266-1*) Douglas & McIntyre, Ltd. CAN. *Dist:* Publishers Group West.

—Uncle Ronald. 1998. 144p. (J). (gr. 4-7). pap. 4.95 (*0-88899-309-9*) Groundwood Bks. CAN. *Dist:* Publishers Group West.

—Uncle Ronald. 1997. 144p. (J). pap. (*0-88899-267-X*) Publishers Group West.

Durbin, William. The Broken Blade. 1997. 176p. (gr. 5-9). text 14.95 o.s.i (*0-385-32224-0*, Dell Books for Young Readers) Random Hse. Children's Bks.

—The Broken Blade. 1998. (J). 10.55 (*0-606-13228-7*) Turtleback Bks.

—Wintering. 208p. (YA). (gr. 5-7). 2000. (Illus.). pap. 4.50 (*0-440-22759-3*, Yearling); 1999. 14.95 (*0-385-32598-3*, Dell Books for Young Readers) Random Hse. Children's Bks.

Eckert, Allan W. Return to Hawk's Hill. (J). 2000. 208p. (gr. 7 up). pap. 6.99 (*0-316-00689-0*); 1999. 192p. pap. 4.99 (*0-316-20341-6*); 1998. (Illus.). 160p. (gr. 7-12). 15.95 o.p. (*0-316-21593-7*) Little Brown & Co.

—Return to Hawk's Hill. 2000. 12.00 (*0-606-17850-3*) Turtleback Bks.

Ellis, Kathryn. A Stroke of Luck. 1995. (Sports Novels Ser.). 84p. (J). (gr. 3-8). pap. 5.50 (*1-55028-506-8*) Lorimer, James & Co. CAN. *Dist:* Orca Bk. Pubs.

Ellis, Sarah. Next-Door Neighbors. 1992. 160p. (J). (gr. 4-7). pap. 3.25 o.s.i (*0-440-40620-X*) Dell Publishing.

—Next-Door Neighbors. 1990. 160p. (J). (gr. 4-7). 16.00 (*0-689-50495-0*, McElderry, Margaret K.) Simon & Schuster Children's Publishing.

Ferris, Sean. Children of the Great Muskeg. 1991. (Illus.). 84p. (J). (gr. 3-5). pap. 12.95 o.p. (*0-88753-128-8*) Black Moss Pr. CAN. *Dist:* Firefly Bks., Ltd.

Fleck, Earl. Chasing Bears: A Canoe Country Adventure. 2004. (Illus.). 135p. (YA). (gr. 7-12). pap. 12.95 (*0-930100-90-5*) Holy Cow! Pr.

Foggo, Cheryl. One Thing That's True. unabr. ed. 2002. (Illus.). 120p. (YA). (gr. 5-9). pap. 5.95 (*1-55074-377-5*); 1998. 260p. (J). (gr. 4-7). (*1-55074-411-9*) Kids Can Pr., Ltd.

—Sam Finds a Monster. 2003. (Kids Can Read Ser.). (Illus.). 32p. (J). (gr. k-1). 14.95 (*1-55337-351-0*) Kids Can Pr., Ltd.

Freedman, Benedict. Mrs. Mike. 1981. (J). (gr. 8-12). reprint ed. lib. bdg. 35.95 (*0-89966-396-6*) Buccaneer Bks., Inc.

Freedman, Benedict, et al. Mrs. Mike. 1987. 288p. (YA). (gr. 8-12). mass mkt. 4.99 (*0-425-10328-5*) Berkley Publishing Group.

Freedman, Nancy. Mrs. Mike. 9999. (J). pap. 1.95 o.s.i (*0-590-03445-6*) Scholastic, Inc.

Freeman, Bill. First Spring on the Grand Banks. 1978. (Bains Ser.). (Illus.). 215p. (J). mass mkt. 9.95 (*0-88862-220-1*); bds. 16.95 (*0-88862-221-X*) Lorimer, James & Co. CAN. *Dist:* Formac Distributing, Ltd.

—First Spring on the Grand Banks, Grades 5-10. 1981. (Bains Ser.). (Illus.). 80p. tchr. ed., spiral bd. 6.95 (*0-88862-431-X*) Lorimer, James & Co. CAN. *Dist:* Formac Distributing, Ltd.

Gale, Donald. Francie & the Basket Women. 2000. (Illus.). 56p. pap. (*1-55081-149-5*) Breakwater Bks., Ltd.

Garrigue, Sheila. The Eternal Spring of Mr. Ito. 1998. (J). pap. 3.95 (*0-87628-340-7*) Ctr. for Applied Research in Education, The.

—The Eternal Spring of Mr. Ito. 176p. (J). 1985. (gr. 5-7). lib. bdg. 14.95 o.s.i (*0-02-737300-2*, Atheneum/Richard Jackson Bks.); 1994. (gr. 3-7). reprint ed. pap. 4.99 (*0-689-71809-8*, Aladdin) Simon & Schuster Children's Publishing.

—The Eternal Spring of Mr. Ito. 1994. (J). 11.04 (*0-606-06363-3*) Turtleback Bks.

Garvie, Maureen McCallum & Beaty, Mary. George Johnson's War. (Illus.). (YA). (gr. 7 up). 2003. 248p. pap. 8.95 (*0-88899-468-0*); 2002. 224p. 15.95 (*0-88899-465-6*) Groundwood Bks. CAN. *Dist:* Publishers Group West.

Gilmore, Rachna. A Group of One, ERS. 2001. 192p. (YA). (gr. 6-9). 16.95 (*0-8050-6475-3*, Holt, Henry & Co. Bks. For Young Readers) Holt, Henry & Co.

—Roses for Gita. 1996. (Illus.). 24p. (J). (gr. k-3). 12.95 (*0-929005-86-4*); pap. 5.95 (*0-929005-85-6*) Second Story Pr. CAN. *Dist:* Univ. of Toronto Pr.

—Roses for Gita. 2001. (Illus.). 24p. (J). (gr. 1-5). pap. 7.95 (*0-88448-224-3*, Harpswell Pr.) Tilbury Hse. Pubs.

Goodman, Joan Elizabeth. Paradise: A Tale of Survival. 2002. 224p. (J). (gr. 7 up). tchr. ed. 16.00 (*0-618-11450-5*) Houghton Mifflin Co.

Gostick, Adrian R. Jessica's Search: The Secret of Ballycater Cove. 1998. (J). 1.99 (*1-57345-436-2*) Deseret Bk. Co.

Greenwood, Barbara. Spy in the Shadows 1867. 1990. 130p. (J). pap. text (*1-55074-018-0*) Kids Can Pr., Ltd.

Griek, Susan Vande. The Art Room. 2002. (Illus.). 24p. (J). (ps-2). 15.95 (*0-88899-449-4*) Groundwood Bks. CAN. *Dist:* Publishers Group West.

Guenter, Clarence A. God's Children. 1998. (Illus.). 106p. (J). (gr. 5-7). pap. text 8.00 (*1-58345-027-0*) Domhan Bks.

Guillot, Rene. Boy & Five Huskies. 1965. (Illus.). (J). (gr. 6-7). lib. bdg. 4.69 o.p. (*0-394-90972-0*, Pantheon) Knopf Publishing Group.

Harlow, Joan Hiatt. Star in the Storm. 2001. (Illus.). 160p. (J). (gr. 3-7). pap. 4.99 (*0-689-84621-5*, Aladdin) Simon & Schuster Children's Publishing.

Hebert-Collins, Sheila. Jean-Paul Hebert Was There. 2003. Tr. of Jean-Paul Hebert Etait La. (ENG & FRE., Illus.). (J). (*1-56554-928-7*) Pelican Publishing Co., Inc.

Hemon, Louis. Maria Chapdelaine. Brown, Alan, tr. from FRE. 1989. (Illus.). 96p. (YA). (gr. 5 up). reprint ed. 19.95 o.s.i (*0-88776-236-0*) Tundra Bks. of Northern New York.

Heneghan, James. Flood, RS. 2002. 192p. (YA). (gr. 7 up). 16.00 (*0-374-35057-4*, Farrar, Straus & Giroux (BYR)) Farrar, Straus & Giroux.

—Torn Away. 2003. 256p. (YA). (gr. 7 up). pap. 6.95 (*1-55143-263-3*) Orca Bk. Pubs.

—Torn Away. 192p. (J). 1996. (gr. 5-9). pap. 4.99 o.s.i (*0-14-036646-6*, Puffin Bks.); 1994. (Illus.). (gr. 7 up). 14.99 o.s.i (*0-670-85180-9*, Viking Children's Bks.) Penguin Putnam Bks. for Young Readers.

—Torn Away. 1996. 10.09 o.p. (*0-606-09984-0*) Turtleback Bks.

Henty, G. A. With Wolfe in Canada: The Winning of a Continent. 2001. (Illus.). 353p. (J). pap. 13.99 (*0-921100-87-6*); text 19.99 (*0-921100-86-8*) Inheritance Pubns.

—With Wolfe in Canada: The Winning of a Continent. (Illus.). 353p. 2000. (gr. 8-12). pap. 14.99 (*1-887159-30-4*); 1998. (J). lib. bdg. 20.99 (*1-887159-18-5*) Preston-Speed Pubns.

Holeman, Linda. Raspberry House Blues. 2000. 248p. (J). (gr. 6-9). pap. 6.95 (*0-88776-493-2*) Tundra Bks. of Northern New York.

Holubitsky, Katherine. Alone at Ninety Foot. (YA). (gr. 7 up). 2001. 194p. mass mkt. 6.95 (*1-55143-204-8*); 1999. 224p. 14.95 o.s.i (*1-55143-127-0*); 1999. 224p. pap. 5.95 (*1-55143-129-7*) Orca Bk. Pubs.

—Alone at Ninety Foot. 1999. (Illus.). (J). 12.00 (*0-606-18327-2*) Turtleback Bks.

Hope, Laura Lee. The Bobbsey Twins & the Cedar Camp Mystery. 1967. (Bobbsey Twins Ser.). (J). (gr. 3-5). 4.50 o.p. (*0-448-08014-1*, Grosset & Dunlap) Penguin Putnam Bks. for Young Readers.

—The Bobbsey Twins & the Talking Fox Mystery. 1970. (Bobbsey Twins Ser.). (Illus.). (J). (gr. 3-5). 4.50 o.s.i (*0-448-08063-X*, Grosset & Dunlap) Penguin Putnam Bks. for Young Readers.

Houston, James R. River Runners: A Tale of Hardship & Bravery. 1992. 160p. (J). (gr. 5 up). pap. 4.50 o.s.i (*0-14-036093-X*, Puffin Bks.) Penguin Putnam Bks. for Young Readers.

Hughes, Monica. Blaine's Way. l.t. ed. 1989. 334p. lib. bdg. 11.95 o.p. (*1-85057-581-9*, Macmillan Reference USA) Gale Group.

—Blaine's Way. 1996. 224p. (YA). (gr. 7 up). mass mkt. 4.95 (*0-7736-7445-4*) Stoddart Kids CAN. *Dist:* Fitzhenry & Whiteside, Ltd.

—The Crystal Drop. 1993. (J). (gr. 5-9). pap. 14.00 o.s.i (*0-671-79195-8*, Simon & Schuster Children's Publishing) Simon & Schuster Children's Publishing.

—Jan on the Trail. 2000. (New First Novels Ser.). (Illus.). 64p. (J). pap. 3.99 (*0-88780-502-7*); (gr. 1-4). (*0-88780-503-5*) Formac Publishing Co., Ltd. CAN. *Dist:* Orca Bk. Pubs., Formac Distributing, Ltd.

Hume, Stephen Eaton. Red Moon Follows Truck. 2001. (Illus.). 32p. (J). (gr. k-3). 16.95 (*1-55143-218-8*) Orca Bk. Pubs.

Hutchins, Hazel J. Within a Painted Past. 1994. (Illus.). 120p. (J). (gr. 5-7). lib. bdg. 14.95 (*1-55037-369-2*) Annick Pr., Ltd. CAN. *Dist:* Firefly Bks., Ltd.

Jackson, Lorna. Dressing for Hope. 1996. 148p. (J). pap. (*0-86492-167-5*) Goose Lane Editions.

Jam, Teddy. The Kid Line. 2001. (Illus.). 32p. (J). (gr. k-3). 16.95 (*0-88899-432-X*) Groundwood Bks. CAN. *Dist:* Publishers Group West.

—The Stoneboat. 2nd ed. 1999. (Illus.). 32p. (J). (ps-2). 15.95 (*0-88899-368-4*) Groundwood-Douglas & McIntyre CAN. *Dist:* Publishers Group West.

—The Year of Fire. 1992. (Illus.). (J). (gr. 2-5). (*0-88899-154-1*) Groundwood Bks.

—The Year of Fire. 1993. (Illus.). 48p. (J). (gr. 1-5). per. 14.95 (*0-689-50566-3*, McElderry, Margaret K.) Simon & Schuster Children's Publishing.

Johnston, Gordon. Inscription Rock. 1982. (Illus.). 70p. (J). 7.95 (*0-920806-20-1*) Penumbra Pr. CAN. *Dist:* Univ. of Toronto Pr.

Johnston, Julie. Hero of Lesser Causes. 1993. (J). 15.95 o.p. (*0-316-46988-2*, Joy Street Bks.) Little Brown & Co.

—Hero of Lesser Causes. 1994. 208p. (YA). (gr. 5 up). pap. 3.99 o.p. (*0-14-036998-8*, Puffin Bks.) Penguin Putnam Bks. for Young Readers.

—Hero of Lesser Causes. pap. 6.95 (*0-7737-5850-X*) Stoddart Kids CAN. *Dist:* Fitzhenry & Whiteside, Ltd.

—Hero of Lesser Causes. 2003. 232p. (J). (gr. 6). pap. 9.95 (*0-88776-649-8*) Tundra Bks. of Northern New York.

—Hero of Lesser Causes. 1994. (J). 9.09 o.p. (*0-606-07005-2*) Turtleback Bks.

Juby, Susan. Alice, I Think. 2003. (Illus.). 304p. (YA). 15.99 (*0-06-051543-0*, HarperTempest) HarperCollins Children's Bk. Group.

Katz, Welwyn W., ed. Time Ghost. 1995. 144p. (J). (gr. 4-7). per. 16.00 (*0-689-80027-4*, McElderry, Margaret K.) Simon & Schuster Children's Publishing.

Keep, Linda Lowery. Trouble on Ice. 1999. (Hannah & the Angels Ser.: No. 7). (Illus.). 144p. (YA). (gr. 5-8). pap. 3.99 o.s.i (*0-375-80112-X*, Random Hse. Bks. for Young Readers) Random Hse. Children's Bks.

Kinsey-Warnock, Natalie. Wilderness Cat. 1992. (Illus.). 32p. (J). (ps-3). 14.99 o.s.i (*0-525-65068-7*, Dutton Children's Bks.) Penguin Putnam Bks. for Young Readers.

Kositsky, Lynne. Claire by Moonlight. 2001. (On Time's Wing Ser.). 224p. (J). pap. 8.95 (*1-896184-03-0*) Roussan Pubs., Inc./Roussan Editeur, Inc. CAN. *Dist:* Orca Bk. Pubs.

Kouhi, Elizabeth. North Country Spring. 1980. (Illus.). 54p. (J). (ps-8). 6.95 (*0-920806-10-4*) Penumbra Pr. CAN. *Dist:* Univ. of Toronto Pr.

Kusugak, Michael Arvaarluk. Arctic Stories. 1998. (Illus.). 40p. (J). (gr. k-6). pap. 6.95 (*1-55037-452-4*); lib. bdg. 18.95 (*1-55037-453-2*) Firefly Bks., Ltd.

—Arctic Stories. 1999. 13.10 (*0-606-16482-0*) Turtleback Bks.

Lawson, Julie. Danger Game: A Novel. 1996. 214p. (YA). (gr. 5 up). 15.95 o.p. (*0-316-51728-3*) Little Brown & Co.

—White Jade Tiger. rev. ed. 2000. 165p. (J). (gr. 3-8). reprint ed. pap. 5.95 (*0-88878-332-9*, Sandcastle Bks.) Beach Holme Pubs., Ltd. CAN. *Dist:* Strauss Consultants.

Leavey, Peggy Dymond. Finding My Own Way. 2001. 184p. (YA). (gr. 8 up). pap. 7.95 (*0-929141-83-0*, Napoleon Publishing) Napoleon Publishing/ Rendezvous Pr. CAN. *Dist:* Words Distributing Co.

Leavitt, Martine. Heck, Superhero. 2003. 172p. (J). 16.95 (*1-886910-94-4*, Front Street) Front Street, Inc.

Lingard, Joan. Between Two Worlds. 1991. 192p. (YA). (gr. 7 up). 14.95 o.p. (*0-525-67360-1*, Dutton Children's Bks.) Penguin Putnam Bks. for Young Readers.

Little, Jean. The Belonging Place. 1997. 128p. (J). (gr. 3-7). 13.99 o.p. (*0-670-87593-7*, Viking Children's Bks.) Penguin Putnam Bks. for Young Readers.

—Spring Begins in March. 1966. (Illus.). (J). (gr. 4-6). 7.95 o.p. (*0-316-52785-8*) Little Brown & Co.

London, Jack. White Fang: A Scribner Illustrated Classic. 2000. (Scribner Illustrated Classics Ser.). (Illus.). 272p. (J). 25.00 (*0-689-82431-9*, Atheneum) Simon & Schuster Children's Publishing.

—White Fang: With a Discussion of Resilience. 2003. (Values in Action Illustrated Classics Ser.). (J). (*1-59203-038-6*) Learning Challenge, Inc.

—The Whole Story: White Fang. 1999. (Whole Story Ser.). (Illus.). 248p. (J). (gr. 7-12). 25.99 o.s.i (*0-670-88479-0*); pap. 18.99 (*0-670-88480-4*) Penguin Putnam Bks. for Young Readers. (Viking).

London, Jonathan. The Sugaring-Off Party. 1995. (Illus.). 32p. (J). 15.99 o.s.i (*0-525-45187-0*, Dutton Children's Bks.) Penguin Putnam Bks. for Young Readers.

—The Sugaring-Off Party. 1999. (J). pap. 5.99 (*0-14-056360-1*) Viking Penguin.

Lunn, Janet. Laura Secord: A Story of Courage. 2001. (Illus.). 32p. (J). (gr. 3-4). 16.95 (*0-88776-538-6*) Tundra Bks. of Northern New York.

—The Root Cellar. 1996. 240p. (J). (gr. 5-9). pap. 5.99 (*0-14-038036-1*); 1985. 256p. (YA). (gr. 7 up). pap. 3.99 o.p. (*0-14-031835-6*) Penguin Putnam Bks. for Young Readers. (Puffin Bks.).

—The Root Cellar. 1983. 256p. (YA). (gr. 5 up). lib. bdg. 17.00 (*0-684-17855-9*, Atheneum) Simon & Schuster Children's Publishing.

—The Root Cellar. 1996. (J). 12.04 (*0-606-03439-0*) Turtleback Bks.

—Shadow in Hawthorn Bay. 1988. 192p. (J). (gr. 5-9). pap. 3.95 o.p. (*0-14-032436-4*, Puffin Bks.) Penguin Putnam Bks. for Young Readers.

—Shadow in Hawthorn Bay. 1987. 192p. (YA). (gr. 7 up). 13.95 o.s.i (*0-684-18843-0*, Atheneum) Simon & Schuster Children's Publishing.

MacGregor, Roy. The Ghost of the Stanley Cup, No. 11. 1999. (Screech Owls Ser.: No. 11). 128p. (J). (gr. 4-7). mass mkt. 3.95 (*0-7710-5622-2*) McClelland & Stewart/Tundra Bks.

Maracle, Lee. Will's Gardens. 2002. (Illus.). 224p. (YA). (gr. 7 up). pap. 9.95 (*1-894778-02-2*) Theytus Bks., Ltd. CAN. *Dist:* Orca Bk. Pubs.

Matas, Carol. Rebecca. 2000. (Illus.). 160p. (J). mass mkt. (*0-439-98718-0*) Scholastic, Inc.

—Sparks Fly Upward. 2002. 192p. (YA). (gr. 5-9). 15.00 (*0-618-15964-9*, Clarion Bks.) Houghton Mifflin Co. Trade & Reference Div.

McNicoll, Sylvia. Grave Secrets. l.t. ed. 1999. (Illus.). 176p. (J). (gr. 7-9). pap. 8.95 (*0-7737-6015-6*) Stoddart Kids CAN. *Dist:* Fitzhenry & Whiteside, Ltd.

—Grave Secrets. 1999. 15.00 (*0-606-19641-2*) Turtleback Bks.

Montgomery, L. M. Anne of Green Gables. 2002. pap. 4.50 (*1-59109-388-0*) Booksurge, LLC.

—Anne of Green Gables. 2002. (Cageworld Ser.). (Illus.). (J). pap. 9.99 (*0-14-250102-6*, Puffin Bks.) Penguin Putnam Bks. for Young Readers.

—Anne of Green Gables. 2002. (Illus.). 256p. (J). 16.99 (*0-517-22111-X*, Random Hse. Bks. for Young Readers) Random Hse. Children's Bks.

—Anne of Green Gables. 2001. (Children's Classics). 288p. (J). pap. 3.95 (*1-85326-139-4*) Wordsworth Editions, Ltd. GBR. *Dist:* Advanced Global Distribution Services.

—The Complete Anne of Green Gables: Anne of Green Gables; Anne of the Island; Anne of Avonlea; Anne of Windy Poplars; Anne's House of Dreams; Anne of Ingleside; Rainbow Valley; Rilla of Ingleside, 8 vols. gif. ed. 1997. (J). (gr. 4-7). mass mkt. 36.00 (*0-553-60941-6*) Bantam Bks.

—Emily Climbs. 1976. 336p. (YA). 25.95 (*0-8488-0588-7*) Amereon, Ltd.

—Emily Climbs. 1984. 336p. (YA). mass mkt. 4.99 (*0-7704-2032-X*) Bantam Bks.

—Emily Climbs. 1996. 336p. (J). (gr. 7 up). mass mkt. 4.95 (*0-7710-9980-0*) McClelland & Stewart/ Tundra Bks.

—Emily Climbs. 1983. 336p. (YA). (gr. 7 up). mass mkt. 4.99 (*0-553-26214-9*, Starfire) Random Hse. Children's Bks.

—Emily of New Moon. 1976. 360p. (J). 25.95 (*0-8488-0589-5*) Amereon, Ltd.

—Emily of New Moon. unabr. ed. Set. 1989. (YA). (gr. 8 up). 47.95 incl. audio; Set 1999. (J). (gr. 5-6). pap. 47.95 incl. audio (*1-55685-579-6*) Audio Bk. Contractors, Inc.

—Emily of New Moon. 1983. 352p. (YA). mass mkt. 4.99 (*0-7704-1798-1*); (gr. 4-7). mass mkt. 4.99 (*0-553-23370-X*) Bantam Bks.

—Emily of New Moon. unabr. ed. 1999. (YA). (gr. 4-7). audio 62.95 (*0-7861-1488-6*, 118471) Blackstone Audio Bks., Inc.

—Emily of New Moon, Set. unabr. ed. 1999. (J). audio 62.95 Highsmith Inc.

—Emily of New Moon. 1996. 368p. (J). (gr. 4-7). mass mkt. 4.95 (*0-7710-9979-7*) McClelland & Stewart/ Tundra Bks.

—Emily of New Moon. 1999. 144p. (gr. 2-5). pap. text 3.99 (*0-440-41613-2*, Dell Books for Young Readers) Random Hse. Children's Bks.

—Emily of New Moon. l.t. ed. 1980. (Ulverscroft Large Print Ser.). 29.99 o.p. (*0-7089-0401-7*, Ulverscroft) Thorpe, F. A. Pubs. GBR. *Dist:* Ulverscroft Large Print Bks., Ltd., Ulverscroft Large Print Canada, Ltd.

—Emily's Quest. 1976. 236p. (J). 21.95 (*0-8488-0590-9*) Amereon, Ltd.

—Emily's Quest. 1984. 240p. (YA). mass mkt. 4.99 (*0-7704-2060-5*); 1983. (J). mass mkt. 2.95 o.s.i (*0-553-23323-8*); 1983. 240p. (YA). (gr. 4-7). mass mkt. 4.99 (*0-553-26493-1*) Bantam Bks.

—Emily's Quest. 1982. reprint ed. lib. bdg. 16.95 o.p. (*0-89966-418-0*) Buccaneer Bks., Inc.

—Emily's Quest. 1996. 248p. (J). (gr. 7 up). mass mkt. 4.95 (*0-7710-9981-9*) McClelland & Stewart/ Tundra Bks.

Moorhouse, Karin. A Child's Story of Canada. 1987. 72p. (J). (ps-8). pap. 8.95 (*0-920806-50-3*) Penumbra Pr. CAN. *Dist:* Univ. of Toronto Pr.

Mowat, Farley. Lost in the Barrens. 1956. (Illus.). (J). (gr. 7 up). 15.95 o.p. (*0-316-58638-2*, Joy Street Bks.) Little Brown & Co.

—Lost in the Barrens. 1987. 256p. mass mkt. 6.99 (*0-7710-6681-3*) McClelland & Stewart/Tundra Bks.

—Lost in the Barrens. 1985. 208p. (YA). (gr. 4-7). mass mkt. 5.50 (*0-553-27525-9*, Starfire) Random Hse. Children's Bks.

—Lost in the Barrens. 1956. 11.55 (*0-606-00513-7*) Turtleback Bks.

Napoli, Donna Jo. North. 2004. (J). (*0-06-057987-0*); lib. bdg. (*0-06-057988-9*) HarperCollins Children's Bk. Group. (Greenwillow Bks.).

Oke, Janette. Drums of Change. 2003. (Classics for Girls Ser.). (Illus.). 176 p. (J). 9.99 (*0-7642-2714-9*) Bethany Hse. Pubs.

Page, Katherine Hall. Bon Voyage, Christie & Company. 1998. (Christie & Company Ser.). 288p. (YA). (gr. 6-8). 14.00 (*0-380-97398-7*) HarperCollins Pubs.

—Bon Voyage, Christie & Company. 1999. (Christie & Company Ser.). (Illus.). (YA). (gr. 6-8). pap. 3.99 (*0-380-78035-6*, Avon Bks.) Morrow/Avon.

Paulsen, Gary. Hatchet. l.t. ed. 1989. 232p. (YA). reprint ed. lib. bdg. 15.95 o.p. (*1-55736-117-7*) Bantam Doubleday Dell Large Print Group, Inc.

—Hatchet. 2002. (Illus.). (J). 14.47 (*0-7587-0017-2*) Book Wholesalers, Inc.

—Hatchet. 1999. 235p. (J). (*0-03-054626-5*) Holt, Rinehart & Winston.

—Hatchet. 1995. (YA). (gr. 6 up). 9.28 (*0-395-73261-1*) Houghton Mifflin Co.

—Hatchet. l.t. ed. 2000. (LRS Large Print Cornerstone Ser.). 205p. (YA). (gr. 4-12). lib. bdg. 28.95 (*1-58118-055-1*, 23469) LRS.

—Hatchet. 2003. 151p. (J). pap. (*0-330-31045-3*) Macmillan Children's Bks.

—Hatchet. 208p. 1989. (J). (gr. 4-7). pap. 4.99 o.s.i (*0-14-034371-7*); 1988. (YA). (gr. 5-9). pap. 4.99 o.p. (*0-14-032724-X*) Penguin Putnam Bks. for Young Readers. (Puffin Bks.).

—Hatchet. 195p. (J). (gr. 4-6). pap. 4.99 (*0-8072-8320-7*, Listening Library) Random Hse. Audio Publishing Group.

—Hatchet. 2000. (Illus.). (J). 16.95 (*0-689-84092-6*, Atheneum/Richard Jackson Bks.); 1999. 208p. (YA). (gr. 5-9). mass mkt. 5.99 (*0-689-82699-0*, 076714004993, Simon Pulse); 1999. (J). pap. 2.99 o.p. (*0-689-82965-5*, Aladdin); 1998. 208p. (J). pap. 2.65 (*0-689-82167-0*, Aladdin); 1996. 208p. (YA). (gr. 5-9). pap. 5.99 (*0-689-80882-8*, Aladdin); 1987. 208p. (YA). (gr. 5-9). text 16.95 (*0-02-770130-1*, Atheneum/Richard Jackson Bks.) Simon & Schuster Children's Publishing.

—Hatchet. 1996. (J). 11.04 (*0-606-10206-X*) Turtleback Bks.

Paulsen, Gary, et al. Hatchet/Robinson Crusoe: Curriculum Unit — Novel Series — Grades 6-12. 1996. (Novel Ser.). 79p. tchr. ed., spiral bd. 18.95 (*1-56077-457-6*) Ctr. for Learning, The.

Pearce, Jacqueline. The Reunion. 2003. (Illus.). 96p. (J). (gr. 2-6). pap. 4.99 (*1-55143-230-7*) Orca Bk. Pubs.

Rees, Celia. Sorceress. 2003. 352p. (YA). bds. 8.99 (*0-7636-2183-8*); 2002. 336p. (J). (gr. 7-11). 15.99 (*0-7636-1847-0*) Candlewick Pr.

Reitz, Ric. The Journey of Sir Douglas Fir: A Reader's Musical. Bell, Suzanne, ed. 1999. (Illus.). 48p. (J). (gr. 2-6). per. 19.95 (*0-9670160-0-2*, Sir Fir Bks. & Music) Sir Fir Enterprises, LLC.

Reynolds, Marilynn. The Prairie Fire. (Illus.). 32p. (J). (ps-3). 2001. pap. 7.95 (*1-55143-175-0*); 1999. pap. 14.95 o.s.i (*1-55143-137-8*) Orca Bk. Pubs.

Rispin, Karen. Tianna, the Terrible. 1992. (Anika Scott Ser.: No. 2). (J). (gr. 3-7). 4.99 o.p. (*0-8423-2031-8*) Tyndale Hse. Pubs.

Sage, Elizabeth. Finding Home. 2002. (Five Star First Edition Women's Fiction Ser.). 225p. (J). 25.95 (*0-7862-4111-X*, Five Star) Gale Group.

Schwartz, Virginia Frances. Messenger. 2002. vii, 277p. (J). tchr. ed. 17.95 (*0-8234-1716-6*) Holiday Hse., Inc.

Scrimger, Richard. The Nose from Jupiter. 1998. 160p. (J). (gr. 3-7). pap. 7.95 (*0-88776-428-2*) Tundra Bks. of Northern New York.

Silverthorne, Judith. The Secret of Sentinel Rock. 1997. 160p. (J). (gr. 3-7). pap. 5.95 (*1-55050-103-8*) Coteau Bks. CAN. *Dist:* General Distribution Services, Inc.

—The Secret of Sentinel Rock. 1998. (J). 12.00 (*0-606-19022-8*) Turtleback Bks.

Slade, Arthur G. Draugr. 1998. (Northern Frights Ser.). (Illus.). 144p. (J). (gr. 4-7). pap. 6.95 o.p. (*1-55143-094-0*) Orca Bk. Pubs.

—Tribes. 2002. 144p. (YA). (gr. 7). 15.95 (*0-385-73003-9*, Lamb, Wendy) Random Hse. Children's Bks.

Spalding, Andrea. The Keeper & the Crows. 2000. (Young Reader Ser.). (Illus.). 112p. (J). (gr. 3-4). pap. 4.99 (*1-55143-141-6*) Orca Bk. Pubs.

—Sarah May & the New Red Dress. ed. 2000. (J). (gr. 2). spiral bd. (*0-616-01782-0*) Canadian National Institute for the Blind/Institut National Canadien pour les Aveugles.

—Sarah May & the New Red Dress. 2000. (Illus.). 32p. (J). (ps-3). 14.95 (*1-55143-117-3*); pap. 6.95 (*1-55143-119-X*) Orca Bk. Pubs.

—Sarah May & the New Red Dress. 2000. 13.10 (*0-606-18329-9*) Turtleback Bks.

Stafford, Liliana. Snow Bear. 2001. (Illus.). 32p. (J). (gr. 1-3). 15.95 (*0-439-26977-6*) Scholastic, Inc.

Stafford, Liliana & Davis, Lambert. Snow Bear. (Illus.). 32p. (J). (*0-88899-441-9*) Groundwood Bks.

Stanley, George Edward. Moose Master: Adam Sharp Spy School. 2004. (Illus.). (J). (gr. 1-4). 48p. pap. 3.99 (*0-375-82688-2*); lib. bdg. 11.99 (*0-375-92688-7*) Random Hse. Children's Bks. (Random Hse. Bks. for Young Readers).

Steiner, Barbara A. Mystery at Chilkoot Pass. 2002. (American Girl Collection: Bk. 17). (Illus.). 176p. (J). (gr. 4-6). pap. 6.95 (*1-58485-487-1*); trans. 10.95 (*1-58485-488-X*) Pleasant Co. Pubns. (American Girl).

Stenhouse, Ted. Across the Steel River. 2003. (Illus.). 224p. pap. 6.95 (*1-55337-015-5*); (YA). (gr. 5). 16.95 (*1-55074-891-2*) Kids Can Pr., Ltd.

Stewart, Sharon. Spider's Web. 1998. 160p. (YA). (gr. 4-9). pap. 7.95 (*0-88995-177-2*) Red Deer Pr. CAN. *Dist:* Fitzhenry & Whiteside, Ltd.

Stuchner, Joan Betty. The Kugel Valley Klezmer Band. 2001. (Illus.). 32p. (J). (ps-3). 15.95 (*1-56656-430-1*, Crocodile Bks.) Interlink Publishing Group, Inc.

Taylor, Drew Hayden. The Boy in the Treehouse/The Girl Who Loved Her Horses. 2001. 218p. (J). pap. 12.95 (*0-88922-441-2*) Talonbooks, Ltd. CAN. *Dist:* General Distribution Services, Inc.

Thien, Madeleine. The Chinese Violin. 2001. (Illus.). 32p. (J). (gr. k-3). 15.95 (*1-55285-205-9*) Whitecap Bks., Ltd. CAN. *Dist:* Graphic Arts Ctr. Publishing Co.

Toye, William. How Summer Came to Canada. ed. 1983. (J). (gr. 2). spiral bd. (*0-616-01794-4*) Canadian National Institute for the Blind/Institut National Canadien pour les Aveugles.

Trottier, Maxine. A Circle of Silver. 2000. (Circle of Silver Chronicles Ser.). 220p. (J). (gr. 7-12). pap. 7.95 (*0-7737-6055-5*) Stoddart Kids CAN. *Dist:* Fitzhenry & Whiteside, Ltd.

—Storm at Batoche. 2001. (Illus.). 24p. (J). (ps-3). 15.95 (*0-7737-3248-9*) Stoddart Kids CAN. *Dist:* Fitzhenry & Whiteside, Ltd.

—Under a Shooting Star. 2002. (Circle of Silver Chronicles Ser.). 212p. (YA). (gr. 5-8). pap. 7.95 (*0-7737-6228-0*) Stoddart Kids CAN. *Dist:* Fitzhenry & Whiteside, Ltd.

Valgardson, W. D. Frances. (gr. 6-9). 2002. 172p. (YA). pap. 5.95 (*0-88899-397-8*); 2000. 190p. (J). 15.95 (*0-88899-386-2*) Groundwood Bks. CAN. *Dist:* Publishers Group West.

—Sarah & the People of Sand River. 1996. (Illus.). 44p. (J). (ps-3). 16.95 (*0-88899-255-6*) Groundwood Bks. CAN. *Dist:* Publishers Group West.

Van Stockum, Hilda. Canadian Summer. 1996. (Mitchells Ser.: Vol. 2). (Illus.). 208p. (J). (ps up). reprint ed. pap. 11.95 o.p. (*1-883937-14-0*, 14-0) Bethlehem Bks.

Villeneuve, Jocelyne. The Legend of Greenmantle. 1988. (Illus.). 80p. (J). (ps-8). 9.95 (*0-920806-95-3*) Penumbra Pr. CAN. *Dist:* Univ. of Toronto Pr.

—Nanna Bijou: The Legend of the Sleeping Giant. 1984. (Illus.). 46p. (J). (ps-8). 6.95 (*0-920806-26-0*) Penumbra Pr. CAN. *Dist:* Univ. of Toronto Pr.

Wallace, Ian. Trapper Jack's Missing Toe. 2001. (Illus.). (J). (*0-7894-7666-5*) Dorling Kindersley Publishing, Inc.

—The True Story of Trapper Jack's Left Big Toe. 2002. (Illus.). 40p. (gr. 1-5). 24.90 (*0-7613-2405-4*); (J). 17.95 (*0-7613-1493-8*) Millbrook Pr., Inc. (Roaring Brook Pr.).

Walsh, Ann. Your Time, My Time. 2000. 156p. (J). (gr. 3-8). reprint ed. pap. 5.95 (*0-88878-219-5*, Sandcastle Bks.) Beach Holme Pubs., Ltd. CAN. *Dist:* Strauss Consultants.

Walters, Eric. Caged Eagles. 2001. 244p. (gr. 7-11). (J). pap. 7.95 (*1-55143-139-4*); (YA). 15.95 (*1-55143-182-3*) Orca Bk. Pubs.

Warnant-Cote, Marie-Andree. The Diabolicave. McConnell, Sylvia, tr. from FRE. 1992. 120p. (YA). (gr. 5-8). pap. 5.95 (*0-929141-16-4*, Napoleon Publishing) Napoleon Publishing/ Rendezvous Pr. CAN. *Dist:* Words Distributing Co.

Warner, Gertrude Chandler. The Mystery of the Screech Owl. 2001. (Boxcar Children Special Ser.: No. 16). (Illus.). 144p. (J). (gr. 2-5). pap. 3.95 (*0-8075-5482-0*); lib. bdg. 13.95 (*0-8075-5481-2*) Whitman, Albert & Co.

Whitehead, Catherine. Skookumchuck. 2002. (Illus.). 156p. (J). (gr. 5-12). pap. 11.95 (*1-58151-064-0*) BookPartners, Inc.

Wieler, Diana. Ran Van: The Defender. 1997. 171p. (YA). (gr. 7 up). 16.95 (*0-88899-270-X*) Groundwood Bks. CAN. *Dist:* Publishers Group West.

—Ranvan: Magic Nation. 1998. (J). (gr. 7-12). 229p. pap. 5.95 (*0-88899-316-1*); 232p. text 14.95 (*0-88899-317-X*) Groundwood Bks. CAN. *Dist:* Publishers Group West.

—Ranvan: The Defender. 1998. 172p. (YA). (gr. 7-12). pap. 5.95 (*0-88899-184-3*) Groundwood Bks. CAN. *Dist:* Publishers Group West.

Wilson, Budge. The Dandelion Garden & Other Stories. 1995. 168p. (YA). (gr. 7 up). 15.95 o.p. (*0-399-22768-7*, Philomel) Penguin Putnam Bks. for Young Readers.

Wilson, Eric G. Vampires of Ottawa. 2001. (Liz Austen Mystery Ser.). (Illus.). 108p. (J). (gr. 3-7). 4.99 (*1-55143-228-5*) Orca Bk. Pubs.

—Vancouver Nightmare: A Tom Austin Mystery. 2000. (Tom Austin Mysteries Ser.). (Illus.). 112p. (J). pap. 4.99 (*1-55143-149-1*) Orca Bk. Pubs.

Woodbury, Mary. Brad's Universe. 1998. 192p. (YA). (gr. 7-11). pap. 7.95 (*1-55143-120-3*) Orca Bk. Pubs.

Wyeth, Sharon Dennis. Message in the Sky: Corey's Underground Railroad Diary, Bk. 3. 2003. (My America Ser.). 112p. (J). pap. 10.95 (*0-439-37057-4*); mass mkt. 4.99 (*0-439-37058-2*) Scholastic, Inc. (Scholastic Pr.).

Wynne-Jones, Tim. The Boy in the Burning House. braille ed. 2003. (gr. 2). spiral bd. (*0-616-15275-2*) Canadian National Institute for the Blind/Institut National Canadien pour les Aveugles.

—The Boy in the Burning House. 2000. (*0-7894-5621-4*) Dorling Kindersley Publishing, Inc.

—The Boy in the Burning House, RS. 224p. (J). 2003. pap. 5.95 (*0-374-40887-4*, Sunburst); 2001. (gr. 5-9). 16.00 (*0-374-30930-2*, Farrar, Straus & Giroux (BYR)) Farrar, Straus & Giroux.

—The Boy in the Burning House. l.t. ed. 2002. (Young Adult Ser.). 332p. (J). 23.95 (*0-7862-4435-6*) Thorndike Pr.

—Lord of the Fries: And Other Stories. 1999. (Illus.). 224p. (J). (gr. 5-9). pap. 17.95 (*0-7894-2623-4*, D K Ink) Dorling Kindersley Publishing, Inc.

Yee, Paul. Breakaway. 1997. (J). text (*0-88899-289-0*) Groundwood Bks.

—Breakaway. 2000. 144p. (YA). (gr. 4-7). pap. 5.95 (*0-88899-201-7*) Groundwood Bks. CAN. *Dist:* Publishers Group West.

—The Jade Necklace. 2002. (Illus.). 32p. (J). (ps-3). 15.95 (*1-56656-455-7*, Crocodile Bks.) Interlink Publishing Group, Inc.

Zagwyn, Deborah Turney. The Pumpkin Blanket. 2003. (Illus.). 32p. (J). (gr. k-3). pap. 7.95 (*1-883672-59-7*) Tricycle Pr.

Zeman, Ludmila. The First Red Maple Leaf. (Illus.). 24p. (J). (gr. k-3). 1997. 15.95 (*0-88776-372-3*); 1999. reprint ed. pap. 9.99 (*0-88776-419-3*) Tundra Bks. of Northern New York.

CANARY ISLANDS—FICTION

Baglio, Ben M. Following the Rainbow. 2003. (Dolphin Diaries: No. 7). (Illus.). 160p. (J). (gr. 3-6). mass mkt. 4.50 (*0-439-44614-7*, Scholastic Paperbacks) Scholastic, Inc.

CAPE COD (MASS.)—FICTION

Adkins, Jan E. A Storm Without Rain. 1993. 192p. (YA). (gr. 7 up). reprint ed. pap. 3.95 o.p. (*0-688-11852-6*, Morrow, William & Co.) Morrow/Avon.

Adler, C. S. The Lump in the Middle. 1991. 160p. (YA). pap. 3.50 (*0-380-71176-1*, Avon Bks.) Morrow/Avon.

—Mismatched Summer. 1991. 144p. (YA). 14.95 o.p. (*0-399-21776-2*, G. P. Putnam's Sons) Penguin Group (USA) Inc.

Bliss, Corinne Demas. The Disappearing Island. 2000. (Illus.). 32p. (J). (ps-3). 16.00 (*0-689-80539-X*, Simon & Schuster Children's Publishing) Simon & Schuster Children's Publishing.

Chenoweth, Russ. Shadow Walkers. 1993. 176p. (YA). (gr. 5 up). lib. bdg. 13.95 o.s.i (*0-684-19447-3*, Atheneum) Simon & Schuster Children's Publishing.

Feil, Hila. Blue Moon. 1990. 208p. (J). (gr. 5-9). lib. bdg. 14.95 o.s.i (*0-689-31607-0*, Atheneum) Simon & Schuster Children's Publishing.

Guy, Rosa. The Music of Summer. 1992. 12.95 (*0-385-30704-7*) Doubleday Publishing.

Johnson, Angela. Looking for Red. 128p. 2003. (Illus.). (YA). mass mkt. 4.99 (*0-689-86388-8*, Simon Pulse); 2002. (J). (gr. 7 up). 15.95 (*0-689-83253-2*, Simon & Schuster Children's Publishing) Simon & Schuster Children's Publishing.

—Looking for Red. l.t. ed. 2003. 117p. (J). 24.95 (*0-7862-5603-6*) Thorndike Pr.

Markham, Gretchen. Dempsey's Hot Summer: The July Adventures of a Cape Cod Dog. 1995. (Illus.). 30p. (Orig.). (J). (gr. 1-3). pap. 9.95 (*1-887146-01-6*) Ark Works, Inc.

—A Gift for Dempsey: The Christmas Adventure of a Cape Cod Dog. 1995. (Illus.). 30p. (Orig.). (J). (gr. 1-3). pap. 9.95 (*1-887146-00-8*) Ark Works, Inc.

Murphy, T. M. The Secrets of Belltown. 2001. (Belltown Mystery Ser.: Vol. 1). 176p. (J). (gr. 4-7). pap. 9.95 (*1-880158-34-5*) Townsend, J.N. Publishing.

—The Secrets of Cranberry Beach. 2001. (Belltown Mystery Ser.). (Illus.). 156p. (J). 9.95 (*1-880158-36-1*) Townsend, J.N. Publishing.

—The Secrets of Pilgrim Pond. 2001. (Belltown Mystery Ser.). 144p. (J). (gr. 4-7). pap. 9.95 (*1-880158-39-6*) Townsend, J.N. Publishing.

Rouillard, Wendy W. Barnaby's Cape Cod Coloring Book. 1996. 16p. (J). (ps-4). pap. 2.50 (*0-9642836-4-6*) Barnaby & Co.

Rue, Nancy. The Caper. 2000. (Christian Heritage Ser.). (Illus.). 192p. (J). (gr. 3-7). pap. 5.99 (*1-56179-837-1*) Bethany Hse. Pubs.

Trull, Peter. Billy's Bird-Day: A Young Boy's Adventures on the Beaches of Cape Cod. 1997. (Illus.). 36p. (J). (gr. 1-5). 14.95 (*1-888959-26-6*) Shank Painter Publishing Co.

Weller, Frances Ward. Boat Song. 1987. 180p. (J). (gr. 3-7). 13.95 o.p. (*0-02-792611-7*, Simon & Schuster Children's Publishing) Simon & Schuster Children's Publishing.

Wittlinger, Ellen. Razzle. 2001. (Illus.). 256p. (J). (gr. 7-10). 17.00 (*0-689-83565-5*, Simon & Schuster Children's Publishing) Simon & Schuster Children's Publishing.

CARIBBEAN AREA—FICTION

Ada, Alma Flor, et al. Choices & Other Stories from the Caribbean. 1993. (J). (gr. 3-5). pap. 6.95 (*0-377-00257-7*) Friendship Pr.

Agard, John. The Calypso Alphabet, ERS. 1989. (Illus.). 32p. (J). (ps-2). 13.95 o.p. (*0-8050-1177-3*, Holt, Henry & Co. Bks. For Young Readers) Holt, Henry & Co.

Applegate, K. A. Climb Aboard If You Dare! Stories from the Pirates of the Caribbean. 1996. (Illus.). 80p. (J). (gr. 2-6). pap. 3.50 o.s.i (*0-7868-4061-7*); lib. bdg. 14.49 (*0-7868-5033-7*) Disney Pr.

Baglio, Ben M. Chasing the Dream. 2003. (Dolphin Diaries: No. 5). 160p. (J). (gr. 3-6). mass mkt. 4.50 (*0-439-31951-X*) Scholastic, Inc.

Bosse. The Barracuda Gang. 1982. 9.95 o.p. (*0-525-66737-7*, Dutton Children's Bks.) Penguin Putnam Bks. for Young Readers.

Buffett, Jimmy. The Jolly Mon. Buffett, Savannah Jane, ed. 1988. (Illus.). 32p. (J). (ps-3). 16.00 (*0-15-240530-5*) Harcourt Children's Bks.

—The Jolly Mon. 1988. (J). 12.15 (*0-606-05894-X*) Turtleback Bks.

—Trouble Dolls. 1997. (J). 12.15 (*0-606-12012-2*) Turtleback Bks.

Buffett, Jimmy & Buffett, Savannah Jane. The Jolly Mon. 1993. (Illus.). 32p. (J). (ps-3). pap. 6.00 (*0-15-240538-0*, Voyager Bks./Libros Viajeros) Harcourt Children's Bks.

Bunting, Eve. How Many Days to America? A Thanksgiving Story. (Illus.). 32p. (J). (ps-3). 1990. pap. 5.95 (*0-395-54777-6*); 1988. lib. bdg., tchr. ed. 16.00 (*0-89919-521-0*) Houghton Mifflin Co. Trade & Reference Div. (Clarion Bks.).

—How Many Days to America? A Thanksgiving Story. 1988. (J). 12.10 (*0-606-03816-7*) Turtleback Bks.

Carlstrom, Nancy White. Baby-O. 1992. (Illus.). 32p. (J). (ps-3). 14.95 o.p. (*0-316-12851-1*) Little Brown & Co.

Cherry, Lynne. The Sea, the Storm, & the Mangrove Tangle, RS. 2004. (Illus.). (J). (*0-374-36482-6*, Farrar, Straus & Giroux (BYR)) Farrar, Straus & Giroux.

Cohen, Miriam. Down in the Subway. 1998. (Illus.). 32p. (J). (ps-2). pap. 16.95 o.p. (*0-7894-2510-6*) Dorling Kindersley Publishing, Inc.

—Down in the Subway. 2003. (Illus.). (J). (gr. k-3). pap. 5.95 (*1-932065-24-5*); 40p. mass mkt. 15.95 (*1-932065-08-3*) Star Bright Bks., Inc.

Cooper, Marva. Livingston's Vision. 1993. (Illus.). (J). (gr. 1-7). pap. 3.95 (*1-882185-08-0*) Cornerstone Publishing.

Crowe, Carole. Waiting for Dolphins. 2003. 144p. (YA). pap. 9.95 (*1-59078-073-6*); (Illus.). (gr. 7-9). 16.95 (*1-56397-847-4*) Boyds Mills Pr.

Donovan, Rosalind. Come to My Island. 1996. (Illus.). 32p. (J). (ps-2). 15.95 (*1-881316-30-0*) A & B Distributors & Pubs. Group.

—Come to My Island. Taylor, Maxwell, ed. 1996. (Illus.). 32p. (J). (ps-2). pap. 7.95 (*1-881316-47-5*) A & B Distributors & Pubs. Group.

Dorros, Arthur. Isla. Orig. Title: The Island. (Illus.). (ps-1). 1999. 40p. pap. 5.99 (*0-14-056505-1*, Puffin Bks.); 1995. (SPA., 48p. (J). 16.99 (*0-525-45149-8*, Dutton Children's Bks.) Penguin Putnam Bks. for Young Readers.

—Isla. 1999. Orig. Title: The Island. 13.14 (*0-606-16811-7*); 12.14 (*0-606-16810-9*) Turtleback Bks.

—La Isla. 1999. (Picture Puffins Ser.). (SPA., Illus.). 32p. (J). (gr. k-3). pap. 6.99 (*0-14-056541-8*, DT8806, Puffin Bks.) Penguin Putnam Bks. for Young Readers.

Farley, Walter. The Island Stallion. 1948. (Black Stallion Ser.). (J). (gr. 4-6). 10.09 o.p. (*0-606-01731-3*) Turtleback Bks.

Garne, S. T. One White Sail: A Caribbean Counting Book. 1992. (Illus.). 32p. (J). 14.00 (*0-671-75579-X*, Simon & Schuster Children's Publishing) Simon & Schuster Children's Publishing.

Gershator, Phillis. Sambalena Show-Off. 1995. (Illus.). 32p. (J). (gr. k-3). 15.00 o.p. (*0-689-80314-1*, Simon & Schuster Children's Publishing) Simon & Schuster Children's Publishing.

—Sweet, Sweet Fig Banana. 1996. (Illus.). 32p. (J). (ps-2). lib. bdg. 14.95 o.p. (*0-8075-7693-X*) Whitman, Albert & Co.

Gershator, Phyllis. Rata-Pata-Scata-Fata: A Caribbean Story. 1994. (Illus.). (J). 15.95 o.s.i (*0-316-30470-0*, Joy Street Bks.) Little Brown & Co.

Godard, Alex. Mama, Across the Sea, ERS. Wen, George, tr. from FRE. 2000. (Illus.). 48p. (J). (ps-3). 16.95 (*0-8050-6161-4*, Holt, Henry & Co. Bks. For Young Readers) Holt, Henry & Co.

Gottlieb, Dale. Where Jamaica Go? 1996. (Illus.). 32p. (J). (ps-3). pap. 14.95 (*0-531-09525-8*); lib. bdg. 15.99 (*0-531-08875-8*) Scholastic, Inc. (Orchard Bks.).

Haynes, Betsy. A Caribbean Adventure. 1990. (Fabulous Five Super Ser.: No. 2). 192p. (J). (gr. 4-7). pap. 2.95 o.s.i (*0-553-15831-7*, Skylark) Random Hse. Children's Bks.

Hodge, Merle. For the Life of Laetitia, RS. (Aerial Fiction Ser.). 224p. (YA). (gr. 7 up). 1994. pap. 6.95 (*0-374-42444-6*, Aerial); 1993. 15.00 o.p. (*0-374-32447-6*, Farrar, Straus & Giroux (BYR)) Farrar, Straus & Giroux.

Holland, Isabelle. The Island. 1986. 176p. (J). mass mkt. 2.50 o.s.i (*0-449-70138-7*, Fawcett) Ballantine Bks.

—The Island. 1984. 240p. (J). (gr. 6 up). 14.95 o.p. (*0-316-36993-4*) Little Brown & Co.

Hulser, Andrea. Henry in the Caribbean. 1993. (Illus.). 40p. (J). pap. 9.95 (*0-89825-007-2*) Publishing Resources, Inc.

Huth, Holly Y. Darkfright. 1996. (Illus.). 32p. (J). (ps-3). 16.00 (*0-689-80188-2*, Atheneum) Simon & Schuster Children's Publishing.

Isadora, Rachel. Caribbean Dream. 1998. (Illus.). 32p. (J). (ps-3). 15.99 o.p. (*0-399-23230-3*) Penguin Group (USA) Inc.

—Caribbean Dream. 2002. (Illus.). 32p. (J). pap. 6.99 (*0-698-11944-4*, PaperStar) Penguin Putnam Bks. for Young Readers.

Kaserman, James F. & Kaserman, Sarah Jane. The Legend of Gasparilla: A Tale for All Ages. 2000. 304p. (YA). pap. 14.95 (*0-9674081-1-3*) Pirate Publishing International.

Keens-Douglas, Richardo. La Diablesse et le Bebe. 1994. Tr. of Diablesse & the Baby. (FRE., Illus.). 24p. (J). (gr. 1-3). pap. 6.95 (*1-55037-994-1*); (ps-2). lib. bdg. 15.95 (*1-55037-995-X*) Annick Pr., Ltd. CAN. *Dist:* Firefly Bks., Ltd.

—La Diablesse et le Bebe. ed. 1994. Tr. of Diablesse & the Baby. (J). (gr. 1). spiral bd. (*0-616-01836-3*) Canadian National Institute for the Blind/Institut National Canadien pour les Aveugles.

Lawrence, Iain. The Buccaneers. (Illus.). 256p. (gr. 5-9). 2003. pap. 5.50 (*0-440-41671-X*, Yearling); 2001. text 15.95 (*0-385-32736-6*, Dell Books for Young Readers) Random Hse. Children's Bks.

—The Buccaneers. l.t. ed. 2001. (Illus.). 320p. (J). 23.95 (*0-7862-3464-4*) Thorndike Pr.

—Ghost Boy. (YA). (gr. 7-12). 2000. (Illus.). 336p. 15.95 (*0-385-32739-0*, Dell Books for Young Readers); 2002. 352p. reprint ed. mass mkt. 5.99 (*0-440-41668-X*, Laurel Leaf) Random Hse. Children's Bks.

—Ghost Boy. l.t. ed. 2001. (Young Adult Ser.). 413p. (J). (gr. 8-12). 23.95 (*0-7862-3243-9*) Thorndike Pr.

Linden, Ann M. One Smiling Grandma: A Caribbean Counting Book. 1992. (Illus.). 32p. (J). (ps-3). 15.00 o.s.i (*0-8037-1132-8*, Dial Bks. for Young Readers) Penguin Putnam Bks. for Young Readers.

Linden, Anne Marie. Emerald Blue. 1994. (Illus.). 32p. (J). 15.95 o.s.i (*0-689-31946-0*, Atheneum) Simon & Schuster Children's Publishing.

London, Jonathan. The Village Basket Weaver. 1996. (Illus.). 32p. (J). (ps-3). 14.99 o.p. (*0-525-45314-8*, Dutton Children's Bks.) Penguin Putnam Bks. for Young Readers.

Lucas, Eileen. Abdu the Fisherman. 1995. (Illus.). 24p. (Orig.). (J). (ps). pap. (*977-5325-45-5*) Hoopoe Bks. EGY. *Dist:* AMIDEAST.

—Belia's Ball. 1995. (Illus.). 24p. (J). (ps). pap. (*977-5325-43-9*) Hoopoe Bks. EGY. *Dist:* AMIDEAST.

—The New Baby. 1995. (Illus.). 24p. (Orig.). (J). (ps). pap. (*977-5325-46-3*) Hoopoe Bks. EGY. *Dist:* AMIDEAST.

—Tofaha's Basket. 1995. (Illus.). 24p. (Orig.). (J). (ps). pap. (*977-5325-44-7*) Hoopoe Bks. EGY. *Dist:* AMIDEAST.

Milstein, Linda B. Coconut Mon. 1995. (Illus.). 32p. (J). (ps up). 16.00 o.p. (*0-688-12862-9*); lib. bdg. 15.93 o.p. (*0-688-12863-7*) Morrow/Avon. (Morrow, William & Co.).

Mitchell, Rita Phillips. Hue Boy. 1999. (Illus.). 32p. (J). (gr. k-3). pap. 11.95 (*0-14-056354-7*) Penguin Bks., Ltd. GBR. *Dist:* Trafalgar Square.

—Hue Boy. (Picture Puffin Ser.). (J). (gr. k-3). 1997. 32p. pap. 4.99 o.s.i (*0-14-055995-7*); 1993. (Illus.). 320p. 13.99 o.s.i (*0-8037-1448-3*, Dial Bks. for Young Readers) Penguin Putnam Bks. for Young Readers.

—Hue Boy. 1997. (Picture Puffin Ser.). (J). 10.19 o.p. (*0-606-11487-4*) Turtleback Bks.

Morgan, Trudy J. Whatcha Doin Alex? 1994. (J). mass mkt. 5.99 o.p. (*0-8280-0849-3*) Review & Herald Publishing Assn.

Nixon, Joan Lowery. Playing for Keeps. 208p. (YA). (gr. 7). 2003. mass mkt. 5.50 (*0-440-22867-0*); 2001. 15.95 (*0-385-32759-5*); 2001. lib. bdg. 17.99 (*0-385-90014-7*) Random Hse. Children's Bks. (Dell Books for Young Readers).

Powell, Pamela. The Turtle Watchers. 1992. 160p. (J). (gr. 3-7). 13.00 o.s.i (*0-670-84294-X*, Viking Children's Bks.) Penguin Putnam Bks. for Young Readers.

Rau, Dana Meachen. Undersea City: A Story of a Caribbean Coral Reef. 1997. (Nature Conservancy Habitat Ser.). (Illus.). 36p. (J). (gr. 1-4). 15.95 (*1-56899-433-8*); pap. 5.95 (*1-56899-434-6*);Incl. toy. pap. 16.95 (*1-56899-438-9*) Soundprints.

—Undersea City: A Story of a Carribean Coral Reef. 1997. (Habitat Ser.). (Illus.). 36p. (J). (gr. 1-4). 19.95 incl. audio (*1-56899-435-4*, BC7002) Soundprints.

Santomenna, Joan E. & Santomenna, Marco D. Caribbean Capers. 2003. (Illus.). 144p. (YA). (gr. 3-9). pap. 9.95 (*0-9643407-2-0*) WindSpirit Publishing.

Sisnett, Ana. Grannie Jus' Come! 1997. (Illus.). 32p. (YA). (gr. 1-3). 15.95 (*0-89239-150-2*) Children's Bk. Pr.

Spillane, Mickey. The Day the Sea Rolled Back. 1979. (Illus.). (J). 7.95 o.p. (*0-525-61589-X*, Dutton) Dutton/Plume.

Stevenson, Robert Louis. Treasure Island. 2002. (Illustrated Library for Children). (Illus.). 272p. (J). 12.99 (*0-517-22114-4*, Random Hse. Bks. for Young Readers) Random Hse. Children's Bks.

Taylor, Theodore. Timothy of the Cay: A Prequel-Sequel. abr. ed. 1993. 176p. (YA). (gr. 7 up). 16.00 (*0-15-288358-4*) Harcourt Children's Bks.

—Timothy of the Cay: A Prequel-Sequel. 1994. 160p. (J). (gr. 7 up). pap. 5.99 (*0-380-72119-8*, Avon Bks.) Morrow/Avon.

Vance, Susanna. Deep. 2003. 272p. (YA). lib. bdg. 17.99 (*0-385-90080-5*, Delacorte Pr.) Dell Publishing.

—Deep. 2003. 272p. (YA). (gr. 7-12). 15.95 (*0-385-73057-8*, Delacorte Bks. for Young Readers) Random Hse. Children's Bks.

CASTLE OF SEVEN TOWERS (IMAGINARY PLACE)—FICTION

Nix, Garth. Aenir, No. 3. 2001. (Seventh Tower Ser.: Bk. 3). 72p. (J). (gr. 8). mass mkt. 4.99 (*0-439-17684-0*) Scholastic, Inc.

—Aenir. 2000. (Seventh Tower Ser.: Bk. 3). 11.04 (*0-606-19610-2*) Turtleback Bks.

—Castle, No. 2. 2000. (Seventh Tower Ser.: Bk. 2). (Illus.). 208p. (J). (gr. 3-7). mass mkt. 4.99 (*0-439-17683-2*) Scholastic, Inc.

—Castle. 2000. (Seventh Tower Ser.: Bk. 2). 11.04 (*0-606-19609-9*) Turtleback Bks.

—The Fall. 2000. (Seventh Tower Ser.: Bk. 1). 190p. (J). (gr. 4-7). mass mkt. 4.99 (*0-439-17682-4*) Scholastic, Inc.

CHAMPLAIN, LAKE—FICTION

Arnosky, Jim. Little Champ. 1995. (Illus.). 69p. (J). (ps-3). 13.95 o.s.i (*0-399-22759-8*, G. P. Putnam's Sons) Penguin Group (USA) Inc.

Arnosky, Jim, illus. Little Champ. 2001. (J). pap. 6.95 (*0-9657144-5-4*) Onion River Pr.

CHARLESTON (S.C.)—FICTION

Brouwer, Sigmund. Legend of the Gilded Saber. 2002. (Accidental Detectives Ser.). 144p. (J). pap. 5.99 (*0-7642-2566-9*) Bethany Hse. Pubs.

—Out of the Shadows. l.t. ed. 2003. (Christian Mystery Ser.). 26.95 (*0-7862-4879-3*) Thorndike Pr.

—Out of the Shadows. E-Book 15.00 (*0-8423-5655-X*); 2002. 352p. pap. 12.99 (*0-8423-4240-0*) Tyndale Hse. Pubs.

Clary, Margie Willis. Make It Three: The Story of the CSS H. L. Hunley, Civil War Submarine. 2001. (Illus.). 110p. (J). 9.95 (*0-87844-158-1*) Sandlapper Publishing Co., Inc.

Curtis, Alice Turner. Yankee Girl at Fort Sumter. 2004. (Yankee Girl Ser.). 190p. (J). (gr. 4-7). pap. text 9.95 (*1-55709-525-6*) Applewood Bks.

Love, D. Anne. Three Against the Tide. 1998. 162p. (J). (gr. 4-7). tchr. ed. 15.95 (*0-8234-1400-0*) Holiday Hse., Inc.

—Three Against the Tide. 2000. (Illus.). 192p. (gr. 4-7). pap. text 4.50 (*0-440-41634-5*, Yearling) Random Hse. Children's Bks.

—Three Against the Tide. 2000. 10.55 (*0-606-18909-2*) Turtleback Bks.

Roberts, Nancy. Blackbeard's Cat. 1998. (Cat of Nine Tales Ser.: Vol. 1). (Illus.). 96p. (J). pap. 9.95 (*1-886391-41-6*, Shipwreck Pr.) Narwhal Pr., Inc.

Rue, Nancy. The Escape. 1998. (Christian Heritage Ser.). 192p. (J). (gr. 3-7). pap. 5.99 (*1-56179-639-5*) Bethany Hse. Pubs.

—The Hostage. 1998. (Christian Heritage Ser.). 208p. (J). (gr. 3-7). pap. 5.99 (*1-56179-638-7*) Bethany Hse. Pubs.

Smith, Bruce. The Silver Locket: A Charleston Christmas Storybook. 1994. (Illus.). 110p. pap. 11.95 (*0-9642620-0-2*) Marsh Wind Pr.

Smith, Sally. Rosebud Roams Charleston: A Child 's Clippity-Clop Guide to the City. 1999. (Illus.). (J). (*0-933101-19-8*) Legacy Pubns.

Thompson, Laura J. Joseph's Charleston Adventure. 1998. (Illus.). 32p. (J). (ps-4). 16.95 (*0-9607854-1-8*) Junior League of Charleston, South Carolina, Inc.

Weathers, Andrea. Hermy the Hermit Crab Goes Shopping. 2001. (Illus.). 40p. (J). 15.99 (*0-933101-20-1*) Legacy Pubns.

Settings

Cipriano, A. G. Bertie. 1999. 294p. (YA). (gr. 6-12). pap. 5.99 (*0-9672074-0-1*) Gold Lace Publishing, LLC.

Clyde, Ahmad. Cheng Ho's Voyage. 1981. (Illus.). 32p. (Orig.). (J). (gr. 3-7). pap. 2.50 (*0-89259-021-1*) American Trust Pubns.

Collins, David R. Kim Soo & His Tortoise. 1971. (Illus.). 48p. (J). (gr. k-3). lib. bdg. 6.59 o.p. (*0-87460-227-0*) Lion Bks.

Compestine, Ying Chang. The Story of Chopsticks. 2001. (Illus.). (J). (ps-2). tchr. ed. 16.95 (*0-8234-1526-0*) Holiday Hse., Inc.

—The Story of Kites. 2003. 32p. (J). tchr. ed. 16.95 (*0-8234-1715-8*) Holiday Hse., Inc.

—The Story of Noodles. 2002. (Illus.). 32p. (J). (gr. k-3). tchr. ed. 16.95 (*0-8234-1600-3*) Holiday Hse., Inc.

—The Story of Paper. 2003. (Illus.). (J). (gr. k-3). tchr. ed. 16.95 (*0-8234-1705-0*) Holiday Hse., Inc.

Cooley, Regina F. The Magic Christmas Pony. 1991. (Illus.). 36p. (J). (gr. 1-5). 19.95 (*1-880450-04-6*) Capstone Publishing, Inc.

Czernecki, Stefan. Paper Lanterns. 2001. (Illus.). (J). (ps-13). 15.95 (*1-57091-411-7*, Talewinds); 32p. 15.95 (*1-57091-410-9*) Charlesbridge Publishing, Inc.

—Paper Lanterns. 2002. (J). E-Book (*1-59019-575-2*); 2001. E-Book (*1-59019-576-0*); 2001. E-Book (*1-59019-577-9*) ipicturebooks, LLC.

D'Antonio, Nancy. You Were Born in China: An Adoption Story. 1997. (J). o.p. (*0-8075-9437-7*) Whitman, Albert & Co.

Davol, Marguerite W. The Paper Dragon. 1997. (Illus.). 60p. (J). (gr. k-3). 19.95 (*0-689-31992-4*, Atheneum) Simon & Schuster Children's Publishing.

DeJong, Meindert. The House of Sixty Fathers. 1956. (Illus.). 208p. (J). (gr. 6 up). lib. bdg. 16.89 (*0-06-021481-3*) HarperCollins Children's Bk. Group.

Demi. The Greatest Power in the World. 2004. (Illus.). 40p. (J). 19.95 (*0-689-84503-0*, McElderry, Margaret K.) Simon & Schuster Children's Publishing.

Demi, Hitz. The Artist & the Architect. 1991. (Illus.). 32p. (J). (ps-2). 15.89 o.p. (*0-8050-1685-6*);ERS. 15.95 o.p. (*0-8050-1580-9*, Holt, Henry & Co. Bks. For Young Readers) Holt, Henry & Co.

Fabian, Erika. Adventure in Splendid China. 1994. (Illus.). 64p. (J). (gr. 4 up). per. 16.95 (*0-9638417-0-X*) Eriako Assocs.

Flack, Marjorie. Story about Ping. (StoryTape Ser.). (J). 1989. 6.95 o.p. (*0-14-095038-9*, Puffin Bks.); 1933. (Illus.). 32p. 15.99 (*0-670-67223-8*, Viking Children's Bks.) Penguin Putnam Bks. for Young Readers.

—Story about Ping. 1977. (Picture Puffin Ser.). (J). 12.14 (*0-606-05022-1*) Turtleback Bks.

—Story about Ping. abr. ed. 1978. (Illus.). pap., tchr. ed. incl. audio (*0-670-67225-4*); (J). pap. incl. audio (*0-670-67226-2*) Viking Penguin.

—Story of Ping. 2000. (Reading Railroad Books Ser.). (Illus.). 32p. (J). (ps-3). mass mkt. 3.49 (*0-448-42165-8*, Grosset & Dunlap) Penguin Putnam Bks. for Young Readers.

Flack, Marjorie & Wiese, Kurt. Story about Ping. 1993. (StoryTape Ser.). (Illus.). 1p. (J). (ps-3). 9.99 (*0-14-095117-2*, Puffin Bks.) Penguin Putnam Bks. for Young Readers.

Fleischman, Sid. The Wooden Cat Man. 1972. (Illus.). 48p. (J). (gr. k-3). 6.95 o.p. (*0-316-28581-1*) Little Brown & Co.

Fontenay, Charles L. Kipton & the I Ching. 1997. (Kipton Chronicles Ser.: No. 9). (Illus.). 178p. (YA). (gr. 5 up). pap. 9.99 (*0-88092-385-7*, 3857) Royal Fireworks Publishing Co.

Fritz, Jean. China Homecoming. 1985. (Illus.). 144p. (J). (gr. 5 up). 19.99 (*0-399-21182-9*, G. P. Putnam's Sons) Penguin Group (USA) Inc.

—Homesick: My Own Story. 1986. 176p. (J). pap. 2.95 o.s.i (*0-440-73683-8*) Dell Publishing.

—Homesick: My Own Story. l.t. ed. 1987. (Illus.). 184p. (J). (gr. 3-9). reprint ed. lib. bdg. 16.95 o.s.i (*1-55736-070-7*, Cornerstone Bks.) Pages, Inc.

—Homesick: My Own Story. 1982. (Illus.). (J). (gr. 3-7). 16.99 (*0-399-20933-6*, G. P. Putnam's Sons) Penguin Group (USA) Inc.

—Homesick: My Own Story. 1999. (Illus.). 192p. (J). (gr. 3-7). pap. 5.99 (*0-698-11782-4*) Penguin Putnam Bks. for Young Readers.

—Homesick: My Own Story. 1984. 176p. (gr. k-6). pap. text 4.99 o.s.i (*0-440-43683-4*, Yearling) Random Hse. Children's Bks.

—Homesick: My Own Story. l.t. ed. 2001. (Illus.). 222p. (J). 22.95 (*0-7862-3603-5*) Thorndike Pr.

—Homesick: My Own Story. (J). 1999. 12.04 (*0-606-16799-4*); 1982. 10.09 o.p. (*0-606-03168-5*) Turtleback Bks.

Frost, Lesley. Digging down to China. 1968. (Illus.). 64p. (J). (gr. 1-4). 9.95 (*0-8159-5306-2*) Devin-Adair Pubs., Inc.

Guillot, Claude. The Ghost of Shanghai. 1999. (Illus.). 48p. (ps-4). 16.95 o.p. (*0-8109-4129-5*) Abrams, Harry N. , Inc.

Guo, Tony & Cheung, Euphine. Er-Lang & the Suns: A Tale from China. 1994. (Mondo Folktales Ser.). (Illus.). 24p. (J). (gr. k-4). pap. 4.95 (*1-879531-21-6*); lib. bdg. 9.95 (*1-879531-42-9*) Mondo Publishing.

Handforth, Thomas. Mei Li. 1955. (Illus.). 48p. (J). (gr. k-3). 14.95 o.s.i (*0-385-07401-8*); 15.99 o.s.i (*0-385-07639-8*) Doubleday Publishing.

Henty, G. A. With the Allies to Pekin: A Tale of the Relief of the Legations. 2000. 252p. (J). E-Book 3.95 (*0-594-02423-4*) 1873 Pr.

Hergé. The Blue Lotus. (Illus.). (J). 19.95 (*0-8288-5480-7*) French & European Pubns., Inc.

—The Blue Lotus. (Adventures of Tintin Ser.). (Illus.). (J). 1992. 64p. 12.95 o.p. (*0-316-35891-6*); 1984. 62p. (gr. 2 up). pap. 9.99 (*0-316-35856-8*) Little Brown & Co. (Joy Street Bks.).

—El Loto Azul.Tr. of Blue Lotus. (SPA., Illus.). 62p. (J). 19.95 (*0-8288-5049-6*) French & European Pubns., Inc.

—El Loto Azul. (Tintin Ser.).Tr. of Blue Lotus. (SPA.). 64p. (J). 14.95 (*84-261-1418-0*) Juventud, Editorial ESP. *Dist:* Distribooks, Inc.

—Le Lotus Bleu. 1999. (Tintin Ser.).Tr. of Blue Lotus. (FRE.). (gr. 4-7). 19.95 (*2-203-00104-6*) Casterman, Editions FRA. *Dist:* Distribooks, Inc.

—Le Lotus Bleu.Tr. of Blue Lotus. (FRE.). (J). (gr. 2-9). 19.95 (*0-8288-5050-X*) French & European Pubns., Inc.

Hill, Elizabeth Starr. Chang & the Bamboo Flute, RS. 2002. (Illus.). 64p. (J). (gr. 3 up). 15.00 (*0-374-31238-9*, Farrar, Straus & Giroux (BYR)) Farrar, Straus & Giroux.

Hillman, Elizabeth. Min-Yo & the Moon Dragon. (Illus.). 32p. (J). (ps-3). 1992. 14.95 o.s.i (*0-15-254230-2*); 1996. pap. 5.00 (*0-15-200985-X*) Harcourt Children's Bks.

—Min-Yo & the Moon Dragon. 1996. 10.20 o.p. (*0-606-09617-5*) Turtleback Bks.

Hong, Lily T. The Empress & the Silkworm. 1995. (Illus.). (J). (ps-3). lib. bdg. 16.95 (*0-8075-2009-8*) Whitman, Albert & Co.

Hsiao, Ellen. A Chinese Year. 1970. (Two World Bks.). (Illus.). 64p. (gr. 4-6). 3.95 o.p. (*0-87131-095-3*) Evans, M. & Co., Inc.

Huang, Benrei. A Visit to China. 1991. (Golden Look-Look Bks.). (Illus.). 24p. (J). (ps-3). pap. 3.29 o.s.i (*0-307-12633-1*, Golden Bks.) Random Hse. Children's Bks.

Huggins, Alice M. The Red Chair Waits. 1948. (Illus.). (J). (gr. 4-6). 3.95 o.p. (*0-664-32047-3*) Westminster John Knox Pr.

Hwa-I Publishing Co., Staff. Chinese Children's Stories Vol. 10: The Money Tree, The Coxcomb. Ching, Emily et al, eds. Wonder Kids Publications Staff, tr. from CHI. 1991. (Tales about Plants Ser.). (Illus.). 28p. (J). (gr. 3-6). reprint ed. 7.95 o.p. (*1-56162-010-6*) Wonder Kids Pubns.

—Chinese Children's Stories Vol. 12: The Snail & the Ox, Sparrows Can't Walk. Ching, Emily et al, eds. Wonder Kids Publications Staff, tr. from CHI. 1991. (Animal Tales Ser.). (Illus.). 28p. (J). (gr. 3-6). reprint ed. 7.95 o.p. (*1-56162-012-2*) Wonder Kids Pubns.

—Chinese Children's Stories Vol. 13: Rooster Summons the Sun, The White-Haired Bird. Ching, Emily et al, eds. Wonder Kids Publications Staff, tr. from CHI. 1991. (Animal Tales Ser.). (Illus.). 28p. (J). (gr. 3-6). reprint ed. 7.95 o.p. (*1-56162-013-0*) Wonder Kids Pubns.

—Chinese Children's Stories Vol. 14: Weasel Steals the Chickens, Why is the Crow Black? Ching, Emily et al, eds. Wonder Kids Publications Staff, tr. from CHI. 1991. (Animal Tales Ser.). (Illus.). 28p. (J). (gr. 3-6). reprint ed. 7.95 o.p. (*1-56162-014-9*) Wonder Kids Pubns.

—Chinese Children's Stories Vol. 15: Jiggle in the Wind, The Bat Can't See the Sun. Ching, Emily et al, eds. Wonder Kids Publications Staff, tr. from CHI. 1991. (Animal Tales Ser.). (Illus.). 28p. (J). (gr. 3-6). reprint ed. 7.95 o.p. (*1-56162-015-7*) Wonder Kids Pubns.

—Chinese Children's Stories Vol. 18: The Little Bamboo Pole, The Wise Old Man. Ching, Emily et al, eds. Wonder Kids Publications Staff, tr. from CHI. 1991. (Fables Ser.). (Illus.). 28p. (J). (gr. 3-6). reprint ed. 7.95 o.p. (*1-56162-018-1*) Wonder Kids Pubns.

—Chinese Children's Stories Vol. 19: Crow Moves Away, Baby Lion & Baby Rhino. Ching, Emily et al, eds. Wonder Kids Publications Staff, tr. from CHI. 1991. (Fables Ser.). (Illus.). 28p. (J). (gr. 3-6). reprint ed. 7.95 o.p. (*1-56162-019-X*) Wonder Kids Pubns.

—Chinese Children's Stories Vol. 20: Ah-Liu Picks Corn, Cuckoo's Winter. Ching, Emily et al, eds. Wonder Kids Publications Staff, tr. from CHI. 1991. (Fables Ser.). (Illus.). 28p. (J). (gr. 3-6). reprint ed. 7.95 o.p. (*1-56162-020-3*) Wonder Kids Pubns.

—Chinese Children's Stories Vol. 23: Dummy Afa, The Fox in a Tiger's Suit. Ching, Emily et al, eds. Wonder Kids Publications Staff, tr. from CHI. 1991. (Idioms Ser.). (Illus.). 28p. (J). (gr. 3-6). reprint ed. 7.95 o.p. (*1-56162-023-8*) Wonder Kids Pubns.

—Chinese Children's Stories Vol. 25: The Blindmen & the Elephant, Little Frog in the Well. Ching, Emily et al, eds. Wonder Kids Publications Staff, tr. from CHI. 1991. (Idioms Ser.). (Illus.). 28p. (J). (gr. 3-6). reprint ed. 7.95 o.p. (*1-56162-025-4*) Wonder Kids Pubns.

—Chinese Children's Stories Vol. 28: Mih-Ro River, The Herder & the Seamstress. Ching, Emily et al, eds. Wonder Kids Publications Staff, tr. from CHI. 1991. (Festivals Ser.). (Illus.). 28p. (J). (gr. 3-6). reprint ed. 7.95 o.p. (*1-56162-028-9*) Wonder Kids Pubns.

—Chinese Children's Stories Vol. 29: Moon Cake, Fei's Adventure. Ching, Emily et al, eds. Wonder Kids Publications Staff, tr. from CHI. 1991. (Festivals Ser.). (Illus.). 28p. (J). (gr. 3-6). reprint ed. 7.95 o.p. (*1-56162-029-7*) Wonder Kids Pubns.

—Chinese Children's Stories Vol. 30: La-Ba Porridge, The Stove God. Ching, Emily et al, eds. Wonder Kids Publications Staff, tr. from CHI. 1991. (Festivals Ser.). (Illus.). 28p. (J). (gr. 3-6). reprint ed. 7.95 o.p. (*1-56162-030-0*) Wonder Kids Pubns.

—Chinese Children's Stories Vol. 33: Noodles over the Bridge, Steamed Bread. Ching, Emily et al, eds. Wonder Kids Publications Staff, tr. from CHI. 1991. (Tales about Food Ser.). (Illus.). 28p. (J). (gr. 3-6). reprint ed. 7.95 o.p. (*1-56162-033-5*) Wonder Kids Pubns.

—Chinese Children's Stories Vol. 34: The Stuffed Steamed Bao, Miss Freckle's Tofu. Ching, Emily et al, eds. Wonder Kids Publications Staff, tr. from CHI. 1991. (Tales about Food Ser.). (Illus.). 28p. (J). (gr. 3-6). reprint ed. 7.95 o.p. (*1-56162-034-3*) Wonder Kids Pubns.

—Chinese Children's Stories Vol. 39: Brush Pen, Duan's Ink-Slab. Ching, Emily et al, eds. Wonder Kids Publications Staff, tr. from CHI. 1991. (Inventions Ser.). (Illus.). 28p. (J). (gr. 3-6). reprint ed. 7.95 o.p. (*1-56162-039-4*) Wonder Kids Pubns.

—Chinese Children's Stories Vol. 40: The Ink-Stick, Shiuan Paper. Ching, Emily et al, eds. Wonder Kids Publications Staff, tr. from CHI. 1991. (Inventions Ser.). (Illus.). 28p. (J). (gr. 3-6). reprint ed. 7.95 o.p. (*1-56162-040-8*) Wonder Kids Pubns.

—Chinese Children's Stories Vol. 43: The Bunny's Tail, Fox, Monkey, Rabbit & Horse. Ching, Emily et al, eds. Wonder Kids Publications Staff, tr. from CHI. 1991. (Twelve Beasts & the Years Ser.). (Illus.). 28p. (J). (gr. 3-6). reprint ed. 7.95 o.p. (*1-56162-043-2*) Wonder Kids Pubns.

—Chinese Children's Stories Vol. 44: Snake's Lost Drum, Ox & Buffalo Change Clothes. Ching, Emily et al, eds. Wonder Kids Publications Staff, tr. from CHI. 1991. (Twelve Beasts & the Years Ser.). (Illus.). 28p. (J). (gr. 3-6). reprint ed. 7.95 o.p. (*1-56162-044-0*) Wonder Kids Pubns.

—Chinese Children's Stories Vol. 45: The Goat & the Camel, The Wolf & the Pig. Ching, Emily et al, eds. Wonder Kids Publications Staff, tr. from CHI. 1991. (Twelve Beasts & the Years Ser.). (Illus.). 28p. (J). (gr. 3-6). reprint ed. 7.95 o.p. (*1-56162-045-9*) Wonder Kids Pubns.

—Chinese Children's Stories Vol. 47: The Crane-Riding Immortal, Lyu Dungbin & Guanyin. Ching, Emily et al, eds. Wonder Kids Publications Staff, tr. from CHI. 1991. (Fairy Tales Ser.). (Illus.). 28p. (J). (gr. 3-6). reprint ed. 7.95 o.p. (*1-56162-047-5*) Wonder Kids Pubns.

—Chinese Children's Stories Vol. 48: Sir Thunder & Lady Lightning, The Door Guards. Ching, Emily et al, eds. Wonder Kids Publications Staff, tr. from CHI. 1991. (Folklore Ser.). (Illus.). 28p. (J). (gr. 3-6). reprint ed. 7.95 o.p. (*1-56162-048-3*) Wonder Kids Pubns.

—Chinese Children's Stories Vol. 49: The Slippery Nose Deity, Under the Moonlight. Ching, Emily et al, eds. Wonder Kids Publications Staff, tr. from CHI. 1991. (Fairy Tales Ser.). (Illus.). 28p. (J). (gr. 3-6). reprint ed. 7.95 o.p. (*1-56162-049-1*) Wonder Kids Pubns.

—Chinese Children's Stories Vol. 50: Zung Kuei & the Little Ghost, Earth God & Earth Goddess. Ching, Emily et al, eds. Wonder Kids Publications Staff, tr. from CHI. 1991. (Fairy Tales Ser.). (Illus.). 28p. (J). (gr. 3-6). reprint ed. 7.95 o.p. (*1-56162-050-5*) Wonder Kids Pubns.

—Chinese Children's Stories Vol. 53: Meeting an Angel, The Child in the Deer Skin. Ching, Emily et al, eds. Wonder Kids Publications Staff, tr. from CHI. 1991. (Filial Piety Ser.). (Illus.). 28p. (J). (gr. 3-6). reprint ed. 7.95 o.p. (*1-56162-053-X*) Wonder Kids Pubns.

—Chinese Children's Stories Vol. 54: The Story of Shun, Village of Filial Piety. Ching, Emily et al, eds. Wonder Kids Publications Staff, tr. from CHI. 1991. (Filial Piety Ser.). (Illus.). 28p. (J). (gr. 3-6). reprint ed. 7.95 o.p. (*1-56162-054-8*) Wonder Kids Pubns.

—Chinese Children's Stories Vol. 55: Two Baskets of Mulberries, Trun's Little Daughter. Ching, Emily et al, eds. Wonder Kids Publications Staff, tr. from CHI. 1991. (Filial Piety Ser.). (Illus.). 28p. (J). (gr. 3-6). reprint ed. 7.95 o.p. (*1-56162-055-6*) Wonder Kids Pubns.

—Chinese Children's Stories Vol. 57: The Little-Boy God, A Rooster's Egg. Ching, Emily et al, eds. Wonder Kids Publications Staff, tr. from CHI. 1991. (Wonder Kids Ser.). (Illus.). 28p. (J). (gr. 3-6). reprint ed. 7.95 o.p. (*1-56162-057-2*) Wonder Kids Pubns.

—Chinese Children's Stories Vol. 59: A Tankful of Water, The Little Hero. Ching, Emily et al, eds. Wonder Kids Publications Staff, tr. from CHI. 1991. (Wonder Kids Ser.). (Illus.). 28p. (J). (gr. 3-6). reprint ed. 7.95 o.p. (*1-56162-059-9*) Wonder Kids Pubns.

—Chinese Children's Stories Vol. 60: Weighing an Elephant, The Distant Homeland. Ching, Emily et al, eds. Wonder Kids Publications Staff, tr. from CHI. 1991. (Wonder Kids Ser.). (Illus.). 28p. (J). (gr. 3-6). reprint ed. 7.95 o.p. (*1-56162-060-2*) Wonder Kids Pubns.

—Chinese Children's Stories Vol. 62: To Catch the Suns, Two Quarrelsome Brothers. Ching, Emily et al, eds. Wonder Kids Publications Staff, tr. from CHI. 1991. (Mythology Ser.). (Illus.). 28p. (J). (gr. 3-6). reprint ed. 7.95 o.p. (*1-56162-062-9*) Wonder Kids Pubns.

—Chinese Children's Stories Vol. 63: To Speak or Not, The Dark Village. Ching, Emily et al, eds. Wonder Kids Publications Staff, tr. from CHI. 1991. (Mythology Ser.). (Illus.). 28p. (J). (gr. 3-6). reprint ed. 7.95 o.p. (*1-56162-063-7*) Wonder Kids Pubns.

—Chinese Children's Stories Vol. 64: Why Is the Sky So High?, Turning into Stone. Ching, Emily et al, eds. Wonder Kids Publications Staff, tr. from CHI. 1991. (Mythology Ser.). (Illus.). 28p. (J). (gr. 3-6). reprint ed. 7.95 o.p. (*1-56162-064-5*) Wonder Kids Pubns.

—Chinese Children's Stories Vol. 65: Lugging Mountains, What's a Life Span? Ching, Emily et al, eds. Wonder Kids Publications Staff, tr. from CHI. 1991. (Mythology Ser.). (Illus.). 28p. (J). (gr. 3-6). reprint ed. 7.95 o.p. (*1-56162-065-3*) Wonder Kids Pubns.

—Chinese Children's Stories Vol. 67: The After-Meal Bell, Passing the Three Gorges. Ching, Emily et al, eds. Wonder Kids Publications Staff, tr. from CHI. 1991. (Literature Ser.). (Illus.). 28p. (J). (gr. 3-6). reprint ed. 7.95 o.p. (*1-56162-067-X*) Wonder Kids Pubns.

—Chinese Children's Stories Vol. 68: The Donkey-Riding Poet, The Backyard Song. Ching, Emily et al, eds. Wonder Kids Publications Staff, tr. from CHI. 1991. (Literature Ser.). (Illus.). 28p. (J). (gr. 3-6). reprint ed. 7.95 o.p. (*1-56162-068-8*) Wonder Kids Pubns.

—Chinese Children's Stories Vol. 69: The Young Family, Tsuei's Beautiful Bride. Ching, Emily et al, eds. Wonder Kids Publications Staff, tr. from CHI. 1991. (Literature Ser.). (Illus.). 28p. (J). (gr. 3-6). reprint ed. 7.95 o.p. (*1-56162-069-6*) Wonder Kids Pubns.

—Chinese Children's Stories Vol. 70: Ji's Jokes, The Scrooge. Ching, Emily et al, eds. Wonder Kids Publications Staff, tr. from CHI. 1991. (Literature Ser.). (Illus.). 28p. (J). (gr. 3-6). reprint ed. 7.95 o.p. (*1-56162-070-X*) Wonder Kids Pubns.

—Chinese Children's Stories Vol. 98: Ai-Yu Jello, Granny & the Fox. Ching, Emily et al, eds. Wonder Kids Publications Staff, tr. from CHI. 1991. (Taiwanese Folklore Ser.). (Illus.). 28p. (J). (gr. 3-6). reprint ed. 7.95 o.p. (*1-56162-098-X*) Wonder Kids Pubns.

—Chinese Children's Stories Vol. 99: The Underground People, Half-Street Lai. Ching, Emily et al, eds. Wonder Kids Publications Staff, tr. from CHI. 1991. (Taiwanese Folklore Ser.). (Illus.). 28p. (J). (gr. 3-6). reprint ed. 7.95 o.p. (*1-56162-099-8*) Wonder Kids Pubns.

—Chinese Children's Stories Vol. 100: From Rice into Flowers, The Shy Rainbow. Ching, Emily et al, eds. Wonder Kids Publications Staff, tr. from CHI. 1991. (Taiwanese Folklore Ser.). (Illus.). 28p. (J). (gr. 3-6). reprint ed. 7.95 o.p. (*1-56162-100-5*) Wonder Kids Pubns.

—Chinese Children's Stories Vol.24: Running Fifty vs. One-Hundred Strides, Atu Yanks the Rice Seedlings. Ching, Emily et al, eds. Wonder Kids Publications Staff, tr. from CHI. 1991. (Idioms Ser.). (Illus.). 28p. (J). (gr. 3-6). reprint ed. 7.95 o.p. (*1-56162-024-6*) Wonder Kids Pubns.

—Chinese Children's Stories, Vol. 17: The Monkey & the Fire, Lazy Wife & the Bread Ring. Ching, Emily et al, eds. Wonder Kids Publications Staff, tr. from CHI. 1991. (Fables Ser.). (Illus.). 28p. (J). (gr. 3-6). reprint ed. 7.95 o.p. (*1-56162-017-3*) Wonder Kids Pubns.

—Chinese Children's Stories, Vol. 22: The Steal a Bell, The Dropout. Ching, Emily et al, eds. Wonder Kids Publications Staff, tr. from CHI. 1991. (Idioms Ser.). (Illus.). 28p. (J). (gr. 3-6). reprint ed. 7.95 o.p. (*1-56162-022-X*) Wonder Kids Pubns.

—Chinese Children's Stories, Vol. 27: Sky-Mending Festival, Decorative Paper for Graves. Ching, Emily et al, eds. Wonder Kids Publications Staff, tr. from CHI. 1991. (Festivals Ser.). (Illus.). 28p. (J). (gr. 3-6). reprint ed. 7.95 o.p. (*1-56162-027-0*) Wonder Kids Pubns.

—Chinese Children's Stories, Vol. 32: Dumplings, Ham. Ching, Emily et al, eds. Wonder Kids Publications Staff, tr. from CHI. 1991. (Tales about Food Ser.). (Illus.). 28p. (J). (gr. 3-6). reprint ed. 7.95 o.p. (*1-56162-032-7*) Wonder Kids Pubns.

—Chinese Children's Stories, Vol. 35: Monks' Beef Stew, Yue's Tofu Store. Ching, Emily et al, eds. Wonder Kids Publications Staff, tr. from CHI. 1991. (Tales about Food Ser.). (Illus.). 28p. (J). (gr. 3-6). reprint ed. 7.95 o.p. (*1-56162-035-1*) Wonder Kids Pubns.

—Chinese Children's Stories, Vol. 37: Confucius' Bookkeeping, The Scissors Shop. Ching, Emily et al, eds. Wonder Kids Publications Staff, tr. from CHI. 1991. (Inventions Ser.). (Illus.). 28p. (J). (gr. 3-6). reprint ed. 7.95 o.p. (*1-56162-037-8*) Wonder Kids Pubns.

—Chinese Children's Stories, Vol. 38: The Peace Drum, Comb. Ching, Emily et al, eds. Wonder Kids Publications Staff, tr. from CHI. 1991. (Inventions Ser.). (Illus.). 28p. (J). (gr. 3-6). reprint ed. 7.95 o.p. (*1-56162-038-6*) Wonder Kids Pubns.

—Chinese Children's Stories, Vol. 42: Tiger Seeks a Master, Why Are Cats Afraid of Dogs? Ching, Emily et al, eds. Wonder Kids Publications Staff, tr. from CHI. 1991. (Twelve Beasts & the Years Ser.). (Illus.). 28p. (J). (gr. 3-6). reprint ed. 7.95 o.p. (*1-56162-042-4*) Wonder Kids Pubns.

—Chinese Children's Stories, Vol. 52: Joining the Army, Beating up the Tiger. Ching, Emily et al, eds. Wonder Kids Publications Staff, tr. from CHI. 1991. (Filial Piety Ser.). (Illus.). 28p. (J). (gr. 3-6). reprint ed. 7.95 o.p. (*1-56162-052-1*) Wonder Kids Pubns.

—Chinese Children's Stories, Vol. 58: Three Princes & the Firewood, Wang's Memory. Ching, Emily et al, eds. Wonder Kids Publications Staff, tr. from CHI. 1991. (Wonder Kids Ser.). (Illus.). 28p. (J). (gr. 3-6). reprint ed. 7.95 o.p. (*1-56162-058-0*) Wonder Kids Pubns.

—Chinese Children's Stories, Vol. 7: Dragon Eye & Cassia Circle, The Conceited Barber. Ching, Emily et al, eds. Wonder Kids Publications Staff, tr. from CHI. 1991. (Tales about Plants Ser.). (Illus.). 28p. (J). (gr. 3-6). reprint ed. 7.95 o.p. (*1-56162-007-6*) Wonder Kids Pubns.

—Chinese Children's Stories, Vol. 72: The Lotus Child, The Ghost in the Basin. Ching, Emily et al, eds. Wonder Kids Publications Staff, tr. from CHI. 1991. (Popular Narratives Ser.). (Illus.). 28p. (J). (gr. 3-6). reprint ed. 7.95 o.p. (*1-56162-072-6*) Wonder Kids Pubns.

—Chinese Children's Stories, Vol. 73: Walking through Walls, Who Is the Real Lord Ji? Ching, Emily et al, eds. Wonder Kids Publications Staff, tr. from CHI. 1991. (Popular Narratives Ser.). (Illus.). 28p. (J). (gr. 3-6). reprint ed. 7.95 o.p. (*1-56162-073-4*) Wonder Kids Pubns.

—Chinese Children's Stories, Vol. 74: Chaos in the Heavenly Palace, Eating the Ginseng Fruit. Ching, Emily et al, eds. Wonder Kids Publications Staff, tr. from CHI. 1991. (Popular Narratives Ser.). (Illus.). 28p. (J). (gr. 3-6). reprint ed. 7.95 o.p. (*1-56162-074-2*) Wonder Kids Pubns.

—Chinese Children's Stories, Vol. 75: Tang's Strange Journey, Dwarfs & Giants. Ching, Emily et al, eds. Wonder Kids Publications Staff, tr. from CHI. 1991. (Popular Narratives Ser.). (Illus.). 28p. (J). (gr. 3-6). reprint ed. 7.95 o.p. (*1-56162-075-0*) Wonder Kids Pubns.

—Chinese Children's Stories, Vol. 77: Sir Guan's Big Red Face, Turning Cranes into Words. Ching, Emily et al, eds. Wonder Kids Publications Staff, tr. from CHI. 1991. (Heroes Ser.). (Illus.). 28p. (J). (gr. 3-6). reprint ed. 7.95 o.p. (*1-56162-077-7*) Wonder Kids Pubns.

—Chinese Children's Stories, Vol. 78: Tang Buohu's Drawings, The General & the Water Tank. Ching, Emily et al, eds. Wonder Kids Publications Staff, tr. from CHI. 1991. (Heroes Ser.). (Illus.). 28p. (J). (gr. 3-6). reprint ed. 7.95 o.p. (*1-56162-078-5*) Wonder Kids Pubns.

—Chinese Children's Stories, Vol. 79: Black-Faced Sir Bao, Doctor Hwa-Tuo. Ching, Emily et al, eds. Wonder Kids Publications Staff, tr. from CHI. 1991. (Heroes Ser.). (Illus.). 28p. (J). (gr. 3-6). reprint ed. 7.95 o.p. (*1-56162-079-3*) Wonder Kids Pubns.

—Chinese Children's Stories, Vol. 8: The Millets Won't Go Home, The Immortal Palm. Ching, Emily et al, eds. Wonder Kids Publications Staff, tr. from CHI. 1991. (Tales about Plants Ser.). (Illus.). 28p. (J). (gr. 3-6). reprint ed. 7.95 o.p. (*1-56162-008-4*) Wonder Kids Pubns.

—Chinese Children's Stories, Vol. 80: The Dwarf Minister, The Fabulous Chimera's Gift. Ching, Emily et al, eds. Wonder Kids Publications Staff, tr. from CHI. 1991. (Heroes Ser.). (Illus.). 28p. (J). (gr. 3-6). reprint ed. 7.95 o.p. (*1-56162-080-7*) Wonder Kids Pubns.

—Chinese Children's Stories, Vol. 82: The Fish Minister, The Hidden Sword. Ching, Emily et al, eds. Wonder Kids Publications Staff, tr. from CHI. 1991. (Historical Accounts Ser.). (Illus.). 28p. (J). (gr. 3-6). reprint ed. 7.95 o.p. (*1-56162-082-3*) Wonder Kids Pubns.

—Chinese Children's Stories, Vol. 83: The Revenge of Chao's Orphan, Tien's Wonderful Strategies. Ching, Emily et al, eds. Wonder Kids Publications Staff, tr. from CHI. 1991. (Historical Accounts Ser.). (Illus.). 28p. (J). (gr. 3-6). reprint ed. 7.95 o.p. (*1-56162-083-1*) Wonder Kids Pubns.

—Chinese Children's Stories, Vol. 84: Who Is the Real Liu Bong?, Kong Borrows the East Wind. Ching, Emily et al, eds. Wonder Kids Publications Staff, tr. from CHI. 1991. (Historical Accounts Ser.). (Illus.). 28p. (J). (gr. 3-6). reprint ed. 7.95 o.p. (*1-56162-084-X*) Wonder Kids Pubns.

—Chinese Children's Stories, Vol. 85: The Battle of the Fei River, The Princess' Engagement. Ching, Emily et al, eds. Wonder Kids Publications Staff, tr. from CHI. 1991. (Historical Accounts Ser.). (Illus.). 28p. (J). (gr. 3-6). reprint ed. 7.95 o.p. (*1-56162-085-8*) Wonder Kids Pubns.

—Chinese Children's Stories, Vol. 87: Fan Bridge & Escape Alley, The Stream of Flowers. Ching, Emily et al, eds. Wonder Kids Publications Staff, tr. from CHI. 1991. (Chinese Sites Ser.). (Illus.). 28p. (J). (gr. 3-6). reprint ed. 7.95 o.p. (*1-56162-087-4*) Wonder Kids Pubns.

—Chinese Children's Stories, Vol. 88: Five Stone Goats, Six-Foot Street. Ching, Emily et al, eds. Wonder Kids Publications Staff, tr. from CHI. 1991. (Chinese Sites Ser.). (Illus.). 28p. (J). (gr. 3-6). reprint ed. 7.95 o.p. (*1-56162-088-2*) Wonder Kids Pubns.

—Chinese Children's Stories, Vol. 89: Peach Blossom Cave, Mt. Lee. Ching, Emily et al, eds. Wonder Kids Publications Staff, tr. from CHI. 1991. (Chinese Sites Ser.). (Illus.). 28p. (J). (gr. 3-6). reprint ed. 7.95 o.p. (*1-56162-089-0*) Wonder Kids Pubns.

—Chinese Children's Stories, Vol. 9: The Story of Rice, The Cows & the Trumpet. Ching, Emily et al, eds. Wonder Kids Publications Staff, tr. from CHI. 1991. (Tales about Plants Ser.). (Illus.). 28p. (J). (gr. 3-6). reprint ed. 7.95 o.p. (*1-56162-009-2*) Wonder Kids Pubns.

—Chinese Children's Stories, Vol. 90: The Dragon Who Puts out Fires, The Golden Hairpin Well. Ching, Emily et al, eds. Wonder Kids Publications Staff, tr. from CHI. 1991. (Chinese Sites Ser.). (Illus.). 28p. (J). (gr. 3-6). reprint ed. 7.95 o.p. (*1-56162-090-4*) Wonder Kids Pubns.

—Chinese Children's Stories, Vol. 92: White-Rice Magic Cave, Sun-Moon Lake. Ching, Emily et al, eds. Wonder Kids Publications Staff, tr. from CHI. 1991. (Taiwanese Sites Ser.). (Illus.). 28p. (J). (gr. 3-6). reprint ed. 7.95 o.p. (*1-56162-092-0*) Wonder Kids Pubns.

—Chinese Children's Stories, Vol. 93: Mt. Anvil & the Sword Well, Two Waters. Ching, Emily et al, eds. Wonder Kids Publications Staff, tr. from CHI. 1991. (Taiwanese Sites Ser.). (Illus.). 28p. (J). (gr. 3-6). reprint ed. 7.95 o.p. (*1-56162-093-9*) Wonder Kids Pubns.

—Chinese Children's Stories, Vol. 94: Muddy Water Stream, Sister Lakes & Brother Trees. Ching, Emily et al, eds. Wonder Kids Publications Staff, tr. from CHI. 1991. (Taiwanese Sites Ser.). (Illus.). 28p. (J). (gr. 3-6). reprint ed. 7.95 o.p. (*1-56162-094-7*) Wonder Kids Pubns.

—Chinese Children's Stories, Vol. 95: Half-Shield Mountain, The Adopted Daughter Lake. Ching, Emily et al, eds. Wonder Kids Publications Staff, tr. from CHI. 1991. (Taiwanese Sites Ser.). (Illus.). 28p. (J). (gr. 3-6). reprint ed. 7.95 o.p. (*1-56162-095-5*) Wonder Kids Pubns.

—Chinese Children's Stories, Vol. 97: Tiger Aunty, Ah-Long & Ah-Hwa. Ching, Emily et al, eds. Wonder Kids Publications Staff, tr. from CHI. 1991. (Taiwanese Folklore Ser.). (Illus.). 28p. (J). (gr. 3-6). reprint ed. 7.95 o.p. (*1-56162-097-1*) Wonder Kids Pubns.

—Chinese Sites Vols. 86-90: Chinese Children's Stories. Ching, Emily et al, eds. Wonder Kids Publications Staff, tr. from CHI. 1991. (Chinese Sites Ser.). (Illus.). 28p. (J). (gr. 3-6). reprint ed. 7.95 (*1-56162-086-6*) Wonder Kids Pubns.

—Festivals Vols. 26-30: Chinese Children's Stories. Ching, Emily et al, eds. Wonder Kids Publications Staff, tr. from CHI. 1991. (Festivals Ser.). (Illus.). 28p. (J). (gr. 3-6). reprint ed. 39.75 o.p. (*1-56162-026-2*) Wonder Kids Pubns.

Jackson, Dave & Jackson, Neta. Shanghaied to China: Hudson Taylor. 1993. (Trailblazer Bks.: Vol. 9). (Illus.). 144p. (J). (gr. 3-7). pap. 5.99 (*1-55661-271-0*) Bethany Hse. Pubs.

Jaynes, Ruth. Yo-Ho & Kim. 1965. 58p. (J). (gr. 1-6). 2.50 (*0-89986-386-8*) Oriental Bk. Store, The.

—Yo-Ho & Kim at Sea. 1965. 58p. (J). (gr. 1-6). 2.50 (*0-89986-387-6*) Oriental Bk. Store, The.

Kendall, Carol & Li, Yao-Wen. Sweet & Sour: Tales from China. 2nd ed. 1990. 112p. (J). (gr. 4-6). pap. 7.95 (*0-395-54798-9*, Clarion Bks.) Houghton Mifflin Co. Trade & Reference Div.

Krakauer, Hoong Y. One Chinese Dragon in New York City. 1996. (J). (*0-316-50323-1*) Little Brown & Co.

Lasky, Kathryn. Lady of Ch'iao Kuo: Warrior of the South, China 531 A.D. 2001. (Royal Diaries Ser.). (Illus.). 304p. (J). (gr. 4-9). 12.95 (*0-439-16483-4*) Scholastic, Inc.

Lattimore, Deborah Nourse. The Dragon's Robe. 1990. (Illus.). 32p. (J). (gr. 1-5). lib. bdg. 14.89 o.p. (*0-06-023723-6*) HarperCollins Children's Bk. Group.

—Dragons Robe. 1990. (Illus.). 32p. (J). (gr. 1-5). 15.00 o.s.i (*0-06-023719-8*) HarperCollins Children's Bk. Group.

Lattimore, Eleanor F. Little Pear. D'Andrade, Diane, ed. 1991. (Odyssey Ser.). (Illus.). 144p. (J). (gr. 4-7). pap. 6.00 (*0-15-246685-1*) Harcourt Children's Bks.

—Little Pear. (Illus.). (J). (gr. 2-5). 1931. 7.50 o.p. (*0-15-246682-7*); 1968. reprint ed. pap. 3.95 o.p. (*0-15-652799-5*, Voyager Bks./Libros Viajeros) Harcourt Children's Bks.

—Little Pear & His Friends. (Odyssey Ser.). (Illus.). 1991. 144p. (YA). (gr. 4-7). pap. 4.95 o.s.i (*0-15-246863-3*, Odyssey Classics); 1934. (J). (gr. k-3). 5.95 o.p. (*0-15-246861-7*) Harcourt Children's Bks.

Lawson, Julie. The Dragon's Pearl. 1993. (Illus.). 32p. (J). (ps-3). 15.95 o.p. (*0-395-63623-X*, Clarion Bks.) Houghton Mifflin Co. Trade & Reference Div.

Lawson, Julie & Morin, Paul. The Dragon's Pearl. 1992. 32p. (J). (*0-19-540843-8*) Oxford Univ. Pr., Inc.

Lee, Jeanne M. Bitter Dumplings, RS. 2002. (Illus.). 32p. (J). (gr. 2-5). 16.00 (*0-374-39966-2*, Farrar, Straus & Giroux (BYR)) Farrar, Straus & Giroux.

Lewis, Elizabeth F. Young Fu of the Upper Yangtze. 1990. 288p. (gr. 4-7). pap. text 5.99 (*0-440-49043-X*, Yearling) Random Hse. Children's Bks.

Li, Xu. Trouble on Black Wind Mountain. 1985. (Monkey Ser.: No. 4). (Illus.). 54p. (J). (gr. 3 up). pap. 6.95 o.p. (*0-8351-1366-3*) China Bks. & Periodicals, Inc.

Lin, Grace. Kite Flying. 2002. 32p. (J). 14.95 (*0-375-81520-1*); lib. bdg. 16.99 (*0-375-91520-6*) Knopf, Alfred A. Inc.

Lobel, Arnold. Ming lo Moves the Mountain. 1986. (J). (ps-3). mass mkt. 3.95 o.p. (*0-590-42902-7*) Scholastic, Inc.

—Ming Lo Moves the Mountain. 1993. (Illus.). 32p. (J). (ps-3). pap. 5.99 (*0-688-10995-0*, Harper Trophy) HarperCollins Children's Bk. Group.

—Ming lo Moves the Mountain. 1983. (Illus.). 32p. (J). (ps-3). reprint ed. pap. 2.95 o.p. (*0-590-33273-2*) Scholastic, Inc.

Lu Meng. Three Precious Pearls. 1983. (Illus.). 19p. (J). (gr. 3-6). pap. 1.95 o.p. (*0-8351-1253-5*) China Bks. & Periodicals, Inc.

Mahy, Margaret. The Seven Chinese Brothers. (Illus.). 40p. (J). (ps-3). 1994. (SPA.). pap. 3.95 (*0-590-25211-9*); 1990. pap. 15.95 o.p. (*0-590-42055-0*) Scholastic, Inc.

—Seven Chinese Brothers. 1989. (Blue Ribbon Bks.). (J). 12.14 (*0-606-01945-6*) Turtleback Bks.

McCoy-Miller, Judith. The Journey of Yung Lee: From China to America. (Immigrants Chronicles Ser.). 132p. (J). (gr. 3-7). pap. 5.99 (*0-7814-3285-5*) Cook Communications Ministries.

McCully, Emily Arnold. Beautiful Warrior: The Legend of the Nun's Kung Fu. 2nd ed. 1998. (Illus.). 40p. (J). (ps-3). pap. 16.95 (*0-590-37487-7*) Scholastic, Inc.

McLean, Jacqueline. Grace from China. 2003. (J). (*0-9638472-8-7*) Yeong & Yeong Bk. Co.

Merrill, Jean. The Superlative Horse. 1986. (J). (gr. 4-7). lib. bdg. o.p. (*0-201-09357-X*) Addison-Wesley Longman, Inc.

Monjo, F. N. Prisoners of the Scrambling Dragon, ERS. 1980. (Illus.). 96p. (gr. 2-5). o.p. (*0-03-016656-X*, Holt, Henry & Co. Bks. For Young Readers) Holt, Henry & Co.

Morimoto, Junko. The Two Bullies. Morimoto, Isao, tr. from JPN. 1999. (Illus.). 32p. (J). (ps-2). 17.00 o.s.i (*0-517-80061-6*); lib. bdg. 18.99 o.s.i (*0-517-80062-4*) Random Hse. Children's Bks. (Random Hse. Bks. for Young Readers).

Nagda, Ann Whitehead. Bamboo Valley: A Story of a Chinese Bamboo Forest. 1997. (Habitat Ser.). (J). (gr. 1-4). 5.00 (*1-56899-497-4*, B7006); (Illus.). 32p. 19.95 incl. audio (*1-56899-493-1*, BC7006); (Illus.). 32p. 15.95 (*1-56899-491-5*); (Illus.). 32p. pap. 5.95 (*1-56899-492-3*);Incl. toy. (Illus.). 36p. 35.95 incl. audio (*1-56899-494-X*);Incl. toy. (Illus.). 32p. 26.95 (*1-56899-498-2*);Incl. toy. (Illus.). 32p. pap. 16.95 (*1-56899-495-8*);Incl. toy. (Illus.). 36p. pap. 19.95 incl. audio (*1-56899-496-6*) Soundprints.

Namioka, Lensey. The Laziest Boy in the World. 1998. (Illus.). 32p. (J). (ps-3). tchr. ed. 16.95 (*0-8234-1330-6*) Holiday Hse., Inc.

—Ties That Bind, Ties That Break. 160p. (YA). (gr. 7 up). 2000. mass mkt. 4.99 (*0-440-41599-3*, Laurel Leaf); 1999. 15.95 o.s.i (*0-385-32666-1*, Dell Books for Young Readers) Random Hse. Children's Bks.

—Ties That Bind, Ties That Break. l.t. ed. 2003. 185p. (J). 24.95 (*0-7862-5922-1*) Thorndike Pr.

Neville, Emily C. The China Year. 256p. (J). 1999. pap. 4.95 (*0-06-440407-2*); 1991. (gr. 5-9). 15.95 (*0-06-024383-X*); 1991. (gr. 5-9). lib. bdg. 15.89 o.p. (*0-06-024384-8*) HarperCollins Children's Bk. Group.

Okimoto, Jean Davies & Aoki, Elaine Mei. The White Swan Express: A Story about Adoption. 2002. (Illus.). 32p. (J). (ps-3). lib. bdg., tchr. ed. 16.00 (*0-618-16453-7*, Clarion Bks.) Houghton Mifflin Co. Trade & Reference Div.

Osborne, Mary Pope. Day of the Dragon King. 1998. (Magic Tree House Ser.: No. 14). (Illus.). 96p. (gr. k-3). lib. bdg. 11.99 (*0-679-99051-8*, Random Hse. Bks. for Young Readers) Random Hse. Children's Bks.

—Day of the Dragon King. 14th ed. 1998. (Magic Tree House Ser.: No. 14). (Illus.). 96p. (J). (gr. k-3). pap. 3.99 (*0-679-89051-3*) Random Hse., Inc.

—Day of the Dragon King. 1998. (Magic Tree House Ser.: No. 14). (Illus.). (J). (gr. k-3). 10.04 (*0-606-13958-3*) Turtleback Bks.

Pacilio, V. J. Ling Cho & His Three Friends, RS. 2000. (Illus.). 32p. (J). (ps-3). 16.00 (*0-374-34545-7*, Farrar, Straus & Giroux (BYR)) Farrar, Straus & Giroux.

Partridge, Elizabeth. Oranges on Golden Mountain. (Illus.). 40p. 2003. (YA). pap. 6.99 (*0-14-250033-X*, Puffin Bks.); 2001. (J). (gr. 1-4). 16.99 (*0-525-46453-0*, Dutton Children's Bks.) Penguin Putnam Bks. for Young Readers.

Paterson, Katherine. Rebels of the Heavenly Kingdom. 1983. 224p. (YA). (gr. 12 up). 14.99 o.s.i (*0-525-66911-6*, Dutton Children's Bks.) Penguin Putnam Bks. for Young Readers.

Pferdehirt, Julia, et al. Hudson Taylor: Shanghaied to China. 2000. (Trailblazer Bks.). (Illus.). 24p. pap., stu. ed. 4.99 o.p. (*0-7642-2344-5*) Bethany Hse. Pubs.

Pilegard, Virginia Walton. The Warlord's Fish. 2002. (Illus.). 32p. (J). 14.95 (*1-56554-964-3*) Pelican Publishing Co., Inc.

—The Warlord's Puppeteers. 2003. (Illus.). 32p. (J). 14.95 (*1-58980-077-X*) Pelican Publishing Co., Inc.

—The Warlord's Puzzle. 2000. (Illus.). 32p. (J). (ps-4). 14.95 (*1-56554-495-1*) Pelican Publishing Co., Inc.

Pittman, Helena Clare. A Grain of Rice. 1986. (Illus.). (J). (gr. k-4). 12.95 o.p. (*0-8038-2728-8*); lib. bdg. 12.95 o.p. (*0-8038-9289-6*) Hastings Hse. Daytrips Pubs.

Piumini, Roberto. Doctor Me Di Cin. 2001. (Illus.). (J). (gr. 2-4). 15.95 (*1-886910-67-7*, Front Street) Front Street, Inc.

Porte, Barbara Ann. Ma Jiang & the Orange Ants. 2000. (Illus.). 32p. (J). pap. 16.95 (*0-531-30241-5*); lib. bdg. 17.99 (*0-531-33241-1*) Scholastic, Inc. (Orchard Bks.).

Poter, Wesley. Dragons of Peking. 1979. (Illus.). (gr. k-3). 2.95 o.p. (*0-531-02500-4*); lib. bdg. 6.90 o.p. (*0-531-04079-8*) Scholastic Library Publishing. (Watts, Franklin).

Provensen, Alice. The Master Swordsman & the Magic Doorway: Two Legends from Ancient China. 2001. (Illus.). 40p. (J). (gr. k-2). 16.95 (*0-689-83232-X*, Simon & Schuster Children's Publishing) Simon & Schuster Children's Publishing.

Pyne, K. D. All the Way to China. 1993. (Illus.). 16p. (J). (ps). pap. 4.95 (*1-882185-06-4*) Cornerstone Publishing.

Ransome, Arthur. Missee Lee: The Swallows & Amazons in the China Seas. 2002. (Godine Storyteller Ser.). (Illus.). 352p. (J). pap. 14.95 (*1-56792-196-5*) Godine, David R. Pub.

Ricci, Regolo, illus. The Nightingale. 1992. Orig. Title: Nattergalen. 32p. (J). (gr. k-4). 15.45 o.p. (*0-395-60819-8*, Clarion Bks.) Houghton Mifflin Co. Trade & Reference Div.

Roome, Diana Reynolds. The Elephant's Pillow, RS. 2003. (Illus.). 32p. (J). 16.00 (*0-374-32015-2*, Farrar, Straus & Giroux (BYR)) Farrar, Straus & Giroux.

Rumford, James. The Cloudmakers. 1996. (Illus.). 32p. (J). (ps-3). tchr. ed. 17.00 (*0-395-76505-6*) Houghton Mifflin Co.

Russell, Ching Yeung. Child Bride. 136p. (J). (gr. 3-7). 2003. pap. 9.95 (*1-59078-024-8*); 1999. (Illus.). 15.95 (*1-56397-748-6*) Boyds Mills Pr.

Schlein, Miriam. The Year of the Panda. 1990. (Illus.). 96p. (J). (gr. 3-7). 13.00 (*0-690-04864-5*) Harper-Collins Children's Bk. Group.

Schlesinger, Marian C. San Bao & His Adventures in Peking. 2nd ed. 1998. (Illus.). 75p. (J). (gr. 3-7). reprint ed. pap. 15.00 (*0-9645809-1-8*) Gale Hill Bks.

Scott, Mavis. Little Ho & the Golden Kites. 1993. (Illus.). 32p. (Orig.). (J). (gr. k-3). pap. 6.95 o.p. (*0-04-442242-3*) Allen & Unwin Pty., Ltd. AUS. *Dist:* Independent Pubs. Group.

Seven Chinese Brothers. 2001. (Fun with Math Ser.). lib. bdg. (*1-59054-490-0*) Fitzgerald Bks.

Shemie, Bonnie. Houses of China. 1996. (Illus.). 24p. (J). (gr. 3-7). 13.95 (*0-88776-369-3*) Tundra Bks. of Northern New York.

Shepard, Aaron. The Magic Brocade: A Tale of China. 2000. (Illus.). 32p. (J). (gr. 3-7). 16.95 (*1-57227-064-0*) Pan Asia Pubns. (USA), Inc.

—The Magic Brocade: A Tale of China. Araujo, Frank P., tr. 2000. (ENG & SPA., Illus.). 32p. (J). (gr. 3-7). 16.95 (*1-57227-065-9*) Pan Asia Pubns. (USA), Inc.

—The Magic Brocade: A Tale of China. Chen, Isabella, tr. from ENG. 2000. (CHI & ENG., Illus.). 32p. (J). (gr. 3-7). 16.95 (*1-57227-066-7*) Pan Asia Pubns. (USA), Inc.

—The Magic Brocade: A Tale of China. Vu, Khanh Yen, tr. 2000. (ENG & VIE., Illus.). 32p. (J). (gr. 3-7). 16.95 (*1-57227-067-5*) Pan Asia Pubns. (USA), Inc.

Shufen, Li. Why Tomorrow? 1983. (Illus.). 49p. (Orig.). (J). (gr. 3-5). pap. 3.95 o.p. (*0-8351-1094-X*) China Bks. & Periodicals, Inc.

Singer, Isaac Bashevis. The Topsy-Turvy Emperor of China, RS. Singer, Isaac Bashevis & Shub, Elizabeth, trs. 1996. (Illus.). 32p. (J). (ps-3). pap. 5.95 o.p. (*0-374-47588-1*, Sunburst) Farrar, Straus & Giroux.

Singer, Marilyn. The Painted Fan. 1994. (Illus.). 40p. (J). 15.00 o.p. (*0-688-11742-2*); lib. bdg. 14.93 o.p. (*0-688-11743-0*) Morrow/Avon. (Morrow, William & Co.).

Stone, Kazuko G., illus. The Butterfly's Dream: Children's Stories from China. 2003. 32p. (J). 15.95 (*0-8048-3480-6*) Tuttle Publishing.

Story about Ping. 2001. (Early Readers Ser.: Vol. 1). (J). lib. bdg. (*1-59054-325-4*) Fitzgerald Bks.

Talley, Linda. Thank You, Meiling. 1999. (Key Concepts in Personal Development Ser.). (Illus.). 32p. (J). (gr. k-4). 16.95 (*1-55942-118-5*, 7666) Marsh Media.

Tan, Amy. The Chinese Siamese Cat. abr. ed. 1994. (ps-3). 8.95 o.p. (*0-7871-0202-4*) NewStar Media, Inc.

—The Chinese Siamese Cat. 1994. (Illus.). 32p. (J). (gr. k-3). 16.95 (*0-02-788835-5*, Simon & Schuster Children's Publishing) Simon & Schuster Children's Publishing.

—The Moon Lady. (Illus.). 32p. (J). 1995. (ps-3). pap. 6.99 (*0-689-80616-7*, Aladdin); 1992. (gr. 1 up). lib. bdg. 16.95 (*0-02-788830-4*, Simon & Schuster Children's Publishing) Simon & Schuster Children's Publishing.

—The Moon Lady. 1995. 11.15 o.p. (*0-606-07886-X*) Turtleback Bks.

Tompert, Ann. The Jade Horse, the Cricket & the Peachstone. 2001. (Illus.). 32p. (J). 14.95 o.s.i (*1-56397-239-5*) Boyds Mills Pr.

Treffinger, Carolyn. Li Lun, Lad of Courage. 1995. (Newbery Honor Roll Ser.). 11.15 o.p. (*0-606-09553-5*) Turtleback Bks.

—Li Lun, Lad of Courage. 1995. (Newbery Honor Roll Ser.). (Illus.). 96p. (J). (gr. 4-7). pap. 5.95 (*0-8027-7468-7*) Walker & Co.

Tseng, Grace. White Tiger, Blue Serpent. 1999. (Illus.). 32p. (J). (gr. 1 up). lib. bdg. 16.89 (*0-688-12516-6*) HarperCollins Children's Bk. Group.

—White Tiger, Blue Serpent. 1999. (Illus.). 32p. (J). (ps-3). 16.00 (*0-688-12515-8*, Morrow, William & Co.) Morrow/Avon.

Tsubakiyama, Margaret. Mei-Mei Loves the Morning. 1999. (Illus.). 32p. (J). (ps-3). lib. bdg. 15.95 (*0-8075-5039-6*) Whitman, Albert & Co.

Tucker, Kathy. The Seven Chinese Sisters. 2003. (Illus.). 32p. (J). (gr. k-3). 15.95 (*0-8075-7309-4*) Whitman, Albert & Co.

Va, Leong. A Letter to the King. Anderson, James, tr. from CHI. 1991. (Illus.). 32p. (J). (gr. k-3). lib. bdg. 14.89 (*0-06-020070-7*); 14.95 o.p. (*0-06-020079-0*) HarperCollins Children's Bk. Group.

Vander Els, Betty. Leaving Point, RS. 1987. 176p. (YA). (gr. 7-12). 15.00 o.p. (*0-374-34376-4*, Farrar, Straus & Giroux (BYR)) Farrar, Straus & Giroux.

Vollbracht, James. The Way of the Circle. 1993. (Illus.). 48p. (J). (gr. 4-8). pap. 6.95 o.p. (*0-915166-76-3*, Little Imp Bks.) Impact Pubs., Inc.

Wallace, Karen. Raspberries on the Yangtze. 2002. 144p. (YA). (gr. 7). 15.95 (*0-385-72963-4*, Delacorte Bks. for Young Readers) Random Hse. Children's Bks.

Wenjing, Yan, et al. Favorite Children's Stories from China. 1983. (Illus.). 270p. (J). (gr. 5-7). pap. 4.95 o.p. (*0-8351-1064-8*) China Bks. & Periodicals, Inc.

Whelan, Gloria. Chu Ju's House. 2004. 240p. (J). 15.99 (*0-06-050724-1*); lib. bdg. 16.89 (*0-06-050725-X*) HarperCollins Pubs.

Wilson, Barbara Ker. Wishbones: A Folk Tale from China. (Illus.). 32p. (J). (ps-2). pap. 9.99 (*0-7112-1415-8*) Lincoln, Frances Ltd. GBR. *Dist:* Antique Collectors' Club.

Wolff, Ferida. The Emperor's Garden. 1994. (Illus.). (J). 15.00 o.p. (*0-688-11651-5*); 32p. lib. bdg. 14.93 o.p. (*0-688-11652-3*) Morrow/Avon. (Morrow, William & Co.).

Wolkstein, Diane. White Wave: A Chinese Tale. 1979. (Illus.). (J). (gr. 2 up). 13.95 o.p. (*0-690-03893-3*); lib. bdg. 12.89 (*0-690-03894-1*) HarperCollins Children's Bk. Group.

Wonder Kids Publications Staff, et al. Folklore: Chinese Children's Stories, 100 vols., Set, Vols. 1-5. Ching, Emily et al, eds. 1991. (Illus.). 28p. (J). (gr. 3-6). reprint ed. 795.00 o.p. (*1-56162-120-X*) Wonder Kids Pubns.

Ye, Ting-Xing. Share the Sky. 1999. (Illus.). 32p. (J). (gr. k-3). lib. bdg. 17.95 (*1-55037-579-2*) Annick Pr., Ltd. CAN. *Dist:* Firefly Bks., Ltd.

—Weighing the Elephant. 1998. (Illus.). 32p. (J). (ps-3). pap. 6.95 (*1-55037-526-1*); lib. bdg. 16.95 (*1-55037-527-X*) Annick Pr., Ltd. CAN. *Dist:* Firefly Bks., Ltd.

—Weighing the Elephant. 1998. 13.10 (*0-606-16262-3*) Turtleback Bks.

Yee, Paul. The Jade Necklace. 2002. (Illus.). 32p. (J). (ps-3). 15.95 (*1-56656-455-7*, Crocodile Bks.) Interlink Publishing Group, Inc.

Yep, Laurence. The City of Dragons. 1995. (Illus.). 32p. (J). (gr. k-4). pap. 14.95 (*0-590-47865-6*) Scholastic, Inc.

—The Ghost Fox. 80p. (J). 1997. (gr. 2-5). mass mkt. 2.99 (*0-590-47205-4*, Scholastic Paperbacks); 1994. (Illus.). (gr. 4-6). pap. 13.95 (*0-590-47204-6*) Scholastic, Inc.

—The Ghost Fox. 1997. (J). 9.65 (*0-606-11369-X*) Turtleback Bks.

—Mountain Light, 1855. 1997. (Golden Mountain Chronicles: Vol. 1855). 288p. (J). (gr. 5 up). pap. 6.95 (*0-06-440667-9*, Harper Trophy) HarperCollins Children's Bk. Group.

—Spring Pearl: The Last Flower. 2002. (Girls of Many Lands Ser.). (Illus.). 224p. (J). (gr. 4-7). 12.95 (*1-58485-595-9*); pap. 7.95 (*1-58485-519-3*) Pleasant Co. Pubns. (American Girl).

Yin. Coolies. (Illus.). 40p. 2003. pap. 7.99 (*0-14-250055-0*, Puffin Bks.); 2001. (J). 16.99 (*0-399-23227-3*, Philomel) Penguin Putnam Bks. for Young Readers.

Young, Ed. The Lost Horse: A Chinese Folktale. 2004. (Illus.). 32p. (J). pap. (*0-15-205023-X*, Voyager Bks./Libros Viajeros) Harcourt Children's Bks.

—The Monkey King. 2001. (Illus.). 40p. (J). (gr. k-3). 16.95 (*0-06-027919-2*); lib. bdg. 16.89 (*0-06-027950-8*) HarperCollins Children's Bk. Group.

Ziner, Feenie & Young, Ed. Cricket Boy: A Chinese Tale Retold. 1977. (gr. 3 up). lib. bdg. 6.95 o.p. (*0-385-12507-0*) Doubleday Publishing.

CHINA (PEOPLE'S REPUBLIC OF CHINA)—FICTION

Behrens, June. Soo Ling Finds a Way. 1965. (Illus.). 32p. (J). (gr. k-3). lib. bdg. 7.95 o.p. (*0-516-08739-8*, Children's Pr.) Scholastic Library Publishing.

McLenighan, Valjean. People's Republic of China. 1984. (Illus.). 128p. (J). (gr. 5-9). lib. bdg. 32.00 o.p. (*0-516-02781-6*, Children's Pr.) Scholastic Library Publishing.

CHISHOLM TRAIL—FICTION

Rogers, Lisa Waller. Get along Little Dogies: The Chisholm Trail Diary of Hallie Lou Wells. 2001. (Lone Star Journals: Vol. 1). (Illus.). 174p. (J). (gr. 4-7). 14.50 (*0-89672-446-8*) Texas Tech Univ. Pr.

—Get along, Little Dogies: The Chisholm Trail Diary of Hallie Lou Wells, South Texas 1878. 2001. (Lone Star Journals). (Illus.). 174p. (J). (gr. 4-7). 8.95 (*0-89672-448-4*) Texas Tech Univ. Pr.

Sargent, Dave & Sargent, Pat. Flash (Strawberry Roan) Speed Counts #25. 2001. (Saddle Up Ser.). 36p. (J). pap. 6.95 (*1-56763-614-4*); lib. bdg. 22.60 (*1-56763-613-6*) Ozark Publishing.

CLEVELAND (OHIO)—FICTION

Fleischman, Paul. Seedfolks. 1997. (Joanna Cotler Bks.). (Illus.). 80p. (J). (gr. 5 up). 14.99 (*0-06-027471-9*); lib. bdg. 15.89 (*0-06-027472-7*) HarperCollins Children's Bk. Group.

Holbrook, Sara. What's So Big about Cleveland, Ohio? 1997. (Illus.). 36p. (J). (gr. k-5). 17.95 (*1-886228-02-7*) Gray & Co., Pubs.

Manry, Douglas. The Land the Cleves Built. Sloan, Stephen, ed. 1989. (Illus.). 32p. (J). (gr. 2-5). (*0-9622316-0-6*) Sloan/Manry Pubs.

COLOMBIA—FICTION

Becerra de Jenkins, Lyll. Celebrating the Hero. 1993. (Illus.). 192p. (YA). (gr. 7 up). 15.99 o.p. (*0-525-67399-7*, Dutton Children's Bks.) Penguin Putnam Bks. for Young Readers.

Elwood, Roger. Forbidden River. 1991. (J). (gr. 3-7). pap. 4.99 o.p. (*0-8499-3304-8*) W Publishing Group.

Kendall, Sarita H. Ransom for a River Dolphin. 1993. 128p. (J). (gr. 3-6). lib. bdg. 19.95 o.p. (*0-8225-0735-8*, Lerner Pubns.) Lerner Publishing Group.

Vallejo, Fernando. Our Lady of the Assassins. Hammond, Paul, tr. from SPA. 2001. 144p. pap. 13.99 (*1-85242-647-0*) Serpent's Tail Ltd. GBR. *Dist:* Consortium Bk. Sales & Distribution.

Windle, Jeanette. Captured in Colombia. 2002. (Parker Twins Ser.: No. 3). 176p. (J). (gr. 3-8). pap. 5.99 (*0-8254-4147-1*) Kregel Pubns.

COLORADO—FICTION

Aigner-Clark, Julie. In the Rain with Jane, No. 1. 2003. (Baby Einstein Ser.). (Illus.). 6p. (J). 6.99 (*0-7868-1903-0*) Hyperion Bks. for Children.

Avi. The Good Dog. l.t. ed. 2003. 176p. (J). 23.95 (*0-7862-5600-1*) Thorndike Pr.

—Prairie School. (I Can Read Chapter Bks.). (Illus.). 48p. (J). (gr. 3-4). 2001. 15.99 (*0-06-027664-9*); 2001. lib. bdg. 16.89 (*0-06-027665-7*); Bk. 4. 2003. pap. 3.99 (*0-06-051318-7*) HarperCollins Children's Bk. Group.

—The Secret School. 2001. 160p. (J). (gr. 3-7). 16.00 (*0-15-216375-1*) Harcourt Children's Bks.

—The Secret School. 2003. (Illus.). 168p. (J). (gr. 3-6). pap. 5.95 (*0-15-204699-2*, 53582853) Harcourt Trade Pubs.

Ayres, Katherine. Silver Dollar Girl. 2002. (Illus.). 208p. (gr. 3-7). pap. text 4.99 (*0-440-41705-8*, Laurel Leaf) Random Hse. Children's Bks.

Barker, Jane Valentine & Downing, Sybil. Beauty in the Rockies. 1980. (Colorado Heritage Ser.: Bk. 10). (Illus.). 50p. (J). (gr. 3-4). pap. 2.50 o.p. (*0-87108-226-8*) Pruett Publishing Co.

—Colorado Heritage Series, 10 vols., Set. (Illus.). (J). (ps-8). reprint ed. pap. 9.50 (*1-878611-00-3*) Silver Rim Pr.

Barron, T. A. The Story of a Brave Young Girl & a Mountain Guide. Lewin, Ted, tr. & illus. by. 2004. (J). 16.99 (*0-399-23704-6*, Philomel) Penguin Putnam Bks. for Young Readers.

Bograd, Larry & Hubbard, Coleen. Colorado Summer. l.t. ed. 1999. (Treasured Horses Collection). (Illus.). 128p. (J). (gr. 4 up). lib. bdg. 22.60 (*0-8368-2277-3*) Stevens, Gareth Inc.

Courtney, Dayle. Operation Doomsday. 1981. (Thorne Twins Adventure Bks.). (Illus.). 192p. (Orig.). (J). (gr. 5 up). pap. 2.98 o.p. (*0-87239-466-2*, 2711) Standard Publishing.

Danneberg, Julie. Margaret's Magnificent Colorado Adventure. 1999. (Illus.). 47p. (J). (gr. 4-7). pap. 14.95 (*1-56579-329-3*) Westcliffe Pubs.

Downing, Sybil & Barker, Jane Valentine. Happy Harvest. (Colorado Heritage Ser.). (Illus.). 43p. (J). reprint ed. pap. text 7.95 (*1-878611-02-X*) Silver Rim Pr.

—Mesas to Mountains. (Colorado Heritage Ser.). (Illus.). 47p. (J). (ps-8). reprint ed. pap. 7.95 (*1-878611-04-6*) Silver Rim Pr.

Duey, Kathleen. Agnes May Gleason: Walsenburg, Colorado, 1933. 1998. (American Diaries Ser.: No. 11). 144p. (J). (gr. 3-7). pap. 4.50 (*0-689-82329-0*, Aladdin) Simon & Schuster Children's Publishing.

—Agnes May Gleason: Walsenburg, Colorado, 1933. 1998. (American Diaries Ser.: No. 11). (J). (gr. 3-7). 10.04 (*0-606-16133-3*) Turtleback Bks.

Duey, Kathleen & Bale, Karen A. Blizzard, Estes Park, Colorado, 1886. 1998. (Survival! Ser.: No. 3). (J). (gr. 4-7). 10.55 (*0-606-13827-7*) Turtleback Bks.

Ernst, Kathleen. Whistler in the Dark. 2002. (American Girl Collection: Bk. 16). (Illus.). 176p. (J). 10.95 (*1-58485-486-3*); pap. 6.95 (*1-58485-485-5*) Pleasant Co. Pubns. (American Girl).

Finley, Mary Pearce. Little Fox's Secret: The Mystery of Bent's Fort. 1999. (Illus.). 68p. (J). (gr. 3-4). lib. bdg. 15.95 (*0-86541-049-6*) Filter Pr., LLC.

Henty, G. A. In the Heart of the Rockies: A Story of Adventure in Colorado. E-Book 3.95 (*0-594-01719-X*) 1873 Pr.

—In the Heart of the Rockies: A Story of Adventure in Colorado. 2002. 370p. 29.95 (*1-59087-073-5*, GAH073); per. 19.95 (*1-59087-072-7*, GAH072) Althouse Pr.

—In the Heart of the Rockies: A Story of Adventure in Colorado. 1998. (Illus.). 385p. (YA). (gr. 4 up). reprint ed. pap. 16.95 (*1-890623-08-3*) Lost Classics Bk. Co.

—In the Heart of the Rockies: A Story of Adventure in Colorado. collector's ed. 2002. (Illus.). im. lthr. 38.85 (*1-4115-1341-X*); pap. 19.95 (*1-4115-0577-8*); 25.95 (*1-4115-0949-8*); pap. 17.95 (*1-4115-0174-8*) Polyglot Pr., Inc.

Hutchens, Paul. Colorado Kidnapping. (Sugar Creek Gang Ser.: No. 27). (J). (gr. 3-7). mass mkt. 3.99 o.p. (*0-8024-4827-5*, 627) Moody Pr.

—The Colorado Kidnapping. rev. ed. 1998. (Sugar Creek Gang Ser.: Vol. 24). 128p. (Orig.). (J). (gr. 4-7). mass mkt. 4.99 (*0-8024-7028-9*) Moody Pr.

Jackson, Helen Hunt. Nelly's Silver Mine: A Story of Colorado Life. 1977. (Classics of Children's Literature, 1621-1932: Vol. 46). (Illus.). (J). reprint ed. lib. bdg. 46.00 o.p. (*0-8240-2295-5*) Garland Publishing, Inc.

Jones, J. Syndey. Frankie. 1997. 192p. (YA). (gr. 5-9). 16.99 o.s.i (*0-525-67574-4*, Dutton Children's Bks.) Penguin Putnam Bks. for Young Readers.

Ladd, Louise. The Anywhere Ring Book No. 3: Lost Valley. 1996. 144p. (Orig.). (J). (gr. 3-7). mass mkt. 4.50 o.s.i (*0-425-15192-1*) Berkley Publishing Group.

Lawlor, Laurie. Gold in the Hills. 1995. 196p. (J). (gr. 4-7). 15.95 (*0-8027-8371-6*) Walker & Co.

Montgomery, Dan. The Mystery of the Aspen Bandits: A Kimmy O'Keefe Mystery. 1996. (Kimmy O'Keefe Mystery Ser.: Vol. 1). 204p. (YA). (gr. 8-11). pap. 6.95 (*0-8198-4788-7*) Pauline Bks. & Media.

Moore, Beverly. Echo's Song. 1993. (Illus.). 40p. (J). (gr. k-3). lib. bdg. 13.95 (*0-9637288-7-3*) River Walker Bks.

Myers, Edward. Climb or Die. 192p. (J). 1996. pap. 4.95 (*0-7868-1181-1*); 1994. (gr. 5-9). 14.95 (*0-7868-0026-7*); 1994. (gr. 5-9). lib. bdg. 14.89 o.p. (*0-7868-2021-7*) Hyperion Bks. for Children.

—Climb or Die. 1997. 180p. (J). (gr. 5-9). lib. bdg. 14.49 (*0-7868-2350-X*) Hyperion Pr.

—Climb or Die. 1996. (J). 11.00 (*0-606-10162-4*) Turtleback Bks.

—Climb or Die: A Test of Survival. 1996. 192p. (J). (gr. 4-7). pap. 4.95 (*0-7868-1129-3*) Disney Pr.

Nixon, Joan Lowery. Fat Chance, Claude. 1989. (Illus.). 32p. (J). (ps-3). pap. 4.99 o.s.i (*0-14-050679-9*, Puffin Bks.) Penguin Putnam Bks. for Young Readers.

Samantha's Colorado Adventure. 1998. (Illus.). 2p. (J). (ps-1). 15.00 (*1-888074-85-X*) Pockets of Learning.

Savage, Nancy. Nickel, the Baby Buffalo Who Thought He Was a Dog. 1999. (Illus.). 31p. (J). pap. (*0-9669130-0-0*) Savage Parks Pr.

Schaller, Bob. Crime in a Colorado Cave. 2000. (X-Country Adventures Ser.). (Illus.). 128p. (J). (gr. 3-6). pap. 5.99 o.p. (*0-8010-4453-7*) Baker Bks.

Shirley, Gayle C. C Is for Colorado. 1989. (Illus.). 40p. (J). (gr. k-3). 7.95 o.p. (*0-937959-85-5*, Falcon) Globe Pequot Pr., The.

Steiner, Barbara. Oliver Dibbs & the Dinosaur Cause. 1988. 160p. (J). pap. 2.95 (*0-380-70466-8*, Avon Bks.) Morrow/Avon.

—Oliver Dibbs & the Dinosaur Cause. 1986. (Illus.). 160p. (J). (gr. 3-7). text 13.95 o.s.i (*0-02-787880-5*, Simon & Schuster Children's Publishing) Simon & Schuster Children's Publishing.

Strand, Keith. Grandfather's Christmas Tree. 1999. (Illus.). 32p. (J). (ps-3). 16.00 (*0-15-201821-2*, Silver Whistle) Harcourt Children's Bks.

—Grandfather's Christmas Tree. 2002. (Illus.). 32p. (J). (gr. k-3). pap. 6.00 (*0-15-216374-3*, Voyager Bks./Libros Viajeros) Harcourt Children's Bks.

Taylor, Kim. Cissy Funk. 2001. 224p. (J). (gr. 5 up). 15.95 (*0-06-029041-2*); lib. bdg. 15.89 (*0-06-029042-0*) HarperCollins Children's Bk. Group.

Turner, Barbara. Treasure in Ghost Town. 2001. 126p. (J). pap. 11.95 (*1-55517-540-6*, Bonneville Bks.) Cedar Fort, Inc./CFI Distribution.

Weber, Lenora Mattingly. How Long Is Always? 1970. 226p. (YA). (gr. 7 up). 14.95 o.p. (*0-690-40680-0*) HarperCollins Children's Bk. Group.

COLORADO RIVER AND VALLEY—FICTION

Honig, Donald. An End of Innocence. 1972. (J). (gr. 4-9). 5.75 o.p. (*0-399-20254-4*) Putnam Publishing Group, The.

CONFEDERATE STATES OF AMERICA—FICTION

Bennett, Cherie. A Heart Divided. 2004. (YA). lib. bdg. 17.99 (*0-385-90039-2*, Delacorte Bks. for Young Readers) Random Hse. Children's Bks.

Connell, Kate. Yankee Blue or Rebel Grey: The Civil War Adventures of Sam Shaw. 2003. (I Am American Ser.). (Illus.). 40p. (J). pap. 6.99 (*0-7922-5179-2*) National Geographic Society.

Daringer, Helen F. Mary Montgomery, Rebel. 1948. (Illus.). (J). (gr. 7 up). 4.95 o.p. (*0-15-252231-X*) Harcourt Children's Bks.

Gibboney, Douglas Lee. Stonewall Jackson at Gettysburg. 2002. (Illus.). 132p. (YA). pap. 12.95 (*1-57249-317-8*, Burd Street Pr.) White Mane Publishing Co., Inc.

Hahn, Stephen. Pike McCallister. 1998. 253p. (YA). (gr. 6 up). per. 14.95 (*1-888125-29-2*) Publication Consultants.

Page, Thomas Nelson. Two Little Confederates. 1888. (YA). reprint ed. pap. text 28.00 (*1-4047-4689-7*) Classic Textbooks.

—Two Little Confederates. 1999. (Illus.). 180p. (J). (gr. 4-7). pap. 14.95 (*1-56554-574-5*) Pelican Publishing Co., Inc.

Sappey, Maureen S. Dreams of Ships, Dreams of Julia: At Sea with the Monitor & the Merrimack-Virginia, 1862. 1998. (Young American Ser.: Vol. 2). (Illus.). 140p. (YA). (gr. 4-7). 5.99 (*1-57249-134-5*) White Mane Publishing Co., Inc.

Schoenherr, John. Rebel. 1998. (Illus.). 32p. (J). (ps-1). pap. 5.99 o.s.i (*0-698-11619-4*, PaperStar) Penguin Putnam Bks. for Young Readers.

Smiley, Brad & Smiley, Barbara. The Stone Wall: The Story of a Confederate Soldier. 1998. (Illus.). 355p. 23.00 (*0-9664424-1-5*) Kennesaw Publishing.

CONGO (BRAZZAVILLE)—FICTION

Clair, Andree. Bemba: An African Adventure. Ponsot, Marie, tr. 1966. (Illus.). (J). (gr. 4-6). pap. 0.60 o.p. (*0-15-611816-5*, AVB37, Voyager Bks./Libros Viajeros) Harcourt Children's Bks.

CONGO (DEMOCRATIC REPUBLIC)—FICTION

Elting, Mary & McKown, Robin. A Mongo Homecoming. 1969. (Two Worlds Bks.). (Illus.). 64p. (J). (gr. 4-6). 3.95 o.p. (*0-87131-099-6*) Holt, Henry & Co.

Hergé. Tintin au Congo. 1999. (Tintin Ser.). (FRE.). (gr. 4-7). 19.95 (*2-203-00101-1*) Casterman, Editions FRA. *Dist:* Distribooks, Inc.

—Tintin au Congo. (FRE., Illus.). (J). (gr. 7-9). 24.95 (*0-8288-5090-9*) French & European Pubns., Inc.

—Tintin en el Congo. (SPA., Illus.). 62p. (J). 24.95 (*0-8288-5095-X*) French & European Pubns., Inc.

—Tintin en el Congo. (Tintin Ser.). (SPA.). 64p. (J). 14.95 (*84-261-1401-6*) Juventud, Editorial ESP. *Dist:* Distribooks, Inc.

—Tintin im Kongo. (GER., Illus.). 62p. (J). pap. 24.95 (*0-8288-4998-6*) French & European Pubns., Inc.

Stanley, Sanna. Monkey for Sale, RS. 2002. (Illus.). 32p. (J). 17.00 (*0-374-35017-5*, Farrar, Straus & Giroux (BYR)) Farrar, Straus & Giroux.

CONNECTICUT—FICTION

Boehm, Bruce & Winn, Janet. Connecticut Low, 001. 1980. (J). (gr. 7 up). 6.95 o.p. (*0-395-29518-1*) Houghton Mifflin Co.

Collier, James Lincoln. Jump Ship to Freedom. 1996. (J). pap. 5.99 (*0-440-91158-3*, Dell Books for Young Readers) Random Hse. Children's Bks.

—Jump Ship to Freedom. 1987. (Arabus Family Saga Ser.). (J). 11.55 (*0-606-02265-1*) Turtleback Bks.

Collier, James Lincoln & Collier, Christopher. Jump Ship to Freedom. 1981. 192p. (J). (gr. 4-6). pap. 13.95 o.s.i (*0-385-28484-5*, Delacorte Pr.) Dell Publishing.

—Jump Ship to Freedom. 1987. (Arabus Family Saga Ser.: Vol. 2). 208p. (gr. 4-7). pap. text 5.50 (*0-440-44323-7*, Yearling) Random Hse. Children's Bks.

Curtis, Alice Turner. A Little Maid of Old Connecticut. 2004. (Little Maid Ser.). (Illus.). 192p. (J). (gr. 4-7). reprint ed. pap. 9.95 (*1-55709-328-8*) Applewood Bks.

Eager, Edward. Magic or Not? (Odyssey Classics). (Illus.). 1999. 208p. (YA). (gr. 3-7). pap. 6.00 (*0-15-202080-2*, Odyssey Classics); 1989. 208p. (J). (gr. 3-7). pap. 3.95 o.p. (*0-15-251160-1*, Odyssey Classics); 1959. (J). (gr. 4-6). 5.95 o.p. (*0-15-251157-1*); 1979. 192p. (J). (gr. 3-6). reprint ed. pap. 4.95 o.p. (*0-15-655121-7*, Voyager Bks./Libros Viajeros) Harcourt Children's Bks.

—Magic or Not? 1984. (Illus.). 125p. (J). (gr. 4-6). 17.55 o.p. (*0-8446-6154-6*) Smith, Peter Pub., Inc.

—Magic or Not? 1999. (J). 12.05 (*0-606-19001-5*) Turtleback Bks.

Estes, Eleanor. The Middle Moffat. 2001. (Young Classics). (Illus.). 256p. (YA). (gr. 3 up). 17.00 (*0-15-202525-5*); pap. 6.00 (*0-15-202529-4*) Harcourt Children's Bks. (Odyssey Classics).

—The Moffat Museum. 2001. (Young Classics). (Illus.). 256p. (YA). (gr. 3 up). 17.00 (*0-15-202547-2*); pap. 6.00 (*0-15-202553-7*) Harcourt Children's Bks.

—The Moffats. 2001. (Young Classics). (Illus.). 224p. (YA). (gr. 3 up). 17.00 (*0-15-202535-9*, Odyssey Classics) Harcourt Children's Bks.

—Rufus M. 2001. (Young Classics). (Illus.). 256p. (YA). (gr. 3 up). 17.00 (*0-15-202571-5*, Odyssey Classics); pap. 6.00 (*0-15-202577-4*) Harcourt Children's Bks.

Estes, Eleanor & Slobodkin, Louis. The Moffats. 2001. (Odyssey Classics). (Illus.). 224p. (YA). (gr. 3 up). pap. 6.00 (*0-15-202541-3*, Odyssey Classics) Harcourt Children's Bks.

Hominick, Judy & Spreier, Jeanne. Ride for Freedom: The Story of Sybil Ludington. 2001. (Heroes to Remember Ser.). (Illus.). 52p. (J). 14.95 (*1-893110-24-9*) Silver Moon Pr.

Hurst, Carol Otis. Through the Lock. 2001. 172p. (J). (gr. 5-9). tchr. ed. 15.00 (*0-618-03036-0*) Houghton Mifflin Co.

Janeczko, Paul B. Worlds Afire: The Hartford Circus Fire of 1944. 2004. 112p. (J). 15.99 (*0-7636-2235-4*) Candlewick Pr.

Leigh, Tina. Groundhog Day for Essex Ed. 2001. (Illus.). 32p. (J). pap. 14.95 (*0-9715673-0-1*) Leigh, Tina Illustrator.

Louthain, J. A. Tagger: Alone along the Mystic River. 2002. (Illus.). 215p. (YA). per. 14.95 (*0-9679416-0-1*, 0-1) Alexie Bks.

Rinaldi, Ann. The Education of Mary: A Little Miss of Color, 1832. 2000. 256p. (J). (gr. 6-8). 15.99 (*0-7868-0532-3*, Jump at the Sun) Hyperion Bks. for Children.

—The Education of Mary: A Little Miss of Color, 1832. 2000. 254p. (J). pap. (*0-7868-1377-6*) Hyperion Pr.

Seidler, Tor. The Silent Spillbills. 1998. 224p. (J). (gr. 3-7). 14.95 (*0-06-205180-6*); lib. bdg. 14.89 (*0-06-205181-4*) HarperCollins Children's Bk. Group.

CORNWALL (ENGLAND: COUNTY)—FICTION

Blyton, Enid. Five Go down to the Sea. l.t. ed. 1997. (J). 16.95 o.p. (*0-7451-6972-4*, Galaxy Children's Large Print) BBC Audiobooks America.

Cooper, Susan. Greenwitch. (Dark Is Rising Sequence Ser.). (J). 2000. 144p. (gr. 4-7). pap. 4.99 (*0-689-84034-9*, Aladdin); 1985. (Illus.). 148p. (gr. 4-7). 18.00 (*0-689-30426-9*, McElderry, Margaret K.); 1977. pap. 3.95 o.s.i (*0-689-70431-3*, Simon & Schuster Children's Publishing); 1986. 148p. (gr. 4-7). reprint ed. pap. 4.99 (*0-689-71088-7*, Simon Pulse) Simon & Schuster Children's Publishing.

—Greenwitch. l.t. ed. 2001. (Dark Is Rising Sequence Ser.). 131p. (J). 21.95 (*0-7862-2923-3*) Thorndike Pr.

—Greenwitch. (J). 2000. 11.04 (*0-606-19710-9*); 1974. 9.05 (*0-606-00700-8*) Turtleback Bks.

—Over Sea, under Stone. 1979. (Dark Is Rising Sequence Ser.). (Illus.). (J). (gr. 4-7). pap. 5.95 o.p. (*0-15-670542-7*, Voyager Bks./Libros Viajeros) Harcourt Children's Bks.

—Over Sea, under Stone. 2000. (Dark Is Rising Sequence Ser.). 208p. (J). (gr. 4-7). pap. 4.99 (*0-689-84035-7*, Aladdin) Simon & Schuster Children's Publishing.

—Over Sea, under Stone. 1989. (Dark Is Rising Sequence Ser.). (J). 11.04 (*0-606-04293-8*) Turtleback Bks.

—Over Sea, Under Stone. 1966. (Dark Is Rising Sequence Ser.). (Illus.). 252p. (J). (gr. 4-7). 18.00 (*0-15-259034-X*) Harcourt Children's Bks.

—Over Sea, under Stone. unabr. ed. 2001. (Dark Is Rising Ser.: Vol. 1). (YA). (gr. 4 up). audio 40.00 (*0-8072-0519-2*, Listening Library) Random Hse. Audio Publishing Group.

—Over Sea, under Stone. 1989. (Dark Is Rising Sequence Ser.). 256p. (J). (gr. 4-7). reprint ed. pap. 4.99 (*0-02-042785-9*, Simon Pulse) Simon & Schuster Children's Publishing.

—Over Sea, under Stone. l.t. ed. 2000. (Dark Is Rising Sequence Ser.). 332p. (J). (gr. 4-7). 22.95 (*0-7862-2918-7*) Thorndike Pr.

—Over Sea, under Stone: The Dark Is Rising Sequence. unabr. ed. 2001. (Dark Is Rising Ser.: Vol. 1). (YA). (gr. 4 up). audio 30.00 (*0-8072-0480-3*, Listening Library) Random Hse. Audio Publishing Group.

Grow, Mary L. Chester Meets the Walker House Ghost, No. 1. 2000. (Illus.). 72p. (Orig.). (J). (gr. 8-12). pap. 12.00 (*0-9700777-0-X*) Studio 17.

Leach, Christopher. The Great Book Raid. 1979. (J). (gr. 5-7). 7.95 o.p. (*0-7232-6174-1*, Warne, Frederick) Penguin Putnam Bks. for Young Readers.

Mayne, William. A Year & a Day. 2000. (Candlewick Treasures Ser.). (Illus.). 72p. (J). (gr. 3-7). 11.99 o.p. (*0-7636-0850-5*) Candlewick Pr.

—A Year & a Day. 1976. 112p. (J). (gr. 4-6). lib. bdg. 6.95 o.p. (*0-525-43450-X*, Dutton) Dutton/Plume.

—A Year & a Day. 1990. (J). (gr. 4-7). 19.25 (*0-8446-6431-6*) Smith, Peter Pub., Inc.

Zemach, Harve. Duffy & the Devil: A Cornish Tale. 1986. (J). 13.10 (*0-606-03189-8*) Turtleback Bks.

COSTA RICA—FICTION

Banks, Joan. Song of La Selva: A Story of a Costa Rican Rain Forest. 1998. (Habitat Ser.: No. 9). (Illus.). 36p. (J). (gr. 1-4). 15.95 (*1-56899-586-5*); 19.95 incl. audio (*1-56899-588-1*, BC7009); pap. 5.95 (*1-56899-587-3*); pap. 10.95 incl. audio (*1-56899-589-X*);Incl. toy. 26.95 (*1-56899-590-3*);Incl. toy. 31.95 incl. audio (*1-56899-592-X*);Incl. toy. pap. 16.95 (*1-56899-591-1*);Incl. toy. pap. 19.95 incl. audio (*1-56899-593-8*) Soundprints.

—Song of La Selva: A Story of a Costa Rican Rain Forest. 1998. 12.10 (*0-606-16857-5*) Turtleback Bks.

Franklin, Kristine L. Cuando Regresaron los Monos. Zubizarreta, Rosa, tr. from ENG. 1994. (Libros Colibri Ser.).Tr. of When the Monkeys Came Back. (SPA., Illus.). 32p. (J). (ps-3). mass mkt. 14.95 (*0-689-31950-9*, Atheneum) Simon & Schuster Children's Publishing.

—When the Monkeys Came Back. 1994. (Illus.). 32p. (J). (gr. k-3). 14.95 (*0-689-31807-3*) Central Bureau voor Schimmelcultures NLD. *Dist:* Lubrecht & Cramer, Ltd.

Henderson, Aileen Kilgore. The Monkey Thief. 1997. (Illus.). 176p. (J). (gr. 3-8). 14.95 (*1-57131-612-4*); pap. 6.95 (*1-57131-613-2*) Milkweed Editions.

Keister, Douglas. El Regalo de Fernando.Tr. of Fernando's Gift. (SPA., Illus.). 32p. (J). (ps-3). 1998. pap. 6.95 (*0-87156-927-2*); 1995. 16.95 (*0-87156-414-9*) Sierra Club Bks.

—El Regalo de Fernando. 1998. (Sierra Club Bks.).Tr. of Fernando's Gift. (J). 13.10 (*0-606-13382-8*) Turtleback Bks.

Russell, Barbara T. Remembering Stone. 1999. (Illus.). (J). (*0-7894-2583-1*) Dorling Kindersley Publishing, Inc.

—The Remembering Stone, RS. 2004. (J). 16.00 (*0-374-36242-4*, Farrar, Straus & Giroux (BYR)) Farrar, Straus & Giroux.

Tennyson, Michael. Morpha: A Rain Forest Story. 2002. (CMC Wilderness Kids Ser.). (Illus.). 40p. (J). 14.95 (*0-9671466-8-2*) Colorado Mountain Club Pr., The.

Wax, Wendy. The Night Before Easter. 2004. (Wild Thornberrys Ser.: Vol. 8). 24p. (J). pap. 3.99 (*0-689-86493-0*, Simon Spotlight/Nickelodeon) Simon & Schuster Children's Publishing.

CRETE (GREECE)—FICTION

Bolton, James. Ancient Crete & Mycenae. Reeves, Marjorie, ed. 1968. (Then & There Ser.). (Illus.). 96p. (YA). (gr. 7-12). reprint ed. pap. text 4.95 o.p. (*0-582-20415-1*) Longman Publishing Group.

Cheney, David M. Son of Minos. 1970. (J). (gr. 7). 22.00 (*0-8196-0142-X*) Biblo & Tannen Booksellers & Pubs., Inc.

Sreenivasan, Jyotsna. The Moon over Crete. 1994. (Illus.). 128p. (Orig.). (J). pap. 8.95 o.p. (*0-930100-58-1*) Holy Cow! Pr.

—The Moon over Crete. 1996. (Illus.). 128p. (Orig.). (J). (gr. 3-7). reprint ed. pap. 6.95 (*0-9619401-6-6*) Smooth Stone Pr.

CUBA—FICTION

Ada, Alma Flor. Barquitos de Papel. 1993. (Cuentos con Alma Ser.). (SPA., Illus.). 24p. (J). (gr. 3-9). 16.95 (*1-56492-118-2*) Laredo Publishing Co., Inc.

Figueredo, D. H. The Road to Santiago. 2003. (Illus.). (J). 16.95 (*1-58430-059-0*) Lee & Low Bks., Inc.

Gonzalez-Cruz, Luis F. Olorun's Rainbow: Anatomy of a Cuban Dreamer. 2001. 188p. pap. 19.95 (*0-7596-3401-7*) 1stBooks Library.

Leiner, Katherine. Mama Does the Mambo. 2001. (Illus.). 40p. (J). (gr. k-4). 15.99 (*0-7868-0646-X*) Hyperion Bks. for Children.

Perera, Hilda. Cuentos de Apolo. 3rd ed. 1975. (SPA., Illus.). 103p. (YA). (gr. 6 up). pap. 5.00 (*0-89729-438-6*) Ediciones Universal.

Veciana-Suarez, Ana. The Flight to Freedom. 2002. (First Person Fiction Ser.). 208p. (J). (gr. 6-9). pap. 16.95 (*0-439-38199-1*, Orchard Bks.) Scholastic, Inc.

CUTTER GAP (TENN.: IMAGINARY PLACE)—FICTION

Marshall, Catherine. The Angry Intruder. 1995. (Christy Fiction Ser.: No. 3). 128p. (J). (gr. 4-8). pap. 4.99 o.s.i (*0-8499-3688-8*) Nelson, Tommy.

—The Bridge to Cutter Gap. 1995. (Christy Fiction Ser.: No. 1). 128p. (J). (gr. 4-8). mass mkt. 4.99 (*0-8499-3686-1*) Nelson, Tommy.

—Brotherly Love. 1997. (Christy Fiction Ser.: No. 12). 128p. (Orig.). (J). (gr. 4-8). mass mkt. 4.99 (*0-8499-3963-1*) Nelson, Tommy.

—Goodbye, Sweet Prince. 1997. (Christy Fiction Ser.: No. 11). 128p. (Orig.). (J). (gr. 4-8). pap. 4.99 (*0-8499-3962-3*) Nelson, Tommy.

—Midnight Rescue. 1995. (Christy Fiction Ser.: No. 4). 128p. (J). (gr. 4-8). pap. 4.99 o.s.i (*0-8499-3689-6*) Nelson, Tommy.

—Mountain Madness. adapted ed. 1997. (Christy Fiction Ser.: No. 9). 128p. (Orig.). (J). (gr. 4-8). mass mkt. 4.99 (*0-8499-3960-7*) Nelson, Tommy.

—The Princess Club. 1996. (Christy Fiction Ser.: No. 7). 128p. (J). (gr. 4-8). pap. text 4.99 (*0-8499-3958-5*) Nelson, Tommy.

—The Proposal. 1995. (Christy Fiction Ser.: No. 5). 128p. (J). (gr. 4-8). mass mkt. 4.99 (*0-8499-3918-6*) Nelson, Tommy.

—Silent Superstitions. 1995. (Christy Fiction Ser.: No. 2). 128p. (J). (gr. 4-8). pap. 4.99 o.s.i (*0-8499-3687-X*) Nelson, Tommy.

—Stage Fright. 1997. (Christy Fiction Ser.: No. 10). (Illus.). 128p. (J). (gr. 4-8). mass mkt. 4.99 (*0-8499-3961-5*) Nelson, Tommy.

CYPRUS—FICTION

Rasp-Nuri, Grace. Yusuf, Boy of Cyprus. 1958. (Illus.). (gr. 5-9). 9.95 o.p. (*0-87599-095-9*) Phillips, S.G. Inc.

CZECHOSLOVAKIA—FICTION

Isaacs, Anne. Torn Thread. 2002. 192p. (YA). mass mkt. 4.99 (*0-590-60364-7*, Scholastic Paperbacks); 2000. (Illus.). 188p. (J). (gr. 5-9). pap. 15.95 o.p. (*0-590-60363-9*, Scholastic Reference) Scholastic, Inc.

Kacer, Kathy. Clara's War. 2001. (Holocaust Remembrance Ser.). (Illus.). 128p. (YA). (gr. 5 up). pap. 5.95 (*1-896764-42-8*) Second Story Pr. CAN. *Dist:* Univ. of Toronto Pr.

Kanefield, Teri. Rivka's Way. 2001. (Illus.). 137p. (J). (gr. 5-9). 15.95 (*0-8126-2870-5*) Cricket Bks.

Melnikoff, Pamela. Prisoner in Time. 2001. 142p. (J). (gr. 5-8). pap. 9.95 (*0-8276-0735-0*) Jewish Pubn. Society.

Sis, Peter. The Three Golden Keys. 1994. (Illus.). 64p. (J). (ps-3). 22.50 o.s.i (*0-385-47292-7*) Doubleday Publishing.

D

DALEMARK (IMAGINARY PLACE)—FICTION

Jones, Diana Wynne. Cart & Cwidder. (Dalemark Quartet Ser.: Vol. 1). (gr. 7 up). 2001. 224p. (J). 16.95 (*0-06-623745-9*, Greenwillow Bks.); 2001. (Illus.). 240p. (J). pap. 6.95 (*0-06-447313-9*, Harper Trophy); 1995. 40p. (J). pap. 4.95 (*0-688-13399-1*, Greenwillow Bks.); 1995. (Illus.). 224p. (YA). 15.00 (*0-688-13360-6*, Greenwillow Bks.) HarperCollins Children's Bk. Group.

—Cart & Cwidder. 1995. (Dalemark Quartet Ser.: No. 1). (J). 10.05 o.p. (*0-606-07342-6*) Turtleback Bks.

—The Crown of Dalemark. (Dalemark Quartet Ser.). (J). (gr. 7 up). 2001. 480p. 16.95 (*0-06-029874-X*); 2001. (Illus.). 496p. pap. 6.95 (*0-06-447316-3*, Harper Trophy); 1996. (Illus.). 480p. pap. 5.95 (*0-688-13402-5*, Greenwillow Bks.); 1995. (Illus.). 480p. 17.00 (*0-688-13363-0*, Greenwillow Bks.) HarperCollins Children's Bk. Group.

—The Crown of Dalemark. 1996. (Dalemark Quartet Ser.: Bk. 4). (J). 10.05 o.p. (*0-606-10166-7*) Turtleback Bks.

—Drowned Ammet. (Dalemark Quartet Ser.). (J). (gr. 7 up). 2001. 320p. 16.95 (*0-06-029872-3*, Greenwillow Bks.); 2001. 336p. pap. 6.95 (*0-06-447314-7*, Harper Trophy); 1995. (Illus.). 40p. 15.00 (*0-688-13361-4*, Greenwillow Bks.) HarperCollins Children's Bk. Group.

—Drowned Ammet. 1995. (Dalemark Quartet Ser.: No. 2). (Illus.). 320p. (J). (gr. 7 up). pap. 4.95 (*0-688-13400-9*, Morrow, William & Co.) Morrow/Avon.

—Drowned Ammet. 1995. (Dalemark Quartet Ser.). (J). 10.05 o.p. (*0-606-07455-4*) Turtleback Bks.

—The Spellcoats. (Dalemark Quartet Ser.). (gr. 7 up). 2001. 288p. (J). 16.95 (*0-06-029873-1*, Greenwillow Bks.); 2001. 304p. (J). pap. 6.99 (*0-06-447315-5*, Harper Trophy); 1995. (Illus.). 288p. (J). pap. 4.95 (*0-688-13401-7*, Greenwillow Bks.); 1995. (Illus.). 288p. (YA). 15.00 (*0-688-13362-2*, Greenwillow Bks.) HarperCollins Children's Bk. Group.

—The Spellcoats. 1980. pap. 2.25 o.s.i (*0-671-83599-8*, Pocket) Simon & Schuster.

—The Spellcoats. 1979. (Dalemark Quartet Ser.: No. 3). (YA). (gr. 7 up). 7.95 o.p. (*0-689-30712-8*, Atheneum) Simon & Schuster Children's Publishing.

—The Spellcoats. 1995. (Dalemark Quartet Ser.: No. 3). (J). 10.05 o.p. (*0-606-08191-7*) Turtleback Bks.

DELAWARE—FICTION

Hesse, Karen. A Light in the Storm: The Civil War Diary of Amelia Martin, Fenwick Island, Delaware, 1861. (Dear America Ser.). 2002. (YA). E-Book 9.95 (*0-439-42541-7*); 1999. (Illus.). 169p. (J). (gr. 4-9). pap. 10.95 (*0-590-56733-0*, Scholastic Pr.) Scholastic, Inc.

Laird, Marnie. Water Rat. 2001. 192p. (J). (gr. 4-7). pap. 5.95 (*1-58837-002-X*) Winslow Pr.

Maxson, H. A. & Young, Claudia H. Kalmar Nyckel & Fort Christina. 2002. (J). per. 8.95 (*0-9704692-6-8*) Bay Oak Pubs., Ltd.

—Lenapehoking: Land of the Delawares. 2001. 64p. (J). per. 8.95 (*0-9704692-1-7*) Bay Oak Pubs., Ltd.

Rodowsky, Colby. Spindrift, RS. 2000. (Illus.). 144p. (J). (gr. 4-7). 16.00 (*0-374-37155-5*, Farrar, Straus & Giroux (BYR)) Farrar, Straus & Giroux.

—Spindrift. 2002. 144p. (J). (gr. 4-7). pap. 5.95 (*0-06-440991-0*, Harper Trophy) HarperCollins Children's Bk. Group.

Zeises, Lara M. Contents under Pressure. 2004. (YA). 256p. 15.95 (*0-385-73047-0*); 192p. lib. bdg. (*0-385-90162-3*) Dell Publishing. (Delacorte Pr.).

DELTORA (IMAGINARY PLACE)—FICTION

Rodda, Emily. Cavern of Fear. 2002. (Deltora Quest Ser.: No. 1). (Illus.). 144p. (J). (gr. 3-7). pap. 4.99 (0-439-39491-0) Scholastic, Inc.

—City of the Rats. 2001. (Deltora Quest Ser.: No. 3). (Illus.). 128p. (J). (gr. 3-7). pap. 4.99 (0-439-25325-X) Scholastic, Inc.

—Deltora Book of Monsters. 2002. (Deltora Quest Ser.). (Illus.). 48p. (J). (gr. 3-7). mass mkt. 7.99 o.s.i (0-439-39084-2) Scholastic, Inc.

—Dread Mountain. 2001. (Deltora Quest Ser.: No. 5). (Illus.). 128p. (J). pap. 4.99 (0-439-25327-6, Scholastic Paperbacks) Scholastic, Inc.

—The Forests of Silence. 2001. (Deltora Quest Ser.: No. 1). (Illus.). 128p. (gr. 3-7). pap. 4.50 (0-439-25323-3) Scholastic, Inc.

—The Isle of Illusion. 2002. (Deltora Quest Ser.: No. 2). 144p. (J). pap. 4.99 (0-439-39492-9, Scholastic Paperbacks) Scholastic, Inc.

—The Lake of Tears. 2001. (Deltora Quest Ser.: No. 2). (Illus.). 128p. (gr. 3-7). pap. 4.50 (0-439-25324-1) Scholastic, Inc.

—The Maze of the Beast. 2001. (Deltora Quest Ser.: No. 6). (Illus.). 128p. (J). pap. 4.99 (0-439-25328-4, Scholastic Paperbacks) Scholastic, Inc.

—Return to Del. (Illus.). (J). 2002. 136p. (0-439-41951-4); 2001. (Deltora Quest Ser.: No. 8). 128p. (gr. 8). pap. 4.99 (0-439-25330-6) Scholastic, Inc.

—The Shadowlands. 2002. (Deltora Quest Ser.: No. 3). 256p. (YA). (gr. 4-9). pap. 4.99 (0-439-39493-7, Scholastic Paperbacks) Scholastic, Inc.

—The Shifting Sands. 2001. (Deltora Quest Ser.: No. 4). (Illus.). 128p. (J). (gr. 4-7). pap. 4.99 (0-439-25326-8) Scholastic, Inc.

—The Valley of the Lost. 2001. (Deltora Quest Ser.: No. 7). (Illus.). 128p. pap. 4.99 (0-439-25329-2, Scholastic Paperbacks) Scholastic, Inc.

DENMARK—FICTION

Deedy, Carmen Agra. The Yellow Star: The Legend of King Christian X of Denmark. 2000. (Illus.). 32p. (J). (gr. 3-7). 16.95 (1-56145-208-4) Peachtree Pubs., Ltd.

Elmer, Robert. Chasing the Wind. 1996. (Young Underground Ser.: Vol. 5). 192p. (Orig.). (J). (gr. 3-8). pap. 5.99 o.s.i (1-55661-658-9, Bethany Backyard) Bethany Hse. Pubs.

—Far from the Storm. 1995. (Young Underground Ser.: Bk. 4). 176p. (J). (gr. 3-8). pap. 5.99 (1-55661-377-6) Bethany Hse. Pubs.

—Follow the Star. 1997. (Young Underground Ser.: Vol. 7). 176p. (J). (gr. 3-8). pap. 5.99 (1-55661-660-0) Bethany Hse. Pubs.

—Into the Flames. 1995. (Young Underground Ser.: Bk. 3). 192p. (J). (gr. 3-8). pap. 5.99 (1-55661-376-8) Bethany Hse. Pubs.

Haugaard, Erik Christian. Untold Tale, 001. 1971. (Illus.). (J). (gr. 5 up). 4.95 o.p. (0-395-12366-6) Houghton Mifflin Co.

Levitin, Sonia. Room in the Heart. 2003. 304p. (J). 16.99 (0-525-46871-4, Dutton Children's Bks.) Penguin Putnam Bks. for Young Readers.

Lowry, Lois. Number the Stars. (J). 1996. 144p. mass mkt. 2.49 o.s.i (0-440-22033-5); 1994. 144p. pap. 3.99 (0-440-91002-1); 1992. 144p. (gr. 4-7). mass mkt. 1.99 o.s.i (0-440-21372-X); 1990. 144p. pap. 3.50 o.s.i (0-440-70031-0); 1990. pap. o.p. (0-440-80164-8) Dell Publishing.

—Number the Stars. 1996. (J). pap. 5.60 (0-87129-711-6, N45) Dramatic Publishing Co.

—Number the Stars. (J). 1995. (gr. 6). 9.28 (0-395-73270-0); 1992. (gr. 6). pap. 11.04 (0-395-61834-7); 1989. 144p. (gr. 4-6). tchr. ed. 16.00 (0-395-51060-0) Houghton Mifflin Co.

—Number the Stars. 1992. (J). pap. 3.50 (0-440-80291-1, Dell Books for Young Readers); 1990. 144p. (gr. 5-9). pap. text 5.99 (0-440-40327-8, Yearling); 1998. 144p. (YA). (gr. 4-7). reprint ed. mass mkt. 5.99 (0-440-22753-4, Laurel Leaf) Random Hse. Children's Bks.

—Number the Stars. (J). 1998. 12.04 (0-606-13670-3); 1989. 12.04 (0-606-04493-0) Turtleback Bks.

—Number the Stars - Musical. 1998. 33p. pap. 5.95 (0-87129-834-1, N03) Dramatic Publishing Co.

—Quien Cuenta las Estrellas. 5th ed. 1998. (SPA., Illus.). 152p. (J). 8.95 (84-239-8867-8) Espasa Calpe, S.A. ESP. *Dist:* Continental Bk. Co., Inc.

Lutzen, Hanna. Vlad the Undead. 192p. (YA). (gr. 8 up). 2001. pap. 5.95 (0-88899-342-0); 1998. 15.95 (0-88899-341-2) Groundwood Bks. CAN. *Dist:* Publishers Group West.

Reuter, Bjarne. The Boys from St. Petri. 1994. 224p. (YA). (gr. 6 up). 15.99 o.s.i (0-525-45121-8, Dutton Children's Bks.) Penguin Putnam Bks. for Young Readers.

—Boys from St. Petri. 1996. 11.04 (0-606-08704-4) Turtleback Bks.

Shakespeare, William. William Shakespeare's Hamlet. 2004. (Illus.). 40p. (J). 16.99 (0-8037-2708-9, Dial Bks. for Young Readers) Penguin Putnam Bks. for Young Readers.

Sorenson, Virginia. Lotte's Locket. 1964. (Illus.). (J). (gr. 4-6). 5.95 o.p. (0-15-249457-X) Harcourt Children's Bks.

DETROIT (MICH.)—FICTION

Burgess, Barbara H. The Fred Field. 1995. 192p. (J). pap. 3.99 o.s.i (0-440-41067-3) Dell Publishing.

—Oren Bell. 192p. (J). (ps-3). 1992. pap. 3.50 o.s.i (0-440-40747-8); 1991. 15.00 o.s.i (0-385-30325-4, Delacorte Pr.) Dell Publishing.

Fisher, Marcy Heller. The Outdoor Museum: The Magic of Michigan's Marshall M. Fredericks. 2001. (Great Lakes Bks.). (Illus.). 72p. (J). (gr. 3-7). 16.95 (0-8143-2969-1, Great Lakes Bks.); 27.95 (0-8143-2932-2) Wayne State Univ. Pr.

DOMINICAN REPUBLIC—FICTION

Alvarez, Julia. Antes de Ser Libre. 2004. (SPA.). 176p. (YA). (gr. 7). mass mkt. 5.99 (0-375-81545-7, Laurel Leaf) Random Hse. Children's Bks.

—Before We Were Free. 2002. (Illus.). 176p. (J). (gr. 7-10). 15.95 (0-375-81544-9); lib. bdg. 17.99 (0-375-91544-3) Knopf, Alfred A. Inc.

—Before We Were Free. 2004. 192p. (YA). (gr. 7). mass mkt. 5.99 (0-440-23784-X, Laurel Leaf) Random Hse. Children's Bks.

Mi Abuelita. 2001. (SPA.). (J). pap. 14.95 (0-9630310-5-8) Will Hall Bks.

Moore, Robin. The Man with the Silver Oar. 2002. 192p. (J). (gr. 5 up). 15.95 (0-380-97877-6) HarperCollins Children's Bk. Group.

—The Man with the Silver Oar. 2002. 192p. (J). (gr. 5 up). lib. bdg. 15.89 (0-06-000048-1) HarperCollins Pubs.

DROON (IMAGINARY PLACE)—FICTION

Abbott, Tony. The Coiled Viper. 2003. (Secrets of Droon Ser.: Vol. 19). 128p. (J). (gr. 2-5). pap. 3.99 (0-439-42080-6) Scholastic, Inc.

—Dream Thief. 2003. (Secrets of Droon Ser.: No. 17). (Illus.). 128p. (J). (gr. 2-5). pap. 3.99 (0-439-42078-4, Scholastic Paperbacks) Scholastic, Inc.

—The Moon Scroll. 2002. (Secrets of Droon Ser.: No. 15). (Illus.). 144p. (J). (gr. 2-5). pap. 3.99 (0-439-30608-6) Scholastic, Inc.

—Search for the Dragon Ship. 2003. (Secrets of Droon Ser.: Vol. 18). 128p. (J). (gr. 2-5). pap. 3.99 (0-439-42079-2, Scholastic Paperbacks) Scholastic, Inc.

—The Secrets of Droon, 4 vols. 2002. (Secrets of Droon Ser.: Bks. 1-4). (Illus.). 144p. (J). per. 15.96 (0-439-45747-5, Scholastic Paperbacks) Scholastic, Inc.

DUBLIN (IRELAND)—FICTION

Bulla, Clyde Robert. New Boy in Dublin: A Story of Ireland. 1969. (Stories from Many Lands Ser.). (Illus.). (J). (gr. k-3). 7.95 o.p. (0-690-57756-7) HarperCollins Children's Bk. Group.

Lynch, Patricia. Shane Comes to Dublin. 1958. (Illus.). (gr. 4-7). 9.95 o.p. (0-87599-070-3) Phillips, S.G. Inc.

Parkinson, Siobhan. Kathleen: The Celtic Knot. 2003. (Girls of Many Lands Ser.). (YA). (gr. 5-9). pap. 15.95 (1-58485-830-3); pap. 7.95 (1-58485-748-X) Pleasant Co. Pubns. (American Girl).

Regan, Peter. Riverside: The Curse. 2003. (Illus.). 112p. (J). pap. 8.95 (1-901737-46-2) Anvil Bks., Ltd. IRL. *Dist:* Dufour Editions, Inc.

Thompson, Kate. Switchers. 1999. 224p. (J). (gr. 7-12). pap. 5.99 (0-7868-1396-2) Disney Pr.

—Switchers. 1998. 224p. (gr. 7-12). (J). 14.95 (0-7868-0380-0); (YA). lib. bdg. 15.49 (0-7868-2328-3) Hyperion Bks. for Children.

—Switchers. 220p. (J). (gr. 4-7). pap. 5.99 (0-8072-1553-8); 1999. (Switchers Ser.: Vol. 1). pap. 37.00 incl. audio (0-8072-8138-7, YA115SP) Random Hse. Audio Publishing Group. (Listening Library).

—Switchers. 1999. 12.04 (0-606-17387-0) Turtleback Bks.

DUSTLAND (IMAGINARY PLACE)—FICTION

Hamilton, Virginia. Dustland. 1989. (Justice Cycle Ser.: Vol. 2). 224p. (YA). (gr. 7 up). pap. 3.95 o.p. (0-15-224315-1, Odyssey Classics) Harcourt Children's Bks.

—Dustland. 1980. (Justice Cycle Ser.: Vol. 2). 192p. (J). (gr. 7 up). 13.00 o.p. (0-688-80228-1); lib. bdg. 12.88 o.p. (0-688-84228-3) HarperCollins Children's Bk. Group. (Greenwillow Bks.).

—Dustland. 1985. (J). pap. 1.95 o.p. (0-380-56127-1, 56127-1, Avon Bks.) Morrow/Avon.

—Dustland. 1998. (Justice Cycle Ser.: Bk. 2). 214p. (YA). (gr. 6-12). mass mkt. 4.50 (0-590-36217-8) Scholastic, Inc.

—Dustland. (Justice Cycle Ser.). 1998. 10.55 (0-606-12927-8); 1989. 9.05 o.p. (0-606-00822-5) Turtleback Bks.

—The Gathering. 1981. (Justice Cycle Ser.: Vol. 3). 192p. (J). (gr. 7 up). 12.95 o.p. (0-688-80269-9); lib. bdg. 12.88 o.p. (0-688-84269-0) HarperCollins Children's Bk. Group. (Greenwillow Bks.).

—The Gathering. 1985. 160p. pap. 1.95 o.p. (0-380-56135-2, 56135-2, Avon Bks.) Morrow/Avon.

—The Gathering. 1998. (Justice Cycle Ser.: Bk. 3). 214p. (J). (gr. 6-12). mass mkt. 4.50 (0-590-36216-X) Scholastic, Inc.

—The Gathering. (Justice Cycle Ser.). 1998. 10.55 (0-606-13414-X); 1989. (J). 9.05 o.p. (0-606-01140-4) Turtleback Bks.

—The Gathering Bk. 3. 1989. (Justice Cycle Ser.: Vol. 3). 224p. (YA). (gr. 7 up). pap. 3.95 o.p. (0-15-230592-0, Odyssey Classics) Harcourt Children's Bks.

—Justice & Her Brothers. 1989. (Justice Cycle Ser.: Vol. 1). 290p. (YA). (gr. 7 up). pap. 3.95 o.p. (0-15-241640-4, Odyssey Classics) Harcourt Children's Bks.

—Justice & Her Brothers. 1978. (Justice Cycle Ser.: Vol. 1). 224p. (J). (gr. 7 up). lib. bdg. 12.88 o.p. (0-688-84182-1, Greenwillow Bks.) HarperCollins Children's Bk. Group.

—Justice & Her Brothers. 1985. pap. 1.95 o.p. (0-380-56119-0, 56119-0, Avon Bks.) Morrow/Avon.

—Justice & Her Brothers. 1998. (Justice Cycle Ser.: Vol. 1). 214p. (J). (gr. 6-12). mass mkt. 4.99 (0-590-36214-3, Scholastic Paperbacks) Scholastic, Inc.

—Justice & Her Brothers. 1992. (J). (gr. 4-7). 17.55 o.p. (0-8446-6577-0) Smith, Peter Pub., Inc.

—Justice & Her Brothers. (Justice Cycle Ser.: Vol. 1). 1998. 11.04 (0-606-12973-1); 1989. 9.05 o.p. (0-606-01602-3) Turtleback Bks.

E

ECUADOR—FICTION

Meyer, Jane G. Hands Across the Moon. 2003. 224p. (J). pap. 10.99 (0-8423-8286-0) Tyndale Hse. Pubs.

EGYPT—FICTION

Abuan, Natalye, adapted by. The Emperor's New Groove. 2000. (Read-Aloud Book Ser.). (Illus.). 64p. (J). (ps-2). 6.99 (0-7364-0196-2) Mouse Works.

Adinolfi, JoAnn. The Egyptian Polar Bear. 1994. (Illus.). 32p. (J). (ps-3). tchr. ed. 14.95 o.p. (0-395-68074-3) Houghton Mifflin Co.

Adler, David A. Brothers in Egypt. 1998. (Prince of Egypt Ser.). (Illus.). 64p. (J). (gr. 2-5). pap. 3.99 o.p. (0-14-130218-6, Puffin Bks.) Penguin Putnam Bks. for Young Readers.

Austin, Judith M. The Secret Egyptian Code. 1996. (GlobalFriends Adventures Ser.). (Illus.). 64p. (J). (gr. 2-6). pap. 5.95 (1-58056-000-8, GlobalFriends Pr.) GlobalFriends Collection, Inc.

Banks, Lynne Reid. Prince of Egypt: The Novel. 1998. (Illus.). 128p. (gr. 5-9). pap. 4.99 o.p. (0-14-130217-8, Puffin Bks.) Penguin Putnam Bks. for Young Readers.

—Prince of Egypt: The Novel. 1998. 11.04 (0-606-15685-2) Turtleback Bks.

Bott, Elizabeth. Vinnie in Egypt. l.t. ed. 2000. (Laugh & Learn Travel Ser.: No. 1). (Illus.). 54p. (J). (gr. k-8). 15.95 (0-9704678-0-X) Pageturner Bks.

Bradshaw, Gillian. The Dragon & the Thief. 1991. (Illus.). (J). (gr. 5 up). 12.95 o.p. (0-688-10575-0, Greenwillow Bks.) HarperCollins Children's Bk. Group.

Campbell, Jeff, et al. Raiders of the Lost Ark. 1998. (Mighty Chronicles Ser.). (Illus.). 320p. (gr. 3-7). 9.95 o.p. (0-8118-2209-5) Chronicle Bks. LLC.

Carter, Dorothy S. His Majesty, Queen Hatshepsut. 1987. (Illus.). 256p. (J). (gr. 5 up). 13.95 (0-397-32178-3); lib. bdg. 16.89 (0-397-32179-1) HarperCollins Children's Bk. Group.

Caselli, Giovanni, illus. Dotto & the Pharaoh's Mask: An Interactive Connect-the-Dots Adventure. 1997. 48p. (gr. 3). pap. 10.95 (0-8109-2783-7) Abrams, Harry N., Inc.

Cianos, Elizabeth A., et al. Peter & the Pyramid. 1977. 4.50 o.p. (0-533-03080-3) Vantage Pr., Inc.

Clements, Andrew. Temple Cat. 2001. (J). 12.10 (0-606-21484-4) Turtleback Bks.

Climo, Shirley. The Egyptian Cinderella. 1992. (J). 12.10 (0-606-00411-4) Turtleback Bks.

Cooney, Caroline B. For All Time. 2001. (Illus.). 272p. (J). (gr. 7 up). 15.95 (0-385-32773-0, Delacorte Pr.) Dell Publishing.

—For All Time. 272p. (YA). (gr. 7). 2003. mass mkt. 4.99 (0-440-22931-6, Laurel Leaf); 2001. lib. bdg. 17.99 (0-385-90019-8, Dell Books for Young Readers) Random Hse. Children's Bks.

Curry, Jane Louise. The Egyptian Box. 2002. (Illus.). 192p. (J). (gr. 4-7). 16.00 (0-689-84273-2, McElderry, Margaret K.) Simon & Schuster Children's Publishing.

—The Egyptian Box. l.t. ed. 2002. 216p. (J). (0-7862-4896-3) Thorndike Pr.

Cushman, Doug. The Mystery of King Karfu. 1996. (Illus.). (J). (ps-3). 32p. 14.95 o.p. (0-06-024796-7); 80p. lib. bdg. 14.89 o.p. (0-06-024797-5) HarperCollins Children's Bk. Group.

de Paola, Tomie. Bill & Pete Go down the Nile. 1987. (Illus.). 32p. (J). (ps-3). 16.99 (0-399-21395-3, G. P. Putnam's Sons) Penguin Group (USA) Inc.

—Bill & Pete Go down the Nile. 1996. (Illus.). 32p. (J). (ps-3). pap. 5.99 (0-698-11401-9, PaperStar) Penguin Putnam Bks. for Young Readers.

—Bill & Pete Go down the Nile. 1990. (Illus.). 32p. (J). (ps-3). 5.95 o.s.i (0-399-22003-8, Sandcastle Bks.) Putnam Publishing Group, The.

—Bill & Pete Go down the Nile. 1996. (J). 12.14 (0-606-19072-4) Turtleback Bks.

Dexter, Catherine. The Gilded Cat. 1992. 208p. (J). (gr. 4 up). 14.00 o.p. (0-688-09425-2, Morrow, William & Co.) Morrow/Avon.

Ellerby, Leona. King Tut's Game Board. 1980. (Books for Adults & Young Adults). 120p. (J). (gr. 4 up). 13.50 o.p. (0-8225-0765-X, Lerner Pubns.) Lerner Publishing Group.

Ford, George Cephas, illus. A Camel Called Bump-Along. 1997. (0-7802-8030-X) Wright Group, The.

Gantos, Jack. Rotten Ralph Helps Out, RS. 2004. (Illus.). (J). pap. (0-374-46355-7) Farrar, Straus & Giroux.

Gantos, Jack & Rubel, Nicole. Rotten Ralph Helps Out, RS. 2001. (Illus.). 48p. (J). (gr. 1-3). 15.00 (0-374-36355-2, Farrar, Straus & Giroux (BYR)) Farrar, Straus & Giroux.

Geller, Norman. Farfel, the Cat That Left Egypt. 1987. (Illus.). 31p. (Orig.). (J). (gr. 3-7). pap. text 6.95 (0-915753-12-X) Geller, Norman Pubs.

Gormley, Beatrice. Miriam. (J). 1999. 180p. (gr. 4-9). pap. 6.00 (0-8028-5156-8, Eerdmans Bks For Young Readers); 1998. (0-8028-5153-3) Eerdmans, William B. Publishing Co.

Hall, Margaret & Jones, Dawn L. Sebastian in Egypt. 2001. (Suitcase Bear Adventures Ser.). (Illus.). (J). (0-9713174-2-9, Bear & Co.) Bear & Co.

Heide, Florence P. & Gilliland, Judith Heide. Day of Ahmed's Secret. 1995. (Illus.). 32p. (J). (ps-3). reprint ed. pap. 6.99 (0-688-14023-8, Harper Trophy) HarperCollins Children's Bk. Group.

Hergé. Les Cigares du Pharaon. 1999. (Tintin Ser.).Tr. of Cigars of the Pharaoh. (FRE.). (gr. 4-7). 19.95 (2-203-00103-8) Casterman, Editions FRA. *Dist:* Distribooks, Inc.

—Les Cigares du Pharaon.Tr. of Cigars of the Pharaoh. (FRE.). (J). (gr. 7-9). ring bd. 19.95 o.p. (0-8288-5018-6); 1992. 64p. reprint ed. (0-7859-4560-1) French & European Pubns., Inc.

—Cigars of the Pharaoh.Tr. of Cigares du Pharaon. (Illus.). 62p. (J). 19.95 (0-8288-5021-6); pap. 4.95 o.p. (0-416-83610-0) French & European Pubns., Inc.

—Cigars of the Pharaoh. 1975. (Adventures of Tintin Ser.).Tr. of Cigares du Pharaon. 62p. (J). (gr. 2 up). pap. 9.99 (0-316-35836-3, Joy Street Bks.) Little Brown & Co.

Hope, Laura Lee. The Bobbsey Twins & Their Camel Adventure. 1978. (Bobbsey Twins Ser.). (J). (gr. 3-5). 3.29 o.p. (0-448-18059-6, Grosset & Dunlap) Penguin Putnam Bks. for Young Readers.

Houghton Mifflin Company Staff. Pyramid. 1992. (Literature Experience 1993 Ser.). (J). (gr. 6). pap. 11.04 (0-395-61836-3) Houghton Mifflin Co.

Hutchins, Pat. The Curse of the Egyptian Mummy. l.t. ed. 1996. (J). 16.95 o.p. (0-7451-4958-8, Galaxy Children's Large Print) BBC Audiobooks America.

Jacobson, Sheldon A. Fleet Surgeon to Pharaoh. 1971. 300p. (YA). (gr. 9 up). lib. bdg. 12.95 (0-87071-316-7) Educare Pr.

Johnson-Davies, Denys, tr. Maarouf & the Dream Caravan. 1996. (Tales from Egypt & the Arab World Ser.). (ARA., Illus.). 48p. (Orig.). (J). (gr. 3-8). pap. 6.95 (977-5325-42-0) Hoopoe Bks. EGY. *Dist:* AMIDEAST.

Kalman, Maira. Hey Willy, See the Pyramids. 1988. (Illus.). 32p. (J). (ps-3). 16.99 (0-670-82163-2, Viking Children's Bks.) Penguin Putnam Bks. for Young Readers.

Karr, Kathleen. Bone Dry. (J). 2003. 5.99 (0-7868-1594-9); 2002. (Illus.). 240p. (gr. 5-9). 15.99 (0-7868-0776-8) Hyperion Bks. for Children.

Katz, Fred E. Tuck Me in, Mummy. 1997. (Spinechillers Mysteries Ser.: Vol. 9). (Illus.). 144p. (Orig.). (J). (gr. 3-7). pap. 4.99 (0-8499-4052-4) Nelson, Tommy.

Kendrick, Rosalyn. Bride of the Nile. 1998. 176p. (YA). (gr. 9 up). pap. 6.95 (0-86327-622-9) Wolfhound Pr. IRL. *Dist:* Irish American Bk. Co.

Korman, Gordon. Your Mummy Is a Nose Picker. 2000. (L.A.F. Bks.). (Illus.). 153p. (J). (gr. 4-7). pap. 4.99 (0-7868-1446-2) Disney Pr.

—Your Mummy Is a Nose Picker. 2000. (L.A.F. Bks.). (Illus.). 144p. (J). (gr. 4-7). pap. 14.49 (0-7868-2587-1) Hyperion Bks. for Children.

Lattimore, Deborah Nourse. The Winged Cat: A Tale of Ancient Egypt. 1992. (Illus.). 40p. (J). (gr. 2-5). 15.00 (0-06-023635-3); lib. bdg. 14.89 o.s.i (0-06-023636-1) HarperCollins Children's Bk. Group.

—Winged Cat: And Other Tales of Ancient Civilization. 2002. (Illus.). 80p. (J). pap. 4.25 (*0-06-442154-6*, Harper Trophy) HarperCollins Children's Bk. Group.

L'Engle, Madeleine. Moses, Prince of Egypt: Storyteller's Edition. 1998. 48p. 15.99 (*0-525-46051-9*, Puffin Bks.) Penguin Putnam Bks. for Young Readers.

Lepon, Shoshana. The Ten Plagues of Egypt. Goldstein-Alpern, Neva, ed. 1988. (Illus.). 32p. (J). (gr. k-4). 12.95 (*0-910818-77-0*); pap. 9.95 (*0-910818-76-2*) Judaica Pr., Inc., The.

Lewin, Betsy. What's the Matter, Habibi? 2004. (Illus.). 32p. (J). (ps-3). pap. 4.95 (*0-618-43242-6*, Clarion Bks.) Houghton Mifflin Co. Trade & Reference Div.

Lewin, Betsy, illus. What's the Matter, Habibi? 1997. 32p. (J). (ps-ps). tchr. ed. 15.00 (*0-395-85816-X*, Clarion Bks.) Houghton Mifflin Co. Trade & Reference Div.

Lewis, Tommi. Prince of Egypt: The Movie Scrapbook. 1998. (Illus.). 64p. (YA). (gr. 3 up). pap. 8.99 o.p. (*0-14-056474-8*, Puffin Bks.) Penguin Putnam Bks. for Young Readers.

Logan, Claudia. The 5,000-Year-Old Puzzle: Solving a Mystery at Giza. 2001. (Illus.). (J). (*0-7894-2635-8*) Dorling Kindersley Publishing, Inc.

—The 5,000-Year-Old Puzzle: Solving a Mystery of Ancient Egypt, RS. 2002. (Illus.). 48p. (J). 17.00 (*0-374-32335-6*, Farrar, Straus & Giroux (BYR)) Farrar, Straus & Giroux.

London, Victoria. Lucy & the Beauty Queen. 2002. (Gifted Girls Ser.). 64p. (J). (gr. 2-7). per. 6.95 (*0-9714776-1-2*) Sparklesoup Studios, Inc.

Long. Secret of the Nile. 1987. (J). 13.27 o.p. (*0-516-09752-0*, Children's Pr.) Scholastic Library Publishing.

Macaulay, David. Pyramid. 1982. (Illus.). 80p. (J). (gr. 5-9). pap. 9.95 (*0-395-32121-2*) Houghton Mifflin Co.

Marcellino, Fred. I, Crocodile. (Illus.). 32p. (J). 2002. (ps-3). pap. 6.99 (*0-06-008859-1*, Harper Trophy); 1999. (gr. 1-3). lib. bdg. 15.89 (*0-06-205199-7*); 1999. (gr. k-3). 15.95 (*0-06-205168-7*) HarperCollins Children's Bk. Group.

—I, Crocodile. (J). (gr. 1-2). 6.95 net. (*1-55592-982-6*) Weston Woods Studios, Inc.

Marston, Elsa. The Ugly Goddess. 2002. 218p. (YA). (gr. 5-8). 16.95 (*0-8126-2667-2*) Cricket Bks.

Matthews, Mary. Magid Fasts for Ramadan. (Illus.). 48p. (J). (gr. 4-6). 2000. pap. 6.95 (*0-618-04035-8*); 1996. tchr. ed. 16.00 (*0-395-66589-2*) Houghton Mifflin Co. Trade & Reference Div. (Clarion Bks.).

—Magid Fasts for Ramadan. 1996. 13.10 (*0-606-18044-3*) Turtleback Bks.

Matze, Claire Sidhom. The Stars in My Geddoh's Sky. 1999. (Concept Book Ser.). (Illus.). 32p. (J). (gr. k-3). pap. 14.95 (*0-8075-5332-8*) Whitman, Albert & Co.

May, Scott. Sten Gizzle, Time Traveler: The Egyptian Adventure. 2000. (Illus.). 24p. (J). (gr. 1-3). pap. (*0-9701450-4-7*) Long Hill Productions, Inc.

McCaughrean, Geraldine. Casting the Gods Adrift: A Tale of Ancient Egypt. 2003. (Illus.). 112p. (J). (gr. 4-7). 15.95 (*0-8126-2684-2*) Cricket Bks.

McGraw, Eloise Jarvis. Mara: Daughter of the Nile. 1953. (Illus.). (J). (gr. 5-8). 7.95 o.p. (*0-698-20087-X*) Putnam Publishing Group, The.

—Mara, Daughter of the Nile. 1985. 288p. (J). (gr. 4-7). pap. 5.99 (*0-14-031929-8*, Puffin Bks.) Penguin Putnam Bks. for Young Readers.

Mika, Andre. Prince of Egypt. abr. ed. 1998. (Illus.). 24p. (J). (ps-3). pap. text 8.99 o.p. incl. audio (*0-14-088862-4*, Puffin Bks.) Penguin Putnam Bks. for Young Readers.

Moore, Ishbel. Xanthe's Pyramid. 1998. 120p. (YA). (gr. 7-12). pap. 6.95 (*1-896184-34-0*) Roussan Pubs., Inc./Roussan Editeur, Inc. CAN. *Dist:* Orca Bk. Pubs.

Myers, Walter Dean. Tales of a Dead King. 1983. 128p. (J). (gr. 5-9). 11.95 o.p. (*0-688-02413-0*, Morrow, William & Co.) Morrow/Avon.

Norton, Andre. Shadow Hawk. 1960. (J). 5.50 o.p. (*0-15-273170-9*) Harcourt Children's Bks.

Oppenheim, Shulamith Levey. The Hundredth Name. 2003. (Illus.). 32p. (J). (ps-3). pap. 9.95 (*1-56397-694-3*) Boyds Mills Pr.

Paton Walsh, Jill. Pepi & the Secret Names. 1995. (Illus.). 32p. (J). (ps-3). 15.00 (*0-688-13428-9*) HarperCollins Children's Bk. Group.

Peck, Richard. Blossom Culp & the Sleep of Death. 1986. 224p. (J). (gr. 4-6). 14.95 o.s.i (*0-385-29433-6*, Delacorte Pr.) Dell Publishing.

—Blossom Culp & the Sleep of Death. 1994. 192p. (J). (gr. k-6). reprint ed. pap. 3.99 o.s.i (*0-440-40676-5*, Yearling) Random Hse. Children's Bks.

—Blossom Culp & the Sleep of Death. 1986. (J). 9.09 o.p. (*0-606-03552-4*) Turtleback Bks.

Pond, Roy. Mummy's Tomb. 1996. (J). 8.60 (*0-606-09645-0*) Turtleback Bks.

Rayyan, Omar, illus. Lilacs, Lotuses & Ladybugs. 1997. (*0-7802-8033-4*) Wright Group, The.

Rockwell, Anne F. Boy Who Became an Egyptian Scribe. 2003. (J). 15.99 (*0-06-029507-4*); lib. bdg. 16.89 (*0-06-029508-2*) HarperCollins Pubs.

Roden, Katie. The Mummy. 1996. (In the Footsteps of Ser.). 12.15 o.p. (*0-606-09462-8*) Turtleback Bks.

Rubalcaba, Jill. A Place in the Sun. 1997. 96p. (J). (gr. 4-6). tchr. ed. 15.00 (*0-395-82645-4*) Houghton Mifflin Co.

—A Place in the Sun. 1998. 11.14 (*0-606-17147-9*) Turtleback Bks.

—Place in the Sun. 1998. (Puffin Novel Ser.). 96p. (J). (gr. 3-7). pap. 4.99 (*0-14-130123-6*) Penguin Putnam Bks. for Young Readers.

Sabuda, Robert. Tutankhamen's Gift. 1997. 13.14 (*0-606-13101-9*) Turtleback Bks.

Schwartz, Stephen. Through Heaven's Eyes: The Prince of Egypt in Story & Song. deluxe ed. 1998. (Prince of Egypt Ser.). (Illus.). 32p. (gr. 1-3). 14.99 o.p. (*0-525-46128-0*, Puffin Bks.) Penguin Putnam Bks. for Young Readers.

Scieszka, Jon. Tut, Tut Twt Promo. 2003. (Time Warp Trio Ser.). (Illus.). 76p. pap. 2.66 (*0-14-250133-6*, Puffin Bks.) Penguin Putnam Bks. for Young Readers.

Smart, Andy. The Legend of Lotfiya: Who's after You? 1997. (Illus.). 32p. (J). (gr. 2-6). pap. 6.95 (*977-5325-71-4*) Hoopoe Bks. EGY. *Dist:* AMIDEAST.

Smith, Parker. The Mummy's Curse. 1992. (Young Indiana Jones Chronicles: No. 1). (Illus.). 24p. (J). (gr. 2-4). pap. 3.29 o.s.i (*0-307-12689-7*, 12689, Golden Bks.) Random Hse. Children's Bks.

Snyder, Zilpha Keatley. The Egypt Game. 2002. (Illus.). (J). 14.47 (*0-7587-0259-0*) Book Wholesalers, Inc.

—The Egypt Game. 1997. mass mkt. 2.69 o.p. (*0-440-22724-0*); 1996. 224p. (J). mass mkt. 2.49 o.s.i (*0-440-22025-4*); 1994. 224p. (J). (gr. 4-7). pap. 1.99 o.s.i (*0-440-21943-4*) Dell Publishing.

—The Egypt Game. 1991. (J). pap. o.s.i (*0-440-80245-8*, Dell Books for Young Readers); 1985. (Illus.). 240p. (gr. 5-9). pap. text 5.99 (*0-440-42225-6*, Yearling) Random Hse. Children's Bks.

—The Egypt Game. 1972. (Illus.). 224p. (J). (gr. 3-7). 18.95 (*0-689-30006-9*, Atheneum) Simon & Schuster Children's Publishing.

—The Egypt Game. 1967. (J). 12.04 (*0-606-03131-6*) Turtleback Bks.

Sommers, Stephen. The Mummy. novel ed. 1999. (Illus.). 142p. (J). mass mkt. 3.99 (*0-439-05015-4*) Scholastic, Inc.

Somper, J. Pyramid Plot. 1992. (Puzzle Adventures Ser.). (Illus.). 48p. (J). (gr. 3-8). pap. 5.95 (*0-7460-0506-7*); lib. bdg. 13.95 (*0-88110-403-5*, Usborne) EDC Publishing.

Steiner, Barbara. Mummy. 1995. (J). 8.60 o.p. (*0-606-07899-1*) Turtleback Bks.

Stilton, Geronimo. The Curse of the Cheese Pyramid. 2004. (Geronimo Stilton Ser.: No. 2). (Illus.). 128p. (J). mass mkt. 5.99 (*0-439-55964-2*) Scholastic, Inc.

Stine, H. William, ed. The Mummy's Curse. 1992. (Young Indiana Jones Chronicles: No. 1). (Illus.). 136p. (J). (gr. 4-6). pap. 3.50 o.s.i (*0-679-82774-9*, Random Hse. Bks. for Young Readers) Random Hse. Children's Bks.

Stolz, Mary. Cat in the Mirror. 1975. 256p. (J). (gr. 5 up). o.p. (*0-06-025832-2*); lib. bdg. 11.89 o.p. (*0-06-025833-0*) HarperCollins Pubs.

—Zekmet, the Stone Carver: A Tale of Ancient Egypt. 1988. (Illus.). 32p. (J). (gr. 2-5). 16.00 o.s.i (*0-15-299961-2*) Harcourt Trade Pubs.

Strong, Jeremy. There's a Pharaoh in Our Bath! l.t. ed. 1997. (J). 16.95 o.p. (*0-7451-6904-X*, Galaxy Children's Large Print) BBC Audiobooks America.

Syfret, Anne. Mot, Ybbat & Little Pharoah. 1976. (Illus.). (J). (gr. 4-6). lib. bdg. o.p. (*0-07-062647-2*) McGraw-Hill Cos., The.

Talley, Linda. Bastet. (Key Concepts in Personal Development Ser.). (Illus.). 2001. 32p. pap., tchr. ed. 79.95 incl. VHS (*1-55942-176-2*, 9390K3); 2000. 30p. (J). 79.95 incl. VHS (*1-55942-161-4*) Marsh Media.

Trout, Richard E. Falcon of Abydos: Oracle of the Nile, Vol. 3. 2000. (Harbor Lights Ser.: No. 3). 220p. (J). (gr. 5-12). pap. 9.95 (*1-880292-73-4*) LangMarc Publishing.

Welsh, Theresa. Tara: Initiate of Heliopolis: A Young Girl's Journey Back in Time to Cleopatra's Egypt. 2000. (Illus.). 148p. (YA). (gr. 4-7). pap. 13.95 (*1-58736-002-0*, Hats Off Bks.) Wheatmark, Inc.

Whitman, John. The Mummy Returns. 2001. (Illus.). 176p. (gr. 3-7). pap. text 4.99 (*0-553-48753-1*, Skylark) Random Hse. Children's Bks.

Williams, Jeff E. The Unknown Priestess. 1998. (J). 25.25 (*1-56763-342-0*); pap. (*1-56763-343-9*) Ozark Publishing.

Wynne-Jones, Tim. Zoom Upstream. 1994. (Laura Geringer Bks.). (Illus.). 32p. (J). (ps-2). 15.00 o.p. (*0-06-022977-2*); lib. bdg. 14.89 o.p. (*0-06-022978-0*) HarperTrade.

Yates, Philip. Ten Little Mummies: An Egyptian Counting Book. 2003. (Illus.). 40p. (J). (ps-2). 15.99 (*0-670-03641-2*, Viking) Viking Penguin.

Yolen, Jane. The Prince of Egypt. 1998. (Illus.). 80p. (J). (ps-4). 8.99 o.p. (*0-525-46050-0*, Puffin Bks.) Penguin Putnam Bks. for Young Readers.

Zindel, Paul. Egyptian Mystery. 2002. 192p. (YA). (gr. 6 up). 15.95 (*0-06-028508-7*) HarperCollins Children's Bk. Group.

—Egyptian Mystery. Date not set. 192p. (YA). (gr. 6 up). lib. bdg. 16.89 (*0-06-028509-5*) HarperCollins Pubs.

Zoehfeld, Kathleen Weidner, adapted by. The Emperor's New Groove: Junior Novel. 2000. (Illus.). 96p. (J). (gr. 3-7). pap. 4.99 (*0-7868-4429-9*) Disney Pr.

EL SALVADOR—FICTION

Argueta, Jorge. Zipitio. Amado, Elisa, tr. from SPA. 2003. (Illus.). 32p. (J). 16.95 (*0-88899-487-7*) Groundwood Bks. CAN. *Dist:* Publishers Group West.

Buss, Fran L. Journey of the Sparrows. 1993. 160p. (J). (gr. 4-7). pap. text 4.50 o.s.i (*0-440-40785-0*) Dell Publishing.

—Journey of the Sparrows. 1991. 160p. (J). (gr. 5-9). 15.00 o.p. (*0-525-67362-8*, Dutton Children's Bks.) Penguin Putnam Bks. for Young Readers.

—Journey of the Sparrows. 1993. (J). pap. o.p. (*0-440-90012-3*, Dell Books for Young Readers) Random Hse. Children's Bks.

—Journey of the Sparrows. 1993. (J). 9.60 o.p. (*0-606-05389-1*) Turtleback Bks.

ELLIS ISLAND (N.J. AND N.Y.)—FICTION

Holub, Joan. Tatiana Comes to America: An Ellis Island Story. 2002. (Doll Hospital Ser.: No. 1). 112p. (J). (gr. 2-4). mass mkt. 3.99 (*0-439-40178-X*, Scholastic Paperbacks) Scholastic, Inc.

Lasky, Kathryn. Hope in My Heart: Sofia's Immigrant Diary, Bk. 1. 2003. (My America Ser.). 112p. (J). pap. 12.95 (*0-439-18875-X*) Scholastic, Inc.

Woodruff, Elvira. The Memory Coat. 1999. (Illus.). 32p. (J). (gr. 2-5). pap. 15.95 (*0-590-67717-9*) Scholastic, Inc.

—The Orphan of Ellis Island: A Time Travel Adventure. (J). 2000. pap. 4.50 (*0-590-48246-7*); 1997. 160p. (gr. 4-7). pap. 15.95 (*0-590-48245-9*) Scholastic, Inc.

ENCHANTED FOREST (IMAGINARY PLACE: WREDE)—FICTION

Wrede, Patricia C. Calling on Dragons. (Enchanted Forest Chronicles: Bk. 3). (YA). 2003. (Illus.). 272p. pap. 5.95 (*0-15-204692-5*, Magic Carpet Bks.); Vol. 3. 1993. 240p. (gr. 7 up). 16.95 o.s.i (*0-15-200950-7*) Harcourt Children's Bks.

—Calling on Dragons. unabr. ed. 2002. (Enchanted Forest Ser.: Vol 3). (YA). 244p. pap. 37.00 incl. audio (*0-8072-0792-6*, LYA 347 SP);3. (gr. 5 up). audio 26.00 (*0-8072-0635-0*) Random Hse. Audio Publishing Group. (Listening Library).

—Calling on Dragons. 1994. 256p. (YA). (gr. 7-9). mass mkt. 4.99 (*0-590-48467-2*) Scholastic, Inc.

—Calling on Dragons. 1993. (Enchanted Forest Chronicles Ser.). 11.04 (*0-606-06950-X*) Turtleback Bks.

—Dealing with Dragons. (Enchanted Forest Chronicles: Bk. 1). (YA). 2002. (Illus.). 240p. (gr. 5 up). pap. 5.95 (*0-15-204566-X*, Magic Carpet Bks.); 1990. 224p. (gr. 7-12). 17.00 (*0-15-222900-0*) Harcourt Children's Bks.

—Dealing with Dragons. unabr. ed. (Enchanted Forest Ser.: Bk. 1). (J). 2001. (gr. 5 up). audio 25.00 (*0-8072-6190-4*); 1996. (gr. 7-12). audio 32.00 (*0-8072-7634-0*, YA906CX) Random Hse. Audio Publishing Group. (Listening Library).

—Dealing with Dragons. 1992. (Enchanted Forest Chronicles Ser.: Vol. 1). 212p. (YA). (gr. 7-12). mass mkt. 4.99 (*0-590-45722-5*, Scholastic Paperbacks) Scholastic, Inc.

—Dealing with Dragons. 1990. (Enchanted Forest Chronicles Ser.). (J). 11.04 (*0-606-01813-1*) Turtleback Bks.

—Dealing with Dragons. unabr. ed. 1996. (Enchanted Forest Ser.: Bk. 1). 212p. (J). (gr. 3-6). pap. 37.00 incl. audio (*0-8072-7635-9*, YA906SP, Listening Library) Random Hse. Audio Publishing Group.

—Dealing with Dragons, Set. unabr. ed. 1999. (YA). audio 29.98 Highsmith Inc.

—Searching for Dragons. abr. ed. 1991. (Enchanted Forest Chronicles Ser.: Bk. 2). 256p. (YA). (gr. 7-12). 16.95 (*0-15-200898-5*) Harcourt Children's Bks.

—Searching for Dragons. 1992. (Enchanted Forest Chronicles Ser.). 242p. (YA). (gr. 7-12). mass mkt. 4.99 (*0-590-45721-7*, 071, Scholastic Paperbacks) Scholastic, Inc.

—Searching for Dragons. 1991. (Enchanted Forest Chronicles Ser.). (J). 11.04 (*0-606-01941-3*) Turtleback Bks.

—Talking to Dragons. 1985. (MagicQuest Ser.: No. 13). 240p. (J). 2.25 o.s.i (*0-441-79591-9*) Ace Bks.

—Talking to Dragons. (Enchanted Forest Chronicles: Bk. 4). 272p. 2003. (Illus.). (YA). pap. 5.95 (*0-15-204691-7*, Magic Carpet Bks.); 1993. (J). (gr. 7 up). 16.95 (*0-15-284247-0*) Harcourt Children's Bks.

—Talking to Dragons, 4. unabr. ed. 2002. (J). (gr. 3 up). audio 26.00 (*0-8072-0638-5*, Listening Library) Random Hse. Audio Publishing Group.

—Talking to Dragons. 1995. 272p. (J). (gr. 7-9). mass mkt. 4.99 (*0-590-48475-3*) Scholastic, Inc.

—Talking to Dragons. 1995. (Enchanted Forest Chronicles Ser.). (J). 11.04 (*0-606-08267-0*) Turtleback Bks.

ENGLAND—FICTION

Aber, Linda Williams. The Clue in the Castle Wall. 2004. (Barbie Mystery Ser.). 48p. (J). pap. 3.99 (*0-439-55709-7*, Scholastic Paperbacks) Scholastic, Inc.

Adone, Claudio. My Grandfather Jack the Ripper. 2000. Tr. of Mio Nonno Jack Lo Squartatore. (Illus.). 304p. (J). (gr. 7-10). 19.00 (*1-928746-16-0*) Herodias.

Ahlberg, Allan. My Brother's Ghost. 2001. 87p. (J). (gr. 6 up). 9.99 o.s.i (*0-670-89290-4*, Viking Children's Bks.) Penguin Putnam Bks. for Young Readers.

Aiken, Joan. Cold Shoulder Road. 1996. (J). (gr. 5). 15.95 (*0-03-853218-2*, Delacorte Pr.) Dell Publishing.

—Cold Shoulder Road. (gr. 5 up). 1997. 288p. pap. text 4.50 o.s.i (*0-440-41341-9*, Yearling); 1996. 192p. (YA). 15.95 o.s.i (*0-385-32182-1*, Dell Books for Young Readers) Random Hse. Children's Bks.

—Cold Shoulder Road. 1997. 10.55 (*0-606-11218-9*) Turtleback Bks.

—The Cuckoo Tree. 2000. (Illus.). 297p. (J). (gr. 5-9). 16.00 (*0-618-07024-9*); pap. 5.95 (*0-618-07023-0*) Houghton Mifflin Co. Trade & Reference Div.

—The Cuckoo Tree. 1988. 320p. (J). (gr. k-6). pap. 3.50 o.s.i (*0-440-40046-5*, Yearling) Random Hse. Children's Bks.

—The Cuckoo Tree. 1989. (J). (gr. 4-6). 15.25 o.p. (*0-8446-6380-8*) Smith, Peter Pub., Inc.

—Midnight Is a Place. 2002. 304p. (J). (gr. 5 up). reprint ed. 16.00 (*0-618-19626-9*); pap. 5.95 (*0-618-19625-0*) Houghton Mifflin Co.

—Midnight Is a Place. 1985. (J). pap. 3.50 o.s.i (*0-440-45634-7*, Yearling) Random Hse. Children's Bks.

—Midnight Is a Place. 1993. 288p. (J). (gr. 4-7). pap. 2.95 (*0-590-45496-X*) Scholastic, Inc.

—Midnight Is a Place. 1975. pap. 1.50 o.p. (*0-671-78937-6*, Pocket) Simon & Schuster.

—Midnight Is a Place. 1974. (J). 8.05 o.p. (*0-606-05466-9*) Turtleback Bks.

—Midnight Is a Place. 1974. 288p. (J). (gr. 7 up). 9.95 o.p. (*0-670-47483-5*) Viking Penguin.

—Midwinter Nightingale. 2003. 256p. (J). (gr. 5). text 15.95 (*0-385-73081-0*); lib. bdg. 17.99 (*0-385-90103-8*) Dell Publishing. (Delacorte Pr.).

—The Stolen Lake. 1981. 256p. (YA). (gr. 7 up). 10.95 o.s.i (*0-385-28982-0*, Delacorte Pr.) Dell Publishing.

—The Stolen Lake. 1988. 304p. (J). (gr. k-6). pap. 3.25 o.s.i (*0-440-40037-6*, Yearling) Random Hse. Children's Bks.

—The Stolen Lake. 1989. (J). (gr. 4-6). 15.00 o.p. (*0-8446-6417-0*) Smith, Peter Pub., Inc.

Alcock, Vivien. The Haunting of Cassie Palmer. 1997. 192p. (YA). (gr. 7-9). pap. 6.95 (*0-395-81653-X*) Houghton Mifflin Co.

—The Stonewalkers. 1998. 176p. (YA). (gr. 7-9). pap. 4.95 (*0-395-81652-1*) Houghton Mifflin Co.

—The Trial of Anna Cotman. 1997. 224p. (YA). (gr. 7-9). pap. 6.95 (*0-395-81649-1*) Houghton Mifflin Co.

Almond, David. Counting Stars. 2002. 224p. (gr. 7 up). text 16.95 (*0-385-72946-4*); lib. bdg. 18.99 (*0-385-90034-1*) Dell Publishing. (Delacorte Pr.).

—Kit's Wilderness. l.t. ed. 2000. pap. 16.95 (*0-7540-6115-9*, Galaxy Children's Large Print) BBC Audiobooks America.

—Kit's Wilderness. 2000. (J). audio 24.00 (*0-7366-9017-4*) Books on Tape, Inc.

—Kit's Wilderness. unabr. ed. 2000. (J). (gr. 4-6). 240p. pap. 35.00 incl. audio (*0-8072-8216-2*); audio 30.00 (*0-8072-8215-4*, LL0166) Random Hse. Audio Publishing Group. (Listening Library).

—Kit's Wilderness. (YA). (gr. 7). 2001. (Illus.). 256p. mass mkt. 4.99 (*0-440-41605-1*, Laurel Leaf); 2000. 240p. 15.95 (*0-385-32665-3*, Dell Books for Young Readers) Random Hse. Children's Bks.

—Kit's Wilderness. l.t. ed. 2001. (Illus.). 272p. (J). (gr. 4-7). 22.95 (*0-7862-2772-9*) Thorndike Pr.

—Skellig. 2001. E-Book 3.99 (*1-59061-419-4*) Adobe Systems, Inc.

—Skellig. 1999. (J). 16.95 (*0-7540-6066-7*) BBC Audiobooks America.

—Skellig. 2000. (J). audio 18.00 (*0-7366-9025-5*) Books on Tape, Inc.

—Skellig. 1999. 192p. (gr. 3 up). text 16.95 (*0-385-32653-X*, Delacorte Pr.) Dell Publishing.

—Skellig. 2001. (Illus.). 208p. (gr. 5). mass mkt. 5.99 (*0-440-22908-1*, Laurel Leaf) Random Hse. Children's Bks.

—Skellig. Wojtyla, Karen, ed. 2000. (Illus.). 192p. (gr. 5-7). pap. text 4.99 (*0-440-41602-7*, Yearling) Random Hse. Children's Bks.

—Skellig. l.t. ed. 2000. (Young Adult Ser.). 205p. (J). 21.95 o.p. (*0-7862-2344-8*) Thorndike Pr.

—Skellig. 2000. 11.04 (*0-606-19192-5*) Turtleback Bks.

—Skellig. abr. ed. 1999. (J). audio 15.00 (*1-84032-224-1*) Ulverscroft Audio (U.S.A.).

Alphin, Elaine Marie. Tournament of Time. 1994. 125p. (Orig.). (J). (gr. 4-6). pap. 3.95 (*0-9643683-0-7*) Bluegrass Bks.

Alton, Steve. The Malifex. 2002. (Middle Readers Ser.). (Illus.). 182p. (J). (gr. 3-7). lib. bdg. 14.95 (*0-8225-0959-8*, Carolrhoda Bks.) Lerner Publishing Group.

Anderson, Rachel. Black Water, ERS. 1995. 88p. (J). (gr. 5-8). 14.95 o.p. (*0-8050-3847-7*, Holt, Henry & Co. Bks. For Young Readers) Holt, Henry & Co.

—Black Water. 1996. 180p. (J). (gr. 5-9). pap. 5.95 o.s.i (*0-698-11421-3*, PaperStar) Penguin Putnam Bks. for Young Readers.

—Black Water. 1996. 10.05 o.p. (*0-606-11141-7*) Turtleback Bks.

—The Bus People, ERS. 1992. 112p. (YA). (gr. 5 up). 13.95 o.p. (*0-8050-2297-X*, Holt, Henry & Co. Bks. For Young Readers) Holt, Henry & Co.

Anson-Weber, Joan. Snuffles Goes to Scotland Yard. 2001. (J). 16.95 (*0-87797-293-1*) Cherokee Publishing Co.

Ashley, Bernard. Little Soldier: A Novel. 240p. (J). 2003. mass mkt. 5.99 (*0-439-28502-X*); 2002. (Illus.). (gr. 9 up). pap. 16.95 (*0-439-22424-1*, Scholastic Pr.) Scholastic, Inc.

Austen, Jane. Pride & Prejudice. 1999. (YA). 11.95 (*1-56137-767-8*) Novel Units, Inc.

—Pride & Prejudice, Level 6. Hedge, Tricia, ed. 2000. (Bookworms Ser.). (Illus.). 121p. (YA). pap. text 5.95 (*0-19-423093-7*) Oxford Univ. Pr., Inc.

—Pride & Prejudice. 1979. (Now Age Illustrated V Ser.). (Illus.). 64p. (gr. 4-12). (J). stu. ed. 1.25 o.p. (*0-88301-419-X*); (J). text 5.00 o.p. (*0-88301-407-6*); pap. text 1.95 o.p. (*0-88301-395-9*) Pendulum Pr., Inc.

—Pride & Prejudice. (Illustrated Junior Library). (Illus.). 384p. 1984. (J). (gr. 4 up). 10.95 o.s.i (*0-448-06032-9*, Grosset & Dunlap); 1995. (YA). (gr. 7 up). pap. 4.99 (*0-14-037337-3*, Puffin Bks.) Penguin Putnam Bks. for Young Readers.

—Pride & Prejudice. abr. l.t. ed. 1996. (Great Illustrated Classics Ser.: Vol. 52). (Illus.). 240p. (J). (gr. 3-7). 9.95 (*0-86611-871-3*) Playmore, Inc., Pubs.

—Pride & Prejudice. (J). 1998. 47p. pap. 6.95 (*0-8114-6836-4*); 1996. (Illus.). 48p. (gr. 4 up). lib. bdg. 22.83 o.p. (*0-8172-1673-1*); 1988. (gr. 4 up). 22.00 (*0-8172-2188-3*); 1983. (Illus.). 48p. (gr. 4 up). pap. 9.27 o.p. (*0-8172-2018-6*) Raintree Pubs.

—Pride & Prejudice. 1996. (J). pap. 2.25 (*0-590-08576-X*) Scholastic, Inc.

—Pride & Prejudice. 1994. (Enriched Classics Ser.). (YA). (gr. 9-12). 3.95 o.p. (*0-671-00601-0*, Pocket) Simon & Schuster.

—Pride & Prejudice. 1994. 9.04 (*0-606-18651-4*) Turtleback Bks.

—Pride & Prejudice: Penguin Readers Level 5. 1998. 80p. pap. 7.00 (*0-14-081507-4*) Viking Penguin.

Austen, Jane & Kerrigan, Michael. Pride & Prejudice. 1999. (Literature Made Easy Ser.). (Illus.). 96p. (YA). pap. 4.95 (*0-7641-0834-4*) Barron's Educational Series, Inc.

Avery, Gillian. A Likely Lad. 1994. (YA). 16.00 o.p. (*0-671-79867-7*, Simon & Schuster Children's Publishing) Simon & Schuster Children's Publishing.

—Maria Escapes. 1992. (Illus.). 272p. (J). (gr. 4-8). pap. 15.00 (*0-671-77074-8*, Simon & Schuster Children's Publishing) Simon & Schuster Children's Publishing.

Avi. Beyond the Western Sea Bk. 1: The Escape from Home. 1996. 304p. (J). (gr. 7 up). pap. 18.95 (*0-531-09513-4*); lib. bdg. 19.99 (*0-531-08863-4*) Scholastic, Inc. (Orchard Bks.).

—Beyond the Western Sea Bk. 2: Lord Kirkle's Money. 1996. 400p. (J). (gr. 6-9). pap. 19.99 (*0-531-09520-7*); (Beyond the Western Sea Ser.: Vol. 2). lib. bdg. 19.99 (*0-531-08870-7*) Scholastic, Inc. (Orchard Bks.).

Awdry, Wilbert V. Down at the Docks. 2003. (Thomas & Friends Ser.). (Illus.). 24p. (J). 3.25 (*0-375-82592-4*) Random Hse. Children's Bks.

—Thomas & Toby. 2003. (Illus.). 32p. (J). 11.99 (*0-375-82593-2*) Random Hse. Children's Bks.

Bagnold, Enid. National Velvet. 1991. 272p. (J). mass mkt. 4.99 (*0-380-71235-0*, Avon Bks.) Morrow/Avon.

Banks, Lynne Reid. Alice-by-Accident. 2000. (Avon Camelot Bks.). 144p. (J). (gr. 4-7). 14.95 (*0-380-97865-2*) HarperCollins Children's Bk. Group.

—My Darling Villain. 1977. 240p. (YA). (gr. 7 up). 11.25 (*0-06-020392-7*); lib. bdg. 11.89 o.p. (*0-06-020393-5*) HarperCollins Children's Bk. Group.

Barkan, Joanne. A Pup in King Arthur's Court. 1998. (Adventures of Wishbone Ser.: No. 15). (Illus.). 164p. (J). (gr. 2-5). pap. 3.99 o.p. (*1-57064-325-3*) Lyrick Publishing.

—A Pup in King Arthur's Court. l.t. ed. 1999. (Adventures of Wishbone Ser.: No. 15). (Illus.). 164p. (J). (gr. 2-5). lib. bdg. 22.60 (*0-8368-2593-4*) Stevens, Gareth Inc.

Barklem, Jill. Autumn Story. (Seasons of Brambly Hedge Ser.). (J). 1989. (gr. k up). 8.95 o.s.i (*0-399-21754-1*); 1980. (Illus.). 32p. (gr. 1 up). 10.95 o.p. (*0-399-20745-7*, Philomel) Penguin Putnam Bks. for Young Readers.

—Autumn Story. 1999. (Brambly Hedge Ser.). (Illus.). 32p. (J). (ps-3). 9.95 (*0-689-83054-8*, Atheneum) Simon & Schuster Children's Publishing.

—The Secret Staircase. (J). (ps-3). 1992. 32p. 10.95 o.s.i (*0-399-21865-3*); 1983. (Illus.). 13.95 o.p. (*0-399-20994-8*) Penguin Putnam Bks. for Young Readers. (Philomel).

—The Secret Staircase. 1989. (Illus.). 32p. (J). (ps-3). 5.95 o.s.i (*0-399-21726-6*, Sandcastle Bks.) Putnam Publishing Group, The.

—The Secret Staircase. 1999. (Brambly Hedge Ser.). (Illus.). 32p. (J). (ps-3). 9.95 (*0-689-83090-4*, Atheneum) Simon & Schuster Children's Publishing.

—Winter Story. (Seasons of Brambly Hedge Ser.). (J). 1989. (ps-3). 8.95 o.s.i (*0-399-21752-5*); 1980. (Illus.). 32p. (gr. 1 up). 6.99 o.p. (*0-399-61158-4*); 1980. (Illus.). 32p. (gr. 1 up). 10.95 o.p. (*0-399-20748-1*) Penguin Putnam Bks. for Young Readers. (Philomel).

—Winter Story. 1999. (Brambly Hedge Ser.). (Illus.). 32p. (J). (ps-3). 9.95 (*0-689-83057-2*, Atheneum) Simon & Schuster Children's Publishing.

Bassett, Jennifer, ed. Black Beauty. 1995. (Illus.). 80p. (J). pap. text 5.95 o.p. (*0-19-422754-5*) Oxford Univ. Pr., Inc.

—The Children of the New Forest. 1996. (Illus.). 48p. (J). pap. text 5.95 o.p. (*0-19-422748-0*) Oxford Univ. Pr., Inc.

Bawden, Nina. The Peppermint Pig. l.t. ed. 1987. (J). 16.95 o.p. (*0-7451-0447-9*, Galaxy Children's Large Print) BBC Audiobooks America.

—The Peppermint Pig. 1988. 160p. (J). (gr. 5 up). pap. 4.95 o.s.i (*0-440-40122-4*) Dell Publishing.

—The Peppermint Pig. 1975. 192p. (J). (gr. 3-6). lib. bdg. 13.89 (*0-397-31618-6*) HarperCollins Children's Bk. Group.

—The Peppermint Pig. 1977. (Story Bks.). 160p. (J). (gr. 2-7). pap. 2.95 o.p. (*0-14-030944-6*, Penguin Bks.) Viking Penguin.

Beardshaw, Rosalind. Grandpa's Surprise. 2004. (J). 15.95 (*1-58234-934-7*) Bloomsbury Publishing.

Beere, Peter. At Gehenna's Door. l.t. ed. 2000. 304p. pap. 18.99 (*0-7089-9500-4*) Harlequin Mills & Boon, Ltd. GBR. *Dist:* Ulverscroft Large Print Bks., Ltd., Ulverscroft Large Print Canada, Ltd.

Bellairs, John. The Secret of the Underground Room. (Johnny Dixon Ser.). (Illus.). (J). 1992. 144p. (gr. 3-7). pap. 4.99 o.p. (*0-14-034932-4*, Puffin Bks.); 1990. 12p. (ps-3). 13.89 o.p. (*0-8037-0864-5*, Dial Bks. for Young Readers); 1990. 160p. (ps-3). 14.00 o.s.i (*0-8037-0863-7*, Dial Bks. for Young Readers) Penguin Putnam Bks. for Young Readers.

—The Secret of the Underground Room. 1992. (J). 9.09 (*0-606-01744-5*) Turtleback Bks.

—The Vengeance of the Witch-Finder. (Illus.). 1995. 160p. (J). (gr. 4-7). pap. 5.99 (*0-14-037511-2*, Puffin Bks.); 1993. 176p. (YA). (gr. 5 up). 14.89 o.p. (*0-8037-1451-3*, Dial Bks. for Young Readers); 1993. 160p. (YA). (gr. 5 up). 14.99 o.s.i (*0-8037-1450-5*, Dial Bks. for Young Readers) Penguin Putnam Bks. for Young Readers.

—The Vengeance of the Witch-Finder. 1995. (J). 11.04 (*0-606-08343-X*) Turtleback Bks.

Bemelmans, Ludwig. Madeline in London. 2002. (Madeline Ser.). (Illus.). (J). 14.04 (*0-7587-5002-1*) Book Wholesalers, Inc.

—Madeline in London. unabr. ed. 1995. (Madeline Ser.). (Illus.). (J). (ps-3). pap. 15.95 incl. audio (*0-670-44655-6*) Live Oak Media.

—Madeline in London. (Madeline Ser.). (Illus.). 64p. (J). (ps-3). 2000. pap. 6.99 (*0-14-056649-X*, Puffin Bks.); 1977. pap. 5.99 o.s.i (*0-14-050199-1*, Puffin Bks.); 1961. 16.99 (*0-670-44648-3*, Viking Children's Bks.) Penguin Putnam Bks. for Young Readers.

—Madeline in London. (Madeline Ser.). (J). (ps-3). 2000. (Illus.). 13.14 (*0-606-18429-5*); 1978. 10.19 o.p. (*0-606-03875-2*) Turtleback Bks.

Berry, Liz. The China Garden, RS. 1996. 288p. (YA). (gr. 7 up). 18.00 o.p. (*0-374-31248-6*, Farrar, Straus & Giroux (BYR)) Farrar, Straus & Giroux.

—The China Garden. 1999. 288p. (J). pap. 6.99 (*0-380-73228-9*, Avon Bks.) Morrow/Avon.

Birney, Betty, adapted by. Black Beauty: Adapted from the Screenplay. 1999. (Golden Look-Look Bks.). (Illus.). 24p. (J). (ps-3). pap. 3.29 o.s.i (*0-307-12838-5*, Golden Bks.) Random Hse. Children's Bks.

Blackmore, Richard D. Lorna Doone, Level 4. Hedge, Tricia, ed. 2000. (Bookworms Ser.). (Illus.). 96p. (J). pap. text 5.95 (*0-19-423038-4*) Oxford Univ. Pr., Inc.

Blyton, Enid. Five Go down to the Sea. l.t. ed. 1997. (J). 16.95 o.p. (*0-7451-6972-4*, Galaxy Children's Large Print) BBC Audiobooks America.

Bodger, Joan. The Forest Family. (Illus.). 112p. (J). (gr. 3-7). 2001. pap. 7.95 (*0-88776-579-3*); 1999. 16.95 (*0-88776-485-1*) Tundra Bks. of Northern New York.

Bond, Michael. Paddington on Top. 1991. (Paddington Ser.). (Illus.). 128p. (J). (ps-3). pap. 3.25 o.s.i (*0-440-46818-3*) Dell Publishing.

—Paddington on Top, 001. (Paddington Ser.). (Illus.). (J). 1975. 128p. (ps-3). 13.95 o.p. (*0-395-21897-7*); 2002. 144p. (gr. 3-7). pap. 4.95 (*0-618-25072-7*) Houghton Mifflin Co.

—Paddington on Top. rev. ed. 2000. (Paddington Ser.). (Illus.). 128p. (J). (gr. 4-6). 15.00 (*0-618-07041-9*) Houghton Mifflin Co. Trade & Reference Div.

—Paddington Treasury. 1999. (Paddington Ser.). (Illus.). 416p. (J). (gr. 4-6). 29.95 (*0-395-90507-9*) Houghton Mifflin Co.

Booth, Martin. Panther. 2001. (Illus.). 96p. (J). (gr. 3-7). 15.00 (*0-689-82976-0*, McElderry, Margaret K.) Simon & Schuster Children's Publishing.

Boston, Lucy M. The Children of Green Knowe. l.t. unabr. ed. 1987. (J). (gr. 4-6). lib. bdg. 15.95 o.p. (*0-7451-0626-9*, Macmillan Reference USA) Gale Group.

—The Children of Green Knowe. (Voyager/HBJ Book Ser.). (Illus.). (J). 1989. 192p. (gr. 4-7). pap. 6.00 o.s.i (*0-15-217151-7*, Odyssey Classics); 1977. (gr. 4-7). pap. 3.95 o.p. (*0-15-616870-7*, Voyager Bks./Libros Viajeros); 2002. 192p. (gr. 3 up). reprint ed. 17.00 (*0-15-202462-X*, Harcourt Young Classics); 2002. 192p. (gr. 4-7). reprint ed. pap. 6.00 (*0-15-202468-9*, Odyssey Classics) Harcourt Children's Bks.

—The Children of Green Knowe. 1979. (Illus.). (J). reprint ed. o.p. Harcourt Trade Pubs.

—The Children of Green Knowe. 1990. (Illus.). (J). (gr. 3-6). 17.30 o.p. (*0-8446-6288-7*) Smith, Peter Pub., Inc.

—The Children of Green Knowe. 1977. (Voyager/HBJ Bks.). (J). 12.05 (*0-606-01092-0*) Turtleback Bks.

—An Enemy at Green Knowe. 2002. (Green Knowe Ser.). (Illus.). 192p. (YA). (gr. 4-7). reprint ed. pap. 6.00 (*0-15-202481-6*, Odyssey Classics) Harcourt Children's Bks.

—An Enemy at Green Knowe. 1984. (Illus.). (J). (gr. 3-6). 17.30 o.p. (*0-8446-6152-X*) Smith, Peter Pub., Inc.

—The River at Green Knowe. 1989. 176p. (J). (gr. 4-7). pap. 3.95 o.s.i (*0-15-267450-0*, Odyssey Classics); 1966. (Illus.). 153p. (J). (gr. 4-6). pap. 2.95 o.p. (*0-15-677701-0*, Voyager Bks./Libros Viajeros); 1959. (Illus.). (J). (gr. 4-7). 5.95 o.p. (*0-15-267446-2*); 2002. (Illus.). 176p. (YA). (gr. 3 up). reprint ed. 17.00 (*0-15-202613-4*, Harcourt Young Classics); 2002. (Illus.). 176p. (YA). (gr. 4-7). reprint ed. pap. 6.00 (*0-15-202607-X*, Odyssey Classics) Harcourt Children's Bks.

—The River at Green Knowe. 1979. (Illus.). (J). reprint ed. o.p. Harcourt Trade Pubs.

—The River at Green Knowe. 1984. (Illus.). (J). (gr. 3-6). 17.55 o.p. (*0-8446-6153-8*) Smith, Peter Pub., Inc.

—The River at Green Knowe. 1959. 10.00 (*0-606-02244-9*) Turtleback Bks.

—The Stones of Green Knowe. 1976. (Illus.). 128p. (J). (gr. 5-9). 7.95 o.p. (*0-689-50058-0*, McElderry, Margaret K.) Simon & Schuster Children's Publishing.

—A Stranger at Green Knowe. 2002. (Green Knowe Ser.). (Illus.). 208p. (YA). reprint ed. (gr. 3 up). 17.00 (*0-15-202583-9*, Harcourt Young Classics); (gr. 4-7). pap. 6.00 (*0-15-202589-8*, Odyssey Classics) Harcourt Children's Bks.

—The Treasure of Green Knowe. (Illus.). 1989. 224p. (J). (gr. 4-7). pap. 3.95 (*0-15-289982-0*, Odyssey Classics); 1978. (J). (gr. 4-7). pap. 1.95 o.p. (*0-15-691302-X*, Voyager Bks./Libros Viajeros); 1958. (J). (gr. 4-6). 8.95 o.s.i (*0-15-289979-0*); 2002. 224p. (YA). (gr. 3 up). reprint ed. 17.00 (*0-15-202595-2*, Harcourt Young Classics) Harcourt Children's Bks.

—The Treasure of Green Knowe. 1979. (J). reprint ed. o.p. Harcourt Trade Pubs.

—The Treasure of Green Knowe. 1990. (Illus.). (J). (gr. 3-6). 17.30 o.p. (*0-8446-6275-5*) Smith, Peter Pub., Inc.

Boston, Lucy M. & Boston, Peter. The Treasure of Green Knowe. 2002. (Green Knowe Ser.). (Illus.). 224p. (YA). (gr. 4-7). reprint ed. pap. 6.00 (*0-15-202601-0*, Odyssey Classics) Harcourt Children's Bks.

Bouchard, David. The Mermaid's Muse. 2000. (Chinese Legends Trilogy). (Illus.). 223p. (J). (gr. 3-6). 15.95 (*1-55192-248-7*) Raincoast Bk. Distribution CAN. *Dist:* Publishers Group West.

Bray, Libba. A Great & Terrible Beauty. 2003. 416p. (YA). lib. bdg. 18.99 (*0-385-90161-5*); (gr. 9). 16.95 (*0-385-73028-4*) Random Hse. Children's Bks. (Delacorte Bks. for Young Readers).

Brennan, Herbie. Fairy Nuff. 2002. (Illus.). 121p. (J). (gr. 2-4). 13.95 (*1-58234-770-0*, Bloomsbury Children) Bloomsbury Publishing.

—Nuff Said: Another Tale of Bluebell Wood. 2002. (Illus.). (J). (gr. 2-5). 128p. pap. 6.95 (*1-58234-807-3*); 159p. 13.95 (*1-58234-771-9*) Bloomsbury Publishing. (Bloomsbury Children).

Bronte, Charlotte. Jane Eyre. 1997. (Classics Illustrated Study Guides). (Illus.). 64p. (YA). (gr. 7 up). mass mkt., stu. ed. 4.99 o.p. (*1-57840-005-8*) Acclaim Bks.

—Jane Eyre. Farr, Naunerle C., ed. 1977. (Illus.). (J). (gr. 4-12). stu. ed. 1.25 (*0-88301-290-1*); text 7.50 o.p. (*0-88301-278-2*); pap. text 2.95 (*0-88301-266-9*) Pendulum Pr., Inc.

—Jane Eyre. 1999. (gr. 4-7). pap. 2.99 o.s.i (*0-14-130537-1*, Puffin Bks.); 1995. (Illus.). 656p. (YA). (gr. 4-7). pap. 4.99 (*0-14-036678-4*, Puffin Bks.); 1992. 448p. (J). (gr. 5 up). pap. 3.50 o.p. (*0-14-035131-0*, Puffin Bks.); 1983. (Illus.). 576p. (J). (gr. 4-7). 19.99 (*0-448-06031-0*, Grosset & Dunlap) Penguin Putnam Bks. for Young Readers.

—Jane Eyre. 1983. (Illus.). 48p. (J). (gr. 4 up). pap. 9.27 o.p. (*0-8172-2012-7*) Raintree Pubs.

—Jane Eyre. 1997. (Step into Classics Ser.). 112p. (J). (gr. 3-5). pap. 3.99 (*0-679-88618-4*) Random Hse., Inc.

—Jane Eyre. (Saddleback Classics). 1999. (Illus.). (J). 13.10 (*0-606-21557-3*); 1997. 10.04 (*0-606-11517-X*) Turtleback Bks.

—Jane Eyre. 1981. (Illus.). 48p. (J). (gr. 4 up). lib. bdg. 24.26 o.p. (*0-8172-1661-8*) Raintree Pubs.

—Jane Eyre. 2003. (Illus.). 48p. 16.95 (*0-7502-3668-X*) Hodder Wayland GBR. *Dist:* Trafalgar Square.

—Jane Eyre. 2nd ed. 1998. (Illustrated Classic Book Ser.). (Illus.). 61p. (J). (gr. 3 up). reprint ed. pap. text 4.95 (*1-56767-267-1*) Educational Insights, Inc.

—Jane Eyre. adapted ed. (YA). (gr. 5-12). pap. text 9.95 (*0-8359-0215-3*) Globe Fearon Educational Publishing.

—Jane Eyre. unabr. ed. 1998. (Wordsworth Classics Ser.). (YA). (gr. 6-12). 5.27 (*0-89061-020-7*, R0207WW) Jamestown.

—Jane Eyre, Level 6. Hedge, Tricia, ed. 2000. (Bookworms Ser.). (Illus.). 128p. pap. text 5.95 (*0-19-423088-0*) Oxford Univ. Pr., Inc.

—Jane Eyre Promo. 2003. (Parallel Text Ser.). 656p. pap. 3.99 o.p. (*0-14-250090-9*, Puffin Bks.) Penguin Putnam Bks. for Young Readers.

—Jane Eyre Readalong. 1994. (Illustrated Classics Collection). 64p. pap. 14.95 incl. audio (*0-7854-0739-1*, 40458); (J). pap. 13.50 o.p. incl. audio (*1-56103-536-X*) American Guidance Service, Inc.

Bronte, Emily. Wuthering Heights. abr. ed. (Classics Illustrated Ser.). (Illus.). 52p. (YA). pap. 4.95 (*1-57209-011-1*) Classics International Entertainment, Inc.

—Wuthering Heights. Farr, Naunerle C., ed. abr. ed. 1977. (Now Age Illustrated III Ser.). (Illus.). (YA). (gr. 4-12). text 7.50 o.p. (*0-88301-284-7*); pap. text 2.95 (*0-88301-272-3*) Pendulum Pr., Inc.

—Wuthering Heights. 1995. (Classics for Young Readers Ser.). (Illus.). 464p. (YA). (gr. 4-7). pap. 4.99 (*0-14-036694-6*, Puffin Bks.) Penguin Putnam Bks. for Young Readers.

—Wuthering Heights. 2003. (Scholastic Classics Ser.). 416p. (J). mass mkt. 4.99 (*0-439-22891-3*) Scholastic, Inc.

—Wuthering Heights: Abridged for Children, Level 5. Hedge, Tricia, ed. 2000. (Bookworms Ser.). (Illus.). 112p. (YA). pap. text 5.95 (*0-19-423075-9*) Oxford Univ. Pr., Inc.

—Wuthering Heights: Abridged for Children. (gr. 4-7). 1998. (Illus.). 48p. (YA). pap. text 6.95 (*0-8114-6847-X*); 1988. (YA). 22.00 o.p. (*0-8172-2199-9*); 1982. (Illus.). 48p. (J). 22.83 o.p. (*0-8172-1682-0*); 1982. (Illus.). 48p. (YA). pap. 9.27 o.p. (*0-8172-2029-1*) Raintree Pubs.

Brooks, Kevin. Lucas. (J). 2004. 368p. mass mkt. 7.99 (*0-439-53063-6*, Scholastic Paperbacks); 2003. 432p. 16.95 (*0-439-45698-3*, Chicken Hse., The) Scholastic, Inc.

Brown, Janet Allison & Burnett, Frances Hodgson. The Secret Garden. 2001. (Storytime Classics Ser.). (Illus.). 32p. (J). (ps-3). 15.99 o.p. (*0-670-89911-9*, Puffin Bks.) Penguin Putnam Bks. for Young Readers.

Brown, Janet Allison & Rust, Graham. The Secret Garden. 2001. (Storytime Classics Ser.). (Illus.). 32p. (J). (ps-3). pap. 5.99 (*0-14-131201-7*, Puffin Bks.) Penguin Putnam Bks. for Young Readers.

Burgess, Melvin. An Angel for May. l.t. ed. 1994. (J). (gr. 1-8). 16.95 o.p. (*0-7451-2086-5*, Galaxy Children's Large Print) BBC Audiobooks America.

—An Angel for May. 1995. (J). 15.00 o.s.i (*0-671-89004-2*, Simon & Schuster Children's Publishing) Simon & Schuster Children's Publishing.

—Burning Issy. 1994. (YA). (gr. 5 up). 15.00 o.s.i (*0-671-89003-4*, Simon & Schuster Children's Publishing) Simon & Schuster Children's Publishing.

—Kite, RS. 2000. 192p. (J). (gr. 5-8). 16.00 (*0-374-34228-8*, Farrar, Straus & Giroux (BYR)) Farrar, Straus & Giroux.

—Lady: My Life As a Bitch. 2003. (Illus.). 272p. (J). pap. 6.99 (*0-06-054033-8*) HarperCollins Children's Bk. Group.

—Lady: My Life As a Bitch, ERS. 2002. 256p. (YA). 16.95 (*0-8050-7148-2*, Holt, Henry & Co. Bks. For Young Readers) Holt, Henry & Co.

—Smack, ERS. 1998. 288p. (YA). (gr. 9-13). 16.95 (*0-8050-5801-X*, Holt, Henry & Co. Bks. For Young Readers) Holt, Henry & Co.

—Smack. (J). 2003. 384p. pap. 6.99 (*0-06-052187-2*); 1999. 304p. (gr. 7-12). pap. 6.99 (*0-380-73223-8*) Morrow/Avon. (Avon Bks.).

—Smack. 1999. 13.04 (*0-606-16355-7*) Turtleback Bks.

Burnett, Frances Hodgson. Little Lord Fauntleroy. (J). E-Book 3.95 (*0-594-06327-2*) 1873 Pr.

—Little Lord Fauntleroy. (J). 21.95 (*0-8488-0792-8*) Amereon, Ltd.

—Little Lord Fauntleroy. 1987. (Classics Ser.). 192p. mass mkt. 2.95 o.s.i (*0-553-21202-8*, Bantam Classics) Bantam Bks.

—Little Lord Fauntleroy. (J). 1977. 21.95 o.p. (*0-89967-002-4*); 1981. (Illus.). 252p. (gr. 5-7). reprint ed. lib. bdg. 21.95 (*0-89966-288-9*) Buccaneer Bks., Inc.

—Little Lord Fauntleroy. 1990. 224p. (J). (gr. k-6). pap. 3.50 o.s.i (*0-440-44764-X*) Dell Publishing.

—Little Lord Fauntleroy. 2002. (Evergreen Classics). (Illus.). 176p. (J). pap. 2.50 (*0-486-42368-9*) Dover Pubns., Inc.

—Little Lord Fauntleroy. 1976. (Classics of Children's Literature, 1621-1932: Vol. 53). (Illus.). (J). reprint ed. lib. bdg. 46.00 o.p. (*0-8240-2302-1*) Garland Publishing, Inc.

—Little Lord Fauntleroy. 1993. (Illus.). 160p. (YA). (gr. 5 up). 18.95 (*0-87923-958-1*) Godine, David R. Pub.

—Little Lord Fauntleroy. l.t. ed. 706p. pap. 57.20 (*0-7583-3718-3*); 574p. pap. 48.96 (*0-7583-3717-5*); 819p. pap. 73.10 (*0-7583-3719-1*); 365p. pap. 32.98 (*0-7583-3715-9*); 285p. pap. 26.48 (*0-7583-3714-0*); 208p. pap. 21.07 (*0-7583-3713-2*); 160p. pap. 18.06 (*0-7583-3712-4*); 467p. pap. 40.77 (*0-7583-3716-7*); 160p. lib. bdg. 24.06 (*0-7583-3704-3*); 819p. lib. bdg. 85.10 (*0-7583-3711-6*); 706p. lib. bdg. 63.20 (*0-7583-3710-8*); 574p. lib. bdg. 54.96 (*0-7583-3709-4*); 208p. lib. bdg. 27.07 (*0-7583-3705-1*); 285p. lib. bdg. 32.48 (*0-7583-3706-X*); 365p. lib. bdg. 38.98 (*0-7583-3707-8*); 467p. lib. bdg. 46.77 (*0-7583-3708-6*) Huge Print Pr.

—Little Lord Fauntleroy. 2002. 164p. 93.99 (*1-4043-1340-0*); per. 88.99 (*1-4043-1341-9*) IndyPublish-.com.

—Little Lord Fauntleroy. 1995. (Everyman's Library Children's Classics Ser.). (Illus.). (J). (gr. 4-7). 13.95 (*0-679-44474-2*, Everyman's Library) Knopf Publishing Group.

—Little Lord Fauntleroy. l.t. ed. 1997. (Large Print Heritage Ser.). 272p. (YA). (gr. 7-12). lib. bdg. 28.95 (*1-58118-002-0*, 21965) LRS.

—Little Lord Fauntleroy. E-Book 1.95 (*1-57799-840-5*) Logos Research Systems, Inc.

—Little Lord Fauntleroy. 1992. 224p. (YA). mass mkt. 2.95 o.s.i (*0-451-52559-0*, Signet Classics) NAL.

—Little Lord Fauntleroy. 1993. (Oxford World's Classics Ser.). 208p. (J). pap. 7.95 o.p. (*0-19-282961-0*) Oxford Univ. Pr., Inc.

—Little Lord Fauntleroy. (Puffin Classics Ser.). 1996. (Illus.). 238p. (YA). (gr. 5-9). 4.99 (*0-14-036753-5*); 1985. 176p. (YA). (gr. 7 up). pap. 3.50 o.p. (*0-14-035025-X*); 1981. pap. 2.50 o.p. (*0-14-031411-3*) Penguin Putnam Bks. for Young Readers. (Puffin Bks.).

—Little Lord Fauntleroy, Homework Set. unabr. ed. 1997. (J). (gr. 5). 56.24 incl. audio (*0-7887-1840-1*, 40620) Recorded Bks., LLC.

—Little Lord Fauntleroy. (Illus.). (J). pap. 21.95 (*0-590-74607-3*) Scholastic, Inc.

—Little Lord Fauntleroy. E-Book 5.00 (*0-7410-0417-8*) SoftBook Pr.

—Little Lord Fauntleroy. 1994. (Puffin Classics). (J). 11.04 (*0-606-09560-8*) Turtleback Bks.

—Little Lord Fauntleroy. 1998. (Children's Library). (J). (gr. 4-7). pap. 3.95 (*1-85326-130-0*, 1300WW) Wordsworth Editions, Ltd. GBR. *Dist:* Combined Publishing.

—A Little Princess. (J). 16.95 (*0-8488-1253-0*) Amereon, Ltd.

—A Little Princess. 1987. (Classics Ser.). 208p. (J). mass mkt. 2.95 o.s.i (*0-553-21203-6*, Bantam Classics) Bantam Bks.

—A Little Princess. 2000. per. 12.50 (*1-58396-000-7*) Blue Unicorn Editions.

—A Little Princess. (J). 1977. 300p. lib. bdg. 15.95 (*0-89967-005-9*, Harmony Raine & Co.); 1981. 232p. reprint ed. lib. bdg. 15.95 (*0-89966-327-3*) Buccaneer Bks., Inc.

—A Little Princess. 1995. 256p. (J). (gr. 5-8). pap. 3.50 (*0-87406-739-1*) Darby Creek Publishing.

—A Little Princess. 1990. 240p. (J). pap. 3.99 o.s.i (*0-440-40386-3*) Dell Publishing.

—A Little Princess. abr. ed. (Children's Thrift Classics Ser.). (Illus.). (J). 1996. 96p. (gr. 1). pap. 1.00 (*0-486-29171-5*); 2000. 240p. pap. 2.00 (*0-486-41446-9*) Dover Pubns., Inc.

—A Little Princess. 2000. (Illus.). 192p. (YA). (gr. 4-7). reprint ed. 18.95 (*0-87923-784-8*) Godine, David R. Pub.

—A Little Princess. (Illus.). (J). 2000. 32p. (ps-3). 16.95 (*0-06-027891-9*); 2000. 32p. (ps-3). lib. bdg. 16.89 (*0-06-029010-2*); 1999. 336p. (gr. 4 up). 17.99 (*0-397-30693-8*); 1963. 80p. (gr. 4-6). lib. bdg. 15.89 o.p. (*0-397-31339-X*); 1987. 336p. (gr. 4 up). reprint ed. pap. 5.99 (*0-06-440187-1*, Harper Trophy) HarperCollins Children's Bk. Group.

—A Little Princess. l.t. ed. 330p. pap. 30.77 (*0-7583-1386-1*); 818p. pap. 65.40 (*0-7583-1390-X*); 541p. pap. 45.77 (*0-7583-1388-8*); 949p. pap. 74.67 (*0-7583-1391-8*); 193p. pap. 20.92 (*0-7583-1384-5*); 241p. pap. 24.55 (*0-7583-1385-3*); 665p. pap. 54.57 (*0-7583-1389-6*); 423p. pap. 37.40 (*0-7583-1387-X*); 949p. lib. bdg. 94.49 (*0-7583-1383-7*); 241p. lib. bdg. 30.64 (*0-7583-1377-2*); 193p. lib. bdg. 26.92 (*0-7583-1376-4*); 818p. lib. bdg. 85.54 (*0-7583-1382-9*); 665p. lib. bdg. 62.21 (*0-7583-1381-0*); 541p. lib. bdg. 52.95 (*0-7583-1380-2*); 330p. lib. bdg. 36.77 (*0-7583-1378-0*); 423p. lib. bdg. 44.12 (*0-7583-1379-9*) Huge Print Pr.

—A Little Princess. 2002. 196p. (gr. 4-7). 24.99 (*1-4043-1548-9*); per. 19.99 (*1-4043-1549-7*) IndyPublish.com.

—A Little Princess. l.t. ed. 1998. (Large Print Heritage Ser.). 324p. (YA). lib. bdg. 31.95 (*1-58118-021-7*, 21998) LRS.

—A Little Princess. (Signet Classics). 240p. 1995. (YA). mass mkt. 3.95 o.s.i (*0-451-52622-8*); 1990. (J). mass mkt. 3.95 o.s.i (*0-451-52509-4*) NAL. (Signet Classics).

—A Little Princess. 1998. (Illus.). 44p. pap. text 5.25 o.p. (*0-19-422875-4*) Oxford Univ. Pr., Inc.

—A Little Princess. Lindskoog, Kathryn, ed. 2002. (Classics for Young Readers Ser.). (Illus.). 208p. (J). pap. text 7.99 (*0-87552-727-2*) P&R Publishing.

—A Little Princess. (Puffin Classics Ser.). (gr. 4-7). 1995. (Illus.). 304p. (YA). pap. 4.99 (*0-14-036688-1*, Puffin Bks.); 1995. (Illus.). 288p. (J). 15.99 (*0-448-40949-6*, Grosset & Dunlap); 1989. (Illus.). 288p. (J). 13.95 o.p. (*0-448-09299-9*, Grosset & Dunlap); 1984. 224p. (J). pap. 3.50 o.p. (*0-14-035028-4*, Puffin Bks.) Penguin Putnam Bks. for Young Readers.

—A Little Princess. 1981. (Illus.). 288p. (J). (gr. 3-7). 7.95 o.p. (*0-448-40083-9*) Putnam Publishing Group, The.

—A Little Princess. 1975. 240p. (J). (gr. 3-7). pap. 1.25 o.s.i (*0-440-44767-4*, Yearling) Random Hse. Children's Bks.

—A Little Princess. 1990. (Children's Classics Ser.). (J). 12.99 o.s.i (*0-517-01480-7*) Random Hse. Value Publishing.

—A Little Princess. 1994. (Step into Classics Ser.). 112p. (J). (gr. 3-8). pap. 3.99 (*0-679-85090-2*) Random Hse., Inc.

—A Little Princess. (Courage Unabridged Classics Ser.). 1997. 224p. (YA). pap. 6.00 o.p. (*0-7624-0548-1*); 1996. 224p. (J). 5.98 o.p. (*1-56138-742-8*); 1997. 480p. (J). reprint ed. text 8.98 o.p. (*0-7624-0115-X*) Running Pr. Bk. Pubs. (Courage Bks.).

—A Little Princess. (Illus.). (J). text 22.95 (*0-590-24079-X*); 2000. (Illus.). 272p. (gr. 4-7). mass mkt. 3.99 (*0-439-10137-9*); 1995. 88p. (J). (gr. 3-7). mass mkt. 3.50 o.p. (*0-590-48628-4*); 1995. (Illus.). 256p. (J). (gr. 4-7). mass mkt. 3.99 (*0-590-54307-5*, Scholastic Paperbacks); 1987. 256p. (J). (gr. 4-6). mass mkt. 3.25 o.p. (*0-590-40719-8*, Scholastic Paperbacks) Scholastic, Inc.

—A Little Princess. deluxe ed. 1995. 48p. (J). (gr. 4-7). pap. 12.95 (*0-590-48627-6*) Scholastic, Inc.

—A Little Princess. l.t. ed. 2003. 342p. (J). 28.95 (*0-7862-5842-X*) Thorndike Pr.

—A Little Princess. abr. ed. 1997. (Children's Classics Ser.). (J). pap. 16.95 o.p. incl. audio (*1-85998-751-6*) Trafalgar Square.

—A Little Princess. unabr. ed. 1992. 11.00 (*0-606-16620-3*) Turtleback Bks.

—A Little Princess. Knoepflmacher, U. C., ed. & intro. by. 2002. (Classics Ser.). 272p. (J). 10.00 (*0-14-243701-8*, Penguin Classics) Viking Penguin.

—A Little Princess. 1997. (J). pap. 12.95 (*0-14-086079-7*, Puffin Bks.) Viking Penguin.

—A Little Princess. 1998. (Children's Classics). 192p. (J). (gr. 4-7). pap. 3.95 (*1-85326-136-X*, 136XWW) Wordsworth Editions, Ltd. GBR. *Dist:* Advanced Global Distribution Services.

—A Little Princess. Lindskoog, Kathryn, ed. & abr. by. 1993. (gr. 3 up). pap. 6.99 o.p. (*0-88070-527-2*) Zonderkidz.

—A Little Princess: Picture Book. 1995. (Illus.). 32p. (J). (gr. k-2). mass mkt. 2.95 (*0-590-55204-X*) Scholastic, Inc.

—A Little Princess & The Secret Garden. 2002. 480p. (J). (gr. 4-7). reprint ed. 9.00 o.p. (*0-7624-0564-3*) Running Pr. Bk. Pubs.

—A Little Princess Book & Charm. 1999. (Charming Classic Bks.). (Illus.). 336p. (J). (gr. 4 up). pap. 6.99 (*0-694-01236-X*, Harper Festival) HarperCollins Children's Bk. Group.

—The Secret Garden. 2002. (Great Illustrated Classics). (Illus.). 240p. (J). (gr. 3-8). lib. bdg. 21.35 (*1-57765-809-4*, ABDO & Daughters) ABDO Publishing Co.

—The Secret Garden. 1999. (Illus.). 288p. (J). pap. text 2.50 (*0-486-40784-5*) Dover Pubns., Inc.

—The Secret Garden. 2003. 288p. (J). mass mkt. 3.95 (*0-451-52883-2*, Signet Classics) NAL.

—The Secret Garden. 2003. (Illus.). (J). pap. 3.99 o.p. (*0-14-250099-2*, Puffin Bks.) Penguin Putnam Bks. for Young Readers.

—The Secret Garden. 2003. 288p. pap. 6.95 (*0-8129-6998-7*, Modern Library) Random House Adult Trade Publishing Group.

—The Secret Garden. 2002. (Illustrated Children's Library). (Illus.). 288p. (J). 16.99 (*0-517-22115-2*, Random Hse. Bks. for Young Readers) Random Hse. Children's Bks.

—The Secret Garden. 1996. pap. 12.00 o.s.i (*0-517-20019-8*) Random Hse. Value Publishing.

—The Secret Garden. 2002. (Illus.). 56p. (J). (ps up). text 9.98 (*0-7624-0572-4*) Running Pr. Bk. Pubs.

—The Secret Garden. 2002. (Classics Ser.). 288p. (J). pap. 7.00 (*0-14-243705-0*, Penguin Classics) Viking Penguin.

—The Secret Garden. 2000. (Books of Wonder). (Illus.). 352p. (J). (ps up). 21.95 (*0-688-14582-5*) HarperCollins Children's Bk. Group.

—The Secret Garden. ed. 2003. (gr. 1). spiral bd. (*0-616-14565-9*); (gr. 2). spiral bd. (*0-616-14566-7*) Canadian National Institute for the Blind/Institut National Canadien pour les Aveugles.

—The Secret Garden. abr. ed. 1996. (Ultimate Classics Ser.). (J). 19.95 o.p. (*0-7871-0745-X*); (gr. 4-7). 6.95 o.p. (*0-7871-0744-1*) NewStar Media, Inc.

—The Secret Garden. abr. ed. 1993. (J). 16.00 incl. audio (*0-453-00840-2*) Penguin/HighBridge.

—The Secret Garden. unabr. ed. 1990. (J). (gr. 3-5). pap. 17.00 incl. audio (*0-8072-1124-9*, Listening Library) Random Hse. Audio Publishing Group.

—The Secret Garden. abr. ed. 1993. (Step into Classics Ser.). (Illus.). 112p. (J). (gr. 3-8). pap. 3.99 (*0-679-84751-0*, Random Hse. Bks. for Young Readers) Random Hse. Children's Bks.

—The Secret Garden. abr. ed. 1997. (Children's Classics Ser.). (J). pap. 16.95 incl. audio (*1-85998-748-6*) Trafalgar Square.

—The Secret Garden: With a Discussion of Compassion. 2003. (Values in Action Illustrated Classics Ser.). (Illus.). 191p. (J). (*1-59203-037-8*) Learning Challenge, Inc.

—The Secret Garden; A Little Princess; Little Lord Fauntleroy. 1995. 576p. (J). 11.99 o.s.i (*0-517-14748-3*) Random Hse. Value Publishing.

—The Secret Garden Book Includes Charm. adapted ed. 1998. (Charming Classics Ser.). (Illus.). 368p. (J). (gr. 5 up). pap. 6.99 (*0-694-01110-X*) HarperCollins Pubs.

Burnett, Frances Hodgson & Burnett, Constance B. The Secret Garden. 1996. (Literary Classics Ser.). 272p. (J). text 5.98 o.p. (*1-56138-713-4*, Courage Bks.) Running Pr. Bk. Pubs.

Burnett, Frances Hodgson & Cockcroft, Jason. The Secret Garden. 2002. (Kingfisher Classics Ser.). (Illus.). 384p. (J). (*0-7534-0602-0*) Kingfisher Publications, plc.

Burnett, Frances Hodgson, et al. The Secret Garden. 2001. (Young Classics Ser.). (Illus.). 48p. (J). (gr. 1-3). pap. 9.95 (*0-7894-4943-9*, D K Ink) Dorling Kindersley Publishing, Inc.

Butler, Charles. Timon's Tide. 2000. (Illus.). 192p. (YA). (gr. 7-12). 16.00 (*0-689-82593-5*, McElderry, Margaret K.) Simon & Schuster Children's Publishing.

Byng, Georgia. Molly Moon's Incredible Book of Hypnotism. 2004. (Illus.). 400p. (J). pap. 6.99 (*0-06-051409-4*, Harper Trophy) HarperCollins Children's Bk. Group.

—Molly Moon's Incredible Book of Hypnotism. 2003. (Illus.). 384p. (J). (gr. 3-7). 16.99 (*0-06-051406-X*); (Illus.). 384p. (J). (gr. 3-7). lib. bdg. 17.89 (*0-06-051407-8*); 135.92 (*0-06-057217-5*) HarperCollins Pubs.

—Molly Moon's Incredible Book of Hypnotism. 2002. 330p. (J). (gr. 3-7). 24.95 (*0-333-98489-7*) Macmillan Children's Bks. GBR. *Dist:* Trans-Atlantic Pubns., Inc.

Cann, Kate. Diving In. 1997. (Livewire Ser.). 238p. (YA). (gr. 7-11). pap. 9.95 (*0-7043-4937-X*) Women's Pr., Ltd., The GBR. *Dist:* Trafalgar Square.

—Go! 2001. (Love Trilogy). 240p. (gr. 7 up). (YA). pap. 6.95 (*0-06-440868-X*, HarperTempest);Vol. 3. (J). lib. bdg. 15.89 (*0-06-028939-2*) HarperCollins Children's Bk. Group.

—Ready? 2001. (Love Trilogy). 256p. (YA). (gr. 9 up). pap. 6.95 (*0-06-440869-8*, HarperTempest);Vol. 1. (J). (gr. 7 up). lib. bdg. 15.89 (*0-06-028938-4*) HarperCollins Children's Bk. Group.

—Sex. 2001. 240p. (gr. 7 up). (Love Trilogy Ser.: Vol. 2). (J). lib. bdg. 15.89 (*0-06-028937-6*); (Love Trilogy). (YA). pap. 6.95 (*0-06-440870-1*, Harper-Tempest) HarperCollins Children's Bk. Group.

Canterbury Tales. 1999. (YA). 9.95 (*1-56137-919-0*); 11.95 (*1-56137-920-4*) Novel Units, Inc.

Carabetta, Natalie, illus. A Little Princess. 1996. (All Aboard Reading Ser.: Level 3). 48p. (J). (gr. 2-3). 13.99 o.s.i (*0-448-41329-9*, Grosset & Dunlap) Penguin Putnam Bks. for Young Readers.

—The Secret Garden. 1995. (All Aboard Reading Ser.). 48p. (J). (gr. 2-3). 10.99 o.p. (*0-448-40737-X*); (gr. 4-7). 3.99 (*0-448-40736-1*) Penguin Putnam Bks. for Young Readers. (Grosset & Dunlap).

Carter, Peter. Madatan. 1979. (Illus.). (J). (gr. 6 up). reprint ed. 7.95 o.p. (*0-19-271359-0*) Oxford Univ. Pr., Inc.

CH Classics: Secret Garden/Little Princess. 1995. (Illus.). 448p. (Orig.). (J). (gr. 3-5). 12.98 o.p. (*0-8317-1213-9*) Smithmark Pubs., Inc.

Cheaney, Janie B. The Playmaker. Siscoe, Nancy, ed. 2000. 320p. (J). (gr. 5-7). lib. bdg. 17.99 (*0-375-90577-4*, Knopf Bks. for Young Readers) Random Hse. Children's Bks.

Childs, Rob. Big Cup Collection Omnibus. 2003. (Illus.). 169p. (J). pap. (*0-552-54764-6*, Corgi) Bantam Bks.

Christie, Agatha. Nemesis. 1992. (J). 12.04 (*0-606-12448-9*) Turtleback Bks.

Christopher, John. The White Mountains. 2nd ed. 1988. (Tripods Trilogy Ser.: Vol. 2). (Illus.). 192p. (YA). (gr. 7 up). mass mkt. 4.99 (*0-02-042711-5*, Simon Pulse) Simon & Schuster Children's Publishing.

—The White Mountains: The Tripods Trilogy. l.t. ed. 1990. 256p. (J). (gr. 3 up). 16.95 (*0-7451-1043-6*, Macmillan Reference USA) Gale Group.

—The White Mountains: The Tripods Trilogy. 1967. 192p. (J). (gr. 4-7). 17.95 (*0-02-718360-2*, Simon & Schuster Children's Publishing) Simon & Schuster Children's Publishing.

—The White Mountains: The Tripods Trilogy. l.t. ed. 2000. (Science Fiction Ser.). 168p. 25.95 (*0-7838-9170-9*) Thorndike Pr.

—The White Mountains: The Tripods Trilogy. 1970. (J). 11.04 (*0-606-05083-3*) Turtleback Bks.

Clark, Walter V. The Ox-Bow Incident. 1943. 224p. (YA). (gr. 9-12). mass mkt. 3.95 o.p. (*0-451-52386-5*, CE1497, Signet Classics) NAL.

Clarke, Judith. Starry Nights. 2003. 152p. (J). 15.95 (*1-886910-82-0*, Front Street) Front Street, Inc.

Clymer, Eleanor. A Search for Two Bad Mice. 1980. (Illus.). 80p. (J). (gr. 2-5). 9.95 o.s.i (*0-689-30771-3*, Atheneum) Simon & Schuster Children's Publishing.

Coats, Lucy, et al. A Little Princess. 2001. (Young Classics Ser.). (Illus.). 48p. (J). (gr. 1-3). pap. 9.95 o.p. (*0-7894-6679-1*) Dorling Kindersley Publishing, Inc.

Cobb, Vicki. Lots of Rot. 1981. (Illus.). 40p. (J). (gr. 1-3). lib. bdg. 15.89 o.p. (*0-397-31939-8*) HarperCollins Children's Bk. Group.

Colfer, Eoin. The Arctic Incident. l.t. ed. 2003. (Artemis Fowl Ser.: Bk. 2). (J). (gr. 3-6). 16.95 (*0-7540-7839-6*, Galaxy Children's Large Print) BBC Audiobooks America.

—The Arctic Incident. (Artemis Fowl Ser.: Bk. 1). (J). (gr. 3-6). 2003. 304p. pap. 7.99 (*0-7868-1708-9*); 2002. 288p. 16.99 (*0-7868-0855-1*) Hyperion Bks. for Children.

—The Arctic Incident. l.t. ed. 2003. (Artemis Fowl Ser.: Bk. 2). 313p. (J). (gr. 3-6). 25.95 (*0-7862-4825-4*) Thorndike Pr.

—Artemis Fowl. 2002. (Artemis Fowl Ser.: Bk. 1). 288p. (J). (gr. 4-7). pap. 7.99 (*0-7868-1707-0*) Disney Pr.

—Artemis Fowl. l.t. ed. 2001. (Artemis Fowl Ser.: Bk. 1). 312p. (J). (gr. 3-6). 27.95 (*1-58724-092-0*, Wheeler Publishing, Inc.) Gale Group.

—Artemis Fowl. 2003. (Artemis Fowl Ser.: Bk. 1). (Illus.). 304p. (J). (gr. 3-6). mass mkt. 5.99 (*0-7868-1787-9*) Hyperion Bks. for Children.

—Artemis Fowl. 2001. (Artemis Fowl Ser.: Bk. 1). 288p. (gr. 4-7). 16.95 (*0-7868-0801-2*) Talk Miramax Bks.

—The Eternity Code. 2003. (Artemis Fowl Ser.: Bk. 3). 288p. (J). (gr. 3-6). 16.95 (*0-7868-1914-6*) Hyperion Bks. for Children.

Cooper, Susan. The Dark Is Rising. 244p. (YA). (gr. 5 up). pap. 4.99 (*0-8072-1533-3*, Listening Library) Random Hse. Audio Publishing Group.

Settings

Settings

—The Dark Is Rising. (Dark Is Rising Sequence Ser.). 1999. (Illus.). 232p. (J). (gr. 7 up). mass mkt. 4.99 (*0-689-82983-3*, Aladdin); 1999. pap. 2.99 (*0-689-82989-2*, Aladdin); 1976. (YA). (gr. 7 up). pap. 3.95 o.s.i (*0-689-70420-8*, Simon & Schuster Children's Publishing); 1973. (Illus.). 232p. (J). (gr. 5-9). 18.95 (*0-689-30317-3*, McElderry, Margaret K.); 1986. 232p. (J). (gr. 7 up). reprint ed. mass mkt. 4.99 (*0-689-71087-9*, Simon Pulse) Simon & Schuster Children's Publishing.

—The Dark Is Rising. l.t. ed. 2001. 395p. (J). (gr. 4-7). 21.95 (*0-7862-2920-9*) Thorndike Pr.

—The Dark Is Rising. (Dark Is Rising Sequence Ser.). 1986. (J). 11.04 (*0-606-00687-7*); 1973. 11.04 (*0-606-17313-7*) Turtleback Bks.

—The Dark Is Rising Sequence: Over Sea, under Stone; The Dark Is Rising; Greenwitch; The Grey King; Silver on the Tree, 5 bks. 2000. (J). (gr. 3-6). reprint ed. pap. 24.95 (*0-02-042565-1*, Simon Pulse) Simon & Schuster Children's Publishing.

—The Dark Is Rising Sequence Box Set, Set. 1987. (Dark Is Rising Sequence Ser.: 4 bks.). 874p. (YA). (gr. 6 up). reprint ed. pap. 15.75 (*0-689-71155-7*, Simon Pulse) Simon & Schuster Children's Publishing.

—Greenwitch. (Dark Is Rising Sequence Ser.). (J). 2000. 144p. (gr. 4-7). pap. 4.99 (*0-689-84034-9*, Aladdin); 1985. (Illus.). 148p. (gr. 4-7). 18.00 (*0-689-30426-9*, McElderry, Margaret K.); 1977. pap. 3.95 o.s.i (*0-689-70431-3*, Simon & Schuster Children's Publishing); 1986. 148p. (gr. 4-7). reprint ed. pap. 4.99 (*0-689-71088-7*, Simon Pulse) Simon & Schuster Children's Publishing.

—Greenwitch. l.t. ed. 2001. (Dark Is Rising Sequence Ser.). 131p. (J). 21.95 (*0-7862-2923-3*) Thorndike Pr.

—Greenwitch. (J). 2000. 11.04 (*0-606-19710-9*); 1974. 9.05 (*0-606-00700-8*) Turtleback Bks.

—The Grey King. 2002. 224p. (J). E-Book 6.99 (*0-689-84783-1*, McElderry, Margaret K.); 1999. (Dark Is Rising Sequence Ser.). (Illus.). 176p. (J). (gr. 4-7). pap. 4.99 (*0-689-82984-1*, Aladdin); 1978. (Dark Is Rising Sequence Ser.). (Illus.). (YA). (gr. 7 up). pap. 3.95 o.s.i (*0-689-70448-8*, Simon & Schuster Children's Publishing); 1975. (Grey King Ser.: Vol. 1). (Illus.). 224p. (J). 18.95 (*0-689-50029-7*, McElderry, Margaret K.); 1986. (Dark Is Rising Sequence Ser.). 224p. (YA). (gr. 4-7). reprint ed. mass mkt. 4.99 (*0-689-71089-5*, Simon Pulse); Vol. 1. 1999. (Dark Is Rising Sequence Ser.). 165p. (gr. 5-9). pap. 2.99 (*0-689-82988-4*, Aladdin) Simon & Schuster Children's Publishing.

—The Grey King. (Dark Is Rising Sequence Ser.). 1986. (J). 11.04 (*0-606-01150-1*); 1975. 11.04 (*0-606-17326-9*) Turtleback Bks.

—King of Shadows. (Illus.). 192p. (gr. 5-9). 2001. (J). pap. 4.99 (*0-689-84445-X*, Aladdin); 1999. (YA). 16.00 (*0-689-82817-9*, McElderry, Margaret K.) Simon & Schuster Children's Publishing.

—King of Shadows. l.t. ed. 2000. (Thorndike Press Large Print Juvenile Ser.). (Illus.). 246p. (J). (gr. 8-12). 21.95 (*0-7862-2706-0*) Thorndike Pr.

—Over Sea, under Stone. 1979. (Dark Is Rising Sequence Ser.). (Illus.). (J). (gr. 4-7). pap. 5.95 o.p. (*0-15-670542-7*, Voyager Bks./Libros Viajeros) Harcourt Children's Bks.

—Over Sea, under Stone. 2000. (Dark Is Rising Sequence Ser.). 208p. (J). (gr. 4-7). pap. 4.99 (*0-689-84035-7*, Aladdin) Simon & Schuster Children's Publishing.

—Over Sea, under Stone. 1989. (Dark Is Rising Sequence Ser.). (J). 11.04 (*0-606-04293-8*) Turtleback Bks.

—Over Sea, Under Stone. 1966. (Dark Is Rising Sequence Ser.). (Illus.). 252p. (J). (gr. 4-7). 18.00 (*0-15-259034-X*) Harcourt Children's Bks.

—Over Sea, under Stone. unabr. ed. 2001. (Dark Is Rising Ser.: Vol. 1). (YA). (gr. 4 up). audio 40.00 (*0-8072-0519-2*, Listening Library) Random Hse. Audio Publishing Group.

—Over Sea, under Stone. 1989. (Dark Is Rising Sequence Ser.). 256p. (J). (gr. 4-7). reprint ed. pap. 4.99 (*0-02-042785-9*, Simon Pulse) Simon & Schuster Children's Publishing.

—Over Sea, under Stone. l.t. ed. 2000. (Dark Is Rising Sequence Ser.). 332p. (J). (gr. 4-7). 22.95 (*0-7862-2918-7*) Thorndike Pr.

—Over Sea, under Stone: The Dark Is Rising Sequence. unabr. ed. 2001. (Dark Is Rising Ser.: Vol. 1). (YA). (gr. 4 up). audio 30.00 (*0-8072-0480-3*, Listening Library) Random Hse. Audio Publishing Group.

—Silver on the Tree. 1980. (Dark Is Rising Sequence Ser.). 256p. (J). (gr. 4-8). 4.95 o.s.i (*0-689-70467-4*, Simon Pulse) Simon & Schuster Children's Publishing.

Cooper, Susan & Houghton Mifflin Company Staff. The Dark Is Rising. 1992. (Literature Experience 1993 Ser.). (J). (gr. 8). pap., stu. ed. 11.04 (*0-395-61880-0*) Houghton Mifflin Co.

Copping, Harold & Dickens, Charles. Children's Stories from Dickens. 1993. (Illus.). 128p. (J). 5.99 o.s.i (*0-517-08485-6*) Random Hse. Value Publishing.

Cowan, Andrew. Pig. 1997. 224p. pap. 12.00 o.s.i (*0-15-600545-X*, Harvest Bks.) Harcourt Trade Pubs.

Creech, Sharon. Pleasing the Ghost, 2000. (J). (gr. 3 up). pap., stu. ed. 25.20 incl. audio (*0-7887-3852-6*, 41050X4) Recorded Bks., LLC.

Cross, Gillian. Pictures in the Dark. 1996. 208p. (J). (gr. 7-12). 16.95 (*0-8234-1267-9*) Holiday Hse., Inc.

—Pictures in the Dark. 1998. 208p. (J). (gr. 5-9). pap. 5.99 o.s.i (*0-14-038958-X*) Penguin Putnam Bks. for Young Readers.

—Pictures in the Dark. 1998. 10.09 (*0-606-13703-3*) Turtleback Bks.

—Tightrope. 2001. (Harper Trophy Bks.). 304p. (J). (gr. 7 up). pap. 5.95 (*0-06-447272-8*, Harper Trophy) HarperCollins Children's Bk. Group.

—Tightrope. 1999. 208p. (YA). (gr. 7-12). 16.95 (*0-8234-1512-0*) Holiday Hse., Inc.

—Tightrope. 1999. 210p. (YA). (*0-19-271804-5*) Oxford Univ. Pr., Inc.

Cubbage, Jenny. Close Encounters with an English Mind. 1986. (Illus.). 64p. (Orig.). (J). (gr. 5-12). pap. 6.95 o.p. (*0-913853-05-4*, 115-065, Upstart Bks.) Highsmith Inc.

Cunliffe, John. Postman Pat: Paints & Ceiling Books. 1997. (Postman Pat Ser.: Vol. 7). (J). 12.95 incl. audio (*1-85998-914-4*) Hodder Headline Audiobooks GBR. *Dist:* Trafalgar Square.

—Postman Pat & the Beast of Greendale. 1997. (Postman Pat Ser.: Vol. 12). (J). text 12.95 incl. audio (*1-85998-919-5*) Hodder Headline Audiobooks GBR. *Dist:* Trafalgar Square.

—Postman Pat & the Mystery Tour, Bk. 13. (Illus.). 32p. (J). text 17.95 o.p. (*0-340-67817-8*) Hodder & Stoughton, Ltd. GBR. *Dist:* Lubrecht & Cramer, Ltd., Trafalgar Square.

—Postman Pat Has Too Many Parcels. (Illus.). 32p. (J). text 17.95 (*0-340-67812-7*) Hodder & Stoughton, Ltd. GBR. *Dist:* Lubrecht & Cramer, Ltd., Trafalgar Square.

—Postman Pat Has Too Many Parcels. 1997. (Postman Pat Ser.: Vol. 8). 12.95 incl. audio (*1-85998-915-2*) Hodder Headline Audiobooks GBR. *Dist:* Trafalgar Square.

Cushman, Karen. Catherine, Called Birdy. 2002. (Illus.). (J). 15.00 (*0-7587-0246-9*) Book Wholesalers, Inc.

—Catherine, Called Birdy. 1995. 224p. (J). (gr. 7 up). pap. 6.50 (*0-06-440584-2*, Harper Trophy) HarperCollins Children's Bk. Group.

—Catherine, Called Birdy. 1995. (YA). (gr. 6 up). pap. 3.95 o.p. (*0-06-449683-X*) HarperCollins Pubs.

—Catherine, Called Birdy. 1994. 176p. (YA). (gr. 7 up). tchr. ed. 16.00 (*0-395-68186-3*, Clarion Bks.) Houghton Mifflin Co. Trade & Reference Div.

—Catherine, Called Birdy. 1995. (YA). (gr. 6 up). 12.00 (*0-606-07355-8*) Turtleback Bks.

—Catherine, Called Birdy: And The Midwife's Apprentice. 1999. (YA). (gr. 3-7). pap. text 7.50 o.p. (*0-06-449365-2*) HarperCollins Pubs.

—Matilda Bone. 2002. 13.94 (*1-4046-1906-2*) Book Wholesalers, Inc.

—Matilda Bone. 2000. (Illus.). 167p. (YA). (gr. 5-9). tchr. ed. 15.00 (*0-395-88156-0*, Clarion Bks.) Houghton Mifflin Co. Trade & Reference Div.

—Matilda Bone. unabr. ed. 2000. (J). (gr. 4-8). audio 30.00 (*0-8072-8737-7*, YA252CX, Listening Library) Random Hse. Audio Publishing Group.

—Matilda Bone. 2002. 176p. (J). (gr. 5-7). reprint ed. pap. 5.50 (*0-440-41822-4*, Yearling) Random Hse. Children's Bks.

—Matilda Bone. l.t. ed. 2001. (Young Adult Ser.). 184p. (J). (gr. 8-12). 23.95 (*0-7862-3212-9*) Thorndike Pr.

Cusick, Richie Tankersley. Silent Stalker. MacDonald, Patricia, ed. 1993. 224p. (YA). (gr. 7 up). mass mkt. 3.99 (*0-671-79402-7*, Simon Pulse) Simon & Schuster Children's Publishing.

—Silent Stalker. 1993. 9.09 o.p. (*0-606-05601-7*) Turtleback Bks.

Dahl, Roald. The Witches. 2002. (J). pap. 29.95 incl. audio (*0-7540-6247-3*) BBC Audiobooks America.

—The Witches. 1999. (gr. 3-7). pap. 13.55 (*0-8085-7491-4*) Econo-Clad Bks.

—The Witches, RS. 1983. (Illus.). 208p. (J). (gr. 3-7). 17.00 (*0-374-38457-6*); 35.00 o.p. (*0-374-38458-4*) Farrar, Straus & Giroux. (Farrar, Straus & Giroux (BYR)).

—The Witches. (Illus.). (J). 1999. 200p. (gr. 3-7). pap. 3.95 (*0-14-031730-9*, Viking Children's Bks.); 1998. 208p. (gr. 3-7). pap. 5.99 (*0-14-130110-4*, Puffin Bks.); 1989. 208p. pap. 4.99 o.s.i (*0-14-034020-3*, Puffin Bks.) Penguin Putnam Bks. for Young Readers.

—The Witches. 1985. (J). 11.04 (*0-606-00540-4*) Turtleback Bks.

Daniels, Lucy. Goat in the Garden. 1996. (Animal Ark Ser.: No. 4). (Illus.). 160p. (J). (gr. 3-5). pap. 3.95 o.p. (*0-8120-9662-2*) Barron's Educational Series, Inc.

—Pony on the Porch. 1996. (Animal Ark Ser.: No. 2). (Illus.). 160p. (J). (gr. 3-5). pap. 3.95 o.p. (*0-8120-9664-9*) Barron's Educational Series, Inc.

Davoll, Barbara. To London to See the Queen. 1999. (New Christopher Churchmouse Adventures Ser.: Vol. 4). (Illus.). 24p. (J). (ps-3). 9.99 (*0-8024-5399-6*) Moody Pr.

De Angeli, Marguerite. The Door in the Wall. 1996. (J). pap. 4.99 (*0-440-91164-8*, Dell Books for Young Readers); 1998. (Illus.). 128p. (YA). (gr. 5-9). reprint ed. mass mkt. 4.99 (*0-440-22779-8*, Laurel Leaf) Random Hse. Children's Bks.

—The Door in the Wall. 1984. (J). mass mkt. 2.50 o.p. (*0-590-40968-9*) Scholastic, Inc.

—The Door in the Wall. 1995. (J). (gr. 3-6). 20.25 (*0-8446-6834-6*) Smith, Peter Pub., Inc.

—The Door in the Wall. 1998. 11.04 (*0-606-13344-5*); 1977. (J). 11.04 (*0-606-03234-7*) Turtleback Bks.

—The Door in the Wall: Story of Medieval London. 1990. (Yearling Newbery Ser.). (Illus.). 128p. (J). (gr. 5-9). reprint ed. pap. text 5.50 (*0-440-40283-2*) Dell Publishing.

—The Door in the Wall: Story of Medieval London. 1989. (Illus.). 128p. (gr. 4-7). text 16.95 (*0-385-07283-X*) Doubleday Publishing.

Dean, Jan. Finders. 1995. 176p. (J). (gr. 4-7). per. 15.00 (*0-689-50612-0*, McElderry, Margaret K.) Simon & Schuster Children's Publishing.

Delton, Judy. Royal Escapade. 1996. (Lottery Luck Ser.: Bk. 7). (Illus.). 96p. (J). (gr. 2-5). pap. 5.95 (*0-7868-1024-6*) Hyperion Paperbacks for Children.

Dennard, Deborah. Hedgehog Haven: The Story of an English Hedgerow Community. 2001. (Wild Habitats Ser.). (Illus.). 36p. 19.95 incl. audio (*1-56899-989-5*); 36p. (J). (gr. 1-4). 15.95 (*1-56899-987-9*); 36p. (J). (gr. 1-4). 26.95 (*1-56899-991-7*); 27p. (J). (gr. 1-4). pap. 5.95 (*1-56899-988-7*); 36p. (J). (gr. 1-4). pap. 16.95 (*1-56899-992-5*) Soundprints.

Dent, Grace. It's a Girl Thing. 2003. 192p. (YA). 15.99 (*0-399-24187-6*, G. P. Putnam's Sons) Penguin Putnam Bks. for Young Readers.

Derwent, Lavinia. Tale of Greyfriar's Bobby. 1986. (Illus.). 80p. (J). (gr. 3-6). pap. 7.95 (*0-14-031181-5*) Penguin Bks., Ltd. GBR. *Dist:* Trafalgar Square.

Dhondy, Farrukh. Black Swan. 1993. 208p. (YA). (gr. 6 up). 14.95 o.p. (*0-395-66076-9*) Houghton Mifflin Co.

Dickens, Charles. The Baron of Grogzwig. Greenway, Shirley, ed. 1993. (Illus.). 32p. (J). (gr. 4-7). 14.95 o.p. (*1-879085-81-X*, Whispering Coyote) Charlesbridge Publishing, Inc.

—Children's Classics: A Christmas Carol & Other Christmas Stories. 1990. (J). 12.99 o.s.i (*0-517-64126-7*) Random Hse. Value Publishing.

—A Christmas Carol. 1963. (YA). (gr. 7 up). mass mkt. 2.25 (*0-8049-0026-4*, CL-26) Airmont Publishing Co., Inc.

—A Christmas Carol. 1985. (Illus.). 80p. (J). (ps up). 1.50 o.p. (*0-8120-5705-8*) Barron's Educational Series, Inc.

—A Christmas Carol. 1990. (YA). (gr. 1-12). 3.75 o.s.i (*0-425-12334-0*, Classics Illustrated) Berkley Publishing Group.

—A Christmas Carol. 1993. (Illus.). 48p. (J). (ps-3). 15.95 o.p. (*1-56402-204-8*) Candlewick Pr.

—A Christmas Carol. (Illus.). (YA). 1990. 152p. (gr. 1 up). lib. bdg. 46.65 (*0-88682-327-7*, 97200-098, Creative Editions); 1984. 78p. (gr. 4 up). lib. bdg. 13.95 o.p. (*0-87191-955-9*, Creative Education) Creative Co., The.

—A Christmas Carol. 1990. (Classics Ser.). (Illus.). 128p. (YA). (gr. 2-12). mass mkt. 2.99 (*0-8125-0434-8*, Tor Classics) Doherty, Tom Assocs., LLC.

—A Christmas Carol. 1996. (Illus.). 152p. (J). lib. bdg. 35.00 (*0-15-100200-2*, Red Wagon Bks.) Harcourt Children's Bks.

—A Christmas Carol. 2001. (Illus.). 80p. (J). (gr. 1-5). 17.95 (*0-06-028577-X*); (gr. 2-5). lib. bdg. 17.89 (*0-06-028578-8*) HarperCollins Children's Bk. Group.

—A Christmas Carol. 1983. (Illus.). 128p. (J). (gr. 2-12). tchr. ed. 18.95 (*0-8234-0486-2*) Holiday Hse., Inc.

—A Christmas Carol. 1992. (J). pap. 10.95 o.p. (*0-395-60726-4*) Houghton Mifflin Co.

—A Christmas Carol. 1987. (Illus.). 88p. (J). 6.95 o.p. (*0-89783-046-6*) Larlin Corp.

—A Christmas Carol. 1985. (J). audio 4.95 (*0-913675-40-7*) McGraw-Hill Cos., The.

—A Christmas Carol. 1996. (Books of Wonder). (Illus.). 64p. (J). (gr. 4-7). 18.00 (*0-688-13606-0*, Morrow, William & Co.) Morrow/Avon.

—A Christmas Carol. 1997. 128p. pap. 2.95 (*0-89375-356-4*) NAL.

—A Christmas Carol. 1990. (Illus.). 48p. (YA). (gr. 7-12). 14.95 (*0-88289-812-4*) Pelican Publishing Co., Inc.

—A Christmas Carol. Fagan, Tom, ed. 1978. (Now Age Illustrated IV Ser.). (Illus.). (gr. 4-12). (J). stu. ed. 1.25 (*0-88301-337-1*); (J). pap. text 2.95 (*0-88301-313-4*); (YA). text 7.50 o.p. (*0-88301-325-8*) Pendulum Pr., Inc.

—A Christmas Carol. (Classic Ser.). (Illus.). 56p. (J). 1996. (gr. 2-4). 2.99 o.s.i (*0-7214-5677-4*); 1994. text 3.50 (*0-7214-1729-9*) Penguin Group (USA) Inc. (Ladybird Bks.).

—A Christmas Carol. (Whole Story Ser.). 2000. (Illus.). 112p. (YA). (gr. 7-12). pap. 17.99 (*0-670-88879-6*, Viking Children's Bks.); 1995. (Illus.). 144p. (YA). (gr. 5 up). pap. 3.99 o.p. (*0-14-036723-3*, Puffin Bks.); 1984. 112p. (J). (gr. 7). pap. 2.99 o.p. (*0-14-035027-6*, Puffin Bks.); 1983. (Illus.). 128p. (J). (gr. 6). 12.95 o.p. (*0-8037-0032-6*, Dial Bks. for Young Readers) Penguin Putnam Bks. for Young Readers.

—A Christmas Carol. 1965. 96p. (J). (gr. 6 up). 6.95 o.p. (*0-88088-125-9*) Peter Pauper Pr. Inc.

—A Christmas Carol. 1997. (Illus.). 144p. (gr. 4-7). pap. text 3.99 (*0-440-41421-0*, Dell Books for Young Readers) Random Hse. Children's Bks.

—A Christmas Carol. 1993. (Christmas Treasury Pop-Up Ser.). (J). 4.99 o.s.i (*0-517-08787-1*) Random Hse. Value Publishing.

—A Christmas Carol. (Everyman's Library Children's Classics Ser.). (Illus.). (gr. 2-12). 1994. 180p. 13.95 (*0-679-43639-1*); 1984. (J). 4.99 o.s.i (*0-517-23159-X*) Random Hse., Inc.

—A Christmas Carol. 1996. (Illus.). 128p. (J). (gr. 4-7). text 4.95 (*0-7624-0831-6*) Running Pr. Bk. Pubs.

—A Christmas Carol. (J). (gr. 4-7). 2000. (Illus.). 144p. mass mkt. 2.99 (*0-439-10133-6*); 1987. (Illus.). 128p. pap. 3.50 (*0-590-43527-2*, Scholastic Paperbacks); 1986. pap. 1.95 o.p. (*0-590-02102-8*) Scholastic, Inc.

—A Christmas Carol. 1983. (Illus.). 240p. mass mkt. 3.99 (*0-671-47369-7*, Pocket) Simon & Schuster.

—A Christmas Carol. (Illus.). (J). 1995. 144p. mass mkt. 19.95 o.s.i (*0-689-80213-7*, McElderry, Margaret K.); 1995. 68p. 19.95 (*0-88708-069-3*, Simon & Schuster Children's Publishing); 1983. 128p. pap. 16.00 o.p. (*0-671-45599-0*, Simon & Schuster Children's Publishing) Simon & Schuster Children's Publishing.

—A Christmas Carol. (Children's Classics Ser.). (J). 1998. audio 10.95 o.p. (*1-55935-212-4*); 1972. pap. 5.95 o.p. incl. audio (*0-88142-364-5*, 364) Soundelux Audio Publishing.

—A Christmas Carol. (Illus.). 1997. 164p. 19.95 (*1-55670-648-0*); 1990. 152p. (J). 30.00 o.p. (*1-55670-161-6*) Stewart, Tabori & Chang.

—A Christmas Carol. 1997. 10.04 (*0-606-13273-2*) Turtleback Bks.

—A Christmas Carol. (Through the Magic Window Ser.). (Illus.). (J). (ps-2). 1991. 48p. 6.95 o.p. (*0-88101-160-6*); 1990. 11.95 o.p. (*0-88101-108-8*) Unicorn Publishing Hse., Inc., The.

—A Christmas Carol. 1998. (Children's Classics). (Illus.). 96p. (YA). (ps up). pap. 3.95 (*1-85326-121-1*, 1211WW) Wordsworth Editions, Ltd. GBR. *Dist:* Advanced Global Distribution Services.

—A Christmas Carol. 1995. (Illus.). 4p. (J). cd-rom 17.95 (*0-7611-0036-9*, 10036) Workman Publishing Co., Inc.

—A Christmas Carol. 1986. (Illus.). 48p. (J). (ps up). lib. bdg. 16.95 o.s.i (*0-02-730310-1*, Simon & Schuster Children's Publishing) Simon & Schuster Children's Publishing.

—A Christmas Carol, Set. unabr. ed. 1984. (J). audio 20.95 (*1-55685-048-4*) Audio Bk. Contractors, Inc.

—A Christmas Carol. unabr. ed. (J). audio 16.95 (*1-55686-138-9*, 138) Books in Motion.

—A Christmas Carol. unabr. collector's ed. 1979. (J). audio 18.00 (*0-7366-0953-9*, 1897) Books on Tape, Inc.

—A Christmas Carol. reprint ed. 1981. (Illus.). 191p. (YA). lib. bdg. 15.95 (*0-89966-344-3*); 1980. 150p. (J). lib. bdg. 15.95 (*0-89967-017-2*, Harmony Raine & Co.) Buccaneer Bks., Inc.

—A Christmas Carol. 1996. (Illus.). 48p. (J). (gr. 3-7). reprint ed. bds. 6.99 o.p. (*1-56402-977-8*) Candlewick Pr.

—A Christmas Carol. abr. ed. (J). 1992. audio 4.99 (*0-88646-654-7*); 1986. (gr. 5-7). audio 29.95 o.p. (*0-88646-798-5*, R 7051) Durkin Hayes Publishing Ltd.

—A Christmas Carol. 2nd ed. 1998. (Illustrated Classic Book Ser.: Vol. III). (Illus.). 61p. (J). reprint ed. pap. text 4.95 (*1-56767-241-8*) Educational Insights, Inc.

—A Christmas Carol. abr. ed. 1980. (J). audio 8.98 o.p. (*0-89845-103-5*, CP 1657, Caedmon) HarperTrade.

—A Christmas Carol. 2nd ed. 1993. (Illus.). 78p. pap. text 5.95 (*0-19-585258-3*) Oxford Univ. Pr., Inc.

—A Christmas Carol. abr. ed. 1988. (Illus.). (gr. 4-7). audio 9.99 (*0-553-45146-4*, RH Audio) Random Hse. Audio Publishing Group.

—A Christmas Carol, unabr. ed. 1981. (J). (gr. 6 up). audio 18.00 (*1-55690-101-1*, 80200E7) Recorded Bks., LLC.

—A Christmas Carol. 1987. (Illus.). 128p. (J). (gr. 4-6). reprint ed. pap. 2.50 o.p. (*0-590-41293-0*, Scholastic Paperbacks) Scholastic, Inc.

—A Christmas Carol. abr. ed. 1997. (J). audio 14.95 o.p. (*1-85998-304-9*) Trafalgar Square.

—A Christmas Carol. Wendt, Michael & Pizar, Kathleen, eds. abr. ed. 1988. (Little Unicorn Classic Ser.). (Illus.). 80p. (J). (gr. 2-5). 5.95 o.p. (*0-88101-087-1*) Unicorn Publishing Hse., Inc., The.

—A Christmas Carol. abr. ed. 1995. 2p. pap. 16.95 incl. audio (*0-14-086178-5*, Penguin AudioBooks) Viking Penguin.

—A Christmas Carol: A Changing Picture & Lift-the-Flap Book. 1989. (Illus.). 320p. (J). (ps-3). 14.95 o.p. (*0-670-82694-4*, Viking Children's Bks.) Penguin Putnam Bks. for Young Readers.

—A Christmas Carol: A Young Reader's Edition of the Classic Holiday Tale. 2002. (Illus.). 56p. (J). (gr. 4-7). text 9.98 (*0-7624-0848-0*) Running Pr. Bk. Pubs.

—A Christmas Carol: Charles Dickens' Tale. 1997. (Eyewitness Classics Ser.). (Illus.). 64p. (J). (gr. 3-6). pap. 14.95 (*0-7894-2070-8*, D K Ink) Dorling Kindersley Publishing, Inc.

—A Christmas Carol & Other Christmas Stories. 1984. (Signet Classics). (Illus.). 224p. (YA). mass mkt. 3.95 (*0-451-52283-4*, Signet Classics) NAL.

—A Christmas Carol & Other Christmas Stories. 1984. (Signet Classics Ser.). 10.00 (*0-606-04893-6*) Turtleback Bks.

—A Christmas Carol & The Cricket on the Hearth. 1973. (Dent's Illustrated Children's Classics Ser.). (Illus.). 220p. (J). reprint ed. 9.00 o.p. (*0-460-05059-1*) Biblio Distribution.

—A Christmas Carol Book & Charm. 2002. (Charming Classics Ser.). 160p. (J). (ps-2). 6.99 (*0-694-01583-0*) HarperCollins Children's Bk. Group.

—David Copperfield. 1965. (Classics Ser.). (YA). (gr. 9 up). mass mkt. 3.95 o.p. (*0-8049-0065-5*) Airmont Publishing Co., Inc.

—David Copperfield. 2000. (SPA., Illus.). (J). pap. 7.95 (*84-406-8898-9*) B Ediciones S.A. ESP. *Dist:* Distribooks, Inc.

—David Copperfield. 1981. 832p. (gr. 7 up). mass mkt. 5.99 (*0-553-21189-7*, Bantam Classics) Bantam Bks.

—David Copperfield. 1985. (Barron's Book Notes Ser.). (YA). (gr. 10-12). pap. 3.95 (*0-8120-3509-7*) Barron's Educational Series, Inc.

—David Copperfield. 2002. (Classics for Young Readers Ser.). (SPA.). (YA). 14.95 (*84-392-0933-9*, EV30653) Gaviota Ediciones ESP. *Dist:* Lectorum Pubns., Inc.

—David Copperfield, 001. Ford, G. H., ed. 1958. (YA). (gr. 7 up). pap. 13.16 o.p. (*0-395-05122-3*, Riverside Editions) Houghton Mifflin Co.

—David Copperfield. 1962. (Signet Classics). 880p. (J). (gr. 7). mass mkt. 5.95 (*0-451-52292-3*, Signet Classics) NAL.

—David Copperfield. abr. ed. 1995. (Illus.). 64p. (J). (gr. 3-7). 18.95 o.p. (*1-55858-453-6*) North-South Bks., Inc.

—David Copperfield. Vogel, Malvina, ed. 1992. (Great Illustrated Classics Ser.: Vol. 23). (Illus.). 240p. (J). (gr. 3-7). 9.95 (*0-86611-974-4*) Playmore, Inc., Pubs.

—David Copperfield. 2002. (SPA.). (J). 6.95 (*84-243-0468-3*) Publicaciones Fher, S.A. ESP. *Dist:* AIMS International Bks., Inc.

—David Copperfield. 1997. (Penguin Classics Ser.). (Illus.). 896p. pap. 7.95 (*0-14-043494-1*, Penguin Classics) Viking Penguin.

—Great Expectations. 1997. (Classics Illustrated Study Guides). (Illus.). 64p. (YA). (gr. 7 up). mass mkt., stu. ed. 4.99 o.p. (*1-57840-011-2*) Acclaim Bks.

—Great Expectations. Seward, Tim, ed. 1995. (Literature Ser.). (Illus.). 512p. (gr. 9 up). pap. text 11.95 o.p. (*0-521-48472-3*) Cambridge Univ. Pr.

—Great Expectations. (Classics Illustrated Ser.). (Illus.). 52p. (YA). pap. 4.95 (*1-57209-001-4*) Classics International Entertainment, Inc.

—Great Expectations. Klischer, Beth, ed. rev. ed. 1989. (Literature for Christian Schools Ser.). (Illus.). 610p. (YA). (gr. 10 up). pap. 11.06 (*0-89084-504-2*, 046516) Jones, Bob Univ. Pr.

—Great Expectations. abr. ed. 1950. (Bridge Ser.). (Illus.). 172p. (YA). pap. text 4.46 o.p. (*0-582-53003-2*) Longman Publishing Group.

—Great Expectations. 1961. 536p. (YA). (gr. 9). mass mkt. 4.95 o.s.i (*0-451-52524-8*, Signet Classics) NAL.

—Great Expectations. 1979. (Now Age Illustrated V Ser.). (Illus.). 64p. (J). (gr. 4-12). 1.25 (*0-88301-412-2*); text 7.50 o.p. (*0-88301-400-9*); pap. text 2.95 (*0-88301-388-6*) Pendulum Pr., Inc.

—Great Expectations. (Classics for Young Readers Ser.). 1992. 464p. (J). (gr. 5 up). pap. 3.50 o.p. (*0-14-035130-2*); 1995. (Illus.). 432p. (YA). (gr. 4-7). pap. 4.99 (*0-14-036681-4*) Penguin Putnam Bks. for Young Readers. (Puffin Bks.).

—Great Expectations. Vogel, Malvina, ed. 1992. (Great Illustrated Classics Ser.: Vol. 21). (Illus.). 240p. (J). (gr. 3-6). 9.95 (*0-86611-972-8*) Playmore, Inc., Pubs.

—Great Expectations. (Short Classics Ser.). (Illus.). 48p. (J). (gr. 4 up). 1989. lib. bdg. 22.83 o.p. (*0-8172-2762-8*); 1988. pap. 9.27 o.p. (*0-8172-2766-0*) Raintree Pubs.

—Great Expectations. 1992. (Literary Classics Ser.). 536p. (J). text 8.98 o.p. (*1-56138-170-5*, Courage Bks.) Running Pr. Bk. Pubs.

—Great Expectations. 2003. (Scholastic Classics Ser.). (Illus.). 40p. (YA). mass mkt. 4.99 (*0-439-29128-3*, Scholastic Paperbacks) Scholastic, Inc.

—Great Expectations. (Saddleback Classics). 1999. (Illus.). (J). 13.10 (*0-606-21552-2*); 1981. 11.00 (*0-606-13450-6*) Turtleback Bks.

—A Tale of Two Cities. 1995. (Fiction Ser.). (YA). pap. text 7.88 o.p. (*0-582-08466-0*, 79830) Longman Publishing Group.

—Whole Story Christmas Carol. 2000. (Whole Story Ser.). (Illus.). 112p. (YA). (gr. 7-12). 25.99 o.s.i (*0-670-88878-8*, Viking Children's Bks.) Penguin Putnam Bks. for Young Readers.

Dickens, Charles & Skarmeas, Nancy J. A Christmas Carol. abr. ed. 1998. (Illus.). 48p. (J). (gr. 4-7). 14.00 (*0-8249-4096-2*, Candy Cane Pr.) Ideals Pubns.

Dickens, Charles & Sweaney, A. A Christmas Carol: Retold by A. Sweaney. 1976. (Oxford Progressive English Readers Ser.). (J). (gr. k-6). pap. text 4.95 o.p. (*0-19-580724-3*) Oxford Univ. Pr., Inc.

Dickens, Charles & Wheatcroft, Andrew. A Christmas Carol. (Classics Ser.). (Illus.). 64p. (J). 2001. pap. 9.99 (*0-7894-6246-X*, D K Ink); 2000. pap. incl. cd-rom (*0-7894-6363-6*) Dorling Kindersley Publishing, Inc.

Dickens, Charles, et al. A Christmas Carol. unabr. ed. 1994. (J). audio 11.00 o.s.i (*0-89845-755-6*, CPN 1135, Caedmon) HarperTrade.

Dickinson, Peter. Chuck & Danielle. 2000. (J). audio 18.00 (*0-7366-4969-7*) Books on Tape, Inc.

—Chuck & Danielle. 1996. 20.95 (*0-385-31720-4*) Doubleday Publishing.

—Chuck & Danielle. 115p. (J). (gr. 3-5). pap. 3.99 (*0-8072-1504-X*, Listening Library) Random Hse. Audio Publishing Group.

—Chuck & Danielle. (Illus.). 2001. 128p. (gr. 4-7). pap. text 12.00 (*0-375-89505-1*, Random Hse. Bks. for Young Readers); 1996. 96p. (YA). (gr. 5 up). 14.95 o.s.i (*0-385-32188-0*, Yearling) Random Hse. Children's Bks.

—Chuck & Danielle. 1997. (J). 9.09 o.p. (*0-606-11206-5*) Turtleback Bks.

Dickinson, Peter, ed. Chuck & Danielle, Set. unabr. ed. 1997. (J). (gr. 8 up). 21.98 incl. audio (*0-8072-7835-1*, YA929SP, Listening Library) Random Hse. Audio Publishing Group.

Dickinson, Peter & De Kiefte, Kees. Chuck & Danielle. 1997. (Illus.). 128p. pap. text 3.99 o.s.i (*0-440-41087-8*, Yearling) Random Hse. Children's Bks.

Dixon, Andy. Los Caballeros del Rey Arturo. 2001. (SPA., Illus.). 32p. (YA). (gr. 3 up). pap. 8.95 (*0-7460-3896-8*); lib. bdg. 16.95 (*1-58086-318-3*) EDC Publishing. (Usborne).

Doherty, Berlie. Granny Was a Buffer Girl. 1993. (Illus.). 144p. (YA). (gr. 8 up). reprint ed. pap. 3.95 o.p. (*0-688-11863-1*, Morrow, William & Co.) Morrow/Avon.

—Holly Starcross. 2002. 192p. (J). (gr. 7 up). 15.99 (*0-06-001341-9*); 17.89 (*0-06-001342-7*) HarperCollins Children's Bk. Group. (Greenwillow Bks.).

Doherty, Bertie. White Peak Farm. 1993. 112p. (YA). (gr. 8 up). pap. 3.95 o.p. (*0-688-11864-X*, Morrow, William & Co.) Morrow/Avon.

Doyle, Arthur Conan. The Adventures of Sherlock Holmes. 1986. 304p. (YA). (gr. 4-7). mass mkt. 4.99 (*0-425-09838-9*) Berkley Publishing Group.

—The Adventures of Sherlock Holmes. 1994. 144p. (J). 12.98 o.p. (*0-86112-972-5*) Brimax Bks., Ltd.

—The Adventures of Sherlock Holmes. 1989. (Illus.). 259p. (YA). (gr. 7-12). mass mkt. 4.99 (*0-8125-0424-0*, Tor Classics) Doherty, Tom Assocs., LLC.

—The Adventures of Sherlock Holmes. 1992. (Books of Wonder: Vol. 1). (Illus.). 352p. (J). (gr. 2 up). 24.99 (*0-688-10782-6*) HarperCollins Children's Bk. Group.

—The Adventures of Sherlock Holmes. 1998. (Wordsworth Classics Ser.). (YA). (gr. 6-12). 5.27 (*0-89061-033-9*, R0339WW) Jamestown.

—The Adventures of Sherlock Holmes. 1981. (Illus.). (J). (gr. 4-7). Book 1. 140p. pap. 3.50 o.p. (*0-380-78089-5*); Book 2. 156p. pap. 2.95 (*0-380-78097-6*); Book 3. 112p. pap. 2.95 (*0-380-78105-0*); Book 4. 112p. pap. 3.50 (*0-380-78113-1*) Morrow/Avon. (Avon Bks.).

—The Adventures of Sherlock Holmes. abr. ed. 1998. 2p. audio 16.95 o.p. (*0-14-086600-0*, Penguin AudioBooks) Viking Penguin.

—The Hound of the Baskervilles. 1965. (Airmont Classics Ser.). (J). (gr. 8 up). mass mkt. 2.50 (*0-8049-0062-0*, CL-62) Airmont Publishing Co., Inc.

—The Hound of the Baskervilles. 1996. (Andre Deutsch Classics). 204p. (J). (gr. 5-8). 11.95 (*0-233-99035-6*) Andre Deutsch GBR. *Dist:* Trafalgar Square, Trans-Atlantic Pubns., Inc.

—The Hound of the Baskervilles. 1987. 176p. (J). (gr. 10 up). mass mkt. 4.99 (*0-425-10405-2*) Berkley Publishing Group.

—The Hound of the Baskervilles. 1994. 208p. (YA). (gr. 5 up). pap. 2.99 (*0-87406-698-0*) Darby Creek Publishing.

—The Hound of the Baskervilles. unabr. ed. 1994. (Thrift Editions Ser.). 128p. (J). pap. 1.50 (*0-486-28214-7*) Dover Pubns., Inc.

—The Hound of the Baskervilles. 2002. (YA). (gr. 5-12). pap. 7.95 (*0-8359-0963-8*) Globe Fearon Educational Publishing.

—The Hound of the Baskervilles. 1995. (Fiction Ser.). (YA). pap. text 7.88 (*0-582-09679-0*, 79819) Longman Publishing Group.

—The Hound of the Baskervilles. 1986. (YA). (gr. 7 up). 256p. mass mkt. 4.95 o.s.i (*0-451-52478-0*); mass mkt. 2.95 o.p. (*0-451-52385-7*) NAL. (Signet Classics).

—The Hound of the Baskervilles. (Oxford Progressive English Readers Ser.). (Illus.). (gr. k-6). 1982. (J). pap. 4.95 o.p. (*0-19-581211-5*); 2nd ed. 1993. 94p. pap. text 5.95 (*0-19-585432-2*) Oxford Univ. Pr., Inc.

—The Hound of the Baskervilles. Fago, John N., ed. abr. ed. 1977. (Now Age Illustrated III Ser.). (Illus.). (J). (gr. 4-12). text 7.50 o.p. (*0-88301-276-6*); pap. text 2.95 (*0-88301-264-2*) Pendulum Pr., Inc.

—The Hound of the Baskervilles. 1991. (Horror Classics Ser.: No. 841-5). (Illus.). (J). (gr. 4 up). pap. 3.50 o.p. (*0-7214-0719-6*, Ladybird Bks.) Penguin Group (USA) Inc.

—The Hound of the Baskervilles. (Whole Story Ser.). 2004. pap. 25.99 (*0-670-03653-6*, Viking Children's Bks.); 1995. (Illus.). 256p. (YA). (gr. 4-7). pap. 4.99 (*0-14-036699-7*, Puffin Bks.); 1986. 176p. (J). (gr. 4-6). pap. 3.50 o.p. (*0-14-035064-0*, Puffin Bks.) Penguin Putnam Bks. for Young Readers.

—The Hound of the Baskervilles. 1959. (Laurel-Leaf Bks.). 224p. (YA). (gr. 7-12). mass mkt. 4.50 (*0-440-93758-2*, Laurel Leaf) Random Hse. Children's Bks.

—The Hound of the Baskervilles. (Children's Classics Ser.). (Illus.). 272p. 1992. (J). (gr. 4 up). 12.99 o.p. (*0-517-07770-1*); 1988. (YA). 9.99 o.s.i (*0-517-67028-3*) Random Hse. Value Publishing.

—The Hound of the Baskervilles. 1972. (J). reprint ed. pap. 1.50 o.p. (*0-590-01355-6*) Scholastic, Inc.

—The Hound of the Baskervilles. 2000. (Aladdin Classics Ser.). 256p. (J). (gr. 4-11). pap. 3.99 (*0-689-83571-X*, Aladdin) Simon & Schuster Children's Publishing.

—The Memoirs of Sherlock Holmes. 1987. (YA). (gr. 10 up). mass mkt. 2.75 o.p. (*0-425-10402-8*) Berkley Publishing Group.

—The Mysteries of Sherlock Holmes. 1994. (Bullseye Step into Classics Ser.). (Illus.). 96p. (J). (gr. 2-6). pap. 3.50 (*0-679-85086-4*, Random Hse. Bks. for Young Readers) Random Hse. Children's Bks.

—The Return of Sherlock Holmes. l.t. ed. 1998. (Large Print Heritage Ser.). 278p. (YA). (gr. 7-12). lib. bdg. 29.95 (*1-58118-038-1*) LRS.

—Sherlock Holmes Reader. (Courage Unabridged Classics Ser.). 224p. (YA). 1998. pap. 6.00 o.p. (*0-7624-0553-8*); 1994. text 5.98 o.p. (*1-56138-429-1*) Running Pr. Bk. Pubs. (Courage Bks.).

—A Study in Scarlet. 1986. (Illus.). 336p. (J). (gr. 7-12). 12.95 o.p. (*0-89577-254-X*) Reader's Digest Assn., Inc., The.

—A Study in Scarlet & The Sign of the Four. 1986. 256p. (YA). (gr. 10 up). mass mkt. 4.99 (*0-425-10240-8*) Berkley Publishing Group.

Doyle, Arthur Conan & Vogel, Malvina, eds. The Adventures of Sherlock Holmes. 1993. (Great Illustrated Classics Ser.: Vol. 25). (Illus.). 240p. (J). (gr. 3-6). 9.95 (*0-86611-976-0*) Playmore, Inc., Pubs.

Dubowski, Cathy. Scrooge: Adapted from Charles Dickens' "A Christmas Carol" 1994. (All Aboard Reading Ser.). (Illus.). 48p. (J). (gr. 1-3). 3.99 o.p. (*0-448-40221-1*, Grosset & Dunlap) Penguin Putnam Bks. for Young Readers.

—Scrooge: Adapted from Charles Dickens' A Christmas Carol. 1994. (All Aboard Reading Ser.). (Illus.). 32p. (J). (gr. 1-3). 10.99 o.p. (*0-448-40222-X*, Grosset & Dunlap) Penguin Putnam Bks. for Young Readers.

Duncan, Kathleen M. Crispin's Castle. 1979. (Pathfinder Ser.). (Illus.). (J). (gr. 2-6). reprint ed. pap. 2.95 o.p. (*0-310-37821-4*) Zondervan.

Edwards, Julie Andrews. Mandy. 1981. 224p. (gr. 4-8). pap. 2.25 o.p. (*0-553-24620-8*) Bantam Bks.

—Mandy. (Illus.). (J). 1990. 192p. (gr. 4-7). lib. bdg. 14.89 o.s.i (*0-06-021803-7*); 1989. 288p. (gr. 3-7). pap. 5.99 (*0-06-440296-7*, Harper Trophy); 1971. 192p. (gr. 3-7). 13.95 (*0-06-021802-9*) HarperCollins Children's Bk. Group.

—Mandy. 1989. 11.00 (*0-606-12413-6*) Turtleback Bks.

Eliot, George. Silas Marner, Level 4. Hedge, Tricia, ed. 2000. (Bookworms Ser.). (Illus.). 96p. (J). pap. text 5.95 (*0-19-423044-9*) Oxford Univ. Pr., Inc.

Ewing, Juliana H. Lob-Lie-by-the-Fire, Repr. Of 1874 Ed. 1977. (Classics of Children's Literature, 1621-1932: Vol. 41). (Illus.). (J). lib. bdg. 46.00 o.p. (*0-8240-2290-4*) Garland Publishing, Inc.

Farjeon, Eleanor. Elsie Piddock Skips in Her Sleep. (Illus.). (J). 2000. 48p. (ps-3). 16.99 (*0-7636-0790-8*); 1997. 96p. (gr. 3-9). 11.99 o.p. (*0-7636-0133-0*) Candlewick Pr.

Farmer, Penelope. Thicker Than Water. 1993. 208p. (J). (gr. 6-10). 16.95 o.p. (*1-56402-178-5*) Candlewick Pr.

—Year King. 1977. 228p. (J). (gr. 9 up). 1.98 o.p. (*0-689-50090-4*, McElderry, Margaret K.) Simon & Schuster Children's Publishing.

Fearnley, Jan. Colin & the Curly Claw. 2001. (Blue Bananas Ser.). (Illus.). 48p. (J). (gr. 1-2). pap. 4.95 (*0-7787-0886-1*); lib. bdg. 19.96 (*0-7787-0840-3*) Crabtree Publishing Co.

Fine, Anne. Up on Cloud Nine. l.t. ed. 2003. (Illus.). (J). pap. 16.95 incl. audio (*0-7540-7878-7*, Galaxy Children's Large Print) BBC Audiobooks America.

—Up on Cloud Nine. 2003. 160p. (gr. 5). pap. text 4.99 (*0-440-41916-6*, Dell Books for Young Readers); 2003. 176p. pap. (*0-552-54840-5*, Yearling); 2002. 160p. (gr. 5-7). text 15.95 (*0-385-73009-8*, Delacorte Bks. for Young Readers); 2002. 160p. (gr. 5-7). lib. bdg. 17.99 (*0-385-90058-9*, Delacorte Bks. for Young Readers) Random Hse. Children's Bks.

Fisk, Pauline. The Secret of Sabrina Fludde. 2002. 256p. (J). (gr. 5 up). 15.95 (*1-58234-754-9*, Bloomsbury Children) Bloomsbury Publishing.

Forrest, Emma. Namedropper: A Novel. 2000. 240p. (J). pap. 12.00 (*0-684-86538-6*, Touchstone) Simon & Schuster.

Furlong, Monica. Robin's Country. 1995. (J). lib. bdg. o.p. (*0-679-94332-3*); (Illus.). 15.00 o.s.i (*0-679-84332-9*) Knopf, Alfred A. Inc.

Garfield, Leon. Black Jack. 2000. (J). 13.00 (*0-606-21673-1*) Turtleback Bks.

Garner, Alan. Elidor. 1999. 20p. (J). pap. 6.00 (*0-15-201797-6*, Magic Carpet Bks.) Harcourt Children's Bks.

—Elidor. 1981. (J). (gr. 5 up). 9.95 o.p. (*0-399-20809-7*) Putnam Publishing Group, The.

—Elidor. 192p. (YA). (gr. 5 up). pap. 6.00 (*0-8072-1545-7*); 1997. (J). pap. 29.00 incl. audio (*0-8072-7791-6*, YA921SP) Random Hse. Audio Publishing Group. (Listening Library).

Gates, Susan. Bill's Baggy Pants. 2002. (Read-It! Readers Ser.). (Illus.). 32p. (J). (ps-3). lib. bdg. 18.60 (*1-4048-0050-6*) Picture Window Bks.

Geras, Adele. Pictures of the Night. Stearns, Michael, ed. 1998. (Egerton Hall Trilogy Ser.: Vol. 3). (Illus.). 192p. (gr. 7-12). pap. 6.00 o.s.i (*0-15-201519-1*, Harcourt Paperbacks) Harcourt Children's Bks.

—Pictures of the Night. 1993. 192p. (YA). (gr. 7 up). 16.95 (*0-15-261588-1*) Harcourt Trade Pubs.

Gili, Phillida. Fanny & Charles: A Regency Escapade. 1984. (Illus.). 28p. (J). (gr. 5). 7.95 o.p. (*0-670-30697-5*, Viking Children's Bks.) Penguin Putnam Bks. for Young Readers.

Glasser, Robin Preiss, illus. Doctor Dolittle's Journey. 1999. (Doctor Dolittle Chapter Bks.). 128p. (gr. 1-4). pap. text 3.99 o.s.i (*0-440-41547-0*, Dell Books for Young Readers) Random Hse. Children's Bks.

Glassman, Peter. A Little Princess. 1924. (J). o.s.i (*0-688-14585-X*, Morrow, William & Co.) Morrow/Avon.

Gleitzman, Morris. Misery Guts. l.t. ed. 2003. (Illus.). (J). pap. 16.95 incl. audio (*0-7540-7867-1*, Galaxy Children's Large Print) BBC Audiobooks America.

—Misery Guts. 1995. 160p. (YA). (gr. 4-7). pap. 5.00 o.s.i (*0-15-200026-7*, Harcourt Paperbacks) Harcourt Children's Bks.

—Misery Guts. (J). 1993. 160p. (gr. 3-7). 12.95 o.s.i (*0-15-254768-1*); 94th ed. 1994. text 20.30 (*0-15-302254-X*) Harcourt Trade Pubs.

—Misery Guts. 1995. (J). (gr. 3-7). 11.05 (*0-606-07874-6*) Turtleback Bks.

—Two Weeks with the Queen. 1991. 144p. (YA). 14.95 o.p. (*0-399-22249-9*, G. P. Putnam's Sons) Penguin Group (USA) Inc.

Gleitzman, Morris & Levers, John, illus. Misery Guts: And, Worry Warts. 2003. 121p. (J). mass mkt. 8.00 (*0-330-39103-8*) Macmillan Children's Bks.

Globe-Fearon Staff. Jane Eyre. 1985. pap. 6.95 o.p. (*0-671-55577-4*) Alpha Bks.

Globe-Fearon Staff, ed. Jane Eyre, Grades 5-12. pap. text, tchr. ed. 4.95 (*0-8359-0109-2*) Globe Fearon Educational Publishing.

Godden, Rumer. The Diddakoi. unabr. ed. 1989. (YA). audio 24.95 (*0-7451-8497-9*, CCA3091, Chivers Children's Audio Bks.) BBC Audiobooks America.

—The Diddakoi. 1988. 144p. (J). (gr. 5-9). pap. 3.95 o.p. (*0-14-030753-2*, Puffin Bks.) Penguin Putnam Bks. for Young Readers.

—The Diddakoi. 1992. (J). 16.50 o.p. (*0-8446-6534-7*) Smith, Peter Pub., Inc.

—The Diddakoi. 1972. 160p. (J). 9.95 o.p. (*0-670-27220-5*) Viking Penguin.

—Gypsy Girl. 2002. Orig. Title: The Diddakoi. (Illus.). 176p. (J). lib. bdg. 15.89 (*0-06-029192-3*); (gr. 5 up). pap. 5.95 (*0-06-440937-6*, Harper Trophy) HarperCollins Children's Bk. Group.

—Listen to the Nightingale. (J). 1994. 208p. (gr. 3-7). pap. 4.99 o.s.i (*0-14-036091-3*, Puffin Bks.); 1992. 192p. (gr. 5 up). 15.00 o.p. (*0-670-84517-5*, Viking Children's Bks.) Penguin Putnam Bks. for Young Readers.

—Listen to the Nightingale. 1994. 9.09 o.p. (*0-606-07026-5*) Turtleback Bks.

—Miss Happiness & Miss Flower. 2002. (Illus.). 128p. (J). (gr. 3-7). lib. bdg. 14.89 (*0-06-029193-1*); pap. 4.95 (*0-06-440938-4*, Harper Trophy) HarperCollins Children's Bk. Group.

—Miss Happiness & Miss Flower. 1987. (Illus.). 112p. (J). (gr. 2-6). pap. 3.95 o.p. (*0-14-030273-5*, Puffin Bks.) Penguin Putnam Bks. for Young Readers.

Goudge, Elizabeth. Linnets & Valerians. 1981. (J). lib. bdg. 12.95 o.p. (*0-8398-2750-4*, Macmillan Reference USA) Gale Group.

—Linnets & Valerians. 1985. (YA). (gr. 7 up). pap. 1.75 o.p. (*0-380-01934-5*, 37838, Avon Bks.) Morrow/Avon.

—Linnets & Valerians. 2001. 256p. (J). pap. 5.99 (*0-14-230026-8*, Puffin Bks.) Penguin Putnam Bks. for Young Readers.

—The Little White Horse. 1976. (J). 24.95 (*0-8488-1416-9*) Amereon, Ltd.

—The Little White Horse. unabr. collector's ed. 1988. audio 56.00 (*0-7366-1401-X*, 2290) Books on Tape, Inc.

—The Little White Horse. 1976. (J). (ps up). 35.95 (*0-89966-474-1*) Buccaneer Bks., Inc.

—The Little White Horse. 1980. (J). lib. bdg. 10.50 o.p. (*0-8398-2607-9*, Macmillan Reference USA) Gale Group.

—The Little White Horse. 1978. (YA). (gr. 7 up). pap. 1.75 o.p. (*0-380-01875-6*, 52050, Avon Bks.) Morrow/Avon.

—The Little White Horse. 2001. 240p. (J). pap. 5.99 (*0-14-230027-6*, Puffin Bks.) Penguin Putnam Bks. for Young Readers.

—The Little White Horse. 1992. 272p. (YA). (gr. 5 up). pap. 3.50 o.s.i (*0-440-40734-6*, Yearling) Random Hse. Children's Bks.

Graham, Harriet & McElderry, Margaret K. A Boy & His Bear. 1996. 192p. (J). (gr. 4-7). 16.00 (*0-689-80943-3*, McElderry, Margaret K.) Simon & Schuster Children's Publishing.

Grahame, Kenneth. Dream Days. 1993. (Illus.). 240p. (YA). (gr. 5 up). 18.95 o.s.i (*0-89815-546-0*) Ten Speed Pr.

—The Golden Age. 2000. (J). E-Book 2.49 (*1-58744-126-8*) Electric Umbrella Publishing.

—The Golden Age. l.t. ed. 421p. pap. 37.29 (*0-7583-0942-2*); 488p. pap. 42.06 (*0-7583-0943-0*); 342p. pap. 31.72 (*0-7583-0941-4*); 170p. pap. 19.52 (*0-7583-0938-4*); 217p. pap. 22.88 (*0-7583-0939-2*); 278p. pap. 27.19 (*0-7583-0940-6*); 99p. pap. 14.50 (*0-7583-0936-8*); 124p. pap. 16.27 (*0-7583-0937-6*); 124p. lib. bdg. 23.18 (*0-7583-0929-5*); 170p. lib. bdg. 27.81 (*0-7583-0930-9*); 99p. lib. bdg. 20.60 (*0-7583-0928-7*); 342p. lib. bdg. 42.97 (*0-7583-0933-3*); 488p. lib. bdg. 53.31 (*0-7583-0935-X*); 217p. lib. bdg. 33.37 (*0-7583-0931-7*); 278p. lib. bdg. 38.44 (*0-7583-0932-5*); 421p. lib. bdg. 48.54 (*0-7583-0934-1*) Huge Print Pr.

—The Golden Age. 2002. 124p. (gr. 4-7). 22.99 (*1-4043-0572-6*); per. 18.99 (*1-4043-0573-4*) IndyPublish.com.

—The Golden Age. 1993. (Illus.). 264p. (YA). (gr. 5 up). 18.95 o.s.i (*0-89815-545-2*) Ten Speed Pr.

—Mr. Toad. Johnson, Joe, tr. from FRE. 1998. (Wind in the Willows Ser.: Vol. 2). (Illus.). 32p. (J). (gr. 4-7). 15.95 (*1-56163-218-X*) NBM Publishing Co.

—The Open Road. 1990. (Shaped Board Bks. Ser.). (Illus.). 10p. (J). 2.99 o.s.i (*0-517-02028-9*, Random Hse. Bks. for Young Readers) Random Hse. Children's Bks.

—The Open Road. 1986. (Illus.). 48p. (J). (ps-3). 9.95 o.s.i (*0-671-61095-3*, Simon & Schuster Children's Publishing) Simon & Schuster Children's Publishing.

—El Viento en los Sauces. (SPA.). 192p. (J). I. 9.50 (*84-372-1882-9*); II. 9.50 (*84-372-1883-7*) Santillana USA Publishing Co., Inc.

—The Wild Wood. Johnson, Joe, tr. from FRE. 1997. (Wind in the Willows Ser.: Vol. 1). (Illus.). 32p. (J). (gr. 4-7). 15.95 (*1-56163-196-5*) NBM Publishing Co.

—The Wind in the Willows. 2002. (Great Illustrated Classics). (Illus.). 240p. (J). (gr. 3-8). lib. bdg. 21.35 (*1-57765-808-6*, ABDO & Daughters) ABDO Publishing Co.

—The Wind in the Willows. 1999. (Abbeville Classics Ser.). (Illus.). 192p. (J). 12.95 (*0-7892-0559-9*); pap. 7.95 (*0-7892-0549-1*) Abbeville Pr., Inc. (Abbeville Kids).

—The Wind in the Willows. 1966. (Airmont Classics Ser.). (J). (gr. 4 up). mass mkt. 2.75 (*0-8049-0105-8*, CL-105) Airmont Publishing Co., Inc.

—The Wind in the Willows. 253p. (J). (gr. 5-6). reprint ed. lib. bdg. 22.95 (*0-88411-877-0*) Amereon, Ltd.

—The Wind in the Willows. 1983. (Illus.). 256p. (J). (gr. 4-12). mass mkt. 1.95 o.s.i (*0-553-21129-3*); (gr. 7 up). mass mkt. 3.95 (*0-553-21368-7*) Bantam Bks. (Bantam Classics).

—The Wind in the Willows. (Longmeadow Press Children's Library). (Illus.). (J). 1995. 256p. 10.95 o.p. (*0-681-00768-0*); 1987. 352p. (gr. 4 up). 11.95 o.p. (*0-681-40057-9*) Borders Pr.

—The Wind in the Willows. (Classics for Children 8 & Younger Ser.). (J). (ps-3). 1997. (Illus.). 48p. 6.98 (*1-85854-601-X*); 1994. 64p. 5.98 o.p. (*0-86112-823-0*); 1994. 160p. 9.98 o.p. (*0-86112-354-9*) Brimax Bks., Ltd.

—The Wind in the Willows. 1981. 234p. (J). reprint ed. lib. bdg. 17.95 (*0-89966-305-2*) Buccaneer Bks., Inc.

—The Wind in the Willows. 2000. (Illus.). 180p. 4.50 o.p. (*0-7445-7553-2*) Candlewick Pr.

—The Wind in the Willows. Moore, Inga, ed. & illus. by. 1999. (YA). (gr. 3-7). 39.99 o.p. (*0-7636-0980-3*) Candlewick Pr.

—The Wind in the Willows. 2003. 192p. (J). 4.99 (*1-57759-567-X*) Dalmatian Pr.

—The Wind in the Willows. 1990. (Illus.). 256p. (gr. 2 up). pap. text 4.99 (*0-440-40385-5*) Dell Publishing.

—The Wind in the Willows. 1989. mass mkt. 3.25 o.s.i (*0-8125-0511-5*); (Illus.). 224p. (J). (gr. 4-7). mass mkt. 2.99 (*0-8125-0510-7*) Doherty, Tom Assocs., LLC. (Tor Classics).

—The Wind in the Willows. (Illus.). (J). 1999. 256p. pap. text 3.00 (*0-486-40785-3*); 1998. 96p. pap. text 1.00 (*0-486-28600-2*) Dover Pubns., Inc.

—The Wind in the Willows. (J). E-Book 2.49 (*0-7574-0469-3*) Electric Umbrella Publishing.

—The Wind in the Willows. 1996. (Illus.). 185p. (J). (gr. 3-5). pap. 15.95 (*0-575-06209-6*) Gollancz, Victor GBR. *Dist:* Trafalgar Square.

—The Wind in the Willows. collector's ed. 2002. (Illus.). 240p. (YA). 24.00 (*0-15-216807-9*) Harcourt Children's Bks.

—The Wind in the Willows. (J). ERS. 2003. (Illus.). 224p. (gr. 1 up). 25.95 (*0-8050-7237-3*); Vol. 1. 1980. 17.95 o.p. (*0-03-056294-5*) Holt, Henry & Co. (Holt, Henry & Co. Bks. For Young Readers).

—The Wind in the Willows. 1991. (J). pap. 12.95 o.p. (*0-395-60728-0*) Houghton Mifflin Co.

—The Wind in the Willows. l.t. ed. 211p. pap. 21.18 (*0-7583-3377-3*); 830p. pap. 66.19 (*0-7583-3383-8*); 715p. pap. 57.46 (*0-7583-3382-X*); 581p. pap. 48.64 (*0-7583-3381-1*); 473p. pap. 40.94 (*0-7583-3380-3*); 369p. pap. 33.14 (*0-7583-3379-X*); 162p. pap. 18.16 (*0-7583-3376-5*); 289p. pap. 26.62 (*0-7583-3378-1*); 369p. lib. bdg. 39.14 (*0-7583-3371-4*); 715p. lib. bdg. 63.46 (*0-7583-3374-9*); 289p. lib. bdg. 32.62 (*0-7583-3370-6*); 830p. lib. bdg. 85.40 (*0-7583-3375-7*); 581p. lib. bdg. 55.19 (*0-7583-3373-0*); 473p. lib. bdg. 46.97 (*0-7583-3372-2*); 162p. (J). lib. bdg. 24.16 (*0-7583-3368-4*); 211p. (J). lib. bdg. 27.18 (*0-7583-3369-2*) Huge Print Pr.

—The Wind in the Willows. 1993. (Everyman's Library Children's Classics Ser.). (Illus.). 260p. (gr. 5 up). 13.95 (*0-679-41802-4*) Knopf, Alfred A. Inc.

—The Wind in the Willows. l.t. ed. 2000. (LRS Large Print Heritage Ser.). 271p. (J). (gr. 3-8). lib. bdg. 29.95 (*1-58118-066-7*, 23661) LRS.

—The Wind in the Willows. 1985. (Illus.). 224p. (J). (gr. 2 up). 12.95 o.p. (*0-915361-32-9*) Lambda Pubs., Inc.

—The Wind in the Willows. (YA). E-Book 2.95 (*1-57799-886-3*) Logos Research Systems, Inc.

—The Wind in the Willows. (Classics Ser.). (J). pap. 3.95 o.p. 1989. (Illus.). pap. text 7.87 (*0-582-54142-5*, TG7244) Longman Publishing Group.

—The Wind in the Willows. 1988. (Illus.). 196p. (YA). pap. 7.95 o.p. (*0-8092-4489-6*) McGraw-Hill/Contemporary.

—The Wind in the Willows. 1924. (J). 22.99 o.s.i (*0-688-12422-4*, Morrow, William & Co.) Morrow/Avon.

—The Wind in the Willows. 1969. (J). mass mkt. 1.95 o.p. (*0-451-51733-4*); (Illus.). 224p. (YA). (gr. 2 up). mass mkt. 3.95 (*0-451-52462-4*); (Illus.). 224p. (J). (gr. 4). mass mkt. 2.50 o.p. (*0-451-52164-1*, Signet Classics) NAL.

—The Wind in the Willows. l.t. ed. (Large Print Ser.). reprint ed. 1997. 284p. lib. bdg. 25.00 (*0-939495-18-X*); 1998. 185p. lib. bdg. 24.00 (*1-58287-080-2*) North Bks.

—The Wind in the Willows. 2002. (Illus.). 208p. (J). 19.95 (*1-58717-204-6*) North-South Bks., Inc.

—The Wind in the Willows. 1999. (Oxford World's Classics Ser.). 192p. (J). pap. 9.95 (*0-19-283515-7*) Oxford Univ. Pr., Inc.

—The Wind in the Willows. Bassett, Jennifer, ed. 1995. (Illus.). 64p. (J). pap. text 5.95 o.p. (*0-19-422753-7*) Oxford Univ. Pr., Inc.

—The Wind in the Willows. 1983. (Oxford World's Classics Ser.). 224p. (YA). (gr. 5 up). pap. 4.95 o.p. (*0-19-281640-3*) Oxford Univ. Pr., Inc.

—The Wind in the Willows, Level 3. Hedge, Tricia, ed. 2000. (Bookworms Ser.). (Illus.). 74p. (J). pap. text 5.95 (*0-19-423022-8*) Oxford Univ. Pr., Inc.

—The Wind in the Willows. (Illus.). 192p. 2000. pap. 8.95 (*1-85793-914-X*); 1992. (J). (gr. 3-6). 24.95 o.p. (*1-85145-603-1*) Pavilion Bks., Ltd. GBR. *Dist:* Trafalgar Square.

—The Wind in the Willows. (Illus.). (J). 9999. (Children's Classics Ser.: No. 740-13). (gr. 3-5). pap. 3.50 o.p. (*0-7214-0757-9*); 1996. (Classic Ser.). 52p. (gr. 2-4). 2.99 o.s.i (*0-7214-5608-1*); 1994. (Classics Ser.). 56p. text 3.50 (*0-7214-1653-5*) Penguin Group (USA) Inc. (Ladybird Bks.).

—The Wind in the Willows. (Puffin Classics Ser.). 1995. (Illus.). 220p. (YA). (gr. 4-7). 4.99 (*0-14-036685-7*, Puffin Bks.); 1988. 224p. (J). pap. 3.50 o.p. (*0-14-035087-X*, Puffin Bks.); 1985. (Illus.). 224p. (J). (gr. 3-9). 12.95 o.p. (*0-399-20944-1*, Grosset & Dunlap); 1984. (Illus.). 240p. (J). (gr. 4-6). pap. 2.95 o.p. (*0-14-031544-6*, Viking Children's Bks.); 1983. (Illus.). 240p. (J). (gr. 1 up). 15.75 o.p. (*0-670-77120-1*, Viking Children's Bks.); 1989. 128p. (J). (gr. 2-6). 2.95 o.p. (*0-448-11079-2*, Platt & Munk); 1981. (Illus.). (J). (gr. 3-9). reprint ed. 6.95 o.p. (*0-448-11028-8*, Grosset & Dunlap); 1967. (Illus.). 224p. (J). reprint ed. 15.99 (*0-448-06028-0*, Grosset & Dunlap) Penguin Putnam Bks. for Young Readers.

—The Wind in the Willows. Hanft, Joshua, ed. (Great Illustrated Classics Ser.: Vol. 39). (Illus.). 240p. (J). (gr. 3-6). 9.95 (*0-86611-990-6*) Playmore, Inc., Pubs.

—The Wind in the Willows. 1966. (Illus.). (J). 12.95 o.p. (*0-529-00119-5*) Putnam Publishing Group, The.

—The Wind in the Willows. 1969. (Illus.). 256p. (J). (gr. 1 up). pap. 3.25 o.s.i (*0-440-49555-5*, Yearling) Random Hse. Children's Bks.

—The Wind in the Willows. (J). 1996. 9.99 o.s.i (*0-517-16023-4*); 1991. 2.99 o.s.i (*0-517-02026-2*); 1991. 2.99 o.s.i (*0-517-02027-0*); 1988. 12.99 o.s.i (*0-517-63230-6*); 1988. 7.99 o.s.i (*0-517-49284-9*) Random Hse. Value Publishing.

—The Wind in the Willows. (J). 2000. 6.00 o.p. (*0-7624-0558-9*); 1994. 176p. text 5.98 o.p. (*1-56138-455-0*, Courage Bks.) Running Pr. Bk. Pubs.

—The Wind in the Willows. 208p. (J). (gr. 4-7). 1988. pap. 2.75 o.p. (*0-590-43404-7*); 1987. (Illus.). mass mkt. 4.50 (*0-590-44774-2*, Scholastic Paperbacks) Scholastic, Inc.

—The Wind in the Willows. 1987. (YA). 3.98 (*0-671-08895-5*) Simon & Schuster.

—The Wind in the Willows. 1991. (Illus.). 264p. (YA). (gr. 3 up). 25.00 o.s.i (*0-684-19345-0*, Atheneum); 1972. (Wind in the Willows Ser.: Vol. 1). (Illus.). 272p. (J). (gr. 2 up). 17.00 (*0-684-12819-5*, Atheneum); 1950. (J). pap. 7.95 o.s.i (*0-684-71788-3*, Simon & Schuster Children's Publishing); 1989. (Illus.). 272p. (J). (gr. 2 up). reprint ed. pap. 5.99 (*0-689-71310-X*, Aladdin); 75th anniv. ed. 1983. (Illus.). 256p. (J). (gr. 2 up). 19.95 (*0-684-17957-1*, Atheneum) Simon & Schuster Children's Publishing.

—The Wind in the Willows. 1991. (J). pap. 9.95 (*0-8045-1033-4*) Spoken Arts, Inc.

—The Wind in the Willows. (Illus.). 272p. 3rd ed. 1995. (J). (gr. 2 up). 19.95 (*0-312-13624-2*); 5th ed. 1996. (gr. 4-7). pap. 11.95 (*0-312-14826-7*, Saint Martin's Griffin) St. Martin's Pr.

—The Wind in the Willows. l.t. ed. 1996. 248p. (J). lib. bdg. 21.95 (*0-7838-1874-2*) Thorndike Pr.

—The Wind in the Willows. l.t. ed. 1981. (Classics Ser.). 260p. (J). 13.95 o.p. (*0-7089-8007-4*, Charnwood) Thorpe, F. A. Pubs. GBR. *Dist:* Ulverscroft Large Print Bks., Ltd.

—The Wind in the Willows. 1969. (Signet Classics Ser.). (J). 10.00 (*0-606-01976-6*) Turtleback Bks.

—The Wind in the Willows. 1985. (J). 15.95 o.p. (*0-670-80764-8*) Viking Penguin.

—The Wind in the Willows. 1998. (Children's Classics). (Illus.). 192p. (YA). (ps up). pap. 3.95 (*1-85326-122-X*, 122XWW); 160p. (J). (gr. 4-7). pap. 3.95 (*1-85326-017-7*, 0177WW) Wordsworth Editions, Ltd. GBR. *Dist:* Advanced Global Distribution Services, Combined Publishing.

—The Wind in the Willows: A Young Reader's Edition of the Classic Story. abr. ed. 1993. (Children's Illustrated Classics Ser.). (Illus.). 56p. (J). (gr. 3-7). 9.98 (*1-56138-276-0*, Courage Bks.) Running Pr. Bk. Pubs.

—The Wind in the Willows: Anniversary Edition. 1960. (J). 16.95 o.s.i (*0-684-20838-5*, Atheneum) Simon & Schuster Children's Publishing.

—The Wind in the Willows Vol. 3: The Gates of Dawn. Johnson, Joe, tr. 1999. (Illus.). 31p. (J). (gr. 4-7). 15.95 (*1-56163-245-7*) NBM Publishing Co.

—A Wind in the Willows Christmas. 2000. (Illus.). 41p. (J). (ps-3). lib. bdg. 16.50 (*1-58717-007-8*) North-South Bks., Inc.

—A Wind in the Willows Christmas. 2000. (Illus.). 41p. (J). (ps-3). 15.95 o.p. (*1-58717-006-X*) SeaStar Bks.

—The Wind in the Willows Pop-up-Book, ERS. 1983. (Illus.). 12p. (J). (gr. k-4). o.p. (*0-03-063862-3*, Holt, Henry & Co. Bks. For Young Readers) Holt, Henry & Co.

Grahame, Kenneth & Cooper, intros. The Wind in the Willows. 1999. (Aladdin Classics Ser.). (Illus.). 304p. (J). (gr. 4-7). pap. 3.99 (*0-689-83140-4*, Aladdin) Simon & Schuster Children's Publishing.

Grahame, Kenneth & Golden Books Staff. The Wind in the Willows. 1987. (Golden Classics Ser.). (Illus.). 128p. (J). pap. 8.95 o.s.i (*0-307-17117-5*, Golden Bks.) Random Hse. Children's Bks.

Grahame, Kenneth, et al. The Wind in the Willows. abr. ed. 1997. (Children's Classics Ser.). (J). audio 10.95 (*0-14-086243-9*, Puffin Bks.) Viking Penguin.

Gray, Nigel. The Deserter. 1977. (Illus.). (J). (gr. 4-7). o.p. (*0-06-022061-9*); lib. bdg. 7.40 o.p. (*0-06-022062-7*) HarperCollins Pubs.

—I'll Take You to Mrs. Cole. 1992. (Illus.). 32p. (J). (gr. k-5). 12.95 o.p. (*0-916291-39-1*) Kane/Miller Bk. Pubs.

Green, Roger J. They Watched Him Die. 1988. (Illus.). 208p. (J). (gr. 6 up). 13.95 o.p. (*0-19-271573-9*) Oxford Univ. Pr., Inc.

Green, Roger Lancelyn. King Arthur & His Knights of the Round Table. 1993. (Everyman's Library Children's Classics Ser.). 368p. (gr. 2 up). 14.95 (*0-679-42311-7*) Knopf, Alfred A. Inc.

—King Arthur & His Knights of the Round Table. (Puffin Classics Ser.). (J). 1995. (Illus.). 352p. (gr. 4-7). pap. 4.99 (*0-14-036670-9*, Puffin Bks.); 1990. 288p. (gr. 5 up). pap. 3.99 o.p. (*0-14-035100-0*, Puffin Bks.); 1974. 288p. (gr. 5-7). pap. 2.95 o.p. (*0-14-030073-2*, Viking Children's Bks.) Penguin Putnam Bks. for Young Readers.

—King Arthur & His Knights of the Round Table. abr. ed. 1997. (Children's Classics Ser.). 2p. (J). pap. 10.95 o.s.i incl. audio (*0-14-086369-9*, Penguin AudioBooks) Viking Penguin.

Greene, Graham. The Destructors. 1993. (Short Stories Ser.). 32p. (YA). (gr. 3 up). lib. bdg. 18.60 (*0-88682-348-X*, 97213-098, Creative Education) Creative Co., The.

Greene, Janice. Jane Eyre. Hagerty, Carol, ed. 1998. (Classics Ser.: Set II). (Illus.). 77p. (YA). (gr. 5-12). pap. text 7.95 (*1-56254-268-0*, SP2680) Saddleback Publishing, Inc.

Greenwood, Marie, contrib. by. The Hound of the Baskervilles. 2000. (Dorling Kindersley Classics Ser.). (Illus.). 64p. (J). (gr. 2-5). pap. 14.95 o.p. (*0-7894-6108-0*) Dorling Kindersley Publishing, Inc.

Gregory, Kristiana. Eleanor: Crown Jewel of Aquitaine. 2002. (Royal Diaries Ser.). 112p. (YA). (gr. 4-9). 10.95 (*0-439-16484-2*, Scholastic Pr.) Scholastic, Inc.

Haahr, Berit I. The Minstrel's Tale. 2000. (Illus.). 256p. (YA). (gr. 7 up). 15.95 (*0-385-32713-7*, Dell Books for Young Readers) Random Hse. Children's Bks.

Hague, Michael. The Wind in the Willows, ERS. 1980. (Illus.). 216p. (YA). (gr. 2 up). 25.95 o.s.i (*0-8050-0213-8*, Holt, Henry & Co. Bks. For Young Readers) Holt, Henry & Co.

Haley, Gail E. Dream Peddler. 1993. (Illus.). 32p. (J). (ps-3). 14.99 o.p. (*0-525-45153-6*, Dutton Children's Bks.) Penguin Putnam Bks. for Young Readers.

Hall, Donald. Ox-Cart Man. Cooney, Barbara, tr. 1984. (Illus.). (J). (gr. k-3). pap., tchr. ed. 31.95 incl. audio (*0-941078-41-8*) Live Oak Media.

Hall, Margaret & Jones, Dawn L. Sebastian at the Tower of London. 2001. (Suitcase Bear Adventures Ser.). (Illus.). (J). (*0-9713174-1-0*, Bear & Co.) Bear & Co.

Hardy, Thomas. The Return of the Native. 1964. (Airmont Classics Ser.). (YA). (gr. 10 up). mass mkt. 3.50 o.p. (*0-8049-0038-8*, CL-38) Airmont Publishing Co., Inc.

—The Return of the Native. 1982. 384p. (gr. 9-12). mass mkt. 4.95 (*0-553-21269-9*, Bantam Classics) Bantam Bks.

—The Return of the Native. 1922. 485p. (YA). reprint ed. pap. text 28.00 (*1-4047-7548-X*) Classic Textbooks.

—The Return of the Native. Litz, A. Walton, ed. 1967. (YA). (gr. 9 up). pap. 16.36 (*0-395-05201-7*, Riverside Editions) Houghton Mifflin Co.

—The Return of the Native. Calhoun, Dorothy, ed. 1978. (Now Age Illustrated IV Ser.). (Illus.). (J). (gr. 4-12). stu. ed. 1.25 (*0-88301-343-6*); text 7.50 o.p. (*0-88301-331-2*); pap. text 2.95 (*0-88301-319-3*) Pendulum Pr., Inc.

—The Return of the Native. 1983. (Enriched Classics Ser.). 528p. (gr. 9 up). mass mkt. 1.75 o.s.i (*0-671-48917-8*, Pocket) Simon & Schuster.

Harris, Ruth Elwin. Frances' Story: Sisters of the Quantock Hills. 2002. 304p. (YA). (gr. 7 up). bds. 5.99 (*0-7636-1704-0*) Candlewick Pr.

—Gwen's Story. 2002. 304p. (YA). (gr. 7 up). bds. 5.99 (*0-7636-1705-9*) Candlewick Pr.

—Julia's Story. 2002. 304p. (YA). (gr. 7 up). bds. 5.99 (*0-7636-1706-7*) Candlewick Pr.

—Sarah's Story. 2002. 304p. (YA). (gr. 7 up). bds. 5.99 (*0-7636-1707-5*) Candlewick Pr.

Hatfield, Kate. Drowning in Honey. 2000. 333p. (J). pap. 12.95 o.p. (*0-552-99694-7*) Transworld Publishers Ltd. GBR. *Dist:* Trafalgar Square.

Hayes, Sheila. Zoe's Gift. 1994. 160p. (J). 14.99 o.p. (*0-525-67484-5*, Dutton Children's Bks.) Penguin Putnam Bks. for Young Readers.

Hearne, Betsy. Eliza's Dog. 1996. (Illus.). 160p. (J). (gr. 4-7). 16.00 (*0-689-80704-X*, McElderry, Margaret K.) Simon & Schuster Children's Publishing.

Hendry, Diana. Double Vision. (gr. 7-11). 1995. (YA). bds. 6.99 o.p. (*1-56402-436-9*); 1993. 272p. (J). 14.95 o.p. (*1-56402-125-4*) Candlewick Pr.

—Double Vision. 1995. 12.09 o.p. (*0-606-08729-X*) Turtleback Bks.

Henry, Marguerite. King of the Wind. 2002. (Illus.). (J). 13.40 (*0-7587-0197-7*) Book Wholesalers, Inc.

—King of the Wind. 2000. (J). audio 30.00 (*0-7366-9038-7*) Books on Tape, Inc.

—King of the Wind. unabr. ed. (J). 2000. 173p. (gr. 4-6). pap. 37.00 incl. audio (*0-8072-8697-4*, YA239SP); 1998. audio 25.00 (*0-553-47829-X*, 395671) Random Hse. Audio Publishing Group. (Listening Library).

—King of the Wind. unabr. ed. 1993. (J). (gr. 4). audio 27.00 (*1-55690-959-4*, 93445E7) Recorded Bks., LLC.

—King of the Wind. 1985. (J). 17.30 o.p. (*0-516-09862-4*, Children's Pr.) Scholastic Library Publishing.

—King of the Wind. (J). 2001. (Illus.). 192p. 21.00 (*0-689-84697-5*, Simon & Schuster Children's Publishing); 2001. 176p. pap. 2.99 o.s.i (*0-689-84513-8*, Aladdin); 1995. 3.95 o.s.i (*0-689-80408-3*, Aladdin); 2nd ed. 1991. (Illus.). 176p. (gr. 3-7). reprint ed. pap. 4.99 (*0-689-71486-6*, Aladdin); Vol. 1. 1999. pap. 2.99 (*0-689-82990-6*, Aladdin) Simon & Schuster Children's Publishing.

—King of the Wind. l.t. ed. 2001. (Illus.). 216p. (J). (gr. 4-7). 21.95 (*0-7862-2848-2*) Thorndike Pr.

—King of the Wind. 1991. (J). 11.04 (*0-606-01888-3*) Turtleback Bks.

—King of the Wind: The Story of the Godolphin Arabian. (Illus.). 176p. (J). (gr. 3-7). 1990. lib. bdg. 2.95 o.p. (*0-528-80174-0*, Simon & Schuster Children's Publishing); 1987. pap. 3.95 (*0-02-688758-4*, Simon Pulse); 2nd ed. 1990. 17.95 (*0-02-743629-2*, Simon & Schuster Children's Publishing) Simon & Schuster Children's Publishing.

Henty, G. A. Beric the Briton: A Story of the Roman Invasion. 1996. (Illus.). 398p. (YA). 20.99 (*1-887159-06-1*) Preston-Speed Pubns.

—Both Sides of the Border: A Tale of Hotspur & Glendower. 2000. 252p. (J). pap. 9.95 (*0-594-01504-9*); E-Book 3.95 (*0-594-02365-3*) 1873 Pr.

—In the Reign of Terror: The Adventures of a Westminster Boy. 2000. 252p. E-Book 3.95 (*0-594-02393-9*); pap. 9.95 (*0-594-01344-5*) 1873 Pr.

—In the Reign of Terror: The Adventures of a Westminster Boy. 2002. 370p. 29.95 (*1-59087-077-8*, GAH077); per. 19.95 (*1-59087-076-X*, GAH076) Althouse Pr.

—In the Reign of Terror: The Adventures of a Westminster Boy. 2002. 228p. 24.99 (*1-4043-0996-9*); per. 19.99 (*1-4043-0997-7*) IndyPublish.com.

—In the Reign of Terror: The Adventures of a Westminster Boy. collector's ed. 2002. (Illus.). im. lthr. 38.85 (*1-4115-1378-9*); pap. 19.95 (*1-4115-0618-9*); 25.95 (*1-4115-0946-3*); pap. 17.95 (*1-4115-0128-4*) Polyglot Pr., Inc.

Hill, Pamela Smith. The Last Grail Keeper. 2001. 288p. (J). (gr. 6-8). tchr. ed. 17.95 (*0-8234-1574-0*) Holiday Hse., Inc.

Hilton, James. Goodbye, Mr. Chips. 1976. 124p. (YA). 17.95 (*0-8488-0364-7*) Amereon, Ltd.

—Goodbye, Mr. Chips. 1982. (YA). (gr. 7 up). mass mkt. 2.75 o.s.i (*0-553-25613-0*); 144p. mass mkt. 4.99 o.s.i (*0-553-27321-3*) Bantam Bks.

—Goodbye, Mr. Chips. 1982. (YA). reprint ed. lib. bdg. 21.95 (*0-89966-413-X*) Buccaneer Bks., Inc.

—Goodbye, Mr. Chips. 1962. (Illus.). 132p. (gr. 4-7). 22.00 (*0-316-36420-7*) Little Brown & Co.

—Goodbye, Mr. Chips. 1986. (J). mass mkt. o.p. (*0-553-16698-0*, Dell Books for Young Readers) Random Hse. Children's Bks.

—Goodbye, Mr. Chips. 1957. (YA). 10.55 (*0-606-00727-X*) Turtleback Bks.

—Goodbye, Mr. Chips & to You, Mr. Chips. l.t. ed. 1995. 266p. (YA). 22.95 (*0-7838-1231-0*) Thorndike Pr.

Holeman, Linda. Search of the Moon King's Daughter. 320p. (YA). (gr. 6). 2003. pap. 9.95 (*0-88776-609-9*); 2002. 17.95 o.s.i (*0-88776-592-0*) Tundra Bks. of Northern New York.

Hollinshead, Marilyn. The Nine Days Wonder. 1994. (Illus.). 32p. (J). (ps-3). 14.95 o.s.i (*0-399-21967-6*, Philomel) Penguin Putnam Bks. for Young Readers.

Hooper, Mary. Amy. 2002. 176p. (J). (gr. 5 up). 14.95 (*1-58234-793-X*, Bloomsbury Children) Bloomsbury Publishing.

Horowitz, Anthony. The Devil & His Boy. 2000. 182p. (J). (gr. 5-9). 16.99 (*0-399-23432-2*, Philomel) Penguin Putnam Bks. for Young Readers.

—Skeleton Key. 2003. 208p. (YA). 17.99 (*0-399-23777-1*, Philomel) Penguin Putnam Bks. for Young Readers.

—Stormbreaker. 2002. 208p. pap. 5.99 (*0-698-11934-7*, Puffin Bks.); 2002. (Illus.). (J). (gr. 4-7). 5.99 (*0-698-11932-0*, Puffin Bks.); 2001. (Illus.). 208p. (YA). (gr. 5). 16.99 (*0-399-23620-1*, Philomel) Penguin Putnam Bks. for Young Readers.

—Stormbreaker. unabr. ed. 2001. (YA). (gr. 5-8). audio 22.00 (*0-8072-0479-X*, Listening Library) Random Hse. Audio Publishing Group.

Horwood, William. The Willows at Christmas. 2001. (J). 21.95 (*0-312-28386-5*) St. Martin's Pr.

—The Willows in Winter. 304p. (gr. 4-7). 1996. pap. 11.95 (*0-312-14825-9*, Saint Martin's Griffin); 1994. (Illus.). (J). 18.95 o.p. (*0-312-11354-4*) St. Martin's Pr.

Howard, Ellen. The Gate in the Wall. 1999. (Illus.). 160p. (J). (gr. 3-7). 16.00 (*0-689-82295-2*, Atheneum) Simon & Schuster Children's Publishing.

Howarth, Lesley. Weather Eye. 1995. (Illus.). 224p. (YA). (gr. 7-10). 16.99 o.p. (*1-56402-616-7*) Candlewick Pr.

Howe, D. H., adapted by. Pickwick Papers: Simplified Edition. 1995. (Illus.). 94p. pap. text 5.95 (*0-19-586308-9*) Oxford Univ. Pr., Inc.

Howe, D. H., ed. Wuthering Heights: Abridged for Children. 2nd ed. 1993. (Illus.). 126p. (J). pap. text 5.95 (*0-19-585474-8*) Oxford Univ. Pr., Inc.

Howker, Janni. Badger on the Barge & Other Stories. 1985. 208p. (J). (gr. 5-9). 12.95 o.p. (*0-688-04215-5*, Greenwillow Bks.) HarperCollins Children's Bk. Group.

—Isaac Campion. Pacheco, Laura E., tr. 1992. (SPA., Illus.). 128p. (YA). pap. 6.99 (*968-16-3783-6*) Fondo de Cultura Economica MEX. *Dist:* Continental Bk. Co., Inc.

—Isaac Campion. 1990. 96p. (J). (gr. k-6). pap. 2.95 o.s.i (*0-440-40280-8*, Yearling) Random Hse. Children's Bks.

—The Nature of the Beast. 1985. 137p. (J). (gr. 7-9). 11.95 o.p. (*0-688-04233-3*, Greenwillow Bks.) HarperCollins Children's Bk. Group.

—The Nature of the Beast. 1987. (Novels Ser.). (J). (gr. 5-9). pap. 4.95 o.p. (*0-14-032254-X*, Puffin Bks.) Penguin Putnam Bks. for Young Readers.

Hubbard, Coleen. A Horse for Hannah. l.t. ed. 1999. (Treasured Horses Collection). (Illus.). 128p. (J). (gr. 4 up). lib. bdg. 22.60 (*0-8368-2402-4*) Stevens, Gareth Inc.

Hughes, Shirley. An Evening at Alfie's. 1985. (Illus.). 32p. (J). (ps-1). 16.00 o.p. (*0-688-04122-1*); lib. bdg. 15.93 o.p. (*0-688-04123-X*) HarperCollins Children's Bk. Group.

—The Lion & the Unicorn. 1999. (Illus.). 64p. (J). (gr. 2-6). pap. 17.95 o.p. (*0-7894-2555-6*, D K Ink) Dorling Kindersley Publishing, Inc.

Hughes, Thomas. Tom Brown's School Days. 1969. (Illus.). pap. 2.50 o.p. (*0-312-80885-2*, Saint Martin's Griffin) St. Martin's Pr.

—Tom Brown's School Days. 1998. lib. bdg. 22.95 (*1-56723-061-X*) Yestermorrow, Inc.

—Tom Brown's Schooldays. 1972. (J). pap. 1.45 o.p. (*0-14-030534-3*, Puffin Bks.) Penguin Putnam Bks. for Young Readers.

—Tom Brown's Schooldays. 2002. (Children's Classics). 352p. (J). (gr. 3-6). pap. 3.95 (*1-85326-108-4*) Wordsworth Editions, Ltd. GBR. *Dist:* Advanced Global Distribution Services.

Ibbotson, Eva. Dial-a-Ghost. l.t. ed. 2002. 212p. (J). 22.95 (*0-7862-3927-1*) Gale Group.

—Dial-a-Ghost. (Illus.). 2003. 224p. (J). pap. 5.99 (*0-14-250018-6*, Puffin Bks.); 2001. 256p. (YA). (gr. 3-7). 15.99 (*0-525-46693-2*, Dutton Children's Bks.) Penguin Putnam Bks. for Young Readers.

—The Great Ghost Rescue. 2002. (J). pap. 29.95 incl. audio (*0-7540-6253-8*) BBC Audiobooks America.

—The Great Ghost Rescue. 2003. 192p. (J). pap. 5.99 (*0-14-250087-9*, Puffin Bks.); 2002. (Illus.). 144p. (YA). (gr. 3-9). 15.99 (*0-525-46769-6*, Dutton Children's Bks.) Penguin Putnam Bks. for Young Readers.

—The Great Ghost Rescue. l.t. ed. 2002. (Illus.). 185p. (J). 22.95 (*0-7862-3967-0*) Thorndike Pr.

James, Henry. The Portrait of a Lady. 1966. (Airmont Classics Ser.). (YA). (gr. 11 up). mass mkt. 2.50 o.p. (*0-8049-0098-1*, CL-98) Airmont Publishing Co., Inc.

—The Portrait of a Lady. Edel, Leon, ed. 1972. (YA). (gr. 9 up). pap. 16.36 (*0-395-05106-1*, Riverside Editions) Houghton Mifflin Co.

—The Portrait of a Lady. Dixson, Robert James, ed. rev. ed. 1987. (American Classics: Bk. 7). (gr. 9 up). pap. text 5.75 o.p. (*0-13-024571-2*, 18126) Prentice Hall, ESL Dept.

—The Turn of the Screw. 1998. (gr. 4-7). pap. 6.95 o.p. (*0-8114-6845-3*) Raintree Pubs.

James, Simon. Leon & Bob. 1997. (Illus.). 32p. (J). (gr. 1-4). 15.99 o.s.i (*1-56402-991-3*) Candlewick Pr.

Jane Eyre. 1988. (Short Classics Learning Files Ser.). (J). (gr. 4 up). 22.00 o.p. (*0-8172-2182-4*) Raintree Pubs.

Jeffries, Roderic. Trapped. 1973. (Trophy Bk.). 160p. (J). (gr. 4-6). pap. 3.50 o.p. (*0-06-440035-2*, Harper Trophy) HarperCollins Children's Bk. Group.

Jones, Diana Wynne. Wild Robert. 2003. 112p. (J). 15.99 (*0-06-055530-0*); lib. bdg. 16.89 (*0-06-055531-9*) HarperCollins Children's Bk. Group. (Greenwillow Bks.).

—Witch's Business. (J). 2004. 224p. pap. 5.99 (*0-06-008784-6*, Harper Trophy); 2002. 208p. (gr. 3 up). 15.99 (*0-06-008782-X*); 2002. 208p. (gr. 3 up). lib. bdg. 17.89 (*0-06-008783-8*) HarperCollins Children's Bk. Group.

Jordan, Sherryl. The Hunting of the Last Dragon. (J). (gr. 7 up). 2003. 256p. pap. 5.99 (*0-06-447231-0*); 2002. 192p. 15.95 (*0-06-028902-3*); 2002. 192p. lib. bdg. 15.89 (*0-06-028903-1*) HarperCollins Children's Bk. Group.

Keene, Carolyn. Mystery at Moorsea Manor. 1999. (Nancy Drew Mystery Stories Ser.: No. 150). 160p. (J). (gr. 3-6). pap. 4.99 (*0-671-02787-5*, Aladdin) Simon & Schuster Children's Publishing.

—Mystery at Moorsea Manor. 1999. (Nancy Drew Mystery Stories Ser.: No. 150). (J). (gr. 3-6). 10.04 (*0-606-19038-4*) Turtleback Bks.

Kennemore, Tim. Circle of Doom, RS. 2003. 208p. (J). 16.00 (*0-374-31284-2*, Farrar, Straus & Giroux (BYR)) Farrar, Straus & Giroux.

King-Smith, Dick. The Crowstarver. l.t. ed. 2000. (J). (Illus.). pap. (*0-7540-6095-0*); 216p. pap. incl. audio (*0-7540-6228-7*, RA029, Chivers Children's Audio Bks.) BBC Audiobooks America.

—Funny Frank. 2002. (Illus.). 112p. (J). (gr. 2-5). 14.95 (*0-375-81460-4*); lib. bdg. 16.99 (*0-375-91460-9*) Knopf, Alfred A. Inc.

—Funny Frank. 2003. (Illus.). 112p. (gr. 2-5). pap. text 4.99 (*0-440-41880-1*, Yearling) Random Hse. Children's Bks.

—Harriet's Hare. 1995. 104p. (gr. 4-7). 16.99 o.s.i (*0-517-59831-0*) Crown Publishing Group.

—Harriet's Hare. 1995. (Illus.). 104p. (J). (gr. 4-7). 15.00 o.s.i (*0-517-59830-2*, Random Hse. Bks. for Young Readers) Random Hse. Children's Bks.

—Harriet's Hare. 1997. 11.04 (*0-606-11441-6*) Turtleback Bks.

—Lady Daisy. 144p. (J). 1995. pap. 3.99 o.s.i (*0-440-40998-5*); 1993. (Illus.). 14.00 o.s.i (*0-385-30891-4*, Delacorte Pr.) Dell Publishing.

—The Roundhill. 2001. (Illus.). (J). 16.95 (*0-7540-6168-X*) BBC Audiobooks America.

—The Roundhill. 2002. (Illus.). 96p. (YA). (gr. 5-8). pap. 4.99 (*0-440-41844-5*) Random Hse., Inc.

—Sophie's Snail. unabr. ed. 1997. (Sophie Ser.: Vol. 1). (J). audio 9.95 (*1-85549-721-2*, CTC 112, Chivers Children's Audio Bks.) BBC Audiobooks America.

—Sophie's Snail. 1999. (Sophie Bks.). (Illus.). 96p. (J). (ps-3). bds. 4.99 o.p. (*0-7636-0484-4*) Candlewick Pr.

—Sophie's Snail. 1989. (Illus.). 80p. (J). (gr. k-4). 11.95 o.s.i (*0-385-29824-2*, Delacorte Pr.) Dell Publishing.

—Sophie's Snail. 1991. 96p. (J). pap. 3.25 o.s.i (*0-440-40482-7*, Yearling) Random Hse. Children's Bks.

—Sophie's Snail. 1999. (Sophie Bks). 11.14 (*0-606-16402-2*) Turtleback Bks.

—Spider Sparrow. unabr. ed. 2000. (J). (gr. 4-6). audio 30.00 (*0-8072-8406-8*, Listening Library) Random Hse. Audio Publishing Group.

—Spider Sparrow. 2001. 176p. (gr. 5 up). pap. text 4.99 (*0-440-41664-7*, Yearling) Random Hse. Children's Bks.

—Titus Rules! 2003. (Illus.). 96p. (J). (gr. 2-4). lib. bdg. 17.99 (*0-375-91461-7*); 15.95 (*0-375-81461-2*) Random Hse. Children's Bks. (Knopf Bks. for Young Readers).

Kipling, Rudyard. The Haunting of Holmescroft. 1998. (Classic Frights Ser.). Orig. Title: The House Surgeon. (Illus.). 64p. (J). (gr. 4-7). pap. 5.95 o.p. (*0-929605-81-0*, Classic Frights) Books of Wonder.

Kirwan, Anna. Juliet: A Dream Takes Flight, England, 1339. 1997. (Girlhood Journeys Ser.: Bk. 2). (Orig.). (J). 12.95 (*0-689-81203-5*, Simon & Schuster Children's Publishing) Simon & Schuster Children's Publishing.

—Juliet: A Secret Takes Flight, England, 1339. 1996. (Girlhood Journeys Ser.). (Illus.). 72p. (J). mass mkt. 5.99 (*0-689-80983-2*, Aladdin) Simon & Schuster Children's Publishing.

—Juliet: Midsummer at Greenchapel, Bk. 3. 1997. (Girlhood Journeys Ser.: No. 3). (Illus.). 72p. (J). (gr. 2-6). pap. 5.99 (*0-689-81560-3*, Simon Pulse) Simon & Schuster Children's Publishing.

—Juliet: Rescue at Marlehead Manor, England. 1997. (Girlhood Journeys Ser.: Bks. 2). (Illus.). 72p. (J). (gr. 2-6). per. 5.99 (*0-689-80987-5*, Aladdin) Simon & Schuster Children's Publishing.

Kulling, Monica. Great Expectations. 1996. (Bullseye Step into Classics Ser.). 10.04 (*0-606-10832-7*) Turtleback Bks.

Kulling, Monica & Dickens, Charles. Great Expectations. 1996. (Step into Classics Ser.). 112p. (gr. 2-7). pap. 3.99 (*0-679-87466-6*) Random Hse., Inc.

Laden, Janis. Bewitching Minx. 1988. mass mkt. 3.95 o.s.i (*0-8217-2532-7*, Zebra Bks.) Kensington Publishing Corp.

Lankester-Brisley, Joyce. Milly-Molly-Mandy Stories. 2002. (Kingfisher Modern Classics Ser.). (Illus.). 224p. (J). tchr. ed. 15.95 (*0-7534-5559-5*, Kingfisher) Houghton Mifflin Co. Trade & Reference Div.

Lawrence, Iain. Lord of the Nutcracker Men. 2001. 224p. (gr. 5 up). text 15.95 (*0-385-72924-3*, Delacorte Pr.) Dell Publishing.

—Lord of the Nutcracker Men. l.t. ed. 2002. 280p. (J). 24.95 (*0-7862-4155-1*) Gale Group.

—Lord of the Nutcracker Men. (gr. 5). 2003. 240p. pap. 5.99 (*0-440-41812-7*, Laurel Leaf); 2001. 224p. lib. bdg. 17.99 (*0-385-90024-4*, Delacorte Bks. for Young Readers) Random Hse. Children's Bks.

—The Smugglers. 2000. (Illus.). 208p. (YA). (gr. 4-7). pap. 5.50 (*0-440-41596-9*, Yearling) Dell Bks. for Young Readers CAN. *Dist:* Random Hse. of Canada, Ltd.

—The Smugglers. 1999. (Illus.). 192p. (gr. 5-9). text 15.95 (*0-385-32663-7*, Dell Books for Young Readers) Random Hse. Children's Bks.

—The Smugglers. 2000. (YA). pap., stu. ed. 59.95 incl. audio (*0-7887-4348-1*, 41142); (gr. 7). audio compact disk 48.00 (*0-7887-4734-7*, C1263E7); audio 204.80 (*0-7887-4448-8*, 47139) Recorded Bks., LLC.

—The Smugglers. l.t. ed. 2001. (Illus.). 246p. (J). 22.95 (*0-7862-3465-2*) Thorndike Pr.

—The Smugglers. 2000. (J). 11.04 (*0-606-19693-5*) Turtleback Bks.

—The Wreckers. 1998. 208p. (gr. 8-12). text 15.95 (*0-385-32535-5*, Delacorte Pr.) Dell Publishing.

—The Wreckers. 1999. (Dell Yearling Book Ser.). 224p. (gr. 5-9). reprint ed. pap. 5.50 (*0-440-41545-4*, Dell Books for Young Readers) Random Hse. Children's Bks.

—The Wreckers. 2000. (YA). (gr. 7). pap., stu. ed. 59.95 incl. audio (*0-7887-4195-0*, 41097) Recorded Bks., LLC.

—The Wreckers. l.t. ed. 1999. (Young Adult Ser.). (Illus.). 232p. (YA). (gr. 7-12). 22.95 (*0-7862-2189-5*) Thorndike Pr.

—The Wreckers. 1999. 11.04 (*0-606-17565-2*) Turtleback Bks.

Layton, George. The Swap. 1997. 192p. (YA). (gr. 4 up). 16.95 o.s.i (*0-399-23148-X*, G. P. Putnam's Sons) Penguin Group (USA) Inc.

Le Feuvre, Amy. Probable Sons, No. 2. 1996. (Golden Inheritance Ser.). (J). pap. 5.90 (*0-921100-81-7*) Inheritance Pubns.

—Probable Sons. 1997. (Classic Ser.). 128p. (J). (gr. 4-7). pap. 6.00 (*0-7188-2818-6*) Lutherworth Pr., The GBR. *Dist:* Parkwest Pubns., Inc.

—Teddy's Button. 2002. (Golden Inheritance Ser.: Vol. 6). (Illus.). 93p. (J). 6.90 (*0-921100-83-3*) Inheritance Pubns.

—Teddy's Button. 1997. (Classic Ser.). 128p. (J). (gr. 4-7). pap. 6.00 (*0-7188-2803-8*) Lutherworth Pr., The GBR. *Dist:* Parkwest Pubns., Inc.

Leavitt, Caroline. The Prince & the Pooch. 1997. (Adventures of Wishbone Ser.: No. 3). (Illus.). 128p. (J). (gr. 2-5). mass mkt. 3.99 o.p. (*1-57064-196-X*, Big Red Chair Bks.) Lyrick Publishing.

—The Prince & the Pooch. l.t. ed. 1999. (Adventures of Wishbone Ser.: No. 3). (Illus.). 144p. (J). (gr. 4 up). lib. bdg. 22.60 (*0-8368-2299-4*) Stevens, Gareth Inc.

Lerman, Rory S. Charlie's Checklist. 1997. (Illus.). 32p. (J). (ps-3). pap. 14.95 (*0-531-30001-3*, Orchard Bks.) Scholastic, Inc.

Lewis, J. Patrick. The Christmas of the Reddle Moon. 1994. (Illus.). 32p. (J). 15.99 o.s.i (*0-8037-1566-8*); 15.89 o.p. (*0-8037-1567-6*) Penguin Putnam Bks. for Young Readers. (Dial Bks. for Young Readers).

Lillington, Kenneth, text. A Christmas Carol. 1988. (Easy Piano Picture Bks.). (Illus.). 32p. (Orig.). (J). (gr. k up). pap. 9.95 o.p. (*0-571-10093-7*) Faber & Faber, Inc.

Love, D. Anne. The Puppeteer's Apprentice. 2003. 192p. (J). 16.95 (*0-689-84424-7*, McElderry, Margaret K.) Simon & Schuster Children's Publishing.

Lutzen, Hanna. Vlad the Undead. 192p. (YA). (gr. 8 up). 2001. pap. 5.95 (*0-88899-342-0*); 1998. 15.95 (*0-88899-341-2*) Groundwood Bks. CAN. *Dist:* Publishers Group West.

Magorian, Michelle. Not a Swan. 1992. (Laura Geringer Bks.). 416p. (YA). (gr. 7 up). 18.00 o.p. (*0-06-024214-0*); lib. bdg. 17.89 (*0-06-024215-9*) HarperCollins Children's Bk. Group.

Malory, Thomas. Le Morte D'Arthur, 2 vols., 2. Cowen, Janet, ed. 1970. (Classics Ser.). 554p. 13.00 (*0-14-043044-X*, Penguin Classics) Viking Penguin.

Manley, Seon. A Present for Charles Dickens. 1983. (Illus.). 124p. (J). (gr. 5 up). 12.95 o.p. (*0-664-32706-0*) Westminster John Knox Pr.

Manns, Nick. Operating Codes. 2001. (Illus.). 192p. (J). (gr. 5 up). 15.95 (*0-316-60465-8*) Little Brown Children's Bks.

Mark, Jan. Thunder & Lightnings. l.t. ed. 1987. (J). 16.95 o.p. (*0-7451-0496-7*, Galaxy Children's Large Print) BBC Audiobooks America.

—Thunder & Lightnings. 1979. (Illus.). (YA). (gr. 5 up). 11.95 o.p. (*0-690-03901-8*) HarperCollins Children's Bk. Group.

Mason, Simon. The Quigleys. 160p. 2003. (YA). pap. 4.99 (*0-440-41898-4*, Dell Books for Young Readers); 2002. (Illus.). (J). 14.95 (*0-385-75006-4*, Fickling, David Bks.) Random Hse. Children's Bks.

Matthews, Andrew. The Flip Side. 2003. 160p. (YA). lib. bdg. 17.99 (*0-385-90126-7*); (gr. 7). 15.95 (*0-385-73096-9*) Dell Publishing. (Delacorte Pr.).

Maxwell, Katie. The Year My Life Went down the Loo. (YA). 2004. mass mkt. 5.99 (*0-8439-5313-6*); 2003. mass mkt. 5.99 o.p. (*0-8439-5251-2*, SMOOCH) Dorchester Publishing Co., Inc.

Mayne, William. A Year & a Day. 2000. (Candlewick Treasures Ser.). (Illus.). 125p. (J). (gr. 3-7). 11.99 o.p. (*0-7636-0850-5*) Candlewick Pr.

—A Year & a Day. 1976. 112p. (J). (gr. 4-6). lib. bdg. 6.95 o.p. (*0-525-43450-X*, Dutton) Dutton/Plume.

—A Year & a Day. 1990. (J). (gr. 4-7). 19.25 (*0-8446-6431-6*) Smith, Peter Pub., Inc.

McAllister, Margaret. The Octave of Angels. 2002. (J). 128p. (gr. 4 up). 16.00 (*0-8028-5245-9*); 119p. pap. 8.00 (*0-8028-5240-8*) Eerdmans, William B. Publishing Co. (Eerdmans Bks For Young Readers).

McCully, Emily Arnold. Little Kit, or, the Industrious Flea Circus Girl. 1995. (Illus.). 32p. (J). (gr. k-3). 14.99 o.p. (*0-8037-1671-0*); 14.89 o.s.i (*0-8037-1674-5*) Penguin Putnam Bks. for Young Readers. (Dial Bks. for Young Readers).

—Popcorn at the Palace. 1997. (Illus.). 40p. (J). (gr. k-3). 16.00 (*0-15-277699-0*) Harcourt Children's Bks.

McCutcheon, Elsie. Summer of the Zeppelin, RS. 1985. 168p. (J). (gr. 5 up). 11.95 o.p. (*0-374-37294-2*, Farrar, Straus & Giroux (BYR)) Farrar, Straus & Giroux.

McKay, Hilary. The Amber Cat. 1999. (YA). pap., stu. ed. 41.00 incl. audio (*0-7887-3635-3*, 41000) Recorded Bks., LLC.

—The Amber Cat. 1997. 144p. (J). 15.00 (*0-689-81360-0*, McElderry, Margaret K.) Simon & Schuster Children's Publishing.

—The Amber Cat. 1999. 'p. 10.55 (*0-606-16326-3*) Turtleback Bks.

—Dog Friday. 1995. 144p. (J). (gr. 4-7). 15.00 (*0-689-80383-4*, McElderry, Margaret K.) Simon & Schuster Children's Publishing.

—Dolphin Luck. l.t. ed. 2003. (Illus.). (J). pap. 16.95 incl. audio (*0-7540-7865-5*, Galaxy Children's Large Print) BBC Audiobooks America.

—Dolphin Luck. 160p. (J). (gr. 3-7). 2000. (Illus.). pap. 4.99 o.s.i (*0-689-83889-1*, Aladdin); 1999. 16.00 (*0-689-82376-2*, McElderry, Margaret K.) Simon & Schuster Children's Publishing.

—Dolphin Luck. l.t. ed. 2001. (Illus.). 198p. (J). (gr. 4-7). 21.95 (*0-7862-2703-6*) Thorndike Pr.

—Dolphin Luck. 2000. (J). 11.04 (*0-606-20086-X*) Turtleback Bks.

—The Exiles at Home. 208p. (J). (gr. 4-8). 1997. (Illus.). pap. 3.99 (*0-689-81403-8*, Aladdin); 1994. 15.95 (*0-689-50610-4*, McElderry, Margaret K.) Simon & Schuster Children's Publishing.

—The Exiles in Love. 176p. (J). (gr. 3-7). 1999. pap. 4.50 (*0-689-82013-5*, Aladdin); 1998. (Illus.). 16.00 o.s.i (*0-689-81752-5*, McElderry, Margaret K.) Simon & Schuster Children's Publishing.

—The Exiles in Love. 1999. 10.55 (*0-606-17315-3*) Turtleback Bks.

—Indigo's Star. 2004. (J). 15.95 (*0-689-86563-5*, McElderry, Margaret K.) Simon & Schuster Children's Publishing.

—Saffy's Angel. unabr. ed. 2002. (J). (gr. 13 up). audio 25.00 (*0-8072-0823-X*, Listening Library) Random Hse. Audio Publishing Group.

—Saffy's Angel. 160p. (J). 2003. (Illus.). pap. 4.99 (*0-689-84934-6*, Aladdin); 2002. (gr. 4-7). 16.00 (*0-689-84933-8*, McElderry, Margaret K.) Simon & Schuster Children's Publishing.

—Saffy's Angel. 2003. (Juvenile Ser.). 227p. (J). 21.95 (*0-7862-5500-5*) Thorndike Pr.

—Was That Christmas? 2002. (Illus.). 32p. (J). 16.00 (*0-689-84765-3*, McElderry, Margaret K.) Simon & Schuster Children's Publishing.

McKay, Hilary & Piazza, Gail. The Amber Cat. 1999. 144p. (J). pap. 4.50 (*0-689-82557-9*, Aladdin) Simon & Schuster Children's Publishing.

Melnikoff, Pamela. Plots & Players. 1996. (Illus.). 160p. (YA). (gr. 8 up). pap. 9.95 (*0-8276-0576-5*) Jewish Pubn. Society.

—Plots & Players. 1989. 160p. (J). 9.95 o.p. (*0-87226-406-8*, Bedrick, Peter Bks.) McGraw-Hill Children's Publishing.

Meyer, Carolyn. Doomed Queen Anne. 2004. (Young Royals Ser.). (Illus.). 256p. (J). pap. 5.95 (*0-15-205086-8*, Gulliver Bks.) Harcourt Children's Bks.

—Mary, Bloody Mary. 2001. (Young Royals Ser.). (Illus.). 240p. (YA). (gr. 7 up). pap. 6.00 (*0-15-216456-1*, Gulliver Bks.) Harcourt Children's Bks.

Milne, A. A., pseud. The Red House Mystery. 2001. 202p. (J). per. 6.49 (*1-57924-702-4*) Jones, Bob Univ. Pr.

Mitchell, Mark. The Curious Knighthood of Sir Pellimore. Kemnitz, Myrna, ed. 1996. (Chronicles of the House of Chax Ser.: Bk. 1). 62p. (J). (gr. 3-6). pap. 9.99 (*0-88092-139-0*, 1390) Royal Fireworks Publishing Co.

Montgomery, Raymond A. Castle of Darkness. 1996. (Choose Your Own Nightmare Ser.: No. 4). (J). (gr. 4-8). 8.60 o.p. (*0-606-09140-8*) Turtleback Bks.

—The Castle of Darkness. 1995. (Choose Your Own Nightmare Ser.: No. 4). 96p. (J). (gr. 4-8). pap. 3.50 o.s.i (*0-553-48232-7*) Bantam Bks.

—Castle of Darkness. l.t. ed. 1996. (Illus.). 96p. (J). (gr. 4 up). lib. bdg. 22.60 o.p. (*0-8368-1513-0*) Stevens, Gareth Inc.

Moon, Nicola. Something Special. 1997. (Illus.). 32p. (J). (ps-1). 14.95 (*1-56145-137-1*) Peachtree Pubs., Ltd.

Morpurgo, Michael. The Butterfly Lion. 1997. (Illus.). 96p. (J). (gr. 3-7). 14.99 o.s.i (*0-670-87461-2*) Penguin Putnam Bks. for Young Readers.

—Escape from Shangri-La. 1998. 192p. (J). (gr. 5-8). 16.99 o.s.i (*0-399-23311-3*, Philomel) Penguin Putnam Bks. for Young Readers.

—Farm Boy. 1999. (Illus.). 74p. (YA). pap. 16.95 (*1-86205-192-5*) Pavilion Bks., Ltd. GBR. *Dist:* Trafalgar Square.

Morris, Gerald. Parsifal's Page. 240p. (J). (gr. 5-9). 2004. pap. 5.95 (*0-618-43237-X*); 2001. (Illus.). tchr. ed. 15.00 (*0-618-05509-6*) Houghton Mifflin Co.

—The Savage Damsel & the Dwarf. 224p. (gr. 5-9). 2004. (YA). pap. 5.95 (*0-618-19681-1*); 2000. (J). tchr. ed. 16.00 (*0-395-97126-8*) Houghton Mifflin Co.

—The Savage Damsel & the Dwarf. l.t. ed. 2001. (Illus.). 248p. (J). 22.95 (*0-7862-3037-1*) Thorndike Pr.

—The Savage Damsel & the Dwarf. 2000. E-Book 15.00 (*0-585-36843-0*) netLibrary, Inc.

—The Squire & His Knight. l.t. ed. 2001. (Young Adult Ser.). (Illus.). 257p. (J). (gr. 4-7). 21.95 (*0-7862-3039-8*) Thorndike Pr.

—The Squire, His Knight, & His Lady. 1999. 232p. (J). (gr. 5-9). tchr. ed. 15.00 (*0-395-91211-3*) Houghton Mifflin Co.

—The Squire, His Knight & His Lady. 2001. 240p. (YA). (gr. 7 up). reprint ed. mass mkt. 4.99 o.s.i (*0-440-22885-9*, Laurel Leaf) Random Hse. Children's Bks.

—The Squire's Tale. 1998. 224p. (J). (gr. 5-9). tchr. ed 15.00 (*0-395-86959-5*) Houghton Mifflin Co.

—The Squire's Tale. 2000. (Sister Frevisse Medieval Mysteries Ser.). (Illus.). 224p. (YA). (gr. 5 up). mass mkt. 4.99 (*0-440-22823-9*, Laurel Leaf) Random Hse. Children's Bks.

—The Squire's Tale. l.t. ed. 2000. (Young Adult Ser.). (Illus.). 213p. (J). 19.95 (*0-7862-3038-X*) Thorndike Pr.

Morris, Gilbert. Buckingham Palace & the Crown Jewels - Travels in England Vol. 2: Adventures of the Kerrigan Kids. 2001. (Illus.). 128p. (J). (gr. 3-7). pap. 5.99 (*0-8024-1579-2*) Moody Pr.

Mould, Wendy. Ants in My Pants. 2001. (Illus.). 32p. (J). (ps-3). tchr. ed. 15.00 (*0-618-09640-X*, Clarion Bks.) Houghton Mifflin Co. Trade & Reference Div.

Mullin, Caryl Cude. A Riddle of Roses. 2000. (Illus.). 222p. (YA). (gr. 5-8). pap. 6.95 (*1-896764-28-2*) Second Story Pr. CAN. *Dist:* Orca Bk. Pubs.

Napoli, Donna Jo. Crazy Jack. 1999. 144p. (YA). (gr. 7-12). 15.95 (*0-385-32627-0*, Delacorte Pr.) Dell Publishing.

—Crazy Jack. 2001. 144p. (YA). (gr. 7). mass mkt. 5.50 (*0-440-22788-7*, Laurel Leaf) Random Hse. Children's Bks.

—Crazy Jack. 2000. (YA). pap., stu. ed. 51.95 incl. audio (*0-7887-4159-4*, 41099) Recorded Bks., LLC.

—Crazy Jack. l.t. ed. 2000. (Young Adult Ser.). 183p. (YA). (gr. 8-12). 20.95 (*0-7862-3047-9*) Thorndike Pr.

Naylor, Phyllis Reynolds. Footprints at the Window. 2002. (York Trilogy Ser.: Vol. 3). (Illus.). 173p. (J). pap. 4.99 (*0-689-84963-X*, Aladdin) Simon & Schuster Children's Publishing.

Nesbit, Edith. The Deliverers of Their Country. 1996. (Illus.). 32p. (J). (ps-3). pap. 6.95 o.p. (*1-55858-612-1*); 16.95 o.p. (*1-55858-623-7*) North-South Bks., Inc.

—Five Children & It. 207p. 20.95 (*0-8488-2523-3*) Amereon, Ltd.

—Five Children & It. 1981. 182p. (J). reprint ed. lib. bdg. 21.95 (*0-89967-036-9*, Harmony Raine & Co.) Buccaneer Bks., Inc.

—Five Children & It. 2002. (Dover Evergreen Classics Ser.). (Illus.). 160p. (J). pap. 2.50 (*0-486-42366-2*) Dover Pubns., Inc.

—Five Children & It. 1999. (Books of Wonder). (Illus.). 256p. (J). (gr. 4-7). 22.95 (*0-688-13545-5*) HarperCollins Children's Bk. Group.

—Five Children & It. l.t. ed. 461p. pap. 40.00 (*0-7583-3207-6*); 397p. pap. 36.00 (*0-7583-3206-8*); 323p. pap. 30.00 (*0-7583-3205-X*); 263p. pap. 26.00 (*0-7583-3204-1*); 160p. pap. 19.00 (*0-7583-3202-5*); 205p. pap. 22.00 (*0-7583-3203-3*); 90p. pap. 14.00 (*0-7583-3200-9*); 117p. pap. 16.00 (*0-7583-3201-7*); 90p. lib. bdg. 20.00 (*0-7583-3192-4*); 160p. lib. bdg. 27.00 (*0-7583-3194-0*); 205p. lib. bdg. 33.00 (*0-7583-3195-9*); 323p. lib. bdg. 42.00 (*0-7583-3197-5*); 397p. lib. bdg. 47.00 (*0-7583-3198-3*); 461p. lib. bdg. 51.00 (*0-7583-3199-1*); 117p. lib. bdg. 23.00 (*0-7583-3193-2*); 263p. lib. bdg. 37.00 (*0-7583-3196-7*) Huge Print Pr.

—Five Children & It. 2002. 160p. (gr. 4-7). per. 88.99 (*1-4043-0285-9*) IndyPublish.com.

—Five Children & It. 1959. 224p. (J). pap. 2.95 o.p. (*0-14-030128-3*, Puffin Bks.) Penguin Putnam Bks. for Young Readers.

—Five Children & It. E-Book 5.00 (*0-7410-0796-7*) SoftBook Pr.

—Five Children & It. 2002. 192p. pap. 14.95 (*1-59224-938-8*); lib. bdg. 24.95 (*1-59224-942-6*) Wildside Pr.

—The Railway Children. 1998. (J). pap. text 7.00 o.p. (*0-582-40140-2*) Addison-Wesley Longman, Inc.

—The Railway Children. 1996. (Andre Deutsch Classics). 223p. (J). (gr. 5-8). 11.95 (*0-233-99037-2*) Andre Deutsch GBR. *Dist:* Trafalgar Square, Trans-Atlantic Pubns., Inc.

—The Railway Children. 1993. 272p. (J). (gr. 4 up). mass mkt. 3.25 o.s.i (*0-553-21415-2*, Bantam Classics) Bantam Bks.

—The Railway Children. 1975. (Dent's Illustrated Children's Classics Ser.). (Illus.). 208p. (J). 9.00 o.p. (*0-460-05094-X*) Biblio Distribution.

—The Railway Children. 1994. (Classics for Young Readers Ser.). 64p. (J). 5.98 o.p. (*0-86112-983-0*) Brimax Bks., Ltd.

—The Railway Children. 1992. 224p. (J). (gr. 4-7). pap. 3.50 o.s.i (*0-440-40602-1*) Dell Publishing.

—The Railway Children. (J). E-Book 2.49 (*1-58627-659-X*) Electric Umbrella Publishing.

—The Railway Children. Dryhurst, Dinah, tr. & illus. by. 2003. (J). 18.95 (*1-56792-261-9*) Godine, David R. Pub.

—The Railway Children. 1999. (Chapter Book Charmers Ser.). (Illus.). 80p. (J). (gr. 2-5). 2.99 o.p. (*0-694-01285-8*) HarperCollins Children's Bk. Group.

—The Railway Children. 1993. (Children's Classics Ser.). (J). (gr. 2-7). 12.95 (*0-679-42534-9*, Everyman's Library) Knopf Publishing Group.

—The Railway Children. 1992. 256p. mass mkt. 2.95 o.s.i (*0-451-52561-2*, Signet Classics) NAL.

—The Railway Children. 1991. (Oxford World's Classics Ser.). (Illus.). 224p. (J). pap. 4.95 o.p. (*0-19-282659-X*, 11912) Oxford Univ. Pr., Inc.

—The Railway Children. 2000. (Illus.). 224p. pap. 8.95 (*1-86205-235-2*) Pavilion Bks., Ltd. GBR. *Dist:* Trafalgar Square.

—The Railway Children. (Illus.). (J). (gr. 3-5). 9999. (Children's Classics Ser.: No. 740-19). pap. 3.50 o.p. (*0-7214-0824-9*); 1997. (Classic Ser.). 54p. 2.99 o.s.i (*0-7214-5708-8*) Penguin Group (USA) Inc. (Ladybird Bks.).

—The Railway Children. (Classics for Young Readers Ser.). (Illus.). 1994. 288p. (J). (gr. 4-7). pap. 3.99 (*0-14-036671-7*, Puffin Bks.); 1991. 192p. (YA). 16.95 o.s.i (*0-399-21819-X*, Philomel); 1983. 240p. (J). (gr. 3-7). pap. 3.50 o.p. (*0-14-035005-5*, Puffin Bks.) Penguin Putnam Bks. for Young Readers.

—The Railway Children. (Children's Library Ser.). 1996. (J). 1.10 o.s.i (*0-517-14153-1*); 1991. (Illus.). 192p. (YA). 9.99 o.s.i (*0-517-07011-1*) Random Hse. Value Publishing.

—The Railway Children. 9999. (Illus.). (J). 19.95 o.p. (*0-590-74000-8*) Scholastic, Inc.

—The Railway Children. 1988. (J). (gr. 5-8). 16.30 o.p. (*0-8446-6345-X*) Smith, Peter Pub., Inc.

—The Railway Children. E-Book 5.00 (*0-7410-0817-3*) SoftBook Pr.

—The Railway Children. 1961. (Illus.). (J). (gr. 2-5). pap. 1.95 o.p. (*0-14-030147-X*, Penguin Bks.) Viking Penguin.

—The Railway Children. 1998. (Children's Classics). 208p. (J). (gr. 4-7). pap. 3.95 (*1-85326-107-6*, 1076WW) Wordsworth Editions, Ltd. GBR. *Dist:* Advanced Global Distribution Services.

—Railway Children. 2000. (Juvenile Classics). (Illus.). iii, 188p. (J). pap. 2.50 (*0-486-41022-6*) Dover Pubns., Inc.

—Railway Children. (J). 3.50 (*0-340-71497-2*) Hodder & Stoughton, Ltd. GBR. *Dist:* Lubrecht & Cramer, Ltd., Trafalgar Square.

—The Railway Children, ERS. 1994. (J). 14.95 o.p. (*0-8050-3129-4*, Holt, Henry & Co. Bks. For Young Readers) Holt, Henry & Co.

—The Railway Children, Level 2. 2000. (C). pap. 7.66 (*0-582-41790-2*) Longman Publishing Group.

—The Railway Children. abr. ed. 1996. (J). audio 13.98 (*962-634-585-3*, NA208514, Naxos AudioBooks) Naxos of America, Inc.

—The Railway Children, Level 3. Hedge, Tricia, ed. 2000. (Bookworms Ser.). (Illus.). 74p. pap. text 5.95 (*0-19-423013-9*) Oxford Univ. Pr., Inc.

—The Railway Children. l.t. ed. 1987. (Charnwood Large Print Ser.). 288p. 29.99 o.p. (*0-7089-8382-0*, Charnwood) Thorpe, F. A. Pubs. GBR. *Dist:* Ulverscroft Large Print Bks., Ltd., Ulverscroft Large Print Canada, Ltd.

—The Railway Children. abr. ed. (Children's Classics Ser.). (J). 1997. pap. 15.95 o.p. incl. audio (*1-85998-750-8*); 1994. audio 14.95 (*1-85998-081-3*) Trafalgar Square.

Newbery, Linda. The Shell House. 2002. 352p. (J). (gr. 7-11). 15.95 (*0-385-75011-0*) Doubleday Publishing.

—The Shell House. 2004. 352p. (YA). (gr. 7-11). mass mkt. 6.50 (*0-440-23786-6*, Laurel Leaf) Random Hse. Children's Bks.

Newman, Robert. Merlin's Mistake. 2001. (Lost Treasures Ser.: No. 5). (Illus.). 352p. (J). pap. 4.99 (*0-7868-1546-9*); (gr. 3-7). pap. 1.99 (*0-7868-1545-0*) Hyperion Bks. for Children. (Volo).

—Merlin's Mistake. 1990. (Illus.). (J). (gr. 5-9). 18.75 (*0-8446-6187-2*) Smith, Peter Pub., Inc.

Nimmo, Jenny. Midnight for Charlie Bone. 2003. 352p. (J). (gr. 4-6). 9.95 (*0-439-47429-9*, Orchard Bks.) Scholastic, Inc.

Norman, Shane. The Adventures of Melton Greengrass. (J). E-Book 12.95 (*1-930756-53-4*, Bookmice) McGraw Publishing, Inc.

Northway, Jennifer. Get Lost, Laura! 1995. (Illus.). 32p. (J). (ps-2). pap. 10.95 o.s.i (*0-307-17520-0*, Golden Bks.) Random Hse. Children's Bks.

Norton, Mary. The Borrowers. unabr. ed. 1993. (Borrowers Ser.). (J). (gr. 3-7). 24.95 incl. audio (*0-7451-8551-7*, CCA 3002, Chivers Children's Audio Bks.) BBC Audiobooks America.

—The Borrowers. l.t. unabr. ed. 1986. (Borrowers Ser.). (J). (gr. 3-7). lib. bdg. 12.95 o.p. (*0-7451-0331-6*, Macmillan Reference USA) Gale Group.

—The Borrowers. (Illus.). 2003. 192p. (YA). pap. 5.95 (*0-15-204737-9*, Odyssey Classics); 1991. 160p. (J). (gr. 3-7). 22.95 o.s.i (*0-15-209991-3*); 1989. 192p. (YA). (gr. 3-7). pap. 6.00 o.s.i (*0-15-209990-5*, Odyssey Classics); 1965. 192p. (J). (gr. 3-7). pap. 4.95 o.p. (*0-15-613600-7*, Voyager Bks./Libros Viajeros); 1953. 192p. (J). (gr. 3-7). 17.00 (*0-15-209987-5*); 50th anniv. ed. 2003. 176p. (J). 19.95 (*0-15-204928-2*) Harcourt Children's Bks.

—The Borrowers. 1993. (Borrowers Ser.). (Illus.). 180p. (J). (gr. 3-7). pap. 6.00 (*0-15-200086-0*) Harcourt Trade Pubs.

—The Borrowers. 1981. (Borrowers Ser.). (J). (gr. 3-7). 12.05 (*0-606-02413-1*) Turtleback Bks.

—The Borrowers Afield. unabr. ed. 1993. (Borrowers Ser.). (J). (gr. 3-7). 32.95 incl. audio (*0-7451-8552-5*, CCA 3143, Chivers Children's Audio Bks.) BBC Audiobooks America.

—The Borrowers Afield. l.t. ed. 1987. (Borrowers Ser.). (J). (gr. 3-7). lib. bdg. 15.95 o.p. (*0-7451-0549-1*, Macmillan Reference USA) Gale Group.

—The Borrowers Afield. (Illus.). 2003. 224p. (YA). pap. 5.95 (*0-15-204732-8*, Odyssey Classics); 1990. 224p. (YA). (gr. 3-7). pap. 6.00 o.s.i (*0-15-210535-2*, Odyssey Classics); 1955. 224p. (J). (gr. 3-7). 17.00 (*0-15-210166-7*); 1970. (J). (gr. 3-7). reprint ed. pap. 4.95 o.p. (*0-15-613601-5*, Voyager Bks./Libros Viajeros) Harcourt Children's Bks.

—The Borrowers Afield. 1983. (Borrowers Ser.). (J). (gr. 3-7). 12.05 (*0-606-02414-X*) Turtleback Bks.

—The Borrowers Afloat. l.t. ed. 1988. (Borrowers Ser.). 216p. (J). (gr. 3-7). 13.95 o.p. (*0-8161-4441-9*, Macmillan Reference USA) Gale Group.

—The Borrowers Afloat. (Illus.). 192p. 2003. (YA). pap. 5.95 (*0-15-204733-6*, Odyssey Classics); 1990. (YA). (gr. 3-7). pap. 6.00 o.s.i (*0-15-210534-4*, Odyssey Classics); 1959. (J). (gr. 3-7). 17.00 (*0-15-210345-7*); 1973. (J). (gr. 3-7). reprint ed. pap. 4.95 o.p. (*0-15-613603-1*, Voyager Bks./Libros Viajeros) Harcourt Children's Bks.

—The Borrowers Afloat. 1987. (Borrowers Ser.). (J). (gr. 3-7). 12.05 (*0-606-02417-4*) Turtleback Bks.

—The Borrowers Aloft. (Borrowers Ser.). (Illus.). (gr. 3-7). reprint ed. 1990. 224p. (YA). pap. 6.00 o.s.i (*0-15-210533-6*, Odyssey Classics); 1974. 192p. (J). pap. 4.95 o.p. (*0-15-613604-X*, Voyager Bks./Libros Viajeros) Harcourt Children's Bks.

—The Borrowers Aloft. 1961. (Borrowers Ser.). (J). (gr. 3-7). 12.05 (*0-606-02416-6*) Turtleback Bks.

—The Borrowers Aloft: Plus the Short Tale, Poor Stainless. 1961. (Borrowers Ser.). (Illus.). 224p. (J). (gr. 3-7). reprint ed. 17.00 (*0-15-210524-7*) Harcourt Children's Bks.

—The Borrowers Avenged. (Illus.). 2003. 304p. (YA). pap. 5.95 (*0-15-204731-X*, Odyssey Classics); 1990. 304p. (YA). (gr. 3-7). pap. 6.00 o.s.i (*0-15-210532-8*, Odyssey Classics); 1984. 300p. (J). (gr. 3-7). pap. 4.95 o.p. (*0-15-210531-X*, Voyager Bks./Libros Viajeros); 1982. 304p. (J). (gr. 3-7). 17.00 (*0-15-210530-1*) Harcourt Children's Bks.

—The Borrowers Avenged. 1988. (Borrowers Ser.). (J). (gr. 3-7). 18.05 o.p. (*0-8446-6358-1*) Smith, Peter Pub., Inc.

—The Borrowers Avenged. 1982. (Borrowers Ser.). (J). (gr. 3-7). 12.05 (*0-606-03322-X*) Turtleback Bks.

O'Brien, Patrick. The Making of a Knight: How Sir James Earned His Armor. 1998. (Illus.). 32p. (J). (gr. 1-4). 15.95 (*0-88106-354-1*) Charlesbridge Publishing, Inc.

Orde, Lewis. The Proprietor's Daughter. 1988. 18.95 (*0-316-67340-4*) Little Brown & Co.

Osborne, Mary Pope. Stage Fright on a Summer Night. 2002. (Illus.). 96p. (J). (gr. 1-4). pap. 3.99 (*0-375-80611-3*); lib. bdg. 11.99 (*0-375-90611-8*) Random Hse., Inc.

Overton, Jenny. The Thirteen Days of Christmas. 1987. (Illus.). 144p. (J). (gr. 5 up). 12.95 o.p. (*0-688-07321-2*, Greenwillow Bks.) HarperCollins Children's Bk. Group.

Paine, Penelope C. Time for Horatio. 2001. 48p. (J). per. 17.95 (*0-9707944-7-9*) Paper Posie.

Pascal, Francine, creator. Love & Death in London. 1996. (Sweet Valley High Ser.: No. 104). 208p. (YA). (gr. 7 up). mass mkt. 2.49 o.s.i (*0-553-57036-6*) Bantam Bks.

Paton Walsh, Jill. Gaffer Samson's Luck, RS. 1984. (Illus.). 112p. (YA). (gr. 5 up). 14.00 o.p. (*0-374-32498-0*, Farrar, Straus & Giroux (BYR)) Farrar, Straus & Giroux.

—Grace, RS. 1992. 256p. (YA). (gr. 7 up). 16.00 o.p. (*0-374-32758-0*, Farrar, Straus & Giroux (BYR)) Farrar, Straus & Giroux.

—A Parcel of Patterns, RS. (gr. 7 up). 1992. 144p. (YA). pap. 5.95 (*0-374-45743-3*, Aerial); 1983. 139p. (J). 11.95 o.p. (*0-374-35750-1*, Farrar, Straus & Giroux (BYR)) Farrar, Straus & Giroux.

—A Parcel of Patterns. 1995. (J). 20.75 (*0-8446-6819-2*) Smith, Peter Pub., Inc.

Pearce, Philippa. Minnow on the Say. 2000. (Illus.). 256p. (J). (gr. 5 up). 16.95 (*0-688-17098-6*, Greenwillow Bks.) HarperCollins Children's Bk. Group.

Peck, Richard. Amanda/Miranda. 1981. 544p. (YA). (gr. 7 up). pap. 2.95 o.p. (*0-380-53850-4*, 53850-5, Avon Bks.) Morrow/Avon.

—Amanda/Miranda. Kane, Cindy, ed. abr. ed. 1999. (Illus.). 176p. (YA). (gr. 7-12). 16.99 (*0-8037-2489-6*, Dial Bks. for Young Readers) Penguin Putnam Bks. for Young Readers.

—Amanda/Miranda. 2001. (J). 12.04 (*0-606-21025-3*) Turtleback Bks.

—Amanda/Miranda. 1980. 12.95 o.p. (*0-670-11530-4*) Viking Penguin.

Peyton, K. M. Blind Beauty. Brooks, Donna, ed. 2001. (Illus.). 368p. (J). (gr. 7). 18.99 (*0-525-46652-5*) Penguin Putnam Bks. for Young Readers.

—Darkling. 1989. 16.95 o.p. (*0-385-26963-3*) Doubleday Publishing.

—A Pattern of Roses. 1973. (Illus.). 132p. (J). (gr. 6 up). o.p. (*0-690-61199-4*) HarperCollins Children's Bk. Group.

—Snowfall. 1998. 344p. (YA). (gr. 7-9). tchr. ed. 16.00 (*0-395-89598-7*) Houghton Mifflin Co.

Phillips, Ann. A Haunted Year. 1994. (Illus.). 176p. (J). (gr. 4-8). text 14.95 o.s.i (*0-02-774605-4*, Simon & Schuster Children's Publishing) Simon & Schuster Children's Publishing.

—The Peace Child. 1988. (Illus.). 160p. (J). (gr. 5 up). 15.00 o.p. (*0-19-271560-7*) Oxford Univ. Pr., Inc.

Post, Douglas. The Wind in the Willows - Musical. 1987. 87p. (J). pap. 5.95 (*0-87129-172-X*, W05) Dramatic Publishing Co.

The Prince & the Pauper. 1988. mass mkt. 2.25 (*0-938819-24-0*, Aerie) Doherty, Tom Assocs., LLC.

Pringle, Eric. Big George. 2001. (Illus.). 160p. (J). (gr. 3-7). 18.95 (*1-55037-713-2*); pap. 9.95 (*1-55037-712-4*) Annick Pr., Ltd. CAN. *Dist:* Firefly Bks., Ltd.

Pullein-Thompson, Josephine. Black Beauty's Family. 1989. (J). 7.98 o.p. (*0-671-08724-X*) Simon & Schuster.

Pullein-Thompson, Josephine, et al. Black Beauty's Clan. 1981. (Illus.). 288p. (J). (gr. 7-9). text 8.95 o.p. (*0-07-050913-1*) McGraw-Hill Cos., The.

—Black Beauty's Family. 1980. (Illus.). 288p. (J). (gr. 7-9). text 8.95 o.p. (*0-07-050914-X*) McGraw-Hill Cos., The.

Pullman, Philip. Count Karstein. 2000. (J). pap. 8.95 (*0-440-86266-3*) Transworld Publishers Ltd. GBR. *Dist:* Trafalgar Square.

—I Was a Rat!: or The Scarlet Slippers. l.t. unabr. ed. 2001. (Read-Along Ser.). 224p. (J). 29.95 incl. audio (*0-7540-6233-3*, RA034); (YA). audio 24.95 (*0-7540-5193-5*, CCA3631) BBC Audiobooks America. (Chivers Children's Audio Bks.).

—I Was a Rat!: or The Scarlet Slippers. 2000. (Illus.). 176p. (gr. 3-5). text 15.95 (*0-375-80176-6*); lib. bdg. 17.99 (*0-375-90176-0*) Random Hse. Children's Bks. (Knopf Bks. for Young Readers).

Raintree Steck-Vaughn Staff. Jane Eyre, 5 vols., Set. 1991. (Short Classics Ser.). (Illus.). (J). pap. 32.69 (*0-8114-6966-2*) Raintree Pubs.

—Pride & Prejudice, 5 vols., Set. 1991. (Short Classics Ser.). (Illus.). (J). pap. 32.69 (*0-8114-6972-7*) Raintree Pubs.

—Wuthering Heights: Abridged for Children, 5 vols., Set. 1991. (Short Classics Ser.). (Illus.). (J). pap. 32.69 (*0-8114-6983-2*) Raintree Pubs.

Random House Value Publishing Staff & Dickens, Charles. Children's Stories from Dickens. 1998. (Illustrated Stories for Children Ser.). (Illus.). 128p. (J). 7.99 (*0-517-20301-4*) Random Hse. Value Publishing.

Ransome, Arthur. The Big Six. 2000. (Swallows & Amazons Ser.). (Illus.). 368p. (YA). (gr. 5 up). reprint ed. pap. 14.95 (*1-56792-119-1*) Godine, David R. Pub.

—Coot Club. 1990. (Swallows & Amazons Ser.). (Illus.). 352p. (J). (gr. 4-6). reprint ed. pap. 14.95 (*0-87923-787-2*) Godine, David R. Pub.

—Secret Water. 1995. (Swallows & Amazons Ser.). (Illus.). 376p. (J). (gr. 5-8). pap. 14.95 (*1-56792-064-0*) Godine, David R. Pub.

Reed, Neil, illus. Black Beauty. 1997. 96p. (J). (gr. 1-6). 9.98 (*1-85854-549-8*) Brimax Bks., Ltd.

Rennison, Louise. Angus, Thongs & Full-Frontal Snogging: Confessions of Georgia Nicolson. (J). (gr. 7 up). 2001. 272p. pap. 6.99 (*0-06-447227-2*, HarperTempest); 2000. 256p. 15.99 (*0-06-028814-0*); 2000. (Illus.). 256p. lib. bdg. 15.89 (*0-06-028871-X*) HarperCollins Children's Bk. Group.

—Dancing in My Nuddy-Pants: Even Further Confessions of Georgia Nicolson. (J). 2004. (Illus.). 240p. pap. 6.99 (*0-06-009748-5*); 2003. 224p. 15.99 (*0-06-009746-9*); 2003. 224p. lib. bdg. 16.89 (*0-06-009747-7*) HarperCollins Children's Bk. Group. (HarperTempest).

—Knocked Out by My Nunga-Nungas: Further, Further Confessions of Georgia Nicolson. 2002. 192p. (J). (gr. 8-10). 15.99 (*0-06-623656-8*); lib. bdg. 15.89 (*0-06-623695-9*) HarperCollins Pubs.

—On the Bright Side, I'm Now the Girlfriend of a Sex God: Further Confessions of Georgia Nicolson. 2001. 256p. (J). (gr. 7 up). 15.99 (*0-06-028813-2*); lib. bdg. 15.89 (*0-06-028872-8*) HarperCollins Children's Bk. Group.

—On the Bright Side, I'm Now the Girlfriend of a Sex God: Further Confessions of Georgia Nicolson. 2002. 272p. (J). pap. 6.99 (*0-06-447226-4*) HarperCollins Pubs.

—On the Bright Side, I'm Now the Girlfriend of a Sex God: Further Confessions of Georgia Nicolson. 2003. 256p. (J). mass mkt. 6.99 (*0-06-052185-6*, Avon Bks.) Morrow/Avon.

Riordan, James. Great Expectations. 2002. (Illus.). 96p. (J). (gr. 3-9). 19.95 (*0-19-274190-X*) Oxford Univ. Pr., Inc.

Rose, Malcolm. The Highest Form of Killing. 1992. 240p. (YA). (gr. 9 up). 16.95 (*0-15-234270-2*) Harcourt Children's Bks.

Rowling, J. K. Harry Potter & the Chamber of Secrets. braille ed. 1999. (Harry Potter Ser.: Year 2). 520p. (YA). (gr. 3 up). pap. 17.99 (*0-939173-35-2*) National Braille Pr.

—Harry Potter & the Chamber of Secrets. unabr. ed. 2000. (Harry Potter Ser.: Year 2). (YA). (gr. 3 up). audio 44.00 (*0-8072-8207-3*, YA137SP, Listening Library) Random Hse. Audio Publishing Group.

—Harry Potter & the Chamber of Secrets. (Harry Potter Ser.). 2003. 352p. (J). 24.95 (*0-439-55489-6*, Levine, Arthur A. Bks.); 2002. (Illus.). 352p. (J). pap. 6.99 (*0-439-42010-5*, Levine, Arthur A. Bks.); 2000. (Illus.). 352p. (YA). (gr. 3 up). pap. 6.99 (*0-439-06487-2*); 1999. (Illus.). viii, 341p. (J). (gr. 3 up). 19.95 (*0-439-06486-4*, Levine, Arthur A. Bks.); 2002. (Illus.). 352p. (J). 75.00 (*0-439-20353-8*, Levine, Arthur A. Bks.) Scholastic, Inc.

—Harry Potter & the Chamber of Secrets. l.t. ed. 2000. (Harry Potter Ser.: Year 2). (Illus.). 464p. (J). (gr. 3 up). 24.95 (*0-7862-2273-5*) Thorndike Pr.

—Harry Potter & the Goblet of Fire. unabr. collector's ed. 2000. (Harry Potter Ser.: Year 4). (YA). (gr. 3 up). audio compact disk 33.95 (*0-7366-5848-3*) Books on Tape, Inc.

—Harry Potter & the Goblet of Fire. braille ed. 2000. (Harry Potter Ser.: Year 4). 650p. (YA). (gr. 3 up). pap. 25.95 (*0-939173-37-9*) National Braille Pr.

—Harry Potter & the Goblet of Fire. (Harry Potter Ser.). 2003. 752p. (J). 30.95 (*0-439-55490-X*); 2002. 752p. (J). (gr. 3 up). pap. 8.99 (*0-439-13960-0*); 2000. (Illus.). xi, 734p. (YA). (gr. 3 up). 25.95 (*0-439-13959-7*) Scholastic, Inc. (Levine, Arthur A. Bks.).

—Harry Potter & the Goblet of Fire. l.t. ed. 2000. (Harry Potter Ser.: Year 4). (Illus.). 936p. (J). (gr. 3 up). 25.95 (*0-7862-2927-6*) Thorndike Pr.

—Harry Potter & the Prisoner of Azkaban. braille ed. 1999. (Harry Potter Ser.: Year 3). (YA). (gr. 3 up). pap. 19.95 (*0-939173-36-0*) National Braille Pr.

—Harry Potter & the Prisoner of Azkaban. 2000. tchr. ed. 9.95 (*1-58130-656-3*); stu. ed. 11.95 (*1-58130-657-1*) Novel Units, Inc.

—Harry Potter & the Prisoner of Azkaban. (Harry Potter Ser.: Year 3). (Illus.). (J). (gr. 3 up). 2001. 448p. pap. 7.99 (*0-439-13636-9*, Levine, Arthur A. Bks.); 1999. ix, 435p. 19.95 (*0-439-13635-0*) Scholastic, Inc.

—Harry Potter & the Prisoner of Azkaban. l.t. ed. 2000. (Harry Potter Ser.: Year 3). (Illus.). 592p. (YA). (gr. 3 up). 24.95 (*0-7862-2274-3*) Thorndike Pr.

—Harry Potter & the Sorcerer's Stone. 1997. (Harry Potter Ser.: Year 1). (Illus.). 223p. (YA). (gr. 3 up). pap. (*0-7475-3274-5*) Bloomsbury Publishing, Ltd. GBR. *Dist:* Raincoast Bk. Distribution.

—Harry Potter & the Sorcerer's Stone. unabr. ed. (Harry Potter Ser.: Year 1). (YA). (gr. 3 up). 320p. pap. 62.00 incl. audio (*0-8072-1547-3*); 2000. pap. 44.00 incl. audio (*0-8072-8119-0*, YYA108SP) Random Hse. Audio Publishing Group. (Listening Library).

—Harry Potter & the Sorcerer's Stone. (Harry Potter Ser.: Year 1). (YA). (gr. 3 up). 2001. 384p. mass mkt. 6.99 (*0-439-36213-X*); 1999. (Illus.). 312p. pap. 6.99 (*0-590-35342-X*); 1998. (Illus.). 320p. 19.95 (*0-590-35340-3*, Levine, Arthur A. Bks.); 2000. 320p. 75.00 (*0-439-20352-X*) Scholastic, Inc.

—Harry Potter & the Sorcerer's Stone. l.t. ed. 1999. (Harry Potter Ser.: Year 1). (Illus.). 422p. (YA). (gr. 3 up). 24.95 (*0-7862-2272-7*) Thorndike Pr.

—Harry Potter & the Sorcerer's Stone. 1999. (Harry Potter Ser.: Year 1). (Illus.). (YA). (gr. 3 up). 12.95 o.p. (*0-606-17233-5*) Turtleback Bks.

—Harry Potter Boxed Set: Harry Potter & the Sorcerer's Stone; Harry Potter & the Chamber of Secrets; Harry Potter & the Prisoner of Azkaban, 3 vols. (Harry Potter Ser.: Years 1-3). (Illus.). (YA). 2002. pap. 21.97 (*0-439-32466-1*); 1999. (gr. 3 up). 55.85 (*0-439-13316-5*) Scholastic, Inc. (Levine, Arthur A. Bks.).

—Harry Potter Boxed Set: Harry Potter & the Sorcerer's Stone; Harry Potter & the Chamber of Secrets; Harry Potter & the Prisoner of Azkaban; Harry Potter & the Goblet of Fire, 4 vols. (Harry Potter Ser.: Years 1-4). 2002. 752p. (YA). (gr. 3 up). pap. 30.96 (*0-439-43486-6*, Levine, Arthur A. Bks.); 2001. 85.80 (*0-439-24954-6*); 2000. (YA). (gr. 3 up). 85.80 (*0-641-06631-7*, Levine, Arthur A. Bks.) Scholastic, Inc.

—Harry Potter Boxed Set: Harry Potter & the Sorcerer's Stone; Harry Potter & the Chamber of Secrets; Harry Potter & the Prisoner of Azkaban; Harry Potter & the Goblet of Fire; Harry Potter & the Order of the Phoenix, 5 vols. ltd. ed. 2003. (Harry Potter Ser.). 2000p. (J). 99.95 (*0-439-61255-1*) Scholastic, Inc.

—Harry Potter Coffret: Harry Potter a l'Ecole des Sorciers; Harry Potter et la Chambre des Secrets; Harry Potter et le Prisonnier d'Azkaban. 1999. (Harry Potter Ser.: Years 1-3). Tr. of Harry Potter Boxed Set: Harry Potter & the Chamber of Secrets; Harry Potter & the Sorcerer's Stone; Harry Potter & the Prisoner of Azkaban. (FRE.). 1400p. (YA). (gr. 3 up). 34.95 (*0-320-03843-2*) French & European Pubns., Inc.

—Harry Potter Coffret: Harry Potter a l'Ecole des Sorciers; Harry Potter et la Chambre des Secrets; Harry Potter et le Prisonnier d'Azkaban. 1999. (Harry Potter Ser.: Years 1-3). Tr. of Harry Potter Boxed Set: Harry Potter & the Chamber of Secrets; Harry Potter & the Sorcerer's Stone; Harry Potter & the Prisoner of Azkaban. (FRE.). (YA). (gr. 3 up). pap. 43.95 (*2-07-052929-0*) Gallimard, Editions FRA. *Dist:* Distribooks, Inc.

—Harry Potter et la Chambre des Secrets. 1999. (Harry Potter Ser.: Year 2). Tr. of Harry Potter & the Chamber of Secrets. (FRE.). (YA). (gr. 3 up). pap. 13.95 (*0-320-03778-9*) French & European Pubns., Inc.

—Harry Potter et la Chambre des Secrets. 1999. (Harry Potter Ser.: Year 2). Tr. of Harry Potter & the Chamber of Secrets. (FRE., Illus.). (YA). (gr. 3 up). pap. 14.95 (*2-07-052455-8*) Gallimard, Editions FRA. *Dist:* Distribooks, Inc.

—Harry Potter et le Prisonnier d'Azkaban. 1999. (Harry Potter Ser.: Year 3). Tr. of Harry Potter & the Prisoner of Azkaban. (FRE.). (YA). (gr. 3 up). pap. (*2-07-052818-9*) Gallimard, Editions.

—Harry Potter et l'Ecole des Sorciers. 3rd ed. 1998. (Harry Potter Ser.: Year 1). Tr. of Harry Potter & the Sorcerer's Stone. (FRE., Illus.). (YA). (gr. 3 up). pap. 14.95 (*2-07-050142-6*) Distribooks, Inc.

—Harry Potter et l'Ecole des Sorciers. 1999. (Harry Potter Ser.: Year 1). Tr. of Harry Potter & the Sorcerer's Stone. (FRE.). (YA). (gr. 3 up). pap. 16.95 (*0-320-03780-0*) French & European Pubns., Inc.

—Harry Potter und der Gefangene von Azkaban. 1999. (Harry Potter Ser.: Year 3). Tr. of Harry Potter & the Prisoner of Azkaban. (GER.). (YA). (gr. 3 up). 28.95 (*3-551-55169-3*) Carlsen Verlag DEU. *Dist:* Distribooks, Inc.

—Harry Potter und der Stein de Weisen. 1999. (Harry Potter Ser.: Year 1). Tr. of Harry Potter & the Sorcerer's Stone. (GER.). 335p. (YA). (gr. 3 up). 28.95 (*3-551-55167-7*) Carlsen Verlag DEU. *Dist:* Distribooks, Inc.

—Harry Potter und die Kammer des Schreckens. 1999. (Harry Potter Ser.: Year 2). Tr. of Harry Potter & Chamber of Secrets. (GER.). (YA). (gr. 3 up). 28.95 (*3-551-55168-5*) Carlsen Verlag DEU. *Dist:* Distribooks, Inc.

—Harry Potter y el Prisionero de Azkaban. 2000. (Harry Potter Ser.: Year 3). (SPA., Illus.). 360p. (YA). (gr. 3 up). 15.95 (*84-7888-519-6*, SAL1889) Emece Editores ESP. *Dist:* Lectorum Pubns., Inc.

—Harry Potter y el Prisionero de Azkaban. 2000. (Harry Potter Ser.: Year 3). (SPA.). (YA). (gr. 3 up). 16.95 (*0-320-03783-5*) French & European Pubns., Inc.

—Harry Potter y la Camara Secreta. (Harry Potter Ser.: Year 2). (SPA., Illus.). (YA). 2000. 288p. (gr. 3 up). (*84-7888-495-5*, SAL4595); 1999. 256p. (gr. 7 up). 15.95 (*84-7888-445-9*, SAL2819) Emece Editores ESP. *Dist:* Lectorum Pubns., Inc., Lectorum Pubns., Inc., Libros Sin Fronteras.

—Harry Potter y la Camara Secreta. 1999. (Harry Potter Ser.: Year 2). (SPA.). (YA). (gr. 3 up). 14.95 (*0-320-03781-9*) French & European Pubns., Inc.

—Harry Potter y la Piedra Filosofal. 1999. (Harry Potter Ser.: Year 1). (SPA.). (YA). (gr. 3 up). 14.95 (*0-320-03782-7*) French & European Pubns., Inc.

San Souci, Robert D. Young Guinevere. 1996. (Illus.). 32p. (J). (ps-3). pap. 7.99 o.s.i (*0-440-41291-9*) Dell Publishing.

Scherer, Catherine W. Simon & Barklee in England: Fun Book. Scherer, Catherine W., ed. 2001. (Another Country Calling Ser.). (Illus.). 32p. (J). (gr. 2-6). pap. 4.00 (*0-9704661-5-3*, Explorer Media) Simon & Barklee, Inc./ExplorerMedia.

Schlee, Ann. Ask Me No Questions. 1982. 228p. (J). (gr. 5 up). o.p. (*0-03-061523-2*) Holt, Henry & Co.

Scott, Deborah. The California Kid Fights Back. 1998. (J). (gr. 3-7). pap. 3.99 (*0-380-72851-6*, Avon Bks.) Morrow/Avon.

Scullard, Sue, illus. The Flyaway Pantaloons. (J). (gr. 2-4). 22.95 o.p. incl. audio (*0-87499-257-5*); pap. 14.95 o.p. incl. audio (*0-87499-256-7*); pap. 33.95 o.p. incl. audio (*0-87499-258-3*) Live Oak Media.

Sedgwick, Marcus. Floodland. 2001. (Illus.). 160p. (gr. 3-7). text 15.95 o.s.i (*0-385-32801-X*, Delacorte Bks. for Young Readers) Random Hse. Children's Bks.

—Floodland: Library Edition. unabr. ed. 2001. (J). (gr. 4-6). audio 23.00 (*0-8072-8864-0*, Listening Library) Random Hse. Audio Publishing Group.

—Witch Hill. 2001. (Illus.). 160p. (YA). (gr. 5-9). 15.95 o.s.i (*0-385-32802-8*, Dell Books for Young Readers) Random Hse. Children's Bks.

Sewell, Anna. The Annotated Black Beauty. 1990. 500p. 140.00 (*0-85131-438-4*) Allen, J. A. & Co., Ltd. GBR. *Dist:* State Mutual Bk. & Periodical Service, Ltd.

—Black Beauty. 2002. (Great Illustrated Classics). (Illus.). 240p. (J). (gr. 3-8). lib. bdg. 21.35 (*1-57765-681-4*, ABDO & Daughters) ABDO Publishing Co.

—Black Beauty. 1963. (YA). (gr. 5 up). mass mkt. 1.50 (*0-8049-0023-X*, CL-23) Airmont Publishing Co., Inc.

—Black Beauty. (J). 21.95 (*0-88411-065-6*) Amereon, Ltd.

—Black Beauty. 1996. 224p. (J). (gr. 5-8). 11.95 (*0-233-99039-9*) Andre Deutsch GBR. *Dist:* Trafalgar Square, Trans-Atlantic Pubns., Inc.

—Black Beauty. 1986. (J). mass mkt. 9.95 o.p. (*0-553-35502-3*) Bantam Bks.

—Black Beauty. adapted ed. 1997. (Living Classics Ser.). (Illus.). 32p. (J). (gr. 3-7). 14.95 o.p. (*0-7641-7050-3*) Barron's Educational Series, Inc.

—Black Beauty. 1977. (Dent's Illustrated Children's Classics Ser.). (Illus.). 237p. (J). (gr. 4 up). reprint ed. 11.00 o.p. (*0-460-05012-5*, BKA 01620) Biblio Distribution.

—Black Beauty. (J). 2000. per. 12.50 (*1-58396-361-8*); 2001. per. 15.50 (*1-58396-383-9*) Blue Unicorn Editions.

—Black Beauty. (Longmeadow Press Paperback Classics Ser.). (J). 1994. 196p. pap. 2.95 o.p. (*0-681-00680-3*); 1994. (Illus.). 288p. 10.95 o.p. (*0-681-00586-6*); 1986. (Illus.). 226p. (gr. 4 up). 10.95 o.p. (*0-681-40058-7*) Borders Pr.

—Black Beauty. 1994. 96p. (J). 7.98 (*0-86112-830-3*) Brimax Bks., Ltd.

—Black Beauty. 1995. reprint ed. lib. bdg. 24.95 o.p. (*1-56849-661-3*) Buccaneer Bks., Inc.

—Black Beauty. (J). reprint ed. lib. bdg. 48.00 (*0-7426-1042-X*); 2001. (Illus.). pap. text 28.00 (*0-7426-6042-7*) Classic Bks.

—Black Beauty. 1988. o.s.i (*0-517-62431-1*) Crown Publishing Group.

—Black Beauty. 1990. 224p. (J). (gr. 4 up). pap. 3.99 o.s.i (*0-440-40355-3*) Dell Publishing.

—Black Beauty. 1989. (J). mass mkt. 3.25 o.s.i (*0-8125-0429-1*, Tor Classics); 1989. (Illus.). 196p. (gr. 4-7). mass mkt. 2.99 (*0-8125-0428-3*, Tor Classics); 1988. (J). mass mkt. 4.95 (*1-55902-005-9*, Aerie); Level 3. 1988. mass mkt. 2.25 (*0-938819-72-0*, Aerie) Doherty, Tom Assocs., LLC.

—Black Beauty. 2000. (Read & Listen Ser.). (Illus.). (J). 64p. (gr. 4-7). pap. 9.99 (*0-7894-5461-0*); 48p. (gr. 2-4). pap. 3.99 (*0-7894-5388-6*); 32p. (gr. 2-4). pap. 12.95 (*0-7894-5702-4*) Dorling Kindersley Publishing, Inc. (D K Ink).

—Black Beauty. (Illus.). 1999. 208p. pap. text 2.00 (*0-486-40788-8*); 1993. 96p. (J). (gr. 1-9). reprint ed. pap. 1.00 (*0-486-27570-1*) Dover Pubns., Inc.

—Black Beauty. 2nd ed. 1998. (Illustrated Classic Book Ser.). (Illus.). 61p. (J). (gr. 3 up). reprint ed. pap. text 4.95 (*1-56767-253-1*) Educational Insights, Inc.

—Black Beauty. (J). E-Book 2.49 (*1-58627-495-3*) Electric Umbrella Publishing.

—Black Beauty, RS. 1990. (Illus.). 216p. (YA). (gr. 5 up). 19.95 o.p. (*0-374-30776-8*, Farrar, Straus & Giroux (BYR)) Farrar, Straus & Giroux.

—Black Beauty. l.t. ed. 2001. 186p. (J). 27.95 (*0-7838-9522-4*, Macmillan Reference USA) Gale Group.

—Black Beauty. 1997. (Books of Wonder). (Illus.). 256p. (J). (gr. 5-7). 24.99 (*0-688-14714-3*) Harper-Collins Children's Bk. Group.

—Black Beauty, ERS. 1993. (Little Classics Ser.). (Illus.). 208p. (J). (gr. 4-8). 14.95 o.p. (*0-8050-2772-6*, Holt, Henry & Co. Bks. For Young Readers) Holt, Henry & Co.

—Black Beauty. 2001. (Kingfisher Classics Ser.). 352p. (J). (gr. 4-6). tchr. ed. 15.95 (*0-7534-5379-7*, Kingfisher) Houghton Mifflin Co. Trade & Reference Div.

—Black Beauty. l.t. ed. 193p. lib. bdg. 28.92 (*0-7583-0497-8*); 193p. (J). pap. 21.15 (*0-7583-0505-2*); 264p. (J). pap. 26.21 (*0-7583-0506-0*); 338p. (J). pap. 31.44 (*0-7583-0507-9*); 433p. (J). pap. 38.15 (*0-7583-0508-7*); 533p. (J). pap. 45.20 (*0-7583-0509-5*); 655p. (J). pap. 53.87 (*0-7583-0510-9*); 760p. (J). pap. 61.29 (*0-7583-0511-7*); 154p. (J). pap. 18.42 (*0-7583-0504-4*); 655p. (J). lib. bdg. 65.12 (*0-7583-0502-8*); 154p. (J). lib. bdg. 24.74 (*0-7583-0496-X*); 264p. (J). lib. bdg. 34.70 (*0-7583-0498-6*); 338p. (J). lib. bdg. 41.64 (*0-7583-0499-4*); 433p. (J). lib. bdg. 49.40 (*0-7583-0500-1*); 533p. (J). lib. bdg. 56.45 (*0-7583-0501-X*); 760p. (J). lib. bdg. 89.97 (*0-7583-0503-6*) Huge Print Pr.

—Black Beauty. 2001. (J). (gr. 4-7). 17.95 (*0-8249-5400-9*) Ideals Pubns.

—Black Beauty. 2002. 188p. (gr. 3-7). per. 12.99 (*1-58827-861-1*); 17.99 (*1-58827-860-3*) IndyPublish.com.

—Black Beauty. Stemach, Jerry, ed. (J). 2000. text 65.00 incl. audio, cd-rom (*1-58702-312-1*); 2002. text 150.00 (*1-58702-023-8*); 2000. text 50.00 (*1-58702-508-6*) Johnston, Don Inc.

—Black Beauty. (Illus.). 192p. (J). 9.95 (*1-56156-310-2*) Kidsbooks, Inc.

—Black Beauty. 1993. (Children's Classics Ser.). 312p. (gr. 2 up). 14.95 (*0-679-42811-9*, Everyman's Library) Knopf Publishing Group.

—Black Beauty. l.t. ed. 1999. (Large Print Heritage Ser.). 260p. (YA). (gr. 7-12). lib. bdg. 29.95 (*1-58118-042-X*, 22511) LRS.

—Black Beauty. 1992. (Illus.). 220p. (J). reprint ed. 25.00 (*0-88363-200-4*) Levin, Hugh Lauter Assocs.

—Black Beauty. (YA). E-Book 1.95 (*1-57799-807-3*) Logos Research Systems, Inc.

—Black Beauty. (English As a Second Language Bk.). (J). pap. o.p. 1989. pap. text 4.46 net. o.p. (*0-582-53522-0*, 74111) Longman Publishing Group.

—Black Beauty. 240p. 2002. (J). mass mkt. 4.95 (*0-451-52865-4*); 1994. (YA). mass mkt. 3.95 o.s.i (*0-451-52596-5*); 1986. (J). mass mkt. 4.95 o.s.i (*0-451-52295-8*) NAL. (Signet Classics).

—Black Beauty, 2 vols., Set. l.t. ed. (YA). (gr. 8 up). reprint ed. 10.00 (*0-89064-017-3*) National Assn. for Visually Handicapped.

—Black Beauty. 2001. (Twelve-Point Ser.). (J). lib. bdg. 24.00 (*1-58287-132-9*); 269p. lib. bdg. 26.00 (*1-58287-619-3*) North Bks.

—Black Beauty. 1994. (Read-Along Ser.). (YA). pap., stu. ed. 34.95 incl. audio (*0-88432-963-1*, S23920) Norton Pubs., Inc., Jeffrey /Audio-Forum.

—Black Beauty. (Oxford World's Classics Ser.). 1993. 240p. (J). pap. 7.95 o.p. (*0-19-282812-6*); 1988. (Illus.). pap. text 3.50 o.p. (*0-19-421725-6*) Oxford Univ. Pr., Inc.

—Black Beauty, Level 4. Hedge, Tricia, ed. 2000. (Bookworms Ser.). (Illus.). 90p. (J). pap. text 5.95 (*0-19-423028-7*) Oxford Univ. Pr., Inc.

—Black Beauty. 2002. (Classics for Young Readers Ser.). (Illus.). 208p. (J). per. 7.99 (*0-87552-728-0*) P&R Publishing.

—Black Beauty. 2000. (Illus.). 224p. (J). pap. 8.95 (*1-86205-240-9*) Pavilion Bks., Ltd. GBR. *Dist:* Trafalgar Square.

—Black Beauty. Farr, Naunerle C., ed. 1973. (Illus.). 64p. (J). (gr. 5-10). 7.50 o.p. (*0-88301-224-3*); pap. 2.95 (*0-88301-094-1*) Pendulum Pr., Inc.

—Black Beauty. (Illus.). (J). 9999. (Children's Classics Ser.: No. 740-22). (gr. 3-5). pap. 3.50 o.p. (*0-7214-0956-3*); 1996. (Classic Ser.). 56p. (gr. 2-4). 2.99 o.s.i (*0-7214-5633-2*) Penguin Group (USA) Inc. (Ladybird Bks.).

—Black Beauty. Daly, Audrey, ed. 1994. (Classics Ser.). (Illus.). 56p. (J). text 3.50 o.p. (*0-7214-1660-8*, Ladybird Bks.) Penguin Group (USA) Inc.

—Black Beauty. 2003. (Illus.). 224p. (J). pap. 3.99 o.p. (*0-14-250101-8*, Puffin Bks.); 2001. (Illus.). (YA). 17.99 (*0-670-89497-4*, Puffin Bks.); 2001. (Illus.). 208p. (YA). text 25.99 (*0-670-89496-6*, Puffin Bks.); 1999. pap. 2.99 o.p. (*0-14-130540-1*, Puffin Bks.); 1995. (Illus.). 320p. (J). (gr. 4-7). 16.99 (*0-448-40942-9*, Grosset & Dunlap); 1994. (Illus.). 272p. (J). (gr. 4-7). pap. 4.99 (*0-14-036684-9*, Puffin Bks.); 1983. (Illus.). 208p. (J). (gr. 3-7). pap. 3.50 o.p. (*0-14-035006-3*, Puffin Bks.) Penguin Putnam Bks. for Young Readers.

—Black Beauty. Vogel, Malvina, ed. 1989. (Great Illustrated Classics Ser.: Vol. 2). (Illus.). 240p. (J). (gr. 3-6). 9.95 (*0-86611-953-1*) Playmore, Inc., Pubs.

—Black Beauty. (J). 8.97 (*0-13-052329-1*) Prentice Hall PTR.

—Black Beauty. (J). 1989. 96p. (gr. 2-6). 2.95 o.p. (*0-448-11077-6*); 1981. (Illus.). 320p. (gr. 4 up). 7.95 o.s.i (*0-448-11007-5*); 1945. (Illus.). 320p. (gr. 4 up). 14.95 o.p. (*0-448-06007-8*) Putnam Publishing Group, The.

—Black Beauty. 1999. (J). E-Book 3.99 incl. cd-rom (*1-891595-95-4*) Quiet Vision Publishing.

—Black Beauty. (Illus.). 2000. 240p. (gr. 5-7). pap. text 4.50 (*0-440-41645-0*, Yearling); 1994. 128p. (J). (ps-3). 3.50 o.p. (*0-307-12420-7*, Golden Bks.); 1990. 96p. (J). (gr. 1-4). pap. 3.99 (*0-679-80370-X*, Random Hse. Bks. for Young Readers); 1987. 72p. (J). (ps-5). 17.95 o.s.i (*0-394-89228-3*, Random Hse. Bks. for Young Readers) Random Hse. Children's Bks.

—Black Beauty. Vance, Eleanor G., ed. 1986. (Illus.). 72p. (J). (ps-5). 20.99 o.s.i (*0-394-96575-2*, Random Hse. Bks. for Young Readers) Random Hse. Children's Bks.

—Black Beauty. 1986. (Illus.). 256p. (J). (ps-3). o.p. (*0-307-17112-4*, Golden Bks.) Random Hse. Children's Bks.

—Black Beauty. (Children's Classics Ser.). (J). 1998. (Illus.). 240p. 5.99 (*0-517-18958-5*); 1996. 4.99 o.s.i (*0-517-14148-5*); 1995. (Illus.). 20.98 o.s.i (*0-517-15113-8*, Gramercy); 1990. 7.99 o.p. (*0-517-05739-5*); 1988. 240p. 12.99 o.s.i (*0-517-61884-2*) Random Hse. Value Publishing.

—Black Beauty. 176p. 2001. 6.00 o.p. (*0-7624-0543-0*); 1995. (J). text 5.98 o.p. (*1-56138-651-0*, Courage Bks.) Running Pr. Bk. Pubs.

—Black Beauty. (Scholastic Junior Classics Ser.). (J). 2003. (Illus.). 272p. mass mkt. 3.99 (*0-439-22890-5*, Scholastic Paperbacks); 2000. 256p. (gr. 4-7). pap. 4.50 (*0-590-42354-1*, Scholastic Paperbacks); 1997. (Illus.). pap. 21.95 (*0-590-24078-1*); 1994. 256p. (gr. 4-6). mass mkt. 3.50 o.p. (*0-590-48610-1*) Scholastic, Inc.

—Black Beauty. 1988. (J). 2.98 o.p. (*0-671-92200-9*, Pocket) Simon & Schuster.

—Black Beauty. 2001. (Classics Ser.). (Illus.). 224p. (J). (gr. 4-7). pap. 3.99 (*0-689-84255-4*, Aladdin) Simon & Schuster Children's Publishing.

—Black Beauty. Barish, Wendy, ed. 1982. (Illus.). 240p. (J). pap. 15.95 o.s.i (*0-671-43789-5*, Simon & Schuster Children's Publishing) Simon & Schuster Children's Publishing.

—Black Beauty. (Classic Pop-Up Ser.). (J). 1990. 3.98 o.p. (*0-8317-1482-4*); 1994. (Illus.). 64p. 4.98 o.p. (*0-8317-6578-X*) Smithmark Pubs., Inc.

—Black Beauty. (J). E-Book 9.95 (*1-930767-02-1*); 1990. (Illus.). 128p. reprint ed. pap. 11.95 (*0-9623072-2-X*) Storytellers Ink, Inc.

—Black Beauty. l.t. ed. 1987. 272p. (J). 15.95 o.p. (*0-7089-8394-4*, Ulverscroft) Thorpe, F. A. Pubs. GBR. *Dist:* Ulverscroft Large Print Bks., Ltd.

—Black Beauty. (Bullseye Step into Classics Ser.). (J). 1993. 9.09 o.p. (*0-606-09081-9*); 1989. (Illus.). 9.04 (*0-606-18636-0*); 1986. 10.00 (*0-606-01814-X*) Turtleback Bks.

—Black Beauty. 1993. (Illus.). 298p. (J). reprint ed. 29.95 o.p. (*1-877767-86-7*) University Publishing Hse., Inc.

—Black Beauty. 1998. (Children's Classics). 208p. (YA). (ps up). pap. 3.95 (*1-85326-109-2*, 1092WW) Wordsworth Editions, Ltd. GBR. *Dist:* Advanced Global Distribution Services.

—Black Beauty. Lindskoog, Kathryn, ed. 1992. (Young Reader's Library). (gr. 3 up). reprint ed. pap. 12.99 o.p. (*0-88070-498-5*) Zonderkidz.

—Black Beauty: His Groom & Companions. 1995. (J). E-Book 5.98 (*0-585-23465-5*) netLibrary, Inc.

—Black Beauty: Level 2. (Illus.). 72p. (YA). (gr. 4 up). pap. 7.95 (*0-931334-51-9*, EDN201B) AV Concepts Corp.

—Black Beauty: Timeless Classic Stories for Today. 1997. (Eyewitness Classics Ser.). (Illus.). 64p. (J). (gr. 3-6). pap. 14.95 (*0-7894-1488-0*, D K Ink) Dorling Kindersley Publishing, Inc.

—Black Beauty Level 3. 1999. (Penguin Readers Ser.: Level 3). (Orig.). pap. text 7.00 o.p. (*0-582-40166-6*) Longman Publishing Group.

—Black Beauty Book & Charm. 1998. (Charming Classics Ser.). 288p. (J). (gr. 3-7). 6.99 (*0-694-01243-2*) HarperCollins Pubs.

—Black Beauty Readalong. 1994. (Illustrated Classics Collection). 64p. (J). pap. 13.50 o.p. incl. audio (*1-56103-416-9*); pap. 14.95 incl. audio (*0-7854-0703-0*, 40333) American Guidance Service, Inc.

Sewell, Anna, intro. Black Beauty. 1978. (Illus.). (J). (gr. 6-9). 2.95 o.p. (*0-448-14940-0*) Putnam Publishing Group, The.

Sewell, Anna, et al. Black Beauty. 2001. (Young Reader's Classics Ser.). (Illus.). 95p. 16.95 (*1-55263-322-5*, Key Porter kids) Key Porter Bks. CAN. *Dist:* Firefly Bks., Ltd.

Seymour, Peter S., adapted by. Wuthering Heights. 1971. (Hallmark Editions Ser.). 61p. (YA). (*0-87529-213-5*) Hallmark Card, Inc.

Shadwell, Thomas. Time Tours No. 4: The Dinosaurs Trackers. 1991. 160p. mass mkt. 3.50 o.p. (*0-06-106053-4*, HarperTorch) Morrow/Avon.

Shulman, Dee. Roaring Billy. 1992. (Illus.). 32p. (J). (ps). 15.95 o.p. (*0-370-31585-5*) Bodley Head, The GBR. *Dist:* Trafalgar Square.

Simon & Barklee in England. 2001. (Another Country Calling Ser.). (Illus.). 64p. (J). (gr. 3-5). pap. text 12.00 (*0-9704661-1-0*, Explorer Media) Simon & Barklee, Inc./ExplorerMedia.

Skurzynski, Gloria. Spider's Voice. 1999. (Illus.). (J). 11.04 (*0-606-21446-1*) Turtleback Bks.

Slater, Teddy. Disney's the Prince & the Pauper. 1993. (Animated Film Picture Bks.). (Illus.). 48p. (J). lib. bdg. 13.49 o.p. (*1-56282-512-7*) Disney Pr.

—Disney's The Prince & the Pauper. 1993. (Animated Film Picture Bks.). (Illus.). 48p. (J). 12.95 (*1-56282-511-9*) Disney Pr.

Smith, Dodie. Starlight Barking. 1997. (Wyatt Book Ser.). (Illus.). 160p. (J). pap. 8.95 (*0-312-15664-2*, Saint Martin's Griffin) St. Martin's Pr.

Smith, Kathryn. Elusive Passion. 2001. 384p. mass mkt. 5.99 (*0-380-81610-5*, Avon Bks.) Morrow/Avon.

Smith, Sherwood. The Borrowers: Movie Tie-In. 1997. (Borrowers Ser.). (J). (gr. 3-7). pap. 4.99 o.s.i (*0-15-201779-8*) Harcourt Trade Pubs.

Smithmark Staff. Black Beauty - Rebecca of Sunnybrook Farm. 1995. (Illus.). 440p. (J). 12.98 o.p. (*0-8317-6695-6*) Smithmark Pubs., Inc.

Spalding, Andrea. Phoebe & the Gypsy. 1999. (Young Reader Ser.). (Illus.). 96p. (J). (gr. 3-6). pap. 4.99 (*1-55143-135-1*) Orca Bk. Pubs.

—Phoebe & the Gypsy. 1999. (Young Reader Ser.). 10.04 (*0-606-19478-9*) Turtleback Bks.

Springer, Nancy. I Am Mordred: A Tale from Camelot. (Firebird Ser.). (YA). (gr. 7 up). 2002. 192p. pap. 5.99 (*0-698-11841-3*, Firebird); 1998. 184p. 16.99 (*0-399-23143-9*, Philomel) Penguin Putnam Bks. for Young Readers.

—I Am Mordred: A Tale from Camelot. unabr. ed. 2000. (YA). pap. 68.99 incl. audio (*0-7887-3006-1*, 40888X4) Recorded Bks., LLC.

—I Am Morgan Le Fay: A Tale from Camelot. 2001. ix, 227p. (J). (gr. 7 up). 17.99 (*0-399-23451-9*, Philomel) Penguin Putnam Bks. for Young Readers.

—I Am Morgan le Fay: A Tale from Camelot. 2002. (Firebird Ser.). 240p. (J). pap. 5.99 (*0-698-11974-6*, Firebird) Penguin Putnam Bks. for Young Readers.

St. George, Judith S. The Mysterious Girl in the Garden. 1981. (Illus.). 64p. (J). 7.95 o.p. (*0-399-20822-4*) Putnam Publishing Group, The.

St. John, Patricia M. The Tanglewoods' Secret. 2001. (Illus.). 167p. (J). 6.99 (*0-8024-6576-5*) Moody Pr.

Stanley, George Edward. Adam Sharp, the Spy Who Barked. 2002. (Road to Reading Ser.). (Illus.). 48p. (J). (gr. 2-4). pap. 3.99 (*0-307-26412-2*); lib. bdg. 11.99 (*0-307-46412-1*) Random Hse. Children's Bks. (Golden Bks.).

Stewart, Paul. The Weather Witch. 2002. 179p. pap. (*0-440-86504-2*, Corgi) Bantam Bks.

Stoker, Bram. Dracula. unabr. ed. 1965. (Classics Ser.). (YA). (gr. 7 up). mass mkt. 2.25 (*0-8049-0072-8*, CL-72) Airmont Publishing Co., Inc.

—Dracula. 1983. (Bantam Classics Ser.). 432p. (gr. 9-12). mass mkt. 4.95 (*0-553-21271-0*) Bantam Bks.

—Dracula. 1965. 416p. (YA). (gr. 7 up). pap. 2.50 o.s.i (*0-440-92148-1*, Laurel) Dell Publishing.

—Dracula. 1997. (Eyewitness Classics Ser.). (Illus.). 64p. (J). (gr. 3-6). pap. 14.95 o.p. (*0-7894-1489-9*) Dorling Kindersley Publishing, Inc.

—Dracula. 1997. (Children's Thrift Classics Ser.). (Illus.). 96p. (J). reprint ed. pap. text 1.00 (*0-486-29567-2*) Dover Pubns., Inc.

—Dracula. unabr. ed. 1998. (Wordsworth Classics Ser.). (YA). (gr. 6-12). 5.27 o.p. (*0-89061-086-X*, R086XWW) Jamestown.

—Dracula. 1986. (Signet Classics). 400p. (YA). (gr. 10). mass mkt. 4.95 (*0-451-52337-7*, Signet Classics) NAL.

—Dracula. Farr, Naunerle C., ed. 1973. (Now Age Illustrated Ser.). (Illus.). 64p. (J). (gr. 5-10). stu. ed. 1.25 (*0-88301-175-1*); pap. 2.95 (*0-88301-100-X*) Pendulum Pr., Inc.

—Dracula. (Puffin Classics Ser.). 1995. (Illus.). 528p. (YA). (gr. 4-7). pap. 3.99 (*0-14-036717-9*, Puffin Bks.); 1994. (Illus.). 432p. (J). 15.95 o.p. (*0-448-40559-8*, Grosset & Dunlap); 1986. 448p. (J). (gr. 4-6). pap. 3.50 o.p. (*0-14-035048-9*, Puffin Bks.) Penguin Putnam Bks. for Young Readers.

—Dracula. Lafreniere, Kenneth, ed. 1982. (Stepping Stone Bks.: No. 1). (Illus.). 96p. (J). (gr. 3-7). pap. 3.99 (*0-394-84828-4*, Random Hse. Bks. for Young Readers) Random Hse. Children's Bks.

—Dracula. abr. ed. 1992. (J). mass mkt. 3.99 (*0-590-46029-3*, 067, Scholastic Paperbacks) Scholastic, Inc.

Streatfield, Noel. Dancing Shoes. 1994. (Illus.). 224p. (J). (gr. 3-7). pap. 4.99 (*0-679-85428-2*, Golden Bks.) Random Hse. Children's Bks.

Stretton, Hesba. Jessica's First Prayer & Jessica's Mother. 1995. (Illus.). 123p. (Orig.). (J). pap. 7.90 (*0-921100-63-9*) Inheritance Pubns.

—Little Meg's Children. 2000. (Golden Inheritance Ser.: Vol. 5). (Illus.). 88p. (J). pap. 7.90 (*0-921100-92-2*) Inheritance Pubns.

Swindells, Robert. A Serpent's Tooth. 1989. 144p. (J). (gr. 6 up). 13.95 o.p. (*0-8234-0743-8*) Holiday Hse., Inc.

Sword in Stone. 1996. (J). mass mkt. o.s.i (*0-440-91295-4*, Dell Books for Young Readers) Random Hse. Children's Bks.

Symons, Geraldine. Crocuses Were Over, Hitler Was Dead. 1978. (J). (gr. 5-12). 7.95 o.p. (*0-397-31814-6*) HarperCollins Children's Bk. Group.

Talbot, Bryan. The Tale of One Bad Rat. 2002. (Illus.). (YA). 23.19 (*1-4046-2391-4*) Book Wholesalers, Inc.

—The Tale of One Bad Rat. 1995. (Illus.). 136p. (YA). (gr. 7 up). pap. 14.95 (*1-56971-077-5*) Dark Horse Comics.

Talley, Linda. Toad in Town. 2001. (Key Concepts in Personal Development Ser.). (Illus.). (gr. k-4). 30p. (J). 79.95 incl. VHS (*1-55942-165-7*); 32p. pap., tchr. ed. 79.95 incl. VHS (*1-55942-168-1*, 9387K3) Marsh Media.

Tarkington, Booth. Monsieur Beaucaire & the Beautiful Lady. 1968. (YA). (gr. 6 up). mass mkt. 0.95 (*0-8049-0158-9*) Airmont Publishing Co., Inc.

Thomas, Frances. Polly's Really Secret Diary. 2003. (Illus.). 96p. (gr. 1-4). pap. text 4.50 (*0-440-41704-X*, Yearling) Random Hse. Children's Bks.

Thomas, Ruth. The Runaways. 1989. 304p. (J). (gr. 3-7). 13.95 (*0-397-32344-1*); lib. bdg. 13.89 (*0-397-32345-X*) HarperCollins Children's Bk. Group.

Thompson, Caroline, retold by. Black Beauty. 1994. (Illus.). 24p. (J). (gr. k-6). audio 7.98 o.p. (*1-57042-154-4*, KR18, Warner Audio Video Entertainment (WAVE)) Time Warner AudioBooks.

Thomson, Sarah L. The Dragon's Son. 2001. (Illus.). 181p. (J). (gr. 7 up). pap. 17.95 (*0-531-30333-0*, Orchard Bks.) Scholastic, Inc.

Townsend, John R. Downstream. 1987. 224p. (YA). (gr. 7 up). lib. bdg. 12.89 (*0-397-32189-9*) Harper-Collins Children's Bk. Group.

—The Persuading Stick. 1987. 96p. (J). (gr. 3-7). 11.95 o.p. (*0-688-07260-7*) HarperCollins Children's Bk. Group.

Travers, Pamela L. Mary Poppins & the House Next Door. 1992. (Illus.). 96p. (J). (gr. 4-7). pap. 3.50 o.s.i (*0-440-40656-0*, Yearling) Random Hse. Children's Bks.

—Mary Poppins in Cherry Tree Lane. 1992. 96p. (J). (gr. 3-7). pap. 3.50 o.s.i (*0-440-40637-4*, Yearling) Random Hse. Children's Bks.

Traynor, Shauwn. Little Man in England. 1989. 112p. (J). pap. 6.95 (*1-85371-032-6*) Poolbeg Pr. IRL. *Dist:* Dufour Editions, Inc.

Turnbull, Ann. Room for a Stranger. 1996. 128p. (J). (gr. 5-9). 15.99 o.p. (*1-56402-868-2*) Candlewick Pr.

—Speedwell. 1994. 128p. (J). (gr. 5-9). bds. 3.99 o.p. (*1-56402-281-1*) Candlewick Pr.

Ure, Jean. Muddy Four Paws. 1999. (We Love Animals Bks.). (Illus.). 128p. (J). (gr. 4-7). pap. 3.95 (*0-7641-0968-5*) Barron's Educational Series, Inc.

—Plague. 1991. 160p. (YA). (gr. 5 up). 16.95 (*0-15-262429-5*) Harcourt Children's Bks.

—Plague. 1993. 224p. (J). (gr. 7 up). pap. 4.99 o.s.i (*0-14-036283-5*, Puffin Bks.) Penguin Putnam Bks. for Young Readers.

—Plague. 1993. (J). 10.09 o.p. (*0-606-05548-7*) Turtleback Bks.

Van Hook, Beverly. The Villainous Vicar. 1996. (Supergranny Ser.: No. 7). (Illus.). (J). (gr. 3-6). pap. 3.25 (*0-916761-25-8*); lib. bdg. (*0-916761-26-6*) Holderby & Bierce.

Vanice, Eleanor Grah, adapted by. Black Beauty. 1949. (J). 5.95 o.s.i (*0-394-80637-9*) Random Hse., Inc.

Wallace, Barbara Brooks. Sparrows in the Scullery. 2000. (J). pap., stu. ed. 49.75 incl. audio (*0-7887-3842-9*, 41053X4) Recorded Bks., LLC.

Watts, Irene N. Finding Sophie. 2002. 144p. (YA). (gr. 5). pap. 6.95 (*0-88776-613-7*) Tundra Bks. of Northern New York.

Waugh, Sylvia. Earthborn. 2002. 288p. (gr. 5 up). text 15.95 (*0-385-72964-2*, Delacorte Bks. for Young Readers) Random Hse. Children's Bks.

—Earthborn. 2002. 288p. lib. bdg. 17.99 (*0-385-90060-0*) Random Hse., Inc.

—Earthborn. l.t. ed. 2003. 331p. (J). 23.95 (*0-7862-5647-8*) Thorndike Pr.

—The Mennyms. (Illus.). (gr. 5-7). 1994. 32p. (YA). 16.00 (*0-688-13070-4*, Greenwillow Bks.); 1995. 224p. (J). reprint ed. pap. 4.99 (*0-380-72528-2*, Harper Trophy) HarperCollins Children's Bk. Group.

—The Mennyms. 1995. (J). 11.04 (*0-606-07858-4*) Turtleback Bks.

—Mennyms Alive. 224p. (J). (gr. 3-7). 1999. pap. 4.50 (*0-380-72943-1*, Harper Trophy); 1997. 16.00 (*0-688-15201-5*, Greenwillow Bks.) HarperCollins Children's Bk. Group.

—Mennyms Alone. 1998. 224p. (J). (gr. 3-7). pap. 4.50 (*0-380-78867-5*, Harper Trophy); 1996. (Illus.). 196p. (YA). (gr. 5 up). 16.00 o.s.i (*0-688-14702-X*, Greenwillow Bks.) HarperCollins Children's Bk. Group.

—Mennyms in the Wilderness. 1995. (Illus.). 32p. (YA). (ps-3). 15.00 o.s.i (*0-688-13820-9*, Greenwillow Bks.) HarperCollins Children's Bk. Group.

—Mennyms in the Wilderness. 1996. 272p. (J). (gr. 5-7). mass mkt. 4.50 (*0-380-72529-0*, Avon Bks.) Morrow/Avon.

—Mennyms in the Wilderness. 1996. (J). 10.55 (*0-606-08821-0*) Turtleback Bks.

—Mennyms under Seige. 1997. 256p. (J). (gr. 5-7). pap. 4.50 (*0-380-72584-3*, Harper Trophy) HarperCollins Children's Bk. Group.

—Mennyms under Siege. 1996. 224p. (J). (gr. 3-7). 16.00 o.p. (*0-688-14372-5*, Greenwillow Bks.) HarperCollins Children's Bk. Group.

—Mennyms under Siege. 1997. 10.55 (*0-606-11617-6*) Turtleback Bks.

—Space Race. 256p. (gr. 5 up). 2001. pap. text 4.99 (*0-440-41714-7*, Yearling); 2000. (Illus.). text 15.95 o.s.i (*0-385-32766-8*, Dell Books for Young Readers) Random Hse. Children's Bks.

—Space Race. l.t. ed. 2001. 300p. (J). 20.95 (*0-7862-3606-X*) Thorndike Pr.

—Who Goes Home? 2004. (J). 224p. text 15.95 (*0-385-72965-0*); lib. bdg. (*0-385-90160-7*) Dell Publishing. (Delacorte Pr.).

Wells, H. G. The Invisible Man. 1994. (Illustrated Classics Collection). 64p. (J). pap. 4.95 (*0-7854-0718-9*, 40400) American Guidance Service, Inc.

—The Invisible Man. 1986. (Illus.). (YA). (gr. 10 up). 2.50 o.p. (*0-425-10043-X*, Classics Illustrated) Berkley Publishing Group.

—The Invisible Man. 1992. 178p. (YA). mass mkt. 3.99 (*0-8125-0467-4*, Tor Classics) Doherty, Tom Assocs., LLC.

—The Invisible Man. Hanft, Joshua, ed. 1995. (Great Illustrated Classics Ser.: Vol. 44). (Illus.). 240p. (J). (gr. 3-6). 9.95 (*0-86611-995-7*) Playmore, Inc., Pubs.

—The Invisible Man. 1990. 208p. (J). (gr. 7-9). pap. 3.99 o.p. (*0-590-44016-0*) Scholastic, Inc.

—The Invisible Man. 1985. (gr. 10-12). pap. 0.60 o.s.i (*0-671-46119-2*, Washington Square Pr.) Simon & Schuster.

Wells, H. G. & Geary, Rick. The Invisible Man. (Classics Illustrated Ser.). (Illus.). 52p. (YA). pap. 4.95 (*1-57209-020-0*) Classics International Entertainment, Inc.

Wells, Rosemary. Lassie Come Home, ERS. 1995. (Illus.). 48p. (J). (gr. 2 up). reprint ed. 16.95 (*0-8050-3794-2*, Holt, Henry & Co. Bks. For Young Readers) Holt, Henry & Co.

—Lassie Come Home: Eric Knight's Original Classic, ERS. 1998. (Illus.). 48p. (YA). (ps up). reprint ed. pap. 7.95 (*0-8050-5995-4*, Holt, Henry & Co. Bks. For Young Readers) Holt, Henry & Co.

Wells, Rosemary & Knight, Eric. Lassie Come Home, ERS. 2000. (Illus.). 64p. (J). (gr. 2-5). 15.95 (*0-8050-6423-0*, Holt, Henry & Co. Bks. For Young Readers) Holt, Henry & Co.

Westall, Robert. Christmas Spirit: Two Stories, RS. (Illus.). 160p. (J). 1996. (gr. 4-7). pap. 4.95 o.p. (*0-374-41125-5*, Sunburst); 1994. 15.00 o.p. (*0-374-31260-5*, Farrar, Straus & Giroux (BYR)) Farrar, Straus & Giroux.

—Christmas Spirit: Two Stories. 1996. (YA). (gr. 3 up). 10.05 o.p. (*0-606-10158-6*) Turtleback Bks.

—Falling into Glory, RS. 1995. 304p. (J). (gr. 7 up). 18.00 o.p. (*0-374-32256-2*, Farrar, Straus & Giroux (BYR)) Farrar, Straus & Giroux.

—A Place to Hide. 1994. 208p. (YA). (gr. 5 up). 13.95 (*0-590-47748-X*) Scholastic, Inc.

—The Scarecrows. 1981. 192p. (YA). (gr. 7 up). 12.95 o.p. (*0-688-00612-4*, Greenwillow Bks.) HarperCollins Children's Bk. Group.

—Stormsearch, RS. 1992. 128p. (J). (gr. 4-7). 14.00 o.p. (*0-374-37272-1*, Farrar, Straus & Giroux (BYR)) Farrar, Straus & Giroux.

—Time of Fire. 1997. 176p. (J). (gr. 5-9). 15.95 (*0-590-47746-3*) Scholastic, Inc.

Wilde, Oscar. The Canterville Ghost. Date not set. (Nelson Readers Ser.). (J). pap. text (*0-17-557035-3*) Addison-Wesley Longman, Inc.

—The Canterville Ghost. 1997. (Candlewick Treasures Ser.). (Illus.). 128p. (J). (gr. 3-9). 11.99 o.p. (*0-7636-0132-2*) Candlewick Pr.

—The Canterville Ghost. 2nd ed. 2000. (Reading & Training Ser.). 112p. (YA). pap. (*1-57159-012-9*) Los Andes Publishing Co.

—The Canterville Ghost. 1996. (Illus.). 44p. (J). (gr. 2-4). 16.95 o.p. (*1-55858-624-5*); (ps-3). pap. 6.95 (*1-55858-611-3*) North-South Bks., Inc.

—The Canterville Ghost. 1991. (Illus.). 36p. (J). (gr. 4 up). pap. 15.95 o.s.i (*0-88708-027-8*, Simon & Schuster Children's Publishing) Simon & Schuster Children's Publishing.

—The Picture of Dorian Gray. 2002. (Great Illustrated Classics). (Illus.). 240p. (J). (gr. 3-8). lib. bdg. 21.35 (*1-57765-821-3*, ABDO & Daughters) ABDO Publishing Co.

—The Picture of Dorian Gray. 1964. 172p. (YA). (gr. 7 up). pap. 44.95 o.p. (*3-418-00018-5*) Adler's Foreign Bks., Inc.

—The Picture of Dorian Gray, 2 vols. l.t. ed. (YA). (gr. 10 up). reprint ed. 10.00 (*0-89064-049-1*) National Assn. for Visually Handicapped.

—The Picture of Dorian Gray, Level 3. Hedge, Tricia, ed. 2000. (Bookworms Ser.). (Illus.). 77p. (J). pap. text 5.95 (*0-19-423011-2*) Oxford Univ. Pr., Inc.

—The Picture of Dorian Gray. 2001. (Whole Story Ser.). (Illus.). 272p. (YA). (gr. 10 up). 25.99 (*0-670-89494-X*); pap. 17.99 (*0-670-89495-8*) Penguin Putnam Bks. for Young Readers. (Viking Children's Bks.).

—The Picture of Dorian Gray. 1998. 13.00 (*0-606-17247-5*) Turtleback Bks.

Willard, Barbara. The Lark & the Laurel. 1970. (J). (gr. 7 up). 5.95 o.p. (*0-15-243604-9*) Harcourt Children's Bks.

Willis, Jeanne. The Truth or Something, ERS. 2002. 272p. (YA). (gr. 9 up). 16.95 (*0-8050-7079-6*, Holt, Henry & Co. Bks. For Young Readers) Holt, Henry & Co.

—The Wind in the Willows. 1998. (Illus.). 32p. (J). (ps-1). 15.95 (*0-86264-782-7*) Andersen Pr., Ltd. GBR. *Dist:* Trafalgar Square.

Wilson, Jacqueline. Bad Girls. 2002. (Illus.). 176p. (gr. 3-7). pap. text 4.99 (*0-440-41806-2*, Random Hse. Bks. for Young Readers) Random Hse. Children's Bks.

—Bad Girls: American Edition. 2001. (Illus.). 176p. (gr. 3-7). text 15.95 o.s.i (*0-385-72916-2*, Delacorte Pr.) Dell Publishing.

—The Bed & Breakfast Star. l.t. ed. 2000. (J). (Illus.). pap. (*0-7540-6090-X*); 242p. pap. 29.95 incl. audio (*0-7540-6231-7*, RA032, Chivers Children's Audio Bks.) BBC Audiobooks America.

—The Bed & Breakfast Star. 2000. 32p. (J). pap. 6.95 (*0-440-86324-4*, Delacorte Pr.) Dell Publishing.

—Girls in Tears. 2003. 176p. (J). lib. bdg. 11.99 (*0-385-90104-6*); (gr. 7). 9.95 (*0-385-73082-9*) Dell Publishing. (Delacorte Pr.).

—Girls in Tears. 2004. 192p. (YA). (gr. 7). mass mkt. 4.99 (*0-440-23807-2*, Laurel Leaf) Random Hse. Children's Bks.

—Vicky Angel. 2001. (J). 16.95 (*0-7540-6165-5*) BBC Audiobooks America.

—Vicky Angel. 2002. 144p. (J). pap. (*0-440-86415-1*, Corgi) Bantam Bks.

—Vicky Angel. (Illus.). 176p. (gr. 3-7). 2003. pap. text 4.99 (*0-440-41808-9*, Yearling); 2001. text 15.95 (*0-385-72920-0*, Dell Books for Young Readers) Random Hse. Children's Bks.

Windsor, Patricia. The Blooding. (gr. 7-12). 1999. 288p. mass mkt. 4.50 (*0-590-43308-3*); 1996. 272p. (YA). pap. 15.95 (*0-590-43309-1*) Scholastic, Inc.

Wise, William. Nell of Branford Hall. Arico, Diane, ed. 1999. 192p. (YA). (gr. 5-9). 16.99 o.s.i (*0-8037-2393-8*, Dial Bks. for Young Readers) Penguin Putnam Bks. for Young Readers.

Wiseman, David. Thimbles, 001. 1982. (J). (gr. 4 up). 7.95 o.p. (*0-395-31867-X*) Houghton Mifflin Co.

Wodehouse, P. G. Mike at Wrykyn. reprint ed. lib. bdg. 98.00 (*0-7426-3265-2*); 2001. pap. text 28.00 (*0-7426-8265-X*) Classic Bks.

—Mike at Wrykyn. 1998. 192p. pap. 9.95 o.s.i (*0-14-012454-3*) Penguin Group (USA) Inc.

Wood, Kenneth. Shining Armour. 1982. (Julia MacRae Blackbird Bks.). 144p. (J). (gr. 7). 9.95 o.p. (*0-531-04434-3*, Watts, Franklin) Scholastic Library Publishing.

Wu, William F. Time Tours No. 1: Robin Hood Ambush. 1990. 160p. (YA). mass mkt. 3.50 o.p. (*0-06-106003-8*, HarperTorch) Morrow/Avon.

Young Guinevere. 1995. (J). o.p. (*0-440-91059-5*, Dell Books for Young Readers) Random Hse. Children's Bks.

Zephaniah, Benjamin. Face. 2002. 207p. (J). (gr. 5-10). 15.95 (*1-58234-774-3*, Bloomsbury Children) Bloomsbury Publishing.

—Refugee Boy. 2002. 291p. (J). 15.95 (*1-58234-763-8*, Bloomsbury Children) Bloomsbury Publishing.

ERIE, LAKE—FICTION

Armbruster, Ann. Lake Erie. 1996. (True Bks.). (Illus.). 48p. (J). (gr. 3-5). lib. bdg. 23.50 (*0-516-20011-9*, Children's Pr.) Scholastic Library Publishing.

Lawrence, Mildred. Peachtree Island. 1966. (Illus.). (J). (gr. 3-6). pap. 2.95 o.p. (*0-15-671560-0*, Voyager Bks./Libros Viajeros) Harcourt Children's Bks.

Panagopoulos, Janie Lynn. Erie Trail West: A Dream-Quest Adventure. 1995. 184p. (J). (gr. 3-7). 14.95 o.p. (*0-938682-35-0*) River Road Pubns., Inc.

ERIE CANAL—FICTION

Abbott, Jacob. Marco Paul's Travels on the Erie Canal. 1987. (Illus.). 203p. (J). (gr. 4-8). reprint ed. pap. 6.95 o.p. (*0-932334-99-7*, NY70056, Empire State Bks.) Heart of the Lakes Publishing.

Adams, Samuel Hopkins. Chingo Smith of the Erie Canal. 1963. (Illus.). (J). (gr. 6-11). lib. bdg. 5.49 o.p. (*0-394-91020-6*, Random Hse. Bks. for Young Readers) Random Hse. Children's Bks.

Breed, Nancy L. The Van Wies of Nine Mile Creek: A Story of the Erie Canal. 1995. (J). pap. 12.50 (*0-925168-12-2*) North Country Bks., Inc.

Kimmel, Eric A. The Erie Canal Pirates. 2002. (Illus.). 32p. (J). (gr. k-3). tchr. ed. 16.95 (*0-8234-1657-7*) Holiday Hse., Inc.

Reber, Jack. Eerie Canal: An Historical Adventure. 1990. pap. 9.99 (*0-88092-310-5*) Royal Fireworks Publishing Co.

Rizzo, Kay D. Old Friends & New. 2003. 96p. (J). (*0-8163-1975-8*) Pacific Pr. Publishing Assn.

Seguin, Marilyn Weymouth. Silver Ribbon Skinny. Caso, Adolph, ed. 1996. (Illus.). 96p. (J). (gr. 4-10). pap. 12.95 (*0-8283-2020-9*) Branden Bks.

ESTONIA—FICTION

Brodtkorb, Reidar. Gold Coin. Kingsland, L. W., tr. 1966. (Illus.). (YA). (gr. 5 up). 4.95 o.p. (*0-15-231155-6*) Harcourt Children's Bks.

ETHIOPIA—FICTION

Araujo, Frank P. The Perfect Orange: A Tale from Ethiopia. 1994. (Toucan Tales Ser.: Vol. 2). (Illus.). 32p. (J). (ps-8). 16.95 (*1-877810-94-0*, ORAN) Rayve Productions, Inc.

Bohrer, Dick. They Called Him Shifta. 1981. 320p. pap. 4.95 o.p. (*0-8024-7910-3*) Moody Pr.

Coatsworth, Elizabeth. Princess & the Lion. 1963. (Illus.). (J). (gr. 3-7). lib. bdg. 5.99 o.p. (*0-394-91520-8*, Pantheon) Knopf Publishing Group.

Dunckel, Mona. Escape. 1999. 101p. (J). (gr. 1-2). pap. 6.49 (*1-57924-068-2*, 113100) Jones, Bob Univ. Pr.

Kendall, Jonathan P. My Name Is Rachamim. 1987. (Illus.). (J). (ps-3). 7.95 (*0-8074-0321-0*, 123925) UAHC Pr.

Kurtz, Jane. Faraway Home. 2000. (Illus.). 32p. (J). (gr. 1-5). 16.00 (*0-15-200036-4*, Gulliver Bks.) Harcourt Children's Bks.

—Fire on the Mountain. 1998. (Illus.). 40p. (J). (ps-3). pap. 6.99 (*0-689-81896-3*, Aladdin) Simon & Schuster Children's Publishing.

—Pulling the Lion's Tail. 1995. (Illus.). (J). (ps-3). 32p. pap. 15.00 (*0-689-80324-9*); pap. 14.00 (*0-671-88183-3*) Simon & Schuster Children's Publishing. (Simon & Schuster Children's Publishing).

—Saba: Under the Hyena's Foot. 2003. (Girls of Many Lands Ser.). (Illus.). 207p. (J). pap. 15.95 (*1-58485-829-X*); pap. 7.95 (*1-58485-747-1*) Pleasant Co. Pubns. (American Girl).

—The Storyteller's Beads. Van Doren, Liz, ed. 1998. (Illus.). 160p. (J). (gr. 3-7). 15.00 (*0-15-201074-2*, Gulliver Bks.) Harcourt Children's Bks.

Kurtz, Jane & Kurtz, Christopher. Only a Pigeon. 1997. (Illus.). 40p. (J). (ps-3). per. 16.00 (*0-689-80077-0*, Simon & Schuster Children's Publishing) Simon & Schuster Children's Publishing.

Laird, Elizabeth. The Garbage King. 2003. 336p. (J). pap. 5.95 (*0-7641-2626-1*); (YA). 14.95 (*0-7641-5679-9*) Barron's Educational Series, Inc.

Levitin, Sonia. The Return. 1988. 192p. (gr. 7 up). mass mkt. 5.99 (*0-449-70280-4*, Fawcett) Ballantine Bks.

—The Return. 1987. 224p. (YA). (gr. 5 up). 16.00 (*0-689-31309-8*, Atheneum) Simon & Schuster Children's Publishing.

Schlee, Ann. Guns of Darkness. 1974. 240p. (J). (gr. 5-9). 1.79 o.p. (*0-689-30145-6*, Atheneum) Simon & Schuster Children's Publishing.

Schrier, Jeffrey. On the Wings of Eagles. 1998. (Single Titles Ser.). (Illus.). 32p. (J). (ps up). 21.90 o.p. (*0-7613-0004-X*) Millbrook Pr., Inc.

Schur, Maxine R. Day of Delight: A Jewish Sabbath in Ethiopia. 1994. (Illus.). 40p. (J). (gr. k-4). 15.99 o.s.i (*0-8037-1413-0*); 15.89 o.p. (*0-8037-1414-9*) Penguin Putnam Bks. for Young Readers. (Dial Bks. for Young Readers).

Zephaniah, Benjamin. Refugee Boy. 2002. 291p. (J). 15.95 (*1-58234-763-8*, Bloomsbury Children) Bloomsbury Publishing.

EUROPE—FICTION

Alexander, Lloyd. The Illyrian Adventure. 1990. (J). pap. o.p. (*0-440-80161-3*); 144p. (gr. 7 up). reprint ed. pap. text 3.99 o.s.i (*0-440-40297-2*) Dell Publishing.

—The Illyrian Adventure. (Illus.). (gr. 5-9). 2000. 144p. (J). pap. 5.99 (*0-14-130313-1*, Puffin Bks.); 1986. 14p. (YA). 13.95 o.s.i (*0-525-44250-2*, Dutton Children's Bks.) Penguin Putnam Bks. for Young Readers.

—The Illyrian Adventure. (J). 1995. pap. 4.50 (*0-440-91042-0*, Dell Books for Young Readers); 1987. 144p. mass mkt. 3.50 o.s.i (*0-440-94018-4*, Laurel Leaf) Random Hse. Children's Bks.

—The Illyrian Adventure. 1999. 12.04 (*0-606-16832-X*); 1986. (J). 9.99 o.p. (*0-606-02191-4*) Turtleback Bks.

Cohen, Barbara. Here Come the Purim Players! 1984. (Illus.). 32p. (J). (gr. 1-4). 12.00 o.p. (*0-688-02106-9*); lib. bdg. 12.88 o.p. (*0-688-02108-5*) HarperCollins Children's Bk. Group.

—Here Come the Purim Players! 1998. (Illus.). (J). (ps-3). 12.95 (*0-8074-0645-7*, 101251) UAHC Pr.

Collingwood, Lucy. Postcards from Europe, 5 bks., Set. Kratoville, Betty Lou, ed. Incl. Postcards from Europe: Reproducible Activity Workbook. (Illus.). 64p. 1995. pap., tchr. ed., wbk. ed. 15.00 (*0-87879-995-8*, HN9958); (Postcards Ser.). (Illus.). 1994. Set pap. 19.00 (*0-87879-976-1*, HN9761) High Noon Bks.

de Trevino, Elizabeth Borton. Turi's Poppa, RS. 1968. (Illus.). (J). (gr. 4 up). 3.95 o.p. (*0-374-37887-8*, Farrar, Straus & Giroux (BYR)) Farrar, Straus & Giroux.

Dickinson, Peter. Shadow of a Hero. 1995. 9.09 o.p. (*0-606-09847-X*) Turtleback Bks.

Dickinson, Peter & Kiefte, Kees De. Shadow of a Hero. 1995. 295p. (YA). (gr. 7 up). mass mkt. 3.99 o.s.i (*0-440-21963-9*, Laurel Leaf) Random Hse. Children's Bks.

Dunrea, Olivier. The Trow-Wife's Treasure, RS. 1998. (Illus.). 32p. (J). (ps-3). 16.00 o.p. (*0-374-37792-8*, Farrar, Straus & Giroux (BYR)) Farrar, Straus & Giroux.

Englehart, Steve & Englehart, Terry. The DNAgers. 1997. 9.09 o.p. (*0-606-10787-8*) Turtleback Bks.

—The DNAgers. 2000. 128p. (gr. 4-7). per. 9.95 (*0-595-16697-0*) iUniverse, Inc.

Finklea, Michael. The Worldwide Adventures of Winston Churchill Bk. 1: Europe. 1998. (Illus.). (J). 19.95 (*1-56763-406-0*); pap. (*1-56763-407-9*) Ozark Publishing.

Flynn, Gerard. The Mysteries of Mr. Garibaldi Patch & How He Hated Children: A Baroque Novel for Children. 1996. (Illus.). 128p. (Orig.). (YA). pap. 8.95 (*1-56002-493-3*, University Editions) Aegina Pr., Inc.

Freymann-Weyr, Garret. The Kings Are Already Here. 2003. 160p. (YA). (gr. 7). tchr. ed. 15.00 (*0-618-26363-2*) Houghton Mifflin Co.

Hughes, Virginia E. Anna: The Little Peasant Girl. 1994. (Illus.). 64p. (J). (gr. 4 up). pap. 8.00 (*1-56002-264-7*, University Editions) Aegina Pr., Inc.

Johnston, Norma. Return to Monocco. 1999. 200p. (YA). (gr. 5-12). reprint ed. pap. 16.00 (*1-892323-49-4*, Pierce Harris Press) Vivisphere Publishing.

Mooney, Bel. Voices of Silence. 1998. 11.04 (*0-606-13887-0*) Turtleback Bks.

Ross, Stewart. Only a Matter of Time: A Story from Kosova. 2002. (Survivors Ser.). (Illus.). 96p. (J). (gr. 5-8). 12.95 (0-7641-5524-5) Barron's Educational Series, Inc.

Standish, Burt L. Frank Merriwell in Europe. Rudman, Jack, ed. (Frank Merriwell Ser.). (YA). (gr. 9 up). 29.95 (0-8373-9308-6); pap. 9.95 (0-8373-9008-7, FM-008) Merriwell, Frank Inc.

Tolstoy, Leo. Philipok. 2002. (Illus.). 32p. (J). pap. 6.99 (0-698-11966-5, PaperStar) Penguin Putnam Bks. for Young Readers.

EVERGLADES (FLA.)—FICTION

Buffett, Jimmy. Trouble Dolls. 1997. (Illus.). 32p. (J). pap. 7.00 (0-15-201501-9, Harcourt Paperbacks) Harcourt Children's Bks.

Buffett, Jimmy & Buffett, Savannah Jane. Trouble Dolls. 1991. (Illus.). 32p. (J). (ps-3). 16.00 (0-15-290790-4) Harcourt Children's Bks.

DeFelice, Cynthia C. Lostman's River. 1995. 160p. (J). (gr. 4-7). pap. 4.95 (0-380-72396-4, Avon Bks.) Morrow/Avon.

—Lostman's River. 1994. 160p. (YA). (gr. 7 up). lib. bdg. 15.00 (0-02-726466-1, Atheneum) Simon & Schuster Children's Publishing.

—Lostman's River. 1995. (J). 10.55 (0-606-07810-X) Turtleback Bks.

Douglas, Marjory Stoneman. Alligator Crossing. 2003. (Illus.). 192p. (J). (gr. 3-8). 16.95 (1-57131-640-X); pap. 6.95 (1-57131-644-2) Milkweed Editions.

Everglades Environmental Storybook: Coastal Creatures. l.t. ed. 1999. (Voices of the Earth Ser.: Vol. I). (Illus.). 48p. (J). (gr. k-4). pap. 6.95 (0-9666720-1-1) Earthwing Pubns.

Fedotonsky, Alex. Dingle Dorts in the Everglades Vacation Adventure. 1994. (Illus.). 32p. (Orig.). (J). (gr. 3-7). pap. 2.95 (0-9638756-1-2) Skylight Studios.

Hall, Nancy & Packard, Mary. Spike & Mike. 1993. (Better World Ser.). (Illus.). 40p. (J). (ps-4). mass mkt. 16.30 o.p. (0-516-00830-7, Children's Pr.) Scholastic Library Publishing.

Packard, Mary. Fairest of All. 1993. (Better World Ser.). (Illus.). 40p. (J). (ps-4). mass mkt. 16.30 o.p. (0-516-00826-9, Children's Pr.) Scholastic Library Publishing.

—Playing by the Rules. 1993. (Better World Ser.). (Illus.). 40p. (J). (ps-4). mass mkt. 16.30 o.p. (0-516-00827-7, Children's Pr.) Scholastic Library Publishing.

—Safe & Sound. 1993. (Better World Ser.). (Illus.). 40p. (J). (ps-4). mass mkt. 16.30 o.p. (0-516-00828-5, Children's Pr.) Scholastic Library Publishing.

—Save the Swamp. 1993. (Better World Ser.). (Illus.). 40p. (J). (ps-4). mass mkt. 16.30 o.p. (0-516-00829-3, Children's Pr.) Scholastic Library Publishing.

—Spike & Mike & the Treasure Hunt. (Pictureback Ser.). (Illus.). (J). 1994. pap. 2.25 o.p. (0-679-83936-4); 1993. o.p. (0-679-93936-9) Random Hse. Children's Bks. (Random Hse. Bks. for Young Readers).

—Starting Over. 1993. (Better World Ser.). (Illus.). 40p. (J). (ps-4). mass mkt. 16.30 o.p. (0-516-00831-5, Children's Pr.) Scholastic Library Publishing.

Rorby, Ginny. Dolphin Sky. 1996. 246p. (J). (gr. 5-9). 16.95 o.s.i (0-399-22905-1, G. P. Putnam's Sons) Penguin Group (USA) Inc.

Rust, Ann O'Connell. Torry Island. Rust, Allen F., ed. 2002. (Nonie of the Everglades Ser.: Vol. II). 94p. (J). (gr. 4-7). pap. 7.95 (1-883203-06-6) Amaro Bks.

EVERWORLD (IMAGINARY PLACE)—FICTION

Applegate, K. A. Brave the Betrayal. 2000. (Ever World Ser.: No. 8). (Illus.). 208p. (J). (gr. 4-7). mass mkt. 4.99 (0-590-87854-9) Scholastic, Inc.

—Brave the Betrayal. 2000. (Ever World Ser.: No. 8). (Illus.). (J). (gr. 4-7). 11.04 (0-606-18541-0) Turtleback Bks.

—Discover the Destroyer. 2000. (Ever World Ser.: No. 5). (Illus.). 192p. (J). (gr. 4-7). mass mkt. 4.99 (0-590-87762-3) Scholastic, Inc.

—Discover the Destroyer. 1999. (Ever World Ser.: No. 5). (Illus.). (J). (gr. 4-7). 11.04 (0-606-18539-9) Turtleback Bks.

—Enter the Enchanted, 3rd ed. 1999. (Ever World Ser.: No. 3). 169p. (J). (gr. 4-7). mass mkt. 4.99 (0-590-87754-2) Scholastic, Inc.

—Enter the Enchanted. 1999. (Ever World Ser.: No. 3). (J). (gr. 4-7). 11.04 (0-606-17279-3) Turtleback Bks.

—Fear the Fantastic. 2000. (Ever World Ser.: No. 6). (Illus.). 208p. (J). (gr. 4-7). mass mkt. 4.99 (0-590-87764-X) Scholastic, Inc.

—Fear the Fantastic. 2000. (Ever World Ser.: No. 6). (Illus.). (J). (gr. 4-7). 11.04 (0-606-18540-2) Turtleback Bks.

—Gateway to the Gods. 7th ed. 2000. (Ever World Ser.: No. 7). (Illus.). 208p. (J). (gr. 4-7). mass mkt. 4.99 (0-590-87766-6) Scholastic, Inc.

—Gateway to the Gods. 2000. (Ever World Ser.: No. 7). (Illus.). (J). (gr. 4-7). 11.04 (0-606-18872-X) Turtleback Bks.

—Inside the Illusion. 2000. (Ever World Ser.: No. 9). (Illus.). 208p. (J). (gr. 4-7). mass mkt. 4.99 (0-590-87855-7) Scholastic, Inc.

—Inside the Illusion. 2000. (Ever World Ser.: No. 9). (J). (gr. 4-7). 11.04 (0-606-19558-0) Turtleback Bks.

—Land of Loss. 1999. (Ever World Ser.: No. 2). 208p. (J). (gr. 4-7). mass mkt. 4.99 (0-590-87751-8) Scholastic, Inc.

—Land of Loss. 1999. (Ever World Ser.: No. 2). (J). (gr. 4-7). 11.04 (0-606-16927-X) Turtleback Bks.

—Realm of the Reaper, 1999. (Ever World Ser.: No. 4). 173p. (J). (gr. 4-7). mass mkt. 4.99 (0-590-87760-7) Scholastic, Inc.

—Realm of the Reaper. 1999. (Ever World Ser.: No. 4). (J). (gr. 4-7). 11.04 (0-606-17541-5) Turtleback Bks.

—Search for Senna. 1999. (Ever World Ser.: No. 1). 208p. (J). (gr. 4-7). mass mkt. 4.99 (0-590-87743-7) Scholastic, Inc.

—Search for Senna. 1999. (Ever World Ser.: No. 1). (J). (gr. 4-7). 11.04 (0-606-16926-1) Turtleback Bks.

—Understand the Unknown, No. 10. 2000. (Ever World Ser.: No. 10). 208p. (J). (gr. 4-7). mass mkt. 4.99 (0-590-87986-3) Scholastic, Inc.

—Understand the Unknown. 2000. (Ever World Ser.: No. 10). (J). (gr. 4-7). 11.04 (0-606-19557-2); 11.04 (0-606-19917-9) Turtleback Bks.

F

FINCAYRA (IMAGINARY PLACE)—FICTION

Barron, T. A. The Fires of Merlin. 1998. (Lost Years of Merlin Ser.: Vol. 3). (Illus.). 272p. (YA). (gr. 5-9). 19.99 (0-399-23020-3, Philomel) Penguin Putnam Bks. for Young Readers.

—The Fires of Merlin Bk. 3. 2000. (Lost Years of Merlin Ser.: Vol. 3). (Illus.). 304p. (J). (gr. 4-7). reprint ed. mass mkt. 6.99 (0-441-00713-9) Ace Bks.

—The Lost Years of Merlin, Bk. 1. 1999. (Lost Years of Merlin Ser.). 304p. (J). (gr. 4-7). reprint ed. mass mkt. 6.99 (0-441-00668-X) Ace Bks.

—The Lost Years of Merlin. 1996. (Lost Years of Merlin Ser.: No. 1). 336p. (J). (gr. 5-9). 19.99 (0-399-23018-1, Philomel) Penguin Putnam Bks. for Young Readers.

—The Seven Songs of Merlin. 1997. (Lost Years of Merlin Ser.: Bk. 2). 320p. (J). (gr. 5-9). 19.99 (0-399-23019-X, Philomel) Penguin Putnam Bks. for Young Readers.

—The Seven Songs of Merlin. unabr. ed. 2002. (J). (gr. 4-7). audio 30.00 (0-8072-0958-9, Listening Library) Random Hse. Audio Publishing Group.

—Wings of Merlin. 2000. (Lost Years of Merlin Ser.: Vol. 5). (Illus.). 272p. (J). (gr. 6-9). 19.99 (0-399-23456-X, Philomel) Penguin Putnam Bks. for Young Readers.

FINLAND—FICTION

Dick, Lois Hoadley. Mercy at Midnight: How One Courageous Woman Set Prisoners Free. 2002. 214p. (J). pap. 8.99 (0-8024-2647-6) Moody Pr.

Lilius, Irmelin S. Gold Crown Lane. Helweg, Marianne, tr. 1980. (J). (gr. 5 up). 7.95 o.s.i (0-440-04231-3); lib. bdg. 7.45 o.s.i (0-440-04232-1) Dell Publishing. (Delacorte Pr.).

—The Goldmaker's House. Helweg, Marianne, tr. 1980. (J). (gr. 5 up). 7.95 o.s.i (0-440-04200-3); lib. bdg. 7.45 o.s.i (0-440-04201-1) Dell Publishing. (Delacorte Pr.).

Sharp, Mary & Niemi, Matt. Bobbi, Father of the Finnish White Tailed Deer. 1979. (Illus.). (Orig.). (J). (gr. 4-6). pap. 5.95 (0-9603200-0-8) Bobbi Enterprises.

Shepard, Aaron. The Maiden of Northland: A Hero Tale of Finland. 1996. (Illus.). 40p. (J). (gr. 4-7). 16.00 (0-689-80485-7, Atheneum) Simon & Schuster Children's Publishing.

FIRE ISLAND (N.Y.)—FICTION

Chambers, John W. Fire Island Forfeit. 1984. 192p. (J). (gr. 4-6). 11.95 o.s.i (0-689-31043-9, Atheneum) Simon & Schuster Children's Publishing.

Estes, Eleanor. Pinky Pye. 1958. (Illus.). 192p. (J). (gr. 3-7). 12.95 o.s.i (0-15-262076-1) Harcourt Children's Bks.

Farrell, Vivian. Robert's Tall Friend: A Story of the Fire Island Lighthouse. 1988. (Illus.). 64p. (J). (gr. 4-7). 11.50 (0-9619832-0-5) Island-Metro Pubns., Inc.

—Robert's Tall Friend: A Story of the Fire Island Lighthouse. Wood, Jean, ed. 1997. (Illus.). 64p. (J). (gr. 3-6). text 24.00 (0-9657524-1-0); pap. text 16.00 (0-9657524-7-X) Logan, Tracy Pubns.

Howe, James. The Watcher. 2001. 192p. (YA). (gr. 8-12). mass mkt. 4.99 (0-689-83533-7, Simon Pulse) Simon & Schuster Children's Publishing.

Martin, Ann M. Eleven Kids, One Summer. 1991. 160p. (J). (gr. 3-7). 15.95 o.p. (0-8234-0912-0) Holiday Hse., Inc.

—Eleven Kids, One Summer. 1993. 160p. (J). (gr. 4-7). pap. 4.50 (0-590-45917-1) Scholastic, Inc.

—Eleven Kids, One Summer. 1991. (J). 10.55 (0-606-05264-X) Turtleback Bks.

Shub, Elizabeth. Cutlass in the Snow. 1986. (Illus.). 48p. (J). (gr. 1-4). 12.95 o.p. (0-688-05927-9); lib. bdg. 14.93 o.p. (0-688-05928-7) HarperCollins Children's Bk. Group. (Greenwillow Bks.).

FLORENCE (ITALY)—FICTION

Barbeau, Clayton C. Dante & Gentucca: A Love Story. 2nd ed. 1996. (Illus.). 43p. reprint ed. pap. 5.95 (0-9633157-4-9) Ikon Pr.

Sabuda, Robert. Uh Oh Leonardo. 2003. (Illus.). 48p. (J). 16.95 (0-689-81160-8, Atheneum) Simon & Schuster Children's Publishing.

FLORIDA—FICTION

Acierno, Maria A. Children of Flight Pedro Pan. 1994. (Stories of the States Ser.). (Illus.). 80p. (J). (gr. 4-7). lib. bdg. 13.95 o.p. (1-881889-52-1) Silver Moon Pr.

Amato, Carol A. Chessie, the Meandering Manatee. 1997. (Young Readers' Ser.). (Illus.). 48p. (J). (gr. 2-4). pap. 5.95 (0-8120-9850-1) Barron's Educational Series, Inc.

Anderson, Laurie Halse. Manatee Blues. 2000. (American Girl Wild at Heart Ser.: Bk. 4). (Illus.). 110p. (J). (gr. 5 up). pap. 4.95 (1-58485-049-3, American Girl) Pleasant Co. Pubns.

—Manatee Blues. 2003. (Wild at Heart Ser.). (Illus.). 114p. (J). (gr. 4 up). lib. bdg. 22.60 (0-8368-3258-2) Stevens, Gareth Inc.

—Manatee Blues. 2000. (American Girl Wild at Heart Ser.: Bk. 4). (Illus.). (YA). 11.10 (0-606-20455-5) Turtleback Bks.

Bloor, Edward. Tangerine. 1997. 304p. (YA). (gr. 6 up). 17.00 (0-15-201246-X) Harcourt Children's Bks.

—Tangerine. 1998. (Apple Signature Edition Ser.). 304p. (YA). (gr. 6 up). mass mkt. 4.99 (0-590-43277-X, Scholastic Paperbacks) Scholastic, Inc.

Brink, Carol R. The Pink Motel. 1993. (Illus.). 224p. (J). (gr. 3-7). reprint ed. mass mkt. 3.95 (0-689-71677-X, Aladdin) Simon & Schuster Children's Publishing.

Brooks, Walter R. Freddy Goes to Florida. 1997. (Freddy Ser.). (Illus.). 208p. (YA). (gr. 3-7). 23.95 (0-87951-808-1) Overlook Pr., The.

—Freddy Goes to Florida. 2001. (Illus.). 208p. (J). (gr. 4-7). pap. 7.99 (0-14-131233-5) Penguin Putnam Bks. for Young Readers.

—Freddy Goes to Florida. 1987. (Knopf Children's Paperbacks Ser.). (Illus.). 208p. (J). (gr. 3-7). 3.95 o.s.i (0-394-88886-3, Knopf Bks. for Young Readers) Random Hse. Children's Bks.

—Freddy Goes to Florida. unabr. ed. 2001. (YA). (gr. 5-8). audio compact disk 48.00; 1998. (J). (gr. 3). audio 35.00 (0-7887-2064-3, 95417E7) Recorded Bks., LLC.

—Freddy the Detective/Freddy Goes to Florida Flip-Over Book. 2002. (Illus.). pap. 6.99 (0-14-230162-0) Penguin Putnam Bks. for Young Readers.

Brouwer, Sigmund. Hurricane Power: Track. 1999. (Sigmund Brouwer's Sports Mystery Ser.: Vol. 6). 128p. (J). (gr. 5-9). pap. 5.99 o.s.i (0-8499-5818-0) Nelson, Tommy.

Carlson, Nancy. A Visit to Grandma's. 1993. (Illus.). 32p. (J). (ps-3). pap. 4.99 o.s.i (0-14-054243-4, Puffin Bks.) Penguin Putnam Bks. for Young Readers.

Carter, Dorothy. Grandma's General Store: The Ark, RS. 2004. (J). (0-374-32766-1, Farrar, Straus & Giroux (BYR)) Farrar, Straus & Giroux.

Cavanagh, Helen. Panther Glade. 1993. 160p. (J). (gr. 5-9). mass mkt. 16.00 (0-671-75617-6, Simon & Schuster Children's Publishing) Simon & Schuster Children's Publishing.

Christelow, Eileen. The Great Pig Search. 2001. (Illus.). 32p. (J). (ps-3). lib. bdg., tchr. ed. 15.00 (0-618-04910-X, Clarion Bks.) Houghton Mifflin Co. Trade & Reference Div.

Clague, Mary H. Fort Brooke Drummer Boy: A Story of Old Florida. 1998. 93p. (J). pap. 6.99 (1-57502-747-X, PO2075) Morris Publishing.

Crane, Carol. Sunny Numbers: A Florida Counting Book. 2001. (Illus.). 40p. (J). 16.95 (1-58536-050-3) Sleeping Bear Pr.

Cray, Jordan. Dead Man's Hand. 1998. (Danger.com Ser.: No. 8). 224p. (YA). (gr. 6 up). mass mkt. 3.99 (0-689-82383-5, Simon Pulse) Simon & Schuster Children's Publishing.

Crews, Donald. Bigmama's. 2001. (J). (gr. k-3). pap. 16.90 incl. audio (0-8045-6840-5, 6840) Spoken Arts, Inc.

Crist-Evans, Craig. Amaryllis. 2003. 208p. (YA). 15.99 (0-7636-1863-2) Candlewick Pr.

Crocker, Carter. The Tale of the Swamp Rat. 2003. 240p. (YA). (gr. 3-8). 16.99 (0-399-23964-2, Philomel) Penguin Putnam Bks. for Young Readers.

Day, Robert & Day, Linda. There's a Frog on a Log in the Bog. 2002. (Florida Tales Ser.: Vol. 1). (Illus.). 112p. (J). (gr. 4-6). pap. 7.95 (1-890905-20-8) Day to Day Enterprises.

DeFelice, Cynthia C. Lostman's River. 1995. 160p. (J). (gr. 4-7). pap. 4.95 (0-380-72396-4, Avon Bks.) Morrow/Avon.

—Lostman's River. 1994. 160p. (YA). (gr. 7 up). lib. bdg. 15.00 (0-02-726466-1, Atheneum) Simon & Schuster Children's Publishing.

—Lostman's River. 1995. (J). 10.55 (0-606-07810-X) Turtleback Bks.

DiCamillo, Kate. Because of Winn-Dixie. (gr. 3 up). 2001. 192p. (YA). pap. 5.99 (0-7636-1605-2); 2000. 184p. (J). 15.99 (0-7636-0776-2) Candlewick Pr.

—Because of Winn-Dixie. l.t. ed. 2002. 125p. (J). 23.95 (0-7862-3665-5) Gale Group.

—Because of Winn-Dixie. unabr. ed. 2001. (J). (gr. 3-5). audio 23.00 (0-8072-8856-X, LL0219); (YA). (gr. 4-7). audio 18.00 (0-8072-6186-6) Random Hse. Audio Publishing Group. (Listening Library).

—The Tiger Rising. (Illus.). 128p. (gr. 5-12). 2002. (YA). pap. 5.99 (0-7636-1898-5); 2001. (J). 14.99 (0-7636-0911-0) Candlewick Pr.

—The Tiger Rising. unabr. ed. 2001. (YA). audio 18.00 (0-8072-6198-X, Listening Library) Random Hse. Audio Publishing Group.

Doerr, Bonnie J. Kenzie's Key. 2003. 211p. (J). 16.95 (0-9619155-6-0) Laurel & Herbert, Inc.

Dole, Mayra L. Drum, Chavi, Drum ! / Toca, Chavi, Toca! 2003. Tr. of Toca, Chavi, Toca!. (ENG & SPA., Illus.). 32p. (J). 16.95 (0-89239-186-3) Children's Bk. Pr.

Douglas, Marjory S. Freedom River. 1994. (Illus.). 240p. (J). (gr. 4 up). 19.95 (0-9633461-4-8); pap. 14.95 (0-9633461-5-6) Valiant Pr., Inc.

Douglas, Marjory Stoneman. Alligator Crossing. 2003. (Illus.). 192p. (J). (gr. 3-8). 16.95 (1-57131-640-X); pap. 6.95 (1-57131-644-2) Milkweed Editions.

Dubowski, Cathy. The Case of the Sea World Adventure. 1996. (Adventures of Mary-Kate & Ashley Ser.). (Illus.). 80p. (J). (gr. 2-7). mass mkt. 3.99 (0-590-86369-X) Scholastic, Inc.

Englehart, Steve & Englehart, Terry. The DNAgers: The Legend of Crossbones Key. 1997. (J). pap. 3.99 (0-380-78419-X, Avon Bks.) Morrow/Avon.

—The DNAgers: The Legend of Crossbones Key. 2000. 132p. (gr. 4-7). per. 9.95 (0-595-16696-2) iUniverse, Inc.

Farley, Steven. Wild Spirit. 1999. (Young Black Stallion Ser.: No. 4). 122p. (J). (Illus.). (gr. 4-6). lib. bdg. 11.99 o.s.i (0-679-99359-2); 4th ed. (gr. 5-8). pap. 3.99 o.s.i (0-679-89359-8) Random Hse. Children's Bks. (Random Hse. Bks. for Young Readers).

—Wild Spirit. 1999. (Young Black Stallion Ser.: No. 4). (J). (gr. 4-6). 10.04 (0-606-16963-6) Turtleback Bks.

—The Yearling. 1999. (Young Black Stallion Ser.: No. 5). (Illus.). (J). 128p. (gr. 5-8). pap. 3.99 o.s.i (0-375-80091-3); 144p. (gr. 4-6). lib. bdg. 11.99 (0-375-90091-8) Random Hse. Children's Bks. (Random Hse. Bks. for Young Readers).

—The Yearling. 1999. (Young Black Stallion Ser.: No. 5). (J). (gr. 4-6). 10.04 (0-606-16964-4) Turtleback Bks.

Ferris, Jean. All That Glitters, RS. 1996. 192p. (YA). (gr. 7 up). 16.00 (0-374-30204-9, Farrar, Straus & Giroux (BYR)) Farrar, Straus & Giroux.

Flinn, Alex. Nothing to Lose. 2004. 288p. (J). 15.99 (0-06-051750-6); lib. bdg. 16.89 (0-06-051751-4) HarperCollins Children's Bk. Group. (HarperTempest).

Fogelin, Adrian. Anna Casey's Place in the World. 224p. (J). (gr. 3-6). 2003. pap. 6.95 (1-56145-295-5); 2001. 14.95 (1-56145-249-1, Peachtree Junior) Peachtree Pubs., Ltd.

—My Brother's Hero. 2002. (Peachtree Junior Publication Ser.). 224p. (J). (gr. 3-7). 14.95 (1-56145-274-2, Peachtree Junior) Peachtree Pubs., Ltd.

Forney, Melissa. Oonawassee Summer: Something is Lurking Beneath the Surface... 2000. (Illus.). 126p. (J). (gr. 4-8). pap. 14.95 (1-928961-04-5) Barker Creek Publishing, Inc.

Gantos, Jack. Jack on the Tracks: Four Seasons of Fifth Grade, RS. 1999. (Illus.). 192p. (J). (gr. 5-9). 16.00 (0-374-33665-2, Farrar, Straus & Giroux (BYR)) Farrar, Straus & Giroux.

—Jack on the Tracks: Four Seasons of Fifth Grade. l.t. ed. 2002. 210p. (J). 22.95 (0-7862-4394-5) Thorndike Pr.

George, Jean Craighead. The Missing Gator of Gumbo Limbo. 1992. 176p. (J). (gr. 3-7). lib. bdg. 14.89 o.p. (0-06-020397-8); (gr. 4-7). 15.95 o.p. (0-06-020396-X) HarperCollins Children's Bk. Group.

Golden Books Staff. Shipwreck Fever. 2003. (Road to Reading Ser.). (Illus.). 48p. (J). (gr. 2-4). pap. 3.99 (0-307-26416-5); lib. bdg. 11.99 (0-307-46416-4) Random Hse. Children's Bks. (Golden Bks.).

Greenberg, Dan. How to Speak Dolphin in Three Easy Lessons. (Zack Files Ser.: No. 11). (Illus.). (J). (gr. 2-5). 2015. 3.99 o.s.i (*0-448-41737-5*); 1997. 64p. 4.99 (*0-448-41736-7*) Penguin Putnam Bks. for Young Readers. (Grosset & Dunlap).

Griffith, Helen V. Foxy. 1984. 144p. (J). (gr. 7 up). 15.00 (*0-688-02567-6*, Greenwillow Bks.) HarperCollins Children's Bk. Group.

—Foxy. 1997. 144p. (J). (gr. 3-7). mass mkt. 4.95 o.p. (*0-688-15489-1*, Morrow, William & Co.) Morrow/Avon.

—Foxy. 1997. 10.05 o.p. (*0-606-11350-9*) Turtleback Bks.

Harvey, Dean. The Secret Elephant of Harlan Kooter. 1992. (Illus.). 160p. (J). (gr. 2-5). 13.95 o.s.i (*0-395-62523-8*) Houghton Mifflin Co.

Haynes, Betsy. Deadly Deception. 224p. (YA). (gr. 6 up). 1995. mass mkt. 3.99 o.s.i (*0-440-21947-7*); 1994. 14.95 o.s.i (*0-385-32067-1*, Delacorte Pr.) Dell Publishing.

—Deadly Deception. 1995. (YA). (gr. 7-10). 9.09 o.p. (*0-606-07423-6*) Turtleback Bks.

Hays, Wilma P. Siege: The Story of St. Augustine in 1702. 1976. (Illus.). 96p. (J). (gr. 3-6). 6.95 o.p. (*0-698-20357-7*) Putnam Publishing Group, The.

Hest, Amy. Travel Tips from Harry: A Guide to Family Vacations in the Sun. 1989. (Illus.). 64p. (J). (gr. 2 up). 11.95 o.p. (*0-688-07972-5*); lib. bdg. 11.88 o.p. (*0-688-09291-8*) Morrow/Avon. (Morrow, William & Co.).

Hiaasen, Carl. Hoot. unabr. ed. 2002. (J). (gr. 4-7). audio 26.00 (*0-8072-0922-8*, Listening Library) Random Hse. Audio Publishing Group.

—Hoot. 304p. (J). (gr. 5). 2004. pap. 8.95 (*0-375-82916-4*); 2002. (Illus.). 15.95 (*0-375-82181-3*); 2002. (Illus.). lib. bdg. 17.99 (*0-375-92181-8*) Random Hse. Children's Bks. (Knopf Bks. for Young Readers).

—Hoot. 2003. (Young Adult Ser.). 25.95 (*0-7862-5014-3*) Thorndike Pr.

Hoff, Syd. Irving & Me. 1967. (J). (gr. 6 up). 8.95 o.p. (*0-06-022498-3*) HarperCollins Pubs.

Holland, Marion. No Children, No Pets. 1965. (Illus.). (J). (gr. 3-7). lib. bdg. 4.99 o.p. (*0-394-91447-3*, Knopf Bks. for Young Readers) Random Hse. Children's Bks.

Holmes, Mary Z. Dear Dad. 1992. (History's Children Ser.). (Illus.). 48p. (J). (gr. 4-5). pap. o.p. (*0-8114-6428-8*); lib. bdg. 21.36 o.p. (*0-8114-3503-2*) Raintree Pubs.

Jackson, C. Paul. Stepladder Steve Plays Basketball. 1969. (Illus.). (J). (gr. 4-6). lib. bdg. 6.95 o.p. (*0-8038-6688-7*) Hastings Hse. Daytrips Pubs.

Joseph, Daniel M. All Dressed up & Nowhere to Go. 1993. 32p. (J). (ps-3). 14.95 o.p. (*0-395-60196-7*) Houghton Mifflin Co.

Katschke, Judy. Shore Thing. 2001. (Two of a Kind Ser.: No. 17). (Illus.). 112p. (gr. 3-7). mass mkt. 4.99 (*0-06-106657-5*, HarperEntertainment) Morrow/Avon.

Kennedy, Barbara. The Boy Who Loved Alligators. 1994. 144p. (J). (gr. 3-7). text 15.00 (*0-689-31876-6*, Atheneum) Simon & Schuster Children's Publishing.

Klima, Charlene H. Give Me Five. 2000. 106p. (YA). (gr. 4-9). pap. 12.00 (*1-883911-36-2*) Brandylane Pubs., Inc.

Konigsburg, E. L. T-Backs, T-Shirts, Coat, & Suit. 1993. 176p. (J). (gr. 4-7). 16.95 (*0-689-31855-3*, Atheneum) Simon & Schuster Children's Publishing.

—T-Backs, T-Shirts, Coat & Suit. 1995. 176p. (J). (gr. 4-7). pap. 3.95 (*0-7868-1027-0*) Disney Pr.

—T-Backs, T-Shirts, Coat & Suit. 2003. (Illus.). 176p. (J). pap. 4.99 (*0-689-85682-2*, Aladdin) Simon & Schuster Children's Publishing.

Lasky, Kathryn. Shadows in the Water. 1992. (Starbuck Family Adventure Ser.: Vol. 2). 224p. (J). (gr. 4-7). pap. 8.00 (*0-15-273534-8*, Harcourt Paperbacks) Harcourt Children's Bks.

—Shadows in the Water: A Starbuck Family Adventure, Vol. 2. 1992. 224p. (J). (gr. 3-7). 16.95 o.s.i (*0-15-273533-X*) Harcourt Children's Bks.

Lawrence, Mildred. Inside the Gate. 1968. (J). (gr. 7 up). 5.95 o.p. (*0-15-238728-5*) Harcourt Children's Bks.

—The Treasure & the Song. 1966. (J). (gr. 7 up). 4.95 o.p. (*0-15-289950-2*) Harcourt Children's Bks.

Leppard, Lois Gladys. Mandie & the Seaside Rendezvous. 2000. (Mandie Bks.: No. 32). 176p. (J). (gr. 4-7). pap. 4.99 (*1-55661-673-2*) Bethany Hse. Pubs.

—Mandie & the Seaside Rendezvous. 2000. (Mandie Bks.: No. 32). (J). (gr. 4-7). 11.04 (*0-606-18919-X*) Turtleback Bks.

Lippincott, Joseph W. Phantom Deer. 1954. (Illus.). (YA). (gr. 7-9). 11.95 (*0-397-30278-9*) HarperCollins Children's Bk. Group.

—Wahoo Bobcat. 1950. (Illus.). (J). (gr. 7-9). o.p. (*0-397-30198-7*) HarperCollins Children's Bk. Group.

McDaniel, Lurlene. The Girl Death Left Behind. 1999. 192p. (YA). (gr. 7-12). mass mkt. 4.99 (*0-553-57091-9*, Dell Books for Young Readers) Random Hse. Children's Bks.

—The Girl Death Left Behind. 1999. 11.04 (*0-606-16371-9*) Turtleback Bks.

—The Time Capsule. 2003. 224p. (YA). (gr. 7). 9.95 (*0-553-57096-X*, Bantam Bks. for Young Readers) Random Hse. Children's Bks.

—The Time Capsule. 2003. 224p. (YA). (gr. 7). lib. bdg. 11.99 (*0-553-13051-X*) Random Hse., Inc.

McDonald, Joyce. Devil on My Heels. 2004. 272p. (YA). lib. bdg. 17.99 (*0-385-90133-X*); (gr. 7). 15.95 (*0-385-73107-8*) Random Hse. Children's Bks. (Delacorte Bks. for Young Readers).

McDonald, Megan. Beezy. 1997. (Illus.). 48p. (J). (gr. 1-3). pap. 13.95 (*0-531-30046-3*); lib. bdg. 14.99 o.p. (*0-531-33046-X*) Scholastic, Inc. (Orchard Bks.).

—Beezy & Funnybone. 2000. (Illus.). 48p. (J). (gr. 1-4). pap. 14.95 (*0-531-30211-3*); lib. bdg. 15.99 (*0-531-33211-X*) Scholastic, Inc. (Orchard Bks.).

—Beezy & Funnybone. 2000. 11.10 (*0-606-19481-9*) Turtleback Bks.

—Beezy at Bat. (Illus.). 48p. (J). (gr. 1-4). 2000. mass mkt. 4.95 (*0-531-07164-2*); 1998. pap. 13.95 (*0-531-30085-4*); 1998. lib. bdg. 14.99 (*0-531-33085-0*) Scholastic, Inc. (Orchard Bks.).

—Beezy at Bat. 2000. (J). 11.10 (*0-606-20453-9*) Turtleback Bks.

McKay, Kathleen C. Hearts of Rosewood: A Novel. unabr. ed. 1997. 122p. (J). (gr. 5-12). 18.95 o.p. (*0-936389-46-X*) Tudor Pubs., Inc.

Mikaelsen, Ben. Stranded. 1996. 288p. (J). (gr. 4-8). pap. 4.95 (*0-7868-1109-9*) Disney Pr.

—Stranded. 1995. 256p. (J). (gr. 4-8). 15.99 (*0-7868-0072-0*); (ps-3). lib. bdg. 16.49 (*0-7868-2059-4*) Hyperion Bks. for Children.

—Stranded. 1996. (J). 11.00 (*0-606-08882-2*) Turtleback Bks.

Nixon-Weaver, Elizabeth. Rooster. 2001. (Illus.). 320p. (J). (gr. 7 up). 16.95 (*1-58837-001-1*) Winslow Pr.

Nolan, Peggy. The Spy Who Came in from the Sea. 2000. 129p. (J). (gr. 5-9). 14.95 (*1-56164-186-3*) Pineapple Pr., Inc.

Peck, Robert. Bro. 2004. (J). (*0-06-052974-1*); lib. bdg. (*0-06-052975-X*) HarperCollins Pubs.

Peck, Robert Newton. Arly. 1989. (History Series for Young People). 160p. (J). (gr. 5 up). 16.95 (*0-8027-6856-3*) Walker & Co.

—Arly's Run. 1991. 160p. (J). (gr. 4-7). 16.95 (*0-8027-8120-9*) Walker & Co.

—Cowboy Ghost. 208p. (gr. 7 up). 2000. (J). pap. 4.95 (*0-06-447228-0*, Harper Trophy); 1999. (J). lib. bdg. 15.89 (*0-06-028211-8*); 1999. (YA). 15.95 (*0-06-028168-5*, Harper Trophy) HarperCollins Children's Bk. Group.

—Cowboy Ghost. 1999. (YA). pap., stu. ed. 52.95 incl. audio (*0-7887-3189-0*, 40924); (gr. 5). audio 30.00 (*0-7887-3208-0*, 95795E7);Class set. audio 197.80 (*0-7887-3235-8*, 46891) Recorded Bks., LLC.

—Cowboy Ghost. 2000. (Illus.). (J). 11.00 (*0-606-18684-0*) Turtleback Bks.

—The Horse Thief. 2002. 192p. (J). (gr. 7 up). lib. bdg. 16.89 (*0-06-623792-0*) HarperCollins Children's Bk. Group.

—The Horse Thief. 2002. 240p. (J). (gr. 7 up). 16.95 (*0-06-623791-2*) HarperCollins Pubs.

Pilius, Nancy A. A Manatee Recovers. 1994. (J). 7.95 o.p. (*0-533-10835-7*) Vantage Pr., Inc.

Prather, Ray. Fish & Bones. 1992. 272p. (J). (gr. 5-9). 14.00 o.p. (*0-06-025121-2*); lib. bdg. 14.89 o.p. (*0-06-025122-0*) HarperCollins Children's Bk. Group.

Rawlings, Marjorie Kinnan. The Yearling. abr. ed. 1995. (J). (gr. 7-12). audio 16.95 (*1-55927-358-5*, 393213) Audio Renaissance.

—The Yearling. 1991. 250p. (YA). reprint ed. lib. bdg. 27.95 (*0-89966-841-0*) Buccaneer Bks., Inc.

—The Yearling. abr. ed. 1984. (J). audio 15.95 (*1-55994-076-X*, CPN 2057, Caedmon) HarperTrade.

—The Yearling. 1999. (Illus.). 444p. (J). (*0-03-054778-4*) Holt, Rinehart & Winston.

—The Yearling, Level 3. 2001. pap. 7.66 (*0-582-34439-5*) Longman Publishing Group.

—The Yearling. unabr. ed. (YA). 2000. pap. 104.20 incl. audio (*0-7887-3661-2*, 41027X4); 2000. (gr. 7). audio 90.00 (*0-7887-3530-6*, 95919E7); Class Set. 1999. audio 170.30 (*0-7887-3690-6*, 46994) Recorded Bks., LLC.

—The Yearling. 2002. 480p. pap. 14.00 (*0-7432-2525-2*, Scribner) Simon & Schuster.

—The Yearling. (Aladdin Classics Ser.). 2001. (Illus.). 528p. (J). pap. 5.99 (*0-689-84623-1*, Aladdin); 1985. (Illus.). 416p. (YA). (gr. 7-12). 28.00 (*0-684-18461-3*, Atheneum); 1982. 428p. (YA). pap. 4.95 o.s.i (*0-684-17617-3*, Simon & Schuster Children's Publishing); 1930. (YA). 20.00 o.s.i (*0-684-20922-5*, Atheneum); 1930. 428p. (YA). pap. 9.95 o.s.i (*0-684-71878-2*, Simon & Schuster Children's Publishing); deluxe ltd. ed. 1985. (Illus.). 416p. (J). 75.00 o.s.i (*0-684-18508-3*, Atheneum); 50th annot. ed. 1988. (Illus.). 416p. (YA). (gr. 7-12). mass mkt. 5.95 (*0-02-044931-3*, Simon Pulse) Simon & Schuster Children's Publishing.

—The Yearling. l.t. ed. 1994. 559p. (YA). lib. bdg. 23.95 (*0-8161-5992-0*) Thorndike Pr.

—The Yearling. 1988. (YA). 12.00 (*0-606-00109-3*) Turtleback Bks.

Rogers, Kirby. Operation Dewey. 2002. (Illus.). ix, 100p. (J). pap. (*1-877633-65-8*) Luthers.

Roy, Ron. The Goose's Gold. (Stepping Stone Book Ser.: No. 7). (Illus.). 96p. (J). (gr. 2-5). 1999. lib. bdg. 11.99 (*0-679-99078-X*); 1998. pap. 3.99 (*0-679-89078-5*) Random Hse. Children's Bks. (Random Hse. Bks. for Young Readers).

—The Goose's Gold. 1999. (A to Z Mysteries Ser.: No. 7). (J). (gr. k-3). 10.04 (*0-606-15977-0*) Turtleback Bks.

Rust, Ann O'Connell. Nonie of the Everglades. Rust, Allen F., ed. 1998. 72p. (J). (gr. 4-7). pap. 7.95 (*1-883203-04-X*) Amaro Bks.

—Walking with Irma. 1999. 248p. pap. 14.95 (*1-883203-05-8*) Amaro Bks.

Samantha's Florida Adventure. 1998. (Illus.). 2p. (J). (ps-1). 15.00 (*1-888074-86-8*) Pockets of Learning.

Schaller, Bob. The Great Florida Chase. 2002. (X-Country Adventures Ser.: Bk. 8). (Illus.). 128p. (J). (gr. 4-7). pap. 5.99 o.p. (*0-8010-4494-4*) Baker Bks.

Schreengost, Maity. Tasso of Tarpon Springs. 1998. (Illus.). 118p. (J). (gr. 3-6). pap. 5.95 (*0-929895-24-X*, Hoot Owl Bks.) Maupin Hse. Publishing.

Scott, Kieran. While You Were Gone. 1999. (Love Stories Ser.). 192p. (gr. 7-12). mass mkt. 3.99 o.s.i (*0-553-49277-2*, Dell Books for Young Readers) Random Hse. Children's Bks.

Siegelson, Kim L. Escape South. 2000. (Road to Reading Ser.). (Illus.). (J). (gr. 2-5). 78p. pap. 3.99 (*0-307-26504-8*); 80p. lib. bdg. 11.99 o.s.i (*0-307-46504-7*) Random Hse. Children's Bks. (Golden Bks.).

—Escape South. 2000. (J). 10.14 (*0-606-18931-9*) Turtleback Bks.

Smith, Patrick D. A Land Remembered, 2 vols. 2001. (Illus.). Vol. 1. 235p. (J). (gr. 5-12). pap., stu. ed. 7.95 (*1-56164-223-1*); Vol. 1. 240p. (YA). (gr. 5-12). stu. ed. 14.95 (*1-56164-230-4*); Vol. 2. 235p. (J). pap., stu. ed. 7.95 (*1-56164-224-X*); Vol. 2. 200p. (YA). (gr. 5-12). 14.95 (*1-56164-231-2*) Pineapple Pr., Inc.

Stevenson, James. The Worst Goes South. 1995. (Illus.). 32p. (J). (gr. k up). 15.00 o.p. (*0-688-13059-3*); lib. bdg. 14.93 o.s.i (*0-688-13060-7*) HarperCollins Children's Bk. Group. (Greenwillow Bks.).

Stolz, Mary. Coco Grimes. (Trophy Bk.). (J). 1995. 96p. (gr. 4-7). pap. 4.50 o.p. (*0-06-440512-5*, Harper Trophy); 1994. 128p. (gr. 3-6). lib. bdg. 13.89 o.p. (*0-06-024233-7*); 1994. 128p. (gr. 3-6). 14.00 o.p. (*0-06-024232-9*) HarperCollins Children's Bk. Group.

—Coco Grimes. 1996. (J). 9.70 o.p. (*0-606-08507-6*) Turtleback Bks.

—Stealing Home. 160p. (J). (gr. 3-6). 1994. (Illus.). pap. 5.99 (*0-06-440528-1*, Harper Trophy); 1992. lib. bdg. 14.89 o.p. (*0-06-021157-1*); 1992. 15.95 (*0-06-021154-7*) HarperCollins Children's Bk. Group.

—Stealing Home. 1994. 11.00 (*0-606-06767-1*) Turtleback Bks.

Strickland, Brad. The Wrath of the Grinning Ghost. Moore, Lisa, ed. 2001. (Johnny Dixon Ser.). 176p. (J). (gr. 3-7). pap. 5.99 (*0-14-131103-7*, Puffin Bks.) Penguin Putnam Bks. for Young Readers.

—The Wrath of the Grinning Ghost. Sherry, Toby, ed. 1999. (Johnny Dixon Mystery Ser.). (Illus.). 192p. (YA). (gr. 5-9). 16.99 o.s.i (*0-8037-2222-2*, Dial Bks. for Young Readers) Penguin Putnam Bks. for Young Readers.

Sweeney, Joyce. Head Lock. 2002. 200p. (YA). (gr. 7 up). 16.95 (*1-58837-010-0*) Winslow Pr.

—The Spirit Window. 1998. 256p. (YA). 15.95 o.s.i (*0-385-32510-X*, Delacorte Pr.) Dell Publishing.

—The Spirit Window. 1999. (Laurel-Leaf Bks.). 256p. (YA). (gr. 7 up). mass mkt. 4.50 o.s.i (*0-440-22711-9*, Dell Books for Young Readers) Random Hse. Children's Bks.

Tylander, Robert. Mystery at Manatee Creek. 2000. 182p. (J). pap. 11.95 (*1-56315-204-5*) Sterling-House Pubs., Inc.

Veciana-Suarez, Ana. The Flight to Freedom. 2002. (First Person Fiction Ser.). 208p. (J). (gr. 6-9). pap. 16.95 (*0-439-38199-1*, Orchard Bks.) Scholastic, Inc.

Whittaker, Dorothy. Angels of the Swamp. 1992. 160p. (J). (gr. 6-9). 17.95 (*0-8027-8129-2*) Walker & Co.

Yorinks, Arthur. The Miami Giant. 1999. (Illus.). 36p. (J). (gr. 5-8). text 16.00 (*0-7881-6464-3*) DIANE Publishing Co.

—The Miami Giant. 1995. (Michael di Capua Bks.). (Illus.). 40p. (J). (ps up). 15.95 o.p. (*0-06-205068-0*); lib. bdg. 15.89 o.s.i (*0-06-205069-9*) HarperCollins Children's Bk. Group.

FRANCE—FICTION

Agee, Jon. The Return of Freddy LeGrand, RS. 32p. (J). (ps-3). 1994. (Illus.). pap. 4.95 o.p. (*0-374-46230-5*, Sunburst); 1992. 15.00 o.p. (*0-374-36249-1*, Farrar, Straus & Giroux (BYR)) Farrar, Straus & Giroux.

Anderson, Margaret J. Children of Summer, RS. 1997. (Illus.). 112p. (J). (gr. 3 up). 15.00 o.p. (*0-374-31243-5*, Farrar, Straus & Giroux (BYR)) Farrar, Straus & Giroux.

Anholt, Laurence. Camille & the Sunflowers. 1994. (Illus.). 32p. (J). (ps-2). 14.95 (*0-8120-6409-7*) Barron's Educational Series, Inc.

—The Magical Garden of Claude Monet. 2003. (Illus.). 32p. (J). 14.95 (*0-7641-5574-1*) Barron's Educational Series, Inc.

Arnold, Marsha D. & Davis, Jack E. Metro Cat. 2001. (Storybook Ser.). (Illus.). 40p. (J). (ps-3). 9.95 o.s.i (*0-307-10213-0*, Golden Bks.) Random Hse. Children's Bks.

Auerbach, Marjorie. Seven Uncles Come to Dinner. 1963. (Illus.). (J). (gr. 5 up). lib. bdg. 4.99 o.p. (*0-394-91606-9*, Knopf Bks. for Young Readers) Random Hse. Children's Bks.

Aurum Press & Van der Meer, Frank. The Phantom of the Opera Pop-Up Book. 1989. 19.95 o.p. (*0-06-016012-8*) HarperTrade.

Austin, Judith M. Discovery in a French Garden. 1997. (GlobalFriends Adventures Ser.). (Illus.). 64p. (J). (gr. 2-6). pap. 5.95 (*1-58056-007-5*, GlobalFriends Pr.) GlobalFriends Collection, Inc.

Bagwell, Stella. Madeline's Song. 1987. (Harlequin Romance Ser.). pap. (*0-373-08543-5*, Silhouette) Harlequin Enterprises, Ltd.

Banks, Kate. The Cat Who Walked Across France, RS. 2004. (J). 16.00 (*0-374-39968-9*, Farrar, Straus & Giroux (BYR)) Farrar, Straus & Giroux.

Banks, Lynne Reid. Melusine: A Mystery. (YA). (gr. 7 up). 1997. 256p. pap. 4.99 (*0-380-79135-8*, Harper Trophy); 1991. 224p. mass mkt. 3.95 (*0-06-447054-7*, Harper Trophy); 1989. 256p. 12.95 (*0-06-020394-3*); 1989. 256p. lib. bdg. 12.89 o.p. (*0-06-020395-1*) HarperCollins Children's Bk. Group.

—Melusine: A Mystery. 1997. 11.04 (*0-606-13604-5*) Turtleback Bks.

Bemelmans, Ludwig. Madeline. 1995. (Madeline Ser.). (J). (ps-3). reprint ed. lib. bdg. 25.95 (*1-56849-657-5*) Buccaneer Bks., Inc.

—Madeline, 2 bks. Grosman, Ernesto Livon, tr. from ENG. unabr. ed. 1999. (Madeline Ser.). (SPA., Illus.). (J). (ps-3). pap. 29.95 incl. audio (*0-87499-570-1*) Live Oak Media.

—Madeline. unabr. ed. 1997. (Madeline Ser.). (SPA., Illus.). (J). (ps-3). 24.95 incl. audio (*0-87499-409-8*); pap. 15.95 incl. audio (*0-87499-408-X*, LK7307) Live Oak Media.

—Madeline. 2000. (Madeline Ser.). (Illus.). 48p. (J). (ps-3). pap. 6.99 (*0-14-056439-X*, Puffin Bks.) Penguin Putnam Bks. for Young Readers.

—Madeline. Grosman, Ernesto L., tr. 1996. (Madeline Ser.). (SPA., Illus.). 48p. (J). (ps-3). pap. 6.99 (*0-14-055761-X*, VK1051) Penguin Putnam Bks. for Young Readers.

—Madeline. 1993. (Madeline Ser.). (Illus.). 1p. (J). (ps-3). 9.99 (*0-14-095121-0*) Penguin Putnam Bks. for Young Readers.

—Madeline. Grosman, Ernesto L., tr. 1993. (Madeline Ser.). (SPA., Illus.). 64p. (J). (ps-3). 16.99 (*0-670-85154-X*, PG54X, Viking Children's Bks.) Penguin Putnam Bks. for Young Readers.

—Madeline. (Madeline Ser.). (Illus.). (J). (ps-3). 1993. 32p. pap. 19.99 o.s.i (*0-14-054845-9*, Puffin Bks.); 1977. 48p. pap. 5.99 o.s.i (*0-14-050198-3*, Puffin Bks.); 1958. 48p. 16.99 (*0-670-44580-0*, Viking Children's Bks.) Penguin Putnam Bks. for Young Readers.

—Madeline. (Madeline Ser.). (J). (ps-3). 1996. 12.14 (*0-606-08812-1*); 1977. 10.19 o.p. (*0-606-03874-4*) Turtleback Bks.

—Madeline: A Pop-Up Book. 1987. (Madeline Ser.). (Illus.). 12p. (J). (ps-3). 17.99 (*0-670-81667-1*, Viking Children's Bks.) Penguin Putnam Bks. for Young Readers.

—Madeline: A Pop-Up Carousel. 1994. (Madeline Ser.). (Illus.). 5p. (J). (ps-3). 10.99 o.s.i (*0-670-85602-9*) Penguin Putnam Bks. for Young Readers.

—Madeline & the Bad Hat. 2002. (Madeline Ser.). (Illus.). (J). 14.04 (*0-7587-4084-0*) Book Wholesalers, Inc.

—Madeline & the Bad Hat. (Madeline Ser.). (Illus.). 64p. (J). (ps-3). 2000. pap. 6.99 (*0-14-056648-1*); 1977. pap. 5.99 o.s.i (*0-14-050206-8*) Penguin Putnam Bks. for Young Readers. (Puffin Bks.).

—Madeline & the Gypsies. (Madeline Ser.). (Illus.). (J). (ps-3). 2000. 64p. pap. 6.99 (*0-14-056647-3*, Puffin Bks.); 1977. 64p. pap. 5.99 o.s.i (*0-14-050261-0*, Puffin Bks.); 1959. 56p. 16.99 (*0-670-44682-3*, Viking Children's Bks.) Penguin Putnam Bks. for Young Readers.

—Madeline & the Gypsies. (Madeline Ser.). (J). (ps-3). 2000. (Illus.). 13.14 (*0-606-18428-7*); 1959. 10.19 o.p. (*0-606-01010-6*) Turtleback Bks.

Settings

—Madeline Book & Toy Box. 1991. (Madeline Ser.). 64p. (J). (ps-3). 24.99 (*0-14-034880-8*, Puffin Bks.) Penguin Putnam Bks. for Young Readers.

—Madeline, Grades Preschool-3. 1997. (Madeline Ser.). (SPA., Illus.). pap., tchr. ed. 31.95 incl. audio (*0-87499-410-1*) Live Oak Media.

—Madeline in America & Other Holiday Tales. 2002. (Madeline Ser.). (Illus.). (J). 18.68 (*0-7587-4186-3*) Book Wholesalers, Inc.

—Madeline in America & Other Holiday Tales. 1999. (Madeline Ser.). (J). (ps-3). (Illus.). 111p. pap. 19.95 o.s.i (*0-590-03910-5*, Levine, Arthur A. Bks.); pap. 125.00 (*0-439-09633-2*) Scholastic, Inc.

—Madeline Playtime Activity Book. 1997. (Madeline Ser.). (Illus.). 16p. (J). (ps-3). pap. 7.99 (*0-670-87464-7*) Penguin Putnam Bks. for Young Readers.

—Madeline Storybook Collection Snap & Fold Away. 1994. (J). 14.98 (*0-670-77188-0*) Penguin Putnam Bks. for Young Readers.

—Madeline's Christmas. (Madeline Ser.). 32p. (J). (ps-3). 1993. (Illus.). pap. 9.99 incl. audio (*0-14-095108-3*, Puffin Bks.); 1988. pap. 5.99 o.s.i (*0-14-050666-7*, Puffin Bks.); 1985. (Illus.). 15.99 (*0-670-80666-8*, Viking Children's Bks.) Penguin Putnam Bks. for Young Readers.

—Madeline's Christmas. 1984. (Madeline Ser.). (J). (ps-3). 12.14 (*0-606-03983-X*) Turtleback Bks.

—Madeline's House: Madeline; Madeline's Rescue; Madeline & the Bad Hat. 1989. (Madeline Ser.). (Illus.). (J). (ps-3). pap. 12.99 (*0-14-095028-1*) Penguin Putnam Bks. for Young Readers.

—Madeline's Rescue. (Madeline Ser.). (J). (ps-3). 2000. (Illus.). 64p. pap. 6.99 (*0-14-056651-1*, Puffin Bks.); 1993. (Illus.). 9.99 (*0-14-095122-9*, Puffin Bks.); 1989. 6.95 o.p. (*0-14-095034-6*, Puffin Bks.); 1977. (Illus.). 64p. pap. 5.99 o.s.i (*0-14-050207-6*, Puffin Bks.); 1953. (Illus.). 56p. 16.99 (*0-670-44716-1*, Viking Children's Bks.) Penguin Putnam Bks. for Young Readers.

—Madeline's Rescue. 1977. (Madeline Ser.). (J). (ps-3). 10.19 o.p. (*0-606-03876-0*) Turtleback Bks.

—Madeline's Velcro. 1997. (Madeline Ser.). (J). (ps-3). pap. 14.98 (*0-670-78126-6*) NAL.

Bemelmans, Ludwig & Outlet Book Company Staff. Madeline & the Bad Hat. 1988. (Madeline Ser.). (J). (ps-3). 0.75 o.s.i (*0-517-18388-9*) Random Hse. Value Publishing.

Berson, Harold. The Thief Who Hugged a Moonbeam, 001. 1979. (Illus.). 40p. (J). (ps-3). 7.95 o.p. (*0-395-28767-7*, Clarion Bks.) Houghton Mifflin Co. Trade & Reference Div.

Birchman, David F. Victorious Paints the Great Balloon. 1991. (Illus.). 64p. (J). (gr. 2-6). text 13.95 o.p. (*0-02-710111-8*, Simon & Schuster Children's Publishing) Simon & Schuster Children's Publishing.

Bott, Elizabeth. Vinnie in France. 2001. (Vinnie Ser.: Vol. 2). (Illus.). 54p. (YA). (gr. 5 up). 15.95 (*0-9704678-1-8*) Pageturner Bks.

Brow, Thea J. The Secret Cross of Lorraine, 001. 1981. (J). (gr. 5-8). 8.95 o.p. (*0-395-30344-3*) Houghton Mifflin Co.

Capodanno, Sophie & Neff, Lisi, illus. The Misadventures of Sophie. 2002. 163p. (J). (gr. 2 up). per. 9.95 (*0-9719396-0-8*) Neff, Lisi A.

Carlson, Natalie S. Brother for the Orphelines. 1959. (Illus.). (J). (gr. 2-6). lib. bdg. 10.89 o.p. (*0-06-020961-5*) HarperCollins Pubs.

—Carnival in Paris. 1962. (Illus.). (J). (gr. 2-6). lib. bdg. 13.89 o.p. (*0-06-020971-2*) HarperCollins Children's Bk. Group.

—Happy Orpheline. 1957. (Illus.). 112p. (J). (gr. 3-6). lib. bdg. 13.89 o.p. (*0-06-021007-9*) HarperCollins Children's Bk. Group.

—Orphelines in the Enchanted Castle. 1964. (Illus.). (J). (gr. 3-7). lib. bdg. 10.89 o.p. (*0-06-021046-X*) HarperCollins Pubs.

—Pet for the Orphelines. 1962. (Illus.). (J). (gr. 3-7). lib. bdg. 10.89 o.p. (*0-06-021056-7*) HarperCollins Pubs.

Carter, Peter. The Hunted, RS. 1994. 320p. (J). 17.00 o.p. (*0-374-33520-6*, Farrar, Straus & Giroux (BYR)) Farrar, Straus & Giroux.

Chall, Marsha W. Bonaparte. 2000. (Illus.). 32p. (J). (ps-3). pap. 16.95 (*0-7894-2617-X*, D K Ink) Dorling Kindersley Publishing, Inc.

Chester, Deborah. The Sign of the Owl. 1984. 256p. (J). (gr. 5-9). 12.95 o.s.i (*0-02-718140-5*, Simon & Schuster Children's Publishing) Simon & Schuster Children's Publishing.

Christopher, John. The White Mountains. 2nd ed. 1988. (Tripods Trilogy Ser.: Vol. 2). (Illus.). 192p. (YA). (gr. 7 up). mass mkt. 4.99 (*0-02-042711-5*, Simon Pulse) Simon & Schuster Children's Publishing.

—The White Mountains: The Tripods Trilogy. l.t. ed. 1990. 256p. (J). (gr. 3 up). 16.95 (*0-7451-1043-6*, Macmillan Reference USA) Gale Group.

—The White Mountains: The Tripods Trilogy. 1967. 192p. (J). (gr. 4-7). 17.95 (*0-02-718360-2*, Simon & Schuster Children's Publishing) Simon & Schuster Children's Publishing.

—The White Mountains: The Tripods Trilogy. l.t. ed. 2000. (Science Fiction Ser.). 168p. 25.95 (*0-7838-9170-9*) Thorndike Pr.

—The White Mountains: The Tripods Trilogy. 1970. (J). 11.04 (*0-606-05083-3*) Turtleback Bks.

Clements, Bruce. A Chapel of Thieves, RS. 2002. 224p. (J). (gr. 6-9). 16.00 (*0-374-37701-4*, Farrar, Straus & Giroux (BYR)) Farrar, Straus & Giroux.

Clewes, Dorothy. Missing from Home. 1978. (J). (gr. 7 up). 6.95 o.p. (*0-15-254882-3*) Harcourt Children's Bks.

Collier, Peter & Collier, Mary Jo. The King's Giraffe. 1996. (J). 14.00 (*0-671-88133-7*); (Illus.). 40p. 16.00 (*0-689-80679-5*) Simon & Schuster Children's Publishing. (Simon & Schuster Children's Publishing).

Cowley, Marjorie. Anooka's Answer. 1998. (Illus.). 152p. (J). (gr. 5-9). tchr. ed. 16.00 (*0-395-88530-2*, Clarion Bks.) Houghton Mifflin Co. Trade & Reference Div.

Cunningham, Julia. Burnish Me Bright. 1970. (Illus.). (J). (gr. 5-8). lib. bdg. 6.99 o.s.i (*0-394-90851-1*, Pantheon) Knopf Publishing Group.

de Paola, Tomie & Lear, Edward. Bonjour Mr. Satie. 1991. (Illus.). 32p. (J). (ps-3). 16.99 (*0-399-21782-7*, G. P. Putnam's Sons) Penguin Group (USA) Inc.

Dickens, Charles. A Tale of Two Cities. 1997. (Classics Illustrated Study Guides). (Illus.). 64p. (YA). (gr. 7 up). mass mkt., stu. ed. 4.99 o.p. (*1-57840-003-1*) Acclaim Bks.

Donahue, John. Till Tomorrow, RS. 2001. 176p. (J). (gr. 3-7). 16.00 (*0-374-37580-1*, Farrar, Straus & Giroux (BYR)) Farrar, Straus & Giroux.

Dubowski, Cathy. Bonjour Alex! 1997. (Secret World of Alex Mack Ser.: No. 17). 160p. (J). (gr. 4-7). pap. 3.99 (*0-671-01373-4*, Aladdin) Simon & Schuster Children's Publishing.

Dumas, Alexandre. The Man in the Iron Mask. 1967. (Airmont Classics Ser.). (YA). (gr. 9 up). mass mkt. 2.75 o.p. (*0-8049-0150-3*, CL-150) Airmont Publishing Co., Inc.

—The Man in the Iron Mask. 1994. (Illustrated Classics Collection). 64p. pap. 3.60 o.p. (*1-56103-591-2*) American Guidance Service, Inc.

—The Man in the Iron Mask. Farr, Naunerle C., ed. 1978. (Now Age Illustrated IV Ser.). (Illus.). (J). (gr. 4-12). stu. ed. 1.25 (*0-88301-340-1*); text 7.50 o.p. (*0-88301-328-2*); pap. text 2.95 (*0-88301-316-9*) Pendulum Pr., Inc.

—The Man in the Iron Mask. 1998. (Bullseye Step into Classics Ser.). (Illus.). 128p. (J). (gr. 3-5). pap. 3.99 (*0-679-89433-0*, Random Hse. Bks. for Young Readers) Random Hse. Children's Bks.

—The Man in the Iron Mask. 1998. 11.04 (*0-606-13594-4*) Turtleback Bks.

—The Man in the Iron Mask Readalong. 1994. (Illustrated Classics Collection). 64p. pap. 14.95 incl. audio (*0-7854-0766-9*, 40505); pap. 13.50 o.p. incl. audio (*1-56103-593-9*) American Guidance Service, Inc.

—The Three Musketeers. 1966. (Airmont Classics Ser.). (YA). (gr. 8 up). mass mkt. 3.95 o.p. (*0-8049-0127-9*, CL-127) Airmont Publishing Co., Inc.

—The Three Musketeers. abr. ed. (Classics Illustrated Bks.). (J). audio 5.95. (Illus.). audio Audio Bk. Co.

—The Three Musketeers. 1993. (Junior Novelization Ser.). (Illus.). (J). (gr. 4-7). pap. 3.50 o.p. (*1-56282-590-9*) Disney Pr.

—The Three Musketeers. 2nd ed. 1998. (Illustrated Classic Book Ser.). (Illus.). 61p. (J). (gr. 3 up). reprint ed. pap. text 4.95 (*1-56767-251-5*) Educational Insights, Inc.

—The Three Musketeers. Bair, Lowell, tr. 1998. (Books of Wonder). (Illus.). 656p. (J). (gr. 4-7). 25.00 (*0-688-14583-3*, Morrow, William & Co.) Morrow/Avon.

—The Three Musketeers. (Classics Ser.). 56p. (J). text 3.50 (*0-7214-1753-1*, Ladybird Bks.) Penguin Group (USA) Inc.

—The Three Musketeers. 9999. (Children's Classics Ser.: No. 740-5). (Illus.). (J). (gr. 3-5). pap. 3.50 o.p. (*0-7214-0633-5*, Ladybird Bks.) Penguin Group (USA) Inc.

—The Three Musketeers. 1996. (Classic Ser.). (Illus.). 56p. (J). (gr. 2-4). 2.99 o.s.i (*0-7214-5610-3*, Ladybird Bks.) Penguin Group (USA) Inc.

—The Three Musketeers. (Illustrated Junior Library). (Illus.). (gr. 4-6). 1982. (J). 6.95 o.p. (*0-448-11024-5*, Grosset & Dunlap); 1953. 320p. (J). 16.99 (*0-448-06024-8*, Grosset & Dunlap); 1995. 464p. (YA). pap. 4.99 (*0-14-036747-0*, Puffin Bks.) Penguin Putnam Bks. for Young Readers.

—The Three Musketeers. Vogel, Malvina, ed. 1990. (Great Illustrated Classics Ser.: Vol. 15). (Illus.). 240p. (J). (ps up). 9.95 (*0-86611-966-3*) Playmore, Inc., Pubs.

—The Three Musketeers. Le Clercq, Jacques, tr. from ENG. 1999. (Modern Library Ser.). 624p. (gr. 4-11). 24.95 (*0-679-60332-8*) Random Hse., Inc.

—The Three Musketeers. 2001. (Saddleback Classics). (Illus.). (J). 13.10 (*0-606-21573-5*) Turtleback Bks.

—The Three Musketeers Readalong. 1994. (Illustrated Classics Collection). 64p. pap. 13.50 o.p. incl. audio (*1-56103-511-4*); pap. 14.95 incl. audio (*0-7854-0691-3*, 40423) American Guidance Service, Inc.

—Los Tres Mosqueteros. (SPA.). (J). 2.49 (*968-890-125-3*) Editorial Diana, S.A. MEX. *Dist:* Continental Bk. Co., Inc.

—Los Tres Mosqueteros. 2002. (Classics for Young Readers Ser.). (SPA.). (YA). 14.95 (*84-392-0928-2*, EV30622) Lectorum Pubns., Inc.

Edwards, Julie Andrews. Little Bo in France. 2002. (Illus.). 128p. (J). (ps-2). 18.99 (*0-7868-0658-3*) Hyperion Bks. for Children.

—Little Bo in France. 2000. (Illus.). 144p. (J). (gr. 2-4). lib. bdg. 19.49 (*0-7868-2540-5*) Hyperion Pr.

Elliott, L. M. Under a War-Torn Sky. 2001. 288p. (gr. 5-9). (J). lib. bdg. 16.49 (*0-7868-2485-9*); 15.99 (*0-7868-0755-5*) Hyperion Bks. for Children.

Ferris, Jean. Signs of Life, RS. 1995. 160p. (J). (gr. 7 up). 14.00 o.p. (*0-374-36909-7*, Farrar, Straus & Giroux (BYR)) Farrar, Straus & Giroux.

Filion, Pierre. Pikolo: L'Arbre aux Mille Tresors (Pikolo's Night Voyage) 1994. (FRE., Illus.). 32p. (J). (ps-3). 15.95 (*1-55037-367-6*); pap. 6.95 (*1-55037-366-8*) Annick Pr., Ltd. CAN. *Dist:* Firefly Bks., Ltd.

Francoise. The Adventures of Jeanne-Marie: Three Complete Stories. 1999. (Illus.). 96p. (J). (ps-3). 12.98 (*0-7651-1684-7*) Smithmark Pubs., Inc.

Garland, Michael. Dinner at Magritte's. 1995. (Young Readers' History of the Civil War Ser.). (Illus.). 32p. (J). (gr. 1-4). 14.99 o.s.i (*0-525-45336-9*, Dutton Children's Bks.) Penguin Putnam Bks. for Young Readers.

Giono, Jean. The Man Who Planted Trees. (Illus.). 1990. (J). 21.95 incl. audio (*0-930031-35-0*); 1985. audio compact disk 15.98 (*0-930031-76-8*); 1985. 56p. (YA). (gr. 3-12). 16.95 (*0-930031-02-4*); 1987. 56p. (YA). (gr. 3-12). reprint ed. pap. 7.95 (*0-930031-06-7*); 1999. 80p. pap. 8.95 (*1-890132-32-2*) Chelsea Green Publishing.

—The Man Who Planted Trees. Roberts, Jean, tr. from FRE. 1996. (Illus.). 56p. (J). (gr. k-12). pap. 16.95 (*0-7737-5733-3*) Direct Cinema, Ltd.

—The Man Who Planted Trees. 1996. (Illus.). 96p. (J). (*1-86046-293-6*) Harvill Pr., The.

—The Man Who Planted Trees. 2000. 74p. pap. 6.00 (*1-57062-538-7*) Shambhala Pubns., Inc.

Guillot, Rene. Wind of Chance. Dale, Norman, tr. 1958. (Illus.). (J). (gr. 6-9). 26.95 (*0-87599-048-7*) Phillips, S.G. Inc.

Hatton, Caroline K. Vero & Philippe. 2001. (Illus.). 120p. (J). (gr. 3-7). 14.95 (*0-8126-2940-X*) Cricket Bks.

Hergé. Les Bijoux de la Castafiore. 1999. (Tintin Ser.).Tr. of Castafiore Emerald. (FRE.). (gr. 4-7). 19.95 (*2-203-00120-8*) Casterman, Editions FRA. *Dist:* Distribooks, Inc.

—Les Bijoux de la Castafiore.Tr. of Castafiore Emerald. (FRE., Illus.). 62p. (J). (gr. 7-9). ring bd. 19.95 o.p. (*0-8288-5011-9*) French & European Pubns., Inc.

—The Castafiore Emerald. (Illus.). 62p. (J). 19.95 (*0-8288-5016-X*); pap. 4.95 o.p. (*0-416-77400-8*) French & European Pubns., Inc.

—The Castafiore Emerald. 1975. (Adventures of Tintin Ser.). 62p. (J). (gr. 2 up). pap. 9.99 (*0-316-35842-8*, Joy Street Bks.) Little Brown & Co.

Hite, Sid. The King of Slippery Falls. 2004. 208p. (YA). pap. 16.95 (*0-439-34257-0*) Scholastic, Inc.

Hugo, Victor. Les Miserables. adapted ed. 2001. (Stepping Stone Bks.). (Illus.). (J). 10.04 (*0-606-21560-3*) Turtleback Bks.

Isom, Joan Shaddox. The First Starry Night. (Illus.). 32p. (J). (gr. k-7). 2001. pap. 6.95 (*1-58089-027-X*); 1998. 16.95 (*1-879085-96-8*) Charlesbridge Publishing, Inc. (Whispering Coyote).

Knight, Joan MacPhail. Charlotte in Giverny. Rock, Victoria, ed. 2000. (Illus.). 64p. (J). (gr. 4-7). 15.95 (*0-8118-2383-0*) Chronicle Bks. LLC.

Ladybird Books Staff, ed. Three Musketeers. 1998. (Ladybird Picture Classics Ser.). (Illus.). 32p. (J). (gr. 2 up). pap. 4.99 o.p. (*0-7214-7383-0*, Ladybird Bks.) Penguin Group (USA) Inc.

Lamensdorf, Len. The Crouching Dragon. 1999. (Will to Conquer Ser.: Bk. 1). (Illus.). 278p. (YA). (gr. 7-12). 19.95 (*0-9669741-5-8*) SeaScape Pr., Ltd.

Lawrence, Iain. Lord of the Nutcracker Men. 2001. 224p. (gr. 5 up). text 15.95 (*0-385-72924-3*, Delacorte Pr.) Dell Publishing.

—Lord of the Nutcracker Men. l.t. ed. 2002. 280p. (J). 24.95 (*0-7862-4155-1*) Gale Group.

—Lord of the Nutcracker Men. (gr. 5). 2003. 240p. pap. 5.99 (*0-440-41812-7*, Laurel Leaf); 2001. 224p. lib. bdg. 17.99 (*0-385-90024-4*, Delacorte Bks. for Young Readers) Random Hse. Children's Bks.

Leitch, Michael & Dumas, Alexandre, contrib. by. The Three Musketeers. 2000. (Dorling Kindersley Classics Ser.). (Illus.). 64p. (J). (gr. 2-5). pap. 14.95 o.p. (*0-7894-5456-4*) Dorling Kindersley Publishing, Inc.

Leroux, Gaston. The Phantom of the Opera. l.t. ed. 1999. (Large Print Heritage Ser.). 420p. (J). (gr. 7-12). lib. bdg. 35.95 (*1-58118-043-8*, 22512) LRS.

—The Phantom of the Opera. 1994. (Classics for Young Readers Ser.). (Illus.). 336p. (YA). (gr. 4-7). pap. 4.99 (*0-14-036813-2*, Puffin Bks.) Penguin Putnam Bks. for Young Readers.

—The Phantom of the Opera. 1989. (Bullseye Chillers Ser.). (Illus.). 96p. (J). (gr. 3-7). 5.99 o.s.i (*0-394-93847-X*); (gr. 2-5). pap. 3.99 (*0-394-83847-5*) Random Hse. Children's Bks. (Random Hse. Bks. for Young Readers).

—The Phantom of the Opera. Bair, Lowell, tr. abr. ed. 1998. 336p. (YA). (gr. 7-12). mass mkt. 3.99 (*0-440-22774-7*, Dell Books for Young Readers) Random Hse. Children's Bks.

—The Phantom of the Opera. abr. ed. 1998. 10.04 (*0-606-15677-1*) Turtleback Bks.

—The Phantom of the Opera. 1988. (Illus.). (J). (gr. 4 up). 14.95 o.p. (*0-88101-082-0*); 208p. (YA). (gr. 7 up). 9.95 o.p. (*0-88101-121-5*) Unicorn Publishing Hse., Inc., The.

Lingard, Joan. Snake Among the Sunflowers. 1977. (J). 6.95 o.p. (*0-525-66570-6*, Dutton Children's Bks.) Penguin Putnam Bks. for Young Readers.

Lisle, Janet Taylor. Sirens & Spies. 1985. 192p. (J). (gr. 7 up). lib. bdg. 14.95 o.p. (*0-02-759150-6*, Simon & Schuster Children's Publishing) Simon & Schuster Children's Publishing.

Littlesugar, Amy. Lisette's Angel. 2002. (Illus.). 32p. (J). (gr. 2-4). 15.99 (*0-8037-2435-7*, Dial Bks. for Young Readers) Penguin Putnam Bks. for Young Readers.

Lloyd, Emily. Truffle Trouble: The Case of Fungus among Us. 1998. (Kinetic City Super Crew Ser.: No. 10). (Illus.). 160p. (J). (gr. 4-7). pap. 4.25 o.p. (*0-07-079397-2*) McGraw-Hill Cos., The.

Loggia, Wendy. Ever After: A Cinderella Story. 1998. 192p. (YA). mass mkt. 4.99 (*0-440-22815-8*, Delacorte Pr.) Dell Publishing.

—Ever After: A Cinderella Story. 1998. 11.04 (*0-606-16172-4*) Turtleback Bks.

Mantell, Paul. The Man in the Iron Mask. 1998. (Bullseye Step into Classics Ser.). (J). 10.04 (*0-606-13965-6*) Turtleback Bks.

Marcellino, Fred. I, Crocodile. (Illus.). 32p. (J). 2002. (ps-3). pap. 6.99 (*0-06-008859-1*, Harper Trophy); 1999. (gr. 1-3). lib. bdg. 15.89 (*0-06-205199-7*); 1999. (gr. k-3). 15.95 (*0-06-205168-7*) HarperCollins Children's Bk. Group.

—I, Crocodile. (J). (gr. 1-2). 6.95 net. (*1-55592-982-6*) Weston Woods Studios, Inc.

Martin, Nora. The Stone Dancers. 1995. (Illus.). 32p. (J). (ps-3). 15.00 (*0-689-80312-5*, Atheneum) Simon & Schuster Children's Publishing.

McCann, Helen. What's French for Help, George? 1993. (Illus.). 460p. (J). (gr. 5-9). pap. 13.00 o.s.i (*0-671-74689-8*, Simon & Schuster Children's Publishing) Simon & Schuster Children's Publishing.

McGraw, Sheila. Je T'Aimera Toujours. 1988. (FRE., Illus.). 32p. (ps-3). pap. 4.95 (*0-920668-49-6*) Firefly Bks., Ltd.

McGrory, Arlene A. & McGrory, Anik. Mouton's Impossible Dream. 2000. (Illus.). 32p. (J). (ps-3). 16.00 o.s.i (*0-15-202195-7*, Gulliver Bks.) Harcourt Children's Bks.

McLaren, Chesley, illus. Zat Cat! A Haute Couture Tail. 2002. 40p. (J). (ps-3). pap. 16.95 (*0-439-27316-1*, Scholastic Pr.) Scholastic, Inc.

Montgomery, R. A. Tour de France. 1992. (J). mass mkt. o.s.i (*0-553-54063-7*, Dell Books for Young Readers) Random Hse. Children's Bks.

Morgenstern, Susie. Three Days Off. Rosner, Gill, tr. from FRE. 2001. Tr. of Trois Jours Sans. 96p. (YA). 14.99 (*0-670-03511-4*, Puffin Bks.) Penguin Putnam Bks. for Young Readers.

Mosher, Richard. Zazoo. 2001. 224p. (YA). (gr. 7 up). tchr. ed. 16.00 (*0-618-13534-0*, Clarion Bks.) Houghton Mifflin Co. Trade & Reference Div.

Nascimbene, Yan. Day in September. 2002. (J). (*0-89812-328-3*, Creative Paperbacks) Creative Co., The.

Neumeyer, Peter. The Phantom of the Opera. abr. ed. 1988. (Illus.). 48p. (J). 14.95 o.p. (*0-87905-330-5*) Smith, Gibbs Pub.

Niedermayer, Walter. Into the Deep Misty Woods of the Ardennes. 1990. (Illus.). 170p. (Orig.). (YA). pap. text 13.50 (*0-935648-30-5*) Halldin, A. G. Publishing Co.

Noonan, Diana. The Shepherd Who Planted a Forest. 1994. (Illus.). (J). (*0-383-03774-3*) SRA/McGraw-Hill.

Parenteau, Shirley. Secrets of Scarlet. 1979. (Illus.). (J). (gr. 2-5). lib. bdg. 7.95 o.p. (*0-516-03614-9*, Children's Pr.) Scholastic Library Publishing.

Pietri, Annie & Temerson, Catherine, trs. from FRE. The Orange Trees of Versailles. 2004. 144p. (J). text (*0-385-73103-5*); lib. bdg. (*0-385-90130-5*) Dell Publishing. (Delacorte Pr.).

Polacco, Patricia. The Butterfly. 2000. (Illus.). 48p. (J). (ps-3). 16.99 (0-399-23170-6, Philomel) Penguin Putnam Bks. for Young Readers.

Potter, Giselle. Chloe's Birthday— & Me. 2005. (J). 16.95 (0-689-86230-X, Atheneum/Anne Schwartz Bks.) Simon & Schuster Children's Publishing.

Richardson, Kara. Simon & Barklee in France. 2000. (Another Country Calling Ser.: No. 1). (Illus.). 48p. (J). (gr. 2-5). 12.00 (0-9704661-0-2, Explorer Media) Simon & Barklee, Inc./ExplorerMedia.

Roberts, Michele. The Looking Glass: A Novel. 2001. 288p. 23.00 o.s.i (0-8050-6700-0) Holt, Henry & Co.

Sand, George. The Wings of Courage. Bloom, Margaret, tr. from FRE. 1998. (Illus.). 70p. (YA). (gr. 4-7). 12.95 (0-8076-1434-3) Braziller, George Inc.

Scalora, Suza. The Witches & Wizards of Oberin. 2001. (Ageless Bks.). (Illus.). 48p. (J). 19.95 (0-06-029535-X, Cotler, Joanna Bks.) HarperCollins Children's Bk. Group.

Scherer, Catherine W. Simon & Barklee in France: Fun Book. 2001. (Another Country Calling Ser.). (Illus.). 32p. (J). (gr. 2-6). pap. 4.00 (0-9704661-3-7, Explorer Media) Simon & Barklee, Inc./ExplorerMedia.

Schnur, Steven. The Shadow Children. 1994. (Illus.). 96p. (J). (gr. 3 up). 16.99 (0-688-13281-2) HarperCollins Children's Bk. Group.

—The Shadow Children. 1994. (Illus.). 192p. (J). (gr. 4-7). 15.89 o.p. (0-688-13831-4, Morrow, William & Co.) Morrow/Avon.

Sempe, Jean-Jacques. Chronicles of Little Nicholas, RS. 1992. (J). 15.00 o.p. (0-374-31275-3, Farrar, Straus & Giroux (BYR)) Farrar, Straus & Giroux.

Smith, Duncan. Fred Goes to France. (Fred the Ted Ser.). (Illus.). (J). o.p. (1-85435-162-1) Cavendish, Marshall Corp.

—Fred Goes to France. 1991. (Fred the Ted Ser.). (Illus.). 25p. (J). (gr. k-2). 11.95 o.p. (0-237-51125-8) Evans Brothers, Ltd. GBR. *Dist:* Trafalgar Square.

Spirn, Michele Sobel. The Bridges in Paris. 2000. (Going to Ser.). (Illus.). 121p. (J). (gr. 4-8). pap. 5.99 (1-893577-04-X) Four Corners Publishing Co., Inc.

Stephens, Becky & Jeanes, Steve. Me Again! (And Charlie) A Snowy State of Mind. 2003. (Me (and Charlie) Ser.). 160p. (J). (gr. 3-6). mass mkt. 4.99 (0-439-51270-0, Chicken Hse., The) Scholastic, Inc.

Stock, Catherine. A Spree in Paree. 2003. (J). (0-8234-1720-4) Holiday Hse., Inc.

Stoneberg, Diana. French Lessons. 1995. (Illus.). 19p. (J). (gr. k-3). (0-9642796-2-2) Snapping Turtle Pr.

Storr, Catherine, as told by. The Three Musketeers. 1985. (Legends & Folktales Ser.). (Illus.). 32p. (J). (gr. k-5). pap. 9.27 o.p. (0-8172-2508-0); lib. bdg. 19.97 o.p. (0-8172-2500-5) Raintree Pubs.

Stevens, Biddy. Toto in France. 1994. (Toto in... Ser.). (FRE., Illus.). 24p. (J). (gr. 4-7). 12.95 o.p. (0-8442-9180-3, National Textbook Co.) McGraw-Hill/Contemporary.

Sweeney, Joan. Suzette & the Puppy: A Story about Mary Cassatt. 2000. (Illus.). 28p. (J). (ps-3). pap. 14.95 (0-7641-5294-7) Barron's Educational Series, Inc.

Talley, Linda. Bea's Own Good. 1997. (Key Concepts in Personal Development Ser.). (Illus.). 32p. (J). (gr. k-4). 16.95 (1-55942-092-8, 7663) Marsh Media.

Thompson, Kay. Eloise a Paris. 5th ed. 1999. Orig. Title: Eloise in Paris. (FRE., Illus.). (J). (ps-3). pap. 13.95 (2-07-052625-9) Gallimard, Editions FRA. *Dist:* Distribooks, Inc.

—Eloise in Paris. 1991. (Eloise Ser.). (Illus.). 66p. (J). reprint ed. lib. bdg. 35.95 (0-89966-834-8) Buccaneer Bks., Inc.

—Eloise in Paris. 1999. (J). (ps-3). (Illus.). 72p. 17.00 (0-689-82704-0); 64p. 100.00 o.s.i (0-689-82960-4) Simon & Schuster Children's Publishing. (Simon & Schuster Children's Publishing).

Titus, Eve & Galdone, Paul. Anatole & the Pied Piper. 1979. (J). text 9.95 o.p. (0-07-064897-2) McGraw-Hill Cos., The.

Vanderjagt, A. The Escape: Adventures of Three Huguenot Children Fleeing Persecution. 1993. (Illus.). 197p. (J). pap. 9.95 (0-921100-04-3) Inheritance Pubns.

Waldron, Ann. The French Detection. 1979. (Illus.). (J). (gr. 4-7). 7.95 o.p. (0-525-30190-9, Dutton) Dutton/Plume.

—The French Detection. 2000. 140p. (gr. 4-7). pap. 10.95 (0-595-00066-5) iUniverse, Inc.

Weinberg, Larry. Universal Monsters: The Phantom of the Opera. 1993. (J). (gr. 4-7). pap. o.p. (0-307-22334-5, Golden Bks.) Random Hse. Children's Bks.

Weinberger, Jane. The Little Ones. 1987. (ENG & FRE., Illus.). 54p. (Orig.). (J). (ps-4). pap. 3.95 (0-932433-29-4) Windswept Hse. Pubs.

Weiss, Jim, reader. Three Musketeers. (J). audio NewSound, LLC.

Wheeler, Jody. Madeline Christmas Activity Book: With Reusable Vinyl Stickers. 1998. (Madeline Ser.). (Illus.). 16p. (J). (ps-3). 7.99 (0-670-88204-6, Viking Children's Bks.) Penguin Putnam Bks. for Young Readers.

—Madeline Paper Dolls. 1994. (Madeline Ser.). (Illus.). 24p. (J). (ps-3). 6.99 (0-670-85601-0) Penguin Putnam Bks. for Young Readers.

—Madeline's Birthday Activity Book. 1999. (Madeline Ser.). (Illus.). 16p. (J). (ps-3). pap. 7.99 (0-670-88767-6, Viking Children's Bks.) Penguin Putnam Bks. for Young Readers.

Yorinks, Arthur. Harry & Lulu. braille ed. 2001. (J). (gr. 1). spiral bd. (0-616-07249-X); (gr. 2). spiral bd. (0-616-07250-3) Canadian National Institute for the Blind/Institut National Canadien pour les Aveugles.

—Harry & Lulu. 1999. (Illus.). 32p. (J). (ps-2). 16.49 (0-7868-2276-7); 15.99 (0-7868-0335-5) Hyperion Bks. for Children.

—Harry & Lulu. Date not set. (Illus.). 32p. (J). (ps-2). pap. 4.99 (0-7868-1221-4) Hyperion Paperbacks for Children.

G

GEORGE WASHINGTON BRIDGE (NEW YORK, N.Y.)—FICTION

Swift, Hildegarde H. & Ward, Lynd. The Little Red Lighthouse & the Great Gray Bridge. 1942. (Illus.). 56p. (J). (ps-3). 17.00 o.s.i (0-15-247040-9) Harcourt Children's Bks.

GEORGIA—FICTION

Armstrong, William H. Sounder. (Trophy Bk.). (Illus.). 128p. 1996. (YA). (gr. 7 up). pap. 2.25 o.p. (0-06-447153-5, Harper Trophy); 1969. (J). (gr. 5 up). 15.99 (0-06-020143-6); 1969. (J). (gr. 5 up). lib. bdg. 16.89 (0-06-020144-4); 1972. (J). (gr. 5 up). reprint ed. pap. 5.99 (0-06-440020-4, Harper Trophy) HarperCollins Children's Bk. Group.

—Sounder. 1978. pap. 4.50 o.p. (0-06-080379-7, P379, Perennial) HarperTrade.

—Sounder. l.t. ed. 1999. (LRS Large Print Cornerstone Ser.). (Illus.). 230p. (YA). (gr. 6-12). lib. bdg. 27.95 (1-58118-054-3, 22768) LRS.

—Sounder. l.t. ed. 1987. (Illus.). 99p. (J). (gr. 2-6). reprint ed. lib. bdg. 16.95 o.s.i (1-55736-003-0, Cornerstone Bks.) Pages, Inc.

—Sounder. 9999. 116p. (YA). (gr. 7 up). pap. 2.50 o.p. (0-590-40212-9) Scholastic, Inc.

—Sounder. 1972. (J). 12.00 (0-606-04962-2) Turtleback Bks.

—Sounder Ri. 1989. 128p. (YA). (gr. 4-7). reprint ed. pap. 6.00 (0-06-080975-2, P 975, Perennial) HarperTrade.

Banks, Sarah Harrell. A Net to Catch Time. 1996. (Illus.). 32p. (J). (ps-3). 17.99 o.s.i (0-679-96673-0) Random Hse., Inc.

Beatty, Patricia. Turn Homeward, Hannalee. 1984. (Illus.). 208p. (J). (gr. 4-7). 16.99 (0-688-03871-9) HarperCollins Children's Bk. Group.

Blackburn, Joyce. Suki & the Magic Sand Dollar. unabr. ed. 1998. (J). (gr. 2). audio 31.70 (0-7887-1928-9, 46476); (gr. 2). audio 179.00 (0-7887-3152-1, 46476); audio 10.00 (0-7887-1900-9, 95321E7) Recorded Bks., LLC.

Blackburn, Joyce K. The Bloody Summer of Seventeen Forty-Two: A Colonial Boy's Journal. 1985. (Illus.). 64p. (J). (gr. 5-8). pap. 7.95 (0-930803-00-0) Fort Frederica Assn., Inc.

—Suki & the Magic Sand Dollar. rev. ed. 1996. (Suki Ser.). (Illus.). 64p. (J). (ps-3). 14.95 (1-881576-70-1) Providence Hse. Pubs.

Brady, Laurel. Say You Are My Sister. 2000. (Illus.). 224p. (J). (gr. 5 up). lib. bdg. 16.89 (0-06-028308-4); 15.95 (0-06-028307-6) HarperCollins Children's Bk. Group.

Burch, Robert. Ida Early Comes over the Mountain. 1982. 152p. (J). (gr. 3-7). pap. 2.50 (0-380-57091-2, Avon Bks.) Morrow/Avon.

—Ida Early Comes over the Mountain. 1990. 160p. (J). (gr. 4-7). pap. 4.99 (0-14-034534-5, Puffin Bks.) Penguin Putnam Bks. for Young Readers.

—Ida Early Comes over the Mountain. 1990. (J). 11.04 (0-606-04701-8) Turtleback Bks.

—Ida Early Comes Over the Mountain. 1980. (J). (gr. 5-9). 14.99 o.p. (0-670-39169-7, Viking Children's Bks.) Penguin Putnam Bks. for Young Readers.

—Ida Early Comes Over the Mountain. 2001. (J). (gr. 3-6). 20.25 (0-8446-7171-1) Smith, Peter Pub., Inc.

—Skinny. 1964. (Illus.). (J). (gr. 4-7). 6.95 o.p. (0-670-64999-6) Viking Penguin.

—Tyler, Wilkin, & Skee. 1971. 160p. (gr. 2-6). pap. 1.25 o.p. (0-440-49144-4) Dell Publishing.

—Wilkin's Ghost. 1978. (Illus.). (J). (gr. 5-9). 9.95 o.p. (0-670-76897-9) Viking Penguin.

Charbonneau, Eileen. The Connor Emerald. 1995. 224p. (J). mass mkt. 3.99 o.p. (0-8217-4823-8) Kensington Publishing Corp.

—The Connor Emerald. Williams, Lori, ed. 1999. (YA). 170p. pap. 9.99 (1-58365-753-3, Timeless Romance); E-Book 2.99 (1-58365-754-1, Timeless Treasures) Sierra Raconteur Publishing.

Engel, Beth B. Ride the Pine Sapling. 1978. (J). (gr. 5-9). 12.70 o.p. (0-06-021815-0); lib. bdg. 11.89 o.p. (0-06-021816-9) HarperCollins Children's Bk. Group.

Gibbons, Faye. The Day the Picture Man Came. 2003. (Illus.). 32p. (J). (gr. k up). 16.95 (1-56397-161-5) Boyds Mills Pr.

—Full Steam Ahead. 2003. (Illus.). 32p. (J). (gr. k-3). 15.95 (1-56397-858-X) Boyds Mills Pr.

—Hook Moon Night. 1997. (Illus.). 112p. (J). (gr. 3-7). 14.95 (0-688-14504-3) HarperCollins Children's Bk. Group.

Griffith, Helen V. Georgia Music. 1990. (Illus.). 24p. (J). (ps-3). mass mkt. 6.95 (0-688-09931-9, Morrow, William & Co.) Morrow/Avon.

—Georgia Music. 1990. 13.10 (0-606-04679-8) Turtleback Bks.

Hahn, Stephen. Pike McCallister. 1998. 253p. (YA). (gr. 6 up). per. 14.95 (1-888125-29-2) Publication Consultants.

Hall, Marjory. Mystery at October House. 1977. (J). (gr. 6 up). 7.95 o.p. (0-664-32606-4) Westminster John Knox Pr.

Hammer, Loretta C. & Karwoski, Gail Langer. The Tree That Owns Itself: And Other Adventure Tales from Out of the Past. 1996. (Illus.). 160p. (Orig.). (J). (gr. 3-7). pap. 8.95 (1-56145-120-7) Peachtree Pubs., Ltd.

Harper, Jon. Blue Ridge. 1995. (Illus.). 160p. (J). pap. 8.95 (0-9611872-7-1) Our Child Pr.

Harrell, Sara G. Mallory's Island: Puppy Love. 1986. (Christian Reader Ser.). (Illus.). 80p. (Orig.). (J). (gr. 4-7). pap. 3.95 o.s.i (0-570-03637-2, 39-1099) Concordia Publishing Hse.

Hewett, Lorri. Lives of Our Own. (gr. 7-12). 1998. 192p. (J). 15.99 (0-525-45959-6); 2000. (Illus.). 196p. (YA). reprint ed. pap. 5.99 o.s.i (0-14-130589-4, Puffin Bks.) Penguin Putnam Bks. for Young Readers.

—Lives of Our Own. 2000. 12.04 (0-606-19695-1) Turtleback Bks.

Jacobs, Jimmy. Moonlight Through the Pines: Tales of the Georgia Evenings. 2000. (Illus.). x, 116p. (J). (gr. 7-12). pap. 11.95 (0-9637477-3-8) Franklin-Sarrett Pubs.

Kadohata, Cynthia. Kira-kira. 2004. (Illus.). 256p. (J). 15.95 (0-689-85639-3, Atheneum) Simon & Schuster Children's Publishing.

Krisher, Trudy B. Kinship. 1997. 304p. (YA). (gr. 7). 15.95 o.s.i (0-385-32272-0, Delacorte Pr.) Dell Publishing.

—Kinship. 1997. mass mkt. 15.95 (0-385-44695-0) Doubleday Publishing.

—Kinship. 1999. 304p. (YA). (gr. 7 up). mass mkt. 4.50 o.s.i (0-440-22023-8, Dell Books for Young Readers) Random Hse. Children's Bks.

—Kinship. 1999. 10.55 (0-606-16170-8) Turtleback Bks.

—Spite Fences. 1994. 288p. (J). (gr. 6 up). 15.95 o.p. (0-385-32088-4, Delacorte Pr.) Dell Publishing.

—Spite Fences. 1995. 18.95 (0-385-30978-3) Doubleday Publishing.

—Spite Fences. 1996. 10.55 (0-606-09882-8) Turtleback Bks.

Lee, Mildred. The Skating Rink. 9999. pap. 1.95 o.s.i (0-590-05185-7) Scholastic, Inc.

L'Engle, Madeleine. The Other Side of the Sun. 1971. 344p. (J). 6.95 o.s.i (0-374-22805-1) Farrar, Straus & Giroux.

Luttrell, Wanda. Hannah's Sojourn. 2000. (Immigrants Chronicles Ser.). 132p. (J). (gr. 3-7). pap. 5.99 (0-7814-3082-8) Cook Communications Ministries.

Matthews, Kezi. Scorpio's Child. 2001. 160p. (J). (gr. 6-8). 15.95 (0-8126-2890-X) Cricket Bks.

—Scorpio's Child. 2004. 160p. (J). 6.99 (0-14-240079-3, Puffin Bks.) Penguin Putnam Bks. for Young Readers.

McDaniel, Lurlene. Garden of Angels. 2003. (Illus.). 288p. (YA). (gr. 7). 9.95 (0-553-57093-5, Starfire) Random Hse. Children's Bks.

Murphy, Rita. Black Angels. 2002. 176p. (gr. 4). pap. text 4.99 (0-440-22934-0) Random Hse., Inc.

O'Connor, Barbara. Moonpie & Ivy, RS. 2004. (Illus.). pap. (0-374-45320-9); 2001. 160p. (YA). (gr. 5 up). 16.00 (0-374-35059-0, Farrar, Straus & Giroux (BYR)) Farrar, Straus & Giroux.

Oughton, Jerrie. The War in Georgia. 1997. 192p. (J). (gr. 7-10). tchr. ed. 14.95 o.p. (0-395-81568-1) Houghton Mifflin Co.

—The War in Georgia. 1999. 192p. (YA). (gr. 7 up). mass mkt. 4.50 o.s.i (0-440-22752-6, Dell Books for Young Readers) Random Hse. Children's Bks.

—The War in Georgia. 1999. 10.55 (0-606-16444-8) Turtleback Bks.

Schunk, Laurel. Black & Secret Midnight. 1998. 239p. (YA). (gr. 6-8). 24.99 (0-9661879-0-3, SKP98-41) St Kitts Pr.

Siegelson, Kim L. Dancing the Ring Shout. 2000. (Illus.). 32p. (J). lib. bdg. 16.49 (0-7868-2396-8) Disney Pr.

—Dancing the Ring Shout. 2000. (Illus.). 32p. (J). 15.99 (0-7868-0453-X, Jump at the Sun) Hyperion Bks. for Children.

—Dancing the Ring Shout. 2000. (J). 16.00 (0-689-81699-5, Simon & Schuster Children's Publishing) Simon & Schuster Children's Publishing.

Smith, Doris B. Dreams & Drummers. 1978. 192p. (YA). (gr. 6 up). lib. bdg. 12.89 o.p. (0-690-03843-7) HarperCollins Children's Bk. Group.

Smith, Doris Buchanan. Dreams & Drummers. 1978. (J). (gr. 4 up). 11.20 (0-690-01381-7) HarperCollins Children's Bk. Group.

Thomas Young, Ronder. Moving Mama to Town. 1997. 224p. (J). (gr. 3-8). pap. 17.95 (0-531-30025-0, Orchard Bks.) Scholastic, Inc.

Wilkinson, Brenda. Ludell. 1985. 176p. mass mkt. 2.50 o.s.i (0-553-26433-8) Bantam Bks.

—Ludell. (Trophy Bk.). 176p. (J). 1992. (gr. 5 up). pap. 3.95 o.p. (0-06-440419-6, Harper Trophy); 1975. (gr. 7 up). lib. bdg. 14.89 o.p. (0-06-026492-6) HarperCollins Children's Bk. Group.

—Ludell & Willie. 1985. (Skylark Ser.). 144p. (J). (gr. 6 up). mass mkt. 2.25 o.s.i (0-553-24995-9) Bantam Bks.

—Ludell & Willie. 1977. (YA). (gr. 7 up). lib. bdg. 14.89 o.p. (0-06-026488-8) HarperCollins Children's Bk. Group.

Young, Ronder T. Moving Mama to Town. 1997. 224p. (J). (gr. 3-8). lib. bdg. 18.99 (0-531-33025-7, Orchard Bks.) Scholastic, Inc.

GERMANY—FICTION

Austin, Judith M. The Ghostly German Castle. 1997. (GlobalFriends Adventures Ser.). (Illus.). 64p. (J). (gr. 2-6). pap. 5.95 (1-58056-008-3, GlobalFriends Pr.) GlobalFriends Collection, Inc.

Baer, Edith. Walk the Dark Streets, RS. 1998. 272p. (YA). (gr. 4-7). 18.00 o.p. (0-374-38229-8, Farrar, Straus & Giroux (BYR)) Farrar, Straus & Giroux.

—Walk the Dark Streets. 1996. lib. bdg. 10.00 o.p. (0-394-90596-2, Random Hse. Bks. for Young Readers) Random Hse. Children's Bks.

Balaguae, Lin & Long, Robert, contrib. by. Hansel y Gretel: Hansel & Gretel. 2000. (Cuentos y Leyendas Bilingues Ser.). (ENG & SPA.). (J). 21.20 (0-658-01037-9, National Textbook Co.) McGraw-Hill/Contemporary.

Balague, Lin & Long, Robert. Hansel y Gretel (Hansel & Gretel) 2000. (Cuentos y Leyendas Bilingues Ser.). (ENG & SPA., Illus.). (J). (0-658-01038-7) McGraw-Hill/Contemporary.

Benary-Isbert, Margot. Ark. 1953. (J). (gr. 7 up). 6.50 o.p. (0-15-203901-5) Harcourt Children's Bks.

—Blue Mystery. (Illus.). (J). (gr. 4-7). 1965. pap. 3.95 o.p. (0-15-613225-7, Voyager Bks./Libros Viajeros); 1957. 5.95 o.p. (0-15-209092-4) Harcourt Children's Bks.

—Castle on the Border. 1956. (J). 5.95 o.p. (0-15-214999-6) Harcourt Children's Bks.

—Under a Changing Moon. 1964. (J). 5.95 o.p. (0-15-292800-6) Harcourt Children's Bks.

Brodmann, Aliana. Gift. 1993. (Illus.). 40p. (J). (ps-3). pap. 15.00 (0-671-75110-7, Simon & Schuster Children's Publishing) Simon & Schuster Children's Publishing.

Carter, Peter. Bury the Dead, RS. 1987. 374p. (J). (gr. 6 up). 17.00 o.p. (0-374-31011-4, Farrar, Straus & Giroux (BYR)) Farrar, Straus & Giroux.

Craddock, Sonia. Sleeping Boy. 1999. (Illus.). 40p. (J). (gr. 1-4). 16.95 (0-689-81763-0, Atheneum) Simon & Schuster Children's Publishing.

Degens, T. Freya on the Wall. 1997. 288p. (J). 19.00 o.s.i (0-15-200210-3) Harcourt Trade Pubs.

—On the Third Ward. 1990. 256p. (J). (gr. 6 up). 14.95 o.p. (0-06-021428-7); lib. bdg. 14.89 o.p. (0-06-021429-5) HarperCollins Children's Bk. Group.

Doyle, Peter R. Escape from Black Forest. 1995. (Daring Adventure Ser.: Vol. 8). (J). (gr. 4). pap. 5.99 o.p. (1-56179-397-3) Focus on the Family Publishing.

French, Simon. Where in the World. 2003. 208p. (J). (gr. 3-6). 14.95 (1-56145-292-0) Peachtree Pubs., Ltd.

Friedrich, Joachim. 4 1/2 Friends & the Disappearing Bio Teacher. Crawford, Elizabeth D., tr. from GER. 2001. 156p. (J). (0-7868-2588-X, Volo) Hyperion Bks. for Children.

—4 1/2 Friends & the Disappearing Bio Teacher, Bk. 2. 2001. (Illus.). 156p. (J). (gr. 3-7). 15.99 (0-7868-0698-2, Volo) Hyperion Bks. for Children.

Heyduck-Huth, Hilde. In the Village. 1971. Orig. Title: Thomas in Dorf. (Illus.). (J). (ps-1). 3.50 o.p. (0-15-238751-X) Harcourt Children's Bks.

Holub, Josef. The Robber & Me, ERS. Crawford, Elizabeth D., tr. from GER. 1997. 210p. (J). (gr. 3-7). 16.95 (0-8050-5599-1, Holt, Henry & Co. Bks. For Young Readers) Holt, Henry & Co.

Settings

—The Robber & Me. Crawford, Elizabeth D., tr. 1999. 224p. (gr. 5-9). pap. text 4.50 o.s.i (*0-440-41540-3*, Dell Books for Young Readers) Random Hse. Children's Bks.

—The Robber & Me. 1999. (gr. 4-7). 19.25 (*0-8446-7007-3*) Smith, Peter Pub., Inc.

—The Robber & Me. 1999. 10.55 (*0-606-15909-6*) Turtleback Bks.

Hoobler, Dorothy & Hoobler, Thomas. The 1930s: Directions. 2000. (Century Kids Ser.). (Illus.). 160p. (YA). (gr. 5-8). 22.90 (*0-7613-1603-5*) Millbrook Pr., Inc.

—The 1930s: Directions. 2000. E-Book 21.90 (*0-585-34213-X*) netLibrary, Inc.

Hutsell-Manning, Linda. Jason & the Wonder Horn. 2002. (In the Same Boat Ser.). (Illus.). 288p. (J). pap. (*1-55050-214-X*) Coteau Bks.

Kerr, M. E. Gentlehands. 1982. 144p. (gr. 8 up). mass mkt. 2.75 o.s.i (*0-553-26677-2*) Bantam Bks.

—Gentlehands. (Ursula Nordstrom Bk.). (gr. 7 up). 1990. (Illus.). 208p. (J). pap. 5.99 (*0-06-447067-9*, Harper Trophy); 1978. (YA). lib. bdg. 16.89 o.p. (*0-06-023177-7*) HarperCollins Children's Bk. Group.

—Gentlehands. 1990. 11.00 (*0-606-04678-X*) Turtleback Bks.

Ketcham, Sallie. Bach's Big Adventure. 1999. (Illus.). 32p. (J). (gr. k-4). lib. bdg. 17.99 (*0-531-33140-7*, Orchard Bks.) Scholastic, Inc.

Kordon, Klaus. Brothers Like Friends. 2015. (Illus.). (J). 14.95 (*0-399-22100-X*, Philomel) Penguin Putnam Bks. for Young Readers.

—Brothers Like Friends. Crawford, Elizabeth D., tr. from GER. 1992. 192p. (J). (gr. 5 up). 14.95 o.s.i (*0-399-22137-9*, Philomel) Penguin Putnam Bks. for Young Readers.

Napoli, Donna Jo. Stones in Water. 224p. (YA). (gr. 5-9). 1997. 16.99 o.s.i (*0-525-45842-5*, Dutton Children's Bks.); 1999. (Illus.). reprint ed. pap. 5.99 (*0-14-130600-9*, Puffin Bks.) Penguin Putnam Bks. for Young Readers.

—Stones in Water. 1999. 11.04 (*0-606-17262-9*) Turtleback Bks.

O'Sullivan, Mark. Angels Without Wings. 1997. 160p. (*0-86327-591-5*) Wolfhound Pr.

Parma, Clemens. Wandering Shoe. 1966. (Foreign Lands Bks.). (Illus.). (J). (gr. k-5). lib. bdg. 3.95 o.p. (*0-8225-0358-1*) Lerner Publishing Group.

Roland, Donna. More of Grandfather's Stories from Germany. 1984. (J). (gr. k-3). pap. 5.95 (*0-941996-04-2*) Open My World Publishing.

Savery, Constance. Enemy Brothers. 2001. (Living History Library). 304p. (J). (gr. 5-12). reprint ed. pap. 13.95 (*1-883937-50-7*, 50-7) Bethlehem Bks.

Simon & Barklee in Germany. 2001. (Another Country Calling Ser.). (Illus.). 64p. (J). (gr. 3-5). pap. text 12.00 (*0-9704661-2-9*, Explorer Media) Simon & Barklee, Inc./ExplorerMedia.

Steinhofel, Andreas. The Middle of the World. Skofield, James, tr. 2002. (YA). 16.95 (*0-385-72943-X*, Delacorte Pr.) Dell Publishing.

Townsend, Tom. Trader Wooly & the Ghost in the Colonel's Jeep. 1991. (Illus.). 110p. (J). (gr. 6-7). 13.95 (*0-89015-807-X*) Eakin Pr.

—Trader Wooly & the Terrorist. 1988. (J). (gr. 6-7). pap. 13.95 (*0-89015-670-0*) Eakin Pr.

Tunnell, Michael O. Brothers in Valor: Story of Resistance. 2001. 260p. (J). (gr. 6-10). tchr. ed. 16.95 (*0-8234-1541-4*) Holiday Hse., Inc.

Watts, Irene N. Good-Bye, Marianne: A Story of Growing up in Nazi Germany. 1998. 112p. (J). (gr. 3-7). pap. 7.95 (*0-88776-445-2*) Tundra Bks. of Northern New York.

Wilhelm, Doug. Shadow of the Swastika. 1995. (Choose Your Own Adventure Ser.: No. 163). (J). (gr. 4-8). 8.60 o.p. (*0-606-08148-8*) Turtleback Bks.

GHANA—FICTION

Glasser, Margaret D. Kofi's Story. 1999. (Illus.). 28p. (J). (gr. k-3). pap. text 8.95 (*1-58521-003-X*) Books for Black Children, Inc.

Medearis, Angela Shelf. Seven Spools of Thread: A Kwanzaa Story. 2000. (Illus.). 40p. (J). (gr. 2-5). lib. bdg. 15.95 (*0-8075-7315-9*) Whitman, Albert & Co.

Simmons, Lesley Anne. Meet Kofi, Maria & Sunita: Family Life in Ghana, Peru & India. 1996. (Stories from the World Bank Ser.: Vol. 1). (Illus.). 80p. (J). (gr. 2-4). 14.95 (*0-942389-12-3*) Cobblestone Publishing Co.

GLOBE THEATRE (SOUTHWARK, LONDON, ENGLAND)—FICTION

Cooper, Susan. King of Shadows. (Illus.). 192p. (gr. 5-9). 2001. (J). pap. 4.99 (*0-689-84445-X*, Aladdin); 1999. (YA). 16.00 (*0-689-82817-9*, McElderry, Margaret K.) Simon & Schuster Children's Publishing.

—King of Shadows. l.t. ed. 2000. (Thorndike Press Large Print Juvenile Ser.). (Illus.). 246p. (J). (gr. 8-12). 21.95 (*0-7862-2706-0*) Thorndike Pr.

GRAND CANYON (ARIZ.)—FICTION

Allen, Julia. Sixty Word Grand Canyon Series, 6 bks., Set. 1994. (Illus.). (J). (gr. k-3). pap. 23.70 (*0-89868-240-1*, Reading Research) ARO Publishing Co.

Chandler, Mitzi. I See Something Grand. 1995. (Illus.). 32p. (J). (ps-1). pap. 8.95 (*0-938216-50-3*) Grand Canyon Assn.

Cuyler, Margery. That's Good! That's Bad! In the Grand Canyon, ERS. 2002. (Illus.). 32p. (J). (ps-2). 16.95 (*0-8050-5975-X*, Holt, Henry & Co. Bks. For Young Readers) Holt, Henry & Co.

Davinroy, Paul V. Dusty & the Grand Canyon. 1996. 40p. (J). (gr. k-2). pap. 8.00 o.p. (*0-8059-3898-2*) Dorrance Publishing Co., Inc.

Hautman, Pete. Hole in the Sky. 2001. (Illus.). 192p. (J). 16.00 (*0-689-83118-8*, Simon & Schuster Children's Publishing) Simon & Schuster Children's Publishing.

Henry, Marguerite. Brighty of the Grand Canyon. 2002. (Illus.). (YA). 13.40 (*1-4046-1351-X*) Book Wholesalers, Inc.

—Brighty of the Grand Canyon. Scholastic, Inc. Staff, ed. 1992. (J). pap. 2.25 (*0-590-02354-3*) Scholastic, Inc.

—Brighty of the Grand Canyon. 224p. (J). 2001. (Kids' Picks Ser.). pap. 2.99 o.s.i (*0-689-84522-7*, Aladdin); 1991. (Illus.). (gr. 3-7). lib. bdg. 15.00 o.s.i (*0-02-743664-0*, Simon & Schuster Children's Publishing); 2nd ed. 1991. (Marguerite Henry Horseshoe Library: Vol. 5). (Illus.). (gr. 3-7). reprint ed. pap. 4.99 (*0-689-71485-8*, Aladdin) Simon & Schuster Children's Publishing.

—Brighty of the Grand Canyon. 2001. (J). (gr. 3-6). 20.25 (*0-8446-7176-2*) Smith, Peter Pub., Inc.

—Brighty of the Grand Canyon. 1987. (Marguerite Henry Horseshoe Library). (J). 11.04 (*0-606-02444-1*) Turtleback Bks.

Hobbs, William. Downriver. 1991. 208p. (YA). (gr. 7 up). 17.00 (*0-689-31690-9*, Atheneum) Simon & Schuster Children's Publishing.

—River Thunder: A Companion the Downriver. 1999. 224p. (YA). (gr. 7-12). mass mkt. 5.50 (*0-440-22681-3*, Dell Books for Young Readers) Random Hse. Children's Bks.

Hogg, Gary. Happy Hawk Series, 6 bks., Set. 1991. (Illus.). (J). (gr. k-6). 83.70 (*0-89868-243-6*); pap. 29.70 (*0-89868-242-8*) ARO Publishing Co.

Lind, Heidemarie. Mowgli in Grand Canyon. 1997. (Illus.). 38p. (J). (ps-8). 15.95 (*1-891126-11-3*); pap. 7.95 (*1-891126-05-9*) Rocky Mountain West Co.

Reese, Bob. Abert & Kaibab: Big Book. 1987. (Grand Canyon Ser.). (Illus.). (J). (gr. k-6). 9.95 (*0-89868-226-6*); pap. 3.95 (*0-89868-227-4*) ARO Publishing Co.

—Cocos Berry Party. 1987. (Grand Canyon Ser.). (Illus.). (J). (gr. k-6). 9.95 (*0-89868-193-6*); pap. 3.95 (*0-89868-194-4*) ARO Publishing Co.

—Raven's Roost. 1987. (Grand Canyon Ser.). (Illus.). (J). (gr. k-6). 9.95 (*0-89868-195-2*); pap. 3.95 (*0-89868-196-0*) ARO Publishing Co.

—Ravens Roost. 1988. (Grand Canyon Critters Ser.). (J). pap. 2.95 o.p. (*0-516-42433-5*, Children's Pr.) Scholastic Library Publishing.

—Sixty Word Grand Canyon Series, 6 bks., Set. 1987. (Illus.). (J). (gr. k-6). 59.70 (*0-89868-241-X*) ARO Publishing Co.

—Surefoot Mule. 1987. (Grand Canyon Ser.). (Illus.). (J). (gr. k-6). 9.95 (*0-89868-197-9*); pap. 9.95 (*0-89868-198-7*) ARO Publishing Co.

—Wild Turkey Run. 1987. (Grand Canyon Critters Ser.). (Illus.). (J). (gr. k-6). 24p. 9.95 (*0-89868-199-5*); pap. 3.95 (*0-89868-225-8*) ARO Publishing Co.

Thompson-Hoffman, Susan. Tassel's Mission. 1989. (Illus.). 32p. (J). (gr. 2-5). 11.95 o.p. (*0-924483-00-8*); 16.95 o.p. incl. audio (*0-924483-03-2*); 39.95 o.p. incl. audio (*0-924483-06-7*); audio o.p. (*0-924483-09-1*);Incl. toy. 39.95 o.p. incl. audio (*0-924483-41-5*) Soundprints.

GRAND CENTRAL TERMINAL (NEW YORK, N.Y.)—FICTION

Kalman, Maira. Next Stop, Grand Central. 1999. (Illus.). 32p. (YA). (gr. k-3). 16.99 (*0-399-22926-4*) Penguin Group (USA) Inc.

GREAT BRITAIN—FICTION

Alcott, Louisa May. The Inheritance. l.t. ed. 1997. 26.95 o.p. (*1-56895-505-7*, Wheeler Publishing, Inc.) Gale Group.

—The Inheritance. 1998. 192p. mass mkt. 5.99 o.s.i (*0-14-027729-3*) Penguin Group (USA) Inc.

—The Inheritance. Myerson, Joel & Shealy, Daniel, eds. 1997. 160p. (YA). 18.00 o.s.i (*0-525-45756-9*) Penguin Putnam Bks. for Young Readers.

—The Inheritance. 1998. (Illus.). (J). 12.04 (*0-606-18412-0*) Turtleback Bks.

—The Inheritance. Myerson, Joel & Shealy, Daniel, eds. 1998. (Classics Ser.). 192p. 13.00 (*0-14-043666-9*, Penguin Classics) Viking Penguin.

Anno, Mitsumasa. Anno's Britian. rev. ed. 2015. (J). 8.95 (*0-399-21795-9*) Penguin Putnam Bks. for Young Readers.

Austen, Jane. Persuasion. 1966. (Classics Ser.). (YA). (gr. 10 up). mass mkt. 2.50 o.p. (*0-8049-0107-4*, CL-107) Airmont Publishing Co., Inc.

—Sense & Sensibility. 1982. (Bantam Classics Ser.). 352p. (gr. 9-12). mass mkt. 4.95 (*0-553-21334-2*, Bantam Classics) Bantam Bks.

Baker, Margaret J. Home from the Hill, RS. 1969. (Illus.). (J). (gr. 4 up). 3.95 o.p. (*0-374-33300-9*, Farrar, Straus & Giroux (BYR)) Farrar, Straus & Giroux.

Blackmore, Richard D. Lorna Doone. 1984. (Classics for Young Readers Ser.). 272p. (J). (gr. 4-6). pap. 3.50 o.p. (*0-14-035021-7*, Puffin Bks.) Penguin Putnam Bks. for Young Readers.

Blackwood, Gary L. The Shakespeare Stealer. 1998. 208p. (J). (gr. 4-6). 15.99 (*0-525-45863-8*, Dutton Children's Bks.) Penguin Putnam Bks. for Young Readers.

—The Shakespeare Stealer. 2000. 12.04 (*0-606-17870-8*) Turtleback Bks.

—Shakespeare's Scribe. 2000. (Illus.). 224p. (J). (gr. 4-6). 15.99 (*0-525-46444-1*, Dutton Children's Bks.) Penguin Putnam Bks. for Young Readers.

Bond, Michael. More about Paddington, rev. ed. 1979. (Paddington Ser.). (Illus.). 144p. (J). (gr. 4-6). 15.00 (*0-395-06640-9*) Houghton Mifflin Co.

—Paddington at Large, 001. 1998. (Paddington Ser.). (Illus.). 128p. (J). (ps-3). 15.00 o.p. (*0-395-06641-7*) Houghton Mifflin Co.

—Paddington at Work, 001. 1967. (Paddington Ser.). (Illus.). 128p. (J). (ps-3). 15.00 o.p. (*0-395-06637-9*) Houghton Mifflin Co.

—Paddington Goes to Town, 001. 1977. (Paddington Ser.). (Illus.). 128p. (J). (ps-3). 15.00 o.p. (*0-395-06635-2*) Houghton Mifflin Co.

—Paddington Goes to Town. 1972. (Paddington Ser.). (Illus.). 128p. (J). (ps-3). pap. 0.75 o.s.i (*0-440-46793-4*, Yearling) Random Hse. Children's Bks.

—Paddington Helps Out, 001. 1973. (Paddington Ser.). (Illus.). 128p. (J). (ps-3). 15.00 o.p. (*0-395-06639-5*) Houghton Mifflin Co.

—Paddington Marches On. 1965. (Paddington Ser.). (SPA., Illus.). 128p. (J). (ps-3). 12.00 (*0-395-06642-5*) Houghton Mifflin Co.

—Paddington Takes the Air, 001. 1971. (Paddington Ser.). (Illus.). 128p. (J). (ps-3). 14.95 o.p. (*0-395-10909-4*) Houghton Mifflin Co.

Borden, Louise. The Little Ships: The Heroic Rescue at Dunkirk in World War II. 2003. (Illus.). 32p. (J). (gr. 4 up). pap. 6.99 (*0-689-85396-3*, Aladdin) Simon & Schuster Children's Publishing.

Boston, Lucy M. A Stranger at Green Knowe. 1961. (Illus.). (YA). (gr. 5-9). 9.95 o.p. (*0-15-281752-2*) Harcourt Children's Bks.

Brouwer, Sigmund. Barbarians from the Isle. 1992. (Winds of Light Ser.: No. 2). 132p. (J). (gr. 5-8). pap. 5.99 (*0-89693-116-1*, 6-1116) Cook Communications Ministries.

—Barbarians from the Isle. 2002. (Winds of Light Ser.). 202p. (YA). pap. 5.99 (*1-55305-033-9*) Cygnet Publishing Group, Inc./Coolreading.com CAN. *Dist:* Orca Bk. Pubs.

—Wings of an Angel. 1992. (Winds of Light Ser.: No. 1). 132p. (J). (gr. 5-8). pap. 5.99 (*0-89693-115-3*, 6-1115) Cook Communications Ministries.

—Wings of an Angel. 2002. (Winds of Light Ser.). 214p. (YA). pap. 5.99 (*1-55305-032-0*) Cygnet Publishing Group, Inc./Coolreading.com CAN. *Dist:* Orca Bk. Pubs.

Brown, Alan. The Windhover. 1997. (Illus.). 32p. (J). (gr. k-3). 17.00 (*0-15-201187-0*) Harcourt Children's Bks.

Browne, N. M. Warriors of Camlann. 2003. (Illus.). 275p. (YA). 16.95 (*1-58234-817-0*, Bloomsbury Children) Bloomsbury Publishing.

Burgess, Melvin. The Ghost Behind the Wall, ERS. 2003. (Illus.). 176p. (YA). (gr. 4-7). 16.95 (*0-8050-7149-0*, Holt, Henry & Co. Bks. For Young Readers) Holt, Henry & Co.

—The Ghost Behind the Wall. l.t. ed. 2003. 160p. (J). 22.95 (*0-7862-5774-1*) Thorndike Pr.

Butler, Samuel. The Way of All Flesh. 1965. (Airmont Classics Ser.). (J). (gr. 11 up). mass mkt. 2.50 o.p. (*0-8049-0090-6*, CL-90) Airmont Publishing Co., Inc.

Carnegie, Dale. Tess of the d'Urbervilles. Hardy, Thomas, ed. 1998. (Enriched Classics Ser.). (Illus.). 480p. reprint ed. mass mkt. 5.99 (*0-671-01546-X*, Pocket) Simon & Schuster.

Clarke, Pauline. The Return of the Twelve. 1963. (Illus.). (J). (gr. 4-6). 7.95 o.p. (*0-698-20117-5*) Putnam Publishing Group, The.

Cohen, Barbara. Robin Hood & Little John. 1998. 12.14 (*0-606-13744-0*) Turtleback Bks.

Cooper, Susan. Dawn of Fear. 1989. (Illus.). 224p. (J). (gr. 4-7). reprint ed. pap. 4.99 (*0-689-71327-4*, Aladdin) Simon & Schuster Children's Publishing.

—Dawn of Fear. 1970. (J). 11.04 (*0-606-04195-8*) Turtleback Bks.

Crossley-Holland, Kevin. The Seeing Stone. (Illus.). (J). 2002. (Arthur Trilogy: Bk. 1). 352p. (gr. 4-7). pap. 6.99 (*0-439-26327-1*); 2001. 368p. (gr. 5-8). trans. 17.95 (*0-439-26326-3*) Scholastic, Inc. (Levine, Arthur A. Bks.).

Dalgliesh, Alice. The Silver Pencil. 1991. (Newbery Library Ser.). (Illus.). 256p. (YA). (gr. 7 up). pap. 5.99 (*0-14-034792-5*, Puffin Bks.) Penguin Putnam Bks. for Young Readers.

Davis, Todd & Frey, Marc E. Classics Literary Gift Set 2: The Visual Desk Reference, 6 vols. 2002. (Illus.). 1248p. (J). 35.00 o.p. (*0-7624-0868-5*) Running Pr. Bk. Pubs.

De Angeli, Marguerite. The Door in the Wall. 2002. (Illus.). (J). 13.94 (*0-7587-0181-0*) Book Wholesalers, Inc.

—The Door in the Wall. 1997. 128p. (J). mass mkt. 2.69 o.p. (*0-440-22740-2*) Dell Publishing.

—The Door in the Wall. unabr. ed. (J). (gr. 4-6). 2000. 121p. pap. 28.00 incl. audio (*0-8072-8691-5*, YA237SP); 1998. pap. 18.00 incl. audio (*0-553-52522-0*) Random Hse. Audio Publishing Group. (Listening Library).

—The Door in the Wall. 1983. (J). pap. 1.95 o.p. (*0-590-02980-0*); pap. 2.25 o.p. (*0-590-33853-6*) Scholastic, Inc.

Dickens, Charles. Great Expectations. unabr. ed. 1963. (Classics Ser.). (YA). (gr. 9 up). mass mkt. 3.95 (*0-8049-0068-X*, CL-68) Airmont Publishing Co., Inc.

—Listen & Read Charles Dickens' A Christmas Carol. 1996. 96p. (J). pap. 5.95 incl. audio (*0-486-29103-0*) Dover Pubns., Inc.

—Nicholas Nickleby. 1982. 816p. (YA). (gr. 10-12). mass mkt. 5.95 o.s.i (*0-553-21265-6*, Bantam Classics) Bantam Bks.

—Quilp: The Old Curiosity Shop: Movie Edition. 1975. (Movie Editions Ser.). 320p. (YA). (gr. 9). mass mkt. 1.25 o.p. (*0-451-06420-8*, Y6420, Signet Bks.) NAL.

Dietrich, William, tr. Hadrian's Wall: A Novel. 2004. pap. (*0-06-056372-9*) HarperCollins Pubs.

Dorre, Pamela. Wind Over Stonehenge. 1978. (Pacesetters Ser.). (Illus.). 64p. (J). (gr. 4 up). lib. bdg. 9.25 o.p. (*0-516-02175-3*, Children's Pr.) Scholastic Library Publishing.

—Wind Over Stonehenge. 1977. (Bestsellers II Ser.). (J). 16.60 o.p. (*0-606-02449-2*) Turtleback Bks.

D'Ottari, Francesca. The Legend of King Arthur: A Young Reader's Edition of the Classic Story by Howard Pyle. 1996. (Illus.). 56p. (J). text 9.98 o.p. (*1-56138-503-4*, Courage Bks.) Running Pr. Bk. Pubs.

Eliot, George. The Mill on the Floss. 1964. (Airmont Classics Ser.). (YA). (gr. 10 up). mass mkt. 2.95 o.s.i (*0-8049-0043-4*, CL-43) Airmont Publishing Co., Inc.

—The Mill on the Floss, 001. Haight, G. S., ed. 1972. (YA). (gr. 9 up). pap. 14.76 o.p. (*0-395-05151-7*, Riverside Editions) Houghton Mifflin Co.

Fairweather, Eileen. French Leave: Maxine Harrison Moves Out! 1997. (Livewire Ser.). 132p. (YA). (gr. 7-11). pap. 7.95 (*0-7043-4916-7*) Women's Pr., Ltd., The GBR. *Dist:* Trafalgar Square.

Farmer, Penelope. Emma in Winter. 1966. (Illus.). (J). (gr. 5-7). 5.75 o.p. (*0-15-225700-4*) Harcourt Children's Bks.

Fielding, Henry. Tom Jones. 1967. (Airmont Classics Ser.). (YA). (gr. 11 up). mass mkt. 2.50 o.p. (*0-8049-0135-X*, CL-135) Airmont Publishing Co., Inc.

Finkel, Irving. The Lewis Chessman & What Happened to Them. 1999. (J). (gr. 4-7). pap. text 16.95 (*0-7141-0592-9*) Brimax Bks., Ltd.

Freeman, Don. The Guard Mouse. 1967. (Illus.). (J). (ps-2). 12.95 o.p. (*0-670-35639-5*, Viking Children's Bks.) Penguin Putnam Bks. for Young Readers.

Gardam, Jane. A Long Way from Verona. 1988. 192p. (YA). (gr. 7 up). 13.95 o.p. (*0-02-735781-3*, Simon & Schuster Children's Publishing) Simon & Schuster Children's Publishing.

Garfield, Leon. Mister Corbett's Ghost. 1968. (Illus.). (J). (gr. 5 up). lib. bdg. 5.99 o.p. (*0-394-91601-8*, Pantheon) Knopf Publishing Group.

Gerrard, Roy. Sir Cedric Rides Again, RS. 1986. (Illus.). 32p. (J). (ps up). 15.00 o.p. (*0-374-36961-5*, Farrar, Straus & Giroux (BYR)) Farrar, Straus & Giroux.

Goldsmith, Oliver. The Vicar of Wakefield. 1964. (Airmont Classics Ser.). (YA). (gr. 10 up). mass mkt. 1.25 o.p. (*0-8049-0052-3*, CL-52) Airmont Publishing Co., Inc.

—The Vicar of Wakefield. 1981. (gr. 10 up). pap. 0.95 o.s.i (*0-671-47869-9*, Pocket) Simon & Schuster.

Hardy, Thomas. The Return of the Native: A Facsimile of the Manuscript, with Related Materials. Gatrell, Simon, ed. 1986. (Thomas Hardy Archives Ser.). 512p. lib. bdg. 100.00 o.p. (*0-8240-7475-0*) Garland Publishing, Inc.

—Under the Greenwood Tree. 1998. (Penguin Readers Ser.: Level 2). 144p. (J). pap. 7.66 (*0-582-40161-5*) Longman Publishing Group.

—The Woodlanders. Pinion, F. B., ed. 1975. (Students' Hardy Ser.). 494p. (J). 12.50 (*0-333-17265-5*) Macmillan U.K. GBR. *Dist:* Trans-Atlantic Pubns., Inc.

—The Woodlanders. 1974. 416p. (J). 12.50 (*0-333-16883-6*) Macmillan U.K. GBR. *Dist:* Trans-Atlantic Pubns., Inc.

Hardy, Thomas, ed. Tess of the d'Urbervilles. 1963. (Airmont Classics Ser.). (gr. 11 up). mass mkt. 3.50 (*0-8049-0082-5*, CL-82) Airmont Publishing Co., Inc.

—Tess of the d'Urbervilles. 1984. (Bantam Classics Ser.). 448p. (gr. 9-12). mass mkt. 4.95 (*0-553-21168-4*, Bantam Classics) Bantam Bks.

Hardy, Thomas & Buckler, William E., eds. Tess of the d'Urbervilles. 1960. (YA). (gr. 9 up). pap. 16.36 (*0-395-05144-4*, Riverside Editions) Houghton Mifflin Co.

Harnett, Cynthia. The Writing on the Hearth. 1973. (Illus.). 320p. (J). (gr. 7 up). 9.95 o.p. (*0-670-79119-9*) Viking Penguin.

Hatfield, Kate. Drowning in Honey. 2000. 333p. (J). pap. 12.95 o.p. (*0-552-99694-7*) Transworld Publishers Ltd. GBR. *Dist:* Trafalgar Square.

Henty, G. A. The Dragon & the Raven: Or the Days of King Alfred. 2000. (Illus.). 238p. (J). pap. 14.99 (*1-887159-31-2*) Preston-Speed Pubns.

Hersom, Kathleen. The Half Child. (gr. 5 up). 1993. 104p. (J). pap. 4.95 o.s.i (*0-671-86696-6*, Aladdin); 1991. 176p. (YA). ring bd. 15.00 o.s.i (*0-671-74225-6*, Simon & Schuster Children's Publishing) Simon & Schuster Children's Publishing.

Holt, Victoria. Paragon Revels. 1962. 10.95 o.s.i (*0-385-00061-8*) Doubleday Publishing.

Howarth, Lesley. Weather Eye. 1997. (Illus.). 224p. (YA). (gr. 7-10). reprint ed. bds. 4.99 o.p. (*0-7636-0243-4*) Candlewick Pr.

Huang, Benrei. A Visit to Great Britain. 1991. (Golden Look-Look Bks.). (Illus.). 24p. (J). (ps-3). pap. 3.29 o.s.i (*0-307-12631-5*, Golden Bks.) Random Hse. Children's Bks.

Ivanhoe. 1988. (Short Classics Ser.). (Illus.). 48p. (J). (gr. 4 up). pap. 9.27 o.p. (*0-8172-2769-5*) Raintree Pubs.

John, Mary. A Shilling for the Gate. 1991. 68p. (YA). pap. 23.00 (*0-86383-763-8*) Gomer Pr. GBR. *Dist:* State Mutual Bk. & Periodical Service, Ltd.

Johnson, Jane. Bertie on the Beach. 1984. (Illus.). 32p. (J). (gr. k-3). 9.95 o.s.i (*0-02-747840-8*, Simon & Schuster Children's Publishing) Simon & Schuster Children's Publishing.

King-Smith, Dick. Pigs Might Fly. 1990. (Illus.). 160p. (J). (gr. 3-7). pap. 5.99 (*0-14-034537-X*, Puffin Bks.) Penguin Putnam Bks. for Young Readers.

Kipling, Rudyard. The Light That Failed. 1969. (Airmont Classics Ser.). (YA). (gr. 8 up). mass mkt. 1.50 (*0-8049-0199-6*, CL-199) Airmont Publishing Co., Inc.

Kirwan, Anna. Victoria: May Blossom of Britannia England, 1829. 2001. (Royal Diaries Ser.). (Illus.). 144p. (J). (gr. 4-9). 10.95 (*0-439-21598-6*) Scholastic, Inc.

Lassie Come Home. 1970. (Grow-up Books Ser.). (J). (gr. 2-7). 1.95 o.p. (*0-448-02139-0*) Putnam Publishing Group, The.

Lewis, Kim. The Last Train. 1996. (Illus.). 32p. (J). (ps-3). reprint ed. bds. 5.99 o.p. (*1-56402-969-7*) Candlewick Pr.

Maccarone, Grace. The Sword in the Stone. 1992. (Hello Reader! Ser.). (J). 10.14 (*0-606-01957-X*) Turtleback Bks.

Maddock, Reginald. The Pit. 1968. (Illus.). (J). (gr. 7 up). 5.95 o.p. (*0-316-54316-0*) Little Brown & Co.

Marryat, Frederick. Mr. Midshipman Easy. 1991. 424p. (J). (gr. 2 up). pap. 2.95 o.p. (*0-14-035118-3*, Puffin Bks.) Penguin Putnam Bks. for Young Readers.

Mathur-Kamat, Ambika. Miss Panda in England. 2001. (Miss Panda Ser.). (Illus.). 40p. (J). (ps-5). pap. 11.95 (*1-883573-01-7*, Little Blue Works) Windstorm Creative Ltd.

Maugham, W. Somerset. Of Human Bondage. 1955. 576p. 22.50 o.s.i (*0-385-04899-8*) Doubleday Publishing.

Mills, Frank. The Boggarts of Britain. 2001. pap. 13.95 (*1-84243-005-X*) No Exit Pr. GBR. *Dist:* Trafalgar Square.

Morpurgo, Michael. Mr. Nobody's Eyes. 1990. 144p. (YA). (gr. 5 up). 12.95 o.p. (*0-670-83022-4*, Viking Children's Bks.) Penguin Putnam Bks. for Young Readers.

—The Wreck of the Zanzibar. l.t. ed. 2003. (J). 16.95 (*0-7540-7846-9*, Galaxy Children's Large Print) BBC Audiobooks America.

—The Wreck of the Zanzibar. 1995. (Illus.). 80p. (J). (gr. 3-5). 14.99 o.s.i (*0-670-86360-2*, Viking Children's Bks.) Penguin Putnam Bks. for Young Readers.

Nesbit, Edith. House of Arden. 1968. (J). (gr. 4-8). 4.50 o.p. (*0-525-32331-7*, Dutton) Dutton/Plume.

North, Elizabeth. Ancient Enemies. 1986. 240p. reprint ed. 15.95 o.p. (*0-89733-215-6*); (J). pap. 14.00 (*0-89733-214-8*) Academy Chicago Pubs., Ltd.

Parker, Dorothy D. Liam's Catch. 1972. (Illus.). (J). (gr. k-3). 8.95 o.p. (*0-670-42744-6*) Viking Penguin.

Peyton, K. M. Flambards. 1967. (Illus.). (J). (gr. 6 up). 4.99 o.p. (*0-529-00507-7*) Putnam Publishing Group, The.

Pockets Learning Staff. Victorian Advent. 1998. (Illus.). (J). 45.00 (*1-888074-68-X*) Pockets of Learning.

—Victorian Stocking. 1998. (Illus.). (J). 20.00 (*1-888074-21-3*) Pockets of Learning.

Potter, Beatrix. The Tailor of Gloucester. 1989. (Beatrix Potter Book & Storytape Collection). (Illus.). (J). (ps-3). 6.95 o.p. (*0-7232-3668-2*, Warne, Frederick) Penguin Putnam Bks. for Young Readers.

—The Tailor of Gloucester Model Book. 1987. (Illus.). 20p. (J). (ps-3). pap. 3.95 o.p. (*0-7232-3455-8*, Warne, Frederick) Penguin Putnam Bks. for Young Readers.

Pyle, Howard. The Story of King Arthur & His Knights. 1986. (Signet Classics Ser.). (J). 12.00 (*0-606-01952-9*) Turtleback Bks.

Random House Staff, ed. Sir Cumference. 1998. (J). lib. bdg. 11.99 (*0-679-98378-3*) Random Hse., Inc.

Running Press Staff. Classics Literary Gift Set, 6 vols. 2002. text 35.00 o.p. (*0-7624-0867-7*) Running Pr. Bk. Pubs.

Scott, Walter, Sr. Ivanhoe. 2nd ed. 2000. (Historias de Siempre Ser.). (SPA., Illus.). 168p. (YA). (gr. 5-8). 12.95 (*84-204-5721-3*) Alfaguara, Ediciones, S.A.-Grupo Santillana ESP. *Dist:* Santillana USA Publishing Co., Inc.

Sharp, Evelyn. A Child's Christmas. 1991. (Children's Classics Ser.). (J). 12.99 o.s.i (*0-517-03369-0*) Random Hse. Value Publishing.

Shaw, Margret. A Wider Tomorrow. 1990. 144p. (YA). 13.95 o.p. (*0-8234-0837-X*) Holiday Hse., Inc.

Springer, Nancy. Lionclaw: A Tale of Rowan Hood. 2002. 160p. (J). (gr. 4-7). 16.99 (*0-399-23716-X*, G. P. Putnam's Sons) Penguin Putnam Bks. for Young Readers.

Sterne, Laurence. Tristram Shandy. 1967. (Airmont Classics Ser.). (YA). (gr. 11 up). mass mkt. 1.95 o.p. (*0-8049-0152-X*, CL-152) Airmont Publishing Co., Inc.

Stevenson, Robert Louis. The Black Arrow. 1964. (Airmont Classics Ser.). (J). (gr. 6 up). mass mkt. 2.95 o.p. (*0-8049-0020-5*, CL-20) Airmont Publishing Co., Inc.

—The Black Arrow. 1967. (Dent's Illustrated Children's Classics Ser.). (Illus.). (J). reprint ed. 9.00 o.p. (*0-460-05040-0*) Biblio Distribution.

—The Black Arrow. 1990. 288p. (J). (gr. 4 up). pap. 3.50 o.s.i (*0-440-40359-6*) Dell Publishing.

—The Black Arrow. 1998. 269p. (YA). (gr. 7 up). pap. text 3.99 (*0-8125-6562-2*, Tor Classics) Doherty, Tom Assocs., LLC.

—The Black Arrow. 2001. (Juvenile Classics). 272p. (J). pap. 3.00 (*0-486-41820-0*) Dover Pubns., Inc.

—The Black Arrow. 1997. (J). 8.05 o.p. (*0-606-12193-5*) Turtleback Bks.

—The Black Arrow. 2003. (Children's Classics). 304p. (J). (gr. 3-6). pap. 3.95 (*1-85326-161-0*) Wordsworth Editions, Ltd. GBR. *Dist:* Advanced Global Distribution Services.

—The Black Arrow: A Tale of the Two Roses. 1987. (Illustrated Classics Ser.). (Illus.). 336p. (J). (gr. 4-7). 28.00 (*0-684-18877-5*, Atheneum) Simon & Schuster Children's Publishing.

Thackeray, William Makepeace. Vanity Fair. (Modern Library Ser.). (J). E-Book 4.95 (*1-58945-016-7*) Adobe Systems, Inc.

—Vanity Fair. 1967. (Airmont Classics Ser.). (YA). (gr. 11 up). mass mkt. 2.50 o.p. (*0-8049-0138-4*, CL-138) Airmont Publishing Co., Inc.

—Vanity Fair. Shefter, Harry et al, eds. rev. ed. 1980. (Illus.). (YA). pap. 1.25 o.p. (*0-671-48119-3*, Washington Square Pr.) Simon & Schuster.

Tingle, Rebecca. The Edge on the Sword. 2001. (Illus.). 288p. (J). (gr. 7 up). 18.99 (*0-399-23580-9*) Penguin Group (USA) Inc.

—The Edge on the Sword. 2003. (Sailing Mystery Ser.). 288p. (J). pap. 6.99 (*0-14-250058-5*, Puffin Bks.) Penguin Putnam Bks. for Young Readers.

Tomlinson, Theresa. Child of the May. 1998. (YA). (gr. 5 up). 120p. mass mkt. 16.99 o.p. (*0-531-33118-0*); (Illus.). 128p. pap. 15.95 (*0-531-30118-4*) Scholastic, Inc. (Orchard Bks.).

Townsend, John R. Good Night, Prof, Dear. 1971. 224p. (YA). (gr. 7-9). 11.95 (*0-397-31355-1*) HarperCollins Children's Bk. Group.

—The Intruder. 1970. (Illus.). (J). (gr. 4-9). 9.57 o.p. (*0-397-31126-5*) HarperCollins Children's Bk. Group.

—The Intruder. 1987. (Illus.). 182p. (J). 13.95 o.p. (*0-19-271304-3*) Oxford Univ. Pr., Inc.

Turnbull, Ann. No Friend of Mine. 1995. (Illus.). 128p. (J). (gr. 5-9). 15.95 o.p. (*1-56402-565-9*) Candlewick Pr.

Twain, Mark. A Connecticut Yankee in King Arthur's Court. 1997. (Classics Illustrated Study Guides). (Illus.). 64p. (YA). (gr. 7 up). mass mkt., stu. ed. 4.99 o.p. (*1-57840-016-3*) Acclaim Bks.

—A Connecticut Yankee in King Arthur's Court. 1964. (Airmont Classics Ser.). (J). (gr. 5 up). mass mkt. 3.25 (*0-8049-0029-9*, CL-29) Airmont Publishing Co., Inc.

—A Connecticut Yankee in King Arthur's Court. unabr. collector's ed. 1979. (J). audio 80.00 (*0-7366-0192-9*, 1192) Books on Tape, Inc.

—A Connecticut Yankee in King Arthur's Court. 1999. (YA). reprint ed. pap. text 28.00 (*1-4047-1121-X*) Classic Textbooks.

—A Connecticut Yankee in King Arthur's Court. 1991. 333p. (gr. 4-7). mass mkt. 3.99 (*0-8125-0436-4*, Tor Classics) Doherty, Tom Assocs., LLC.

—A Connecticut Yankee in King Arthur's Court. deluxe ltd. ed. 1988. (Books of Wonder). (Illus.). 384p. (YA). (gr. 5 up). 100.00 o.p. (*0-688-08258-0*, Morrow, William & Co.) Morrow/Avon.

—A Connecticut Yankee in King Arthur's Court. 1963. (Signet Classics). 336p. (YA). mass mkt. 4.95 (*0-451-52475-6*, Signet Classics) NAL.

—A Connecticut Yankee in King Arthur's Court. abr. ed. 2001. (Junior Classics Ser.). (YA). audio compact disk 15.98 (*962-634-218-8*, NA221812); (gr. 5 up). audio 13.98 (*962-634-718-X*, NA221814) Naxos of America, Inc. (Naxos AudioBooks).

—A Connecticut Yankee in King Arthur's Court. Fago, John N., ed. abr. ed. 1977. (Now Age Illustrated III Ser.). (Illus.). (gr. 4-12). (J). pap. text 2.95 (*0-88301-263-4*); (YA). text 7.50 o.p. (*0-88301-275-8*) Pendulum Pr., Inc.

—A Connecticut Yankee in King Arthur's Court, unabr. ed. 1988. (YA). (gr. 10 up). audio 78.00 (*1-55690-120-8*, 88997E7) Recorded Bks., LLC.

—A Connecticut Yankee in King Arthur's Court. abr. ed. 1979. (Mind's Eye Ser.). (J). audio 29.95 o.p. (*0-88142-106-5*, 365) Soundelux Audio Publishing.

—The Tragedy of Pudd'nhead Wilson. 1964. (Signet Classics Ser.). (J). 10.00 (*0-606-01273-7*) Turtleback Bks.

Umansky, Kaye. Dobbin. 1994. (Illus.). 32p. (J). (ps-1). o.p. (*0-370-31910-9*) Random Hse., Inc.

Westall, Robert. The Kingdom by the Sea, RS. 1991. 176p. (J). (gr. 4-7). 15.00 o.p. (*0-374-34205-9*, Farrar, Straus & Giroux (BYR)) Farrar, Straus & Giroux.

—Yaxley's Cat. 1992. 208p. (J). 13.95 o.p. (*0-590-45175-8*) Scholastic, Inc.

Willard, Barbara. Richleighs of Tantamount. 1901. (Illus.). (J). (gr. 6-8). 5.50 o.p. (*0-15-266750-4*) Harcourt Children's Bks.

Wilson, John. And in the Morning. 2003. 200p. (YA). (gr. 5 up). 16.95 (*1-55337-400-2*) Kids Can Pr., Ltd.

GREAT BRITAIN—POLITICS AND GOVERNMENT—FICTION

Stewart, Josie & Salem, Lynn. The Royal Family. 1995. (Illus.). 8p. (J). (gr. k-2). pap. 3.75 (*1-880612-37-2*) Seedling Pubns., Inc.

Willard, Barbara. If All the Swords in England. 2000. (Living History Library). (Illus.). x, 181p. (J). (gr. 8-12). reprint ed. pap. 12.95 (*1-883937-49-3*, 49-3) Bethlehem Bks.

GREAT LAKES—FICTION

Agee, Jonis. Acts of Love on Indigo Road: New & Selected Stories. 2003. 336p. pap. 16.95 (*1-56689-138-8*) Coffee Hse. Pr.

Briggs-Bunting, Jane. Laddie of the Light, Grades 3-6. 1997. (Barnyard Tales Ser.). (Illus.). 48p. tchr. ed. 17.00 (*0-9649083-1-X*) Black River Trading Co.

Holling, Holling C. Paddle-to-the-Sea. (Illus.). 64p. (J). (gr. 4-6). 1980. pap. 11.95 (*0-395-29203-4*); 1941. tchr. ed. 20.00 (*0-395-15082-5*) Houghton Mifflin Co.

Winters, Donna. Isabelle's Inning: Encore Edition. 1997. (Great Lakes Romances Ser.: No. 1). 240p. pap. 9.95 (*0-923048-85-5*) Bigwater Publishing.

GREAT SMOKY MOUNTAINS (N.C. AND TENN.)—FICTION

Clark, Mindy Starns. A Dime a Dozen. 2003. (Million Dollar Mysteries Ser.). 300p. pap. 10.99 (*0-7369-0995-8*) Harvest Hse. Pubs.

Horstman, Lisa. The Great Smoky Mountain Salamander Ball. Kemp, Steve, ed. 1997. (Illus.). 32p. (Orig.). (J). (gr. k-2). pap. 5.99 (*0-937207-21-7*, 1291) Great Smoky Mountains Natural History Assn.

Youmans, Marly. The Curse of the Raven Mocker, RS. 2003. 288p. 18.00 (*0-374-31667-8*, Farrar, Straus & Giroux (BYR)) Farrar, Straus & Giroux.

GREECE—FICTION

Alcock, Vivien. Singer to the Sea God. 1995. 208p. (J). (gr. 7-12). pap. 3.99 o.s.i (*0-440-41003-7*) Dell Publishing.

—Singer to the Sea God. 1996. (YA). (gr. 9-12). 18.75 (*0-8446-6887-7*) Smith, Peter Pub., Inc.

Allen, Judy. Seal. 1996. (Illus.). 32p. (J). (gr. k-5). reprint ed. bds. 5.99 o.p. (*1-56402-956-5*) Candlewick Pr.

—Seal. 1996. 11.19 o.p. (*0-606-10299-X*) Turtleback Bks.

Bawden, Nina. The Real Plato Jones. 1993. 176p. (YA). (gr. 7-7). tchr. ed. 15.00 (*0-395-66972-3*, Clarion Bks.) Houghton Mifflin Co. Trade & Reference Div.

—The Real Plato Jones. 1996. 176p. (J). (gr. 5-9). pap. 4.99 o.s.i (*0-14-037947-9*, Puffin Bks.) Penguin Putnam Bks. for Young Readers.

—The Real Plato Jones. 1996. (J). 10.09 o.p. (*0-606-10907-2*) Turtleback Bks.

Blacklock, Dyan. Pankration: The Ultimate Game. 192p. (J). (gr. 5-9). 2001. pap. 5.95 (*0-8075-6324-2*); 1999. (Illus.). lib. bdg. 15.95 o.p. (*0-8075-6323-4*) Whitman, Albert & Co.

Bunting, Eve. I Have an Olive Tree. 1999. (Joanna Cotler Bks.). (Illus.). 32p. (J). (ps-3). lib. bdg. 15.89 (*0-06-027574-X*, Cotler, Joanna Bks.) HarperCollins Children's Bk. Group.

Cann, Kate. Grecian Holiday: Or, How I Turned down the Best Possible Thing Only to Have the Time of My Life. 2002. 352p. (J). (gr. 9 up). pap. 5.99 (*0-06-447302-3*, Avon Bks.) Morrow/Avon.

Cargill, Linda. Jason & Medea. 2001. 157p. (YA). (gr. 7 up). 9.99 (*0-88092-548-5*, 5485) Royal Fireworks Publishing Co.

Case, Cassandra. Run with Me, Nike! The Olympics in 420, B.C. 1999. (Smithsonian Odyssey Ser.: No. 12). (Illus.). 32p. (J). (gr. 2-4). 14.95 (*1-56899-604-7*); pap. 5.95 (*1-56899-605-5*); 19.95 o.p. incl. audio (*1-56899-606-3*) Soundprints.

Colum, Padraic. The Children's Homer: The Adventures of Odysseus & the Tale of Troy. 1994. (Illus.). 248p. (J). pap. (*0-86315-529-4*) Floris Bks. GBR. *Dist:* SteinerBooks, Inc.

—The Children's Homer: The Adventures of Odysseus & the Tale of Troy. 1982. (Illus.). 256p. (J). (gr. 3-7). pap. 9.95 (*0-02-042520-1*, Simon Pulse) Simon & Schuster Children's Publishing.

Coville, Bruce. William Shakespeare's A Midsummer Night's Dream. 2003. (Illus.). 48p. 7.99 (*0-14-250168-9*, Puffin Bks.) Penguin Putnam Bks. for Young Readers.

Daringer, Helen F. Yesterday's Daughter. 1964. (Illus.). (J). (gr. 7 up). 4.95 o.p. (*0-15-299821-7*) Harcourt Children's Bks.

Delton, Judy. Angel Spreads Her Wings. (Illus.). (J). 2002. 160p. (gr. 2-5). pap. 4.95 (*0-618-21617-0*); 1999. 144p. (gr. 4-6). tchr. ed. 15.00 (*0-395-91006-4*) Houghton Mifflin Co.

Fenton, Edward. The Refugee Summer. 1982. 272p. (J). (gr. 7 up). pap. 10.95 o.s.i (*0-385-28854-9*, Delacorte Pr.) Dell Publishing.

Fox, Paula. Lily & the Lost Boy. 1987. 160p. (J). (gr. 6-8). lib. bdg. 17.99 (*0-531-08320-9*); (YA). (gr. 7-12). pap. 16.95 (*0-531-05720-8*) Scholastic, Inc. (Orchard Bks.).

Galloway, Priscilla. Aleta et Penelope: Un Recit de la Grece Antique. Asselin, Michelle, tr. 1997. Tr. of Aleta & the Queen. (FRE., Illus.). 160p. (J). (gr. 5 up). pap. 19.95 (*1-55037-420-6*) Annick Pr., Ltd. CAN. *Dist:* Firefly Bks., Ltd.

—The Courtesan's Daughter. 2004. 272p. (YA). (gr. 7). mass mkt. 5.50 (*0-440-22902-2*, Laurel Leaf) Random Hse. Children's Bks.

—The Courtesan's Daughter. 2002. 272p. (YA). lib. bdg. 18.99 (*0-385-90052-X*); (gr. 7-12). 16.95 (*0-385-72907-3*) Random Hse., Inc.

Gigeroff, Alex K. Baba's Macedonian Socks. 1994. (Illus.). 32p. (J). per. 7.50 (*0-921369-14-X*) George, J. C. Enterprises.

Gramatky, Hardie. Nikos & the Sea God. 1963. (Illus.). (J). (gr. 1-3). 4.76 o.p. (*0-399-60492-8*) Putnam Publishing Group, The.

Green, Roger Lancelyn. The Luck of Troy. 1991. 176p. (J). (gr. 5 up). pap. 2.25 o.p. (*0-14-035103-5*, Puffin Bks.) Penguin Putnam Bks. for Young Readers.

—Tales of the Greek Heroes. 1995. (Puffin Classics Ser.). (Illus.). 288p. (YA). (gr. 4-7). pap. 4.99 (*0-14-036683-0*, Puffin Bks.) Penguin Putnam Bks. for Young Readers.

Guner, Kagan. The Children of Atlantis. 2002. (Illus.). 32p. 7.95 (*1-84059-325-3*) Milet Publishing, Ltd. GBR. *Dist:* Consortium Bk. Sales & Distribution.

—Icarus. 2002. (Illus.). 32p. 7.95 (*1-84059-326-1*) Milet Publishing, Ltd. GBR. *Dist:* Consortium Bk. Sales & Distribution.

Hazen, Lynn E. Mermaid Mary Margaret. 2003. (J). 15.95 (*1-58234-842-1*) Bloomsbury Publishing.

Hort, Lenny. Goatherd & the Shepherdess. 1995. (Illus.). 32p. (J). 15.99 o.p. (*0-8037-1352-5*); 15.89 o.p. (*0-8037-1353-3*) Penguin Putnam Bks. for Young Readers. (Dial Bks. for Young Readers).

Iliad. 1999. (YA). 9.95 (*1-56137-752-X*) Novel Units, Inc.

Jones, Allan Frewin. Blood Stone, Vol. 6. 2003. 176p. (J). pap. (*0-330-37476-1*) Macmillan Children's Bks.

Keene, Carolyn. Greek Odyssey: Passport to Romance #3. Greenberg, Anne, ed. 1992. (Nancy Drew Files: No. 74). 160p. (Orig.). (YA). (gr. 6 up). pap. 3.75 (*0-671-73078-9*, Simon Pulse) Simon & Schuster Children's Publishing.

Keep, Linda Lowery. Missing Piece in Greece. 2000. (Hannah & the Angels Ser.: No. 9). (Illus.). 128p. (gr. 3-7). pap. text 3.99 o.s.i (*0-375-80257-6*, Random Hse. Bks. for Young Readers) Random Hse. Children's Bks.

Kerisel, Francoise. Diogenes' Lantern. Mansot, Frederick, tr. from FRE. & illus. by. 2004. (J). (*0-89236-738-5*) Getty Pubns.

Kindl, Patrice. Lost in the Labyrinth: A Novel. 2002. 194p. (J). (gr. 5-9). tchr. ed. 16.00 (*0-618-16684-X*) Houghton Mifflin Co.

Korman, Susan. Megan in Ancient Greece. 1998. (Magic Attic Club Ser.). (Illus.). 80p. (gr. 2-6). 18.90 o.p. (*1-57513-143-9*, Magic Attic Pr.) Millbrook Pr., Inc.

—Megan in Ancient Greece. Bodnar, Judit, ed. 1998. (Magic Attic Club Ser.). (Illus.). 80p. (gr. 2-6). (J). 13.95 (*1-57513-128-5*); pap. 5.95 o.p. (*1-57513-127-7*) Millbrook Pr., Inc. (Magic Attic Pr.).

—Megan in Ancient Greece. 1998. (Magic Attic Club Ser.). (J). (gr. 2-6). 12.10 (*0-606-17141-X*) Turtleback Bks.

Lang, Andrew. Tales of Troy & Greece. 1978. (Illus.). 300p. (J). (gr. 5-8). pap. o.p. (*0-571-04984-2*) Faber & Faber Ltd.

—Tales of Troy & Greece. 2002. (Children's Classics). 256p. (J). (gr. 3-6). pap. 3.95 (*1-85326-172-6*) Wordsworth Editions, Ltd. GBR. *Dist:* Advanced Global Distribution Services.

Leighton, Margaret. Other Island, RS. 1971. 192p. (J). (gr. 7 up). 4.50 o.p. (*0-374-35671-8*, Farrar, Straus & Giroux (BYR)) Farrar, Straus & Giroux.

Lexau, Joan M. Archimedes Takes a Bath. 1969. (Illus.). (J). (gr. 2-5). lib. bdg. 6.89 o.p. (*0-690-09900-2*) HarperCollins Children's Bk. Group.

Lillington, Kenneth. Young Man of Morning. 1979. 176p. (J). (gr. 6-9). o.p. (*0-571-11421-0*) Faber & Faber Ltd.

Malam, John. Indiana Jones Explores Ancient Greece. 1996. (Illus.). 47p. (J). (gr. 5-8). 19.95 (*0-237-51221-1*) Evans Brothers, Ltd. GBR. *Dist:* Trafalgar Square.

Mara, Pam. The Greeks Pop-Up. 1997. (Ancient Civilizations Pop-Ups Ser.). (Illus.). 32p. (J). (gr. 4-9). pap. 9.00 (*0-906212-33-2*) Tarquin Pubns. GBR. *Dist:* Parkwest Pubns., Inc.

Mayer, Albert I., Jr. Olympiad. 1938. (Illus.). (YA). (gr. 7 up). 22.00 (*0-8196-0115-2*) Biblo & Tannen Booksellers & Pubs., Inc.

Mayne, William. Glass Ball. 1962. (J). (gr. 3-7). 5.50 o.p. (*0-525-30686-2*, Dutton) Dutton/Plume.

McCaughrean, Geraldine. The Odyssey. 1997. (Oxford Illustrated Classics Ser.). (Illus.). 96p. (J). (gr. 2-9). pap. 12.95 o.p. (*0-19-274153-5*) Oxford Univ. Pr., Inc.

McLaren, Clemence. Waiting for Odysseus. (Illus.). (YA). 2004. 192p. mass mkt. 5.99 (*0-689-86705-0*, Simon Pulse); 2000. 160p. (gr. 7-12). 16.95 (*0-689-82875-6*, Atheneum) Simon & Schuster Children's Publishing.

McMullan, Kate. Get to Work, Hercules! 2003. (Myth-o-Mania Ser.: Vol. 7). (Illus.). 160p. (J). pap. 4.99 (*0-7868-1670-8*, Volo) Hyperion Bks. for Children.

—Keep the Lid on It Pandora! 2003. (Myth-o-Mania Ser.: Vol. 6). (Illus.). 160p. (J). pap. 4.99 (*0-7868-1669-4*, Volo) Hyperion Bks. for Children.

Norfolk. In the Shape of a Boar. 2003. pap. 13.00 (*0-8021-3967-1*) Grove/Atlantic, Inc.

O'Malley, Kevin. Mount Olympus Basketball. 2003. (Illus.). 32p. (J). (gr. 2-6). 15.95 (*0-8027-8844-0*); lib. bdg. 16.95 (*0-8027-8845-9*) Walker & Co.

Oppenheim, Shulamith Levey. Yanni Rubbish. 2003. (Illus.). 32p. (J). (gr. k-3). 15.95 (*1-56397-668-4*) Boyds Mills Pr.

Orgel, Doris. Ariadne, Awake! 1999. (Illus.). 74p. (gr. 6-11). reprint ed. text 16.00 (*0-7881-6477-5*) DIANE Publishing Co.

—Ariadne, Awake! 1994. (Illus.). 80p. (J). 15.99 o.p. (*0-670-85158-2*, Viking) Penguin Putnam Bks. for Young Readers.

—We Goddesses: Athena, Aphrodite, Hera. 1999. (Illus.). 144p. (J). (gr. 5-9). pap. 22.95 o.p. (*0-7894-2586-6*) Dorling Kindersley Publishing, Inc.

Osborne, Mary Pope. Hour of the Olympics. unabr. ed. 2002. (Magic Tree House Ser. : Vol. 16). 70p. (J). (gr. k-4). pap. 17.00 incl. audio (*0-8072-0785-3*, LFTR 244 SP, Listening Library) Random Hse. Audio Publishing Group.

—Hour of the Olympics. 1998. (Magic Tree House Ser.: No. 16). (Illus.). 96p. (J). (gr. k-3). lib. bdg. 11.99 (*0-679-99062-3*); pap. 3.99 (*0-679-89062-9*) Random Hse., Inc.

—Hour of the Olympics. 1998. 10.04 (*0-606-15575-9*) Turtleback Bks.

Packard, Edward. Olympus: What Is the Secret of the Oracle. 1988. (Earth Inspectors Ser.). 112p. (J). pap. text 3.95 o.p. (*0-07-047995-X*) McGraw-Hill Cos., The.

Pike, Christopher, pseud. The Immortal. MacDonald, Patricia, ed. 1993. 224p. (J). (gr. 7 up). mass mkt. 3.99 (*0-671-74510-7*, Simon Pulse); (YA). (gr. 9 up). 14.00 o.p. (*0-671-87039-4*, Simon & Schuster Children's Publishing) Simon & Schuster Children's Publishing.

Ray, Mary. Eastern Beacon, RS. 1966. (Illus.). (J). (gr. 7 up). 3.50 o.p. (*0-374-31947-2*, Farrar, Straus & Giroux (BYR)) Farrar, Straus & Giroux.

—Standing Lions. 1979. (Fanfares Ser.). (Illus.). 170p. (J). (gr. 4 up). pap. o.p. (*0-571-11267-6*) Faber & Faber Ltd.

Richards, Jean. The First Olympic Games: A Gruesome Greek Myth with a Happy Ending. 2004. 32p. pap. 6.95 (*0-7613-2443-7*) Millbrook Pr., Inc.

Richards, Jean & Thacker, Kat, illus. The First Olympic Games: A Gruesome Greek Myth with a Happy Ending. 2000. 40p. (J). (gr. k-3). 23.90 (*0-7613-1311-7*) Millbrook Pr., Inc.

Rosen, Billi. Andi's War. 1989. 144p. (YA). (gr. 7 up). 13.95 o.p. (*0-525-44473-4*, Dutton Children's Bks.) Penguin Putnam Bks. for Young Readers.

Skolnick, Evan. My Fill of Phil. 1997. (Disney's Action Club Ser.). pap. text 4.50 (*1-57840-076-7*) Acclaim Bks.

Sophocles. Oedipus the King. 1983. (Enriched Classics Ser.). (J). (gr. 10 up). pap. 2.95 (*0-671-49946-7*, Washington Square Pr.) Simon & Schuster.

Steig. The Greek Project. 2000. (J). pap. 5.95 (*0-06-443576-8*) HarperCollins Children's Bk. Group.

Steig, William, illus. A Gift from Zeus: Sixteen Favorite Myths. 2001. 176p. (J). (gr. 9 up). 17.95 (*0-06-028405-6*); lib. bdg. 17.89 (*0-06-028406-4*) HarperCollins Children's Bk. Group. (Cotler, Joanna Bks.).

Talley, Linda. Plato's Journey. 1998. (Key Concepts in Personal Development Ser.). (Illus.). 32p. (J). (gr. k-4). 16.95 (*1-55942-100-2*, 7664) Marsh Media.

Yolen, Jane & Harris, Robert J. Hippolyta & the Curse of the Amazons. 2002. (Young Heroes Ser.: Bk. 2). 256p. (J). (gr. k-3). lib. bdg. 15.89 (*0-06-028737-3*) HarperCollins Children's Bk. Group.

—Odysseus in the Serpent Maze. 2001. (Young Heroes Ser.: Bk. 1). 256p. (J). (gr. 3-7). 15.95 (*0-06-028734-9*); (gr. 5 up). lib. bdg. 16.89 (*0-06-028735-7*) HarperCollins Children's Bk. Group.

—Odysseus in the Serpent Maze. 2002. (Young Heroes Ser.). 256p. (J). (gr. 7 up). pap. 5.99 (*0-06-440847-7*) HarperCollins Pubs.

GREECE, MODERN—FICTION

Forman, James. Ring the Judas Bell, RS. 1965. 224p. (J). (gr. 7 up). 4.95 o.p. (*0-374-36304-8*, Farrar, Straus & Giroux (BYR)) Farrar, Straus & Giroux.

—Shield of Achilles, RS. 1966. 224p. (J). (gr. 7 up). 3.95 o.p. (*0-374-36798-1*, Farrar, Straus & Giroux (BYR)) Farrar, Straus & Giroux.

Hairfield, Judy L. When the Dancing Ends. 1996. 163p. (Orig.). (YA). (gr. 7-12). pap. text 8.95 (*0-943864-79-8*) Davenport, May Pubs.

Hope, Laura Lee. The Bobbsey Twins & the Greek Hat Mystery. 1964. (Bobbsey Twins Ser.). (J). (gr. 3-5). 4.50 o.s.i (*0-448-08057-5*, Grosset & Dunlap) Penguin Putnam Bks. for Young Readers.

Rosen, Billi. Andi's War. 1991. (Illus.). 144p. (J). pap. 3.95 o.p. (*0-14-034404-7*, Puffin Bks.) Penguin Putnam Bks. for Young Readers.

Rydberg, Ernie & Rydberg, Lou. The Shadow Army. 1976. 160p. (J). 7.95 o.p. (*0-525-66493-9*, Dutton Children's Bks.) Penguin Putnam Bks. for Young Readers.

Sarton, May. Joanna & Ulysses. 1963. (Illus.). (J). (gr. 8 up). 4.95 o.p. (*0-393-08494-9*) Norton, W. W. & Co., Inc.

Storr, Catherine. Kate & the Island. 1978. (Illus.). 87p. (J). o.p. (*0-571-10119-4*) Faber & Faber Ltd.

Valencak, Hannelore. When Half-Gods Go. Crampton, Patricia, tr. from GER. 1976. 192p. (Orig.). (J). (gr. 7 up). 9.50 o.p. (*0-688-22077-0*); lib. bdg. 12.88 o.p. (*0-688-32077-5*) Morrow/Avon. (Morrow, William & Co.).

GREENLAND—FICTION

Conrad, Pam. Call Me Ahnighito. 1995. (Laura Geringer Bks.). (Illus.). 32p. (J). (gr. 1-4). lib. bdg. 14.89 o.p. (*0-06-023323-0*); (ps-4). 16.95 (*0-06-023322-2*, Geringer, Laura Bk.) HarperCollins Children's Bk. Group.

Hertz, Ole. Tobias Has a Birthday. Tobias, Tobi, tr. from DAN. 1984. Tr. of Tobias har Fodselsdag. (Illus.). 32p. (J). (gr. k-3). lib. bdg. 7.95 o.p. (*0-87614-261-7*, Carolrhoda Bks.) Lerner Publishing Group.

Newth, Mette. The Transformation, RS. Ingwersen, Faith, tr. from NOR. 2000. 208p. (J). (gr. 7-12). 16.00 (*0-374-37752-9*, Farrar, Straus & Giroux (BYR)) Farrar, Straus & Giroux.

GUAM—FICTION

Holt, Kimberly Willis. Keeper of the Night, ERS. 2003. (Illus.). 180p. (J). (gr. 6-12). 16.95 (*0-8050-6361-7*, Holt, Henry & Co. Bks. For Young Readers) Holt, Henry & Co.

—Keeper of the Night. unabr. ed. 2003. (J). (gr. 7). audio 25.00 (*0-8072-1570-8*, Listening Library) Random Hse. Audio Publishing Group.

Kerley, Barbara Kelly. Songs of Papa's Island. 1995. (Illus.). 64p. (J). (gr. 4-6). 14.95 o.p. (*0-395-71548-2*) Houghton Mifflin Co.

GUATEMALA—FICTION

Cameron, Ann. Colibri, RS. 2003. 240p. (J). 17.00 (*0-374-31519-1*, 53501559, Farrar, Straus & Giroux (BYR)) Farrar, Straus & Giroux.

Carling, Amelia Lau. Mama & Papa Have a Store. 1998. (Illus.). 32p. (J). (ps-3). 15.99 (*0-8037-2044-0*); 15.89 o.p. (*0-8037-2045-9*) Penguin Putnam Bks. for Young Readers. (Dial Bks. for Young Readers).

Czernecki, Stefan & Rhodes, Timothy. The Sleeping Bread. 1992. (Illus.). 40p. (J). (gr. k-4). 14.95 (*1-56282-183-0*) Hyperion Bks. for Children.

Franklin, Kristine L. Iguana Beach. 1997. (Illus.). (J). (gr. 1-4). 18.99 o.s.i (*0-517-70901-5*) Crown Publishing Group.

Ichikawa, Satomi. My Pig Amarillo: A Tale from Guatemala. 2003. (Illus.). 32p. (J). 15.99 (*0-399-23768-2*, Philomel) Penguin Putnam Bks. for Young Readers.

Martin, Marilyn S., tr. & illus. Pedro of Guatemala. 1997. Tr. of Pedro de Guatemala. (SPA.). 160p. (J). (gr. 3-6). pap. 5.35 (*0-7399-0084-6*, 2340.1) Rod & Staff Pubs., Inc.

Mikaelsen, Ben. Red Midnight. 224p. (J). (gr. 5 up). 2003. pap. 5.99 (*0-380-80561-8*); 2002. 15.95 (*0-380-97745-1*) HarperCollins Pubs.

Mikaelson, Ben. Red Midnight. 2002. 256p. (J). (gr. 5 up). lib. bdg. 15.89 (*0-06-001228-5*) HarperCollins Children's Bk. Group.

Palmer, Bernard. Danny Orlis & the Guatemala Adventure. 1963. (J). (gr. 5-10). pap. 1.50 o.p. (*0-8024-7221-4*) Moody Pr.

H

HAITI—FICTION

Bontemps, Arna & Hughes, Langston. Popo & Fifina. 2000. (Iona & Peter Opie Library of Children's Literature). (Illus.). 128p. (YA). pap. 8.95 o.p. (*0-19-513939-9*) Oxford Univ. Pr., Inc.

Bontemps, Arna W. & Hughes, Langston. Popo & Fifina. 1993. (Iona & Peter Opie Library of Children's Literature). (Illus.). 128p. (YA). (gr. 3 up). 16.95 o.p. (*0-19-508765-8*) Oxford Univ. Pr., Inc.

Danticat, Edwidge. Behind the Mountains: The Diary of Celiane Esperance. (First Person Fiction Ser.). (J). 2004. 192p. mass mkt. 16.95 (*0-439-37300-X*); 2002. 176p. (gr. 5-9). pap. 16.95 (*0-439-37299-2*) Scholastic, Inc. (Orchard Bks.).

Dunn, Stephen. The Wonderful Way Home: An Adventure in Haiti, One. 1990. (Illus.). 16p. (J). (ps-5). pap. 6.95 (*0-9679937-2-5*, 20520) Baptist Haiti Mission.

Lauture, Denize. Running the Road to ABC. 1996. (Illus.). 32p. (J). (gr. 1-5). 16.00 (*0-689-80507-1*, Simon & Schuster Children's Publishing) Simon & Schuster Children's Publishing.

Montero, Mayra. In the Palm of Darkness: A Novel. 1998. 192p. pap. 13.00 (*0-06-092906-5*, Perennial) HarperTrade.

Moore, Robin. The Man with the Silver Oar. 2002. 192p. (J). (gr. 5 up). 15.95 (*0-380-97877-6*) HarperCollins Children's Bk. Group.

—The Man with the Silver Oar. 2002. 192p. (J). (gr. 5 up). lib. bdg. 15.89 (*0-06-000048-1*) HarperCollins Pubs.

Sorenson, Jane B. In Another Land. 1985. (Jennifer Bks.). 128p. (J). (gr. 5-8). 4.99 o.p. (*0-87239-934-6*, 2984) Standard Publishing.

Stuart, Morna. Marassa & Midnight. 1969. (gr. 5-8). pap. 1.25 o.p. (*0-440-45322-4*) Dell Publishing.

Temple, Frances. Taste of Salt. 1994. (Trophy Bk.). 192p. (YA). (gr. 7 up). pap. 5.99 (*0-06-447136-5*, Harper Trophy) HarperCollins Children's Bk. Group.

—A Taste of Salt: A Story of Modern Haiti. 1992. 192p. (YA). (gr. 6-12). pap. 16.95 (*0-531-05459-4*); (gr. 7 up). lib. bdg. 17.99 (*0-531-08609-7*) Scholastic, Inc. (Orchard Bks.).

—A Taste of Salt: A Story of Modern Haiti. 1994. (J). 11.00 (*0-606-07117-2*) Turtleback Bks.

—Tonight, by Sea. 1997. (Illus.). 160p. (J). (gr. 5 up). pap. 5.99 (*0-06-440670-9*, Harper Trophy) HarperCollins Children's Bk. Group.

—Tonight, by Sea. 1995. 160p. (J). (gr. 7 up). (J). lib. bdg. 16.99 (*0-531-08749-2*); (YA). pap. 15.95 (*0-531-06899-4*) Scholastic, Inc. (Orchard Bks.).

—Tonight, by Sea. 1997. 11.00 (*0-606-10955-2*) Turtleback Bks.

Van Laan, Nancy. Mama Rocks, Papa Sings. 1994. (Illus.). 40p. (J). (ps-2). 15.00 o.s.i (*0-679-84016-8*, Knopf Bks. for Young Readers) Random Hse. Children's Bks.

Williams, Karen L. Painted Dreams. 1998. (Illus.). 40p. (J). (gr. k-3). 16.99 (*0-688-13901-9*) HarperCollins Children's Bk. Group.

—Painted Dreams. 1998. (Illus.). 40p. (J). (gr. k-3). 15.89 (*0-688-13902-7*, Morrow, William & Co.) Morrow/Avon.

Williams, Karen Lynn. Tap-Tap. (Carry-Along Book & Cassette Favorites Ser.). (Illus.). (J). (ps-3). 1996. 32p. pap. 9.95 o.p. incl. audio (*0-395-72087-7*, 111767); 1995. 48p. pap. 6.95 (*0-395-72086-9*); 1994. 48p. lib. bdg., tchr. ed. 16.00 (*0-395-65617-6*) Houghton Mifflin Co. Trade & Reference Div. (Clarion Bks.).

—Tap-Tap. 1994. (J). 11.15 o.p. (*0-606-08268-9*) Turtleback Bks.

HARLEM (NEW YORK, N.Y.)—FICTION

Childress, Alice. A Hero Ain't Nothin' but a Sandwich. 1977. 128p. (YA). (gr. 7 up). pap. 4.50 o.p. (*0-380-00132-2*, Avon Bks.) Morrow/Avon.

—A Hero Ain't Nothin' but a Sandwich. l.t. ed. 1989. 144p. (J). lib. bdg. 16.95 o.s.i (*1-55736-112-6*, Cornerstone Bks.) Pages, Inc.

—A Hero Ain't Nothin' but a Sandwich. 2000. 128p. (J). (gr. 7-12). pap. 5.99 (*0-698-11854-5*) Penguin Putnam Bks. for Young Readers.

—A Hero Ain't Nothin' but a Sandwich. 1973. 128p. (YA). (gr. 5-9). 15.95 o.p. (*0-698-20278-3*, Coward-McCann) Putnam Publishing Group, The.

—A Hero Ain't Nothin' but a Sandwich. 2000. 11.04 (*0-606-17821-X*); 1973. (YA). 9.60 o.p. (*0-606-03528-1*) Turtleback Bks.

Coleman, Evelyn. Mystery of the Dark Tower. 2000. (American Girl Collection: Bk. 6). (Illus.). 160p. (J). (gr. 5-9). pap. 5.95 (*1-58485-084-1*); 9.95 (*1-58485-085-X*) Pleasant Co. Pubns. (American Girl).

—Mystery of the Dark Tower. 2000. (History Mysteries Ser.). 12.00 (*0-606-18356-6*) Turtleback Bks.

Collier, Bryan. Uptown, ERS. (Illus.). 32p. (J). 2004. pap. 6.95 (*0-8050-7399-X*); 2000. 16.95 (*0-8050-5721-8*) Holt, Henry & Co. (Holt, Henry & Co. Bks. For Young Readers).

Creary, Eve M. A Silent Witness in Harlem. 2002. (Mysteries in Time Ser.: Vol. 10). (Illus.). 96p. (J). (gr. 3-8). lib. bdg. 14.95 (*1-893110-27-3*) Silver Moon Pr.

Grimes, Nikki. Jazmin's Notebook. 2002. (Illus.). (J). 12.34 (*0-7587-0368-6*) Book Wholesalers, Inc.

—Jazmin's Notebook. 112p. (YA). 1998. (gr. 8-12). 15.99 (*0-8037-2224-9*, Dial Bks. for Young Readers); 2000. (gr. 5-9). reprint ed. pap. 5.99 (*0-14-130702-1*, Puffin Bks.) Penguin Putnam Bks. for Young Readers.

—Jazmin's Notebook. 2000. (Illus.). (J). 11.04 (*0-606-18414-7*) Turtleback Bks.

Guy, Rosa. New Guys Around the Block. 1983. 192p. (J). (gr. 7 up). 11.95 o.s.i (*0-385-29247-3*, Delacorte Pr.) Dell Publishing.

—New Guys Around the Block. 1987. 208p. (J). (gr. k-12). mass mkt. 2.95 o.s.i (*0-440-95888-1*, Laurel Leaf) Random Hse. Children's Bks.

—Ruby. 1979. pap. 2.25 o.p. (*0-553-23367-X*) Bantam Bks.

—Ruby. 1991. 192p. (YA). mass mkt. 3.99 o.s.i (*0-440-21130-1*) Dell Publishing.

—Ruby. 1976. 192p. (YA). 8.95 o.p. (*0-670-61023-2*) Viking Penguin.

Kuklin, Susan & Byrd, Donald. Harlem Nutcracker. 2001. (Illus.). 48p. (J). 19.99 (*0-7868-0633-8*) Disney Pr.

Levine, Gail Carson. Dave at Night. 288p. (J). 2001. (gr. 3-7). pap. 5.99 (*0-06-440747-0*, Harper Trophy); 1999. (Illus.). (gr. k-3). lib. bdg. 16.89 (*0-06-028154-5*); 1999. (gr. k-4). 16.99 (*0-06-028153-7*) HarperCollins Children's Bk. Group.

—Dave at Night. unabr. ed. 2001. 278p. (J). (gr. 4-6). pap. 37.00 incl. audio (*0-8072-8379-7*, YA174SP, Listening Library) Random Hse. Audio Publishing Group.

—Dave at Night. (YA). 1999. pap., stu. ed. 69.95 incl. audio (*0-7887-3794-5*, 41038); 2001. (gr. 5-8). audio compact disk 58.00 Recorded Bks., LLC.

—Dave at Night. l.t. ed. 2001. (Illus.). 295p. (J). (gr. 4-7). 22.95 (*0-7862-2972-1*) Thorndike Pr.

Lewis, Zoe. Keisha Discovers Harlem. 1998. (Magic Attic Club Ser.). (Illus.). 80p. (gr. 2-6). 18.90 (*1-57513-144-7*, Magic Attic Pr.) Millbrook Pr., Inc.

—Keisha Discovers Harlem. Bodnar, Judit, ed. 1998. (Magic Attic Club Ser.). (Illus.). 80p. (gr. 2-6). (J). 13.95 (*1-57513-130-7*); pap. 5.95 o.p. (*1-57513-129-3*) Millbrook Pr., Inc. (Magic Attic Pr.).

—Keisha Discovers Harlem. 1998. (Magic Attic Club Ser.). (J). (gr. 2-6). 12.10 (*0-606-16855-9*) Turtleback Bks.

Littlesugar, Amy. Tree of Hope. 1999. (Illus.). 40p. (J). (ps-3). 16.99 o.s.i (*0-399-23300-8*, Philomel) Penguin Putnam Bks. for Young Readers.

Mohr, Nicholasa. Nilda. 2nd ed. 1986. 292p. (YA). (ps up). pap. 11.95 (*0-934770-61-1*) Arte Publico Pr.

—Nilda. 1973. (Illus.). 272p. (YA). (gr. 5 up). 8.96 o.p. (*0-06-024331-7*); lib. bdg. 13.89 o.p. (*0-06-024332-5*) HarperCollins Children's Bk. Group.

Myers, Walter Dean. Bearer Of Dreams. 2003. 192p. (J). (gr. 5 up). lib. bdg. 16.89 (*0-06-029522-8*, Amistad Pr.) HarperTrade.

—Beast. 2003. 224p. (J). pap. 16.95 (*0-439-36841-3*) Scholastic, Inc.

—The Dream Bearer. 2003. 192p. (J). (gr. 5 up). 15.99 (*0-06-029521-X*, Amistad Pr.) HarperTrade.

—The Dream Bearer. l.t. ed. 2003. 207p. (J). 25.95 (*0-7862-5923-X*) Thorndike Pr.

—Handbook for Boys: A Novel. 2002. (Illus.). 192p. (J). (gr. 5 up). 15.95 (*0-06-029146-X*); lib. bdg. 15.89 (*0-06-029147-8*) HarperCollins Children's Bk. Group.

—Handbook for Boys: A Novel. 2003. (Amistad Ser.). 224p. (J). (gr. 5 up). pap. 5.99 (*0-06-440930-9*) HarperCollins Pubs.

—Handbook for Boys: A Novel. unabr. ed. 2002. (gr. 5 up). pap. 24.00 incl. audio (*0-06-008968-7*, HarperAudio) HarperTrade.

—Motown & Didi: A Love Story. 2002. (Illus.). (J). 13.40 (*0-7587-0384-8*) Book Wholesalers, Inc.

—Motown & Didi: A Love Story. 1984. 192p. (YA). (gr. 7 up). 14.95 o.p. (*0-670-49062-8*, Viking Children's Bks.) Penguin Putnam Bks. for Young Readers.

—Motown & Didi: A Love Story. 1987. (Laurel-Leaf Contemporary Fiction Ser.). 176p. (YA). (gr. 7 up). mass mkt. 4.99 o.s.i (*0-440-95762-1*, Laurel Leaf) Random Hse. Children's Bks.

—Motown & Didi: A Love Story. 1987. (Laurel-Leaf Contemporary Fiction Ser.). (J). 11.04 (*0-606-03623-7*) Turtleback Bks.

—The Mouse Rap. Bacha, Andy, ed. & contrib. by by. 1992. (Trophy Bk.). 192p. (J). (gr. 5-9). pap. 5.99 (*0-06-440356-4*, Harper Trophy) HarperCollins Children's Bk. Group.

—The Mouse Rap. 1990. 192p. (J). (gr. 5-9). 14.95 o.p. (*0-06-024343-0*); lib. bdg. 14.89 o.s.i (*0-06-024344-9*) HarperCollins Children's Bk. Group.

—The Mouse Rap. 3rd ed. pap. text 3.95 (*0-13-800087-5*) Prentice Hall (Schl. Div.).

—Scorpions. (Trophy Bk.). 224p. (J). (gr. 7 up). 1996. pap. 5.99 (*0-06-440623-7*, Harper Trophy); 1990. pap. 5.99 (*0-06-447066-0*, Harper Trophy); 1988. 16.99 (*0-06-024364-3*); 1988. (Illus.). lib. bdg. 16.89 (*0-06-024365-1*) HarperCollins Children's Bk. Group.

—Scorpions. unabr. ed. 1997. (J). Class Set. 105.30 incl. audio (*0-7887-2585-8*, 46431); Homework Set. 48.20 incl. audio (*0-7887-1599-2*, 40630) Recorded Bks., LLC.

—Scorpions. 1990. 12.00 (*0-606-09833-X*); (J). 12.00 (*0-606-04533-3*) Turtleback Bks.

—The Young Landlords. 1980. (YA). pap. 1.95 o.p. (*0-380-52191-1*, 67561-7, Avon Bks.) Morrow/Avon.

—The Young Landlords. (ALA Notable Bk.). 1989. 208p. (J). (gr. 4-7). pap. 5.99 (*0-14-034244-3*, Puffin Bks.); 1979. (YA). (gr. 7 up). 11.50 o.p. (*0-670-79454-6*, Viking Children's Bks.) Penguin Putnam Bks. for Young Readers.

—The Young Landlords. 1992. (J). (gr. 6-10). 20.75 (*0-8446-6569-X*) Smith, Peter Pub., Inc.

—The Young Landlords. 1979. (J). 12.04 (*0-606-04432-9*) Turtleback Bks.

—145th Street: Short Stories. 2000. 160p. (YA). (gr. 7-12). 15.95 (*0-385-32137-6*, Delacorte Pr.) Dell Publishing.

—145th Street: Short Stories. 2001. 160p. (YA). (gr. 7 up). mass mkt. 5.50 (*0-440-22916-2*, Laurel Leaf) Random Hse. Children's Bks.

—145th Street: Short Stories. 2001. 11.55 (*0-606-22414-9*) Turtleback Bks.

Nishiyama, Yuriko. Harlem Beat 2. 1999. (Harlem Beat Ser.: Vol. 2). (Illus.). 192p. (J). (gr. 7-12). mass mkt. 9.95 (*1-892213-17-6*, Pocket Mixx) Mixx Entertainment, Inc.

Ringgold, Faith. Tar Beach. 2002. (Illus.). (J). 14.79 (*0-7587-5352-7*) Book Wholesalers, Inc.

—Tar Beach. (Book & Doll Packages Ser.). (Illus.). 32p. (ps-4). 1994. (J). 10.00 o.s.i (*0-517-59961-9*, Random Hse. Bks. for Young Readers); 1991. (J). lib. bdg. 18.99 (*0-517-58031-4*, Knopf Bks. for Young Readers); 1991. 18.00 (*0-517-58030-6*, Random Hse. Bks. for Young Readers) Random Hse. Children's Bks.

—Tar Beach. 1996. (ps-3). (Illus.). 32p. pap. 6.99 (*0-517-88544-1*); (J). 5.99 o.s.i (*0-517-58984-2*) Random Hse. Value Publishing.

—Tar Beach. 1996. (J). 13.14 (*0-606-10950-1*) Turtleback Bks.

Smalls, Irene. Don't Say Ain't. (Illus.). 32p. (J). (gr. k-3). 2004. pap. 6.95 (*1-57091-382-X*); 2003. 15.95 (*1-57091-381-1*) Charlesbridge Publishing, Inc.

—Irene & the Big, Fine Nickel. (J). (ps-3). 1996. (Illus.). 32p. pap. 5.95 o.p. (*0-316-79898-3*); 1994. pap. (*0-316-79879-7*); 2nd ed. 2003. (Illus.). 32p. pap. 5.99 (*0-316-69832-6*); Vol. 1. 1991. (Illus.). 15.95 o.p. (*0-316-79871-1*) Little Brown & Co.

—Irene & the Big, Fine Nickel. 1991. (J). 11.15 o.p. (*0-606-08783-4*) Turtleback Bks.

Taylor, Debbie. A Special Day in Harlem. Morrison, Frank, tr. & illus. by. 2004. (J). (*1-58430-165-1*) Lee & Low Bks., Inc.

Wright, Richard. Rite of Passage. (Trophy Bk.). 1996. (Illus.). 160p. (J). (gr. 7 up). pap. 5.99 (*0-06-447111-X*, Harper Trophy); 1994. 128p. (YA). lib. bdg. 13.89 o.p. (*0-06-023420-2*); 1994. 128p. (YA). (gr. 7 up). 12.95 o.p. (*0-06-023419-9*) HarperCollins Children's Bk. Group.

—Rite of Passage. 1996. 11.00 (*0-606-08592-0*) Turtleback Bks.

HAWAII—FICTION

Aloha Bear - Footprint Detective. 2002. (J). pap. 8.99 (*0-89610-290-4*) Island Heritage Publishing.

Arkin, Anthony D. Captain Hawaii. 1997. 256p. (YA). (gr. 6-9). pap. 3.95 (*0-06-440583-4*, Harper Trophy); 1994. 224p. (J). (gr. 3-7). lib. bdg. 14.89 o.p. (*0-06-021509-7*); 1994. 256p. (J). (gr. 6-9). 15.00 o.p. (*0-06-021508-9*) HarperCollins Children's Bk. Group.

Asato, Dennis. A Dolphin Day in Hawaii. (Illus.). 50p. (J). (ps-1). 2001. pap. 9.95 (*0-9702618-2-9*); 1999. 12.00 (*0-9653971-8-1*) Anoai Pr.

Ay, Joy Mitsu. Paniolo Pete & the Wild Pua'a. 2001. (J). 8.99 (*0-89610-348-X*) Island Heritage Publishing.

Bates, Gale. The Jewel in the Forest. 2000. (J). 10.99 (*0-89610-440-0*) Island Heritage Publishing.

Bikle, Edie. Kapono & the Turtle. 2001. (J). 10.99 (*0-89610-199-1*) Island Heritage Publishing.

Bridgman, C. A. My Hawaiian Smile. 1996. (Illus.). 32p. (J). (ps-4). 14.95 (*0-9659382-1-2*) Immanuel Pr.

—Santa's Hawaiian Vacation. (J). 14.95 (*0-681-32827-4*) Booklines Hawaii, Ltd.

—Santa's Hawaiian Vacation. 1996. (Illus.). 32p. (J). (ps-4). 14.95 (*0-9659382-0-4*) Immanuel Pr.

Brouwer, Sigmund. The Volcano of Doom. 2002. (Accidental Detectives). 144p. (J). pap. 5.99 (*0-7642-2564-2*) Bethany Hse. Pubs.

Budar, Valjeanne, ed. Ke Ahiahi Mamua O Kalikimaka Vol. II: 'Twas the Night Before Christmas in Hawaii. Roy, Lynette A., tr. 1994. (Illus.). 48p. (J). (gr. k-6). 12.95 (*1-880188-92-9*) Bess Pr., Inc.

Bunting, Eve. Yesterday's Island. 1979. (Illus.). (J). (gr. 5-9). 6.95 o.p. (*0-7232-6166-0*, Warne, Frederick) Penguin Putnam Bks. for Young Readers.

Cadwallader, Sharon. Cookie McCorkle & the Case of the King's Ghost. 1991. (J). pap. 2.99 (*0-380-76350-8*, Avon Bks.) Morrow/Avon.

Carolan, Joanna F., illus. Ten Days in Hawaii. 2002. 32p. (J). 19.95 (*0-9715333-4-2*) Banana Patch Pr.

Corcoran, Barbara. Make No Sound. 1977. (J). (gr. 5-8). 6.95 o.p. (*0-689-30580-X*, Atheneum) Simon & Schuster Children's Publishing.

—The Shadowed Path. 1985. (Moonstone Novels Ser.: No. 2). 160p. (Orig.). (J). (gr. 5 up). pap. (*0-671-50781-8*, Simon Pulse) Simon & Schuster Children's Publishing.

Courtney, Dayle. Escape from Eden. 1981. (Thorne Twins Adventure Bks.). (Illus.). 192p. (Orig.). (J). (gr. 5 up). pap. 2.98 o.p. (*0-87239-467-0*, 2712) Standard Publishing.

Dano, Helen M. The Little Makana. 1994. (Illus.). 32p. (J). (gr. k-3). 8.95 (*1-880188-93-7*) Bess Pr., Inc.

Davids, Hollace & Davids, Paul. The Fires of Pele: Mark Twain's Legendary Lost Journal. 1986. (Illus.). 56p. (Orig.). (YA). pap. 9.95 (*0-939031-00-0*) Pictorial Legends.

Denenberg, Barry. Early Sunday Morning: The Pearl Harbor Diary of Amber Billows, Hawaii, 1941. 2001. (Dear America Ser.). (Illus.). 192p. (J). (gr. 4-9). pap. 10.95 (*0-439-32874-8*) Scholastic, Inc.

Duey, Kathleen. Janey G. Blue: Pearl Harbor 1941. 2001. (American Diaries Ser.: No. 18). (Illus.). 144p. (J). (gr. 3-7). pap. 4.99 (*0-689-84404-2*, Aladdin) Simon & Schuster Children's Publishing.

Ehlers, Sabine. The Bossy Hawaiian Moon. 1980. (Illus.). 32p. (J). (ps-1). pap. 3.95 (*0-930492-15-3*) Hawaiian Service, Inc.

Entz, Susan & Galarza, Sheri. Menehune Mischief. 1999. (Hawaiian Values Ser.: Vol. 5). (Illus.). 24p. (J). (ps-2). pap. 3.71 (*1-57306-091-7*) Bess Pr., Inc.

—The Mystery of the Shark & the Poi. 1999. (Hawaiian Values Ser.: Vol. 1). (Illus.). 24p. (J). (ps-2). pap. 3.71 (*1-57306-087-9*) Bess Pr., Inc.

Feeney, Stephanie. Hawaii Is a Rainbow. 1985. (Kolowalu Bks.). (Illus.). 64p. (J). (ps-3). 12.95 (*0-8248-1007-4*, Kolowalu Bk.) Univ. of Hawaii Pr.

Feeney, Stephanie & Fielding, Ann. Ka Pili Kahakai: Na Mea Ola o ke Kai o Hawai'i Nei. Wilson, William H., tr. from ENG. 1993. Orig. Title: Sand to Sea. (HAW.). 64p. (J). (gr. 4-7). reprint ed. pap. 8.95 (*0-9645646-2-9*) Aha Punana Leo.

Fellows, Rebecca N. A Lei for Tutu. 1998. (Illus.). 32p. (J). (gr. 1-3). lib. bdg. 14.95 o.p. (*0-8075-4426-4*) Whitman, Albert & Co.

Funai, Mamoru. Moke & Poki in the Rain Forest. 1972. (I Can Read Bks.). (Illus.). 64p. (J). (ps-3). lib. bdg. 9.89 o.p. (*0-06-021927-0*) HarperCollins Children's Bk. Group.

George, Jean Craighead. Dear Katie, the Volcano Is a Girl. 32p. (J). pap. (*0-7868-1178-1*); 1998. (Illus.). (gr. 2-5). 14.95 (*0-7868-0314-2*); 1998. (Illus.). (gr. 2-5). lib. bdg. 15.49 (*0-7868-2254-6*) Hyperion Bks. for Children.

Goodman, Robert & Spicer, Robert A. Urashima Taro. 2nd ed. (Illus.). 72p. (J). 15.95 o.p. (*0-89610-276-9*, 24019-000) Island Heritage Publishing.

Goudge, Eileen. Hawaiian Christmas. 1986. (Super Seniors Ser.: No. 2). (J). (gr. 6 up). mass mkt. 2.95 o.s.i (*0-440-93649-7*, Laurel Leaf) Random Hse. Children's Bks.

Guback, Georgia. Luka's Quilt. 1994. (Illus.). 32p. (J). (ps-3). 16.99 (*0-688-12154-3*); lib. bdg. 13.93 o.p. (*0-688-12155-1*) HarperCollins Children's Bk. Group. (Greenwillow Bks.).

Gunn, Robin Jones. Island Dreamer. rev. ed. 1999. (Christy Miller Ser.: Vol. 5). 176p. (J). (gr. 7-12). pap. 6.99 (*1-56179-718-9*) Bethany Hse. Pubs.

—Island Dreamer. 1998. (Christy Miller Ser.: Vol. 5). 184p. (YA). (gr. 7-11). pap. 5.99 o.p. (*1-56179-072-9*) Focus on the Family Publishing.

Hale, Chaika P. Mama Is Hapai. l.t. ed. 1998. (Illus.). 32p. (J). (gr. 1-6). 14.00 (*0-9653971-2-2*) Anoai Pr.

Hall, Pat. The Kona Town Musicians. 1998. (Illus.). 32p. (J). (ps-5). 9.95 (*0-9633493-6-8*) Pacific Greetings.

Hamilton, Elizabeth L. Date with Responsibility. 2003. (Character-in-Action Ser.: Bk. 2). 384p. (YA). per. 19.95 (*0-9713749-0-2*) Quiet Impact, Inc.

Hamilton, Gail. Love Comes to Eunice K. O'Herlihy. 1977. (J). (gr. 5-8). 5.95 o.p. (*0-689-30584-2*, Atheneum) Simon & Schuster Children's Publishing.

Han, C. C. Ponopono. 2002. pap. 8.99 (*0-89610-151-7*) Island Heritage Publishing.

Harder, Ethel & Fujimoto, Janne. Spunky: A Kona Nightingale. 1995. (Illus.). 11p. spiral bd. 6.50 (*1-881161-14-5*) Japanese American National Museum.

Harwood, Pearl A. Widdles. 1966. (Illus.). (J). (gr. k-5). lib. bdg. 3.95 o.p. (*0-8225-0257-7*) Lerner Publishing Group.

Hayashi, Leslie Ann. Fables from the Garden. 1998. (Illus.). 40p. (J). (gr. 3-6). 14.95 (*0-8248-2036-3*, Kolowalu Bk.) Univ. of Hawaii Pr.

—Fables from the Sea. 2000. (Kolowalu Bks.). (Illus.). 40p. (J). (ps-5). 14.95 (*0-8248-2224-2*) Univ. of Hawaii Pr.

Herndon, Ernest. Trouble at Bamboo Bay. 1996. (Eric Sterling, Secret Agent Ser.: Bk. 6). 128p. (YA). (gr. 8-12). pap. 5.99 (*0-310-20730-4*) Zondervan.

Holder, Nancy. Pearl Harbor 1941. 2001. (Illus.). 208p. (YA). (gr. 9-12). pap. 4.99 (*0-671-03927-X*, Simon Pulse) Simon & Schuster Children's Publishing.

Hope, Laura Lee. The Bobbsey Twins in Volcano Land. 1961. (Bobbsey Twins Ser.). (Illus.). (J). (gr. 3-5). 4.50 o.s.i (*0-448-08054-0*, Grosset & Dunlap) Penguin Putnam Bks. for Young Readers.

Hossack, Sylvie A. Green Mango Magic. (Avon Camelot Bks.). 128p. (J). (gr. 3-7). 1998. 14.00 (*0-380-97613-7*); Vol. 1. 1999. pap. 4.95 (*0-380-79601-5*, Harper Trophy) HarperCollins Children's Bk. Group.

—Green Mango Magic. 1998. 10.04 (*0-606-17328-5*) Turtleback Bks.

Hughes, Dean. Lucky in Love. 1993. (Lucky Ladd Ser.: No. 9). 161p. (Orig.). (J). (gr. 3-7). pap. 4.95 (*0-87579-805-5*, Cinnamon Tree) Deseret Bk. Co.

Kapono, Henry. A Beautiful Hawaiian Day. 2000. 32p. (J). bds. 9.95 (*1-56647-346-2*) Booklines Hawaii, Ltd.

Keene, Carolyn. Mystery on Maui. 1998. (Nancy Drew Mystery Stories Ser.: No. 143). (J). (gr. 3-6). 10.04 (*0-606-13645-2*) Turtleback Bks.

Kelly, Jack. Keoni's Dream. 1999. 17.95 (*0-9662777-1-6*) Pleiades Publishing.

Kiehm, Eve B. Plantation Child & Other Stories. 1995. (Illus.). 80p. (J). (gr. 3-6). 9.95 (*0-8248-1596-3*, Kolowalu Bk.) Univ. of Hawaii Pr.

Koski, Mary B. The Stowaway Fairy in Hawaii. 1991. (Illus.). 36p. (J). (gr. k-5). 12.95 (*0-89610-225-4*) Island Heritage Publishing.

Kremer, Marcia. Aloha Love. 1995. (Sweet Dreams Ser.: No. 226). 160p. (YA). pap. 3.50 o.s.i (*0-553-56680-6*) Bantam Bks.

Krulik, Nancy E., et al. Hawaiian Beach Party. 1997. (You're Invited to Mary-Kate & Ashley's Ser.). 48p. (J). (gr. 2-4). pap. 12.95 (*0-590-88012-8*) Scholastic, Inc.

Kulling, Monica. Go, Stitch, Go! 2002. (Step into Reading Ser.). (Illus.). 32p. (J). (ps-1). pap. 3.99 (*0-7364-1350-2*); lib. bdg. 11.99 (*0-7364-8010-2*) Random Hse. Children's Bks. (RH/Disney).

Lantz, Francess L. Luna Bay: Hawaii Five-Go!, No. 5. 2003. 176p. mass mkt. 4.99 (*0-06-057374-0*, HarperEntertainment) Morrow/Avon.

Lapka, Fay S. The Sea, the Song & the Trumpetfish. 1991. (Young Adult Fiction Ser.). 160p. (Orig.). (YA). (gr. 7-12). pap. 6.99 o.p. (*0-87788-754-3*, Shaw) WaterBrook Pr.

Lipkind, William. Boy of the Islands. 1955. (Illus.). (J). (gr. 2-5). 5.95 o.p. (*0-15-211061-5*) Harcourt Children's Bks.

Matsumoto, Lisa. Beyond 'Ohi'a Valley: Adventures in a Hawaiian Rainforest. 1996. (Illus.). 36p. (J). (gr. 3-6). 16.95 (*0-9647491-2-2*) Lehua, Inc.

Matsuura, Richard & Matsuura, Ruth. Ali'i Kai. (Illus.). (J). 7.95 (*1-887916-05-9*) Orchid Isle Publishing Co.

—Hawaiian Christmas Story. (Illus.). (J). 8.95 (*1-887916-01-6*) Orchid Isle Publishing Co.

Mccann, Jesse Leo. Scooby-Doo & the Tiki's Curse. 2004. (Scooby-Doo Ser.). 24p. (J). mass mkt. 3.50 (*0-439-54604-4*, Scholastic Paperbacks) Scholastic, Inc.

McGrath, E. J. The Magic of Believing. 2002. pap. 8.99 (*0-89610-200-9*) Island Heritage Publishing.

McLaren, Clemence. Dance for the Land. 1999. 128p. (J). (gr. 5-9). 16.00 (*0-689-82393-2*, Atheneum) Simon & Schuster Children's Publishing.

Momi Tropical Water Hide & Seek. 2002. (J). 8.99 (*0-89610-349-8*) Island Heritage Publishing.

Mower, Nancy A. Tutu Kane & Granpa. 1989. (Illus.). 32p. (J). (ps). 8.95 (*0-916630-66-8*) Press Pacifica, Ltd.

Napoleon, Kawika. 'Ai'ai. Wilson, William & Cleeland, Hokulani, eds. 1993. (HAW., Illus.). 36p. (J). (gr. 3-5). pap. 3.95 incl. audio (*0-9645646-9-6*) Aha Punana Leo.

Nimori, Tomoe, et al. Kona Coffee Days. 1995. 25p. spiral bd. 7.50 (*1-881161-13-7*) Japanese American National Museum.

Nunes, Shiho S. The Power of the Stone. 2002. mass mkt. 4.99 (*0-89610-283-1*) Island Heritage Publishing.

O'Connor, Maura. Flowing to the Sea. Wong, Keola, tr. from HAW. 1994. (Illus.). (J). (gr. 4-6). pap. 14.95 (*1-882163-19-2*) Moanalua Gardens Foundation.

Oetting, Rae. Keiki of the Islands. 1970. (Illus.). 96p. (J). (gr. 3 up). lib. bdg. 10.95 (*0-87783-018-5*); pap. 3.94 (*0-87783-096-7*) Oddo Publishing, Inc.

Olsen, E. A. Killer in the Trap. 1970. (Oceanography Ser.). (Illus.). 48p. (J). (gr. 3 up). pap. 10.60 incl. audio (*0-87783-190-4*); lib. bdg. 10.95 (*0-87783-019-3*); pap. 3.94 (*0-87783-097-5*) Oddo Publishing, Inc.

Olsen, Mary-Kate & Olsen, Ashley. Island Girls. 2002. (Two of a Kind Ser.: 23). 112p. (gr. 3-7). mass mkt. 4.99 (*0-06-106663-X*) HarperCollins Pubs.

Osborne, Mary Pope. High Tide in Hawaii. 2003. (Magic Tree House Ser.). (Illus.). 96p. (gr. 1-4). lib. bdg. 11.99 (*0-375-90616-9*, Random Hse. Bks. for Young Readers) Random Hse. Children's Bks.

Pike, Christopher, pseud. Bury Me Deep. 2001. (J). 10.55 (*0-606-21093-8*) Turtleback Bks.

Pitchford, Gene. Young Folks' Hawaiian Time. 1965. (Illus.). (J). (ps). pap. 3.00 o.p. (*0-87505-275-4*) Borden Publishing Co.

Rand, Gloria. Aloha, Salty!, ERS. 1996. (Illus.). 32p. (J). (ps-2). 15.95 o.p. (*0-8050-3429-3*, Holt, Henry & Co. Bks. For Young Readers) Holt, Henry & Co.

Random House Books for Young Readers Staff, ed. Hawaiian Shirt. 1998. (J). pap. 3.25 (*0-679-89413-6*, Random Hse. Bks. for Young Readers) Random Hse. Children's Bks.

Rappolt, Miriam E. One Paddle, Two Paddle: Hawaiian Teen Age Mystery & Suspense Stories. Pultz, Jane W., ed. 1993. (Illus.). 190p. (YA). (gr. 7-12). 10.95 o.p. (*0-916630-30-7*); tchr. ed. 2.00 o.p. (*0-916630-33-1*); stu. ed. 4.00 o.p. (*0-916630-32-3*); pap. 10.95 (*0-916630-69-2*) Press Pacifica, Ltd.

—Queen Emma: A Woman of Vision. 1991. (Illus.). (Orig.). (YA). pap. 12.95 (*0-916630-68-4*) Press Pacifica, Ltd.

Rattigan, Jama K. Dumpling Soup. 1993. (Illus.). 32p. (J). (gr. 4-8). 16.95 o.p. (*0-316-73445-4*) Little Brown & Co.

Reid, Mary C. Big Island Search. 1996. (Backpack Mystery Ser.: No. 2). (Illus.). 80p. (J). (gr. 2-5). pap. 3.99 o.p. (*1-55661-716-X*) Bethany Hse. Pubs.

Rivenburgh, Viola K. Tales of the Menehune, the Little Pixie Folk of Hawaii. 1980. (Illus.). 48p. (J). pap. 3.50 o.p. (*0-918146-19-4*) Peninsula Publishing, Inc.

Roddy, Lee. The Legend of Fire. 1989. (Ladd Family Adventure Ser.: Vol. 2). 148p. (J). (gr. 3-6). reprint ed. pap. 5.99 o.p. (*0-929608-17-8*) Focus on the Family Publishing.

—Panic in the Wild Waters. 1995. (Ladd Family Adventure Ser.: No. 12). (J). (gr. 3-7). pap. 5.99 o.p. (*1-56179-392-2*) Focus on the Family Publishing.

—Terror at Forbidden Falls. 1993. (Ladd Family Adventure Ser.: Vol. 8). (J). (gr. 3-7). pap. 5.99 o.p. (*1-56179-137-7*) Focus on the Family Publishing.

Rodriquez, Mary D. Hawaiian Spelling Bee. 1980. (Illus.). (J). (gr. 1-5). lib. bdg. 6.19 o.p. (*0-8313-0084-1*) Lantern Pr., Inc., Pubs.

Roop, Peter. The Cry of the Conch. 1984. (Treasury of Children's Hawaiian Stories Ser.). (Illus.). (J). (gr. 3-5). 8.95 o.p. (*0-916630-39-0*) Press Pacifica, Ltd.

Salisbury, Graham. Blue Skin of the Sea. 1997. 224p. pap. text 3.99 o.s.i (*0-440-41359-1*, Yearling); 1994. (J). mass mkt. o.s.i (*0-440-90121-9*, Dell Books for Young Readers) Random Hse. Children's Bks.

—Blue Skin of the Sea: A Novel in Stories. 1994. 224p. (gr. 5 up). mass mkt. 4.99 (*0-440-21905-1*) Dell Publishing.

—Blue Skin of the Sea: A Novel in Stories. 1992. 224p. (J). (gr. 4-7). 15.95 (*0-385-30596-6*) Doubleday Publishing.

—Blue Skin of the Sea: A Novel in Stories. 1997. (J). 10.04 (*0-606-11144-1*) Turtleback Bks.

—Island Boyz. 272p. (YA). 2003. (gr. 5). mass mkt. 5.99 (*0-440-22955-3*); 2002. (gr. 7-12). lib. bdg. 18.99 (*0-385-90037-6*) Random Hse. Children's Bks. (Dell Books for Young Readers).

—Island Boyz: Short Stories. 2002. 272p. (YA). (gr. 7-12). 16.95 (*0-385-72970-7*, Dell Books for Young Readers) Random Hse. Children's Bks.

—Jungle Dogs. 1999. 192p. (gr. 4-8). pap. text 4.99 (*0-440-41573-X*) Bantam Bks.

—Jungle Dogs. 1998. 192p. (gr. 4-8). text 15.95 o.s.i (*0-385-32187-2*) Doubleday Publishing.

—Jungle Dogs. 2000. (YA). (gr. 5 up). pap., stu. ed. 59.95 incl. audio (*0-7887-4336-8*, 41131) Recorded Bks., LLC.

—Jungle Dogs. 1999. 11.04 (*0-606-17837-6*) Turtleback Bks.

—Lord of the Deep. braille ed. 2003. (gr. 2). spiral bd. (*0-616-15872-6*) Canadian National Institute for the Blind/Institut National Canadien pour les Aveugles.

—Lord of the Deep. 192p. (YA). 2003. (gr. 5). mass mkt. 5.50 (*0-440-22911-1*); 2001. (gr. 7 up). lib. bdg. 17.99 (*0-385-90013-9*); 2001. (Illus.). (gr. 7 up). 15.95 (*0-385-72918-9*) Random Hse. Children's Bks. (Dell Books for Young Readers).

—Shark Bait. 1999. 160p. (YA). (gr. 5-9). mass mkt. 4.50 (*0-440-22803-4*, Dell Books for Young Readers) Random Hse. Children's Bks.

—Shark Bait. 1999. 10.55 (*0-606-16449-9*) Turtleback Bks.

—Under the Blood Red Sun. 1994. 256p. (gr. 6-8). text 15.95 o.s.i (*0-385-32099-X*, Delacorte Pr.) Dell Publishing.

—Under the Blood Red Sun. 1995. 256p. (gr. 5-8). pap. text 5.50 (*0-440-41139-4*, Yearling) Random Hse. Children's Bks.

—Under the Blood Red Sun. 1995. (J). 11.04 (*0-606-08654-4*) Turtleback Bks.

Salter-Mathieson, Nigel. Little Chief Mischief. 1962. (Illus.). (J). (gr. 2-7). 14.95 (*0-8392-3020-6*) Astor-Honor, Inc.

Samantha's Hawaii Adventure. 1998. (Illus.). 2p. (J). (ps-1). 15.00 (*1-888074-87-6*) Pockets of Learning.

Samuels, Barbara. Aloha, Dolores. 2000. (Melanie Kroupa Bks.). (Illus.). 32p. (J). (ps-2). pap. 15.95 (*0-7894-2508-4*, D K Ink) Dorling Kindersley Publishing, Inc.

Skurzynski, Gloria & Ferguson, Alane. Rage of Fire. 160p. (J). (gr. 3-7). 2001. (Mysteries in Our National Parks Ser.). pap. 5.95 (*0-7922-7653-1*); 1999. (National Parks Mysteries Ser.: No. 2). (Illus.). 15.95 (*0-7922-7035-5*) National Geographic Society.

Slepian, Jan. The Broccoli Tapes. 1989. 160p. (J). (gr. 4-7). 15.99 (*0-399-21712-6*, Philomel) Penguin Putnam Bks. for Young Readers.

Stender, Joyce C. Noodle Mouse Goes to Hawaii. 1997. (Illus.). 32p. (J). (ps-3). 9.95 (*1-890557-27-7*) Cadelle Publishing.

Stevenson, Robert Louis. The Bottle Imp. 1996. (Illus.). 64p. (J). (gr. 4-7). 16.95 o.p. (*0-395-72101-6*, Clarion Bks.) Houghton Mifflin Co. Trade & Reference Div.

Swanson, Helen M. Angel of Rainbow Gulch. 1992. (Illus.). 128p. (J). (gr. 3-6). pap. 5.21 o.p. (*1-880188-08-2*) Bess Pr., Inc.

—The Secret of Petroglyph Cave. 1995. 128p. (J). (gr. 3-6). pap. 6.95 o.p. (*1-880188-97-X*) Bess Pr., Inc.

Sweeney, Jacqueline. Aloha! 2002. (We Can Read! Ser.). (Illus.). 32p. (J). 14.95 (*0-7614-1510-6*) Benchmark Investigative Group.

—Lava. 2002. (We Can Read! Ser.). (Illus.). 32p. (J). 14.95 (*0-7614-1511-4*) Benchmark Investigative Group.

—Little Honu. 2002. (We Can Read! Ser.). (Illus.). 32p. (J). 14.95 (*0-7614-1512-2*) Benchmark Investigative Group.

Tabrah, Ruth M. Emily's Hawaii. 1986. Orig. Title: Hawaiian Heart. (Illus.). 191p. (J). (gr. 4-6). reprint ed. pap. 8.95 (*0-916630-45-5*) Press Pacifica, Ltd.

—The Red Shark. 2nd ed. 1991. (Illus.). 224p. (J). (gr. 5-10). reprint ed. pap. 8.95 (*0-916630-67-6*) Press Pacifica, Ltd.

Vigil-Pianon, Evangelina & Torrecilla, Pablo. Marina's Muumuu: El Muumuu de Marina. 2001. (ENG & SPA., Illus.). (J). pap. 9.95 (*1-55885-351-0*, Piñata Books) Arte Publico Pr.

Vigil-Pion, Evangelina. Marina's Muumuu. 2001. Tr. of Muumuu de Marina. (ENG & SPA., Illus.). 32p. (J). (ps-3). 14.95 (*1-55885-350-2*, Piñata Books) Arte Publico Pr.

Von Tempski, Armine. Bright Spurs. 1992. (Illus.). x, 284p. (YA). reprint ed. pap. 14.95 (*0-918024-95-1*) Ox Bow Pr.

—Pam's Paradise Ranch: A Story of Hawaii. 1992. (Illus.). viii, 334p. (YA). reprint ed. pap. 14.95 (*0-918024-96-X*) Ox Bow Pr.

Wallace, Bill. Aloha Summer. 1997. 208p. (J). (gr. 3-7). tchr. ed. 15.95 (*0-8234-1306-3*) Holiday Hse., Inc.

Walls, Pamela June. Lost at Sea. 2000. (Abby Ser.: No. 1). (Illus.). 224p. (J). (gr. 3-7). mass mkt. 2.99 (*0-8423-3626-5*, Tyndale Kids) Tyndale Hse. Pubs.

—Maui Mystery. 2002. (Abby & the South Seas Adventures Ser.: Vol. 8). (Illus.). 192p. (J). mass mkt. 5.99 (*0-8423-3633-8*) Tyndale Hse. Pubs.

Warren, Bonnie. Aloha from Hawaii. 1987. (Illus.). 24p. (J). (ps-3). 8.95 (*0-9643494-0-X*) Warren Assocs.

Warren, Jean. Huff & Puff's Hawaiian Rainbow. 1995. (Totline Teaching Tales Ser.). (Illus.). (J). (ps-2). pap. 5.95 o.p. (*1-57029-019-9*, WPH 2015, Totline Pubns.) McGraw-Hill Children's Publishing.

White, Ellen Emerson. Kaiulani: The People's Princess, Hawaii, 1889. 2002. E-Book 9.95 (*0-439-42548-4*); 2002. E-Book 9.95 (*0-439-42549-2*); 2001. (Illus.). 240p. (J). (gr. 4-8). 10.95 (*0-439-12909-5*) Scholastic, Inc.

Williams, Julie S. From the Mountains to the Sea: Early Hawaiian Life. 1997. (Kamehameha Schools Intermediate Reading Program Ser.). (Illus.). xi, 177p. (Orig.). (J). (gr. 3-7). pap. 11.95 (*0-87336-030-3*) Kamehameha Schools Pr.

Williams, Laura E. Torch Fishing with the Sun. 2003. (Illus.). 32p. (J). (gr. k-3). 15.95 (*1-56397-685-4*) Boyds Mills Pr.

Yamanaka, Lois-Ann. Name Me Nobody. 2000. 229p. (J). (gr. 7-12). mass mkt. 5.99 (*0-7868-1466-7*) Disney Pr.

Yee, T. Leilani's Hula. 2002. (J). pap. 3.99 (*0-89610-379-X*) Island Heritage Publishing.

HIMALAYA MOUNTAINS—FICTION

Bond, Ruskin. Panther's Moon. 1969. (Illus.). (J). (gr. 3-5). lib. bdg. 4.69 o.p. (*0-394-91497-X*, Random Hse. Bks. for Young Readers) Random Hse. Children's Bks.

Corbalis, Judy. The Ice Cream Heroes. 1989. (Illus.). 144p. (J). (gr. 4-7). 13.95 o.s.i (*0-316-15648-5*) Little Brown & Co.

Healey, Larry. The Hoard of the Himalayas. 1981. 160p. (J). (gr. 7 up). 7.95 o.p. (*0-396-07978-4*) Putnam Publishing Group, The.

Lama, Nurbu Tenzing. Himalaya. Tanaka, Shelley, tr. from FRE. 2002. (Illus.). 40p. (J). 16.95 (*0-88899-480-X*) Groundwood Bks. CAN. *Dist:* Publishers Group West.

Thorpe, Kiki. Snowbound. 2000. (Wild Thornberrys Ready-to-Read Ser. : Vol. 3). (Illus.). 32p. (J). (gr. k-3). pap. 3.99 (*0-689-83429-2*, Simon Spotlight/ Nickelodeon) Simon & Schuster Children's Publishing.

Vandersteen, Willy. Sagarmatha. 1998. (Greatest Adventures of Spike & Suzy Ser.: Vol. 1). (Illus.). 56p. (J). (gr. 2-9). 11.95 (*0-9533178-0-3*) Intes International (UK) Ltd. GBR. *Dist:* Diamond Book Distributors, Inc.

Yorkins, Arthur. Harry & Lulu Go to the Himalayas. 2002. (Illus.). 32p. (J). (*0-7868-0794-6*) Disney Pr.

HIROSHIMA-SHI (JAPAN)—FICTION

Morimoto, Junko. My Hiroshima. 1990. (Illus.). 320p. (J). (ps up). 13.95 o.p. (*0-670-83181-6*, Viking Children's Bks.) Penguin Putnam Bks. for Young Readers.

Yep, Laurence. Hiroshima. unabr. ed. 1997. (J). (gr. 2). pap. 21.24 incl. audio (*0-7887-1269-1*, 40515); (gr. 2). audio. (gr. 4). audio 10.00 (*0-7887-1111-3*, 95104E7) Recorded Bks., LLC.

—Hiroshima. 64p. (J). (gr. 4-7). 1996. mass mkt. 2.99 (*0-590-20833-0*); 1995. pap. 9.95 (*0-590-20832-2*) Scholastic, Inc.

—Hiroshima: A Novella. 1996. (J). 10.65 (*0-606-09414-8*) Turtleback Bks.

HOGWARTS SCHOOL OF WITCHCRAFT AND WIZARDRY (IMAGINARY PLACE)—FICTION

Magical Movie Scenes from Harry Potter & the Sorcerer's Stone: A Poster Book. movie tie-in ed. 2001. (Illus.). 32p. (YA). (gr. 1 up). mass mkt. 6.99 (*0-439-34256-2*) Scholastic, Inc.

Rowling, J. K. Harry Potter & the Chamber of Secrets. collector's ed. (Harry Potter Ser.: Year 2). (YA). (gr. 3 up). 1999. audio 38.00 (*0-7366-9130-8*); 2000. audio compact disk 60.00 (*0-7366-5091-1*) Books on Tape, Inc.

—Harry Potter & the Chamber of Secrets. 2003. 464p. (J). pap. 13.95 (*1-59413-001-9*, Wheeler Publishing, Inc.) Gale Group.

—Harry Potter & the Chamber of Secrets. braille ed. 1999. (Harry Potter Ser.: Year 2). 520p. (YA). (gr. 3 up). pap. 17.99 (*0-939173-35-2*) National Braille Pr.

—Harry Potter & the Chamber of Secrets. unabr. ed. (Harry Potter Ser.: Year 2). (gr. 3 up). 2001. (YA). audio compact disk 60.00 (*0-8072-8601-X*); 2000. (YA). audio 44.00 (*0-8072-8207-3*, YA137SP); 2000. (YA). audio 40.00 (*0-8072-8206-5*, LL0160); 1999. (J). audio 35.00 (*0-8072-8191-3*); 1999. (J). audio compact disk 49.95 (*0-8072-8194-8*) Random Hse. Audio Publishing Group. (Listening Library).

—Harry Potter & the Chamber of Secrets. (Harry Potter Ser.). 2003. 352p. (J). 24.95 (*0-439-55489-6*, Levine, Arthur A. Bks.); 2002. (Illus.). 352p. (J). pap. 6.99 (*0-439-42010-5*, Levine, Arthur A. Bks.); 2000. (Illus.). 352p. (YA). (gr. 3 up). pap. 6.99 (*0-439-06487-2*); 1999. (Illus.). viii, 341p. (J). (gr. 3 up). 19.95 (*0-439-06486-4*, Levine, Arthur A. Bks.); 2002. (Illus.). 352p. (J). 75.00 (*0-439-20353-8*, Levine, Arthur A. Bks.) Scholastic, Inc.

—Harry Potter & the Chamber of Secrets. l.t. ed. 2000. (Harry Potter Ser.: Year 2). (Illus.). 464p. (J). (gr. 3 up). 24.95 (*0-7862-2273-5*) Thorndike Pr.

—Harry Potter & the Chamber of Secrets. 2000. (Harry Potter Ser.: Year 2). (YA). (gr. 3 up). 13.04 (*0-606-19181-X*) Turtleback Bks.

—Harry Potter & the Chamber of Secrets with Poster. 2000. (Harry Potter Ser.: Year 2). (Illus.). 16p. (YA). (gr. 3 up). pap. 5.95 (*0-439-21114-X*) Scholastic, Inc.

—Harry Potter & the Goblet of Fire. unabr. ed. 2000. (Harry Potter Ser.: Year 4). (YA). (gr. 3 up). audio 60.00 Blackstone Audio Bks., Inc.

—Harry Potter & the Goblet of Fire. collector's ed. 2000. (Harry Potter Ser.: Year 4). (YA). (gr. 3 up). audio 39.95 (*0-7366-5519-0*); audio 36.00 (*0-7366-5847-5*); audio compact disk 33.95 (*0-7366-5848-3*) Books on Tape, Inc.

—Harry Potter & the Goblet of Fire. 2003. 936p. pap. 14.95 (*1-59413-003-5*, Wheeler Publishing, Inc.) Gale Group.

—Harry Potter & the Goblet of Fire. braille ed. 2000. (Harry Potter Ser.: Year 4). 650p. (YA). (gr. 3 up). pap. 25.95 (*0-939173-37-9*) National Braille Pr.

—Harry Potter & the Goblet of Fire. unabr. ed. (Harry Potter Ser.: Year 4). (gr. 3 up). 2001. (YA). audio compact disk 80.00 (*0-8072-8603-6*); 2000. (J). audio compact disk 69.95 (*0-8072-8259-6*); 2000. (YA). audio 39.95 (*0-8072-8258-8*); 2000. (YA). audio 55.00 (*0-8072-8793-8*, LL0190) Random Hse. Audio Publishing Group. (Listening Library).

—Harry Potter & the Goblet of Fire. (Harry Potter Ser.). 2003. 752p. (J). 30.95 (*0-439-55490-X*, Levine, Arthur A. Bks.); 2002. 752p. (J). (gr. 3 up). pap. 8.99 (*0-439-13960-0*, Levine, Arthur A. Bks.); 2000. (Illus.). 24p. (YA). (gr. 3 up). pap. 5.95 (*0-439-23194-9*); 2000. (Illus.). xi, 734p. (YA). (gr. 3 up). 25.95 (*0-439-13959-7*, Levine, Arthur A. Bks.) Scholastic, Inc.

—Harry Potter & the Goblet of Fire. l.t. ed. 2000. (Harry Potter Ser.: Year 4). (Illus.). 936p. (J). (gr. 3 up). 25.95 (*0-7862-2927-6*) Thorndike Pr.

—Harry Potter & the Order of the Phoenix, 13 vols. braille ed. 2003. (Harry Potter Ser.: 5). (YA). 29.99 (*0-939173-38-7*) National Braille Pr.

—Harry Potter & the Order of the Phoenix. unabr. ed. 2003. audio 45.00 (*0-8072-2030-2*); (J). audio compact disk 90.00 (*0-8072-2031-0*, Listening Library); (Harry Potter Ser.: Year 5). (J). audio 45.00 (*0-8072-2028-0*, Listening Library); (Harry Potter Ser.: Year 5). (J). audio compact disk 75.00 (*0-8072-2029-9*, Listening Library) Random Hse. Audio Publishing Group.

—Harry Potter & the Order of the Phoenix. 2003. (Harry Potter Ser.: Year 5). (Illus.). 896p. (J). (gr. 3-6). 34.99 (*0-439-56761-0*); 29.99 (*0-439-35806-X*); 60.00 (*0-439-56762-9*) Scholastic, Inc.

—Harry Potter & the Order of the Phoenix. l.t. ed. 2003. (Sequel to Harry Potter & the Goblet of Fire Ser.). 1093p. 29.95 (*0-7862-5778-4*) Thorndike Pr.

—Harry Potter & the Prisoner of Azkaban. unabr. ed. 2000. (Harry Potter Ser.: Year 3). (YA). (gr. 3 up). audio 38.00 Blackstone Audio Bks., Inc.

—Harry Potter & the Prisoner of Azkaban. unabr. ed. 2000. (Harry Potter Ser.: Year 3). (YA). (gr. 3 up). audio compact disk 49.46 (*0-7366-5096-2*); audio 31.50 (*0-7366-9131-6*) Books on Tape, Inc.

—Harry Potter & the Prisoner of Azkaban. 2003. 592p. (J). pap. 13.95 (*1-59413-002-7*, Wheeler Publishing, Inc.) Gale Group.

—Harry Potter & the Prisoner of Azkaban. braille ed. 1999. (Harry Potter Ser.: Year 3). (YA). (gr. 3 up). pap. 19.95 (*0-939173-36-0*) National Braille Pr.

—Harry Potter & the Prisoner of Azkaban. 2000. tchr. ed. 9.95 (*1-58130-656-3*); stu. ed. 11.95 (*1-58130-657-1*) Novel Units, Inc.

—Harry Potter & the Prisoner of Azkaban. unabr. ed. (Harry Potter Ser.: Year 3). (YA). (gr. 3 up). 2001. audio compact disk 65.00 (*0-8072-8602-8*); 2000. audio 46.00 (*0-8072-8315-0*, LL0164); 2000. audio compact disk 54.95 (*0-8072-8232-4*); 2000. audio 35.00 (*0-8072-8231-6*) Random Hse. Audio Publishing Group. (Listening Library).

—Harry Potter & the Prisoner of Azkaban. (Harry Potter Ser.: Year 3). (Illus.). (J). (gr. 3 up). 2001. 448p. pap. 7.99 (*0-439-13636-9*, Levine, Arthur A. Bks.); 1999. ix, 435p. 19.95 (*0-439-13635-0*) Scholastic, Inc.

—Harry Potter & the Prisoner of Azkaban. l.t. ed. 2000. (Harry Potter Ser.: Year 3). (Illus.). 592p. (YA). (gr. 3 up). 24.95 (*0-7862-2274-3*) Thorndike Pr.

—Harry Potter & the Sorcerer's Stone. unabr. ed. 1999. (Harry Potter Ser.: Year 1). (YA). (gr. 3 up). audio 37.98 BBC Audiobooks America.

—Harry Potter & the Sorcerer's Stone. unabr. ed. 2000. (Harry Potter Ser.: Year 1). (YA). (gr. 3 up). audio 38.00 Blackstone Audio Bks., Inc.

—Harry Potter & the Sorcerer's Stone. 1997. (Harry Potter Ser.: Year 1). (Illus.). 223p. (YA). (gr. 3 up). pap. (*0-7475-3274-5*) Bloomsbury Publishing, Ltd. GBR. *Dist:* Raincoast Bk. Distribution.

—Harry Potter & the Sorcerer's Stone. unabr. ed. (Harry Potter Ser.: Year 1). (YA). (gr. 3 up). 2000. audio compact disk 49.95 (*0-7366-5092-X*); 1999. audio 33.95 (*0-7366-9000-X*, 4195) Books on Tape, Inc.

—Harry Potter & the Sorcerer's Stone. 2003. 423p. pap. 13.95 (*1-59413-000-0*, Wheeler Publishing, Inc.) Gale Group.

—Harry Potter & the Sorcerer's Stone. unabr. ed. 1999. (Harry Potter Ser.: Year 1). (YA). (gr. 3 up). audio 37.98 Highsmith Inc.

—Harry Potter & the Sorcerer's Stone. unabr. ed. (Harry Potter Ser.: Year 1). 320p. (YA). (gr. 3 up). pap. 62.00 incl. audio (*0-8072-1547-3*); 2001. (Harry Potter Ser.: Year 1). (YA). (gr. 3 up). audio compact disk 60.00 (*0-8072-8600-1*); 2000. (Harry Potter Ser.: Year 1). (YA). (gr. 3 up). pap. 44.00 incl. audio (*0-8072-8119-0*, YYA108SP); 1999. (J). audio 33.00 o.s.i (*0-8072-8161-1*); 1999. (Harry Potter Ser.: Year 1). (J). (gr. 3 up). audio compact disk 49.95 (*0-8072-8195-6*); 1999. (Harry Potter Ser.: Year 1). (J). (gr. 3 up). audio 35.00 (*0-8072-8175-1*, YA108CXR); 1999. (Harry Potter Ser.: Year 1). (YA). (gr. 3 up). audio 40.00 (*0-8072-8118-2*, LL0146) Random Hse. Audio Publishing Group. (Listening Library).

—Harry Potter & the Sorcerer's Stone. (Harry Potter Ser.: Year 1). (YA). (gr. 3 up). 2001. 384p. mass mkt. 6.99 (*0-439-36213-X*); 2000. (Illus.). 16p. pap. 5.95 (*0-439-21116-6*); 1999. (Illus.). 312p. pap. 6.99 (*0-590-35342-X*); 1998. (Illus.). 320p. 19.95 (*0-590-35340-3*, Levine, Arthur A. Bks.); 2000. 320p. 75.00 (*0-439-20352-X*) Scholastic, Inc.

—Harry Potter & the Sorcerer's Stone. l.t. ed. 1999. (Harry Potter Ser.: Year 1). (Illus.). 422p. (YA). (gr. 3 up). 24.95 (*0-7862-2272-7*) Thorndike Pr.

—Harry Potter & the Sorcerer's Stone. (Harry Potter Ser.: Year 1). (YA). (gr. 3 up). 1999. (Illus.). 12.95 o.p. (*0-606-17233-5*); 1998. 13.04 (*0-606-17097-9*) Turtleback Bks.

—Harry Potter Boxed Set: Harry Potter & the Sorcerer's Stone; Harry Potter & the Chamber of Secrets; Harry Potter & the Prisoner of Azkaban, 3 vols. (Harry Potter Ser.: Years 1-3). (Illus.). (YA). 2002. pap. 21.97 (*0-439-32466-1*); 1999. (gr. 3 up). 55.85 (*0-439-13316-5*) Scholastic, Inc. (Levine, Arthur A. Bks.).

—Harry Potter Boxed Set: Harry Potter & the Sorcerer's Stone; Harry Potter & the Chamber of Secrets; Harry Potter & the Prisoner of Azkaban; Harry Potter & the Goblet of Fire, 4 vols. (Harry Potter Ser.: Years 1-4). 2002. 752p. (YA). (gr. 3 up). pap. 30.96 (*0-439-43486-6*, Levine, Arthur A. Bks.); 2001. 85.80 (*0-439-24954-6*); 2000. (YA). (gr. 3 up). 85.80 (*0-641-06631-7*, Levine, Arthur A. Bks.) Scholastic, Inc.

—Harry Potter Boxed Set: Harry Potter & the Sorcerer's Stone; Harry Potter & the Chamber of Secrets; Harry Potter & the Prisoner of Azkaban; Harry Potter & the Goblet of Fire; Harry Potter & the Order of the Phoenix, 5 vols. ltd. ed. 2003. (Harry Potter Ser.). 2000p. (J). 99.95 (*0-439-61255-1*) Scholastic, Inc.

—Harry Potter Coffret: Harry Potter a l'Ecole des Sorciers; Harry Potter et la Chambre des Secrets; Harry Potter et le Prisonnier d'Azkaban. 1999. (Harry Potter Ser.: Years 1-3). Tr. of Harry Potter Boxed Set: Harry Potter & the Chamber of Secrets; Harry Potter & the Sorcerer's Stone; Harry Potter & the Prisoner of Azkaban. (FRE.). 1400p. (YA). (gr. 3 up). 34.95 (*0-320-03843-2*) French & European Pubns., Inc.

—Harry Potter Coffret: Harry Potter a l'Ecole des Sorciers; Harry Potter et la Chambre des Secrets; Harry Potter et le Prisonnier d'Azkaban. 1999. (Harry Potter Ser.: Years 1-3). Tr. of Harry Potter Boxed Set: Harry Potter & the Chamber of Secrets; Harry Potter & the Sorcerer's Stone; Harry Potter & the Prisoner of Azkaban. (FRE.). (YA). (gr. 3 up). pap. 43.95 (*2-07-052929-0*) Gallimard, Editions FRA. *Dist:* Distribooks, Inc.

—Harry Potter et la Chambre des Secrets. 1999. (Harry Potter Ser.: Year 2). Tr. of Harry Potter & the Chamber of Secrets. (FRE.). (YA). (gr. 3 up). pap. 13.95 (0-320-03778-9) French & European Pubns., Inc.

—Harry Potter et la Chambre des Secrets. 1999. (Harry Potter Ser.: Year 2). Tr. of Harry Potter & the Chamber of Secrets. (FRE., Illus.). (YA). (gr. 3 up). pap. 14.95 (2-07-052455-8) Gallimard, Editions FRA. Dist: Distribooks, Inc.

—Harry Potter et la Coupe de Feu. 2001. (Harry Potter Ser.: Year 4). Tr. of Harry Potter & the Goblet of Fire. (FRE.). (YA). (gr. 3 up). pap. 34.95 (0-320-03932-3) French & European Pubns., Inc.

—Harry Potter et le Prisonnier d'Azkaban. 1999. (Harry Potter Ser.: Year 3). Tr. of Harry Potter & the Prisoner of Azkaban. (FRE.). (YA). (gr. 3 up). pap. (2-07-052818-9) Gallimard, Editions.

—Harry Potter et l'Ecole des Sorciers. 3rd ed. 1998. (Harry Potter Ser.: Year 1). Tr. of Harry Potter & the Sorcerer's Stone. (FRE., Illus.). (YA). (gr. 3 up). pap. 14.95 (2-07-050142-6) Distribooks, Inc.

—Harry Potter et l'Ecole des Sorciers. 1999. (Harry Potter Ser.: Year 1). Tr. of Harry Potter & the Sorcerer's Stone. (FRE.). (YA). (gr. 3 up). pap. 16.95 (0-320-03780-0) French & European Pubns., Inc.

—Harry Potter et l'Ecole des Sorciers. 2000. Tr. of Harry Potter & the Sorcerer's Stone. (FRE.). (J). pap. 14.95 (2-07-051426-9) Gallimard, Editions FRA. Dist: Distribooks, Inc.

—Harry Potter und der Gefangene von Azkaban. 1999. (Harry Potter Ser.: Year 3). Tr. of Harry Potter & the Prisoner of Azkaban. (GER.). (YA). (gr. 3 up). 28.95 (3-551-55169-3) Carlsen Verlag DEU. Dist: Distribooks, Inc.

—Harry Potter und der Stein de Weisen. 1999. (Harry Potter Ser.: Year 1). Tr. of Harry Potter & the Sorcerer's Stone. (GER.). 335p. (YA). (gr. 3 up). 28.95 (3-551-55167-7) Carlsen Verlag DEU. Dist: Distribooks, Inc.

—Harry Potter und die Kammer des Schreckens. 1999. (Harry Potter Ser.: Year 2). Tr. of Harry Potter & Chamber of Secrets. (GER.). (YA). (gr. 3 up). 28.95 (3-551-55168-5) Carlsen Verlag DEU. Dist: Distribooks, Inc.

—Harry Potter y el Prisionero de Azkaban. 2000. (Harry Potter Ser.: Year 3). (SPA.). 359p. (YA). (gr. 3 up). 16.95 (84-7888-568-4) Baker & Taylor Bks.

—Harry Potter y el Prisionero de Azkaban. 2000. (Harry Potter Ser.: Year 3). (SPA., Illus.). 360p. (YA). (gr. 3 up). 15.95 (84-7888-519-6, SAL1889) Emece Editores ESP. Dist: Lectorum Pubns., Inc.

—Harry Potter y el Prisionero de Azkaban. 2000. (Harry Potter Ser.: Year 3). (SPA.). (YA). (gr. 3 up). 16.95 (0-320-03783-5) French & European Pubns., Inc.

—Harry Potter y el Prisionero de Azkaban. 2001. (Harry Potter Ser.: Year 3). (SPA.). (YA). (gr. 3 up). 17.00 (0-606-88519-6) Turtleback Bks.

—Harry Potter y la Camara Secreta. (Harry Potter Ser.: Year 2). (SPA., Illus.). (YA). 2000. 288p. (gr. 3 up). (84-7888-495-5, SAL4595); 1999. 256p. (gr. 7 up). 15.95 (84-7888-445-9, SAL2819) Emece Editores ESP. Dist: Lectorum Pubns., Inc., Lectorum Pubns., Inc., Libros Sin Fronteras.

—Harry Potter y la Camara Secreta. 1999. (Harry Potter Ser.: Year 2). (SPA.). (YA). (gr. 3 up). 14.95 (0-320-03781-9) French & European Pubns., Inc.

—Harry Potter y la Camara Secreta. 2001. (Harry Potter Ser.: Year 2). (SPA.). (YA). (gr. 3 up). 16.83 (0-606-88495-5) Turtleback Bks.

—Harry Potter y la Piedra Filosofal. 1999. (Harry Potter Ser.: Year 1). (SPA.). (YA). (gr. 3 up). 14.95 (0-320-03782-7) French & European Pubns., Inc.

—Harry Potter y la Piedra Filosofal. 2001. (Harry Potter Ser.: Year 1). (SPA.). (YA). (gr. 3 up). 15.00 (0-606-88445-9) Turtleback Bks.

Scholastic, Inc. Staff. Harry Potter & the Chamber of Secrets: A Deluxe Pop-Up Book. 2002. (Harry Potter Ser.). (Illus.). 5p. (J). pap. 17.95 (0-439-45193-0, Levine, Arthur A. Bks.) Scholastic, Inc.

HOLLAND (MICH.)—FICTION

Bowman, Crystal. Windmills & Woodenshoes. 1999. (Illus.). 40p. (J). (gr. 2-6). 15.00 (0-9636050-2-X) Cygnet Publishing Co.

HOLLYWOOD (LOS ANGELES, CALIF.)—FICTION

Blair, Cynthia. The Popcorn Project. 1989. (J). (gr. 5 up). mass mkt. 3.99 o.s.i (0-449-70309-6, Fawcett) Ballantine Bks.

Gregory, Deborah. Hey, Ho, Hollywood. 2000. (Cheetah Girls Ser.: No. 4). 135p. (J). (gr. 3-7). pap. 4.00 (0-7868-1387-3) Disney Pr.

Ianaeken, Philippa. Jan & Ann in Hollywood. 1997. 180p. (YA). pap. 9.95 (0-9658267-0-8, 10457) Socks, Inc.

Jones, Adrienne. A Matter of Spunk. 1983. (Charlotte Zolotow Bk.). 320p. (YA). (gr. 7 up). lib. bdg. 13.89 o.p. (0-06-023054-1) HarperCollins Children's Bk. Group.

Kalman, Maira. Max in Hollywood, Baby. 1992. (Illus.). 400p. (J). (gr. 2 up). 17.99 (0-670-84479-9, Viking Children's Bks.) Penguin Putnam Bks. for Young Readers.

Kendall, Jane, et al. Miranda Goes to Hollywood. 1999. 256p. (YA). (gr. 5-9). 16.00 o.s.i (0-15-202059-4) Harcourt Children's Bks.

Morgan, Allen. Matthew & the Midnight Movie. 2002. (Matthew's Midnight Adventures Ser.). (Illus.). 32p. (YA). pap. 6.99 (0-7737-6273-6) Stoddart Kids CAN. Dist: Fitzhenry & Whiteside, Ltd.

Paterson, Aileen. Maisie Goes to Hollywood. 2001. (Illus.). 32p. (J). (ps-3). pap. (1-871512-40-9) Glowworm Bks., Ltd.

Pfeffer, Susan Beth. Revenge of the Aztecs: A Story of the Jazz Age. (American Portraits Ser.). (Illus.). 114p. (YA). (gr. 5-8). 2001. 12.64 (0-8092-0586-6); 2000. pap. 5.95 (0-8092-0627-7, 06277E) Jamestown.

Savage, Derek. Cool Cat Goes to Hollywood. 2001. (Cool Cat Ser.: Vol. 2). 32p. (J). pap. 9.95 (0-9673000-4-5) Savage Bks.

Schultz, Marion. Going Hollywood. 1989. (J). (gr. 6 up). mass mkt. 2.95 o.s.i (0-449-70281-2, Fawcett) Ballantine Bks.

Schulz, Charles M. Peanuts Gang in Hollywood. 9999. (J). pap. 1.50 o.s.i (0-590-32495-0) Scholastic, Inc.

Sharmat, Marjorie Weinman. Dog - Gone Hollywood. 2000. (Duz Shedd Stories Ser.: Vol. 3). (Illus.). 80p. (J). (gr. k-3). pap. 3.99 o.s.i (0-375-80529-X, Random Hse. Bks. for Young Readers) Random Hse. Children's Bks.

—Dog-Gone Hollywood. 2000. (Duz Shedd Stories Ser.: Vol. 3). (Illus.). 80p. (J). (gr. k-3). lib. bdg. 11.99 o.s.i (0-375-90529-4, Random Hse. Bks. for Young Readers) Random Hse. Children's Bks.

—Dog-Gone Hollywood. 2000. (Illus.). (J). 10.14 (0-606-18853-3) Turtleback Bks.

Suzanne, Jamie. The Twins Hit Hollywood. 1997. (Sweet Valley Twins Ser.: No. 107). (Illus.). 144p. (gr. 3-7). pap. text 3.50 o.s.i (0-553-48438-9, Sweet Valley) Random Hse. Children's Bks.

Van Draanen, Wendelin. Sammy Keyes & the Hollywood Mummy. unabr. ed. 2001. (Sammy Keyes Ser.). (J). audio 23.95 (0-87499-799-2, OAK011) Live Oak Media.

—Sammy Keyes & the Hollywood Mummy. 2001. (Sammy Keyes Ser.). 272p. (gr. 5-8). text 15.95 (0-375-80266-5, Knopf Bks. for Young Readers); lib. bdg. 17.99 (0-375-90266-X, Random Hse. Bks. for Young Readers) Random Hse. Children's Bks.

Vaughan, Christina. Artie Goes to Hollywood. 2000. (Artie Stories Ser.: Vol. 2). (Illus.). 34p. (J). (gr. 1-5). spiral bd. 12.95 (0-9641697-6-2, You-Draw-It Bks.) Castlebrook Pubns.

Weaver, Lydia. Child Star: When Talkies Came to Hollywood. 1992. (Once upon America Ser.). (Illus.). 64p. (J). (gr. 2-6). 12.00 o.p. (0-670-84039-4, Viking Children's Bks.) Penguin Putnam Bks. for Young Readers.

Wojciechowska, Maia. The Hollywood Kid. 1966. (YA). (gr. 7 up). lib. bdg. 11.89 o.p. (0-06-026573-6) HarperCollins Children's Bk. Group.

Zindel, Bonnie. Hollywood Dream Machine. 1984. (J). 12.95 o.p. (0-670-23220-3) Viking Penguin.

HONG KONG (CHINA)—FICTION

Dixon, Franklin W. The Clue of the Hissing Serpent. 1974. (Hardy Boys Mystery Stories Ser.: No. 53). (Illus.). 180p. (J). (gr. 3-6). 5.99 (0-448-08953-X, Grosset & Dunlap) Penguin Putnam Bks. for Young Readers.

Markie, Uncle. Piglette & BoBo See Hong Kong. l.t. ed. 2002. 46p. ring bd. 9.95 (0-9633943-8-X) Studio 403.

Martin, Patricia M. The Dog & the Boat Boy. 1969. (Illus.). (J). (gr. k-3). 4.69 o.p. (0-399-60130-9) Putnam Publishing Group, The.

McOmber, Rachel B., ed. McOmber Phonics Storybooks: A Package from Hong Kong. rev. ed. (Illus.). (J). (0-944991-61-0) Swift Learning Resources.

Morris, Gilbert. Nine-Story Pagodas & Double Decker Buses - Travels in Hong Kong No. 4: Adventures of the Kerrigan Kids. 2001. (Illus.). 121p. (J). (gr. 3-7). pap. 5.99 (0-8024-1581-4) Moody Pr.

HUNGARY—FICTION

Biro, Val. Hungarian Folk-Tales. 1987. (Illus.). 192p. (J). (gr. 1-5). 14.95 o.p. (0-19-274126-8) Oxford Univ. Pr., Inc.

Cheng, Andrea. Marika. 2002. 168p. (J). (gr. 5 up). 16.95 (1-886910-78-2, Front Street) Front Street, Inc.

Eyerly, Jeannette. Goodbye to Budapest. 1974. (J). (gr. 5 up). 12.95 (0-397-31496-5) HarperCollins Children's Bk. Group.

Hippely, Hilary Horder. A Song for Lena. 1996. (Illus.). 40p. (J). (ps-3). 16.00 o.s.i (0-689-80763-5, Simon & Schuster Children's Publishing) Simon & Schuster Children's Publishing.

Marx, Trish. Hanna's Cold Winter. 1993. (Illus.). 32p. (J). (ps-3). lib. bdg. 15.95 o.s.i (0-87614-772-4, Carolrhoda Bks.) Lerner Publishing Group.

Sawyer, Ruth. Christmas Anna Angel. 1944. (Illus.). (J). (gr. 2-6). 5.95 o.p. (0-670-22039-6) Viking Penguin.

Seredy, Kate. The Good Master. (Puffin Newbery Library). (Illus.). (J). (gr. 4-7). 1986. 192p. pap. 5.99 (0-14-030133-X, Puffin Bks.); 1935. 13.95 o.s.i (0-670-34592-X, Viking Children's Bks.) Penguin Putnam Bks. for Young Readers.

—The Singing Tree. 1990. (Puffin Newbery Library). 256p. (J). (gr. 4-7). pap. 5.99 (0-14-034543-4, Puffin Bks.) Penguin Putnam Bks. for Young Readers.

—The White Stag. 1937. (Illus.). 9p. (J). (gr. 7 up). 14.99 o.s.i (0-670-76375-6, Viking Children's Bks.) Penguin Putnam Bks. for Young Readers.

Szablya, Helen M. & Anderson, Peggy King. The Fall of the Red Star. 2003. 168p. (YA). (gr. 5 up). pap. 9.95 (1-56397-977-2) Boyds Mills Pr.

Watkins, Dawn L. Zoli's Legacy: Inheritance. 1991. (Zolis Ser.: Vol. 1). 190p. (YA). (gr. 7 up). pap. 6.49 (0-89084-596-4, 055699) Jones, Bob Univ. Pr.

Wiseman, Eva. My Canary Yellow Star. 2001. (Illus.). 240p. (J). (gr. 3-7). pap. 6.95 (0-88776-533-5) Tundra Bks. of Northern New York.

—A Place Not Home. unabr. ed. 1997. 192p. (YA). (gr. 7 up). pap. 7.95 (0-7737-5834-8) Stoddart Kids CAN. Dist: Fitzhenry & Whiteside, Ltd.

—A Place Not Home. 1996. 12.00 (0-606-16559-2) Turtleback Bks.

I

ICELAND—FICTION

Boucher, Alan. The Land Seekers, RS. 1968. (J). (gr. 7 up). 3.50 o.p. (0-374-34323-3, Farrar, Straus & Giroux (BYR)) Farrar, Straus & Giroux.

Hauger, Torill Thorstad. Escape from the Vikings. Hamnes, Lisa, ed. Born, Anne, tr. from NOR. 2000. Orig. Title: Flukten Fra Vikingene. (Illus.). 175p. (J). (gr. 4-12). pap. (1-57534-013-5) Skandisk, Inc.

Ruepp, Krista. Winter Pony. James, J. Alison, tr. from GER. 2002. (Illus.). 32p. (J). 15.95 (0-7358-1691-3); lib. bdg. 16.50 (0-7358-1692-1) North-South Bks., Inc.

Stefansson, Thorsteinn. The Golden Future. 1977. (J). (gr. 6-12). 6.95 o.p. (0-8407-6520-7, Dutton Children's Bks.) Penguin Putnam Bks. for Young Readers.

Yates, Elizabeth. Iceland Adventures. 1997. 144p. (J). (gr. 4-6). pap. 6.49 (0-89084-935-8, 110031) Jones, Bob Univ. Pr.

IDAHO—FICTION

Beatty, Patricia. Bonanza Girl. 1993. 224p. (J). (gr. 5 up). 16.00 o.p. (0-688-12361-9); pap. 4.95 o.p. (0-688-12280-9) Morrow/Avon. (Morrow, William & Co.).

—Bonanza Girl. 1993. 10.05 o.p. (0-606-05164-3) Turtleback Bks.

Bergera, Janet. Vital Signs: A Mission of the Heart. 1995. (J). pap. 9.95 (1-55503-773-9, 01111817) Covenant Communications, Inc.

Creech, Sharon. Walk Two Moons. 2002. (Illus.). (J). 15.00 (0-7587-0223-X) Book Wholesalers, Inc.

—Walk Two Moons. 2004. 304p. (J). pap. 6.50 (0-06-056013-4, Harper Trophy) HarperCollins Children's Bk. Group.

—Walk Two Moons. 1999. (J). 9.95 (1-56137-770-8) Novel Units, Inc.

Duey, Kathleen. Celou Sudden Shout: Idaho, 1826. 1998. (American Diaries Ser.: No. 9). 144p. (J). (gr. 3-7). pap. 4.50 o.s.i (0-689-81622-7, Aladdin) Simon & Schuster Children's Publishing.

—Celou Sudden Shout: Idaho, 1826. 1998. (American Diaries Ser.: No. 9). (J). (gr. 3-7). 10.55 (0-606-13121-3) Turtleback Bks.

George, Jean Craighead. Avalanche. 2004. (J). (0-06-050595-8); lib. bdg. (0-06-050596-6) HarperCollins Pubs.

George, Jean Craighead & Minor, Wendell. Firestorm. 2003. (Outdoor Adventures Ser.). (Illus.). 32p. (J). 15.99 (0-06-000263-8); lib. bdg. 16.89 (0-06-000264-6) HarperCollins Children's Bk. Group. (Tegen, Katherine Bks.).

Hamilton, Morse. The Garden of Eden Motel. 1999. (Illus.). 160p. (J). (gr. 5 up). 16.00 (0-688-16814-0, Greenwillow Bks.) HarperCollins Children's Bk. Group.

Hite, Sid. The King of Slippery Falls. 2004. 208p. (YA). pap. 16.95 (0-439-34257-0) Scholastic, Inc.

Ingold, Jeanette. The Big Burn. (YA). 2003. 320p. pap. 6.95 (0-15-204924-X, Harcourt Paperbacks); 2002. 304p. 17.00 (0-15-216470-7) Harcourt Children's Bks.

Littke, Lael. Searching for Selene. 2003. 203p. (J). pap. 13.95 (1-59038-179-3) Deseret Bk. Co.

Murphy, Jim. West to a Land of Plenty: The Diary of Teresa Angelino Viscardi, New York to Idaho Territory, 1883. 1998. (Dear America Ser.). (Illus.). 204p. (YA). (gr. 4-9). pap. 10.95 (0-590-73888-7) Scholastic, Inc.

Patneaude, David. Colder Than Ice. 2003. 168p. (J). (gr. 3-6). 14.95 (0-8075-8135-6) Whitman, Albert & Co.

Peek, P. Cary. One Winter in the Wilderness. 1998. (Living the West Ser.). (Illus.). 224p. 24.95 (0-89301-210-6) Univ. of Idaho Pr.

Plowhead, Ruth G. Mile High Cabin. 1945. (Illus.). 299p. (J). (gr. 6-8). 2.50 o.p. (0-87004-121-5) Caxton Pr.

Wyss, Thelma H. A Stranger Here. 1993. (YA). (gr. 7 up). 144p. 14.00 o.p. (0-06-021438-4); 80p. lib. bdg. 13.89 o.p. (0-06-021439-2) HarperCollins Children's Bk. Group.

ILLINOIS—FICTION

Baker, Camy. Camy Baker's Love You Like a Sister: Thirty Cool Rules for Making & Being a Better Best Friend! 1998. 176p. (gr. 2-7). pap. text 3.99 o.s.i (0-553-48656-X) Bantam Bks.

—Camy Baker's Love You Like a Sister: Thirty Cool Rules for Making & Being a Better Best Friend! 1998. 10.04 (0-606-15475-2) Turtleback Bks.

Brokaw, Nancy Steele. Leaving Emma. 1999. 144p. (J). (gr. 4-6). tchr. ed. 15.00 (0-395-90699-7, Clarion Bks.) Houghton Mifflin Co. Trade & Reference Div.

Courtney, Dayle. The Ivy Plot. 1981. (Thorne Twins Adventure Bks.). (Illus.). 192p. (Orig.). (J). (gr. 5 up). pap. 2.98 o.p. (0-87239-469-7, 2714) Standard Publishing.

Dell, Pamela. Liam's Watch: A Strange Story of the Great Chicago Fire. 2002. (Illus.). 48p. (J). (gr. 3-8). lib. bdg. 27.07 (1-59187-014-3) Child's World, Inc.

Dower, Laura. Just Visiting, Vol. 9. 2002. (From the Files of Madison Finn Ser.). 176p. (J). pap. 4.99 (0-7868-1683-X, Volo) Hyperion Bks. for Children.

Fenner, Carol. Yolonda's Genius. unabr. ed. 2002. 211p. pap. 37.00 incl. audio (0-8072-0462-5, Listening Library) Random Hse. Audio Publishing Group.

Hunt, Irene. Across Five Aprils. (J). 1985. 2.50 o.s.i (0-441-00318-4); 1984. 2.25 o.s.i (0-441-00317-6); 1983. 2.25 o.s.i (0-441-00316-8) Ace Bks.

—Across Five Aprils. 2002. 224p. (J). mass mkt. 4.99 (0-425-18278-9); 1986. 192p. (gr. 4-7). mass mkt. 4.99 (0-425-10241-6) Berkley Publishing Group.

—Across Five Aprils. 1999. (J). pap. 1.95 (0-590-05178-4) Scholastic, Inc.

—Across Five Aprils. 1986. 11.04 (0-606-00289-8) Turtleback Bks.

Lems, Kristin. Piano Teacher's Daughter. 2002. (Illus.). pap. 18.00 (0-9637048-2-6) Lems-Dworkin, Carol Pubs.

Marsh, Carole. Uncle Rebus: Illinois Picture Stories for Computer Kids. 1994. (Carole Marsh Illinois Bks.). (Illus.). (J). (gr. k-3). pap. 19.95 (0-7933-4541-3); lib. bdg. 29.95 (0-7933-4540-5); cd-rom 29.95 (0-7933-4542-1) Gallopade International.

Moranville, Sharelle Byars. Over the River, ERS. 2002. 192p. (YA). (gr. 4-9). 16.95 (0-8050-7049-4, Holt, Henry & Co. Bks. For Young Readers) Holt, Henry & Co.

Noble, Kate. The Dragon of Navy Pier. 1996. (Illus.). 32p. (J). (ps-4). 15.95 (0-9631798-5-3) Silver Seahorse Pr.

O'Rourke, Kelly. The Mad House. 1998. (Halloween Ser.: Vol. 3). 160p. (YA). (gr. 7-12). mass mkt. 4.50 o.s.i (1-57297-342-0) Boulevard Bks.

—The Old Myers Place. 1997. (Halloween Ser.: No. 2). 160p. (YA). mass mkt. 4.50 o.s.i (1-57297-341-2) Boulevard Bks.

O'Rourke, Michael. The Scream Factory. 1997. (Halloween Ser.: No. 1). 160p. (YA). (gr. 5-11). mass mkt. 4.50 o.s.i (1-57297-298-X) Boulevard Bks.

Peck, Richard. A Long Way from Chicago. 2002. (Illus.). (J). 13.19 (0-7587-6520-7) Book Wholesalers, Inc.

—A Long Way from Chicago. 2004. (Illus.). 160p. pap. 5.99 (0-14-240110-2, Puffin Bks.); 2000. (Illus.). 176p. (YA). (gr. 5-9). pap. 5.99 (0-14-130352-2, Puffin Bks.); 1998. 192p. (J). (gr. 4-7). 15.99 (0-8037-2290-7, Dial Bks. for Young Readers) Penguin Putnam Bks. for Young Readers.

—A Long Way from Chicago. unabr. ed. 2000. (ps up). audio 25.00 (0-8072-6162-9, LL0153, Listening Library) Random Hse. Audio Publishing Group.

—A Long Way from Chicago. 2000. 11.04 (0-606-19769-9) Turtleback Bks.

—A Year down Yonder. 2002. (Illus.). (YA). 13.19 (1-4046-1795-7) Book Wholesalers, Inc.

—A Year down Yonder. 144p. (gr. 5-8). 2002. (YA). pap. 5.99 (0-14-230070-5, Puffin Bks.); 2000. (J). 16.99 (0-8037-2518-3, Dial Bks. for Young Readers) Penguin Putnam Bks. for Young Readers.

Settings

—A Year down Yonder. unabr. ed. 2000. (J). (gr. 4-6). audio 23.00 (*0-8072-8750-4*, LL0222); (ps up). audio 18.00 (*0-8072-6167-X*, LL0222) Random Hse. Audio Publishing Group. (Listening Library).
—A Year down Yonder. l.t. ed. 2001. 160p. (J). 24.95 (*0-7862-3282-X*) Thorndike Pr.
Rogo, Thomas Paul. The Surfrider: A Midwestern Odyssey. 1999. (Illus.). 80p. (J). (gr. 3 up). 19.95 (*1-57306-082-8*); pap. 11.21 (*1-57306-110-7*) Bess Pr., Inc.
Rosales, Melodye. The Adventures of Minnie, Bk. 2. 2003. (J). (*0-316-75688-1*) Little Brown Children's Bks.
—The Adventures of Minny, Bk. 3. 2000. (J). (*0-316-75633-4*) Little Brown & Co.
Rosales, Melodye Benson. Minnie Saves the Day! 2001. (Adventures of Minnie Merriweather Ser.). (Illus.). 96p. (J). (gr. 1-4). 12.95 (*0-316-75605-9*) Little Brown Children's Bks.
Schraff, Anne. Freedom Knows No Color. 2000. 118p. (J). (*0-7807-9270-X*); pap. (*0-7891-5136-7*) Perfection Learning Corp.
Sinclair, Upton. The Jungle. 1965. (Airmont Classics Ser.). (YA). (gr. 11 up). mass mkt. 2.95 o.p. (*0-8049-0086-8*, CL-86) Airmont Publishing Co., Inc.
Sinclair, Upton, et al. The Jungle. (Classics Illustrated Ser.). (Illus.). 52p. (YA). pap. 4.95 (*1-57209-025-1*) Classics International Entertainment, Inc.
Smith, Greg Leitich. Ninjas, Piranhas, & Galileo. 2003. 192p. (J). (gr. 3-6). 15.95 (*0-316-77854-0*) Little Brown & Co.
Stark, Ken, illus. Oh, Brother! 2003. 32p. (J). 15.99 (*0-399-23766-6*) Putnam Publishing Group, The.
Van Steenwyk, Elizabeth. Maggie in the Morning. 144p. (gr. 4-9). 2002. (YA). pap. 6.00 (*0-8028-5219-X*); 2001. (J). 16.00 (*0-8028-5222-X*) Eerdmans, William B. Publishing Co. (Eerdmans Bks For Young Readers).

INCAS—FICTION

Clark, Ann Nolan. Secret of the Andes. (Puffin Newbery Library). (Illus.). (J). (gr. 4-7). 1976. 128p. pap. 4.99 (*0-14-030926-8*, Puffin Bks.); 1952. 14.99 o.s.i (*0-670-62975-8*, Viking Children's Bks.) Penguin Putnam Bks. for Young Readers.
—Secret of the Andes. 2001. (YA). (gr. 5-9). 20.25 (*0-8446-7172-X*) Smith, Peter Pub., Inc.
—Secret of the Andes. 1976. (J). (gr. 4-8). 11.04 (*0-606-01802-6*) Turtleback Bks.
Cussler, Clive. Inca Gold. abr. ed. 1998. (Dirk Pitt Adventure Ser.). 400p. (YA). (gr. 5 up). mass mkt. 4.99 (*0-671-02056-0*, Simon Pulse) Simon & Schuster Children's Publishing.
Lehtinen, Ritva & Nurmi, Kari E. The Grandchildren of the Incas. 1992. (Illus.). (J). (gr. 3-6). pap. 6.95 o.p. (*0-87614-566-7*, Carolrhoda Bks.) Lerner Publishing Group.
Malkus, Alida A. Young Inca Prince. 1966. (Illus.). (J). (gr. 7-10). lib. bdg. 4.39 o.s.i (*0-394-91845-2*, Knopf Bks. for Young Readers) Random Hse. Children's Bks.
Plenk, Dagmar. Sophie & the Incas. 1991. 72p. (Orig.). (J). (gr. 3-7). pap. 9.00 (*1-56002-039-3*) Aegina Pr., Inc.
Vandersteen, Willy. The Secret of the Incas. 1998. (Greatest Adventures of Spike & Suzy Ser.: Vol. 3). (Illus.). 56p. (J). (gr. 2-9). 11.95 (*0-9533178-2-X*) Intes International (UK) Ltd. GBR. *Dist:* Diamond Book Distributors, Inc.
Villoldo, Alberto. The First Story Ever Told. 1996. (Illus.). (J). (ps-3). 40p. 16.00 (*0-689-80515-2*); 16.00 (*0-671-89729-2*) Simon & Schuster Children's Publishing. (Simon & Schuster Children's Publishing).

INDIA—FICTION

Anand, Mulk Raj. Maya of Mohenjo-Daro. 3rd ed. 1980. (Illus.). 24p. (Orig.). (J). (gr. k-3). pap. 2.50 o.p. (*0-89744-214-8*) Children's Bk. Trust IND. *Dist:* Random Hse. of Canada, Ltd.
Arnold, Marsha D. Heart of a Tiger. 1995. (Illus.). 32p. (J). (ps-2). 14.89 o.s.i (*0-8037-1696-6*); 16.99 (*0-8037-1695-8*) Penguin Putnam Bks. for Young Readers. (Dial Bks. for Young Readers).
Atkins, Jeannine. Aani & the Tree Huggers. 2000. (Illus.). 32p. (J). (ps-5). pap. 6.95 (*1-58430-004-3*); 15.95 (*1-880000-24-5*) Lee & Low Bks., Inc.
—Aani & the Tree Huggers. 2000. (Illus.). (J). 13.10 (*0-606-18245-4*) Turtleback Bks.
Ballard, John H. SoulMates: A Novel to End World Hunger, 2 bks. in 1. Ellen, Joan, ed. 1998. (Soul to Soul Adventure Ser.). 524p. (YA). (gr. 7 up). 19.95 (*0-932279-06-6*); (Illus.). (gr. 4-7). pap. 14.95 (*0-932279-05-8*) World Citizens.
Bannerman, Helen. Little Black Sambo. 1978. (Panda-back Bks.). (Illus.). (J). (gr. 1-3). 1.25 o.p. (*0-448-49608-9*, Grosset & Dunlap) Penguin Putnam Bks. for Young Readers.
—The Story of Little Babaji. ed. 2003. (gr. 2). spiral bd. (*0-616-14615-9*) Canadian National Institute for the Blind/Institut National Canadien pour les Aveugles.
—The Story of Little Babaji. (Illus.). 72p. (J). (ps up). 2002. pap. 7.95 (*0-06-008093-0*, Harper Trophy); 1996. 15.95 (*0-06-205064-8*); 1996. lib. bdg. 14.89 (*0-06-205065-6*) HarperCollins Children's Bk. Group.
—The Story of Little Black Sambo. 2004. (Wee Books for Wee Folks). (Illus.). 64p. (J). (gr. 1-3). reprint ed. 6.95 (*1-55709-414-4*) Applewood Bks.
—The Story of Little Black Sambo. 1994. (Illus.). (J). (gr. k-4). 32p. 16.95 (*0-87797-265-6*); 24p. lib. bdg. 14.95 o.p. (*0-87797-266-4*) Cherokee Publishing Co.
—The Story of Little Black Sambo. (J). E-Book 2.49 (*1-58627-192-X*) Electric Umbrella Publishing.
—The Story of Little Black Sambo. (Illus.). 58p. (J). 1996. 25.00 (*0-9616844-8-8*); 1986. pap. 12.95 (*0-9616844-1-0*) Greenhouse Publishing Co.
—The Story of Little Black Sambo. 2003. (Illus.). 40p. (J). 17.95 (*1-929766-55-6*) Handprint Bks.
—The Story of Little Black Sambo. 2003. (Illus.). 64p. (J). (gr. k-3). 15.99 (*0-397-30006-9*) HarperTrade.
—The Story of Little Black Sambo. 1999. (J). E-Book 1.95 (*1-58515-118-1*) MesaView, Inc.
—The Story of Little Black Sambo. E-Book 2.00 (*0-7410-1435-1*) SoftBook Pr.
Barker, Carol. Arjun & His Village in India. 1979. (Illus.). (J). (gr. 4-6). 10.95 o.p. (*0-19-279734-4*) Oxford Univ. Pr., Inc.
Basu, Romen. The Street Corner Boys. Hauge, Veronica, tr. 1992. 154p. (YA). (gr. 9-10). 14.95 (*0-932377-40-8*) Facet Bks. International, Inc.
Bond, Ruskin. Cherry Tree. 2003. (Illus.). 32p. (J). (ps-3). pap. 8.95 (*1-56397-621-8*) Boyds Mills Pr.
—Cherry Tree. 1996. 14.10 (*0-606-15478-7*) Turtleback Bks.
—Tigers Forever. 1984. (Redwing Bks.). (Illus.). 48p. 6.95 o.p. (*0-531-03764-9*, Watts, Franklin) Scholastic Library Publishing.
Bonnici, Peter. The Festival. 1985. (Arjuna Bks.). (Illus.). 32p. (J). (ps-3). lib. bdg. 9.95 o.p. (*0-87614-229-3*, Carolrhoda Bks.) Lerner Publishing Group.
Bosse, Malcolm. Ganesh. 1981. 192p. (YA). (gr. 7 up). o.p. (*0-690-04102-0*); lib. bdg. 11.89 (*0-690-04103-9*) HarperCollins Children's Bk. Group.
—Tusk & Stone. 2004. 224p. (J). pap. (*1-886910-74-X*); 1995. 244p. (YA). (gr. 4-7). 15.95 (*1-886910-01-4*) Front Street, Inc.
—Tusk & Stone. 1996. 256p. (J). (gr. 5-9). pap. 4.99 o.s.i (*0-14-038217-8*) Penguin Putnam Bks. for Young Readers.
—Tusk & Stone. 1996. (J). 10.09 o.p. (*0-606-12017-3*) Turtleback Bks.
Bothwell, Jean. Dancing Princess. 1965. (J). (gr. 7 up). 4.50 o.p. (*0-15-221637-5*) Harcourt Children's Bks.
—Defiant Bride. 1969. (J). (gr. 7 up). 5.95 o.p. (*0-15-223090-4*) Harcourt Children's Bks.
—Promise of the Rose. 1958. (J). 4.50 o.p. (*0-15-263687-0*) Harcourt Children's Bks.
Champagne, Maurice. The Mysterious Valley. Bucko, Bill, tr. from FRE. 1994. (Illus.). 256p. (J). pap. 19.95 (*0-9626854-9-6*); (gr. 3 up). 29.95 (*0-9626854-6-1*) Atlantean Pr.
Cherrington, Janelle. Drawing the Line. 2000. (Wild Thornberrys Ready-to-Read Ser.: Vol. 2). (Illus.). 32p. (J). (gr. 4-6). pap. 3.99 (*0-689-83231-1*, Simon Spotlight/Nickelodeon) Simon & Schuster Children's Publishing.
Chidvilasananda, Gurumayi, narrated by. The Great Hiss. 2001. (J). pap. 18.95 incl. audio compact disk (*0-911307-90-7*, 205221, Siddha Yoga Publication) SYDA Foundation.
Clifford, Mary L. Bisha of Burundi. 1973. (Illus.). 160p. (J). (gr. 5 up). 7.95 o.p. (*0-690-14596-9*) HarperCollins Children's Bk. Group.
Corry, Beatrice J. Old Friends. 2002. (Babu the Buffalo, Tales of India Ser.: Bk. 1). (Illus.). 21p. (J). (*0-9722880-0-7*); pap. (*0-9722880-1-5*) Babu Bks.
Cowcher, Helen. La Tigresa, RS. Marcuse, Aida E., tr. 1993. (SPA.). 32p. (J). (ps-3). pap. 5.95 o.p. (*0-374-47779-5*, Mirasol/Libros Juveniles) Farrar, Straus & Giroux.
—La Tigresa. 1993. (SPA.). (J). 12.10 (*0-606-05902-4*) Turtleback Bks.
—La Tigresa: Tigress, RS. 1993. (SPA.). 32p. (J). (ps-3). 16.00 o.p. (*0-374-37565-8*, Mirasol/Libros Juveniles) Farrar, Straus & Giroux.
—Tigress. (BEN, CHI, ENG, GRE & GUJ., Illus.). 40p. 16.95 (*1-84059-025-4*); 16.95 (*1-84059-030-0*); 2001. (YA). 16.95 (*1-84059-024-6*); 2001. (YA). 16.95 (*1-84059-026-2*); 2001. (YA). 16.95 (*1-84059-027-0*); 2001. (YA). 16.95 (*1-84059-028-9*); 2001. (YA). 16.95 (*1-84059-029-7*) Milet Publishing, Ltd. GBR. *Dist:* Pan Asia Pubns. (USA), Inc., Consortium Bk. Sales & Distribution.
—Tigress. (Illus.). 34p. (J). 3.98 o.p. (*0-8317-2263-0*) Smithmark Pubs., Inc.
—Tigress. 1990. (Illus.). 32p. (J). (gr. k-3). 19.95 o.p. incl. audio (*0-924483-33-4*) Soundprints.
—Tigress. 1993. 11.15 o.p. (*0-606-06060-X*) Turtleback Bks.
Cowcher, Helen, illus. Tigress, RS. 32p. (J). (ps-3). 1993. pap. 5.95 (*0-374-47781-7*, Sunburst); 1991. 14.95 o.p. (*0-374-37567-4*, Farrar, Straus & Giroux (BYR)) Farrar, Straus & Giroux.
Divakaruni, Chitra Banerjee. Neela: Victory Song. 2002. (Girls of Many Lands Ser.). (Illus.). 198p. (J). 12.95 (*1-58485-597-5*); pap. 7.95 (*1-58485-521-5*) Pleasant Co. Pubns. (American Girl).
Dutta, S. & Hemalata. Harishchandra. 1979. (Illus.). (J). (gr. 1-8). pap. 3.00 o.p. (*0-89744-155-9*) Auromere, Inc.
Ellis, Ella Thorp. The Year of My Indian Prince. 2002. 224p. (YA). (gr. 7). mass mkt. 5.50 (*0-440-22950-2*, Random Hse. Bks. for Young Readers) Random Hse. Children's Bks.
Forman, James. Follow the River, RS. 1975. 192p. (J). (gr. 7 up). 6.95 o.p. (*0-374-32424-7*, Farrar, Straus & Giroux (BYR)) Farrar, Straus & Giroux.
Gavin, Jamila. Fine Feathered Friend. 2002. (Yellow Bananas Ser.). (Illus.). 48p. (J). (gr. 3-4). pap. 4.95 (*0-7787-0985-X*); lib. bdg. 19.96 (*0-7787-0939-6*) Crabtree Publishing Co.
Godden, Rumer. The Peacock Spring. 1976. 286p. (YA). 10.95 o.p. (*0-670-54558-9*) Viking Penguin.
—Premlata & the Festival of Lights. 1997. (Illus.). 64p. (J). (gr. 2 up). 15.00 o.s.i (*0-688-15136-1*, Greenwillow Bks.) HarperCollins Children's Bk. Group.
Golden Books Family Entertainment Staff. Walt Disney's Jungle Book. (Illus.). (J). o.p. (*0-307-01138-0*, Golden Bks.) Random Hse. Children's Bks.
Grant, Eva. A Cow for Jaya. 1973. (Break-of-Day Bks.). (Illus.). 64p. (J). (gr. 1-3). 4.69 o.p. (*0-698-30484-5*) Putnam Publishing Group, The.
Guillot, Rene. The Three Hundred Ninety-Seventh White Elephant. 1957. (Illus.). (J). (gr. 3-7). 20.95 o.p. (*0-87599-043-6*) Phillips, S.G. Inc.
Gunda, Kavita & Baruah, Sangita. What Is That? 1999. (Illus.). (J). (gr. k-5). 14.95 (*1-882792-89-0*) Proctor Pubns.
Hammerslough, Jane. Langur Monkey's Day. Buelt, Laura, tr. & illus. by. 2003. (J). (*1-59249-141-3*); pap. (*1-59249-142-1*) Soundprints.
Henty, G. A. Through the Sikh War: A Tale of the Conquest of the Punjaub. (J). E-Book 3.95 (*0-594-02405-6*) 1873 Pr.
Highwater, Jamake. Rama: A Legend. 1997. 238p. (J). reprint ed. lib. bdg. 24.95 (*0-7351-0001-2*) Replica Bks.
Hirshkowith, Sandra. Premlata & the Festival of Lights. 1999. (Chapter Bks.). (Illus.). 96p. (J). (gr. 2-5). pap. 4.25 (*0-06-442091-4*, Harper Trophy) HarperCollins Children's Bk. Group.
Hoff, Syd. Mahatma. 1969. (Illus.). (J). (gr. k-2). 4.69 o.p. (*0-399-60440-5*) Putnam Publishing Group, The.
Howard, Ginger. A Basket of Bangles: How a Business Begins. 2002. (Around the World Ser.). (Illus.). 32p. (J). (gr. k-3). 21.90 (*0-7613-1902-6*) Millbrook Pr., Inc.
Jacob, Helen P. A Garland for Gandhi, 001. 1968. (Illus.). (J). (gr. 2-5). 5.95 o.p. (*0-395-27651-9*) Houghton Mifflin Co.
Jaffrey, Madhur. Robi Dobi: The Marvellous Adventures of an Indian Elephant. 2001. (Illus.). 64p. (YA). (gr. 1 up). pap. 13.00 (*1-86205-160-7*) Pavilion Bks., Ltd. GBR. *Dist:* Trafalgar Square.
Jekel, Pamela. The Third Jungle Book. 1992. (Illus.). 220p. (J). (ps-12). 19.95 (*1-879373-22-X*) Rinehart, Roberts Pubs.
Kalman, Maira. Swami on Rye: Max in India. 1995. (Illus.). 40p. (J). (ps-3). 16.00 o.p. (*0-670-85646-0*, Viking) Penguin Putnam Bks. for Young Readers.
Kamal, Aleph. The Bird Who Was an Elephant. 1989. 32p. text o.p. (*0-521-36614-3*) Cambridge Univ. Pr.
—The Bird Who Was an Elephant. 1990. (Illus.). 32p. (J). (gr. k-4). 14.95 (*0-397-32445-6*); lib. bdg. 14.89 (*0-397-32446-4*) HarperCollins Children's Bk. Group.
Kipling, Rudyard. The Complete Just So Stories. Philip, Neil, ed. & intro. by. 1993. (Illus.). 160p. (J). 19.99 o.s.i (*0-670-85196-5*, Viking Children's Bks.) Penguin Putnam Bks. for Young Readers.
—The Jungle Book. 2002. (Great Illustrated Classics). (Illus.). 240p. (J). (gr. 3-8). lib. bdg. 21.35 (*1-57765-812-4*, ABDO & Daughters) ABDO Publishing Co.
—The Jungle Book. 1999. (Classics Ser.). (Illus.). 160p. (J). 12.95 (*0-7892-0558-0*); pap. 7.95 (*0-7892-0548-3*) Abbeville Pr., Inc. (Abbeville Kids).
—The Jungle Book. 2000. (Juvenile Classics). 160p. (J). pap. 2.00 (*0-486-41024-2*) Dover Pubns., Inc.
—The Jungle Book. 1994. 28p. (J). (gr. 2-8). pap. 4.00 (*1-57514-250-3*, 1163) Encore Performance Publishing.
—The Jungle Book. 1995. (Books of Wonder: Vol. 1). (Illus.). 272p. (J). (ps-3). 24.99 (*0-688-09979-3*) HarperCollins Children's Bk. Group.
—The Jungle Book. 1984. (Illus.). 224p. (J). (gr. 2-9). 12.95 o.s.i (*0-8052-3906-5*, Schocken) Knopf Publishing Group.
—The Jungle Book. 1994. (Everyman's Library Children's Classics Ser.). (Illus.). 272p. (J). (gr. 2 up). 14.95 (*0-679-43637-5*) Knopf, Alfred A. Inc.
—The Jungle Book. 1995. (Classics Ser.). (Illus.). (YA). pap. text 7.87 (*0-582-03587-2*) Longman Publishing Group.
—The Jungle Book. Robson, W. W., ed. & intro. by. 1992. (Oxford World's Classics Ser.). 420p. (J). pap. 5.95 o.p. (*0-19-282901-7*) Oxford Univ. Pr., Inc.
—The Jungle Book. (Whole Story Ser.). (Illus.). 1996. 216p. (YA). (gr. 7-12). 22.99 o.s.i (*0-670-86919-8*, Viking Children's Bks.); 1995. 294p. (J). 16.99 (*0-448-40948-8*, Grosset & Dunlap); 1995. 224p. (YA). (gr. 4-7). pap. 3.99 (*0-14-036686-5*, Puffin Bks.); 1987. 176p. (J). (gr. 5-9). 16.00 o.p. (*0-670-80241-7*, Viking Children's Bks.) Penguin Putnam Bks. for Young Readers.
—The Jungle Book. Hanft, Joshua, ed. 1994. (Great Illustrated Classics Ser.: Vol. 37). (Illus.). 240p. (J). (gr. 3-6). 9.95 (*0-86611-988-4*) Playmore, Inc., Pubs.
—The Jungle Book. (Children's Classics Ser.). (Illus.). (J). 1989. xv, 303p. 12.99 o.s.i (*0-517-67902-7*); 1988. 48p. 5.99 o.p. (*0-517-67006-2*) Random Hse. Value Publishing.
—The Jungle Book. 1995. (J). mass mkt. 3.50 (*0-590-50323-5*, Scholastic Paperbacks) Scholastic, Inc.
—The Jungle Book. 1995. (J). 7.98 o.p. (*0-8317-0747-X*) Smithmark Pubs., Inc.
—The Jungle Book. 1998. (Children's Classics). 192p. (J). (gr. 4-7). pap. 3.95 (*1-85326-119-X*, 119XWW) Wordsworth Editions, Ltd. GBR. *Dist:* Advanced Global Distribution Services.
—The Jungle Book. 1996. (Little Golden Bks.). (Illus.). 24p. (J). (ps-3). bds. 2.99 (*0-307-00326-4*, Golden Bks.) Random Hse. Children's Bks.
—The Jungle Book. 2001. (Young Classics Ser.). (Illus.). 48p. (J). (gr. 1-3). pap. 9.95 o.p. (*0-7894-4944-7*) Dorling Kindersley Publishing, Inc.
—The Jungle Book. l.t. ed. 1997. (Large Print Heritage Ser.). 240p. (YA). (gr. 7-12). lib. bdg. 28.95 (*1-58118-006-3*, 21966) LRS.
—The Jungle Book. l.t. ed. 1998. (Large Print Ser.). 265p. lib. bdg. 25.00 (*0-939495-58-9*) North Bks.
—The Jungle Book. deluxe ed. 1996. (Whole Story Ser.). (Illus.). 45p. (YA). (gr. 7-12). pap. 18.99 o.p. (*0-670-86797-7*, Viking Children's Bks.) Penguin Putnam Bks. for Young Readers.
—The Jungle Book. l.t. ed. 1999. (Classics for Children 8 & Younger Ser.). (Illus.). 48p. (J). (ps-3). (*1-85854-684-2*) Brimax Bks., Ltd.
—The Jungle Book. (J). reprint ed. lib. bdg. 24.95 (*0-88411-819-3*) Amereon, Ltd.
—The Jungle Book. unabr. ed. 1982. (J). audio 29.95 o.p. (*0-7861-0510-0*, 2010) Blackstone Audio Bks., Inc.
—The Jungle Book. unabr. ed. 1990. (J). audio 16.99 (*0-88646-375-0*, 7375) Durkin Hayes Publishing Ltd.
—The Jungle Book, Level 2. Hedge, Tricia, ed. 2000. (Bookworms Ser.). (Illus.). 64p. (J). pap. text 5.95 (*0-19-422977-7*) Oxford Univ. Pr., Inc.
—The Jungle Book: A Young Reader's Edition of the Classic Story. 1994. (Illus.). 56p. (J). (ps up). 9.98 (*1-56138-475-5*, Courage Bks.) Running Pr. Bk. Pubs.
—The Jungle Book: BBC. abr. ed. 1996. (BBC Radio Presents Ser.). (J). audio 16.99 o.s.i (*0-553-47799-4*, 394319, Listening Library) Random Hse. Audio Publishing Group.
—The Jungle Book I. 1994. 400p. mass mkt. 4.99 o.s.i (*0-06-106286-3*) HarperCollins Pubs.
—The Jungle Book I. 1950. (Illus.). 294p. (J). (gr. 4-6). 12.95 o.s.i (*0-448-06014-0*) Putnam Publishing Group, The.
—The Jungle Book I. 1987. 8.98 (*0-671-09226-X*) Simon & Schuster.
—The Jungle Book II. 1995. 177p. (YA). mass mkt. 2.99 (*0-8125-2278-8*, Tor Classics) Doherty, Tom Assocs., LLC.
—The Jungle Books. 1966. (Classics Ser.). (YA). (gr. 5 up). mass mkt. 1.95 o.p. (*0-8049-0109-0*, CL-109) Airmont Publishing Co., Inc.
—The Jungle Books. 1961. 368p. (YA). (gr. 4-7). mass mkt. 4.95 (*0-451-52340-7*, Signet Classics) NAL.
—The Jungle Books. abr. ed. 1995. (J). (gr. 4-7). audio 17.98 (*962-634-535-7*, NA303514); audio compact disk 19.98 (*962-634-035-5*, NA303512) Naxos of America, Inc. (Naxos AudioBooks).
—Kim. 1965. (Airmont Classics Ser.). (YA). (gr. 8 up). pap. 1.95 o.p. (*0-8049-0075-2*, CL75) Airmont Publishing Co., Inc.
—Kim, Set. unabr. ed. 1998. (J). audio 64.95 (*1-85549-974-6*, CTC135) BBC Audiobooks America.
—Kim. 1992. 384p. (J). (gr. 5 up). pap. 3.50 o.s.i (*0-440-40695-1*) Dell Publishing.
—Kim. 1985. (gr. 11 up). 6.95 o.p. (*0-385-07361-5*) Doubleday Publishing.

—Kim. abr. ed. (J). audio 15.95 o.p. (*0-88646-138-3*, 7139) Durkin Hayes Publishing Ltd.

—Kim. abr. ed. (J). audio 9.95 o.p. (*0-694-50821-7*, CDL5 1480, HarperAudio) HarperTrade.

—Kim. unabr. ed. 1998. (Wordsworth Classics Ser.). (YA). (gr. 6-12). 5.27 (*0-89061-099-1*, R0991WW) Jamestown.

—Kim. abr. ed. 1994. audio compact disk 15.98 (*962-634-018-5*, NA201812, Naxos AudioBooks) Naxos of America, Inc.

—Kim. l.t. ed. 1992. (Large Print Ser.). 519p. (J). reprint ed. lib. bdg. 26.00 (*0-939495-39-2*) North Bks.

—Kim. unabr. ed. (Read-Along Ser.). (J). audio 34.95 Norton Pubs., Inc., Jeffrey /Audio-Forum.

—Kim. 1996. (Illus.). 400p. (YA). (gr. 5-9). pap. 4.99 (*0-14-036744-6*, Viking) Penguin Putnam Bks. for Young Readers.

—Kim, unabr. ed. 1988. (J). (gr. 4). audio 85.00 (*1-55690-285-9*, 88720E7) Recorded Bks., LLC.

—The Maltese Cat. 1991. (Short Story Library). (Illus.). 48p. (YA). (gr. 4 up). lib. bdg. 13.95 o.p. (*0-88682-475-3*, Creative Education) Creative Co., The.

—The Miracle of Purun Bhagat. 1986. (Short Story Library). (Illus.). 40p. (YA). (gr. 5 up). lib. bdg. 13.95 o.p. (*0-88682-052-9*, Creative Education) Creative Co., The.

—Mowgli. 1924. lib. bdg. o.s.i (*0-688-04643-6*); (J). o.s.i (*0-688-04642-8*) HarperCollins Children's Bk. Group.

—Mowgli Stories. 1994. (Illus.). 128p. (J). pap. 1.00 (*0-486-28030-6*) Dover Pubns., Inc.

—Mowgli's Brothers. 1995. (Illus.). 64p. (J). (gr. 1-5). 19.95 o.p. (*0-15-200933-7*) Harcourt Trade Pubs.

—Rikki-Tikki-Tavi. 1997. (Candlewick Treasures Ser.). (Illus.). 64p. (J). (gr. 3-9). 11.99 o.p. (*0-7636-0135-7*) Candlewick Pr.

—Rikki-Tikki-Tavi. (Creative Short Stories Ser.). (gr. 4-12). 1993. 47p. (YA). lib. bdg. 18.60 (*0-88682-126-6*, 1078-4); 1986. (Illus.). 48p. (J). lib. bdg. 8.95 o.p. (*0-88682-002-2*) Creative Co., The. (Creative Education).

—Rikki-Tikki-Tavi. 1993. 20p. (J). (gr. 2-7). pap. 4.00 (*1-57514-258-9*, 1115) Encore Performance Publishing.

—Rikki-Tikki-Tavi. 1997. (Illus.). 48p. (J). (ps-3). 16.99 (*0-688-14320-2*); lab manual ed. 15.89 (*0-688-14321-0*) HarperCollins Children's Bk. Group.

—Rikki-Tikki-Tavi. (J). (gr. k-5). 1985. 5.95 o.p. (*0-8249-8117-0*); 1982. (Illus.). 48p. 4.95 o.p. (*0-8249-8041-7*) Ideals Pubns.

—Rikki-Tikki-Tavi. 1982. (Illus.). (J). (ps-3). lib. bdg. 11.95 o.p. (*0-516-09223-5*, Children's Pr.) Scholastic Library Publishing.

—Rudyard Kipling Collected Short Stories. 2001. (Great Author Ser.). (J). (*0-9709033-6-7*) Peterson Publishing Co., Inc.

—The Second Jungle Book. 1923. (J). (gr. 7-11). 4.50 o.s.i (*0-385-07483-2*) Doubleday Publishing.

—Tales from The Jungle Book. 9999. (Children's Classics Ser.: No. 740-26). (Illus.). (J). (gr. 3-5). pap. 3.50 o.p. (*0-7214-0997-0*, Ladybird Bks.) Penguin Group (USA) Inc.

—The Two Jungle Books. 2000. 252p. (J). E-Book 9.95 (*0-594-05381-1*) 1873 Pr.

Kipling, Rudyard & Said, Edward W. Kim. 1987. 384p. (J). (gr. 5 up). pap. 3.99 o.p. (*0-14-035076-4*, Puffin Bks.) Penguin Putnam Bks. for Young Readers.

Krishnaswami, Uma. Chachaji's Cup. 2003. (Illus.). 32p. (J). (gr. 1 up). 16.95 (*0-89239-178-2*) Children's Bk. Pr.

—Monsoon, RS. 2003. (Illus.). 32p. (J). 16.00 (*0-374-35015-9*, Farrar, Straus & Giroux (BYR)) Farrar, Straus & Giroux.

—Naming Maya, RS. 2004. (J). 16.00 (*0-374-35485-5*, Farrar, Straus & Giroux (BYR)) Farrar, Straus & Giroux.

Linam, Gail. Kind Doctor, Missionary Friend. 1981. (J). (gr. 1-3). 5.95 o.p. (*0-8054-4274-X*) Broadman & Holman Pubs.

McDonald, Megan. Baya, Baya, Lulla-by-A. 2003. (Illus.). 32p. (J). 16.95 (*0-689-84932-X*, Atheneum/Richard Jackson Bks.) Simon & Schuster Children's Publishing.

Mehta, Lila. The Enchanted Anklet: A Cinderella Story from India. 2nd ed. 1985. (Illus.). 32p. (J). (gr. 3-7). 15.95 (*0-9692729-0-1*) Lilmur Publishing CAN. *Dist:* Shen's Bks.

Mouse Works Staff. Disney's The Jungle Book: Mowgli Makes a Friend. 1995. (Tiny Changing Pictures Bk.). (Illus.). 10p. (J). (ps-k). 4.95 o.p. (*0-7868-3068-9*) Disney Pr.

—El Libro de la Selva (The Jungle Book) 1995. (SPA., Illus.). 96p. (J). 7.98 o.p. (*1-57082-223-9*) Mouse Works.

Mukerji, Dhan G. Kari, the Elephant. 1922. (Illus.). (J). (gr. 5-7). lib. bdg. 7.95 o.p. (*0-525-33008-9*, Dutton) Dutton/Plume.

Namjoshi, Suniti. Aditi & the One-Eyed Monkey. 1989. (Night Lights Ser.). (Illus.). 96p. (J). (gr. 2-5). reprint ed. pap. 3.95 o.p. (*0-8070-8315-1*); lib. bdg. 10.95 o.p. (*0-8070-8314-3*) Beacon Pr.

Osborne, Mary Pope. Tigers at Twilight. 1999. (Magic Tree House Ser.: No. 19). (Illus.). 96p. (J). (gr. k-3). lib. bdg. 11.99 (*0-679-99065-8*); pap. 3.99 (*0-679-89065-3*) Random Hse. Children's Bks. (Random Hse. Bks. for Young Readers).

—Tigers at Twilight. 1999. (Magic Tree House Ser.: No. 18). (J). (gr. k-3). 10.14 (*0-606-16957-1*) Turtleback Bks.

Parkison, Jami. Amazing Mallika. Talley, Carol, ed. 1996. (Key Concepts in Personal Development Ser.). (Illus.). 32p. (J). (gr. k-4). 16.95 (*1-55942-087-1*) Marsh Media.

Patel, Mickey. Story of a Panther. 1998. 14.00 (*81-7530-020-5*) Dayal, Ravi Pub. IND. *Dist:* South Asia Bks.

Pinkney, Jerry. Rikki-Tikki-Tavi. 2004. (Illus.). 48p. (J). pap. 6.99 (*0-06-058785-7*, Harper Trophy) HarperCollins Children's Bk. Group.

Precious Moments: An Adventure in Wellmore. 2001. 132p. (J). pap. 10.95 (*0-595-19555-5*, Writers Club Pr.) iUniverse, Inc.

Rana, Indi. The Roller Birds of Rampur. 1994. 320p. mass mkt. 3.99 o.s.i (*0-449-70434-3*, Fawcett) Ballantine Bks.

—The Roller Birds of Rampur, ERS. 1993. 304p. (YA). (gr. 7 up). 15.95 o.p. (*0-8050-2670-3*, Holt, Henry & Co. Bks. For Young Readers) Holt, Henry & Co.

Rankin, Louise. Daughter of the Mountains. 1993. (Puffin Newbery Library). (Illus.). 192p. (J). (gr. 3-7). pap. 6.99 (*0-14-036335-1*, Puffin Bks.) Penguin Putnam Bks. for Young Readers.

—Daughter of the Mountains. 1980. (J). (gr. 4-6). pap. 1.25 o.p. (*0-671-29517-9*, Archway Paperbacks) Pocket Bks.

—Daughter of the Mountains. 1996. (J). (gr. 5-9). 21.25 (*0-8446-6895-8*) Smith, Peter Pub., Inc.

—Daughter of the Mountains. 1993. (Puffin Newbery Library). (J). 11.04 (*0-606-02585-5*) Turtleback Bks.

Rumford, James. The Nine Animals & the Well. 2003. (Illus.). 32p. (J). (gr. k-5). tchr. ed. 16.00 (*0-618-30915-2*) Houghton Mifflin Co.

Sharma, Partap. The Surangini Tales. 1973. (Illus.). 128p. (J). (gr. 4-7). 5.75 o.p. (*0-15-283200-9*) Harcourt Children's Bks.

Shivkumar. Krishna & Sudama. 1979. (Illus.). (J). (gr. 1-8). pap. 2.00 o.p. (*0-89744-156-7*) Auromere, Inc.

Silverstone, Marilyn & Miller, Luree. Bala: Child of India. 1968. (Children Everywhere Ser.: No. 4). (Illus.). (J). (gr. 2-4). lib. bdg. 3.33 o.p. (*0-8038-0670-1*) Hastings Hse. Daytrips Pubs.

Simmons, Lesley Anne. Meet Kofi, Maria & Sunita: Family Life in Ghana, Peru & India. 1996. (Stories from the World Bank Ser.: Vol. 1). (Illus.). 80p. (J). (gr. 2-4). 14.95 (*0-942389-12-3*) Cobblestone Publishing Co.

Smarananda, Swami. Story of Sarada Devi. 1987. (Illus.). 31p. (Orig.). (J). (gr. k-4). pap. 2.00 (*0-87481-229-1*) Advaita Ashrama IND. *Dist:* Vedanta Pr.

Sreenivasan, Jyotsna. Aruna's Journeys. 1997. (Illus.). 136p. (Orig.). (J). (gr. 1-4). pap. 6.95 (*0-9619401-7-4*) Smooth Stone Pr.

Staples, Suzanne Fisher. Shiva's Fire, RS. (J). o.p. (*0-374-31686-4*); 2000. (Illus.). 288p. (YA). (gr. 7-12). 18.00 (*0-374-36824-4*) Farrar, Straus & Giroux. (Farrar, Straus & Giroux (BYR)).

—Shiva's Fire. 2001. 288p. (J). (gr. 5 up). pap. 5.99 (*0-06-440979-1*, Harper Trophy) HarperCollins Children's Bk. Group.

—Shiva's Fire. 2001. (YA). pap., stu. ed. 82.00 incl. audio. (gr. 7). audio compact disk 58.00 (*0-7887-5222-7*, C1370E7); (gr. 7). audio 56.00 Recorded Bks., LLC.

—Shiva's Fire. l.t. ed. 2000. (Young Adult Ser.). 316p. (J). (gr. 8-12). 21.95 (*0-7862-2902-0*) Thorndike Pr.

Stewart, Mollie D. Noah's Land. 1991. (J). 12.95 o.p. (*0-533-09336-8*) Vantage Pr., Inc.

Stone, Susheila. Nadeem Makes Samosas. 1991. (Duets Ser.). (Illus.). 25p. (J). (gr. 2-4). 15.95 o.p. (*0-237-60155-9*) Evans Brothers, Ltd. GBR. *Dist:* Trafalgar Square.

Sucksdorff, A. B., photos by. Tooni, the Elephant Boy. 1971. (Illus.). 48p. (J). (gr. 3 up). 5.95 o.p. (*0-15-289426-8*) Harcourt Children's Bks.

Thornhill, Jan. The Rumor: A Jataka Tale from Indian. 2003. (Illus.). 32p. (J). (ps-3). 17.95 (*1-894379-39-X*) Maple Tree Pr. CAN. *Dist:* Firefly Bks., Ltd.

Towle, Faith M. The Magic Cooking Pot, 001. 1975. (Illus.). 48p. (J). (gr. k-3). 6.95 o.p. (*0-395-20273-6*) Houghton Mifflin Co.

Trimble, Irene. Jungle Friends. 2003. (Step into Reading Ser.). 32p. (J). 3.99 (*0-7364-2089-4*, RH/Disney) Random Hse. Children's Bks.

—Jungle Friends. 2003. (Step into Reading Ser.). 32p. (J). lib. bdg. 11.99 (*0-7364-8017-X*) Random Hse., Inc.

Watts, Mabel. Elephant That Became a Ferry Boat. 1971. (Illus.). (J). (gr. k-4). lib. bdg. 6.19 o.p. (*0-8313-0102-3*) Lantern Pr., Inc., Pubs.

Whelan, Gloria. Homeless Bird. l.t. ed. 2002. 147p. (J). 23.95 (*0-7862-4060-1*) Gale Group.

—Homeless Bird. (J). (gr. 5 up). 2001. 192p. pap. 5.99 (*0-06-440819-1*); 2000. 240p. 15.95 (*0-06-028454-4*); 2000. 240p. lib. bdg. 16.89 (*0-06-028452-8*) HarperCollins Children's Bk. Group.

—Homeless Bird. unabr. ed. 2001. (J). 240p. pap. 28.00 incl. audio (*0-8072-8859-4*, Listening Library); audio 18.00 (*0-8072-6181-5*, RH Audio) Random Hse. Audio Publishing Group.

White, Rosalyn, illus. The Best of Friends. 1989. (Jataka Tales Ser.). 32p. (Orig.). (J). (ps-3). pap. 7.95 (*0-89800-187-0*) Dharma Publishing.

Wright, Meg, illus. Three Stories from India. 1984. (J). (gr. 1-8). pap. text 10.00 (*0-86508-166-2*) BCM Pubns., Inc.

Yolen, Jane. Children of the Wolf. 1984. 144p. (J). (gr. 7 up). 11.95 o.p. (*0-670-21763-8*, Viking Children's Bks.) Penguin Putnam Bks. for Young Readers.

INDIANA—FICTION

Blakeslee, Ann R. Summer Battles. 2000. (Illus.). 128p. (YA). (gr. 5-9). 14.95 (*0-7614-5064-5*, Cavendish Children's Bks.) Cavendish, Marshall Corp.

Bradley, Kimberly Brubaker. Ruthie's Gift. 1998. (Illus.). 160p. (gr. 2-7). text 14.95 o.s.i (*0-385-32525-8*, Dell Books for Young Readers) Random Hse. Children's Bks.

Carroll, Jenny. When Lightning Strikes. E-Book 4.99 (*1-58945-631-9*) Adobe Systems, Inc.

—When Lightning Strikes. 2001. (1-800-Where-R-You Ser.: Vol. 1). (YA). (Illus.). 272p. (gr. 7-12). pap. 4.99 (*0-7434-1139-0*); reprint ed. E-Book 4.99 (*0-7434-2324-0*) Simon & Schuster Children's Publishing. (Simon Pulse).

Clifford, Eth. Search for the Crescent Moon, 001. 1974. (Illus.). 256p. (J). (gr. 7-12). 5.95 o.p. (*0-395-16035-9*) Houghton Mifflin Co.

—The Year of the Three-Legged Deer. Cuffari, Richard, tr. & illus. by. 2003. (Library of Indiana Classics). xix, 164p. (YA). 32.95 (*0-253-34251-1*); pap. 14.95 (*0-253-21604-4*) Indiana Univ. Pr.

Cullen, Lynn. Diary of Nelly Vandorn. 2002. (Nelly in the Wilderness Ser.). 192p. (J). (gr. 3-6). lib. bdg. 15.89 (*0-06-029134-6*); 15.95 (*0-06-029133-8*) HarperCollins Children's Bk. Group.

—Diary of Nelly Vandorn. Date not set. 128p. (gr. 3 up). mass mkt. 4.99 (*0-06-440926-0*) HarperCollins Pubs.

Ford, Mike. The Eerie Triangle. 1997. (Eerie Indiana Ser.: No. 3). 144p. (J). (gr. 3-7). pap. 3.99 (*0-380-79776-3*, Avon Bks.) Morrow/Avon.

—Return to Foreverware. 1997. (Eerie Indiana Ser.: No. 1). (J). (gr. 3-7). pap. 0.99 (*0-380-79774-7*, Avon Bks.) Morrow/Avon.

—Who Framed Alice Prophet? 2003. (Illus.). 140p. (J). pap. o.p. (*0-330-37074-X*) Macmillan Children's Bks.

Haddix, Margaret Peterson. Running Out of Time. unabr. ed. 1998. (J). (gr. 4-7). audio 32.00 (*0-8072-8031-3*, YA972CX, Listening Library) Random Hse. Audio Publishing Group.

—Running Out of Time. 192p. (J). 1997. (gr. 3-7). pap. 4.99 (*0-689-81236-1*, Aladdin); 1995. (gr. 4-7). 16.00 (*0-689-80084-3*, Simon & Schuster Children's Publishing) Simon & Schuster Children's Publishing.

—Running Out of Time. 1997. (J). 11.04 (*0-606-11007-0*) Turtleback Bks.

Hamilton, Dorothy. Rosalie at Eleven. 1980. (Illus.). 112p. (J). (gr. 3-8). pap. 3.95 o.p. (*0-8361-1931-2*) Herald Pr.

Henry, Joanne Landers. A Clearing in the Forest: A Story about a Real Settler Boy. 1992. (Illus.). 64p. (J). (gr. 3-6). lib. bdg. 14.95 (*0-02-743671-3*, Simon & Schuster Children's Publishing) Simon & Schuster Children's Publishing.

Holl, Kristi. 4Give & 4Get. 2001. (TodaysGirls.com Ser.: Vol. 9). (Illus.). 144p. (J). (gr. 5-9). pap. 5.99 o.s.i (*0-8499-7712-6*) Nelson, Tommy.

Kornblatt, Marc. Izzy's Place. 2003. (Illus.). 128p. (J). 16.95 (*0-689-84639-8*, McElderry, Margaret K.) Simon & Schuster Children's Publishing.

Lasky, Kathryn. Christmas after All: The Great Depression Diary of Minnie Swift, Indianapolis, Indiana, 1932. 2001. (Dear America Ser.). (Illus.). 192p. (J). (gr. 4-9). pap. 10.95 (*0-439-21943-4*) Scholastic, Inc.

Lawlor, Laurie. Crooked Creek. Himler, Ronald, tr. & illus. by. 2004. (J). (*0-8234-1812-X*) Holiday Hse., Inc.

Metz, Alberta R. Toughy. 1980. (Illus.). 94p. (Orig.). (J). (gr. 4-7). pap. 4.99 (*0-89827-009-X*, BKF63) Wesleyan Publishing Hse.

—"Toughy" Learns to Fight. 1988. (Illus.). 101p. (Orig.). (J). (gr. 4-7). pap. 4.99 (*0-89827-056-1*, BKF64) Wesleyan Publishing Hse.

Mildred Keith. 2001. (Mildred Classics Ser.: Vol. 1). 288p. pap. 5.95 (*1-58182-227-8*) Cumberland Hse. Publishing.

Naylor, Phyllis Reynolds. The Bodies in the Bessledorf Hotel. 1988. pap. 2.99 (*0-380-70485-4*, Avon Bks.) Morrow/Avon.

—The Bodies in the Bessledorf Hotel. 1986. 144p. (J). (gr. 3-7). lib. bdg. 15.00 (*0-689-31304-7*, Atheneum) Simon & Schuster Children's Publishing.

Peel, John. Bureau of Lost, No. 2. 1997. (Eerie Indiana Ser.: No. 2). 144p. (J). (gr. 3-7). pap. 3.99 (*0-380-79775-5*, Avon Bks.) Morrow/Avon.

—Simon & Marshall's Excellent Adventure. 1997. (Eerie Indiana Ser.: No. 4). 128p. (J). (gr. 3-7). pap. 3.99 (*0-380-79777-1*, Avon Bks.) Morrow/Avon.

—Simon & Marshall's Excellent Adventure. 2003. (Illus.). 121p. (J). pap. o.p. (*0-330-37070-7*) Macmillan Children's Bks.

Shoup, Barbara. Stranded in Harmony. 2001. 194p. (YA). pap. 15.95 (*1-57860-094-4*) Emmis Bks.

—Stranded in Harmony. 1997. 192p. (YA). (gr. 7 up). 17.95 (*0-7868-0287-1*); lib. bdg. 18.49 (*0-7868-2284-8*) Hyperion Bks. for Children.

Stratton-Porter, Gene. A Daughter of the Land. 1997. (Library of Indiana Classics). 352p. pap. 11.95 (*0-253-21138-7*); (J). 20.00 (*0-253-33305-9*) Indiana Univ. Pr.

—Freckles. (J). reprint ed. lib. bdg. 24.95 (*0-89190-949-4*, Rivercity Pr.) Amereon, Ltd.

—Freckles. (J). 1977. 21.95 (*0-89967-003-2*, Harmony Raine & Co.); 1980. 254p. reprint ed. lib. bdg. 25.95 (*0-89966-224-2*) Buccaneer Bks., Inc.

—Freckles. l.t. ed. 2000. (Illus.). (J). o.p. (*1-58547-004-X*) Ctr. Point Large Print.

—Freckles. 1990. 272p. (J). pap. 3.50 o.s.i (*0-440-40050-3*) Dell Publishing.

—Freckles. (J). E-Book 2.49 (*1-58627-576-3*) Electric Umbrella Publishing.

—Freckles. l.t. ed. 2000. (Focus on the Family Great Stories Ser.). (Illus.). 320p. (J). pap. 9.99 o.p. (*1-56179-796-0*) Focus on the Family Publishing.

—Freckles. 1986. (Library of Indiana Classics). (Illus.). 362p. (J). 30.00 (*0-253-32471-8*) Indiana Univ. Pr.

—Freckles. 2002. 228p. 94.99 (*1-4043-0332-4*); per. 89.99 (*1-4043-0333-2*) IndyPublish.com.

—Freckles. (J). E-Book 1.95 (*1-57799-854-5*) Logos Research Systems, Inc.

—Freckles. 2000. (Penguin Readers Lv. 2). (J). pap. 7.66 (*0-582-42655-3*) Longman Publishing Group.

—Freckles. 1990. 256p. (J). mass mkt. 2.95 o.p. (*0-451-52451-9*, Signet Classics) NAL.

—Freckles. 1992. 272p. (J). (gr. 5 up). pap. 4.99 o.s.i (*0-14-035144-2*, Puffin Bks.) Penguin Putnam Bks. for Young Readers.

—Freckles. 1971. reprint ed. 49.00 (*0-403-01156-6*) Scholarly Pr., Inc.

—Freckles. 2000. (J). pap. text 17.99 (*1-930142-10-2*); 467p. (gr. 4-7). 24.99 (*1-930142-11-0*) Write Together Publishing.

—A Girl of the Limberlost. (J). reprint ed. lib. bdg. 33.95 (*0-89190-948-6*, Rivercity Pr.) Amereon, Ltd.

—A Girl of the Limberlost. 2000. (J). per. 14.50 (*1-58396-473-8*) Blue Unicorn Editions.

—A Girl of the Limberlost. (J). E-Book 2.49 (*1-58627-577-1*) Electric Umbrella Publishing.

—A Girl of the Limberlost. 1984. (Library of Indiana Classics). (Illus.). 494p. (J). 25.00 (*0-253-13320-3*); (gr. 4-7). pap. 14.95 (*0-253-20331-7*, MB-331) Indiana Univ. Pr.

—A Girl of the Limberlost. 2002. 340p. (gr. 4-7). 26.99 (*1-4043-0508-4*); per. 21.99 (*1-4043-0509-2*) IndyPublish.com.

—A Girl of the Limberlost. 1988. 384p. mass mkt. 4.95 o.p. (*0-451-52181-1*, Signet Classics) NAL.

—A Girl of the Limberlost. 2003. (Twelve-Point Ser.). (J). lib. bdg. 25.00 (*1-58287-232-5*); lib. bdg. 26.00 (*1-58287-716-5*) North Bks.

—A Girl of the Limberlost. 1961. (J). 4.95 o.p. (*0-448-01243-X*) Putnam Publishing Group, The.

—A Girl of the Limberlost. l.t. ed. 1995. 452p. (J). 22.95 (*0-7838-1450-X*) Thorndike Pr.

—A Girl of the Limberlost. 1991. 352p. (J). pap. 9.99 o.p. (*0-8423-1015-0*) Tyndale Hse. Pubs.

—A Girl of the Limberlost. 2000. (J). Vol. 1. 22.99 (*1-930142-13-7*); Vol. 1. (Illus.). 452p. (gr. 4-7). pap. 15.99 (*1-930142-12-9*); Vol. 2. 22.99 (*1-930142-15-3*); Vol. 2. (Illus.). 399p. pap. 15.99 (*1-930142-14-5*) Write Together Publishing.

—The Harvester. 1977. 560p. (YA). lib. bdg. 35.95 (*0-89966-225-0*) Buccaneer Bks., Inc.

—The Harvester, 2 vols. 2000. Vol. 1. 516p. (gr. 7-12). 23.99 (*1-930142-25-0*); Vol. 1. (Illus.). 502p. (YA). pap. 16.99 (*1-930142-20-X*); Vol. 2. (Illus.). (YA). pap. 16.99 (*1-930142-26-9*) Write Together Publishing.

—Laddie: A True Blue Story. 1988. (Library of Indiana Classics). 416p. (J). 24.95 (*0-253-33113-7*); (YA). pap. 12.95 (*0-253-20458-5*, MB-458) Indiana Univ. Pr.

—Laddie: A True Blue Story. (J). E-Book 1.95 (1-57799-876-6) Logos Research Systems, Inc.

Stratton-Porter, Gene & Falkoff, Marc D. A Girl of the Limberlost. 1999. (Chapter Book Charmers Ser.). 69p. (J). (gr. 2-5). 2.99 o.p. (0-694-01286-6) HarperCollins Children's Bk. Group.

Stratton-Porter, Gene & Outlet Book Company Staff. Freckles. 1994. 320p. (J). 8.99 o.s.i (0-517-10126-2) Random Hse. Value Publishing.

Stratton-Porter, Gene, et al. Freckles. 1986. (Library of Indiana Classics). (Illus.). 362p. (J). (gr. 3-7). pap. 12.95 (0-253-20363-5, MB-363) Indiana Univ. Pr.

Swain, Gwenyth. Chig & the Second Spread. 2003. 208p. (gr. 3-7). (J). 14.95 (0-385-73065-9, Delacorte Bks. for Young Readers); lib. bdg. 16.99 (0-385-90094-5) Random Hse. Children's Bks.

Waters, Kate. Andrew McClure & the Headless Horseman: An Adventure in Prairietown, Indiana, 1836. 1984. (Illus.). 40p. (J). (gr. 1-4). pap. 15.95 (0-590-45503-6) Scholastic, Inc.

Wyman, Andrea. Red Sky at Morning. 1991. 240p. (J). (gr. 4-7). 15.95 o.p. (0-8234-0903-1) Holiday Hse., Inc.

—Red Sky at Morning. 1997. pap. 3.99 o.p. (0-380-72877-X, Avon Bks.) Morrow/Avon.

—Red Sky at Morning. 1997. 9.09 o.p. (0-606-10908-0) Turtleback Bks.

INDONESIA—FICTION

Conrad, Joseph. Lord Jim. Hedge, Tricia, ed. abr. ed. 2000. (Bookworms Ser.). (Illus.). 112p. (J). pap. text 5.95 (0-19-423037-6) Oxford Univ. Pr., Inc.

—Lord Jim. 1979. (Now Age Illustrated V Ser.). (Illus.). 64p. (J). (gr. 4-12). stu. ed. 1.25 (0-88301-415-7); text 7.50 o.p. (0-88301-403-3); pap. text 2.95 (0-88301-391-6) Pendulum Pr., Inc.

Fama, Elizabeth. Overboard. 2002. (Illus.). 192p. (YA). (gr. 6-9). 15.95 (0-8126-2652-4) Cricket Bks.

Leigh, Frances. The Lost Boy. 1976. (J). (gr. 3-5). 6.95 o.p. (0-525-34221-4, Dutton) Dutton/Plume.

Richards, Kitty. The Bird Who Cried Wolf. 2000. (Wild Thornberrys Ready-to-Read Ser. : Vol. 1). (Illus.). 32p. (J). (gr. k-4). pap. 3.99 (0-689-83234-6, Simon Spotlight/Nickelodeon) Simon & Schuster Children's Publishing.

Taylor, Diane. Singapore Children's Favorite Stories. 2003. (Illus.). 96p. (J). (gr. 1-5). 16.95 (0-7946-0097-2, PeriplusEdition) Tuttle Publishing.

Thoene, Jake & Thoene, Luke. The Giant Rat of Sumatra. 1998. (Baker Street Mysteries Ser.: Vol. 2). 168p. (J). (gr. 4-7). pap. 5.99 (0-7852-7079-5) Nelson, Thomas Pubs.

Vogelaar-Van Amersfoort, Alie. Tekko Returns. 1997. (Tekko Ser.). (Illus.). (J). pap. 6.90 (0-921100-75-2) Inheritance Pubns.

—Tekko the Fugitive. Van Brugge, Jean, tr. from DUT. 1995. (Tekko Ser.: No. 2). (Illus.). 93p. (Orig.). pap. 6.90 (0-921100-74-4) Inheritance Pubns.

Youngberg, Norma. The Tiger of Bitter Valley. 2000. (Illus.). 250p. (J). (gr. 3-6). reprint ed. pap. 11.95 (1-57258-186-7) TEACH Services, Inc.

Zuverink, Mary & Haskin, Georgette, compiled by. Listen to a Shadow. 1976. (J). (gr. k-3). pap. 2.95 o.p. (0-377-00046-9) Friendship Pr.

IOWA—FICTION

Adee, Donna J. Miriam & Timothy Face Life, Vol. 3. 2000. (Illus.). 384p. (J). pap. 12.95 (0-9654272-3-4) Harvest Pubns.

Andersen, C. B. The Book of Mormon Sleuth. 2000. v, 279p. (J). pap. 9.95 (1-57345-664-0) Deseret Bk. Co.

Bauer, Joan. Squashed! 2001. 208p. (J). 16.99 (0-399-23750-X, Putnam & Grosset) Penguin Group (USA) Inc.

Eyerly, Jeannette. More Than a Summer Love. 1962. (J). (gr. 7-9). 8.95 o.p. (0-397-30618-0) HarperCollins Children's Bk. Group.

Hall, Lynn. Dagmar Schultz & the Angel Edna. 1992. 96p. (J). (gr. 3-7). reprint ed. pap. 3.95 o.s.i (0-689-71615-X, Aladdin) Simon & Schuster Children's Publishing.

—Dagmar Schultz & the Powers of Darkness. 1992. 80p. (J). (gr. 3-7). reprint ed. pap. 3.95 o.s.i (0-689-71547-1, Aladdin) Simon & Schuster Children's Publishing.

Hewitt, William. Across the Wide River. 2003. 104p. (J). 11.95 (0-8263-2978-0) Univ. of New Mexico Pr.

Heynen, Jim. Cosmos Coyote & William the Nice. 2002. 352p. (J). (gr. 7 up). pap. 7.99 (0-06-447256-6, HarperTempest) HarperCollins Children's Bk. Group.

Johnson, Tim. Never So Green, RS. 2002. 240p. (YA). 18.00 (0-374-35509-6, Farrar, Straus & Giroux (BYR)) Farrar, Straus & Giroux.

Lawlor, Laurie. Addie's Forever Friend. 1997. (Illus.). 128p. (J). (gr. 2-5). lib. bdg. 13.95 (0-8075-0164-6) Whitman, Albert & Co.

Mackall, Dandi Daley. Kyra's Story. 2003. (Degrees of Guilt Ser.). 225p. (YA). pap. 12.99 (0-8423-8284-4) Tyndale Hse. Pubs.

Marlow, Herb. Twisters, Bronc Riders & Cherry Pie. 1996. (Illus.). 118p. (J). pap. 8.95 (0-9666858-9-X, TW100); lib. bdg. 18.95 (0-9666858-8-1, TW100) Four Seasons Bks., Inc.

—Twisters, Bronc Riders & Cherry Pie. 1997. (Illus.). (J). 25.25 (1-56763-273-4); pap. (1-56763-274-2) Ozark Publishing.

Naylor, Phyllis Reynolds & Reynolds, Lura Schield. Maudie in the Middle. 1988. (Illus.). 176p. (J). (gr. 2-6). lib. bdg. 16.00 (0-689-31395-0, Atheneum) Simon & Schuster Children's Publishing.

Pfeiffer, Joseph R. & Pfeiffer, Robert J. Billy's Unusual Adventure. l.t. ed. 1998. (Illus.). 32p. (J). (gr. k-4). 11.95 (0-9659772-1-8); pap. 5.95 (0-9659772-2-6) Chessmore Publishing.

Rayyan, Omar, illus. Lilacs, Lotuses & Ladybugs. 1997. (0-7802-8033-4) Wright Group, The.

Rylant, Cynthia. Old Town in the Green Groves: Laura Ingalls Wilder's Lost Little House Years. 2002. (Little House Ser.). (Illus.). 176p. (J). (gr. 3-7). lib. bdg. 16.89 (0-06-029562-7); (ps-1). 15.99 (0-06-029561-9) HarperCollins Children's Bk. Group.

IRAN—FICTION

Fardjam, Faridah & Azaad, Meyer. Uncle New Year. 1972. (Illus.). (J). (gr. k-5). lib. bdg. 4.95 o.p. (0-87614-014-2, Carolrhoda Bks.) Lerner Publishing Group.

Fletcher, Susan. Shadow Spinner. 1999. (J). (gr. 5). pap., stu. ed. 59.24 incl. audio (0-7887-3007-X, 40889) Recorded Bks., LLC.

—Shadow Spinner. 1998. 224p. (J). (gr. 5-9). 17.00 (0-689-81852-1, Atheneum) Simon & Schuster Children's Publishing.

—Shadow Spinner. 1999. 11.04 (0-606-17195-9) Turtleback Bks.

Fletcher, Susan & Kramer, Dave. Shadow Spinner. 1999. (Jean Karl Bks.). 224p. (YA). (gr. 5-9). pap. 4.99 (0-689-83051-3, Aladdin) Simon & Schuster Children's Publishing.

Laird, Elizabeth. Kiss the Dust. 288p. (J). (gr. 5 up). 1994. pap. 6.99 (0-14-036855-8, Puffin Bks.); 1992. 15.00 o.p. (0-525-44893-4, Dutton Children's Bks.) Penguin Putnam Bks. for Young Readers.

—Kiss the Dust. 1994. 12.04 (0-606-06513-X) Turtleback Bks.

Napoli, Donna Jo. Beast. 272p. (YA). 2002. (gr. 7 up). pap. 8.00 (0-689-83590-6, Simon Pulse); 2000. (Illus.). (gr. 8 up). 17.00 (0-689-83589-2, Atheneum) Simon & Schuster Children's Publishing.

Pakulak, Eric. At the Side of Esther: A Multiple-Ending Bible Adventure. 2000. (Illus.). 96p. (J). pap. 6.95 (0-8198-0769-9) Pauline Bks. & Media.

Rizzi, Timothy. The Phalanx Dragon. 1995. E-Book 9.95 (0-585-29807-6) netLibrary, Inc.

Wolkstein, Diane. The Red Lion: A Persian Story. 1977. (J). (gr. k-3). 8.61 o.p. (0-690-01346-9); lib. bdg. 11.89 (0-690-01347-7) HarperCollins Children's Bk. Group.

IRELAND—FICTION

Armstrong, Gerry & Armstrong, George. The Fairy Thorn. 1969. (Illus.). (gr. 2-4). 5.95 o.p. (0-8075-2241-4) Whitman, Albert & Co.

Banks, Lynne Reid. Maura's Angel. (J). (gr. 3-7). 1999. 160p. pap. 4.99 (0-380-79514-0, Harper Trophy); 1998. 128p. 14.00 (0-380-97590-4) HarperCollins Children's Bk. Group.

—Maura's Angel. 1999. 11.04 (0-606-16353-0) Turtleback Bks.

Bateman, Teresa. The Ring of Truth. 1997. (Illus.). 32p. (J). (ps-3). tchr. ed. 16.95 (0-8234-1255-5) Holiday Hse., Inc.

Bell, Sam H. The Hollow Ball. 1990. 248p. (Orig.). (YA). (gr. 10-12). reprint ed. pap. 12.95 (0-85640-452-7) Blackstaff Pr., The IRL. *Dist:* Dufour Editions, Inc.

Blazek, Sarah K. A Leprechaun's St. Patrick's Day. 1997. (Illus.). 32p. (J). (gr. 1-4). 14.95 (1-56554-237-1) Pelican Publishing Co., Inc.

Bo, Ben. Skullcrack. 2003. pap. 6.95 (0-8225-3311-1, Carolrhoda Bks.); 2000. 168p. (YA). (gr. 9-12). lib. bdg. 14.95 (0-8225-3308-1, LernerSports) Lerner Publishing Group.

Branson, Karen. The Potato Eaters. 1979. (Illus.). (J). (gr. 6-8). 8.95 o.p. (0-399-20678-7) Putnam Publishing Group, The.

Brightfield, Richard. The Irish Rebellion. 1993. (Young Indiana Jones Chronicles Choose Your Own Adventure Ser.: No.8). 144p. (YA). (gr. 5-8). pap. 3.25 o.s.i (0-553-56349-1) Bantam Bks.

Bulla, Clyde Robert. New Boy in Dublin: A Story of Ireland. 1969. (Stories from Many Lands Ser.). (Illus.). (J). (gr. k-3). 7.95 o.p. (0-690-57756-7) HarperCollins Children's Bk. Group.

Bunting, Eve. Ghost of Summer. 1977. (Illus.). (J). (gr. 5 up). 7.95 o.p. (0-7232-6141-5, Warne, Frederick) Penguin Putnam Bks. for Young Readers.

—The Haunting of Kildoran Abbey. 1978. (J). (gr. 5 up). 7.95 o.p. (0-7232-6152-0, Warne, Frederick) Penguin Putnam Bks. for Young Readers.

—Just Like Everyone Else. 1978. (Creative's Young Romance Ser.). (Illus.). (J). (gr. 3-9). pap. 3.95 o.p. (0-89812-062-4); lib. bdg. 6.95 o.p. (0-87191-630-4) Creative Co., The. (Creative Education).

—Market Day. (Trophy Picture Book Ser.). (Illus.). 32p. (J). (ps-3). 1999. pap. 5.95 o.s.i (0-06-443517-2, Harper Trophy); 1996. lib. bdg. 16.89 (0-06-025368-1, Harper Trophy); 1996. 15.95 o.p. (0-06-025364-9) HarperCollins Children's Bk. Group.

—Market Day. 1999. 12.10 (0-606-14263-0) Turtleback Bks.

—Spying on Miss Muller. 1996. 160p. (gr. 4-7). mass mkt. 6.99 (0-449-70455-6, Fawcett) Ballantine Bks.

—Spying on Miss Muller. 1995. 192p. (J). (gr. 4-6). 15.00 (0-395-69172-9, Clarion Bks.) Houghton Mifflin Co. Trade & Reference Div.

—Spying on Miss Muller. 1996. 10.55 (0-606-14320-3) Turtleback Bks.

Casey, Maude. Over the Water. 1990. (Wildfire Bks.). 224p. text 13.95 o.p. (0-521-38557-1) Cambridge Univ. Pr.

—Over the Water, ERS. 1994. 88p. (J). 15.95 o.p. (0-8050-3276-2, Holt, Henry & Co. Bks. For Young Readers) Holt, Henry & Co.

—Over the Water. 1996. 10.09 o.p. (0-606-08841-5) Turtleback Bks.

Casey, Maude & Paterson, Katherine. Over the Water. 1996. 256p. (YA). (gr. 7 up). pap. 4.99 o.s.i (0-14-037589-9, Puffin Bks.) Penguin Putnam Bks. for Young Readers.

Clark, Ann Nolan. Hoofprint on the Wind. 1972. (Illus.). 160p. (J). (gr. 4-6). 8.95 o.p. (0-670-37874-7) Viking Penguin.

Colum, Padraic. Kate Mary Ellen & the Fairies. 1999. (Illus.). (J). lib. bdg. (0-7868-2149-3) Hyperion Pr.

Conlon-McKenna, Marita. Under the Hawthorn Tree. 1990. (Illus.). 160p. (J). (gr. 4-7). 13.95 o.p. (0-8234-0838-8) Holiday Hse., Inc.

—Under the Hawthorn Tree. 2001. (Illus.). 160p. pap. 5.95 (0-86278-206-6) O'Brien Pr., Ltd., The IRL. *Dist:* Independent Pubs. Group.

—Under the Hawthorn Tree: Children of the Famine. 1992. 128p. (YA). (gr. 5 up). pap. 4.99 o.s.i (0-14-036031-X, Puffin Bks.) Penguin Putnam Bks. for Young Readers.

Considine, June. When the Luvenders Came to Merrick Town. 1990. 240p. (Orig.). pap. 6.95 (1-85371-055-5) Dufour Editions, Inc.

Cowley, Joy. The Wishing of Biddy Malone. 2004. (Illus.). 40p. (J). 15.99 (0-399-23404-7, Philomel) Penguin Putnam Bks. for Young Readers.

de Paola, Tomie. Jamie O'Rourke & the Pooka. Frith, Margaret, ed. 2000. (Illus.). 32p. (J). (ps-3). 16.99 (0-399-23467-5, G. P. Putnam's Sons) Penguin Group (USA) Inc.

Devine, Pauline. Riders by the Grey Lake. 1997. 144p. pap. 8.95 (0-947962-99-9) Dufour Editions, Inc.

Dhuibhne, Ellis Ni. Hugo & the Sunshine Girl. 1991. (Illus.). 129p. (Orig.). (J). (gr. 5-9). pap. 7.95 (1-85371-160-8) Poolbeg Pr. IRL. *Dist:* Dufour Editions, Inc.

Donovan, Anna & Lizatovic, Josip. Cuchulainn: A Storybook to Color. 1997. (Illus.). 32p. (J). pap. 5.95 (0-86278-454-9) Irish American Bk. Co.

Doyle, Malachy. Who Is Jesse Flood? 2002. 176p. (J). (gr. 5-10). 14.95 (1-58234-776-X, Bloomsbury Children) Bloomsbury Publishing.

Duane, Diane. A Wizard Abroad. (Young Wizards Ser.: Bk. 4). (YA). (gr. 5 up). 2001. 368p. pap. 6.95 (0-15-216238-0, Magic Carpet Bks.); 1997. 352p. 15.00 o.s.i (0-15-201209-5) Harcourt Children's Bks.

—A Wizard Abroad. 1999. (Young Wizards Ser.: Bk. 4). 352p. (YA). (gr. 5 up). pap. 6.00 o.p. (0-15-201207-9) Harcourt Trade Pubs.

Dunlop, Eileen. Tales of St. Patrick. 1996. 144p. (J). (gr. 4-7). tchr. ed. 15.95 (0-8234-1218-0) Holiday Hse., Inc.

Edwards, Pamela Duncan. The Leprechaun's Gold. 2004. 32p. (J). 15.99 (0-06-623974-5); lib. bdg. 16.89 (0-06-623975-3) HarperCollins Pubs.

Flegg, Aubrey. Katie's War. A Story of the Irish Civil War. 2000. 192p. (YA). (gr. 5 up). pap. 7.95 (0-86278-525-1) O'Brien Pr., Ltd., The IRL. *Dist:* Independent Pubs. Group, Irish American Bk. Co.

Forman, James. A Fine, Soft Day, RS. 1978. 224p. (J). (gr. 7 up). 12.95 o.p. (0-374-32301-1, Farrar, Straus & Giroux (BYR)) Farrar, Straus & Giroux.

Friel, Maeve. Charlie's Story. 1997. 112p. (YA). (gr. 7-11). 14.95 (1-56145-167-3) Peachtree Pubs., Ltd.

Fry, Rosalie. Secret of Roan Inish. 1995. (Junior Novels Ser.). (Illus.). 144p. (J). (gr. 3-7). pap. 4.95 o.s.i (0-7868-1063-7) Hyperion Paperbacks for Children.

Fullen, Dave. A Nest in the Gale. unabr. ed. 1993. (Learning Disability Ser.). (Illus.). 72p. (J). (gr. 2-6). pap. 18.95 incl. audio (1-881650-01-4) Mountain Bks. & Music.

Giff, Patricia Reilly. The Great Shamrock Disaster. 1993. (Lincoln Lions Band Ser.: No. 6). 80p. (J). (ps-3). pap. 3.25 o.s.i (0-440-40778-8) Dell Publishing.

—Maggie's Door. unabr. ed. 2003. (J). (gr. 3). audio 18.00 (0-8072-1797-2, Listening Library) Random Hse. Audio Publishing Group.

—Maggie's Door. 2003. (Illus.). 176p. (J). (gr. 3-7). 15.95 (0-385-32658-0); lib. bdg. 17.99 (0-385-90095-3) Random Hse. Children's Bks. (Lamb, Wendy).

—Nory Ryan's Song. unabr. ed. 2000. (J). (gr. 3-7). audio 22.00 (0-8072-6163-7, Listening Library) Random Hse. Audio Publishing Group.

—Nory Ryan's Song. Lamb, Wendy, ed. 2000. 160p. (gr. 5-9). text 15.95 (0-385-32141-4, Dell Books for Young Readers) Random Hse. Children's Bks.

—Nory Ryan's Song. 2002. 176p. (gr. 3-7). pap. text 5.99 (0-440-41829-1) Random Hse., Inc.

—Nory Ryan's Song. l.t. ed. 2001. 176p. (J). 23.95 (0-7862-3459-8) Thorndike Pr.

Grossman, Patricia. Disney's the Lion King: Roar! 1997. (Disney First Reader Ser.). (Illus.). 24p. (J). (gr. k-1). pap. 2.95 o.p. (0-7868-4076-5) Disney Pr.

Harrison, Cora. The Famine Secret. 1998. (Drumshee Timeline Ser.: Bk. 5). (Illus.). 128p. (J). (gr. 4-8). pap. 6.95 (0-86327-649-0) Wolfhound Pr. IRL. *Dist:* Irish American Bk. Co.

—Milleniumdrumshee. 1999. (Drumshee Timeline Ser.). (Illus.). 143p. (J). (0-86327-715-2) Wolfhound Pr.

—Nuala & Her Secret Wolf. 1998. (Drumshee Timeline Ser.: Bk. 1). (Illus.). 128p. (J). (gr. 4-8). pap. 6.95 (0-86327-585-0) Wolfhound Pr. IRL. *Dist:* Irish American Bk. Co.

—The Secret of Drumshee Castle. 1998. (Drumshee Timeline Ser.: Bk. 3). (Illus.). 128p. (J). (gr. 3-9). pap. 6.95 (0-86327-632-6) Wolfhound Pr. IRL. *Dist:* Interlink Publishing Group, Inc., Irish American Bk. Co.

—The Secret of the Seven Crosses. 1998. (Drumshee Timeline Ser.: Bk. 2). (Illus.). 128p. (J). (gr. 4-8). pap. 6.95 (0-86327-616-4) Wolfhound Pr. IRL. *Dist:* Irish American Bk. Co.

—The Secret of 1798. 1998. (Drumshee Timeline Ser.: Bk. 4). (Illus.). 128p. (J). (gr. 4-8). pap. 6.95 (0-86327-638-5) Wolfhound Pr. IRL. *Dist:* Irish American Bk. Co.

—Secret Spy from Drumshee. 2003. (Drumshee Timeline Ser.: No. 13). 144p. (J). pap. 6.95 (0-86327-902-3) Wolfhound Pr. IRL. *Dist:* Interlink Publishing Group, Inc.

—Titanic: Voyage From Drumshee. 1999. (Drumshee Timeline Ser.: 6). (Illus.). 130p. (J). (gr. 3-7). pap. text (0-86327-679-2) Wolfhound Pr.

Hazen, Barbara Shook. Katie's Wish. 2002. (Illus.). 32p. (J). (gr. k up). 15.99 (0-8037-2478-0, Dial Bks. for Young Readers) Penguin Putnam Bks. for Young Readers.

Hearne, Betsy. Eliza's Dog. 1996. (Illus.). 160p. (J). (gr. 4-7). 16.00 (0-689-80704-X, McElderry, Margaret K.) Simon & Schuster Children's Publishing.

Heneghan, James. The Grave, RS. 2000. 256p. (YA). (gr. 7-12). 17.00 (0-374-32765-3, Farrar, Straus & Giroux (BYR)) Farrar, Straus & Giroux.

—The Grave. 2000. (Illus.). 236p. (J). (gr. 7-10). pap. 7.95 (0-88899-414-1) Groundwood Bks. CAN. *Dist:* Publishers Group West.

—Torn Away. 2003. 256p. (YA). (gr. 7 up). pap. 6.95 (1-55143-263-3) Orca Bk. Pubs.

—Torn Away. 192p. (J). 1996. (gr. 5-9). pap. 4.99 o.s.i (0-14-036646-6, Puffin Bks.); 1994. (Illus.). (gr. 7 up). 14.99 o.s.i (0-670-85180-9, Viking Children's Bks.) Penguin Putnam Bks. for Young Readers.

—Torn Away. 1996. 10.09 o.p. (0-606-09984-0) Turtleback Bks.

Henning, Ann, et al. The Connemara Champion. 1995. 184p. (J). (gr. 4-7). pap. 8.95 (1-85371-335-X) Poolbeg Pr. IRL. *Dist:* Dufour Editions, Inc.

Henty, G. A. Orange & Green: A Tale of the Boyne & Limerick. 2000. 252p. (J). E-Book 3.95 (0-594-02884-1) 1873 Pr.

Hickey, Tony. Flip 'n' Flop in Kerry. 1997. 94p. (J). pap. 6.95 (0-947962-93-X) Dufour Editions, Inc.

Hodges, Margaret & Root, Kimberly Bulcken. The Wee Christmas Cabin. 2001. (Illus.). (J). (0-8234-1528-7) Holiday Hse., Inc.

Hoyal, Dawna T. Pat & the Leprechaun. 1992. (J). 7.95 o.p. (0-533-10158-1) Vantage Pr., Inc.

Hunt, Angela Elwell. The Secret of Cravenhill Castle. 1994. (Nicki Holland Mystery Ser.: Vol. 8). (J). pap. 4.99 o.p. (0-8407-6305-0) Nelson, Thomas Inc.

Hunter, Mollie. The Smartest Man in Ireland. 1996. 128p. (YA). (gr. 7 up). pap. 5.00 (0-15-200993-0, Magic Carpet Bks.) Harcourt Children's Bks.

—The Smartest Man in Ireland. 1996. 11.05 (0-606-11852-7) Turtleback Bks.

Janoski, Elizabeth. What's Wrong with Eddie? 1995. 92p. (J). (gr. 5-8). lib. bdg. 15.00 o.p. *(0-88092-041-6)*; pap. 9.99 *(0-88092-040-8)* Royal Fireworks Publishing Co.

Jones, Shelagh & Myler, Terry. Save the Unicorns. 1989. 144p. pap. 8.95 o.p. *(0-947962-50-6)* Anvil Bks., Ltd. IRL. *Dist:* Dufour Editions, Inc.

Joyce, James. An Encounter. 1982. (Classics Ser.). (Illus.). 32p. (YA). (gr. 5 up). lib. bdg. 13.95 o.p. *(0-87191-896-X*, 1061-1, Creative Education) Creative Co., The.

Keep, Linda Lowery. Saving Uncle Sean. 1999. (Hannah & the Angels Ser.: No. 5). (Illus.). 128p. (J). (gr. 5-8). pap. 3.99 o.s.i *(0-375-80095-6)* Random Hse., Inc.

King-Smith, Dick. Paddy's Pot of Gold. 1992. (Illus.). 128p. (J). (gr. 2-7). 14.00 o.s.i *(0-517-58136-1*, Random Hse. Bks. for Young Readers) Random Hse. Children's Bks.

Kissane, Dan. Jimmy's Leprechaun Trap. 2001. (Illus.). 95p. (gr. 8-12). pap. 5.95 *(0-86278-512-X)* O'Brien Pr., Ltd., The IRL. *Dist:* Independent Pubs. Group.

Krull, Kathleen. Irish Anthology. 2002. 96p. (J). lib. bdg. 20.49 *(0-7868-2539-1)* Hyperion Bks. for Children.

—A Pot O' Gold: A Treasury of Irish Stories, Poetry, Folklore & (of Course) Blarney. 2001. 96p. (J). 16.99 *(0-7868-0625-7)* Hyperion Pr.

Ladd, Louise. The Anywhere Ring No.. 2: Castle in Time. 1995. (Illus.). 160p. (J). mass mkt. 4.50 o.s.i *(0-425-15048-8)* Berkley Publishing Group.

Langford, Sondra G. Red Bird of Ireland. 1983. 192p. (J). (gr. 4-7). 10.95 o.s.i *(0-689-50270-2*, McElderry, Margaret K.) Simon & Schuster Children's Publishing.

Lavin, Kevin. Desiroscope. 2002. 288p. (J). (gr. 3-9). pap. 6.95 *(0-86327-885-X)* Interlink Publishing Group, Inc.

Lenihan, Edmund. Humorous Irish Tales for Children. 1998. pap. text *(1-85635-238-2)* Irish American Bk. Co.

Leppard, Lois Gladys. Mandie & the Fiery Rescue. 1993. (Mandie Bks.: No. 21). 160p. (J). (gr. 4-7). pap. 4.99 *(1-55661-289-3)* Bethany Hse. Pubs.

—Mandie & the Fiery Rescue. 1993. (Mandie Bks.: No. 21). (J). (gr. 4-7). 11.04 *(0-606-06127-4)* Turtleback Bks.

Lingard, Joan. Across the Barricades. 1973. 160p. (J). (gr. 7 up). 7.95 o.p. *(0-525-66280-4*, Dutton Children's Bks.) Penguin Putnam Bks. for Young Readers.

—The Twelfth Day of July. 1972. 160p. (J). (gr. 6 up). 6.95 o.p. *(0-8407-6254-2*, Dutton Children's Bks.) Penguin Putnam Bks. for Young Readers.

Llywelyn, Morgan. Brian Boru: Emperor of the Irish. 1997. 192p. (gr. 7-12). mass mkt. 4.99 *(0-8125-4461-7)*; 1995. (Illus.). 160p. (J). (gr. 5-10). 14.95 o.p. *(0-312-85623-7)* Doherty, Tom Assocs., LLC. (Tor Bks.).

Lutzeier, Elizabeth. The Coldest Winter. 1991. 160p. (YA). (gr. 5-9). 13.95 o.p. *(0-8234-0899-X)* Holiday Hse., Inc.

Lynch, Patricia. Back of Beyond. 1993. 180p. (J). (gr. 4 up). pap. 9.95 *(1-85371-206-X)* Poolbeg Pr. IRL. *Dist:* Dufour Editions, Inc.

Lyons, Mary E. Knockabeg: A Famine Tale. 2001. (Illus.). 128p. (J). (gr. 4-6). tchr. ed. 15.00 *(0-618-09283-8)* Houghton Mifflin Co.

MacGill-Callahan, Sheila. The Last Snake in Ireland. 2000. (Illus.). (J). (ps-3). pap. 6.95 *(0-8234-1555-4)* Holiday Hse., Inc.

MacGrory, Yvonne. Emma & the Ruby Ring. 2002. (Illus.). 160p. (J). (gr. 4-7). 17.95 *(1-57131-635-3)*; pap. 6.95 *(1-57131-634-5)* Milkweed Editions.

—The Secret of the Ruby Ring. 1994. (Illus.). (J). reprint ed. 189p. 14.95 o.p. *(0-915943-88-3)*; 192p. (gr. 4-8). pap. 6.95 *(0-915943-92-1)* Milkweed Editions.

MacMahon, Bryan. Brendan of Ireland. 1967. (Children Everywhere Ser.). (Illus.). (J). (gr. 2-4). lib. bdg. 4.95 o.p. *(0-8038-0705-8)* Hastings Hse. Daytrips Pubs.

MacUistin, Liam & Cronin, Laura. The Hunt for Diarmaid & Grainne. 1997. (Illus.). 80p. pap. 6.95 *(0-86278-480-8)* Irish American Bk. Co.

Malterre, Elona. The Last Wolf of Ireland. 1990. 144p. (J). (gr. 4-6). tchr. ed. 15.00 *(0-395-54381-9*, Clarion Bks.) Houghton Mifflin Co. Trade & Reference Div.

Mannion, Sean. Ireland's Friendly Dolphin. 1991. (Illus.). 128p. (Orig.). (YA). (gr. 7-11). pap. 9.95 o.p. *(0-86322-122-X)* Brandon Bk. Pubs., Ltd. IRL. *Dist:* Irish Bks. & Media, Inc.

McCaughren, Tom. Rainbows of the Moon. 1989. 160p. (YA). (gr. 9-12). pap. 7.95 *(0-947962-51-4)* Children's Pr., Ltd. IRL. *Dist:* Irish Bks. & Media, Inc.

—Ride a Pale Horse. 1998. 144p. (YA). (gr. 4 up). 13.95 *(1-901737-08-X)* Anvil Bks., Ltd. IRL. *Dist:* Irish Bks. & Media, Inc.

—Run with the Wind. 2002. pap. 7.95 *(0-86327-568-0)* Interlink Publishing Group, Inc.

—The Silent Sea. 1988. (Illus.). 111p. (Orig.). (YA). reprint ed. pap. 7.95 *(0-947962-20-4)* Children's Pr., Ltd. IRL. *Dist:* Irish Bks. & Media, Inc.

McDermott, Gerald. Tim O'Toole & the Wee Folk. 1992. (Picture Puffins Ser.). (Illus.). 32p. (J). (ps-3). pap. 5.99 *(0-14-050675-6*, Puffin Bks.) Penguin Putnam Bks. for Young Readers.

McGinley, Carol. Allyn's Embarrassing & Mysterious Irish Adventures. 1999. (Illus.). 202p. (J). (gr. 4-6). pap. 7.95 *(1-892671-00-X)* AGA Publishing.

Moll, Linda J. A Poison Tree: A Children's Fairy Tale. 1994. (Illus.). 40p. (J). (gr. 1). 12.95 *(0-9641641-1-6)* Punking Pr.

Molloy, Anne. Shaun & the Boat. 1965. (Illus.). (J). (gr. 1-4). 6.95 o.p. *(0-8038-6655-0)* Hastings Hse. Daytrips Pubs.

Monoghan, Nancy. The Spirit Stone: A Tale of Ireland. 2000. (YA). (gr. 4-7). E-Book 10.00 *(0-9679076-5-9)* E-Pub2000.

Morpurgo, Michael. Twist of Gold. 1993. 224p. (J). (gr. 5-9). 14.99 o.p. *(0-670-84851-4*, Viking Children's Bks.) Penguin Putnam Bks. for Young Readers.

Mullen, Michael. The Four Masters. 1992. 153p. (YA). (gr. 5 up). pap. 9.95 *(1-85371-204-3)* Poolbeg Pr. IRL. *Dist:* Dufour Editions, Inc.

Mulrooney, Gretta. A Nest of Vipers. 1994. (J). *(1-85371-412-7)* Poolbeg Pr.

Murphy, T. M. The Secrets of Cain's Castle. 2001. (Belltown Mystery Ser.). 144p. (J). 9.95 *(1-880158-38-8)* Townsend, J.N. Publishing.

Newman, Roger C. Murtagh the Warrior. 1997. 144p. pap. 8.95 *(0-947962-98-0)* Dufour Editions, Inc.

Newsham, Ian, illus. A Treasury of Irish Stories. 1995. 160p. (J). (ps-4). pap. 5.95 o.s.i *(1-85697-595-9)* Larousse Kingfisher Chambers, Inc.

Nixon, Joan Lowery. The Gift. 1983. (Illus.). 96p. (J). (gr. 4-7). lib. bdg. 13.95 o.s.i *(0-02-768160-2*, Simon & Schuster Children's Publishing) Simon & Schuster Children's Publishing.

Nolan, Janet. The St. Patrick's Day Shillelagh. 2002. (Illus.). 32p. (J). (gr. 2-4). lib. bdg. 15.95 *(0-8075-7344-2)* Whitman, Albert & Co.

Nye, Robert. Wishing Gold. 1971. (Illus.). 112p. (J). (gr. 5 up). 3.95 o.p. *(0-8090-9774-5*, Hill & Wang) Farrar, Straus & Giroux.

O'Connor, Frank. First Confession. 1993. (Short Stories Ser.). 32p. (YA). (gr. 5 up). lib. bdg. 18.60 *(0-88682-058-8*, Creative Education) Creative Co., The.

Osborne, Mary Pope. Viking Ships at Sunrise. unabr. ed. 2002. (Magic Tree House Ser. : Vol. 15). 71p. (J). (gr. k-4). pap. 17.00 incl. audio *(0-8072-0784-5*, LFTR 243 SP, Listening Library) Random Hse. Audio Publishing Group.

—Viking Ships at Sunrise. 1998. (Magic Tree House Ser.: No. 15). (J). (gr. k-3). 10.14 *(0-606-15755-7)* Turtleback Bks.

O'Shaughnessy, Peter. Con's Fabulous Journey to the Land of Gobel O'Glug. rev. ed. 1992. (Illus.). 104p. (J). (gr. 6-10). reprint ed. pap. 5.95 *(0-947962-68-9)* Anvil Bks., Ltd. IRL. *Dist:* Irish Bks. & Media, Inc.

Paine, Penelope C. Molly's Magic. 1995. (Key Concepts in Personal Development Ser.). (Illus.). 32p. (J). (gr. 1-4). 16.95 *(1-55942-068-5*, 7660) Marsh Media.

Pastore, Clare. Journey to America, Vol. 1. 2002. 192p. mass mkt. 5.99 *(0-425-18735-7)* Berkley Publishing Group.

Paulsen, Brendan P. The Luck of the Irish. (J). 1995. pap. text 4.95 o.p. *(0-8114-6347-8)*; 1988. (Illus.). 32p. (gr. 2-4). 29.28 o.p. incl. audio *(0-8172-2467-X)* Raintree Pubs.

Reeve, Phyllis Cardoze. One for Sorrow, Two for Joy. 2002. 150p. (YA). (gr. 6-9). pap. 14.95 *(0-9725590-0-0)* Reeve, Phyllis.

Regan, Peter. The Street-League. 1996. (Riverside Ser.). 112p. pap. 6.95 *(0-947962-46-8)* Dufour Editions, Inc.

Robertson, Ivan T. Jack & the Leprechaun. 2000. (Pictureback Ser.). (Illus.). 24p. (J). (gr. k-3). pap. 3.25 *(0-375-80328-9*, Random Hse. Bks. for Young Readers) Random Hse. Children's Bks.

Rose, Deborah Lee. The People Who Hugged the Trees: An Environmental Folk Tale. 1999. (Illus.). 64p. (gr. 4-7). pap. 7.95 *(1-879373-50-5)* Rinehart, Roberts Pubs.

Rose-Paradise, Helen. Timothy O'Toole: Irish Stories for Little Folk. 1994. (Illus.). 136p. (J). 14.95 *(1-56002-431-3*, University Editions) Aegina Pr., Inc.

Ryan, Joan & Snell, Gordon, eds. Land of Tales: Stories of Ireland for Children. 1983. (Illus.). 160p. (J). 12.00 o.p. *(0-8023-1276-4)* Dufour Editions, Inc.

Schmidt, Gary D. Anson's Way. 1999. 224p. (J). (gr. 5-9). tchr. ed. 15.00 *(0-395-91529-5*, Clarion Bks.) Houghton Mifflin Co. Trade & Reference Div.

—Anson's Way. 2001. (J). 12.04 *(0-606-21039-3)* Turtleback Bks.

—The Wonders of Donal O'Donnell: A Folktale of Ireland, ERS. 2002. (Illus.). 40p. (J). (gr. 3-6). 17.95 *(0-8050-6516-4*, Holt, Henry & Co. Bks. For Young Readers) Holt, Henry & Co.

Schneider, Mical. Annie Quinn in America. 2001. (J). 6.95 *(1-57505-535-X)* Carolrhoda Bks.

—Annie Quinn in America. 2001. (Adventures in Time Ser.). (Illus.). 252p. (J). (gr. 4-7). lib. bdg. 15.95 *(1-57505-510-4*, Carolrhoda Bks.) Lerner Publishing Group.

Scott, Michael. October Moon. 1994. 160p. (J). (gr. 7-12). 14.95 o.p. *(0-8234-1110-9)* Holiday Hse., Inc.

—October Moon. 1995. 160p. (J). (gr. 7-9). pap. 3.50 *(0-590-26591-1)* Scholastic, Inc.

So Far from Home: The Diary of Mary Driscoll, an Irish Mill Girl. 2003. (J). lib. bdg. 12.95 *(0-439-55506-X)* Scholastic, Inc.

Stevens, Kathleen. Molly, McCullough & Tom the Rogue. 1991. (Trophy Picture Bk.). (Illus.). 32p. (J). (gr. 1-5). 4.95 o.p. *(0-06-443261-0*, Harper Trophy) HarperCollins Children's Bk. Group.

Stuart, Chad. The Ballymara Flood: A Tale from Old Ireland. 1996. (Illus.). 40p. (J). (gr. k-3). 15.00 *(0-15-205698-X)* Harcourt Trade Pubs.

Swift, Carolyn. Bugsy Goes to Cork. 1990. 190p. (J). (gr. 3-7). pap. 7.95 *(1-85371-071-7)* Poolbeg Pr. IRL. *Dist:* Dufour Editions, Inc.

Tail of Three Tails. 1975. (J). (gr. 1-6). pap. 1.95 o.p. *(0-8431-0563-1*, Price Stern Sloan) Penguin Putnam Bks. for Young Readers.

Tannen, Mary. The Lost Legend of Finn. 1983. 154p. (J). (gr. 4-7). pap. 2.25 o.p. *(0-380-63354-X*, 63354-X, Avon Bks.) Morrow/Avon.

—The Wizard Children of Finn. 1981. (Illus.). 256p. (J). (gr. 3 up). 8.95 o.p. *(0-394-84744-X*, Knopf Bks. for Young Readers) Random Hse. Children's Bks.

Thesman, Jean. Sea So Far. 2001. 224p. (J). (gr. 5-9). 15.99 *(0-670-89278-5*, Viking Children's Bks.) Penguin Putnam Bks. for Young Readers.

—A Sea So Far. 2003. 224p. (YA). pap. 6.99 *(0-14-230059-4*, Puffin Bks.) Penguin Putnam Bks. for Young Readers.

Thompson, Kate. Switchers. 1999. 224p. (J). (gr. 7-12). pap. 5.99 *(0-7868-1396-2)* Disney Pr.

—Switchers. 1998. 224p. (YA). (gr. 7-12). lib. bdg. 15.49 *(0-7868-2328-3)* Hyperion Bks. for Children.

—Switchers. 220p. (J). (gr. 4-7). pap. 5.99 *(0-8072-1553-8)*; 1999. (Switchers Ser.: Vol. 1). pap. 37.00 incl. audio *(0-8072-8138-7*, YA115SP) Random Hse. Audio Publishing Group. (Listening Library).

—Switchers. 1999. 12.04 *(0-606-17387-0)* Turtleback Bks.

—Wild Blood. 2000. (J). (gr. 5-9). 261p. 15.99 *(0-7868-0572-2)*; 240p. lib. bdg. 16.49 *(0-7868-2497-2)* Hyperion Bks. for Children.

—Wild Blood. 2002. 240p. (J). pap. 5.99 *(0-7868-1422-5)* Hyperion Paperbacks for Children.

Todd, Justin, photos by. The Starlight Cloak. 1993. (Illus.). 320p. (J). (ps-3). 14.99 o.p. *(0-8037-1508-0*, Dial Bks. for Young Readers) Penguin Putnam Bks. for Young Readers.

Trevor, William. Juliet's Story. 1994. (J). pap. 15.00 o.s.i *(0-671-87442-X*, Simon & Schuster Children's Publishing) Simon & Schuster Children's Publishing.

Van Stockum, Hilda. Pegeen. 1996. (Bantry Bay Ser.). (Illus.). 176p. (J). (gr. 4-7). pap. 11.95 *(1-883937-20-5*, 20-5) Bethlehem Bks.

Vaughan-Jackson, Genevieve. Carramore. 1968. (Illus.). (J). (gr. 4-6). 5.95 o.p. *(0-8038-1083-0)*; lib. bdg. 6.95 o.p. *(0-8038-1084-9)* Hastings Hse. Daytrips Pubs.

Wall, Bill. The Slave Coast. 1998. 144p. (YA). (gr. 4-7). pap. 7.95 *(1-85635-196-3)* Mercier Pr., Ltd., The IRL. *Dist:* Irish Bks. & Media, Inc.

Welling, Peter J. Shawn O'Hisser, the Last Snake in Ireland. 2002. (Illus.). 32p. (J). (gr. k-3). 14.95 *(1-58980-014-1)* Pelican Publishing Co., Inc.

Wetterer, Margaret K. Patrick & the Fairy Thief. 1980. (Illus.). 32p. (J). (gr. 1-4). 7.95 o.p. *(0-689-50160-9*, McElderry, Margaret K.) Simon & Schuster Children's Publishing.

Whelan, Gerard. A Winter of Spies. 1999. 191p. (YA). (gr. 5 up). pap. 6.95 *(0-86278-566-9)* O'Brien Pr., Ltd., The IRL. *Dist:* Independent Pubs. Group.

Wilson, Laura. The Great Hunger. 2000. (Time Travellers Ser.). (Illus.). 36p. (J). (ps up). pap. 9.95 *(0-688-17750-6*, Harper Trophy) HarperCollins Children's Bk. Group.

—How I Survived the Irish Famine: Journal of Mary O'Flynn. 2000. (Time Travellers Ser.). (Illus.). 36p. (J). (ps-3). lib. bdg. 14.89 *(0-06-029534-1)* HarperCollins Pubs.

ISLAM—FICTION

Lewis, Richard. The Flame Tree. 2004. (J). *(0-689-86333-0*, Simon & Schuster Children's Publishing) Simon & Schuster Children's Publishing.

Matthews, Mary. Magid Fasts for Ramadan. (Illus.). 48p. (J). (gr. 4-6). 2000. pap. 6.95 *(0-618-04035-8)*; 1996. tchr. ed. 16.00 *(0-395-66589-2)* Houghton Mifflin Co. Trade & Reference Div. (Clarion Bks.).

—Magid Fasts for Ramadan. 1996. 13.10 *(0-606-18044-3)* Turtleback Bks.

Oppenheim, Shulamith Levey. The Hundredth Name. 2003. (Illus.). 32p. (J). (ps-3). pap. 9.95 *(1-56397-694-3)* Boyds Mills Pr.

Yamani, Muhammad Abdo. A Boy from Makkah, Vol. 1. Mohiuddin, Khadija & De Backer, Talha, eds. novel ed. 2002. (Illus.). 149p. (J). 10.00 *(1-56316-057-9)* IQRA International Educational Foundation.

ISLANDS OF THE PACIFIC—FICTION

Bates, Gale. Tales of Tutu Nene & Nele. 1991. (Illus.). 36p. (J). (ps-4). 10.95 *(0-89610-193-2)* Island Heritage Publishing.

Conrad, Joseph. An Outcast of the Islands. 1966. (Airmont Classics Ser.). (YA). (gr. 9 up). mass mkt. 1.50 *(0-8049-0113-9*, CL-113) Airmont Publishing Co., Inc.

Gittins, Anne. Tales from the South Pacific Islands. 1977. (Illus.). 96p. (J). (gr. 3 up). 12.95 *(0-916144-02-X)* Stemmer Hse. Pubs., Inc.

Jackson, Dave & Jackson, Neta. Sinking the Dayspring: John G. Paton. 2001. (Trailblazer Bks.: Vol. 35). (Illus.). 144p. (J). (gr. 3-7). pap. 5.99 *(0-7642-2268-6)* Bethany Hse. Pubs.

Keeping, Charles. Adam & Paradise Island. 1989. (Illus.). 36p. (J). (gr. 3-6). 13.95 o.p. *(0-19-279842-1)* Oxford Univ. Pr., Inc.

Lang, W. Harold. Islands of the Pacific. Kubat, Frank J., Jr., ed. 1988. (Illus.). 168p. (YA). 44.95 *(0-945201-00-1)* Gannam/Kubat Pubs.

Taylor, Theodore. The Bomb. abr. ed. 1995. 208p. (YA). (gr. 7 up). 15.00 *(0-15-200867-5)* Harcourt Children's Bks.

—The Bomb. 1997. 176p. (J). (gr. 7 up). pap. 5.99 *(0-380-72723-4*, Harper Trophy) HarperCollins Children's Bk. Group.

—The Bomb. 1997. 11.04 *(0-606-11146-8)* Turtleback Bks.

Von Tempski, Armine. Judy of the Islands: A Story of the South Seas. 1992. (Illus.). viii, 280p. (YA). reprint ed. pap. 14.95 *(0-918024-97-8)* Ox Bow Pr.

Walls, Pamela June. Abby King's Ransom. 2001. (South Seas Adventure Ser.: Vol. 5). (Illus.). 192p. (J). mass mkt. 5.99 *(0-8423-3630-3*, Tyndale Kids) Tyndale Hse. Pubs.

—Into the Dragon's Den. 2001. (South Seas Adventures Ser.: 6). (Illus.). 224p. (J). mass mkt. 5.99 *(0-8423-3631-1*, Tyndale Kids) Tyndale Hse. Pubs.

Williams, Laura E. Island Rose. Bodnar, Judit, ed. 1998. (Magic Attic Club Ser.). (Illus.). 80p. (gr. 2-6). (J). 13.95 *(1-57513-126-9)*; pap. 5.95 o.p. *(1-57513-125-0)* Millbrook Pr., Inc. (Magic Attic Pr.).

ISLE OF ECHOES (IMAGINARY PLACE)—FICTION

Roberts, Katherine. Crystal Mask. (J). 2003. 272p. pap. 4.99 *(0-439-44083-1*, Chicken Hse., The); 2003. (Echorium Sequence Ser.: Vol. 2). 272p. mass mkt. 4.99 *(0-439-51147-X)*; 2002. (Echorium Sequence Ser.: Vol. 2). (Illus.). 256p. (gr. 4 up). pap. 15.95 *(0-439-33864-6*, Chicken Hse., The) Scholastic, Inc.

—Dark Quetzal. 256p. (J). 2004. mass mkt. 5.99 *(0-439-52309-5)*; Bk. 3. 2003. (Echorium Sequence Ser.: Vol. 3). pap. 15.95 *(0-439-45697-5)* Scholastic, Inc. (Chicken Hse., The).

—Song Quest. (J). (gr. 5 up). 2000. (Illus.). 240p. pap. 5.95 *(1-902618-94-7)*; 1999. 236p. 16.95 *(1-902618-28-9)* Element Children's Bks.

—Song Quest. 2002. (Echorium Sequence Ser.: Vol. 1). 256p. (YA). (gr. 4 up). mass mkt. 4.99 *(0-439-33892-1*, Chicken Hse., The) Scholastic, Inc.

ISRAEL—FICTION

Alexander, Sue. Behold the Trees. 2001. (Illus.). 48p. (J). (ps-3). pap. 16.95 *(0-590-76211-7*, Levine, Arthur A. Bks.) Scholastic, Inc.

Almagor, Gila. Under the Domim Tree. Schenker, Hillel, tr. 1995. 176p. (J). (gr. 7 up). 15.00 *(0-671-89020-4*, Simon & Schuster Children's Publishing) Simon & Schuster Children's Publishing.

Banks, Lynne Reid. Broken Bridge. 1996. 336p. (J). (gr. 7 up). pap. 6.99 *(0-380-72384-0*, Harper Trophy) HarperCollins Children's Bk. Group.

—Broken Bridge. 1995. (Illus.). 336p. (YA). (gr. 5 up). 16.00 *(0-688-13595-1*, Morrow, William & Co.) Morrow/Avon.

—Broken Bridge. 1996. 10.55 *(0-606-09105-X)* Turtleback Bks.

—One More River. 1996. (YA). (gr. 7 up). pap. 4.50 *(0-380-72755-2*, Avon Bks.); 1993. 256p. (J). (gr. 4-7). pap. 5.99 *(0-380-71563-5*, Avon Bks.); 1992. 256p. (YA). (gr. 5 up). 14.00 *(0-688-10893-8*, Morrow, William & Co.) Morrow/Avon.

—One More River. 1992. 11.04 *(0-606-05525-8)* Turtleback Bks.

Bergman, Tamar. The Boy from over There. Halkin, Hillel, tr. from HEB. 1988. 192p. (J). (gr. 3-7). 13.95 o.p. *(0-395-43077-1)* Houghton Mifflin Co.

—Boy from over There. 1992. (J). (gr. 4-7). pap. 4.95 o.p. *(0-395-64370-8)* Houghton Mifflin Co.

Carmi, Daniella. Samir & Yonatan. Lotan, Yael, tr. from HEB. 2002. 160p. (J). (gr. 3-7). mass mkt. 4.99 *(0-439-13523-0,* Scholastic Paperbacks) Scholastic, Inc.

—Samir & Yonatan. 2000. (Illus.). 183p. (J). (gr. 3-7). pap. 15.95 *(0-439-13504-4,* Levine, Arthur A. Bks.) Scholastic, Inc.

Chaikin, Miriam. Aviva's Piano. 1986. (Illus.). 48p. (J). (gr. 2-4). 12.20 o.p. *(0-89919-367-6,* Clarion Bks.) Houghton Mifflin Co. Trade & Reference Div.

Clinton, Cathryn. A Stone in My Hand. 2002. 208p. (J). (gr. 5-12). 15.99 *(0-7636-1388-6)* Candlewick Pr.

Cohen, Susan J., illus. The Donkey's Story. 1988. 32p. (J). (gr. k-5). 12.95 o.p. *(0-688-04104-3)*; lib. bdg. 12.88 o.p. *(0-688-04105-1)* HarperCollins Children's Bk. Group.

Collins, Alan. Joshua. 1995. 130p. (YA). pap. 14.95 *(0-7022-2809-5)* Univ. of Queensland Pr. AUS. *Dist:* International Specialized Bk. Services.

Edwards, Michelle. Chicken Man. 1991. (J). (ps-3). lib. bdg. 13.88 o.p. *(0-688-09709-X)*; (Illus.). 32p. 13.95 *(0-688-09708-1)* HarperCollins Children's Bk. Group.

—Chicken Man. 1994. (Illus.). 32p. (J). (ps up). reprint ed. pap. 4.95 o.p. *(0-688-13106-9,* Morrow, William & Co.) Morrow/Avon.

Goldreich, Gloria. Lori, ERS. 1979. (gr. 6 up). o.p. *(0-03-044646-5,* Holt, Henry & Co. Bks. For Young Readers) Holt, Henry & Co.

Goodman, Ruth F. Pen Pals: What It Means to Be Jewish in Israel & America. 1996. 96p. (YA). (gr. 7 up). 14.95 *(1-56474-159-1)* Fithian Pr.

Hoban, Lillian. I Met a Traveler. 1977. 192p. (J). (gr. 5 up). 6.95 o.p. *(0-06-022373-1)*; lib. bdg. 10.89 o.p. *(0-06-022374-X)* HarperCollins Pubs.

Ingermanson, Randall Scott. Transgression. 2000. 406p. (J). pap. 10.99 o.p. *(0-7369-0195-7)* Harvest Hse. Pubs.

Kalechofsky, Roberta. A Boy, a Chicken & the Lion of Judah: How Ari Became a Vegetarian. 1995. (Illus.). 45p. (J). (gr. 2-5). pap. 8.00 *(0-916288-39-0)* Micah Pubns.

Levine, Anna. Running on Eggs. 1999. 128p. (YA). (gr. 5-9). 15.95 *(0-8126-2875-6)* Cricket Bks.

Levitin, Sonia. The Singing Mountain. (YA). (gr. 7-12). 1998. 272p. 17.00 *(0-689-80809-7,* Simon & Schuster Children's Publishing); 2000. 304p. reprint ed. mass mkt. 4.99 *(0-689-83523-X,* Simon Pulse) Simon & Schuster Children's Publishing.

McOmber, Rachel B., ed. McOmber Phonics Storybooks: Razz Visits Raz in Israel. rev. ed. (Illus.). (J). *(0-944991-75-0)* Swift Learning Resources.

Meir, Mira. Alina: A Russian Girl Comes to Israel. Shapiro, Zeva, tr. from HEB. 1982. (Illus.). 48p. (J). (gr. 2-4). 9.95 o.p. *(0-8276-0208-1)* Jewish Pubn. Society.

Orlev, Uri. The Lady with the Hat. Halkin, Hillel, tr. 1995. 192p. (YA). (gr. 7 up). tchr. ed. 16.00 *(0-395-69957-6)* Houghton Mifflin Co.

—The Lady with the Hat. Halkin, Hillel, tr. from HEB. 1997. (Illus.). 192p. (J). (gr. 5-9). pap. 4.99 o.s.i *(0-14-038571-1)* Penguin Putnam Bks. for Young Readers.

—The Lady with the Hat. 1997. 10.09 o.p. *(0-606-13562-6)* Turtleback Bks.

—Lydia: Queen of Palestine. Halkin, Hillel, tr. from HEB. 1993. Tr. of Lidyah: Malkat Erest Yisrael. 176p. (J). 13.95 o.p. *(0-395-65660-5)* Houghton Mifflin Co.

—Lydia, Queen of Palestine. Halkin, Hillel, tr. 1995. (Illus.). 176p. (J). (gr. 5-9). pap. 4.99 o.s.i *(0-14-037089-7,* Puffin Bks.) Penguin Putnam Bks. for Young Readers.

—Lydia, Queen of Palestine. 1995. 9.09 o.p. *(0-606-07817-7)* Turtleback Bks.

Oz, Amos. Soumchi. Oz, Amos & Farmer, Penelope, trs. from HEB. 1995. (Harvest Book Ser.). (Illus.). 96p. (J). (gr. 4 up). pap. 10.00 o.s.i *(0-15-600193-4,* Harvest Bks.) Harcourt Trade Pubs.

Peterseil, Tehila. The Safe Place. 1996. (Illus.). 144p. (J). (gr. 5-9). 16.95 *(0-943706-71-8)*; pap. 12.95 *(0-943706-72-6)* Pitspopany Pr.

Ramsay, Elizabeth. The Burning Light. 2002. (Illus.). 128p. (YA). (gr. 4-9). 14.95 *(1-930143-43-5)*; pap. 9.95 *(1-930143-44-3)* Pitspopany Pr.

Rouss, Sylvia A. Sammy Spider's First Israel: A Book about the Five Senses. 2002. (Illus.). (J). pap. *(1-58013-035-6)* Kar-Ben Publishing.

Segal, Sheila F. Joshua's Dream. 1985. (Illus.). 32p. (J). (gr. 1-3). pap. 6.95 o.p. *(0-8074-0272-9,* 101060) UAHC Pr.

—Joshua's Dream: A Journey to the Land of Israel. 1992. (Illus.). 26p. (J). (ps-3). 12.95 *(0-8074-0476-4,* 101062) UAHC Pr.

Semel, Nava. Becoming Gershona. Simckes, Seymour, tr. 160p. (J). 1990. (gr. 4 up). 12.95 o.p. *(0-670-83105-0,* Viking Children's Bks.); 1992. (gr. 5 up). reprint ed. pap. 4.50 o.p. *(0-14-036071-9,* Puffin Bks.) Penguin Putnam Bks. for Young Readers.

—Flying Lessons. Halkin, Hillel, tr. 1995. Orig. Title: Moris Havivel Melamid La-uf. (Illus.). 112p. (YA). (gr. 5 up). 14.00 o.p. *(0-689-80161-0,* Simon & Schuster Children's Publishing) Simon & Schuster Children's Publishing.

Shalant, Phyllis. Shalom, Geneva Peace. 1992. 160p. (J). (gr. 7 up). 15.00 o.p. *(0-525-44868-3,* Dutton Children's Bks.) Penguin Putnam Bks. for Young Readers.

Spector, Shoshannah. Five Young Heroes of Israel. 1970th ed. 1983. (Illus.). (J). (gr. 1-3). 3.95 o.p. *(0-88400-032-X,* Shengold Bks.) Schreiber Publishing, Inc.

Steiner, Connie C. On Eagles Wings & Other Things. 1987. 32p. (J). (gr. k-4). 16.95 o.p. *(0-8276-0274-X)* Jewish Pubn. Society.

Story, Bettie W. The Other Side of the Tell. 1976. (gr. 3-7). pap. 1.95 o.p. *(0-912692-92-8)* Cook, David C. Publishing Co.

Waldman, Neil. The Never-Ending Greenness. 1997. (Illus.). 40p. (J). 16.00 *(0-688-14479-9)*; lib. bdg. 15.93 o.p. *(0-688-14480-2)* Morrow/Avon. (Morrow, William & Co.).

ISTANBUL (TURKEY)—FICTION

Gustaveson, Dave. The Lost Diary. 1996. (Reel Kids Adventures Ser.: Bk. 7). 160p. (Orig.). (J). (gr. 5-7). pap. 5.99 *(0-927545-88-8)* YWAM Publishing.

Whitney, Phyllis A. Mystery of the Golden Horn. 1962. (Illus.). (J). (gr. 5-9). 4.95 o.p. *(0-664-32288-3)* Westminster John Knox Pr.

ITALY—FICTION

Anno, Mitsumasa. Anno's Italy. 2015. (J). 8.95 *(0-399-21796-7)* Penguin Putnam Bks. for Young Readers.

Balit, Christina. Escape from Pompeii, ERS. 2003. (Illus.). 32p. (J). 16.95 *(0-8050-7324-8,* Holt, Henry & Co. Bks. For Young Readers) Holt, Henry & Co.

Bellissimo, Cinzia C., et al. Benvenuti All' Italiano. 1992. (ITA., Illus.). 370p. (J). (gr. 7-9). pap. text 29.95 *(0-9645107-0-7)* Cima Pubns.

Bettina. Pantaloni. 1957. (Illus.). 32p. (J). (gr. k-3). lib. bdg. 12.89 o.p. *(0-06-020506-7)* HarperCollins Children's Bk. Group.

Boccaccio, Giovanni. Chichibo & the Crane. 1961. (Illus.). (J). (gr. 1-6). 14.95 *(0-8392-3004-4)* Astor-Honor, Inc.

Bolognese, Don. The War Horse. 2003. (Illus.). 176p. (J). (gr. 5-9). 16.95 *(0-689-85458-7,* Simon & Schuster Children's Publishing) Simon & Schuster Children's Publishing.

Bosca, Francesca. Christmas Cakes. 2003. 32p. (J). lib. bdg. 16.50 *(0-7358-1886-X)*; (Illus.). 15.95 *(0-7358-1885-1)* North-South Bks., Inc.

Bowen, Marjorie. Viper of Milan. 2000. 252p. pap. 9.95 *(0-594-00198-6)* 1873 Pr.

—Viper of Milan. 1965. (J). (gr. 4-8). 14.95 *(0-8023-1014-1)* Dufour Editions, Inc.

—The Viper of Milan. 2000. 252p. E-Book 3.95 *(0-594-01895-1)* 1873 Pr.

—The Viper of Milan. 1963. pap. 1.25 o.p. *(0-14-047018-2,* Puffin Bks.) Penguin Putnam Bks. for Young Readers.

Brown, Regina. Little Brother. 1962. (Illus.). (J). (gr. 3-7). 12.95 *(0-8392-3019-2)* Astor-Honor, Inc.

Bufalari, Giuseppe. Devil's Boat. 1971. (Illus.). (J). (gr. 5 up). lib. bdg. 5.69 o.p. *(0-394-92289-1,* Knopf Bks. for Young Readers) Random Hse. Children's Bks.

Caselli, Giovanni. A Roman Soldier. 1991. (Everyday Life of Ser.). (Illus.). 32p. (J). (gr. 3-6). lib. bdg. 12.95 o.p. *(0-87226-106-9,* Bedrick, Peter Bks.) McGraw-Hill Children's Publishing.

Cazzola, Gus. The Bells of Santa Lucia. 1991. (Illus.). 32p. (J). (ps-3). 14.95 o.s.i *(0-399-21804-1,* Philomel) Penguin Putnam Bks. for Young Readers.

Collodi, Carlo. Las Aventuras de Pinocho. (SPA., Illus.). 160p. (YA). 14.95 *(84-7281-190-5,* AF1905) Auriga, Ediciones S.A. ESP. *Dist:* Continental Bk. Co., Inc.

—Las Aventuras de Pinocho. 1995. (SPA.). 196p. (gr. 4-7). per. *(950-581-271-X)* Colihue.

—Las Aventuras de Pinocho. (Coleccion Cuentos Universales). (SPA.). (YA). (gr. 4 up). *(84-261-3145-X,* JV30301) Juventud, Editorial ESP. *Dist:* Lectorum Pubns., Inc.

—Las Aventuras de Pinocho. 2002. (Classics for Young Readers Ser.). (SPA.). (YA). 14.95 *(84-392-0916-9,* EV30602) Lectorum Pubns., Inc.

Daly, Maureen. The Small War of Sergeant Donkey. 2000. (Living History Library). (Illus.). 104p. (J). (gr. 5-9). reprint ed. pap. 11.95 *(1-883937-47-7)* Bethlehem Bks.

de Paola, Tomie. Big Anthony: His Story. 1998. (Illus.). 32p. (J). (ps-3). 16.99 *(0-399-23189-7)* Penguin Group (USA) Inc.

—Big Anthony: His Story. 3.70 *(0-399-24873-0)*; 22.25 *(0-399-24925-7)*; 22.25 *(0-399-24926-5)* Putnam Publishing Group, The.

—Big Anthony: His Story. 2001. 12.14 *(0-606-21064-4)* Turtleback Bks.

—The Days of the Blackbird: A Tale of Northern Italy. 1997. (Illus.). 32p. (J). (ps-3). 16.99 *(0-399-22929-9,* G. P. Putnam's Sons) Penguin Group (USA) Inc.

—Jingle, the Christmas Clown. 1992. (Illus.). 40p. (J). (ps-3). 16.95 o.s.i *(0-399-22338-X,* G. P. Putnam's Sons) Penguin Group (USA) Inc.

Dixon, Franklin W. The Lure of the Italian Treasure. 1999. (Hardy Boys Mystery Stories Ser.: No. 157). 160p. (J). (gr. 3-6). pap. 3.99 *(0-671-03445-6,* Aladdin) Simon & Schuster Children's Publishing.

Fienberg, Anna. The Witch in the Lake. 2002. 220p. (J). (gr. 5-9). pap. 7.95 *(1-55037-722-1)*; lib. bdg. 18.95 *(1-55037-723-X)* Annick Pr., Ltd. CAN. *Dist:* Firefly Bks., Ltd.

French, Simon. Change the Locks. 1993. 112p. (J). (gr. 3-7). pap. 13.95 *(0-590-45593-1)* Scholastic, Inc.

—Change the Locks. 1991. (J). 8.05 o.p. *(0-606-06955-0)* Turtleback Bks.

Funke, Cornelia. The Thief Lord. Latsch, Oliver, tr. from GER. 2002. (Illus.). 352p. (J). (gr. 4-7). pap. 16.95 *(0-439-40437-1,* Chicken Hse., The) Scholastic, Inc.

—The Thief Lord. 2003. 376p. (J). (gr. 3-6). reprint ed. pap. 6.99 *(0-439-42089-X,* Chicken Hse., The) Scholastic, Inc.

Gallico, Paul. Paul Gallico's the Small Miracle, ERS. 2003. (Illus.). 32p. (J). (ps-3). 16.95 *(0-8050-6745-0,* Holt, Henry & Co. Bks. For Young Readers) Holt, Henry & Co.

Gutman, Anne. Gaspard on Vacation: Lisa's Airplane Trip. 2001. (Illus.). 32p. (J). (ps-1). 9.95 o.p. *(0-375-81115-X,* Knopf Bks. for Young Readers) Random Hse. Children's Bks.

Haugaard, Erik Christian. The Little Fishes. 1967. (Illus.). (J). (gr. 6-8). 6.95 o.p. *(0-395-06802-9)* Houghton Mifflin Co.

Heidenreich, Elke. Nero Corleone: A Cat's Story. Orgel, Doris, tr. from GER. 1997. 96p. (J). (gr. 2-6). 15.99 o.s.i *(0-670-87395-0)* Penguin Putnam Bks. for Young Readers.

Henry, Marguerite. Gaudenzia Pride of the Palio. 1989. (J). 12.95 o.s.i *(0-02-689416-5,* Simon & Schuster Children's Publishing) Simon & Schuster Children's Publishing.

Heuston, Kimberley Burton. Dante's Daughter. 2003. (J). 16.95 *(1-886910-97-9,* Front Street) Front Street, Inc.

Hope, Laura Lee. The Bobbsey Twins & the Mystery of the King's Puppet. 1967. (Bobbsey Twins Ser.). (J). (gr. 3-5). 4.50 o.s.i *(0-448-08060-5,* Grosset & Dunlap) Penguin Putnam Bks. for Young Readers.

Lawrence, Caroline. Roman Mysteries #2: Secrets of Vesuvius. 2004. 192p. pap. 5.99 *(0-14-240118-8,* Puffin Bks.) Penguin Putnam Bks. for Young Readers.

—The Secrets of Vesuvius. 2002. (Roman Mysteries Ser.). 192p. (YA). (gr. 6-9). 22.90 *(0-7613-2603-0)*; (J). (gr. 5-9). 15.95 *(0-7613-1583-7)* Millbrook Pr., Inc. (Roaring Brook Pr.).

Leppard, Lois Gladys. Mandie & the Silent Catacombs. 1990. (Mandie Bks.: No. 16). 160p. (J). (gr. 4-7). pap. 4.99 *(1-55661-148-X)* Bethany Hse. Pubs.

Masini, Beatrice. The Wedding Dress Mess. 2003. (Illus.). 32p. (J). 15.95 *(0-8230-1738-9)* Watson-Guptill Pubns., Inc.

McCully, Emily Arnold. The Orphan Singer. 2001. (Illus.). 32p. (J). (gr. k-2). pap. 16.95 *(0-439-19274-9,* Levine, Arthur A. Bks.) Scholastic, Inc.

Mele, Michael. A Gift for the Contessa. 1997. (Illus.). 40p. (J). 15.95 *(1-56554-216-9)* Pelican Publishing Co., Inc.

Morpurgo, Michael. Jo-Jo, & the Melon Donkey. 2002. (Yellow Bananas Ser.). (Illus.). 48p. (J). (gr. 3-4). pap. 4.95 *(0-7787-0988-4)*; lib. bdg. 19.96 *(0-7787-0942-6)* Crabtree Publishing Co.

Napoli, Donna Jo. Three Days. 2003. (Illus.). 160p. pap. 5.99 *(0-14-250025-9,* Puffin Bks.); 2001. 136p. (J). (gr. 4-6). 15.99 *(0-525-46790-4,* Dutton Children's Bks.) Penguin Putnam Bks. for Young Readers.

Nobisso, Josephine. In English, of Course. 2002. Tr. of En Ingles, Por Supuesto. (Illus.). 32p. (J). (SPA.). 16.95 *(0-940112-07-8)*; pap. 8.95 *(0-940112-08-6)* Gingerbread Hse.

O'Dell, Scott. The Road to Damietta. 1987. 240p. (gr. 7 up). mass mkt. 6.50 *(0-449-70233-2,* Fawcett) Ballantine Bks.

—The Road to Damietta, 001. 1985. 256p. (J). (gr. 6 up). 14.95 o.p. *(0-395-38923-2)* Houghton Mifflin Co.

—The Road to Damietta. 1985. (J). 12.04 *(0-606-04403-5)* Turtleback Bks.

Osborne, Mary Pope. Vacation under the Volcano. unabr. ed. 2002. (Magic Tree House Ser. : Vol. 13). 74p. (J). (gr. k-4). pap. 17.00 incl. audio *(0-8072-0782-9,* LFTR 241 SP, Listening Library) Random Hse. Audio Publishing Group.

—Vacation under the Volcano. 1998. (Magic Tree House Ser.: No. 13). (Illus.). 96p. (J). (gr. k-3). lib. bdg. 11.99 *(0-679-99050-X,* Random Hse. Bks. for Young Readers) Random Hse. Children's Bks.

—Vacation under the Volcano. 1998. (Magic Tree House Ser.: No. 13). (Illus.). 80p. (J). (gr. k-3). pap. 3.99 *(0-679-89050-5)* Random Hse., Inc.

—Vacation under the Volcano, 13. 1998. (Magic Tree House Ser.: No. 13). (Illus.). (J). (gr. k-3). 10.04 *(0-606-13972-9)* Turtleback Bks.

Outlet Book Company Staff. Pinocchio. 1987. o.s.i *(0-517-64691-9)* Crown Publishing Group.

Parillo, Tony. Michelangelo's Surprise, RS. 1998. 32p. (YA). (ps-3). 16.00 o.p. *(0-374-34961-4,* Farrar, Straus & Giroux (BYR)) Farrar, Straus & Giroux.

Pinocho: The Human Body, Sea Life, the Bedroom. 1999. Tr. of Pinocchio. (ENG & SPA., Illus.). (J). (ps-5). pap. 4.95 *(88-8148-253-3)* European Language Institute ITA. *Dist:* Midwest European Pubns.

Rosen, Michael & Shakespeare, William. Shakespeare's Romeo & Juliet. Ray, Jane, tr. & illus. by. 2003. 80p. (J). 17.99 *(0-7636-2258-3)* Candlewick Pr.

Sabuda, Robert. Uh Oh Leonardo. 2003. (Illus.). 48p. (J). 16.95 *(0-689-81160-8,* Atheneum) Simon & Schuster Children's Publishing.

Shakespeare, William. Romeo & Juliet: Adaptation. 2002. (Shakespeare Collection). (Illus.). 46p. (J). text 9.95 o.p. *(0-19-521798-5)* Oxford Univ. Pr., Inc.

Strangis, Joel. Grandfather's Rock. 1993. (Illus.). (J). 14.95 o.p. *(0-395-65367-3)* Houghton Mifflin Co.

Stevens, Biddy. Toto in Italy. 1994. (Toto in... Ser.). (ITA., Illus.). 24p. (J). (gr. 4-7). 12.95 *(0-8442-9289-3,* 92893, National Textbook Co.) McGraw-Hill/Contemporary.

Titus, Eve. Anatole in Italy. 1973. (Adventures of Anatole Ser.). (Illus.). 40p. (J). (gr. k-3). lib. bdg. o.p. *(0-07-064899-9)* McGraw-Hill Cos., The.

Valens, Amy. Danilo the Fruit Man. 1993. (Illus.). 320p. (J). (ps-3). 12.99 o.p. *(0-8037-1151-4)*; 12.89 o.p. *(0-8037-1152-2)* Penguin Putnam Bks. for Young Readers. (Dial Bks. for Young Readers).

Ventura, Piero & Ventura, Marisa M. The Painter's Trick. 1977. (Illus.). (J). (gr. k-2). 5.95 o.p. *(0-394-83320-1,* Random Hse. Bks. for Young Readers) Random Hse. Children's Bks.

Vigna, Judith. Zio Pasquale's Zoo. 1993. (J). o.p. *(0-8075-9488-1)* Whitman, Albert & Co.

Weaver, Tess. Opera Cat. 2002. (Illus.). 32p. (J). (gr. k-3). lib. bdg. 15.00 *(0-618-09635-3,* Clarion Bks.) Houghton Mifflin Co. Trade & Reference Div.

Weston, Carol. The Diary of Melanie Martin: How I Survived Matt the Brat, Michelangelo & the Leaning Tower of Pizza. 2000. (Illus.). 160p. (gr. 3-5). lib. bdg. 17.99 o.s.i *(0-375-90509-X,* Knopf Bks. for Young Readers) Random Hse. Children's Bks.

—The Diary of Melanie Martin: Or How I Survived Matt the Brat, Michelangelo & the Leaning Tower of Pizza. 2000. (Illus.). 160p. (gr. 3-5). text 15.95 o.s.i *(0-375-80509-5,* Knopf Bks. for Young Readers) Random Hse. Children's Bks.

Winterson, Jeanette. The King of Capri. 2003. (Illus.). 32p. (J). 16.95 *(1-58234-830-8,* Bloomsbury Children) Bloomsbury Publishing.

J

JAMAICA—FICTION

Belafonte, Harry. Island in the Sun. 2001. 13.14 *(0-606-21254-X)* Turtleback Bks.

Berry, James. A Thief in the Village & Other Stories. 1988. 160p. (YA). (gr. 6 up). lib. bdg. 12.95 o.p. *(0-531-05745-3)*; mass mkt. 12.99 o.p. *(0-531-08345-4)* Scholastic, Inc. (Orchard Bks.).

Berry, James R. Ajeemah & His Son. (Willa Perlman Bks.). 96p. (gr. 7 up). 1994. (J). pap. 4.99 *(0-06-440523-0,* Harper Trophy); 1992. (YA). 13.95 o.p. *(0-06-021043-5)*; 1992. (YA). lib. bdg. 13.89 o.p. *(0-06-021044-3)* HarperCollins Children's Bk. Group.

—Ajeemah & His Son. 1994. (J). 11.10 *(0-606-05726-9)* Turtleback Bks.

Buckley, Owen & Mahoney, Sharon. Jam in Jamaica. 1997. (Illus.). 24p. (J). (gr. k-1). pap. 7.00 o.p. *(0-8059-4153-3)* Dorrance Publishing Co., Inc.

Hanson, Regina. The Face at the Window. 1997. (Illus.). 32p. (J). (ps-3). lib. bdg., tchr. ed. 14.95 *(0-395-78625-8,* Clarion Bks.) Houghton Mifflin Co. Trade & Reference Div.

—The Tangerine Tree. 1995. (Illus.). 32p. (J). (ps-3). lib. bdg. 16.00 *(0-395-68963-5,* Clarion Bks.) Houghton Mifflin Co. Trade & Reference Div.

Hausman, Gerald. Doctor Bird: Three Lookin' up Tales from Jamaica. 1998. (Illus.). 40p. (J). (ps-3). 15.99 o.s.i *(0-399-22744-X,* Philomel) Penguin Putnam Bks. for Young Readers.

Hausman, Gerald & Hinds, Uton. The Jacob Ladder. 2001. (Illus.). 120p. (J). (gr. 5-8). pap. 15.95 (*0-531-30331-4*, Orchard Bks.) Scholastic, Inc.

McKenzie, Earl. A Boy Named Ossie: A Jamaican Childhood. 1991. (Caribbean Writers Ser.). (Illus.). 104p. (Orig.). (C). pap. 8.95 (*0-435-98816-6*, 98816) Heinemann.

Pomerantz, Charlotte. The Chalk Doll. (Illus.). 32p. (J). (ps-3). 1993. pap. 6.99 (*0-06-443333-1*, Harper Trophy); 1989. 15.00 (*0-397-32318-2*); 1989. lib. bdg. 14.89 o.p. (*0-397-32319-0*) HarperCollins Children's Bk. Group.

—The Chalk Doll. 1993. (J). 13.10 (*0-606-05196-1*) Turtleback Bks.

Strickland, Brad. Mutiny! 2002. (Illus.). 208p. (J). (gr. 3-6). pap. 4.99 (*0-689-85296-7*, Aladdin) Simon & Schuster Children's Publishing.

Temple, Frances. Tiger Soup: An Anansi Story from Jamaica. 1998. (J). 13.10 (*0-606-13850-1*) Turtleback Bks.

Van West, Patricia E. The Crab Man. 1998. (Illus.). 40p. (J). (ps-3). 15.95 (*1-890515-08-6*) Turtle Bks.

JAMESTOWN (VA.)—FICTION

Hermes, Patricia. The Starving Time Bk. 2: Elizabeth's Jamestown Colony Diary. (My America Ser.: Bk. 2). (Illus.). 112p. (J). (gr. 2-5). 2002. mass mkt. 4.99 (*0-439-36902-9*); 2001. pap. 8.95 (*0-439-19998-0*) Scholastic, Inc. (Scholastic Pr.).

Karwoski, Gail Langer. Surviving Jamestown: The Adventures of Young Sam Collier. 2001. (Illus.). 192p. (J). (gr. 3-7). 14.95 (*1-56145-239-4*); pap. 8.95 (*1-56145-245-9*) Peachtree Pubs., Ltd.

O'Dell, Scott. The Serpent Never Sleeps: A Novel of Jamestown & Pocahontas. 1988. 192p. (gr. 7 up). mass mkt. 6.50 (*0-449-70328-2*, Fawcett) Ballantine Bks.

Ruemmler, John D. Smoke on the Water: A Novel of Jamestown & the Powhatans. 1992. (Illus.). 176p. (YA). (gr. 7 up). pap. 6.95 o.p. (*1-55870-239-3*, Betterway Bks.) F&W Pubns., Inc.

Strigenz, Geri K., illus. Two Chimneys. 1992. (History's Children Ser.). 48p. (J). (gr. 4-5). pap. o.p. (*0-8114-6431-8*); lib. bdg. 21.36 o.p. (*0-8114-3506-7*) Raintree Pubs.

JAPAN—FICTION

Austin, Judith M. The Missing Japanese Festival Dolls. 1997. (GlobalFriends Adventures Ser.). (Illus.). 64p. (J). (gr. 2-6). pap. 5.95 (*1-58056-004-0*, GlobalFriends Pr.) GlobalFriends Collection, Inc.

Baker, Keith. The Magic Fan. (gr. k-5). 1997. (Illus.). 32p. (J). pap. 8.00 (*0-15-200983-3*, Harcourt Paperbacks); 1989. (Illus.). 32p. (J). 16.00 (*0-15-250750-7*); 93rd ed. 1993. pap. text 19.60 (*0-15-300334-0*) Harcourt Children's Bks.

Baruch, Dorothy W. Kobo & the Wishing Pictures: A Story from Japan. 1964. (gr. 1-4). bds. 3.75 o.p. (*0-8048-0347-1*) Tuttle Publishing.

Bauld, Jane Scoggins. Journey of the Third Seed. 2001. (Illus.). 32p. (J). (gr. k-2). pap. 9.95 (*1-57168-429-8*); 16.95 (*1-57168-428-X*) Eakin Pr.

Bell, Lili. The Sea Maidens of Japan. 2001. (Illus.). 32p. (J). (ps-3). 14.95 (*0-8249-5426-2*, Ideals Children's Bks.) Ideals Pubns.

Blumberg, Rhoda. Commodore Perry in the Land of Shogun. 2003. (Illus.). 144p. (J). (gr. 3 up). pap. 7.99 (*0-06-008625-4*, Harper Trophy) HarperCollins Children's Bk. Group.

Brenner, T., et al. Chibi: A True Story from Japan. 1999. (Illus.). 64p. (J). (ps-3). pap. 7.95 (*0-395-72088-5*, Clarion Bks.) Houghton Mifflin Co. Trade & Reference Div.

Brightfield, Richard. A Master of Judo. 1994. (Choose Your Own Adventure Ser.: No. 148). (Illus.). 128p. (J). (gr. 4-8). pap. 3.50 o.s.i (*0-553-56397-1*) Bantam Bks.

—Master of Karate. l.t. ed. 1995. (Choose Your Own Adventure Ser.: No. 108). (Illus.). 128p. (J). (gr. 4-8). lib. bdg. 21.27 o.p. (*0-8368-1403-7*) Stevens, Gareth Inc.

Brouwer, Sigmund. Terror on Kamikaze Run. 2003. (Accidental Detectives Ser.). 144p. (YA). pap. 5.99 (*0-7642-2573-1*) Bethany Hse. Pubs.

—Terror on Kamikaze Run. 1994. (Accidental Detective Ser.: Vol. 12). 132p. (J). (gr. 3-7). pap. 5.99 o.p. (*1-56476-381-1*, 6-3381) Cook Communications Ministries.

Buck, Pearl S. The Big Wave. 1985. (Illus.). (J). pap. 1.95 o.s.i (*0-590-08512-3*) Scholastic, Inc.

Compher, Catherine. Shoes on, Shoes Off. Gross, Karen, ed. 1993. (Illus.). 24p. (J). (ps). pap. text 3.99 (*1-56309-076-7*, N938101, New Hope) Woman's Missionary Union.

Crofford, Emily. Born in the Year of Courage. 1991. (Adventures in Time Ser.). 184p. (J). (ps up). lib. bdg. 21.27 o.p. (*0-87614-679-5*, Carolrhoda Bks.) Lerner Publishing Group.

Dalkey, Kara. The Heavenward Path. 1998. 240p. (J). (gr. 7-12). 17.00 o.s.i (*0-15-201652-X*) Harcourt Children's Bks.

—Little Sister. 1996. (Jane Yolen Bks.). 208p. (J). (gr. 7-12). 17.00 o.s.i (*0-15-201392-X*) Harcourt Trade Pubs.

—Little Sister. 1998. 208p. (J). (gr. 5-9). pap. 4.99 o.s.i (*0-14-038631-9*) Penguin Putnam Bks. for Young Readers.

Davis, Emmett. See No Evil. 1983. (Adventure Diaries). (Illus.). 32p. (J). (gr. 3-6). lib. bdg. 14.65 o.p. (*0-940742-14-4*) Raintree Pubs.

Dobrin, Arnold. Taro & the Sea Turtles. 1967. (Illus.). (J). (gr. k-3). 4.39 o.p. (*0-698-30352-0*) Putnam Publishing Group, The.

Esterl, Arnica. Okino & the Whales. abr. ed. 1995. Tr. of Okino und die Wale. (Illus.). 32p. (J). (ps-3). 16.00 (*0-15-200377-0*) Harcourt Trade Pubs.

Faulkner, Matt. Black Belt. 2000. (Illus.). 40p. (J). (gr. k-3). lib. bdg. 17.99 (*0-375-90157-4*, Knopf Bks. for Young Readers) Random Hse. Children's Bks.

Frew, Andrew W. The Invisible Seam. 2003. (Illus.). 32p. (J). (gr. 1-5). 15.95 (*1-931659-02-8*) Moon Mountain Publishing, Inc.

Friedman, Ina R. How My Parents Learned to Eat. (Carry-Along Book & Cassette Favorites Ser.). (J). (ps-3). 1993. 1p. pap. 9.95 incl. audio (*0-395-66488-8*, 485871); 1987. (Illus.). 32p. pap. 5.95 (*0-395-44235-4*); 1984. (Illus.). 32p. lib. bdg., tchr. ed. 15.00 (*0-395-35379-3*) Houghton Mifflin Co.

—How My Parents Learned to Eat. 1984. (J). 12.10 (*0-606-03692-X*) Turtleback Bks.

Gibson, William. Idoru. 1997. 400p. mass mkt. 7.50 (*0-425-15864-0*) Berkley Publishing Group.

—Idoru. 1996. 304p. 24.95 o.s.i (*0-399-14130-8*, G. P. Putnam's Sons) Penguin Group (USA) Inc.

—Idoru. 1998. 4.98 o.p. (*0-7651-0900-X*) Smithmark Pubs., Inc.

Gollub, Matthew. Ten Oni Drummers. 2000. (ENG & JPN., Illus.). 32p. (J). (ps-3). 15.95 (*1-58430-011-6*) Lee & Low Bks., Inc.

Haugaard, Erik Christian. The Boy & the Samurai. 1991. 256p. (YA). (gr. 7-7). tchr. ed. 16.00 (*0-395-56398-4*) Houghton Mifflin Co.

—The Boy & the Samurai. 2000. (Illus.). 256p. (YA). (gr. 7-9). pap. 7.95 (*0-618-07039-7*) Houghton Mifflin Co. Trade & Reference Div.

—The Revenge of the Forty-Seven Samurai. 1995. 240p. (YA). (gr. 7 up). tchr. ed. 16.00 (*0-395-70809-5*) Houghton Mifflin Co.

—The Samurai's Tale. 1990. 256p. (YA). (gr. 7-12). pap. 6.95 (*0-395-54970-1*) Houghton Mifflin Co.

—The Samurai's Tale. 2001. (YA). 20.25 (*0-8446-7175-4*) Smith, Peter Pub., Inc.

—The Samurai's Tale. 1984. 13.00 (*0-606-04791-3*) Turtleback Bks.

Hoobler, Dorothy & Hoobler, Thomas. The Demon in the Teahouse. (J). 2002. 192p. pap. 5.99 (*0-698-11971-1*, PaperStar); 2001. 181p. (gr. 5-8). 17.99 (*0-399-23499-3*, G. P. Putnam's Sons) Penguin Putnam Bks. for Young Readers.

—The Ghost in the Tokaido Inn. 1999. 214p. (J). (gr. 5-9). 17.99 (*0-399-23330-X*, G. P. Putnam's Sons) Penguin Putnam Bks. for Young Readers.

Hope, Laura Lee. The Bobbsey Twins & the Goldfish Mystery. 1962. (Bobbsey Twins Ser.). (Illus.). (J). (gr. 3-5). 4.50 o.s.i (*0-448-08055-9*, Grosset & Dunlap) Penguin Putnam Bks. for Young Readers.

Hosozawa-Nagano, Elaine. Chopsticks from America. 1994. (Illus.). 64p. (YA). (gr. 5 up). 16.95 (*1-879965-11-9*) Polychrome Publishing Corp.

Hughes, Dean. Nutty & the Case of the Ski-Slope Spy. 1990. (Nutty Ser.). 128p. (J). (gr. 3-7). reprint ed. pap. 3.95 o.s.i (*0-689-71438-6*, Aladdin) Simon & Schuster Children's Publishing.

Iijima, Geneva Cobb. The Way We Do It in Japan. 2002. (Illus.). 32p. (J). (gr. k-4). lib. bdg. 14.95 (*0-8075-7822-3*) Whitman, Albert & Co.

Ikeda, Daisaku. The Cherry Tree. McCaughrean, Geraldine, tr. 1992. (Illus.). 32p. (J). (ps-3). 15.00 o.s.i (*0-679-82669-6*); 15.99 o.s.i (*0-679-92669-0*) Random Hse. Children's Bks. (Knopf Bks. for Young Readers).

—Kanta & the Deer. 1997. (Illus.). 64p. (J). 15.95 (*0-8348-0406-9*) Weatherhill, Inc.

James, J. Alison. The Drums of Noto Hanto. 1999. (Illus.). 40p. (J). (ps-3). pap. 16.95 o.p. (*0-7894-2574-2*) Dorling Kindersley Publishing, Inc.

Jordan, June. Kimako's Story. 1991. (Illus.). 42p. (J). (gr. k-3). pap. 3.95 (*0-395-60338-2*) Houghton Mifflin Co. Trade & Reference Div.

Kajikawa, Kimiko & Heo, Yumi, illus. Yoshi's Feast. 2000. (Melanie Kroupa Bks.). 32p. (J). (ps-3). pap. 15.99 (*0-7894-2607-2*, D K Ink) Dorling Kindersley Publishing, Inc.

Kako, Satoshi. Little Daruma & Little Daikoku: A Japanese Children's Tale. McNamara, Richard B. & Howlett, Peter, trs. 2003. (Illus.). 32p. (J). (ps-3). 10.95 (*0-8048-3351-6*) Tuttle Publishing.

Kako, Satoshi, et al, trs. from JPN. Little Daruma & the Little Rabbits. 2003. (Little Daruma Ser.). (Illus.). 32p. (J). 10.95 (*0-8048-3349-4*) Tuttle Publishing.

Kalman, Maira. Sayonara, Mrs. Kackleman. 1989. (Illus.). 40p. (J). (ps-5). 16.99 o.p. (*0-670-82945-5*, Viking Children's Bks.) Penguin Putnam Bks. for Young Readers.

Kasuya, Masahiro. The Smallest Christmas Tree. 1981. 24p. (J). (gr. k-2). 6.95 o.p. (*0-8170-0921-3*) Judson Pr.

Kimmel, Eric A. Sword of the Samurai: Adventure Stories from Japan. 1999. 128p. (J). 15.00 (*0-15-201985-5*) Harcourt Children's Bks.

—Sword of the Samurai: Adventure Stories from Japan. 2000. (Trophy Chapter Bks.). (Illus.). 112p. (J). (gr. 2-5). pap. 4.25 (*0-06-442131-7*, Harper Trophy) HarperCollins Children's Bk. Group.

—Sword of the Samurai: Adventure Stories from Japan. 2000. 10.30 (*0-606-19999-3*) Turtleback Bks.

Kroll, Virginia L. A Carp for Kimiko. 1993. (Illus.). 32p. (J). (ps-3). 14.95 (*0-88106-412-2*, Talewinds); lib. bdg. 15.88 o.p. (*0-88106-413-0*) Charlesbridge Publishing, Inc.

Kudler, David. The Seven Gods of Luck. 1997. (Illus.). 32p. (J). (ps-3). tchr. ed. 15.00 o.p. (*0-395-78830-7*) Houghton Mifflin Co.

Lattimore, Deborah Nourse. The Fool & the Phoenix: A Tale of Old Japan. 1997. (Joanna Cotler Bks.). (Illus.). 40p. (J). (gr. 1-6). lib. bdg. 14.89 (*0-06-026211-7*); 14.95 o.s.i (*0-06-026209-5*) HarperCollins Children's Bk. Group.

Levinson, Riki. Boys Here - Girls There. 1993. (Illus.). 112p. (J). 13.00 o.p. (*0-525-67374-1*, Dutton Children's Bks.) Penguin Putnam Bks. for Young Readers.

Libster, Bernard. The Bonsai Bear. 1999. (Illus.). 32p. (J). (ps-3). 15.95 (*0-935699-15-5*) Illumination Arts Publishing Co., Inc.

Liebold, Jay. Secret of the Ninja. l.t. ed. 1995. (Choose Your Own Adventure Ser.: No. 66). (Illus.). 128p. (J). (gr. 4-8). lib. bdg. 21.27 o.p. (*0-8368-1405-3*) Stevens, Gareth Inc.

Lifton, Betty J. Joji & the Dragon. 1989. (Illus.). 64p. (J). (gr. 1-3). reprint ed. lib. bdg. 17.50 o.p. (*0-208-02245-7*, Linnet Bks.) Shoe String Pr., Inc.

Lobel, Anita. The Dwarf Giant. 1996. (Illus.). 32p. (J). (gr. k up). 16.00 o.p. (*0-688-14407-1*, Greenwillow Bks.) HarperCollins Children's Bk. Group.

Lolling, Atsuko G. Aki & the Banner of Names: And Other Stories from Japan. 1991. (Orig.). (J). (gr. 1-6). pap. 4.95 (*0-377-00218-6*) Friendship Pr.

London, Jonathan. Moshi Moshi. 1998. (Around the World Ser.). (Illus.). 32p. (gr. k-4). lib. bdg. 23.90 o.p. (*0-7613-0110-0*) Millbrook Pr., Inc.

Manz, L. B. Noshi's Special Gift. 2003. (Illus.). (J). (*0-9710278-9-7*) All About Kids Publishing.

Markie, Uncle. Piglette & BoBo Do Tokyo. l.t. ed. 2002. 28p. 9.95 (*0-9633943-7-1*) Studio 403.

Martin, Patricia M. Kumi & the Pearl. 1968. (Illus.). (J). (gr. 2-4). 3.86 o.p. (*0-399-60343-3*) Putnam Publishing Group, The.

Marton, Jirina, illus. Lady Kaguya's Secret: A Japanese Tale. 1997. 48p. (YA). (ps up). lib. bdg. 19.95 (*1-55037-441-9*) Annick Pr., Ltd. CAN. *Dist:* Firefly Bks., Ltd.

Matsuno, Masako. A Pair of Red Clogs. 2002. 32p. (J). 16.95 (*1-930900-20-1*) Purple Hse. Pr.

—A Pair of Red Clogs. 1981. (Illus.). (J). (gr. 1-4). 3.95 o.p. (*0-399-20796-1*) Putnam Publishing Group, The.

Mayer, Mercer. Shibumi & the Kitemaker. (Illus.). 48p. 2003. pap. 5.95 (*0-7614-5145-5*); 1999. (J). 18.95 (*0-7614-5054-8*, Cavendish Children's Bks.) Cavendish, Marshall Corp.

McCann, Jesse Leon. The Case of the Karate Kitty-Nappers. 2000. (Illus.). 57p. (J). (ps-3). mass mkt. 3.99 (*0-439-20654-5*) Scholastic, Inc.

—The Case of the Karate Kitty-Nappers. 2000. (Ace Ventura Chapter Bk.: Vol. 1). 10.14 (*0-606-19525-4*) Turtleback Bks.

Melmed, Laura Krauss. Little Oh. 1997. (Illus.). 32p. (J). (ps-3). 16.99 (*0-688-14208-7*); lib. bdg. 17.89 (*0-688-14209-5*) HarperCollins Children's Bk. Group.

Merrill, Jean. The Girl Who Loved Caterpillars: A Twelfth-Century Tale from Japan. 1992. (Illus.). 32p. (J). (ps-3). 16.99 (*0-399-21871-8*, Philomel) Penguin Putnam Bks. for Young Readers.

Miller, Elizabeth K. Seven Lucky Gods & Ken-Chan. 1969. (Illus.). (gr. k-5). bds. 4.35 o.p. (*0-8048-0520-2*) Tuttle Publishing.

Miyazawa, Kenji. Winds from Afar. Bester, John, tr. from JPN. 1972. (Illus.). 204p. 15.50 o.s.i (*0-87011-171-X*) Kodansha America, Inc.

Mori, Hana, et al. Jirohattan. Kurosaki, Tamiko & Crowe, Elizabeth, trs. from JPN. 1993. (Illus.). 80p. (Orig.). (YA). (gr. 4-8). pap. 6.95 (*1-880188-69-4*) Bess Pr., Inc.

Mori, Kyoko. One Bird. 1996. 256p. (gr. 8 up). mass mkt. 6.50 (*0-449-70453-X*, Fawcett) Ballantine Bks.

—One Bird, ERS. 1995. (Edge Bks.). 242p. (YA). (gr. 7 up). 15.95 o.p. (*0-8050-2983-4*, Holt, Henry & Co. Bks. For Young Readers) Holt, Henry & Co.

—One Bird. 1996. 10.55 (*0-606-16246-1*) Turtleback Bks.

—Shizuko's Daughter. 1994. 224p. (gr. 7-12). mass mkt. 6.99 (*0-449-70433-5*, Fawcett) Ballantine Bks.

—Shizuko's Daughter, ERS. 1993. 240p. (YA). (gr. 7-12). 15.95 o.s.i (*0-8050-2557-X*, Holt, Henry & Co. Bks. For Young Readers) Holt, Henry & Co.

—Shizuko's Daughter. 1994. (J). 11.55 (*0-606-07153-9*) Turtleback Bks.

Morimoto, Junko. The Two Bullies. Morimoto, Isao, tr. from JPN. 1999. (Illus.). 32p. (J). (ps-2). 17.00 o.s.i (*0-517-80061-6*); lib. bdg. 18.99 o.s.i (*0-517-80062-4*) Random Hse. Children's Bks. (Random Hse. Bks. for Young Readers).

Mosel, Arlene. The Funny Little Woman. 2002. (Illus.). (J). 13.19 (*0-7587-0033-4*) Book Wholesalers, Inc.

—The Funny Little Woman. (Illus.). 40p. (J). (ps-3). 1993. pap. 5.99 (*0-14-054753-3*, Puffin Bks.); 1977. 3.95 o.p. (*0-525-45036-X*, Dutton Children's Bks.); 1972. 16.00 o.s.i (*0-525-30265-4*, 01258-370, Dutton Children's Bks.) Penguin Putnam Bks. for Young Readers.

Myers, Steven. The Enchanted Sticks. 1979. (Illus.). (J). (gr. 3 up). 6.95 o.p. (*0-698-20483-2*) Putnam Publishing Group, The.

Myers, Tim. Basho & the Fox. 2000. (Illus.). 32p. (J). (gr. k-3). 15.95 (*0-7614-5068-8*, Cavendish Children's Bks.) Cavendish, Marshall Corp.

Nakawatari, Harutaka. The Sea & I, RS. 1992. (Illus.). 32p. (J). (ps-3). 15.00 o.p. (*0-374-36428-1*, Farrar, Straus & Giroux (BYR)) Farrar, Straus & Giroux.

Namioka, Lensey. The Coming of the Bear. 1992. 192p. (YA). (gr. 7 up). 14.00 (*0-06-020288-2*); lib. bdg. 14.89 o.p. (*0-06-020289-0*) HarperCollins Children's Bk. Group.

—Den of the White Fox. 1997. 256p. (YA). 14.00 o.s.i (*0-15-201282-6*); (J). pap. 6.00 (*0-15-201283-4*) Harcourt Trade Pubs.

—Den of the White Fox. 1997. 12.05 (*0-606-11250-2*) Turtleback Bks.

—The Hungriest Boy in the World. 2001. (Illus.). 32p. (J). (ps-3). tchr. ed. 16.95 (*0-8234-1542-2*) Holiday Hse., Inc.

—Island of Ogres. 1989. 208p. (YA). (gr. 7 up). 13.95 (*0-06-024372-4*); lib. bdg. 13.89 o.p. (*0-06-024373-2*) HarperCollins Children's Bk. Group.

—Samurai & the Long-Nosed Devils. 1976. (gr. 7 up). 6.95 o.p. (*0-679-20361-3*) McKay, David Co., Inc.

—Valley of the Broken Cherry Trees. 176p. (YA). (gr. 6 up). reprint ed. pap. 8.95 o.p. (*0-936085-32-0*) Blue Heron Publishing.

—Valley of the Broken Cherry Trees. 1980. (YA). (gr. 7 up). 8.95 o.s.i (*0-440-09325-2*, Delacorte Pr.) Dell Publishing.

—Village of the Vampire Cat: A Novel. 1995. 192p. (YA). pap. 8.95 o.p. (*0-936085-29-0*) Blue Heron Publishing.

—Village of the Vampire Cat: A Novel. 1981. 224p. (YA). (gr. 8-12). 9.95 o.s.i (*0-440-09377-5*, Delacorte Pr.) Dell Publishing.

—White Serpent Castle. 1976. (J). (gr. 7 up). 6.95 o.p. (*0-679-20362-1*) McKay, David Co., Inc.

Neurath, Marie. They Lived Like This in Old Japan. 1967. (They Lived Like This Ser.). (Illus.). (gr. 4-6). lib. bdg. 3.90 o.p. (*0-531-01387-1*, Watts, Franklin) Scholastic Library Publishing.

Newman, Leslea. Hachi-Ko Waits. 2004. (J). 15.95 (*0-8050-7336-1*, Holt, Henry & Co. Bks. For Young Readers) Holt, Henry & Co.

Nomura, Takaaki. Grandpa's Town. Stinchecum, Amanda M., tr. from JPN. (Illus.). 32p. (J). (ps-3). 1995. pap. 7.95 (*0-916291-57-X*); 1991. 13.95 o.p. (*0-916291-36-7*) Kane/Miller Bk. Pubs.

Osborne, Mary Pope. Night of the Ninjas. 1995. (Magic Tree House Ser.: No. 5). (Illus.). 80p. (J). (gr. k-3). lib. bdg. 11.99 (*0-679-96371-5*, Random Hse. Bks. for Young Readers) Random Hse. Children's Bks.

—Night of the Ninjas. 1995. (Magic Tree House Ser.: No. 5). (Illus.). 80p. (J). (gr. k-3). pap. 3.99 (*0-679-86371-0*) Random Hse., Inc.

—Night of the Ninjas. 1995. (Magic Tree House Ser.: No. 5). (Illus.). (J). (gr. k-3). 10.14 (*0-606-07947-5*) Turtleback Bks.

Otey-Little, Mimi. Yoshiko & the Foreigner, RS. 1996. 40p. (J). (ps-3). 16.00 (*0-374-32448-4*, Farrar, Straus & Giroux (BYR)) Farrar, Straus & Giroux.

Paterson, Katherine. The Master Puppeteer. 1976. (Illus.). 192p. (J). (gr. 6 up). 15.00 o.p. (*0-690-00913-5*) HarperCollins Children's Bk. Group.

—Of Nightingales That Weep. (Illus.). (J). 1974. (gr. 5 up). 14.00 o.s.i (*0-690-00485-0*); 1989. 192p. (gr. 7 up). reprint ed. pap. 5.99 (*0-06-440282-7*, Harper Trophy) HarperCollins Children's Bk. Group.

—Of Nightingales That Weep. 1980. (Illus.). 172p. (J). (gr. 5 up). pap. 2.50 o.p. (*0-380-51110-X*, Avon Bks.) Morrow/Avon.

—The Sign of the Chrysanthemum. 1980. (Illus.). 132p. (J). (gr. 6 up). pap. 2.25 o.p. (*0-380-49288-1*, Avon Bks.) Morrow/Avon.

Peck, Helen E. & Dearmin, Jennie T. The Smiling Dragon. 1984. (Second Grade Bk.). (Illus.). (gr. 2-3). lib. bdg. 5.95 o.p. (*0-513-00409-2*) Denison, T. S. & Co., Inc.

Settings

Peers, Judi. Sayonara Sharks. 2001. (Sports Stories Ser.). (Illus.). 128p. (J). (gr. 3-7). pap. 5.50 (*1-55028-730-3*) Lorimer, James & Co. CAN. *Dist:* Orca Bk. Pubs.

Perkins, Lucy F. Japanese Twins. 1968. (Walker's Twins Ser.). (Illus.). (J). (gr. 2-5). lib. bdg. 4.85 o.p. (*0-8027-6036-8*) Walker & Co.

Pirotta, Saviour. Turtle Bay, RS. 1997. (Illus.). 32p. (J). (ps-3). 15.00 o.p. (*0-374-37888-6*, Farrar, Straus & Giroux (BYR)) Farrar, Straus & Giroux.

Powers, Daniel T. Jiro's Pearl. 1997. (Illus.). (J). (gr. 1-4). 15.99 o.p. (*1-56402-631-0*) Candlewick Pr.

Pray, Ralph. Jingu: The Hidden Princess. 2002. (Illus.). 80p. (J). 14.95 (*1-885008-21-X*, 188500821x) Shen's Bks.

Sakade, Florence. Kintaro's Adventures & Other Japanese Children's Stories. 1989. (Illus.). 60p. (J). (gr. 1-5). pap. 9.95 (*0-8048-0343-9*) Tuttle Publishing.

—Little One-Inch & Other Japanese Children's Favorite Stories. 1989. (Illus.). 64p. (J). (gr. 5-7). pap. 9.95 o.s.i (*0-8048-0384-6*) Tuttle Publishing.

—Peach Boy & Other Japanese Children's Favorite Stories. 1989. (Illus.). 58p. (J). (ps-3). pap. 9.95 (*0-8048-0469-9*) Tuttle Publishing.

Sakade, Florence, ed. Urashima Taro & Other Japanese Children's Stories. 1989. (Illus.). 58p. (J). (gr. 1-6). pap. 9.95 (*0-8048-0609-8*) Tuttle Publishing.

San Souci, Robert D. The Samurai's Daughter. 1997. 13.14 (*0-606-13756-4*) Turtleback Bks.

Say, Allen. The Feast of Lanterns. 1976. (Illus.). (J). (gr. k-4). 9.95 (*0-06-025213-8*); lib. bdg. 4.79 o.p. (*0-06-025214-6*) HarperCollins Children's Bk. Group.

—Grandfather's Journey. 1993. (Illus.). 32p. (J). (ps-3). lib. bdg., tchr. ed. 16.95 (*0-395-57035-2*) Houghton Mifflin Co.

—The Ink-Keeper's Apprentice. 1979. (YA). (gr. 7 up). lib. bdg. 12.89 o.p. (*0-06-025209-X*) HarperCollins Children's Bk. Group.

—The Ink-Keeper's Apprentice. 1994. (Illus.). 160p. (YA). (gr. 7-7). tchr. ed. 13.95 (*0-395-70562-2*) Houghton Mifflin Co.

—Tea with Milk. 2002. (Illus.). (J). 24.36 (*0-7587-3768-8*) Book Wholesalers, Inc.

—Tea with Milk. 1999. (Illus.). 32p. (J). (ps-3). lib. bdg., tchr. ed. 17.00 (*0-395-90495-1*) Houghton Mifflin Co.

—Tree of Cranes. 2002. (Illus.). 25.28 (*0-7587-3857-9*) Book Wholesalers, Inc.

—Tree of Cranes. 1991. (Illus.). 32p. (J). (ps-3). tchr. ed. 17.95 (*0-395-52024-X*) Houghton Mifflin Co. Trade & Reference Div.

Scieszka, Jon. Sam Samurai. (Time Warp Trio Ser.). (Illus.). 2004. 112p. pap. 4.99 (*0-14-240088-2*); Vol. 10. 2002. 112p. (J). pap. 4.99 (*0-14-230213-9*); Vol. 10. 2001. 80p. (J). (gr. 2-5). 14.99 (*0-670-89915-1*) Penguin Putnam Bks. for Young Readers. (Puffin Bks.).

Sogabe, Aki, illus. The Loyal Cat. 1995. 40p. (J). (ps-3). 15.00 o.s.i (*0-15-200092-5*) Harcourt Children's Bks.

Soto, Gary. Pacific Crossing. 1992. 144p. (YA). (gr. 4-7). 17.00 (*0-15-259187-7*) Harcourt Children's Bks.

Steiber, Ellen. Shadow of the Fox. 1994. (Bullseye Chillers Ser.). 108p. (J). (gr. 2-6). pap. 3.50 o.s.i (*0-679-86667-1*, Random Hse. Bks. for Young Readers) Random Hse. Children's Bks.

Suyeoka, George. Momotaro. Tabrah, Ruth, ed. 1972. (Illus.). (J). (gr. 1-7). 5.95 o.s.i (*0-89610-009-X*) Island Heritage Publishing.

Talley, Carol. Hana's Year. 1992. (Key Concepts in Personal Development Ser.). (Illus.). 32p. (J). (gr. 1-4). 16.95 (*1-55942-034-0*, 7652); tchr. ed. 79.95 incl. VHS (*1-55942-037-5*, 9371) Marsh Media.

Tamaki, Donna, tr. Hats for the Jizos. l.t. ed. 1995. Tr. of Kasa Jizo. (ENG & JPN., Illus.). 16p. (J). (ps-12). 35.00 (*1-893533-04-2*, 5) Kamishibai for Kids.

The Tongue-Cut Sparrow, a Japanese Fairy Tale. 2001. audio compact disk 7.99 (*0-923586-53-9*) Data Systems.

Tung, Angela. Song of the Stranger. Artenstein, Michael, ed. 1999. (Roxbury Park Bks.). (J). 192p. (gr. 3-7). pap. 4.95 (*1-56565-948-1*, 09481W); 96p. (gr. 5-8). 12.95 (*1-56565-774-8*, 07748W) Lowell Hse. (Roxbury Park).

Watkins, Yoko Kawashima. So Far from the Bamboo Grove. 1994. (Illus.). 192p. (J). (gr. 3-6). reprint ed. pap. 5.99 (*0-688-13115-8*, HarperTempest) HarperCollins Children's Bk. Group.

Williams, Laura E. The Long Silk Strand: A Grandmother's Legacy to Her Granddaughter. 2003. (Illus.). 32p. (J). (ps-3). pap. 7.95 (*1-56397-856-3*) Boyds Mills Pr.

—The Long Silk Strand: A Grandmother's Legacy to Her Granddaughter. 2000. (Illus.). (J). 14.10 (*0-606-18013-3*) Turtleback Bks.

Wisniewski, David. Sumo Mouse. 2002. (Illus.). 32p. (J). (ps-3). 16.95 (*0-8118-3492-1*) Chronicle Bks. LLC.

Yashima, Taro. Crow Boy. 2000. (J). pap. 19.97 incl. audio (*0-7366-9208-8*) Books on Tape, Inc.

—Crow Boy. (Picture Puffins Ser.). (Illus.). (J). (ps-3). 1976. 40p. pap. 5.99 (*0-14-050172-X*, Puffin Bks.); 1955. 32p. 17.99 (*0-670-24931-9*, Viking Children's Bks.) Penguin Putnam Bks. for Young Readers.

—Crow Boy. 1983. (Picture Puffin Ser.). (Illus.). (J). 12.14 (*0-606-02075-6*) Turtleback Bks.

Yep, Laurence. Hiroshima. unabr. ed. 1997. (J). (gr. 2). pap. 21.24 incl. audio (*0-7887-1269-1*, 40515); (gr. 2). audio. (gr. 4). audio 10.00 (*0-7887-1111-3*, 95104E7) Recorded Bks., LLC.

—Hiroshima. 64p. (J). (gr. 4-7). 1996. mass mkt. 2.99 (*0-590-20833-0*); 1995. pap. 9.95 (*0-590-20832-2*) Scholastic, Inc.

—Hiroshima: A Novella. 1996. (J). 10.65 (*0-606-09414-8*) Turtleback Bks.

Yumoto, Kazumi. The Friends, RS. Hirano, Cathy, tr. from JPN. 1996. 176p. (J). (gr. 5-9). 15.00 (*0-374-32460-3*, Farrar, Straus & Giroux (BYR)) Farrar, Straus & Giroux.

—The Letters, RS. Hirano, Cathy, tr. from JPN. 2002. 176p. (YA). (gr. 9 up). 16.00 (*0-374-34383-7*, Farrar, Straus & Giroux (BYR)) Farrar, Straus & Giroux.

—The Letters. 2003. 176p. (YA). (gr. 7). mass mkt. 5.50 (*0-440-23822-6*, Dell Books for Young Readers) Random Hse. Children's Bks.

—The Spring Tone, RS. 1999. (JPN.). 176p. (J). (gr. 7-12). 16.00 o.p. (*0-374-37153-9*, Farrar, Straus & Giroux (BYR)) Farrar, Straus & Giroux.

—The Spring Tone. Hirano, Cathy, tr. 2001. 176p. (YA). (gr. 7 up). mass mkt. 4.99 (*0-440-22855-7*, Laurel Leaf) Random Hse. Children's Bks.

—The Spring Tone. Hirano, Cathy, tr. 2000. (YA). pap., stu. ed. 52.00 incl. audio (*0-7887-4189-6*, 41112);Class Set. audio 197.30 (*0-7887-4190-X*, 47105) Recorded Bks., LLC.

JAVA (INDONESIA)—FICTION

Lewis, Richard. The Flame Tree. 2004. (J). (*0-689-86333-0*, Simon & Schuster Children's Publishing) Simon & Schuster Children's Publishing.

JAVA SEA—FICTION

Catherall, Arthur M. Death of an Oil Rig. 1969. (Illus.). (J). (gr. 5-8). 9.95 o.p. (*0-87599-159-9*) Phillips, S.G. Inc.

JERUSALEM—FICTION

da Costa, Deborah. Snow in Jerusalem: A Junior Library Guild Book. 2001. (Illus.). 32p. (J). (gr. 1-5). 15.95 (*0-8075-7521-6*) Whitman, Albert & Co.

Dennis, Jeanne Gowen & Seifert, Sheila. Escape! Hohn, David, tr. & illus. by. 2003. (Strive to Thrive Ser.). (J). pap. 4.99 (*0-7814-3895-0*) Cook Communications Ministries.

Drewery, Mary. Hamid & the Palm Sunday Donkey. 1968. (Illus.). (J). (gr. 4-6). 6.95 o.p. (*0-8038-2962-0*); lib. bdg. 7.95 o.p. (*0-8038-2963-9*) Hastings Hse. Daytrips Pubs.

Ganz, Yaffa. Savta Simcha & the Roundabout Journey to Jerusalem. 2000. (Illus.). (J). 15.95 (*1-58330-452-5*) Feldheim, Philipp Inc.

—Savta Simcha, Uncle Nechemya & the Very Strange Stone in the Garden. 1992. (Illus.). (J). 14.95 (*0-87306-618-9*) Feldheim, Philipp Inc.

Geras, Adele. Golden Windows: And Other Stories of Jerusalem. 1993. (Willa Perlman Bks.). 160p. (J). (gr. 3-7). 14.95 o.p. (*0-06-022941-1*); lib. bdg. 13.89 o.p. (*0-06-022942-X*) HarperCollins Children's Bk. Group.

Hawse, Alberta. Encounter Christ Through the Dramatic Story of Vinegar Boy. 2002. 222p. (J). 9.99 (*0-8024-6588-9*) Moody Pr.

Heimerdinger, Chris. Tennis Shoes & the Seven Churches. 1997. (J). pap. 6.95 (*1-57734-217-8*, 01113275) Covenant Communications, Inc.

Henty, G. A. For the Temple: A Tale of the Fall of Jerusalem. 2000. 252p. (J). E-Book 3.95 (*0-594-02385-8*) 1873 Pr.

Kelly, Clint. Escape Underground. 2001. (KidWitness Tales Ser.). 128p. (J). (gr. 3-8). pap. 5.99 (*1-56179-964-5*) Bethany Hse. Pubs.

Kelly, Clint & Ware, Jim. Escape Underground & the Prophet's Kid. 2001. (KidWitness Tales Ser.). 128p. (J). (gr. 3-8). pap. 5.99 (*1-56179-965-3*) Bethany Hse. Pubs.

Kimmel, Eric A. Asher & the Capmakers: A Hanukkah Story. 1993. (Illus.). 32p. (J). (ps-3). tchr. ed. 15.95 (*0-8234-1031-5*) Holiday Hse., Inc.

Mackall, Dandi Daley. Off to Bethlehem! 2002. (Illus.). 24p. (J). (ps-2). 8.99 (*0-694-01505-9*) HarperCollins Pubs.

Nye, Naomi Shihab. Habibi. unabr. ed. 2000. (YA). pap. 49.24 incl. audio (*0-7887-3642-6*, 41008X4) Recorded Bks., LLC.

—Habibi. 272p. (YA). (gr. 5 up). 1999. mass mkt. 5.99 (*0-689-82523-4*, Simon Pulse); 1997. 16.00 (*0-689-80149-1*, Simon & Schuster Children's Publishing) Simon & Schuster Children's Publishing.

Oz, Amos. Soumchi. Oz, Amos & Farmer, Penelope, trs. from HEB. 1995. (Harvest Book Ser.). (Illus.). 96p. (J). (gr. 4 up). pap. 10.00 o.s.i (*0-15-600193-4*, Harvest Bks.) Harcourt Trade Pubs.

—Soumchi. Farmer, Penelope, tr. from HEB. 1981. (Illus.). 96p. (J). (gr. 4-7). 8.95 o.p. (*0-06-024621-9*); lib. bdg. 8.79 o.p. (*0-06-024622-7*) HarperCollins Children's Bk. Group.

Paris, Alan. Jerusalem, 3000: Kids Discover the City of Gold. 1995. (Illus.). 47p. (J). (gr. 4-8). 16.95 (*0-943706-59-9*) Pitspopany Pr.

Rouss, Sylvia. Tali's Jerusalem Scrapbook. 2003. (Illus.). 32p. (J). 14.95 (*1-930143-68-0*); pap. 9.95 (*1-930143-69-9*) Pitspopany Pr.

Turley, Reid P. Benjamin's Gift. 3rd ed. 1996. (Illus.). 48p. reprint ed. pap. 5.95 (*0-9651494-0-4*) Turley, Reid P.

Weil, Judith. School for One. 1992. (J). (gr. 4 up). 11.95 o.p. (*0-87306-620-0*); pap. 9.95 (*0-87306-621-9*) Feldheim, Philipp Inc.

Wheeler, Gerald, ed. Return to Jerusalem. 1988. 160p. (Orig.). (J). pap. 6.95 o.p. (*0-8280-0426-9*) Review & Herald Publishing Assn.

K

KANSAS—FICTION

Brenner, Barbara. Wagon Wheels. (I Can Read Bks.). (Illus.). 64p. (J). (gr. k-3). 1978. 15.95 (*0-06-020668-3*); 1978. lib. bdg. 15.89 (*0-06-020669-1*); unabr. ed. 1995. pap. 8.99 incl. audio (*0-694-70001-0*); 97th ed. 1997. pap. 3.99 (*0-06-444052-4*, Harper Trophy) HarperCollins Children's Bk. Group.

—Wagon Wheels. 1978. (I Can Read Bks.). (J). (gr. 2-4). 10.10 (*0-606-02372-0*) Turtleback Bks.

Brown, Irene Bennett. Willow Whip. (Sunflower Editions Ser.). 208p. (Orig.). (YA). (gr. 5 up). reprint ed. pap. 8.95 o.p. (*0-936085-23-1*) Blue Heron Publishing.

—Willow Whip. l.t. ed. 2002. 253p. (Orig.). (J). 21.95 (*0-7862-4392-9*) Gale Group.

Francis, Dorothy Brenner. The Jayhawk Horse Mystery. 2001. (Cover-to-Cover Novel Ser.). (Illus.). 80p. (J). (*0-7807-9728-0*); pap. (*0-7891-5349-1*) Perfection Learning Corp.

Gaeddert, LouAnn Bigge. Friends & Enemies. 2000. (Illus.). 176p. (J). (gr. 5-9). 16.00 (*0-689-82822-5*, Atheneum) Simon & Schuster Children's Publishing.

Garretson, Jerri. Johnny Kaw: The Pioneer Spirit of Kansas. 1997. (Illus.). 32p. (Orig.). (J). (ps-4). pap. 4.00 (*0-9659712-0-1*) Ravenstone Pr.

—Kansas Katie: A Sunflower Tale. 2000. (Illus.). 48p. (J). (gr. 1-5). pap. 6.95 (*0-9659712-3-6*) Ravenstone Pr.

—Twister Twyla: The Kansas Cowgirl. 2003. 32p. (J). 5.95 (*0-9659712-5-2*) Ravenstone Pr.

Graef, Renee, illus. Hard Times on the Prairie. adapted ed. 1998. (Little House Ser.: No. 8). 80p. (J). (gr. 3-6). pap. 4.25 (*0-06-442077-9*, Harper Trophy); lib. bdg. 15.89 (*0-06-027792-0*) HarperCollins Children's Bk. Group.

Gregory, Kristiana. A Journey of Faith. 2003. (Prairie River Ser.: No. 1). 224p. (J). (gr. 3-8). mass mkt. 4.99 (*0-439-43991-4*, Scholastic Paperbacks) Scholastic, Inc.

—Prairie River 2: A Grateful Harvest. 2003. (Prairie River Ser.: No. 2). 208p. (J). mass mkt. 4.99 (*0-439-43993-0*) Scholastic, Inc.

—Prairie River 3. 2004. (Prairie River Ser.: No. 3). (J). per. (*0-439-44001-7*) Scholastic, Inc.

—Prairie River 4. 2004. (Prairie River Ser.: No. 4). (J). per. (*0-439-44003-3*) Scholastic, Inc.

Guile, Gill, illus. The Wizard of Oz. 1997. (Classics for Children 8 & Younger Ser.). 48p. (J). (ps-3). 6.98 (*1-85854-644-3*) Brimax Bks., Ltd.

Holland, Isabelle. The Promised Land. 1996. 176p. (J). (gr. 3-7). pap. 15.95 (*0-590-47176-7*) Scholastic, Inc.

Hopkinson, Deborah. Prairie Skies: Cabin in the Snow. 2002. (Ready-for-Chapters Ser.). 80p. (J). pap. 3.99 (*0-689-84351-8*, Aladdin); lib. bdg. 11.89 (*0-689-84352-6*, Aladdin Library) Simon & Schuster Children's Publishing.

Irwin, Hadley. Jim Dandy. 1994. 144p. (J). (gr. 5-9). 15.00 (*0-689-50594-9*, McElderry, Margaret K.) Simon & Schuster Children's Publishing.

Jennings, Richard W. The Great Whale of Kansas. 2001. (Illus.). 160p. (J). (gr. 5-9). tchr. ed. 15.00 (*0-618-10228-0*, Lorraine, A. Walter) Houghton Mifflin Co. Trade & Reference Div.

Kochenderfer, Lee. The Victory Garden. Date not set. 176p. (J). pap. text 4.99 (*0-440-41703-1*, Yearling) Dell Bks. for Young Readers CAN. *Dist:* Random Hse. of Canada, Ltd.

—The Victory Garden. 2002. (Illus.). 176p. (gr. 3-7). text 14.95 (*0-385-32788-9*, Delacorte Pr.) Dell Publishing.

McAfee, Joan K. Riddle of the Lost Gold. 2002. (Illus.). 162p. (YA). pap. 9.95 (*0-89745-262-3*) Sunflower Univ. Pr.

McMullan, Kate. For This Land: Meg's Prairie Diary, Bk. 2. 2003. (My America Ser.). (Illus.). 112p. (J). pap. 10.95 (*0-439-37059-0*); mass mkt. 4.99 (*0-439-37060-4*) Scholastic, Inc. (Scholastic Pr.).

Moss, Marissa. Rose's Journal: The Story of a Girl in the Great Depression. (Young American Voices Ser.). (Illus.). 56p. (J). 2003. pap. 7.00 (*0-15-204605-4*); 2001. (gr. 3-7). 15.00 (*0-15-202423-9*) Harcourt Children's Bks. (Silver Whistle).

Nixon, Joan Lowery. In the Face of Danger. 160p. (YA). 1996. (Orphan Train Adventures Ser.: Vol. 3). (gr. 4-7). mass mkt. 4.99 (*0-440-22705-4*, Dell Books for Young Readers); 1989. (Orphan Train Quartet Ser.: Bk. 3). (gr. 7 up). mass mkt. 4.50 o.p. (*0-553-28196-8*, Starfire); 1988. (Orphan Train Quartet Ser.: Bk. 3). (gr. 7 up). 16.00 o.s.i (*0-553-05490-2*, Starfire) Random Hse. Children's Bks.

—In the Face of Danger. 1988. (Orphan Train Quartet Ser.). (J). 10.55 (*0-606-01526-4*) Turtleback Bks.

Osborne, Mary Pope. Twister on Tuesday. 2001. (Magic Tree House Ser.: No. 23). (Illus.). 96p. (J). (gr. k-3). pap. 3.99 (*0-679-89069-6*); lib. bdg. 11.99 (*0-679-99069-0*) Random Hse. Children's Bks. (Random Hse. Bks. for Young Readers).

—Twister on Tuesday. 2001. (Magic Tree House Ser.). (Illus.). (J). 10.04 (*0-606-21498-4*) Turtleback Bks.

Prigger, Mary Skillings. Aunt Minnie & the Twister. 2002. (Illus.). 32p. (J). (ps-3). lib. bdg. 15.00 (*0-618-11136-0*, Clarion Bks.) Houghton Mifflin Co. Trade & Reference Div.

Reiss, Kathryn. Riddle of the Prairie Bride. 2001. (American Girl Collection: Bk. 12). (Illus.). 176p. (J). (gr. 3-6). pap. 5.95 (*1-58485-308-5*); 9.95 o.p. (*1-58485-309-3*) Pleasant Co. Pubns. (American Girl).

—Riddle of the Prairie Bride. 2001. (American Girl Collection). (Illus.). (J). 12.00 (*0-606-21400-3*) Turtleback Bks.

Rossiter, Phyllis. Moxie. 1990. 192p. (J). (gr. 5 up). 14.95 (*0-02-777831-2*, Simon & Schuster Children's Publishing) Simon & Schuster Children's Publishing.

Ruby, Lois. Steal Away Home. 1997. pap. 1.95 o.p. (*0-590-03322-0*) Scholastic, Inc.

—Steal Away Home. 1999. 208p. (J). (gr. 3-7). pap. 4.99 (*0-689-82435-1*, Aladdin) Simon & Schuster Children's Publishing.

—Steal Away Home. 1999. 11.04 (*0-606-15921-5*) Turtleback Bks.

Rumbaut, Hendle. Dove Dream. 1994. (J). 13.95 o.p. (*0-395-68393-9*) Houghton Mifflin Co.

Ryland, Cynthia. The Van Gogh Cafe. 1999. (J). pap., stu. ed. 24.24 incl. audio (*0-7887-2669-2*, 40829) Recorded Bks., LLC.

Seely, Debra. Grasslands. 2002. (Illus.). 170p. (J). (gr. 5-9). tchr. ed. 16.95 (*0-8234-1731-X*) Holiday Hse., Inc.

Shannon, George. Climbing Kansas Mountains. 1993. (Illus.). 32p. (J). (ps-3). lib. bdg. 15.95 o.s.i (*0-02-782181-1*, Simon & Schuster Children's Publishing) Simon & Schuster Children's Publishing.

—Climbing Kansas Mountains. 1996. 13.14 (*0-606-09153-X*) Turtleback Bks.

Smith, Florence B. Painted Eagle's Dream. 2001. 220p. pap. 8.00 (*1-893463-41-9*) Prickly Pr.

Thomas, Carroll. Blue Creek Farm: A Matty Trescott Novel. 2000. (Illus.). 185p. (J). pap. 9.95 (*1-57525-243-0*) Smith & Kraus Pubs., Inc.

—Riding by Starlight: A Matty Trescott Novel. 2002. (Illus.). ix, 173p. (J). 9.95 (*1-57525-315-1*) Smith & Kraus Pubs., Inc.

Vogt, Esther Loewen. Harvest Gold. 1978. (gr. 4-6). pap. 2.25 o.p. (*0-89191-105-7*) Cook, David C. Publishing Co.

Wilder, Laura Ingalls. Little House on the Prairie. 1991. (Little House Ser.). 250p. (J). (gr. 3-6). reprint ed. lib. bdg. 19.95 (*0-89966-868-2*) Buccaneer Bks., Inc.

—Little House on the Prairie. (Little House Ser.). (J). 2003. 272p. pap. 5.99 (*0-06-052237-2*); 1999. (Illus.). 320p. (gr. 3-6). 29.95 (*0-06-028244-4*); 1953. (Illus.). 352p. (gr. 3-6). pap. 6.99 (*0-06-440002-6*, Harper Trophy); 1997. (Illus.). 352p. (gr. 3-6). 24.95 o.s.i (*0-06-027723-8*); 1953. (Illus.). 320p. (gr. k-3). lib. bdg. 17.89 (*0-06-026446-2*); 1953. (Illus.). 352p. (ps-2). 16.99 (*0-06-026445-4*) HarperCollins Children's Bk. Group.

—Little House on the Prairie. 1975. (Little House Ser.). (J). (gr. 3-6). pap. 5.50 o.p. (*0-06-080357-6*, P357, Perennial) HarperTrade.

—Little House on the Prairie. l.t. ed. 1999. (Little House Ser.). (Illus.). 420p. (J). (gr. 3-6). lib. bdg. 35.95 (*1-58118-051-9*, 22771) LRS.

—Little House on the Prairie. 1998. (Little House Ser.). (Illus.). 256p. (J). (gr. 3-6). 9.99 o.p. (*1-897954-27-1*) M Q Pubns. GBR. *Dist:* Independent Pubs. Group.

—Little House on the Prairie. 1990. (Little House Ser.). (J). (gr. 3-6). pap. 3.50 (*0-06-107006-8*, HarperTorch) Morrow/Avon.
—Little House on the Prairie. 1999. (Little House Ser.). (J). (gr. 3-6). 11.95 (*1-56137-834-8*) Novel Units, Inc.
—Little House on the Prairie. 9999. (Little House Ser.). (J). (gr. 3-6). pap. 2.50 o.s.i (*0-590-02111-7*) Scholastic, Inc.
Williams, Jeanne. Freedom Trail. 1973. 160p. (YA). (gr. 6 up). 5.95 o.p. (*0-399-20336-2*) Putnam Publishing Group, The.

KENOSKA (IMAGINARY PLACE)—FICTION

Heide, Florence P. & Heide, Roxanne. Mystery at Keyhole Carnival. Rubin, Caroline, ed. 1976. (Spotlight Club Mysteries Ser.). (Illus.). (J). (gr. 3-8). 7.95 o.p. (*0-8075-5361-1*) Whitman, Albert & Co.
—Mystery at Southport Cinema. Pacini, Kathy, ed. 1978. (Spotlight Club Mysteries Ser.). (Illus.). (J). (gr. 3-8). lib. bdg. 9.95 o.p. (*0-8075-5363-8*) Whitman, Albert & Co.
—The Mystery of the Bewitched Bookmobile. 1975. (Pilot Bks.). (Illus.). (J). (gr. 3-8). lib. bdg. 8.95 o.p. (*0-8075-5375-1*) Whitman, Albert & Co.
—Mystery of the Forgotten Island. 1983. (Spotlight Club Mysteries Ser.). (Illus.). (J). (gr. 3-7). pap. (*0-671-43983-9*, Simon Pulse) Simon & Schuster Children's Publishing.
—Mystery of the Forgotten Island. Tucker, Kathleen, ed. 1980. (Spotlight Club Mysteries Ser.). (Illus.). (J). (gr. 3-8). lib. bdg. 8.95 o.p. (*0-8075-5376-X*) Whitman, Albert & Co.
—The Mystery of the Lonely Lantern. Rubin, Caroline, ed. 1976. (Spotlight Club Mysteries Ser.). (Illus.). 128p. (J). 7.50 o.p. (*0-8075-5377-8*) Whitman, Albert & Co.
—Mystery of the Melting Snowman. 1974. (Spotlight Club Mysteries Ser.). (Illus.). 128p. (J). (gr. 3-8). lib. bdg. 9.95 o.p. (*0-8075-5378-6*) Whitman, Albert & Co.
—Mystery of the Midnight Message, No. 3. 1982. (Spotlight Club Mysteries Ser.). (Illus.). (J). (gr. 3-6). pap. (*0-671-43980-4*, Simon Pulse) Simon & Schuster Children's Publishing.
—Mystery of the Midnight Message. Rubin, Caroline, ed. 1977. (Spotlight Club Mysteries Ser.). (Illus.). (J). (gr. 3-8). lib. bdg. 8.95 o.p. (*0-8075-5381-6*) Whitman, Albert & Co.
—Mystery of the Mummy's Mask. 1982. (Spotlight Club Mysteries Ser.: No. 1). (Illus.). (J). (gr. 3-7). reprint ed. pap. (*0-671-43982-0*, Simon Pulse) Simon & Schuster Children's Publishing.
—Mystery of the Mummy's Mask. Pacini, Kathy, ed. 1979. (Spotlight Club Mysteries Ser.). (Illus.). (J). (gr. 3-8). lib. bdg. 8.95 o.p. (*0-8075-5384-0*) Whitman, Albert & Co.
—The Mystery of the Vanishing Visitor. 1982. (Spotlight Club Mysteries Ser.: No. 2). (Illus.). (J). (gr. 3-7). pap. (*0-671-43977-4*, Simon Pulse) Simon & Schuster Children's Publishing.
—The Mystery of the Vanishing Visitor. Rubin, Caroline, ed. 1975. (Pilot Bks.). (Illus.). 128p. (J). (gr. 3-8). lib. bdg. 8.95 o.p. (*0-8075-5388-3*) Whitman, Albert & Co.
—Mystery on Danger Road. Fay, Ann, ed. 1983. (High-Low Mysteries Ser.). (Illus.). 128p. (J). (gr. 3-8). lib. bdg. 8.95 o.p. (*0-8075-5396-4*) Whitman, Albert & Co.
Heide, Florence P. & Van Clief, Sylvia. Hidden Box Mystery. 1973. (Pilot Bks.). (Illus.). 128p. (J). (gr. 3-6). 7.50 o.p. (*0-8075-3270-3*) Whitman, Albert & Co.
—Mystery at Macadoo Zoo. 1973. (Spotlight Club Mysteries Ser.). (Illus.). 128p. (J). (gr. 3-7). lib. bdg. 8.95 o.p. (*0-8075-5358-1*) Whitman, Albert & Co.
—The Mystery of the Missing Suitcase. 1972. (Spotlight Club Mysteries Ser.). (Illus.). 128p. (J). (gr. 3-8). lib. bdg. 9.95 o.p. (*0-8075-5382-4*) Whitman, Albert & Co.
—Mystery of the Silver Tag. 1972. (Spotlight Club Mysteries Ser.). (Illus.). 128p. (J). (gr. 3-7). lib. bdg. 8.95 o.p. (*0-8075-5387-5*) Whitman, Albert & Co.
—Mystery of the Whispering Voice. 1974. (Spotlight Club Mysteries Ser.). (Illus.). 128p. (J). (gr. 3-7). lib. bdg. 8.95 o.p. (*0-8075-5389-1*) Whitman, Albert & Co.
Heide, Florence P. & Worth Van Clief, Sylvia. Mystery of the Whispering Voice. 1983. (Spotlight Club Mysteries Ser.). (Illus.). (J). (gr. 3-7). pap. (*0-671-43973-1*, Simon Pulse) Simon & Schuster Children's Publishing.

KENTUCKY—FICTION

Borden, Louise. Just in Time for Christmas. (J). 2000. mass mkt. 5.99 (*0-590-45356-4*); 1994. (Illus.). 32p. pap. 14.95 (*0-590-45355-6*) Scholastic, Inc.
Brouwer, Sigmund. Cobra Threat: Football. 1998. (Sigmund Brouwer's Sports Mystery Ser.: Vol. 3). 128p. (J). (gr. 5-9). 5.99 (*0-8499-5815-6*) Nelson, Tommy.
Bunin, Sherry. Dear Great American Writers School. 1995. 176p. (YA). (gr. 7 up). tchr. ed. 15.00 (*0-395-71645-4*) Houghton Mifflin Co.
Byars, Betsy C. Keeper of the Doves. 2004. (Illus.). 112p. (J). pap. 5.99 (*0-14-240063-7*, Puffin Bks.) Penguin Putnam Bks. for Young Readers.
—Keeper of the Doves. 2002. 112p. (J). (gr. 3-7). 14.99 (*0-670-03576-9*, Viking) Viking Penguin.
Campbell, Joanna. Ashleigh's Promise. 2001. (Ashleigh Ser.: No. 11). 176p. mass mkt. 4.99 (*0-06-106827-6*) HarperCollins Pubs.
—Melanie's Last Ride. 1998. (Thoroughbred Ser.: No. 29). 192p. (gr. 4-7). mass mkt. 4.99 (*0-06-106531-5*, HarperEntertainment) Morrow/Avon.
Cannon, Bettie. A Bellsong for Sarah Raines. 1987. 192p. (YA). (gr. 7 up). text 14.95 o.s.i (*0-684-18839-2*, Atheneum) Simon & Schuster Children's Publishing.
Clark, Billy C. Goodbye Kate. 1994. (Illus.). 288p. (J). (gr. 6 up). reprint ed. 20.00 (*0-945084-41-2*) Stuart, Jesse Foundation, The.
—Mooneyed Hound. Gifford, James M. & Hall, Patricia A., eds. 2nd ed. 1995. (Illus.). 128p. (J). (gr. 4 up). pap. 8.50 (*0-945084-49-8*) Stuart, Jesse Foundation, The.
—Song of the River. Gifford, James M. et al, eds. rev. ed. 1993. (Illus.). 176p. (YA). (gr. 7 up). reprint ed. 15.00 o.p. (*0-945084-35-8*) Stuart, Jesse Foundation, The.
—Trail of the Hunter's Horn. Gifford, James M. & Hall, Patricia A., eds. 2nd ed. 1995. (Illus.). 80p. (J). (gr. 4 up). pap. 6.00 (*0-945084-48-X*) Stuart, Jesse Foundation, The.
Crum, Shutta. Spitting Image. 2003. 224p. (J). tchr. ed. 15.00 (*0-618-23477-2*, Clarion Bks.) Houghton Mifflin Co. Trade & Reference Div.
Dadey, Debbie. Whistler's Stump. 2002. 111p. (J). 14.95 (*1-58234-789-1*, Bloomsbury Children) Bloomsbury Publishing.
Hart, Alison. Danger at the Wild West Show. 2003. (History Mysteries Ser.: Vol. 19). (Illus.). 163p. (J). 10.95 (*1-58485-718-8*); pap. 6.95 (*1-58485-717-X*) Pleasant Co. Pubns. (American Girl).
Havill, Juanita. Kentucky Troll. 1993. (Illus.). (J). (ps-3). 13.00 o.p. (*0-688-10457-6*); lib. bdg. 12.93 o.p. (*0-688-10458-4*) HarperCollins Children's Bk. Group.
—Kentucky Troll. (Illus.). 2001. (J). E-Book (*1-59019-498-5*); 1993. E-Book (*1-59019-499-3*) ipicturebooks, LLC.
Henson, Heather. Making the Run. 2002. 240p. (J). (gr. k-4). lib. bdg. 15.89 (*0-06-029797-2*); (gr. 10 up). 15.95 (*0-06-029796-4*) HarperCollins Children's Bk. Group. (HarperTempest).
Johnson, Annie F. Two Little Knights of Kentucky: The Little Colonel's Neighbors. 2004. (Little Colonel Ser.). (Illus.). 192p. (J). (gr. 4-7). reprint ed. pap. 9.95 (*1-55709-316-4*) Applewood Bks.
Johnston, Annie F. The Little Colonel. 2004. (Little Colonel Ser.). (Illus.). 192p. (J). (gr. 4-7). reprint ed. pap. 9.95 (*1-55709-315-6*) Applewood Bks.
—The Little Colonel. 1974. (Illus.). (J). 145p. (gr. 5-9). 8.95 o.p. (*0-88289-050-6*); 168p. (gr. 4-7). pap. 16.95 (*1-56554-542-7*) Pelican Publishing Co., Inc.
Johnston, Annie Fellows. The Little Colonel. l.t. ed. 57p. pap. 12.11 (*0-7583-3696-9*); 74p. pap. 14.37 (*0-7583-3697-7*); 102p. pap. 16.74 (*0-7583-3698-5*); 130p. pap. 19.03 (*0-7583-3699-3*); 166p. pap. 21.96 (*0-7583-3700-0*); 205p. pap. 25.05 (*0-7583-3701-9*); 252p. pap. 28.85 (*0-7583-3702-7*); 292p. pap. 32.09 (*0-7583-3703-5*); 57p. lib. bdg. 18.11 (*0-7583-3688-8*); 74p. lib. bdg. 20.37 (*0-7583-3689-6*); 102p. lib. bdg. 24.45 (*0-7583-3690-X*); 130p. lib. bdg. 27.94 (*0-7583-3691-8*); 166p. lib. bdg. 30.52 (*0-7583-3692-6*); 205p. lib. bdg. 33.22 (*0-7583-3693-4*); 252p. lib. bdg. 36.55 (*0-7583-3694-2*); 292p. lib. bdg. 39.40 (*0-7583-3695-0*) Huge Print Pr.
—Two Little Knights of Kentucky: Who Were the "Little Colonel's" Neighbours. 1999. (Cosy Corner Ser.). (Illus.). 196p. (J). (gr. 4-7). pap. 16.95 (*1-56554-624-5*) Pelican Publishing Co., Inc.
Luttrell, Wanda. Home on Stoney Creek. 208p. (gr. 4-7). (Sarah's Journey Ser.: Vol. 1). (J). pap. 6.99 (*0-7814-0901-2*); 1995. (YA). 12.99 (*0-7814-0234-4*) Cook Communications Ministries.
—Reunion in Kentucky. (Illus.). 208p. (J). (Sarah's Journey Ser.: Vol. 3). (gr. 4-7). pap. 6.99 (*0-7814-0907-1*); 1995. 12.99 (*0-7814-0236-0*) Cook Communications Ministries.
Lyon, George Ella. Borrowed Children. 1990. 176p. (YA). mass mkt. 3.99 o.p. (*0-553-28380-4*) Bantam Bks.
—Borrowed Children. 1988. 160p. (J). (gr. 5-7). 15.95 o.p. (*0-531-05751-8*); mass mkt. 16.99 o.p. (*0-531-08351-9*) Scholastic, Inc. (Orchard Bks.).
Pryor, Bonnie. Joseph: 1861 - A Rumble of War. 2000. (Illus.). (J). 10.55 (*0-606-17975-5*) Turtleback Bks.
—Joseph: 1861 - a Rumble of War. 1999. (American Adventures Ser.). (Illus.). 176p. (J). (gr. 3-7). 14.95 (*0-688-15671-1*) HarperCollins Children's Bk. Group.
—Joseph: 1861—A Rumble of War. 2000. (American Adventures Ser.). (Illus.). 176p. (J). (gr. 3-7). pap. 4.50 (*0-380-73103-7*, Harper Trophy) HarperCollins Children's Bk. Group.
Rinaldi, Ann. Numbering All the Bones. 2002. (Illus.). 176p. (J). (gr. 5-9). 15.99 (*0-7868-0533-1*, Jump at the Sun) Hyperion Bks. for Children.
Shore, June L. Summer Storm. 1977. (J). (gr. 7 up). 4.95 o.p. (*0-687-40609-9*) Abingdon Pr.
Snelling, Lauraine. Kentucky Dreamer. 1992. (Golden Filly Ser.: No. 4). 176p. (Orig.). (J). (gr. 4-7). pap. 5.99 (*1-55661-234-6*) Bethany Hse. Pubs.
Stiles, Martha Bennett. Kate of Still Waters. 1990. 240p. (J). (gr. 3-7). lib. bdg. 14.95 o.p. (*0-02-788395-7*, Simon & Schuster Children's Publishing) Simon & Schuster Children's Publishing.
Strigenz, Geri K. Year of the Sevens. 1992. (History's Children Ser.). (Illus.). 48p. (J). (gr. 4-5). pap. o.p. (*0-8114-6430-X*) Raintree Pubs.
Strigenz, Geri K., illus. Year of the Sevens. 1992. (History's Children Ser.). 48p. (J). (gr. 4-5). lib. bdg. 21.36 o.p. (*0-8114-3505-9*) Raintree Pubs.
Stuart, Jesse H. Hie to the Hunters. 5th ed. 1988. 270p. (YA). (gr. 8 up). reprint ed. 20.00 o.p. (*0-945084-06-4*); pap. 10.00 o.s.i (*0-945084-07-2*) Stuart, Jesse Foundation, The.
—Hie to the Hunters. Herndon, Jerry A., ed. 6th ed. 1996. (Illus.). 272p. (YA). reprint ed. 22.00 (*0-945084-58-7*); (gr. 9-12). pap. 12.00 (*0-945084-59-5*) Stuart, Jesse Foundation, The.
—A Penny's Worth of Character. Herndon, Jerry A. et al, eds. 3rd ed. 1993. (Jesse Stuart Foundation Juvenile Ser.). (Illus.). 62p. (J). (gr. 3-6). reprint ed. pap. 4.00 (*0-945084-32-3*) Stuart, Jesse Foundation, The.
—Plowshare in Heaven. Herndon, Jerry A. et al, eds. 2nd ed. 1991. (Illus.). 268p. (YA). (gr. 7 up). reprint ed. 22.00 (*0-945084-21-8*) Stuart, Jesse Foundation, The.
—Red Mule. 2nd ed. 1993. (Jesse Stuart Foundation Juvenile Ser.). (Illus.). 96p. (J). (gr. 3-6). reprint ed. pap. text 6.00 (*0-945084-33-1*) Stuart, Jesse Foundation, The.
—Red Mule. Herndon, Jerry A., ed. 2nd ed. 1993. (Jesse Stuart Foundation Juvenile Ser.). (Illus.). 96p. (J). (gr. 3-6). reprint ed. 12.00 (*0-945084-34-X*) Stuart, Jesse Foundation, The.
White, Ruth. Tadpole, RS. 2003. 208p. (J). 16.00 (*0-374-31002-5*, Farrar, Straus & Giroux (BYR)) Farrar, Straus & Giroux.
—Tadpole. l.t. ed. 2003. 201p. (J). 24.95 (*0-7862-5813-6*) Thorndike Pr.
Wood, James P. Kentucky Time. 1977. 144p. (J). 6.95 o.s.i (*0-201-09344-8*, 9344) Addison-Wesley Longman, Inc.
Woodson, Jacqueline. Lena. 1999. 128p. (YA). (gr. 5-9). 15.95 o.s.i (*0-385-32308-5*, Dell Books for Young Readers) Random Hse. Children's Bks.

KENYA—FICTION

Andersen, Laurie H. Ndito Runs, ERS. 1996. (Illus.). 32p. (J). (ps-2). 15.95 o.s.i (*0-8050-3265-7*, Holt, Henry & Co. Bks. For Young Readers) Holt, Henry & Co.
Arensen, Shel. The Carjackers. 2003. (Rugendo Rhino Ser.). 128p. (J). pap. 5.99 (*0-8254-2042-3*) Kregel Pubns.
—The Hidden Treasure of Lamu. 2000. 120p. (gr. 4-7). pap. 9.95 o.p. (*0-595-15843-9*) iUniverse, Inc.
—Poachers Beware! 2003. (Rugendo Rhino Ser.). 112p. (J). pap. 5.99 (*0-8254-2039-3*) Kregel Pubns.
—The Poison Arrow Tree. 2003. (Rugendo Rhino Ser.). (Illus.). 128p. (J). pap. 5.99 (*0-8254-2041-5*) Kregel Pubns.
—The Secret Oath. 2003. (Rugendo Rhino Ser.). 128p. (J). pap. 5.99 (*0-8254-2040-7*) Kregel Pubns.
—The Test of the Tribal Challenge. 2000. 132p. (gr. 4-7). pap. 9.95 o.p. (*0-595-15779-3*) iUniverse, Inc.
Arensen, Sheldon. Kenyan Chronicles Bk. 1: The Secret Oath. 2000. 108p. (gr. 4-7). pap. 9.95 o.p. (*0-595-15844-7*) iUniverse, Inc.
Austin, Judith M. Rescue in Kenya. 1997. (Global-Friends Adventures Ser.). (Illus.). 64p. (J). (gr. 2-6). pap. 5.95 (*1-58056-006-7*, GlobalFriends Pr.) GlobalFriends Collection, Inc.
Brady, Jennifer. Jambi & the Lions. Thatch, Nancy R., ed. 1992. (Books for Students by Students). (Illus.). 26p. (J). (gr. 4-7). lib. bdg. 15.95 (*0-933849-41-9*) Landmark Editions, Inc.
Carr, Josephine. No Regrets. 1982. 192p. (J). (gr. 7 up). 10.95 o.p. (*0-8037-6721-8*, Dial Bks. for Young Readers) Penguin Putnam Bks. for Young Readers.
Chaikin, Linda L. Endangered. 1997. (Portraits Ser.). 256p. pap. 8.99 o.p. (*1-55661-977-4*) Bethany Hse. Pubs.
Crippen, David. Two Sides of the River. 1976. (J). (gr. 1-4). 4.25 o.p. (*0-687-42783-5*) Abingdon Pr.
Dinneen, Betty. A Tale of Three Leopards. 1980. (Illus.). 7.95 o.p. (*0-385-14848-8*); lib. bdg. o.p. (*0-385-14849-6*) Doubleday Publishing.
Dobkins, Lucy M. Daddy, There's a Hippo in the Grapes. 1992. (Illus.). 88p. (J). (gr. 5-7). 13.95 (*0-88289-889-2*) Pelican Publishing Co., Inc.
James, Ellen Foley. Little Bull: Growing up in Africa's Elephant Kingdom. 1998. (Discovery Kids Ser.). (Illus.). 48p. (J). (gr. 4-7). 13.95 (*0-8069-2098-X*) Sterling Publishing Co., Inc.
Johnston, Tony. A Kenya Christmas. 2003. (Illus.). (J). (gr. k-3). tchr. ed. 16.95 (*0-8234-1623-2*) Holiday Hse., Inc.
Matthews, Ron. Nandi's Magic Garden. 1997. (Illus.). (YA). (gr. 3-7). 16.95 (*1-881316-21-1*); pap. 7.95 (*1-881316-34-3*) A & B Distributors & Pubs. Group.
Mbuthia, Waithira. My Sister's Wedding: A Story of Kenya. 2002. (Make Friends Around the World Ser.). (Illus.). 32p. (J). (gr. k-3). 15.95 (*1-56899-896-1*, B8006); 19.95 incl. audio (*1-56899-898-8*, BC8006); pap. 5.95 (*1-56899-897-X*, S8006) Soundprints.
McDaniel, Lurlene. Angel of Mercy. 1999. (Mercy Trilogy Ser.). 224p. (YA). (gr. 7-12). 8.95 (*0-553-57145-1*, Dell Books for Young Readers) Random Hse. Children's Bks.
—Angel of Mercy. 1999. (Illus.). (J). 14.30 o.p. (*0-606-17992-5*) Turtleback Bks.
Ngumy, James. The Boy Who Rode a Lion. 1992. (Junior African Writers Ser.). (Illus.). 30p. (J). (gr. 4-8). pap. text 2.50 o.p. (*0-435-89168-5*) Heinemann.
Rispin, Karen. Ambush at Amboseli. 1994. (Anika Scott Ser.: Vol. 4). 136p. (J). (gr. 5-7). 4.99 o.p. (*0-8423-1295-1*) Tyndale Hse. Pubs.
—Sabrina the Schemer. 1994. (Anika Scott Ser.: Vol. 5). 130p. (J). (gr. 3-7). pap. 4.99 o.p. (*0-8423-1296-X*) Tyndale Hse. Pubs.
—Tianna, the Terrible. 1992. (Anika Scott Ser.: No. 2). (J). (gr. 3-7). 4.99 o.p. (*0-8423-2031-8*) Tyndale Hse. Pubs.
Smith, Laura L. Sophisticated Josephine: The East African Bush Elephant. 1993. (Illus.). 24p. (J). (gr. 3-5). pap. 6.95 o.p. (*0-8059-3311-5*) Dorrance Publishing Co., Inc.
Smith, Roland. Thunder Cave. 1997. 256p. (J). (gr. 5-9). pap. 5.95 (*0-7868-1159-5*) Disney Pr.
—Thunder Cave. (YA). (gr. 5 up). 1997. (Illus.). 272p. lib. bdg. 17.49 (*0-7868-2055-1*); 1995. 277p. 16.95 o.s.i (*0-7868-0068-2*) Hyperion Bks. for Children.
—Thunder Cave. 1997. (J). 12.00 (*0-606-11987-6*) Turtleback Bks.
Talbott, Hudson. Safari Journal. 2003. (Illus.). 64p. (J). 18.00 (*0-15-216393-X*) Harcourt Children's Bks.
Travers, Bill. The Elephant Truck. 1998. (Born Free Wildlife Ser.). (Illus.). 40p. (gr. 2-6). 22.90 o.p. (*0-7613-0408-8*) Millbrook Pr., Inc.

KLONDIKE GOLD FIELDS—FICTION

Czuchna-Curl, Ardyce. Days of Gold. 2002. (Illus.). 128p. (J). pap. text 12.95 (*0-88196-012-8*) Oak Woods Media.
Dell, Pamela. Half-Breed: The Story of Two Boys During the Klondike Gold Rush. 2003. (J). (*1-59187-044-5*) Tradition Publishing Co.
Greenwood, Barbara. Gold Rush Fever: A Story of the Klondike, 1898. 2001. (Illus.). 160p. (J). (gr. 3-7). 18.95 (*1-55074-852-1*); pap. 12.95 (*1-55074-850-5*) Kids Can Pr., Ltd.
Hobbs, William. Jason's Gold. 240p. (J). 2000. (gr. 6 up). pap. 5.99 (*0-380-72914-8*); 1999. (Illus.). (gr. 5-9). 16.99 (*0-688-15093-4*, Morrow, William & Co.) Morrow/Avon.
—Jason's Gold. unabr. ed. 2000. (YA). (gr. 5-7). audio 32.00 (*0-8072-8228-6*, LL0168, Listening Library) Random Hse. Audio Publishing Group.

KOREA—FICTION

Adams, Edward B. Herdboy & Weaver. 1981. (Korean Folk Story for Children Ser.). (Illus.). 32p. (J). (gr. 3). 10.95 (*0-8048-1470-8*) Seoul International Tourist Publishing Co. KOR. *Dist:* Tuttle Publishing.
—Woodcutter & Nymph. 1982. (Korean Folk Story for Children Ser.). (Illus.). 32p. (J). (gr. 3). 10.95 (*0-8048-1471-6*) Seoul International Tourist Publishing Co. KOR. *Dist:* Tuttle Publishing.
Brightfield, Richard. Master of Tae Kwon Do. l.t. ed. 1995. (Choose Your Own Adventure Ser.: No. 102). (Illus.). 128p. (J). (gr. 4-8). lib. bdg. 24.27 o.p. (*0-8368-1404-5*) Stevens, Gareth Inc.
Burkholder, Ruth C. Mi Jun's Difficult Decision. 1984. (Illus.). 14p. (Orig.). (J). (gr. 4-6). pap. 4.95 o.p. (*0-377-00139-2*) Friendship Pr.
Choi, Sook-Nyul. Echoes of the White Giraffe. 1995. 144p. (J). (gr. 4-7). pap. text 4.50 o.s.i (*0-440-40970-5*) Dell Publishing.
—Echoes of the White Giraffe. 1993. 144p. (YA). (gr. 7 up). tchr. ed. 16.00 (*0-395-64721-5*) Houghton Mifflin Co.
—Echoes of the White Giraffe. 1995. 10.55 (*0-606-07464-3*) Turtleback Bks.
—Yunmi & Halmoni's Trip. 1997. (Illus.). 32p. (J). (ps-3). tchr. ed. 15.00 o.s.i (*0-395-81180-5*) Houghton Mifflin Co.

Choi, Yangsook. Peach Heaven. 2005. (J). *(0-374-35761-7*, Farrar, Straus & Giroux (BYR)) Farrar, Straus & Giroux.

Farley, Carol. The King's Secret. 2001. (Illus.). 32p. (J). (gr. 1 up). 15.95 *(0-688-12776-2)*; lib. bdg. 15.89 *(0-688-12777-0)* HarperCollins Children's Bk. Group.

—Ms Isabelle Cornell, Herself. 1980. (J). (gr. 5-7). 7.95 o.p. *(0-689-30740-3*, Atheneum) Simon & Schuster Children's Publishing.

Gukova, Julia, illus. The Mole's Daughter: An Adaptation of a Korean Folktale. 1998. 24p. (J). (ps-3). 15.95 *(1-55037-525-3)*; pap. 6.95 *(1-55037-524-5)* Annick Pr., Ltd. CAN. *Dist:* Firefly Bks., Ltd.

Hyun, Peter, ed. Korean Children's Favorite Folk Tales. 1996. (Illus.). 70p. (J). (gr. 1-7). 16.95 *(1-56591-064-8)* Hollym International Corp.

—Korean Children's Stories & Songs. 1996. (Illus.). 62p. (J). (gr. 1-7). 16.95 *(1-56591-065-6)* Hollym International Corp.

Ilyon. The Birth of Tangun: The Legend of Korea's First King. Adams, Edward B., tr. from KOR. 1986. (Children's Stories from Korean History Ser.: Vol. 1). (Illus.). (J). (gr. 5). pap. *(0-00-000006-X)* HarperCollins Pubs.

—The Death of Echadon: How Buddhism Came to Silla. Adams, Edward B., tr. 1986. (Children's Stories from Korean History Ser.: Vol. 3). (Illus.). 28p. (J). (gr. 5). pap. *(0-00-000004-3)* HarperCollins Pubs.

—The Three Good Events. Adams, Edward B., tr. from KOR. 1986. (Children's Stories from Korean History Ser.: Vol. 4). (Illus.). 30p. (J). (gr. 5). 8.95 o.p. *(0-00-000009-4)* Seoul International Tourist Publishing Co. KOR. *Dist:* Tuttle Publishing.

Kim, Helen S. The Long Season of Rain. 1997. 256p. (gr. 7-12). mass mkt. 6.50 o.s.i *(0-449-70462-9*, Fawcett) Ballantine Bks.

—The Long Season of Rain, ERS. 1996. 288p. (YA). (gr. 7 up). 15.95 o.s.i *(0-8050-4758-1*, Holt, Henry & Co. Bks. For Young Readers) Holt, Henry & Co.

—The Long Season of Rain. 1997. 10.55 *(0-606-14258-4)* Turtleback Bks.

Lee, Gus. Tiger's Tail. 1997. (Illus.). 370p. mass mkt. 6.99 *(0-8041-1326-2*, Ivy Bks.) Ballantine Bks.

—Tiger's Tail. 1996. 288p. 24.00 o.s.i *(0-679-43855-6)* Knopf, Alfred A. Inc.

Lee, Uk-Bae. Sori's Harvest Moon Day: A Story of Korea. 1999. Orig. Title: Sori's Chu-Suk. (Illus.). 32p. (J). (ps-3). 15.95 *(1-56899-687-X)*; pap. 5.95 *(1-56899-688-8)* Soundprints.

Neilan, Eujin Kim, illus. The Rabbit & the Dragon King: Based on a Korean Folk Tale. 2003. 32p. (J). (gr. 1-4). 15.95 *(1-56397-880-6)* Boyds Mills Pr.

Neuberger, Anne E. The Girl-Son. 1994. (Adventures in Time Ser.). 132p. (J). (gr. 4-7). lib. bdg. 15.95 *(0-87614-846-1*, Carolrhoda Bks.) Lerner Publishing Group.

Paek, Min. Aekyung's Dream. 1992. (J). mass mkt. 18.60 o.p. *(0-516-80042-6*, Children's Pr.) Scholastic Library Publishing.

Park, Frances & Park, Ginger. Where on Earth Is My Bagel? 2001. (Illus.). 32p. (J). (ps-4). 16.00 *(1-58430-033-7)* Lee & Low Bks., Inc.

Park, Linda Sue. The Firekeeper's Son. 2004. (Illus.). 40p. (J). (ps-3). 16.00 *(0-618-13337-2*, Clarion Bks.) Houghton Mifflin Co. Trade & Reference Div.

—The Kite Fighters. 2000. (Illus.). 144p. (J). (gr. 5-9). tchr. ed. 15.00 *(0-395-94041-9*, Clarion Bks.) Houghton Mifflin Co. Trade & Reference Div.

—Seesaw Girl. 1999. (Illus.). 96p. (J). (gr. 4-6). tchr. ed. 14.00 *(0-395-91514-7*, Clarion Bks.) Houghton Mifflin Co. Trade & Reference Div.

—Seesaw Girl. 2001. (Illus.). 112p. (gr. 4-7). pap. text 4.50 *(0-440-41672-8*, Dell Books for Young Readers) Random Hse. Children's Bks.

—Seesaw Girl. 1999. (Illus.). (J). 10.55 *(0-606-20902-6)* Turtleback Bks.

—A Single Shard. braille ed. 2001. (YA). (gr. 2). spiral bd. *(0-616-08848-5)* Canadian National Institute for the Blind/Institut National Canadien pour les Aveugles.

—A Single Shard. 2001. (Illus.). 160p. (J). (gr. 5-9). tchr. ed. 15.00 *(0-395-97827-0*, Clarion Bks.) Houghton Mifflin Co. Trade & Reference Div.

—A Single Shard. 2002. (J). (gr. 5-6). stu. ed. *(1-58130-771-3)* Novel Units, Inc.

—A Single Shard. unabr. ed. 2002. (J). (gr. 5 up). audio 25.00 *(0-8072-0701-2*, Listening Library) Random Hse. Audio Publishing Group.

—A Single Shard. 2003. 192p. (gr. 5 up). pap. 5.99 *(0-440-41851-8*, Yearling) Random Hse. Children's Bks.

—A Single Shard. l.t. ed. 2002. (Young Adult Ser.). 175p. (YA). 24.95 *(0-7862-4305-8)* Thorndike Pr.

—When My Name Was Keoko. 2002. 208p. (YA). (gr. 5-9). 16.00 *(0-618-13335-6*, Clarion Bks.) Houghton Mifflin Co. Trade & Reference Div.

—When My Name Was Keoko. 2004. (Illus.). 208p. (gr. 5). pap. 5.50 *(0-440-41944-1*, Yearling) Random Hse. Children's Bks.

Wong, Janet S. The Trip Back Home. 2000. (Illus.). 32p. (J). (ps-2). 16.00 *(0-15-200784-9)* Harcourt Children's Bks.

KOREA, REPUBLIC OF—FICTION

Watkins, Yoko Kawashima. So Far from the Bamboo Grove. 1994. (Illus.). 192p. (J). (gr. 3-6). reprint ed. pap. 5.99 *(0-688-13115-8*, HarperTempest) HarperCollins Children's Bk. Group.

L

LANCASTER COUNTY (PA.)—FICTION

De Angeli, Marguerite. Henner's Lydia. 1936. (Illus.). 76p. (gr. 2-5). 9.95 o.p. *(0-385-07318-6)* Doubleday Publishing.

—Henner's Lydia. 1998. (Illus.). 74p. (J). (ps-3). pap. 15.99 *(0-8361-9093-9)* Herald Pr.

LAPLAND—FICTION

D'Aulaire, Ingri & D'Aulaire, Edgar P. Children of the Northlights. 1935. (Illus.). (J). (gr. k-4). 8.95 o.p. *(0-670-21741-7)* Viking Penguin.

Hallard, Peter. Puppy Lost in Lapland. 1971. (Illus.). (gr. 3-7). 5.90 o.p. *(0-531-01998-5*, Watts, Franklin) Scholastic Library Publishing.

Lindman, Maj. Snipp, Snapp, Snurr & the Reindeer. 1995. (Illus.). (J). (ps-3). pap. 6.95 *(0-8075-7497-X)* Whitman, Albert & Co.

LATIN AMERICA—FICTION

Ada, Alma Flor. Barquitos de Papel. 1993. (Cuentos con Alma Ser.). (SPA., Illus.). 24p. (J). (gr. 3-9). 16.95 *(1-56492-118-2)* Laredo Publishing Co., Inc.

—Barriletes. 1993. (Cuentos con Alma Ser.). (SPA., Illus.). 24p. (J). (gr. 3-9). 16.95 *(1-56492-126-3)* Laredo Publishing Co., Inc.

—Dias de Circo. 1993. (Cuentos con Alma Ser.). (SPA., Illus.). 24p. (J). (gr. 3-9). 16.95 *(1-56492-127-1)* Laredo Publishing Co., Inc.

—The Gold Coin. Randall, Bernice, tr. from SPA. (Illus.). 32p. (J). (gr. k-3). 1994. pap. 6.99 *(0-689-71793-8*, Aladdin); 1991. lib. bdg. 16.00 *(0-689-31633-X*, Atheneum) Simon & Schuster Children's Publishing.

—The Gold Coin. Randall, Bernice, tr. 1994. (J). 12.14 *(0-606-05846-X)* Turtleback Bks.

—Pin, Pin, Sarabin. 1993. (Cuentos con Alma Ser.). (SPA., Illus.). 24p. (J). (gr. 3-9). 16.95 *(1-56492-130-1)* Laredo Publishing Co., Inc.

—Pregones. 1993. (Cuentos con Alma Ser.).Tr. of Merchants. (SPA., Illus.). 24p. (J). (gr. 3-4). 16.95 *(1-56492-110-7)* Laredo Publishing Co., Inc.

Asturias, Miguel Ángel. El Senor Presidente. 1998. (Leer en Espanol Ser.: Level 6). (SPA., Illus.). 142p. (YA). (gr. 9-12). 12.48 *(84-294-3590-5*, EM341) Santillana USA Publishing Co., Inc.

Baez, Josefina. Por Que Mi Nombre es Marisol? Un Cuento de la Republica Dominicana. 1993. (Marisol Ser.: Vol. 1). (SPA., Illus.). 24p. (Orig.). (J). (gr. k-3). pap. 12.95 *(1-882161-01-7)* Latinarte.

—Why Is My Name Marisol? A Dominican Children's Story. 1993. (Marisol Ser.: Vol. 1). (Illus.). 24p. (Orig.). (J). (gr. k-3). pap. 12.95 *(1-882161-02-5)* Latinarte.

Carle, Eric. What's for Lunch? 1982. 10p. (J). (ps-1). 4.95 o.p. *(0-399-20897-6*, Philomel) Penguin Putnam Bks. for Young Readers.

Carlson, Lori M. Where Angels Glide at Dawn: New Stories from Latin America. 1993. 9.05 o.p. *(0-606-02982-6)* Turtleback Bks.

Carlson, Lori M. & Ventura, Cynthia L. Where Angels Glide at Dawn: New Stories from Latin America. 1993. (Trophy Bk.). 128p. (J). (gr. 5 up). pap. 4.50 o.p. *(0-06-440464-1*, Harper Trophy) HarperCollins Children's Bk. Group.

Carlson, Lori M. & Ventura, Cynthia L., eds. Where Angels Glide at Dawn: New Stories from Latin America. 1990. (Illus.). 128p. (YA). (gr. 5 up). 14.00 *(0-397-32424-3)* HarperCollins Children's Bk. Group.

De Jenkins, Lyll. So Loud a Silence. 1996. 160p. (YA). (gr. 7 up). 16.99 o.s.i *(0-525-67538-8)* NAL.

De Jenkins, Lyll B. The Honorable Prison. (YA). (gr. 7 up). 1989. 208p. pap. 4.99 o.s.i *(0-14-032952-8*, Puffin Bks.); 1988. 192p. 14.95 o.p. *(0-525-67238-9*, Dutton Children's Bks.) Penguin Putnam Bks. for Young Readers.

Delacre, Lulu, contrib. by. Salsa Stories. 2000. (SPA., Illus.). 105p. (J). (gr. 2-6). pap. 15.95 *(0-590-63118-7*, Scholastic Reference) Scholastic, Inc.

Diaz, Gloria Cecilia. El Sol de los Venados. 1996. (SPA.). 128p. (J). (gr. 5-8). 6.95 net. *(84-348-3976-8)* Lectorum Pubns., Inc.

Gauthier, Gilles & Derome, Pierre-Andre. Babucha Esta Celosa. 1994. (Primeros Lectores Ser.). (SPA., Illus.). 60p. (J). (gr. 5 up). pap. 5.95 *(958-07-0075-3)* Firefly Bks., Ltd.

Highwater, Jamake. Journey to the Sky: A Novel about the True Adventures of Two Men in Search of the Lost Maya Kingdom. 258p. 2000. pap. 16.95 *(0-7351-0506-5)*; 1999. reprint ed. lib. bdg. 33.95 *(0-7351-0131-0)* Replica Bks.

Higuero, Cristina M. Los Payasos y Otros Cuentos. 1993. (SPA., Illus.). 21p. (Orig.). (J). (gr. 1-3). pap. 10.00 *(0-9605082-4-4)* Allied Enterprises.

Hurwitz, Johanna. New Shoes for Silvia. 1993. (Illus.). 32p. (J). (ps-3). 16.99 *(0-688-05286-X)*; 16.89 *(0-688-05287-8)* HarperCollins Children's Bk. Group.

Joseph, Lynn. The Color of My Words. 144p. (J). 2002. (gr. 5 up). pap. 5.99 *(0-06-447204-3*, Harper Trophy); 2000. (Illus.). (gr. 3-7). lib. bdg. 15.89 *(0-06-028233-9*, Cotler, Joanna Bks.) HarperCollins Children's Bk. Group.

Reiser, Lynn W. Tortillas & Lullabies, Tortillas y Cancioncitas. 1998. (ENG & SPA., Illus.). 48p. (J). (ps-3). lib. bdg. 17.89 *(0-688-14629-5)* HarperCollins Children's Bk. Group.

—Tortillas & Lullabies, Tortillas y Cancioncitas. 1998. (ENG & SPA., Illus.). 48p. (J). (ps-3). 16.99 *(0-688-14628-7*, Rayo) HarperTrade.

Skármeta, Antonio. The Composition. 2003. (Illus.). 32p. (J). (gr. 3 up). 5.95 *(0-88899-550-4)* Groundwood Bks. CAN. *Dist:* Publishers Group West.

—The Composition. Amado, Elisa, tr. from SPA. 2003. (Illus.). 32p. (J). (gr. 2-6). 16.95 *(0-88899-390-0*, Libros Tigrillo) Groundwood Bks. CAN. *Dist:* Publishers Group West.

Torres, Leyla. Liliana's Grandmothers, RS. 1998. (Illus.). 32p. (J). (ps-5). 16.00 *(0-374-35105-8*, Farrar, Straus & Giroux (BYR)) Farrar, Straus & Giroux.

LEBANON—FICTION

Heide, Florence Parry & Gilliland, Judith Heide. Sami & the Time of the Troubles. 1995. (Illus.). 40p. (J). (ps-3). pap. 6.95 *(0-395-72085-0)* Houghton Mifflin Co.

Heide, Florence Parry & Gilliland, Judith Heide. Sami & the Time of the Troubles. (Illus.). (J). (ps-3). 2002. pap. 9.95 incl. audio *(0-618-22998-1)*; 1992. 40p. lib. bdg., tchr. ed. 16.00 *(0-395-55964-2)* Houghton Mifflin Co. Trade & Reference Div. (Clarion Bks.).

Rugh, Belle D. Lost Waters. 1967. (J). (gr. 5-6). 3.50 o.p. *(0-395-07084-8)* Houghton Mifflin Co.

LIBERIA—FICTION

Allen, C. William. The African Interior Mission. 2001. (J). pap. *(0-9653308-5-0)* Africana Homestead Legacy Pubs.

Chandler, Edna W. Five Cent, Five Cent (Liberia) 1967. (Illus.). (J). (gr. 1-3). lib. bdg. 9.50 o.p. *(0-8075-2463-8)* Whitman, Albert & Co.

McCully, Emily Arnold. Starring Mirette & Bellini. 1997. (Illus.). 32p. (J). (ps-3). 15.99 *(0-399-22636-2*, G. P. Putnam's Sons) Penguin Group (USA) Inc.

Zemser, Amy Bronwen. Beyond the Mango Tree. (Illus.). (gr. 5 up). 2000. 176p. (J). pap. 5.99 *(0-06-440786-1*, Harper Trophy); 1998. 156p. (YA). 14.95 *(0-688-16005-0*, Greenwillow Bks.) HarperCollins Children's Bk. Group.

—Beyond the Mango Tree. 2000. 11.00 *(0-606-17879-1)* Turtleback Bks.

LIVERPOOL (ENGLAND)—FICTION

Heneghan, James. The Grave. 2000. (Illus.). 236p. (J). (gr. 7-10). pap. 7.95 *(0-88899-414-1)* Groundwood Bks. CAN. *Dist:* Publishers Group West.

LONDON (ENGLAND)—FICTION

Adone, Claudio. My Grandfather Jack the Ripper. 2000. Tr. of Mio Nonno Jack Lo Squartatore. (Illus.). 304p. (J). (gr. 7-10). 19.00 *(1-928746-16-0)* Herodias.

Alcock, Vivien. The Cuckoo Sister. l.t. ed. 1987. 256p. (J). (gr. 3-7). 16.95 o.p. *(0-7451-0586-6*, Galaxy Children's Large Print) BBC Audiobooks America.

—The Cuckoo Sister. 1986. 158p. (J). (gr. 4-6). 14.95 o.s.i *(0-385-29467-0*, Delacorte Pr.) Dell Publishing.

—The Cuckoo Sister. 1997. 240p. (YA). (gr. 7-7). pap. 4.95 *(0-395-81651-3)* Houghton Mifflin Co.

—The Stranger at the Window. 1998. 208p. (YA). (gr. 7-9). 16.00 *(0-395-81661-0)* Houghton Mifflin Co.

—The Stranger at the Window. 1999. 208p. (J). (gr. 5-9). pap. 4.95 *(0-395-94329-9)* Houghton Mifflin Co. Trade & Reference Div.

Andrew, Ian, illus. Oliver Twist. abr. ed. 1999. (Eyewitness Classics Ser.). 64p. (J). (gr. 3-9). pap. 14.95 o.p. *(0-7894-3959-X)* Dorling Kindersley Publishing, Inc.

Arnaud, Rayne. Getaway. (J). E-Book *(1-84045-034-7)* Online Originals.

—Jamaica Street. (YA). E-Book *(1-84045-003-7)* Online Originals.

Ashley, Bernard. Little Soldier: A Novel. 240p. (J). 2003. mass mkt. 5.99 *(0-439-28502-X)*; 2002. (Illus.). (gr. 9 up). pap. 16.95 *(0-439-22424-1*, Scholastic Pr.) Scholastic, Inc.

—Terry on the Fence. 1977. (Illus.). (J). (gr. 5-9). 26.95 *(0-87599-222-6)* Phillips, S.G. Inc.

—Your Guess Is As Good As Mine. 1984. (Redwing Bks.). (Illus.). 48p. (gr. 7-11). 6.95 o.p. *(0-531-03765-7*, Watts, Franklin) Scholastic Library Publishing.

Bawden, Nina. The Robbers. 1979. (Illus.). 160p. (J). (gr. 4-7). reprint ed. 12.95 o.p. *(0-688-41902-X)*; lib. bdg. 12.88 o.p. *(0-688-51902-4)* HarperCollins Children's Bk. Group.

Bemelmans, Ludwig. Madeline in London. 2002. (Madeline Ser.). (Illus.). (J). 14.04 *(0-7587-5002-1)* Book Wholesalers, Inc.

—Madeline in London. ed. 1998. (J). (gr. 2). spiral bd. *(0-616-01545-3)* Canadian National Institute for the Blind/Institut National Canadien pour les Aveugles.

—Madeline in London. unabr. ed. 1995. (Madeline Ser.). (Illus.). (J). (ps-3). pap. 15.95 incl. audio *(0-670-44655-6)* Live Oak Media.

—Madeline in London. (Madeline Ser.). (Illus.). 64p. (J). (ps-3). 2000. pap. 6.99 *(0-14-056649-X*, Puffin Bks.); 1977. pap. 5.99 o.s.i *(0-14-050199-1*, Puffin Bks.); 1961. 16.99 *(0-670-44648-3*, Viking Children's Bks.) Penguin Putnam Bks. for Young Readers.

—Madeline in London. (Madeline Ser.). (J). (ps-3). 2000. (Illus.). 13.14 *(0-606-18429-5)*; 1978. 10.19 o.p. *(0-606-03875-2)* Turtleback Bks.

Birmingham, Christian, illus. Oliver Twist. 1996. 144p. (J). (gr. 4-7). 19.99 o.s.i *(0-8037-1995-7*, Dial Bks. for Young Readers) Penguin Putnam Bks. for Young Readers.

Blacker, Terence. The Angel Factory. (Illus.). 224p. (J). 2004. pap. 4.99 *(0-689-86413-2*, Aladdin); 2002. (gr. 6-9). 16.95 *(0-689-85171-5*, Simon & Schuster Children's Publishing) Simon & Schuster Children's Publishing.

—Homebird. 1993. 144p. (J). (gr. 7 up). text 13.95 o.s.i *(0-02-710685-3*, Simon & Schuster Children's Publishing) Simon & Schuster Children's Publishing.

Bond, Michael. Paddington Meets the Queen. 1993. (Paddington Ser.). (Illus.). 32p. (J). (ps-3). 3.95 *(0-694-00460-X*, Harper Festival) HarperCollins Children's Bk. Group.

Bond, Nancy. The Love of Friends. 1997. 304p. (YA). (gr. 7 up). 17.00 *(0-689-81365-1*, McElderry, Margaret K.) Simon & Schuster Children's Publishing.

Borlenghi, Patricia. Chaucer the Cat & the Animal Pilgrims. 2001. (Illus.). 80p. (J). (gr. 3-6). 22.95 *(0-7475-4491-3)* Bloomsbury Publishing, Ltd. GBR. *Dist:* Trafalgar Square.

Bray-Moffatt, Naia, adapted by. Oliver Twist. 2000. (Read & Listen Ser.). (Illus.). 64p. (J). (gr. 4-7). pap. 7.95 *(0-7894-5463-7*, D K Ink) Dorling Kindersley Publishing, Inc.

Brown, Janet Allison & Burnett, Frances Hodgson. A Little Princess. 2001. (Storytime Classics Ser.). (Illus.). 32p. (J). (ps-3). 15.99 o.p. *(0-670-89913-5*, Viking Children's Bks.) Penguin Putnam Bks. for Young Readers.

Brundige, Patricia. Traveling with Aunt Patty: Aunt Patty Visits London. Wright, Cindy, ed. Date not set. (Illus.). (J). (gr. 1-4). text 12.95 *(0-9659668-0-1)* Aunt Patty's Travels-London.

Bulla, Clyde Robert. A Lion to Guard Us. (Trophy Bk.). (Illus.). (J). 1989. 128p. (gr. 3 up). pap. 4.99 *(0-06-440333-5*, Harper Trophy); 1981. (gr. 2-5). 14.00 o.p. *(0-690-04096-2)*; 1981. 128p. (gr. 7 up). lib. bdg. 16.89 *(0-690-04097-0)* HarperCollins Children's Bk. Group.

—A Lion to Guard Us. 1983. (Illus.). 128p. (J). reprint ed. pap. 2.25 o.p. *(0-590-33788-2)* Scholastic, Inc.

—A Lion to Guard Us. 1989. (J). 11.00 *(0-606-04267-9)* Turtleback Bks.

Burgess, Melvin. The Baby & Fly Pie: Could a Kidnapped Baby be the Key to a Better Life for Three Homeless Kids? 1996. 192p. (YA). (gr. 7 up). mass mkt. 16.00 o.p. *(0-689-80489-X*, Simon & Schuster Children's Publishing) Simon & Schuster Children's Publishing.

—The Ghost Behind the Wall, ERS. 2003. (Illus.). 176p. (YA). (gr. 4-7). 16.95 *(0-8050-7149-0*, Holt, Henry & Co. Bks. For Young Readers) Holt, Henry & Co.

—The Ghost Behind the Wall. l.t. ed. 2003. 160p. (J). 22.95 *(0-7862-5774-1)* Thorndike Pr.

Burnett, Frances Hodgson. A Little Princess. (J). 16.95 *(0-8488-1253-0)* Amereon, Ltd.

—A Little Princess. unabr. ed. 2000. (YA). (gr. 3 up). audio 24.95 *(0-945353-94-4*, H90394u, Audio Editions Bks. on Cassette) Audio Partners Publishing Corp.

—A Little Princess. 1987. (Classics Ser.). 208p. (J). mass mkt. 2.95 o.s.i *(0-553-21203-6*, Bantam Classics) Bantam Bks.

—A Little Princess. 2000. per. 12.50 *(1-58396-000-7)* Blue Unicorn Editions.

—A Little Princess. (J). 1977. 300p. lib. bdg. 15.95 (*0-89967-005-9*, Harmony Raine & Co.); 1981. 232p. reprint ed. lib. bdg. 15.95 (*0-89966-327-3*) Buccaneer Bks., Inc.

—A Little Princess. 1995. 256p. (J). (gr. 5-8). pap. 3.50 (*0-87406-739-1*) Darby Creek Publishing.

—A Little Princess. 1990. 240p. (J). pap. 3.99 o.s.i (*0-440-40386-3*) Dell Publishing.

—A Little Princess. abr. ed. (Children's Thrift Classics Ser.). (Illus.). (J). 1996. 96p. (gr. 1). pap. 1.00 (*0-486-29171-5*); 2000. 240p. pap. 2.00 (*0-486-41446-9*) Dover Pubns., Inc.

—A Little Princess. 2000. (Illus.). 192p. (YA). (gr. 4-7). reprint ed. 18.95 (*0-87923-784-8*) Godine, David R. Pub.

—A Little Princess. (Illus.). (J). 2000. 32p. (ps-3). 16.95 (*0-06-027891-9*); 2000. 32p. (ps-3). lib. bdg. 16.89 (*0-06-029010-2*); 1999. 336p. (gr. 4 up). 17.99 (*0-397-30693-8*); 1963. 80p. (gr. 4-6). lib. bdg. 15.89 o.p. (*0-397-31339-X*); 1987. 336p. (gr. 4 up). reprint ed. pap. 5.99 (*0-06-440187-1*, Harper Trophy) HarperCollins Children's Bk. Group.

—A Little Princess. l.t. ed. 423p. pap. 37.40 (*0-7583-1387-X*); 193p. pap. 20.92 (*0-7583-1384-5*); 241p. pap. 24.55 (*0-7583-1385-3*); 949p. pap. 74.67 (*0-7583-1391-8*); 818p. pap. 65.40 (*0-7583-1390-X*); 665p. pap. 54.57 (*0-7583-1389-6*); 541p. pap. 45.77 (*0-7583-1388-8*); 330p. pap. 30.77 (*0-7583-1386-1*); 241p. lib. bdg. 30.64 (*0-7583-1377-2*); 193p. lib. bdg. 26.92 (*0-7583-1376-4*); 330p. lib. bdg. 36.77 (*0-7583-1378-0*); 423p. lib. bdg. 44.12 (*0-7583-1379-9*); 949p. lib. bdg. 94.49 (*0-7583-1383-7*); 541p. lib. bdg. 52.95 (*0-7583-1380-2*); 665p. lib. bdg. 62.21 (*0-7583-1381-0*); 818p. lib. bdg. 85.54 (*0-7583-1382-9*) Huge Print Pr.

—A Little Princess. 2002. 196p. (gr. 4-7). 24.99 (*1-4043-1548-9*); per. 19.99 (*1-4043-1549-7*) IndyPublish.com.

—A Little Princess. l.t. ed. 1998. (Large Print Heritage Ser.). 324p. (YA). lib. bdg. 31.95 (*1-58118-021-7*, 21998) LRS.

—A Little Princess. (Signet Classics). 240p. 1995. (YA). mass mkt. 3.95 o.s.i (*0-451-52622-8*); 1990. (J). mass mkt. 3.95 o.s.i (*0-451-52509-4*) NAL. (Signet Classics).

—A Little Princess. 1998. (Illus.). 44p. pap. text 5.25 o.p. (*0-19-422875-4*) Oxford Univ. Pr., Inc.

—A Little Princess. Lindskoog, Kathryn, ed. 2002. (Classics for Young Readers Ser.). (Illus.). 208p. (J). pap. text 7.99 (*0-87552-727-2*) P&R Publishing.

—A Little Princess. (Puffin Classics Ser.). (gr. 4-7). 1995. (Illus.). 304p. (YA). pap. 4.99 (*0-14-036688-1*, Puffin Bks.); 1995. (Illus.). 288p. (J). 15.99 (*0-448-40949-6*, Grosset & Dunlap); 1989. (Illus.). 288p. (J). 13.95 o.p. (*0-448-09299-9*, Grosset & Dunlap); 1984. 224p. (J). pap. 3.50 o.p. (*0-14-035028-4*, Puffin Bks.) Penguin Putnam Bks. for Young Readers.

—A Little Princess. 1981. (Illus.). 288p. (J). (gr. 3-7). 7.95 o.p. (*0-448-40083-9*) Putnam Publishing Group, The.

—A Little Princess. 1975. 240p. (J). (gr. 3-7). pap. 1.25 o.s.i (*0-440-44767-4*, Yearling) Random Hse. Children's Bks.

—A Little Princess. 1990. (Children's Classics Ser.). (J). 12.99 o.s.i (*0-517-01480-7*) Random Hse. Value Publishing.

—A Little Princess. 1994. (Step into Classics Ser.). 112p. (J). (gr. 3-8). pap. 3.99 (*0-679-85090-2*) Random Hse., Inc.

—A Little Princess. (Courage Unabridged Classics Ser.). 1997. 224p. (YA). pap. 6.00 o.p. (*0-7624-0548-1*); 1996. 224p. (J). 5.98 o.p. (*1-56138-742-8*); 1997. 480p. (J). reprint ed. text 8.98 o.p. (*0-7624-0115-X*) Running Pr. Bk. Pubs. (Courage Bks.).

—A Little Princess. (Illus.). (J). text 22.95 (*0-590-24079-X*); 2000. (Illus.). 272p. (gr. 4-7). mass mkt. 3.99 (*0-439-10137-9*); 1995. 88p. (J). (gr. 3-7). mass mkt. 3.50 o.p. (*0-590-48628-4*); 1995. (Illus.). 256p. (J). (gr. 4-7). mass mkt. 3.99 (*0-590-54307-5*, Scholastic Paperbacks); 1987. 256p. (J). (gr. 4-6). mass mkt. 3.25 o.p. (*0-590-40719-8*, Scholastic Paperbacks) Scholastic, Inc.

—A Little Princess. deluxe ed. 1995. 48p. (J). (gr. 4-7). pap. 12.95 (*0-590-48627-6*) Scholastic, Inc.

—A Little Princess. l.t. ed. 2003. 342p. (J). 28.95 (*0-7862-5842-X*) Thorndike Pr.

—A Little Princess. abr. ed. 1997. (Children's Classics Ser.). (J). pap. 16.95 o.p. incl. audio (*1-85998-751-6*) Trafalgar Square.

—A Little Princess. unabr. ed. 1992. 11.00 (*0-606-16620-3*) Turtleback Bks.

—A Little Princess. Knoepflmacher, U. C., ed. & intro. by. 2002. (Classics Ser.). 272p. (J). 10.00 (*0-14-243701-8*, Penguin Classics) Viking Penguin.

—A Little Princess. 1997. (J). pap. 12.95 (*0-14-086079-7*, Puffin Bks.) Viking Penguin.

—A Little Princess. 1998. (Children's Classics). 192p. (J). (gr. 4-7). pap. 3.95 (*1-85326-136-X*, 136XWW) Wordsworth Editions, Ltd. GBR. *Dist:* Advanced Global Distribution Services.

—A Little Princess. Lindskoog, Kathryn, ed. & abr. by. 1993. (gr. 3 up). pap. 6.99 o.p. (*0-88070-527-2*) Zonderkidz.

—A Little Princess: Picture Book. 1995. (Illus.). 32p. (J). (gr. k-2). mass mkt. 2.95 (*0-590-55204-X*) Scholastic, Inc.

—A Little Princess: With a Discussion of Generosity. Gribbon, Sean & Jael, trs. 2003. (Values in Action Illustrated Classics Ser.). (J). (*1-59203-050-5*) Learning Challenge, Inc.

—A Little Princess & The Secret Garden. 2002. 480p. (J). (gr. 4-7). reprint ed. 9.00 o.p. (*0-7624-0564-3*) Running Pr. Bk. Pubs.

—A Little Princess Book & Charm. 1999. (Charming Classic Bks.). (Illus.). 336p. (J). (gr. 4 up). pap. 6.99 (*0-694-01236-X*, Harper Festival) HarperCollins Children's Bk. Group.

Cage, Elizabeth. License to Thrill. 1998. (Spy Girls Ser.: No. 1). 192p. (YA). (gr. 7 up). mass mkt. 4.50 (*0-671-02286-5*, Simon Pulse) Simon & Schuster Children's Publishing.

Carabetta, Natalie, illus. A Little Princess. 1996. (All Aboard Reading Ser.: Level 3). 48p. (J). (gr. 2-3). 13.99 o.s.i (*0-448-41329-9*); (ps-3). 3.99 (*0-448-41327-2*) Penguin Putnam Bks. for Young Readers. (Grosset & Dunlap).

Carillo, Fred, illus. Oliver Twist. 1979. (Now Age Illustrated V Ser.). 64p. (J). (gr. 4-12). text 7.50 o.p. (*0-88301-406-8*) Pendulum Pr., Inc.

Carrick, Malcolm. Tramp. 1977. (J). (gr. 2-5). 5.95 o.p. (*0-06-021117-2*); lib. bdg. 5.79 o.p. (*0-06-021118-0*) HarperCollins Pubs.

Causley, Charles. Dick Whittington: A Story from England. 1979. (Puffin Folktales of the World Ser.). (Illus.). (J). (gr. 2-6). pap. 1.95 o.p. (*0-14-030801-6*, Penguin Bks.) Viking Penguin.

Center for Learning Network Staff. Oliver Twist: Curriculum Unit —Novel Series. 2001. (Novel Ser.). 65p. (YA). tchr. ed., spiral bd. 18.95 (*1-56077-684-6*) Ctr. for Learning, The.

Cheaney, Janie B. The Playmaker. Siscoe, Nancy, ed. 2000. 320p. (J). (gr. 5-7). lib. bdg. 17.99 (*0-375-90577-4*, Knopf Bks. for Young Readers) Random Hse. Children's Bks.

Chute, Marchette. The Wonderful Winter. 1954. (J). (gr. 5-9). lib. bdg. 5.95 o.p. (*0-525-43208-6*, Dutton) Dutton/Plume.

—The Wonderful Winter. 2002. 256p. (J). 12.95 (*0-9714612-1-X*) Green Mansion Pr. LLC.

Coats, Lucy, et al. A Little Princess. 2001. (Young Classics Ser.). (Illus.). 48p. (J). (gr. 1-3). pap. 9.95 o.p. (*0-7894-6679-1*) Dorling Kindersley Publishing, Inc.

Collins, Suzanne. Fire Proof. 1999. (Mystery Files of Shelby Woo Ser.: No. 11). 144p. (J). (gr. 4-6). pap. 3.99 (*0-671-02695-X*, Aladdin) Simon & Schuster Children's Publishing.

Cooney, Caroline B. The Terrorist. (YA). 1997. 208p. pap. 15.95 o.p. (*0-590-22853-6*); 1999. 198p. (gr. 7-12). reprint ed. mass mkt. 4.50 (*0-590-22854-4*) Scholastic, Inc.

Cooper, Susan. King of Shadows. (Illus.). 192p. (gr. 5-9). 2001. (J). pap. 4.99 (*0-689-84445-X*, Aladdin); 1999. (YA). 16.00 (*0-689-82817-9*, McElderry, Margaret K.) Simon & Schuster Children's Publishing.

—King of Shadows. l.t. ed. 2000. (Thorndike Press Large Print Juvenile Ser.). (Illus.). 246p. (J). (gr. 8-12). 21.95 (*0-7862-2706-0*) Thorndike Pr.

Cutler, Lynn W. Baggage to London. 2003. (Annikins Ser.: Vol. 13). (Illus.). 12p. (Orig.). (J). (ps-1). pap. 1.25 (*1-55037-345-5*) Annick Pr., Ltd. CAN. *Dist:* Firefly Bks., Ltd.

Danziger, Paula. Thames Doesn't Rhyme with James. 1995. 192p. (J). (gr. 5-9). mass mkt. 4.50 o.s.i (*0-425-15015-1*) Berkley Publishing Group.

—Thames Doesn't Rhyme with James. 1994. 176p. (YA). 15.95 o.s.i (*0-399-22526-9*, G. P. Putnam's Sons) Penguin Group (USA) Inc.

—Thames Doesn't Rhyme with James. 1999. (Illus.). 160p. (YA). (gr. 5-9). pap. 4.99 (*0-698-11788-3*, PaperStar) Penguin Putnam Bks. for Young Readers.

—Thames Doesn't Rhyme with James. 153p. pap. 3.99 (*0-8072-1473-6*, Listening Library) Random Hse. Audio Publishing Group.

—Thames Doesn't Rhyme with James. 1995. 10.55 (*0-606-17332-3*) Turtleback Bks.

—You Can't Eat Your Chicken Pox, Amber Brown. 1995. (Amber Brown Ser.: No. 2). (Illus.). 80p. (J). (gr. 3-6). 14.99 (*0-399-22702-4*, G. P. Putnam's Sons) Penguin Group (USA) Inc.

—You Can't Eat Your Chicken Pox, Amber Brown. 1996. (Amber Brown Ser.: No. 2). (Illus.). 101p. (J). (gr. 3-6). mass mkt. 4.50 (*0-590-50207-7*, Scholastic Paperbacks) Scholastic, Inc.

—You Can't Eat Your Chicken Pox, Amber Brown. 1996. (Amber Brown Ser.: No. 2). (J). (gr. 3-6). 10.04 (*0-606-08911-X*) Turtleback Bks.

Davoll, Barbara. To London to See the Queen. 1999. (New Christopher Churchmouse Adventures Ser.: Vol. 4). (Illus.). 24p. (J). (ps-3). 9.99 (*0-8024-5399-6*) Moody Pr.

Dickens, Charles. A Christmas Carol. l.t. ed. 420p. pap. 42.42 (*0-7583-3607-1*); (Illus.). 82p. pap. 15.16 (*0-7583-3600-4*); (Illus.). 107p. pap. 17.15 (*0-7583-3601-2*); (Illus.). 146p. pap. 20.33 (*0-7583-3602-0*); (Illus.). 187p. pap. 23.63 (*0-7583-3603-9*); (Illus.). 239p. pap. 27.85 (*0-7583-3604-7*); (Illus.). 294p. pap. 32.29 (*0-7583-3605-5*); (Illus.). 362p. pap. 37.75 (*0-7583-3606-3*); (Illus.). 239p. lib. bdg. 35.68 (*0-7583-3596-2*); (Illus.). 294p. lib. bdg. 39.57 (*0-7583-3597-0*); (Illus.). 362p. lib. bdg. 44.36 (*0-7583-3598-9*); (Illus.). 420p. lib. bdg. 48.46 (*0-7583-3599-7*); (Illus.). 107p. lib. bdg. 25.47 (*0-7583-3593-8*); (Illus.). 146p. lib. bdg. 29.08 (*0-7583-3594-6*); (Illus.). 187p. lib. bdg. 31.98 (*0-7583-3595-4*); (Illus.). 82p. lib. bdg. 22.64 (*0-7583-3592-X*) Huge Print Pr.

—A Christmas Carol. l.t. ed. 1999. (Large Print Heritage Ser.). 140p. (YA). (gr. 7-12). lib. bdg. 24.95 (*1-58118-041-1*, 22510) LRS.

—Cuento de Navidad. 2002. (Classics for Young Readers Ser.). (SPA.). (YA). 14.95 (*84-392-0913-4*, EV30594) Gaviota Ediciones ESP. *Dist:* Lectorum Pubns., Inc.

—Dombey & Son. 1990. (J). (ps-8). reprint ed. lib. bdg. 29.95 o.p. (*0-89966-678-7*) Buccaneer Bks., Inc.

—Little Dorrit. 1990. (J). (ps-8). reprint ed. lib. bdg. 39.95 o.p. (*0-89966-680-9*) Buccaneer Bks., Inc.

—Little Dorrit. 1987. (Illus.). 858p. (J). 17.95 (*0-19-254512-4*) Oxford Univ. Pr., Inc.

—Oliver Twist. 2002. (Classics for Young Readers Ser.). (SPA.). (YA). 14.95 (*84-392-0919-3*, EV30603) Gaviota Ediciones ESP. *Dist:* Lectorum Pubns., Inc.

—Oliver Twist. 1979. (Now Age Illustrated V Ser.). (Illus.). 64p. (J). (gr. 4-12). stu. ed. 1.25 (*0-88301-418-1*) Pendulum Pr., Inc.

—Oliver Twist. 1990. (Spanish Children's Classics Ser.: No. 800-4). (SPA.). (J). 3.50 (*0-7214-1398-6*, Ladybird Bks.) Penguin Group (USA) Inc.

—Oliver Twist. 2000. (SPA.). 287p. (gr. 4-7). pap. 14.95 (*0-595-13258-8*) iUniverse, Inc.

—Oliver Twist. 1992. (Illus.). 110p. pap. text 5.95 o.p. (*0-19-422683-2*) Oxford Univ. Pr., Inc.

—Oliver Twist. abr. ed. Date not set. (Nelson Readers Ser.). (J). pap. text (*0-17-557020-5*) Addison-Wesley Longman, Inc.

—Oliver Twist. abr. ed. (J). 9.95 (*1-56156-372-2*) Kidsbooks, Inc.

—Oliver Twist. abr. ed. 1991. (Bridge Ser.). 137p. (YA). pap. text 5.95 o.p. (*0-582-53014-8*) Longman Publishing Group.

—Oliver Twist. 2nd abr. ed. 2000. (Green Apple). 96p. (YA). pap. (*1-57159-008-0*) Los Andes Publishing Co.

—Oliver Twist. Hedge, Tricia, ed. abr. ed. 2000. (Bookworms Ser.). (Illus.). 128p. (YA). (gr. 6 up). pap. text 5.95 (*0-19-423092-9*) Oxford Univ. Pr., Inc.

—Oliver Twist. abr. ed. 1979. (Now Age Illustrated V Ser.). (Illus.). 64p. (J). (gr. 4-12). pap. text 2.95 (*0-88301-394-0*) Pendulum Pr., Inc.

—Oliver Twist. abr. ed. 1997. (Classic Ser.). 54p. (J). (gr. 3-6). 2.99 o.s.i (*0-7214-5653-7*, Ladybird Bks.) Penguin Group (USA) Inc.

—Oliver Twist. abr. ed. 1994. (Classics for Young Readers Ser.). (Illus.). 352p. (YA). (gr. 4-7). pap. 4.99 (*0-14-036814-0*, Puffin Bks.) Penguin Putnam Bks. for Young Readers.

—Oliver Twist. Vogel, Malvina, ed. abr. ed. 1989. (Great Illustrated Classics Ser.: Vol. 5). (Illus.). 240p. (J). (gr. 3-6). 9.95 (*0-86611-956-6*) Playmore, Inc., Pubs.

—Oliver Twist: Level 3. (Illus.). 72p. (YA). (gr. 4 up). pap. 7.95 (*1-55576-325-1*, EDN308B) AV Concepts Corp.

—Oliver Twist: With a Discussion of Honesty. 2003. (Values in Action Illustrated Classics Ser.). (J). (*1-59203-051-3*) Learning Challenge, Inc.

Disney Staff. Oliver & Company. 1990. (Disney Classics Ser.). 96p. (J). (ps-3). 6.98 o.p. (*0-8317-6574-7*, Viking Children's Bks.) Penguin Putnam Bks. for Young Readers.

—Oliver & Company: A Picture Book. 1996. 32p. (J). pap. 4.95 o.p. (*0-7868-4120-6*) Disney Pr.

Dixon, Franklin W. The London Deception. 1999. (Hardy Boys Mystery Stories Ser.: No. 158). 160p. (J). (gr. 3-6). pap. 3.99 (*0-671-03496-0*, Aladdin) Simon & Schuster Children's Publishing.

—The London Deception. 1999. (Hardy Boys Mystery Stories Ser.: No. 158). (J). (gr. 3-6). 10.04 (*0-606-19052-X*) Turtleback Bks.

Doherty, Berlie. Street Child. l.t. ed. 1994. (Illus.). (J). (gr. 1-8). 16.95 o.p. (*0-7451-2225-6*, Galaxy Children's Large Print) BBC Audiobooks America.

—Street Child. 1996. 160p. (J). (gr. 5-9). pap. 4.99 o.s.i (*0-14-037936-3*, Puffin Bks.) Penguin Putnam Bks. for Young Readers.

—Street Child. 1994. 160p. (J). (gr. 4-7). pap. 17.95 (*0-531-06864-1*); lib. bdg. 18.99 (*0-531-08714-X*) Scholastic, Inc. (Orchard Bks.).

—Street Child. 1996. 10.09 o.p. (*0-606-08883-0*) Turtleback Bks.

Doyle, Arthur Conan. Listen & Read Sherlock Holmes Stories. unabr. ed. 1997. 112p. (J). 6.95 incl. audio (*0-486-29827-2*) Dover Pubns., Inc.

—Selected Adventures of Sherlock Holmes. Marshall, Michael J., ed. abr. ed. 1997. (Core Classics Ser.: Vol. 5). (Illus.). 160p. (J). (gr. 4-6). pap. 5.95 (*1-890517-08-9*); lib. bdg. 10.95 (*1-890517-09-7*) Core Knowledge Foundation.

Escott, John, adapted by. Oliver Twist. 1995. (Classics for Young Readers Ser.). 64p. (J). 5.98 o.p. (*0-86112-981-4*) Brimax Bks., Ltd.

Estrada, Ric, illus. Oliver Twist. 2002. (Great Illustrated Classics). 240p. (J). (gr. 3-8). lib. bdg. 21.35 (*1-57765-697-0*, ABDO & Daughters) ABDO Publishing Co.

Eure, Wesley. Red Wings of Christmas. 1992. (Illus.). 176p. (YA). (gr. 7 up). 19.95 (*0-88289-902-3*) Pelican Publishing Co., Inc.

—The Red Wings of Christmas. abr. ed. 1992. (Illus.). 160p. (J). (gr. 3-7). pap. 14.95 incl. audio (*0-88289-998-8*) Pelican Publishing Co., Inc.

Fearnley, Jan. Colin & the Curly Claw. 2001. (Blue Bananas Ser.). (Illus.). 48p. (J). (gr. 1-2). pap. 4.95 (*0-7787-0886-1*); lib. bdg. 19.96 (*0-7787-0840-3*) Crabtree Publishing Co.

Ferguson, Sarah. The Royal Switch. 1996. (Illus.). 112p. (J). 14.95 (*0-385-32177-5*, Delacorte Pr.) Dell Publishing.

—The Royal Switch. 1997. (Illus.). 176p. (gr. 2-6). pap. text 4.99 o.s.i (*0-440-41213-7*, Dell Books for Young Readers) Random Hse. Children's Bks.

Gaiman, Neil. Books of Magic. 2004. (Books of Magic Ser.: No. 4). 192p. (J). pap. 5.99 (*0-06-447382-1*, Eos) Morrow/Avon.

Gleitzman, Morris. Puppy Fat. 1996. 192p. (YA). (gr. 3-7). pap. 5.00 o.s.i (*0-15-200052-6*, Harcourt Paperbacks); (gr. 4-7). 11.00 o.s.i (*0-15-200047-X*) Harcourt Children's Bks.

—Puppy Fat. 1995. 10.10 o.p. (*0-606-09771-6*) Turtleback Bks.

Godden, Rumer. An Episode of Sparrows. 1989. 256p. (YA). (gr. 7 up). pap. 4.95 o.p. (*0-14-034024-6*, Puffin Bks.) Penguin Putnam Bks. for Young Readers.

—The Kitchen Madonna. 1967. (Illus.). (J). 5.95 o.p. (*0-670-41399-2*) Viking Penguin.

Gordon, Patricia. The Boy Jones. 1980. (J). lib. bdg. 6.95 o.p. (*0-8398-2608-7*, Macmillan Reference USA) Gale Group.

Hall, Margaret & Jones, Dawn L. Sebastian at the Tower of London. 2001. (Suitcase Bear Adventures Ser.). (Illus.). (J). (*0-9713174-1-0*, Bear & Co.) Bear & Co.

Haunting of Alaizabel Cray. 2004. (J). pap. 16.95 (*0-439-54656-7*) Scholastic, Inc.

Hautzig, Deborah. A Little Princess. 1996. (All Aboard Reading Ser.). (J). 10.14 (*0-606-11570-6*) Turtleback Bks.

Hayner, Linda K. The Foundling. 1997. 352p. (YA). (gr. 10 up). pap. 9.95 (*0-89084-941-2*, 108951) Jones, Bob Univ. Pr.

Haynes, Betsy. The Scapegoat. 1991. (Fabulous Five Ser.: No. 27). 128p. (J). (gr. 4-7). pap. 2.99 o.s.i (*0-553-15872-4*) Bantam Bks.

Hope, Laura Lee. The Bobbsey Twins at London Tower. 1959. (Bobbsey Twins Ser.). (Illus.). (J). (gr. 3-5). 4.50 o.s.i (*0-448-08052-4*, Grosset & Dunlap) Penguin Putnam Bks. for Young Readers.

Horowitz, Anthony. The Devil & His Boy. 2000. 182p. (J). (gr. 5-9). 16.99 (*0-399-23432-2*, Philomel) Penguin Putnam Bks. for Young Readers.

Johns, Michael-Anne, et al. What a Girl Wants. novel ed. 2003. 80p. (J). mass mkt. 4.99 (*0-439-53062-8*) Scholastic, Inc.

Joy, Margaret. Allotment Lane in London. 1990. (Illus.). 96p. (J). (gr. 3-7). bds. 10.95 o.p. (*0-571-15403-4*) Faber & Faber, Inc.

Kenney, Cindy. The Star of Christmas: A Very Veggie Christmas Story. 2002. (Illus.). 40p. (J). (gr. k-3). 14.99 (*0-310-70504-5*) Zondervan.

Kincaid, Eric, illus. Oliver Twist. 1994. (Children's Classics Ser.). 112p. (J). 9.98 o.p. (*0-86112-452-9*) Brimax Bks., Ltd.

MacDonald, George. At the Back of the North Wind. 1966. (Airmont Classics Ser.). (Illus.). (YA). (gr. 5 up). mass mkt. 1.50 o.p. (*0-8049-0100-7*, CL-100) Airmont Publishing Co., Inc.

—At the Back of the North Wind. (Young Reader's Christian Library). 1991. (Illus.). 224p. (J). (gr. 3-7). pap. 1.39 o.p. (*1-55748-188-1*); 1988. 384p. 8.97 o.p. (*1-55748-024-9*) Barbour Publishing, Inc.

—At the Back of the North Wind. 1987. (Illus.). (YA). (gr. 5 up). reprint ed. pap. 8.95 o.s.i (*0-8052-0595-0*, Schocken) Knopf Publishing Group.

—At the Back of the North Wind. 1985. (Classics for Young Readers Ser.). 336p. (J). (gr. 4-6). pap. 3.50 o.p. (*0-14-035030-6*, Puffin Bks.) Penguin Putnam Bks. for Young Readers.

—At the Back of the North Wind. 1990. 352p. (J). 12.99 o.s.i (*0-517-69120-5*) Random Hse. Value Publishing.

—At the Back of the North Wind. Watson, Jean, ed. 1981. (Illus.). 128p. (J). (gr. 3-7). reprint ed. 7.95 o.p. (*0-310-42340-6*, 9065P) Zondervan.

Marshak, Samuel. The Absent Minded Fellow, RS. Pevear, Richard, tr. from RUS. 1999. (Illus.). 32p. (YA). (ps-3). 16.00 o.p. (*0-374-30013-5*, Farrar, Straus & Giroux (BYR)) Farrar, Straus & Giroux.

Mattern, Joanne, retold by. Oliver Twist. 1996. (Wishbone Classics Ser.: No. 5). (J). (gr. 3-7). 10.04 (*0-606-10368-6*) Turtleback Bks.

McClintock, Barbara, illus. Goldilocks & the Three Bears. 2003. 192p. (J). pap. 15.95 (*0-439-28133-4*) Scholastic, Inc.

Morgan, Geoffrey. A Small Piece of Paradise. 1968. (Illus.). (J). (gr. 5 up). lib. bdg. 5.69 o.s.i (*0-394-91635-2*, Knopf Bks. for Young Readers) Random Hse. Children's Bks.

Murray, Millie. Cairo Hughes. 1997. (Livewire Ser.). 110p. (YA). (gr. 7-11). pap. 7.95 (*0-7043-4936-1*) Women's Pr., Ltd., The GBR. *Dist:* Trafalgar Square.

Naidoo, Beverley. The Other Side of Truth. 2001. 272p. (J). (gr. 5 up). 16.99 (*0-06-029628-3*); lib. bdg. 17.89 (*0-06-029629-1*) HarperCollins Children's Bk. Group.

—The Other Side of Truth. 2000. 208p. (J). pap. (*0-14-130476-6*, Puffin Bks.) Penguin Putnam Bks. for Young Readers.

Nicholson, Louise. Look Out London. 1995. (Illus.). 48p. (J). (gr. 1-4). pap. o.p. (*1-898304-84-X*) Random Hse. of Canada, Ltd. CAN. *Dist:* Random Hse., Inc.

O'Bryan, Caitlin. Tarnished Dream. 2001. 180p. pap. 13.95 o.p. (*0-595-17713-1*, Writers Club Pr.) iUniverse, Inc.

Oliver & Company. (Read-Along Ser.). (J). 7.99 incl. audio (*1-55723-024-2*) Walt Disney Records.

Paine, Penelope C. Time for Horatio. Stryker, Sandy, ed. 1990. (Illus.). 48p. (J). (ps up). 14.95 (*0-911655-33-6*) Advocacy Pr.

—Time for Horatio. 2001. 48p. (J). per. 17.95 (*0-9707944-7-9*) Paper Posie.

Parker, Ed & Yingling, Kathryn, illus. Oliver Twist. 1996. (Wishbone Classics Ser.: No. 5). 128p. (J). (gr. 3-7). mass mkt. 3.99 (*0-06-106419-X*, Harper-Entertainment) Morrow/Avon.

Pascal, Francine. London Calling. 2001. (Elizabeth Ser.). 240p. (YA). (gr. 9-12). mass mkt. 4.50 o.s.i (*0-553-49354-X*, Sweet Valley) Random Hse. Children's Bks.

Pascal, Francine, creator. Love & Death in London. 1994. (Sweet Valley High Ser.: No. 104). 224p. (YA). (gr. 7 up). mass mkt. 3.50 o.s.i (*0-553-56227-4*) Bantam Bks.

Penguin Books Staff, ed. Oliver Twist: Abridged for Children. 9999. (Classics Ser.). 56p. (J). text 3.50 o.p. (*0-7214-1754-X*, Ladybird Bks.) Penguin Group (USA) Inc.

Prince, Maggie. The House on Hound Hill. (YA). 2003. 256p. (gr. 5). pap. 6.95 (*0-618-33124-7*); 1998. 242p. (gr. 7-9). tchr. ed. 16.00 (*0-395-90702-0*) Houghton Mifflin Co.

Prior, Natalie Jane. London Calling. 1997. 200p. (YA). pap. 12.95 (*0-7022-2948-2*) Univ. of Queensland Pr. AUS. *Dist:* International Specialized Bk. Services.

Pullman, Philip. I Was a Rat!: or The Scarlet Slippers. l.t. unabr. ed. 2001. (Read-Along Ser.). 224p. (J). 29.95 incl. audio (*0-7540-6233-3*, RA034); (YA). audio 24.95 (*0-7540-5193-5*, CCA3631) BBC Audiobooks America. (Chivers Children's Audio Bks.).

—I Was a Rat!: or The Scarlet Slippers. 2000. (Illus.). 176p. (gr. 3-5). text 15.95 (*0-375-80176-6*); lib. bdg. 17.99 (*0-375-90176-0*) Random Hse. Children's Bks. (Knopf Bks. for Young Readers).

—Spring-Heeled Jack: A Story of Bravery & Evil. 1991. (Illus.). 112p. (J). (gr. 3-6). 10.99 o.s.i (*0-679-91057-3*, Knopf Bks. for Young Readers) Random Hse. Children's Bks.

Rabley, Stephen. Dino's Day in London. Date not set. pap. text 38.00 (*0-582-03146-X*) Addison-Wesley Longman, Ltd. GBR. *Dist:* Trans-Atlantic Pubns., Inc.

Regan, Peter. Riverside: The London Trip. 1999. (Illus.). 112p. (YA). (gr. 3 up). pap. 7.95 (*1-901737-16-0*) Anvil Bks., Ltd. IRL. *Dist:* Dufour Editions, Inc.

Richardson, I. M. Charles Dickens' A Christmas Carol. 1988. (J). 10.10 (*0-606-03559-1*) Turtleback Bks.

Richemont, Enid. The Magic Skateboard. (Illus.). (J). 1995. bds. 3.99 o.p. (*1-56402-449-0*); 1993. 80p. (gr. 3-6). 14.95 o.p. (*1-56402-132-7*) Candlewick Pr.

Saksena, Kate. Hang on in There, Shelley. 2003. 219p. (J). 16.95 (*1-58234-822-7*, Bloomsbury Children) Bloomsbury Publishing.

Shaw-Larkman, Neil. The Great London Adventure. 2001. 216p. (J). pap. (*0-9540371-0-3*) International Media Developments Publishing Ltd.

Simmons, Steven J. Percy to the Rescue. 1998. (Illus.). 32p. (J). (ps-3). 15.95 (*0-88106-390-8*, Talewinds) Charlesbridge Publishing, Inc.

Slobodkin, Louis. The Space Ship Returns to the Apple Tree. 2nd ed. 1994. (Illus.). 128p. (J). (gr. 3-7). reprint ed. pap. 3.95 o.s.i (*0-689-71768-7*, Aladdin) Simon & Schuster Children's Publishing.

Spirn, Michele Sobel. The Bridges in London. 2000. (Going to Ser.). (Illus.). 96p. pap. 7.95 (*1-893577-00-7*) Four Corners Publishing Co., Inc.

Stanley, George Edward. Adam Sharp, the Spy Who Barked. 2002. (Road to Reading Ser.). (Illus.). 48p. (J). (gr. 2-4). pap. 3.99 (*0-307-26412-2*); lib. bdg. 11.99 (*0-307-46412-1*) Random Hse. Children's Bks. (Golden Bks.).

Stevenson, Robert Louis. Dr. Jekyll & Mr. Hyde. (Illus.). 72p. (YA). (gr. 4 up). pap. 7.95 (*0-931334-50-0*, EDN402B) AV Concepts Corp.

—Dr. Jekyll & Mr. Hyde. 1990. 82p. (J). mass mkt. 2.99 (*0-8125-0448-8*, Tor Classics) Doherty, Tom Assocs., LLC.

—Dr. Jekyll & Mr. Hyde. (YA). (gr. 5-12). pap. 7.95 (*0-8224-9255-5*) Globe Fearon Educational Publishing.

—Dr. Jekyll & Mr. Hyde. 2002. 208p. (YA). mass mkt. 3.99 (*0-439-29575-0*) Scholastic, Inc.

Stretton, Hesba. Little Meg's Children. 2000. (Golden Inheritance Ser.: Vol. 5). (Illus.). 88p. (J). pap. 7.90 (*0-921100-92-2*) Inheritance Pubns.

Stroud, Jonathan. The Amulet of Samarkand. 2003. (Bartimaeus Trilogy: Bk. 1). (Illus.). 464p. (J). (gr. 5 up). 17.95 (*0-7868-1859-X*) Hyperion Bks. for Children.

—The Amulet of Samarkand, No. 1. unabr. ed. 2003. (J). audio 35.00 (*0-8072-1953-3*, Listening Library) Random Hse. Audio Publishing Group.

Theroux, Paul. London Snow: A Christmas Story, 001. 1980. (J). (gr. k-10). 6.95 o.p. (*0-395-29458-4*) Houghton Mifflin Co.

Thoene, Jake & Thoene, Luke. The Jewelled Peacock of Persia. 1996. (Baker Street Mysteries Ser.: No. 3). 160p. pap. 5.99 o.s.i (*0-345-39559-X*, Ballantine Bks.) Ballantine Bks.

—The Mystery of the Yellow Hands. 1995. (Baker Street Brigade Ser.: No. 1). 160p. pap. 5.99 o.s.i (*0-345-39561-1*, Ballantine Bks.) Ballantine Bks.

Thomas, Jerry D. Detective Zack Trapped in Darkmoor Manor. 1997. (Detective Zack Ser.: Vol. 9). (J). pap. 6.99 (*0-8163-1394-6*) Pacific Pr. Publishing Assn.

Tourret, Gwen, illus. Oliver Twist. 9999. (Children's Classics Ser.: No. 740-18). (J). (gr. 3-5). pap. 3.50 o.p. (*0-7214-0823-0*, Ladybird Bks.) Penguin Group (USA) Inc.

Updale, Eleanor. Montmorency. 2004. 240p. (J). 16.95 (*0-439-58035-8*, Orchard Bks.) Scholastic, Inc.

Ure, Jean. The Children Next Door. l.t. ed. 1994. (Illus.). (J). (gr. 1-8). 16.95 o.p. (*0-7451-2271-X*, Galaxy Children's Large Print) BBC Audiobooks America.

—The Children Next Door. 1996. 135p. (J). (gr. 3-6). pap. 14.95 (*0-590-22293-7*) Scholastic, Inc.

—Plague. 1991. 160p. (YA). (gr. 5 up). 16.95 (*0-15-262429-5*) Harcourt Children's Bks.

—Plague. 1993. 224p. (J). (gr. 7 up). pap. 4.99 o.s.i (*0-14-036283-5*, Puffin Bks.) Penguin Putnam Bks. for Young Readers.

—Plague. 1993. (J). 10.09 o.p. (*0-606-05548-7*) Turtleback Bks.

Usher, Frances. The Hermit Shell. 1998. (Cambridge Reading Ser.). (Illus.). 160p. pap. text 10.25 (*0-521-55666-X*);Set. 6p. 53.00 (*0-521-64914-5*) Cambridge Univ. Pr.

Vernon, Louise A. A Heart Strangely Warmed. 1994. 130p. (J). (gr. 4-8). pap. 7.95 (*1-882514-14-9*) Greenleaf Pr.

—A Heart Strangely Warmed. (Illus.). 128p. (J). (gr. 4-9). 2002. pap. 7.99 (*0-8361-1769-7*); 1975. 4.95 o.p. (*0-8361-1768-9*) Herald Pr.

Warner, Gertrude Chandler, creator. The Mystery of the Queen's Jewels. 1998. (Boxcar Children Special Ser.: No. 11). (Illus.). 144p. (J). (gr. 2-5). lib. bdg. 13.95 (*0-8075-5450-2*); mass mkt. 3.95 (*0-8075-5451-0*) Whitman, Albert & Co.

Whelan, Gloria. Farewell to the Island. 208p. (gr. 4 up). 1999. (Illus.). (YA). pap. 5.99 (*0-06-440821-3*, Harper Trophy); 1998. (J). 16.95 (*0-06-027751-3*) HarperCollins Children's Bk. Group.

White, Ellen Emerson. Voyage on the Great Titanic: The Diary of Margaret Ann Brady, R. M. S. Titanic, 1912. 1998. (Illus.). 197p. (YA). (gr. 4-9). pap. 10.95 (*0-590-96273-6*, Scholastic Pr.) Scholastic, Inc.

William, Kate. Love & Death in London. 1994. (Sweet Valley High Ser.: No. 104). (YA). (gr. 7 up). 9.55 (*0-606-06027-8*) Turtleback Bks.

Wilson, Jacqueline. Girls Out Late. 2003. 224p. (YA). (gr. 7). mass mkt. 4.99 (*0-440-22959-6*, Laurel Leaf) Random Hse. Children's Bks.

—Girls Out Late. 2002. 224p. (YA). (gr. 7). 9.95 (*0-385-72976-6*); lib. bdg. 11.99 (*0-385-90042-2*) Random Hse., Inc.

—Girls Out Late. 2003. (Illus.). 192p. (YA). mass mkt. (*0-552-54523-6*) Transworld Publishers Ltd. GBR. *Dist:* Random Hse. of Canada, Ltd.

Wolff, Ashley. The Bells of London. 1984. (J). (gr. k-3). 12.95 o.s.i (*0-396-08485-0*, G. P. Putnam's Sons) Penguin Putnam Bks. for Young Readers.

Woodruff, Elvira. The Christmas Doll. 160p. (J). 2002. mass mkt. 4.50 (*0-590-31879-9*, Scholastic Paperbacks); 2000. (Illus.). (gr. 4-7). pap. 15.95 (*0-590-31872-1*) Scholastic, Inc.

Wrede, Patricia C. & Stevermer, Caroline. Sorcery & Cecelia: or the Enchanged Chocolate Pot: Magical Misadventures of Two Lady Cousins in Regency England. 2003. (Illus.). 336p. (YA). 17.00 (*0-15-204615-1*) Harcourt Children's Bks.

Zallinger, Jean Day, illus. Oliver Twist. 1990. (Step into Classics Ser.). 96p. (gr. 2-7). pap. 3.99 (*0-679-80391-2*, Random Hse. Bks. for Young Readers) Random Hse. Children's Bks.

—Oliver Twist. 1994. (Bullseye Step into Classics Ser.). (J). 10.04 (*0-606-09705-8*) Turtleback Bks.

LONG ISLAND (N.Y.)—FICTION

Blume, Judy. Quiza No lo Haga. Orig. Title: Then Again, Maybe I Won't. (SPA.). 162p. (J). 8.50 o.p. (*84-204-4626-2*) Santillana USA Publishing Co., Inc.

—Then Again, Maybe I Won't, Set. unabr. ed. 1999. (YA). audio 23.98 Highsmith Inc.

—Then Again, Maybe I Won't. 125p. (J). pap. 3.99 (*0-8072-1445-0*); 2002. 164p. (YA). (gr. 5 up). pap. 28.00 incl. audio (*0-8072-0796-9*, LYA 354 SP); 2002. (YA). (gr. 7 up). audio 18.00 (*0-8072-0699-7*); 1990. (YA). (gr. 7 up). pap. 28.98 incl. audio (*0-8072-7296-5*, YA827SP); 1990. (YA). (gr. 7 up). pap. 29.00 incl. audio (*0-8072-7306-6*, YA827SP) Random Hse. Audio Publishing Group. (Listening Library).

—Then Again, Maybe I Won't. 1971. (J). 11.04 (*0-606-05069-8*) Turtleback Bks.

Fitzhugh, Louise. The Long Secret. 1965. (Illus.). (YA). (gr. 5 up). 15.00 (*0-06-021410-4*); lib. bdg. 14.89 o.p. (*0-06-021411-2*) HarperCollins Children's Bk. Group.

—The Long Secret: Harriet the Spy Adventure. 2001. (Illus.). 288p. (gr. 5 up). text 15.95 (*0-385-32784-6*, Delacorte Bks. for Young Readers); 1978. (J). mass mkt. 1.50 o.s.i (*0-440-94977-7*, Dell Books for Young Readers) Random Hse. Children's Bks.

Forman, James. Cow Neck Rebels, RS. 1969. 256p. (J). (gr. 7 up). 3.95 o.p. (*0-374-31617-1*, Farrar, Straus & Giroux (BYR)) Farrar, Straus & Giroux.

Karr, Kathleen. Playing with Fire, RS. 2001. 192p. (J). (gr. 5 up). 16.00 (*0-374-23453-1*, Farrar, Straus & Giroux (BYR)) Farrar, Straus & Giroux.

LOS ANGELES (CALIF.)—FICTION

Block, Francesca Lia. Dangerous Angels: The 5 Weetzie Bat Books. 1998. (Weetzie Bat Bks.). 496p. (J). (gr. 7-12). pap. 12.00 (*0-06-440697-0*, Harper Trophy) HarperCollins Children's Bk. Group.

—The Hanged Man. 1994. (YA). 144p. (ps-2). lib. bdg. 15.89 (*0-06-024537-9*, Cotler, Joanna Bks.); 128p. (gr. 7 up). 14.00 o.p. (*0-06-024536-0*) HarperCollins Children's Bk. Group.

—I Was a Teenage Fairy. 192p. (gr. 7 up). 1998. (J). lib. bdg. 14.89 (*0-06-027748-3*); 1998. (YA). 14.95 (*0-06-027747-5*, Cotler, Joanna Bks.); 2000. (J). reprint ed. pap. 7.99 (*0-06-440862-0*, Harper Trophy) HarperCollins Children's Bk. Group.

—I Was a Teenage Fairy. 2000. (Illus.). (J). 14.00 (*0-606-18903-3*) Turtleback Bks.

—Wasteland. 2003. 160p. (J). 15.99 (*0-06-028644-X*, Cotler, Joanna Bks.) HarperCollins Children's Bk. Group.

—Weetzie Bat. (Charlotte Zolotow Bk.). 1991. 96p. (J). (gr. 12 up). pap. 4.50 o.s.i (*0-06-447068-7*, Harper Trophy); 1989. 96p. (YA). (gr. 7 up). lib. bdg. 14.89 o.p. (*0-06-020536-9*); 10th anniv. ed. 1999. 128p. (J). (gr. 5 up). pap. 7.99 (*0-06-440818-3*, Harper Trophy) HarperCollins Children's Bk. Group.

—Weetzie Bat. 1991. (J). 14.00 (*0-606-05688-2*) Turtleback Bks.

—Weetzie Bat: 10th Anniversary Edition. 10th anniv. ed. 1999. (Charlotte Zolotow Book Ser.). 128p. (YA). (gr. 7-k). 14.95 (*0-06-020534-2*) HarperCollins Children's Bk. Group.

—Witch Baby. 1991. (Charlotte Zolotow Bk.). 112p. (YA). (gr. 7 up). 14.95 o.p. (*0-06-020547-4*); lib. bdg. 14.89 o.s.i (*0-06-020548-2*) HarperCollins Children's Bk. Group.

Bray, Marian F. Stars over East L. A. 1993. (Young Adult Fiction Ser.). 216p. (Orig.). (YA). (gr. 8-12). pap. 6.99 o.p. (*0-87788-798-5*, Shaw) WaterBrook Pr.

Brian, Kate. The Princess & the Pauper. 2003. (Illus.). 272p. (YA). (gr. 5-9). 14.95 (*0-689-86173-7*, Simon & Schuster Children's Publishing) Simon & Schuster Children's Publishing.

Brouwer, Sigmund. Shroud of the Lion. 2003. (Accidental Detectives Ser.). (Illus.). 128p. (J). pap. 5.99 (*0-7642-2568-5*) Bethany Hse. Pubs.

Bunting, Eve. Noche de Humo. Andujar, Gloria de Aragón, tr. 1999. (SPA., Illus.). 36p. (J). (gr. 2-4). pap. 6.00 (*0-15-201946-4*, Voyager Bks./Libros Viajeros) Harcourt Children's Bks.

—Noche de Humo. 1999. 12.15 (*0-606-16516-9*) Turtleback Bks.

—Smoky Night. 2002. (Illus.). (J). 13.19 (*0-7587-0073-3*) Book Wholesalers, Inc.

—Smoky Night. 1994. (Illus.). 28p. (YA). (gr. 5-8). reprint ed. 15.00 (*0-7567-6337-1*) DIANE Publishing Co.

—Smoky Night. (J). (ps-3). 1999. (Illus.). 40p. pap. 6.00 (*0-15-201884-0*, Harcourt Paperbacks); 1996. 15.00 o.s.i (*0-15-201541-8*); 1994. (Illus.). 40p. 16.00 (*0-15-269954-6*) Harcourt Children's Bks.

—Smoky Night. 1995. (Illus.). 15.00 o.p. (*0-15-201035-1*) Harcourt Trade Pubs.

—Smoky Night. 1999. 12.15 (*0-606-16515-0*) Turtleback Bks.

Byng, Georgia. Molly Moon, Vol. 2. 2004. (Illus.). 384p. (J). 16.99 (*0-06-051410-8*); lib. bdg. 17.89 (*0-06-051413-2*) HarperCollins Pubs.

Cannell, Stephen J. The Tin Collectors. 2002. 384p. reprint ed. mass mkt. 6.99 (*0-312-97951-7*, St. Martin's Paperbacks) St. Martin's Pr.

Ciencin, Scott & Jolley, Dan. Vengeance. 2002. (Angel Ser.: Bk. 14). 352p. (YA). (gr. 11 up). pap. 5.99 (*0-7434-2754-8*, Simon Pulse) Simon & Schuster Children's Publishing.

Conn, Nicole. Angel Wings. 1997. 208p. 22.50 (*0-684-83205-4*, Simon & Schuster) Simon & Schuster.

English, Karen. Strawberry Moon, RS. 2001. 128p. (J). (gr. 4-6). 16.00 (*0-374-47122-3*, Farrar, Straus & Giroux (BYR)) Farrar, Straus & Giroux.

Escandon, Maria Amparo. Esperanza's Box of Saints: A Novel. 1999. 256p. pap. 12.00 (*0-684-85614-X*, Touchstone) Simon & Schuster.

—Esperanza's Box of Saints: A Novel. 1999. 18.05 (*0-606-16079-5*) Turtleback Bks.

Espenson, Jane. Haunted. 2002. (Buffy the Vampire Slayer Ser.). (Illus.). 96p. (YA). pap. 12.95 (*1-56971-737-0*) Dark Horse Comics.

Eulo, Ken & Mauck, Joe. Claw. 320p. 3.98 o.p. (*0-7651-0133-5*) Smithmark Pubs., Inc.

Ewing, Lynne. The Choice. 2003. (Daughters of the Moon Ser.: No. 9). 192p. (J). 9.99 (*0-7868-0851-9*, Volo) Hyperion Bks. for Children.

—Daughters of the Moon. 2000. 160p. (YA). pap. 4.99 (*0-7868-1409-8*);Vol. 2. pap. 4.99 (*0-7868-1410-1*) Disney Pr.

—Goddess of the Night. 2000. (Daughters of the Moon Ser.: Vol. 1). 294p. (J). (gr. 5-9). 9.99 (*0-7868-0653-2*) Disney Pr.

—Into the Cold Fire. 2000. (Daughters of the Moon Ser.: Vol. 2). (Illus.). 264p. (J). (gr. 5-9). 9.99 (*0-7868-0654-0*) Hyperion Bks. for Children.

—The Lost One. 2001. (Daughters of the Moon Ser.: No. 6). 288p. (J). 9.99 (*0-7868-0707-5*, Volo) Hyperion Bks. for Children.

—Moon Demon. 2002. (Daughters of the Moon Ser.: No. 7). 288p. (J). 9.99 (*0-7868-0849-7*, Volo) Hyperion Bks. for Children.

—Night Shade. 2001. (Daughters of the Moon Ser.: Vol. 3). 288p. (J). (gr. 5-9). 9.99 (*0-7868-0708-3*, Volo) Hyperion Bks. for Children.

—Party Girl. 1998. (gr. 9-12). 144p. (J). 17.99 o.s.i (*0-679-99285-5*); 128p. (YA). 16.00 o.s.i (*0-679-89285-0*) Random Hse. Children's Bks. (Random Hse. Bks. for Young Readers).

—Party Girl. 1999. 128p. (gr. 9-11). mass mkt. 4.99 (*0-375-80210-X*) Random Hse., Inc.

—Party Girl. 1999. 11.04 (*0-606-17373-0*) Turtleback Bks.

—The Sacrifice. 2001. (Daughters of the Moon Ser.: Bk. 5). 288p. (J). (gr. 7 up). 9.99 (*0-7868-0706-7*, Volo) Hyperion Bks. for Children.

—The Secret Scroll. 2001. (Daughters of the Moon Ser.: Vol. 4). 288p. (J). (gr. 5-9). reprint ed. pap. 9.99 (*0-7868-0709-1*, Volo) Hyperion Bks. for Children.

Fitch, Janet. Kicks. 1996. (J). (gr. 7). mass mkt. 4.50 o.s.i (*0-449-70452-1*, Fawcett) Ballantine Bks.

—Kicks. 1995. 192p. (J). (gr. 7 up). tchr. ed. 14.95 o.p. (*0-395-69624-0*, Clarion Bks.) Houghton Mifflin Co. Trade & Reference Div.

Fleischman, Paul. Breakout. 2003. (YA). 16.95 (*0-8126-2696-6*) Cricket Bks.

Fleischman, Sid. Disappearing Act. 2003. (Illus.). 144p. (J). (gr. 3-7). 15.99 (*0-06-051962-2*); lib. bdg. 16.89 (*0-06-051963-0*) HarperCollins Children's Bk. Group. (Greenwillow Bks.).

Francesca, Lia. Wasteland. 2003. 160p. (J). lib. bdg. 16.89 (*0-06-028645-8*, Cotler, Joanna Bks.) HarperCollins Children's Bk. Group.

Garcia, Victor A. Con Safos. 1997. 88p. (YA). (gr. 9-12). pap. 10.00 o.p. (*0-8059-4029-4*) Dorrance Publishing Co., Inc.

Haugaard, Kay. No Place. 1999. (Illus.). 208p. (J). (gr. 3-8). 15.95 (*1-57131-616-7*); pap. 6.95 (*1-57131-617-5*) Milkweed Editions.

—No Place. 1999. (J). 13.00 (*0-606-19034-1*) Turtleback Bks.

Holder, Nancy. City of Angel. 1999. (Angel Ser.: No. 1). 192p. (YA). (gr. 7 up). pap. 4.99 (*0-671-04144-4*, Simon Pulse) Simon & Schuster Children's Publishing.

—Not Forgotten. 2000. (Angel Ser.: No. 2). 256p. (YA). (gr. 7 up). mass mkt. 5.99 (*0-671-04145-2*, Simon Pulse) Simon & Schuster Children's Publishing.

Johnston, Tony. Angel City. 2002. (Illus.). (J). (*0-399-23405-5*, Philomel) Penguin Putnam Bks. for Young Readers.

—Any Small Goodness: A Novel of the Barrio. 128p. (J). 2003. mass mkt. 4.99 (*0-439-23384-4*, Scholastic Paperbacks); 2001. (Illus.). (gr. 4 up). pap. 15.95 (*0-439-18936-5*, Blue Sky Pr., The) Scholastic, Inc.

Klass, David. Screen Test. 1997. 256p. (J). (gr. 7-12). pap. 16.95 (*0-590-48592-X*) Scholastic, Inc.

Koertge, Ronald. Harmony Arms. 1992. (YA). 15.95 o.p. (*0-316-50104-2*, Joy Street Bks.) Little Brown & Co.

Lachtman, Ofelia Dumas. The Summer of El Pintor. 2001. (Illus.). 234p. (J). (gr. 11 up). pap. 9.95 (*1-55885-327-8*) Arte Publico Pr.

Mariotte, Jeff. Haunted. 2002. (Angel Ser.: Vol. 11). (Illus.). 336p. (YA). pap. 5.99 (*0-7434-2748-3*, Simon Pulse) Simon & Schuster Children's Publishing.

—Stranger to the Sun. 2002. (Angel Ser.: Bk. 13). (Illus.). 304p. (YA). (gr. 11 up). pap. 5.99 (*0-7434-2752-1*, Simon Pulse) Simon & Schuster Children's Publishing.

Miklowitz, Gloria D. The Enemy Has a Face. (YA). 2004. 143p. pap. 8.00 (*0-8028-5261-0*); 2003. 148p. 16.00 (*0-8028-5243-2*) Eerdmans, William B. Publishing Co. (Eerdmans Bks For Young Readers).

Mills, Bart. Melrose Place - Off the Record. 1992. 79p. (YA). mass mkt. 3.99 o.p. (*0-06-106787-3*, Harper-Torch) Morrow/Avon.

Myers, Bill. The Scream: Forbidden Doors 09. 1998. (Forbidden Doors Ser.: Vol. 9). 160p. mass mkt. 4.99 o.p. (*0-8423-5970-2*) Tyndale Hse. Pubs.

Nelson, Peter. Melrose Place. 1992. 79p. (YA). mass mkt. 3.99 o.p. (*0-06-106788-1*, HarperTorch) Morrow/Avon.

Odom, Mel. Image. 2002. (Angel Ser.: Bk. 12). (Illus.). 336p. (YA). pap. 5.99 (*0-7434-2750-5*, Simon Pulse) Simon & Schuster Children's Publishing.

Reed, Philip. Low Rider. 1999. 320p. pap. 6.50 (*0-671-00167-1*, Pocket) Simon & Schuster.

Reeve, Kirk. Lolo & Red-Legs. 1998. 100p. (J). (gr. 2-5). lib. bdg. 12.95 o.p. (*0-87358-683-2*) Northland Publishing.

—Lolo & Red Legs. 1998. (Illus.). 100p. (J). (gr. 3-6). pap. 6.95 o.p. (*0-87358-684-0*, Rising Moon Bks. for Young Readers) Northland Publishing.

Riefe, Barbara. Amelia Dale Archer Story. 1998. 304p. (YA). (gr. 8 up). 22.95 o.p. (*0-312-86077-3*, Forge Bks.) Doherty, Tom Assocs., LLC.

Rocklin, Joanne. Jace the Ace. 1990. (Illus.). 112p. (J). (gr. 2-6). lib. bdg. 13.95 o.s.i (*0-02-777445-7*, Simon & Schuster Children's Publishing) Simon & Schuster Children's Publishing.

Sisters in Crime, Los Angeles Chapter Staff. Murder by Thirteen. English, Priscilla et al, eds. 1997. 176p. pap. 10.95 (*0-9647945-3-5*, Intrigue Pr.) Corvus Publishing.

Somtow, S. P. The Wizard's Apprentice. 1993. (Dragonflight Ser.: No. 7). (Illus.). 144p. (YA). (gr. 7 up). 14.95 o.s.i (*0-689-31576-7*, Atheneum) Simon & Schuster Children's Publishing.

—The Wizard's Apprentice. 2002. (J). E-Book (*1-58824-702-3*); 1993. E-Book (*1-58824-703-1*); 1993. E-Book (*1-58824-908-5*) ipicturebooks, LLC.

Sones, Sonya. Miserably Yours, Ruby. 2004. (J). (*0-689-85820-5*, Simon & Schuster Children's Publishing) Simon & Schuster Children's Publishing.

Soto, Gary. Chato & the Party Animals. 2000. (Illus.). 32p. (J). (ps-3). 15.99 (*0-399-23159-5*, G. P. Putnam's Sons) Penguin Group (USA) Inc.

—Chato & the Party Animals. 2004. (Illus.). 32p. (J). 6.99 (*0-14-240032-7*, Puffin Bks.) Penguin Putnam Bks. for Young Readers.

—Chato y los Amigos Pachangueros. 2004. Tr. of Chato & the Party Animals. (Illus.). 32p. 7.99 (*0-14-240033-5*, Puffin Bks.) Penguin Putnam Bks. for Young Readers.

—Chato y Su Cena. Ada, Alma Flor, tr. 1998. (SPA., Illus.). (gr. k-3). pap., tchr. ed. 37.95 incl. audio (*0-87499-439-X*); (J). pap. 15.95 incl. audio (*0-87499-437-3*) Live Oak Media.

—Summer on Wheels. 1995. 176p. (J). (gr. 4-6). pap. 13.95 (*0-590-48365-X*) Scholastic, Inc.

Talbert, Marc. Star of Luis. 1999. 192p. (J). (gr. 5-9). tchr. ed. 15.00 (*0-395-91423-X*, Clarion Bks.) Houghton Mifflin Co. Trade & Reference Div.

Weisberg, Valerie H. Three Jolly Stories Include - Three Jollys, Jollys Visit L. A., Jolly Gets Mugged: An ESL Adult-Child Reader. 1985. (Jolly Ser.). (Illus.). 76p. (Orig.). (J). (gr. 4 up). pap. text 6.95 (*0-9610912-4-X*) VHW Publishing.

Woods, Brenda. The Red Rose Box. 2002. 160p. (J). (gr. 4-6). 16.99 (*0-399-23702-X*) Putnam Publishing Group, The.

LOUISIANA—FICTION

Burnett, Frances Hodgson. Louisiana. 2000. 252p. (J). E-Book 3.95 (*0-594-05578-4*) 1873 Pr.

Callen, Larry. Pinch. 1976. (Illus.). (J). (gr. 5 up). 14.95 o.p. (*0-316-12495-8*, Joy Street Bks.) Little Brown & Co.

Collins, Sheila Hebert. Cajun Fairy Tales, 3 vols. Incl. Jolie Blonde & the Three Herberts: A Cajun Twist to an Old Tale. 1993. lib. bdg. 14.95 o.p. (*1-884725-00-7*); Petite Rouge: Little Red Riding Hood - A Cajun Twist to an Old Tale. 1994. lib. bdg. 14.95 o.p. (*1-884725-02-3*); Trois Cochons: The Three Little Pigs - A Cajun Twist to an Old Tale. 1995. lib. bdg. 14.95 o.p. (*1-884725-09-0*); 32p. (J). (ps-7). (Illus.). 1995. 46.00 o.p. (*1-884725-16-3*) Blue Heron Pr.

—Jolie Blonde & the Three Heberts: A Cajun Twist to an Old Tale. 1999. 32p. (J). (gr. k-3). pap. 14.95 (*1-56554-324-6*) Pelican Publishing Co., Inc.

—Les Trois Cochons: The Three Little Pigs - A Cajun Twist to an Old Tale. 1995. (Cajun Fairy Tales Ser.: No. 3). (Illus.). 32p. (J). (ps-7). lib. bdg. 14.95 o.p. (*1-884725-09-0*) Blue Heron Pr.

Connolly, John. Every Dead Thing. 2000. 480p. reprint ed. pap. 6.99 (*0-671-02731-X*, Pocket) Simon & Schuster.

Couvillon, Alice W. & Moore, Elizabeth. Mimi & Jean-Paul's Cajun Mardi Gras. 1996. (Illus.). 32p. (J). (ps-3). 14.95 (*1-56554-069-7*) Pelican Publishing Co., Inc.

Crockem, Linda. 1 2 3 Louisiana & Me. 1989. 12p. (J). (ps). 14.99 (*1-887637-01-X*, TX378468) First Bk. Productions.

Cusick, Richie Tankersley. Evil on the Bayou. 1992. 160p. (J). (gr. 7 up). mass mkt. 3.50 o.s.i (*0-440-92431-6*, Laurel Leaf) Random Hse. Children's Bks.

Davis, David. Jazz Cats. 2001. (Illus.). 32p. (J). (gr. 2-4). 14.95 (*1-56554-859-0*) Pelican Publishing Co., Inc.

Doucet, Sharon Arms. Fiddle Fever. l.t. ed. 2001. 174p. (J). 20.95 (*0-7862-3548-9*) Gale Group.

—Fiddle Fever. 2000. (Illus.). 176p. (J). (gr. 5-9). tchr. ed. 15.00 (*0-618-04324-1*, Clarion Bks.) Houghton Mifflin Co. Trade & Reference Div.

Duey, Kathleen. Louisiana Hurricane, 1860. 2000. (Illus.). (J). 11.04 (*0-606-18802-9*) Turtleback Bks.

—Louisiana Hurricane 1860. 2000. (Historical Romance Ser.). 256p. (YA). pap. 4.99 (*0-671-03926-1*, Simon Pulse) Simon & Schuster Children's Publishing.

Duey, Kathleen & Bale, Karen. Swamp, Bayou Teche, Louisiana, 1851. 1999. (Survival! Ser.: No. 11). 10.04 (*0-606-16302-6*) Turtleback Bks.

Duey, Kathleen & Bale, Karen A. Swamp: Bayou Teche, Louisiana 1851. 1999. (Survival! Ser.: No. 11). 160p. (J). (gr. 4-7). pap. 4.50 (*0-689-82929-9*, 076714004504, Aladdin) Simon & Schuster Children's Publishing.

Elder, Tim. Crawfish-Man Rescues Ron Guidry. deluxe ed. 1980. (Louisiana Crawfish-Man's Tales from the Atchafalaya Ser.). (Illus.). (J). (gr. k-8). spiral bd. 8.00 (*0-931108-05-5*) Little Cajun Bks.

—Crawfish-Man Rescues the Ol' Beachcomber. deluxe ed. 1985. (Louisiana Crawfish-Man's Tales from the Atchafalaya Ser.). (Illus.). 32p. (J). (gr. k-8). spiral bd. 8.00 (*0-931108-13-6*) Little Cajun Bks.

Finley, Martha. Elsie's True Love. 2000. (Elsie Dinsmore: Bk. 5). 224p. (J). (gr. 5-9). 9.99 (*1-928749-05-4*) Mission City Pr., Inc.

Fontenot, Mary Alice. Clovis Crawfish & Batiste Bete Puante. 1993. (Illus.). 32p. (J). (ps-3). 14.95 (*0-88289-952-X*) Pelican Publishing Co., Inc.

—Clovis Crawfish & Bertile's Bon Voyage. 1991. (Clovis Crawfish Ser.). (Illus.). 32p. (J). (ps-3). 14.95 (*0-88289-825-6*) Pelican Publishing Co., Inc.

—Clovis Crawfish & Bidon Box Turtle. 1996. (Clovis Crawfish Ser.: Vol. 14). (ENG & FRE., Illus.). 32p. (J). (ps-3). 14.95 (*1-56554-057-3*) Pelican Publishing Co., Inc.

—Clovis Crawfish & Echo Gecko. 2003. (Illus.). 32p. (J). 14.95 (*1-56554-708-X*) Pelican Publishing Co., Inc.

—Clovis Crawfish & Etienne Escargot. 2nd ed. 1992. (Clovis Crawfish Ser.). (Illus.). 32p. (J). (ps-3). 14.95 (*0-88289-826-4*) Pelican Publishing Co., Inc.

—Clovis Crawfish & Paillasse Poule d'Eau. 1997. (ENG & FRE., Illus.). 32p. (J). (gr. 1-4). 14.95 (*1-56554-144-8*) Pelican Publishing Co., Inc.

—Clovis Crawfish & Raoul Raccoon. 1999. (Clovis Crawfish Ser.). (Illus.). 32p. (J). (gr. k-3). 14.95 (*1-56554-369-6*) Pelican Publishing Co., Inc.

—Clovis Crawfish & Silvie Sulphur. 2003. (Illus.). 32p. (J). 15.95 (*1-56554-864-7*) Pelican Publishing Co., Inc.

—Clovis Crawfish & Simeon Suce-Fleur. 1990. (Clovis Crawfish Ser.). (Illus.). 32p. (J). (ps-3). 14.95 (*0-88289-751-9*) Pelican Publishing Co., Inc.

—Clovis Ecrevisse et Bidon Tortue Terrestre. 1996. (Clovis Crawfish Ser.). (FRE., Illus.). 32p. (J). (gr. k-3). 15.95 (*1-56554-218-5*) Pelican Publishing Co., Inc.

—Clovis Ecrevisse et l'Araignee Qui File. Landry, Julie F., tr. 1996. (Clovis Crawfish Ser.). (ENG & FRE., Illus.). 32p. (J). (gr. 1-4). 15.95 (*1-56554-220-7*) Pelican Publishing Co., Inc.

—Clovis Ecrevisse et l'Oiseau Orphelin. Landry, Julie F., tr. 1996. (Clovis Crawfish Ser.). (ENG & FRE., Illus.). 32p. (J). (gr. 1-4). 15.95 (*1-56554-219-3*) Pelican Publishing Co., Inc.

—Mardi Gras in the Country. 1994. (Illus.). 40p. (J). (ps-3). 12.95 (*1-56554-033-6*) Pelican Publishing Co., Inc.

Garrett, Ann. El Guardian del Pantano. 2001. (SPA., Illus.). 40p. (J). (gr. 3-5). pap. 8.95 (*1-890515-28-0*, TK30971) Turtle Bks.

—El Guardian del Pantano. Gutiérrez, Guillermo, tr. 1999. (SPA., Illus.). 40p. (J). (gr. 3-5). 16.95 (*1-890515-13-2*, TK2991) Turtle Bks.

—Keeper of the Swamp. (Illus.). 40p. 2001. (ps-3). pap. 8.95 (*1-890515-27-2*); 1999. (SPA., (J). (gr. 1-4). 16.95 (*1-890515-12-4*) Turtle Bks.

Gates, Susan. Cry Wolf. l.t. ed. 2000. pap. 16.95 (*0-7540-6105-1*, Galaxy Children's Large Print) BBC Audiobooks America.

Gutman, Dan. The Million Dollar Shot. (J). 1997. (Illus.). 120p. (gr. 3-7). 13.95 o.p. (*0-7868-0334-7*); 1997. (Illus.). 120p. (gr. 3-7). lib. bdg. 14.49 o.p. (*0-7868-2275-9*); 2003. 128p. pap. 5.99 (*0-7868-1746-1*) Hyperion Bks. for Children.

—The Million Dollar Shot. 1997. 120p. (J). (gr. 3-7). pap. 4.99 (*0-7868-1220-6*) Hyperion Pr.

—The Million Dollar Shot. 1997. 11.04 (*0-606-15635-6*) Turtleback Bks.

Hebert-Collins, Sheila. Jean-Paul Hebert Was There. 2003. Tr. of Jean-Paul Hebert Etait La. (ENG & FRE., Illus.). (J). (*1-56554-928-7*) Pelican Publishing Co., Inc.

Holt, Kimberly Willis. Mister & Me. 1998. (Illus.). 80p. (J). (gr. 2-6). 13.99 (*0-399-23215-X*) Penguin Group (USA) Inc.

—My Louisiana Sky, ERS. 1998. 176p. (J). (gr. 4-7). 16.95 (*0-8050-5251-8*, Holt, Henry & Co. Bks. For Young Readers) Holt, Henry & Co.

—My Louisiana Sky. 208p. (YA). (gr. 5 up). 4.99 (*0-8072-8291-X*); 2000. 208p. (J). pap. 35.00 incl. audio (*0-8072-8290-1*, YA152SP); 1999. (J). (gr. 4-7). audio 22.00 (*0-553-52598-0*) Random Hse. Audio Publishing Group. (Listening Library).

—My Louisiana Sky. 2000. 208p. (gr. 5-9). pap. text 5.50 (*0-440-41570-5*, Yearling) Random Hse. Children's Bks.

—My Louisiana Sky. 2000. 11.04 (*0-606-17562-8*) Turtleback Bks.

Hughes, Alice D. Cajun Columbus. rev. ed. 1991. (Illus.). 40p. (J). (gr. k-4). 14.95 (*0-88289-875-2*) Pelican Publishing Co., Inc.

Johnson, Zenobia M. & Broussard, Lucretia-del J. Louisiana Reading Adventures. 1984. (Illus.). 32p. (Orig.). (J). (gr. 4-7). 3.50 (*0-9617411-0-4*) Johnson, Zenobia M.

Kovacs, Deborah. Brewster's Courage. 1992. (Illus.). 112p. (J). (gr. 2-6). pap. 14.00 o.p. (*0-671-74016-4*, Simon & Schuster Children's Publishing) Simon & Schuster Children's Publishing.

Kroll, Virginia L. Sweet Magnolia. 1995. (Illus.). 32p. (J). (ps-3). 15.95 (*0-88106-415-7*, Talewinds); pap. 6.95 (*0-88106-414-9*, Talewinds); lib. bdg. 15.88 o.p. (*0-88106-416-5*) Charlesbridge Publishing, Inc.

—Sweet Magnolia. 1995. (J). 13.10 (*0-606-09919-0*) Turtleback Bks.

LaFaye, A. Nissa's Place. 256p. (gr. 3-7). 2001. pap. 4.99 (*0-689-84250-3*, Aladdin); 1999. (Illus.). (J). 16.00 (*0-689-82610-9*, Simon & Schuster Children's Publishing) Simon & Schuster Children's Publishing.

—The Strength of Saints. 2002. 192p. (J). (gr. 4-9). 16.95 (*0-689-83200-1*, Simon & Schuster Children's Publishing) Simon & Schuster Children's Publishing.

—The Year of the Sawdust Man. 224p. (J). (gr. 3-7). 1999. (Illus.). pap. 4.99 (*0-689-83106-4*, Aladdin); 1998. 16.00 (*0-689-81513-1*, Simon & Schuster Children's Publishing) Simon & Schuster Children's Publishing.

—The Year of the Sawdust Man. 1999. 11.04 (*0-606-17947-X*) Turtleback Bks.

Lane, Dakota. Johnny Voodoo. 1996. 224p. (J). (gr. 7 up). 15.95 o.s.i (*0-385-32230-5*, Delacorte Pr.) Dell Publishing.

Louisiana Crawfish-Man. The Ballad of Tont Lala. deluxe ed. (Illus.). 32p. (J). (gr. k-8). 6.00 o.p. (*0-931108-11-X*) Little Cajun Bks.

MacBride, Roger Lea. On the Banks of the Bayou. 1998. (Little House Ser.: Vol. 1). (Illus.). 240p. (J). (gr. 3-7). 15.95 (*0-06-024973-0*) HarperCollins Children's Bk. Group.

—On the Banks of the Bayou. 1998. (Little House Ser.). 11.00 (*0-606-15660-7*) Turtleback Bks.

Mire, Betty. T-Pierre Frog & T-Felix Frog Go to School. 1994. (Illus.). 32p. (Orig.). (J). (gr. 1-3). lib. bdg. 6.95 (*0-9639378-0-4*) Cajun Bayou Pr.

Moore, Diane M. Martin's Quest. 1995. (Illus.). (Orig.). (J). (gr. 5-12). 10.00 (*1-884725-12-0*) Blue Heron Pr.

Nixon, Joan Lowery. The Haunting. 1998. 192p. (YA). (gr. 7-12). 15.95 o.s.i (*0-385-32247-X*) Doubleday Publishing.

—The Haunting. Horowitz, Beverly, ed. 2000. 192p. (YA). (gr. 7-12). mass mkt. 4.99 (*0-440-22008-4*, Laurel Leaf) Random Hse. Children's Bks.

—The Haunting. l.t. ed. 2000. (Illus.). 224p. (J). (ps up). 21.95 (*0-7862-2739-7*) Thorndike Pr.

—The Haunting. 2000. (YA). 11.04 (*0-606-19191-7*) Turtleback Bks.

Perales, Andre P. Fanfou dans les Bayous: The Adventures of a Bilingual Elephant in Louisiana. 1982. (Illus.). 40p. (J). (gr. 1-7). pap. 7.95 o.s.i (*0-88289-378-5*); audio 11.95 (*0-88289-410-2*) Pelican Publishing Co., Inc.

Pockets Learning Staff. Samantha's Louisiana Adventure. 1998. (Illus.). 2p. (YA). (ps-1). 15.00 (*1-888074-92-2*) Pockets of Learning.

Raphael, Morris. The Loup-Garou of Cote Gelee. 1990. (Illus.). 48p. (J). (gr. 3-9). 19.95 (*0-9608866-7-2*) Raphael, Morris Bks.

—Maria: Goddess of the Teche. 1991. (Illus.). 48p. (J). (gr. 4-9). 19.95 (*0-9608866-8-0*) Raphael, Morris Bks.

—Ti-Nute, the Angel of Devil's Pond. 2000. (Illus.). 47p. (J). (*0-8187-0332-6*) Harlo Pr.

Rice, James. Gaston Goes to Mardi Gras Coloring Book. 2000. (Illus.). 32p. (J). (ps-3). pap. 3.25 (*1-56554-773-X*) Pelican Publishing Co., Inc.

—The Ghost of Pont Diable. 1996. (Illus.). 176p. (J). (gr. 5-8). 14.95 o.p. (*1-57168-109-4*); pap. 8.95 o.p. (*1-57168-130-2*) Eakin Pr.

Schadler, Cherie D. Welcome to Bayou Town! 1996. (Illus.). 32p. (J). (gr. 1-4). 14.95 (*1-56554-161-8*) Pelican Publishing Co., Inc.

Shaik, Fatima. Melitte. 160p. (J). (gr. 5-9). 1999. (Illus.). pap. 4.99 o.s.i (*0-14-130420-0*, Puffin Bks.); 1997. 15.99 o.s.i (*0-8037-2106-4*, Dial Bks. for Young Readers) Penguin Putnam Bks. for Young Readers.

—Melitte. 2000. 11.04 (*0-606-18432-5*) Turtleback Bks.

Smith, Debra. Hattie Marshall & the Mysterious Strangers. 1996. (Hattie Marshall Frontier Adventure Ser.: Vol. 3). 128p. (J). (gr. 7 up). pap. 4.99 o.p. (*0-89107-878-9*) Crossway Bks.

Smith, Debra West. Yankees on the Doorstep: The Story of Sarah Morgan. 2001. (Illus.). 176p. (J). (gr. 3-7). pap. 10.95 (*1-56554-872-8*) Pelican Publishing Co., Inc.

Snellings, M. L. Jessie Strikes Louisiana Gold. 1969. (J). (gr. 3-7). 3.95 (*0-87511-116-5*) Claitor's Publishing Div.

Stonecipher, Philiip. Boudreau of de Bayou. Perez Sanchez, Delia, tr. from ENG. 1999. (ENG & SPA., Illus.). ii, 22p. (J). (gr. 2-3). 6.95 (*0-943864-92-5*) Davenport, May Pubs.

Thomassie, Tynia. Cajun Through & Through. 2000. (Illus.). 32p. (J). (ps-3). 14.95 o.p. (*0-316-84189-7*) Little Brown & Co.

—Cajun Through & Through. 2000. (Illus.). E-Book (*1-58824-630-2*); E-Book (*1-58824-631-0*); E-Book 9.99 (*1-58824-872-0*) ipicturebooks, LLC.

—Feliciana Feydra LeRoux: A Cajun Tall Tale. 1995. (Illus.). 32p. (J). (ps-3). 14.95 o.p. (*0-316-84125-0*) Little Brown & Co.

—Feliciana Feydra LeRoux: A Cajun Tall Tale. 1998. (J). 11.10 (*0-606-13380-1*) Turtleback Bks.

—Feliciana Feydra LeRoux Meets d'Loup Garou: A Cajun Tall Tale. 1998. (Illus.). 32p. (J). (ps-3). 15.95 o.p. (*0-316-84133-1*) Little Brown & Co.

Walker, Mary A. To Catch a Zombi. 1979. 204p. (J). (gr. 7-10). 8.95 o.s.i (*0-689-30725-X*, Atheneum) Simon & Schuster Children's Publishing.

Wallace, Bill. Blackwater Swamp. 1994. 208p. (J). (gr. 4-7). tchr. ed. 15.95 (*0-8234-1120-6*) Holiday Hse., Inc.

—Blackwater Swamp. MacDonald, Patricia, ed. 1995. 192p. (YA). (gr. 3 up). pap. 4.50 (*0-671-51156-4*, Aladdin) Simon & Schuster Children's Publishing.

—Blackwater Swamp. 1995. 10.55 (*0-606-07294-2*) Turtleback Bks.

Walter, Mildred Pitts. Trouble's Child. 1985. 128p. (J). (gr. 4 up). 11.95 o.p. (*0-688-04214-7*) HarperCollins Children's Bk. Group.

White, Jack N. The Canebrake Kids: The Trip to Texas. 1996. (Illus.). 120p. (J). (gr. 4-6). 12.95 o.p. (*1-57168-111-6*) Eakin Pr.

Woods, Brenda. The Red Rose Box. 2002. 160p. (J). (gr. 4-6). 16.99 (*0-399-23702-X*) Putnam Publishing Group, The.

M

MACKINAC ISLAND (MICH.)—FICTION

Hale, Anna W. Mystery on Mackinac Island. 5th rev. ed. 1997. (Illus.). 183p. (J). (gr. 4-7). pap. 10.95 (*1-882376-48-X*) Thunder Bay Pr.

Lytle, Robert A. Mackinac Passage: The General's Treasure. 1997. (Illus.). 172p. (YA). (gr. 4-7). pap. 12.95 (*1-882376-45-5*) Thunder Bay Pr.

Panagopoulos, Janie Lynn. A Castle at the Straits. 2003. (Illus.). 48p. (J). (gr. 1-6). 18.95 (*0-911872-83-3*) Mackinac State Historic Parks.

Whelan, Gloria. Farewell to the Island. 1998. 208p. (J). (gr. 4 up). 16.95 (*0-06-027751-3*) HarperCollins Children's Bk. Group.

—Once on This Island. (Trophy Bk.). 192p. (J). 1996. (gr. 3-7). pap. 5.99 (*0-06-440619-9*, Harper Trophy); 1995. (gr. k-3). 16.99 (*0-06-026248-6*); 1995. (gr. 3-7). lib. bdg. 14.89 (*0-06-026249-4*) HarperCollins Children's Bk. Group.

—Once on This Island. 1996. (J). 11.00 (*0-606-09709-0*) Turtleback Bks.

—Return to the Island. 2000. 192p. (J). (gr. 4). lib. bdg. 15.89 (*0-06-028254-1*); 14.95 (*0-06-028253-3*) HarperCollins Children's Bk. Group.

—Return to the Island. 2002. 192p. (J). (gr. 4-7). pap. 5.95 (*0-06-440761-6*) HarperCollins Pubs.

MADAGASCAR—FICTION

Dennard, Deborah. Lemur Landing: A Story of a Madagascan Dry Tropical Forest. 2001. (Wild Habitats Ser.). (Illus.). 36p. (J). (gr. 1-4). 15.95 (*1-56899-978-X*); 19.95 incl. audio (*1-56899-980-1*); 26.95 (*1-56899-982-8*); pap. 16.95 (*1-56899-983-6*) Soundprints.

Dennard, Deborah & Kest, Kristin. Lemur Landing: A Story of a Madagascan Dry Tropical Forest. 2001. (Wild Habitats Ser.). (Illus.). 36p. (J). (gr. 1-4). pap. 5.95 (*1-56899-979-8*) Soundprints.

McCaughrean, Geraldine. The Pirate's Son. 1998. 224p. (YA). (gr. 5-9). 16.95 o.s.i (*0-590-20344-4*) Scholastic, Inc.

MAINE—FICTION

Agell, Charlotte, illus. Welcome Home or Someplace Like It, ERS. 2003. 240p. (J). 16.95 (*0-8050-7083-4*, Holt, Henry & Co. Bks. For Young Readers) Holt, Henry & Co.

Austad, Julie. Uncle's Trunk: A Shadows in the Dark Book. 2001. 134p. pap. 20.99 (*0-7388-9943-7*) Xlibris Corp.

Austin, Heather. Visiting Aunt Sylvia's: A Maine Adventure. 2002. (Illus.). 32p. (J). (gr. k-3). 15.95 (*0-89272-523-0*) Down East Bks.

Bartlett, Susan. Seal Island School. Bonnell, J., ed. 2001. (Chapter Ser.). (Illus.). 80p. (J). (gr. 2-5). pap. 4.99 (*0-14-131104-5*, Puffin Bks.) Penguin Putnam Bks. for Young Readers.

—Seal Island School. 1999. (Illus.). 80p. (J). (gr. 2-5). 15.99 (*0-670-88349-2*) Penguin Putnam Bks. for Young Readers.

Beckhorn, Susan Williams. Sarey by Lantern Light. 2003. (Illus.). 160p. (J). pap. 10.95 (*0-89272-612-1*) Down East Bks.

Brown, Margaret Wise. The Little Island. (Illus.). 48p. (J). Date not set. 14.95 (*0-385-74640-7*); 2003. lib. bdg. 16.99 (*0-385-90872-5*) Doubleday Bks. for Young Readers CAN. *Dist:* Random Hse. of Canada, Ltd.

Brown, Margaret Wise & MacDonald, Golden. The Little Island. 1973. (Dell Picture Yearling Ser.). (J). 13.14 (*0-606-05908-3*) Turtleback Bks.

Bryant, Sally S. Here's Juggins. 1996. (Illus.). 176p. (J). (gr. 4-7). 19.95 (*0-945980-62-0*) North Country Pr.

Buzzeo, Toni. The Sea Chest. 2002. (Illus.). 32p. (J). (gr. k up). 16.99 (*0-8037-2703-8*, Dial Bks. for Young Readers) Penguin Putnam Bks. for Young Readers.

Chetkowski, Emily. Mabel Takes a Sail. 1999. (Illus.). 64p. (J). (ps-3). pap. 10.50 (*1-880158-26-4*) Townsend, J.N. Publishing.

—Mabel Takes the Ferry. 2001. (Illus.). 40p. (J). 11.95 (*1-880158-37-X*) Townsend, J.N. Publishing.

Cooney, Barbara. The Kellyhorns. 2001. (Lost Treasures Ser.: No. 1). 352p. (J). (Illus.). (gr. 3-7). reprint ed. pap. 1.99 (*0-7868-1522-1*);Bk. 3. pap. 4.99 (*0-7868-1523-X*) Hyperion Bks. for Children. (Volo).

Copeland, Cynthia L. Elin's Island. 2003. (Single Titles Ser.: up). 144p. lib. bdg. 22.90 (*0-7613-2522-0*) Millbrook Pr., Inc.

Crossman, David A. The Secret of the Missing Grave. 1999. (Bean & Ab Mystery Ser.). 184p. (YA). (gr. 4-10). 16.95 (*0-89272-456-0*) Down East Bks.

Deans, Sis Boulos. Every Day & All the Time, ERS. 2003. 240p. (J). 16.95 (*0-8050-7337-X*, Holt, Henry & Co. Bks. For Young Readers) Holt, Henry & Co.

Du Jardin, Rosamond. Someone to Count On. 1962. (J). (gr. 4-9). lib. bdg. 6.95 o.p. (*0-397-30636-9*) HarperCollins Children's Bk. Group.

Flanagan, James M. Builders of Maine. 1994. 400p. (YA). pap. 10.00 (*0-932433-86-3*) Windswept Hse. Pubs.

Futcher, Jane. Promise Not to Tell. 1991. 192p. (J). (gr. 4-5). pap. 2.95 (*0-380-76037-1*, Avon Bks.) Morrow/Avon.

Garden, Nancy. Meeting Melanie, RS. 2002. 208p. (J). (gr. 5 up). 16.00 (*0-374-34943-6*, Farrar, Straus & Giroux (BYR)) Farrar, Straus & Giroux.

Garfield, Henry. Tartabull's Throw. (Illus.). 2003. 304p. (YA). pap. 5.99 (*0-689-85671-7*, Simon Pulse); 2001. 272p. (J). (gr. 7 up). 16.00 (*0-689-83840-9*, Atheneum/Richard Jackson Bks.) Simon & Schuster Children's Publishing.

Goodrich, Beatrice. Happy Hollow Stories. (gr. k-6). Bk. 1. 1987. (Illus.). 54p. (J). pap. 5.95 (*0-932433-20-0*); Bk. 2. 1988. pap. 5.95 o.s.i (*0-932433-35-9*) Windswept Hse. Pubs.

—Happy Hollow Stories, Bk. 3. Weinberger, Jane, ed. 1989. (Illus.). 84p. pap. 5.95 (*0-932433-51-0*) Windswept Hse. Pubs.

Hahn, Mary Downing. Look for Me by Moonlight. 1997. 192p. (J). (gr. 7 up). pap. 5.99 (*0-380-72703-X*, Harper Trophy) HarperCollins Children's Bk. Group.

—Look for Me by Moonlight. 1995. (YA). 208p. (gr. 7 up). tchr. ed. 16.00 (*0-395-69843-X*); E-Book 16.00 (*0-618-15205-9*) Houghton Mifflin Co.

—Look for Me by Moonlight. 1997. (J). 10.55 (*0-606-11573-0*) Turtleback Bks.

Harlow, Joan Hiatt. Shadows on the Sea. 2003. (Illus.). 256p. (J). (gr. 3-6). 16.95 (*0-689-84926-5*, McElderry, Margaret K.) Simon & Schuster Children's Publishing.

—Shadows on the Sea. 2004. (J). (*0-7862-6145-5*) Thorndike Pr.

Holmes, Barbara Ware. Following Fake Man. 2001. (Illus.). 240p. (gr. 5-9). text 15.95 (*0-375-81266-0*); lib. bdg. 17.99 (*0-375-91266-5*) Random Hse. Children's Bks. (Knopf Bks. for Young Readers).

Hopkinson, Deborah. Birdie's Lighthouse. 1996. 16.00 (*0-679-86998-0*) Random Hse., Inc.

—Birdie's Lighthouse. (Illus.). 32p. (J). (ps-3). 2000. pap. 5.99 (*0-689-83529-9*, Aladdin); 1997. 16.00 (*0-689-81052-0*, Atheneum/Anne Schwartz Bks.) Simon & Schuster Children's Publishing.

—Birdie's Lighthouse. 2000. (Illus.). (J). 12.14 (*0-606-17913-5*) Turtleback Bks.

Horvath, Polly. The Canning Season, RS. 2003. 208p. (YA). 16.00 (*0-374-39956-5*, Farrar, Straus & Giroux (BYR)) Farrar, Straus & Giroux.

—The Canning Season. 2004. (J). (*0-7862-6144-7*) Thorndike Pr.

Hotze, Sollace. Acquainted with the Night. 1992. 256p. (J). (gr. 4-7). 15.00 o.p. (*0-395-61576-3*, Clarion Bks.) Houghton Mifflin Co. Trade & Reference Div.

Howland, Ethan. The Lobster War. 2001. (Illus.). 146p. (J). (gr. 7 up). 15.95 (*0-8126-2800-4*) Cricket Bks.

Irwin, Hadley. The Original Freddie Ackerman. (Illus.). 192p. (YA). 1996. (gr. 4-7). pap. 4.50 (*0-689-80389-3*, Simon Pulse); 1992. (gr. 5 up). 15.00 (*0-689-50562-0*, McElderry, Margaret K.) Simon & Schuster Children's Publishing.

Janover, Caroline. How Many Days until Tomorrow? 2000. (Illus.). 173p. (J). (gr. 4-8). pap. 11.95 (*1-890627-22-4*) Woodbine Hse.

Jones, Dorothy H. & Sargent, Ruth S. Abbie Burgess: Lighthouse Heroine. 1976. (Illus.). 190p. (J). (gr. 7 up). pap. 3.75 o.p. (*0-89272-018-2*) Down East Bks.

Keizer, Garret. God of Beer. 256p. (J). 2003. pap. 6.99 (*0-06-447276-0*); 2002. (gr. 8 up). 15.95 (*0-06-029456-6*); 2002. (gr. 8 up). lib. bdg. 15.89 (*0-06-029457-4*) HarperCollins Children's Bk. Group.

Koller, Jackie French. The Last Voyage of the Misty Day. 1992. 160p. (J). (gr. 7-12). 14.00 (*0-689-31731-X*, Atheneum) Simon & Schuster Children's Publishing.

Kroll, Steven. Patrick's Tree House. 1994. (Illus.). 64p. (J). (gr. 2-5). mass mkt. 13.95 o.p. (*0-02-751005-0*, Simon & Schuster Children's Publishing) Simon & Schuster Children's Publishing.

Levin, Betty. Fire in the Wind. (J). 1997. (Illus.). 144p. (gr. 3-7). pap. 4.95 (*0-688-15495-6*, Harper Trophy); 1995. 176p. (gr. 7 up). 15.00 o.s.i (*0-688-14299-0*, Greenwillow Bks.) HarperCollins Children's Bk. Group.

—Fire in the Wind. 1997. 11.00 (*0-606-11327-4*) Turtleback Bks.

—Island Bound. 1997. 224p. (YA). (gr. 5-9). 15.00 o.s.i (*0-688-15217-1*, Greenwillow Bks.) HarperCollins Children's Bk. Group.

—That'll Do, Moss. 2002. (Illus.). 128p. (J). (gr. 3 up). 15.89 (*0-06-000532-7*); 15.95 (*0-06-000531-9*) HarperCollins Children's Bk. Group. (Greenwillow Bks.).

Love, Pamela. A Loon Alone. 2002. (J). (ps-2). (Illus.). 32p. 14.95 (*0-89272-571-0*); 29p. pap. text 9.95 (*0-89272-526-5*, 1078) Down East Bks.

Mariconda, Barbara. Turn the Cup Around. 1997. 160p. (J). (gr. 3-7). text 15.95 o.s.i (*0-385-32292-5*, Delacorte Pr.) Dell Publishing.

—Turn the Cup Around. 1998. 160p. (gr. 3-7). reprint ed. pap. text 3.99 o.s.i (*0-440-41311-7*, Yearling) Random Hse. Children's Bks.

—Turn the Cup Around. 1998. 10.04 (*0-606-13878-1*) Turtleback Bks.

Martin, Jacqueline Briggs. Grandmother Bryant's Pocket. (Illus.). 48p. (J). (ps-3). 2000. pap. 5.95 (*0-618-03309-2*); 1996. tchr. ed. 14.95 (*0-395-68984-8*) Houghton Mifflin Co.

—Grandmother Bryant's Pocket. 2000. (Illus.). (J). 12.10 (*0-606-18209-8*) Turtleback Bks.

McCloskey, Robert. Blueberries for Sal. 2002. (Illus.). (J). 14.04 (*0-7587-0097-0*) Book Wholesalers, Inc.

—Blueberries for Sal. 2000. (J). pap. 19.97 incl. audio (*0-7366-9193-6*) Books on Tape, Inc.

—Blueberries for Sal. ed. 1980. (J). (gr. 2). spiral bd. (*0-616-01715-4*) Canadian National Institute for the Blind/Institut National Canadien pour les Aveugles.

—Blueberries for Sal. (StoryTape Ser.). (Illus.). (J). 1993. 9.99 (*0-14-095110-5*, Puffin Bks.); 1989. 6.95 o.p. (*0-14-095032-X*, Puffin Bks.); 1976. 64p. pap. 6.99 (*0-14-050169-X*, Puffin Bks.); 1948. 56p. 16.99 (*0-670-17591-9*, Viking Children's Bks.) Penguin Putnam Bks. for Young Readers.

—Blueberries for Sal. 1976. (Picture Puffin Ser.). (Illus.). (J). 12.14 (*0-606-01675-9*) Turtleback Bks.

—Blueberries for Sal. (J). (ps-k). pap. text 12.95 incl. audio Weston Woods Studios, Inc.

—Burt Dow: Deep-Water Man. 1963. (Illus.). 64p. (J). (gr. 4-6). 19.99 (*0-670-19748-3*, Viking Children's Bks.) Penguin Putnam Bks. for Young Readers.

—Burt Dow: Deep-Water Man. 2001. (J). (gr. 1-4). 12.00 (*0-7887-5510-2*) Recorded Bks., LLC.

—Burt Dow: Deep-Water Man. 1990. (J). (ps-4). pap. text 12.95 incl. audio (*1-56008-101-5*, RAC262) Weston Woods Studios, Inc.

—One Morning in Maine. (Picture Puffin Bks.). (J). (ps-3). 1976. 62p. pap. 6.99 (*0-14-050174-6*, Puffin Bks.); 1952. (Illus.). 64p. 17.99 (*0-670-52627-4*, Viking Children's Bks.) Penguin Putnam Bks. for Young Readers.

—One Morning in Maine. 1976. (Picture Puffin Ser.). (Illus.). (J). 12.14 (*0-606-04247-4*) Turtleback Bks.

—Time of Wonder. 1957. (Illus.). 64p. (J). (ps-3). 19.99 (*0-670-71512-3*, Viking Children's Bks.) Penguin Putnam Bks. for Young Readers.

—Time of Wonder. 2001. (J). pap., stu. ed. 25.24 incl. audio Recorded Bks., LLC.

—Time of Wonder. 2000. (J). (ps-4). pap. 12.95 incl. audio Weston Woods Studios, Inc.

Mead, Alice. Walking the Edge. 1995. 192p. (J). (gr. 4-7). lib. bdg. 14.95 (*0-8075-8649-8*) Whitman, Albert & Co.

Molloy, Anne S. Girl from Two Miles High. 1967. (Illus.). (J). (gr. 4-6). lib. bdg. 6.95 o.p. (*0-8038-2602-8*) Hastings Hse. Daytrips Pubs.

Murphy, Catherine F. Songs in the Silence. 1994. 192p. (J). (gr. 3-7). 14.95 o.p. (*0-02-767730-3*, Simon & Schuster Children's Publishing) Simon & Schuster Children's Publishing.

Nugent, Matthew A. The Legend of Goose Rocks Beach. 2001. (Illus.). 84p. (YA). (gr. 3-8). pap. 14.95 (*0-9705812-0-3*) CBI Pr.

Packie, Robert M. Storm Treasure. 1981. (Illus.). 160p. (Orig.). (J). (gr. 6). 8.95 o.p. (*0-89272-082-4*) Down East Bks.

Page, Katherine Hall. Down East. (Christie & Company Ser.). (YA). (gr. 6-8). 1997. 160p. mass mkt. 14.00 o.p. (*0-380-97396-0*); 1998. reprint ed. pap. 3.99 (*0-380-78033-X*) Morrow/Avon. (Avon Bks.).

—Down East. 1998. (Christie & Company Ser.). (YA). (gr. 6-8). 9.09 o.p. (*0-606-13271-6*) Turtleback Bks.

Perrow, Angeli. Captain's Castaway. 1998. (Illus.). 32p. (J). (ps-3). 15.95 (*0-89272-419-6*) Down East Bks.

—Lighthouse Dog to the Rescue. (Illus.). (J). 2003. 30p. pap. 9.95 (*0-89272-600-8*); 2000. 32p. 14.95 (*0-89272-487-0*) Down East Bks.

Pickford, Susan B. The Fairy Houses of Monhegan Island. 1995. (Illus.). 8p. (Orig.). (J). (ps-6). pap. 5.95 (*1-889664-01-4*) SBP Collaboratioin Works.

Pochocki, Ethel. A Penny for a Hundred. 1996. (Illus.). 32p. (J). (gr. 3-6). 14.95 (*0-89272-392-0*) Down East Bks.

Rich, Louise D. Three of a Kind. 1970. (gr. 4-6). lib. bdg. 4.90 o.p. (*0-531-01837-7*, Watts, Franklin) Scholastic Library Publishing.

Sawyer, Ruth. Year of Jubilo. 1970. (gr. 4-7). pap. 1.50 o.p. (*0-440-49754-X*) Dell Publishing.

Simpson, Dorothy. Island in the Bay. 1993. 184p. (Orig.). (YA). (gr. 7-12). 9.95 (*0-942396-62-6*) Blackberry Maine.

Stengel, Joyce A. Mystery at Kittiwake Bay. 2001. 176p. (J). pap. 4.99 (*0-689-84595-2*, Aladdin) Simon & Schuster Children's Publishing.

Stolz, Mary. Seagulls Woke Me. 1951. (J). (gr. 8 up). lib. bdg. 12.89 o.p. (*0-06-026006-8*) HarperCollins Pubs.

Stone, Bruce. Autumn of the Royal Tar. 1995. (Laura Geringer Bks.). 168p. (YA). (gr. 5 up). 13.95 o.s.i (*0-06-021492-9*) HarperCollins Children's Bk. Group.

Sylvester, Natalie. Summer on Cleo's Island, RS. 1977. (Illus.). 48p. (J). (ps-3). 7.95 o.p. (*0-374-37295-0*, Farrar, Straus & Giroux (BYR)) Farrar, Straus & Giroux.

Testa, Maria. Some Kind of Pride. 128p. (gr. 3-7). 2003. pap. text 4.99 (*0-440-41669-8*, Laurel Leaf); 2001. (Illus.). text 14.95 (*0-385-32782-X*, Random Hse. Bks. for Young Readers) Random Hse. Children's Bks.

Voigt, Cynthia. Tree by Leaf. 1989. 176p. (J). (gr. 7 up). mass mkt. 4.50 o.s.i (*0-449-70334-7*, Fawcett) Ballantine Bks.

—Tree by Leaf. (J). (gr. 4-7). 2000. 240p. pap. 4.99 (*0-689-83527-2*, Aladdin); 1988. 208p. 15.95 (*0-689-31403-5*, Atheneum) Simon & Schuster Children's Publishing.

—Tree by Leaf. 1989. (J). 9.60 o.p. (*0-606-01223-0*) Turtleback Bks.

Wait, Lea. Stopping to Home. 160p. 2003. pap. 4.99 (*0-689-83849-2*, Aladdin); 2001. (Illus.). (J). (gr. 3-7). 16.00 (*0-689-83832-8*, McElderry, Margaret K.) Simon & Schuster Children's Publishing.

—Wintering Well. 2004. (J). (*0-689-85646-6*, McElderry, Margaret K.) Simon & Schuster Children's Publishing.

Waters, John F. Summer of the Seals. 1978. (Illus.). (J). (gr. 3-6). 6.95 o.p. (*0-7232-6155-5*, Warne, Frederick) Penguin Putnam Bks. for Young Readers.

Weber, Susan Bartlett. The Seal Island Seven. 2002. (Illus.). 80p. (J). (gr. 2-5). 15.99 (*0-670-03533-5*, Viking) Viking Penguin.

Wiggin, Eric. The Lesson of the Ancient Bones. 1996. (Hannah's Island Ser.: Bk. 4). 150p. (Orig.). (J). (gr. 3-7). pap. 5.99 (*1-883002-27-3*) Emerald Bks.

—Maggie: Life at the Elms. 1994. (Maggie Ser.). (J). mass mkt. 3.99 o.p. (*1-56507-133-6*) Harvest Hse. Pubs.

—Maggie's Homecoming. 1994. (Maggie Ser.). (J). mass mkt. 3.99 o.p. (*1-56507-134-4*) Harvest Hse. Pubs.

—Maggie's Secret Longing. 1995. (Maggie's World Ser.: Vol. 3). 165p. (Orig.). (J). (gr. 5-9). mass mkt. 3.99 o.p. (*1-56507-266-9*) Harvest Hse. Pubs.

—The Secret of the Old Well. 1996. (Hannah's Island Ser.: Bk. 5). 158p. (Orig.). (J). (gr. 3-7). pap. 5.99 (*1-883002-28-1*) Emerald Bks.

Woodruff, Elvira. The Ghost of Lizard Light. 1999. (Illus.). 192p. (YA). (gr. 5-8). 14.95 (*0-679-89281-8*); lib. bdg. 16.99 (*0-679-99281-2*) Knopf, Alfred A. Inc.

—The Ghost of Lizard Light. 2001. (Illus.). 192p. (gr. 3-7). pap. text 4.99 (*0-440-41655-8*, Yearling) Random Hse. Children's Bks.

MALAYA—FICTION

Conrad, Joseph. Lord Tim. unabr. ed. 1965. (Classics Ser.). (YA). (gr. 10 up). mass mkt. 1.95 o.p. (*0-8049-0054-X*, CL-54) Airmont Publishing Co., Inc.

—An Outcast of the Islands. (J). E-Book 2.49 (*0-7574-3104-6*) Electric Umbrella Publishing.

Means, Nathalie T. Aminah. 1979. 97p. (J). (gr. 6-8). 5.95 o.p. (*0-8059-2685-2*) Dorrance Publishing Co., Inc.

MALAYSIA—FICTION

Wingeier, Carol. Where the Jungle Meets the Street. Barth, Claire H., ed. 1976. (J). (gr. 4-5). pap. 2.95 o.p. (*0-377-00048-5*) Friendship Pr.

MALI—FICTION

Burns, Khephra. Mansa Musa: The Lion of Mali. 2001. (Illus.). 56p. (J). (gr. 3-5). 18.00 (*0-15-200375-4*, Gulliver Bks.) Harcourt Children's Bks.

Linklater, Andro. Amazing Maisie & the Cold Porridge Brigade. 1979. (Illus.). (J). (gr. 2-5). 5.95 o.p. (*0-394-84009-7*); lib. bdg. 5.99 o.p. (*0-394-94009-1*) Knopf Publishing Group. (Pantheon).

Winter, Jeanette. My Baby, RS. 2001. (Illus.). 32p. (J). (ps-1). 16.00 (*0-374-35103-1*, Farrar, Straus & Giroux (BYR)) Farrar, Straus & Giroux.

MALTA—FICTION

Clizbe, Kent. Xrina at Hagar Qim: The Temple Builders of Malta. 1998. (Children of Malta Ser.: Vol. 1). (Illus.). 40p. (J). (gr. k-5). pap. 12.95 (*0-9656252-1-4*, MAL001) O.T.S.

MARTHA'S VINEYARD (MASS.)—FICTION

Cross, Gilbert B. A Witch Across Time. 1990. 224p. (J). (gr. 6-9). lib. bdg. 14.95 o.p. (*0-689-31602-X*, Atheneum) Simon & Schuster Children's Publishing.

DeFelice, Cynthia C. Death at Devil's Bridge, RS. 2000. 192p. (J). (gr. 3-7). 16.00 (*0-374-31723-2*, Farrar, Straus & Giroux (BYR)) Farrar, Straus & Giroux.

—Death at Devil's Bridge. 2002. 192p. (J). (gr. 3-7). pap. 5.95 (*0-06-441037-4*, Harper Trophy) HarperCollins Children's Bk. Group.

Sanger, Richard. Holly's Hurricane. 1976. (Illus.). (J). (gr. 1-6). pap. 3.75 o.p. (*0-932384-02-1*) Tashmoo Pr., The.

MARTINIQUE—FICTION

Cendrillon.Tr. of Cinderella. (FRE.). 48p. pap. 12.95 incl. audio compact disk (*2-89558-065-0*) Coffragants CAN. *Dist:* Penton Overseas, Inc.

Perrault, Charles. Cendrillon. 2000. (FRE., Illus.). 32p. (J). 11.95 (*2-09-202114-1*) Nathan, Fernand FRA. *Dist:* Distribooks, Inc.

Stengel, Joyce A. Mystery of the Island Jewels. 2002. 208p. (J). (gr. 3-7). pap. 4.99 (*0-689-85049-2*, Aladdin) Simon & Schuster Children's Publishing.

MARYLAND—FICTION

Carbone, Elisa. Stealing Freedom. 272p. (gr. 5-8). 2001. (Illus.). (YA). pap. 5.50 (*0-440-41707-4*, Dell Books for Young Readers); 1998. lib. bdg. 18.99 o.s.i (*0-679-99307-X*, Random Hse. Bks. for Young Readers); 1998. (Illus.). (YA). 17.00 o.s.i (*0-679-89307-5*, Random Hse. Bks. for Young Readers) Random Hse. Children's Bks.

Conly, Jane Leslie. While No One Was Watching. 2000. 240p. (J). (gr. 7 up). pap. 5.99 (*0-06-440787-X*, Harper Trophy) HarperCollins Children's Bk. Group.

—While No One Was Watching. 2000. 11.00 (*0-606-18728-6*) Turtleback Bks.

Cummings, Priscilla. A Face First. 2003. 208p. (J). pap. 5.99 (*0-14-230247-3*, Puffin Bks.) Penguin Putnam Bks. for Young Readers.

—A Face First. Brooks, Donna, ed. 2001. 224p. (J). 16.99 (*0-525-46522-7*, Dutton Children's Bks.) Penguin Putnam Bks. for Young Readers.

Fuqua, Jonathon Scott. The Reappearance of Sam Webber. 1999. (Illus.). 232p. (YA). 23.95 (*1-890862-03-7*) Bancroft Pr.

—The Reappearance of Sam Webber. 2001. (Illus.). 288p. (J). reprint ed. bds. 9.99 (*0-7636-1424-6*) Candlewick Pr.

Hahn, Mary. Anna on the Farm. 2003. (Illus.). 160p. (J). pap. 5.99 (*0-06-441100-1*, Harper Trophy) HarperCollins Children's Bk. Group.

Hahn, Mary Downing. Anna All Year Round. 2001. (Illus.). 144p. (J). (gr. 4-7). pap. 4.95 (*0-380-73317-X*, Harper Trophy) HarperCollins Children's Bk. Group.

—Promises to the Dead. 2002. 208p. (J). (gr. 3 up). pap. 5.95 (*0-06-440982-1*, Harper Trophy) HarperCollins Children's Bk. Group.

Kimball, K. M. The Star Spangled Secret. 2001. (Mystery Ser.). 240p. (J). (gr. 5-7). pap. 4.99 (*0-689-84550-2*, Aladdin) Simon & Schuster Children's Publishing.

Leatherman, Diane. Rebecca, a Maryland Farm Girl. 2002. (J). (gr. 3-7). per. 7.95 (*0-9665861-1-5*) Leatherman, Diane.

Lockhart, Lynne N. & Lockhart, Barbara M. Rambling Raft. 1989. (Illus.). 30p. (J). (gr. 2 up). 7.95 (*0-87033-392-5*, Tidewater Pubs.) Cornell Maritime Pr., Inc.

McCully, Emily Arnold. The Battle for St. Michaels. 2002. (I Can Read Chapter Bks.). (Illus.). 64p. (J). (gr. 3 up). 15.99 (*0-06-028728-4*); lib. bdg. 17.89 (*0-06-028729-2*) HarperCollins Children's Bk. Group.

—The Battle for St. Michaels. 2004. (I Can Read Book 4 Ser.). 64p. (J). (gr. k-3). pap. 3.99 (*0-06-444278-0*) HarperCollins Pubs.

Mills, Charles. Storm on Shadow Mountain. 2003. (J). (*0-8163-1993-6*) Pacific Pr. Publishing Assn.

Troeger, Virginia B. Secret along the St. Mary's. Swisher, Michael-Che, tr. & illus. by. 2003. (Mysteries in Time Ser.). (J). (*1-893110-35-4*) Silver Moon Pr.

Williams, Barbara. Making Waves. 2000. (Illus.). 215p. (J). (gr. 4-8). 17.99 o.s.i (*0-8037-2515-9*, Dial Bks. for Young Readers) Penguin Putnam Bks. for Young Readers.

Winstead, Amy. The Star-Spangled Banner. Dacey, Bob & Bandelin, Debra, trs. 2003. (Illus.). 32p. (J). 16.95 (*0-8249-5462-9*, Ideals Pr.) Ideals Pubns.

MASSACHUSETTS—FICTION

Albrecht, Lillie V. Spinning Wheel Secret. 1965. (Illus.). (J). (gr. 4-6). lib. bdg. 3.99 o.p. (*0-8038-6668-2*) Hastings Hse. Daytrips Pubs.

Arciero, Susan. Nantucket 1, 2, 3. l.t. ed. 2000. (Illus.). (J). (ps). 7.95 (*0-9677548-2-8*) Pigtail Publishing.

Avi. Emily Upham's Revenge: Or How Deadwood Dick Saved the Banker's Niece. 1992. (Illus.). 192p. (J). 16.00 o.p. (*0-688-11898-4*, Morrow, William & Co.) Morrow/Avon.

—Emily Upham's Revenge: Or How Deadwood Dick Saved the Banker's Niece. ALC Staff, ed. 1992. (Illus.). 192p. (YA). (gr. 5 up). pap. 3.95 o.p. (*0-688-11899-2*, Morrow, William & Co.) Morrow/Avon.

Beckhorn, Susan Williams. The Kingfisher's Gift. 2002. (Illus.). 208p. (J). 17.99 (*0-399-23712-7*) Putnam Publishing Group, The.

Bulla, Clyde Robert. White Sails to China. 1955. (Illus.). (J). (gr. 2-5). 8.95 o.p. (*0-690-88712-4*); lib. bdg. 7.89 o.p. (*0-690-88713-2*) HarperCollins Children's Bk. Group.

Chetkowski, Emily. Amasa Walker's Spendid Garment. 2003. (Illus.). 48p. (J). (gr. 5-8). reprint ed. pap. 9.95 (*0-911469-21-4*) Hood, Alan C. & Co., Inc.

Christian, Mary Blount. Goody Sherman's Pig. 1991. (Illus.). 48p. (J). (gr. 2-6). text 12.95 o.p. (*0-02-718251-7*, Simon & Schuster Children's Publishing) Simon & Schuster Children's Publishing.

Cleveland-Peck, Patricia. City Cat, Country Cat. 1992. (Illus.). 32p. (J). (ps). lib. bdg. 13.93 o.p. (*0-688-11645-0*, Morrow, William & Co.) Morrow/Avon.

Cocca-Leffler, Maryann. Bus Route to Boston. 2003. (Illus.). 32p. (J). (gr. k-3). 15.95 (*1-56397-723-0*) Boyds Mills Pr.

Cohn, Rachel. Pop Princess. 2004. (Illus.). 320p. (J). 15.95 (*0-689-85205-3*, Simon & Schuster Children's Publishing) Simon & Schuster Children's Publishing.

Corcoran, Barbara. The Hideaway. 1987. 128p. (J). (gr. 5-9). 13.95 o.p. (*0-689-31353-5*, Atheneum) Simon & Schuster Children's Publishing.

Cormier, Robert. The Rag & Bone Shop. 2001. 160p. (YA). (gr. 7 up). lib. bdg. 17.99 (*0-385-90027-9*, Delacorte Pr.) Dell Publishing.

—The Rag & Bone Shop. l.t. ed. 2002. 141p. (J). 24.95 (*0-7862-3873-9*) Gale Group.

—The Rag & Bone Shop. 2001. (Illus.). 160p. (YA). (gr. 7 up). 15.95 (*0-385-72962-6*, Delacorte Bks. for Young Readers) Random Hse. Children's Bks.

Crowley, Maude. Azor & the Blue-Eyed Cow. 1980. (G. K. Hall Children's Literature Ser.). (J). lib. bdg. 7.95 o.p. (*0-8398-2605-2*, Macmillan Reference USA) Gale Group.

Curtis, Alice Turner. A Little Maid of Massachusetts Bay Colony. 2004. (Little Maid Ser.). (Illus.). 192p. (J). (gr. 4-7). reprint ed. pap. 9.95 (*1-55709-329-6*) Applewood Bks.

DeFelice, Cynthia C. Death at Devil's Bridge, RS. 2000. 192p. (J). (gr. 3-7). 16.00 (*0-374-31723-2*, Farrar, Straus & Giroux (BYR)) Farrar, Straus & Giroux.

—Death at Devil's Bridge. 2002. 192p. (J). (gr. 3-7). pap. 5.95 (*0-06-441037-4*, Harper Trophy) HarperCollins Children's Bk. Group.

Dell, Pamela. Giles & Metacom: A Story about Plimouth Colony & the Wampanoag. 2002. (Illus.). 48p. (J). (gr. 3-8). lib. bdg. 27.07 (*1-59187-012-7*) Child's World, Inc.

Duey, Kathleen & Bale, Karen A. Hurricane, New Bedford, Massachusetts, 1784. 1999. (Survival! Ser.: No. 9). 160p. (J). (gr. 4-7). per. 4.50 (*0-689-82544-7*, Simon Pulse) Simon & Schuster Children's Publishing.

Fast, Howard. April Morning. 1983. 208p. (gr. 6 up). mass mkt. 6.99 (*0-553-27322-1*) Bantam Bks.

—April Morning. unabr. ed. 1988. (J). (gr. 6). audio 35.00 (*1-55690-026-0*, 88320E7) Recorded Bks., LLC.

—April Morning. 9999. (J). pap. 2.25 o.p. (*0-590-02283-0*) Scholastic, Inc.

Golden, Christopher. Body Bags. 1999. (Body of Evidence Ser.: Vol. 1). 272p. (YA). (gr. 7-12). mass mkt. 4.99 (*0-671-03492-8*, Simon Pulse) Simon & Schuster Children's Publishing.

—Head Games. 2000. (Body of Evidence Ser.: No. 5). (Illus.). 256p. (YA). (gr. 7-12). mass mkt. 4.99 (*0-671-77582-0*, Simon Pulse) Simon & Schuster Children's Publishing.

—Meets the Eye. 2000. (Body of Evidence Ser.: No. 4). 256p. (YA). (gr. 7 up). mass mkt. 4.99 (*0-671-03495-2*, Simon Pulse) Simon & Schuster Children's Publishing.

—Skin Deep. 2000. (Body of Evidence Ser.: Vol. 6). (Illus.). 288p. (YA). mass mkt. 5.99 o.s.i (*0-671-77583-9*, Simon Pulse) Simon & Schuster Children's Publishing.

—Soul Survivor. 1999. (Body of Evidence Ser.: Vol. 3). 256p. (YA). (gr. 7-12). pap. 4.99 (*0-671-03494-4*, Simon Pulse) Simon & Schuster Children's Publishing.

—Thief of Hearts. 1999. (Body of Evidence Ser.: Vol. 2). (Illus.). 272p. (YA). (gr. 8-12). pap. 4.99 (*0-671-03493-6*, Simon Pulse) Simon & Schuster Children's Publishing.

Griffin, Adele. Amandine. 2001. 224p. (J). trans. 15.99 (*0-7868-0618-4*) Hyperion Bks. for Children.

Hansen, Joyce. The Captive. 192p. (YA). 1995. (gr. 5 up). pap. 4.50 (*0-590-41624-3*); 1994. (Illus.). (gr. 7 up). pap. 13.95 (*0-590-41625-1*) Scholastic, Inc.

—The Captive. 1994. 8.60 o.p. (*0-606-07339-6*) Turtleback Bks.

Hawthorne, Nathaniel. The House of the Seven Gables. abr. ed. 1994. (Illustrated Classics Collection). (Illus.). 64p. pap. 4.95 (*0-7854-0697-2*, 40453); (J). pap. 3.60 o.p. (*1-56103-531-9*) American Guidance Service, Inc.

—The House of the Seven Gables. (YA). reprint ed. 1999. pap. text 28.00 (*1-4047-1350-6*); 1851. pap. text 28.00 (*1-4047-3039-7*) Classic Textbooks.

—The House of the Seven Gables, Set. abr. ed. 1997. (Ultimate Classics Ser.). (YA). (gr. 9 up). 19.95 o.p. (*0-7871-0924-X*, 694868) NewStar Media, Inc.

—The House of the Seven Gables. Farr, Naunerle C., ed. abr. ed. 1977. (Now Age Illustrated III Ser.). (Illus.). (J). (gr. 4-12). text 7.50 o.p. (*0-88301-277-4*); pap. text 2.95 (*0-88301-265-0*) Pendulum Pr., Inc.

—The Scarlet Letter. unabr. ed. 1962. (Classics Ser.). (YA). (gr. 9 up). mass mkt. 3.95 (*0-8049-0007-8*, CL-7) Airmont Publishing Co., Inc.

—The Scarlet Letter. 1965. (Bantam Classics Ser.). 256p. reprint ed. mass mkt. 3.95 (*0-553-21009-2*, Bantam Classics) Bantam Bks.

—The Scarlet Letter. Cockcroft, Susan, ed. 1997. (Cambridge Literature Ser.). (Illus.). 320p. pap. text 11.95 (*0-521-56783-1*) Cambridge Univ. Pr.

—The Scarlet Letter. 1989. 277p. (YA). (gr. 8-12). mass mkt. 3.99 (*0-8125-0483-6*, Tor Classics) Doherty, Tom Assocs., LLC.

—The Scarlet Letter. 1972. 106p. (YA). (gr. 10 up). pap. 5.60 (*0-87129-921-6*, SB6) Dramatic Publishing Co.

—The Scarlet Letter. adapted ed. (YA). (gr. 5-12). pap. text 9.95 (*0-8359-0262-5*) Globe Fearon Educational Publishing.

—The Scarlet Letter. Levin, Harry T., ed. 1960. (YA). (gr. 9 up). pap. 16.36 (*0-395-05142-8*, Riverside Editions) Houghton Mifflin Co.

—The Scarlet Letter. 1995. (Illus.). 288p. (YA). pap. 12.95 (*0-7868-8093-7*) Hyperion Pr.

—The Scarlet Letter. l.t. ed. 2000. (LRS Large Print Heritage Ser.). 379p. (YA). (gr. 7-12). lib. bdg. 34.95 (*1-58118-065-9*, 23660) LRS.

—The Scarlet Letter. 1981. 256p. (YA). mass mkt. 4.95 o.p. (*0-451-51908-6*, Signet Classics) NAL.

—The Scarlet Letter. 1998. (YA). 32p. 9.95 (*1-56137-338-9*, NU3389); 40p. 11.95 (*1-56137-339-7*, NU3397SP) Novel Units, Inc.

—The Scarlet Letter. 1987. (Portland House Illustrated Classics Ser.). (Illus.). 312p. (YA). 9.99 o.s.i (*0-517-64302-2*) Random Hse. Value Publishing.

—The Scarlet Letter. 1999. (Courage Unabridged Classics Ser.). 208p. (YA). pap. 6.00 o.p. (*0-7624-0552-X*, Courage Bks.) Running Pr. Bk. Pubs.

—The Scarlet Letter. (YA). 1994. 11.04 (*0-606-13027-6*); 1981. 10.00 (*0-606-13760-2*) Turtleback Bks.

Howe, Janet R. The Mystery of the Marmalade Cat. l.t. ed. 1969. (Illus.). (J). (gr. 4-9). 4.25 o.p. (*0-664-32439-8*) Westminster John Knox Pr.

Howells, William Dean. The Rise of Silas Lapham. 1968. (Airmont Classics Ser.). (J). (gr. 11 up). mass mkt. 2.95 o.p. (*0-8049-0165-1*, CL-165) Airmont Publishing Co., Inc.

—The Rise of Silas Lapham. Cady, Edwin H., ed. 1957. (YA). (gr. 9 up). pap. 13.56 o.p. (*0-395-05126-6*, Riverside Editions) Houghton Mifflin Co.

—The Rise of Silas Lapham. 1963. (YA). (gr. 9). 352p. mass mkt. 7.95 o.s.i (*0-451-52496-9*, CE1850); mass mkt. 3.50 o.p. (*0-451-52198-6*) NAL. (Signet Classics).

Hurst, Carol Otis. In Plain Sight. 2002. 160p. (YA). (gr. 5-9). 15.00 (*0-618-19699-4*) Houghton Mifflin Co.

Hurst, Carol Otis & Otis, Rebecca. A Killing in Plymouth Colony. 2003. 160p. (J). (gr. 5-9). tchr. ed. 15.00 (*0-618-27597-5*) Houghton Mifflin Co.

Hyppolite, Joanne. Ola Shakes It Up. 1998. (Illus.). 176p. (gr. 2-6). text 14.95 o.s.i (*0-385-32235-6*, Delacorte Pr.) Dell Publishing.

—Ola Shakes It Up. 1999. (Illus.). 176p. (gr. 4-7). pap. text 4.50 o.s.i (*0-440-41204-8*, Dell Books for Young Readers) Random Hse. Children's Bks.

A Journey to the New World: The Diary of Remember Patience Whipple, Mayflower, 1620. 2003. (J). lib. bdg. 12.95 (*0-439-55504-3*) Scholastic, Inc.

Kirkpatrick, Katherine. The Voyage of the Continental. 2002. (Illus.). 297p. (J). (gr. 7 up). tchr. ed. 16.95 (*0-8234-1580-5*) Holiday Hse., Inc.

Klass, Sheila S. Little Women Next Door. 2000. (Illus.). 188p. (J). (gr. 3-7). tchr. ed. 15.95 (*0-8234-1472-8*) Holiday Hse., Inc.

Koller, Jackie French. Someday. 2002. 224p. (J). (gr. 5 up). pap. 16.95 (*0-439-29317-0*, Orchard Bks.) Scholastic, Inc.

Lewis, Maggie. Morgy Makes His Move. (Illus.). (J). 2002. 80p. (gr. 1-4). pap. 4.95 (*0-618-19680-3*); 1999. 74p. (gr. 4-6). tchr. ed. 15.00 (*0-395-92284-4*) Houghton Mifflin Co.

Lynch, Chris. Blood Relations. 1996. (Blue Eyed Son Ser.: No. 2). (Illus.). (YA). 224p. (gr. 12 up). lib. bdg. 13.89 o.s.i (*0-06-025399-1*); 192p. (gr. 7 up). pap. 4.50 o.s.i (*0-06-447122-5*) HarperCollins Children's Bk. Group. (Harper Trophy).

—Blood Relations. 1996. (Blue-Eyed Son Ser.: 2). (J). 9.60 o.p. (*0-606-09090-8*) Turtleback Bks.

—Mick. 1996. (Blue-Eyed Son Ser.: Bk. 1). (Illus.). 160p. (YA). (gr. 12 up). lib. bdg. 13.89 o.p. (*0-06-025397-5*); mass mkt. 4.50 o.s.i (*0-06-447121-7*, Harper Trophy) HarperCollins Children's Bk. Group.

—Mick. 1996. (Blue-Eyed Son Ser.). (YA). 9.60 o.p. (*0-606-09089-4*) Turtleback Bks.

Matchette, Katharine E. Libby's Choice. 1995. 157p. (YA). (gr. 6-12). pap. 8.75 (*0-9645045-0-2*) Deka Pr.

Moody, Ralph. Mary Emma & Company. 1976. (J). 26.95 (*0-8488-1513-0*) Amereon, Ltd.

—Mary Emma & Company. 1991. 340p. (J). reprint ed. lib. bdg. 25.95 o.p. (*0-89966-830-5*) Buccaneer Bks., Inc.

—Mary Emma & Company. 1961. (Illus.). (J). (gr. 8 up). 11.95 o.p. (*0-393-08382-9*) Norton, W. W. & Co., Inc.

—Mary Emma & Company. 1994. (Illus.). 235p. (J). pap. 11.95 (*0-8032-8211-7*, Bison Bks.) Univ. of Nebraska Pr.

Murphy, T. M. The Secrets of the Twisted Cross. 2002. (Belltown Mystery Ser.). (Illus.). 176p. (J). 9.95 (*1-880158-43-4*) Townsend, J.N. Publishing.

Owens, Tom. Flames of Freedom. 2001. (Cover-to-Cover Bks.). (Illus.). 54p. (J). (*0-7807-9040-5*) Perfection Learning Corp.

Paterson, John & Kath. Blueberries for the Queen. 2004. (Illus.). (J). lib. bdg. (*0-06-623943-5*) HarperCollins Pubs.

Paterson, John & Paterson, Katherine. Blueberries for the Queen. Jeffers, Susan, tr. & illus. by. 2004. (J). (*0-06-623942-7*) HarperCollins Pubs.

Paterson, Katherine. Lyddie. 1999. (Espasa Juvenil Ser.: Vol. 18). (SPA., Illus.). (J). (gr. 9-12). pap. 9.95 (*84-239-9015-X*, EC6561) Espasa Calpe, S.A. ESP. *Dist:* Lectorum Pubns., Inc., Planeta Publishing Corp.

—Lyddie. (YA). 1995. 192p. (gr. 7-12). pap. 6.99 (*0-14-037389-6*, Puffin Bks.); 1992. 192p. (gr. 5-12). pap. 5.99 (*0-14-034981-2*, Puffin Bks.); 1991. 240p. (gr. 7-12). 17.99 (*0-525-67338-5*, Dutton Children's Bks.) Penguin Putnam Bks. for Young Readers.

—Lyddie. 1996. 16.00 (*0-606-16067-1*); 1992. (J). 12.04 (*0-606-00880-2*) Turtleback Bks.

Pedicini, John G. Slow Moe. Serino, John, ed. 1991. (Nantucket Nanny & Friends Ser.). (Illus.). 32p. (J). (gr. k-2). 9.95 (*0-9627436-7-4*) Je Suis Derby Publishing.

Pfeffer, Susan Beth. Beth's Story. 2001. (Portraits of Little Women Ser.). (Illus.). (J). 10.55 (*0-606-21063-6*) Turtleback Bks.

—A Gift for Jo. 1999. (Portraits of Little Women Ser.: No. 10). (Illus.). 112p. (gr. 3-7). text 9.95 o.s.i (*0-385-32668-8*, Dell Books for Young Readers) Random Hse. Children's Bks.

Pfeffer, Susan Beth & Alcott, Louisa May. Amy Makes a Friend. 1998. (Portraits of Little Women Ser.). (Illus.). 112p. (gr. 3-7). text 9.95 o.s.i (*0-385-32584-3*, Dell Books for Young Readers) Random Hse. Children's Bks.

—A Gift for Beth. 1999. (Portraits of Little Women Ser.: No. 11). (Illus.). 112p. (gr. 3-7). text 9.95 o.s.i (*0-385-32667-X*, Dell Books for Young Readers) Random Hse. Children's Bks.

—Jo Makes a Friend. 1998. (Portraits of Little Women Ser.). (Illus.). 112p. (gr. 3-7). text 9.95 (*0-385-32581-9*, Dell Books for Young Readers) Random Hse. Children's Bks.

—Jo's Story. 1997. (Portraits of Little Women Ser.). 112p. (gr. 3-7). text 9.95 o.s.i (*0-385-32523-1*, Dell Books for Young Readers) Random Hse. Children's Bks.

—Meg Makes a Friend. 1998. (Portraits of Little Women Ser.). (Illus.). 112p. (gr. 3-7). text 9.95 (*0-385-32580-0*, Delacorte Pr.) Dell Publishing.

Pyne, Patricia P. The Magic Chopsticks. l.t. ed. 1996. (Illus.). 24p. (J). (gr. 1-8). lib. bdg. 14.95 (*0-9655465-9-4*) Pelican Publishing.

Rees, Douglas. Vampire High. 2003. 240p. (YA). (gr. 7). 15.95 (*0-385-73117-5*); lib. bdg. 17.99 (*0-385-90143-7*) Random Hse. Children's Bks. (Delacorte Bks. for Young Readers).

Rice, Alice H. Mrs. Wiggs of the Cabbage Patch. 1984. 96p. (J). pap. 3.95 o.s.i (*0-671-52476-3*, Pocket) Simon & Schuster.

Rosenberg, Liz. Seventeen: A Novel in Prose Poems. 2002. 160p. (YA). (gr. 9 up). 16.95 (*0-8126-4915-X*) Cricket Bks.

Rue, Nancy. The Accused. 1998. (Christian Heritage Ser.). 224p. (J). (gr. 3-7). pap. 5.99 (*1-56179-398-1*) Focus on the Family Publishing.

Schaller, Bob. Mystery in Massachusetts. 2001. (X-Country Adventures Ser.). 128p. (J). (gr. 3-6). pap. 5.99 o.p. (*0-8010-4491-X*) Baker Bks.

Smith, L. J. The Initiation. 1995. 79p. (J). mass mkt. 1.99 o.p. (*0-06-106399-1*, HarperTorch) Morrow/Avon.

—Secret Circle: The Initiation. 1992. (Secret Circle Ser.: Vol. 1). 320p. (gr. 7-12). mass mkt. 4.99 (*0-06-106712-1*, HarperTorch) Morrow/Avon.

Smith, Patricia Clark. Weetamoo Heart of the Pocassets: Chief of the Pocassets, Massachusetts, 1653. 2003. (Royal Diaries Ser.). (Illus.). 208p. (J). 10.95 (*0-439-12910-9*) Scholastic, Inc.

Speare, Elizabeth George. The Witch of Blackbird Pond. l.t. ed. 1989. 280p. (J). reprint ed. lib. bdg. 15.95 o.s.i (*1-55736-138-X*) Bantam Doubleday Dell Large Print Group, Inc.

Settings

—The Witch of Blackbird Pond. 2002. (Illus.). (J). 14.47 (*0-7587-0227-2*) Book Wholesalers, Inc.

—The Witch of Blackbird Pond. 1997. mass mkt. 2.69 o.p. (*0-440-22721-6*) Dell Publishing.

—The Witch of Blackbird Pond. 2001. (Illus.). 288p. (YA). (gr. 7-9). tchr. ed. 22.00 (*0-395-91367-5*) Houghton Mifflin Co.

—The Witch of Blackbird Pond. 2002. (J). (gr. 4-7). 32.00 incl. audio (*0-8072-0749-7*); (gr. 4-7). pap., tchr.'s planning gde. ed. 37.00 incl. audio (*0-8072-0862-0*); (gr. 3-7). audio 26.00 (*0-8072-0748-9*) Random Hse. Audio Publishing Group. (Listening Library).

—The Witch of Blackbird Pond. 1987. (YA). (gr. 7 up). 12.04 (*0-606-00107-7*) Turtleback Bks.

Spykman, Elizabeth C. Lemon & a Star. 1955. (J). (gr. 5 up). 5.95 o.p. (*0-15-244713-X*) Harcourt Children's Bks.

Stanley, Diane. Being Thankful at Plymouth Plantation. 2003. (Illus.). (J). 15.99 (*0-06-027069-1*); lib. bdg. 16.89 (*0-06-027076-4*) HarperCollins Children's Bk. Group. (Cotler, Joanna Bks.).

Terris, Susan. Nell's Quilt, RS. 1996. 176p. (YA). (gr. 7 up). pap. 5.95 (*0-374-45497-3*, Sunburst) Farrar, Straus & Giroux.

—Nell's Quilt. 1988. 192p. (J). (gr. 7-9). pap. 2.50 o.p. (*0-590-41914-5*) Scholastic, Inc.

—Nell's Quilt. 1996. 12.00 (*0-606-10892-0*) Turtleback Bks.

Terry, Wendy, illus. The Cape Cod Summer Home: A Family Adventure in the Town of Chatham. 2001. 40p. (YA). 10.00 (*0-9676082-1-X*) Stage Harbor Pr.

Trimble, Marcia. Witchy's Turned-Around House. 1998. (Illus.). 32p. (J). (ps-5). 15.95 (*1-891577-27-1*) Images Pr.

Voigt, Cynthia. The Callender Papers. 1994. 192p. (YA). (gr. 7 up). mass mkt. 4.50 o.s.i (*0-449-70184-0*, Fawcett) Ballantine Bks.

—The Callender Papers. (J). (gr. 4-8). 2000. (Illus.). 272p. pap. 5.99 (*0-689-83283-4*, Aladdin); 1983. 224p. lib. bdg. 15.95 o.s.i (*0-689-30971-6*, Atheneum) Simon & Schuster Children's Publishing.

—The Callender Papers. 2001. (J). (gr. 4-8). 20.75 (*0-8446-7192-4*) Smith, Peter Pub., Inc.

Wallace-Brodeur, Ruth. Blue Eyes Better. (J). 2003. (Illus.). 112p. pap. 5.99 (*0-14-250086-0*, Puffin Bks.); 2002. 128p. (gr. 4-6). 15.99 (*0-525-46836-6*, Dutton Children's Bks.) Penguin Putnam Bks. for Young Readers.

Weber, Judith E. Forbidden Friendship. 1993. (Stories of the States Ser.). (Illus.). 80p. (J). (gr. 4-7). lib. bdg. 14.95 (*1-881889-42-4*) Silver Moon Pr.

The Wednesday Afternoon Witch Club. 2001. 162p. per. 12.00 (*0-9712428-3-6*) Black Cat Bks.

Weller, Frances Ward. Madaket Millie. 1999. (Illus.). 32p. (J). (ps-3). pap. 5.99 o.s.i (*0-698-11774-3*) Penguin Putnam Bks. for Young Readers.

Werlin, Nancy. The Killer's Cousin. 1998. 240p. (YA). (gr. 9-12). 15.95 (*0-385-32560-6*) Bantam Bks.

—The Killer's Cousin. 2000. 240p. (YA). (gr. 9-12). mass mkt. 5.50 (*0-440-22751-8*) Dell Publishing.

—The Killer's Cousin. l.t. ed. 1999. (Young Adult Ser.). 277p. (YA). (gr. 9-12). 21.95 (*0-7862-2188-7*) Thorndike Pr.

—The Killer's Cousin. 2000. 11.04 (*0-606-17820-1*) Turtleback Bks.

Wharton, Edith. Ethan Frome, Level 3. Hedge, Tricia, ed. 2000. (Bookworms Ser.). (Illus.). 80p. (YA). pap. text 5.95 (*0-19-423002-3*) Oxford Univ. Pr., Inc.

Wiley, Melissa. Little House by Boston Bay. 1999. (Little House Ser.). (Illus.). 208p. (J). (gr. 3-7). 15.95 (*0-06-027011-X*); (gr. 3-7). pap. 5.99 (*0-06-440737-3*, Harper Trophy); (ps-3). lib. bdg. 16.89 (*0-06-028201-0*) HarperCollins Children's Bk. Group.

—On Tide Mill Lane, No. 2. 2001. (Little House Ser.). (Illus.). 272p. (J). (gr. k-4). 16.95 (*0-06-027013-6*); (gr. 3-7). lib. bdg. 16.89 (*0-06-027014-4*) HarperCollins Children's Bk. Group.

Wilson, Nancy Hope. Becoming Felix, RS. 1996. 192p. (J). (gr. 3-7). 16.00 o.p. (*0-374-30664-8*, Farrar, Straus & Giroux (BYR)) Farrar, Straus & Giroux.

Wittlinger, Ellen. What's in a Name. 2000. 160p. (J). (gr. 7-12). 16.00 (*0-689-82551-X*, Simon & Schuster Children's Publishing) Simon & Schuster Children's Publishing.

—What's in a Name. l.t. ed. 2001. 199p. (J). 22.95 (*0-7862-3505-5*) Thorndike Pr.

Yolen, Jane. Letting Swift River Go. 1995. (Illus.). 32p. (J). (ps-3). pap. 6.99 (*0-316-96860-9*) Little Brown & Co.

—Letting Swift River Go. 1992. (J). 12.10 (*0-606-07783-9*) Turtleback Bks.

MEDITERRANEAN REGION—FICTION

Napoli, Donna Jo. Sirena. (gr. 7-12). 2000. 224p. (J). mass mkt. 5.99 (*0-590-38389-2*); 1998. 256p. (YA). pap. 15.95 (*0-590-38388-4*) Scholastic, Inc.

METROPOLITAN AREAS—FICTION

Haynes, Henry L. Squarehead & Me. 1980. (J). (gr. 4-7). pap. 8.95 o.p. (*0-664-32663-3*) Westminster John Knox Pr.

Hostetler, Marian. Secret in the City. 1980. (Illus.). 104p. (J). (gr. 4-8). pap. 3.95 o.p. (*0-8361-1932-0*) Herald Pr.

METROPOLITAN MUSEUM OF ART (NEW YORK, N.Y.)—FICTION

Konigsburg, E. L. From the Mixed-up Files of Mrs. Basil E. Frankweiler. 1977. (Yearling Newbery Ser.). (Illus.). 176p. (gr. 4-7). pap. text 4.99 o.s.i (*0-440-43180-8*, Yearling) Random Hse. Children's Bks.

—From the Mixed-Up Files of Mrs. Basil E. Frankweiler. 1970. (Illus.). 168p. (J). (gr. 3-7). 17.00 (*0-689-20586-4*, Atheneum) Simon & Schuster Children's Publishing.

—From the Mixed up Files of Mrs. Basil E. Frankweiler. 2002. 208p. (YA). mass mkt. 5.99 (*0-689-85354-8*, Simon Pulse) Simon & Schuster Children's Publishing.

—From the Mixed up Files of Mrs. Basil E. Frankweiler: 35th Anniversary Edition. anniv. ed. 2002. (Illus.). 176p. (J). (gr. 3-7). 16.95 (*0-689-85322-X*, Atheneum) Simon & Schuster Children's Publishing.

MEXICO—FICTION

Aardema, Verna. Borreguita & the Coyote. 1998. (Illus.). 32p. (gr. k-3). pap. 6.99 (*0-679-88936-1*, Random Hse. Bks. for Young Readers) Random Hse. Children's Bks.

Agustin, Jose. La Panza del Tepozteco. 1998. (SPA., Illus.). 118p. (YA). (gr. 9-12). pap. 16.95 (*968-29-4573-9*) Secretaria de Educacion Publica MEX. *Dist:* Santillana USA Publishing Co., Inc.

Amado, Elisa. Barrilete: A Kite for the Day of the Dead. 1999. (SPA., Illus.). 32p. (ps-3). pap. 6.95 (*0-88899-381-1*) Groundwood Bks. CAN. *Dist:* Publishers Group West.

Anaya, Rudolfo A. Maya's Children: The Story of la Llorona. 1997. (Illus.). 32p. (J). (gr. k-4). 14.95 o.p. (*0-7868-0152-2*); lib. bdg. 15.49 o.p. (*0-7868-2124-8*) Hyperion Bks. for Children.

Ancona, George. The Pinata Maker. 1994. Tr. of Pinatero. (SPA., Illus.). 40p. (J). (ps-3). pap. 9.00 (*0-15-200060-7*) Harcourt Children's Bks.

Baker, Betty. Walk the World's Rim. 1965. (J). (gr. 5 up). pap. 2.95 o.p. (*0-06-440026-3*) HarperCollins Pubs.

Bang, Molly Garrett. Tiger's Fall, ERS. 2001. (Illus.). 112p. (J). (gr. 4-7). 15.95 (*0-8050-6689-6*, Holt, Henry & Co. Bks. For Young Readers) Holt, Henry & Co.

Behn, Harry. Two Uncles of Pablo. 1959. (Illus.). (J). (gr. 4-6). 4.95 o.p. (*0-15-292306-3*) Harcourt Children's Bks.

Bernard, Virginia. Eliza & the Sacred Mountain. 2000. (Going to Ser.). (Illus.). 128p. (J). (gr. 4-8). pap. 5.99 (*1-893577-05-8*) Four Corners Publishing Co., Inc.

Best, Cari. Montezuma's Revenge. 1999. (Illus.). 32p. (J). (ps-2). pap. 15.95 (*0-531-30198-2*); lib. bdg. 16.99 (*0-531-33198-9*) Scholastic, Inc. (Orchard Bks.).

Bontemps, Arna & Hughes, Langston. The Pasteboard Bandit. 1997. (Iona & Peter Opie Library of Children's Literature). (Illus.). 96p. (J). (gr. 3-7). 16.95 o.p. (*0-19-511476-0*) Oxford Univ. Pr., Inc.

Bovaird, Anne. Goodbye U. S. A. - Ola Mexico! 1994. (ENG & SPA., Illus.). 48p. (J). (gr. 3-7). 12.95 (*0-8120-6374-0*); pap. 5.95 (*0-8120-1388-3*) Barron's Educational Series, Inc.

Brammer, Ethriam Cash. Alla en el Rancho Grande: The Rowdy, Rowdy Ranch. Cruz, D. Nina, tr. & illus. by. 2003. (ENG & SPA.). (J). (*1-55885-409-6*, Piñata Books) Arte Publico Pr.

Brenner, Anita. A Hero by Mistake. 1953. (J). (gr. 1-5). lib. bdg. 4.95 o.p. (*0-201-09223-9*) Addison-Wesley Longman, Inc.

Bulla, Clyde Robert. The Poppy Seeds. 1955. (Illus.). (J). (gr. k-3). o.p. (*0-690-64856-1*) HarperCollins Children's Bk. Group.

Bunting, Eve. Going Home. (Trophy Picture Book Ser.). (Illus.). 32p. (J). (ps-3). 1998. pap. 6.99 (*0-06-443509-1*, Harper Trophy); 1996. 15.99 (*0-06-026296-6*, Cotler, Joanna Bks.); 1996. lib. bdg. 15.89 (*0-06-026297-4*) HarperCollins Children's Bk. Group.

—Going Home. 1998. 13.10 (*0-606-15551-1*) Turtleback Bks.

—A Part of the Dream. 1992. (Eve Bunting Collection). (Illus.). 48p. (J). (gr. 2-6). lib. bdg. 12.79 o.p. (*0-89565-771-6*) Child's World, Inc.

Cahill, Doris. Nina. 2001. (Illus.). 80p. (J). 15.95 (*0-9713224-0-6*) Johnson, J LLC.

Cohen, Dan. The Case of the Spanish Stamps. 1980. (Carolrhoda Mini-Mysteries Ser.). (Illus.). (J). (gr. 1-4). lib. bdg. 4.95 o.p. (*0-87614-117-3*, Carolrhoda Bks.) Lerner Publishing Group.

Cohn, Diana. Dream Carver. 2002. (Illus.). 40p. (J). o.p. (*0-8118-3357-7*); 15.95 (*0-8118-1244-8*) Chronicle Bks. LLC.

Corpi, Lucha. Where Fireflies Dance (Ahi, Donde Bailan las Luciernagas) (Illus.). 32p. (J). (gr. 1 up). 2002. pap. 7.95 (*0-89239-177-4*); 1997. (ENG & SPA., 15.95 (*0-89239-145-6*) Children's Bk. Pr.

de Trevino, Elizabeth Borton. El Guero: A True Adventure Story, RS. (Illus.). 112p. (J). 1991. (gr. 4-7). pap. 4.95 (*0-374-42028-9*, Sunburst); 1989. (gr. 3 up). 14.00 o.p. (*0-374-31995-2*, Farrar, Straus & Giroux (BYR)) Farrar, Straus & Giroux.

Delgado, Maria I. Chave's Memories: Los Recuerdos de Chave. 1996. (SPA., Illus.). 32p. (ps-3). 14.95 (*1-55885-084-8*, Piñata Books) Arte Publico Pr.

D'Harnoncourt, Rene, illus. The Painted Pig: A Mexican Picture Book. 2001. 37p. (J). 19.95 (*0-8263-2769-9*) Univ. of New Mexico Pr.

Dralle, Elizabeth. Angel in the Tower, RS. 1962. (Illus.). 101p. (J). (gr. 7 up). 2.75 o.p. (*0-374-30330-4*, Farrar, Straus & Giroux (BYR)) Farrar, Straus & Giroux.

Estes, Kristyn. Manuela's Gift. 1999. (Illus.). 32p. (J). (ps-3). 15.95 (*0-8118-2085-8*) Chronicle Bks. LLC.

Ets, Marie Hall. Gilberto & the Wind. 1978. (Picture Puffin Bks.). (Illus.). 32p. (J). (ps-3). pap. 5.99 (*0-14-050276-9*, Puffin Bks.) Penguin Putnam Bks. for Young Readers.

Farnes, Catherine. Out of Hiding. 2000. 174p. (YA). (gr. 9 up). pap. 6.49 (*1-57924-329-0*, 122085) Jones, Bob Univ. Pr.

Fine, Edith Hope. Bajo la Luna de Limon. ed. 2000. (SPA.). (J). (gr. 1). spiral bd. (*0-616-03089-4*) Canadian National Institute for the Blind/Institut National Canadien pour les Aveugles.

—Bajo la Luna de Limon. de la Vega, Eida, tr. from ENG. 1999. (SPA., Illus.). 32p. (J). (gr. 1-3). pap. 6.96 (*1-880000-91-1*, LW2628); lib. bdg. 15.95 (*1-880000-90-3*, LW5634) Lee & Low Bks., Inc.

—Bajo la Luna de Limon. 1999. (SPA., Illus.). 13.10 (*0-606-17377-3*) Turtleback Bks.

—Under the Lemon Moon.Tr. of Bajo la Luna de Limon. (Illus.). 32p. (J). 2002. pap. 6.95 (*1-58430-051-5*); 1999. 16.95 (*1-880000-69-5*) Lee & Low Bks., Inc.

Flora, James. The Fabulous Firework Family. 2nd ed. 1994. (Illus.). 32p. (J). (ps-3). 14.95 (*0-689-50596-5*, McElderry, Margaret K.) Simon & Schuster Children's Publishing.

Forsman, Bettie. From Lupita's Hill. 1973. 272p. (J). (gr. 4-6). 1.49 o.p. (*0-689-30085-9*, Atheneum) Simon & Schuster Children's Publishing.

Geeslin, Campbell. Elena's Serenade. 2004. (Illus.). 40p. (J). 16.95 (*0-689-84908-7*, Atheneum/Anne Schwartz Bks.) Simon & Schuster Children's Publishing.

—How Nanita Learns to Make Flan. 1999. (Illus.). 32p. (J). (ps-3). 16.00 (*0-689-81546-8*, Atheneum/Anne Schwartz Bks.) Simon & Schuster Children's Publishing.

—In Rosa's Mexico. 1996. (Illus.). (J). (ps-3). 18.99 o.s.i (*0-679-96721-4*); 1.99 o.s.i (*0-679-86721-X*) Random Hse. Children's Bks. (Knopf Bks. for Young Readers).

—On Ramon's Farm: Five Tales of Mexico. 1998. (Illus.). 48p. (J). (ps-2). 16.00 o.s.i (*0-689-81134-9*, Atheneum/Anne Schwartz Bks.) Simon & Schuster Children's Publishing.

George, Jean Craighead. Shark Beneath the Reef. 1989. 192p. (YA). (gr. 7 up). 13.95 (*0-06-021992-0*); lib. bdg. 13.89 o.p. (*0-06-021993-9*) HarperCollins Children's Bk. Group.

Gollub, Matthew. La Luna se Fue de Fiesta. Guzman, Martin L., tr. 1997. (Illus.). 32p. (J). (gr. k-6). (SPA.). pap. 6.95 (*1-889910-14-7*, TOR7579); 15.95 (*1-889910-12-0*, TOR7576) Tortuga Pr.

—The Moon Was at a Fiesta. 1994. (Illus.). 32p. (J). 15.00 o.p. (*0-688-11637-X*); lib. bdg. 14.93 o.p. (*0-688-11638-8*) Morrow/Avon. (Morrow, William & Co.).

—The Moon Was at a Fiesta. Guzman, Martin L., tr. rev. ed. 1997. (Illus.). 32p. (J). (gr. k-6). 15.95 (*1-889910-11-2*) Tortuga Pr.

—The Twenty-Five Mixtec Cats. 1993. (Illus.). 32p. (J). (ps-3). 15.95 (*0-688-11639-6*) HarperCollins Children's Bk. Group.

—The Twenty-Five Mixtec Cats. 1993. (Illus.). 32p. (J). (gr. 1 up). lib. bdg. 15.93 o.s.i (*0-688-11640-X*, Morrow, William & Co.) Morrow/Avon.

—Los Veinticinco Gatos Mixtecos. Ferrer, Martin Luis Guzmán, tr. l.t. ed. 1997. (SPA., Illus.). 32p. (J). (gr. 2-4). 15.95 (*1-889910-00-7*, TOR7577); pap. 6.95 (*1-889910-01-5*, TOR7580) Tortuga Pr.

Gonzalez Jensen, Margarita. And Then It Was Sugar. 1997. (Illus.). (*0-7802-8318-X*) Wright Group, The.

Grace, Nancy. Earrings for Celia. 1963. (Illus.). (J). (gr. 3-6). 3.69 o.s.i (*0-394-91103-2*, Pantheon) Knopf Publishing Group.

Grey, Zane. Ken Ward in the Jungle. l.t. ed. 1999. (J). 272p. (*0-7540-3607-3*); pap. (*0-7540-3608-1*) BBC Audiobooks America.

Grifalconi, Ann, illus. The Toy Trumpet. 2nd ed. 1995. (J). (ps-3). 15.95 (*0-316-32858-8*) Little Brown & Co.

Harper, Jo. The Legend of Mexicatl. 1998. (Illus.). 40p. (J). (ps up). 15.95 (*1-890515-05-1*) Turtle Bks.

—La Leyenda de Mexicatl. Lans, Tatiana, tr. 1998. (SPA., Illus.). 40p. (J). (gr. 2-4). 15.95 (*1-890515-06-X*, TK8484) Turtle Bks.

Hays, Jim, illus. Marigolds for Dona Remedios. 1997. (*0-7802-8302-3*) Wright Group, The.

Herbst, Judith. Ivy's Journal. 2000. (Illus.). 32p. (J). (gr. 3-7). 15.95 (*1-57255-839-3*) Mondo Publishing.

Herbst, Judith & O'Gorman, Molly. Ivy's Journal. 2000. (J). o.p. (*1-57255-840-0*) Mondo Publishing.

Hill, Pamela Smith. A Voice from the Border. 2000. 256p. (J). (gr. 5 up). pap. 4.95 (*0-380-73231-9*, Harper Trophy) HarperCollins Children's Bk. Group.

Jennings, Patrick. Faith & the Electric Dogs. 1996. 128p. (J). (gr. 1-7). pap. 15.95 (*0-590-69768-4*) Scholastic, Inc.

Johnston, Terry C. Lorenzo the Naughty Parrot. 1992. (Illus.). 32p. (C). (ps-3). 14.95 o.s.i (*0-15-249350-6*) Harcourt Children's Bks.

Johnston, Tony. Day of the Dead. 1997. (Illus.). 56p. (J). (ps-3). 14.00 (*0-15-222863-2*) Harcourt Children's Bks.

—Day of the Dead. 2000. 12.15 (*0-606-20323-0*) Turtleback Bks.

—Isabel's House of Butterflies. 2003. (Illus.). 32p. (J). (ps-3). 15.95 (*0-87156-409-2*) Sierra Club Bks. for Children.

—Magic Maguey. 1996. (Illus.). 32p. (J). (ps-3). 16.00 o.s.i (*0-15-250988-7*) Harcourt Children's Bks.

—My Mexico - Mexico Mio. 1999. (SPA., Illus.). 32p. (J). (gr. k-3). pap. 6.99 (*0-698-11757-3*, PaperStar) Penguin Putnam Bks. for Young Readers.

—The Old Lady & the Birds. abr. ed. 1994. (Illus.). 32p. (J). (ps-3). 14.95 (*0-15-257769-6*) Harcourt Children's Bks.

Joosse, Barbara M. Ghost Wings. 2001. (Illus.). 40p. (J). (ps-3). 15.95 (*0-8118-2164-1*) Chronicle Bks. LLC.

Kirwan, Anna. Lady of Palenque: Flower of Bacal, Mesoamerica, A.D. 2004. 10.95 (*0-439-40971-3*) Scholastic, Inc.

Krull, Kathleen. Maria Molina & the Days of the Dead. 1994. (Illus.). 32p. (J). (gr. k-3). mass mkt. 15.95 o.p. (*0-02-750999-0*, Simon & Schuster Children's Publishing) Simon & Schuster Children's Publishing.

Labastida, Aurora & Ets, Marie Hall. Nine Days to Christmas. 1959. (Illus.). 48p. (J). (ps-3). 16.99 o.s.i (*0-670-51350-4*, Viking Children's Bks.) Penguin Putnam Bks. for Young Readers.

Lauria, Frank. The Mask of Zorro. 1998. 176p. (J). (gr. 4-7). pap. 4.50 (*0-671-51967-0*, Aladdin) Simon & Schuster Children's Publishing.

Lee, Marie G. Night of the Chupacabras. (gr. 3-7). 1999. 128p. pap. 3.99 (*0-380-79773-9*); 1998. 144p. (J). 14.00 o.p. (*0-380-97706-0*) Morrow/Avon. (Avon Bks.).

—Night of the Chupacabras. 1999. 10.04 (*0-606-17336-6*) Turtleback Bks.

Levy, Janice. The Spirit of Tio Fernando. Fuenmayor, Morella, tr. 1995. Tr. of Espiritu de Tio Fernando: Una Historia del Dia de los Muertos. (ENG & SPA., Illus.). 32p. (J). (ps-3). pap. 6.95 (*0-8075-7586-0*) Whitman, Albert & Co.

—The Spirit of Tio Fernando. Mlawer, Teresa, tr. 1995. Tr. of Espiritu de Tio Fernando: Una Historia del Dia de los Muertos. (ENG & SPA., Illus.). 32p. (J). (ps-3). 14.95 (*0-8075-7585-2*) Whitman, Albert & Co.

Lewis, Thomas P. Here Comes the Strikeout!, Level 2. 1987. (I Can Read Bks.). (Illus.). 64p. (J). (gr. 1-3). 5.98 o.p. incl. audio (*0-694-00175-9*, JC-168, Harper Trophy) HarperCollins Children's Bk. Group.

—Hill of Fire. 2001. (First Readers Ser.). lib. bdg. (*1-59054-064-6*) Fitzgerald Bks.

—Hill of Fire. (I Can Read Bks.). (Illus.). 64p. (J). (gr. k-3). 1983. pap. 3.99 (*0-06-444040-0*, Harper Trophy); 1971. lib. bdg. 17.89 (*0-06-023804-6*) HarperCollins Children's Bk. Group.

—Hill of Fire. unabr. ed. 1990. (I Can Read Bks.). (Illus.). 64p. (J). (gr. k-3). 8.99 incl. audio (*1-55994-232-0*, TBC 2320, HarperAudio) HarperTrade.

—Hill of Fire. 1987. (I Can Read Bks.). (J). (gr. 2-4). 10.10 (*0-606-03198-7*) Turtleback Bks.

—La Montana de Fuego. Blanco, Osvaldo J., tr. 1997. (Ya Se Leer Ser.). Orig. Title: Hill of Fire. (SPA., Illus.). 64p. (J). (ps-3). pap. 4.95 o.p. (*0-06-444199-7*) HarperCollins Children's Bk. Group.

—La Montana de Fuego. 1997. Orig. Title: Hill of Fire. 10.15 o.p. (*0-606-10858-0*) Turtleback Bks.

Lewis, Thomas P. & Sandin, Joan. Hill of Fire. 9999. (I Can Read Bks.). (Illus.). (J). (gr. 2-4). 14.89 o.s.i (*0-06-023803-8*, 568868) HarperCollins Children's Bk. Group.

Madrigal, Antonio H. Erandi's Braids. Peskin, Joy, ed. 2001. (Illus.). 32p. (J). (ps-3). pap. 6.99 (*0-698-11885-5*, PaperStar) Penguin Putnam Bks. for Young Readers.

Madrigal, Antonio Hernandez. Erandi's Braids. 1999. (Illus.). 32p. (J). (ps-3). 15.99 (*0-399-23212-5*) Penguin Group (USA) Inc.

Maitland, Katherine. Ashes for Gold: A Tale from Mexico. 1994. (Mondo Folktales Ser.). (Illus.). 24p. (J). (gr. k-4). pap. 4.95 (*1-879531-22-4*) Mondo Publishing.

Manning, Brennan. The Boy Who Cried Abba: A Parable of Trust & Acceptance. 2001. 85p. pap. 13.95 (*1-879290-19-7*) PageMill Pr.

Mardis, Lloyd. The Burro & the Basket. 1997. (Illus.). 32p. (J). 13.95 (*1-57168-178-7*) Eakin Pr.

Marzollo, Jean. Soccer Cousins. 1997. (Hello Reader! Ser.). (Illus.). (J). (gr. 2-4). mass mkt. 3.99 (*0-590-74254-X*) Scholastic, Inc.

Matthews, Billie P. & Chichester, A. Lee. Secret of the Cibolo. Roberts, Melissa, ed. 1988. (Illus.). 88p. (J). (gr. 6-7). 9.95 (*0-89015-638-7*) Eakin Pr.

McColley, Kevin. The Walls of Pedro Garcia. 1993. 112p. (YA). 15.00 o.s.i (*0-385-30806-X*) Doubleday Publishing.

McCunney, Michelle. Mario's Mayan Journey. 1996. (Illus.). 32p. (J). (gr. 2-6). pap. 4.95 (*1-57255-203-4*) Mondo Publishing.

McGee, Charmayne. So Sings the Blue Deer. 1994. 160p. (J). (gr. 3-7). 14.95 (*0-689-31888-X*, Atheneum) Simon & Schuster Children's Publishing.

Merino, Jose M. The Gold of Dreams, RS. Lane, Helen, tr. 1992. 224p. (YA). (gr. 7 up). 15.00 o.p. (*0-374-32692-4*, Farrar, Straus & Giroux (BYR)) Farrar, Straus & Giroux.

Merino, Jose Maria. Beyond the Ancient Cities, RS. Lane, Helen, tr. from SPA. 1994. Tr. of Tierra del Tiempo Perdido. 208p. (J). 16.00 o.p. (*0-374-34307-1*, Farrar, Straus & Giroux (BYR)) Farrar, Straus & Giroux.

Mills, Elise, illus. Ashes for Gold: A Tale from Mexico. 1994. (Mondo Folktales ser.). 24p. (J). (gr. k-4). lib. bdg. 9.95 (*1-879531-43-7*) Mondo Publishing.

Mora, Pat & Berg, Charles R. The Gift of the Poinsettia - El Regalo de la Flor de Nochebuena. 1995. (ENG & SPA., Illus.). 32p. (J). (ps-3). 14.95 (*1-55885-137-2*, Piñata Books) Arte Publico Pr.

Navarro, Laura. Marcelo el Murcielago (Marcelo the Bat) 1997 (ENG & SPA., Illus.). 40p. (J). (ps-2). pap. 8.95 (*0-292-75567-8*) Bat Conservation International, Inc.

Oppenheim, Joanne. El Milagro de la Primera Flora de Nochebuena: Un Cuento Mexicano Sobre la Navidad. 2003. (SPA., Illus.). 32p. (J). 16.99 (*1-84148-308-7*) Barefoot Bks., Inc.

—The Miracle of the First Poinsettia: A Mexican Christmas Story. 2003. (Illus.). 32p. (J). 16.99 (*1-84148-245-5*) Barefoot Bks., Inc.

Patrick, Denise Lewis. The Adventures of Midnight Son, ERS. 1997. 128p. (J). (gr. 4-7). 16.00 (*0-8050-4714-X*, Holt, Henry & Co. Bks. For Young Readers) Holt, Henry & Co.

Peck, Richard. Unfinished Portrait of Jessica. 1991. 176p. (J). 15.00 o.s.i (*0-385-30500-1*, Delacorte Pr.) Dell Publishing.

Polley, Judith. Val Verde. 1974. pap. 6.95 o.s.i (*0-440-06092-3*, Delacorte Pr.) Dell Publishing.

Poulet, Virginia. Blue Bug Visits Mexico. 1990. (Blue Bug Bks.). (Illus.). 32p. (J). (ps-2). lib. bdg. 11.85 o.p. (*0-516-03429-4*); mass mkt. 3.95 o.p. (*0-516-43429-2*) Scholastic Library Publishing. (Children's Pr.).

Rhoads, Dorothy. The Corn Grows Ripe. 1993. (Puffin Newbery Library). (Illus.). 96p. (YA). (gr. 3-7). pap. 4.99 (*0-14-036313-0*, Puffin Bks.) Penguin Putnam Bks. for Young Readers.

—The Corn Grows Ripe. 1994. (J). 19.75 (*0-8446-6756-0*) Smith, Peter Pub., Inc.

—The Corn Grows Ripe. 1993. (J). 11.14 (*0-606-05215-1*) Turtleback Bks.

Richardson, Arleta. Across the Border. (Orphans' Journey Ser.: Vol. 4). (J). 128p. (gr. 3-7). pap. 5.99 (*0-7814-3535-8*); 1996. 144p. (gr. 4-7). 4.99 (*0-7814-0193-3*) Cook Communications Ministries.

Richardson, Kara, illus. Simon & Barklee in Mexico. 2002. (Simon & Barklee in Mexico). 64p. (J). 12.00 (*0-9714502-0-X*, Explorer Media) Simon & Barklee, Inc./ExplorerMedia.

Riecken, Nancy. Today Is the Day. 1996. (Illus.). 32p. (J). (ps-3). 14.95 o.p. (*0-395-73917-9*) Houghton Mifflin Co.

Ritchie, Marilynne K. Ramon Makes a Trade, 001. 1959. (ENG & SPA., Illus.). (J). (gr. 3-8). 7.95 o.p. (*0-395-28955-9*) Houghton Mifflin Co.

Roy, Cal. The Legend & the Storm, RS. 1975. (Illus.). 224p. (J). (gr. 7 up). 6.95 o.p. (*0-374-34367-5*, Farrar, Straus & Giroux (BYR)) Farrar, Straus & Giroux.

Ryan, Pam Muñoz. Mice & Beans. 2001. (Illus.). 32p. (J). (ps-2). pap. 15.95 (*0-439-18303-0*, Levine, Arthur A. Bks.) Scholastic, Inc.

Sanroman, Susana. Senora Reganona: A Mexican Bedtime Story. 1997. (Illus.). 20p. (J). (ps). reprint ed. 15.00 (*0-7567-6389-4*) DIANE Publishing Co.

—Senora Reganona: A Mexican Bedtime Story. (Illus.). (J). (ps-k). 2000. 32p. pap. 5.95 (*0-88899-389-7*); 1998. (SPA., 24p. pap. 14.95 (*0-88899-320-X*) Groundwood Bks. CAN. *Dist:* Publishers Group West.

—Senora Reganona: A Mexican Bedtime Story. 2000. 12.10 (*0-606-18344-2*) Turtleback Bks.

Schrade, Arlene O. Gabriel the Happy Ghost in Mexico. 1979. Tr. of Gabriel el Fantasmita Simpatico en Mexico. (ENG & SPA.). (J). 11.80 (*0-606-01277-X*) Turtleback Bks.

Shura, Mary Francis. Pornada. 1970. (Illus.). (J). (gr. 2-6). 1.19 o.s.i (*0-689-20617-8*, Atheneum) Simon & Schuster Children's Publishing.

Simon & Barklee in Mexico. 2002. 70p. tchr. ed. 20.00 (*0-9714502-2-6*, Explorer Media) Simon & Barklee, Inc./ExplorerMedia.

Soros, Barbara. Grandmother's Song. 1998. (Illus.). 32p. (J). (gr. 3-7). 15.95 (*1-902283-02-3*) Barefoot Bks., Inc.

Stolz, Mary. Dragons of the Queen. 1969. (Illus.). (J). (gr. 3-7). lib. bdg. 9.89 o.p. (*0-06-025973-6*) HarperCollins Pubs.

—Juan. 1970. (Illus.). (J). (gr. 3-7). 8.79 o.p. (*0-06-025914-0*) HarperCollins Pubs.

Strasser, Todd. The Diving Bell. 1992. 176p. (J). (gr. 4-6). pap. 13.95 (*0-590-44620-7*) Scholastic, Inc.

Talbert, Marc. Small Change. 2000. (Richard Jackson Bks.). (Illus.). 192p. (J). (gr. 4-7). pap. 16.95 o.p. (*0-7894-2531-9*, D K Ink) Dorling Kindersley Publishing, Inc.

Tenorio-Coscarelli, Jane. The Tortilla Quilt. 1996. (Illus.). 52p. (J). (ps-6). pap. 11.95 (*0-9653422-1-2*); 15.95 (*0-9653422-0-4*) Quarter-Inch Publishing.

Thompson, Carol. The Case of the Volcano Mystery. 1997. (Adventures of Mary-Kate & Ashley Ser.). 64p. (J). (gr. 2-7). mass mkt. 3.99 (*0-590-88014-4*, Scholastic Paperbacks) Scholastic, Inc.

Toepperwein, Emilie & Toepperwein, Fritz A. Jose & the Mexican Jumping Bean. 1965. (Illus.). (J). (gr. 4-7). lib. bdg. 2.95 (*0-910722-05-6*) Highland Pr.

Turner, Anna & Kitching, Beth. El Pato Paco. (Illus.). (J). (ps-1). 1994. 27p. pap. 5.49 (*0-89084-722-3*, 076398); Set. 2000. (SPA., pap. 9.98 incl. audio (*0-89084-900-5*, 078865) Jones, Bob Univ. Pr.

Villasenor, Victor. Los Trece Sentidos. 2001. 512p. 26.00 (*0-06-621297-9*, Rayo) HarperTrade.

Villicana, Eugenio. Viva Morelia. 1972. (Two Worlds Bks.). (Illus.). 64p. (J). (gr. 4-6). 3.95 o.p. (*0-87131-098-8*) Holt, Henry & Co.

West, Tracey. The Day of the Dead. 2004. (Scream Shop Ser.). (Illus.). 144p. mass mkt. 4.99 (*0-448-43360-5*, Grosset & Dunlap) Penguin Putnam Bks. for Young Readers.

Whitman, John. The Mask of Zorro. 1998. (Mighty Chronicles Ser.). (Illus.). 320p. (J). (gr. 3-7). 9.95 o.p. (*0-8118-2036-X*) Chronicle Bks. LLC.

Williams, Jeanne. Mission in Mexico. 2000. 196p. pap. 12.95 (*0-595-14642-2*, Backinprint.com) iUniverse, Inc.

—Tame the Wild Stallion. 1985. (Chaparral Bks.). (Illus.). 182p. (YA). (gr. 6 up). 14.95 (*0-87565-002-3*); (ps up). pap. 8.95 (*0-87565-009-0*) Texas Christian Univ. Pr.

Winter, Jeanette. Josefina. 1996. (Illus.). 36p. (J). (ps-3). 16.00 (*0-15-201091-2*) Harcourt Children's Bks.

Witton, Dorothy. Teen-Age Mexican Stories. 1973. 192p. (J). (gr. 7-12). lib. bdg. 6.19 o.p. (*0-8313-0106-6*) Lantern Pr., Inc., Pubs.

Woodman, Nancy. Sea-Fari Deep. 1998. (Illus.). 48p. (J). (gr. 3-7). 17.95 (*0-7922-7340-0*) National Geographic Society.

Yacowitz, Caryn. Pumpkin Fiesta. 1998. (Illus.). 32p. (J). (ps-1). 15.99 (*0-06-027658-4*) HarperCollins Children's Bk. Group.

MICHIGAN—FICTION

Bellairs, John. The House with a Clock in Its Walls. (Lewis Barnavelt Ser.). (Illus.). 192p. (J). 1993. (gr. 3-7). pap. 5.99 (*0-14-036336-X*, Puffin Bks.); 1984. (gr. 4-7). 13.95 o.p. (*0-8037-3821-8*, Dial Bks. for Young Readers); 1984. (gr. 4-7). 13.89 o.p. (*0-8037-3823-4*, Dial Bks. for Young Readers) Penguin Putnam Bks. for Young Readers.

—The House with a Clock in Its Walls. 179p. (J). (gr. 4-6). pap. 4.50 (*0-8072-1423-X*, Listening Library) Random Hse. Audio Publishing Group.

—The House with a Clock in Its Walls. 1974. 192p. (J). (gr. 3 up). pap. 3.50 o.s.i (*0-440-43742-3*, Yearling) Random Hse. Children's Bks.

—The House with a Clock in Its Walls, unabr. ed. 1992. (J). (gr. 5). audio 27.00 (*1-55690-587-4*, 92124E7) Recorded Bks., LLC.

—The House with a Clock in Its Walls. 1994. (J). 20.50 (*0-8446-6758-7*) Smith, Peter Pub., Inc.

—The House with a Clock in Its Walls. 1993. (J). 11.04 (*0-606-05353-0*) Turtleback Bks.

—The Letter, the Witch & the Ring. (Lewis Barnavelt Ser.). (Illus.). (J). 1993. 208p. (gr. 3 up). pap. 5.99 (*0-14-036338-6*, Puffin Bks.); 1985. (gr. 4-7). 7.45 o.p. (*0-8037-4741-1*, Dial Bks. for Young Readers); 1976. (gr. 4-7). 13.95 o.p. (*0-8037-4740-3*, Dial Bks. for Young Readers) Penguin Putnam Bks. for Young Readers.

—The Letter, the Witch & the Ring. 1977. 192p. (J). (gr. 3-6). pap. 3.25 o.s.i (*0-440-44722-4*, Yearling) Random Hse. Children's Bks.

—The Letter, the Witch & the Ring. 1993. (J). 12.04 (*0-606-05424-3*) Turtleback Bks.

Blos, Joan W. Brothers of the Heart: A Story of the Old Northwest, 1837-1838. 2nd ed. 1993. 176p. (J). (gr. 3-7). reprint ed. pap. 4.99 (*0-689-71724-5*, Aladdin) Simon & Schuster Children's Publishing.

—Brothers of the Heart: A Story of the Old Northwest, 1837-1838. 1993. (J). 11.04 (*0-606-12203-6*) Turtleback Bks.

Brill, Ethel C. Copper Country Adventure. 1988. 213p. (J). (gr. 4 up). 26.00 (*0-933249-05-5*) Mid-Peninsula Library Cooperative.

Bury, Laurie D. The Adventures of Dalbert Juan: Enjoying Michigan. 2000. (Illus.). 12.95 (*0-9702319-1-1*) Rhette Enterprises, Inc.

Center for Learning Network Staff & Arnow, Harriette Louisa Simpson. The Dollmaker: Curriculum Unit — Novel Series — Grades 8-12. 1996. (Novel Ser.). 74p. (YA). tchr. ed., spiral bd. 18.95 (*1-56077-490-8*) Ctr. for Learning, The.

Cory, Kim Delmar. Lilly's Way. Austin, Jane G., ed. 1998. 187p. (J). (gr. 4 up). pap. 9.99 (*0-88092-363-6*, 3636) Royal Fireworks Publishing Co.

Costello, Emily. Calling the Shots. 1999. (Soccer Stars Ser.: No. 7). 144p. (gr. 3-7). pap. text 3.99 o.s.i (*0-553-48683-7*, Dell Books for Young Readers) Random Hse. Children's Bks.

—Calling the Shots. 1999. (Soccer Stars Ser.: No. 7). (J). (gr. 3-7). 10.04 (*0-606-17152-5*) Turtleback Bks.

Curtis, Christopher Paul. Bud, Not Buddy. 1999. (Illus.). 256p. (gr. 4-7). text 16.95 (*0-385-32306-9*, Delacorte Pr.) Dell Publishing.

—Bud, Not Buddy. l.t. ed. 2000. (Young Adult Ser.). (Illus.). 279p. (J). (gr. 8-12). 22.95 (*0-7862-2574-2*) Thorndike Pr.

—The Watsons Go to Birmingham - 1963. 1999. 240p. (gr. 5-8). mass mkt. 2.99 o.s.i (*0-440-22836-0*) Bantam Bks.

—The Watsons Go to Birmingham - 1963. 1998. 15p. pap., stu. ed., tchr.'s training gde. ed. 15.95 (*1-58303-068-9*) Pathways Publishing.

—The Watsons Go to Birmingham - 1963. 210p. (YA). (gr. 5 up). pap. 5.50 (*0-8072-8336-3*); 2000. (J). pap. 37.00 incl. audio (*0-8072-8335-5*, YA166SP) Random Hse. Audio Publishing Group. (Listening Library).

—The Watsons Go to Birmingham - 1963. 2000. 224p. (YA). (gr. 5-7). mass mkt. 5.99 (*0-440-22800-X*, Laurel Leaf); 1997. 224p. (gr. 4-10). pap. text 6.50 (*0-440-41412-1*, Dell Books for Young Readers); 1997. (YA). pap. o.s.i (*0-440-41431-8*, Dell Books for Young Readers) Random Hse. Children's Bks.

—The Watsons Go to Birmingham - 1963. l.t. ed. 2000. (Illus.). 260p. (J). (ps up). 22.95 (*0-7862-2741-9*) Thorndike Pr.

—The Watsons Go to Birmingham - 1963. 1997. (YA). 12.04 (*0-606-10993-5*) Turtleback Bks.

—The Watsons Go to Birmingham—1963. 1995. 224p. (gr. 4-7). text 16.95 (*0-385-32175-9*, Dell Books for Young Readers) Random Hse. Children's Bks.

Curtis, Rebecca S. Charlotte Avery on Isle Royale. 1995. 192p. (J). 14.95 o.p. (*1-883953-09-X*) Midwest Traditions, Inc.

De Angeli, Marguerite. Copper-Toed Boots. 1938. (gr. k-4). 5.95 o.p. (*0-385-07264-3*) Doubleday Publishing.

Denboer, Helen. Pieter's & Anna's Trek. (Immigrants Chronicles Ser.). 132p. (J). (gr. 3-7). pap. 5.99 (*0-7814-3083-6*) Cook Communications Ministries.

Farley, Carol. Sergeant Finney's Family. 1969. (Illus.). (gr. 4-6). lib. bdg. 4.90 o.p. (*0-531-01915-2*, Watts, Franklin) Scholastic Library Publishing.

Lytle, Robert A. Three Rivers Crossing. 2000. 161p. (J). pap. 8.95 (*0-938682-60-1*); (gr. 4-8). 15.95 (*0-938682-55-5*) River Road Pubns., Inc.

Martin, Terri L. A Family Trait. 1999. 192p. (J). (gr. 3-7). tchr. ed. 15.95 (*0-8234-1467-1*) Holiday Hse., Inc.

Murray, Anna. Sarah's Page. 1998. (Illus.). 120p. (gr. 4-7). 14.00 (*1-886947-58-9*) Sleeping Bear Pr.

Orton, Helen F. Secret of the Rosewood Box. 1937. (Illus.). (J). (gr. 4-6). 8.95 o.p. (*0-397-31596-1*) HarperCollins Children's Bk. Group.

Panagopoulos, Janie Lynn. A Castle at the Straits. 2003. (Illus.). 48p. (J). (gr. 1-6). 18.95 (*0-911872-83-3*) Mackinac State Historic Parks.

—A Place Called Home: Michigan's Mill Creek Story. 2001. (Illus.). 48p. (J). 18.95 (*1-58536-054-6*) Sleeping Bear Pr.

—Traders in Time: A Dream-Quest Adventure. (J). (gr. 3-6). 1994. pap. 7.95 (*0-938682-27-X*); 1993. 200p. 14.95 o.p. (*0-938682-24-5*) River Road Pubns., Inc.

Pfitsch, Patricia C. Keeper of the Light. 1997. 137p. (YA). (gr. 5-9). 16.00 (*0-689-81492-5*, Simon & Schuster Children's Publishing) Simon & Schuster Children's Publishing.

Polacco, Patricia. The Calhoun Club. 2015. (Illus.). 48p. (J). 15.99 o.s.i (*0-399-23171-4*, Philomel) Penguin Putnam Bks. for Young Readers.

—Mrs. Mack. 2001. (J). 13.14 (*0-606-20813-5*) Turtleback Bks.

—My Ol' Man. 1995. (Illus.). 40p. (J). (gr. k-3). 16.99 (*0-399-22822-5*, Philomel) Penguin Putnam Bks. for Young Readers.

—The Trees of the Dancing Goats. 2002. (Illus.). (J). 25.11 (*0-7587-3858-7*) Book Wholesalers, Inc.

—The Trees of the Dancing Goats. 32p. (J). 2000. (Illus.). (gr. k-3). pap. 6.99 (*0-689-83857-3*, Aladdin); 1997. (gr. k-5). pap. 22.00 incl. audio compact disk (*0-689-81193-4*, Simon & Schuster Children's Publishing); 1996. (Illus.). (gr. 4-7). 16.00 (*0-689-80862-3*, Simon & Schuster Children's Publishing) Simon & Schuster Children's Publishing.

—The Trees of the Dancing Goats. 2000. 13.14 (*0-606-20094-0*) Turtleback Bks.

Rand, Jonathan. Dinosaurs Destroy Detroit. 2001. (Michigan Chillers: Vol. 8). 215p. (YA). pap. 5.99 (*1-893699-14-5*) AudioCraft Publishing, Inc.

Richardson, Arleta. The Grandma's Attic Storybook. 1993. 256p. (J). pap. 10.99 (*0-7814-0070-8*) Cook Communications Ministries.

Wagner, Jerri. Jako's Vacation. 2001. 58p. pap. 9.95 (*0-7414-0704-3*) Buy Bks. on the Web.Com.

Wargin, Kathy-Jo. The Michigan Reader. 2001. (Illus.). 90p. (J). 12.95 (*1-58536-042-2*) Sleeping Bear Pr.

Whelan, Gloria. Farewell to the Island. 208p. (gr. 4 up). 1999. (Illus.). (YA). pap. 5.99 (*0-06-440821-3*, Harper Trophy); 1998. (J). 16.95 (*0-06-027751-3*) HarperCollins Children's Bk. Group.

—Forgive the River, Forgive the Sky. 1998. 166p. (J). (gr. 4-7). 15.00 o.p. (*0-8028-5155-X*, Eerdmans Bks For Young Readers) Eerdmans, William B. Publishing Co.

—Night of the Full Moon. 1993. (Illus.). 64p. (J). (gr. 2-4). 15.00 o.s.i (*0-679-84464-3*); (gr. 4-7). 15.99 o.s.i (*0-679-94464-8*) Random Hse. Children's Bks. (Knopf Bks. for Young Readers).

—Night of the Full Moon. 1996. (Illus.). 64p. (J). (gr. 2-4). pap. 3.99 (*0-679-87276-0*) Random Hse., Inc.

—Once on This Island. (Trophy Bk.). 192p. (J). 1996. (gr. 3-7). pap. 5.99 (*0-06-440619-9*, Harper Trophy); 1995. (gr. k-3). 16.99 (*0-06-026248-6*); 1995. (gr. 3-7). lib. bdg. 14.89 (*0-06-026249-4*) HarperCollins Children's Bk. Group.

—Once on This Island. 1996. (J). 11.00 (*0-606-09709-0*) Turtleback Bks.

—The Pathless Woods: Ernest Hemingway's Sixteenth Summer in Northern Michigan. 2nd rev. ed. 1998. (Illus.). (J). (gr. 6-10). 16.95 (*1-882376-63-3*); 176p. (gr. 7-12). pap. 11.95 (*1-882376-44-7*) Thunder Bay Pr.

—Return to the Island. 2000. 192p. (J). (gr. 4). lib. bdg. 15.89 (*0-06-028254-1*); 14.95 (*0-06-028253-3*) HarperCollins Children's Bk. Group.

—Return to the Island. 2002. 192p. (J). (gr. 4-7). pap. 5.95 (*0-06-440761-6*) HarperCollins Pubs.

—The Wanigan: A Life on the River. (Illus.). 144p. (gr. 3-7). 2003. (YA). pap. 4.99 (*0-440-41882-8*, Dell Books for Young Readers); 2002. (J). 14.95 (*0-375-81429-9*, Knopf Bks. for Young Readers); 2002. (J). lib. bdg. 16.99 (*0-375-91429-3*, Knopf Bks. for Young Readers) Random Hse. Children's Bks.

White, Ruth. Memories of Summer, RS. 2000. 144p. (J). (gr. 7-10). 16.00 (*0-374-34945-2*, Farrar, Straus & Giroux (BYR)) Farrar, Straus & Giroux.

—Memories of Summer. 2002. 160p. (YA). (gr. 7 up). mass mkt. 5.99 (*0-440-22921-9*, Dell Books for Young Readers) Random Hse. Children's Bks.

—Memories of Summer. l.t. ed. 2001. (Illus.). 144p. (J). (gr. 5-9). 21.95 (*0-7862-3084-3*) Thorndike Pr.

MICHIGAN, LAKE—FICTION

Bergel, Colin. Mail by the Pail. 2000. (Great Lakes Bks.). (Illus.). (J). pap. 16.95 (*0-8143-2891-1*); 32p. (gr. 1-4). 16.95 (*0-8143-2890-3*, Great Lakes Bks.) Wayne State Univ. Pr.

Winter, Jeanette. The Christmas Tree Ship. 1998. (Illus.). 32p. (J). (ps-3). pap. 5.99 o.s.i (*0-698-11653-4*, PaperStar) Penguin Putnam Bks. for Young Readers.

MIDDLE EARTH (IMAGINARY PLACE)—FICTION

The Hobbit. 1999. (YA). 9.95 (*1-56137-253-6*) Novel Units, Inc.

The Lord of the Rings. (Lord of the Rings Ser.). (J). audio o.p. HarperTrade.

Tolkien, J. R. R. The Hobbit. 2002. 16.60 (*0-7587-7961-5*) Book Wholesalers, Inc.

—The Hobbit. (YA). 2002. 320p. (gr. 5). pap. 10.00 (*0-618-26030-7*); 1997. (Illus.). 289p. (gr. 7). 35.00 (*0-395-87346-0*); 1984. (Illus.). 304p. (gr. 7 up).

29.95 (*0-395-36290-3*); 1973. (Illus.). 320p. (gr. 7). 35.00 (*0-395-17711-1*); 1938. (Illus.). 320p. (gr. 7). 16.00 (*0-395-07122-4*) Houghton Mifflin Co.

—The Hobbit. 1989. (Illus.). 304p. (YA). (gr. 7-5). pap. 17.95 (*0-395-52021-5*) Houghton Mifflin Co. Trade & Reference Div.

—The Hobbit. unabr. ed. 2000. (YA). audio 25.95 (*0-8072-8883-7*, Listening Library) Random Hse. Audio Publishing Group.

—The Hobbit. (J). 1984. pap. 29.95 o.p. incl. audio (*0-88142-269-X*, 269); 1994. audio compact disk 29.95 (*1-55935-119-5*) Soundelux Audio Publishing.

—The Hobbit: A 3-D Pop-Up Adventure. 1999. (Illus.). 12p. (J). (gr. 2 up). 9.98 o.s.i (*0-694-01436-2*) HarperCollins Children's Bk. Group.

—The Lord of the Rings. unabr. ed. 2002. 129.99 incl. audio compact disk (*1-4025-1627-4*, 00312) Recorded Bks., LLC.

—The Lord of the Rings. abr. ed. (Lord of the Rings Ser.). 2001. audio compact disk 59.95 (*1-55935-120-9*); 1979. 12p. pap. 59.95 o.p. incl. audio (*0-88142-270-3*, 102629) Soundelux Audio Publishing.

MIDDLE EAST—FICTION

Alexander, Lloyd. The Jedera Adventure. 1994. 160p. (J). pap. 3.99 (*0-440-91004-8*) Dell Publishing.

—The Jedera Adventure. (gr. 5-9). 2001. (Illus.). 160p. (YA). pap. 5.99 (*0-14-131238-6*); 1989. 16p. (J). 13.95 o.p. (*0-525-44481-5*, Dutton Children's Bks.) Penguin Putnam Bks. for Young Readers.

—The Jedera Adventure. 1989. (J). 10.55 (*0-606-04442-6*) Turtleback Bks.

Alrawi, Karim. The Girl Who Lost Her Smile. 2000. (Illus.). 32p. (J). (ps-3). 16.95 (*1-890817-17-1*) Winslow Pr.

Alta, C. Allah Created Everything. 1995. (Illus.). 28p. (J). (gr. 1-3). 14.95 (*1-884187-09-9*) AMICA Publishing Hse.

Balaguae, Lin & Long, Robert, contrib. by. Alai Babaa y los 40 Ladrones: Ali Baba & the 40 Thieves. 2000. (Cuentos y Leyendas Bilingues Ser.). (ENG & SPA.). (J). 21.20 (*0-658-01023-9*, National Textbook Co.) McGraw-Hill/Contemporary.

Balague, Lin & Long, Robert. Ali Baba y los 40 Ladrones (Ali Baba & the 40 Thieves) 2000. (Cuentos y Leyendas Bilingues Ser.). (ENG & SPA., Illus.). (J). 17.68 (*0-658-01024-7*) McGraw-Hill/Contemporary.

Climo, Shirley. The Persian Cinderella. 2001. (Illus.). 32p. (J). (gr. k-4). pap. 5.95 (*0-06-443853-8*, Harper Trophy) HarperCollins Children's Bk. Group.

Hernandez, David, creator. The Crumbling Wall of Jericho. 2003. (Adventures of Toby Digz Ser.: Bk. 3). (Illus.). 96p. (J). pap. 5.99 (*1-4003-0285-4*) Nelson, Tommy.

Italia, Bob. Armed Forces. Wallner, Rosemary, ed. 1991. (War in the Gulf Ser.). (Illus.). (J). (gr. 5). lib. bdg. 25.65 (*1-56239-026-0*, ABDO & Daughters) ABDO Publishing Co.

Kyuchukov, Hristo. My Name Was Hussein. 2004. (J). pap. 15.95 (*1-56397-964-0*) Boyds Mills Pr.

Matze, Claire Sidhom. The Stars in My Geddoh's Sky. 32p. (J). 2002. pap. 6.95 (*0-8075-7610-7*, Prairie Paperbacks); 1999. (Illus.). pap. 14.95 (*0-8075-5332-8*) Whitman, Albert & Co.

Qadri, Maulana. Three-D Stories. 1985. 200p. (YA). (gr. 10-12). 12.00 o.p. (*1-56744-404-0*) Kazi Pubns., Inc.

Rose, Anne. Hamid & the Sultan's Son. 1975. (Illus.). 48p. (J). (gr. 2-5). 6.25 o.p. (*0-15-270101-X*) Harcourt Children's Bks.

Sabu, Jasmine. Moonshadow: The Adventures of the Thief of Bagdad. 1997. 278p. (Orig.). (J). (gr. 8-12). pap. 5.25 (*0-9655666-0-9*) UBASFILM, Ltd.

Schami, Rafik. A Hand Full of Stars. Lesser, Rika, tr. from GER. (gr. 7 up). 1992. 208p. (YA). pap. 4.99 o.s.i (*0-14-036073-5*, Puffin Bks.); 1990. 20p. (J). 14.95 o.p. (*0-525-44535-8*, Dutton Children's Bks.) Penguin Putnam Bks. for Young Readers.

Skolnick, Evan. Monkey Business. 1997. (Disney's Action Club Ser.). pap. text 4.50 (*1-57840-084-8*) Acclaim Bks.

Temple, Frances. The Beduins' Gazelle. 1998. (Harper Trophy Bks.). (Illus.). 160p. (J). (gr. 7 up). pap. 5.99 (*0-06-440669-5*, Harper Trophy) HarperCollins Children's Bk. Group.

—The Beduins' Gazelle. 1996. 160p. (YA). (gr. 7 up). pap. 15.95 (*0-531-09519-3*); lib. bdg. 16.99 (*0-531-08869-3*) Scholastic, Inc. (Orchard Bks.).

Thomas, Jerry D. Detective Zack & the Red Hat Mystery. 121p. (J). pap. 5.99 (*0-7814-3802-0*) Cook Communications Ministries.

—Detective Zack & the Red Hat Mystery. 1993. (Detective Zack Ser.: Vol. 3). 126p. (J). (gr. 4-7). pap. 6.99 (*0-8163-1169-2*) Pacific Pr. Publishing Assn.

—Detective Zack & the Secrets in the Sand. 124p. (J). pap. 5.99 (*0-7814-3803-9*) Cook Communications Ministries.

—Detective Zack & the Secrets in the Sand. 1993. (Detective Zack Ser.: No. 2). 127p. (J). (gr. 4-7). pap. 6.99 (*0-8163-1129-3*) Pacific Pr. Publishing Assn.

Ulwani, Abd-al-Wahid. Ma'ajim Marhalat Al-Hadanah: Dalil al-Murabbi. 1994. (Majalis Bi'r 'Ajam Ser.: Al-Hadanah). 288p. (J). 47.95 (*1-57547-002-0*) Dar Al-Fikr Al-Mouaser.

Ware, Cheryl. Sea Monkey Summer. 1996. 144p. (J). (gr. 4-6). mass mkt. 15.99 o.p. (*0-531-08868-5*, Orchard Bks.) Scholastic, Inc.

MIDDLE WEST—FICTION

Fleischman, Sid. Chancy & the Grand Rascal. 1997. (Illus.). 192p. (YA). (gr. 3 up). pap. 4.95 o.s.i (*0-688-14924-3*); reprint ed. 15.00 (*0-688-14923-5*) HarperCollins Children's Bk. Group. (Greenwillow Bks.).

—Chancy & the Grand Rascal. 1989. (Illus.). 190p. (J). (gr. 3-7). 14.95 (*0-316-28575-7*); mass mkt. 4.95 (*0-316-26012-6*) Little Brown & Co. (Joy Street Bks.).

Hubalek, Linda K. Butter in the World: A Scandinavian Woman's Tale of Light on the Praiire. 1994. (Butter in the Well Ser.: Bk. 1). (Illus.). 148p. reprint ed. pap. 9.95 (*1-886652-00-7*) Butterfield Bks., Inc.

—Looking Back: The Final Tale of Life on the Prairie. 1995. (Butter in the Well Ser.: Bk. 4). (Illus.). 140p. (J). (gr. 4-12). reprint ed. pap. 9.95 (*1-886652-03-1*) Butterfield Bks., Inc.

—Prarieblomman: The Prairie Blossoms for an Immigrant's Daughter. 1994. (Butter in the Well Ser.: Bk. 2). (Illus.). 144p. (J). reprint ed. pap. 9.95 (*1-886652-01-5*) Butterfield Bks., Inc.

Lawlor, Laurie. Addie's Long Summer. 1995. (Illus.). 176p. (J). (gr. 3-7). reprint ed. pap. 3.50 (*0-671-52607-3*, Aladdin) Simon & Schuster Children's Publishing.

—Addie's Long Summer. 1995. (J). 9.55 (*0-606-07178-4*) Turtleback Bks.

—Addie's Long Summer. Tucker, Kathleen, ed. 1992. (Illus.). 176p. (J). (gr. 7 up). 13.95 o.p. (*0-8075-0167-0*) Whitman, Albert & Co.

MacLachlan, Patricia. Caleb's Story. 2001. (Sarah, Plain & Tall Ser.). 128p. (J). (gr. 3-5). 14.95 (*0-06-023605-1*); (gr. 7 up). lib. bdg. 15.89 (*0-06-023606-X*) HarperCollins Children's Bk. Group. (Cotler, Joanna Bks.).

McGugan, Jim. Josepha: A Prairie Boy's Story. 1993. (Northern Lights Books for Children Ser.). (Illus.). 32p. (YA). (gr. 2 up). text 14.95 (*0-88995-101-2*) Red Deer Pr. CAN. *Dist:* General Distribution Services, Inc.

Rapp, Adam. 33 Snowfish. 2003. (Illus.). 192p. (YA). (gr. 10 up). 15.99 (*0-7636-1874-8*) Candlewick Pr.

Sherman, Eileen B. The Violin Players. 1998. 130p. (YA). (gr. 5 up). 14.95 (*0-8276-0595-1*) Jewish Pubn. Society.

Wilder, Laura Ingalls. A Little House Birthday. 1998. (My First Little House Bks.). (Illus.). 40p. (J). (ps-3). pap. 5.99 (*0-06-443494-X*) HarperCollins Pubs.

—A Little House Birthday. 1997. (My First Little House Bks.). 12.10 (*0-606-15617-8*) Turtleback Bks.

—A Little Prairie House. (My First Little House Bks.). (Illus.). (J). (ps-3). 1999. 32p. pap. 5.99 (*0-06-443526-1*, Harper Trophy); 1998. 40p. 14.99 (*0-06-025907-8*) HarperCollins Children's Bk. Group.

—A Little Prairie House. 1998. (My First Little House Bks.). 12.10 (*0-606-16687-4*) Turtleback Bks.

MILWAUKEE (WIS.)—FICTION

Wilkins, Celia. Little City by the Lake. 2003. (Little House Ser.). (Illus.). 320p. (J). (gr. 3-7). 16.99 (*0-06-027006-3*); (gr. 5 up). pap. 5.99 (*0-06-440735-7*) HarperCollins Children's Bk. Group.

MINNESOTA—FICTION

Bauer, Marion Dane. Land of the Buffalo Bones: The Diary of Mary Elizabeth Rodgers, an English Girl in Minnesota. 2003. (Dear America Ser.). (Illus.). 240p. (J). pap. 12.95 (*0-439-22027-0*) Scholastic, Inc.

Blair, Yogi. Minnesota Fortune Cookies. 5th ed. 1993. 26p. (YA). (gr. 11 up). pap. 8.95 (*0-930366-73-5*) Northcountry Publishing Co.

Brock, Emma L. Topsy-Turvy Family. 1962. (Illus.). (J). (gr. 3-7). lib. bdg. 4.99 o.p. (*0-394-91760-X*, Knopf Bks. for Young Readers) Random Hse. Children's Bks.

Casanova, Mary. When Eagles Fall. 2002. 144p. (J). 15.99 (*0-7868-0665-6*); lib. bdg. 16.49 (*0-7868-2557-X*) Hyperion Bks. for Children.

—Wolf Shadows. 144p. (J). (gr. 3-7). 1999. pap. 5.99 (*0-7868-1340-7*); 1997. (Illus.). 14.95 o.p. (*0-7868-0325-8*); 1997. (Illus.). lib. bdg. 15.49 (*0-7868-2269-4*) Hyperion Bks. for Children.

—Wolf Shadows. 1999. 144p. (J). pap. 5.99 (*0-7868-1415-2*) Little Brown & Co.

Clark, Ann Nolan. All This Wild Land. 1976. (J). (gr. 7-12). 7.95 o.p. (*0-670-11444-8*) Viking Penguin.

Dean, Pamela. Juniper, Gentian & Rosemary. 1999. 352p. (J). pap. 14.95 (*0-312-85970-8*, Tor Bks.) Doherty, Tom Assocs., LLC.

Delton, Judy. Wild, Wild West. 1999. (Pee Wee Scouts Ser.: No. 37). (Illus.). 112p. (gr. 2-5). pap. text 3.99 o.s.i (*0-440-41342-7*, Dell Books for Young Readers) Random Hse. Children's Bks.

—Wild, Wild West. 1999. (Pee Wee Scouts Ser.: No. 37). (J). (gr. 2-5). 10.04 (*0-606-16585-1*) Turtleback Bks.

Dines, Carol. Talk to Me: Stories & a Novella. 1999. (Laurel-Leaf Bks.). 240p. (YA). (gr. 7 up). mass mkt. 4.50 o.s.i (*0-440-22026-2*, Dell Books for Young Readers) Random Hse. Children's Bks.

—Talk to Me: Stories & a Novella. 1999. 10.55 (*0-606-16451-0*) Turtleback Bks.

Duey, Kathleen & Bale, Karen. Forest Fire, Hinckley, Minnesota, 1894. 1999. (Survival! Ser.: No. 10). (J). (gr. 4-7). 10.04 (*0-606-16301-8*) Turtleback Bks.

Duey, Kathleen & Bale, Karen A. Forest Fire, Hinckley, Minnesota, 1894, 1999. (Survival! Ser.: No. 10). 160p. (J). (gr. 3-7). mass mkt. 3.99 (*0-689-82928-0*, 076714004504, Aladdin) Simon & Schuster Children's Publishing.

Durbin, William. Blackwater Ben. 2003. 208p. (gr. 5). text 15.95 (*0-385-72928-6*); lib. bdg. 17.99 (*0-385-90149-6*) Random Hse. Children's Bks. (Delacorte Bks. for Young Readers).

—The Journal of Otto Peltonen: A Finnish Immigrant: Hibbing, Minnesota, 1905. 2000. (My Name Is America Ser.). (Illus.). 163p. (J). (gr. 4-8). pap. 10.95 (*0-439-09254-X*) Scholastic, Inc.

—Song of Sampo Lake. 2002. 224p. (gr. 4-7). lib. bdg. 17.99 (*0-385-90055-4*); (gr. 5 up). text 15.95 (*0-385-32731-5*) Dell Publishing. (Delacorte Pr.).

—Song of Sampo Lake. 2004. 224p. (gr. 5). pap. text 5.50 (*0-440-22899-9*, Yearling) Random Hse. Children's Bks.

Ellsworth, Loretta. The Shrouding Woman, ERS. 2002. 160p. (YA). (gr. 5-8). 16.95 (*0-8050-6651-9*, Holt, Henry & Co. Bks. For Young Readers) Holt, Henry & Co.

Fleck, Earl. Chasing Fire: Danger in Canoe Country. 2004. (Illus.). 173p. (J). pap. 12.95 (*0-930100-53-0*) Holy Cow! Pr.

Hassler, Jon. Four Miles to Pinecone. 1989. 128p. (gr. 7-12). mass mkt. 5.99 (*0-449-70323-1*, Fawcett) Ballantine Bks.

—Four Miles to Pinecone. 1977. (Illus.). (J). (gr. 5 up). 6.95 o.p. (*0-7232-6143-1*, Warne, Frederick) Penguin Putnam Bks. for Young Readers.

Hutchens, Paul. The Lost Campers. (Sugar Creek Gang Ser.: Vol. 4). (J). 1968. (gr. 3-7). mass mkt. 3.99 o.p. (*0-8024-4804-6*); rev. ed. 1989. (gr. 2-7). pap. 4.99 o.p. (*0-8024-6959-0*); 4th rev. ed. 1997. 128p. (gr. 4-7). mass mkt. 4.99 (*0-8024-7008-4*, 659) Moody Pr.

Kirsten Saves the Day: A Summer Story. 2001. (Frequently Requested Ser.). lib. bdg. (*1-59054-094-8*) Fitzgerald Bks.

Kresel, Maryann. Thoughts of Yesterday. 1989. (Illus.). 106p. (Orig.). (J). pap. 9.95 (*0-944958-37-0*) Elfin Cove Pr.

Lane, Rose Wilder. Young Pioneers. 1998. (Little House Ser.). (Illus.). 192p. (J). (gr. 3 up). pap. 5.99 (*0-06-440698-9*, Harper Trophy) HarperCollins Children's Bk. Group.

—Young Pioneers. 1998. (Little House Ser.). (YA). (gr. 3 up). 12.00 (*0-606-17778-7*) Turtleback Bks.

Lasky, Kathryn. Marven of the Great North Woods. (Illus.). 48p. (J). (gr. 1-4). 2002. pap. 7.00 (*0-15-216826-5*, Voyager Bks./Libros Viajeros); 1997. 16.00 (*0-15-200104-2*) Harcourt Children's Bks.

Lee, Marie G. Necessary Roughness. 1998. 240p. (J). (gr. 7 up). pap. 5.99 (*0-06-447169-1*, Harper Trophy) HarperCollins Children's Bk. Group.

—Necessary Roughness. 1998. (J). 11.00 (*0-606-13000-4*) Turtleback Bks.

Lovelace, Maud Hart. Betsy & Joe. 1948. (Illus.). 256p. (YA). (gr. 5 up). 14.95 o.s.i (*0-690-13378-2*) HarperCollins Children's Bk. Group.

—Betsy & Tacy Go Downtown. 1966. (Illus.). 192p. (J). (gr. 2-5). lib. bdg. 14.89 o.p. (*0-690-13450-9*) HarperCollins Children's Bk. Group.

—Betsy & Tacy Go over the Big Hill. 1966. (Illus.). 176p. (J). (gr. 2-5). lib. bdg. 14.89 o.p. (*0-690-13521-1*) HarperCollins Children's Bk. Group.

—Betsy in Spite of Herself. 1946. (Illus.). 272p. (J). (gr. 5 up). 14.95 (*0-690-13662-5*) HarperCollins Children's Bk. Group.

—Betsy-Tacy. 1966. (Illus.). 128p. (J). (gr. 2-5). lib. bdg. 14.89 o.p. (*0-690-13805-9*) HarperCollins Children's Bk. Group.

—Betsy-Tacy & Tib. 1966. (Illus.). 144p. (J). (gr. 2-5). lib. bdg. 14.89 o.p. (*0-690-13876-8*) HarperCollins Children's Bk. Group.

—Betsy's Wedding. 1955. (Illus.). 241p. (J). (gr. 5 up). 14.95 o.s.i (*0-690-13733-8*) HarperCollins Children's Bk. Group.

—Heaven to Betsy. 1945. (Illus.). 268p. (J). (gr. 5-11). 14.95 (*0-690-37449-6*) HarperCollins Children's Bk. Group.

Marsh, Carole. Minnesota Coastales. 1994. (Carole Marsh Minnesota Bks.). (Illus.). (J). (gr. 3 up). pap. 19.95 (*1-55609-655-0*); lib. bdg. 29.95 (*1-55609-654-2*); cd-rom 29.95 (*1-55609-656-9*) Gallopade International.

—Minnesota Silly Football Sportsmysteries, Vol. II. 1994. (Carole Marsh Minnesota Bks.). (Illus.). (J). (gr. 3 up). pap. 19.95 (*1-55609-652-6*); lib. bdg. 29.95 (*1-55609-651-8*); cd-rom 29.95 (*1-55609-653-4*) Gallopade International.

Marvin, Isabel R. A Bride for Anna's Papa. 1994. (Illus.). 144p. (J). 14.95 o.p. (*0-915943-89-1*); (gr. 3-8). pap. 6.95 (*0-915943-93-X*) Milkweed Editions.

—The Tenth Rifle. Date not set. (Illus.). 128p. (Orig.). (J). (gr. 3-8). pap. 9.95 (*0-89896-109-2*) Larksdale.

McColley, Kevin. Pecking Order. 224p. (YA). 2000. (gr. 12 up). pap. 4.95 (*0-06-440516-8*); 1994. (gr. 7 up). 16.00 o.p. (*0-06-023554-3*); 1994. (gr. 7 up). lib. bdg. 15.89 o.p. (*0-06-023555-1*) HarperCollins Children's Bk. Group.

Miller, Susan Martins. Lights for Minneapolis. 27th ed. 1998. (American Adventure Ser.: No. 27). (Illus.). (J). (gr. 3-7). pap. 3.97 (*1-57748-289-1*) Barbour Publishing, Inc.

Nichols, James. Boundary Waters. 1986. 176p. (YA). (gr. 7 up). 12.95 o.p. (*0-8234-0616-4*) Holiday Hse., Inc.

Nixon, Joan Lowery. Land of Dreams. l.t. ed. 2001. (Ellis Island Stories Ser.). 153p. (J). (gr. 4 up). lib. bdg. 22.60 (*0-8368-2810-0*) Stevens, Gareth Inc.

—Land of Dreams. 1994. (Ellis Island Ser.). 9.09 o.p. (*0-606-07160-1*) Turtleback Bks.

Okimoto, Jean Davies. Blumpoe the Grumpoe Meets Arnold the Cat. 2nd ed. 1997. (Illus.). 28p. (J). (gr. k-5). reprint ed. (*0-9661149-0-6*, 1) Partners/West.

Paulsen, Gary. Popcorn Days & Buttermilk Nights. (J). 1989. 112p. (gr. 4-7). pap. 4.99 (*0-14-034204-4*, Puffin Bks.); 1983. 160p. (gr. 7 up). 10.95 o.p. (*0-525-66770-9*, Dutton Children's Bks.) Penguin Putnam Bks. for Young Readers.

—Popcorn Days & Buttermilk Nights. 1989. (J). 11.04 (*0-606-02250-3*) Turtleback Bks.

—The Winter Room. 1989. 128p. (J). (gr. 6-9). lib. bdg. 16.99 (*0-531-08439-6*); (YA). (gr. 7 up). pap. 15.95 (*0-531-05839-5*) Scholastic, Inc. (Orchard Bks.).

Qualey, Marsha. Come in from the Cold. 1994. 224p. (YA). (gr. 7 up). tchr. ed. 16.00 (*0-395-68986-4*) Houghton Mifflin Co.

—One Night. 176p. 2003. (YA). pap. 5.99 (*0-14-250150-6*, Puffin Bks.); 2002. (Illus.). (J). 16.99 (*0-8037-2602-3*, Dial Bks. for Young Readers) Penguin Putnam Bks. for Young Readers.

Riddell, Ruth. Ice Warrior. 1992. 144p. (J). (gr. 4-7). lib. bdg. 15.00 o.s.i (*0-689-31710-7*, Atheneum) Simon & Schuster Children's Publishing.

Rylant, Cynthia. Old Town in the Green Groves: Laura Ingalls Wilder's Lost Little House Years. 2002. (Little House Ser.). (Illus.). 176p. (J). (gr. 3-7). lib. bdg. 16.89 (*0-06-029562-7*); (ps-1). 15.99 (*0-06-029561-9*) HarperCollins Children's Bk. Group.

Schultz, Jan Neubert. Firestorm. 2002. (Adventures in Time Ser.). 204p. (J). (gr. 4-7). lib. bdg. 15.95 (*0-87614-276-5*, Carolrhoda Bks.) Lerner Publishing Group.

—Horse Sense: The Story of Will Sasse, His Horse Star & the Outlaw Jesse James. 2001. (Adventures in Time Ser.). 180p. (J). (gr. 4-7). lib. bdg. 15.95 (*1-57505-998-3*, Carolrhoda Bks.) Lerner Publishing Group.

Shaw, Janet Beeler. Changes for Kirsten: A Winter Story. 1988. (American Girls Collection: Bk. 6). (Illus.). 65p. (YA). (gr. 2 up). 12.95 o.p. (*0-937295-44-2*) Pleasant Co. Pubns.

—Changes for Kirsten: A Winter Story. Thieme, Jeanne, ed. 1988. (American Girls Collection: Bk. 6). (Illus.). 80p. (J). (gr. 2 up). pap. 5.95 (*0-937295-45-0*); lib. bdg. 12.95 (*0-937295-94-9*) Pleasant Co. Pubns. (American Girl).

—Changes for Kirsten: A Winter Story. 1988. (American Girls Collection: Bk. 6). (Illus.). (YA). (gr. 2 up). 12.10 (*0-606-03749-7*) Turtleback Bks.

—Happy Birthday, Kirsten! A Springtime Story. Thieme, Jeanne, ed. 1987. (American Girls Collection: Bk. 4). (Illus.). 72p. (gr. 2 up). (J). 12.95 (*0-937295-88-4*, American Girl); (J). pap. 5.95 (*0-937295-33-7*, American Girl); (YA). 12.95 o.p. (*0-937295-32-9*) Pleasant Co. Pubns.

—Happy Birthday, Kirsten! A Springtime Story. 1987. (American Girls Collection: Bk. 4). (Illus.). (YA). (gr. 2 up). 12.10 (*0-606-03798-5*) Turtleback Bks.

—Kirsten & the Chippewa. 2002. (American Girls Short Stories Ser.). (Illus.). 56p. (J). 4.95 (*1-58485-479-0*, American Girl) Pleasant Co. Pubns.

—Kirsten Learns a Lesson: A School Story. Thieme, Jeanne, ed. 1986. (American Girls Collection: Bk. 2). (Illus.). (gr. 2 up). 80p. (J). pap. 5.95 (*0-937295-10-8*, American Girl); 72p. (YA). 12.95 o.p. (*0-937295-09-4*) Pleasant Co. Pubns.

—Kirsten Learns a Lesson: A School Story. 1986. (American Girls Collection: Bk. 2). (Illus.). (YA). (gr. 2 up). 12.10 (*0-606-02289-9*) Turtleback Bks.

—Kirsten Saves the Day: A Summer Story. Thieme, Jeanne, ed. 1988. (American Girls Collection: Bk. 5). (Illus.). (gr. 2 up). 80p. (J). pap. 5.95 (*0-937295-39-6*, American Girl); 66p. (J). lib. bdg. 12.95 (*0-937295-91-4*, American Girl); 72p. (YA). 12.95 o.p. (*0-937295-38-8*) Pleasant Co. Pubns.

—Kirsten Saves the Day: A Summer Story. 1988. (American Girls Collection: Bk. 5). (Illus.). (YA). (gr. 2 up). 12.10 (*0-606-03840-X*) Turtleback Bks.

—Kirsten Snowbound! 2001. (American Girls Short Stories Ser.). (Illus.). 56p. (J). (gr. 2). 3.95 (*1-58485-273-9*, American Girl) Pleasant Co. Pubns.

—Kirsten's Boxed Set: Meet Kirsten; Kirsten Learns a Lesson; Kirsten's Surprise; Happy Birthday, Kirsten!; Kirsten Saves the Day; Changes for Kirsten. 1991. (American Girls Collection: Bks. 1-6). (Illus.). 400p. (YA). (gr. 2 up). 74.95 o.p. (*1-56247-012-4*) Pleasant Co. Pubns.

—Kirsten's Boxed Set: Meet Kirsten; Kirsten Learns a Lesson; Kirsten's Surprise; Happy Birthday, Kirsten!; Kirsten Saves the Day; Changes for Kirsten, 6 bks. Thieme, Jeanne, ed. 1990. (American Girls Collection: Bks. 1-6). (Illus.). (J). 388p. (gr. 2 up). 74.95 (*1-56247-049-3*); 400p. (gr. 3-7). pap. 34.95 (*0-937295-76-0*) Pleasant Co. Pubns. (American Girl).

—Kirsten's Promise. 2003. (American Girls Collection). (Illus.). 38p. (J). pap. 4.95 (*1-58485-696-3*, American Girl) Pleasant Co. Pubns.

—Kirsten's Story Collection. 2001. (American Girls Collection). (Illus.). 366p. (J). (gr. 2 up). 29.95 (*1-58485-443-X*, American Girl) Pleasant Co. Pubns.

—Kirsten's Surprise: A Christmas Story. Thieme, Jeanne, ed. 1986. (American Girls Collection: Bk. 3). (Illus.). 72p. (gr. 2 up). (J). pap. 5.95 (*0-937295-19-1*, American Girl); (J). lib. bdg. 12.95 (*0-937295-85-X*, American Girl); (YA). 12.95 o.p. (*0-937295-18-3*) Pleasant Co. Pubns.

—Kirsten's Surprise: A Christmas Story. 1986. (American Girls Collection: Bk. 3). (Illus.). (YA). (gr. 2 up). 12.10 (*0-606-02290-2*) Turtleback Bks.

—Meet Kirsten: An American Girl. Thieme, Jeanne, ed. 1986. (American Girls Collection: Bk. 1). (Illus.). 72p. (gr. 2 up). (J). lib. bdg. 12.95 (*0-937295-79-5*, American Girl); (YA). pap. 5.95 (*0-937295-01-9*, American Girl); (YA). 12.95 o.p. (*0-937295-00-0*) Pleasant Co. Pubns.

—Meet Kirsten: An American Girl. 1986. (American Girls Collection: Bk. 1). (Illus.). (YA). (gr. 2 up). 12.10 (*0-606-02754-8*) Turtleback Bks.

Sorensen, Henri. New Hope. 1998. 32p. (J). pap. 5.99 o.p. (*0-14-056359-8*, Puffin Bks.) Penguin Putnam Bks. for Young Readers.

Thomas, Jane Resh. Courage at Indian Deep. 1984. (Illus.). 128p. (J). (gr. 3-7). 13.95 o.p. (*0-89919-181-9*, Clarion Bks.) Houghton Mifflin Co. Trade & Reference Div.

Travis, L. The Redheaded Orphan. 1995. (Ben & Zack Ser.: Vol. 3). 154p. (J). (gr. 3-8). pap. 5.99 o.p. (*0-8010-4023-X*) Baker Bks.

Weaver, Will. Claws: A Novel. 2004. 240p. (J). pap. 6.99 (*0-06-009475-3*, HarperTempest) HarperCollins Children's Bk. Group.

—Claws: A Novel. 2003. 240p. (J). 15.99 (*0-06-009473-7*); lib. bdg. 16.89 (*0-06-009474-5*) HarperCollins Pubs.

—Farm Team. 288p. 1999. (J). (gr. 6 up). pap. 5.99 (*0-06-447118-7*, Harper Trophy); 1995. (YA). (gr. 7 up). 14.95 o.p. (*0-06-023588-8*); 1995. (Illus.). (YA). (gr. 6 up). lib. bdg. 15.89 (*0-06-023589-6*) HarperCollins Children's Bk. Group.

—Farm Team. 1999. 11.00 (*0-606-15860-X*) Turtleback Bks.

—Hard Ball. (gr. 6 up). 1999. 256p. (J). pap. 5.99 (*0-06-447208-6*, Harper Trophy); 1998. 240p. (YA). 15.95 (*0-06-027121-3*); 1998. 240p. (YA). lib. bdg. 15.89 (*0-06-027122-1*) HarperCollins Children's Bk. Group.

—Hard Ball. 1999. 11.00 (*0-606-16706-4*) Turtleback Bks.

—Hard Ball: A Billy Baggs Novel. l.t. ed. 2000. (Illus.). 270p. (YA). (gr. 8-12). 20.95 (*0-7862-2752-4*) Thorndike Pr.

—Striking Out. (J). 1995. (Illus.). 304p. (gr. 6 up). pap. 6.99 (*0-06-447113-6*, Harper Trophy); 1993. 288p. (gr. 5 up). 15.00 o.p. (*0-06-023346-X*); 1993. 288p. (gr. 5 up). lib. bdg. 14.89 o.p. (*0-06-023347-8*) HarperCollins Children's Bk. Group.

—Striking Out. 1995. (J). 11.00 (*0-606-08211-5*) Turtleback Bks.

Welch, Catherine A. Clouds of Terror. (On My Own History Ser.). (Illus.). (J). (gr. 1-3). 1994. 56p. pap. 6.95 (*0-87614-639-6*); 1993. 48p. lib. bdg. 21.27 (*0-87614-771-6*) Lerner Publishing Group. (Carolrhoda Bks.).

Wells, Rosemary. Wingwalker. 2002. (Illus.). 80p. (J). (gr. 2-5). 15.99 (*0-7868-0397-5*); lib. bdg. 16.49 (*0-7868-2347-X*) Hyperion Bks. for Children.

Wilder, Laura Ingalls. On the Banks of Plum Creek. (Little House Ser.). (J). 2003. 304p. pap. 5.99 (*0-06-052239-9*); 1953. (Illus.). 352p. (gr. 3-7). pap. 6.99 (*0-06-440004-2*, Harper Trophy); rev. ed. 1953. (Illus.). 352p. (gr. 3-7). lib. bdg. 17.89 (*0-06-026471-3*); 32nd rev. ed. 1953. (Illus.). 352p. (gr. 3-7). 16.99 (*0-06-026470-5*) HarperCollins Children's Bk. Group.

—On the Banks of Plum Creek. l.t. ed. 2002. (LRS Large Print Cornerstone Ser.). (Illus.). (J). lib. bdg. 35.95 (*1-58118-099-3*, 25531) LRS.

—On the Banks of Plum Creek. 1971. (Little House Ser.). (J). (gr. 3-6). 12.00 (*0-606-04233-4*) Turtleback Bks.

Wilson, Pauline Hutchens & Dengler, Sandy. The Case of the Loony Cruise. 2001. (New Sugar Creek Gang Ser.: Vol. 5). 144p. (J). mass mkt. 5.99 (*0-8024-8665-7*) Moody Pr.

Wosmek, Frances. A Brown Bird Singing. 1993. (Illus.). 128p. (J). (gr. 5 up). pap. 4.95 o.p. (*0-688-04596-0*, Morrow, William & Co.) Morrow/Avon.

Ylvisaker, Anne. Dear Papa. 2002. 192p. (J). (gr. 5-8). 15.99 (*0-7636-1618-4*) Candlewick Pr.

MISSISSIPPI—FICTION

Applegate, Stanley. The Devil's Highway. 1998. (Illus.). 224p. (YA). (gr. 3-7). pap. 8.95 (*1-56145-184-3*, Peachtree Junior) Peachtree Pubs., Ltd.

—The Devil's Highway. 1998. (J). 15.00 (*0-606-19042-2*) Turtleback Bks.

Armistead, John. The Return of Gabriel. 2002. (Illus.). 240p. (J). (gr. 3-8). 17.95 (*1-57131-637-X*); pap. 6.95 (*1-57131-638-8*) Milkweed Editions.

Ball, Zachary. Bristle Face. 1962. (Illus.). 206p. (J). (gr. 5 up). 9.95 o.p. (*0-8234-0013-1*) Holiday Hse., Inc.

—Bristle Face. 1993. 208p. (J). (gr. 5 up). pap. 3.99 o.p. (*0-14-036444-7*, Puffin Bks.) Penguin Putnam Bks. for Young Readers.

—Kep. 1961. 208p. (J). (gr. 7-9). 4.95 o.p. (*0-8234-0064-6*) Holiday Hse., Inc.

Burman, Ben L. Blow a Bugle at Catfish Bend. 1981. 132p. (J). (gr. 3-5). pap. 1.95 o.p. (*0-380-53504-1*, 53504-1, Avon Bks.) Morrow/Avon.

—High Treason at Catfish Bend. 1981. 144p. (J). (gr. 3-5). pap. 1.95 o.p. (*0-380-53512-2*, 53512-2, Avon Bks.) Morrow/Avon.

—High Water at Catfish Bend. 1981. 132p. (J). (gr. 3-5). pap. 1.95 o.p. (*0-380-53470-3*, 53470-3, Avon Bks.) Morrow/Avon.

—The Owl Hoots Twice at Catfish Bend. 1981. 132p. (J). (gr. 3-5). pap. 1.95 o.p. (*0-380-53496-7*, 53496-7, Avon Bks.) Morrow/Avon.

—Seven Stars for Catfish Bend. 1981. (Illus.). 88p. (J). (gr. 3-5). pap. 1.95 o.p. (*0-380-53488-6*, 53488-6, Avon Bks.) Morrow/Avon.

—The Strange Invasion of Catfish Bend. 1981. 156p. (J). (gr. 3-5). pap. 1.95 o.p. (*0-380-53520-3*, 53520-3, Avon Bks.) Morrow/Avon.

Butterworth, W. E., pseud. Leroy & the Old Man. 1982. 168p. (J). (gr. 7 up). pap. 2.50 o.p. (*0-590-40573-X*, Scholastic Paperbacks) Scholastic, Inc.

Cannon, Taffy. Mississippi Treasure Hunt. 1996. (J). (gr. 7). mass mkt. 4.50 o.s.i (*0-449-70450-5*, Fawcett) Ballantine Bks.

Coleman, Evelyn. White Socks Only. (Prairie Paperback Bks.). (Illus.). 32p. (J). (gr. k-4). 1999. pap. 6.95 (*0-8075-8956-X*); 1996. lib. bdg. 15.95 (*0-8075-8955-1*) Whitman, Albert & Co.

Cooper, Jason. The Mississippi Delta. 1995. (Natural Wonders Ser.). (J). (gr. 2-6). lib. bdg. 13.95 (*1-57103-016-6*) Rourke Publishing, LLC.

Crowe, Chris. The Mississippi Trial, 1955. 2003. 240p. pap. 5.99 (*0-14-250192-1*, Puffin Bks.) Penguin Putnam Bks. for Young Readers.

Duey, Kathleen. Emma Eileen Grove: Mississippi, 1865. 1996. (American Diaries Ser.: No. 2). (Illus.). 144p. (J). (gr. 3-7). pap. 4.99 (*0-689-80385-0*, Aladdin) Simon & Schuster Children's Publishing.

—Emma Eileen Grove: Mississippi, 1865. 1996. (American Diaries Ser.: No. 2). (J). (gr. 3-7). 10.55 (*0-606-08986-1*) Turtleback Bks.

Ernst, Kathleen. Ghosts of Vicksburg. 2003. (White Main Kids Ser.: 13). (Illus.). 180p. (J). pap. 8.95 (*1-57249-322-4*, WM Kids) White Mane Publishing Co., Inc.

Faulkner, William. Go down, Moses. 1973. 416p. (YA). (gr. 9-12). pap. 8.95 o.p. (*0-394-71884-4*, Random Hse. Bks. for Young Readers) Random Hse. Children's Bks.

—The Portable Faulkner. Cowley, Malcolm, ed. rev. ed. 1977. (Viking Portable Library: No. 18). 768p. (J). (gr. 10 up). pap. 15.95 o.s.i (*0-14-015018-8*, Penguin Bks.) Penguin Group (USA) Inc.

Greenberg, Polly. Oh Lord, I Wish I Was a Buzzard. (Illus.). 32p. (J). (gr. k-3). 2003. pap. 5.95 (*1-58717-220-8*); 2002. 15.95 (*1-58717-122-8*); 2002. lib. bdg. 16.50 (*1-58717-123-6*) North-South Bks., Inc.

Herschler, Mildred Barger. The Darkest Corner. 2000. 240p. (J). (gr. 7-12). 16.95 (*1-886910-54-5*, Front Street) Front Street, Inc.

Johnson, Angela. I Dream of Trains. 2003. (Illus.). 32p. (J). (gr. k-2). 16.95 (*0-689-82609-5*, Simon & Schuster Children's Publishing) Simon & Schuster Children's Publishing.

Littlesugar, Amy & Cooper, Floyd. Freedom School, Yes! 2001. (Illus.). 40p. (J). (ps-3). 16.99 (*0-399-23006-8*) Penguin Putnam Bks. for Young Readers.

Mandrake the Wild Mallard Duck. 2000. (Illus.). 133p. (YA). (gr. 10 up). pap. 13.95 (*0-9616701-0-X*) Oak Hill Bks.

Masters, Susan Rowan. Night Journey to Vicksburg. Killcoyne, Hope L., ed. 2003. (J). 14.95 (*1-893110-30-3*) Silver Moon Pr.

Matas, Carol. The War Within: A Novel of the Civil War. 2001. (Illus.). 160p. (J). (gr. 5-8). 16.00 (*0-689-82935-3*, Simon & Schuster Children's Publishing) Simon & Schuster Children's Publishing.

—The War Within: A Novel of the Civil War. 2003. (J). 22.95 (*0-7862-5499-8*) Thorndike Pr.

Naylor, Phyllis Reynolds. Night Cry. 1984. (Night Cry CL Nrf Ser.: Vol. 1). 168p. (YA). (gr. 4-7). 17.95 (*0-689-31017-X*, Atheneum) Simon & Schuster Children's Publishing.

Peters, Nancy L. Wishmagic. 1998. 24p. (J). (gr. k-4). pap. 6.00 (*0-8059-4304-8*) Dorrance Publishing Co., Inc.

Ploog, Mike, illus. The Adventures of Tom Sawyer. 1990. 43p. (J). 3.75 o.s.i (*0-425-12241-7*, Classics Illustrated) Berkley Publishing Group.

Robinet. Mississippi Chariot. 1998. (J). pap. 3.99 (*0-87628-571-X*) Ctr. for Applied Research in Education, The.

Robinet, Harriette Gillem. Mississippi Chariot. 128p. (J). (gr. 4-7). 1997. per. 3.99 (*0-689-80632-9*, Aladdin); 1994. 14.95 (*0-689-31960-6*, Atheneum) Simon & Schuster Children's Publishing.

Rodman, Mary Ann. Yankee Girl, RS. 2004. (J). 16.00 (*0-374-38661-7*, Farrar, Straus & Giroux (BYR)) Farrar, Straus & Giroux.

Skates, Craig. Mississippi Stories for Young People: A Look at the Past. 1999. 112p. (YA). pap. 6.95 (*1-893062-07-4*) Quail Ridge Pr., Inc.

Spears, Britney & Spears, Lynne. A Mother's Gift: A Novel. 2003. 240p. (YA). (gr. 5 up). mass mkt. 5.99 (*0-440-23799-8*, Laurel Leaf) Random Hse. Children's Bks.

Stark, Lynette. Escape from Heart. 2000. 224p. (YA). (gr. 7-10). 17.00 o.s.i (*0-15-202385-2*) Harcourt Children's Bks.

Taulbert, Clifton L. Little Cliff & the Porch People. Kane, Cindy, ed. 1999. (Illus.). 32p. (J). (ps-3). 16.99 (*0-8037-2174-9*, Dial Bks. for Young Readers) Penguin Putnam Bks. for Young Readers.

Taylor, Mildred D. Elements of Literature: Roll of Thunder, Hear My Cry. 1989. pap. text, stu. ed. 15.33 (*0-03-023434-4*) Holt, Rinehart & Winston.

—The Friendship. (Illus.). 56p. 1998. (gr. 2-6). pap. 4.99 (*0-14-038964-4*, Puffin Bks.); 1987. (J). (gr. 2-6). 13.89 o.p. (*0-8037-0418-6*, Dial Bks. for Young Readers); 1987. (J). (gr. 4-7). 16.99 (*0-8037-0417-8*, Dial Bks. for Young Readers) Penguin Putnam Bks. for Young Readers.

—The Friendship. 1998. 10.14 (*0-606-12938-3*) Turtleback Bks.

—Mississippi Bridge. 2002. (J). 12.87 (*0-7587-9586-6*) Book Wholesalers, Inc.

—Mississippi Bridge. (Illus.). 2000. 64p. (YA). (gr. 4-7). pap. 4.99 (*0-14-130817-6*, Puffin Bks.); 1990. 64p. (J). 15.99 o.s.i (*0-8037-0426-7*, Dial Bks. for Young Readers); 1990. 6p. (J). 13.89 o.p. (*0-8037-0427-5*, Dial Bks. for Young Readers) Penguin Putnam Bks. for Young Readers.

—Mississippi Bridge. 1992. (Illus.). 64p. (gr. 2-6). pap. text 4.50 (*0-553-15992-5*, Skylark); (J). pap. o.s.i (*0-553-54058-0*, Dell Books for Young Readers) Random Hse. Children's Bks.

—Mississippi Bridge. 2002. (J). (gr. 2-6). 19.75 (*0-8446-7213-0*) Smith, Peter Pub., Inc.

—Mississippi Bridge. 2000. 11.14 (*0-606-18434-1*); 1992. 9.19 o.p. (*0-606-00528-5*) Turtleback Bks.

—The Road to Memphis. 1992. 304p. (YA). (gr. 7-12). pap. 6.99 (*0-14-036077-8*, Puffin Bks.) Penguin Putnam Bks. for Young Readers.

—The Road to Memphis. Fogelman, Phyllis J., ed. 1990. (Illus.). 30p. (YA). (gr. 7 up). 16.99 (*0-8037-0340-6*, Dial Bks. for Young Readers) Penguin Putnam Bks. for Young Readers.

—Roll of Thunder, Hear My Cry. 1984. 224p. (YA). (gr. 8-12). mass mkt. 3.50 o.s.i (*0-553-25450-2*) Bantam Bks.

—Roll of Thunder, Hear My Cry. 1993. (Golden Leaf Classics). 48p. (YA). (gr. 5 up). stu. ed. 9.95 (*1-56872-003-3*) Incentives For Learning.

—Roll of Thunder, Hear My Cry. l.t. ed. 2000. (LRS Large Print Cornerstone Ser.). 348p. (YA). (gr. 5-12). lib. bdg. 32.95 (*1-58118-057-8*, 23471) LRS.

—Roll of Thunder, Hear My Cry. l.t. ed. 1989. 304p. (YA). reprint ed. lib. bdg. 16.95 o.s.i (*1-55736-140-1*, Cornerstone Bks.) Pages, Inc.

—Roll of Thunder, Hear My Cry. 1999. (Masterpiece Series Access Editions). xvii, 205p. (J). pap. 10.95 (*0-8219-1985-7*, 35335) Paradigm Publishing, Inc.

—Roll of Thunder, Hear My Cry. (gr. 5-8). 1997. 288p. (YA). pap. 6.99 (*0-14-038451-0*, Puffin Bks.); 1991. 288p. (J). pap. 6.99 (*0-14-034893-X*); 1976. (Illus.). 290p. (YA). 16.99 o.s.i (*0-8037-7473-7*, Dial Bks. for Young Readers); 25th anniv. ed. 2001. (Illus.). 296p. (J). 17.99 (*0-8037-2647-3*, Fogelman, Phyllis Bks.) Penguin Putnam Bks. for Young Readers.

—Roll of Thunder, Hear My Cry. 1999. 60p. (gr. 6-8). stu. ed., ring bd. 12.99 (*1-58609-152-2*) Progeny Pr.

—Roll of Thunder, Hear My Cry. 1998. (J). (gr. 5). pap. 3.95 (*0-439-04476-6*) Scholastic, Inc.

—Roll of Thunder, Hear My Cry. (YA). 1997. 12.04 (*0-606-11807-1*); 1991. 12.04 (*0-606-00720-2*) Turtleback Bks.

—Roll of Thunder, Hear My Cry: Let the Circle Be Unbroken, 3 vols., Set. 1996. (J). (gr. 4-7). 13.99 o.p. (*0-14-774347-8*, Puffin Bks.) Penguin Putnam Bks. for Young Readers.

Twain, Mark. The Adventures of Huckleberry Finn: Long Classic Stage Four. 1995. (Longman Classics Ser.). (Illus.). (J). (gr. 4-7). pap. text 7.87 (*0-582-03585-6*) Longman Publishing Group.

—The Adventures of Tom Sawyer. deluxe ed. 1989. (Books of Wonder). (Illus.). 272p. (J). (gr. 8-12). 24.99 (*0-688-07510-X*, Morrow, William & Co.) Morrow/Avon.

—The Adventures of Tom Sawyer: Stage 3. 1995. (Classics Ser.). 1p. (YA). pap. text 7.87 (*0-582-03588-0*) Longman Publishing Group.

—Les Aventures de Tom Sawyer. 5th ed. 1997. Tr. of Adventures of Tom Sawyer. (FRE., Illus.). (J). (gr. 4-7). pap. 15.95 (*2-07-051431-5*) Gallimard, Editions FRA. *Dist:* Distribooks, Inc.

Vander Zee, Ruth. Mississippi Morning. 2003. (J). (*0-8028-5211-4*, Eerdmans Bks For Young Readers) Eerdmans, William B. Publishing Co.

Wiles, Deborah. Love, Ruby Lavender. (YA). (gr. 3-7). 2002. 216p. pap. 5.95 (*0-15-204568-6*); 2001. (Illus.). 200p. 16.00 (*0-15-202314-3*) Harcourt Children's Bks. (Gulliver Bks.).

—Love, Ruby Lavender. unabr. ed. 2002. (gr. 3-7). audio 25.00 (*0-8072-0717-9*, Listening Library) Random Hse. Audio Publishing Group.

MISSISSIPPI RIVER—FICTION

Abbott, Tony. Mississippi River Blues: The Adventures of Tom Sawyer, Vol. 2. 2002. (Cracked Classics Ser.). (Illus.). 144p. (J). (gr. 3-7). pap. 4.99 (*0-7868-1325-3*, Volo) Hyperion Bks. for Children.

The Adventures of Tom Sawyer. 1987. mass mkt. 1.95 (*0-938819-01-1*, Aerie) Doherty, Tom Assocs., LLC.

The Adventures of Tom Sawyer. 2003. (Classic Retelling Ser.). (J). (*0-618-12053-X*) McDougal Littell Inc.

The Adventures of Tom Sawyer. 1998. 44p. (YA). stu. ed. 11.95 (*1-56137-528-4*, NU5284SP) Novel Units, Inc.

The Adventures of Tom Sawyer. 2004. (Literature Units Ser.). (Illus.). 48p. 7.99 (*1-57690-637-X*) Teacher Created Materials, Inc.

Bulla, Clyde Robert. Down the Mississippi. 1954. (Illus.). (J). (gr. 2-5). o.p. (*0-690-24383-9*) HarperCollins Children's Bk. Group.

Burman, Ben L. Blow a Wild Bugle for Catfish Bend. 1967. (Illus.). (J). (gr. 6 up). 3.95 o.s.i (*0-8008-0825-8*) Taplinger Publishing Co., Inc.

—Three from Catfish Bend. Incl. High Water at Catfish Bend. o.p. Owl Hoots Twice at Catfish Bend. o.p. Seven Stars for Catfish Bend. o.p. (Illus.). 1967. 6.95 o.s.i (*0-8008-7676-8*) Taplinger Publishing Co., Inc.

Center for Learning Network Staff & Twain, Mark. The Adventures of Huckleberry Finn: Curriculum Unit. 1990. (Novel Ser.). 83p. (YA). (gr. 9-12). reprint ed. spiral bd. 18.95 (*1-56077-123-2*) Ctr. for Learning, The.

Clements, Bruce. I Tell a Lie Every So Often, RS. (Sunburst Ser.). 160p. (J). 2001. (gr. 7 up). pap. 5.95 (*0-374-43539-1*, Sunburst); 1974. (gr. 5 up). 9.95 o.p. (*0-374-33619-9*, Farrar, Straus & Giroux (BYR)) Farrar, Straus & Giroux.

Duey, Kathleen & Bale, Karen A. Flood, Mississippi, 1927. 1998. (Survival! Ser.: No. 5). (J). (gr. 4-7). 10.04 (*0-606-13829-3*) Turtleback Bks.

—Flood, Mississippi 1927. 1998. (Survival! Ser.: No. 5). 176p. (J). (gr. 4-7). pap. 3.99 (*0-689-82116-6*, Aladdin) Simon & Schuster Children's Publishing.

Esbaum, Jill. Ste-e-e-e-eamboat A-Comin! 2005. (J). (*0-374-37236-5*, Farrar, Straus & Giroux (BYR)) Farrar, Straus & Giroux.

Fichter, George S. First Steamboat down the Mississippi. 1989. (Illus.). 112p. (J). (gr. 4-7). 12.95 (*0-88289-715-2*) Pelican Publishing Co., Inc.

Holling, Holling C. Minn of the Mississippi. 1978. (Illus.). 88p. (J). (gr. 4-6). pap. 11.95 (*0-395-27399-4*) Houghton Mifflin Co.

Koste, Virginia G. The Trial of Tom Sawyer. 1978. (J). (gr. 4 up). 6.00 (*0-87602-213-1*) Anchorage Pr.

Meigs, Cornelia. Swift Rivers. 1994. (Newbery Honor Roll Ser.). (YA). 13.00 (*0-606-06792-2*) Turtleback Bks.

—Swift Rivers. 1994. (Newbery Honor Roll Ser.). (Illus.). 288p. (J). (gr. 4-7). reprint ed. pap. 7.95 (*0-8027-7419-9*) Walker & Co.

Robinet, Harriette Gillem. Mississippi Chariot. 1997. 9.09 (*0-606-11629-X*) Turtleback Bks.

Shalant, Phyllis. Bartleby of the Mighty Mississippi. 2000. (Illus.). 164p. (J). (gr. 3-6). 15.99 (*0-525-46033-0*, Dutton Children's Bks.) Penguin Putnam Bks. for Young Readers.

Stevermer, Caroline. River Rats. (YA). (gr. 7-12). 1996. 320p. pap. 6.00 (*0-15-201411-X*, Magic Carpet Bks.); 1992. 224p. 17.00 (*0-15-200895-0*) Harcourt Children's Bks.

Tom Sawyer. 1980. (Tempo Classics Ser.). (J). (gr. 5 up). 1.50 o.s.i (*0-448-17136-8*) Ace Bks.

Tom Sawyer. 1990. (Spanish Children's Classics Ser.: No. 800-1). (SPA.). (J). 3.50 (*0-7214-1395-1*, Ladybird Bks.) Penguin Group (USA) Inc.

Tom Sawyer. 1988. (Short Classics Learning Files Ser.). (J). (gr. 4 up). 22.00 o.p. (*0-8172-2195-6*) Raintree Pubs.

Twain, Mark. The Adventures of Huckleberry Finn. (World Digital Library). (J). 2002. E-Book 3.95 (*0-594-08343-5*); 2000. 252p. E-Book 9.95 (*0-594-05327-7*) 1873 Pr.

—The Adventures of Huckleberry Finn. 2002. (Great Illustrated Classics). (Illus.). 240p. (J). (gr. 3-8). lib. bdg. 21.35 (*1-57765-676-8*, ABDO & Daughters) ABDO Publishing Co.

—The Adventures of Huckleberry Finn. 1962. (Classics Ser.). (YA). (gr. 5 up). mass mkt. 2.75 (*0-8049-0004-3*, CL-4) Airmont Publishing Co., Inc.

—The Adventures of Huckleberry Finn. 2001. 7.95 (*0-8010-1220-1*) Baker Bks.

—The Adventures of Huckleberry Finn. 1981. (Bantam Classics Ser.). 320p. reprint ed. mass mkt. 4.95 (*0-553-21079-3*, Bantam Classics) Bantam Bks.

—The Adventures of Huckleberry Finn. rev. ed. 2000. 250p. (J). per. 9.90 (*1-58396-056-2*) Blue Unicorn Editions.

—The Adventures of Huckleberry Finn. 1982. (J). reprint ed. lib. bdg. 15.95 (*0-89967-047-4*, Harmony Raine & Co.) Buccaneer Bks., Inc.

—The Adventures of Huckleberry Finn. pap. 4.95 (*0-7910-4108-5*) Chelsea Hse. Pubs.

—The Adventures of Huckleberry Finn. 1992. (Children's Classics Ser.). (Illus.). 224p. (YA). 12.99 o.s.i (*0-517-08128-8*) Crown Publishing Group.

—The Adventures of Huckleberry Finn. 2002. (Spot the Classics Ser.). (Illus.). 192p. (J). (gr. k-5). 4.99 (*1-57759-553-X*) Dalmatian Pr.

—The Adventures of Huckleberry Finn. 1987. mass mkt. 2.25 (*0-938819-00-3*, Aerie) Doherty, Tom Assocs., LLC.

—The Adventures of Huckleberry Finn. (Children's Thrift Classics Ser.). (J). 1998. (Illus.). 80p. pap. 1.00 (*0-486-40349-1*); 1994. 224p. reprint ed. pap. 2.00 (*0-486-28061-6*) Dover Pubns., Inc.

—The Adventures of Huckleberry Finn. 2nd ed. 1998. (Illustrated Classic Book Ser.). (Illus.). 61p. (J). (gr. 3 up). reprint ed. pap. text 4.95 (*1-56767-255-8*) Educational Insights, Inc.

—The Adventures of Huckleberry Finn. (J). E-Book 2.49 (*1-929120-49-4*) Electric Umbrella Publishing.

—The Adventures of Huckleberry Finn. 1994. (Books of Wonder: Vol. 1). (Illus.). 368p. (J). (gr. 4-7). 24.99 (*0-688-10656-0*) HarperCollins Children's Bk. Group.

—The Adventures of Huckleberry Finn. deluxe ed. (Illus.). (J). lib. bdg. 9.87 o.p. (*0-06-014377-0*); 1942. reprint ed. 11.95 o.p. (*0-06-014376-2*) HarperTrade.

—The Adventures of Huckleberry Finn. Smith, Henry N., ed. 1972. (YA). (gr. 4-7). pap. 13.96 o.s.i (*0-395-05114-2*, Riverside Editions) Houghton Mifflin Co.

—The Adventures of Huckleberry Finn. 1999. 318p. (J). pap. 9.95 o.p. (*1-930128-06-1*, JNMedia Bks.) JNMedia, Inc.

—The Adventures of Huckleberry Finn. 1998. (Cloth Bound Pocket Ser.). 240p. 7.95 (*3-89508-210-4*, 521309) Konemann.

—The Adventures of Huckleberry Finn. 1977. (American Classics). (J). (gr. 9-12). 6.12 o.p. (*0-88343-416-4*); pap. 8.92 o.p. (*0-88343-415-6*); audio 89.08 o.p. (*0-88343-426-1*) McDougal Littell Inc.

—The Adventures of Huckleberry Finn. 1959. 288p. (YA). (gr. 7). mass mkt. 1.75 o.p. (*0-451-51912-4*, Signet Classics) NAL.

—The Adventures of Huckleberry Finn. 2003. (Illus.). 288p. (J). pap. 3.99 o.p. (*0-14-250098-4*, Puffin Bks.); 1999. pap. 2.99 o.s.i (*0-14-130543-6*, Puffin Bks.); 1995. (Illus.). 400p. (J). (gr. 4-7). pap. 4.99 (*0-14-036676-8*, Puffin Bks.); 1983. 288p. (J). (gr. 3-7). pap. 3.50 o.p. (*0-14-035007-1*, Puffin Bks.); 1981. (Illus.). 448p. (J). (gr. 4-6). reprint ed. 7.95 o.p. (*0-448-11000-8*, Grosset & Dunlap); 1948. (Illus.). 448p. (J). (gr. 4-7). reprint ed. 17.99 (*0-448-06000-0*, Grosset & Dunlap) Penguin Putnam Bks. for Young Readers.

—The Adventures of Huckleberry Finn. 1978. (Illus.). (J). (gr. 6-9). 2.95 o.p. (*0-448-14922-2*) Putnam Publishing Group, The.

—The Adventures of Huckleberry Finn. 2001. (Illus.). pap. (*1-57646-254-4*) Quiet Vision Publishing.

—The Adventures of Huckleberry Finn. 1986. (Running Press Classics Ser.). 256p. (J). (gr. 4 up). pap. 4.95 o.p. (*0-89471-476-7*); lib. bdg. 12.90 o.p. (*0-89471-477-5*) Running Pr. Bk. Pubs.

—The Adventures of Huckleberry Finn. (J). 1987. 384p. (gr. 4-6). 1.25 o.p. (*0-590-40662-0*, Scholastic Paperbacks); 1987. 384p. (gr. 4-6). pap. 2.50 o.p. (*0-590-40801-1*, Scholastic Paperbacks); 1987. 384p. (gr. 4-6). pap. 4.99 (*0-590-43389-X*); 1983. pap. 2.25 o.p. (*0-590-02426-4*) Scholastic, Inc.

—The Adventures of Huckleberry Finn. 1989. (Enriched Classics Ser.). 432p. (YA). (gr. 5-12). mass mkt. (*0-671-70136-3*, 46198, Washington Square Pr.) Simon & Schuster.

—The Adventures of Huckleberry Finn. 1999. 10.04 (*0-606-17508-3*); 1994. 11.04 (*0-606-12869-7*); 1982. (J). 11.00 (*0-606-13112-4*) Turtleback Bks.

—The Adventures of Huckleberry Finn. Fischer, Victor et al, eds. 2001. (Mark Twain Library). (Illus.). (J). 535p. 45.00 (*0-520-22806-5*); xxvii, 561p. pap. 14.95 (*0-520-22838-3*) Univ. of California Pr.

—The Adventures of Huckleberry Finn. 1999. 230p. (YA). reprint ed. pap. 9.95 (*1-57002-098-1*) University Publishing Hse., Inc.

—The Adventures of Huckleberry Finn. 2002. (Classics Ser.). (Illus.). 368p. pap. 6.00 (*0-14-243717-4*, Penguin Classics) Viking Penguin.

—The Adventures of Huckleberry Finn. Seelye, John, ed. & intro. by. 1986. (Penguin Classics Ser.). 368p. (J). (gr. 4). pap. 5.95 o.s.i (*0-14-039046-4*) Viking Penguin.

—The Adventures of Huckleberry Finn: With a Discussion of Friendship. Lauter, Richard, tr. & illus. by. 2003. (Values in Action Illustrated Classics Ser.). (J). (*1-59203-042-4*) Learning Challenge, Inc.

—The Adventures of Tom Sawyer. (YA). E-Book 3.95 (*0-594-05730-2*); 2002. (J). E-Book 3.95 (*0-594-09149-7*) 1873 Pr.

—The Adventures of Tom Sawyer. 2002. (Great Illustrated Classics). (Illus.). 240p. (J). (gr. 3-8). lib. bdg. 21.35 (*1-57765-679-2*, ABDO & Daughters) ABDO Publishing Co.

—The Adventures of Tom Sawyer. 1962. (Airmont Classics Ser.). (YA). (gr. 5 up). mass mkt. 2.95 (*0-8049-0006-X*, CL-6) Airmont Publishing Co., Inc.

—The Adventures of Tom Sawyer, Vol. 1. 1995. (Adventures of Tom Sawyer Ser.: Vol. 1). 224p. mass mkt. 5.50 (*0-553-21128-5*, Bantam Classics) Bantam Bks.

—The Adventures of Tom Sawyer. 1999. (YA). reprint ed. pap. text 28.00 (*1-4047-1117-1*) Classic Textbooks.

—The Adventures of Tom Sawyer. 2002. (Kingfisher Classics Ser.). (Illus.). 352p. (J). tchr. ed. 15.95 (*0-7534-5478-5*, Kingfisher) Houghton Mifflin Co. Trade & Reference Div.

—The Adventures of Tom Sawyer. (Young Collector's Illustrated Classics Ser.). (Illus.). 192p. (J). (gr. 3-7). 9.95 (*1-56156-453-2*) Kidsbooks, Inc.

—The Adventures of Tom Sawyer. l.t. ed. 1997. (Large Print Heritage Ser.). 357p. (YA). (gr. 7-12). lib. bdg. 30.95 (*1-58118-014-4*, 21488) LRS.

—The Adventures of Tom Sawyer. 1995. (Fiction Ser.). (YA). pap. text 7.88 o.p. (*0-582-09677-4*, 79814) Longman Publishing Group.

—The Adventures of Tom Sawyer. 1997. (Wishbone Classics Ser.: No. 11). (Illus.). 144p. (gr. 3-7). mass mkt. 4.25 (*0-06-106498-X*, HarperEntertainment) Morrow/Avon.

—The Adventures of Tom Sawyer. (J). 2002. (Illus.). 544p. mass mkt. 5.95 (*0-451-52864-6*, Signet Bks.); 1959. 224p. (gr. 7). mass mkt. 3.95 o.p. (*0-451-52355-5*, Signet Classics) NAL.

—The Adventures of Tom Sawyer. abr. ed. 1996. (J). audio 13.98 (*962-634-580-2*, NA208014, Naxos AudioBooks) Naxos of America, Inc.

—The Adventures of Tom Sawyer. 2000. (J). audio 12.95 (*0-19-422879-7*) Oxford Univ. Pr., Inc.

—The Adventures of Tom Sawyer, Level 1. Hedge, Tricia, ed. 2000. (Bookworms Ser.). (Illus.). 57p. (J). pap. text 5.95 (*0-19-422936-X*) Oxford Univ. Pr., Inc.

—The Adventures of Tom Sawyer. (J). (*0-448-41455-4*); 1999. (gr. 4-7). pap. 2.99 o.p. (*0-14-130544-4*, Puffin Bks.); 1996. (Illus.). 288p. (YA). (gr. 7-12). 23.99 o.s.i (*0-670-86984-8*); 1994. (Illus.). 336p. (J). (gr. 4-7). 16.99 (*0-448-40560-1*, Grosset & Dunlap); 1983. 224p. (J). (gr. 3-7). pap. 3.50 o.p. (*0-14-035003-9*, Puffin Bks.); 1996. (Illus.). 288p. (J). (gr. 7-12). 19.99 (*0-670-86985-6*); 1981. (Illus.). (J). (gr. 4-6). reprint ed. 7.95 o.p. (*0-448-11002-4*, Grosset & Dunlap); 1946. (Illus.). 336p. (J). (gr. 4-6). reprint ed. 13.95 o.p. (*0-448-06002-7*, Grosset & Dunlap) Penguin Putnam Bks. for Young Readers.

—The Adventures of Tom Sawyer. 1978. (Illus.). (J). (gr. 6-9). 2.95 o.p. (*0-448-14921-4*) Putnam Publishing Group, The.

—The Adventures of Tom Sawyer. 2001. (Paperback Classics Ser.). (Illus.). 304p. pap. 6.95 (*0-375-75681-7*, Modern Library) Random House Adult Trade Publishing Group.

—The Adventures of Tom Sawyer. (Illustrated Library for Children). (Illus.). (J). 2002. 224p. 16.99 (*0-517-22108-X*, Random Hse. Bks. for Young Readers); 1986. 304p. o.p. (*0-307-17110-8*, Golden Bks.) Random Hse. Children's Bks.

—The Adventures of Tom Sawyer. (Children's Library Ser.). (J). 1995. 1.10 o.s.i (*0-517-14155-8*); 1989. (Illus.). 288p. 12.99 o.s.i (*0-517-68813-1*) Random Hse. Value Publishing.

—The Adventures of Tom Sawyer. 1995. (Step into Classics Ser.). (Illus.). 112p. (gr. 2-7). pap. 3.99 (*0-679-88070-4*) Random Hse., Inc.

—The Adventures of Tom Sawyer. 1985. (Illus.). 223p. (YA). (gr. 7-12). 12.95 o.p. (*0-89577-217-5*) Reader's Digest Assn., Inc., The.

—The Adventures of Tom Sawyer. (Literary Classics Ser.). 2002. (Illus.). 176p. 6.00 o.p. (*0-7624-0542-2*); 1987. 160p. (J). (gr. 4 up). pap. 4.95 o.p. (*0-89471-541-0*); 1987. 160p. (J). (gr. 4 up). lib. bdg. 12.90 o.p. (*0-89471-542-9*) Running Pr. Bk. Pubs.

—The Adventures of Tom Sawyer. 1987. 320p. (J). (gr. 4-6). 1.25 o.p. (*0-590-40663-9*); pap. 2.50 o.p. (*0-590-40800-3*); mass mkt. 3.50 (*0-590-43352-0*) Scholastic, Inc. (Scholastic Paperbacks).

—The Adventures of Tom Sawyer. 1982. (Silver Classic Ser.). (Illus.). 246p. (J). (*0-382-03437-6*) Silver, Burdett & Ginn, Inc.

—The Adventures of Tom Sawyer. (Aladdin Classics Ser.). 2001. 272p. (J). (gr. 4-7). pap. 3.99 (*0-689-84224-4*, Aladdin); 1981. (Illus.). (YA). (gr. 7-12). pap. 2.95 (*0-671-44135-3*, Simon Pulse) Simon & Schuster Children's Publishing.

—The Adventures of Tom Sawyer. 1997. (Wishbone Classics Ser.: No. 11). (J). (gr. 3-7). 10.30 (*0-606-12104-8*) Turtleback Bks.

—The Adventures of Tom Sawyer. Gise, Joanne, ed. 1990. (Troll Illustrated Classics). (J). 12.10 (*0-606-00298-7*) Turtleback Bks.

—The Adventures of Tom Sawyer. (Illus.). 292p. pap. 14.95 (*0-520-23575-4*) Univ. of California Pr.

—The Adventures of Tom Sawyer. 2001. 184p. pap. 9.95 (*1-57002-169-4*) University Publishing Hse., Inc.

—The Adventures of Tom Sawyer: With a Discussion of Imagination. 2003. (Values in Action Illustrated Classics Ser.). (Illus.). 190p. (J). (*1-59203-027-0*) Learning Challenge, Inc.

—The Adventures of Tom Sawyer & the Adventures of Huckleberry Finn. 1979. 288p. (J). (gr. 4-7). mass mkt. 4.95 (*0-451-52272-9*) NAL.

—The Adventures of Tom Sawyer & the Adventures of Huckleberry Finn. 2001. (Giant Courage Classics Ser.). 384p. (YA). 9.00 o.p. (*0-7624-0568-6*, Courage Bks.) Running Pr. Bk. Pubs.

—Les Aventures de Tom Sawyer. 1987. (Folio - Junior Ser.: No. 449). Tr. of Adventures of Tom Sawyer. (FRE., Illus.). 296p. (J). (gr. 5-10). pap. 9.95 (*2-07-033449-X*) Schoenhof's Foreign Bks., Inc.

—The Boys' Ambition. 1975. (Seedling Bks.). (Illus.). 32p. (J). (gr. 2-6). lib. bdg. 4.95 o.p. (*0-8225-0283-6*) Lerner Publishing Group.

—Huckleberry Finn. 1997. (Classics Illustrated Study Guides). (Illus.). 64p. (YA). (gr. 7 up). mass mkt., stu. ed. 4.99 o.p. (*1-57840-008-2*) Acclaim Bks.

—Huckleberry Finn. 1995. (Classroom Reading Plays Ser.). 32p. (YA). (gr. 6-12). pap. 3.95 (*0-7854-1122-4*, 40210); pap. 2.40 o.p. (*1-56103-110-0*) American Guidance Service, Inc.

—Huckleberry Finn, unabr. ed. 1965. (J). audio 41.95 (*1-55685-353-X*) Audio Bk. Contractors, Inc.

—Huckleberry Finn. 1977. (Dent's Illustrated Children's Classics Ser.). (Illus.). 338p. (J). reprint ed. 10.00 o.p. (*0-460-05031-1*) Biblio Distribution.

—Huckleberry Finn. 1999. (YA). reprint ed. pap. text 28.00 (*1-4047-1118-X*) Classic Textbooks.

—Huckleberry Finn. 6th ed. 1997. (FRE., Illus.). (J). (gr. 4-7). pap. 13.95 (*2-07-051625-3*) Gallimard, Editions FRA. *Dist:* Distribooks, Inc.

—Huckleberry Finn. 1988. (Study Texts Ser.). (YA). (gr. 7 up). pap. text 3.97 o.p. (*0-582-00264-8*, 73957) Longman Publishing Group.

—Huckleberry Finn. 1940. (J). audio 7.95 National Recording Co.

—Huckleberry Finn. Bassett, Jennifer, ed. 1995. (Illus.). 48p. (J). pap. text 5.95 o.p. (*0-19-422724-3*) Oxford Univ. Pr., Inc.

—Huckleberry Finn. Teresa Agnes, ed. Heller, Rudolf, tr. 1979. (SPA., Illus.). 64p. (YA). stu. ed. 1.50 (*0-88301-570-6*) Pendulum Pr., Inc.

—Huckleberry Finn. Farr, Naunerle C., ed. 1973. (Now Age Illustrated Ser.). (Illus.). 64p. (J). (gr. 5-10). 7.50 o.p. (*0-88301-207-3*); pap. 2.95 (*0-88301-098-4*) Pendulum Pr., Inc.

—Huckleberry Finn. (American Collection Short Classics). (J). (gr. 4-7). 1993. 32p. pap. 4.95 o.p. (*0-8114-6826-7*); 1988. 22.00 o.p. (*0-8172-2179-4*); 1983. (Illus.). 48p. pap. 9.27 o.p. (*0-8172-2009-7*); 1983. (Illus.). 48p. lib. bdg. 24.26 o.p. (*0-8172-1651-0*); Set. 1991. (Illus.). 48p. pap. 34.00 (*0-8114-6962-X*) Raintree Pubs.

—Huckleberry Finn. 1990. (Folio - Junior Ser.: No. 230). (FRE., Illus.). 380p. (J). (gr. 5-10). pap. 10.95 (*2-07-033230-6*) Schoenhof's Foreign Bks., Inc.

—Huckleberry Finn, unabr. ed. 2002. (YA). audio compact disk 39.95 (*1-58472-259-2*, 076); pap. incl. audio compact disk (*1-58472-261-4*) Sound Room Pubs., Inc. (In Audio).

—Tom Sawyer. 1997. (Classics Illustrated Study Guides). (Illus.). 64p. (YA). (gr. 7 up). mass mkt., stu. ed. 4.99 (*1-57840-001-5*) Acclaim Bks.

—Tom Sawyer. abr. adapted ed. 1998. (Children's Thrift Classics Ser.). (Illus.). 96p. (J). (gr. 1 up). pap. 1.00 (*0-486-29156-1*) Dover Pubns., Inc.

—Tom Sawyer. 2nd ed. 1998. (Illustrated Classic Book Ser.). (Illus.). 61p. (J). (gr. 3 up). reprint ed. pap. text 4.95 (*1-56767-263-9*) Educational Insights, Inc.

—Tom Sawyer. 1992. (Children's Classics Ser.). (Illus.). 272p. (J). (*0-89434-127-8*, Ferguson Publishing Co.) Facts on File Inc.

—Tom Sawyer. adapted ed. (YA). (gr. 5-12). pap. text 9.95 (*0-8359-0212-9*) Globe Fearon Educational Publishing.

—Tom Sawyer. 1998. (Cloth Bound Pocket Ser.). 240p. (J). 7.95 (*3-89508-463-8*, 520258) Konemann.

—Tom Sawyer. (Coleccion Clasicos de la Juventud). (SPA., Illus.). 220p. (J). 12.95 (*84-7189-029-1*, ORT310) Ortells, Alfredo Editorial S.L. ESP. *Dist:* Continental Bk. Co., Inc.

—Tom Sawyer. Shapiro, Irwin, ed. 1973. (Now Age Illustrated Ser.). (Illus.). 64p. (J). (gr. 5-10). 7.50 o.p. (*0-88301-220-0*); stu. ed. 1.25 (*0-88301-179-4*); pap. 2.95 (*0-88301-103-4*) Pendulum Pr., Inc.

—Tom Sawyer. 9999. (Children's Classics Ser.: No. 740-24). (Illus.). (J). (gr. 3-5). text 3.50 o.p. (*0-7214-0977-6*, Ladybird Bks.) Penguin Group (USA) Inc.

—Tom Sawyer. (American Short Classics Ser.). (J). (gr. 4-7). 1993. 32p. pap. 4.95 o.p. (*0-8114-6843-7*); 1983. (Illus.). 48p. pap. 9.27 o.p. (*0-8172-2025-9*); 1983. (Illus.). 48p. lib. bdg. 24.26 o.p. (*0-8172-1665-0*) Raintree Pubs.

—Tom Sawyer. 1999. (Illus.). 336p. (gr. 4-7). mass mkt. 3.99 (*0-439-09940-4*) Scholastic, Inc.

—Tom Sawyer. 1994. (Classic Story Bks.). (J). 4.98 o.p. (*0-8317-1646-0*) Smithmark Pubs., Inc.

—Tom Sawyer. 1996. 16.00 (*0-606-16016-7*) Turtleback Bks.

—Tom Sawyer Abroad. 1999. (YA). reprint ed. pap. text 28.00 (*1-4047-1125-2*) Classic Textbooks.

—Tom Sawyer Abroad. 1993. 112p. mass mkt. 2.50 (*0-8125-2334-2*, Tor Classics) Doherty, Tom Assocs., LLC.

—Tom Sawyer Abroad, Set. unabr. ed. 1996. (J). pap. 46.20 incl. audio (*0-7887-1442-2*, 40272) Recorded Bks., LLC.

—Tom Sawyer Abroad & Tom Sawyer, Detective. 1966. (Classics Ser.). (YA). (gr. 5 up). mass mkt. 1.50 o.s.i (*0-8049-0126-0*, CI-126) Airmont Publishing Co., Inc.

—Tom Sawyer Abroad & Tom Sawyer, Detective. 1985. 224p. (J). (ps-8). mass mkt. 1.95 o.p. (*0-451-51961-2*, Signet Classics) NAL.

—Tom Sawyer Abroad; Tom Sawyer, Detective. l.t. ed. 1999. (Large Print Heritage Ser.). 265p. (YA). (gr. 7-12). lib. bdg. 29.95 (*1-58118-046-2*, 22515) LRS.

—Tom Sawyer & Huckleberry Finn. unabr. ed. 1998. (Wordsworth Classics Ser.). (YA). (gr. 6-12). 5.27 (*0-89061-011-8*, R0118WW) Jamestown.

Twain, Mark & Price, David. The Adventures of Tom Sawyer & the Adventures of Huckleberry Finn. 1995. (Illus.). 560p. (J). (gr. 3-5). 12.98 o.p. (*0-8317-1211-2*) Smithmark Pubs., Inc.

Warner, Gertrude Chandler, creator. The Haunted Cabin Mystery. 1991. (Boxcar Children Ser.: No. 20). (Illus.). 121p. (J). (gr. 2-5). lib. bdg. 13.95 (*0-8075-3179-0*); mass mkt. 3.95 (*0-8075-3178-2*) Whitman, Albert & Co.

MISSOURI—FICTION

The Adventures of Tom Sawyer. 1987. mass mkt. 1.95 (*0-938819-01-1*, Aerie) Doherty, Tom Assocs., LLC.

The Adventures of Tom Sawyer. 2003. (Classic Retelling Ser.). (J). (*0-618-12053-X*) McDougal Littell Inc.

The Adventures of Tom Sawyer. 1998. 44p. (YA). stu. ed. 11.95 (*1-56137-528-4*, NU5284SP) Novel Units, Inc.

The Adventures of Tom Sawyer. 2004. (Literature Units Ser.). (Illus.). 48p. 7.99 (*1-57690-637-X*) Teacher Created Materials, Inc.

Blackwood, Gary L. Moonshine. 1999. (Accelerated Reader Bks.). 158p. (J). (gr. 3-7). 14.95 (*0-7614-5056-4*, Cavendish Children's Bks.) Cavendish, Marshall Corp.

Bornstein, Ruth Lercher. Butterflies & Lizards, Beryl & Me. 2002. (Illus.). 160p. (J). (gr. 3-7). lib. bdg. 14.95 (*0-7614-5118-8*, Cavendish Children's Bks.) Cavendish, Marshall Corp.

Byers, Stephen P. Lost River Bridge. 2001. 165p. pap. 12.95 (*1-929663-02-1*) Books By Byers.

Center for Learning Network Staff & Twain, Mark. The Adventures of Huckleberry Finn: Curriculum Unit. 1990. (Novel Ser.). 83p. (YA). (gr. 9-12). reprint ed. spiral bd. 18.95 (*1-56077-123-2*) Ctr. for Learning, The.

Champlin, Tim. Swift Thunder. 1998. (Western Ser.). 230p. 19.95 (*0-7862-1160-1*, Five Star) Gale Group.

Clements, Bruce. I Tell a Lie Every So Often, RS. (Sunburst Ser.). 160p. (J). 2001. (gr. 7 up). pap. 5.95 (*0-374-43539-1*, Sunburst); 1974. (gr. 5 up). 9.95 o.p. (*0-374-33619-9*, Farrar, Straus & Giroux (BYR)) Farrar, Straus & Giroux.

Crofford, Emily. When the River Ran Backward. 2000. (Adventures in Time Ser.). 80p. (J). (gr. 4-7). pap. 6.95 (*1-57505-488-4*); lib. bdg. 15.95 (*1-57505-305-5*) Lerner Publishing Group. (Carolrhoda Bks.).

—When the River Ran Backward. 2000. E-Book 21.27 (*0-585-31372-5*) netLibrary, Inc.

Ford, Laura. Misfit Heroes: The Adventures of Buster Brown & Tige. 2002. (J). 19.95 (*1-881554-28-7*) Skyward Publishing Co.

Grove, Vicki. Reaching Dustin. 2000. (Illus.). 208p. (YA). (gr. 4-9). pap. 5.99 (*0-698-11839-1*, Puffin Bks.) Penguin Putnam Bks. for Young Readers.

—Reaching Dustin. 2000. 12.04 (*0-606-18844-4*) Turtleback Bks.

Hill, Pamela Smith. A Voice from the Border. 1998. 320p. (YA). (gr. 7-12). tchr. ed. 16.95 (*0-8234-1356-X*) Holiday Hse., Inc.

Hoffman, Allen. Big League Dreams. 1999. (Small Worlds Ser.). 296p. pap. 12.95 (*0-7892-0583-1*) Abbeville Pr., Inc.

Horvath, Polly. The Happy Yellow Car, RS. (J). 2004. (Illus.). pap. 5.95 (*0-374-42879-4*); 1994. 128p. (gr. 4-7). 15.00 o.p. (*0-374-32845-5*, Farrar, Straus & Giroux (BYR)) Farrar, Straus & Giroux.

Hughes, Pat. Guerilla Season, RS. 2003. 336p. (J). 18.00 (*0-374-32811-0*, Farrar, Straus & Giroux (BYR)) Farrar, Straus & Giroux.

Kerr, M. E. Deliver Us from Evie. 1994. 224p. (YA). 15.00 o.p. (*0-06-024475-5*) HarperCollins Children's Bk. Group.

MacBride, Roger Lea. The Adventures of Rose & Swiney. 2000. (Little House Chapter Bks.: No. 4). (Illus.). 80p. (J). (gr. 2-5). lib. bdg. 14.89 (*0-06-028553-2*) HarperCollins Children's Bk. Group.

—In the Land of the Big Red Apple. 1995. (Little House Ser.). (Illus.). 352p. (J). (gr. 3-6). pap. 5.99 (*0-06-440574-5*, Harper Trophy); lib. bdg. 15.89 (*0-06-024964-1*) HarperCollins Children's Bk. Group.

—In the Land of the Big Red Apple. 1995. (Little House Ser.). (Illus.). 352p. (J). (gr. 3-6). 15.95 (*0-06-024963-3*) HarperCollins Pubs.

—In the Land of the Big Red Apple. 1995. (Little House Ser.). (Illus.). (J). (gr. 3-6). 11.00 (*0-606-07702-2*) Turtleback Bks.

—Little House on Rocky Ridge. 1993. (Little House). (Illus.). 368p. (J). (gr. 3-6). lib. bdg. 15.89 o.s.i (*0-06-020843-0*); pap. 5.99 (*0-06-440478-1*, Harper Trophy); 305th ed. 16.95 (*0-06-020842-2*) HarperCollins Children's Bk. Group.

—Little House on Rocky Ridge. 1993. (Little House Ser.). (Illus.). (J). (gr. 3-6). 11.00 (*0-606-05432-4*) Turtleback Bks.

—Little Town in the Ozarks. 1996. (Little House Ser.). (Illus.). 352p. (J). (gr. k-4). lib. bdg. 16.89 (*0-06-024970-6*); (gr. 3-6). 15.95 o.p. (*0-06-024977-3*) HarperCollins Children's Bk. Group.

—Missouri School Days. 2001. (Little House Chapter Bks.). (Illus.). 80p. (J). (gr. 2-5). pap. 4.25 (*0-06-442110-4*, Harper Trophy); lib. bdg. 14.89 (*0-06-028555-9*) HarperCollins Children's Bk. Group.

—New Dawn on Rocky Ridge. 1997. (Little House Ser.). (Illus.). 384p. (J). (gr. 3-7). pap. 6.99 (*0-06-440581-8*, Harper Trophy) HarperCollins Children's Bk. Group.

—New Dawn on Rocky Ridge. 1997. (Little House). (Illus.). 384p. (J). (gr. 3-7). 15.95 (*0-06-024971-4*) HarperCollins Pubs.

—On the Other Side of the Hill. 1995. (Little House Ser.). (Illus.). (J). (gr. 3-6). 368p. 16.95 (*0-06-024967-6*); 356p. lib. bdg. 14.89 o.p. (*0-06-024968-4*) HarperCollins Children's Bk. Group.

—Rose & Alva. 2000. (Little House Chapter Bks.: No. 3). (Illus.). 80p. (J). (gr. 2-5). pap. 4.25 (*0-06-442095-7*, Harper Trophy) HarperCollins Children's Bk. Group.

—Rose & Alva. 1999. (Little House Chapter Bks.). (J). (gr. 2-5). 10.40 (*0-606-18718-9*) Turtleback Bks.

Marsh, Carole. Missouri Silly Basketball Sportsmysteries, Vol. I. (Carole Marsh Missouri Bks.). (Illus.). (J). (gr. 3 up). 1997. cd-rom 29.95 (*0-7933-0679-5*); 1994. pap. 19.95 (*0-7933-0677-9*); 1994. lib. bdg. 29.95 (*0-7933-0678-7*) Gallopade International.

McCaughrean, Geraldine. One Bright Penny. 2002. (Illus.). 32p. (J). (gr. k-3). 15.99 (*0-670-03588-2*) Penguin Putnam Bks. for Young Readers.

Nixon, Joan Lowery. A Dangerous Promise. 1995. (Orphan Train Adventures Ser.: Vol. 5). 160p. (YA). (gr. 4-7). mass mkt. 4.99 (*0-440-21965-5*, Laurel Leaf) Random Hse. Children's Bks.

—Keeping Secrets. 1995. (Orphan Train Adventures Ser.). 176p. (J). 15.95 o.s.i (*0-385-32139-2*, Delacorte Pr.) Dell Publishing.

Potter, Marian. A Chance Wild Apple. 1982. 224p. (J). (gr. 4-6). 12.95 o.p. (*0-688-01075-X*, Morrow, William & Co.) Morrow/Avon.

Rabe, Berniece. Hiding Mr. McMulty. 1997. 256p. (YA). (gr. 5-9). 18.00 (*0-15-201330-X*) Harcourt Trade Pubs.

Roberts, Laura Peyton. New Beginnings. 1999. (Clearwater Crossing Ser.: No. 7). 224p. (gr. 5-8). mass mkt. 3.99 o.s.i (*0-553-49256-X*, Dell Books for Young Readers) Random Hse. Children's Bks.

—One Real Thing. 1999. (Clearwater Crossing Ser.: No. 8). 208p. (gr. 7-8). mass mkt. 3.99 o.s.i (*0-553-49257-8*, Dell Books for Young Readers) Random Hse. Children's Bks.

Ross, Rhea B. The Bet's on Lizzie Bingman! 1992. (YA). pap. 4.95 o.p. (*0-395-64375-9*); 1988. 192p. (J). (gr. 5-9). 13.95 o.p. (*0-395-44472-1*) Houghton Mifflin Co.

Russ, Lavinia. Over the Hills & Far Away. 1968. (J). (gr. 5 up). 5.50 o.p. (*0-15-258946-5*) Harcourt Children's Bks.

Shelby, Kermit. Big Shake & the Night of Terror. 1981. (Voyager Ser.). (J). (gr. 4-6). pap. 2.95 o.p. (*0-8010-8209-9*) Baker Bks.

Sherman, Eileen B. The Violin Players. 1998. 130p. (YA). (gr. 5 up). 14.95 (*0-8276-0595-1*) Jewish Pubn. Society.

Simmons, Marc. Millie Cooper's Ride: A True Story from History. 2002. (Illus.). 56p. (J). 16.95 (*0-8263-2925-X*) Univ. of New Mexico Pr.

Tate, Eleanora E. Front Porch Stories at the One-Room School. 1992. 112p. (YA). 15.00 o.s.i (*0-553-08384-8*) Bantam Bks.

—Front Porch Stories at the One-Room School. 1993. (Illus.). 112p. (gr. 4-7). pap. text 4.99 (*0-440-40901-2*) Dell Publishing.

—Front Porch Stories at the One-Room School. 1993. (J). pap. o.p. (*0-440-90061-1*, Dell Books for Young Readers) Random Hse. Children's Bks.

—Front Porch Stories at the One-Room School. 1992. (J). 11.04 (*0-606-05838-9*) Turtleback Bks.

—The Minstrel's Melody. 2001. (American Girl Collection: Bk. 11). (Illus.). 160p. (J). (gr. 5-9). pap. 5.95 (*1-58485-310-7*, American Girl) Pleasant Co. Pubns.

—The Minstrel's Melody. 2001. (American Girl Collection). (Illus.). (J). 12.00 (*0-606-21331-7*) Turtleback Bks.

Tedrow, T. L. Days of Laura Ingalls Wilder, Vol. 2: Children of Promise. 1992. (J). pap. 4.99 o.p. (*0-8407-3398-4*) Nelson, Thomas Inc.

—Days of Laura Ingalls Wilder, Vol. 3: Good Neighbors. 1992. (J). pap. 4.99 o.p. (*0-8407-3399-2*) Nelson, Thomas Inc.

—Days of Laura Ingalls Wilder, Vol. 4: Home to the Prairie. 1992. (J). pap. 4.99 o.p. (*0-8407-3401-8*) Nelson, Thomas Inc.

—Land of Promise. 1992. (Days of Laura Ingalls Wilder Ser.: Bk. 8). (J). 4.99 o.p. (*0-8407-7735-3*) Nelson, Thomas Inc.

Tedrow, Thomas L. The Legend of the Missouri Mud Monster. 1996. (Younguns Ser.: Vol. 4). 224p. (J). (gr. 5-9). pap. 5.99 o.p. (*0-8407-4135-9*) Nelson, Thomas Inc.

Tom Sawyer. 1980. (Tempo Classics Ser.). (J). (gr. 5 up). 1.50 o.s.i (*0-448-17136-8*) Ace Bks.

Tom Sawyer. 1990. (Spanish Children's Classics Ser.: No. 800-1). (SPA.). (J). 3.50 (*0-7214-1395-1*, Ladybird Bks.) Penguin Group (USA) Inc.

Tom Sawyer. 1988. (Short Classics Learning Files Ser.). (J). (gr. 4 up). 22.00 o.p. (*0-8172-2195-6*) Raintree Pubs.

Twain, Mark. The Adventures of Huckleberry Finn. (World Digital Library). (J). 2002. E-Book 3.95 (*0-594-08343-5*); 2000. 252p. E-Book 9.95 (*0-594-05327-7*) 1873 Pr.

—The Adventures of Huckleberry Finn. 2002. (Great Illustrated Classics). (Illus.). 240p. (J). (gr. 3-8). lib. bdg. 21.35 (*1-57765-676-8*, ABDO & Daughters) ABDO Publishing Co.

—The Adventures of Huckleberry Finn. 1962. (Classics Ser.). (YA). (gr. 5 up). mass mkt. 2.75 (*0-8049-0004-3*, CL-4) Airmont Publishing Co., Inc.

—The Adventures of Huckleberry Finn. 2001. 7.95 (*0-8010-1220-1*) Baker Bks.

—The Adventures of Huckleberry Finn. 1981. (Bantam Classics Ser.). 320p. reprint ed. mass mkt. 4.95 (*0-553-21079-3*, Bantam Classics) Bantam Bks.

—The Adventures of Huckleberry Finn. rev. ed. 2000. 250p. (J). per. 9.90 (*1-58396-056-2*) Blue Unicorn Editions.

—The Adventures of Huckleberry Finn. 1982. (J). reprint ed. lib. bdg. 15.95 (*0-89967-047-4*, Harmony Raine & Co.) Buccaneer Bks., Inc.

—The Adventures of Huckleberry Finn. 1992. (Children's Classics Ser.). (Illus.). 224p. (YA). 12.99 o.s.i (*0-517-08128-8*) Crown Publishing Group.

—The Adventures of Huckleberry Finn. 2002. (Spot the Classics Ser.). (Illus.). 192p. (J). (gr. k-5). 4.99 (*1-57759-553-X*) Dalmatian Pr.

—The Adventures of Huckleberry Finn. (Children's Thrift Classics Ser.). (J). 1998. (Illus.). 80p. pap. 1.00 (*0-486-40349-1*); 1994. 224p. reprint ed. pap. 2.00 (*0-486-28061-6*) Dover Pubns., Inc.

—The Adventures of Huckleberry Finn. 2nd ed. 1998. (Illustrated Classic Book Ser.). (Illus.). 61p. (J). (gr. 3 up). reprint ed. pap. text 4.95 (*1-56767-255-8*) Educational Insights, Inc.

—The Adventures of Huckleberry Finn. (J). E-Book 2.49 (*1-929120-49-4*) Electric Umbrella Publishing.

—The Adventures of Huckleberry Finn. 1994. (Books of Wonder: Vol. 1). (Illus.). 368p. (J). (gr. 4-7). 24.99 (*0-688-10656-0*) HarperCollins Children's Bk. Group.

—The Adventures of Huckleberry Finn. deluxe ed. (Illus.). (J). lib. bdg. 9.87 o.p. (*0-06-014377-0*); 1942. reprint ed. 11.95 o.p. (*0-06-014376-2*) HarperTrade.

—The Adventures of Huckleberry Finn. Smith, Henry N., ed. 1972. (YA). (gr. 4-7). pap. 13.96 o.s.i (*0-395-05114-2*, Riverside Editions) Houghton Mifflin Co.

—The Adventures of Huckleberry Finn. l.t. ed. 1182p. pap. 83.02 (*0-7583-0030-1*); 961p. pap. 72.45 (*0-7583-0029-8*); 781p. pap. 61.96 (*0-7583-0028-X*); 610p. pap. 43.97 (*0-7583-0027-1*); 1371p. pap. 93.15 (*0-7583-0031-X*); 348p. pap. 28.70 (*0-7583-0025-5*); 278p. pap. 24.74 (*0-7583-0024-7*); 477p. pap. 35.64 (*0-7583-0026-3*); 1371p. lib. bdg. 105.15 (*0-7583-0023-9*); 477p. lib. bdg. 41.64 (*0-7583-0018-2*); 1182p. lib. bdg. 95.02 (*0-7583-0022-0*); 961p. lib. bdg. 84.45 (*0-7583-0021-2*); 781p. lib. bdg. 73.96 (*0-7583-0020-4*); 610p. lib. bdg. 49.97 (*0-7583-0019-0*); 348p. lib. bdg. 34.70 (*0-7583-0017-4*); 2000. 278p. 30.74 (*0-7583-0016-6*) Huge Print Pr.

—The Adventures of Huckleberry Finn. 1999. 318p. (J). pap. 9.95 o.p. (*1-930128-06-1*, JNMedia Bks.) JNMedia, Inc.

—The Adventures of Huckleberry Finn. l.t. ed. 1997. (Large Print Heritage Ser.). 491p. lib. bdg. 35.95 (*1-58118-015-2*, 21489) LRS.

—The Adventures of Huckleberry Finn. 1977. (American Classics). (J). (gr. 9-12). 6.12 o.p. (*0-88343-416-4*); pap. 8.92 o.p. (*0-88343-415-6*); audio 89.08 o.p. (*0-88343-426-1*) McDougal Littell Inc.

—The Adventures of Huckleberry Finn. 1959. 288p. (YA). (gr. 7). mass mkt. 1.75 o.p. (*0-451-51912-4*, Signet Classics) NAL.

—The Adventures of Huckleberry Finn, Level 2. Hedge, Tricia, ed. 2000. (Bookworms Ser.). (Illus.). 64p. (J). pap. text 5.95 (*0-19-422976-9*) Oxford Univ. Pr., Inc.

—The Adventures of Huckleberry Finn. 2003. (Illus.). 288p. (J). pap. 3.99 o.p. (*0-14-250098-4*, Puffin Bks.); 1999. pap. 2.99 o.s.i (*0-14-130543-6*, Puffin Bks.); 1995. (Illus.). 400p. (J). (gr. 4-7). pap. 4.99 (*0-14-036676-8*, Puffin Bks.); 1983. 288p. (J). (gr. 3-7). pap. 3.50 o.p. (*0-14-035007-1*, Puffin Bks.); 1981. (Illus.). 448p. (J). (gr. 4-6). reprint ed. 7.95 o.p. (*0-448-11000-8*, Grosset & Dunlap); 1948. (Illus.). 448p. (J). (gr. 4-7). reprint ed. 17.99 (*0-448-06000-0*, Grosset & Dunlap) Penguin Putnam Bks. for Young Readers.

—The Adventures of Huckleberry Finn. 1978. (Illus.). (J). (gr. 6-9). 2.95 o.p. (*0-448-14922-2*) Putnam Publishing Group, The.

—The Adventures of Huckleberry Finn. 2001. (Illus.). pap. (*1-57646-254-4*) Quiet Vision Publishing.

—The Adventures of Huckleberry Finn. 1986. (Running Press Classics Ser.). 256p. (J). (gr. 4 up). pap. 4.95 o.p. (*0-89471-476-7*); lib. bdg. 12.90 o.p. (*0-89471-477-5*) Running Pr. Bk. Pubs.

—The Adventures of Huckleberry Finn. 1987. 384p. (J). (gr. 4-6). 1.25 o.p. (*0-590-40662-0*, Scholastic Paperbacks); pap. 2.50 o.p. (*0-590-40801-1*, Scholastic Paperbacks); pap. 4.99 (*0-590-43389-X*) Scholastic, Inc.

—The Adventures of Huckleberry Finn. 1989. (Enriched Classics Ser.). 432p. (YA). (gr. 5-12). mass mkt. (*0-671-70136-3*, 46198, Washington Square Pr.) Simon & Schuster.

—The Adventures of Huckleberry Finn. abr. ed. 1972. (J). pap. 11.95 o.p. incl. audio (*0-88142-325-4*) Soundelux Audio Publishing.

—The Adventures of Huckleberry Finn. l.t. ed. 1996. (Perennial Bestsellers Ser.). 420p. (J). 24.95 (*0-7838-1609-X*) Thorndike Pr.

—The Adventures of Huckleberry Finn. 1999. 10.04 (*0-606-17508-3*); 1994. 11.04 (*0-606-12869-7*); 1982. (J). 11.00 (*0-606-13112-4*) Turtleback Bks.

—The Adventures of Huckleberry Finn. Fischer, Victor et al, eds. 2001. (Mark Twain Library). (Illus.). (J). 535p. 45.00 (*0-520-22806-5*); xxvii, 561p. pap. 14.95 (*0-520-22838-3*) Univ. of California Pr.

—The Adventures of Huckleberry Finn. 2002. (Classics Ser.). (Illus.). 368p. pap. 6.00 (*0-14-243717-4*, Penguin Classics) Viking Penguin.

—The Adventures of Huckleberry Finn. Seelye, John, ed. & intro. by. 1986. (Penguin Classics Ser.). 368p. (J). (gr. 4). pap. 5.95 o.s.i (*0-14-039046-4*) Viking Penguin.

—The Adventures of Huckleberry Finn: With a Discussion of Friendship. Lauter, Richard, tr. & illus. by. 2003. (Values in Action Illustrated Classics Ser.). (J). (*1-59203-042-4*) Learning Challenge, Inc.

—The Adventures of Tom Sawyer. (YA). E-Book 3.95 (*0-594-05730-2*); 2002. (J). E-Book 3.95 (*0-594-09149-7*) 1873 Pr.

—The Adventures of Tom Sawyer. 2002. (Great Illustrated Classics). (Illus.). 240p. (J). (gr. 3-8). lib. bdg. 21.35 (*1-57765-679-2*, ABDO & Daughters) ABDO Publishing Co.

—The Adventures of Tom Sawyer. 1962. (Airmont Classics Ser.). (YA). (gr. 5 up). mass mkt. 2.95 (*0-8049-0006-X*, CL-6) Airmont Publishing Co., Inc.

—The Adventures of Tom Sawyer, Vol. 1. 1995. (Adventures of Tom Sawyer Ser.: Vol. 1). 224p. mass mkt. 5.50 (*0-553-21128-5*, Bantam Classics) Bantam Bks.

—The Adventures of Tom Sawyer. 2002. 12.17 (*0-7587-7968-2*) Book Wholesalers, Inc.

—The Adventures of Tom Sawyer. 1999. (YA). reprint ed. pap. text 28.00 (*1-4047-1117-1*) Classic Textbooks.

—The Adventures of Tom Sawyer. 2003. 192p. (J). 4.99 (*1-57759-556-4*) Dalmatian Pr.

—The Adventures of Tom Sawyer. 2002. (Kingfisher Classics Ser.). (Illus.). 352p. (J). tchr. ed. 15.95 (*0-7534-5478-5*, Kingfisher) Houghton Mifflin Co. Trade & Reference Div.

—The Adventures of Tom Sawyer. l.t. ed. 205p. pap. 20.60 (*0-7583-0056-5*); 256p. pap. 23.48 (*0-7583-0057-3*); 1008p. pap. 79.44 (*0-7583-0063-8*); 869p. pap. 69.01 (*0-7583-0062-X*); 351p. pap. 29.38 (*0-7583-0058-1*); 449p. pap. 36.45 (*0-7583-0059-X*); 575p. pap. 44.94 (*0-7583-0060-3*); 707p. pap. 53.86 (*0-7583-0061-1*); 351p. lib. bdg. 35.38 (*0-7583-0050-6*); 449p. lib. bdg. 42.45 (*0-7583-0051-4*); 1008p. lib. bdg. 91.44 (*0-7583-0055-7*); 256p. lib. bdg. 29.48 (*0-7583-0049-2*); 869p. lib. bdg. 82.83 (*0-7583-0054-9*); 575p. lib. bdg. 50.94 (*0-7583-0052-2*); 205p. lib. bdg. 26.60 (*0-7583-0048-4*); 707p. lib. bdg. 59.86 (*0-7583-0053-0*) Huge Print Pr.

—The Adventures of Tom Sawyer. (Young Collector's Illustrated Classics Ser.). (Illus.). 192p. (J). (gr. 3-7). 9.95 (*1-56156-453-2*) Kidsbooks, Inc.

—The Adventures of Tom Sawyer. l.t. ed. 1997. (Large Print Heritage Ser.). 357p. (YA). (gr. 7-12). lib. bdg. 30.95 (*1-58118-014-4*, 21488) LRS.

—The Adventures of Tom Sawyer. 1995. (Fiction Ser.). (YA). pap. text 7.88 o.p. (*0-582-09677-4*, 79814) Longman Publishing Group.

—The Adventures of Tom Sawyer. 1997. (Wishbone Classics Ser.: No. 11). (Illus.). 144p. (gr. 3-7). mass mkt. 4.25 (*0-06-106498-X*, HarperEntertainment) Morrow/Avon.

—The Adventures of Tom Sawyer. (J). 2002. (Illus.). 544p. mass mkt. 5.95 (*0-451-52864-6*, Signet Bks.); 1959. 224p. (gr. 7). mass mkt. 3.95 o.p. (*0-451-52355-5*, Signet Classics) NAL.

—The Adventures of Tom Sawyer. abr. ed. 1996. (J). audio 13.98 (*962-634-580-2*, NA208014, Naxos AudioBooks) Naxos of America, Inc.

—The Adventures of Tom Sawyer. 2000. (J). audio 12.95 (*0-19-422879-7*) Oxford Univ. Pr., Inc.

—The Adventures of Tom Sawyer, Level 1. Hedge, Tricia, ed. 2000. (Bookworms Ser.). (Illus.). 57p. (J). pap. text 5.95 (*0-19-422936-X*) Oxford Univ. Pr., Inc.

—The Adventures of Tom Sawyer. 2003. (Illus.). 228p. (J). pap. 3.99 o.p. (*0-14-250097-6*, Puffin Bks.); 1999. (gr. 4-7). pap. 2.99 o.p. (*0-14-130544-4*, Puffin Bks.); 1996. (Illus.). 288p. (YA). (gr. 7-12). 23.99 o.s.i (*0-670-86984-8*); 1994. (Illus.). 336p. (J). (gr. 4-7). 16.99 (*0-448-40560-1*, Grosset & Dunlap); 1983. 224p. (J). (gr. 3-7). pap. 3.50 o.p. (*0-14-035003-9*, Puffin Bks.); 1996. (Illus.). 288p. (J). (gr. 7-12). 19.99 (*0-670-86985-6*); 1981. (Illus.). (J). (gr. 4-6). reprint ed. 7.95 o.p. (*0-448-11002-4*, Grosset & Dunlap); 1946. (Illus.). 336p. (J). (gr. 4-6). reprint ed. 13.95 o.p. (*0-448-06002-7*, Grosset & Dunlap) Penguin Putnam Bks. for Young Readers.

—The Adventures of Tom Sawyer. Vogel, Malvina, ed. 1989. (Great Illustrated Classics Ser.: Vol. 6). (Illus.). 240p. (J). (gr. 3-6). 9.95 (*0-86611-957-4*) Playmore, Inc., Pubs.

—The Adventures of Tom Sawyer. 1978. (Illus.). (J). (gr. 6-9). 2.95 o.p. (*0-448-14921-4*) Putnam Publishing Group, The.

—The Adventures of Tom Sawyer. 2001. (Paperback Classics Ser.). (Illus.). 304p. pap. 6.95 (*0-375-75681-7*, Modern Library) Random House Adult Trade Publishing Group.

—The Adventures of Tom Sawyer. (Illustrated Library for Children). (Illus.). (J). 2002. 224p. 16.99 (*0-517-22108-X*, Random Hse. Bks. for Young Readers); 1986. 304p. o.p. (*0-307-17110-8*, Golden Bks.) Random Hse. Children's Bks.

—The Adventures of Tom Sawyer. (Children's Library Ser.). (J). 1995. 1.10 o.s.i (*0-517-14155-8*); 1989. (Illus.). 288p. 12.99 o.s.i (*0-517-68813-1*) Random Hse. Value Publishing.

—The Adventures of Tom Sawyer. 1995. (Step into Classics Ser.). (Illus.). 112p. (gr. 2-7). pap. 3.99 (*0-679-88070-4*) Random Hse., Inc.

—The Adventures of Tom Sawyer. 1985. (Illus.). 223p. (YA). (gr. 7-12). 12.95 o.p. (*0-89577-217-5*) Reader's Digest Assn., Inc., The.

—The Adventures of Tom Sawyer. (Literary Classics Ser.). 2002. (Illus.). 176p. 6.00 o.p. (*0-7624-0542-2*); 1987. 160p. (J). (gr. 4 up). pap. 4.95 o.p. (*0-89471-541-0*); 1987. 160p. (J). (gr. 4 up). lib. bdg. 12.90 o.p. (*0-89471-542-9*) Running Pr. Bk. Pubs.

—The Adventures of Tom Sawyer. 1987. 320p. (J). (gr. 4-6). 1.25 o.p. (*0-590-40663-9*); pap. 2.50 o.p. (*0-590-40800-3*) Scholastic, Inc. (Scholastic Paperbacks).

—The Adventures of Tom Sawyer. 1982. (Silver Classic Ser.). (Illus.). 246p. (J). (*0-382-03437-6*) Silver, Burdett & Ginn, Inc.

—The Adventures of Tom Sawyer. abr. ed. 2000. (J). audio compact disk 20.00 (*0-7435-0634-0*, Simon & Schuster Audioworks) Simon & Schuster Audio.

—The Adventures of Tom Sawyer. 2001. (Aladdin Classics Ser.). 272p. (J). (gr. 4-7). pap. 3.99 (*0-689-84224-4*, Aladdin) Simon & Schuster Children's Publishing.

—The Adventures of Tom Sawyer. Barish, Wendy, ed. 1982. (Illus.). 279p. (J). 14.50 o.p. (*0-671-43791-7*, Atheneum) Simon & Schuster Children's Publishing.

—The Adventures of Tom Sawyer. rev. ed. 1981. (Illus.). (YA). (gr. 7-12). pap. 2.95 (*0-671-44135-3*, Simon Pulse) Simon & Schuster Children's Publishing.

—The Adventures of Tom Sawyer. l.t. ed. 1996. (Perennial Bestsellers Ser.). 285p. (J). 24.95 (*0-7838-1705-3*) Thorndike Pr.

—The Adventures of Tom Sawyer. 1997. (Wishbone Classics Ser.: No. 11). (J). (gr. 3-7). 10.30 (*0-606-12104-8*) Turtleback Bks.

—The Adventures of Tom Sawyer. Gise, Joanne, ed. 1990. (Troll Illustrated Classics). (J). 12.10 (*0-606-00298-7*) Turtleback Bks.

—The Adventures of Tom Sawyer. (Illus.). 292p. pap. 14.95 (*0-520-23575-4*) Univ. of California Pr.

—The Adventures of Tom Sawyer: With a Discussion of Imagination. 2003. (Values in Action Illustrated Classics Ser.). (Illus.). 190p. (J). (*1-59203-027-0*) Learning Challenge, Inc.

—The Adventures of Tom Sawyer & the Adventures of Huckleberry Finn. 1979. 288p. (J). (gr. 4-7). mass mkt. 4.95 (*0-451-52272-9*) NAL.

—Huckleberry Finn. 1997. (Classics Illustrated Study Guides). (Illus.). 64p. (YA). (gr. 7 up). mass mkt., stu. ed. 4.99 o.p. (*1-57840-008-2*) Acclaim Bks.

—Huckleberry Finn. 1995. (Classroom Reading Plays Ser.). 32p. (YA). (gr. 6-12). pap. 3.95 (*0-7854-1122-4*, 40210); pap. 2.40 o.p. (*1-56103-110-0*) American Guidance Service, Inc.

—Huckleberry Finn. unabr. ed. 1965. (J). audio 41.95 (*1-55685-353-X*) Audio Bk. Contractors, Inc.

—Huckleberry Finn. 1977. (Dent's Illustrated Children's Classics Ser.). (Illus.). 338p. (J). reprint ed. 10.00 o.p. (*0-460-05031-1*) Biblio Distribution.

—Huckleberry Finn. 1999. (YA). reprint ed. pap. text 28.00 (*1-4047-1118-X*) Classic Textbooks.

—Huckleberry Finn. 1988. (Study Texts Ser.). (YA). (gr. 7 up). pap. text 3.97 o.p. (*0-582-00264-8*, 73957) Longman Publishing Group.

—Huckleberry Finn. 1940. (J). audio 7.95 National Recording Co.

—Huckleberry Finn. Bassett, Jennifer, ed. 1995. (Illus.). 48p. (J). pap. text 5.95 o.p. (*0-19-422724-3*) Oxford Univ. Pr., Inc.

—Huckleberry Finn. Teresa Agnes, ed. Heller, Rudolf, tr. 1979. (SPA., Illus.). 64p. (YA). stu. ed. 1.50 (*0-88301-570-6*) Pendulum Pr., Inc.

—Huckleberry Finn. Farr, Naunerle C., ed. 1973. (Now Age Illustrated Ser.). (Illus.). 64p. (J). (gr. 5-10). 7.50 o.p. (*0-88301-207-3*); pap. 2.95 (*0-88301-098-4*) Pendulum Pr., Inc.

—Huckleberry Finn. (American Collection Short Classics). (J). (gr. 4-7). 1993. 32p. pap. 4.95 o.p. (*0-8114-6826-7*); 1988. 22.00 o.p. (*0-8172-2179-4*); 1983. (Illus.). 48p. pap. 9.27 o.p. (*0-8172-2009-7*); 1983. (Illus.). 48p. lib. bdg. 24.26 o.p. (*0-8172-1651-0*); Set. 1991. (Illus.). 48p. pap. 34.00 (*0-8114-6962-X*) Raintree Pubs.

—Huckleberry Finn. 1990. (Folio - Junior Ser.: No. 230). (FRE., Illus.). 380p. (J). (gr. 5-10). pap. 10.95 (*2-07-033230-6*) Schoenhof's Foreign Bks., Inc.

—Huckleberry Finn. unabr. ed. 2002. (YA). audio compact disk 39.95 (*1-58472-259-2*, 076); pap. incl. audio compact disk (*1-58472-261-4*) Sound Room Pubs., Inc. (In Audio).

—Tom Sawyer. 1997. (Classics Illustrated Study Guides). (Illus.). 64p. (YA). (gr. 7 up). mass mkt., stu. ed. 4.99 (*1-57840-001-5*) Acclaim Bks.

—Tom Sawyer. abr. adapted ed. 1998. (Children's Thrift Classics Ser.). (Illus.). 96p. (J). (gr. 1 up). pap. 1.00 (*0-486-29156-1*) Dover Pubns., Inc.

—Tom Sawyer. 2nd ed. 1998. (Illustrated Classic Book Ser.). (Illus.). 61p. (J). (gr. 3 up). reprint ed. pap. text 4.95 (*1-56767-263-9*) Educational Insights, Inc.

—Tom Sawyer. 1992. (Children's Classics Ser.). (Illus.). 272p. (J). (*0-89434-127-8*, Ferguson Publishing Co.) Facts on File Inc.

—Tom Sawyer. adapted ed. (YA). (gr. 5-12). pap. text 9.95 (*0-8359-0212-9*) Globe Fearon Educational Publishing.

—Tom Sawyer. 1998. (Cloth Bound Pocket Ser.). 240p. (J). 7.95 (*3-89508-463-8*, 520258) Konemann.

—Tom Sawyer. (Coleccion Clasicos de la Juventud). (SPA., Illus.). 220p. (J). 12.95 (*84-7189-029-1*, ORT310) Ortells, Alfredo Editorial S.L. ESP. *Dist:* Continental Bk. Co., Inc.

—Tom Sawyer. Shapiro, Irwin, ed. 1973. (Now Age Illustrated Ser.). (Illus.). 64p. (J). (gr. 5-10). 7.50 o.p. (*0-88301-220-0*); stu. ed. 1.25 (*0-88301-179-4*); pap. 2.95 (*0-88301-103-4*) Pendulum Pr., Inc.

—Tom Sawyer. 9999. (Children's Classics Ser.: No. 740-24). (Illus.). (J). (gr. 3-5). text 3.50 o.p. (*0-7214-0977-6*, Ladybird Bks.) Penguin Group (USA) Inc.

—Tom Sawyer. (American Short Classics Ser.). (J). (gr. 4-7). 1993. 32p. pap. 4.95 o.p. (*0-8114-6843-7*); 1983. (Illus.). 48p. pap. 9.27 o.p. (*0-8172-2025-9*); 1983. (Illus.). 48p. lib. bdg. 24.26 o.p. (*0-8172-1665-0*) Raintree Pubs.

—Tom Sawyer. 1999. (Illus.). 336p. (gr. 4-7). mass mkt. 3.99 (*0-439-09940-4*) Scholastic, Inc.

—Tom Sawyer. 1994. (Classic Story Bks.). (J). 4.98 o.p. (*0-8317-1646-0*) Smithmark Pubs., Inc.

—Tom Sawyer. unabr. ed. 2002. (YA). pap. incl. audio compact disk (*1-58472-341-6*, In Audio) Sound Room Pubs., Inc.

—Tom Sawyer. 1996. 16.00 (*0-606-16016-7*) Turtleback Bks.

—Tom Sawyer Abroad. 1999. (YA). reprint ed. pap. text 28.00 (*1-4047-1125-2*) Classic Textbooks.

—Tom Sawyer Abroad. 1993. 112p. mass mkt. 2.50 (*0-8125-2334-2*, Tor Classics) Doherty, Tom Assocs., LLC.

—Tom Sawyer Abroad, Set. unabr. ed. 1996. (J). pap. 46.20 incl. audio (*0-7887-1442-2*, 40272) Recorded Bks., LLC.

—Tom Sawyer Abroad & Tom Sawyer, Detective. 1966. (Classics Ser.). (YA). (gr. 5 up). mass mkt. 1.50 o.s.i (*0-8049-0126-0*, CL-126) Airmont Publishing Co., Inc.

—Tom Sawyer Abroad & Tom Sawyer, Detective. 1985. 224p. (J). (ps-8). mass mkt. 1.95 o.p. (*0-451-51961-2*, Signet Classics) NAL.

—Tom Sawyer Abroad; Tom Sawyer, Detective. l.t. ed. 1999. (Large Print Heritage Ser.). 265p. (YA). (gr. 7-12). lib. bdg. 29.95 (*1-58118-046-2*, 22515) LRS.

—Tom Sawyer & Huckleberry Finn. 1972. reprint ed. 14.95 o.p. (*0-460-00976-1*) Biblio Distribution.

—Tom Sawyer & Huckleberry Finn. unabr. ed. 1998. (Wordsworth Classics Ser.). (YA). (gr. 6-12). 5.27 (*0-89061-011-8*, R0118WW) Jamestown.

Twain, Mark & Price, David. The Adventures of Tom Sawyer & the Adventures of Huckleberry Finn. 1995. (Illus.). 560p. (J). (gr. 3-5). 12.98 o.p. (*0-8317-1211-2*) Smithmark Pubs., Inc.

Walter, Mildred Pitts. Justin & the Best Biscuits in the World. 2002. (Illus.). (J). 13.40 (*0-7587-0371-6*) Book Wholesalers, Inc.

—Justin & the Best Biscuits in the World. 1986. (Illus.). 128p. (J). (gr. 4-7). 15.95 (*0-688-06645-3*) HarperCollins Children's Bk. Group.

—Justin & the Best Biscuits in the World. 1995. (Illus.). (J). (gr. 4). 9.00 (*0-395-73245-X*) Houghton Mifflin Co.

—Justin & the Best Biscuits in the World. 1999. (Illus.). 128p. (J). (gr. 3-5). pap. 4.99 (*0-679-89448-9*) Knopf, Alfred A. Inc.

—Justin & the Best Biscuits in the World. 1986. (J). 11.04 (*0-606-04714-X*) Turtleback Bks.

MONGOLIA—FICTION

Aldridge, James. The Marvellous Mongolian. 2003. 144p. (J). (gr. 4-7). pap. (*1-55041-820-3*) Fitzhenry & Whiteside, Ltd.

MONSTERVILLE (IMAGINARY PLACE)—FICTION

Noonan, R. A. Beware the Claw! 1996. (Monsterville Ser.: 5). 144p. (J). pap. 3.95 o.p. (*0-689-71867-5*, Simon Pulse) Simon & Schuster Children's Publishing.

—Don't Go into the Graveyard! 1995. (Monsterville USA Ser.: No. 2). 144p. (J). (gr. 4-5). pap. 3.95 o.p. (*0-689-71864-0*, Simon Pulse) Simon & Schuster Children's Publishing.

—Enter at Your Own Risk. 1995. (Monsterville USA Ser.: 1). 160p. (J). (gr. 4-5). mass mkt. 3.95 o.p. (*0-689-71863-2*, Simon Pulse) Simon & Schuster Children's Publishing.

—My Teacher Is a Zombie. 1995. (Monsterville USA Ser.: No. 3). 144p. (J). pap. 3.95 o.p. (*0-689-71865-9*, Simon Pulse) Simon & Schuster Children's Publishing.

—New Grrrl in Town. 1996. (Monsterville USA Ser.: Vol. 6). (Illus.). 144p. (J). (gr. 3-7). pap. 3.99 (*0-689-71868-3*, Simon Pulse) Simon & Schuster Children's Publishing.

—Wild Ghost Chase. 1996. (Monsterville USA Ser.: 4). 144p. (J). pap. 3.95 o.p. (*0-689-71866-7*, Simon Pulse) Simon & Schuster Children's Publishing.

MONTANA—FICTION

Bly, Stephen A. & Bly, Janet. Crystal's Blizzard Trek. 1901. (Crystal Blake Ser.). (J). (gr. 7-10). pap. 3.95 o.p. (*1-55513-055-0*) Cook Communications Ministries.

Campbell, Joanna. Star's Chance. 2001. (Thoroughbred Ser.: No. 45). 176p. (gr. 4-7). mass mkt. 4.99 (*0-06-106669-9*, HarperEntertainment) Morrow/Avon.

Corcoran, Barbara. Long Journey. 1970. (Illus.). (J). (gr. 3-7). lib. bdg. 5.50 o.p. (*0-689-20596-1*, Atheneum) Simon & Schuster Children's Publishing.

—Wolf at the Door. 1993. 192p. (J). (gr. 3-7). 17.00 (*0-689-31870-7*, Atheneum) Simon & Schuster Children's Publishing.

Eunson, Dale. Up on the Rim, RS. 1970. (J). (gr. 7 up). 4.50 o.p. (*0-374-38053-8*, Farrar, Straus & Giroux (BYR)) Farrar, Straus & Giroux.

Farnes, Catherine. Over the Divide. 2001. 146p. (J). (gr. 7-12). 6.49 (*1-57924-646-X*) Jones, Bob Univ. Pr.

Fradin, Dennis Brindell. Montana. 1995. (From Sea to Shining Sea Ser.). (Illus.). 64p. (J). (gr. 3-5). pap. 7.95 (*0-516-43826-3*, Children's Pr.) Scholastic Library Publishing.

Gilliland, Hap. Alone in the Wilderness. 2001. (Illus.). 158p. (YA). (gr. 6-10). pap. 14.95 (*0-87961-257-6*) Naturegraph Pubs., Inc.

Guthrie, Alfred B., Jr. The Big Sky. 1984. 384p. (ps up). mass mkt. 6.50 o.s.i (*0-553-26683-7*) Bantam Bks.

Hamilton, Gail. Love Comes to Eunice K. O'Herlihy. 1977. (J). (gr. 5-8). 5.95 o.p. (*0-689-30584-2*, Atheneum) Simon & Schuster Children's Publishing.

Hill, Janet Muirhead. Starlight's Shooting Star. 2003. (Illus.). 192p. (J). (gr. 3-8). per. 9.00 (*0-9714161-3-3*) Raven Publishing of Montana.

Ingold, Jeanette. The Big Burn. (YA). 2003. 320p. pap. 6.95 (*0-15-204924-X*, Harcourt Paperbacks); 2002. 304p. 17.00 (*0-15-216470-7*) Harcourt Children's Bks.

—Mountain Solo. 2003. 320p. (J). 17.00 (*0-15-202670-3*) Harcourt Children's Bks.

Johnson, Annabel & Johnson, Edgar. Bearcat. 1960. (J). (gr. 7 up). lib. bdg. 10.89 o.p. (*0-06-022836-9*) HarperCollins Pubs.

—Black Symbol. 1959. (J). (gr. 7 up). lib. bdg. 10.89 o.p. (*0-06-022846-6*) HarperCollins Pubs.

Katschke, Judy. The Case of the Wild Wolf River. 1998. (New Adventures of Mary-Kate & Ashley Ser.). 87p. (J). (gr. 2-7). mass mkt. 3.99 (*0-590-29401-6*) Scholastic, Inc.

Larson, Dorothy W. Bright Shadows. 1992. (Illus.). 96p. (J). (gr. 4-6). 14.95 (*0-9621779-0-3*) Sandstone Publishing.

Lasky, Kathryn. The Bone Wars. 1988. 378p. (J). (gr. 7 up). 12.95 o.p. (*0-688-07433-2*, Morrow, William & Co.) Morrow/Avon.

Martin, Nora. A Perfect Snow. 2002. 144p. (J). 16.95 (*1-58234-788-3*, Bloomsbury Children) Bloomsbury Publishing.

Mikaelsen, Ben. Rescue Josh McGuire. (J). 1993. 266p. (gr. 5-9). pap. 5.95 (*1-56282-523-2*); 1991. 272p. (gr. 5-9). 14.95 o.s.i (*1-56282-099-0*); 1991. 272p. (gr. 7 up). lib. bdg. 14.89 (*1-56282-100-8*) Hyperion Bks. for Children.

—Rescue Josh McGuire. 1993. (J). 12.00 (*0-606-05987-3*) Turtleback Bks.

Mills, Charles. Attack of the Angry Legend. 1998. (Shadow Creek Ranch Ser.: Vol. 10). 160p. (YA). (gr. 5-7). pap. 5.99 o.p. (*0-8280-1267-9*) Review & Herald Publishing Assn.

—Heart of the Warrior. 1994. (Shadow Creek Ranch Ser.: Vol. 6). 144p. (YA). (gr. 4-7). pap. 5.99 (*0-8280-0861-2*) Review & Herald Publishing Assn.

—Stranger in the Shadows. 1998. (Shadow Creek Ranch Ser.: Vol. 11). 151p. (Orig.). (J). (gr. 4-7). pap. 5.99 (*0-8280-1316-0*) Review & Herald Publishing Assn.

Place, Marian T. Mystery of the Wild Horse Trap. 2001. (Classic Ser.). (Illus.). 212p. (J). (gr. 4-7). pap. 15.95 (*0-87004-411-7*) Caxton Pr.

Richard, Adrienne. Pistol. 1989. 256p. (YA). 14.95 o.s.i (*0-316-74324-0*, Joy Street Bks.); 1969. (J). (gr. 7 up). 7.95 o.p. (*0-316-74320-8*) Little Brown & Co.

Rodriguez, Francisco E. Pancho Montana: Un Viaje Inesperado. 1996. (SPA., Illus.). 55p. (Orig.). (J). (gr. 4-6). pap. 7.95 (*1-887578-45-5*) SpanPr., Inc.

Sargent, Dave & Sargent, Pat. Sweetpea: Be Happy. 2003. (Saddle Up Ser.: Vol. 58). (Illus.). 42p. (J). pap. 6.95 (*1-56763-816-3*) Ozark Publishing.

—Sweetpea (Purple Corn Welsh) Be Happy. 2003. (Saddle Up Ser.: Vol. 58). (Illus.). 42p. (J). lib. bdg. 22.60 (*1-56763-815-5*) Ozark Publishing.

Scary, R. U. Ten Scary Monsters. 1995. (Illus.). 20p. (J). 8.99 o.s.i (*0-679-87414-3*) Random Hse., Inc.

Schaller, Bob. Mysterious Message in Montana. 2000. (X-Country Adventures Ser.). (Illus.). 128p. (J). (gr. 3-6). pap. 5.99 o.p. (*0-8010-4454-5*) Baker Bks.

Stein, Charlotte M. The Stained Glass Window. Sakurai, Jennifer, ed. (Illus.). 150p. (Orig.). (YA). 1996. pap., stu. ed. 11.95 (*0-916634-12-4*); 1994. 16.95 o.p. (*0-916634-13-2*) Rose Window Pr., The.

Wallace, Bill. Eye of the Great Bear. 1999. 176p. (J). (gr. 3-6). pap. 4.99 (*0-671-02502-3*, Aladdin); (Illus.). 16.00 (*0-671-02504-X*, Simon & Schuster Children's Publishing) Simon & Schuster Children's Publishing.

—Eye of the Great Bear. 1999. (J). 11.04 (*0-606-19050-3*) Turtleback Bks.

Wier, Ester. Loner. 1963. (Illus.). (J). (gr. 7-9). 5.95 o.p. (*0-679-20097-5*) McKay, David Co., Inc.

—Loner. 1992. 160p. (J). (gr. 4-7). pap. 4.50 (*0-590-44352-6*) Scholastic, Inc.

Yep, Laurence. When the Circus Came to Town. 128p. (J). 2004. pap. 5.99 (*0-06-440965-1*, Harper Trophy); 2001. (Illus.). 14.95 (*0-06-029325-X*); 2001. (Illus.). lib. bdg. 14.89 (*0-06-029326-8*) HarperCollins Children's Bk. Group.

Yorinks, Arthur. Whitefish Will Rides Again! 1996. (Michael di Capua Bks.). (Illus.). 32p. (YA). pap. 5.95 o.s.i (*0-06-205921-1*, Harper Trophy) HarperCollins Children's Bk. Group.

MONTEREY (CALIF.)—FICTION

Gregory, Kristiana. The Stowaway: A Tale of California Pirates. 1995. (Illus.). 144p. (J). (gr. 4 up). pap. 3.99 (*0-590-48822-8*) Scholastic, Inc.

Lehr, Norma. The Secret of the Floating Phantom. 1994. 1p. (J). (gr. 4-7). lib. bdg. 14.95 o.s.i (*0-8225-0736-6*, Lerner Pubns.) Lerner Publishing Group.

MONTREAL (QUEBEC)—FICTION

Frechette, Carole. In the Key of Do. Ouriou, Susan, tr. from FRE. 2002. 196p. (YA). (gr. 8 up). pap. 9.95 (*0-88995-254-X*) Red Deer Pr. CAN. *Dist:* General Distribution Services, Inc.

Mark, Jan. Mr. Dickens Hits Town. (Illus.). 72p. (J). (gr. 4). 2001. pap. 7.95 (*0-88776-578-5*); 1999. 16.95 (*0-88776-468-1*) Tundra Bks. of Northern New York.

Poulin, Stephane. Ah Belle Cite-A Beautiful City ABC. 1985. (ENG & FRE., Illus.). 28p. (J). (gr. k-3). 14.95 o.s.i (*0-88776-175-5*) Kitchen Sink Pr., Inc.

Richardson, Grace. Douglas. 1966. (J). (gr. 7 up). lib. bdg. 10.89 o.p. (*0-06-025011-9*) HarperCollins Pubs.

MOORS (WETLANDS)—FICTION

Blyton, Enid. Five Go to Mystery Moor. l.t. ed. 1997. (J). 16.95 o.p. (*0-7451-5491-3*, Galaxy Children's Large Print) BBC Audiobooks America.

MOROCCO—FICTION

Cory, Lynda. Boys Who Became Prophets. 1992. (Illus.). vii, 80p. (J). pap. 8.95 o.p. (*0-87579-664-8*) Deseret Bk. Co.

Czernecki, Stefan. Zorah's Magic Carpet. 1996. (Illus.). 32p. (J). (gr. k-4). 14.95 (*0-7868-0081-X*); lib. bdg. 15.49 (*0-7868-2066-7*) Hyperion Bks. for Children.

Jackson, Dave & Jackson, Neta. Risking the Forbidden Game: Maude Cary. 2002. (Trailblazers Ser.). (Illus.). 160p. (J). (gr. 3-7). pap. 5.99 (*0-7642-2234-1*) Bethany Hse. Pubs.

Johnston, Norma. Return to Morocco. 1988. 176p. (YA). (gr. 7 up). 13.95 o.p. (*0-02-747712-6*, Simon & Schuster Children's Publishing) Simon & Schuster Children's Publishing.

Klaus, Sandra. Mustafas Geheimnis: Ein Moslemischer Junge auf der Suche nach Gott. Date not set. Tr. of Mustapha's Secret - A Muslim Boy's Search to Know God. (GER., Illus.). (J). (gr. 2-7). pap. *(0-9617490-6-7)* Gospel Missionary Union.

—Mustapha's Secret: A Muslim Boy's Search to Know God. 2nd ed. 1997. (Illus.). 42p. (J). (gr. 2-7). spiral bd. 11.95 *(1-890940-00-3)* Gospel Missionary Union.

—Tainata na Mustapha. Date not set. Tr. of Mustapha's Secret. (BUL.). (J). (gr. 2-7). pap. *(1-890940-04-6)* Gospel Missionary Union.

Lewin, Ted. The Storytellers. 1998. (Illus.). 40p. (J). (gr. k-3). 16.00 *(0-688-15178-7)* HarperCollins Children's Bk. Group.

Myers, Walter Dean. Duel in the Desert. 1986. (Puffin Novels-Arrow Adventure Ser.). 96p. (J). (gr. 5-9). pap. 3.95 o.p. *(0-14-032101-2*, Penguin Bks.) Viking Penguin.

Sales, Francesc. Ibrahim. Simont, Marc, tr. from CAT. 1989. (Illus.). 32p. (J). (gr. k-3). 11.95 *(0-397-32146-5)*; lib. bdg. 11.89 o.p. *(0-397-32147-3)* HarperCollins Children's Bk. Group.

St. John, Patricia M. Star of Light. 2002. (Illus.). 256p. (J). pap. 6.99 *(0-8024-6577-3)* Moody Pr.

MOSCOW (RUSSIA)—FICTION

Thompson, Kay. Eloise in Moscow. 2000. 80p. (J). ltd. ed. 150.00 *(0-689-83328-8)*; 40th ed. (Illus.). 17.00 *(0-689-83211-7)* Simon & Schuster Children's Publishing. (Simon & Schuster Children's Publishing).

MOUNTAIN LIFE—SOUTHERN STATES—FICTION

Axsom, Dora & Pelham, Erra. Mountain Mama: Courageous Backwoods Mistress. 3rd rev. ed. 1990. (Orig.). (YA). pap. 10.00 *(0-9621669-1-X)* Little Red Hen.

—No Lace for Cricket: Sequel to Mountain Mama. (Orig.). (YA). 1991. 216p. (gr. 10 up). pap. 5.50 *(0-9621669-2-8)*; 2nd ed. 1997. 207p. reprint ed. pap. 10.00 *(0-9621669-3-6)* Little Red Hen.

Beatty, Patricia. Charley Skedaddle. 1987. 192p. (YA). (gr. 5-9). 16.00 o.p. *(0-688-06687-9*, Morrow, William & Co.) Morrow/Avon.

—Charley Skedaddle. 1997. (Literature Units Ser.). (Illus.). 48p. (gr. 5-8). pap., tchr. ed. 7.99 *(1-55734-565-1*, TCA0565) Teacher Created Materials, Inc.

—Charley Skedaddle. 1987. (J). 11.00 *(0-606-04029-3)* Turtleback Bks.

Buck, Charles Neville. The Code of Mountains. 2000. 252p. E-Book 3.95 *(0-594-06339-6)* 1873 Pr.

Clark, Billy C. Mooneyed Hound. Gifford, James M. & Hall, Patricia A., eds. 2nd ed. 1995. (Illus.). 128p. (J). (gr. 4 up). pap. 8.50 *(0-945084-49-8)* Stuart, Jesse Foundation, The.

—Trail of the Hunter's Horn. Gifford, James M. & Hall, Patricia A., eds. 2nd ed. 1995. (Illus.). 80p. (J). (gr. 4 up). pap. 6.00 *(0-945084-48-X)* Stuart, Jesse Foundation, The.

Collier, James Lincoln. Wild Boy. 2002. 176p. (J). (gr. 4-7). 15.95 *(0-7614-5126-9)* Cavendish, Marshall Corp.

Credle, Ellis. Down, Down the Mountain. 1934. (Illus.). (J). (gr. k-3). 8.25 o.p. *(0-525-66020-8*, 0801-240, Dutton Children's Bks.) Penguin Putnam Bks. for Young Readers.

Dragonwagon, Crescent. The Itch Book. 1990. (Illus.). 32p. (J). (gr. k-3). lib. bdg. 13.95 *(0-02-733121-0*, Atheneum) Simon & Schuster Children's Publishing.

Garland, Sherry. Letters from the Mountain. 1996. 256p. (YA). (gr. 7 up). 12.00 *(0-15-200661-3)* Harcourt Children's Bks.

George, Jean Craighead. My Side of the Mountain. 1997. (My Side of the Mountain Gift Set Ser.). (Illus.). (J). (gr. 3-7). pap. 9.99 *(0-14-774425-3*, Puffin Bks.) Penguin Putnam Bks. for Young Readers.

Gibbons, Faye. Hook Moon Night. 1997. (Illus.). 112p. (J). (gr. 3-7). 14.95 *(0-688-14504-3)* HarperCollins Children's Bk. Group.

Harper, Jon. Blue Ridge. 1995. (Illus.). 160p. (J). pap. 8.95 *(0-9611872-7-1)* Our Child Pr.

Harshman, Marc & Collins, Bonnie. Rocks in My Pockets. 2002. (Illus.). 36p. (J). per. 6.95 *(1-891852-23-X)* Quarrier Pr.

Hermes, Patricia. When Snow Lay Soft on the Mountains. 1996. (Illus.). 32p. (J). (ps-3). 15.95 o.p. *(0-316-36005-8)* Little Brown & Co.

Houston, Gloria M. Littlejim's Dream. 1997. (Illus.). 240p. (J). (gr. 3-7). 16.00 *(0-15-201509-4)* Harcourt Children's Bks.

Johnston, Tony. Amber on the Mountain. 1998. (Picture Puffin Bks.). (Illus.). 32p. (J). (ps-3). pap. 6.99 *(0-14-056408-X*, Puffin Bks.) Penguin Putnam Bks. for Young Readers.

—Amber on the Mountain. 1998. (Picture Puffin Ser.). (J). 12.14 *(0-606-13119-1)* Turtleback Bks.

Lenski, Lois. Blue Ridge Billy. 1946. (Regional Stories Ser.). (Illus.). (J). (gr. 4-6). lib. bdg. 9.79 o.p. *(0-397-30120-0)* HarperCollins Children's Bk. Group.

Lewis, J. Patrick. The Moonbow of Mr. B. Bones. 1992. (Illus.). 40p. (J). (ps-4). 16.00 o.s.i *(0-394-85365-2*, Knopf Bks. for Young Readers) Random Hse. Children's Bks.

Lyon, George Ella. Borrowed Children. 1990. 176p. (YA). mass mkt. 3.99 o.p. *(0-553-28380-4)* Bantam Bks.

—Borrowed Children. 1988. 160p. (J). (gr. 5-7). 15.95 o.p. *(0-531-05751-8)*; mass mkt. 16.99 o.p. *(0-531-08351-9)* Scholastic, Inc. (Orchard Bks.).

Marshall, Catherine. Goodbye, Sweet Prince. 1997. (Christy Fiction Ser.: No. 11). 128p. (Orig.). (J). (gr. 4-8). pap. 4.99 *(0-8499-3962-3)* Nelson, Tommy.

—Mountain Madness. adapted ed. 1997. (Christy Fiction Ser.: No. 9). 128p. (Orig.). (J). (gr. 4-8). mass mkt. 4.99 *(0-8499-3960-7)* Nelson, Tommy.

—The Princess Club. 1996. (Christy Fiction Ser.: No. 7). 128p. (J). (gr. 4-8). pap. text 4.99 *(0-8499-3958-5)* Nelson, Tommy.

—Stage Fright. 1997. (Christy Fiction Ser.: No. 10). (Illus.). 128p. (J). (gr. 4-8). mass mkt. 4.99 *(0-8499-3961-5)* Nelson, Tommy.

Murphy, Rita. Harmony. 2004. 160p. (YA). (gr. 7). mass mkt. 5.99 *(0-440-22923-5*, Laurel Leaf) Random Hse. Children's Bks.

—Harmony. 2002. 144p. (YA). lib. bdg. 17.99 *(0-385-90069-4)*; (gr. 7). 15.95 *(0-385-72938-3)* Random Hse., Inc.

Murray, Cleitus O. Stories of the Southern Mountains & Swamps. 1992. (Illus.). 192p. (Orig.). (YA). pap. 9.95 *(0-9632132-0-2)* Murray Pubns.

O'Dell, Scott. Thunder Rolling in the Mountains. 1993. 144p. (J). (gr. 7 up). pap. text 5.50 *(0-440-40879-2)* Dell Publishing.

O'Dell, Scott & Hall, Elizabeth. Thunder Rolling in the Mountains, Set. unabr. ed. 1997. (J). (gr. 4). pap. 48.70 incl. audio *(0-7887-2196-8*, 40267) Recorded Bks., LLC.

Partridge, Elizabeth. Clara & the Hoodoo Man. 176p. (gr. 3-7). 1998. pap. 4.99 o.s.i *(0-14-038348-4)*; 1996. (J). 14.99 o.s.i *(0-525-45403-9*, Dutton Children's Bks.) Penguin Putnam Bks. for Young Readers.

Ransom, Candice F. When the Whippoorwill Calls. 1995. (Illus.). 32p. (J). (gr. 2-5). 16.00 *(0-688-12729-0)*; lib. bdg. 15.93 o.p. *(0-688-12730-4)* Morrow/Avon. (Morrow, William & Co.).

Smyers, Jacquelyn. The Time a Cloud Came into the Cabin (A Mountain Tale for Boys) 1986. (Illus.). 12p. (Orig.). (J). (ps-6). pap. 3.98 *(0-9615130-3-9)* Very Idea, The.

—The Time a Cloud Came into the Cabin (A Mountain Tale for Girls) 1986. (Illus.). 12p. (Orig.). (J). (ps-6). pap. 3.98 *(0-9615130-4-7)* Very Idea, The.

Steele, William O. No-Name Man of the Mountain. 1964. (Illus.). (J). (gr. 1-5). 4.50 o.p. *(0-15-257501-4)*; 3.33 o.p. *(0-15-257502-2)* Harcourt Children's Bks.

Stuart, Jesse. Penny's Worth of Character. 1964. (Illus.). (J). (gr. 3-5). lib. bdg. o.p. *(0-07-062301-5)* McGraw-Hill Cos., The.

Stuart, Jesse H. Hie to the Hunters. Herndon, Jerry A., ed. 6th ed. 1996. (Illus.). 272p. (YA). reprint ed. 22.00 *(0-945084-58-7)*; (gr. 9-12). pap. 12.00 *(0-945084-59-5)* Stuart, Jesse Foundation, The.

Welches School, Jeanine Boldt's English Class. The Mountaineer, Vol. 2, No. 1. 1984. (Illus.). 58p. (J). pap. 7.00 *(0-89904-018-7)* Crumb Elbow Publishing.

White, Alana. Come Next Spring. 1990. 170p. (J). (gr. 6 up). 13.95 o.p. *(0-395-52593-4*, Clarion Bks.) Houghton Mifflin Co. Trade & Reference Div.

Yolen, Jane. Uncle Lemon's Spring. 1981. (Illus.). (J). (gr. 2-6). 9.25 o.p. *(0-525-41830-X*, Dutton) Dutton/Plume.

N

NANTUCKET ISLAND (MASS.)—FICTION

Arciero, Susan. Nantucket 1, 2, 3. l.t. ed. 2000. (Illus.). (J). (ps). 7.95 *(0-9677548-2-8)* Pigtail Publishing.

Barnes, Peter W. & Barnes, Cheryl Shaw. Nat, Nat, the Nantucket Cat. 1993. (Illus.). 30p. (J). 15.95 *(0-9637688-0-8)* Vacation Spot Publishing.

—Nat, Nat, the Nantucket Cat Goes to the Beach. 2001. (Illus.). 32p. 15.95 *(1-893622-05-3*, VSP Bks.) Vacation Spot Publishing.

Brett, Jan. Comet's Nine Lives. 1996. (Illus.). 32p. (J). (ps-3). 16.99 *(0-399-22931-0*, G. P. Putnam's Sons) Penguin Group (USA) Inc.

Corcoran, Barbara. The Faraway Island. 1977. (J). (gr. 5-9). lib. bdg. 6.95 o.p. *(0-689-30550-8*, Atheneum) Simon & Schuster Children's Publishing.

Cunningham, Bradley S. Tucket Teddy's Day at Work. 7.95 *(0-9653674-0-1)* Nantucket Cobblestones, Ltd.

Finley, Martha. Elsie at Nantucket. (J). reprint ed. 1981. 301p. lib. bdg. 32.95 o.s.i *(0-89966-333-8)*; 1980. 302p. lib. bdg. 17.95 o.s.i *(0-89967-011-3*, Harmony Raine & Co.) Buccaneer Bks., Inc.

—Elsie at Nantucket. 2001. (Elsie Books: Vol. 10). 234p. (J). pap. 5.99 *(1-931343-01-2)* Hibbard Pubns., Inc.

Mathews, Francine. Death in Rough Water: A Merry Folger Mystery. 1996. 288p. mass mkt. 5.50 *(0-380-72335-2*, Avon Bks.) Morrow/Avon.

Miles, Mary. Benjamin's Secret Sea Dragon: A Nantucket Adventure. 2002. pap. 17.50 *(1-59109-320-1)* Booksurge, LLC.

—What's So Special about Nantucket? 1993. (Illus.). 36p. (J). (ps up). lib. bdg. 17.00 *(0-9636885-0-2)* Faraway Publishing Group.

Parvey, Karen G. A Katie Dog Day on Nantucket. 1995. (Illus.). 34p. (J). (ps-3). 15.95 *(0-9648685-5-5)* Island Dog Pr.

Rouillard, Wendy W. Barnaby-Seasons in the Park. Rouillard, Wendy W., ed. 2000. (Barnaby Ser.: Vol. 5). (Illus.). 32p. (J). 15.95 *(0-9642836-9-7)* Barnaby & Co.

—Barnaby's Faraway Land. 1993. (Illus.). 28p. (J). (ps-4). pap. 8.95 *(0-9642836-0-3)* Barnaby & Co.

Snedeker, Caroline Dale. Downright Dencey. 1927. (J). (gr. 3-7). 3.95 o.p. *(0-385-07284-8)* Doubleday Publishing.

Stowe, Cynthia. The Second Escape of Arthur Cooper. 2000. (Illus.). 110p. (J). (gr. 5-9). lib. bdg. 14.95 *(0-7614-5069-6*, Cavendish Children's Bks.) Cavendish, Marshall Corp.

Trimble, Marcia. Malinda Martha & Her Skipping Stones. 1999. (Illus.). 32p. (J). (ps-3). 15.95 *(1-891577-72-7)* Images Pr.

—The Smiling Stone. 1998. (Illus.). 32p. (J). (ps-2). lib. bdg. 15.95 *(1-891577-37-9)* Images Pr.

Trimble, Marcia & Grell, Susi. Serendipity Says to Know Me Is to Love Me. 2000. (Illus.). 32p. (J). (ps-3). 15.95 *(1-891577-77-8)* Images Pr.

Turkle, Brinton. Rachel & Obadiah. (Unicorn Paperbacks Ser.). (Illus.). 32p. (J). 1987. (gr. 1-3). pap. 4.95 o.s.i *(0-525-44303-7)*; 1978. (gr. k-3). 15.00 o.s.i *(0-525-38020-5)* Penguin Putnam Bks. for Young Readers. (Dutton Children's Bks.).

Watkins, Dawn L. Nantucket Cats. 1998. (Illus.). 32p. (J). (ps-1). pap. 5.49 *(0-89084-975-7)* Jones, Bob Univ. Pr.

Weller, Frances Ward. Madaket Millie. 1999. (Illus.). 32p. (J). (ps-3). pap. 5.99 o.s.i *(0-698-11774-3)* Penguin Putnam Bks. for Young Readers.

NARNIA (IMAGINARY PLACE)—FICTION

The Chronicles of Narnia. unabr. ed. Incl. Horse & His Boy. Lewis, C. S. (J). (gr. 4-8). audio Last Battle. York, Michael, reader. (J). (gr. 4-8). audio Lion, the Witch & the Wardrobe. Lewis, C. S. (J). (gr. 4-8). audio Magician's Nephew. Lewis, C. S. (J). (gr. 4-8). audio Prince Caspian. Lewis, C. S. (J). (gr. 4-8). audio Silver Chair. Lewis, C. S. (gr. 3 up). 1989. audio compact disk 11.95 *(0-89845-875-7*, CPN 1631); Voyage of the Dawn Treader. Chronicles of Narnia. Lewis, C. S. (gr. 3 up). 1989. audio compact disk 11.95 *(0-89845-874-9)*; 1985. Set audio 9.95 HarperTrade.

The Chronicles of Narnia, Set. audio 99.95 Random Hse. Audio Publishing Group.

The Chronicles of Narnia, Set. 2003. (Radio Theatre Ser.). audio 99.99 *(1-58997-150-7)*; audio compact disk 99.99 *(1-58997-149-3)* Tyndale Hse. Pubs.

Lewis, C. S. L'Armoire Magique. 6th ed. 1999. Orig. Title: The Lion, the Witch & the Wardrobe. (FRE.). (J). (gr. 4-7). pap. 12.95 *(2-08-164414-2)* Distribooks, Inc.

—Aslan. 1998. (World of Narnia Ser.: Bk. 3). (Illus.). 40p. (J). (gr. k-4). 15.95 *(0-06-027636-3)* HarperCollins Pubs.

—Aslan's Triumph. 1998. (World of Narnia Ser.). (Illus.). 40p. (J). (gr. k-4). 14.95 o.s.i *(0-06-027638-X)* HarperCollins Pubs.

—Aslan's Triumph. 1999. (World of Narnia Ser.). (Illus.). 40p. (J). (gr. k-4). pap. 5.95 o.p. *(0-06-443575-X)* HarperCollins Pubs.

—Aslan's Triumph. 1999. (Illus.). (J). 12.10 *(0-606-18675-1)* Turtleback Bks.

—El Caballo y Su Jinete. 1995. Tr. of Horse & His Boy. (SPA.). 200p. 11.95 o.p. *(84-204-4609-2)* Santillana USA Publishing Co., Inc.

—The Chronicles of Narnia, 7 vols. l.t. ed. 1986. (Chronicles of Narnia Ser.: Bks. 1-7). (J). (gr. 4-8). 97.65 o.p. *(0-8161-4188-6*, Macmillan Reference USA) Gale Group.

—The Chronicles of Narnia, 7 vols. (Illus.). (J). 2002. (Chronicles of Narnia Ser.: Bks. 1-7). (gr. 3 up). mass mkt. 41.93 *(0-06-447119-5*, Harper Trophy); 2001. (Narnia Ser.). 768p. (ps-k). pap. 19.95 *(0-06-623850-1)* HarperCollins Children's Bk. Group.

—The Chronicles of Narnia. (Chronicles of Narnia Ser.: Bks. 1-7). (Illus.). (J). (gr. 4-8). 1988. lib. bdg. 97.00 o.p. *(0-02-758801-7)*; 1983. pap. 79.95 o.p. *(0-02-757740-6)* Simon & Schuster Children's Publishing. (Simon & Schuster Children's Publishing).

—The Chronicles of Narnia. unabr. ed. Incl. Lion, the Witch & the Wardrobe. audio Prince Caspian. audio Silver Chair. audio Voyage of the Dawn Treader. audio (J). (gr. 4-8). 1985. Set audio 29.95 *(0-89845-027-6*, SBC 123, Caedmon) HarperTrade.

—The Chronicles of Narnia, 7 vols., Set. 1994. (Chronicles of Narnia Ser.: Bks. 1-7). (Illus.). 336p. (J). (gr. 3 up). pap. 55.93 *(0-06-440537-0*, Harper Trophy) HarperCollins Children's Bk. Group.

—The Chronicles of Narnia, 7 bks., Set. 1994. (Chronicles of Narnia Ser.: Bks. 1-7). (Illus.). (J). (gr. 3 up). 118.93 *(0-06-024488-7)* Zondervan.

—The Chronicles of Narnia: The Complete Collection. 2001. audio 99.95 Lodestone Catalog, The.

—The Chronicles of Narnia Audio Collection. unabr. ed. 1991. (Narnia Ser.). (gr. 3 up). audio 25.00 *(1-55994-501-X*, SBN 123, HarperAudio) HarperTrade.

—The Chronicles of Narnia Box Set: Full-Color Collector's Edition. 2000. (Chronicles of Narnia Ser.: Bks. 1-7). (Illus.). (J). (gr. 3 up). 59.99 *(0-06-440939-2*, Harper Trophy) HarperCollins Children's Bk. Group.

—The Chronicles of Narnia Super-Soundbook. unabr. ed. Incl. Horse & His Boy. (J). (gr. 4-8). audio Horse & His Boy. Baynes, Pauline, illus. (gr. 3 up). 1989. audio compact disk 12.00 *(0-89845-876-5)*; Last Battle. (J). (gr. 4-8). audio Lion, the Witch & the Wardrobe. York, Michael, reader. (J). (gr. 4-8). 2000. audio 50.00 Magician's Nephew. (J). (gr. 4-8). audio Silver Chair. (J). (gr. 4-8). audio Voyage of the Dawn Treader. (J). (gr. 4-8). audio 1985. Set audio 49.95 *(0-89845-049-7*, SSBC 701, Caedmon) HarperTrade.

—The Complete Chronicles of Narnia. deluxe ed. 1998. (Chronicles of Narnia Ser.). (Illus.). 528p. (J). (gr. 3 up). 50.00 *(0-06-028137-5)* HarperCollins Children's Bk. Group.

—Edmund & the White Witch. 1997. (World of Narnia Ser.: Bk. 2). (Illus.). 40p. (J). (gr. k-4). 12.95 *(0-06-027516-2)* HarperCollins Children's Bk. Group.

—Edmund & the White Witch. (World of Narnia Ser.). (Illus.). 40p. (J). (gr. k-4). 1998. pap. 5.95 o.s.i *(0-06-443506-7)*; 1997. lib. bdg. 12.89 o.p. *(0-06-027517-0)* HarperCollins Pubs.

—The Horse & His Boy. abr. ed. 2002. (Chronicles of Narnia: Bk.5). (J). (gr. 4-8). audio 16.99 Blackstone Audio Bks., Inc.

—The Horse & His Boy. l.t. ed. 1986. (Chronicles of Narnia Ser.: Bk. 5). 224p. (J). (gr. 4-8). 13.95 o.p. *(0-8161-4093-6*, Macmillan Reference USA) Gale Group.

—The Horse & His Boy. (Chronicles of Narnia Ser.: Bk. 5). (Illus.). (J). (gr. 3 up). 1994. 240p. 16.99 *(0-06-023488-1)*; 1994. 240p. pap. 7.99 *(0-06-440501-X*, Harper Trophy); 1994. 240p. lib. bdg. 17.89 *(0-06-023489-X*, Harper Trophy); 1994. 256p. mass mkt. 5.99 *(0-06-447106-3*, Harper Trophy); 2000. 240p. pap. 8.95 *(0-06-440940-6*, Harper Trophy) HarperCollins Children's Bk. Group.

—The Horse & His Boy. (Chronicles of Narnia Ser.: Bk.5). (J). (gr. 4-8). audio. (J). (gr. 4-8). audio. 1989. (gr. 3 up). audio compact disk 12.00 *(0-89845-876-5)* HarperTrade. (Caedmon).

—The Horse & His Boy. 2001. (Chronicles of Narnia Ser.: Vol. 5). audio 16.99 Lodestone Catalog, The.

—The Horse & His Boy. (Chronicles of Narnia Ser.: Bk.5). (J). (gr. 4-8). 1999. audio 16.99; 1997. audio 18.00 o.s.i *(0-553-47884-2*, Listening Library) Random Hse. Audio Publishing Group.

—The Horse & His Boy. 2nd ed. 1988. (Chronicles of Narnia Ser.: Bk. 5). (Illus.). 208p. (J). (gr. 4-8). 13.95 o.p. *(0-02-757650-7*, Simon & Schuster Children's Publishing) Simon & Schuster Children's Publishing.

—The Horse & His Boy. l.t. ed. 2000. (Chronicles of Narnia Ser.: Bk. 5). (Illus.). 253p. (J). (gr. 4-8). 21.95 *(0-7862-2233-6)* Thorndike Pr.

—The Horse & His Boy. (Chronicles of Narnia Ser.: Bk.5). (J). (gr. 4-8). 2000. 14.00 *(0-606-19976-4)*; 1994. 13.00 *(0-606-06470-2)*; 1994. 11.00 *(0-606-06471-0)* Turtleback Bks.

—The Last Battle. unabr. ed. (Chronicles of Narnia: Bk.7). (J). (gr. 4-8). audio 16.99 Blackstone Audio Bks., Inc.

—The Last Battle. l.t. ed. (Chronicles of Narnia Ser.: Bk. 7). (J). (gr. 4-8). 2001. (Illus.). 237p. 22.95 *(0-7862-2237-9)*; 1986. 208p. 13.95 o.p. *(0-8161-4095-2)* Gale Group. (Macmillan Reference USA).

Settings

—The Last Battle. (Chronicles of Narnia Ser.: Bk. 7). (Illus.). (J). (gr. 3 up). 1994. 224p. 16.99 (*0-06-023493-8*); 1994. 224p. pap. 7.99 (*0-06-440503-6*, Harper Trophy); 1994. 224p. lib. bdg. 17.89 (*0-06-023494-6*); 1994. 240p. mass mkt. 5.99 (*0-06-447108-X*, Harper Trophy); 2000. 224p. pap. 7.95 (*0-06-440941-4*, Harper Trophy) HarperCollins Children's Bk. Group.

—The Last Battle. (Chronicles of Narnia Ser.: Bk.7). (J). (gr. 4-8). audio. 2004. audio 24.00 (*0-06-059783-6*, HarperAudio); 2004. audio compact disk 27.50 (*0-06-059782-8*, HarperAudio); 1989. (Chronicles of Narnia Ser.: Bk.7). 122p. (gr. 3 up). audio compact disk 11.95 (*0-89845-878-1*, Harper-Audio) HarperTrade.

—The Last Battle. 2001. (Chronicles of Narnia Ser.: Vol. 7). (J). audio 16.99 Lodestone Catalog, The.

—The Last Battle. abr. unabr. ed. (Chronicles of Narnia Ser.: Bk. 7). (J). (gr. 4-7). 1998. audio 16.99 o.s.i (*0-553-52550-6*, Listening Library); Set. 1999. audio 16.99 Random Hse. Audio Publishing Group.

—The Last Battle. (Chronicles of Narnia Ser.: Bk. 7). (YA). (gr. 4-8). 1988. (Illus.). 184p. lib. bdg. 13.95 o.p. (*0-02-757900-X*); 1969. pap. 11.95 o.p. (*0-02-757890-9*) Simon & Schuster Children's Publishing. (Simon & Schuster Children's Publishing).

—The Last Battle. (Chronicles of Narnia Ser.: Bk.7). (gr. 4-8). 2000. (J). 14.00 (*0-606-19980-2*); 1994. (YA). 11.00 (*0-606-06518-0*); 1994. (YA). 13.00 (*0-606-06517-2*) Turtleback Bks.

—The Last Battle. unabr. ed. 2003. (Radio Theatre Ser.). (J). audio compact disk 21.97 o.p. (*1-56179-842-8*) Tyndale Hse. Pubs.

—El Leon, la Bruja y el Armario. 1995. (SPA., Illus.). 176p. (YA). (gr. 5-8). 11.95 (*84-204-4564-9*) Alfaguara, Ediciones, S.A.- Grupo Santillana ESP. *Dist:* Santillana USA Publishing Co., Inc.

—The Lion, the Witch & the Wardrobe. 1976. (Chronicles of Narnia Ser.: Bk. 1). (J). (gr. 4-8). 20.95 (*0-8488-0823-1*) Amereon, Ltd.

—The Lion, the Witch & the Wardrobe. unabr. ed. (Chronicles of Narnia: Bk.1). (J). (gr. 4-8). audio 24.00 Blackstone Audio Bks., Inc.

—The Lion, the Witch & the Wardrobe. 1989. (Chronicles of Narnia Ser.: Bk. 1). (J). (gr. 4-8). pap. 5.95 (*0-87129-265-3*, L62) Dramatic Publishing Co.

—The Lion, the Witch & the Wardrobe. 2003. (Chronicles of Narnia Ser.: Bk.1). (gr. 4-8). (J). audio compact disk 18.97 (*1-56179-700-6*); (YA). audio compact disk 18.97 (*1-56179-699-9*) Focus on the Family Publishing.

—The Lion, the Witch & the Wardrobe. l.t. ed. 1986. (Chronicles of Narnia Ser.: Bk.1). (Illus.). 227p. (J). (gr. 4-8). 13.95 o.p. (*0-8161-4089-8*, Macmillan Reference USA) Gale Group.

—The Lion, the Witch & the Wardrobe. (J). 2003. 208p. (gr. 3 up). 29.99 incl. audio compact disk (*0-06-055649-8*); 2002. (Narnia Ser.). (Illus.). 48p. pap. 7.99 (*0-06-443695-0*); 2002. (Narnia Ser.). (SPA., Illus.). 208p. (gr. 3 up). pap. 7.99 (*0-06-008661-0*); 2000. (Chronicles of Narnia Ser.: Bk.1). (gr. 4-8). pap., tchr. ed. (*0-06-447260-4*, Harper Trophy); 1997. (Chronicles of Narnia Ser.: Bk. 1). (gr. 4-8). pap. 187.65 o.p. (*0-06-449498-5*); 2000. (Chronicles of Narnia Ser.). (Illus.). 48p. (gr. 5 up). 15.95 (*0-06-029011-0*); 1995. (Chronicles of Narnia Ser.: Bk.1). (Illus.). 64p. (gr. 3 up). pap. 11.95 (*0-06-443399-4*, Harper Trophy); 1994. (Chronicles of Narnia Ser.: Bk. 1). (Illus.). 208p. (gr. 3 up). 16.99 (*0-06-023481-4*); 1994. (Chronicles of Narnia Ser.: Bk. 1). (Illus.). 208p. (gr. 3 up). pap. 7.99 (*0-06-440499-4*); 1994. (Chronicles of Narnia Ser.: Bk. 1). (Illus.). 208p. (gr. 3 up). lib. bdg. 17.89 (*0-06-023482-2*); 1994. (Chronicles of Narnia Ser.: Bk. 1). (Illus.). 224p. (gr. 3 up). mass mkt. 5.99 (*0-06-447104-7*, Harper Trophy); 2000. (Chronicles of Narnia Ser.: Bk.1). (Illus.). 208p. (gr. 3 up). pap. 8.99 (*0-06-440942-2*, Harper Trophy); 2000. (Chronicles of Narnia Ser.: Bk. 1). (Illus.). 176p. (ps up). 24.95 (*0-06-027724-6*); 2002. (Narnia Ser.). 192p. pap. 20.00 (*0-06-008240-2*) HarperCollins Children's Bk. Group.

—The Lion, the Witch & the Wardrobe. (J). 2004. (*0-06-055650-1*); 2004. lib. bdg. (*0-06-055651-X*); 2000. (Chronicles of Narnia Ser.: Bk.1). 28p. (gr. 4-8). 10.95 o.p. (*0-694-01479-6*); 2003. (Narnia Ser.). (Illus.). 112p. 19.99 (*0-06-053083-9*) Harper-Collins Pubs.

—The Lion, the Witch & the Wardrobe. (Chronicles of Narnia Ser.: Bk.1). (J). (gr. 4-8). audio. (J). (gr. 4-8). audio. 2000. (J). (gr. 4-8). audio 50.00. 1989. (gr. 3 up). audio compact disk 12.00 (*0-89845-159-0*, HarperAudio) HarperTrade.

—The Lion, the Witch & the Wardrobe. 2001. (Chronicles of Narnia Ser.: Vol. 1). (J). audio 18.00 Lodestone Catalog, The.

—The Lion, the Witch & the Wardrobe. 1999. (Chronicles of Narnia Ser.: Bk. 1). (J). (gr. 4-8). 11.95 (*1-56137-704-X*); 40p. 9.95 (*1-56137-243-9*) Novel Units, Inc.

—The Lion, the Witch & the Wardrobe. (Chronicles of Narnia Ser.: Bk.1). (J). (gr. 4-8). 1999. audio 18.00; 1996. audio 18.00 o.s.i (*0-553-47656-4*, 394128, Listening Library) Random Hse. Audio Publishing Group.

—The Lion, the Witch & the Wardrobe. (Chronicles of Narnia Ser.: Bk. 1). (J). (gr. 4-8). 1988. (Illus.). 192p. 13.95 o.p. (*0-02-758120-9*); 1988. (Illus.). 160p. lib. bdg. 22.95 (*0-02-758200-0*); 1968. pap. 11.95 o.p. (*0-02-758110-1*) Simon & Schuster Children's Publishing. (Simon & Schuster Children's Publishing).

—The Lion, the Witch & the Wardrobe. 1999. (Chronicles of Narnia Ser.: Bk.1). 112p. (J). (gr. 4-8). pap. 10.95 (*1-84002-049-0*) Theatre Communications Group, Inc.

—The Lion, the Witch & the Wardrobe. l.t. ed. 2000. (Chronicles of Narnia Ser.: Bk.1). (Illus.). 208p. (J). (gr. 4-8). 21.95 (*0-7862-2232-8*) Thorndike Pr.

—The Lion, the Witch & the Wardrobe. (Chronicles of Narnia Ser.: Bk.1). (J). (gr. 4-8). 2000. 14.00 (*0-606-19981-0*); 1995. 18.10 (*0-606-07791-X*); 1994. 11.00 (*0-606-06533-4*); 1994. 13.00 (*0-606-06532-6*) Turtleback Bks.

—The Lion, the Witch & the Wardrobe Vol. 1. 1998. (Chronicles of Narnia Ser.). pap. 14.99 o.p. (*0-88070-482-9*) Multnomah Pubs., Inc.

—The Lion, the Witch & the Wardrobe - One Act - Two Character. 1989. 30p. pap. 5.95 (*0-87129-668-3*, L54) Dramatic Publishing Co.

—Lucy Steps Through the Wardrobe. (World of Narnia Ser.). (Illus.). 40p. (J). (gr. k-4). 1998. pap. 5.95 o.s.i (*0-06-443505-9*); 1997. lib. bdg. 12.89 o.p. (*0-06-027451-4*); 1997. 12.95 o.p. (*0-06-027450-6*) HarperCollins Pubs.

—The Magician's Nephew. abr. ed. (Chronicles of Narnia: Bk.6). (J). (gr. 4-8). audio 18.00 Blackstone Audio Bks., Inc.

—The Magician's Nephew. 1985. pap. 5.95 (*0-87129-368-4*, M86); 1984. (Chronicles of Nanrnia Ser.: Bk.6). (J). (gr. 4-8). 5.95 (*0-87129-541-5*, M57) Dramatic Publishing Co.

—The Magician's Nephew. abr. ed. 2003. (Focus on the Family Great Stories Ser.: Bk.6). (J). (gr. 4-8). audio compact disk 18.97 (*1-56179-701-4*) Focus on the Family Publishing.

—The Magician's Nephew. l.t. ed. 1986. (Chronicles of Narnia Ser.: Bk. 6). 192p. (J). (gr. 4-8). 13.95 o.p. (*0-8161-4094-4*, Macmillan Reference USA) Gale Group.

—The Magician's Nephew. (Chronicles of Narnia Ser.: Bk. 6). (J). (gr. 3 up). 1994. (Illus.). 208p. 16.99 (*0-06-023497-0*); 1994. (Illus.). 208p. pap. 7.99 (*0-06-440505-2*, Harper Trophy); 1994. (Illus.). 240p. mass mkt. 5.99 (*0-06-447110-1*, Harper Trophy); 2000. (Illus.). 208p. pap. 8.99 (*0-06-440943-0*, Harper Trophy); 2001. 176p. 24.95 (*0-06-623826-9*) HarperCollins Children's Bk. Group.

—The Magician's Nephew. gif. ed. 2003. (Narnia Ser.). (Illus.). 208p. (J). 19.99 (*0-06-053084-7*) Harper-Collins Pubs.

—The Magician's Nephew. (Chronicles of Narnia Ser.: Bk.6). (J). (gr. 4-8). audio. (J). (gr. 4-8). audio. 1989. (gr. 3 up). audio compact disk 12.00 (*0-89845-877-3*, HarperAudio) HarperTrade.

—The Magician's Nephew. 2001. (Chronicles of Narnia Ser.: Bk.6). (J). (gr. 4-8). audio 18.00 Lodestone Catalog, The.

—The Magician's Nephew. (Chronicles of Narnia Ser.: Bk.6). (J). (gr. 4-8). audio 18.00. 1997. audio 18.00 o.s.i (*0-553-47768-4*, Listening Library) Random Hse. Audio Publishing Group.

—The Magician's Nephew. (Chronicles of Narnia Ser.: Bk. 6). (J). (gr. 4-8). 1970. 192p. pap. 3.50 o.p. (*0-02-044230-0*); 1969. pap. 11.95 o.p. (*0-02-758360-0*); 2nd ed. 1988. (Illus.). 176p. lib. bdg. 13.95 o.p. (*0-02-758340-6*) Simon & Schuster Children's Publishing. (Simon & Schuster Children's Publishing).

—The Magician's Nephew. l.t. ed. 2000. (Chronicles of Narnia Ser.: Bk.6). 224p. (J). (gr. 4-8). 21.95 (*0-7862-2231-X*) Thorndike Pr.

—The Magician's Nephew. 1994. (Chronicles of Narnia Ser.: Bk. 6). (J). (gr. 4-8). 11.00 (*0-606-06554-7*); 13.00 (*0-606-06553-9*); 14.10 (*0-606-20308-7*) Turtleback Bks.

—The Narnia Journal. 1997. (Narnia Ser.). (Illus.). 160p. (J). (gr. 3-7). 12.95 o.p. (*0-694-00695-5*, Harper Festival) HarperCollins Children's Bk. Group.

—Prince Caspian. unabr. ed. (Chronicles of Narnia: Bk.2). (J). (gr. 4-8). audio 16.99 Blackstone Audio Bks., Inc.

—Prince Caspian. l.t. ed. 1986. (Chronicles of Narnia Ser.: Bk. 2). 224p. (J). (gr. 4-8). 13.95 o.p. (*0-8161-4090-1*, Macmillan Reference USA) Gale Group.

—Prince Caspian. (Chronicles of Narnia Ser.: Bk. 2). 1994. (Illus.). 240p. (J). (gr. 3 up). 16.99 (*0-06-023483-0*); 1994. (Illus.). 240p. (J). (gr. 3 up). pap. 7.99 (*0-06-440500-1*, Harper Trophy); 1994. (Illus.). 240p. (J). (gr. 3 up). lib. bdg. 17.89 (*0-06-023484-9*); 1994. (Illus.). 256p. (J). (gr. 3 up). mass mkt. 5.99 (*0-06-447105-5*, Harper Trophy); 2000. (Illus.). 240p. (J). (gr. 3 up). pap. 8.95 (*0-06-440944-9*, Harper Trophy); 2003. audio compact disk 27.50 (*0-06-056440-7*) HarperCollins Children's Bk. Group.

—Prince Caspian. (Chronicles of Narnia Ser.: Bk.2). (J). (gr. 4-8). audio. (Chronicles of Narnia Ser.: Bk.2). (J). (gr. 4-8). audio. 1989. (Chronicles of Narnia Ser.: Bk. 2). 240p. (gr. 3 up). audio compact disk 12.00 (*0-89845-090-X*, CPN 1603, HarperAudio); 2003. audio 24.00 (*0-06-056439-3*, HarperAudio) HarperTrade.

—Prince Caspian. 2001. (Chronicles of Narnia Ser.: Vol. 2). (J). audio 16.99 Lodestone Catalog, The.

—Prince Caspian. (Chronicles of Narnia Ser.: Bk.2). (J). (gr. 4-8). 1999. audio 16.99; 1998. audio 16.99 o.s.i (*0-553-47917-2*, 390037, Listening Library) Random Hse. Audio Publishing Group.

—Prince Caspian. (Chronicles of Narnia Ser.: Bk. 2). (J). (gr. 4-8). 1969. pap. 11.95 o.p. (*0-02-758550-6*); 2nd ed. 1988. (Illus.). 192p. lib. bdg. 13.95 o.p. (*0-02-758580-8*) Simon & Schuster Children's Publishing. (Simon & Schuster Children's Publishing).

—Prince Caspian. l.t. ed. 2000. (Chronicles of Narnia Ser.: Bk. 2). (Illus.). 262p. (J). (gr. 4-8). 21.95 (*0-7862-2234-4*) Thorndike Pr.

—Prince Caspian. (Chronicles of Narnia Ser.: Bk.2). (J). (gr. 4-8). 2000. 14.00 (*0-606-19995-0*); 1994. 11.00 (*0-606-06681-0*); 1994. 13.00 (*0-606-06680-2*) Turtleback Bks.

—Prince Caspian. 1998. (Chronicles of Narnia Ser.: Bk. 2). (J). (gr. 4-8). lib. bdg. 18.95 (*1-56723-072-5*) Yestermorrow, Inc.

—El Principe Caspian. 1995. (SPA.). 208p. 11.95 o.p. (*84-204-4630-0*) Santillana USA Publishing Co., Inc.

—El Sillon de Plata. 1995. Tr. of Silver Chair. (SPA.). 240p. 11.95 o.p. (*84-204-4699-8*) Santillana USA Publishing Co., Inc.

—The Silver Chair. unabr. ed. (Chronicles of Narnia). (J). (gr. 4-8). audio 18.00 Blackstone Audio Bks., Inc.

—The Silver Chair. l.t. ed. 1986. (Chronicles of Narnia Ser.: Bk. 4). 312p. (J). (gr. 4-8). 13.95 o.p. (*0-8161-4092-8*, Macmillan Reference USA) Gale Group.

—The Silver Chair. (Chronicles of Narnia Ser.: Bk. 4). (Illus.). (J). 1994. 256p. (gr. 3 up). 16.99 (*0-06-023495-4*); 1994. 272p. (gr. 3 up). pap. 7.99 (*0-06-440504-4*, Harper Trophy); 1994. 272p. (gr. 3 up). mass mkt. 5.99 (*0-06-447109-8*, Harper Trophy); 1994. 256p. (gr. 4-8). lib. bdg. 14.89 o.s.i (*0-06-023496-2*); 2000. 256p. (gr. 3 up). pap. 7.95 (*0-06-440945-7*, Harper Trophy) HarperCollins Children's Bk. Group.

—The Silver Chair. (Chronicles of Narnia Ser.). (J). (gr. 4-8). audio. (Chronicles of Narnia Ser.). (J). (gr. 4-8). audio. 2004. audio 24.00 (*0-06-058256-1*, HarperAudio); 2004. audio compact disk 27.50 (*0-06-058257-X*, HarperAudio); 1989. (Chronicles of Narnia Ser.: Bk.4). (gr. 3 up). audio compact disk 11.95 (*0-89845-875-7*, CPN 1631, Caedmon) HarperTrade.

—The Silver Chair. (Chronicles of Narnia Ser.: Bk.4). (J). (gr. 4-8). audio 16.99. 1998. audio 18.00 o.s.i (*0-553-52570-0*, Listening Library) Random Hse. Audio Publishing Group.

—The Silver Chair. (Chronicles of Narnia Ser.: Bk. 4). (J). (gr. 4-8). 1969. pap. 11.95 o.p. (*0-02-758770-3*); 2nd ed. 1988. (Illus.). 216p. reprint ed. lib. bdg. 13.95 o.p. (*0-02-758780-0*) Simon & Schuster Children's Publishing. (Simon & Schuster Children's Publishing).

—The Silver Chair. l.t. ed. 1950. (Chronicles of Narnia Ser.: Bk. 4). (Illus.). 272p. (J). (gr. 4-8). 22.95 o.p. (*0-7862-2236-0*) Thorndike Pr.

—The Silver Chair. (Chronicles of Narnia Ser.: Bk.4). (J). (gr. 4-8). 2000. 14.00 (*0-606-19997-7*); 1994. 13.00 (*0-606-06737-X*); 1994. 11.00 (*0-606-06738-8*) Turtleback Bks.

—The Silver Chair Vol. 3. (Chronicles of Narnia Ser.). (J). (gr. 4-8). 14.99 o.p. incl. VHS (*0-88070-480-2*) Multnomah Pubs., Inc.

—El Sobrino del Mago. 2003. (SPA.). pap. (*956-13-1674-9*, AB4755) Bello, Andres CHL. *Dist:* Lectorum Pubns., Inc.

—El Sobrino del Mago. 1995. pap. text 11.95 o.p. (*84-204-4510-X*) Santillana USA Publishing Co., Inc.

—El Sobrino del Mago. 2001. 15.00 (*0-606-22692-3*) Turtleback Bks.

—La Ultima Batalla. 2003. (SPA.). pap. (*956-13-1675-7*, AB3856) Bello, Andres CHL. *Dist:* Lectorum Pubns., Inc.

—La Ultima Batalla. 1995. pap. text 11.95 o.p. (*84-204-4698-X*) Santillana USA Publishing Co., Inc.

—La Ultima Batalla. 2001. 15.00 (*0-606-22702-4*) Turtleback Bks.

—The Voyage of the Dawn Treader. abr. ed. (Chronicles of Narnia: Bk.3). (J). (gr. 4-8). audio 16.99 Blackstone Audio Bks., Inc.

—The Voyage of the Dawn Treader. l.t. ed. 1986. (Chronicles of Narnia Ser.: Bk. 3). 240p. (J). (gr. 4-8). 13.95 o.p. (*0-8161-4091-X*, Macmillan Reference USA) Gale Group.

—The Voyage of the Dawn Treader. (Chronicles of Narnia Ser.: Bk. 3). (Illus.). (J). 1994. 256p. (gr. 3 up). 16.99 (*0-06-023486-5*); 1994. 256p. (gr. 3 up). pap. 7.99 (*0-06-440502-8*, Harper Trophy); 1994. 288p. (gr. 3 up). mass mkt. 5.99 (*0-06-447107-1*, Harper Trophy); 1994. 80p. (gr. 4-8). lib. bdg. 14.89 o.p. (*0-06-023487-3*); 2000. 256p. (gr. 3 up). pap. 8.99 (*0-06-440946-5*, Harper Trophy) Harper-Collins Children's Bk. Group.

—The Voyage of the Dawn Treader. (Chronicles of Narnia Ser.: Bk.3). (J). (gr. 4-8). audio. audio HarperTrade.

—The Voyage of the Dawn Treader. 2001. (Chronicles of Narnia Ser.: Vol. 3). audio 16.99 Lodestone Catalog, The.

—The Voyage of the Dawn Treader. (Chronicles of Narnia Ser.: Bk.3). (J). (gr. 4-8). 1999. audio 16.99; 1998. audio 16.99 o.s.i (*0-553-52495-X*, Listening Library) Random Hse. Audio Publishing Group.

—The Voyage of the Dawn Treader. (Chronicles of Narnia Ser.: Bk. 3). (J). (gr. 4-8). 1969. pap. 11.95 o.p. (*0-02-758800-9*); 2nd ed. 1988. (Illus.). 216p. reprint ed. 13.95 o.p. (*0-02-758820-3*) Simon & Schuster Children's Publishing. (Simon & Schuster Children's Publishing).

—The Voyage of the Dawn Treader. l.t. ed. 1950. (Chronicles of Narnia Ser.: Bk. 3). (Illus.). 278p. (J). (gr. 4-8). 20.95 (*0-7862-2235-2*) Thorndike Pr.

—The Voyage of the Dawn Treader. (Chronicles of Narnia Ser.: Bk.3). (J). (gr. 4-8). 2000. 14.00 (*0-606-20005-3*); 1994. 11.00 (*0-606-06852-X*); 1994. 13.00 (*0-606-06851-1*) Turtleback Bks.

—The Voyage of the Dawn Treader: Chronicles of Narnia. unabr. ed. 1989. (Chronicles of Narnia Ser.: Bk.3). (gr. 3 up). audio compact disk 11.95 (*0-89845-874-9*, Caedmon) HarperTrade.

—The Wisdom of Narnia. 2001. (Narnia Ser.). (Illus.). 64p. (J). (ps-3). 10.95 (*0-06-623851-X*) HarperCollins Children's Bk. Group.

—The Wood Between the Worlds. (World of Narnia Ser.). (Illus.). 40p. (J). (gr. k-4). 2000. pap. 5.95 (*0-06-443641-1*, Harper Trophy); 1999. 14.95 o.p. (*0-06-027640-1*) HarperCollins Children's Bk. Group.

—The Wood Between the Worlds. 2000. 12.10 (*0-606-18732-4*) Turtleback Bks.

Lewis, C. S., adapted by. The Last Battle. 2003. (Radio Theatre Ser.). (J). audio compact disk 21.97 o.p. (*1-56179-843-6*) Tyndale Hse. Pubs.

Lewis, C. S. & Baynes, Pauline. The Magician's Nephew. 1994. (Chronicles of Narnia Ser.: Bk. 6). (Illus.). 208p. (J). (gr. 4-8). lib. bdg. 15.89 o.s.i (*0-06-023498-9*) HarperCollins Children's Bk. Group.

Lewis, C. S. & Clausen, Andrew. The Lion, the Witch & the Wardrobe. 1993. (Chronicles of Narnia Ser.: Bk.1). 56p. (J). (gr. 4-8). stu. ed., ring bd. 12.99 (*1-58609-136-0*) Progeny Pr.

Lewis, C. S. & Lawrie, Robin. The Magician's Nephew. abr. ed. 1999. (Chronicles of Narnia Ser.: Bk. 6). (Illus.). 64p. (J). (gr. 4-8). pap. 10.95 o.s.i (*0-06-443515-6*, Harper Trophy) HarperCollins Children's Bk. Group.

Lewis, C. S. & Maze, Deborah. Aslan. 1999. (World of Narnia Ser.). (Illus.). 40p. (J). (gr. k-4). pap. 5.95 o.s.i (*0-06-443527-X*) HarperCollins Pubs.

Lewis, C. S. & Scholastic, Inc. Staff. The Lion, the Witch & the Wardrobe. anniv. ed. 1997. (Chronicles of Narnia Ser.: Bk. 1). 16p. (J). (gr. 4-8). mass mkt. 3.95 (*0-590-36647-5*) Scholastic, Inc.

Lewis, C. S. & Shepherd, Michael. The Lion, the Witch & the Wardrobe. 1992. (Chronicles of Narnia Ser.: Bk.1). (Illus.). 48p. (J). (gr. 4-8). pap., tchr. ed. 7.99 (*1-55734-409-4*, TCA0409) Teacher Created Materials, Inc.

Lewis, C. S., et al. The Lion, the Witch & the Wardrobe. 2000. (Chronicles of Narnia Ser.: Bk.1). (Illus.). (J). (gr. 4-8). lib. bdg. 14.89 (*0-06-029013-7*) HarperCollins Pubs.

NEBRASKA—FICTION

Aldrich, Bess S. A Lantern in Her Hand. 1997. 256p. (YA). (gr. 8 up). pap. 6.99 (*0-14-038428-6*) Penguin Putnam Bks. for Young Readers.

Buchanan, Jane. Gratefully Yours, RS. 1997. 128p. (J). (gr. 3-7). 15.00 o.p. (*0-374-32775-0*, Farrar, Straus & Giroux (BYR)) Farrar, Straus & Giroux.

—Gratefully Yours. 1999. 128p. (J). (gr. 3-7). pap. 4.99 o.p. (*0-14-130315-8*, Puffin Bks.) Penguin Putnam Bks. for Young Readers.

Buchannan, Jane. Hank's Story, RS. 2001. 144p. (J). (gr. 3-7). 16.00 o.p. (*0-374-32836-6*, Farrar, Straus & Giroux (BYR)) Farrar, Straus & Giroux.

Bunting, Eve. Dandelions. 1995. (Illus.). 48p. (J). (ps-3). 16.00 (*0-15-200050-X*) Harcourt Children's Bks.

—Dandelions. 2001. 12.15 (*0-606-21135-7*) Turtleback Bks.

Cavanaugh, Kate. Pete & His Elves Series, Set. 1992. (Illus.). 28p. (J). pap. (*0-9622353-4-2*) KAC, Inc.

Conrad, Pam. My Daniel. 1989. 144p. (gr. 5 up). (J). lib. bdg. 16.89 (*0-06-021314-0*); (YA). 13.95 (*0-06-021313-2*) HarperCollins Children's Bk. Group.

—Prairie Songs. (Trophy Book Ser.). (Illus.). 176p. (gr. 5 up). 1987. (YA). pap. 5.99 (*0-06-440206-1*, Harper Trophy); 1985. (J). lib. bdg. 15.89 (*0-06-021337-X*) HarperCollins Children's Bk. Group.

—Prairie Songs. 1985. (Illus.). (J). (gr. 4-7). 14.00 o.s.i (*0-06-021336-1*, 236070) HarperCollins Pubs.

—Prairie Songs. 1995. 19.50 (*0-8446-6812-5*) Smith, Peter Pub., Inc.

—Prairie Songs. 1987. (J). 11.00 (*0-606-03639-3*) Turtleback Bks.

Cross, Gillian. The Great American Elephant Chase. 1993. 160p. (J). (gr. 4-7). 16.95 (*0-8234-1016-1*) Holiday Hse., Inc.

—The Great American Elephant Chase. 1994. 208p. (J). (gr. 5 up). pap. 3.99 o.s.i (*0-14-037014-5*, Puffin Bks.) Penguin Putnam Bks. for Young Readers.

Drake, Jane & Love, Ann. Farming. (America at Work Ser.). (Illus.). (J). (gr. 2-5). 2002. 32p. text 12.95 (*1-55074-451-8*); 2000. 118p. pap. (*1-55074-821-1*); 1996. 340p. text (*1-55074-228-0*) Kids Can Pr., Ltd.

Durbin, William. The Journal of Sean Sullivan: A Transcontinental Railroad Worker: Nebraska & Points West, 1867. 1999. (My Name Is America Ser.). (Illus.). 188p. (J). (gr. 4-8). pap. 10.95 (*0-439-04994-6*, Scholastic Pr.) Scholastic, Inc.

Figley, Marty Rhodes. The Schoolchildren's Blizzard. 2004. (On My Own History Ser.). (J). lib. bdg. 22.60 (*1-57505-586-4*, Carolrhoda Bks.) Lerner Publishing Group.

Gray, Dianne E. Holding up the Earth. 2000. 224p. (J). (gr. 5-9). tchr. ed. 15.00 (*0-618-00703-2*) Houghton Mifflin Co. Trade & Reference Div.

Heath, Jenny, illus. Prairie Meeting. 1998. (Cover-to-Cover Bks.). (J). (*0-7807-6787-X*, Covercraft) Perfection Learning Corp.

Hermes, Patricia. Calling Me Home. 1998. (Avon Camelot Bks.). 144p. (J). (gr. 4-7). 15.00 (*0-380-97451-7*, Eos) Morrow/Avon.

—Calling Me Home. 1999. (Illus.). (J). 10.04 (*0-606-17961-5*) Turtleback Bks.

Jackson, Bill, illus. The Rattlesnake Necklace. 1998. (Cover-to-Cover Bks.). (J). (*0-7807-6789-6*) Perfection Learning Corp.

Miner, Jane C. Margaret. 1988. (Sunfire Ser.: No. 27). 224p. (Orig.). (J). (gr. 7 up). pap. 2.75 o.p. (*0-590-41191-8*) Scholastic, Inc.

Murphy, Jim. My Face to the Wind: The Diary of Sarah Jane Price, a Prairie Teacher. 2001. (Dear America Ser.). (Illus.). 208p. (J). (gr. 4-9). pap. 10.95 (*0-590-43810-7*) Scholastic, Inc.

Ott, Margaret U. Sterling's Carrie. 1989. (Illus.). (Orig.). (J). (gr. 5-12). pap. text 9.95 o.p. (*0-939644-64-9*) Media Publishing.

Richardson, Arleta. Whistle-Stop West. (Orphans' Journey Ser.: Vol. 2). (J). 128p. (gr. 3-7). pap. 5.99 (*0-7814-3537-4*); 1993. 144p. pap. 4.99 (*0-7814-0922-5*) Cook Communications Ministries.

Ritthaler, Shelly. With Love, Amanda. 1997. (YA). pap. 3.99 (*0-380-78375-4*, Avon Bks.) Morrow/Avon.

—With Love, Amanda. 1997. (American Dreams Ser.). (YA). 9.09 o.p. (*0-606-10976-5*) Turtleback Bks.

Ruckman, Ivy. In Care of Cassie Tucker. 1998. 176p. (gr. 5-8). text 14.95 o.s.i (*0-385-32514-2*, Dell Books for Young Readers) Random Hse. Children's Bks.

Saban, Vera. Jennie Barnes: Right Now Forever. 1990. (This Is America Ser.). (Illus.). 130p. (Orig.). (J). (gr. 4-6). pap. 6.95 (*0-914565-34-6*, Timbertrails) Capstan Pubns.

Stahl, Hilda. Sadie Rose & the Mysterious Stranger. 1993. (Sadie Rose Adventure Ser.: No. 11). 128p. (J). (gr. 4-7). pap. 4.99 o.p. (*0-89107-747-2*) Crossway Bks.

Thomasma, Kenneth. Doe Sia: Bannock Girl & the Handcart Pioneer. 1999. (Amazing Indian Children: 8). (J). (gr. 3-8). pap. 7.99 (*1-880114-20-8*); 12.99 (*1-880114-21-6*) Grandview Publishing Co.

NEPAL—FICTION

Cloud, Linda. Meena of Nepal. 1982. (Illus.). 37p. (J). (gr. 1-6). spiral bd. 5.00 (*1-58318-039-7*, WOL018B) Way of Life Literature.

Dixit, Mani. Annapurna Fantasy: Happenings at Shangri-la. 1997. pap. 24.00 (*0-7855-7358-5*) Ratna Pustak Bhandar NPL. *Dist:* State Mutual Bk. & Periodical Service, Ltd.

Lama, Nurbu Tenzing. Himalaya. Tanaka, Shelley, tr. from FRE. 2002. (Illus.). 40p. (J). 16.95 (*0-88899-480-X*) Groundwood Bks. CAN. *Dist:* Publishers Group West.

Lumry, Amanda & Hurwitz, Laura. Tigers in Terai. 2003. (Adventures of Riley Ser.). (Illus.). 36p. 15.95 (*0-9662257-7-5*) Eaglemont Pr.

NETHERLANDS—FICTION

Alcott, Louisa May. Trudel's Siege. 1976. (Illus.). (J). (gr. 4-6). o.p. (*0-07-057791-9*) McGraw-Hill Cos., The.

Andersen, Hans Christian. The Tinder-Box. 1990. (J). (ps-9). 14.95 o.p. (*0-316-03938-1*) Little Brown & Co.

—The Tinder-Box. 1988. (Illus.). 32p. (J). (gr. 1 up). mass mkt. 14.95 o.s.i (*0-689-50458-6*, McElderry, Margaret K.) Simon & Schuster Children's Publishing.

Attema, Martha. Daughter of Light. 2001. (Young Reader Ser.). (Illus.). 144p. (J). (gr. 3-6). pap. 4.99 (*1-55143-179-3*) Orca Bk. Pubs.

—Daughter of Light. 2001. (J). 11.04 (*0-606-22770-9*) Turtleback Bks.

Birchman, David F. A Tale of Tulips, a Tale of Onions. 1994. (Illus.). 40p. (J). (gr. 1-4). lib. bdg. 15.95 o.p. (*0-02-710112-6*, Simon & Schuster Children's Publishing) Simon & Schuster Children's Publishing.

Borden, Louise. The Greatest Skating Race: A WWII Story from the Netherlands. 2003. (J). 18.95 (*0-689-84502-2*, McElderry, Margaret K.) Simon & Schuster Children's Publishing.

Bouhuys, Mies. The Lady of Stavoren: A Story from Holland. Willems-Treeman, Elizabeth, tr. 1979. (Puffin Folktales of the World Ser.). (Illus.). (J). (gr. 2-5). pap. 1.95 o.p. (*0-14-030802-4*, Penguin Bks.) Viking Penguin.

Carle, Eric, illus. The Hole in the Dike. 1993. 32p. (J). (ps-2). pap. 4.95 (*0-590-46146-X*) Scholastic, Inc.

Chambers, Aidan. Postcards from No Man's Land. 2004. pap. 7.99 (*0-14-240145-5*, Puffin Bks.) Penguin Putnam Bks. for Young Readers.

De Vries, Anke. Bruises. Knecht, Stacey, tr. 1995. 174p. (J). (gr. 7 up). 15.95 (*1-886910-03-0*) Front Street, Inc.

—Bruises. 1997. 176p. (YA). (gr. 9-12). mass mkt. 4.50 o.s.i (*0-440-22694-5*, Dell Books for Young Readers) Random Hse. Children's Bks.

DeJong, Meindert. Shadrach. 1953. (Illus.). 80p. (J). (gr. 3-6). lib. bdg. 14.89 o.p. (*0-06-021546-1*) HarperCollins Children's Bk. Group.

—The Wheel on the School. 1954. (Illus.). 256p. (J). (gr. 4-7). 16.99 (*0-06-021585-2*); (gr. k-4). lib. bdg. 16.89 (*0-06-021586-0*) HarperCollins Children's Bk. Group.

Dodge, Mary Mapes. Hans Brinker. (Illus.). (J). (gr. 4-6). 1963. 2.95 o.p. (*0-448-05462-0*); 1945. 12.95 o.s.i (*0-448-06011-6*) Penguin Putnam Bks. for Young Readers. (Grosset & Dunlap).

—Hans Brinker. Hanft, Joshua, ed. 1994. (Great Illustrated Classics Ser.: Vol. 40). (Illus.). 240p. (J). (gr. 3-6). 9.95 (*0-86611-991-4*) Playmore, Inc., Pubs.

—Hans Brinker & the Silver Skates. 2002. (Great Illustrated Classics). (Illus.). 240p. (J). (gr. 3-8). lib. bdg. 21.35 (*1-57765-814-0*, ABDO & Daughters) ABDO Publishing Co.

—Hans Brinker or the Silver Skates. 1966. (Airmont Classics Ser.). (YA). (gr. 5 up). mass mkt. 1.50 o.p. (*0-8049-0099-X*, CL-99) Airmont Publishing Co., Inc.

—Hans Brinker or the Silver Skates. 1993. (Classics Ser.). 256p. (gr. 8-12). mass mkt. 3.99 (*0-8125-3342-9*, Tor Classics) Doherty, Tom Assocs., LLC.

—Hans Brinker or the Silver Skates. (J). E-Book 2.49 (*1-58744-240-X*) Electric Umbrella Publishing.

—Hans Brinker or the Silver Skates. 1986. mass mkt. 2.50 o.p. (*0-451-52020-3*, Signet Classics) NAL.

—Hans Brinker or the Silver Skates. Lindskoog, Kathryn, ed. 2001. (Classics for Young Readers Ser.). (Illus.). 224p. (J). (gr. 3-6). pap. 7.99 (*0-87552-725-6*) P&R Publishing.

—Hans Brinker or the Silver Skates. 1993. (J). (gr. 4 up). pap. 4.99 o.p. (*0-88070-528-0*) Zonderkidz.

—Hans Brinker, or the Silver Skates. Kopito, Janet Baine, ed. 2003. (Dover Evergreen Classics Ser.). 240p. (J). pap. 3.00 (*0-486-42842-7*) Dover Pubns., Inc.

—Hans Brinker or the Silver Skates. l.t. ed. 245p. pap. 22.86 (*0-7583-3744-2*); 319p. pap. 26.47 (*0-7583-3745-0*); 1255p. pap. 87.29 (*0-7583-3751-5*); 436p. pap. 32.96 (*0-7583-3746-9*); 559p. pap. 40.75 (*0-7583-3747-7*); 715p. pap. 50.10 (*0-7583-3748-5*); 879p. pap. 67.92 (*0-7583-3749-3*); 1082p. pap. 77.81 (*0-7583-3750-7*); 436p. lib. bdg. 38.96 (*0-7583-3738-8*); 559p. lib. bdg. 46.75 (*0-7583-3739-6*); 715p. lib. bdg. 56.10 (*0-7583-3740-X*); 879p. lib. bdg. 79.92 (*0-7583-3741-8*); 1082p. lib. bdg. 89.81 (*0-7583-3742-6*); 1255p. lib. bdg. 99.29 (*0-7583-3743-4*); 245p. lib. bdg. 28.86 (*0-7583-3736-1*); 319p. lib. bdg. 32.47 (*0-7583-3737-X*) Huge Print Pr.

—Hans Brinker or the Silver Skates, Set. 1996. (J). (gr. 4). pap. 77.75 incl. audio (*0-7887-1551-8*, 40114) Recorded Bks., LLC.

Evenhuis, Gertie. What About Me? 1976. (Illus.). (J). 6.95 o.p. (*0-525-66524-2*, Dutton Children's Bks.) Penguin Putnam Bks. for Young Readers.

Fennema, Ilona & Apol, Georgette. Dirk's Wooden Shoes. 1970. (Illus.). (J). (gr. k-3). 4.95 o.p. (*0-15-223567-1*) Harcourt Children's Bks.

Flakkeberg, Ardo. Sea Broke Through. 1962. (Illus.). (J). (gr. 5-7). lib. bdg. 5.69 o.p. (*0-394-91591-7*, Knopf Bks. for Young Readers) Random Hse. Children's Bks.

Fleming, Candace. Boxes for Katje, RS. 2003. (Illus.). 40p. (gr. k-3). 16.00 (*0-374-30922-1*, Farrar, Straus & Giroux (BYR)) Farrar, Straus & Giroux.

Forman, James. The Survivor, RS. 1976. 288p. (J). (gr. 7 up). 11.95 o.p. (*0-374-37312-4*, Farrar, Straus & Giroux (BYR)) Farrar, Straus & Giroux.

Gilson, Jamie. Stink Alley. 2002. 192p. (J). (gr. 3 up). 15.95 (*0-688-17864-2*); lib. bdg. 15.89 (*0-06-029217-2*) HarperCollins Children's Bk. Group.

Green, Norma. The Hole in the Dike. 1975. (Illus.). 32p. (J). (gr. k-3). lib. bdg. 15.89 o.p. (*0-690-00676-4*) HarperCollins Children's Bk. Group.

—The Hole in the Dyke. 1975. (Illus.). 32p. (J). (gr. k-3). 14.95 o.p. (*0-690-00734-5*) HarperCollins Children's Bk. Group.

Henty, G. A. By England's Aid: The Freeing of the Netherlands, 1585-1604. 2000. 252p. (J). E-Book 3.95 (*0-594-02371-8*) 1873 Pr.

—By Pike & Dyke: A Tale of the Rise of the Dutch Republic. (J). E-Book 3.95 (*0-594-02373-4*) 1873 Pr.

Howells, Mildred. The Woman Who Lived in Holland, RS. 1973. (Illus.). (J). (ps-3). 3.95 o.p. (*0-374-38460-6*, Farrar, Straus & Giroux (BYR)) Farrar, Straus & Giroux.

Jones, Douglas. Dutch Color. (J). 2000. (Illus.). pap. 9.00 (*1-885767-65-X*); 1999. 144p. (gr. 3-6). pap. 8.50 (*1-885767-52-8*) Canon Pr.

Krasilovsky, Phyllis. The Cow Who Fell in the Canal. 1985. (Illus.). 38p. (J). (gr. k-1). 11.95 o.s.i (*0-385-07585-5*) Doubleday Publishing.

—Cow Who Fell in the Canal. 1985. (Illus.). 38p. (J). (gr. k-1). lib. bdg. o.p. (*0-385-07740-8*) Doubleday Publishing.

Lambregtse, Cornelius. He Gathers the Lambs. 1996. (J). 12.90 (*0-921100-77-9*) Inheritance Pubns.

Monjo, F. N. The Sea Beggar's Son. 1975. (Illus.). 36p. (J). (gr. 3-5). 5.95 o.p. (*0-698-20277-5*) Putnam Publishing Group, The.

Noble, Trinka Hakes. Hansy's Mermaid. 1983. (Illus.). (J). (ps-2). 32p. 10.95 o.p. (*0-8037-3605-3*, 01063-320); 10.89 o.p. (*0-8037-3606-1*) Penguin Putnam Bks. for Young Readers. (Dial Bks. for Young Readers).

Norton, Andre. At Swords' Points. 1954. (J). (gr. 7 up). 5.75 o.p. (*0-15-283893-7*) Harcourt Children's Bks.

Noyes, Deborah. Hana in the Time of the Tulips. 2004. (J). (*0-7636-1875-6*) Candlewick Pr.

Pelgrom, Els. The Winter When Time Was Frozen. Rudnik, Maryka & Rudnik, Raphael, trs. from DUT. 1980. Tr. of De Kinderen Van Het Achtste Woud. 256p. (J). (gr. 4-6). 13.00 o.p. (*0-688-22247-1*); lib. bdg. 12.88 o.p. (*0-688-32247-6*) Morrow/Avon. (Morrow, William & Co.).

Perkins, Lucy F. Dutch Twins. 1968. (Walker's Twins Ser.). (Illus.). (J). (gr. 2-5). lib. bdg. 4.85 o.s.i (*0-8027-6019-8*) Walker & Co.

Prins, Piet. Dispelling the Tyranny, No. 2. Rustenberg-Bootsma, Paulina M., tr. from DUT. 1994. (Struggle for Freedom Ser.: No. 2). (Illus.). 152p. (Orig.). (J). pap. 8.90 (*0-921100-40-X*) Inheritance Pubns.

—Scout: The Secret of the Swamp. 1997. (DUT & ENG.). 176p. (J). pap. 8.90 (*0-921100-50-7*) Inheritance Pubns.

—When the Morning Came. Deboer, Gertrude, tr. from DUT. 1989. (Struggle for Freedom Ser.: No. 1). (Illus.). 158p. (Orig.). (J). pap. 8.90 (*0-921100-12-4*) Inheritance Pubns.

Propp, Vera W. When the Soldiers Were Gone. 1999. 112p. (YA). (gr. 5-9). 14.99 (*0-399-23325-3*) Penguin Group (USA) Inc.

Rang, William R. Salt in His Blood: The Life of Michael de Ruyter. 1996. (J). 9.90 (*0-921100-59-0*) Inheritance Pubns.

Reesink, Maryke & Apol, Georgette. Two Windmills. 1967. (Illus.). (J). (gr. k-3). 5.25 o.p. (*0-15-292350-0*) Harcourt Children's Bks.

Richardson, V. A. The House of Windjammer. 2003. (Illus.). 300p. (J). 17.95 (*1-58234-811-1*, Bloomsbury Children) Bloomsbury Publishing.

Rustenburg-Bootsma, Paulina M. A Mighty Fortress in the Storm. 1992. (Illus.). 174p. (YA). 10.90 (*0-921100-37-X*) Inheritance Pubns.

Shemin, Margaretha. The Little Riders. 1993. (Illus.). 80p. (J). (gr. 4 up). reprint ed. pap. 4.95 (*0-688-12499-2*) HarperCollins Children's Bk. Group.

Shoup, Barbara. Vermeer's Daughter. 2003. 164p. (YA). 16.95 (*1-57860-131-2*, Guild Pr.) Emmis Bks.

Terlouw, Jan. Winter in Wartime. 1976. 144p. (J). (gr. 7-12). lib. bdg. 7.95 o.p. (*0-07-063504-8*) McGraw-Hill Cos., The.

Toast, Sarah, et al. The Little Dutch Boy: A Tale of Perseverance. 1997. (Illus.). (*0-7853-2137-3*) Publications International, Ltd.

Van Steenwyk, Elizabeth. A Traitor among Us. 1999. 143p. (J). (gr. 4-7). pap. 6.00 (*0-8028-5157-6*, Eerdmans Bks For Young Readers) Eerdmans, William B. Publishing Co.

—A Traitor among Us. 1999. 12.05 (*0-606-17601-2*) Turtleback Bks.

Van Stockum, Hilda. A Day on Skates: The Story of a Dutch Picnic. (Illus.). 40p. (J). (gr. 1 up). reprint ed. 1996. pap. 14.95 o.p. (*1-883937-02-7*, 02-7); 1994. 19.95 o.p. (*1-883937-00-0*, 00-0) Bethlehem Bks.

—The Winged Watchman. 1995. (Living History Library). (Illus.). 204p. (J). (gr. 4-7). reprint ed. pap. 12.95 (*1-883937-07-8*, 07-8) Bethlehem Bks.

—Winged Watchman, RS. (Illus.). 228p. (J). (gr. 4 up). 1985. pap. 3.45 o.p. (*0-374-48405-8*, Sunburst); 1963. 6.95 o.p. (*0-374-38448-7*, Farrar, Straus & Giroux (BYR)) Farrar, Straus & Giroux.

Vernon, Louise A. Peter & the Pilgrims. 2nd ed. 2002. (Illus.). 119p. (J). (gr. 4-9). pap. 7.99 (*0-8361-9226-5*) Herald Pr.

Vos, Ida. Anna Is Still Here. Edelstein, Terese & Smidt, Inez, trs. from DUT. 1993. 144p. (J). (gr. 4-6). tchr. ed. 15.00 o.s.i (*0-395-65368-1*) Houghton Mifflin Co.

—Anna Is Still Here. Edelstein, Terese & Smidt, Inez, trs. 1995. 144p. (J). (gr. 4-7). pap. 5.99 (*0-14-036909-0*, Puffin Bks.) Penguin Putnam Bks. for Young Readers.

—Anna is Still Here. 1995. 11.04 (*0-606-07199-7*) Turtleback Bks.

—Dancing on the Bridge of Avignon. Edelstein, Terese & Smidt, Inez, trs. from DUT. 1995. Tr. of Dansen ob de Brug van Avignon. 192p. (YA). (gr. 7-7). 14.95 (*0-395-72039-7*) Houghton Mifflin Co.

—Hide & Seek. Edelstein, Terese & Smidt, Inez, trs. 1991. Orig. Title: Wie Niet Weg Is Word Gezien. 144p. (J). (gr. 4-6). tchr. ed. 16.00 (*0-395-56470-0*) Houghton Mifflin Co.

Weston, Carol. Melanie Martin Goes Dutch: The Private Diary of My Almost Bummer Summer with Cecily, Matt the Brat, & Vincent van Go Go Go. 2002. (Illus.). 240p. (J). (gr. 3-7). 15.95 (*0-375-82195-3*); lib. bdg. 17.99 (*0-375-92195-8*) Knopf, Alfred A. Inc.

—Melanie Martin Goes Dutch: The Private Diary of My Almost Bummer Summer with Cecily, Matt the Brat, & Vincent van Go Go Go. 2003. (Illus.). 240p. (J). (gr. 3-7). pap. 4.99 (*0-440-41899-2*, Yearling) Random Hse. Children's Bks.

Woelfle, Gretchen. Katje, the Windmill Cat. 2001. (Illus.). 32p. (J). (gr. k-4). 15.99 (*0-7636-1347-9*) Candlewick Pr.

Yolan, Jane. The Sea Man. 1998. (Illus.). 48p. (J). (gr. 4-7). 14.99 o.s.i (*0-399-22939-6*, Philomel) Penguin Putnam Bks. for Young Readers.

NEVADA—FICTION

Bly, Stephen A. The Adventures of Nathan T. Riggins, 31 vols., Vol. 1. 2001. 384p. (J). (gr. 4-9). reprint ed. pap. 10.99 (*1-58134-235-7*) Crossway Bks.

—The Adventures of Nathan T. Riggins Bks. 4-6, 31 vols., Vol. 2. 2001. 384p. (J). (gr. 4-9). reprint ed. pap. 10.99 (*1-58134-234-9*) Crossway Bks.

—Coyote True, No. 2. 1992. (Nathan T. Riggins Western Adventure Ser.: Bk. 2). 128p. (J). (gr. 4-7). pap. 4.99 o.p. (*0-89107-680-8*) Crossway Bks.

—You Can Always Trust a Spotted Horse, No. 3. 1993. (Nathan T. Riggins Western Adventure Ser.: Vol. 3). 128p. (J). (gr. 4-7). pap. 4.99 o.p. (*0-89107-716-2*) Crossway Bks.

Cox, Judy. Weird Stories from the Lonesome Cafe. 2000. (Illus.). 80p. (J). (gr. 2-4). 15.00 (*0-15-202134-5*) Harcourt Children's Bks.

Kelso, Mary J. Sierra Summer. 1992. (Lynne Garrett Adventure Ser.: No. 3). (Illus.). 120p. (Orig.). (YA). (gr. 6 up). pap. 4.95 (*0-9621406-3-5*) MarKel Pr.

Lasky, Kathryn. Alice Rose & Sam. 1999. 208p. (J). (gr. 3-7). pap. 5.99 (*0-7868-1222-2*) Disney Pr.

—Alice Rose & Sam. 1998. (Illus.). 208p. (J). (gr. 3-7). 15.95 (*0-7868-0336-3*); lib. bdg. 16.49 (*0-7868-2277-5*) Hyperion Bks. for Children.

—Alice Rose & Sam. 1999. 12.04 (*0-606-17380-3*) Turtleback Bks.

Peel, John. Lost in Vegas! 1998. (Secret World of Alex Mack Ser.: No. 23). 144p. (J). (gr. 4-7). pap. 3.99 (*0-671-00710-6*, Aladdin) Simon & Schuster Children's Publishing.

Rue, Nancy. Don't Count on Homecoming Queen. 1998. (Raise the Flag Ser.: Bk. 1). 224p. (YA). (gr. 7-12). pap. 2.95 o.s.i (*1-57856-032-2*) WaterBrook Pr.

Sargent, Dave & Sargent, Pat. Gus (Slate Grullo) Be Thankful. 2003. (Saddle Up Ser.: Vol.32). (Illus.). 42p. (J). mass mkt. 6.95 (*1-56763-694-2*); lib. bdg. 22.60 (*1-56763-693-4*) Ozark Publishing.

Smith, Roland. Zach's Lie. (J). 2003. 224p. pap. 5.99 (*0-7868-1440-3*); 2001. 211p. (gr. 5-9). 15.99 (*0-7868-0617-6*) Hyperion Bks. for Children.

Snyder, Zilpha Keatley. The Runaways. 1999. 256p. (gr. 3-7). text 15.95 o.s.i (*0-385-32599-1*, Delacorte Pr.) Dell Publishing.

NEVER-NEVER LAND (IMAGINARY PLACE)—FICTION

Barrie, J. M. Peter Pan. 1994. (Illus.). 96p. (J). 14.95 o.p. (*1-56282-638-7*); lib. bdg. 15.49 o.p. (*1-56282-639-5*) Disney Pr.

—Peter Pan. 1998. (Illus.). 144p. (J). 19.95 (*1-85149-702-1*) Antique Collectors' Club.

—Peter Pan. 1985. (Bantam Classics Ser.). 176p. (gr. 4-7). mass mkt. 4.95 (*0-553-21178-1*, Bantam Classics) Bantam Bks.

—Peter Pan. 1994. (Classics for Young Readers Ser.). (J). 64p. 5.98 o.p. (*0-86112-822-2*); 112p. 9.98 o.p. (*0-86112-648-3*) Brimax Bks., Ltd.

—Peter Pan. 1984. (Great 3-D Fairy Tale Bks.). (Illus.). (J). 2.99 o.s.i (*0-517-45984-1*) Crown Publishing Group.

—Peter Pan. (ACE.). (YA). E-Book 2.49 (*1-58627-197-0*) Electric Umbrella Publishing.

—Peter Pan. 1995. (Illus.). (J). mass mkt. 8.95 (*0-340-62664-X*) Hodder & Stoughton, Ltd. GBR. *Dist:* Lubrecht & Cramer, Ltd., Trafalgar Square.

—Peter Pan. 1987. (J). audio 28.00 Jimcin Recordings.

—Peter Pan. 1991. (Illustrated Classics Ser.). (Illus.). 128p. (J). pap. 2.95 o.p. (*1-56156-029-4*) Kidsbooks, Inc.

—Peter Pan. 1992. (Everyman's Library Children's Classics Ser.). (Illus.). 240p. (ps-3). 12.95 (*0-679-41792-3*, Everyman's Library) Knopf Publishing Group.

—Peter Pan. 1987. 208p. (J). mass mkt. 4.95 (*0-451-52088-2*, Signet Classics) NAL.

—Peter Pan. (Classic Ser.). (J). 1997. 56p. (gr. 3-6). 2.99 o.s.i (*0-7214-5681-2*); 1994. (Illus.). 52p. text 3.50 o.p. (*0-7214-1659-4*) Penguin Group (USA) Inc. (Ladybird Bks.).

—Peter Pan. 1996. (Illus.). 256p. (YA). (gr. 5-9). pap. 3.99 (*0-14-036674-1*, Puffin Bks.); 1993. (Illus.). 208p. (J). (gr. 5 up). pap. 3.99 o.p. (*0-14-032007-5*, Puffin Bks.); 1991. (Illus.). 192p. (J). (gr. 4-7). 24.99 (*0-670-84180-3*, Viking Children's Bks.); 1987. (Illus.). (J). (gr. 5 up). 12.95 o.p. (*0-670-80862-8*, Viking Children's Bks.); 1987. (Illus.). 224p. (J). (gr. 4 up). 13.95 o.s.i (*0-448-06033-7*, Grosset & Dunlap); 1987. (J). 10.95 o.p. (*0-448-19209-8*, Platt & Munk); 1986. 224p. (J). pap. 3.50 o.p. (*0-14-035066-7*, Puffin Bks.) Penguin Putnam Bks. for Young Readers.

—Peter Pan. Hanft, Joshua, ed. 1995. (Great Illustrated Classics Ser.: Vol. 46). (Illus.). 240p. (J). (gr. 3-6). 9.95 (*0-86611-997-3*) Playmore, Inc., Pubs.

—Peter Pan. 1970. (Silver Dollar Library Ser.). (Illus.). (J). (gr. 2-6). 1.95 o.p. (*0-448-02137-4*) Putnam Publishing Group, The.

—Peter Pan. (Book & Cassette Classics Ser.). (Illus.). (J). (ps-5). 1987. 72p. 15.95 o.s.i (*0-394-89226-7*); 1985. 1.00 o.s.i (*0-517-48144-8*); 1983. 72p. 8.99 o.s.i (*0-394-95717-2*); 1983. 72p. 8.95 o.s.i (*0-394-85717-8*) Random Hse. Children's Bks. (Random Hse. Bks. for Young Readers).

—Peter Pan. 1996. (Children's Library Ser.). (J). 1.10 o.s.i (*0-517-14151-5*) Random Hse. Value Publishing.

—Peter Pan. 1988. (Folio - Junior Ser.: No. 411). (FRE., Illus.). 239p. (J). (gr. 5-10). pap. 9.95 (*2-07-033411-2*) Schoenhof's Foreign Bks., Inc.

—Peter Pan. (J). 1993. 208p. (gr. 4-7). mass mkt. 3.25 (*0-590-46735-2*, Scholastic Paperbacks); 1978. pap. 1.95 (*0-590-30054-7*) Scholastic, Inc.

—Peter Pan. 1988. 2.98 (*0-671-10162-5*, Fireside) Simon & Schuster.

—Peter Pan. (J). (gr. k up). 1980. (Illus.). 192p. lib. bdg. 19.95 o.s.i (*0-684-16611-9*); 1972. 12.95 o.s.i (*0-684-13214-1*) Simon & Schuster Children's Publishing. (Atheneum).

—Peter Pan. 1999. (J). E-Book 3.25 (*1-58505-994-3*) Treeless Pr.

—Peter Pan. (J). 1990. 16.10 (*0-606-00686-9*); 1985. 11.00 (*0-606-02465-4*) Turtleback Bks.

—Peter Pan. (J). (ps-5). 1988. 5.95 o.p. (*0-88101-080-4*); 1987. 16.95 o.p. (*0-88101-069-3*); 1987. (Illus.). 160p. 14.95 o.p. (*0-88101-270-X*) Unicorn Publishing Hse., Inc., The.

—Peter Pan. 1970. (J). pap. 1.50 o.p. (*0-14-030298-0*) Viking Penguin.

—Peter Pan. 1998. (Children's Classics). 176p. (J). (gr. 4-7). pap. 3.95 (*1-85326-120-3*, 1203WW) Wordsworth Editions, Ltd. GBR. *Dist:* Advanced Global Distribution Services.

—Peter Pan. (Step-up Classic Chillers Ser.). (Illus.). 96p. (J). 2003. (gr. 1-4). 11.99 (*0-679-91044-1*); 1991. (gr. 2-7). pap. 3.99 (*0-679-81044-7*) Random Hse. Children's Bks. (Random Hse. Bks. for Young Readers).

—Peter Pan. abr. ed. 1982. (J). audio 15.95 o.p. (*0-88646-067-0*, TC-LFP 7086) Durkin Hayes Publishing Ltd.

—Peter Pan. abr. ed. 1999. (Story Theatre for Young Readers Ser.). (J). (gr. 4-7). audio 16.95 (*1-56994-518-7*, 337354, Monterey SoundWorks) Monterey Media, Inc.

—Peter Pan. abr. ed. 1996. (Illus.). (J). audio 13.98 (*962-634-602-7*, NA210214); (gr. 4-7). audio compact disk 15.98 (*962-634-102-5*, NA210212) Naxos of America, Inc. (Naxos AudioBooks).

—Peter Pan. abr. ed. 1993. (J). (ps-6). audio 10.95 o.p. (*1-55800-121-2*, 30080, Dove Audio) NewStar Media, Inc.

—Peter Pan. abr. ed. (J). 1999. (gr. 4-7). audio 18.00 o.s.i (*0-553-47771-4*, 396218, Listening Library); 1993. audio 11.00 o.s.i (*0-679-42949-2*, RH Audio) Random Hse. Audio Publishing Group.

—Peter Pan. abr. ed. (Illus.). (J). (gr. 1-4). 1965. 4.79 o.s.i (*0-394-90749-3*); 1957. 3.95 o.s.i (*0-394-80749-9*) Random Hse. Children's Bks. (Random Hse. Bks. for Young Readers).

—Peter Pan, 2 cass. abr. ed. 1979. (J). pap. 11.95 o.p. incl. audio (*0-88142-328-9*) Soundelux Audio Publishing.

—Peter Pan. abr. ed. (Children's Classics Ser.). (J). 1998. pap. 16.95 o.p. incl. audio (*1-85998-588-2*); 1997. audio 14.95 (*1-85998-338-3*) Trafalgar Square.

—Peter Pan. abr. ed. 1997. (Classic Ser.). (J). 10.95 o.s.i incl. audio (*0-14-086460-1*, Penguin Audio-Books) Viking Penguin.

—Peter Pan. l.t. ed. 1999. (Classics for Children 8 & Younger Ser.). (Illus.). 48p. (J). (ps-3). (*1-85854-603-6*) Brimax Bks., Ltd.

—Peter Pan, Set. unabr. ed. 1987. (J). (gr. 3-5). audio 29.95 (*1-55685-075-1*) Audio Bk. Contractors, Inc.

—Peter Pan. unabr. ed. (J). audio 26.95 o.p. (*1-55656-093-1*, DAB 002) BBC Audiobooks America.

—Peter Pan. unabr. ed. 1987. (J). audio 32.95 (*0-7861-0607-7*, 2585) Blackstone Audio Bks., Inc.

—Peter Pan. unabr. ed. 1992. (J). audio 26.95 (*1-55686-439-6*, 439) Books in Motion.

—Peter Pan. unabr. collector's ed. 1993. (J). audio 30.00 (*0-7366-2537-2*, 3289) Books on Tape, Inc.

—Peter Pan. unabr. ed. (J). audio 21.95 o.s.i (*1-55656-042-7*); 1997. pap. 21.95 incl. audio (*1-55656-201-2*) Dercum Audio.

—Peter Pan, ERS. 1987. (Illus.). 144p. (YA). (gr. 2 up). 19.95 o.s.i (*0-8050-0276-6*, Holt, Henry & Co. Bks. For Young Readers) Holt, Henry & Co.

—Peter Pan, Set. 1992. 35.95 incl. audio Olivia & Hill Pr., The.

—Peter Pan. 1988. (Children's Classics Ser.). (Illus.). 304p. (J). (gr. k-5). reprint ed. 12.99 o.s.i (*0-517-63222-5*) Random Hse. Value Publishing.

—Peter Pan, unabr. ed. 1991. (J). (gr. 4). audio 44.00 (*1-55690-409-6*, 91105E7) Recorded Bks., LLC.

—Peter Pan: A Changing Picture & Lift-the-Flap Book. abr. ed. 1992. (Illus.). 320p. (J). (ps-3). 15.95 o.p. (*0-670-83608-7*, Viking Children's Bks.) Penguin Putnam Bks. for Young Readers.

—Peter Pan: Fairy Tales. Tallarico, Tony, ed. 1987. (Tuffy Story Bks.). (Illus.). 32p. (J). (ps-3). 1.95 (*0-89828-339-6*, 83396, Tuffy Bks.) Putnam Publishing Group, The.

—Peter Pan: The Complete Book. 1988. (Illus.). 180p. (J). (gr. 4 up). reprint ed. pap. 4.95 o.p. (*0-88776-206-9*) Tundra Bks. of Northern New York.

—Peter Pan: The Complete Play. 1988. 136p. (J). (gr. 4 up). pap. 4.95 o.p. (*0-88776-207-7*) Tundra Bks. of Northern New York.

—Peter Pan & Other Plays: The Admirable Crichton; Peter Pan; When Wendy Grew Up; What Every Woman Knows; Mary Rose. Hollindale, Peter, ed. & intro. by. 1999. (Oxford World's Classics Ser.). 384p. (J). pap. 14.95 (*0-19-283919-5*) Oxford Univ. Pr., Inc.

—Peter Pan & Other Plays: The Admirable Crichton; Peter Pan; When Wendy Grew Up; What Every Woman Knows; Mary Rose, Vol. 10. reprint ed. 57.50 (*0-404-08790-6*) AMS Pr., Inc.

—Peter Pan & Other Plays: The Admirable Crichton; Peter Pan; When Wendy Grew Up; What Every Woman Knows; Mary Rose. Hollindale, Peter, ed. 1995. (Oxford World's Classics Ser.). 374p. pap. 13.95 o.p. (*0-19-282572-0*); 376p. text 80.00 (*0-19-812162-8*) Oxford Univ. Pr., Inc.

—Peter Pan & Wendy. 1999. (Abbeville Classics Ser.). (Illus.). 176p. (J). 12.95 (*0-7892-0560-2*); pap. 7.95 (*0-7892-0550-5*) Abbeville Pr., Inc. (Abbeville Kids).

—Peter Pan & Wendy. 1988. (Illus.). 160p. (J). (gr. 4-6). 12.95 o.s.i (*0-517-56837-3*, Clarkson Potter) Crown Publishing Group.

—Peter Pan & Wendy. Carruth, Jane, ed. 2000. (Illus.). 92p. (J). (gr. 4-6). reprint ed. 25.00 (*0-7881-9230-2*) DIANE Publishing Co.

—Peter Pan & Wendy. (Illus.). 2000. 176p. pap. 8.95 (*1-85793-909-3*); 1992. 160p. (J). (gr. 3-6). 24.95 o.p. (*1-85145-179-X*); 1992. 160p. (J). (gr. 3-6). pap. 17.95 (*1-85145-449-7*) Pavilion Bks., Ltd. GBR. *Dist:* Trafalgar Square.

—Peter Pan & Wendy. 1988. (J). 7.99 o.s.i (*0-517-66189-6*) Random Hse. Value Publishing.

—Peter Pan Book: Includes Tinker Bell Charm & Necklace. 2000. (Charming Classic Bks.). 240p. (J). (gr. 4-7). pap. 6.99 (*0-694-01318-8*, Harper Festival) HarperCollins Children's Bk. Group.

—Peter Pan in Kensington Gardens. (J). 18.95 (*0-8488-0427-9*) Amereon, Ltd.

—Peter Pan in Kensington Gardens. unabr. ed. 1994. (J). (gr. 1 up). audio 19.95 (*1-55685-337-8*) Audio Bk. Contractors, Inc.

—Peter Pan in Kensington Gardens. (J). reprint ed. 1981. 175p. lib. bdg. 16.95 (*0-89966-328-1*); 1980. 150p. lib. bdg. 16.95 (*0-89967-006-7*, Harmony Raine & Co.) Buccaneer Bks., Inc.

—Peter Pan in Kensington Gardens. (YA). E-Book 2.49 (*1-58627-198-9*) Electric Umbrella Publishing.

—Peter Pan in Kensington Gardens. 1995. 64p. (J). pap. 0.95 o.p. (*0-14-600077-3*) Penguin Group (USA) Inc.

—Peter Pan in Kensington Gardens & Peter & Wendy. Hollingdale, Peter, ed. 1999. (Oxford World's Classics Ser.). (Illus.). 288p. (J). pap. 8.95 (*0-19-283929-2*) Oxford Univ. Pr., Inc.

—Peter Pan in Kensington Gardens & Peter & Wendy. 1991. (Oxford World's Classics Ser.). (Illus.). 276p. (J). pap. 7.95 o.p. (*0-19-282593-3*) Oxford Univ. Pr., Inc.

—Peter Pan in Neverland. 1995. (Illus.). 58p. pap. 4.50 (*0-88680-414-0*) Clark, I. E. Pubns.

—Peter Pan: or The Boy Who Would Not Grow Up. adapted ed. 1994. per. 6.50 (*0-8222-1345-1*) Dramatists Play Service, Inc.

—Peter Pan: or The Boy Who Would Not Grow Up. 1982. 208p. (J). (gr. k up). pap. 2.95 o.p. (*0-380-57752-6*, Avon Bks.) Morrow/Avon.

Johnstone, Michael & Barrie, J. M. Peter Pan. 2001. (Young Classics Ser.). (Illus.). 48p. (J). (gr. 1-3). pap. 9.95 o.p. (*0-7894-3796-1*) Dorling Kindersley Publishing, Inc.

Johnstone, Michael, et al. Peter Pan. 2001. (Read & Listen Ser.). (Illus.). 64p. (J). (gr. 4-7). pap. 9.99 incl. audio (*0-7894-6199-4*, D K Ink) Dorling Kindersley Publishing, Inc.

Martin, Mary. Peter Pan. (J). (ps up). audio 9.98 Music for Little People, Inc.

Strasser, Todd & Barrie, J. M. Peter Pan: Junior Novelization. 1994. (Illus.). 80p. (J). (gr. 2-6). pap. 3.50 o.p. (*1-56282-640-9*) Disney Pr.

NEW ENGLAND—FICTION

Alcott, Louisa May. Eight Cousins. 1971. (Louisa May Alcott Library). (J). (gr. 5-9). reprint ed. 5.95 o.p. (*0-448-02359-8*) Putnam Publishing Group, The.

—Jack & Jill. (J). E-Book 3.95 (*0-594-06550-X*) 1873 Pr.

—Jack & Jill. Date not set. 352p. (YA). 25.95 (*0-8488-2671-X*) Amereon, Ltd.

—Jack & Jill. 1880. (YA). reprint ed. pap. text 28.00 (*1-4047-1638-6*) Classic Textbooks.

—Jack & Jill. 2002. 248p. (gr. 4-7). 24.99 (*1-4043-1058-4*); per. 20.99 (*1-4043-1059-2*) IndyPublish.com.

—Jack & Jill. 1999. (Illus.). 304p. (J). (gr. 5-9). pap. 9.95 (*0-316-03084-8*); 1997. (YA). (*0-316-03778-8*); 1979. (YA). (gr. 5 up). 17.95 o.s.i (*0-316-03092-9*) Little Brown & Co.

—Jack & Jill. 1991. (Illus.). 352p. (YA). (gr. 5 up). pap. 3.50 o.s.i (*0-14-035128-0*, Puffin Bks.) Penguin Putnam Bks. for Young Readers.

—Jack & Jill. 1971. (Louisa May Alcott Library). (YA). (gr. 5-9). reprint ed. 5.95 o.p. (*0-448-02361-X*) Putnam Publishing Group, The.

—Jack & Jill. 1989. (Works of Louisa May Alcott). (YA). reprint ed. lib. bdg. 79.00 (*0-7812-1638-9*) Reprint Services Corp.

—Jo's Boys. 1988. (J). 23.95 (*0-8488-0411-2*) Amereon, Ltd.

—Jo's Boys. 1995. 336p. mass mkt. 4.95 (*0-553-21449-7*) Bantam Bks.

—Jo's Boys. 1886. 366p. (YA). reprint ed. pap. text 28.00 (*1-4047-1642-4*) Classic Textbooks.

—Jo's Boys. (Juvenile Classics). (J). 2002. 292p. 3.00 (*0-486-42226-7*); 1999. (Illus.). 80p. pap. 1.00 (*0-486-40789-6*) Dover Pubns., Inc.

—Jo's Boys. 1987. 304p. (YA). (gr. 7-12). mass mkt. 2.25 o.p. (*0-451-52089-0*, Signet Classics) NAL.

—Jo's Boys. (gr. 4-7). 1996. (Illus.). 350p. (YA). 4.99 (*0-14-036714-4*); 1984. 352p. (J). pap. 3.99 o.p. (*0-14-035015-2*, Puffin Bks.) Penguin Putnam Bks. for Young Readers.

—Jo's Boys. 1949. (Illustrated Junior Library). (J). (gr. 4-6). 5.95 o.p. (*0-448-05813-8*); 8.95 o.p. (*0-448-06013-2*) Putnam Publishing Group, The.

—Jo's Boys. 1994. 320p. (J). (gr. 4-8). 8.99 o.s.i (*0-517-11830-0*) Random Hse. Value Publishing.

—Jo's Boys. 2001. (YA). pap., stu. ed. 87.20 incl. audio Recorded Bks., LLC.

—Jo's Boys. 1989. (Works of Louisa May Alcott). (J). reprint ed. lib. bdg. 79.00 (*0-7812-1642-7*) Reprint Services Corp.

—Jo's Boys. 1992. 344p. (J). mass mkt. 3.25 o.p. (*0-590-45178-2*, Scholastic Paperbacks) Scholastic, Inc.

—Jo's Boys & How They Turned Out. 2000. 252p. (J). pap. 9.95 (*0-594-05147-9*); E-Book 3.95 (*0-594-05150-9*) 1873 Pr.

—Jo's Boys & How They Turned Out. 1994. 336p. (J). (gr. 4-7). pap. 8.95 (*0-316-03103-8*); 1994. 316p. (J). (gr. 7-10). 16.95 o.p. (*0-316-03110-0*); 1986. (YA). (gr. 7 up). 19.95 o.s.i (*0-316-03093-7*) Little Brown & Co.

—Little Men: Life at Plumfield with Jo's Boys. unabr. ed. 1991. (YA). (gr. 4-7). audio 53.95 (*1-55685-200-2*) Audio Bk. Contractors, Inc.

—Little Men: Life at Plumfield with Jo's Boys. (Early Best Sellers Ser.). reprint ed. lib. bdg. 48.00 (*0-7426-1004-7*); 2001. (Illus.). pap. text 28.00 (*0-7426-6004-4*) Classic Bks.

—Little Men: Life at Plumfield with Jo's Boys. 1871. 292p. (YA). reprint ed. pap. text 28.00 (*1-4047-1629-7*) Classic Textbooks.

—Little Men: Life at Plumfield with Jo's Boys. 2001. (Juvenile Classics). 304p. (J). pap. 3.00 (*0-486-41808-1*) Dover Pubns., Inc.

—Little Men: Life at Plumfield with Jo's Boys. l.t. ed. 1470p. pap. 94.00 (*0-7583-3223-8*); 1267p. pap. 84.00 (*0-7583-3222-X*); 837p. pap. 63.00 (*0-7583-3220-3*); 1030p. pap. 73.00 (*0-7583-3221-1*); 287p. pap. 25.00 (*0-7583-3216-5*); 373p. pap. 29.00 (*0-7583-3217-3*); 511p. pap. 36.00 (*0-7583-3218-1*); 654p. pap. 45.00 (*0-7583-3219-X*); 373p. lib. bdg. 35.00 (*0-7583-3209-2*); 511p. lib. bdg. 42.00 (*0-7583-3210-6*); 287p. lib. bdg. 31.00 (*0-7583-3208-4*); 837p. lib. bdg. 75.00 (*0-7583-3212-2*); 1030p. lib. bdg. 85.00 (*0-7583-3213-0*); 1267p. lib. bdg. 96.00 (*0-7583-3214-9*); 654p. lib. bdg. 51.00 (*0-7583-3211-4*); 1470p. lib. bdg. 106.00 (*0-7583-3215-7*) Huge Print Pr.

—Little Men: Life at Plumfield with Jo's Boys. 2002. 284p. 19.99 (*1-4043-1450-4*); per. 14.99 (*1-4043-1451-2*) IndyPublish.com.

—Little Men: Life at Plumfield with Jo's Boys. 1986. mass mkt. 2.95 o.p. (*0-451-51998-1*, Signet Classics) NAL.

—Little Men: Life at Plumfield with Jo's Boys. 1991. o.s.i (*0-517-06050-7*); 224p. (J). 12.99 o.s.i (*0-517-03088-8*) Random Hse. Value Publishing.

—Little Men: Life at Plumfield with Jo's Boys. 1995. (Illus.). 816p. (J). (gr. 3-5). 12.98 o.p. (*0-8317-1212-0*) Smithmark Pubs., Inc.

—Little Men: Life at Plumfield with Jo's Boys. l.t. ed. 1995. 460p. (J). 23.95 (*0-7838-1468-2*) Thorndike Pr.

—Little Women. 2002. (Great Illustrated Classics). (Illus.). 240p. (J). (gr. 3-8). lib. bdg. 21.35 (*1-57765-693-8*, ABDO & Daughters) ABDO Publishing Co.

—Little Women. 1998. (Keepsake Collection Bks.). (J). 3.99 o.p. (*1-57145-101-3*, Thunder Bay Pr.) Advantage Pubs. Group.

—Little Women. 1966. (Airmont Classics Ser.). (Illus.). (YA). (gr. 6 up). pap. 2.95 o.p. (*0-8049-0106-6*, CL-106) Airmont Publishing Co., Inc.

—Little Women. 1996. (Andre Deutsch Classics). 264p. (J). (gr. 5-8). 11.95 (*0-233-99040-2*) Andre Deutsch GBR. *Dist:* Trafalgar Square, Trans-Atlantic Pubns., Inc.

—Little Women. 1983. 480p. (ps up). mass mkt. 3.95 (*0-553-21275-3*, Bantam Classics) Bantam Bks.

—Little Women. 1998. (Young Reader's Christian Library). (Illus.). 192p. (J). (gr. 3-7). pap. 1.39 o.p. (*1-57748-229-8*) Barbour Publishing, Inc.

—Little Women. (Paperback Classics Ser.). (J). 1995. 294p. pap. 2.95 o.p. (*0-681-10333-7*); 1994. (Illus.). 10.95 o.p. (*0-681-00767-2*); 1986. (Illus.). 388p. (gr. 4 up). 12.95 o.p. (*0-681-40055-2*) Borders Pr.

—Little Women. 1995. (Illus.). 93p. (J). 7.98 o.p. (*1-85854-176-X*) Brimax Bks., Ltd.

—Little Women. 1987. 608p. (gr. k-6). pap. text 4.99 o.s.i (*0-440-44768-2*) Dell Publishing.

—Little Women. Gerver, Jane E., ed. 1999. (Eyewitness Classics Ser.). (Illus.). 64p. (J). (gr. 2 up). pap. 14.95 (*0-7894-4767-3*, D K Ink) Dorling Kindersley Publishing, Inc.

—Little Women. 2000. (Juvenile Classics). (Illus.). 608p. (J). pap. 3.00 (*0-486-41023-4*) Dover Pubns., Inc.

—Little Women. 1999. (Focus on the Family Great Stories Ser.). (Illus.). 576p. (J). pap. 9.99 o.p. (*1-56179-744-8*) Focus on the Family Publishing.

—Little Women. (Illus.). 192p. (J). 9.95 (*1-56156-371-4*) Kidsbooks, Inc.

—Little Women. 1994. (Everyman's Library Children's Classics Ser.). 530p. (gr. 4 up). 14.95 (*0-679-43642-1*, Everyman's Library) Knopf Publishing Group.

—Little Women. 1988. (Knopf Book & Cassette Classics Ser.). (Illus.). 512p. (J). 18.95 o.s.i (*0-394-56279-8*) Knopf, Alfred A. Inc.

—Little Women. 1994. 512p. (J). (gr. 4-7). 19.95 (*0-316-03107-0*); 1994. 512p. (J). (gr. 4-7). pap. 9.99 (*0-316-03105-4*); 1968. (Illus.). 524p. (YA). (gr. 7 up). 19.95 (*0-316-03095-3*) Little Brown & Co.

—Little Women. (J). E-Book 1.95 (*1-58515-196-3*) MesaView, Inc.

Howard, Ginger. William's House. 2001. (Illus.). 32p. (J). (gr. k-3). 22.90 (*0-7613-1674-4*) Millbrook Pr., Inc.

Howell, Troy, illus. Little Men: Life at Plumfield with Jo's Boys. 1991. (Children's Classics Ser.). 202p. (J). (gr. 4 up). 11.95 o.p. (*0-681-41080-9*) Borders Pr.

Jewett, Sarah Orne. A White Heron. 1997. (Candlewick Treasures Ser.). (Illus.). 64p. (J). (gr. 3-9). 11.99 o.s.i (*0-7636-0205-1*) Candlewick Pr.

—A White Heron. 1983. (Short Story Library). (Illus.). 32p. (YA). (gr. 5 up). lib. bdg. 19.93 o.p. (*0-87191-966-4*, 1075-9, Creative Education) Creative Co., The.

Kinkade, Thomas. Girls of Lighthouse Lane. 2004. (Girls of Lighthouse Lane Ser.). (J). No. 1. 176p. 12.99 (*0-06-054341-8*); No. 1. 176p. lib. bdg. 13.89 (*0-06-054342-6*); No. 2. (*0-06-054344-2*); No. 2. lib. bdg. (*0-06-054345-0*) HarperCollins Pubs.

Levin, Betty. Shoddy Cove. 2003. 208p. (J). (gr. 5 up). 15.99 (*0-06-052271-2*); lib. bdg. 16.89 (*0-06-052272-0*) HarperCollins Children's Bk. Group. (Greenwillow Bks.).

Lorimer, Janet. Trouble with Buster: A Day in the Life of a Pilgrim Girl. 1990. (J). mass mkt. 2.50 o.p. (*0-590-42641-9*) Scholastic, Inc.

Merrill, Frank T., illus. Little Men: Life at Plumfield with Jo's Boys. 1995. (Everyman's Library Children's Classics Ser.). (J). 13.95 o.s.i (*0-679-44503-X*, Everyman's Library) Knopf Publishing Group.

Pfeffer, Susan Beth & Alcott, Louisa May. Jo Makes a Friend. 1998. (Portraits of Little Women Ser.). (Illus.). 112p. (gr. 3-7). text 9.95 (*0-385-32581-9*, Dell Books for Young Readers) Random Hse. Children's Bks.

Pfeffer, Susan Beth & Ramsey, Marcy Dunn. Ghostly Tales. Bui, Francoise, ed. 2000. (Portraits of Little Women Ser.). (Illus.). 192p. (gr. 3-7). text 9.95 (*0-385-32741-2*, Delacorte Bks. for Young Readers) Random Hse. Children's Bks.

Rees, Celia. Sorceress. 2003. 352p. (YA). bds. 8.99 (*0-7636-2183-8*); 2002. 336p. (J). (gr. 7-11). 15.99 (*0-7636-1847-0*) Candlewick Pr.

Richardson, Judith Benet. David's Landing. 1984. (Illus.). 150p. (J). (gr. 3-7). 10.95 (*0-9611374-1-X*) Woods Hole Historical Collection.

Ross, Pat. Hannah's Fancy Notions: A Story of Industrial New England. 1992. (Once upon America Ser.). (Illus.). 64p. (J). (gr. 2-6). pap. 4.99 o.s.i (*0-14-032389-9*, Puffin Bks.) Penguin Putnam Bks. for Young Readers.

—Hannah's Fancy Notions: A Story of Industrial New England. 1992. (Once upon America Ser.). (J). (gr. 2-6). 11.14 (*0-606-02662-2*) Turtleback Bks.

San Souci, Robert D. Feathertop: Based on the Tale by Nathaniel Hawthorne. 1995. (J). 12.14 (*0-606-07506-2*) Turtleback Bks.

—The Red Heels. 1996. (Illus.). 32p. (YA). (gr. k up). 15.99 o.s.i (*0-8037-1133-6*); 15.89 o.s.i (*0-8037-1134-4*) Penguin Putnam Bks. for Young Readers. (Dial Bks. for Young Readers).

The Scarlet Letter. 1988. mass mkt. 2.25 (*0-938819-11-9*, Aerie) Doherty, Tom Assocs., LLC.

Scharnhorst, Gary, ed. The Lost Tales of Horatio Alger: Adventure, Romance & Moral Intrigue, the Best of Alger's Early Tales. 1990. 240p. (YA). (gr. 10 up). 6.95 (*0-934745-11-0*) Acadia Publishing Co.

Seidler, Tor. The Dulcimer Boy. 2003. (Illus.). 160p. (J). lib. bdg. 16.89 (*0-06-623610-X*, Geringer, Laura Bk.) HarperCollins Children's Bk. Group.

—The Dulcimer Boy. 2003. (Illus.). 160p. (J). reprint ed. 15.99 (*0-06-623609-6*) HarperCollins Pubs.

—The Dulcimer Boy. 1979. (Illus.). (J). 8.95 o.p. (*0-670-28609-5*) Viking Penguin.

Shaffer, Elizabeth N. Hannah & the Indian King, Vol. 2. Pratt, Fran, ed. 2002. (Historical Novel Ser.). pap. 9.95 (*0-936369-35-3*) Son-Rise Pubns. & Distribution Co.

Shetterly, Susan H. The Tinker of Salt Cove. 1990. (Illus.). 48p. (YA). 13.95 o.p. (*0-88448-080-1*) Tilbury Hse. Pubs.

Smithmark Staff. Black Beauty - Rebecca of Sunnybrook Farm. 1995. (Illus.). 440p. (J). 12.98 o.p. (*0-8317-6695-6*) Smithmark Pubs., Inc.

Speare, Elizabeth George. Witch Blackbird Pond. 1993. (J). mass mkt. o.p. (*0-440-90051-4*) Dell Publishing.

Swicord, Robin. Little Women: The Children's Picture Book. 2004. (Illus.). 96p. (gr. 2 up). 15.95 (*1-55704-216-0*) Newmarket Pr.

Tentas, Jane Grant. Alice & the Bird Lady. 2002. 36p. per. 13.95 (*0-9658983-6-9*) Book Nook Pr.

Thorson, Robert & Thorson, Kristine. Stone Wall Secrets. 1998. (Illus.). 40p. (J). (gr. 3-6). 16.95 (*0-88448-195-6*) Tilbury Hse. Pubs.

Tudor, Tasha. The Great Corgiville Kidnapping. 1997. (Illus.). 48p. (J). (ps-3). 15.95 o.p. (*0-316-85583-9*) Little Brown & Co.

Ward Weller, Frances. The Angel of Mill Street. 1998. (Illus.). 32p. (J). (ps-3). 15.99 o.p. (*0-399-23133-1*, G. P. Putnam's Sons) Penguin Putnam Bks. for Young Readers.

Weller, Frances Ward. Matthew Wheelock's Wall. 1992. (Illus.). 40p. (J). (gr. k-3). 14.95 o.p. (*0-02-792612-5*, Simon & Schuster Children's Publishing) Simon & Schuster Children's Publishing.

Wiggen, Kate D. Rebecca of Sunnybrook Farm. 1991. 272p. (J). mass mkt. 3.95 o.s.i (*0-451-52483-7*, Signet Classics) NAL.

Wiggin, Kate Douglas. Rebecca of Sunnybrook Farm. 1994. (Books of Wonder). (Illus.). 304p. (J). (gr. 4-7). 24.99 (*0-688-13481-5*) HarperCollins Children's Bk. Group.

—Rebecca of Sunnybrook Farm. 1980. (J). (gr. 7-9). 1.75 o.s.i (*0-448-17238-0*) Ace Bks.

—Rebecca of Sunnybrook Farm. 1967. (Airmont Classics Ser.). (YA). (gr. 5 up). mass mkt. 1.50 o.p. (*0-8049-0144-9*, CL-144) Airmont Publishing Co., Inc.

—Rebecca of Sunnybrook Farm. (J). 23.95 (*0-8488-0854-1*) Amereon, Ltd.

—Rebecca of Sunnybrook Farm, unabr. ed. 1991. (J). (gr. 3-5). audio 35.95 (*1-55685-198-7*) Audio Bk. Contractors, Inc.

—Rebecca of Sunnybrook Farm. unabr. ed. 1993. audio 39.95 (*1-55686-473-6*, 473) Books in Motion.

—Rebecca of Sunnybrook Farm. 1981. (J). reprint ed. 239p. (gr. 4-7). lib. bdg. 25.95 (*0-89966-354-0*); 259p. lib. bdg. 21.95 o.s.i (*0-89967-028-8*, Harmony Raine & Co.) Buccaneer Bks., Inc.

—Rebecca of Sunnybrook Farm. 1993. (J). 12.99 o.s.i (*0-517-09275-1*) Crown Publishing Group.

—Rebecca of Sunnybrook Farm. 1993. 288p. (J). (gr. 5-8). pap. 2.99 o.p. (*0-87406-655-7*) Darby Creek Publishing.

—Rebecca of Sunnybrook Farm. 1986. 256p. (gr. k-6). pap. text 3.99 o.s.i (*0-440-47533-3*) Dell Publishing.

—Rebecca of Sunnybrook Farm. 1999. 241p. (gr. 4-7). pap. text 2.99 (*0-8125-6590-8*, Tor Classics) Doherty, Tom Assocs., LLC.

—Rebecca of Sunnybrook Farm. 1976. (Classics of Children's Literature, 1621-1932: Vol. 63). (Illus.). (J). reprint ed. lib. bdg. 38.00 o.p. (*0-8240-2312-9*) Garland Publishing, Inc.

—Rebecca of Sunnybrook Farm. (Charming Classics Ser.). (Illus.). (J). 2001. 336p. (gr. 3-7). pap. 6.99 (*0-694-01528-8*, Harper Festival); 1999. 80p. (gr. 2-5). 2.99 o.p. (*0-694-01290-4*) HarperCollins Children's Bk. Group.

—Rebecca of Sunnybrook Farm. abr. ed. 1984. (J). audio 9.95 (*0-89845-481-6*, CDL5 1637, Caedmon) HarperTrade.

—Rebecca of Sunnybrook Farm, 001. 9999. (J). (gr. 4-7). 5.95 o.p. (*0-395-07074-0*); 2003. 304p. (YA). (gr. 5 up). tchr. ed. 20.00 (*0-618-34694-5*) Houghton Mifflin Co.

—Rebecca of Sunnybrook Farm. l.t. ed. (J). 893p. pap. 70.69 (*0-7583-1990-8*); 263p. pap. 26.11 (*0-7583-1985-1*); 210p. pap. 22.36 (*0-7583-1984-3*); 360p. pap. 32.99 (*0-7583-1986-X*); 461p. pap. 40.13 (*0-7583-1987-8*); 1036p. pap. 88.30 (*0-7583-1991-6*); 590p. pap. 49.27 (*0-7583-1988-6*); 726p. pap. 58.87 (*0-7583-1989-4*); 210p. lib. bdg. 29.44 (*0-7583-1976-2*); 1036p. lib. bdg. 100.37 (*0-7583-1983-5*); 893p. lib. bdg. 90.77 (*0-7583-1982-7*); 726p. lib. bdg. 66.76 (*0-7583-1981-9*); 590p. lib. bdg. 56.82 (*0-7583-1980-0*); 461p. lib. bdg. 47.35 (*0-7583-1979-7*); 360p. lib. bdg. 39.46 (*0-7583-1978-9*); 263p. lib. bdg. 32.88 (*0-7583-1977-0*) Huge Print Pr.

—Rebecca of Sunnybrook Farm. l.t. ed. 1999. (Large Print Heritage Ser.). 340p. (YA). (gr. 7-12). lib. bdg. 33.95 (*1-58118-045-4*, 22514) LRS.

—Rebecca of Sunnybrook Farm. (YA). E-Book 1.95 (*1-57799-885-5*) Logos Research Systems, Inc.

—Rebecca of Sunnybrook Farm. (Puffin Classics Ser.). 288p. (YA). 1995. (Illus.). (gr. 4-7). 4.99 (*0-14-036759-4*); 1986. (gr. 5 up). pap. 2.95 o.p. (*0-14-035046-2*) Penguin Putnam Bks. for Young Readers. (Puffin Bks.).

—Rebecca of Sunnybrook Farm. 1969. (Thrushwood Bks.). (J). (gr. 7-9). 3.95 o.p. (*0-448-02527-2*) Putnam Publishing Group, The.

—Rebecca of Sunnybrook Farm, unabr. ed. 1997. (J). (gr. 5). audio 51.00 (*0-7887-0888-0*, 95026E7) Recorded Bks., LLC.

—Rebecca of Sunnybrook Farm. 1988. 288p. (J). (gr. 4-6). mass mkt. 3.50 o.p. (*0-590-41343-0*) Scholastic, Inc.

—Rebecca of Sunnybrook Farm. 2003. (Aladdin Classics Ser.). (Illus.). 368p. (J). pap. 3.99 (*0-689-86001-3*, Aladdin) Simon & Schuster Children's Publishing.

—Rebecca of Sunnybrook Farm. (J). E-Book 5.00 (*0-7410-0426-7*) SoftBook Pr.

—Rebecca of Sunnybrook Farm. l.t. ed. 2002. (Perennial Bestsellers Ser.). 374p. 28.95 (*0-7862-4625-1*) Thorndike Pr.

—Rebecca of Sunnybrook Farm. 1995. (J). 11.04 (*0-606-12495-0*) Turtleback Bks.

—Rebecca of Sunnybrook Farm. unabr. ed. 1997. 175p. (J). reprint ed. pap. 14.95 o.p. (*1-57002-021-3*) University Publishing Hse., Inc.

—Rebecca of Sunnybrook Farm. 1998. (Children's Classics). 208p. (YA). (ps up). pap. 3.95 (*1-85326-134-3*, 1343WW) Wordsworth Editions, Ltd. GBR. *Dist:* Advanced Global Distribution Services.

Wiggin, Kate Douglas Smith. Rebecca of Sunnybrook Farm. 2002. (Great Illustrated Classics). (Illus.). 240p. (J). (gr. 3-8). lib. bdg. 21.35 (*1-57765-823-X*, ABDO & Daughters) ABDO Publishing Co.

—Rebecca of Sunnybrook Farm. 2003. (Dover Evergreen Classics Ser.). 208p. (J). 2.50 (*0-486-42845-1*) Dover Pubns., Inc.

The Witch of Blackbird Pond. 1988. (J). pap. o.p. (*0-440-80074-9*) Dell Publishing.

NEW GUINEA—FICTION

Dillman, Bradford. That Air Forever Dark: An Adventure. 2001. 192p. pap. 14.95 (*1-56474-371-3*) Fithian Pr.

Tabrah, Ruth. The Old Man & the Astronauts. 1975. (Illus.). (J). (gr. 1-7). 5.95 o.p. (*0-89610-015-4*) Island Heritage Publishing.

NEW HAMPSHIRE—FICTION

Bailey, Carolyn S. Miss Hickory. (Newbery Library Ser.). (Illus.). (J). (ps-3). 1977. 128p. pap. 5.99 (*0-14-030956-X*, Puffin Bks.); 1946. 12p. 16.99 (*0-670-47940-3*, Viking Children's Bks.) Penguin Putnam Bks. for Young Readers.

Banks, Kate. Dillon Dillon, RS. 2002. 160p. (J). (gr. 3-6). 16.00 (*0-374-31786-0*, Farrar, Straus & Giroux (BYR)) Farrar, Straus & Giroux.

Bertrand, Lynne. Granite Baby. 2005. (J). (*0-374-32761-0*, Farrar, Straus & Giroux (BYR)) Farrar, Straus & Giroux.

Bruchac, Joseph. The Heart of a Chief. 1998. 160p. (J). (gr. 4-7). 16.99 o.p. (*0-8037-2276-1*, Dial Bks. for Young Readers) Penguin Putnam Bks. for Young Readers.

—The Heart of a Chief. l.t. ed. 2002. 175p. (J). 21.95 (*0-7862-4453-4*) Thorndike Pr.

Buckey, Sarah Masters. Enemy in the Fort. (American Girl Collection: Bk. 13). (Illus.). 176p. (J). (gr. 4-7). 2001. 9.95 o.p. (*1-58485-307-7*); 2000. pap. 5.95 (*1-58485-306-9*) Pleasant Co. Pubns. (American Girl).

—Enemy in the Fort. 2001. (American Girl Collection). (Illus.). (J). 12.00 (*0-606-21180-2*) Turtleback Bks.

Cameron, Eleanor. To the Green Mountains. 1975. 224p. (J). (gr. 5 up). 9.95 o.p. (*0-525-41355-3*, Dutton) Dutton/Plume.

Corcoran, Barbara. The Sky Is Falling. 1990. 192p. (J). pap. 2.95 (*0-380-70837-X*, Avon Bks.) Morrow/Avon.

—Stay Tuned. 1991. 208p. (J). (gr. 3-7). lib. bdg. 14.95 o.p. (*0-689-31673-9*, Atheneum) Simon & Schuster Children's Publishing.

Crandell, Myra C. Molly & the Regicides. 1968. (Illus.). (J). (gr. 6 up). lib. bdg. 3.79 o.p. (*0-671-65015-7*, Simon & Schuster Children's Publishing) Simon & Schuster Children's Publishing.

Curry, Jane Louise. Moon Window. 1996. 170p. (J). (gr. 4-7). 16.00 (*0-689-80945-X*, McElderry, Margaret K.) Simon & Schuster Children's Publishing.

Duffy, James. The Graveyard Gang. 1993. 192p. (J). (gr. 5-7). text 14.95 o.s.i (*0-684-19449-X*, Atheneum) Simon & Schuster Children's Publishing.

Fleischman, Paul. Rear-View Mirror. 1986. (Charlotte Zolotow Bk.). 128p. (YA). (gr. 7 up). 12.95 o.s.i (*0-06-021866-5*); lib. bdg. 12.89 o.p. (*0-06-021867-3*) HarperCollins Children's Bk. Group.

Hall, Donald. Lucy's Summer. abr. ed. 1995. (Illus.). 40p. (J). (ps-3). 15.00 o.s.i (*0-15-276873-4*) Harcourt Children's Bks.

Harrar, George. The Trouble with Jeremy Change. 2003. (Illus.). 176p. (YA). pap. 6.95 (*1-57131-646-9*); (J). 16.95 (*1-57131-647-7*) Milkweed Editions.

Hawthorne, Nathaniel. The Great Stone Face & Other Tales of the White Mountains, 001. 9999. (Illus.). (J). (gr. 7 up). 6.95 o.p. (*0-395-07787-7*) Houghton Mifflin Co.

Hoppe, Joanne. Pretty Penny Farm. 1987. 224p. (YA). (gr. 7 up). 12.95 o.p. (*0-688-07201-1*, Morrow, William & Co.) Morrow/Avon.

Kingman, Lee. The Refiner's Fire, 001. 1981. (J). (gr. 7 up). 8.95 o.p. (*0-395-31606-5*) Houghton Mifflin Co.

Meader, Stephen W. Red Horse Hill. 1930. (Illus.). (J). (gr. 6 up). 6.95 o.p. (*0-15-266193-X*) Harcourt Children's Bks.

—Who Rides in the Dark? 1966. (Illus.). (J). (gr. 7 up). pap. 0.75 o.p. (*0-15-696315-9*, Voyager Bks./Libros Viajeros) Harcourt Children's Bks.

Yates, Elizabeth. American Haven. 2002. (Illus.). 112p. (J). (*1-57924-896-9*) Jones, Bob Univ. Pr.

—Hue & Cry: Sequel. 1990. 182p. (YA). (gr. 7 up). pap. 6.49 (*0-89084-536-0*, 048561) Jones, Bob Univ. Pr.

NEW JERSEY—FICTION

Avi. Captain Grey. 1977. (Illus.). (J). (gr. 5 up). 5.95 o.p. (*0-394-83484-4*); lib. bdg. 6.99 o.s.i (*0-394-93484-9*) Knopf Publishing Group. (Pantheon).

—Captain Grey. 1993. 160p. (YA). (gr. 5-9). pap. 4.95 (*0-688-12234-5*, Morrow, William & Co.) Morrow/Avon.

—Captain Grey. 1993. (J). 11.00 (*0-606-05780-3*) Turtleback Bks.

—Captain Grey. 1993. (Illus.). 160p. (J). (ps-3). 16.00 o.p. (*0-688-12233-7*, Morrow, William & Co.) Morrow/Avon.

Blume, Judy. Are You There God? It's Me, Margaret. 2002. (J). 13.94 (*0-7587-9131-3*) Book Wholesalers, Inc.

—Are You There God? It's Me, Margaret. l.t. ed. 2002. (LRS Large Print Cornerstone Ser.). (J). lib. bdg. 28.95 (*1-58118-088-8*, 24873) LRS.

—Are You There God? It's Me, Margaret. unabr. ed. 2000. (YA). (gr. 4-7). audio 18.00 (*0-8072-7859-9*, 396013, Listening Library) Random Hse. Audio Publishing Group.

—Quiza No lo Haga. Orig. Title: Then Again, Maybe I Won't. (SPA.). 162p. (J). 8.50 o.p. (*84-204-4626-2*) Santillana USA Publishing Co., Inc.

—Then Again, Maybe I Won't, Set. unabr. ed. 1999. (YA). audio 23.98 Highsmith Inc.

—Then Again, Maybe I Won't. 125p. (J). pap. 3.99 (*0-8072-1445-0*); 2002. 164p. (YA). (gr. 5 up). pap. 28.00 incl. audio (*0-8072-0796-9*, LYA 354 SP); 2002. (YA). (gr. 7 up). audio 18.00 (*0-8072-0699-7*); 1990. (YA). (gr. 7 up). pap. 28.98 incl. audio (*0-8072-7296-5*, YA827SP); 1990. (YA). (gr. 7 up). pap. 29.00 incl. audio (*0-8072-7306-6*, YA827SP) Random Hse. Audio Publishing Group. (Listening Library).

—Then Again, Maybe I Won't. 1971. (J). 11.04 (*0-606-05069-8*) Turtleback Bks.

Bryant, Jennifer. The Trial. 2004. 108p. (J). (gr. 3-7). lib. bdg. 16.99 (*0-375-92752-2*, Knopf Bks. for Young Readers) Random Hse. Children's Bks.

Buckey, Sarah Masters. Gangsters at the Grand Atlantic. 2003. (History Mysteries Ser.: Vol. 20). (Illus.). 163p. (J). 10.95 (*1-58485-720-X*); pap. 6.95 (*1-58485-719-6*) Pleasant Co. Pubns. (American Girl).

Cohen, Barbara. Make a Wish, Molly. 1995. 48p. (gr. 4-7). pap. text 3.99 (*0-440-41058-4*); 1994. (Illus.). 40p. (J). 14.95 o.s.i (*0-385-31079-X*, Delacorte Pr.) Dell Publishing.

—Make a Wish, Molly. 1993. (J). o.s.i (*0-385-44599-7*) Doubleday Publishing.

—Make a Wish, Molly. 1994. (J). pap. 4.50 (*0-440-91018-8*, Dell Books for Young Readers) Random Hse. Children's Bks.

—Make a Wish, Molly. 1995. (J). 10.14 (*0-606-07831-2*) Turtleback Bks.

—Make a Wish Molly. 1995. (Illus.). (J). 10.55 (*0-7857-5404-0*) Econo-Clad Bks.

Cuyler, Margery. The Battlefield Ghost. (Illus.). (J). 2002. 112p. mass mkt. 3.99 (*0-590-10849-2*, Scholastic Paperbacks); 1999. 103p. (gr. 2-4). pap. 15.95 (*0-590-10848-4*) Scholastic, Inc.

Dahlstedt, Marden. The Stopping Place. 1976. (Illus.). 160p. (J). (gr. 5 up). 6.95 o.p. (*0-399-20496-2*) Putnam Publishing Group, The.

Danziger, Paula. Amber Brown is Green with Envy. 2003. (Illus.). 160p. (J). 15.99 (*0-399-23181-1*, G. P. Putnam's Sons) Penguin Putnam Bks. for Young Readers.

Davidson, Neil. The Sweet Revenge of Melissa Chavez: A Novel. 1995. 178p. (YA). (gr. 9 up). lib. bdg. 18.95 o.p. (*0-936389-39-7*) Tudor Pubs., Inc.

Finale, Frank. A Gull's Story: A Tale of Learning about Life, the Shore & the ABCs. Valente, George C., ed. 2002. (Illus.). 36p. (J). 22.00 (*0-9632906-3-0*) Jersey Shore Pubns.

Gauch, Patricia L. This Time, Tempe Wick? 1992. (Illus.). 48p. (J). (ps-3). 15.99 o.p. (*0-399-21880-7*, G. P. Putnam's Sons) Penguin Group (USA) Inc.

Golding, Theresa Martin. The Secret Within. 2003. 240p. (YA). (gr. 5-8). 16.95 (*1-56397-995-0*) Boyds Mills Pr.

Gutman, Dan. The Edison Mystery. 2001. (Qwerty Stevens Ser.). (Illus.). 208p. (J). (gr. 4-8). 16.00 (*0-689-84124-8*, Simon & Schuster Children's Publishing) Simon & Schuster Children's Publishing.

High, Linda Oatman. The Girl on the High Diving Horse: An Adventure in Atlantic City. 2003. (Illus.). 40p. (J). (gr. k-4). 16.99 (*0-399-23649-X*, Philomel) Penguin Putnam Bks. for Young Readers.

Ismail, Suzy. The BFF Sisters: Jennah's New Friends. 2001. 64p. (J). (*1-59008-005-X*) amana-pubns.

Johnston, Norma. Feather in the Wind. 2001. (Illus.). 172p. (J). (gr. 5-9). 14.95 (*0-7614-5063-7*, Cavendish Children's Bks.) Cavendish, Marshall Corp.

Lubar, David. Dunk. 2002. 256p. (YA). (gr. 7-10). tchr. ed. 15.00 (*0-618-19455-X*, Clarion Bks.) Houghton Mifflin Co. Trade & Reference Div.

Mazzeo Zocchi, Judy. Circus or Not - Here We Come. 1998. (Adventures of Paulie & Sasha Ser.). (Illus.). 32p. (J). (gr. k-4). 15.95 (*1-891997-00-9*, THC 01, Treehouse Court) Dingles & Co.

McDonald, Joyce. Shades of Simon Gray. 2001. 256p. (YA). (gr. 7 up). lib. bdg. 17.99 (*0-385-90026-0*, Delacorte Pr.) Dell Publishing.

—Shades of Simon Gray. (YA). (gr. 7). 2003. 272p. mass mkt. 5.50 (*0-440-22804-2*, Dell Books for Young Readers); 2001. 256p. 15.95 (*0-385-32659-9*, Delacorte Bks. for Young Readers) Random Hse. Children's Bks.

Moore, Ruth N. Danger in the Pines. 1983. 160p. (J). (gr. 4-9). pap. 4.95 o.p. (*0-8361-3314-5*); text 7.95 o.p. (*0-8361-3313-7*) Herald Pr.

Myers, Robert J. When the Monarchs Fly. 2001. (Illus.). 64p. (J). 11.95 (*0-945582-76-5*) Down The Shore Publishing.

Myers, Walter Dean. Me, Mop & the Moondance Kid. 1990. (J). pap. o.s.i (*0-440-80215-6*) Bantam Bks.

—Me, Mop & the Moondance Kid. Foresmman, Scoot, ed. 1994. 160p. (J). pap. 3.50 (*0-440-91005-6*) Dell Publishing.

—Me, Mop & the Moondance Kid. 1988. (Illus.). 128p. (J). (gr. 3-7). 13.95 o.s.i (*0-440-50065-6*, Delacorte Pr.); 1990. 160p. (gr. 4-7). reprint ed. pap. text 4.99 (*0-440-40396-0*) Dell Publishing.

—Me, Mop & the Moondance Kid. 1988. 160p. (J). (gr. 4-7). 13.95 o.s.i (*0-385-30147-2*) Doubleday Publishing.

—Me, Mop & the Moondance Kid. (J). 1996. pap. 4.99 (*0-440-91093-5*); 1995. pap. 4.99 (*0-440-91071-4*) Random Hse. Children's Bks. (Dell Books for Young Readers).

—Me, Mop & the Moondance Kid. 1988. (J). 11.04 (*0-606-04745-X*) Turtleback Bks.

Pinkwater, Daniel M. The Hoboken Chicken Emergency. (Illus.). (J). (gr. 3-7). 1984. 4.95 o.s.i (*0-13-392499-8*); 1977. 10.95 o.s.i (*0-13-392514-5*) Prentice Hall PTR.

—The Hoboken Chicken Emergency. 1978. (J). (gr. 4-6). reprint ed. pap. 1.50 o.p. (*0-590-11856-0*) Scholastic, Inc.

—The Hoboken Chicken Emergency. (Illus.). (J). 1999. 96p. (gr. 1-4). 15.00 (*0-689-83060-2*, Atheneum); 1999. 112p. (gr. 1-4). pap. 4.99 (*0-689-82889-6*, Aladdin); 1990. 94p. (gr. k-3). pap. 12.95 o.s.i (*0-671-73980-8*, Simon & Schuster Children's Publishing); 1977. 94p. (gr. k-3). pap. 4.95 (*0-671-66447-6*, Aladdin) Simon & Schuster Children's Publishing.

—The Hoboken Chicken Emergency. 1997. (J). 11.20 (*0-606-03344-0*) Turtleback Bks.

Repp, Gloria. Night Flight: Sequel. 1991. 164p. (YA). (gr. 7 up). pap. 6.49 (*0-89084-563-8*, 052191) Jones, Bob Univ. Pr.

Rinaldi, Ann. A Ride into Morning: The Story of Tempe Wick. Grove, Karen, ed. 1991. (Great Episodes Ser.). 368p. (YA). (gr. 7 up). 15.95 (*0-15-200573-0*, Gulliver Bks.) Harcourt Children's Bks.

Robertson, Keith. Henry Reed, Inc. 1958. (Illus.). 240p. (J). (gr. 4-6). 14.95 o.p. (*0-670-36796-6*, Viking Children's Bks.) Penguin Putnam Bks. for Young Readers.

—Henry Reed, Inc. abr. ed. (J). (gr. 4-7). pap. 15.95 incl. audio (*0-670-36801-6*);Set. 24.95 incl. audio (*0-670-36800-8*) Live Oak Media.

—Henry Reed, Inc. 1989. (Illus.). 240p. (J). (gr. 4-7). pap. 5.99 (*0-14-034144-7*, Puffin Bks.) Penguin Putnam Bks. for Young Readers.

—Henry Reed, Inc. 1973. 224p. (J). (gr. 2-5). pap. 0.95 o.s.i (*0-440-43552-8*, Yearling) Random Hse. Children's Bks.

—Henry Reed, Inc. 1989. (J). 11.04 (*0-606-04244-X*) Turtleback Bks.

—Henry Reed's Baby-Sitting Service. (Illus.). (J). 1989. 208p. (gr. 4-7). pap. 5.99 (*0-14-034146-3*, Puffin Bks.); 1966. (gr. 5-8). 14.95 o.p. (*0-670-36825-3*, Viking Children's Bks.) Penguin Putnam Bks. for Young Readers.

—Henry Reed's Baby-Sitting Service. 1974. 206p. (J). (gr. 2-5). pap. 3.25 o.s.i (*0-440-43565-X*, Yearling) Random Hse. Children's Bks.

—Henry Reed's Baby-Sitting Service. 1989. (J). 11.04 (*0-606-04245-8*) Turtleback Bks.

Ruby, Laura. Lily's Ghost. 2003. 272p. (J). (gr. 5 up). 16.99 (*0-06-051829-4*); lib. bdg. 17.89 (*0-06-051830-8*) HarperCollins Children's Bk. Group.

Waldron, Ann. The Bluebury Collection. 1981. (J). (gr. 4-7). 9.25 o.p. (*0-525-26739-5*, 0898-270, Dutton) Dutton/Plume.

—The Bluebury Collection. 2000. 132p. (gr. 4-7). pap. 9.95 (*0-595-00065-7*) iUniverse, Inc.

Walker, Sally M. The 18 Penny Goose. 1998. (I Can Read Bks.). (Illus.). 64p. (J). (gr. k-3). lib. bdg. 15.89 (*0-06-027557-X*) HarperCollins Children's Bk. Group.

—The 18 Penny Goose. 1998. (I Can Read Bks.). (Illus.). 64p. (J). (ps-4). 14.95 o.p. (*0-06-027556-1*) HarperCollins Pubs.

Whitney, Phyllis A. Mystery of the Crimson Ghost. 1969. (J). (gr. 5-9). 5.50 o.p. (*0-664-32440-1*) Westminster John Knox Pr.

Wolfe, Hillary. Dead Asleep. 1994. (You-Solve-It Mysteries Ser.: No. 2). 224p. (YA). mass mkt. 3.50 o.s.i (*0-8217-4581-6*) Kensington Publishing Corp.

—Death Spirit. 1994. (You-Solve-It Mysteries Ser.: No. 8). 224p. (YA). mass mkt. 3.50 (*0-8217-4766-5*, Zebra Bks.) Kensington Publishing Corp.

NEW MEXICO—FICTION

Anaya, Rudolfo A. Farolitos for Abuelo. 1999. (Illus.). 32p. (J). (gr. k-4). pap. 15.99 (*0-7868-0237-5*); lib. bdg. 16.49 (*0-7868-2186-8*) Hyperion Bks. for Children.

—The Farolitos of Christmas. 1995. (Illus.). 32p. (J). (gr. k-4). lib. bdg. 16.49 (*0-7868-2047-0*); 16.95 (*0-7868-0060-7*) Hyperion Bks. for Children.

Atwood, Marjorie, Jr. Galisteo Legend: A Story. Smith, James C., ed. 1992. (Illus.). 48p. (J). pap. 6.95 (*0-86534-154-0*) Sunstone Pr.

Blume, Judy. Tiger Eyes. 2003. 256p. (J). 16.00 (*0-689-85872-8*, Atheneum/Richard Jackson Bks.) Simon & Schuster Children's Publishing.

Burroughs, Jean M. Children of Destiny: True Adventures of Three Cultures. 2001. (Illus.). 108p. (J). pap. 12.95 (*0-913270-75-X*) Sunstone Pr.

Courtney, Dayle. Omen of the Flying Light. 1981. (Thorne Twins Adventure Bks.). (Illus.). 192p. (Orig.). (J). (gr. 5 up). pap. 2.98 o.p. (*0-87239-470-0*, 2715) Standard Publishing.

Creel, Ann H. Water at the Blue Earth. 1998. (Illus.). (gr. 5-9). 148p. (YA). 14.95 o.p. (*1-57098-209-0*, Rinehart, Roberts International); 112p. pap. 8.95 (*1-57098-224-4*) Rinehart, Roberts Pubs.

Ellison, Suzanne Pierson. The Best of Enemies. 1998. (YA). 200p. (gr. 7 up). 12.95 o.p. (*0-87358-714-6*); pap. 8.95 o.p. (*0-87358-717-0*) Northland Publishing.

Elster, Alayne. Julio & His New Amigo. 1988. (Illus.). 27p. (J). (gr. 2-4). 4.95 o.p. (*0-533-07646-3*) Vantage Pr., Inc.

Hiscock, Bruce. Coyote & Badger: Desert Hunters of the Southwest. 2003. (Illus.). 32p. (J). (gr. 2-5). 15.95 (*1-56397-848-2*) Boyds Mills Pr.

Hobbs, William. Kokopelli's Flute. 1995. 160p. (J). (gr. 4-9). 16.00 (*0-689-31974-6*, Atheneum) Simon & Schuster Children's Publishing.

Holmes, Mary Z. Cross of Gold. 1992. (History's Children Ser.). (Illus.). 48p. (J). (gr. 4-5). pap. o.p. (*0-8114-6432-6*); lib. bdg. 21.36 o.p. (*0-8114-3507-5*) Raintree Pubs.

Hulme, Joy N. Climbing the Rainbow. 2004. 224p. (J). 15.99 (*0-380-81572-9*); lib. bdg. 16.89 (*0-06-054304-3*) HarperCollins Pubs.

—Through the Open Door. 2000. 176p. (J). (gr. 4-6). 14.95 (*0-380-97870-9*) HarperCollins Children's Bk. Group.

Krumgold, Joseph. And Now Miguel. 1987. (Illus.). 245p. (J). (gr. 5 up). lib. bdg. 15.89 o.s.i (*0-690-04696-0*) HarperCollins Children's Bk. Group.

—...And Now Miguel. 1953. (Illus.). 256p. (J). (gr. 5 up). 17.99 (*0-690-09118-4*) HarperCollins Children's Bk. Group.

Lasky, Kathryn. Voice in the Wind: A Starbuck Family Adventure. 1993. (Illus.). 224p. (J). (gr. 3-7). 10.95 (*0-15-294102-9*); pap. 3.95 o.s.i (*0-15-294103-7*) Harcourt Children's Bks.

Lehr, Norma. Dance of the Crystal Skull. 1999. (Illus.). (J). (gr. 3-7). 115p. pap. 6.95 o.p. (*0-87358-725-1*); 238p. lib. bdg. 15.95 o.p. (*0-87358-724-3*) Northland Publishing. (Rising Moon Bks. for Young Readers).

—Dance of the Crystal Skull. 1999. (Illus.). (J). 13.00 (*0-606-18310-8*) Turtleback Bks.

Little, Kimberley Griffiths. The Last Snake Runner. 2002. 208p. (J). (gr. 6-9). 15.95 (*0-375-81539-2*); lib. bdg. 17.99 (*0-375-91539-7*) Random Hse., Inc.

Mazzio, Joann. The One Who Came Back. 1992. 192p. (YA). (gr. 7-7). tchr. ed. 17.00 (*0-395-59506-1*) Houghton Mifflin Co.

Mendel, Kathleen Lee. Whispering Clay. Valentine, Candy K., ed. 1992. (Illus.). 30p. (J). spiral bd. 11.00 (*1-878142-29-1*) Telstar.

Metz, Melinda. The Dark One. (Roswell High Ser.: No. 9). (YA). (gr. 6 up). 2000. 176p. mass mkt. 5.99 (*0-671-03563-0*); 2001. reprint ed. E-Book 5.90 (*0-7434-3450-1*) Simon & Schuster Children's Publishing. (Simon Pulse).

—The Intruder. (Roswell High Ser.: No. 5). (YA). (gr. 6 up). 2001. E-Book 4.99 (*0-7434-3446-3*); 2000. 160p. pap. 5.99 (*0-671-77459-X*); 1999. 176p. mass mkt. 4.50 (*0-671-02378-0*) Simon & Schuster Children's Publishing. (Simon Pulse).

—The Outsider. (Roswell High Ser.: No. 1). (YA). (gr. 6 up). 1999. 176p. pap. 5.99 (*0-671-77466-2*); 1998. 176p. mass mkt. 1.99 (*0-671-02374-8*); 2001. reprint ed. E-Book 5.99 (*0-7434-3442-0*) Simon & Schuster Children's Publishing. (Simon Pulse).

—The Rebel. (Roswell High Ser.: No. 8). (YA). (gr. 6 up). 2000. 176p. pap. 5.99 (*0-671-03562-2*); 2001. reprint ed. E-Book 5.99 (*0-7434-3449-8*) Simon & Schuster Children's Publishing. (Simon Pulse).

—The Salvation. (Roswell High Ser.: No. 10). (YA). (gr. 6 up). 2000. 176p. pap. 5.99 (*0-671-03564-9*); 2001. reprint ed. E-Book 5.99 (*0-7434-3451-X*) Simon & Schuster Children's Publishing. (Simon Pulse).

—The Seeker. (Roswell High Ser.: No. 3). (YA). (gr. 6 up). 2000. 176p. pap. 5.99 (*0-671-77464-6*); 1998. 176p. mass mkt. 4.50 (*0-671-02376-4*); 2001. reprint ed. E-Book 4.99 (*0-7434-3444-7*) Simon & Schuster Children's Publishing. (Simon Pulse).

—The Stowaway. (Roswell High Ser.: No. 6). (YA). (gr. 6 up). 2000. 176p. pap. 5.99 (*0-671-02379-9*); 2001. reprint ed. E-Book 4.99 (*0-7434-3447-1*) Simon & Schuster Children's Publishing. (Simon Pulse).

—The Vanished. (Roswell High Ser.: No. 7). (YA). (gr. 6 up). 2000. 176p. mass mkt. 5.99 (*0-671-03561-4*); 2001. reprint ed. E-Book 5.99 (*0-7434-3448-X*) Simon & Schuster Children's Publishing. (Simon Pulse).

—The Watcher. (Roswell High Ser.: No. 4). 176p. (YA). (gr. 6 up). 2000. pap. 5.99 (*0-671-77463-8*); 1999. per. 4.50 (*0-671-02377-2*); 2001. reprint ed. E-Book 5.99 (*0-7434-3445-5*) Simon & Schuster Children's Publishing. (Simon Pulse).

—The Wild One. (Roswell High Ser.: No. 2). (YA). (gr. 6 up). 1999. 176p. mass mkt. 5.99 (*0-671-77465-4*); 2001. reprint ed. E-Book 5.99 (*0-7434-3443-9*); No. 2. 1998. 176p. pap. 3.99 (*0-671-02375-6*) Simon & Schuster Children's Publishing. (Simon Pulse).

Meyer, Carolyn. Rio Grande Stories. 1994. (Illus.). 280p. (YA). (gr. 5-9). 12.00 o.s.i (*0-15-200548-X*); pap. 6.00 (*0-15-200066-6*) Harcourt Children's Bks. (Gulliver Bks.).

—Rio Grande Stories. 1994. 12.05 (*0-606-09791-0*) Turtleback Bks.

Momaday, N. Scott. Circle of Wonder: A Native American Christmas Story. 1993. (Illus.). 42p. (J). (gr. 4-7). 17.95 o.p. (*0-940666-32-4*) Clear Light Pubs.

—Circle of Wonder: A Native American Christmas Story. 1999. (Illus.). 44p. (gr. 4-7). 19.95 (*0-8263-2149-6*) Univ. of New Mexico Pr.

Mora, Pat. Maria Paints the Hills. 2002. (J). 19.95 o.p. (*0-89013-401-4*); pap. 9.95 (*0-89013-410-3*) Museum of New Mexico Pr.

Ortega, Cristina. Los Ojos del Tejedor: Through the Eyes of the Weaver. 1997. (Illus.). 64p. (YA). (gr. 4-7). pap. 14.95 (*0-940666-81-2*) Clear Light Pubs.

Pancho & the Power. 2000. 15.95 o.p. (*0-9678566-4-7*) Barbed Wire Publishing.

Pijoan, Teresa. Stories from a Dark & Evil World. Sharon, Franco, tr. 1999. (Bilingual Ser.).Tr. of Cuentos del Mundo Malevolo. (SPA., Illus.). 229p. (YA). (gr. 8-12). pap. text 14.95 (*1-878610-71-6*) Red Crane Bks., Inc.

Pleasant Company Staff. Meet the American Girls, 6 bks., Set. 1997. (American Girls Collection Ser.). (YA). (gr. 2 up). pap. 34.95 o.p. (*1-56247-542-8*) Pleasant Co. Pubns.

Rue, Nancy. The Choice. 2002. (Christian Heritage Ser.). 192p. (Orig.). (J). pap. 5.99 (*1-56179-896-7*) Focus on the Family Publishing.

—The Discovery. 2001. (Christian Heritage Ser.). (Illus.). 192p. (J). (gr. 3-7). pap. 5.99 (*1-56179-862-2*) Focus on the Family Publishing.

Rue, Nancy N. The Struggle. 2002. (Christian Heritage Ser.). 192p. (J). pap. 5.99 (*1-56179-895-9*) Bethany Hse. Pubs.

Ruiz, Joseph J. The Little Ghost Who Wouldn't Go Away: A Story for Children. Lucero, Juan S., tr. 2000. (ENG & SPA., Illus.). 96p. (J). (gr. 2-4). pap. 10.95 (*0-86534-303-9*) Sunstone Pr.

Sagel, Jim. Always the Heart. 1998. (Red Crane Literature Ser.).Tr. of Siempre el Corazon. (ENG & SPA., Illus.). 168p. (YA). (gr. 8-12). pap. 12.95 (*1-878610-68-6*) Red Crane Bks., Inc.

Scruggs, Sandy. Ode to the Wart Hog. 1999. (Illus.). 56p. (YA). (gr. 3 up). pap. 11.95 (*0-9660239-7-8*) Azro Pr., Inc.

Simmons, Marc. Josi's Buffalo Hunt: A Story from History. Kil, Ron, tr. & illus. by. 2003. 62p. (J). 17.95 (*0-8263-3315-X*) Univ. of New Mexico Pr.

Skurzynski, Gloria & Ferguson, Alane. Running Scared. 2002. (Mysteries in Our National Parks Ser.: Vol. 11). 160p. (J). 15.95 (*0-7922-8232-9*);Vol. 11. pap. 5.95 (*0-7922-6948-9*) National Geographic Society.

Slate, Joseph. The Secret Stars. (Illus.). (J). 2003. 5.95 (*0-7614-5152-8*); 1998. 32p. 15.95 (*0-7614-5027-0*) Cavendish, Marshall Corp. (Cavendish Children's Bks.).

Smith, Dean Wesley & Rusch, Kristine K. No Good Deed. 2001. (Roswell Ser.: No. 2). 256p. (YA). pap. 6.99 (*0-7434-1835-2*, Simon Pulse) Simon & Schuster Children's Publishing.

Stevens, Jan Romero. Carlos & the Cornfield. Davison, Patricia, tr. 1995. Tr. of Carlos y la Milpa de Maiz. (ENG & SPA., Illus.). 32p. (J). (gr. k-3). lib. bdg. 14.95 (*0-87358-596-8*, NP968, Rising Moon Bks. for Young Readers) Northland Publishing.

—Carlos & the Skunk. 1997. Tr. of Carlos y el Zorrillo. (ENG & SPA., Illus.). 32p. (J). (gr. k-3). lib. bdg. 14.95 (*0-87358-591-7*, Rising Moon Bks. for Young Readers) Northland Publishing.

Stoddard, Michael Eugene. The Porthole to Time. 1999. 176p. (YA). pap. 9.95 (*0-9675924-0-2*) Stoddard, Michael Eugene.

Talbert, Marc. Star of Luis. 1999. 192p. (J). (gr. 5-9). tchr. ed. 15.00 (*0-395-91423-X*, Clarion Bks.) Houghton Mifflin Co. Trade & Reference Div.

Thomasma, Kenneth. Amee-nah: Zuni Boy Runs the Race of His Life. 1995. (Amazing Indian Children Ser.). (Illus.). 160p. (J). (gr. 6-9). pap. 5.99 o.p. (*0-8010-4054-X*) Baker Bks.

Tripp, Valerie. Again, Josefina! 2000. (American Girls Short Stories Ser.). (Illus.). 56p. (YA). (gr. 2 up). 3.95 (*1-58485-032-9*, American Girl) Pleasant Co. Pubns.

—Asi es Josefina: Una Nina Americana. 1998. (American Girls Collection: Bk. 1). (SPA.). 432p. (J). (gr. 2 up). pap. 34.95 (*1-56247-706-4*) Pleasant Co. Pubns.

—Asi es Josefina: Una Nina Americana. Moreno, Jose, tr. 1997. (American Girls Collection: Bk. 1). (SPA., Illus.). 96p. (J). (gr. 2 up). pap. 5.95 (*1-56247-496-0*, PE6901, American Girl) Pleasant Co. Pubns.

—Asi es Josefina: Una Nina Americana. 1997. (American Girls Collection: Bk. 1). (SPA., Illus.). (YA). (gr. 2 up). 12.10 (*0-606-11060-7*) Turtleback Bks.

—Cambios para Josefina: Un Cuento de Invierno. 1998. (American Girls Collection: Bk. 6). (SPA., Illus.). 80p. (J). (gr. 2 up). pap. 5.95 (*1-56247-595-9*, BT5959, American Girl) Pleasant Co. Pubns.

—Changes for Josefina: A Winter Story. 1998. (American Girls Collection: Bk. 6). (Illus.). 80p. (J). (gr. 2 up). 12.95 (*1-56247-592-4*); pap. 5.95 (*1-56247-591-6*) Pleasant Co. Pubns. (American Girl).

—Changes for Josefina: A Winter Story. 1998. (American Girls Collection: Bk. 6). (Illus.). (YA). (gr. 2 up). 12.10 (*0-606-13264-3*) Turtleback Bks.

—Feliz Cumpleanos, Josefina! Un Cuento de Primavera. 1998. (American Girls Collection: Bk. 4). (SPA., Illus.). 80p. (J). (gr. 2 up). pap. 5.95 (*1-56247-593-2*, BT5932, American Girl) Pleasant Co. Pubns.

—Happy Birthday, Josefina! A Springtime Story. 1998. (American Girls Collection: Bk. 4). (Illus.). 80p. (J). (gr. 2 up). 12.95 (*1-56247-588-6*); pap. 5.95 (*1-56247-587-8*) Pleasant Co. Pubns. (American Girl).

—Happy Birthday, Josefina! A Springtime Story. 1998. (American Girls Collection: Bk. 4). (Illus.). (YA). (gr. 2 up). 12.10 (*0-606-13456-5*) Turtleback Bks.

—Josefina Aprende une Leccion: Un Cuento de la Escuela. Moreno, Jose, tr. 1997. (American Girls Collection: Bk. 2). (SPA., Illus.). 80p. (J). (gr. 2 up). pap. 5.95 (*1-56247-497-9*, BT4979, American Girl) Pleasant Co. Pubns.

—Josefina Entra en Accion: Un Cuento de Verano. Morano, Jose, tr. 1998. (American Girls Collection: Bk. 5). (SPA., Illus.). 80p. (J). (gr. 2 up). pap. 5.95 (*1-56247-594-0*, BT5940, American Girl) Pleasant Co. Pubns.

—Josefina Entra en Accion: Un Cuento de Verano. 1998. (American Girls Collection: Bk. 5). (SPA., Illus.). (YA). (gr. 2 up). 12.10 (*0-606-13540-5*) Turtleback Bks.

—Josefina Learns a Lesson: A School Story. 1997. (American Girls Collection: Bk. 2). (Illus.). 80p. (J). (gr. 2 up). pap. 5.95 (*1-56247-517-7*); lib. bdg. 12.95 (*1-56247-518-5*) Pleasant Co. Pubns. (American Girl).

—Josefina Learns a Lesson: A School Story. 1997. (American Girls Collection: Bk. 2). (Illus.). (YA). (gr. 2 up). 12.10 (*0-606-11524-2*) Turtleback Bks.

—Josefina Saves the Day: A Summer Story. 1998. (American Girls Collection: Bk. 5). (Illus.). 80p. (J). (gr. 2 up). 12.95 (*1-56247-590-8*); pap. 5.95 (*1-56247-589-4*) Pleasant Co. Pubns. (American Girl).

—Josefina Saves the Day: A Summer Story. 1998. (American Girls Collection: Bk. 5). (Illus.). (YA). (gr. 2 up). 12.10 (*0-606-13541-3*) Turtleback Bks.

—Josefina's Short Story Set: A Reward for Josefina; Again, Josefina!; Just Josefina, 3 vols. 2002. (American Girls Short Stories Ser.). (Illus.). (YA). (gr. 2). 11.95 (*1-58485-495-2*, American Girl) Pleasant Co. Pubns.

—Josefina's Song. 2001. (American Girls Short Stories Ser.). (Illus.). 56p. (YA). (gr. 2 up). 3.95 (*1-58485-272-0*, American Girl) Pleasant Co. Pubns.

—Josefina's Story Collection. 2001. (American Girls Collection). (Illus.). 406p. (J). (gr. 2 up). 29.95 (*1-58485-442-1*, American Girl) Pleasant Co. Pubns.

—Josefina's Surprise: A Christmas Story. 1997. (American Girls Collection: Bk. 3). (Illus.). 80p. (J). (gr. 2 up). pap. 5.95 (*1-56247-519-3*); lib. bdg. 12.95 (*1-56247-520-7*) Pleasant Co. Pubns. (American Girl).

—Josefina's Surprise: A Christmas Story. 1997. (American Girls Collection: Bk. 3). (Illus.). (YA). (gr. 2 up). 12.10 (*0-606-11525-0*) Turtleback Bks.

—Just Josefina. 2002. (American Girls Short Stories Ser.). (Illus.). 64p. (J). 4.95 (*1-58485-478-2*, American Girl) Pleasant Co. Pubns.

—Meet Josefina: An American Girl. 1997. (American Girls Collection: Bk. 1). (Illus.). 96p. (J). (gr. 2 up). pap. 5.95 (*1-56247-515-0*); lib. bdg. 12.95 (*1-56247-516-9*) Pleasant Co. Pubns. (American Girl).

—Meet Josefina: An American Girl. 1997. (American Girls Collection: Bk. 1). (Illus.). (YA). (gr. 2 up). 12.10 (*0-606-11614-1*) Turtleback Bks.

—A Reward for Josefina. 1999. (American Girls Short Stories Ser.). (Illus.). 56p. (YA). (gr. 2 up). 3.95 (*1-56247-763-3*, American Girl) Pleasant Co. Pubns.

—Una Sorpresa para Josefina: Un Cuento de Navidad. Moreno, Jose, tr. 1997. (American Girls Collection: Bk. 3). (SPA., Illus.). 80p. (J). (gr. 2 up). pap. 5.95 (*1-56247-498-7*, BT4987, American Girl) Pleasant Co. Pubns.

—Una Sorpresa para Josefina: Un Cuento de Navidad. 1997. (American Girls Collection: Bk. 3). (SPA.). (YA). (gr. 2 up). 12.10 (*0-606-12025-4*) Turtleback Bks.

—Thanks to Josefina. 2003. (American Girls Collection). (Illus.). 39p. (J). pap. 4.95 (*1-58485-698-X*, American Girl) Pleasant Co. Pubns.

Zindel, Paul. The Gadget. 2001. 192p. (J). (gr. 6 up). lib. bdg. 16.89 (*0-06-028255-X*) HarperCollins Children's Bk. Group.

—The Gadget. 2003. (Illus.). 192p. (YA). (gr. 7). mass mkt. 5.50 (*0-440-22951-0*, Laurel Leaf) Random Hse. Children's Bks.

NEW ORLEANS (LA.)—FICTION

Buckey, Sarah Masters. The Smuggler's Treasure. 1999. (American Girl Collection: Bk. 1). (Illus.). 176p. (YA). (gr. 5 up). 9.95 (*1-56247-813-3*); pap. 5.95 (*1-56247-757-9*) Pleasant Co. Pubns. (American Girl).

Buckley, Sarah Masters. The Smuggler's Treasure. 1999. (American Girl Collection Ser.). 12.00 (*0-606-17520-2*) Turtleback Bks.

Couvillon, Alice W. & Moore, Elizabeth. Mimi's First Mardi Gras. 1992. (Illus.). 32p. (J). (ps-3). 14.95 (*0-88289-840-X*) Pelican Publishing Co., Inc.

Cushman, Jerome. Tom B. & the Joyful Noise. 1970. (Illus.). (J). (gr. 4-7). 4.25 o.p. (*0-664-32467-3*) Westminster John Knox Pr.

Dartez, Cecilia Casrill. Jenny Giraffe & the Streetcar Party. 1993. (Illus.). 32p. (J). (gr. k-3). 14.95 (*0-88289-962-7*) Pelican Publishing Co., Inc.

—Jenny Giraffe Discovers the French Quarter. 1991. (Illus.). 32p. (J). (gr. 4-7). 14.95 (*0-88289-819-1*) Pelican Publishing Co., Inc.

Davis, David. Jazz Cats. 2001. (Illus.). 32p. (J). (gr. 2-4). 14.95 (*1-56554-859-0*) Pelican Publishing Co., Inc.

Flettrich, Terry. House in the Bend of Bourbon Street: A Child's Walking Tour of the French Quarter. 1974. (Illus.). 52p. (J). (gr. 1-6). pap. 5.95 o.p. (*0-88289-015-8*, Firebird Pr.) Pelican Publishing Co., Inc.

Hill, Elizabeth S. The Banjo Player. 1993. 208p. (J). (gr. 5-9). 14.99 o.p. (*0-670-84967-7*, Viking Children's Bks.) Penguin Putnam Bks. for Young Readers.

—The Banjo Player. 1999. pap. 4.99 (*0-14-036422-6*) Viking Penguin.

Keene, Carolyn. Nightmare in New Orleans. 1997. (Nancy Drew & Hardy Boys Super Mystery Ser.: No. 30). 224p. (YA). (gr. 6 up). pap. 3.99 (*0-671-53749-0*, Simon Pulse) Simon & Schuster Children's Publishing.

—Nightmare in New Orleans. 1997. (Nancy Drew & Hardy Boys Super Mystery Ser.: No. 30). (YA). (gr. 6 up). 9.09 o.p. (*0-606-11667-2*) Turtleback Bks.

MacBride, Roger Lea. On the Banks of the Bayou. 1998. (Little House Ser.: Vol. 1). (Illus.). 240p. (J). (gr. 3-7). 15.95 (*0-06-024973-0*) HarperCollins Children's Bk. Group.

—On the Banks of the Bayou. 1998. (Little House Ser.). 11.00 (*0-606-15660-7*) Turtleback Bks.

Martin, Valerie. Alexandra. 1979. 192p. 8.95 o.p. (*0-374-10264-3*) Farrar, Straus & Giroux.

—Alexandra. 1991. 192p. reprint ed. pap. 10.00 (*0-671-73688-4*, Pocket) Simon & Schuster.

McConduit, Denise W. D. J. & the Jazz Fest. 1997. (Illus.). 32p. (J). 14.95 (*1-56554-239-8*) Pelican Publishing Co., Inc.

—D. J. & the Zulu Parade. 1994. (Illus.). 32p. (J). (ps-3). 8.95 (*1-56554-063-8*) Pelican Publishing Co., Inc.

Medearis, Angela Shelf. Rum-a-Tum-Tum. 1997. (Illus.). 32p. (J). (ps-3). tchr. ed. 16.95 (*0-8234-1143-5*) Holiday Hse., Inc.

Miller, William. Rent Party Jazz. 2001. (Illus.). 32p. (J). (gr. 1-5). 16.95 (*1-58430-025-6*) Lee & Low Bks., Inc.

Muldrow, Diane. Recipe for Trouble, Vol. 7. 2003. (Dish Ser.: No. 7). (Illus.). 160p. (J). mass mkt. 4.99 (*0-448-42898-9*, Grosset & Dunlap) Penguin Putnam Bks. for Young Readers.

Phillips, Betty Lou. Emily Goes Wild. 2003. (Illus.). 32p. (J). (ps-3). 16.95 (*1-58685-268-X*) Smith, Gibbs Pub.

Pisano, Mary B. Going to New Orleans to Visit Weezie Anna. 1994. (Illus.). 24p. (J). (ps-3). 8.95 o.p. (*0-937552-52-6*) Quail Ridge Pr., Inc.

Rice, James. Gaston Goes to Mardi Gras. (Illus.). 40p. (J). 1977. (gr. 1-6). reprint ed. 14.95 (*0-88289-158-8*); 2nd ed. 1999. (ps-3). 14.95 (*1-56554-286-X*) Pelican Publishing Co., Inc.

Schroeder, Alan. Satchmo's Blues. 1996. (Illus.). 32p. (J). (gr. k-3). 15.95 o.s.i (*0-385-32046-9*) Doubleday Publishing.

Shaik, Fatima. The Jazz of Our Street. 1998. (Illus.). 32p. (J). (ps-3). 15.99 o.s.i (*0-8037-1885-3*); 15.89 o.s.i (*0-8037-1886-1*) Penguin Putnam Bks. for Young Readers. (Dial Bks. for Young Readers).

—On Mardi Gras Day. Kane, Cindy, ed. (Illus.). 32p. (J). (ps-3). 2015. 16.89 o.s.i (*0-8037-1443-2*); 1999. 16.99 o.p. (*0-8037-1442-4*) Penguin Putnam Bks. for Young Readers. (Dial Bks. for Young Readers).

Stewart, Whitney. Jammin' on the Avenue. Barstow, Susannah Driver, ed. 2001. (Going to Ser.). 96p. (J). (gr. 4-8). pap. 7.95 (*1-893577-06-6*) Four Corners Publishing Co., Inc.

Tang, Charles, illus. The Mystery Bookstore. 1995. (Boxcar Children Ser.: No. 48). (J). (gr. 2-5). lib. bdg. 13.95 (*0-8075-5421-9*); mass mkt. 3.95 (*0-8075-5422-7*) Whitman, Albert & Co.

Wright, Mildred W. Henrietta Goes to the Mardi Gras. 1971. (Illus.). (J). (gr. k-3). 3.97 o.p. (*0-399-60233-X*) Putnam Publishing Group, The.

NEW YORK (N.Y.)—FICTION

Abagnalo, George. Boy on a Pony. 2001. 288p. 25.95 (*0-9706677-0-1*) Moreland Pr., Inc.

Alda, Arlene. Morning Glory Monday. 2003. (Illus.). 32p. (J). (gr. k-3). 17.95 (*0-88776-620-X*) Tundra Bks. of Northern New York.

Allan, Mabel E. Kraymer Mystery. 1969. (J). (gr. 5-9). 4.95 o.p. (*0-200-71994-7*, 342330) Criterion Bks., Inc.

—Mystery on the Fourteenth Floor. 1965. (Illus.). (J). (gr. 7 up). 6.95 o.p. (*0-200-00088-8*, 368060) Criterion Bks., Inc.

Arrhenius, Peter. The Penguin Quartet. 1998. (Picture Bks.). (Illus.). 28p. (J). (ps-3). lib. bdg. 15.95 (*1-57505-252-0*, Carolrhoda Bks.) Lerner Publishing Group.

Auch, Mary Jane. Ashes of Roses, ERS. 2002. 256p. (YA). (gr. 7-10). 16.95 (*0-8050-6686-1*, Holt, Henry & Co. Bks. For Young Readers) Holt, Henry & Co.

—Ashes of Roses. 2004. 256p. (YA). (gr. 7). mass mkt. 5.99 (*0-440-23851-X*, Laurel Leaf) Random Hse. Children's Bks.

Auchincloss, Louis. Manhattan Monologues: Stories. 2002. 240p. tchr. ed. 25.00 (*0-618-15289-X*) Houghton Mifflin Co.

Avi. Abigail Takes the Wheel. (I Can Read Chapter Bks.). (Illus.). 64p. (J). (gr. 3 up). 2000. pap. 3.95 (*0-06-444281-0*, Harper Trophy); 1999. 14.95 (*0-06-027662-2*); 1999. 15.89 (*0-06-027663-0*) HarperCollins Children's Bk. Group.

—Abigail Takes the Wheel. 2000. (Illus.). (J). 10.10 (*0-606-18672-7*) Turtleback Bks.

—Don't You Know There's a War On? 2003. 208p. (J). pap. 5.99 (*0-380-81544-3*, Harper Trophy) HarperCollins Children's Bk. Group.

—Silent Movie. 2003. (Illus.). 64p. (J). (gr. k-3). 16.95 (*0-689-84145-0*, Atheneum/Anne Schwartz Bks.) Simon & Schuster Children's Publishing.

Barracca, Debra. The Adventures of Taxi Dog. 2002. (Illus.). (J). 13.19 (*0-7587-1907-8*) Book Wholesalers, Inc.

—Maxi, the Hero. 2002. (Illus.). (J). 14.04 (*0-7587-3112-4*) Book Wholesalers, Inc.

—Maxi, the Hero. 1994. (J). 11.19 o.p. (*0-606-07850-9*) Turtleback Bks.

Barracca, Debra & Barracca, Sal. The Adventures of Taxi Dog. 2000. (Illus.). 32p. (J). (ps-3). pap. 5.99 (*0-14-056665-1*, Puffin Bks.) Penguin Putnam Bks. for Young Readers.

—The Adventures of Taxi Dog. Fogelman, Phyllis J., ed. 1990. (Illus.). 32p. (J). (ps-3). 13.89 o.p. (*0-8037-0672-3*); 15.99 (*0-8037-0671-5*) Penguin Putnam Bks. for Young Readers. (Dial Bks. for Young Readers).

—The Adventures of Taxi Dog. 2000. (Illus.). (J). 11.44 (*0-606-18386-8*) Turtleback Bks.

—Maxi, the Hero. 1991. (Illus.). 32p. (J). (ps-3). 15.99 o.p. (*0-8037-0939-0*); 12.89 o.p. (*0-8037-0940-4*) Penguin Putnam Bks. for Young Readers. (Dial Bks. for Young Readers).

Barrie, Barbara. Adam Zigzag. 1995. 192p. (YA). (gr. 7 up). mass mkt. 3.99 o.s.i (*0-440-21964-7*, Laurel Leaf) Random Hse. Children's Bks.

—Adam Zigzag. 1996. 10.04 (*0-606-08968-3*) Turtleback Bks.

Bartone, Elisa. Peppe the Lamplighter. 1993. (Illus.). 32p. (J). (ps-3). 16.95 (*0-688-10268-9*); lib. bdg. 16.89 (*0-688-10269-7*) HarperCollins Children's Bk. Group.

—Peppe the Lamplighter. 1997. (Illus.). 32p. (J). (gr. k-3). pap. 5.99 (*0-688-15469-7*, Morrow, William & Co.) Morrow/Avon.

Bennett, Helen S. Jack's Amazing Magic Bed. 1994. (Illus.). 32p. (J). (gr. 2). 9.95 (*0-9638747-1-3*); pap. 9.95 (*0-9638747-0-5*) Tomac Publishing.

Betancourt, Jeanne. Exposed. 2003. (Three Girls in the City Ser.). 160p. (J). mass mkt. 4.99 (*0-439-49840-6*, Scholastic Paperbacks) Scholastic, Inc.

—Self-Portrait. 2003. (Three Girls in the City Ser.: No. 1). 176p. (J). (gr. 3-7). mass mkt. 4.99 (*0-439-49839-2*, 53517295, Scholastic Paperbacks) Scholastic, Inc.

Bethancourt, T. Ernesto. Doris Fein: Superspy. 1980. 160p. (gr. 9 up). 10.95 o.p. (*0-8234-0407-2*) Holiday Hse., Inc.

Birenbaum, Barbara. Lady Liberty's Light. 1986. (Historical Adventure Ser.: No. 3). (Illus.). 50p. (J). (gr. 3-5). 12.95 (*0-935343-12-1*); pap. 5.95 (*0-935343-11-3*) Peartree.

Block, Francesca Lia. Missing Angel Juan. 1993. (Illus.). 144p. (YA). (gr. 12 up). 14.89 o.s.i (*0-06-023007-X*); (gr. 7 up). 14.95 o.p. (*0-06-023004-5*) HarperCollins Children's Bk. Group.

Borisoff, Norman. Bird Seed & Lightning. 1973. (Mystery & Adventure Ser.). (J). (gr. 2-4). lib. bdg. 7.95 o.p. (*0-87191-206-6*, Creative Education) Creative Co., The.

Brouwer, Sigmund. The Downtown Desperados. 1991. (Accidental Detective Ser.). 132p. (J). (gr. 3-7). pap. 4.99 o.s.i (*0-89693-860-3*) Cook Communications Ministries.

—Lost Beneath Manhattan. 1994. (Accidental Detective Ser.: Vol. 1). 132p. (J). (gr. 3-7). pap. 5.99 (*1-56476-370-6*, 6-3370) Cook Communications Ministries.

Bryant, Bonnie. Horse Show. l.t. ed. 1996. (Saddle Club Ser.: No. 8). 144p. (J). (gr. 4-6). lib. bdg. 21.27 o.p. (*0-8368-1530-0*) Stevens, Gareth Inc.

Buchan, Stuart. Guys Like Us. 1986. (YA). (gr. 7 up). 14.95 o.s.i (*0-385-29448-4*, Delacorte Pr.) Dell Publishing.

—Guys Like Us. 1988. (J). (gr. k-12). mass mkt. 2.95 o.s.i (*0-440-20244-2*, Laurel Leaf) Random Hse. Children's Bks.

Buck, Nola & Godwin, Laura. Central Park Serenade. 2002. (Illus.). 32p. (J). (ps-k). 15.95 (*0-06-025891-8*); lib. bdg. 15.89 (*0-06-025892-6*) HarperCollins Children's Bk. Group. (Cotler, Joanna Bks.).

Burleigh, Robert, et al. Edna. 2000. (Illus.). 32p. (J). (gr. k-4). pap. 15.95 (*0-531-30246-6*, Orchard Bks.) Scholastic, Inc.

Byalick, Marcia. Quit It. 2004. 176p. (gr. 3-7). pap. text 5.50 (*0-440-41865-8*, Yearling) Random Hse. Children's Bks.

—Quit It. 2002. 176p. (gr. 3-7). lib. bdg. 17.99 (*0-385-90061-9*); (gr. 4-8). text 15.95 (*0-385-72997-9*) Random Hse., Inc.

Byng, Georgia. Molly Moon's Incredible Book of Hypnotism. 2004. (Illus.). 400p. (J). pap. 6.99 (*0-06-051409-4*, Harper Trophy) HarperCollins Children's Bk. Group.

—Molly Moon's Incredible Book of Hypnotism. 2003. (Illus.). 384p. (J). (gr. 3-7). 16.99 (*0-06-051406-X*); (Illus.). 384p. (J). (gr. 3-7). lib. bdg. 17.89 (*0-06-051407-8*); 135.92 (*0-06-057217-5*) HarperCollins Pubs.

—Molly Moon's Incredible Book of Hypnotism. 2002. 330p. (J). (gr. 3-7). 24.95 (*0-333-98489-7*) Macmillan Children's Bks. GBR. *Dist:* Trans-Atlantic Pubns., Inc.

Cabell, Suzy McKee. The Bronze King. 2001. 212p. pap. 14.95 (*1-58715-478-1*) Wildside Pr.

Cabot, Meg. The Princess Diaries: A Novel. l.t. ed. 2002. 325p. (J). 24.95 (*0-7862-4058-X*) Gale Group.

—The Princess Diaries: A Novel. (J). (gr. 7 up). 2000. (Princess Diaries: Vol. I). 224p. lib. bdg. 16.89 (*0-06-029210-5*); 2001. (Princess Diaries). 304p. pap. 6.99 (*0-380-81402-1*, Harper Trophy); 2000. (Princess Diaries). (Illus.). 240p. 15.99 (*0-380-97848-2*) HarperCollins Children's Bk. Group.

—The Princess Diaries: A Novel, Vol. 5. 2004. (Princess Diaries: Vol. 5). 272p. (J). lib. bdg. 16.89 (*0-06-009611-X*) HarperCollins Pubs.

—The Princess Diaries: A Novel. unabr. ed. 2001. (Princess Diaries: Vol. I). (YA). (gr. 6 up). pap. 37.00 incl. audio (*0-8072-0669-5*); (gr. 5-9). audio 26.00 (*0-8072-0431-5*) Random Hse. Audio Publishing Group. (Listening Library).

—The Princess Diaries: A Novel. 2001. (Illus.). (J). 12.00 (*0-606-21844-0*) Turtleback Bks.

—Princess in Love. 2002. (Princess Diaries: Vol. 3). 240p. (J). (gr. 7 up). 15.99 (*0-06-029467-1*); lib. bdg. 16.89 (*0-06-029468-X*) HarperCollins Children's Bk. Group.

—Princess in Pink. 2004. (Princess Diaries: Vol. 5). 272p. (J). 15.99 (*0-06-009610-1*) HarperCollins Pubs.

—Princess in the Spotlight. 2001. (Princess Diaries: Vol. 2). 240p. (J). (gr. 7 up). lib. bdg. 16.89 (*0-06-029466-3*); 15.95 (*0-06-029465-5*) HarperCollins Children's Bk. Group.

Campbell Bartoletti, Susan, et al. The Journal of Finn Reardon, a Newsie. 2003. (My Name Is America Ser.). (Illus.). 192p. (J). pap. 10.95 (*0-439-18894-6*, Scholastic Pr.) Scholastic, Inc.

Campbell, Louisa. Gargoyles' Christmas. 1994. (Illus.). 32p. (J). 19.95 o.p. (*0-87905-587-1*) Smith, Gibbs Pub.

Cao, Glen. Beijinger in New York. 1994. 220p. (J). (gr. 10-12). pap. 14.95 (*0-8351-2526-2*) China Bks. & Periodicals, Inc.

Carlesimo, Cheryl & Sorel, Edward. The Saturday Kid. 2000. (Illus.). 40p. (J). (gr. k-3). 18.00 (*0-689-82399-1*, McElderry, Margaret K.) Simon & Schuster Children's Publishing.

Carlson, Lorentz. The Littles Visit the Statue of Liberty. 1986. (Illus.). 24p. (Orig.). (J). (gr. k-3). pap. 1.95 o.p. (*0-590-33908-7*) Scholastic, Inc.

Carr, Jan. The Elf of Union Square. 2004. (J). 15.99 (*0-399-24180-9*) Penguin Putnam Bks. for Young Readers.

Chambers, Roland. The Rooftop Rocket Party. 2003. (Illus.). 32p. (ps-2). (J). 16.95 (*0-7613-1888-7*); lib. bdg. 23.90 (*0-7613-2744-4*) Millbrook Pr., Inc. (Roaring Brook Pr.).

Charbonneau, Eileen. Honor to the Hills. (J). 1997. (Woods Family Saga: Vol. 3). (FRE.). 238p. (gr. 8-12). mass mkt. 3.99 (*0-8125-5187-7*); 1996. 192p. (gr. 7-12). 18.95 (*0-312-86094-3*) Doherty, Tom Assocs., LLC. (Tor Bks.).

—Honor to the Hills, 3. 1997. (Woods Family Saga). 10.04 (*0-606-11477-7*) Turtleback Bks.

Charnas, Suzy M. The Bronze King. 1988. 208p. (J). mass mkt. 2.95 o.s.i (*0-553-27104-0*, Starfire) Random Hse. Children's Bks.

Chastain, Madye L. Emmy Keeps a Promise. (Illus.). (J). (gr. 4-6). 1956. 4.50 o.p. (*0-15-225739-X*); 1901. pap. 0.75 o.p. (*0-15-628776-5*, AVB21, Voyager Bks./Libros Viajeros) Harcourt Children's Bks.

—Plippen's Palace. 1961. (Illus.). (J). (gr. 4-7). 4.50 o.p. (*0-15-262792-8*) Harcourt Children's Bks.

Chetwin, Grace. Collidescope. 1990. 240p. (J). (gr. 5-9). lib. bdg. 14.95 o.s.i (*0-02-718316-5*, Simon & Schuster Children's Publishing) Simon & Schuster Children's Publishing.

Christopher, Matt. Fairway Phenom. 2003. 144p. (J). (gr. 4-6). pap. 4.50 (*0-316-07551-5*); (Illus.). 15.95 (*0-316-07550-7*) Little Brown Children's Bks.

Coburn, Jake. Prep. 2003. 176p. (YA). 15.99 (*0-525-47135-9*, Dutton Children's Bks.) Penguin Putnam Bks. for Young Readers.

Cohen, Miriam. Down in the Subway. 1998. (Illus.). 32p. (J). (ps-2). pap. 16.95 o.p. (*0-7894-2510-6*) Dorling Kindersley Publishing, Inc.

—Down in the Subway. 2003. (Illus.). (J). (gr. k-3). pap. 5.95 (*1-932065-24-5*); 40p. mass mkt. 15.95 (*1-932065-08-3*) Star Bright Bks., Inc.

Cohen, Ron. My Dad's Baseball. 1994. (Illus.). 32p. (J). (gr. k up). 15.00 o.p. (*0-688-12390-2*); lib. bdg. 14.93 o.p. (*0-688-12391-0*) HarperCollins Children's Bk. Group.

Collier, James Lincoln. Rich & Famous. 2001. (Lost Treasures Ser.: No. 6). (Illus.). 240p. (J). pap. 4.99 (*0-7868-1520-5*); (gr. 3-7). pap. 1.99 (*0-7868-1519-1*) Hyperion Bks. for Children. (Volo).

—The Teddy Bear Habit or How I Became a Winner. 2001. (Lost Treasures Ser.: No. 3). (Illus.). 240p. (J). pap. 4.99 (*0-7868-1544-2*); (gr. 3-7). reprint ed. pap. 1.99 (*0-7868-1543-4*) Hyperion Bks. for Children. (Volo).

Collier, James Lincoln & Collier, Christopher. Who Is Carrie? 1984. 192p. (J). (gr. 4-6). 14.95 o.s.i (*0-385-29295-3*, Delacorte Pr.) Dell Publishing.

—Who Is Carrie? 1987. (Arabus Family Saga Ser.: Vol. 3). 176p. (gr. 5-7). pap. text 4.99 o.s.i (*0-440-49536-9*, Yearling) Random Hse. Children's Bks.

—Who Is Carrie? 1987. (Arabus Family Saga Ser.). (J). 11.04 (*0-606-03505-2*) Turtleback Bks.

Colman, Hila. Claudia, Where Are You? 1969. (J). (gr. 7 up). lib. bdg. 6.96 o.p. (*0-688-31174-1*, Morrow, William & Co.) Morrow/Avon.

—The Double Life of Angela Jones. 1989. 128p. mass mkt. 2.95 o.s.i (*0-449-70336-3*, Fawcett) Ballantine Bks.

—The Double Life of Angela Jones. 1988. 160p. (J). (gr. 7 up). 12.95 o.p. (*0-688-06781-6*, Morrow, William & Co.) Morrow/Avon.

Connolly, John. Every Dead Thing. 2000. 480p. reprint ed. pap. 6.99 (*0-671-02731-X*, Pocket) Simon & Schuster.

Cooney, Barbara. Hattie & the Wild Waves: A Story from Brooklyn. (Picture Puffins Ser.). (Illus.). (J). (ps-3). 1993. 40p. pap. 6.99 (*0-14-054193-4*, Puffin Bks.); 1990. 400p. 16.99 (*0-670-83056-9*, Viking Children's Bks.) Penguin Putnam Bks. for Young Readers.

—Hattie & the Wild Waves: A Story from Brooklyn. 1993. (Picture Puffin Ser.). (Illus.). (J). 12.14 (*0-606-05343-3*) Turtleback Bks.

Settings

Cooper, Ilene. No-Thanks Thanksgiving, Bk. 5. 1996. (Holiday Five Ser.). 128p. (J). (gr. 3-8). 14.99 o.s.i (*0-670-85657-6*, Viking) Penguin Putnam Bks. for Young Readers.

Courtney, Dayle. The House That Ate People. rev. ed. 1991. (Thorne Twins Adventure Bks.). 160p. (Orig.). (J). (gr. 6-9). reprint ed. pap. 4.99 o.p. (*0-87403-832-4*, 24-03882) Standard Publishing.

Cowley, Joy. Gracias, the Thanksgiving Turkey. 1996. (Illus.). 32p. (J). (ps-3). pap. 15.95 (*0-590-46976-2*) Scholastic, Inc.

Crane, Stephen. Maggie, a Girl of the Streets & Other New York Writings. 2001. (Paperback Classics Ser.). 288p. pap. 8.95 (*0-375-75689-2*, Modern Library) Random House Adult Trade Publishing Group.

Cummings, Pat. C.L.O.U.D.S. 1986. (Illus.). 32p. (J). (ps-3). 12.95 o.p. (*0-688-04682-7*); lib. bdg. 12.88 o.p. (*0-688-04683-5*) HarperCollins Children's Bk. Group.

Cunningham, Michael. The Hours. 1998. pap. o.s.i (*0-374-93947-0*) Farrar, Straus & Giroux.

Czuchlewski, David. The Muse Asylum. 2002. 240p. 13.00 (*0-14-200060-4*) Viking Penguin.

Daly-Weir, Catherine. A Simple Wish: Make a Simple Wish of Your Very Own. 1997. (Simple Wish Ser.). (Illus.). 24p. (J). (gr. 3-5). 4.95 o.s.i (*0-448-41635-2*, Grosset & Dunlap) Penguin Putnam Bks. for Young Readers.

Daniel, Barlette. I'll Take Manhattan. 1984. (Mirrors Ser.). 144p. (J). (gr. 7 up). 2.25 (*0-448-47725-4*) Putnam Publishing Group, The.

Danticat, Edwidge. Behind the Mountains: The Diary of Celiane Esperance. (First Person Fiction Ser.). (J). 2004. 192p. mass mkt. 16.95 (*0-439-37300-X*); 2002. 176p. (gr. 5-9). pap. 16.95 (*0-439-37299-2*) Scholastic, Inc. (Orchard Bks.).

Danziger, Paula. Remember Me to Harold Square. 1987. 168p. (J). (gr. 7 up). 13.95 o.s.i (*0-385-29610-X*, Delacorte Pr.) Dell Publishing.

—Remember Me to Harold Square. 1999. (Illus.). 160p. (YA). (gr. 5-9). pap. 4.99 (*0-698-11694-1*, PaperStar) Penguin Putnam Bks. for Young Readers.

—Remember Me to Harold Square. 139p. (YA). (gr. 6 up). pap. 3.99 (*0-8072-1472-8*); 1995. (J). (gr. 7 up). pap. 23.00 incl. audio (*0-8072-7526-3*, YA874SP) Random Hse. Audio Publishing Group. (Listening Library).

—Remember Me to Harold Square. 1988. 144p. (J). (gr. k-12). mass mkt. 3.99 o.p. (*0-440-20153-5*, Laurel Leaf) Random Hse. Children's Bks.

—Remember Me to Harold Square. 1999. 10.04 (*0-606-16795-1*) Turtleback Bks.

Davies, Valentine. Miracle on 34th Street. 1996. 76p. pap. 5.60 (*0-87129-707-8*, M96) Dramatic Publishing Co.

—Miracle on 34th Street. 2002. 80p. pap. 6.25 (*0-573-62892-0*) French, Samuel Inc.

—Miracle on 34th Street. fac. ed. 2001. 136p. (YA). 12.95 (*0-15-216377-8*) Harcourt Children's Bks.

—Miracle on 34th Street. gif. ed. 1991. (Illus.). 146p. pap. 9.95 (*0-15-660455-8*, Harvest Bks.) Harcourt Trade Pubs.

Davis, Edward E. Bruno the Pretzel Man. 1984. (Illus.). 64p. (J). (gr. 2-5). 11.50 (*0-06-021398-1*); lib. bdg. 12.89 o.p. (*0-06-021399-X*) HarperCollins Children's Bk. Group.

de Brunhoff, Laurent. Babar a New York. 1975. (Babar Ser.). (FRE., Illus.). (J). (ps-3). bds. 15.95 (*0-7859-5281-0*, 2010025520) French & European Pubns., Inc.

De Montano, Marty K. Coyote in Love with a Star. 1998. (Tales of the People Ser.). (Illus.). 30p. (J). (ps up). 14.95 (*0-7892-0162-3*, Abbeville Kids) Abbeville Pr., Inc.

de Paola, Tomie. Nana Upstairs & Nana Downstairs. 1997. (Illus.). 32p. (J). (ps-3). 16.99 (*0-399-23108-0*, G. P. Putnam's Sons) Penguin Group (USA) Inc.

Dell, Pamela. The Gold Coin: A Story about New York City's Lower East Side. 2002. (Illus.). 48p. (J). (gr. 3-8). lib. bdg. 27.07 (*1-59187-017-8*) Child's World, Inc.

Delton, Judy. Prize-Winning Private Eyes. 1995. (Lottery Luck Ser.: Bk. 2). (Illus.). 96p. (J). (gr. 4-7). pap. 3.95 (*0-7868-1019-X*) Hyperion Paperbacks for Children.

Desaix, Frank. Hilary & the Lions, RS. 1990. 32p. (J). (ps-3). 15.00 o.p. (*0-374-33237-1*, Farrar, Straus & Giroux (BYR)) Farrar, Straus & Giroux.

—Hilary & the Lions. 1996. 11.15 o.p. (*0-606-10843-2*) Turtleback Bks.

DeSaix, Frank. Hilary & the Lions, RS. 1996. (Illus.). 32p. (J). (ps-3). pap. 5.95 o.p. (*0-374-43065-9*, Sunburst) Farrar, Straus & Giroux.

Donovan, John. I'll Get There: It Better Be Worth the Trip. 1969. (YA). (gr. 7 up). lib. bdg. 12.89 o.p. (*0-06-021718-9*) HarperCollins Children's Bk. Group.

Dorros, Arthur. Abuela. 2002. (Illus.). (J). 14.04 (*0-7587-1901-9*) Book Wholesalers, Inc.

—Abuela. (Picture Puffin Bks.). (J). (ps-1). 1997. (SPA.). 40p. pap. 6.99 (*0-14-056226-5*); 1997. (Illus.). 40p. pap. 6.99 (*0-14-056225-7*, Puffin Bks.); 1995. (SPA., Illus.). 48p. 15.99 (*0-525-45438-1*, Dutton Children's Bks.); 1991. (Illus.). 40p. 16.99 (*0-525-44750-4*, Dutton Children's Bks.) Penguin Putnam Bks. for Young Readers.

—Abuela. 1997. (Picture Puffin Ser.). 13.14 (*0-606-11019-4*); (J). 13.14 (*0-606-11018-6*) Turtleback Bks.

Dreams in the Golden Country: The Diary of Zipporah Feldman, a Jewish Immmigrant Girl. 2003. (J). lib. bdg. 12.95 (*0-439-55502-7*) Scholastic, Inc.

Dreyer, Ellen. Speechless in New York. (Going to Ser.). (Illus.). (J). 2000. 96p. pap. 7.95 (*1-893577-01-5*); 2nd rev. ed. 2003. 121p. (gr. 4-8). pap. 6.95 (*1-893577-09-0*) Four Corners Publishing Co., Inc.

Drummond, Allan. Liberty!, RS. 2002. (Illus.). 40p. (J). (ps-3). 17.00 (*0-374-34385-3*, Farrar, Straus & Giroux (BYR)) Farrar, Straus & Giroux.

Egielski, Richard. The Gingerbread Boy. 1997. (Laura Geringer Bks.). (Illus.). 32p. (J). (ps-2). 15.99 (*0-06-026030-0*, Geringer, Laura Bk.) HarperCollins Children's Bk. Group.

Ehrlich, Amy. Annie: The Storybook Based on the Movie. 1982. (Movie Storybooks Ser.). (Illus.). 64p. (J). (gr. 5 up). 5.95 o.p. (*0-394-85087-4*); lib. bdg. 6.99 o.p. (*0-394-95087-9*) Random Hse. Children's Bks. (Random Hse. Bks. for Young Readers).

Elish, Dan. The Great Squirrel Uprising. 1992. (Illus.). 128p. (J). (gr. 4 up). 14.95 o.p. (*0-531-05995-2*); mass mkt. 14.99 o.p. (*0-531-08595-3*) Scholastic, Inc. (Orchard Bks.).

Enderle, Judith R. & Tessler, Stephanie G. Where Are You, Little Zack? 1997. (Illus.). 32p. (J). (ps-3). tchr. ed. 14.95 o.s.i (*0-395-73092-9*) Houghton Mifflin Co.

Enright, Elizabeth. The Saturdays. (Illus.). 1941. (gr. 4-6). 5.95 o.p. (*0-03-089690-8*); ERS. 2002. (Melendy Quartet Ser.: Bk. 1). 176p. (J). (gr. 3-6). 16.95 (*0-8050-7060-5*, Holt, Henry & Co. Bks. For Young Readers); ERS. 1988. 196p. (YA). (gr. 4-7). 12.95 o.s.i (*0-8050-0291-X*, Holt, Henry & Co. Bks. For Young Readers) Holt, Henry & Co.

—The Saturdays. 1997. (Melendy Family Ser.). (Illus.). 192p. (J). (gr. 3-7). pap. 4.99 o.s.i (*0-14-038395-6*) Penguin Putnam Bks. for Young Readers.

—The Saturdays. 1923. (Illus.). 176p. (J). (gr. k-6). pap. 0.65 o.p. (*0-440-47615-1*, Yearling) Random Hse. Children's Bks.

Ferguson, Sarah. Bright Lights. 1996. (Illus.). 112p. (J). 14.95 (*0-385-32178-3*, Delacorte Pr.) Dell Publishing.

Fitzgerald, Frank. Where's Kevin? 1992. 24p. (J). (gr. 4-7). pap. 7.99 o.s.i (*0-553-37199-1*) Bantam Bks.

Fitzhugh, Louise. Harriet the Spy. 1975. (J). pap. 2.95 o.s.i (*0-440-73447-9*) Dell Publishing.

—Harriet the Spy. (Illus.). 1996. 304p. (J). (gr. 4-7). pap. 5.95 o.p. (*0-06-440660-1*, Harper Trophy); 1996. 224p. (YA). (gr. 5 up). mass mkt. 4.50 o.s.i (*0-06-447165-9*, Harper Trophy); 1996. 224p. (YA). (gr. 5 up). pap. 2.25 o.p. (*0-06-447154-3*, Harper Trophy); 1990. 304p. (J). (gr. 3-7). pap. 5.95 o.p. (*0-06-440331-9*, Harper Trophy); 1964. 304p. (J). (gr. 4-7). 15.95 o.p. (*0-06-021910-6*); 1964. 304p. (J). (gr. 4-7). lib. bdg. 15.89 o.p. (*0-06-021911-4*) HarperCollins Children's Bk. Group.

—Harriet the Spy. l.t. ed. 1987. (Illus.). 282p. (J). (gr. 2-6). reprint ed. lib. bdg. 16.95 o.s.i (*1-55736-012-X*, Cornerstone Bks.) Pages, Inc.

—Harriet the Spy. 298p. (J). (gr. 3-5). pap. 5.95 (*0-8072-1535-X*); 1999. pap. 37.00 incl. audio (*0-8072-8069-0*, YA993SP) Random Hse. Audio Publishing Group. (Listening Library).

—Harriet the Spy. (gr. 5-7). 2001. (Illus.). 320p. pap. 5.99 (*0-440-41679-5*, Yearling); 2000. (Illus.). 304p. text 15.95 (*0-385-32783-8*, Delacorte Bks. for Young Readers); 1978. 304p. (YA). mass mkt. 1.50 o.s.i (*0-440-93447-8*, Laurel Leaf) Random Hse. Children's Bks.

—Harriet the Spy. 1964. (J). 10.05 o.p. (*0-606-03426-9*) Turtleback Bks.

—Harriet the Spy: The Long Secret. 1999. (J). (gr. 3-7). pap. o.p. (*0-06-449363-6*) HarperCollins Pubs.

—Sport. 1980. 224p. (J). (gr. 7 up). mass mkt. 3.25 o.s.i (*0-440-98350-9*, Laurel Leaf) Random Hse. Children's Bks.

Ford, Barbara. The Eagles' Child. 1990. 160p. (J). (gr. 3-7). lib. bdg. 13.95 o.p. (*0-02-735405-9*, Simon & Schuster Children's Publishing) Simon & Schuster Children's Publishing.

Fox, Paula. Monkey Island. (American Library Association Notable Bks.). 1993. 160p. (YA). (gr. 5-9). pap. text 5.50 (*0-440-40770-2*); 1992. pap. o.p. (*0-440-80344-6*) Dell Publishing.

—Monkey Island. 1991. 160p. (YA). (gr. 4-7). lib. bdg. 16.99 (*0-531-08562-7*); (gr. 5 up). pap. 15.95 (*0-531-05962-6*) Scholastic, Inc. (Orchard Bks.).

—Monkey Island. 1991. 11.55 (*0-606-02756-4*) Turtleback Bks.

Frank, Lucy. I Am an Artichoke. 1995. 192p. (J). (gr. 7 up). tchr. ed. 14.95 o.p. (*0-8234-1150-8*) Holiday Hse., Inc.

—Just Ask Iris. (Illus.). 224p. (J). 2003. pap. 4.99 (*0-689-84454-9*, Aladdin); 2001. (gr. 5-9). 17.00 (*0-689-84406-9*, Atheneum/Richard Jackson Bks.) Simon & Schuster Children's Publishing.

—Will You Be My Brussels Sprout? 1996. 160p. (YA). (gr. 7-12). tchr. ed. 15.95 (*0-8234-1220-2*) Holiday Hse., Inc.

French, Fiona. Snow White in New York. 1990. (Illus.). 32p. (YA). (gr. 2 up). pap. 8.95 (*0-19-272210-7*) Oxford Univ. Pr., Inc.

Freymann-Weyr, Garret. When I Was Older. 2000. (Illus.). 176p. (YA). (gr. 5-9). tchr. ed. 15.00 (*0-618-05545-2*) Houghton Mifflin Co. Trade & Reference Div.

—When I Was Older. 2002. 176p. (J). pap. 5.99 (*0-14-230093-4*, Puffin Bks.) Penguin Putnam Bks. for Young Readers.

Gaeddert, Lou Ann. Noisy Nancy & Nick. 1970. (ps-3). lib. bdg. 8.95 o.p. (*0-385-01542-9*) Doubleday Publishing.

Giff, Patricia Reilly. Advent: Molly Maguire, No. 2. 1999. (J). pap. 12.95 (*0-670-81410-5*, Viking Children's Bks.) Penguin Putnam Bks. for Young Readers.

—Advent: Molly Maguire, No. 1. 1989. 320p. (J). (ps-2). 12.95 o.p. (*0-670-81409-1*) Viking Penguin.

—Good Dog, Bonita. 1998. (Friends & Amigos Ser.: No. 5). (ENG & SPA., Illus.). 86p. (J). (gr. 3 up). lib. bdg. 22.60 (*0-8368-2053-3*) Stevens, Gareth Inc.

—Next Stop, New York City! 1997. (Polk Street Special Ser.). 10.04 (*0-606-11682-6*) Turtleback Bks.

Going, Kelly. Fat Kid Rules the World. 2003. 192p. (YA). 17.99 (*0-399-23990-1*, G. P. Putnam's Sons) Penguin Putnam Bks. for Young Readers.

Gonzalez, Gloria. Gaucho. 1977. (Illus.). (J). (gr. 4-7). 5.95 o.p. (*0-394-83389-9*, Knopf Bks. for Young Readers) Random Hse. Children's Bks.

Gray, Genevieve. The Dark Side of Nowhere. 1977. (Time of Danger, Time for Courage Ser.). (Illus.). (J). (gr. 3-9). pap. 3.95 o.p. (*0-88436-391-0*, 35298) Paradigm Publishing, Inc.

Gray, Luli. Falcon & the Charles Street Witch. 2002. 144p. (J). (gr. 5-9). 15.00 (*0-618-16410-3*) Houghton Mifflin Co.

—Falcon's Egg. 1997. 144p. (J). (gr. 3-6). pap. text 4.50 o.s.i (*0-440-41247-1*) Dell Publishing.

—Falcon's Egg. 1995. 144p. (J). (gr. 4-6). tchr. ed. 16.00 (*0-395-71128-2*) Houghton Mifflin Co.

—Falcon's Egg. 1997. 10.55 (*0-606-11311-8*) Turtleback Bks.

Greenberg, Jan. Just the Two of Us, RS. 128p. (J). (gr. 4-7). 1991. pap. 3.95 o.p. (*0-374-43982-6*, Sunburst); 1988. 14.00 o.p. (*0-374-36198-3*, Farrar, Straus & Giroux (BYR)) Farrar, Straus & Giroux.

Greene, Constance C. Al(exandra) the Great. 1983. 144p. (J). (gr. 5-9). pap. 2.95 o.s.i (*0-440-40350-2*, Yearling) Random Hse. Children's Bks.

—I & Sproggy. 1978. (Illus.). (J). (gr. 3-7). 11.50 o.p. (*0-670-38980-3*, Viking Children's Bks.) Penguin Putnam Bks. for Young Readers.

Greenwald, Sheila. My Fabulous New Life. 1993. (Illus.). (gr. 3-7). 176p. (J). pap. 3.95 o.s.i (*0-15-276716-9*); 128p. (YA). 10.95 o.s.i (*0-15-277693-1*) Harcourt Children's Bks.

—Stucksville. 2001. (Illus.). 112p. (J). (gr. 2-6). pap. 15.95 o.p. (*0-7894-2675-7*) Dorling Kindersley Publishing, Inc.

—Valentine Rosy. 1984. (Illus.). 89p. (J). (gr. 4 up). 11.95 o.s.i (*0-316-32708-5*, Joy Street Bks.) Little Brown & Co.

Griffin, Adele. The Other Shepards. 1998. (J). (gr. 4-9). 224p. 14.95 (*0-7868-0423-8*); 218p. lib. bdg. 15.49 (*0-7868-2370-4*) Disney Pr.

—The Other Shepards. 1999. 224p. (J). (gr. 5-9). pap. 5.99 (*0-7868-1333-4*) Hyperion Bks. for Children.

—The Other Shepards. l.t. ed. 2000. (Illus.). 209p. (J). (gr. 4-7). 20.95 (*0-7862-2914-4*) Thorndike Pr.

—The Other Shepards. 1999. 12.04 (*0-606-17144-4*) Turtleback Bks.

Grimes, Nikki. Bronx Masquerade. 176p. (J). 2003. pap. 5.99 (*0-14-250189-1*, Puffin Bks.); 2001. (Illus.). (gr. 8 up). 16.99 (*0-8037-2569-8*, Dial Bks. for Young Readers) Penguin Putnam Bks. for Young Readers.

Gutman, Anne. Lisa in New York. 2002. (Illus.). 32p. (J). (gr. k-3). 9.95 (*0-375-81119-2*, Knopf Bks. for Young Readers) Random Hse. Children's Bks.

Guy, Rosa. Paris, Pee Wee & Big Dog. 1988. 112p. (J). (gr. 3 up). pap. 2.95 o.s.i (*0-440-40072-4*) Dell Publishing.

Hall, Bruce Edward. Henry & the Kite Dragon. Low, William, tr. & illus. by. 2004. (J). 15.99 (*0-399-23727-5*, Philomel) Penguin Putnam Bks. for Young Readers.

Hall, Margaret. Sebastian in Central Park. 2001. (Suitcase Bear Adventures Ser.: Vol. 1). (Illus.). (J). (*0-9713174-0-2*, Bear & Co.) Bear & Co.

Hamilton, Virginia. Bluish: A Novel. (gr. 4-6). 2002. 128p. (J). mass mkt. 4.99 (*0-439-36786-7*, Scholastic Paperbacks); 1999. 127p. (YA). pap. 15.95 (*0-590-28879-2*, Blue Sky Pr., The) Scholastic, Inc.

—The Planet of Junior Brown. 1998. (J). pap. 4.50 (*0-87628-347-4*) Ctr. for Applied Research in Education, The.

—The Planet of Junior Brown. l.t. unabr. ed. 1988. 400p. (YA). (gr. 5 up). 13.95 o.p. (*0-8161-4642-X*, Macmillan Reference USA) Gale Group.

—The Planet of Junior Brown. 240p. 2002. (J). E-Book 6.99 (*0-689-84805-6*, Simon & Schuster Children's Publishing); 1971. (YA). (gr. 5-9). 18.00 (*0-02-742510-X*, Simon & Schuster Children's Publishing); 2nd ed. 1993. (YA). (gr. 5-9). reprint ed. mass mkt. 4.99 (*0-689-71721-0*, Simon Pulse); 3rd ed. 1986. (Illus.). (YA). (gr. 5-9). mass mkt. 4.99 (*0-02-043540-1*, Simon Pulse) Simon & Schuster Children's Publishing.

—The Planet of Junior Brown. 1993. (YA). 11.04 (*0-606-05975-X*) Turtleback Bks.

Hansen, Joyce. Home Boy. 1994. (YA). pap. 4.95 o.p. (*0-395-69625-9*); 1982. 160p. (J). (gr. 6 up). 13.95 o.p. (*0-89919-114-2*) Houghton Mifflin Co. Trade & Reference Div. (Clarion Bks.).

—Home Boy. 1982. 10.05 o.p. (*0-606-06466-4*) Turtleback Bks.

Heilbrun, Robert. Offer of Proof. 2003. 304p. 24.95 (*0-06-053812-0*, Morrow, William & Co.) Morrow/Avon.

Herold, Maggie R. A Very Important Day. 1995. (Illus.). 40p. (J). (ps-3). 16.99 (*0-688-13065-8*) HarperCollins Children's Bk. Group.

—A Very Important Day. 1995. (Illus.). 40p. (J). (ps-3). 15.89 o.p. (*0-688-13066-6*, Morrow, William & Co.) Morrow/Avon.

Hest, Amy. Gabby Growing Up. 1998. (Illus.). 32p. (J). (gr. k-3). 16.00 (*0-689-80573-X*, Simon & Schuster Children's Publishing) Simon & Schuster Children's Publishing.

—Love You, Soldier. 1993. 4p. (J). (gr. 4-7). pap. 4.99 o.p. (*0-14-036174-X*, Puffin Bks.) Penguin Putnam Bks. for Young Readers.

—Love You, Soldier. 1991. 48p. (J). (gr. 2-5). text 13.95 o.p. (*0-02-743635-7*, Simon & Schuster Children's Publishing) Simon & Schuster Children's Publishing.

—Love You, Soldier. 1993. 11.14 (*0-606-02730-0*) Turtleback Bks.

—Weekend Girl. 1993. (Illus.). 32p. (J). (gr. k up). lib. bdg. 14.93 o.p. (*0-688-09690-5*, Morrow, William & Co.) Morrow/Avon.

Hest, Amy & Lamut, Sonja. Love You, Soldier. 2000. (Illus.). 80p. (J). (gr. 3-7). 14.99 o.s.i (*0-7636-0943-9*) Candlewick Pr.

Heyes, Eileen. O'Dwyer & Grady Starring in Acting Innocents. 2002. 176p. (J). (gr. 4-7). pap. 4.99 (*0-689-84911-7*, Aladdin) Simon & Schuster Children's Publishing.

Hildick, E. Wallace. Manhattan Is Missing. 1969. (gr. 4-7). 4.95 o.p. (*0-385-02776-1*); lib. bdg. o.p. (*0-385-03095-9*) Doubleday Publishing.

Hiller, B. B. Teenage Mutant Ninja Turtles. 1990. 96p. (J). pap. 2.95 o.s.i (*0-440-40322-7*) Dell Publishing.

—Teenage Mutant Ninja Turtles II: The Secret of the Ooze. 1991. (Teenage Mutant Ninja Turtles Ser.: No. 2). 112p. (J). (gr. 4-7). pap. 3.50 o.s.i (*0-440-40451-7*) Dell Publishing.

Holland, Isabelle. Paperboy. 1999. 144p. (J). (gr. 3-7). tchr. ed. 15.95 (*0-8234-1422-1*) Holiday Hse., Inc.

Holt, Rinehart and Winston Staff. Wish You Well. 3rd ed. 2002. pap. text, stu. ed. 13.20 (*0-03-068009-3*) Holt, Rinehart & Winston.

—Wish You Well: With Connections. 3rd ed. 2002. text 14.64 (*0-03-068008-5*) Holt, Rinehart & Winston.

Hope, Laura Lee. The Bobbsey Twins' Search in the Great City. 1930. (Bobbsey Twins Ser.). (J). (gr. 3-6). 4.50 o.s.i (*0-448-08009-5*, Grosset & Dunlap) Penguin Putnam Bks. for Young Readers.

Hopper, Nancy J. Cassandra Live at Carnegie Hall! 1998. 160p. (J). (gr. 5-8). 15.99 o.s.i (*0-8037-2329-6*, Dial Bks. for Young Readers) Penguin Putnam Bks. for Young Readers.

Howe, Fanny. Radio City. 1984. 128p. (YA). (gr. 7 up). pap. 2.25 o.p. (*0-380-86025-2*, 86025, Avon Bks.) Morrow/Avon.

Hunt, Angela Elwell. Star Light, Star Bright. 1993. (Cassie Perkins Ser.: Vol. 7). (YA). pap. 4.99 o.p. (*0-8423-1117-3*) Tyndale Hse. Pubs.

—Star Light, Star Bright. 2000. (Cassie Perkins Ser.: Vol. 7). 180p. (gr. 4-7). pap. 11.95 (*0-595-08996-8*, Backinprint.com) iUniverse, Inc.

Hurwitz, Johanna. Ali Baba Bernstein, Lost & Found. 1992. (Illus.). 96p. (J). (gr. 3-7). 13.93 o.p. (*0-688-11455-5*, Morrow, William & Co.) Morrow/Avon.

—Ali Baba Bernstein, Lost & Found. 1995. 8.70 o.p. (*0-606-07180-6*) Turtleback Bks.

—Busybody Nora. (Illus.). 64p. (J). 1976. (gr. 1-5). lib. bdg. 11.88 o.p. (*0-688-32057-0*); 1990. (ps up). 15.00 o.p. (*0-688-09092-3*); 1990. (ps up). lib. bdg. 15.93 o.p. (*0-688-09093-1*) Morrow/Avon. (Morrow, William & Co.).

—Busybody Nora. 1991. (Illus.). 64p. (J). (gr. 2-5). pap. 3.99 o.s.i (*0-14-034592-2*, Puffin Bks.) Penguin Putnam Bks. for Young Readers.

—Busybody Nora. 1982. (Illus.). 64p. (J). (gr. 1-5). pap. 1.50 o.s.i (*0-440-41019-3*, Yearling) Random Hse. Children's Bks.

—Busybody Nora. 1991. (J). 9.19 o.p. (*0-606-04621-6*) Turtleback Bks.

—Dear Emma. 2002. (Illus.). 160p. (J). (ps-3). lib. bdg. 17.89 (*0-06-029841-3*) HarperCollins Children's Bk. Group.

—Lexi's Tale. (Park Pals Adventure Ser.). (Illus.). 112p. (J). (gr. 2-5). 2002. pap. 3.95 (*1-58717-160-0*); 2001. 14.95 (*1-58717-091-4*) SeaStar Bks.

—New Neighbors for Nora. 2001. (Riverside Kids Ser.). (Illus.). 96p. (J). (gr. 1-8). pap. 4.25 (*0-06-442169-4*, Harper Trophy) HarperCollins Children's Bk. Group.

—New Neighbors for Nora. 1979. (Illus.). 80p. (J). (gr. k-3). 11.95 o.p. (*0-688-22173-4*, Morrow, William & Co.) Morrow/Avon.

—Pee Wee & Plush. 2002. (Park Pals Adventure Ser.). (Illus.). 144p. (J). (gr. 2-5). 14.95 (*1-58717-191-0*) SeaStar Bks.

—Pee-Wee's Tale. (Park Pals Adventure Ser.). (Illus.). (J). 2001. 112p. (gr. 2-5). pap. 3.95 (*1-58717-111-2*); 2000. 104p. pap. 14.95 (*1-58717-028-0*) SeaStar Bks.

Jackson, Jesse. Tessie. 1969. (Illus.). (gr. 2-8). pap. 1.50 o.p. (*0-440-48624-6*) Dell Publishing.

—Tessie. 1968. (Illus.). (J). (gr. 6 up). lib. bdg. 8.79 o.p. (*0-06-022802-4*) HarperCollins Pubs.

James, Henry. Washington Square. unabr. ed. 1970. (Classics Ser.). (YA). (gr. 10 up). mass mkt. 1.50 o.p. (*0-8049-0210-0*, CL-210) Airmont Publishing Co., Inc.

—Washington Square. 1880. 270p. (YA). reprint ed. pap. text 28.00 (*1-4047-3377-9*) Classic Textbooks.

—Washington Square, Level 2. 1999. 144p. (J). pap. 7.66 (*0-582-40162-3*) Longman Publishing Group.

—Washington Square, Level 4. Hedge, Tricia, ed. 2000. (Bookworms Ser.). (Illus.). 96p. (YA). pap. text 5.95 (*0-19-423052-X*) Oxford Univ. Pr., Inc.

—Washington Square. 2001. (Washington Square Press Enriched Classic Ser.). (Illus.). (J). 13.04 (*0-606-21510-7*) Turtleback Bks.

Jane, Pamela. Winky Blue Goes Wild! 2003. (J). 64p. 13.95 (*1-59034-588-6*); pap. (*1-59034-589-4*) Mondo Publishing.

Jocelyn, Marthe. Earthly Astonishments. (J). 2000. 192p. (gr. 3-7). 15.99 o.p. (*0-525-46263-5*, Dutton); 2nd ed. 2001. (Illus.). 15.99 o.p. (*0-525-46496-4*, Dutton Children's Bks.) Penguin Putnam Bks. for Young Readers.

—The Invisible Day. (Illus.). 144p. (gr. 3-7). 1997. (J). 15.99 o.s.i (*0-525-45908-1*, Dutton Children's Bks.); Vol. 1. 1999. pap. 4.99 o.s.i (*0-14-130641-6*, Puffin Bks.) Penguin Putnam Bks. for Young Readers.

—The Invisible Day. (J). (gr. 3-7). 1997. 144p. 14.99 o.p. (*0-88776-412-6*); 1999. (Illus.). 160p. reprint ed. pap. 6.99 (*0-88776-477-0*) Tundra Bks. of Northern New York.

—The Invisible Day. 1999. (Illus.). (J). 11.04 (*0-606-18413-9*) Turtleback Bks.

—The Invisible Enemy. 2002. (Illus.). 144p. (J). (gr. 3-7). 15.99 (*0-525-46831-5*, Dutton Children's Bks.) Penguin Putnam Bks. for Young Readers.

Jones, Chuck, illus. & adapted by. The Cricket in Times Square. 1984. (Chester Cricket Ser.). 48p. (J). (gr. 3-6). 5.95 o.p. (*0-8249-8074-3*) Ideals Pubns.

Jones, Elizabeth McDavid. Secrets on 26th Street. 1999. (American Girl Collection: Bk. 5). (Illus.). 160p. (YA). (gr. 5 up). pap. 5.95 (*1-56247-760-9*); 9.95 (*1-56247-816-8*) Pleasant Co. Pubns. (American Girl).

—Secrets on 26th Street. 1999. (American Girl Collection Ser.). 12.00 (*0-606-17519-9*) Turtleback Bks.

Joosse, Barbara M. The Morning Chair. 1995. (Illus.). 32p. (J). (ps-3). tchr. ed. 14.95 o.p. (*0-395-62337-5*, Clarion Bks.) Houghton Mifflin Co. Trade & Reference Div.

Kalman, Maira. Next Stop, Grand Central. 1999. (Illus.). 32p. (YA). (gr. k-3). 16.99 (*0-399-22926-4*) Penguin Group (USA) Inc.

Kaplow, Robert. Two in the City, 001. 1979. (J). 6.95 o.p. (*0-395-27813-9*) Houghton Mifflin Co.

Karlins, Mark. Music over Manhattan. 1999. (Illus.). 32p. (ps-3). pap. 6.99 o.s.i (*0-440-41187-4*, Dell Books for Young Readers) Random Hse. Children's Bks.

—Music over Manhattan. 1999. 13.14 (*0-606-16712-9*) Turtleback Bks.

Karr, Kathleen. The Boxer, RS. 2000. (Illus.). 144p. (YA). (gr. 7 up). 16.00 (*0-374-30921-3*, Farrar, Straus & Giroux (BYR)) Farrar, Straus & Giroux.

Klein, Norma. A Honey of a Chimp. 1980. (J). (gr. 3-7). 6.95 o.p. (*0-394-84412-2*, Pantheon) Knopf Publishing Group.

—A Honey of a Chimp. 1983. (J). (gr. 5-7). pap. (*0-671-49614-X*, Simon Pulse) Simon & Schuster Children's Publishing.

—Snapshots. 1986. 128p. (J). mass mkt. 2.50 o.s.i (*0-449-70157-3*, Fawcett) Ballantine Bks.

—Snapshots. 1984. (J). (gr. 7 up). 12.95 o.p. (*0-8037-0129-2*, 01258-370, Dial Bks. for Young Readers) Penguin Putnam Bks. for Young Readers.

Konigsburg, E. L. Amy Elizabeth Explores Bloomingdale's. 1992. (Illus.). 32p. (J). (ps-3). 14.95 (*0-689-31766-2*, Atheneum) Simon & Schuster Children's Publishing.

—Amy Elizabeth Explores Bloomingdale's. 1999. 12.14 (*0-606-17201-7*) Turtleback Bks.

—From the Mixed-Up Files of Mrs. Basil E. Frankweiler. 1998. (Illus.). 168p. (J). (gr. 3-7). pap. 5.99 (*0-689-71181-6*, Aladdin) Simon & Schuster Children's Publishing.

Korman, Gordon. Invasion of the Nose Pickers. 2001. (L.A.F. Ser.). (Illus.). 144p. (J). (gr. 4-7). pap. 4.99 (*0-7868-1447-0*) Hyperion Bks. for Children.

—Invasion of the Nose Pickers. 2000. (L.A.F. Bks.). (Illus.). 138p. (J). (gr. 2-6). lib. bdg. 14.49 (*0-7868-2590-1*) Hyperion Paperbacks for Children.

Kovalski, Maryann. Jingle Bells. 1988. (Illus.). 32p. (J). (ps-3). 12.95 o.p. (*0-316-50258-8*) Little Brown & Co.

Krakauer, Hoong Y. One Chinese Dragon in New York City. 1996. (J). (*0-316-50323-1*) Little Brown & Co.

Krulik, Nancy E. The First Cut. 2001. (Illus.). 140p. (J). (gr. 7-12). mass mkt. 5.99 o.p. (*0-448-42580-7*, Grosset & Dunlap) Penguin Putnam Bks. for Young Readers.

—In the Spotlight. 2001. (Illus.). 153p. (J). (gr. 7 up). mass mkt. 5.99 o.p. (*0-448-42583-1*, Grosset & Dunlap) Penguin Putnam Bks. for Young Readers.

—Sneaking Around. 2001. (Illus.). 157p. (J). (gr. 7 up). mass mkt. 5.99 o.p. (*0-448-42581-5*, Grosset & Dunlap) Penguin Putnam Bks. for Young Readers.

—Spring Fever, Vol. 3. 2001. (Illus.). 128p. (J). (gr. 7 up). mass mkt. 5.99 o.p. (*0-448-42582-3*, Grosset & Dunlap) Penguin Putnam Bks. for Young Readers.

Krupinski, Loretta. Christmas in the City. 2002. (Illus.). 44p. (J). (ps-3). 15.99 (*0-7868-0834-9*) Time Warner Bk. Group.

Krupinski, Loretta. Away in a Manger in New York City. 2002. (Illus.). 32p. (J). (gr. k-2). 16.49 (*0-7868-2652-5*) Time Warner Bk. Group.

Kushner, Ellen. Statue of Liberty Adventure. 1986. (Choose Your Own Adventure Ser.: No. 58). (J). (gr. 4-8). pap. 2.25 o.s.i (*0-553-25813-3*); 128p. pap. 2.75 o.s.i (*0-553-28176-3*) Bantam Bks.

LaBate, Jim. Mickey Mantle Day in Amsterdam: Another Novella by Jim LaBate. 1999. (Illus.). 61p. (YA). (gr. 7-12). pap. 7.95 (*0-9662100-7-7*) Mohawk River Pr.

Lakin, Pat. Subway Sonata. 2001. (Illus.). 32p. (J). (gr. k-4). 22.90 (*0-7613-1464-4*) Millbrook Pr., Inc.

Lakin, Patricia. Fat Chance Thanksgiving. 2001. (Illus.). 32p. (J). (gr. 2-5). lib. bdg. 14.95 (*0-8075-2288-0*) Whitman, Albert & Co.

Landis, J. D. Daddy's Girl. 1984. 208p. (J). (gr. 7 up). 11.95 o.p. (*0-688-02763-6*, Morrow, William & Co.) Morrow/Avon.

—Daddy's Girl. 1985. (YA). (gr. 8 up). pap. (*0-671-55823-4*, Simon Pulse) Simon & Schuster Children's Publishing.

Laser, Michael. 6-321. 2001. 144p. (J). (gr. 5). 15.00 (*0-689-83372-5*, Atheneum) Simon & Schuster Children's Publishing.

Lasky, Kathryn. Hope in My Heart. 2003. (My America Ser.). 112p. (J). mass mkt. 4.99 (*0-439-44962-6*) Scholastic, Inc.

Lauber, Patricia. Clarence Goes to Town. 1967. (Gateway Bks.). (Illus.). (J). (gr. 3-5). lib. bdg. 5.99 o.p. (*0-394-90145-2*, Random Hse. Bks. for Young Readers) Random Hse. Children's Bks.

Lebowitz, Fran. Mr. Chas & Lisa Sue Meet the Pandas. 1994. (Illus.). 72p. (J). (gr. 2-7). 15.00 o.s.i (*0-679-86052-5*, Knopf Bks. for Young Readers) Random Hse. Children's Bks.

Lehman, Yvonne. Picture Perfect. 1997. (White Dove Romances Ser.: No. 4). 176p. (J). (gr. 7-12). mass mkt. 4.99 o.p. (*1-55661-708-9*) Bethany Hse. Pubs.

Lehrman, Robert. Separations. 1993. 224p. (J). (gr. 5-9). pap. 3.99 o.p. (*0-14-032322-8*, Puffin Bks.) Penguin Putnam Bks. for Young Readers.

Leppard, Lois Gladys. Mandie & Jonathan's Predicament. 1997. (Mandie Bks.: No. 28). 176p. (J). (gr. 3-9). pap. 4.99 (*1-55661-555-8*) Bethany Hse. Pubs.

—Mandie & Jonathan's Predicament. 1998. (Mandie Bks.: No. 28). (J). (gr. 4-7). 11.04 (*0-606-18915-7*) Turtleback Bks.

LeRoy, Gen. Emma's Dilemma. 1975. (Illus.). (J). (gr. 5 up). pap. 1.50 o.p. (*0-06-440078-6*) HarperCollins Pubs.

Levine, Gail Carson. Dave at Night. 288p. (J). 2001. (gr. 3-7). pap. 5.99 (*0-06-440747-0*, Harper Trophy); 1999. (Illus.). (gr. k-3). lib. bdg. 16.89 (*0-06-028154-5*); 1999. (gr. k-4). 16.99 (*0-06-028153-7*) HarperCollins Children's Bk. Group.

—Dave at Night. unabr. ed. 2001. 278p. (J). (gr. 4-6). pap. 37.00 incl. audio (*0-8072-8379-7*, YA174SP, Listening Library) Random Hse. Audio Publishing Group.

—Dave at Night. (YA). 1999. pap., stu. ed. 69.95 incl. audio (*0-7887-3794-5*, 41038); 2001. (gr. 5-8). audio compact disk 58.00 Recorded Bks., LLC.

—Dave at Night. l.t. ed. 2001. (Illus.). 295p. (J). (gr. 4-7). 22.95 (*0-7862-2972-1*) Thorndike Pr.

Levoy, Myron. Kelly 'n' Me. 1992. (Charlotte Zolotow Bk.). 208p. (YA). (gr. 7 up). 15.00 (*0-06-020838-4*); lib. bdg. 14.89 o.p. (*0-06-020839-2*) HarperCollins Children's Bk. Group.

—Kelly 'n' Me. 2000. 202p. (gr. 7-12). pap. 13.95 (*0-595-09356-6*) iUniverse, Inc.

—The Witch of Fourth Street & Other Stories. 1972. (Illus.). 128p. (J). (gr. 4-7). o.p. (*0-06-023795-3*); lib. bdg. 5.79 o.p. (*0-06-023796-1*) HarperCollins Children's Bk. Group.

Levy, Elizabeth. Gorgonzola Zombies in the Park. 1993. (Illus.). 96p. (J). (gr. 2-5). 14.00 o.p. (*0-06-021461-9*); lib. bdg. 14.89 o.p. (*0-06-021460-0*) HarperCollins Children's Bk. Group.

—Vampire State Building. 2002. (Illus.). 112p. (J). lib. bdg. 16.89 (*0-06-000053-8*); (gr. 2-5). 14.99 (*0-06-000054-6*) HarperCollins Pubs.

Lewiton, Mina. Candita's Choice. 1959. (Illus.). (J). (gr. 3-6). lib. bdg. 8.79 o.p. (*0-06-023821-6*) HarperCollins Pubs.

—Rachel. 1954. (Illus.). (gr. 4-6). lib. bdg. 3.90 o.p. (*0-531-01908-X*, Watts, Franklin) Scholastic Library Publishing.

—That Bad Carlos. 1964. (Illus.). (J). (gr. 2-6). lib. bdg. 8.79 o.p. (*0-06-023846-1*) HarperCollins Pubs.

Ling, Bettina. The Big City. 1999. (Scholastic At-Home Phonics Reading Program Ser.: Vol. 32). (Illus.). 24p. (J). (*0-590-68780-8*) Scholastic, Inc.

Lipsyte, Robert. The Brave. (Charlotte Zolotow Bk.). (gr. 7 up). 1993. 240p. (J). pap. 5.99 (*0-06-447079-2*, Harper Trophy); 1991. 208p. (YA). 15.00 o.p. (*0-06-023915-8*); 1991. 208p. (YA). lib. bdg. 14.89 o.p. (*0-06-023916-6*) HarperCollins Children's Bk. Group.

—Brave. 1993. (J). 11.00 (*0-606-02539-1*) Turtleback Bks.

Locker, Thomas. In Blue Mountains: An Artist's Return to America's First Wilderness. 2000. (Illus.). 32p. (J). (ps-3). 18.00 (*0-88010-471-6*, Bell Pond Bks.) SteinerBooks, Inc.

Low, William. Chinatown, ERS. 1997. (Illus.). 32p. (J). (ps-3). 16.95 (*0-8050-4214-8*, Holt, Henry & Co. Bks. For Young Readers) Holt, Henry & Co.

Luna, Rachel Nickerson. Darinka, the Little Artist Deer. 1999. (Illus.). 36p. (J). (gr. 3-4). 12.95 (*1-886551-06-5*) Howard, Emma Bks.

Lundell, Margo & Terhune, Albert Pason. Lad, a Dog: Lad Is Lost. 1997. (Lad a Dog Ser.). (Illus.). 48p. (J). (gr. 2-4). mass mkt. 3.99 (*0-590-92978-X*) Scholastic, Inc.

Machlin, Mikki. My Name Is Not Gussie. 1999. (Illus.). 32p. (J). (ps-3). lib. bdg., tchr. ed. 16.00 (*0-395-95646-3*) Houghton Mifflin Co.

Mack, Tracy. Birdland. 2003. 224p. (J). pap. 16.95 (*0-439-53590-5*) Scholastic, Inc.

Mackler, Carolyn. The Earth, My Butt, & Other Big, Round Things. 2003. (Illus.). 256p. (YA). 15.99 (*0-7636-1958-2*) Candlewick Pr.

Maizlish, Lisa. The Ring. 1996. (Illus.). 24p. (J). (ps-3). 15.00 (*0-688-14217-6*, Greenwillow Bks.) HarperCollins Children's Bk. Group.

Mak, Kam. Chinatown. Date not set. 32p. (J). (gr. k-3). pap. 5.99 (*0-06-443732-9*) HarperCollins Pubs.

—My Chinatown: One Year in Poems. 2001. (Illus.). 32p. (J). (gr. 2-4). 16.99 (*0-06-029190-7*); lib. bdg. 17.89 (*0-06-029191-5*) HarperCollins Children's Bk. Group.

Maloney, Peter. Redbird at Rockefeller Center. 1997. (Illus.). 32p. (J). (ps-3). 14.89 o.p. (*0-8037-2257-5*, Dial Bks. for Young Readers) Penguin Putnam Bks. for Young Readers.

Mancini, Kitty. Goatina Goes to New York. 1999. (Illus.). 72p. (J). (gr. k-3). pap. 10.00 (*0-9648010-7-8*) Hypertext Publishing Group.

Mango, Karin N. Portrait of Miranda. 1993. (Charlotte Zolotow Bk.). 240p. (YA). (gr. 7 up). 16.00 (*0-06-021777-4*); lib. bdg. 15.89 (*0-06-021778-2*) HarperCollins Children's Bk. Group.

Mann, Peggy. The Street of the Flower Boxes. 1966. (Illus.). (J). (gr. 4-6). 4.49 o.p. (*0-698-30341-5*) Putnam Publishing Group, The.

—When Carlos Closed the Street. 1969. (Illus.). (J). (gr. 3-5). 4.97 o.p. (*0-698-30401-2*) Putnam Publishing Group, The.

Marciano, John Bemelmans. Harold's Tail. 2003. (Illus.). 160p. (J). (gr. 3-6). 15.99 (*0-670-03660-9*, Viking) Viking Penguin.

Marsh, Carole. The Mystery in New York City. (Carole Marsh Mysteries Ser.). (J). pap. 5.95 (*0-635-02099-8*) Gallopade International.

Marsh, Fabienne. The Moralist of the Alphabet Streets. 1991. 252p. (YA). (gr. 10 up). 17.95 o.p. (*0-945575-47-5*) Algonquin Bks. of Chapel Hill.

Martel, Cruz. Yagua Days. 1995. (Illus.). (J). (gr. 3). 8.60 (*0-395-73235-2*) Houghton Mifflin Co.

—Yagua Days. 1987. (Pied Piper Bks.). (Illus.). 40p. (J). (ps-3). 11.89 o.p. (*0-8037-9766-4*); pap. 4.95 o.p. (*0-8037-0457-7*) Penguin Putnam Bks. for Young Readers. (Dial Bks. for Young Readers).

Martin, Ann M. New York, New York! 1991. (Baby-Sitters Club Super Special Ser.: No. 6). 256p. (J). (gr. 3-7). mass mkt. 4.50 (*0-590-43576-0*) Scholastic, Inc.

—New York, New York! 1991. (Baby-Sitters Club Super Special Ser.: No. 6). (J). (gr. 3-7). 10.55 (*0-606-04991-6*) Turtleback Bks.

—Stacey's Mistake. (Baby-Sitters Club Ser.: No. 18). (J). (gr. 3-7). 1996. mass mkt. 3.99 (*0-590-60534-8*); 1988. 192p. mass mkt. 3.99 (*0-590-43718-6*); 1988. pap. 2.75 o.p. (*0-590-41584-0*) Scholastic, Inc.

—Stacey's Mistake. l.t. ed. 1993. (Baby-Sitters Club Ser.: No. 18). 176p. (J). (gr. 3-7). lib. bdg. 19.93 o.p. (*0-8368-1022-8*) Stevens, Gareth Inc.

—Stacey's Mistake. 1987. (Baby-Sitters Club Ser.: No. 18). (J). (gr. 3-7). 10.04 (*0-606-04091-9*) Turtleback Bks.

Marx, David F. See the City Level A. 2001. (Rookie Readers Ser.). (Illus.). 24p. (J). (gr. k-1). lib. bdg. 16.00 (*0-516-22254-6*, Children's Pr.) Scholastic Library Publishing.

Matas, Carol. Rosie in New York City: Gotcha! 2003. (Illus.). 128p. (J). (gr. 3-6). pap. 4.99 (*0-689-85714-4*, Aladdin) Simon & Schuster Children's Publishing.

Mays, Lucinda. The Other Shore. 1979. (J). (gr. 5-10). 8.95 o.p. (*0-689-30717-9*, Atheneum) Simon & Schuster Children's Publishing.

Mazer, Harry. Cave under the City. 1986. 160p. (J). (gr. 3-7). 13.95 o.p. (*0-690-04557-3*); lib. bdg. 13.89 o.p. (*0-690-04559-X*) HarperCollins Children's Bk. Group.

McDonald, Janet. Chill Wind, RS. 2002. 144p. (YA). (gr. 7 up). 16.00 (*0-374-39958-1*, Farrar, Straus & Giroux (BYR)) Farrar, Straus & Giroux.

—Chill Wind. 2003. 165p. (J). 24.95 (*0-7862-5502-1*) Thorndike Pr.

McDonnell, Virginia. Trouble at Mercy Hospital. 1968. (gr. 7-8). 5.95 o.p. (*0-385-08948-1*) Doubleday Publishing.

McGarrahan, Margaret. Nessie's Manhattan Holiday. 2000. (Illus.). 57p. (J). (gr. k-5). pap. 12.50 (*0-9672639-1-3*) Smith Lane Pubs.

McGuigan, Mary Ann. Where You Belong. (J). (gr. 5-9). 1998. 192p. per. 4.50 (*0-689-82318-5*, Simon Pulse); 1997. 176p. 16.95 (*0-689-81250-7*, Atheneum) Simon & Schuster Children's Publishing.

—Where You Belong. 1998. 10.55 (*0-606-15763-8*) Turtleback Bks.

McHargue, Georgess. Stoneflight. 1982. (Illus.). (J). (gr. 3-9). pap. 1.25 o.p. (*0-380-00632-4*, 28514, Avon Bks.) Morrow/Avon.

McKeever, Gracie. Miles to Go. 2000. 180p. (YA). E-Book 4.75 incl. disk (*1-58749-025-0*); E-Book 4.75 (*1-58749-026-9*) Awe-Struck E-Bks. (Byte/Me Book).

McNulty, John. This Place on Third Avenue. 2002. 240p. pap. text 12.50 (*1-58243-213-9*, Counterpoint Pr.) Basic Bks.

Metaxas, Eric & Peck, Everett. Mose the Fireman. 1996. (Illus.). 48p. (J). (ps up). pap. 19.95 o.p. incl. audio (*0-689-80227-7*, Simon & Schuster Children's Publishing) Simon & Schuster Children's Publishing.

Metzger, Lois. Ellen's Case. 1995. 208p. (YA). (gr. 7 up). 16.00 (*0-689-31934-7*, Atheneum) Simon & Schuster Children's Publishing.

Mezek, Karen. Katie Goes to New York. 1991. (Illus.). 58p. (Orig.). (J). (gr. 2-6). pap. 4.99 o.p. (*0-89081-864-9*) Harvest Hse. Pubs.

Mickey's New York Xmas. 2000. (J). 15.99 (*0-7868-3153-7*) Hyperion Bks. for Children.

Miller-Lachmann, Lyn. Hiding Places. 1987. 206p. (Orig.). (YA). (gr. 9-12). pap. 4.95 (*0-938961-00-4*, Stamp Out Sheep Pr.) Square 1 Pubs., Inc.

Mohr, Nicholasa. El Bronx Remembered. 1993. (Trophy Keypoint Bks.). (Illus.). 272p. (J). (gr. 7 up). pap. 5.99 (*0-06-447100-4*, Harper Trophy) HarperCollins Children's Bk. Group.

—El Bronx Remembered: A Novella & Stories. 1975. (J). 11.00 (*0-606-05255-0*) Turtleback Bks.

—In Nueva York. 2nd ed. 1988. 194p. (YA). (gr. 8-12). reprint ed. pap. 10.95 o.p. (*0-934770-78-6*) Arte Publico Pr.

—In Nueva York. 1977. (J). (gr. 7 up). 7.95 o.p. (*0-8037-4044-1*, Dial Bks. for Young Readers) Penguin Putnam Bks. for Young Readers.

—In Nueva York. 1988. 17.00 (*0-606-16041-8*) Turtleback Bks.

Mosher, Richard. The Taxi Navigator. 1996. 144p. (J). (gr. 4-7). 15.95 o.s.i (*0-399-23104-8*, Philomel) Penguin Putnam Bks. for Young Readers.

Moskin, Marietta. Waiting for Mama. 1975. (Illus.). 98p. (J). (gr. 2-6). 7.95 o.p. (*0-698-20319-4*) Putnam Publishing Group, The.

Mundis, Hester. My Chimp Friday: The Nana Banana Chronicles. 2002. (Illus.). 176p. (J). (gr. 4-6). 16.00 (*0-689-83837-9*, Simon & Schuster Children's Publishing) Simon & Schuster Children's Publishing.

Mungin, Horace. Sleepy Willie. Orange, Charlotte, ed. 1991. 128p. (Orig.). (YA). (gr. 8-12). pap. 8.95 (*0-936026-24-3*) R&M Publishing Co.

Munro, Roxie. The Inside-Outside Book of New York City. 1994. (Illus.). 48p. (J). (gr. k-3). pap. 4.99 o.s.i (*0-14-050454-0*, Puffin Bks.) Penguin Putnam Bks. for Young Readers.

Murphy, Barbara Beasley. Tripping the Runner. 2000. 192p. (gr. 4-7). pap. 12.95 (*0-595-15398-4*, Backinprint.com) iUniverse, Inc.

Myers, Walter Dean. Fast Sam, Cool Clyde & Stuff. 1978. (YA). (gr. 7 up). pap. 1.50 o.p. (*0-380-01943-4*, 52761-8, Avon Bks.) Morrow/Avon.

—Fast Sam, Cool Clyde & Stuff. 192p. 1988. (J). (gr. 5-9). pap. 5.99 (*0-14-032613-8*, Puffin Bks.); 1975. (YA). (gr. 7 up). 12.95 o.p. (*0-670-30874-9*, Viking Children's Bks.) Penguin Putnam Bks. for Young Readers.

—Fast Sam, Cool Clyde & Stuff. 1995. (J). 20.25 (*0-8446-6798-6*) Smith, Peter Pub., Inc.

—Fast Sam, Cool Clyde & Stuff. 1975. (J). 11.04 (*0-606-03575-3*) Turtleback Bks.

—Fast Sam, Cool Clyde & Stuff. 1999. 12.40 (*0-8335-0206-9*) Univ. of Oklahoma Pr.

Nathan, Robert. One More Spring. 1981. (Keith Jennison Large Type Bks.). (gr. 6 up). lib. bdg. 7.95 o.p. (*0-531-00255-1*, Watts, Franklin) Scholastic Library Publishing.

Nentwig, Wendy L. Cabs, Cameras & Catastrophes. 2000. (Unmistakably Cooper Ellis Ser.: Vol. 4). 160p. (J). (gr. 7-12). pap. 5.99 o.p. (*0-7642-2068-3*) Bethany Hse. Pubs.

—Moonstruck in Manhattan. 1998. (Unmistakably Cooper Ellis Ser.: Vol. 2). 160p. (J). (gr. 7-12). pap. 5.99 o.p. (*0-7642-2066-7*) Bethany Hse. Pubs.

Neville, Emily. It's Like This, Cat. (Trophy Bk.). (Illus.). 192p. (J). 1975. (gr. 5-9). pap. 5.99 (*0-06-440073-5*, Harper Trophy); 1964. (gr. k-3). lib. bdg. 16.89 (*0-06-024391-0*); 1963. (ps-2). 15.95 (*0-06-024390-2*) HarperCollins Children's Bk. Group.

—It's Like This, Cat. 1999. (J). 9.95 (*1-56137-101-7*) Novel Units, Inc.

—It's Like This, Cat. 1963. (J). 12.00 (*0-606-01732-1*) Turtleback Bks.

Neville, Emily C. Seventeenth-Street Gang. 1966. (Illus.). (J). (gr. 5-7). lib. bdg. 9.89 o.p. (*0-06-024395-3*) HarperCollins Pubs.

Nixon, Joan Lowery. David's Search. 1998. (Orphan Train Children Ser.: No. 4). 144p. (gr. 2-6). text 9.95 o.s.i (*0-385-32296-8*, Delacorte Pr.) Dell Publishing.

Norwich, Billy. Molly & the Magical Dress. 2002. (Illus.). 40p. (J). (ps-3). 16.95 o.p. (*0-385-32745-5*, Doubleday Bks. for Young Readers) Random Hse. Children's Bks.

O'Connor, Ilett. A Born Leader - Our Francine. 2002. 32p. pap. 10.00 (*0-9717003-1-1*) O'Connor, Ilett K.

Odom, Mel. I'll Zap Manhattan. 1999. (Sabrina, the Teenage Witch Ser.: No. 18). 176p. (YA). (gr. 5 up). pap. 4.50 (*0-671-02702-6*, Simon Pulse) Simon & Schuster Children's Publishing.

Orden, J. Hannah. In Real Life. 1990. 224p. (YA). (gr. 7 up). 12.95 o.p. (*0-670-82679-0*, Viking Children's Bks.) Penguin Putnam Bks. for Young Readers.

Orgel, Doris. Crack in the Heart. 1989. (YA). (gr. 7 up). mass mkt. 2.95 o.s.i (*0-449-70204-9*, Fawcett) Ballantine Bks.

Osborne, Mary Pope. New York's Bravest. 2002. (Illus.). 32p. (J). (gr. k-3). 15.95 (*0-375-82196-1*); lib. bdg. 17.99 (*0-375-92196-6*) Random Hse. Children's Bks. (Knopf Bks. for Young Readers).

Palatini, Margie. Ding Dong Ding Dong. 1999. (Illus.). 32p. (J). (ps-3). 15.99 (*0-7868-0420-3*) Disney Pr.

—Ding Dong Ding Dong. 1999. (Illus.). 32p. (J). (ps-3). lib. bdg. 16.49 (*0-7868-2367-4*) Hyperion Pr.

—Mary Had a Little Ham. 2003. (Illus.). 32p. (J). lib. bdg. 16.49 (*0-7868-2491-3*) Hyperion Bks. for Children.

Panetta, George. Sea Beach Express. 1966. (Illus.). (J). (gr. 3-6). lib. bdg. 5.79 o.p. (*0-06-024620-0*) HarperCollins Pubs.

Paraskevas, Betty. On the Day the Tall Ships Sailed. 2000. Orig. Title: Did You See That Eagle?. (Illus.). 32p. (J). (ps-3). 16.00 (*0-689-82864-0*, Simon & Schuster Children's Publishing) Simon & Schuster Children's Publishing.

Pascal, Francine, creator. Escape to New York. 1998. (Sweet Valley University Ser.: No. 41). 240p. (gr. 7 up). mass mkt. 3.99 o.s.i (*0-553-57029-3*, Sweet Valley) Random Hse. Children's Bks.

—Jessica Takes Manhattan. 1997. (Sweet Valley High Super Edition Ser.). 240p. (gr. 7 up). mass mkt. 4.50 o.s.i (*0-553-57001-3*, Sweet Valley) Random Hse. Children's Bks.

Pass, Erica. New York Nightmare! 1998. (Secret World of Alex Mack Ser.: No. 31). 144p. (J). (gr. 4-7). pap. 3.99 (*0-671-01957-0*, Aladdin) Simon & Schuster Children's Publishing.

Peck, Richard. Voices after Midnight. 1989. 192p. (J). (gr. 5-9). 14.95 o.s.i (*0-385-29779-3*, Delacorte Pr.) Dell Publishing.

Pfeffer, Susan Beth. Beth's Story. 2001. (Portraits of Little Women Ser.). (Illus.). (J). 10.55 (*0-606-21063-6*) Turtleback Bks.

—Fantasy Summer. 1984. (Perfect Image Ser.). 192p. (J). (gr. 7 up). 12.95 o.p. (*0-399-21086-5*, G. P. Putnam's Sons) Penguin Putnam Bks. for Young Readers.

Pfeffer, Susan Beth & Alcott, Louisa May. Beth's Story. 1997. (Portraits of Little Women Ser.). 112p. (gr. 3-7). text 9.95 o.s.i (*0-385-32526-6*, Delacorte Pr.) Dell Publishing.

Pinkwater, Jill. Tails of the Bronx. 176p. (J). (gr. 3-7). 1993. pap. 3.95 o.s.i (*0-689-71671-0*, Aladdin); 1991. lib. bdg. 14.95 o.p. (*0-02-774652-6*, Atheneum) Simon & Schuster Children's Publishing.

Pool, Eugene. The Captain of Battery Park. 1978. (Illus.). (J). lib. bdg. 7.95 o.p. (*0-201-05857-X*) Addison-Wesley Longman, Inc.

Priest, Robert. The Old Pirate of Central Park. 1999. (Illus.). 30p. (J). (ps-3). tchr. ed. 16.00 (*0-395-90505-2*) Houghton Mifflin Co.

Provensen, Alice. Punch in New York. (J). 1996. (Illus.). 32p. pap. 4.99 o.p. (*0-14-054067-9*, Puffin Bks.); 1991. 14.95 o.p. (*0-670-82790-8*, Viking Children's Bks.) Penguin Putnam Bks. for Young Readers.

Quackenbush, Robert M. Daughter of Liberty: A True Story of the American Revolution. 1999. 64p. (J). (gr. 2-4). pap. 4.99 (*0-7868-1286-9*) Hyperion Pr.

Queen, Ellery, ed. Redbird at Rockefeller Center. 1997. (Illus.). 32p. (J). (ps-3). 15.99 o.p. (*0-8037-2256-7*, Dial Bks. for Young Readers) Penguin Putnam Bks. for Young Readers.

Quin-Harkin, Janet. Dream Come True, No. 16. 1988. (Sugar & Spice Ser.: No. 16). (YA). (gr. 6 up). mass mkt. 2.95 o.s.i (*0-8041-0334-8*, Ivy Bks.) Ballantine Bks.

Quirk, Anne. Dancing with Great-Aunt Cornelia. 1997. 160p. (J). (gr. 3-7). 14.95 o.p. (*0-06-027332-1*) HarperCollins Children's Bk. Group.

Rael, Elsa Okon. What Zeesie Saw on Delancey Street. (Illus.). 40p. (J). (ps-3). 2000. pap. 6.99 (*0-689-83535-3*, Aladdin); 1996. 16.00 (*0-689-80549-7*, Simon & Schuster Children's Publishing) Simon & Schuster Children's Publishing.

—What Zeesie Saw on Delancey Street. 2000. 12.14 (*0-606-17943-7*) Turtleback Bks.

Raphael, Marie. Streets of Gold. rev. ed. 2001. (Illus.). 224p. (J). (gr. 5 up). pap. 9.95 (*0-89255-256-5*) Persea Bks., Inc.

—Streets of Gold: A Novel. Sena, Jerry, ed. 1998. (Illus.). 216p. (J). (gr. 6-9). per. 7.95 (*1-883088-05-4*) Source Productions, Inc.

Rapin, William. A Penguin in New York. 1984. (Illus.). 29p. (J). (gr. 2 up). 9.95 o.p. (*0-918273-04-8*) Coffee Hse. Pr.

Reilly Giff, Patricia. Next Stop, New York City! The Polk Street Kids on Tour. 1997. (Polk Street Special Ser.: No. 9). (Illus.). 128p. (gr. 1-4). pap. text 3.99 (*0-440-41362-1*) Dell Publishing.

Reiss, Mike. Late for School. 2003. (Illus.). (J). (gr. 1-5). 16.95 (*1-56145-286-6*) Peachtree Pubs., Ltd.

Ringgold, Faith. Cassie's Word Quilt. (Illus.). 32p. (J). 2004. pap. 6.99 (*0-553-11233-3*, Dragonfly Bks.); 2002. lib. bdg. 15.99 (*0-375-91200-2*, Knopf Bks. for Young Readers); 2002. 13.95 (*0-375-81200-8*, Random Hse. Bks. for Young Readers) Random Hse. Children's Bks.

Ritter, John H. Over the Wall. 2002. 320p. pap. 6.99 (*0-698-11931-2*, Puffin Bks.); 2000. (Illus.). 312p. (YA). (gr. 5 up). 17.99 (*0-399-23489-6*, Philomel) Penguin Putnam Bks. for Young Readers.

Roberts, Willo Davis. The Kidnappers. 1998. 144p. (J). (gr. 3-7). 15.00 (*0-689-81394-5*, Atheneum) Simon & Schuster Children's Publishing.

Ronan, Anne M. Muffles in New York. 1999. (Illus.). 32p. (J). (ps-4). pap. 8.00 (*1-930248-00-8*) Polka Dot Pr. Corp., The.

Roth-Hano, Renee. Safe Harbors. 1993. 224p. (YA). (gr. 12 up). 16.95 o.p. (*0-02-777795-2*, Simon & Schuster Children's Publishing) Simon & Schuster Children's Publishing.

Roth, Susan L. It's a Dog's New York. 2001. (Illus.). 32p. (J). (ps-3). 16.95 (*0-7922-7054-1*) National Geographic Society.

Rouillard, Wendy W. Barnaby-Seasons in the Park. Rouillard, Wendy W., ed. 2000. (Barnaby Ser.: Vol. 5). (Illus.). 32p. (J). 15.95 (*0-9642836-9-7*) Barnaby & Co.

Roy, Ron. The Jaguar's Jewel. 2000. (Stepping Stone Book Ser.: No. 10). (Illus.). 96p. (J). (gr. 2-5). lib. bdg. 11.99 (*0-679-99458-0*); pap. 3.99 (*0-679-89458-6*) Random Hse. Children's Bks. (Random Hse. Bks. for Young Readers).

—The Jaguar's Jewel. 2000. (A to Z Mysteries Ser.: No. 10). (Illus.). (J). (gr. k-3). 10.04 (*0-606-18480-5*) Turtleback Bks.

Rush, Ken. Friday's Journey. 1994. (Illus.). 32p. (J). (ps-1). 15.95 o.p. (*0-531-06821-8*); mass mkt. 16.99 o.p. (*0-531-08671-2*) Scholastic, Inc. (Orchard Bks.).

Russo, Marisabina. House of Sports. 2002. 192p. (J). (gr. 3 up). 15.95 (*0-06-623803-X*); lib. bdg. 16.89 (*0-06-623804-8*) HarperCollins Children's Bk. Group. (Greenwillow Bks.).

Rylant, Cynthia. An Angel for Solomon Singer. 1992. (Illus.). 32p. (J). mass mkt. 16.99 o.p. (*0-531-08578-3*); 15.95 o.p. (*0-531-05978-2*) Scholastic, Inc. (Orchard Bks.).

—An Angel for Solomon Singer. 1996. (J). 13.10 (*0-606-10741-X*) Turtleback Bks.

Sachs, Marilyn. Amy & Laura. 1966. (gr. 4-7). lib. bdg. 6.95 o.p. (*0-385-06984-7*) Doubleday Publishing.

—Call Me Ruth. 1995. 224p. (J). (gr. 4-7). pap. 4.95 (*0-688-13737-7*, Harper Trophy) HarperCollins Children's Bk. Group.

—Call Me Ruth. 1996. (J). (gr. 3 up). 18.75 o.p. (*0-8446-6905-9*) Smith, Peter Pub., Inc.

—Call Me Ruth. 1995. 11.00 (*0-606-07333-7*) Turtleback Bks.

Sargent, Dave & Sargent, Pat. Ring (Silver Grullo) Grace & Pride #50. 2001. 36p. (J). pap. (*1-56763-662-4*); lib. bdg. 22.60 (*1-56763-661-6*) Ozark Publishing.

Sattler, Jennifer Gordon. Bella's Saratoga Summer. 2002. (Illus.). (J). (*0-9713069-4-X*); 32p. pap. 10.95 (*0-9713069-3-1*) Burns, Nicholas K. Publishing.

Sawyer, Ruth. Roller Skates. (Puffin Newbery Library). (J). (gr. 4-7). 1986. (Illus.). 176p. pap. 5.99 (*0-14-030358-8*, Puffin Bks.); 1936. 184p. 16.99 (*0-670-60310-4*) Penguin Putnam Bks. for Young Readers.

—Roller Skates. 1923. (Illus.). 192p. (J). (gr. 4-7). pap. 3.50 o.s.i (*0-440-47499-X*, Yearling) Random Hse. Children's Bks.

—Roller Skates. 1988. (J). (gr. 5-7). 18.75 o.p. (*0-8446-6343-3*) Smith, Peter Pub., Inc.

—Roller Skates. 1986. (Puffin Newbery Library). (J). 12.04 (*0-606-04607-0*) Turtleback Bks.

Schade, Susan & Buller, Jon. Hawk Talk. 2002. (Danger Joe Show Ser.: No. 3). (Illus.). 112p. (J). mass mkt. 3.99 (*0-439-40977-2*, Scholastic Paperbacks) Scholastic, Inc.

Schantz, Daniel D. Wheeler's Swap. 1989. (Wheeler's Adventures Ser.). (Illus.). 96p. (J). (gr. 3-6). pap. 4.99 o.p. (*0-87403-573-2*, 3953) Standard Publishing.

Scher, Paula. The Brownstone. 1973. (Illus.). (J). (gr. 1-3). lib. bdg. 5.69 o.p. (*0-394-92487-8*, Pantheon) Knopf Publishing Group.

Scieszka, Jon. Hey Kid, Want to Buy a Bridge? 2004. (Time Warp Trio Ser.). (Illus.). 96p. pap. 4.99 (*0-14-240089-0*, Puffin Bks.) Penguin Putnam Bks. for Young Readers.

—2095 Twt Promo. 2003. (Time Warp Trio Ser.). (Illus.). 76p. pap. 2.66 (*0-14-250128-X*, Puffin Bks.) Penguin Putnam Bks. for Young Readers.

Scrimger, Richard. A Nose for Adventure. 2000. 184p. (J). (gr. 3-7). pap. 7.95 (*0-88776-499-1*) Tundra Bks. of Northern New York.

Seidler, Tor. A Rat's Tale, RS. 187p. 1990. pap. 6.95 o.p. (*0-374-46204-6*, Sunburst); 1986. (Illus.). (J). (gr. 1-8). 16.00 o.p. (*0-374-36185-1*, Farrar, Straus & Giroux (BYR)) Farrar, Straus & Giroux.

—A Rat's Tale. 1999. (Illus.). 192p. (J). (gr. 5 up). pap. 6.95 (*0-06-440779-9*, Harper Trophy) HarperCollins Children's Bk. Group.

—The Revenge of Randal Reese Rat, RS. 2001. (Illus.). 240p. (J). (gr. 3 up). 16.00 (*0-374-36257-2*, Farrar, Straus & Giroux (BYR)) Farrar, Straus & Giroux.

—The Revenge of Randal Reese Rat. 2004. (Illus.). (J). pap. (*0-06-050867-1*, Harper Trophy) HarperCollins Children's Bk. Group.

Selden, George. Chester Cricket's Pigeon Ride, RS. 1981. (Chester Cricket Ser.). (Illus.). 64p. (J). (gr. 3-6). 15.00 o.s.i (*0-374-31239-7*, Farrar, Straus & Giroux (BYR)) Farrar, Straus & Giroux.

—Chester Cricket's Pigeon Ride. 1983. (Chester Cricket Ser.). (Illus.). 80p. (gr. 3-6). pap. text 3.50 o.s.i (*0-440-41389-3*, Yearling) Random Hse. Children's Bks.

—Chester Cricket's Pigeon Ride. 1983. (Chester Cricket Ser.). (J). (gr. 3-6). 9.65 (*0-606-01151-X*) Turtleback Bks.

—The Cricket in Times Square. 1999. (Chester Cricket Ser.). 176p. (gr. 3-6). mass mkt. 2.99 o.s.i (*0-440-22889-1*) Bantam Bks.

—The Cricket in Times Square. (Chester Cricket Ser.). 160p. (J). (gr. 3-6). 1996. mass mkt. 2.49 o.s.i (*0-440-22022-X*); 1993. pap. 1.99 o.s.i (*0-440-21622-2*) Dell Publishing.

—The Cricket in Times Square, RS. 1960. (Chester Cricket Ser.). (Illus.). 144p. (J). (gr. 3-6). 16.00 (*0-374-31650-3*, Farrar, Straus & Giroux (BYR)) Farrar, Straus & Giroux.

—The Cricket in Times Square. 1999. (Chester Cricket Ser.). 32p. (J). (gr. 3-6). 9.95 (*1-56137-396-6*) Novel Units, Inc.

—The Cricket in Times Square. l.t. ed. 1990. (Chester Cricket Ser.). 192p. (J). (gr. 3-6). reprint ed. lib. bdg. 16.95 o.s.i (*1-55736-170-3*, Cornerstone Bks.) Pages, Inc.

—The Cricket in Times Square. (Chester Cricket Ser.). 151p. (J). (gr. 3-6). pap. 5.50 (*0-8072-8311-8*); 2000. pap. 23.00 incl. audio (*0-8072-8310-X*, YA158SP) Random Hse. Audio Publishing Group. (Listening Library).

—The Cricket in Times Square. 1997. (Chester Cricket Ser.). (J). (gr. 3-6). o.s.i (*0-440-70015-9*, Dell Books for Young Readers) Random Hse. Children's Bks.

—The Cricket in Times Square. 1985. (Chester Cricket Ser.). (Illus.). (J). (gr. 3-6). pap. 11.93 o.p. (*0-516-09162-X*, Children's Pr.) Scholastic Library Publishing.

—The Cricket in Times Square. 1960. (Chester Cricket Ser.). (J). (gr. 3-6). 11.55 (*0-606-02883-8*) Turtleback Bks.

—The Cricket in Times Square: All about Animals. 1970. (Chester Cricket Ser.). (Illus.). 160p. (gr. 3-6). pap. text 5.99 (*0-440-41563-2*, Yearling) Random Hse. Children's Bks.

—The Cricket of Time Square. 1988. (Illus.). (J). pap. o.p. (*0-440-80083-8*) Dell Publishing.

—Cricket Time Square. 1996. (J). pap. 6.99 (*0-440-91095-1*, Dell Books for Young Readers) Random Hse. Children's Bks.

—The Genie of Sutton Place, RS. 1973. 192p. (J). (gr. 3 up). 12.95 o.p. (*0-374-32527-8*, Farrar, Straus & Giroux (BYR)) Farrar, Straus & Giroux.

—Un Grillo en Times Square, RS. 1994. (ENG & SPA.). 144p. (J). (gr. 4-7). pap. 5.95 (*0-374-48060-5*, FS5908, Mirasol/Libros Juveniles) Farrar, Straus & Giroux.

—Un Grillo en Times Square. 1994. 13.48 (*0-606-10522-0*) Turtleback Bks.

—Harry Kitten & Tucker Mouse, RS. (Chester Cricket Ser.). (Illus.). 80p. (J). (gr. 3-6). 1986. 16.00 (*0-374-32860-9*, Farrar, Straus & Giroux (BYR)); 2001. reprint ed. pap. 5.95 (*0-374-42895-6*, Sunburst) Farrar, Straus & Giroux.

Shange, Ntozake. Whitewash. 1997. (Illus.). 32p. (J). (gr. 2-5). 15.95 (*0-8027-8490-9*); lib. bdg. 16.85 (*0-8027-8491-7*) Walker & Co.

Shotwell, Louisa R. Magdalena. 1971. (Illus.). (J). (gr. 4-6). 5.95 o.p. (*0-670-44799-4*) Viking Penguin.

Shreve, Susan Richards. Amy Dunn Quits School. 1993. (Illus.). 96p. (J). (gr. 3 up). 13.00 o.p. (*0-688-10320-0*, Morrow, William & Co.) Morrow/Avon.

Shulman, Irving. West Side Story. (Orig.). 1990. 160p. mass mkt. 5.99 (*0-671-72566-1*); 1983. (J). (gr. 8 up). mass mkt. 2.95 (*0-671-50448-7*); 1981. pap. 2.50 o.s.i (*0-671-44142-6*) Simon & Schuster. (Pocket).

Shusterman, Neal. Downsiders. l.t. ed. 2000. 336p. (YA). (gr. 6-12). lib. bdg. 29.95 (*1-58118-071-3*) LRS.

—Downsiders. 256p. 2001. (J). (gr. 8-12). mass mkt. 4.99 (*0-689-83969-3*, Simon Pulse); 1999. (Illus.). (YA). (gr. 5-9). 16.95 (*0-689-80375-3*, Simon & Schuster Children's Publishing) Simon & Schuster Children's Publishing.

—Downsiders. 2001. (YA). 11.04 (*0-606-20637-X*) Turtleback Bks.

Simon, Carly. The Nightime Chauffeur. 1993. (Illus.). (J). 16.00 o.s.i (*0-385-47009-6*) Doubleday Publishing.

Singer, A. L. Sing. 1989. 144p. (J). (gr. 7 up). pap. 2.75 (*0-590-42151-4*) Scholastic, Inc.

Sis, Peter. Madelenka, RS. 2000. (Illus.). 48p. (J). (ps-3). 17.00 (*0-374-39969-7*, Farrar, Straus & Giroux (BYR)) Farrar, Straus & Giroux.

—Madlenka. 2000. (Illus.). 48p. (J). (gr. k-3). 19.95 (*0-88899-412-5*) Groundwood Bks. CAN. *Dist:* Publishers Group West.

Skolsky, Mindy Warshaw. Hannah & the Whistling Tea Kettle. 2000. (Richard Jackson Bks.). (Illus.). 40p. (J). (gr. k-3). pap. 15.95 o.p. (*0-7894-2602-1*) Dorling Kindersley Publishing, Inc.

—The Whistling Teakettle & Other Stories about Hannah. 1977. (Illus.). (J). (gr. 2-5). 10.89 o.p. (*0-06-025688-5*); lib. bdg. 11.89 o.p. (*0-06-025689-3*) HarperCollins Children's Bk. Group.

Slade, Michael. The Horses of Central Park. 1992. 96p. (J). 12.95 o.p. (*0-590-44659-2*) Scholastic, Inc.

Settings

Snyder, Carol. Ike & Mama & Trouble at School. 1983. (Illus.). (J). (gr. 4-7). 9.95 o.s.i (*0-698-20570-7*, Coward-McCann) Putnam Publishing Group, The.

Southgate, Martha. Another Way to Dance. 1996. 192p. (YA). (gr. 7-12). 15.95 o.s.i (*0-385-32191-0*, Delacorte Pr.) Dell Publishing.

—Another Way to Dance. 1998. 208p. (YA). (gr. 7-12). reprint ed. mass mkt. 4.99 o.s.i (*0-440-21968-X*, Laurel Leaf) Random Hse. Children's Bks.

—Another Way to Dance. 1998. 10.55 (*0-606-12878-6*) Turtleback Bks.

Spaziante, Patrick, illus. Look Out! It's Turtle Titan! 2004. (Teenage Mutant Ninja Turtles Ser.). 24p. (J). pap. 3.99 (*0-689-86900-2*, Simon Spotlight) Simon & Schuster Children's Publishing.

—Meet Casey Jones. 2004. (Teenage Mutant Ninja Turtles Ser.). 24p. (J). pap. 3.99 (*0-689-86899-5*, Simon Spotlight) Simon & Schuster Children's Publishing.

Spinner, Stephanie & Weiss, Ellen. Bright Lights, Little Gerbil. 1997. (Weebie Zone Ser.: No. 4). (Illus.). 80p. (J). (gr. 2-4). pap. 3.95 o.p. (*0-06-442067-1*); lib. bdg. 13.89 o.p. (*0-06-027589-8*) HarperCollins Pubs.

Stainton, Sue. Santa's Snow Cat. 2001. (Illus.). 32p. (J). (ps-2). 15.95 (*0-06-623827-7*); lib. bdg. 15.89 (*0-06-623828-5*) HarperCollins Children's Bk. Group.

Stevens, Carla. Lily & Miss Liberty. 80p. (J). 1993. (gr. 4-7). pap. 3.99 (*0-590-44920-6*); 1992. 12.95 o.p. (*0-590-44919-2*) Scholastic, Inc.

—Lily & Miss Liberty. 1992. (J). 10.14 (*0-606-05907-5*) Turtleback Bks.

Stevenson, James. Runaway Horse! A Novel. Date not set. (J). 15.99 (*0-06-051978-9*); lib. bdg. 16.89 (*0-06-051979-7*) HarperCollins Children's Bk. Group. (Greenwillow Bks.).

Stewart, Melanie. Picture Perfect? 1999. (Generation Girl Ser.: Vol. 5). (Illus.). 128p. (gr. 2-5). pap. 3.99 o.s.i (*0-307-23454-1*, Golden Bks.) Random Hse. Children's Bks.

Stoehr, Shelley. Weird on the Outside. 1995. 224p. (J). 14.95 o.s.i (*0-385-32090-6*, Delacorte Pr.) Dell Publishing.

Stolz, Mary. Ivy Larkin. 1986. 224p. (YA). (gr. 7 up). 13.95 (*0-15-239366-8*) Harcourt Children's Bks.

—Ivy Larkin. 1989. (J). (gr. k-6). reprint ed. pap. 3.25 o.s.i (*0-440-40175-5*, Yearling) Random Hse. Children's Bks.

—Ready or Not. 1953. (J). (gr. 9 up). lib. bdg. 12.89 o.p. (*0-06-025991-4*) HarperCollins Pubs.

Strasser, Todd, tr. Can't Get There from Here. 2004. 208p. (YA). 15.95 (*0-689-84169-8*, Simon & Schuster Children's Publishing) Simon & Schuster Children's Publishing.

Swift, Hildegarde H. The Little Red Lighthouse & the Great Gray Bridge. 1974. (Voyager Bks.). (Illus.). 56p. (J). (ps-3). reprint ed. pap. 8.00 o.s.i (*0-15-652840-1*, Voyager Bks./Libros Viajeros) Harcourt Children's Bks.

Swift, Hildegarde H. & Ward, Lynd. The Little Red Lighthouse & the Great Gray Bridge. 1942. (Illus.). 56p. (J). (ps-3). 17.00 o.s.i (*0-15-247040-9*) Harcourt Children's Bks.

Takabayashi, Mari, tr. & illus. I Live in Brooklyn. 2004. 32p. (J). (ps-3). 16.00 (*0-618-30899-7*) Houghton Mifflin Co.

Talbot, Charlene J. A Home with Aunt Florry. 1974. 208p. (J). (gr. 5-8). 7.25 o.p. (*0-689-30440-4*, Atheneum) Simon & Schuster Children's Publishing.

Tamar, Erika. Alphabet City Ballet. 176p. (J). (gr. 3-7). 1996. lib. bdg. 14.89 o.p. (*0-06-027329-1*); 1996. 14.95 o.p. (*0-06-027328-3*); 1997. (Illus.). reprint ed. pap. 5.99 (*0-06-440668-7*, Harper Trophy) HarperCollins Children's Bk. Group.

—Alphabet City Ballet. 1997. (J). 11.00 (*0-606-11032-1*) Turtleback Bks.

—Donnatalee: A Mermaid Adventure. 1998. (Illus.). 40p. (J). (ps-3). 16.00 o.s.i (*0-15-200386-X*) Harcourt Children's Bks.

—The Truth about Kim O'Hara. 1992. 192p. (J). (gr. 6-9). 14.95 o.p. (*0-689-31789-1*, Atheneum) Simon & Schuster Children's Publishing.

Tang, Charles, illus. The Mystery in New York. 1999. (Boxcar Children Special Ser.: No. 13). 121p. (J). (gr. 2-5). lib. bdg. 13.95 (*0-8075-5459-6*); mass mkt. 3.95 (*0-8075-5460-X*) Whitman, Albert & Co.

Tanner, Louise. Reggie & Nilma: A New York City Story, RS. 1971. (J). (gr. 7 up). 4.50 o.p. (*0-374-36244-0*, Farrar, Straus & Giroux (BYR)) Farrar, Straus & Giroux.

Taylor, Sydney. All-of-a-Kind Family. 2002. 13.94 (*0-7587-9169-0*) Book Wholesalers, Inc.

—All-of-a-Kind Family. (Illus.). 189p. (J). reprint ed. 2000. (gr. 4-7). pap. 12.95 (*0-929093-08-9*); 1988. (gr. 3-6). 16.95 o.p. (*0-929093-00-3*) GRM Assocs. (Taylor Productions).

—All-of-a-Kind Family. 1984. (All-Of-A-Kind Family Ser.). (Illus.). 192p. (gr. 3-7). pap. text 5.50 (*0-440-40059-7*, Yearling) Random Hse. Children's Bks.

—All-of-a-Kind Family. 1990. (J). (gr. 2-6). 20.50 (*0-8446-6253-4*) Smith, Peter Pub., Inc.

—All-of-a-Kind Family. 1979. (J). 11.04 (*0-606-01942-1*) Turtleback Bks.

—All-of-a-Kind Family Downtown. (All-of-a-Kind Family Ser.). (Illus.). 187p. reprint ed. 2001. (YA). (gr. 5 up). pap. 12.95 (*0-929093-07-0*); 1988. (J). 16.95 (*0-929093-01-1*) GRM Assocs. (Taylor Productions).

—All-of-a-Kind Family Downtown. 1973. 188p. (J). (gr. k-6). pap. 3.50 o.s.i (*0-440-42032-6*, Yearling) Random Hse. Children's Bks.

—All-of-a-Kind Family Uptown. (All-of-a-Kind Family Ser.). (Illus.). 160p. 2001. (YA). (gr. 5 up). pap. 12.95 (*0-929093-09-7*); 1988. (J). reprint ed. 16.95 (*0-929093-03-8*) GRM Assocs. (Taylor Productions).

—All-of-a-Kind Family Uptown. 1980. (Illus.). 160p. (J). (gr. 4-7). pap. 3.25 o.s.i (*0-440-40091-0*, Yearling) Random Hse. Children's Bks.

—Ella of All-of-a-Kind Family. 1980. 144p. (J). (gr. k-6). pap. 3.25 o.s.i (*0-440-42252-3*, Yearling) Random Hse. Children's Bks.

—Ella of All of a Kind Family. 1978. (Illus.). 144p. (J). (gr. 4-7). 9.95 o.p. (*0-525-29238-1*, Dutton Children's Bks.) Penguin Putnam Bks. for Young Readers.

—Ella of All-of-a-Kind Family. (All-of-a-Kind Family Ser.). (J). (gr. 4-7). reprint ed. 2000. 144p. pap. 12.95 (*0-929093-05-4*); 1988. (Illus.). 133p. 16.95 o.p. (*0-929093-04-6*, 91417) GRM Assocs. (Taylor Productions).

—More All-of-a-Kind Family. 160p. (YA). (gr. 5 up). 2000. (Illus.). pap. 12.95 (*0-929093-10-0*); 2001. reprint ed. 16.95 (*0-929093-02-X*) GRM Assocs. (Taylor Productions).

—More All-of-a-Kind Family. 1923. (Illus.). 160p. (J). (gr. 3-7). pap. 3.25 o.s.i (*0-440-45813-7*, Yearling) Random Hse. Children's Bks.

Teitelbaum, Michael, adapted by. An American Tail: The Mott Street Maulers. 1986. (Illus.). 24p. (J). (ps-3). 2.25 o.s.i (*0-448-48618-0*, Grosset & Dunlap) Penguin Putnam Bks. for Young Readers.

Thoene, Bodie. Say to This Mountain. 1993. (Shiloh Legacy Ser.: Vol. 3). 448p. (J). pap. 12.99 (*1-55661-191-9*) Bethany Hse. Pubs.

Thomas, Piri. Stories from el Barrio. 1980. 110p. (YA). (gr. 9 up). pap. 1.75 o.p. (*0-380-50013-2*, 50013-2, Avon Bks.) Morrow/Avon.

Thompson, Kay. Eloise. 2001. (Illus.). 64p. (ps). 22.00 incl. audio compact disk (*0-689-84311-9*, Simon & Schuster Children's Publishing) Simon & Schuster Children's Publishing.

—Eloise: The Ultimate Edition. 2000. (Illus.). 304p. (J). (ps-3). 35.00 (*0-689-83990-1*, Simon & Schuster Children's Publishing) Simon & Schuster Children's Publishing.

Tripp, Valerie. Changes for Samantha: A Winter Story. Thieme, Jeanne, ed. 1988. (American Girls Collection: Bk. 6). (Illus.). (YA). (gr. 2 up). 80p. pap. 5.95 (*0-937295-47-7*, American Girl); 80p. lib. bdg. 12.95 (*0-937295-95-7*, American Girl); 72p. 12.95 o.p. (*0-937295-46-9*) Pleasant Co. Pubns.

—Changes for Samantha: A Winter Story. 1988. (American Girls Collection: Bk. 6). (Illus.). (YA). (gr. 2 up). 12.10 (*0-606-03751-9*) Turtleback Bks.

—Happy Birthday, Samantha! A Springtime Story. Thieme, Jeanne, ed. 1987. (American Girls Collection: Bk. 4). (Illus.). 72p. (gr. 2 up). (YA). pap. 5.95 (*0-937295-35-3*, American Girl); (J). 12.95 (*0-937295-89-2*, American Girl); (YA). 12.95 o.p. (*0-937295-34-5*) Pleasant Co. Pubns.

—Happy Birthday, Samantha! A Springtime Story. 1987. (American Girls Collection: Bk. 4). (Illus.). (YA). (gr. 2 up). 12.10 (*0-606-03801-9*) Turtleback Bks.

Twentieth Century Fox Film Corporation Staff. Home Alone Two: Lost in New York. 1993. (Comes to Life Bks.). 16p. (J). (ps-2). (*1-883366-14-3*) YES! Entertainment Corp.

Vampire State Building. 1992. (J). pap. o.s.i (*0-553-54059-9*, Dell Books for Young Readers) Random Hse. Children's Bks.

Van de Wetering, Janwillem. Hugh Pine & Something Else. 1989. (Illus.). 96p. (J). (gr. 3 up). 13.95 o.p. (*0-395-49216-5*) Houghton Mifflin Co.

—Hugh Pine & Something Else. ALC Staff, ed. 1992. (Illus.). 80p. (J). (gr. 2 up). pap. 3.95 o.p. (*0-688-11800-3*, Morrow, William & Co.) Morrow/Avon.

Van Leeuwen, Jean. The Great Googlestein Museum Mystery. 2003. (Illus.). 208p. (J). 16.99 (*0-8037-2765-8*) Penguin Putnam Bks. for Young Readers.

Vogel, Amos. How Little Lori Visited Times Square. 2001. (Sendak Reissues Ser.). (Illus.). 64p. (J). (gr. 4 up). lib. bdg. 14.89 (*0-06-028463-3*); (ps-3). 14.95 (*0-06-028462-5*) HarperCollins Children's Bk. Group.

Von-Zeigesar, Cecily. Gossip Girl, No. 5. 2004. (Illus.). 224p. (J). pap. 8.99 (*0-316-73518-3*) Little Brown & Co.

Von Ziegesar, Cecily. Gossip Girl. 2002. 208p. (J). (gr. 9). pap. 8.99 (*0-316-91033-3*) Little Brown Children's Bks.

Von Ziegesar, Cecily, contrib. by. Gossip Girl. 2003. (Illus.). (J). 107.88 (*0-316-73797-6*, Tingley, Megan Bks.) Little Brown Children's Bks.

Warner, Gertrude Chandler. The Mystery in New York. 1999. (Boxcar Children Special Ser.: No.13). (Illus.). (J). (gr. 2-5). 10.00 (*0-606-18771-5*) Turtleback Bks.

Waters, Kate. Lion Dancer: Ernie Wan's Chinese New Year. 1991. (Reading Rainbow Bks.). 40p. (J). (ps-2). mass mkt. 4.99 (*0-590-43047-5*) Scholastic, Inc.

—Lion Dancer: Ernie Wan's Chinese New Year. 1990. (Reading Rainbow Bks.). (J). 11.14 (*0-606-04729-8*) Turtleback Bks.

Waters, Kate & Slovenz-Low, Madeline. Lion Dancer: Ernie Wan's Chinese New Year. 1990. (Illus.). 40p. (J). (ps-2). pap. 14.95 o.p. (*0-590-43046-7*) Scholastic, Inc.

Wax, Wendy. Empire Dreams. 2000. (Adventures in America Ser.). (Illus.). 96p. (J). (gr. 4-7). lib. bdg. 14.95 (*1-893110-19-2*) Silver Moon Pr.

Weitzman, Jacqueline Preiss. You Can't Take a Balloon into the Metropolitan Museum. 1998. (Illus.). 40p. (J). (gr. k-3). 17.99 (*0-8037-2301-6*, Dial Bks. for Young Readers) Penguin Putnam Bks. for Young Readers.

—You Can't Take a Balloon into the Metropolitan Museum. 2001. (Illus.). (J). 13.14 (*0-606-21004-0*) Turtleback Bks.

Weller, Frances Ward. The Day the Animals Came: A Story of Saint Francis Day. 2003. (Illus.). 48p. (J). 16.99 (*0-399-23630-9*, 53247533, Philomel) Penguin Putnam Bks. for Young Readers.

Wersba, Barbara. You'll Never Guess the End. 1992. (Charlotte Zolotow Bk.). 144p. (YA). (gr. 7 up). 14.00 (*0-06-020448-6*); lib. bdg. 13.89 o.p. (*0-06-020449-4*) HarperCollins Children's Bk. Group.

Whitney, Phyllis A. Secret of the Emerald Star. 1964. (Illus.). (J). (gr. 5-9). 4.95 o.p. (*0-664-32337-5*) Westminster John Knox Pr.

Wibberley, Leonard. The Mouse That Roared. 1984. (YA). (gr. 6-12). mass mkt. 2.95 o.s.i (*0-553-24969-X*) Bantam Bks.

Wiesner, David. Sector 7. 2002. (Illus.). (J). 23.40 (*0-7587-0142-X*) Book Wholesalers, Inc.

—Sector 7. 1999. (Illus.). 48p. (J). (ps-3). lib. bdg., tchr. ed. 16.00 (*0-395-74656-6*, Clarion Bks.) Houghton Mifflin Co. Trade & Reference Div.

Wilkinson, Brenda. Ludell's New York Time. 1980. 192p. (YA). (gr. 7 up). 11.95 (*0-06-026497-7*); lib. bdg. 12.89 o.p. (*0-06-026498-5*) HarperCollins Children's Bk. Group.

Williams-Garcia, Rita. Every Time a Rainbow Dies. (Amistad Ser.). 176p. (J). 2002. (Illus.). pap. 6.95 (*0-06-447303-1*, HarperTempest); 2001. (gr. 5 up). lib. bdg. 17.89 (*0-06-029202-4*); 2001. (Illus.). (gr. 9 up). 15.95 (*0-688-16245-2*) HarperCollins Children's Bk. Group.

—Fast Talk on a Slow Track. 1992. 192p. (YA). mass mkt. 3.99 o.p. (*0-553-29594-2*) Bantam Bks.

—Fast Talk on a Slow Track. (YA). (gr. 7-12). 1998. 190p. 5.99 (*0-14-130231-3*, Puffin Bks.); 1991. 176p. 15.00 o.s.i (*0-525-67334-2*, Dutton Children's Bks.) Penguin Putnam Bks. for Young Readers.

—No Laughter Here. 2004. 144p. (J). 15.99 (*0-688-16247-9*); lib. bdg. 16.89 (*0-688-16248-7*) HarperCollins Pubs.

Winters, Kay. How Will the Bunny Know? 1999. (Illus.). 48p. (J). (gr. k-3). 13.95 o.s.i (*0-385-32596-7*, Dell Books for Young Readers) Random Hse. Children's Bks.

Wood, Marcia. Always, Julia. 1993. 128p. (J). (gr. 5-9). lib. bdg. 13.95 o.s.i (*0-689-31728-X*, Atheneum) Simon & Schuster Children's Publishing.

Woodson, Jacqueline. If You Come Softly. 192p. (YA). (gr. 5 up). 2000. pap. 5.99 (*0-698-11862-6*); 1998. 15.99 (*0-399-23112-9*) Putnam Publishing Group, The.

—If You Come Softly. 2000. 11.04 (*0-606-17863-5*) Turtleback Bks.

—Miracle's Boys. 2000. 192p. (YA). (gr. 5 up). 15.99 (*0-399-23113-7*) Penguin Group (USA) Inc.

Yektai, Niki. The Secret Room. 1992. 192p. (J). (gr. 4-7). 14.95 o.p. (*0-531-05456-X*); mass mkt. 14.99 o.p. (*0-531-08606-2*) Scholastic, Inc. (Orchard Bks.).

Zarin, Cynthia. Albert, the Dog Who Liked to Ride in Taxis. 2004. (Illus.). 32p. (J). 16.95 (*0-689-84762-9*, Atheneum/Richard Jackson Bks.) Simon & Schuster Children's Publishing.

Zindel, Paul. The Scream Museum. l.t. ed. 2002. (Young Adult Ser.). (Illus.). 175p. (J). 22.95 (*0-7862-4473-9*) Thorndike Pr.

NEW YORK (STATE)—FICTION

Auch, Mary Jane. Frozen Summer, ERS. 1998. 224p. (YA). (gr. 4-8). 16.95 (*0-8050-4923-1*, Holt, Henry & Co. Bks. For Young Readers) Holt, Henry & Co.

—Frozen Summer. 2000. (Illus.). 208p. (gr. 5-9). pap. text 4.50 (*0-440-41624-8*, Yearling) Random Hse. Children's Bks.

—Frozen Summer. 2000. (Illus.). (J). 10.55 (*0-606-18783-9*) Turtleback Bks.

—The Road to Home, ERS. 2000. 224p. (YA). (gr. 5-8). 16.95 (*0-8050-4921-5*, Holt, Henry & Co. Bks. For Young Readers) Holt, Henry & Co.

—The Road to Home. 2002. 224p. (gr. 5). pap. text 4.99 (*0-440-41805-4*, Random Hse. Bks. for Young Readers) Random Hse. Children's Bks.

Banim, Lisa. Drums at Saratoga. 1993. (Stories of the States Ser.). (Illus.). 64p. (J). (gr. 4-7). lib. bdg. 14.95 (*1-881889-20-3*) Silver Moon Pr.

Bat-Ami, Miriam. Two Suns in the Sky. 1999. 208p. (YA). (gr. 7-12). 17.95 (*0-8126-2900-0*) Cricket Bks.

—Two Suns in the Sky. 2001. 208p. (YA). pap. 6.99 (*0-14-230036-5*, Puffin Bks.) Penguin Putnam Bks. for Young Readers.

Benton, Amanda. Silent Stranger. 1998. pap. 3.99 (*0-380-79222-2*, Avon Bks.) Morrow/Avon.

—Silent Stranger. 1998. 10.04 (*0-606-16165-1*) Turtleback Bks.

Bergen, Lara Rice, adapted by. Washington Irving's Rip Van Winkle. 1997. (All Aboard Reading Ser.). (Illus.). 48p. (J). (gr. 1-3). 3.95 o.p. (*0-448-41136-9*, Grosset & Dunlap) Penguin Putnam Bks. for Young Readers.

Blumenthal, Deborah. Ice Palace. 2003. (Illus.). 32p. (J). (ps-3). lib. bdg. 16.00 (*0-618-15960-6*, Clarion Bks.) Houghton Mifflin Co. Trade & Reference Div.

Bruchac, Joseph. Hidden Roots. 2004. (J). pap. 16.95 (*0-439-35358-0*) Scholastic, Inc.

Burns, Paula. Abby's Search for Cooper. 1996. (Illus.). 32p. (J). (gr. k-3). pap. 7.95 (*0-925168-48-3*) North Country Bks., Inc.

Cannon, A. E. Sam's Gift. 1997. 97p. (J). pap. 7.95 (*1-57345-289-0*, Shadow Mountain) Deseret Bk. Co.

Collier, James Lincoln. The Teddy Bear Habit or How I Became a Winner. 2001. (Lost Treasures Ser.: No. 3). (Illus.). 240p. (J). pap. 4.99 (*0-7868-1544-2*); (gr. 3-7). reprint ed. pap. 1.99 (*0-7868-1543-4*) Hyperion Bks. for Children. (Volo).

Collier, James Lincoln & Collier, Christopher. Who Is Carrie? 1984. 192p. (J). (gr. 4-6). 14.95 o.s.i (*0-385-29295-3*, Delacorte Pr.) Dell Publishing.

—Who Is Carrie? 1987. (Arabus Family Saga Ser.: Vol. 3). 176p. (gr. 5-7). pap. text 4.99 o.s.i (*0-440-49536-9*, Yearling) Random Hse. Children's Bks.

—Who Is Carrie? 1987. (Arabus Family Saga Ser.). (J). 11.04 (*0-606-03505-2*) Turtleback Bks.

Conrad, Pam. Our House: The Stories of Levittown. 1995. (Illus.). 80p. (J). (gr. 3-7). pap. 14.95 (*0-590-46523-6*) Scholastic, Inc.

Cook, Donald, illus. The Headless Horseman. 2003. (Step into Reading Step 2 Bks.). 48p. (J). (gr. 1-3). lib. bdg. 11.99 (*0-679-91241-X*, Random Hse. Bks. for Young Readers) Random Hse. Children's Bks.

Cooper, James Fenimore. The Pioneers. 1964. (Airmont Classics Ser.). (J). (gr. 8 up). mass mkt. 1.95 o.p. (*0-8049-0049-3*, CL-49) Airmont Publishing Co., Inc.

—The Pioneers. 1823. 477p. (YA). reprint ed. pap. text 28.00 (*1-4047-2371-4*) Classic Textbooks.

—The Pioneers. 1964. 448p. (YA). mass mkt. 6.95 (*0-451-52521-3*); mass mkt. 4.50 o.p. (*0-451-52339-3*) NAL. (Signet Classics).

Crowe, Carole. Groover's Heart. 2003. (Illus.). 144p. (J). (gr. 4-6). 15.95 (*1-56397-953-5*) Boyds Mills Pr.

Curtis, Alice Turner. A Little Maid of Old New York. 2004. (Little Maid Ser.). (Illus.). 192p. (J). (gr. 4-7). reprint ed. pap. 9.95 (*1-55709-326-1*) Applewood Bks.

de Paola, Tomie. Tomie de Lit Miracle. (J). 8.95 (*0-399-21343-0*) Penguin Group (USA) Inc.

DeFelice, Cynthia C. Under the Same Sky, RS. 2003. 224p. (J). 16.00 (*0-374-38032-5*, Farrar, Straus & Giroux (BYR)) Farrar, Straus & Giroux.

Drummond, Allan. Liberty!, RS. 2002. (Illus.). 40p. (J). (ps-3). 17.00 (*0-374-34385-3*, Farrar, Straus & Giroux (BYR)) Farrar, Straus & Giroux.

Edmonds, Walter D. The Night Raider & Other Stories. 1980. 96p. (J). (gr. 7 up). o.p. (*0-316-21141-9*) Little Brown & Co.

Farrell, Vivian. Robert's Tall Friend: A Story of the Fire Island Lighthouse. 1988. (Illus.). 64p. (J). (gr. 4-7). 11.50 (*0-9619832-0-5*) Island-Metro Pubns., Inc.

—Robert's Tall Friend: A Story of the Fire Island Lighthouse. Wood, Jean, ed. 1997. (Illus.). 64p. (J). (gr. 3-6). text 24.00 (*0-9657524-1-0*); pap. text 16.00 (*0-9657524-7-X*) Logan, Tracy Pubns.

Feder, Harriet K. Death on Sacred Ground. 2001. (Young Adult Fiction Ser.). (Illus.). 192p. (J). (gr. 7-12). lib. bdg. 14.95 (*0-8225-0741-2*, Lerner Pubns.) Lerner Publishing Group.

George, Jean Craighead. Frightful's Mountain. 1999. (Illus.). 176p. (J). (gr. 4-7). 15.99 (*0-525-46166-3*) Penguin Putnam Bks. for Young Readers.

NEW ZEALAND—FICTION

Settings

—The Fat Man. 192p. (YA). (gr. 7-12). 1999. (Illus.). mass mkt. 4.50 (0-689-82459-9, Simon Pulse); 1997. 16.00 o.s.i (0-689-81182-9, Simon & Schuster Children's Publishing) Simon & Schuster Children's Publishing.

—The Fire-Raiser. 1992. 176p. (J). (gr. 4-6). 16.00 (0-395-62428-2) Houghton Mifflin Co.

—Orchard Street. 1998. 137p. pap. (0-670-88367-0) Viking.

Hamilton, Elizabeth L. Passport to Courage. 2002. (Character-in-Action Ser.: Bk. 1). 384p. (YA). per. 19.95 (0-9713749-3-7) Quiet Impact, Inc.

Ihimaera, Witi. The Whale Rider. 2003. 168p. (YA). (gr. 3-6). pap. 8.00 (0-15-205016-7, Harcourt Paperbacks) Harcourt Children's Bks.

Lattimore, Deborah Nourse. Punga: The Goddess of Ugly. 1993. (Illus.). 32p. (J). (ps-3). 14.95 o.s.i (0-15-292862-6) Harcourt Trade Pubs.

Mahy, Margaret. The Changeover: A Supernatural Romance. l.t. unabr. ed. 1988. (Illus.). (YA). 13.95 o.p. (0-8161-4440-0, Macmillan Reference USA) Gale Group.

—The Changeover: A Supernatural Romance. 1985. (YA). pap. 2.25 o.p. (0-590-33798-X); 264p. (gr. 7 up). reprint ed. pap. 2.50 o.p. (0-590-41289-2, Scholastic Paperbacks) Scholastic, Inc.

—The Changeover: A Supernatural Romance. 1984. 224p. (YA). (gr. 7 up). 16.00 (0-689-50303-2, McElderry, Margaret K.) Simon & Schuster Children's Publishing.

—The Changeover: A Supernatural Romance. 1994. (YA). 10.09 o.p. (0-606-05784-6) Turtleback Bks.

—The Good Fortunes Gang Bk. 1: Cousins Quartet. l.t. ed. 1994. (Illus.). (J). (gr. 1-8). 16.95 o.p. (0-7451-2222-1, Galaxy Children's Large Print) BBC Audiobooks America.

—The Great Piratical Rumbustification & the Librarian & The Robbers. 1993. (Illus.). 64p. (YA). (gr. 5 up). pap. 3.95 o.p. (0-688-12469-0, Morrow, William & Co.) Morrow/Avon.

—The Great Piratical Rumbustification, the Librarian & the Robbers. 2000. (Illus.). 64p. (J). pap. 6.95 (1-56792-169-8) Godine, David R. Pub.

—Tangled Fortunes. (Cousins Quartet Ser.: Bk. 4). 112p. (J). 1996. (gr. 4-7). pap. 3.99 o.s.i (0-440-41163-7); 1994. (Illus.). (gr. 3-6). 14.95 (0-385-32066-3, Delacorte Pr.) Dell Publishing.

—Tangled Fortunes. 1995. 18.95 (0-385-30979-1) Doubleday Publishing.

—The Tricksters. 272p. 1999. (Illus.). (J). (gr. 7-12). per. 8.00 (0-689-82910-8, Simon Pulse); 1987. (YA). (gr. 9 up). text 16.00 o.s.i (0-689-50400-4, McElderry, Margaret K.) Simon & Schuster Children's Publishing.

—24 Hours. (J). 2001. 208p. pap. 10.00 (0-689-83903-0, Simon Pulse); 2000. (Illus.). 192p. (gr. 7-12). 17.00 (0-689-83884-0, McElderry, Margaret K.) Simon & Schuster Children's Publishing.

Morgan, Stacy Towle. New Zealand Shake-Up, + 1997. (Ruby Slippers School Ser.: Vol. 6). 80p. (J). (gr. 2-5). pap. 3.99 o.p. (1-55661-605-8) Bethany Hse. Pubs.

Savage, Deborah. A Stranger Calls Me Home. 1992. 240p. (J). (gr. 4-7). 14.95 (0-395-59424-3) Houghton Mifflin Co.

Stokoe, Julian & Chambers, Brent. Tamatoa & the Big Wind. 2000. (Illus.). (J). pap. 12.95 (1-86950-345-7) HarperCollins NZL. Dist: Antipodes Bks. & Beyond.

Sutherland, Margaret. Hello, I'm Karen. 1976. (Illus.). 96p. (J). (gr. k-5). 4.95 o.p. (0-698-20371-2) Putnam Publishing Group, The.

Taylor, William. The Blue Lawn. 1999. 16.00 (0-606-19431-2) Turtleback Bks.

Van Rynbach, Iris. Captain Cook's Christmas Pudding. 1997. (Illus.). 32p. (J). (gr. k-4). 14.95 (1-56397-644-7) Boyds Mills Pr.

NEWFOUNDLAND AND LABRADOR—FICTION

Butler, Geoff. The Hangashore. 1998. (Illus.). 32p. (YA). (gr. 3-7). 15.95 (0-88776-444-4) Tundra Bks. of Northern New York.

—The Killick: A Newfoundland Story. 1998. (Illus.). 32p. (J). (gr. 5-9). reprint ed. pap. 8.95 (0-88776-449-5) Tundra Bks. of Northern New York.

Carlson, Natalie S. Sailor's Choice. 1966. (Illus.). (J). (gr. 3-7). lib. bdg. 7.89 o.p. (0-06-021067-2) HarperCollins Pubs.

Dorion, Betty F. Bay Girl. 1998. (Illus.). (J). 12.00 (0-606-19010-4) Turtleback Bks.

Gostick, Adrian R. Jessica's Search: The Secret of Ballycater Cove. 1998. (J). 1.99 (1-57345-436-2) Deseret Bk. Co.

Harlow, Joan Hiatt. Star in the Storm. (Illus.). 160p. (J). (gr. 3-7). 2001. pap. 4.99 (0-689-84621-5, Aladdin); 2000. 16.00 (0-689-82905-1, McElderry, Margaret K.) Simon & Schuster Children's Publishing.

Jackson, Lawrence. Newfoundland & Labrador. 1995. (Hello Canada Ser.). (Illus.). 76p. (J). (gr. 3-6). lib. bdg. 19.93 (0-8225-2757-X, Lerner Pubns.) Lerner Publishing Group.

Katz, Welwyn W. Out of the Dark. 1996. 192p. (YA). (gr. 4). pap. 5.95 (0-88899-262-9) Groundwood Bks. CAN. Dist: Publishers Group West.

—Out of the Dark. 1996. 192p. (J). (gr. 6-9). 16.00 (0-689-80947-6, McElderry, Margaret K.) Simon & Schuster Children's Publishing.

Major, Kevin. Thirty-Six Exposures. 1984. (J). (gr. 7 up). 14.95 o.s.i (0-385-29347-X, Delacorte Pr.) Dell Publishing.

McNaughton, Janet. Make or Break Spring. 1999. 192p. (YA). (gr. 7 up). pap. (1-895387-93-0) Creative Bk. Publishing.

Reed, Don C. The Kraken. 2003. (Illus.). 224p. (YA). (gr. 5-9). pap. 7.95 (1-56397-693-5) Boyds Mills Pr.

—The Kraken. 1997. lib. bdg. 14.00 (0-606-14348-3) Turtleback Bks.

Walsh, Alice. Heroes of Isle Aux Morts. 2001. (Illus.). 32p. (J). (gr. 3-7). 17.95 (0-88776-501-7) Tundra Bks. of Northern New York.

—Heroes of Isle aux Morts. ed. 2001. (gr. 1). spiral bd. (0-616-11138-X); (gr. 2). spiral bd. (0-616-11139-8) Canadian National Institute for the Blind/Institut National Canadien pour les Aveugles.

NIGERIA—FICTION

Adimora-Ezeigbo, Akachi. The Buried Treasure. 1992. (Junior African Writers Ser.). (Illus.). 30p. (J). (gr. 4-8). pap. text 2.50 o.p. (0-435-89169-3) Heinemann.

Echewa, O. T. The Ancestor Tree. 1994. (Illus.). 32p. (J). (gr. k-3). 13.99 o.p. (0-525-67467-5, Dutton Children's Bks.) Penguin Putnam Bks. for Young Readers.

Emecheta, Buchi. The Moonlight Bride. 1983. 77p. (gr. 6-10). (J). 7.95 (0-8076-1062-3); (YA). pap. 8.95 (0-8076-1063-1) Braziller, George Inc.

—The Wrestling Match. 1983. 74p. (YA). (gr. 6-10). 7.95 (0-8076-1060-7); pap. 6.95 (0-8076-1061-5) Braziller, George Inc.

Gamble, Kim. Come the Terrible Tiger. 1995. (Illus.). 32p. (J). (ps-2). pap. 6.95 o.p. (1-86373-473-2); 14.95 o.p. (1-86373-236-5) Independent Pubs. Group.

Hurd, Thacher. The Quiet Evening. (J). (ps up). 1992. 15.00 o.p. (0-688-10526-2); 1991. lib. bdg. 13.93 o.p. (0-688-10527-0) HarperCollins Children's Bk. Group. (Greenwillow Bks.).

Low, Alice, ed. Spooky Stories for a Dark & Stormy Night. 1996. (Illus.). 128p. (J). (gr. 3 up). pap. 7.95 o.s.i (0-7868-1114-5) Disney Pr.

Olaleye, Isaac. Bikes for Rent! 2000. (Illus.). 32p. (J). (gr. k-4). pap. 16.95 (0-531-30290-3, Orchard Bks.) Scholastic, Inc.

—Bitter Bananas. 1996. (Illus.). 32p. (J). pap. 5.99 o.s.i (0-14-055710-5, Puffin Bks.) Penguin Putnam Bks. for Young Readers.

—Bitter Bananas. 1996. (J). 11.19 (0-606-09080-0) Turtleback Bks.

Onyefulu, Ifeoma. Grandfather's Work: A Traditional Healer in Nigeria. 1998. (Around the World Ser.). (Illus.). 32p. (gr. 2-4). lib. bdg. 22.90 o.p. (0-7613-0412-6) Millbrook Pr., Inc.

Rupert, Janet E. The African Mask. 1994. 144p. (J). (gr. 4-7). tchr. ed. 16.00 o.p. (0-395-67295-3, Clarion Bks.) Houghton Mifflin Co. Trade & Reference Div.

Vesey, Amanda. Duncan's Tree House. 1993. (J). (ps-3). lib. bdg. 18.95 o.s.i (0-87614-784-8, Carolrhoda Bks.) Lerner Publishing Group.

Welch, Leona N. Kai: Lost Statue: Girlhood Journey. 1997. (Girlhood Journeys Ser.: No. 3). (Illus.). 71p. (J). (gr. 2-6). per. 5.99 (0-689-81571-9, Simon Pulse) Simon & Schuster Children's Publishing.

NORTH CAROLINA—FICTION

Ballard, C. R. A Child of the Veil. 2001. 126p. (J). pap. 7.99 (1-889893-64-1) Emerald Hse. Group, Inc.

Bledsoe, Jerry. The Angel Doll: A Christmas Story. 1996. (Illus.). 125p. 14.95 (1-878086-54-5) Down Home Pr.

—The Angel Doll: A Christmas Story. 1999. 112p. 13.95 (0-312-17104-8) St. Martin's Pr.

Bradfield, Carl. The Sullivans of Little Horsepen Creek: A Tale of Colonial North Carolina's Regulator Era, Circa: 1760s. (Illus.). 350p. (YA). (gr. 8-12). (0-9632319-2-8) ASDA Publishing, Inc.

Campbell, Donna. An Independent Spirit: The Tale of Betsy Dowdy & Black Bess. 2002. (Legends of the Carolinas Ser.). 200p. (J). 8.95 (1-928556-35-3) Coastal Carolina Pr.

Carbone, Elisa. Storm Warriors. 2001. 176p. (gr. 5-8). text 16.95 (0-375-80664-4, Knopf Bks. for Young Readers) Random Hse. Children's Bks.

—The Surfmen of Pea Island. 2001. 176p. (gr. 5-8). lib. bdg. 18.99 (0-375-90664-9) Random Hse., Inc.

Carris, Joan D. A Ghost of a Chance. 1992. (Illus.). 160p. (J). (gr. 3-7). 14.95 o.p. (0-316-13016-8) Little Brown & Co.

Carris, Joan Davenport. Ghost of a Chance. 2003. (Legends of the Carolinas Ser.). 155p. (J). 8.95 (1-928556-40-X) Coastal Carolina Pr.

Countess, Mary Alice. Cowpath Days. Fallis, Janet M., ed. 2001. (Illus.). 128p. (J). (gr. 4-8). pap. 6.95 (0-9662431-1-0) Viewpoint Pr., Inc.

Credle, Ellis. Big Fraid, Little Fraid. 1964. (Illus.). (J). 6.95 o.p. (0-525-66007-0, Dutton Children's Bks.) Penguin Putnam Bks. for Young Readers.

Davis, C. L. The Christmas Barn. 2001. 200p. (J). 12.95 (1-58485-414-6, American Girl) Pleasant Co. Pubns.

Davis, Donald. Listening for the Crack of Dawn: A Master Storyteller Recalls the Appalachia of the 1950's & 60's. 1991. 18.00 (0-606-12397-0) Turtleback Bks.

Dowell, Frances O'Roark. Dovey Coe. 192p. (J). 2001. (Illus.). pap. 4.99 (0-689-84667-3, Aladdin); 2000. (gr. 4-7). 16.00 (0-689-83174-9, Atheneum) Simon & Schuster Children's Publishing.

—Dovey Coe. l.t. ed. 2001. 171p. (J). 22.95 (0-7862-3590-X) Thorndike Pr.

—Dovey Coe. 2001. 11.04 (0-606-22127-1) Turtleback Bks.

Fripp, Jon, et al. Kinnakeet & the Lighthouse. 2000. (Illus.). 33p. 5.50 (0-9638258-4-4) Bicast, Inc.

Gantos, Jack. Jack Adrift: Fourth Grade Without a Clue, RS. 2003. (Jack Henry Ser.). (Illus.). 208p. (J). 16.00 o.s.i (0-374-39987-5, Farrar, Straus & Giroux (BYR)) Farrar, Straus & Giroux.

Gutman, Dan. Race for the Sky: The Kitty Hawk Diaries of Johnny Moore. 2003. (Illus.). 192p. (J). (gr. 3-6). 15.95 (0-689-84554-5, Simon & Schuster Children's Publishing) Simon & Schuster Children's Publishing.

Hallman, Ruth. Secrets of a Silent Stranger. 1976. (Hiway Book). (J). 6.95 o.p. (0-664-32598-X) Westminster John Knox Pr.

Houston, Gloria M. Littlejim. 1993. (Illus.). 176p. (J). (gr. 5 up). pap. 4.95 (0-688-12112-8, Harper Trophy) HarperCollins Children's Bk. Group.

—Littlejim's Dream. 1997. (Illus.). 240p. (J). (gr. 3-7). 16.00 (0-15-201509-4) Harcourt Children's Bks.

Hyman, John H. The Relationship. 1995. (Illus.). 251p. (YA). (gr. 7 up). 16.95 (1-880664-14-3) E. M. Productions.

Janney, Rebecca P. Secret of the Lost Colony. 2002. (Impossible Dreamers Ser.: Vol. 1). 128p. (gr. 4-7). pap. 5.99 o.p. (1-57673-018-2) Multnomah Pubs., Inc.

Jones, Elizabeth McDavid. The Night Flyers. 1999. (American Girl Collection: Bk. 3). (Illus.). 160p. (J). (gr. 5-9). pap. 5.95 (1-56247-759-5, American Girl) Pleasant Co. Pubns.

—The Night Flyers. 1999. 12.00 (0-606-17518-0) Turtleback Bks.

Klaveness, Jan O. Keeper of the Light. 1990. 224p. (YA). (gr. 7 up). 12.95 o.p. (0-688-06996-7, Morrow, William & Co.) Morrow/Avon.

Lenski, Lois. Blue Ridge Billy. 1946. (Regional Stories Ser.). (Illus.). (J). (gr. 4-6). lib. bdg. 9.79 o.p. (0-397-30120-0) HarperCollins Children's Bk. Group.

Lentz, Alice B. Tweetsie Adventure. 1995. (Illus.). 32p. (J). (ps-3). 9.95 (1-57072-025-8) Overmountain Pr.

Leppard, Lois Gladys. Mandie & Her Missing Kin. 1995. (Mandie Bks.: No. 25). 160p. (J). (gr. 4-7). pap. 4.99 (1-55661-511-6) Bethany Hse. Pubs.

—Mandie & Her Missing Kin. 1995. (Mandie Bks.: No. 25). (J). (gr. 4-7). 11.04 (0-606-10868-8) Turtleback Bks.

—Mandie & the Buried Stranger. 1999. (Mandie Bks.: No. 31). 176p. (J). (gr. 4-7). pap. 4.99 (1-55661-384-9) Bethany Hse. Pubs.

—Mandie & the Buried Stranger. 1999. (Mandie Bks.: No. 31). (J). (gr. 4-7). 11.04 (0-606-18918-1) Turtleback Bks.

—Mandie & the Unwanted Gift, 29. 1997. (Mandie Bks.: No. 29). 176p. (J). (gr. 4-7). pap. 4.99 (1-55661-556-6) Bethany Hse. Pubs.

—Mandie & the Unwanted Gift. 1998. (Mandie Bks.: No. 29). (J). (gr. 4-7). 11.04 (0-606-18916-5) Turtleback Bks.

Littleton, Mark. Tracks in the Sand. 2001. (Ally OConnor Adventures Ser.: Vol. 1). 128p. (J). (gr. 4-7). pap. 5.99 (0-8010-4490-1) Baker Bks.

Longmeyer, Carole M. North Carolina Football Mystery. 1994. (Sportsmystery Ser.). (Illus.). (Orig.). (J). (gr. 3 up). pap. 19.95 (0-935326-29-4) Gallopade International.

Moses, Shelia P. The Legend of Buddy Bush. 2004. (Illus.). 224p. (YA). 15.95 (0-689-85839-6, McElderry, Margaret K.) Simon & Schuster Children's Publishing.

Newton, Suzanne. Where Are You When I Need You? 208p. 1993. (YA). (gr. 7 up). pap. 3.99 o.s.i (0-14-034454-3, Puffin Bks.); 1991. (J). 14.00 o.p. (0-670-81702-3, Viking Children's Bks.) Penguin Putnam Bks. for Young Readers.

O'Connor, Barbara. Me & Rupert Goody, RS. 1999. 112p. (J). (gr. 4-7). 15.00 (0-374-34904-5, Farrar, Straus & Giroux (BYR)) Farrar, Straus & Giroux.

—Me & Rupert Goody. l.t. ed. 2000. (Illus.). 126p. (J). (gr. 8-12). 21.95 (0-7862-2767-2) Thorndike Pr.

O'Leary, Patsy Baker. With Wings As Eagles. 1997. 272p. (YA). (gr. 7-12). tchr. ed. 15.00 (0-395-70557-6) Houghton Mifflin Co.

Osborne, Mary Pope. Best Wishes, Joe Brady. 1984. (J). (gr. 5 up). 12.95 o.p. (0-8037-0067-9, 01258-370, Dial Bks. for Young Readers) Penguin Putnam Bks. for Young Readers.

—Best Wishes, Joe Brady. 1994. 192p. (YA). (gr. 7 up). pap. 4.99 (0-679-84560-7, Random Hse. Bks. for Young Readers) Random Hse. Children's Bks.

—Best Wishes, Joe Brady. 1985. 192p. (J). (gr. 7 up). reprint ed. pap. 2.25 o.p. (0-590-33215-5, Scholastic Paperbacks) Scholastic, Inc.

Penn, Audrey. The Whistling Tree. 2003. 32p. (J). 16.95 (0-87868-852-8, Child & Family Pr.) Child Welfare League of America, Inc.

Pinkney, Gloria J. Back Home. 1992. (Illus.). (J). (gr. k-4). 400p. 14.89 o.p. (0-8037-1169-7); 40p. 16.99 (0-8037-1168-9) Penguin Putnam Bks. for Young Readers. (Dial Bks. for Young Readers).

—Back Home. 1999. 13.14 (0-606-16773-0) Turtleback Bks.

Ransom, Candice F. Rescue on the Outer Banks. 2002. (On My Own History Ser.). (Illus.). 48p. (J). (gr. 2-5). pap. 5.95 (0-87614-815-1, First Avenue Editions); (gr. 1-3). lib. bdg. 21.27 (0-87614-460-1, Carolrhoda Bks.) Lerner Publishing Group.

Russell, Anne. Seabiscuit: Wild Pony of the Outer Banks. 2001. (Illus.). 32p. (J). (gr. k-8). 14.95 (1-928556-28-0) Coastal Carolina Pr.

Tate, Suzanne. Holly from Hatteras: A Tale of Saving Lives. 1998. (Suzanne Tate's History Ser.: No. 1). (Illus.). 32p. (J). (ps-4). pap. 4.95 (1-878405-22-5) Nags Head Art, Inc.

Taylor, Theodore. Teetoncey & Ben O'Neal, Bk. 2. 1991. (Illus.). 192p. (J). (gr. 5-7). pap. 3.99 (0-380-71025-0, Avon Bks.) Morrow/Avon.

Teague, Bobbie T. Simon's Gold. 2001. (Illus.). 94p. (J). per. 13.00 (1-887774-09-2, Wynden) Canmore Pr.

Warner, Gertrude Chandler, creator. The Mystery of the Wild Ponies. 2000. (Boxcar Children Ser.: No. 77). (Illus.). 135p. (J). (gr. 2-5). lib. bdg. 13.95 (0-8075-5465-0); mass mkt. 3.95 (0-8075-5466-9) Whitman, Albert & Co.

Weatherford, Carole Boston. Freedom on the Menu: The Greensboro Sit-Ins. 2004. (J). (0-8037-2860-3, Dial Bks. for Young Readers) Penguin Putnam Bks. for Young Readers.

—Princeville: The 500 Year Flood. 2001. (Illus.). 32p. 14.95 (1-928556-32-9) Coastal Carolina Pr.

Wechter, Nell W. Taffy of Torpedo Junction. (Illus.). 134p. (gr. 5-9). 1979. 6.95 o.p. (0-910244-08-1); 1990. (J). reprint ed. pap. 7.95 o.p. (0-89587-076-2) Blair, John F. Pub.

Wellman, Manly W. Settlement on Shocco: Adventures in Colonial Carolina. 1963. (gr. 4-8). lib. bdg. 6.95 o.p. (0-910244-35-9) Blair, John F. Pub.

Wilson, Dawn. Saint Jude. 2000. (Illus.). 171p. (YA). (gr. 6-12). pap. 15.95 (0-936389-68-0) Tudor Pubs., Inc.

Wolfe, Thomas. Look Homeward, Angel. 1920. 544p. pap. 13.95 o.s.i (0-684-71941-X, Macmillan Reference USA) Gale Group.

Wood, Frances. Becoming Rosemary. 2001. 256p. pap. text 12.00 (0-375-89504-3) Random Hse. Children's Bks.

Wood, Frances M. Becoming Rosemary. 1998. 256p. (gr. 7-12). pap. text 3.99 o.s.i (0-440-41238-2) Dell Publishing.

—Becoming Rosemary. 1997. 192p. (gr. 5-9). text 14.95 o.s.i (0-385-32248-8, Dell Books for Young Readers) Random Hse. Children's Bks.

—Becoming Rosemary. 1998. (J). 10.04 (0-606-13186-8) Turtleback Bks.

Wyche, Blonnie Bunn. The Anchor: P. Moore, Proprietor. 2003. 224p. pap. 12.00 (1-889199-05-2) Banks Channel Bks.

NORTH DAKOTA—FICTION

Brooke, Peggy. Jake's Orphan. 2000. (Illus.). 272p. (J). (gr. 5-9). pap. 16.99 (0-7894-2628-5, D K Ink) Dorling Kindersley Publishing, Inc.

—Jake's Orphan. 2001. 272p. (J). reprint ed. pap. 4.99 (0-7434-2703-3, Aladdin) Simon & Schuster Children's Publishing.

Johnson, Rodney. The Curse of the Royal Ruby: A Rinnah Two Feathers Mystery. 2002. (J). 10.95 (0-9663473-9-0) UglyTown.

—The Secret of Dead Man's Mine: A Rinnah Two Feathers Mystery. 2001. (Illus.). 241p. (J). (gr. 4-7). pap. 12.00 (0-9663473-3-1) UglyTown.

Kremer, Kevin. Spaceship over North Dakota. 1996. (Illus.). (J). (gr. 2-8). pap. 7.99 (0-9632837-4-X) Sweetgrass Communications, Inc.

Kurtz, Jane. Jakarta Missing. 2001. 272p. (J). (gr. 5 up). 15.99 (0-06-029401-9); lib. bdg. 16.89 (0-06-029402-7) HarperCollins Children's Bk. Group. (Greenwillow Bks.).

—River Friendly, River Wild. 2000. (Illus.). 40p. (J). (ps-3). 16.00 (0-689-82049-6, Simon & Schuster Children's Publishing) Simon & Schuster Children's Publishing.

Marsh, Carole. North Dakota Silly Basketball Sportsmysteries, Vol. 2. (Carole Marsh North Dakota Bks.). (Illus.). (J). 1997. lib. bdg. 29.95 (*0-7933-1845-9*); 1994. pap. 19.95 (*0-7933-1846-7*); 1994. cd-rom 29.95 (*0-7933-1847-5*) Gallopade International.

—North Dakota Silly Football Sportsmysteries, Vol. 1. 1994. (Carole Marsh North Dakota Bks.). (Illus.). (J). pap. 19.95 (*1-55609-949-5*); lib. bdg. 29.95 (*1-55609-948-7*) Gallopade International.

Naylor, Phyllis Reynolds. Blizzard's Wake. 2004. (Illus.). 192p. (YA). mass mkt. 5.99 (*0-689-85221-5*, Simon Pulse); 2002. 224p. (J). 16.95 (*0-689-85220-7*, Atheneum) Simon & Schuster Children's Publishing.

—Blizzard's Wake. l.t. ed. 2003. 260p. (J). 22.95 (*0-7862-5815-2*) Thorndike Pr.

Reese, John. Big Mutt. 1982. (J). (gr. 5-7). pap. (*0-671-43921-9*, Simon Pulse) Simon & Schuster Children's Publishing.

Schuman, Burt E. Chanukah on the Prairie. 2002. (J). 12.95 (*0-8074-0814-X*) UAHC Pr.

Sypher, Lucy J. Cousins & Circuses. 1991. (Illus.). 256p. (J). (gr. 3-7). pap. 3.95 o.p. (*0-14-034551-5*, Puffin Bks.) Penguin Putnam Bks. for Young Readers.

—The Edge of Nowhere. 1991. (Illus.). 211p. (J). (gr. 3-7). pap. 3.95 o.p. (*0-14-034550-7*, Puffin Bks.) Penguin Putnam Bks. for Young Readers.

—The Edge of Nowhere. 1993. (J). (gr. 5-9). 17.25 o.p. (*0-8446-6645-9*) Smith, Peter Pub., Inc.

Wilder, Laura Ingalls. By the Shores of Silver Lake. (Little House Ser.). (J). (gr. 3-6). lib. bdg. 23.95 (*0-8488-2117-3*) Amereon, Ltd.

—By the Shores of Silver Lake. (Little House Ser.). 304p. (J). 2003. pap. 5.99 (*0-06-052240-2*); 1953. (Illus.). (gr. 3-6). 16.99 (*0-06-026416-0*); 1953. (Illus.). (gr. 3-7). lib. bdg. 17.89 (*0-06-026417-9*) HarperCollins Children's Bk. Group.

—By the Shores of Silver Lake. 2002. (LRS Large Print Cornerstone Ser.). (J). lib. bdg. 35.95 (*1-58118-098-5*) LRS.

—By the Shores of Silver Lake. l.t. ed. 1990. (Little House Ser.). (J). (gr. 3-6). reprint ed. lib. bdg. 16.95 o.p. (*1-55736-176-2*, Cornerstone Bks.) Pages, Inc.

—By the Shores of Silver Lake. 1981. (Little House Ser.). (J). (gr. 3-6). 11.00 (*0-606-02488-3*) Turtleback Bks.

NORTH POLE—FICTION

Ashman, Linda. Sailing off to Sleep. 2001. (Illus.). 32p. (J). 12.95 (*0-689-82971-X*, Simon & Schuster Children's Publishing) Simon & Schuster Children's Publishing.

Brooks, Walter R. Freddy Goes to the North Pole. 2002. (Illus.). 320p. (J). pap. 7.99 (*0-14-230206-6*, Puffin Bks.) Penguin Putnam Bks. for Young Readers.

Bunson, Rick. Rudolph. 2001. 32p. (J). (ps-2). 9.99 (*0-307-11270-5*, Golden Bks.) Random Hse. Children's Bks.

Christie, Michael G. Olive the Orphan Reindeer. 2000. (Illus.). 50p. (J). (gr. 4-7). pap. 7.95 (*1-889658-16-2*) New Canaan Publishing Co., Inc.

—The Story of Olive. 1999. (Illus.). 50p. (J). (gr. 4-7). 14.95 (*1-889658-18-9*) New Canaan Publishing Co., Inc.

Cornetta, Fred. Holly Snow. 1997. (Illus.). 32p. (Orig.). (J). (ps-6). pap. 5.95 (*0-9658318-2-5*) Icicle Publishing.

Howard, Pam. At the North Pole. 1996. (Big Bks.). (Illus.). 8p. (J). (ps-k). pap. text 10.95 (*1-57332-043-9*) HighReach Learning, Inc.

Johnson, Crockett. Harold at the North Pole. 1998. (Harold & the Purple Crayon Ser.). (Illus.). 48p. (J). (ps-3). 14.95 (*0-06-028073-5*); lib. bdg. 14.89 (*0-06-028074-3*) HarperCollins Children's Bk. Group.

Posner, Andrea. Helping Holiday Hands. 1999. (Rudolph Ser.). (Illus.). 18p. (J). (ps). bds. 3.99 (*0-307-14526-3*, Golden Bks.) Random Hse. Children's Bks.

—Santa from Head to Toe. 1999. (Golden Book Ser.). (Illus.). 12p. (J). (ps). bds. 3.99 (*0-307-14527-1*, Golden Bks.) Random Hse. Children's Bks.

Primavera, Elise. Auntie Claus. (Illus.). 40p. (J). (ps-3). 1999. 16.00 (*0-15-201909-X*); 2001. 24.95 o.s.i incl. audio compact disk (*0-15-216259-3*) Harcourt Children's Bks. (Silver Whistle).

—Auntie Claus & the Key to Christmas. 2002. (Illus.). 40p. (J). (gr. k-3). 16.00 (*0-15-202441-7*, Silver Whistle) Harcourt Children's Bks.

—Ralph's Frozen Tale. 1991. (Illus.). 32p. (J). 14.95 o.p. (*0-399-22252-9*, G. P. Putnam's Sons) Penguin Group (USA) Inc.

Shealy, Dennis. Rudolph the Red-Nosed Reindeer: Oh, Nose! 2001. 24p. (J). (ps-k). 2.99 o.p. (*0-307-96005-6*, Golden Bks.) Random Hse. Children's Bks.

Stickland, Paul. Santa's Workshop: A Magical Three-Dimensional Tour. 1995. (Illus.). 8p. (J). (ps-3). 18.99 o.p. (*0-525-45343-1*, Dutton Children's Bks.) Penguin Putnam Bks. for Young Readers.

Thompson, R. W., Jr. The Christmas Eve Tradition. 1993. (Illus.). 16p. (J). (ps-3). 8.95 o.p. (*0-9636442-7-0*) North Pole Chronicles.

Thompson, R. W. The Star on the Pole. 1996. (Illus.). 16p. (J). 8.95 (*0-9636442-3-8*) North Pole Chronicles.

Tiller, Steve. Rudolf the Red Nose Rocket. 2002. (Illus.). 28p. (J). (gr. k-3). 15.95 (*0-9704597-9-3*) MichaelsMind LLC.

Tullus & the Vandals of the North. 1974. (Illus.). 112p. (gr. 5-8). pap. 1.25 o.p. (*0-912692-44-8*) Cook, David C. Publishing Co.

Wynne-Jones, Tim. Zoom Away. 1993. (Laura Geringer Bks.). (Illus.). 32p. (J). (ps-2). 15.00 o.p. (*0-06-022962-4*); lib. bdg. 14.89 o.p. (*0-06-022963-2*) HarperCollins Pubs.

NORTHWEST, PACIFIC—FICTION

Baker, Betty. The Pig War. 1969. (I Can Read Bks.). (Illus.). 64p. (J). (ps-3). lib. bdg. 13.89 o.p. (*0-06-020333-1*) HarperCollins Children's Bk. Group.

Challenger, Robert James. Eagle's Reflection & Other Westcoast Stories. 1995. 48p. (J). pap. (*1-895811-07-4*) Heritage Hse. Publishing Co., Ltd.

Creedon, Catherine. Blue Wolf. 2003. (Julie Andrews Collection). 192p. (J). 15.99 (*0-06-050868-X*); lib. bdg. 16.89 (*0-06-050869-8*) HarperCollins Pubs.

Hobbs, William. Ghost Canoe. 1997. (Illus.). 208p. (J). (gr. 5-9). 15.95 (*0-688-14193-5*) HarperCollins Children's Bk. Group.

—Ghost Canoe. 1998. (Avon Camelot Bks.). 208p. (J). (gr. 5-9). pap. 5.99 (*0-380-72537-1*, Avon Bks.) Morrow/Avon.

—Ghost Canoe. 1998. (J). 11.00 (*0-606-13420-4*) Turtleback Bks.

Killingsworth, Monte. Circle Within a Circle. 1994. 176p. (YA). (gr. 7 up). pap. 14.95 (*0-689-50598-1*, McElderry, Margaret K.) Simon & Schuster Children's Publishing.

LaMear, Arline. Lewis & Clark, the Astoria Cats. 2002. (Illus.). 32p. (J). (gr. 3-7). pap. 9.95 (*0-9720394-0-6*) Lucky Cat Publishing.

Moody, Skye Kathleen. K Falls: Pacific Northwest Mystery. 2001. (Pacific Northwest Mysteries Ser.). 324p. 24.95 (*0-312-26609-X*, Saint Martin's Minotaur) St. Martin's Pr.

Nickerson, Sara. How to Disappear Completely & Never Be Found. (Illus.). 288p. (J). (gr. 5 up). 2003. pap. 5.99 (*0-06-441027-7*); 2002. 15.95 (*0-06-029771-9*); 2002. lib. bdg. 15.89 (*0-06-029772-7*) HarperCollins Children's Bk. Group.

Okimoto, Jean Davies. No Dear, Not Here: The Marbled Murrelets' Quest for a Nest in the Pacific Northwest. 1995. (Illus.). 32p. (J). (ps-2). 14.95 (*1-57061-019-3*) Sasquatch Bks.

RH Disney Staff. Bear with Me. 2003. (Illus.). (J). pap. 3.99 (*0-7364-2174-2*, RH/Disney) Random Hse. Children's Bks.

Shaw, Janet Beeler. Changes for Kaya: A Winter Story. 2002. (American Girls Collection: Bk. 6). (Illus.). 80p. (J). (gr. 2-7). 12.95 (*1-58485-434-0*); pap. 5.95 (*1-58485-433-2*) Pleasant Co. Pubns. (American Girl).

—Kaya: An American Girl. 2002. (American Girls Collection). (Illus.). (J). 74.95 o.p. (*1-56247-512-6*); (YA). (gr. 2). pap. 34.95 (*1-58485-511-8*, American Girl) Pleasant Co. Pubns.

—Kaya & Lone Dog: A Friendship Story. 2002. (American Girls Collection: Bk. 4). (Illus.). 96p. (J). (gr. 2-7). 12.95 (*1-58485-430-8*); pap. 5.95 (*1-58485-429-4*) Pleasant Co. Pubns. (American Girl).

—Kaya & the River Girl. 2003. (American Girls Collection). (Illus.). 38p. (J). pap. 4.95 (*1-58485-792-7*, American Girl) Pleasant Co. Pubns.

—Kaya Shows the Way: A Sister Story. 2002. (American Girls Collection: Bk. 5). (Illus.). 88p. (J). (gr. 2-7). 12.95 (*1-58485-432-4*); pap. 5.95 (*1-58485-431-6*) Pleasant Co. Pubns. (American Girl).

—Kaya's Escape! A Survival Story. 2002. (American Girls Collection: Bk. 2). (Illus.). 88p. (J). (gr. 2-7). 12.95 (*1-58485-426-X*); pap. 5.95 (*1-58485-425-1*) Pleasant Co. Pubns. (American Girl).

—Kaya's Hero: A Story of Giving. 2002. (American Girls Collection: Bk. 3). (Illus.). 88p. (J). (gr. 2-7). 12.95 (*1-58485-428-6*); pap. 5.95 (*1-58485-427-8*) Pleasant Co. Pubns. (American Girl).

Sloat, Teri. There Was an Old Lady Who Swallowed a Trout! 2002. (Illus.). (J). 26.47 (*0-7587-3781-5*) Book Wholesalers, Inc.

—There Was an Old Lady Who Swallowed a Trout!, ERS. 1998. (Illus.). (J). (ps-2). 16.95 (*0-8050-4294-6*, Holt, Henry & Co. Bks. For Young Readers) Holt, Henry & Co.

—There Was an Old Lady Who Swallowed a Trout, ERS. 2002. (Illus.). 32p. (J). (gr. k-2). pap. 6.95 (*0-8050-6900-3*, Holt, Henry & Co. Bks. For Young Readers) Holt, Henry & Co.

Suzuki, David & Ellis, Sarah. The Salmon Forest. 2003. (Illus.). 32p. (J). (gr. k-2). (*1-55054-937-5*) Greystone Bks., Ltd.

Tjepkema, Edith R. Lost in Paradise. 1991. (Northwest Paradise Ser.: Vol. 4). 125p. (Orig.). (YA). (gr. 8-12). pap. 4.95 (*0-9620280-3-7*) Northland Pr.

Vaughan, Richard Lee. Eagle Boy: A Pacific Northwest Native Tale. 2000. (Illus.). 32p. (J). (gr. 1-5). 16.95 (*1-57061-171-8*) Sasquatch Bks.

NORTHWEST TERRITORIES—FICTION

Van Camp, Richard. What's the Most Beautiful Thing You Know about Horses? 1998. (Illus.). 32p. (J). (gr. 1 up). 15.95 (*0-89239-154-5*) Children's Bk. Pr.

Wilson, John. Across Frozen Seas. 2000. 124p. (J). (gr. 3-8). pap. 5.95 (*0-88878-381-7*, Sandcastle Bks.) Beach Holme Pubs., Ltd. CAN. *Dist:* Strauss Consultants.

NORTHWESTERN STATES—FICTION

Perkins, Stanley C. Arvilla & the Tattler Tree: The Fur Trader. 1994. (Illus.). 702p. (J). 30.00 (*0-9614640-9-7*); pap. 25.00 (*0-9620249-4-5*) Broadblade Pr.

NORWAY—FICTION

Aamundsen, Nina R. Two Short & One Long. 1990. 112p. (J). (gr. 4-8). 13.95 o.p. (*0-395-52434-2*) Houghton Mifflin Co.

Archer, Marion F. There Is a Happy Land. 1963. (Illus.). (gr. 5-7). 5.95 o.p. (*0-8075-7861-4*) Whitman, Albert & Co.

Asbjornsen, Peter C. East of the Sun & West of the Moon. 2001. (Children's Classics). 256p. (J). pap. 3.95 (*1-85326-164-5*) Wordsworth Editions, Ltd. GBR. *Dist:* Advanced Global Distribution Services.

D'Aulaire, Ingri & D'Aulaire, Edgar P. Ola. 1939. (gr. k-4). 6.95 o.p. (*0-385-07670-3*) Doubleday Publishing.

Egner, Thorbjorn. Karius & Baktus. Sevig, Mike, tr. from NOR. 2nd ed. 2002. (Illus.). 41p. (J). (gr. 1-3). 10.95 (*0-9615394-1-0*) Skandisk, Inc.

Hamre, Leif. Leap into Danger. Ramsden, Evelyn, tr. 1966. (J). pap. 0.60 o.p. (*0-15-649483-3*, AVB42, Voyager Bks./Libros Viajeros) Harcourt Children's Bks.

—Leap into Danger. 1959. (J). 4.50 o.p. (*0-15-244355-X*) Harcourt Children's Bks.

Marron, Carol A. Last Look from the Mountain. 1983. (Adventure Diaries). (Illus.). 32p. (J). (gr. 3-6). lib. bdg. 14.65 o.p. (*0-940742-17-9*) Raintree Pubs.

McSwigan, Marie. Snow Treasure. 1967. (Illus.). (J). (gr. 3-7). 9.95 o.p. (*0-525-39556-3*, Dutton) Dutton/Plume.

—Snow Treasure. 2000. (J). pap., stu. ed. 40.24 incl. audio (*0-7887-3001-0*, 40883X4) Recorded Bks., LLC.

—Snow Treasure. (Illus.). (J). 9999. (gr. 6-9). pap. 2.50 o.p. (*0-590-41148-9*); 1986. 156p. (gr. 4-6). reprint ed. pap. 2.25 o.p. (*0-590-33992-3*, Scholastic Paperbacks) Scholastic, Inc.

Newth, Mette. The Dark Light, RS. 2004. pap. 5.95 (*0-374-41688-5*) Farrar, Straus & Giroux.

—The Dark Light, RS. Ingwersen, Faith, tr. 1998. 256p. (YA). (gr. 7-12). 18.00 (*0-374-31701-1*, Farrar, Straus & Giroux (BYR)) Farrar, Straus & Giroux.

Parkison, Jami. Inger's Promise. 1995. (Key Concepts in Personal Development Ser.). (Illus.). 32p. (J). (gr. 1-5). 16.95 (*1-55942-080-4*) Marsh Media.

Perkins, Lucy F. Norwegian Twins. 1969. (Walker's Twins Ser.). (Illus.). (J). (gr. 2-5). lib. bdg. 4.85 o.s.i (*0-8027-6045-7*) Walker & Co.

Rongen, Bjorn. Anna of the Bears, RS. 1967. (Illus.). 128p. (J). (gr. 4 up). 3.75 o.p. (*0-374-30363-0*, Farrar, Straus & Giroux (BYR)) Farrar, Straus & Giroux.

Wiesner, William. Turnabout, 001. 1979. (Illus.). 40p. (J). (ps-3). 5.95 o.p. (*0-395-28832-0*, Clarion Bks.) Houghton Mifflin Co. Trade & Reference Div.

Wuorio, Eva-Lis. To Fight in Silence. 1973. 240p. (gr. 5-9). 5.95 o.p. (*0-03-080241-5*) Holt, Henry & Co.

NOVA SCOTIA—FICTION

Amoss, Berthe. The Loup-Garou. 1979. (Illus.). 48p. (J). (gr. 5-7). 11.95 o.s.i (*0-88289-189-8*) Pelican Publishing Co., Inc.

Carey, Mary. A Place for Allie. 1985. (J). (gr. 3-7). 12.95 o.p. (*0-396-08583-0*, G. P. Putnam's Sons) Penguin Putnam Bks. for Young Readers.

Choyce, Lesley. Good Idea Gone Bad. 1998. 128p. (J). (gr. 6-11). pap. (*0-88780-239-7*) Formac Distributing, Ltd.

—Good Idea Gone Bad. 1998. 151p. (J). (gr. 7-12). pap. 4.95 (*0-88780-470-5*); 1995. 128p. (YA). (gr. 6 up). 16.95 (*0-88780-241-9*) Formac Publishing Co., Ltd. CAN. *Dist:* Formac Distributing, Ltd.

Cook, Lyn. Flight from the Fortress. 2003. 152p. (YA). (*1-55041-790-8*) Fitzhenry & Whiteside, Ltd.

Cooper, Gordon. A Second Springtime. 1975. 160p. (J). 7.50 o.p. (*0-525-66428-9*, Dutton Children's Bks.) Penguin Putnam Bks. for Young Readers.

Couvillon, Alice W., et al. Evangeline for Children. 2002. (Illus.). 32p. (J). (gr. k-3). 14.95 (*1-56554-709-8*) Pelican Publishing Co., Inc.

Fox, Paula. The Moonlight Man. 1988. 192p. (YA). (gr. 7 up). reprint ed. mass mkt. 4.99 o.s.i (*0-440-20079-2*, Laurel Leaf) Random Hse. Children's Bks.

—The Moonlight Man. 2003. (Illus.). 176p. (J). pap. 4.99 (*0-689-85886-8*, Aladdin); 1986. 192p. (YA). (gr. 7 up). lib. bdg. 14.95 (*0-02-735480-6*, Simon & Schuster Children's Publishing) Simon & Schuster Children's Publishing.

—The Moonlight Man. 1986. (J). 10.55 (*0-606-03864-7*) Turtleback Bks.

Gillard, Denise. Music from the Sky. 2001. (Illus.). 32p. (J). (gr. k-2). 15.95 (*0-88899-311-0*) Groundwood Bks. CAN. *Dist:* Publishers Group West.

James, Janet C. Jeremy Gates & the Magic Key. 1986. 101p. (YA). (gr. 9-12). 7.95 (*0-920806-32-5*) Penumbra Pr. CAN. *Dist:* Univ. of Toronto Pr.

Murray, Marguerite. Like Seabirds Flying Home. 1988. 192p. (YA). lib. bdg. 13.95 o.s.i (*0-689-31459-0*, Atheneum) Simon & Schuster Children's Publishing.

—The Sea Bears. 1984. 168p. (J). (gr. 4-9). 10.95 o.s.i (*0-689-31050-1*, Atheneum) Simon & Schuster Children's Publishing.

Sauer, Julia L. Fog Magic. 1986. (Newbery Library). (Illus.). 128p. (J). (gr. 4-7). pap. 5.99 (*0-14-032163-2*, Puffin Bks.) Penguin Putnam Bks. for Young Readers.

—Fog Magic. 1988. 20.75 (*0-8446-6344-1*) Smith, Peter Pub., Inc.

—Fog Magic. 1943. (J). 11.04 (*0-606-01269-9*) Turtleback Bks.

—Fog Magic. 1943. 3.37 o.p. (*0-670-32304-7*, Viking); (Illus.). (J). (gr. 4-6). 5.95 o.p. (*0-670-32303-9*) Viking Penguin.

Trottier, Maxine. There Have Always Been Foxes. 2001. (Illus.). 18p. (J). (ps-4). 15.95 (*0-7737-3278-0*) Stoddart Kids CAN. *Dist:* Fitzhenry & Whiteside, Ltd.

Vazquez, Diana. Hannah. l.t. ed. 1998. 144p. (YA). (gr. 4-7). pap. 5.95 (*1-55050-149-6*) Coteau Bks. CAN. *Dist:* Fitzhenry & Whiteside, Ltd.

Wallace, Ian. Boy of the Deeps. 1999. (Illus.). 40p. (J). (gr. 3-6). pap. 16.95 o.p. (*0-7894-2569-6*, D K Ink) Dorling Kindersley Publishing, Inc.

Wilson, Budge. The Leaving. 1992. 208p. (J). (gr. 6 up). 14.95 o.p. (*0-399-21878-5*, Philomel) Penguin Putnam Bks. for Young Readers.

—The Leaving. 1993. 208p. (J). (gr. 7-9). pap. 3.50 (*0-590-46933-9*, Scholastic Paperbacks) Scholastic, Inc.

—The Leaving. 176p. (J). mass mkt. 6.95 (*0-7736-7363-6*) Stoddart Kids CAN. *Dist:* Fitzhenry & Whiteside, Ltd.

—Leaving, & Other Stories. 1990. (J). 8.60 o.p. (*0-606-05421-9*) Turtleback Bks.

O

OCEAN—FICTION

A la Mer. 1992. (Raconte et Chante Ser.). (FRE., Illus.). 28p. (J). (gr. k-2). pap. 18.95 (*88-85148-63-8*) European Language Institute ITA. *Dist:* Midwest European Pubns.

Agell, Charlotte. The Sailor's Book. 1995. (Illus.). 32p. (J). pap. 5.00 (*0-15-200297-9*, Voyager Bks./Libros Viajeros) Harcourt Children's Bks.

Alcock, Vivien. Singer to the Sea. 1994. (J). pap. o.s.i (*0-440-91010-2*, Dell Books for Young Readers) Random Hse. Children's Bks.

Applegate, K. A. August Magic. 1995. (Summer Ser.: Vol. 3). 240p. (YA). (gr. 7 up). per. 3.99 (*0-671-51032-0*, Simon Pulse) Simon & Schuster Children's Publishing.

Avi. Captain Grey. 1993. 144p. (J). pap. 4.95 (*0-380-73244-0*, Harper Trophy) HarperCollins Children's Bk. Group.

Banks, Kate. A Gift from the Sea, RS. 2001. (Illus.). 40p. (J). (gr. 3-6). 16.00 (*0-374-32566-9*, Farrar, Straus & Giroux (BYR)) Farrar, Straus & Giroux.

Barklem, Jill. Sea Story. (Illus.). (J). 2015. 14.95 o.s.i (*0-399-21836-X*); 1991. 32p. 9.95 o.p. (*0-399-21844-0*) Penguin Putnam Bks. for Young Readers. (Philomel).

—Sea Story. 2000. (Brambly Hedge Ser.). (Illus.). 32p. (J). (ps-1). 9.95 (*0-689-83171-4*, Atheneum) Simon & Schuster Children's Publishing.

Batten, Mary. The Winking, Blinking Sea. 2001. 4. (Illus.). 32p. (J). (gr. 2-4). pap. 7.95 (*0-7613-1484-9*) Millbrook Pr., Inc.

Bishop, Gavin. Conejito y el Mar. Acevedo, Pilar, tr. from ENG. 2000. (SPA., Illus.). 32p. (J). (ps-1). 15.95 (*0-7358-1313-2*, NS0105); pap. 6.95 (*0-7358-1314-0*, NS7070) North-South Bks., Inc.

—Conejito y el Mar. 2000. (SPA., Illus.). (J). 13.10 (*0-606-18317-5*) Turtleback Bks.

—Little Rabbit & the Sea. (Illus.). 32p. (J). (ps-1). 2000. pap. 6.95 (*0-7358-1312-4*); 1997. 15.95 o.p. (*1-55858-809-4*); 1997. 16.50 o.p. (*1-55858-810-8*) North-South Bks., Inc.

—Little Rabbit & the Sea. 2000. (Illus.). (J). 13.10 (*0-606-18322-1*) Turtleback Bks.

Bozanich, Tony L. Captain Flounder, His Sole Brothers & Friends. Isaksen, Patricia, ed. 1984. (Illus.). 16p. (J). (ps-4). pap. 4.95 (*0-930655-00-1*) Antarctic Pr.

Brin, Susannah. Mean Waters. 1992. 10.10 (*0-606-11609-5*) Turtleback Bks.

Bunney, Ron. Sink or Swim. 1999. 200p. (J). pap. 12.95 (*1-86368-238-4*) Fremantle Arts Centre Pr. AUS. *Dist:* International Specialized Bk. Services.

Burchard, Peter. Sea Change, RS. 1984. (Illus.). 116p. (J). (gr. 7 up). 9.95 o.p. (*0-374-36460-5*, Farrar, Straus & Giroux (BYR)) Farrar, Straus & Giroux.

Bush, Timothy. Three at Sea. 1994. (Illus.). 32p. (J). (ps-2). 14.00 o.s.i (*0-517-59299-1*, Random Hse. Bks. for Young Readers) Random Hse. Children's Bks.

Cain, Sheridan. Little Turtle & the Song of the Sea. 2000. (Illus.). 32p. (J). (ps-3). 15.95 (*1-56656-355-0*, Crocodile Bks.) Interlink Publishing Group, Inc.

Champlin, Dale, illus. Down by the Bay Big Book: Black & White Nellie Edge I Can Read & Sing Big Book. 1988. (J). (ps-2). pap. text 20.00 (*0-922053-02-2*) Nellie Edge Resources, Inc.

Choyce, Lesley. Wave Watch. 2nd ed. 1994. 120p. (J). (gr. 6-9). reprint ed. pap. 6.95 (*0-88780-300-8*); text 16.95 (*0-88780-081-5*) Formac Publishing Co., Ltd. CAN. *Dist:* Formac Distributing, Ltd., Orca Bk. Pubs., Formac Distributing, Ltd.

Clark, James I. Three Years on the Ocean. 1982. (Quest, Adventure, Survival Ser.). (Illus.). 48p. (J). (gr. 4-9). pap. 9.27 o.p. (*0-8172-2072-0*) Raintree Pubs.

Clownfish Reef. 2002. (Oceanic Mini Bks.). (Illus.). 32p. (J). (*1-59069-011-7*, H1012) Studio Mouse LLC.

Coles, Allison. Michael & the Sea. 1985. (Michael & Mandy Ser.). (Illus.). 28p. (J). (ps up). 3.95 o.p. (*0-88110-268-7*) EDC Publishing.

Cosgrove, Stephen. Serendipity. rev. ed. 1995. (Serendipity Bks.). (Illus.). 32p. (J). (ps-3). 4.99 (*0-8431-3819-X*, Price Stern Sloan) Penguin Putnam Bks. for Young Readers.

—Serendipity. 1995. 11.14 (*0-606-02428-X*) Turtleback Bks.

Cowan, Catherine. My Life with the Wave. ed. 2000. (J). (gr. 2). spiral bd. (*0-616-01621-2*) Canadian National Institute for the Blind/Institut National Canadien pour les Aveugles.

—My Life with the Wave. 2004. (Illus.). 32p. (J). pap. 6.99 (*0-06-056200-5*, Harper Trophy) HarperCollins Children's Bk. Group.

Cowan, Catherine & Paz, Octavio. My Life with the Wave. 1997. (Illus.). 32p. (J). (ps-3). 16.99 (*0-688-12660-X*); 16.89 (*0-688-12661-8*) HarperCollins Children's Bk. Group.

Davidson, Amanda. Teddy at the Seashore, ERS. 1984. (Illus.). 24p. (J). (gr. k-2). pap. o.p. (*0-03-071026-X*, Holt, Henry & Co. Bks. For Young Readers) Holt, Henry & Co.

De Beer, Hans. Al Mar, Al Mar, Osito Polar. Antresyan, Augustin, tr. 1999. (SPA., Illus.). 14p. (J). (gr. k-3). bds. 6.95 (*0-7358-1091-5*, NS0147) North-South Bks., Inc.

Denney, John M. The Sailor. Denney, Rose M., ed. 1996. (Illus.). 24p. (Orig.). (YA). (gr. 9-12). pap. 4.95 (*0-9654698-3-2*) Denney Literary Services.

Disney Staff. Under the Sea. 2001. (Illus.). 12p. (J). pap. 6.99 (*0-7364-1275-1*, RH/Disney) Random Hse. Children's Bks.

Dodd, Lynley. Smallest Turtle. 1985. (Gold Star First Readers Ser.). (Illus.). 29p. (J). (gr. 1-2). lib. bdg. 18.60 o.p. (*0-918831-07-5*) Stevens, Gareth Inc.

Domanska, Janina. If All the Seas Were One Sea. (Illus.). 32p. (J). (ps-2). 1996. pap. 5.95 (*0-689-80343-5*, Aladdin); 1987. lib. bdg. 17.95 (*0-02-732540-7*, Simon & Schuster Children's Publishing) Simon & Schuster Children's Publishing.

—If All the Seas Were One Sea. 1996. 12.10 (*0-606-09456-3*) Turtleback Bks.

Farmer Bob Oceans Series. 2001. (*1-883772-86-9*); (J). (*1-883772-78-8*) Flying Rhinoceros, Inc.

Finding Nemo. 2003. 128p. (J). 19.95 (*0-7868-5400-6*) Disney Pr.

Fisher, Leonard Everett. Sky, Sea, the Jetty, & Me. 2001. (Illus.). 32p. (J). (gr. k-3). 15.95 (*0-7614-5082-3*, Cavendish Children's Bks.) Cavendish, Marshall Corp.

Follow the Fish: A Touch & Say ABC Book. 2002. (DK Ladybird Ser.). 12p. (J). bds. 6.95 (*0-7894-8470-6*) Dorling Kindersley Publishing, Inc.

Fontes, Justine. Who's in the Ocean. 2000. (Wiggly Tab Bks.). (Illus.). 6p. (J). (ps-k). bds. 5.99 (*1-57584-354-4*, Reader's Digest Children's Bks.) Reader's Digest Children's Publishing, Inc.

Frasier, Debra. Out of the Ocean. 1998. (Illus.). 40p. (J). (ps-3). 16.00 (*0-15-258849-3*, Red Wagon Bks.) Harcourt Children's Bks.

Graziadio, Stephanie. Sea Splash! 2000. (Groovy Tube Bks.). (Illus.). 24p. (J). (gr. k-7). bds. 17.99 (*1-58476-019-2*, IKIDS) Innovative Kids.

Greene, Jacqueline Dembar. Out of Many Waters. 1993. 208p. (J). (gr. 5 up). pap. 8.95 (*0-8027-7401-6*) Walker & Co.

Groves. Bee & the Sea, Bk. 9. Date not set. (J). pap. text 129.15 (*0-582-18770-2*) Addison-Wesley Longman, Ltd. GBR. *Dist:* Trans-Atlantic Pubns., Inc.

Guiberson, Brenda Z. Into the Sea, ERS. 1996. (Illus.). 32p. (YA). (gr. 4-7). 16.95 (*0-8050-2263-5*, Holt, Henry & Co. Bks. For Young Readers) Holt, Henry & Co.

Hamilton, Harriet E. The Sunbeam & the Wave. 2000. (Illus.). 33p. (J). (gr. 4-7). 17.95 (*0-87159-250-9*) Unity Schl. of Christianity.

Henderson, Kathy. The Little Boat. 1995. (Illus.). 32p. (J). (ps-3). 15.95 o.p. (*1-56402-420-2*) Candlewick Pr.

Hendra, Sue, illus. Quien Soy? Oceano (Oceans) 2002. (Puzzle Play Ser.). 10p. (J). 10.95 (*968-5308-57-8*) Silver Dolphin Spanish Editions MEX. *Dist:* Publishers Group West.

Hoffman, Basia. The Ocean & Pebbles. l.t. ed. (Illus.). 32p. (J). (ps-2). 1999. pap. (*1-890582-02-6*); 1997. 15.95 (*1-890582-01-8*) Creations by Basia.

Holling, Holling C. Paddle-to-the-Sea. 1980. 16.10 (*0-606-12471-3*) Turtleback Bks.

Huddy, Delia. Puffin at Sea. 1992. (Illus.). 32p. (J). (ps-1). o.s.i (*1-85681-161-1*) Random Hse. of Canada, Ltd. CAN. *Dist:* Random Hse., Inc.

Jackson, Shelley. The Old Woman & the Wave. 1998. (Illus.). 32p. (J). (ps-2). pap. 15.95 o.p. (*0-7894-2484-3*) Dorling Kindersley Publishing, Inc.

Jaynes, Ruth. Yo Ho & Kim at Sea. 1978. (J). (gr. 1-4). o.p. (*0-87505-320-3*) Borden Publishing Co.

Jordan, Polly, illus. In the Ocean. 1993. (What's Missing Ser.). 24p. (J). (ps-2). pap. text 2.95 (*1-56293-319-1*, McClanahan Bk.) Learning Horizons, Inc.

Kalan, Robert. Blue Sea. 2002. (Illus.). (J). 14.43 (*0-7587-2127-7*) Book Wholesalers, Inc.

—Blue Sea. (Illus.). 24p. (J). (ps up). 1992. pap. 5.99 (*0-688-11509-8*, Harper Trophy); 1979. lib. bdg. 15.93 o.p. (*0-688-84184-8*, Greenwillow Bks.) HarperCollins Children's Bk. Group.

—Blue Sea. 1992. 12.10 (*0-606-01330-X*) Turtleback Bks.

Karas, G. Brian. Atlantic. 2002. (Illus.). 32p. (J). 15.99 (*0-399-23632-5*) Penguin Group (USA) Inc.

Keens-Douglas, Richardo. Freedom Child of the Sea. 1995. (Illus.). 24p. (YA). (gr. 1 up). lib. bdg. 16.95 (*1-55037-373-0*); (gr. 4 up). pap. 6.95 (*1-55037-372-2*) Annick Pr., Ltd. CAN. *Dist:* Firefly Bks., Ltd.

Kempton, Kate & Trehearn, Carol. The World Beyond the Waves: An Environmental Adventure. Anderson, David, ed. 1995. (Illus.). 164p. (J). (gr. 4-9). pap. 8.95 (*0-9641330-1-6*) Portunus Publishing Co.

Kranking, Kathy. The Ocean Is, ERS. 2003. (Illus.). 32p. (J). (ps-2). 16.95 (*0-8050-7097-4*, Holt, Henry & Co. Bks. For Young Readers) Holt, Henry & Co.

Le Tord, Bijou. The Deep Blue Sea. 1996. (Illus.). 32p. (J). (ps-2). pap. 4.99 o.s.i (*0-440-41063-0*) Dell Publishing.

Levinson, Riki. Our Home Is the Sea. (Illus.). 32p. (J). (gr. k-3). 1992. pap. 5.99 o.s.i (*0-14-054552-2*, Puffin Bks.); 1988. 13.95 o.s.i (*0-525-44406-8*, Dutton Children's Bks.) Penguin Putnam Bks. for Young Readers.

Locker, Thomas. The Boy Who Held Back the Sea. 1993. 32p. (J). (gr. 2 up). pap. 6.99 (*0-14-054613-8*, Puffin Bks.) Penguin Putnam Bks. for Young Readers.

Long, Susan Hill. Hide & Seek. 2003. (Illus.). 16p. (J). (ps-2). pap. 3.99 (*1-59014-110-5*) Night Sky Bks.

Lost at Sea. 1996. (Ready Readers Series II Stage II). (Illus.). 32p. (J). (gr. 1-3). pap. (*1-56144-951-2*, Honey Bear Bks.) Modern Publishing.

Lottridge, Celia Barker. Music for the Tsar of the Sea. 1998. (Illus.). 32p. (J). (ps-2). 16.95 (*0-88899-328-5*) Groundwood-Douglas & McIntyre CAN. *Dist:* Publishers Group West.

MacGregor, Ellen & Pantell, Dora. Miss Pickerell Harvests the Sea. 1968. (Illus.). (J). (gr. 3-7). lib. bdg. o.p. (*0-07-044572-9*) McGraw-Hill Cos., The.

Machado, Ed. One Tree Island. 1994. 264p. (J). (gr. 5-10). pap. 5.99 (*0-9642652-0-6*) Reef Publishing.

Marshak, Susanna. I Am the Ocean. 1992. (J). 14.95 o.p. (*0-316-54719-0*) Little Brown & Co.

Marshall, Edward. Three by the Sea. 1994. (Puffin Easy-to-Read Ser.). (J). 10.14 (*0-606-00604-4*) Turtleback Bks.

Marshall, Edward & Marshall, James. Three by the Sea. 48p. (J). (gr. k-3). pap. 3.99 (*0-8072-1342-X*, Listening Library) Random Hse. Audio Publishing Group.

Marsoli, Lisa A. Ocean Playmates. 1996. (Playtime Pals Ser.). (Illus.). 12p. (J). (gr. k-3). bds. 6.99 o.p. (*1-57584-022-7*, Reader's Digest Young Families, Inc.) Reader's Digest Children's Publishing, Inc.

Mayne, William. Low Tide. 1994. (J). pap. o.p. (*0-440-90075-1*, Dell Books for Young Readers) Random Hse. Children's Bks.

McClear, Preston. The Sailor & the Sea Witch. 1999. (Illus.). 31p. (J). (gr. k-5). 16.95 (*1-929084-00-5*); pap. 12.95 (*1-929084-01-3*) Malibu Bks. for Children.

McCloskey, Robert. Burt Dow, Deep-Water Man: A Tale of the Sea in the Classic Tradition. 1989. (Picture Puffin Ser.). (J). 12.14 (*0-606-04004-8*) Turtleback Bks.

Morris, Deborah. Long Way Home. 1998. (Real Kids, Real Adventures Ser.: No. 7). 112p. (J). (gr. 4-7). mass mkt. 4.50 o.s.i (*0-425-16190-0*) Berkley Publishing Group.

—Long Way Home. 2000. (Real Kids, Real Adventures Ser.: No. 7). 104p. (J). (gr. 4-7). pap. 4.99 o.p. (*1-928591-02-7*) Real Kids Real Adventures.

Morris, John D. A Trip to the Ocean. 2000. (DJ & Tracker John Ser.). (Illus.). 40p. (J). (ps-3). 11.99 (*0-89051-285-X*) Master Bks.

Mullican, Judy. Under the Sea. 1998. (Big Bks.). (Illus.). 8p. (J). (ps-k). pap. text 10.95 (*1-57332-093-5*) HighReach Learning, Inc.

Nakawatari, Harutaka. Sea & I. 1992. (J). 12.10 (*0-606-08140-2*) Turtleback Bks.

—The Sea & I, RS. Matsui, Susan, tr. 1994. (Illus.). 32p. (J). (ps-3). pap. 5.95 o.p. (*0-374-46454-5*, Sunburst) Farrar, Straus & Giroux.

Navarro, Dawn E., et al. Chelonia: El Retorno de la Tortuga Marina. 2002. (SPA., Illus.). (J). (gr. 3-5). 16.95 (*0-930118-35-9*, SCH31403) Sea Challengers, Inc.

Nilsen, Anna. Under the Sea. 1998. (Illus.). 16p. (Orig.). (J). (ps-k). bds. 3.99 o.s.i (*0-7636-0434-8*) Candlewick Pr.

O'Neill, Michael Patrick. Fishy Friends: A Journey Through the Coral Kingdom. 2003. (Illus.). 64p. (J). 19.95 (*0-9728653-0-6*) Batfish Bks.

O'Rourke, Carol J. Sea Critters Vol. 1: The Case of the Stolen Pearl. 1998. (Illus.). 14p. (J). (gr. k-4). pap. 2.95 (*0-9665692-0-2*) Sea Critters.

—Sea Critters Vol. 2: The Splangywangba Adventure. 1998. (Illus.). 14p. (J). (gr. k-4). pap. 2.95 (*0-9665692-1-0*) Sea Critters.

Page, P. K. A Flask of Sea Water. 1989. (Illus.). 34p. (J). (gr. 2 up). text 17.00 o.p. (*0-19-540704-0*) Oxford Univ. Pr., Inc.

Pallotta, Jerry. Dory Story. (Illus.). 32p. (J). (gr. k-2). 2004. pap. 7.95 (*0-88106-076-3*); 2000. 15.95 (*0-88106-075-5*, Talewinds) Charlesbridge Publishing, Inc.

—Dory Story. 2000. (Illus.). E-Book (*1-59019-578-7*); E-Book (*1-59019-579-5*) ipicturebooks, LLC.

Paterson, Diane. The Bathtub Ocean. 1979. (Illus.). (J). (ps-2). 6.95 o.p. (*0-8037-0460-7*, Dial Bks. for Young Readers) Penguin Putnam Bks. for Young Readers.

Patkau, Karen. In the Sea. 1990. (Illus.). 24p. (J). (ps). 15.95 o.p. (*1-55037-067-7*); pap. 5.95 o.p. (*1-55037-066-9*) Annick Pr., Ltd. CAN. *Dist:* Firefly Bks., Ltd.

Patrick, Denise L. Disney's The Little Mermaid: Ariel's Secret. 1992. (Golden Sturdy Bks.). (Illus.). 14p. (J). (ps). bds. o.p. (*0-307-12393-6*, 12393, Golden Bks.) Random Hse. Children's Bks.

Pechter, Alese. What's in the Deep: An Underwater Adventure for Children. rev. ed. 1991. (J). 14.95 o.p. (*0-87491-983-5*) Acropolis Bks., Inc.

Peck, Jan. Way down Deep in the Deep Blue Sea. 2005. (Illus.). (J). 15.95 (*0-689-85110-3*, Simon & Schuster Children's Publishing) Simon & Schuster Children's Publishing.

Peretti, Frank E. Trapped at the Bottom of the Sea. 1990. (Cooper Kids Adventures Ser.: No. 4). (J). (gr. 4-7). pap. 5.99 (*0-89107-594-1*) Crossway Bks.

Plourde, Lynn. The First Feud: Between the Mountain & the Sea. 2003. (Illus.). 32p. (J). 15.95 (*0-89272-611-3*) Down East Bks.

Ponsolle, Danielle. What Lives in the Water? 1997. (Life with Sylvie Ser.: Bk. 6). (Illus.). 24p. (J). (ps-k). 12.95 o.p. (*0-9655782-5-9*, Tern Bks.) Tern Bk. Co., Inc., The.

Pratt, Kristin J. A Swim Through the Sea. 1994. (Illus.). 40p. (YA). (gr. 4-7). 16.95 (*1-883220-03-3*); (ps-3). pap. 7.95 (*1-883220-04-1*) Dawn Pubns.

Ready Reader Staff. A Sea Star, 6 bks., set, Level 6, Bk. 21. 1996. (J). (ps-3). pap. text 30.95 (*0-8136-2042-2*) Modern Curriculum Pr.

Ryan, Pam Muñoz. Hello, Ocean. 2001. Tr. of Hola Mar. (Illus.). 32p. (J). (ps-3). 16.95 (*0-88106-987-6*, Talewinds); pap. 6.95 (*0-88106-988-4*) Charlesbridge Publishing, Inc.

—Hello, Ocean. 2001. Tr. of Hola Mar. (Illus.). (J). 13.10 (*0-606-20698-1*) Turtleback Bks.

—Hello Ocean/Hola Mar. Canetti, Yanitzia, tr. from ENG. 2003. (ENG & SPA., Illus.). (J). (gr. k-3). pap. 7.95 (*1-57091-372-2*) Charlesbridge Publishing, Inc.

Rylant, Cynthia. Henry & Mudge & the Forever Sea. (Henry & Mudge Ser.). (Illus.). 48p. (J). (gr. k-3). 1997. pap. 3.99 (*0-689-81017-2*, Aladdin); 1996. 15.00 (*0-689-81016-4*, Simon & Schuster Children's Publishing); 1989. text 12.95 o.s.i (*0-02-778007-4*, Simon & Schuster Children's Publishing); 1993. reprint ed. pap. 3.95 (*0-689-71701-6*, Aladdin) Simon & Schuster Children's Publishing.

—Henry & Mudge & the Forever Sea. 1993. (Henry & Mudge Ser.). (J). (gr. k-3). 10.14 (*0-606-02669-X*) Turtleback Bks.

Sargent, Ruth. The Tunnel Beneath the Sea. Weinberger, Jane, ed. 1993. (Illus.). 120p. (J). (gr. 3-6). pap. 9.95 (*0-932433-11-1*) Windswept Hse. Pubs.

Scripture Union. Man up a Tree (Zacchaeus) 1978. (J). pap. 0.49 o.p. (*0-87508-932-1*) Christian Literature Crusade, Inc.

Seymour, Peter. What's in the Deep Blue Sea? 1991. (GRE.). (J). 11.99 (*0-85953-851-6*) Child's Play of England GBR. *Dist:* Child's Play-International.

Shepard, Aaron. The Sea King's Daughter. (Illus.). (ps-3). 2001. 40p. pap. 6.99 (*0-689-84259-7*, Aladdin); 1999. 28p. per. 17.00 (*0-689-82743-1*, Simon & Schuster Children's Publishing) Simon & Schuster Children's Publishing.

Shih, Bernadette L. Follow the Sea. Turner, Francia, tr. & illus. by. 1998. 32p. (J). (ps-3). (ENG & SPA.). 16.95 (*1-889736-07-4*); pap. (*1-889736-06-6*) Ridyl Publishing.

Simpson, Dorothy. Visitors from the Sea. Date not set. 188p. (J). 20.95 (*0-8488-2632-9*) Amereon, Ltd.

Slawski, Wolfgang. Captain Jonathan Sails the Sea. Lanning, Rosemary, tr. from GER. 1997. (Illus.). 32p. (J). (gr. k-3). 16.50 o.p. (*1-55858-814-0*) North-South Bks., Inc.

Smith, Geof. Sponge Bob Square Pants: A Christmas Coral. 2001. (Little Golden Bks.). 32p. pap. 3.99 (*0-307-29055-7*, Golden Bks.) Random Hse. Children's Bks.

Solomon, Joan. A Day by the Sea. 1978. (Illus.). (J). (ps-3). text 9.50 o.p. (*0-241-89782-3*) Trafalgar Square.

Spirin, Gennady, illus. The Sea King's Daughter. 1997. 40p. (J). (gr. 1-4). 17.00 (*0-689-80759-7*, Atheneum) Simon & Schuster Children's Publishing.

Tibbetts, Emily. Ocean, Ocean in the Shell. 1992. 24p. (J). (gr. k-6). pap. 5.00 (*1-886210-02-0*) Tyketoon Young Author Publishing Co.

Tomkins, Jasper. The Hole in the Ocean. 1991. (Illus.). 60p. (J). pap. 7.95 o.s.i (*0-671-74974-9*, Aladdin) Simon & Schuster Children's Publishing.

Under the Sea Carnival. (J). pap. 0.99 o.p. (*0-307-09203-8*, 09203, Golden Bks.) Random Hse. Children's Bks.

Verne, Jules. 20,000 Leagues under the Sea. Vogel, Malvina, ed. 1992. (Great Illustrated Classics Ser.: Vol. 18). (Illus.). 240p. (J). (gr. 3-6). 9.95 (*0-86611-969-8*) Playmore, Inc., Pubs.

Verne, Jules & Golden Books Staff. 20,000 Leagues under the Sea: A First Chapter Book. 1997. (Crayola Kids Adventures Ser.). 64p. (J). pap. 3.99 o.s.i (*0-307-20200-3*, Golden Bks.) Random Hse. Children's Bks.

—20,000 Leagues under the Sea: With Stickers. 1997. (Crayola Kids Adventures Ser.). 48p. (J). pap., wbk. ed. 3.99 o.s.i (*0-307-20700-5*, Golden Bks.) Random Hse. Children's Bks.

Weller, Frances Ward. I Wonder If I'll See a Whale. 1998. (Illus.). 32p. (J). (ps-3). pap. 5.99 o.p. (*0-698-11677-1*, PaperStar) Penguin Putnam Bks. for Young Readers.

Whalen, Erin T. Charlie Goes to Sea! Grant, Stacey, ed. l.t. ed. 2001. (Charlie's Head Ser.). (Illus.). 32p. (J). (gr. 1-3). 16.95 (*1-929265-02-6*); pap. 8.95 (*1-929265-03-4*) Lily & Co. Publishing.

Wild, Margaret. There's a Sea in My Bedroom. 1987. (Illus.). 32p. (J). (ps-3). 3.50 o.p. (*0-87406-255-1*, 16-14576-4) Darby Creek Publishing.

Williams, Jay & Abrashkin, Raymond. Danny Dunn on the Ocean Floor. 1964. (J). (gr. 4-7). lib. bdg. o.p. (*0-07-070524-0*) McGraw-Hill Cos., The.

—Danny Dunn on the Ocean Floor. 1981. (Danny Dunn Ser.: No. 9). (Illus.). (J). (gr. 4-6). pap. (*0-671-43679-1*, Simon Pulse) Simon & Schuster Children's Publishing.

Wood, Jakki. Across the Big Blue Sea: An Ocean Wildlife Book. 1998. (Illus.). 32p. (J). (ps-3). 14.95 (*0-7922-7308-7*) National Geographic Society.

Wright, Glen. Snatched by a Killer Wave. Murphy, Carol, ed. 1981. (Illus.). (J). (gr. 3-6). pap. text 4.95 o.p. (*0-89868-121-9*); lib. bdg. 6.95 o.p. (*0-89868-114-6*) ARO Publishing Co. (Reading Research).

Ziefert, Harriet. Under the Water. 1993. (Puffin Easy-to-Read Ser.). (Illus.). 32p. (J). (ps-3). pap. 3.99 o.s.i (*0-14-036535-4*, Puffin Bks.) Penguin Putnam Bks. for Young Readers.

OHIO—FICTION

Anderson, Sherwood. Winesburg, Ohio. unabr. ed. 1998. audio 29.95 (*1-55685-596-6*) Audio Bk. Contractors, Inc.

—Winesburg, Ohio. 1919. E-Book (*1-58734-001-1*) Bartleby.com.

—Winesburg, Ohio. unabr. ed. 1995. 160p. (J). pap. 2.00 (*0-486-28269-4*) Dover Pubns., Inc.

—Winesburg, Ohio. 1976. (Penguin Twentieth-Century Classics Ser.). 15.00 (*0-606-01787-9*) Turtleback Bks.

—Winesburg, Ohio: Text & Criticism. Feres, John H., ed. 1996. (Viking Critical Library). 512p. pap. 16.00 (*0-14-024779-3*, Penguin Bks.) Penguin Group (USA) Inc.

—Winesburg, Ohio: Text & Criticism. Ferres, John H., ed. (Critical Studies: No. 1). 1977. 512p. pap. 13.95 o.p. (*0-14-015501-5*, Viking); 1960. (J). (gr. 9-12). 15.00 o.p. (*0-670-77269-0*) Viking Penguin.

Borntrager, Mary Christner. Andy. 1993. (Ellie's People Ser.: Vol. 6). 144p. (J). (gr. 7 up). pap. 8.99 (*0-8361-3633-0*); (gr. 5-7). pap. 8.99 o.p. (*0-8361-3641-1*) Herald Pr.

—Annie. 1997. (Ellie's People Ser.: Vol. 10). 144p. (J). (gr. 7-12). pap. 8.99 (*0-8361-9070-X*); (gr. 5-7). pap. 8.99 o.p. (*0-8361-9071-8*) Herald Pr.

—Ellie. (Ellie's People Ser.: Vol. 1). 168p. (J). 1988. (gr. 3-7). pap. 8.99 (*0-8361-3468-0*); 1993. (gr. 4-7). pap. 8.99 o.p. (*0-8361-3636-5*) Herald Pr.

—Ellie's People Series. (J). (ps up). 1995. pap. 89.90 (*0-8361-9003-3*); 1993. pap. 89.90 o.p. (*0-8361-9004-1*) Herald Pr.

—Mandy. 1996. (Ellie's People Ser.: Vol. 9). 144p. (Orig.). (J). (gr. 4-7). pap. 8.99 (*0-8361-9046-7*); (gr. 5-7). pap. 8.99 o.p. (*0-8361-9048-3*) Herald Pr.

—Rebecca. (Ellie's People Ser.: Vol. 2). 176p. (J). 1989. (gr. 4-7). pap. 8.99 (*0-8361-3500-8*); 1993. (gr. 7 up). pap. 8.99 o.p. (*0-8361-3637-3*) Herald Pr.

—Reuben. (Ellie's People Ser.: Vol. 5). 160p. (J). 1992. (gr. 7 up). pap. 8.99 (*0-8361-3593-8*); 1993. (gr. 5-7). pap. 8.99 o.p. (*0-8361-3640-3*) Herald Pr.

—Sarah. 1995. (Ellie's People Ser.: Vol. 8). 144p. (J). (gr. 4-7). pap. 8.99 (*0-8361-9019-X*); pap. 8.99 o.p. (*0-8361-9020-3*) Herald Pr.

Carroll, Betty Casbeer. The Foothill Spirits! Frontier Life & the Shawnees. 2001. 137p. pap. 17.95 (*0-595-17708-5*, Writer's Showcase Pr.) iUniverse, Inc.

Christopher, Debbonnaire. The Day the Ohio Canal Turned Eerie. 1993. (Illus.). (J). 3.00 (*1-880443-10-4*) Roscoe Village Foundation, Inc.

Cockley, David H. Over the Falls: A Child's Storybook Guide to Chagrin Falls. Ascherman, Herbert, Jr., tr. 2000. (Illus.). 24p. (J). (ps-10). pap. 5.95 (*0-9700846-1-7*) Fireside Book Shop, Inc.

Drake, Jane & Love, Ann. Farming. (America at Work Ser.). (Illus.). (J). (gr. 2-5). 2002. 32p. text 12.95 (*1-55074-451-8*); 2000. 118p. pap. (*1-55074-821-1*); 1996. 340p. text (*1-55074-228-0*) Kids Can Pr., Ltd.

Draper, Sharon M. Double Dutch. 192p. (J). 2004. pap. 4.99 (*0-689-84231-7*, Aladdin); 2002. (gr. 7 up). 16.00 (*0-689-84230-9*, Atheneum) Simon & Schuster Children's Publishing.

Fleischman, Paul. The Borning Room. 1991. (Charlotte Zolotow Bk.). 80p. (YA). (gr. 6 up). 14.95 o.s.i (*0-06-023762-7*); lib. bdg. 14.89 o.p. (*0-06-023785-6*) HarperCollins Children's Bk. Group.

Greegor, Katherine. Trouble - Of the Northwest Territory. 1992. (Illus.). 100p. (Orig.). (J). (gr. 3-8). pap. 5.95 (*0-9633091-7-X*) Promise Land Pubs.

Gundisch, Karin. How I Became an American. Skofield, James, tr. from GER. 2001. 128p. (J). (gr. 3-7). 15.95 (*0-8126-4875-7*) Cricket Bks.

Hamilton, Virginia. The Great M. C. Higgins, 6 vols. 3rd ed. (J). pap. text 23.70 (*0-13-620220-9*); pap. text 3.95 (*0-13-800137-5*) Prentice Hall (Schl. Div.).

—The House of Dies Drear. l.t. ed. 2001. 305p. lib. bdg. 29.95 (*1-58118-087-X*) LRS.

—The House of Dies Drear. 1998. 32p. 9.95 (*1-56137-516-0*, NU5168) Novel Units, Inc.

—The House of Dies Drear. 2001. (Assessment Packs Ser.). 15p. pap. text 15.95 (*1-58303-122-7*) Pathways Publishing.

—The House of Dies Drear. 8.97 (*0-13-437491-6*) Prentice Hall PTR.

—The House of Dies Drear. (Illus.). 256p. (YA). 1984. (gr. 7 up). mass mkt. 5.99 (*0-02-043520-7*, Simon Pulse); 1968. (gr. 4-7). 18.95 (*0-02-742500-2*, Simon & Schuster Children's Publishing) Simon & Schuster Children's Publishing.

—The House of Dies Drear. 1984. (Dies Drear Chronicle Ser.). (J). 11.04 (*0-606-03314-9*) Turtleback Bks.

—M. C. Higgins, the Great. l.t. ed. 1988. 320p. (J). (gr. 3-7). reprint ed. lib. bdg. 15.95 o.p. (*1-55736-075-8*) Bantam Doubleday Dell Large Print Group, Inc.

—M. C. Higgins, the Great. 1998. (J). pap. 4.50 (*0-87628-568-X*) Ctr. for Applied Research in Education, The.

—M. C. Higgins, the Great. l.t. ed. 1976. 400 p. lib. bdg. 10.95 o.p. (*0-8161-6356-1*, Macmillan Reference USA) Gale Group.

—M. C. Higgins, the Great. pap. text, stu. ed. (*0-13-620246-2*) Prentice Hall (Schl. Div.).

—M. C. Higgins, the Great. 1976. 240p. (J). (gr. 7 up). pap. 2.50 o.s.i (*0-440-95598-X*, Laurel Leaf) Random Hse. Children's Bks.

—M. C. Higgins, the Great. 2003. (J). E-Book 6.99 (*0-689-84806-4*, Simon & Schuster Children's Publishing); 1998. (J). pap. 2.65 o.p. (*0-689-82168-9*, Aladdin); 1974. 288p. (YA). (gr. 7 up). lib. bdg. 17.00 (*0-02-742480-4*, Simon & Schuster Children's Publishing); 1987. 288p. (YA). (gr. 5-9). reprint ed. pap. 4.99 (*0-02-043490-1*, Simon Pulse); 2nd ed. 1993. 288p. (J). (gr. 4-7). reprint ed. mass mkt. 4.99 (*0-689-71694-X*, Simon Pulse); 25th anniv. ed. 1999. (Illus.). 240p. (J). (gr. 7). 18.00 (*0-689-83074-2*, Simon & Schuster Children's Publishing) Simon & Schuster Children's Publishing.

—M. C. Higgins, the Great. 1987. (J). 11.04 (*0-606-02497-2*) Turtleback Bks.

—M. C. Higgins, the Great & Newbery Summer. 2003. 288p. (J). pap. 2.99 (*0-689-86228-8*, Aladdin) Simon & Schuster Children's Publishing.

—Willie Bea & the Time the Martians Landed. 1983. 224p. (J). (gr. 5-9). 16.00 o.s.i (*0-688-02390-8*, Greenwillow Bks.) HarperCollins Children's Bk. Group.

—Willie Bea & the Time the Martians Landed. 1989. 224p. (J). (gr. 4-7). reprint ed. pap. 3.95 o.p. (*0-689-71328-2*, Simon Pulse) Simon & Schuster Children's Publishing.

Hickman, Janet. Susannah. (gr. 5 up). 2000. (Illus.). 192p. (J). mass mkt. 4.95 (*0-380-73224-6*, Harper Trophy); 1998. 144p. (YA). 15.00 (*0-688-14854-9*, Greenwillow Bks.) HarperCollins Children's Bk. Group.

—Susannah. 2001. (J). 11.00 (*0-606-20934-4*) Turtleback Bks.

Lutz, Norma Jean. Escape from Slavery: A Family's Fight for Freedom. 1999. (American Adventure Ser.: No. 16). 144p. (J). (gr. 3-7). lib. bdg. 15.95 (*0-7910-5590-6*) Chelsea Hse. Pubs.

Lyon, George Ella. Gina, Jamie, Father, Bear. 2002. 144p. (J). (gr. 6-9). 15.95 (*0-689-84370-4*, Atheneum/Richard Jackson Bks.) Simon & Schuster Children's Publishing.

Morehead, Don & Morehead, Ann. A Short Season: Story of a Montana Childhood. 1998. (Illus.). 190p. pap. 13.00 (*0-8032-8244-3*, A Bison Original) Univ. of Nebraska Pr.

Rinaldi, Ann. The Second Bend in the River. (J). 1999. 288p. (gr. 5-9). mass mkt. 4.99 (*0-590-74259-0*); 1997. pap. 15.95 (*0-590-74258-2*) Scholastic, Inc.

—The Second Bend in the River. 1999. 11.04 (*0-606-16581-9*) Turtleback Bks.

Roos, Stephen. Recycling George. 144p. (J). 2003. (Illus.). pap. 4.99 (*0-689-86351-9*, Aladdin); 2002. 16.00 (*0-689-83146-3*, Simon & Schuster Children's Publishing) Simon & Schuster Children's Publishing.

—Recycling George. 2003. (Young Adult Ser.). 22.95 (*0-7862-5015-1*) Thorndike Pr.

Sanders, Scott R. Aurora Means Dawn. 1998. 12.14 (*0-606-13155-8*) Turtleback Bks.

Sanders, Scott Russell. Warm As Wool. 1992. (Illus.). 32p. (J). (gr. k-5). mass mkt. 16.00 (*0-02-778139-9*, Atheneum) Simon & Schuster Children's Publishing.

—Warm As Wool. 1998. 12.14 (*0-606-15877-4*) Turtleback Bks.

Schraff, Anne. Darkness. 2000. 119p. (J). (*0-7807-9367-6*); pap. (*0-7891-5183-9*) Perfection Learning Corp.

—Wait until Spring. 2000. 125p. (J). (*0-7807-9282-3*); pap. (*0-7891-5139-1*) Perfection Learning Corp.

Schumacher, Julie. Grass Angel. 2004. 144p. lib. bdg. 17.99 (*0-385-90163-1*); 208p. (gr. 5-9). text 15.95 (*0-385-73073-X*) Dell Publishing. (Delacorte Pr.).

Sherwood, Anderson. Winesburg, Ohio. (Modern Library Ser.). (J). E-Book 4.95 (*1-931208-07-7*) Adobe Systems, Inc.

Tripp, Valerie. Changes for Kit: A Winter Story. 2001. (American Girls Collection: Bk. 6). (Illus.). 80p. (J). (gr. 2 up). 12.95 (*1-58485-027-2*); pap. 5.95 (*1-58485-026-4*) Pleasant Co. Pubns. (American Girl).

—Changes for Kit: A Winter Story. 2001. (American Girls Collection). (Illus.). (J). 12.10 (*0-606-21107-1*) Turtleback Bks.

—Kit's Home Run. 2002. (American Girls Short Stories Ser.). (Illus.). 64p. (J). 4.95 (*1-58485-482-0*) Pleasant Co. Pubns.

Willis, Donald B. Mystery of the Waterloo Bagpipes. 2001. 196p. (YA). pap. 9.95 (*0-9707845-0-3*) Anubis Publishing.

Willis, Patricia. Out of the Storm. 1995. 192p. (J). (gr. 4-6). tchr. ed. 15.00 (*0-395-68708-X*, Clarion Bks.) Houghton Mifflin Co. Trade & Reference Div.

Woodson, Jacqueline. Lena. 1999. 128p. (YA). (gr. 5-9). 15.95 o.s.i (*0-385-32308-5*, Dell Books for Young Readers) Random Hse. Children's Bks.

Woodyard, Chris. Haunted Ohio Vol. 1: Ghostly Tales from the Buckeye State. 1991. 224p. (YA). (gr. 6 up). pap. 10.95 (*0-9628472-0-8*) Kestrel Pubns.

Zinnen, Linda. The Truth about Rats, Rules, & Seventh Grade. 2001. 160p. (J). (gr. 3-7). 14.95 (*0-06-028799-3*); (gr. 4-7). lib. bdg. 15.89 (*0-06-028800-0*) HarperCollins Children's Bk. Group.

OHIO RIVER AND VALLEY—FICTION

Lutz, Norma Jean. Trouble on the Ohio River: Drought Shuts Down a City. 15th ed. 1998. (American Adventure Ser.: No. 15). (Illus.). (J). (gr. 3-7). pap. 3.97 (*1-57748-232-8*) Barbour Publishing, Inc.

Nolan, Jeannette. Getting to Know the Ohio River. 1974. (Getting to Know Ser.). (Illus.). (J). (gr. 3-4). 3.97 o.p. (*0-698-30497-7*) Putnam Publishing Group, The.

Willis, Patricia. Danger along the Ohio. 1999. 192p. (J). (gr. 3-7). pap. 5.99 (*0-380-73151-7*, Harper Trophy) HarperCollins Children's Bk. Group.

—Danger along the Ohio. 1999. 10.04 (*0-606-16343-3*) Turtleback Bks.

OKEFENOKEE SWAMP (GA. AND FLA.)—FICTION

George, Jean Craighead. Tree Castle Island. 2002. (Illus.). 256p. (J). (gr. 3-7). 15.95 (*0-06-000254-9*); (gr. 4-7). lib. bdg. 16.89 (*0-06-000255-7*) HarperCollins Children's Bk. Group.

Talley, Linda. Jackson's Plan. 1998. (Key Concepts in Personal Development Ser.). (Illus.). 32p. (J). (gr. k-4). 16.95 (*1-55942-104-5*, 7665) Marsh Media.

OKLAHOMA—FICTION

Antle, Nancy. Hard Times: A Story of the Great Depression. 1993. (Once upon America Ser.). (Illus.). 64p. (J). (gr. 2-6). 12.99 o.p. (*0-670-84665-1*, Viking Children's Bks.) Penguin Putnam Bks. for Young Readers.

—Playing Solitaire. 2000. (Illus.). 112p. (YA). (gr. 7 up). 16.99 o.p. (*0-8037-2406-3*, Dial Bks. for Young Readers) Penguin Putnam Bks. for Young Readers.

Beard, Darleen Bailey. The Babbs Switch Story, RS. 2002. 176p. (J). 16.00 (*0-374-30475-0*, Farrar, Straus & Giroux (BYR)) Farrar, Straus & Giroux.

—The Flim-Flam Man, RS. (Illus.). 96p. (J). 2003. pap. 5.95 (*0-374-42345-8*, Sunburst); 1998. (gr. 2-6). 15.00 (*0-374-32346-1*, Farrar, Straus & Giroux (BYR)) Farrar, Straus & Giroux.

Constant, Alberta W. Miss Charity Comes to Stay. 1959. (Illus.). (J). (gr. 5-9). 8.95 o.p. (*0-690-54490-1*) HarperCollins Children's Bk. Group.

Durbin, William. The Journal of C. J. Jackson: A Dust Bowl Migrant, Oklahoma to California, 1935. 2002. (My Name Is America Ser.). (Illus.). 144p. (J). (gr. 4-9). pap. 10.95 (*0-439-15306-9*, Scholastic Pr.) Scholastic, Inc.

Goins, Ellen H. Big Diamond's Boy. 1977. (J). 6.95 o.p. (*0-525-66528-5*, Dutton Children's Bks.) Penguin Putnam Bks. for Young Readers.

Griffis, Molly Levite. The Feester Filibuster. 2002. (Illus.). vi, 236p. (J). pap. 8.95 (*1-57168-694-0*, Eakin Pr.) Eakin Pr.

—The Rachel Resistance. 2001. 224p. (J). 16.95 (*1-57168-541-3*, Eakin Pr.) Eakin Pr.

Grove, Vicki. The Starplace. 1999. 214p. (YA). (gr. 5-9). 17.99 (*0-399-23207-9*) Penguin Group (USA) Inc.

—The Starplace. 2000. (Illus.). 224p. (J). (gr. 5-9). pap. 5.99 (*0-698-11868-5*, Puffin Bks.) Penguin Putnam Bks. for Young Readers.

—The Starplace. 2000. 12.04 (*0-606-20373-7*); (J). 12.04 (*0-606-20257-9*) Turtleback Bks.

Hall, Lynn. Uphill All the Way. 1984. 121p. (YA). (gr. 7 up). 11.95 o.s.i (*0-684-18066-9*, Atheneum) Simon & Schuster Children's Publishing.

Hesse, Karen. Out of the Dust. 2002. (Illus.). (J). 13.19 (*0-7587-0207-8*) Book Wholesalers, Inc.

—Out of the Dust. 240p. (YA). (gr. 5 up). pap. 4.99 (*0-8072-1526-0*); 2000. (YA). (gr. 4-7). audio 18.00 (*0-8072-8050-X*, YA967CXR); 1998. 240p. (J). (gr. 5 up). pap. 28.00 incl. audio (*0-8072-8013-5*, YA967SP) Random Hse. Audio Publishing Group. (Listening Library).

—Out of the Dust. (Apple Signature Edition Ser.). (J). 1999. 176p. (gr. 4-7). mass mkt. 4.99 (*0-590-37125-8*); 1997. 227p. (gr. 6-8). pap. 15.95 (*0-590-36080-9*) Scholastic, Inc.

—Out of the Dust. 1999. 11.04 (*0-606-15665-8*) Turtleback Bks.

Hinton, S. E. The Outsiders. 1967. 192p. (YA). (gr. 7-12). text 16.99 (*0-670-53257-6*, Viking Children's Bks.) Penguin Putnam Bks. for Young Readers.

Hurmence, Belinda. Dixie in the Big Pasture. 1994. (J). (gr. 4 up). 13.95 o.s.i (*0-395-52002-9*) Clarion IND. *Dist:* Houghton Mifflin Co.

Jerman, Jerry. The Secret of Whispering Woods: The Journeys of Jessie Land. 1996. 132p. (J). (gr. 3-7). mass mkt. 5.99 (*1-56476-552-0*) Cook Communications Ministries.

Myers, Anna. Captain's Command. 1999. 144p. (YA). (gr. 5-9). 15.95 (*0-8027-8706-1*) Walker & Co.

—Ethan Between Us. 2000. (Illus.). (J). 14.00 (*0-606-18742-1*) Turtleback Bks.

—Ethan Between Us. 160p. (YA). (gr. 7-12). 2000. pap. 7.95 (*0-8027-7584-5*); 1998. (Illus.). 15.95 (*0-8027-8670-7*) Walker & Co.

—Fire in the Hills. 1996. 192p. (YA). (gr. 7 up). 15.95 (*0-8027-8421-6*) Walker & Co.

—The Fire in the Hills. 1998. (Puffin Novel Ser.). 176p. (J). (gr. 7-12). pap. 5.99 o.s.i (*0-14-130074-4*, Puffin Bks.) Penguin Putnam Bks. for Young Readers.

—Red Dirt Jessie. 1992. 107p. (YA). 13.95 (*0-8027-8172-1*) Walker & Co.

—Rosie's Tiger. 1994. 128p. (J). (gr. 4-7). 14.95 (*0-8027-8305-8*) Walker & Co.

—Spotting the Leopard. 1996. 176p. (J). (gr. 4-7). 15.95 (*0-8027-8459-3*) Walker & Co.

Porter, Tracey. Treasures in the Dust. (J). 1999. 160p. (gr. 5 up). pap. 5.99 (*0-06-440770-5*, Harper Trophy); 1997. (Illus.). 128p. (gr. 4-8). lib. bdg. 14.89 (*0-06-027564-2*); 1997. (Illus.). 160p. (gr. 3-7). 15.95 (*0-06-027563-4*) HarperCollins Children's Bk. Group.

—Treasures in the Dust. l.t. ed. 2000. (Juvenile Ser.). (Illus.). 135p. (J). (gr. 4-7). 20.95 (*0-7862-2751-6*) Thorndike Pr.

—Treasures in the Dust. 1999. 11.00 (*0-606-16702-1*) Turtleback Bks.

Rawls, Wilson. Summer of the Monkeys. 1992. (Bantam Starfire Bks.). 304p. (YA). (gr. 4-7). mass mkt. 5.99 (*0-553-29818-6*) Bantam Bks.

—Summer of the Monkeys. 1992. (Bantam Starfire Bks.). (J). 12.04 (*0-606-00432-7*) Turtleback Bks.

Thomas, Joyce Carol. Bright Shadow. 1983. (Avon Flare Book Ser.). 128p. (gr. 7 up). mass mkt. 4.99 (*0-380-84509-1*, Avon Bks.) Morrow/Avon.

—Bright Shadow. 1983. (Avon/Flare Bks.). 9.60 o.p. (*0-606-03029-8*) Turtleback Bks.

—Marked by Fire. 1982. (J). (gr. 7 up). pap. 4.50 o.s.i (*0-380-79327-X*, Avon Bks.) Morrow/Avon.

Tomlinson, Sylvia. Maddie. 2002. (Illus.). 124p. (J). (gr. 3-7). 12.95 (*0-9720293-0-3*) Redbud Publishing Co.

Townsend, Una Belle. Grady's in the Silo. 2003. (Illus.). 32p. (J). 14.95 (*1-58980-098-2*) Pelican Publishing Co., Inc.

Wallace, Bill. Aloha Summer. 1997. 208p. (J). (gr. 3-7). tchr. ed. 15.95 (*0-8234-1306-3*) Holiday Hse., Inc.

—Coyote Autumn. 2002. 208p. pap. 4.99 (*0-7434-2836-6*, Aladdin) Simon & Schuster Children's Publishing.

—Journey into Terror. 1996. 176p. (J). (gr. 3-6). 14.00 (*0-671-00114-0*, Simon & Schuster Children's Publishing) Simon & Schuster Children's Publishing.

Whitworth, Artie. Turkey John. 1996. (Illus.). 175p. (J). 25.25 (*1-56763-190-8*); pap. 4.95 o.p. (*1-56763-191-6*) Ozark Publishing.

OLD FORT NIAGARA (N.Y.)—FICTION

Orton, Helen F. The Gold-Laced Coat. rev. ed. 1988. (Illus.). 226p. (J). (gr. 4-8). reprint ed. pap. 5.95 (*0-941967-07-7*) Old Fort Niagara Assn., Inc.

ONTARIO—FICTION

Buja, John E. Race to Freedom. 2002. (Illus.). 132p. 7.95 (*1-894303-24-5*) RRP Pubs.

Cook, Lyn. Pegeen & the Pilgrim. 2002. (Illus.). 288p. (J). (gr. 5 up). pap. 7.95 (*0-88776-593-9*) Tundra Bks. of Northern New York.

Dabcovich, Lydia, illus. The Ghost on the Hearth. 2003. (Family Heritage Ser.). 32p. (J). (gr. 1-5). 15.95 (*0-916718-18-2*) Vermont Folklife Ctr.

Fleck, Earl. Chasing Fire: Danger in Canoe Country. 2004. (Illus.). 173p. (J). pap. 12.95 (*0-930100-53-0*) Holy Cow! Pr.

Johnston, Julie. The Only Outcast. (YA). (gr. 6-9). 1998. 232p. 14.95 (*0-88776-441-X*); 1999. 248p. reprint ed. pap. 6.95 (*0-88776-488-6*) Tundra Bks. of Northern New York.

—The Only Outcast. 1999. (J). 13.00 (*0-606-19122-4*) Turtleback Bks.

McCurdy, J. Fitzgerald. The Serpent's Egg. 2001. (Illus.). 280p. (J). (gr. 9-13). (*0-9688713-0-5*) Saratime, Inc.

McNamee, Graham. Acceleration. 2003. 224p. (YA). (gr. 7). 15.95 (*0-385-73119-1*); lib. bdg. 17.99 (*0-385-90144-5*) Random Hse. Children's Bks. (Lamb, Wendy).

Nugent, Matthew A. The Legend of Timber Island. 2001. (Illus.). (YA). (gr. 4-9). pap. 14.95 (*0-9705812-1-1*) CBI Pr.

Posesorski, Sherie. Escape Plans. 2001. (Illus.). 272p. (YA). (gr. 5). pap. 8.95 (*1-55050-177-1*) Coteau Bks. CAN. *Dist:* General Distribution Services, Inc.

Wilson, Eric G. The Lost Treasure of Casa Loma. 6th ed. 2001. (Tom & Liz Austen Mysteries Ser.). (Illus.). 102p. (J). (gr. 3-6). mass mkt. 5.95 (*0-7736-7492-6*) Stoddart Kids CAN. *Dist:* Fitzhenry & Whiteside, Ltd.

Woods, Shirley. Black Nell: The Adventures of a Coyote. 2000. (Illus.). 96p. (J). (gr. 3-7). pap. 6.95 (*0-88899-319-6*) Groundwood Bks. CAN. *Dist:* Publishers Group West.

—Black Nell: The Adventures of a Coyote. 2000. (Illus.). (J). 13.10 (*0-606-21882-3*) Turtleback Bks.

OREGON—FICTION

Allen, T. D. Doctor in Buckskin. 1951. lib. bdg. 9.87 o.p. (*0-06-010096-6*) HarperCollins Pubs.

Biggar, Joan R. High Desert Secrets. 1992. (Adventure Quest Ser.). 160p. (Orig.). (J). (gr. 5-8). pap. 4.99 o.s.i (*0-570-04711-0*, 56-1670) Concordia Publishing Hse.

Carson, Drew. Summer Discovery. Thatch, Nancy R., ed. 1998. (Books for Students by Students). (Illus.). 29p. (J). (gr. 2-4). lib. bdg. 15.95 (*0-933849-68-0*) Landmark Editions, Inc.

Cleary, Beverly. Emily's Runaway Imagination. 2002. (J). 13.83 (*0-7587-9141-0*) Book Wholesalers, Inc.

—Emily's Runaway Imagination. 1988. mass mkt. o.s.i (*0-440-80049-8*) Dell Publishing.

—Emily's Runaway Imagination. (Cleary Reissue Ser.). (Illus.). (J). (gr. 4-7). 1990. 240p. pap. 5.99 (*0-380-70923-6*, Harper Trophy); 1961. 224p. lib. bdg. 16.89 (*0-688-31267-5*) HarperCollins Children's Bk. Group.

—Emily's Runaway Imagination. 1961. (Illus.). 224p. (J). (gr. 3-7). 16.00 o.p. (*0-688-21267-0*, Morrow, William & Co.) Morrow/Avon.

—Emily's Runaway Imagination. (J). (gr. 2-4). 221p. pap. 4.95 (*0-8072-1416-7*); 1986. audio 15.98 (*0-8072-1140-0*, SWR48SP) Random Hse. Audio Publishing Group. (Listening Library).

—Emily's Runaway Imagination, unabr. ed. 1992. (J). (gr. 4). audio 35.00 (*1-55690-609-9*, 92302E7) Recorded Bks., LLC.

—Emily's Runaway Imagination. 1990. (J). 11.00 (*0-606-04665-8*) Turtleback Bks.

Corbin, William. Smoke. 1967. (J). (gr. 5-9). 7.95 o.p. (*0-698-20131-0*) Putnam Publishing Group, The.

Crew, Linda. Brides of Eden: A True Story Imagined. 2001. (Illus.). 240p. (J). (gr. 7 up). 15.95 (*0-06-028750-0*); (YA). (gr. 5 up). lib. bdg. 15.89 (*0-06-028751-9*) HarperCollins Children's Bk. Group.

—Brides of Eden: A True Story Imagined. 2003. 256p. (J). (gr. 5 up). pap. 6.99 (*0-06-447217-5*) HarperCollins Pubs.

—Fire on the Wind. 1997. 208p. (YA). (gr. 7 up). mass mkt. 3.99 o.s.i (*0-440-21961-2*, Yearling); 1995. 208p. (YA). pap. 12.00 (*0-375-89512-4*); 1995. 176p. (YA). (gr. 7 up). 14.95 o.s.i (*0-385-32185-6*, Dell Books for Young Readers); 1995. (J). 20.95 (*0-385-31003-X*, Dell Books for Young Readers) Random Hse. Children's Bks.

—Fire on the Wind. 1997. 10.04 (*0-606-11326-6*) Turtleback Bks.

—Nekomah Creek Christmas. 1995. (Illus.). 160p. (J). (gr. 4-7). pap. 3.99 o.s.i (*0-440-41099-1*, Yearling) Random Hse. Children's Bks.

—Nekomah Creek Christmas. 1995. (J). 9.34 o.p. (*0-606-07940-8*) Turtleback Bks.

Hermes, Patricia. A Perfect Place: Joshua's Oregon Trail Diary, Bk. 2. 2002. (My America Ser.: Bk. 2). 128p. (J). (gr. 2-5). pap. 10.95 (*0-439-19999-9*); mass mkt. 4.99 (*0-439-38900-3*) Scholastic, Inc. (Scholastic Pr.).

—The Wild Year: Joshua's Oregon Trail Diary. 2003. (My America Ser.). 112p. (J). mass mkt. 4.99 (*0-439-37056-6*);Bk. 3. pap. 12.95 (*0-439-37055-8*) Scholastic, Inc.

Holcomb, Jerry K. The Chinquapin Tree. 1998. (Accelerated Reader Bks.). 192p. (J). (gr. 3-7). 14.95 (*0-7614-5028-9*, Cavendish Children's Bks.) Cavendish, Marshall Corp.

Hough, Emerson. 54-40 or Fight. 2000. 252p. (J). E-Book 3.95 (*0-594-02461-7*) 1873 Pr.

Karr, Kathleen. Oregon Sweet Oregon. (Petticoat Party Ser.: Vol. 3). 160p. (gr. 5 up). 1998. (J). pap. 4.95 o.p. (*0-06-440497-8*, Harper Trophy); 1997. (YA). 14.95 (*0-06-027233-3*); 1997. (YA). lib. bdg. 14.89 (*0-06-027234-1*) HarperCollins Children's Bk. Group.

Kehret, Peg. Escaping the Giant Wave. 2003. (Illus.). 160p. (J). 15.95 (*0-689-85272-X*, Simon & Schuster Children's Publishing) Simon & Schuster Children's Publishing.

—Escaping the Giant Wave. l.t. ed. 2003. 152p. (J). 21.95 (*0-7862-5985-X*) Thorndike Pr.

Killingsworth, Monte. Eli's Songs. 1991. 144p. (YA). (gr. 5 up). 13.95 o.s.i (*0-689-50527-2*, McElderry, Margaret K.) Simon & Schuster Children's Publishing.

Kimmel, Eric A. One Good Turn Deserves Another. 1994. 160p. (J). (gr. 4-7). tchr. ed. 14.95 o.p. (*0-8234-1138-9*) Holiday Hse., Inc.

Lampman, Evelyn S. Treasure Mountain. 2nd ed. 2000. (Eager Beaver Bks.). (Illus.). 220p. (J). (gr. 4). reprint ed. pap. 5.95 o.p. (*0-87595-231-3*) Oregon Historical Society Pr.

Love, D. Anne. Bess's Log Cabin Quilt. 1996. (Illus.). 128p. (J). (gr. 4-7). pap. text 4.50 (*0-440-41197-1*) Dell Publishing.

—Bess's Log Cabin Quilt. 1995. (Illus.). 123p. (J). (gr. 4-7). tchr. ed. 15.95 (*0-8234-1178-8*) Holiday Hse., Inc.

—Bess's Log Cabin Quilt. 1996. (Illus.). (J). pap. 4.99 (*0-440-91154-0*, Dell Books for Young Readers) Random Hse. Children's Bks.

—Bess's Log Cabin Quilt. 1996. 10.55 (*0-606-11115-8*) Turtleback Bks.

Love, Glen A., ed. The World Begins Here: An Anthology of Oregon Short Fiction. 1993. (Oregon Literature Ser.: Vol. 1). (Illus.). 320p. (Orig.). (YA). pap. 21.95 (*0-87071-370-1*); pap. text 35.95 (*0-87071-369-8*) Oregon State Univ. Pr.

McDonald, Megan. The Sisters Club. 2003. (Pleasant Company Publications). (Illus.). (J). pap. 15.95 (*1-58485-782-X*, American Girl) Pleasant Co. Pubns.

McGraw, Eloise Jarvis. Greensleeves. 1968. (J). (gr. 7 up). 6.50 o.p. (*0-15-232564-6*) Harcourt Children's Bks.

—The Moccasin Trail. 1952. (Illus.). (J). (gr. 5-8). 8.50 o.p. (*0-698-20092-6*, Coward-McCann) Putnam Publishing Group, The.

Nelson, Blake. New Rules of High School. 2003. 244p. (YA). text 16.99 (*0-670-03644-7*, Viking) Viking Penguin.

Nicholas, Jay. Down to the Sea: The Story of a Little Salmon & His Neighborhood. 1999. (Illus.). 47p. (J). (ps-3). 35.00 o.s.i (*1-58151-038-1*); pap. 15.00 o.s.i (*1-58151-036-5*) BookPartners, Inc.

O'Brien, Kevin. Only Son. 1997. 304p. 21.95 o.p. (*1-57566-091-1*, Kensington Bks.) Kensington Publishing Corp.

Shands, Linda I. Blind Fury. 2001. (Wakara of Eagle Lodge Ser.: Vol. 2). (Illus.). 176p. (YA). (gr. 7-9). pap. 5.99 (*0-8007-5747-5*) Revell, Fleming H. Co.

—White Water. 2001. (Wakara of Eagle Lodge Ser.).Tr. of Juv033010. (Illus.). 176p. (YA). (gr. 7-9). pap. 5.99 (*0-8007-5772-6*, Spire) Revell, Fleming H. Co.

—Wild Fire. 2001. (Wakara of Eagle Lodge Ser.: Vol. 1). (Illus.). 176p. (YA). (gr. 7-9). pap. 5.99 (*0-8007-5746-7*) Revell, Fleming H. Co.

Van Leeuwen, Jean. Bound for Oregon. (Illus.). 176p. 1996. (J). (gr. 3-7). pap. 5.99 (*0-14-038319-0*); 1994. (YA). (gr. 4 up). 14.99 o.s.i (*0-8037-1526-9*, Dial Bks. for Young Readers) Penguin Putnam Bks. for Young Readers.

—Bound for Oregon. 1996. (YA). (gr. 4 up). 11.04 (*0-606-11159-X*) Turtleback Bks.

Wolff, Virginia Euwer. Bat 6. 256p. (J). (gr. 4-6). pap. 4.99 (*0-8072-8223-5*); 2000. pap. 35.00 incl. audio (*0-8072-8222-7*, YYA144SP) Random Hse. Audio Publishing Group. (Listening Library).

—Bat 6. 240p. (YA). (gr. 5-9). 2000. (Illus.). mass mkt. 4.99 o.s.i (*0-590-89800-0*, Scholastic Reference); 1998. pap. 16.95 (*0-590-89799-3*) Scholastic, Inc.

—Bat 6. 2000. (Illus.). (J). 11.04 (*0-606-18516-X*) Turtleback Bks.

Wood, Elizabeth L. Long Rope. 1955. (Illus.). (J). (gr. 5-11). 5.95 o.p. (*0-8323-0174-4*) Binford & Mort Publishing.

—Many Horses. 1953. (Illus.). (J). (gr. 5-11). 7.95 o.p. (*0-8323-0175-2*) Binford & Mort Publishing.

OUTER SPACE—FICTION

Abbott, Tony. Orbit Wipeout! 1995. (J). mass mkt. 4.75 (*0-553-54235-4*, Dell Books for Young Readers) Random Hse. Children's Bks.

—Space Bingo. 1996. (J). mass mkt. 4.75 (*0-553-54230-3*, Dell Books for Young Readers) Random Hse. Children's Bks.

—Zombie Surf Commandos from Mars. 1996. (Weird Zone Ser.). 8.09 o.p. (*0-606-10030-X*) Turtleback Bks.

Act-Two Staff. Space Mission. 2004. (Illus.). (J). pap. 8.99 incl. cd-rom (*0-7868-3418-8*) Hyperion Bks. for Children.

Adams, Renee. Cosmic Kate: The First Mission. 1999. (Illus.). 23p. (J). (ps-2). pap. (*0-9675994-0-7*) Make Believe Publishing.

Alexander, Alec. My Fantastic Dream of the Marshmallow Martians. 2000. (Marshmallow Martian Ser.: Vol. 1). (Illus.). 32p. (J). (ps-5). 5.95 (*0-9670091-0-3*) Smart Alec Toys Publishing.

—My Magical Christmas Dream of the Marshmallow Martians. 2000. (Marshmallow Martian Ser.: Vol. 2). (Illus.). 32p. (J). (ps-5). 5.95 (*0-9670091-1-1*) Smart Alec Toys Publishing.

Alfonsi, Alice. Jedi Knights & Heroes Coloring Book. 2000. (Star Wars). (Illus.). 80p. (J). (ps-3). pap. 2.99 o.s.i (*0-375-80526-5*, Random Hse. Bks. for Young Readers) Random Hse. Children's Bks.

Amodeo, John, et al. The Crystal Planet: Zenda #3. 2004. (Zenda Ser.). 144p. mass mkt. 4.99 (*0-448-43255-2*, Grosset & Dunlap) Penguin Putnam Bks. for Young Readers.

Anthony, Piers. Bio of A Space Tyrant, 4 vols., Set. 1986. pap. 14.00 (*0-380-75246-8*, Avon Bks.) Morrow/Avon.

Archer, Chris. Alien Blood. 1997. (Mindwarp Ser.: No. 2). 144p. (YA). (gr. 6-8). pap. 3.99 (*0-671-01483-8*, Simon Pulse) Simon & Schuster Children's Publishing.

—Alien Blood. 1997. (Mindwarp Ser.: No. 2). (YA). (gr. 6-8). 10.04 (*0-606-12771-2*) Turtleback Bks.

—Alien Terror. 1997. (Mindwarp Ser.: No. 1). (YA). (gr. 6-8). 10.04 (*0-606-12770-4*) Turtleback Bks.

Arnold, Caroline. My Friend from Outer Space. 1981. (Easy-Read Story Bks.). (Illus.). 32p. (J). (gr. k-3). 9.40 o.p. (*0-531-04192-1*, Watts, Franklin) Scholastic Library Publishing.

Baldry, Cherith. Surfers Mutiny in Space. (Illus.). 128p. (J). pap. 7.95 (*0-14-038489-8*) Penguin Bks., Ltd. GBR. *Dist:* Trafalgar Square.

Barlow, Steve & Skidmore, Steve. The Hunt. 2003. (Outernet Ser.: No. 5). 176p. (J). mass mkt. 4.99 (*0-439-43018-6*, Chicken Hse., The) Scholastic, Inc.

Barlow, Steve L. & Skidmore, Steve. Control! 2002. (Outernet Ser.: No. 2). (Illus.). 176p. (J). (gr. 3-7). mass mkt. 4.99 (*0-439-34352-6*) Scholastic, Inc.

—Friend or Foe? 2002. (Outernet Ser.: No. 1). (Illus.). 176p. (J). (gr. 3-7). mass mkt. 4.99 (*0-439-34351-8*) Scholastic, Inc.

—Odyssey. 2002. (Outernet Ser.: No. 3). 144p. (J). (gr. 3-7). mass mkt. 4.99 (*0-439-34353-4*, Chicken Hse., The) Scholastic, Inc.

Barlowe, Wayne D., illus. Star Wars. 1978. (Star Wars Episode I Ser.). (J). (gr. 1-4). 5.95 o.p. (*0-394-83754-1*, Random Hse. Bks. for Young Readers) Random Hse. Children's Bks.

Barton, Byron. I Want to Be an Astronaut. 2002. (Illus.). (J). 15.49 (*0-7587-4224-X*) Book Wholesalers, Inc.

—I Want to Be an Astronaut. 1992. (J). 13.10 (*0-606-00516-1*) Turtleback Bks.

Beatty, Jerome. Matthew Looney & the Space Pirates. 1972. (Young Scott Bks.). (Illus.). (J). 9.95 (*0-201-09282-4*) HarperCollins Children's Bk. Group.

Beechen, Adam. Scrambled Planets! 2003. 32p. (J). pap. 6.99 (*0-689-85493-5*, Simon Spotlight/Nickelodeon) Simon & Schuster Children's Publishing.

Bell, Lucille H. Trip to the Planets. 1990. (Glow in the Dark Ser.). (J). (ps-3). 5.99 o.s.i (*0-307-06250-3*, Golden Bks.) Random Hse. Children's Bks.

Biemiller, Carl L. The Hydronaut Adventures. 1981. (Fatback Ser.). (Illus.). 408p. (gr. 6-8). mass mkt. 4.95 o.p. (*0-385-15536-0*) Doubleday Publishing.

Bisson, Terry. Crossfire. 2003. (Star Wars Ser.). 144p. (J). mass mkt. 4.99 (*0-439-39002-8*) Scholastic, Inc.

Black, Christopher. The Cosmic Funhouse. 1984. (Star Challenge Ser.: No. 3). (gr. 4-8). pap. 2.50 o.p. (*0-440-41615-9*) Dell Publishing.

Blackman. Space Race. 2000. (Illus.). 63p. pap. 6.95 (*0-552-54542-2*) Transworld Publishers Ltd. GBR. *Dist:* Trafalgar Square.

Boston, Lucy M. An Enemy at Green Knowe. 1979. (Illus.). reprint ed. o.p. Harcourt Trade Pubs.

—An Enemy at Green Knowe. 1979. (Voyager/HBJ Bks.). 9.05 o.p. (*0-606-01590-6*) Turtleback Bks.

Boys' Life Magazine Editors. Boys' Life Book of Outer Space Stories. 1964. (Boys' Life Library: No. 5). (Illus.). (J). (gr. 5-9). 2.95 o.p. (*0-394-81015-5*) Random Hse., Inc.

Branley, Franklyn M. Floating in Space: Stage 2. 1998. (J). 11.10 (*0-606-12934-0*) Turtleback Bks.

Branzei, Sylvia. The Outer Space Place: Welcome To Eurekaville. 2001. (Illus.). 32p. (J). 9.99 (*0-8431-7683-0*, Price Stern Sloan) Penguin Putnam Bks. for Young Readers.

Brookes, Diane. The Man in the Moon. 1998. (Illus.). 32p. (ps-3). pap. (*0-9683234-0-5*) Raven Rock Publishing.

Brooks, Walter R. Freddy & the Flying Saucer Plans. 1998. (Freddy Ser.). (Illus.). 256p. (J). (gr. 3-7). 23.95 (*0-87951-883-9*) Overlook Pr., The.

Buller, Jon & Schade, Susan. Space Mall. 1997. (Illus.). (J). (gr. 1-4). 11.99 o.s.i (*0-679-97919-0*); 63p. pap. 3.99 o.s.i (*0-679-87919-6*) Random Hse. Children's Bks. (Random Hse. Bks. for Young Readers).

Cameron, Eleanor. Mr. Bass's Planetoid. 1958. (Illus.). (J). (gr. 3-7). 14.95 (*0-316-12525-3*, Joy Street Bks.) Little Brown & Co.

—The Wonderful Flight to the Mushroom Planet. 1954. (Illus.). (J). (gr. 4-6). 15.95 o.p. (*0-316-12537-7*) Little Brown & Co.

—The Wonderful Flight to the Mushroom Planet. 2002. (Mushroom Planet Ser.). 214p. (J). (gr. 4-7). pap. 7.95 (*0-316-12540-7*) Little Brown Children's Bks.

—The Wonderful Flight to the Mushroom Planet. 1988. 13.75 (*0-606-12581-7*) Turtleback Bks.

Canatella, Ray. Saucer Sam. Bowser, Milton, ed. 1992. (Cartoon Ser.). (Illus.). 72p. (J). 10.00 o.s.i (*0-940178-38-9*) Sitare, Ltd.

Carballido, Emilio. La Historia de Sputnik y David (The Story of Sputnik & David) 1992. (SPA., Illus.). 48p. (J). (gr. 3-4). reprint ed. pap. 5.99 (*968-16-3678-3*) Fondo de Cultura Economica MEX. *Dist:* Continental Bk. Co., Inc.

Carter, Polly. Telescope. 1996. (J). 15.00 (*0-671-87310-5*, Simon & Schuster Children's Publishing) Simon & Schuster Children's Publishing.

Cecil, Laura. Noah & the Space Ark. 1998. (Picture Bks.). (Illus.). 32p. (J). (gr. k-3). lib. bdg. 15.95 o.s.i (*1-57505-255-5*, Carolrhoda Bks.) Lerner Publishing Group.

Clark, Margaret G. Barney in Space. 1981. (Illus.). 160p. (J). (gr. 3-7). 8.95 o.p. (*0-396-08001-4*, G. P. Putnam's Sons) Penguin Putnam Bks. for Young Readers.

Clarke, Arthur C. Tales of Ten Worlds. 1962. 6.95 o.s.i (*0-15-187980-X*) Harcourt Trade Pubs.

—Tales of Ten Worlds. 1981. mass mkt. 2.50 o.p. (*0-451-11093-5*); 1973. mass mkt. 0.95 o.p. (*0-451-05452-0*); 1973. mass mkt. 1.25 o.p. (*0-451-07241-3*); 1973. mass mkt. 1.50 o.p. (*0-451-08328-8*); 1973. mass mkt. 2.50 o.p. (*0-451-12780-3*); 1973. mass mkt. 2.95 o.p. (*0-451-13233-5*) NAL. (ROC).

Coffelt, Nancy. Dogs in Space. 1993. (Illus.). 32p. (J). (ps-3). 14.95 (*0-15-200440-8*, Gulliver Bks.) Harcourt Children's Bks.

—The Great Space Doghouse. Eagle, Lynnea & Siegel, Joseph, eds. 2000. (Illus.). 36p. (J). pap. 9.95 (*1-883772-53-2*) Flying Rhinoceros, Inc.

Cosmo & the Robot Solar System Belt. 2000. (J). (*0-688-18010-8*) HarperCollins Children's Bk. Group.

Coville, Bruce. Aliens Stole My Body. 1998. (Bruce Coville's Alien Adventures Ser.: Vol. 4). 192p. (J). (gr. 4-7). pap. 4.50 (*0-671-79835-9*, Aladdin) Simon & Schuster Children's Publishing.

—The Saber-Toothed Poodnoobie. 1997. (Space Brat Ser.: No. 5). (J). (gr. 4-7). 10.04 (*0-606-12817-4*) Turtleback Bks.

—Space Station Ice-3. 1996. 192p. (YA). (gr. 6 up). per. 3.99 (*0-671-53641-9*, Simon Pulse) Simon & Schuster Children's Publishing.

Cox, Greg. Devil in the Sky. 1995. (Star Trek Deep Space Nine Ser.: No. 11). (Illus.). 288p. (J). mass mkt. 5.50 (*0-671-88114-0*, Star Trek) Simon & Schuster.

Dadey, Debbie. Mrs. Jeepers in Outer Space. 1999. (Adventures of the Bailey School Kids Super Special Ser.: No. 4). (J). (gr. 2-4). 10.04 (*0-606-19912-8*) Turtleback Bks.

Dadey, Debbie & Jones, Marcia Thornton. Martians Don't Take Temperatures. 1995. (Adventures of the Bailey School Kids Ser.: No. 18). (J). (gr. 2-4). 10.14 (*0-606-08565-3*) Turtleback Bks.

—Mrs. Jeepers in Outer Space. 1999. (Adventures of the Bailey School Kids Super Special Ser.: No. 4). (Illus.). 124p. (J). (gr. 2-4). mass mkt. 3.99 (*0-439-04396-4*) Scholastic, Inc.

Dahl, Roald. Charlie & the Great Glass Elevator. 2001. (Illus.). 176p. (J). (gr. 3-7). lib. bdg. 17.99 (*0-375-91525-7*) Knopf, Alfred A. Inc.

Davies, Tristan, et al. Crackers in Space. 2000. (Illus.). 48p. (J). mass mkt. 8.95 (*0-340-71290-2*); 15.95 (*0-340-71289-9*) Hodder & Stoughton, Ltd. GBR. *Dist:* Lubrecht & Cramer, Ltd., Trafalgar Square.

Deem, James M. How to Catch a Flying Saucer. 1991. (Illus.). 192p. (J). (gr. 5-9). 16.95 o.p. (*0-395-51958-6*) Houghton Mifflin Co.

Delton, Judy. Planet Pee Wee. 1998. (Pee Wee Scouts Ser.: No. 34). (J). (gr. 2-5). 10.04 (*0-606-13699-1*) Turtleback Bks.

DeWeese, Gene. Black Suits from Outer Space. 1989. 144p. (J). (gr. k-6). reprint ed. pap. 2.95 o.s.i (*0-440-40196-8*) Dell Publishing.

—Black Suits from Outer Space. 1985. (Illus.). 160p. (J). (gr. 4-8). 13.95 o.p. (*0-399-21261-2*, G. P. Putnam's Sons) Penguin Putnam Bks. for Young Readers.

Dickens, Frank. Albert Herbert Hawkins, the Naughtiest Boy in the World, & the Space Rocket. 1978. 5.95 o.p. (*0-385-13327-8*); lib. bdg. o.p. (*0-385-14416-4*) Doubleday Publishing.

Disney Staff. The Smartest Guy in the Galaxy. 2002. (Illus.). 24p. (J). pap. 3.25 (*0-7364-2007-X*, RH/Disney) Random Hse. Children's Bks.

Dodd, Quentin. Beatnik Rutabagas from Beyond the Stars, RS. 2001. (Illus.). 224p. (J). (gr. 4-6). 17.00 (*0-374-30515-3*, Farrar, Straus & Giroux (BYR)) Farrar, Straus & Giroux.

Dong, Claxton. Save Our Star. 2002. 144p. (YA). (gr. 5-9). pap. 5.99 (*0-9717993-0-X*) Brown Swan Pubs.

Edick, Grant. Space Station: A Two Boys Adventure Story. 2003. (J). (*0-9677839-9-2*) Wysteria Publishing.

Encyclopedia Galactica: From the Fleet Library of Battlestar Galactica. 1979. (J). 5.95 o.p. (*0-525-61039-1*, Dutton) Dutton/Plume.

Etra, Jonathan. Aliens for Breakfast. 2002. (Illus.). (J). 11.91 (*0-7587-5970-3*) Book Wholesalers, Inc.

—Aliens for Breakfast. 1988. (J). (gr. 3-5). 10.14 (*0-606-03709-8*) Turtleback Bks.

—Aliens for Lunch. 1991. (Stepping Stone Bks.). 10.14 (*0-606-04859-6*) Turtleback Bks.

Random House Staff. Star Wars: Episode II: Attack of the Clones. 2002. (Illus.). 80p. (J). pap. 2.99 (*0-375-82244-5*, Random Hse. Bks. for Young Readers) Random Hse. Children's Bks.

—Star Wars: Episode II: Attack of the Clones Trivia Challenge. 2002. (Illus.). 96p. (gr. 3). pap. 3.99 (*0-375-82245-3*, Random Hse. Bks. for Young Readers) Random Hse. Children's Bks.

Rau, Dana Meachen. One Giant Leap: The First Moon Landing. 1996. (Smithsonian Odyssey Ser.). (Illus.). 32p. (J). (gr. 2-5). 19.95 incl. audio (*1-56899-360-9*, BC6001);Incl. toy. 29.95 (*1-56899-345-5*);Incl. toy. 35.95 incl. audio (*1-56899-347-1*);Incl. toy. pap. 17.95 (*1-56899-346-3*) Soundprints.

Rauch, Sidney J. Barnaby Brown: Home from Erehwon. 1990. (Barnaby Brown Bks.: Bk. 5). (Illus.). 80p. (Orig.). (J). (gr. 2-4). pap. 4.95 (*1-55743-162-0*) Berrent Pubns., Inc.

—The Further Adventures of Barnaby Brown. 1990. (Barnaby Brown Bks.: Bk. 4). (Illus.). 63p. (Orig.). (J). (gr. 2-4). pap. 4.95 (*1-55743-159-0*) Berrent Pubns., Inc.

—The Return of B. B. 1989. (Barnaby Brown Bks.: Bk. 2). (Illus.). 48p. (Orig.). (J). (gr. 2-4). pap. 4.95 (*1-55743-153-1*) Berrent Pubns., Inc.

—A Visit to B. B.'s Planet. 1989. (Barnaby Brown Bks.: Bk. 3). (Illus.). 64p. (Orig.). (J). (gr. 2-4). pap. 4.95 (*1-55743-156-6*) Berrent Pubns., Inc.

—The Visitor from Outer Space. 1989. (Barnaby Brown Bks.: Bk. 1). (Illus.). 48p. (Orig.). (J). (gr. 2-4). pap. 4.95 (*1-55743-150-7*) Berrent Pubns., Inc.

Razzi, James. The Empire Strikes Back Punch-Out & Make-It Book. 1980. (Star Wars Ser.). (Illus.). 32p. (J). (gr. 2-6). 3.95 o.p. (*0-394-84515-3*) Random Hse., Inc.

Riding, Julia. Space Traders Unlimited. 1988. 160p. (YA). (gr. 6 up). lib. bdg. 13.95 o.s.i (*0-689-31409-4*, Atheneum) Simon & Schuster Children's Publishing.

Riley. Fantastic Space Stories. 2000. (Illus.). 184p. pap. 6.95 (*0-552-52767-X*) Transworld Publishers Ltd. GBR. *Dist:* Trafalgar Square.

Rodriguez, Lisa M. Bopo Gets Lost in Space (Bopo Se Pierde en el Espacio) Rodriguez, David A., ed. & tr. by. 2000. (ENG & SPA., Illus.). 32p. (J). (ps-3). 14.95 (*0-9665575-2-2*) BOPO Biligual Bks.

Rotsler, William. Star Trek III: Short Stories. Barish, Wendy, ed. 1984. (Star Trek Ser.). 160p. (Orig.). (J). (gr. 3 up). pap. 3.85 o.s.i (*0-671-50139-9*, Simon & Schuster Children's Publishing) Simon & Schuster Children's Publishing.

—The Vulcan Treasure: The Search for Spock Plot-It-Yourself Adventure Stories. Barish, Wendy, ed. 1984. (Star Trek Ser.). 128p. (Orig.). (J). (gr. 3 up). pap. 3.85 o.p. (*0-671-50138-0*, Simon & Schuster Children's Publishing) Simon & Schuster Children's Publishing.

Rouss, Sylvia. Reach for the Stars. 2004. 40p. (J). (gr. 3-7). 16.95 (*1-930143-82-6*); pap. 9.95 (*1-930143-83-4*) Pitspopany Pr.

Rowe, Alan. Aliens on Earth: Puzzles, Jokes, & Things to Make & Do. 1994. (Illus.). 32p. (J). (ps-3). bds. 2.99 o.p. (*1-56402-407-5*) Candlewick Pr.

Ryan, Kevin. Unleashed in Space. 2000. (Illus.). (J). (gr. 4-7). pap. text 3.99 o.p. (*1-57064-968-5*) Lyrick Publishing.

Ryder, Joanne. The Incredible Space Machines. 1982. (Three-Two-One Contact Bk.). (Illus.). 32p. (J). (gr. 4-7). pap. 4.95 o.p. (*0-394-85201-X*) Random Hse., Inc.

Sadler, Marilyn. Alistair in Outer Space. (J). 1989. pap. 6.95 o.s.i (*0-671-67938-4*, Aladdin); 1984. pap. 15.00 (*0-671-66678-9*, Simon & Schuster Children's Publishing) Simon & Schuster Children's Publishing.

—Bobo Crazy. 2001. (Zenon Ser.: No. 1). (Illus.). 96p. (J). (gr. k-3). lib. bdg. 11.99 (*0-679-99249-9*, Random Hse. Bks. for Young Readers) Random Hse. Children's Bks.

Schade, Susan. Space Mall. 1997. (Stepping Stone Bks.). 10.14 (*0-606-11864-0*) Turtleback Bks.

—Space Rock. 1988. (Step into Reading Step 3 Bks.). (Illus.). 48p. (J). (gr. 2-3). pap. 3.99 (*0-394-89384-0*, Random Hse. Bks. for Young Readers) Random Hse. Children's Bks.

Schade, Susan & Buller, Jon. Space Dog Jack. 2001. (Hello Reader! Ser.). (Illus.). 32p. (J). (ps-1). mass mkt. (*0-439-20541-7*) Scholastic, Inc.

Scholastic, Inc. Staff. Lost in Space Deluxe Storybook. 1998. (Illus.). 48p. (J). (ps-3). mass mkt. 5.98 (*0-590-18935-2*, Cartwheel Bks.) Scholastic, Inc.

—Lost in Space Hello Reader. 1998. (Hello Reader! Ser.). (Illus.). 48p. (J). (gr. 1-3). pap. text 3.99 (*0-590-18937-9*, Cartwheel Bks.) Scholastic, Inc.

Senn, Steve. Ralph Fozbek & the Amazing Black Hole Patrol. 1986. 112p. (J). (gr. 3-7). pap. 2.50 o.p. (*0-380-89905-1*, Avon Bks.) Morrow/Avon.

Seuss, Dr. There's No Place Like Space. 1999. (Cat in the Hat's Learning Library). (Illus.). 48p. (J). (gr. k-3). 8.99 (*0-679-89115-3*); lib. bdg. 11.99 (*0-679-99115-8*) Random Hse. Children's Bks. (Random Hse. Bks. for Young Readers).

Shields, Carol Diggory. Martian Rock. 1999. (Illus.). 40p. (J). (ps-3). 15.99 (*0-7636-0598-0*) Candlewick Pr.

Silbert, Jack. Santa in Space. 2001. 24p. (J). pap. 3.29 o.p. (*0-307-20410-3*, Golden Bks.) Random Hse. Children's Bks.

Simmons, Monica. Aster City: 2Kul4Skul - The Hyperspace Hero. 1998. (Aster Planet Chronicles Ser.: Vol. 5). (Illus.). 32p. (J). (gr. k-4). 15.95 (*0-9658128-6-3*) Long Wind Publishing.

—Uniworld: The Construction of Asterplanet. 1998. (Aster Planet Chronicles Ser.: Vol. 1). (Illus.). 32p. (J). (gr. k-4). 15.95 o.p. (*0-9658128-2-0*) Long Wind Publishing.

Simons, Jeff. Starships. 1983. (Illus.). 24p. (J). (gr. 4-7). pap. 1.95 o.p. (*0-89954-222-0*) Antioch Publishing Co.

Siracusa, Catherine. The Banana Split from Outer Space. 1995. (Illus.). 48p. (J). (gr. 1-3). pap. 3.95 o.s.i (*0-7868-1062-9*, Disney Editions) Disney Pr.

—The Banana Split from Outer Space. 1995. (Illus.). 48p. (J). (gr. 1-3). 13.95 (*0-7868-0040-2*) Hyperion Bks. for Children.

Smith, Claire. Forced Earth Landing. 1996. (Illus.). 32p. (J). (gr. k-3). 19.95 (*0-85236-334-6*); pap. 9.95 (*0-85236-335-4*) Diamond Farm Bk. Pubs.

Smith, Dona. My Favorite Martian. 1999. (Disney's Junior Novel Ser.). (Illus.). 92p. (J). (gr. 3-7). pap. 4.99 o.p. (*0-7868-4239-3*) Hyperion Pr.

Snyder, Margaret. Rebel Heroes & Galactic Villains. 1999. (Sticker Fun Bks.). (Illus.). 24p. (J). pap. 4.99 o.s.i (*0-307-15733-4*, Golden Bks.) Random Hse. Children's Bks.

Snyder, Margaret & Kantor, Susan. Pilots & Spacecraft. 1999. (Golden Book Ser.). (Illus.). 16p. (J). (ps-3). pap. 3.99 o.s.i (*0-307-13480-6*, 13480, Golden Bks.) Random Hse. Children's Bks.

Stamper, Judith Bauer & Blevins, Wiley. Boom! Zoom!, Level 1. 1997. (Hello Reader! Science Ser.). (Illus.). 32p. (J). (gr. 1-2). 3.99 (*0-590-76264-8*) Scholastic, Inc.

—Space Race. 1998. (Hello Reader! Ser.). (Illus.). 32p. (J). (gr. 1-2). mass mkt. 3.99 (*0-590-76267-2*) Scholastic, Inc.

Standiford, Natalie. Space Dog & Roy. 1998. (Space Dog Ser.). (Illus.). 74p. (J). (gr. k-3). pap. 3.99 o.s.i (*0-679-88903-5*) Random Hse., Inc.

Steele, Alexander. Unleashed in Space. Ryan, Kevin, ed. 1999. (Super Adventures of Wishbone Ser.: Vol. No. 3). (Illus.). 252p. (J). (ps-3). pap. 3.99 o.p. (*1-57064-329-6*) Lyrick Publishing.

—Unleashed in Space. 1999. (Super Adventures of Wishbone Ser.: No. 3). (J). (gr. 4-7). 10.04 (*0-606-19032-5*) Turtleback Bks.

Stephenson, T. S. The Cosmos Kids. 1992. (J). pap. 8.95 o.p. (*0-533-10206-5*) Vantage Pr., Inc.

Stern, Leonard & Price, Roger. Mad Libs from Outer Space. 1989. (Mad Libs Ser.). (Illus.). 48p. (Orig.). (J). (gr. 4-7). 3.99 (*0-8431-2443-1*, Price Stern Sloan) Penguin Putnam Bks. for Young Readers.

Stine, R. L. Losers in Space. 1991. (Space Cadets Ser.: No. 2). 144p. (J). mass mkt. 2.75 o.p. (*0-590-44746-7*, Scholastic Paperbacks) Scholastic, Inc.

—Zapped in Space. 1997. (Give Yourself Goosebumps Ser.: No. 23). (J). (gr. 3-7). mass mkt. 3.99 (*0-590-39774-5*) Scholastic, Inc.

Strickland, Brad & Strickland, Barbara. Crisis on Vulcan. 1996. (Starfleet Academy Ser.: No. 1). 128p. (J). (gr. 4-7). mass mkt. 3.99 (*0-671-00078-0*, Aladdin) Simon & Schuster Children's Publishing.

—Crisis on Vulcan. 1996. (Star Trek: No. 1). (J). (gr. 4-7). 10.04 (*0-606-10942-0*) Turtleback Bks.

Sweeny, Sheila & Golden Books Staff. Luke Skywalker's Battle with Darth Vader: Star Wars Reading Story Workbook. 1999. (Star Wars Ser.). 48p. (J). pap., wbk. ed. 3.99 o.s.i (*0-307-21305-6*, Golden Bks.) Random Hse. Children's Bks.

Sykes, Julie. Little Rocket's Special Star. 2000. (Illus.). 32p. (J). (ps-1). 15.99 o.s.i (*0-525-46494-8*, Dutton Children's Bks.) Penguin Putnam Bks. for Young Readers.

Tauscher, Donna. Hero for Hire: By Han Solo. 1998. (Star Wars Journals). 104p. (J). (gr. 4-7). mass mkt. 3.99 (*0-590-18901-8*) Scholastic, Inc.

Thomas, Frances. One Day, Daddy. 2001. (Illus.). 32p. (J). (ps-2). 15.99 (*0-7868-0732-6*) Hyperion Bks. for Children.

Tinkler, David. Lucasta Smirk Goes Beserk! l.t. ed. 1997. (Illus.). (J). 16.95 (*0-7451-5493-X*, Galaxy Children's Large Print) BBC Audiobooks America.

Vaz, Mark Cotta. The Star Wars Trilogy Scrapbook: The Galactic Empire. 1997. 48p. (gr. 4-7). mass mkt. 6.99 (*0-590-12052-2*) Scholastic, Inc.

Viney, Peter. Space Affair. 1998. (Illus.). 24p. (J). (gr. k). pap. text 6.00 (*0-19-421968-2*) Oxford Univ. Pr., Inc.

Von Stemm, Antje. Bertie & Gertie: Space Detectives. 1996. 12p. (J). (ps-5). 12.95 o.p. (*0-8118-1461-0*) Chronicle Bks. LLC.

Vornholt, John. Crossfire. 1996. (Star Trek, The Next Generation: No. 11). 112p. (J). (gr. 3-6). per. 3.99 (*0-671-55305-4*, Aladdin) Simon & Schuster Children's Publishing.

Walt Disney Productions Staff. Walt Disney Productions Presents "The Black Hole" 1979. (Walt Disney's Wonderful World of Reading Ser.: No. 47). (Illus.). (J). (ps-3). lib. bdg. 4.99 o.p. (*0-394-94279-5*, Random Hse. Bks. for Young Readers) Random Hse. Children's Bks.

Walters, Hugh. The Blue Aura. 1979. 128p. (J). (gr. 5-8). o.p. (*0-571-11423-7*) Faber & Faber Ltd.

—The Last Disaster. 1979. 128p. (J). (gr. 5-8). o.p. (*0-571-11153-X*) Faber & Faber Ltd.

Warner, Gertrude Chandler, creator. The Outer Space Mystery. 1997. (Boxcar Children Ser.: No. 59). (J). (gr. 2-5). 10.00 (*0-606-11162-X*) Turtleback Bks.

—The Outer Space Mystery. 1997. (Boxcar Children Ser.: No. 59). (J). (gr. 2-5). lib. bdg. 13.95 (*0-8075-6286-6*); mass mkt. 3.95 (*0-8075-6287-4*) Whitman, Albert & Co.

Washington, T. Edward. Crash Crater: Intergalactic Space Warrior. 1997. (Illus.). 16p. (J). (gr. 7-8). pap. 6.00 o.p. (*0-8059-4221-1*) Dorrance Publishing Co., Inc.

Watson, Jude. Captive to Evil: By Princess Leia Organa. 1998. (Star Wars Journals). 91p. (J). (gr. 4-7). mass mkt. 3.99 (*0-590-18900-X*) Scholastic, Inc.

—Captive to Evil: By Princess Leia Organa. 1998. (Star Wars Journals). (J). (gr. 4-7). 10.14 (*0-606-13808-0*) Turtleback Bks.

—Journey Across Planet X. 1999. (Star Wars Science Adventures Ser.). 10.04 (*0-606-16616-5*) Turtleback Bks.

—Queen Amidala. 1999. (Star Wars Ser.). (Illus.). 111p. (J). (gr. 4-7). mass mkt. 5.99 (*0-590-52101-2*) Scholastic, Inc.

—The Shadow Trap. 2003. (Star Wars Jedi Quest Ser.: No. 6). 144p. (J). mass mkt. 4.99 (*0-439-33922-7*) Scholastic, Inc.

Watson, Jude & Burkett, K. D. Journey Across Planet X. 1999. (Star Wars Science Adventures Ser.). 96p. (J). (gr. 3-7). mass mkt. 3.99 (*0-590-20228-6*) Scholastic, Inc.

Wells, H. G. War of the Worlds. 2004. (Scholastic Classics Ser.). 304p. (J). pap. 3.99 (*0-439-51849-0*, Scholastic Paperbacks) Scholastic, Inc.

Whitman, John. Army of Terror. l.t. ed. 1998. (Star Wars Ser.: No. 6). 144p. (J). (gr. 4 up). lib. bdg. 22.60 (*0-8368-2240-4*) Stevens, Gareth Inc.

—Army of Terror. 1997. (Star Wars: Bk. 6). (J). (gr. 4-7). 11.04 (*0-606-13804-8*) Turtleback Bks.

—The Brain Spiders. 1997. (Star Wars: No. 7). (J). (gr. 4-8). 11.04 (*0-606-13805-6*) Turtleback Bks.

—City of the Dead. l.t. ed. 1998. (Star Wars Ser.: No. 2). 144p. (J). (gr. 4 up). lib. bdg. 22.60 (*0-8368-2236-6*) Stevens, Gareth Inc.

—Eaten Alive. ltd. ed. 1997. (Star Wars: No. 1). 160p. (gr. 4-7). pap. text 4.99 o.s.i (*0-553-48450-8*, Skylark) Random Hse. Children's Bks.

—Eaten Alive. l.t. ed. 1998. (Star Wars Ser.: No. 1). 144p. (J). (gr. 4 up). lib. bdg. 22.60 (*0-8368-2235-8*) Stevens, Gareth Inc.

—Eaten Alive. 1997. (Star Wars: No. 1). (J). (gr. 4-7). 10.09 o.p. (*0-606-11888-8*) Turtleback Bks.

—Ghost of the Jedi. l.t. ed. 1998. (Star Wars Ser.: No. 5). 144p. (J). (gr. 4 up). lib. bdg. 22.60 (*0-8368-2239-0*) Stevens, Gareth Inc.

—Ghost of the Jedi. 1997. (Star Wars: No. 5). (J). (gr. 4-7). 11.04 (*0-606-11892-6*) Turtleback Bks.

—The Nightmare Machine. 1997. (Star Wars: No. 4). 144p. (gr. 3-7). pap. text 4.99 o.s.i (*0-553-48453-2*, Skylark) Random Hse. Children's Bks.

—The Nightmare Machine. l.t. ed. 1998. (Star Wars Ser.: No. 4). 144p. (J). (gr. 4 up). lib. bdg. 22.60 (*0-8368-2238-2*) Stevens, Gareth Inc.

—The Nightmare Machine. 1997. (Star Wars: No. 4). (J). (gr. 4-7). 10.09 (*0-606-11891-8*) Turtleback Bks.

—Planet Plague. 1997. (Star Wars: No. 3). (J). (gr. 4-7). mass mkt. 4.99 (*0-553-54298-2*); 144p. (gr. 3-7). pap. text 4.99 o.s.i (*0-553-48452-4*) Random Hse. Children's Bks. (Skylark).

—Planet Plague. l.t. ed. 1998. (Star Wars Ser.: No. 3). 144p. (J). (gr. 4 up). lib. bdg. 22.60 (*0-8368-2237-4*) Stevens, Gareth Inc.

—Planet Plague. 1997. (Star Wars: No. 3). (J). (gr. 4-7). 10.09 (*0-606-11890-X*) Turtleback Bks.

—Spore. 1998. (Star Wars: No. 9). 144p. (gr. 3-7). pap. text 4.50 o.s.i (*0-553-48639-X*, Skylark) Random Hse. Children's Bks.

—Spore. 1998. (Star Wars: No. 9). (J). (gr. 4-7). 10.55 (*0-606-13807-2*) Turtleback Bks.

—The Swarm. 1998. (Star Wars: No. 8). 144p. (gr. 3-7). pap. text 4.50 o.s.i (*0-553-48638-1*, Skylark) Random Hse. Children's Bks.

—The Swarm. 1998. (Star Wars: No. 8). (J). (gr. 4-7). 9.85 (*0-606-13806-4*) Turtleback Bks.

Wilkinson, Philip. Spacebusters: Level 3: Reading Alone. 2001. (Dk Readers Big Book Ser.). (Illus.). 48p. (J). pap. 19.95 (*0-7894-5085-2*, D K Ink) Dorling Kindersley Publishing, Inc.

Williams, Geoff. Aliens Next Door: Book & Cassette in 3-D Sound. 1989. (Illus.). 32p. (J). (gr. 2-5). 2.95 o.p. (*0-8431-2376-1*); 6.95 o.p. (*0-8431-2746-5*) Penguin Putnam Bks. for Young Readers. (Price Stern Sloan).

Williams, Jay & Abrashkin, Raymond. Danny Dunn & the Voice from Space. (Danny Dunn Ser.: No. 12). (Illus.). (J). (gr. 4-6). 1982. pap. (*0-671-47235-6*); 1981. pap. (*0-671-42684-2*) Simon & Schuster Children's Publishing. (Simon Pulse).

Williams, Lawrence. Space. 1990. (Last Frontiers Ser.). (Illus.). 48p. (J). (gr. 4-8). lib. bdg. 9.95 o.p. (*1-85435-174-5*) Cavendish, Marshall Corp.

Wilson, Sarah. Good Zap, Little Grog! (Illus.). 32p. (J). (ps-3). 1995. 15.95 o.p. (*1-56402-286-2*); 1997. reprint ed. bds. 6.99 (*0-7636-0294-9*) Candlewick Pr.

World Book, Inc. Staff. Professor Spacey Discovers Photography. 1997. (J). 16.95 o.p. (*0-7166-0316-0*) World Bk., Inc.

Wright, Walter, illus. The Maverick Moon. 1979. (Star Wars Episode I Ser.). (J). (gr. 3-5). lib. bdg. 3.99 o.p. (*0-394-94087-3*, Random Hse. Bks. for Young Readers) Random Hse. Children's Bks.

XYZ Group Staff. Battle for Hyperspace Colony (Includes Toy) 1998. (Build n Play Ser.). (Illus.). 24p. (J). (ps-2). pap. text 12.95 o.p. (*1-879332-85-X*) Futech Interactive Products, Inc.

—Space Fun. 1998. (Glow in Dark Posterbook Ser.). (J). (ps-2). pap. text 2.99 o.p. (*1-879332-79-5*) Futech Interactive Products, Inc.

Yamamoto, Neal, illus. 50 Nifty Space Aliens to Draw. 1999. (Fifty Nifty Ser.). 79p. (J). (gr. 2-7). pap. 6.95 (*0-7373-0163-5*, 01635W) McGraw-Hill/Contemporary.

Yolen, Jane. Commander Toad & the Big Black Hole. 1996. (Break-Of-Day Book Ser.). (Illus.). 64p. (J). (ps-3). pap. 5.99 (*0-698-11403-5*, PaperStar) Penguin Putnam Bks. for Young Readers.

—Commander Toad & the Big Black Hole. 1983. (Illus.). (J). (gr. 1-4). 10.99 o.s.i (*0-698-30741-0*); 64p. 6.95 o.s.i (*0-698-20594-4*) Putnam Publishing Group, The. (Coward-McCann).

—Commander Toad & the Big Black Hole. 1996. (Break-of-Day Bks.). (J). 11.14 (*0-606-02547-2*) Turtleback Bks.

—Commander Toad & the Dis-Asteroid. 1996. (Illus.). 64p. (J). (ps-3). pap. 5.99 (*0-698-11404-3*, PaperStar) Penguin Putnam Bks. for Young Readers.

—Commander Toad & the Dis-Asteroid. 1985. (Commander Toad Bks.). (Illus.). 64p. (J). (gr. 4). 10.99 o.s.i (*0-698-30744-5*); 6.95 o.s.i (*0-698-20620-7*) Putnam Publishing Group, The. (Coward-McCann).

—Commander Toad & the Dis-Asteroid. 1985. 11.14 (*0-606-00779-2*) Turtleback Bks.

—Commander Toad & the Intergalactic Spy. 1997. (Illus.). 64p. (J). (gr. 2-5). pap. 5.99 (*0-698-11418-3*, PaperStar) Penguin Putnam Bks. for Young Readers.

—Commander Toad & the Intergalactic Spy. 1986. (Commander Toad Bks.). (Illus.). 64p. (J). (ps-4). 10.99 o.s.i (*0-698-30747-X*); 6.95 o.s.i (*0-698-20623-1*) Putnam Publishing Group, The. (Coward-McCann).

—Commander Toad & the Intergalactic Spy. 1997. (J). 12.14 (*0-606-11220-0*) Turtleback Bks.

—Commander Toad & the Planet of the Grapes. 1996. (Illus.). 64p. (J). (ps-3). pap. 5.99 (*0-698-11353-5*, PaperStar) Penguin Putnam Bks. for Young Readers.

—Commander Toad in Space. 1996. (J). 12.14 (*0-606-09159-9*) Turtleback Bks.

—Moonball. 1999. (Illus.). 40p. (J). (ps-3). 16.00 o.s.i (*0-689-81095-4*, Simon & Schuster Children's Publishing) Simon & Schuster Children's Publishing.

OZ (IMAGINARY PLACE)—FICTION

Baum, L. Frank. Dorothy & the Wizard in Oz. (Oz Ser.). (YA). (gr. 5 up). 1979. mass mkt. 1.95 o.p. (*0-345-28226-4*); No. 4. 1984. mass mkt. 2.25 o.p. (*0-345-31948-6*) Ballantine Bks.

—Dorothy & the Wizard in Oz. l.t. ed. 2002. per. 15.50 (*1-58396-161-5*); 2000. 200p. per. 12.50 (*1-58396-073-2*) Blue Unicorn Editions.

—Dorothy & the Wizard in Oz. 1984. (Oz Ser.). (Illus.). 256p. (YA). (gr. 5 up). reprint ed. pap. 8.95 (*0-486-24714-7*) Dover Pubns., Inc.

—Dorothy & the Wizard in Oz. (Oz Ser.: Vol. 4). (YA). (gr. 5 up). E-Book 2.49 (*1-58627-035-4*) Electric Umbrella Publishing.

—Dorothy & the Wizard in Oz. 1990. (Books of Wonder). (Illus.). 272p. (J). (gr. 2 up). reprint ed. 24.99 (*0-688-09826-6*) HarperCollins Children's Bk. Group.

—Dorothy & the Wizard in Oz. (Oz Ser.). (Illus.). 288p. (YA). (gr. 5 up). reprint ed. 12.95 o.p. (*1-56852-228-2*, Konecky & Konecky) Konecky, William S. Assocs., Inc.

—Dorothy & the Wizard in Oz. 1999. (Wizard of Oz Ser.: Vol. 4). (Illus.). (J). (ps up). E-Book 5.99 incl. cd-rom (*1-891595-17-2*) Quiet Vision Publishing.

—Dorothy & the Wizard in Oz. 1990. (Oz Ser.). (YA). (gr. 5 up). 25.25 (*0-8446-6141-4*) Smith, Peter Pub., Inc.

—Dorothy & the Wizard in Oz. (J). E-Book 5.00 (*0-7410-0609-X*) SoftBook Pr.

—Dorothy & the Wizard of Oz. 2003. pap. 14.95 (*1-58726-036-0*, For Your Knowledge) Ann Arbor Media Group, LLC.

—Dorothy & the Wizard of Oz. l.t. ed. (Oz Ser.). (YA). (gr. 5-8). 580p. pap. 48.54 (*0-7583-0783-7*); 120p. pap. 15.80 (*0-7583-0776-4*); 150p. pap. 18.11 (*0-7583-0777-2*); 205p. pap. 22.00 (*0-7583-0778-0*); 261p. pap. 25.97 (*0-7583-0779-9*); 333p. pap. 31.06 (*0-7583-0780-2*); 407p. pap. 36.30 (*0-7583-0781-0*); 500p. pap. 42.88 (*0-7583-0782-9*); 205p. lib. bdg. 29.43 (*0-7583-0770-5*); 261p. lib. bdg. 35.32 (*0-7583-0771-3*); 333p. lib. bdg. 42.31 (*0-7583-0772-1*); 407p. lib. bdg. 47.55 (*0-7583-0773-X*); 500p. lib. bdg. 54.13 (*0-7583-0774-8*); 120p. lib. bdg. 21.80 (*0-7583-0768-3*); 150p. lib. bdg. 24.53 (*0-7583-0769-1*); 580p. lib. bdg. 59.79 (*0-7583-0775-6*) Huge Print Pr.

—Emerald City: Wonderful Wizard of Oz. 1991. (Wonderful Wizard of Oz Pop-Ups Ser.). (Illus.). 6p. (J). 2.99 o.s.i (*0-517-05266-0*) Random Hse. Value Publishing.

—The Emerald City of Oz. 2002. 294p. (YA). per. (*1-58726-023-9*, Mundus) Ann Arbor Media Group, LLC.

—The Emerald City of Oz. l.t. ed. 2000. (Oz Ser.). (YA). (gr. 5-8). per. 15.50 (*1-58396-165-8*); 200p. per. 12.50 (*1-58396-077-5*) Blue Unicorn Editions.

—The Emerald City of Oz. 2002. (Illus.). 296p. (YA). pap. 17.00 (*0-7567-6271-5*) DIANE Publishing Co.

—The Emerald City of Oz. (Oz Ser.). (YA). (gr. 5-8). E-Book 2.49 (*1-58627-036-2*) Electric Umbrella Publishing.

—The Emerald City of Oz. unabr. ed. 1995. (Oz Ser.). (YA). (gr. 5-8). audio 24.95 (*1-886354-06-5*) Piglet Pr., Inc.

—The Emerald City of Oz. 1999. (Wizard of Oz Ser.). (Illus.). (YA). (gr. 5-8). E-Book 5.99 incl. cd-rom (*1-891595-19-9*) Quiet Vision Publishing.

—The Emerald City of Oz. (Oz Ser.). (YA). (gr. 5-8). E-Book 5.00 (*0-7410-0510-7*) SoftBook Pr.

—Glinda of Oz. (Oz Ser.). (YA). (gr. 5-8). 21.95 (*0-8488-0784-7*) Amereon, Ltd.

—Glinda of Oz. 2002. 276p. (YA). per. (*1-58726-024-7*, Mundus) Ann Arbor Media Group, LLC.

—Glinda of Oz, Set. 1997. (Oz Ser.). (YA). (gr. 5-8). audio 24.95 (*1-55685-483-8*) Audio Bk. Contractors, Inc.

—Glinda of Oz. 1985. (Oz Ser.). 272p. (gr. 5-8). mass mkt. 5.99 (*0-345-33394-2*, Del Rey) Ballantine Bks.

—Glinda of Oz. l.t. ed. (Oz Ser.). (YA). (gr. 5-8). 2000. per. 15.50 (*1-58396-162-3*); 2001. 200p. per. 12.50 (*1-58396-074-0*) Blue Unicorn Editions.

—Glinda of Oz. 2000. (Oz Ser.). (Illus.). 288p. (YA). (gr. 5-8). pap. 7.95 (*0-486-41018-8*) Dover Pubns., Inc.

—Glinda of Oz. (Oz Ser.). (YA). (gr. 5-8). E-Book 2.49 (*1-58627-037-0*) Electric Umbrella Publishing.

—Glinda of Oz. 2002. 136p. (gr. 4-7). 16.99 (*1-4043-0448-7*); per. 12.99 (*1-4043-0449-5*) IndyPublish.com.

—Glinda of Oz. 1999. (Wizard of Oz Ser.). (Illus.). (YA). (gr. 5-8). E-Book 5.99 incl. cd-rom (*1-891595-27-X*) Quiet Vision Publishing.

—Glinda of Oz. (Oz Ser.). (YA). (gr. 5-8). E-Book 5.00 (*0-7410-0557-3*) SoftBook Pr.

—The Land of Oz. 1985. (Wonderful Oz Bks.: Vol. 2). 288p. (gr. 5-8). mass mkt. 6.99 (*0-345-33568-6*) Ballantine Bks.

—The Land of Oz. abr. ed. 1979. (Oz Ser.). (YA). (gr. 5-8). audio 9.95 o.s.i (*0-694-50839-X*, CDL5 1618, Caedmon) HarperTrade.

—The Land of Oz. 1989. (Oz Ser.). (YA). (gr. 5-8). audio 18.00 Jimcin Recordings.

—The Land of Oz. 1999. (Oz Ser.). (Illus.). 320p. (YA). (gr. 5-8). reprint ed. 12.95 (*1-56852-226-6*, Konecky & Konecky) Konecky, William S. Assocs., Inc.

—The Land of Oz. 1997. (Oz Ser.). (YA). (gr. 5-8). pap. 2.95 (*0-89375-992-9*) NAL.

—The Land of Oz, unabr. ed. 1980. (Oz Ser.). (YA). (gr. 5-8). audio 27.00 (*1-55690-295-6*, 80121E7) Recorded Bks., LLC.

—The Land of Oz. (Oz Ser.). (YA). (gr. 5-8). E-Book (*1-58824-058-4*) ipicturebooks, LLC.

—Little Wizard Stories of Oz. 1994. (Books of Wonder). (Illus.). 192p. (J). (gr. 2 up). 22.95 (*0-688-12126-8*) HarperCollins Children's Bk. Group.

—Little Wizard Stories of Oz. 1985. (Illus.). 160p. (J). (ps-4). reprint ed. 14.95 o.s.i (*0-8052-4005-5*, Schocken) Knopf Publishing Group.

—Little Wizard Stories of Oz. 1988. (Illus.). 96p. (J). pap. 2.95 o.s.i (*0-553-15617-9*, Skylark) Random Hse. Children's Bks.

—The Lost Princess of Oz. (Oz Ser.). (YA). (gr. 5-8). 22.95 (*0-8488-0786-3*) Amereon, Ltd.

—The Lost Princess of Oz. 2002. 302p. (YA). per. (*1-58726-022-0*, Mundus) Ann Arbor Media Group, LLC.

—The Lost Princess of Oz. 1985. (Wonderful Oz Bks.: Vol. 11). 304p. (YA). (gr. 5-8). mass mkt. 5.99 (*0-345-33367-5*, Del Rey) Ballantine Bks.

—The Lost Princess of Oz. l.t. ed. 2000. (Oz Ser.). (YA). (gr. 5-8). per. 15.50 (*1-58396-166-6*); 200p. per. 12.50 (*1-58396-078-3*) Blue Unicorn Editions.

—The Lost Princess of Oz. 2002. (Illus.). 312p. (J). (gr. 3-6). pap. 17.00 (*0-7567-6273-1*) DIANE Publishing Co.

—The Lost Princess of Oz. unabr. ed. 1999. (Oz Ser.). (Illus.). 332p. (YA). (gr. 5-8). pap. 9.95 (*0-486-40344-0*) Dover Pubns., Inc.

—The Lost Princess of Oz, No. 11. (Oz Ser.). (YA). (gr. 5-8). E-Book 2.49 (*1-58744-075-X*) Electric Umbrella Publishing.

—The Lost Princess of Oz. 2002. 152p. (gr. 4-7). 23.99 (*1-4043-1500-4*); per. 18.99 (*1-4043-1501-2*) IndyPublish.com.

—The Lost Princess of Oz. 1999. (Wizard of Oz Ser.). (Illus.). 289p. (YA). (gr. 5-8). E-Book 5.99 incl. cd-rom (*1-891595-24-5*, 786-39570024) Quiet Vision Publishing.

—The Magic of Oz. 1996. (Oz Ser.). (YA). (gr. 5-8). 20.95 (*0-8488-0787-1*) Amereon, Ltd.

—The Magic of Oz. 1985. (Oz Ser.). (Illus.). 256p. (gr. 5-8). mass mkt. 5.99 o.s.i (*0-345-33288-1*, Del Rey) Ballantine Bks.

—The Magic of Oz. l.t. ed. 2000. (Oz Ser.). (YA). (gr. 5-8). per. 15.50 (*1-58396-167-4*); 200p. per. 12.50 (*1-58396-079-1*) Blue Unicorn Editions.

—The Magic of Oz. 1998. (Oz Ser.). (Illus.). 284p. (YA). (gr. 5-8). pap. 8.95 (*0-486-40019-0*) Dover Pubns., Inc.

—The Magic of Oz. 1999. (Oz Ser.). (YA). (gr. 5-8). E-Book 2.49 (*1-58627-042-7*) Electric Umbrella Publishing.

—The Magic of Oz. 2002. 140p. (gr. 4-7). 23.99 (*1-4043-1600-0*) IndyPublish.com.

—The Magic of Oz. l.t. ed. 1999. (Oz Ser.). (YA). (gr. 5-8). E-Book 24.95 incl. cd-rom (*1-929077-41-6*, Books OnScreen) PageFree Publishing, Inc.

—The Magic of Oz. 1999. (Wizard of Oz Ser.). (Illus.). (YA). (gr. 5). E-Book 5.99 incl. cd-rom (*1-891595-26-1*) Quiet Vision Publishing.

—The Magic of Oz. (Oz Ser.). (YA). (gr. 5-8). E-Book 5.00 (*0-7410-0570-0*) SoftBook Pr.

—The Magic of Oz. (Oz Ser.). (YA). (gr. 5-8). E-Book (*1-58824-135-1*) ipicturebooks, LLC.

—The Magical World of Oz, 4 vols. 1986. (YA). 11.10 o.p. (*0-345-34048-5*, Del Rey) Ballantine Bks.

—El Mago de Oz. 1987. (Oz Ser.).Tr. of Wizard of Oz. (YA). (gr. 5-8). 15.05 o.p. (*0-606-10414-3*) Turtleback Bks.

—El Maravilloso Mago de Oz. (Oz Ser.). (SPA., Illus.). 160p. (YA). (gr. 5-8). 14.95 (*84-7281-184-0*, AF1184) Auriga, Ediciones S.A. ESP. *Dist:* Continental Bk. Co., Inc.

—El Maravilloso Mago de Oz. 1996. (Oz Ser.). (SPA., Illus.). 160p. (YA). (gr. 5-8). pap. 2.95 (*0-486-28968-0*) Dover Pubns., Inc.

—El Maravilloso Mago de Oz. 3rd ed. 2002. (Clover Ser.). (SPA., Illus.). 264p. (YA). 11.50 (*84-392-8002-5*, EV3454) Lectorum Pubns., Inc.

—The Marvelous Land of Oz, Set. unabr. ed. 1993. (Oz Ser.). (YA). (gr. 5-8). audio 24.95 (*1-55685-290-8*) Audio Bk. Contractors, Inc.

—The Marvelous Land of Oz. 1975. (Oz Ser.). (Illus.). 176p. (YA). (gr. 5-8). 11.00 o.p. (*0-460-05078-8*) Biblio Distribution.

—The Marvelous Land of Oz. rev. ed. 2001. (Oz Ser.). 200p. (YA). (gr. 5-8). per. 12.50 (*1-58396-080-5*) Blue Unicorn Editions.

—The Marvelous Land of Oz. l.t. ed. (Oz Ser.). (YA). (gr. 5-8). 727p. pap. 62.96 (*0-7583-3783-3*); 414p. pap. 39.32 (*0-7583-3780-9*); 510p. pap. 46.52 (*0-7583-3781-7*); 627p. pap. 55.38 (*0-7583-3782-5*); 142p. pap. 18.74 (*0-7583-3776-0*); 185p. pap. 21.92 (*0-7583-3777-9*); 253p. pap. 27.12 (*0-7583-3778-7*); 324p. pap. 32.47 (*0-7583-3779-5*); 185p. lib. bdg. 27.92 (*0-7583-3769-8*); 253p. lib. bdg. 33.80 (*0-7583-3770-1*); 324p. lib. bdg. 40.56 (*0-7583-3771-X*); 142p. lib. bdg. 25.04 (*0-7583-3768-X*); 627p. lib. bdg. 63.10 (*0-7583-3774-4*); 414p. lib. bdg. 48.07 (*0-7583-3772-8*); 510p. lib. bdg. 54.81 (*0-7583-3773-6*); 727p. lib. bdg. 70.20 (*0-7583-3775-2*) Huge Print Pr.

—The Marvelous Land of Oz. l.t. ed. 1998. (Oz Ser.). 231p. (YA). (gr. 5-8). lib. bdg. 28.95 (*1-58118-022-5*, 21999) LRS.

—The Marvelous Land of Oz. (Oz Ser.). (YA). (gr. 5-8). E-Book 1.95 (*1-58515-192-0*) MesaView, Inc.

—The Marvelous Land of Oz. 1970. (Oz Ser.). (YA). (gr. 5-8). pap. 1.95 o.p. (*0-590-08565-4*) Scholastic, Inc.

—The Marvelous Land of Oz. 1985. (Oz Ser.). (YA). (gr. 5-8). 13.50 o.p. (*0-8446-6197-X*) Smith, Peter Pub., Inc.

—Oz Boxed Set, 3 vols. 2000. (Oz Ser.). 272p. (YA). (gr. 5-8). pap. 19.50 (*0-06-440947-3*, Harper Trophy) HarperCollins Children's Bk. Group.

—The Oz Read Aloud Collection, 14 CDs, Set. 1999. (Wizard of Oz Ser.). (Illus.). (J). (ps up). E-Book 144.00 incl. cd-rom (*1-891595-44-X*) Quiet Vision Publishing.

—Ozma of Oz. 1996. (Oz Ser.). (YA). (gr. 5-8). 22.95 (*0-8488-0706-5*) Amereon, Ltd.

—Ozma of Oz. 2003. pap. 14.95 (*1-58726-035-2*, For Your Knowledge) Ann Arbor Media Group, LLC.

—Ozma of Oz. unabr. ed. 1998. (Oz Ser.). (YA). (gr. 5-8). audio 24.95 (*1-55685-546-X*) Audio Bk. Contractors, Inc.

—Ozma of Oz. 1986. (Wonderful Oz Bks.). 264p. (gr. 5-8). mass mkt. 6.99 (*0-345-33589-9*, Del Rey) Ballantine Bks.

—Ozma of Oz. l.t. ed. 2000. (Oz Ser.). (YA). (gr. 5-8). per. 15.50 (*1-58396-163-1*) Blue Unicorn Editions.

—Ozma of Oz. 1985. (Oz Ser.). (Illus.). 288p. (YA). (gr. 5-8). reprint ed. pap. 8.95 (*0-486-24779-1*) Dover Pubns., Inc.

—Ozma of Oz. (Books of Wonder). (Illus.). 272p. (J). 2001. (gr. 3 up). pap. 7.95 (*0-06-440962-7*, Harper Trophy); 1989. (gr. 5-8). 24.99 (*0-688-06632-1*) HarperCollins Children's Bk. Group.

—Ozma of Oz. 1999. (Oz Ser.). (Illus.). 288p. (YA). (gr. 5-8). reprint ed. 12.95 o.p. (*1-56852-227-4*, Konecky & Konecky) Konecky, William S. Assocs., Inc.

—Ozma of Oz. 1976. (Oz Ser.). (YA). (gr. 5-8). pap. o.p. (*0-8092-7974-6*) McGraw-Hill/Contemporary.

—Ozma of Oz. 1992. (Oz Ser.). 160p. (YA). (gr. 5-8). pap. 2.95 o.p. (*0-14-035119-1*, Puffin Bks.) Penguin Putnam Bks. for Young Readers.

—Ozma of Oz. 1999. (Wizard of Oz Ser.). (Illus.). 251p. (YA). (gr. 5-8). E-Book 5.99 incl. cd-rom (*1-891595-16-4*) Quiet Vision Publishing.

—Ozma of Oz. 1985. (Oz Ser.). (YA). (gr. 5-8). 18.75 o.p. (*0-8446-6180-5*) Smith, Peter Pub., Inc.

—Ozma of Oz. l.t. ed. 2003. 288p. (J). 28.95 (*0-7862-5888-8*) Thorndike Pr.

—Ozma of Oz. 2000. (Oz Ser.). (YA). (gr. 5-8). pap. 9.95 o.p. (*1-58348-486-8*) iUniverse, Inc.

—Ozma of Oz. (Oz Ser.). (YA). (gr. 5-8). E-Book (*1-58824-062-2*) ipicturebooks, LLC.

—The Patchwork Girl of Oz. (Oz Ser.). (YA). (gr. 5-8). 25.95 (*0-8488-0705-7*) Amereon, Ltd.

—The Patchwork Girl of Oz. 2003. pap. 14.95 (*1-58726-038-7*, For Your Knowledge) Ann Arbor Media Group, LLC.

—The Patchwork Girl of Oz. l.t. ed. 2001. (Oz Ser.). (YA). (gr. 5-8). per. 15.50 (*1-58396-169-0*); 200p. per. 12.50 (*1-58396-081-3*) Blue Unicorn Editions.

—The Patchwork Girl of Oz. 1990. (Oz Ser.). (Illus.). 336p. (YA). (gr. 5-8). pap. 7.95 (*0-486-26514-5*) Dover Pubns., Inc.

—The Patchwork Girl of Oz, No. 7. (Oz Ser.). (YA). (gr. 5-8). E-Book 2.49 (*1-58744-039-3*) Electric Umbrella Publishing.

—The Patchwork Girl of Oz. 1995. (Books of Wonder). (Illus.). 352p. (J). (gr. 5-8). 24.99 (*0-688-13354-1*) HarperCollins Children's Bk. Group.

—The Patchwork Girl of Oz. 1999. (Wizard of Oz Ser.). (Illus.). 332p. (YA). (gr. 5-8). E-Book 5.99 incl. cd-rom (*1-891595-20-2*) Quiet Vision Publishing.

—The Patchwork Girl of Oz. 1992. (Oz Ser.). (YA). (gr. 5-8). 25.50 (*0-8446-6495-2*) Smith, Peter Pub., Inc.

—The Patchwork Girl of Oz. (Oz Ser.). (YA). (gr. 5-8). E-Book 5.00 (*0-7410-0532-8*) SoftBook Pr.

—The Patchwork Girl of Oz. (Oz Ser.). (YA). (gr. 5-8). E-Book (*1-58824-055-X*) ipicturebooks, LLC.

—Rinkitink in Oz. (Oz Ser.). (YA). (gr. 5-8). 22.95 (*0-8488-0735-9*) Amereon, Ltd.

—Rinkitink in Oz. 1985. (Oz Ser.). 304p. (YA). (gr. 5-8). mass mkt. 5.99 o.s.i (*0-345-33317-9*, Del Rey) Ballantine Bks.

—Rinkitink in Oz. l.t. ed. 2000. (Oz Ser.). (YA). (gr. 5-8). per. 15.50 (*1-58396-164-X*); 200p. per. 12.50 (*1-58396-076-7*) Blue Unicorn Editions.

—Rinkitink in Oz. 1993. (Oz Ser.). (Illus.). 336p. (YA). (gr. 5-8). reprint ed. pap. text 6.95 (*0-486-27756-9*) Dover Pubns., Inc.

—Rinkitink in Oz. 1998. (Oz Ser.). (Illus.). 352p. (J). (gr. 5-8). 24.99 (*0-688-14720-8*, Morrow, William & Co.) Morrow/Avon.

—Rinkitink in Oz. 1999. (Wizard of Oz Ser.). (Illus.). (YA). (gr. 5-8). E-Book 5.99 incl. cd-rom (*1-891595-23-7*) Quiet Vision Publishing.

—Rinkitink in Oz. (Oz Ser.). (YA). (gr. 5-8). E-Book 5.00 (*0-7410-0559-X*) SoftBook Pr.

—The Road to Oz. (Oz Ser.). (YA). (gr. 5-8). 20.95 (*0-8488-0788-X*) Amereon, Ltd.

—The Road to Oz. 2003. pap. 14.95 (*1-58726-037-9*, For Your Knowledge) Ann Arbor Media Group, LLC.

—The Road to Oz. unabr. ed. 1982. (Oz Ser.). (YA). (gr. 5-8). audio 24.95 (*1-55685-545-1*) Audio Bk. Contractors, Inc.

—The Road to Oz. 1986. (Oz Ser.). 272p. (gr. 5-8). mass mkt. 6.99 (*0-345-33467-1*, Del Rey) Ballantine Bks.

—The Road to Oz. l.t. ed. 2001. (Oz Ser.). (YA). (gr. 5-8). per. 15.50 (*1-58396-170-4*); 200p. per. 12.50 (*1-58396-082-1*) Blue Unicorn Editions.

—The Road to Oz. 1986. (Oz Ser.). (Illus.). 272p. (YA). (gr. 5-8). reprint ed. pap. 8.95 (*0-486-25208-6*) Dover Pubns., Inc.

—The Road to Oz. (Oz Ser.). (YA). (gr. 5-8). E-Book 2.49 (*0-7574-0393-X*) Electric Umbrella Publishing.

—The Road to Oz. 1991. (Books of Wonder). (Illus.). 272p. (J). (gr. 5-8). reprint ed. 24.99 (*0-688-09997-1*) HarperCollins Children's Bk. Group.

—The Road to Oz. 1993. (Oz Ser.). 160p. (YA). (gr. 5-8). pap. 2.99 o.p. (*0-14-035121-3*, Puffin Bks.) Penguin Putnam Bks. for Young Readers.

—The Road to Oz. 1999. (Wizard of Oz Ser.). (Illus.). (YA). (gr. 5-8). E-Book 5.99 incl. cd-rom (*1-891595-18-0*) Quiet Vision Publishing.

—The Road to Oz. 1990. (Oz Ser.). (Illus.). (YA). (gr. 5-8). 23.50 (*0-8446-6250-X*) Smith, Peter Pub., Inc.

—The Road to Oz. (Oz Ser.). (YA). (gr. 5-8). E-Book 5.00 (*0-7410-1129-8*) SoftBook Pr.

—The Road to Oz. (Oz Ser.). E-Book (*1-58824-063-0*) ipicturebooks, LLC.

—The Royal Book of Oz. Thompson, Ruth Plumly, ed. enl. ed. 2001. (Oz Ser.). (Illus.). 332p. (J). (gr. 5-8). 9.95 (*0-486-41766-2*) Dover Pubns., Inc.

—The Scarecrow of Oz. (Oz Ser.). (YA). (gr. 5-8). 20.95 (*0-8488-0707-3*) Amereon, Ltd.

—The Scarecrow of Oz. l.t. ed. 2000. (Oz Ser.). (YA). (gr. 5-8). per. 15.50 (*1-58396-174-7*); 200p. per. 12.50 (*1-58396-086-4*) Blue Unicorn Editions.

—The Scarecrow of Oz. 1999. (Oz Ser.). (Illus.). 304p. (YA). (gr. 5-8). pap. 9.95 (*0-486-40548-6*) Dover Pubns., Inc.

—The Scarecrow of Oz. 1997. (Books of Wonder). (Illus.). 304p. (J). (gr. 5-7). 24.99 (*0-688-14719-4*) HarperCollins Children's Bk. Group.

—The Scarecrow of Oz. 1999. (Wizard of Oz Ser.). (Illus.). (YA). (gr. 5-8). E-Book 5.99 incl. cd-rom (*1-891595-22-9*) Quiet Vision Publishing.

—The Scarecrow of Oz. (Oz Ser.). (YA). (gr. 5-8). E-Book 5.00 (*0-7410-0534-4*) SoftBook Pr.

—Tik-Tok of Oz. 1996. (gr. 4-7). 20.95 (*0-8488-0708-1*) Amereon, Ltd.

—Tik-Tok of Oz. 2003. pap. 14.95 (*1-58726-039-5*, For Your Knowledge) Ann Arbor Media Group, LLC.

—Tik-Tok of Oz. 1985. (Wonderful Oz Bks.: Vol. 8). 272p. (YA). (gr. 5-8). mass mkt. 5.99 o.s.i (*0-345-33435-3*, Del Rey) Ballantine Bks.

—Tik-Tok of Oz. l.t. ed. (Oz Ser.). (YA). (gr. 5-8). 2000. per. 15.50 (*1-58396-173-9*); 2001. 200p. per. 12.50 (*1-58396-085-6*) Blue Unicorn Editions.

—Tik-Tok of Oz, No. 8. (Oz Ser.). (YA). (gr. 5-8). E-Book 2.49 (*1-58744-041-5*) Electric Umbrella Publishing.

—Tik-Tok of Oz. 1996. (Books of Wonder). (Illus.). 304p. (J). (gr. 5-8). 25.95 (*0-688-13355-X*) HarperCollins Children's Bk. Group.

—Tik-Tok of Oz. 1991. (Oz Ser.). (Illus.). 192p. (YA). (gr. 5-8). pap. 2.25 o.p. (*0-14-035124-8*, Puffin Bks.) Penguin Putnam Bks. for Young Readers.

—Tik-Tok of Oz. 1999. (Wizard of Oz Ser.). (Illus.). 297p. (YA). (gr. 5-8). E-Book 5.99 incl. cd-rom (*1-891595-21-0*) Quiet Vision Publishing.

—Tik-Tok of Oz. (Oz Ser.). (YA). (gr. 5-8). E-Book 5.00 (*0-7410-0537-9*) SoftBook Pr.

—Tik-Tok of Oz. (Oz Ser.). (YA). (gr. 5-8). E-Book (*1-58824-057-6*) ipicturebooks, LLC.

—The Tin Woodman of Oz. 20.95 (*0-8488-0709-X*) Amereon, Ltd.

—The Tin Woodman of Oz. 1980. mass mkt. 2.25 o.p. (*0-345-28234-5*, Del Rey) Ballantine Bks.

—The Tin Woodman of Oz. l.t. ed. (Oz Ser.). (YA). (gr. 5-8). 2000. per. 15.50 (*1-58396-171-2*); 2001. 200p. per. 12.50 (*1-58396-083-X*) Blue Unicorn Editions.

—The Tin Woodman of Oz. 2000. (Oz Ser.). (Illus.). 288p. (J). (gr. 5-8). pap. 8.95 (*0-486-41302-0*) Dover Pubns., Inc.

—The Tin Woodman of Oz. 1999. (Books of Wonder). (Illus.). 336p. (J). (gr. 5). 24.99 (*0-688-14976-6*) HarperCollins Children's Bk. Group.

—The Tin Woodman of Oz. 2003. (Twelve-Point Ser.). lib. bdg. 24.00 (*1-58287-257-0*); lib. bdg. 25.00 (*1-58287-741-6*) North Bks.

—The Tin Woodman of Oz. 1999. (Wizard of Oz Ser.). (Illus.). (YA). (gr. 5-8). E-Book 5.99 incl. cd-rom (*1-891595-25-3*) Quiet Vision Publishing.

—The Tin Woodman of Oz. (Oz Ser.). (YA). (gr. 5-8). E-Book 5.00 (*0-7410-0619-7*) SoftBook Pr.

—The Wizard of Oz. 2002. (Great Illustrated Classics). (Illus.). 240p. (J). (gr. 3-8). lib. bdg. 21.35 (*1-57765-807-8*, ABDO & Daughters) ABDO Publishing Co.

Settings

—The Wizard of Oz. 1994. (Illus.). 30p. (J). pap. 7.95 (1-55859-820-0) Abbeville Pr., Inc.

—The Wizard of Oz. 1996. (Pocket Play Bks.). (Illus.). 24p. (J). (ps-2). 9.95 (0-8362-0953-2) Andrews McMeel Publishing.

—The Wizard of Oz. 1986. 240p. mass mkt. 5.99 (0-345-33590-2); 1983. (J). mass mkt. 2.25 o.p. (0-345-31363-1) Ballantine Bks. (Del Rey).

—The Wizard of Oz. 2002. (Illus.). 208p. (J). (gr. 5-7). 25.00 (0-7567-5917-X) DIANE Publishing Co.

—The Wizard of Oz. 1995. (Children's Thrift Classics Ser.). (Illus.). 96p. (J). pap. text 1.00 (0-486-28585-5) Dover Pubns., Inc.

—The Wizard of Oz. 1983. (J). audio 11.00 (0-89856-082-9) HarperChildren's Audio.

—The Wizard of Oz. 1988. (Children's Classics Ser.). (Illus.). 32p. (J). (gr. k-3). 5.95 o.p. (0-8249-8264-9) Ideals Pubns.

—The Wizard of Oz. (Paint with Water Fairy Tales Ser.). (Illus.). (J). (gr. k-2). 1994. 32p. pap. (1-56144-489-8, Honey Bear Bks.); 1990. 8p. pap. 6.95 o.p. (0-87449-883-X) Modern Publishing.

—The Wizard of Oz. 1984. (Signet Classics). (Illus.). 240p. (YA). mass mkt. 3.95 (0-451-51864-0, Signet Classics) NAL.

—The Wizard of Oz. 1996. (Illus.). 105p. (J). (ps-3). 19.95 (1-55858-638-5) North-South Bks., Inc.

—The Wizard of Oz. 9999. (Illus.). (J). (Well-Loved Tales Ser.: Level 3, No. 606D-11). (gr. 2-4). 3.50 o.p. (0-7214-0828-1); (Read It Yourself Ser.: Level 4, No. 777-6). (ps-2). pap. 3.50 o.p. (0-7214-5127-6) Penguin Group (USA) Inc. (Ladybird Bks.).

—The Wizard of Oz. 1999. pap. 2.99 o.p. (0-14-130546-0); 1995. (Illus.). 208p. (J). (gr. 4-7). pap. 4.99 (0-14-036693-8) Penguin Putnam Bks. for Young Readers. (Puffin Bks.).

—The Wizard of Oz. Denslow, W. W., ed. 1994. (Illustrated Junior Library). (Illus.). 224p. (J). (gr. 4-7). 15.99 (0-448-40561-X, Grosset & Dunlap) Penguin Putnam Bks. for Young Readers.

—The Wizard of Oz. (J). 1984. (gr. k-3). 238.80 o.s.i (0-8431-4184-0, Grosset & Dunlap); 1983. (Illus.). 176p. (gr. 3-7). pap. 2.99 o.p. (0-14-035001-2, Puffin Bks.); 1981. (Illus.). 224p. (gr. 3-9). 6.95 o.s.i (0-448-11026-1, Grosset & Dunlap); 1963. (Illus.). (gr. 4-6). 2.95 o.p. (0-448-05470-1, Grosset & Dunlap); 1956. (Illus.). 224p. (gr. 4-6). 12.95 o.p. (0-448-06026-4, Grosset & Dunlap); 1956. (Illus.). (gr. 4-6). 5.95 o.p. (0-448-05826-X, Grosset & Dunlap) Penguin Putnam Bks. for Young Readers.

—The Wizard of Oz. Vogel, Malvina, ed. 1989. (Great Illustrated Classics Ser.: Vol. 8). (Illus.). 240p. (J). (gr. 3-6). 9.95 (0-86611-959-0) Playmore, Inc., Pubs.

—The Wizard of Oz. 1993. (Look & Find Ser.). (Illus.). 24p. (J). 7.98 (0-7853-0066-X); 12.98 (0-7853-0129-1) Publications International, Ltd.

—The Wizard of Oz. (Crazy Games Ser.). 1999. (Illus.). 3.99 o.p. (0-8431-7500-1, Wee Sing Bks.); 1978. (Illus.). (J). 2.95 o.p. (0-448-16305-5); 1976. (J). 2.95 o.p. (0-448-12432-7) Putnam Publishing Group, The.

—The Wizard of Oz. 1987. (Radiobook Ser.). (J). audio 4.98 (0-929541-01-4) Radiola Co.

—The Wizard of Oz. (Golden Sound Story Bks.). (ps up). 1992. (Illus.). 20p. (J). o.p. (0-307-74706-9, 64706, Golden Bks.); 1991. o.s.i (0-517-07034-0, Random Hse. Bks. for Young Readers); 1986. (Illus.). 176p. (J). o.p. (0-307-17115-9, Golden Bks.); 1984. (Illus.). 64p. (J). 8.99 o.s.i (0-394-95331-2, Random Hse. Bks. for Young Readers) Random Hse. Children's Bks.

—The Wizard of Oz. Chaffee, Allen, ed. 1963. (Illus.). (J). (gr. k-3). 4.95 o.p. (0-394-80689-1); lib. bdg. 4.99 o.p. (0-394-90689-6) Random Hse. Children's Bks. (Random Hse. Bks. for Young Readers).

—The Wizard of Oz. 1991. (Illus.). 96p. (J). 15.00 o.s.i (0-517-69506-5) Random Hse. Value Publishing.

—The Wizard of Oz. 1995. audio 31.98 (1-56826-542-5) Rhino Entertainment.

—The Wizard of Oz. (SPA.). 256p. (J). 9.95 (84-204-3509-0) Santillana USA Publishing Co., Inc.

—The Wizard of Oz. (J). 2001. mass mkt. 10.95 (0-439-23641-X); 1989. (gr. 3-5). pap. 2.50 o.p. (0-590-41746-0, Scholastic Paperbacks); 1989. 160p. (gr. 4-7). mass mkt. 4.50 (0-590-44089-6, Scholastic Paperbacks) Scholastic, Inc.

—The Wizard of Oz. audio 3.98 (1-55886-112-2, BB/PT 439) Smarty Pants.

—The Wizard of Oz. 2002. (J). audio compact disk 26.95 (1-58472-349-1, 065, In Audio) Sound Room Pubs., Inc.

—The Wizard of Oz. 1999. 10.04 (0-606-17516-4); 1982. (J). 10.04 (0-606-04376-4) Turtleback Bks.

—The Wizard of Oz. 1985. (Illus.). 160p. (J). 14.95 o.p. (0-88101-273-4) Unicorn Publishing Hse., Inc., The.

—The Wizard of Oz. 1998. (Children's Classics). 144p. (J). (gr. 4-7). pap. 3.95 (1-85326-112-2, 1122WW) Wordsworth Editions, Ltd. GBR. *Dist:* Advanced Global Distribution Services.

—The Wizard of Oz. 1988. (J). (ps-3). 5.95 o.p. (0-88101-076-6) Unicorn Publishing Hse., Inc., The.

—The Wizard of Oz. 1985. (J). 17.95 o.p. (0-671-60509-7, Atheneum) Simon & Schuster Children's Publishing.

—The Wizard of Oz. abr. ed. (J). audio 12.95 (0-89926-138-8, 826); audio 23.80 Audio Bk. Co.

—The Wizard of Oz. adapted ed. 1997. (Living Classics Ser.). (Illus.). 32p. (J). (gr. 3-7). 14.95 o.p. (0-7641-7046-5) Barron's Educational Series, Inc.

—The Wizard of Oz. unabr. ed. 2002. audio compact disk 32.00 (0-7861-9586-X); 1980. (J). audio 23.95 Blackstone Audio Bks., Inc.

—The Wizard of Oz. unabr. collector's ed. 1996. (J). audio 24.00 (0-7366-3403-7, 4049) Books on Tape, Inc.

—The Wizard of Oz. Escott, John, ed. abr. ed. 1996. (Classics for Young Readers Ser.). (Illus.). 64p. (J). (gr. 1-4). 5.98 (1-85854-286-3) Brimax Bks., Ltd.

—The Wizard of Oz. Kincaid, Lucy, ed. 1997. (Illus.). 45p. (J). (gr. k-2). reprint ed. 18.00 (0-7567-5963-3) DIANE Publishing Co.

—The Wizard of Oz. 1993. (Illus.). 143p. (C). reprint ed. pap. 15.00 (0-7567-5186-1) DIANE Publishing Co.

—The Wizard of Oz. abr. ed. 1984. (J). audio 15.95 o.p. (0-88646-091-3, TC-LFP 7022) Durkin Hayes Publishing Ltd.

—The Wizard of Oz. abr. ed. 1984. (J). audio 9.95 (0-89845-900-1, CPN 1512, Caedmon) HarperTrade.

—The Wizard of Oz, ERS. 1982. (Illus.). 240p. (YA). (gr. 2 up). 29.95 o.s.i (0-8050-0221-9, Holt, Henry & Co. Bks. For Young Readers) Holt, Henry & Co.

—The Wizard of Oz. 1999. (Illus.). 272p. (YA). (gr. 3 up). reprint ed. 12.95 (1-56852-225-8, Konecky & Konecky) Konecky, William S. Assocs., Inc.

—The Wizard of Oz. 1992. 48p. (J). No. 175. pap. 5.95 (0-7935-1637-4, 00243140); No. 282. pap. 6.95 (0-7935-1635-8, 00102256) Leonard, Hal Corp.

—The Wizard of Oz, Set. unabr. ed. 2000. audio 16.95 Monterey Media, Inc.

—The Wizard of Oz. ltd. ed. 1996. (Illus.). 105p. (J). (gr. 2-6). 200.00 (1-55858-657-1) North-South Bks., Inc.

—The Wizard of Oz, Level 1. Hedge, Tricia, ed. 2000. (Bookworms Ser.). (Illus.). 64p. pap. text 5.95 (0-19-422958-0) Oxford Univ. Pr., Inc.

—The Wizard of Oz. Kilgras, Heidi, ed. anniv. ed. 2000. (Illus.). 96p. (J). (ps-3). 21.95 (0-375-81137-0, Random Hse. Bks. for Young Readers) Random Hse. Children's Bks.

—The Wizard of Oz, unabr. ed. 1980. (J). (gr. 4). audio 27.00 (1-55690-570-X, 80120E7) Recorded Bks., LLC.

—The Wizard of Oz. 1984. (Illus.). (J). (gr. 2-4). reprint ed. pap. 2.25 o.p. (0-590-40442-3) Scholastic, Inc.

—The Wizard of Oz, Set. Lewis, Bob & Mortensen, Patti, eds. abr. ed. 1972. (Dramatized Classics Ser.). (J). (gr. 3-8). pap. 11.95 o.p. incl. audio (0-88142-336-X, 392926) Soundelux Audio Publishing.

—The Wizard of Oz. abr. unabr. ed. 1997. (Classic Ser.). (J). audio 10.95 o.s.i (0-14-086438-5, Penguin AudioBooks) Viking Penguin.

—The Wizard of Oz: Centennial Edition, ERS. 100th anniv. ed. 2000. (Illus.). xiv, 220p. (J). (gr. 4-7). 29.95 (0-8050-6430-3, Holt, Henry & Co. Bks. For Young Readers) Holt, Henry & Co.

—The Wizard of Oz & The Land of Oz. unabr. ed. (J). audio 48.00 o.p. audio o.p. Books on Tape, Inc.

—The Wizard of Oz Collection. 1999. E-Book 11.99 o.p. incl. cd-rom (1-891595-08-3) Quiet Vision Publishing.

—The Wizard of Oz Color Book. 1978. (J). pap. 2.95 (0-486-20452-9) Dover Pubns., Inc.

—The Wizard of Oz Frieze. Corso, Heidi K., ed. 1986. (Oz Ser.). (Illus.). 30p. (YA). (gr. 5-8). 4.95 o.p. (0-88101-060-X) Unicorn Publishing Hse., Inc., The.

—The Wizard of Oz Waddle Book. 1993. (Illus.). (J). reprint ed. 85.00 (1-55709-203-6) Applewood Bks.

—The Wonderful Wizard of Oz. 1965. (Oz Ser.). (Illus.). (YA). (gr. 5-8). mass mkt. 1.75 o.p. (0-8049-0069-8, CL-69) Airmont Publishing Co., Inc.

—The Wonderful Wizard of Oz. (Oz Ser.). (YA). (gr. 5-8). 20.95 (0-88411-772-3) Amereon, Ltd.

—The Wonderful Wizard of Oz. 1990. (Oz Ser.). 176p. (YA). (gr. 5-8). mass mkt. 2.25 o.s.i (0-553-21384-9) Bantam Bks.

—The Wonderful Wizard of Oz. 1975. (Oz Ser.). (Illus.). 159p. (YA). (gr. 5-8). reprint ed. 11.00 o.p. (0-460-05068-0, BKA 01574) Biblio Distribution.

—The Wonderful Wizard of Oz. unabr. ed. 1980. (Oz Ser.). (YA). (gr. 5-8). audio 23.95 (0-7861-0586-0, 2075) Blackstone Audio Bks., Inc.

—The Wonderful Wizard of Oz. rev. ed. 2001. (Oz Ser.). 200p. (YA). (gr. 5-8). per. 12.50 (1-58396-084-8) Blue Unicorn Editions.

—The Wonderful Wizard of Oz. 1981. (Oz Ser.). (YA). (gr. 5-8). reprint ed. 193p. lib. bdg. 11.95 (0-89967-021-0, Harmony Raine & Co.); 139p. lib. bdg. 15.95 (0-89966-347-8) Buccaneer Bks., Inc.

—The Wonderful Wizard of Oz. 1995. (Oz Ser.). (Illus.). (YA). (gr. 5-8). 12.99 o.s.i (0-517-12204-9) Crown Publishing Group.

—The Wonderful Wizard of Oz. 2002. (Spot the Classics Ser.). (Illus.). 192p. (J). (gr. k-5). 4.99 (1-57759-551-3) Dalmatian Pr.

—The Wonderful Wizard of Oz. l.t. unabr. ed. (Dover Large Print Classics Ser.). (Illus.). 2002. 256p. (J). pap. 9.95 (0-486-42248-8); 1960. 267p. (YA). (gr. 5-8). reprint ed. pap. 9.95 (0-486-20691-2); 1996. 128p. (YA). (gr. 5-8). reprint ed. pap. text 1.50 (0-486-29116-2) Dover Pubns., Inc.

—The Wonderful Wizard of Oz. (Oz Ser.). (YA). (gr. 5-8). E-Book 2.49 (0-7574-0473-1) Electric Umbrella Publishing.

—The Wonderful Wizard of Oz. 2001. (Books of Wonder Ser.). (Illus.). 320p. (J). pap. 7.99 (0-688-16677-6, Harper Trophy) HarperCollins Children's Bk. Group.

—The Wonderful Wizard of Oz, Set. abr. ed. 1999. (Oz Ser.). (YA). (gr. 5-8). audio 16.95 Highsmith Inc.

—The Wonderful Wizard of Oz. l.t. ed. (Oz Ser.). (YA). (gr. 5-8). 283p. pap. 31.38 (0-7583-2918-0); 68p. pap. 14.03 (0-7583-2912-1); 85p. pap. 15.41 (0-7583-2913-X); 116p. pap. 17.91 (0-7583-2914-8); 231p. pap. 27.18 (0-7583-2917-2); 148p. pap. 20.49 (0-7583-2915-6); 329p. pap. 35.09 (0-7583-2919-9); 189p. pap. 23.79 (0-7583-2916-4); 283p. lib. bdg. 38.77 (0-7583-2910-5); 68p. lib. bdg. 21.72 (0-7583-2904-0); 85p. lib. bdg. 24.76 (0-7583-2905-9); 116p. lib. bdg. 26.96 (0-7583-2906-7); 189p. lib. bdg. 32.12 (0-7583-2908-3); 329p. lib. bdg. 42.03 (0-7583-2911-3); 148p. lib. bdg. 29.22 (0-7583-2907-5); 231p. lib. bdg. 35.09 (0-7583-2909-1) Huge Print Pr.

—The Wonderful Wizard of Oz. unabr. ed. 1979. (Oz Ser.). (YA). (gr. 5-8). audio 21.00 Jimcin Recordings.

—The Wonderful Wizard of Oz. 1992. (Everyman's Library Children's Classics Ser.). (Illus.). 240p. (gr. 5-8). 12.95 (0-679-41794-X, Everyman's Library) Knopf Publishing Group.

—The Wonderful Wizard of Oz. l.t. ed. 1997. (Oz Ser.). 198p. (YA). (gr. 5-8). lib. bdg. 26.95 (1-58118-011-X, 21511) LRS.

—The Wonderful Wizard of Oz. (Oz Ser.). (YA). (gr. 5-8). E-Book 2.95 (1-57799-887-1); E-Book 2.95 (1-57799-977-0) Logos Research Systems, Inc.

—The Wonderful Wizard of Oz. 1992. (Fun-to-Read Fairy Tales Ser.). (Illus.). 24p. (J). (gr. k-3). pap. 2.50 o.s.i (1-56144-174-0, Honey Bear Bks.) Modern Publishing.

—The Wonderful Wizard of Oz. (Oz Ser.). (YA). (gr. 5-8). 1987. (Illus.). 316p. 21.95 (0-688-06944-4); 1924. lib. bdg. 99.98 o.p. (0-688-06945-2) Morrow/Avon. (Morrow, William & Co.).

—The Wonderful Wizard of Oz. abr. ed. 2001. (J). audio 13.98 (962-634-714-7, NA221414); (YA). (gr. 3 up). audio compact disk 15.98 (962-634-214-5, NA221412) Naxos of America, Inc. (Naxos AudioBooks).

—The Wonderful Wizard of Oz. abr. ed. 1977. (Oz Ser.). (YA). (gr. 5-8). audio 6.95 (0-7871-1202-X, 686086, Dove Audio) NewStar Media, Inc.

—The Wonderful Wizard of Oz. Wolstenholme, Susan & Denslow, W. W., eds. 2000. (Oz Ser.). (Illus.). 336p. (YA). (gr. 5-8). pap. 11.95 (0-19-283930-6) Oxford Univ. Pr., Inc.

—The Wonderful Wizard of Oz. Wolstenholme, Susan, ed. 1997. (Oz Ser.). (Illus.). 330p. (YA). (gr. 5-8). pap. 9.95 o.p. (0-19-282400-7) Oxford Univ. Pr., Inc.

—The Wonderful Wizard of Oz. l.t. ed. 1987. (Oz Ser.). (Illus.). 188p. (YA). (gr. 5-8). lib. bdg. 16.95 o.s.i (1-55736-013-8, Cornerstone Bks.) Pages, Inc.

—The Wonderful Wizard of Oz. 2003. (Illus.). 160p. (J). 16.95 (1-84365-007-X) Pavilion Bks., Ltd. GBR. *Dist:* Trafalgar Square.

—The Wonderful Wizard of Oz. Wright, W. R., ed. unabr. ed. 1995. (Oz Ser.). (YA). (gr. 5-8). audio 19.95 (1-886354-01-4) Piglet Pr., Inc.

—The Wonderful Wizard of Oz. 1999. (Wizard of Oz Ser.). (Illus.). 244p. (YA). (gr. 5-8). E-Book 5.99 incl. cd-rom (1-891595-14-8) Quiet Vision Publishing.

—The Wonderful Wizard of Oz. abr. ed. 1994. (Oz Ser.). (YA). (gr. 5-8). audio 11.00 o.s.i (0-679-43441-0, RH Audio) Random Hse. Audio Publishing Group.

—The Wonderful Wizard of Oz. 1991. (Oz Ser.). (YA). (gr. 5-8). 12.99 o.s.i (0-517-06094-9) Random Hse. Value Publishing.

—The Wonderful Wizard of Oz. 2000. (Classic Collectible Pop-Up Ser.). (Illus.). 16p. (J). (ps-3). 24.95 (0-689-81751-7); (YA). (gr. 5-8). 150.00 o.s.i (0-689-84014-4) Simon & Schuster Children's Publishing. (Little Simon).

—The Wonderful Wizard of Oz. 1990. (Oz Ser.). (Illus.). (YA). (gr. 5-8). 24.00 (0-8446-1610-9) Smith, Peter Pub., Inc.

—The Wonderful Wizard of Oz. 1986. (Oz Ser.). (Illus.). (YA). (gr. 5-8). 29.95 o.p. (0-520-05822-4) Univ. of California Pr.

—The Wonderful Wizard of Oz. Leach, William R., ed. 1991. (Oz Ser.). 188p. (YA). (gr. 5-8). 19.25 o.p. (0-534-14736-4) Wadsworth.

—The Wonderful Wizard of Oz. 2001. E-Book (1-58824-419-9); E-Book (1-58824-392-3) ipicturebooks, LLC.

—The Wonderful Wizard of Oz: The Centennial Edition. 2000. (Oz Ser.). (Illus.). 160p. (YA). (gr. 5-8). 29.95 (1-86205-343-X) Pavilion Bks., Ltd. GBR. *Dist:* Trafalgar Square.

—The Wonderful Wizard of Oz: 100th Anniversary Edition. 100th anniv. ed. 2000. (Books of Wonder). (Illus.). 272p. (J). (gr. 5-8). 24.99 (0-06-029323-3) HarperCollins Children's Bk. Group.

—The Wonderful World of Oz: The Wizard of Oz, The Emerald City of Oz & Glinda of Oz. 2001. (J). (ps up). Vol. 1. audio 9.95 o.p. (1-56015-688-0); Vol. 2. audio 9.95 o.p. (1-56015-689-9) Penton Overseas, Inc. (Penton Kids).

Baum, L. Frank, contrib. by. The Wonderful Wizard of Oz. abr. ed. 1998. (Oz Ser.). 120p. (YA). (gr. 5-8). audio 16.95 (1-56994-501-2, 339994, Monterey SoundWorks) Monterey Media, Inc.

Baum, L. Frank & Denslow, W. W. Oz-Story 5. Maxine, David, ed. 1999. (Oz Ser.:). (Illus.). 128p. (Orig.). (YA). (gr. 5-8). pap. 14.95 (1-929527-00-4) Hungry Tiger Pr.

Baum, L. Frank & Glassman, Peter. Glinda of Oz. 2000. (Books of Wonder). (Illus.). 288p. (J). (gr. 5-8). 24.99 (0-688-14978-2) HarperCollins Children's Bk. Group.

—The Lost Princess of Oz. 1998. (Books of Wonder). (Illus.). 352p. (J). (gr. 5-8). 24.99 (0-688-14975-8) HarperCollins Children's Bk. Group.

—The Magic of Oz. 1999. (Books of Wonder). (Illus.). 272p. (J). (gr. 5-8). 24.95 (0-688-14977-4) HarperCollins Children's Bk. Group.

Baum, L. Frank & McGraw, Eloise Jarvis, illus. The Wizard of Oz. 1999. (Aladdin Classics Ser.). 224p. (J). (gr. 4-7). pap. 3.99 (0-689-83142-0, Aladdin) Simon & Schuster Children's Publishing.

Baum, L. Frank & Mitchell, Kathy. The Wizard of Oz. 1986. (Illus.). 174p. (J). (0-307-67115-1) Whitman Publishing LLC.

Baum, L. Frank & Santore, Charles. The Wizard of Oz. 1991. (Illus.). 96p. (J). 15.99 o.s.i (0-517-06655-6) Random Hse. Value Publishing.

Baum, L. Frank, et al. Oz-Story 4. Maxine, David, ed. 1998. (Oz Ser.). (Illus.). 128p. (Orig.). (YA). (gr. 5-8). pap. 14.95 (0-9644988-7-1) Hungry Tiger Pr.

Baum, Roger S. Dorothy of Oz. 1989. (Books of Wonder). (Illus.). 176p. (J). (gr. 5-10). 22.95 (0-688-07848-6) HarperCollins Children's Bk. Group.

—The Lion of Oz & the Badge of Courage. (Illus.). (J). 24.95 (1-57072-255-2) Overmountain Pr.

—The Rewolf of Oz. 1991. (Oz Ser.). (Illus.). (YA). (gr. 5-8). pap. 13.95 o.p. (0-671-74982-X, Simon & Schuster Children's Publishing) Simon & Schuster Children's Publishing.

Carr, M. J. & Baum, L. Frank. The Wizard of Oz. novel ed. 1993. 96p. (J). (ps-3). mass mkt. 3.25 (0-590-46993-2) Scholastic, Inc.

Einhorn, Edward A. Paradox in Oz. 2000. (Illus.). 238p. (J). (gr. 3 up). 24.95 (1-929527-01-2) Hungry Tiger Pr.

Gardner, Richard A. Dorothy & the Lizard of Oz: What Happened to Dorothy & Her Friends after They Lived Happily Ever After? 1980. (Illus.). 108p. (J). (gr. 1-6). 10.99 (0-933812-03-5) Creative Therapeutics, Inc.

Garland, Judy. The Wizard of Oz. (J). audio 7.95 National Recording Co.

Glassman, Peter. Oz: The 100th Anniversary Celebration. 2000. (Books of Wonder). (Illus.). 64p. (J). (gr. 4-7). 24.95 (0-688-15915-X) HarperCollins Children's Bk. Group.

Glassman, Peter, ed. Oz: The Hundredth Anniversary Celebration. 2000. (Illus.). 55p. (YA). reprint ed. 25.00 (0-7567-5499-2) DIANE Publishing Co.

Hague, Michael. Wizard of Oz, Vol. 1. ltd. ed. 1983. (J). 100.00 o.p. (0-03-062426-6, Holt, Henry & Co. Bks. For Young Readers) Holt, Henry & Co.

Houghton Mifflin Company Staff. The Wonderful Wizard of Oz. 1992. (Literature Experience 1993 Ser.). (J). (gr. 4). pap. 10.24 (0-395-61804-5) Houghton Mifflin Co.

The Land of Oz. (Oz Ser.). (YA). (gr. 5-8). audio HarperTrade.

Landes, William-Alan & Standish, Marilyn. The Wizard of Oz. rev. ed. 1985. (Wondrawhopper Ser.). 40p. (J). (gr. 3-12). pap. 6.00 (*0-88734-105-5*) Players Pr., Inc.

McGraw, Eloise Jarvis, et al. Merry Go Round in Oz. (Oz Ser.). (Illus.). 313p. (YA). 1989. (gr. 5-8). 24.95 o.p. (*0-929605-06-3*); 1996. (gr. 3-10). reprint ed. pap. 12.95 o.p. (*0-929605-60-8*) Books of Wonder.

Mitchell, Adrian. The Patchwork Girl of Oz. 1994. (Oz Ser.). (YA). (gr. 5-8). pap. 5.95 (*0-87129-335-8*, P09) Dramatic Publishing Co.

Morris, Kimberly & Baum, L. Frank. The Wizard of Oz. 2001. (Young Classics Ser.). (Illus.). 48p. (J). (gr. 1-3). pap. 9.95 (*0-7894-4444-5*, D K Ink) Dorling Kindersley Publishing, Inc.

Neill, John R. Lucky Bucky in Oz. 1992. (Oz Ser.). (Illus.). 289p. (YA). (gr. 5-8). 24.95 o.p. (*0-929605-17-9*) Books of Wonder.

—Wonder City of Oz. (Oz Ser.). (Illus.). 318p. (YA). (gr. 5-8). 1990. 24.95 o.p. (*0-929605-07-1*); 1996. reprint ed. pap. 12.95 o.p. (*0-929605-61-6*) Books of Wonder.

Neill, John R. & Baum, L. Frank. The Runaway in Oz. 1995. (Oz Ser.). (Illus.). 254p. (YA). (gr. 5-8). 24.95 o.p. (*0-929605-39-X*) Books of Wonder.

Outlet Book Company Staff & Baum, L. Frank. Journeys Through Oz. 1985. (Oz Ser.). (YA). (gr. 5-8). 7.99 o.p. (*0-517-29490-7*) Random Hse. Value Publishing.

Santore, Charles & Aesop. Aesop's Fables. 1997. (Illus.). 64p. (J). (ps-1). 20.00 o.s.i (*0-679-88758-X*, Random Hse. Bks. for Young Readers) Random Hse. Children's Bks.

Smath, Jerry. The Wizard of Oz. 1999. (Jewel Sticker Stories Ser.). (Illus.). 24p. (J). (ps-2). 3.99 (*0-448-41978-5*, Grosset & Dunlap) Penguin Putnam Bks. for Young Readers.

Snow, Jack. The Magical Mimics in Oz. 1991. (Oz Ser.). (Illus.). (YA). (gr. 5-8). 240p. 24.95 o.p. (*0-929605-08-X*); 243p. pap. 14.95 (*0-929605-09-8*) Books of Wonder.

—The Shaggy Man of Oz. 1991. (Oz Ser.). (Illus.). (YA). (gr. 5-8). 256p. 24.95 o.p. (*0-929605-10-1*); 255p. pap. 14.95 (*0-929605-11-X*) Books of Wonder.

Stillman, William & Scarfone, Jay. The Wizard of Oz: The Film Classic Comes to Life with Music & Stunning 3-Dimension! 2000. (Illus.). 10p. (J). (gr. 4-7). 24.95 (*1-58117-058-0*, Piggy Toes Pr.) Intervisual Bks., Inc.

Thompson, Ruth P. Captain Salt in Oz. 1996. (Oz Ser.). (Illus.). 304p. (YA). (gr. 5-8). reprint ed. pap. 12.95 o.p. (*0-929605-48-9*) Books of Wonder.

—Handy Mandy in Oz. 1996. (Oz Ser.). (Illus.). 256p. (YA). (gr. 5-8). pap. 12.95 o.p. (*0-929605-49-7*) Books of Wonder.

—Ozoplaning with the Wizard of Oz. 1996. (Oz Ser.). (Illus.). 256p. (YA). (gr. 5-8). pap. 14.95 (*0-929605-57-8*) Books of Wonder.

—The Silver Princess in Oz. 1996. (Oz Ser.). (Illus.). 304p. (YA). (gr. 5-8). reprint ed. pap. 14.95 (*0-929605-56-X*) Books of Wonder.

Thomson, Ruth P. The Royal Book of Oz. 1997. (Oz Ser.). (Illus.). 312p. (YA). (gr. 5-8). reprint ed. 22.95 o.p. (*0-929605-67-5*) Books of Wonder.

Vrato, Elizabeth. The Wonderful Wizard of Oz. 2003. (Illus.). 64p. (J). 9.98 (*0-7624-1628-9*) Running Pr. Bk. Pubs.

The Wizard of Oz: Original Motion Picture Soundtrack. (J). 2002. audio 7.98 (*1-56826-802-5*, 72755); 2001. audio compact disk 11.98 Rhino Entertainment.

Zeder, Suzan L. Ozma of Oz: A Tale of Time. 1981. (Oz Ser.). (YA). (gr. 5-8). 6.50 (*0-87602-233-6*) Anchorage Pr.

OZARK MOUNTAINS REGION—FICTION

Blackwood, Gary L. Moonshine. 1999. (Accelerated Reader Bks.). 158p. (J). (gr. 3-7). 14.95 (*0-7614-5056-4*, Cavendish Children's Bks.) Cavendish, Marshall Corp.

Bowman, Eddie. Roddy the Rooster. 1997. (Illus.). (J). 17.25 (*1-56763-326-9*); pap. (*1-56763-327-7*) Ozark Publishing.

Branscum, Robbie. Old Blue Tilley. 1991. 96p. (J). (gr. 5-9). text 13.95 o.p. (*0-02-711931-9*, Simon & Schuster Children's Publishing) Simon & Schuster Children's Publishing.

Byers, Stephen P. Lost River Bridge. 2001. 165p. pap. 12.95 (*1-929663-02-1*) Books By Byers.

Calif, Ruth. The Over-the-Hill Witch. 1990. (Illus.). 144p. (J). (gr. 5). 11.95 o.s.i (*0-88289-754-3*) Pelican Publishing Co., Inc.

Chittum, Ida. The Hermit Boy. 1972. (Illus.). 160p. (J). (gr. 4-6). 4.95 o.p. (*0-440-03557-0*, Delacorte Pr.) Dell Publishing.

Dengler, Marianna. Fiddlin' Sam. 1999. (Illus.). 32p. (J). (ps-3). 15.95 (*0-87358-742-1*, Rising Moon Bks. for Young Readers) Northland Publishing.

Hershenhorn, Esther. There Goes Lowell's Party! 1998. (Illus.). 32p. (J). (ps-k). tchr. ed. 15.95 (*0-8234-1313-6*) Holiday Hse., Inc.

Lipe, Riki. Sooty. Spears-Stewart, Reta, ed. 1998. (Illus.). 34p. (J). (ps-6). 10.00 (*0-9659381-3-1*) Hoot N' Cackle Pr.

MacBride, Roger Lea. Little Farm in the Ozarks. 1994. (Little House). (Illus.). (J). (gr. 3-6). 256p. lib. bdg. 15.89 o.p. (*0-06-024246-9*); 304p. 15.95 o.s.i (*0-06-024245-0*) HarperCollins Children's Bk. Group.

—Rose & Alva. 2000. (Little House Chapter Bks.: No. 3). (Illus.). 80p. (J). (gr. 2-5). pap. 4.25 (*0-06-442095-7*, Harper Trophy) HarperCollins Children's Bk. Group.

—Rose & Alva. 1999. (Little House Chapter Bks.). (J). (gr. 2-5). 10.40 (*0-606-18718-9*) Turtleback Bks.

MacBride, Roger Lea & Ettlinger, Doris, illus. Rose & Alva. 2000. (Little House Chapter Bks.: No. 3). 80p. (J). (gr. 2-5). lib. bdg. 14.89 (*0-06-028158-8*) HarperCollins Children's Bk. Group.

McMurtry, Larry & Ossana, Diana. Zeke & Ned. 1997. 592p. 24.50 o.p. (*0-684-81152-9*, Simon & Schuster) Simon & Schuster.

Morris, Gilbert. The Bucks of Goober Hollow. 1994. (Ozark Adventures Ser.: Vol. 1). 225p. (J). (gr. 3-7). pap. 3.99 o.p. (*0-8423-4392-X*) Tyndale Hse. Pubs.

Phillips, Joy. The Rooster Crowed Early: In the Ozarks. 1997. (Illus.). ix, 66p. (Orig.). (YA). (gr. 6 up). pap. 6.00 (*0-9621669-5-2*) Little Red Hen.

Rawls, Wilson. Where the Red Fern Grows. unabr. ed. 1997. (J). audio 40.00 BBC Audiobooks America.

—Where the Red Fern Grows. 1997. 256p. (YA). (gr. 3-7). mass mkt. 6.50 (*0-553-27429-5*); 1984. 256p. (J). (gr. 5-10). mass mkt. 2.95 o.s.i (*0-553-25585-1*); 1989. (YA). (gr. 4-7). audio 18.00 o.s.i (*0-553-45132-4*) Bantam Bks.

—Where the Red Fern Grows. l.t. ed. 1987. 280p. (YA). (gr. 5 up). reprint ed. lib. bdg. 14.95 o.p. (*1-55736-057-X*) Bantam Doubleday Dell Large Print Group, Inc.

—Where the Red Fern Grows, Set. unabr. ed. 1999. (J). audio 44.95 Blackstone Audio Bks., Inc.

—Where the Red Fern Grows. unabr. ed. 1996. (J). (gr. 4-8). audio 42.00 (*0-7366-3503-3*, 4143) Books on Tape, Inc.

—Where the Red Fern Grows. 1996. (Illus.). 208p. (gr. 4-7). pap. text 5.99 (*0-440-41267-6*) Dell Publishing.

—Where the Red Fern Grows. 25th anniv. ed. 1961. 216p. (J). (gr. 5 up). pap. 11.95 o.s.i (*0-385-05619-2*); 11.95 o.s.i (*0-385-02059-7*) Doubleday Publishing.

—Where the Red Fern Grows, Set. unabr. ed. 1999. (YA). audio 37.98 Highsmith Inc.

—Where the Red Fern Grows. 1999. (Masterpiece Series Access Editions). (Illus.). xvii, 235p. (J). 10.95 (*0-8219-1987-3*, 35337) Paradigm Publishing, Inc.

—Where the Red Fern Grows. 249p. (YA). (gr. 5 up). pap. 5.99 (*0-8072-1358-6*); 249p. (YA). (gr. 5 up). pap. 5.99 (*0-8072-1467-1*); 2000. (YA). (gr. 4-7). audio 9.99 o.s.i (*0-8072-8279-0*); 2001. (YA). (gr. 5-9). audio 26.00 (*0-8072-0468-4*); 1995. (J). (gr. 4-7). audio 32.00 (*0-8072-7512-3*, LL0048); 1995. 249p. (YA). (gr. 5 up). pap. 37.00 incl. audio (*0-8072-7513-1*, YA 868 SP); 1984. (J). (gr. 5 up). audio 15.98 (*0-8072-1804-9*, JRH 102 SP) Random Hse. Audio Publishing Group. (Listening Library).

—Where the Red Fern Grows. 2000. 272p. (gr. 3-7). mass mkt. 2.99 o.s.i (*0-375-80681-4*, Random Hse. Bks. for Young Readers); 1998. 272p. mass mkt. 2.99 o.s.i (*0-440-22814-X*, Yearling); 1996. 208p. (YA). (gr. 4-7). 16.95 (*0-385-32330-1*, Dell Books for Young Readers); 1992. 208p. (YA). (gr. 7 up). 16.95 o.s.i (*0-553-08900-5*, Starfire) Random Hse. Children's Bks.

—Where the Red Fern Grows, unabr. ed. 1995. (J). (gr. 5). audio 51.00 (*0-7887-0185-1*, 94410E7) Recorded Bks., LLC.

—Where the Red Fern Grows. (J). 1996. 12.04 (*0-606-10972-2*); 1974. 12.55 (*0-606-00108-5*) Turtleback Bks.

P

PAKISTAN—FICTION

Davis, Emmett. Clues in the Desert. 1983. (Adventure Diaries). (Illus.). 32p. (J). (gr. 3-6). lib. bdg. 14.65 o.p. (*0-940742-29-2*) Raintree Pubs.

DeLoach, Sylvia & Massey, Barbara. A Is for Aleeya. 1999. (Child Like Me Ser.). (Illus.). 30p. (J). (gr. 1-5). 10.99 (*1-56309-366-9*, New Hope) Woman's Missionary Union.

Ellis, Deborah. Mud City. 2003. 176p. (YA). (gr. 5-9). 15.95 (*0-88899-518-0*) Groundwood Bks. CAN. *Dist:* Publishers Group West.

Khan, Rukhsana. The Roses in My Carpets. 1998. (Illus.). 32p. (J). (ps-3). 15.95 (*0-8234-1399-3*) Holiday Hse., Inc.

—The Roses in My Carpets. (Illus.). 29p. 16.95 (*0-7737-3092-3*) Stoddart Kids CAN. *Dist:* Fitzhenry & Whiteside, Ltd.

—Ruler of the Courtyard. 2003. (Illus.). 32p. (J). 15.99 (*0-670-03583-1*, Viking) Viking Penguin.

Shaw, Denis J. Pakistani Twins. 1965. (Twins Ser.). (Illus.). (J). (gr. 6-9). 12.95 (*0-8023-1094-X*) Dufour Editions, Inc.

Shea, Pegi Deitz. The Carpet Boy's Gift. 2003. (Illus.). 40p. (J). (gr. 3-6). 16.95 (*0-88448-248-0*) Tilbury Hse. Pubs.

Staples, Suzanne Fisher. Haveli. 1993. (YA). o.p. (*0-06-798443-6*) Knopf, Alfred A. Inc.

—Haveli. 1995. 336p. (gr. 7 up). mass mkt. 5.50 (*0-679-86569-1*) Random Hse., Inc.

—Haveli. 1995. (J). 11.04 (*0-606-07634-4*) Turtleback Bks.

—Shabanu: Daughter of the Wind. 3rd ed. (J). pap. text 3.99 (*0-13-800053-0*) Prentice Hall (Schl. Div.).

—Shabanu: Daughter of the Wind. 2003. 288p. pap. 6.50 (*0-440-23856-0*, Dell Books for Young Readers) Random Hse. Children's Bks.

PALESTINE—FICTION

Abdul-Baki, Kathryn K. Fields of Fig & Olive: Ameera & Other Stories of the Middle East. 1991. 217p. (YA). (gr. 10 up). 14.00 o.s.i (*0-89410-725-9*); pap. 14.00 o.p. (*0-89410-726-7*) Rienner, Lynne Pubs., Inc. (Three Continents).

Carmi, Daniella. Samir & Yonatan. Lotan, Yael, tr. from HEB. 2002. 160p. (J). (gr. 3-7). mass mkt. 4.99 (*0-439-13523-0*, Scholastic Paperbacks) Scholastic, Inc.

—Samir & Yonatan. 2000. (Illus.). 183p. (J). (gr. 3-7). pap. 15.95 (*0-439-13504-4*, Levine, Arthur A. Bks.) Scholastic, Inc.

Elmer, Robert. Brother Enemy. 2001. (Promise of Zion Ser.). 176p. (J). (gr. 3-8). pap. 5.99 o.s.i (*0-7642-2298-8*) Bethany Hse. Pubs.

—Freedom Trap. 2002. (Promise of Zion Ser.: Vol. 5). (Illus.). 160p. (J). pap. 5.99 (*0-7642-2313-5*) Bethany Hse. Pubs.

—Peace Rebel. 2000. (Promise of Zion Ser.: Vol. 2). 160p. (J). (gr. 3-7). pap. 5.99 (*0-7642-2297-X*) Bethany Hse. Pubs.

—Promise Breaker. 2000. (Promise of Zion Ser.: Vol. 1). 176p. (J). (gr. 3-7). pap. 5.99 (*0-7642-2296-1*) Bethany Hse. Pubs.

—True Betrayer: A Close Call or a Sinister Coincidence???? 2002. (Promise of Zion Ser.). 160p. (J). (gr. 3-8). pap. 5.99 (*0-7642-2314-3*) Bethany Hse. Pubs.

Matas, Carol. The Garden. 1998. 144p. (gr. 7-12). per. 4.99 (*0-689-80723-6*, Simon Pulse) Simon & Schuster Children's Publishing.

—The Garden. 1998. 11.04 (*0-606-15542-2*) Turtleback Bks.

Ray, Mary. Beyond the Desert Gate. 2001. (Young Adult Bookshelf Ser.). (Illus.). 190p. (YA). (gr. 3-9). 11.95 (*1-883937-54-X*, 54-X) Bethlehem Bks.

—Beyond the Desert Gate. 1977. (Illus.). 160p. (J). o.p. (*0-571-10988-8*) Faber & Faber Ltd.

Roskey, William. Fifth Gospel: The Odyssey of a Time Traveler in First Century Palestine. 1984. 240p. (J). 12.95 (*0-9612112-0-2*) Elghund Enterprises.

Speare, Elizabeth George. The Bronze Bow. 2002. (J). 14.74 (*0-7587-0173-X*) Book Wholesalers, Inc.

—The Bronze Bow, 001. 1997. (Illus.). 256p. (J). (gr. 4-6). pap. 6.95 (*0-395-13719-5*) Houghton Mifflin Co. Trade & Reference Div.

—Bronze Bow, 001. 1961. 256p. (YA). (gr. 6 up). 16.00 o.p. (*0-395-07113-5*) Houghton Mifflin Co.

Stewart, Dana. Friends from Galilee: A Bible-Times Visit with Micah & Hannah. 1994. (Little Deer Bks.). (Illus.). 28p. (J). (ps). 5.49 o.p. (*0-7847-0003-6*, 03869) Standard Publishing.

Travis, Lucille. Tirzah. Garber, S. David, ed. 1991. 160p. (Orig.). (J). (gr. 4-7). pap. 5.99 (*0-8361-3546-6*) Herald Pr.

PANAMA—FICTION

Chambers, Veronica. Marisol & Magdalena: The Sound of Our Sisterhood. 2001. 176p. (J). (gr. 3-7). pap. 5.99 (*0-7868-1304-0*) Hyperion Bks. for Children.

—Marisol & Magdalena: The Sound of Our Sisterhood. 1998. 141p. (gr. 3-7). (J). 14.95 (*0-7868-0437-8*); (YA). lib. bdg. 15.49 (*0-7868-2385-2*) Hyperion Pr.

Griffin, Adele. Rainy Season. 1998. 208p. (J). (gr. 5-9). reprint ed. pap. 5.95 (*0-7868-1241-9*) Disney Pr.

—Rainy Season. 1996. (Illus.). 208p. (J). (gr. 4-7). tchr. ed. 14.95 o.p. (*0-395-81181-3*) Houghton Mifflin Co.

Head, Judith. Culebra Cut. 1995. (Adventures in Time Ser.). 153p. (J). (gr. 5-9). lib. bdg. 21.27 o.p. (*0-87614-878-X*, Carolrhoda Bks.) Lerner Publishing Group.

Markun, Patricia Maloney. The Little Painter of Sabana Grande. 1993. (Illus.). 32p. (J). (ps-2). text 14.95 (*0-02-762205-3*, Simon & Schuster Children's Publishing) Simon & Schuster Children's Publishing.

Monjo, Ferdinand N. Pirates in Panama. 1970. (Illus.). (J). (gr. 3 up). 4.50 o.p. (*0-671-65119-6*, Simon & Schuster Children's Publishing) Simon & Schuster Children's Publishing.

Palacios, Argentina. A Christmas Surprise for Chabelita. 1993. 10.10 (*0-606-06278-5*) Turtleback Bks.

PAPUA NEW GUINEA—FICTION

Herndon, Ernest. Deathbird of Paradise. 1997. (Eric Sterling, Secret Agent Ser.: Bk. 7). 128p. (J). (gr. 3-7). pap. 5.99 (*0-310-20732-0*) Zondervan.

Repp, Gloria. A Question of Yams. 1992. 67p. (J). (gr. 1-2). pap. 6.49 (*0-89084-614-6*, 057885) Jones, Bob Univ. Pr.

PARIS (FRANCE)—FICTION

Arnold, Marsha D. & Davis, Jack E. Metro Cat. 2001. (Storybook Ser.). (Illus.). 40p. (J). (ps-3). 9.95 o.s.i (*0-307-10213-0*, Golden Bks.) Random Hse. Children's Bks.

Aurum Press & Van der Meer, Frank. The Phantom of the Opera Pop-Up Book. 1989. 19.95 o.p. (*0-06-016012-8*) HarperTrade.

Bagwell, Stella. Madeline's Song. 1987. (Harlequin Romance Ser.). pap. (*0-373-08543-5*, Silhouette) Harlequin Enterprises, Ltd.

Baker, Leslie A. Paris Cat. 1999. (Illus.). 32p. (J). (ps-3). 15.95 o.p. (*0-316-07309-1*) Little Brown & Co.

—Paris Cat. 1999. E-Book (*1-58824-662-0*); E-Book (*1-58824-663-9*); E-Book (*1-58824-888-7*) ipicturebooks, LLC.

Bemelmans, Ludwig. Mad about Madeline: The Complete Tales. 1993. (Madeline Ser.). (Illus.). 32p. (J). (ps-3). 35.00 o.s.i (*0-670-85187-6*, Viking Children's Bks.) Penguin Putnam Bks. for Young Readers.

—Madeline. 1995. (Madeline Ser.). (J). (ps-3). reprint ed. lib. bdg. 25.95 (*1-56849-657-5*) Buccaneer Bks., Inc.

—Madeline, 2 bks. Grosman, Ernesto Livon, tr. from ENG. unabr. ed. 1999. (Madeline Ser.). (SPA., Illus.). (J). (ps-3). pap. 29.95 incl. audio (*0-87499-570-1*) Live Oak Media.

—Madeline. unabr. ed. 1997. (Madeline Ser.). (SPA., Illus.). (J). (ps-3). 24.95 incl. audio (*0-87499-409-8*); pap. 15.95 incl. audio (*0-87499-408-X*, LK7307) Live Oak Media.

—Madeline. 2000. (Madeline Ser.). (Illus.). 48p. (J). (ps-3). pap. 6.99 (*0-14-056439-X*, Puffin Bks.) Penguin Putnam Bks. for Young Readers.

—Madeline. Grosman, Ernesto L., tr. 1996. (Madeline Ser.). (SPA., Illus.). 48p. (J). (ps-3). pap. 6.99 (*0-14-055761-X*, VK1051) Penguin Putnam Bks. for Young Readers.

—Madeline. 1993. (Madeline Ser.). (Illus.). 1p. (J). (ps-3). 9.99 (*0-14-095121-0*) Penguin Putnam Bks. for Young Readers.

—Madeline. Grosman, Ernesto L., tr. 1993. (Madeline Ser.). (SPA., Illus.). 64p. (J). (ps-3). 16.99 (*0-670-85154-X*, PG54X, Viking Children's Bks.) Penguin Putnam Bks. for Young Readers.

—Madeline. (Madeline Ser.). (Illus.). (J). (ps-3). 1993. 32p. pap. 19.99 o.s.i (*0-14-054845-9*, Puffin Bks.); 1977. 48p. pap. 5.99 o.s.i (*0-14-050198-3*, Puffin Bks.); 1958. 48p. 16.99 (*0-670-44580-0*, Viking Children's Bks.) Penguin Putnam Bks. for Young Readers.

—Madeline. (Madeline Ser.). (J). (ps-3). 1996. 12.14 (*0-606-08812-1*); 1977. 10.19 o.p. (*0-606-03874-4*) Turtleback Bks.

—Madeline: A Pop-Up Book. 1987. (Madeline Ser.). (Illus.). 12p. (J). (ps-3). 17.99 (*0-670-81667-1*, Viking Children's Bks.) Penguin Putnam Bks. for Young Readers.

—Madeline: A Pop-Up Carousel. 1994. (Madeline Ser.). (Illus.). 5p. (J). (ps-3). 10.99 o.s.i (*0-670-85602-9*) Penguin Putnam Bks. for Young Readers.

—Madeline & the Bad Hat. 2002. (Madeline Ser.). (Illus.). (J). 14.04 (*0-7587-4084-0*) Book Wholesalers, Inc.

—Madeline & the Bad Hat. (Madeline Ser.). (Illus.). 64p. (J). (ps-3). 2000. pap. 6.99 (*0-14-056648-1*); 1977. pap. 5.99 o.s.i (*0-14-050206-8*) Penguin Putnam Bks. for Young Readers. (Puffin Bks.).

—Madeline & the Gypsies. (Madeline Ser.). (Illus.). (J). (ps-3). 2000. 64p. pap. 6.99 (*0-14-056647-3*, Puffin Bks.); 1977. 64p. pap. 5.99 o.s.i (*0-14-050261-0*, Puffin Bks.); 1959. 56p. 16.99 (*0-670-44682-3*, Viking Children's Bks.) Penguin Putnam Bks. for Young Readers.

—Madeline & the Gypsies. (Madeline Ser.). (J). (ps-3). 2000. (Illus.). 13.14 (*0-606-18428-7*); 1959. 10.19 o.p. (*0-606-01010-6*) Turtleback Bks.

—Madeline Book & Toy Box. 1991. (Madeline Ser.). 64p. (J). (ps-3). 24.99 (*0-14-034880-8*, Puffin Bks.) Penguin Putnam Bks. for Young Readers.

—Madeline, Grades Preschool-3. 1997. (Madeline Ser.). (SPA., Illus.). pap., tchr. ed. 31.95 incl. audio (*0-87499-410-1*) Live Oak Media.

—Madeline in America & Other Holiday Tales. 2002. (Madeline Ser.). (Illus.). (J). 18.68 (*0-7587-4186-3*) Book Wholesalers, Inc.

—Madeline in America & Other Holiday Tales. 1999. (Madeline Ser.). (J). (ps-3). (Illus.). 111p. pap. 19.95 o.s.i (*0-590-03910-5*, Levine, Arthur A. Bks.); pap. 125.00 (*0-439-09633-2*) Scholastic, Inc.

—Madeline Playtime Activity Book. 1997. (Madeline Ser.). (Illus.). 16p. (J). (ps-3). pap. 7.99 (*0-670-87464-7*) Penguin Putnam Bks. for Young Readers.

—Madeline Storybook Collection Snap & Fold Away. 1994. (J). 14.98 (*0-670-77188-0*) Penguin Putnam Bks. for Young Readers.

—Madeline's Christmas. (Madeline Ser.). 32p. (J). (ps-3). 1993. (Illus.). pap. 9.99 incl. audio (*0-14-095108-3*, Puffin Bks.); 1988. pap. 5.99 o.s.i (*0-14-050666-7*, Puffin Bks.); 1985. (Illus.). 15.99 (*0-670-80666-8*, Viking Children's Bks.) Penguin Putnam Bks. for Young Readers.

—Madeline's Christmas. 1984. (Madeline Ser.). (J). (ps-3). 12.14 (*0-606-03983-X*) Turtleback Bks.

—Madeline's House: Madeline; Madeline's Rescue; Madeline & the Bad Hat. 1989. (Madeline Ser.). (Illus.). (J). (ps-3). pap. 12.99 (*0-14-095028-1*) Penguin Putnam Bks. for Young Readers.

—Madeline's Rescue. (Madeline Ser.). (J). (ps-3). 2000. (Illus.). 64p. pap. 6.99 (*0-14-056651-1*, Puffin Bks.); 1993. (Illus.). 9.99 (*0-14-095122-9*, Puffin Bks.); 1989. 6.95 o.p. (*0-14-095034-6*, Puffin Bks.); 1977. (Illus.). 64p. pap. 5.99 o.s.i (*0-14-050207-6*, Puffin Bks.); 1953. (Illus.). 56p. 16.99 (*0-670-44716-1*, Viking Children's Bks.) Penguin Putnam Bks. for Young Readers.

—Madeline's Rescue. 1977. (Madeline Ser.). (J). (ps-3). 10.19 o.p. (*0-606-03876-0*) Turtleback Bks.

—Madeline's Velcro. 1997. (Madeline Ser.). (J). (ps-3). pap. 14.98 (*0-670-78126-6*) NAL.

Bemelmans, Ludwig & Outlet Book Company Staff. Madeline & the Bad Hat. 1988. (Madeline Ser.). (J). (ps-3). 0.75 o.s.i (*0-517-18388-9*) Random Hse. Value Publishing.

Bennett, Cherie. Anne Frank & Me. 2002. 352p. (J). pap. 6.99 (*0-698-11973-8*, PaperStar) Penguin Putnam Bks. for Young Readers.

Bennett, Cherie & Gottesfeld, Jeff. Anne Frank & Me. 2001. 291p. (J). (gr. 7 up). 18.99 (*0-399-23329-6*, G. P. Putnam's Sons) Penguin Group (USA) Inc.

Bishop, Claire Huchet. Georgette. 1974. (Break-of-Day Bks.). (Illus.). 64p. (J). (gr. k-3). 4.69 o.p. (*0-698-30512-4*) Putnam Publishing Group, The.

Carlson, Natalie S. Family under the Bridge. 1958. (Illus.). 112p. (J). (gr. k-3). lib. bdg. 16.89 (*0-06-020991-7*) HarperCollins Children's Bk. Group.

—Family under the Bridge. 1989. (J). 12.00 (*0-606-04031-5*) Turtleback Bks.

Cawley, Rhya N. Pongee Goes to Paris. 1996. (Illus.). 70p. (Orig.). (J). pap. 4.95 (*1-57502-282-6*, PO985) Morris Publishing.

Cazet, Denys. Minnie & Moo Go to Paris. 2002. (Minnie & Moo Ser.). (Illus.). (J). 11.45 (*0-7587-1442-4*) Book Wholesalers, Inc.

—Minnie & Moo Go to Paris. 1999. (Minnie & Moo Ser.: Vol. 4). (Illus.). 48p. (J). (gr. 1-3). pap. 3.99 (*0-7894-3928-X*);Vol. 4. pap. 12.99 (*0-7894-2595-5*) Dorling Kindersley Publishing, Inc. (D K Ink).

—Minnie & Moo Go to Paris. 2001. (J). (gr. 1-3). 24.95 incl. audio (*0-87499-767-4*) Live Oak Media.

Clements, Bruce. A Chapel of Thieves, RS. 2002. 224p. (J). (gr. 6-9). 16.00 (*0-374-37701-4*, Farrar, Straus & Giroux (BYR)) Farrar, Straus & Giroux.

Cunningham, Julia. Flight of the Sparrow. 1980. 144p. (J). (gr. 5-9). 6.95 o.p. (*0-394-84501-3*, Pantheon) Knopf Publishing Group.

—Flight of the Sparrow. 1982. 128p. (YA). (gr. 7 up). pap. 1.95 o.p. (*0-380-57653-8*, 57653-8, Avon Bks.) Morrow/Avon.

—The Silent Voice. 1981. 176p. (J). (gr. 5-9). 11.95 o.p. (*0-525-39295-5*, Dutton) Dutton/Plume.

—The Silent Voice. 1983. (J). pap. 2.50 o.s.i (*0-440-48404-9*, Dell Books for Young Readers) Random Hse. Children's Bks.

Devlin, Wende & Devlin, Harry. The Trouble with Henriette. 1995. (J). 15.00 o.s.i (*0-02-729937-6*, Simon & Schuster Children's Publishing) Simon & Schuster Children's Publishing.

Dickens, Charles. A Tale of Two Cities. Vogel, Malvina, ed. 1993. (Great Illustrated Classics Ser.: Vol. 26). (Illus.). 240p. (J). (gr. 3-6). 9.95 (*0-86611-977-9*) Playmore, Inc., Pubs.

Disney Staff. The Aristocats Join Scat Cat's Band. 1988. (J). bds. 5.98 o.p. (*0-8317-0396-2*) Smithmark Pubs., Inc.

Donovan, Donna. Countdown on the Metro. 1988. (BePuzzled Junior Ser.). (Illus.). 14p. (J). (gr. 3-7). 9.95 o.p. (*0-922242-07-0*) Bepuzzled.

Dragonwagon, Crescent. Winter Holding Spring. 1990. (Illus.). 32p. (J). (gr. 4-7). 15.00 (*0-02-733122-9*, Atheneum) Simon & Schuster Children's Publishing.

Dunrea, Olivier. The Tale of Hilda Louise, RS. 1996. 32p. (J). (ps-3). 16.00 o.p. (*0-374-37380-9*, Farrar, Straus & Giroux (BYR)) Farrar, Straus & Giroux.

Eisenstein, Marilyn. Periwinkle Isn't Paris. 2001. (Illus.). 24p. (J). pap. 7.95 (*0-88776-571-8*) Tundra Bks. of Northern New York.

Fagan, Cary. Daughter of the Great Zandini. 2001. (Illus.). 64p. (J). (gr. 3-7). 16.95 (*0-88776-534-3*) Tundra Bks. of Northern New York.

Fender, Kay. Odette: A Springtime in Paris. 1991. (Illus.). 32p. (J). (ps-3). 10.95 o.p. (*0-916291-33-2*) Kane/Miller Bk. Pubs.

Fine, illus. French Kitty Goes to Paris. 2003. 48p. 12.95 (*0-8109-4447-2*) Abrams, Harry N. , Inc.

Fleming, Candace. Madame LaGrande & Her So High, to the Sky, Uproarious Pompadour. 1996. (Illus.). 40p. (J). 16.99 o.s.i (*0-679-95835-5*, Knopf Bks. for Young Readers) Random Hse. Children's Bks.

Forever Free. 1996. 10p. (J). 7.98 o.p. (*1-57082-322-7*) Mouse Works.

Friedman, Michael Jan. Hunchdog of Notre Dame. l.t. ed. 1999. (Adventures of Wishbone Ser.: No. 5). (Illus.). 139p. (J). (gr. 4 up). lib. bdg. 22.60 (*0-8368-2301-X*) Stevens, Gareth Inc.

Goode, Diane. Mama's Perfect Present. 1999. (Illus.). 32p. (J). (ps-3). pap. 5.99 o.s.i (*0-14-056549-3*, Puffin Bks.) Penguin Putnam Bks. for Young Readers.

—Where's Our Mama? 1991. (Illus.). 32p. (J). (ps-2). 13.95 o.s.i (*0-525-44770-9*, Dutton Children's Bks.) Penguin Putnam Bks. for Young Readers.

Greene, Bette. Morning Is a Long Time Coming. 1993. 272p. (YA). (gr. 7-12). mass mkt. 4.99 o.s.i (*0-440-21893-4*) Dell Publishing.

—Morning Is a Long Time Coming. 1978. (J). (gr. 9 up). 10.95 o.p. (*0-8037-5496-5*, Dial Bks. for Young Readers) Penguin Putnam Bks. for Young Readers.

—Morning Is a Long Time Coming. 1988. (YA). mass mkt. 2.95 o.s.i (*0-553-27354-X*, Starfire) Random Hse. Children's Bks.

—Morning Is a Long Time Coming. (gr. 7-9). 1983. (Illus.). pap. (*0-671-47618-1*); 1980. (J). pap. (*0-671-42456-4*) Simon & Schuster Children's Publishing. (Simon Pulse).

—Morning Is a Long Time Coming. 1978. 9.60 o.p. (*0-606-05928-8*) Turtleback Bks.

Grimes, Nikki. On the Road to Paris. 2003. (Illus.). 224p. (J). 16.99 (*0-8037-2817-4*, Dial Bks. for Young Readers) Penguin Putnam Bks. for Young Readers.

Hatton, Caroline K. Vero & Philippe. 2001. (Illus.). 120p. (J). (gr. 3-7). 14.95 (*0-8126-2940-X*) Cricket Bks.

Hawthorne, Rachel. Paris: Alex & Dana. 2000. (Love Stories Ser.). 192p. (YA). (gr. 7-12). mass mkt. 4.50 o.s.i (*0-553-49327-2*) Random Hse. Children's Bks.

Hoestlandt, Jo. Star of Fear, Star of Hope. Polizzotti, Mark, tr. from FRE. Tr. of Grande Peur sous les Etoiles. (Illus.). 32p. (J). (gr. 2-5). 1995. lib. bdg. 16.85 (*0-8027-8374-0*); 2000. reprint ed. 16.95 (*0-8027-8373-2*); 2000. reprint ed. pap. 8.95 (*0-8027-7588-8*) Walker & Co.

Hugo, Victor. The Hunchback of Notre Dame: With a Discussion of Compassion. Butterfield, Ned, tr. & illus. by. 2003. (Values in Action Illustrated Classics Ser.). (J). (*1-59203-049-1*) Learning Challenge, Inc.

The Hunchback of Notre Dame. (Read-Along Ser.). (J). 7.99 incl. audio (*1-55723-992-4*) Walt Disney Records.

Hutchins, Pat. The Mona Lisa Mystery. l.t. ed. 1997. (Illus.). (J). 16.95 (*0-7451-8926-1*, Galaxy Children's Large Print) BBC Audiobooks America.

Ichikawa, Satomi. La-La Rose. 2004. 40p. (J). 15.99 (*0-399-24029-2*, Philomel) Penguin Putnam Bks. for Young Readers.

Ingman, Bruce. A Night on the Tiles. 1999. (Illus.). 32p. (J). (ps-3). 15.00 o.s.i (*0-395-93655-1*) Houghton Mifflin Co.

Kirby, David & Woodman, Allen. The Cows Are Going to Paris. 2003. (Illus.). 32p. (J). (gr. k-3). pap. 8.95 (*1-56397-781-8*) Boyds Mills Pr.

Knight, Joan. Bon Appetit, Bertie! 1993. (Illus.). 32p. (J). (ps-1). pap. 13.95 o.p. (*1-56458-195-0*) Dorling Kindersley Publishing, Inc.

Kudlinski, Kathleen V. Marie: An Invitation to Dance. 1996. (Girlhood Journeys Ser.: No. 3). 72p. (J). pap. 5.99 (*0-689-80985-9*, Aladdin) Simon & Schuster Children's Publishing.

Kusan, Ivan. The Mystery of the Stolen Painting. Willen, Drenka, tr. 1975. (Illus.). 256p. (J). (gr. 5 up). 7.95 o.p. (*0-15-243353-8*, 15-243353) Harcourt Children's Bks.

Lamorisse, Albert. The Red Balloon. 1990. (Short Story Library). (Illus.). 32p. (YA). (gr. 5 up). lib. bdg. 13.95 o.p. (*0-88682-304-8*, Creative Education) Creative Co., The.

—The Red Balloon. 1957. (J). (ps-3). 9.95 o.p. (*0-385-08289-4*) Doubleday Publishing.

—The Red Balloon. 1978. 19.10 (*0-606-12496-9*) Turtleback Bks.

Leblanc, Louise. Maddie Goes to Paris. 1994. (First Novels Ser.). (Illus.). 64p. (J). (gr. 1-4). pap. 3.99 (*0-88780-278-8*) Formac Publishing Co., Ltd. CAN. *Dist:* Formac Distributing, Ltd., Orca Bk. Pubs.

Leblanc, Louise. Maddie Goes to Paris. 1995. (First Novels Ser.). (Illus.). 64p. (J). (gr. 1-4). (*0-88780-279-6*) Formac Publishing Co., Ltd.

Leroux, Gaston. The Phantom of the Opera. l.t. ed. 1999. (Large Print Heritage Ser.). 420p. (J). (gr. 7-12). lib. bdg. 35.95 (*1-58118-043-8*, 22512) LRS.

—The Phantom of the Opera. 1994. (Classics for Young Readers Ser.). (Illus.). 336p. (YA). (gr. 4-7). pap. 4.99 (*0-14-036813-2*, Puffin Bks.) Penguin Putnam Bks. for Young Readers.

—The Phantom of the Opera. 1989. (Bullseye Chillers Ser.). (Illus.). 96p. (J). (gr. 3-7). 5.99 o.s.i (*0-394-93847-X*); (gr. 2-5). pap. 3.99 (*0-394-83847-5*) Random Hse. Children's Bks. (Random Hse. Bks. for Young Readers).

—The Phantom of the Opera. Bair, Lowell, tr. abr. ed. 1998. 336p. (YA). (gr. 7-12). mass mkt. 3.99 (*0-440-22774-7*, Dell Books for Young Readers) Random Hse. Children's Bks.

—The Phantom of the Opera. abr. ed. 1998. 10.04 (*0-606-15677-1*) Turtleback Bks.

—The Phantom of the Opera. 1988. (Illus.). (J). (gr. 4 up). 14.95 o.p. (*0-88101-082-0*); 208p. (YA). (gr. 7 up). 9.95 o.p. (*0-88101-121-5*) Unicorn Publishing Hse., Inc., The.

McClintock, Barbara. The Fantastic Drawings of Danielle. (Illus.). 32p. (J). (ps-3). 2004. pap. 5.95 (*0-618-43230-2*); 1996. tchr. ed. 17.00 o.p. (*0-395-73980-2*) Houghton Mifflin Co.

McLaren, Chesley, illus. Zat Cat! A Haute Couture Tail. 2002. 40p. (J). (ps-3). pap. 16.95 (*0-439-27316-1*, Scholastic Pr.) Scholastic, Inc.

Morgenstern, Susie. Secret Letters from 0 to 10. 2000. (Illus.). 144p. (J). (gr. 3-7). pap. 4.99 (*0-14-130819-2*, Puffin Bks.) Penguin Putnam Bks. for Young Readers.

—Secret Letters from 0 to 10. Rosner, Gill, tr. 1998. 208p. (J). (gr. 4-7). 16.99 (*0-670-88007-8*, Viking) Penguin Putnam Bks. for Young Readers.

—Secret Letters from 0 to 10. 2000. 11.04 (*0-606-18846-0*) Turtleback Bks.

Mouse Works Staff. The Hunchback of Notre Dame. 1996. (Classic Storybook Ser.). 96p. (J). (ps-4). 7.98 o.p. (*1-57082-173-9*) Mouse Works.

—El Jorodado de Notre Dame. 1996. 96p. (J). 7.98 o.p. (*1-57082-267-0*) Mouse Works.

Nascimbene, Yan. Day in September. 2002. (J). (*0-89812-328-3*, Creative Paperbacks) Creative Co., The.

Neumeyer, Peter. The Phantom of the Opera. abr. ed. 1988. (Illus.). 48p. (J). 14.95 o.p. (*0-87905-330-5*) Smith, Gibbs Pub.

Pascal, Francine, creator. The Twins Take Paris. 1996. (Sweet Valley Twins Super Edition Ser.: No. 6). 192p. (gr. 3-7). pap. text 3.99 o.s.i (*0-553-48390-0*) Bantam Bks.

Paterson, Aileen. Maisie Loves Paris. 2001. (Illus.). 32p. (J). pap. (*1-871512-05-0*) Glowworm Bks., Ltd.

Patterson, Paul. Anastasia: A Princess in Paris. 1997. (Disney Ser.). 14p. (J). (ps-3). o.p. (*0-307-75702-1*, Golden Bks.) Random Hse. Children's Bks.

Peterson, Melissa & Golden Books Staff. Together in Paris. 1997. (Golden Book Ser.). 32p. (J). pap. 2.99 o.s.i (*0-307-20013-2*, Golden Bks.) Random Hse. Children's Bks.

Poulet, Virginia. Blue Bug Goes to Paris. 1986. (Blue Bug Bks.). (Illus.). 32p. (J). (ps-3). pap. 3.95 o.p. (*0-516-43480-2*); mass mkt. 15.00 o.p. (*0-516-03480-4*) Scholastic Library Publishing. (Children's Pr.).

Rabley, Stephen. Marcel & the Mona Lisa. Date not set. pap. text 73.13 (*0-582-06075-3*) Addison-Wesley Longman, Ltd. GBR. *Dist:* Trans-Atlantic Pubns., Inc.

—Marcel & the Mona Lisa. 2002. (Illus.). 16p. pap. (*0-582-40173-9*) Penguin Putnam Bks. for Young Readers.

Reisfeld, Randi. An American Betty in Paris. 1996. (Clueless Ser.). 160p. (YA). (gr. 6 up). pap. 4.99 (*0-671-56869-8*, Simon Pulse) Simon & Schuster Children's Publishing.

Ringgold, Faith. Bonjour, Lonnie. 1996. (Illus.). 32p. (J). (gr. k-4). 15.95 (*0-7868-0076-3*); (gr. 4-7). lib. bdg. 16.49 (*0-7868-2062-4*) Hyperion Bks. for Children.

Robertson, Bruce. Marguerite Makes a Book. 1999. (Getty Trust Publications). (Illus.). 44p. (J). (gr. 3 up). 18.95 (*0-89236-372-X*) Getty Pubns.

Rue, Nancy N. Lily's Passport to Paris. 2003. 160p. pap. 4.99 (*0-310-70555-X*) Zondervan.

Schotter, Roni. That Extraordinary Pig of Paris. 1994. (Illus.). 32p. (J). (ps-3). 14.95 o.p. (*0-399-22023-2*, Philomel) Penguin Putnam Bks. for Young Readers.

—That Extraordinary Pig of Paris. 1994. E-Book (*1-58824-279-X*) ipicturebooks, LLC.

Schwartz, Stephen, et al. Out There. 1996. (Illus.). 48p. (J). (ps-3). 9.95 (*0-7868-6224-6*) Hyperion Pr.

Skolnick, Evan. Veiled Beauty. 1997. (Hunchback of Notre Dame Ser.). (J). pap. text 4.50 (*1-57840-156-9*) Acclaim Bks.

Spirn, Michele Sobel. The Bridges in Paris. 2000. (Going to Ser.). (Illus.). 121p. (J). (gr. 4-8). pap. 5.99 (*1-893577-04-X*) Four Corners Publishing Co., Inc.

Stock, Catherine. A Spree in Paree. 2003. (J). (*0-8234-1720-4*) Holiday Hse., Inc.

Suzanne, Jamie. The Twins Take Paris. 1996. (Sweet Valley Twins Super Edition Ser.: No. 6). (J). (gr. 3-7). 9.09 o.p. (*0-606-09938-7*) Turtleback Bks.

Thompson, Kay. Eloise a Paris. 5th ed. 1999. Orig. Title: Eloise in Paris. (FRE., Illus.). (J). (ps-3). pap. 13.95 (*2-07-052625-9*) Gallimard, Editions FRA. *Dist:* Distribooks, Inc.

—Eloise en Paris. 2002. (SPA.). 64p. 18.95 (*1-4000-0174-9*) Random Hse., Inc.

—Eloise in Paris. 1991. (Eloise Ser.). (Illus.). 66p. (J). reprint ed. lib. bdg. 35.95 (*0-89966-834-8*) Buccaneer Bks., Inc.

—Eloise in Paris. 1999. (Illus.). 72p. (J). (ps-3). 17.00 (*0-689-82704-0*, Simon & Schuster Children's Publishing) Simon & Schuster Children's Publishing.

Thorpe, Kiki. Rugrats in Paris Movie Storybook. 2000. (Rugrats Ser.). (Illus.). 32p. (J). (ps-2). 5.99 (*0-689-84198-1*, Simon Spotlight/Nickelodeon) Simon & Schuster Children's Publishing.

Titus, Eve. Anatole over Paris. 1991. (Illus.). 32p. (J). (ps-8). pap. 4.99 o.s.i (*0-553-35240-7*) Bantam Bks.

—Anatole over Paris. 1991. (J). mass mkt. o.p. (*0-553-53067-4*, Dell Books for Young Readers) Random Hse. Children's Bks.

Weinberg, Larry. Universal Monsters: The Phantom of the Opera. 1993. (J). (gr. 4-7). pap. o.p. (*0-307-22334-5*, Golden Bks.) Random Hse. Children's Bks.

Wheeler, Jody. Madeline Christmas Activity Book: With Reusable Vinyl Stickers. 1998. (Madeline Ser.). (Illus.). 16p. (J). (ps-3). 7.99 (*0-670-88204-6*, Viking Children's Bks.) Penguin Putnam Bks. for Young Readers.

—Madeline Paper Dolls. 1994. (Madeline Ser.). (Illus.). 24p. (J). (ps-3). 6.99 (*0-670-85601-0*) Penguin Putnam Bks. for Young Readers.

—Madeline's Birthday Activity Book. 1999. (Madeline Ser.). (Illus.). 16p. (J). (ps-3). pap. 7.99 (*0-670-88767-6*, Viking Children's Bks.) Penguin Putnam Bks. for Young Readers.

Wolf, Conor & Publications International Staff. Disney's The Hunchback of Notre Dame. 1996. (YA). (*0-7853-1641-8*) Publications International, Ltd.

Young, Amy. Belinda in Paris. 2004. 32p. 15.99 (*0-670-03693-5*, Viking) Viking Penguin.

Zolotow, Charlotte. The Moon Was the Best. 1993. (Illus.). 32p. (J). (ps up). lib. bdg. 14.93 o.p. (*0-688-09941-6*, Greenwillow Bks.) HarperCollins Children's Bk. Group.

PENNSYLVANIA—FICTION

Ammon, Richard & Patrick, Pamela, illus. Amish Horses. 2001. 40p. (J). (gr. k-3). 17.00 (*0-689-82623-0*, Atheneum) Simon & Schuster Children's Publishing.

Anderson, Laurie Halse. Fear of Falling. 2001. (American Girl Wild at Heart Ser.: Bk. 9). (Illus.). 144p. (J). pap. 4.95 (*1-58485-059-0*, American Girl) Pleasant Co. Pubns.

—Fever, 1793. 256p. (J). 2000. (gr. 5-9). 16.00 (*0-689-83858-1*, Simon & Schuster Children's Publishing); 2002. (Illus.). reprint ed. pap. 5.99 (*0-689-84891-9*, Aladdin) Simon & Schuster Children's Publishing.

—Fever, 1793. l.t. ed. 2001. 22.95 (*0-7862-3408-3*) Thorndike Pr.

—Time to Fly. 2002. (American Girl Wild at Heart Ser.: Bk. 10). 128p. (J). pap. 4.95 (*1-58485-061-2*, American Girl) Pleasant Co. Pubns.

—Time to Fly. 2003. (Wild at Heart Ser.). (Illus.). 113p. (J). (gr. 4 up). lib. bdg. 22.60 (*0-8368-3262-0*) Stevens, Gareth Inc.

Avi. Encounter at Easton. 1980. (J). (gr. 5-8). 6.95 o.p. (*0-394-84342-8*); lib. bdg. 6.99 o.p. (*0-394-94342-2*) Knopf Publishing Group. (Pantheon).

—Encounter at Easton. 1994. 144p. (gr. 5 up). (YA). 15.00 o.p. (*0-688-05295-9*); (J). reprint ed. pap. 4.95 o.p. (*0-688-05296-7*) Morrow/Avon. (Morrow, William & Co.).

—Encounter at Easton. 2000. (Illus.). (J). 11.04 (*0-606-17969-0*); 1994. 10.05 o.p. (*0-606-06362-5*) Turtleback Bks.

—Night Journeys. 160p. (J). 2000. (Illus.). (gr. 3-7). pap. 5.99 (*0-380-73242-4*, Harper Trophy); 1994. (gr. 5 up). reprint ed. pap. 4.95 (*0-688-13628-1*) HarperCollins Children's Bk. Group.

—Night Journeys. 1994. 160p. (YA). (gr. 5 up). reprint ed. 15.00 o.p. (*0-688-05298-3*, Morrow, William & Co.) Morrow/Avon.

PERU—FICTION

PHILADELPHIA (PA.)—FICTION

PHILADELPHIA (PA.)—HISTORY—FICTION

Gutman, Dan. Qwerty Stevens, Stuck in Time with Benjamin Franklin. 2002. (Illus.). 192p. (J). (gr. 5-8). 16.95 (0-689-84553-7, Simon & Schuster Children's Publishing) Simon & Schuster Children's Publishing.

Thomas Jefferson: Letters from a Philadelphia Bookworm. 2002. (Dear Mr. President Series). (J). (gr. 4-7). 25.95 incl. audio (0-87499-989-8) Live Oak Media.

PHILIPPINES—FICTION

Arcellana, Francisco. The Mats. 1999. (Illus.). 24p. (J). (ps-3). 13.95 (0-916291-86-3) Kane/Miller Bk. Pubs.

Brown, Fletch. Street Boy: When a Street Boy Steals a Wallet in Manila, Money Is Not All That He Finds. . . 3rd ed. 2001. reprint ed. pap. text 5.99 (1-884543-64-2) Gabriel Publishing.

Fuentes, Vilma M. Pearl Makers: Six Stories about Children in the Philippines. 1989. (Illus.). 60p. (Orig.). (J). (gr. 1-6). pap. 4.95 (0-377-00191-0) Friendship Pr.

Hertenstein, Jane. Beyond Paradise. 1999. (Illus.). 168p. (YA). (gr. 7 up). 16.00 (0-688-16381-5, Morrow, William & Co.) Morrow/Avon.

Richardson, Arleta. Andrew's Secret. Payne, Peggy & Yoder, Tamra, eds. 1989. (Illus.). 30p. (Orig.). (J). (gr. 1-3). pap. 3.00 o.p. (0-89367-143-6) Light & Life Communications.

Robles, Al. Looking for Ifugao Mountain: Bilingual, Pilipino & English. 1977. (Fifth World Tales Ser.). (Illus.). 24p. (J). (gr. k-6). pap. 5.95 o.p. (0-89239-012-3) Children's Bk. Pr.

POLAND—FICTION

Boraks-Nemetz, Lillian. The Old Brown Suitcase: A Teenager's Story of War & Peace. 1994. 210p. (Orig.). (YA). (gr. 8-12). pap. 9.50 (0-914539-10-8) Ben-Simon Pubns.

Carey, Valerie S. Tsugele's Broom. 1993. (Laura Geringer Bks.). (Illus.). 48p. (J). (gr. k-3). 15.00 o.p. (0-06-020986-0); lib. bdg. 14.89 (0-06-020987-9) HarperCollins Children's Bk. Group.

Drucker, Malka. Jacob's Rescue: A Holocaust Story. 1993. 128p. (J). 15.95 o.s.i (0-385-32519-3, Dell Books for Young Readers) Random Hse. Children's Bks.

—Jacob's Rescue: A Holocaust Story. 1993. 10.55 (0-606-06504-0) Turtleback Bks.

Drucker, Malka & Halperin. Jacob's Rescue: A Holocaust Story. 1994. (J). pap. o.p. (0-440-90106-5) Dell Publishing.

Drucker, Malka & Halperin, Michael. Jacob's Rescue: A Holocaust Story. 1993. 128p. (J). (gr. 4-7). 15.95 o.s.i (0-553-08976-5, Skylark) Random Hse. Children's Bks.

Drucker, Malka, et al. Jacob's Rescue: A Holocaust Story. 1994. 128p. (gr. 2-6). pap. text 4.99 (0-440-40965-9) Dell Publishing.

Hautzig, Esther Rudomin. A Picture of Grandmother, RS. 2002. (Illus.). 80p. (J). (gr. 2-5). 15.00 (0-374-35920-2, Farrar, Straus & Giroux (BYR)) Farrar, Straus & Giroux.

Ish-Kishor, Sulamith. Boy of Old Prague. 1963. (Illus.). (J). (gr. 4-9). lib. bdg. 5.99 o.p. (0-394-90978-X, Pantheon) Knopf Publishing Group.

Kelly, Eric P. The Trumpeter of Krakow. 224p. 1992. (Illus.). (YA). (gr. 7 up). reprint ed. mass mkt. 4.99 (0-689-71571-4, Simon Pulse); 1968. (Illus.). (YA). (gr. 7 up). reprint ed. 17.95 (0-02-750140-X, Simon & Schuster Children's Publishing); Vol. 1. 1999. (J). (gr. 4-7). mass mkt. 2.99 o.s.i (0-689-82992-2, Aladdin) Simon & Schuster Children's Publishing.

—The Trumpeter of Krakow. 1973. (J). 11.04 (0-606-05074-4) Turtleback Bks.

Kimmel, Eric A. The Jar of Fools: Eight Hanukkah Stories from Chelm. 2000. (Illus.). 56p. (J). (gr. 1-5). tchr. ed. 18.95 (0-8234-1463-9) Holiday Hse., Inc.

Kirk, Heather. Warsaw Spring. 2001. 256p. (YA). (gr. 9 up). pap. 8.95 (0-929141-86-5, Napoleon Publishing) Napoleon Publishing/Rendezvous Pr. CAN. *Dist:* Words Distributing Co.

Laird, Christa. But Can the Phoenix Sing? 1995. 224p. (YA). (gr. 7 up). 16.00 o.s.i (0-688-13612-5, Greenwillow Bks.) HarperCollins Children's Bk. Group.

—Shadow of the Wall. 1990. 144p. (YA). (gr. 7 up). 12.95 o.p. (0-688-09336-1, Greenwillow Bks.) HarperCollins Children's Bk. Group.

—Shadow of the Wall. 1997. 144p. (gr. 6-12). mass mkt. 4.95 (0-688-15291-0, Morrow, William & Co.) Morrow/Avon.

—Shadow of the Wall. 1997. 11.00 (0-606-11832-2) Turtleback Bks.

Nerlove, Miriam. Flowers on the Wall. 1996. (Illus.). 32p. (J). (gr. k-3). 16.00 (0-689-50614-7, McElderry, Margaret K.) Simon & Schuster Children's Publishing.

Orlev, Uri. The Island on Bird Street. Halkin, Hillel, tr. from HEB. 176p. (J). (gr. 4-6). 1992. pap. 6.95 (0-395-61623-9); 1984. tchr. ed. 16.00 (0-395-33887-5, 5-92515) Houghton Mifflin Co.

—The Island on Bird Street. Halkin, Hillel, tr. from HEB. 1984. (J). 12.00 (0-606-00521-8) Turtleback Bks.

—The Man from the Other Side. Halkin, Hillel, tr. from HEB. 1991. 192p. (YA). (gr. 7-7). tchr. ed. 16.00 (0-395-53808-4) Houghton Mifflin Co.

—The Man from the Other Side. Halkin, Hillel, tr. from HEB. 1995. (Illus.). 192p. (J). (gr. 5-9). pap. 5.99 (0-14-037088-9, Puffin Bks.) Penguin Putnam Bks. for Young Readers.

—The Man from the Other Side. Halkin, Hillel, tr. from HEB. 1995. 11.04 (0-606-07834-7) Turtleback Bks.

—Run Boy, Run. Halkin, Hillel, tr. from HEB. 2003. 192p. (YA). (gr. 5 up). tchr. ed. 15.00 (0-618-16465-0, Lorraine, A. Walter) Houghton Mifflin Co. Trade & Reference Div.

Pastore, Clare. Journey to America: Aniela Kaminski's Story, Vol. 2. 2002. 192p. mass mkt. 5.99 (0-425-18816-7) Berkley Publishing Group.

Pellowski, Anne. The Nine Crying Dolls. 1980. (Illus.). 32p. (J). (gr. k-3). 5.95 o.p. (0-399-20752-X); 5.99 o.p. (0-399-61162-2) Putnam Publishing Group, The.

Pressler, Mirjam. Malka. Murdoch, Brian, tr. from GER. 2003. 286p. (YA). (gr. 9-12). 18.99 (0-399-23984-7, Philomel) Penguin Putnam Bks. for Young Readers.

Schur, Maxine R. Sacred Shadows. (J). (gr. 6-9). 1999. 14.99 (0-8037-1800-4); 1997. 224p. 15.99 o.p. (0-8037-2295-8) Penguin Putnam Bks. for Young Readers. (Dial Bks. for Young Readers).

Seidler, Babara. The Legend of King Piast. Kedron, Jane, tr. 1977. (Kosciuszko Young People's Ser.). (Illus.). (J). (gr. 2-8). pap. 2.00 (0-917004-08-6) Kosciuszko Foundation.

Singer, Isaac Bashevis. The Fools of Chelm & Their History, RS. Shub, Elizabeth, tr. from YID. 1973. (Illus.). 64p. (J). (gr. 3 up). 14.00 o.s.i (0-374-32444-1, Farrar, Straus & Giroux (BYR)) Farrar, Straus & Giroux.

Skurzynski, Gloria. Manwolf. 1981. 192p. (J). (gr. 6 up). 10.95 o.p. (0-395-30079-7, Clarion Bks.) Houghton Mifflin Co. Trade & Reference Div.

Treseder, Terry W. Hear O Israel: A Story of the Warsaw Ghetto. 1990. (Illus.). 48p. (J). (gr. 3 up). text 13.95 o.s.i (0-689-31456-6, Atheneum) Simon & Schuster Children's Publishing.

Yolen, Jane. The Devil's Arithmetic. 2002. (J). 13.19 (0-7587-9594-7) Book Wholesalers, Inc.

—The Devil's Arithmetic. 176p. 2004. (Illus.). pap. 5.99 (0-14-240109-9, Puffin Bks.); 1990. (YA). (gr. 5-9). pap. 5.99 (0-14-034535-3, Puffin Bks.); 1988. (YA). 15.99 (0-670-81027-4, Viking Children's Bks.) Penguin Putnam Bks. for Young Readers.

—The Devil's Arithmetic. 1990. (YA). 11.04 (0-606-04653-4) Turtleback Bks.

Zyskind, Sara. Struggle. 1989. 288p. (J). lib. bdg. 22.95 o.p. (0-8225-0772-2, Lerner Pubns.) Lerner Publishing Group.

POLAR REGIONS—FICTION

DeRubertis, Barbara. Wally Walrus. 1998. (Let's Read Together Ser.). (Illus.). 32p. (J). (ps-3). pap. 4.95 (1-57565-046-0) Kane Pr., The.

Henkel, Donald G. A Legend of Santa & His Brother Fred. 2000. (Illus.). 46p. (J). 20.50 (0-9673504-0-9) Quillpen.

Howard, Pam & Crowell, Knox. A Flight to Polar Bay. l.t. ed. 2002. (Illus.). 8p. (J). (ps-1). pap. text 10.95 (1-57332-220-2); pap. text 10.95 (1-57332-221-0) HighReach Learning, Inc.

Howland, Deborah. Heart of the Arctic: The Story of a Polar Bear Family. (Smithsonian Wild Heritage Collection). (Illus.). (J). (ps-3). 1996. 32p. pap. 4.95 (1-56899-210-6); 1994. 32p. 11.95 o.p. (1-56899-064-2); 32p. 16.95 o.p. incl. audio (1-56899-065-0); 32p. 39.95 o.p. incl. audio (1-56899-067-7); 32p. 25.95 o.p. incl. audio (1-56899-066-9); audio o.p. (1-56899-068-5); Incl. small toy. 1996. 32p. pap. 15.95 (1-56899-212-2) Soundprints.

Newton, Jill. Polar Bear Scare. 1992. (Illus.). (J). (ps-3). 15.00 o.p. (0-688-11232-3) HarperCollins Children's Bk. Group.

Osborne, Mary Pope. Polar Bears Past Bedtime. 1998. (Magic Tree House Ser.: No. 12). (Illus.). 96p. (J). (gr. k-3). 11.99 (0-679-98341-4); pap. 3.99 (0-679-88341-X) Random Hse. Children's Bks. (Random Hse. Bks. for Young Readers).

Plante, Raymond & Favreau, Marie-Claude. Marilou Polaire et l'Iguane des Neiges. 2002. (La Courte Echelle Premier Roman Ser.). (FRE., Illus.). 64p. (J). (gr. 2-5). pap. 8.95 (2-89021-336-6) La Courte Echelle CAN. *Dist:* Firefly Bks., Ltd.

Pledger, Maurice, illus. Adventure with Polly Polar Bear, , 1997. (Peek & Find Ser.). 18p. (J). (ps-k). 12.95 o.p. (1-57145-077-7, Silver Dolphin Bks.) Advantage Pubs. Group.

POLYNESIA—FICTION

Schields, Gretchen. The Water Shell. 1995. (Illus.). 40p. (J). (ps-3). 16.00 (0-15-200404-1, Gulliver Bks.) Harcourt Children's Bks.

Stevenson, Robert Louis. The Bottle Imp. 1996. (Illus.). 64p. (J). (gr. 4-7). 16.95 o.p. (0-395-72101-6, Clarion Bks.) Houghton Mifflin Co. Trade & Reference Div.

POMPEII (EXTINCT CITY)—FICTION

Osborne, Mary Pope. Vacation under the Volcano. unabr. ed. 2002. (Magic Tree House Ser. : Vol. 13). 74p. (J). (gr. k-4). pap. 17.00 incl. audio (0-8072-0782-9, LFTR 241 SP, Listening Library) Random Hse. Audio Publishing Group.

—Vacation under the Volcano. 1998. (Magic Tree House Ser.: No. 13). (Illus.). 96p. (J). (gr. k-3). lib. bdg. 11.99 (0-679-99050-X, Random Hse. Bks. for Young Readers) Random Hse. Children's Bks.

—Vacation under the Volcano. 1998. (Magic Tree House Ser.: No. 13). (Illus.). 80p. (J). (gr. k-3). pap. 3.99 (0-679-89050-5) Random Hse., Inc.

—Vacation under the Volcano, 13. 1998. (Magic Tree House Ser.: No. 13). (Illus.). (J). (gr. k-3). 10.04 (0-606-13972-9) Turtleback Bks.

Tuttle, Howard N. Fire Night: A Story of Pompeii, August 24, 79 A.D. 1978. (J). 4.50 o.p. (0-533-02947-3) Vantage Pr., Inc.

PORTUGAL—FICTION

Balet, Jan. Joanjo, a Portuguese Tale. 1967. (Illus.). (J). (ps-2). 4.95 o.p. (0-440-04236-4); lib. bdg. 4.58 o.s.i (0-440-04233-X) Dell Publishing. (Delacorte Pr.).

Doyle, Peter R. Lost in the Secret Cave. 1996. (Daring Adventure Ser.: Bk. 10). (J). (gr. 4). pap. 5.99 o.p. (1-56179-481-3) Focus on the Family Publishing.

Hope, Laura Lee. The Bobbsey Twins' Search for the Green Rooster. 1964. (Bobbsey Twins Ser.). (J). (gr. 3-5). 4.50 o.s.i (0-448-08058-3, Grosset & Dunlap) Penguin Putnam Bks. for Young Readers.

L'Engle, Madeleine. The Arm of the Starfish, RS. 1965. 256p. (J). (gr. 7 up). 18.00 o.s.i (0-374-30396-7, Farrar, Straus & Giroux (BYR)) Farrar, Straus & Giroux.

—The Arm of the Starfish. 1979. (Laurel-Leaf Suspense Ser.). 288p. (YA). (gr. 7 up). mass mkt. 4.99 (0-440-90183-9, Laurel Leaf) Random Hse. Children's Bks.

Walden, Amelia. A Spy Case Built for Two. 1969. (J). (gr. 7 up). 3.95 o.p. (0-664-32433-9) Westminster John Knox Pr.

PRINCE EDWARD ISLAND—FICTION

Conkie, Heather. Dreamer of Dreams. 1993. (Road to Avonlea Ser.: No. 18). 144p. (J). (gr. 4-6). pap. 3.99 o.s.i (0-553-48044-8) Bantam Bks.

—Old Quarrels, Old Love. 1993. (Road to Avonlea Ser.: No. 15). 128p. (J). (gr. 4-6). pap. 3.99 o.s.i (0-553-48041-3) Bantam Bks.

Dalmatian Press Staff, adapted by. Anne of Green Gables. 2002. (Spot the Classics Ser.). (Illus.). 192p. (J). (gr. k-5). 4.99 (1-57759-543-2) Dalmatian Pr.

Dussling, Jennifer. Anne of Green Gables. 2001. (All Aboard Reading Ser.). (Illus.). 48p. (J). (gr. 4-7). 13.89 o.s.i (0-448-42460-6); pap. 3.99 (0-448-42459-2) Penguin Putnam Bks. for Young Readers. (Philomel).

Glassman, Peter. Ann of the Green Gables. 1924. (J). o.s.i (0-688-13352-5, Morrow, William & Co.) Morrow/Avon.

Helldorfer, Mary-Claire. Anne of Green Gables. 2003. (Illus.). 32p. (J). pap. 6.99 (0-440-41614-0, Dragonfly Bks.) Random Hse. Children's Bks.

McAugh, Fiona. Quarantine at Alexander Abraham's. 1992. (Road to Avonlea Ser.: No. 5). 128p. (J). (gr. 3-7). pap. 3.99 o.s.i (0-553-48031-6) Bantam Bks.

McHugh, Fiona, adapted by. The Anne of Green Gables Storybook. 2003. (Illus.). 80p. (J). (gr. 2-7). 19.95 (0-920668-43-7); pap. 9.95 (0-920668-42-9) Firefly Bks., Ltd.

Montgomery. Story Girl of Avonlea: Dreams Scheme. 2004. 96p. pap. 4.99 (0-310-70601-7) Zondervan.

—Summer Shenanigans. 2004. (Story Girl Ser.: Bk. 3). 96p. pap. 4.99 (0-310-70600-9) Zondervan.

Montgomery, L. M. After Many Days: Tales of Time Passed. 1992. 320p. (YA). (gr. 4-7). mass mkt. 4.99 o.s.i (0-553-29184-X, Dell Books for Young Readers) Random Hse. Children's Bks.

—Along the Shore: Tales by the Sea. (YA). 22.95 (0-8488-2655-8) Amereon, Ltd.

—Along the Shore: Tales by the Sea. 1990. 288p. (YA). (gr. 4-7). mass mkt. 4.99 o.s.i (0-553-28589-0, Dell Books for Young Readers) Random Hse. Children's Bks.

—Among the Shadows. 1991. 304p. (YA). mass mkt. 4.99 o.s.i (0-553-28959-4) Bantam Bks.

—Ana la de Alamos Ventosos. 2001. (Coleccion "Ana, la de Tejas Verdes"). (SPA.). (gr. 4-7). (84-7888-201-4, SAL3944) Emece Editores ESP. *Dist:* Lectorum Pubns., Inc.

—Ana la de Isla. 2001. (SPA.). 240p. (gr. 4-7). 10.95 (84-7888-161-1) Scholastic, Inc.

—Ana, la de la Isla. 4th ed. (Coleccion "Ana, la de Tejas Verdes").Tr. of Anne of the Island. (SPA., Illus.). 240p. (YA). (gr. 5-8). (84-7888-635-4, SAL5036) Emece Editores ESP. *Dist:* Lectorum Pubns., Inc.

—Ana, la de la Isla. 2001. Tr. of Anne of the Island. (J). 17.00 (0-606-22674-5) Turtleback Bks.

—Anne of Avonlea. 1984. (Avonlea Ser.: No. 2). (YA). (gr. 5-8). mass mkt. 2.95 o.p. (0-8049-0219-4, CL219) Airmont Publishing Co., Inc.

—Anne of Avonlea. 1976. (Avonlea Ser.: No. 2). 376p. (YA). (gr. 5-8). 22.95 (0-89190-155-8) Amereon, Ltd.

—Anne of Avonlea. unabr. ed. 1987. (Avonlea Ser.: No. 2). (YA). (gr. 5-8). audio 41.95 (1-55685-089-1) Audio Bk. Contractors, Inc.

—Anne of Avonlea. (Avonlea Ser.: No. 2). (gr. 5-8). 1992. 288p. (YA). pap. 3.25 o.s.i (0-553-15114-2); 1984. 288p. (J). mass mkt. 2.95 o.s.i (0-553-24740-9); 1984. 288p. (YA). mass mkt. 3.95 (0-7704-2206-3); No. 2. 1984. 304p. (YA). mass mkt. 4.50 (0-553-21314-8) Bantam Bks.

—Anne of Avonlea. unabr. ed. (Avonlea Ser.: No. 2). (YA). (gr. 5-8). 1998. audio (0-7861-1428-2, 896061); 1992. audio 49.95 (0-7861-0314-0, 2289) Blackstone Audio Bks., Inc.

—Anne of Avonlea. unabr. ed. 1992. (Avonlea Ser.: Bk. 2). (YA). (gr. 5-8). audio 49.95 (1-55686-448-5, 448) Books in Motion.

—Anne of Avonlea. 1992. (Avonlea Ser.: No. 2). (Illus.). xiv, 204p. (YA). (gr. 5-8). 12.99 o.s.i (0-517-08127-X) Crown Publishing Group.

—Anne of Avonlea. 1995. (Avonlea Ser.: No. 2). 291p. (YA). (gr. 5-8). mass mkt. 2.99 (0-8125-5196-6, Tor Classics); 1994. mass mkt. 2.50 (1-55902-905-6, Aerie) Doherty, Tom Assocs., LLC.

—Anne of Avonlea. unabr. ed. 2002. (Juvenile Classics). 272p. (J). pap. 3.00 (0-486-42239-9) Dover Pubns., Inc.

—Anne of Avonlea. 1997. (Avonlea Ser.: No. 2). (YA). (gr. 5-8). pap. 5.60 (0-87129-791-4, A72) Dramatic Publishing Co.

—Anne of Avonlea, RS. 1950. (Avonlea Ser.: No. 2). (YA). (gr. 5-8). o.p. (0-374-30354-1, Farrar, Straus & Giroux (BYR)) Farrar, Straus & Giroux.

—Anne of Avonlea, unabr. ed. 1999. (Avonlea Ser.: No. 2). (YA). (gr. 5-8). audio 49.95 Highsmith Inc.

—Anne of Avonlea. l.t. ed. (Avonlea Ser.: No. 2). (YA). (gr. 5-8). 311p. pap. 28.60 (0-7583-0217-7); 1225p. pap. 92.89 (0-7583-0223-1); 1056p. pap. 82.79 (0-7583-0222-3); 859p. pap. 68.25 (0-7583-0221-5); 698p. pap. 53.79 (0-7583-0220-7); 545p. pap. 43.82 (0-7583-0219-3); 426p. pap. 35.52 (0-7583-0218-5); 249p. pap. 23.08 (0-7583-0216-9); 249p. lib. bdg. 29.08 (0-7583-0208-8); 311p. lib. bdg. 34.60 (0-7583-0209-6); 426p. lib. bdg. 41.52 (0-7583-0210-X); 545p. lib. bdg. 49.82 (0-7583-0211-8); 698p. lib. bdg. 59.79 (0-7583-0212-6); 859p. lib. bdg. 84.25 (0-7583-0213-4); 1056p. lib. bdg. 94.79 (0-7583-0214-2); 1225p. lib. bdg. 104.89 (0-7583-0215-0) Huge Print Pr.

—Anne of Avonlea. l.t. ed. 1998. (Avonlea Ser.: No. 2). 401p. (YA). (gr. 5-8). lib. bdg. 35.95 (1-58118-039-X, 22507) LRS.

—Anne of Avonlea. (Avonlea Ser.: No. 2). (YA). (gr. 5-8). E-Book 1.95 (1-57799-878-2) Logos Research Systems, Inc.

—Anne of Avonlea. 1987. (Avonlea Ser.: No. 2). 288p. (YA). (gr. 5-8). mass mkt. 3.95 o.s.i (0-451-52113-7, Signet Classics) NAL.

—Anne of Avonlea. abr. ed. 1999. (Avonlea Ser.: No. 2). (YA). (gr. 5-8). audio 13.98 (962-634-669-8, NA216914); audio compact disk 15.98 (962-634-169-6, NA216912) Naxos of America, Inc. (Naxos AudioBooks).

—Anne of Avonlea. l.t. ed. (Avonlea Ser.: No. 2). (YA). (gr. 5-8). reprint ed. 1993. 435p. lib. bdg. 26.00 (0-939495-26-0); 1998. 270p. lib. bdg. 25.00 (1-58287-013-6) North Bks.

—Anne of Avonlea. (Avonlea Ser.: No. 2). (YA). (gr. 5-8). 1997. (Illus.). 336p. pap. 4.99 (0-14-036798-5); 1992. 240p. pap. 2.99 o.p. (0-14-032565-4, Puffin Bks.); 1990. (Illus.). 320p. 15.99 (0-448-40063-4, Grosset & Dunlap) Penguin Putnam Bks. for Young Readers.

—Anne of Avonlea. (YA). (gr. 5-8). 1999. (Avonlea Ser.: No. 2). E-Book 8.99 o.p. incl. cd-rom (1-57646-053-3); 2000. (Anne of Green Gables Ser.: Vol. 2). 366p. pap. 24.99 (1-57646-306-0); 2000. (Anne of Green Gables Ser.: Vol. No. 2). 366p. lib. bdg. 34.99 (1-57646-307-9) Quiet Vision Publishing.

—Anne of Avonlea. abr. unabr. ed. 1989. (Avonlea Ser.: No. 2). (J). (gr. 4-7). audio 18.00 (0-553-45200-2, Listening Library) Random Hse. Audio Publishing Group.

—Anne of Avonlea. (Avonlea Ser.: No. 2). (YA). (gr. 5-8). 1994. pap. o.s.i (0-553-85021-0); 1993. pap. o.s.i (0-553-56709-8) Random Hse. Children's Bks. (Dell Books for Young Readers).

—Anne of Avonlea, unabr. ed. 2001. (Avonlea Ser.: No. 2). (YA). (gr. 5-8). audio 62.00 (0-7887-0535-0, 94730E7) Recorded Bks., LLC.

—Anne of Avonlea. 1994. (Avonlea Ser.: No. 2). 256p. (YA). (gr. 5-8). text 5.98 o.p. (1-56138-368-6, Courage Bks.) Running Pr. Bk. Pubs.

—Anne of Avonlea. 1991. (Avonlea Ser.: No. 2). 336p. (YA). (gr. 5-8). mass mkt. 4.50 (*0-590-44556-1*, Scholastic Paperbacks) Scholastic, Inc.

—Anne of Avonlea. 1976. (Avonlea Ser.: No. 2). (YA). (gr. 5-8). 10.04 (*0-606-00791-1*) Turtleback Bks.

—Anne of Green Gables. 2002. (Great Illustrated Classics). (Illus.). 240p. (J). (gr. 3-7). lib. bdg. 21.35 (*1-57765-816-7*, ABDO & Daughters) ABDO Publishing Co.

—Anne of Green Gables. 1984. (Avonlea Ser.: No. 1). (YA). (gr. 5-8). mass mkt. 1.95 o.p. (*0-8049-0218-6*, CL218) Airmont Publishing Co., Inc.

—Anne of Green Gables. 1976. (Avonlea Ser.: No. 1). 244p. (YA). (gr. 5-8). 23.95 (*0-8488-0584-4*) Amereon, Ltd.

—Anne of Green Gables, 3 vols. (Avonlea Ser.: No. 1). (YA). (gr. 5-8). 1997. mass mkt. 13.50 (*0-553-33307-0*); 1987. mass mkt. 8.85 o.s.i (*0-553-30838-6*); 1986. mass mkt. o.s.i (*0-553-16646-8*); 1983. 320p. pap. 3.95 (*0-7704-2205-5*); 1982. 320p. mass mkt. 2.95 o.s.i (*0-553-24295-4*); 1982. 336p. mass mkt. 4.50 (*0-553-21313-X*, Bantam Classics) Bantam Bks.

—Anne of Green Gables. 1998. (J). E-Book 5.00 (*0-7607-1341-3*) Barnes & Noble, Inc.

—Anne of Green Gables. 2001. (J). per. 12.50 (*1-891355-34-1*) Blue Unicorn Editions.

—Anne of Green Gables. 2002. pap. 4.50 (*1-59109-388-0*) Booksurge, LLC.

—Anne of Green Gables. (Avonlea Ser.: No. 1). (Illus.). (YA). (gr. 5-8). 1995. 352p. o.p. (*0-681-00770-2*); 1988. 240p. 11.95 o.p. (*0-681-40501-5*) Borders Pr.

—Anne of Green Gables. 2000. (Avonlea Ser.: No. 1). 280p. (YA). (gr. 5-8). pap. text 15.00 (*0-7881-9155-1*) DIANE Publishing Co.

—Anne of Green Gables. 1995. (Avonlea Ser.: No. 1). 307p. (YA). (gr. 5-8). pap. text 2.99 (*0-8125-5152-4*, Tor Classics); 1994. mass mkt. 2.50 (*1-55902-906-4*, Aerie) Doherty, Tom Assocs., LLC.

—Anne of Green Gables. (Avonlea Ser.: No. 1). (YA). (gr. 5-8). 2000. 320p. pap. 3.00 (*0-486-41025-0*); 1995. (Illus.). iv, 91p. pap. text 1.00 (*0-486-28366-6*) Dover Pubns., Inc.

—Anne of Green Gables. 1989. (Avonlea Ser.: No. 1). (YA). (gr. 5-8). pap. 5.60 (*0-87129-242-4*, A41) Dramatic Publishing Co.

—Anne of Green Gables. (J). E-Book 2.49 (*0-7574-3112-7*) Electric Umbrella Publishing.

—Anne of Green Gables. 1999. (Focus on the Family Great Stories Ser.). (Illus.). 368p. (J). (gr. 4-7). 15.99 o.p. (*1-56179-625-5*) Focus on the Family Publishing.

—Anne of Green Gables. 1999. (Avonlea Ser.: No. 1). (YA). (gr. 5-8). 23.95 (*0-8057-8090-4*, Macmillan Reference USA) Gale Group.

—Anne of Green Gables. 1989. (Avonlea Ser.: No. 1). (Illus.). 320p. (YA). (gr. 5-8). 19.95 o.s.i (*0-87923-783-X*) Godine, David R. Pub.

—Anne of Green Gables. (Avonlea Ser.: No. 1). (YA). (gr. 5-8). 2000. (*0-06-028227-4*); 1999. (Illus.). 80p. 2.99 o.s.i (*0-694-01284-X*, Harper Festival) HarperCollins Children's Bk. Group.

—Anne of Green Gables. (Avonlea Ser.: No. 1). (YA). (gr. 5-8). pap. 3.50 (*0-340-71500-6*) Hodder & Stoughton, Ltd. GBR. *Dist:* Lubrecht & Cramer, Ltd., Trafalgar Square.

—Anne of Green Gables. Greenwood, Barbara, ed. 2001. (Avonlea Ser.: No. 1). 94p. (YA). (gr. 5-8). pap. 9.95 (*1-55013-431-0*) Key Porter Bks. CAN. *Dist:* Firefly Bks., Ltd.

—Anne of Green Gables. 1995. (Avonlea Ser.: No. 1). (Illus.). 416p. (gr. 5-8). 14.95 (*0-679-44475-0*, Everyman's Library) Knopf Publishing Group.

—Anne of Green Gables. 1994. (Avonlea Ser.: No. 1). (Illus.). 256p. (YA). (gr. 5-8). 25.00 (*0-88363-994-7*) Levin, Hugh Lauter Assocs.

—Anne of Green Gables. (Avonlea Ser.: No. 1). (YA). (gr. 5-8). E-Book 1.95 (*1-57799-946-0*) Logos Research Systems, Inc.

—Anne of Green Gables. MQ Publications Staff, ed. 1998. (Little Brown Notebooks Ser.). (Illus.). 256p. 9.99 (*1-84072-063-8*) M Q Pubns. GBR. *Dist:* Watson-Guptill Pubns., Inc.

—Anne of Green Gables. 1992. (Avonlea Ser.: No. 1). 338p. (YA). (gr. 5-8). mass mkt. 4.95 (*0-7710-9883-9*) McClelland & Stewart/Tundra Bks.

—Anne of Green Gables. (Avonlea Ser.: No. 1). (YA). (gr. 5-8). E-Book 1.95 (*1-58515-198-X*) MesaView, Inc.

—Anne of Green Gables. 1987. (Avonlea Ser.: No. 1). 320p. (YA). (gr. 5-8). mass mkt. 4.95 o.p. (*0-451-52112-9*, Signet Classics) NAL.

—Anne of Green Gables. 1998. 354p. (J). pap. (*1-55109-249-2*) Nimbus Publishing, Ltd.

—Anne of Green Gables. Bassett, Jennifer, ed. 1995. (Avonlea Ser.: No. 1). (Illus.). 48p. (YA). (gr. 5-8). pap. text 5.95 o.p. (*0-19-422725-1*) Oxford Univ. Pr., Inc.

—Anne of Green Gables. 2002. (Cageworld Ser.). (Illus.). (J). pap. 9.99 (*0-14-250102-6*, Puffin Bks.); 1996. (Avonlea Ser.: No. 1). (Illus.). 384p. (YA). (gr. 5-8). 4.99 (*0-14-036741-1*, Puffin Bks.); 1994. (Avonlea Ser.: No. 1). 256p. (YA). (gr. 5-8). pap. 2.99 o.p. (*0-14-035148-5*, Puffin Bks.); 1993. (Avonlea Ser.: No. 1). (Illus.). 16p. (YA). (gr. 5-8). o.p. (*0-525-45173-0*); 1992. (Avonlea Ser.: No. 1). 256p. (YA). (gr. 5-8). pap. 2.99 o.p. (*0-14-032462-3*, Puffin Bks.); 1983. (Avonlea Ser.: No. 1). (Illus.). 384p. (YA). (gr. 5-8). 17.99 (*0-448-06030-2*, Grosset & Dunlap) Penguin Putnam Bks. for Young Readers.

—Anne of Green Gables. Hanft, Joshua, ed. 1995. (Great Illustrated Classics Ser.: Vol. 42). (Illus.). 240p. (J). (gr. 3-6). 9.95 (*0-86611-993-0*) Playmore, Inc., Pubs.

—Anne of Green Gables. (YA). (gr. 5-8). 2000. (Anne of Green Gables Ser.: Vol. No. 1). 220p. pap. 12.99 (*1-57646-300-1*); 2000. (Anne of Green Gables Ser.: Vol. No.1). 220p. lib. bdg. 32.99 (*1-57646-301-X*); 1999. (Avonlea Ser.: No. 1). E-Book 8.99 o.p. incl. cd-rom (*1-57646-052-5*) Quiet Vision Publishing.

—Anne of Green Gables. 2004. 112p. (J). (gr. 3-5). lib. bdg. 11.99 (*0-679-99428-9*, Random Hse. Bks. for Young Readers); 2002. (Illus.). 256p. (J). 16.99 (*0-517-22111-X*, Random Hse. Bks. for Young Readers); 1999. (Avonlea Ser.: No. 1). (Illus.). 112p. (gr. 5-8). pap. text 3.99 (*0-440-41356-7*, Dell Books for Young Readers); 1998. (Avonlea Ser.: No. 1). 352p. (gr. 5-8). mass mkt. 2.99 o.s.i (*0-440-22787-9*, Yearling); 1994. (Avonlea Ser.: No. 1). (YA). (gr. 5-8). mass mkt. o.s.i (*0-553-85018-0*, Dell Books for Young Readers); 1994. (Step into Classics Ser.). (Illus.). 112p. (J). (gr. 3-5). pap. 3.99 (*0-679-85467-3*, Random Hse. Bks. for Young Readers); 1993. (Avonlea Ser.: No. 1). (YA). (gr. 5-8). pap. o.s.i (*0-553-56712-8*, Dell Books for Young Readers) Random Hse. Children's Bks.

—Anne of Green Gables. (Children's Classics Ser.: No. 1). 1998. (Illus.). 256p. (J). (gr. 4-7). 5.99 (*0-517-18968-2*); 1995. (YA). (gr. 5-8). 1.10 o.s.i (*0-517-14154-X*); 1988. (Illus.). xvi, 240p. (YA). (gr. 5-8). 12.99 o.s.i (*0-517-65958-1*) Random Hse. Value Publishing.

—Anne of Green Gables. 1993. (Avonlea Ser.: No.1). 287p. (YA). (gr. 5-8). text 5.98 o.p. (*1-56138-324-4*, Courage Bks.) Running Pr. Bk. Pubs.

—Anne of Green Gables. (YA). 2002. (Scholastic Classic Ser.). 400p. mass mkt. 4.99 (*0-439-29577-7*); 1989. (Avonlea Ser.: No. 1). 384p. (gr. 5-8). mass mkt. 4.50 (*0-590-42243-X*, Scholastic Paperbacks) Scholastic, Inc.

—Anne of Green Gables, 3 vol. set. 1997. (YA). (*0-7704-2218-7*) Seal Bks. CAN. *Dist:* Random Hse. of Canada, Ltd.

—Anne of Green Gables. 2001. (Aladdin Classics Ser.). (Illus.). 480p. (J). pap. 3.99 (*0-689-84622-3*, Aladdin) Simon & Schuster Children's Publishing.

—Anne of Green Gables. 1994. (Avonlea Ser.: No. 1). (Illus.). 256p. (YA). (gr. 5-8). 9.99 o.p. (*1-897954-26-3*) Sterling Publishing Co., Inc.

—Anne of Green Gables. 2000. (Avonlea Ser.: No. 1). (Illus.). 328p. (J). (gr. 5-8). 24.95 (*0-88776-515-7*) Tundra Bks. of Northern New York.

—Anne of Green Gables. Morgan, Sally, ed. 1994. (Avonlea Ser.: No. 1). (YA). (gr. 5-8). 9.09 o.p. (*0-606-09006-1*) Turtleback Bks.

—Anne of Green Gables. 1987. (Avonlea Ser.: No. 1). (YA). (gr. 5-8). 10.55 (*0-606-00282-0*) Turtleback Bks.

—Anne of Green Gables. 2001. (Children's Classics). 288p. (J). pap. 3.95 (*1-85326-139-4*) Wordsworth Editions, Ltd. GBR. *Dist:* Advanced Global Distribution Services.

—Anne of Green Gables. 2001. (Illus.). 40p. (J). (gr. k-3). 15.95 o.p. (*0-385-32715-3*, Doubleday Bks. for Young Readers) Random Hse. Children's Bks.

—Anne of Green Gables, unabr. ed. 1986. (Avonlea Ser.: No. 1). (YA). (gr. 5-8). audio 53.95 (*1-55685-045-X*) Audio Bk. Contractors, Inc.

—Anne of Green Gables. abr. ed. 1986. (Avonlea Ser.: No. 1). (YA). (gr. 5-8). pap. 12.95 incl. audio (*1-882071-07-7*, 009) B&B Audio, Inc.

—Anne of Green Gables, Vol. 1. 1984. (Avonlea Ser.: Vol. 1). 320p. (gr. 5-8). pap. text 4.50 (*0-553-15327-7*) Bantam Bks.

—Anne of Green Gables. unabr. ed. (Avonlea Ser.: No. 1). (YA). (gr. 5-8). 1998. audio 56.95 (*0-7861-1315-4*, 2240); 1991. audio 62.95 (*0-7861-0247-0*, 1216) Blackstone Audio Bks., Inc.

—Anne of Green Gables. l.t. ed. 2001. (Avonlea Ser.: No. 1). (YA). (gr. 5-8). per. 15.50 (*1-58396-202-6*) Blue Unicorn Editions.

—Anne of Green Gables. unabr. ed. 1992. (Avonlea Ser.: Bk. 1). (J). audio 49.95 (*1-55686-447-7*, 447) Books in Motion.

—Anne of Green Gables. unabr. collector's ed. 1998. (Avonlea Ser.: No. 1). (YA). (gr. 5-8). audio 56.00 (*0-7366-4150-5*, 896035) Books on Tape, Inc.

—Anne of Green Gables. 1977. (Avonlea Ser.: No. 1). 429p. (YA). (gr. 5-8). reprint ed. lib. bdg. 27.95 (*0-89966-262-5*) Buccaneer Bks., Inc.

—Anne of Green Gables. abr. ed. 1997. (Avonlea Ser.: No. 1). (YA). (gr. 5-8). audio 4.99 (*0-88646-954-6*, 7954) Durkin Hayes Publishing Ltd.

—Anne of Green Gables, RS. 1950. (Avonlea Ser.: No. 1). (YA). (gr. 5-8). pap. o.p. (*0-374-40403-8*, Sunburst) Farrar, Straus & Giroux.

—Anne of Green Gables. unabr. ed. 1999. (Avonlea Ser.: No. 1). (YA). (gr. 5-8). audio 56.95 Highsmith Inc.

—Anne of Green Gables, ERS. 1994. (Avonlea Ser.: No. 1). (FRE., Illus.). xx, 486p. (YA). (gr. 5-8). 15.95 o.p. (*0-8050-3126-X*, Holt, Henry & Co. Bks. For Young Readers) Holt, Henry & Co.

—Anne of Green Gables. l.t. ed. (Avonlea Ser.: No. 1). (YA). (gr. 5-8). 350p. pap. 28.82 (*0-7583-0233-9*); 614p. pap. 44.14 (*0-7583-0235-5*); 1379p. pap. 93.47 (*0-7583-0239-8*); 1189p. pap. 83.30 (*0-7583-0238-X*); 966p. pap. 72.70 (*0-7583-0237-1*); 480p. pap. 35.78 (*0-7583-0234-7*); 280p. pap. 24.84 (*0-7583-0232-0*); 786p. pap. 62.17 (*0-7583-0236-3*); 350p. lib. bdg. 34.82 (*0-7583-0225-8*); 480p. lib. bdg. 41.78 (*0-7583-0226-6*); 280p. lib. bdg. 30.84 (*0-7583-0224-X*); 786p. lib. bdg. 74.17 (*0-7583-0228-2*); 966p. lib. bdg. 84.70 (*0-7583-0229-0*); 1189p. lib. bdg. 95.30 (*0-7583-0230-4*); 1379p. lib. bdg. 105.47 (*0-7583-0231-2*); 614p. lib. bdg. 50.14 (*0-7583-0227-4*) Huge Print Pr.

—Anne of Green Gables. l.t. ed. 1991. (Avonlea Ser.: No. 1). 376p. (YA). (gr. 5-8). 17.95 o.p. (*1-85089-895-2*) ISIS Large Print Bks. GBR. *Dist:* Transaction Pubs.

—Anne of Green Gables. Sternach, Jerry, ed. l.t. ed. 2002. text 150.00 (*1-58702-021-1*) Johnston, Don Inc.

—Anne of Green Gables. l.t. ed. 1998. (Avonlea Ser.: No. 1). 472p. (YA). (gr. 5-8). lib. bdg. 35.95 (*1-58118-035-7*, 22019) LRS.

—Anne of Green Gables. abr. ed. 1997. (Junior Classics Ser.: No. 1). (YA). (gr. 4-7). audio 13.98 (*962-634-623-X*, NA212314); (gr. 5-8). audio compact disk 15.98 (*962-634-123-8*, NA212312) Naxos of America, Inc. (Naxos AudioBooks).

—Anne of Green Gables. abr. ed. 1997. (Avonlea Ser.: No. 1). (YA). (gr. 5-8). audio 7.00 (*0-7871-1221-6*); audio 20.00 (*0-7871-1222-4*) NewStar Media, Inc. (Dove Audio).

—Anne of Green Gables. 1998. (Avonlea Ser.). 352p. (YA). (gr. 5-8). reprint ed. (*1-55109-013-9*) Nimbus Publishing, Ltd.

—Anne of Green Gables. l.t. ed. (Avonlea Ser.: No. 1). (YA). (gr. 5-8). reprint ed. 1993. 494p. lib. bdg. 26.00 (*0-939495-25-2*); 1998. 310p. lib. bdg. 25.00 (*1-58287-014-4*) North Bks.

—Anne of Green Gables, Level 2. Hedge, Tricia, ed. 2000. (Bookworms Ser.). (Illus.). 64p. (J). pap. text 5.95 (*0-19-422965-3*) Oxford Univ. Pr., Inc.

—Anne of Green Gables. l.t. ed. 2000. (Anne of Green Gables Ser.: Vol. 1). 414p. (YA). (gr. 5-8). pap. 24.99 (*1-57646-302-8*); lib. bdg. 37.99 (*1-57646-303-6*) Quiet Vision Publishing.

—Anne of Green Gables. abr. ed. 1991. (Avonlea Ser.: No. 1). (YA). (gr. 5-8). 27.99 o.s.i incl. audio (*0-7704-2492-9*, RH Audio); 1987. (Avonlea Ser.: No. 1). (YA). (gr. 4-7). audio 18.00 (*0-553-45091-3*, 390221, Listening Library); 2001. audio 32.00 (*0-8072-0646-6*, Listening Library); 2000. (Avonlea Ser.: No. 1). 38p. (YA). (gr. 5-8). audio 9.99 o.s.i (*0-8072-8278-2*, Listening Library); Set. 1991. (Avonlea Ser.: No. 1). (J). (gr. 5-8). 24.99 o.s.i incl. audio (*0-553-47020-5*, RH Audio) Random Hse. Audio Publishing Group.

—Anne of Green Gables, Set. 1992. (Avonlea Ser.: No. 1). (YA). (gr. 5-8). 16.24 o.p. (*0-553-62867-4*, Dell Books for Young Readers) Random Hse. Children's Bks.

—Anne of Green Gables, unabr. ed. 1989. (Avonlea Ser.: No. 1). (YA). (gr. 5-8). audio 60.00 (*1-55690-022-8*, 89150E7) Recorded Bks., LLC.

—Anne of Green Gables, 8 vols., Set. 1997. (YA). (*0-7704-2407-4*) Seal Bks. CAN. *Dist:* Random Hse. of Canada, Ltd.

—Anne of Green Gables. abr. ed. 1997. (Avonlea Ser.: No. 1). (YA). (gr. 5-8). mass mkt. 16.95 o.p. incl. audio (*1-85998-749-4*); audio 14.95 (*1-85998-080-5*) Trafalgar Square.

—Anne of Green Gables. abr. ed. 1997. (Avonlea Ser.: No. 1). (YA). (gr. 5-8). 2p. audio 10.95 o.s.i (*0-14-086331-1*, Penguin AudioBooks); (Illus.). 112p. 22.95 o.p. (*0-670-87031-5*) Viking Penguin.

—Anne of Green Gables: Address & Birthday Book, 2 vols., Set. 2001. (Illus.). 238p. (J). 12.95 (*1-55263-180-X*) Key Porter Bks. CAN. *Dist:* Firefly Bks., Ltd.

—Anne of Green Gables: Anne of Avonlea. 1996. (Avonlea Ser.: No. 1). (YA). (gr. 5-8). 12.98 o.p. (*0-7651-9979-3*) Smithmark Pubs., Inc.

—Anne of Green Gables: Anne of Avonlea; Anne of the Island; Anne of Green Gables. 1997. (Avonlea Ser.: No. 1). (YA). (gr. 5-8). mass mkt. 13.50 (*0-553-33306-2*) Bantam Bks.

—Anne of Green Gables: Seal Edition. abr. ed. 1987. (Avonlea Ser.: No. 1). (YA). (gr. 5-8). audio 18.99 o.s.i (*0-7704-3998-5*, RH Audio) Random Hse. Audio Publishing Group.

—Anne of Green Gables Book & Charm. 1999. (Charming Classic Bks.). 400p. (J). (ps up). pap. 6.99 (*0-694-01251-3*, Harper Festival) HarperCollins Children's Bk. Group.

—The Anne of Green Gables Collection. 1999. (Workhorse Library Ser.). E-Book 19.99 incl. cd-rom (*1-891595-36-9*) Quiet Vision Publishing.

—Anne of Green Gables Promo. 384p. 2003. pap. 3.99 o.p. (*0-14-250092-5*); 2000. pap. 2.99 o.p. (*0-14-130935-0*) Penguin Putnam Bks. for Young Readers. (Puffin Bks.).

—Anne of Ingleside. (Avonlea Ser.: No. 10). (YA). (gr. 5-8). 23.95 (*0-8488-0890-8*); 1976. 286p. 23.95 (*0-8488-1101-1*) Amereon, Ltd.

—Anne of Ingleside. 1984. (Avonlea Ser.: No. 10). (YA). (gr. 5-8). 288p. mass mkt. 2.95 o.s.i (*0-553-24648-8*); mass mkt. 3.50 o.s.i (*0-7704-2144-X*); 6th ed. 304p. mass mkt. 3.95 (*0-7704-2207-1*);No. 6. 304p. mass mkt. 4.50 (*0-553-21315-6*, Bantam Classics) Bantam Bks.

—Anne of Ingleside. (Avonlea Ser.: No. 10). (Illus.). 341p. (YA). (gr. 5-8). 6.98 (*0-7710-6180-3*) McClelland & Stewart/Tundra Bks.

—Anne of Ingleside. 1999. (Avonlea Ser.: No. 10). 320p. (YA). (gr. 5-8). mass mkt. 3.95 (*0-451-52643-0*, Signet Classics) NAL.

—Anne of Ingleside, Vol. 6. 1999. 384p. (J). pap. 3.99 (*0-14-036801-9*, Puffin Bks.) Penguin Putnam Bks. for Young Readers.

—Anne of Ingleside. 1970. (Avonlea Ser.: No. 10). (YA). (gr. 5-8). 6.95 o.p. (*0-448-02546-9*) Putnam Publishing Group, The.

—Anne of Ingleside. 1967. (Avonlea Ser.: No. 10). (YA). (gr. 5-8). 10.55 (*0-606-00375-4*) Turtleback Bks.

—Anne of the Island. 1976. (Avonlea Ser.: No. 4). 252p. (YA). (gr. 5-8). 22.95 (*0-8488-0585-2*) Amereon, Ltd.

—Anne of the Island, unabr. ed. 1999. (Avonlea Ser.: No. 4). (YA). (gr. 5-8). audio 35.95 (*1-55685-580-X*) Audio Bk. Contractors, Inc.

—Anne of the Island. (Avonlea Ser.: No. 4). (YA). 1992. 256p. (gr. 3-7). pap. 4.50 o.s.i (*0-553-48066-9*); 1983. 256p. (gr. 5-8). mass mkt. 2.95 o.s.i (*0-553-24158-3*); 1983. 272p. (gr. 5-8). mass mkt. 4.50 (*0-553-21317-2*, Bantam Classics); 1983. 274p. (gr. 5-8). mass mkt. 3.95 (*0-7704-2204-7*) Bantam Bks.

—Anne of the Island, unabr. ed. 1999. (Avonlea Ser.: No. 4). (YA). (gr. 5-8). audio 44.95 (*0-7861-1905-5*, P2698) Blackstone Audio Bks., Inc.

—Anne of the Island. unabr. ed. 1993. (Avonlea Ser.: Bk. 4). (YA). (gr. 5-8). audio 39.95 (*1-55686-461-2*, 461) Books in Motion.

—Anne of the Island, RS. 1950. (Avonlea Ser.: No. 4). (YA). (gr. 5-8). pap. o.p. (*0-374-40404-6*, Sunburst) Farrar, Straus & Giroux.

—Anne of the Island, unabr. ed. 1999. (Avonlea Ser.: No. 4). (YA). (gr. 5-8). audio 49.95 Highsmith Inc.

—Anne of the Island. l.t. ed. (Avonlea Ser.: No. 4). (YA). (gr. 5-8). 1095p. pap. 90.63 (*0-7583-0255-X*); 944p. pap. 74.29 (*0-7583-0254-1*); 768p. pap. 61.80 (*0-7583-0253-3*); 624p. pap. 51.65 (*0-7583-0252-5*); 488p. pap. 41.99 (*0-7583-0251-7*); 381p. pap. 34.45 (*0-7583-0250-9*); 278p. pap. 27.17 (*0-7583-0249-5*); 222p. pap. 22.58 (*0-7583-0248-7*); 944p. lib. bdg. 92.78 (*0-7583-0246-0*); 278p. lib. bdg. 33.74 (*0-7583-0241-X*); 222p. lib. bdg. 28.58 (*0-7583-0240-1*); 1095p. lib. bdg. 102.63 (*0-7583-0247-9*); 381p. lib. bdg. 40.49 (*0-7583-0242-8*); 488p. lib. bdg. 48.59 (*0-7583-0243-6*); 624p. lib. bdg. 58.30 (*0-7583-0244-4*); 768p. lib. bdg. 82.51 (*0-7583-0245-2*) Huge Print Pr.

—Anne of the Island. l.t. ed. 1998. (Avonlea Ser.: No. 4). 376p. (YA). (gr. 5-8). lib. bdg. 34.95 (*1-58118-036-5*, 22020) LRS.

—Anne of the Island. (Avonlea Ser.: No. 4). (YA). (gr. 5-8). E-Book 1.95 (*1-57799-879-0*) Logos Research Systems, Inc.

—Anne of the Island. l.t. ed. 1991. (Avonlea Ser.: No. 4). 256p. (YA). (gr. 5-8). mass mkt. 2.95 o.p. (*0-451-52534-5*, Signet Classics) NAL.

—Anne of the Island. (Avonlea Ser.: No. 4). (YA). (gr. 5-8). 1998. 304p. pap. 4.99 (*0-14-036777-2*); 1992. 304p. pap. 2.99 o.p. (*0-14-032567-0*, Puffin Bks.); 1992. (Illus.). 282p. 14.95 o.s.i (*0-448-40311-0*, Grosset & Dunlap); 1956. 3.95 o.p. (*0-448-02513-2*, Planet Dexter) Penguin Putnam Bks. for Young Readers.

—Anne of the Island. 1970. (Avonlea Ser.: No. 4). (YA). (gr. 5-8). 6.95 o.p. (*0-448-02547-7*) Putnam Publishing Group, The.

—Anne of the Island. (YA). (gr. 5-8). 1999. (Avonlea Ser.: No. 4). E-Book 8.99 o.p. incl. cd-rom (*1-57646-054-1*); 2000. (Anne of Green Gables Ser.: Vol. 3). 336p. pap. 24.99 (*1-57646-310-9*); 2000. (Anne of Green Gables Ser.: Vol. No. 3). 336p. lib. bdg. 33.99 (*1-57646-311-7*) Quiet Vision Publishing.

—Anne of the Island. abr. ed. 1990. (Avonlea Ser.: No. 4). (J). (gr. 4-7). audio 18.00 (*0-553-45201-0*, Listening Library) Random Hse. Audio Publishing Group.

—Anne of the Island. 1994. (Avonlea Ser.: No. 4). (YA). (gr. 5-8). pap. o.s.i (*0-553-85024-5*, Dell Books for Young Readers) Random Hse. Children's Bks.

—Anne of the Island, unabr. ed. 1996. (Avonlea Ser.: No. 4). (YA). (gr. 5-8). audio 53.00 (*0-7887-0598-9*, 94776E7) Recorded Bks., LLC.

—Anne of the Island. 1994. (Avonlea Ser.: No. 4). 239p. (YA). (gr. 5-8). text 5.98 o.p. (*1-56138-369-4*, Courage Bks.) Running Pr. Bk. Pubs.

—Anne of the Island. 1993. (Avonlea Ser.: No. 4). 320p. (YA). (gr. 5-8). mass mkt. 3.25 (*0-590-46163-X*, Scholastic Paperbacks) Scholastic, Inc.

—Anne of the Island. 1976. (Avonlea Ser.: No. 4). (YA). (gr. 5-8). 10.04 (*0-606-00792-X*) Turtleback Bks.

—Anne of the Islands & Tales of Avonlea. 1991. (Avonlea Ser.: No. 4). (Illus.). xv, 573p. (YA). (gr. 5-8). 11.99 o.s.i (*0-517-03705-X*) Random Hse. Value Publishing.

—Anne of Windy Poplars. 1976. (Avonlea Ser.: No. 9). 268p. (YA). (gr. 5-8). 22.95 (*0-8488-0586-0*) Amereon, Ltd.

—Anne of Windy Poplars. (Avonlea Ser.: No. 9). (YA). (gr. 5-8). 1992. 288p. pap. 3.99 o.s.i (*0-553-48065-0*); 1983. 288p. mass mkt. 4.50 (*0-553-21316-4*, Bantam Classics); 1983. 272p. mass mkt. 2.95 o.s.i (*0-553-24397-7*); 4th ed. 1983. 288p. mass mkt. 3.95 (*0-7704-2167-9*) Bantam Bks.

—Anne of Windy Poplars. (Avonlea Ser.: No. 9). 274p. (YA). (gr. 5-8). pap. 4.98 o.p. (*0-7710-6164-1*) McClelland & Stewart/Tundra Bks.

—Anne of Windy Poplars, Vol. 4. 1999. 336p. (J). pap. 3.99 (*0-14-036800-0*, Puffin Bks.) Penguin Putnam Bks. for Young Readers.

—Anne of Windy Poplars. 1970. (Avonlea Ser.: No. 9). (YA). (gr. 5-8). 6.95 o.p. (*0-448-02548-5*) Putnam Publishing Group, The.

—Anne of Windy Poplars. 1987. (Avonlea Ser.: No. 9). (YA). (gr. 5-8). 10.04 (*0-606-02371-2*) Turtleback Bks.

—Anne's House of Dreams. 1976. (Avonlea Ser.: No. 5). 192p. (YA). (gr. 5-8). 20.95 (*0-8488-0587-9*) Amereon, Ltd.

—Anne's House of Dreams, unabr. ed. 1999. (Avonlea Ser.: No. 5). (YA). (gr. 5-8). audio 35.95 (*1-55685-586-9*) Audio Bk. Contractors, Inc.

—Anne's House of Dreams. 1983. (Avonlea Ser.: No. 5). (YA). (gr. 5-8). 256p. mass mkt. 4.50 (*0-553-21318-0*, Bantam Classics); 5th ed. 256p. mass mkt. 3.95 (*0-7704-2210-1*);No. 5. 240p. mass mkt. 2.95 o.s.i (*0-553-24195-8*) Bantam Bks.

—Anne's House of Dreams, unabr. ed. 1997. (Avonlea Ser.: No. 5). (YA). (gr. 5-8). audio 44.95 (*0-7861-1230-1*, 1976) Blackstone Audio Bks., Inc.

—Anne's House of Dreams, unabr. ed. 1999. (Avonlea Ser.: No. 5). (YA). (gr. 5-8). audio 44.95 Highsmith Inc.

—Anne's House of Dreams. l.t. ed. 1999. (Avonlea Ser.: No. 5). 364p. (YA). (gr. 5-8). lib. bdg. 34.95 (*1-58118-048-9*, 22517) LRS.

—Anne's House of Dreams. (Avonlea Ser.: No. 5). (YA). (gr. 5-8). E-Book 1.95 (*1-57799-880-4*) Logos Research Systems, Inc.

—Anne's House of Dreams. 1989. (J). pap. o.p. (*0-7710-6161-7*) McClelland & Stewart/Tundra Bks.

—Anne's House of Dreams. 1989. (Avonlea Ser.: No. 5). (YA). (gr. 5-8). mass mkt. 2.95 o.p. (*0-451-52319-9*, Signet Classics) NAL.

—Anne's House of Dreams. 1992. (Avonlea Ser.: No. 5). 304p. (YA). (gr. 5-8). pap. 2.99 o.p. (*0-14-032569-7*, Puffin Bks.); 1970. (Avonlea Ser.: No. 5). (YA). (gr. 5-8). 6.95 o.p. (*0-448-02549-3*, Grosset & Dunlap); Vol. 5. 1999. 320p. (J). pap. 3.99 (*0-14-036799-3*, Puffin Bks.) Penguin Putnam Bks. for Young Readers.

—Anne's House of Dreams. (YA). (gr. 5-8). 2000. (Anne of Green Gables Ser.: Vol. No. 5). 182p. pap. 14.99 (*1-57646-312-5*); 2000. (Anne of Green Gables Ser.: Vol. No. 5). 182p. lib. bdg. 30.99 (*1-57646-313-3*); 1999. (Avonlea Ser.: No. 5). E-Book 8.99 o.p. incl. cd-rom (*1-57646-055-X*); 2000. (Anne of Green Gables Ser.: Vol. 5). 336p. pap. 24.99 (*1-57646-314-1*); 2000. (Anne of Green Gables Ser.: Vol. No. 5). 336p. lib. bdg. 33.99 (*1-57646-315-X*) Quiet Vision Publishing.

—Anne's House of Dreams. 1994. (Avonlea Ser.: No. 5). (YA). (gr. 5-8). o.s.i (*0-553-85030-X*, Dell Books for Young Readers) Random Hse. Children's Bks.

—Anne's House of Dreams. 1996. (Avonlea Ser.: No. 5). viii, 193p. (YA). (gr. 5-8). 8.99 o.s.i (*0-517-14820-X*) Random Hse. Value Publishing.

—Anne's House of Dreams. 1994. (Avonlea Ser.: No. 5). 238p. (YA). (gr. 5-8). text 5.98 o.p. (*1-56138-430-5*, Courage Bks.) Running Pr. Bk. Pubs.

—Anne's House of Dreams. 1972. (Avonlea Ser.: No. 5). (YA). (gr. 5-8). 10.55 (*0-606-00376-2*) Turtleback Bks.

—The Annotated Anne of Green Gables. Jones, Mary E. Doody et al, eds. annot. ed. 1997. (Illus.). 504p. (J). 39.95 (*0-19-510428-5*) Oxford Univ. Pr., Inc.

—Avonlea Boxed Set: Anne of the Island; Anne's House of Dreams. (Avonlea Ser.: No. 4-5). 464p. (YA). (gr. 5-8). reprint ed. 2000. 9.00 o.p. (*0-7624-0561-9*); 1997. text 8.98 o.p. (*0-7624-0113-3*, Courage Bks.) Running Pr. Bk. Pubs.

—Chronicles of Avonlea. 1988. (Avonlea Ser.: No. 3). 192p. (YA). (gr. 5-8). mass mkt. 3.99 (*0-553-21378-4*, Dell Books for Young Readers) Random Hse. Children's Bks.

—Chronicles of Avonlea. 1988. (Avonlea Ser.: No. 3). (YA). (gr. 5-8). 10.04 (*0-606-03755-1*) Turtleback Bks.

—The Chronicles of Avonlea. 1987. (Avonlea Ser.: No. 3). 192p. (YA). (gr. 5-8). mass mkt. 3.99 (*0-7704-2161-X*) Bantam Bks.

—The Complete Anne of Green Gables: Anne of Green Gables; Anne of the Island; Anne of Avonlea; Anne of Windy Poplars; Anne's House of Dreams; Anne of Ingleside; Rainbow Valley; Rilla of Ingleside, 8 vols. gif. ed. 1997. (J). (gr. 4-7). mass mkt. 36.00 (*0-553-60941-6*) Bantam Bks.

—Further Chronicles of Avonlea. 1987. (Avonlea Ser.: No. 7). 208p. (YA). (gr. 5-8). mass mkt. 3.95 (*0-7704-2162-8*) Bantam Bks.

—Further Chronicles of Avonlea. 1970. (Avonlea Ser.: No. 7). (YA). (gr. 5-8). 6.95 o.p. (*0-448-02551-5*) Putnam Publishing Group, The.

—Further Chronicles of Avonlea. 1989. (Avonlea Ser.: No. 7). 208p. (YA). (gr. 5-8). mass mkt. 3.99 (*0-553-21381-4*, Starfire) Random Hse. Children's Bks.

—The Golden Road. 1976. 382p. (J). 23.95 (*0-8488-0720-0*) Amereon, Ltd.

—The Golden Road. 224p. (J). 1989. (gr. 4-7). mass mkt. 4.50 o.s.i (*0-553-21367-9*, Bantam Classics); 1987. mass mkt. 3.95 o.s.i (*0-7704-2182-2*) Bantam Bks.

—The Golden Road. unabr. ed. 1999. (YA). audio 44.95 (*0-7861-1489-4*, 897841) Blackstone Audio Bks., Inc.

—The Golden Road, Set. unabr. ed. 1999. audio 44.95 Highsmith Inc.

—The Golden Road. 2002. 236p. per. 19.99 (*1-4043-0523-8*) IndyPublish.com.

—The Golden Road. (YA). E-Book 1.95 (*1-57799-898-7*) Logos Research Systems, Inc.

—The Golden Road. 2000. (Sara Stanley of Avonlea Series: Vol. 2). 180p. (YA). lib. bdg. 19.99 (*1-57646-317-6*); 2000. (Sara Stanley of Avonlea Series: Vol. 2). 180p. (YA). pap. 10.99 (*1-57646-316-8*); 1999. E-Book 3.99 o.p. incl. cd-rom (*1-57646-056-8*); 2000. (Sara Stanley of Avonlea Ser.: Vol. 2). 328p. (YA). pap. 24.99 (*1-57646-318-4*); 2000. (Sara Stanley of Avonlea Ser.: Vol. 2). 328p. (YA). lib. bdg. 32.99 (*1-57646-319-2*) Quiet Vision Publishing.

—The Golden Road. E-Book 5.00 (*0-7410-1094-1*) SoftBook Pr.

—Jane of Lantern Hill. (YA). 1989. 224p. mass mkt. 2.95 o.s.i (*0-553-28049-X*); 1988. 288p. mass mkt. 3.99 (*0-7704-2314-0*) Bantam Bks.

—Jane of Lantern Hill. 1989. (J). pap. o.p. (*0-7710-6165-X*) McClelland & Stewart/Tundra Bks.

—Kilmeny of the Orchard. 1976. 264p. (J). 22.95 (*0-8488-0721-9*) Amereon, Ltd.

—Kilmeny of the Orchard. 144p. (J). 1989. (gr. 4-7). mass mkt. 4.50 (*0-553-21377-6*); 1987. mass mkt. 3.95 o.s.i (*0-7704-2181-4*) Bantam Bks.

—Pat of Silver Bush. 1988. 288p. (YA). (gr. 4-7). mass mkt. 4.99 (*0-7704-2247-0*) Bantam Bks.

—Pat of Silver Bush. (Illus.). 380p. (J). pap. 4.98 (*0-7710-6167-6*) McClelland & Stewart/Tundra Bks.

—Rainbow Valley. 1976. (Avonlea Ser.: No. 6). 234p. (YA). (gr. 5-8). 21.95 (*0-8488-0591-7*) Amereon, Ltd.

—Rainbow Valley. (Avonlea Ser.: No. 6). (gr. 5-8). 1987. 256p. (J). mass mkt. 4.99 (*0-7704-2268-3*); 1985. 240p. (YA). mass mkt. 2.95 o.s.i (*0-553-25213-5*) Bantam Bks.

—Rainbow Valley, unabr. ed. 1995. (Avonlea Ser.: No. 6). (YA). (gr. 5-8). audio 44.95 (*0-7861-0913-0*, 1704) Blackstone Audio Bks., Inc.

—Rainbow Valley. unabr. ed. 1999. (Avonlea Ser.: No. 6). (YA). (gr. 5-8). audio 44.95 Highsmith Inc.

—Rainbow Valley. (Avonlea Ser.: No. 6). (YA). (gr. 5-8). E-Book 1.95 (*1-57799-881-2*) Logos Research Systems, Inc.

—Rainbow Valley. 1985. (Avonlea Ser.: No. 6). 256p. (YA). (gr. 5-8). mass mkt. 4.50 (*0-553-26921-6*, Dell Books for Young Readers) Random Hse. Children's Bks.

—Rainbow Valley. 1985. (Avonlea Ser.: No. 6). (YA). (gr. 5-8). 10.04 (*0-606-02613-4*) Turtleback Bks.

—Rilla of Ingleside. 1976. (Avonlea Ser.: No. 8). 286p. (YA). (gr. 5-8). 23.95 (*0-8488-0592-5*) Amereon, Ltd.

—Rilla of Ingleside. (Avonlea Ser.: No. 8). (YA). (gr. 5-8). 1987. 288p. mass mkt. 3.99 (*0-7704-2185-7*); 1985. 304p. mass mkt. 4.50 (*0-553-26922-4*) Bantam Bks.

—Rilla of Ingleside. unabr. ed. 1998. (Avonlea Ser.: No. 8). (YA). (gr. 5-8). audio 56.95 (*0-7861-1275-1*, 2172) Blackstone Audio Bks., Inc.

—Rilla of Ingleside. 1985. (Avonlea Ser.: No. 8). 288p. (YA). (gr. 5-8). mass mkt. 2.95 o.s.i (*0-553-25241-0*, Starfire) Random Hse. Children's Bks.

—Rilla of Ingleside. 1997. (Avonlea Ser.: No. 8). (Illus.). (YA). (gr. 5-8). 7.99 (*0-517-18083-9*) Random Hse. Value Publishing.

—Rilla of Ingleside. 1985. (Avonlea Ser.: No. 8). (YA). (gr. 5-8). 10.04 (*0-606-00747-4*) Turtleback Bks.

—The Road to Yesterday. 1993. 416p. (YA). (gr. 4-7). mass mkt. 4.99 (*0-553-56068-9*) Bantam Bks.

—The Rock to Yesterday. 1993. 416p. (J). mass mkt. 4.50 o.s.i (*0-7704-2551-8*) Bantam Bks.

—The Story Girl. Date not set. 22.95 (*0-8488-2372-9*) Amereon, Ltd.

—The Story Girl. 272p. 1988. (J). mass mkt. 4.50 o.s.i (*0-553-21366-0*, Bantam Classics); 1987. (YA). mass mkt. 4.99 (*0-7704-2285-3*) Bantam Bks.

—The Story Girl. unabr. ed. 1997. audio 49.95 Blackstone Audio Bks., Inc.

—The Story Girl, Set. unabr. ed. 1999. (J). audio 49.95 Highsmith Inc.

—The Story Girl. 1991. 288p. (YA). mass mkt. 3.95 o.s.i (*0-451-52532-9*, Signet Classics) NAL.

—The Story Girl. 2000. (Sara Stanley of Avonlea Series: Vol. vol 1). (YA). 178p. pap. 10.99 (*1-57646-321-4*); 178p. lib. bdg. 19.99 (*1-57646-322-2*); 453p. E-Book 3.99 incl. cd-rom (*1-57646-320-6*); 370p. pap. 24.99 (*1-57646-323-0*); 370p. lib. bdg. 34.99 (*1-57646-324-9*) Quiet Vision Publishing.

—The Story Girl. 1996. vi, 231p. 8.99 o.s.i (*0-517-14818-8*) Random Hse., Inc.

Montgomery, L. M. & Outlet Book Company Staff. Rainbow Valley. 1995. (Avonlea Ser.: No. 6). (Illus.). xi, 256p. (YA). (gr. 5-8). 7.99 o.s.i (*0-517-10192-0*) Random Hse. Value Publishing.

Montgomery, L. M. & Tanaka, Shelley. Anne of Green Gables. 1998. (Avonlea Ser.: No. 1). 112p. (gr. 5-8). text 12.95 o.s.i (*0-385-32333-6*, Dell Books for Young Readers) Random Hse. Children's Bks.

Perry, Katy. The Laughing Lighthouse. Lyons Graphic Design Staff, ed. 1995. (Illus.). 16p. (Orig.). (J). (gr. 1-4). pap. 7.50 (*0-9626823-6-5*) Perry Publishing.

Peterson. Anne of Green Gables. 1999. (Avonlea Ser.: No. 1). 32p. (YA). (gr. 5-8). pap. 4.95 (*0-06-443535-0*) HarperCollins Children's Bk. Group.

Tanaka, Shelley. Anne of Green Gables. 1998. (Avonlea Ser.: No. 1). 112p. (gr. 5-8). mass mkt. 5.99 (*0-7704-2744-8*) Bantam Bks.

PRYDAIN (IMAGINARY PLACE)—FICTION

Alexander, Lloyd. The Black Cauldron. 1999. (Chronicles of Prydain Ser.). 256p. (gr. 5-7). mass mkt. 2.99 o.s.i (*0-440-22883-2*) Bantam Bks.

—The Black Cauldron. 1997. (Chronicles of Prydain Ser.). (J). mass mkt. 2.69 o.p. (*0-440-22743-7*) Dell Publishing.

—The Black Cauldron, ERS. (Chronicles of Prydain). 224p. (J). 1965. (gr. 4-6). 17.95 o.s.i (*0-8050-0992-2*); 1999. (Illus.). (gr. 3-7). 19.95 (*0-8050-6131-2*) Holt, Henry & Co. (Holt, Henry & Co. Bks. For Young Readers).

—The Black Cauldron. (Chronicles of Prydain Ser.). 1993. (J). mass mkt. o.p. (*0-440-90052-2*, Dell Books for Young Readers); 1985. 240p. (gr. 5-9). pap. text 5.99 (*0-440-40649-8*, Yearling); 1980. 220p. (J). mass mkt. 3.50 (*0-440-90649-0*, Laurel Leaf) Random Hse. Children's Bks.

—The Black Cauldron. 1965. (Chronicles of Prydain Ser.). (J). 11.55 (*0-606-02354-2*) Turtleback Bks.

—The Book of Three. 1995. (Chronicles of Prydain Ser.). (J). 5.99 (*0-440-91069-2*) Dell Publishing.

—The Book of Three. (Chronicles of Prydain Ser.). (J). ERS. 1996. o.p. (*0-03-046205-3*); ERS. 1964. 224p. (gr. 4-6). 16.95 o.p. (*0-8050-0874-8*); ERS. 1999. (Illus.). 224p. (gr. 3-7). 19.95 (*0-8050-6132-0*); Vol. 1. 1964. 11.95 o.p. (*0-03-089821-8*) Holt, Henry & Co. (Holt, Henry & Co. Bks. For Young Readers).

—The Book of Three. unabr. ed. 1991. (YA). (gr. 5 up). pap. 37.00 incl. audio (*0-8072-7348-1*, YA 834 SP, Listening Library) Random Hse. Audio Publishing Group.

—The Book of Three. (Chronicles of Prydain Ser.). 1993. (J). pap. o.p. (*0-440-90054-9*, Dell Books for Young Readers); 1980. 224p. (gr. 5-9). mass mkt. 3.99 o.s.i (*0-440-90702-0*, Laurel Leaf); 1978. 224p. (gr. 5-9). pap. text 5.99 (*0-440-40702-8*, Yearling) Random Hse. Children's Bks.

—The Book of Three. 1964. (Chronicles of Prydain Ser.). (J). 12.04 (*0-606-02410-7*) Turtleback Bks.

—The Castle of Llyr, ERS. (Chronicles of Prydain Ser.). 208p. (J). 1999. (Illus.). (gr. 3-7). 19.95 (*0-8050-6133-9*); 1966. (gr. 4-6). 16.95 o.p. (*0-8050-1115-3*) Holt, Henry & Co. (Holt, Henry & Co. Bks. For Young Readers).

—The Castle of Llyr. (Chronicles of Prydain Ser.). 1993. (J). mass mkt. o.p. (*0-440-90053-0*, Dell Books for Young Readers); 1980. 208p. (gr. 5-9). mass mkt. 3.50 o.s.i (*0-440-91125-7*, Laurel Leaf); 1969. 208p. (gr. 5-9). pap. text 5.99 (*0-440-41125-4*, Yearling) Random Hse. Children's Bks.

—The Castle of Llyr. 1966. (Chronicles of Prydain Ser.). (J). 11.55 (*0-606-02572-3*) Turtleback Bks.

—The Foundling: And Other Tales of Prydain, ERS. 1999. (Illus.). 96p. (J). (gr. 3-7). 19.95 (*0-8050-6130-4*, Holt, Henry & Co. Bks. For Young Readers) Holt, Henry & Co.

—The Foundling: And Other Tales of Prydain. 1996. 128p. (J). (gr. 4-7). pap. 4.99 (*0-14-037825-1*, Puffin Bks.) Penguin Putnam Bks. for Young Readers.

—The Foundling: And Other Tales of Prydain. 1982. 128p. (YA). (gr. 5 up). pap. 3.50 o.s.i (*0-440-42536-0*, Yearling) Random Hse. Children's Bks.

—The Foundling: And Other Tales of Prydain. 1992. (J). 17.00 o.p. (*0-8446-6546-0*) Smith, Peter Pub., Inc.

—The High King. 1996. (Chronicles of Prydain Ser.). 304p. (J). mass mkt. 2.49 o.s.i (*0-440-22030-0*) Dell Publishing.

—The High King, ERS. (Chronicles of Prydain). (J). 1968. 288p. (gr. 4-6). 16.95 o.p. (*0-8050-1114-5*); 1999. (Illus.). 253p. (gr. 3-7). 19.95 (*0-8050-6135-5*) Holt, Henry & Co. (Holt, Henry & Co. Bks. For Young Readers).

—The High King. (Chronicles of Prydain Ser.). 1980. 288p. (YA). (gr. 5-9). mass mkt. 3.99 (*0-440-93574-1*, Laurel Leaf); 1969. 304p. (gr. 4-7). pap. text 5.99 (*0-440-43574-9*, Yearling) Random Hse. Children's Bks.

—The High King. 1968. (Chronicles of Prydain Ser.). (J). 11.55 (*0-606-03530-3*) Turtleback Bks.

—Taran Wanderer, ERS. (Chronicles of Prydain Ser.). (J). 1967. 11.95 o.p. (*0-03-089732-7*); 1967. 256p. (gr. 4-6). 16.95 o.p. (*0-8050-1113-7*); 1999. 222p. (gr. 3-7). 19.95 (*0-8050-6134-7*) Holt, Henry & Co. (Holt, Henry & Co. Bks. For Young Readers).

—Taran Wanderer. (Chronicles of Prydain Ser.). 1993. (J). mass mkt. o.p. (*0-440-90057-3*, Dell Books for Young Readers); 1980. 256p. (gr. 5-9). mass mkt. 1.75 o.s.i (*0-440-98483-1*, Laurel Leaf); 1969. 272p. (gr. 7 up). pap. text 5.99 (*0-440-48483-9*, Yearling) Random Hse. Children's Bks.

—Taran Wanderer. 1967. (Chronicles of Prydain Ser.). (J). 12.04 (*0-606-00482-3*) Turtleback Bks.

Mouse Works Staff & Alexander, Lloyd. The Black Cauldron. 1997. (Chronicles of Prydain Ser.). (J). (*1-57082-796-6*) Mouse Works.

PUERTO RICO—FICTION

Barry, Robert. Ramon & the Pirate Gull. 1971. (J). (gr. k-3). lib. bdg. o.p. (*0-07-003833-3*) McGraw-Hill Cos., The.

Barsy, Kalman. Del Nacimiento de la Isla de Boriken. 1982. (Coleccion Sur). (SPA., Illus.). 76p. (J). (gr. 6). pap. 8.75 (*0-940238-01-2*) Ediciones Huracan, Inc.

Belpré, Pura. Santiago. 1969. (Illus.). (J). (gr. k-3). 7.95 o.p. (*0-7232-6019-2*, Warne, Frederick) Penguin Putnam Bks. for Young Readers.

Bernier-Grand, Carmen T. In the Shade of the Nispero Tree. 2001. 192p. (gr. 4-7). pap. text 4.50 o.s.i (*0-440-41660-4*, Dell Books for Young Readers) Random Hse. Children's Bks.

—In the Shade of the Nispero Tree. 1999. 192p. (J). (gr. 4-7). pap. 15.95 (*0-531-30154-0*); lib. bdg. 16.99 (*0-531-33154-7*) Scholastic, Inc. (Orchard Bks.).

Delace, Lulu. Rafi & Rosi Coqui. 2004. (I Can Read Book 3 Ser.). 64p. (J). lib. bdg. 16.89 (*0-06-009896-1*) HarperCollins Pubs.

Delacre, Lulu. Rafi & Rosi Coqui. 2004. (I Can Read Book 3 Ser.). 64p. (J). 15.99 (*0-06-009895-3*) HarperCollins Pubs.

Green, Yuko. Marisol from Puerto Rico. 1998. pap. 1.00 (*0-486-40319-X*) Dover Pubns., Inc.

Heron, Virginia. Pedro's Gift. 1980. (Third Grade Bk.). (Illus.). (gr. 3-4). lib. bdg. 4.95 o.p. (*0-513-00507-2*) Denison, T. S. & Co., Inc.

Ichikawa, Satomi. Isabela's Ribbons. 1995. (Illus.). 32p. (J). (gr. 1-3). 15.95 o.p. (*0-399-22772-5*, Philomel) Penguin Putnam Bks. for Young Readers.

London, Jonathan. The Hurricane. 1924. (Illus.). (J). o.s.i (*0-688-08117-7*) HarperCollins Children's Bk. Group.

—Island Hurricane. 1924. (Illus.). (J). lib. bdg. o.s.i (*0-688-08118-5*) HarperCollins Children's Bk. Group.

Martel, Cruz. Yagua Days. 1995. (Illus.). (J). (gr. 3). 8.60 (*0-395-73235-2*) Houghton Mifflin Co.

—Yagua Days. 1987. (Pied Piper Bks.). (Illus.). 40p. (J). (ps-3). 11.89 o.p. (*0-8037-9766-4*); pap. 4.95 o.p. (*0-8037-0457-7*) Penguin Putnam Bks. for Young Readers. (Dial Bks. for Young Readers).

Merced De Mendez, Ana T. Tales from the Island: Puerto Rican Stories. 1995. (Illus.). (J). (gr. 6-10). 60p. 20.00 (*0-9627442-1-2*); 70p. wbk. ed. 12.95 (*0-9627442-2-0*) Merced de Mendez, Ana T.

Misla, Victor M. Little Anabo from Boriken. 1987. (Illus.). 28p. (Orig.). (YA). (gr. 6-7). pap. 5.00 (*0-9626870-0-6*) Northwest Monarch Pr.

Settings

Nodar, Carmen M. Abuelita's Paradise. Mathews, Judith, ed. 1992. (Illus.). 32p. (J). (ps-3). lib. bdg. 14.95 o.p. (0-8075-0129-8) Whitman, Albert & Co.

Nodar, Carmen S. El Paraiso de Abuelita. Mathews, Judith, ed. Mlawer, Teresa, tr. 1992. (SPA., Illus.). 32p. (J). (gr. k-3). lib. bdg. 14.95 o.p. (0-8075-6346-3, WT4618) Whitman, Albert & Co.

Nodar, Carmen Santiago. Abuelita's Paradise. unabr. ed. 2001. (J). (gr. k-3). 25.90 incl. audio (0-8045-6847-2, 6847) Spoken Arts, Inc.

Picó, Fernando. The Red Comb. 1994. 11.10 (0-606-08064-3) Turtleback Bks.

Pomerantz, Charlotte. The Outside Dog. (I Can Read Bks.). (Illus.). 64p. (J). 1995. (gr. k-3). pap. 3.99 (0-06-444187-3, Harper Trophy); 1993. (gr. k-3). lib. bdg. 15.89 (0-06-024783-5); 1993. (gr. 2-4). 14.95 o.p. (0-06-024782-7) HarperCollins Children's Bk. Group.

—The Outside Dog. 1995. (I Can Read Bks.). (J). (gr. 2-4). 10.10 (0-606-07983-1) Turtleback Bks.

Scharde, Arlene O. Gabriel the Happy Ghost in Puerto Rico. 1985. Tr. of Gabriel el Fantasmita Simpatico en Puerto Rico. (ENG & SPA.). (J). 11.80 (0-606-01275-3) Turtleback Bks.

Wallner, Alexandra. Sergio & the Hurricane, ERS. 2000. (Illus.). 32p. (J). (ps-2). 16.00 (0-8050-6203-3, Holt, Henry & Co. Bks. For Young Readers) Holt, Henry & Co.

PUGET SOUND (WASH.)—FICTION

Thesman, Jean. Moonstones. 208p. (YA). (gr. 5-9). 2000. (Illus.). pap. 5.99 (0-14-130809-5, Puffin Bks.); 1998. 15.99 o.s.i (0-670-87959-2) Penguin Putnam Bks. for Young Readers.

Q

QUEBEC (PROVINCE)—FICTION

Bruchac, Joseph. The Winter People. 2002. (Illus.). 176p. (J). 16.99 (0-8037-2694-5, Dial Bks. for Young Readers) Penguin Putnam Bks. for Young Readers.

Carrier, Roch. The Longest Home Run. braille ed. 1994. Orig. Title: Le Plus Long Circuit. (J). (gr. 2). spiral bd. (0-616-01614-X) Canadian National Institute for the Blind/Institut National Canadien pour les Aveugles.

—The Longest Home Run. Fischman, Sheila, tr. from FRE. Orig. Title: Le Plus Long Circuit. (Illus.). 24p. (J). (gr. 3). 2001. pap. 7.95 (0-88776-312-X); 1993. 15.95 (0-88776-300-6) Tundra Bks. of Northern New York.

Downie, Mary Alice & Downie, John. Danger in Disguise. 2001. (On Time's Wing Ser.). (Illus.). 178p. (J). (gr. 4-7). pap. 6.95 (1-896184-72-3) Roussan Pubs., Inc./Roussan Editeur, Inc. CAN. *Dist:* Orca Bk. Pubs.

Dubois, Muriel L. Abenaki Captive. 16.00 (0-9723410-0-5) Apprentice Shop Bks., LLC.

—Abenaki Captive. 1994. (J). (gr. 4-7). lib. bdg. 15.95 o.s.i (0-87614-753-8, Carolrhoda Bks.) Lerner Publishing Group.

Mangin, Marie-France. Suzette & Nicholas & the Seasons Clock. 1982. (Illus.). 32p. (J). (ps). 8.95 o.p. (0-399-20832-1, Philomel) Penguin Putnam Bks. for Young Readers.

Warner, Gertrude Chandler. The Mystery of the Screech Owl. 2001. (Boxcar Children Special Ser.: No. 16). (Illus.). 144p. (J). (gr. 2-5). pap. 3.95 (0-8075-5482-0); lib. bdg. 13.95 (0-8075-5481-2) Whitman, Albert & Co.

Wilson, Eric G. Cold Midnight in Old Quebec. 2002. (Eric Wilson Mysteries Ser.). Orig. Title: Cold Midnight in Vieux Quebec. 121p. (J). 4.99 (1-55143-191-2) Orca Bk. Pubs.

QUEBEC (QUEBEC)—FICTION

Page, Katherine Hall. Bon Voyage, Christie & Company. 1998. (Christie & Company Ser.). 288p. (YA). (gr. 6-8). 14.00 (0-380-97398-7) HarperCollins Pubs.

—Bon Voyage, Christie & Company. 1999. (Christie & Company Ser.). (Illus.). (YA). (gr. 6-8). pap. 3.99 (0-380-78035-6, Avon Bks.) Morrow/Avon.

R

REDWALL ABBEY (IMAGINARY PLACE)—FICTION

Jacques, Brian. The Bellmaker. 1996. (Redwall Ser.). (Illus.). 416p. (J). (gr. 4-8). mass mkt. 6.99 (0-441-00315-X) Ace Bks.

—The Bellmaker. 1995. (Redwall Ser.). (Illus.). 352p. (J). (gr. 4-8). 23.99 (0-399-22805-5, Philomel) Penguin Putnam Bks. for Young Readers.

—The Bellmaker. 1996. (Redwall Ser.). (J). (gr. 4-8). 13.04 (0-606-12888-3) Turtleback Bks.

—Build Your Own Redwall Abbey. 1998. (Illus.). 16p. (J). (gr. 4-7). 19.99 o.p. (0-399-23379-2, Philomel) Penguin Putnam Bks. for Young Readers.

—The Great Redwall Feast. (Redwall Ser.). (Illus.). 64p. (J). (gr. 4-8). 2000. pap. 6.99 (0-698-11876-6, Puffin Bks.); 1996. 18.99 (0-399-22707-5, G. P. Putnam's Sons) Penguin Putnam Bks. for Young Readers.

—The Great Redwall Feast. 2000. (Redwall Ser.). (J). (gr. 4-8). 13.14 (0-606-20236-6); 13.14 (0-606-20360-5) Turtleback Bks.

—The Legend of Luke. 2001. (Redwall Ser.). 368p. (J). (gr. 4-8). reprint ed. mass mkt. 6.99 (0-441-00773-2) Ace Bks.

—The Legend of Luke. abr. ed. 1999. (Redwall Ser.). 3p. (J). (gr. 4-8). audio 17.95 o.p. (0-399-14605-9, Putnam Berkley Audio) Penguin Group (USA) Inc.

—The Legend of Luke. 2000. (Redwall Ser.). (Illus.). 374p. (J). (gr. 4-8). 22.95 (0-399-23490-X, Philomel) Penguin Putnam Bks. for Young Readers.

—The Legend of Luke. l.t. ed. 2000. (Redwall Ser.). (Illus.). 534p. (J). (gr. 4-8). 23.95 (0-7862-2662-5) Thorndike Pr.

—The Long Patrol. 1999. (Redwall Ser.). (Illus.). 336p. (J). (gr. 4-8). reprint ed. mass mkt. 6.99 (0-441-00599-3) Ace Bks.

—The Long Patrol. 1998. (Redwall Ser.). (J). (gr. 4-8). (Illus.). 368p. 22.99 (0-399-23165-X, Philomel); audio 17.95 o.p. (0-399-14384-X, Putnam Berkley Audio) Penguin Putnam Bks. for Young Readers.

—The Long Patrol. 1999. (Redwall Ser.). (J). (gr. 4-8). 13.04 (0-606-15882-0) Turtleback Bks.

—Lord Brocktree. 2000. (Redwall Ser.: Vol. 13). (Illus.). 370p. (J). (gr. 4-8). 22.95 (0-399-23590-6, G. P. Putnam's Sons) Penguin Putnam Bks. for Young Readers.

—Lord Brocktree. abr. ed. 2000. (Redwall Ser.). (J). (gr. 4-8). audio 18.95 (0-399-14679-2, Putnam Berkley Audio) Putnam Publishing Group, The.

—Mariel of Redwall. 2000. (Redwall Ser.). (Illus.). 384p. (J). (gr. 4-8). mass mkt. 6.99 (0-441-00694-9) Ace Bks.

—Mariel of Redwall. 1999. (Redwall Ser.). (Illus.). 400p. (gr. 4-8). mass mkt. 5.99 o.s.i (0-380-71922-3, Avon Bks.) Morrow/Avon.

—Mariel of Redwall. (Redwall Ser.). (Illus.). 400p. (J). 2003. pap. 7.99 (0-14-230239-2, Firebird); 1992. (gr. 4-8). 23.99 (0-399-22144-1, Philomel) Penguin Putnam Bks. for Young Readers.

—Mariel of Redwall. 1991. (Redwall Ser.). (J). (gr. 4-8). 13.04 (0-606-18010-9) Turtleback Bks.

—Marlfox. 2000. (Redwall Ser.). (Illus.). 384p. (J). (gr. 4-8). reprint ed. mass mkt. 6.99 (0-441-00693-0) Ace Bks.

—Marlfox. (Redwall Ser.). (J). (gr. 4-8). 1998. (Illus.). 386p. 22.99 (0-399-23307-5, Philomel); 1999. audio 17.95 o.p. (0-399-14479-X, 396220) Penguin Putnam Bks. for Young Readers.

—Martin the Warrior. 1995. (Redwall Ser.). (Illus.). 384p. (J). (gr. 4-8). mass mkt. 6.99 (0-441-00186-6) Ace Bks.

—Martin the Warrior. unabr. ed. 1999. (Redwall Ser.). (J). (gr. 4-8). audio 52.00 BBC Audiobooks America.

—Martin the Warrior. 1998. (Redwall Ser.: Bk. 2). (J). (gr. 4-8). audio 17.95 Blackstone Audio Bks., Inc.

—Martin the Warrior. 2000. (Redwall Ser.). (J). (gr. 4-8). audio 50.00 Books on Tape, Inc.

—Martin the Warrior. 1994. (Redwall Ser.). (J). (gr. 4-8). o.p. (0-03-992267-7); (Illus.). 400p. 23.99 (0-399-22670-2) Penguin Putnam Bks. for Young Readers. (Philomel).

—Martin the Warrior. unabr. ed. 1999. (Redwall Ser.). (Illus.). (J). (gr. 4-8). 35.00 incl. audio (0-8072-8182-4, YA124CXR, Listening Library) Random Hse. Audio Publishing Group.

—Martin the Warrior. 1996. (Redwall Ser.). (J). (gr. 4-8). 13.04 (0-606-12990-1) Turtleback Bks.

—Martin the Warrior Bk. 1: The Prisoner & the Tyrant. unabr. ed. 1999. (Redwall Ser.). (J). (gr. 4-8). audio 19.95 (0-8072-8150-6, BWYA111CXR); audio 23.98 (0-8072-8128-X, BWYA111CX) Random Hse. Audio Publishing Group. (Listening Library).

—Martin the Warrior Bk. 2: Actors & Searchers. unabr. ed. 1999. (Redwall Ser.). (J). (gr. 4-8). audio 23.98 Random Hse. Audio Publishing Group.

—Martin the Warrior Bk. 3: The Battle of Marshank. unabr. ed. 1999. (Redwall Ser.). (J). (gr. 4-8). audio 23.98 (0-8072-8159-X, BWYA122CX, Listening Library) Random Hse. Audio Publishing Group.

—Martin the Warrior Bks. 1-3: The Prisoner & the Tyrant; Actors & Searchers; The Battle of Marshank. unabr. ed. 1999. (Redwall Ser.). (J). (gr. 4-8). audio 59.98 Highsmith Inc.

—Martin the Warrior Bks. 1-3: The Prisoner & the Tyrant; Actors & Searchers; The Battle of Marshank. unabr. ed. 1999. (Redwall Ser.). (J). (gr. 4-8). 376p. pap. 56.00 incl. audio (0-8072-8178-6, YA124SP); 10p. audio 50.00 (0-8072-8177-8, YA124CX) Random Hse. Audio Publishing Group. (Listening Library).

—Mattimeo. 1999. (Redwall Ser.). (Illus.). 448p. (J). (gr. 4-8). mass mkt. 6.99 (0-441-00610-8) Ace Bks.

—Mattimeo. 1991. (Redwall Ser.). (Illus.). 448p. (gr. 4-8). mass mkt. 5.99 (0-380-71530-9, Avon Bks.) Morrow/Avon.

—Mattimeo. (Firebird Ser.). (Illus.). 448p. (J). 2003. pap. 7.99 (0-14-230240-6, Firebird); 1990. (gr. 4-8). 23.99 (0-399-21741-X, Philomel) Penguin Putnam Bks. for Young Readers.

—Mattimeo. 1991. (Redwall Ser.). (J). (gr. 4-8). 12.04 (0-606-05456-1) Turtleback Bks.

—Mossflower. 1998. (Redwall Ser.). (Illus.). 384p. (J). (gr. 4-8). reprint ed. mass mkt. 6.99 (0-441-00576-4) Ace Bks.

—Mossflower. 1990. (Redwall Ser.). 384p. (J). (gr. 4-8). mass mkt. 5.99 (0-380-70828-0, Avon Bks.) Morrow/Avon.

—Mossflower. 2002. (Firebird Ser.). (Illus.). 432p. pap. 7.99 (0-14-230238-4) Penguin Group (USA) Inc.

—Mossflower. 1988. (Redwall Ser.). (Illus.). 432p. (J). (gr. 4-8). 23.99 (0-399-21549-2, Philomel) Penguin Putnam Bks. for Young Readers.

—Mossflower. unabr. ed. 1997. (Redwall Ser.). (J). (gr. 4-8). audio 87.00 (0-7887-0538-5, 94733E7) Recorded Bks., LLC.

—Mossflower. 1998. (Redwall Ser.). (J). (gr. 4-8). 13.04 (0-606-15640-2) Turtleback Bks.

—Outcast of Redwall. 1997. (Redwall Ser.). (Illus.). 384p. (J). (gr. 4-8). mass mkt. 6.99 (0-441-00416-4) Ace Bks.

—Outcast of Redwall. 1996. (Redwall Ser.). (Illus.). 360p. (J). (gr. 4-8). 23.99 (0-399-22914-0, Philomel) Penguin Putnam Bks. for Young Readers.

—Outcast of Redwall. 1997. (Redwall Ser.). (J). (gr. 4-8). 13.04 (0-606-13011-X) Turtleback Bks.

—Pearls of Lutra. 1998. (Redwall Ser.). (Illus.). 368p. (J). (gr. 4-8). mass mkt. 6.99 (0-441-00508-X) Ace Bks.

—Pearls of Lutra. 1997. (Redwall Ser.). (J). (gr. 4-8). (Illus.). 416p. 23.99 (0-399-22946-9, Philomel); 17.95 o.p. incl. audio (0-399-23178-1, 395054) Penguin Putnam Bks. for Young Readers.

—Pearls of Lutra. 1998. (Redwall Ser.). (J). (gr. 4-8). 13.04 (0-606-13015-2) Turtleback Bks.

—Redwall. 10th anniv. ed. 1998. (Redwall Ser.). (Illus.). 352p. (J). (gr. 4-8). mass mkt. 6.99 (0-441-00548-9) Ace Bks.

—Redwall. 2001. (Redwall Ser.). 352p. (J). (gr. 4-8). 1.99 (0-441-00817-8) Berkley Publishing Group.

—Redwall. 2000. (Redwall Ser.). (J). (gr. 4-8). audio 50.00 (0-7366-9097-2) Books on Tape, Inc.

—Redwall. 1990. (Redwall Ser.). (Illus.). 352p. (J). (gr. 4-8). mass mkt. 5.99 o.p. (0-380-70827-2, Avon Bks.) Morrow/Avon.

—Redwall. (Firebird Ser.). 2002. (Illus.). 352p. pap. 7.99 (0-14-230237-6); 1997. (J). (gr. 4-8). 22.95 (0-399-23073-4, Perigee Bks.) Penguin Group (USA) Inc.

—Redwall. (Redwall Ser.). (Illus.). (J). (gr. 4-8). 2000. 368p. pap. 12.95 (0-399-23629-5); 1987. 351p. 23.99 (0-399-21424-0); 1997. 368p. 22.95 o.p. (0-399-23160-9) Penguin Putnam Bks. for Young Readers. (Philomel).

—Redwall. (Redwall Ser.). (J). (gr. 4-8). 2001. audio compact disk 49.95 (0-8072-6204-8); 2001. audio compact disk 55.00 (0-8072-8610-9); Bks. 1-3. 2000. audio 35.00 (0-8072-8190-5) Random Hse. Audio Publishing Group. (Listening Library).

—Redwall. unabr. ed. 1997. (Redwall Ser.). (J). (gr. 4-8). audio 77.00 (0-7887-0382-X, 94573E7) Recorded Bks., LLC.

—Redwall. 1998. (Redwall Ser.). (J). (gr. 4-8). 13.04 (0-606-13734-3) Turtleback Bks.

—Redwall Bk. 1: The Wall. 1999. (Redwall Ser.). (J). (gr. 4-8). audio 15.98 NewSound, LLC.

—Redwall Bk. 1: The Wall. unabr. ed. 1997. (Redwall Ser.). (J). (gr. 4-8). audio 19.95 (0-8072-7840-8, 495624, Listening Library) Random Hse. Audio Publishing Group.

—Redwall Bk. 2: The Quest. 1999. (Redwall Ser.). (J). (gr. 4-8). audio 15.98 NewSound, LLC.

—Redwall Bk. 2: The Quest. unabr. ed. 1998. (Redwall Ser.). (J). (gr. 4-8). audio 19.95 (0-8072-7965-X, YA943CXR, Listening Library) Random Hse. Audio Publishing Group.

—Redwall Bk. 3: The Warrior. (Redwall Ser.). (J). (gr. 4-8). audio 12.78 NewSound, LLC.

—Redwall Bk. 3: The Warrior. unabr. ed. 1998. (Redwall Ser.). (J). (gr. 4-8). audio 15.95 (0-8072-7968-4, 395746, Listening Library) Random Hse. Audio Publishing Group.

—Redwall Bks. 1, 2, 3: The Wall; The Quest; The Warrior. unabr. ed. 1998. (Redwall Ser.). (J). (gr. 4-8). audio 56.95 Blackstone Audio Bks., Inc.

—Redwall Bks. 1, 2, 3: The Wall; The Quest; The Warrior. unabr. ed. 1999. (Redwall Ser.). (J). (gr. 4-8). audio 52.00 (0-7366-4489-X, 4928) Books on Tape, Inc.

—Redwall Bks. 1, 2, 3: The Wall; The Quest; The Warrior. unabr. ed. 1999. (Redwall Ser.). (J). (gr. 4-8). audio 59.98 Highsmith Inc.

—Redwall Bks. 1, 2, 3: The Wall; The Quest; The Warrior. unabr. ed. 1997. 351p. (J). (gr. 4-8). pap. 56.00 incl. audio (0-8072-7879-3, YA940SP, Listening Library) Random Hse. Audio Publishing Group.

—Redwall Bks. 1-3: The Wall; The Quest; The Warrior. unabr. ed. 1997. 43p. (J). (gr. 4-8). audio 50.00 (0-8072-7878-5, YA940CX, Listening Library) Random Hse. Audio Publishing Group.

—Redwall Friend & Foe. 2000. (Redwall Ser.). (Illus.). 16p. (J). (gr. 4-7). 8.99 (0-399-23589-2, Philomel) Penguin Putnam Bks. for Young Readers.

—Redwall Map & Riddle Book: Includes the Redwall Riddler! 1998. (Redwall Ser.). (J). (gr. 4-8). 8.99 (0-399-23248-6, Philomel) Penguin Putnam Bks. for Young Readers.

—A Redwall Winter's Tale. 2001. (Redwall Ser.). (Illus.). 80p. (J). (gr. 4-8). mass mkt. 18.99 (0-399-23346-6, G. P. Putnam's Sons) Penguin Putnam Bks. for Young Readers.

—Salamandastron. 1994. (Redwall Ser.). (Illus.). 368p. (J). (gr. 4-8). mass mkt. 6.99 (0-441-00031-2) Ace Bks.

—Salamandastron. 1993. (Redwall Ser.). (Illus.). 400p. (J). (gr. 4-8). 23.99 (0-399-21992-7, Philomel) Penguin Putnam Bks. for Young Readers.

—Salamandastron. 1994. (Redwall Ser.). (J). (gr. 4-8). 13.04 (0-606-06708-6) Turtleback Bks.

—Salamandastron. 2003. (Redwall Ser.). (Illus.). 400p. (YA). pap. 7.99 (0-14-250152-2, Puffin Bks.) Penguin Putnam Bks. for Young Readers.

—Seven Strange & Ghostly Tales. unabr. ed. 1999. (YA). audio 23.98 Highsmith Inc.

—Seven Strange & Ghostly Tales. 1993. 144p. (YA). pap. 3.99 (0-380-71906-1, Avon Bks.) Morrow/Avon.

—Seven Strange & Ghostly Tales, 1 vol. (Illus.). (J). 1999. 144p. (gr. 4-7). pap. 5.99 (0-698-11808-1, PaperStar); 1991. 160p. (gr. 3 up). 15.99 o.p. (0-399-22103-4, G. P. Putnam's Sons) Penguin Putnam Bks. for Young Readers.

—Seven Strange & Ghostly Tales. (J). 144p. (gr. 3-5). pap. 5.99 (0-8072-1486-8); 1996. (gr. 4-7). audio 30.00 (0-8072-7612-X, YA899CX) Random Hse. Audio Publishing Group. (Listening Library).

—Seven Strange & Ghostly Tales. 1999. (Illus.). (J). 12.04 (0-606-16802-8) Turtleback Bks.

—Taggerung. 2001. (Redwall Ser.: Bk. 14). 448p. (J). (gr. 3-6). 23.99 (0-399-23720-8) Putnam Publishing Group, The.

—Taggerung. 2003. (Redwall Ser.). (Illus.). 448p. (YA). pap. 7.99 (0-14-250154-9, Puffin Bks.) Penguin Putnam Bks. for Young Readers.

—Taggerung. 2002. 416p. (J). reprint ed. mass mkt. 7.99 (0-441-00968-9) Ace Bks.

—Taggerung. l.t. ed. 2002. (Redwall Ser.: Vol. 2). (Illus.). 683p. (J). 25.95 (0-7862-4014-8) Gale Group.

—Tribes of Redwall: Badgers. 2002. (Illus.). (J). E-Book 8.99 (0-399-23852-2, G. P. Putnam's Sons) Penguin Putnam Bks. for Young Readers.

—Tribes of Redwall: Otters. 2003. (Illus.). (J). 8.99 (0-399-23961-8, G. P. Putnam's Sons) Penguin Putnam Bks. for Young Readers.

—Triss. 2002. (Redwall Ser.: Bk. 15). (Illus.). 432p. (J). 23.99 (0-399-23723-2) Putnam Publishing Group, The.

Jacques, Brian, ed. & reader. Seven Strange & Ghostly Tales. unabr. ed. 1996. (J). (gr. 3-5). pap. 35.00 incl. audio (0-8072-7613-8, YA899SP, Listening Library) Random Hse. Audio Publishing Group.

Jacques, Brian & Jacques, Brian. Mossflower. audio 29.99 (1-4025-0529-9) Recorded Bks., LLC.

RHINE RIVER AND VALLEY—FICTION

Schaad, Hans P. Rhine Pirates. Crawford, Elizabeth D., tr. 1968. (Illus.). (J). (gr. k-3). 4.75 o.p. (0-15-266680-X) Harcourt Children's Bks.

RHODE ISLAND—FICTION

Avi. Something Upstairs: A Tale of Ghosts. 1997. 128p. (J). (gr. 5 up). pap. 4.99 (0-380-79086-6, Harper Trophy) HarperCollins Children's Bk. Group.

—Something Upstairs: A Tale of Ghosts. 1990. 128p. (J). (gr. 4-7). reprint ed. pap. 4.99 (0-380-70853-1, Avon Bks.) Morrow/Avon.

—Something Upstairs: A Tale of Ghosts. 1997. 11.00 (0-606-11860-8) Turtleback Bks.

Curtis, Alice Turner. A Little Maid of Narragansett Bay. 2004. (Little Maid Ser.). (Illus.). 210p. (J). (gr. 1-6). reprint ed. pap. 9.95 (1-55709-334-2) Applewood Bks.

—A Little Maid of Virginia. 2004. (Little Maid Ser.). (Illus.). 192p. (J). (gr. 1-3). reprint ed. pap. 9.95 (1-55709-333-4) Applewood Bks.

Lisle, Janet Taylor. The Art of Keeping Cool. (Illus.). (J). (gr. 5-9). 2002. 256p. pap. 4.99 (0-689-83788-7, Aladdin); 2000. 216p. 17.00 (0-689-83787-9, Atheneum/Richard Jackson Bks.) Simon & Schuster Children's Publishing.

—The Art of Keeping Cool. l.t. ed. 2001. 207p. (J). 21.95 (0-7862-3427-X) Thorndike Pr.

—The Crying Rocks. 2003. (Illus.). 208p. (YA). 16.95 (0-689-85319-X, Atheneum/Richard Jackson Bks.) Simon & Schuster Children's Publishing.

Manes, Stephen. Some of the Adventures of Rhode Island Red. (Trophy Bk.). (Illus.). 128p. (J). (gr. 3-7). 1993. pap. 3.95 o.p. (0-06-440358-0, Harper Trophy); 1990. 10.95 o.p. (0-397-32347-6); 1990. lib. bdg. 11.89 o.p. (0-397-32348-4) HarperCollins Children's Bk. Group.

Nicholson, Peggy & Warner, John F. The Case of the Squeaky Thief. 1994. (Kerry Hill Casecrackers Ser.: No. 3). 120p. (J). (gr. 3-6). lib. bdg. 13.27 (0-8225-0711-0, Lerner Pubns.) Lerner Publishing Group.

Shea, Pegi Deitz. Tangled Threads: A Hmong Girl's Story. 2003. 240p. (J). (gr. 5-9). tchr. ed. 15.00 (0-618-24748-3, Clarion Bks.) Houghton Mifflin Co. Trade & Reference Div.

Stainer, M. L. The Lyon's Roar. 1997. (Lyon Saga Ser.: Bk. 1). (Illus.). 160p. (YA). (gr. 5-9). pap. 6.95 (0-9646904-3-8) Chicken Soup Pr., Inc.

RHODES (GREECE)—FICTION

Henty, G. A. A Knight of the White Cross: A Tale of the Siege of Rhodes. (J). E-Book 3.95 (0-594-02397-1) 1873 Pr.

ROCKY MOUNTAINS—FICTION

Baker, Elizabeth. Tammy Camps in the Rocky Mountains. 1970. (Illus.). (J). (gr. 2-5). 3.95 o.p. (0-395-06589-5); lib. bdg. 4.95 o.p. (0-395-06590-9) Houghton Mifflin Co.

Bender, Carrie. Chestnut Ridge Acres. 2001. 288p. (J). 23.95 (0-7862-3416-4, Five Star) Gale Group.

—Chestnut Ridge Acres. 1997. (Whispering Brook Ser.: Vol. 3). (Illus.). 176p. (J). (gr. 4-8). pap. 8.99 (0-8361-9077-7) Herald Pr.

—Chestnut Ridge Acres. 1997. E-Book 7.99 (0-585-26298-5) netLibrary, Inc.

James, Will. Cowboy in the Making. 2001. (Illus.). 92p. (J). 15.00 (0-87842-439-3) Mountain Pr. Publishing Co., Inc.

Kabel, Larassa, illus. Rocky Mountain Summer. 1998. (Cover-to-Cover Bks.). (J). (0-7807-6790-X) Perfection Learning Corp.

Kroll, Virginia L. & Jones, Dawn L. Bluffy's Mighty Mountain. 2001. (Illus.). (J). (0-9712840-3-2) Boyds Collection Ltd., The.

MacDougall, Mary-Katherine. Black Jupiter. Gruver, Kate E., ed. 1983. (Illus.). 181p. (YA). (gr. 5 up). 8.95 (0-940175-01-0) Now Communications Co.

Sargent, Dave & Sargent, Pat. Stinky (sorrel) Don't Be Mischievous #56: Don't Be Mischievous #56. 2001. (Saddle Up Ser.). 36p. (J). pap. (1-56763-666-7); lib. bdg. 22.60 (1-56763-665-9) Ozark Publishing.

Warner, Gertrude Chandler. The Ghost Town Mystery. 1999. (Boxcar Children Ser.: No. 71). (J). (gr. 2-5). 10.00 (0-606-18764-2) Turtleback Bks.

Warner, Gertrude Chandler, creator. The Ghost Town Mystery. 1999. (Boxcar Children Ser.: No. 71). (Illus.). 128p. (J). (gr. 2-5). lib. bdg. 13.95 (0-8075-2858-7); mass mkt. 3.95 (0-8075-2859-5) Whitman, Albert & Co.

Woods, Becky. Rocky Mountain Rabbit. 1991. (Illus.). 86p. (J). (gr. 4-8). 12.95 (0-932433-65-0) Windswept Hse. Pubs.

ROMANIA—FICTION

Abbott, Tony. Trapped in Transylvania: Dracula. 2002. (Cracked Classics Ser.). (Illus.). 144p. (J). (gr. 4-7). pap. 4.99 (0-7868-1324-5, Volo) Hyperion Bks. for Children.

Bell, Mary Reeves. Checkmate in the Carpathians. 2000. (Passport to Danger Ser.: Vol. 4). (Illus.). 208p. (J). (gr. 7-12). pap. 5.99 o.p. (1-55661-551-5) Bethany Hse. Pubs.

Gundisch, Karin. How I Became an American. Skofield, James, tr. from GER. 2001. 128p. (J). (gr. 3-7). 15.95 (0-8126-4875-7) Cricket Bks.

Mooney, Bel. Voices of Silence. 1997. 192p. text 14.95 o.s.i (0-385-32326-3, Dell Books for Young Readers) Random Hse. Children's Bks.

Orlev, Uri. Lydia, Queen of Palestine. Halkin, Hillel, tr. 1995. (Illus.). 176p. (J). (gr. 5-9). pap. 4.99 o.s.i (0-14-037089-7, Puffin Bks.) Penguin Putnam Bks. for Young Readers.

—Lydia, Queen of Palestine. 1995. 9.09 o.p. (0-606-07817-7) Turtleback Bks.

Pullein-Thompson, Christine. The Long Search. 1993. 160p. (J). (gr. 5-9). 13.95 o.p. (0-02-775445-6, Simon & Schuster Children's Publishing) Simon & Schuster Children's Publishing.

Stoker, Bram. Dracula. unabr. ed. 1965. (Classics Ser.). (YA). (gr. 7 up). mass mkt. 2.25 (0-8049-0072-8, CL-72) Airmont Publishing Co., Inc.

—Dracula. 1983. (Bantam Classics Ser.). 432p. (gr. 9-12). mass mkt. 4.95 (0-553-21271-0) Bantam Bks.

—Dracula. 1965. 416p. (YA). (gr. 7 up). pap. 2.50 o.s.i (0-440-92148-1, Laurel) Dell Publishing.

—Dracula. 1997. (Eyewitness Classics Ser.). (Illus.). 64p. (J). (gr. 3-6). pap. 14.95 o.p. (0-7894-1489-9) Dorling Kindersley Publishing, Inc.

—Dracula. 1997. (Children's Thrift Classics Ser.). (Illus.). 96p. (J). reprint ed. pap. text 1.00 (0-486-29567-2) Dover Pubns., Inc.

—Dracula. unabr. ed. 1998. (Wordsworth Classics Ser.). (YA). (gr. 6-12). 5.27 o.p. (0-89061-086-X, R086XWW) Jamestown.

—Dracula. 1986. (Signet Classics). 400p. (YA). (gr. 10). mass mkt. 4.95 (0-451-52337-7, Signet Classics) NAL.

—Dracula. Farr, Naunerle C., ed. 1973. (Now Age Illustrated Ser.). (Illus.). 64p. (J). (gr. 5-10). stu. ed. 1.25 (0-88301-175-1); pap. 2.95 (0-88301-100-X) Pendulum Pr., Inc.

—Dracula. (Puffin Classics Ser.). 1995. (Illus.). 528p. (YA). (gr. 4-7). pap. 3.99 (0-14-036717-9, Puffin Bks.); 1994. (Illus.). 432p. (J). 15.95 o.p. (0-448-40559-8, Grosset & Dunlap); 1986. 448p. (J). (gr. 4-6). pap. 3.50 o.p. (0-14-035048-9, Puffin Bks.) Penguin Putnam Bks. for Young Readers.

—Dracula. Lafreniere, Kenneth, ed. 1982. (Stepping Stone Bks.: No. 1). (Illus.). 96p. (J). (gr. 3-7). pap. 3.99 (0-394-84828-4, Random Hse. Bks. for Young Readers) Random Hse. Children's Bks.

—Dracula. abr. ed. 1992. (J). mass mkt. 3.99 (0-590-46029-3, 067, Scholastic Paperbacks) Scholastic, Inc.

ROME—FICTION

Bretecher, Claire. Agrippina. 1992. (Illus.). 50p. (C). (gr. 3 up). pap. 9.95 o.p. (0-7493-0812-5, A0649) Heinemann.

Burrell, Roy. The Romans. 1998. (Rebuilding the Past Ser.). (Illus.). 112p. (J). (gr. 4-8). reprint ed. pap. text 14.95 o.p. (0-19-917102-5) Oxford Univ. Pr., Inc.

Gerrard, Roy. The Roman Twins, RS. 1998. (Illus.). 32p. (J). (ps-3). 16.00 (0-374-36339-0, Farrar, Straus & Giroux (BYR)) Farrar, Straus & Giroux.

Goodman, Joan Elizabeth. Songs from Home. 1994. 224p. (YA). (gr. 5 up). pap. 4.95 (0-15-203591-5); (Illus.). 10.95 o.s.i (0-15-203590-7) Harcourt Trade Pubs.

—Songs from Home. 1994. 10.10 o.p. (0-606-09875-5) Turtleback Bks.

Hull, Robert. Roman Stories. 1993. (Tales from Around the World Ser.). (Illus.). 48p. (J). (gr. 4-6). ring bd. 24.26 (1-56847-105-X, AS105-X) Raintree Pubs.

Jansen, Susan Estelle. The Lizzie McGuire Movie. novel ed. 2003. (Illus.). 48p. (J). (gr. 3-6). pap. 4.99 (0-7868-4584-8) Disney Pr.

Lawrence, Carol. The Assassins of Rome, No. 4. 2003. (Roman Mysteries Ser.: Bk. 4). 176p. lib. bdg. 22.90 (0-7613-2605-7); (Illus.). 15.95 (0-7613-1940-9) Millbrook Pr., Inc. (Roaring Brook Pr.).

Malam, John. Indiana Jones Explores Ancient Rome. 1996. (Illus.). 47p. (J). (gr. 5-8). 22.95 (0-237-51223-8) Evans Brothers, Ltd. GBR. *Dist:* Trafalgar Square.

McKee, David. Mr. Benn, Gladiator. 2002. (Illus.). 33p. (J). (ps-3). 16.95 (1-84270-024-3) Andersen Pr., Ltd. GBR. *Dist:* Trafalgar Square.

Nolan, Dennis. Androcles & the Lion. 1997. (Illus.). 32p. (J). (gr. 1-5). 15.00 o.s.i (0-15-203355-6) Harcourt Children's Bks.

Odom, Mel. Sabrina Goes to Rome. 1998. (Sabrina, the Teenage Witch Ser.). 176p. (YA). (gr. 5 up). mass mkt. 4.50 (0-671-02772-7, Simon Pulse) Simon & Schuster Children's Publishing.

Ray, Mary. Rain from the West. 1980. 192p. (J). (gr. 5-8). o.p. (0-571-11532-2) Faber & Faber Ltd.

Ross, Stewart. Down with the Romans! 1996. (Illus.). 62p. (J). 17.95 (0-237-51634-9); pap. 8.95 (0-237-51635-7) Evans Brothers, Ltd. GBR. *Dist:* Trafalgar Square.

Scieszka, Jon. See You Later, Gladiator. (Illus.). 2004. (Time Warp Trio Ser.). 112p. pap. 4.99 (0-14-240117-X, Puffin Bks.); 2002. (Time Warp Trio Ser.: Vol. 9). 112p. pap. 4.99 (0-14-230069-1); 2000. (Time Warp Trio Ser.: Vol. 9). 80p. (J). (gr. 2-5). 14.99 (0-670-89340-4, Viking Children's Bks.) Penguin Putnam Bks. for Young Readers.

Simon, Les. The Secret of the Red Silk Pouch. 1998. 157p. (J). (gr. 5-8). pap. 9.99 (0-88092-362-8, 3628) Royal Fireworks Publishing Co.

Vida Publishers Staff, contrib. by. Los Guarda Historias, Bk. 2. 1998. (SPA., Illus.). 64p. (J). (ps-3). pap. 2.49 (0-8297-2228-9) Vida Pubs.

Winterfeld, Henry. Detectives in Togas. Winston, Richard & Winston, Clara, trs. from GER. 2002. (Illus.). 272p. (YA). (gr. 3 up). 17.00 (0-15-216292-5, Harcourt Young Classics); pap. 5.95 (0-15-216280-1, Odyssey Classics) Harcourt Children's Bks.

—Detectives in Togas. (Illus.). (J). (gr. 4-7). 1990. 272p. pap. 6.00 o.s.i (0-15-223415-2, Odyssey Classics); 1966. pap. 2.25 o.p. (0-15-625315-1, Voyager Bks./Libros Viajeros) Harcourt Children's Bks.

—Detectives in Togas. 1990. (J). 12.05 (0-606-03200-2) Turtleback Bks.

—Mystery of the Roman Ransom. McCormick, Edith Rockefeller, tr. from GER. 2002. Tr. of Caius Geht ein Licht Auf. (Illus.). 240p. (YA). (gr. 3). 17.00 (0-15-216313-1, Harcourt Young Classics); pap. 5.95 (0-15-216268-2, Odyssey Classics) Harcourt Children's Bks.

—Mystery of the Roman Ransom. McCormick, Edith, tr. from GER. Tr. of Caius Geht ein Licht Auf. (Illus.). (J). (gr. 5-9). 1977. pap. 1.75 o.p. (0-15-662340-4, Voyager Bks./Libros Viajeros); 1971. 5.50 o.p. (0-15-256612-0) Harcourt Children's Bks.

Wood. Roman Palace. (Illus.). 32p. (J). 13.95 o.p. (0-7136-3812-5, 93339) A & C Black GBR. *Dist:* Lubrecht & Cramer, Ltd., Talman Co.

ROSWELL HIGH (N. M.: IMAGINARY PLACE)—FICTION

Mangels, Andy. Pursuit. 2003. (Roswell Ser.). (Illus.). 256p. (YA). mass mkt. 5.99 (0-689-85522-2, Simon Pulse) Simon & Schuster Children's Publishing.

Mangels, Andy & Martin, Michael A. Turnabout. 2003. (Roswell Ser.). (Illus.). 272p. (YA). mass mkt. 5.99 (0-689-86410-8, Simon Pulse) Simon & Schuster Children's Publishing.

Metz, Melinda. The Dark One. (Roswell High Ser.: No. 9). (YA). (gr. 6 up). 2000. 176p. mass mkt. 5.99 (0-671-03563-0); 2001. reprint ed. E-Book 5.90 (0-7434-3450-1) Simon & Schuster Children's Publishing. (Simon Pulse).

—The Intruder. (Roswell High Ser.: No. 5). (YA). (gr. 6 up). 2001. E-Book 4.99 (0-7434-3446-3); 2000. 160p. pap. 5.99 (0-671-77459-X); 1999. 176p. mass mkt. 4.50 (0-671-02378-0) Simon & Schuster Children's Publishing. (Simon Pulse).

—The Outsider. (Roswell High Ser.: No. 1). (YA). (gr. 6 up). 1999. 176p. pap. 5.99 (0-671-77466-2); 1998. 176p. mass mkt. 1.99 (0-671-02374-8); 2001. reprint ed. E-Book 5.99 (0-7434-3442-0) Simon & Schuster Children's Publishing. (Simon Pulse).

—The Rebel. (Roswell High Ser.: No. 8). (YA). (gr. 6 up). 2000. 176p. pap. 5.99 (0-671-03562-2); 2001. reprint ed. E-Book 5.99 (0-7434-3449-8) Simon & Schuster Children's Publishing. (Simon Pulse).

—The Salvation. (Roswell High Ser.: No. 10). (YA). (gr. 6 up). 2000. 176p. pap. 5.99 (0-671-03564-9); 2001. reprint ed. E-Book 5.99 (0-7434-3451-X) Simon & Schuster Children's Publishing. (Simon Pulse).

—The Seeker. (Roswell High Ser.: No. 3). (YA). (gr. 6 up). 2000. 176p. pap. 5.99 (0-671-77464-6); 1998. 176p. mass mkt. 4.50 (0-671-02376-4); 2001. reprint ed. E-Book 4.99 (0-7434-3444-7) Simon & Schuster Children's Publishing. (Simon Pulse).

—The Stowaway. (Roswell High Ser.: No. 6). (YA). (gr. 6 up). 2000. 176p. pap. 5.99 (0-671-02379-9); 2001. reprint ed. E-Book 4.99 (0-7434-3447-1) Simon & Schuster Children's Publishing. (Simon Pulse).

—The Vanished. (Roswell High Ser.: No. 7). (YA). (gr. 6 up). 2000. 176p. mass mkt. 5.99 (0-671-03561-4); 2001. reprint ed. E-Book 5.99 (0-7434-3448-X) Simon & Schuster Children's Publishing. (Simon Pulse).

—The Watcher. (Roswell High Ser.: No. 4). 176p. (YA). (gr. 6 up). 2000. pap. 5.99 (0-671-77463-8); 1999. per. 4.50 (0-671-02377-2); 2001. reprint ed. E-Book 5.99 (0-7434-3445-5) Simon & Schuster Children's Publishing. (Simon Pulse).

—The Wild One. (Roswell High Ser.: No. 2). (YA). (gr. 6 up). 1999. 176p. mass mkt. 5.99 (0-671-77465-4); 2001. reprint ed. E-Book 5.99 (0-7434-3443-9); No. 2. 1998. 176p. pap. 3.99 (0-671-02375-6) Simon & Schuster Children's Publishing. (Simon Pulse).

Ryan, Kevin. Roswell a New Beginning. 2003. (Roswell Ser.). (Illus.). 256p. (YA). mass mkt. 5.99 (0-689-85520-6, Simon Pulse) Simon & Schuster Children's Publishing.

S

SAHARA—FICTION

Kaufmann, Herbert. Adventure in the Desert. 1961. (Illus.). (J). (gr. 7 up). 12.95 (0-8392-3000-1) Astor-Honor, Inc.

—Lost Sahara Trail. 1962. (J). (gr. 7 up). 12.95 (0-8392-3022-2) Astor-Honor, Inc.

Kessler, Cristina. One Night: A Story from the Desert. 1995. (Illus.). 28p. (J). (gr. 4-8). 15.95 o.p. (0-399-22726-1, Philomel) Penguin Putnam Bks. for Young Readers.

London, Jonathan. Ali, Child of the Desert. 1997. (Illus.). 32p. (J). (gr. 1 up). 16.00 o.p. (0-688-12560-3); lib. bdg. 15.89 (0-688-12561-1) HarperCollins Children's Bk. Group.

Saint-Exupéry, Antoine de. The Little Prince. 1992. (J). reprint ed. lib. bdg. 18.95 (0-89968-299-5, Lightyear Pr.) Buccaneer Bks., Inc.

—The Little Prince. Woods, Katherine, tr. 1943. (Illus.). 97p. (J). (gr. 4-7). 16.00 o.p. (0-15-246503-0) Harcourt Children's Bks.

—The Little Prince. Woods, Katherine, tr. (J). 1993. 160p. 50.00 o.s.i (0-15-243820-3); 1968. (Illus.). 128p. (gr. 3 up). pap. 6.00 (0-15-652820-7); Large-Format, Color Edition. 1982. (Illus.). 97p. (gr. 4-7). pap. 10.00 o.s.i (0-15-646511-6, Harvest Bks.) Harcourt Trade Pubs.

—The Little Prince. 1971. (J). 12.05 (0-606-03815-9) Turtleback Bks.

—The Little Prince. 1998. (Children's Library). (J). pap. 3.95 Wordsworth Editions, Ltd. GBR. *Dist:* Combined Publishing.

Wells, Rosemary. Abdul. 1975. (Illus.). 40p. (J). (ps-2). 8.95 o.p. (0-8037-4461-7); 5.47 o.s.i (0-8037-4462-5) Penguin Putnam Bks. for Young Readers. (Dial Bks. for Young Readers).

SAINT LAWRENCE RIVER—FICTION

Holling, Holling C. Paddle-to-the-Sea. (Illus.). 64p. (J). (gr. 4-6). 1980. pap. 11.95 (0-395-29203-4); 1941. tchr. ed. 20.00 (0-395-15082-5) Houghton Mifflin Co.

SAINT LOUIS (MO.)—FICTION

Betancourt, Jeanne. Sweet Sixteen & Never . . . 1987. 144p. (YA). (gr. 7-12). mass mkt. 2.75 o.s.i (0-553-25534-7, Starfire) Random Hse. Children's Bks.

Cutler, Jane. The Song of the Molimo, RS. 1998. (Illus.). 160p. (YA). (gr. 4-7). 16.00 (0-374-37141-5, Farrar, Straus & Giroux (BYR)) Farrar, Straus & Giroux.

Duey, Kathleen. Evie Peach: St. Louis, 1857. 1997. (American Diaries Ser.: No. 8). (J). (gr. 3-7). 10.55 (0-606-12615-5) Turtleback Bks.

Erwin, Vicki B. & Powell, Jennifer, eds. A Midwinter Knight's Dream: A St. Louis Tail. 2000. (Illus.). 64p. (J). (gr. 1-7). 15.99 (0-7383-0000-4) Booksource, The.

Hoffman, Allen. Big League Dreams. 1999. (Small Worlds Ser.). 296p. pap. 12.95 (0-7892-0583-1) Abbeville Pr., Inc.

Schroeder, Alan. Ragtime Tumpie. (J). (ps-3). 1993. 32p. pap. 6.99 (0-316-77504-5); 1989. (Illus.). 16.95 o.p. (0-316-77497-9, Joy Street Bks.) Little Brown & Co.

SAN ANTONIO (TEX.)—FICTION

Bruni, Mary-Ann S. Rosita's Christmas Wish. 1985. (Texas Ser.). (Illus.). 48p. (J). (gr. k-8). 13.95 (0-935857-00-1); (0-935857-09-5); pap. (0-935857-01-X); pap. (0-935857-10-9); 125.00 (0-935857-03-6) TexArt Services, Inc.

Griffin, Peni R. A Dig in Time. 1992. 160p. (J). (gr. 3-7). pap. 3.99 o.p. (0-14-036001-8, Puffin Bks.) Penguin Putnam Bks. for Young Readers.

—The Music Thief, ERS. 2002. 160p. (YA). (gr. 5-8). 16.95 (0-8050-7055-9, Holt, Henry & Co. Bks. For Young Readers) Holt, Henry & Co.

—The Music Thief. l.t. ed. 2003. 190p. (J). 21.95 (0-7862-5606-0) Thorndike Pr.

—Switching Well. 1994. 224p. (J). (gr. 5 up). pap. 5.99 (0-14-036910-4, Puffin Bks.) Penguin Putnam Bks. for Young Readers.

—Switching Well. 1994. (J). 11.04 (0-606-07115-6) Turtleback Bks.

Maruca, Mary. A Kid's Guide to Exploring San Antonio Missions. 2000. (Illus.). 12p. (J). (gr. 3-6). pap. 3.95 (1-58369-002-6, E1018) Western National Parks Assn.

Warner, Gertrude Chandler, creator. The Mystery at the Alamo. 1997. (Boxcar Children Ser.: No. 58). (J). (gr. 2-5). lib. bdg. 13.95 (0-8075-5436-7); mass mkt. 3.95 (0-8075-5437-5) Whitman, Albert & Co.

SAN FRANCISCO (CALIF.)—FICTION

Alef, Daniel. Centennial Stories: A Living History of San Francisco. 2nd ed. 2000. (Illus.). 227p. (J). pap. 15.95 (0-9700174-2-1) Maxit Publishing, Inc.

Argueta, Jorge. Xochitl & the Flowers / Xochitl, la Nina de Las Flores. 2003. Tr. of Xochitl, la Nina de Las Flores. (ENG & SPA., Illus.). 32p. (J). 16.95 (0-89239-181-2) Children's Bk. Pr.

Bethancourt, T. Ernesto. The Tomorrow Connection. 1984. 144p. (YA). (gr. 7 up). 10.95 o.p. (0-8234-0543-5) Holiday Hse., Inc.

Caen, Herb. The Cable Car & the Dragon. 1986. (Illus.). 40p. (J). (ps-3). 12.95 (0-87701-390-X) Chronicle Bks. LLC.

Child of the Owl. pap. text, stu. ed. (0-13-053125-1) Prentice Hall (Schl. Div.).

Child of the Owl. 8.97 (0-13-437497-5) Prentice Hall PTR.

Cruise, Beth. It's the Thought That Counts. 1995. (Saved by the Bell: No. 8). 128p. (YA). (gr. 5-8). pap. 3.95 (0-689-80195-5, Aladdin) Simon & Schuster Children's Publishing.

Dell, Pamela. A Song for Sung Li: A Story of the 1906 San Francisco Earthquake. 2002. (Illus.). 48p. (J). lib. bdg. 27.07 (1-59187-015-1) Child's World, Inc.

Duey, Kathleen. Alexia Ellery Finsdale: San Francisco, 1905. 1997. (American Diaries Ser.: No. 7). 144p. (J). (gr. 3-7). pap. 4.50 (*0-689-81620-0*, Aladdin) Simon & Schuster Children's Publishing.

—Alexia Ellery Finsdale: San Francisco, 1905. 1997. (American Diaries Ser.: No. 7). (J). (gr. 3-7). 10.55 (*0-606-12614-7*) Turtleback Bks.

—San Francisco Earthquake 1906. 1999. (Historical Romance Ser.). 208p. (YA). (gr. 7-12). pap. 4.99 (*0-671-03602-5*, Simon Pulse) Simon & Schuster Children's Publishing.

Duey, Kathleen & Bale, Karen A. Earthquake, San Francisco, 1906. 1998. (Survival! Ser.: No. 2). 176p. (J). (gr. 4-7). mass mkt. 4.50 (*0-689-81308-2*, Aladdin) Simon & Schuster Children's Publishing.

—Earthquake, San Francisco, 1906. 1997. (Survival! Ser.: No. 2). (J). (gr. 4-7). 10.55 (*0-606-13048-9*) Turtleback Bks.

Elmore, Patricia. Susannah & the Purple Mongoose Mystery. 1992. (Illus.). 120p. (J). (gr. 3-7). 15.00 o.p. (*0-525-44907-8*, Dutton Children's Bks.) Penguin Putnam Bks. for Young Readers.

Enderle, Judith R. & Gordon, Stephanie Jacob. Francis the Earthquake Dog. 1996. (Illus.). 32p. (J). (ps-3). 13.95 o.p. (*0-8118-0630-8*) Chronicle Bks. LLC.

English, Karen. Speak to Me, RS. 2004. (J). (*0-374-37156-3*, Farrar, Straus & Giroux (BYR)) Farrar, Straus & Giroux.

Fischer, Jackie. An Egg on Three Sticks. 2004. 272p. pap. 23.95 (*0-312-31774-3*) St. Martin's Pr.

Fraser, Kathleen & Levy, Miriam. Adam's World: San Francisco. 1971. (Illus.). (J). (gr. k-2). 5.75 o.p. (*0-8075-0174-3*) Whitman, Albert & Co.

Freeman, Don. Fly High, Fly Low. (J). 2004. 16.99 (*0-670-03685-4*, Viking); 1957. (Illus.). 8.95 o.p. (*0-670-32218-0*) Viking Penguin.

Freeman, Martha. The Trouble with Babies. 2002. (Illus.). 80p. (J). (gr. 1-4). tchr. ed. 15.95 (*0-8234-1698-4*) Holiday Hse., Inc.

—The Trouble with Cats. 2000. (Illus.). 77p. (J). (gr. 1-5). tchr. ed. 15.95 (*0-8234-1479-5*) Holiday Hse., Inc.

—The Trouble with Cats. 2003. (Illus.). 80p. (gr. 4-7). pap. text 4.99 (*0-440-41809-7*, Yearling) Random Hse. Children's Bks.

The Girl of the Golden Gate. 1981. 48p. (J). pap. 1.50 o.p. (*0-8431-0730-8*, Price Stern Sloan) Penguin Putnam Bks. for Young Readers.

Goodger, Jane. Into the Wild Wind. 1999. 320p. mass mkt. 5.99 o.s.i (*0-451-40894-2*, Topaz) NAL.

Gordon, Jeffie R. Nora, No. 26. 1987. 224p. (Orig.). (YA). (gr. 7 up). pap. 2.75 o.p. (*0-590-41012-1*) Scholastic, Inc.

Gregory, Kristiana & Campbell, Mary Exa Atkins. Earthquake at Dawn. 2003. (Great Episodes Ser.). (Illus.). 224p. (J). pap. 5.95 (*0-15-204681-X*) Harcourt Children's Bks.

Hinman, Bonnie. San Francisco Earthquake. 32nd ed. 1998. (American Adventure Ser.: No. 32). (Illus.). (J). (gr. 3-7). pap. 3.97 (*1-57748-393-6*) Barbour Publishing, Inc.

Jackson, Dave & Jackson, Neta. Journey to the End of the Earth: William Seymour. 2000. (Trailblazer Bks.: Vol. 33). (Illus.). 160p. (J). (gr. 3-7). pap. 5.99 (*0-7642-2266-X*) Bethany Hse. Pubs.

Jennings, Patrick. Faith & the Rocket Cat. 1998. (Illus.). 224p. (J). (gr. 3-6). pap. 15.95 (*0-590-11004-7*) Scholastic, Inc.

Karr, Kathleen. Gold-Rush Phoebe. 1998. (Petticoat Party Ser.: No. 4). (Illus.). 208p. (YA). (gr. 5 up). pap. 4.95 o.s.i (*0-06-440498-6*) HarperCollins Pubs.

Kudlinski, Kathleen V. Earthquake! A Story of Old San Francisco. (Once upon America Ser.). (Illus.). 64p. (J). (gr. 2-6). 1995. pap. 4.99 (*0-14-036390-4*, Puffin Bks.); 1993. 12.99 o.p. (*0-670-84874-3*, Viking Children's Bks.) Penguin Putnam Bks. for Young Readers.

—Shannon: A Chinatown Adventure, San Francisco, 1880. unabr. ed. 1996. (Girlhood Journeys Ser.). (Illus.). 71p. (J). (gr. 6-8). pap. 32.99 (*1-887327-06-1*) Aladdin Paperbacks.

—Shannon: A Chinatown Adventure, San Francisco, 1880. (Girlhood Journeys Ser.: Bk. 2). (J). 1997. 12.95 (*0-689-81204-3*, Simon & Schuster Children's Publishing); 1996. (Illus.). 72p. mass mkt. 5.99 (*0-689-80984-0*, Aladdin) Simon & Schuster Children's Publishing.

—Shannon: A Chinatown Adventure, San Francisco, 1880. 1996. (Girlhood Journeys Ser.: 2). (J). 11.19 o.p. (*0-606-10824-6*) Turtleback Bks.

—Shannon: Lost & Found, San Francisco, 1880. 1997. (Girlhood Journeys Ser.: Bk. 2). (Illus.). 72p. (J). (gr. 2-6). per. 5.99 (*0-689-80988-3*, Simon Pulse) Simon & Schuster Children's Publishing.

—Shannon: The Schoolmarm Mysteries, San Francisco, 1880. 1997. (Girlhood Journeys Ser.: No. 3). (Illus.). 72p. (J). (gr. 2-6). mass mkt. 5.99 (*0-689-81561-1*, Simon Pulse) Simon & Schuster Children's Publishing.

Kudlinski, Kathleen V. & Farnsworth, Bill. Shannon: A Chinatown Adventure, San Francisco, 1880. 1996. (Girlhood Journeys Ser.: 2). (Illus.). 72p. (J). (gr. 4-7). 13.00 o.s.i (*0-689-81138-1*, Simon & Schuster Children's Publishing) Simon & Schuster Children's Publishing.

Lee, Milly. Earthquake, RS. 2001. (Illus.). 32p. (J). (gr. k-2). 16.00 (*0-374-39964-6*, Farrar, Straus & Giroux (BYR)) Farrar, Straus & Giroux.

Levy, Marc. If Only It Were True. 2000. 224p. mass mkt. 6.99 (*0-7434-1717-8*); 2001. 256p. reprint ed. mass mkt. 6.99 (*0-7434-0618-4*) Simon & Schuster. (Pocket).

—If Only It Were True. abr. ed. 2000. audio 26.00 (*0-7435-0545-X*); audio compact disk 32.00 (*0-7435-0546-8*) Simon & Schuster Audio. (Simon & Schuster Audioworks).

Martin, Patricia M. Rice Bowl Pet. 1962. (Illus.). (J). (gr. k-3). lib. bdg. 8.79 o.p. (*0-690-69969-7*) HarperCollins Children's Bk. Group.

Molarsky, Osmond. A Sky Full of Kites. 1996. (Illus.). 32p. (J). (gr. k-2). 12.95 (*1-883672-26-0*) Tricycle Pr.

Osborne, Mary Pope. Earthquake in the Early Morning. 2001. (Magic Tree House Ser.: No. 24). (Illus.). 96p. (J). (gr. k-3). pap. 3.99 (*0-679-89070-X*); lib. bdg. 11.99 (*0-679-99070-4*) Random Hse. Children's Bks. (Random Hse. Bks. for Young Readers).

—Earthquake in the Early Morning. 2001. (Magic Tree House Ser.). (Illus.). (J). 10.04 (*0-606-21166-7*) Turtleback Bks.

Partridge, Elizabeth. Oranges on Golden Mountain. (Illus.). 40p. 2003. (YA). pap. 6.99 (*0-14-250033-X*, Puffin Bks.); 2001. (J). (gr. 1-4). 16.99 (*0-525-46453-0*, Dutton Children's Bks.) Penguin Putnam Bks. for Young Readers.

Polese, James. Tales from the Iron Triangle: Boyhood Days in the San Francisco Bay Area of the 1920's. Polese, Richard L., ed. 1995. (Illus.). 96p. (YA). (gr. 6-12). pap. 9.95 (*0-943734-12-6*) Ocean Tree Bks.

Reiss, Kathryn. The Strange Case of Baby H. 2002. (American Girl Collection: Bk. 18). (Illus.). 176p. (J). (gr. 4-7). 10.95 (*1-58485-534-7*); pap. 6.95 (*1-58485-533-9*) Pleasant Co. Pubns. (American Girl).

Robles, Anthony D. Lakas & the Manilatown Fish / Si Lakas at Ang Isdang Manilatown. de Jesus, Eloisa D. & de Guzman, Magdalena, trs. 2003. Tr. of Si Lakas at Ang Isdang Manilatown. (ENG & TAG., Illus.). 32p. (J). 16.95 (*0-89239-182-0*) Children's Bk. Pr.

Rovetch, Lissa. Cora & the Elephants. 1995. (Illus.). 32p. (J). (gr. 3 up). 14.99 o.p. (*0-670-84335-0*, Viking) Penguin Putnam Bks. for Young Readers.

Salat, Cristina. Living in Secret. 3rd ed. 1999. 183p. (YA). (gr. 5-10). reprint ed. pap. 7.95 (*0-916020-02-9*) Books Marcus.

Salat, Cristina. Living in Secret. 1994. 192p. (J). (gr. 4-7). pap. 3.99 o.s.i (*0-440-40950-0*) Dell Publishing.

Sanders, Evelin. Janine. 1999. 221p. (YA). (gr. 9 up). pap. 9.99 (*0-88092-444-6*) Royal Fireworks Publishing Co.

Sargent, Dave & Sargent, Pat. Hank (Black Sabino) Be Responsible #33. 2001. (Saddle Up Ser.). 36p. (J). pap. (*1-56763-656-X*); lib. bdg. 22.60 (*1-56763-655-1*) Ozark Publishing.

Schiller, Gerald A. Two Dogs, an Emperor, & Me. 2000. (Illus.). 108p. (J). (gr. 4-7). pap. 7.50 (*1-881164-92-6*) Intercontinental Publishing, Inc.

Schulte, Elaine L. Daniel Colton Kidnapped. 2002. (Colton Cousins Adventure Ser.: Bk. 4). (Illus.). 138p. (J). 6.49 (*1-57924-566-8*) Jones, Bob Univ. Pr.

—Daniel Colton Kidnapped. 1993. (Colton Cousins Adventure Ser.: Vol. 4). (Illus.). 144p. (J). (gr. 3-7). pap. 5.99 o.p. (*0-310-57261-4*) Zondervan.

Thesman, Jean. Rising Tide. 2003. 224p. (YA). 16.99 (*0-670-03656-0*, Viking) Viking Penguin.

—Sea So Far. 2001. 224p. (J). (gr. 5-9). 15.99 (*0-670-89278-5*, Viking Children's Bks.) Penguin Putnam Bks. for Young Readers.

—A Sea So Far. 2003. 224p. (YA). pap. 6.99 (*0-14-230059-4*, Puffin Bks.) Penguin Putnam Bks. for Young Readers.

Warner, Gertrude Chandler, creator. The Mystery in San Francisco. 1997. (Boxcar Children Ser.: No. 57). (J). (gr. 2-5). 10.00 (*0-606-11160-3*) Turtleback Bks.

—The Mystery in San Francisco. 1997. (Boxcar Children Ser.: No. 57). (J). (gr. 2-5). mass mkt. 3.95 (*0-8075-5434-0*) Whitman, Albert & Co.

Williams, Carol Lynch. Victoria's Courage. 1998. (Latter-Day Daughters Ser.). (J). 5.95 (*1-57345-434-6*) Deseret Bk. Co.

Wintz, Jack. St. Francis in San Francisco. 2001. (Illus.). 32p. (J). (gr. k-3). 12.95 (*0-8091-6684-4*) Paulist Pr.

Wong, Jade S. Fifth Chinese Daughter. 1950. (Illus.). lib. bdg. o.p. (*0-06-014731-8*) HarperCollins Pubs.

Yep, Laurence. Child of the Owl. (Golden Mountain Chronicles). (J). (gr. 7 up). 1990. 288p. pap. 6.99 (*0-06-440336-X*, Harper Trophy); 1977. 224p. lib. bdg. 16.89 (*0-06-026743-7*) HarperCollins Children's Bk. Group.

—Child of the Owl. 1977. (YA). (gr. 7-12). 16.12 (*0-06-026739-9*, 972926) HarperCollins Pubs.

—Child of the Owl. 1977. (J). 11.00 (*0-606-04634-8*) Turtleback Bks.

—The Imp That Ate My Homework. (Illus.). 96p. (J). (gr. 3-7). 2000. pap. 4.99 (*0-06-440840-X*, Harper Trophy); 1998. lib. bdg. 14.89 (*0-06-027689-4*) HarperCollins Children's Bk. Group.

—The Imp That Ate My Homework. 1998. (Illus.). 96p. (J). (gr. 3-7). 14.95 (*0-06-027688-6*) HarperCollins Pubs.

—The Imp That Ate My Homework. 2000. 11.10 (*0-606-17671-3*) Turtleback Bks.

—The Magic Paintbrush. 2000. (Illus.). 96p. (J). (gr. 7 up). 14.95 (*0-06-028199-5*); lib. bdg. 13.89 (*0-06-028200-2*) HarperCollins Children's Bk. Group.

—The Magic Paintbrush. 2003. (Illus.). 96p. (J). (gr. 3-7). pap. 4.99 (*0-06-440852-3*) HarperCollins Pubs.

—Thief of Hearts. 1995. (Illus.). 208p. (J). (gr. 5-9). 14.95 o.p. (*0-06-025341-X*) HarperTrade.

—Tiger's Apprentice. 2003. 192p. (J). (gr. 5 up). lib. bdg. 16.89 (*0-06-001014-2*) HarperCollins Children's Bk. Group.

—The Tiger's Apprentice. 2003. 192p. (J). (gr. 5 up). 15.99 (*0-06-001013-4*) HarperCollins Children's Bk. Group.

—The Tiger's Apprentice. l.t. ed. 2003. 221p. (J). 22.95 (*0-7862-5731-8*) Thorndike Pr.

SANTA FE NATIONAL HISTORIC TRAIL—FICTION

Bartlow, Evelyn A. Emily & the Santa Fe Trail. unabr. ed. 1998. (Illus.). 64p. (J). (gr. 4-7). pap. 8.00 (*1-890826-04-9*) Rock Creek Pr., LLC.

Holling, Holling C. Tree in the Trail. (Illus.). 64p. (J). (gr. 4-6). 1990. pap. 11.95 (*0-395-54534-X*); 1964. tchr. ed. 20.00 (*0-395-18228-X*) Houghton Mifflin Co.

—Tree in the Trail. 1970. (J). 14.15 o.p. (*0-606-04565-1*) Turtleback Bks.

Joosse, Barbara M. Lewis & Papa: Adventure on the Santa Fe Trail. 1998. (Illus.). 40p. (J). (ps-3). 15.95 (*0-8118-1959-0*) Chronicle Bks. LLC.

McDonald, Megan, et al. All the Stars in the Sky: The Santa Fe Trail Diary of Florrie Ryder. 2003. (Dear America Ser.). 192p. (J). pap. 10.95 (*0-439-16963-1*) Scholastic, Inc.

Mian, Mary. The Net to Catch War, 001. 1975. (J). (gr. 4-6). 6.95 o.p. (*0-395-20491-7*) Houghton Mifflin Co.

Oliphant, Pat, illus. Peter Becomes a Trail Man: The Story of a Boy's Journey on the Santa Fe Trail. 2002. 191p. (J). 12.95 (*0-8263-2895-4*) Univ. of New Mexico Pr.

Sargent, Dave & Sargent, Pat. Chub (Dappled Black) Be Dependable #17. 2001. (Saddle Up Ser.). 36p. (J). 22.60 (*1-56763-645-4*); pap. 6.95 (*1-56763-646-2*) Ozark Publishing.

Sperry, Armstrong. Wagons Westward: The Old Trail to Santa Fe. 2000. (Illus.). 208p. (YA). pap. 14.95 (*1-56792-128-0*) Godine, David R. Pub.

Wadsworth, Ginger. Scenes along the Santa Fe Trail. 1993. (Illus.). (J). o.p. (*0-8075-7258-6*) Whitman, Albert & Co.

SCILLY, ISLES OF (ENGLAND)—FICTION

Morpurgo, Michael. Why the Whales Came. (J). 1992. 144p. pap. 2.75 o.p. (*0-590-42912-4*, Scholastic Paperbacks); 1990. (gr. 5-7). pap. 10.95 o.p. (*0-590-42911-6*) Scholastic, Inc.

—The Wreck of the Zanzibar. l.t. ed. 2003. (J). 16.95 (*0-7540-7846-9*, Galaxy Children's Large Print) BBC Audiobooks America.

—The Wreck of the Zanzibar. 1995. (Illus.). 80p. (J). (gr. 3-5). 14.99 o.s.i (*0-670-86360-2*, Viking Children's Bks.) Penguin Putnam Bks. for Young Readers.

Stevenson, Robert Louis. Dr. Jekyll & Mr. Hyde. 1995. 32p. (YA). (gr. 6-12). pap. 3.95 (*0-7854-1117-8*, 40205) American Guidance Service, Inc.

SCOTLAND—FICTION

Anderson, Ken. Nessie & the Little Blind Boy of Loch Ness. deluxe ed. 1992. (Illus.). 72p. (J). 49.95 o.p. (*0-941613-27-5*) Stabur Pr., Inc.

Barrie, J. M. The Little Minister. 1968. (Airmont Classics Ser.). (J). (gr. 10 up). mass mkt. 0.75 o.p. (*0-8049-0187-2*, CL-187) Airmont Publishing Co., Inc.

Batten, H. Mortimer. Singing Forest. 1964. (Illus.). 214p. (J). (gr. 6 up). 3.95 o.p. (*0-374-26468-6*) Farrar, Straus & Giroux.

Bawden, Nina. The Witch's Daughter. 1966. (Illus.). (J). (gr. 4-6). 12.95 o.p. (*0-397-30922-8*) Harper-Collins Children's Bk. Group.

—The Witch's Daughter. 1991. 192p. (J). (gr. 3-7). 13.95 o.s.i (*0-395-58635-6*, Clarion Bks.) Houghton Mifflin Co. Trade & Reference Div.

Blackmore, R. D. Lorna Doone. 1999. lib. bdg. 21.95 (*1-56723-172-1*) Yestermorrow, Inc.

Blackmore, Richard D. Lorna Doone. 1996. (Andre Deutsch Classics). 319p. (J). (gr. 5-8). 11.95 (*0-233-99076-3*) Andre Deutsch GBR. *Dist:* Trafalgar Square, Trans-Atlantic Pubns., Inc.

—Lorna Doone: A Romance of Exmoor. Shuttleworth, Sally, ed. 1999. (Oxford World's Classics Ser.). 720p. pap. 11.95 (*0-19-283627-7*) Oxford Univ. Pr., Inc.

Blyton, Enid. The Sea of Adventure. 2003. 192p. (J). o.p. (*0-333-73271-5*) Macmillan U.K. GBR. *Dist:* Trafalgar Square.

—The Sea of Adventure. 2003. (Adventure Series [3] Ser.). 185p. (J). pap. (*0-330-30173-X*) Pan Macmillan.

Bond, Nancy. The Love of Friends. 1997. 304p. (YA). (gr. 7 up). 17.00 (*0-689-81365-1*, McElderry, Margaret K.) Simon & Schuster Children's Publishing.

Brown, Ruth, illus. & retold by. The Ghost of Greyfriar's Bobby. 1996. 32p. (J). (ps-3). 14.99 o.s.i (*0-525-45581-7*, Dutton Children's Bks.) Penguin Putnam Bks. for Young Readers.

Brown, Ruth, retold by. The Ghost of Greyfriar's Bobby. 1999. (Illus.). (J). pap. 5.99 (*0-14-056190-0*, Puffin Bks.) Penguin Putnam Bks. for Young Readers.

Calvert, Patricia. Hadder MacColl. 1985. 160p. (J). (gr. 6-8). 12.95 o.s.i (*0-684-18447-8*, Macmillan Reference USA) Gale Group.

Cameron, Eleanor. Beyond Silence. 1980. 208p. (J). (gr. 5-9). 9.95 o.p. (*0-525-26463-9*, Dutton Children's Bks.) Penguin Putnam Bks. for Young Readers.

Cassinari, Ramon P. The Legend of Little Nessie. 1997. (Illus.). 24p. (J). (gr. k-4). 14.95 (*0-9654002-0-4*) Little Lochness Publishing.

Cavanagh, Helen. The Last Piper. 1996. (Illus.). 128p. (J). (gr. 4-7). 16.00 o.p. (*0-689-80481-4*, Simon & Schuster Children's Publishing) Simon & Schuster Children's Publishing.

Clement-Davies, David. Fire Bringer. 2000. (Illus.). 480p. (YA). (gr. 5-9). 19.95 (*0-525-46492-1*, Dutton Children's Bks.) Penguin Putnam Bks. for Young Readers.

Cooper, Susan. The Boggart. 1995. (J). 11.04 (*0-606-07305-1*) Turtleback Bks.

—The Boggart & the Monster. unabr. ed. 1997. (Boggart Ser.). (J). (gr. 4-7). audio 30.00 (*0-8072-7820-3*, YA925CX, Listening Library) Random Hse. Audio Publishing Group.

Courtney, Dayle. The Knife with Eyes. 1981. (Thorne Twins Adventure Bks.). (Illus.). 192p. (Orig.). (J). (gr. 5 up). pap. 2.98 o.p. (*0-87239-471-9*, 2716) Standard Publishing.

Del Negro, Janice. Lucy Dove. (Illus.). 32p. (J). (gr. 3-6). 2001. pap. 6.95 (*0-7894-8084-0*, D K Ink); 1998. pap. 16.95 o.p. (*0-7894-2514-9*) Dorling Kindersley Publishing, Inc.

Del Negro, Janice & Gore, Leonid. Lucy Dove. 1999. (Illus.). 32p. (J). pap. 19.95 o.p. (*0-7737-3107-5*) Dorling Kindersley Publishing, Inc.

Dickinson, Peter. Inside Grandad. 2004. 128p. (gr. 4-7). lib. bdg. 17.99 (*0-385-90873-3*, Lamb, Wendy) Random Hse. Children's Bks.

Duncan, Jane. Janet Reachfar & the Kelpie. 2002. (Illus.). 32p. (J). (gr. k-3). pap. 7.95 (*1-84158-210-7*) Birlinn, Ltd. GBR. *Dist:* Interlink Publishing Group, Inc.

Dunlop, Eileen. Finn's Search. 1994. 160p. (J). (gr. 4-7). 14.95 (*0-8234-1099-4*) Holiday Hse., Inc.

—Fox Farm, ERS. 1979. (gr. 6 up). o.p. (*0-03-049051-0*, Holt, Henry & Co. Bks. For Young Readers) Holt, Henry & Co.

—The Ghost by the Sea. 1996. 192p. (J). (gr. 4-7). tchr. ed. 15.95 (*0-8234-1264-4*) Holiday Hse., Inc.

—Green Willow. 1993. 160p. (J). (gr. 4-7). 14.95 o.p. (*0-8234-1021-8*) Holiday Hse., Inc.

—Websters' Leap. 1995. (Illus.). 176p. (J). (gr. 4-7). 15.95 (*0-8234-1193-1*) Holiday Hse., Inc.

Duquennoy, Jacques. The Ghosts' Trip to Loch Ness. 2001. (Illus.). 48p. (J). (ps-2). pap. 6.00 (*0-15-216303-4*, Voyager Bks./Libros Viajeros) Harcourt Children's Bks.

—The Ghosts' Trip to Loch Ness. 1996. (Illus.). 52p. (J). (ps-3). 11.00 (*0-15-201440-3*) Harcourt Trade Pubs.

Gafford, Deborah. Swept Away Stories: Secret in Scotland. (J). E-Book 5.95 (*1-930756-49-6*, Bookmice) McGraw Publishing, Inc.

—Swept Away Stories - Secret in Scotland. 2000. (J). E-Book 4.50 (*1-930364-32-6*, Bookmice) McGraw Publishing, Inc.

Glencoe McGraw-Hill Staff. Topics from the Restless, Bk. 2. unabr. ed. 1999. (Wordsworth Classics Ser.). (YA). (gr. 10 up). pap. 21.00 (*0-89061-117-3*, R1173WW) Jamestown.

Gliori, Debi. Pure Dead Magic. 2001. 192p. (J). (gr. 5 up). 15.95 o.s.i (*0-375-81410-8*) Knopf, Alfred A. Inc.

—Pure Dead Magic. 2001. (Illus.). 192p. (J). (gr. 5). lib. bdg. 17.99 o.s.i (*0-375-91410-2*, Knopf Bks. for Young Readers) Random Hse. Children's Bks.

—Pure Dead Magic. 2002. 208p. (gr. 5). pap. 4.99 (*0-440-41849-6*) Random Hse., Inc.

—Pure Dead Magic. 2002. (Juvenile Ser.). (Illus.). (J). 21.95 (*0-7862-4869-6*) Thorndike Pr.

—Pure Dead Wicked. 224p. (gr. 5 up). 2003. pap. 4.99 (*0-440-41936-0*, Yearling); 2002. (J). lib. bdg. 17.99 (*0-375-91411-0*, Knopf Bks. for Young Readers); 2002. (Illus.). (J). 15.95 (*0-375-81411-6*, Knopf Bks. for Young Readers) Random Hse. Children's Bks.

Goode, Diane. Mama's Perfect Present. 1996. (Illus.). 32p. (J). (ps-3). 15.99 o.p. (*0-525-45493-4*) Penguin Putnam Bks. for Young Readers.

Greiman, Lois. The MacGowan Betrothal: Highland Rogues. 2001. 384p. mass mkt. 5.99 (*0-380-81541-9*, Avon Bks.) Morrow/Avon.

Heaven, Constance. The Fires of Glenlochy. 1976. 240p. 8.95 o.p. (*0-698-10726-8*) Putnam Publishing Group, The.

Hedderwick, Mairi. Katie Morag & the Riddles. 2002. (Illus.). 32p. pap. (*0-09-941418-X*) Random Hse. of Canada, Ltd. CAN. *Dist:* Random Hse., Inc.

—Katie Morag & the Riddles. 2001. (Illus.). 32p. (J). o.p. (*0-370-32713-6*) Random Hse., Inc.

Hendry, Frances M. Quest for a Maid, RS. 288p. (gr. 4-7). 1992. (YA). pap. 5.95 (*0-374-46155-4*, Sunburst); 1990. 14.95 o.p. (*0-374-36162-2*, Farrar, Straus & Giroux (BYR)) Farrar, Straus & Giroux.

Hergé. The Black Island. (Illus.). 62p. (J). 19.95 (*0-8288-5012-7*); pap. 4.95 o.p. (*0-416-24040-2*) French & European Pubns., Inc.

—The Black Island. 1975. (Adventures of Tintin Ser.). 62p. (J). (gr. 4-7). pap. 9.99 (*0-316-35835-5*, Joy Street Bks.) Little Brown & Co.

—The Black Island. 1975. 27.71 (*0-416-92640-1*) Routledge.

—L' Ile Noire. 1999. (Tintin Ser.).Tr. of Black Island. (FRE.). (gr. 4-7). 19.95 (*2-203-00106-2*) Casterman, Editions FRA. *Dist:* Distribooks, Inc.

—L' Ile Noire.Tr. of Black Island. (FRE., Illus.). (J). (gr. 7-9). ring bd. 19.95 (*0-8288-5039-9*) French & European Pubns., Inc.

Hunter, Mollie. Cat, Herself. 1986. (Charlotte Zolotow Bk.). Orig. Title: I'll Go My Own Way. 288p. (J). (gr. 6-9). lib. bdg. 12.89 o.p. (*0-06-022635-8*) HarperCollins Children's Bk. Group.

—The Kelpie's Pearls. 1976. (Illus.). (J). (gr. 3-7). o.p. (*0-06-022656-0*); lib. bdg. 8.79 o.p. (*0-06-022659-5*) HarperCollins Pubs.

—The King's Swift Rider: A Novel on Robert the Bruce. 1999. (YA). pap., stu. ed. 67.95 incl. audio (*0-7887-3010-X*, 40892X4); (gr. 7). audio 44.00 (*0-7887-2980-2*, 95662E7);Class set. audio 221.80 (*0-7887-3040-1*, 46857) Recorded Bks., LLC.

—A Sound of Chariots. 1972. 256p. (J). (gr. 7 up). 12.95 o.p. (*0-06-022668-4*); (Illus.). lib. bdg. 12.89 o.p. (*0-06-022669-2*) HarperCollins Children's Bk. Group.

—The Third Eye. 1979. (YA). (gr. 8 up). 11.95 o.p. (*0-06-022676-5*); lib. bdg. 12.89 o.p. (*0-06-022677-3*) HarperCollins Children's Bk. Group.

—The Walking Stones. 1996. (Jackson Friends Bk.). 176p. (J). (gr. 3 up). pap. 5.00 (*0-15-200995-7*, Magic Carpet Bks.) Harcourt Children's Bks.

—The Wicked One. 1977. (Story of Suspense Ser.). 128p. (J). (gr. 5-8). lib. bdg. 12.89 o.p. (*0-06-022648-X*) HarperCollins Children's Bk. Group.

Jezard, Alison. Albert in Scotland. 1969. o.p. (*0-575-00368-5*) David & Charles Pubs.

Jones, Douglas. Scottish Seas. 1997. 144p. (J). (gr. 2-6). pap. 8.50 (*1-885767-28-5*) Canon Pr.

Kantenwein, Louise. A True Scotsman. 1996. (Illus.). (J). (gr. 2-4). 8.95 o.p. (*0-533-11643-0*) Vantage Pr., Inc.

Kellerhals-Stewart, Heather. Brave Highland Heart. ed. 2000. (J). (gr. 2). spiral bd. (*0-616-01688-3*) Canadian National Institute for the Blind/Institut National Canadien pour les Aveugles.

—Brave Highland Heart. 1998. (Illus.). 32p. (J). (gr. k-3). 15.95 (*0-7737-3099-0*) Stoddart Kids CAN. *Dist:* Fitzhenry & Whiteside, Ltd., Stoddart Publishing.

Kidnapped. 9999. (Children's Classics Ser.: No. 740-20). (Illus.). (J). (gr. 3-5). text 3.50 o.p. (*0-7214-0862-1*, Ladybird Bks.) Penguin Group (USA) Inc.

King-Smith, Dick. The Merman. (Illus.). (gr. 3-5). 1999. 102p. (J). 16.00 o.s.i (*0-517-80030-6*, Random Hse. Bks. for Young Readers); 2001. 112p. reprint ed. pap. text 4.99 (*0-440-41718-X*, Yearling) Random Hse. Children's Bks.

—Sophie's Lucky. 1996. (Illus.). 108p. (J). (gr. k-4). 14.99 o.p. (*1-56402-869-0*) Candlewick Pr.

—The Water Horse. 1998. (Illus.). 108p. (J). (gr. 2-5). 17.99 o.s.i (*0-517-80027-6*); (gr. 3-5). 16.00 o.s.i (*0-517-80026-8*) Crown Publishing Group.

—The Water Horse. l.t. ed. 1992. (Children's Lythway Ser.). (Illus.). 124p. (YA). 13.95 (*0-7451-1610-8*, Macmillan Reference USA) Gale Group.

—The Water Horse. 2000. (Illus.). 128p. (gr. 3-5). pap. text 4.99 (*0-375-80352-1*, Knopf Bks. for Young Readers) Random Hse. Children's Bks.

—The Water Horse. 2000. 11.04 (*0-606-19026-0*) Turtleback Bks.

Knight, Eric. Lassie Come-home, ERS. 2003. (Illus.). 256p. (J). (gr. 4-12). 17.95 (*0-8050-7206-3*, Holt, Henry & Co. Bks. For Young Readers) Holt, Henry & Co.

Leitch, Patricia. Jumping Lessons. 1996. (Horseshoes Ser.: Vol. 2). 128p. (J). (gr. 3-7). (Illus.). lib. bdg. 13.89 o.p. (*0-06-027288-0*);Bk. 2. pap. 3.95 o.p. (*0-06-440635-0*) HarperCollins Children's Bk. Group. (Harper Trophy).

—The Perfect Horse. 1996. (Horseshoes Ser.: Vol. 1). 112p. (J). (gr. 3-7). (Illus.). lib. bdg. 13.89 o.p. (*0-06-027289-9*);Bk. 1. pap. 3.95 o.p. (*0-06-440634-2*, Harper Trophy) HarperCollins Children's Bk. Group.

Lingard, Joan. The Clearance. 1974. 160p. (J). (gr. 7 up). 6.95 o.p. (*0-525-66400-9*, Dutton Children's Bks.) Penguin Putnam Bks. for Young Readers.

Little, Jean. The Belonging Place. 1997. 128p. (J). (gr. 3-7). 13.99 o.p. (*0-670-87593-7*, Viking Children's Bks.) Penguin Putnam Bks. for Young Readers.

MacDonald, George. Sir Gibbie. Lindskoog, Kathryn, ed. 1992. (Illus.). 200p. (J). (gr. 3-7). pap. 9.99 o.p. (*0-88070-414-4*, Multnomah Bks.) Multnomah Pubs., Inc.

—Sir Gibbie. Lindskoog, Kathryn, ed. 2001. (Classics for Young Readers Ser.). (Illus.). 224p. (J). (gr. 3-6). pap. 7.99 (*0-87552-726-4*) P&R Publishing.

—Wee Sir Gibbie of the Highlands. Phillips, Michael R., ed. 1990. (George MacDonald Classics Ser.). 240p. (J). (gr. 2-7). text 10.99 o.p. (*1-55661-139-0*) Bethany Hse. Pubs.

MacPhail, Catherine. Dark Waters. 2003. 177p. (J). (gr. 5 up). 15.95 (*1-58234-846-4*, Bloomsbury Children) Bloomsbury Publishing.

MacPherson, Margaret M. Ponies for Hire. 1967. (Illus.). (J). (gr. 6-7). 4.50 o.p. (*0-15-263165-8*) Harcourt Children's Bks.

—Rough Road. 1966. (Illus.). (J). (gr. 7 up). 4.75 o.p. (*0-15-269147-2*) Harcourt Children's Bks.

Maddux, Marlaine. The Loch Pt.1: Facing the Future, 3 vols. 2000. (Mythics Ser.). (Illus.). 64p. (J). (gr. 3-6). 17.95 (*0-9673683-3-2*) Penny-Farthing Pr., Inc.

Masters, Anthony. The Klondyker. 1992. (YA). pap. 15.00 o.s.i (*0-671-79173-7*, Simon & Schuster Children's Publishing) Simon & Schuster Children's Publishing.

Maxwell, Katie. They Wear What under Their Kilts? 2004. (Illus.). (YA). mass mkt. 5.99 (*0-8439-5258-X*, Leisure Bks.) Dorchester Publishing Co., Inc.

McAllister, Margaret. Hold My Hand & Run. 2000. (Illus.). 160p. (J). (gr. 5-9). 15.99 o.p. (*0-525-46391-7*, Dutton Children's Bks.) Penguin Putnam Bks. for Young Readers.

Monaghan, Nancy. The Isle of Mist: A Tale of Scotland. 2000. (YA). (gr. 4-7). E-Book 10.00 (*0-9679076-6-7*) E-Pub2000.

Ollivant, Alfred. Bob, Son of Battle. 1967. (Airmont Classics Ser.). (YA). (gr. 5 up). mass mkt. 2.50 o.p. (*0-8049-0141-4*, CL-141) Airmont Publishing Co., Inc.

—Bob, Son of Battle. 1988. (Illus.). 306p. (YA). (gr. 5 up). 19.95 o.p. (*0-9616844-2-9*) Greenhouse Publishing Co.

Paton Walsh, Jill. Birdy & the Ghosties, RS. 48p. 1991. (Illus.). (gr. 4-7). pap. 4.95 o.p. (*0-374-40675-8*, Sunburst); 1989. 10.95 o.p. (*0-374-30716-4*, Farrar, Straus & Giroux (BYR)) Farrar, Straus & Giroux.

—Matthew & the Sea Singer, RS. 1993. (Illus.). 48p. (J). (ps-3). 13.00 o.p. (*0-374-34869-3*, Farrar, Straus & Giroux (BYR)) Farrar, Straus & Giroux.

Pelley, Kathleen. The Giant King. Manning, Maurie, tr. & illus. by. 2003. 32p. (J). (ps-4). 14.95 (*0-87868-880-3*, Child & Family Pr.) Child Welfare League of America, Inc.

Perkins, Lucy F. Scotch Twins. 1969. (Walker's Twins Ser.). (Illus.). (J). (gr. 3-5). reprint ed. lib. bdg. 4.85 o.s.i (*0-8027-6062-7*) Walker & Co.

Quigley, John. Queen's Royal. 1977. 10.95 o.p. (*0-698-10756-X*) Putnam Publishing Group, The.

Ransome, Arthur. Great Northern: A Scottish Adventure of Swallows & Amazons. 2003. (Swallows & Amazons Ser.). 352p. (J). 14.95 (*1-56792-259-7*) Godine, David R. Pub.

Robertson, Jenny. Fear in the Glen. 1990. 128p. (J). (gr. 5-8). pap. 4.99 o.p. (*0-7459-1874-3*) Lion Publishing.

Smith, Alison. Come Away Home. 1991. (Illus.). 112p. (J). (gr. 3-5). lib. bdg. 12.95 o.p. (*0-684-19283-7*, Atheneum) Simon & Schuster Children's Publishing.

Stevenson, Robert Louis. Kidnapped. unabr. ed. 1963. (Classics Ser.). (YA). (gr. 8 up). mass mkt. 1.95 (*0-8049-0010-8*, CL-10) Airmont Publishing Co., Inc.

—Kidnapped. unabr. ed. 2002. (YA). (gr. 6 up). audio 41.95 (*1-55685-675-X*,) Audio Bk. Contractors, Inc.

—Kidnapped. 1982. 240p. (J). mass mkt. 1.50 o.s.i (*0-553-21067-X*, Bantam Classics) Bantam Bks.

—Kidnapped. 1974. (Dent's Illustrated Children's Classics Ser.). (Illus.). (J). reprint ed. 5.50 o.p. (*0-460-05045-1*) Biblio Distribution.

—Kidnapped. unabr. collector's ed. 1977. (YA). audio 42.00 (*0-7366-0059-0*, 1071) Books on Tape, Inc.

—Kidnapped. 1991. 222p. (J). (ps up). mass mkt. 3.99 (*0-8125-0473-9*, Tor Classics) Doherty, Tom Assocs., LLC.

—Kidnapped. abr. ed. (Children's Thrift Classics Ser.). (Illus.). (J). 1996. 89p. reprint ed. pap. text 1.00 (*0-486-29354-8*); 2000. vi, 230p. pap. 2.50 (*0-486-41026-9*) Dover Pubns., Inc.

—Kidnapped. 1996. (Illus.). 352p. (YA). (gr. 10 up). pap. 14.95 (*0-9652952-4-9*) Doyle Studio Pr.

—Kidnapped. abr. ed. (J). audio 15.95 o.p. (*0-88646-033-6*, 7049); 1986. (YA). (gr. 7-9). audio 29.95 o.p. (*0-88646-797-7*, R 7049) Durkin Hayes Publishing Ltd.

—Kidnapped. abr. ed. (J). audio 9.95 o.p. (*1-55994-063-8*, CPN 1636, Caedmon) HarperTrade.

—Kidnapped. Stemach, Jerry et al, eds. 2002. (Start-to-Finish Books). (J). (gr. 2-3). audio 100.00 (*1-58702-945-6*); audio (*1-58702-806-9*); audio (*1-58702-791-7*) Johnston, Don Inc.

—Kidnapped. 1994. (Everyman's Library Children's Classics Ser.). (Illus.). 340p. (gr. 2 up). 13.95 (*0-679-43638-3*, Everyman's Library) Knopf Publishing Group.

—Kidnapped. 1985. (J). audio 4.95 (*0-87188-166-7*) McGraw-Hill Cos., The.

—Kidnapped. 1988. (Illus.). xii, 306p. (YA). pap. 7.95 o.p. (*0-8092-4486-1*) McGraw-Hill/Contemporary.

—Kidnapped. 1959. (Signet Classics). 240p. (YA). mass mkt. 3.95 o.s.i (*0-451-52504-3*); (J). (gr. 6). mass mkt. 2.25 o.p. (*0-451-52333-4*, CW1754) NAL. (Signet Classics).

—Kidnapped. abr. ed. 1997. 27p. audio compact disk 15.98 (*962-634-117-3*, NA211712); (YA). audio 13.98 (*962-634-617-5*, NA211714) Naxos of America, Inc. (Naxos AudioBooks).

—Kidnapped. abr. ed. 1997. (J). audio 7.00 (*0-7871-1303-4*, Dove Audio) NewStar Media, Inc.

—Kidnapped. 1995. (Illus.). 64p. (J). pap. text 5.95 o.p. (*0-19-422751-0*) Oxford Univ. Pr., Inc.

—Kidnapped. 1995. (Illus.). 336p. (YA). (gr. 4-7). pap. 4.99 (*0-14-036690-3*, Puffin Bks.); 1983. 240p. (J). (gr. 3-7). pap. 3.50 o.p. (*0-14-035012-8*, Puffin Bks.); 1965. (Illus.). (J). (gr. 4-6). 2.95 o.p. (*0-448-05474-4*, Grosset & Dunlap); 1948. (Illus.). (J). (gr. 4-6). 12.95 o.s.i (*0-448-06015-9*, Grosset & Dunlap); 1948. (Illus.). (J). (gr. 4-6). 5.95 o.p. (*0-448-05815-4*, Grosset & Dunlap) Penguin Putnam Bks. for Young Readers.

—Kidnapped. Vogel, Malvina, ed. 1992. (Great Illustrated Classics Ser.: Vol. 20). (Illus.). 240p. (J). (gr. 3-6). 9.95 (*0-86611-971-X*) Playmore, Inc., Pubs.

—Kidnapped. 1994. (Step into Classics Ser.). 112p. (J). (gr. 1-4). pap. 3.99 o.s.i (*0-679-85091-0*, Random Hse. Bks. for Young Readers) Random Hse. Children's Bks.

—Kidnapped. 1989. (Children's Classics Ser.). (Illus.). xiii, 241p. (J). 12.99 o.s.i (*0-517-68783-6*) Random Hse. Value Publishing.

—Kidnapped. 1986. (Illus.). 240p. (J). (gr. 7-12). 12.95 o.p. (*0-89577-232-9*) Reader's Digest Assn., Inc., The.

—Kidnapped, unabr. ed. 1999. (J). audio 44.00 (*1-55690-281-6*, 79030E7) Recorded Bks., LLC.

—Kidnapped. 1993. (N. C. Wyeth Illustrated Classics Ser.). (Illus.). 290p. (YA). (gr. 6 up). reprint ed. text 16.95 o.p. (*1-56138-262-0*) Running Pr. Bk. Pubs.

—Kidnapped. 1971. (J). (gr. 5 up). pap. 0.75 o.s.i (*0-671-47188-0*, Washington Square Pr.) Simon & Schuster.

—Kidnapped. unabr. ed. 2002. (YA). audio compact disk 29.95 (*1-58472-273-8*, 075, In Audio) Sound Room Pubs., Inc.

—Kidnapped. abr. ed. (J). audio 10.95 (*0-8045-1058-X*, SAC1058) Spoken Arts, Inc.

—Kidnapped. 1981. (J). 10.00 (*0-606-01889-1*) Turtleback Bks.

—Kidnapped. McFarlan, Donald, ed. & intro. by. 1995. (Penguin Classics Ser.). (Illus.). 272p. (J). pap. 7.95 (*0-14-043401-1*, Penguin Classics) Viking Penguin.

—Kidnapped: The Adventures of David Balfour. 1982. (Illus.). 289p. (J). (gr. 4-7). 28.00 (*0-684-17634-3*, Atheneum) Simon & Schuster Children's Publishing.

Stewart, A. C. Ossian House. 1976. (J). (gr. 6 up). lib. bdg. 26.95 (*0-87599-219-6*) Phillips, S.G. Inc.

—Silas & Con. 1977. 132p. (J). (gr. 4-7). 1.98 o.p. (*0-689-50086-6*, McElderry, Margaret K.) Simon & Schuster Children's Publishing.

Thomas, Jerry D. Detective Zack Secret of Blackloch Castle. 1998. (Detective Zack Ser.: Vol. 10). (Illus.). 126p. (J). (gr. 3-6). pap. 6.99 (*0-8163-1399-7*) Pacific Pr. Publishing Assn.

The Travels of Jimm Pigg. 2001. 32p. (J). per. 9.95 (*0-9713900-0-2*) Hynes Enterprises, Inc.

Wallace, Barbara Brooks. Argyle. 1987. (Illus.). (J). (gr. k-3). pap. text 10.95 o.p. (*0-687-01724-6*) Abingdon Pr.

Wallace, Randall. Braveheart. 1998. (SPA.). 164p. (*84-08-02152-4*) GeoPlaneta, Editorial, S. A.

—Braveheart. 1995. (Illus.). 288p. (J). mass mkt. 6.99 (*0-671-52281-7*, Pocket) Simon & Schuster.

Way, Irene. Armada Quest. 1979. (Pathfinder Ser.). (Illus.). (J). (gr. 2-6). reprint ed. pap. 2.50 o.p. (*0-310-37841-9*) Zondervan.

Weems, David B. Son of an Earl . . . Sold for a Slave. 1992. (Illus.). 136p. (J). (gr. 5 up). 11.95 o.s.i (*0-88289-921-X*) Pelican Publishing Co., Inc.

Wiley, Melissa. Beyond the Heather Hills. 2003. (Little House Ser.). (Illus.). 208p. (J). pap. 5.99 (*0-06-440715-2*) HarperCollins Pubs.

—Down to the Bonny Glen: Martha Years. 2001. (Martha Years Ser.). (Illus.). (J). 12.00 (*0-606-21160-8*) Turtleback Bks.

—The Far Side of the Loch. (Little House). (Illus.). (J). (gr. 3-6). 2001. lib. bdg. (*0-06-028556-7*); 2000. 256p. pap. 5.99 (*0-06-440713-6*, Harper Trophy); 2000. 256p. 15.95 (*0-06-027984-2*); 2000. 256p. lib. bdg. 15.89 (*0-06-028203-7*) HarperCollins Children's Bk. Group.

—The Far Side of the Loch. 2000. (Little House Ser.). (Illus.). (J). 11.00 (*0-606-18689-1*) Turtleback Bks.

—Little House in the Highlands. 1999. (Little House Ser.). (Illus.). (J). 288p. (gr. 3-7). pap. 5.99 (*0-06-440712-8*, Harper Trophy); 271p. (gr. 4-7). lib. bdg. 15.89 (*0-06-028202-9*) HarperCollins Children's Bk. Group.

—Little House in the Highlands. 1999. (Little House Ser.). 11.00 (*0-606-15838-3*) Turtleback Bks.

Wiley, Melissa, et al. Little House in the Highlands. 1999. (Little House Ser.). (Illus.). 288p. (J). (gr. 3-7). 16.95 (*0-06-027983-4*) HarperCollins Children's Bk. Group.

Yolen, Jane. The Bagpiper's Ghost. (Tartan Magic Ser.: Bk. 3). 144p. 2003. (Illus.). (J). pap. 5.95 (*0-15-204913-4*, Magic Carpet Bks.); 2002. (YA). (gr. 4-7). 16.00 (*0-15-202310-0*) Harcourt Children's Bks.

—The Wizard's Map. 1999. (Tartan Magic Ser.: Bk. 1). 144p. (YA). (gr. 3-7). 16.00 (*0-15-202067-5*) Harcourt Children's Bks.

Yolen, Jane & Harris, Robert J. Girl in a Cage. 2002. (Illus.). 240p. (J). (gr. 6-10). 18.99 (*0-399-23627-9*, Philomel) Penguin Putnam Bks. for Young Readers.

SCOTLAND—KINGS AND RULERS—FICTION

Porter, Jane. The Scottish Chiefs. Smith, Nora A. & Wiggin, Kate Douglas, eds. & trs. by. from SCO. 1991. (Scribner Illustrated Classics Ser.). (Illus.). 520p. (YA). (gr. 7 up). 29.00 (*0-684-19340-X*, Atheneum) Simon & Schuster Children's Publishing.

—The Scottish Chiefs. deluxe ltd. ed. 1991. (Scribners Illustrated Classics Ser.). (Illus.). 528p. (J). 75.00 o.s.i (*0-684-19339-6*, Atheneum) Simon & Schuster Children's Publishing.

SEATTLE (WASH.)—FICTION

Ennis, Judith. Kalakala Comes Home: No Dream Is Too Big! McCoy, Lisa et al, eds. Ingram, Dean, tr. l.t. ed. 2000. (Illus.). 50p. 18.95 (*0-9660092-7-4*) Puget Sound Pr.

Hobbs, William. Jackie's Wild Seattle. (J). 2004. 208p. pap. 5.99 (*0-380-73311-0*, Harper Trophy); 2003. 192p. (gr. 5 up). 15.99 (*0-688-17474-4*); 2003. 192p. (gr. 5 up). lib. bdg. 16.89 (*0-06-051631-3*) HarperCollins Children's Bk. Group.

Kirkpatrick, Katherine. The Voyage of the Continental. 2002. (Illus.). 297p. (J). (gr. 7 up). tchr. ed. 16.95 (*0-8234-1580-5*) Holiday Hse., Inc.

Mochizuki, Ken. Beacon Hill Boys. 2002. 201p. (YA). pap. 4.95 (*0-439-24906-6*); 208p. (J). (gr. 9 up). pap. 16.95 (*0-439-26749-8*, Scholastic Pr.) Scholastic, Inc.

Powell, Randy. Run If You Dare, RS. 2001. 192p. (J). (gr. 7 up). 16.00 (*0-374-39981-6*, Farrar, Straus & Giroux (BYR)) Farrar, Straus & Giroux.

—Run If You Dare. l.t. ed. 2001. 216p. (J). 22.95 (*0-7862-3716-3*) Thorndike Pr.

Wilbee, Brenda. Sweetbriar Spring. 1989. (Pioneer Romance Ser.). 224p. (Orig.). (YA). (gr. 11 up). pap. 6.99 o.p. (*0-89081-661-1*) Harvest Hse. Pubs.

Wilson, Barbara. A Clear Spring. 2004. (Girls First! Ser.: Vol. 1). 173p. (J). pap. 12.50 (*1-55861-277-7*) Feminist Pr. at The City Univ. of New York.

SIBERIA (RUSSIA)—FICTION

Cross, Gillian. Phoning a Dead Man. 2002. 256p. (J). (gr. 7 up). 16.95 (*0-8234-1685-2*) Holiday Hse., Inc.

Guillot, Rene. Grishka & the Bear. March, Gwenn, tr. 1960. (Illus.). (J). (gr. 3-6). o.p. (*0-200-00000-4*, 329050) Criterion Bks., Inc.

Kalashnikoff, Nicholas. The Defender. 1993. (Newbery Honor Roll Ser.). (Illus.). 144p. (J). (gr. 4-7). reprint ed. pap. 6.95 (*0-8027-7397-4*) Walker & Co.

—Toyon: A Dog of the North & His People. 1950. (J). lib. bdg. o.p. (*0-06-012241-2*) HarperCollins Pubs.

Linevski, A. An Old Tale Carved Out of Stone. Polushkin, Maria, tr. 1973. (ENG & RUS.). 256p. (J). (gr. 7 up). 1.49 o.p. (*0-517-50263-1*, Crown) Crown Publishing Group.

Piumini, Roberto. The Knot in the Tracks. 1994. Tr. of Patrisciuz e el Diavolo Racso. (Illus.). (J). (ps-3). 14.00 o.p. (*0-688-11166-1*); 32p. lib. bdg. 13.93 o.p. (*0-688-11167-X*) Morrow/Avon. (Morrow, William & Co.).

—The Knot in the Tracks. Holmes, Olivia, tr. from ITA. 1924. Tr. of Patrisciuz e el Diavolo Racso. (Illus.). 32p. (J). 14.00 o.s.i (*0-688-11353-2*); lib. bdg. 13.93 o.s.i (*0-688-11354-0*) Morrow/Avon. (Morrow, William & Co.).

Schuch, Steve. A Symphony of Whales. 2002. (Illus.). 32p. (J). (gr. 1-4). pap. 6.00 (*0-15-216548-7*, Voyager Bks./Libros Viajeros) Harcourt Children's Bks.

Whelan, Gloria. The Impossible Journey. 2004. 256p. (J). pap. 5.99 (*0-06-441083-8*, Harper Trophy) HarperCollins Children's Bk. Group.

—The Impossible Journey. 2003. 256p. (J). (gr. 5 up). 15.99 (*0-06-623811-0*); lib. bdg. 16.89 (*0-06-623812-9*) HarperCollins Pubs.

SICILY (ITALY)—FICTION

Valens, Amy. Danilo the Fruit Man. 1993. (Illus.). 320p. (J). (ps-3). 12.99 o.p. (*0-8037-1151-4*); 12.89 o.p. (*0-8037-1152-2*) Penguin Putnam Bks. for Young Readers. (Dial Bks. for Young Readers).

SIERRA LEONE—FICTION

Kessler, Christina. No Condition Is Permanent. 2000. (Illus.). 183p. (J). (gr. 5-9). 17.99 (*0-399-23486-1*, Philomel) Penguin Putnam Bks. for Young Readers.

SIERRA NEVADA (CALIF. AND NEV.)—FICTION

Nesbit, Jeffrey A. Mountaintop Rescue. 1994. (High Sierra Adventure Ser.: Vol. 4). (J). (gr. 4 up). pap. 5.99 o.p. (*0-8407-9257-3*) Nelson, Thomas Inc.

—Setting the Trap. 1994. (High Sierra Adventure Ser.: Vol. 3). 162p. (J). (gr. 7 up). pap. 5.99 o.p. (*0-8407-9256-5*) Nelson, Thomas Inc.

Nesbit, Jeffrey A. Cougar Chase. 1994. (High Sierra Adventure Ser.). (J). (gr. 5-9). pap. 5.99 o.p. (*0-8407-9255-7*) Nelson, Thomas Inc.

—The Legend of the Great Grizzly. 1994. (High Sierra Adventure Ser.: Bk. 1). (J). (gr. 5-9). pap. 5.99 o.p. (*0-8407-9254-9*) Nelson, Thomas Inc.

Roddy, Lee. The City Bears Adventures. 1985. (D. J. Dillon Adventure Ser.: No. 2). 144p. (J). (gr. 3-7). pap. 5.99 o.p. (*0-88207-496-2*, 6-2496) Cook Communications Ministries.

—Dooger, the Grasshopper Hound. (D. J. Dillon Adventure Ser.). (J). 1996. 132p. pap. 4.99 o.p. (*1-56476-504-0*, 6-3504); 1985. (Illus.). 144p. (gr. 3-7). pap. 5.99 (*0-88207-497-0*, 6-2497) Cook Communications Ministries.

—Escape down the Raging Rapids. (D. J. Dillon Adventure Ser.). 132p. (J). 1996. pap. 5.99 o.p. (*1-56476-511-3*, 6-3511); 1988. (gr. 3-7). pap. 5.99 (*0-89693-477-2*, 6-1477) Cook Communications Ministries.

—The Ghost Dog of Stoney Ridge. (D. J. Dillon Adventure Ser.: No. 4). (J). 1985. 144p. (gr. 3-7). pap. 5.99 (*0-88207-498-9*, 6-2498); 1996. 132p. pap. 4.99 o.p. (*1-56476-505-9*, 6-3505) Cook Communications Ministries.

—Ghost of the Moaning Mansion. 1987. (D. J. Dillon Adventure Ser.: No. 8). 132p. (J). (gr. 3-7). pap. 5.99 o.p. (*0-89693-349-0*, 6-1349) Cook Communications Ministries.

—The Hair-Pulling Bear Dog. (D. J. Dillon Adventure Ser.: No. 1). (J). 1985. 144p. (gr. 3-7). pap. 5.99 (*0-88207-499-7*, 6-2499); 1996. 132p. (gr. 4-7). pap. 4.99 o.p. (*1-56476-502-4*, 6-3502) Cook Communications Ministries.

—The Legend of the White Raccoon. 1986. (D. J. Dillon Adventure Ser.: No. 6). 144p. (J). (gr. 3-7). pap. 5.99 (*0-89693-500-0*, 6-2500) Cook Communications Ministries.

—The Mad Dog of Lobo Mountain. (D. J. Dillon Adventure Ser.: No. 5). 132p. (J). 1986. (gr. 3-7). pap. 4.99 o.p. (*0-89693-482-9*); 1996. pap. 5.99 (*1-56476-506-7*, 6-3506) Cook Communications Ministries.

—The Mystery of the Black Hole Mine. (D. J. Dillon Adventure Ser.). 132p. (J). 1996. pap. 5.99 (*1-56476-508-3*, 6-3508); 1987. (gr. 3-7). pap. 4.99 o.p. (*0-89693-320-2*) Cook Communications Ministries.

—The Secret of Mad River. 1996. (D. J. Dillon Adventure Ser.: No. 9). 132p. (J). (gr. 3-7). pap. 5.99 o.p. (*1-56476-510-5*, 6-3510) Cook Communications Ministries.

Wood, Phyllis A. Pass Me a Pine Cone. 1982. (Hiway Book). 160p. (J). (gr. 7-9). 11.95 o.p. (*0-664-32692-7*) Westminster John Knox Pr.

SOUTH AFRICA—FICTION

Abramson, Ruth. The Cresta Adventure. 1989. (J). (gr. 4-7). 8.95 o.p. (*0-87306-493-3*) Feldheim, Philipp Inc.

Both, Zilpha. Stories on Rocks. Weinberger, Jane, ed. 1994. (Illus.). 80p. (J). (gr. 4-8). pap. 8.00 (*1-883650-08-9*) Windswept Hse. Pubs.

Brain, Helen. Fly Cemetery & Other Juicy Stories. 1999. (Illus.). 92p. (J). (*0-7981-3987-0*) Human & Rousseau.

Case, Dianne. Love, David. 1991. (Illus.). 128p. (J). (gr. 3-7). 14.95 o.p. (*0-525-67350-4*, Dutton Children's Bks.) Penguin Putnam Bks. for Young Readers.

—Ninety-Two Queens Road, RS. 1995. 176p. (J). (gr. 4-7). 16.00 o.p. (*0-374-35518-5*, Farrar, Straus & Giroux (BYR)) Farrar, Straus & Giroux.

Coman, Carolyn. Many Stones. 2000. (Illus.). 158p. (J). (gr. 7-12). 15.95 (*1-886910-55-3*, Front Street) Front Street, Inc.

—Many Stones. 2002. 160p. (J). pap. 5.99 (*0-14-230148-5*, Puffin Bks.) Penguin Putnam Bks. for Young Readers.

—Many Stones. l.t. ed. 2001. 24.95 (*0-7862-3399-0*) Thorndike Pr.

Cousins, Linda. Huggy Bean: We Happened upon a Beautiful Place. 1992. (Series 2). (Illus.). 28p. (J). pap. 5.95 o.p. (*0-936073-13-6*) Gumbs & Thomas Pubs., Inc.

Daly, Niki. Jamela's Dress, RS. (Illus.). (J). 2004. pap. 6.95 (*0-374-43720-3*); 1999. 32p. 16.00 (*0-374-33667-9*, Farrar, Straus & Giroux (BYR)) Farrar, Straus & Giroux.

—Jamela's Dress. 2001. (J). (ps-2). 26.95 incl. audio (*0-8045-6878-2*, 6878) Spoken Arts, Inc.

—Not So Fast, Songololo. 1998. (J). pap. 4.95 (*0-87628-975-8*) Ctr. for Applied Research in Education, The.

—Not So Fast, Songololo. 1987. 32p. (J). (ps-3). pap. 4.99 o.p. (*0-14-050715-9*, Puffin Bks.) Penguin Putnam Bks. for Young Readers.

—Not So Fast, Songololo. (Illus.). 32p. (J). (gr. k-3). 1996. pap. 6.99 (*0-689-80154-8*, Aladdin); 1986. 16.00 (*0-689-50367-9*, McElderry, Margaret K.) Simon & Schuster Children's Publishing.

—Not So Fast, Songololo. 1996. (J). 10.15 o.p. (*0-606-09700-7*) Turtleback Bks.

—Oh Jamela!, RS. 2001. (Illus.). 32p. (J). (ps-2). 16.00 (*0-374-35602-5*, Farrar, Straus & Giroux (BYR)) Farrar, Straus & Giroux.

Daly, Niki, illus. & text. Once upon a Time, RS. 2003. 40p. (J). (gr. k-3). 16.00 (*0-374-35633-5*, Farrar, Straus & Giroux (BYR)) Farrar, Straus & Giroux.

Ferreira, Anton. Zulu Dog, RS. 2002. (Illus.). 208p. (J). (gr. 5 up). 16.00 (*0-374-39223-4*, Farrar, Straus & Giroux (BYR)) Farrar, Straus & Giroux.

Gordon, Sheila. The Middle of Somewhere: A Story of South Africa. 1992. 160p. (J). (gr. 4-7). pap. 3.50 o.s.i (*0-553-15991-7*) Bantam Bks.

—The Middle of Somewhere: A Story of South Africa. 1990. 160p. (J). (gr. 4-6). mass mkt. 16.99 o.p. (*0-531-08508-2*, Orchard Bks.) Scholastic, Inc.

Haarhoff, Dorian. Desert December. 1992. (Illus.). 32p. (J). (ps-3). 13.95 o.s.i (*0-395-61300-0*, Clarion Bks.) Houghton Mifflin Co. Trade & Reference Div.

Haggard, H. Rider. King Solomon's Mines. 1997. (J). pap. text o.p. (*0-17-556582-1*) Addison-Wesley Longman, Inc.

—King Solomon's Mines. unabr. ed. 1967. (Classics Ser.). mass mkt. 1.95 o.p. (*0-8049-0140-6*, CL-140) Airmont Publishing Co., Inc.

—King Solomon's Mines. 1985. 236p. mass mkt. 3.99 o.s.i (*0-8125-8356-6*, Tor Classics) Doherty, Tom Assocs., LLC.

—King Solomon's Mines. 1979. (Blackie Chosen Classics Ser.). 320p. (J). (gr. 6 up). 3.95 o.p. (*0-216-88516-7*) Hippocrene Bks., Inc.

—King Solomon's Mines. (Puffin Classics Ser.). (Illus.). 1996. 304p. (YA). (gr. 5-9). 3.99 (*0-14-036687-3*); 1983. 256p. (J). (gr. 3-7). pap. 3.50 o.p. (*0-14-035014-4*) Penguin Putnam Bks. for Young Readers. (Puffin Bks.).

—King Solomon's Mines. 1994. (Puffin Classics). (J). 10.04 (*0-606-03596-6*) Turtleback Bks.

Howe, D. H., ed. King Solomon's Mines. 2nd ed. 1993. (Illus.). 110p. pap. text 5.95 (*0-19-585461-6*) Oxford Univ. Pr., Inc.

Isadora, Rachel. At the Crossroads. 1991. (Illus.). 32p. (J). (ps up). 16.00 o.s.i (*0-688-05270-3*); lib. bdg. 15.93 o.p. (*0-688-05271-1*) HarperCollins Children's Bk. Group. (Greenwillow Bks.).

—At the Crossroads. 1994. (Illus.). 32p. (J). (ps-3). reprint ed. pap. 5.95 (*0-688-13103-4*, Morrow, William & Co.) Morrow/Avon.

—At the Crossroads. 1994. 11.10 (*0-606-06192-4*) Turtleback Bks.

—Over the Green Hills. 1992. 32p. (J). (ps up). lib. bdg. 13.93 o.p. (*0-688-10510-6*); (Illus.). 17.99 (*0-688-10509-2*) HarperCollins Children's Bk. Group. (Greenwillow Bks.).

—A South African Night. 1998. (Illus.). 24p. (J). (ps-3). 15.00 (*0-688-11389-3*); lib. bdg. 14.89 (*0-688-11390-7*) HarperCollins Children's Bk. Group. (Greenwillow Bks.).

Jones, Toeckey. Go Well, Stay Well. 1980. 208p. (YA). (gr. 7 up). lib. bdg. 12.89 o.p. (*0-06-023062-2*) HarperCollins Children's Bk. Group.

—Skindeep. 1986. (Charlotte Zolotow Bk.). 256p. (YA). (gr. 7 up). 12.95 (*0-06-023051-7*); lib. bdg. 12.89 o.p. (*0-06-023052-5*) HarperCollins Children's Bk. Group.

Kahn, Milne. Grandma's Hat. 1999. (Illus.). (J). pap. (*0-14-054402-X*) NAL.

Komai, Felicia, ed. Cry, the Beloved Country. 1954. (J). (gr. 9 up). pap. 1.35 o.p. (*0-377-80501-7*) Friendship Pr.

Lewin, Hugh. Jafta. (Picture Bks.). (Illus.). 24p. (J). (ps-3). 2000. lib. bdg. 15.95 (*0-87614-207-2*); 1997. reprint ed. pap. 9.60 (*0-87614-494-6*) Lerner Publishing Group. (Carolrhoda Bks.).

—Jafta's Father. (Jafta Collection). (Illus.). 24p. (J). (gr. 1-3). 1983. lib. bdg. 15.95 (*0-87614-209-9*); 1989. reprint ed. pap. 4.95 (*0-87614-496-2*) Lerner Publishing Group. (Carolrhoda Bks.).

—Jafta's Mother. 24p. (J). (gr. 1-3). 1983. lib. bdg. 15.95 (*0-87614-208-0*); 1989. (Illus.). reprint ed. pap. 4.95 (*0-87614-495-4*) Lerner Publishing Group. (Carolrhoda Bks.).

Maartens, Maretha. Paper Bird: A Novel of South Africa. 1991. 144p. (J). (gr. 4-9). 13.95 o.s.i (*0-395-56490-5*, Clarion Bks.) Houghton Mifflin Co. Trade & Reference Div.

Mennen, Ingrid. Somewhere in Africa. 1997. (Illus.). 32p. (J). (ps-3). pap. 4.99 o.s.i (*0-14-056242-7*) Penguin Putnam Bks. for Young Readers.

Mennen, Ingrid & Daly, Niki. Somewhere in Africa. 1992. (Illus.). 32p. (J). (gr. 2-7). 15.99 o.p. (*0-525-44848-9*, Dutton Children's Bks.) Penguin Putnam Bks. for Young Readers.

Naidoo, Beverley. Chain of Fire. (Trophy Bk.). (Illus.). (J). (gr. 6 up). 1993. 224p. pap. 5.99 (*0-06-440468-4*, Harper Trophy); 1990. 256p. 14.00 (*0-397-32426-X*); 1990. 256p. lib. bdg. 14.89 o.p. (*0-397-32427-8*) HarperCollins Children's Bk. Group.

—Chain of Fire. 1993. 11.00 (*0-606-02551-0*) Turtleback Bks.

—Journey to Jo'burg: A South African Story. (Illus.). 96p. (J). (gr. 4-7). 1986. 14.95 o.p. (*0-397-32168-6*); 1986. lib. bdg. 16.89 (*0-397-32169-4*); 1988. reprint ed. pap. 4.99 (*0-06-440237-1*, Harper Trophy) HarperCollins Children's Bk. Group.

—Journey to Jo'burg: A South African Story. 1986. (J). 11.10 (*0-606-03834-5*) Turtleback Bks.

—No Turning Back: A Novel of South Africa. (J). (gr. 3-7). 1999. 208p. pap. 5.99 (*0-06-440749-7*); 1997. 208p. 15.89 (*0-06-027506-5*); 1996. 160p. 14.95 o.p. (*0-06-027505-7*) HarperCollins Children's Bk. Group. (Harper Trophy).

—No Turning Back: A Novel of South Africa. 1999. 12.00 (*0-606-15856-1*) Turtleback Bks.

Naidoo, Beverly. Journey to Jo'burg: A South African Story. 1995. (Longman Literature Ser.). pap. text 50.95 (*0-582-25402-7*) Addison-Wesley Longman, Ltd. GBR. *Dist:* Trans-Atlantic Pubns., Inc.

—Out of Bounds: Seven Stories of Conflict & Hope. 2003. 192p. (J). (gr. 5 up). 16.99 (*0-06-050799-3*); lib. bdg. 17.89 (*0-06-050800-0*) HarperCollins Pubs.

Owen, Phyllis. The Farm Children. 1984. (J). 5.95 o.p. (*0-533-05986-0*) Vantage Pr., Inc.

Paton, Alan. Tales from a Troubled Land. 1996. 128p. pap. 11.95 (*0-684-82584-8*, Scribner); 1985. pap. 7.95 o.s.i (*0-684-18494-X*, Scribner Paper Fiction); 1977. 128p. 20.00 o.s.i (*0-684-15135-9*, Scribner) Simon & Schuster.

Rochman, Hazel, ed. Somehow Tenderness Survives: Stories of Southern Africa. (Charlotte Zolotow Bk.). (gr. 7 up). 1990. 208p. (J). mass mkt. 5.99 (*0-06-447063-6*, Harper Trophy); 1988. 160p. (YA). 12.95 (*0-06-025022-4*); 1988. 160p. (YA). lib. bdg. 14.89 o.p. (*0-06-025023-2*) HarperCollins Children's Bk. Group.

—Somehow Tenderness Survives: Stories of Southern Africa. 1990. 11.00 (*0-606-04802-2*) Turtleback Bks.

Romain, Trevor. The Other Side of the Invisible Fence. Willerman, Benne, ed. 1994. 96p. (J). (gr. 3-11). pap. 7.95 (*1-880092-17-4*) Bright Bks., Inc.

Sacks, Margaret. Beyond Safe Boundaries. 1990. 160p. (J). (gr. 4-7). pap. 4.99 o.s.i (*0-14-034407-1*, Puffin Bks.); 1989. 16p. (YA). (gr. 7 up). 13.95 o.p. (*0-525-67281-8*, Dutton Children's Bks.) Penguin Putnam Bks. for Young Readers.

—Themba. 1992. (Illus.). 48p. (J). (gr. 2-5). 12.00 o.p. (*0-525-67414-4*, Dutton Children's Bks.) Penguin Putnam Bks. for Young Readers.

Silver, Norman. An Eye for Color. 1993. 192p. (YA). (gr. 8 up). 14.99 o.p. (*0-525-44859-4*, Dutton Children's Bks.) Penguin Putnam Bks. for Young Readers.

—Python Dance. 1993. 240p. (YA). 14.99 o.p. (*0-525-45161-7*) Penguin Putnam Bks. for Young Readers.

Sisulu, Elinor B. The Day Gogo Went to Vote: South Africa, April 1994. (Illus.). 32p. (J). (ps-3). 1999. pap. 5.95 (*0-316-70271-4*); 1996. 15.95 o.p. (*0-316-70267-6*) Little Brown & Co.

Stewart, Dianne. The Dove. 1993. (Illus.). 32p. (J). (ps up). 14.00 o.p. (*0-688-11264-1*); lib. bdg. 13.93 o.p. (*0-688-11265-X*) HarperCollins Children's Bk. Group. (Greenwillow Bks.).

—El Regalo del Sol. 2001. (SPA., Illus.). 28p. (J). (ps-3). pap. 6.99 (*980-257-258-6*, EK(1977)) Ekare, Ediciones VEN. *Dist:* Kane/Miller Bk. Pubs., Lectorum Pubns., Inc.

—El Regalo del Sol, RS. 1996. (SPA., Illus.). 32p. (J). (gr. k up). 15.00 o.p. (*0-374-32425-5*, Farrar, Straus & Giroux (BYR)) Farrar, Straus & Giroux.

Williams, Michael. Crocodile Burning. 208p. (gr. 7 up). 1994. (J). pap. 3.99 o.s.i (*0-14-036793-4*, Puffin Bks.); 1992. (YA). 15.00 o.p. (*0-525-67401-2*, Dutton Children's Bks.) Penguin Putnam Bks. for Young Readers.

—The Genuine Half-Moon Kid. 1994. 208p. (J). (gr. 7 up). 15.99 o.p. (*0-525-67470-5*, Dutton Children's Bks.) Penguin Putnam Bks. for Young Readers.

—Into the Valley. 1992. 176p. (J). (gr. 5-9). 14.95 o.p. (*0-399-22516-1*, Philomel) Penguin Putnam Bks. for Young Readers.

SOUTH AMERICA—FICTION

Alphin, Elaine Marie. A Bear for Miguel. 1996. (I Can Read Bks.). (Illus.). 64p. (J). (gr. 2-4). lib. bdg. 14.89 o.p. (*0-06-024522-0*) HarperCollins Children's Bk. Group.

—A Bear for Miguel. 1997. (I Can Read Bks.). (J). (gr. 2-4). 10.10 (*0-606-11098-4*) Turtleback Bks.

Baglio, Ben M. Racing the Wind. 2003. (Dolphin Diaries: No. 6). 160p. (J). mass mkt. 4.50 (*0-439-31952-8*) Scholastic, Inc.

Biebow, Natascha. Eleonora: Natascha Biebow. 1995. (Illus.). 32p. (J). text 15.95 o.p. (*0-7167-6614-0*) Freeman, W. H. & Co.

Campoy, F. Isabel. Rosa Raposa. 2002. (Illus.). 32p. (J). (gr. k-2). 16.00 (*0-15-202161-2*, Gulliver Bks.) Harcourt Children's Bks.

Fraggalosch, Audrey. Land of the Wild Llama: A Story of the Patagonian Andes. 2002. (Wild Habitats Ser.). (Illus.). (J). 36p. pap. 5.95 (*1-931465-82-7*, S7022); 36p. (gr. 1-4). 15.95 (*1-931465-81-9*, B7022); 46p. (gr. 1-4). 19.95 incl. audio (*1-931465-83-5*, BC7022) Soundprints.

—Land of the Wild Llama: A Story of the Patagonian Andes, Including 10" Toy. 2002. (Wild Habitats Ser.). (Illus.). 36p. (J). (gr. 1-4). 26.95 (*1-931465-85-1*, PB7022); pap. 16.95 (*1-931465-86-X*, PS7022) Soundprints.

Guebel, Daniel. Cuerpo Cristiano. 1994. Tr. of Christians. 16.05 (*0-606-17629-2*) Turtleback Bks.

Hergé. The Broken Ear. (Illus.). 62p. (J). 24.95 (*0-8288-5086-0*); pap. 4.95 o.p. (*0-416-57030-5*) French & European Pubns., Inc.

—The Broken Ear. 1978. (Adventures of Tintin Ser.). 62p. (J). (gr. 2 up). pap. 9.99 (*0-316-35850-9*, Joy Street Bks.) Little Brown & Co.

—The Broken Ear. 1993. 27.71 (*0-416-14872-7*); 1985. 10.95 (*0-416-83450-7*) Routledge.

—L' Oreille Cassee. 1999. (Tintin Ser.).Tr. of Broken Ear. (FRE.). (gr. 4-7). 19.95 (*2-203-00105-4*) Casterman, Editions FRA. *Dist:* Distribooks, Inc.

—L' Oreille Cassee.Tr. of Broken Ear. (FRE., Illus.). 62p. (J). 19.95 (*0-8288-5054-2*) French & European Pubns., Inc.

Hudson, William Henry. Green Mansions: A Romance of the Tropical Forest. 1998. (Illus.). (J). 15.00 (*0-606-18337-X*) Turtleback Bks.

Jackson, Dave & Jackson, Neta. Ambushed in Jaguar Swamp: Barbrooke Grubb. 1999. (Trailblazer Bks.: Vol. 30). 144p. (J). (gr. 3-7). pap. 5.99 (*0-7642-2014-4*) Bethany Hse. Pubs.

—Race for the Record: Joy Ridderhof. 1999. (Trailblazer Bks.: Vol. 29). 144p. (J). (gr. 3-7). pap. 5.99 (*0-7642-2013-6*) Bethany Hse. Pubs.

Lester, Alison. Isabella's Bed. 1993. (Illus.). 32p. (J). (ps-3). reprint ed. tchr. ed. 14.95 o.p. (*0-395-65565-X*) Houghton Mifflin Co.

Lumry, Amanda. Safari in South Africa. 2003. (Adventures of Riley Ser.: Bk. 2). (Illus.). 36p. (J). (gr. k-3). 15.95 (*0-9662257-8-3*) Eaglemont Pr.

Milliron, Kerry. Xena Warrior Princess: Queen of the Amazons. 1996. (Xena, Warrior Princess Ser.). 23p. (ps-3). pap. 3.25 o.s.i (*0-679-88296-0*) Random Hse., Inc.

Schaefer, Jackie. El Dia de Miranda para Bailar. Blanco, Alberto, tr. 1994. (SPA., Illus.). 32p. (J). 14.95 (*0-02-781112-3*, Atheneum) Simon & Schuster Children's Publishing.

Siembieda, Kevin & Carella, C. J. Rifts South America, Vol. 2. Kirsten, Kevin & Osten, James, eds. 1995. (Rifts Worldbook Ser.: Vol. 9). (Illus.). 192p. (Orig.). (YA). (gr. 8 up). pap. 20.95 (*0-916211-89-4*, 819) Palladium Bks., Inc.

Torres, Leyla. Saturday Sancocho, RS. 1995. 32p. (J). (ps-3). 16.00 o.p. (*0-374-36418-4*, Farrar, Straus & Giroux (BYR)) Farrar, Straus & Giroux.

Windle, Jeanette. Adventures in South America. 1994. 154p. pap. 8.99 o.p. (*0-88070-647-3*, Multnomah Bks.) Multnomah Pubs., Inc.

SOUTH CAROLINA—FICTION

Arrington, Aileen. Camp of the Angel. 2003. 160p. (J). 16.99 (*0-399-23882-4*, Philomel) Penguin Putnam Bks. for Young Readers.

Bodie, Idella. Ghost in the Capitol. 1986. (Illus.). 116p. (J). (gr. 5 up). pap. 6.95 (*0-87844-072-0*) Sandlapper Publishing Co., Inc.

Clary, Margie Willis. A Sweet, Sweet Basket. Stone, Barbara, ed. 1995. (Illus.). 40p. (J). (gr. k-7). 15.95 (*0-87844-127-1*) Sandlapper Publishing Co., Inc.

Clinton, Cathryn. The Calling. 2001. 176p. (J). (gr. 5 up). 15.99 (*0-7636-1387-8*) Candlewick Pr.

Flood, Pansie Hart. Secret Holes. 2003. (Illus.). 122p. (J). 15.95 (*0-87614-923-9*, Carolrhoda Bks.) Lerner Publishing Group.

—Sylvia & Miz Lula Maye. 2002. (Middle Grade Fiction Ser.). (Illus.). 120p. (J). (gr. 3-6). lib. bdg. 15.95 (*0-87614-204-8*, Carolrhoda Bks.) Lerner Publishing Group.

Fuqua, Jonathon Scott. Darby. 2002. 256p. (J). (gr. 5 up). 15.99 (*0-7636-1417-3*) Candlewick Pr.

Hansen, Joyce. The Heart Calls Home. 2002. 256p. (J). (gr. 7 up). pap. 5.95 (*0-380-73294-7*, Harper Trophy) HarperCollins Children's Bk. Group.

—The Heart Calls Home. 1999. viii, 175p. (J). (gr. 7-12). 16.95 (*0-8027-8636-7*) Walker & Co.

Haskins, James. The March on Washington. 2003. 192p. (YA). (gr. 5 up). pap. 10.95 (*0-940975-93-9*) Just Us Bks., Inc.

Hogan, Stephen. Johnny Lynch. 1991. (Illus.). 165p. (J). (gr. 5-6). lib. bdg. 13.00 (*0-945253-07-9*) Thornsbury Bailey & Brown.

Houston, Gloria M. Young Will: A Sunny Land with a Sunny Brook. 1995. (Illus.). (J). o.p. (*0-399-22740-7*, Philomel) Penguin Putnam Bks. for Young Readers.

Jones, Elizabeth McDavid. Mystery on Skull Island. 2001. (American Girl Collection: Bk. 15). (Illus.). 192p. (J). 9.95 (*1-58485-342-5*); pap. 5.95 (*1-58485-341-7*) Pleasant Co. Pubns. (American Girl).

Monte, Emily C. The Lost Sword of the Confederate Ghost: A Mystery in Two Centuries. 1999. 116p. (J). (gr. 4-7). 5.99 (*1-57249-132-9*) White Mane Publishing Co., Inc.

Myers, Anna. The Keeping Room. 1999. (Illus.). 128p. (J). (gr. 3-7). pap. 5.99 (*0-14-130468-5*) Penguin Putnam Bks. for Young Readers.

—The Keeping Room. 1999. 11.04 (*0-606-16786-2*) Turtleback Bks.

—The Keeping Room. 1997. 144p. (J). (gr. 3-7). 16.95 (*0-8027-8641-3*) Walker & Co.

Myers, Walter Dean. The Glory Field. 1999. 420p. (J). 15.60 (*0-03-054616-8*) Holt, Rinehart & Winston.

—The Glory Field. 1996. 288p. (YA). (gr. 7-12). mass mkt. 4.99 (*0-590-45898-1*) Scholastic, Inc.

—The Glory Field. 1994. (J). 11.04 (*0-606-08527-0*) Turtleback Bks.

O'Connor, Barbara. Beethoven in Paradise, RS. 160p. (gr. 5-8). 1999. (Illus.). (YA). pap. 4.95 (*0-374-40588-3*, Sunburst); 1997. (J). 16.00 o.p. (*0-374-30666-4*, Farrar, Straus & Giroux (BYR)) Farrar, Straus & Giroux.

—Beethoven in Paradise. 1997. (YA). Class Set. 97.30 incl. audio (*0-7887-2777-X*, 46097); Homework Set. (gr. 7). 40.20 incl. audio (*0-7887-1845-2*, 40625) Recorded Bks., LLC.

Plowden, Sally H. Turtle Tracks. 2002. (Illus.). 32p. (J). (gr. 4-6). 14.95 (*0-9679016-6-9*) Palmetto Conservation Foundation.

Richardson, Sandy. The Girl Who Ate Chicken Feet & Other Stories. (J). 1999. pap. 14.89 (*0-8037-2255-9*); 1998. 144p. (gr. 5-9). 16.99 o.s.i (*0-8037-2254-0*) Penguin Putnam Bks. for Young Readers. (Dial Bks. for Young Readers).

Rinaldi, Ann. Cast Two Shadows: The American Revolution in the South. (Great Episodes Ser.). (YA). 2004. (Illus.). 304p. pap. (*0-15-205077-9*); 2000. (Illus.). 288p. (gr. 7-12). pap. 6.00 (*0-15-200882-9*); 1998. 288p. (gr. 7-12). 16.00 (*0-15-200881-0*) Harcourt Children's Bks. (Gulliver Bks.).

—Cast Two Shadows: The American Revolution in the South. 2000. (Illus.). (J). 12.05 (*0-606-18805-3*) Turtleback Bks.

Rue, Nancy. The Ally. 1998. (Christian Heritage Ser.). 192p. (J). (gr. 3-7). pap. 5.99 (*1-56179-561-5*) Focus on the Family Publishing.

—The Escape. 1998. (Christian Heritage Ser.). 192p. (J). (gr. 3-7). pap. 5.99 (*1-56179-639-5*) Bethany Hse. Pubs.

—The Hostage. 1998. (Christian Heritage Ser.). 208p. (J). (gr. 3-7). pap. 5.99 (*1-56179-638-7*) Bethany Hse. Pubs.

—The Misfit. 1998. (Christian Heritage Ser.). 192p. (J). (gr. 3-7). pap. 5.99 (*1-56179-560-7*) Focus on the Family Publishing.

—The Trap. 1998. (Christian Heritage Ser.). 208p. (J). (gr. 3-7). pap. 5.99 (*1-56179-567-4*) Focus on the Family Publishing.

Schroeder, Alan. Carolina Shout! 1995. (Illus.). 32p. (J). 14.89 o.s.i (*0-8037-1678-8*); 14.99 o.s.i (*0-8037-1676-1*) Penguin Putnam Bks. for Young Readers. (Dial Bks. for Young Readers).

Seabrooke, Brenda. The Bridges of Summer. 1992. 160p. (J). (gr. 5 up). 14.99 o.p. (*0-525-65094-6*, Dutton Children's Bks.) Penguin Putnam Bks. for Young Readers.

Tallent, Mary. The Secret at Robert's Roost. 1988. 161p. (J). (gr. 4-7). pap. 3.95 o.p. (*0-941711-05-6*) Wyrick & Co.

Tate, Eleanora E. A Blessing in Disguise. 1995. 192p. (J). 14.95 o.s.i (*0-385-32103-1*, Delacorte Pr.) Dell Publishing.

—A Blessing in Disguise. 1996. 192p. (gr. 3-7). pap. text 3.99 o.s.i (*0-440-41209-9*, Yearling) Random Hse. Children's Bks.

—A Blessing in Disguise. 1996. (J). 9.09 o.p. (*0-606-09086-X*) Turtleback Bks.

—Blessing in Disguise. 1996. (J). 18.95 (*0-385-30997-X*, Dell Books for Young Readers) Random Hse. Children's Bks.

—The Secret of Gumbo Grove. 1996. 208p. (J). pap. 3.99 o.s.i (*0-440-41273-0*) Dell Publishing.

—The Secret of Gumbo Grove. 1988. 208p. (YA). mass mkt. 5.50 (*0-440-22716-X*, Dell Books for Young Readers); (gr. 7 up). mass mkt. 4.50 o.s.i (*0-553-27226-8*, Starfire) Random Hse. Children's Bks.

—The Secret of Gumbo Grove. 1987. (Illus.). 256p. (YA). (gr. 7-12). 12.95 o.p. (*0-531-15051-8*); lib. bdg. 12.90 o.p. (*0-531-10298-X*) Scholastic Library Publishing. (Watts, Franklin).

—The Secret of Gumbo Grove. 1998. (J). (gr. 4-7). 18.25 o.p. (*0-8446-6977-6*) Smith, Peter Pub., Inc.

—The Secret of Gumbo Grove. (J). 1997. 11.04 (*0-606-04041-2*); 1996. 9.09 o.p. (*0-606-10926-9*) Turtleback Bks.

Williams, G. Walton. Of Mice & Bells. unabr. ed. 1999. (Illus.). 674p. (J). (gr. k-3). pap. 6.95 (*0-9703570-1-X*) Barksdale Hse. Pr.

Wisler, G. Clifton. The King's Mountain. 2002. 160p. (J). (gr. 5 up). lib. bdg. 15.89 (*0-06-623793-9*) HarperCollins Children's Bk. Group.

SOUTH DAKOTA—FICTION

Armstrong, Jennifer. Black-Eyed Susan. 1995. (Illus.). 128p. (J). (gr. 4-7). 15.00 o.s.i (*0-517-70107-3*) Random Hse., Inc.

Arrington, Frances. Prairie Whispers. 2003. 176p. (YA). (gr. 5-9). 17.99 (*0-399-23975-8*, Philomel) Penguin Putnam Bks. for Young Readers.

Brouwer, Sigmund. Tyrant of the Badlands. 2002. (Accidental Detectives Ser.: Bk. 4). 144p. (J). (gr. 3-8). pap. 5.99 (*0-7642-2567-7*) Bethany Hse. Pubs.

—Tyrant of the Badlands. 1996. (Accidental Detective Ser.: Bk. 4). 132p. (J). (gr. 3-7). mass mkt. 5.99 o.p. (*1-56476-160-6*) Cook Communications Ministries.

Dixon, Franklin W. Dead Man in Deadwood. Greenberg, Anne, ed. 1994. (Hardy Boys Casefiles Ser.: No. 87). 160p. (YA). (gr. 6 up). pap. 3.99 (*0-671-79471-X*, Simon Pulse) Simon & Schuster Children's Publishing.

—Dead Man in Deadwood. 1994. (Hardy Boys Casefiles Ser.: Vol. 87). (Illus.). (J). mass mkt. 3.99 (*0-671-89281-9*, Simon Pulse) Simon & Schuster Children's Publishing.

—Dead Man in Deadwood. 1994. (Hardy Boys Casefiles Ser.: No. 87). (YA). (gr. 6 up). 9.09 o.p. (*0-606-06444-3*) Turtleback Bks.

Geisert, Bonnie. Prairie Summer. 2002. (Illus.). 96p. (YA). (gr. 3-7). 15.00 (*0-618-21293-0*, Lorraine, A. Walter) Houghton Mifflin Co. Trade & Reference Div.

Hill, Pamela Smith. Ghost Horses. 1996. (Illus.). 224p. (YA). (gr. 4-7). tchr. ed. 15.95 (*0-8234-1229-6*) Holiday Hse., Inc.

—Ghost Horses. 1999. 224p. (J). (gr. 4-7). pap. 4.50 (*0-380-72942-3*, Avon Bks.) Morrow/Avon.

—Ghost Horses. 1999. 10.55 (*0-606-16340-9*) Turtleback Bks.

Karr, Kathleen. The Cave, RS. 1994. 176p. (J). (gr. 4-7). 16.00 o.p. (*0-374-31230-3*, Farrar, Straus & Giroux (BYR)) Farrar, Straus & Giroux.

Kinyon, Jeannette. Over Home. 1992. 244p. (J). (gr. 4-8). 24.95 (*1-880531-01-1*); pap. 13.95 (*1-880531-02-X*) East Eagle Pr.

Kotzwinkle, William. The Return of Crazy Horse. 2001. (Illus.). 32p. (J). (ps-3). 16.95 (*1-58394-047-2*) Frog, Ltd.

Love, D. Anne. A Year Without Rain. 2000. (Illus.). vii, 118p. (J). (gr. 3-7). tchr. ed. 15.95 (*0-8234-1488-4*) Holiday Hse., Inc.

Richardson, Arleta. Prairie Homestead. (Orphans' Journey Ser.: Vol. 3). (J). 141p. (gr. 3-7). pap. 5.99 (*0-7814-3536-6*); 1994. 144p. (gr. 4-7). pap. 4.99 (*0-7814-0091-0*) Cook Communications Ministries.

Thomasma, Kenneth. Kunu: Winnebago Boy Escapes. 1989. (J). 12.99 (*1-880114-04-6*); pap. 7.99 (*1-880114-03-8*) Grandview Publishing Co.

Wilder, Laura Ingalls. The First Four Years. (Little House Ser.). (J). 2003. 144p. pap. 5.99 (*0-06-052243-7*); 1971. (Illus.). 160p. (gr. 3-7). lib. bdg. 17.89 (*0-06-026427-6*); 1971. (Illus.). 160p. (ps-2). 16.99 (*0-06-026426-8*); 1953. (Illus.). 160p. (gr. 5 up). pap. 6.99 (*0-06-440031-X*, Harper Trophy) HarperCollins Children's Bk. Group.

—The First Four Years. l.t. ed. 2002. (LRS Large Print Cornerstone Ser.). (Illus.). (J). lib. bdg. 27.95 (*1-58118-103-5*, 25535) LRS.

—The First Four Years. 1971. (Little House Ser.). (J). (gr. 3-6). 11.00 (*0-606-03250-9*) Turtleback Bks.

—Little Town on the Prairie. (Little House Ser.). (J). 2003. 320p. pap. 5.99 (*0-06-052242-9*); 2000. (gr. 3-6). pap. 9.90 (*0-06-449101-3*, Harper Trophy); 1953. (Illus.). 320p. (gr. 3-7). pap. 6.99 (*0-06-440007-7*, Harper Trophy); 1953. (Illus.). 320p. (gr. 3-7). 16.99 (*0-06-026450-0*); 1953. (Illus.). 320p. (gr. 3-7). lib. bdg. 17.89 (*0-06-026451-9*) HarperCollins Children's Bk. Group.

—Little Town on the Prairie. l.t. ed. 2002. (LRS Large Print Cornerstone Ser.). (Illus.). (J). lib. bdg. 35.95 (*1-58118-101-9*, 25533) LRS.

—Little Town on the Prairie. 1981. (Little House Ser.). (J). (gr. 3-6). 12.00 (*0-606-03820-5*) Turtleback Bks.

—The Long Winter. (Little House Ser.). (J). 2003. 368p. pap. 5.99 (*0-06-052241-0*); 1953. (Illus.). 352p. (gr. 3-7). pap. 6.99 (*0-06-440006-9*, Harper Trophy); 1953. (Illus.). 352p. (gr. k-3). lib. bdg. 17.89 (*0-06-026461-6*); 1953. (Illus.). 352p. (ps-2). 16.99 (*0-06-026460-8*) HarperCollins Children's Bk. Group.

—The Long Winter. l.t. ed. 2002. (LRS Large Print Cornerstone Ser.). (Illus.). (J). lib. bdg. 35.95 (*1-58118-100-0*) LRS.

—The Long Winter. 1995. (Little House Ser.). (J). (gr. 3-6). pap. 2.50 (*0-590-30094-6*) Scholastic, Inc.

—The Long Winter. 1981. (Little House Ser.). (J). (gr. 3-6). 12.00 (*0-606-03846-9*) Turtleback Bks.

—These Happy Golden Years. (Little House Ser.). (J). 2003. 336p. pap. 5.99 (*0-06-052315-8*); 1953. (Illus.). 304p. (gr. 3-7). pap. 6.99 (*0-06-440008-5*, Harper Trophy); 1953. (Illus.). 304p. (gr. 3-7). 16.99 (*0-06-026480-2*); 1953. (Illus.). 304p. (gr. 3-7). lib. bdg. 17.89 (*0-06-026481-0*) HarperCollins Children's Bk. Group.

—These Happy Golden Years. l.t. ed. (J). (gr. 3-6). 35.95 (*1-58118-102-7*) LRS.

—These Happy Golden Years. 1971. (Little House Ser.). (J). (gr. 3-6). 11.00 (*0-606-05071-X*) Turtleback Bks.

SOUTH POLE—FICTION

Heidenreich, Elke. Some Folk Say the South Pole's Hot. 2001. (Illus.). 64p. (J). 17.95 (*1-56792-170-1*) Godine, David R. Pub.

Spinelli, Eileen. Something to Tell the Grandcows. Slavin, Bill, tr. & illus. by. 2004. (J). (*0-8028-5236-X*, Eerdmans Bks For Young Readers) Eerdmans, William B. Publishing Co.

Taylor, Barbara. Pole to Pole. 1999. (Natural World Ser.). (Illus.). 31p. (J). (gr. 5-9). pap. 5.95 (*0-7641-0639-2*) Barron's Educational Series, Inc.

SOUTHERN STATES—FICTION

Battle-Lavert, Gwendolyn. Papa's Mark. 2003. (Illus.). (J). (gr. k-3). tchr. ed. 16.95 (*0-8234-1650-X*) Holiday Hse., Inc.

Bennett, Cherie. A Heart Divided. 2004. (YA). lib. bdg. 17.99 (*0-385-90039-2*); 320p. (gr. 7). 15.95 (*0-385-32749-8*) Random Hse. Children's Bks. (Delacorte Bks. for Young Readers).

Bernardini, Robert. Southern Love for Christmas. 1993. (Illus.). 32p. (J). (gr. 4-7). reprint ed. 14.95 (*0-88289-974-0*) Pelican Publishing Co., Inc.

—A Southern Time Christmas. 1991. (Illus.). 32p. (J). (gr. 4-7). reprint ed. 14.95 (*0-88289-828-0*) Pelican Publishing Co., Inc.

Bond, Adrienne. Sugarcane House: And Other Stories about Mr. Fat. 1997. (Illus.). 96p. (J). (gr. 3-7). 16.00 (*0-15-201446-2*) Harcourt Children's Bks.

Bond, Adrienne Moore. Sugarcane House. 1997. pap. 5.00 (*0-15-201447-0*) Harcourt Trade Pubs.

Brewer, Tony G. Catfish Don't Jump: And Other Stories of the South. l.t. ed. 1996. (Illus.). 1p. (YA). (gr. 8 up). 15.95 (*1-889005-00-2*, 101) Temco Publishing.

Brown, Virginia P. Cochula's Journey. 1996. 160p. (J). (gr. 5-8). 18.00 (*1-881320-40-5*, Black Belt Pr.) River City Publishing.

Butler, Mary Nyegard. Palmetto Who?, 4 vols. 2001. (Illus.). 27p. (J). (ps-3). per. 7.95 (*0-9701497-9-4*) Bay Tree Enterprises.

Capote, Truman. Children on Their Birthdays. 1992. (J). o.p. (*0-88682-491-5*, Creative Education) Creative Co., The.

—Children on Their Birthdays. abr. ed. audio 12.95 o.p. (*0-694-50960-4*, SWC 1771, HarperAudio) HarperTrade.

Coleman, Lonnie. Orphan Jim. 1975. 216p. 6.95 o.p. (*0-385-11085-5*) Doubleday Publishing.

Comor-Jacobs, Annie. Reesy: A Little Girl Learning Life's Lessons: Reesy Learning about Divorce; Reesy Learning about the Deep South; Reesy Learning about Deafness; Reesy Learning about Death, 4 vols. 2000. (Illus.). 40p. (J). (gr. 2-5). pap. 30.00 (*1-889743-18-6*) Robbie Dean Pr.

Dadey, Debbie. Cherokee Sister. 128p. (gr. 3-7). 2001. pap. text 4.50 o.s.i (*0-440-41568-3*, Yearling); 2000. text 14.95 o.s.i (*0-385-32703-X*, Delacorte Bks. for Young Readers) Random Hse. Children's Bks.

Duey, Kathleen. Evie Peach: St. Louis, 1857. 1997. (American Diaries Ser.: No. 8). 144p. (J). (gr. 3-7). pap. 4.99 (*0-689-81621-9*, Simon Pulse) Simon & Schuster Children's Publishing.

—Evie Peach: St. Louis, 1857. 1997. (American Diaries Ser.: No. 8). (J). (gr. 3-7). 10.55 (*0-606-12615-5*) Turtleback Bks.

Duke, Mary A. Victoria Scarlett Jones. 1993. (Illus.). 55p. (Orig.). (J). (gr. 3-5). pap. 5.95 o.p. (*1-883241-05-7*) Cognitive Pr.

Finley, Martha. Elsie's Endless Wait. 1999. (Elsie Dinsmore: Bk. 1). (Illus.). 224p. (J). (gr. 5-9). 9.99 (*1-928749-01-1*) Mission City Pr., Inc.

Foreman, Wilmoth. Summer of the Skunks. 2003. 156p. (J). 15.95 (*1-886910-80-4*, Front Street) Front Street, Inc.

Forrester, Sandra. My Home Is over Jordan: Sequel to "Sound the Jubilee" 1997. Orig. Title: Fire & Shadow. 160p. (J). (gr. 5-9). 15.99 o.s.i (*0-525-67568-X*, Dutton Children's Bks.) Penguin Putnam Bks. for Young Readers.

Graham, Lorenz. South Town. 2003. 188p. (YA). (gr. 7 up). 16.95 (*1-59078-161-9*) Boyds Mills Pr.

—South Town. 1970. mass mkt. 0.60 o.p. (*0-451-04409-6*); 1965. mass mkt. 0.95 o.p. (*0-451-06244-2*); 1965. mass mkt. 1.25 o.p. (*0-451-07915-9*); 1965. (J). (gr. 6). mass mkt. 1.75 o.p. (*0-451-11483-3*, AE1483) NAL. (Signet Bks.).

Gray, Genevieve. Two Tickets to Memphis. 1977. (Time of Danger, Time for Courage Ser.). (Illus.). 40p. (J). (gr. 3-9). pap. 3.95 o.p. (*0-88436-389-9*, 35301); lib. bdg. 6.95 o.p. (*0-88436-388-0*, 35483) Paradigm Publishing, Inc.

Haley, Gail E. Jack Jouett's Ride. 1976. (Seafarer Ser.). (Illus.). (J). (gr. 1-4). 2.95 o.p. (*0-670-05102-0*, Penguin Bks.) Viking Penguin.

Hall, Marjory. Beneath Another Sun. 1970. (J). (gr. 7-10). 4.75 o.p. (*0-664-32472-X*) Westminster John Knox Pr.

Hanna, James M. Southern Tales. Toscano, Filippo M., tr. l.t. ed. 1999. (ENG & SPA., Illus.). 190p. (Orig.). (YA). (gr. 8-12). pap. text 19.95 (*0-9640458-6-9*) Cherokee Bks.

Harrington, Janice N. Going North, RS. 2004. (J). (*0-374-32681-9*, Farrar, Straus & Giroux (BYR)) Farrar, Straus & Giroux.

Hearne, Betsy. Listening for Leroy. 1998. 224p. (J). (gr. 4-7). 16.00 (*0-689-82218-9*, McElderry, Margaret K.) Simon & Schuster Children's Publishing.

Hermes, Patricia. Fly Away Home: The Novelization & Story Behind the Film. novel ed. 1996. (Medallion Edition Ser.). (Illus.). 160p. (J). pap. 6.95 (*1-55704-303-5*) Newmarket Pr.

Hinson, Robert. Of Fairfield Plantation. 1997. 64p. (YA). (gr. 7-12). pap. 5.95 (*1-890424-00-5*) D-N Publishing.

Hite, Sid. An Even Break, ERS. 1995. (Illus.). 96p. (J). (gr. 2-4). 14.95 o.p. (*0-8050-3837-X*, Holt, Henry & Co. Bks. For Young Readers) Holt, Henry & Co.

—An Even Break. 1997. 96p. (gr. 4-7). pap. text 3.99 o.s.i (*0-440-41323-0*, Yearling) Random Hse. Children's Bks.

Holloway Lambe, Jennifer. Kudzu Chaos. 2003. (Illus.). 32p. (J). 14.95 (*1-58980-157-1*) Pelican Publishing Co., Inc.

Hooks, William H. Crossing the Line. 1978. (YA). 6.95 o.p. (*0-394-83938-2*); lib. bdg. 6.99 o.p. (*0-394-93938-7*) Random Hse. Children's Bks. (Knopf Bks. for Young Readers).

Jablonski, Carla. Southern Fried Makeover. 1999. (Clueless Ser.). 160p. (YA). (gr. 6 up). pap. 4.99 (*0-671-03437-5*, Simon Pulse) Simon & Schuster Children's Publishing.

Jackson, Dave & Jackson, Neta. Defeat of the Ghost Riders: Mary McLeod Bethune. 1997. (Trailblazer Bks.: Vol. 23). 144p. (J). (gr. 3-7). pap. 5.99 (*1-55661-742-9*) Bethany Hse. Pubs.

Justus, Adalu. The Storyteller House. 1999. 180p. (YA). (gr. 5-12). per. (*0-937109-11-8*) Ike, J. Bks.

Lawlor, Laurie. Old Crump: The True Story of a Trip West. 2002. (Illus.). 32p. (J). (gr. 2-4). tchr. ed. 16.95 (*0-8234-1608-9*) Holiday Hse., Inc.

L'Engle, Madeleine. The Other Side of the Sun. 1971. 344p. (J). 6.95 o.s.i (*0-374-22805-1*) Farrar, Straus & Giroux.

Littlesugar, Amy. Jonkonnu: A Story from the Sketchbook of Winslow Homer. 1997. (Illus.). 32p. (J). (ps-3). 15.95 o.s.i (*0-399-22831-4*, Philomel) Penguin Putnam Bks. for Young Readers.

Marino, Jan. The Day That Elvis Came to Town. 1993. 208p. (J). (gr. 5). reprint ed. pap. 3.50 (*0-380-71672-0*, Avon Bks.) Morrow/Avon.
Marshall, James. A Summer in the South. (Illus.). (J). 1999. 98p. (gr. 4-6). pap. 5.95 (*0-395-91361-6*); 1977. (gr. 1 up). 13.95 o.p. (*0-395-25840-5*) Houghton Mifflin Co.
Martin, Ann M. Belle Teal. 2001. 256p. (YA). (gr. 5-9). pap. 15.95 (*0-439-09823-8*) Scholastic, Inc.
Martin, JoAn W. Pine Cones & Magnolia Blossoms. 1999. (Illus.). 100p. pap. text 8.95 (*1-58521-005-6*) Books for Black Children, Inc.
McKissack, Patricia C. Run Away Home. 1997. 128p. (J). (gr. 3-7). pap. 14.95 (*0-590-46751-4*) Scholastic, Inc.
Page, Thomas Nelson. Two Little Confederates, Repr. Of 1888 Ed. 1976. (Classics of Children's Literature, 1621-1932: Vol. 56). (J). lib. bdg. 42.00 o.p. (*0-8240-2305-6*) Garland Publishing, Inc.
Peck, Robert Newton. Extra Innings. 2001. 192p. (J). (gr. 7 up). 16.99 (*0-06-028867-1*) HarperCollins Children's Bk. Group.
—Extra Innings. 2003. 224p. (J). (gr. 7 up). pap. 5.99 (*0-06-447229-9*) HarperCollins Pubs.
Pyrnelle, Louise Clarke. Diddie, Dumps & Tot. 1963. (Illus.). 240p. (J). (gr. 4-8). 15.95 (*0-911116-17-6*) Pelican Publishing Co., Inc.
Reaver, Chap. Bill. 1994. 224p. (YA). 14.95 o.s.i (*0-385-31175-3*, Delacorte Pr.) Dell Publishing.
—Bill. 1996. 224p. (YA). (gr. 5 up). pap. 3.99 o.s.i (*0-440-41153-X*, Yearling) Random Hse. Children's Bks.
—Bill. 1996. (J). 9.09 o.p. (*0-606-09076-2*) Turtleback Bks.
Rinaldi, Ann. The Coffin Quilt: The Feud Between the Hatfields & the McCoys. 2001. (Great Episodes Ser.). 240p. (YA). (gr. 5-9). pap. 6.00 (*0-15-216450-2*, Gulliver Bks.) Harcourt Children's Bks.
—The Last Silk Dress. 1999. 352p. (YA). (gr. 7). mass mkt. 5.99 (*0-440-22861-1*) Bantam Dell Publishing Group.
Rue, Nancy. The Threat. 1998. (Christian Heritage Ser.). 208p. (J). (gr. 3-7). pap. 5.99 (*1-56179-566-6*) Focus on the Family Publishing.
Sorensen. Curious Missie C. 2003. (J). (*0-15-204717-4*) Harcourt Trade Pubs.
—Curious Missie P. 2003. (J). pap. (*0-15-204716-6*) Harcourt Trade Pubs.
Sorensen, Virginia. Curious Missie. 1953. (Illus.). (J). (gr. 3-6). 5.50 o.p. (*0-15-221085-7*) Harcourt Children's Bks.
Standish, Burt L. Frank Merriwell down South. Rudman, Jack, ed. (Frank Merriwell Ser.). (YA). (gr. 9 up). 29.95 (*0-8373-9305-1*); 2003. pap. 9.95 (*0-8373-9005-2*, FM-005) Merriwell, Frank Inc.
Stowe, Harriet Beecher. La Cabana del Tio Tom. 2002. (Classics for Young Readers Ser.). (SPA.). (YA). 14.95 (*84-392-0905-3*, EV30595) Lectorum Pubns., Inc.
—La Cabana del Tio Tom. 1999. (Coleccion "Clasicos Juveniles" Ser.). (SPA., Illus.). 477p. (J). pap. 21.95 (*1-58348-829-4*) iUniverse, Inc.
—Uncle Tom's Cabin. 1967. (Airmont Classics Ser.). (YA). (gr. 9 up). mass mkt. 3.50 (*0-8049-0143-0*, CL-143) Airmont Publishing Co., Inc.
—Uncle Tom's Cabin. 1852. (YA). reprint ed. pap. text 28.00 (*1-4047-8957-X*) Classic Textbooks.
—Uncle Tom's Cabin. 1966. 496p. (C). mass mkt. 5.95 o.s.i (*0-451-52302-4*) NAL.
—Uncle Tom's Cabin. 1981. (Penguin American Library). (J). 14.05 o.p. (*0-606-01538-8*) Turtleback Bks.
Stroud, Bettye. Down Home at Miss Dessa's. 1996. (Illus.). 32p. (J). (ps up). 14.95 (*1-880000-39-3*) Lee & Low Bks., Inc.
Tate, Eleanora E. Don't Split the Pole: Tales of down Home Folk Wisdom. 1997. (Illus.). 144p. (J). (gr. 2-6). text 14.95 o.s.i (*0-385-32302-6*, Delacorte Pr.) Dell Publishing.
Taylor, Mildred D. Friendship & the Gold Cadillac. 1989. 96p. (J). (gr. 2-6). pap. 3.99 o.s.i (*0-553-15765-5*, Skylark) Random Hse. Children's Bks.
—The Gold Cadillac. (Illus.). (J). 1998. 48p. (gr. 2-6). pap. 4.99 (*0-14-038963-6*); 1987. 4p. (gr. 2-6). 12.89 o.p. (*0-8037-0343-0*, Dial Bks. for Young Readers); 1987. 4p. (gr. 4-7). 16.99 (*0-8037-0342-2*, Dial Bks. for Young Readers) Penguin Putnam Bks. for Young Readers.
—The Gold Cadillac. 1998. 11.14 (*0-606-13433-6*) Turtleback Bks.
—The Land. 2001. 392p. (J). (gr. 7 up). 17.99 (*0-8037-1950-7*); 1999. pap. 15.89 (*0-8037-1951-5*) Penguin Putnam Bks. for Young Readers. (Dial Bks. for Young Readers).
—Land. 2003. 384p. (YA). pap. 6.99 (*0-14-250146-8*, Puffin Bks.) Penguin Putnam Bks. for Young Readers.
Turner, Ann Warren. Nettie's Trip South. 1998. (J). pap. 4.95 (*0-87628-955-3*) Ctr. for Applied Research in Education, The.
—Nettie's Trip South. 1995. (Illus.). 32p. (J). (gr. 4-7). pap. 5.99 (*0-689-80117-3*, Aladdin) Simon & Schuster Children's Publishing.
Twain, Mark. The Adventures of Huckleberry Finn. (Washington Square Press Enriched Classic Ser.). 1994. 11.04 (*0-606-12869-7*); 1982. (J). 11.00 (*0-606-13112-4*) Turtleback Bks.
—The Adventures of Tom Sawyer. 1997. (J). 11.00 (*0-606-01797-6*) Turtleback Bks.
Wiles, Deborah. Freedom Summer. 2001. (Illus.). 32p. (J). (ps-3). 16.95 (*0-689-83016-5*, Atheneum/Anne Schwartz Bks.) Simon & Schuster Children's Publishing.
Williams, Rozanne L. Way down South, Vol. 3691. 1995. (Emergent Reader Big Bks.). (Illus.). 46p. (J). (gr. k-2). pap. 12.98 (*1-57471-074-5*) Creative Teaching Pr., Inc.
Woodson, Jacqueline. The House You Pass on the Way. 1999. 128p. (YA). (gr. 7-12). mass mkt. 4.50 o.s.i (*0-440-22797-6*, Dell Books for Young Readers) Random Hse. Children's Bks.
—The House You Pass on the Way. 1999. 10.55 (*0-606-16085-X*) Turtleback Bks.
Woodtor, Dee P. Big Meeting. 1996. (Illus.). 40p. (J). (gr. k-3). 16.00 (*0-689-31933-9*, Atheneum) Simon & Schuster Children's Publishing.
Youmans, Marly. Little Jordan. 1995. 112p. 18.95 (*1-56792-029-2*) Godine, David R. Pub.
—Little Jordan. 1999. 112p. (YA). (gr. 7-12). pap. 6.99 (*0-380-73136-3*, Avon Bks.) Morrow/Avon.
Young, Ronder T. Learning by Heart. 1995. 176p. (J). pap. 3.99 o.s.i (*0-14-037252-0*, Puffin Bks.) Penguin Putnam Bks. for Young Readers.
Young, Ronder Thomas. Learning by Heart. 1993. 176p. (J). (gr. 4-6). 14.95 (*0-395-65369-X*) Houghton Mifflin Co.

SOUTHWEST, NEW—FICTION

Anaya, Rudolfo A. Roadrunner's Dance. 2000. (Illus.). 32p. (J). (gr. k-4). 15.99 (*0-7868-0254-5*); lib. bdg. 16.49 (*0-7868-2209-0*) Disney Pr.
Baker, Betty. Treasure of the Padres. 1964. (Illus.). (J). (gr. 3-7). lib. bdg. 8.79 o.p. (*0-06-020366-8*) HarperCollins Pubs.
Baylor, Byrd. I'm in Charge of Celebrations. (Illus.). 32p. (J). (ps-3). 1995. pap. 5.99 (*0-689-80620-5*, Aladdin); 1986. 17.95 (*0-684-18579-2*, Atheneum) Simon & Schuster Children's Publishing.
—I'm in Charge of Celebrations. 1995. 12.14 (*0-606-07693-X*) Turtleback Bks.
Burks, Brian. Walks Alone. 1998. 128p. (YA). (gr. 6-12). 16.00 (*0-15-201612-0*) Harcourt Children's Bks.
Cook, Jean Thor. Los Amiguitos' Fiesta. Wilson, Lincoln, ed. l.t. ed. 2001. Tr. of Little Friends' Fiesta. (SPA., Illus.). 28p. (J). (ps-3). 17.00 (*0-9708940-0-7*) Gently Worded Bks., LLC.
Cordova, Amy. Abuelita's Heart. 1997. (ENG & SPA., Illus.). 32p. (J). (ps-3). 16.00 (*0-689-80181-5*, Simon & Schuster Children's Publishing) Simon & Schuster Children's Publishing.
Curry, Jane Louise. The Egyptian Box. 2002. (Illus.). 192p. (J). (gr. 4-7). 16.00 (*0-689-84273-2*, McElderry, Margaret K.) Simon & Schuster Children's Publishing.
—The Egyptian Box. l.t. ed. 2002. 216p. (J). (*0-7862-4896-3*) Thorndike Pr.
Greer, Mary L. & Van Bebber, Charlotte. 'Twas the Night Before Christmas on the Desert. 1987. (Illus.). 32p. (J). (gr. 3 up). pap. 7.50 o.p. (*0-918080-07-X*) Treasure Chest Bks.
Hobbs, William. The Big Wander. 1994. 192p. (J). (gr. 4-7). reprint ed. pap. 5.95 (*0-380-72140-6*, Avon Bks.) Morrow/Avon.
—The Big Wander. unabr. ed. 1997. (J). Class Set. (gr. 5). pap. 100.80 incl. audio (*0-7887-3498-9*, 46110); Homework Set. 47.75 incl. audio (*0-7887-1848-7*, 40628) Recorded Bks., LLC.
—The Big Wander. 1992. 160p. (J). (gr. 4-7). 17.00 (*0-689-31767-0*, Atheneum) Simon & Schuster Children's Publishing.
—The Big Wander. 1992. 11.00 (*0-606-06231-9*) Turtleback Bks.
Lattimore, Deborah Nourse. Frida Maria: A Story of the Old Southwest. (Illus.). (J). (gr. k-3). 1997. 32p. pap. 6.00 (*0-15-201515-9*, Harcourt Paperbacks); 1994. 28p. 14.95 (*0-15-276636-7*) Harcourt Children's Bks.
—Frida Maria: Un Cuento del Sudoeste de Antes. Marcuse, Aida E., tr. 1997. (SPA., Illus.). 32p. (J). (gr. k-3). pap. 7.00 (*0-15-201487-X*, Voyager Bks./Libros Viajeros) Harcourt Children's Bks.
Lowell, Susan. The Three Little Javelinas. 1992. (Reading Rainbow Bks.). (Illus.). 32p. (J). (ps-3). lib. bdg. 15.95 (*0-87358-542-9*, Rising Moon Bks. for Young Readers) Northland Publishing.
Oberman, Sheldon. The White Stone in the Castle Wall. 1995. (Illus.). 24p. (J). (gr. 1-3). 15.95 (*0-88776-333-2*) Tundra Bks. of Northern New York.
Paulsen, Gary. Tucket's Ride. 1997. (Tucket Adventures Ser.: Vol. 3). 112p. (gr. 5-9). text 15.95 o.s.i (*0-385-32199-6*, Dell Books for Young Readers) Random Hse. Children's Bks.
Roach, Joyce Gibson. Horned Toad Canyon. 2003. 48p. (J). 17.95 (*1-931721-01-7*) Bright Sky Pr.
Stein, R. Conrad. On the Old Western Frontier. 1999. (How We Lived Ser.). (Illus.). 72p. (J). (gr. 4-8). lib. bdg. 27.07 (*0-7614-0909-2*, Benchmark Bks.) Cavendish, Marshall Corp.
Taylor, Bonnie Highsmith. Kodi's Mare. 2000. (Cover-to-Cover Novel Ser.). (Illus.). 82p. (J). (*0-7807-8962-8*); pap. (*0-7891-2929-9*) Perfection Learning Corp.
Thesz, Fredda. Pueblo Suite. 1994. 200p. (Orig.). 10.99 o.p. (*1-881542-22-X*) Book World, Inc.
White, Robb. Deathwatch. 1973. (Laurel-Leaf Bks.). 224p. (YA). (gr. 7-12). mass mkt. 5.50 (*0-440-91740-9*) Dell Publishing.
—Deathwatch. 1972. (gr. 9-12). 6.95 o.p. (*0-385-02510-6*); lib. bdg. o.p. (*0-385-02612-9*) Doubleday Publishing.
—Deathwatch. 1973. (J). 11.55 (*0-606-01160-9*) Turtleback Bks.
Wright, Randall. A Hundred Days from Home, ERS. 2002. 160p. (YA). (gr. 6 up). 15.95 (*0-8050-6885-6*, Holt, Henry & Co. Bks. For Young Readers) Holt, Henry & Co.

SOUTHWEST, OLD—FICTION

Lattimore, Deborah Nourse. Frida Maria: A Story of the Old Southwest. 1997. (J). 12.15 (*0-606-11354-1*) Turtleback Bks.
—Frida Maria: Un Cuento del Sudoeste de Antes. 1997. (J). 12.15 (*0-606-11355-X*) Turtleback Bks.

SOVIET UNION—FICTION

Almedingen, E. M. Anna, RS. 1972. 192p. (J). (gr. 7 up). 5.95 o.p. (*0-374-30361-4*, Farrar, Straus & Giroux (BYR)) Farrar, Straus & Giroux.
—Young Mark, RS. 1968. (Illus.). (J). (gr. 7 up). 3.75 o.p. (*0-374-38745-1*, Farrar, Straus & Giroux (BYR)) Farrar, Straus & Giroux.
Bograd, Larry. The Kolokol Papers, RS. 1981. 196p. (J). (gr. 7 up). 11.95 o.p. (*0-374-34277-6*, Farrar, Straus & Giroux (BYR)) Farrar, Straus & Giroux.
—The Kolokol Papers. 1983. (J). mass mkt. 2.25 o.s.i (*0-440-94552-6*, Dell Books for Young Readers) Random Hse. Children's Bks.
Brewster, Hugh. Anastasia's Album: The Last Tsar's Youngest Daughter. 1999. 64p. (J). pap. 7.99 (*0-7868-1395-4*) Disney Pr.
Burstein, Chaya M. Rifka Bangs the Teakettle. 1970. (Illus.). (J). (gr. 4-6). 4.95 o.p. (*0-15-266944-2*) Harcourt Children's Bks.
Chukofky, Kornei. The Silver Crest: My Russian Boyhood, ERS. Stillman, Beatrice, tr. from RUS. 1976. 192p. (J). (gr. 5 up). o.p. (*0-03-014241-5*, Holt, Henry & Co. Bks. For Young Readers) Holt, Henry & Co.
Clark, Margery. Poppy Seed Cakes. 1986. (Books for Young Readers). (ps-1). (J). 9.95 (*0-385-07457-3*); lib. bdg. o.p. (*0-385-03834-8*) Doubleday Publishing.
Cole, Joanna. Bony-Legs. 1984. (Illus.). 48p. (J). (ps-3). lib. bdg. 16.00 (*0-02-722970-X*, Simon & Schuster Children's Publishing) Simon & Schuster Children's Publishing.
Corcoran, Barbara. The Clown. 1975. 192p. (J). (gr. 5-9). 8.95 o.s.i (*0-689-30465-X*, Atheneum) Simon & Schuster Children's Publishing.
—Meet Me at Tamerlane's Tomb. 1975. (Illus.). 160p. (J). (gr. 5-9). 6.95 o.p. (*0-689-30446-3*, Atheneum) Simon & Schuster Children's Publishing.
Currier, Alvin Alexsi. Old Maria: A Grandfather's Tale of Spiritual Warfare Once upon a Time in Old Russia. 2002. (Illus.). 28p. (J). (gr. 2-6). 14.95 (*0-9723411-0-2*) Currier, Alvin Alexsi.
Deutsch, Babette & Yarmolinsky, Avrahm. Steel Flea. 1964. (J). (gr. 2-6). lib. bdg. 6.89 o.p. (*0-06-021616-6*) HarperCollins Pubs.
Deyneka, Anita. Alexi & the Mountain Treasure. 1979. (Illus.). (J). (gr. 4-7). pap. 1.75 o.p. (*0-89191-062-X*) Cook, David C. Publishing Co.
Dostoyevsky, Fyodor. The Brothers Karamazov: A Dramatization. 1995. per. 6.50 (*0-8222-1425-3*) Dramatists Play Service, Inc.
—The Brothers Karamazov: A Novel in Four Parts with Epilogue. Pevear, Richard & Volokhonsky, Larissa, trs. from RUS. 1990. 832p. 40.00 o.s.i (*0-86547-422-2*, North Point Pr.) Farrar, Straus & Giroux.
Gernyet, N. & Jagdfeld, G. Katya & the Crocodile. Corrin, Stephen, tr. 1969. (Illus.). (J). (gr. 1-4). 4.00 o.p. (*0-900675-09-8*) Transatlantic Arts, Inc.
Gogol, Nikolai. Dead Souls. 1966. (Airmont Classics Ser.). (YA). (gr. 11 up). mass mkt. 1.95 o.p. (*0-8049-0122-8*, CL-122) Airmont Publishing Co., Inc.
Goldberg, Yaffa G. A Gift of Challahs. Zakutinsky, Ruth, ed. 1981. (Illus.). 32p. (Orig.). (J). (gr. k-6). pap. 3.95 o.p. (*0-911643-00-1*) Aura Printing, Inc.
Grant, Myrna. Ivan & the Moscow Circus. 1980. (J). (gr. 4-8). pap. 3.50 o.p. (*0-8423-1843-7*) Tyndale Hse. Pubs.
—Ivan & the Secret in the Suitcase. 1975. (Ivan Ser.). (J). (gr. 3-8). pap. 3.50 o.p. (*0-8423-1849-6*) Tyndale Hse. Pubs.
Gross, Sukey S. Passport to Russia. 1989. (Girls of Riukah Gross Academy Ser.). (Illus.). 158p. (J). (gr. 5-8). 13.95 (*0-935063-59-5*, CJR108H); pap. 10.95 (*0-935063-60-9*, CJR108S) CIS Communications, Inc.
Hergé. L' Affaire Tournesol. 1999. (Tintin Ser.).Tr. of Calculus Affair. (FRE.). (gr. 4-7). 19.95 (*2-203-00117-8*) Casterman, Editions FRA. *Dist:* Distribooks, Inc.
—L' Affaire Tournesol.Tr. of Calculus Affair. (FRE., Illus.). (J). (gr. 7-9). lib. bdg. 19.95 o.p. (*0-8288-6087-4*, FC867); 1992. 64p. reprint ed. (*0-7859-4692-6*) French & European Pubns., Inc.
—The Calculus Affair. (Illus.). 62p. (J). 19.95 (*0-8288-5014-3*); pap. 4.95 o.p. (*0-416-77390-7*) French & European Pubns., Inc.
—The Calculus Affair. 1976. (Adventures of Tintin Ser.). 62p. (J). (gr. 2 up). pap. 9.99 (*0-316-35847-9*, Joy Street Bks.) Little Brown & Co.
—Tintin au Pays des Soviets. 1999. (Tintin Ser.). (FRE.). (gr. 4-7). 19.95 (*2-203-01101-7*) Midwest European Pubns.
—Tintin in the Land of the Soviets. 1992. 116p. (J). 39.95 (*0-7859-0978-8*, 2203020016) French & European Pubns., Inc.
—Tintin in the Land of the Soviets. fac. ed. 2003. 128p. (J). reprint ed. 19.95 (*0-86719-903-2*) Last Gasp Eco-Funnies, Inc.
Holman, Felice. The Wild Children. 1985. 160p. (J). (gr. 5-9). pap. 5.99 (*0-14-031930-1*, Puffin Bks.) Penguin Putnam Bks. for Young Readers.
Huang, Benrei. A Visit to the Soviet Union. 1991. (Golden Look-Look Bks.). (Illus.). 24p. (J). (ps-3). pap. 3.29 o.s.i (*0-307-12632-3*, Golden Bks.) Random Hse. Children's Bks.
Kassil, Lev & White, Anne T. Brother of the Hero. 1968. (J). (gr. 4-6). 3.95 o.s.i (*0-8076-0444-5*) Braziller, George Inc.
Krasnopolsky, Fara L. I Remember. 1995. (Illus.). 176p. (J). 15.95 o.p. (*0-395-67401-8*, Clarion Bks.) Houghton Mifflin Co. Trade & Reference Div.
Langford, Sondra Gordon. Mishka & Plishka. 1996. (J). 16.00 (*0-689-80244-7*, Simon & Schuster Children's Publishing) Simon & Schuster Children's Publishing.
Margolin, Miriam. Little Stories for Little Children. 1986. (Illus.). 32p. (J). (gr. k-3). reprint ed. 11.75 o.p. (*0-918825-55-5*) Moyer Bell.
Matas, Carol. Sworn Enemies. 1994. 144p. (YA). mass mkt. 3.99 o.s.i (*0-440-21900-0*) Dell Publishing.
—Sworn Enemies. 1993. (J). mass mkt. o.p. (*0-440-90069-7*, Dell Books for Young Readers) Random Hse. Children's Bks.
—Sworn Enemies. 1993. 9.09 o.p. (*0-606-06043-X*) Turtleback Bks.
Mazzeo Zocchi, Judy. Circus or Not - Here We Come. 1998. (Adventures of Paulie & Sasha Ser.). (Illus.). 32p. (J). (gr. k-4). 15.95 (*1-891997-00-9*, THC 01, Treehouse Court) Dingles & Co.
Pargment, Lila & Titiev, Estelle, adapted by. How the Moolah Was Taught a Lesson & Other Tales from Russia. 1985. (Illus.). 56p. (J). lib. bdg. 5.47 o.s.i (*0-8037-5746-8*, Dial Bks.) Dell Publishing.
—How the Moolah Was Taught a Lesson & Other Tales from Russia. 1985. (Illus.). 56p. (J). 5.95 o.p. (*0-8037-5744-1*, Dial Bks. for Young Readers) Penguin Putnam Bks. for Young Readers.
Polacco, Patricia. Babushka Baba Yaga. (Illus.). 32p. (ps-3). 1999. pap. 6.99 (*0-698-11633-X*); 1993. (J). 16.99 (*0-399-22531-5*, Philomel) Penguin Putnam Bks. for Young Readers.
—Babushka Baba Yaga. 1999. lib. bdg. 13.14 (*0-606-16844-3*) Turtleback Bks.
—Rechenka's Eggs. 2002. (Illus.). (J). 14.04 (*0-7587-3502-2*) Book Wholesalers, Inc.
—Rechenka's Eggs. (ps-3). 1996. (Illus.). 32p. (J). pap. 6.99 (*0-698-11385-3*, PaperStar); 1988. (Illus.). 32p. (J). 16.99 (*0-399-21501-8*, Philomel); 1987. 13.95 o.p. (*0-399-21497-6*, Philomel) Penguin Putnam Bks. for Young Readers.
—Rechenka's Eggs. unabr. ed. 1993. (J). (ps-4). pap. 17.95 incl. audio (*0-8045-6586-4*, 6586) Spoken Arts, Inc.
—Rechenka's Eggs. 1996. 12.14 (*0-606-09782-1*) Turtleback Bks.
Posell, Elsa. Homecoming. 1987. 224p. (YA). (gr. 7 up). 14.95 o.p. (*0-15-235160-4*) Harcourt Children's Bks.
Price, Susan. Ghost Dance, RS. 1995. 228p. (J). (gr. 4-7). 16.00 o.p. (*0-374-32537-5*, Farrar, Straus & Giroux (BYR)) Farrar, Straus & Giroux.
—Ghost Song, RS. 1992. 160p. (YA). (gr. 7 up). 15.00 o.p. (*0-374-32544-8*, Farrar, Straus & Giroux (BYR)) Farrar, Straus & Giroux.
Samstag, Nicholas. Kay Kay Comes Home. 1962. (Illus.). (J). (gr. 5-7). 12.95 (*0-8392-3015-X*) Astor-Honor, Inc.
Sandman, Rochel. As Big As an Egg: A Story about Giving. Rosenfeld, Dina, ed. 1995. (Illus.). 32p. (J). (gr. 2 up). 9.95 (*0-922613-77-X*) Hachai Publishing.

—Perfect Porridge: A Story about Kindness. 2000. (Illus.). 32p. (J). (ps-2). 9.95 (*0-922613-92-3*) Hachai Publishing.

Schloneger, Florence E. Sara's Trek. 1982. (Illus.). 100p. (YA). (gr. 7 up). pap. 4.95 o.p. (*0-87303-071-0*) Faith & Life Pr.

Schur, Maxine R. The Circlemaker. 192p. (YA). (gr. 5 up). 1996. pap. 5.99 (*0-14-037997-5*, Puffin Bks.); 1994. 14.99 o.s.i (*0-8037-1354-1*, Dial Bks. for Young Readers) Penguin Putnam Bks. for Young Readers.

—The Circlemaker. 1996. (YA). (gr. 5 up). 11.04 (*0-606-09149-1*) Turtleback Bks.

Segal, Jerry. The Place Where Nobody Stopped. Cohn, Amy, ed. 1994. (Illus.). 160p. (J). (gr. 5 up). reprint ed. pap. 4.95 o.p. (*0-688-12567-0*, Morrow, William & Co.) Morrow/Avon.

Sesemann, Dimitri. V Moskve Vse Spokoino (All Is Calm in Moscow) Roman (A Novel) Jurovskii, A. & Rybakov, V., eds. 1990. (RUS.). 222p. (Orig.). (YA). (gr. 9-12). pap. 12.50 (*0-911971-47-5*) Effect Publishing, Inc.

Sevela, Ephraim. Why There Is No Heaven on Earth. Lourie, Richard, tr. 1982. (RUS.). 224p. (YA). (gr. 7 up). o.p. (*0-06-025502-1*); lib. bdg. 10.89 o.p. (*0-06-025503-X*) HarperCollins Children's Bk. Group.

Shepard, Aaron. The Sea King's Daughter. 2001. (Illus.). 40p. (ps-3). pap. 6.99 (*0-689-84259-7*, Aladdin) Simon & Schuster Children's Publishing.

Shulevitz, Uri. Soldier & Tsar in the Forest: A Russian Tale, RS. Lourie, Richard, tr. from RUS. 1972. (Illus.). 32p. (J). (ps-3). 16.00 (*0-374-37126-1*, Farrar, Straus & Giroux (BYR)) Farrar, Straus & Giroux.

Shulman, Colette, ed. We the Russians: Voices from Russia. 1971. (Illus.). 320p. (J). pap. 2.95 o.p. (*0-275-88550-X*, Praeger Pubs.) Greenwood Publishing Group, Inc.

Shusterman, Neal. Dissidents. 1989. 224p. (YA). (gr. 7 up). 13.95 (*0-316-78904-6*) Little Brown & Co.

Singer, Isaac Bashevis. When Shlemiel Went to Warsaw & Other Stories, RS. Shub, Elizabeth, tr. from YID. 1969. (Illus.). 128p. (J). (gr. 4-7). 13.95 o.p. (*0-374-38316-2*, Farrar, Straus & Giroux (BYR)) Farrar, Straus & Giroux.

Solzhenitsyn, Aleksandr. One Day in the Life of Ivan Denisovich. Hingley, Ronald, tr. 1963. 234p. (gr. 10 up). pap. 2.95 o.p. (*0-275-62300-9*, P169, Praeger Pubs.) Greenwood Publishing Group, Inc.

Thompson, Kay. Eloise in Moscow. 2000. 80p. (J). ltd. ed. 150.00 (*0-689-83328-8*); 40th ed. (Illus.). 17.00 (*0-689-83211-7*) Simon & Schuster Children's Publishing. (Simon & Schuster Children's Publishing).

Tompert, Ann. The Tzar's Bird. 1990. (Illus.). 32p. (J). (gr. k-3). 14.95 o.p. (*0-02-789401-0*, Simon & Schuster Children's Publishing) Simon & Schuster Children's Publishing.

Townsend, Tom. Nadia of the Night Witches. Kemnitz, Myrna, ed. 1998. 153p. (J). pap. 9.99 (*0-88092-273-7*, 2737) Royal Fireworks Publishing Co.

Trivas, Irene. Annie ... Anya: A Month in Moscow. 1992. (Illus.). 32p. (J). (gr. k-2). 15.95 o.p. (*0-531-05452-7*); mass mkt. 16.99 o.p. (*0-531-08602-X*) Scholastic, Inc. (Orchard Bks.).

Trottier, Maxine. Pavlova's Gift. unabr. ed. 1997. (Illus.). 32p. (J). (ps-3). 14.95 (*0-7737-2969-0*) Stoddart Kids CAN. *Dist:* Fitzhenry & Whiteside, Ltd.

Ushinsky, Konstantin. How a Shirt Grew in the Field. 1992. (Illus.). 32p. (J). (ps-3). 13.95 o.p. (*0-395-59761-7*, Clarion Bks.) Houghton Mifflin Co. Trade & Reference Div.

Verne, Jules. Michael Strogoff. deluxe ed. 1997. (Scribner Classics Ser.). 416p. (J). 75.00 (*0-689-81097-0*, Atheneum) Simon & Schuster Children's Publishing.

Whelan, Gloria. The Impossible Journey. 2004. 256p. (J). pap. 5.99 (*0-06-441083-8*, Harper Trophy) HarperCollins Children's Bk. Group.

—The Impossible Journey. 2003. 256p. (J). (gr. 5 up). 15.99 (*0-06-623811-0*); lib. bdg. 16.89 (*0-06-623812-9*) HarperCollins Pubs.

Zheleznikov, Vladimir. Scarecrow. Bouis, Antonina W., tr. from RUS. 1990. 160p. (J). (gr. 5 up). 12.95 o.p. (*0-397-32316-6*); lib. bdg. 12.89 (*0-397-32317-4*) HarperCollins Children's Bk. Group.

SPAIN—FICTION

Ardizzone, Edward, illus. Exploits of Don Quixote. 1985. (Children's Classics from World Literature Ser.). (YA). (gr. 5 up). 12.95 o.p. (*0-87226-025-9*); pap. 5.95 o.p. (*0-87226-026-7*) McGraw-Hill Children's Publishing. (Bedrick, Peter Bks.).

Armstrong, Wm. Las Aventuras De Pepito. Armstrong, Wm., tr. Igartua, Arturo, tr. & illus. by. Bradley, Arlene, illus. 1973. (Armstrong Spanish Cartoons Ser.: Vol. 1). (ENG & SPA.). 48p. (Orig.). (J). (gr. 1-10). pap. 1.00 o.p. (*0-913452-23-8*) Jesuit Bks.

Braun, Lutz. Faster Than the Bull. 1992. (Publish-a-Book Ser.). (Illus.). 32p. (J). (gr. 1-6). lib. bdg. 22.83 (*0-8114-3580-6*) Raintree Pubs.

Cann, Kate. Spanish Holiday. 2004. (Illus.). 352p. (J). pap. 5.99 (*0-06-056160-2*, Avon Bks.) Morrow/Avon.

Carlson, Natalie S. Song of the Lop-Eared Mule. 1961. (Illus.). (J). (gr. 2-6). lib. bdg. 7.89 o.p. (*0-06-021071-0*) HarperCollins Pubs.

Cervantes Saavedra, Miguel de. The Adventures of Don Quixote de la Mancha. Barret, Leighton, ed. 1962. (Illus.). (YA). (gr. 5 up). lib. bdg. 5.99 o.p. (*0-394-90892-9*, Knopf Bks. for Young Readers) Random Hse. Children's Bks.

—Don Quijote de la Mancha. 2002. (Classics for Young Readers Ser.). (SPA.). (YA). 14.95 (*84-392-0926-6*, EV30621) Lectorum Pubns., Inc.

—Don Quijote de la Mancha, Pt. 2. 1971. (SPA., Illus.). (YA). (gr. 11-12). pap. 3.95 o.p. (*0-88345-138-7*) Prentice Hall, ESL Dept.

—Don Quixote. Harrison, Michael, ed. 1999. (Oxford Illustrated Classics Ser.). (Illus.). 96p. (YA). pap. 12.95 o.p. (*0-19-274182-9*) Oxford Univ. Pr., Inc.

—Don Quixote. 1979. (Now Age Illustrated V Ser.). (Illus.). 64p. (J). (gr. 4-12). text 7.50 o.p. (*0-88301-399-1*); pap. text 2.95 (*0-88301-387-8*); stu. ed. 1.25 (*0-88301-411-4*) Pendulum Pr., Inc.

—Don Quixote. 1972. (Enriched Classics Ser.). (J). (gr. 9 up). pap. 0.95 o.s.i (*0-671-47873-7*, Washington Square Pr.) Simon & Schuster.

—Don Quixote. 1993. (Illus.). 32p. (J). (gr. 2 up). 13.95 o.p. (*1-56402-174-2*) Candlewick Pr.

—Don Quixote. 1995. (Oxford Illustrated Classics Ser.). (Illus.). 96p. (J). (gr. 4 up). 22.95 o.p. (*0-19-274165-9*) Oxford Univ. Pr., Inc.

—Don Quixote. Marshall, Michael J., ed. abr. ed. 1999. (Core Classics Ser.: Vol. 6). (Illus.). (J). (gr. 4-6). 264p. pap. 7.95 (*1-890517-10-0*); 256p. lib. bdg. 9.95 o.p. (*1-890517-11-9*) Core Knowledge Foundation.

—Don Quixote: Illustrated Classics. 1994. (Illustrated Classics Collection). 64p. (J). pap. 3.60 o.p. (*1-56103-621-8*) American Guidance Service, Inc.

—Don Quixote: Wishbone Classics. 1996. (Wishbone Classics Ser.: No. 1). (Illus.). 128p. (gr. 3-7). mass mkt. 4.25 (*0-06-106416-5*, HarperEntertainment) Morrow/Avon.

—Don Quixote: Wishbone Classics. 1996. (Wishbone Classics Ser.: No. 1). (J). (gr. 3-7). 10.30 (*0-606-10364-3*) Turtleback Bks.

—Don Quixote of Mancha. 1999. (Everyman's Library Children's Classics). (Illus.). 256p. (gr. 8-12). 14.95 (*0-375-40659-X*) Random Hse., Inc.

Comella, Maria Angeles, et al. Buenos Dias, Senor Tapies! 2001. Tr. of Good Day, Mr. Tapies!. (Illus.). 32p. (J). (CAT.). (gr. k-2). 14.95 (*84-95040-97-2*); (SPA., (gr. 2-5). 14.95 (*84-95040-96-4*) Serres, Ediciones, S. L. ESP. *Dist:* Lectorum Pubns., Inc.

de Trevino, Elizabeth Borton. Yo, Juan de Pareja, RS. Borton, Enrique T., tr. 1996. (SPA.). 192p. (YA). (gr. 7 up). pap. 5.95 (*0-374-49292-1*, FS2729, Mirasol/Libros Juveniles) Farrar, Straus & Giroux.

Fisher, Leonard Everett, illus. Don Quixote & the Windmills, RS. 2004. (J). 16.00 (*0-374-31825-5*, Farrar, Straus & Giroux (BYR)) Farrar, Straus & Giroux.

Hahn, Mary Downing. The Spanish Kidnapping Disaster. Giblin, James C., ed. 1991. 144p. (J). (gr. 5-9). tchr. ed. 16.00 (*0-395-55696-1*, Clarion Bks.) Houghton Mifflin Co. Trade & Reference Div.

—The Spanish Kidnapping Disaster. 1993. 144p. (YA). (gr. 4-7). pap. 4.50 (*0-380-71712-3*, Avon Bks.) Morrow/Avon.

—The Spanish Kidnapping Disaster. 1991. (J). 10.55 (*0-606-02901-X*) Turtleback Bks.

Hemingway, Ernest. The Sun Also Rises. unabr. ed. 2002. (YA). (gr. 10 up). audio 35.95 (*1-55685-686-5*) Audio Bk. Contractors, Inc.

—The Sun Also Rises. unabr. collector's ed. 1989. (J). audio 42.00 (*0-7366-2165-2*, 2964) Books on Tape, Inc.

—The Sun Also Rises. abr. ed. 1995. (A+ Audio Ser.). audio 8.00 (*1-57042-166-8*, 4-521668) Time Warner AudioBooks.

Hunter, Mollie. Spanish Letters. 1990. (Kelpie Ser.). 173p. (J). (gr. 5-8). pap. 6.95 o.p. (*0-86241-057-6*) Trafalgar Square.

I, Juan de Pareja. 3rd ed. (J). pap. text, stu. ed. (*0-13-667452-6*) Prentice Hall (Schl. Div.).

Jessup, Jack. A Donkey Named Rico. 2001. 497p. lib. bdg. (*0-7541-1539-9*) Minerva Pr.

Jiménez, Juan Ramón. Platero & I. 2003. (Illus.). 64p. (J). (gr. 4-6). pap. 5.95 (*0-618-37838-3*, Clarion Bks.) Houghton Mifflin Co. Trade & Reference Div.

—Platero & I. 1960. mass mkt. 0.50 o.p. (*0-451-50017-2*); mass mkt. 0.60 o.p. (*0-451-50302-3*); mass mkt. 0.75 o.p. (*0-451-50370-8*); mass mkt. 0.95 o.p. (*0-451-50849-1*, CQ849) NAL. (Signet Classics).

—Platero & I. Roach, Eloise, tr. from SPA. (Illus.). 1983. 218p. (C). pap. 14.95 (*0-292-76479-0*); 1957. 228p. pap. 12.95 o.p. (*0-292-73328-3*) Univ. of Texas Pr.

—Platero & I. 2000. (Illus.). 200p. pap. 12.95 (*0-595-00345-1*) iUniverse, Inc.

—Platero y Yo. (SPA.). 192p. 13.95 (*84-206-1851-9*, AZ1851); (Illus.). 159p. 9.95 (*84-206-3408-5*) Alianza Editorial, S. A. ESP. *Dist:* Continental Bk. Co., Inc., Distribooks, Inc., Distribooks, Inc.

—Platero y Yo. (SPA.). pap. 9.95 (*968-432-357-3*, PM223) Editorial Porrua MEX. *Dist:* Continental Bk. Co., Inc.

—Platero y Yo. Cardwell, Richard A., ed. 1991. (Nueva Austral Ser.: Vol. 58). (SPA.). 288p. 24.95 (*84-239-1858-0*) Elliot's Bks.

—Platero y Yo. annot. ed. (SPA., Illus.). 232p. 15.95 (*84-207-2636-2*, ANY010) Grupo Anaya, S.A. ESP. *Dist:* Continental Bk. Co., Inc.

—Platero y Yo. (SPA.). (YA). (gr. 5-8). pap. (*958-30-0744-7*, PV0560) Panamericana Editorial COL. *Dist:* Lectorum Pubns., Inc.

—Platero y Yo (Platero & I) (SPA.). pap. 9.95 (*968-416-022-4*, AOR01) Fernandez USA Publishing.

Jiménez, Juan Ramón & Dominguez, Joseph P. Platero & I. Livingston, Myra C., tr. 1994. (ENG & SPA., Illus.). 64p. (J). (gr. 4-6). tchr. ed. 15.00 (*0-395-62365-0*, BT3650, Clarion Bks.) Houghton Mifflin Co. Trade & Reference Div.

Johnson, Jane. La Princesa y el Pintor. 1996. (SPA., Illus.). 30p. (J). (ps-3). pap. 14.95 (*1-56014-618-4*, SAN6184) Santillana USA Publishing Co., Inc.

—La Princesa y el Pintor. 1999. (Illus.). (J). (gr. 4-7). (SPA.). 12p. 14.95 (*84-88061-30-7*); (CAT., 38p. 14.95 (*84-95040-23-9*) Serres, Ediciones, S. L. ESP. *Dist:* Lectorum Pubns., Inc.

—The Princess & the Painter, RS. 1994. 32p. (J). (ps-3). 15.00 o.p. (*0-374-36118-5*, Farrar, Straus & Giroux (BYR)) Farrar, Straus & Giroux.

Kaserman, James F. & Kaserman, Sarah Jane. The Legend of Gasparilla: A Tale for All Ages. 2000. 304p. (YA). pap. 14.95 (*0-9674081-1-3*) Pirate Publishing International.

Kimmel, Eric A. Bernal & Florinda: A Spanish Tale. 1994. (Illus.). 32p. (J). (ps-3). tchr. ed. 15.95 (*0-8234-1089-7*) Holiday Hse., Inc.

Levinson, Riki. Mira Como Salen las Estrellas. 1992. (SPA., Illus.). 32p. (J). (ps-3). 15.99 o.s.i (*0-525-44958-2*, Dutton Children's Bks.) Penguin Putnam Bks. for Young Readers.

Lewin, Waldtraut. Freedom Beyond the Sea. Crawford, Elizabeth D., tr. 2001. 272p. (YA). (gr. 9 up). 15.95 (*0-385-32705-6*, Delacorte Pr.) Dell Publishing.

—Freedom Beyond the Sea. 2003. 272p. (YA). (gr. 9-12). mass mkt. 5.50 (*0-440-22868-9*, Laurel Leaf) Random Hse. Children's Bks.

Marchesi, Stephen, illus. Don Quixote & Sancho Panza. 1992. 80p. (YA). (gr. 6 up). 16.95 (*0-684-19235-7*, Atheneum) Simon & Schuster Children's Publishing.

O'Dell, Scott. The Spanish Smile, 001. 1982. (J). (gr. 7 up). 13.95 o.p. (*0-395-32867-5*) Houghton Mifflin Co.

Palacios, Argentina. The Adventures of Don Quixote de la Mancha. 1999. (Children's Thrift Classics Ser.). (Illus.). 80p. (J). pap. text 1.00 (*0-486-40791-8*) Dover Pubns., Inc.

Paul, Sherry. Two-B 7 the Space Visitor. 1981. (See How I Read Bks.). (Illus.). 32p. (J). (gr. k-3). 9.95 o.p. (*0-516-02356-X*, Children's Pr.) Scholastic Library Publishing.

Pelgrom, Els. The Acorn Eaters, RS. Prins, Johanna H. & Prins, Johanna W., trs. from DUT. 1997. Tr. of Eikelvreters. 224p. (J). (gr. 7-12). 16.00 o.p. (*0-374-30029-1*, Farrar, Straus & Giroux (BYR)) Farrar, Straus & Giroux.

Perkins, Lucy F. Spanish Twins. 1969. (Walker's Twins Ser.). (Illus.). (J). (gr. 4-6). lib. bdg. 4.85 o.s.i (*0-8027-6070-8*) Walker & Co.

Rabley, Stephen. The Barcelona Game. 2002. (Illus.). 16p. pap. (*0-582-42771-1*) Penguin Putnam Bks. for Young Readers.

Schrade, Arlene O. Gabriel the Happy Ghost in Spain. 1986. Tr. of Gabriel el Fantasmita Simpatico en Espana. (ENG & SPA.). (J). 13.59 (*0-606-01276-1*) Turtleback Bks.

Sherrow, Victoria. Los Puerquitos Se Escaparon. Writer, C. C. & Nielsen, Lisa C., trs. 1992. (Hippy Ser.). (SPA., Illus.). 24p. (Orig.). (J). (ps). pap. text 3.00 o.p. (*1-56134-171-1*, McGraw-Hill/Dushkin) McGraw-Hill Higher Education.

Stevens, Biddy. Toto in Spain. 1995. (Toto in... Ser.). (ENG & SPA., Illus.). 24p. (J). 12.95 o.s.i (*0-8442-9170-6*, 91706, National Textbook Co.) McGraw-Hill/Contemporary.

Talley, Linda. Following Isabella. 2001. (Illus.). 30p. (J). pap. 16.95 (*1-55942-163-0*) Marsh Media.

—Following Isabella, Grades K-4. 2001. (Key Concepts in Personal Development Ser.). (Illus.). 32p. pap., tchr. ed. 79.95 incl. VHS (*1-55942-170-3*, 9388K3) Marsh Media.

Weston, Carol. With Love from Spain, Melanie Martin. 2004. (Illus.). 256p. (J). (gr. 3-7). 15.95 (*0-375-82646-7*); lib. bdg. 17.99 (*0-375-92646-1*) Random Hse. Children's Bks. (Knopf Bks. for Young Readers).

Williams, Marcia, illus. & retold by. Don Quixote. 1995. (J). (gr. 2 up). bds. 5.99 o.p. (*1-56402-070-3*) Candlewick Pr.

Wojciechowska, Maia. Shadow of a Bull. 1972. (Illus.). 176p. (YA). (gr. 5 up). 16.95 (*0-689-30042-5*, Atheneum); 2nd ed. 1987. 160p. (J). (gr. 4). reprint ed. pap. 3.95 o.s.i (*0-689-71132-8*, Aladdin); 3rd ed. 1992. 176p. (J). (gr. 4-7). reprint ed. pap. 4.99 (*0-689-71567-6*, Aladdin) Simon & Schuster Children's Publishing.

—Single Light. 1968. (J). (gr. 7 up). lib. bdg. 7.89 o.p. (*0-06-026575-2*) HarperCollins Pubs.

Wuorio, Eva-Lis. Detour to Danger: A Novel. 1981. 192p. (YA). (gr. 7 up). 12.95 o.s.i (*0-385-28206-0*, Delacorte Pr.) Dell Publishing.

Zamorano, Ana. Let's Eat! 1997. (Illus.). 32p. (J). (ps-2). pap. 15.95 (*0-590-13444-2*) Scholastic, Inc.

SPANISH MAIN—FICTION

Henty, G. A. Under Drake's Flag: A Tale of the Spanish Main. 2000. 252p. (J). E-Book 9.95 (*0-594-02411-0*) 1873 Pr.

Jordan, Apple. Simon Says: A Spanish-English Word Book. 2002. (ENG & SPA., Illus.). 24p. (J). (gr. k-3). pap. 3.25 (*0-375-81527-9*, Random Hse. Bks. for Young Readers) Random Hse. Children's Bks.

SRI LANKA—FICTION

Lipp, Frederick. Tea Leaves. Coloma, Lester, tr. & illus. by. 2003. (J). 32p. (gr. 1-6). 15.95 (*1-59034-998-9*); pap. (*1-59034-999-7*) Mondo Publishing.

Williams, Harry. Twins of Ceylon. 1965. (Twins Ser.). (Illus.). (J). (gr. 6-9). 12.95 (*0-8023-1108-3*) Dufour Editions, Inc.

STATEN ISLAND (NEW YORK, N.Y.)—FICTION

Hoff, B. J. The Winds of Graystone Manor. 1995. (St Clare Trilogy Ser.: No. 1). pap. 15.99 o.p. incl. audio (*1-55661-827-1*); 320p. pap. 10.99 o.p. (*1-55661-435-7*) Bethany Hse. Pubs.

—The Winds of Graystone Manor. l.t. ed. 1996. 504p. 22.95 o.s.i (*0-7838-1703-7*, Macmillan Reference USA) Gale Group.

SUPERIOR, LAKE—FICTION

Erdrich, Louise. The Birchbark House. 1999. (Illus.). 256p. (J). (gr. 4 up). 17.99 (*0-7868-0300-2*) Hyperion Bks. for Children.

—The Birchbark House. 2002. (Illus.). 256p. (J). (gr. 4 up). pap. 6.99 (*0-7868-1454-3*) Hyperion Paperbacks for Children.

—The Birchbark House. l.t. ed. 2000. (Young Adult Ser.). 272p. (YA). (gr. 7-12). 20.95 (*0-7862-2178-X*) Thorndike Pr.

Ernst, Kathleen. Trouble at Fort la Pointe. 2000. (American Girl Collection: Bk. 7). (Illus.). 176p. (J). (gr. 5-9). pap. 5.95 (*1-58485-086-8*); 9.95 (*1-58485-087-6*) Pleasant Co. Pubns. (American Girl).

—Trouble at Fort la Pointe. 2000. (American Girl Collection). (Illus.). (J). 12.00 (*0-606-20956-5*) Turtleback Bks.

Martin, Jacqueline Briggs. On Sand Island. 2003. (Illus.). 32p. (J). (ps-3). tchr. ed. 16.00 (*0-618-23151-X*) Houghton Mifflin Co.

Seymour, Tres. The Gulls of the Edmund Fitzgerald. 1996. (Illus.). 32p. (J). (gr. k-3). mass mkt. 16.99 o.p. (*0-531-08859-6*); pap. 15.95 (*0-531-09509-6*) Scholastic, Inc. (Orchard Bks.).

SWEDEN—FICTION

Anckarsvard, Karin. Aunt Vinnie's Invasion. 1962. (Illus.). 128p. (J). (gr. 5 up). 4.50 o.p. (*0-15-204621-6*) Harcourt Children's Bks.

—Doctor's Boy. MacMillan, Annabelle, tr. 1965. (Illus.). (J). (gr. 4-7). 5.50 o.p. (*0-15-223925-1*) Harcourt Children's Bks.

—Madcap Mystery. MacMillan, Annabelle, tr. (Illus.). (J). 1962. (gr. 5 up). 5.95 o.p. (*0-15-250175-4*); 1970. (gr. 4-7). reprint ed. pap. 2.75 o.p. (*0-15-655108-X*, Voyager Bks./Libros Viajeros) Harcourt Children's Bks.

—Mysterious Schoolmaster. MacMillan, Annabelle, tr. (Illus.). (J). (gr. 3-7). 1965. pap. 2.95 o.p. (*0-15-663971-8*, Voyager Bks./Libros Viajeros); 1959. 6.50 o.p. (*0-15-256527-2*) Harcourt Children's Bks.

—Robber Ghost. MacMillan, Annabelle, tr. (Illus.). (J). 1901. (gr. 3-7). 6.50 o.p. (*0-15-267804-2*); 1968. (gr. 4-6). reprint ed. pap. 3.95 o.p. (*0-15-678350-9*, Voyager Bks./Libros Viajeros) Harcourt Children's Bks.

Beckman, Gunnel. The Girl Without a Name. Parker, Anne, tr. from SWE. 1970. (Illus.). (J). (gr. 4-6). 5.50 o.p. (*0-15-230980-2*) Harcourt Children's Bks.

—A Room of His Own. Tate, Joan, tr. 1974. 128p. (J). (gr. 7 up). 5.95 o.p. (*0-670-60695-2*) Viking Penguin.

Beskow, Elsa. Pelle's New Suit. 1929. (Illus.). 16p. (J). (ps-1). lib. bdg. 13.89 o.p. (*0-06-020496-6*) HarperCollins Children's Bk. Group.

Dexter, Catherine. Safe Return. (Illus.). 96p. (J). (gr. 4-7). 1998. bds. 4.99 o.s.i (*0-7636-0486-0*); 1996. 16.99 (*0-7636-0005-9*) Candlewick Pr.

Gripe, Maria. The Glassblower's Children. La Farge, Sheila, tr. 1973. (Illus.). 160p. (J). (gr. 3-7). lib. bdg. 6.46 o.p. (*0-440-03065-X*, Delacorte Pr.) Dell Publishing.

—Hugo & Josephine. Austin, Paul B., tr. 1970. (Illus.). (J). (gr. 4-6). 4.95 o.p. (*0-440-04283-6*, Delacorte Pr.) Dell Publishing.

—The Night Daddy. Bothmer, Gerry, tr. 1971. (Illus.). (J). (gr. 3-6). lib. bdg. 7.45 o.p. (*0-440-06391-4*, Delacorte Pr.) Dell Publishing.

Hickox, Rebecca. Per & the Dala Horse. (Picture Yearling Ser.). (Illus.). 32p. (ps-3). 1997. pap. text 5.99 o.s.i (*0-440-41425-3*, Dell Books for Young Readers); 1995. (J). 15.95 o.s.i (*0-385-32075-2*, Doubleday Bks. for Young Readers) Random Hse. Children's Bks.

Lagerlof, Selma. The Wonderful Adventures of Nils. Howard, Velma S., tr. from SWE. 1995. (Illus.). xii, 219p. (J). (gr. 4-12). pap. text 6.95 (*0-486-28611-8*) Dover Pubns., Inc.

Lengstrand, Rolf. Horse Astray in Stockholm. 1965. (Foreign Lands Bks.). (Illus.). (J). (gr. k-5). lib. bdg. 3.95 o.p. (*0-8225-0354-9*) Lerner Publishing Group.

Lindgren, Astrid. A Calf for Christmas. Lucas, Barbara, tr. 1991. (Illus.). 32p. (J). (ps up). 13.95 (*91-29-59920-2*) R & S Bks. SWE. *Dist:* Farrar, Straus & Giroux, Holtzbrinck Pubs.

—The Children of Noisy Village. 1988. (Illus.). 128p. (J). (gr. 4-7). pap. 5.99 (*0-14-032609-X*, Puffin Bks.) Penguin Putnam Bks. for Young Readers.

—The Children of Noisy Village. Lamborn, Florence, tr. 1962. (Illus.). 128p. (J). (gr. 1-5). 10.95 o.p. (*0-670-21674-7*, Viking Children's Bks.) Penguin Putnam Bks. for Young Readers.

—The Children of Noisy Village. 1988. (J). 9.09 o.p. (*0-606-03557-5*) Turtleback Bks.

—Christmas in Noisy Village. Lamborn, Florence, tr. 1964. (Illus.). (J). (gr. 1-4). 6.50 o.p. (*0-670-22106-6*); 784p. audio 14.95 o.p. (*0-670-90526-7*) Viking Penguin.

—Do You Know Pippi Longstocking? Dyssegaard, Elisabeth Kallick, tr. from SWE. 1999. (Pippi Longstocking Storybooks). (Illus.). 32p. (J). (gr. k-2). 9.95 (*91-29-64661-8*) R & S Bks. SWE. *Dist:* Holtzbrinck Pubs.

—Karlsson-on-the-Roof. Turner, Marianne, tr. 1971. (Illus.). (J). (gr. k-3). 3.95 o.p. (*0-670-41176-0*) Viking Penguin.

—Mischievous Meg. 1962. (Illus.). (J). (gr. 4-6). 5.50 o.p. (*0-670-47806-7*) Viking Penguin.

—Pippi's Extraordinary Ordinary Day. 2001. (Illus.). (J). 12.14 (*0-606-21381-3*) Turtleback Bks.

—The Tomten. (Illus.). (J). (gr. 1-3). reprint ed. 1979. 6.95 o.s.i (*0-698-20487-5*); 1961. 32p. 15.95 o.s.i (*0-698-20147-7*) Putnam Publishing Group, The. (Coward-McCann).

—The Tomten & the Fox. 1965. (Illus.). (J). (gr. k-3). 7.99 o.s.i (*0-698-30371-7*, Coward-McCann) Putnam Publishing Group, The.

Lindman, Maj. Flicka, Ricka, Dicka & a Little Dog. 1995. (J). (ps-2). 6.95 o.p. (*0-8075-2486-7*) Whitman, Albert & Co.

—Flicka, Ricka, Dicka & the Big Red Hen. (ps-3). 1995. (J). pap. 6.95 (*0-8075-2493-X*); 1960. (Illus.). 5.75 o.p. (*0-8075-2481-6*) Whitman, Albert & Co.

—Flicka, Ricka, Dicka & the Girl Next Door. 1982. (Illus.). (gr. k-2). 5.75 o.p. (*0-8075-2483-2*) Whitman, Albert & Co.

—Flicka, Ricka, Dicka & the New Dotted Dresses. (Albert Whitman Prairie Bks.). (Illus.). (ps-3). 1994. 32p. (J). pap. 6.95 (*0-8075-2494-8*); 1983. 5.75 o.p. (*0-8075-2482-4*) Whitman, Albert & Co.

—Flicka, Ricka, Dicka & the Strawberries. (Illus.). (gr. k-2). 1944. lib. bdg. 6.50 o.p. (*0-8075-2489-1*); 1996. 32p. (J). reprint ed. pap. 6.95 (*0-8075-2499-9*) Whitman, Albert & Co.

—Flicka, Ricka, Dicka & the Three Kittens. 1941. (Illus.). (gr. k-2). 5.75 o.p. (*0-8075-2490-5*) Whitman, Albert & Co.

—Flicka, Ricka, Dicka & Their New Friend. (Illus.). (ps-3). 1995. (J). pap. 6.95 (*0-8075-2498-0*); 1942. lib. bdg. 6.50 o.p. (*0-8075-2487-5*) Whitman, Albert & Co.

—Flicka, Ricka, Dicka & Their New Skates. 1950. (Illus.). (gr. k-2). 5.75 o.p. (*0-8075-2488-3*) Whitman, Albert & Co.

—Flicka, Ricka, Dicka Bake a Cake. 1995. (J). (ps-2). 6.95 o.p. (*0-8075-2480-8*); pap. 6.95 (*0-8075-2492-1*) Whitman, Albert & Co.

—Flicka, Ricka, Dicka Go to Market. 1958. (Illus.). (gr. k-2). lib. bdg. 6.50 o.p. (*0-8075-2485-9*) Whitman, Albert & Co.

—Snipp, Snapp, Snurr & the Big Farm. 1946. (Illus.). (gr. k-2). 5.25 o.p. (*0-8075-7501-1*) Whitman, Albert & Co.

—Snipp, Snapp, Snurr & the Big Surprise. 1937. (Illus.). (gr. k-2). 5.75 o.p. (*0-8075-7503-8*) Whitman, Albert & Co.

—Snipp, Snapp, Snurr & the Buttered Bread. 1995. (J). (ps-2). pap. 6.95 o.p. (*0-8075-7504-6*); pap. 6.95 (*0-8075-7491-0*) Whitman, Albert & Co.

—Snipp, Snapp, Snurr & the Gingerbread. 1936. (Illus.). (gr. k-2). lib. bdg. 6.50 o.p. (*0-8075-7505-4*) Whitman, Albert & Co.

—Snipp, Snapp, Snurr & the Red Shoes. 1980. (Illus.). (gr. k-2). 5.25 o.p. (*0-8075-7509-7*) Whitman, Albert & Co.

—Snipp, Snapp, Snurr & the Seven Dogs. 1959. (Illus.). (gr. k-2). 5.75 o.p. (*0-8075-7512-7*) Whitman, Albert & Co.

—Snipp, Snapp, Snurr & the Yellow Sled. 1995. (J). (ps-3). pap. 6.95 (*0-8075-7499-6*) Whitman, Albert & Co.

—Snipp, Snapp, Snurr Learn to Swim. 1954. (Illus.). (gr. k-2). 5.75 o.p. (*0-8075-7506-2*) Whitman, Albert & Co.

Meyer, Carolyn. Kristina, the Girl King. 2003. (Royal Diaries Ser.). 176p. (J). 10.95 (*0-439-24976-7*, Scholastic Pr.) Scholastic, Inc.

Nilsson, Per. Heart's Delight. Chace, Tara, tr. from SWE. 2003. 160p. (YA). 16.95 (*1-886910-92-8*, Front Street) Front Street, Inc.

Nilsson, Ulf. If You Didn't Have Me. Blecher, Lone T. & Blecher, George, trs. 1987. (Illus.). 128p. (J). (gr. 2-5). 16.00 (*0-689-50406-3*, McElderry, Margaret K.) Simon & Schuster Children's Publishing.

Schwartz, David M. Supergrandpa. 1991. (Illus.). (J). (ps-3). 17.00 o.p. (*0-688-09898-3*) HarperCollins Children's Bk. Group.

—Supergrandpa. 1998. 11.10 (*0-606-15728-X*) Turtleback Bks.

Svendsen, Carol. Hulda. 1974. (Illus.). 32p. (J). (gr. k-3). 5.95 o.p. (*0-395-19497-0*) Houghton Mifflin Co.

Wallin, Marie-Louise. Tangles. Bothmer, Gerry, tr. 1977. (J). (gr. 7 up). 7.95 o.p. (*0-440-08502-0*, Delacorte Pr.) Dell Publishing.

SWITZERLAND—FICTION

Buff, Conrad & Buff, Mary. The Apple & the Arrow. 2001. (Illus.). 80p. (J). (gr. 4-6). tchr. ed. 16.00 (*0-618-12807-7*); pap. 7.95 (*0-618-12809-3*) Houghton Mifflin Co.

Buff, Mary & Buff, Conrad. Apple & the Arrow. 1974. (Illus.). (J). (gr. 3-7). 6.95 o.p. (*0-395-18591-2*) Houghton Mifflin Co.

Coats, Lucy & Spyri, Johanna. Heidi. 2000. (Classic Readers Ser.). (Illus.). 32p. (J). (gr. 2-3). pap. 12.95 (*0-7894-5703-2*); pap. 3.95 (*0-7894-5390-8*) Dorling Kindersley Publishing, Inc. (D K Ink).

Creech, Sharon. Bloomability. 288p. (J). 1999. (Illus.). (gr. 3-7). pap. 5.99 (*0-06-440823-X*, Harper Trophy); 1998. (gr. 4 up). lib. bdg. 16.89 (*0-06-026994-4*, Cotler, Joanna Bks.); 1998. (gr. 3 up). 16.99 (*0-06-026993-6*, Cotler, Joanna Bks.) HarperCollins Children's Bk. Group.

—Bloomability. unabr. ed. 2000. (J). pap. 37.00 incl. audio (*0-8072-8754-7*, YA257SP); (gr. 4-7). audio 25.00 (*0-8072-6152-1*) Random Hse. Audio Publishing Group. (Listening Library).

—Bloomability. 1999. 12.00 (*0-606-17460-5*) Turtleback Bks.

Dalmatian Press Staff, adapted by. Heidi. (SPA., Illus.). (YA). 11.95 (*84-7281-082-8*, AF1082) Auriga, Ediciones S.A. ESP. *Dist:* Continental Bk. Co., Inc.

—Heidi. 2002. (Spot the Classics Ser.). (Illus.). 192p. (J). (gr. k-5). 4.99 (*1-57759-546-7*) Dalmatian Pr.

—Heidi. (Young Collector's Illustrated Classics Ser.). (Illus.). 192p. (J). (gr. 3-7). 9.95 (*1-56156-455-9*) Kidsbooks, Inc.

—Heidi. 1993. (Fun-to-Read Fairy Tales Ser.). (Illus.). 24p. (J). (gr. k-3). pap. 2.50 (*1-56144-296-8*, Honey Bear Bks.) Modern Publishing.

—Heidi. 1988. (Illus.). pap. text 3.50 o.p. (*0-19-421761-2*) Oxford Univ. Pr., Inc.

—Heidi. (Illus.). (J). 9999. (Read It Yourself Ser.: Level 5, No. 777-4). (ps-2). 3.50 o.p. (*0-7214-5169-1*); 1990. (Children's Classics Ser.: No. 740-29). (gr. 3-5). pap. 3.50 o.p. (*0-7214-1210-6*) Penguin Group (USA) Inc. (Ladybird Bks.).

Gallaz, Christophe. The Wolf Who Loved Music. Logue, Mary, tr. from FRE. 2003. (Illus.). 32p. (YA). lib. bdg. 17.95 (*1-56846-178-X*, Creative Editions) Creative Co., The.

Grindley, Sally & Spyri, Johanna. Heidi. 2001. (Young Classics Ser.). (Illus.). 48p. (J). (gr. 1-3). pap. 9.95 o.p. (*0-7894-3596-9*) Dorling Kindersley Publishing, Inc.

Gudel, Helen. Dear Alexandra: A Story of Switzerland. 1999. Orig. Title: Leiber Alex. (Illus.). 32p. (J). (ps-3). 15.95 (*1-56899-739-6*); pap. 5.95 (*1-56899-740-X*) Soundprints.

H. D. The Hedgehog. 1988. (Illus.). 96p. (J). (ps up). 12.95 (*0-8112-1069-3*) New Directions Publishing Corp.

Hergé. L' Affaire Tournesol. 1999. (Tintin Ser.).Tr. of Calculus Affair. (FRE.). (gr. 4-7). 19.95 (*2-203-00117-8*) Casterman, Editions FRA. *Dist:* Distribooks, Inc.

—L' Affaire Tournesol.Tr. of Calculus Affair. (FRE., Illus.). (J). (gr. 7-9). lib. bdg. 19.95 o.p. (*0-8288-6087-4*, FC867); 1992. 64p. reprint ed. (*0-7859-4692-6*) French & European Pubns., Inc.

—The Calculus Affair. (Illus.). 62p. (J). 19.95 (*0-8288-5014-3*); pap. 4.95 o.p. (*0-416-77390-7*) French & European Pubns., Inc.

—The Calculus Affair. 1976. (Adventures of Tintin Ser.). 62p. (J). (gr. 2 up). pap. 9.99 (*0-316-35847-9*, Joy Street Bks.) Little Brown & Co.

Hicyilmaz, Gaye. The Frozen Waterfall, RS. 1994. 288p. (J). (gr. 7 up). 17.00 o.p. (*0-374-32482-4*, Farrar, Straus & Giroux (BYR)) Farrar, Straus & Giroux.

Humphrey, L. Spencer. Heidi. 1994. 32p. (J). (gr. 4-7). pap. text 2.95 (*0-8125-2323-7*, Tor Bks.) Doherty, Tom Assocs., LLC.

Krupinski, Loretta & Spyri, Johanna. Heidi. 1996. (Illus.). 32p. (J). (gr. k-4). lib. bdg. 14.89 o.p. (*0-06-023439-3*); 14.95 o.p. (*0-06-023438-5*) HarperCollins Children's Bk. Group.

Ladybird Books Staff. Heidi. 1997. (Read It Yourself Ser.). 48p. (J). 3.50 o.s.i (*0-7214-5795-9*) Penguin Group (USA) Inc.

Ladybird Books Staff, ed. Heidi. 1998. (Ladybird Read It Yourself Ser.). (Illus.). 48p. (J). text 2.99 o.p. (*0-7214-1978-X*, Ladybird Bks.) Penguin Group (USA) Inc.

Leppard, Lois Gladys. Mandie & the Singing Chalet. 1991. (Mandie Bks.: No. 17). 176p. (J). (gr. 4-7). pap. 4.99 (*1-55661-198-6*) Bethany Hse. Pubs.

—Mandie & the Singing Chalet. 1991. (Mandie Bks.: No. 17). (J). (gr. 4-7). 11.04 (*0-606-06141-X*) Turtleback Bks.

Montgomery, Raymond A. Behind the Wheel. Lt. ed. 1995. (Choose Your Own Adventure Ser.: No. 121). (Illus.). 128p. (J). (gr. 4-8). lib. bdg. 21.27 o.p. (*0-8368-1402-9*) Stevens, Gareth Inc.

Nascimbene, Yan. Ocean Deep. 1999. 40p. (J). 17.95 (*1-56846-161-5*, Creative Editions) Creative Co., The.

Obligado, Lilian. The Chocolate Cow. 1993. (Illus.). 48p. (J). (ps-2). pap. 14.00 o.p. (*0-671-73852-6*, Simon & Schuster Children's Publishing) Simon & Schuster Children's Publishing.

Outlet Book Company Staff. Heidi. 1988. o.s.i (*0-517-62434-6*) Crown Publishing Group.

Pacinelli, Donna, illus. Heidi. 1991. (Gateway Classic Ser.). 48p. (J). (gr. 2-5). 6.95 o.p. (*0-88101-112-6*) Unicorn Publishing Hse., Inc., The.

Pullman, Philip. Count Karlstein. 2000. (Illus.). 256p. (YA). (gr. 5-8). pap. 5.99 (*0-375-80348-3*) Knopf, Alfred A. Inc.

—Count Karlstein. 1998. 176p. (J). (gr. 3-7). 18.99 o.s.i (*0-679-99255-3*); (gr. 5-8). 17.00 (*0-679-89255-9*) Random Hse. Children's Bks. (Random Hse. Bks. for Young Readers).

—Count Karlstein. 2000. 11.04 (*0-606-17845-7*) Turtleback Bks.

Random House Value Publishing Staff. Heidi. 1998. (Children's Classics Ser.). (Illus.). 352p. (J). (gr. 5-9). 5.99 (*0-517-18967-4*) Random Hse. Value Publishing.

Read, Beryl J. Pip's Mountain. 1980. (Pathfinder Ser.). (Illus.). 96p. (J). pap. 1.95 o.p. (*0-310-37901-6*) Zondervan.

Ruiz, Celia & Spyri, Johanna. Heidi. 2001. (SPA., Illus.). 184p. 15.95 (*84-372-2237-0*) Altea, Ediciones, S.A. - Grupo Santillana ESP. *Dist:* Santillana USA Publishing Co., Inc.

Spyri, Johanna. Heidi. 2002. (Great Illustrated Classics). (Illus.). 240p. (J). (gr. 3-8). lib. bdg. 21.35 (*1-57765-688-1*, ABDO & Daughters) ABDO Publishing Co.

—Heidi. 1964. (Airmont Classics Ser.). (YA). (gr. 5 up). mass mkt. 1.95 o.p. (*0-8049-0018-3*, CL-18) Airmont Publishing Co., Inc.

—Heidi. 2002. (SPA., Illus.). 96p. (YA). (gr. 5-8). 9.95 (*84-204-5788-4*) Alfaguara, Ediciones, S.A.- Grupo Santillana ESP. *Dist:* Santillana USA Publishing Co., Inc.

—Heidi. (J). 24.95 (*0-8488-1179-8*) Amereon, Ltd.

—Heidi. 1994. (Illustrated Classics Collection). 64p. (J). pap. 4.95 (*0-7854-0778-2*, 40553) American Guidance Service, Inc.

—Heidi. 1999. (Andre Deutsch Classics). 316p. 9.95 (*0-233-99227-8*) Andre Deutsch GBR. *Dist:* Trafalgar Square, Trans-Atlantic Pubns., Inc.

—Heidi. 1995. (Young Reader's Christian Library). (Illus.). 224p. (J). (gr. 3-7). pap. text 1.39 o.p. (*1-55748-670-0*) Barbour Publishing, Inc.

—Heidi. 1974. (Dent's Illustrated Children's Classics Ser.). (Illus.). 327p. (J). reprint ed. 9.00 o.p. (*0-460-05013-3*) Biblio Distribution.

—Heidi. (Children's Library). (Illus.). (J). 1994. (gr. 1-8). 10.95 o.p. (*0-681-00766-4*); 1986. 350p. (gr. 4 up). 11.95 o.p. (*0-681-40060-9*) Borders Pr.

—Heidi. abr. rev. ed. 1991. (Illus.). 96p. (J). (gr. 1-5). 9.99 o.p. (*0-89107-600-X*) Crossway Bks.

—Heidi. 1993. 336p. (J). (gr. 5-8). pap. 2.99 o.p. (*0-87406-640-9*) Darby Creek Publishing.

—Heidi. 1990. 304p. (J). (gr. 4 up). pap. text 3.50 o.s.i (*0-440-40357-X*) Dell Publishing.

—Heidi. unabr. ed. 2000. (Juvenile Classics). (Illus.). 304p. (J). pap. 2.50 (*0-486-41235-0*) Dover Pubns., Inc.

—Heidi. 2nd ed. (Coleccion Clasicos en Accion). (SPA., Illus.). 80p. (YA). (gr. 5-8). 15.95 (*84-241-5784-2*, EV0790) Everest de Ediciones y Distribucion, S.L. ESP. *Dist:* Lectorum Pubns., Inc.

—Heidi. (Chapter Book Charmers Ser.). (Illus.). (J). 1999. 80p. (gr. 2-5). 2.99 o.p. (*0-694-01281-5*, Harper Festival); 1996. 384p. (gr. 1 up). 24.95 (*0-688-14519-1*) HarperCollins Children's Bk. Group.

—Heidi. 2002. (Kingfisher Classics Ser.). (Illus.). 352p. (J). tchr. ed. 15.95 (*0-7534-5494-7*, Kingfisher) Houghton Mifflin Co. Trade & Reference Div.

—Heidi. 2001. (Young Reader's Classics Ser.). 94p. pap. 9.95 (*1-55013-971-1*, Key Porter kids) Key Porter Bks. CAN. *Dist:* Firefly Bks., Ltd.

—Heidi. (YA). E-Book 1.95 (*1-58515-176-9*) MesaView, Inc.

—Heidi. 2002. (Twelve-Point Ser.). lib. bdg. 25.00 (*1-58287-183-3*) North Bks.

—Heidi. 1979. (Now Age Illustrated V Ser.). (Illus.). 64p. (J). (gr. 4-12). text 7.50 o.p. (*0-88301-401-7*); pap. text 2.95 (*0-88301-389-4*); stu. ed. 1.25 (*0-88301-413-0*) Pendulum Pr., Inc.

—Heidi. (Whole Story Ser.). 1996. 208p. (YA). (gr. 7 up). 22.99 o.p. (*0-670-86986-4*); 1995. (Illus.). 304p. (J). (gr. 4-7). pap. 4.99 (*0-14-036679-2*, Puffin Bks.) Penguin Putnam Bks. for Young Readers.

—Heidi. Dole, Helen B., tr. 1994. (Illustrated Junior Library). (Illus.). 336p. (J). (gr. 4-7). 16.99 (*0-448-40563-6*, Grosset & Dunlap) Penguin Putnam Bks. for Young Readers.

—Heidi. (J). 1983. (gr. k-3). 0.99 o.s.i (*0-8431-4178-6*, Price Stern Sloan); 1983. (Illus.). 240p. (gr. 3-7). pap. 3.50 o.p. (*0-14-035002-0*, Puffin Bks.); 1981. (Illus.). 336p. (gr. 3-7). 7.95 o.s.i (*0-448-11012-1*, Grosset & Dunlap); 1957. (Illus.). pap. 1.95 o.p. (*0-14-030097-X*, Puffin Bks.); 1996. (Illus.). 208p. (gr. 7-12). pap. 18.99 (*0-670-86987-2*); 1945. (Illus.). 336p. (gr. 3-7). 13.95 o.p. (*0-448-06012-4*, Grosset & Dunlap) Penguin Putnam Bks. for Young Readers.

—Heidi. Vogel, Malvina, ed. 1990. (Great Illustrated Classics Ser.: Vol. 12). (Illus.). 240p. (J). (gr. 3-6). 9.95 (*0-86611-963-9*) Playmore, Inc., Pubs.

—Heidi. (J). 1990. o.s.i (*0-385-30291-6*, Dell Books for Young Readers); 1984. (Illus.). (gr. 4-7). 18.95 o.p. (*0-394-53820-X*, Knopf Bks. for Young Readers) Random Hse. Children's Bks.

—Heidi. (J). 1995. 1.10 o.s.i (*0-517-14149-3*); 1988. 12.99 o.s.i (*0-517-61814-1*); 1988. (Illus.). 2.99 o.s.i (*0-517-30779-0*) Random Hse. Value Publishing.

—Heidi. (J). 9999. pap. text 1.50 o.p. (*0-590-08541-7*); 1988. (Illus.). 240p. (gr. 4-6). mass mkt. 3.25 o.p. (*0-590-42046-1*) Scholastic, Inc.

—Heidi. 2000. (Aladdin Classics Ser.). (Illus.). 304p. (J). (gr. 4-7). pap. 3.99 (*0-689-83962-6*, Aladdin) Simon & Schuster Children's Publishing.

—Heidi. Barish, Wendy, ed. 1982. (Illus.). 336p. (J). 14.50 o.p. (*0-671-43790-9*, Atheneum) Simon & Schuster Children's Publishing.

—Heidi. abr. ed. 1974. (J). pap. 5.95 o.p. incl. audio (*0-88142-324-6*) Soundelux Audio Publishing.

—Heidi. 1986. (J). (ps-3). 16.95 o.p. (*0-88101-059-6*) Unicorn Publishing Hse., Inc., The.

—Heidi. abr. ed. 1997. (Children's Classics Ser.). (J). pap. 10.95 o.s.i incl. audio (*0-14-086241-2*, Penguin AudioBooks) Viking Penguin.

—Heidi. 1998. (Children's Classics). 240p. (J). pap. 3.95 (*1-85326-125-4*, 1254WW) Wordsworth Editions, Ltd. GBR. *Dist:* Advanced Global Distribution Services.

—Heidi: With a Discussion of Optimism. 2003. (Values in Action Illustrated Classics Ser.). (J). (*1-59203-030-0*) Learning Challenge, Inc.

—Heidi Book & Charm. 2000. (Charming Classics Ser.). 432p. (J). (gr. 3-7). 6.99 (*0-694-01453-2*, Harper Festival) HarperCollins Children's Bk. Group.

—Heidi (Holt Little Classic), ERS. 1994. (Illus.). (J). (gr. 4-7). 14.95 o.p. (*0-8050-3565-6*, Holt, Henry & Co. Bks. For Young Readers) Holt, Henry & Co.

—Moni, the Goat Boy: And Other Stories. (Illus.). (J). 1993. 218p. pap. 5.95 (*1-883453-00-3*); 2000. 219p. reprint ed. pap. 6.95 (*1-883453-09-7*) Deutsche Buchhandlung-James Lowry.

Spyri, Johanna, intro. Heidi. 1978. (Nancy Drew's Favorite Classics). (Illus.). (J). (gr. 6-9). 2.95 o.p. (*0-448-14941-9*) Penguin Putnam Bks. for Young Readers.

Spyri, Johanna & Blaisdell, Robert. Heidi. 1998. (Illus.). (J). 1.00 (*0-486-40166-9*) Dover Pubns., Inc.

Spyri, Johanna & Golden Books Staff. Heidi. 1986. (Golden Classics Ser.). (Illus.). 128p. (J). (gr. k-12). pap. 8.95 o.s.i (*0-307-17114-0*, Golden Bks.) Random Hse. Children's Bks.

Stephen, Sarah. Heidi. 2002. (Scholastic Junior Classics Ser.). (Illus.). 128p. (J). mass mkt. 3.99 (*0-439-22506-X*) Scholastic, Inc.

Taylor, Sally. Mountain Express. 1984. (Starters Ser.). (J). lib. bdg. 4.35 o.p. (*0-382-06505-0*) Silver, Burdett & Ginn, Inc.

Yates, Elizabeth. Swiss Holiday. 1996. 160p. (J). (gr. 4-7). pap. 6.49 (*0-89084-889-0*, 100537) Jones, Bob Univ. Pr.

T

TAHITI—FICTION

Fremantle, Anne. Island of Cats. 1964. (Illus.). (J). (gr. 1-4). 12.95 (*0-8392-3011-7*) Astor-Honor, Inc.

Walls, Pamela June. Trouble in Tahiti. 2002. (Abby & the South Seas Adventures Ser.: Vol. 7). 208p. (J). mass mkt. 5.99 (*0-8423-3632-X*) Tyndale Hse. Pubs.

TAIWAN—FICTION

Anderson, Joy. Pai-Pai Pig. 1967. (Illus.). (J). (gr. 4-6). 4.50 o.p. (*0-15-259415-9*); 4.50 o.p. (*0-15-259416-7*) Harcourt Children's Bks.

Brammer, Deb. Peanut Butter Friends in a Chop Suey World. 1994. 177p. (J). (gr. 4-7). pap. 6.49 (*0-89084-751-7*, 082685) Jones, Bob Univ. Pr.

Hwa-I Publishing Co., Staff. Taiwanese Sites Vol. 91-95: Chinese Children's Stories. Ching, Emily et al, eds. Wonder Kids Publications Staff, tr. from CHI. 1991. (Taiwanese Sites Ser.). (Illus.). 28p. (J). (gr. 3-6). reprint ed. 39.75 (*1-56162-091-2*) Wonder Kids Pubns.

Wu, Priscilla. The Abacus Contest: Stories from Taiwan & China. 1996. (Fulcrum Kids Ser.). (Illus.). 64p. (J). (ps up). 15.95 (*1-55591-243-5*) Fulcrum Publishing.

TANGIER (MOROCCO)—FICTION

Baraadah, Muohammad. Fugitive Light: A Novel. Boullata, Issa J., tr. from ENG. & frwd. by. 2002. (Middle East Literature in Translation Ser.). (ARA & ENG.). xi, 171p. 24.95 (*0-8156-0749-0*) Syracuse Univ. Pr.

TANZANIA—FICTION

Campbell, Eric. Papa Tembo. 1998. 288p. (YA). (gr. 5-9). 16.00 (*0-15-201727-5*) Harcourt Children's Bks.

—The Year of the Leopard Song. 1992. 224p. (YA). (gr. 5 up). 16.95 o.s.i (*0-15-299806-3*) Harcourt Children's Bks.

—The Year of the Leopard Song. 1995. 224p. (C). (gr. 5 up). pap. 5.00 o.s.i (*0-15-200873-X*) Harcourt Trade Pubs.

—The Year of the Leopard Song. 1995. (J). 10.10 o.p. (*0-606-08406-1*) Turtleback Bks.

Mollel, Tololwa M. Kele's Secret. 1997. (Illus.). 32p. (J). 14.99 o.s.i (*0-525-67500-0*, Dutton) Dutton/Plume.

—Kele's Secret. 2000. (Illus.). (J). pap. 5.99 (*0-14-055649-4*, Puffin Bks.) Penguin Putnam Bks. for Young Readers.

—My Rows & Piles of Coins. 2002. (Illus.). (J). 22.45 (*0-7587-0385-6*) Book Wholesalers, Inc.

—My Rows & Piles of Coins. 1999. (Illus.). 32p. (J). (ps-3). lib. bdg., tchr. ed. 15.00 (*0-395-75186-1*) North-South Bks., Inc.

Stuve-Bodeen, Stephanie. Babu's Song. 2003. (Illus.). 32p. (J). 16.95 (*1-58430-058-2*) Lee & Low Bks., Inc.

—Elizabeti's Doll. 2002. (Illus.). (J). 23.19 (*0-7587-2449-7*) Book Wholesalers, Inc.

—Elizabeti's Doll. (Illus.). 32p. (YA). 2002. pap. 6.95 (*1-58430-081-7*); 2000. 15.95 (*1-880000-70-9*) Lee & Low Bks., Inc.

—Elizabeti's School. 2002. (Illus.). 32p. (J). (gr. k-3). 16.95 (*1-58430-043-4*) Lee & Low Bks., Inc.

—Mama Elizabeti. 2000. (Illus.). 32p. (J). (ps up). 12.76 (*1-58430-002-7*) Lee & Low Bks., Inc.

—La Muneca de Elizabeti. Sarfatti, Esther, tr. from ENG. 2000. (SPA., Illus.). 32p. (J). (gr. k-1). pap. 6.95 (*1-58430-001-9*, LW5012); lib. bdg. 15.95 (*1-58430-000-0*, LW5352) Lee & Low Bks., Inc.

—La Muneca de Elizabeti. 2000. 13.10 (*0-606-17847-3*) Turtleback Bks.

Trimble, Marcia. Hello Sun: A True African Travel Tale. 2000. (Illus.). 32p. (J). (gr. k-2). 12.95 (*1-891577-50-6*); pap. 6.95 (*1-891577-51-4*) Images Pr.

TASMANIA—FICTION

Baker, Jeannie. The Hidden Forest. 2000. (Illus.). (J). (gr. k up). 32p. 16.95 (*0-688-15760-2*); 40p. lib. bdg. 16.89 (*0-688-15761-0*) HarperCollins Children's Bk. Group. (Greenwillow Bks.).

Darling, Kathy. Tasmanian Devil. 1992. (On Location Ser.: Vol. 1). (Illus.). 40p. (J). (ps-3). 16.95 (*0-688-09726-X*) HarperCollins Children's Bk. Group.

—Tasmanian Devil: On Location. 1992. (Illus.). 40p. (J). (gr. 2 up). lib. bdg. 15.93 o.p. (*0-688-09727-8*) HarperCollins Children's Bk. Group.

TENNESSEE—FICTION

Applegate, Stanley. The Devil's Highway. 1998. (Illus.). 224p. (YA). (gr. 3-7). pap. 8.95 (*1-56145-184-3*, Peachtree Junior) Peachtree Pubs., Ltd.

—The Devil's Highway. 1998. (J). 15.00 (*0-606-19042-2*) Turtleback Bks.

Barrett, Tracy. Cold in Summer, ERS. 2003. (Illus.). 208p. (J). (gr. 5-9). 16.95 (*0-8050-7052-4*, Holt, Henry & Co. Bks. For Young Readers) Holt, Henry & Co.

Bradley, Kimberly Brubaker. Weaver's Daughter. l.t. ed. 2002. 173p. (J). 21.95 (*0-7862-3763-5*) Gale Group.

—Weaver's Daughter. 2000. (Illus.). 160p. (gr. 3-7). text 14.95 (*0-385-32769-2*, Delacorte Bks. for Young Readers) Random Hse. Children's Bks.

Brummett, Nancy Parker. Journey of Elisa: From Switzerland to America. (Immigrants Chronicles Ser.). 132p. (J). (gr. 3-7). pap. 5.99 (*0-7814-3286-3*) Cook Communications Ministries.

Burchard, S. H. Sports Star: Chris Evert Lloyd. 1901. (Sports Star Ser.). (Illus.). (J). (gr. 1-5). pap. 2.95 o.p. (*0-15-278008-4*, Voyager Bks./Libros Viajeros) Harcourt Children's Bks.

Coleman, Evelyn. Circle of Fire. 2001. (American Girl Collection: Bk. 14). (Illus.). 160p. (J). 9.95 o.p. (*1-58485-340-9*); pap. 5.95 (*1-58485-339-5*) Pleasant Co. Pubns. (American Girl).

—Circle of Fire. 2001. (American Girl Collection). (Illus.). (J). 12.00 (*0-606-21249-3*) Turtleback Bks.

Crist-Evans, Craig. Moon over Tennessee: A Boy's Civil War Journal. (Illus.). (J). 2003. 64p. pap. 6.95 (*0-618-31107-6*); 1999. 62p. (gr. 4-6). tchr. ed. 15.00 (*0-395-91208-3*) Houghton Mifflin Co.

Dowell, Frances O'Roark. Where I'd Like to Be. 2003. (Illus.). 240p. (J). (gr. 5-9). 15.95 (*0-689-84420-4*, Atheneum) Simon & Schuster Children's Publishing.

—Where I'd Like to Be. l.t. ed. 2003. 162p. (J). 22.95 (*0-7862-5741-5*) Thorndike Pr.

Eady, Ellen. Pardon Me. . . Is That the Grand Ole Opry? 2001. 28p. (J). 15.95 (*0-9679065-2-0*) Majestic Publishing.

—Pardon Me, Is That the Chattanooga Choo-Choo? 2000. (Illus.). (J). pap. 9.95 (*0-9679065-1-2*) Majestic Publishing.

Gage, Wilson. Ghost of Five Owl Farm. 1966. (Illus.). (J). (gr. 4-6). 5.99 o.p. (*0-529-03889-7*) Putnam Publishing Group, The.

Hermes, Patricia. Sweet by & By. 2002. 208p. (J). (gr. 3-6). 15.99 (*0-380-97452-5*) HarperCollins Pubs.

Hopkinson, Deborah. A Band of Angels: A Story Inspired by the Jubilee Singers. 1999. (Anne Schwartz Bks.). (Illus.). 40p. (J). (gr. 1-4). 16.00 (*0-689-81062-8*, Atheneum/Anne Schwartz Bks.) Simon & Schuster Children's Publishing.

Isaacs, Anne. Swamp Angel. 2002. (Illus.). (J). 14.04 (*0-7587-0152-7*) Book Wholesalers, Inc.

—Swamp Angel. (Illus.). 48p. (J). (ps-3). 2000. pap. 6.99 (*0-14-055908-6*); 1994. 16.99 (*0-525-45271-0*, Dutton Children's Bks.) Penguin Putnam Bks. for Young Readers.

—Swamp Angel. 2000. 13.14 (*0-606-18453-8*) Turtleback Bks.

—Swamp Angel. 2001. (J). (gr. k-4). 6.95 (*1-55592-985-0*) Weston Woods Studios, Inc.

Jukes, Mavis. No One Is Going to Nashville. 1987. (Borzoi Sprinters Ser.). (Illus.). 48p. (J). (gr. 2-5). pap. 2.95 o.s.i (*0-394-89264-X*, Knopf Bks. for Young Readers) Random Hse. Children's Bks.

Kalamvocas, Patty O. Another Underserved Lickin' Kindle, Judy & Variety Printing Staff, eds. ltd. ed. 1995. 280p. (Orig.). pap. 13.95 (*0-9648412-0-7*) Kalamvocas, Patricia Osborne.

Ketteman, Helen. Luck with Potatoes. 1995. (Illus.). 32p. (J). (ps-3). pap. 14.95 (*0-531-09473-1*); lib. bdg. 15.99 (*0-531-08773-5*) Scholastic, Inc. (Orchard Bks.).

Lyon, George Ella. Borrowed Children. 1990. 176p. (YA). mass mkt. 3.99 o.p. (*0-553-28380-4*) Bantam Bks.

—Borrowed Children. 1988. 160p. (J). (gr. 5-7). 15.95 o.p. (*0-531-05751-8*); mass mkt. 16.99 o.p. (*0-531-08351-9*) Scholastic, Inc. (Orchard Bks.).

Marshall, Catherine. The Angry Intruder. 1995. (Christy Fiction Ser.: No. 3). 128p. (J). (gr. 4-8). pap. 4.99 o.s.i (*0-8499-3688-8*) Nelson, Tommy.

—The Bridge to Cutter Gap. 1995. (Christy Fiction Ser.: No. 1). 128p. (J). (gr. 4-8). mass mkt. 4.99 (*0-8499-3686-1*) Nelson, Tommy.

—Brotherly Love. 1997. (Christy Fiction Ser.: No. 12). 128p. (Orig.). (J). (gr. 4-8). mass mkt. 4.99 (*0-8499-3963-1*) Nelson, Tommy.

—Family Secrets. 1996. (Christy Fiction Ser.: No. 8). (Illus.). 128p. (Orig.). (J). (gr. 4-8). mass mkt. 4.99 (*0-8499-3959-3*) Nelson, Tommy.

—Goodbye, Sweet Prince. 1997. (Christy Fiction Ser.: No. 11). 128p. (Orig.). (J). (gr. 4-8). pap. 4.99 (*0-8499-3962-3*) Nelson, Tommy.

—Midnight Rescue. 1995. (Christy Fiction Ser.: No. 4). 128p. (J). (gr. 4-8). pap. 4.99 o.s.i (*0-8499-3689-6*) Nelson, Tommy.

—Mountain Madness. adapted ed. 1997. (Christy Fiction Ser.: No. 9). 128p. (Orig.). (J). (gr. 4-8). mass mkt. 4.99 (*0-8499-3960-7*) Nelson, Tommy.

—The Princess Club. 1996. (Christy Fiction Ser.: No. 7). 128p. (J). (gr. 4-8). pap. text 4.99 (*0-8499-3958-5*) Nelson, Tommy.

—The Proposal. 1995. (Christy Fiction Ser.: No. 5). 128p. (J). (gr. 4-8). mass mkt. 4.99 (*0-8499-3918-6*) Nelson, Tommy.

—Silent Superstitions. 1995. (Christy Fiction Ser.: No. 2). 128p. (J). (gr. 4-8). pap. 4.99 o.s.i (*0-8499-3687-X*) Nelson, Tommy.

—Stage Fright. 1997. (Christy Fiction Ser.: No. 10). (Illus.). 128p. (J). (gr. 4-8). mass mkt. 4.99 (*0-8499-3961-5*) Nelson, Tommy.

McDaniel, Lurlene. The Girl Death Left Behind. 1999. 192p. (YA). (gr. 7-12). mass mkt. 4.99 (*0-553-57091-9*, Dell Books for Young Readers) Random Hse. Children's Bks.

—The Girl Death Left Behind. 1999. 11.04 (*0-606-16371-9*) Turtleback Bks.

McKissack, Patricia C. Color Me Dark: The Diary of Nellie Lee Love, the Great Migration North, Chicago, Illinois, 1919. 2000. (Dear America Ser.). (Illus.). 218p. (J). (gr. 4-9). pap. 10.95 (*0-590-51159-9*, Scholastic Pr.) Scholastic, Inc.

—Goin' Someplace Special. 2001. (Illus.). 40p. (J). (ps-3). 16.00 (*0-689-81885-8*, Atheneum/Anne Schwartz Bks.) Simon & Schuster Children's Publishing.

—Tippy Lemmey. 2003. (Ready-for-Chapters Ser.). (Illus.). 64p. (J). lib. bdg. 11.89 (*0-689-85594-X*, Aladdin Library) Simon & Schuster Children's Publishing.

Merrifield, Juanita, illus. The Little Purple Cow of Murphysboro. 1995. 18p. (Orig.). (J). (ps-6). pap. 6.00 (*0-9656822-0-X*) Purple Cow, The.

Murphy, Rita. Harmony. 2004. 160p. (YA). (gr. 7). mass mkt. 5.99 (*0-440-22923-5*, Laurel Leaf) Random Hse. Children's Bks.

—Harmony. 2002. 144p. (YA). lib. bdg. 17.99 (*0-385-90069-4*); (gr. 7). 15.95 (*0-385-72938-3*) Random Hse., Inc.

Partridge, Elizabeth. Clara & the Hoodoo Man. 176p. (gr. 3-7). 1998. pap. 4.99 o.s.i (*0-14-038348-4*); 1996. (J). 14.99 o.s.i (*0-525-45403-9*, Dutton Children's Bks.) Penguin Putnam Bks. for Young Readers.

Peach, Bill. The South Side of Boston. 1995. 128p. (Orig.). (J). pap. 11.95 (*1-881576-42-6*, Hillsboro Pr.) Providence Hse. Pubs.

Steele, William O. Andy Jackson's Water-Well. 1959. (Illus.). (J). (gr. 1-5). 4.50 o.p. (*0-15-203364-5*) Harcourt Children's Bks.

—Far Frontier. 1959. (Illus.). (J). (gr. 3-7). 5.50 o.p. (*0-15-227171-6*) Harcourt Children's Bks.

—Flaming Arrows. (J). (gr. 4-7). 1990. 192p. pap. 3.95 (*0-15-228427-3*, Odyssey Classics); 1957. (Illus.). 5.95 o.p. (*0-15-228424-9*); 1972. (Illus.). reprint ed. pap. 1.15 o.p. (*0-15-631550-5*, Voyager Bks./Libros Viajeros) Harcourt Children's Bks.

—Flaming Arrows. 1992. (J). 17.50 o.p. (*0-8446-6506-1*) Smith, Peter Pub., Inc.

—The Lone Hunt. 1956. (Illus.). (J). (gr. 4-6). 6.75 o.p. (*0-15-248293-8*) Harcourt Children's Bks.

—The Perilous Road. (Illus.). (J). (gr. 3-7). 1965. pap. 3.95 o.p. (*0-15-671696-8*, Voyager Bks./Libros Viajeros); 1958. 9.95 o.p. (*0-15-260644-0*) Harcourt Children's Bks.

Street, Jane. Snow Baby. 2002. (Illus.). 30p. (J). 11.95 (*1-887905-56-1*) Parkway Pubs., Inc.

Taylor, Mildred D. The Road to Memphis. 1992. 304p. (YA). (gr. 7-12). pap. 6.99 (*0-14-036077-8*, Puffin Bks.) Penguin Putnam Bks. for Young Readers.

—The Road to Memphis. Fogelman, Phyllis J., ed. 1990. (Illus.). 30p. (YA). (gr. 7 up). 16.99 (*0-8037-0340-6*, Dial Bks. for Young Readers) Penguin Putnam Bks. for Young Readers.

Turner, Thomas N. Country Music Night Before Christmas. 2003. (Illus.). 32p. (J). 14.95 (*1-58980-148-2*) Pelican Publishing Co., Inc.

Weathers, Anah D. Secrets of the Cave. unabr. ed. 2000. (Treasures from the Past Ser.). (Illus.). x, 104p. (J). (gr. 4-8). pap. 7.98 (*0-9702584-0-2*) Creative Services.

Wells, Rosemary. The Small World of Binky Braverman. 2003. (Illus.). 40p. (J). (gr. k-3). 15.99 (*0-670-03636-6*, Viking) Viking Penguin.

Wisler, G. Clifton. Jericho's Journey. 144p. (J). 1995. (gr. 4-7). pap. 5.99 (*0-14-037065-X*, Puffin Bks.); 1993. (gr. 5-9). 13.99 o.s.i (*0-525-67428-4*, Dutton Children's Bks.) Penguin Putnam Bks. for Young Readers.

—Jericho's Journey. 1995. 11.04 (*0-606-07737-5*) Turtleback Bks.

TEXAS—FICTION

Abernathy, Francis E. How the Critters Created Texas. 2nd rev. ed. 1998. (Illus.). 46p. (J). (gr. 1-6). lib. bdg. 14.95 (*0-936650-14-1*) Temple, Ellen C. Publishing, Inc.

Abernethy, Francis Edward. How the Critters Created Texas. 1998. (Illus.). 40p. (J). (gr. 1-5). pap. 13.95 o.p. (*0-936650-01-X*) Temple, Ellen C. Publishing, Inc.

Alter, Judy. After Pa Was Shot. 1991. (Illus.). 192p. (Orig.). (J). (gr. 3-10). reprint ed. pap. 5.95 (*0-936650-12-5*) Temple, Ellen C. Publishing, Inc.

—Sam Houston Is My Hero. 2003. (Chaparral Book for Young Readers Ser.). 140p. (J). pap. 15.95 (*0-87565-277-8*) Texas Christian Univ. Pr.

Anzaldua, Gloria. Friends from the Other Side (Amigos del Otro Lado) (Illus.). 32p. (J). 1995. (ENG & SPA.). (gr. 1 up). pap. 7.95 (*0-89239-130-8*); 1993. (SPA., (ps-3). 17.50 (*0-89239-113-8*, CBP1138) Children's Bk. Pr.

—Prietita & the Ghost Woman (Prietita y la Llorona) 1996. (ENG & SPA., Illus.). 32p. (J). (gr. 1 up). 17.50 (*0-89239-136-7*, CBP367) Children's Bk. Pr.

—Prietita & the Ghost Woman (Prietita y la Llorona) 1996. (Illus.). 32p. (J). (gr. 2-4). 19.90 (*0-516-20000-3*, Children's Pr.) Scholastic Library Publishing.

Arbuckle, Scott. Zeb, the Cow's on the Roof Again! And Other Tales of Early Texas Dwellings. 1996. (Illus.). 120p. (J). (gr. 4-8). 15.95 (*1-57168-102-7*) Eakin Pr.

Axelrod, Amy. The News Hounds in the Great Balloon Race: A Geography Adventure. 2000. (News Hounds Geography Ser.). (Illus.). 40p. (J). (gr. 1-4). 13.00 o.s.i (*0-689-82409-2*, Simon & Schuster Children's Publishing) Simon & Schuster Children's Publishing.

Ballard, Todhunter. Home to Texas. 1974. (Western Ser.). 159p. (J). o.p. (*0-385-09595-3*) Doubleday Publishing.

Bauer, Joan. Rules of the Road. 1998. 208p. (YA). (gr. 7-12). 16.99 (*0-399-23140-4*) Penguin Group (USA) Inc.

—Rules of the Road. 2000. (Chapters Ser.). (Illus.). 208p. (YA). (gr. 7 up). reprint ed. pap. 6.99 (*0-698-11828-6*, Puffin Bks.) Penguin Putnam Bks. for Young Readers.

—Rules of the Road. l.t. ed. 2000. (Young Adult Ser.). 245p. (YA). (gr. 8-12). 21.95 (*0-7862-2888-1*) Thorndike Pr.

—Rules of the Road. 2000. 11.04 (*0-606-20370-2*); (YA). 11.04 (*0-606-20252-8*) Turtleback Bks.

Bauld, Jane S. Hector's Escapades: The First Night Out. 1997. (Illus.). 39p. (J). 14.95 (*1-57168-185-X*) Eakin Pr.

Baurys, Florence. Spur for Christmas. 1999. (Illus.). 218p. (J). pap. 16.95 (*0-88415-300-2*, 5300) Lone Star Bks.

Baylor, Byrd. The Best Town in the World. 1986. (Illus.). 32p. (J). (gr. 2 up). reprint ed. mass mkt. 5.99 (*0-689-71086-0*, Aladdin) Simon & Schuster Children's Publishing.

—The Best Town in the World. 1986. (J). 12.14 (*0-606-03181-2*) Turtleback Bks.

Bear Paw. 2001. 180p. per. 11.95 (*1-891929-63-1*) Four Seasons Pubs.

Beecher, Jo. Texas Beau. 1999. (Illus.). 32p. (J). (gr. 3-5). 14.95 (*1-57168-204-X*) Eakin Pr.

Benner, J. A. Uncle Comanche. 1996. (Chaparral Book for Young Readers Ser.). 174p. (Orig.). (J). (gr. 7 up). pap. 12.95 (*0-87565-152-6*) Texas Christian Univ. Pr.

Bertrand, Diane Gonzales. Trino's Choice. 1999. 124p. (J). (gr. 4-7). 16.95 (*1-55885-279-4*); (Illus.). (gr. 5-11). pap. 9.95 (*1-55885-268-9*) Arte Publico Pr. (Piñata Books).

—Trino's Choice. 1999. 16.00 (*0-606-17956-9*) Turtleback Bks.

Borntrager, Mary Christner. Polly. l.t. ed. 2002. 165p. (J). 25.95 (*0-7862-4030-X*) Gale Group.

—Polly. 1994. (Ellie's People Ser.: Vol. 7). 144p. (J). (gr. 4-7). pap. 8.99 (*0-8361-3670-5*); pap. 8.99 o.p. (*0-8361-9008-4*) Herald Pr.

Brett, Jan. Armadillo Rodeo. 2002. (Illus.). (J). 23.64 (*0-7587-1968-X*) Book Wholesalers, Inc.

—Armadillo Rodeo. 1995. (Illus.). 32p. (J). (ps-3). 16.99 (*0-399-22803-9*, G. P. Putnam's Sons) Penguin Group (USA) Inc.

Burandt, Harriet, et al. Tales from the Home Place: Adventures of a Texas Farm Girl, ERS. 1997. 160p. (YA). (gr. 4-7). 15.95 o.s.i (*0-8050-5075-2*, Holt, Henry & Co. Bks. For Young Readers) Holt, Henry & Co.

Carey, Mary. Two for Texas: The Extraordinary Story of Kian & Jane Long. 1999. (J). 14.95 (*1-57168-292-9*) Eakin Pr.

Casad, Dede W. My Fellow Texans: Governors of Texas in the 20th Century. 1997. (Illus.). 128p. (J). 13.95 (*0-89015-996-3*) Eakin Pr.

Casad, Mary Brooke. Bluebonnet at the State Fair. 1995. (Bluebonnet Bks.: No. 3). (Illus.). 40p. (J). (gr. 4-5). pap. 6.95 (*1-57168-069-1*) Eakin Pr.

—Bluebonnet at the Texas State Capitol. 1997. (Illus.). 32p. (J). (ps-3). 14.95 (*1-56554-232-0*) Pelican Publishing Co., Inc.

—Bluebonnet of the Hill Country. 1995. (Illus.). 40p. (J). (gr. 4-5). pap. 6.95 (*1-57168-028-4*) Eakin Pr.

Cheadle, J. A. A Donkey's Life: A Story for Children. 1979. iii, 88p. (Orig.). (J). (gr. 2-6). pap. 7.00 (*0-9604244-0-7*) Heahstan Pr., The.

Cherry, Lynne. The Armadillo from Amarillo. 1994. (Illus.). 40p. (J). (gr. k-4). 17.00 (*0-15-200359-2*, Gulliver Bks.) Harcourt Children's Bks.

Chrismer, Melanie. Phoebe Clappsaddle & the Tumbleweed Gang. 2002. (Illus.). 32p. (J). 14.95 (*1-56554-966-X*) Pelican Publishing Co., Inc.

—Phoebe Clappsaddle for Sheriff. 2003. (Illus.). 32p. (J). 14.95 (*1-58980-127-X*) Pelican Publishing Co., Inc.

Cole, Barbara H. Texas Star. 1990. (Illus.). 32p. (J). (ps-2). 14.95 o.p. (*0-531-05820-4*); mass mkt. 14.99 o.p. (*0-531-08420-5*) Scholastic, Inc. (Orchard Bks.).

Cooner, Donna D. Twelve Days in Texas. 1994. (Illus.). 32p. (J). (ps up). pap. 12.95 (*0-937460-85-0*) Hendrick-Long Publishing Co.

Crawford, Ann Fears. Vangie: The Ghost of the Pines. 2002. 142p. (J). 17.95 (*1-57168-710-6*, Eakin Pr.) Eakin Pr.

Crockem, Linda. Counting from 1-10 in the Lone Star State Texas. 1995. 12p. (J). (ps). 14.99 (*1-887637-02-8*, TX3-993-328) First Bk. Productions.

Darby, Maribeth. The Land of the Magic Sand: Salt, Yesterday & Today. 1994. 120p. (J). (gr. 5-6). 12.95 o.p. (*0-89015-973-4*) Eakin Pr.

Dean, Carolee. Comfort. 2002. 240p. (J). (gr. 7 up). 15.00 (*0-618-13846-3*) Houghton Mifflin Co.

Dearen, Patrick. Comanche Peace Pipe. 2001. (Lone Star Heroes Ser.). 300p. (J). (ps-3). pap. 8.95 (*1-55622-831-7*, Republic of Texas Pr.) Wordware Publishing, Inc.

—The Hidden Treasure of the Chisos. 2001. (Lone Star Heroes Ser.). 128p. (J). pap. 8.95 (*1-55622-829-5*, Republic of Texas Pr.) Wordware Publishing, Inc.

—On the Pecos Trail. 2001. (Lone Star Heroes Ser.). 128p. (J). (gr. 4-7). pap. 8.95 (*1-55622-830-9*, Republic of Texas Pr.) Wordware Publishing, Inc.

Dell, Pamela. Blood in the Water: A Story of Friendship During the Mexican War. 2003. (J). (*1-59187-042-9*) Tradition Publishing Co.

Dionne, Wanda. The Couturiere of Galvez. 1993. (Illus.). (J). (gr. 6-7). 176p. 15.95 o.p. (*0-89015-860-6*); pap. 9.95 (*1-57168-161-2*) Eakin Pr.

—The Couturiere of Galvez. 1993. E-Book 9.95 (*0-585-23700-X*) netLibrary, Inc.

Duey, Kathleen. Ellen Elizabeth Hawkins: Mobeetie, Texas, 1886. 1997. (American Diaries Ser.: No. 6). (Illus.). 144p. (J). (gr. 3-7). pap. 4.99 (*0-689-81409-7*, Aladdin) Simon & Schuster Children's Publishing.

—Ellen Elizabeth Hawkins: Mobeetie, Texas, 1886. 1997. (American Diaries Ser.: No. 6). (J). (gr. 3-7). 10.55 (*0-606-11037-2*) Turtleback Bks.

Epner, Paul. Herbert Hilligan's Lone Star Adventure. 2002. (Illus.). (J). 15.95 (*1-57168-678-9*, Eakin Pr.) Eakin Pr.

—Herbert Hilligan's Lone Star Adventure. 2003. (J). 15.95 (*0-9743335-3-0*) Imaginative Publishing, LTD.

Erickson, John R. Moonshiner's Gold. (J). 2003. (Illus.). 208p. pap. 6.99 (*0-14-250023-2*, Puffin Bks.); 2001. 176p. (gr. 5-9). 15.99 (*0-670-03502-5*, Viking) Penguin Putnam Bks. for Young Readers.

Evans, Max. My Pardner. 1984. (Zia Bks.). (Illus.). 111p. (J). reprint ed. pap. 5.95 o.p. (*0-8263-0699-3*) Univ. of New Mexico Pr.

Evey, Ethel L. Stowaway to Texas. Darst, Shelia S., ed. 1986. 201p. (J). (gr. 4-7). 11.95 (*0-89896-102-5*); pap. 6.95 (*0-89896-101-7*) Larksdale. (Post Oak Pr.).

—Thistles & Bluebonnets. 1996. (Illus.). 128p. (J). (gr. 5-6). 14.95 (*1-57168-037-3*) Eakin Pr.

Eytcheson, Pat. Catch a Winner. 1997. (Illus.). 40p. (J). 4.95 (*0-89015-740-5*) Eakin Pr.

Farish, Terry. The Cat Who Liked Potato Soup. 2003. (Illus.). 40p. (J). (ps-3). 15.99 (*0-7636-0834-3*) Candlewick Pr.

Fowler, Zinita. The Last Innocent Summer. 1990. (Chaparral Book for Young Readers Ser.). 144p. (J). (gr. 4-7). pap. 11.95 (*0-87565-045-7*) Texas Christian Univ. Pr.

Freeman, Peggy P. Swept Back to a Texas Future: An Original Historical Musical. 1991. (Illus.). 38p. (J). (gr. 4-7). pap. 5.95 (*0-937460-72-9*) Hendrick-Long Publishing Co.

Gaard, Betty. Jericho Ride. 2003. (Illus.). 165p. (J). pap. (*1-57924-968-X*) Jones, Bob Univ. Pr.

Garland, Sherry. A Line in the Sand: The Alamo Diary of Lucinda Lawrence, Gonzales, Texas, 1836. 1998. (Dear America Ser.). (Illus.). 201p. (YA). (gr. 4-9). pap. 10.95 (*0-590-39466-5*, Scholastic Pr.) Scholastic, Inc.

—The Silent Storm. 1995. 288p. (J). (gr. 4-7). pap. 6.00 (*0-15-200016-X*, Harcourt Paperbacks) Harcourt Children's Bks.

—The Silent Storm. 1993. 288p. (J). (gr. 4-7). 14.95 (*0-15-274170-4*) Harcourt Trade Pubs.

—The Silent Storm: Scholastic Edition. 1996. pap. 5.00 o.s.i (*0-15-201336-9*) Harcourt Trade Pubs.

Giff, Patricia Reilly. Shark in School. 1994. 112p. (J). (gr. 1 up). 14.95 o.s.i (*0-385-32029-9*, Delacorte Pr.) Dell Publishing.

Gipson, Fred. Hound-Dog Man. 1966. (J). o.p. (*0-06-011540-8*) HarperCollins Pubs.

—Old Yeller. Date not set. 192p. (J). 20.95 (*0-8488-2273-0*) Amereon, Ltd.

—Old Yeller. abr. ed. 1995. (J). audio 16.95 (*1-55927-347-X*, 393873) Audio Renaissance.

—Old Yeller. unabr. ed. 1989. (J). (gr. 4-7). audio 30.00 (*0-7366-1648-9*, 2500) Books on Tape, Inc.

—Old Yeller. 1992. 192p. (YA). (gr. 8-12). reprint ed. 25.95 (*0-89966-906-9*) Buccaneer Bks., Inc.

—Old Yeller. 1956. (Illus.). 176p. (gr. 7 up). 23.00 (*0-06-011545-9*); 1956. (Illus.). (J). (gr. 7-9). lib. bdg. 14.89 o.p. (*0-06-011546-7*); 1942. (YA). mass mkt. 4.50 o.p. (*0-06-080002-X*, Perennial) Harper-Trade.

—Old Yeller. 1995. (J). (gr. 5). 9.32 (*0-395-73259-X*) Houghton Mifflin Co.

—Old Yeller. 1990. (YA). pap. 3.50 o.p. (*0-06-107008-4*, HarperTorch) Morrow/Avon.

—Old Yeller, unabr. ed. 1991. (J). (gr. 5). audio 27.00 (*1-55690-389-8*, 91104E7) Recorded Bks., LLC.

—Old Yeller. 9999. (J). pap. 1.75 o.p. (*0-590-02310-1*) Scholastic, Inc.

—Old Yeller. 1989. (J). 11.55 (*0-606-01189-7*) Turtleback Bks.

—Old Yeller. 1999. (J). lib. bdg. 21.95 (*1-56723-204-3*) Yestermorrow, Inc.

Gonzales Bertrand, Diane, et al. Close to the Heart. 2001. (Illus.). 144p. (J). pap. 9.95 (*1-55885-319-7*, Piñata Books) Arte Publico Pr.

Gonzalez, Catherine G. Cherub in Stone. 1995. (Chaparral Book for Young Readers Ser.). 116p. (J). (gr. 7 up). pap. 12.95 (*0-87565-139-9*) Texas Christian Univ. Pr.

Greene, Thomas J. I Want to Be a Texas Aggie. 1999. (Illus.). 28p. (J). (ps-2). 15.95 (*0-9670607-0-2*) Chalk Stream Publishing.

Griffin, Kitty & Combs, Kathy. The Foot-Stomping Adventures of Clementine Sweet. Wohnoutka, Mike, tr. & illus. by. 2004. 32p. (J). (ps-3). 15.00 (*0-618-24746-7*, Clarion Bks.) Houghton Mifflin Co. Trade & Reference Div.

Griffin, Peni R. The Treasure Bird. 1994. 144p. (J). (gr. 3-7). pap. 3.99 o.p. (*0-14-036653-9*, Puffin Bks.) Penguin Putnam Bks. for Young Readers.

—The Treasure Bird. 1992. (Illus.). 144p. (J). (gr. 4-7). pap. 14.00 (*0-689-50554-X*, McElderry, Margaret K.) Simon & Schuster Children's Publishing.

Gurasich, Marjorie A. A House Divided. 1994. (Chaparral Book Ser.). 170p. (J). (gr. 7 up). pap. 9.95 (*0-87565-122-4*) Texas Christian Univ. Pr.

Guzman, Lila. Green Slime & Jam. 2001. (Illus.). (J). v, 168p. pap. 11.95 (*1-57168-555-3*); 174p. pap. 16.95 (*1-57168-483-2*) Eakin Pr. (Eakin Pr.).

Hardy, Robin. Sammy: Dallas Detective. 1997. 224p. (YA). pap. 9.99 o.p. (*1-56384-134-7*, Vital Issue Pr.) Huntington Hse. Pubs.

Harman, Betty & Meador, Nancy. The Moon Rock Heist. 1988. 112p. (J). (gr. 6-7). 13.95 (*0-89015-667-0*) Eakin Pr.

—Paco & the Lion of the North. Roberts, Melissa, ed. 1987. 112p. (J). (gr. 4-7). 10.95 o.p. (*0-89015-598-4*) Eakin Pr.

Harper, Jo. Delfino's Journey. 2000. viii, 184p. (J). (gr. 8-12). 15.95 (*0-89672-437-9*) Texas Tech Univ. Pr.

—Delfino's Journey, Grades 8-12. 2000. (Illus.). viii, 184p. (J). tchr. ed. 5.95 (*0-89672-442-5*) Texas Tech Univ. Pr.

—Jalapeno Hal. Date not set. (Illus.). 40p. (J). (gr. 4). pap. 7.95 (*1-57168-206-6*) Eakin Pr.

—Jalapeno Hal. 1993. (Illus.). 40p. (J). (ps-2). 14.95 o.p. (*0-02-742645-9*, Simon & Schuster Children's Publishing) Simon & Schuster Children's Publishing.

—Mayor Jalapeno Hal from Presidio, Texas. 2003. (Illus.). (J). (*1-57168-767-X*, Eakin Pr.) Eakin Pr.

Hart, Jan S. The Many Adventures of Minnie. 1992. (Illus.). 96p. (J). (gr. 4-7). 12.95 o.p. (*0-89015-859-2*) Eakin Pr.

—The Many Adventures of Minnie. 1997. (Illus.). 111p. (J). (gr. 3-6). reprint ed. 12.95 (*0-9644559-2-7*) Hart Publishing.

Henderson, Aileen Kilgore. The Treasure of Panther Peak. 1998. (Illus.). 160p. (J). (gr. 3-8). 15.95 (*1-57131-618-3*); pap. 6.95 (*1-57131-619-1*) Milkweed Editions.

—The Treasure of Panther Peak. 1998. (J). 13.00 (*0-606-19037-6*) Turtleback Bks.

Hernandez, Irene B. The Secret of Two Brothers. 1995. 182p. (YA). (gr. 7-12). pap. 9.95 (*1-55885-142-9*, Piñata Books) Arte Publico Pr.

—The Secret of Two Brothers. 1995. 16.00 (*0-606-16039-6*) Turtleback Bks.

Hest, Amy. The Private Notebook of Katie Roberts, Age 11. (Illus.). 80p. (J). 1996. (gr. 4-7). bds. 4.99 o.s.i (*1-56402-859-3*); 1995. (gr. 3-6). 14.99 o.s.i (*1-56402-474-1*) Candlewick Pr.

—The Private Notebook of Katie Roberts, Age 11. 1996. 10.14 (*0-606-09768-6*) Turtleback Bks.

Hicks, Grace R. The Critters of Gazink. 1992. (Illus.). 64p. (J). (gr. 4-7). 11.95 o.p. (*0-89015-816-9*) Eakin Pr.

Higman, Anita. The Living Darkness: Texas Caves. 2nd ed. 2003. (J). (*1-57168-783-1*, Eakin Pr.) Eakin Pr.

—Texas Twisters. 1999. (Illus.). viii, 47 p. (J). 13.95 (*1-57168-316-X*) Eakin Pr.

—Texas Twisters. 1999. E-Book 13.95 (*0-585-16342-1*) netLibrary, Inc.

Hill, William. The Vampire Hunters. 1998. (YA). (gr. 7-11). 286p. pap. 12.95 (*1-890611-02-6*); 288p. 19.95 (*1-890611-05-0*) Otter Creek Pr., Inc.

Hoff, Carol. Johnny Texas. 1992. (Illus.). (J). reprint ed. 160p. (gr. 3 up). pap. 13.95 (*0-937460-81-8*); 150p. (gr. 4 up). lib. bdg. 15.95 o.p. (*0-937460-80-X*) Hendrick-Long Publishing Co.

Holt, Kimberly Willis. Dancing in Cadillac Light. 2002. 176p. (YA). (gr. 5 up). pap. 5.99 (*0-698-11970-3*, PaperStar) Penguin Putnam Bks. for Young Readers.

—Dancing in Cadillac Light. unabr. ed. 2001. (J). (gr. 5-7). audio 25.00 (*0-8072-6194-7*, Listening Library) Random Hse. Audio Publishing Group.

—Dancing in Cadillac Light. l.t. ed. 2002. 195p. (J). 23.95 (*0-7862-4395-3*) Thorndike Pr.

—When Zachary Beaver Came to Town, ERS. 1999. 227p. (YA). (gr. 5-9). 16.95 (*0-8050-6116-9*, Holt, Henry & Co. Bks. For Young Readers) Holt, Henry & Co.

—When Zachary Beaver Came to Town. 2000. tchr. ed. 9.95 (*1-58130-674-1*); (YA). stu. ed. 11.95 (*1-58130-675-X*) Novel Units, Inc.

—When Zachary Beaver Came to Town. unabr. ed. 2000. 227p. pap. 35.00 incl. audio (*0-8072-8394-0*); (YA). (gr. 5-9). audio 22.00 (*0-8072-8247-2*, LL0202); (YA). (gr. 5 up). audio 30.00 (*0-8072-8393-2*, YA200CX) Random Hse. Audio Publishing Group. (Listening Library).

—When Zachary Beaver Came to Town. (YA). (gr. 5 up). 2003. (Illus.). 256p. pap. 5.99 (*0-440-23841-2*, Laurel Leaf); 2001. 240p. pap. 5.50 (*0-440-22904-9*, Yearling) Random Hse. Children's Bks.

—When Zachary Beaver Came to Town. l.t. ed. 2000. (Young Adult Ser.). 224p. (YA). 22.95 (*0-7862-2515-7*) Thorndike Pr.

—When Zachary Beaver Came to Town. 2000. 11.55 (*0-606-20113-0*); (J). 6.20 (*0-606-20114-9*) Turtleback Bks.

Holt, Kimberly Willis & Colon, Raul. Dancing in Cadillac Light. 2001. 167p. (J). (gr. 5-8). 16.99 (*0-399-23402-0*, G. P. Putnam's Sons) Penguin Group (USA) Inc.

Horan, Evelyn. Jeannie, a Texas Frontier Girl, Bk. 1. 2001. 134p. (gr. 4-7). per. 14.95 (*1-58851-705-5*) PublishAmerica, Inc.

Horgan, Paul. Whitewater. 1970. 337p. (YA). (gr. 8 up). 6.95 o.p. (*0-374-28970-0*) Farrar, Straus & Giroux.

Horowitz, Jordan. The Big Green - Junior: Junior Novelization. 1995. (Illus.). 112p. (J). (gr. 4-7). pap. 4.95 o.p. (*0-7868-4058-7*) Disney Pr.

Howard, Jo Ann. The Little Boy Who Made a Difference. 2001. 41p. per. 8.95 (*0-7414-0575-X*) Infinity Publishing.com.

Janke, Katelan. Survival in the Storm: The Dust Bowl Diary of Grace Edwards. 2002. (Dear America Ser.). (Illus.). 192p. (J). (gr. 4-9). pap. 10.95 (*0-439-21599-4*, Scholastic Pr.) Scholastic, Inc.

Johnston, Tony. The Cowboy & the Black-Eyed Pea. 1992. (Illus.). 32p. (J). (ps-3). 15.99 o.s.i (*0-399-22330-4*, G. P. Putnam's Sons) Penguin Group (USA) Inc.

Jones, Martha Tannery. Terror from the Gulf: A Hurricane in Galveston. 1999. (Illus.). 134p. (YA). (gr. 4-7). 17.95 (*1-885777-21-3*) Hendrick-Long Publishing Co.

—Terror from the Gulf: Hurricane in Gavelston. 1999. (Illus.). (J). o.p. (*1-885777-23-X*) Hendrick-Long Publishing Co.

Kaderli, Janet. Molasses Cookies. 1988. (Illus.). 64p. (J). (gr. 4 up). 16.95 (*1-885777-05-1*) Hendrick-Long Publishing Co.

Kahn, Lisa. The Calf Who Fell in Love with a Wolf: And Other Calf Stories from Round Top, Texas. von Schweinitz, Helga, tr. from GER. 1999. (J). (*1-57168-346-1*, Eakin Pr.) Eakin Pr.

Karr, Kathleen. Oh, Those Harper Girls!, RS. 1992. 176p. (YA). (gr. 7 up). 16.00 o.p. (*0-374-35609-2*, Farrar, Straus & Giroux (BYR)) Farrar, Straus & Giroux.

Kerr, Rita. Buttercup & Bully Goat. 1995. (Illus.). 64p. (J). (gr. 3-4). 13.95 (*1-57168-056-X*) Eakin Pr.

—The Good Old Days. 1999. (Illus.). 110p. (J). 13.95 (*1-57168-362-3*) Eakin Pr.

—Texas Cavalier: The Story of James Butler Bonham. Roberts, Melissa, ed. 1989. (Illus.). 64p. (J). (gr. 4-7). 10.95 o.p. (*0-89015-714-6*) Eakin Pr.

—The Texas Cowboy. 1996. (Illus.). 96p. (J). (gr. 2-4). 13.95 (*1-57168-105-1*) Eakin Pr.

—Texas Footprints. 1988. 96p. (J). (gr. 4-5). 13.95 (*0-89015-676-X*) Eakin Pr.

—The Texas Orphans: A Story of the Orphan Trail Children. 1994. (Illus.). (J). 13.95 (*0-89015-962-9*) Eakin Pr.

—Texas Rose: Dilue Rose Harris. 1986. 64p. (J). (gr. 4-5). 13.95 (*0-89015-578-X*) Eakin Pr.

—A Wee Bit of Texas. 1991. (Illus.). 80p. (J). (gr. 1-4). 13.95 (*0-89015-809-6*) Eakin Pr.

Ketner, Mary G. Ganzy Remembers. 1991. (Illus.). 32p. (J). (gr. k-3). lib. bdg. 13.95 o.p. (*0-689-31610-0*, Atheneum) Simon & Schuster Children's Publishing.

Ketteman, Helen. Bubba the Cowboy Prince: A Fractured Texas Tale. 1997. (Illus.). 32p. (J). (gr. k-3). pap. 15.95 (*0-590-25506-1*) Scholastic, Inc.

—Shoeshine Whittaker. 1999. (Illus.). 32p. (J). (gr. k-3). 15.95 (*0-8027-8714-2*); lib. bdg. 16.85 (*0-8027-8715-0*) Walker & Co.

King, C. Richard. A Birthday in Texas. 1980. (Illus.). 64p. (J). (gr. 3-6). 6.95 o.p. (*0-88319-051-6*) Shoal Creek Pubs.

Knapik, Jane A. Sarah's Flag for Texas. 1994. (Illus.). 96p. (J). (gr. 6-7). 13.95 (*0-89015-900-9*) Eakin Pr.

Komechak, Marilyn Gilbert. Paisano Pete: Snake-Killer Bird. 2003. (J). 9.95 (*1-57168-770-X*, Eakin Pr.) Eakin Pr.

Kudlinski, Kathleen V. Lone Star: A Story of the Texas Rangers. (Once upon America Ser.). (Illus.). 64p. (J). (gr. 2-6). 1996. pap. 3.99 o.s.i (*0-14-036645-8*, Puffin Bks.); 1994. 12.99 o.p. (*0-670-85179-5*, Viking Children's Bks.) Penguin Putnam Bks. for Young Readers.

—Lone Star: A Story of the Texas Rangers. 1996. (Once upon America Ser.). (J). (gr. 2-6). 9.19 o.p. (*0-606-09571-3*) Turtleback Bks.

Kutchinski, Marjorie. Liberty, Justice & F'Rall: The Dog Heroes of the Texas Republic. 1998. 152p. (J). (gr. k-5). 15.95 (*1-57168-217-1*) Eakin Pr.

Lake, Julie. Galveston's Summer of the Storm. 2003. (Chaparral Book for Young Readers Ser.). 210p. (J). 16.95 (*0-87565-272-7*) Texas Christian Univ. Pr.

Landrey, Wanda A. The Ghost of Spindletop Hill. 2000. (Illus.). xiii, 140p. (J). 15.95 (*1-57168-449-2*) Eakin Pr.

Laronde, Gary, illus. Hector Visits His Country Cousin. 2002. 25p. (J). 14.95 (*1-57168-601-0*); pap. (*1-57168-676-2*) Eakin Pr. (Eakin Pr.).

Legrand. Why Cowboys Sing in Texas. 1984. (Illus.). (J). (gr. 1-5). 3.25 o.p. (*0-687-45424-7*) Abingdon Pr.

Lester, Jim. Fallout. 1997. 224p. (J). (gr. 7 up). mass mkt. 3.99 o.s.i (*0-440-22683-X*) Dell Publishing.

—Fallout. 1996. 224p. (YA). (gr. 7 up). 15.95 o.s.i (*0-385-32168-6*, Dell Books for Young Readers) Random Hse. Children's Bks.

—Fallout. 1997. 9.09 o.p. (*0-606-11312-6*) Turtleback Bks.

Lewis, Preston. Blanca Is My Name: Or, How I Saved the Buffalo on the Texas Plains. 2002. (Animal Legends Ser.: Vol. 2). (Illus.). x, 174p. (J). (*1-57168-699-1*); pap. (*1-57168-700-9*) Eakin Pr. (Eakin Pr.).

—They Called Me Old Blue: Or How I Helped Charles Goodnight Invent the Chuck Wagon. 2001. 188p. (J). pap. 12.95 (*1-57168-636-3*); (Illus.). 15.95 (*1-57168-493-X*) Eakin Pr. (Eakin Pr.).

Liles, Maurine W. Boy of Blossom Prairie. 1997. (Illus.). 128p. (J). pap. 5.95 o.p. (*0-89015-941-6*) Eakin Pr.

—Dona Maria, la Ranchera. 2000. (Illus.). viii, 152p. (J). 15.95 (*1-57168-381-X*) Eakin Pr.

—Kitty of Blossom Prairie. 1997. 128p. (J). pap. 5.95 o.s.i (*0-89015-890-8*) Eakin Pr.

—The Littlest Vaquero: A Story of the First Texas Cowboys, Longhorns, & the American Revolution. 1996. (Illus.). 120p. (J). (gr. 4-6). 15.95 (*1-57168-103-5*) Eakin Pr.

—Rebecca of Blossom Prairie. 1997. 105p. (J). pap. 5.95 o.p. (*0-89015-892-4*) Eakin Pr.

—Rebecca of Blossom Prairie: Grandmother of a Vice President. Roberts, M., ed. 1990. (Illus.). 105p. (J). (gr. 5-6). 15.95 (*0-89015-754-5*) Eakin Pr.

Love, D. Anne. I Remember the Alamo. 1999. 156p. (J). (gr. 3-7). tchr. ed. 15.95 (*0-8234-1426-4*) Holiday Hse., Inc.

—I Remember the Alamo. 2001. 176p. (gr. 4-7). pap. text 4.50 (*0-440-41697-3*, Yearling) Random Hse. Children's Bks.

—My Lone Star Summer. 1996. 192p. (J). (gr. 4-7). tchr. ed. 15.95 (*0-8234-1235-0*) Holiday Hse., Inc.

Marlow, Herb. Dillon's Revenge. 1997. (Illus.). (J). (*1-56763-275-0*); pap. (*1-56763-276-9*) Ozark Publishing.

Marvin, Isabel R. Josefina & the Hanging Tree. 1992. (Chaparral Book Ser.). 128p. (YA). (gr. 7 up). pap. 9.95 (*0-87565-103-8*) Texas Christian Univ. Pr.

—Shipwrecked on Padre Island. 1993. (Illus.). 160p. (J). (gr. 4 up). 14.95 o.p. (*0-937460-83-4*) Hendrick-Long Publishing Co.

Settings

Mason, Lynn. As I Am. 1999. (Love Stories Ser.). 192p. (gr. 7-12). mass mkt. 3.99 o.s.i (0-553-49274-8, Dell Books for Young Readers) Random Hse. Children's Bks.

Mayhar, Ardath. Carrots & Miggle. 1986. (J). pap. 12.95 o.s.i (0-689-31184-2, Atheneum) Simon & Schuster Children's Publishing.

McBride-Smith, Barbara. Greek Myths, Western Style: Toga Tales with an Attitude. 128p. (J). (ps-3). 2001. pap. 6.95 (0-87483-617-4); 1998. 14.95 (0-87483-524-0) August Hse. Pubs., Inc.

McCullough, William E. Listen to the Howl of the Wolf. 1996. 160p. (J). (gr. 6-7). 15.95 (1-57168-026-8) Eakin Pr.

McDonald, Archie. When the Corn Grows Tall in Texas. 1991. (Illus.). 96p. (J). (gr. 4-5). 13.95 (0-89015-808-8) Eakin Pr.

McMurtry, Larry. The Last Picture Show. 1999. (Last Picture Show Trilogy: Bk. 1). pap. (0-7540-2238-2) BBC Audiobooks America.

McPhail, David M. Hermanas. 1998. Tr. of Sisters. (SPA.). (J). 14.10 (0-606-21671-5) Turtleback Bks.

Meyer, Carolyn. White Lilacs. 1993. (Illus.). 256p. (J). (gr. 4-7). pap. 6.00 (0-15-295876-2); (YA). (gr. 5-9). 13.00 (0-15-200641-9) Harcourt Children's Bks. (Gulliver Bks.).

—White Lilacs. 1993. 12.05 (0-606-17360-9) Turtleback Bks.

Michaels, Vaughn. Dodi's Prince. 2003. (Illus.). 96p. (J). 15.99 (0-525-47034-4, Dutton Children's Bks.) Penguin Putnam Bks. for Young Readers.

Michener, James A. The Eagle & the Raven. 1990. (Illus.). 228p. (J). 19.95 (0-938349-57-0); 100.00 o.p. (0-938349-58-9) State Hse. Pr.

Moore, Martha. Angels on the Roof. 192p. (YA). (gr. 7 up). 1997. 15.95 o.s.i (0-385-32278-X, Delacorte Pr.); 1999. reprint ed. mass mkt. 4.99 (0-440-22806-9) Dell Publishing.

—Angels on the Roof. 1999. 11.04 (0-606-17346-3) Turtleback Bks.

—Matchit. 2002. 208p. (gr. 3-7). text 15.95 (0-385-72906-5); lib. bdg. 17.99 (0-385-90023-6) Dell Publishing. (Delacorte Pr.).

—Matchit. 2003. (Illus.). 208p. (gr. 3-7). pap. text 4.99 (0-440-41716-3, Dell Books for Young Readers) Random Hse. Children's Bks.

Moore, Martha A. Under the Mermaid Angel. (YA). (gr. 7 up). 1997. 176p. mass mkt. 3.99 o.s.i (0-440-22682-1, Laurel Leaf); 1995. 192p. 14.95 o.s.i (0-385-32160-0, Dell Books for Young Readers) Random Hse. Children's Bks.

Munson, Sammye. Hej Texas, Goodbye Sweden. 1994. 128p. (J). (gr. 5-6). 13.95 (0-89015-948-3) Eakin Pr.

Myers, Anna. Stolen by the Sea. 2001. 160p. (J). (gr. 3-7). 16.95 (0-8027-8787-8) Walker & Co.

Naylor, Phyllis Reynolds. The Healing of Texas Jake. 1998. (Illus.). 128p. (J). (gr. 3-7). pap. 4.50 (0-689-82243-X, Aladdin) Simon & Schuster Children's Publishing.

—The Healing of Texas Jake. 1998. 10.55 (0-606-15566-X) Turtleback Bks.

Neugeboren, Jay. Poli - A Mexican Boy in Early Texas. (Multicultural Texas Ser.). (Illus.). 120p. (YA). (gr. 7 up). 1992. pap. 7.95 (0-931722-74-8); 1989. 13.95 o.p. (0-931722-72-1) Corona Publishing, Co.

Nixon, Joan Lowery. If You Say So, Claude. 1980. (Illus.). 48p. (J). (gr. 1-4). 9.95 o.p. (0-7232-6183-0); pap. 5.95 o.p. (0-7232-6250-0) Penguin Putnam Bks. for Young Readers. (Warne, Frederick).

—Search for the Shadowman. 1996. 160p. (gr. 3-7). text 15.95 o.s.i (0-385-32203-8, Delacorte Pr.) Dell Publishing.

—Shadowmaker. 1994. 208p. (J). 15.95 o.s.i (0-385-32030-2, Delacorte Pr.) Dell Publishing.

—The Trap. 2002. 176p. (J). (gr. 7). 15.95 (0-385-32762-5, Delacorte Pr.) Dell Publishing.

—The Trap. 2002. 176p. (YA). (gr. 7). lib. bdg. 17.99 (0-385-90063-5) Random Hse., Inc.

Patrick, Denise Lewis. The Adventures of Midnight Son, ERS. 1997. 128p. (J). (gr. 4-7). 16.00 (0-8050-4714-X, Holt, Henry & Co. Bks. For Young Readers) Holt, Henry & Co.

Paulsen, Gary. Canyons. 192p. 1991. (J). (gr. 4-7). mass mkt. 5.99 (0-440-21023-2); 1990. (YA). 15.95 o.s.i (0-385-30153-7, Delacorte Pr.) Dell Publishing.

—Canyons. 1991. (J). mass mkt. o.s.i (0-440-80233-4); 1990. (YA). o.s.i (0-385-30201-0) Random Hse. Children's Bks. (Dell Books for Young Readers).

—Canyons. 1992. (J). (gr. 4-8). 17.75 o.p. (0-8446-6590-8) Smith, Peter Pub., Inc.

—Canyons. 1990. 11.55 (0-606-04884-7) Turtleback Bks.

Pella, Judith. Frontier Lady. 1993. (Lone Star Legacy Ser.: Bk. 1). 400p. (Orig.). (gr. 7-12). pap. 10.99 o.p. (1-55661-293-1) Bethany Hse. Pubs.

Pennebaker, Ruth. Both Sides Now, ERS. 2000. 208p. (YA). (gr. 6-9). 16.95 (0-8050-6105-3, Holt, Henry & Co. Bks. For Young Readers) Holt, Henry & Co.

Penson, Mary. You're an Orphan, Mollie Brown. 1993. (Illus.). 122p. (J). pap. 9.95 o.p. (0-87565-111-9) Texas Christian Univ. Pr.

Pringle, Terry. The Preacher's Boy. 1988. 280p. (YA). 15.95 o.p. (0-912697-77-6) Algonquin Bks. of Chapel Hill.

—The Preacher's Boy. 1989. 288p. (YA). mass mkt. 4.95 o.s.i (0-345-36045-1) Ballantine Bks.

Rice, David L. Crazy Loco: Stories about Growing up Chicano in Southern Texas. 2001. (Illus.). 160p. (J). (gr. 7 up). 16.99 (0-8037-2598-1, Dial Bks. for Young Readers) Penguin Putnam Bks. for Young Readers.

Rice, James. Trail Drive. 1996. (Illus.). 32p. (J). (gr. 1-4). 14.95 (1-56554-163-4) Pelican Publishing Co., Inc.

—Victor Lopez at the Alamo. 2001. (Illus.). 128p. (J). (gr. 3-7). pap. 12.95 (1-56554-866-3) Pelican Publishing Co., Inc.

Rice, Mel. Messenger on the Battlefield. 2001. (Lone Star Heroine Ser.). (Illus.). 108p. (J). (gr. 4-7). pap. 8.95 (1-55622-788-4, Republic of Texas Pr.) Wordware Publishing, Inc.

—Secrets in the Sky. 2001. (Lone Star Heroine Ser.). (Illus.). 106p. (J). (gr. 4-7). pap. 8.95 (1-55622-787-6, Republic of Texas Pr.) Wordware Publishing, Inc.

Rice, Melinda. Fire on the Hillside. 2001. (Lone Star Heroine Ser.). (Illus.). 250p. (J). (gr. 4-7). pap. 8.95 (1-55622-789-2, Republic of Texas Pr.) Wordware Publishing, Inc.

Richardson, Jean. Tag-Along Timothy Tours Texas. 1992. (Illus.). (J). 10.95 o.p. (0-89015-817-7) Eakin Pr.

—When Grandpa Had Fangs. 1997. (Illus.). 32p. (J). (gr. 2-3). 14.95 (1-57168-175-2) Eakin Pr.

Roach, Joyce Gibson, tr. Cowgirl of the Rocking R. 2003. (J). (0-9726573-0-4) Crosswinds Bks.

Roberts, Sally A. The Legend of Crystal Lake. (Illus.). vi, 135p. (J). 2001. pap. (1-57168-557-X, Eakin Pr.); 2000. 16.95 (1-57168-369-0) Eakin Pr.

Roberts, Willo Davis. Jo & the Bandit. 1992. 192p. (J). (gr. 4-7). 16.00 (0-689-31745-X, Atheneum) Simon & Schuster Children's Publishing.

Roderus, Frank. Duster. 1987. (Chaparral Books for Young Readers). (Illus.). 266p. (J). (gr. 6 up). reprint ed. 14.95 o.p. (0-87565-055-4); pap. 10.95 (0-87565-095-3) Texas Christian Univ. Pr.

Rogers, Lisa Waller. The Great Storm: The Hurricane Diary of J. T. King, Galveston, Texas, 1900. 2002. (Lone Star Journals). (Illus.). 192p. (J). text 14.50 (0-89672-478-6) Texas Tech Univ. Pr.

—Remember the Alamo! The Runaway Scrape Diary of Belle Wood. 2003. (Lone Star Journals: Bk. 3). 176p. (J). 15.95 (0-89672-497-2) Texas Tech Univ. Pr.

Rubel, Nicole. A Cowboy Named Ernestine. 2001. (Illus.). 32p. (J). (ps-3). 15.99 (0-8037-2152-8, Dial Bks. for Young Readers) Penguin Putnam Bks. for Young Readers.

Ruby, Lois. The Moxie Kid. 2002. 15.95 (1-57168-677-0); 2001. (J). pap. 15.95 (1-57168-608-8) Eakin Pr. (Eakin Pr.).

—Swindletop. 2000. (Illus.). 127p. (J). 15.95 (1-57168-393-3) Eakin Pr.

Rumbley, Rose-Mary. What? No Chili? rev. ed. 2000. (Illus.). 144p. (J). (gr. 6-8). pap. 16.95 (0-89015-992-0) Eakin Pr.

Sachar, Louis. Holes, RS. 1998. 240p. (J). (gr. 4-7). 17.00 (0-374-33265-7, Farrar, Straus & Giroux (BYR)) Farrar, Straus & Giroux.

—Holes. 240p. (J). (gr. 4-6). pap. 5.99 (0-8072-8073-9, Listening Library) Random Hse. Audio Publishing Group.

—Holes. 2003. (Newbery Ser.). (Illus.). 240p. (gr. 5-6). reprint ed. pap. 6.50 (0-440-41480-6, Yearling) Random Hse. Children's Bks.

Saldana, Rene, Jr. The Jumping Tree. 2002. (Illus.). 192p. (YA). (gr. 5). mass mkt. 5.50 (0-440-22881-6, Laurel Leaf) Random Hse. Children's Bks.

—The Jumping Tree: A Novel. 2001. (Illus.). 192p. (YA). (gr. 5-9). 14.95 (0-385-32725-0, Delacorte Bks. for Young Readers) Random Hse. Children's Bks.

Sargent, Dave & Sargent, Pat. Grady (Dappled Grey) Proud to Be an American. 2003. (Saddle Up Ser.: Vol. 30). 42p. (J). lib. bdg. 22.60 (1-56763-813-9); mass mkt. 6.95 (1-56763-814-7) Ozark Publishing.

Saunders, Susan. Lucky Lady. 128p. (J). 2002. pap. 4.95 (0-380-80756-4, Harper Trophy); 2000. (gr. 4-7). 14.95 (0-380-97784-2) HarperCollins Children's Bk. Group.

Savage, Derek. Cool Cat Goes to Texas. 2001. (Cool Cat Ser.: Vol. 3). 32p. (J). pap. 9.95 (0-9673000-5-3) Savage Bks.

Schaller, Bob. Treasure in Texas. 2001. (X-Country Adventures Ser.). 128p. (J). (gr. 3-6). pap. 5.99 o.p. (0-8010-4492-8) Baker Bks.

Searle, Don L. Light in the Harbor. 1991. viii, 245p. (Orig.). (J). pap. 8.95 o.p. (0-87579-528-5) Deseret Bk. Co.

Shefelman, Janice J. A Paradise Called Texas. 1983. (Illus.). 128p. (J). (gr. 4-5). 13.95 (0-89015-409-0); pap. 6.95 (0-89015-506-2) Eakin Pr.

—Spirit of Iron. 1997. 136p. (J). pap. 6.95 (0-89015-889-4) Eakin Pr.

—Spirit of Iron. Eakin, Edwin M., ed. 1987. (Mina Jordan Ser.: No. 3). (Illus.). 136p. (J). (gr. 4-7). pap. 5.95 o.p. (0-89015-624-7); 13.95 (0-89015-636-0) Eakin Pr.

—Willow Creek Home. 1997. (J). pap. 6.95 (0-89015-637-9) Eakin Pr.

Shefelman, Janice J., et al. Comanche Song. 2000. (Illus.). 255p. (J). (gr. 4-7). 17.95 (1-57168-397-6) Eakin Pr.

Shope, Kimberly A. The Apache Blessing: A Modern Tale of Texas Indians. 1992. 24p. (J). (gr. 3-8). pap. 5.00 (1-886210-03-9) Tyketoon Young Author Publishing Co.

Simmons, Marc. Josi's Buffalo Hunt: A Story from History. Kil, Ron, tr. & illus. by. 2003. 62p. (J). 17.95 (0-8263-3315-X) Univ. of New Mexico Pr.

Smith, Beatrice S. The Road to Galveston. 1973. (Books for Adults & Young Adults). (Illus.). 132p. (J). (gr. 4 up). lib. bdg. 10.95 o.p. (0-8225-0755-2, Lerner Pubns.) Lerner Publishing Group.

Smith, Debra. Hattie Marshall & the Prowling Panther. 1995. (Hattie Marshall Frontier Adventure Ser.: Vol. 1). 144p. (J). (gr. 3-7). pap. 4.99 o.p. (0-89107-831-2) Crossway Bks.

Smith, Debra West. Hattie Marshall & the Prowling Panther. 2002. (J). 6.95 (1-56554-940-6) Pelican Publishing Co., Inc.

Spellman, Paul N. Race to Velasco. 1995. 128p. (YA). (gr. 4 up). pap. 4.95 (1-885777-01-9) Hendrick-Long Publishing Co.

Spinner, Stephanie & Weiss, Ellen. We're Off to See the Lizard. 1998. (Weebie Zone Ser.: Vol. 6). (Illus.). 80p. (J). (gr. 2-4). pap. 3.95 o.p. (0-06-442069-8) HarperCollins Pubs.

Stem, Jacqueline. The Borrowed Grave. 2001. (Illus.). (J). 160p. 16.95 (1-57168-451-4); v, 153p. pap. (1-57168-556-1) Eakin Pr. (Eakin Pr.).

—Dangerous Games. 2002. (Illus.). v, 141p. (J). 16.95 (1-57168-701-7); pap. (1-57168-702-5) Eakin Pr. (Eakin Pr.).

—The Ghosts of Goliad. 2003. iii, 165p. (J). 17.95 (1-57168-785-8, Eakin Pr.) Eakin Pr.

—The Haunted Tunnel. 1994. 96p. (J). (gr. 5-6). 12.95 o.p. (0-89015-959-9) Eakin Pr.

—The Secret of Little Creek Farm. 1999. (Illus.). 130p. (J). 14.95 (1-57168-293-7) Eakin Pr.

Stem, Jacqueline & Laronde, Gary. The Secret of Little Creek Farm. 1999. E-Book 14.95 (0-585-16340-5) netLibrary, Inc.

Stevens, Diane. Liza's Star Wish. 1997. (Illus.). 320p. (YA). (gr. 5 up). 15.00 o.s.i (0-688-15310-0, Greenwillow Bks.) HarperCollins Children's Bk. Group.

Stewart, Elisabeth J. Bimmi Finds a Cat. 1996. (Illus.). 48p. (J). (gr. 1-5). tchr. ed. 14.95 o.p. (0-395-64652-9, Clarion Bks.) Houghton Mifflin Co. Trade & Reference Div.

Stone, B. J. Girl on the Bluff. 1999. (Illus.). 124p. (J). (gr. 4-6). 14.95 (1-57168-280-5) Eakin Pr.

Stover, Jill. Alamo Across Texas. 1993. (Illus.). 32p. (J). (ps up). 14.00 o.p. (0-688-11712-0) HarperCollins Children's Bk. Group.

Tex. 1999. 17p. (YA). (gr. 7-12). 9.95 (1-56137-146-7, BK8619) Novel Units, Inc.

Tilli Comes to Texas. 1987. (J). (gr. k up). lib. bdg. 15.95 o.p. (0-937460-57-5); audio 6.95 o.p. (0-937460-56-7) Hendrick-Long Publishing Co.

Tolliver, Ruby C. Boomer's Kids. 1992. (Illus.). 128p. (YA). (gr. 4 up). pap. 7.95 (1-885777-22-1) Hendrick-Long Publishing Co.

—Have Gun - Need Bullets. 1991. (Chaparral Bks.). (Illus.). 120p. (J). (gr. 4 up). 10.95 (0-87565-085-6); pap. 10.95 o.p. (0-87565-089-9) Texas Christian Univ. Pr.

—I Love You, Daisy Phew. 1994. (Illus.). 168p. (J). (gr. 4 up). lib. bdg. 12.95 (0-937460-86-9) Hendrick-Long Publishing Co.

—Muddy Banks. 1987. (Chaparral Book for Young Readers Ser.). (Illus.). 154p. (J). (gr. 4). pap. 11.95 (0-87565-049-X); 14.95 o.p. (0-87565-062-7) Texas Christian Univ. Pr.

—Sarita, Be Brave. 1999. 128p. (J). (gr. 3-6). 14.95 (1-57168-184-1) Eakin Pr.

—Sarita, Be Brave. 1999. E-Book 14.95 (0-585-23975-4) netLibrary, Inc.

Torres, David M. A Whooper Named Frank. 1999. (J). (1-57168-329-1) Eakin Pr.

Townsend, Tom. Fair Wind to Glory. 1994. (Illus.). 136p. (J). (gr. 4-7). lib. bdg. 6.95 (0-89015-975-0) Eakin Pr.

Von Rosenberg, Marjorie. Cowboy Bob's Critters Visit Texas Heroes. 1993. (Illus.). 76p. (J). (gr. 4-5). 12.95 o.p. (0-89015-905-X) Eakin Pr.

Wallace, Bill. Eye of the Great Bear. 1999. 176p. (J). (gr. 3-6). pap. 4.99 (0-671-02502-3, Aladdin); (Illus.). 16.00 (0-671-02504-X, Simon & Schuster Children's Publishing) Simon & Schuster Children's Publishing.

—Eye of the Great Bear. 1999. (J). 11.04 (0-606-19050-3) Turtleback Bks.

Warner, Gertrude Chandler, creator. The Mystery at the Alamo. 1997. (Boxcar Children Ser.: No. 58). (J). (gr. 2-5). lib. bdg. 13.95 (0-8075-5436-7); mass mkt. 3.95 (0-8075-5437-5) Whitman, Albert & Co.

Weatherford, Carole Boston. Juneteenth Jamboree. 1995. (Illus.). 24p. (J). (ps-3). 15.95 (1-880000-18-0) Lee & Low Bks., Inc.

Webber, Earlynne. The Secret of the Big Thicket. 1994. (J). pap. 7.95 o.p. (0-89015-958-0) Eakin Pr.

Wesley, Valerie Wilson. Freedom's Child. 1997. (Illus.). 32p. (J). (gr. 3-7). 16.00 (0-689-80269-2, Simon & Schuster Children's Publishing) Simon & Schuster Children's Publishing.

White, Jack N. The Canebrake Kids: The Trip to Texas. 1996. (Illus.). 120p. (J). (gr. 4-6). 12.95 o.p. (1-57168-111-6) Eakin Pr.

Wilburn, Garlyn Webb. The Donkey Boy. 2002. (Illus.). 207p. (J). 17.95 (1-57168-697-5); pap. 12.95 (1-57168-698-3) Eakin Pr. (Eakin Pr.).

Williams, Jeanne. Tame the Wild Stallion. 1985. (Chaparral Bks.). (Illus.). 182p. (YA). (gr. 6 up). 14.95 (0-87565-002-3); (ps up). pap. 8.95 (0-87565-009-0) Texas Christian Univ. Pr.

Williams, Lori Aurelia. When Kambia Elaine Flew in from Neptune. unabr. ed. 2001. 256p. (YA). (gr. 7 up). pap. 50.00 incl. audio (0-8072-8851-9, Listening Library) Random Hse. Audio Publishing Group.

—When Kambia Elaine Flew in from Neptune. (Illus.). 256p. 2001. (J). pap. 10.00 (0-689-84593-6, Simon Pulse); 2000. (YA). (gr. 8 up). 17.00 (0-689-82468-8, Simon & Schuster Children's Publishing) Simon & Schuster Children's Publishing.

—When Kambia Elaine Flew in from Neptune. 2002. 16.05 (0-606-22109-3) Turtleback Bks.

Wilson, Linda Miller. A Few Days Journey. 1998. 124p. (J). (gr. 6-9). pap. 9.99 (0-88092-402-0, 4020) Royal Fireworks Publishing Co.

Wisler, G. Clifton. Mustang Flats. 1997. 128p. (YA). (gr. 5-9). 14.99 o.s.i (0-525-67544-2, Dutton Children's Bks.) Penguin Putnam Bks. for Young Readers.

—Piper's Ferry. 1990. 14p. (J). (gr. 5-9). 14.95 o.p. (0-525-67303-2, Dutton Children's Bks.) Penguin Putnam Bks. for Young Readers.

Woolley, Bryan. Mr. Green's Magnificent Machine. 2003. (Illus.). 29p. (J). 15.95 (1-57168-606-1, Eakin Pr.) Eakin Pr.

Young, K. A. Man in the Moon. 2001. (Illus.). 120p. (J). per. 10.00 (0-9708999-5-5) Whyte Dove Pr.

THAILAND—FICTION

Ayer, Jacqueline. Wish for Little Sister. 1960. (Illus.). (J). (gr. k-3). 6.50 o.p. (0-15-298213-2) Harcourt Children's Bks.

Coerr, Eleanor. Mystery of the Golden Cat. 1968. (Illus.). (gr. 1-5). 3.85 o.p. (0-8048-0413-3) Tuttle Publishing.

Dobrin, Arnold. Little Monk & the Tiger: A Tale of Thailand. 1965. (Illus.). (J). (gr. k-3). 3.86 o.p. (0-698-30222-2) Putnam Publishing Group, The.

Giles, Gail. Breath of the Dragon. 1998. 10.04 (0-606-15465-5) Turtleback Bks.

—The Breath of the Dragon. 1997. (Illus.). 112p. (J). (gr. 4-6). tchr. ed. 14.95 (0-395-76476-9) Houghton Mifflin Co.

—Breath of the Dragon. 1998. (Illus.). 112p. (gr. 4-7). reprint ed. pap. text 3.99 o.s.i (0-440-41496-2) Dell Publishing.

Glass, Tom. Even a Little Is Something: Stories of Nong. 1997. (Illus.). viii, 119p. (J). (gr. 4 up). lib. bdg. 19.50 (0-208-02457-3, Linnet Bks.) Shoe String Pr., Inc.

Ho, Minfong. Rice Without Rain. 1990. (Illus.). 256p. (J). (gr. 7 up). 16.99 (0-688-06355-1) HarperCollins Children's Bk. Group.

Luangpraseut, Khamchong. Laos & Laotians. 1995. (ENG & LAO., Illus.). 96p. (Orig.). (J). (gr. 2-5). pap. 14.95 (1-879600-41-2) Pacific Asia Pr.

Marsden, Carolyn. Silk Umbrellas. 2004. 144p. (J). 15.99 (0-7636-2257-5) Candlewick Pr.

Maugham, W. Somerset. Princess September & the Nightingale. 1998. (Iona & Peter Opie Library of Children's Literature). (Illus.). 48p. (YA). (gr. k-6). 16.95 o.p. (0-19-512480-4) Oxford Univ. Pr., Inc.

Sleator, William. Dangerous Wishes. 1995. (Illus.). 192p. (J). (gr. 4-6). 14.99 o.s.i (0-525-45283-4, Dutton Children's Bks.) Penguin Putnam Bks. for Young Readers.

TIBET (CHINA)—FICTION

Carlson, Dale. The Mountain of Truth. 1972. (Illus.). (J). (gr. 5-9). 5.95 o.p. (0-689-30023-9, Atheneum) Simon & Schuster Children's Publishing.

Dickinson, Peter. Tulku. 1979. (J). (gr. 7 up). 9.95 o.p. (0-525-41571-8, Dutton) Dutton/Plume.

Gerstein, Mordicai. The Mountains of Tibet. (Trophy Picture Bk.). (Illus.). 32p. (J). (gr. 2 up). 1989. pap. 6.99 (0-06-443211-4, Harper Trophy); 1987. 15.95 o.p. (0-06-022144-5); 1987. lib. bdg. 13.89 o.p. (0-06-022149-6) HarperCollins Children's Bk. Group.

Hergé. Tintin au Tibet. 1999. (Tintin Ser.).Tr. of Tintin in Tibet. (FRE.). (gr. 4-7). 19.95 (*2-203-00119-4*) Casterman, Editions FRA. *Dist:* Distribooks, Inc.

—Tintin au Tibet.Tr. of Tintin in Tibet. (J). (gr. 7-9). ring bd. 24.95 (*0-8288-5092-5*) French & European Pubns., Inc.

—Tintin en Tibet. (SPA., Illus.). 62p. (J). 24.95 (*0-8288-4996-X*) French & European Pubns., Inc.

—Tintin en Tibet. (Tintin Ser.). (SPA.). 64p. (J). 14.95 (*84-261-1403-2*) Juventud, Editorial ESP. *Dist:* Distribooks, Inc.

—Tintin in Tibet. Orig. Title: Tintin au Tibet. (Illus.). 62p. (J). 24.95 (*0-8288-5001-1*); pap. 4.95 o.p. (*0-416-24090-9*) French & European Pubns., Inc.

—Tintin in Tibet. (Adventures of Tintin Ser.). Orig. Title: Tintin au Tibet. (J). 1992. (Illus.). 64p. 12.95 o.p. (*0-316-35863-0*); 1975. 62p. (gr. 2 up). pap. 9.99 (*0-316-35839-8*) Little Brown & Co. (Joy Street Bks.).

Nicholas, Charles, illus. Lost Horizon. 1979. (Contemporary Motivators Ser.). 32p. (Orig.). (J). (gr. 3-5). pap. text 2.25 (*0-88301-309-6*) Pendulum Pr., Inc.

Rankin, Louise. Daughter of the Mountains. 1993. (Puffin Newbery Library). (Illus.). 192p. (J). (gr. 3-7). pap. 6.99 (*0-14-036335-1*, Puffin Bks.) Penguin Putnam Bks. for Young Readers.

—Daughter of the Mountains. 1980. (J). (gr. 4-6). pap. 1.25 o.p. (*0-671-29517-9*, Archway Paperbacks) Pocket Bks.

—Daughter of the Mountains. 1996. (J). (gr. 5-9). 21.25 (*0-8446-6895-8*) Smith, Peter Pub., Inc.

—Daughter of the Mountains. 1993. (Puffin Newbery Library). (J). 11.04 (*0-606-02585-5*) Turtleback Bks.

Suzanne, Jamie. Cammi's Crush. 1997. (Sweet Valley Twins Ser.: No. 108). 144p. (gr. 3-7). pap. text 3.50 o.s.i (*0-553-48439-7*, Sweet Valley) Random Hse. Children's Bks.

Trottier, Maxine. Little Dog Moon. 2000. (Illus.). 32p. (J). (ps-3). 14.95 (*0-7737-3220-9*) Stoddart Kids CAN. *Dist:* Fitzhenry & Whiteside, Ltd.

Whitesel, Cheryl Aylward. Rebel: A Tibetan Odyssey. 2000. 208p. (J). (gr. 5 up). 15.95 (*0-688-16735-7*) HarperCollins Children's Bk. Group.

TREASURE ISLAND (IMAGINARY PLACE)—FICTION

Stevenson, Robert Louis. Kidnapped. 2002. (Scholastic Classics Ser.). 288p. (J). (gr. 5). mass mkt. 3.99 (*0-439-29578-5*) Scholastic, Inc.

—Treasure Island. 1979. (Illus.). (J). 35.00 o.p. (*0-913870-78-1*) Abaris Bks.

—Treasure Island. 1999. (Abbeville Classics Ser.). (Illus.). 176p. (J). 12.95 (*0-7892-0561-0*); pap. 7.95 (*0-7892-0551-3*) Abbeville Pr., Inc. (Abbeville Kids).

—Treasure Island. 1962. (Classics Ser.). (YA). (gr. 7 up). mass mkt. 2.95 (*0-8049-0002-7*, CL-2) Airmont Publishing Co., Inc.

—Treasure Island. 1995. (Classroom Reading Plays Ser.). (YA). (gr. 6-12). 31p. pap. 2.40 o.p. (*1-56103-108-9*); 32p. pap. 3.95 (*0-7854-1120-8*, 40208) American Guidance Service, Inc.

—Treasure Island. 1996. (Andre Deutsch Classics). 253p. (J). (gr. 5-8). 11.95 (*0-233-99038-0*) Andre Deutsch GBR. *Dist:* Trafalgar Square, Trans-Atlantic Pubns., Inc.

—Treasure Island. 1982. 208p. (J). mass mkt. 1.75 o.s.i (*0-553-21099-8*, Bantam Classics) Bantam Bks.

—Treasure Island. 1991. (Illus.). 45p. (J). 3.75 (*0-425-12335-9*, Classics Illustrated) Berkley Publishing Group.

—Treasure Island. 2002. (YA). 12.34 (*0-7587-7947-X*) Book Wholesalers, Inc.

—Treasure Island. 1995. (Longmeadow Press Children's Library). (Illus.). 224p. (J). (gr. 2-5). 10.95 o.p. (*0-681-00769-9*) Borders Pr.

—Treasure Island. McGuinn, Nicholas, ed. 1995. (Literature Ser.). (Illus.). 256p. pap. text 9.95 (*0-521-48568-1*) Cambridge Univ. Pr.

—Treasure Island. 2003. 192p. (J). 4.99 (*1-57759-557-2*) Dalmatian Pr.

—Treasure Island. 1988. mass mkt. 2.25 (*0-938819-26-7*, Aerie) Doherty, Tom Assocs., LLC.

—Treasure Island. 1996. 304p. (YA). (gr. 10 up). pap. 14.95 (*0-9652952-3-0*) Doyle Studio Pr.

—Treasure Island. 2002. (Illus.). 48p. pap. 6.95 (*0-237-52282-9*) Evans Brothers, Ltd. GBR. *Dist:* Trafalgar Square.

—Treasure Island. 2001. (YA). (gr. 5-12). pap. text 9.95 (*0-8359-0234-X*) Globe Fearon Educational Publishing.

—Treasure Island. 1980. (Pocket Pop-Ups Ser.). (Illus.). 16p. (J). (ps-5). 2.95 o.s.i (*0-89346-143-1*) Heian International Publishing, Inc.

—Treasure Island. 1997. text 8.25 (*0-03-051503-3*) Holt, Rinehart & Winston.

—Treasure Island. (Young Collector's Illustrated Classics Ser.). (Illus.). 192p. (J). (gr. 3-7). 9.95 (*1-56156-456-7*) Kidsbooks, Inc.

—Treasure Island. 1992. (Everyman's Library Children's Classics Ser.). (Illus.). 320p. (gr. 2 up). 14.95 (*0-679-41800-8*, Everyman's Library) Knopf Publishing Group.

—Treasure Island. 1998. (Cloth Bound Pocket Ser.). 240p. 7.95 (*3-89508-458-1*, 521307) Konemann.

—Treasure Island. 1977. (McKay Illustrated Classics Ser.). (J). (gr. 7 up). 7.95 o.p. (*0-679-20393-1*) McKay, David Co., Inc.

—Treasure Island. 1998. (Signet Classic Shakespeare Ser.). 224p. (J). mass mkt. 3.95 (*0-451-52704-6*) NAL.

—Treasure Island. 1994. (Read-Along Ser.). (YA). pap., stu. ed. 34.95 incl. audio (*0-88432-972-0*, S23919) Norton Pubs., Inc., Jeffrey /Audio-Forum.

—Treasure Island. 1993. (Illus.). 80p. (J). pap. text 5.95 o.p. (*0-19-422722-7*) Oxford Univ. Pr., Inc.

—Treasure Island. Letley, Emma, ed. & intro. by. 1985. (WC-P Ser.). 240p. (YA). (gr. 7-12). pap. 5.95 o.p. (*0-19-281681-0*) Oxford Univ. Pr., Inc.

—Treasure Island. 1996. (Classic Ser.). (Illus.). 56p. (J). (gr. 2-4). 2.99 o.s.i (*0-7214-5609-X*, Ladybird Bks.) Penguin Group (USA) Inc.

—Treasure Island. (Whole Story Ser.). 1996. (Illus.). 304p. (YA). (gr. 7 up). 23.99 o.s.i (*0-670-86920-1*, Viking Children's Bks.); 1994. (Illus.). 342p. (J). (gr. 4-7). 17.99 (*0-448-40562-8*, Grosset & Dunlap); 1975. (J). pap. 2.25 o.p. (*0-14-030036-8*, Puffin Bks.) Penguin Putnam Bks. for Young Readers.

—Treasure Island. Vogel, Malvina, ed. 1989. (Great Illustrated Classics Ser.: Vol. 7). (Illus.). 240p. (J). (gr. 3-6). 9.95 (*0-86611-958-2*) Playmore, Inc., Pubs.

—Treasure Island. (Short Classics Learning Files Ser.). (J). (gr. 4 up). 1988. 22.00 o.p. (*0-8172-2196-4*); 1983. (Illus.). lib. bdg. 22.80 o.p. (*0-8172-1655-3*) Raintree Pubs.

—Treasure Island. 1990. (Step into Classics Ser.). (Illus.). 96p. (J). (gr. 3-5). pap. 3.99 (*0-679-80402-1*, Random Hse. Bks. for Young Readers) Random Hse. Children's Bks.

—Treasure Island. 1995. (Children's Library Ser.). (J). 1.10 o.s.i (*0-517-14145-0*) Random Hse. Value Publishing.

—Treasure Island. 2001. (Courage Unabridged Classics Ser.). 208p. (YA). pap. 6.00 o.p. (*0-7624-0555-4*, Courage Bks.) Running Pr. Bk. Pubs.

—Treasure Island. (Aladdin Classics Ser.). 2000. 368p. (J). (gr. 3-7). pap. 3.99 (*0-689-83212-5*, Aladdin); 1981. (Illus.). 273p. (YA). (gr. 4-7). 28.00 (*0-684-17160-0*, Atheneum) Simon & Schuster Children's Publishing.

—Treasure Island. 1981. (Bantam Classics Ser.). (J). 10.00 (*0-606-02469-7*) Turtleback Bks.

—Treasure Island. Seelye, John, ed. & intro. by. 1999. (Classics Ser.). (Illus.). 224p. (J). pap. 5.95 (*0-14-043768-1*, Penguin Classics) Viking Penguin.

—Treasure Island. 1998. (Children's Classics). 224p. (J). (gr. 3-7). pap. 3.95 (*1-85326-103-3*, 1033WW) Wordsworth Editions, Ltd. GBR. *Dist:* Advanced Global Distribution Services.

—Treasure Island. 1991. 64p. (Orig.). (YA). (gr. 6-12). pap. 6.00 (*0-88734-412-7*) Players Pr., Inc.

—Treasure Island. 1975. (Dent's Illustrated Children's Classics Ser.). 281p. (J). reprint ed. text 11.00 o.p. (*0-460-05001-X*) Biblio Distribution.

—Treasure Island. Marshall, Michael J., ed. abr. ed. 1997. (Core Classics Ser.). (Illus.). 160p. (J). (gr. 4-6). lib. bdg. 10.95 (*1-890517-05-4*); pap. 5.95 (*1-890517-04-6*) Core Knowledge Foundation.

—Treasure Island. 1993. (Thrift Editions Ser.). 160p. (J). reprint ed. pap. 1.50 (*0-486-27559-0*) Dover Pubns., Inc.

—Treasure Island. 2nd ed. 1998. (Illustrated Classic Book Ser.). (Illus.). 61p. (J). (gr. 3 up). reprint ed. pap. text 4.95 (*1-56767-239-6*) Educational Insights, Inc.

—Treasure Island. abr. ed. 2001. (YA). (gr. 7 up). audio 13.95 (*1-84032-412-0*) Hodder Headline Audiobooks GBR. *Dist:* Trafalgar Square.

—Treasure Island, ERS. 1993. (Little Classics Ser.). (Illus.). xx, 379p. (J). (gr. 4-8). 15.95 o.p. (*0-8050-2773-4*, Holt, Henry & Co. Bks. For Young Readers) Holt, Henry & Co.

—Treasure Island. unabr. ed. 1998. (Wordsworth Classics Ser.). (YA). (gr. 6-12). 5.27 (*0-89061-103-3*, R1033WW) Jamestown.

—Treasure Island. Stemach, Jerry et al, eds. abr. ed. 2000. (Start-to-Finish Books: Vol. 1). (J). (gr. 2-3). audio 7.00 (*1-893376-09-5*, FO4K2) Johnston, Don Inc.

—Treasure Island. 1999. (Illus.). 240p. (YA). (gr. 3 up). reprint ed. 7.95 (*1-56852-233-9*, Konecky & Konecky) Konecky, William S. Assocs., Inc.

—Treasure Island. l.t. ed. 1997. (Large Print Heritage Ser.). 323p. (YA). (gr. 7-12). lib. bdg. 30.95 (*1-58118-008-X*, 21494) LRS.

—Treasure Island. abr. ed. 1996. (J). audio 13.98 (*962-634-601-9*, NA210114, Naxos AudioBooks) Naxos of America, Inc.

—Treasure Island. abr. ed. 1996. pap. 19.95 o.s.i incl. audio (*0-7871-0016-1*, NewStar Pr.) NewStar Media, Inc.

—Treasure Island. 1998. (Twelve-Point Ser.). 204p. reprint ed. lib. bdg. 25.00 (*1-58287-075-6*) North Bks.

—Treasure Island. abr. ed. 1996. (Children's Classics Ser.). (J). (gr. 4-7). pap. 6.95 o.p. incl. audio (*0-7871-1071-X*, 651804) Penguin Group (USA) Inc.

—Treasure Island. 1989. (Illus.). 273p. (YA). reprint ed. text 12.98 o.p. (*0-89471-778-2*, Courage Bks.) Running Pr. Bk. Pubs.

—Treasure Island. abr. ed. 2003. (Scribner Storybook Classic Ser.). (Illus.). 64p. (J). 18.95 (*0-689-85468-4*, Atheneum) Simon & Schuster Children's Publishing.

—Treasure Island. unabr. ed. 2002. (YA). pap. incl. audio compact disk (*1-58472-361-0*, In Audio) Sound Room Pubs., Inc.

—Treasure Island, Set. Lewis, Bob, ed. abr. ed. 1972. (Dramatized Classics Ser.). (J). (gr. 3-8). pap. 11.95 o.p. incl. audio (*0-88142-333-5*, 391802) Soundelux Audio Publishing.

—Treasure Island: With Story of the Treasure of Normon Island. Date not set. (J). (gr. 5-6). reprint ed. lib. bdg. 22.95 (*0-89190-236-8*, American Reprint Co.) Amereon, Ltd.

—Treasure Island: With Story of the Treasure of Normon Island. 1982. (Bantam Classics Ser.). (Illus.). 208p. (gr. 7-12). mass mkt. 3.95 (*0-553-21249-4*, Bantam Classics) Bantam Bks.

—Treasure Island: With Story of the Treasure of Normon Island. 1989. (Illus.). 192p. (J). (gr. 4 up). 1.50 o.p. (*0-8120-5942-5*) Barron's Educational Series, Inc.

—Treasure Island: With Story of the Treasure of Normon Island. 1986. (Children's Classics Ser.). (Illus.). 258p. (J). (gr. 4 up). 11.95 o.p. (*0-681-40059-5*) Borders Pr.

—Treasure Island: With Story of the Treasure of Normon Island. 1990. 252p. (YA). (gr. 4-7). mass mkt. 3.99 (*0-8125-0508-5*, Tor Classics) Doherty, Tom Assocs., LLC.

—Treasure Island: With Story of the Treasure of Normon Island. 1988. 224p. (J). (gr. 4-7). pap. 2.50 o.p. (*0-590-41617-0*) Dramatists Play Service, Inc.

—Treasure Island: With Story of the Treasure of Normon Island. 1992. (Illus.). (J). (*0-89434-128-6*, Ferguson Publishing Co.) Facts on File Inc.

—Treasure Island: With Story of the Treasure of Normon Island. 1987. (Illus.). (J). (gr. 5-12). reprint ed. lib. bdg. 9.95 o.s.i (*0-8052-3707-0*, Schocken) Knopf Publishing Group.

—Treasure Island: With Story of the Treasure of Normon Island. 1965. 224p. (J). (gr. 6). mass mkt. 3.95 o.s.i (*0-451-52189-7*); (YA). (gr. 7 up). mass mkt. 1.75 o.p. (*0-451-51917-5*) NAL. (Signet Classics).

—Treasure Island: With Story of the Treasure of Normon Island. 1982. (Oxford Progressive English Readers Ser.). (Illus.). (YA). (gr. 7-12). pap. 4.95 o.p. (*0-19-581379-0*) Oxford Univ. Pr., Inc.

—Treasure Island: With Story of the Treasure of Normon Island. (Illus.). 192p. 1995. (YA). (gr. 5 up). pap. 19.95 (*1-85793-488-1*); 1994. (J). (gr. 4 up). 24.95 (*1-85145-962-6*) Pavilion Bks., Ltd. GBR. *Dist:* Trafalgar Square.

—Treasure Island: With Story of the Treasure of Normon Island. (Illus.). (J). 9999. (Children's Classics Ser.: No. 740-1). (gr. 3-5). pap. 3.50 o.p. (*0-7214-0597-5*); 1994. (Classics Ser.). 56p. text 3.50 (*0-7214-1658-6*) Penguin Group (USA) Inc. (Ladybird Bks.).

—Treasure Island: With Story of the Treasure of Normon Island. (Puffin Classics Ser.). 1994. (Illus.). 320p. (YA). (gr. 4-7). pap. 4.99 (*0-14-036672-5*, Puffin Bks.); 1992. (Illus.). 176p. (J). 20.00 o.p. (*0-670-84685-6*, Viking Children's Bks.); 1984. 240p. (J). (gr. 2-5). pap. 3.50 o.p. (*0-14-035016-0*, Puffin Bks.); 1996. (Illus.). 304p. (J). (gr. 7-12). 19.99 (*0-670-86795-0*, Viking Children's Bks.); 1947. (Illus.). 352p. (J). (gr. 1-9). 13.95 o.p. (*0-448-06025-6*, Grosset & Dunlap) Penguin Putnam Bks. for Young Readers.

—Treasure Island: With Story of the Treasure of Normon Island. 1987. (Regents Illustrated Classics Ser.). (YA). (gr. 7-12). pap. text 3.75 o.p. (*0-13-930629-3*, 20521) Prentice Hall, ESL Dept.

—Treasure Island: With Story of the Treasure of Normon Island. 1978. (Illus.). (J). (gr. 6-9). 2.95 o.p. (*0-448-14920-6*) Putnam Publishing Group, The.

—Treasure Island: With Story of the Treasure of Normon Island. (J). (gr. 4-7). 1993. 32p. pap. 4.95 (*0-8114-6844-5*); 1983. (Illus.). pap. 9.27 o.p. (*0-8172-2026-7*) Raintree Pubs.

—Treasure Island: With Story of the Treasure of Normon Island. 1988. (Illustrated Classics Ser.). (Illus.). (J). 3.99 o.s.i (*0-517-65587-X*, Random Hse. Bks. for Young Readers) Random Hse. Children's Bks.

—Treasure Island: With Story of the Treasure of Normon Island. 1989. (Children's Classics Ser.). 272p. (J). 12.99 o.s.i (*0-517-61816-8*) Random Hse. Value Publishing.

—Treasure Island: With Story of the Treasure of Normon Island. 1987. (Illus.). 224p. (YA). (gr. 5 up). 12.95 o.p. (*0-89577-262-0*) Reader's Digest Assn., Inc., The.

—Treasure Island: With Story of the Treasure of Normon Island. 1993. (N. C. Wyeth Illustrated Classics Ser.). (Illus.). 274p. (YA). (gr. 5 up). reprint ed. text 16.95 o.p. (*1-56138-264-7*) Running Pr. Bk. Pubs.

—Treasure Island: With Story of the Treasure of Normon Island. 1988. 224p. (J). (gr. 4-7). mass mkt. 4.50 (*0-590-44501-4*, Scholastic Paperbacks); 1972. (YA). (gr. 7-12). reprint ed. pap. 2.25 o.p. (*0-590-40105-X*) Scholastic, Inc.

—Treasure Island: With Story of the Treasure of Normon Island. 1994. (Classic Story Bks.). (J). (gr. 4 up). 4.98 o.p. (*0-8317-1649-5*) Smithmark Pubs., Inc.

—Treasure Island: With Story of the Treasure of Normon Island. 1989. (Kelpie Ser.). (Illus.). 256p. (J). (gr. 5-8). pap. 5.95 o.p. (*0-86241-190-4*) Trafalgar Square.

—Treasure Island Promotion. 2003. 224p. (J). pap. 3.99 o.p. (*0-14-250091-7*, Puffin Bks.) Penguin Putnam Bks. for Young Readers.

TRINIDAD AND TOBAGO—FICTION

Binch, Caroline. Gregory Cool. 1994. 32p. (J). 14.99 o.s.i (*0-8037-1577-3*, Dial Bks. for Young Readers) Penguin Putnam Bks. for Young Readers.

Dalgliesh, Alice. The Silver Pencil. 1991. (Newbery Library Ser.). (Illus.). 256p. (YA). (gr. 7 up). pap. 5.99 (*0-14-034792-5*, Puffin Bks.) Penguin Putnam Bks. for Young Readers.

Joseph, Lynn. An Island Christmas. 1996. (Illus.). 40p. (J). (ps-3). pap. 7.95 (*0-395-81310-7*) Houghton Mifflin Co.

—An Island Christmas. 1992. (Illus.). 32p. (J). (ps-3). tchr. ed. 14.95 o.p. (*0-395-58761-1*, Clarion Bks.) Houghton Mifflin Co. Trade & Reference Div.

—An Island Christmas. 1992. 12.10 (*0-606-10122-5*) Turtleback Bks.

—Island Christmas. unabr. ed. 1997. (Illus.). 32p. (J). (gr. k-3). 9.95 o.p. incl. audio (*0-395-85811-9*, 11211, Clarion Bks.) Houghton Mifflin Co. Trade & Reference Div.

—Jasmine's Parlour Day. 1994. (Illus.). (J). (ps-3). 15.00 o.p. (*0-688-11487-3*); 32p. lib. bdg. 14.93 o.p. (*0-688-11488-1*) HarperCollins Children's Bk. Group.

Joseph, Lynn & Keller, Laurie. Jump-Up Time: A Trinidad Carnival Story. 1998. (Illus.). 32p. (J). (gr. k-3). tchr. ed. 16.00 o.p. (*0-395-65012-7*, Clarion Bks.) Houghton Mifflin Co. Trade & Reference Div.

Rahaman, Vashanti. A Little Salmon for Witness. 1997. (Illus.). 32p. (J). 15.99 o.s.i (*0-525-67521-3*, Dutton Children's Bks.) Penguin Putnam Bks. for Young Readers.

TROY (EXTINCT CITY)—FICTION

Gates, Doris. A Fair Wind for Troy. 1976. (Viking Kestrel Greek Myths Ser.). (Illus.). (J). (gr. 4-6). 9.95 o.p. (*0-670-30505-7*) Viking Penguin.

Geras, Adele. Troy. (Illus.). 352p. (YA). 2002. (gr. 9 up). pap. 6.95 (*0-15-204570-8*, Harcourt Paperbacks); 2001. (gr. 10-12). 17.00 (*0-15-216492-8*) Harcourt Children's Bks.

Green, Roger Lancelyn. The Luck of Troy. 1964. (J). (gr. 4-8). 4.75 o.p. (*0-8023-1050-8*) Dufour Editions, Inc.

—The Tale of Troy. (Puffin Classics Ser.). 1995. (Illus.). 224p. (YA). (gr. 7 up). pap. 4.99 (*0-14-036745-4*); 1974. (Illus.). (J). (gr. 5-7). pap. 3.95 o.p. (*0-14-030120-8*); 1958. 224p. (J). pap. 3.99 o.p. (*0-14-035102-7*) Penguin Putnam Bks. for Young Readers. (Puffin Bks.).

Lang, Andrew. The Tales of Troy: Ulysses the Sacker of Cities. (J). E-Book 2.49 (*1-58627-831-2*) Electric Umbrella Publishing.

McLaren, Clemence. Inside the Walls of Troy. 1996. 208p. (YA). (gr. 7-12). 17.00 (*0-689-31820-0*, Atheneum) Simon & Schuster Children's Publishing.

—Inside the Walls of Troy: A Novel of the Women Who Lived the Trojan War. 1998. 208p. (YA). (gr. 7 up). reprint ed. mass mkt. 5.50 (*0-440-22749-6*, Laurel Leaf) Random Hse. Children's Bks.

—Inside the Walls of Troy: A Novel of the Women Who Lived the Trojan War. 1998. (J). 11.04 (*0-606-13519-7*) Turtleback Bks.

TUNISIA—FICTION

Colfer, Eoin. Benny & Omar. 2001. 240p. (YA). (gr. 5 up). pap. 7.95 (*0-86278-567-7*) O'Brien Pr., Ltd., The IRL. *Dist:* Independent Pubs. Group.

Lloyd, Norris. The Village That Allah Forgot. 1973. (Illus.). 128p. (J). (gr. 4-7). 7.95 o.p. (*0-8038-7746-3*) Hastings Hse. Daytrips Pubs.

Powe-Allred, Alexandra. Ambassador to Tunis. 1996. 82p. (YA). pap. 7.00 o.p. (*0-8059-3977-6*) Dorrance Publishing Co., Inc.

TURKEY—FICTION

Bagdasarian, Adam. Forgotten Fire. 2002. 304p. (YA). (gr. 9 up). mass mkt. 5.99 (*0-440-22917-0*, Laurel Leaf) Random Hse. Children's Bks.

Blatter, Dorothy. Cap & Candle. 1961. (J). (gr. 7-10). 3.95 o.s.i (*0-664-32255-7*) Westminster John Knox Pr.

Bruni, Mary-Ann S. Elif: Child of Turkey. 1988. (Middle Eastern Magic Ser.: Vol. 1). (Illus.). 48p. (J). (gr. k-8). 12.95 (*0-935857-13-3*); pap. text (*0-935857-14-1*) TexArt Services, Inc.

Bunting, Eve. A Turkey for Thanksgiving. 2002. (Illus.). (J). 13.79 (*0-7587-3875-7*) Book Wholesalers, Inc.

—A Turkey for Thanksgiving. 1991. (Illus.). 32p. (J). (ps-ps). lib. bdg., tchr. ed. 15.00 (*0-89919-793-0*, Clarion Bks.) Houghton Mifflin Co. Trade & Reference Div.

Croutier, Alev Lytle. Leyla: The Black Tulip. 2003. (Girls of Many Lands Ser.). (Illus.). 196p. (J). pap. 15.95 (*1-58485-831-1*); pap. 7.95 (*1-58485-749-8*) Pleasant Co. Pubns. (American Girl).

Feder, Harriet K. Mystery of the Kaifeng Scroll: A Vivi Hartman Adventure. 1995. (Lerner Mysteries Ser.). 144p. (YA). (gr. 5-8). lib. bdg. 14.95 (*0-8225-0739-0*, Lerner Pubns.) Lerner Publishing Group.

Hicyilmaz, Gaye. Against the Storm. 1992. 176p. (YA). (gr. 7 up). 14.95 o.p. (*0-316-36078-3*, Joy Street Bks.) Little Brown & Co.

Jackson, Ellen B. A Tale of Two Turkeys. 1996. (J). 7.70 (*0-606-08262-X*) Turtleback Bks.

Johnston, Norma. The Delphic Choice. 1989. 208p. (YA). (gr. 7 up). lib. bdg. 14.95 o.p. (*0-02-747711-8*, Simon & Schuster Children's Publishing) Simon & Schuster Children's Publishing.

—The Delphic Choice. 1999. 200p. (YA). (gr. 5-12). reprint ed. pap. 16.00 (*1-892323-48-6*, Pierce Harris Press) Vivisphere Publishing.

Klevin, Jill R. Turtles Together Forever! 1983. (Illus.). 160p. (gr. 3-7). pap. 2.25 o.p. (*0-440-48918-0*) Dell Publishing.

Schwarz, Joanie & Keene, Carolyn. Turkey Trouble. 2003. (Nancy Drew Notebooks Ser.). (Illus.). 80p. (J). pap. 3.99 (*0-689-85696-2*, Aladdin) Simon & Schuster Children's Publishing.

St. Pierre, Stephanie. Where's That Turkey Lurking? Book & Cookie Cutter Pack. 1990. 16p. (Orig.). (J). (gr. k-3). mass mkt. 3.95 (*0-590-68984-3*) Scholastic, Inc.

Wangerin, Walter, Jr. Paul: A Novel. 2000. 512p. 22.99 (*0-310-21892-6*) Zondervan.

Wickstrom, Sylvie K. Turkey On the Loose! 1990. 32p. (J). (ps-3). 10.95 o.p. (*0-8037-0818-1*); 10.89 o.p. (*0-8037-0820-3*) Penguin Putnam Bks. for Young Readers. (Dial Bks. for Young Readers).

U

UKRAINE—FICTION

DeSena, Bronwen & Zucker, Linda. Babu's Babushka. 2000. (Publish-a-Book Ser.). (Illus.). 24p. (J). (ps-3). 7.95 (*0-7398-2368-X*) Raintree Pubs.

Hale, Irina. The Naughty Crow. 1992. (Illus.). 32p. (J). (gr. k-4). lib. bdg. 14.95 (*0-689-50546-9*, McElderry, Margaret K.) Simon & Schuster Children's Publishing.

Kimmel, Eric A. The Tartar's Sword. 1974. 288p. (J). (gr. 6 up). 6.95 o.p. (*0-698-20243-0*) Putnam Publishing Group, The.

Larysa & Andrijko Series, Set. 1991. (ENG & UKR., Illus.). (J). (gr. 3 up). 11.75 (*1-882406-04-4*) M.A.K. Pubns., Inc.

Maxwell, Cassandre. Yosef's Gift of Many Colors: An Easter Story. 1993. (Illus.). 32p. (J). (ps-3). 16.99 o.p. (*0-8066-2627-5*, 9-2627) Augsburg Fortress, Pubs.

Posell, Elsa. Homecoming. 1987. 224p. (YA). (gr. 7 up). 14.95 o.p. (*0-15-235160-4*) Harcourt Children's Bks.

Yolen, Jane. And Twelve Chinese Acrobats. 1995. (Illus.). 50p. (J). 15.95 o.p. (*0-399-22691-5*, Philomel) Penguin Putnam Bks. for Young Readers.

UNITED STATES—FICTION

Bader, Bonnie. East Side Story. (Stories of the States Ser.). (J). (gr. 4-7). 1995. (Illus.). 108p. pap. 5.95 (*1-881889-71-8*); 1993. 80p. lib. bdg. 14.95 (*1-881889-22-X*) Silver Moon Pr.

—East Side Story. 1995. 12.10 (*0-606-14384-X*) Turtleback Bks.

—Golden Quest. 1995. (Stories of the States Ser.). (Illus.). 96p. (J). (gr. 4-7). pap. 5.95 (*1-881889-74-2*) Silver Moon Pr.

—Golden Quest. 1995. 12.10 (*0-606-14378-5*) Turtleback Bks.

Banim, Lisa. American Dreams. (Stories of the States Ser.). (J). (gr. 4-7). 1995. (Illus.). 108p. pap. 5.95 (*1-881889-68-8*); 1993. 80p. lib. bdg. 14.95 (*1-881889-34-3*) Silver Moon Pr.

—American Dreams. 1995. 12.10 (*0-606-14374-2*) Turtleback Bks.

—Drums at Saratoga. 1995. (Stories of the States Ser.). (Illus.). 108p. (J). (gr. 4-7). pap. 5.95 (*1-881889-70-X*) Silver Moon Pr.

—Drums at Saratoga. 1995. 12.10 (*0-606-14375-0*) Turtleback Bks.

Barracca, Sal & Barracca, Debra. Maxi, the Star. 1993. (Illus.). 32p. (J). (ps-3). 13.99 o.p. (*0-8037-1348-7*); 13.89 o.p. (*0-8037-1349-5*) Penguin Putnam Bks. for Young Readers. (Dial Bks. for Young Readers).

Bunting, Eve. How Many Days to America? A Thanksgiving Story. 1992. (Literature Experience 1993 Ser.). (J). (gr. 5). pap. 10.24 (*0-395-61811-8*) Houghton Mifflin Co.

Chin-Lee, Cynthia & De la Pena, Terri. A Is for the Americas. 1999. (Illus.). 32p. (J). (gr. k-4). lib. bdg. 16.99 (*0-531-33194-6*, Orchard Bks.) Scholastic, Inc.

Danziger, Paula. United Tates of America. 2002. (J). (gr. 4-7). lib. bdg. 20.00 incl. audio (*0-9717540-5-5*, 02002) Full Cast Audio.

Danziger, Paula, et al. United Tates of America. 2003. 144p. (J). mass mkt. 5.99 (*0-590-69222-4*, Scholastic Paperbacks) Scholastic, Inc.

Griswold, Jerry. Classic American Children's Story: Novels of the Golden Age. 1996. 304p. pap. 12.95 o.p. (*0-14-025639-3*, Penguin Bks.) Penguin Group (USA) Inc.

Grosset and Dunlap Staff. Stuck on the U. S. A. 1994. (Books & Stuff Ser.). (Illus.). 64p. (J). (ps-3). 7.99 o.s.i (*0-448-40179-7*, Grosset & Dunlap) Penguin Putnam Bks. for Young Readers.

Hergé. Tintin en Amerique. 1999. (Tintin Ser.). Orig. Title: Tintin in America. (FRE.). (gr. 4-7). 19.95 (*2-203-00102-X*) Casterman, Editions FRA. *Dist:* Distribooks, Inc.

—Tintin en Amerique. Orig. Title: Tintin in America. (Illus.). 62p. (J). (FRE.). 24.95 (*0-8288-5093-3*); (SPA., 24.95 (*0-8288-5094-1*) French & European Pubns., Inc.

—Tintin en Amerique. (Tintin Ser.). Orig. Title: Tintin in America. (SPA.). 64p. (J). 14.95 (*84-261-1400-8*) Juventud, Editorial ESP. *Dist:* Distribooks, Inc.

—Tintin in America. Orig. Title: Tintin en Amerique. (Illus.). 62p. (J). 24.95 (*0-8288-5000-3*) French & European Pubns., Inc.

—Tintin in America. 1979. (Adventures of Tintin Ser.). Orig. Title: Tintin en Amerique. 62p. (J). (gr. 2 up). pap. 9.99 (*0-316-35852-5*) Little Brown & Co.

Higgins, Robert & Flaming, Doug. Roast Beef in April: An Autobiographical Sketch of the 30's & 40's. 1993. 165p. pap. 9.95 (*0-9637936-2-4*) Western New York Wares, Inc.

Holt, Rinehart and Winston Staff. The Coffin Quilt: The Feud Between the Hatfields & the McCoys. 2nd ed. 2002. (J). text 4.80 (*0-03-073522-X*) Holt, Rinehart & Winston.

Icenoggle, Jodi. America's Betrayal. 2001. 208p. (J). (gr. 7 up). 7.95 (*1-57249-252-X*, WM Kids) White Mane Publishing Co., Inc.

Johnson, Angela. Those Building Men. 2001. (Illus.). 32p. (J). (ps-3). pap. 16.95 (*0-590-66521-9*, Blue Sky Pr., The) Scholastic, Inc.

Katzakian, Norma. Naomi - A First Generation American. Chidester, Ardis & Folchi, Robert A., eds. l.t. ed. 2000. (Illus.). (J). (gr. 4-7). pap. 12.95 (*0-9662228-1-4*) Dab Publishing Co.

Keller, Laurie. The Scrambled States of America, ERS. 2002. (Illus.). 40p. (J). (ps-4). pap. 6.95 (*0-8050-6831-7*, Holt, Henry & Co. Bks. For Young Readers) Holt, Henry & Co.

Kellogg, Steven, illus. Yankee Doodle. 1996. 40p. (J). (ps-3). pap. 6.99 (*0-689-80726-0*, Aladdin) Simon & Schuster Children's Publishing.

LaFaye, A. Edith Shay. 2001. (J). 11.04 (*0-606-21170-5*) Turtleback Bks.

Loomis, Christine. Across America, I Love You. 2000. (Illus.). 32p. (J). (ps-3). lib. bdg. 16.49 (*0-7868-2314-3*);Vol. 1. 15.99 (*0-7868-0366-5*) Hyperion Bks. for Children.

Martin, Joseph P. Yankee Doodle Boy. Scheer, George F., ed. 1995. (Illus.). (YA). (gr. 7 up). pap. 8.95 (*0-8234-1180-X*) Holiday Hse., Inc.

Meltzer, Milton. American Promise. 1990. (J). o.p. (*0-553-53050-X*, Dell Books for Young Readers) Random Hse. Children's Bks.

Mullin, Penn. Postcards from America, 5 bks., Set. Incl. Postcards from America: Reproducible Activity Workbook. (Illus.). 64p. pap., tchr. ed., wbk. ed. 15.00 (*0-87879-974-5*, HN9745); (Postcards Ser.). (Illus.). 1992. Set pap. 19.00 (*0-87879-957-5*, HN9575) High Noon Bks.

Naipaul, V. S. In a Free State. 1984. 256p. mass mkt. 10.00 o.s.i (*0-394-72205-1*, Vintage) Knopf Publishing Group.

—In a Free State. 1977. 256p. pap. 3.95 o.p. (*0-14-003711-X*, Penguin Bks.) Viking Penguin.

Nelson, Ray & Kelly, Douglas. Greetings from America. McLane, Mike & Siegal, Joseph, eds. rev. ed. 1997. (Illus.). 48p. (J). (gr. 3-6). 16.95 (*1-883772-13-3*) Flying Rhinoceros, Inc.

Peckham, Howard. Lew Wallace: Boy Writer. Underdown, Harold, ed. 2nd ed. 2001. (Young Patriots Ser.: Vol. 3). (Illus.). 112p. (J). (gr. 3 up). pap. 9.95 (*1-882859-06-5*); 14.95 (*1-882859-05-7*) Patria Pr., Inc.

Peel, John & Golden Books Staff. Where in the U. S. A. Is Carmen Sandiego? 1993. (J). (gr. 4-7). pap. 3.95 o.s.i (*0-307-22304-3*, Golden Bks.) Random Hse. Children's Bks.

Reed, Patrick. Theodore Elijah Bear Explores the United States. 1998. (Illus.). 40p. (J). pap. 12.00 (*1-891989-02-2*) Fundbuilder$, U.S.A.

Rinaldi, Ann. The Coffin Quilt: The Feud Between the Hatfields & the McCoys. 2001. (J). 12.05 (*0-606-20507-1*) Turtleback Bks.

Robertson, Keith. Henry Reed's Journey. 1963. (Illus.). (J). (gr. 4-6). 13.95 o.p. (*0-670-36854-7*, Viking Children's Bks.) Penguin Putnam Bks. for Young Readers.

Romain, Trevor. Jemma's Journey. 2003. (Illus.). 32p. (J). (gr. k-3). 15.95 (*1-56397-937-3*) Boyds Mills Pr.

Rylant, Cynthia. Tulip Sees America. (Illus.). 32p. (ps up). 2002. (YA). mass mkt. 5.99 (*0-439-39978-5*); 1998. (J). pap. 15.95 (*0-590-84744-9*, Blue Sky Pr., The) Scholastic, Inc.

Sherrill, Ronda. The Year of the New Barn. 2002. 132p. (J). pap. 19.95 (*1-59129-140-2*) PublishAmerica, Inc.

Sonnenmark, Laura A. Something's Rotten in the State of Maryland. 1993. 176p. (YA). (gr. 7-9). mass mkt. 2.95 (*0-590-42877-2*) Scholastic, Inc.

Twain, Mark, et al. Pudd'nhead Wilson: Curriculum Unit. 2000. (Novel Ser.). 60p. (YA). (gr. 9-12). spiral bd. 18.95 (*1-56077-648-X*) Ctr. for Learning, The.

Van Leeuwen, Jean. Hannah's Winter of Hope. 2001. (Pioneer Daughters Ser.). (Illus.). (J). 11.04 (*0-606-21780-0*) Turtleback Bks.

Villasenor, Victor. Los Trece Sentidos. 2001. 512p. 26.00 (*0-06-621297-9*, Rayo) HarperTrade.

Wanttaja, Ronald. The Price of Command: Nate Lawton's War of 1812. Kemnitz, Myrna, ed. 1998. (Illus.). 330p. (J). pap. 9.99 (*0-88092-286-9*, 2869) Royal Fireworks Publishing Co.

West, Tracey. Voyage of the Half Moon. 1995. (Stories of the States Ser.). (Illus.). 96p. (J). (gr. 4-7). pap. 5.95 (*1-881889-76-9*) Silver Moon Pr.

—Voyage of the Half Moon. 1995. 12.10 (*0-606-14382-3*) Turtleback Bks.

Wood, Frances. The Daughter of Madrugada. 2002. 176p. (gr. 5-7). text 15.95 (*0-385-32719-6*, Delacorte Bks. for Young Readers) Random Hse. Children's Bks.

—Daughter of Madrugada. 176p. (gr. 5). 2003. pap. text 4.99 (*0-440-41644-2*, Dell Books for Young Readers); 2002. lib. bdg. 17.99 (*0-385-90038-4*, Delacorte Bks. for Young Readers) Random Hse. Children's Bks.

UNITED STATES MILITARY ACADEMY, WEST POINT—FICTION

Efaw, Amy. Battle Dress. (J). (gr. 7 up). 2003. 400p. pap. 6.99 (*0-06-053520-2*); 2000. (Illus.). 304p. 16.99 (*0-06-027943-5*); 2000. (Illus.). 304p. lib. bdg. 16.89 (*0-06-028411-0*) HarperCollins Children's Bk. Group.

Fleming, Thomas J. Band of Brothers. 1988. (J). (gr. 8 up). 13.95 (*0-8027-6740-0*); lib. bdg. 14.85 (*0-8027-6741-9*) Walker & Co.

UTAH—FICTION

Adrian, Mary. Mystery of the Dinosaur Bones. 1967. (Illus.). (J). (gr. 4-6). lib. bdg. 6.95 o.p. (*0-8038-4644-4*) Hastings Hse. Daytrips Pubs.

Anderson, Launi K. Ellie's Gold. 1995. (Latter-Day Daughters Ser.). (J). pap. 4.95 (*1-56236-505-3*) Aspen Bks.

—Gracie's Angel. Utley, Jennifer, ed. 1996. (Latter-Day Daughters Ser.). (Illus.). 80p. (J). (gr. 3-9). pap. 4.95 (*1-56236-508-8*) Aspen Bks.

—Violet's Garden. 1996. (Latter-Day Daughters Ser.). (Illus.). 80p. (J). (gr. 3-9). pap. 4.95 (*1-56236-506-1*) Aspen Bks.

Fitzgerald, John D. The Great Brain. 1985. (Great Brain Ser.). (Illus.). (J). (gr. 4-8). 192p. 12.95 o.s.i (*0-8037-3074-8*); 11.89 o.p. (*0-8037-3076-4*) Penguin Putnam Bks. for Young Readers. (Dial Bks. for Young Readers).

—Me & My Little Brain. 1985. (Great Brain Ser.). (Illus.). 144p. (J). (gr. 4-7). 14.99 o.s.i (*0-8037-5531-7*); 11.89 o.p. (*0-8037-5532-5*) Penguin Putnam Bks. for Young Readers. (Dial Bks. for Young Readers).

—Me & My Little Brain. 1972. 144p. (J). (gr. 4-7). pap. 4.50 o.s.i (*0-440-45533-2*, Yearling) Random Hse. Children's Bks.

—Me & My Little Brain. 1971. (J). 10.04 (*0-606-03953-8*) Turtleback Bks.

—More Adventures of the Great Brain. (Great Brain Ser.). (Illus.). 2004. 160p. pap. 4.99 (*0-14-240065-3*, Puffin Bks.); 1985. (J). (gr. 4-8). 11.89 o.p. (*0-8037-5821-9*, Dial Bks. for Young Readers); 1969. (J). (gr. 4-8). 12.95 o.s.i (*0-8037-5819-7*, 01160-350, Dial Bks. for Young Readers) Penguin Putnam Bks. for Young Readers.

—More Adventures of the Great Brain. 2002. (J). pap., tchr.'s training gde. ed. 35.00 incl. audio (*0-8072-0860-4*, Listening Library) Random Hse. Audio Publishing Group.

—More Adventures of the Great Brain. 1971. (Yearling Ser.). 160p. (gr. 4-7). pap. text 4.50 o.s.i (*0-440-45822-6*, Yearling) Random Hse. Children's Bks.

—More Adventures of the Great Brain. 1969. (Dell Yearling Bks.). (J). 10.55 (*0-606-02183-3*) Turtleback Bks.

Fitzgerald, John D. & Mayer, Mercer. More Adventures of the Great Brain. 2000. (Great Brain Ser.). (Illus.). 160p. (J). (ps-3). 6.99 (*0-8037-2591-4*, Dial Bks. for Young Readers) Penguin Putnam Bks. for Young Readers.

Harrison, Mette Ivie. The Monster in Me. 2003. 176p. (J). tchr. ed. 16.95 (*0-8234-1713-1*) Holiday Hse., Inc.

Hobbs, William. The Maze. (J). (gr. 5 up). 1999. 256p. pap. 5.99 (*0-380-72913-X*, Harper Trophy); 1998. 208p. 15.95 (*0-688-15092-6*) HarperCollins Children's Bk. Group.

—The Maze. 1999. (YA). pap., stu. ed. 59.00 incl. audio (*0-7887-3990-5*, 41062X4) Recorded Bks., LLC.

—The Maze. 1999. 11.00 (*0-606-16369-7*) Turtleback Bks.

Hubbard, Louise G. Grandfather's Gold Watch. 1997. (Illus.). 32p. (J). (ps-3). 11.95 (*1-57345-242-4*, Shadow Mountain) Deseret Bk. Co.

Johnson, Annabel & Johnson, Edgar. Wilderness Bride. 2003. 232p. (YA). 12.95 (*0-9714612-7-9*) Green Mansion Pr. LLC.

Johnson, Sherrie. A House with Wings. 1995. (J). pap. 7.95 (*1-56236-309-3*) Aspen Bks.

London, Jonathan & London, Aaron. White Water. 2001. (Illus.). 32p. (J). (gr. 2-4). 15.99 o.p. (*0-670-89286-6*, Viking Children's Bks.) Penguin Putnam Bks. for Young Readers.

McKendrick, Lisa. On a Whim. 2001. 156p. (J). (*1-57734-896-6*) Covenant Communications.

Nielsen, Gwyn English. Torey the Turkey Goes Skiing. 1998. (Illus.). 24p. (Orig.). (J). (ps-4). pap. 5.99 (*0-9660726-0-X*) C.G.S. Pr.

Rees, Shirley. Hannah Stands Tall. 2002. 130p. (J). pap. 10.95 (*1-55517-652-6*, 76526, Bonneville Bks.) Cedar Fort, Inc./CFI Distribution.

Richardson, Boyd C. Danger Trail: Knife Thrower's Journey West. 1995. (J). pap. 9.95 o.p. (*1-55503-777-1*, 01111795) Covenant Communications, Inc.

Rostkowski, Margaret I. Moon Dancer. 1995. (YA). (gr. 7 up). 224p. 11.00 o.s.i (*0-15-276638-3*); 192p. pap. 6.00 (*0-15-200194-8*) Harcourt Children's Bks.

Rowley, B. J. Missing Children. 2000. (Light Traveler Adventure Ser.: Vol. 3). 252p. (YA). (gr. 6-12). pap. 13.95 (*0-9700103-3-8*) Golden Wings Enterprises.

Rowley, Brent. My Body Fell Off! A Novel. 1997. (J). 9.95 o.p. (*1-57734-130-9*) Covenant Communications, Inc.

Sargent, Dave & Sargent, Pat. Bashful: Be Brave. 2003. (Saddle Up Ser.: Vol. 1). 42p. (J). mass mkt. 6.95 (*1-56763-684-5*) Ozark Publishing.

—Bashful (Dusty Dun) Be Brave. 2003. (Saddle Up Ser.: Vol. 1). 42p. (J). lib. bdg. 22.60 (*1-56763-683-7*) Ozark Publishing.

Skurzynski, Gloria. Rockbuster. 2001. (Illus.). 272p. (J). 16.00 (*0-689-83991-X*, Atheneum) Simon & Schuster Children's Publishing.

Skurzynski, Gloria & Ferguson, Alane. Ghost Horses. 2000. (National Parks Mysteries Ser.: Vol. 6). (Illus.). 145p. (J). (gr. 4-7). 15.95 (*0-7922-7055-X*) National Geographic Society.

Thayne, Emma L. Never Past the Gate. 1975. 250p. (J). 7.95 o.p. (*0-87905-047-0*) Smith, Gibbs Pub.

Ury, Allen B. Lost in Horror Valley. 1996. (Scary Stories for Sleep-Overs Ser.: Vol. 2). 128p. (J). (gr. 4-7). pap. 4.95 o.s.i (*1-56565-522-2*, 05222W) Lowell Hse. Juvenile.

Williams, Carol Lynch. Esther's Celebration. 1996. (Latter-Day Daughters Ser.). (Illus.). 80p. (J). (gr. 3-9). pap. 4.95 (*1-56236-507-X*) Aspen Bks.

—A Mother to Embarrass Me. 2002. 144p. lib. bdg. 17.99 (*0-385-90028-7*); (gr. 3-7). text 15.95 o.p. (*0-385-72922-7*) Dell Publishing. (Delacorte Pr.).

—A Mother to Embarrass Me. 2003. 144p. (gr. 3-7). pap. text 4.99 (*0-440-41810-0*, Yearling) Random Hse. Children's Bks.

Wunderli, Stephen. The Blue Between the Clouds, ERS. 1996. (J). (gr. 4-7). pap. 5.95 o.p. (*0-8050-4819-7*); 1992. 80p. (YA). (gr. 5 up). 13.95 o.p. (*0-8050-1772-0*) Holt, Henry & Co. (Holt, Henry & Co. Bks. For Young Readers).

Yates, Alma J. Nick. 1995. (Orig.). (YA). (gr. 7 up). pap. 9.95 (*1-57345-062-6*) Deseret Bk. Co.

Young, Joseph R. Legend of the Lost Josephine Mine: A Fascinating Adventure. 2001. 221p. (J). pap. 13.95 (*1-55517-550-3*, Bonneville Bks.) Cedar Fort, Inc./CFI Distribution.

Zindel, Paul. Raptor, No. 1. 1999. (Raptor Ser.: Vol. 1). 176p. (J). (gr. 5-9). pap. 4.99 (*0-7868-1224-9*) Disney Pr.

—Raptor. 1998. (J). (gr. 4-7). 170p. lib. bdg. 15.49 (*0-7868-2374-7*);No. 1. (Raptor Ser.: Vol. 1). 176p. 14.95 (*0-7868-0338-X*) Hyperion Bks. for Children.

—Raptor. 2000. (J). pap., stu. ed. 42.24 incl. audio (*0-7887-4185-3*, 41098) Recorded Bks., LLC.

—Raptor. 1999. 11.04 (*0-606-17385-4*) Turtleback Bks.

—Raptor Paperback Club. 1999. (Illus.). 176p. (J). pap. 4.99 (*0-7868-1471-3*) Disney Pr.

V

VENEZUELA—FICTION

Cowcher, Helen. Jaguar. (Illus.). 40p. (BEN, CHI, ENG, GRE & GUJ.). (J). 16.95 (*1-84059-014-9*); 2001. (BEN, CHI, ENG, GRE & GUJ., (YA). 16.95 (*1-84059-008-4*); 2001. (BEN, CHI, ENG, GRE & GUJ., (YA). 16.95 (*1-84059-010-6*); 2001. (BEN, CHI, ENG, GRE & GUJ., (YA). 16.95 (*1-84059-011-4*); 2001. (BEN, CHI, ENG, GRE & GUJ., (YA). 16.95 (*1-84059-012-2*); 2001. (BEN, CHI, ENG, GRE & GUJ., (YA). 16.95 (*1-84059-013-0*); 2001. (TUR., (YA). 16.95 (*1-84059-015-7*) Milet Publishing, Ltd. GBR. *Dist:* Pan Asia Pubns. (USA), Inc., Consortium Bk. Sales & Distribution.

—Jaguar. (J). (gr. 1-2). (*0-590-36037-X*); (SPA., Illus.). (gr. 1-3). pap. 3.96 net. (*0-590-87599-X*, SO30738, Scholastic Pr.); 2002. 32p. mass mkt. 5.99 (*0-439-39470-8*); 1997. (Illus.). 32p. (ps-5). pap. 15.95 (*0-590-29937-9*) Scholastic, Inc.

Hudson, William Henry. Green Mansions: A Romance of the Tropical Forest. 1965. (Airmont Classics Ser.). (J). (gr. 8 up). mass mkt. 1.95 o.p. (*0-8049-0087-6*, CL-87) Airmont Publishing Co., Inc.

Johnson, Lissa Halls & Wierenga, Kathy. Croutons for Breakfast. 2003. (Brio Girls Ser.). (Illus.). 192p. (J). (gr. 6-11). pap. 6.99 (*1-58997-080-2*) Focus on the Family Publishing.

Kurusa. The Streets Are Free. 2003. (Illus.). 50p. (J). (gr. k-3). reprint ed. pap. 7.95 (*1-55037-370-6*) Annick Pr., Ltd. CAN. *Dist:* Firefly Bks., Ltd.

Talbott, Hudson & Greenberg, Mark. Amazon Diary: The Jungle Adventures of Alex Winters. 1996. (Illus.). 48p. (J). (gr. 4-7). 15.95 o.s.i (*0-399-22916-7*, G. P. Putnam's Sons) Penguin Group (USA) Inc.

—Amazon Diary: The Jungle Adventures of Alex Winters. 1998. (Illus.). 48p. (J). (gr. k up). reprint ed. pap. 6.99 o.s.i (*0-698-11699-2*, PaperStar) Penguin Putnam Bks. for Young Readers.

VENICE (ITALY)—FICTION

Bjork, Christina. Eugenia en Venecia. 2000. (Illus.). (J). (gr. 3-5). (CAT.). 96p. 17.95 (*84-95040-39-5*); (SPA., 94p. 17.95 (*84-95040-38-7*, RR2897) Serres, Ediciones, S. L. ESP. *Dist:* Lectorum Pubns., Inc.

—Vendela in Venice. Crampton, Patricia, tr. from SWE. 1999. (Illus.). 96p. (YA). (gr. 4-7). 18.00 (*91-29-64559-X*) R & S Bks. SWE. *Dist:* Holtzbrinck Pubs.

Fleming, Candace. Gabriella's Song. 1997. (Illus.). 32p. (J). (ps-3). 16.00 (*0-689-80973-5*, Atheneum/Anne Schwartz Bks.) Simon & Schuster Children's Publishing.

Funke, Cornelia. The Thief Lord. Latsch, Oliver, tr. from GER. 2002. (Illus.). 352p. (J). (gr. 4-7). pap. 16.95 (*0-439-40437-1*, Chicken Hse., The) Scholastic, Inc.

—The Thief Lord. 2003. 376p. (J). (gr. 3-6). reprint ed. pap. 6.99 (*0-439-42089-X*, Chicken Hse., The) Scholastic, Inc.

Gutman, Anne. Gaspard on Vacation: Lisa's Airplane Trip. 2001. (Illus.). 32p. (J). (ps-1). 9.95 o.p. (*0-375-81115-X*, Knopf Bks. for Young Readers) Random Hse. Children's Bks.

Jaffe, Michele. The Stargazer. l.t. ed. 2000. (G. K. Hall Core Ser.). 567p. 28.95 (*0-7838-8931-3*, Macmillan Reference USA) Gale Group.

Kraus, Robert. The Gondolier of Venice. 1976. (Illus.). 30p. (J). (gr. 1 up). 5.95 o.p. (*0-671-96176-4*, Atheneum) Simon & Schuster Children's Publishing.

Maurer, Claudia & Smalley, Elisa. Zoe Sophia's Scrapbook: An Adventure in Venice. 2003. (Illus.). 40p. (J). (ps-1). 14.95 (*0-8118-3606-1*) Chronicle Bks. LLC.

Miano, Sarah E. The Venetian. 1999. (Illus.). (J). (gr. 3-4). E-Book (*1-929776-00-4*) Chapter & Verse Publishing for Children.

Morpurgo, Michael. Jo-Jo, & the Melon Donkey. 2002. (Yellow Bananas Ser.). (Illus.). 48p. (J). (gr. 3-4). pap. 4.95 (*0-7787-0988-4*); lib. bdg. 19.96 (*0-7787-0942-6*) Crabtree Publishing Co.

Napoli, Donna Jo. Daughter of Venice. 2003. 288p. (YA). (gr. 7). mass mkt. 5.50 (*0-440-22928-6*, Dell Books for Young Readers) Random Hse. Children's Bks.

—For the Love of Venice. 1998. 256p. (YA). (gr. 8 up). 15.95 o.s.i (*0-385-32531-2*, Delacorte Pr.) Dell Publishing.

—For the Love of Venice. 2000. 256p. (YA). (gr. 7-12). mass mkt. 4.99 (*0-440-41411-3*, Laurel Leaf) Random Hse. Children's Bks.

—For the Love of Venice. 2000. (Illus.). (J). 10.55 (*0-606-17998-4*) Turtleback Bks.

Pressler, Mirjam. Shylock's Daughter. Murdoch, Brian, tr. from GER. 2001. (Illus.). 272p. (J). (gr. 9 up). 17.99 (*0-8037-2667-8*, Dial Bks. for Young Readers) Penguin Putnam Bks. for Young Readers.

VERMONT—FICTION

Alvarez, Julia. How Tia Lola Came to (Visit) Stay. 160p. (gr. 3-7). 2004. (J). lib. bdg. 17.99 (*0-375-91552-4*, Knopf Bks. for Young Readers); 2004. (SPA., Illus.). pap. text 5.50 (*0-375-81552-X*, Yearling); 2002. (Illus.). pap. text 5.50 (*0-440-41870-4*, Laurel Leaf) Random Hse. Children's Bks.

—How Tia Lola Came to (Visit) Stay. Cascardi, Andrea, ed. 2001. (Illus.). 160p. (gr. 3-5). text 15.95 (*0-375-80215-0*); lib. bdg. 17.99 (*0-375-90215-5*) Random Hse. Children's Bks. (Knopf Bks. for Young Readers).

Arnosky, Jim. Little Champ. 1995. (Illus.). 69p. (J). (ps-3). 13.95 o.s.i (*0-399-22759-8*, G. P. Putnam's Sons) Penguin Group (USA) Inc.

Arnosky, Jim, illus. Little Champ. 2001. (J). pap. 6.95 (*0-9657144-5-4*) Onion River Pr.

Baker, Carin Greenberg. Pride of the Green Mountains, 3. 1998. (Treasured Horses Ser.). (J). 10.55 (*0-606-13863-3*) Turtleback Bks.

Bennett, Cherie. Sunset Fling. 1995. 224p. mass mkt. 3.99 o.s.i (*0-425-15026-7*) Berkley Publishing Group.

Carty, Margaret F. Christmas in Vermont: Three Stories. 1983. (Illus.). 48p. (Orig.). (J). (gr. 5 up). pap. 2.95 (*0-933050-21-6*) New England Pr., Inc., The.

Cray, Jordan. Shiver. 1998. (Danger.com Ser.: No. 9). 224p. (YA). (gr. 6 up). per. 3.99 (*0-689-82384-3*, Simon Pulse) Simon & Schuster Children's Publishing.

Curtis, Alice Turner. A Little Maid of Ticonderoga. 2004. (Little Maid Ser.). (Illus.). 192p. (J). (gr. 4-7). reprint ed. pap. 9.95 (*1-55709-330-X*) Applewood Bks.

Doyle, Eugenie. Stray Voltage. 2002. 136p. (J). (gr. 5-7). 16.95 (*1-886910-86-3*, Front Street) Front Street, Inc.

—Stray Voltage. 2004. pap. 5.99 (*0-14-240153-6*, Puffin Bks.) Penguin Putnam Bks. for Young Readers.

Fairless, Caroline. Hambone. 2001. (Illus.). 48p. (J). pap. 10.95 (*0-89869-361-6*) Church Publishing, Inc.

—Hambone. 1980. (Illus.). 48p. (J). (gr. 3 up). 8.95 o.p. (*0-912766-97-2*) Tundra Bks. of Northern New York.

Fisher, Dorothy Canfield. Understood Betsy, ERS. 1999. (Illus.). 229p. (J). (gr. 4-6). 17.95 (*0-8050-6073-1*, Holt, Henry & Co. Bks. For Young Readers) Holt, Henry & Co.

Gauthier, Gail. The Hero of Ticonderoga. 2001. 231p. (J). (gr. 5 up). 16.99 (*0-399-23559-0*) Penguin Group (USA) Inc.

—The Hero of Ticonderoga. 2002. 240p. (YA). (gr. 5-9). pap. 6.99 (*0-698-11968-1*, PaperStar) Penguin Putnam Bks. for Young Readers.

Graff, Nancy Price. A Long Way Home. 2001. 192p. (J). (gr. 5-9). tchr. ed. 15.00 (*0-618-12042-4*, Clarion Bks.) Houghton Mifflin Co. Trade & Reference Div.

Haas, Jessie. Westminster West. 1997. (Illus.). 176p. (J). (gr. 5 up). 15.00 (*0-688-14883-2*, Greenwillow Bks.) HarperCollins Children's Bk. Group.

Hesse, Karen. Witness. unabr. ed. 2001. audio 18.00 (*0-8072-0592-3*, Listening Library) Random Hse. Audio Publishing Group.

—Witness. (*0-439-36634-8*, Scholastic Pr.); 2003. (Illus.). 168p. (J). pap. 5.99 (*0-439-27200-9*, Scholastic Paperbacks); 2001. (Illus.). 176p. (YA). (gr. 4-7). pap. 16.95 (*0-439-27199-1*) Scholastic, Inc.

Hurwitz, Johanna. Bunk Mates. 1987. (Illus.). 128p. (J). (gr. 7 up). reprint ed. pap. 2.50 o.p. (*0-590-40418-0*) Scholastic, Inc.

—A Llama in the Family. 1994. (Illus.). 112p. (J). (gr. 2 up). 16.00 (*0-688-13388-6*) HarperCollins Children's Bk. Group.

—A Llama in the Family. 1996. (J). 8.60 o.p. (*0-606-09568-3*) Turtleback Bks.

—Yellow Blue Jay. 1993. (Illus.). 128p. (J). (ps-3). reprint ed. pap. 4.95 (*0-688-12278-7*, Harper Trophy) HarperCollins Children's Bk. Group.

—Yellow Blue Jay. 1993. (Illus.). (J). 11.00 (*0-606-22072-0*) Turtleback Bks.

Jackson, Edgar N. Green Mountain Hero. 1988. 192p. (YA). (gr. 6 up). reprint ed. pap. 10.95 (*0-933050-61-5*) New England Pr., Inc., The.

Jackson, Jacqueline. The Taste of Spruce Gum. 1966. (Illus.). (J). (gr. 6-8). 6.95 o.p. (*0-316-45476-1*) Little Brown & Co.

Jaspersohn, William. The Two Brothers. 2000. (Family Heritage Ser.). (Illus.). 32p. (J). (gr. 1-5). text 14.95 (*0-916718-16-6*) Vermont Folklife Ctr.

Johnson, Allen, Jr. The Christmas Tree Express. (Illus.). (J). (gr. 4-8). 12.95 o.s.i (*1-878561-21-9*) Seacoast Publishing, Inc.

Kinsey-Warnock, Natalie. As Long as There Are Mountains. 1997. 144p. (YA). (gr. 5-9). 14.99 o.s.i (*0-525-65236-1*) Penguin Putnam Bks. for Young Readers.

—A Doctor Like Papa. (Illus.). 80p. (J). 2003. pap. 4.99 (*0-06-444291-8*, Harper Trophy); 2002. 14.95 (*0-06-029319-5*); 2002. lib. bdg. 14.89 (*0-06-029320-9*) HarperCollins Children's Bk. Group.

—A Farm of Her Own. 2001. (Illus.). 32p. (J). (gr. k-3). 15.99 (*0-525-46507-3*, Dutton Children's Bks.) Penguin Putnam Bks. for Young Readers.

—From Dawn till Dusk: A Vermont Farm Year. 2002. (Illus.). 40p. (J). (gr. k-4). lib. bdg., tchr. ed. 16.00 (*0-618-18655-7*) Houghton Mifflin Co.

—In the Language of Loons. 1998. 112p. (J). (gr. 5-9). 15.99 (*0-525-65237-X*, Dutton Children's Bks.) Penguin Putnam Bks. for Young Readers.

—The Night the Bells Rang. 1991. (Illus.). 80p. (J). (gr. 4 up). 13.99 o.s.i (*0-525-65074-1*, Dutton Children's Bks.) Penguin Putnam Bks. for Young Readers.

—The Night the Bells Rang. 2001. (J). (gr. 1-5). 19.75 (*0-8446-7180-0*) Smith, Peter Pub., Inc.

—The Night the Bells Rang. 2000. 11.04 (*0-606-20367-2*) Turtleback Bks.

Kirkpatrick. Honey in the Rock. 1979. (J). 8.95 o.p. (*0-525-66643-5*) NAL.

Klass, Sheila S. Next Stop: Nowhere. 1995. (Illus.). 176p. (YA). (gr. 7-9). pap. 14.95 (*0-590-46686-0*) Scholastic, Inc.

Lange, Willem. John & Tom. 2001. (Family Heritage Ser.). (Illus.). 32p. (J). (ps-2). text 14.95 (*0-916718-17-4*) Vermont Folklife Ctr.

Littlefield, William. The Circus in the Woods. 2001. 240p. (J). (gr. 4-6). tchr. ed. 15.00 (*0-618-06642-X*) Houghton Mifflin Co.

London, Sara. Firehorse Max. 1997. (Michael di Capua Bks.). (Illus.). 32p. (J). (ps up). lib. bdg. 14.89 (*0-06-205095-8*); 14.95 o.s.i (*0-06-205094-X*) HarperCollins Children's Bk. Group.

Lunn, Janet. Hollow Tree. 2000. (Illus.). 208p. (J). (gr. 5-9). 15.99 (*0-670-88949-0*, Viking) Penguin Putnam Bks. for Young Readers.

Maguire, Gregory. Four Stupid Cupids. 2001. (Hamlet Chronicles Ser.). 192p. (J). (gr. 5 up). pap. 4.95 (*0-06-441072-2*, Harper Trophy) HarperCollins Children's Bk. Group.

—Four Stupid Cupids. 2001. (Illus.). 160p. (J). (gr. 4-6). tchr. ed. 15.00 (*0-395-83895-9*, Clarion Bks.) Houghton Mifflin Co. Trade & Reference Div.

—Four Stupid Cupids. l.t. ed. 2001. 225p. (J). 21.95 (*0-7862-3547-0*) Thorndike Pr.

—Six Haunted Hairdos. 1999. (Hamlet Chronicles Ser.). (Illus.). 160p. (J). (gr. 3-7). pap. 4.95 (*0-06-440720-9*, Harper Trophy) HarperCollins Children's Bk. Group.

—Six Haunted Hairdos. 1997. (Illus.). 160p. (J). (gr. 4-6). tchr. ed. 15.00 (*0-395-78626-6*, Clarion Bks.) Houghton Mifflin Co. Trade & Reference Div.

—Six Haunted Hairdos. l.t. ed. 2002. 178p. (J). 21.95 (*0-7862-4421-6*) Thorndike Pr.

—Six Haunted Hairdos. 1999. 11.00 (*0-606-17470-2*) Turtleback Bks.

—Three Rotten Eggs. 2002. (Illus.). 192p. (J). (gr. 4-6). 16.00 (*0-618-09655-8*, Clarion Bks.) Houghton Mifflin Co. Trade & Reference Div.

Mather, Melissa. One Summer in Between. 1967. 9.95 o.p. (*0-06-012837-2*) HarperCollins Pubs.

—One Summer in Between. 2000. 228p. pap. 14.95 (*0-595-09384-1*, Backinprint.com) iUniverse, Inc.

Medearis, Michael & Medearis, Angela Shelf. Daisy & the Doll. 2000. (Family Heritage Ser.). (Illus.). 32p. (J). (gr. 1-5). text 14.95 (*0-916718-15-8*) Vermont Folklife Ctr.

Page, Marion. The Printer's Devil. 2002. (Illus.). 171p. (YA). (gr. 5 up). pap. 9.99 (*0-88092-464-0*, 4640) Royal Fireworks Publishing Co.

Paterson, Katherine. Preacher's Boy. 2001. 192p. (J). (gr. 5 up). pap. 4.95 (*0-06-447233-7*, Harper Trophy) HarperCollins Children's Bk. Group.

—Preacher's Boy. 1999. (Illus.). 160p. (J). (gr. 5-9). tchr. ed. 15.00 (*0-395-83897-5*, Clarion Bks.) Houghton Mifflin Co. Trade & Reference Div.

—Preacher's Boy. l.t. ed. 2000. (Juvenile Ser.). 228p. (J). (gr. 4-7). 21.95 (*0-7862-2717-6*) Thorndike Pr.

Pearson, Tracey Campbell. Where Does Joe Go?, RS. 2002. (Illus.). 32p. (J). pap. 5.95 (*0-374-48366-3*, Sunburst) Farrar, Straus & Giroux.

Peck, Robert Newton. A Day No Pigs Would Die. 139p. (YA). (gr. 7 up). pap. 4.99 (*0-8072-1384-5*); pap. 4.99 (*0-8072-1357-8*) Random Hse. Audio Publishing Group. (Listening Library).

—Justice Lion. 1981. 264p. (J). (gr. 7 up). 13.95 o.s.i (*0-316-69658-7*) Little Brown & Co.

—A Part of the Sky. 1997. 176p. (J). (gr. 5-9). mass mkt. 4.99 (*0-679-88696-6*, Random Hse. Bks. for Young Readers) Random Hse. Children's Bks.

—Soup Ahoy. 1994. (Illus.). 144p. (J). (gr. 2-6). 15.99 o.s.i (*0-679-94978-X*, Knopf Bks. for Young Readers) Random Hse. Children's Bks.

—Soup Ahoy. 1995. 9.60 o.p. (*0-606-08610-2*) Turtleback Bks.

—Soup in Love. 1992. (J). 17.95 (*0-385-30703-9*) Doubleday Publishing.

—Soup on Ice. 128p. (J). 1988. (gr. k-6). pap. 2.75 o.s.i (*0-440-40115-1*, Yearling); 1985. (Illus.). (gr. 3-7). 13.99 o.s.i (*0-394-97613-4*, Knopf Bks. for Young Readers) Random Hse. Children's Bks.

—Soup 1776. 1995. (Illus.). 160p. (J). (gr. 4-7). 17.99 o.s.i (*0-679-97320-6*); 16.00 o.s.i (*0-679-87320-1*) Knopf, Alfred A. Inc.

—Soup's Hoop. 1990. 144p. (J). 13.95 o.s.i (*0-385-29808-0*) Doubleday Publishing.

—Soup's Hoop. 1992. 144p. (gr. 4-7). pap. text 4.50 o.s.i (*0-440-40589-0*, Yearling) Random Hse. Children's Bks.

—Soup's Hoop. 1990. 9.09 o.p. (*0-606-00926-4*) Turtleback Bks.

—Soup's Uncle. 1990. (J). pap. o.p. (*0-440-80166-4*) Dell Publishing.

—Trig. 1979. 64p. (J). (gr. 4-6). pap. 2.25 o.s.i (*0-440-49098-7*, Yearling) Random Hse. Children's Bks.

Pitkin, Dorothy. Wiser Than Winter. 1965. (J). (gr. 7-9). lib. bdg. 5.69 o.p. (*0-394-91828-2*, Pantheon) Knopf Publishing Group.

Rossiter, Nan Parson. Sugar on Snow. 2003. (Illus.). 32p. (J). (gr. k-4). 15.99 (*0-525-46910-9*, Dutton Children's Bks.) Penguin Putnam Bks. for Young Readers.

Samantha's Vermont Adventure. 1998. (Illus.). 2p. (J). (ps-1). 15.00 (*1-888074-89-2*) Pockets of Learning.

Seidler, Tor. Brothers below Zero. (Illus.). 144p. (J). 2003. (gr. 5 up). pap. 5.99 (*0-06-440936-8*, Harper Trophy); 2002. (gr. 3 up). 14.95 (*0-06-029179-6*, Geringer, Laura Bk.); 2002. (gr. 5 up). lib. bdg. 14.89 (*0-06-029180-X*, Geringer, Laura Bk.) HarperCollins Children's Bk. Group.

Stolz, Mary. Cider Days. 1978. (Ursula Nordstrom Bk.). (J). (gr. 3-7). lib. bdg. 12.89 o.p. (*0-06-025838-1*) HarperCollins Children's Bk. Group.

—Ferris Wheel. 1977. (Ursula Nordstrom Bk.). 144p. (J). (gr. 4-7). lib. bdg. 12.89 o.p. (*0-06-025860-8*) HarperCollins Children's Bk. Group.

Thompson, Julian F. Ghost Story, ERS. 1997. 224p. (J). 15.95 o.p. (*0-8050-4870-7*, Holt, Henry & Co. Bks. For Young Readers) Holt, Henry & Co.

—The Trials of Molly Sheldon, ERS. 1995. 176p. (YA). (gr. 7 up). 16.95 o.p. (*0-8050-3382-3*, Holt, Henry & Co. Bks. For Young Readers) Holt, Henry & Co.

—The Trials of Molly Sheldon. 1997. 192p. (gr. 7 up). pap. 4.99 o.s.i (*0-14-038425-1*) Penguin Putnam Bks. for Young Readers.

—The Trials of Molly Sheldon. 1997. (J). 10.09 o.p. (*0-606-12006-8*) Turtleback Bks.

Walker, Mildred. A Piece of the World. 2001. (Illus.). 218p. (J). pap. 12.95 (*0-8032-9823-4*, Bison Bks.) Univ. of Nebraska Pr.

Wells, Rosemary. Waiting for the Evening Star. 1993. (Illus.). (J). (gr. k-3). 400p. 15.00 o.s.i (*0-8037-1398-3*); 32p. 14.89 o.p. (*0-8037-1399-1*) Penguin Putnam Bks. for Young Readers. (Dial Bks. for Young Readers).

Williams, G. Walton. The Beavers Build a Dam. Kollock, John, ed. unabr. ed. 2000. (Illus.). 64p. (Orig.). (J). pap. 6.95 (*0-9703570-0-1*) Barksdale Hse. Pr.

Wilson, Nancy Hope. Mountain Pose, RS. 2001. 240p. (J). (gr. 5 up). 17.00 (*0-374-35078-7*, Farrar, Straus & Giroux (BYR)) Farrar, Straus & Giroux.

—Mountain Pose. 2003. 240p. (J). mass mkt. 4.50 (*0-439-44153-6*, Scholastic Paperbacks) Scholastic, Inc.

VIENNA (AUSTRIA)—FICTION

Dahlberg, Mavrine E. Play to the Angel. 2002. 192p. (J). pap. 5.99 (*0-14-230145-0*, Puffin Bks.) Penguin Putnam Bks. for Young Readers.

Dahlberg, Mavrine F. Play to the Angel, RS. 2000. 192p. (J). (gr. 3-7). 16.00 (*0-374-35994-6*, Farrar, Straus & Giroux (BYR)) Farrar, Straus & Giroux.

Death in Vienna. Date not set. (Nelson Readers Ser.). (J). pap. text (*0-17-557027-2*) Addison-Wesley Longman, Inc.

Settings

Henry, Marguerite. White Stallion of Lipizza. 1994. (Illus.). (J). (gr. 3-7). reprint ed. 111p. text 14.95 (0-02-743628-4); 112p. lib. bdg. o.p. (0-528-80154-6) Simon & Schuster Children's Publishing. (Simon & Schuster Children's Publishing).

Orgel, Doris. The Devil in Vienna. 1988. 256p. (J). (gr. 4-7). pap. 5.99 (0-14-032500-X, Puffin Bks.) Penguin Putnam Bks. for Young Readers.

Von Canon, Claudia. The Moonclock, 001. 1979. (J). (gr. 7 up). 6.95 o.p. (0-395-27810-4) Houghton Mifflin Co.

VIETNAM—FICTION

Acker, Rick. The Case of the Autumn Rose. 2003. (Davis Detective Mysteries Ser.). 204p. (J). pap. 6.99 (0-8254-2004-0) Kregel Pubns.

Baillie, Allan. Little Brother. 144p. (J). 1994. (gr. 5 up). pap. 3.99 o.s.i (0-14-036862-0, Puffin Bks.); 1992. (gr. 3-7). 14.00 o.s.i (0-670-84381-4, Viking Children's Bks.) Penguin Putnam Bks. for Young Readers.

—Little Brother. 1994. 9.09 o.p. (0-606-06535-0) Turtleback Bks.

Coe, Charles. Young Man in Vietnam. 1990. mass mkt. 2.75 o.p. (0-590-43298-2) Scholastic, Inc.

Garland, Sherry. The Lotus Seed. (Illus.). 32p. (J). 1997. pap. 7.00 (0-15-201483-7, Harcourt Paperbacks); 1993. (gr. 3 up). 16.00 (0-15-249465-0) Harcourt Children's Bks.

—Song of the Buffalo Boy. (YA). (gr. 7 up). 1994. 288p. pap. 6.00 (0-15-200098-4, Harcourt Paperbacks); 1992. 192p. 16.00 o.s.i (0-15-277107-7) Harcourt Children's Bks.

—Song of the Buffalo Boy. 1992. 12.05 (0-606-06751-5) Turtleback Bks.

Gibbons, Alan. Jaws of the Dragon. 1994. 156p. (J). (gr. 4-7). lib. bdg. 19.93 o.p. (0-8225-0737-4, Lerner Pubns.) Lerner Publishing Group.

Huynh, Quang Nhuong. The Land I Lost: Adventures of a Boy in Vietnam. 1986. (Trophy Bk.). (Illus.). 144p. (J). (gr. 5 up). pap. 4.99 (0-06-440183-9, Harper Trophy) HarperCollins Children's Bk. Group.

Keller, Holly. Grandfather's Dream. 1994. (Illus.). 32p. (J). (ps-3). 16.99 (0-688-12339-2); lib. bdg. 15.93 o.p. (0-688-12340-6) HarperCollins Children's Bk. Group. (Greenwillow Bks.).

McKay, Lawrence, Jr. Journey Home. 2000. (Illus.). 32p. (J). (ps-5). 15.95 (1-880000-65-2); pap. 6.95 (1-58430-005-1) Lee & Low Bks., Inc.

—Journey Home. 1998. (Illus.). (J). 13.10 (0-606-18247-0) Turtleback Bks.

Minh Tang, Eric & Ifkovic, Ed. The Minh Man Rules. 2000. (J). (gr. 7-9). pap. 9.99 (0-88092-419-5) Royal Fireworks Publishing Co.

Nhat Hanh, Thich. The Hermit & the Well. 2003. (Illus.). 32p. (J). pap. 15.00 (1-888375-31-0) Parallax Pr.

Nhuong, Nuynh Q. Land I Lost. 1982. (J). 12.95 (0-06-024592-1); 144p. 12.89 (0-06-024593-X) Harper-Collins Children's Bk. Group.

Pastore, Clare. Journey to America: Chantrea's Voyage, Vol. 3. 2002. 192p. mass mkt. 5.99 (0-425-18857-4) Berkley Publishing Group.

Pevsner, Stella & Tang, Fay. Sing for Your Father, Su Phan. 1997. (Illus.). 112p. (J). (gr. 4-6). 14.00 o.s.i (0-395-82267-X, Clarion Bks.) Houghton Mifflin Co. Trade & Reference Div.

—Sing for Your Father, Su Phan. 1999. 10.55 (0-606-16709-9) Turtleback Bks.

Pomerantz, Charlotte. The Princess & the Admiral. (Illus.). 48p. (gr. 4-7). 2004. (YA). pap. 8.95 (1-55861-061-8); 1992. (J). 17.95 (1-55861-060-X) Feminist Pr. at The City Univ. of New York.

Sherlock, Patti. Letters to Wolfie. 2004. 16.99 (0-670-03694-3, Viking) Viking Penguin.

Tran, Truong. Going Home, Coming Home / Ve Nha Tham Que Hu'O'Ng. 2003. Tr. of Ve Nha Tham Que Hu'O'Ng. (ENG & VIE., Illus.). 32p. (J). 16.95 (0-89239-179-0) Children's Bk. Pr.

Whelan, Gloria. Goodbye, Vietnam. (gr. 3-9). 1993. 144p. pap. 4.99 (0-679-82376-X, Random Hse. Bks. for Young Readers); 1992. 112p. (J). 13.99 o.s.i (0-679-92263-6, Knopf Bks. for Young Readers); 1992. 112p. (J). 13.00 o.s.i (0-679-82263-1, Knopf Bks. for Young Readers) Random Hse. Children's Bks.

—Goodbye, Vietnam. 1993. 10.04 (0-606-05848-6) Turtleback Bks.

Wolitzer, Meg. Caribou. 1984. 176p. (J). (gr. 7 up). 11.95 o.p. (0-688-03991-X, Greenwillow Bks.) HarperCollins Children's Bk. Group.

VIRGIN ISLANDS OF THE UNITED STATES—FICTION

Gershator, Phillis. Someday Cyril. 2000. (MONDO Chapter Books). (Illus.). 46p. (J). (1-57255-748-6) Mondo Publishing.

Howard, Ellen. When Daylight Comes. 1985. 192p. (J). (gr. 5-9). lib. bdg. 14.95 o.p. (0-689-31133-8, Atheneum) Simon & Schuster Children's Publishing.

Skurzynski, Gloria & Ferguson, Alane. Escape from Death, No. 9. 2002. (Mysteries in Our National Parks Ser.: Vol. 9). 160p. (J). pap. 5.95 (0-7922-6782-6) National Geographic Society.

—Escape from Fear. 2002. (Mysteries in Our National Parks Ser.: Vol. 9). 160p. (J). 15.95 (0-7922-6780-X) National Geographic Society.

VIRGINIA—FICTION

Alford, Katherine. Home Again, Home Again. 1996. (Illus.). 31p. (Orig.). (J). (gr. 2-7). pap. 12.00 (0-9652438-0-X) Little City Bks.

Beatty, Patricia. Charley Skedaddle. 1987. 192p. (YA). (gr. 5-9). 16.00 o.p. (0-688-06687-9, Morrow, William & Co.) Morrow/Avon.

—Charley Skedaddle. 1997. (Literature Units Ser.). (Illus.). 48p. (gr. 5-8). pap., tchr. ed. 7.99 (1-55734-565-1, TCA0565) Teacher Created Materials, Inc.

—Charley Skedaddle. 1987. (J). 11.00 (0-606-04029-3) Turtleback Bks.

Beiler, Edna. Mattie Mae. (Illus.). (J). 1967. 128p. (gr. 4-7). pap. 5.99 (0-8361-1789-1); 2nd ed. 2000. 112p. (ps-4). pap. 6.99 (0-8361-9141-2) Herald Pr.

Belle Prater's Boy. 1999. (Pathways to Critical Thinking Ser.). 32p. (YA). pap. text, stu. ed., tchr.'s training gde. ed. 19.95 (1-58303-081-6) Pathways Publishing.

Beukema, George D. Stories from Below the Poverty Line: Urban Lessons for Today's Mission. 2000. 112p. (J). pap. 9.99 (0-8361-9143-9) Herald Pr.

Brantley, Steven & Brantley, Judi. Molly's Christmas Mystery. l.t. ed. 2001. 40p. (J). 16.95 (1-892570-06-8) Spring Hse. Bks.

Brenaman, Miriam. Evvy's Civil War. 2002. 224p. (J). (gr. 7-10). 18.99 (0-399-23713-5) Penguin Group (USA) Inc.

—Evvy's Civil War. 2004. (Illus.). 224p. pap. 6.99 (0-14-240039-4, Puffin Bks.) Penguin Putnam Bks. for Young Readers.

Brooke, Lauren. After the Storm, No. 2. 2000. (Heartland Ser.: No. 2). (Illus.). 128p. (J). (gr. 3-6). mass mkt. 4.50 (0-439-13022-0) Scholastic, Inc.

—Coming Home. 2000. (Heartland Ser.: No. 1). (Illus.). 144p. (J). (gr. 3-6). mass mkt. 4.50 (0-439-13020-4) Scholastic, Inc.

Bryant, Bonnie. Changing Leads. 1999. (Pine Hollow Ser.: No. 4). 240p. (gr. 7 up). mass mkt. 4.50 o.s.i (0-553-49245-4, Dell Books for Young Readers) Random Hse. Children's Bks.

—Conformation Faults. 1999. (Pine Hollow Ser.: No. 5). 272p. (gr. 7 up). mass mkt. 4.50 o.s.i (0-553-49246-2, Dell Books for Young Readers) Random Hse. Children's Bks.

—Conformation Faults. 1999. (Pine Hollow Ser.: No. 5). (YA). (gr. 7 up). 10.55 (0-606-18958-0) Turtleback Bks.

—Reining In. 1998. (Pine Hollow Ser.: No. 3). 240p. (gr. 7 up). mass mkt. 4.50 o.s.i (0-553-49244-6) Bantam Bks.

—Secret Horse. 1999. (Saddle Club Ser.: No. 86). 160p. (gr. 4-6). pap. text 3.99 o.s.i (0-553-48671-3, Dell Books for Young Readers) Random Hse. Children's Bks.

—Show Jumper. 1999. (Saddle Club Ser.: No. 87). 176p. (gr. 4-6). pap. text 3.99 o.s.i (0-553-48672-1, Dell Books for Young Readers) Random Hse. Children's Bks.

—Stevie: The Inside Story. 1999. (Illus.). 304p. (gr. 4-6). pap. text 4.50 o.s.i (0-553-48674-8, Dell Books for Young Readers) Random Hse. Children's Bks.

—Stevie: The Inside Story. 1999. 10.55 (0-606-17154-1) Turtleback Bks.

Bulla, Clyde Robert. A Lion to Guard Us. (Trophy Bk.). (Illus.). (J). 1989. 128p. (gr. 3 up). pap. 4.99 (0-06-440333-5, Harper Trophy); 1981. (gr. 2-5). 14.00 o.p. (0-690-04096-2); 1981. 128p. (gr. 7 up). lib. bdg. 16.89 (0-690-04097-0) HarperCollins Children's Bk. Group.

—A Lion to Guard Us. 1983. (Illus.). 128p. (J). reprint ed. pap. 2.25 o.p. (0-590-33788-2) Scholastic, Inc.

—A Lion to Guard Us. 1989. (J). 11.00 (0-606-04267-9) Turtleback Bks.

Butler, Amy. Virginia Bound. 2003. 192p. (J). (gr. 5-9). tchr. ed. 15.00 (0-618-24752-1, Clarion Bks.) Houghton Mifflin Co. Trade & Reference Div.

Coombs, Karen M. Sarah on Her Own. 1996. (American Dreams Ser.). 9.09 o.p. (0-606-09818-6) Turtleback Bks.

Coombs, Karen Mueller. Sarah on Her Own. 1996. (American Dreams Ser.). 240p. (YA). (gr. 7 up). mass mkt. 3.99 (0-380-78275-8, Avon Bks.) Morrow/Avon.

Crane, Stephen. The Red Badge of Courage. (Modern Library Ser.). (J). E-Book 4.95 (1-931208-32-8) Adobe Systems, Inc.

—The Red Badge of Courage. unabr. ed. 1962. (Classics Ser.). (YA). (gr. 7 up). mass mkt. 2.50 (0-8049-0003-5, CL-3) Airmont Publishing Co., Inc.

—The Red Badge of Courage. 1971. (Dent's Illustrated Children's Classics Ser.). (Illus.). (J). 9.00 o.p. (0-460-05090-7) Biblio Distribution.

—The Red Badge of Courage. 1990. 162p. (YA). mass mkt. 3.99 (0-8125-0479-8, Tor Classics) Doherty, Tom Assocs., LLC.

—The Red Badge of Courage. unabr. ed. 1998. (Wordsworth Classics Ser.). (YA). (gr. 6-12). 5.27 o.p. (0-89061-567-5, R5675WW) Jamestown.

—The Red Badge of Courage. 1996. (Wishbone Classics Ser.: No. 10). 128p. (gr. 3-7). mass mkt. 4.25 (0-06-106497-1, HarperEntertainment) Morrow/Avon.

—The Red Badge of Courage. 1999. (Masterpiece Series Access Editions). (J). 10.95 (0-8219-1981-4) Paradigm Publishing, Inc.

—The Red Badge of Courage. Shapiro, Irwin, ed. 1973. (Now Age Illustrated Ser.). (Illus.). 64p. (J). (gr. 5-10). 7.50 o.p. (0-88301-214-6); pap. 2.95 (0-88301-101-8) Pendulum Pr., Inc.

—The Red Badge of Courage. 1995. (Puffin Classics Ser.). (Illus.). 224p. (YA). (gr. 4-7). pap. 4.99 (0-14-036710-1, Puffin Bks.) Penguin Putnam Bks. for Young Readers.

—The Red Badge of Courage. Hanft, Joshua, ed. 1993. (Great Illustrated Classics Ser.: Vol. 27). (Illus.). 240p. (J). (gr. 3-6). 9.95 (0-86611-978-7) Playmore, Inc., Pubs.

—The Red Badge of Courage. (J). (gr. 4-7). 1993. 32p. pap. 4.95 (0-8114-6837-2); 1983. (Illus.). 48p. pap. 9.27 o.p. (0-8172-2019-4); 1983. (Illus.). 48p. lib. bdg. 24.26 o.p. (0-8172-1670-7) Raintree Pubs.

—The Red Badge of Courage. 1988. (Portland House Illustrated Classics Ser.). (Illus.). 224p. (YA). 9.99 o.s.i (0-517-66844-0) Random Hse. Value Publishing.

—The Red Badge of Courage. 1972. 180p. (YA). (gr. 7-12). reprint ed. 1.25 o.p. (0-590-40678-7); pap. 2.25 (0-590-02117-6) Scholastic, Inc.

—The Red Badge of Courage. 1996. (Wishbone Classics Ser.: No. 10). (J). (gr. 3-7). 10.04 (0-606-10974-9) Turtleback Bks.

—The Red Badge of Courage & Other Stories. unabr. ed. 1999. (J). (gr. 1-8). audio 40.00 BBC Audiobooks America.

—The Red Badge of Courage & Other Writings. Chase, Richard, ed. 1972. (YA). (gr. 9 up). pap. 16.36 (0-395-05143-6, Riverside Editions) Houghton Mifflin Co.

Curry, Jane Louise. A Stolen Life. 1999. (Illus.). 192p. (J). (gr. 5-9). 16.00 (0-689-82932-9, McElderry, Margaret K.) Simon & Schuster Children's Publishing.

Denenberg, Barry. When Will This Cruel War Be Over? The Civil War Diary of Emma Simpson, Gordonsville, Virginia, 1864. 1996. (Dear America Ser.). (Illus.). 156p. (YA). (gr. 4-9). pap. 10.95 (0-590-22862-5) Scholastic, Inc.

Destiny Calls - Pocahontas. 1995. (Picture Window Ser.). (Illus.). 30p. (J). (ps-4). 9.98 o.p. (1-57082-241-7) Mouse Works.

Doss, Rodger. Killing of a Court: 1912 Hillsville Massacre. 1994. 140p. (J). (gr. 5-12). pap. 12.95 (0-9641867-0-5) Docar Publishing.

Doyon, Stephanie. Buying Time. 1999. (On the Road Ser.: Vol. 2). 235p. (J). (gr. 7-12). pap. 4.50 (0-689-82108-5, 076714004504, Simon Pulse) Simon & Schuster Children's Publishing.

—Buying Time. 1999. (On the Road Ser.: No. 2). 10.55 (0-606-18898-3) Turtleback Bks.

Duey, Kathleen. Summer MacCleary: Virginia, 1749. 1998. (American Diaries Ser.: Vol. 10). (J). (gr. 3-7). 10.04 (0-606-13120-5) Turtleback Bks.

—Summer McCleary: Virginia, 1749. 1998. (American Diaries Ser.: No. 10). 144p. (J). (gr. 3-7). pap. 4.50 o.s.i (0-689-81623-5, Aladdin) Simon & Schuster Children's Publishing.

Elliott, Laura. Flying South. 2003. 160p. (J). (gr. 4 up). 15.99 (0-06-001214-5); lib. bdg. 16.89 (0-06-001215-3) HarperCollins Pubs.

Farnsworth, Bill. My Misty Diary. 1997. (Illus.). 160p. (J). (gr. 2-7). per. 12.95 (0-689-81769-X, Little Simon) Simon & Schuster Children's Publishing.

Flournoy, Valerie. Tanya's Reunion. 1995. (Illus.). 40p. (J). 15.89 o.p. (0-8037-1605-2); 16.99 (0-8037-1604-4) Penguin Putnam Bks. for Young Readers. (Dial Bks. for Young Readers).

Forrester, Sandra. Wheel of the Moon. 2000. 176p. (J). (gr. 5 up). lib. bdg. 15.89 (0-06-029203-2); (Illus.). 15.95 (0-688-17149-4) HarperCollins Children's Bk. Group.

Fradin, Dennis Brindell. Virginia. 1995. (From Sea to Shining Sea Ser.). (Illus.). 64p. (J). (gr. 4-7). pap. 7.95 (0-516-43846-8, Children's Pr.) Scholastic Library Publishing.

Fugate, Clara T. The Legend of Natural Tunnel: La Leyenda del Tunel Natural. Calvera, Elizabeth C., ed. Socarras-Roufagalas, Gilda, tr. 1986. (Tales of the Virginia Wilderness Ser.: No. 1). (ENG & SPA., Illus.). 78p. (Orig.). (YA). (gr. 6-12). pap. 5.95 (0-936015-02-0) Pocahontas Pr., Inc.

Fuqua, Jonathon Scott. The Willoughby Spit Wonder. 2004. 160p. (J). 15.99 (0-7636-1776-8) Candlewick Pr.

Griffin, Adele. Witch Twins at Camp Bliss. (J). 2003. 144p. pap. 5.99 (0-7868-1583-3); 2002. (Illus.). 128p. (gr. 2-5). 15.99 (0-7868-0763-6) Hyperion Bks. for Children.

Haislip, Phyllis Hall. Lottie's Courage: A Contraband Slave's Story. 2003. (Illus.). 120p. (J). pap. 7.95 (1-57249-311-9, WM Kids) White Mane Publishing Co., Inc.

Hays, Wilma P. The Scarlet Badge. 1963. (Young Readers Ser.). (Illus.). (gr. 4-7). 3.95 o.p. (0-910412-67-7) Colonial Williamsburg Foundation.

Henry, Marguerite. Marguerite Henry's Horseshoe Library: Stormy, Misty's Foal, Sea Star, Orphan of Chincoteague; Misty of Chincoteague, 3 bks., Set. 1992. (Illus.). (J). (gr. 4-7). pap. 11.85 (0-689-71624-9, Aladdin) Simon & Schuster Children's Publishing.

—Misty of Chincoteague. 1991. pap. 3.95 o.p. (0-689-71483-1) Aladdin Paperbacks.

—Misty of Chincoteague. 2002. (Illus.). (J). 13.40 (0-7587-0291-4) Book Wholesalers, Inc.

—Misty of Chincoteague. 1995. (Illus.). (J). (gr. 4). 9.00 (0-395-73241-7) Houghton Mifflin Co.

—Misty of Chincoteague. 1986. (J). 19.95 o.p. (0-516-09863-2, Children's Pr.) Scholastic Library Publishing.

—Misty of Chincoteague. 9999. 160p. (J). (gr. 4-6). pap. 1.75 o.s.i (0-590-02388-8) Scholastic, Inc.

—Misty of Chincoteague. 2003. 176p. (J). pap. o.s.i (0-689-86224-5, Aladdin); 2001. 176p. mass mkt. 2.99 (0-689-84512-X, Aladdin); 1998. (J). pap. 2.65 (0-689-82170-0, Aladdin); 1997. (J). 100.00 (0-689-81377-5, Simon & Schuster Children's Publishing); 1995. (J). 3.95 o.s.i (0-689-80407-5, Aladdin); 1990. (Illus.). 176p. (J). (gr. 3-7). 17.95 (0-02-743622-5, Simon & Schuster Children's Publishing); 2000. (Illus.). 176p. (J). (gr. 3-7). 21.95 o.s.i (0-689-83926-X, Simon & Schuster Children's Publishing); 1991. (Illus.). 176p. (J). (gr. 3-7). reprint ed. pap. 4.99 (0-689-71492-0, Aladdin); Vol. 1. 1999. pap. 2.99 (0-689-82993-0, Aladdin) Simon & Schuster Children's Publishing.

—Misty of Chincoteague. l.t. ed. 2001. (Illus.). 195p. (J). (gr. 4-7). 21.95 (0-7862-2847-4) Thorndike Pr.

—Misty of Chincoteague. 1991. (J). 11.04 (0-606-04009-9) Turtleback Bks.

—Stormy: Misty's Foal. 1987. (Illus.). 224p. (J). (gr. 2-9). 8.95 o.p. (0-528-82083-4) Aladdin Paperbacks.

—Stormy: Misty's Foal. 2002. (Illus.). (J). 13.40 (0-7587-6608-4) Book Wholesalers, Inc.

—Stormy: Misty's Foal. 1986. (J). pap. 17.30 o.p. (0-516-09864-0, Children's Pr.) Scholastic Library Publishing.

—Stormy: Misty's Foal. (Kids' Picks Ser.). (J). 2001. 224p. pap. 2.99 o.s.i (0-689-84517-0, Aladdin); 1995. 3.95 o.s.i (0-689-80405-9, Aladdin); 1987. (Illus.). 224p. (gr. 2-9). pap. 3.95 o.s.i (0-02-688762-2, Simon & Schuster Children's Publishing); 2nd ed. 1991. (Illus.). 224p. (gr. 3-7). reprint ed. pap. 4.99 (0-689-71487-4, Aladdin) Simon & Schuster Children's Publishing.

—Stormy: Misty's Foal. 1996. (J). 20.25 (0-8446-6880-X) Smith, Peter Pub., Inc.

—Stormy: Misty's Foal. 1986. (J). 11.04 (0-606-01939-1) Turtleback Bks.

Henty, G. A. With Lee in Virginia: A Story of the American Civil War. 2000. 252p. (J). E-Book 3.95 (0-594-02419-6) 1873 Pr.

Hermes, Patricia. Our Strange New Land: Elizabeth's Jamestown Colony Diary. 2000. (My America Ser.). (Illus.). 112p. (J). (gr. 2-5). pap. 8.95 (0-439-11208-7, Scholastic Pr.) Scholastic, Inc.

—Our Strange New Land Bk. 1: Elizabeth's Jamestown Colony Diary. 2002. (My America Ser.: Bk. 1). (Illus.). 112p. (J). (gr. 2-5). mass mkt. 4.99 (0-439-36898-7, Scholastic Pr.) Scholastic, Inc.

—Season of Promise: Elizabeth's Jamestown Colony Diary. 2002. (My America Ser.: Bk. 3). (Illus.). (J). (gr. 2-5). 128p. pap. 10.95 (0-439-38898-8); 144p. mass mkt. 4.99 (0-439-27206-8) Scholastic, Inc. (Scholastic Pr.).

—The Starving Time Bk. 2: Elizabeth's Jamestown Colony Diary. (My America Ser.: Bk. 2). (Illus.). 112p. (J). (gr. 2-5). 2002. mass mkt. 4.99 (0-439-36902-9); 2001. pap. 8.95 (0-439-19998-0) Scholastic, Inc. (Scholastic Pr.).

Hite, Sid. Dither Farm, ERS. 1992. 224p. (YA). (gr. 7 up). 15.95 o.s.i (0-8050-1871-9, Holt, Henry & Co. Bks. For Young Readers) Holt, Henry & Co.

—A Hole in the World. 208p. (J). 2004. (gr. 5 up). mass mkt. 4.99 (0-439-09831-9, Scholastic Pr.); 2001. (Illus.). pap. 16.95 (0-439-09830-0) Scholastic, Inc.

—It's Nothing to a Mountain, ERS. 1994. (YA). (gr. 6 up). 15.95 o.p. (0-8050-2769-6, Holt, Henry & Co. Bks. For Young Readers) Holt, Henry & Co.

—It's Nothing to a Mountain. 1995. 224p. (YA). (gr. 6 up). mass mkt. 3.99 o.s.i (0-440-21945-0, Laurel Leaf) Random Hse. Children's Bks.

—It's Nothing to a Mountain. 1995. (YA). (gr. 6 up). 9.09 o.p. (0-606-07721-9) Turtleback Bks.

—Those Darn Dithers, ERS. 1996. 192p. (YA). (gr. 7-12). 15.95 o.s.i (0-8050-3838-8, Holt, Henry & Co. Bks. For Young Readers) Holt, Henry & Co.

Howard-Douglas, Daisy. Jad & Old Ananias. 1999. (Illus.). (J). (gr. 3-6). 12.95 o.p. (0-533-13028-X) Vantage Pr., Inc.

Johnston, Mary. To Have & to Hold. 1976. lib. bdg. 18.95 (0-89968-149-2, Lightyear Pr.); 1977. 403p. reprint ed. lib. bdg. 16.95 (0-89966-252-8) Buccaneer Bks., Inc.

—To Have & to Hold. reprint ed. lib. bdg. 48.00 (0-7426-1112-4); 2001. pap. text 28.00 (0-7426-6112-1) Classic Bks.

—To Have & to Hold, 001. 1969. 5.95 o.p. (0-395-07835-0) Houghton Mifflin Co.

Jones, Elizabeth McDavid. Watcher in the Piney Woods. 2000. (American Girl Collection: Bk. 9). (Illus.). 160p. (gr. 5-7). (J). pap. 5.95 (1-58485-090-6); (YA). 9.95 (1-58485-091-4) Pleasant Co. Pubns. (American Girl).

—Watcher in the Piney Woods. 2000. (American Girl Collection). (Illus.). (J). 12.00 (0-606-20981-6) Turtleback Bks.

Konz, Helen S. Builders of the Nation. 1999. 212p. reprint ed. o.p. (0-9658183-2-2) Heloukon Publishing.

Loggia, Wendy. Summer Love. 1999. (Love Stories Super Edition Ser.). 224p. (gr. 7-12). mass mkt. 4.50 o.s.i (0-553-49276-4, Dell Books for Young Readers) Random Hse. Children's Bks.

Marsh, Carole. Pocahontas. 2002. (One Thousand Readers Ser.). (Illus.). 12p. (J). (gr. 2-6). pap. 2.95 (0-635-01506-4, 15064) Gallopade International.

—Pocahontas. 1995. (Classics Ser.). (Illus.). (ps-4). 96p. (J). 7.98 o.p. (1-57082-114-3); 40p. (YA). 5.98 o.p. (1-57082-115-1) Mouse Works.

—Pocahontas. (Biographical Stories Ser.). (J). (gr. 1-5). pap. 5.72 o.p. (0-8114-8304-5); audio 8.49 o.p. (0-8114-8339-8) Raintree Pubs.

—Pocahontas. (Read-Along Ser.). (J). 7.99 incl. audio (1-55723-739-5); audio 11.99 (1-55723-741-7); audio compact disk 19.99 (1-55723-743-3); 1995. 11.99 incl. audio (1-55723-745-X); 1995. audio 11.99 (1-55723-740-9); 1995. audio compact disk 19.99 (1-55723-742-5) Walt Disney Records.

—The Virginia Experience! A Virginia Mystery Musical! 2000. (Virginia Experience! Ser.). (Illus.). pap. 20.00 (0-7933-9496-1) Gallopade International.

McDonald, Megan. Judy Moody Saves the World. (Illus.). 160p. (J). 2004. pap. 5.99 (0-7636-2087-4); 2002. (gr. 1-5). 15.99 (0-7636-1446-7) Candlewick Pr.

—Shadows in the Glasshouse. 2000. (American Girl Collection: Bk. 10). (Illus.). 160p. (J). (gr. 4-6). 9.95 (1-58485-093-0); pap. 5.95 (1-58485-092-2) Pleasant Co. Pubns. (American Girl).

—Shadows in the Glasshouse. 2000. (American Girl Collection). (Illus.). (J). 12.00 (0-606-20906-9) Turtleback Bks.

McKissack, Patricia C. & McKissack, Fredrick L. Christmas in the Big House, Christmas in the Quarters. (Illus.). 80p. (J). 2002. pap. 6.99 (0-590-43028-9); 1994. (gr. 3-8). pap. 17.95 (0-590-43027-0) Scholastic, Inc.

Nixon, Joan Lowery. John's Story 1775: Colonial Williamsburg. 2001. (Young Americans Ser.). (Illus.). 176p. (gr. 3-7). text 9.95 (0-385-32688-2, Dell Books for Young Readers) Random Hse. Children's Bks.

—Maria's Story, 1773. 2001. (Young Americans). (Illus.). 176p. (gr. 2-6). text 9.95 (0-385-32685-8, Delacorte Bks. for Young Readers) Random Hse. Children's Bks.

—Nancy's Story 1765. 2000. (Young Americans). (Illus.). 160p. (gr. 2-6). text 9.95 o.s.i (0-385-32679-3, Delacorte Bks. for Young Readers) Random Hse. Children's Bks.

Olasky, Susan. Annie Henry: Adventures in the American Revolution. 2003. (Illus.). 528p. (J). pap. 16.99 (1-58134-521-6) Crossway Bks.

—Annie Henry & the Mysterious Stranger. 1996. (Adventures of the American Revolution Ser.: Vol. 3). 144p. (J). (gr. 3-7). pap. 5.99 (0-89107-907-6) Crossway Bks.

—Annie Henry & the Secret Mission. 1995. (Adventures of the American Revolution Ser.: Vol. 1). 128p. (J). (gr. 3-7). pap. 5.99 (0-89107-830-4) Crossway Bks.

Pinkney, Andrea Davis. Silent Thunder: A Civil War Story. 2001. 224p. (J). (gr. 3-7). pap. 5.99 (0-7868-1569-8, Jump at the Sun); 1999. (Illus.). 208p. (J). (gr. 4-7). 15.99 (0-7868-0439-4); 1999. (Illus.). 208p. (YA). (gr. 4-7). lib. bdg. 16.49 (0-7868-2388-7) Hyperion Bks. for Children.

Pistole, Katy. Flying High. 2003. (Illus.). 126p. (J). 7.99 (0-8163-1942-1) Pacific Pr. Pubns.

—The Palomino. 2002. (Sonrise Farm Ser.). (Illus.). 128p. (J). 7.99 (0-8163-1863-8) Pacific Pr. Publishing Assn.

—Stolen Gold, Vol. 2. 2002. (Illus.). 127p. (J). pap. 7.99 (0-8163-1882-4) Pacific Pr. Publishing Assn.

Ransom, Candice F. Liberty Street. 2003. (J). lib. bdg. 17.85 (0-8027-8871-8); (Illus.). 16.95 (0-8027-8869-6) Walker & Co.

—The Promise Quilt. 2002. (Illus.). 32p. (J). (gr. k-3). pap. 6.95 (0-8027-7648-5) Walker & Co.

—When the Whippoorwill Calls. 1995. (Illus.). 32p. (J). (gr. 2-5). 16.00 (0-688-12729-0); lib. bdg. 15.93 o.p. (0-688-12730-4) Morrow/Avon. (Morrow, William & Co.).

Ray, Delia. Ghost Girl: A Blue Ridge Mountain Story. 2003. (Illus.). 224p. (YA). (gr. 5-9). tchr. ed. 15.00 (0-618-33377-0, Clarion Bks.) Houghton Mifflin Co. Trade & Reference Div.

Reeder, Carolyn. Across the Lines. 1998. 224p. (J). (gr. 4-7). pap. 5.99 (0-380-73073-1, Harper Trophy) HarperCollins Children's Bk. Group.

—Across the Lines. 1997. 224p. (J). (gr. 3-7). 17.00 (0-689-81133-0, Atheneum) Simon & Schuster Children's Publishing.

—Across the Lines. 1998. 11.00 (0-606-15426-4) Turtleback Bks.

—Grandpa's Mountain. 1993. 176p. (J). (gr. 4-7). reprint ed. pap. 4.95 (0-380-71914-2, Avon Bks.) Morrow/Avon.

—Grandpa's Mountain. 176p. (J). 2002. (Illus.). pap. 4.99 (0-689-84867-6, Aladdin); 1991. (gr. 3-7). text 14.95 o.p. (0-02-775811-7, Simon & Schuster Children's Publishing) Simon & Schuster Children's Publishing.

—Grandpa's Mountain. 1991. (J). 11.04 (0-606-05321-2) Turtleback Bks.

—Moonshiner's Son. 2003. (Illus.). 208p. (J). pap. 4.99 (0-689-85550-8, Aladdin) Simon & Schuster Children's Publishing.

—Shades of Gray. 1991. 160p. (YA). (gr. 4-9). pap. 4.99 o.p. (0-380-71232-6, Avon Bks.) Morrow/Avon.

—Shades of Gray. 3rd ed. 1994. pap. text 3.50 (0-13-800046-8) Prentice Hall (Schl. Div.).

—Shades of Gray. 1999. 160p. (J). (gr. 3-7). pap. 4.99 (0-689-82696-6, 076714004993, Aladdin); 1989. 176p. (YA). (gr. 7 up). lib. bdg. 16.00 (0-02-775810-9, Simon & Schuster Children's Publishing) Simon & Schuster Children's Publishing.

—Shades of Gray. 1991. 9.60 o.p. (0-606-04873-1) Turtleback Bks.

Rinaldi, Ann. Or Give Me Death: A Novel of Patrick Henry's Family. 2003. (Great Episodes Ser.). 240p. (J). 17.00 (0-15-216687-4) Harcourt Children's Bks.

Roddy, Lee. Risking the Dream. 2000. (Between Two Flags Ser.: Vol. 6). (Illus.). 176p. (J). (gr. 6-9). pap. 5.99 o.p. (0-7642-2030-6) Bethany Hse. Pubs.

—Road to Freedom. 1999. (Between Two Flags Ser.: Vol. 4). 160p. (J). (gr. 6-9). pap. 5.99 o.p. (0-7642-2028-4) Bethany Hse. Pubs.

Roop, Peter & Roop, Connie. An Eye for an Eye: A Story of the American Revolution. 2001. (Jamestown Classics Ser.). (Illus.). 168p. (YA). (gr. 5-8). 12.64 (0-8092-0587-4) Jamestown.

Rosenberg, Liz. Heart & Soul. 1996. 224p. (YA). (gr. 7 up). pap. 5.00 o.s.i (0-15-201270-2, Harcourt Paperbacks) Harcourt Children's Bks.

—Heart & Soul. 1996. 224p. (YA). (gr. 7 up). 11.00 (0-15-200942-6) Harcourt Trade Pubs.

Sappey, Maureen S. A Rose at Bull Run: Romance & Realities at First Bull Run. 1999. (Young American Ser.: Vol. 1). (Illus.). 100p. (YA). (gr. 4-7). 5.99 (1-57249-133-7) White Mane Publishing Co., Inc.

—Yankee Spy. 1999. (Young American Ser.: Vol. 3). (Illus.). 140p. (J). (gr. 4-7). 5.99 (1-57249-135-3) White Mane Publishing Co., Inc.

Scheer, Julian. A Thanksgiving Turkey. 2001. (Illus.). 32p. (J). (ps-2). tchr. ed. 16.95 (0-8234-1674-7) Holiday Hse., Inc.

Schurfranz, Vivian. A Message for General Washington. 1998. (Stories of the States Ser.: Vol. 10). 92p. (J). (gr. 4-7). lib. bdg. 14.95 (1-881889-89-0) Silver Moon Pr.

Seabrooke, Brenda. The Haunting of Holroyd Hill. 144p. 1997. (YA). (gr. 5-9). pap. 4.99 o.s.i (0-14-038540-1); 1995. (J). (ps-3). 14.99 o.p. (0-525-65167-5, Dutton Children's Bks.) Penguin Putnam Bks. for Young Readers.

—The Haunting of Holroyd Hill. 1997. (J). 11.04 (0-606-10987-0) Turtleback Bks.

Sharpe, Susan. Waterman's Boy. 1990. 96p. (J). (gr. 3-7). pap. 16.00 (0-02-782351-2, Simon & Schuster Children's Publishing) Simon & Schuster Children's Publishing.

Stolz, Mary. A Ballad of the Civil War. 1997. (Illus.). (J). 64p. (gr. 3-5). 14.95 (0-06-027362-3); 80p. (gr. 2-6). lib. bdg. 13.89 (0-06-027363-1) HarperCollins Children's Bk. Group.

Strigenz, Geri K., illus. Two Chimneys. 1992. (History's Children Ser.). 48p. (J). (gr. 4-5). pap. o.p. (0-8114-6431-8); lib. bdg. 21.36 o.p. (0-8114-3506-7) Raintree Pubs.

Susi, Geraldine Lee. Looking Back: A Boy's Civil War Memories. 2001. (Illus.). 128p. (J). (gr. 3-7). pap. 11.95 (1-880664-34-8) E. M. Productions.

—Looking for Pa: A Civil War Journey from Catlett to Manassas, 1861. 1995. (Illus.). 128p. (J). (gr. 5-7). pap. 9.95 (0-939009-87-0, EPM Pubns.) Howell Pr.

—My Father, My Companion: Life at the Hollow, Chief Justice John Marshall's Boyhood Home in Virginia. 2001. (Illus.). 96p. (J). (gr. 4-9). pap. 10.95 (1-889324-22-1) EPM Pubns., Inc.

Szymanski, Lois. Sea Feather. 1999. (Illus.). 80p. (J). (gr. 3-7). pap. 3.99 (0-380-80566-9, Avon Bks.) Morrow/Avon.

Tripp, Valerie. Felicity Discovers a Secret. 2002. (American Girls Short Stories Ser.). (Illus.). 56p. (J). 4.95 (1-58485-477-4, American Girl) Pleasant Co. Pubns.

—Felicity's Story Collection. 2001. (American Girls Collection). (Illus.). 390p. (J). (gr. 2 up). 29.95 (1-58485-441-3, American Girl) Pleasant Co. Pubns.

Turner, Barbara F. Charles T. Bear & the Big Flood. 1994. (Illus.). iv, 29p. (J). (gr. k-3). pap. 6.00 (1-892614-06-5, SC-CBF-5, Sassy Cat Bks.) Briarwood Pubns.

—Ghost Fire. 1998. (J). pap. 6.00 (1-892614-08-1) Briarwood Pubns.

Turner, Louise. Yesterday to Color at Gunston Hall. 1990. (Illus.). 15p. (Orig.). (J). pap. 3.95 (1-884085-05-9) Board of Regents, Gunston Hall.

Warmuth, Donna Akers & Gobble, DeAnna Akers, illus. Plumb Full of History: A Story of Abingdon, Virginia. 2003. 64p. (J). 9.95 (1-932158-78-2) High Country Pubs., Ltd.

Waters, Kate. Mary Geddy's Day: A Colonial Girl in Williamsburg. 1999. (Illus.). 40p. (J). (gr. 1-4). pap. 16.95 (0-590-92925-9) Scholastic, Inc.

White, Ruth. Belle Prater's Boy, RS. 1996. 208p. (J). (gr. 5-9). 17.00 (0-374-30668-0, Farrar, Straus & Giroux (BYR)) Farrar, Straus & Giroux.

—Belle Prater's Boy. unabr. ed. 2000. 196p. (J). (gr. 4-6). pap. 37.00 incl. audio (0-8072-8682-6, YA234SP, Listening Library) Random Hse. Audio Publishing Group.

—Belle Prater's Boy. 1997. (YA). pap., tchr. ed. o.s.i (0-440-41497-0, Dell Books for Young Readers); 1998. 224p. (gr. 5-9). reprint ed. pap. text 5.50 (0-440-41372-9, Yearling) Random Hse. Children's Bks.

—Belle Prater's Boy. l.t. ed. 2000. (Illus.). 221p. (YA). (gr. 4-7). 21.95 (0-7862-2885-7) Thorndike Pr.

—Belle Prater's Boy. 1998. (YA). 11.04 (0-606-12610-4) Turtleback Bks.

—Memories of Summer, RS. 2000. 144p. (J). (gr. 7-10). 16.00 (0-374-34945-2, Farrar, Straus & Giroux (BYR)) Farrar, Straus & Giroux.

—Memories of Summer. 2002. 160p. (YA). (gr. 7 up). mass mkt. 5.99 (0-440-22921-9, Dell Books for Young Readers) Random Hse. Children's Bks.

—Memories of Summer. l.t. ed. 2001. (Illus.). 144p. (J). (gr. 5-9). 21.95 (0-7862-3084-3) Thorndike Pr.

Wister, Owen. Virginian. 1998. (Classics Library). pap. 3.95 (1-85326-560-8, 5608WW) Wordsworth Editions, Ltd. GBR. *Dist:* Combined Publishing.

Yolen, Jane. Miz Berlin Walks. 1997. (Illus.). 32p. (J). (ps-3). 15.99 o.p. (0-399-22938-8, Philomel) Penguin Putnam Bks. for Young Readers.

VIRGINIA CITY (NEV.)—FICTION

Lasky, Kathryn. Alice Rose & Sam. 1999. 208p. (J). (gr. 3-7). pap. 5.99 (0-7868-1222-2) Disney Pr.

—Alice Rose & Sam. 1998. (Illus.). 208p. (J). (gr. 3-7). 15.95 (0-7868-0336-3); lib. bdg. 16.49 (0-7868-2277-5) Hyperion Bks. for Children.

—Alice Rose & Sam. 1999. 12.04 (0-606-17380-3) Turtleback Bks.

W

WALES—FICTION

Alexander, Lloyd. The Foundling: And Other Tales of Prydain, ERS. 1999. (Illus.). 96p. (J). (gr. 3-7). 19.95 (0-8050-6130-4, Holt, Henry & Co. Bks. For Young Readers) Holt, Henry & Co.

Bawden, Nina. Carrie's War. l.t. ed. 1985. (J). 16.95 o.p. (0-7451-0129-1, Galaxy Children's Large Print) BBC Audiobooks America.

—Carrie's War. 1989. 160p. (J). reprint ed. pap. 4.95 o.s.i (0-440-40142-9) Dell Publishing.

—Carrie's War. l.t. ed. 1976. (J). lib. bdg. 9.95 o.p. (0-8161-6355-3, Macmillan Reference USA) Gale Group.

—Carrie's War. 1973. 160p. (J). (gr. 4-7). lib. bdg. 14.89 (0-397-31450-7) HarperCollins Children's Bk. Group.

—Carrie's War. 1975. (Illus.). 144p. (J). (gr. 4-6). pap. 1.95 o.p. (0-14-030689-7, Penguin Bks.) Viking Penguin.

Bond, Nancy. A String in the Harp. 1976. (String in the Harp Ser.). 384p. (J). (gr. 4-7). 19.00 (0-689-50036-X, McElderry, Margaret K.) Simon & Schuster Children's Publishing.

Cameron, Eleanor. Time & Mr. Bass. 1967. (Illus.). (J). (gr. 4-6). 14.95 o.s.i (0-316-12536-9, Joy Street Bks.) Little Brown & Co.

Cooper, Susan. The Grey King. l.t. ed. 2002. (Dark Is Rising Sequence Ser.). 262p. (J). 21.95 (0-7862-2919-5) Gale Group.

—The Grey King. 2002. 224p. (J). E-Book 6.99 (0-689-84783-1, McElderry, Margaret K.); 1999. (Dark Is Rising Sequence Ser.). (Illus.). 176p. (J). (gr. 4-7). pap. 4.99 (0-689-82984-1, Aladdin); 1978. (Dark Is Rising Sequence Ser.). (Illus.). (YA). (gr. 7 up). pap. 3.95 o.s.i (0-689-70448-8, Simon & Schuster Children's Publishing); 1975. (Grey King Ser.: Vol. 1). (Illus.). 224p. (J). 18.95 (0-689-50029-7, McElderry, Margaret K.); 1986. (Dark Is Rising Sequence Ser.). 224p. (YA). (gr. 4-7). reprint ed. mass mkt. 4.99 (0-689-71089-5, Simon Pulse); Vol. 1. 1999. (Dark Is Rising Sequence Ser.). 165p. (gr. 5-9). pap. 2.99 (0-689-82988-4, Aladdin) Simon & Schuster Children's Publishing.

—The Grey King. (Dark Is Rising Sequence Ser.). 1986. (J). 11.04 (0-606-01150-1); 1975. 11.04 (0-606-17326-9) Turtleback Bks.

—Silver on the Tree. l.t. ed. 2002. (Dark Is Rising Sequence Ser.). (Illus.). 430p. (J). 23.95 (0-7862-2921-7) Gale Group.

—Silver on the Tree. unabr. ed. 2002. (YA). (gr. 3 up). audio 30.00 (0-8072-6209-9, Listening Library) Random Hse. Audio Publishing Group.

—Silver on the Tree. 2000. (Dark Is Rising Sequence Ser.). 288p. (J). (gr. 4-7). pap. 4.99 (0-689-84033-0, Aladdin); 1986. (J). pap. 2.95 o.s.i (0-689-71090-9, Simon & Schuster Children's Publishing); 1977. (Silver on the Tree Ser.: Vol. 1). 256p. (J). (gr. 4-7). 18.00 (0-689-50088-2, McElderry, Margaret K.); 1987. (Dark Is Rising Sequence Ser.). 256p. (YA). (gr. 4-7). reprint ed. pap. 4.99 (0-689-71152-2, Simon Pulse) Simon & Schuster Children's Publishing.

—Silver on the Tree. 1986. (Dark Is Rising Sequence Ser.). (J). 10.00 (0-606-02257-0) Turtleback Bks.

Cronin, A. J. The Citadel. 1983. (J). 16.95 (0-316-16158-6); 368p. pap. 19.99 (0-316-16183-7) Little Brown & Co.

Evans, Christine, ed. Old Enough & Other Stories. 1997. (YA). (gr. 6-12). pap. 13.95 (0-8464-4601-4) Beekman Pubs., Inc.

Evans, Dilys. Looking for Merlyn. 1997. (Illus.). (J). 14.95 (0-590-60191-1) Scholastic, Inc.

Fry, Rosalie K. Whistler in the Mist, RS. 1968. (Illus.). 144p. (J). (gr. 4 up). 3.75 o.p. (0-374-38382-0, Farrar, Straus & Giroux (BYR)) Farrar, Straus & Giroux.

Garner, Alan. The Owl Service. 1981. 192p. mass mkt. 1.95 o.s.i (0-345-29044-5, Del Rey) Ballantine Bks.

—The Owl Service. 1999. 240p. (YA). (gr. 7 up). pap. 6.00 (0-15-201798-4, Magic Carpet Bks.) Harcourt Children's Bks.

—The Owl Service. 1979. 156p. 7.95 (0-529-05520-1) Penguin Putnam Bks. for Young Readers.

—The Owl Service. 1981. (J). 9.95 o.p. (0-399-20805-4) Putnam Publishing Group, The.

—The Owl Service. 1992. 160p. (YA). (gr. 5 up). pap. 3.50 o.s.i (0-440-40735-4, Yearling) Random Hse. Children's Bks.

Henty, G. A. Both Sides of the Border: A Tale of Hotspur & Glendower. 2000. 252p. (J). pap. 9.95 (0-594-01504-9); E-Book 3.95 (0-594-02365-3) 1873 Pr.

Johnson, Catherine. The Last Welsh Summer. 2nd ed. 1997. 114p. (J). (gr. 4). reprint ed. pap. 11.95 (0-8464-4813-0) Beekman Pubs., Inc.

Jones, Brenda W. Giant Tales from Wales. Saer, Ann, tr. from WEL. 1998. (Illus.). (J). (gr. 1-5). pap. 13.95 (0-8464-4930-7) Beekman Pubs., Inc.

Kimmel, Elizabeth Cody. In the Stone Circle. 1998. 225p. (J). (gr. 5-9). pap. 15.95 (0-590-21308-3) Scholastic, Inc.

Kimmel, Margaret M. Magic in the Mist. 1975. (Illus.). 32p. (J). (gr. k-4). 15.00 (0-689-50026-2, McElderry, Margaret K.) Simon & Schuster Children's Publishing.

Lawrence, Louise. The Patchwork People. 1994. 240p. (YA). (gr. 7 up). 14.95 (0-395-67892-7, Clarion Bks.) Houghton Mifflin Co. Trade & Reference Div.

Meyrick, Bette. Invasion. 1991. (J). (gr. 4). pap. 7.95 (0-8464-4879-3, Gomer Pr.) Beekman Pubs., Inc.

Mitchley, Richard, reader. The Grey King. unabr. ed. 2001. 165p. (YA). (gr. 5 up). pap. 37.00 incl. audio (0-8072-8878-0, Listening Library) Random Hse. Audio Publishing Group.

Morpurgo, Michael. The Sandman & the Turtles. 1994. 80p. (J). (gr. 3-7). 14.95 o.p. (0-399-22672-9, Philomel) Penguin Putnam Bks. for Young Readers.

Nimmo, Jenny. Branwen. 1998. (Legends from Wales Ser.: Vol. 2). (Illus.). (J). (gr. 2-5). pap. 11.95 (0-8464-4602-2) Beekman Pubs., Inc.

—Griffin's Castle. 1997. 208p. (J). (gr. 5-9). pap. 16.95 (0-531-30006-4); lib. bdg. 17.99 (0-531-33006-0) Scholastic, Inc. (Orchard Bks.).

—Orchard of the Crescent Moon. 1989. 176p. (J). (gr. 5 up). 13.95 o.p. (0-525-44438-6, Dutton Children's Bks.) Penguin Putnam Bks. for Young Readers.

O'Connor, Jane. Dragon Breath. 1997. (Eek! Stories to Make You Shriek Ser.). (Illus.). 48p. (J). (gr. 1-3). 13.99 o.s.i (0-448-41608-5); 3.99 (0-448-41558-5) Penguin Putnam Bks. for Young Readers. (Grosset & Dunlap).

Pullman, Philip. The Broken Bridge. (gr. 7 up). 1994. (Illus.). 224p. mass mkt. 5.50 (0-679-84715-4, Random Hse. Bks. for Young Readers); 1992. 256p. (YA). 15.99 o.s.i (0-679-91972-4, Knopf Bks. for Young Readers) Random Hse. Children's Bks.

—The Broken Bridge. 2002. (YA). 20.25 (0-8446-7229-7) Smith, Peter Pub., Inc.

—The Broken Bridge. 1994. 11.04 (0-606-06945-3) Turtleback Bks.

Sullivan, Jenny. The Back End of Nowhere. 1997. (J). pap. 23.00 (1-85902-497-1) Gomer Pr. GBR. *Dist:* State Mutual Bk. & Periodical Service, Ltd.

Thomas, Dylan. A Conversation about Christmas. 1991. (Illus.). 32p. (YA). (gr. 5 up). lib. bdg. 13.95 o.p. (0-88682-468-0, Creative Education) Creative Co., The.

Trefor, Eirlys. The Old Man of Gilfach. 2nd ed. 1997. 108p. (J). (gr. 4). reprint ed. pap. 11.95 (0-8464-4845-9) Beekman Pubs., Inc.

Zaring, Jane. The Return of the Dragon, 001. 1981. (Illus.). (J). (gr. 5-8). 7.95 o.p. (0-395-30350-8) Houghton Mifflin Co.

WALL STREET (NEW YORK, N.Y.)—FICTION

Brande, Michael. Shelby Goes to Wall Street. 1983. (Career Guidance Ser.). (Illus.). (J). (gr. 3-6). lib. bdg. 2.00 o.p. (0-513-00407-6) Denison, T. S. & Co., Inc.

WARSAW (POLAND)—FICTION

Laird, Christa. Shadow of the Wall. 1990. 144p. (YA). (gr. 7 up). 12.95 o.p. (0-688-09336-1, Greenwillow Bks.) HarperCollins Children's Bk. Group.

—Shadow of the Wall. 1997. 144p. (gr. 6-12). mass mkt. 4.95 (0-688-15291-0, Morrow, William & Co.) Morrow/Avon.

—Shadow of the Wall. 1997. 11.00 (0-606-11832-2) Turtleback Bks.

Nerlove, Miriam. Flowers on the Wall. 1996. (Illus.). 32p. (J). (gr. k-3). 16.00 (0-689-50614-7, McElderry, Margaret K.) Simon & Schuster Children's Publishing.

Orlev, Uri. The Island on Bird Street. Halkin, Hillel, tr. from HEB. 176p. (J). (gr. 4-6). 1992. pap. 6.95 (0-395-61623-9); 1984. tchr. ed. 16.00 (0-395-33887-5, 5-92515) Houghton Mifflin Co.

—The Island on Bird Street. Halkin, Hillel, tr. from HEB. 1984. (J). 12.00 (0-606-00521-8) Turtleback Bks.

—The Man from the Other Side. Halkin, Hillel, tr. from HEB. 1991. 192p. (YA). (gr. 7-7). tchr. ed. 16.00 (0-395-53808-4) Houghton Mifflin Co.

—The Man from the Other Side. Halkin, Hillel, tr. from HEB. 1995. (Illus.). 192p. (J). (gr. 5-9). pap. 5.99 (0-14-037088-9, Puffin Bks.) Penguin Putnam Bks. for Young Readers.

—The Man from the Other Side. Halkin, Hillel, tr. from HEB. 1995. 11.04 (0-606-07834-7) Turtleback Bks.

Singer, Isaac Bashevis. A Day of Pleasure: Stories of a Boy Growing up in Warsaw. 1994. (J). 17.75 o.p. (0-8446-6778-1) Smith, Peter Pub., Inc.

Spinelli, Jerry. Milkweed. 2003. (Illus.). 224p. (J). (gr. 5). lib. bdg. 17.99 (0-375-91374-2) Random Hse. Children's Bks.

Treseder, Terry W. Hear O Israel: A Story of the Warsaw Ghetto. 1990. (Illus.). 48p. (J). (gr. 3 up). text 13.95 o.s.i (0-689-31456-6, Atheneum) Simon & Schuster Children's Publishing.

WASHINGTON (D.C.)—FICTION

Barnes, Peter W. Woodrow, the White House Mouse. 2nd rev. ed. 1998. (Illus.). 32p. (J). (gr. 1-3). 15.95 (0-9637688-9-1) Vacation Spot Publishing.

Barnes, Peter W. & Barnes, Cheryl Shaw. Woodrow, the White House Mouse. 2000. 32p. (J). (gr. k-3). pap. 5.99 (0-439-12952-4) Scholastic, Inc.

—Woodrow, the White House Mouse. 1995. (Illus.). 32p. (J). (gr. k-6). 15.95 o.p. (0-9637688-2-4) Vacation Spot Publishing.

Blair, Margaret W. House of Spies: Danger in the Civil War. 1999. (White Mane Kids Ser.: Vol. 7). (Illus.). 169p. (YA). (ps up). pap. 8.95 (1-57249-161-2, WM Kids) White Mane Publishing Co., Inc.

Cabot, Meg. All-American Girl. (J). (gr. 7 up). 2003. (Illus.). 416p. pap. 6.99 (0-06-447277-9); 2002. 256p. 15.99 (0-06-029469-8); 2002. (Illus.). 256p. lib. bdg. 17.89 (0-06-029470-1) HarperCollins Children's Bk. Group.

—All-American Girl. unabr. ed. 2002. (J). (gr. 4-7). audio 28.00 (0-8072-0901-5, Listening Library) Random Hse. Audio Publishing Group.

Chavez, Michael A., Jr. The Adventures of Tom Turkey: Thanksgiving in the White House. 2001. 8.00 (0-8059-5079-6) Dorrance Publishing Co., Inc.

Delton, Judy. Next Stop, the White House! 1995. (Lottery Luck Ser.: No. 6). (Illus.). 96p. (J). (gr. 2-5). pap. 3.95 (0-7868-1023-8) Hyperion Paperbacks for Children.

Emmer, E. R. Me, Minerva & the Flying Car. 2000. (Going to Ser.). (Illus.). 96p. (J). pap. 5.99 (1-893577-03-1) Four Corners Publishing Co., Inc.

Giff, Patricia Reilly. Look Out Washington, D. C.! 1996. (J). pap. 4.99 (0-440-91166-4); pap. 4.99 (0-440-91142-7); pap. 4.99 (0-440-91121-4) Random Hse. Children's Bks. (Dell Books for Young Readers).

Harness, Cheryl. Ghosts of the White House. 2002. (Illus.). 48p. (J). (gr. 2-5). pap. 6.99 (0-689-84892-7, Aladdin) Simon & Schuster Children's Publishing.

Hope, Laura Lee. The Bobbsey Twins' Adventure in Washington. rev. ed. 1963. (Bobbsey Twins Ser.). (J). (gr. 3-5). 5.90 o.p. (0-448-40118-5, Grosset & Dunlap) Penguin Putnam Bks. for Young Readers.

Jolin, Dominique. Merry Christmas, Washington! Perkes, Carolyn, tr. from FRE. 2000. (Illus.). 16p. (ps-k). bds. (1-894363-63-9) Dominique & Friends.

—Washington Loves Washington. Perkes, Carolyn, tr. from FRE. 2000. (Illus.). 16p. (ps). bds. (1-894363-62-0) Dominique & Friends.

Lasky, Kathryn. A Time for Courage: The Suffragette Diary of Kathleen Bowen, Washington D. C., 1917. 2002. (Dear America Ser.). (Illus.). 176p. (J). (gr. 4-9). pap. 10.95 (0-590-51141-6, Scholastic Pr.) Scholastic, Inc.

Lindbergh, Anne M. The People in Pineapple Place. 2003. 192p. (J). bds. 5.99 (0-7636-1739-3) Candlewick Pr.

McMullan, Kate. Fluffy Goes to Washington. 2002. (Hello Reader! Level 3 Ser.). (Illus.). (J). 3.99 (0-439-31943-9) Scholastic, Inc.

Mills, Charles. Stranger in the Shadows. 1998. (Shadow Creek Ranch Ser.: Vol. 11). 151p. (Orig.). (J). (gr. 4-7). pap. 5.99 (0-8280-1316-0) Review & Herald Publishing Assn.

Morris, Judy K. Crazies & Sam. 1985. (J). (gr. 4-6). pap. 3.95 o.p. (0-14-031833-X, Puffin Bks.) Penguin Putnam Bks. for Young Readers.

Oestreicher, James. Monumental Discovery. 1992. (Choice Adventures Ser.: Vol. 6). 160p. (J). pap. 4.99 o.p. (0-8423-5030-6) Tyndale Hse. Pubs.

Osborne, Mary Pope. After the Rain: Virginia's Civil War Diary, Bk. 2. 2002. (My America Ser.). 112p. (J). (gr. 2-5). pap. 8.95 o.s.i (0-439-20138-1); (Illus.). mass mkt. 4.99 (0-439-36904-5) Scholastic, Inc. (Scholastic Pr.).

Quattlebaum, Mary. Underground Train. 1999. (Illus.). 32p. (gr. k-3). pap. text 5.99 o.s.i (0-440-41325-7, Dell Books for Young Readers) Random Hse. Children's Bks.

Random, Candice F. Jimmy Crack Corn. 1994. (Illus.). (J). (gr. 2-5). lib. bdg. 19.95 (0-87614-786-4, Carolrhoda Bks.) Lerner Publishing Group.

Rinaldi, Ann. Girl in Blue. 2001. (Illus.). 272p. (J). (gr. 4-9). pap. 15.95 (0-439-07336-7) Scholastic, Inc.

Robinet, Harriette Gillem. Washington City Is Burning. 1996. 160p. (J). (gr. 3-7). 16.95 (0-689-80773-2, Atheneum) Simon & Schuster Children's Publishing.

Roosevelt, Anna. Scamper: Bunny Who Went to the White House. 2000. (Illus.). 72p. (J). (gr. 3-6). pap. 11.95 (1-888683-20-1) Wooster Bk. Co., The.

Roy, Ron. The Skeleton in the Smithsonian. 2003. (Capital Mysteries Ser.: Vol. 3). (Illus.). 96p. (J). (gr. 2-5). pap. 3.99 (0-307-26517-X); lib. bdg. 11.99 (0-307-46517-9) Random Hse., Inc.

Sappey, Maureen S. A Rose at Bull Run: Romance & Realities at First Bull Run. 1999. (Young American Ser.: Vol. 1). (Illus.). 100p. (YA). (gr. 4-7). 5.99 (1-57249-133-7) White Mane Publishing Co., Inc.

Sargent, Dave & Sargent, Pat. Whiskers (Roan) Pride & Peace. 2002. (Saddle Up Ser.: Vol. 59). (Illus.). 42p. (J). lib. bdg. 22.60 (1-56763-805-8) Ozark Publishing.

Service, Pamela F. Stinker's Return. 1994. 96p. mass mkt. 3.99 o.s.i (0-449-70438-6, Fawcett) Ballantine Bks.

—Stinker's Return. 1993. 96p. (J). (gr. 4-6). 12.95 (0-684-19542-9, Atheneum) Simon & Schuster Children's Publishing.

Thomas, Jim. Learning the Ropes. 2001. (7th Heaven Ser.). 144p. (gr. 5-8). mass mkt. 4.99 (0-375-81160-5, Random Hse. Bks. for Young Readers) Random Hse. Children's Bks.

Van Stockum, Hilda. The Mitchells: Five for Victory. 1995. (Mitchells Ser.: Vol. 1). (Illus.). 250p. (J). (gr. 4-7). reprint ed. pap. 12.95 (1-883937-05-1, 05-1) Bethlehem Bks.

Warner, Gertrude Chandler, creator. The Mystery in Washington, D. C. 1994. (Boxcar Children Special Ser.: No. 2). 110p. (J). (gr. 2-5). lib. bdg. 13.95 (0-8075-5409-X); mass mkt. 3.95 (0-8075-5410-3) Whitman, Albert & Co.

Weiss, Ellen. Voting Rights Days. 2002. (Hitty's Travels Ser.: No. 3). (Illus.). 64p. (J). pap. 3.99 (0-689-84912-5, Aladdin) Simon & Schuster Children's Publishing.

Weitzman, Jacqueline Preiss. You Can't Take a Balloon into the National Gallery. 2002. (Illus.). 40p. (YA). pap. 7.99 (0-14-230131-0, Puffin Bks.) Penguin Putnam Bks. for Young Readers.

WASHINGTON (STATE)—FICTION

Beatty, Patricia. The Nickel-Plated Beauty. 1993. 272p. (YA). (gr. 5 up). 16.00 o.p. (0-688-12360-0, Morrow, William & Co.) Morrow/Avon.

—8 Mules From Monterey. 1993. 224p. (J). reprint ed. mass mkt. 4.95 o.p. (0-688-12281-7, Morrow, William & Co.) Morrow/Avon.

Biggar, Joan R. Missing on Castaway Island. 1997. (Megan Parnell Mysteries Ser.: Vol. 1). 160p. (J). (gr. 5-9). pap. text 5.99 (0-570-05015-4, 56-1842) Concordia Publishing Hse.

—Mystery at Camp Galena. 1997. (Megan Parnell Mysteries Ser.: Vol. 2). 160p. (J). (gr. 5-9). pap. text 5.99 (0-570-05016-2, 56-1843) Concordia Publishing Hse.

—Trouble in Yakima Valley. 1998. (Megan Parnell Mysteries Ser.: Vol. 3). 160p. (J). (gr. 5-9). 5.99 (0-570-05031-6, 56-1855) Concordia Publishing Hse.

Boutwell, Florence. Love According to Teresa. 2000. (Illus.). 190p. (J). (0-87062-298-6, Millwood Publishing) Clark, Arthur H. Co.

—Teresa of Northwood Prairie: An Historical Adventure Story for Young & Old. 1998. (Illus.). 175p. (J). 17.95 (0-87062-284-6) Clark, Arthur H. Co.

Caletti, Deb. The Queen of Everything. 2002. 384p. (YA). (gr. 9 up). pap. 6.99 (0-7434-3684-9, Simon Pulse) Simon & Schuster Children's Publishing.

Cecotti, Loralie. Seattle Center. 1983. (Color-A-Story Ser.). (Illus.). 24p. (Orig.). (J). (gr. 1-4). pap. 2.75 (0-933992-30-0) Coffee Break Pr.

Drake, Jane & Love, Ann. Forestry. (America at Work Ser.). (Illus.). (J). (gr. 2-5). 2002. 32p. text 12.95 (1-55074-462-3); 2000. 118p. pap. (1-55074-819-X); 1996. 340p. text (1-55074-227-2) Kids Can Pr., Ltd.

Duey, Kathleen. Josie Poe Palouse: Washington, 1943. 1999. (American Diaries Ser.: No. 13). (J). (gr. 3-7). 10.55 (0-606-16304-2) Turtleback Bks.

—Josie Poe Palouse: Washington 1943. 1999. (American Diaries Ser.: No. 13). (Illus.). 144p. (J). (gr. 3-7). pap. 4.99 (0-689-82930-2, 076714004504, Aladdin) Simon & Schuster Children's Publishing.

Dumond, Val. Visiting Olympia. 1983. (Color-A-Story Ser.). (Illus.). 24p. (Orig.). (J). (gr. 1-4). pap. 2.75 (0-933992-39-4) Coffee Break Pr.

Franklin, Kristine L. The Grape Thief. 2003. 304p. (J). 16.99 (0-7636-1325-8) Candlewick Pr.

Hamm, Diane J. Daughter of Suqua. 1997. 160p. (J). (gr. 5-7). lib. bdg. 14.95 o.p. (0-8075-1477-2) Whitman, Albert & Co.

Helstrom, David C. My Tacoma Dome. 1983. (Color-A-Story Ser.). (Illus.). 24p. (Orig.). (J). (gr. 1-4). pap. 2.75 (0-933992-29-7) Coffee Break Pr.

—Visiting Mt. Rainier. 1984. (Color-A-Story Ser.). (Illus.). 28p. (Orig.). (J). (gr. 1-4). pap. 2.75 (0-933992-37-8) Coffee Break Pr.

Henry, Chad. Dogbreath Victorious. 1999. 188p. (YA). (gr. 7-12). tchr. ed. 16.95 (0-8234-1458-2) Holiday Hse., Inc.

Holm, Jennifer L. Boston Jane: An Adventure. 2001. (Boston Jane Ser.). 288p. (J). (gr. 5 up). 16.95 (0-06-028738-1); (Illus.). lib. bdg. 17.89 (0-06-028739-X) HarperCollins Children's Bk. Group.

—Boston Jane: An Adventure. 2002. (Boston Jane Ser.). 288p. (J). (gr. 5 up). pap. 6.99 (0-06-440849-3) HarperCollins Pubs.

—Boston Jane: Wilderness Days. (Boston Jane Ser.). 256p. (J). 2004. pap. 5.99 (0-06-440881-7, Harper Trophy); 2002. (gr. 5 up). 16.99 (0-06-029043-9); 2002. (gr. 5 up). lib. bdg. 18.89 (0-06-029044-7) HarperCollins Children's Bk. Group.

—Our Only May Amelia. (Harper Trophy Bks.). (Illus.). 272p. (gr. 4 up). 2001. (J). pap. 5.99 (0-06-440856-6, Harper Trophy); 1999. (J). 16.99 (0-06-027822-6); 1999. (YA). lib. bdg. 15.89 (0-06-028354-8) HarperCollins Children's Bk. Group.

—Our Only May Amelia. unabr. ed. 2001. 253p. (J). (gr. 4-6). pap. 35.00 incl. audio (0-8072-8366-5, YA191SP); 2000. (YA). (gr. 5-9). audio 22.00 (0-8072-8234-0, LL0195) Random Hse. Audio Publishing Group. (Listening Library).

—Our Only May Amelia. l.t. ed. 2000. (Illus.). 261p. (J). (ps up). 21.95 (0-7862-2742-7) Thorndike Pr.

—Our Only May Amelia. 2001. (Illus.). (J). 12.00 (0-606-21371-6) Turtleback Bks.

Holsather, Kent. Henry of York: The Secret of Juan de Vega. 2003. 176p. (YA). (Illus.). (gr. 5 up). 22.95 (0-9729101-0-7); 2nd ed. per. 12.95 (0-9729101-1-5) Lonejack Mountain Pr.

Kehret, Peg. The Stranger Next Door. 2003. (Illus.). 176p. pap. 5.99 (0-14-250178-6, Puffin Bks.); 2002. 160p. (J). (gr. 4-8). 15.99 (0-525-46829-3, Dutton Children's Bks.) Penguin Putnam Bks. for Young Readers.

Luenn, Nancy, ed. A Horse's Tale: Ten Adventures in One Hundred Years. (Illus.). 96p. (J). 1989. (gr. 1-7). pap. 9.95 (0-943990-50-5); 1988. (gr. 4-7). lib. bdg. 16.95 (0-943990-51-3) Parenting Pr., Inc.

Nelson, Marg. Mystery on a Full Moon, RS. 1970. 176p. (J). (gr. 7 up). 3.50 o.p. (0-374-35280-1, Farrar, Straus & Giroux (BYR)) Farrar, Straus & Giroux.

Parkhurst, Carole. Visiting Tacoma. 1983. (Color-A-Story Ser.). (Illus.). 24p. (Orig.). (J). (gr. 1-4). pap. 2.75 (0-933992-38-6) Coffee Break Pr.

Pierson, Jan. The Carson Kids & the Mystery of Five Finger Island. 2000. (Carson Kids Ser.: Vol. 1). (Illus.). 128p. (gr. 4-7). pap. 9.95 (0-595-09075-3, Backinprint.com) iUniverse, Inc.

Platt, Randall. The Likes of Me. 2000. 256p. (YA). (gr. 9 up). 15.95 o.s.i (0-385-32692-0, Delacorte Pr.) Dell Publishing.

—The Likes of Me. 2001. 256p. (YA). (gr. 9 up). reprint ed. mass mkt. 5.50 o.s.i (0-440-22880-8, Laurel Leaf) Random Hse. Children's Bks.

Reece, Colleen L. Saturday Scare. 1998. (Juli Scott, Super Sleuth Ser.: Bk. 6). 176p. (J). pap. 2.97 o.p. (1-57748-217-4) Barbour Publishing, Inc.

—Saturday Scare. l.t. ed. 2002. (Juli Scott, Super Sleuth Ser.). (Illus.). 211p. (J). 24.95 (0-7862-3195-5) Gale Group.

—Thursday Trials. 1998. (Juli Scott, Super Sleuth Ser.: Bk. 4). 176p. (J). (gr. 4-10). pap. 2.97 (1-57748-180-1) Barbour Publishing, Inc.

—Thursday Trials. l.t. ed. 2001. (Juli Scott, Super Sleuth Ser.). (Illus.). 204p. (J). 23.95 (0-7862-3201-3) Thorndike Pr.

Sargent, Dave & Sargent, Pat. Whiskers (Roan) Pride & Peace. 2003. (Saddle Up Ser.: Vol. 59). (Illus.). 42p. (J). mass mkt. 6.95 (1-56763-806-6) Ozark Publishing.

Sharpe, Susan. Spirit Quest. 1993. 128p. (J). (gr. 4-7). pap. 4.99 o.s.i (0-14-036282-7, Puffin Bks.) Penguin Putnam Bks. for Young Readers.

—Spirit Quest. 1991. (Illus.). 128p. (J). (gr. 4-6). lib. bdg. 13.95 (0-02-782355-5, Simon & Schuster Children's Publishing) Simon & Schuster Children's Publishing.

—Spirit Quest. 1993. 11.04 (0-606-02904-4) Turtleback Bks.

Thesman, Jean. In the House of Queen's Beasts. 2001. 32p. (J). (gr. 6-9). 15.99 o.s.i (0-670-89285-8, Viking Children's Bks.) Penguin Putnam Bks. for Young Readers.

—Moonstones. 208p. (YA). (gr. 5-9). 2000. (Illus.). pap. 5.99 (0-14-130809-5, Puffin Bks.); 1998. 15.99 o.s.i (0-670-87959-2) Penguin Putnam Bks. for Young Readers.

Warren, Robert L. How Could You, Danny?! Samantha Challenges Hunting. 1997. (Illus.). (J). (0-9658526-0-1) Natural Highs.

WATERSHIP DOWN (IMAGINARY PLACE)—FICTION

Adams, Richard. Tales from Watership Down. unabr. ed. 1997. (YA). audio 51.00 (0-7887-1056-7, 95083E7) Recorded Bks., LLC.

—Watership Down. 2001. (Perennial Classics Ser.). (Illus.). 512p. pap. 13.00 (0-06-093545-6, Perennial) HarperTrade.

—Watership Down. 1993. (J). audio 68.20 (1-56544-017-X, 450002); audio Literate Ear, Inc.

—Watership Down. abr. ed. (Dramatized Classics Ser.). (J). 1985. (gr. 3-8). audio 19.95 o.p. (0-88142-559-1); Set. 1998. 253p. audio 19.95 (1-55935-231-0, 493215) Soundelux Audio Publishing.

WEST (U.S.)—FICTION

Adams, Jean Ekman. Clarence & the Great Surprise. 2001. (Illus.). 32p. (J). (gr. k-2). 15.95 (0-87358-795-2, Rising Moon Bks. for Young Readers) Northland Publishing.

Adler, David A. Wild Pill Hickok & Other Old West Riddles. 1988. (Illus.). 64p. (J). (gr. 4-7). tchr. ed. 14.95 o.p. (0-8234-0718-7) Holiday Hse., Inc.

Anderson, Leone C. Sean's War. 1998. (Illus.). 192p. (J). (gr. 3-9). 16.95 (0-9638819-4-9) ShadowPlay Pr.

Antle, Nancy. Sam's Wild West Christmas. (Dial Easy-to-Read Ser.). (Illus.). 40p. (J). (ps-3). 2000. 13.99 o.p. (0-8037-2199-4, Dial Bks. for Young Readers); 1999. pap. 3.50 o.s.i (0-14-130132-5, Puffin Bks.) Penguin Putnam Bks. for Young Readers.

—Sam's Wild West Show. 1995. (Easy-to-Read Ser.). (Illus.). 40p. (J). (ps-3). 12.99 o.s.i (0-8037-1532-3); 12.89 o.s.i (0-8037-1533-1) Penguin Putnam Bks. for Young Readers. (Dial Bks. for Young Readers).

Appelt, Kathi A. Cowboy Dreams: Sleep Tight, Little Buckaroo. 1999. (Illus.). 32p. (J). (gr. k-2). 14.95 o.s.i (*0-06-027763-7*, Harper Trophy); lib. bdg. 14.89 o.p. (*0-06-027764-5*) HarperCollins Children's Bk. Group.

Arntson, Herbert E. Caravan to Oregon. 1957. (Illus.). (J). (gr. 7-11). 8.95 o.p. (*0-8323-0164-7*) Binford & Mort Publishing.

Ball, Zachary. North to Abilene. 1960. (Illus.). 199p. (J). (gr. 7-9). 3.95 o.p. (*0-8234-0079-4*) Holiday Hse., Inc.

Ballinger, Elizabeth. Prairie Stories of the West. 1993. (Illus.). 124p. (Orig.). (J). (gr. k-8). reprint ed. pap. text 8.95 (*1-879331-39-X*, Classic Publishing) Marciel Publishing & Printing.

Benedict, Rex. The Ballad of Cactus Jack. 1975. 160p. (J). (gr. 4-7). lib. bdg. 5.99 o.p. (*0-394-93085-1*, Pantheon) Knopf Publishing Group.

—Last Stand at Goodbye Gulch. 1974. 144p. (J). (gr. 4-7). lib. bdg. 5.99 o.p. (*0-394-93016-9*, Pantheon) Knopf Publishing Group.

Bickham, Jack M. Katie, Kelly & Keck. 1973. (Western Ser.). 184p. (J). o.p. (*0-385-07501-4*) Doubleday Publishing.

—Showdown at Emerald Canyon. 1975. 183p. (J). o.p. (*0-385-01890-8*) Doubleday Publishing.

Bierhorst, John, ed. The Ring in the Prairie. 1976. (Pied Piper Bks.). (Illus.). (J). (gr. k-3). reprint ed. pap. 1.75 o.p. (*0-8037-7455-9*, Dial Bks. for Young Readers) Penguin Putnam Bks. for Young Readers.

Bird, E. J. The Blizzard of 1896. 1990. (Tall Tales Ser.). (Illus.). 72p. (J). (gr. 2-6). lib. bdg. 14.95 o.p. (*0-87614-651-5*, Carolrhoda Bks.) Lerner Publishing Group.

—Chuck Wagon Stew. (Good Time Library). 1989. (Illus.). 72p. (J). (gr. 4-7). pap. 5.95 o.s.i (*0-87614-498-9*, Carolrhoda Bks.); 1988. lib. bdg. 8.95 o.p. (*0-87614-313-3*) Lerner Publishing Group.

Blackstock, Charity. Ghost Town. 1976. 224p. 7.95 o.p. (*0-698-10735-7*) Putnam Publishing Group, The.

Blakeslee, Ann R. A Different Kind of Hero. 1997. (Accelerated Reader Bks.). (Illus.). 144p. (J). (gr. 5-9). 14.95 (*0-7614-5000-9*, Cavendish Children's Bks.) Cavendish, Marshall Corp.

Bly, Stephen A. The Adventures of Nathan T. Riggins, 31 vols., Vol. 1. 2001. 384p. (J). (gr. 4-9). reprint ed. pap. 10.99 (*1-58134-235-7*) Crossway Bks.

—The Adventures of Nathan T. Riggins Bks. 4-6, 31 vols., Vol. 2. 2001. 384p. (J). (gr. 4-9). reprint ed. pap. 10.99 (*1-58134-234-9*) Crossway Bks.

—The Buffalo's Last Stand. 2002. (Retta Barre's Oregon Trail Ser.: 2). 111p. (J). pap. 5.99 (*1-58134-392-2*) Crossway Bks.

—Coyote True, No. 2. 1992. (Nathan T. Riggins Western Adventure Ser.: Bk. 2). 128p. (J). (gr. 4-7). pap. 4.99 o.p. (*0-89107-680-8*) Crossway Bks.

—The Dog Who Would Not Smile, No. 1. 1992. (Nathan T. Riggins Western Adventure Ser.: Vol. 1). 128p. (J). (gr. 4-7). pap. 4.99 o.p. (*0-89107-656-5*) Crossway Bks.

—The Lost Wagon Train. 2002. (Retta Barre's Oregon Trail Ser.: Vol. 1). 110p. (J). pap. 5.99 (*1-58134-391-4*) Crossway Bks.

—Never Dance with a Bobcat, No. 5. 1994. (Nathan T. Riggins Western Adventure Ser.: Bk. 5). 128p. (J). (gr. 4-8). pap. 4.99 o.p. (*0-89107-771-5*) Crossway Bks.

—The Plain Prairie Princess. 2002. (Retta Barre's Oregon Trail Ser.: 3). 108p. (J). pap. 5.99 (*1-58134-393-0*) Crossway Bks.

—You Can Always Trust a Spotted Horse, No. 3. 1993. (Nathan T. Riggins Western Adventure Ser.: Vol. 3). 128p. (J). (gr. 4-7). pap. 4.99 o.p. (*0-89107-716-2*) Crossway Bks.

Bower, B. M. Cabin Fever. 1981. 290p. (J). reprint ed. lib. bdg. 16.35 o.p. (*0-89966-017-7*) Buccaneer Bks., Inc.

—The Flying U Ranch. 1981. 280p. (J). reprint ed. lib. bdg. 16.95 o.p. (*0-89966-018-5*) Buccaneer Bks., Inc.

Bright, Robert. Georgie Goes West. 1973. 48p. (gr. k-3). lib. bdg. o.p. (*0-385-05277-4*) Doubleday Publishing.

Brimner, Larry Dane. Merry Christmas, Old Armadillo. 2003. (Illus.). 32p. (J). (ps-1). pap. 7.95 (*1-56397-678-1*) Boyds Mills Pr.

—Merry Christmas, Old Armadillo. 1997. 14.10 (*0-606-14268-1*) Turtleback Bks.

Brisson, Pat. Kate Heads West. 1990. (Illus.). 40p. (J). (gr. k-3). lib. bdg. 14.00 (*0-02-714345-7*, Simon & Schuster Children's Publishing) Simon & Schuster Children's Publishing.

Brouwer, Sigmund. Phantom Outlaw at Wolf Creek. 1994. (Accidental Detective Ser.: Vol. 3). 132p. (YA). (gr. 8-12). pap. 4.99 o.p. (*1-56476-372-2*, 6-3372) Cook Communications Ministries.

Brown, Dee. Cavalry Scout. 1988. 224p. (YA). (gr. 7 up). mass mkt. 2.95 o.s.i (*0-440-20227-2*) Dell Publishing.

—Yellow Horse. 1989. 224p. (YA). reprint ed. mass mkt. 2.95 o.s.i (*0-440-20246-9*) Dell Publishing.

Brown, Lois, compiled by. Tales of the Wild West: An Illustrated Collection of Adventure Stories. 1995. (Illus.). 144p. (J). 9.99 o.s.i (*0-517-14703-3*) Random Hse. Value Publishing.

Brown, Towana J. Scottie. 1989. (One Ser.). (Illus.). 150p. (Orig.). (J). (gr. 5-6). pap. 3.50 (*0-9622060-1-6*) Brown, Towana J.

Brownlow, Mike. Way Out West... With a Baby! 2000. (Illus.). 32p. (J). (ps-2). 13.95 (*1-929927-04-5*) Ragged Bears USA.

Bryant, Bonnie. Cutting Horse. 1996. (Saddle Club Ser.: No. 56). 144p. (gr. 4-6). pap. text 3.99 o.s.i (*0-553-48368-4*, Skylark) Random Hse. Children's Bks.

—Cutting Horse. 1996. (Saddle Club Ser.: No. 56). (J). (gr. 4-6). 9.09 o.p. (*0-606-09810-0*) Turtleback Bks.

—Dude Ranch. l.t. ed. 1995. (Saddle Club Ser.). 144p. (J). (gr. 4-6). lib. bdg. 19.93 o.p. (*0-8368-1285-9*) Stevens, Gareth Inc.

—Dude Ranch. 1989. (Saddle Club Ser.: No. 6). (J). (gr. 4-6). 9.09 o.p. (*0-606-08120-8*) Turtleback Bks.

—Stage Coach. 1994. (Saddle Club Ser.: No. 37). 144p. (J). (gr. 4-6). pap. 3.99 o.s.i (*0-553-48153-3*) Bantam Bks.

Bulla, Clyde Robert. Ghost Town Treasure. 1994. (Illus.). 96p. (J). (gr. 2-5). pap. 3.99 o.s.i (*0-14-036732-2*, Puffin Bks.) Penguin Putnam Bks. for Young Readers.

Burgess, Thornton W. Old Mother West Wind's "When" Stories. (J). 21.95 (*0-8488-0387-6*) Amereon, Ltd.

Burn, Doris. The Tale of Lazy Lizard Canyon. 1977. (Illus.). (J). (gr. 3-5). 5.59 o.p. (*0-399-61012-X*) Putnam Publishing Group, The.

Burton, Virginia Lee. Calico the Wonder Horse, or the Saga of Stewy Stinker. (Illus.). 64p. (J). (ps-3). 1997. tchr. ed. 18.00 (*0-395-85735-X*); 1996. pap. 5.95 (*0-395-84541-6*) Houghton Mifflin Co.

Byars, Betsy C. The Golly Sisters Go West: An I Can Read Book. (I Can Read Bks.). (Illus.). 64p. (J). 1989. (gr. k-3). pap. 3.99 (*0-06-444132-6*, Harper Trophy); 1986. (gr. k-3). lib. bdg. 16.89 (*0-06-020884-8*, Harper Trophy); 1986. (gr. 2-4). 11.95 (*0-06-020883-X*); 1995. (ps-3). 8.99 incl. audio (*0-694-70027-4*) HarperCollins Children's Bk. Group.

—The Golly Sisters Go West: An I Can Read Book. 2000. (YA). pap. 23.20 incl. audio (*0-7887-4335-X*, 41130) Recorded Bks., LLC.

—The Golly Sisters Go West: An I Can Read Book. 1985. (I Can Read Bks.). (J). (gr. 2-4). 10.10 (*0-606-04234-2*) Turtleback Bks.

—The Golly Sisters Ride Again: An I Can Read Book. 1994. (I Can Read Bks.). (Illus.). 64p. (J). (gr. k-3). lib. bdg. 15.89 (*0-06-021564-X*); 14.95 o.p. (*0-06-021563-1*) HarperCollins Children's Bk. Group.

—Hooray for the Golly Sisters! An I Can Read Book. 1990. (I Can Read Bks.). (Illus.). 64p. (J). (gr. k-3). lib. bdg. 15.89 (*0-06-020899-6*); (gr. 2-4). 15.95 o.p. (*0-06-020898-8*) HarperCollins Children's Bk. Group.

Campbell, Roy B. Song of the Jackalope. 2002. (Illus.). viii, 108p. (YA). (gr. 4-9). 20.00 (*0-9718282-0-2*) Fireside Bks.

Carabine, Sue. A Cowgirl's Night Before Christmas. 2001. (Illus.). 60p. 5.95 (*1-58685-086-5*); 2nd gif. ed. 5.95 (*1-58685-121-7*) Smith, Gibbs Pub.

Carter, Peter. Borderlands, RS. 432p. 1993. (YA). pap. 4.95 o.p. (*0-374-40883-1*, Aerial); 1990. 17.00 o.p. (*0-374-30895-0*, Farrar, Straus & Giroux (BYR)) Farrar, Straus & Giroux.

—Borderlands. 1993. (Aerial Fiction Ser.). (J). 10.05 o.p. (*0-606-05764-1*) Turtleback Bks.

Cheatham, K. Follis. Bring Home the Ghost. 1980. 325p. (J). (gr. 7 up). 8.95 o.p. (*0-15-212485-3*) Harcourt Children's Bks.

Chodan, Tim. Ghost Stories of the Old West. 2001. (Illus.). 232p. pap. 10.95 (*1-55105-332-2*) Lone Pine Publishing.

Christian, Mary Blount. Go West, Swamp Monsters. 1996. (Puffin Easy-to-Read Ser.). (J). 8.70 o.p. (*0-606-08528-9*) Turtleback Bks.

Christian, Peggy. The Old Coot. 1991. (Illus.). 64p. (J). (gr. 3-5). text 11.95 o.p. (*0-689-31627-5*, Atheneum) Simon & Schuster Children's Publishing.

Cohen, Caron L. Bronco Dogs. 1991. (Illus.). 32p. (J). (ps-3). 12.95 o.p. (*0-525-44721-0*, Dutton Children's Bks.) Penguin Putnam Bks. for Young Readers.

Corbett, Scott. Great McGoniggle Rides Shotgun. 1989. o.p. (*0-316-15729-5*) Little Brown & Co.

Coren, Alan. Arthur the Kid. 1978. (Illus.). (J). (gr. 4-6). 12.95 o.s.i (*0-316-15734-1*) Little Brown & Co.

—Arthur's Last Stand. 1979. (Illus.). (J). (gr. 4-6). o.p. (*0-316-15742-2*) Little Brown & Co.

—Buffalo Arthur. 1978. (Illus.). (J). (gr. 4-6). 7.95 o.p. (*0-316-15738-4*) Little Brown & Co.

—The Lone Arthur. 1978. (Illus.). (J). (gr. 4-6). 10.45 o.p. (*0-316-15739-2*) Little Brown & Co.

—Railroad Arthur. 1978. (Illus.). (J). (gr. 4-6). 7.95 o.p. (*0-316-15737-6*) Little Brown & Co.

Cosgrove, Stephen. Serendipity Boxed Set, No. 1. 1980. (Serendipity Bks.). (J). (gr. 1-6). pap. 9.75 o.p. (*0-8431-0565-8*, Price Stern Sloan) Penguin Putnam Bks. for Young Readers.

Cox, Leona D. Secret of the 2 Bar 4 Ranch. 1994. (Illus.). 153p. (J). (gr. 4-12). pap. 11.95 (*0-9627680-6-5*) Inkwell.

Cummins, Ann F. Cattle Annie. 1988. (Illus.). 182p. (Orig.). (J). pap. 9.95 (*0-943149-04-5*) Alpha Bks.

Cushman, Karen. Rodzina. 2003. 208p. (J). (gr. 5-9). tchr. ed. 16.00 (*0-618-13351-8*, Clarion Bks.) Houghton Mifflin Co. Trade & Reference Div.

—Rodzina. unabr. ed. 2003. (J). (gr. 7-7). audio 26.00 (*0-8072-1576-7*, Listening Library) Random Hse. Audio Publishing Group.

Dana, Barbara. Zucchini Out West. 1997. (Illus.). 160p. (J). (gr. 3-5). 14.95 o.p. (*0-06-024897-1*); lib. bdg. 14.89 o.s.i (*0-06-024898-X*) HarperCollins Children's Bk. Group.

Davis, Tim. More Tales from Dust River Gulch. 2002. (Tales from Dust River Gulch Ser.). (Illus.). 108p. (J). (gr. 4-6). 6.49 (*1-57924-855-1*) Jones, Bob Univ. Pr.

—Tales from Dust River Gulch. (gr. 4-7). 2000. pap. 14.98 incl. audio (*0-89084-956-0*, 110742); 1997. (Illus.). 102p. (J). pap. 6.49 (*0-89084-896-3*, 102517) Jones, Bob Univ. Pr.

De Bevere, Maurice & Goscinny, René. The Stage Coach. 1996. (Illus.). 48p. (J). (gr. 2-7). reprint ed. pap. 8.95 o.p. (*1-887911-52-9*) Fantasy Flight Publishing, Inc.

Degnan, Lawrence. Yosemite Yarns-Stagecoach Stories. 1958. (Illus.). 24p. (YA). (gr. 7 up). pap. 3.50 (*0-915266-04-0*) Awani Pr.

Delton, Judy. Wild, Wild West. 1999. (Pee Wee Scouts Ser.: No. 37). (Illus.). 112p. (gr. 2-5). pap. text 3.99 o.s.i (*0-440-41432-7*, Dell Books for Young Readers) Random Hse. Children's Bks.

—Wild, Wild West. 1999. (Pee Wee Scouts Ser.: No. 37). (J). (gr. 2-5). 10.04 (*0-606-16585-1*) Turtleback Bks.

Denslow, Sharon Phillips. On the Trail with Miss Pace. 1995. (Illus.). 40p. (J). (ps-3). pap. 15.00 (*0-02-728688-6*, Simon & Schuster Children's Publishing) Simon & Schuster Children's Publishing.

Dundy, Melanie Richardson. Westward Ho with Ollie Ox! Date not set. (Illus.). 56p. (J). (gr. k-5). per. 12.95 (*0-9674491-4-6*) MDCT Publishing.

Dutton, June, text. Snoopy & the Gang Out West. 1983. (Illus.). (J). 6.95 (*0-915696-55-X*); 128p. 5.00 (*0-915696-82-7*) Determined Productions, Inc.

Ellison, Douglas W. David Lant: The Vanished Outlaw. 1988. 232p. (Orig.). (YA). pap. text (*0-929918-01-0*) Midstates Publishing.

Erickson, John R. The Case of the Black-Hooded Hangman. 1998. (Hank the Cowdog Ser.: No. 24). (Illus.). 144p. (J). (gr. 2-5). 15.99 (*0-670-88431-6*); pap. 4.99 (*0-14-130400-6*) Penguin Putnam Bks. for Young Readers. (Puffin Bks.).

—The Case of the Black-Hooded Hangman. 1995. (Hank the Cowdog Ser.: No. 24). (Illus.). (J). (gr. 2-5). 11.04 (*0-606-08767-2*) Turtleback Bks.

—The Case of the Burrowing Robot. 2003. (Illus.). 144p. (J). (Hank the Cowdog Ser.: No. 42). pap. 4.99 (*0-14-250063-1*);No. 42. 15.99 (*0-670-03632-3*) Penguin Putnam Bks. for Young Readers. (Puffin Bks.).

—The Case of the Car-Barkaholic Dog, Vol. 17. 1998. (Hank the Cowdog Ser.: No. 17). (Illus.). 144p. (J). (gr. 2-5). pap. 4.99 (*0-14-130393-X*, Puffin Bks.) Penguin Putnam Bks. for Young Readers.

—The Case of the Car-Barkaholic Dog. 1991. (Hank the Cowdog Ser.: No. 17). (Illus.). (J). (gr. 2-5). 11.04 (*0-606-01409-8*) Turtleback Bks.

—The Case of the Double Bumblebee Sting. 1998. (Hank the Cowdog Ser.: No. 22). (Illus.). 144p. (J). (gr. 2-5). 4.99 (*0-14-130398-0*); 14.99 (*0-670-88429-4*) Penguin Putnam Bks. for Young Readers. (Puffin Bks.).

—The Case of the Double Bumblebee Sting. 1994. (Hank the Cowdog Ser.: No. 22). (Illus.). (J). (gr. 2-5). 11.04 (*0-606-06436-2*) Turtleback Bks.

—The Case of the Halloween Ghost. 1990. (Hank the Cowdog Ser.: No. 9). (Illus.). (J). (gr. 2-5). audio 16.95 (*0-87719-149-2*) Lone Star Bks.

—The Case of the Halloween Ghost. 1998. (Hank the Cowdog Ser.: No. 9). (Illus.). 144p. (J). (gr. 2-5). 14.99 (*0-670-88416-2*); pap. 4.99 (*0-14-130385-9*, Puffin Bks.) Penguin Putnam Bks. for Young Readers.

—The Case of the Halloween Ghost. 1989. (Hank the Cowdog Ser.: No. 9). (Illus.). (J). (gr. 2-5). 11.04 (*0-606-01401-2*) Turtleback Bks.

—The Case of the Haystack Kitties. 1998. (Hank the Cowdog Ser.: No. 30). (Illus.). 113p. (J). (gr. 2-5). 14.95 (*0-87719-338-X*) Maverick Bks., Inc.

—The Case of the Haystack Kitties. 1998. (Hank the Cowdog Ser.: No. 30). (Illus.). 144p. (J). (gr. 2-5). pap. 4.99 (*0-14-130406-5*);No. 30. 14.99 (*0-670-88437-5*) Penguin Putnam Bks. for Young Readers. (Puffin Bks.).

—The Case of the Haystack Kitties. 1998. (Hank the Cowdog Ser.: No. 30). (J). (gr. 2-5). 11.04 (*0-606-16821-4*) Turtleback Bks.

—The Case of the Hooking Bull. 1998. (Hank the Cowdog Ser.: No. 18). (Illus.). 144p. (J). (gr. 2-5). 14.99 (*0-670-88425-1*); pap. 4.99 (*0-14-130394-8*) Penguin Putnam Bks. for Young Readers. (Puffin Bks.).

—The Case of the Hooking Bull. 1992. (Hank the Cowdog Ser.: No. 18). (Illus.). (J). (gr. 2-5). 11.04 (*0-606-01410-1*) Turtleback Bks.

—The Case of the Kidnapped Collie. 1998. (Hank the Cowdog Ser.: No. 26). (Illus.). 144p. (J). (gr. 2-5). 14.99 (*0-670-88433-2*); pap. 4.99 (*0-14-130402-2*) Penguin Putnam Bks. for Young Readers. (Puffin Bks.).

—The Case of the Kidnapped Collie. 1999. (Hank the Cowdog Ser.: No. 26). (Illus.). (J). (gr. 2-5). 11.04 (*0-606-09375-3*) Turtleback Bks.

—The Case of the Midnight Rustler. 1992. (Hank the Cowdog Ser.: No. 19). (Illus.). 110 p. (J). (gr. 2-5). 16.95 incl. audio (*0-87719-220-0*, 9220) Lone Star Bks.

—The Case of the Midnight Rustler. 1998. (Hank the Cowdog Ser.: No. 19). (Illus.). 144p. (J). (gr. 2-5). pap. 4.99 (*0-14-130395-6*, Puffin Bks.);Bk. 19. 14.99 (*0-670-88426-X*) Penguin Putnam Bks. for Young Readers.

—The Case of the Midnight Rustler. 1992. (Hank the Cowdog Ser.: No. 19). (Illus.). (J). (gr. 2-5). 11.04 (*0-606-01411-X*) Turtleback Bks.

—The Case of the Missing Bird Dog. 2002. (Hank the Cowdog Ser.). (Illus.). 144p. (J). 14.99 (*0-670-03558-0*, Viking Children's Bks.); pap. 4.99 (*0-14-230141-8*, Puffin Bks.) Penguin Putnam Bks. for Young Readers.

—The Case of the Missing Cat. (Hank the Cowdog Ser.: No. 15). (Illus.). 144p. (J). (gr. 2-5). 2000. 14.99 o.p. (*0-670-88422-7*, Viking); 1998. pap. 4.99 (*0-14-130391-3*, Puffin Bks.) Penguin Putnam Bks. for Young Readers.

—The Case of the Missing Cat. 1990. (Hank the Cowdog Ser.: No. 15). (Illus.). (J). (gr. 2-5). 11.04 (*0-606-01407-1*) Turtleback Bks.

—The Case of the Mopwater Files. 1998. (Hank the Cowdog Ser.: No. 28). (Illus.). 144p. (J). (gr. 2-5). 14.99 (*0-670-88435-9*); pap. 4.99 (*0-14-130404-9*) Penguin Putnam Bks. for Young Readers. (Puffin Bks.).

—The Case of the Night-Stalking Bone Monster. 1996. (Hank the Cowdog Ser.: No. 27). (Illus.). (J). (gr. 2-5). audio 16.95 (*0-87719-305-3*, 9305) Lone Star Bks.

—The Case of the Night-Stalking Bone Monster. 1998. (Hank the Cowdog Ser.: No. 27). (Illus.). (J). (gr. 2-5). 144p. 14.99 (*0-670-88434-0*); 128p. pap. 4.99 (*0-14-130403-0*) Penguin Putnam Bks. for Young Readers. (Puffin Bks.).

—The Case of the Night-Stalking Bone Monster. 1996. (Hank the Cowdog Ser.: No. 27). (J). (gr. 2-5). 11.04 (*0-606-12715-1*) Turtleback Bks.

—The Case of the One-Eyed Killer Stud Horse. 1998. (Hank the Cowdog Ser.: No. 8). (Illus.). 144p. (J). (gr. 2-5). 14.99 (*0-670-88415-4*); pap. 4.99 (*0-14-130384-0*, Puffin Bks.) Penguin Putnam Bks. for Young Readers.

—The Case of the One-Eyed Killer Stud Horse. 1990. (Hank the Cowdog Ser.: No. 8). (Illus.). (J). (gr. 2-5). 11.04 (*0-606-01400-4*) Turtleback Bks.

—The Case of the Raging Rottweiler. 2000. (Hank the Cowdog Ser.: No. 36). (Illus.). (J). (gr. 2-5). 144p. 14.99 (*0-670-89364-1*, Viking Children's Bks.); 160p. pap. 4.99 (*0-14-130668-8*, Puffin Bks.) Penguin Putnam Bks. for Young Readers.

—The Case of the Raging Rottweiler. 2000. (Hank the Cowdog Ser.). (Illus.). (J). 11.04 (*0-606-20460-1*) Turtleback Bks.

—The Case of the Saddle House Robbery. 2000. (Hank the Cowdog Ser.: No. 35). (Illus.). 144p. (J). (gr. 2-5). 14.99 (*0-670-88890-7*, Viking Children's Bks.); pap. 4.99 (*0-14-130678-5*, Puffin Bks.) Penguin Putnam Bks. for Young Readers.

—The Case of the Saddle House Robbery. unabr. ed. 2000. (Hank the Cowdog Ser.: No. 35). (J). (gr. 2-5). pap. 23.00 incl. audio (*0-8072-8376-2*, YA172SP, Listening Library) Random Hse. Audio Publishing Group.

—The Case of the Saddle House Robbery. 2000. (Hank the Cowdog Ser.: No. 35). (Illus.). (J). (gr. 2-5). 11.04 (*0-606-18409-0*) Turtleback Bks.

—The Case of the Shipwrecked Tree. 2003. (Illus.). 144p. (J). 14.99 (*0-670-03603-X*);Vol. 41. pap. 4.99 (*0-14-230225-2*) Penguin Putnam Bks. for Young Readers. (Puffin Bks.).

—The Case of the Swirling Killer Tornado. 1998. (Hank the Cowdog Ser.: No. 25). (Illus.). (J). (gr. 2-5). 144p. 14.99 (*0-670-88432-4*); 128p. pap. 4.99 (*0-14-130401-4*) Penguin Putnam Bks. for Young Readers. (Puffin Bks.).

—The Case of the Swirling Killer Tornado. 1995. (Hank the Cowdog Ser.: No. 25). (Illus.). (J). (gr. 2-5). 11.04 (*0-606-08768-0*) Turtleback Bks.

—The Case of the Vampire Cat. 1998. (Hank the Cowdog Ser.: No. 21). (Illus.). 144p. (J). (gr. 2-5). 14.99 (*0-670-88428-6*); pap. 4.99 (*0-14-130397-2*, Puffin Bks.) Penguin Putnam Bks. for Young Readers.

—The Case of the Vampire Cat. 1993. (Hank the Cowdog Ser.: No. 21). (Illus.). (J). (gr. 2-5). 11.04 (*0-606-05855-9*) Turtleback Bks.

—The Case of the Vampire Vacuum Sweeper. 1998. (Hank the Cowdog Ser.: No. 29). (Illus.). 144p. (J). (gr. 2-5). 14.99 (*0-670-88436-7*); (gr. 3-7). pap. 4.99 (*0-14-130405-7*) Penguin Putnam Bks. for Young Readers. (Puffin Bks.).

—The Case of the Vampire Vacuum Sweeper. 1997. (Hank the Cowdog Ser.: No. 29). (Illus.). (J). (gr. 2-5). 11.04 (*0-606-12717-8*) Turtleback Bks.

—The Case of the Vanishing Fishhook. 1999. (Hank the Cowdog Ser.: No. 31). (Illus.). 144p. (J). (gr. 2-5). 14.99 (*0-670-88438-3*); pap. 4.99 (*0-14-130356-5*, Puffin Bks.) Penguin Putnam Bks. for Young Readers.

—The Curse of the Incredible Priceless Corncob. unabr. ed. 1986. (Hank the Cowdog Ser.: No. 7). (Illus.). (J). (gr. 2-5). 13.95 incl. audio (*0-916941-23-X*) Maverick Bks., Inc.

—The Curse of the Incredible Priceless Corncob. 1998. (Hank the Cowdog Ser.: No. 7). (Illus.). 144p. (J). (gr. 2-5). 14.99 (*0-670-88414-6*);Vol. 7. pap. 4.99 (*0-14-130383-2*, Puffin Bks.) Penguin Putnam Bks. for Young Readers.

—The Curse of the Incredible Priceless Corncob. 1989. (Hank the Cowdog Ser.: No. 7). (Illus.). (J). (gr. 2-5). 11.04 (*0-606-01399-7*) Turtleback Bks.

—Every Dog Has His Day. 1998. (Hank the Cowdog Ser.: No. 10). (Illus.). 144p. (J). (gr. 2-5). 14.99 (*0-670-88417-0*); pap. 4.99 (*0-14-130386-7*, Puffin Bks.) Penguin Putnam Bks. for Young Readers.

—Every Dog Has His Day. 1989. (Hank the Cowdog Ser.: No. 10). (Illus.). (J). (gr. 2-5). 11.04 (*0-606-01402-0*) Turtleback Bks.

—Faded Love. 1991. (Hank the Cowdog Ser.: No. 5). (Illus.). (J). (gr. 2-5). pap. 12.25 (*0-8335-6818-3*) Econo-Clad Bks.

—Faded Love. 1985. (Hank the Cowdog Ser.: No. 5). (Illus.). (J). (gr. 2-5). 9.95 (*0-916941-11-6*); pap. 6.95 (*0-916941-10-8*) Maverick Bks., Inc.

—Faded Love. 1998. (Hank the Cowdog Ser.: No. 5). (Illus.). 144p. (J). (gr. 2-5). 14.99 (*0-670-88412-X*);Vol. 5. pap. 4.99 (*0-14-130381-6*, Puffin Bks.) Penguin Putnam Bks. for Young Readers.

—Faded Love. 1989. (Hank the Cowdog Ser.: No. 5). (Illus.). (J). (gr. 2-5). 11.04 (*0-606-01397-0*) Turtleback Bks.

—The Fling, Vol. 38. 2001. (Hank the Cowdog Ser.: No. 38). (Illus.). 144p. (J). (gr. 2-5). pap. 4.99 (*0-14-131174-6*, Puffin Bks.) Penguin Putnam Bks. for Young Readers.

—The Further Adventures of Hank the Cowdog. 1999. (Hank the Cowdog Ser.: No. 2). (Illus.). (J). (gr. 2-5). pap. 12.25 (*0-8335-6816-7*) Econo-Clad Bks.

—The Further Adventures of Hank the Cowdog. 1983. (Hank the Cowdog Ser.: No. 2). (Illus.). 93p. (J). (gr. 2-5). 9.95 (*0-9608612-7-0*); pap. 6.95 (*0-9608612-5-4*) Maverick Bks., Inc.

—The Further Adventures of Hank the Cowdog. (Hank the Cowdog Ser.: No. 2). (Illus.). 144p. (J). (gr. 2-5). 1998. 14.99 (*0-670-88409-X*); Vol. 2. 1999. pap. 4.99 (*0-14-130378-6*, Puffin Bks.) Penguin Putnam Bks. for Young Readers.

—The Further Adventures of Hank the Cowdog. 1991. (Hank the Cowdog Ser.: No. 2). (Illus.). (J). (gr. 2-5). 11.04 (*0-606-01393-8*) Turtleback Bks.

—The Garbage Monster from Outer Space. 1999. (Hank the Cowdog Ser.: No. 32). (Illus.). 144p. (J). (gr. 2-5). pap. 4.99 (*0-14-130422-7*, Puffin Bks.); 13.99 (*0-670-88488-X*, Viking) Penguin Putnam Bks. for Young Readers.

—The Garbage Monster from Outer Space. 1999. (Hank the Cowdog Ser.: No. 32). (J). (gr. 2-5). 11.04 (*0-606-16827-3*) Turtleback Bks.

—Hank the Cowdog: The Original Adventures of Hank the Cowboy. 2001. (Frequently Requested Ser.). lib. bdg. 17.20 (*1-59054-257-6*) Fitzgerald Bks.

—It's a Dog's Life. (Hank the Cowdog Ser.: No. 3). (Illus.). 100p. (J). (gr. 2-5). 9.95 (*0-916941-04-3*); pap. 5.95 (*0-9608612-9-7*); 1985. pap. text 13.95 incl. audio (*0-916941-03-5*) Maverick Bks., Inc.

—It's a Dog's Life. 1998. (Hank the Cowdog Ser.: No. 3). (Illus.). 144p. (J). (gr. 2-5). 14.99 (*0-670-88410-3*);Vol. 3. pap. 4.99 (*0-14-130379-4*, Puffin Bks.) Penguin Putnam Bks. for Young Readers.

—It's a Dog's Life. 1988. (Hank the Cowdog Ser.: No. 3). (Illus.). (J). (gr. 2-5). 11.04 (*0-606-01394-6*) Turtleback Bks.

—Let Sleeping Dogs Lie. 1989. (Hank the Cowdog Ser.: No. 6). (Illus.). (J). (gr. 2-5). pap. 12.25 (*0-8335-6819-1*) Econo-Clad Bks.

—Let Sleeping Dogs Lie. 1986. (Hank the Cowdog Ser.: No. 6). (Illus.). 19p. (J). (gr. 2-5). 9.95 (*0-916941-15-9*); pap. 6.95 (*0-916941-14-0*); 13.95 incl. audio (*0-916941-16-7*) Maverick Bks., Inc.

—Let Sleeping Dogs Lie, Vol. 6. 1998. (Hank the Cowdog Ser.: No. 6). (Illus.). 144p. (J). (gr. 2-5). pap. 4.99 (*0-14-130382-4*, Puffin Bks.) Penguin Putnam Bks. for Young Readers.

—Let Sleeping Dogs Lie. 1989. (Hank the Cowdog Ser.: No. 6). (Illus.). (J). (gr. 2-5). 11.04 (*0-606-01398-9*) Turtleback Bks.

—Lost in the Blinded Blizzard. 1998. (Hank the Cowdog Ser.: No. 16). (Illus.). 144p. (J). (gr. 2-5). 14.99 (*0-670-88423-5*); pap. 4.99 (*0-14-130392-1*, Puffin Bks.) Penguin Putnam Bks. for Young Readers.

—Lost in the Dark Unchanted Forest. 1998. (Hank the Cowdog Ser.: No. 11). (Illus.). 144p. (J). (gr. 2-5). pap. 4.99 (*0-14-130387-5*, Puffin Bks.) Penguin Putnam Bks. for Young Readers.

—Lost in the Dark Unchanted Forest. 1988. (Hank the Cowdog Ser.: No. 11). (Illus.). (J). (gr. 2-5). 11.04 (*0-606-01403-9*) Turtleback Bks.

—Monkey Business. 1999. (Hank the Cowdog Ser.: No. 14). (Illus.). (J). (gr. 2-5). pap. text 14.50 (*0-8335-6827-2*) Econo-Clad Bks.

—Monkey Business. 1998. (Hank the Cowdog Ser.: No. 14). (Illus.). (J). (gr. 2-5). 144p. 14.99 (*0-670-88421-9*); 128p. pap. 4.99 (*0-14-130390-5*, Puffin Bks.) Penguin Putnam Bks. for Young Readers.

—Monkey Business. 1990. (Hank the Cowdog Ser.: No. 14). (Illus.). (J). (gr. 2-5). 11.04 (*0-606-01406-3*) Turtleback Bks.

—Moonlight Madness. 1994. (Hank the Cowdog Ser.: No. 23). (Illus.). (J). (gr. 2-5). audio 16.95 (*0-87719-253-7*, 9253) Lone Star Bks.

—Moonlight Madness. 1998. (Hank the Cowdog Ser.: No. 23). (Illus.). (J). (gr. 2-5). 144p. 15.99 (*0-670-88430-8*); 128p. pap. 4.99 (*0-14-130399-9*) Penguin Putnam Bks. for Young Readers. (Puffin Bks.).

—Moonlight Madness. 1994. (Hank the Cowdog Ser.: No. 23). (Illus.). (J). (gr. 2-5). 11.04 (*0-606-08766-4*) Turtleback Bks.

—Murder in the Middle Pasture. 1999. (Hank the Cowdog Ser.: No. 4). (Illus.). (J). (gr. 2-5). pap. 14.50 (*0-8335-6817-5*) Econo-Clad Bks.

—Murder in the Middle Pasture. 1989. (Hank the Cowdog Ser.: No. 4). (J). (gr. 2-5). audio 16.95 (*0-87719-135-2*) Lone Star Bks.

—Murder in the Middle Pasture. 1985. (Hank the Cowdog Ser.: No. 4). (Illus.). 91p. (J). (gr. 2-5). 9.95 (*0-916941-08-6*); pap. 6.95 (*0-916941-07-8*) Maverick Bks., Inc.

—Murder in the Middle Pasture. 1998. (Hank the Cowdog Ser.: No. 4). (Illus.). 144p. (J). (gr. 2-5). 14.99 (*0-670-88411-1*, Viking Children's Bks.);Vol. 4. pap. 4.99 (*0-14-130380-8*, Puffin Bks.) Penguin Putnam Bks. for Young Readers.

—Murder in the Middle Pasture. 1988. (Hank the Cowdog Ser.: No. 4). (Illus.). (J). (gr. 2-5). 11.04 (*0-606-01395-4*) Turtleback Bks.

—The Original Adventures of Hank the Cowdog. 1999. (Hank the Cowdog Ser.: No. 1). (Illus.). (J). (gr. 2-5). pap. 12.25 (*0-8335-6815-9*) Econo-Clad Bks.

—The Original Adventures of Hank the Cowdog. unabr. ed. 1983. (Hank the Cowdog Ser.: No. 1). (Illus.). 105p. (J). (gr. 2-5). 13.95 incl. audio (*0-916941-01-9*) Maverick Bks., Inc.

—The Original Adventures of Hank the Cowdog. (Hank the Cowdog Ser.: No. 1). (Illus.). 1998. 144p. (J). (gr. 2-5). pap. 4.99 (*0-14-130377-8*); 2003. 160p. pap. 4.99 (*0-14-250127-1*) Penguin Putnam Bks. for Young Readers. (Puffin Bks.).

—The Original Adventures of Hank the Cowdog. 1988. (Hank the Cowdog Ser.: No. 1). (Illus.). (J). (gr. 2-5). 11.04 (*0-606-01391-1*) Turtleback Bks.

—The Phantom in the Mirror. (Hank the Cowdog Ser.: No. 20). (Illus.). 144p. (J). (gr. 2-5). 2000. 14.99 (*0-670-88427-8*); 1998. pap. 4.99 (*0-14-130396-4*, Puffin Bks.) Penguin Putnam Bks. for Young Readers.

—The Phantom in the Mirror. 1993. (Hank the Cowdog Ser.: No. 20). (Illus.). (J). (gr. 2-5). 11.04 (*0-606-05329-8*) Turtleback Bks.

—The Secret Laundry Monster Files. 2002. (Hank the Cowdog Ser.: Bk. 39). (Illus.). (J). 160p. pap. 4.99 (*0-14-230076-4*); 144p. 14.99 (*0-670-03541-6*) Penguin Putnam Bks. for Young Readers. (Puffin Bks.).

—Slim's Good-Bye. 2000. (Hank the Cowdog Ser.: No. 34). (Illus.). 144p. (J). (gr. 2-5). 14.99 (*0-670-88889-3*); pap. 4.99 (*0-14-130677-7*) Penguin Putnam Bks. for Young Readers. (Puffin Bks.).

—Slim's Good-Bye. 2000. (Hank the Cowdog Ser.: No. 34). (Illus.). (J). (gr. 2-5). 11.04 (*0-606-18408-2*) Turtleback Bks.

Ernst, Lisa Campbell, illus. Hannah Mae O'Hannigan's Wild West Show. 2003. 40p. (J). 16.95 (*0-689-85191-X*, Simon & Schuster Children's Publishing) Simon & Schuster Children's Publishing.

Evans, Jerry. Spur. 1995. 135p. (Orig.). (YA). (gr. 11 up). pap. 7.95 (*0-9623698-2-9*) Magnum Pr.

Farrell, Cliff. Patchsaddle Drive. 1998. 184p. pap. 17.50 (*0-7540-8032-3*) BBC Audiobooks America.

—Patchsaddle Drive. 1972. (Western Ser.). 184p. (J). o.p. (*0-385-08472-2*) Doubleday Publishing.

Faux, Ruth. Golden Dawn. 1994. (Illus.). 192p. (Orig.). (YA). (gr. 7 up). pap. 6.95 o.p. (*1-878893-43-2*) Telcraft Bks.

Finlayson, Ann. Greenhorn on the Frontier. 1974. (Illus.). 196p. (J). (gr. 7-12). 5.95 o.p. (*0-7232-6104-0*, Warne, Frederick) Penguin Putnam Bks. for Young Readers.

—Greenhorn on the Frontier. 2000. (Golden Triangle Bks.). (Illus.). 224p. (J). (gr. 4-7). pap. 9.95 (*0-8229-5722-1*) Univ. of Pittsburgh Pr.

Finley, Mary Pearce. White Grizzly. 2000. (gr. 5-9). (Illus.). 215p. (J). 15.95 (*0-86541-053-4*); 216p. (YA). pap. 8.95 (*0-86541-058-5*) Filter Pr., LLC.

Fleischman, Sid. The Ghost on Saturday Night. 1997. (Beech Tree Chapter Bks.). (Illus.). 64p. (J). (ps-3). pap. 4.95 (*0-688-14920-0*, Harper Trophy); (gr. 3 up). reprint ed. 15.00 o.p. (*0-688-14919-7*, Greenwillow Bks.) HarperCollins Children's Bk. Group.

—The Ghost on Saturday Night. 1974. (Illus.). 64p. (J). (gr. 4-6). 14.95 (*0-316-28583-8*, Joy Street Bks.) Little Brown & Co.

—The Ghost on Saturday Night. 1997. (Beech Tree Chapter Bks.). (J). 11.10 (*0-606-11374-6*) Turtleback Bks.

—Jim Ugly. 1993. 144p. (gr. 4-7). pap. text 4.99 (*0-440-40803-2*) Dell Publishing.

—Jim Ugly. (Illus.). 144p. (J). (gr. 3-6). 2003. pap. 5.99 (*0-06-052121-X*, Harper Trophy); 1992. 16.99 (*0-688-10886-5*, Greenwillow Bks.) HarperCollins Children's Bk. Group.

—Jim Ugly. 1993. (J). pap. o.p. (*0-440-90010-7*, Dell Books for Young Readers) Random Hse. Children's Bks.

—Jim Ugly. 1992. (J). 11.04 (*0-606-05386-7*) Turtleback Bks.

Fleming, Candace. Westward Ho, Carlotta! 1997. (Illus.). (J). 15.00 (*0-679-87182-9*) Random Hse., Inc.

—Westward Ho, Carlotta! 1998. (Illus.). 32p. (J). (ps-3). 16.00 (*0-689-81063-6*, Atheneum/Anne Schwartz Bks.) Simon & Schuster Children's Publishing.

Fontes, Ron & Fontes, Justine. Wild Bill Hickok & the Rebel Raiders. 1993. (Disney's American Frontier Ser.: Bk. 10). (Illus.). 80p. (J). (gr. 1-4). lib. bdg. 12.89 o.s.i (*1-56282-494-5*); pap. 3.50 o.p. (*1-56282-493-7*) Disney Pr.

Garland, Sherry. Rainmaker's Dream. 1997. 336p. (J). (gr. 8 up). pap. 6.00 o.s.i (*0-15-200652-4*, Harcourt Paperbacks) Harcourt Children's Bks.

Gerrard, Roy. Rosie & the Rustlers, RS. 1989. (Illus.). 32p. (J). (ps-3). 15.00 o.p. (*0-374-36345-5*, Farrar, Straus & Giroux (BYR)) Farrar, Straus & Giroux.

—Wagons West!, RS. 32p. (J). (ps-3). 2000. (Illus.). pap. 5.95 (*0-374-48210-1*, Sunburst); 1996. 15.00 (*0-374-38249-2*, Farrar, Straus & Giroux (BYR)) Farrar, Straus & Giroux.

—Wagons West! 2000. (Illus.). (J). 12.10 (*0-606-20401-6*) Turtleback Bks.

Getzinger, Donna. For a Speck of Gold. 2002. pap. 8.95 (*0-87714-828-7*) Denlingers Pubs., Ltd.

Gifaldi, David. Gregory, Maw, & the Mean One. 1992. (Illus.). 144p. (J). (gr. 7 up). 13.95 o.p. (*0-395-60821-X*, Clarion Bks.) Houghton Mifflin Co. Trade & Reference Div.

—Gregory, Maw & the Mean One. 2000. (Illus.). 148p. (gr. 4-7). pap. 10.95 (*0-595-14504-3*, Backinprint-.com) iUniverse, Inc.

Glass, Andrew. The Sweetwater Run: The Story of Buffalo Bill Cody & the Pony Express. 1998. (Picture Yearling Book Ser.). 48p. (gr. 1-5). pap. text 6.99 o.s.i (*0-440-41186-6*) Dell Publishing.

Gold, Brian. The Legend of Cactus Eddie. 1996. (Illus.). 60p. (ps-3). pap. 11.95 (*0-929385-74-8*, Starchild Pr.) Light Technology Publishing.

Golden Books Staff. Pony Express. 2002. (Illus.). 48p. (J). pap. 4.99 (*0-307-27640-6*, Golden Bks.) Random Hse. Children's Bks.

Gonder, Glen W. Deep Woods. Gonder, Sharon J., ed. 1996. (Adventures of Willy Whacker Ser.: Vol. 6). (Illus.). (J). (gr. 3-5). lib. bdg. 8.95 (*0-9626245-8-6*) Osage Bend Publishing Co.

Goscinny, René. Calamity Jane: A Lucky Luke Adventure. 1998. (Lucky Luke Ser.). (Illus.). 48p. (J). (gr. 3-9). pap. 9.95 (*1-902172-02-7*) Glo'worm GBR. *Dist:* Last Gasp Eco-Funnies, Inc.

—Dalton City: A Lucky Luke Adventure. 1998. (Lucky Luke Ser.). (Illus.). 48p. (J). (gr. 3-9). pap. 9.95 (*1-902172-01-9*) Glo'worm GBR. *Dist:* Last Gasp Eco-Funnies, Inc.

—The Dashing White Cowboy: A Lucky Luke Adventure. 2000. (Lucky Luke Ser.). (Illus.). 48p. (J). (gr. 3-9). pap. 9.95 (*1-902172-06-X*) Glo'worm GBR. *Dist:* Last Gasp Eco-Funnies, Inc.

—Jesse James: A Lucky Luke Adventure. 1998. (Lucky Luke Ser.). (Illus.). 48p. (J). (gr. 3-9). pap. 9.95 (*1-902172-00-0*) Glo'worm GBR. *Dist:* Last Gasp Eco-Funnies, Inc.

—Ma Dalton: A Lucky Luke Adventure. 1999. (Lucky Luke Ser.). (Illus.). 48p. (J). (gr. 3-9). pap. 9.95 (*1-902172-04-3*) Glo'worm GBR. *Dist:* Last Gasp Eco-Funnies, Inc.

—The Tenderfoot: A Lucky Luke Adventure. 1999. (Lucky Luke Ser.). (Illus.). 48p. (J). (gr. 3-9). pap. 9.95 (*1-902172-03-5*) Glo'worm GBR. *Dist:* Last Gasp Eco-Funnies, Inc.

—Western Circus: A Lucky Luke Adventure. 2000. (Lucky Luke Ser.). (Illus.). 48p. (J). (gr. 3-9). pap. 9.95 (*1-902172-05-1*) Glo'worm GBR. *Dist:* Last Gasp Eco-Funnies, Inc.

Grattan-Dominguez, Alejandro. Breaking Even. 1997. 250p. (YA). (gr. 9 up). pap. 11.95 (*1-55885-213-1*) Arte Publico Pr.

Greer, Gary & Ruddick, Robert. Billy the Ghost & Me. 1997. (I Can Read Bks.). (Illus.). 48p. (J). (gr. 3-5). 14.95 o.p. (*0-06-026782-8*) HarperCollins Children's Bk. Group.

Greer, Gery. Billy the Ghost & Me. 1997. (I Can Read Chapter Bks.). (J). (gr. 3-5). 10.10 (*0-606-11129-8*) Turtleback Bks.

Greer, Gery & Ruddick, Robert. Billy the Ghost & Me. 1997. (I Can Read Bks.). (Illus.). 48p. (J). (ps-3). lib. bdg. 15.89 (*0-06-026783-6*); reprint ed. pap. 3.95 (*0-06-444214-4*, Harper Trophy) HarperCollins Children's Bk. Group.

—Max & Me & the Wild West. 1989. (Trophy Bk.). 144p. (J). (gr. 3-7). pap. 2.95 o.p. (*0-06-440305-X*, Harper Trophy) HarperCollins Children's Bk. Group.

Greer, Gery, et al. Max & Me & the Wild West. 1988. (Illus.). 144p. (J). (gr. 4-7). 12.95 (*0-15-253136-X*) Harcourt Trade Pubs.

Gregory, Kristiana. The Great Railroad Race: The Diary of Libby West, Utah Territory, 1868. 1999. (Dear America Ser.). (Illus.). 203p. (J). (gr. 4-9). mass mkt. 10.95 (*0-590-10991-X*) Scholastic, Inc.

—Jimmy Spoon & the Pony Express. 1997. 144p. (J). (gr. 4-7). pap. text 4.50 (*0-590-46578-3*) Scholastic, Inc.

—A Journey of Faith. 2003. (Prairie River Ser.: No. 1). 224p. (J). (gr. 3-8). mass mkt. 4.99 (*0-439-43991-4*, Scholastic Paperbacks) Scholastic, Inc.

—Prairie River 2: A Grateful Harvest. 2003. (Prairie River Ser.: No. 2). 208p. (J). mass mkt. 4.99 (*0-439-43993-0*) Scholastic, Inc.

—Prairie River 3. 2004. (Prairie River Ser.: No. 3). (J). per. (*0-439-44001-7*) Scholastic, Inc.

—Prairie River 4. 2004. (Prairie River Ser.: No. 4). (J). per. (*0-439-44003-3*) Scholastic, Inc.

Gregory, Kristiana & Philbrick, Rodman. The Heading West Collection: Seeds of Hope; The Greatest Railroad Race; Across the Wide & Lonesome Prairie; The Journal of Douglas Deeds, 4 vols. 2002. (Dear America Ser.). (J). pap. 19.96 (*0-439-12941-9*) Scholastic, Inc.

Griffin, Kitty, et al. Cowboy Sam & Those Confounded Secrets. 2001. (Illus.). 32p. (J). (ps-3). lib. bdg., tchr. ed. 15.00 (*0-618-08854-7*, Clarion Bks.) Houghton Mifflin Co. Trade & Reference Div.

Grove, Fred. The Child Stealers. 1973. (Western Ser.). 205p. (J). o.p. (*0-385-02596-3*) Doubleday Publishing.

Guthrie, Alfred B., Jr. The Big Sky. 1984. 384p. (ps up). mass mkt. 6.50 o.s.i (*0-553-26683-7*) Bantam Bks.

—The Way West. 1984. 352p. (J). (gr. 8 up). mass mkt. 3.95 o.p. (*0-553-24785-9*) Bantam Bks.

Hahn, Mary Downing. The Gentleman Outlaw & Me, Eli: A Story of the Old West. 1996. (Illus.). 224p. (YA). (gr. 7-7). tchr. ed. 15.00 (*0-395-73083-X*, Clarion Bks.) Houghton Mifflin Co. Trade & Reference Div.

Hancock, Sibyl. Old Blue. 1980. (See & Read Book). (Illus.). 48p. (J). (gr. 1-4). 6.99 o.p. (*0-399-61141-X*, G. P. Putnam's Sons) Penguin Putnam Bks. for Young Readers.

Hardman, Ric L. Sunshine Rider: The First Vegetarian Western. 1999. (Laurel-Leaf Bks.). 352p. (YA). (gr. 7-12). mass mkt. 4.99 (*0-440-22812-3*, Dell Books for Young Readers) Random Hse. Children's Bks.

Hardman, Ric Lynden. Sunshine Rider: The First Vegetarian Western. 1998. 352p. (YA). (gr. 7-12). 15.95 o.s.i (*0-385-32543-6*, Delacorte Pr.) Dell Publishing.

Harper, Jo. Ollie Jolly, Rodeo Clown. 2002. (Illus.). 32p. (J). (gr. k-3). 15.95 (*1-55868-552-9*); pap. 8.95 (*1-55868-553-7*) Graphic Arts Ctr. Publishing Co. (West Winds Pr.).

Harris, Peter. Ordinary Audrey. 2001. (Illus.). (J). tchr. ed. 14.95 (*1-58925-014-1*, Tiger Tales) ME Media LLC.

Harte, Bret. The Outcasts of Poker Flat. 1982. (Short Story Library). (Illus.). 48p. (YA). (gr. 4 up). lib. bdg. 13.95 o.p. (*0-87191-768-8*, Creative Education) Creative Co., The.

—The Outcasts of Poker Flat. 1968. 58p. (YA). (gr. 10 up). pap. 3.60 (*0-87129-547-4*, O27) Dramatic Publishing Co.

—The Outcasts of Poker Flat. 1995. (Jamestown Classics Ser.). (J). pap., stu. ed. 5.99 (*0-89061-052-5*) Jamestown.

Heisler, Jim. Woody, the Adventurous Tumbleweed. 1995. (Illus.). 32p. (J). pap. 6.00 o.p. (*0-8059-3599-1*) Dorrance Publishing Co., Inc.

Henry, Marguerite. Mustang, Wild Spirit of the West. 1992. (Illus.). 224p. (J). (gr. 4-7). pap. 4.99 (*0-689-71601-X*, Aladdin) Simon & Schuster Children's Publishing.

—Mustang, Wild Spirit of the West. 1996. (J). (gr. 3-7). 20.25 (*0-8446-6888-5*) Smith, Peter Pub., Inc.

—San Domingo: The Medicine Hat Stallion. 1989. (J). (ps-3). pap. 3.95 o.p. (*0-02-689415-7*) Checkerboard Pr., Inc.

—San Domingo: The Medicine Hat Stallion. 1992. (Illus.). 224p. (J). (gr. 4-7). reprint ed. pap. 5.99 (*0-689-71631-1*, Aladdin) Simon & Schuster Children's Publishing.

—San Domingo: The Medicine Hat Stallion. 2001. (J). (gr. 4-8). 20.75 (*0-8446-7178-9*) Smith, Peter Pub., Inc.

Henty, G. A. A Tale of the Western Plains: Redskin & Cowboy. 1997. (Illus.). 444p. (YA). (gr. 4 up). reprint ed. pap. 16.95 (*1-890623-00-8*) Lost Classics Bk. Co.

Hergé. Land of Black Gold. Orig. Title: Tintin au Pays de l'Or Noir. (Illus.). 62p. (J). 19.95 (*0-8288-5048-8*); pap. 4.95 o.p. (*0-416-83620-8*) French & European Pubns., Inc.

—Land of Black Gold. 1975. (Adventures of Tintin Ser.). Orig. Title: Tintin au Pays de l'Or Noir. (Illus.). 62p. (J). (gr. 2 up). pap. 9.99 (*0-316-35844-4*, Joy Street Bks.) Little Brown & Co.

—Tintin au Pays de l'Or Noir. 1999. (Tintin Ser.).Tr. of Land of Black Gold. (FRE.). (gr. 4-7). 19.95 (*2-203-00114-3*) Casterman, Editions FRA. *Dist:* Distribooks, Inc.

—Tintin au Pays de l'Or Noir.Tr. of Land of Black Gold. (FRE.). (J). (gr. 7-9). 24.95 (*0-8288-5091-7*) French & European Pubns., Inc.

—Tintin en el Pais del Oro Negro.Tr. of Land of Black Gold. (SPA., Illus.). 62p. (J). 24.95 (*0-8288-4995-1*) French & European Pubns., Inc.

Hermes, Patricia. Westward to Home: Joshua's Oregon Trail Diary, Bk. 1. 2001. (My America Ser.). (J). (gr. 4-8). per. 15.00 (*0-606-19582-3*) Turtleback Bks.

Hite, Sid. Stick & Whittle. 2000. (Illus.). 208p. (J). (gr. 5 up). pap. 16.95 (*0-439-09828-9*) Scholastic, Inc.

Hogan, Ray. Conger's Woman. 1973. (Western Ser.). 188p. (J). o.p. (*0-385-07274-0*) Doubleday Publishing.

Holland, Isabelle. The Journey Home. 1924. (J). o.s.i (*0-688-01576-X*) HarperCollins Children's Bk. Group.

—The Journey Home. 224p. (J). 1993. (gr. 3-7). pap. 2.95 (*0-590-43111-0*, Scholastic Paperbacks); 1990. (gr. 4-7). 13.95 (*0-590-43110-2*) Scholastic, Inc.

Holub, Joan. Cinderdog & the Wicked Stepcat. 2001. (Illus.). 32p. (J). (ps-3). lib. bdg. 14.95 (*0-8075-1178-1*) Whitman, Albert & Co.

Hooff, Sara. Pilgrim, Spirit of the West. 1997. (Illus.). 36p. (Orig.). (J). (gr. 1-8). pap. 12.95 (*0-9659525-0-9*) Hooff Prints Pr.

Hughes, Holly. Hoofbeats of Danger. 1999. (American Girl Collection: Bk. 2). 144p. (YA). (gr. 5 up). 9.95 (*1-56247-814-1*); (Illus.). pap. 5.95 (*1-56247-758-7*) Pleasant Co. Pubns. (American Girl).

—Hoofbeats of Danger. 1999. 12.00 (*0-606-17517-2*) Turtleback Bks.

Hughes, Shirley. Charlie Moon & the Big Bonanza Bust-Up. l.t. ed. 1990. 184p. (J). (gr. 3-7). 14.95 (*0-7451-1151-3*, Macmillan Reference USA) Gale Group.

Hunt, L. J. The Abernathy Boys. 2004. (Abernathy Boys Ser.). 208p. (J). 15.99 (*0-06-440953-8*); (Illus.). lib. bdg. 16.89 (*0-06-029259-8*) HarperCollins Pubs.

Hyde, Dayton O. One Summer in Montana. 1985. 11.95 o.s.i (*0-689-31144-3*, Atheneum) Simon & Schuster Children's Publishing.

Irwin, Ann & Reida, Bernice. Until We Reach the Valley. 1979. (Illus.). 173p. (J). (gr. 4-7). pap. 1.50 o.p. (*0-380-43398-2*, 43398-2, Avon Bks.) Morrow/Avon.

Jackson, Jack. Comanche Moon. 128p. (Orig.). (J). pap. 5.95 o.p. (*0-89620-079-5*) Rip Off Pr., Inc.

James, Will. In the Saddle with Uncle Bill. 2001. (Illus.). xii, 188p. (J). (gr. 4-7). 26.00 (*0-87842-427-X*); pap. 14.00 (*0-87842-428-8*) Mountain Pr. Publishing Co., Inc.

—Look-See with Uncle Bill. 2002. (Illus.). 190p. (J). 26.00 (*0-87842-459-8*); pap. 14.00 (*0-87842-458-X*) Mountain Pr. Publishing Co., Inc.

—Smokey: The Cowhorse. 2000. (Tumbleweed Ser.). (Illus.). (J). (gr. 4-7). xi, 245p. 36.00 (*0-87842-414-8*); 260p. pap. 16.00 (*0-87842-413-X*) Mountain Pr. Publishing Co., Inc.

—Smoky, the Cow Horse. 1997. (J). (gr. 4-7). reprint ed. 37.95 (*1-56849-236-7*) Buccaneer Bks., Inc.

—Smoky, the Cow Horse. 2nd ed. 1993. (Illus.). 324p. (YA). (gr. 7 up). reprint ed. mass mkt. 5.99 (*0-689-71682-6*, Simon Pulse) Simon & Schuster Children's Publishing.

Jan, Calamity. Shadow of Shaniko. 2002. (Ghostowners Ser.: 3). (Illus.). 100p. (Orig.). (J). pap. 10.00 (*0-9721800-2-8*) WildWest Publishing.

Jerman, Jerry. Phantom of Pueblo, No. 3. 1995. (Journeys of Jessie Land Ser.). 132p. (J). pap. 5.99 o.p. (*1-56476-466-4*, 6-3466) Cook Communications Ministries.

Johnson, Annabel & Johnson, Edgar. Golden Touch. 1963. (J). (gr. 7 up). lib. bdg. 12.89 o.p. (*0-06-022856-3*) HarperCollins Pubs.

Johnston, Tony. The Sunsets of the West. 2002. (Illus.). 32p. (J). (gr. k up). 16.99 (*0-399-22659-1*) Putnam Publishing Group, The.

Jones, Katina, et al. Cowdog Caper. 2001. (Little Lucy & Friends Ser.). (Illus.). 24p. (J). (ps-3). 9.99 (*1-57151-701-4*) Playhouse Publishing.

Joyce, Jacqueline. Dust Devil Dan. 1997. (Illus.). 36p. (Orig.). (J). (ps-4). pap. 7.95 (*0-9652211-4-8*, 11129) Bear Path, The.

—Dust Devil Dan. DelMar Communication International Staff, tr. 1997. (SPA., Illus.). 36p. (Orig.). (J). (ps-4). pap. 7.95 (*0-9652211-5-6*, 11130) Bear Path, The.

Kandell, Jonathan. Passage Through El Dorado. 1985. 320p. (J). (gr. 7 up). mass mkt. 5.95 o.p. (*0-380-69959-1*, Avon Bks.) Morrow/Avon.

Karas, G. Brian, illus. Carlita Ropes the Twister. 1999. 27.84 (*0-8172-7256-9*) Raintree Pubs.

Karr, Kathleen. Go West, Young Women!, No. 1. 1996. (Petticoat Party Ser.: Vol. 1). 208p. (gr. 5 up). (J). lib. bdg. 14.89 o.p. (*0-06-027152-3*); (YA). 14.95 o.p. (*0-06-027151-5*) HarperCollins Children's Bk. Group.

—Go West, Young Women! 1997. (Petticoat Party Ser.). 9.60 o.p. (*0-606-11741-5*) Turtleback Bks.

—The Great Turkey Walk, RS. 208p. (J). 2000. (gr. 4-7). pap. 4.95 (*0-374-42798-4*, Sunburst); 1998. (gr. 5-9). 17.00 (*0-374-32773-4*, Farrar, Straus & Giroux (BYR)) Farrar, Straus & Giroux.

—The Great Turkey Walk. unabr. ed. 2000. (YA). (gr. 5 up). pap. 59.00 incl. audio (*0-7887-3631-0*, 41006X4) Recorded Bks., LLC.

—The Great Turkey Walk. l.t. ed. 2001. 216p. (J). 22.95 (*0-7862-3658-2*) Thorndike Pr.

Kay, Verla. Gold Fever. 1999. (Illus.). 32p. (J). (ps-3). 15.99 (*0-399-23027-0*, G. P. Putnam's Sons) Penguin Group (USA) Inc.

—Gold Fever. 2003. (Picture Puffin Ser.). (Illus.). 32p. 6.99 (*0-14-250183-2*, Puffin Bks.) Penguin Putnam Bks. for Young Readers.

—The Orphan Train. 2003. (Illus.). 32p. (J). (ps-3). 15.99 (*0-399-23613-9*) Penguin Group (USA) Inc.

Keller, Charles. Ohm on the Range. 1985. (Illus.). 48p. (J). (gr. 3-7). 4.95 o.p. (*0-13-633546-2*) Prentice Hall PTR.

Kennedy, Richard. The Contests at Cowlick. 1975. (Illus.). 48p. (J). (gr. 1-3). 5.95 o.p. (*0-316-48863-1*) Little Brown & Co.

Kimmel, Eric A. Charlie Drives the Stage. 1989. (Illus.). 32p. (J). (ps-3). lib. bdg. 13.95 o.p. (*0-8234-0738-1*) Holiday Hse., Inc.

King-Smith, Dick. Tumbleweed. unabr. ed. 1993. (J). 18.95 incl. audio (*0-7451-8586-X*, CCA3056, Chivers Children's Audio Bks.) BBC Audiobooks America.

Knowlton, Laurie Lazzaro. Why Cowboys Need a Pardner. 200th ed. 1998. (Illus.). 32p. (J). (gr. k-3). 14.95 (*1-56554-336-X*) Pelican Publishing Co., Inc.

Koertge, Ronald. The Arizona Kid. 1988. (YA). (gr. 9 up). 14.95 o.p. (*0-316-50101-8*, Joy Street Bks.) Little Brown & Co.

Ladd, Justin. Abilene Bk. XI: Hellion. 1989. (J). bds. 2.95 o.s.i (*0-671-68153-2*, Pocket) Simon & Schuster.

Lampman, Evelyn S. Cayuse Courage. 1970. (YA). (gr. 6 up). 5.50 o.p. (*0-15-215539-2*) Harcourt Children's Bks.

Laurance, B. F. Desperate Trail. Laurance, Claire, ed. 1996. 75p. (Orig.). (J). (gr. 3-7). pap. 7.95 (*0-9650660-0-2*) B&C Pubns.

Levine, Ellen. The Journal of Jedediah Barstow, an Emigrant on the Oregon Trail: Overland, 1845. 2002. (My Name Is America Ser.). (Illus.). 192p. (J). (gr. 4-9). 10.95 (*0-439-06310-8*, Scholastic Pr.) Scholastic, Inc.

Levitin, Sonia. Clem's Chances. 2001. (Illus.). 208p. (J). (gr. 2-7). pap. 17.95 (*0-439-29314-6*, Orchard Bks.) Scholastic, Inc.

Levy, Elizabeth. Something Queer in the Wild West. 1997. (Something Queer Ser.: No. 12). (J). (gr. 2-5). 11.10 (*0-606-11859-4*) Turtleback Bks.

Loesch, Joe. The Time Travelers' First Adventure: "The Wild West" with Buffalo Biff. Hutchinson, Cheryl J., ed. l.t. unabr. ed. 1996. (Time Travelers First Adventure - Wild West Vol. 4 Ser.: Vol. 4). (Illus.). 60p. (J). (gr. 1-5). pap. 14.95 incl. audio (*1-887729-14-3*) Toy Box Productions.

Love, D. Anne. Dakota Spring. 1995. (Illus.). 96p. (J). (gr. 4-7). 14.95 o.p. (*0-8234-1189-3*) Holiday Hse., Inc.

—Dakota Spring. 1997. (J). pap. 3.99 (*0-440-91306-3*, Dell Books for Young Readers) Random Hse. Children's Bks.

Loveday, John. Goodbye, Buffalo Sky. 1997. 176p. (J). (gr. 7 up). 16.00 (*0-689-81370-8*, McElderry, Margaret K.) Simon & Schuster Children's Publishing.

Lowell, Susan. Cindy Ellen: A Wild Western Cinderella. 2001. (Illus.). 40p. (J). (ps-3). pap. 6.99 (*0-06-443864-3*, Harper Trophy) HarperCollins Children's Bk. Group.

Lund, Jillian. Way Out West Lives a Coyote Named Frank. (Illus.). 32p. (J). (ps-1). 1997. pap. 5.99 (*0-14-056232-X*, Viking); 1993. 16.99 (*0-525-44982-5*, Dutton Children's Bks.) Penguin Putnam Bks. for Young Readers.

MacLachlan, Patricia. Three Names. 1991. (Charlotte Zolotow Bk.). (Illus.). 32p. (J). (gr. k-4). 14.95 o.p. (*0-06-024035-0*); lib. bdg. 16.89 (*0-06-024036-9*) HarperCollins Children's Bk. Group.

Malcolm, Jahnna N. Ride of Courage, Vol. 2. 1997. (Treasured Horses Ser.: No. 2). (Illus.). (J). (gr. 3-9). mass mkt. 4.50 (*0-590-06865-2*) Scholastic, Inc.

—Spirit of the West. 1997. (Treasured Horses Ser.: No. 1). (Illus.). (J). (gr. 3-7). mass mkt. 4.50 (*0-590-06866-0*) Scholastic, Inc.

—Spirit of the West. 1997. (Treasured Horses Ser.). 10.04 (*0-606-13056-X*) Turtleback Bks.

Mayer, Mercer, et al. Mystery at Big Horn Ranch. 1995. (Little Critter Ser.: No. 6). (Illus.). 72p. (J). (gr. 4-7). pap. 3.99 o.s.i (*0-307-15978-7*, 15978, Golden Bks.) Random Hse. Children's Bks.

McCall, Edith. Message from the Mountains. Nankin, Fran, ed. 1985. (Walker's American History Series for Young People). (Illus.). 122p. (J). (gr. 6-9). 11.95 o.p. (*0-8027-6582-3*) Walker & Co.

McClung, Robert M. Hugh Glass, Mountain Man. 1993. 176p. (YA). (gr. 7 up). pap. 4.95 o.p. (*0-688-04595-2*, Morrow, William & Co.) Morrow/Avon.

McCulley, Johnston. Zorro Rides Again. 1986. (Starfire Ser.). 160p. pap. 2.50 o.p. (*0-553-24671-2*) Bantam Bks.

McCully, Emily Arnold. An Outlaw Thanksgiving. 1998. (Illus.). 40p. (J). (gr. k-3). 16.99 (*0-8037-2197-8*); 15.89 o.s.i (*0-8037-2198-6*) Penguin Putnam Bks. for Young Readers. (Dial Bks. for Young Readers).

McHugh, Elisabet. Wiggie Wins the West. 1991. 160p. (J). (gr. 4-7). pap. 3.25 o.s.i (*0-440-40457-6*) Dell Publishing.

McSherry, Frank D., Jr., et al, eds. Western Ghosts. 1990. (American Ghosts Ser.). 224p. (Orig.). (J). pap. 9.95 (*1-55853-069-X*) Rutledge Hill Pr.

Mercati, Cynthia. Wagons Ho! A Diary of the Oregon Trail. 2000. (Cover-to-Cover Bks.). (Illus.). 56p. (J). 15.95 (*0-7807-9011-1*); pap. (*0-7891-5039-5*) Perfection Learning Corp.

Mitchell, Marianne. Joe Cinders, ERS. 2002. (Illus.). 48p. (J). (ps-3). 16.95 (*0-8050-6529-6*, Holt, Henry & Co. Bks. For Young Readers) Holt, Henry & Co.

Moeri, Louise. Save Queen of Sheba. 112p. (J). 1990. pap. 3.50 (*0-380-71154-0*); 1982. pap. 2.95 (*0-380-58529-4*) Morrow/Avon. (Avon Bks.).

—Save Queen of Sheba. (J). 1994. 128p. (gr. 3-7). pap. 4.99 (*0-14-037148-6*, Puffin Bks.); 1981. 12p. (gr. 4-7). 14.95 o.p. (*0-525-33202-2*, Dutton Children's Bks.) Penguin Putnam Bks. for Young Readers.

Montana Showdown. 1999. (SmartReader Ser.). (J). Level 1. pap. text, tchr. ed. 19.95 incl. audio (*0-7887-0768-X*, 79349T3); Level 2. pap. text, tchr. ed. 19.95 incl. audio (*0-7887-0543-1*, 79330T3) Recorded Bks., LLC.

Mooser, Stephen. Orphan Jeb at the Massacree. 1984. (Borzoi Bks.). (Illus.). 96p. (J). (gr. 3-8). 9.95 o.p. (*0-394-85731-3*); lib. bdg. 9.99 o.p. (*0-394-95731-8*) Random Hse. Children's Bks. (Knopf Bks. for Young Readers).

Morey, Walt. Canyon Winter. 1994. 208p. (YA). (gr. 5-9). pap. 5.99 (*0-14-036856-6*, Puffin Bks.) Penguin Putnam Bks. for Young Readers.

Morris, Neil. Home on the Prairie. 1989. (Tales of the Old West Ser.). (Illus.). 32p. (J). (gr. 4-8). lib. bdg. 9.95 o.p. (*1-85435-165-6*) Cavendish, Marshall Corp.

—Longhorn on the Move. 1989. (Tales of the Old West Ser.). (Illus.). 32p. (J). (gr. 3-8). lib. bdg. 9.95 o.p. (*1-85435-166-4*) Cavendish, Marshall Corp.

—On the Trapping Trail. 1989. (Tales of the Old West Ser.). (Illus.). 32p. (J). (gr. 3-8). lib. bdg. 9.95 o.p. (*1-85435-164-8*) Cavendish, Marshall Corp.

—Tales of the American West. 1989. (J). 5.99 o.s.i (*0-517-68024-6*) Random Hse. Value Publishing.

—Wagon Wheels Roll West. 1989. (Tales of the Old West Ser.). (Illus.). 32p. (J). (gr. 3-8). lib. bdg. 9.95 o.p. (*1-85435-167-2*) Cavendish, Marshall Corp.

Morrow, Honore. On to Oregon! 1991. (Illus.). 240p. (J). (gr. 5-9). reprint ed. pap. 6.99 (*0-688-10494-0*, Harper Trophy) HarperCollins Children's Bk. Group.

Moss, Marissa. Amelia Hits the Road. 1999. (Amelia Ser.). (Illus.). 40p. (YA). (gr. 3 up). 12.95 (*1-56247-791-9*); pap. 5.95 (*1-56247-790-0*) Pleasant Co. Pubns. (American Girl).

—Amelia Hits the Road. 1997. (Amelia Ser.). (Illus.). 40p. (J). (gr. 3-5). 14.95 o.p. (*1-883672-57-0*) Tricycle Pr.

—Amelia Hits the Road. 1999. (Amelia Ser.). (J). (gr. 3-5). 12.10 (*0-606-19867-9*) Turtleback Bks.

—True Heart. 1999. (Illus.). 32p. (J). (gr. k-4). 16.00 (*0-15-201344-X*, Silver Whistle) Harcourt Children's Bks.

Mulford, Clarence E. The Coming of Cassidy. 1992. (Hopalong Cassidy Ser.: No. 1). (Illus.). 288p. mass mkt. 5.99 (*0-8125-2291-5*, Tor Bks.) Doherty, Tom Assocs., LLC.

Myer, John. Silverlock, Bk. 5. 1984. (Illus.). 544p. (Orig.). (J). (gr. 3-5). mass mkt. 6.99 o.s.i (*0-441-76674-9*) Ace Bks.

Myers, Bill. My Life as a Cowboy Cowpie. 2001. (Incredible Worlds of Wally McDoogle Ser.: No. 19). 128p. (J). (gr. 3-7). 5.99 (*0-8499-5990-X*) Nelson, Tommy.

Myers, Walter Dean. The Journal of Joshua Loper: A Black Cowboy: The Chisholm Trail, 1871. 1999. (My Name Is America Ser.). (Illus.). 158p. (J). (gr. 4-8). pap. 10.95 (*0-590-02691-7*) Scholastic, Inc.

—The Righteous Revenge of Artemis Bonner. (Trophy Bk.). 144p. (J). (gr. 5 up). 1994. (Illus.). pap. 5.99 (*0-06-440462-5*, Harper Trophy); 1992. 14.95 o.p. (*0-06-020844-9*); 1992. lib. bdg. 14.89 o.p. (*0-06-020846-5*) HarperCollins Children's Bk. Group.

—The Righteous Revenge of Artemis Bonner. 1994. (YA). 11.00 (*0-606-06698-5*) Turtleback Bks.

Nixon, Joan Lowery. Caught in the Act. 160p. (YA). 1996. (Orphan Train Adventures Ser.: Vol. 2). (gr. 4-7). mass mkt. 4.99 (*0-440-22678-3*, Dell Books for Young Readers); 1988. (Orphan Train Quartet Ser.: Bk. 2). (gr. 9 up). 14.95 o.s.i (*0-553-05443-0*, Starfire) Random Hse. Children's Bks.

—Caught in the Act. 1996. (Orphan Train Quartet Ser.). (J). 10.55 (*0-606-04184-2*) Turtleback Bks.

—A Deadly Promise. 1992. 176p. (J). (gr. 4-7). 16.00 o.s.i (*0-553-08054-7*) Bantam Bks.

—A Deadly Promise. 1991. (J). o.s.i (*0-553-53089-5*, Dell Books for Young Readers) Random Hse. Children's Bks.

Noble, Trinka Hakes. Meanwhile Back at the Ranch. 1992. (Reading Rainbow Bks.). (Illus.). 32p. (J). (ps-3). pap. 6.99 (*0-14-054564-6*, Puffin Bks.) Penguin Putnam Bks. for Young Readers.

Nolte, Elleta. Westward Ha! 1974. 181p. (J). 5.95 o.p. (*0-88289-071-9*) Pelican Publishing Co., Inc.

Norton, Andre. Stand to Horse. 1968. (J). (gr. 7 up). reprint ed. pap. 0.75 o.p. (*0-15-684890-2*, Voyager Bks./Libros Viajeros) Harcourt Children's Bks.

Oliphant, Pat, illus. Peter Becomes a Trail Man: The Story of a Boy's Journey on the Santa Fe Trail. 2002. 191p. (J). 12.95 (*0-8263-2895-4*) Univ. of New Mexico Pr.

Olsen, Theodore V. Mission to the West. 1973. (Western Ser.). 181p. (J). o.p. (*0-385-06021-1*) Doubleday Publishing.

—Starbuck's Brand. 1973. (Western Ser.). 185p. (J). o.p. (*0-385-07012-8*) Doubleday Publishing.

—Starbuck's Brand. l.t. ed. 1992. (Nightingale Ser.). 311p. pap. 14.95 o.p. (*0-8161-5594-1*, Macmillan Reference USA) Gale Group.

Osborne, Mary Pope. Ghost Town at Sundown. unabr. ed. 2001. (Magic Tree House Ser. : No. 10). 73p. (J). (gr. k-4). pap. 17.00 incl. audio (*0-8072-0535-4*, Listening Library) Random Hse. Audio Publishing Group.

—Ghost Town at Sundown. 1997. (Magic Tree House Ser.: No. 10). (Illus.). 96p. (gr. k-3). pap. 3.99 (*0-679-88339-8*);No. 10. lib. bdg. 11.99 (*0-679-98339-2*) Random Hse. Children's Bks. (Random Hse. Bks. for Young Readers).

—Ghost Town at Sundown. 1997. (Magic Tree House Ser.: No. 10). (Illus.). (J). (gr. k-3). 10.04 (*0-606-12709-7*) Turtleback Bks.

Packard, Edward. Greed, Guns & Gold. 1996. (Choose Your Own Adventure Ser.: No. 170). 128p. (J). (gr. 4-8). pap. 3.50 o.s.i (*0-553-56628-8*) Bantam Bks.

—Greed, Guns & Gold. 1996. (Choose Your Own Adventure Ser.: No. 170). (J). (gr. 4-8). 8.60 o.p. (*0-606-09362-1*) Turtleback Bks.

Pamplin, Laurel J. Masquerade on the Western Trail. Roberts, M., ed. 1991. (Illus.). 112p. (J). (gr. 6-7). 13.95 (*0-89015-755-3*) Eakin Pr.

Patten, Lewis B. The Cheyenne Pool. 1972. (Western Ser.). 160p. (J). o.p. (*0-385-02262-X*) Doubleday Publishing.

Paulsen, Gary. Call Me Francis Tucket. 1995. (Tucket Adventures Ser.: Vol. 2). 112p. (gr. 4-7). text 15.95 (*0-385-32116-3*, Delacorte Pr.) Dell Publishing.

—Call Me Francis Tucket. 1996. 10.55 (*0-606-10766-5*) Turtleback Bks.

—Cowpokes & Desperadoes. 1993. (Culpepper Adventures Ser.). 80p. (J). (gr. 3-5). pap. 3.50 o.s.i (*0-440-40902-0*) Dell Publishing.

—Cowpokes & Desperadoes. 1994. (Culpepper Adventures Ser.). (J). (gr. 3-5). 9.65 (*0-606-05793-5*) Turtleback Bks.

—Mr. Tucket. 1994. 176p. text 15.95 (*0-385-31169-9*, Delacorte Pr.) Dell Publishing.

—Mr. Tucket. 2000. (Illus.). 192p. (gr. 5-7). mass mkt. 2.99 o.s.i (*0-375-80680-6*, Random Hse. Bks. for Young Readers); 1996. (J). pap. 5.99 (*0-440-91097-8*, Dell Books for Young Readers); 1995. (Tucket Adventures Ser.: Vol. 1). 192p. (gr. 5 up). pap. text 4.99 (*0-440-41133-5*, Yearling); 1995. (J). pap. 5.99 (*0-440-91053-6*, Dell Books for Young Readers) Random Hse. Children's Bks.

—Mr. Tucket, unabr. ed. 1994. (J). (gr. 6). audio 27.00 (*0-7887-0010-3*, 94209E7) Recorded Bks., LLC.

—Mr. Tucket. 1995. 10.55 (*0-606-07895-9*) Turtleback Bks.

—Tucket's Gold. 1999. (Tucket Adventures Ser.: Vol. 4). 112p. (gr. 4-7). text 15.95 (*0-385-32501-0*) Bantam Bks.

—Tucket's Gold. 2001. (Tucket Adventures Ser.). 112p. (gr. 4-7). pap. text 4.50 (*0-440-41376-1*, Dell Books for Young Readers) Random Hse. Children's Bks.

—Tucket's Gold. 2001. (J). 10.55 (*0-606-20958-1*) Turtleback Bks.

—Tucket's Travels: Francis Tucket's Adventures in the West, 1847-1849, Bks. 1-5. 2003. 560p. (YA). pap. text 6.99 (*0-440-41967-0*, Yearling) Dell Bks. for Young Readers CAN. *Dist:* Random Hse. of Canada, Ltd.

Peart, Jane. Ivy & Allison. 2nd abr. ed. 2000. (Orphan Train West for Young Adults Ser.). (Illus.). 160p. (J). (gr. 5-9). pap. 5.99 o.s.i (*0-8007-5714-9*) Revell, Fleming H. Co.

—Kit. 2nd abr. ed. 2000. (Orphan Train West for Young Adults Ser.). (Illus.). 144p. (J). (gr. 5-9). pap. 5.99 o.s.i (*0-8007-5715-7*) Revell, Fleming H. Co.

—Laurel. 2nd abr. ed. 2000. (Orphan Train West for Young Adults Ser.). (Illus.). 160p. (J). (gr. 5-9). pap. 5.99 o.p. (*0-8007-5713-0*) Revell, Fleming H. Co.

—Orphan Train West Series for Young Readers, 4 vols., Set. abr. ed. 2000. (Illus.). (YA). (gr. 5-9). pap. 19.96 o.p. (*0-8007-6442-0*) Revell, Fleming H. Co.

Peck, Richard. Fair Weather. 2001. (Illus.). 160p. (J). (gr. 4-8). 16.99 (*0-8037-2516-7*, Dial Bks. for Young Readers) Penguin Putnam Bks. for Young Readers.

Peck, Robert Newton. Soup in the Saddle. 1987. 128p. (J). (gr. k-6). pap. 3.25 o.s.i (*0-440-40032-5*, Yearling) Random Hse. Children's Bks.

Piepmeier, Charlotte. Lucy's Journey to the Wild West. 2003. (Illus.). 40p. (J). (gr. k-7). 19.95 (*1-929115-07-5*) Azro Pr., Inc.

Pinkwater, Daniel M. Fat Camp Commandos Go West. 2002. (Illus.). 96p. (J). (gr. 3-8). pap. 14.95 (*0-439-29772-9*, Scholastic Pr.) Scholastic, Inc.

Plowhead, Ruth Gipson. Lucretia Ann in the Golden West. 2001. (Classic Ser.). (Illus.). 246p. (J). (gr. 4-7). pap. 17.95 (*0-87004-409-5*) Caxton Pr.

Postgate, Daniel. Wild West Willy. 2000. (Illus.). 32p. pap. 8.95 (*0-00-664671-9*); (J). 19.95 (*0-00-198317-2*) HarperCollins Pubs. Ltd. GBR. *Dist:* Trafalgar Square.

Quackenbush, Robert. Henry Goes West. 1993. (Illus.). 48p. (J). (gr. 1 up). lib. bdg. 18.60 o.p. (*0-8368-0996-3*) Stevens, Gareth Inc.

Raphael, Elaine & Bolognese, Don. Sam Baker, Gone West. 1977. (Illus.). (J). (gr. k-3). 6.95 o.p. (*0-670-61651-6*) Viking Penguin.

Ratz de Tagyos, Paul. Showdown at Lonesome Pellet. 1994. (Illus.). 32p. (J). 14.95 o.p. (*0-395-67645-2*, Clarion Bks.) Houghton Mifflin Co. Trade & Reference Div.

Reaver, Chap. A Little Bit Dead. 1992. 240p. (YA). (gr. 6 up). 15.00 (*0-385-30801-9*, Delacorte Pr.) Dell Publishing.

Reese, Bob. Calico Jack & the Desert Critters. 1983. (Critterland Readers Ser.). (Illus.). 32p. (J). (ps-2). pap. 3.95 o.p. (*0-516-42321-5*); lib. bdg. 11.93 o.p. (*0-516-02321-7*) Scholastic Library Publishing. (Children's Pr.).

Remkiewicz, Frank. The Bone Stranger. 1994. (Illus.). (J). 15.00 o.p. (*0-688-12041-5*) HarperCollins Children's Bk. Group.

—Bone Stranger. 1994. (Illus.). 32p. (J). lib. bdg. 14.93 o.p. (*0-688-12042-3*) HarperCollins Children's Bk. Group.

Richard, Adrienne. Pistol. 1989. 256p. (YA). 14.95 o.s.i (*0-316-74324-0*, Joy Street Bks.); 1969. (J). (gr. 7 up). 7.95 o.p. (*0-316-74320-8*) Little Brown & Co.

Rizzo, Kay D. Wagon Train West. 2003. 96p. (J). (*0-8163-1986-3*) Pacific Pr. Publishing Assn.

Robinet, Harriette Gillem. Twelve Travelers, Twenty Horses. 2003. (Illus.). 208p. (J). 16.95 (*0-689-84561-8*, Atheneum) Simon & Schuster Children's Publishing.

Rogers, Lisa Waller. Get along Little Dogies: The Chisholm Trail Diary of Hallie Lou Wells. 2001. (Lone Star Journals: Vol. 1). (Illus.). 174p. (J). (gr. 4-7). 14.50 (*0-89672-446-8*) Texas Tech Univ. Pr.

—Get along, Little Dogies: The Chisholm Trail Diary of Hallie Lou Wells, South Texas 1878. 2001. (Lone Star Journals). (Illus.). 174p. (J). (gr. 4-7). 8.95 (*0-89672-448-4*) Texas Tech Univ. Pr.

Ross, Harriet, compiled by. Exciting Western Stories. 2001. (Illus.). 160p. (J). (gr. 4-7). lib. bdg. 12.95 (*0-87460-312-9*) Lion Bks.

Rounds, Glen. Mr. Yowder & the Windwagon. 1983. 48p. (J). (gr. 3-6). 8.95 o.p. (*0-8234-0499-4*) Holiday Hse., Inc.

Rowe, Gordon J. Showdown at Pecos. 2000. (Illus.). 32p. (J). (ps-3). 11.95 o.p. (*1-57197-192-0*) Pentland Pr., Inc.

Rubel, Nicole. Cyrano the Bear. 1995. (Illus.). 32p. (J). 14.99 o.s.i (*0-8037-1444-0*); 14.89 o.p. (*0-8037-1445-9*) Penguin Putnam Bks. for Young Readers. (Dial Bks. for Young Readers).

Rylant, Cynthia. Henry & Mudge & the Tumbling Trip. 2002. (Henry & Mudge Ser.). (J). (gr. k-3). 14.00 (*0-689-81180-2*, Simon & Schuster Children's Publishing) Simon & Schuster Children's Publishing.

Saban, Vera. Test of the Tenderfoot. 1989. (Illus.). 147p. (YA). (gr. 5-8). 6.95 (*0-914565-35-4*, Timbertrails) Capstan Pubns.

Saller, Carol. Pug, Slug, & Doug the Thug. 1994. (Illus.). (J). (ps-3). lib. bdg. 14.95 (*0-87614-803-8*, Carolrhoda Bks.) Lerner Publishing Group.

Sandin, Joan. The Long Way Westward. 1992. (I Can Read Bks.). (J). (gr. 2-4). 8.95 o.p. (*0-606-02304-6*) Turtleback Bks.

Sargent, Dave & Sargent, Pat. Ginger (Lilac Roan) Be Likeable. 2003. (Saddle Up Ser.: Vol. 27). (Illus.). 42p. (J). lib. bdg. 22.60 (*1-56763-811-2*); mass mkt. 6.95 (*1-56763-812-0*) Ozark Publishing.

Sauerwein, Leigh. The Way Home, RS. 1994. 96p. (J). (gr. 7 up). 15.00 o.p. (*0-374-38247-6*, Farrar, Straus & Giroux (BYR)) Farrar, Straus & Giroux.

Savage, Jeff. Gunfighters of the Wild West. 1995. (Trailblazers of the Wild West Ser.). (Illus.). 48p. (YA). (gr. 4-10). lib. bdg. 16.95 (*0-89490-600-3*) Enslow Pubs., Inc.

Schaefer, Jack. Mavericks, 001. 1967. (Illus.). (J). (gr. 5-8). 6.95 o.p. (*0-395-07089-9*) Houghton Mifflin Co.

Schnetzler, Pattie L. Fast 'n Snappy. Manning, Jane K., tr. & illus. by. 2004. (Carolrhoda Picture Books Ser.). (J). lib. bdg. 15.95 (*1-57505-539-2*, Carolrhoda Bks.) Lerner Publishing Group.

—Widdermaker. 2002. (Illus.). 32p. (J). (gr. k-3). lib. bdg. 15.95 (*0-87614-647-7*, Carolrhoda Bks.) Lerner Publishing Group.

Scieszka, Jon. The Good, the Bad & the Goofy. 1992. (Time Warp Trio Ser.). (Illus.). 80p. (J). (gr. 4-7). 14.99 (*0-670-84380-6*, Viking Children's Bks.) Penguin Putnam Bks. for Young Readers.

—The Good, the Bad & the Goofy. 1993. (Time Warp Trio Ser.). (J). 10.14 (*0-606-05847-8*) Turtleback Bks.

—The Good, the Bad, & the Goofy. 2004. (Time Warp Trio Ser.). (Illus.). 80p. pap. 4.99 (*0-14-240046-7*, Puffin Bks.) Penguin Putnam Bks. for Young Readers.

—The Good, the Bad & the Goofy. 1993. (Time Warp Trio Ser.). (Illus.). 80p. (J). (gr. 4-7). reprint ed. pap. 4.99 (*0-14-036170-7*) Penguin Putnam Bks. for Young Readers.

—Good, the Bad, & the Goofy Twt Promo. 2003. (Time Warp Trio Ser.). (Illus.). 76p. pap. 2.66 (*0-14-250132-8*, Puffin Bks.) Penguin Putnam Bks. for Young Readers.

Scott, Bradford. Rider of the Mesquite Trail. 1969. 126 p. (J). (*0-450-00311-6*) New English Library, Ltd.

Scott, J. C. High Ransom: The Story of a Young Man's Struggle for Redemption. 1995. 326p. (Orig.). (YA). (gr. 6-12). pap. 6.95 o.s.i (*1-885591-59-4*) Morris Publishing.

Sewall, Marcia. Riding That Strawberry Roan. 1985. (Illus.). 32p. (J). (ps-2). 9.95 o.p. (*0-670-80623-4*, Viking Children's Bks.) Penguin Putnam Bks. for Young Readers.

Sharmat, Marjorie Weinman. Gila Monsters Meet You at the Airport. 1980. (Illus.). 32p. (J). (ps-3). 16.95 (*0-02-782450-0*, Simon & Schuster Children's Publishing) Simon & Schuster Children's Publishing.

—Gila Monsters Meet You at the Airport. 1990. (Reading Rainbow Bks.). (Illus.). 32p. (J). (ps-3). pap. 5.99 (*0-689-71383-5*, Aladdin) Simon & Schuster Children's Publishing.

—Gila Monsters Meet You at the Airport. 1990. 11.10 (*0-606-13996-6*) Turtleback Bks.

Shub, Elizabeth. The White Stallion. 1982. (Greenwillow Read-Alone Bks.). (Illus.). 56p. (J). (gr. 1-3). 16.00 o.s.i (*0-688-01210-8*); lib. bdg. 15.93 o.p. (*0-688-01211-6*) HarperCollins Children's Bk. Group. (Greenwillow Bks.).

Smith, George S. The Christmas Eve Cattle Drive. 1991. (Illus.). 32p. (J). (gr. 3-4). pap. 3.95 (*0-89015-820-7*) Eakin Pr.

Smith, Janice Lee. Jess & the Stinky Cowboys. 2004. (Dial Easy-To-Read Ser.). (Illus.). 48p. (J). 14.99 (*0-8037-2641-4*, Dial Bks. for Young Readers) Penguin Putnam Bks. for Young Readers.

Smith, Roland. The Captain's Dog: My Journey with the Lewis & Clark Tribe. (Great Episodes Ser.). 296p. 2000. (Illus.). (J). (gr. 4-7). pap. 6.00 (*0-15-202696-7*, Harcourt Paperbacks); 1999. (YA). (gr. 5-9). 17.00 (*0-15-201989-8*, Gulliver Bks.) Harcourt Children's Bks.

—The Captain's Dog: My Journey with the Lewis & Clark Tribe. 2000. (J). 12.05 (*0-606-19000-7*) Turtleback Bks.

Sonberg, Lynn. Wild Horse Country. 1984. (Choose Your Own Adventure Ser.: No. 17). 64p. (J). (gr. 2-4). pap. 2.25 o.s.i (*0-553-15489-3*, Skylark) Random Hse. Children's Bks.

Sperry, Armstrong. Wagons Westward: The Old Trail to Santa Fe. 2000. (Illus.). 208p. (YA). pap. 14.95 (*1-56792-128-0*) Godine, David R. Pub.

Spooner, Michael. Daniel's Walk. 2004. (J). pap. 6.95 (*0-8050-7543-7*); ERS. 2001. (Illus.). 224p. (YA). (gr. 7 up). 16.95 (*0-8050-6750-7*) Holt, Henry & Co. (Holt, Henry & Co. Bks. For Young Readers).

Stahl, Hilda. Sadie Rose Adventure Series, Vols. 1-4. 1991. 512p. (J). (gr. 4-7). 19.96 o.p. (*0-89107-635-2*) Crossway Bks.

—Sadie Rose & the Outlaw Rustlers. 1989. (Sadie Rose Adventure Ser.: No. 3). 128p. (J). (gr. 4-7). pap. 4.99 o.p. (*0-89107-528-3*) Crossway Bks.

Stanley, Diane. Saving Sweetness. 2002. (Illus.). 13.19 (*1-4046-0940-7*) Book Wholesalers, Inc.

—Saving Sweetness. (Illus.). 32p. 2001. pap. 5.99 (*0-698-11767-0*, Puffin Bks.); 1996. (J). 16.99 (*0-399-22645-1*, G. P. Putnam's Sons) Penguin Putnam Bks. for Young Readers.

Steber, Rick. Pacific Coast. 1987. (Tales of the Wild West Ser.: Vol. 2). (Illus.). 60p. (J). pap. 4.95 (*0-945134-02-9*); lib. bdg. 14.95 (*0-945134-80-0*) Bonanza Publishing.

Steig, Jeanne. Tales from Gizzards Grill. 2004. (J). (*0-06-000959-4*); lib. bdg. (*0-06-000960-8*) HarperCollins Children's Bk. Group. (Cotler, Joanna Bks.).

Stern, Mark. It's a Dog's Life. 1978. (Hank the Cowdog Ser.: No. 3). (Illus.). (J). (gr. 2-5). 1.79 o.p. (*0-689-30643-1*, Atheneum) Simon & Schuster Children's Publishing.

Stewart, Molly Mia. The Twins & the Wild West. 1990. (Sweet Valley Kids Ser.: No. 10). (J). (gr. 1-3). 8.70 o.p. (*0-606-04568-6*) Turtleback Bks.

Stine, Megan & Stine, H. William. Young Indiana Jones & the Lost Gold of Durango. 1993. (Young Indiana Jones Ser.: No. 10). 132p. (Orig.). (J). (gr. 4-6). pap. 3.50 o.s.i (*0-679-84926-2*, Random Hse. Bks. for Young Readers) Random Hse. Children's Bks.

Striker, Fran. The Lone Ranger. 1980. (J). lib. bdg. 9.95 o.p. (*0-8398-2676-1*, Macmillan Reference USA) Gale Group.

Swarthout, Glendon F. The Shootist. 1975. 192p. 6.95 o.p. (*0-385-06099-8*) Doubleday Publishing.

Swarthout, Glendon F. & Swarthout, Kathryn. Whichaway. 1966. (Illus.). (J). (gr. 7 up). lib. bdg. 5.39 o.p. (*0-394-91822-3*, Random Hse. Bks. for Young Readers) Random Hse. Children's Bks.

Swobud, I. K. The Battle of the Buzz: Swarm Warning. 1997. (Masked Rider Ser.: No. 2). 96p. (J). (gr. 3-6). mass mkt. 3.99 o.s.i (*1-57297-237-8*) Boulevard Bks.

Teague, Mark. How I Spent My Summer Vacation. 1995. (Illus.). 32p. (J). 16.00 o.s.i (*0-517-59998-8*); 17.99 o.s.i (*0-517-59999-6*) Random Hse. Children's Bks. (Random Hse. Bks. for Young Readers).

Thomas, Rosie. Cowgirl Rosie & Her Five Baby Bison. 2001. (Illus.). 24p. (J). (ps-3). 12.95 (*0-316-64712-8*) Little Brown & Co.

Trixi. It's a Dog's Life. 1995. (Hank the Cowdog Ser.: No. 3). (Illus.). 120p. (Orig.). (J). (gr. 2-5). pap. 15.00 (*0-937953-77-6*) Tiptoe Literary Service.

Vaccaro Associates Staff, illus. Disney's Cowboy Mickey's Pop-Up Book of Games: 4 Rootin' Tootin' Wild West Games. 1994. (J). (ps-3). 11.95 o.p. (*1-56282-510-0*) Disney Pr.

Van Leeuwen, Jean. Going West. 1997. (Picture Puffin Bks.). (Illus.). 48p. (J). (gr. k-3). pap. 5.99 (*0-14-056096-3*) Penguin Putnam Bks. for Young Readers.

Van Steenwyk, Elizabeth. My Name Is York. (Illus.). 32p. 2000. (ps-3). pap. 7.95 (*0-87358-758-8*); 1997. (J). (gr. 1-3). lib. bdg. 14.95 (*0-87358-650-6*) Northland Publishing. (Rising Moon Bks. for Young Readers).

Vande Velde, Vivian. Ghost of a Hanged Man. 1998. (Accelerated Reader Bks.). 95p. (J). (gr. 3-7). 14.95 (*0-7614-5015-7*, Cavendish Children's Bks.) Cavendish, Marshall Corp.

Velde, Vivian Vande. Ghost of a Hanged Man. 2003. (YA). pap. 5.95 (*0-7614-5154-4*, Cavendish Children's Bks.) Cavendish, Marshall Corp.

Vernam, Glenn R. Redman in White Moccasins. 1973. (Western Ser.). 181p. (J). o.p. (*0-385-07448-4*) Doubleday Publishing.

—The Talking Rifle. 1973. (Western Ser.). 184p. (J). o.p. (*0-385-08098-0*) Doubleday Publishing.

Voss, George L. The Man Who Believed in the Code of the West. 1975. 6.95 o.p. (*0-312-51135-3*) St. Martin's Pr.

Waddell, Martin. Little Obie & the Flood. (J). (gr. 3-6). 1996. bds. 4.99 o.p. (*1-56402-857-7*); 1992. (Illus.). 80p. 13.95 o.p. (*1-56402-106-8*) Candlewick Pr.

—Little Obie & the Flood. 1996. 10.19 o.p. (*0-606-09562-4*) Turtleback Bks.

Wallace, Bill. Buffalo Gal. 1992. 192p. (J). (gr. 7 up). tchr. ed. 15.95 (*0-8234-0943-0*) Holiday Hse., Inc.

—Buffalo Gal. MacDonald, Patricia, ed. 1993. 192p. (J). (gr. 4-7). reprint ed. pap. 3.99 (*0-671-79899-5*, Aladdin) Simon & Schuster Children's Publishing.

—Buffalo Gal. 1992. (J). 10.04 (*0-606-05175-9*) Turtleback Bks.

Watson, Esther Pearl. Trouble at Sugar-Dip Well. 2002. (Illus.). 32p. (J). (ps-3). lib. bdg. 15.00 (*0-618-11863-2*) Houghton Mifflin Co.

Weidt, Maryann N. Wild Bill Hickok. (Illus.). (J). 1992. 11.00 o.p. (*0-688-10089-9*); 1924. lib. bdg. o.s.i (*0-688-10090-2*) HarperCollins Children's Bk. Group.

Weinberg, Larry. The Legend of the Lone Ranger Storybook. 1981. (Movie Storybooks Ser.). (Illus.). (J). (gr. 4-7). 6.99 o.s.i (*0-394-94683-9*, Random Hse. Bks. for Young Readers) Random Hse. Children's Bks.

Weinberg, Larry, adapted by. The Legend of the Lone Ranger Storybook. 1981. (Movie Storybooks Ser.). (Illus.). (J). (gr. 4-7). 5.95 o.p. (*0-394-84683-4*, Random Hse. Bks. for Young Readers) Random Hse. Children's Bks.

West, Colin. The Best of West. 1992. (Illus.). 192p. (J). (gr. 5-8). 22.95 o.p. (*0-09-173587-4*) Hutchinson GBR. *Dist:* Trafalgar Square.

Wiggins, VeraLee. Wagons West. 1995. (Young Reader's Christian Library). (Illus.). 224p. (J). (gr. 3-7). pap. text 1.39 o.p. (*1-55748-675-1*) Barbour Publishing, Inc.

The Wild, Wild West: Search & Color. gif. ed. 1990. pap. o.s.i (*0-679-80380-7*, Random Hse. Bks. for Young Readers) Random Hse. Children's Bks.

Williams, Mari. Revolt in the Valley. 1992. (YA). pap. 40.00 (*0-86383-778-6*) Gomer Pr. GBR. *Dist:* State Mutual Bk. & Periodical Service, Ltd.

Williams, Vera B. Stringbean's Trip to the Shining Sea. (Illus.). 48p. (J). (ps-3). 1999. pap. 6.99 (*0-688-16701-2*, Harper Trophy); 1988. 17.89 (*0-688-07162-7*, Greenwillow Bks.); 1988. 16.99 (*0-688-07161-9*, Greenwillow Bks.) HarperCollins Children's Bk. Group.

—Stringbean's Trip to the Shining Sea. 1990. (J). mass mkt. 3.95 o.p. (*0-590-42906-X*); 48p. mass mkt. 5.99 (*0-590-44851-X*) Scholastic, Inc.

—Stringbean's Trip to the Shining Sea. 1999. 11.10 (*0-606-16744-7*); 1988. (J). 11.19 o.p. (*0-606-02682-7*) Turtleback Bks.

Wisler, G. Clifton. Mustang Flats. 1999. (Illus.). 128p. (YA). (gr. 4-7). pap. 5.99 (*0-14-130410-3*, Puffin Bks.) Penguin Putnam Bks. for Young Readers.

—Mustang Flats. 1999. 12.04 (*0-606-16769-2*) Turtleback Bks.

Wu, William F. Hong on the Range. 1989. (Millennium Science Fiction Ser.). (Illus.). 224p. (YA). (gr. 7 up). 17.95 o.p. (*0-8027-6862-8*) Walker & Co.

Yep, Laurence. The Traitor. 2003. (Golden Mountain Chronicles Ser.). 320p. (J). 16.99 (*0-06-027522-7*); (Illus.). lib. bdg. 17.89 (*0-06-027523-5*) HarperCollins Children's Bk. Group.

Yorinks, Arthur. Whitefish Will Rides Again! 1994. (Michael di Capua Bks.). (Illus.). 32p. (J). (gr. 1 up). lib. bdg. 14.89 o.s.i (*0-06-205038-9*) HarperCollins Children's Bk. Group.

—Whitefish Will Rides Again! 1994. (Illus.). 32p. (J). (ps-3). 15.00 o.p. (*0-06-205037-0*) HarperCollins Pubs.

—Whitefish Will Rides Again! 1996. 11.15 o.p. (*0-606-10973-0*) Turtleback Bks.

WEST INDIES—FICTION

Berry, James R. The Future-Telling Lady: And Other Stories. 1993. (Willa Perlman Bks.). 144p. (YA). (gr. 5 up). 14.00 o.p. (*0-06-021434-1*); lib. bdg. 13.89 o.p. (*0-06-021435-X*) HarperCollins Children's Bk. Group.

Coatsworth, Elizabeth. Lonely Maria. 1962. (Illus.). (J). (gr. k-3). lib. bdg. 5.39 o.p. (*0-394-91358-2*, Pantheon) Knopf Publishing Group.

George, Jean Craighead. The Wentletrap Trap. 1978. (Illus.). (J). (ps-3). lib. bdg. 7.95 o.p. (*0-525-42310-9*, Dutton) Dutton/Plume.

Gershator, David & Gershator, Phillis. Palampam Day. 1997. (Accelerated Reader Bks.). (Illus.). 32p. (J). (gr. k-3). 15.95 (*0-7614-5002-5*, Benchmark Bks.) Cavendish, Marshall Corp.

Gershator, Phillis. Tiny & Bigman. 1999. (Accelerated Reader Bks.). (Illus.). 32p. (J). (gr. k-3). 15.95 (*0-7614-5044-0*, Cavendish Children's Bks.) Cavendish, Marshall Corp.

Isadora, Rachel. Caribbean Dream. 1998. (Illus.). 32p. (J). (ps-3). 15.99 o.p. (*0-399-23230-3*) Penguin Group (USA) Inc.

Norton, Andre. Sea Siege. 1957. (J). (gr. 5-8). 5.50 o.p. (*0-15-271738-2*) Harcourt Children's Bks.

Rahaman, Vashanti. O Christmas Tree. 2003. (Illus.). 32p. (J). (ps-3). 14.95 (*1-56397-237-9*) Boyds Mills Pr.

Scott, Michael. Tom Cringle's Log. 1999. (Heart of Oak Sea Classics Ser.). xix, 545p. pap. 16.00 o.s.i (*0-8050-6265-3*, Owl Bks.) Holt, Henry & Co.

Yolen, Jane. Encounter. (Illus.). (J). (gr. 4-7). 1996. 32p. pap. 6.00 (*0-15-201389-X*, Voyager Bks./Libros Viajeros); 1992. 40p. 16.00 (*0-15-225962-7*) Harcourt Children's Bks.

—Encounter. 1996. 12.15 (*0-606-10802-5*) Turtleback Bks.

WEST VIRGINIA—FICTION

Baker, Julie. Up Molasses Mountain. 224p. (YA). 2004. (gr. 5). mass mkt. 5.50 (*0-440-22903-0*, Laurel Leaf); 2002. (gr. 5 up). 15.95 (*0-385-72908-1*, Delacorte Bks. for Young Readers); 2002. (gr. 7). lib. bdg. 17.99 (*0-385-90048-1*, Delacorte Bks. for Young Readers) Random Hse. Children's Bks.

Belton, Sandra. McKendree. 2000. 272p. (J). (gr. 5 up). 16.99 (*0-688-15950-8*, Greenwillow Bks.) HarperCollins Children's Bk. Group.

Cabot, Meg. Project Princess. 2003. (Princess Diaries: Vol. 4). 64p. (J). (gr. 7 up). pap. 2.99 (*0-06-057131-4*) HarperCollins Children's Bk. Group.

Dell, Pamela. Aquila's Drinking Gourd: A Story of the Underground Railroad. 2002. (Illus.). 48p. (J). lib. bdg. 27.07 (*1-59187-013-5*) Child's World, Inc.

Durrant, Linda. Betsy Zane, the Rose of Fort Henry. 2000. 176p. (J). (gr. 5-9). tchr. ed. 15.00 (*0-395-97899-8*, Clarion Bks.) Houghton Mifflin Co. Trade & Reference Div.

Faine, Edward Allan. Little Ned Stories. 1999. (Illus.). 128p. (J). (gr. k-3). pap. 9.99 (*0-9654651-5-2*) IM Pr.

Hedrick, Helen Groves. Baas on the Bus. 2000. (J). 12.00 (*0-8059-5003-6*) Dorrance Publishing Co., Inc.

High, Linda O. Hound Heaven. 1995. 208p. (J). (gr. 4-7). 15.95 (*0-8234-1195-8*) Holiday Hse., Inc.

Holley, Juliette A. Jamie Lemme See. 1975. 113p. (J). 5.95 o.p. (*0-89227-016-0*) Commonwealth Pr., Inc.

Kay, Alan N. On the Trail of John Brown's Body. 2001. (Young Heroes of History Ser.: Vol. 2). (Illus.). 175p. (J). (gr. 4-7). pap. 5.95 (*1-57249-239-2*, 1572492406, Burd Street Pr.) White Mane Publishing Co., Inc.

Lynn, Jodi. Glory. 2003. 176p. (J). pap. 9.99 (*0-14-250038-0*, Puffin Bks.) Penguin Putnam Bks. for Young Readers.

McKenna, Colleen O'Shaughnessy. The Brightest Light. 1992. 208p. (YA). (gr. 7-9). pap. 13.95 (*0-590-45347-5*) Scholastic, Inc.

Mills, Patricia. Until the Cows Come Home. 1945. (Illus.). 32p. (J). (gr. k-3). 14.95 o.p. (*1-55858-190-1*); 15.50 o.p. (*1-55858-191-X*) North-South Bks., Inc.

Naylor, Phyllis Reynolds. Saving Shiloh. 1999. (Shiloh Ser.: No. 3). (J). (gr. 4-7). pap. 12.40 (*0-613-12073-6*) Econo-Clad Bks.

—Saving Shiloh. (Shiloh Ser.: No. 3). 144p. (J). (gr. 4-7). 1997. 15.00 (*0-689-81460-7*, Atheneum); 1999. reprint ed. pap. 5.50 (*0-689-81461-5*, Aladdin) Simon & Schuster Children's Publishing.

—Saving Shiloh. l.t. ed. 2002. 193p. (J). 22.95 (*0-7862-3713-9*) Thorndike Pr.

—Saving Shiloh. 1999. 11.04 (*0-606-14310-6*) Turtleback Bks.

—Send No Blessings. 1992. 240p. (YA). (gr. 5 up). pap. 3.99 o.s.i (*0-14-034859-X*, Puffin Bks.) Penguin Putnam Bks. for Young Readers.

—Send No Blessings. 1990. 240p. (YA). (gr. 7 up). 16.00 (*0-689-31582-1*, Atheneum) Simon & Schuster Children's Publishing.

—Send No Blessings. 1992. 10.09 o.p. (*0-606-00744-X*) Turtleback Bks.

—Shiloh. 1996. (Shiloh Ser.: No. 1). 144p. (J). (gr. 4-7). mass mkt. 2.49 o.s.i (*0-440-21991-4*) Dell Publishing.

—Shiloh. (SPA.). (YA). (gr. 5-8). (*968-16-5805-1*, FC0086) Fondo de Cultura Economica MEX. *Dist:* Lectorum Pubns., Inc.

—Shiloh. l.t. ed. 2000. (Shiloh Ser.: No. 1). 155p. (J). (gr. 4-7). lib. bdg. 27.95 (*1-58118-058-6*, 23472) LRS.

—Shiloh. l.t. ed. 1995. (Shiloh Ser.: No. 1). 160p. (J). (gr. 4-7). lib. bdg. 16.95 o.p. (*1-885885-10-5*, Cornerstone Bks.) Pages, Inc.

—Shiloh. 144p. (J). (gr. 4-7). (Shiloh Ser.: No. 1). pap. 4.99 (*0-8072-8330-4*);No. 1. 2000. pap. 28.00 incl. audio (*0-8072-8329-0*, YA164SP) Random Hse. Audio Publishing Group. (Listening Library).

—Shiloh. 1992. (Shiloh Ser.: No. 1). (gr. 4-7). 160p. pap. text 5.50 o.s.i (*0-440-40752-4*, Yearling); (J). pap. 3.50 (*0-440-80297-0*, Dell Books for Young Readers) Random Hse. Children's Bks.

—Shiloh. (Shiloh Ser.: No. 1). 144p. (J). 2000. (gr. 3-7). pap. 5.99 (*0-689-83582-5*, Aladdin); 1991. (gr. 4-7). 16.00 (*0-689-31614-3*, Atheneum) Simon & Schuster Children's Publishing.

—Shiloh. 2000. (J). 11.55 (*0-606-19724-9*) Turtleback Bks.

—Shiloh Movie Tie-In. 2000. (Shiloh Ser.: No. 6). (Illus.). 144p. (J). (gr. 4-7). pap. 5.50 (*0-689-83583-3*, Aladdin) Simon & Schuster Children's Publishing.

—Shiloh Season. unabr. ed. 2000. (Shiloh Ser.: No. 2). 120p. (J). (gr. 4-7). pap. 28.00 incl. audio (*0-8072-8707-5*, YA242SP, Listening Library) Random Hse. Audio Publishing Group.

—Shiloh Season. (Shiloh Ser.: No. 2). 128p. (J). (gr. 4-7). 2000. mass mkt. 2.99 (*0-689-83862-X*, Aladdin); 1999. (Illus.). pap. 5.50 (*0-689-82931-0*, Aladdin); 1998. pap. 4.99 (*0-689-80646-9*, Aladdin); 1996. 15.00 (*0-689-80647-7*, Atheneum) Simon & Schuster Children's Publishing.

—Shiloh Season. l.t. ed. 2000. (Juvenile Ser.). (Illus.). 164p. (J). (gr. 4-7). 21.95 o.p. (*0-7862-2702-8*) Thorndike Pr.

—Shiloh Season. 1998. (Shiloh Ser.: No. 2). (J). (gr. 4-7). 11.04 (*0-606-13085-3*) Turtleback Bks.

—Shiloh Trilogy: Shiloh; Shiloh Season; Saving Shiloh. (J). 2000. (gr. 3-7). 14.99 (*0-689-01525-9*, Aladdin); 1998. (Shiloh Ser.: Nos. 1-3). (gr. 4-7). 35.00 (*0-689-82327-4*, Atheneum) Simon & Schuster Children's Publishing.

Pool, James M. Among These Hills: A Child's History of Harrison County. 1985. (Illus.). 240p. (J). 12.95 (*0-9615566-0-9*) Clarksburg-Harrison Bicentennial Committee.

Rylant, Cynthia. Missing May. unabr. ed. 2000. 89p. (J). (gr. 4-6). pap. 28.00 incl. audio (*0-8072-8701-6*, YA240SP, Listening Library) Random Hse. Audio Publishing Group.

Seabrooke, Brenda. The Haunting of Swain's Fancy. 2003. 160p. (J). (gr. 5 up). 16.99 (*0-525-46938-9*, Dutton Children's Bks.) Penguin Putnam Bks. for Young Readers.

Slate, Joseph. Crossing the Trestle. 1999. (Accelerated Reader Bks.). 144p. (J). (gr. 3-7). 14.95 (*0-7614-5053-X*, Cavendish Children's Bks.) Cavendish, Marshall Corp.

Ware, Cheryl. Flea Circus Summer. 1997. 144p. (J). (gr. 4-6). pap. 15.95 (*0-531-30032-3*); lib. bdg. 16.99 (*0-531-33032-X*) Scholastic, Inc. (Orchard Bks.).

—Sea Monkey Summer. 1996. 144p. (J). (gr. 4-6). mass mkt. 14.95 o.p. (*0-531-09518-5*, Orchard Bks.) Scholastic, Inc.

Woodruff, Elvira. Ghosts Don't Get Goosebumps. 1995. 176p. (J). (gr. 3-7). pap. text 3.99 o.s.i (*0-440-41033-9*) Dell Publishing.

—Ghosts Don't Get Goosebumps. 1993. 96p. (J). (gr. 4-7). tchr. ed. 16.95 (*0-8234-1035-8*) Holiday Hse., Inc.

—Ghosts Don't Get Goosebumps. 1995. (J). 9.09 o.p. (*0-606-07566-6*) Turtleback Bks.

Yep, Laurence. Dream Soul. 2000. (Illus.). (J). 224p. (gr. 3-7). lib. bdg. 16.89 (*0-06-028390-4*); 256p. (gr. 7 up). 15.95 (*0-06-028389-0*) HarperCollins Children's Bk. Group.

WESTMARK (IMAGINARY PLACE)—FICTION

Alexander, Lloyd. The Beggar Queen. (J). 2002. (Westmark Trilogy: No. 3). (Illus.). 256p. pap. 5.99 (*0-14-131070-7*, Firebird); 1984. 248p. (gr. 6 up). 14.95 o.p. (*0-525-44103-4*, Dutton Children's Bks.) Penguin Putnam Bks. for Young Readers.

—The Beggar Queen. 1985. 256p. (YA). (gr. 7 up). mass mkt. 4.99 (*0-440-90548-6*, Laurel Leaf) Random Hse. Children's Bks.

—The Beggar Queen. 1985. (J). 11.04 (*0-606-00255-3*) Turtleback Bks.

—The Kestrel. 1982. 256p. (J). (gr. 5 up). 14.95 o.s.i (*0-525-45110-2*, Dutton Children's Bks.) Penguin Putnam Bks. for Young Readers.

—The Kestrel. 1983. 256p. (YA). (gr. 7 up). mass mkt. 3.99 o.s.i (*0-440-94393-0*, Laurel Leaf) Random Hse. Children's Bks.

—Westmark. 1981. (J). (gr. 5 up). 15.95 o.s.i (*0-525-42335-4*, Dutton Children's Bks.) Penguin Putnam Bks. for Young Readers.

—Westmark. 1982. 192p. (YA). (gr. 7 up). mass mkt. 4.50 o.s.i (*0-440-99731-3*, Laurel Leaf) Random Hse. Children's Bks.

—Westmark. 1981. (J). 10.55 (*0-606-00638-9*) Turtleback Bks.

WILD ROSE INN (MASS.: IMAGINARY PLACE)—FICTION

Armstrong, Jennifer. Ann of the Wild Rose 1774. 1994. (Wild Rose Inn Ser.: No. 2). 192p. (YA). mass mkt. 3.99 o.s.i (*0-553-29867-4*) Bantam Bks.

—Bridie of the Wild Rose Inn 1695. 1994. (Wild Rose Inn Ser.: No. 1). 192p. (YA). mass mkt. 3.99 o.s.i (*0-553-29866-6*) Bantam Bks.

—Claire of the Wild Rose Inn 1928. 1994. (Wild Rose Inn Ser.: No. 5). 192p. (YA). mass mkt. 3.99 o.s.i (*0-553-29911-5*) Bantam Bks.

—Emily of the Wild Rose Inn 1858. 1994. (Wild Rose Inn Ser.: No. 3). 192p. (YA). (gr. 7 up). mass mkt. 3.99 o.s.i (*0-553-29909-3*) Bantam Bks.

—Grace of the Wild Rose Inn, 1944. 1994. (Wild Rose Inn Ser.: No. 6). 192p. (YA). mass mkt. 3.99 o.p. (*0-553-29912-3*) Bantam Bks.

—Laura of the Wild Rose Inn 1895. 1994. (Wild Rose Inn Ser.: No. 4). 176p. (YA). mass mkt. 3.99 o.s.i (*0-553-29910-7*) Bantam Bks.

—Wild Rose Inn. 1994. (J). mass mkt. 3.95 (*0-553-54154-4*);Vol. 2. mass mkt. o.s.i (*0-553-54155-2*) Random Hse. Children's Bks. (Dell Books for Young Readers).

WILLIAMSBURG (VA.)—FICTION

Cavanna, Betty. Two's Company. 1951. (Illus.). 190p. (J). (gr. 5-9). 7.00 o.p. (*0-664-32080-5*) Westminster John Knox Pr.

Coon, Alma S. Amy, Ben, & Catalpa the Cat: A Fanciful Story of This & That. 1990. (Illus.). 40p. (J). (ps-1). 8.95 (*0-87935-079-2*) Colonial Williamsburg Foundation.

Dwight, Allan. To the Walls of Cartagena. 1967. (Young Readers Ser.). (Illus.). (J). (gr. 4-7). 3.95 o.p. (*0-910412-59-6*) Colonial Williamsburg Foundation.

Luttrell, Wanda. Stranger in Williamsburg. 196p. 2010. (Sarah's Journey Ser.: Vol. 2). (J). (gr. 4-7). pap. 6.99 (*0-7814-0902-0*); 1995. (YA). 12.99 (*0-7814-0235-2*) Cook Communications Ministries.

—Whispers in Williamsburg. (Sarah's Journey Ser.: Vol. 4). (Illus.). 208p. (J). (gr. 3-7). pap. 6.99 (*0-7814-3008-9*) Cook Communications Ministries.

Moore, Eva. Good Children Get Rewards: A Story of Colonial Times. 2001. (Hello Reader! Ser.). (J). 10.14 (*0-606-19563-7*) Turtleback Bks.

Nixon, Joan Lowery. John's Story 1775: Colonial Williamsburg. 2001. (Young Americans Ser.). (Illus.). 176p. (gr. 3-7). text 9.95 (*0-385-32688-2*, Dell Books for Young Readers) Random Hse. Children's Bks.

—Maria's Story, 1773. 2001. (Young Americans). (Illus.). 176p. (gr. 2-6). text 9.95 (*0-385-32685-8*, Delacorte Bks. for Young Readers) Random Hse. Children's Bks.

—Nancy's Story 1765. 2000. (Young Americans). (Illus.). 160p. (gr. 2-6). text 9.95 o.s.i (*0-385-32679-3*, Delacorte Bks. for Young Readers) Random Hse. Children's Bks.

Rue, Nancy. The Burden. 1998. (Christian Heritage Ser.). 192p. (J). (gr. 3-7). pap. 5.99 (*1-56179-517-8*) Focus on the Family Publishing.

—The Invasion. 1998. (Christian Heritage Ser.). 192p. (J). (gr. 3-7). pap. 5.99 (*1-56179-541-0*) Focus on the Family Publishing.

Tripp, Valerie. Changes for Felicity: A Winter Story. 1992. (American Girls Collection: Bk. 6). (Illus.). 80p. (J). (gr. 2 up). 12.95 (*1-56247-038-8*, American Girl) Pleasant Co. Pubns.

—Changes for Felicity: A Winter Story. Johnson, Roberta, ed. 1992. (American Girls Collection: Bk. 6). (Illus.). 80p. (J). (gr. 2 up). pap. 5.95 (*1-56247-037-X*, American Girl) Pleasant Co. Pubns.

—Changes for Felicity: A Winter Story. 1992. (American Girls Collection: Bk. 6). (Illus.). (YA). (gr. 2 up). 12.10 (*0-606-01039-4*) Turtleback Bks.

—Felicity Discovers a Secret. 2002. (American Girls Short Stories Ser.). (Illus.). 56p. (J). 4.95 (*1-58485-477-4*, American Girl) Pleasant Co. Pubns.

—Felicity Learns a Lesson: A School Story. 1991. (American Girls Collection: Bk. 2). (Illus.). 80p. (YA). (gr. 2 up). 12.95 o.p. (*1-56247-006-X*) Pleasant Co. Pubns.

—Felicity Learns a Lesson: A School Story. Thieme, Jeanne, ed. 1991. (American Girls Collection: Bk. 2). (Illus.). 80p. (J). (gr. 2 up). pap. 5.95 (*1-56247-007-8*); 12.95 (*1-56247-008-6*) Pleasant Co. Pubns. (American Girl).

—Felicity Learns a Lesson: A School Story. 1991. (American Girls Collection: Bk. 2). (Illus.). (YA). (gr. 2 up). 12.10 (*0-606-05054-X*) Turtleback Bks.

—Felicity Saves the Day: A Summer Story. 1992. (American Girls Collection: Bk. 5). (Illus.). 80p. (J). (gr. 2 up). 12.95 (*1-56247-035-3*); pap. 5.95 (*1-56247-034-5*) Pleasant Co. Pubns. (American Girl).

—Felicity Saves the Day: A Summer Story. 1992. (American Girls Collection: Bk. 5). (Illus.). (YA). (gr. 2 up). 12.10 (*0-606-01037-8*) Turtleback Bks.

—Felicity Takes a Dare. 2001. (American Girls Short Stories Ser.). (Illus.). 56p. (J). (gr. 2-7). 3.95 (*1-58485-271-2*, American Girl) Pleasant Co. Pubns.

—Felicity's Boxed Set: Meet Felicity; Felicity Learns a Lesson; Felicity's Surprise; Happy Birthday, Felicity!; Felicity Saves the Day; Changes for Felicity, 6 bks. 1992. (American Girls Collection: Bks. 1-6). (Illus.). 412p. (J). (gr. 2 up). 74.95 (*1-56247-045-0*, American Girl) Pleasant Co. Pubns.

—Felicity's Boxed Set: Meet Felicity; Felicity Learns a Lesson; Felicity's Surprise; Happy Birthday, Felicity!; Felicity Saves the Day; Changes for Felicity, 6 bks. Johnson, Roberta et al, eds. 1992. (American Girls Collection: Bks. 1-6). (Illus.). 412p. (J). (gr. 3-7). pap. 34.95 (*1-56247-044-2*, American Girl) Pleasant Co. Pubns.

—Felicity's Dancing Shoes. 2000. (American Girls Short Stories Ser.). (Illus.). 56p. (YA). (gr. 2 up). 3.95 (*1-58485-031-0*, American Girl) Pleasant Co. Pubns.

—Felicity's Story Collection. 2001. (American Girls Collection). (Illus.). 390p. (J). (gr. 2 up). 29.95 (*1-58485-441-3*, American Girl) Pleasant Co. Pubns.

—Felicity's Surprise: A Christmas Story. 1991. (American Girls Collection: Bk. 3). (Illus.). 80p. (YA). (gr. 2 up). 12.95 o.p. (*1-56247-009-4*) Pleasant Co. Pubns.

—Felicity's Surprise: A Christmas Story. Hardesty, Carolyn, ed. 1991. (American Girls Collection: Bk. 3). (Illus.). 80p. (J). (gr. 2 up). 12.95 (*1-56247-011-6*); pap. 5.95 (*1-56247-010-8*) Pleasant Co. Pubns. (American Girl).

—Felicity's Surprise: A Christmas Story. 1991. (American Girls Collection: Bk. 3). (Illus.). (YA). (gr. 2 up). 12.10 (*0-606-05055-8*) Turtleback Bks.

—Happy Birthday, Felicity! A Springtime Story. Hardesty, Carolyn, ed. 1992. (American Girls Collection: Bk. 4). (Illus.). 80p. (J). (gr. 2 up). pap. 5.95 (*1-56247-031-0*); lib. bdg. 12.95 (*1-56247-032-9*) Pleasant Co. Pubns. (American Girl).

—Happy Birthday, Felicity! A Springtime Story. 1992. (American Girls Collection: Bk. 4). (Illus.). (YA). (gr. 2 up). 12.10 (*0-606-01036-X*) Turtleback Bks.

—Meet Felicity: An American Girl. 1991. (American Girls Collection: Bk. 1). (Illus.). 80p. (J). (gr. 2 up). 12.95 o.p. (*1-56247-003-5*); pap. 5.95 (*1-56247-004-3*, American Girl) Pleasant Co. Pubns.

—Meet Felicity: An American Girl. Thieme, Jeanne, ed. 1991. (American Girls Collection: Bk. 1). (Illus.). 80p. (J). (gr. 2 up). lib. bdg. 12.95 (*1-56247-005-1*, American Girl) Pleasant Co. Pubns.

—Meet Felicity: An American Girl. 1991. (American Girls Collection: Bk. 1). (Illus.). (YA). (gr. 2 up). 12.10 (*0-606-05053-1*) Turtleback Bks.

Waters, Kate. Mary Geddy's Day: A Colonial Girl in Williamsburg. 2002. (Illus.). 40p. (J). pap. 5.99 (*0-590-92928-3*, Scholastic Paperbacks) Scholastic, Inc.

WINDING CIRCLE TEMPLE (IMAGINARY PLACE)—FICTION

Pierce, Tamora. Briar's Book. (Circle of Magic Ser.: No. 4). 272p. 2000. (Illus.). (J). mass mkt. 4.99 (*0-590-55411-5*, Scholastic Paperbacks); 1999. (YA). (gr. 6-12). pap. 15.95 (*0-590-55359-3*) Scholastic, Inc.

—Briar's Book. 1999. (Circle of Magic Ser.). (J). 11.04 (*0-606-19550-5*) Turtleback Bks.

—Daja's Book. (Circle of Magic Ser.: No. 3). 2000. (Illus.). 240p. (J). mass mkt. 4.99 (*0-590-55410-7*, Scholastic Paperbacks); 1998. 224p. (YA). (gr. 6-12). pap. 15.95 o.s.i (*0-590-55358-5*) Scholastic, Inc.

—Magic Steps. 2000. (Circle Opens Ser.: No. 1). (Illus.). 264p. (J). (gr. 4-7). pap. 16.95 (*0-590-39588-2*) Scholastic, Inc.

—Sandry's Book. (Circle of Magic Ser.: No. 1). (gr. 6-12). 1999. 252p. (YA). mass mkt. 4.99 (*0-590-55408-5*); 1997. 256p. (J). pap. 15.95 (*0-590-55356-9*) Scholastic, Inc.

—Tris's Book. 1998. (Circle of Magic Ser.). 251p. (J). (gr. 5-10). pap. 15.95 (*0-590-55357-7*) Scholastic, Inc.

WISCONSIN—FICTION

Addy, Sharon Hart. Right Here on This Spot. 1999. (Illus.). 32p. (J). (ps-3). lib. bdg., tchr. ed. 15.00 (*0-395-73091-0*) Houghton Mifflin Co.

Bauer, Joan. Hope Was Here. 2000. (Illus.). 192p. (J). (gr. 7-12). 16.99 (*0-399-23142-0*) Penguin Group (USA) Inc.

Brink, Carol R. Caddie Woodlawn. l.t. ed. 1988. (YA). (gr. 5 up). reprint ed. lib. bdg. 16.95 o.s.i (*1-55736-043-X*, Cornerstone Bks.) Pages, Inc.

—Caddie Woodlawn. (J). 9999. pap. 2.50 o.s.i (*0-590-10121-8*); 1997. (Illus.). 16p. mass mkt. 3.95 (*0-590-37359-5*) Scholastic, Inc.

—Caddie Woodlawn. 1990. (Illus.). 288p. (J). (gr. 3-7). pap. 5.99 (*0-689-71370-3*, Aladdin); 1973. (Illus.). 288p. (J). (gr. 3-7). 17.00 (*0-02-713670-1*, Simon & Schuster Children's Publishing); 2nd ed. 1997. 288p. (YA). (gr. 3-7). mass mkt. 5.50 (*0-689-81521-2*, Simon Pulse); Vol. 1. 1999. pap. 2.99 (*0-689-82969-8*, Aladdin) Simon & Schuster Children's Publishing.

—Caddie Woodlawn. 1970. (J). 11.04 (*0-606-02490-5*) Turtleback Bks.

—Magical Melons. 1990. (Illus.). 208p. (J). (gr. 4-7). reprint ed. pap. 4.99 (*0-689-71416-5*, Aladdin) Simon & Schuster Children's Publishing.

—Magical Melons. 1990. (J). 10.00 (*0-606-04473-6*) Turtleback Bks.

Buchen, Kathryn. Rainmaker. 1995. 153p. (Orig.). (J). pap. 7.50 (*0-9645405-0-9*) Beson, Kathryn.

Cameron, Ann. The Secret Life of Amanda K. Woods, RS. 1998. 208p. (J). (gr. 5 up). 16.00 (*0-374-36702-7*, Farrar, Straus & Giroux (BYR)) Farrar, Straus & Giroux.

—The Secret Life of Amanda K. Woods. l.t. ed. 2000. (Illus.). 204p. (gr. 8-12). 20.95 (*0-7862-2777-X*) Thorndike Pr.

—The Secret Life of Amanda K. Woods. 1999. 11.04 (*0-606-17429-X*) Turtleback Bks.

Carter, Alden R. Bull Catcher. 1997. 288p. (J). (gr. 7-12). pap. 15.95 (*0-590-50958-6*) Scholastic, Inc.

—Crescent Moon. 1999. (J). 15.95 (*0-590-29882-8*) Scholastic, Inc.

—Dogwolf. 1994. 272p. (J). (gr. 7-9). pap. 13.95 (*0-590-46741-7*) Scholastic, Inc.

Chall, Marsha W. Mattie. 1992. (J). (ps-3). 11.00 o.p. (*0-688-09730-8*) HarperCollins Children's Bk. Group.

Clark, Catherine. Wurst Case Scenario. 2001. 320p. (J). (gr. 8 up). pap. 6.95 (*0-06-447287-6*, HarperTempest); lib. bdg. 16.89 (*0-06-029525-2*) HarperCollins Children's Bk. Group.

Clarke, J. Al Capsella Takes a Vacation, ERS. 1993. 144p. (YA). (gr. 7 up). 14.95 o.p. (*0-8050-2685-1*, Holt, Henry & Co. Bks. For Young Readers) Holt, Henry & Co.

Daly, Maureen. Seventeenth Summer. 1981. 288p. (YA). (gr. 7 up). reprint ed. lib. bdg. 19.95 (*0-89967-029-6*, Harmony Raine & Co.) Buccaneer Bks., Inc.

—Seventeenth Summer. (YA). 2003. mass mkt. 5.99 (*0-689-85444-7*, Simon Pulse); 2002. 320p. 17.95 (*0-689-85383-1*, Simon & Schuster Children's Publishing); 1985. 306p. (gr. 7 up). mass mkt. 5.99 (*0-671-61931-4*, Simon Pulse); 1981. (gr. 7 up). pap. (*0-671-44386-0*, Simon Pulse) Simon & Schuster Children's Publishing.

—Seventeenth Summer. 1968. 11.04 (*0-606-04805-7*) Turtleback Bks.

Eccles, Mary. By Lizzie. 128p. (J). 2003. (Illus.). pap. 4.99 (*0-14-250036-4*, Puffin Bks.); 2001. (gr. 3-5). 15.99 o.s.i (*0-8037-2608-2*, Dial Bks. for Young Readers) Penguin Putnam Bks. for Young Readers.

Enright, Elizabeth. Thimble Summer, ERS. 1990. (Illus.). 124p. (J). (gr. 2 up). 19.95 (*0-8050-0306-1*, Holt, Henry & Co. Bks. For Young Readers) Holt, Henry & Co.

—Thimble Summer. 1987. (Yearling Newbery Ser.). 144p. (gr. 4-7). pap. text 4.99 (*0-440-48681-5*, Yearling) Random Hse. Children's Bks.

—Thimble Summer. 1976. 11.04 (*0-606-00764-4*) Turtleback Bks.

Erickson, John R. The Case of the Fiddle-Playing Fox. 1998. (Hank the Cowdog Ser.: No. 12). (Illus.). 144p. (J). (gr. 2-5). pap. 4.99 (*0-14-130388-3*, Puffin Bks.) Penguin Putnam Bks. for Young Readers.

Ferry, Charles. Up in Sister Bay, 001. 1975. (Illus.). 224p. (J). (gr. 7 up). 6.95 o.p. (*0-395-21409-2*) Houghton Mifflin Co.

Gilge, Jeanette. Never Miss a Sunset. 1901. (Wholesome Adventure for Girls Gift Set Ser.). 240p. (Orig.). (J). (gr. 3-7). pap. 2.50 o.p. (*0-912692-56-1*) Cook Communications Ministries.

Hall, Lynn. Flyaway. 1987. 128p. (YA). (gr. 7 up). 12.95 o.s.i (*0-684-18888-0*, Atheneum) Simon & Schuster Children's Publishing.

Hirsch, Phil. One Hundred One Dinosaur Jokes. 1989. (Illus.). 96p. (J). (gr. 4-6). mass mkt. 1.95 o.p. (*0-590-41691-X*) Scholastic, Inc.

Hoehne, Marcia. Emilie's Odyssey. (Immigrants Chronicles Ser.). 132p. (J). (gr. 3-7). pap. 5.99 (*0-7814-3081-X*) Cook Communications Ministries.

Homer, William. Gene Shepard's Wisconsin Hodag. 2001. (Illus.). 32p. (J). (gr. 2-5). lib. bdg. 24.95 (*1-931765-03-0*, BHC501) Badger Hse., LLC.

Konigsburg, E. L. From the Mixed-up Files of Mrs. Basil E. Frankweiler. 1998. 160p. (gr. 4-7). mass mkt. 2.99 o.s.i (*0-440-22802-6*, Yearling) Random Hse. Children's Bks.

Kopetz, Mark. Trolls at the Door: A Door County Story. 1995. (Illus.). 62p. (Orig.). (YA). pap. 8.95 (*0-940473-29-1*) Caxton, Wm Ltd.

LaFaye, A. Edith Shay. 2001. (J). 11.04 (*0-606-21170-5*) Turtleback Bks.

Lansing, Richard D., Jr. The Blue Moose. 1999. 48p. (J). (ps-4). mass mkt. 6.00 (*0-9661844-5-9*) Purple Gorilla, LLC, The.

Levy, Delores G. Branching Out: Emmy's Story. 1995. (Illus.). 136p. (Orig.). (YA). (gr. 7-12). pap. 7.95 (*0-9642639-0-4*) Portraits West.

—Branching Out: Emmy's Story. Levy, Delores G., ed. 1995. (Illus.). (Orig.). (YA). (gr. 8-12). pap. 13.95 (*0-9642639-1-2*) Portraits West.

Liebig, Nelda J. Carrie & the Apple Pie. 1999. 122p. (J). (gr. 3-7). pap. 10.95 (*1-883953-30-8*) Midwest Traditions, Inc.

—Carrie & the Crazy Quilt. 1997. 88p. (Orig.). (J). (gr. 3-7). pap. 7.50 (*1-883953-19-7*) Midwest Traditions, Inc.

—Carrie & the Crazy Quilt. 1996. 96p. (Orig.). (J). pap. 7.50 (*1-883893-40-2*) WinePress Publishing.

Mason, Babbie. Real Monsters: Rosh - O - Monsters. 1997. (Real Monsters Ser.). 64p. (J). (gr. 2-5). 3.99 (*0-689-81155-1*, Simon Spotlight) Simon & Schuster Children's Publishing.

Mason, Jane & Gilmour, H. B. Real Monsters: Spontaneously Combustible. 1997. (Illus.). 64p. (J). (gr. 2-5). 3.99 (*0-689-81154-3*, Simon Spotlight) Simon & Schuster Children's Publishing.

Midfeldt, Linda J. Green As in Springtime. 1994. 128p. (Orig.). (J). pap. 7.99 (*0-8100-0526-3*, 17N1626) Northwestern Publishing Hse.

Pellowski, Anne. Betsy's Up-and-Down Year, Vol. 5. rev. ed. 1997. (Polish American Girls Ser.). (Illus.). 160p. (J). (gr. 3-5). pap. 9.95 (*0-88489-539-4*) St. Mary's Pr.

—First Farm in the Valley: Anna's Story. 1982. (Illus.). 192p. (J). (gr. 3-6). 9.95 o.s.i (*0-399-20887-9*, Philomel) Penguin Putnam Bks. for Young Readers.

—Stairstep Farm Vol. 3: Anna Rose's Story. rev. ed. 1997. (Polish American Girls Ser.). (Illus.). 176p. (J). (gr. 3-6). pap. 9.95 (*0-88489-536-X*) St. Mary's Pr.

—Winding Valley Farm: Annie's Story. 1982. (Illus.). 192p. (J). 9.95 o.s.i (*0-399-20863-1*, Philomel) Penguin Putnam Bks. for Young Readers.

—Winding Valley Farm Vol. 2: Annie's Story. rev. ed. 1997. (Polish American Girls Ser.). 192p. (J). (gr. 3-5). pap. 9.95 (*0-88489-538-6*) St. Mary's Pr.

Peterson, P. Nuzum, et al, contrib. by. The Lucky Kickapoo: A River Tells Its Story. 1997. (Illus.). (J). o.p. (*0-942495-69-1*) Amherst Pr.

Qualey, Marsha. Revolutions of the Heart. 1993. 192p. (YA). (gr. 7 up). 16.00 (*0-395-64168-3*) Houghton Mifflin Co.

—Thin Ice. 1997. 272p. (YA). (gr. 7-12). 14.95 o.s.i (*0-385-32298-4*, Delacorte Pr.) Dell Publishing.

—Thin Ice. 1999. 272p. (YA). (gr. 7-7). mass mkt. 4.99 (*0-440-22037-8*, Dell Books for Young Readers) Random Hse. Children's Bks.

—Thin Ice. 1999. 11.04 (*0-606-17348-X*) Turtleback Bks.

Sweeney, Sandra D. Mystery in Wisdonsin Dells: The Ghost Town of Newport Mystery. 1997. 128p. (J). (gr. 1-6). pap. 3.25 (*0-9659570-0-4*) Adventures for Kids Co.

Sweeten, Sami. Wolf. 1994. 32p. (J). (gr. 1-4). lib. bdg. 14.95 o.p. (*0-8075-9160-2*) Whitman, Albert & Co.

Wanderer, Pauline. Dream Girl at Mystery Lake: A Door County Adventure. 1995. (J). pap. 8.95 (*0-940473-28-3*) Caxton, Wm Ltd.

Wilder, Laura Ingalls. Christmas in the Big Woods. (My First Little House Bks.). (Illus.). (J). (ps-1). 1996. 80p. 3.25 o.p. (*0-694-00877-X*, Harper Festival); 1995. 40p. 14.99 (*0-06-024752-5*); 1995. 40p. lib. bdg. 12.89 o.p. (*0-06-024753-3*) HarperCollins Children's Bk. Group.

—Christmas in the Big Woods. 1995. (My First Little House Bks.). (Illus.). (J). (ps-1). 12.10 (*0-606-10772-X*) Turtleback Bks.

—Dance at Grandpa's. 1994. (My First Little House Bks.). (Illus.). 40p. (J). (ps-1). lib. bdg. 11.89 o.p. (*0-06-023879-8*); 12.95 o.p. (*0-06-023878-X*) HarperCollins Children's Bk. Group.

—The Deer in the Wood. (My First Little House Bks.). (Illus.). (J). (ps-3). 1999. 32p. pap. 5.99 (*0-06-443498-2*, Harper Trophy); 1996. 32p. pap. 3.25 (*0-694-00879-6*, Harper Festival); 1995. 40p. 11.95 o.p. (*0-06-024881-5*); 1995. 40p. lib. bdg. 11.89 o.p. (*0-06-024882-3*) HarperCollins Children's Bk. Group.

—The Deer in the Wood. (My First Little House Bks.). 1999. 12.10 (*0-606-15841-3*); 1996. (Illus.). (J). 8.20 o.p. (*0-606-10780-0*) Turtleback Bks.

—Going to Town. (My First Little House Bks.). (Illus.). (J). (ps-1). 1997. 12p. 3.25 (*0-694-00955-5*, Harper Festival); 1996. 32p. pap. 5.95 (*0-06-443452-4*, Harper Trophy); 1995. 40p. 11.95 o.p. (*0-06-023012-6*); 1995. 40p. lib. bdg. 11.89 o.p. (*0-06-023013-4*) HarperCollins Children's Bk. Group.

—Going to Town. 1995. (My First Little House Bks.). (Illus.). (J). (ps-1). 12.10 (*0-606-09335-4*) Turtleback Bks.

—Little House in the Big Woods. (Little House Ser.). (J). 2003. 176p. pap. 5.99 (*0-06-052236-4*); 1953. (Illus.). 256p. (gr. 3-6). pap. 6.99 (*0-06-440001-8*, Harper Trophy); 1953. (Illus.). 256p. (gr. 3-6). 16.99 (*0-06-026430-6*); 1953. (Illus.). 256p. (gr. 3-6). lib. bdg. 17.89 (*0-06-026431-4*) HarperCollins Children's Bk. Group.

—Little House in the Big Woods. l.t. ed. 1987. (Little House Ser.). 161p. (J). (gr. 3-6). reprint ed. lib. bdg. 14.95 o.p. (*1-85089-913-4*) ISIS Large Print Bks. GBR. *Dist:* Transaction Pubs.

—Little House in the Big Woods. l.t. ed. 2000. (Little House Ser.). (Illus.). 244p. (J). (gr. 3-6). lib. bdg. 28.95 (*1-58118-078-0*, 24070) LRS.

—Little House in the Big Woods. 1990. (Little House Ser.). (J). (gr. 3-6). pap. 3.50 o.p. (*0-06-107005-X*, HarperTorch) Morrow/Avon.

—Little House in the Big Woods. 1971. (Little House). (J). (gr. 3-6). 12.00 (*0-606-03811-6*) Turtleback Bks.

—Little House in the Big Woods A Special Read Aloud Edition. 2001. (Little House Ser.). (Illus.). 256p. (J). (gr. k-4). 19.95 (*0-06-029647-X*) HarperCollins Children's Bk. Group.

—Little House in the Big Woods A Special Read Aloud Edition. 2001. (Little House Ser.). (Illus.). 256p. (J). (gr. 3-5). lib. bdg. 19.89 (*0-06-029648-8*) HarperCollins Pubs.

—Summertime in the Big Woods. 1996. (My First Little House Bks.). (Illus.). (J). (ps-3). 40p. 14.99 (*0-06-025934-5*); 80p. lib. bdg. 11.89 o.p. (*0-06-025937-X*) HarperCollins Children's Bk. Group.

—Winter Days in the Big Woods. 1994. (My First Little House Bks.). (Illus.). 40p. (J). (ps-1). lib. bdg. 11.89 o.p. (*0-06-023022-3*); 12.00 (*0-06-023014-2*) HarperCollins Children's Bk. Group.

Wilder, Laura Ingalls & Graef, Renee. Summertime in the Big Woods. 2000. (My First Little House Bks.). (Illus.). 40p. (J). (ps-3). pap. 5.99 (*0-06-443497-4*, Harper Trophy) HarperCollins Children's Bk. Group.

Wilkes, Maria D. Brookfield Days. 1999. (Little House Chapter Bks.: No. 1). (Illus.). 80p. (J). (gr. 3-6). pap. 4.25 (*0-06-442086-8*, Harper Trophy) HarperCollins Children's Bk. Group.

—Brookfield Days. 1999. (Little House Chapter Bks.: No. 1). (Illus.). 80p. (J). (gr. 3-6). lib. bdg. 14.89 (*0-06-027952-4*) HarperCollins Pubs.

—Brookfield Days. 1999. (Little House Chapter Bks.: No.1). (Illus.). (J). (gr. 3-6). 10.40 (*0-606-18680-8*) Turtleback Bks.

—Brookfield Friends. 2000. (Little House Chapter Bks.: No. 4). (Illus.). 80p. (J). (gr. 3-6). pap. 4.25 (*0-06-442107-4*, Harper Trophy); lib. bdg. 14.89 (*0-06-028552-4*) HarperCollins Children's Bk. Group.

—Little Clearing in the Woods. adapted ed. 1998. (Little House Ser.). (Illus.). 336p. (J). (gr. 3-7). lib. bdg. 15.89 (*0-06-026998-7*) HarperCollins Children's Bk. Group.

—Little Clearing in the Woods. 1998. (Little House Ser.). (Illus.). 336p. (J). (gr. 3-7). 15.95 (*0-06-026997-9*); pap. 5.99 (*0-06-440652-0*) HarperCollins Pubs.

—Little House in Brookfield. 1996. (Little House Ser.). (Illus.). 320p. (J). (gr. 3-7). 16.95 (*0-06-026459-4*); pap. 5.99 (*0-06-440610-5*, Harper Trophy); lib. bdg. 14.89 o.p. (*0-06-026462-4*) HarperCollins Children's Bk. Group.

—Little House in Brookfield. 1996. (Little House Ser.). (Illus.). (J). (gr. 3-6). 11.00 (*0-606-09559-4*) Turtleback Bks.

—A New Little Cabin. 2001. (Little House Chapter Bks.: Vol. 5). (Illus.). 80p. (J). (gr. 2-5). pap. 4.25 (*0-06-442109-0*, Harper Trophy); lib. bdg. 14.89 (*0-06-028554-0*) HarperCollins Children's Bk. Group.

—On Top of Concord Hill. 2000. (Little House Ser.). (Illus.). 288p. (J). (gr. 3-7). 15.95 (*0-06-026999-5*); pap. 5.99 (*0-06-440689-X*, Harper Trophy); lib. bdg. 15.89 (*0-06-027003-9*) HarperCollins Children's Bk. Group.

Wilkins, Celia. Across the Rolling River. 2001. (Little House Ser.). (Illus.). 272p. (J). 16.95 (*0-06-027004-7*); lib. bdg. 16.89 (*0-06-027005-5*); (gr. 5 up). pap. 5.99 (*0-06-440734-9*, Harper Trophy) HarperCollins Children's Bk. Group.

Wright, Betty Ren. Crandall's Castle. 2003. 192p. (J). tchr. ed. 16.95 (*0-8234-1726-3*) Holiday Hse., Inc.

WYOMING—FICTION

Bell, Mary Reeves. Sagebrush Rebellion. 1999. (Passport to Danger Ser.: Vol. 2). 208p. (J). (gr. 7-12). pap. 5.99 o.p. (*1-55661-550-7*) Bethany Hse. Pubs.

—Sagebrush Rebellion. 1999. (J). 12.04 (*0-606-18973-4*) Turtleback Bks.

Calhoun, B. B. Out of Place. 1994. (Dinosaur Detective Ser.: No. 4). (Illus.). 128p. (J). (gr. 3-7). pap. text 3.95 o.p. (*0-7167-6551-9*) Freeman, W. H. & Co.

Cohen, Lane. Down Time. 2003. (YA). pap. 15.95 (*1-932133-67-4*) Writers' Collective, The.

Collier, James Lincoln & Collier, Christopher. The Bloody Country. 1985. 180p. (YA). (gr. 7 up). reprint ed. pap. 2.50 o.p. (*0-590-40948-4*, Scholastic Paperbacks) Scholastic, Inc.

Ehrlich, Gretel. A Blizzard Year. 1999. (Illus.). 122p. (J). (gr. 4). lib. bdg. 15.49 (*0-7868-2309-7*); 14.99 (*0-7868-0364-9*) Disney Pr.

—A Blizzard Year. 2001. 128p. (J). (gr. 4-8). pap. 5.99 (*0-7868-1245-1*) Hyperion Bks. for Children.

—A Blizzard Year. 2001. (J). (gr. 4-8). 12.04 (*0-606-22572-2*) Turtleback Bks.

Gagliano, Eugene. The Secret of the Black Widow. 2002. 67p. (J). pap. 5.95 (*1-57249-286-4*, WM Kids) White Mane Publishing Co., Inc.

George, Jean Craighead. Avalanche. 2004. (J). (*0-06-050595-8*); lib. bdg. (*0-06-050596-6*) HarperCollins Pubs.

Hayden, Jan & Kistler, Mary. Has Anyone Seen Allie? 1991. 128p. (J). (gr. 5 up). 13.95 o.p. (*0-525-65057-1*, Dutton Children's Bks.) Penguin Putnam Bks. for Young Readers.

Johnson, Pamela, illus. A Day for J.J. & Me. 1997. (*0-7802-8031-8*) Wright Group, The.

Keene, Carolyn. The Mystery of the Mother Wolf. l.t. ed. 2002. 159p. (J). 21.95 (*0-7862-4654-5*) Thorndike Pr.

Lippincott, Joseph W. Red Roan Pony. 1951. (Illus.). (J). (gr. 7-9). o.p. (*0-397-30195-2*) HarperCollins Children's Bk. Group.

Malcolm, Jahnna N. The Stallion of Box Canyon. l.t. ed. 1999. (Treasured Horses Collection). (Illus.). 122p. (J). (gr. 4 up). lib. bdg. 22.60 (*0-8368-2283-8*) Stevens, Gareth Inc.

McDonald, Brix. Riding on the Wind. 1998. 243p. (YA). (gr. 5-10). pap. 5.95 (*0-9661306-0-X*) Avenue Publishing.

Naylor, Phyllis Reynolds. Walker's Crossing. 240p. (YA). (gr. 5-9). 2001. pap. 4.99 (*0-689-84261-9*, Aladdin); 1999. (Illus.). 16.00 (*0-689-82939-6*, Atheneum) Simon & Schuster Children's Publishing.

O'Hara, Mary. My Friend Flicka. 1999. (Illus.). 320p. (YA). (gr. 4-7). reprint ed. 37.95 (*1-56849-725-3*) Buccaneer Bks., Inc.

—My Friend Flicka. 2003. (Charming Classics Ser.). (Illus.). 352p. (J). pap. 6.99 (*0-06-052429-4*) HarperCollins Children's Bk. Group.

—My Friend Flicka. 1988. 304p. (gr. 4-7). reprint ed. pap. 6.00 (*0-06-080902-7*, P-902, Perennial) HarperTrade.

—My Friend Flicka. rev. ed. 1973. (Illus.). 272p. (gr. 7-9). (J). text o.p. (*0-397-00008-1*); (YA). 15.95 (*0-397-00981-X*) Lippincott Williams & Wilkins. (Lippincott).

—My Friend Flicka. 1988. (J). 12.05 (*0-606-02855-2*) Turtleback Bks.

—Thunderhead. 1988. 384p. (gr. 4-7). reprint ed. pap. 7.50 (*0-06-080903-5*, P-903, Perennial) HarperTrade.

—Thunderhead. 1967. 320p. (YA). (gr. 5-9). pap. 1.75 o.s.i (*0-440-98875-6*, Laurel Leaf) Random Hse. Children's Bks.

—Thunderhead. 1971. (J). 12.60 o.p. (*0-606-02864-1*) Turtleback Bks.

Paulsen, Gary. The Haymeadow. 1992. 208p. (J). (gr. 4-7). 15.95 o.s.i (*0-385-30621-0*) Doubleday Publishing.

Payne, Richard A. Charlie the Shy Cowboy. 1993. (Illus.). 36p. (J). (gr. 1-9). pap. 4.95 (*0-9636186-2-8*) Blue Sky Graphics, Inc.

Saban, Vera. Johnny Egan of the Paintrock. 1986. (This Is America Ser.). (Illus.). 130p. (Orig.). (J). (gr. 4-8). pap. 6.95 (*0-914565-13-3*, Timbertrails) Capstan Pubns.

Sargent, Dave & Sargent, Pat. Hondo (Silver Dun) Look for Good in Others. 2003. (Saddle Up Ser.: Vol. 34). (Illus.). 42p. (J). lib. bdg. 22.60 (*1-56763-801-5*); mass mkt. 6.95 (*1-56763-802-3*) Ozark Publishing.

Schaefer, Jack. Shane. 1992. (Illus.). 256p. (YA). (gr. 7-12). tchr. ed. 18.00 (*0-395-07090-2*) Houghton Mifflin Co.

Schaller, Bob. Adventure in Wyoming. 2000. (X-Country Adventures Ser.). (Illus.). 128p. (J). (gr. 3-6). pap. 5.99 o.p. (*0-8010-4452-9*) Baker Bks.

Thomasma, Kenneth. Doe Sia: Bannock Girl & the Handcart Pioneer. 1999. (Amazing Indian Children: 8). (J). (gr. 3-8). pap. 7.99 (*1-880114-20-8*); 12.99 (*1-880114-21-6*) Grandview Publishing Co.

—Doe Sia: Bannock Girl & the Handcart Pioneers. 1999. (Amazing Indian Children Ser.). (Illus.). 208p. (J). (gr. 6-9). 9.99 o.p. (*0-8010-4428-6*); pap. 5.99 o.p. (*0-8010-4438-3*) Baker Bks.

—Doe Sia: Bannock Girl & the Handcart Pioneers. 1999. (Illus.). (J). 14.04 (*0-606-21884-X*) Turtleback Bks.

Wallace, Bill. Red Dog. 1987. 192p. (J). (gr. 4-7). tchr. ed. 16.95 (*0-8234-0650-4*) Holiday Hse., Inc.

—Red Dog. 2002. 192p. (J). pap. 4.99 (*0-689-85394-7*, Aladdin); 1989. 176p. (YA). (gr. 4 up). pap. 4.99 (*0-671-70141-X*, Simon Pulse) Simon & Schuster Children's Publishing.

—Red Dog. 1987. 11.04 (*0-606-03899-X*) Turtleback Bks.

Wister, Owen. Virginian. 1964. (Airmont Classics Ser.). (J). (gr. 8 up). mass mkt. 2.95 o.p. (*0-8049-0046-9*, CL-46) Airmont Publishing Co., Inc.

Y

YANGTZE RIVER AND VALLEY—FICTION

Story about Ping. 2001. (Early Readers Ser.: Vol. 1). (J). lib. bdg. (*1-59054-325-4*) Fitzgerald Bks.

YOKNAPATAWPHA COUNTY (IMAGINARY PLACE)—FICTION

Faulkner, William. Go down, Moses. 1973. 416p. (YA). (gr. 9-12). pap. 8.95 o.p. (*0-394-71884-4*, Random Hse. Bks. for Young Readers) Random Hse. Children's Bks.

—The Portable Faulkner. Cowley, Malcolm, ed. rev. ed. 1977. (Viking Portable Library: No. 18). 768p. (J). (gr. 10 up). pap. 15.95 o.s.i (*0-14-015018-8*, Penguin Bks.) Penguin Group (USA) Inc.

YOSEMITE NATIONAL PARK (CALIF.)—FICTION

Sargent, Shirley. Yosemite Tomboy. Browning, Peter, ed. 2nd ed. 1994. (Illus.). 128p. (J). (gr. 4-7). pap. 9.95 (*0-9642244-0-2*) Ponderosa Pr.

YOSEMITE VALLEY (CALIF.)—FICTION

McCully, Emily Arnold. Squirrel & John Muir, RS. 2004. (J). (*0-374-33697-0*, Farrar, Straus & Giroux (BYR)) Farrar, Straus & Giroux.

YUCATAN PENINSULA—FICTION

Hunter, Evan. Find the Feathered Serpent. 1979. (J). lib. bdg. 9.95 o.p. (*0-8398-2519-6*, Macmillan Reference USA) Gale Group.

Keller, Kent. The Mayan Mystery. 1994. (Choice Adventures Ser.: No. 14). (Illus.). 151p. (J). pap. 4.99 o.p. (*0-8423-5132-9*) Tyndale Hse. Pubs.

McCunney, Michelle. Mario's Mayan Journey. 1996. (Illus.). 32p. (J). (gr. 2-6). pap. 4.95 (*1-57255-203-4*) Mondo Publishing.

Strock, Glen T., illus. The Butterfly Pyramid. 1997. (*0-7802-8321-X*) Wright Group, The.

YUGOSLAVIA—FICTION

Cervon, Jacqueline. The Day the Earth Shook. 1969. (J). (gr. 6-8). 4.95 o.p. (*0-698-20029-2*) Putnam Publishing Group, The.

Children of Yugoslavia Staff. I Dream of Peace. 1994. (J). (ps-3). 12.95 o.p. (*0-06-251128-9*) HarperCollins Children's Bk. Group.

Hicyilmaz, Gaye. Smiling for Strangers, RS. 2000. 151p. (J). (gr. 4-7). 16.00 o.p. (*0-374-37081-8*, Farrar, Straus & Giroux (BYR)) Farrar, Straus & Giroux.

Hope-Simpson, Jacynth. Black Madonna. 1977. (J). (gr. 8 up). 6.50 o.p. (*0-8407-6516-9*, Dutton Children's Bks.) Penguin Putnam Bks. for Young Readers.

Kusan, Ivan. The Mystery of Green Hill. Petrovich, Michael B., tr. 1966. (Illus.). (J). (gr. 4-6). pap. 3.95 o.p. (*0-15-663972-6*, Voyager Bks./Libros Viajeros) Harcourt Children's Bks.

Mann, Peggy & Prusina, Katica. A Present for Yanya. 1975. (Illus.). 128p. (J). (gr. 3-6). 4.95 o.p. (*0-394-82425-3*); lib. bdg. 5.99 o.p. (*0-394-92425-8*) Random Hse. Children's Bks. (Random Hse. Bks. for Young Readers).

Mead, Alice. Adem's Cross, RS. 1996. 160p. (YA). (gr. 7-12). 15.00 o.p. (*0-374-30057-7*, Farrar, Straus & Giroux (BYR)) Farrar, Straus & Giroux.

—Adem's Cross. 1998. (Laurel-Leaf Bks.). 144p. (YA). (gr. 5-9). mass mkt. 4.50 o.s.i (*0-440-22735-6*, Laurel Leaf) Random Hse. Children's Bks.

—Adem's Cross. 1998. 10.55 (*0-606-13110-8*) Turtleback Bks.

—Girl of Kosovo, RS. 2001. 113p. (J). (gr. 4-7). 16.00 (*0-374-32620-7*, Farrar, Straus & Giroux (BYR)) Farrar, Straus & Giroux.

—Girl of Kosovo. 2003. (Illus.). 128p. (gr. 5). pap. text 4.99 (*0-440-41853-4*, Yearling) Random Hse. Children's Bks.

YUKON TERRITORY—FICTION

Hill, Kirkpatrick. Toughboy & Sister. 128p. (J). (gr. 3-7). 2000. pap. 4.99 (*0-689-83978-2*, Aladdin); 1990. mass mkt. 15.00 o.s.i (*0-689-50506-X*, McElderry, Margaret K.) Simon & Schuster Children's Publishing.

—Toughboy & Sister. 1992. (J). 9.09 (*0-606-00808-X*) Turtleback Bks.

Hill, Kirkpatrick & Greene, Douglas G. Toughboy & Sister. 1992. (Illus.). 128p. (J). (gr. 3-7). pap. 5.99 (*0-14-034866-2*, Puffin Bks.) Penguin Putnam Bks. for Young Readers.

Hobbs, William. Down the Yukon. 2002. 208p. (J). (gr. 5 up). pap. 5.95 (*0-380-73309-9*) HarperCollins Children's Bk. Group.

London, Jack. The Call of the Wild. 2002. (Great Illustrated Classics). (Illus.). 240p. (J). (gr. 3-8). lib. bdg. 21.35 (*1-57765-682-2*, ABDO & Daughters) ABDO Publishing Co.

—The Call of the Wild. 2002. (Illus.). 48p. pap. 7.50 (*0-237-52285-3*) Evans Brothers, Ltd. GBR. *Dist:* Trafalgar Square.

—The Call of the Wild. 2002. (Kingfisher Classics Ser.). 352p. (J). tchr. ed. 15.95 (*0-7534-5493-9*, Kingfisher) Houghton Mifflin Co. Trade & Reference Div.

—The Call of the Wild. Stemach, Jerry et al, eds. 2002. (Start-to-Finish Books). (J). (gr. 2-3). audio (*1-58702-808-5*) Johnston, Don Inc.

—The Call of the Wild. 2003. (Aladdin Classics Ser.). (Illus.). 160p. (J). pap. 3.99 (*0-689-85674-1*, Aladdin) Simon & Schuster Children's Publishing.

—The Call of the Wild. Clift, Eva, tr. & illus. by. 2003. (Values in Action Illustrated Classics Ser.). (J). (*1-59203-047-5*) Learning Challenge, Inc.

—The Call of the Wild. Stemach, Jerry et al, eds. abr. ed. 2002. (Start-to-Finish Books). (J). (gr. 2-3). audio (*1-58702-793-3*, H09) Johnston, Don Inc.

—The Call of the Wild. unabr. ed. 2002. (YA). pap. incl. audio compact disk (*1-58472-221-5*, In Audio) Sound Room Pubs., Inc.

—Klondike Tales. 2001. (Paperback Classics Ser.). (Illus.). 304p. pap. 11.95 (*0-375-75685-X*, Modern Library) Random House Adult Trade Publishing Group.

—To Build a Fire. 1993. (Short Stories Ser.). 48p. (YA). (gr. 5-9). lib. bdg. 18.60 (*0-87191-769-6*, Creative Education) Creative Co., The.

—To Build a Fire. abr. ed. 1999. mass mkt. 3.99 (*0-8125-6993-8*, Tor Bks.) Doherty, Tom Assocs., LLC.

—White Fang. 2002. (Great Illustrated Classics). (Illus.). 240p. (J). (gr. 3-8). lib. bdg. 21.35 (*1-57765-810-8*, ABDO & Daughters) ABDO Publishing Co.

—White Fang. 2003. 192p. (J). 4.99 (*1-57759-566-1*) Dalmatian Pr.

—White Fang. 2003. (Illus.). 272p. (J). pap. 3.99 o.p. (*0-14-250095-X*, Puffin Bks.) Penguin Putnam Bks. for Young Readers.

Luther, Rebekah S. The Yoda Family. 1994. (Illus.). 16p. (J). (gr. 3). 7.95 o.p. (*0-8059-3486-3*) Dorrance Publishing Co., Inc.

Mosley, Marilyn C. Dachshund Tails down the Yukon. 1988. (Dachshund Tails Ser.: No. 3). (Illus.). 112p. (Orig.). (J). (gr. 5). pap. 5.95 (*0-9614850-2-7*) Mosley, Marilyn C.

Wallace, Ian. Trapper Jack's Missing Toe. 2001. (Illus.). (J). (*0-7894-7666-5*) Dorling Kindersley Publishing, Inc.

—The True Story of Trapper Jack's Left Big Toe. 2002. (Illus.). 40p. (gr. 1-5). 24.90 (*0-7613-2405-4*); (J). 17.95 (*0-7613-1493-8*) Millbrook Pr., Inc. (Roaring Brook Pr.).

Whitehead, Catherine. Skookumchuck. 2002. (Illus.). 156p. (J). (gr. 5-12). pap. 11.95 (*1-58151-064-0*) BookPartners, Inc.

Z

ZENDA (IMAGINARY PLACE)—FICTION

Bassett, Jennifer, ed. The Prisoner of Zenda. 1995. (Illus.). 64p. (J). pap. text 5.95 o.p. (*0-19-422726-X*) Oxford Univ. Pr., Inc.

Hope-Hawkins, Anthony. The Prisoner of Zenda. 1967. (Airmont Classics Ser.). (Illus.). (YA). (gr. 8 up). mass mkt. 1.25 o.p. (*0-8049-0139-2*, CL-139) Airmont Publishing Co., Inc.

—The Prisoner of Zenda. 1974. 176p. (J). (gr. 7). mass mkt. 1.50 o.p. (*0-451-51137-9*, CW1137, Signet Classics) NAL.

—The Prisoner of Zenda, Level 3. Hedge, Tricia, ed. 2000. (Bookworms Ser.). (Illus.). 80p. (J). pap. text 5.95 (*0-19-423012-0*) Oxford Univ. Pr., Inc.

—The Prisoner of Zenda. Fago, John C., ed. 1978. (Now Age Illustrated IV Ser.). (Illus.). (J). (gr. 4-12). stu. ed. 1.25 (*0-88301-342-8*); text 7.50 o.p. (*0-88301-330-4*); pap. text 2.95 (*0-88301-318-5*) Pendulum Pr., Inc.

—The Prisoner of Zenda. 1984. (Classics for Young Readers Ser.). 176p. (J). (gr. 4-6). pap. 3.99 o.p. (*0-14-035032-2*, Puffin Bks.) Penguin Putnam Bks. for Young Readers.

—Rupert of Hentzau. 1970. (Dent's Illustrated Children's Classics Ser.). (Illus.). 251p. (J). reprint ed. 9.00 o.p. (*0-460-05057-5*) Biblio Distribution.

—Rupert of Hentzau. 1984. (Classics for Young Readers Ser.). 256p. (J). (gr. 4-6). pap. 2.25 o.p. (*0-14-035033-0*, Puffin Bks.) Penguin Putnam Bks. for Young Readers.

The Prisoner of Zenda. 1993. (Fiction Ser.). (YA). pap. text 6.50 o.p. (*0-582-09680-4*, 79824) Longman Publishing Group.

ZIMBABWE—FICTION

Farmer, Nancy. Do You Know Me? 1994. (Illus.). 112p. (J). (gr. 3-7). pap. 5.99 (*0-14-036946-5*, Puffin Bks.) Penguin Putnam Bks. for Young Readers.

—Do You Know Me? 1993. (Illus.). 112p. (J). (gr. 3-5). pap. 15.95 (*0-531-05474-8*); (gr. 4-7). lib. bdg. 16.99 (*0-531-08624-0*) Scholastic, Inc. (Orchard Bks.).

—The Ear, the Eye & the Arm: A Novel. 1995. 320p. (YA). (gr. 4-7). pap. 5.99 (*0-14-037641-0*, Puffin Bks.) Penguin Putnam Bks. for Young Readers.

—The Ear, the Eye & the Arm: A Novel. 1994. 320p. (YA). (gr. 7 up). pap. 18.95 (*0-531-06829-3*); lib. bdg. 19.99 (*0-531-08679-8*) Scholastic, Inc. (Orchard Bks.).

—The Ear, the Eye & the Arm: A Novel. 1995. (YA). (gr. 7 up). 12.04 (*0-606-08279-4*) Turtleback Bks.

—A Girl Named Disaster. 1998. 320p. (YA). (gr. 5-9). pap. 5.99 (*0-14-038635-1*, Puffin Bks.) Penguin Putnam Bks. for Young Readers.

—A Girl Named Disaster. 320p. 2003. (J). pap. 9.95 (*0-439-47144-3*); 1996. (YA). (gr. 5 up). pap. 19.95 (*0-531-09539-8*); 1996. (YA). (gr. 6 up). lib. bdg. 20.99 (*0-531-08889-8*) Scholastic, Inc. (Orchard Bks.).

—A Girl Named Disaster. 1998. (J). 12.04 (*0-606-13430-1*) Turtleback Bks.

Mutswairo, Solomon M. Mapondera: Soldier of Zimbabwe. 1978. 133p. 14.00 o.p. (*1-57889-047-0*); pap. 10.00 (*1-57889-046-2*) Passeggiata Pr.

—Mapondera: Soldier of Zimbabwe. 1978. pap. 7.00 o.p. (*0-914478-20-6*, Three Continents) Rienner, Lynne Pubs., Inc.

—Mapondera: Soldier of Zimbabwe. Herdeck, Donald, tr. 1978. (Illus.). 15.00 o.p. (*0-914478-19-2*, Three Continents) Rienner, Lynne Pubs., Inc.

Stock, Catherine. Gugu's House. 2001. (Illus.). 32p. (J). (ps-3). lib. bdg., tchr. ed. 14.00 (*0-618-00389-4*, Clarion Bks.) Houghton Mifflin Co. Trade & Reference Div.

—Where Are You Going, Manyoni. 1993. (Illus.). 48p. (J). (ps-3). 16.99 (*0-688-10352-9*) HarperCollins Children's Bk. Group.

—Where Are You Going, Manyoni. 1993. (Illus.). 48p. (J). (ps-3). lib. bdg. 16.89 o.p. (*0-688-10353-7*, Morrow, William & Co.) Morrow/Avon.

PUBLISHER NAME INDEX

17th Street Productions, An Alloy Online Inc. Co., (*1-931497*) 151 W. 26th St., 11th Flr., New York, NY 10001 Tel 212-244-4307; Fax: 212-244-4311
E-mail: peterlopez@alloy.com
Web site: http://www.alloy.com.

1stBooks Library, (*1-58500; 0-9675669; 1-58721; 1-58820; 0-7596; 1-4033; 1-4107; 1-4140*) Div. of Advanced Marketing Technologies, 2595 Vernal Pike, Bloomington, IN 47403 (SAN 253-7605) Fax: 812-961-1023; Toll Free: 800-839-8640
E-mail: 1stbooks@1stbooks.com
Web site: http://www.1stbooks.com.

21st Century Pr., (*0-9717009; 0-9725719; 0-9728899*) 3308 S. Meadowlark Ave., Springfield, MO 65807 Tel 417-889-4803; Fax: 417-889-2210; Toll Free: 800-658-0284; *Imprints:* Sonship Press (Sonship Pr)
E-mail: lee@21stcenturypress.com
Web site: http://www.21stcenturypress.com.

7 Heads Publishing, (*0-9716596*) 3972 Barranca Pkwy., Suite J, No. 225, Irvine, CA 92606
E-mail: theceo@mindspring.com.

A + Children's Bks. and Music, (*1-888527*) Orders Addr.: 1336 Hwy. 138, Riverdale, GA 30296 (SAN 255-7266) Tel 770-994-4774; Fax: 770-969-1462
E-mail: info@apluschildrensbooks.com
Web site: http://www.apluschildrensbooks.com
Dist(s): **New World Pubns., Inc..**

A & B Books *See* **A & B Distributors & Pubs. Group**

A & B Distributors & Pubs. Group, (*1-881316; 1-886433*) Div. of A&B Distributors, 1000 Atlantic Ave., Brooklyn, NY 11238 (SAN 630-9216) Tel 718-783-7808; Fax: 718-783-7267; Toll Free: 877-542-6657; 146 Lawrence St., Brooklyn, NY 11201 (SAN 631-385X)
E-mail: maxtay@webspan.net
Dist(s): **D&J Bk. Distributors**
Red Sea Pr..

A & C Black (GBR) (*0-245; 0-333; 0-510; 0-7136; 0-85177; 0-85314; 0-212; 0-85146; 0-85147; 0-85317; 0-86019; 0-946716; 0-9507160; 1-85691*) *Dist. by* **Lubrecht & Cramer.**

A & C Black (GBR) (*0-245; 0-333; 0-510; 0-7136; 0-85177; 0-85314; 0-212; 0-85146; 0-85147; 0-85317; 0-86019; 0-946716; 0-9507160; 1-85691*) *Dist. by* **Players Pr.**

A Bison Original Imprint of Univ. of Nebraska Pr.

A+ Bk. Publishing, (*1-929819*) Orders Addr.: P.O. Box 250165, Franklin, MI 48025-0165 Tel 248-223-9322; Fax: 248-223-9161; Edit Addr.: 29233 Wellington Ct., No. 61, Southfield, MI 48034
E-mail: kpcartwright@ameritech.net
Dist(s): **BookMasters, Inc..**

AGA Publishing, (*1-892671*) P.O. Box 513, Apex, NC 27502 Tel 919-387-4568; Fax: 919-303-7111; Toll Free: 800-804-7759
E-mail: aga@pagesz.net
Dist(s): **Quality Bks., Inc..**

AIMS International Bks., Inc., (*0-922852*) 7709 Hamilton Ave., Cincinnati, OH 45231-3103 (SAN 630-270X) Tel 513-521-5590; Fax: 513-521-5592; Toll Free: 800-733-2067
E-mail: aimsbooks@fuse.net
Web site: http://www.aimsbooks.com
Dist(s): **Shen's Bks..**

AMICA Publishing Hse., (*1-884187*) Div. of AMICA International, 844 Industry Dr., No. 20, Seattle, WA 98188-3410 Tel 206-467-1035; Fax: 206-467-1522
E-mail: amica@ix.netcom.com
Web site: http://www.amicaint.com.

†AMS Pr., Inc., (*0-404*) Brooklyn Navy Yard Bldg. 292, Suite 417, 63 Flushing Ave., New York, NY 11205 (SAN 106-6706) Tel 718-875-8100; Fax: 212-995-5413 Do not confuse with companies with the same or similar name in Los Angeles, CA, Pittsburgh, PA
E-mail: amserve@earthlink.net; *CIP.*

A Place to Remember Imprint of deRuyter-Nelson Pubns., Inc.

ARO Publishing Co., (*0-89868*) Box 193, 398 S. 1100 W., Provo, UT 84601 (SAN 212-6370) Tel 801-377-8218; Fax: 801-818-0616; *Imprints:* Reading Research (Read Res)
E-mail: arobook@yahoo.com
Dist(s): **Forest Hse. Publishing Co., Inc..**

A R T L U Publishing, (*0-615*) 5043 SE Dupont Rd., Berryton, KS 66409 Tel 785-379-9533; 785-368-3700 ; Fax: 785-368-3743
E-mail: alancarolhayes@excite.com.

ASDA Publishing, Inc., (*0-9632319*) 904 Forest Lake Dr., Lakeland, FL 33809 Tel 841-859-2194.

Abaris Bks., (*0-89835; 0-913870*) 70 New Canaan Ave., Norwalk, CT 06850-2600 (SAN 206-4588) Tel 203-849-1655; Fax: 203-849-9181
E-mail: abaris@abarisbooks.com; abarisbooks@worldnet.att.net
Web site: http://www.abarisbooks.com.

Abbeville Kids Imprint of Abbeville Pr., Inc.

†Abbeville Pr., Inc., (*0-7892; 0-89659; 1-55859*) 116 W. 23rd St., Suite 500, New York, NY 10011 (SAN 211-4755) Tel 646-375-2039; Fax: 646-375-2040; Toll Free: 800-278-2665; *Imprints:* Artabras (Artabras); Abbeville Kids (Abbeville Kids)
E-mail: service@abbeville.com; abbeville@abbeville.com
Web site: http://www.abbeville.com
Dist(s): **Client Distribution Services;** *CIP.*

Abbey Pr., (*0-87029*) 1 Hill Dr., Saint Meinrad, IN 47577-0128 (SAN 201-2057) Tel 812-357-8215; Fax: 812-357-8388; Toll Free: 800-325-2511
E-mail: customerservice@abbeypress.com
Web site: http://www.abbeypress.com/.

ABDO & Daughters Imprint of ABDO Publishing Co.

Abdo & Daughters Publishing *See* **ABDO Publishing Co.**

†ABDO Publishing Co., (*0-939179; 1-56239; 1-57765; 1-59197*) Div. of the Abdo Consulting Group, Inc., Orders Addr.: P.O. Box 398166, Minneapolis, MN 55439-8166 (SAN 662-9164) Tel 952-831-2120; Fax: 952-831-1632; Toll Free: 800-800-1312; P.O. Box 56510, Vaughan, ON L4 8V3 Tel 905-851-4660; Fax: 905-851-5507; Edit Addr.: 4940 Viking Dr., Suite 622, Edina, MN 55435 (SAN 662-9172) Tel 952-831-2120 ext. 1; Fax: 952-831-1632; 938 Woodbridge Ave., Vaughan, ON L4L 8V3; *Imprints:* ABDO & Daughters (ABDO & Dghtrs)
E-mail: info@abdopub.com
Web site: http://www.abdopub.com; *CIP.*

†Abingdon Pr., (*0-687*) Div. of United Methodist Publishing Hse., Orders Addr.: P.O. Box 801, Nashville, TN 37202-3919 (SAN 201-0054) Tel 615-749-6409; Fax: 615-749-6056; Toll Free Fax: 800-836-7802; Toll Free: 800-251-3320; Edit Addr.: 201 Eighth Ave., S., Nashville, TN 37202 (SAN 699-9956)
E-mail: info@abingdon.org
Web site: http://www.abingdonpress.com/
Dist(s): **CRC Pubns.;** *CIP.*

Aboriginal Studies Pr. (AUS) (*0-85575*) *Dist. by* **Intl Spec Bk.**

Abrams, Harry N. , Inc., (*0-8109*) 100 Fifth Ave., New York, NY 10011 (SAN 200-2434) Tel 212-206-7715; Fax: 212-645-8437
E-mail: webmaster@abramsbooks.com
Web site: http://www.abramsbooks.com
Dist(s): **Time Warner Bk. Group.**

Absey & Co., (*1-888842*) 23011 Northcrest, Spring, TX 77389 Tel 281-257-2340; Fax: 281-251-4676; Toll Free: 888-412-2739
E-mail: Abseyandco@aol.com
Web site: http://www.absey.com
Dist(s): **Baker & Taylor Bks.**
Brodart Co.
Follett Library Resources.

Academic Therapy Pubns., Inc., (*0-87879; 1-57128*) 20 Commercial Blvd., Novato, CA 94949-6191 (SAN 201-2111) Tel 415-883-3314; Fax: 415-883-3720; Toll Free: 800-422-7249; *Imprints:* Ann Arbor Division (Ann Arbor Div)
E-mail: sales@academictherapy.com; customerservice@academictherapy.com
Web site: http://www.academictherapy.com
Dist(s): **PCI Educational Publishing**
PRO-ED, Inc.
Saddleback Publishing, Inc.
Sopris West.

†Academy Chicago Pubs., Ltd., (*0-89733; 0-915864*) 363 W. Erie St., Chicago, IL 60610-3125 (SAN 213-2001) Tel 312-751-7300; Fax: 312-751-7306; Toll Free: 800-248-7323 (Orders, outside Illinois)
E-mail: info@academychicago.com
Web site: http://www.academychicago.com
Dist(s): **Baker & Taylor Bks.**
Brodart Co.; *CIP.*

Acadia Publishing Co., (*0-934745*) Div. of World Three, Inc., P.O. Box 170, Bar Harbor, ME 04609 (SAN 694-1648) Tel 207-288-9025; Fax: 207-288-1132
E-mail: sales@acadiapublishing.com
Web site: http://www.acadiapublishing.com.

Accent Books *See* **Accent Pubns.**

Accent Pubns., *(0-7814; 0-89636; 0-916406; 1-56476)* Div. of Cook Communications Ministries, Orders Addr.: P.O. Box 36640, Colorado Springs, CO 80936 (SAN 208-5097) Tel 719-535-2905; Fax: 719-535-2928; Toll Free: 800-525-5550; Edit Addr.: 4050 Lee Vance View, Colorado Springs, CO 80918 Do not confuse with Accent Pubns. in Kawkawlin, MI
E-mail: connielhawkins@yahoo.com
Web site: http://www.accentcurriculum.com.

Access Pr. Imprint of HarperInformation

Acclaim Bks., *(1-57840)* Div. of Acclaim Comics, Inc., 1 Acclaim Plaza, Glen Cove, NY 11542-2777 Tel 516-656-5000; Fax: 516-656-2037
Dist(s): **Penguin Group (USA) Inc..**

Acclaim Comics, Incorporated *See* **Acclaim Bks.**

†Ace Bks., *(0-441)* Div. of Berkley Publishing Group, Orders Addr.: 405 Murray Hill Pkwy, East Rutherford, NJ 07073 Toll Free: 800-526-0275 (orders); Edit Addr.: 375 Hudson St., New York, NY 10014 (SAN 665-6404) Tel 212-366-2000
Web site: http://www.penguinputnam.com/
Dist(s): **Penguin Group (USA) Inc.**; *CIP.*

Ace Reid Enterprises *See* **Cowpokes Cartoon Bks.**

Ace/Putnam Imprint of Penguin Group (USA) Inc.

Acequia Madre, *(0-940875)* Box 6, El Valle Rte., Chamisal, NM 87521 (SAN 664-7871) Tel 505-689-2200
E-mail: rmms@espanola-nm.com
Dist(s): **Books West**
Sunbelt Pubns., Inc.
Treasure Chest Bks..

Achievers Technology Resource, Inc., *(0-9716113)* PMB No. 455, 442 Rte. 202-206 N., Bedminster, NJ 07921-1522 (SAN 254-2811)
Web site: http://www.achieversrus.com
Dist(s): **Independent Pubs. Group.**

Acorn Publishing *See* **ChoiceSkills, Inc.**

Acropolis Bks., Inc., *(0-87491; 1-889051)* 8601 Dunwoody Pl., Suite 303, Atlanta, GA 30350-2509 (SAN 299-1497) Tel 770-643-1118; Fax: 770-643-1170; Toll Free: 800-773-9923
E-mail: acropolisbooks@mindspring.com
Web site: http://www.acropolisbooks.com
Dist(s): **Internaturally, Inc..**

ACTA Pubns., *(0-87946; 0-914070; 0-915388)* 4848 N. Clark St., Chicago, IL 60640-4711 (SAN 204-7489) Tel 773-271-1030; Fax: 773-271-7399; Toll Free Fax: 800-397-0079; Toll Free: 800-397-2282
E-mail: acta@one.org.

Action Factor, Inc., *(0-9720763)* PMB 218, 3195 Dayton-Xenia Rd., Suite 900, Beavercreek, OH 45434-6390 Tel 937-426-4364 (phone/fax)
E-mail: giffordca@actionfactor.com
Web site: http://www.actionfactor.com.

Action Publishing, LLC, *(0-9617199; 1-883649; 1-888045)* P.O. Box 391, Glendale, CA 91209 (SAN 299-1802) Tel 323-478-1667; Fax: 323-478-1767; Toll Free: 800-705-7482 Do not confuse with companies with the same or similar name in Newport Beach, CA, Burlingame, CA, West Los Angeles, CA, Houstin, TX, Chicago, IL, Ocala, CA, Austin, TX
E-mail: sales@actionpublishing.com
Web site: http://www.politicards.com.

Addax Publishing Group, Inc., *(1-886110; 1-58497)* 8643 Hauser Dr., Suite 235, Lenexa, KS 66215-4543 Tel 913-438-5333; Fax: 913-438-2079; Toll Free: 800-598-5550
E-mail: addax1@addaxpublishing.com
Dist(s): **Baker & Taylor Bks.**
Booksource, The
National Bk. Network.

†Addison-Wesley Longman, Inc., *(0-201; 0-321; 0-582; 0-673; 0-8013; 0-8053; 0-9654123)* Orders Addr.: 200 Old Tappan Rd., Old Tappan, NJ 07675 (SAN 299-4739) Toll Free: 800-922-0579; Edit Addr.: 75 Arlington St., Suite 300, Boston, MA 02116 (SAN 200-2000) Tel 617-848-7500; Toll Free: 800-447-2226
E-mail: pearsoned@eds.com; orderdeptnj@pearsoned.com
Web site: http://www.awl.com
Dist(s): **Continental Bk. Co., Inc.**
Pearson Education
Trans-Atlantic Pubns., Inc.; *CIP.*

Addison-Wesley Longman, Ltd. (GBR) *(0-582) Dist. by* **Trans-Atl Phila.**

Addison-Wesley Publishing Company, Incorporated *See* **Addison-Wesley Longman, Inc.**

Adirondack Kids Pr., *(0-9707044)* 39 Second St., Camden, NY 13316 Tel 315-245-3614; Fax: 315-245-4861
E-mail: gvanriper@aol.com
Web site: http://www.adirondackkids.com.

Adler's Foreign Bks., Inc., *(0-8417)* 915 Foster St., Evanston, IL 60201 (SAN 111-3089) Tel 847-864-0664; Fax: 847-864-0804; Toll Free: 800-235-3771
E-mail: info@afb-adlers.com
Web site: http://www.afb-adlers.com
Dist(s): **Distribooks, Inc..**

Ad-Lib Publications *See* **Open Horizons Publishing Co.**

Adobe Systems, Inc., *(1-58039; 1-930161; 1-931208; 1-58945; 1-59061)* 1601 Trapelo Rd., Waltham, MA 02451 (SAN 663-1975) Fax: 508-544-7053.

Adonis Pr., *(0-932776)* 320 Rte. 21C, Ghent, NY 12075 (SAN 661-9320) Tel 518-672-4736 (phone/fax)
E-mail: adonis@taconic.net
Dist(s): **SteinerBooks, Inc..**

Advaita Ashrama (IND) *(81-85301; 81-7505) Dist. by* **Vedanta Pr.**

Advance Publishers, Incorporated *See* **Advance Pubs. LLC**

Advance Pubs. LLC, *(0-9619525; 1-57973; 1-885222)* 2290 Lucien Way, Suite 280, Maitland, FL 32751 (SAN 244-9226) Tel 407-916-1950; Fax: 407-916-0600; Toll Free: 800-777-2041
E-mail: questions@adv-pub.com; advpublish@aol.com
Web site: http://www.advancepublishers.com.

Advance Publishing, Inc., *(0-9610810; 1-57537)* 6950 Fulton St., Houston, TX 77022 (SAN 263-9572) Tel 713-695-0600; Fax: 713-695-8585; Toll Free: 800-917-9630 Do not confuse with Advance Publishing, Brownburg, IN
E-mail: info@advancepublishing.com
Web site: http://www.advancepublishing.com.

Advanced Global Distribution Services, 5880 Oberlin Dr., San Diego, CA 32121 Toll Free Fax: 800-499-3822; Toll Free: 800-284-3580.

Advanced Marketing Services, Incorporated *See* **Advantage Pubs. Group**

Advantage Books *See* **Advantage Bks., LLC**

Advantage Bks., LLC, *(0-9660366; 0-9714609)* 1001 Spring St., No. 206, Silver Spring, MD 20910 (SAN 253-8237) Tel 301-495-2307; Fax: 301-562-8449; Toll Free: 888-238-8588
E-mail: advantagebooks@aol.com
Web site: http://www.addvance.com.

Advantage Pubs. Group, *(0-934429; 1-57145; 1-59223)* 5880 Oberlin Dr., San Diego, CA 92121 (SAN 630-8090) Toll Free: 800-284-3580; *Imprints:* Thunder Bay Press (Thunder Bay); Silver Dolphin Books (Silver Dolph)
E-mail: janetn@advmkt.com
Web site: http://www.advantagebooksonline.com; http://www.laurelglenbooks.com; http://www.thunderbaypress.com; http://www.bathroomreader.com; http://www.silverdolphinbooks.com
Dist(s): **Publishers Group West.**

Adventure Ink, Company *See* **Real Kids Real Adventures**

Adventure Medical Kits, *(0-9659768)* Orders Addr.: P.O. Box 43309, Oakland, CA 94624 Tel 510-261-7414; Fax: 510-261-7419; Toll Free: 800-324-3517; Edit Addr.: 5555 San Leandro St., Oakland, CA 94621
E-mail: AMKUSA@aol.com.

Adventures for Kids Co., *(0-9659570)* Orders Addr.: P.O. Box 526, Wisconsin Dells, WI 53965 Tel 608-253-6015; Edit Addr.: 426 Vine St., Wisconsin Dells, WI 53965
Dist(s): **Bookmen, Inc..**

Advocacy Pr., *(0-911655)* Div. of Girls Inc. of Greater Santa Barbara, P.O. Box 236, Santa Barbara, CA 93102 (SAN 263-9114) Tel 805-962-2728; Fax: 805-963-3580; Toll Free: 800-676-1480
E-mail: advpress@impulse.net
Web site: http://www.advocacypress.com
Dist(s): **Baker & Taylor Bks.**
Bookpeople
Wieser Educational, Inc..

Aegina Pr., Inc., *(0-916383; 1-56002)* 1905 Madison Ave., Huntington, WV 25704 (SAN 665-469X) Fax: 304-429-7234; *Imprints:* University Editions (Univ Edtns)
E-mail: tommcat28@aol.com.

Aerial Imprint of Farrar, Straus & Giroux

Aerie Imprint of Doherty, Tom Assocs., LLC

Africa World Pr., *(0-86543; 1-59221)* 541 W. Ingham Ave., Trenton, NJ 08638 (SAN 692-3925) Tel 609-695-3200; Fax: 609-695-6466
E-mail: awprsp@africanworld.com
Web site: http://www.africanworld.com.

African American Images, *(0-913543)* 1909 W. 95th St., Chicago, IL 60643 Tel 773-445-0322; Fax: 773-445-9844; Toll Free: 800-552-1991
E-mail: aai@africanamericanimages.com
Web site: http://www.AfricanAmericanImages.com
Dist(s): **Independent Pubs. Group.**

Africana Homestead Legacy Pubs., *(0-9653308)* Orders Addr.: P.O. Box 2957, Cherry Hill, NJ 08034-0265 Tel 856-662-9858; Fax: 856-662-9516; Edit Addr.: 7719 Broad St., No. B, Pennsauken, NJ 08109
E-mail: publisher@ahlpub.com
Web site: http://www.ahlpub.com
Dist(s): **BookMasters, Inc..**

Ageless Treasures, *(0-9705726)* Orders Addr.: 3536 Saint Andrews Village Cir., Louisville, KY 40241-2664 (SAN 253-794X) Tel 502-412-5940; Fax: 502-327-6233
E-mail: carlawebb@agelesstreasures.net; dcw0810@insightbb.com.

Agreka Bks., LLC, *(1-888106)* P.O. Drawer 39, Sandy, UT 84091-0039 Tel 801-733-0708; Toll Free Fax: 888-771-7758; Toll Free: 800-360-5284
E-mail: info@agreka.com
Web site: http://www.utahbooks.com; http://www.agreka.com; http://www.historypreserved.com
Dist(s): **Baker & Taylor Bks.**
Quality Bks., Inc..

Aguilar Editorial (MEX) *(968-19) Dist. by* **Santillana.**

Aha Punana Leo, *(0-9645646; 1-58191; 1-890270)* 928 Nuuanu Ave., Suite 315, Honolulu, HI 96817-5193
E-mail: haawina@leoki.uhh.hawaii.edu
Web site: http://www.ahapunanaleo.org
Dist(s): **Booklines Hawaii, Ltd.**
Native Bks..

AIL Newmedia Publishing, *(1-893798)* Div. of A. L. Labs, Orders Addr.: P.O. Box 147, Park Ridge, NJ 07656 (SAN 253-293X) Tel 201-505-1133; Fax: 815-550-4364; Edit Addr.: 31 Franklin Tpke., Waldwick, NJ 07463 Tel 201-444-5051 (phone/fax)
E-mail: publisher@newmediapublishing.com
Web site: http://www.newmediapublishing.com
Dist(s): **Baker & Taylor Bks.**
Quality Bks., Inc..

Aim Higher Bks., *(0-9713292)* P.O. Box 339, French Camp, CA 95231 Tel 209-983-1904
E-mail: releone@aol.com.

Aim Higher Publishing *See* **Aim Higher Bks.**

Airmont Publishing Co., Inc., *(0-8049)* 160 Madison Ave., New York, NY 10016 (SAN 206-8710) Tel 212-598-0222; Fax: 212-979-1862
E-mail: customerservice@avalonbooks.com; orderdept@avalonbooks.com
Web site: http://www.avalonbooks.com/.

Airplay, *(1-885608)* 110 W. 86th St., 12th Flr., New York, NY 10024-4049 Tel 212-879-1201; Fax: 212-879-1013; Toll Free: 800-459-4925
Dist(s): **Barnes & Noble Bks.-Imports**
Baker & Taylor Bks.
Bookazine Co., Inc.
Borders, Inc.
Brodart Co.
Koen Bk. Distributors.

Akela West Pubs., *(0-9634007; 1-882416)* Orders Addr.: P.O. Box 1646, Deming, NM 88031-1646 (SAN 297-746X); Edit Addr.: San Diego Rd., Deming, NM 88031.

Akiba Pr., *(0-934764)* Box 13086, Oakland, CA 94661 (SAN 212-0666) Tel 510-339-1283 Do not confuse with Akiba Press, Escondido, CA
E-mail: akiba@lemberg.com; paul@lemberg.com.

Aladdin Imprint of Simon & Schuster Children's Publishing

Aladdin Library Imprint of Simon & Schuster Children's Publishing

Aladdin Paperbacks, *(0-02; 0-671; 0-689; 0-7434)* Div. of Simon & Schuster Children's Publishing, 1230 Avenue of the Americas, New York, NY 10020
Web site: http://www.simonsays.com/
Dist(s): **Lectorum Pubns., Inc.**
Libros Sin Fronteras
Simon & Schuster Trade Paperbacks
Simon & Schuster, Inc..

Alaska Native Language Ctr., *(0-933769; 1-55500)* Univ. of Alaska, P.O. Box 757680, Fairbanks, AK 99775-7680 (SAN 692-9796) Tel 907-474-7874; Fax: 907-474-6586
E-mail: fyanlp@uaf.edu
Web site: http://www.uaf.edu/anlc
Dist(s): **Todd Communications.**

Alaska Northwest Bks. Imprint of Graphic Arts Ctr. Publishing Co.

Alcazar Audioworks, *(0-9724995; 0-9746806)* 3032 Alcazar Dr., Burlingame, CA 94010-5814 Tel 650-692-1166; Fax: 650-692-7911
E-mail: bfrohman@pacbell.net
Web site: http://www.alcazaraudioworks.com.

Alchemy Communications Group, Ltd., *(0-934323)* Div. of Alchemy II, Inc., 34341 Amber Lantern St., Dana Point, CA 92629-3011 (SAN 693-5990) Tel 818-700-8300; Fax: 818-882-0840
Dist(s): **Playskool, Inc..**

Alef Design Group, *(1-881283)* 4423 Fruitland Ave., Los Angeles, CA 90058 Tel 323-582-1200; Fax: 323-585-0327; Toll Free: 800-845-0662
E-mail: jane@torahaura.com
Web site: http://www.torahaura.com.

Alexie Bks., *(0-9679416)* Div. of Alexie Enterprises, Inc., P.O. Box 3843, Carmel, IN 46082 Tel 317-844-5638; Fax: 317-846-0788
E-mail: alexie8@aol.com; BusJobs@aol.com; sales@alexiebooks.com
Web site: http://www.alexieenterprises.com
Dist(s): **Baker & Taylor Bks.**
Distributors, The.

Alfaguara, Ediciones, S.A.- Grupo Santillana (ESP) *(84-204; 958-704) Dist. by* **Santillana.**

Alfred Publishing Co., Inc., *(0-7390; 0-88284)* Orders Addr.: P.O. Box 10003, Van Nuys, CA 91410-0003; Edit Addr.: 16320 Roscoe Blvd., Suite 100, Van Nuys, CA 91406 (SAN 201-243X) Tel 818-891-5999; Fax: 818-891-2369; 123 Dry Rd., Oriskany, NY 13424 Tel 315-736-1572; Fax: 315-736-7281
E-mail: customerservice@alfred.com
Web site: http://www.alfred.com.

†Algonquin Bks. of Chapel Hill, *(0-7611; 0-912697; 0-945575; 1-56512)* Div. of Workman Publishing Co., Inc., Orders Addr.: 708 Broadway, New York, NY 10003 Tel 212-254-5900 (orders, customer service); Fax: 212-614-7783; Toll Free Fax: 800-521-1832 (fax orders, customer sevice); Toll Free: 800-722-7202 (orders, customer service); Edit Addr.: P.O. Box 2225, Chapel Hill, NC 27515-2225 (SAN 282-7506) Tel 919-967-0108 (editorial, publicity, marketing); Fax: 919-933-0272 (editorial, publicity, marketing); 127 Kingston Dr., Suite 105, Chapel Hill, NC 27514 (SAN 662-2011)
E-mail: dialogue@algonquin.com
Web site: http://www.booksellerscorner.com; http://www.algonquin.com; *CIP.*

Al-Huda Printing & Publishing Company *See* **Al-Huda Pubs.**

Al-Huda Pubs., *(0-9642101)* 888 S. Greenville, Suite 301, Richardson, TX 75081
E-mail: info@alhudapublishers.com
Web site: http://www.alhudapublishers.com.

Alianza Editorial, S. A. (ESP) *(84-206) Dist. by* **Continental Bk.**

Alianza Editorial, S. A. (ESP) *(84-206) Dist. by* **Distribks Inc.**

All About Kids Publishing, *(0-615; 0-9700863; 0-9710278; 0-9744446)* 6280 San Ignacio Ave., Suite D, San Jose, CA 95119 (SAN 253-8601) Tel 408-578-4026; Fax: 408-578-4029
E-mail: mail@aakp.com
Web site: http://www.aakp.com
Dist(s): **Consortium Bk. Sales & Distribution.**

Allen & Douglas Pubs., *(0-9674281)* 1536 Islamorada Blvd., Punta Gorda, FL 33955-1818 Tel 941-505-1135 (phone/fax, star 51)
E-mail: marstan@nut-n-but.net.

Allen & Unwin Pty., Ltd. (AUS) *(0-04; 0-86861; 1-85242; 1-86373; 1-86448; 1-875680; 1-875889; 0-7299; 1-86508; 1-74114) Dist. by* **IPG Chicago.**

Allen, Hubert & Assocs., *(0-9641694)* 720-25 Tramway Ln., NE, Albuquerque, NM 87122 Tel 505-797-3520; Fax: 505-797-3521
E-mail: hubertaallen@compuserve.com.

Allen, J. A. & Co., Ltd. (GBR) *(0-85131) Dist. by* **St Mut.**

Allied Crafts Pr., *(0-9632305)* 726 Bison Ave., Newport Beach, CA 92660 Tel 949-759-8156; Fax: 949-759-1426
E-mail: mm2yg@aol
Dist(s): **Baker & Taylor Bks..**

Allied Enterprises, *(0-9605082)* P.O. Box 3237, Chicago, IL 60690-3237 (SAN 238-9045) Tel 312-836-0421; Fax: 312-836-0909.

Allied Publishing, *(1-57755)* 107 Nob Hill Park Dr., Reisterstown, MD 21136 Tel 410-833-5278; Fax: 410-833-6193; *Imprints:* Flying Frog Publishing (Flyng Frog) Do not confuse with Allied Publishing, Irving, TX.

Alpha Bks., *(0-943149)* Orders Addr.: P.O. Box 13, Rickreall, OR 97371 (SAN 668-1166); Edit Addr.: 2519 E. Ellendale, Dallas, OR 97338 (SAN 668-1174) Tel 503-623-6889 Do not confuse with companies with the same name in Falls Church, VA, Century City, CA.

Alpha Bks., *(0-02; 0-672; 0-7357; 0-7897; 1-56761; 1-57595; 0-7431; 1-59257)* Div. of Pearson Technology Group, 201 W. 103rd St., Indianapolis, IN 46290 (SAN 219-6298) Tel 317-581-3500 Toll Free: 800-571-5840 (orders)
Web site: http://www.idiotsguides.com
Dist(s): **Libros Sin Fronteras**
Penguin Group (USA) Inc.
Sams Technical Publishing, LLC
netLibrary, Inc..

Alpha-Dolphin Pr., *(1-880485)* Orders Addr.: P.O. Box 206, Fiddletown, CA 95629 Tel 209-296-4680; Fax: 209-298-4961; Toll Free: 800-205-8254; Edit Addr.: 17300 Old River Rd., Fiddletown, CA 95629-0206
E-mail: dolphin@volcano.net
Dist(s): **Baker & Taylor Bks.**
New Leaf Distributing Co., Inc..

†Alpine Pubns., Inc., *(0-931866; 1-57779)* Orders Addr.: P.O. Box 7727, Loveland, CO 80537-0027 (SAN 255-2094); Edit Addr.: 225 S. Madison Ave., Loveland, CO 80537 Tel 970-667-2017; Fax: 970-667-9157; Toll Free: 800-777-7257 (orders only)
E-mail: alpinecsr@aol.com
Web site: http://www.alpinepub.com
Dist(s): **Baker & Taylor Bks.**
Western International, Inc.; *CIP.*

Alpine Publishing, *(1-885624)* 1119 S. Mission Rd., No. 102, Fallbrook, CA 92028 Tel 760-728-3161; Fax: 760-728-3394 Do not confuse with Alpine Publishing, Monroe, OR.

Altea, Ediciones, S.A. - Grupo Santillana (ESP) *(84-372) Dist. by* **Santillana.**

AlterLingo Bks. Imprint of O'Hollow Publishing

Althouse Pr., *(1-59087)* 2251 Dick George Rd., Cave Junction, OR 97523 Tel 541-592-4142; Fax: 541-592-2597
E-mail: noah@oism.org
Web site: http://www.robinsonbooks.org.

Alton Museum of History & Art, Inc., *(0-9678461)* 2809 College Ave., Alton, IL 62002 Tel 618-463-1795.

Alyson Pubns., *(0-932870; 1-55583; 1-59350)* Div. of Liberation Pubns., Inc., Orders Addr.: P.O. Box 4371, Los Angeles, CA 90078 (SAN 213-6546) Tel 323-860-6070; Fax: 323-467-0152; Toll Free: 800-464-4574 (orders only); Edit Addr.: 6922 Hollywood Blvd., Suite 100, Los Angeles, CA 90028; *Imprints:* Alyson Wonderland (Alyson Wonderland)
E-mail: mail@alyson.com
Web site: http://www.alyson.com
Dist(s): **Consortium Bk. Sales & Distribution.**

Alyson Wonderland Imprint of Alyson Pubns.

amana-pubns., *(0-915957; 1-59008)* Div. of amana corp., 10710 Tucker St., Beltsville, MD 20705-2223 (SAN 630-9798) Tel 301-595-5777; Fax: 301-595-5888; Toll Free: 800-660-1777
E-mail: amana@igprinting.com
Web site: http://www.amana-publications.com.

Amaro Bks., *(0-9620556; 1-883203)* 9765-C SW 92nd Ct., Ocala, FL 34481-8623 (SAN 249-2032) Tel 352-237-9840; Fax: 352-237-1810
E-mail: amarobooks@aol.com
Dist(s): **Book Warehouse.**

Amazing Dreams Publishing, *(0-9719628)* P.O. Box 1811, Asheville, NC 28802
E-mail: contact@amazingdreamspublishing.com
Web site: http://www.amazingdreamspublishing.com.

Ambassador Bks., Inc., *(0-9646439; 1-929039)* 91 Prescott St., Worcester, MA 01605 Tel 508-756-2893; Fax: 508-757-7055; Toll Free: 800-577-0909
E-mail: info@ambassadorbooks.com
Web site: http://www.ambassadorbooks.com
Dist(s): **Baker & Taylor Bks.**
Christian Bk. Distributors
Spring Arbor Distributors, Inc..

Amber Bks., *(0-9655064; 0-9702224; 0-9727519)* 1334 E. Chandler Blvd., Suite 5-D67, Phoenix, AZ 85048 Tel 480-460-1660; Fax: 480-283-0991
E-mail: amberbk@aol.com
Web site: http://www.amberbooks.com
Dist(s): **A & B Distributors & Pubs. Group**
Baker & Taylor Bks.
Brodart Co.
Culture Plus Bks.
D&J Bk. Distributors
Follett Library Resources
Koen Bk. Distributors
Midwest Library Service.

Amber Lotus *See* **Amber Lotus Publishing**

Amber Lotus Publishing, *(0-945798; 1-56937; 1-885394)* 537 Castro St., San Francisco, CA 94114 Tel 415-864-7388; 415-664-7388; Fax: 415-864-7399 ; Toll Free: 800-326-2375
E-mail: info@amberlotus.com
Web site: http://www.amberlotus.com
Dist(s): **Banyan Tree Bks..**

Amereon, Ltd., *(0-8488; 0-88411; 0-89190)* Orders Addr.: P.O. Box 1200, Mattituck, NY 11952 (SAN 201-2413) Tel 631-298-5100; Fax: 631-298-5631; Edit Addr.: 800 Wickham Ave., Mattituck, NY 11952; *Imprints:* Rivercity Press (Rivercity Pr); American Reprint Company (Am Repr)
E-mail: amereon@aol.com.

American Biography Service, Incorporated *See* **Reprint Services Corp.**

†American Ceramic Society, The, *(0-916094; 0-934706; 0-944904; 1-57498)* Orders Addr.: P.O. Box 6136, Westerville, OH 43086-6136; Edit Addr.: 735 Ceramic Pl., Westerville, OH 43081-8720 (SAN 201-6958) Tel 614-890-4700; Fax: 614-899-6109
E-mail: customersrvc@acers.org
Web site: http://www.ceramics.org
Dist(s): **World Scientific Publishing Co., Inc.;** *CIP.*

American Education Publishing Imprint of McGraw-Hill Children's Publishing

American Girl Imprint of Pleasant Co. Pubns.

American Guidance Service, Inc., *(0-7854; 0-88671; 0-913476; 0-942277; 1-56269)* 4201 Woodland Rd., Circle Pines, MN 55014-1796 (SAN 201-694X) Tel 763-786-4343; Fax: 763-786-9077; Toll Free: 800-328-2560
E-mail: ags@mr.net
Web site: http://www.agsnet.com.

American Historical Society of Germans from Russia, *(0-914222)* 631 D St., Lincoln, NE 68502-1199 (SAN 204-7543) Tel 402-474-3363; Fax: 402-474-7229
E-mail: ahsgr@aol.com
Web site: http://www.ahsgr.org.

American Literary Pr., Inc., *(1-56167)* 8019 Belair Rd., Suite 10, Baltimore, MD 21236-3711 Tel 410-882-7700; Fax: 410-882-7703; Toll Free: 800-873-2003
E-mail: amerlit@erols.com
Web site: http://www.erols.com/amerlit
Dist(s): **Baker & Taylor Bks.**
Children's Library of Poetry
Temme Haus Pr..

†American Psychological Assn., *(0-912704; 0-945354; 1-55798; 1-59147)* Orders Addr.: P.O. Box 92984, Washington, DC 20090-2984 (SAN 685-3137) Tel 202-336-6123; 202-336-5510; Fax: 202-336-5502 (orders); Toll Free: 800-374-2721; Edit Addr.: 750 First St., NE, Washington, DC 20002-4241 (SAN 255-5921) Tel 202-336-5836; *Imprints:* Magination Press (Magination Press)
E-mail: ghughes@spa.org
Web site: http://www.apa.org; *CIP.*

American Reprint Co. Imprint of Amereon, Ltd.

American Trust Pubns., *(0-89259)* 745 McClintock Dr., Suite 114, Burr Ridge, IN 60521-0857 (SAN 664-6158)
Dist(s): **Islamic Bk. Service.**

Amerotica Imprint of NBM Publishing Co.

Ames Publishing Co., *(0-9615263)* 21172 Aspen Ave., Castro Valley, CA 94546 (SAN 695-1945) Tel 510-537-3250.

Amherst Pr., *(0-910122; 0-942495; 1-930596)* Div. of The Guest Cottage, Inc., Orders Addr.: P.O. Box 848, Woodruff, WI 54568 (SAN 213-9820) Tel 715-358-5195; Fax: 715-358-9456; Toll Free: 800-333-8122; Edit Addr.: 8821 Hwy. 47, Woodruff, WI 54568 (SAN 666-6450) Do not confuse with companies with the same name in Amherst, NY, North Hampton, NH
E-mail: sales@theguestcottage.com
Web site: http://www.theguestcottage.com.

AMIDEAST, *(0-913957)* 1730 M. St. NW, Suite 1100, Washington, DC 20036-4505 (SAN 286-7184) Tel 202-776-9600; Fax: 202-776-7000
E-mail: inquiries@amideast.org
Web site: http://www.amideast.org.

Amirah Publishing, *(1-889720)* Div. of IFNA, Orders Addr.: P.O. Box 541146, Flushing, NY 11354 Tel 917-439-2825; Fax: 718-321-9004; Edit Addr.: a/o IBTS, Inc., P.O. Box 5153, Long Island City, NY 11105 Tel 718-357-3872 (phone/fax)
E-mail: amirahpbco@aol.com
Web site: http://www.ifna.net; http://www.islamiceducation.net
Dist(s): **International Bks. & Tapes Supply.**

Amistad Pr. Imprint of HarperTrade

AmityWorks, *(0-9678923)* 18 Pale Dawn Pl., Spring, TX 77381-6637
Web site: http://www.amityworks.com.

Ammons Communications, Ltd., *(0-9651232)* 29 Regal Ave., Sylva, NC 28779 Tel 828-631-4587 (phone/fax); *Imprints:* Catch the Spirit of Appalachia (CSA)
E-mail: vscopelite@aol.com; CSA@dnet.net
Dist(s): **Baker & Taylor Bks..**

Amon Carter Museum, *(0-88360)* 3501 Camp Bowie Blvd., Fort Worth, TX 76107-2695 (SAN 204-7608) Tel 817-738-1933; Fax: 817-336-1123; Toll Free: 800-573-1933
E-mail: teresa.tucker@cartermuseum.org
Web site: http://www.cartermuseum.org.

Amsea Group, Inc., *(0-9723044)* 441 N. Central Ave., Suite 1, Campbell, CA 95008 Tel 408-378-9200; Fax: 408-379-5621; Toll Free: 800-535-5363
E-mail: tuneman@aol.com
Web site: http://www.amseagroup.com.

Anchor Publishing, *(1-888828)* Orders Addr.: P.O. Box 0992, Muskegon, MI 49443-0992; Edit Addr.: 307 W. Muskegon Ave., Muskegon, MI 49441 Do not confuse with companies with the same or similar name in Anchorage, AK, Landover Hills, MD, Waxhaw, NC, Port Angeles, WA, San Angelo, TX.

Anchorage Pr., *(0-87602)* Orders Addr.: P.O. Box 2901, Louisville, KY 40201-2901 (SAN 203-4727) Tel 502-583-2288; Fax: 502-583-2281 Do not confuse with Anchorage Pr., Houston, TX
E-mail: applays@bellsouth.net.

†Ancient City Pr., Inc., *(0-941270; 1-58096)* Orders Addr.: P.O. Box 5401, Santa Fe, NM 87502 (SAN 164-5552) Tel 505-982-8195; Toll Free Fax: 800-622-8667; Toll Free: 800-249-7737
Dist(s): **Univ. of New Mexico Pr.**; *CIP.*

And Bks., *(0-89708)* 702 S. Michigan, Suite 836, South Bend, IN 46601 (SAN 213-9502) Tel 219-232-3134; Fax: 219-288-4141
E-mail: andbooks@ripco.com
Dist(s): **Distributors, The.**

Andersen Pr., Ltd. (GBR) *(0-86264; 0-905478; 1-84270) Dist. by* **Trafalgar.**

Andre Deutsch (GBR) *(0-233) Dist. by* **Trafalgar.**

Andre Deutsch (GBR) *(0-233) Dist. by* **Trans-Atl Phila.**

†Andrews McMeel Publishing, *(0-8362; 0-7407)* Orders Addr.: c/o Simon & Schuster, Inc., 100 Front St., Riverside, NJ 08075 Toll Free Fax: 800-943-9831 ; Toll Free: 800-943-9839 (Customer Service; 800-897-7650 (Credit Dept.); Edit Addr.: 4520 Main St., Kansas City, MO 64111-7701 (SAN 202-540X) Tel 816-932-6600; Fax: 816-932-6749; Toll Free: 800-851-8923
Web site: http://www.AndrewsMcMeel.com
Dist(s): **AMCAL, Inc.**
Simon & Schuster, Inc.; *CIP.*

Angel Gate Imprint of Left Field Ink

Angel Pubns., *(1-889383)* 3111 Rte. 38, No. 11, Suite 124, Mount Laurel, NJ 08054 Tel 609-235-6896; Fax: 609-235-7167; 310 Timberline Dr., Mount Laurel, NJ 08054 Tel 609-235-6896; Fax: 609-235-7167
E-mail: angelpubs@aol.com
Web site: http://www.angelpubs.com
Dist(s): **Amazon.Com**
Barnes&Noble.com.

Angela's Bookshelf, *(1-881545)* 3039 S. Bagley, Ithaca, MI 48847 Tel 517-875-4985; Fax: 517-875-4988; Toll Free: 800-882-6443
E-mail: abpub@abpub.com.

Angle Publishing Company, Incorporated *See* **Welcome Rain Pubs.**

Animazing Entertainment, Inc., *(1-58083)* 2221 Niagara Falls Blvd., Niagara Falls, NY 14304 Tel 716-731-5137; Fax: 716-731-9180.

Ann Arbor Div. Imprint of Academic Therapy Pubns., Inc.

Ann Arbor Media Group, LLC, *(1-58726)* P.O. Box 1007, Ann Arbor, MI 48106-1007 Tel 734-769-1004 (ext. 1267); Fax: 734-769-0350; *Imprints:* Mundus (Mundus); For Your Knowledge (For Your Knowledge)
E-mail: tbudzinski@annarbormediagroup.com.

Anness Publishing, Inc., *(1-886890)* 27 W. 20th St., Suite 504, New York, NY 10011-3707 (SAN 299-0563) Tel 212-807-6739; Fax: 212-807-6813; Toll Free: 800-354-9657; *Imprints:* Lorenz Books (Lorenz Bks)
E-mail: rwoodcock@anness.com.

Annick Pr., Ltd. (CAN) *(0-920236; 0-920303; 1-55037) Dist. by* **Firefly Bks Limited.**

Anoai Pr., *(0-9653971; 0-9702618)* 3349-A Anoai Pl., Honolulu, HI 96822 Tel 808-988-6109; Fax: 808-988-1119
E-mail: kukui@lava.net
Web site: http://www.anoaipress.com
Dist(s): **Booklines Hawaii, Ltd..**

Antarctic Pr., *(0-930655)* P.O. Box 7134, Bellevue, WA 98008 (SAN 684-2631) Tel 425-885-6853; Fax: 425-867-3905 Do not confuse with Antarctic Pr., San Antonio, TX.

Anthroposophic Press, Incorporated *See* **SteinerBooks, Inc.**

Antioch Publishing Co., *(0-7824; 0-89954; 1-4017)* Div. of The Antioch Co., Orders Addr.: P.O. Box 28, Yellow Springs, OH 45387-0028 (SAN 654-7214) Tel 937-767-7379; Fax: 937-767-6137; Toll Free: 800-543-1515; 800-543-2397; Edit Addr.: 888 Dayton St., Yellow Springs, OH 45387 Do not confuse with Antioch Publishing Co., Torrance, CA
Web site: http://www.antioch.com.

Antioch Publishing Co., *(0-9659551)* Div. of the Optimox Corp., Orders Addr.: P.O. Box 3378, Torrance, CA 90502 Tel 310-618-9370; Fax: 310-618-8748; Toll Free: 800-223-1601; Edit Addr.: 2720 Monterey St., Suite 406, Torrance, CA 90503 Do not confuse with Antioch Publishing Co., Yellow Springs, OH
E-mail: optimox@msn.com
Web site: http://www.optimox.com.

Antipodes Bks. & Beyond, 9707 Fairway Ave., Silver Spring, MD 20901-3001 Tel 301-602-9519; Fax: 301-565-0160
E-mail: Antipode@antipodesbooks.com
Web site: http://www.antipodesbooks.com.

Antique Collectors' Club, *(0-902028; 0-907462; 1-85149)* Orders Addr.: 91 Market St. Industrial Park, Wappingers Falls, NY 12590 (SAN 630-7787) Tel 845-297-0003; Fax: 845-297-0068; Toll Free: 800-252-5231 (orders)
E-mail: info@antiquecc.com
Web site: http://www.antiquecc.com; http://www.antiquecc.com.

Anubis Publishing, *(0-9707845)* 5122 Spencer Rd., Lyndhurst, OH 44124 Tel 440-461-3709; Fax: 440-446-9340; Toll Free: 888-461-3709 Do not confuse with Anubis Publishing in Manorville, NY
E-mail: piperdbw@aol.com; jeoldtp@aol.com
Web site: http://members.aol.com/piperdbw.

Anvil Bks., Ltd. (IRL) *(0-900068; 0-947962; 1-901737) Dist. by* **Dufour.**

Anvil Bks., Ltd. (IRL) *(0-900068; 0-947962; 1-901737) Dist. by* **Irish Bks Media.**

Anythings Possible, Inc., *(1-892186)* Orders Addr.: 1863 N. Farwell Ave., Milwaukee, WI 53202 Fax: 414-226-4901; Toll Free: 800-543-7153
E-mail: info@special-kids.com
Web site: http://www.special-kids.com.

AOL Time Warner Book Group *See* **Time Warner Bk. Group**

Aoyama Publishing *See* **Marble House Editions**

AppleTree Press *See* **Lanton Haas Pr.**

†Applewood Bks., *(0-918222; 1-55709)* 128 The Great Rd., Bedford, MA 01730 (SAN 210-3419) Tel 781-271-0055; Fax: 781-271-0056; Toll Free: 800-277-5312
E-mail: applewood@awb.com
Web site: http://www.awb.com
Dist(s): **Consortium Bk. Sales & Distribution**; *CIP.*

Applied Arts Pubs., *(0-911410)* Div. of Sowers Printing Co., Box 479, Lebanon, PA 17042 (SAN 204-4838) Tel 717-272-9442; Fax: 717-274-2928.

Apprentice Shop Bks., LLC, *(0-9723410)* 18 Wentworth Dr., Bedford, NH 03110-4718 Fax: 603-472-2588
E-mail: mlduboi@aol.com.

AP's Travels *See* **Aunt Patty's Travels-London**

Aquarelle Pr., *(0-9616679)* Orders Addr.: P.O. Box 3676, Baton Rouge, LA 70821-3676 (SAN 659-7270) ; Edit Addr.: 5036 Hyacinth Ave., Baton Rouge, LA 70808 (SAN 659-7289) Tel 504-926-4220; Toll Free: 800-569-2920
Dist(s): **Baker & Taylor Bks..**

†Arcade Publishing, Inc., *(1-55970; 1-58996)* Orders Addr.: c/o Time Warner Trade Publishing, 3 Center Plaza, Boston, MA 02108 Toll Free Fax: 800-890-0875; Toll Free: 800-759-0190; Edit Addr.: 141 Fifth Ave., New York, NY 10010 (SAN 252-2012) Tel 212-475-2633; Fax: 212-353-8148
E-mail: arcadeinfo@arcadepub.com
Web site: http://www.arcadepub.com
Dist(s): **Publishers Group West**
Time Warner Interactive
Time Warner Bk. Group; *CIP.*

Archway Paperbacks Imprint of Pocket Bks.

Argyle Bks., *(0-9642573)* 710 Old Justin Rd., Argyle, TX 76226 Tel 940-464-3368; Fax: 940-380-0151
E-mail: info@argylebooks.com
Web site: http://www.iglobal.net/argyle/
Dist(s): **Hervey's Booklink & Cookbook Warehouse.**

Arizona-Sonora Desert Museum Pr., *(1-886679)* 2021 N. Kinney Rd., Tucson, AZ 85743 Tel 520-883-3028; Fax: 520-883-2500
E-mail: info@desertmuseum.org; asdmpress@desertmuseum.org
Web site: http://www.desertmuseum.org.

Ark Works, Inc., *(1-887146)* Orders Addr.: P.O. Box 1215, Orleans, MA 02653; Edit Addr.: 46 Main St., Orleans, MA 02653 Tel 508-240-1987
E-mail: Sales@ArkWorks.com
Web site: http://www.Arkworks.com.

Arlie Enterprises, *(1-880175)* Orders Addr.: P.O. Box 360933, Strongsville, OH 44136 (SAN 297-4665) Tel 440-238-9397 (phone/fax); Edit Addr.: 17035 Raccoon Trail, Strongsville, OH 44136 (SAN 297-4673)
E-mail: arlieentwarren@juno.com
Web site: http://www.arliebooks.com.

Aromatique, Inc., *(0-9633348)* Orders Addr.: P.O. Box 1500, Heber Springs, AR 72543 Tel 501-362-7511; Fax: 501-362-5361; Toll Free: 800-262-7511.

Aronson, Jason Pubs., *(0-7657; 0-87668; 1-56821)* Orders Addr.: P.O. Box 1539, Fort Lee, NJ 07024-2539 (SAN 665-6536) Fax: 201-840-7242; Toll Free: 800-782-0015; Edit Addr.: 230 Livingston St., Northvale, NJ 07647 (SAN 201-0127) Tel 201-767-4093; Fax: 201-767-4330 Do not confuse with companies with similar name in Highmount, NY, Arcade, NY, Santa Monica, CA
E-mail: editor@aronson.com
Web site: http://www.aronson.com.

Art After Five, *(0-9628710)* P.O. Box 247, Nederland, CO 80466-9537 Tel 303-258-3742; Toll Free: 800-572-7816
Dist(s): **Baker & Taylor Bks..**

†Art Services International, *(0-88397)* 1319 Powhatan St., Alexandria, VA 22314-1342 (SAN 204-0964)
E-mail: office@artservicesintl.org
Web site: http://www.artservicesintl.org; *CIP.*

Artabras Imprint of Abbeville Pr., Inc.

†Arte Publico Pr., *(0-934770; 1-55885)* Univ. of Houston, 452 Cullen Performance Hall, Houston, TX 77204 (SAN 213-4594) Tel 713-743-2841; Fax: 713-743-3080; 713-743-2847; Toll Free: 800-633-2783; *Imprints:* Piñata Books (Pinata Bks)
E-mail: cebaker@uh.edu
Web site: http://www.arte.uh.edu
Dist(s): **Baker & Taylor International**
Bookpeople
Coutts Library Service, Inc.
Empire Publishing Service
Follett Library Resources
Lectorum Pubns., Inc.
Libros Sin Fronteras
Midwest Library Service
Blackwell North America
Quality Bks., Inc.
SPD-Small Pr. Distribution; *CIP.*

Artel Publishing, *(1-889062)* P.O. Box 2123, Cary, NC 27512 Tel 919-387-8972; Fax: 919-387-3340
E-mail: artelpubs@worldnet.att.net.

Artesian Pr., *(1-58659)* Div. of R. F. Dawn, Inc., 7300 Artesia Blvd., Buena Park, CA 90621 (SAN 253-1259) Tel 714-562-0415; Fax: 714-562-0237; Toll Free Fax: 888-462-0226; Toll Free: 888-734-9355
E-mail: MillerEduc@aol.com
Web site: http://www.millereducational.com.

Artisan, *(1-57965; 1-885183)* Div. of Workman Publishing Co., Inc., 708 Broadway, New York, NY 10003 Tel 212-254-5900; Fax: 212-677-6692; Toll Free: 800-967-5630 Do not confuse with Artisan, Wheaton, IL
E-mail: artisan@workman.com.

Artisan House *See* **Artisan**

Artsource Publishing *See* **Markowitz Publishing**

As Simple As That, *(0-9728666)* P.O. Box 31, Montauk, NY 11954 Toll Free: 866-599-7246
Web site: http://www.simpleasthat.com
Dist(s): **Midpoint Trade Bks., Inc..**

Asclepian Pr., *(1-893351)* 386 Quartz Cir., Bailey, CO 80421 Tel 303-816-9618; Fax: 303-816-9619
E-mail: pni@bewellnet.com
Web site: http://www.imeqinationheals.com.

AshleyAlan Enterprises, *(0-9702171; 0-9710145)* Orders Addr.: P.O. Box 1510, Kyle, TX 78640-1510 Tel 512-405-3065; Fax: 512-405-3066; Edit Addr.: 115 Hogan, Kyle, TX 78640
E-mail: celestem@kyle-tx.com
Web site: http://www.ashleyanlan.com.

Names

Aspen Bks., *(1-56236)* Div. of Worldwide Pubs., Inc., P.O. Box 1271, Bountiful, UT 84011-1271 Toll Free: 800-748-4850
E-mail: jasay@qwest.net; prawlins@aspenbook.com
Dist(s): **Origin Bk. Sales, Inc..**

Aspen Pr., Ltd., *(1-882954)* 601 Academy Dr., Northbrook, IL 60062 (SAN 298-7716) Tel 847-291-6600; Fax: 847-291-2261.

†Aspen Pubs., Inc., *(0-444; 0-7896; 0-8342; 0-87189; 0-87622; 0-89443; 0-912862)* Subs. of Wolters Kluwer Nv, Orders Addr.: 7210 McKinney Cir., Frederick, MD 21704 Fax: 301-417-7550; Toll Free Fax: 800-901-9075; Toll Free: 800-638-8437; 800-234-1660 (Customer Service); Edit Addr.: 1185 Avenue of the Americas, 37th Flr., New York, NY 10036 (SAN 203-4999) Tel 212-597-0200; Fax: 212-597-0338
E-mail: customer.service@aspenpubl.com
Web site: http://www.aspenpublishers.com; *CIP.*

Astor-Honor, Inc., *(0-8392)* 16 E. 40th St., Third Flr., New York, NY 10016 (SAN 203-5022) Tel 212-840-8800; Fax: 212-840-7246.

Astoria Productions, *(0-9662378; 0-9715876)* 8260 Eagle Ridge Dr., Concord, OH 44077 Tel 440-392-9041; Fax: 440-392-9042
E-mail: astoriaproductions@att.net.

Asylum Arts, *(1-878580)* 5847 Sawmill Rd., Paradise, CA 95969-5333 (SAN 297-2816) Tel 530-876-1454
E-mail: asyarts@sunset.net
Web site: http://www.asylumartsbooks.com
Dist(s): **SPD-Small Pr. Distribution.**

Atara Publishing, *(1-886611)* 8150 Briarwood St., Stanton, CA 90680-3906 Tel 714-892-7475; Fax: 714-892-7455; Toll Free: 888-366-3537 Do not confuse with Atara Publishing Co. in New York, NY
E-mail: doodle@atara.com
Web site: http://www.atara.com.

Atheneum Imprint of Simon & Schuster Children's Publishing

Atheneum/Anne Schwartz Bks. Imprint of Simon & Schuster Children's Publishing

Atheneum/Richard Jackson Bks. Imprint of Simon & Schuster Children's Publishing

Atlantean Pr., *(0-9626854; 1-885862)* Orders Addr.: P.O. Box 7336, Golden, CO 80403 Tel 303-604-0788; Toll Free: 800-621-5535; Edit Addr.: 44 Rudi Ln., Golden, CO 80403.

Atria Imprint of Simon & Schuster

Atrium Publishing, Incorporated *See* **Trellis Publishing, Inc.**

Attic Pr. (IRL) *(1-85594; 0-946211) Dist. by* **Intl Spec Bk.**

Attic Studio Press *See* **Attic Studio Publishing Hse.**

Attic Studio Publishing Hse., *(1-883551)* Orders Addr.: P.O. Box 75, Clinton Corners, NY 12514 (SAN 298-2838) Tel 845-266-8100; Fax: 845-266-5515; Toll Free: 800-974-5533 (orders); Edit Addr.: 564 Schultzville Rd., Clinton Corners, NY 12514 (SAN 298-2846)
E-mail: atticstudiopress@aol.com; collegeavepress@aol.com
Dist(s): **Baker & Taylor Bks.**
Spring Arbor Distributors, Inc..

Auburn Publishing Co., *(1-889832)* 29 Carrier Ct., Auburn, ME 04210 Tel 207-753-1917 Do not confuse with Auburn Publishing, Auburn, IN
E-mail: auburnpub@aol.com
Web site: http://members.aol.com/auburnpub/index.html.

Audio Bk. Co., *(0-89926)* 125 N. Aspen Ave., Suite 2, Azusa, CA 91702 (SAN 158-1414) Fax: 626-969-6099; Toll Free: 800-423-8273
E-mail: sales@audiobookco.com
Web site: http://www.audiobookco.com.

Audio Bk. Contractors, Inc., *(1-55685)* P.O. Box 40115, Washington, DC 20016-0115 (SAN 687-0376) Tel 202-363-3429 (phone/fax)
E-mail: flogibsonABC@aol.com.

Audio Craft Press *See* **AudioCraft Publishing, Inc.**

Audio Editions Bks. on Cassette Imprint of Audio Partners Publishing Corp.

Audio Language Studies, Incorporated *See* **Durkin Hayes Publishing Ltd.**

Audio Literature, *(0-944993; 1-57453)* 370 W. San Bruno Ave., Suite F, San Bruno, CA 94066 (SAN 245-9825) Tel 650-583-9700; Fax: 650-583-0235; Toll Free: 800-383-0174
E-mail: audiolit@aol.com
Web site: http://www.audiouniverse.com
Dist(s): **Baker & Taylor Bks.**
Landmark Audiobooks
New Leaf Distributing Co., Inc.
Publishers Group West.

Audio Partners, Incorporated *See* **Audio Partners Publishing Corp.**

Audio Partners Publishing Corp., *(0-88690; 0-945353; 1-57270)* P.O. Box 6930, Auburn, CA 95604-6930 (SAN 253-4622) Tel 530-888-7803; Fax: 530-888-1840; Toll Free Fax: 800-882-1840; Toll Free: 800-231-4261 (orders only); *Imprints:* Audio Editions Books on Cassette (Audio Editions)
E-mail: info@audiopartners.com
Web site: http://www.audiopartners.com
Dist(s): **Baker & Taylor Bks.**
Landmark Audiobooks
Publishers Group West.

Audio Renaissance, *(0-940687; 1-55927; 1-59397)* Div. of Holtzbrinck Publishers, Orders Addr.: 16365 James Madison Hwy., Gordonsville, VA 22942-8501 Toll Free Fax: 800-672-2054; Toll Free: 888-330-8477; Edit Addr.: 175 Fifth Ave., Suite 315, New York, NY 10010 (SAN 665-1275) Tel 212-674-5151; Fax: 917-534-0980
Dist(s): **Holtzbrinck Pubs.**
Landmark Audiobooks.

AudioCraft Publishing, Inc., *(1-893699)* Orders Addr.: P.O. Box 281, Topinabee, MI 49791 Tel 231-238-0297 ; Fax: 231-238-0298; Toll Free: 888-420-4244; Edit Addr.: 1416 Patterson, Topinabee, MI 49791
E-mail: boreas@mich.com
Web site: http://www.michiganchillers.com; http://www.americanchillers.com; http://www.audiocraftpublishing.com.

Audio-Forum *See* **Norton Pubs., Inc., Jeffrey /Audio-Forum**

Audioscope, *(1-57375)* Div. of K-tel International (USA), Inc., 2605 Fernbrook Ln., N., No. H-O, Plymouth, MN 55447 Tel 612-559-6888; Fax: 612-559-6848; Toll Free: 800-328-6640
Web site: http://www.ktel.com.

Augsburg Bks. Imprint of Augsburg Fortress, Pubs.

†Augsburg Fortress, Pubs., *(0-8006; 0-8066)* Orders Addr.: P.O. Box 1209, Minneapolis, MN 55440-1209 (SAN 169-4081) Tel 612-330-3300; Fax: 612-330-3455; Toll Free Fax: 800-722-7766; Toll Free: 800-328-4648 (orders only); Edit Addr.: 100 S. Fifth St., Suite 700, Minneapolis, MN 55402; *Imprints:* Augsburg Books (Augsburg Bks)
E-mail: info@augsburgfortress.org; productinfo@augsburgfortress.org; subscriptions@augsburgfortress.org; customerservice@augsburgfortress.com
Web site: http://www.augsburgfortress.org
Dist(s): **CRC Pubns.;** *CIP.*

Augsburg Fortress Publishers, Publishing House of The Evangelical Lutheran Church in America *See* **Augsburg Fortress, Pubs.**

†August Hse. Pubs., Inc., *(0-87483; 0-935304)* Orders Addr.: P.O. Box 3223, Little Rock, AR 72203-3223 (SAN 223-7288) Tel 501-372-5450; Fax: 501-372-5579; Toll Free: 800-284-8784; Edit Addr.: 201 E. Markham St., Little Rock, AR 72201
E-mail: order@augusthouse.com; ahinfo@augusthouse.com
Web site: http://www.augusthouse.com
Dist(s): **Continental Bk. Co., Inc.;** *CIP.*

Augustinians of the Assumption *See* **Ambassador Bks., Inc.**

†Aunt Lute Bks., *(0-918040; 0-933216; 1-879960)* Div. of Aunt Lute Foundation, Orders Addr.: P.O. Box 410687, San Francisco, CA 94141 Tel 415-826-1300; Fax: 415-826-8300; Edit Addr.: 2180 Bryant St., San Francisco, CA 94110-2128
E-mail: books@auntlute.com
Web site: http://www.auntlute.com
Dist(s): **Bookpeople**
Consortium Bk. Sales & Distribution
SPD-Small Pr. Distribution; *CIP.*

Aunt Patty's Travels-London, *(0-9659668)* 4811 Wesleyan Woods Dr., Macon, GA 31210.

Aunt Strawberry Bks., *(0-9669988)* Orders Addr.: P.O. Box 819, Boulder, CO 80306-0819 (SAN 299-9811) Tel 303-449-3574; Fax: 303-444-9221; Edit Addr.: 3255 20th St., Boulder, CO 80304
E-mail: samthe1@hotmail.com.

Aura Printing, Inc., *(0-911643)* 88 Parkville Ave., Brooklyn, NY 11230 (SAN 237-9317) Tel 718-435-9103; Fax: 718-871-9488
Dist(s): **Baker & Taylor Bks.**
Bookazine Co., Inc..

Aurelia Pr., *(0-9670595)* P.O. Box 1426, Richland, WA 99352 (SAN 253-1003) Tel 509-627-0751; Fax: 509-627-0703 Do not confuse with Aurelia Press in Montague, TX
E-mail: info@aureliapress.com
Web site: http://www.aureliapress.com.

Auriga, Ediciones S.A. (ESP) *(84-7281) Dist. by* **Continental Bk.**

Auromere, Inc., *(0-89744)* 2621 W. US Hwy. 12, Lodi, CA 95242-9200 (SAN 169-0043) Fax: 209-339-3715; Toll Free: 800-735-4691
E-mail: sasp@lodinet.com
Web site: http://www.auromere.com
Dist(s): **DeVorss & Co.**
New Leaf Distributing Co., Inc.
Red Wheel/Weiser.

Australian Book Source *See* **Terra Nova Pr.**

Authors Choice Pr. Imprint of iUniverse, Inc.

AV Concepts Corp., *(0-931334; 1-55576)* 30 Montauk Blvd., Oakdale, NY 11769 (SAN 655-5888) Tel 516-567-7227; Fax: 516-567-8745
Dist(s): **Continental Bk. Co., Inc..**

Avalon Publishing Group, *(0-7867; 0-88184; 0-929654; 0-931188; 0-938410; 1-56025; 1-56201; 1-56924; 1-58005; 1-878067)* Div. of Avalon Publishing Group Inc., 161 William St., 16th Flr., New York, NY 10038 Tel 646-375-2570; Fax: 646-375-2571; *Imprints:* Carroll & Graf Publishers (Carr & Graf); Marlowe & Company (Marl & Co)
Web site: http://www.sealpress.com; http://www.carrollandgraf.com; http://www.marlowepub.com; http://www.thundersmouth.com; http://www.avalonpub.com
Dist(s): **Bilingual Pubns. Co., The**
Publishers Group West
netLibrary, Inc..

Avatar Pr., Inc., *(0-9706784; 1-59291)* 9 Triumph Dr., Urbana, IL 61802 Tel 217-384-2211; Fax: 217-384-2216 Do not confuse with companies with the same or similar name in Sunnyside, NY, Atlanta, GA, Brick, NJ
E-mail: william@avatarpress.net
Web site: http://www.avatarpress.com
Dist(s): **Diamond Book Distributors, Inc.**
Diamond Comic Distributors, Inc..

Ave Maria Pr., *(0-87793; 0-939516; 1-59471)* P.O. Box 428, Notre Dame, IN 46556-0428 (SAN 201-1255) Tel 547-287-2831; Fax: 574-239-2908; Toll Free Fax: 800-282-5681; Toll Free: 800-282-1865
E-mail: avemariapress.1@nd.edu
Web site: http://www.avemariapress.com.

Avenue Publishing, *(0-9661306)* 603 Seagaze Dr., PMB 531, Oceanside, CA 92054 Tel 760-720-7189; Fax: 760-720-9544 Do not confuse with Avenue Publishing Co., Hamtramck, MI
E-mail: Nvlwritr13@aol.com
Web site: http://www.Avepub.com.

Avocet Pr., Inc., *(0-9661072; 0-9677346; 0-9705049; 0-9725078)* 19 Paul Ct., Pearl River, NY 10965-1539 (SAN 299-4631) Fax: 845-735-6807; Toll Free: 877-428-6238
E-mail: books@avocetpress.com
Web site: http://www.avocetpress.com
Dist(s): **Words Distributing Co..**

Avon Imprint of HarperCollins Children's Bk. Group

Avon Bks. Imprint of Morrow/Avon

Awani Pr., *(0-915266)* P.O. Box 881, Fredericksburg, TX 78624 (SAN 206-4626) Tel 830-997-5514; Fax: 830-990-0863
E-mail: tupiinc@ktc.com.

Awesome Bks., LLC., *(0-9646302)* 25 Winding Ln., Darien, CT 06820 Tel 203-655-2444; Fax: 203-655-6916
E-mail: miklorelli@aol.com
Web site: http://www.lorelli.net
Dist(s): **Baker & Taylor Bks.**
Partners Pubs. Group, Inc..

Awe-Struck E-Bks., *(1-928670; 1-58749)* 2458 Cherry St., Dubuque, IA 52001-5749; *Imprints:* Byte/Me Book (Byte Me Book)
E-mail: kdstruck@home.com
Web site: http://www.awe-struck.net.

Ayer Co. Pubs., Inc., *(0-88143)* Orders Addr.: c/o IDS, 300 Bedford St., Suite B-213, Manchester, NH 03101 (SAN 211-6936) Fax: 603-669-7945; Toll Free: 888-267-7323
E-mail: cservice@ayerpub.com
Web site: http://www.ayerpub.com.

Azro Pr., Inc., *(0-9660239; 1-929115)* Orders Addr.: 1704 Llano St., Suite B, PMB 342, Sante Fe, NM 87505 Tel 505-989-3272; Fax: 505-989-3832
E-mail: gae@nets.com
Web site: http://www.azropress.com.

B.A.B., Ltd., *(1-928895)* Orders Addr.: P.O. Box 2327, Boston, MA 02107-2327 Tel 617-335-9817; 617-923-9553; Edit Addr.: 8 Westland Rd., Watertown, MA 02174
E-mail: bostonart@hotmail.com
Web site: http://www.BostonArtBoutique.com.

B&B Audio, Inc., *(1-882071)* 3175 Commercial Ave., Suite 107B, Northbrook, IL 60062 (SAN 248-207X) Tel 847-562-9516; Fax: 847-562-9517; Toll Free: 800-354-7836 (orders)
E-mail: info@bandbaudio.com
Web site: http://www.bandbaudio.com
Dist(s): **Landmark Audiobooks.**

B&C Pubns., *(0-9650660)* 4736 Jennifer St., Boise, ID 83704 Tel 208-376-4645
Dist(s): **Writers Pr., Inc..**

BCM Pubns., Inc., *(0-86508)* 237 Fairfield Ave., Upper Darby, PA 19082-2206 (SAN 211-7762) Tel 610-352-7177; Fax: 610-352-5561; Toll Free: 800-226-4685
E-mail: info@bcmintl.org; 103046.613@compuserve.com
Web site: http://www.bcmintl.org
Dist(s): **Christian Literature Crusade, Inc..**

B.C. Publishing, Inc., *(0-926521)* Orders Addr.: Rte. 3, Box 734, Broken Arrow, OK 74014; Edit Addr.: 26520 E. 57th St., Broken Arrow, OK 74014 Tel 918-357-3285.

B Ediciones S.A. (ESP) *(84-406; 84-7735; 84-666)*
Dist. by **Lectorum Pubns.**

B Ediciones S.A. (ESP) *(84-406; 84-7735; 84-666)*
Dist. by **Distribks Inc.**

B G R Publishing *See* **EMG Networks**

BHF Memories Unlimited, *(0-9614108)* 154 E. Tamarack Cir., Parachute, CO 81635 (SAN 685-2998) Tel 970-285-1306
E-mail: FreedancR@aol.com.

BJO's Enterprises, *(0-941381)* 1016 W. 12th Ave., Eugene, OR 97402-4720 (SAN 667-1276).

Babcock Publishing Co., *(1-892161)* P.O. Box 8053, Saginaw, MI 48608 Tel 517-781-4830; Fax: 517-781-4610; 3505 Williamson, Saginaw, MI 48601
E-mail: jerrysps@aol.com
Web site: http://www.swiftsite.com/swm0164/books.htm.

Babu Bks., *(0-9722880)* P.O. Box 2449, Woburn, MA 01888-0849
E-mail: ccryan@attbi.com
Web site: http://www.babubooks.com (under construction).

Baby Hearts Pr., *(0-9652508)* Orders Addr.: 3910 Sierra Blanca, Temple, TX 76502 Tel 254-778-4770; Toll Free: 888-222-4649
E-mail: ajaworski@aol.com
Web site: http://www.babyhearts.com.

Baby Star Productions, LLC, *(0-9705974)* 17847 W. Mequon Rd., Germantown, WI 53022 Tel 262-628-8939; Fax: 262-628-9647
E-mail: burczyk@execpc.com.

Back Bay Imprint of Little Brown & Co.

Back to the Bible Publishing, *(0-8474)* Orders Addr.: P.O. Box 82808, Lincoln, NE 68501 (SAN 211-6901) Tel 402-464-7200; Fax: 402-464-7474; Toll Free: 888-559-7878; Edit Addr.: 6400 Cornhusker Hwy., Lincoln, NE 68507
E-mail: books@backtothebible.org
Web site: http://www.backtothebible.org
Dist(s): **Vision Video.**

Backinprint.com Imprint of iUniverse, Inc.

Backroads, *(0-933294)* P.O. Box 212, Daniel, WY 83115-0212 (SAN 213-831X).

BackYard Bks., *(1-891596)* Orders Addr.: P.O. Box 1403, Rockland, ME 04841 Tel 207-594-4149; Edit Addr.: P.O. Box 1056, Camden, ME 04843 (SAN 299-6774) Tel 207-594-4149; Fax: 207-594-2773; Toll Free Fax: 800-837-0924; Toll Free: 877-669-7233
E-mail: info@imsafe.com; david@imsafe.com
Web site: http://www.imsafe.com
Dist(s): **Baker & Taylor Bks..**

Backyard Pub. Co., Inc., *(0-9646352)* Orders Addr.: P.O. Box 8343, Savannah, GA 31412 Tel 912-239-9300; Fax: 912-234-6009; Toll Free: 800-880-0446; Edit Addr.: 219 W. Bryan St., Savannah, GA 31401.

Bad Cat Bks., *(0-9675214)* P.O. Box 1731, Lahaina, HI 96767-1731 Tel 808-661-1895; Fax: 808-667-5576
E-mail: badcat@aloha.net
Web site: http://www.surfdowns.com
Dist(s): **Diamond Book Distributors, Inc..**

Badger Hse., LLC, *(1-931765)* 1272 Parkview Rd., Green Bay, WI 54304-5619 Tel 920-337-2930; Fax: 920-337-2921; Toll Free Fax: 800-653-5163; Toll Free: 800-242-5585
E-mail: billbadgerhouse@aol.com.

Baha'i Distribution Service, *(0-87743)* Orders Addr.: 4703 Fulton Industrial Blvd., SW, Atlanta, GA 30336-2017 (SAN 213-7496) Toll Free: 800-999-9019 ; Edit Addr.: 415 Linden Ave., Wilmette, IL 60091 Tel 847-251-1854; Fax: 847-251-3652
E-mail: bds@usbnc.org.

Baker & Taylor Bks., *(0-8480)* Orders Addr.: Commerce Service Ctr., 251 Mt. Olive Church Rd., Commerce, GA 30599-9988 (SAN 169-1503) Tel 404-335-5000; Toll Free: 800-775-1800 (orders); 800-775-1200 (customer service); Reno Service Ctr., 1160 Trademark Dr., Reno, NV 89511 (SAN 169-4464) Tel 775-850-3800; Fax: 775-850-3826 (customer service); Toll Free Fax: 800-775-7480 (orders); Edit Addr.: National Sales Hdqtrs., 5 Lakepointe Plaza, Suite 500, 2709 Water Ridge Pkwy., Charlotte, NC 28217 (SAN 169-5606) Fax: 704-329-8989; Toll Free: 800-775-1800 (information) ; 1120 US Hwy. 22, E., Bridgewater, NJ 08807 (SAN 169-4901) Toll Free: 800-775-1500 (customer service)
E-mail: btinfo@btol.com
Web site: http://www.btol.com.

Baker Bks., *(0-8010; 0-913686)* Div. of Baker Bk. Hse., Orders Addr.: P.O. Box 6287, Grand Rapids, MI 49516-6287 (SAN 299-1500) Toll Free Fax: 800-398-3111 (orders only); Toll Free: 800-877-2665 (orders only); Edit Addr.: 6030 E. Fulton, Ada, MI 49301 (SAN 201-4041) Tel 616-676-9185; Fax: 616-676-9573
Web site: http://www.bakerbooks.com
Dist(s): **Baker Bk. Hse., Inc**
CRC Pubns.
Twentieth Century Christian Bks..

Balance Publishing Co., *(1-878298)* 1346 S. Quality Ave., Sanger, CA 93657 Tel 559-876-1577 phone/fax Do not confuse with companies with similar names in Naples, FL, Port Charlotte, FL
E-mail: balance02@sprynet.com
Web site: http://www.balancepublishing.com.

Ballantine Bks. Imprint of Ballantine Bks.

†Ballantine Bks., *(0-345; 0-449; 0-8041; 0-87637; 1-4000)* Div. of Random Hse., Inc., Orders Addr.: 400 Hahn Rd., Westminster, MD 21157 Tel 410-848-1900; Toll Free Fax: 800-767-4465; Toll Free: 800-726-0600 (customer service); 800-733-3000 (orders); Edit Addr.: 1540 Broadway, 11th Flr., New York, NY 10036 (SAN 214-1175) Tel 212-782-9000; Fax: 212-940-7539; Toll Free: 800-733-3000; *Imprints:* Del Rey (Del Rey); Ballantine Books (Ballantine Bks); Fawcett (Fawcett); Ivy Books (Ivy)
E-mail: bfi@randomnhouse.com; thenry@randomhouse.com
Web site: http://www.randomhouse.com
Dist(s): **Random Hse., Inc.**; *CIP.*

Ballantine Publishing Group *See* **Ballantine Bks.**

Banana Patch Pr., *(0-9715333)* P.O. Box 840, Lawai, HI 96765-0840 (SAN 254-3087) Tel 808-332-5944; Fax: 808-332-7311; Toll Free: 800-914-5944
E-mail: carolan@aloha.net
Web site: http://www.bananapatchpress.com.

Banana Peel Bks., *(0-9707509)* 30 River Ct., No. 1601, Jersey City, NJ 07310
Web site: http://www.bananapeelbooks.com.

Bancroft Pr., *(0-9631246; 0-9635376; 1-890862)* P.O. Box 65360, Baltimore, MD 21209-9945 Tel 410-358-0658; Fax: 410-764-1967; Toll Free: 800-637-7377 Do not confuse with Bancroft Pr., San Rafael, CA
E-mail: bruceb@bancroftpress.com
Web site: http://www.bancroftpress.com
Dist(s): **Baker & Taylor Bks.**
Book Hse., Inc., The
Brodart Co.
Fell, Frederick Pubs., Inc.
Yankee Bk. Peddler, Inc..

Banis & Associates *See* **Science & Humanities Pr.**

Banks Channel Bks., *(0-9635967; 1-889199)* 2314 Waverly Dr., Wilmington, NC 28403 Tel 910-762-4677
E-mail: bankschan@ec.rr.com
Dist(s): **Blair, John F. Pub..**

Banner of Truth, The, *(0-85151)* Orders Addr.: P.O. Box 621, Carlisle, PA 17013 Tel 717-249-5747; Fax: 717-249-0604; Toll Free: 800-263-8085; Edit Addr.: 63 E. Louther St., Carlisle, PA 17013 (SAN 112-1553)
E-mail: info@banneroftruth.org
Web site: http://www.banneroftruth.co.uk
Dist(s): **Spring Arbor Distributors, Inc..**

Bantam Bks. for Young Readers Imprint of Random Hse. Children's Bks.

†Bantam Bks., *(0-553; 0-593; 0-7704; 1-4000)* Div. of Bantam Dell Publishing Group, Orders Addr.: 400 Hahn Rd., Westminster, MD 21157 Tel 410-848-1900 ; Toll Free: 800-726-0600; Edit Addr.: 1540 Broadway, New York, NY 10036-4094 Tel 212-354-6500; Fax: 212-492-8941; Toll Free Fax: 800-233-3294; Toll Free: 800-223-6834 (Bulk orders); 800-726-0600 (Orders/Customer service); *Imprints:* Bantam Classics (Bantam Classics); Corgi (Crgi)
E-mail: bantampublicity@randomhouse.com
Web site: http://www.bantam.com
Dist(s): **Random Hse., Inc.**; *CIP.*

Bantam Classics Imprint of Bantam Bks.

†Bantam Dell Publishing Group, *(0-440; 0-553; 0-593; 0-7704; 1-4000)* Div. of Random House, Inc., Orders Addr.: 400 Hahn Rd., Westminster, MD 21157 (SAN 201-3983) Tel 410-848-1900; Toll Free: 800-726-0600 ; Edit Addr.: 1540 Broadway, New York, NY 10036-4094 (SAN 201-0097) Tel 212-354-6500; Fax: 212-492-8941
Dist(s): **Giron Bks.**
Random Hse., Inc.; *CIP.*

Bantam Doubleday Dell Large Print Group, Inc., *(0-385)* Orders Addr.: 2451 S. Wolf Rd., Des Plaines, IL 60018 Toll Free: 800-323-9872 (orders); 800-258-4233 (EDI ordering); Edit Addr.: 1540 Broadway, New York, NY 10036-4094 Tel 212-354-6500; Toll Free: 800-223-5780
Dist(s): **Beeler, Thomas T. Publisher.**

Baptist Haiti Mission, *(0-9679937)* Orders Addr.: P.O. Box 15650, West Palm Beach, FL 33416-5650 Fax: 616-866-1809; Edit Addr.: 118 Courtland, Rockford, MI 49341 Tel 616-866-0111
E-mail: bhmus@bhm.org
Web site: http://www.bhm.org
Dist(s): **Light Messages.**

Barbed Wire Publishing, *(0-9622940; 1-881325; 0-9678566; 0-9711930; 0-9723032)* 270 Avenida De Mesilla, Las Cruces, NM 88005 Tel 505-525-9707; Fax: 505-525-9711; Toll Free: 888-817-1990
E-mail: mschuster@barbed-wire.net
Web site: http://www.barbed-wire.net.

Barbour & Company, Incorporated *See* **Barbour Publishing, Inc.**

Barbour Publishing, Inc., *(0-916441; 1-55748; 1-57748; 1-58660; 1-59310)* P.O. Box 719, Uhrichsville, OH 44683 (SAN 295-7094) Tel 740-922-6045; Fax: 740-922-5948; Toll Free Fax: 800-220-5948; Toll Free: 800-847-8270
E-mail: info@barbourbooks.com
Web site: http://www.barbourbooks.com
Dist(s): **Anchor Distributors**
Appalachian Bk. Distributors
Baker & Taylor Bks.
Riverside
Spring Arbor Distributors, Inc..

Barclay Pr., Inc., *(0-913342; 0-943701; 1-59498)* 211 N. Meridian St., No. 101, Newberg, OR 97132 (SAN 201-7520) Toll Free: 800-962-4014
E-mail: info@barclaypress.com
Web site: http://www.barclaypress.com.

Bardi Consulting, *(0-9660498)* 4237 Brookside Rd., Toledo, OH 43606 Tel 419-536-1719; Fax: 419-536-4527; *Imprints:* Bardi Press (Bardi Pr)
Dist(s): **Typecase, The.**

Bardi Pr. Imprint of Bardi Consulting

Barefoot Bks., Inc., *(1-84148; 1-898000; 1-901223; 1-902283)* 3 Bow St., 3rd Flr., Cambridge, MA 02138 Tel 866-417-2369; Fax: 888-346-9138
E-mail: ussales@barefoot-books.com
Web site: http://www.barefoot-books.com
Dist(s): **American Bk. Ctr.**
Distribution Solutions Group
Lectorum Pubns., Inc.
Ten Speed Pr..

Barker Creek Publishing, Inc., *(0-9639307; 1-928961)* Orders Addr.: P.O. Box 2610, Poulsbo, WA 98370 (SAN 298-4628) Tel 360-692-5833; Fax: 360-613-2542; Toll Free: 800-692-5833
E-mail: marketing@barkercreek.com
Web site: http://www.barkercreek.com
Dist(s): **Appalachian Bk. Distributors**
Baker & Taylor Bks.
Koen Bk. Distributors.

Barksdale Hse. Pr., *(0-9703570)* 1 Tradd St., Charleston, SC 29401 Tel 843-722-3508
E-mail: hpgw@duke.edu
Dist(s): **Saturday Shop.**

Barnaby & Co., *(0-9642836)* P.O. Box 3198, Nantucket, MA 02584 Tel 508-228-5114; Fax: 508-325-0011
E-mail: barnaby@nantucket.net
Web site: http://www.barnabybear.com.

Barnaby Books *See* **Barnaby & Co.**

Barnes & Noble, Inc., *(0-7607; 0-88029; 1-4028)* 122 Fifth Ave., New York, NY 10011 (SAN 141-3651) Tel 212-633-3300
E-mail: staylor@bn.com
Dist(s): **Bookazine Co., Inc.**
Sterling Publishing Co., Inc..

Barnes, Joyce B., *(0-9628493)* R.R. 1, Box 7010, Hornbeck, LA 71439-9801 Tel 318-565-4873.

Barney Bks. Imprint of Lyrick Publishing

Barney Publishing *See* **Lyrick Publishing**

†Barron's Educational Series, Inc., *(0-7641; 0-8120)* 250 Wireless Blvd., Hauppauge, NY 11788-3917 (SAN 201-453X) Tel 631-434-3311; Fax: 631-434-3723; 631-434-3217 (orders); Toll Free: 800-645-3476 Do not confuse with BARRONS, Monroe, WA
E-mail: info@barronseduc.com; barrons@barronseduc.com
Web site: http://www.barronseduc.com
Dist(s): **Continental Bk. Co., Inc.**
Giron Bks.
Lectorum Pubns., Inc.
Production Assocs., Inc.
netLibrary, Inc.; *CIP.*

Barsotti Bks., *(0-9642112)* 2239 Hidden Valley Ln., Camino, CA 95709-9722 Tel 530-622-4629; Fax: 530-642-9703
E-mail: jb@barsottibooks.com
Web site: http://www.barsottibooks.com
Dist(s): **Baker & Taylor Bks..**

Barth Family Ministries, *(0-9624067; 1-891484)* 339 Parkhill Rd., Cornwall, VT 05753 Tel 802-462-2002; Fax: 802-462-2001.

Bartleby.com, *(1-58734)* P.O. Box 13, New York, NY 10034-0013
E-mail: webmaster@bartleby.com
Web site: http://www.bartleby.com.

Bartlett Publishing, *(1-891210)* P.O. Box 56597, Sherman Oaks, CA 91413 Fax: 818-988-8376; Toll Free: 800-553-2061
E-mail: skreng@aol.com
Web site: http://members.aol.com/skreng.

†Basic Bks., *(0-465)* A Member of Perseus Books Group, Orders Addr.: 5500 Central Ave., Boulder, CO 80301-2877 Fax: 303-449-3356 (customer service); Toll Free: 800-386-5656 (customer service); Edit Addr.: 387 Park Ave., S., New York, NY 10016 (SAN 201-4521) Tel 212-340-8100; Fax: 212-340-8135; *Imprints:* Counterpoint Press (Count Pr)
E-mail: westview.orders@perseusbooks.com
Web site: http://www.counterpointpress.com; http://www.perseusbooksgroup.com
Dist(s): **Cobblestone Publishing Co.**
HarperCollins Pubs.; *CIP.*

Baskerville Pubs., Inc., *(0-9627509; 1-880909)* 2711 Park Hill Dr., Fort Worth, TX 76109 Tel 817-923-1064; Fax: 817-921-9114
E-mail: baskerville@baskervillepublishers.com
Web site: http://www.baskervillepublishers.com.

Baskerville Publishing Company, Incorporated *See* **Baskerville Pubs., Inc.**

Bat Conservation International, Inc., *(0-9638248; 0-9742379)* Orders Addr.: P.O. Box 162603, Austin, TX 76716 Tel 512-327-9721; Fax: 512-327-9724; Edit Addr.: 500 N. Capital of Texas Hwy., N., Bldg. 1, Suite 100, Austin, TX 76716
E-mail: pubs@batcon.org
Web site: http://www.batcon.org/
Dist(s): **Univ. of Texas Pr..**

Batfish Bks., *(0-9728653)* Div. of O'Neill, Michael P. Photography, Inc., P.O. Box 32909, Palm Beach Gardens, FL 33420-2909 (SAN 255-1780) Tel 305-577-9984; Fax: 561-840-1939
E-mail: info@batfishbooks.com; mpo@msn.com
Web site: http://www.batfishbooks.com
Dist(s): **Baker & Taylor Bks.**
Southern Bk. Service.

Battledore, Ltd., *(0-9627110)* Orders Addr.: P.O. Box 2288, Kingston, NY 12402-2288 Tel 845-339-6944; Fax: 845-338-0684; Edit Addr.: 77 W. Chestnut St., Kingston, NY 12401-5929
E-mail: battledore@childlit.com
Web site: http://www.childlit.com/battledore/
Dist(s): **Oak Knoll Pr..**

Bauhan, William L. Inc., *(0-87233)* P.O. Box 443, Dublin, NH 03444-0443 (SAN 204-384X) Tel 877-832-3738; 603-563-8020; Fax: 603-563-8026
E-mail: info@bauhanpublishing.com
Web site: http://www.bauhanpublishing.com.

Baxter Pr., *(1-888237)* 700 S. Friendswood Dr., Suite C, Friendswood, TX 77546 Tel 281-992-0628; Fax: 281-992-0615
E-mail: baxter2@flash.net
Dist(s): **FaithWorks.**

Bay Oak Pubs., Ltd., *(0-9704692; 0-9741713)* 34 Wimbledon Dr., Dover, DE 19904 Tel 302-674-5650 (phone/fax)
E-mail: bayoakpublishers@aol.com
Dist(s): **Washington Bk. Distributors.**

Bay Shore Books *See* **Micah Publishing**

Bay Tree Enterprises, *(0-9701497)* 9360 Tonto Dr., Crystal River, FL 34428 Tel 352-795-7205
E-mail: maranda@citrus.infi.net.

BaySailor Bks., *(0-9618461)* P.O. Box 116, Royal Oak, MD 21662 (SAN 667-920X).

†BBC Audiobooks America, *(0-563; 0-7540; 0-7927; 0-89340; 1-55504)* Orders Addr.: P.O. Box 1450, Hampton, NH 03843-1450 (SAN 208-4864) Tel 603-926-8744; Fax: 603-929-3890; Toll Free: 800-621-0182; Edit Addr.: 1 Lafayette Rd., Hampton, NH 03843; *Imprints:* Galaxy Children's Large Print (Galaxy Child Lrg Print); Chivers Children's Audio Books (Chivers Child Audio)
E-mail: customerservice@bbcaudiobooksamerica.com
Web site: http://www.bbcaudiobooksamerica.com
Dist(s): **Landmark Audiobooks**; *CIP.*

BBC Bk. Publishing (GBR) *(0-563) Dist. by* **Ulverscroft US.**

B-Dock Pr., *(0-9621728)* Orders Addr.: P.O. Box 8, Willingboro, NJ 08046 (SAN 252-1962); Edit Addr.: 16 Meadowbrook Pl., Willingboro, NJ 08046 (SAN 252-1970) Tel 609-877-6018.

Beach Holme Pubs., Ltd. (CAN) *(0-88878) Dist. by* **Strauss Cnslts.**

Beach Pebbles Pr., *(0-9641138)* 1187 Coast Village Rd., Suite I-275, Santa Barbara, CA 93108 Tel 805-969-5934
E-mail: beachpeb@silcom.com.

Beachcomber Pr., *(0-9614628)* RR4, Box 2220, Belgrade Rd., Oakland, ME 04963 (SAN 691-8891).

Beachfront Publishing, *(1-892339)* Div. of Words, Words, Words, Inc., Orders Addr.: P.O. Box 811922, Boca Raton, FL 33481
E-mail: info@beachfrontentertainment.com
Web site: http://www.beachfrontentertainment.com
Dist(s): **Biblio Distribution.**

Beacon Hill Bks. Imprint of Meridian Hse.

Beacon Pr., *(0-8070)* 25 Beacon St., Boston, MA 02108-2892 (SAN 201-4483) Tel 617-742-2110; Fax: 617-723-3097
Web site: http://www.beacon.org
Dist(s): **Continental Bk. Co., Inc.**
Houghton Mifflin Co. Trade & Reference Div.
netLibrary, Inc..

Beajo Pub., *(0-9669166)* Orders Addr.: 8545 Balboa Blvd., No. 229, Northridge, CT 91325 Tel 818-700-8504
E-mail: info@beajo.com
Web site: http://www.beajo.com.

Beaman, Joyce Proctor, *(0-9658138)* 8427 Piney Grove Church Rd., Walstonburg, NC 27888 Tel 252-238-3455.

Bean Sprouts Imprint of Standard Publishing

Bear & Co. Imprint of Bear & Co.

†Bear & Co., *(0-939680; 1-879181; 1-59143)* Orders Addr.: One Park St., Rochester, VT 05767 (SAN 216-7174) Tel 802-767-3174; Fax: 802-767-3726; Toll Free: 800-246-8648; *Imprints:* Bear & Company (Bear & Company) Do not confuse with Bear & Co. in Bedford, NH
E-mail: info@innertraditions.com; jeanie@innertraditions.com
Web site: http://www.innertraditions.com
Dist(s): **Ten Speed Pr.**; *CIP.*

Bear & Company *See* **Boyds Collection Ltd., The**

Bear Path, The, *(0-9652211; 1-891317)* 3335 W. Desert Bend Loop, Tucson, AZ 85742-9382 Tel 520-744-6799.

Bear Paw Bks., *(0-9629760)* Div. of Bear Paw Quilts, 748 Chase Rd., NE, Huntsville, AL 35811-1519.

Beascoa, Ediciones S.A. (ESP) *(84-488; 84-7546) Dist. by* **Lectorum Pubns.**

Beaufort Bks., Inc., *(0-8253)* 27 W. 20th St., Suite 1102, New York, NY 10011 (SAN 215-2304) Tel 212-727-0190; Fax: 212-727-0195
E-mail: midpointny@aol.com
Dist(s): **Midpoint Trade Bks., Inc..**

Beautiful America Publishing Co., *(0-89802)* Orders Addr.: P.O. Box 244, Woodburn, OR 97071-0244 (SAN 251-2548) Tel 503-982-4616; Fax: 503-982-2825; Toll Free: 800-874-1233; Edit Addr.: 2600 Progress Way, Woodburn, OR 97071 (SAN 211-4623)
E-mail: bapco@beautifulamericapub.com
Web site: http://www.beautifulamericapub.com
Dist(s): **Baker & Taylor Bks.**
Koen Pacific
Partners/West.

Beautiful Feet Bks., *(0-9643803; 1-893103)* 139 Main St., Sandwich, MA 02563 Tel 508-833-8626; Fax: 508-833-2770; Toll Free: 800-889-1978
E-mail: russell@bfbooks.com
Web site: http://www.bfbooks.com.

Beazley, William O., *(1-884758)* 804 Marsalis, Abilene, TX 79603 Tel 915-673-1549.

Beckham House Publishers, Incorporated *See* **Beckham Pubns. Group, Inc.**

Beckham Pubns. Group, Inc., *(0-931761)* P.O. Box 4066, Silver Spring, MD 20914-4066 (SAN 683-2237) Tel 301-384-7995 (phone/fax)
E-mail: barry@beckhamhouse.com
Web site: http://www.beckhamhouse.com
Dist(s): **BookWorld Services, Inc.**
National Bk. Network.

Bedrick, Peter Bks. Imprint of McGraw-Hill Children's Publishing

Bee & Cee Enterprises, *(0-9662488)* Orders Addr.: P.O. Box 273476, Tampa, FL 33688-3476 Tel 813-948-8887; Fax: 813-948-8682; Edit Addr.: 18808 Chemilee Dr., Lutz, FL 33549
E-mail: dsc27@mindspring.com.

Beehive Pr., The, *(0-88322)* 321 Barnard St., Savannah, GA 31401 (SAN 201-7547) Tel 912-236-4870; Fax: 912-236-4747 Do not confuse with Beehive Pr., Las Vegas, NV
Web site: http://www.beehivepress.org.

BeeJay Enterprises, *(0-9659042)* Orders Addr.: P.O. Box 1373, Alpharetta, GA 30239-1373 Tel 770-346-8626; Fax: 770-410-4995; Edit Addr.: 1306 Cobb Crossing, Smyrna, GA 30080
E-mail: beejaypub@aol.com.

Beekman Pubs., Inc., *(0-8464)* P.O. Box 888, Woodstock, NY 12498-0888 (SAN 170-1622) Tel 845-679-2300; Fax: 845-679-2301; Toll Free: 888-233-5626; *Imprints:* Gomer Press (Gomer Pr)
E-mail: beekman@beekmanpublishers.com
Web site: http://www.beekmanpublishers.comw; http://www.beekman.net.

†Beginner Bks., *(0-394)* Div. of Random Hse., Inc., Orders Addr.: 400 Hahn Rd., Westminster, MD 21157 (SAN 202-3296) Tel 410-848-1900; Toll Free: 800-733-3000 (orders); Edit Addr.: 201 E. 50th St., New York, NY 10022 (SAN 202-3288) Tel 212-751-2600; Fax: 212-872-8026; *CIP.*

Behavenkids Pr., *(0-9714405)* 10333 W. Center Rd., Omaha, NE 68124 Tel 402-926-4373; Fax: 402-926-3898
E-mail: janiep@behavenkids.com.

Behrman Hse., Inc., *(0-87441)* 11 Edison Pl., Springfield, NJ 07081 (SAN 201-4459) Tel 973-379-7200; Fax: 973-379-7280; Toll Free: 800-221-2755
E-mail: webmaster@behrmanhouse.com
Web site: http://www.behrmanhouse.com.

Bell Buckle Pr., *(0-9624100; 1-882845)* P.O. Box 486, Bell Buckle, TN 37020 Tel 931-389-6878.

Bell Pond Bks. Imprint of SteinerBooks, Inc.

Bellerophon Bks., *(0-88388)* Orders Addr.: P.O. Box 21307, Santa Barbara, CA 93121-1307 (SAN 254-7856) Tel 805-965-7034; Fax: 805-965-8286; Toll Free: 800-253-9943
E-mail: bellerophonbooks@bellerophonbooks.com
Web site: http://www.bellerophonbooks.com.

BelleTress Books *See* **BelleTress, Inc.**

BelleTress, Inc., *(0-9634910; 0-9708754)* 2962 N. Middletown Rd., Paris, KY 40361 Tel 859-362-4077; Fax: 859-362-4067
E-mail: friends@belletressbooks.com
Web site: http://www.belletressbooks.com
Dist(s): **Words Distributing Co..**

Bello, Andres (CHL) *(956-13) Dist. by* **AIMS Intl.**

Benchmark Bks. Imprint of Cavendish, Marshall Corp.

Benchmark Education Co., *(1-58344; 1-892393; 1-59000; 1-4108)* 629 Fifth Ave., Pelham, NY 10803 Tel 914-738-6977; Fax: 914-738-5063; Toll Free: 877-236-2465
E-mail: bhaggerty@benchmark.com
Web site: http://www.benchmarkeducation.com.

Names

Benchmark Investigative Group, Div. Plumb Line Press, Incorporated, P.O. Box 717, Estes Park, CO 80517-0717 Tel 970-586-0760; Fax: 970-586-8208 Do not confuse with companies with the same name Benchmark Books in San Marino, CA, Fairfax, VA
E-mail: moses@88truthful.com
Web site: http://www.88truthful.com.

Benes, Veronica, *(0-9662368)* 3964 Southwestern Blvd., Orchard Park, NY 14127 Tel 716-646-1812.

Benmir Bks., *(0-917883)* P.O. Box 515, Walnut Creek, CA 94597 (SAN 656-9641) Tel 510-736-1914; Fax: 510-736-4405.

Bennerson, Denise, *(0-9646279)* Orders Addr.: P.O. Box 3164, Frederiksted, VI 00841
E-mail: justdoit@viaccess.net
Web site:
http://www.homelandcollections.com/children_books.htm
Dist(s): **Century Bk. Distribution.**

Ben-Simon Pubns., *(0-914539)* P.O. Box 2124, Port Angeles, WA 98362 (SAN 289-1492) Tel 250-652-6332; Fax: 360-452-2502
E-mail: bensimon@pinc.com
Web site: http://www.swifty.com/bensimon/index.html.

Benson, W. S. & Co., Inc., *(0-87443)* P.O. Box 1866, Austin, TX 78767 (SAN 202-3989) Tel 512-345-0732 ; Fax: 512-345-6837; Toll Free: 800-835-2197.

Bepuzzled, *(0-922242; 1-57561)* Div. of Lombard Marketing, 780 Farmington Ave., West Hartford, CT 06119-1665 (SAN 251-2041) Tel 860-769-5700; Fax: 860-769-5799; Toll Free: 800-874-6556.

Beraam Publishing Co., *(0-9652751)* 1702 S. Market St., Brenham, TX 77833 Tel 409-836-0523; Fax: 409-836-3519.

Berkeley Major Publishing, *(0-9720691)* 8282 Skyline Cir., Oakland, CA 94605-4230 Fax: 419-791-7109
E-mail: dailon@progidy.net; BMP@berkeleymp.com
Web site: http://www.berkeleymp.com.

†Berkley Publishing Group, *(0-425; 0-515)* Div. of Penguin Putnam, Inc., Orders Addr.: 405 Murray Hill Pkwy., East Rutherford, NJ 07073 Toll Free: 800-788-6262 (individual consumer sales); 800-847-5515 (orders); 800-631-8571 (customer service); Edit Addr.: 375 Hudson St., New York, NY 10014 (SAN 201-3991) Tel 212-366-2000; Fax: 212-366-2385; *Imprints:* Berkley/Pacer (Berkley-Pacer); Splash (Splash); Classics Illustrated (Classics Illus); Prime Crime (Prime Crime); Perigee Books (Perigee Bks); JAM (JAM); Jove (Jove)
E-mail: online@penguinputnam.com
Web site: http://www.penguinputnam.com
Dist(s): **Penguin Group (USA) Inc.**
Perelandra, Ltd.; *CIP.*

Berkley/Pacer Imprint of Berkley Publishing Group

Berkshire Hse. Imprint of Countryman Pr.

Berlitz International, Inc., *(2-8315; 1-59104)* 400 Alexander Park, Princeton, NJ 08540-6306 Tel 609-514-9650; Fax: 609-514-9649; Toll Free: 800-257-9449; *Imprints:* Berlitz Kids (Berlitz Kids)
Web site: http://www.berlitz.com
Dist(s): **Globe Pequot Pr., The**
Langenscheidt Pubs., Inc.
Libros Sin Fronteras.

Berlitz Kids Imprint of Berlitz International, Inc.

Bernard Bks., *(0-9634661)* 157 Shorecliff Rd., Corona del Mar, CA 92625 Tel 714-760-1325.

Bernstein, Susan, *(0-9706596)* 31100 Northwestern Hwy., Farmington Hills, MI 48334-2519 Tel 248-737-8400; Fax: 248-737-4392; Toll Free: 800-225-5726
E-mail: les380414744@aol.com
Web site: http://www.epominonousepstein.com.

Berrent Pubns., Inc., *(0-916259; 1-55743)* 1025 Northern Blvd., Roslyn, NY 11576 (SAN 294-9016) Tel 516-625-6750; Fax: 516-625-6789.

Berry Bks., *(0-9614746; 1-890579)* 61 Cardinal Dr., Whispering Pines, NC 28327 (SAN 692-9214) Tel 910-949-3407 Do not confuse with Berry Bks., Ltd., Columbus, OH
E-mail: bbbooks20@hotmail.com.

Beson, Kathryn, *(0-9645405)* 160 Anton Ct., Appleton, WI 54915 Tel 920-735-9859.

Bess Pr., Inc., *(0-935848; 1-57306; 1-880188)* 3565 Harding Ave., Honolulu, HI 96816 (SAN 239-4111) Tel 808-734-7159; Fax: 808-732-3627; Toll Free: 800-910-2377
E-mail: info@besspress.com
Web site: http://www.besspress.com
Dist(s): **Aha Punana Leo**
Booklines Hawaii, Ltd.
Fell, Frederick Pubs., Inc.
Univ. of Hawaii Pr..

Best of Small Pr. Pubs., *(1-889279)* P.O. Box 47631, Plymouth, MN 55447-0631 Tel 612-559-5578; Fax: 612-559-5497; Toll Free: 800-708-0558.

Best Seller *See* **Best Seller Pubns., Inc.**

Best Seller Pubns., Inc., *(0-9642997)* 12146 Island View Cir., Germantown, MD 20874 (SAN 253-4274) Tel 301-869-0072; Fax: 301-972-4456.

Bethany Backyard Imprint of Bethany Hse. Pubs.

†Bethany Hse. Pubs., *(0-7642; 0-87123; 1-55661; 1-56179; 1-57778; 1-880089; 1-59066)* Div. of Baker Book House, Inc., Orders Addr.: P.O. Box 6287, Grand Rapids, MI 49516-6287 Toll Free: 800-877-2665; Edit Addr.: 11400 Hampshire Ave., S., Bloomington, MN 55438-2455 (SAN 201-4416) Tel 952-829-2500; Fax: 952-996-1393; Toll Free: 800-877-2665; *Imprints:* Bethany Backyard (Bethany Backyard)
E-mail: orders@bakerbooks.com
Web site: http://www.bethanyhouse.com
Dist(s): **Anchor Distributors**
Appalachian Bible Co.
Baker & Taylor Bks.
Baker Bk. Hse., Inc.
Brodart Co.
CRC Pubns.
Follett Library Resources
Permabound Bks.
Riverside Bk. & Bible Resource
Spring Arbor Distributors, Inc.
Beeler, Thomas T. Publisher; *CIP.*

Bethlehem Bks., *(1-883937; 1-932350)* Div. of Bethlehem Community, Orders Addr.: 10194 Garfield St. S., Bathgate, ND 58216-4031 Tel 701-265-3725; Fax: 701-265-3716; Toll Free: 800-757-6831 Do not confuse with bethlehem Books in Richmond, VA
E-mail: inquiry@bethlehembooks.com
Web site: http://www.bethlehembooks.com
Dist(s): **Ignatius Pr.**
Spring Arbor Distributors, Inc..

Better Baby Press, The *See* **Institute for the Achievement of Human Potential**

Better Homes & Gardens Books *See* **Meredith Bks.**

Betterway Bks. Imprint of F&W Pubns., Inc.

Bette's Bks., *(0-9676360)* 8301 S. Pebble Creek Way, No. 48-102, Highlands Ranch, CO 80126 Tel 303-713-9805 (phone/fax); Toll Free: 877-236-7491
E-mail: bettesbooks@msn.com.

Bey, Malik Rasul, *(0-9656137; 1-890301)* 3333 Bailey Ave., Buffalo, NY 14215 Tel 716-838-9221.

Beyond Words Publishing, Inc., *(0-941831; 1-58270; 1-885223)* 20827 NW Cornell Rd., Suite 500, Hillsboro, OR 97124-9808 (SAN 666-4210) Tel 503-531-8700; Fax: 503-531-8773; Toll Free: 800-284-9673
E-mail: sales@beyondword.com; info@beyondword.com
Web site: http://www.beyondword.com
Dist(s): **Graphic Arts Ctr. Publishing Co.**
Publishers Group West.

Biblio Distribution, Div. of National Book Network, Orders Addr.: 15200 NBN Way, Blue Ridge Summit, PA 17214 Toll Free Fax: 800-338-4550; Toll Free: 800-462-6420; Edit Addr.: 4501 Forbes Blvd., Suite 200, Lanham, MD 20706 (SAN 211-724X) Tel 301-459-3366; Fax: 301-429-5746
E-mail: custserv@nbnbooks.com
Web site: http://www.bibliodistribution.com.

Biblio Distribution Center *See* **Biblio Distribution**

Biblo & Tannen Booksellers & Pubs., Inc., *(0-8196)* P.O. Box 302, Cheshire, CT 06410 (SAN 202-4071) Tel 203-250-1647 (phone/fax); Toll Free: 800-272-8778
E-mail: biblo.moser@gte.net.

Bicast, Inc., *(0-9638258; 0-9701008)* Orders Addr.: P.O. Box 2676, Williamsburg, VA 23187 Tel 757-229-3276 ; Fax: 757-253-2273; Toll Free: 800-767-8273; Edit Addr.: 231 K Parkway Dr., Williamsburg, VA 23185
E-mail: bicast@aol.com
Web site: http://lighthousesusa.com.

Biddle Publishing Co., *(1-879418)* Orders Addr.: P.O. Box 1305, Brunswick, ME 04011 Tel 207-833-5016; Toll Free: 888-315-0582 (orders)
Web site: http://www.biddle-audenreed.com
Dist(s): **Baker & Taylor Bks..**

Big Ben Audio, Inc., *(1-885546)* Orders Addr.: P.O. Box 969, Ashland, OR 97520 Tel 541-488-6022; Fax: 541-734-2537; Edit Addr.: 31 Mistletoe, Ashland, OR 97520.

Big Brain Publishing, LLC, *(0-9670636)* Orders Addr.: P.O. Box 8791, Silver Spring, MD 20907 Tel 301-587-7194; Fax: 301-588-8661; Edit Addr.: 8616 Second Ave., Silver Spring, MD 20910
E-mail: bigbrainpb@aol.com.

Big Daddy Press *See* **Buckaroo Bks.**

Big Guy Bks., Inc., *(1-929945)* 7750-F El Camino Real, Carlsbad, CA 92009 (SAN 253-0392) Tel 760-334-1222; Fax: 760-334-1225; Toll Free: 866-836-5879
E-mail: info@bigguybooks.com
Web site: http://www.timesoldiers.com.

Big Red Chair Bks. Imprint of Lyrick Publishing

Bigwater Publishing, *(0-923048)* Orders Addr.: P.O. Box 177, Caledonia, MI 49316 (SAN 251-608X) Tel 616-891-1113; Fax: 616-891-8015
E-mail: bigpub@att.net.

Bilingual Imprint of Star Light Pr.

Bilingual Language Materials, *(0-9624096; 1-893447)* 4912 River Ave., Newport Beach, CA 92663 Tel 949-642-3325 (phone/fax); Toll Free: 800-610-1565.

Billy B Enterprises, *(0-9670394)* 357 W. Via Bacanora, Green Valley, AZ 85614 (SAN 299-8378) Tel 520-648-6163 (phone/fax)
E-mail: cuthbert21@aol.com.

Billy Bee Productions, *(1-886919)* 19 Grace Dr., Nashua, NH 03062 Toll Free Fax: 800-257-0907; Toll Free: 800-327-3227
E-mail: info@billybee.net
Web site: http://www.billybee.net.

Binford & Mort Publishing, *(0-8323)* Orders Addr.: P.O. Box 91580, Portland, OR 97291; Edit Addr.: 5245 NE Elam Young Pkwy., Suite C, Hillsboro, OR 97124 (SAN 201-4386) Tel 503-844-4960; Fax: 503-844-4959; Toll Free: 888-221-4514
Web site: http://www.binfordandmort.com/
Dist(s): **Baker & Taylor Bks.**
Maverick Distributors
Partners/West.

Binford & Mort Publishing; Metropolitan Press *See* **Binford & Mort Publishing**

Binnacle Kids Imprint of Binnacle Publishing Group

Binnacle Publishing Group, *(1-890493)* P.O. Box 3969, Santa Cruz, CA 95063 Tel 408-439-9710 (phone/fax); Toll Free: 800-223-1974; *Imprints:* Binnacle Kids (Binnacle Kids)
E-mail: binnacle@bpgx.com; analogp@ibm.net
Web site: http://www.bpgx.com
Dist(s): **BookMasters, Inc.**
Midpoint Trade Bks., Inc..

Birlinn, Ltd. (GBR) *(1-874744; 1-84158; 1-84341)* *Dist. by* **Interlink Pub.**

Bison Bks. Imprint of Univ. of Nebraska Pr.

Black, Auguste R., *(0-9628010)* 4016 Shelby Ave., SE, Huntsville, AL 35801 Tel 205-534-4006.

Black Belt Communications Group *See* **River City Publishing**

Black Belt Pr. Imprint of River City Publishing

Black Cat Bks., *(0-9712428)* 203 Washington St., PMB 294, Salem, MA 01970
E-mail: jaccomando@compaq.net
Dist(s): **Biblio Distribution.**

Black Cat Pubns., Inc., *(0-9712994)* Orders Addr.: P.O. Box 672, Plainview, NY 11803 Tel 631-273-3545
E-mail: cnamo@blackcatpublications.com
Web site: http://www.blackcatpublications.com.

Black Forest Pr., *(1-58275; 1-881116)* Div. of Black Forest Enterprises, Orders Addr.: P.O. Box 6342, Chula Vista, CA 91909-6342 Fax: 619-482-8704; Toll Free: 888-808-5440 (Book Sales, Marketing and Promotion); 800-451-9404 (General Information, Submission Inquiries and Acquisitions); Edit Addr.: 914 Nolan Way, Chula Vista, CA 91911-2408 (SAN 298-8445) Tel 619-656-8048
E-mail: bfp@blackforestpress.com; dknox@blackforestpress.com
Web site: http://www.blackforestpress.com
Dist(s): **Ingram Bk. Co..**

Black, Judith Storyteller, *(0-9701073)* 33 Prospect St., Marblehead, MA 01941 Tel 781-631-4417
E-mail: jb@storiesalive.com
Web site: http://www.storiesalive.com.

Black Letter Pr., *(0-912382)* 461 Worth Rd., R.1, Moran, MI 49760 (SAN 201-436X) Tel 906-292-5513 ; Fax: 906-292-5626
E-mail: firsteditiontoo@mich.com.

Black Moss Pr. (CAN) *(0-88753)* *Dist. by* **Firefly Bks Limited.**

Black Orb, *(0-9677547)* P.O. Box 5063, Hacienda Heights, CA 91745
E-mail: martine@BlackOrb.com
Web site: http://www.BlackOrb.com
Dist(s): **Seven Locks Pr..**

Names

Black Pyramid Pr., *(0-9656859)* Div. of Black Pyramid Enterprise, P.O. Box 11066, Omaha, NE 68111 Tel 402-342-5481; Fax: 402-393-7745; Toll Free: 800-836-7240
E-mail: pyrapress@aol.com
Web site: http://www.blackpyramid.com
Dist(s): **Baker & Taylor Bks..**

Black River Trading Co., *(0-9649083)* 3550 Hosner Rd., Box 7, Oxford, MI 48371
E-mail: jane@whoopforjoy.com
Web site: http://www.whoopforjoy.com
Dist(s): **Bookmen, Inc..**

Blackberry Maine, *(0-942396)* 617 East Neck Rd., Nobleboro, ME 04555 (SAN 207-7949) Tel 207-729-5083; Fax: 207-729-6783
E-mail: chimfarm@gwi.net
Web site: http://www.blackberrybooksme.com
Dist(s): **SPD-Small Pr. Distribution.**

Blackberry: Salted in the Shell *See* **Blackberry Maine**

Blackbirch Pr., Inc. Imprint of Gale Group

Blackstaff Pr., The (IRL) *(0-85640) Dist. by* **Dufour.**

Blackstone Audio Bks., Inc., *(0-7861)* Orders Addr.: c/o Dept. LJ, P.O. Box 969, Ashland, OR 97520 Tel 541-482-9239; Fax: 541-482-9294; Toll Free: 800-729-2665; Edit Addr.: 31 Mistletoe Rd., Ashland, OR 97520 (SAN 173-2811)
E-mail: sales@blackstoneaudio.com
Web site: http://www.blackstoneaudio.com
Dist(s): **Landmark Audiobooks.**

Blackwell, Donald A., *(0-9650332)* 15402 SW 74th Pl., Miami, FL 33157-2471.

Blackwell Publishers *See* **Blackwell Publishing**

†Blackwell Publishing, *(0-631; 0-7456; 0-85012; 1-55786; 1-57718; 1-878975; 1-4051)* Orders Addr.: c/o AIDC, P.O. Box 20, Williston, VT 05495-0020 (SAN 680-5035) Tel 802-862-0095; Fax: 802-864-7626; Toll Free Fax: 800-864-7626; Toll Free: 800-216-2522; Edit Addr.: 350 Main St., 6th Flr., Malden, MA 02148-5018 (SAN 680-5035) Tel 781-388-8200; Fax: 781-388-8210
E-mail: books@blackwellpub.com
Web site: http://www.blackwellpub.com
Dist(s): **American International Distribution Corp.**
Iowa State Pr.
Lightning Source, Inc.
netLibrary, Inc.; *CIP.*

Blair, John F. Pub., *(0-89587; 0-910244)* 1406 Plaza Dr., Winston-Salem, NC 27103 (SAN 201-4319) Tel 336-768-1374; Fax: 336-768-9194; Toll Free: 800-222-9796
E-mail: blairpub@blairpub.com
Web site: http://www.blairpub.com.

Blessing Our World, Inc., *(1-928777)* 803 Forest Ridge Dr., Suite 109, Bedford, TX 76022 Tel 817-354-2425; Fax: 817-354-8533; Toll Free: 800-729-1130; *Imprints:* BOW Books (BOW Bks)
E-mail: sales@bowbooks.com; gerald@bowbooks.com; sales@blessworld.com
Web site: http://www.blessworld.com; http://www.markyseries.com; http://www.chrismouse.com; http://www.whatgoodis.com; http://www.whydaddywhy.com; http://www.bowbooks.com
Dist(s): **BookWorld Services, Inc..**

Bloch Publishing Co., *(0-8197)* 118 E. 28th St., Suite 501-503, New York, NY 10016-8413 (SAN 214-204X) Tel 212-532-3977; Fax: 212-779-9169
E-mail: BlochPub@worldnet.att.net
Web site: http://www.blochpub.com/.

Bloomsbury Children Imprint of Bloomsbury Publishing

Bloomsbury Publishing, *(1-58234)* Orders Addr.: 16365 James Madison Hwy., Gordonsville, VA 22942-8501 Toll Free: 888-330-8477; Edit Addr.: 175 Fifth Ave., Suite 300, New York, NY 10010 Tel 212-674-5151 (ext. 782); Fax: 212-780-0115; Toll Free: 800-221-7945; *Imprints:* Bloomsbury Children (Bloom Child)
E-mail: alona.fryman@bloomsburyusa.com
Web site: http://www.bloomsbury.com/usa
Dist(s): **St. Martin's Pr..**

Bloomsbury Publishing, Ltd. (GBR) *(0-7475) Dist. by* **Trafalgar.**

BLR Bks., *(0-9721839)* 94 Circle Dr., Waltham, MA 02452.

Blue Crane Bks., Inc., *(0-9628715; 1-886434)* Orders Addr.: P.O. Box 0291, Cambridge, MA 02238 Tel 617-926-8989; Fax: 617-926-0982
E-mail: bluecrane@arrow1.com
Dist(s): **Paul & Co. Pubs. Consortium, Inc..**

Blue Dolphin Publishing, Inc., *(0-931892; 1-57733)* Orders Addr.: P.O. Box 8, Nevada City, CA 95959 (SAN 223-2480) Tel 530-265-6925; Fax: 530-265-0787; Toll Free: 800-643-0765; Edit Addr.: 12428 Nevada City Hwy., Grass Valley, CA 95945 (SAN 696-009X)
E-mail: bdolphin@netshel.net; clemens@netshel.net
Web site: http://www.bluedolphinpublishing.com
Dist(s): **Baker & Taylor Bks.**
Booklines Hawaii, Ltd.
Bookpeople
Koen Bk. Distributors
Koen Pacific
New Concepts Bks. & Tapes Distributors
New Leaf Distributing Co., Inc.
Quality Bks., Inc.
Red Wheel/Weiser
Vision Distributors.

Blue Heron Pr., *(0-9621724; 1-884725)* Orders Addr.: 302 Thoroughbred Park Dr., Thibodaux, LA 70301 (SAN 252-1199) Tel 504-446-8201; Toll Free: 888-273-2352 Do not confuse with companies with the same name in Bellingham, WA, Phoenix, MD, Albuquerque, NM, Shokan, NY, Mercer Island, WA, Commerce Township, MI, Grand Rapids, MI
E-mail: cpgorman@charter.net.

Blue Heron Publishing, *(0-936085)* Orders Addr.: 1234 SW Stark St., Suite 1, Portland, OR 97205 Tel 503-223-2098; Fax: 503-223-9474; Edit Addr.: 4205 SW Washington St., Suite 303, Portland, OR 97204 (SAN 696-6446) Tel 503-221-6841; Fax: 503-221-6843
E-mail: pjt@blueheron.com
Web site: http://www.blueheron.com/.

Blue Horse Mukwa Publishing, *(0-9707770)* 618 Hilltop W., Virginia Beach, VA 23451 Tel 757-425-7992; 757-425-7992; Fax: 757-425-2345
E-mail: yona@infi.net.

Blue Lantern Publishing, *(1-887303)* Orders Addr.: P.O. Box 5833, Kingwood, TX 77325-5833 Tel 281-358-2583; Fax: 281-361-5746; Edit Addr.: 4015 Pecan Pk., Kingwood, TX 77345
E-mail: lanternblu@aol.com
Web site: http://www.geocities.com/SoHo/den/5463.

Blue Marlin Pubns., *(0-9674602)* 823 Aberdeen Rd., West Bay Shore, NY 11706
E-mail: AbigMarlin@aol.com
Web site: http://www.BlueMarlinPubs.com.

Blue Note Pubns., *(1-878398)* Orders Addr.: 400 W. Cocoa Beach Cswy., Ste. 3, Cocoa Beach, FL 32931-5502 Toll Free: 800-624-0401 (order number)
E-mail: bluenote@bv.net
Web site: http://www.bluenotebooks.com
Dist(s): **American Wholesale Bk. Co.**
Baker & Taylor Bks.
Bookazine Co., Inc..

Blue Sky Graphics, Inc., *(0-9636186)* Orders Addr.: P.O. Box 270811, Fort Collins, CO 80527; Edit Addr.: 829 S. Summitview Dr., Fort Collins, CO 80524 Tel 970-484-7585.

Blue Sky Pr., The Imprint of Scholastic, Inc.

Blue Squirrel Concepts, Bk. Div., *(0-9638527)* 7513 N. Armstrong Chapel Rd., West Lafayette, IN 47906-8006 Tel 765-743-0137; Fax: 765-494-9548.

Blue Star Pubs., *(1-882218)* Orders Addr.: P.O. Box 1027, Riverton, WY 82501; Edit Addr.: 1076 Missouri Valley Rd., Riverton, WY 82501 Tel 307-856-7365.

Blue Unicorn Editions, *(1-891355; 1-58396)* 1403 NW Ninth Ave., Gainesville, FL 32605 Fax: 352-371-1154 (orders)
E-mail: blueunicorn@instabook.net
Web site: http://www.blue-unicorn-editions.com/.

Bluegrass Bks., *(0-9643683)* P.O. Box 784, Pewee Valley, KY 40056 Fax: 502-255-7657.

BlueHen Bks. Imprint of Putnam Publishing Group, The

Blushing Rose Publishing, *(1-884807)* 123 Bolinas Rd., Fairfax, CA 94930 Tel 415-458-2090; Fax: 415-458-2091; Toll Free: 800-898-2263
Web site: http://www.blushingrose.com.

Board of Regents, Gunston Hall, *(1-884085)* 10709 Gunston Rd., Lorton, VA 22079-3901 Tel 703-550-9220; Fax: 703-550-9480.

Bobbi Enterprises, *(0-9603200)* 5009 Pemberton, The Colony, TX 75056 (SAN 213-2885) Tel 972-625-3508.

Bodley Head, The (GBR) *(0-370; 1-898304) Dist. by* **Trafalgar.**

Bokmal Pr., *(0-9701441)* 2622 Fenwick Ct., Ann Arbor, MI 48104-6726 Tel 734-971-5823; 734 971 5823
E-mail: kuessner@wccnet.org.

†Bolchazy-Carducci Pubs., *(0-86516)* 1000 Brown St., Unit 101, Wauconda, IL 60084 (SAN 219-7685) Tel 847-526-4344; Fax: 847-526-2867; Toll Free: 800-392-6453
E-mail: info@bolchazy.com
Web site: http://www.bolchazy.com; *CIP.*

Boldt.Entertainment, *(0-9662556)* 5867 Oakland Ave., Minneapolis, MN 55417 Tel 612-869-5999; Fax: 612-869-5995
E-mail: boldt@u-do.com
Web site: http://www.u-do.com.

Bollix Bks., *(1-932188)* 1609 W. Callender Ave., Peoria, IL 61606.

Bonanza Publishing, *(0-945134)* Orders Addr.: P.O. Box 204, Prineville, OR 97754 (SAN 246-0858) Tel 541-447-3115; Fax: 541-416-0822; Edit Addr.: 4393 NE Wainwright Rd., Prineville, OR 97754 (SAN 246-0866)
E-mail: bonanza@transport.com
Web site: http://www.ricksteber.com
Dist(s): **Baker & Taylor Bks.**
Maverick Distributors.

Bongiorno Bks., *(0-9715819)* P.O. Box 83-2345, Richardson, TX 75083 Tel 972-671-6117
E-mail: info@bongiornobooks.com
Web site: http://www.bongiornobooks.com.

Bonneville Bks. Imprint of Cedar Fort, Inc./CFI Distribution

Book Bin - Pacifica, The, *(0-9621818)* 228 SW Third St., Corvallis, OR 97333-4630 Tel 541-752-0045; Fax: 541-754-4115
E-mail: seasia@bookbin.com.

Book Co. Publishing Pty, Ltd., The (AUS) *(1-74047) Dist. by* **Penton Overseas.**

Book Guild, Ltd. (GBR) *(1-85776; 0-86332) Dist. by* **Trans-Atl Phila.**

Book Nook Pr., *(0-9658983)* P.O. Box 598, Block Island, RI 02807 Tel 401-466-2993; Fax: 401-466-9936; Toll Free: 877-284-6665
E-mail: booknook@riconnect.com
Web site: http://www.booknookbi.com.

Book Sales, Inc., *(0-7858; 0-89009; 1-55521)* Orders Addr.: 114 Northfield Ave., Edison, NJ 08837 (SAN 169-488X) Tel 732-225-0530; Fax: 212-779-6058; 732-225-2257; Toll Free: 800-526-7257; Edit Addr.: 276 Fifth Ave., Suite 206, New York, NY 10001 (SAN 299-4062) Tel 212-779-4972; Fax: 212-779-6058
E-mail: booksales@eclipse.net
Web site: http://www.booksales.com
Dist(s): **Continental Bk. Co., Inc..**

Book Wholesalers, Inc., *(0-7587; 1-4046; 1-4131; 1-4155; 1-4156)* 1847 Mercer Rd., Lexington, KY 40511-1001 (SAN 135-5449) Toll Free: 800-888-4478
E-mail: jcarrico@bwibooks.com; nb
Web site: http://www.bwibooks.com.

Book World, Inc., *(1-881542)* 9666 E. Riggs Rd., Box 194, Sun Lakes, AZ 85248 Tel 480-895-7995; Fax: 480-895-6991; Toll Free: 888-472-2665 Do not confuse with companies with the same or similar name in Layfayette, IN, Roanoke, VA
E-mail: bst@bluestarproductions.net
Web site: http://www.bluestarproductions.net
Dist(s): **Bookpeople**
New Leaf Distributing Co., Inc..

Bookcraft, Inc. Imprint of Deseret Bk. Co.

Booklines Hawaii, Ltd., *(1-929844; 1-58849)* 269 Pali'i St., Mililani, HI 96789 (SAN 630-6624) Tel 877-828-4852; Fax: 808-676-2031
E-mail: cynthiar@booklines.com
Web site: http://www.booklineshawaii.com.

Booklocker.com, Inc., *(1-929072; 1-931391; 1-59113)* P.O. Box 2399, Bangor, ME 04402 (SAN 254-363X) Fax: 207-262-5544
E-mail: writersweekly@writersweekly.com; booklocker@booklocker.com
Web site: http://www.booklocker.com; http://www.writersweekly.com.

Bookmice Imprint of McGraw Publishing, Inc.

BookPartners, Inc., *(0-9622269; 1-58151; 1-885221)* Orders Addr.: P.O. Box 345, Portland, OR 97205; Edit Addr.: 620 SW Main, Portland, OR 97205 Tel 503-225-9900; Fax: 503-225-9901
Web site: http://www.arnicapublishing.com
Dist(s): **Arnica Publishing, Inc..**

Bookpublisher.com *See* **Wheatmark, Inc.**

Books By Byers, *(1-929663)* Orders Addr.: 16 Lockerbie Ln., Bella Vista, AR 72715-3501 Tel 501-855-6493
E-mail: spbyers@booksbybyers.com
Web site: http://www.booksbybyers.com.

Books for Black Children, Inc., *(1-58521)* Orders Addr.: P.O. Box 13261, Reading, PA 19612 Tel 610-376-6996; Toll Free Fax: 610-375-0992; Edit Addr.: 1318 Pike St., Reading, PA 19612
E-mail: bbc-inc@att.net
Web site: http://www.booksforblackchildren.com.

Books in Motion, *(1-55686; 1-58116)* Div. of Classic Ventures, Ltd., 9922 E. Montgomery, Suite 31, Spokane, WA 99206 (SAN 677-8909) Tel 509-922-1646; Fax: 509-922-1445; Toll Free: 800-752-3199
E-mail: sales@booksinmotion.com
Dist(s): **Landmark Audiobooks.**

Books Marcus, *(0-916020)* 1840 Tice Creek Dr., No. 2202, Walnut Creek, CA 94595-2459 (SAN 207-9763) Tel 805-646-3945; 67 Meadow View Rd., Orinda, CA 94563 Tel 925-254-2664; Fax: 925-254-2668.

Books of Truth, *(0-939399)* 1742 Orchard Dr., Akron, OH 44333-1853 (SAN 663-1312) Tel 330-666-3852
E-mail: ccrook@mango-bay.com.

Books of Wonder, *(0-929605)* 216 W. 18th St., Rm. 806, New York, NY 10011 (SAN 249-9916) Tel 212-989-3270; 212-989-3475; Fax: 212-989-1203; *Imprints:* Classic Frights (Classic Frights)
E-mail: wholesale@booksofwonder.com
Web site: http://www.booksofwonder.com.

Bks. on Demand, *(0-608; 0-7837; 0-8357; 0-598)* Div. of UMI, 300 N. Zeeb Rd., Ann Arbor, MI 48106-1346 Tel 734-761-4700; Fax: 734-665-5022; Toll Free: 800-521-0600
E-mail: info@umi.com
Web site: http://wwwlib.umi.com/bod; http://www.umi.com.

Books on Tape, Inc., *(0-7366; 0-913369; 1-4159)* Div. of Random House, Inc., Orders Addr.: P.O. Box 25122, Santa Ana, CA 92799-5122 Fax: 714-825-0764 ; Toll Free: 800-541-5525; Edit Addr.: 2910 W. Garry Ave., Santa Ana, CA 92704-6510 (SAN 107-0460) Tel 714-825-0021; Fax: 714-825-0756; Toll Free: 800-626-3333
E-mail: botcs@booksontape.com
Web site: http://www.booksontape.com; http://library.booksontape.com.

Books OnScreen Imprint of PageFree Publishing, Inc.

Books To Remember Imprint of Flyleaf Publishing

Booksource, The, *(0-7383; 0-911891; 0-9641084; 1-890760)* 1230 Macklind Ave., Saint Louis, MO 63110-1432 (SAN 169-4324) Tel 314-647-0600; Fax: 314-647-2622; Toll Free: 800-444-0435
E-mail: vstadts@freewwweb.com
Web site: http://www.booksource.com.

Booksurge, LLC, *(1-59109; 1-59457)* 5341 Dorchester Rd., Suite 16, North Charleston, SC 29418 (SAN 255-2132) Tel 843-579-0000; Fax: 843-577-7506; Toll Free: 866-308-6235
E-mail: editor@booksurge.com; info@imprintbooks.com
Web site: http://www.booksurge.com; http://www.imprintbooks.com
Dist(s): **BookWorld Services, Inc..**

BookWorld Distribution Services, Incorporated *See* **BookWorld Services, Inc.**

BookWorld Services, Inc., *(1-884962)* 1933 Whitfield Pk. Loop, Sarasota, FL 34243 (SAN 173-0568) Tel 941-758-8094; Fax: 941-753-9396; Toll Free Fax: 800-777-2525; Toll Free: 800-444-2524 (orders only)
E-mail: central@bookworld.com; sales@bookworld.com
Web site: http://www.bookworld.com.

BOPO Biligual Bks., *(0-9665575)* P.O. Box 4713, Marietta, GA 30061-4713 Tel 770-432-9859 (phone/fax); Toll Free: 800-251-3423
E-mail: publisher@bopobooks.com
Web site: http://www.bopobooks.com.

Borden Publishing Co., *(0-87505)* 1611-A S. Melrose Dr., N. 108, Vista, CA 92083 (SAN 201-419X) Tel 760-594-0918; Fax: 760-599-4118 (call first)
E-mail: bordenpublishing@msn.com.

Borders Pr., *(0-681)* Div. of Borders Group, Inc., 100 Phoenix Dr., Ann Arbor, MI 48108
Web site: http://www.bordersgroupinc.com; http://www.bordersstores.com; http://www.borders.com.

Borealis Imprint of White Wolf Publishing, Inc.

Boson Bks. Imprint of C&M Online Media, Inc.

Boudelang Pr., *(0-9649742; 1-930124)* Orders Addr.: P.O. Box 12379, Portland, OR 97212-0379 Tel 310-821-2450; Fax: 310-821-5133; Edit Addr.: 1138 Grant Ave., Venice, CA 90291
E-mail: Boudelang@aol.com
Web site: http://www.boudelang.com
Dist(s): **Baker & Taylor Bks.**
Partners/West.

Boulden Publishing, *(1-878076; 1-892421)* P.O. Box 1186, Weaverville, CA 96093-1186 Tel 530-623-5399 ; Fax: 530-623-5525; Toll Free: 800-238-8433
E-mail: jboulden@bouldenpublishing.com
Web site: http://www.bouldenpublishing.com
Dist(s): **MAR*CO Products, Inc.**
Social Studies Schl. Service
Sunburst Communications, Inc..

Boulevard Bks., *(0-399; 0-425; 1-57297)* Div. of Berkley Publishing Group, Orders Addr.: 405 Murray Hill Pkwy., East Rutherford, NJ 07073; Edit Addr.: 200 Madison Ave., 14th Flr., New York, NY 10016 Fax: 212-545-8917; Toll Free: 800-788-6262 Do not confuse with Boulevard Bks. in Topanga, CA
Web site: http://www.penguinputnam.com/
Dist(s): **Penguin Group (USA) Inc..**

Bouregy, Thomas & Co., Inc., *(0-8034)* 160 Madison Ave., New York, NY 10016 (SAN 201-4173) Tel 212-598-0222; Fax: 212-979-1862; Toll Free: 800-223-5251
E-mail: custserv@avalonbooks.com
Web site: http://www.avalonbooks.com.

BOW Bks. Imprint of Blessing Our World, Inc.

Bow Tie Enterprises, *(1-890414)* Div. of Overly-Raker, Inc., 8612 Fairway Pl., Middleton, WI 53562-2504 Tel 717-485-9307; Fax: 717-485-5874; Toll Free: 800-626-9843.

Boxtree, Ltd. (GBR) *(0-7522; 1-85283) Dist. by* **Trafalgar.**

Boxtree, Ltd. (GBR) *(0-7522; 1-85283) Dist. by* **Trans-Atl Phila.**

Boyce Pubns., *(0-918823)* 1023 Oxford, Clovis, CA 93612 (SAN 669-652X) Tel 209-299-8495.

Boyds Collection Ltd., The, *(0-9712840; 0-9713174)* 350 South St., McSherrystown, PA 17344 Tel 717-633-9898
E-mail: alana@boydsstuff.com
Web site: http://www.boydsstuff.com.

Boyds Mills Pr., *(1-56397; 1-878093; 1-59078)* Div. of Highlights For Children, Inc., 815 Church St., Honesdale, PA 18431 Tel 717-253-1164; 570-253-1164; Fax: 570-253-0179; Toll Free: 800-490-5111
E-mail: admin@boydsmillspress.com
Web site: http://www.boydsmillspress.com
Dist(s): **Cheng & Tsui Co.**
Lectorum Pubns., Inc..

Brad Smiley *See* **Kennesaw Publishing**

Brady Computer Books *See* **Brady Publishing**

Brady Publishing, *(0-8359; 0-87618; 0-87619; 0-89303; 0-913486; 1-56686; 0-7440)* Div. of Prentice Hall, 201 W. 103rd St., Indianapolis, IN 46290 Tel 317-581-3500; Fax: 317-705-6290; Toll Free Fax: 800-835-3202; Toll Free: 800-428-5331 (orders); 800-571-5840
E-mail: janet.eshenour@bradygames.com
Web site: http://www.bradygames.com
Dist(s): **Alpha Bks..**

Bragdon, Allen D. Pubs., Inc., *(0-916410)* Orders Addr.: Tupelo Rd., Bass River, MA 02664; Edit Addr.: 252 Great Western Rd., South Yarmouth, MA 02664-2210 (SAN 208-5623) Tel 508-398-4440; Fax: 508-760-2397; Toll Free: 877-876-2787
E-mail: abragdon@brainwaves.com; admin@brainwaves.com
Web site: http://www.brainwaves.com.

Branden Bks., *(0-8283)* P.O. Box 812094, Wellesley, MA 02482 (SAN 201-4106) Tel 781-235-3634; Fax: 781-790-1056
E-mail: branden@branden.com
Web site: http://www.branden.com.

Branden Publishing Company *See* **Branden Bks.**

Brandon Bk. Pubs., Ltd. (IRL) *(0-86322) Dist. by* **Irish Bks Media.**

Brandylane Pubs., Inc., *(0-9627635; 1-883911)* Orders Addr.: P.O. Box 261, White Stone, VA 23223; Edit Addr.: 1711 E. Main St., Suite 9, Richmond, VA 23223 Tel 804-644-3090; Fax: 804-644-3092; Toll Free: 800-553-6922 (orders only)
E-mail: thpruett@hotmail.com; brandy@crosslink.net
Web site: http://www.brandylanepublishers.com
Dist(s): **Baker & Taylor International**
Parnassus Bk. Distributors.

Braziller, George Inc., *(0-8076)* 171 Madison Ave., Suite 1103, New York, NY 10016 (SAN 201-9310) Tel 212-889-0909; Fax: 212-689-5405
Dist(s): **Norton, W. W. & Co., Inc..**

Breakers Palm Beach, Inc., The, *(0-9649743)* Div. of Flagler System, Inc., One S. County Rd., Palm Beach, FL 33480 Tel 407-655-6611; Fax: 407-659-8403; Toll Free: 800-833-3141.

Breakthrough Pubns., Inc., *(0-914327)* 220 White Plains Rd. Ste. 278, Tarrytown, NY 10591-5892 (SAN 287-4946) Toll Free: 800-824-5000 Do not confuse with Breakthrough Pubns., Inc., Spokane, WA
E-mail: webmaster@booksonhorses.com.

Breckenridge Group & Assocs., *(0-9706099)* 4836 Sheffield Dr., Nashville, TN 37211-4510 Tel 615-837-9855; Fax: 615-834-2029
E-mail: p47skelton@home.com
Web site: http://breckenridge-group.com.

Breeding, Robert L. *See* **Thriftecon Publications**

Brenneman, Tim C. *See* **Grand Unification Pr., Inc.**

Breslov Research Institute, *(0-930213; 1-928822)* P.O. Box 587, Monsey, NY 10952-0587 (SAN 670-7890) Tel 845-425-4258; Fax: 845-425-3018; Toll Free: 800-332-7375
E-mail: info@rebbenachman.com
Web site: http://www.rebbenachman.com
Dist(s): **Moznaim Publishing Corp..**

†Brethren Pr., *(0-87178)* Div. of Church of the Brethren, 1451 Dundee Ave., Elgin, IL 60120-1694 (SAN 201-9329) Tel 847-742-5100; 800-441-3712; Fax: 847-742-1407; Toll Free: 800-441-3712
E-mail: brethren_press_gb@brethren.org
Web site: http://www.brethrenpress.com; *CIP.*

Briarwood Pubns., *(1-892614)* 150 W. College St., Rocky Mount, VA 24151 (SAN 299-8068) Tel 540-483-3606; Fax: 540-489-4692 ext. 51; *Imprints:* Sassy Cat Books (Sassy Cat) Do not confuse with Briarwood Pubns., Terre Haute, IN
E-mail: bturner@swva.net
Web site: http://www.briarwoodva.com.

Brickford Lane Pubs., *(0-9656431)* 14 Brickford Ln., Baltimore, MD 21208 Tel 410-653-2299
Dist(s): **Baker & Taylor Bks.**
Koen Bk. Distributors.

Bridge Publishing, Incorporated/LOGOS *See* **Bridge-Logos Pubs.**

Bridge-Logos Pubs., *(0-88270; 0-912106)* Orders Addr.: 17310 NW 32nd Ave., Newberry, FL 32669 Toll Free Fax: 800-935-6467 (orders only); Toll Free: 800-631-5802 (orders only); Edit Addr.: P.O. Box 141630, Gainesville, FL 32614 (SAN 253-5254) Tel 352-472-7900; Fax: 352-472-7908
E-mail: editor@bridgelogos.com; info@bridgelogos.com; mail@bridgelogos.com
Web site: http://www.bridgelogos.com
Dist(s): **Anchor Distributors**
Appalachian Bible Co.
Baker & Taylor Bks.
Riverside
Spring Arbor Distributors, Inc..

Bright Bks., *(0-9605968)* P.O. Box 428, Akron, IN 46910 (SAN 216-7204) Tel 219-893-4113 Do not confuse with companies with the same name in Folsom, CA, Austin, TX.

Bright Bks., Inc., *(1-880092)* 2313 Lake Austin Blvd., Austin, TX 78703 Tel 512-499-4164; Fax: 512-477-9975 Do not confuse with companies with the same name in Akron, IN, Folsom, CA
Dist(s): **Partners Pubs. Group, Inc..**

Bright Eyes Pr., *(0-9728019)* 862 Congressional Rd., Simi Valley, CA 93065 Tel 805-579-0027
E-mail: kassie@kgraves.com
Web site: http://www.brighteyespress.com.

Bright Lamb Pubs., Inc., *(0-9651270; 1-891651)* Orders Addr.: P.O. Box 844, Evans, GA 30809 Tel 706-863-2237; Fax: 706-863-9971; Edit Addr.: 532 McKinne's Line, Evans, GA 30809
E-mail: brightlamb@aol.com
Web site: http://www.brightlamb.com
Dist(s): **Baker & Taylor Bks..**

Bright Sky Pr., *(0-9704729; 0-9709987; 1-931721)* Orders Addr.: P.O. Box 416, Albany, TX 76430 Tel 915-762-3909; Fax: 915-762-3690; Edit Addr.: 340 S. Second St., Albany, TX 76430 Do not confuse with Breakaway Bks., Halcottsville, NY
E-mail: carolcates@brightskypress.com
Web site: http://www.brightskypress.com
Dist(s): **National Bk. Network.**

Bright Sparks Imprint of Parragon, Inc.

Brighton & Lloyd, *(0-922434)* Orders Addr.: P.O. Box 2903, Costa Mesa, CA 92628 (SAN 251-3072); Edit Addr.: 1875 Wren Cir., Costa Mesa, CA 92626 (SAN 251-3080) Tel 714-540-6466.

Brimax Bks., Ltd., *(0-86112; 0-900195; 0-904494; 1-85854)* Member of Reed Elsevier Group, 2284 Black River Rd., Bethlehem, PA 18015
Dist(s): **Libros Sin Fronteras.**

Names

British Bk. Co., Inc., *(1-930468)* 149 Palos Verdes Blvd., Suite B, Redondo Beach, CA 90277 Tel 310-373-5917; Fax: 310-373-7342; Toll Free: 877-990-1299
E-mail: tony310@earthlink.com
Web site: http://www.firstnovels.com.

Broadblade Pr., *(0-9614640; 0-9620249; 0-9713893)* 11314 Miller Rd., Swartz Creek, MI 48473-8570 (SAN 691-9227) Tel 810 635 3156
Dist(s): **Baker & Taylor Bks..**

†Broadman & Holman Pubs., *(0-8054; 0-87981; 1-55819; 1-58640; 0-8400)* Div. of LifeWay Christian Resources of the Southern Baptist Convention, 127 Ninth Ave., N., Nashville, TN 37234 (SAN 201-937X) Tel 615-251-2520; Fax: 615-251-5026 (Books Only); 615-251-2036 (Bibles Only); 615-251-2413 (Gifts/Supplies Only); Toll Free: 800-296-4036 (orders/returns); 800-251-3225; 800-725-5416
E-mail: broadmanholman@lifeway.com
Web site: http://www.broadmanholman.com
Dist(s): **CRC Pubns.**
Christian Bk. Distributors
Twentieth Century Christian Bks.; *CIP.*

Broderbund Software, Inc., *(0-922614; 1-55790; 1-57135; 1-57382; 1-57404)* 500 Redwood Blvd., Novato, CA 94948-6121 (SAN 264-8369) Tel 415-382-4400; Toll Free: 800-527-6263
Web site: http://www.mattelinteractive.com.

Brookfield Reader, Inc., The, *(0-9660172; 1-930093)* 137 Peyton Rd., Sterling, VA 20165-5605 (SAN 299-4445) Tel 703-430-0202; Fax: 703-430-7315; Toll Free: 888-389-2741
E-mail: info@brookfieldreader.com; hbaggett@erols.com
Web site: http://www.brookfieldreader.com
Dist(s): **Book Wholesalers, Inc.**
BookWorld Services, Inc.
Brodart Co.
International Publishers Marketing
Quality Bks., Inc..

†Brookline Bks., Inc., *(0-914797; 1-57129)* Orders Addr.: P.O. Box 97, Newton Upper Falls, MA 02464 (SAN 289-0690) Tel 617-558-8010; Fax: 617-558-8011; Toll Free: 800-666-2665; Edit Addr.: 29 Ware St., Cambridge, MA 02138; *Imprints:* Lumen Editions (Lumen Eds)
E-mail: brbooks@yahoo.com
Web site: http://www.brooklinebooks.com; *CIP.*

Brown Bag Productions, *(1-58193)* 2710 N. Stemmons Freeway, North Tower, Suite 600N, Dallas, TX 75207 Fax: 214-638-7747; Toll Free: 800-686-9484
E-mail: sweingpcico.com
Web site: http://www.childrensplays.com.

Brown, Jack Enterprises, *(1-886290)* 3118 FM 528, Suite 217, Webster, TX 77598 Tel 713-334-5367; Fax: 713-482-3624; Toll Free: 800-356-0375.

Brown Swan Pubs., *(0-9717993)* 760 Redriver Way, Corona, CA 92882
E-mail: cdong@brownswan.com
Web site: http://www.brownswan.com
Dist(s): **Biblio Distribution.**

Brown, Tehane, *(0-9637099)* Orders Addr.: P.O. Box 582, Kula, Maui, HI 96790 Tel 808-878-6609; Fax: 808-878-6949; Edit Addr.: 230 Kahoea Pl., Kula, Maui, HI 96790.

Brown, Towana J., *(0-9622060)* P.O. Box 352, Holly Pond, AL 35083-0352 Tel 205-796-2095.

Brownlow Publishing Co., Inc., *(0-910444; 0-915720; 1-57051; 1-877719; 1-59177)* 6309 Airport Freeway, Fort Worth, TX 76117 (SAN 207-5105) Tel 817-831-3831; Fax: 817-831-7025; Toll Free: 800-433-7610
E-mail: jcerneka@brownlowgift.com; jroser@brownlowgift.com
Web site: http://www.brownlowgift.com
Dist(s): **Appalachian Bible Co.**
Riverside
Spring Arbor Distributors, Inc..

BrownTrout Pubs., Inc., *(0-7631; 0-939027; 1-56313)* Orders Addr.: P.O. Box 280070, San Francisco, CA 94128-0070 (SAN 662-6505) Tel 650-340-9800; Fax: 310-316-1138; 650-340-9450; Toll Free: 800-777-7812; Edit Addr.: 4 W. Fourth Ave., No. 200, San Mateo, CA 94402
E-mail: sales@browntrout.com
Web site: http://browntrout.com.

Bruhn, John G., *(0-9616570)* 8864 E. Surry Ave., Scottsdale, AZ 85260 (SAN 659-9230) Tel 480-767-0755 (phone/fax).

Brunswick Publishing Corp., *(0-931494; 1-55618)* 1386 Lawrenceville Plank Rd., Lawrenceville, VA 23868 (SAN 211-6332) Tel 434-848-3865; Fax: 434-848-0607
E-mail: brunswickbooks@earthlink.net
Web site: http://www.brunswickbooks.com/
Dist(s): **Breakfast Poems.**

Buccaneer Bks., Inc., *(0-89966; 0-89967; 0-89968; 1-56849)* P.O. Box 168, Cutchogue, NY 11935 (SAN 209-1542) Tel 631-734-5724; Fax: 631-734-7920; *Imprints:* Lightyear Press (Lghtyr Pr); Harmony Raine & Company (Harmony Rain)
E-mail: BuccBooks@aol.com
Web site: http://www.BuccaneerBooks.com
Dist(s): **National Bk. Network.**

Buckaroo Bks., *(0-930771)* 1015 N. 7300 E., Huntsville, UT 84317 (SAN 677-6221) Tel 801-745-3102 Do not confuse with Buckaroo Bks. in Seattle, WA.

Buckingham Classics, Limited *See* **B&B Audio, Inc.**

Buddhist Text Translation Society, *(0-88139; 0-917512)* Affil. of Dharma Realm Buddhist Assoc., Orders Addr.: 2001 Talmage Rd., Talmage, CA 95481-0217 Tel 707-462-0939; Fax: 707-462-0949; Edit Addr.: 1777 Murchison Dr., Burlingame, CA 94010-4504 (SAN 281-3556) Tel 650-692-9286 (phone/fax)
E-mail: bttsonline@snetworking.com; transbtts@yahoo.com; drbajgh@jps.net
Web site: http://www.bttsonline.org.

Bunker Hill Publishing, Inc., *(1-59373)* 26 Adams St., Charlestown, MA 02129 Tel 617-242-1518; Fax: 617-242-2429
E-mail: ckitchel@bunkerhillpublishing.com
Web site: http://www.bunkerhillpublishing.com
Dist(s): **Client Distribution Services.**

Bur Oak Pr., Inc., *(0-929326)* 8717 Mockingbird Rd., Platteville, WI 53818 (SAN 249-0463) Tel 608-348-8662
E-mail: buroakpress@yahoo.com
Web site: http://www.geocities.com/buroakpress.

Burd Street Pr. Imprint of White Mane Publishing Co., Inc.

Burke, John Gordon Pub., Inc., *(0-934272)* P.O. Box 1492, Evanston, IL 60204 (SAN 223-7083) Tel 847-866-8625; Fax: 847-866-6639
E-mail: info@jgburkepub.com
Web site: http://www.jgburkepub.com.

Burns, Nicholas K. Publishing, *(0-9713069)* 130 Proctor Blvd., Utica, NY 13501 Tel 315-738-1890; Fax: 315-738-1891; Toll Free: 866-738-1890
E-mail: nkburns@adelphia.net
Dist(s): **Koen Bk. Distributors.**

Bush, Elsie R. *See* **E&R Publishing**

Business Jobs *See* **Alexie Bks.**

Business Word, The, *(0-9636745; 0-9655442; 1-891846)* 11211 E. Arapahoe Rd., Suite 101, Centennial, CO 80112 Tel 303-290-8500; Fax: 303-290-9025; Toll Free: 800-328-3211
E-mail: Richard.Rhinehart@businessword.com
Web site: http://www.businessword.com; http://www.twinsmagazine.com/theBookshelf.shtml.

Butte Pubns., Inc., *(1-884362)* P.O. Box 1328, Hillsboro, OR 97123-1328 (SAN 299-8866) Tel 503-648-9791; Fax: 503-693-9526; Toll Free: 866-312-8883
E-mail: service@buttepublications.com
Web site: http://www.buttepublications.com.

Butterfield Bks., Inc., *(1-886652)* Box 407, Lindsborg, KS 67456 Tel 785-227-2707; Fax: 785-227-2017
E-mail: linda@bookkansas.com
Web site: http://www.bookkansas.com
Dist(s): **Baker & Taylor Bks.**
Booksource, The
Skandisk, Inc..

Butterfly Bks., *(1-889637)* 8236 Maplestar Rd., Las Vegas, NV 89128 Tel 702-256-2798; Toll Free: 800-838-2738 Do not confuse with Butterfly Bks., San Antonio, TX
Web site: http://www.butterflybooks.com.

Butterfly Pr., *(0-9677692)* 18 Cedar St., Old Town, ME 04468-1302 Tel 207-827-5651 Do not confuse with companies with same name in New York, NY, Worcester, MA, Houston, TX, Cochranville, PA, Point Richmond, CA, Phoeniz, AZ, Amherst, MA, Stamford, Ct
E-mail: azames18@aol.com.

Butterworth-Heinemann Imprint of Elsevier Science & Technology Bks.

Buy Bks. on the Web.Com, *(0-9665678; 1-892896; 0-7414)* 519 W. Lancaster Ave., Haverford, PA 19041 Tel 610-520-2500; Fax: 610-519-0261; Toll Free: 877-289-2665
E-mail: info@buybooksontheweb.com
Web site: http://buybooksontheweb.com.

Byte/Me Book Imprint of Awe-Struck E-Bks.

C & C Publishing *See* **Cosmo Starr Bks.**

C&M Online Media, Inc., *(0-917990; 1-886420; 1-932482)* 3905 Meadow Field Ln., Raleigh, NC 27606 Tel 919-233-8164; Fax: 919-233-8578; *Imprints:* Boson Books (Boson Bks)
E-mail: nancy@cmonline.com
Web site: http://www.cmonline.com; http://www.bosonbooks.com; http://www.bosonromances.com
Dist(s): **Amazon.Com**
netLibrary, Inc..

C & M Publications *See* **LCN, Inc.**

C&O Research, 11286 Weatherstone Dr., Waynesboro, PA 17268-8838 (SAN 297-7605)
Dist(s): **Washington Bk. Distributors.**

CBI Pr., *(0-9705812)* 6 Jeffrey Cir., Bedford, MA 01730 Do not confuse with C B I Press, Arlington, VA
E-mail: cbipress@mail.com
Web site: http://www.cbipress.com.

C B P Press *See* **Chalice Pr.**

C C Comics/C C Publishing *See* **C C Publishing**

CC Pubs., *(0-9660099)* Orders Addr.: 114 Branchwood Dr., Deptford, NJ 08096; Edit Addr.: P.O. Box 5213, Deptford, NJ 08096 Tel 609-401-0505 Do not confuse with C C Publishers, Clearwater, FL.

C C Publishing, *(0-9634183)* Orders Addr.: P.O. Box 542, Loveland, OH 45140-0542; Edit Addr.: 6304 Councilridge Ct., Loveland, OH 45140 Tel 513-248-4170
Web site: http://www.mysterypublishers.com/CC
Dist(s): **Spring Arbor Distributors, Inc..**

CEDCO Publishing, *(0-7683; 0-915865; 1-55912)* 100 Pelican Way, San Rafael, CA 94901 (SAN 293-9495) Tel 415-451-3176; Fax: 415-457-4839; Toll Free: 800-227-6162
E-mail: sales@cedco.com
Web site: http://www.cedco.com.

CIS Communications, Inc., *(0-935063; 1-56062)* 180 Park Avenue, Lakewood, NJ 08701 (SAN 694-5953) Tel 732-905-3000; Fax: 732-367-6666.

†CSS Publishing Co., *(0-7880; 0-89536; 1-55673)* Orders Addr.: P.O. Box 4503, Lima, OH 45802-4503 (SAN 207-0707) Tel 419-227-1818; Fax: 419-228-9184; Toll Free: 800-241-4056; Edit Addr.: 517 S. Main St., Lima, OH 45804-4503; *Imprints:* Fairway Press (Fairway Pr) Do not confuse with CSS Publishing in Tularosa, NM
E-mail: editor@csspub.com; csspub@csspub.com; info@csspub.com
Web site: http://www.csspub.com
Dist(s): **BookWorld Services, Inc.**
Spring Arbor Distributors, Inc.; *CIP.*

Cadelle Publishing, *(1-890557)* 255 Weber Dr., Hamilton, MT 59840-3425 Tel 406-363-0195; Fax: 406-363-7401.

Cadence Bks. Imprint of Viz Communications, Inc.

Cadence Pr., *(0-9653018)* P.O. Box 96, Wellesley Island, NY 13640-0096 (SAN 299-2752) Tel 315-655-2253; Toll Free: 888-222-3362 Do not confuse with companies with the same name in Lakewood, CO, Hollywood, CA
Dist(s): **Baker & Taylor Bks..**

Caedmon Imprint of HarperTrade

Cahill Publishing Company *See* **Advance Publishing, Inc.**

Cajun Bayou Pr., *(0-9639378)* Rte. 5, Box 1444, Abbeville, LA 70510 Tel 318-642-9142.

California Artists Radio Theater Productions, 1224 N. Lincoln St., Burbank, CA 91506 Toll Free: 800-200-8868.

Callaway Editions, Inc., *(0-935112)* 54 Seventh Ave. S., New York, NY 10014 (SAN 213-2931) Tel 212-929-5212; Fax: 212-929-8087
E-mail: info@callaway.com
Web site: http://www.callaway.com
Dist(s): **Holt, Henry & Co.**
Simon & Schuster Children's Publishing
Simon & Schuster, Inc.
Viking Penguin.

Names

Calliope Pr., *(0-9649241)* Orders Addr.: P.O. Box 2408, New York, NY 10108-2408 (SAN 298-9026) Tel 212-563-7859; Fax: 212-263-8234; Edit Addr.: 400 W. 43rd St., Apt. 34B, New York, NY 10036 Do not confuse with companies with same name in Silver Springs, MD, San Francisco, CA, North Hollywood, CA, Walnut Creek, CA
E-mail: PWilli1933@aol.com; Information@CalliopePress.com
Web site: http://www.bookwire.com/Bookinfo.Title; http://www.calliopepress.com
Dist(s): **Koen Bk. Distributors**
Partners Pubs. Group, Inc.
Victory Multimedia.

†Cambridge Univ. Pr., *(0-521; 0-511)* Orders Addr.: 100 Brook Hill Dr., West Nyack, NY 10994-2133 (SAN 281-3769) Tel 845-353-7500; Fax: 845-353-4141; Toll Free: 800-872-7423 (orders, returns, credit & accounting); 800-937-9600; Edit Addr.: 40 W. 20th St., New York, NY 10011-4211 (SAN 200-206X) Tel 212-924-3900; Fax: 212-691-3239
E-mail: orders@cup.org; information@cup.org; customer_service@cup.org
Web site: http://www.cup.org
Dist(s): **netLibrary, Inc.**; *CIP.*

Campbell, Tammie Lang, *(0-9623947)* 1219 Kingscreek Trail, Missouri City, TX 77459 Tel 713-499-7966.

Can Family, The, *(0-9665043)* 8491 Imperial Dr., Laurel, MD 20708 Tel 301-490-5114.

Can You Dig It?, Incorporated *See* **Little Spirit Publishing, Inc.**

Canady SW Publishing, *(1-929889)* Orders Addr.: P.O. Box 11361, Chandler, AZ 85248-0007 Tel 480-802-6623; Edit Addr.: 11132 E. Watford Ct., Sun Lakes, AZ 85248
E-mail: grandmacc@uswest.com.

Canal Side Pubs., *(0-9628208; 1-886623)* 3517 State Rd., No. 5, Schuyler, NY 13340 Tel 315-895-7535; Toll Free: 800-493-2501
Web site: http://www.canalsidepublishers.com.

Candle Fly Pr., *(0-9713551)* Orders Addr.: P.O. Box 4561, Spartanburg, SC 29305 Tel 864-585-7250; Edit Addr.: 815 Isom St., Spartanburg, SC 29303
E-mail: candleflypress@aol.com.

CandlePower Communications *See* **Candlepower, Inc.**

Candlepower, Inc., *(0-9677558; 1-932037)* Orders Addr.: P.O. Box 787, New Paltz, NY 12561 (SAN 255-2949) Tel 845-255-4076; Fax: 845-255-7645; Edit Addr.: 64 Plains Rd., New Paltz, NY 12561
E-mail: david@candlepower.org
Web site: http://www.candlepower.org
Dist(s): **BookWorld Services, Inc..**

†Candlewick Pr., *(0-7636; 1-56402)* Div. of Walker Bks., London, England, 2067 Massachusetts Ave., Cambridge, MA 02140 Tel 617-661-3330; Fax: 617-661-0565 Do not confuse with Candlewick Pr., Crystal Lake, IL
E-mail: bigbear@candlewick.com; salesinfo@candlewick.com
Web site: http://www.candlewick.com/
Dist(s): **Lectorum Pubns., Inc.**
Penguin Group (USA) Inc.; *CIP.*

Candy Cane Pr. Imprint of Ideals Pubns.

Canmore Pr., *(1-887774)* Orders Addr.: P.O. Box 510794, Melbourne Beach, FL 32951-0794 Tel 321-729-0078; Fax: 321-724-1162; *Imprints:* Wynden (Wynden)
E-mail: publish@canmorepress.com
Web site: http://www.canmorepress.com.

Canon Pr., *(1-885767; 1-59128)* Div. of Christ Church, Orders Addr.: P.O. Box 8729, Moscow, ID 83843 Toll Free: 800-488-2034 Do not confuse with companies with the same or similar names in Grand Rapids, MI, Centerville, UT
Web site: http://www.canonpress.org.

Canticle Pr., Inc., *(0-9641725)* 385 Watervliet-Shaker Rd., Latham, NY 12110-4799 (SAN 299-268X) Tel 518-783-3604; Fax: 518-783-5209
E-mail: mnoonan45@aol.com.

Capstan Pubns., *(0-914565)* P.O. Box 306, Basin, WY 82410 (SAN 289-162X) Tel 307-568-2604; *Imprints:* Timbertrails (Timbertrails).

Capstone High-Interest Bks. Imprint of Capstone Pr., Inc.

Capstone Pr., Inc., *(0-7368; 1-56065)* 1905 Lookout Dr., North Mankato, MN 56003; Orders Addr.: P.O. Box 669, Mankato, MN 56002-0669 (SAN 254-1815) Tel 507-388-6650; Fax: 507-625-4662; Toll Free Fax: 888-262-0705; Toll Free: 800-747-4992; Edit Addr.: 6117 Blue Circle Dr., Suite 150, Minnetonka, MN 55343; *Imprints:* Capstone High-Interest Books (Caps Hight-Int) Do not confuse with Capstone Pr., Inc. in Decatur, IL
Web site: http://www.capstone-press.com
Dist(s): **Continental Bk. Co., Inc.**
Lectorum Pubns., Inc..

Capstone Publishing, Inc., *(1-880450)* 1376 S. Beach Dr., Camano Island, WA 98292-7601 Do not confuse with Capstone Publishing Co. in New York, NY
Dist(s): **Bookpeople.**

CareMORE, *(1-886990)* Orders Addr.: P.O. Box 4217, Saint George, UT 84770 Tel 435-634-0853; Fax: 435-634-9510; Toll Free: 800-634-2471; Edit Addr.: 845 N. Valleyview, No. 914, Saint George, UT 84770
E-mail: caremore@care-more.com
Web site: http://www.care-more.com
Dist(s): **Origin Bk. Sales, Inc..**

Carlsen Verlag (DEU) *(3-551) Dist. by* **Distribks Inc.**

Carlton Bks., Ltd. (GBR) *(1-85868; 1-84222; 1-84442) Dist. by* **Trafalgar.**

Carolrhoda Bks. Imprint of Lerner Publishing Group

Carolrhoda Bks., *(0-8225; 0-87614; 1-57505)*.

Carousel Pubns., Ltd., *(0-935474)* 1304 Rte. 42, SparrowBush, NY 12780 (SAN 287-7333) Tel 212-758-9399; Fax: 212-758-6453
E-mail: worldntune@aol.com
Web site: http://www.members.aol.com/worldntune/index.html.

Carousel Publishing Corporation *See* **Carousel Pubns., Ltd.**

Carpino Bks., *(1-928675)* 30 Park St., Coventry, RI 02816 Tel 401-828-5589
E-mail: carpino@myexcel.com; topo4@myexcel.com.

Carpino-Weller, Nancy *See* **Carpino Bks.**

Carroll & Graf Pubs. Imprint of Avalon Publishing Group

Carson-Dellosa Publishing Co., Inc., *(0-88724; 1-59441)* Orders Addr.: P.O. Box 35665, Greensboro, NC 27425 Tel 336-632-0084; Fax: 336-856-9414; Toll Free: 800-321-0943; Edit Addr.: 7027 Albert Pick Rd., 3rd Flr., Greensboro, NC 27410
E-mail: dturner@carsondellosa.com
Web site: http://www.carsondellosa.com.

Cartwheel Bks. Imprint of Scholastic, Inc.

Casa Bautista de Publicaciones, *(0-311)* Div. of Southern Baptist Convention, Orders Addr.: P.O. Box 4255, El Paso, TX 79914 (SAN 220-0139) Tel 915-566-9656; Fax: 915-562-6502; Toll Free: 800-755-5958; *Imprints:* Editorial Mundo Hispano (Edit Mundo)
E-mail: epena@casabautista.org
Web site: http://www.casabautista.org.

CasAnanda Publishing, *(1-889131)* P.O. Box 7207, Bayonet Point, FL 34674 Tel 727-819-1082 (phone/fax)
E-mail: idobooks4u@aol.com
Web site: http://www.jansonmedia.com.

Casemate Pubs. & Bk. Distributors, LLC, *(0-9711709; 1-932033)* Orders Addr.: 2114 Darby Rd., 2nd Flr., Havertown, PA 19083 Tel 610-853-9131; Fax: 610-853-9146
E-mail: casemate@casematepublishing.com
Web site: http://www.casematepublishing.com.

Cassette Book Company *See* **Audio Bk. Co.**

Casterman, Editions (FRA) *(2-203) Dist. by* **Distribks Inc.**

Castleberry Farms Pr., *(1-891907)* P.O. Box 337, Poplar, WI 54864 Tel 715-364-8404
E-mail: cbfarmpr@pressenter.com.

Castlebrook Pubns., *(0-9641697)* 1579 Farmers Ln., No. 237, Santa Rosa, CA 95405 Tel 707-539-7583; *Imprints:* You-Draw-It Books (You-Draw-It)
E-mail: youdraw@aol.com
Web site: http://www.youdrawitbooks.com.

Catalpa Pr., *(0-9745665)* P.O. Box 27303, Oakland, CA 94602-0303 Tel 510-569-0796 (phone/fax)
E-mail: catalpapress@aol.com
Web site: http://www.jackschroder.com.

Catch the Spirit of Appalachia Imprint of Ammons Communications, Ltd.

Cauper, Eunice, *(0-9617551)* 8946 Winton Hills Ct., Springboro, OH 45066-9620 (SAN 664-4449).

Cavendish Children's Bks. Imprint of Cavendish, Marshall Corp.

†Cavendish, Marshall Corp., *(0-7614; 0-85685; 0-86307; 1-85435)* Member of Times Publishing Group, 99 White Plains Rd., P.O. Box 2001, Tarrytown, NY 10591-9001 (SAN 238-437X) Tel 914-332-8888; Fax: 914-332-8882; Toll Free: 800-821-9881; *Imprints:* Benchmark Books (Benchmark NY); Cavendish Children's Books (Cav Child Bks)
E-mail: mcc@marshallcavendish.com
Web site: http://www.marshallcavendish.com; *CIP.*

†Caxton Pr., *(0-87004)* Div. of Caxton Printers. Ltd., 312 Main St., Caldwell, ID 83605-3299 (SAN 201-9698) Tel 208-459-7421; Fax: 208-459-7450; Toll Free: 800-657-6465
E-mail: wcornell@caxtonpress.com; sgipson@caxtonpress.com; publish@caxtonprinters.com
Web site: http://www.caxtonpress.com; http://www.caxtonprinters.com; *CIP.*

Caxton Printers, Limited *See* **Caxton Pr.**

Caxton, Wm Ltd., *(0-940473)* P.O. Box 220, Ellison Bay, WI 54210-0220 (SAN 135-1303) Tel 920-854-2955.

CCC of America, *(1-56814)* P.O. Box 166349, Irving, TX 75016-6349 (SAN 298-7546) Toll Free: 800-935-2222
E-mail: customerservice@cccofamerica.com
Web site: http://www.cccofamerica.com
Dist(s): **Liguori Pubns..**

CDA Publishing, *(0-9713985)* P.O. Box 1206, Lombard, IL 60148-1206 Tel 630-261-1884; Fax: 630-261-1886
E-mail: corporatedevelopement@corpdevelopmentassoc.com
Web site: http://www.corpdevelopmentassoc.com.

Cedar Fort, Inc./CFI Distribution, *(0-934126; 1-55517)* 925 N. Main St., Springville, UT 84663-1051 (SAN 170-2858) Tel 801-489-4084; Fax: 801-489-1097; Toll Free Fax: 800-388-3727; Toll Free: 800-759-2665; *Imprints:* Bonneville Books (Bonneville Bks)
E-mail: sales@cedarfort.com; cedarfort@cedarfort.com; editorial@cedarfort.com
Web site: http://www.cedarfort.com
Dist(s): **Todd Communications.**

Cedar Glade Pr., P.O. Box 1664, Jefferson City, MO 65102 (SAN 250-1031) Toll Free: 800-369-9778 (ext. 3333)
E-mail: Jvance@sockets.net
Dist(s): **Cowley Distributing, Inc..**

Cedars Sinai Health System, *(0-9641981)* 8631 W. Third St., Suite 535, Los Angeles, CA 90048 Tel 310-855-6447; Fax: 310-854-6402; Toll Free: 800-319-8111
E-mail: kalifon@smc.edu
Web site: http://www.amazon.com
Dist(s): **PACT Hse. Publishing.**

Cedars Sinai Medical Center *See* **Cedars Sinai Health System**

Celebration Pr., 75 Arlington St., Boston, MA 02116; *Imprints:* Good Year Books (GYB) Do not confuse with Celebration Press in Onalaska WI, Denver CO.

Celebrity Pubs., *(0-9655010)* 9900 Stirling Rd., No. 210, Cooper City, FL 33024 Tel 954-435-9300; Fax: 954-435-9410.

†Celestial Arts Publishing Co., *(0-89087; 0-912310; 1-58761)* Div. of Ten Speed Pr., Orders Addr.: P.O. Box 7123, Berkeley, CA 94707 (SAN 159-8333) Tel 510-559-1600; Fax: 510-559-1637; Toll Free: 800-841-2665; Edit Addr.: 999 Harrison St., Berkeley, CA 94710 Fax: 510-524-1052
E-mail: order@tenspeed.com
Web site: http://www.tenspeed.com; *CIP.*

Celjon Bks., *(1-891612)* 325 Roaumond Ln., Fredericksbrg, TX 78624-6028 (SAN 299-4976); 12470 Starcrest, No. 602, San Antonio, TX 78216-2980
E-mail: kgjz@aol.com; celjonbks@aol.com.

Celo Valley Bks., *(0-923687)* 160 Ohle Rd., Burnsville, NC 28714 (SAN 251-7973) Tel 828-675-5918
E-mail: Marilynb@main.nc.us.

†Ctr. for Applied Research in Education, The, *(0-87628)* Orders Addr.: P.O. Box 11071, Des Moines, IA 50381-1071 (SAN 241-6492) Fax: 515-284-2607; Toll Free: 800-288-4745; Edit Addr.: 240 Frisch Ct., Paramus, NJ 07652-5240 (SAN 206-6424) Tel 201-909-6200
Web site: http://vig.prenhall.com/
Dist(s): **Continental Bk. Co., Inc.**; *CIP.*

Ctr. for Educational Media, *(1-888933)* Orders Addr.: P.O. Box 97, Westwood, NJ 07675 Tel 201-358-1504; Fax: 201-358-9013; Toll Free: 800-221-6116; Edit Addr.: 66 Paluade Ave., Westwood, NJ 07675
E-mail: cenedmedia@aol.com
Web site: http://www.lovesmarts.org.

Names

Ctr. for Learning, The, *(1-56077)* Orders Addr.: P.O. Box 910, Villa Maria, PA 16155 Tel 724-964-8083; Toll Free Fax: 888-767-8080; Toll Free: 800-767-9090 (ordering); Edit Addr.: 24600 Detroit Rd., Suite 201, Westlake, OH 44145 (SAN 248-2029) Tel 440-259-9341; Fax: 440-250-9715
E-mail: cfl@stratos.net
Web site: http://www.centerforlearning.org.

Ctr. Point Large Print, *(1-58547)* P.O. Box 1, Thorndike, ME 04986-0001 Tel 207-568-3717; Fax: 207-568-3727; Toll Free: 800-929-9108; *Imprints:* Premier (Premier)
E-mail: centerpoint@uninets.net.

Center Point Publishing *See* **Ctr. Point Large Print**

Centering Corp., *(1-56123)* P.O. Box 4600, Omaha, NE 68104-0600 (SAN 298-1815) Tel 402-553-1200; Fax: 402-553-0507
E-mail: centering@centering.org; j1200@aol.com
Web site: http://www.centering.org
Dist(s): **Baker & Taylor Bks..**

Centerstage Pr., Inc., *(1-890298)* P.O. Box 36688, Phoenix, AZ 85067 Tel 602-242-1123; Fax: 602-861-2708; Toll Free: 888-836-3453
E-mail: cstage@cstage.com
Web site: http://www.cstage.com.

Centerstream Publishing, *(0-931759; 1-57424)* Orders Addr.: P.O. Box 17878, Anaheim Hills, CA 92817 (SAN 683-8022) Tel 714-779-9390 (phone/fax)
E-mail: centerstrm@aol.com
Web site: http://www.pma-online.org
Dist(s): **Leonard, Hal Corp..**

Central Bureau voor Schimmelcultures (NLD) *(90-70351) Dist. by* **Lubrecht & Cramer.**

Central Conference of American Rabbis/ CCAR Press, *(0-88123; 0-916694)* 355 Lexington Ave., 18th Flr., New York, NY 10017-6603 (SAN 204-3262) Tel 212-972-3636; Fax: 212-692-0819; Toll Free: 800-935-2227
E-mail: info@ccaret.org; ccarpress@ccarnet.org
Web site: http://ccarpress.org
Dist(s): **Fell, Frederick Pubs., Inc..**

Central Park Media Corp., *(1-56219; 1-58664)* 250 W. 57th St., Suite 317, New York, NY 10107 (SAN 631-3191) Tel 212-977-7456; Fax: 212-977-8709; Toll Free: 800-833-7456; *Imprints:* CPM Manga (CPM Manga)
E-mail: info@teamcpm.com; fpannone@teamcpm.com
Web site: http://www.centralparkmedia.com/; http://www.cpmmanga.com/
Dist(s): **Baker & Taylor Bks.**
Diamond Comic Distributors, Inc.
Fantagraphics Bks.
Hobbies Hawaii Distributors.

Century Creations, Inc., *(0-9639984; 1-890939)* 5203 Gateway Dr., Grand Forks, ND 58203 Tel 701-746-4543; Fax: 701-746-0944; Toll Free: 800-746-0201
E-mail: jclayton@cencreations.com
Dist(s): **Aviation Bk. Co..**

Century Pr., *(0-9659417)* Div. of Conservatory of American Letters, P.O. Box 298, Thomaston, ME 04861 Tel 207-354-0998; Fax: 207-354-8953 Do not confuse with companies with the same name in Arroyo Seco, NM, Oklahoma City, OK
E-mail: cal@americanletters.org
Web site: http://www.americanletters.org.

C.G.S. Pr., *(0-9660726)* P.O. Box 1394, Mountainside, NJ 07092 Tel 908-233-8293 (phone/fax)
E-mail: Gwynnic2000@aol.com
Dist(s): **Biblio Distribution.**

Chalice Pr., *(0-8272)* Div. of Christian Board of Pubn., Orders Addr.: P.O. Box 179, Saint Louis, MO 63166-0179 Tel 314-231-8500; Fax: 314-231-8524; Toll Free: 800-366-3383
E-mail: customerservice@cbp21.com
Web site: http://www.chp21.com; http://www.chalicepress.com
Dist(s): **Baker & Taylor Bks.**
Spring Arbor Distributors, Inc..

Chalk Stream Publishing, *(0-9670607)* Orders Addr.: P.O. Box 4007, Temple, TX 76505 (SAN 299-822X) Tel 254-773-6112; Fax: 254-773-6240; Toll Free: 877-288-4606; Edit Addr.: 3215 Buckingham Ct., Temple, TX 76502.

Chambers Kingfisher Graham Publishers, Incorporated *See* **Larousse Kingfisher Chambers, Inc.**

Chamike Pubs., *(1-884876)* 9000 Doris Dr., Fort Washington, MD 20744 Tel 301-248-4034.

Changing Images Art Foundation, Inc., *(0-9665793)* 30 Forest Pl., Towaco, NJ 07082 Tel 973-402-0842; Fax: 973-263-0329
E-mail: ciaf97@aol.com
Web site: http://www.changingimages.org.

Chapel of the Air, *(1-57849; 1-879050)* Orders Addr.: P.O. Box 30, Wheaton, IL 60189 Tel 630-668-7292; Fax: 630-668-9660; Toll Free: 800-224-2735
Web site: http://www.teamsundays.com.

Chapter & Verse Publishing for Children, *(1-929776)* 3528 Wade Ave., PMB 139, Raleigh, NC 27607 Tel 919-787-4895
E-mail: publisher@chapter-verse.com
Web site: http://www.mindspring.com/chapterverse.

Character Lines Publishing, *(0-9663522)* 4501 Bowen Rd., Stockbridge, GA 30281 Tel 770-922-2619.

Charlesbridge Publishing, Inc., *(0-88106; 0-935508; 1-57091; 1-58089; 1-879085)* Orders Addr.: 85 Main St., Watertown, MA 02472 (SAN 240-5474) Tel 617-926-0329; Fax: 617-926-5720; Toll Free Fax: 800-926-5775; Toll Free: 800-225-3214; *Imprints:* Talewinds (Talewinds); Whispering Coyote (Whispering Coyote)
E-mail: books@charlesbridge.com; orders@charlesbridge.com
Web site: http://www.charlesbridge.com
Dist(s): **Continental Bk. Co., Inc.**
Lectorum Pubns., Inc..

Charlotte's Storybooks, *(0-9707920)* Orders Addr.: P.O. Box 1291, Apple Valley, CA 92307 Tel 760-961-2401 (phone/fax); Edit Addr.: 25404 Valley View, Apple Valley, CA 92307
E-mail: charlottestories@aol.com
Web site: http://members.aol.com/charlottestories.

Chase Pubns., *(0-9665699)* 1171 Tellem Dr., Pacific Palisades, CA 90272 Tel 310-454-2344; Fax: 310-459-6021
E-mail: wlarsen421@aol.com.

Chattanooga Regional History Museum, *(0-9648140)* 400 Chestnut St., Chattanooga, TN 37402 Tel 423-265-3247; Fax: 426-266-4280.

†Checkerboard Pr., Inc., *(1-56288)* 1560 Revere Rd., Yardley, PA 19067-4351*; CIP.*

Chelsea Clubhouse Imprint of Chelsea Hse. Pubs.

Chelsea Green Publishing, *(0-930031; 1-890132; 1-931498; 88-86283)* Orders Addr.: P.O. Box 428, White River Junction, VT 05001 (SAN 669-7631) Tel 802-295-6300; Fax: 802-295-6444; Toll Free: 800-639-4099; Edit Addr.: 205 Gates-Briggs Bldg., Main St., White River Junction, VT 05001
Web site: http://www.chelseagreen.com
Dist(s): **Baker & Taylor Bks.**
Koen Bk. Distributors.

†Chelsea Hse. Pubs., *(0-7910; 0-87754; 1-55546)* Div. of Main Line Bk. Co., 1974 Sproul Rd., Suite 400, Broomall, PA 19008-0914 (SAN 206-7609) Tel 610-353-5166; Fax: 610-359-1439; Toll Free: 800-848-2665; *Imprints:* Chelsea Clubhouse (Chel Clubhse)
E-mail: info@chelseahouse.com
Web site: http://www.chelseahouse.com
Dist(s): **Baker & Taylor Bks.**
Brodart Co.
Follett Library Resources
Wolverine Distributing, Inc.*; CIP.*

Cherished Books *See* **Riverpark Publishing Co.**

Chernak, Judy Productions, *(0-944633)* 3114 Hatton Rd., Pikesville, MD 21208-4513 (SAN 244-5859) Tel 410-484-7088; Fax: 410-484-7178
Dist(s): **Baker & Taylor Bks..**

Cherokee Bks., *(0-9640458; 1-930052)* Orders Addr.: P.O. Box 463, Little Creek, DE 19961 Tel 302-734-8782; Fax: 302-734-3198; Edit Addr.: 231 Meadow Ridge Pkwy., Dover, DE 19904 Do not confuse with Cherokee Bks., Ponca City, OK
E-mail: milthanna@aol.com
Web site: http://www.cherokeebooks.com.

†Cherokee Publishing Co., *(0-87797)* Orders Addr.: P.O. Box 1730, Marietta, GA 30061-1730 (SAN 650-0404) Tel 404-467-4189; Fax: 404-237-1062; Toll Free: 800-653-3952; Edit Addr.: 800 Miami Cir., NE, Suite 100, Atlanta, GA 30324-3055 Do not confuse with Cherokee Publishing Co., Antioch, CA
E-mail: books@mgci.com*; CIP.*

Cherokee Publishing Company *See* **Cherokee Bks.**

Cherokee Strip Centennial Foundation, *(0-9638403)* 401 E. Oklahoma, Enid, OK 73701 Tel 405-233-4353 ; Fax: 405-237-9228.

Cherry Lane Books *See* **Cherry Lane Music Co.**

†Cherry Lane Music Co., *(0-89524; 1-57560)* 6 E. 32nd St., 11 Flr., New York, NY 10016 (SAN 219-0788) Tel 212-561-3000
Web site: http://www.cherrylane.com
Dist(s): **Leonard, Hal Corp.***; CIP.*

Cherubic Pr., *(0-9646576; 1-889590)* Orders Addr.: P.O. Box 5036, Johnstown, PA 15904-5036 Tel 814-535-4300; Fax: 814-535-4580; Edit Addr.: 412 Coleman Ave., Johnstown, PA 15902
E-mail: CherubicPr@aol.com.

Cheshire Studio Bks. Imprint of North-South Bks., Inc.

Chessmore Publishing, *(0-9659772)* 6902 River Birch Ct., Bradenton, FL 34202 Tel 941-358-5266; Fax: 941-358-5516
E-mail: jp@chessmorepublishing.com
Web site: http://www.chessmorepublishing.com.

Chestleigh's Bks. Publishing Co., *(1-893240)* Orders Addr.: P.O. Box 2014, Fond DuLac, WI 54936-2014 Tel 920-922-6670; Fax: 920-922-7311; Toll Free: 800-922-6670; Edit Addr.: 45 Sheboyan St., Suite 10, Fond Dulac, WI 54935.

Cheval International, *(0-9640610; 1-885351)* 7600 Anderson Rd., Black Hawk, SD 57718 Tel 605-787-6486; Fax: 605-787-6203
E-mail: cheval@rapidnet.com
Web site: http://www.chevalinternational.com
Dist(s): **Barnes & Noble Bks.-Imports**
Baker & Taylor Bks..

Chiappetta, Joe, *(0-9644323)* 2209 Northgate, North Riverside, IL 60546 Tel 708-447-3437
E-mail: sillydaddy@redweb.com
Web site: http://www.wraithspare.com/sillydaddy
Dist(s): **Diamond Book Distributors, Inc.**
Koen Bk. Distributors
Last Gasp Eco-Funnies, Inc..

†Chicago Review Pr., Inc., *(0-914090; 0-914091; 1-55652; 1-56976)* 814 N. Franklin St., Chicago, IL 60610 (SAN 213-5744) Tel 312-337-0747; Fax: 312-337-5985; Toll Free: 800-888-4741 (orders only) ; *Imprints:* Hill, Lawrence Books (Lawrence Hill); Zephyr Press (ZephPr)
E-mail: orders@ipgbook.com; frontdesk@ipgbook.com
Web site: http://www.ipgbook.com
Dist(s): **Cobblestone Publishing Co.**
Gryphon Hse., Inc.
Independent Pubs. Group*; CIP.*

Chicago Spectrum Pr., *(1-58374; 1-886094)* Div. of Evanston Publishing Inc., 4824 Brownsboro Ctr., Louisville, KY 40207 Tel 502-899-1919; Fax: 502-896-0246; Toll Free: 888-266-5780 (888-BOOKS-80); 800-594-5190
E-mail: info@evanstonpublishing.com; EvanstonPB@aol.com
Web site: http://www.EvanstonPublishing.com
Dist(s): **Baker & Taylor Bks.**
Independent Pubs. Group
Paladin Pr.
Partners/West.

Chicken Hse., The Imprint of Scholastic, Inc.

Chicken Soup Pr., Inc., *(0-9646904; 1-893337)* Orders Addr.: P.O. Box 164, Circleville, NY 10919 (SAN 298-6787) Tel 914-692-6320; Fax: 914-692-7574; Edit Addr.: 17 Todd Dr., Middletown, NY 10941
E-mail: poet@warwick.net
Web site: http://www.chickensouppress.com
Dist(s): **Baker & Taylor Bks.**
Brodart Co.
Hervey's Booklink & Cookbook Warehouse
Quality Bks., Inc..

Child Access Ctr. of Maryland,The, *(0-9677266)* P.O. Box 32834, Pikesville, MD 21282-2834 Tel 410-764-8370; Fax: 410-764-8382
E-mail: rock@childaccesscenter.org
Web site: http://www.childaccesscenter.org.

Child & Family Pr. Imprint of Child Welfare League of America, Inc.

Child Light, *(0-9677511)* P.O. Box 1563, Montpelier, VT 05602-1563 Tel 802-496-5962; Fax: 802-479-5437; Toll Free: 888-780-6258
E-mail: info@childlight.com
Web site: http://www.childlight.com.

†Child Welfare League of America, Inc., *(0-87868; 1-58760)* 440 First St., NW, 3rd Flr., Washington, DC 20001-2085 (SAN 201-9876) Tel 202-638-2952; Fax: 301-206-9789 (orders only); 202-638-4004; Toll Free: 800-407-6273 (orders only); *Imprints:* Child & Family Press (Child-Family Pr)
E-mail: cwla@pmds.com
Web site: http://www.cwla.org
Dist(s): **Baker & Taylor Bks.**
Koen Bk. Distributors
Lectorum Pubns., Inc.
National Bk. Network*; CIP.*

Names

Children's Bk. Pr., *(0-89239)* 2211 Mission St., San Francisco, CA 94110-1811 (SAN 210-7864) Tel 415-821-3080; Fax: 415-821-3081
E-mail: orders@cbookpress.org; catalogs@cbookpress.org; info@cbookpress.org
Web site: http://www.cbookpress.org
Dist(s): **Baker & Taylor Bks.**
Bookpeople
Continental Bk. Co., Inc.
Lectorum Pubns., Inc.
Libros Sin Fronteras
Publishers Group West.

Children's Gallery Pubns., *(0-9636190)* 23 Chambers Ave., Cornelia, GA 30531 Tel 404-778-3745.

Children's Literature, *(1-890920)* 7513 Shadywood Rd., Bethesda, MD 20817 Tel 301-469-2070; Fax: 301-469-2071; Toll Free: 800-469-2070
E-mail: marilyn@childrenslit.com
Web site: http://www.childrenslit.com.

Children's Pictorial Legends, *(0-9661627)* 2010 E. Routt Ave., Pueblo, CO 81004 Tel 719-564-6779; Fax: 719-562-1195.

Children's Pr. Imprint of Scholastic Library Publishing

Children's Pr., Ltd. (IRL) *(0-947962) Dist. by* **Irish Bks Media.**

Child's Play of England (GBR) *(0-85953) Dist. by* **Childs Play.**

†Child's Play-International, *(0-85953)* 67 Minot Ave., Auburn, ME 04210 (SAN 216-2121) Tel 207-784-7252; Fax: 207-784-7358; Toll Free Fax: 800-854-6989; Toll Free: 800-639-6404
E-mail: chpmaine@aol.com; cplay@earthlink.net
Web site: http://www.childs-play.com
Dist(s): **Lectorum Pubns., Inc.**; *CIP.*

†Child's World, Inc., *(0-89565; 0-913778; 1-56766; 1-59296)* Orders Addr.: P.O. Box 326, Chanhassen, MN 55317-0326 (SAN 211-0032) Tel 952-906-3939; Fax: 952-906-3940; Toll Free: 800-599-7323; Edit Addr.: 7081 W. 192nd Ave., Eden Prairie, MN 55346
E-mail: info@childsworld.com
Web site: http://www.childsworld.com; *CIP.*

†China Bks. & Periodicals, Inc., *(0-8351)* 2929 24th St., San Francisco, CA 94110-4126 (SAN 145-0557) Tel 415-282-2994; Fax: 415-282-0994
E-mail: info@chinabooks.com
Web site: http://www.chinabooks.com; *CIP.*

Chivers Children's Audio Bks. Imprint of BBC Audiobooks America

Chivers Large Print (GBR) *(0-7451) Dist. by* **BBC Audiobks.**

Chivers North America *See* **BBC Audiobooks America**

Choctaw Crafts & Bks., *(0-9710250)* Orders Addr.: P.O. Box 668, Durant, OK 74701 Tel 580-931-9144; Fax: 580-920-0864; Toll Free: 888-932-9199; Edit Addr.: 4202 S. Hwy. 69/75, Durant, OK 74701
E-mail: sharbin@choctawcrafts.com
Web site: http://www.choctawcrafts.com.

ChoiceSkills, Inc., *(0-938399)* Orders Addr.: P.O. Box 54, Midvale, UT 84047; Edit Addr.: 7740 Chad Heights Ln., Midvale, UT 84047-5702 (SAN 659-6738) Tel 801-352-7141; Fax: 801-352-7145
E-mail: choiceskills@att.net
Web site: www.choiceskills.com.

Christian Liberty Pr., *(1-930092; 1-930367)* Div. of Church of Christian Liberty, 502 W. Euclid Ave., Arlington Heights, IL 60004 Tel 847-259-4444; Fax: 847-259-2941
E-mail: clplina@starnetwx.net
Web site: http://www.christianlibertypress.com.

Christian Life Workshops *See* **Noble Publishing Assocs.**

Christian Light Pubns., Inc., *(0-87813)* 1066 Chicago Ave., Harrisonburg, VA 22802 (SAN 206-7315) Tel 540-434-0768; Fax: 540-433-8896
E-mail: johnh@clp.org.

Christian Literature Crusade, Inc., *(0-87508)* Div. of CLC Publications, Orders Addr.: P.O. Box 1449, Fort Washington, PA 19034-8449 Tel 215-542-1242; Fax: 215-542-7580; Toll Free: 800-659-1240; Edit Addr.: 701 Pennsylvania Ave., Fort Washington, PA 19034 (SAN 169-7358)
E-mail: joinclc@juno.com
Web site: http://www.clcusa.org
Dist(s): **Anchor Distributors**
Appalachian Bible Co.
Calvary Distribution
Riverside
Spring Arbor Distributors, Inc..

Christian Pubns., Inc., *(0-87509; 0-88965)* 3825 Hartzdale Dr., Camp Hill, PA 17011-7830 (SAN 202-1617) Tel 717-761-7044; Fax: 717-761-7273; Toll Free Fax: 800-865-8799 (orders only); Toll Free: 800-233-4443 (orders only)
E-mail: orders@cpi-horizon.com; salemktg@cpi-horizon.com
Web site: http://www.christianpublications.com
Dist(s): **Christian Literature Crusade, Inc.**
Spring Arbor Distributors, Inc..

Christian Publishing Services, Inc., *(0-88144)* Subs. of Harrison Hse. Pubs., P.O. Box 701434, Tulsa, OK 74155-1388 (SAN 260-0285) Tel 918-494-5966
E-mail: christianpublishingservices@cox.net
Dist(s): **Harrison Hse., Inc..**

Christmas City Distribution, Inc., *(0-9723225)* PMB 352-1041, Honey Creek Rd., Conyers, GA 30013 Tel 770-679-0990 Toll Free: 866-786-4241
E-mail: info@santastories.biz
Web site: http://www.santastories.biz.

†Chronicle Bks. LLC, *(0-8118; 0-87701; 0-938491)* 85 Second St., San Francisco, CA 94105 (SAN 202-165X) Tel 415-537-4200; Fax: 415-537-4460; Toll Free Fax: 800-858-7787; Toll Free: 800-722-6657 (orders only)
E-mail: orders@chroniclebooks.com
Web site: http://www.chroniclebooks.com
Dist(s): **Continental Bk. Co., Inc.**
Lectorum Pubns., Inc.; *CIP.*

Church Hymnal Corporation *See* **Church Publishing, Inc.**

Church Publishing, Inc., *(0-89869)* 445 Fifth Ave., New York, NY 10016-0109 Tel 212-592-1800; Fax: 212-779-3392; Toll Free: 800-242-1918 (orders only)
E-mail: churchpublishing@cpg.org
Web site: http://www.churchpublishing.org.

Cima Pubns., *(0-9645107)* P.O. Box 518, Syosset, NY 11021.

Cimino Publishing Group, *(1-878427)* P.O. Box 174, Carle Place, NY 11514 (SAN 630-3722) Tel 516-997-3721; Fax: 516-997-3420
E-mail: cimpub@juno.com
Dist(s): **CPG Publishing, Inc..**

Cinco Puntos Pr., *(0-938317)* 701 Texas Ave., El Paso, TX 79901 (SAN 661-0080) Tel 915-838-1625; Fax: 915-838-1635; Toll Free: 800-566-9072
E-mail: bbyrd@cincopuntos.com; leebyrd@cincopuntos.com
Web site: http://www.cincopuntos.com
Dist(s): **Consortium Bk. Sales & Distribution.**

Cindy's Books *See* **Beraam Publishing Co.**

Cinnamon Tree Imprint of Deseret Bk. Co.

Cipriani, Nicholas J., *(0-9653570)* 159-44 85th St., Howard Beach, NY 11414 Tel 718-848-4622; Fax: 718-962-1127; Toll Free: 800-464-6873
E-mail: nickc@inhouseinc.com.

Circle Bk. Service, Inc., *(0-87397)* P.O. Box 626, Tomball, TX 77377 (SAN 158-2526) Tel 281-255-6824; Fax: 281-255-8158; Toll Free: 800-227-1591; *Imprints:* Strode Publishers (Strode Pubs)
E-mail: orders@circlebook.com
Web site: http://www.circlebook.com.

Claitor's Publishing Div., *(0-87511; 1-57980)* 3165 S. Acadian, P.O. Box 261333, Baton Rouge, LA 70826-1333 (SAN 206-8346) Tel 504-344-0476; Fax: 504-344-0480; Toll Free: 800-274-1403
E-mail: claitors@claitors.com
Web site: http://www.claitors.com
Dist(s): **Bernan Assocs.**
Brodart Co.
Midpoint Trade Bks., Inc..

Clarion Bks. Imprint of Houghton Mifflin Co. Trade & Reference Div.

†Clark, Arthur H. Co., *(0-87062)* P.O. Box 14707, Spokane, WA 99214 (SAN 201-2006) Tel 509-928-9540; Fax: 509-928-4364; Toll Free: 800-842-9286; *Imprints:* Millwood Publishing (Millwood Pub); Prosperity Press (Prosperity Press)
E-mail: clarkbks@soar.com
Web site: http://www.ahclark.com; *CIP.*

Clark City Pr., *(0-944439)* Orders Addr.: P.O. Box 1358, Livingston, MT 59047 (SAN 243-699X) Tel 406-222-7412; Fax: 406-222-4719; Toll Free: 800-835-0814; Edit Addr.: 109 W. Callender St., Livingston, MT 59047 (SAN 243-7007)
E-mail: sally@russellchatham.com; info@clarkcitypress.com
Web site: http://www.clarkcitypress.com.

Clark, I. E. Pubns., *(0-88680)* P.O. Box 246, Schulenburg, TX 78956-0246 (SAN 282-7433) Tel 979-743-3232; Fax: 979-743-4765
E-mail: ieclark@cvtv.net
Web site: http://www.ieclark.com.

Clark, N. Laurie *See* **Clark Pubs.**

Clark Pubs., *(0-9641197)* 133 Chestnut St., Amherst, MA 01002 Tel 941-255-0431; 413-549-0575
E-mail: ellusmith@aol.com
Dist(s): **Baker & Taylor Bks.**
Brodart Co.
North Country Bks., Inc.
Quality Bks., Inc..

Clarksburg-Harrison Bicentennial Committee, *(0-9615566)* 404 W. Pike St., Clarksburg, WV 26301 (SAN 696-4877) Tel 304-624-6512.

Clarkson Potter Imprint of Crown Publishing Group

Clarus Music, Ltd., *(0-86704)* 150 Clearbrook Rd., Elmsford, NY 10523-1102 (SAN 216-6615).

Classic Bks., *(1-58201; 0-7426)* Orders Addr.: P.O. Box 130, Murrieta, CA 92564-0130 Tel 888-265-3547; Fax: 888-265-3550.

Classic Frights Imprint of Books of Wonder

Classic Publishing Imprint of Marciel Publishing & Printing

Classic Textbooks, *(1-4047)* Div of Classic Books, Orders Addr.: P.O. Box 130, Murrieta, CA 92564-0130 Tel 909-296-9628; Fax: 909-296-3528; Toll Free Fax: 888-265-3550; Edit Addr.: 26111 Ynez B14, Temecula, CA 92591
E-mail: 4classic@gte.net.

Classics Illustrated Imprint of Berkley Publishing Group

Classics International Entertainment, Inc., *(1-57209)* 324 Main Ave., Suite 183, Norwalk, CT 06851 Tel 203-849-8977; Fax: 203-847-5746.

Clear Light Pubs., *(0-940666; 1-57416)* 823 Don Diego, Santa Fe, NM 87501 (SAN 219-7758) Tel 505-989-9590; Fax: 505-989-9519; Toll Free: 800-253-2747 Do not confuse with Clear Light Pub., Seattle, WA
E-mail: service@clearlightbooks.com
Web site: http://www.clearlightbooks.com.

Client Distribution Services, 425 Madison Ave., New York, NY 10017 (SAN 631-760X) Tel 212-223-2969; Fax: 212-223-1504 Do not confuse with Client Distribution Services, Jackson, TN.
E-mail: skail@cds.aeneas.com; tflowers@cdsbooks.com
Web site: http://www.cdsbooks.com/.

Cliff Notes Imprint of Wiley, John & Sons, Inc.

Close Up Foundation, *(0-932765; 1-930810)* 44 Canal Ctr. Plaza, Alexandria, VA 22314 (SAN 679-1980) Tel 703-706-3559; Fax: 703-706-3564; Toll Free: 800-765-3131 (ext. 559)
E-mail: hoye@closeup.org
Web site: http://www.closeup.org/pubs.htm.

Cloudbank Creations, Inc., *(0-9651835)* 11836 N. Blackheath Rd., Scottsdale, AZ 85254-4809 Tel 602-951-3664; Fax: 602-951-5930
E-mail: ses95@aol.com
Web site: http://www.bookworld.com.

Clove Pubns., *(1-889191)* 60 Falcon Hills Dr., Littleton, CO 80162
E-mail: clovepublication@aol.com
Dist(s): **Baker & Taylor Bks..**

Coastal Carolina Pr., *(1-928556)* Orders Addr.: 2231 Wrightville Ave., Wilmington, NC 28403 Tel 910-362-9298; Fax: 910-362-9497
E-mail: books@coastalcarolinapress.org
Web site: http://www.coastalcarolinapress.org
Dist(s): **Baker & Taylor Bks.**
Parnassus Bk. Distributors.

Coastal Publishing Carolina, Inc., *(0-9705727; 1-931650)* 504 Amberjack Way, Summerville, SC 29485 Tel 843-821-6168; 843-870-9352; Fax: 843-851-6949
E-mail: coastalpublishing@earthlink.net
Web site: http://coastalpublishing.net/.

Cobblestone Publishing Co., *(0-382; 0-942389; 0-9607638)* Div. of Cricket Magazine Group, 30 Grove St., Suite C, Peterborough, NH 03458 (SAN 237-9937) Tel 603-924-7209; Fax: 603-924-7380; Toll Free: 800-821-0115
E-mail: custsvc@cobblestone.mv.com
Web site: http://www.cobblestonepub.com
Dist(s): **Americana Publishing, Inc..**

Coffee Break Pr., *(0-933992)* P.O. Box 103, Burley, WA 98322 (SAN 212-341X) Tel 206-851-4074.

Coffee Hse. Pr., *(0-918273; 1-56689)* 27 N. Fourth St., Suite 400, Minneapolis, MN 55401 (SAN 206-3883) Tel 612-338-0125; Fax: 612-338-4004
Web site: http://www.coffeehousepress.org
Dist(s): **Consortium Bk. Sales & Distribution**
SPD-Small Pr. Distribution.

Coffragants (CAN) *(2-921997; 2-89517; 2-89558) Dist. by* **Penton Overseas.**

Cognitive Pr., *(1-883241)* 4014 Southern Manor Ct., Sarasota, FL 34233-1859 (SAN 297-8768) Tel 941-922-1450
E-mail: drmad92@aol.com.

Cold River Pubns., *(0-9712867)* P.O. Box 606, Long Lake, NY 12847-0606 Tel 518-624-3581
E-mail: criver@telenet.net; criver@telenent.net
Web site: http://www.coldriverwoodworks.com.

Cole's, C. Consultant & Pubns., *(0-9640459)* 4126 Cricket Ln., Las Vegas, NV 89031 (SAN 298-1734) Tel 702-645-5786.

Collins Australia (AUS) *(0-207; 0-7322) Dist. by* **Consort Bk Sales.**

Collins Willow (GBR) *(0-00; 0-01) Dist. by* **Trafalgar.**

Collitt, Josephine Fish, *(0-9648441)* 573 Brighton Pl., Mechanicsburg, PA 17055 Tel 717-766-5491
E-mail: Autumnalface@aol.com.

Colonial Pr., *(0-938991; 1-56883)* 5956 Lake Cyrus Dr., Birmingham, AL 35244 (SAN 662-6599) Tel 205-424-9585; Toll Free: 800-264-7541 (orders only).

†Colonial Williamsburg Foundation, *(0-87935; 0-910412)* P.O. Box 3532, Williamsburg, VA 23187-3532 (SAN 128-4630) Fax: 757-565-8999 (orders only); Toll Free: 800-446-9240 (orders only)
Web site: http://www.colonialwilliamsburg.com
Dist(s): **Antique Collectors' Club**
Baker & Taylor Bks.
Koen Bk. Distributors; *CIP.*

Colorado Mountain Club Pr., The, *(0-9671466; 0-9724413)* 710 10th St., No. 200, Golden, CO 80401 Tel 303-279-3080; Fax: 303-279-9690; Toll Free: 800-633-4417
E-mail: cmcpress@cmc.org
Web site: http://www.cmc.org/
Dist(s): **Mountaineers Bks., The.**

Come Alive Pubns., Inc., *(1-882651)* 53 Hillcrest Rd., Concord, MA 01742 Tel 508-369-0680; Fax: 508-369-7291; Toll Free: 800-473-6257.

Common Sense Pr., *(1-880892; 1-929683)* 8786 Hwy. 21, Melrose, FL 32666 Tel 352-475-5757; Fax: 352-475-6105 Do not confuse with companies with the same name in Purcellville, VA, Washington, DC, Neptune, NJ, Sun City, AZ or Common Sense Pr., Inc. in Escondido, CA
E-mail: info@commomsensepress.com; inp@cspress.com
Web site: http://www.cspress.com.

Commonwealth Pr., Inc., *(0-89227)* 415 First St., Radford, VA 24141 (SAN 281-515X) Tel 540-639-2475 Do not confuse with companies with the same or similar name in Oklahoma City, OK, New York, NY, Worcester, MA, San Diego, CA.

Communication Service Corporation *See* **Gryphon Hse., Inc.**

Commuter's Library *See* **Sound Room Pubs., Inc.**

Commuters Library Imprint of Sound Room Pubs., Inc.

Compass Point Bks., *(0-7565)* 3109 W. 50th St., No.115, Minneapolis, MN 55410 (SAN 254-2013) Toll Free Fax: 877-371-1539; Toll Free: 877-371-1536
E-mail: custserv@compasspointbooks.com
Web site: http://www.compasspointbooks.com
Dist(s): **netLibrary, Inc..**

Comprehensive Health Education Foundation, *(0-935529; 1-57021)* 22419 Pacific Hwy. S., Seattle, WA 98198-5106 (SAN 696-3668) Tel 206-824-2907; Fax: 206-824-3072; Toll Free: 800-323-2433
E-mail: chefstaff@chef.org
Web site: http://www.chef.org/.

Computer Press *See* **Page, Andrea**

Concerned Communications, *(0-936785; 1-58938)* Orders Addr.: P.O. Box 1000, Siloam Springs, AR 72761-1000 (SAN 699-8623) Tel 501-594-9000; Fax: 501-549-4002; Toll Free: 800-447-4332; Edit Addr.: 700 E. Granite St., Siloam Springs, AR 72761 (SAN 699-8631)
E-mail: lustwrt@areasonfor.com
Web site: http://www.areasonfor.com.

Concordia Publishing Hse., *(0-570; 0-7586)* Subs. of Lutheran Church Missouri Synod, 3558 S. Jefferson Ave., Saint Louis, MO 63118-3968 (SAN 202-1781) Tel 314-268-1000; Fax: 314-268-1360; Toll Free Fax: 800-490-9889 (orders only); Toll Free: 800-325-0191; 800-325-3040 (orders only)
E-mail: cphorder@cph.org
Web site: http://www.cph.org
Dist(s): **National Bk. Network.**

Conquering Bks., *(1-56411)* 26070 Barhams Hill Rd., Drewyville, VA 23844 (SAN 630-6748) Tel 757-329-7200 (cell phone); 434-658-4934 (phone/fax) ; 210 E. Arrowhead Dr., No. 01, Charlotte, NC 28213 Tel 704-509-2226
E-mail: khalifah@kbabooks.com
Web site: http://www.conqueringbooks.com.

Consortium Bk. Sales & Distribution, Orders Addr.: 1045 Westgate Dr., Suite 90, Saint Paul, MN 55114-1065 (SAN 200-6049) Tel 651-221-9035; Fax: 651-221-0124; Toll Free: 800-283-3572 (orders)
E-mail: consortium@cbsd.com
Web site: http://www.cbsd.com.

Contact/II Pubns., *(0-936556)* 381 E. Tenth St., New York, NY 10009 (SAN 241-6697) Tel 212-674-0911.

Continental Bk. Co., Inc., *(0-9626800)* Eastern Div., 80-00 Cooper Ave., Bldg. No. 29, Glendale, NY 11385 (SAN 169-5436) Tel 718-326-0560; Fax: 718-326-4276; Toll Free: 800-364-0350; Western Div., 625 E. 70th Ave., No. 5, Denver, CO 80229 (SAN 630-2882) Tel 303-289-1761; Fax: 303-289-1764 Do not confuse with Continental Book Company, Denver, CO
E-mail: esl@continentalbook.com; bonjour@continentalbook.com; tag@continentalbook.com; hola@continentalbook.com
Web site: http://www.continentalbook.com.

Cook Communications Ministries, *(0-7459; 0-7814; 0-88207; 0-89191; 0-89693; 0-912692; 1-55513; 1-56476; 983-45027; 983-45018; 983-45031)* 4050 Lee Vance View, Colorado Springs, CO 80918 Tel 719-536-0100; Fax: 719-536-3269; Toll Free: 800-708-5550; 55 Woodslee Ave., Paris, ON N3L 3E5 Toll Free Fax: 800-461-8575; Toll Free: 800-263-2664 Do not confuse with Cook Communications Ministries International, same address
E-mail: bergerj@cookministries.org
Web site: http://www.cookministries.com
Dist(s): **CRC Pubns.**
Libros Sin Fronteras
Twentieth Century Christian Bks..

†Cook, David C. Publishing Co., *(0-7814; 0-88207; 0-89191; 0-89693; 0-912692; 1-55513; 1-56476; 983-45026; 5-503; 983-45027; 983-45023; 983-45019; 983-45018; 983-45013; 983-45012; 983-45016)* Div. of Cook Communications Ministries, 4050 Lee Vance View, Colorado Springs, CO 80918-7102 (SAN 206-0981) Tel 719-536-0100; Fax: 719-536-3202; Toll Free: 800-708-5550
Web site: http://www.davidcook.com; *CIP.*

Cookbooks by Morris Press *See* **Morris Publishing**

Copalis Publishing, *(0-9653703)* Orders Addr.: P.O. Box 339, Copalis Beach, WA 98535 Tel 360-289-0528 ; Fax: 360-289-4045; Toll Free: 800-286-4552; Edit Addr.: 3193 State Rte. 109, Copalis Beach, WA 98535
Web site: http://www.copalis.com.

Copper Beech Bks. Imprint of Millbrook Pr., Inc.

Core Knowledge Foundation, *(1-890517)* 801 E. High St., Charlottesville, VA 22902 Tel 434-977-7550; Fax: 434-977-0021; Toll Free: 800-238-3233
E-mail: coreknow@coreknowledge.org
Web site: http://www.coreknowledge.org.

Corgi Imprint of Bantam Bks.

†Cornell Maritime Pr., Inc., *(0-87033)* P.O. Box 456, Centreville, MD 21617 (SAN 203-5901) Tel 410-758-1075; Fax: 410-758-6849; Toll Free: 800-638-7641; *Imprints:* Tidewater Publishers (Tidewtr Pubs)
E-mail: cornell@crosslink.net
Web site: http://www.cornellmaritimepress.com/
Dist(s): **Hale, Robert & Co., Inc.**; *CIP.*

Cornerstone Bks. Imprint of Pages, Inc.

Cornerstone Pr., *(0-918476)* 1825 Bender Ln., Arnold, MO 63010-0388 (SAN 210-0584) Tel 314-296-9662 Do not confuse with companies with the same name in Edison, NJ, Kents Hill, ME, Pearland, TX, Stevens Point, WI.

Cornerstone Press, Incorporated *See* **Patria Pr., Inc.**

Cornerstone Publishing, *(1-882185)* Div. of Banner Enterprises, Orders Addr.: 2979 W. School House Ln., Suite K-605C, Philadelphia, PA 19144 (SAN 298-735X); P.O. Box 44353, Philadelphia, PA 19144 Do not confuse with companies with the same name in Decatur, GA, Altamonte Springs, FL, Wichita, KS
E-mail: cornerstone@bannerenterprises.org
Web site: http://www.cornerstonepublishing.com
Dist(s): **Book Clearing Hse.**
Follett Library Resources.

Cornwell, Don M. & Co., Inc., *(0-9646734)* 8 S. 300 Blackthorne Ln., Naperville, IL 60540-9503 Tel 630-983-5488.

Corona Pr., *(1-891619)* 4535 Palmer Ct., Niwot, CO 80503 Tel 303-247-1455; Fax: 303-417-0355; Toll Free: 888-648-3877 Do not confuse with Corona Pr., Brooklandville, MD
E-mail: coronapress@aol.com.

Corona Publishing, Co., *(0-931722; 0-9720630)* Orders Addr.: P.O. Box 12407, San Antonio, TX 78212 (SAN 211-8491) Tel 210-828-9532; Fax: 210-828-4947; Edit Addr.: 6714 N. New Braunfels, San Antonio, TX 78209 Do not confuse with Corona Publishing in Long Beach, CA
E-mail: labatt@texas.net
Dist(s): **Hervey's Booklink & Cookbook Warehouse.**

Coronet Bks. & Pubns., *(1-890609)* P.O. Box 957, Eagle Point, OR 97524 Tel 541-830-3040; Fax: 541-858-5595; *Imprints:* Lion's Paw Books (Lions Paw Bks) Do not confuse with Coronet Bks., Philadelphia, PA
E-mail: lions-paw@country.net.

Corporation for Cultural Literacy, *(1-885053)* 17 Blackland Rd., NW, Atlanta, GA 30342-4407 (SAN 299-2132)
E-mail: entgrp@aol.com
Web site: http://www.familybooks.com
Dist(s): **Baker & Taylor Bks..**

Cortland Pr., *(0-9647244)* Div. of Ingraham Graphics, Orders Addr.: 36 Taylor St., Cortland, NY 13045 Tel 607-753-0320; Fax: 607-753-1204; Toll Free: 800-680-1950; Edit Addr.: P.O. Box 5396, Cortland, NY 13045 Do not confuse with Cortland Pr., Apalachicola, FL.

Corvus Publishing, *(1-890768; 0-9725776)* Orders Addr.: P.O. Box 102004, Denver, CO 80210 Tel 303-777-0539; Fax: 303-756-8011; Toll Free: 800-996-9783; *Imprints:* Intrigue Press (Intrigue)
E-mail: derek@corvuspublishing.com; books@corvuspublishing.com
Web site: http://www.intriguepress.com; http://www.corvuspublishing.com; http://www.speckpress.com
Dist(s): **Consortium Bk. Sales & Distribution.**

Corvus Publishing Group *See* **Corvus Publishing**

Cosmic Aye Imprint of Hastings Ende Design Partners

Cosmo Starr Bks., *(0-9650312; 1-930977)* Orders Addr.: P.O. Box 332, Taft, CA 93268 Tel 661-765-2484; Fax: 661-763-1262; Edit Addr.: 221 B St., Taft, CA 93268.

Cotler, Joanna Bks. Imprint of HarperCollins Children's Bk. Group

Cottage Wordsmiths, *(0-9624155)* 6732 Reynolds St., Pittsburgh, PA 15206.

Council for Indian Education, *(0-89992)* Orders Addr.: 1240 Burlington Ave., Billings, MT 59102-4224 Tel 406-248-3465
E-mail: cie@cie-mt.org
Web site: http://www.cie-mt.org.

Council Oak Bks., *(0-933031; 1-57178)* Orders Addr.: 2105 E. 15th St., Suite B, Tulsa, OK 74104 (SAN 689-5522) Toll Free: 800-247-8850 (orders only); Edit Addr.: 5806 S. Perkins Rd., Stillwater, OK 74074
E-mail: sdennison@counciloakbooks.com
Web site: http://www.counciloakbooks.com
Dist(s): **Baker & Taylor Bks.**
Koen Bk. Distributors
New Leaf Distributing Co., Inc..

Counterpoint Pr. Imprint of Basic Bks.

Country Lane Ltd., *(1-879318)* Orders Addr.: 304 Northford Ct., Brandon, MS 39047 Tel 601-992-3245
E-mail: dleedavis@hotmail.com.

Country Lane Limited Edition Books *See* **Country Lane Ltd.**

†Countryman Pr., *(0-88150; 0-914378; 0-936399; 0-942440; 1-58157)* Div. of W. W. Norton & Co., Inc., P.O. Box 748, Woodstock, VT 05091-0748 (SAN 206-4901) Tel 802-457-4826 Toll Free: 800-245-4151 (Orders only); *Imprints:* Berkshire House (BerkHouse)
E-mail: countrymanpress@wwnorton.com
Web site: http://www.countrymanpress.com
Dist(s): **Norton, W. W. & Co., Inc.**; *CIP.*

Courage Bks. Imprint of Running Pr. Bk. Pubs.

Cove Pr. Imprint of U.S. Games Systems, Inc.

†Covenant Communications, *(0-9649122)* 1009 Jones St., Old Hickory, TN 37138 Tel 615-847-2066; Fax: 615-860-3601; Toll Free: 800-979-3882 Do nt oconfuse with Covenant Communications in Old Hickory, TN
Dist(s): **Quality Bks., Inc.**; *CIP.*

Covenant Communications, Inc., *(1-55503; 1-57734; 1-59156)* Orders Addr.: P.O. Box 416, American Fork, UT 84003-0416 (SAN 169-8540) Tel 801-756-9966; Fax: 801-756-1049; Toll Free: 800-662-9545; Edit Addr.: 920 E. State Rd., Suite F, American Fork, UT 84003 Do not confuse with Covenant Communications in American Fork, UT
E-mail: lindao@covenant-lds.com
Web site: http://www.covenant-lds.com.

Names

Cover to Cover Cassettes, Ltd., *(0-941935)* 238 15th St., NE, No. 13, Atlanta, GA 30309 (SAN 666-7910) Tel 404-892-1637.

Covercraft Imprint of Perfection Learning Corp.

Coward-McCann Imprint of Putnam Publishing Group, The

Coward-McCann Imprint of Penguin Group (USA) Inc.

Cowles Creative Publishing, Incorporated *See* **Creative Publishing international, Inc.**

Cowpokes Cartoon Bks., *(0-917207)* P.O. Box 290868, Kerrville, TX 78029-0868 (SAN 656-089X) Tel 830-257-7446 (phone/fax); Toll Free: 800-257-7441 (phone/fax)
E-mail: cartoons@cowpokes.com
Web site: http://www.cowpokes.com.

Cox, Suzy, *(0-9645042)* P.O. Box 31041, Capitol Heights, MD 20731 Tel 301-568-1935 (phone/fax)
E-mail: kittix1958@aol.com.

CPG Publishing, Inc., *(1-931411)* Orders Addr.: c/o CPG Distribution, 7253 Grayson Rd., Harrisburg, PA 17111 Toll Free: 800-501-6883 (orders & customer service); Edit Addr.: P.O. Box 6142, New York, NY 10150 Tel 212-573-9180; Fax: 212-573-9181 Do not confuse with C P G Publishing Company in Gold Canyon, AZ
E-mail: cpgdistribution@juno.com.

CPM Manga Imprint of Central Park Media Corp.

†Crabtree Publishing Co., *(0-7787; 0-86505)* 612 Welland Ave., Saint Catharines, ON L2M 5V6 Tel 905-682-5221; Toll Free: 800-387-7650; PMB 16A, 350 Fifth Ave., Suite 3308, New York, NY 10118 (SAN 251-4796) Tel 212-496-5040; Toll Free Fax: 800-355-7166; Toll Free: 800-387-7650 (returns) Do not confuse with Crabtree Publishing, Federal Way, WA
E-mail: antonsen@crabtreebooks.com
Web site: http://www.crabtreebooks.com*; CIP.*

Crane & Rogers Pubs., *(0-9716515)* 6129 Vista Dr., Falls Church, VA 22041 Tel 703-715-6869.

†Crane Hill Pubs., *(0-9621455; 1-57587; 1-881548)* 3608 Clairmont Ave., Birmingham, AL 35222-3508 Tel 205-714-3007; Fax: 205-714-3008; Toll Free Fax: 800-377-7981; Toll Free: 800-841-2682
E-mail: info@cranehill.com; cranies@cranehill.com
Web site: http://www.cranehill.com
Dist(s): **Blair, John F. Pub.***; CIP.*

Cranky Nell Bks. Imprint of Kane/Miller Bk. Pubs.

Creations by Basia, *(1-890582)* 2219 E. Thousand Oaks Blvd., Suite 370, Thousand Oaks, CA 91362 Tel 818-707-7702; Fax: 818-707-7033
E-mail: creationsbybasia@msn.com
Web site: http://www.basia.com
Dist(s): **Sunbelt Pubns., Inc..**

Creative Co., The, *(0-87191; 0-88682; 1-56660; 1-56846)* 123 S. Broad St., P.O. Box 227, Mankato, MN 56001 Tel 507-388-6273; Fax: 507-388-2746; Toll Free: 800-445-6209; *Imprints:* Creative Editions (Creative Eds); Creative Education (Creat Educ); Creative Paperbacks (Creative Paperbks) Do not confuse with The Creative Co., Lawrenceburg, IN
E-mail: CreativeCo@aol.com.

Creative Editions Imprint of Creative Co., The

Creative Education Imprint of Creative Co., The

Creative Learning Consultants, Incorporated *See* **Pieces of Learning**

Creative Multi-Media, *(0-9625344)* 660 Celebration Ave., Apt. 260, Kissimmee, FL 34747-4928.

Creative Nell Imprint of Kane/Miller Bk. Pubs.

Creative Opportunities, Inc., *(1-881235)* Orders Addr.: P.O. Box 6730, Laguna Niguel, CA 92607-6730 Tel 949-493-7293; Fax: 949-493-8887; Toll Free: 888-493-7293; Edit Addr.: 1 Park Paseo, Laguna Niguel, CA 92677 Do not confuse with Creative Opportunities Publishing Co., Orangevale, CA
E-mail: sbr@home.com
Web site: http://www.C-creativeopportunities.com
Dist(s): **Baker & Taylor Bks..**

Creative Paperbacks Imprint of Creative Co., The

†Creative Publishing Co., Inc., *(0-932702; 1-57208)* Orders Addr.: P.O. Box 9292, College Station, TX 77842 (SAN 209-3499) Tel 979-693-0808; Fax: 979-764-7758; Toll Free: 800-245-5841; Edit Addr.: 407 Timber, College Station, TX 77840 Do not confuse with companies with the same or similar name in Roseboro, NC, Greenville, SC, Lawrenceville, GA, Shrevport, LA, Flower Mound, TX
E-mail: info@creativepublishing.net; creativepublishi@aol.com; earlywest@aol.com
Web site: http://www.creativepublishing.com*; CIP.*

Creative Publishing international, Inc., *(0-86573; 0-942802; 1-55971; 1-85434; 1-58728; 1-58923)* 18705 Lake Dr., E., Chanhassen, MN 55317 (SAN 289-7148) Tel 952-936-4700; Fax: 952-933-1456; Toll Free: 800-328-0590; *Imprints:* Two-Can (Two-Can)
E-mail: sales@creativepub.com
Web site: http://www.two-canpublishing.com; http://www.creativepublishinginternational.com; http://www.northwordpress.com; http:// www.howtobookstore.com; http://www.creativepub.com
Dist(s): **Athena Productions, Inc.**
Book Travelers West
DUX Sales & Marketing
McLemore, Hollern & Assocs.
New England Bk. Reps.
Proe & Proe
Southern Territory Assocs.
Wybel Marketing Group.

Creative Recovery, *(1-878868)* P.O. Box 321, Larkspur, CA 94977-0321.

Creative Services, *(0-9702584)* 1009 Paris Ave., Nashville, TN 37204 Tel 615-385-2881; Fax: 615-298-5309 Do not confuse with Creative Services in Carmichael, CA
E-mail: bose-tennessee@home.com
Dist(s): **Biblio Distribution.**

Creative Teaching Pr., Inc., *(0-88160; 0-916119; 1-57471; 1-59198)* Orders Addr.: P.O. Box 2723, Huntington Beach, CA 92647-0723 Tel 714-895-5047 ; Fax: 714-895-6587; Toll Free Fax: 800-444-4287; Edit Addr.: 15342 Graham St., Huntington Beach, CA 92649-1111 (SAN 294-9180) Tel 714-895-5047; Toll Free Fax: 800-229-9929; Toll Free: 800-444-4287
E-mail: webmaster@creativeteaching.com
Web site: http://www.creativeteaching.com
Dist(s): **Abrams & Co. Pubs., Inc.**
Pacific Learning, Inc..

†Creative Therapeutics, Inc., *(0-933812)* 155 County Rd., P.O. Box 522, Cresskill, NJ 07626-0522 (SAN 212-6508) Tel 201-567-7295; Fax: 201-567-3036; Toll Free: 800-544-6162
E-mail: ct39@erols.com
Web site: http://www.rgardner.com*; CIP.*

Creative Thinkers, Inc., *(1-58237)* 8 South St. Southfield, No. 10, Danbury, CT 06810 Tel 203-778-9749; Fax: 203-778-6492; Toll Free: 800-841-2883
E-mail: thinkkids@aol.com; sftierno@aol.com
Web site: http://www.thinkkids.com.

Cricket Imprint of McGraw-Hill Children's Publishing

Cricket Bks., *(0-8126)* Div. of Carus Publishing Co., 332 S. Michigan Ave., Suite 1100, Chicago, IL 60604 Tel 312-939-1500; Fax: 312-939-8150
E-mail: jpatenaude@caruspub.com; cricketbooks@ureach.com
Web site: http://www.cricketbooks.net
Dist(s): **Cobblestone Publishing Co.**
Publishers Group West.

Cricketfield Pr. Imprint of Picton Pr.

Criqueville Pr., *(0-9705404)* Orders Addr.: P.O. Box 1227, Princeton, NJ 08542-1227 Tel 908-359-7834; Edit Addr.: 2 Dogwood Ln., Princeton, NJ 08542-1227
E-mail: criquevillepress@hotmail.com.

Criterion Bks., Inc., *(0-200)* 1000 Keystone Industrial Pk., Scranton, PA 18512-4621 Tel 717-941-1500.

Critters & Kids Publishing, Incorporated *See* **Froginhood & Friends, Inc.**

Crocodile Bks. Imprint of Interlink Publishing Group, Inc.

†Crossing Pr., Inc., The, *(0-89594; 0-912278; 1-58091)* Orders Addr.: 1201 Shaffer Rd., Suite B, Santa Cruz, CA 95060 (SAN 202-2060) Tel 831-420-1110; Fax: 831-420-1114; Toll Free: 800-777-1048 (orders only)
E-mail: katie@crossingpress.com
Web site: http://www.crossingpress.com
Dist(s): **Baker & Taylor Bks.**
Bookpeople
Koen Bk. Distributors
New Leaf Distributing Co., Inc.
Publishers Group West*; CIP.*

Crossroads Publishing Company *See* **CrossroadsPub.com**

CrossroadsPub.com, *(1-58338)* 505 W. Forest St., Roswell, NM 88203-3728; *Imprints:* CrossroadsPub.Org (CrossroadsPubOrg).

CrossroadsPub.Org Imprint of CrossroadsPub.com

†Crossway Bks., *(0-89107; 1-58134)* Div. of Good News Pubs., 1300 Crescent St., Wheaton, IL 60187 (SAN 211-7991) Tel 630-682-4300; 708-682-4300; Fax: 630-682-4785; Toll Free: 800-323-3890 (sales only)
Web site: http://www.crosswaybooks.org
Dist(s): **LIM Productions, LLC**
Vision Video*; CIP.*

Crosswinds Bks., *(0-9726573)* P.O. Box 143, Keller, TX 76244
E-mail: jroach35@earthlink.net.

Crowder, Jack L., *(0-9616589)* Orders Addr.: P.O. Box 250, Bernalillo, NM 87004 (SAN 659-8064) Tel 505-867-5812 (phone/fax); Edit Addr.: 500 Beehive Ln., Bernalillo, NM 87004 (SAN 659-8072)
E-mail: crowdercon@aol.com.

Crown Imprint of Crown Publishing Group

†Crown Publishing Group, *(0-517; 0-609; 0-676; 1-4000)* Div. of Random Hse., Inc., Orders Addr.: 400 Hahn Rd., Westminster, MD 21157 Tel 410-848-1900; Toll Free Fax: 800-659-2436; Toll Free: 800-733-3000; 800-726-0600; Edit Addr.: 299 Park Ave., New York, NY 10171 (SAN 200-2639) Tel 212-751-2600; Fax: 212-572-2165; *Imprints:* Crown (Crown); Clarkson Potter (Clarkson Potter); Harmony (Harmon); Prima Lifestyles (PrimLife)
E-mail: customerservice@randomhouse.com
Web site: http://www.randomhouse.com/
Dist(s): **Random Hse., Inc.***; CIP.*

Crown Publishing Group, Incorporated *See* **Crown Publishing Group**

Crumb Elbow Publishing, *(0-89904)* P.O. Box 294, Rhododendron, OR 97049 (SAN 679-128X) Tel 503-622-4798.

Cruzane Mountain Publishing, *(0-9711445; 0-9744465)* P.O. Box 670132, Saltese, MT 59867-0132 Tel 406-678-4340; Fax: 406-678-4109
E-mail: hau4109@blackfoot.net
Web site: http://www.cruzanemountain.com.

†Cucumber Island Storytellers, *(1-887813)* Sawin Ln., Hockessin, DE 19707
Web site: http://www.cucumberisland.com*; CIP.*

Culture C.O.-O.P., The, *(0-9644655)* P.O. Box 463, Davis, CA 95616 (SAN 299-3260) Tel 530-792-1334; Fax: 530-753-8511
E-mail: info@CultureCo-Op.com
Web site: http://www.CultureCo-Op.com
Dist(s): **Baker & Taylor Bks.**
Follett Library Resources
Lectorum Pubns., Inc..

Cumberland Hearthside Imprint of Cumberland Hse. Publishing

†Cumberland Hse. Publishing, *(1-58182; 1-888952)* 431 Harding Industrial Park Dr., Nashville, TN 37211-3105 (SAN 254-4172) Tel 615-832-1171; Fax: 615-832-0633; Toll Free Fax: 800-254-6716; Toll Free: 888-439-2665; *Imprints:* Cumberland Hearthside (Cumberland Hearthside) Do not confuse with Cumberland Hse. Publishing. Co., Inc. in Indianapolis, IN
E-mail: twright@cumberlandhouse.com; CumbHouse@aol.com
Web site: http://www.CumberlandHouse.com*; CIP.*

†Curbstone Pr., *(0-915306; 1-880684; 1-931896)* 321 Jackson St., Willimantic, CT 06226 (SAN 209-4282) Tel 860-423-5110; Fax: 860-423-9242
E-mail: info@curbstone.org
Web site: http://www.curbstone.org
Dist(s): **Consortium Bk. Sales & Distribution**
SPD-Small Pr. Distribution*; CIP.*

Current, Inc., *(0-944943; 1-58410)* Div. of Deluxe Corp., Orders Addr.: P.O. Box 2559, Colorado Springs, CO 80901 (SAN 246-0378) Tel 719-594-4100; Fax: 719-534-6259; Toll Free: 800-848-2848; Edit Addr.: 1005 E. Woodmen Rd., Colorado Springs, CO 80920 (SAN 246-0386).

Currier, Alvin Alexsi, *(0-9723411)* 1880 E. Shore Dr., Apt. 212, Saint Paul, MN 55109 Tel 651-772-2788; Fax: 651-772-3151
E-mail: a.currier@juno.com.

Cygnet Publishing Co., *(0-9636050)* 2153 Wealthy, SE, No. 238, East Grand Rapids, MI 49506 Tel 616-459-1258 Do not confuse with Cygnet Publishing, Montecito, CA
E-mail: bowman@grgig.net.

Cygnet Publishing Group, Inc./Coolreading.com (CAN) *(1-55305) Dist. by* **Orca Bk Pubs.**

Cygnet Trumpeter Pubs., *(0-9645976)* Div. of Swanalliance Entertainment, P.O. Box 491626, Los Angeles, CA 90049-8626 Tel 310-915-3559.

Cypress Hill Press *See* **Cypress Pr.**

Cypress Pr., *(0-9638964)* 1623 Morgan Dr., Kingsburg, CA 93631 Tel 209-897-8929.

Names

DAW Bks., Inc., *(0-8099; 0-87997; 0-88677; 0-7564)* Affil. of Penguin Putnam, Inc., Orders Addr.: 405 Murray Hill Pkwy., East Rutherford, NJ 07073 Toll Free: 800-788-6262 (individual consumer sales); 800-526-0275 (reseller sales); 800-631-8571 (reseller customer service); Edit Addr.: 375 Hudson St., New York, NY 10014-3658 (SAN 665-6846) Fax: 212-366-2385; Toll Free: 800-253-6476
E-mail: daw@penguinputnam.com
Web site: http://www.dawbooks.com
Dist(s): **Penguin Group (USA) Inc..**

D&J Arts Pubs., *(0-9634300)* Orders Addr.: P.O. Box 365, Sierra Vista, AZ 85636; Edit Addr.: 5242 Laguna Ave., Sierra Vista, AZ 85635 Tel 602-378-6556; Fax: 520-378-2608
E-mail: shepj@primenet.com.

D K Ink Imprint of Dorling Kindersley Publishing, Inc.

D K Publishing, Incorporated *See* **Dorling Kindersley Publishing, Inc.**

D. R. Eastman, *(0-9640250)* Orders Addr.: P.O. Box 290364, Brooklyn, NY 11229.

Dab Publishing Co., *(0-9662228; 0-9728089)* Orders Addr.: P.O. Box 5554, Fresno, CA 93755-5554 (SAN 254-1416) Tel 559-229-0038; Edit Addr.: 4711 N. Orchard, Fresno, CA 93726
E-mail: phauck@dabpublishing.com
Web site: http://www.dabpublishing.com
Dist(s): **American West Bks.**
Baker & Taylor Bks..

Dageforde Publishing, Inc., *(0-9637515; 1-886225)* 128 E. 13th St., Crete, NE 68333 Tel 402-826-2059; Fax: 402-826-4069; Toll Free: 800-216-8794
E-mail: info@dageforde.com
Web site: http://www.dageforde.com
Dist(s): **Baker & Taylor Bks.**
Quality Bks., Inc.
Unique Bks., Inc..

Dalmatian Pr., *(1-57759; 1-888567; 1-4037)* 118 Seaboard Ln., Suite 118, Franklin, TN 37067-8218 Tel 615-370-9922; Fax: 615-370-8034
E-mail: derekadams@andersonpress.com.

Dandy Creations, *(0-9660574)* Orders Addr.: P.O. Box 51692, Livonia, MI 48150 Tel 313-513-2042; Toll Free: 888-887-7557; Edit Addr.: 29718 Richland, Livonia, MI 48152.

Dar Al-Fikr Al-Mouaser, *(1-57547; 1-59239)* 128 Carondolet Covrt Est., Mobile, AL 36608 Tel 251-344-2848; Fax: 775-417-0836
E-mail: info@fikr.com
Web site: http://www.fikr.com.

†Darby Creek Publishing, *(0-87406; 1-58196)* 7858 Industrial Pkwy., Plain City, OH 43064 (SAN 687-4592) Tel 614-873-7955; *Imprints:* Willowisp Press (Willowisp Pr); Silver Elm Classic (Silver Elm)
E-mail: editorial@darbycreekpublishing.com
Dist(s): **Lerner Publishing Group**; *CIP.*

Dargaud Publishing Co. (FRA) *(0-917201; 2-205)* *Dist. by* **Distribks Inc.**

Daring Child Pr., *(1-892885)* 2343 Timberidge Ln., SE, Rochester, MN 55904 Tel 507-254-1544; Fax: 507-281-4473
E-mail: nortung@aol.com
Dist(s): **Bookmen, Inc..**

Dark Horse Comics, *(1-56971; 1-878574; 1-59307)* 10956 SE Main St., Milwaukie, OR 97222 Tel 503-652-8815; Fax: 503-654-9440
E-mail: daveye@dhorse.com
Web site: http://www.darkhorse.com
Dist(s): **Berkley Publishing Group**
Diamond Book Distributors, Inc.
Diamond Comic Distributors, Inc.
LPC Group
Penguin Group (USA) Inc..

Daryl Ann Pubns., *(1-928641)* Orders Addr.: P.O. Box 7811, Warwick, RI 02887-7811 Tel 401-732-1676; Edit Addr.: 3524 W. Shore Rd., No. 205, Warwick, RI 02887
E-mail: daryl_ann@yahoo.com.

Data Systems, *(0-923586)* 436 I St., SW, Ardmore, OK 73401 (SAN 286-4452)
E-mail: holodga@yahoo.com.

Davenport, May Pubs., *(0-943864; 0-9603118)* 26313 Purissima Rd., Los Altos Hills, CA 94022 (SAN 212-467X) Tel 650-947-1275; Fax: 650-947-1373
E-mail: mdbooks@earthlink.net
Web site: http://www.maydavenportpublishers.com
Dist(s): **Todd Communications.**

David & Charles Children's Bks. (GBR) *(1-86233)* *Dist. by* **Sterling.**

Dawn of Day Childrens Publishing Co., Inc., *(0-9666857)* 73 Ireland Pl., PMB 201, Amityville, NY 11757 (SAN 253-0198) Tel 631-225-5513; Fax: 631-225-5431; Toll Free: 800-575-7040
E-mail: information@dawnofday.com
Web site: http://www.dawnofday.com.

Dawn Pubns., *(0-916124; 1-878265; 1-883220; 1-58469)* P.O. Box 2010, Nevada City, CA 95959 Tel 530-478-0111; Fax: 530-478-0112; Toll Free: 800-545-7475 Do not confuse with Dawn Pubns. in Pasadena, TX
E-mail: info@dawnpub.com; nature@dawnpub.com
Web site: http://www.dawnpub.com
Dist(s): **Baker & Taylor Bks.**
Bookpeople
Brodart Co.
Common Ground Distributors, Inc.
Follett Library Resources
Hervey's Booklink & Cookbook Warehouse
Koen Bk. Distributors
Territory Titles.

Dawn Sign Pr., *(0-915035; 1-58121)* 6130 Nancy Ridge Dr., San Diego, CA 92121-3223 (SAN 289-9183) Tel 858-625-0600; Fax: 858-625-2336; Toll Free: 800-549-5350
E-mail: comments@dawnsign.com
Web site: http://www.dawnsignpress.com
Dist(s): **Gryphon Hse., Inc.**
Independent Pubs. Group.

Day to Day Enterprises, *(1-890905)* Orders Addr.: 1721 Canoe Creek Rd., Oviedo, FL 32766-8533 (SAN 299-7118) Tel 407-359-9356; Fax: 407-359-4323
E-mail: books@daytodayenterprises.com
Web site: http://www.daytodayenterprises.com
Dist(s): **Baker & Taylor Bks.**
Evans Bk. Distribution & Pubs., Inc.
Granite Publishing & Distribution, LLC.

Dayal, Ravi Pub. (IND) *(81-7530)* *Dist. by* **S Asia.**

DC Comics, *(0-930289; 1-56389; 1-4012)* Div. of Warner Bros.- A Time Warner Entertainment Co., 1700 Broadway, New York, NY 10019 Tel 212-636-5400; Fax: 212-636-5979
Web site: http://www.dccomics.com
Dist(s): **Diamond Book Distributors, Inc.**
Eastern News Distributors
Time Warner Bk. Group
Warner Bks., Inc..

Deaconess Press *See* **Fairview Pr.**

Deep River Pr., *(0-9626803)* 1871 S. 155 Cir., Omaha, NE 68144 Tel 402-334-5863 (phone/fax).

Deer Creek Publishing, *(0-9651452)* Orders Addr.: P.O. Box 2594, Nevada City, CA 95959 Tel 530-478-1758 ; Fax: 530-478-1759 Do not confuse with Deer Creek Publishing, Provo, UT
Dist(s): **Baker & Taylor Bks.**
Biblio Distribution.

Deer Pond Pub., *(1-887251)* Div. of Design Etc., Orders Addr.: P.O. Box 467, Hubbardston, MA 01452-0467 Tel 978-928-5907; Fax: 978-928-4208; Toll Free: 800-368-5545; Edit Addr.: 20 Healdville Rd., Hubbardston, MA 01452.

Deerlick Enterprise, *(0-9637936)* 7336 W. Somerset Rd., Appleton, NY 14008 Tel 716-795-3302
Dist(s): **Western New York Wares, Inc..**

Deka Pr., *(0-9645045)* P.O. Box 812, Christmas Valley, OR 97641 Tel 541-576-3900; Fax: 541-576-3909
E-mail: katym@teleport.com.

Del Rey Imprint of Ballantine Bks.

Delacorte Bks. for Young Readers Imprint of Random Hse. Children's Bks.

Delacorte Pr. Imprint of Dell Publishing

Dell Bks. Imprint of Dell Publishing

Dell Books for Young Readers Imprint of Random Hse. Children's Bks.

†Dell Publishing, *(0-440; 1-4000)* Div. of Bantam Dell Publishing Group, Orders Addr.: 400 Hahn Rd., Westminster, MD 21157 Tel 410-848-1900; Toll Free: 800-726-0600; Edit Addr.: 1540 Broadway, New York, NY 10036-4094 Tel 212-782-9000; Fax: 212-492-9698; Toll Free: 800-223-6834 (Bulk orders); 800-223-5780 (Orders only); 800-323-9872 (Customer service); *Imprints:* Dell Books (Dell Bks); Laurel (LE); Delta (Delta); Dial Books (Dial Bks); Delacorte Press (Delacorte Pr)
Web site: http://www.randomhouse.com
Dist(s): **Random Hse., Inc.**; *CIP.*

Delta Imprint of Dell Publishing

Demou, Doris Beck, *(0-9604794)* 2013 Big Oak Dr., Burnsville, MN 55337 (SAN 209-1798) Tel 612-890-3579.

Denison, T. S. & Co., Inc., *(0-513)* Orders Addr.: P.O. Box 1650, Grand Rapids, MI 49501-5431 (SAN 201-3142) Tel 616-802-3000; Fax: 616-802-3009; Toll Free Fax: 800-543-2690; Toll Free: 800-253-5469
Dist(s): **Lectorum Pubns., Inc..**

Denlingers Pubs., Ltd., *(0-87714)* P.O. Box 1030, Edgewater, FL 32132-1030 (SAN 201-3150) Tel 386-424-1737; Fax: 386-428-3534; Toll Free Fax: 800-589-1911; Toll Free: 800-362-1810
E-mail: info@thebookden.com
Web site: http://www.thebookden.com
Dist(s): **Baker & Taylor Bks..**

Denney Literary Services, *(0-9654698; 0-9707469)* 2907 Noah St., Chattanooga, TN 37406-1928 Tel 423-622-0419
E-mail: denney2907@earthlink.net.

Dent, J.M. & Sons (GBR) *(0-460)* *Dist. by* **Trafalgar.**

Dercum Audio, *(1-55656)* 1501 County Hospital Rd., Nashville, TN 37218 (SAN 658-7607) Tel 615-254-2408
E-mail: DawsonC@locc.com
Web site: http://www.bookcase.com/Dercum
Dist(s): **APG Sales and Fulfillment.**

Dercum Press/Dercum Audio *See* **Dercum Audio**

Derrydale Pr., The, *(1-56416; 1-58667)* Div. of Rowman & Littlefield Publishing Group, 4720 Boston Way, Lanham, MD 20706 Tel 301-459-3366; Fax: 301-306-5357
E-mail: sdriver@derrydalepress.com
Web site: http://www.derrydalepress.com
Dist(s): **National Bk. Network.**

deRuyter-Nelson Pubns., Inc., *(0-9650848)* 1885 University Ave., Suite 110, Saint Paul, MN 55104 Tel 612-645-7045; Fax: 612-645-4780; Toll Free: 800-631-0973; *Imprints:* A Place to Remember (A Place to Remember).

†Deseret Bk. Co., *(0-87579; 0-87747; 1-57345; 1-59038)* Div. of Deseret Management Corp., Orders Addr.: P.O. Box 30178, Salt Lake City, UT 84130 (SAN 150-763X) Tel 801-534-1515; 801-517-3165 (Wholesale Dept.); Fax: 801-517-3338; Toll Free: 800-453-3876; Edit Addr.: 40 E. South Temple, Salt Lake City, UT 84111; *Imprints:* Shadow Mountain (Shadow Mount); Cinnamon Tree (Cinnamon Tree); Bookcraft, Incorporated (Bkcraft Inc)
E-mail: dbwhsale@deseretbook.com; wholesale@deseretbook.com
Web site: http://www.deseretbook.com
Dist(s): **BookWorld Services, Inc.**; *CIP.*

Desert Rose Publishing, *(0-9631252)* Div. of RTB Enterprises, Inc., P.O. Box 2078, Tijeras, NM 87059 Tel 505-281-7719 (phone/fax) Do not confuse with companies with the same name in Tucson, AZ, Millen, GA, Eloy, AZ
E-mail: NMRoseB@cs.com; drbi@gcmailbox.com.

Design Enterprises of San Francisco, *(0-932538)* 1007 Castro St., San Francisco, CA 94114 (SAN 211-6359) Tel 415-282-8813
Dist(s): **Blue Feather Products, Inc..**

Destiny Pubns., Inc., *(0-9649522)* 9715 W. Broward Blvd., Suite 110, Plantation, FL 33324 Tel 954-452-1853; Fax: 954-452-8727; 156 NW 98th Terr., Plantation, FL 33324 Do not confuse with companies with the same or similar names in Lacey, WA, Spokane, WA, Flower Mound, TX, Merrimac, MA, Brooklyn, NY, Logandale, NV, North Little Rock, AR, Brooksville, FL, Salem, OR, Hawthorne, FL.

Details Creative, *(0-9679747)* 8175-A Sheridan Blvd., No. 362, Arvada, CO 80003-1928 Tel 303-467-2600; 6090 W. 83rd Pl., Arvada, CO 80003 Tel 303-467-2600; Fax: 303-467-0064
E-mail: details@qwest.net; details@uswest.net.

Determined Productions, Inc., *(0-915696)* P.O. Box 2150, San Francisco, CA 94126-2150 (SAN 212-7385) Tel 415-433-0660; Fax: 415-421-0929.

Detroit Black Writer's Guild, *(0-9613078; 1-888754)* P.O. Box 23100, Detroit, MI 48223-0100 (SAN 294-7315).

Deutsche Buchhandlung-James Lowry, *(1-883453)* 13531 Maugansville Rd., Hagerstown, MD 21740 Tel 301-739-8542.

Developing Resources for Education in America, Inc. (DREAM), *(1-884307)* 310 Airport Rd., Apt. D, Jackson, MS 39208 Tel 601-933-9199; Fax: 601-933-1138; Toll Free: 800-233-7326
E-mail: dream@dreaminc.org; dream@cenaccsys.com
Web site: http://www.dreaminc.org.

†Devil Mountain Bks., *(0-915685)* P.O. Box 4115, Walnut Creek, CA 94596 (SAN 292-4803) Tel 925-939-3415; Fax: 925-937-4883
E-mail: cbsturges@aol.com
Dist(s): **SPD-Small Pr. Distribution**; *CIP.*

Names

†**Devin-Adair Pubs., Inc.,** *(0-8159)* P.O. Box A, Old Greenwich, CT 06870 (SAN 112-062X) Tel 203-531-7755; Fax: 718-359-8568; *CIP.*

Devon Publishing Co., Inc., The, *(0-941402)* 2700 Virginia Ave., NW, Washington, DC 20037 (SAN 238-9703) Tel 202-337-5197
Dist(s): **Baker & Taylor Bks..**

DeVorss & Co., *(0-87516)* Orders Addr.: P.O. Box 1389, Camarillo, CA 93011-1389 (SAN 168-9886) Tel 805-322-9011; Fax: 805-322-9010; Toll Free: 800-843-5743; Edit Addr.: 553 Constitution Ave., Camarillo, CA 93012
E-mail: service@devorss.com
Web site: http://www.devorss.com
Dist(s): **Baker & Taylor Bks.**
Health and Growth Assocs.
New Leaf Distributing Co., Inc..

†**Dharma Publishing,** *(0-89800; 0-913546)* 2910 San Pablo Ave., Berkeley, CA 94702 (SAN 201-2723) Tel 510-548-5407; Fax: 510-548-2230; Toll Free: 800-873-4276
E-mail: info@dharma-publishing.com; Dharma-Publishing@Nyingma.org
Web site: http://www.dharmapublishing.com/
Dist(s): **Bookpeople**
New Leaf Distributing Co., Inc.; *CIP.*

Di Capua, Michael Bks. Imprint of Hyperion Bks. for Children

Dial Bks. Imprint of Dell Publishing

Dial Bks. for Young Readers Imprint of Penguin Putnam Bks. for Young Readers

Dialogus Play Service & Publishing, Incorporated *See* **Brown Bag Productions**

Diamond Book Distributors, Inc., 1966 Greenspring Dr., Suite 300, Timonium, MD 21093 (SAN 110-9502) Tel 410-560-7100; Fax: 410-560-7148; Toll Free: 800-452-6642
E-mail: service@diamondcomics.com; books@diamondcomics.com
Web site: http://www.diamondcomics.com.

Diamond Farm Bk. Pubs., Div. of Yesteryear Toys & Books, Inc., Orders Addr.: P.O. Box 537, Alexandria Bay, NY 13607 (SAN 674-9054) Tel 613-475-1771; Fax: 613-475-3748; Toll Free: 800-481-1353.

DIANE Publishing Co., *(0-7881; 0-941375; 1-56806; 0-7567)* Orders Addr.: P.O. Box 1428, Collingdale, PA 19023-8428 (SAN 667-1217) Tel 610-461-6200; Fax: 610-461-6130; Toll Free: 800-782-3833; Edit Addr.: 330 Pusey Ave., Unit 3 Rear, Collingdale, PA 19023
E-mail: hbdjp220@hotmail.com.

DIMI Pr., *(0-931625)* 3820 Oak Hollow Ln., SE, Salem, OR 97302-4774 (SAN 683-7271) Tel 503-364-7698; Fax: 503-364-9727; Toll Free: 800-644-3464 (orders only)
E-mail: dickbook@earthlink.net
Web site: http://home.earthlink.net/~dickbook.

Dingles & Co., *(1-891997)* 171 Main St., No. 201, Manasquan, NJ 08736-3544; *Imprints:* Treehouse Court (Treehse Ct)
E-mail: info@dingles.com
Dist(s): **Baker & Taylor Bks.**
Humanics Publishing Group.

Dionis Bound Publishing, *(0-9667090)* 18 Bayberry Ln., Nantucket Island, MA 02554 Tel 508-228-5281
E-mail: holden@natucket.net.

Direccion General de Publicaiones (MEX) *(968-29; 970-18) Dist. by* **UPLAAP.**

Direct Cinema, Ltd., *(1-55974)* Orders Addr.: P.O. Box 10003, Santa Monica, CA 90410-1003 (SAN 653-256X) Tel 310-636-8200; Fax: 310-636-8228; Toll Free: 800-525-0000; Edit Addr.: 3200 Airport Ave., No. 6, Santa Monica, CA 90405
E-mail: dcivideo@aol.com; sales@directcinemalimited.com; info@directcinemalimited.com
Web site: http://www.directcinema.com
Dist(s): **Follett Media Distribution**
International Historic Films, Inc.
National Video Resources, Inc..

Discovery Bks., *(0-679; 1-56331; 1-4000)* Orders Addr.: 400 Hahn Rd., Westminster, MD 21157 Tel 410-848-1900; Toll Free: 800-726-0600; Edit Addr.: Star Rte., Mountain View, Owls Heads, NY 12969 (SAN 206-9512)
Web site: http://www.discovery.com; http://www.randomhouse.com
Dist(s): **Libros Sin Fronteras**
Random Hse., Inc..

Discovery Comics, *(1-878181)* P.O. Box 1075, Doylestown, PA 18901 Tel 215-230-7540; Fax: 215-230-7848.

Discovery Enterprises, Ltd., *(1-57960; 1-878668; 1-932663)* 31 Laurelwood Dr., Carlisle, MA 01741-1205 (SAN 297-2611) Tel 978-287-5401; Fax: 978-287-5402; Toll Free: 800-729-1720 Do not confuse with Discovery Enterprises, Ltd. in Sarasota, FL
E-mail: ushistorydocs@aol.com
Web site: http://www.ushistorydocs.com
Dist(s): **Baker & Taylor Bks.**
Brodart Co.
Follett Library Resources.

Discovery Pr., Inc., *(0-944770)* Orders Addr.: P.O. Box 670471, Marietta, GA 30066 (SAN 245-4564) Tel 770-926-2365 Do not confuse with Discovery Pr. Inc., Smithtown, NY.

DiskUs Publishing, *(0-9667995; 1-58495; 0-7572)* Orders Addr.: P.O. Box 43, Albany, IN 47320 Tel 765-789-4064; Fax: 765-789-4993; Edit Addr.: 549 W. First St., Albany, IN 47320
E-mail: editor@diskuspublishing.com; DiskUsMail@aol.com
Web site: http://www.diskuspublishing.com
Dist(s): **netLibrary, Inc..**

Disney Editions Imprint of Disney Pr.

†**Disney Pr.,** *(0-7868; 1-56282)* Div. of Disney Bk. Publishing, Inc., A Walt Disney Co., 114 Fifth Ave., New York, NY 10011 Tel 212-633-4400; Fax: 212-633-4833; Toll Free: 800-759-0190; *Imprints:* Disney Editions (Disney Ed)
Web site: http://www.disney.com/disneybooks/index.html
Dist(s): **Libros Sin Fronteras**
Little Brown & Co.
Time Warner Bk. Group; *CIP.*

Disneyland/Vista Records & Tapes *See* **Walt Disney Records**

Distribooks, Inc., Div. of Midwest European Pubns., Inc., 8120 N. Ridgeway, Skokie, IL 60076 (SAN 630-9763) Tel 847-676-1596; Fax: 847-676-1195
E-mail: info@distribooks.com.

Distribuidora Norma, Inc., *(1-881700)* Div. of Carvajal International, Orders Addr.: P.O. Box 195040, Hato Rey, PR 00919-5040 Tel 809-788-5050 ; Fax: 809-788-7161; Edit Addr.: Carr 869 Km 1.5 Bo. Palmas, Royal Industrial, Catano, PR 00962
E-mail: normapr@caribe.net.

Dixon, S. W., *(0-9652951)* 1550 E. New York Ave., Apt. 3C, Brooklyn, NY 11212-6819 (SAN 298-1505).

D-N Publishing, *(1-890424)* 596 Indian Trail Rd. S., No. 111, Indian Trail, NC 28079 Fax: 704-684-0698
E-mail: hhinsonrw@aol.com.

Docar Publishing, *(0-9641867)* 1660 Blue Bend Rd., Rocky Mount, VA 24151 Tel 540-483-2850.

Dog & Pony Enterprises *See* **Dog & Pony Publishing**

Dog & Pony Publishing, *(0-9646970; 1-890479)* Orders Addr.: P.O. Box 3540, Kill Devil Hills, NC 27948 Tel 252-261-6905; Fax: 252-255-3236; Edit Addr.: 236 Hillcrest Dr., Southern Shores, NC 27949
E-mail: marymadendogpony@interpath.com
Web site: http://www.marymaden.com
Dist(s): **Koen Bk. Distributors**
Mistco, Inc..

Doghouse Publishing, Incorporated *See* **Mess Hall Writers**

Dogwood Pr., *(0-9627049)* Tower Glen, 2 Keppen Trail, Greensboro, NC 27410 Tel 336-299-3447; Fax: 336-218-1114 Do not confuse with companies with the same or similar names in Brandon, MS, Hemphill, TX, Stone Mountain, GA
Dist(s): **Baker & Taylor Bks..**

Doherty, Tom Assocs., LLC, *(0-312; 0-7653; 0-8125)* Div. of Holtzbrinck Publishers, Orders Addr.: 16365 James Madison Hwy., Gordonsville, VA 22942-8501 Toll Free Fax: 800-672-2054; Toll Free: 888-330-8477 ; Edit Addr.: 175 Fifth Ave., New York, NY 10010 Tel 212-674-5151; Fax: 540-672-7540 (customer service); *Imprints:* Aerie (Aerie); Forge Books (Forge Bks); Tor Books (Tor Books); Tor Classics (Tor Class); Starscape (Starscape)
Dist(s): **Holtzbrinck Pubs.**
Libros Sin Fronteras.

Dolls Corp., *(1-889514)* One Sundial Ave., Suite 305, Manchester, NH 03103 Tel 877-365-5638; Fax: 603-645-1472; Toll Free: 800-730-4891
E-mail: customerservice@idolls.com
Web site: http://www.idolls.com
Dist(s): **Baker & Taylor Bks.**
Bookman Bks.
Brodart Co.
Koen Bk. Distributors
Partners Pubs. Group, Inc..

Domhan Bks., *(1-58345)* 9511 Shore Rd., Suite 514, Brooklyn, NY 11209 Tel 718-680-4362; Fax: 888-823-4770
E-mail: domhan@att.net
Web site: http://www.domhanbooks.com.

Dominie Pr., Inc., *(0-7685; 1-56270)* 1949 Kellogg Ave., Carlsbad, CA 92008 (SAN 630-947X) Tel 760-431-8000; Fax: 760-431-8777; Toll Free: 800-232-4570
E-mail: info@dominie.com
Web site: http://www.dominie.com.

Domnick, Howard, *(0-9715419)* 1510 Seneca Dr., Enid, OK 73703 Tel 580-237-7119
E-mail: gankin@enid.com.

Doo Productions *See* **Educational Media Enterprises, Inc.**

Doog Publishing Group, *(0-9646125)* 7100 Sunnyslope Ave., Van Nuys, CA 91405 Tel 818-764-6222; Fax: 818-764-3363
E-mail: Doug@Gribic.com
Web site: http://www.Gribich.com.

Dora Books *See* **Meridian Hse.**

Doral Publishing, Inc., *(0-944875; 0-9745407)* 2501 W. Behrend Dr., No. 43, Phoenix, AZ 85027 (SAN 245-4637) Tel 623-875-2057; Fax: 623-875-2059; Toll Free: 800-633-5385
E-mail: doralpub@mindspring.com
Web site: http://www.doralpub.com
Dist(s): **National Bk. Network.**

Dorchester Publishing Co., Inc., *(0-8439)* 200 Madison Ave., Suite 2000, New York, NY 10016 (SAN 264-0090) Tel 212-725-8811; Fax: 212-532-1054; 610-995-9274 (Single copy orders); Toll Free: 800-481-9191; *Imprints:* Leisure Books (Leisure Bks); SMOOCH (Smooch)
E-mail: dorchesit@aol.com
Web site: http://www.dorchesterpub.com
Dist(s): **Comag Marketing Group**
HarperCollins Pubs..

Dorie Bks., *(0-9703326)* P.O. Box 261, White Stone, VA 22578 Toll Free: 800-553-6922
E-mail: doriethurston@hotmail.com.

†**Dorling Kindersley Publishing, Inc.,** *(0-7894; 1-56458; 1-879431; 0-7566)* Div. of The Penguin Group, 375 Hudson St., 2nd Flr., New York, NY 10014 (SAN 253-0791) Tel 212-213-4800; Fax: 212-213-5240; Toll Free: 877-342-5357 (orders only) ; *Imprints:* D K Ink (D K Ink)
E-mail: customer.service@dk.com; Annemarie.Cancienne@dk.com
Web site: http://www.dk.com
Dist(s): **Continental Bk. Co., Inc.**
Penguin Group (USA) Inc.
Hale, Robert & Co., Inc.
Sunburst Communications, Inc.; *CIP.*

Dorrance Publishing Co., Inc., *(0-8059)* 701 Smithfield St., Pittsburgh, PA 15222 (SAN 201-3363) Tel 412-288-4543; Fax: 412-434-8430; Toll Free: 800-788-7654
E-mail: dorrorder@dorrancepublishing.com
Web site: http://www.dorrancepublishing.com.

DOT Garnet, *(0-9625620)* 2225 Eighth Ave., Oakland, CA 94606 Tel 510-834-6063; Fax: 510-834-7516.

DOT Publishing *See* **DOT Garnet**

Double M Press *See* **Rose Window Pr., The**

Double M Publishing Co., *(0-913379)* 21645 Nadia Dr., Joliet, IL 60436 (SAN 285-872X) Tel 815-741-0576
Dist(s): **Baker & Taylor Bks..**

Double R Publishing, LLC, *(0-9713381; 0-9718696)* 7319 W. Flagler St., Miami, FL 33144 Tel 305-262-4240; Fax: 305-262-4115; Toll Free: 877-262-4240
E-mail: abcsbook@abcsbook.com
Web site: http://www.abcsbook.com
Dist(s): **ABC'S Bk. Supply, Inc..**

Doubleday *See* **Doubleday Publishing**

Doubleday Bks. for Young Readers Imprint of Random Hse. Children's Bks.

Doubleday Canada, Ltd. (CAN) *(0-385) Dist. by* **Random.**

†**Doubleday Publishing,** *(0-385; 1-4000)* Div. of Doubleday Broadway Publishing Group, Orders Addr.: 400 Hahn Rd., Westminster, MD 21157 (SAN 281-6083) Tel 410-848-1900; Toll Free: 800-726-0600 ; Edit Addr.: 1540 Broadway, New York, NY 10036-4094 (SAN 201-0089) Tel 212-782-9000; 212-572-4961 Bulk orders; Toll Free Fax: 800-659-2436 Orders only; Toll Free: 800-726-0600 Customer service; 800-669-1536 Electronic orders; *Imprints:* Image (ImageDD)
Web site: http://www.doubleday.com
Dist(s): **Random Hse., Inc.**; *CIP.*

Names

Douglas & McIntyre, Ltd. (CAN) *(0-88894; 0-920841; 1-55051; 1-55054; 1-55365) Dist. by* **Publishers Group.**

Dove Audio Imprint of NewStar Media, Inc.

Dove Audio, Incorporated *See* **NewStar Media, Inc.**

†Dover Pubns., Inc., *(0-486)* Orders Addr.: 31 E. Second St., Mineola, NY 11501 (SAN 201-338X) Tel 516-294-7000; Fax: 516-742-5049 (orders only); Toll Free: 800-223-3130 (Orders only)
E-mail: http://www.doverpublications.com
Dist(s): **Continental Bk. Co., Inc.**
Beeler, Thomas T. Publisher; *CIP.*

Dovetail Publishing, *(0-9651284)* P.O. Box 19945, Kalamazoo, MI 49019 Tel 616-342-2900; Fax: 616-342-1012; Toll Free: 800-222-0070
E-mail: dovetail@mich.com
Web site: http://www.mich.com/~dovetail
Dist(s): **Baker & Taylor Bks.**
Independent Pubs. Group
Quality Bks., Inc..

Down East Bks., *(0-89272; 0-924357)* Div. of Down East Enterprise, Inc., P.O. Box 679, Camden, ME 04843 (SAN 208-6301) Tel 207-594-9544; Fax: 207-594-0147; Toll Free: 800-766-1670 Wholesale orders; 800-685-7962 Retail orders
E-mail: pblanchard@downeast.com; tbregy@downeast.com
Web site: http://www.downeastbooks.com; http://www.countrysportpress.com.

Down Home Pr., *(0-9624255; 1-878086)* Orders Addr.: P.O. Box 4126, Asheboro, NC 27204 Tel 336-672-6889; Fax: 336-672-2003; Edit Addr.: 1421 Randolph Tabernacle Rd., Asheboro, NC 27203
E-mail: downhomepr@aol.com
Dist(s): **Blair, John F. Pub..**

Down The Shore Publishing, *(0-945582; 0-9615208; 1-59322)* Orders Addr.: P.O. Box 3100, Harvey Cedars, NJ 08008 Tel 609-978-1233; Fax: 609-597-0422; Edit Addr.: 638 Teal St., Cedar Run, NJ 08092 (SAN 661-082X)
E-mail: info@down-the-shore.com; orders@down-the-shore.com; shore@att.net
Web site: http://www.down-the-shore.com
Dist(s): **Koen Bk. Distributors.**

Doyle Studio Pr., *(0-9652952)* 67 Frederick Ave., Medford, MA 02155-5607.

Dr. H Bks. Imprint of Turtle Island Pr., Inc.

Dragonfly Bks. Imprint of Random Hse. Children's Bks.

Dragonfly Publishing, *(0-9667820)* 277 Folly Brook Blvd., Wethersfield, CT 06109 Tel 860-257-7635; Fax: 860-563-1943 Do not confuse with companies with the same name in Mount Enterprise, TX , Sparks, OK , San Antonio, TX
E-mail: mklett@aol.com
Web site: http://www.dragonflypublishing.net.

Dramatic Publishing Co., *(0-87129; 1-58342)* Orders Addr.: P.O. Box 129, Woodstock, IL 60098 Tel 815-338-7170; Fax: 815-338-8981; Toll Free Fax: 800-334-5302; Toll Free: 800-448-7469; Edit Addr.: 311 Washington St., Woodstock, IL 60098 (SAN 201-5676)
E-mail: dramaticpublishing.com
Web site: http://www.dramaticpublishing.com.

Dramatists Play Service, Inc., *(0-8222)* 440 Park Ave., S., New York, NY 10016 (SAN 207-5717) Tel 212-683-8960; Fax: 212-213-1539
E-mail: postmaster@dramatists.com
Web site: http://www.dramatists.com.

Dream Catcher Bks., *(0-9661385)* 135 High St., Berlin, NH 03570-2062 Tel 603-752-3849; Fax: 603-636-3013
E-mail: dcbooks@nciw.net.

Dream Factory Bks., *(0-9701195)* Orders Addr.: P.O. Box 874, Enumclaw, WA 98022 (SAN 253-2611) Tel 360-663-0508; Fax: 360-825-7952; Toll Free Fax: 877-377-7030; Edit Addr.: 58402 114th St., E., Enumclaw, WA 98022-7305
E-mail: sensel@earthlink.net
Web site: http://dreamfactorybooks.com
Dist(s): **Independent Pubs. Group.**

DS-Max USA, Inc., *(1-58805)* Orders Addr.: 19511 Pauling, Foothill Ranch, CA 92610 Tel 949-587-9207 ; Fax: 949-587-9024
E-mail: lizzas@dsmaxgroup.com; jennifer@dsmaxgroup.com.

†Dufour Editions, Inc., *(0-8023)* P.O. Box 7, Chester Springs, PA 19425-0007 (SAN 201-341X) Tel 610-458-5005; Fax: 610-458-7103; Toll Free: 800-869-5677
E-mail: dufour8023@aol.com; info@dufoureditions.com
Web site: http://go.to/Dufour; http://members.aol.com/Dufour8023/index.html; *CIP.*

Durkin Hayes Publishing Ltd., *(0-88625; 0-88646; 1-55204)* 2221 Niagara Falls Blvd., Niagara Falls, NY 14304-1696 (SAN 630-9518) Tel 716-731-9177; Fax: 716-731-9180; Toll Free: 800-962-5200
E-mail: info@dhaudio.com
Web site: http://www.dhaudio.com
Dist(s): **Landmark Audiobooks.**

Dutch Run Publishing, *(0-9632777)* Div. of Dutch Run Designs, Orders Addr.: P.O. Box 839, Soquel, CA 95073; Edit Addr.: 201 Horizon Ave., Mountain View, CA 94043 Tel 408-476-8681.

Dutton Imprint of Penguin Putnam Bks. for Young Readers

Dutton Imprint of Dutton/Plume

Dutton Children's Bks. Imprint of Penguin Putnam Bks. for Young Readers

Dutton/Plume, *(0-525)* Div. of Penguin Putnam, Inc, Orders Addr.: 405 Murray Hill Pkwy., East Rutherford, NJ 07073-2136 Toll Free: 800-631-8571 (reseller customer service); 800-788-6262 (individual consumer sales); 800-526-0275 (reseller sales); Edit Addr.: 375 Hudson St., New York, NY 10014 Tel 212-366-2000; Fax: 212-366-2666; *Imprints:* Dutton (Dutt); Plume (Plume)
E-mail: online@penguinputnam.com
Web site: http://www.penguinputnam.com
Dist(s): **Lectorum Pubns., Inc.**
Penguin Group (USA) Inc..

Dynamics Pr., *(0-9626948)* 519 S. Rogers St., Mason, MI 48854 Tel 517-676-5211; Fax: 517-676-3235.

Dyn-Novel Publishing *See* **D-N Publishing**

E&R Publishing, *(0-9609440)* 29210 Hwy. 41, Coarsegold, CA 93614-9747 (SAN 260-0234) Tel 559-683-6387.

E M C Publishing *See* **EMC/Paradigm Publishing**

EMG Networks, *(1-56843)* Div. of Educational Management Group, 1 Lake St., No. 3B-47, Upper Saddle River, NJ 07458-1813 Tel 602-970-3250; Fax: 602-970-3460; Toll Free: 800-842-6791.

E. M. Press, Incorporated *See* **E. M. Productions**

E. M. Productions, *(1-880664)* 113 Derby Way, Warrenton, VA 20186
E-mail: empress2@erols.com
Web site: http://www.empressinc.com.

EPM Pubns., Inc., *(0-914440; 0-939009; 1-889324)* 8482-A W. Main St., Marshall, VA 20115 (SAN 206-7498) Tel 540-364-6021; Fax: 540-364-6023; Toll Free: 800-289-2339
E-mail: EPMPublications@aol.com.

ETR Assocs., *(0-941816; 1-56071)* Orders Addr.: P.O. Box 1830, Santa Cruz, CA 95061-1830 (SAN 216-2881) Tel 408-438-4060; Fax: 408-438-4284; Toll Free: 800-321-4407; Edit Addr.: 4 Carbonero Way, Scotts Valley, CA 95066.

Eager Minds Pr. Imprint of Warehousing & Fulfillment Specialists, LLC (WFS, LLC)

Eaglemont Pr., *(0-9662257)* 15600 NE 8th, No. B-1, PMB 741, Bellevue, WA 98008-3900 (SAN 254-2102) Tel 425-462-6618; Fax: 425-462-4950
E-mail: info@eaglemontpress.com
Web site: http://www.eaglemontpress.com
Dist(s): **National Bk. Network.**

Eagles 3 Productions, *(0-9638941)* 2277 Jericho Rd., Aurora, IL 60506 Tel 708-844-9873.

Eakin Pr. Imprint of Eakin Pr.

†Eakin Pr., *(0-89015; 1-57168)* P.O. Drawer 90159, Austin, TX 78709-0159 (SAN 207-3633) Tel 512-288-1771; Fax: 512-288-1813; Toll Free: 800-880-8642; *Imprints:* Eakin Press (Eakin Pr)
E-mail: sales@eakinpress.com; tom@eakinpress.com
Web site: http://www.eakinpress.com
Dist(s): **Baker & Taylor Bks.**
Follett Library Resources
Hervey's Booklink & Cookbook Warehouse
Twentieth Century Christian Bks.
Wolverine Distributing, Inc.; *CIP.*

Early Child Consultants, *(0-9624257)* 15121 Regent Dr., Orland Park, IL 60462 Tel 708-403-5869.

Early Learning Assessment 2000, *(0-9667830; 0-9746447)* P.O. Box 21003, Roanoke, VA 24018
E-mail: eanaatwork@aol.com.

Earth Star Pubns., *(0-944851)* P.O. Box 117, Paonia, CO 81428-0117 (SAN 244-9315) Tel 970-527-3257; Fax: 970-527-2305
E-mail: earthstar@tripod.net
Web site: http://earthstar.tripod.com.

Earthen Vessel Production, Inc., *(1-887400)* 3620 Greenwood Dr., Kelseyville, CA 95451 Tel 707-277-7087; Fax: 707-277-7088; Toll Free: 800-233-6367
E-mail: request@earthsn.com; books@earthern.com
Web site: http://www.earthen.com.

Earthkids Publishing, *(0-9704629)* Orders Addr.: 1974 Palo Alto Ave., The Villages, FL 32162 (SAN 253-4592) Tel 352-753-3290
E-mail: mnewek@yahoo.com
Web site: http://www.earthkidspublishing.com
Dist(s): **Baker & Taylor Bks..**

Earthwing Pubns., *(0-9666720)* Orders Addr.: P.O. Box 187, Bonita Springs, FL 34133-0187 Tel 941-498-9369; Edit Addr.: 10255 Pennsylvania Ave., Bonita Springs, FL 34134.

East Eagle Pr., *(0-9605738; 1-880531)* Affil. of Patrick Haley Co., 766 Utah Ave., SE, Huron, SD 57350 Tel 605-352-5875.

East of the Sun Publishing, *(0-9668559)* Orders Addr.: P.O. Box 110063, Naples, FL 34108-0102 Tel 941-566-9676 (phone/fax); Edit Addr.: 75 Mentor Dr., Naples, FL 34110
E-mail: sales@eastofthesun.biz
Web site: http://www.eastofthesun.biz.

Eastern Dakota Publishers, Incorporated *See* **Century Creations, Inc.**

Eastman *See* **D. R. Eastman**

Ebewo's African-American Publishing & Distribution Co., *(0-9634998)* 2219 W. Minister, Parlin, NJ 08859 Fax: 732-316-0327.

Ebner, Adeline R. & Melissa A. Steffes, *(0-9632863)* 3559 Central Ave., NE, Minneapolis, MN 55418 Tel 612-781-3672; Fax: 612-522-7330.

Ebo Ink, *(0-9669230)* 331 Wende Way, Glen Burnie, MD 21061-6285 Tel 410-590-1937
E-mail: pohpoet@aol.com.

EBW Assocs., *(0-9657162)* P.O. Box 2809, South Portland, ME 04106 Tel 207-799-8389.

Econo-Clad Bks., *(0-613; 0-7857; 0-8085; 0-8335; 0-88103)* Div. of American Cos., Inc., Orders Addr.: P.O. Box 1777, Topeka, KS 66601 (SAN 169-2763) Tel 913-233-4252; Toll Free: 800-255-3502; Edit Addr.: 2101 N. Topeka Blvd., Topeka, KS 66608-1830 (SAN 249-2687)
E-mail: hkopperud@sagebrushcorp.com
Web site: http://www.sagebrushcorp.com.

EDC Publishing, *(0-7460; 0-88110; 1-58086; 0-7945)* Div. of Educational Development Corp., Orders Addr.: P.O. Box 470663, Tulsa, OK 74147-0663 (SAN 658-0505); Edit Addr.: 10302 E. 55th Pl., Tulsa, OK 74146-6515 (SAN 107-5322) Tel 918-622-4522; Fax: 918-665-7919; Toll Free: 800-475-4522; *Imprints:* Usborne (Usborne)
E-mail: edc@edcpub.com
Web site: http://www.edcpub.com
Dist(s): **Continental Bk. Co., Inc.**
Lectorum Pubns., Inc.
Libros Sin Fronteras.

Ediciones Destino (ESP) *(84-233) Dist. by* **Lectorum Pubns.**

Ediciones Huracan, Inc., *(0-929157; 0-940238)* Avenida Gonzalez 1002, Rio Piedras, PR 00925 (SAN 217-5134) Tel 809-763-7407
Dist(s): **Continental Bk. Co., Inc.**
Distribuidora Norma, Inc.
Lectorum Pubns., Inc..

Ediciones Norte-Sur Imprint of North-South Bks., Inc.

Ediciones Universal, *(0-89729; 1-59388)* Orders Addr.: P.O. Box 450353, Miami, FL 33245-0353 (SAN 658-0548); Edit Addr.: 3090 SW Eighth St., Miami, FL 33135 (SAN 207-2203) Tel 305-642-3355; Fax: 305-642-7978
E-mail: marta@ediciones.com
Web site: http://www.ediciones.com
Dist(s): **Lectorum Pubns., Inc..**

Editions Alexandre Stanke (CAN) *(2-89558) Dist. by* **Penton Overseas.**

Editions Chouette, Inc. (CAN) *(2-89450; 2-921198; 2-9800909) Dist. by* **Client Dist Srvs.**

Editions du Seuil (FRA) *(2-02) Dist. by* **Continental Bk.**

Editorial Diana, S.A. (MEX) *(968-13) Dist. by* **Continental Bk.**

Editorial Lumen (ESP) *(84-264) Dist. by* **Lectorum Pubns.**

Editorial Mundo Hispano Imprint of Casa Bautista de Publicaciones

Editorial Plaza Mayor, Inc., *(1-56328)* Avenida Ponce De Leon 1527, Barrio El Cinco, Rio Piedras, PR 00926 Tel 787-764-0455; Fax: 787-764-0465
E-mail: patrigut@prtc.net
Dist(s): **Continental Bk. Co., Inc.**
Libros Sin Fronteras.

Editorial Porrua (MEX) *(968-432; 968-452; 970-07) Dist. by* **Continental Bk.**

Names

Editorial Unilit, *(0-7899; 0-945792; 1-56063)* Div. of Spanish Hse., Inc., 1360 NW 88th Ave., Miami, FL 33172-3093 (SAN 247-5979) Tel 305-592-6136; Fax: 305-592-0087; Toll Free: 800-767-7726
E-mail: sales1@unidial.com
Web site: http://www.editorialunilit.com/
Dist(s): **Bethany Hse. Pubs.**
Harrison Hse., Inc.
Lectorum Pubns., Inc..

Educa Vision, *(1-881839; 1-58432)* 7550 NW 47th Ave., Coconut Creek, FL 33073 Tel 954-725-0701; Fax: 954-427-6739; Toll Free: 800-983-3822
E-mail: educa@aol.com
Web site: http://www.educavision.com.

Educare Pr., *(0-944638)* P.O. Box 17222, Seattle, WA 98107 Tel 206-782-4797; Fax: 206-782-4802 Do not confuse with EduCare, Colorado Springs, CO
E-mail: educarepress@hotmail.com
Web site: http://www.educarepress.com
Dist(s): **Baker & Taylor Bks.**
Bookpeople
Midpoint Trade Bks., Inc..

Educational Insights, Inc., *(0-88679; 1-56767)* 16941 Keegan Ave., Carson, CA 90746 (SAN 283-8745) Tel 310-884-2000; Fax: 800-995-0506; Toll Free: 800-933-3277.

Educational Media Enterprises, Inc., *(0-9656279)* Orders Addr.: 51 Whitesville Rd., Jackson, NJ 08527 Tel 732-905-1835; Fax: 732-367-6543
E-mail: thedooples@aol.com
Web site: http://www.dooples.com.

Edupress, Inc., *(1-56472)* 208 Avenida Fabricante, No. 200, San Clemente, CA 92672-7536 Tel 949-366-9499 ; Fax: 949-366-9441; Toll Free: 800-835-7978 Do not confuse with EduPress, Pittsburgh, PA
E-mail: info@edupressinc.com
Web site: http://www.edupressinc.com.

Eerdmans Bks For Young Readers Imprint of Eerdmans, William B. Publishing Co.

†Eerdmans, William B. Publishing Co., *(0-8028)* 255 Jefferson Ave., SE, Grand Rapids, MI 49503-4554 (SAN 220-0058) Tel 616-459-4591; Fax: 616-459-6540; Toll Free: 800-253-7521 (orders); *Imprints:* Eerdmans Books For Young Readers (Eerdmans Bks)
E-mail: info@eerdmans.com; customerservice@eerdmans.com; sales@eerdmans.com
Web site: http://www.eerdmans.com
Dist(s): **CRC Pubns.**; *CIP.*

Effect Publishing, Inc., *(0-911971)* 501 Fifth Ave., Suite 1612, New York, NY 10017 (SAN 264-665X) Tel 212-557-1321; Fax: 212-697-4835; 50 Eastbourne Dr., Chestnut Ridge, NY 10977 (SAN 665-8180) Tel 914-356-6626 Do not confuse with Effect Publishing, Inc., Reno, NV.

Eight Dog Publishing, *(0-9721327)* Orders Addr.: 87 Hillcrest Rd., Warren, NJ 07059-5304
E-mail: info@eightdogpublishing.com; andreac@eightdogpublishing.com
Web site: http://www.eightdogpublishing.com.

1873 Pr., *(0-594)* Div. of Barnes & Noble.com, 76 Ninth Ave., 9th Flr., New York, NY 10011 (SAN 253-0635) Tel 212-414-6000; Fax: 212-414-6320.

Eisch, Beverly, *(0-9724517)* W13211 Cty. C, Athelstane, WI 54104 Toll Free: 888-378-2512
E-mail: bgrandmasbooks@hotmail.com.

Ekare, Ediciones (VEN) *(980-257; 84-8351) Dist. by* **Lectorum Pubns.**

Ekare, Ediciones (VEN) *(980-257; 84-8351) Dist. by* **Kane-Miller Bk.**

Ekare, Ediciones (VEN) *(980-257; 84-8351) Dist. by* **AIMS Intl.**

EKTEK, Inc., *(0-9647830)* 12365 Montsouris Dr., Saint Louis, MO 63141-7450.

Elan Pr., *(0-9658891; 0-9706710)* 10721 W. Mission Ln., Sun City, AZ 85351 Tel 623-977-4515; Fax: 623-977-4493; Toll Free: 800-647-4175 Do not confuse Elan Press with Sunbury, PA Boulder, CO Kaneohe, HI and Toronto, ON.
E-mail: elanpress@aol.com
Web site: http://www.elanpress.com
Dist(s): **Biblio Distribution.**

Elbo Elf, Inc., *(0-9704125)* 3652 N. Amblewood Cliff, Lima, OH 45806 Fax: 419-991-2886
E-mail: customerservice@elboelf.com.

Electric Umbrella, LLC, The *See* **Electric Umbrella Publishing**

Electric Umbrella Publishing, *(0-9671113; 1-929120; 1-58627; 1-58744; 0-7574)* Div. of Mylero Corp., 520 Ericksen Ave., NE, Bainbridge, WA 98110 Tel 206-842-4322; Fax: 206-842-4279
E-mail: chris.vandyk@mylero.com; webmaster@electricumbrella.com; roxy@electricumbrella.com
Web site: http://www.mylero.com; http://www.electricumbrella.com.

Electronic Publishing Services, *(0-9711320)* Div. of eMedix, Inc., P.O. Box 10076, Hattiesburg, MS 39406 Fax: 601-266-5635
E-mail: kariesorrells@emedix.org.

Element Children's Bks., *(1-901881; 1-902618; 1-84207)* 160 N. Washington St., 4th Flr., Boston, MA 02114 Tel 617-598-6500; Fax: 617-248-0909
E-mail: publishers@elementboston.com
Dist(s): **National Bk. Network**
Penguin Group (USA) Inc..

Elfin Cove Pr., *(0-944958)* 1481 130th Ave., NE, Belleuve, WA 98005 (SAN 245-8578) Tel 425-467-6565; Fax: 425-467-6564
E-mail: ecovepress@aol.com
Dist(s): **Baker & Taylor Bks.**
Koen Pacific
Partners/West
Quality Bks., Inc..

Elghund Enterprises, *(0-9612112)* P.O. Box 158, Simpsonville, MD 21150 (SAN 289-0380) Tel 410-997-9127
E-mail: iroskey@aol.com.

Elghund Publishing Company *See* **Elghund Enterprises**

Eller Books *See* **Brethren Pr.**

Elliot's Bks., *(0-911830)* P.O. Box 6, Northford, CT 06472 (SAN 204-1529) Tel 203-484-2184; Fax: 203-484-7644
E-mail: outofprintbooks@mindspring.com.

Elliott & Clark Imprint of River City Publishing

Elsevier Science & Technology Bks., 11830 Westline Industrial Dr., Saint Louis, MO 63146 Tel 314-872-8370; *Imprints:* Butterworth-Heinemann (Butter Sci Hein)
Dist(s): **Elsevier.**

†EMC/Paradigm Publishing, *(0-7638; 0-8219; 0-88436; 0-912022; 1-56118)* Div. of EMC Corp., 875 Montreal Way, Saint Paul, MN 55102-4245 (SAN 201-3800) Tel 651-290-2800; Fax: 651-290-2828
E-mail: publish@emcp.com; educate@emcp.com
Web site: http://www.emcp.com
Dist(s): **Continental Bk. Co., Inc.**; *CIP.*

Emecé Editores S.A. (ARG) *(950-04; 950-519) Dist. by* **Libros Fronteras.**

Emece Editores (ESP) *(84-7888) Dist. by* **Lectorum Pubns.**

Emece Editores (ESP) *(84-7888) Dist. by* **Libros Fronteras.**

Emerald Bks., *(1-880356)* 112 Broad St., Flemington, NJ 08822 Tel 908-654-4266 Do not confuse with Emerald Books, Lynnwood, WA,
E-mail: emeraldbooks@seanet.com.

Emerald Bks., *(1-883002; 1-932096)* Orders Addr.: P.O. Box 635, Lynnwood, WA 98046 (SAN 298-7538) Tel 425-771-1153; Fax: 425-775-2383; Toll Free: 800-922-2143; Edit Addr.: 7825 230th St. SW, Edmonds, WA 98026 Do not confuse with Emerald Bks. in Westfield, NJ
E-mail: emeraldbooks@seanet.com
Web site: http://www.ywampublishing.com
Dist(s): **YWAM Publishing.**

Emerald City Press, Incorporated *See* **Piglet Pr., Inc.**

Emerald Hse. Group, Inc., *(1-889893; 1-932307)* 427 Wade Hampton Blvd., Greenville, SC 29609 Tel 864-235-2434; Fax: 864-235-2491; Toll Free: 800-209-8570
E-mail: info@emeraldhouse.com
Web site: http://www.emeraldhouse.com
Dist(s): **FaithWorks.**

Emmis Bks., *(0-9617367; 1-57860; 1-878208)* 10665 Andrade Dr., Zionsville, IN 46077-9230 (SAN 663-7965) Tel 317-733-4175; Fax: 317-733-4176; Toll Free: 800-913-9563; *Imprints:* Guild Press (GuilPr)
E-mail: info@guildpress.com; nbaxter@indymonthly.emmis.com
Web site: http://www.guildpress.com
Dist(s): **Client Distribution Services**
Distributors, The
Hervey's Booklink & Cookbook Warehouse
Maus Tales
Partners Pubs. Group, Inc..

Empire State Bks. Imprint of Heart of the Lakes Publishing

Emprise Pubns., *(0-938129)* 820 Park Row, Suite 591, Salinas, CA 93901 (SAN 661-2423) Tel 831-422-0415
Dist(s): **Baker & Taylor Bks.**
Sunbelt Pubns., Inc..

Enchante Publishing, *(1-56844)* Div. of Enchante, Ltd., 1250 Sixth St., Suite 403, Santa Monica, CA 90401-1639 Tel 415-529-2100; Fax: 415-851-2229; Toll Free: 800-473-2363
E-mail: web@kideq.com
Web site: http://www.kidseq.com.

Encore Performance Publishing, *(1-57514)* Orders Addr.: P.O. Box 692, Orem, UT 84059 Tel 801-785-9343; Fax: 801-785-9394
E-mail: encoreplay@aol.com
Web site: http://www.encoreplay.com.

End Of The Rainbow Projects, *(0-9706726)* Orders Addr.: P.O. Box 298238, Columbus, OH 43229 Tel 614-806-6204; Edit Addr.: 3754 Eisenhower Rd., Columbus, OH 43224
E-mail: joylynnjossel@aol.com
Web site: http://www.geocities.com/joylynn_j_2000/index.html
Dist(s): **Baker & Taylor Bks..**

Endless Love Productions, Inc., *(0-9634808)* 1500 E. Glenoaks Blvd., Glendale, CA 91206-2709 Tel 818-242-9804; Fax: 818-241-9003.

Ends of the Earth Books.com, *(0-9636652)* P.O. Box 7702, Clearwater, FL 33758-7702.

†Enslow Pubs., Inc., *(0-7660; 0-89490)* Orders Addr.: P.O. Box 398, Berkeley Heights, NJ 07922-0398 (SAN 213-7518) Tel 908-771-9400; Fax: 908-771-0925; Toll Free: 800-398-2504; Edit Addr.: 40 Industrial Rd., Berkeley Heights, NJ 07922-0398
E-mail: mail@enslow.com
Web site: http://www.enslow.com
Dist(s): **Bollett Library Resources**; *CIP.*

Eos Imprint of Morrow/Avon

EPM Pubns. Imprint of Howell Pr.

E-Pub2000, *(0-9679076; 0-9706622)* 1228 Westloop, No. 274, Manhattan, KS 66502 Tel 785-776-1940
E-mail: e_pub_2000@yahoo.com
Web site: http://go.to/E-Pub2000.

ereads.com, *(1-58586; 0-7592)* 171 E. 74th St., New York, NY 10021 Tel 212-772-7363; Fax: 212-772-7393
E-mail: info@e-reads.com
Web site: http://www.e-reads.com.

Eriako Assocs., *(0-9638417)* 1380 Morningside Way, Venice, CA 90291 Tel 310-392-6537; Fax: 310-396-4307.

Eridanos Library Imprint of Marsilio Pubs.

Eridanos Press *See* **Marsilio Pubs.**

E-Rights/E-Reads, Limited *See* **ereads.com**

Ertl Co., Inc., *(1-887327)* Div. of U. S. Industries, Inc., Highways 136 & 20, P.O. Box 500, Dyersville, IA 52040-0500 Tel 319-875-5640; Fax: 319-875-8263
Web site: http://www.rcertl.com.

Eschar Pubns., *(0-9623839; 1-929221)* Orders Addr.: P.O. Box 1196, Waynesboro, VA 22980 (SAN 297-6439) Tel 540-942-2171; Fax: 352-357-9695; Edit Addr.: 435 Alpha St., Waynesboro, VA 22980
E-mail: escharpub@earthlink.net
Web site: http://www.vivianowens.com
Dist(s): **Baker & Taylor Bks.**
Brodart Co..

Espasa Calpe, S.A. (ESP) *(84-239; 84-339; 84-8326; 84-670) Dist. by* **Continental Bk.**

Espasa Calpe, S.A. (ESP) *(84-239; 84-339; 84-8326; 84-670) Dist. by* **Lectorum Pubns.**

Espasa Calpe, S.A. (ESP) *(84-239; 84-339; 84-8326; 84-670) Dist. by* **Libros Fronteras.**

Espasa Calpe, S.A. (ESP) *(84-239; 84-339; 84-8326; 84-670) Dist. by* **Planeta.**

Ethnic Bks., *(0-9630887)* P.O. Box 710352, Houston, TX 77271-0352 Tel 713-726-1044; Fax: 713-726-8948
E-mail: ethnicbooks@lindawaters.com; elkewat@aol.com; ethnicbooks@aol.com
Web site: http://lindawaters.com.

European Language Institute (ITA) *(88-8148; 88-85148) Dist. by* **Midwest European Pubns.**

European Language Institute (ITA) *(88-8148; 88-85148) Dist. by* **Distribks Inc.**

Evanel Assocs., *(0-918948)* 825 Greengate Oval, Sacamore Hills, OH 44067 (SAN 209-4347) Tel 330-467-1750 (phone/fax); Toll Free: 888-678-1701.

Evangel Press *See* **Evangel Publishing Hse.**

Names

Evangel Publishing Hse., *(0-916035; 1-928915)* Div. of Board for Media Ministry of the Brethren in Christ Church, Orders Addr.: P.O. Box 189, Nappanee, IN 46550 (SAN 211-7940) Tel 574-773-3164; Fax: 574-773-5934; Toll Free: 800-253-9315 (order)
E-mail: sales@evangelpublishing.com; editorial@evangelpublishing.com
Web site: http://www.evangelpublishing.com
Dist(s): **Appalachian Bk. Distributors**
Baker & Taylor Bks.
Riverside
Spring Arbor Distributors, Inc..

Evans Brothers, Ltd. (GBR) *(0-237) Dist. by* **Trafalgar.**

†Evans, M. & Co., Inc., *(0-87131; 1-59077)* 216 E. 49th St., New York, NY 10017 (SAN 203-4050) Tel 212-688-2810; Fax: 212-486-4544
E-mail: editorial@mevans.com
Web site: http://www.mevans.com/
Dist(s): **National Bk. Network**; *CIP.*

Evans Pubns., *(0-932715)* Subs. of Eva-Tone, Inc., 4801 Ulmerton Rd., Clearwater, FL 34622 (SAN 687-7419) Tel 813-572-7000; Fax: 813-572-6214 Do not confuse with Evans Pubns., Inola, OK.

Everest de Ediciones y Distribucion, S.L. (ESP) *(84-241) Dist. by* **Lectorum Pubns.**

Evergreen Pacific Publishing, Ltd., *(0-945265; 0-9609036)* 18002 15th Ave., NE, Suite B, Shoreline, WA 98155 (SAN 240-9119) Tel 206-368-8157; Fax: 206-368-7968
E-mail: sales@evergreenpacific.com
Web site: http://www.evergreenpacific.com
Dist(s): **Alpen Bks**
Alpenbooks Pr.
Benjamin News Group
Partners/West
Hale, Robert & Co., Inc..

Evergreen Pr. Imprint of Genesis Communications, Inc.

Evergreen Press *See* **Genesis Communications, Inc.**

Everyman's Classic Library in Paperback Imprint of Tuttle Publishing

Everyman's Library Imprint of Knopf Publishing Group

Ewen Prime Co., *(1-889436)* Orders Addr.: P.O. Box 2061, Natick, MA 01760 Tel 508-628-1891; Edit Addr.: 13 Lankspur Way, No. 1, Natick, MA 01760-4025
E-mail: ewenprime@aol.com
Web site: http://members@aol.com/ewenprime/nepa.html.

Exams Unlimited, Inc., *(1-885343; 1-59132)* 1971 Western Ave., No. 191, Albany, NY 12203-5011 Tel 518-356-1486 (phone/fax)
E-mail: eui@eui.com
Web site: http://www.ebooks-etexts.com.

Excalibur Publishing, Inc., *(0-9627226; 1-885064)* 511 Avenue of the Americas, Suite 392, New York, NY 10011 Tel 212-777-1790; Toll Free: 800-729-6423 (orders) Do not confuse with Excalibur Publishing, Highlands Ranch, CO
E-mail: info@excaliburpublishing.com
Web site: http://www.excaliburpublishing.com
Dist(s): **Lightning Source, Inc.**
SCB Distributors.

Excellence Enterprises, *(0-9627735)* 3040 Aspen Ln., Palmdale, CA 93550-7985 Tel 818-367-8085; Fax: 818-361-2389.

Explorer Media Imprint of Simon & Barklee, Inc./ExplorerMedia

Extra, *(0-9627292)* P.O. Box 1255, Great Neck, NY 11027 Tel 718-224-0302.

Eyrie Pr., *(0-9619465)* Orders Addr.: P.O. Box 805, Gainesville, VA 20156-0805 (SAN 245-016X)
E-mail: dgo@ix.netcom.com.

F&W Pubns., Inc., *(0-89134; 0-89879; 0-932620; 1-55870; 1-58180; 1-58297; 1-884910)* Orders Addr.: 4700 E. Galbraith Rd., Cincinnati, OH 45236 Tel 513-531-2690; Fax: 513-531-4082; Toll Free Fax: 888-590-4082; Toll Free: 800-289-0963; c/o AERO Fulfillment Services, 2800 Henkle Dr., Lebanon, OH 45036; *Imprints:* Betterway Books (Betrwy Bks)
E-mail: marcia.jones@fwpubs.com
Web site: http://www.fwpublications.com; http://www.artistsmagazine.com; http://www.artistsnetwork.com; http://www.davidandcharles.co.uk; http://www.krause.com; http://www.familytreemagazine.com; http://www.howdesign.com; http://www.idonline.com; http://www.memorymakersmagazine.com; http://www.popularwoodworking.com; http://www.writersdigest.com; http://www.writersmarket.com; http://www.writersonlineworkshops.com.

Fabbri - RCS Libri (ITA) *(88-450; 88-451; 88-452; 88-454) Dist. by* **Distribks Inc.**

†Faber & Faber, Inc., *(0-571)* Affil. of Farrar, Straus & Giroux, LLC, Orders Addr.: c/o Van Holtzbrinck Publishing Services, 16365 James Madison Hwy., Gordonsville, VA 22942 Fax: 540-572-7540; Toll Free: 888-330-8477; Edit Addr.: 19 Union Sq., W, New York, NY 10003-3304 (SAN 218-7256) Tel 212-741-6900; Fax: 212-633-9385
Dist(s): **Continental Bk. Co., Inc.**
Holtzbrinck Pubs.; *CIP.*

Face to Face Bks. Imprint of Midwest Traditions, Inc.

Facet Bks. International, Inc., *(0-932377)* 345 E. 69th St., New York, NY 10021 (SAN 687-3839) Tel 212-570-1932
E-mail: ekatra@bol.net.in.

Factor Pr., *(0-9626531; 1-887650)* Orders Addr.: P.O. Box 222, Salisbury, MD 21803 (SAN 631-466X) Toll Free: 800-304-0077; Edit Addr.: 5204 Dove Point Ln., Salisbury, MD 21801 Tel 410-334-6111
E-mail: factorpress@earthlink.net.

†Facts on File Inc., *(0-8160; 0-87196)* 132 W. 31st St., 17th Flr., New York, NY 10001-2006 (SAN 201-4696) Tel 212-967-8800; Fax: 212-967-9196; 212-967-8107 ; Toll Free: 800-322-8755; *Imprints:* Ferguson Publishing Company (Ferg Pub Co)
E-mail: lharris@factsonfile.com
Web site: http://www.factsonfile.com; *CIP.*

Fairfax, C.H. Co., Inc., *(0-935132)* Orders Addr.: P.O. Box 7047, Baltimore, MD 21216-0047 (SAN 221-170X) Tel 410-728-6421 (phone/fax)
E-mail: chfairfaxco@hotmail.com
Web site: http://www.yougetpublished.com.

Fairview Pr., *(0-925190; 1-57749)* 2450 Riverside Ave., Minneapolis, MN 55545 (SAN 298-170X) Tel 612-672-4180; Fax: 612-672-4980; Toll Free: 800-544-8207 Do not confuse with Fairview Pr., in Silver Spring, MD
E-mail: press@webx.fairview.org
Web site: http://www.fairviewpress.org
Dist(s): **National Bk. Network.**

Fairway Pr. Imprint of CSS Publishing Co.

Faith & Life Pr., *(0-87303)* Orders Addr.: P.O. Box 347, Newton, KS 67114-0347 (SAN 658-0637) Tel 316-283-5100; Fax: 316-283-0454; Toll Free: 800-743-2484 (orders only); Edit Addr.: 718 Main St., Newton, KS 67114-0347 (SAN 201-4726)
E-mail: flp@gcmc.org
Web site: http://www.2southwind.net/~gcmc/flp.html
Dist(s): **Spring Arbor Distributors, Inc..**

Falcon Imprint of Globe Pequot Pr., The

Family Connections Publishing Co., *(1-884862)* 1405 E. 2100 S., Salt Lake City, UT 84105 Tel 801-484-2100; Fax: 801-485-5525
Dist(s): **Evans Bk. Distribution & Pubs., Inc..**

Family Learning Center *See* **Common Sense Pr.**

Family Life Publishing *See* **Family Life Publishing/Richard Wainright Bks.**

Family Life Publishing/Richard Wainright Bks., *(0-9619566; 1-928976)* Orders Addr.: P.O. Box 353844, Palm Coast, FL 32135 (SAN 244-9188) Fax: 781-544-2065; Toll Free: 800-633-1357; Edit Addr.: 32 Lago Vista Pl., Palm Coast, FL 32135
Dist(s): **Baker & Taylor Bks..**

Family Of Man Pr., The Imprint of Hutchison, G.F. Pr.

FamilyFinds Imprint of Williford Communications

Fantagraphics Bks., *(0-930193; 1-56097)* 7563 Lake City Way, NE, Seattle, WA 98115 (SAN 251-5571) Tel 206-524-1967; Fax: 206-524-2104; Toll Free: 800-657-1100
E-mail: zura@fantagraphics.com; diva@eroscomix.com
Web site: http://www.fantagraphics.com; http://eroscomix.com
Dist(s): **Norton, W. W. & Co., Inc..**

Fantasy Flight Publishing, Inc., *(1-887911; 1-58994)* 2021 W. County Rd. C, Roseville, MN 55113 Tel 651-639-1905; Fax: 651-639-1764
E-mail: brianw@fantasyflightgames.com
Web site: http://www.fantasyflightgames.com
Dist(s): **Diamond Comic Distributors, Inc..**

Faraway Publishing Group, *(0-9636885; 0-9720457)* P.O. Box 792, Nantucket, MA 02554; 98 Old South Rd., Nantucket, MA 02554.

†Farrar, Straus & Giroux, *(0-374)* Div. of Holtzbrinck Publishers, Orders Addr.: c/o Holtzbrinck Publishers, 16365 James Madison Hwy., Gordonsville, VA 22942 Toll Free Fax: 800-672-2054; Toll Free: 888-330-8477 ; Edit Addr.: 19 Union Sq., W., New York, NY 10003 (SAN 206-782X) Tel 212-741-6900; Fax: 212-463-0641; *Imprints:* Hill & Wang (Hil-Wang); North Point Press (N Point Pr); Aerial (AerFSG); Farrar, Straus & Giroux (BYR) (FSGBYR); Mirasol/Libros Juveniles (Mira Libros); Sunburst (SunbFSG)
E-mail: sales@fsgee.com; fsg.editorial@fsgee.com
Web site: http://www.fsbassociates.com/fsg/index.htm
Dist(s): **Continental Bk. Co., Inc.**
Holtzbrinck Pubs.
Lectorum Pubns., Inc.; *CIP.*

Farrar, Straus & Giroux (BYR) Imprint of Farrar, Straus & Giroux

Fassina, Marene P., *(1-892996)* Orders Addr.: P.O. Box 426, Fultondale, AL 35068 Tel 205-841-7675; Fax: 205-841-7644; Edit Addr.: 1122 Ellard Rd., Fultondale, AL 35068
E-mail: mgtinst@bellsouth.net
Web site: http://www.marene.com.

Fawcett Imprint of Ballantine Bks.

Fearon Teacher Aids Imprint of McGraw-Hill Children's Publishing

Feathertouch Publishing, *(0-9646561)* Div. of Feathertouch Communications, P.O. Box 1990, Lake of the Woods, Lake of the Woods, Frazier Park, CA 93225 Tel 805-245-2925; Fax: 805-245-2926; Toll Free: 800-511-6456.

Feelings Factory, Inc., *(1-882801)* 20 Enterprise St., Raleigh, NC 27607 Tel 919-828-2204; Fax: 919-828-2064; Toll Free: 800-858-2264.

†Feldheim, Philipp Inc., *(0-87306; 1-58330)* 202 Airport Executive Pk., Nanuet, NY 10954 (SAN 106-6307) Tel 845-356-2282; Fax: 845-425-1908; Toll Free: 800-237-7149
E-mail: mike613@netvision.net.il
Web site: http://www.feldheim.com
Dist(s): **Libros Sin Fronteras**; *CIP.*

Feldheim Pubs., 200 Executive Park, Nanuet, NY 10954.

†Feminist Pr. at The City Univ. of New York, *(0-912670; 0-935312; 1-55861)* 365 Fifth Ave., New York, NY 10016 (SAN 213-6813) Tel 212-817-7915; Fax: 212-817-2988
E-mail: lglazer@gc.cuny.edu
Web site: http://www.feministpress.org
Dist(s): **Consortium Bk. Sales & Distribution**
Continental Bk. Co., Inc.
Women Ink; *CIP.*

Feral Pr., Inc., *(0-9649349; 1-930094)* 304 Strawberry Field Rd., Flat Rock, NC 28731 Tel 828-694-0438; Fax: 828-694-0438; *Imprints:* Rivet Books (Rivet Bks)
E-mail: gchet@feralpressinc.com
Web site: http://www.feralpressinc.com.

Ferguson Publishing Co. Imprint of Facts on File Inc.

Fernandez USA Publishing, *(968-416; 970-03)* 203 Argonne Ave., Suite B, PMB 151, Long Beach, CA 90803-1777 Tel 562-901-2370; Fax: 562-901-2372; Toll Free: 800-814-8080
Web site: http://www.fernandezusa.com
Dist(s): **Continental Bk. Co., Inc..**

Fickling, David Bks. Imprint of Random Hse. Children's Bks.

Field Stone Pubs., *(0-9645272)* 331 Fields Hill Rd., Conway, MA 01341 Tel 413-369-4091; Fax: 413-369-4212
E-mail: fieldstn@crocker.com
Web site: http://www.crocker.com/fieldstn.

Filter Pr., LLC, *(0-86541; 0-910584)* P.O. Box 95, Palmer Lake, CO 80133 (SAN 201-484X) Tel 719-481-2420 (phone/fax); Toll Free: 888-570-2663
E-mail: filter.press@prodigy.net.

†Fine, Donald I. Bks., *(0-917657; 1-55611)* Div. of Penguin Putnam, Inc., 375 Hudson St., New York, NY 10014-3658 (SAN 656-9749) Tel 212-366-2000; Fax: 212-366-2933
Web site: http://www.booksnbytes.com/authors/fine_donaldi.htm
Dist(s): **Penguin Group (USA) Inc.**; *CIP.*

FINK, Inc., *(1-930281)* P.O. Box 7562, Santa Monica, CA 90406-7562 Tel 310-384-1334
E-mail: info@studylab.com
Web site: http://www.finkadelic.com; http://www.studylab.com
Dist(s): **Diamond Book Distributors, Inc..**

Finkelstein, Ruth, *(0-9628157)* 216 Private Way, Lakewood, NJ 08701 Tel 732-367-1673.

Fiorello's Pumpkin Patch *See* **Pumpkin Patch Publishing**

Names

Firebird Imprint of Penguin Putnam Bks. for Young Readers

Firebird Pr. Imprint of Pelican Publishing Co., Inc.

Firefly Bks., Ltd., *(0-920668; 1-55209; 1-895565; 1-896284; 1-55297)* 4 Daybreak Ln., Westport, CT 06880-2157
E-mail: service@fireflybooks.com
Web site: http://www.fireflybooks.com/
Dist(s): **Lectorum Pubns., Inc..**

Fireside Imprint of Simon & Schuster

Fireside Book Shop, Inc., *(0-9700846)* 29 N. Franklin St., Chagrin Falls, OH 44022 Tel 440-247-4050; Fax: 440-247-4310.

Fireside Bks., *(0-9718282)* P.O. Box 157, Saint Marys, GA 31558 Tel 912-576-2257 Do not confuse with companies with the same name in St. Louis, MO, Boise, ID, Chicago, IL, Shingle Spring, CA
E-mail: cbyor33@yahoo.com.

Fireweed Pr., *(0-912683)* 7315 Allan Ave., Falls Church, VA 22046-2025 (SAN 277-6839) Tel 703-560-0810 Do not confuse with companies with the same name in Fairbanks, AK, Madison, WI, Evergreen, CO.

First Avenue Editions Imprint of Lerner Publishing Group

First Bk. Productions, *(1-887637)* Orders Addr.: P.O. Box 870128, New Orleans, LA 70128 Tel 504-242-2260; Fax: 504-242-5532; Toll Free: 800-232-8460; Edit Addr.: 14801 Emory Rd., New Orleans, LA 70128.

First Story Pr., *(1-890326)* 1800 Business Park Dr., Clarksville, TN 37040-6023 Tel 931-572-0806; Fax: 931-552-3200; Toll Free: 888-754-0208.

Fithian Pr., *(0-931832; 1-56474)* Div. of Daniel & Daniel Pubs., Inc., P.O. Box 1525, Santa Barbara, CA 93102 (SAN 211-6103) Tel 805-962-1780; Fax: 805-962-8835; Toll Free: 800-662-8351 (orders only)
E-mail: dandd@danielpublishing.com
Web site: http://www.danielpublishing.com
Dist(s): **SCB Distributors.**

Fitzgerald Bks., *(1-887238; 1-59054)* Div. of Central Programs, Inc., Orders Addr.: P.O. Box 505, Bethany, MO 64424 Tel 660-425-7777; Fax: 660-425-3929; Toll Free: 800-821-7199; Edit Addr.: 802 N. 41st St., Bethany, MO 64424
E-mail: wecare@gumdropbooks.com
Web site: http://www.gumdropbooks.com
Dist(s): **Gumdrop Bks..**

Fitzgerald, Clyde C. *See* **Ira Valley Ideas**

Five Star Imprint of Gale Group

Five Star Pubns., Inc., *(0-9619853; 1-877749; 1-58985)* Orders Addr.: P.O. Box 6698, Chandler, AZ 85246-6698 (SAN 246-7429) Tel 480-940-8182; Fax: 480-940-8787; Edit Addr.: 4696 W. Tyson St., Chandler, AZ 85226-2903
E-mail: info@fivestarpublications.com
Web site: http://www.fivestarpublications.com
Dist(s): **Baker & Taylor Bks.**
Distributors, The
Koen Bk. Distributors
Quality Bks., Inc.
Unique Bks., Inc..

Floris Bks. (GBR) *(0-86315; 0-903540) Dist. by* **SteinerBooks Inc.**

Floris Bks. (GBR) *(0-86315; 0-903540) Dist. by* **Gryphon Hse.**

Fly-by-Night Publishing *See* **Awesome Bks., LLC.**

Flying Frog Publishing Imprint of Allied Publishing

Flying Rhino Productions, Incorporated *See* **Flying Rhinoceros, Inc.**

Flying Rhinoceros, Inc., *(1-883772; 1-59168)* 1440 NW Overton St., Portland, OR 97209 Tel 503-552-8700; Fax: 503-221-7282; Toll Free: 800-537-4466
E-mail: flyingrhino@flyingrhino.com
Web site: http://www.flyingrhino.com.

Flyleaf Publishing, *(0-9658246; 1-929262)* Orders Addr.: P.O. Box 287, Lyme, NH 03768-0287 Toll Free: 800-449-7006; *Imprints:* Books To Remember (Bks To Remember)
E-mail: laura@flyleafpublishing.com
Web site: http://www.flyleafpublishing.com.

Flywheel Publishing Co., *(1-930826)* Orders Addr.: The Don Best Bldg., 4875 Nevso Dr., Las Vegas, NV 89103 (SAN 253-2441) Tel 530-269-2020; Fax: 530-579-3385
E-mail: admin@flywheelpublishing.com
Web site: http://www.flywheelpublishing.com
Dist(s): **Baker & Taylor Bks.**
Biblio Distribution
Book Wholesalers, Inc.
Brodart Co.
Quality Bks., Inc..

†**Focus on the Family Publishing,** *(0-929608; 1-56179; 1-58997)* 8605 Explorer Dr., Colorado Springs, CO 80920-1051 (SAN 250-0949) Fax: 719-531-3356; Toll Free: 800-232-6459
E-mail: edresources@fotf.org
Web site: http://www.family.org
Dist(s): **Bethany Hse. Pubs.**
Christian Bk. Distributors
Honor Bks.
Nelson, Tommy
Tyndale Hse. Pubs.
Vision Video
Zondervan; *CIP.*

Focus Publishing, *(1-885904)* Orders Addr.: P.O. Box 665, Bemidji, MN 56619 Tel 218-759-9817; Fax: 218-751-7210; Toll Free: 800-913-6287; Edit Addr.: 502 Third St., NW, Bemidji, MN 56601
Dist(s): **Appalachian Bk. Distributors**
Riverside
Spring Arbor Distributors, Inc..

Fodor's Travel Guides *See* **Fodor's Travel Pubns.**

Fodor's Travel Pubns., *(0-609; 0-676; 0-679; 0-7615; 1-878867; 1-4000)* Div. of Random Hse., Information Group, Orders Addr.: 400 Hahn Rd., Westminster, MD 21157 Tel 410-848-1900; Toll Free: 800-726-0600; Edit Addr.: 280 Park Ave., Tenth Flr., New York, NY 10017 Tel 212-572-8784; Fax: 212-572-2248
Web site: http://www.fodors.com
Dist(s): **Libros Sin Fronteras**
Random Hse., Inc..

Fogelman, Phyllis Bks. Imprint of Penguin Putnam Bks. for Young Readers

Folio One Publishing, *(0-9655753)* 820 Monroe NW, Suite 317, Grand Rapids, MI 49503 Tel 616-356-2580 ; Fax: 616-356-2581
E-mail: mary@folio-one.com
Web site: http://www.adoptiontravel.com.

Fondo de Cultura Economica (MEX) *(968-16) Dist. by* **Continental Bk.**

Fondo de Cultura Economica USA, *(968-16; 950-557; 956-7083; 9972-663)* 2293 Verus St., San Diego, CA 92154 Tel 619-429-0827; Fax: 619-429-0455; Toll Free: 800-532-3872
E-mail: sales@fceusa.com; fceusa@fceusa.com
Web site: http://www.fceusa.com
Dist(s): **Giron Bks.**
Latin American Bk. Source, Inc.
Lectorum Pubns., Inc.
Libros Sin Fronteras
Trucatriche.

Food Allergy & Anaphylaxis Network, *(1-882541)* 10400 Eaton Pl. Suite 107, Fairfax, VA 22030-2208 Tel 703-691-3179; Fax: 703-691-2713; Toll Free: 800-929-4040
E-mail: faan@foodallergy.org
Web site: http://www.foodallergy.org.

Food Allergy Network *See* **Food Allergy & Anaphylaxis Network**

Food Works, *(1-884430)* 64 Main St., Montpelier, VT 05602 Tel 802-223-1515; Fax: 802-229-5277; Toll Free: 800-310-1515
E-mail: foodwork@together.net
Dist(s): **Sewall Co., The.**

For His Kingdom, *(1-889994)* 10425 49th Ave., N., Plymouth, MN 55442 Tel 612-559-7124.

For Your Knowledge Imprint of Ann Arbor Media Group, LLC

Forest Hse. Publishing Co., Inc., *(1-56674; 1-878363)* P.O. Box 738, Lake Forest, IL 60045 Tel 847-295-8287; Fax: 847-295-8201; Toll Free: 800-394-7323; *Imprints:* H T S Books (HTS Bks)
Web site: http://www.forest-house.com.

Forge Bks. Imprint of Doherty, Tom Assocs., LLC

Formac Publishing Co., Ltd. (CAN) *(0-88780; 0-921921) Dist. by* **Orca Bk Pubs.**

Formosan Magazine Pr., Ltd. (CHN) *(957-632) Dist. by* **Shens Bks.**

Fort Frederica Assn., Inc., *(0-930803)* Rte. 9, Box 286-C, Saint Simons Island, GA 31522 (SAN 677-6299) Tel 912-638-3639.

Forword, *(0-9623937)* 16526 W. 78th St., Suite 335, Eden Prairie, MN 55346 Tel 612-944-7761; Fax: 612-944-8674
Dist(s): **Baker & Taylor Bks..**

Foster, Walter Publishing, Inc., *(0-929261; 1-56010)* 23062 La Cadena Dr., Laguna Hills, CA 92653 (SAN 249-051X) Tel 949-380-7510; Fax: 949-380-7575; Toll Free: 800-426-0099
E-mail: info@walterfoster.com
Web site: http://www.walterfoster.com; http://www.mychaoticlife.com.

Foundation Bks., Inc., *(0-934988)* Orders Addr.: P.O. Box 22828, Lincoln, NE 68542-2828 (SAN 201-6567) Tel 402-438-7080; Fax: 402-438-7099
E-mail: foundation@inebraska.com
Web site: http://www.foundationbooks.com
Dist(s): **Baker & Taylor Bks..**

Four Corners Publishing Co., Inc., *(1-893577)* 45 W. Tenth St., New York, NY 10011 Tel 212-673-5226; Fax: 516-771-1243
E-mail: RLutnick@aol.com
Dist(s): **Biblio Distribution.**

Four Directions Publishing, *(0-9645173)* P.O. Box 24671, Minneapolis, MN 55424 Tel 612-922-9322; Fax: 612-922-7163
E-mail: eagleman4@aol.com
Dist(s): **Bookmen, Inc.**
Dakota West Bks.
New Leaf Distributing Co., Inc..

Four Seasons Books, Incorporated *See* **Four Seasons Bks., Inc.**

Four Seasons Bks., Inc., *(0-9666858; 1-893595)* P.O. Box 395, Ben Wheeler, TX 75754 Tel 903-963-1442; Fax: 903-963-1525; Toll Free: 800-852-7484
E-mail: hcmarlow@yahoo.com
Web site: http://www.herbmarlow.com.

Four Seasons Pubs., *(0-9656811; 1-891929; 1-932497)* Orders Addr.: P.O. Box 51, Titusville, FL 32781 Tel 321-267-9800; Fax: 321-267-8076; Edit Addr.: 4350 N. U.S. Hwy. 1, Cocoa, FL 32927
E-mail: fseasons@bellsouth.net
Web site: http://www.fourseasonspub.net
Dist(s): **Baker & Taylor Bks..**

Fowema Publishing Co., *(0-9660136)* Orders Addr.: P.O. Box 51882, Provo, UT 84605-1882 Tel 801-377-6854; Edit Addr.: 86 S. 900 W., Provo, UT 84601.

Fowler Cos., Inc., The, *(0-9661365)* 1417 Alford Ave., Birmingham, AL 35226 Tel 205-822-9252; Fax: 205-822-2140
E-mail: fowlerbook@aol.com.

Fox Chapel Publishing Co., Inc., *(1-56523)* 1970 Broad St., East Petersburg, PA 17520 Tel 717-560-4703; Fax: 717-560-4702; Toll Free Fax: 888-369-2885; Toll Free: 800-457-9112 (orders)
E-mail: sales@carvingworld.com
Web site: http://www.carvingworld.com; http://www.foxchapelpublishing.com/; http://www.scrollsawer.com/
Dist(s): **Independent Pubs. Group.**

Foxhaven Pr., *(0-9651747)* 2425 Foxhaven Dr., Franklin, TN 37069 Tel 615-661-9761; Fax: 615-287-6700; Toll Free: 800-937-8222 (ext. 3424)
E-mail: wibking@juno.com
Web site: http://www.Ingrambook.com
Dist(s): **New Leaf Distributing Co., Inc..**

Frajil Farms, *(1-878689)* Box 13, Mont Vernon, NH 03057; 69 Francestown Tpke., Mont Vernon, NH 03057 Tel 603-673-8041.

Franciscan Herald Pr. Imprint of Franciscan Pr.

Franciscan Pr., *(0-8199)* Orders Addr.: Dept. NL Quincy Univ., 1800 College Ave., Quincy, IL 62301-2699 Tel 217-228-5670; Fax: 217-228-5672; Edit Addr.: Quincy Univ., 1800 College Ave., Quincy, IL 62301-2699; *Imprints:* Franciscan Herald Press (Frncscn Herld)
E-mail: coopebe@quincy.edu
Web site: http://quincy.edu/fpress/index-html.

Franklin, J. Pub., *(0-9616736)* Orders Addr.: P.O. Box 14057, Tulsa, OK 74159 (SAN 661-4302) Tel 918-747-9384; Fax: 918-743-4703; Toll Free Fax: 800-888-6141; Toll Free: 800-234-9384; Edit Addr.: 2705 E. Skelly Dr., No. 306, Tulsa, OK 74105 (SAN 661-4310)
E-mail: lawnhon@ix.netcom.com
Web site: http://www.sellingretail.biz.

Franklin Mason Pr., *(0-9679227)* Orders Addr.: P.O. Box 3808, Trenton, NJ 08629 (SAN 253-1828) Tel 609-396-5473; Fax: 609-396-1534; Edit Addr.: 229 Franklin St., Trenton, NJ 08611
E-mail: franklin@franklinmason.com
Web site: http://www.franklinmason.com.

Franklin-Sarrett Pubs., *(0-9637477)* 3761 Vinyard Trace, Marietta, GA 30062 (SAN 297-9918) Tel 770-578-9410; Fax: 770-973-4243
E-mail: kborden@mindspring.com; info@franklin-sarrett.com
Web site: http://www.franklin-sarrett.com.

†**Free Spirit Publishing, Inc.,** *(0-915793; 1-57542)* 217 Fifth Ave., N., Suite 200, Minneapolis, MN 55401-1299 (SAN 293-9584) Tel 612-338-2068; Fax: 612-337-5050; Toll Free: 800-735-7323
E-mail: help4kids@freespirit.com
Web site: http://www.freespirit.com
Dist(s): **Baker & Taylor Bks.**
Bookmen, Inc.
Quality Bks., Inc.; *CIP.*

Free Will Pr., *(0-9701771)* P.O. Box 12130, San Francisco, CA 94112 Tel 415-337-5494; Fax: 415-586-3787; 631 Naples St., San Francisco, CA 94112
E-mail: michael@freewillpress.com; michaelp@freewillpress.com
Web site: http://www.freewillpress.com.

Freedom Pr. Assocs., *(0-945069)* 18 Old Portland Rd., Freedom, NH 03836 (SAN 245-9558) Tel 603-539-2146; Fax: 603-539-5301; P.O. Box 460, Freedom, NH 03836
E-mail: ghb@worldpath.net
Web site: http://www.riverhaven.org.

†**Freeman, W. H. & Co.,** *(0-7167)* Div. of Holtzbrinck Publishers, Orders Addr.: 16365 James Madison Hwy., Gordonsville, VA 22942 Tel 540-672-7600; Toll Free Fax: 800-672-2054; Toll Free: 888-330-8477 (orders & customer service); Edit Addr.: 41 Madison Ave., 37th Flr., New York, NY 10010 (SAN 290-6864) Tel 212-576-9400; Fax: 212-689-2383; Toll Free: 800-903-3019
E-mail: webmaster@whfreeman.com
Web site: http://www.whfreeman.com
Dist(s): **Holtzbrinck Pubs.**; *CIP.*

Freestone Imprint of Peachtree Pubs., Ltd.

Freestone Publishing Co., *(0-913512)* P.O. Box 398, Monroe, UT 84754 (SAN 206-4154) Tel 435-527-3738
E-mail: freestone@hubwest
Dist(s): **Bookpeople**
New Leaf Distributing Co., Inc..

Fremantle Arts Centre Pr. (AUS) *(1-86368; 0-909144; 0-949206; 1-920731) Dist. by* **Intl Spec Bk.**

French & European Pubns., Inc., *(0-320; 0-7859; 0-8288)* Rockefeller Ctr. Promenade, 610 Fifth Ave., New York, NY 10020-2497 (SAN 206-8109) Tel 212-581-8810; Fax: 212-265-1094
E-mail: frenchbookstore@aol.com
Web site: http://www.frencheuropean.com.

French, Samuel Inc., *(0-573)* 45 W. 25th St., New York, NY 10010-2751 Tel 212-206-8990; Fax: 212-206-1429
E-mail: samuelfrench@earthlink.net
Web site: http://www.samuelfrench.com.

Friedman, Michael Publishing Group, Inc., *(0-9627134; 1-56799; 1-58663; 1-4114)* Div. of Barnes & Noble, Inc., 122 Fifth Ave., Fifth Flr., New York, NY 10011 (SAN 248-9732) Tel 212-685-6610; Fax: 212-633-3327; *Imprints:* MetroBooks (MetroBooks)
E-mail: rlamarche@bn.com
Web site: http://www.metrobooks.com
Dist(s): **Hervey's Booklink & Cookbook Warehouse**
Sterling Publishing Co., Inc..

Friends General Conference *See* **Quaker Press of Friends General Conference**

†**Friends United Pr.,** *(0-913408; 0-944350)* 101 Quaker Hill Dr., Richmond, IN 47374 (SAN 201-5803) Tel 765-962-7573; Fax: 765-966-1293; Toll Free: 800-537-8839
E-mail: friendspress@fum.org; barbaram@fum.org
Web site: http://www.fum.org
Dist(s): **Independent Pubs. Group**; *CIP.*

†**Friendship Pr.,** *(0-377)* Subs. of National Council of the Churches of Christ USA, Orders Addr.: c/o Friendship Pr. Distribution Office, P.O. Box 37844, Cincinnati, OH 45222-0844 (SAN 201-5781) Tel 513-948-8733; Fax: 513-761-3722; Toll Free: 800-889-5733; Edit Addr.: 475 Riverside Dr., Rm. 860, New York, NY 10115 (SAN 201-5773) Tel 212-870-2496; Fax: 212-870-2550 Do not confuse with companies with the same name in Peoria, AZ, Santa Rosa, CA
Web site: http://www.ncccuga.org; *CIP.*

Frog, Ltd., *(1-883319; 1-58394)* Div. of North Atlantic Bks., Orders Addr.: P.O. Box 12327, Berkeley, CA 94712 Tel 510-559-8277; Fax: 510-559-8279; Toll Free: 800-337-2665 (orders only)
E-mail: orders@northatlanticbooks.com
Web site: http://www.northatlanticbooks.com
Dist(s): **Paladin Pr.**
Publishers Group West.

Froginhood & Friends, Inc., *(1-892812)* Orders Addr.: P.O. Box 1745, Safety Harbor, FL 34695 (SAN 299-9277) Tel 727-797-6343; Fax: 727-797-6453; Edit Addr.: 404 Main St., Safety Harbor, FL 34695
E-mail: jonas@froginhood.com
Web site: http://www.froginhood.com
Dist(s): **Biblio Distribution.**

Front Street Imprint of Front Street, Inc.

Front Street, Inc., *(1-886910; 1-932425)* 862 Haywood Rd., Asheville, NC 28806 Tel 828-236-3097; Fax: 828-236-3098; *Imprints:* Front Street (Front Street)
E-mail: contactus@frontstreetbooks.com
Web site: http://www.frontstreetbooks.com
Dist(s): **Lectorum Pubns., Inc.**
Publishers Group West.

Front Street/Cricket Books *See* **Cricket Bks.**

Frontline Communications *See* **YWAM Publishing**

Fulcrum, Incorporated *See* **Fulcrum Publishing**

†**Fulcrum Publishing,** *(0-912347; 1-55591; 1-56373)* 16100 Table Mountain Pkwy., Suite 300, Golden, CO 80403 (SAN 200-2825) Tel 303-277-1623; Fax: 303-279-7111; Toll Free Fax: 800-726-7112; Toll Free: 800-992-2908
E-mail: dianneh@fulcrum-books.com
Web site: http://www.fulcrum-books.com; http://www.fulcrum-gardening.com
Dist(s): **Lone Pine Publishing**; *CIP.*

Full Cast Audio, *(0-9717540; 1-932076)* 618 Westcott St., 1st Flr., Syracuse, NY 13210 Toll Free: 800-871-6809
Web site: http://www.fullcastaudio.com.

Full Quart Pr. Imprint of Holly Hall Pubns., Inc.

Fun With the Law, Inc., *(1-929905)* One Utah Ctr. 201 S. Main St., No. 900, Salt Lake City, UT 84111 Tel 801-535-4335 (phone fax); Fax: 801-621-6953
E-mail: Garth@orijins.com.

Fundbuilder$, U.S.A., *(1-891989)* 2900 N. East St., Lansing, MI 48906 Tel 517-482-1955; Fax: 517-482-6627; Toll Free: 888-880-1955.

Futech Educational Products, Inc., *(0-9627001; 1-889192)* 2999 N. 44th St., Suite 225, Phoenix, AZ 85018-7248 Tel 602-808-8765; Fax: 602-278-5667; Toll Free: 800-597-6278.

Futech Interactive Products, Inc., *(1-58224; 1-879332)* Div. of Futech Interactive Products, N16 W23390 Stoneridge Dr., Waukesha, WI 53188 Tel 414-544-2001; Fax: 414-544-2022; Toll Free: 800-541-2205.

Future Education, Incorporated *See* **Future Horizons, Inc.**

Future Horizons, Inc., *(1-885477; 1-932565)* 721 W. Abram St., Arlington, TX 76013 Tel 817-277-0727; Fax: 817-277-2270; Toll Free: 800-489-0727
E-mail: victoria@futurehorizons-autism.com
Web site: http://www.FutureHorizons-autism.com.

GAGA, *(0-9704202)* 3097 Roberts Ferry Rd., NE, Solon, IA 52333 Tel 319-848-7412
E-mail: jgokio@aol.com.

GAM Pubns., *(0-87377)* P.O. Box 25, Sterling, VA 20167 (SAN 204-6784) Toll Free: 888-689-2243.

GBL Publishing Co., *(0-9638969)* 1275 Pierce Ave., Columbus, OH 43227 Tel 614-239-8596; Fax: 614-338-8702.

G C B Publishing *See* **Holly Hall Pubns., Inc.**

GCT, Inc., *(0-937659; 1-57219)* Orders Addr.: P.O. Box 6448, Mobile, AL 36660-0448 (SAN 659-2325) Tel 334-478-4700; Toll Free: 800-814-1548.

G C T Publishing Company, Incorporated *See* **GCT, Inc.**

G. D. Stewart Publishing, *(0-9712332)* 3735 Mercedes Pl., Canfield, OH 44406
E-mail: nstewart01@sceinet.com.

G. P. Putnam's Sons Imprint of Penguin Group (USA) Inc.

G. P. Putnam's Sons Imprint of Penguin Putnam Bks. for Young Readers

GRM Assocs., *(0-933813; 0-929093)* 290 W. End Ave., 16A, New York, NY 11111 Tel 212-874-5964; Fax: 212-874-6425; *Imprints:* Taylor Productions (Taylor Prods)
Dist(s): **Independent Pubs. Group.**

GR Publishing, *(0-9668530)* 460 Brookside Way, Felton, CA 95018
E-mail: pub@grandmarose.com
Web site: http://www.grandmarose.com.

G Sharp Productions, *(0-9669852)* 220 Oak Meadow Dr., Los Gatos, CA 95032 Tel 408-354-0047; Fax: 408-399-5397
E-mail: gjkiii@aol.com; gikiii@aol.com
Web site: http://www.gsharpproductions.com.

Gabriel Publishing, *(0-9630908; 1-884543)* Orders Addr.: P.O. Box 1047, Waynesboro, GA 30830-2047 Tel 706-554-1594; Fax: 706-554-7444; Toll Free: 866-732-6657; Edit Addr.: 129 Mobilizaiton Dr., Waynesboro, GA 30830
E-mail: info@omlit.om.org
Web site: http://www.gabriel-resources.com
Dist(s): **Gabriel Resources.**

Gabriel's Gatherings, Inc., *(0-9649962)* 10942 Katlian Dr., Eagle River, AK 99577 Tel 907-694-4445; Fax: 907-694-1515.

Galaxy Children's Large Print Imprint of BBC Audiobooks America

Galde Pr., Inc., *(1-880090; 1-931942)* Orders Addr.: P.O. Box 460, Lakeville, MN 55044-460 Tel 952-891-5991; Fax: 952-891-6091; Toll Free: 800-777-3454 (orders only)
E-mail: pgalde@galdepress.com
Web site: http://www.galdepress.com.

†**Gale Group,** *(0-13; 0-7876; 0-8103; 0-936474; 1-57302; 1-878623; 1-59413; 1-59414; 1-59415; 1-4144)* Subs. of The Thomson Corp., Orders Addr.: P.O. Box 9187, Farmington Hills, MI 48333-9187 Toll Free Fax: 800-414-5043; Toll Free: 800-877-4253; Edit Addr.: 27500 Drake Rd., Farmington Hills, MI 48331-3535 (SAN 213-4373) Tel 248-699-4253; a/o Wheeler Publishing, 295 Kennedy Memorial Dr., Waterville, ME 04901 Toll Free: 800-223-1244; *Imprints:* Macmillan Reference USA (Macmillan Ref); Blackbirch Press, Incorporated (Blackbirch Pr); Lucent Books (Lucent Books); Five Star (Five Star ME); Wheeler Publishing, Incorporated (Wheel)
E-mail: galeord@galegroup.com
Web site: http://www.galegroup.com
Dist(s): **netLibrary, Inc.**; *CIP.*

Gale Hill Bks., *(0-9645809)* 109 Irving St., Cambridge, MA 02138 Tel 617-491-3639.

†**Gallaudet Univ. Pr.,** *(0-913580; 0-930323; 1-56368)* 800 Florida Ave., NE, Washington, DC 20002-3695 (SAN 205-261X) Tel 202-651-5488; Fax: 202-651-5489; Toll Free Fax: 800-621-8476; Toll Free: 888-630-9347 (TTY)
E-mail: valencia.simmons@gallaudet.edu
Web site: http://www.gupress.gallaudet.edu/
Dist(s): **Chicago Distribution Ctr.**
Univ. of Chicago Pr.; *CIP.*

Galleon Pubns., *(0-9645810)* 4345 Ileen Cir., Idaho Falls, ID 83406 (SAN 298-5527) Tel 208-523-6252 Do not confuse with Galleon Pubns., Oklahoma City, OK.

Gallery Press *See* **Gallery Press Publishing, Inc.**

Gallery Press Publishing, Inc., *(0-9717117)* 1344 King St., Bellingham, WA 98229 Tel 360-733-1101; Fax: 360-647-2758; Toll Free: 800-237-4762
E-mail: bergsma@bergsma.com
Web site: http://www.bergsma.com.

Gallimard, Editions (FRA) *(2-07) Dist. by* **Distribks Inc.**

Gallopade International, *(0-635; 0-7933; 0-935326; 1-55609)* 665 Highway 74 South, Suite 600, Peachtree City, GA 30269 (SAN 213-8441) Tel 770-631-4222; Toll Free Fax: 800-871-2979; Toll Free: 800-536-2438; *Imprints:* Marsh, Carole Books (C Mrsh Bks)
E-mail: sales@gallopade.com
Web site: http://www.gallopade.com.

Gallopade: Publishing Group *See* **Gallopade International**

Gannam/Kubat Pubs., *(0-945201)* 16200 Trojan Way, La Mirada, CA 90638-5600 (SAN 246-7046) Tel 714-528-8683.

†**Garland Publishing, Inc.,** *(0-8153; 0-8240)* Member of Taylor & Francis, Inc., 29 W. 35th St., Flr. 10, New York, NY 10001-2299 Tel 212-216-7800; Fax: 212-564-7854; Toll Free: 800-627-6273 (orders)
E-mail: info@garland.com
Web site: http://www.garlandscience.com; http://www.garlandpub.com
Dist(s): **Taylor & Francis, Inc.**
netLibrary, Inc.; *CIP.*

Garland S T P M Press *See* **Garland Publishing, Inc.**

†**Garrett Educational Corp.,** *(0-944483; 1-56074)* Orders Addr.: P.O. Box 1588, Ada, OK 74820 (SAN 169-6955) Tel 580-332-6884; Fax: 580-332-1560; Toll Free: 800-654-9366; Edit Addr.: 130 E. 13th St., Ada, OK 74820 (SAN 243-2722)
E-mail: mail@garrettbooks.com
Web site: http://www.garrettbooks.com; *CIP.*

Gato Pr., The, *(0-9647200; 1-930811)* 61 Patillo Rd., Stockbridge, GA 30281 Tel 404-747-7609
E-mail: gatopress@mndspring.com
Web site: http://www.gatopress.com.

Gaviota Ediciones (ESP) *(84-392) Dist. by* **Lectorum Pubns.**

Names

Gayle Publishing Co., *(0-9678436)* 536 Santa Fe Trail, No. 253, Irving, TX 75063 Tel 972-401-1119 Do not confuse with Gayle Publishing, Houston, TX
E-mail: bridgetx@swbell.net
Web site: http://www.grandjuryconnections.com
Dist(s): **Baker & Taylor Bks.**
Hervey's Booklink & Cookbook Warehouse.

Gee, Genese Celeste, *(0-9719935)* 3749 Greenmoor Gardens Ct., Florissant, MO 63034
E-mail: aebballgirl@usa.com.

Gefen Bks., *(0-86343; 965-229)* 12 New St., Hewlett, NY 11557-2012 Tel 516-295-2805; Fax: 516-295-2739; Toll Free: 800-477-5257
E-mail: gefenny@gefenpublishing.com
Web site: http://www.israelbooks.com.

Gefen Publishing Hse., Ltd (ISR) *(965-229) Dist. by* **Gefen Bks.**

Geller, Norman Pubs., *(0-915753)* P.O. Box 73, Newton Centre, MA 02459 (SAN 293-9681) Tel 617-928-0444; Toll Free: 800-261-0081 (phone/fax)
E-mail: ngellerpub@aol.com.

Genesis Communications, Inc., *(0-9637311; 1-58169)* P.O. Box 91011, Mobile, AL 36691-1011 Tel 334-665-0022; Fax: 334-665-4511; Toll Free: 800-367-8203; *Imprints:* Evergreen Press (Evergrn Pr AL)
E-mail: StreamJB@aol.com; GenesisCom@aol.com
Dist(s): **Streamwood Distribution.**

Gently Worded Bks., LLC, *(0-9708940)* Orders Addr.: 211 Old Santa Fe Trail, Santa Fe, NM 87501; Edit Addr.: P.O. Box 1326, Santa Fe, NM 87504-1326 Tel 505-983-6134; Fax: 505-984-7921
E-mail: chasjune@aol.com
Web site: http://www.gentlywordedbooks.com.

George, J. C. Enterprises, *(0-921369)* 2719 Lake Rd., Wilson, NY 14172.

Geringer, Laura Bk. Imprint of HarperCollins Children's Bk. Group

Gerl, Perrine & Brasher Publishing *See* **Gerl Publishing**

Gerl Publishing, *(0-9663820)* 1230 Old Robeline Rd., Apt. C110, Natchitoches, LA 71457 Tel 318-356-0260 ; Fax: 318-352-2782
E-mail: euphoria@cp-tel.net.

Getty, J. Paul Trust Publications *See* **Getty Pubns.**

†Getty Pubns., *(0-89236; 0-941103)* Orders Addr.: P.O. Box 49659, Los Angeles, CA 90049-0659 Tel 310-440-7333; Fax: 818-779-0051; Edit Addr.: 1200 Getty Ctr. Dr., Suite 500, Los Angeles, CA 90049-1682 (SAN 208-2276) Tel 310-440-7365; Fax: 310-440-7706; Toll Free: 800-223-3431
E-mail: pubsinfo@getty.edu
Web site: http://www.getty.edu/publications
Dist(s): **Lectorum Pubns., Inc.**
Libros Sin Fronteras; *CIP.*

Ghost Hunter Productions, *(0-9717234)* P.O. Box 1199, Helena, MT 56924-1199
E-mail: business@theghosthunteronline.com; business@earthacademy7.com
Web site: http://www.theghosthunteronline.com; http://www.earthacademy7.com.

Ghostdancer Press, Incorporated *See* **Grey Ghost Pr., Inc.**

Gibson, C. R. Co., *(0-7667; 0-8378; 0-937970; 0-7053)* 401 BNA Dr., Bldg 200, Suite 600, Nashville, TN 37217 Toll Free: 800-243-6004 (ext. 2895)
E-mail: customerservice@crgibson.com
Web site: http://www.andersonpress.com.

GiNancy Publishing, *(0-9648843)* 2702 N. 96th Ave., Wausau, WI 54401 Tel 715-675-7578.

Gingerbread Hse., *(0-940112)* 602 Montauk Hwy., Westhampton Beach, NY 11978 (SAN 217-0760) Tel 631-288-5119; Fax: 631-288-5179 Do not confuse with Gingerbread House, The, Savannah GA
Web site: http://www.gingerbreadbooks.com
Dist(s): **Independent Pubs. Group.**

Gingham Dog Pr. Imprint of McGraw-Hill Children's Publishing

Gladstone Publishing, *(0-944599; 1-57460)* Div. of The Bruce Hamilton Co., Orders Addr.: P.O. Box 2079, Prescott, AZ 86302 (SAN 244-6197) Tel 602-776-1300; Fax: 602-445-7536 Do not confuse with Gladstone Publishing, Voorhees, NJ
E-mail: info@gladstonepublishing.com
Web site: http://www.brucehamilton.com/gladstone/.

Gladstone Publishing, *(1-928681)* Div. of Direct Konnections, Inc., Orders Addr.: P.O. Box 926, Voorhees, NJ 08043-0926 Tel 856-772-3820; Fax: 856-772-9596; Toll Free: 888-824-3810; Edit Addr.: 2901 Hamilton Dr., Voorhees, NJ 08043-0926 (SAN 254-8410) Do not confuse with Gladstone Publishing, Prescott, AZ
E-mail: info@gladstonepublishing.com
Web site: http://www.gladstonepublishing.com; http://www.kidsbooks2000.com.

Global Age Publishing/Global Academy Pr., *(1-887176)* 16057 Tampa Palms Blvd., W., No. 219, Tampa, FL 33647 Tel 813-991-4982; Fax: 813-973-8166
Dist(s): **Baker & Taylor Bks..**

Global Classroom, The, *(0-9659945; 1-58259)* Orders Addr.: P.O. Box 57218, Washington, DC 20036-9998 Tel 202-496-9780; Fax: 202-496-9781; Toll Free Fax: 888-665-2276; Toll Free: 888-456-2399; Edit Addr.: 1270 New Hampshire Ave., NW, Washington, DC 20036
E-mail: support@globalclassroom.com; info@globalclassroom.com
Web site: http://www.globalclassroom.com.

Global Commitment Publishing, *(1-884931)* Div. of Alpert & Assocs., 3544 Winfield Ln., NW, Washington, DC 20007 Tel 202-338-4975; Fax: 202-835-0668; 5505 Connecticut Ave., Washington, DC 20015.

GlobalFriends Collection, Inc., *(1-58056)* 9255 Sonoma Hwy., Kenwood, CA 95452-9031 Tel 415-345-1200; Fax: 415-345-5561; Toll Free: 800-393-5421 (Customer Service only); *Imprints:* GlobalFriends Press (GlobalFr Pr)
E-mail: traci@globalfriends.com
Web site: http://www.globalfriends.com.

GlobalFriends Pr. Imprint of GlobalFriends Collection, Inc.

Globe Fearon Educational Publishing, *(0-13; 0-8224; 0-8359; 0-87065; 0-88102; 0-912925; 0-915510; 1-55555; 1-55675)* Div. of Pearson Education Corporate Communications, Orders Addr.: 4350 Equity Dr., P.O. Box 2649, Columbus, OH 43216-2649 Toll Free Fax: 800-393-3156; Toll Free: 800-321-3106 (customer service); 800-848-9500; Edit Addr.: One Lake St., Upper Saddle River, NJ 07458
Web site: http://www.globefearon.com/
Dist(s): **Cambridge Bk. Co.**
IFSTA.

†Globe Pequot Pr., The, *(0-7627; 0-87106; 0-88742; 0-914788; 0-933469; 0-934802; 0-941130; 1-56440; 1-57034; 1-58574; 1-59228)* Div. of Morris Communications Corp., Orders Addr.: P.O. Box 480, Guilford, CT 06437-0480 (SAN 201-9892) Toll Free Fax: 800-820-2329 (in Connecticut); Toll Free: 800-243-0495 (24 hours); Edit Addr.: 246 Goose Ln., Guilford, CT 06437 Tel 203-458-4500; Fax: 203-458-4604; *Imprints:* Falcon (Fal)
E-mail: info@globe-pequot.com; adessaint@globe-pequot.com
Web site: http://www.globe-pequot.com
Dist(s): **Paladin Pr.**; *CIP.*

Glo'worm (GBR) *(1-902172) Dist. by* **Last Gasp.**

†Godine, David R. Pub., *(0-87923; 1-56792; 1-57423)* Orders Addr.: P.O. Box 450, Jaffrey, NH 03452 Tel 603-532-4100; Fax: 603-532-5940; Toll Free Fax: 800-226-0934; Toll Free: 800-344-4771; Edit Addr.: 9 Hamilton Pl., Boston, MA 02108-4715 (SAN 213-4381) Tel 617-451-9600; Fax: 617-350-0250; *Imprints:* Pocket Paragon (Pocket Para)
E-mail: info@godine.com; order@godine.com
Web site: http://www.godine.com
Dist(s): **Baker & Taylor International**; *CIP.*

Gold Lace Publishing, LLC, *(0-9672074)* 8049 Rising Ridge Rd., Bethesda, MD 20817 Tel 301-767-0846; Fax: 301-767-0847
E-mail: acv1898@erols.com.

Golden Bks. Imprint of Random Hse. Children's Bks.

Golden Bks. Adult Publishing Group Imprint of St. Martin's Pr.

Golden Rings Publishing Co., *(0-9633607)* 21 Brittany Blvd., Marlton, NJ 08053 Tel 856-596-9190; Fax: 856-596-7391; Toll Free: 800-433-6173
E-mail: grpub@aol.com.

Golden Triangle Bks. Imprint of Univ. of Pittsburgh Pr.

Golden Wings Enterprises, *(0-9700103)* P.O. Box 468, Orem, UT 84059-0468
E-mail: BJ@bjrowley.com; bjrowley@juno.com
Web site: http://www.bjrowley.com.

Goldstar Magic, *(0-9716488)* 611 Pennsylvania Ave., SE, No.121, Washington, DC 20003 Tel 202-675-0684
E-mail: terry@goldstarmagic.com
Web site: http://www.goldstarmagic.com.

Gollancz, Victor (GBR) *(0-575) Dist. by* **Trafalgar.**

Gomer Pr. Imprint of Beekman Pubs., Inc.

Gomer Pr. (GBR) *(0-85088; 0-86383; 1-85902) Dist. by* **St Mut.**

Good Apple Imprint of McGraw-Hill Children's Publishing

†Good Bks., *(0-934672; 1-56148)* Subs. of Good Enterprises, Ltd., Orders Addr.: P.O. Box 419, Intercourse, PA 17534 (SAN 693-9597) Tel 717-768-7171; Fax: 717-768-3433; Toll Free: 800-762-7171; Edit Addr.: 3510 Old Philadelphia Pike, Intercourse, PA 17534-0419
E-mail: custserv@goodbks.com; mgood@goodbks.com
Web site: http://www.goodbks.com
Dist(s): **Baker & Taylor Bks.**
Brodart Co.
Distributors, The
FaithWorks; *CIP.*

Good Growing Bks., *(1-887403)* 1311 Bishop, Grosse Pointe Park, MI 48230 Tel 313-884-8456
E-mail: jpallas@gatecom.com.

Good Year Bks. Imprint of Celebration Pr.

Goodale Publishing, *(0-9662945)* 900 Fort Street Mall, No. 1725, Honolulu, HI 96813-3721 Do not confuse with Goodale Publishing, Minneapolis, MN
E-mail: info@goodalepublishing.com; jhgruenberg@aol.com
Web site: http://www.goodalepublishing.com.

GoodyGoody Bks., *(0-9702546)* P.O. Box 1073, Sun City, AZ 85372-1073
E-mail: goody4u@prodigy.net
Web site: htp://charliethecat.com.

Gospel Light Pubns., *(0-8307)* 2300 Knoll Dr., Ventura, CA 93003 (SAN 299-0873) Tel 805-644-9721; Fax: 805-289-0200; Toll Free: 800-446-7735 (orders only); *Imprints:* Regal Books (Regal Bks) Do not confuse with companies with similar names in Brooklyn, NY, Delight, AR
E-mail: info@gospellight.com; jessieminassian@gospellight.com
Web site: http://www.gospellight.com
Dist(s): **CRC Pubns.**
Christian Bk. Distributors.

Gospel Missionary Union, *(0-9617490; 1-890940)* 10000 N. Oak Trafficway, Kansas City, MO 64155 (SAN 664-1830) Tel 816-734-8500; Fax: 816-734-4601
E-mail: info@gmu.org
Web site: http://www.gmu.org.

†Gospel Publishing Hse., *(0-88243)* Div. of General Council of the Assemblies of God, 1445 N. Boonville Ave., Springfield, MO 65802-1894 (SAN 206-8826) Tel 417-831-8000; Fax: 417-862-5881; Toll Free Fax: 800-328-0294; Toll Free: 800-641-4310 (orders only)
E-mail: webmaster@gph.com
Web site: http://www.gospelpublishing.com
Dist(s): **Appalachian Bible Co.**
Ingram Bk. Co.
Riverside
Spring Arbor Distributors, Inc.; *CIP.*

Gossamer Bks., *(0-9729016)* 444 Eastwood Dr., Petaluma, CA 94954 (SAN 255-2671) Tel 707-765-1992; Fax: 707-765-6507 Do not confuse with Gossamer Books LLC in Belmont, CA
E-mail: dcr530@cs.com.

Gould, Marilyn *See* **Allied Crafts Pr.**

Gramercy Imprint of Random Hse. Value Publishing

Grand Canyon Assn., *(0-938216)* P.O. Box 399, Grand Canyon, AZ 86023 (SAN 215-7675) Tel 520-638-2481; Fax: 520-638-2484; Toll Free: 800-858-2808
E-mail: gcassociation@grandcanyon.org
Web site: http://www.grandcanyon.org
Dist(s): **Yosemite Assn..**

Grand Canyon Natural History Association *See* **Grand Canyon Assn.**

Grand Unification Pr., Inc., *(0-9700453)* 2380 Wayne St., Orrville, OH 44667
E-mail: grandupress@aol.com; info@grandupress.com
Web site: http://www.grandupress.com.

Grandma Dottie Enterprises LLC *See* **PeriWrinkle Productions, Inc.**

Grandview Publishing Co., *(1-880114)* Orders Addr.: P.O. Box 2863, Jackson, WY 83001-2863 Fax: 307-734-0210; Toll Free: 800-525-7344
E-mail: kenthomasma@blissnet.com.

Names

Hampton-Brown Bks., *(0-7362; 0-917837; 1-56334)* Orders Addr.: P.O. Box 369, Marina, CA 93933 Tel 408-384-9695; Fax: 408-384-8940; Edit Addr.: 26385 Carmel Rancho Blvd., Suite 200, Carmel, CA 93923 (SAN 657-145X) Tel 408-625-3666; Fax: 408-625-8619; Toll Free: 800-933-3510
Web site: http://www.hampton-brown.com.

†Hancock Hse. Pubs., *(0-88839; 0-919654)* 1431 Harrison Ave., Blaine, WA 98230-5005 (SAN 665-7079) Tel 604-538-1114; Fax: 604-538-2262; Toll Free Fax: 800-983-2262; Toll Free: 800-938-1114; 19313 Zero Ave., Surrey, BC V3S 9R9
E-mail: sales@hancockhouse.com
Web site: http://www.hancockhouse.com
Dist(s): **Baker & Taylor Bks.**; *CIP.*

Hand-In-Hand Bks. Imprint of Introspect Bks.

Handprint Bks., *(1-929766; 1-59354)* 413 Sixth Ave., Brooklyn, NY 11215
Web site: http://www.handprintbooks.com
Dist(s): **Chronicle Bks. LLC.**

Harbour Bks., *(0-9643672; 1-889535)* 4815 N. 400 W., Park City, UT 84098-6002.

Harcourt Brace & Company *See* **Harcourt Trade Pubs.**

Harcourt Brace Jovanovich College Publishers *See* **Harcourt College Pubs.**

Harcourt Brace School Publishers *See* **Harcourt School Pubs.**

Harcourt Children's Bks. (CAN) *(0-15) Dist. by* **Harcourt.**

Harcourt Children's Bks., *(0-15)* Div. of Harcourt, Inc., Orders Addr.: 6277 Sea Harbor Dr., Orlando, FL 32887 Toll Free Fax: 800-235-0256; Toll Free: 800-543-1918; Edit Addr.: 15 E. 26th St., 15th Flr., New York, NY 10010 Tel 212-592-1000; *Imprints:* Green Light Readers (Green Light Read); Gulliver Books (Gulliver Bks); Harcourt Paperbacks (Harcourt Pbk); Harcourt Young Classics (Harcourt Young); Odyssey Classics (Odyssey Class); Red Wagon Books (Red Wagon Bks); Silver Whistle (Silver Whistle); Voyager Books/Libros Viajeros (Voyage Libros); Magic Carpet Books (Magic Carpet)
E-mail: aporter@harcourt.com
Web site: http://www.HarcourtBooks.com
Dist(s): **Harcourt Trade Pubs..**

Harcourt College Pubs., *(0-03; 0-15)* Div. of Thomson Corp., The, Orders Addr.: 10650 Toebben Dr., Independence, KY 41051 (SAN 250-0086) Toll Free Fax: 800-487-8488 (customer service); Toll Free: 800-354-9706 (orders, inquiries); Edit Addr.: 301 Commerce St., Suite 3700 City Center Tower Two, Fort Worth, TX 76102 (SAN 297-4789) Tel 817-334-7500; Fax: 817-334-7844
E-mail: wlittle@harbrace.com
Web site: http://www.harcourtcollege.com/.

Harcourt Paperbacks Imprint of Harcourt Children's Bks.

Harcourt School Pubs., *(0-15)* Div. of Harcourt, Inc., 6277 Sea Harbor Dr., Orlando, FL 32887 (SAN 299-4585) Tel 407-345-2000; Fax: 407-352-3445; Toll Free Fax: 800-874-6418 (orders); Toll Free: 800-225-5425 (orders)
Web site: http://www.harcourtschool.com.

†Harcourt Trade Pubs., *(0-15)* Div. of Harcourt, Inc., Orders Addr.: 6277 Sea Harbor Dr., Orlando, FL 32887 (SAN 200-285X) Tel 619-699-6707; Toll Free Fax: 800-235-0256; Toll Free: 800-543-1918 (trade orders, inquiries, claims); Edit Addr.: 525 B St., Suite 1900, San Diego, CA 92101-4495 (SAN 200-2736) Tel 619-231-6616; 15 E. 26th St., 15th Flr., New York, NY 10010 Tel 212-592-1000; *Imprints:* Harvest Books (Harvest Bks)
E-mail: apbcs@harcourtbrace.com
Web site: http://www.harcourtbooks.com; *CIP.*

Harcourt Young Classics Imprint of Harcourt Children's Bks.

Hard Shell Word Factory, *(1-58200; 0-7599)* Orders Addr.: P.O. Box 161, Amherst Junction, WI 54407 (SAN 631-4899) Tel 715-824-5542; Fax: 715-824-3875; Edit Addr.: 8941 Loberg Rd., Amherst Junction, WI 54407
E-mail: books@hardshell.com
Web site: http://www.hardshell.com.

Hardscrabble Bks. Imprint of Univ. Pr. of New England

Harlequin Mills & Boon, Ltd. (GBR) *(0-263; 0-373; 0-204) Dist. by* **Ulverscroft US.**

Harlo Pr., *(0-8187)* 50 Victor Ave., Detroit, MI 48203 (SAN 202-2745) Tel 313-883-3600
Dist(s): **Mustard Seed Pubns..**

Harmony Imprint of Crown Publishing Group

Harmony Hse. Pubs., *(0-916509; 1-56469)* Orders Addr.: P.O. Box 90, Prospect, KY 40059 (SAN 298-5446) Tel 502-228-4446; Fax: 502-228-2010; Toll Free: 800-809-9334; Edit Addr.: 1008 Kent Rd., Goshen, KY 40026 (SAN 295-4257)
E-mail: HarmonyPub@aol.com.

Harmony Raine & Co. Imprint of Buccaneer Bks., Inc.

Harper Festival Imprint of HarperCollins Children's Bk. Group

Harper Religious Books *See* **HarperSanFrancisco**

Harper Trophy Imprint of HarperCollins Children's Bk. Group

HarperAudio Imprint of HarperTrade

HarperChildren's Audio Imprint of HarperCollins Children's Bk. Group

HarperChildren's Audio, 10 E. 53rd St., New York, NY 10022-5299 Toll Free: 800-242-7737.

HarperCollins Imprint of HarperTrade

HarperCollins (NZL) *(1-86950) Dist. by* **Antipodes Bks.**

HarperCollins Children's Bk. Group, *(0-06; 0-380; 0-688; 0-690; 0-694)* Div. of HarperCollins US, Orders Addr.: 1000 Keystone Industrial Pk., Scranton, PA 18512-4621 Toll Free Fax: 800-822-4090; Toll Free: 800-242-7737; Edit Addr.: a/o Children's Editorial Dept., 1350 Avenue Of The Americas, New York, NY 10019 Tel 212-261-6500; Fax: 212-207-7192; *Imprints:* Harper Trophy (HarpTrophy); Harper Festival (HarpFestival); Cotler, Joanna Books (J Cotler); Geringer, Laura Book (L Geringer); Greenwillow Books (Greenwillow Bks); HarperTempest (Tempest); Avon (Avon Child); HarperChildren's Audio (HarpChildAudio); Tegen, Katherine Books (K Tegen Bks)
Web site: http://www.harperchildrens.com
Dist(s): **HarperCollins Pubs.**
Lectorum Pubns., Inc..

†HarperCollins Pubs., *(0-00; 0-06; 0-688; 0-690; 0-694; 0-7322)* Div. of News Corp., Orders Addr.: 1000 Keystone Industrial Pk., Scranton, PA 18512-4621 (SAN 215-3742) Tel 570-941-1500; Toll Free Fax: 800-822-4090; Toll Free: 800-242-7737 (orders only); Edit Addr.: 10 E. 53rd St., New York, NY 10022-5299 (SAN 200-2086) Tel 212-207-7000
Web site: http://www.harpercollins.com
Dist(s): **Comag Marketing Group**; *CIP.*

HarperCollins Pubs. Ltd. (GBR) *(0-00; 0-06; 0-261) Dist. by* **Trafalgar.**

HarperEntertainment Imprint of Morrow/Avon

HarperInformation, *(0-06)* Div. of HarperCollins General Bks. Group, Orders Addr.: 1000 Keystone Industrial Pk., Scranton, PA 18512-4021 Toll Free Fax: 800-822-4090; Toll Free: 800-242-7737; Edit Addr.: 10 E. 53rd St., New York, NY 10022-5299 Tel 212-207-7000; *Imprints:* Access Press (Access Pr)
Web site: http://www.harpercollins.com/
Dist(s): **HarperCollins Pubs..**

†HarperSanFrancisco, *(0-06; 0-85924; 0-86683)* Div. of HarperCollins General Bks. Group, Orders Addr.: 1000 Keystone Industrial Pk., Scranton, PA 18512 Toll Free Fax: 800-822-4090; Toll Free: 800-242-7737; Edit Addr.: 353 Sacramento St., Suite 500, San Francisco, CA 94111 Tel 415-477-4400; Fax: 415-477-4444
Web site: http://www.harpercollins.com
Dist(s): **HarperCollins Pubs.**; *CIP.*

HarperTempest Imprint of HarperCollins Children's Bk. Group

HarperTorch Imprint of Morrow/Avon

HarperTrade, *(0-06; 0-688)* Div. of HarperCollins General Bks. Group, Orders Addr.: 1000 Keystone Industrial Pk., Scranton, PA 18512-4021 Toll Free Fax: 800-822-4090; Toll Free: 800-242-7737; Edit Addr.: 10 E. 53rd St., New York, NY 10022 Tel 212-207-7000; Fax: 217-207-7633; Toll Free: 800-242-7737 (orders); *Imprints:* HarperCollins (HarpCollins); Perennial (Perennial); Amistad Press (Amistad); HarperAudio (HarperAudio); Caedmon (Caed); Rayo (Rayo)
Web site: http://www.harpercollins.com/
Dist(s): **Bilingual Pubns. Co., The**
Giron Bks.
HarperCollins Pubs.
Lectorum Pubns., Inc.
Perelandra, Ltd.
Thorndike Pr..

Harpswell Pr. Imprint of Tilbury Hse. Pubs.

Harrington, Denis J. Pub., *(0-9672290)* 6207 Fushsimi Ct., Burke, VA 22015-3451.

Harris, H. E. & Company *See* **Whitman Publishing LLC**

Hart Publishing, *(0-9644559)* 2509 Redwing Dr., Temple, TX 76502 Tel 254-778-2676 Do not confuse with companies with similar names in Spartanburg, SC or Great Falls, VA
E-mail: Cbhart635@aol.com.

†Harvard Common Pr., *(0-87645; 0-916782; 1-55832)* 535 Albany St., Boston, MA 02118 (SAN 208-6778) Tel 617-423-5803; Fax: 617-695-9794; Toll Free: 888-657-3755
E-mail: orders@harvardcommonpress.com
Web site: http://www.harvardcommonpress.com
Dist(s): **National Bk. Network**; *CIP.*

Harvest Bks. Imprint of Harcourt Trade Pubs.

Harvest Hse. Pubs., *(0-7369; 0-89081; 1-56507)* 990 Owen Loop, N., Eugene, OR 97402-9173 (SAN 207-4745) Tel 541-343-0123; Fax: 541-302-0731; Toll Free: 888-501-6991
E-mail: dietzm@harvesthousepubl.com
Web site: http://www.harvesthousepubl.com
Dist(s): **CRC Pubns.**
Twentieth Century Christian Bks..

Harvest Pubns., *(0-9654272)* 1928 Oxbow Rd., Minneapolis, KS 67467 Tel 913-392-2750 Do not confuse with companies with same name in Berkeley, CA, Arlington Heights, IL, Fort Worth, TX, Jacksonville, TX
E-mail: Adharvest@juno.com
Web site: http://www.pma-online.org/list/7345.html.

Hasbro, Inc., *(1-58228; 1-888208)* 1027 Newport Ave., Pawtucket, RI 02862 Tel 401-431-8697; Fax: 401-729-7160; Toll Free: 800-242-7276
Web site: http://www.hasbrocom/home.html.

Hastings Ende Design Partners, *(0-9700306)* 464 Wildwood Ln., Sewanee, TN 37375 Tel 931-598-0660; 615-598-0660; Fax: 931-598-5720; *Imprints:* Cosmic Aye (Cosmic Aye)
E-mail: janda@cafes.net.

Hastings Hse. Daytrips Pubs., *(0-8038)* 2601 Wells Ave., Suite 161, Fern Park, FL 32730 Tel 407-339-3600; Fax: 407-339-5900; Toll Free: 800-206-7822
E-mail: hhousebks@aol.com
Web site: http://www.daytripsbooks.com; http://www.hastingshousebooks.com
Dist(s): **Midpoint Trade Bks., Inc.**
Publishers Group West.

Hastings House Publishers *See* **Hastings Hse. Daytrips Pubs.**

Hats Off Bks. Imprint of Wheatmark, Inc.

Haven Bks., *(0-9659480; 1-58436)* 10153 1/2 Riverside Dr., Suite 629, North Hollywood, CA 91602 Tel 818-503-2518; Fax: 818-508-0299
E-mail: Havenbks@aol.com
Web site: http://www.havenbooks.net.

Havoc Publishing, *(1-57977; 0-7416)* 9808 Waples St., San Diego, CA 92121 Tel 858-638-8211; Fax: 858-638-9118; Toll Free: 800-222-2637
E-mail: mktg@havocpub.com
Web site: http://www.havocpub.com.

Hawaiian Service, Inc., *(0-930492)* 94-527 Puahi St., Waipahu, HI 96797-4208 (SAN 205-0463) Tel 808-676-5026; Fax: 808-676-5156.

Hawk Press *See* **Black Cat Bks.**

Hawkins, Beverly Studio & Gallery, *(0-9608084)* Orders Addr.: 2557E S. Crater Rd., Petersburg, VA 23803 (SAN 665-7087); Edit Addr.: 20104 Halloway Ave., Matoaca, VA 23803 (SAN 240-1495) Tel 804-861-9403.

†Haworth Pr., Inc., The, *(0-7890; 0-86656; 0-917724; 1-56022; 1-56023; 1-56024)* 10 Alice St., Binghamton, NY 13904-1580 (SAN 211-0156) Tel 607-722-5857; Fax: 607-722-6362; 607-722-1424; Toll Free Fax: 800-895-0582; Toll Free: 800-429-6784; *Imprints:* Southern Tier Editions (South Tier Edns)
E-mail: getinfo@haworthpressinc.com
Web site: http://www.haworthpressinc.com; http://www.haworthpressinc.com/journals/dds.asp
Dist(s): **Barnes & Noble, Inc.**
BookWorld Services, Inc.
Bookazine Co., Inc.
Bookpeople
Borders, Inc.
Distributors, The
Koen Bk. Distributors
Matthews Medical Bk. Co.
New Leaf Distributing Co., Inc.
Quality Bks., Inc.
Rittenhouse Bk. Distributors
SPD-Small Pr. Distribution
Unique Bks., Inc.
Waldenbooks, Inc.; *CIP.*

Hayden Imprint of New Riders Publishing

Names

Haypenny Pr., *(0-929885)* 32 Forest St., New Britain, CT 06052-1425 (SAN 250-9571) Fax: 860-832-9566 E-mail: ipsiverba@aol.com.

Hazelden Information & Educational Services *See* **Hazelden Publishing & Educational Services**

†Hazelden Publishing & Educational Services, *(0-89486; 0-89638; 0-935908; 0-942421; 1-56246; 1-56838; 1-59285)* 15215 Pleasant Valley Rd., P.O. Box 176, Center City, MN 55012-0176 (SAN 209-4010) Fax: 651-213-4577; Toll Free: 800-328-9000
E-mail: kbuzick@hazeld.org
Web site: http://www.hazelden.org
Dist(s): **Health Communications, Inc.**; *CIP.*

Heahstan Pr., The, *(0-9604244)* P.O. Box 954, Denton, TX 76202-0954 (SAN 214-3127) Tel 940-387-7730.

†Health Communications, Inc., *(0-922352; 0-932194; 0-941405; 1-55874; 0-7573)* 3201 SW 15th St., Deerfield Beach, FL 33442-8157 (SAN 212-100X) Tel 954-360-0909; Fax: 954-360-0034; Toll Free: 800-851-9100 Do not confuse with Health Communications, Inc., Edison, NJ
E-mail: hci@hcibooks.com; terryy@hcibooks.com; lorig@hcibooks.com
Web site: http://www.hcibooks.com
Dist(s): **Continental Bk. Co., Inc.**
Lectorum Pubns., Inc.
Landmark Audiobooks; *CIP.*

Health Press *See* **Health Pr. NA, Inc.**

Health Pr. NA, Inc., *(0-929173)* P.O. Box 37470, Albuquerque, NM 87176 (SAN 248-5036) Tel 505-888-1394; Fax: 505-888-1521
E-mail: goodbooks@healthpress.com
Web site: http://www.healthpress.com.

Heart Arbor Bks., *(1-891452)* Orders Addr.: P.O. Box 542, Grand River, OH 44045 (SAN 299-6073) Tel 440-257-0722; Toll Free: 877-977-4422.

†Heart of the Lakes Publishing, *(0-932334; 1-55787)* P.O. Box 299, Interlaken, NY 14847-0299 (SAN 213-0769) Tel 607-532-4997; Fax: 607-532-4684; *Imprints:* Empire State Books (Empire State Bks)
E-mail: hlpbooks@aol.com
Web site: http://www.hlpbooks.com
Dist(s): **BUSCA, Inc.**; *CIP.*

Hearth Publishing, *(0-9627947; 1-882420)* Orders Addr.: 212 N. Ash St., Hillsboro, KS 67063-1117 (SAN 631-4503).

HeartMath LLC, *(1-879052; 0-9700286)* 14700 W. Park Ave., Boulder Creek, CA 95006 Tel 831-338-8700; Fax: 831-338-9861; Toll Free: 800-450-9111
E-mail: info@heartmath.com
Web site: http://www.heartmath.com
Dist(s): **Bookpeople.**

†Hebrew Publishing Co., *(0-88482)* P.O. Box 222, Spencertown, NY 12165-0222 (SAN 201-5404) Tel 518-392-3322; Fax: 518-392-4280; *CIP.*

Heian International Publishing, Inc., *(0-89346)* 1815 W. 205th St., Suite 301, Torrance, CA 90501-1518 (SAN 213-2036) Tel 310-782-6268; Fax: 310-782-6269
E-mail: heianemail@heian.com
Web site: http://www.heian.com
Dist(s): **Cheng & Tsui Co.**
SCB Distributors
Weatherhill, Inc..

Heiderscheit, Sara, *(0-9620385)* 519 N. Seventh St., Osage, IA 50461 (SAN 249-3780) Tel 515-732-5619.

†Heinemann, *(0-325; 0-435; 1-59469)* Div. of Greenwood Publishing Group, Inc., Orders Addr.: P.O. Box 5007, Westport, CT 06881-5007 Toll Free: 800-793-2154; Edit Addr.: 361 Hanover St., Portsmouth, NH 03801 (SAN 210-5829) Tel 603-431-7894; Fax: 603-431-7840
E-mail: info@heinemann.com
Web site: http://www.heinemann.com
Dist(s): **National Bk. Network**; *CIP.*

Heinemann Educational Books, Incorporated *See* **Heinemann**

Heiner, Garth *See* **Fun With the Law, Inc.**

Heloukon Publishing, *(0-9658183)* 5022 Debeney Dr., Houston, TX 77039-4813 Tel 281-449-1307; Fax: 281-590-6146
E-mail: heloukom@juno.com.

Hemed Books, Incorporated *See* **Lambda Pubs., Inc.**

Henchanted Bks., *(0-9615756)* Orders Addr.: P.O. Box H, Calpella, CA 95418 (SAN 696-4648) Tel 707-485-7551.

†Hendrick-Long Publishing Co., *(0-937460; 1-885777)* Orders Addr.: P.O. Box 1247, Friendswood, TX 77549 (SAN 281-7756) Tel 281-482-6187; Fax: 281-482-6169; Toll Free: 800-544-3770; Edit Addr.: 3905 Pear St., Suite 130, Pearland, TX 77581 (SAN 281-7748)
E-mail: hendrick-long@worldnet.att.net
Web site: http://www.hendricklongpublishing.com
Dist(s): **Baker & Taylor Bks.**
Brodart Co.
Follett Library Resources
Hervey's Booklink & Cookbook Warehouse
; *CIP.*

Henry Quill Pr., *(1-883960)* 7340 Lake Dr., Fremont, MI 49412-9146 Tel 231-924-3026; Fax: 231-928-2802.

†Herald Pr., *(0-8361)* Div. of Mennonite Publishing Hse., Inc., 616 Walnut Ave., Scottdale, PA 15683-1999 (SAN 202-2915) Tel 412-887-8500; 724-887-8500; Fax: 724-887-3111; Toll Free: 800-245-7894 (orders only) Do not confuse with Herald Pr., Charlotte, NC
E-mail: hp@mph.org
Web site: http://www.mph.org
Dist(s): **Baker & Taylor Bks.**
Spring Arbor Distributors, Inc.; *CIP.*

†Herald Publishing Hse., *(0-8309)* P.O. Box 390, Independence, MO 64051-0390 Tel 816-521-3015; Fax: 816-521-3066; Toll Free: 800-767-8181; 1001W. Walnut St., Independence, MO 64051-0390 (SAN 111-7556); *Imprints:* Independence Press (Indep Pr)
E-mail: hhmark@heraldhouse.org
Web site: http://www.heraldhouse.org; *CIP.*

Herbert, Jo Lynn, *(0-9710595)* 80 Pocosin Rd., Washington, NC 27889 Tel 252-927-3212
E-mail: maherbert@coastalnet.com.

Heritage Bks., *(0-7884; 0-917890; 0-940907; 1-55613; 1-888265; 1-58549)* 1540 E Pointer Ridge Pl., Bowie, MD 20716-1800 (SAN 209-3367) Tel 301-390-7708; Toll Free Fax: 800-276-1760; Toll Free: 800-398-7709
E-mail: info@heritagebooks.com
Web site: http://www.heritagebooks.com; http://www.WillowBendBooks.com.

Herodias, *(1-928746)* Orders Addr.: 1603 79th St., Brooklyn, NY 11214; Edit Addr.: 346 First Ave., New York, NY 10009 Tel 212-995-5332 (phone/fax); Toll Free: 800-219-9116 (orders)
E-mail: greatblue@acninc.net
Web site: http://www.herodias.com
Dist(s): **Mercedes Distribution Ctr., Inc..**

Heyday Bks., *(0-930588; 1-890771)* Orders Addr.: P.O. Box 9145, Berkeley, CA 94709 (SAN 207-2351) Tel 510-549-3564; Fax: 510-549-1889; Edit Addr.: 2054 University Ave., Suite 400, Berkeley, CA 94704
E-mail: heyday@heydaybooks.com
Web site: http://www.heydaybooks.com
Dist(s): **Bookpeople**
SPD-Small Pr. Distribution.

Heyokah Publishing Co., *(0-9656124; 1-930910)* 7244 Lattigo Dr., Nampa, ID 83687 Tel 208-465-5809
E-mail: hiheyokah@aol.com
Dist(s): **MightyWords, Inc.**
New Leaf Distributing Co., Inc..

Hibbard Pubns., Inc., *(1-931343)* P.O. Box 3091, Wilmington, DE 19804-0091 Fax: 302-992-0122
E-mail: info@hibbardpub.com.

Hidden Path Pubn., Inc., *(0-9711534)* 304 Briarwood Rd., Statesville, NC 28677 Tel 704-878-0716; 704-224-4832
E-mail: dkellysteele@aol.com.

High Country Pubs., Ltd., *(0-9713045; 1-932158)* 197 New Market Ctr., No. 135, Boone, NC 28607 (SAN 254-3753) Tel 828-964-0590; Fax: 828-262-1973 Do not confuse with High Country Pubs., Lakewood, CO
E-mail: editor@highcountrypublishers.com
Web site: http://www.highcountrypublishers.com
Dist(s): **Biblio Distribution.**

High Desert Productions, *(0-9652920)* Orders Addr.: P.O. Box 5506, Bisbee, AZ 85603 Tel 520-432-5288; Edit Addr.: 511 Mance St., Bisbee, AZ 85603
Dist(s): **Treasure Chest Bks..**

High Noon Bks., *(0-87879; 1-57128)* Div. of Academic Therapy Pubns., Inc., 20 Commercial Blvd., Novato, CA 94949-6191 Tel 415-883-3314; Fax: 415-883-3720; Toll Free: 800-422-7249
E-mail: atpub@aol.com
Web site: http://www.atpub.com.

Highland Pr., *(0-910722)* 10108 Johns Rd., Boerne, TX 78006 (SAN 204-0522) Do not confuse with companies of the same name or similar in Birmingham, AL, Wilsonville, OR, Tonasket, WA, Bryson City, NC, San Rafael, CA, High Springs, FL.

Highlander Celtic Publications *See* **Paw Prints Pr.**

Highlights for Children, *(0-87534)* Orders Addr.: P.O. Box 269, Columbus, OH 43216-0269 (SAN 281-7810) Tel 614-486-0631; Fax: 614-876-8564; Toll Free: 800-255-9517; Edit Addr.: 803 Church St., Honesdale, PA 18431 (SAN 281-7802) Tel 570-253-1080; Fax: 570-253-1179
Web site: http://www.highlights.com.

HighReach Learning, Inc., *(1-57332)* Orders Addr.: P.O. Box 410647, Charlotte, NC 28241-0647 Fax: 704-357-0608; Toll Free Fax: 800-729-4745; Edit Addr.: 36 Old Shoals Rd., Arden, NC 28704 Tel 828-684-4576; Fax: 828-684-1406; Toll Free: 800-729-4754
E-mail: hrllead@highreach.com
Web site: http://www.highreach.com.

†High/Scope Pr., *(0-929816; 0-931114; 1-57379)* Div. of High/Scope Educational Research Foundation, 600 N. River St., Ypsilanti, MI 48198-2898 (SAN 211-9617) Tel 734-485-2000; Fax: 734-485-0704; Toll Free Fax: 800-442-4329 (orders); Toll Free: 800-407-7377 (orders only)
E-mail: info@highscope.org
Web site: http://www.highscope.org; *CIP.*

Highsmith Inc., *(0-913853; 0-917846; 1-57950; 1-932146)* W5527 Hwy. 106 P.O. Box 800, Fort Atkinson, WI 53538 (SAN 159-8740) Tel 920-563-9571; Fax: 920-563-7395; *Imprints:* Upstart Books (Upstart Bks)
Web site: http://www.highsmith.com
Dist(s): **Women Ink.**

Highsmith Press, LLC *See* **Highsmith Inc.**

Hill & Wang Imprint of Farrar, Straus & Giroux

Hill, Lawrence Bks. Imprint of Chicago Review Pr., Inc.

Hillsboro Pr. Imprint of Providence Hse. Pubs.

Hilltop Publishing Co., *(0-912133)* P.O. Box 654, Sonoma, CA 95476 (SAN 264-6706) Tel 707-938-8110; Fax: 707-938-5438 Do not confuse with companies with similar names in Waco, TX, Geneva, FL
E-mail: Hilltopub@aol.com
Dist(s): **Bookpeople**
Sunbelt Pubns., Inc..

Hindsight, Ltd., *(1-929031)* Orders Addr.: P.O. Box 46406, Eden Prairie, MN 55347
E-mail: hindsightlimited@aol.com
Web site: http://www.hindsightlimited.com
Dist(s): **Baker & Taylor Bks.**
Bookmen, Inc.
Quality Bks., Inc..

†Hippocrene Bks., Inc., *(0-7818; 0-87052; 0-88254)* 171 Madison Ave., New York, NY 10016-1002 (SAN 213-2060) Tel 718-454-2366 (sales); 212-685-4371 (editorial); Fax: 718-454-1391 (sales/order inquiry); 212-779-9338 (editorial)
E-mail: hippocrenebooks.com; hippocre@ix.netcom.com; contact@hippocrenebooks.com
Web site: http://www.hippocrenebooks.com
Dist(s): **Continental Bk. Co., Inc.**; *CIP.*

Hiram Charles Publishing, *(0-9634735)* 860 E. Carson St., Suite 118-63, Carson, CA 90745 Tel 310-768-8964.

Historic Pr.-South, *(0-9645990)* Orders Addr.: P.O. Box 407, Gatlinburg, TN 37738 Tel 423-436-4163; Toll Free: 800-279-2603; Edit Addr.: 367 Buckhorn Rd., Gatlinburg, TN 37738.

†Historical Society of Rockland County, The, *(0-911183)* 20 Zukor Rd., New City, NY 10956 (SAN 211-4488) Tel 845-634-9629; Fax: 845-634-8690
E-mail: HSRockland@aol.com; *CIP.*

Hither Creek Pr., *(0-9700555)* 79 Addison Dr., Short Hills, NJ 07078 Tel 973-258-0338; Fax: 973-389-3366
E-mail: hithercreekpress@aol.com.

Hobby Hse. Pr., Inc., *(0-87588)* One Corporate Dr., Grantsville, MD 21536 (SAN 204-059X) Tel 301-895-3792; Fax: 301-895-5029; Toll Free: 800-554-1447
E-mail: email@hobbyhouse.com
Web site: http://www.hobbyhouse.com.

Hobby Hse. Publishing Group, *(0-9727179)* 48 Hickory Hill Rd., Box 1527, Jackson, NJ 08527 Fax: 732-886-7371
E-mail: thread1@optonline.net
Web site: http:// www.hobbyhousepublishinggroup.com.

Hodder & Stoughton, Ltd. (GBR) *(0-340; 0-450; 0-7122; 0-7131) Dist. by* **Trafalgar.**

Hodder & Stoughton, Ltd. (GBR) *(0-340; 0-450; 0-7122; 0-7131) Dist. by* **Lubrecht & Cramer.**

Hodder & Stoughton, Ltd. (GBR) *(0-340; 0-450; 0-7122; 0-7131) Dist. by* **Distribks Inc.**

Hodder Headline Audiobooks (GBR) *(1-85998; 1-84032) Dist. by* **Trafalgar.**

Hodder Headline Audiobooks (GBR) *(1-85998; 1-84032) Dist. by* **Ulverscroft US.**

Hodder Wayland (GBR) *(0-7500; 0-7502) Dist. by* **Trafalgar.**

Holderby & Bierce, *(0-916761)* P.O. Box 536, Charlottesville, VA 22902 (SAN 654-3979) Tel 434-977-7171
E-mail: lizandutch@aol.com
Web site: http://www.HolderbyandBierce.com
Dist(s): **Baker & Taylor Bks.**
Brodart Co.
Follett Library Resources.

†Holiday Hse., Inc., *(0-8234)* 425 Madison Ave., New York, NY 10017 (SAN 202-3008) Tel 212-688-0085; Fax: 212-688-0395
E-mail: bwalsh@holidayhouse.com
Web site: http://www.holidayhouse.com
Dist(s): **Lectorum Pubns., Inc.**; *CIP.*

Holloway Hse. Publishing Co., *(0-87067; 1-58520)* 8060 Melrose Ave., Los Angeles, CA 90046 (SAN 206-8451) Tel 323-653-8060; Fax: 323-655-9452
E-mail: psi@loop.com
Web site: http://www.hollowayhousebooks.com
Dist(s): **All America Distributors Corp..**

Holly Hall Pubns., Inc., *(0-9645396; 1-888306)* P.O. Box 254, Elkton, MD 21922-0254 Tel 410-392-2300; Fax: 410-620-9877; Toll Free: 800-211-0719; *Imprints:* Full Quart Press (Full Quart Pr)
Dist(s): **Spring Arbor Distributors, Inc..**

Hollym International Corp., *(0-930878; 1-56591)* 18 Donald Pl., Elizabeth, NJ 07208 (SAN 211-0172) Tel 908-353-1655; Fax: 908-353-0255 Do not confuse with Hollym Corporation Pubs., New York, NY
E-mail: hollymint@aol.com
Web site: http://www.hollym.com
Dist(s): **Cheng & Tsui Co..**

Holt, Henry & Co. Bks. For Young Readers Imprint of Holt, Henry & Co.

†Holt, Henry & Co., *(0-03; 0-8050)* Div. of Holtzbrinck Publishers, Orders Addr.: 16365 James Madison Hwy., Gordonsville, VA 22942-8501 Toll Free Fax: 800-672-2054; Toll Free: 888-330-8477; Edit Addr.: 115 W. 18th St., 5th Flr., New York, NY 10011 (SAN 200-6472) Tel 212-886-9200; Fax: 540-672-7540 (customer service); *Imprints:* Owl Books (Owl); Holt, Henry & Company Books For Young Raders (HH Bks Yng Read)
E-mail: info@hholt.com
Web site: http://www.henryholt.com
Dist(s): **Giron Bks.**
Holtzbrinck Pubs.
Lectorum Pubns., Inc.
Weston Woods Studios, Inc.; *CIP.*

Holt, Rinehart & Winston, *(0-03)* Div. of Harcourt, Inc., Orders Addr.: 6277 Sea Harbor Dr., Orlando, FL 32887-0001 Tel 407-345-3800; Fax: 407-352-3395; Toll Free Fax: 800-235-0256; Toll Free: 800-544-6678 ; Edit Addr.: a/o School Div., 10801 N. Mopac Expressway, Bldg. 3, Austin, TX 78759-5415 (SAN 297-4711) Tel 512-721-7000; Toll Free: 800-992-1627
E-mail: holtinfo@hrw.com
Web site: http://www.hrw.com
Dist(s): **Continental Bk. Co., Inc..**

Holt, Rinehart & Winston School Division *See* **Holt, Rinehart & Winston**

†Holy Cow! Pr., *(0-930100)* P.O. Box 3170, Duluth, MN 55803 (SAN 685-3315) Tel 218-724-1653 (phone/fax)
Web site: http://www.holycowpress.org
Dist(s): **Consortium Bk. Sales & Distribution**
SPD-Small Pr. Distribution; *CIP.*

Holy Spirit Pr., *(1-885497)* Div. of JB, Inc., 231 Market Pl., No. 193, San Ramon, CA 94583 Tel 925-833-8122; Fax: 925-833-1792
E-mail: fulgaro@ix.netcom.com.

Home Run Publishing Company *See* **Santa's Publishing**

Home Sales Enhancements *See* **Castlebrook Pubns.**

Honey Bear Bks. Imprint of Modern Publishing

Honor Bks., *(1-56292)* 2448 E. 81st St., Suite 4800, Tulsa, OK 74137-4285 (SAN 631-1687) Tel 918-523-5600; Fax: 918-496-3588; Toll Free: 800-678-2126 Do not confuse with Honor Bks., Rapid City, SD
E-mail: info@honorbooks.com
Web site: http://www.honorbooks.com/
Dist(s): **Cook Communications Ministries.**

Hood, Alan C. & Co., Inc., *(0-911469)* P.O. Box 775, Chambersburg, PA 17201 (SAN 270-8221) Tel 717-267-0867; Fax: 717-267-0572.

Hooff Prints Pr., *(0-9659525)* Washington Farms, G,C & P Rd., Wheeling, WV 26003 Tel 304-232-6223; Fax: 304-232-1137.

Hoopoe Bks. (EGY) *(977-5325) Dist. by* **AMIDEAST.**

Hoot N' Cackle Pr., *(0-9659381)* 1928 S. Mayfair, Springfield, MO 65804 Tel 417-887-0837; Fax: 417-886-3994
E-mail: lrikil@pcis.net
Web site:
http://www./mowrites4kids.drury.edu/authors/lipe/
Dist(s): **Booksource, The.**

Hoot Owl Bks. Imprint of Maupin Hse. Publishing

Hoppa Productions, Inc., *(1-891547)* 100 Horizon Dr., Denver, PA 17517 Tel 717-445-0313; Fax: 717-445-0860; Toll Free: 888-445-2824
E-mail: info@corncob.com
Web site: http://www.corncob.com.

Horizon Pubs. & Distributors, Inc., *(0-88290)* Orders Addr.: P.O. Box 490, Bountiful, UT 84011-0490 Tel 801-295-9451; Fax: 801-295-0196; Toll Free: 800-453-0812
E-mail: horizonp@burgoyne.com
Web site: http://www.horizonpublishers.com
Dist(s): **Cornerstone Publishing & Distribution, Inc..**

†Houghton Mifflin Co., *(0-395; 0-87466; 0-9631591; 1-57630; 1-881527; 0-618)* 222 Berkeley St., Boston, MA 02116 (SAN 215-3793) Tel 617-351-5000; *Imprints:* Riverside Editions (RivEd)
Web site: http://www.hmco.com
Dist(s): **Chelsea Green Publishing**
Cheng & Tsui Co.
Continental Bk. Co., Inc.
Larousse Kingfisher Chambers, Inc.
Lectorum Pubns., Inc.
Perelandra, Ltd.
netLibrary, Inc.; *CIP.*

Houghton Mifflin Company (College Division) *See* **Houghton Mifflin Co. Trade & Reference Div.**

Houghton Mifflin Co. (Schl. Div.), *(0-395; 0-669)* Orders Addr.: 1900 Batavia Ave., Geneva, IL 60134-3399 Toll Free Fax: 800-733-2098; Toll Free: 800-733-2828; 13400 Midway Rd., Dallas, TX 75244-5165 Toll Free: 800-733-2828; Edit Addr.: 222 Berkeley St., Boston, MA 02116 Tel 617-351-5000; Fax: 617-227-5409
E-mail: eduwebmaster@hmco.com
Web site: http://www.eduplace.com.

Houghton Mifflin Co. Trade & Reference Div., *(0-395; 0-618)* Orders Addr.: 181 Ballardvalle St., Wilmington, MA 01887 Tel 978-661-1300; Toll Free: 800-225-3362; Edit Addr.: 222 Berkeley St., Boston, MA 02116 (SAN 200-2388) Tel 617-351-5000; Fax: 617-227-5409; 215 Park Ave., S., New York, NY 10003 Tel 212-420-5800; Fax: 212-420-5855; *Imprints:* Clarion Books (Clarion Bks); Mariner Books (Mariner Bks); Lorraine, A. Walter (W Lorraine); Kingfisher (Kingfisher)
Web site: http://www.hmco.com/
Dist(s): **netLibrary, Inc..**

House of Anansi Pr. (CAN) *(0-88784) Dist. by* **IPG Chicago.**

How I Learn & Grow, *(1-893886)* 120 Saint Mark's Ave., Brooklyn, NY 11217
E-mail: Carola939@aol.com.

Howard, Emma Bks., *(1-886551)* P.O. Box 385, New York, NY 10024-0385 Tel 212-996-2590 (phone/fax)
E-mail: oldhat555@aol.com
Web site: http://www.DarinkaDeer.com
Dist(s): **Baker & Taylor Bks..**

Howell Pr., *(0-943231; 0-9616878; 1-57427)* 1713-2D Allied Ln., Charlottesville, VA 22903-5336 (SAN 661-6607) Tel 804-977-4006; Fax: 804-971-7204; Toll Free Fax: 888-971-7204; Toll Free: 800-868-4512; *Imprints:* E P M Publications (EPM)
E-mail: custserv@howellpress.com
Web site: http://www.howellpress.com
Dist(s): **Naval Institute Pr..**

Howell Publishing Co., *(0-9658089)* 3020 S. Clermont Dr., Denver, CO 80222 Tel 303-756-0692; Fax: 303-757-5225.

Howling at the Moon Pr., *(0-9654333)* P.O. Box 666, Jenks, OK 74037 Toll Free: 877-469-5464
E-mail: hatmpress@aol.com
Web site: http://www.howl4me.com.

HTS Bks. Imprint of Forest Hse. Publishing Co., Inc.

Huckleberry Pr., *(1-887440)* 8191 Defiance Ln., Gig Harbor, WA 98332-1884 Do not confuse with Huckleberry Pr., South Glastonbury, CT.

Huckleberry Pr., *(0-9653035; 1-890570; 1-58584)* Orders Addr.: P.O. Box 573, South Glastonbury, CT 06073 Fax: 646-205-8056; Toll Free: 800-606-0541 Do not confuse with Huckleberry Pr., Gig Harbor, WA
E-mail: HuckleberryPress@HuckleberryPress.com
Web site: http://www.huckleberrypress.com
Dist(s): **Baker & Taylor Bks..**

Hudgins, Lynne, *(1-889203)* 9734 SW 210th Terr., Miami, FL 33189 Fax: 305-235-2147.

Hudson, Anna E., *(0-9703585)* 205 Putters Cir., Dillsburg, PA 17019-1562
E-mail: DBHAES@aol.com.

Huge Print Pr., *(0-7583)* 3052 Casmeg Way, Rancho San Diego, CA 92019 Tel 619-447-2300; Fax: 619-334-7764; Toll Free: 800-825-0057
E-mail: info@hugeprint.com
Web site: http://www.HugePrint.com.

Hulogosi Communications, Inc., *(0-938493)* P.O. Box 1188, Eugene, OR 97440 (SAN 661-4132) Tel 541-688-1199
E-mail: hulogosi@rio.com
Web site: http://www.dead.net/cavenweb.hulogosi.

†Human Kinetics Pubs., *(0-7360; 0-87322; 0-88011; 0-918438; 0-931250)* Orders Addr.: P.O. Box 5076, Champaign, IL 61825-5076 (SAN 211-7088) Tel 217-351-5076 (ext. 2423); Fax: 217-351-2674; Toll Free: 800-747-4457; Edit Addr.: 1607 N. Market St., Champaign, IL 61820 (SAN 658-0866) Tel 217-351-5076; Fax: 217-351-2674; *Imprints:* Y M C A of the U. S. A. (YMCA USA)
E-mail: humank@hkusa.com
Web site: http://www.humankinetics.com; http://www.hkusa.com
Dist(s): **Follett Media Distribution**
Lippincott Williams & Wilkins; *CIP.*

Humanics, Limited *See* **Humanics Publishing Group**

†Humanics Publishing Group, *(0-89334)* Orders Addr.: P.O. Box 7400, Atlanta, GA 30357-0400 (SAN 208-3833) Tel 561-533-6231; Fax: 404-874-1976; Toll Free: 888-874-8844 Do not confuse with Humanics ErgoSystems, Inc., Reseda, CA
E-mail: humanics@mindspring.com
Web site: http://www.humanicslearning.com; http://www.humanicsdealer.com; http://www.humanicspub.com
Dist(s): **Baker & Taylor Bks.**
Bookpeople
Borders, Inc.
New Leaf Distributing Co., Inc.; *CIP.*

Humbug Bks., *(1-881772)* Div. of Humbug Enterprises, 310 College Ave., Watertown, WI 53094-4807 Toll Free: 800-648-6284
E-mail: humbugbk@execpc.com.

Humongous Bks. Imprint of Lyrick Publishing

Hundelrut Studio, *(0-9638293)* 10 Hawthorne St., Plymouth, NH 03264 Tel 603-536-4396
E-mail: hundelrut@earthlink.net
Web site: http://www.hundelrutstudio.com/.

Hungry Tiger Pr., *(0-9644988; 1-929527)* 5995 Dandridge Ln., Suite 121, San Diego, CA 92115-6575
E-mail: books@hungrytigerpress.com
Web site: http://www.hungrytigerpress.com.

Hunter Hse. Pubns., *(0-9662769)* Div. of Hunter & Assocs., 1132 21st St., SE, Cedar Rapids, IA 52403 Tel 319-362-4777; Fax: 319-369-9853
E-mail: hunter.c@mcleodusa.net.

Huntington House *See* **Huntington Hse. Pubs.**

Huntington Hse. Pubs., *(0-910311; 1-56384)* Orders Addr.: P.O. Box 53788, Lafayette, LA 70505 (SAN 241-5208) Tel 337-237-7049; Fax: 337-237-7060; Toll Free: 800-749-4009; Edit Addr.: 104 Row 2, Suite A1 & A2, Lafayette, LA 70508; *Imprints:* Vital Issue Press (Vital Issue Pr)
E-mail: joyced@xspedius.net; admin@alphapublishingonline.com
Web site: http://www.alphapublishingonline.com
Dist(s): **Alpha Publishing, Inc.**
Riverside.

Hutchinson (GBR) *(0-09) Dist. by* **Trafalgar.**

Hutchison, G.F. Pr., *(1-885631)* 319 S. Block, Suite 17, Fayetteville, AR 72701 Tel 479-587-1726; *Imprints:* Family Of Man Press, The (Family Of Man Pr)
E-mail: drwriterguy@netscape.net
Web site: http://www.familypress.com.

Hynes Enterprises, Inc., *(0-9713900)* 8580 E. Bellewood Pl., Denver, CO 80237 Tel 303-221-7012; Fax: 303-221-7015; Toll Free: 800-841-7390
E-mail: thynes6958@aol.com
Web site: http://jimmpigg.com.

†Hyperion Bks. for Children, *(0-7868; 1-56282)* Div. of Disney Bk. Publishing, Inc., A Walt Disney Co., 114 Fifth Ave., New York, NY 10011 Tel 212-633-4400; Fax: 212-633-4833; Toll Free: 800-759-0190 (customer serv.); *Imprints:* Jump at the Sun (Jump at the Sun); Volo (Volo); Di Capua, Michael Books (Michael Di Capua)
Web site: http://www.disney.com
Dist(s): **Little Brown & Co.**
Time Warner Bk. Group; *CIP.*

†**Hyperion Paperbacks for Children,** *(0-7868; 1-56282)* Div. of Disney Bk. Publishing, Inc., A Walt Disney Co., 114 Fifth Ave., New York, NY 10011 Tel 212-633-4400; Fax: 212-633-4833
Web site: http://www.disney.com
Dist(s): **Little Brown & Co.**
Time Warner Bk. Group; *CIP.*

†**Hyperion Pr.,** *(0-7868; 1-56282; 1-4013)* Div. of Disney Bk. Publishing, Inc., A Walt Disney Co., Orders Addr.: 3 Center Plaza, Boston, MA 02108 Toll Free: 800-759-0190; Edit Addr.: 77 W. 66th St., 11th Flr., New York, NY 10023-6298 Tel 212-456-0100; Fax: 212-456-0108
Web site: http://www.hyperionbooks.com
Dist(s): **Time Warner Bk. Group**; *CIP.*

Hypertext Publishing Group, *(0-9648010)* P.O. Box 420686, San Diego, CA 92142 (SAN 298-7651) Tel 619-627-9210; Toll Free: 800-754-9737
E-mail: HPGBooks@aol.com.

I & L Publishing, *(0-9661244; 1-930002)* 174 Oak Dr. Pkwy., Oroville, CA 95966 Tel 530-589-5048; Fax: 530-589-3551; Toll Free: 888-443-4722
E-mail: iolamoore@juno.com
Dist(s): **Morris Publishing.**

i.b.d., Ltd., *(0-88431)* 24 Hudson St., Kinderhook, NY 12106 (SAN 630-7779) Tel 518-758-1755; Fax: 518-758-6702
E-mail: lankhof@ibdltd.com
Web site: http://www.ibdltd.com.

I. J. E. Bk. Publishing, Inc./Kid Stuff, *(0-87660)* Div. of I.J.E., Inc., 812 Kenmore Rd., Chapel Hill, NC 27514-1446 (SAN 294-040X).

ibooks, Inc., *(0-671; 0-7434; 1-58824; 1-59176)* 24 W. 25th St., 11th Flr., New York, NY 10010 Tel 212-645-9870; Fax: 212-645-9874
E-mail: aandrade@ipicturebooks.com
Dist(s): **Simon & Schuster, Inc..**

ibooks, Incorporated/ipictures.com *See* **ibooks, Inc.**

ICAN Press *See* **Black Forest Pr.**

Icicle Publishing, *(0-9658318)* P.O. Box 994, Winchester, MA 01890 Tel 781-721-6011
E-mail: marrcelo15@aol.com
Dist(s): **Quality Bks., Inc..**

Idea & Design Works, LLC, *(0-9712282; 0-9719775; 1-932382)* 2645 Financial Ct., Suite E, San Diego, CA 92117 (SAN 255-1926) Tel 858-270-1315; Fax: 858-270-1308
E-mail: jeff@idwpublishing.com
Web site: http://www.idnpublishing.com
Dist(s): **Diamond Book Distributors, Inc.**
Diamond Comic Distributors, Inc.
LPC Group.

Ideals Imprint of Ideals Pubns.

Ideals Children's Bks. Imprint of Ideals Pubns.

Ideals Pr. Imprint of Ideals Pubns.

Ideals Pubns., *(0-8249; 0-89542)* Div. of Guideposts, 535 Metroplex Dr., Suite 250, Nashville, TN 37211 Tel 615-333-0478; Fax: 615-781-1447; *Imprints:* Ideals (Ideals TN); Candy Cane Press (Candy Cane Pr); Ideals Children's Books (Ideals Chldrns Bks); Ideals Press (Ideals Pr)
E-mail: mflanagan@guideposts.org
Web site: http://www.idealspublications.com
Dist(s): **Appalachian Bk. Distributors**
Baker & Taylor Bks.
Lectorum Pubns., Inc.
Riverside
Spring Arbor Distributors, Inc..

Ideals Publishing Corporation *See* **Ideals Pubns.**

Ike, J. Bks., *(0-937109)* 32 Bland Ave., Sumter, SC 29150-3816 (SAN 658-439X) Tel 803-778-6988
E-mail: bjustus@cpis.net
Dist(s): **Baker & Taylor Bks.**
Southern Bk. Service.

IKIDS Imprint of Innovative Kids

Ikon Pr., *(0-9633157)* 842 Clayton St., San Francisco, CA 94117 Tel 415-661-8643; Fax: 415-731-2937
E-mail: barbeau@aol.com
Web site: http://www.ikonpress.com.

Illumination Arts Publishing Co., Inc., *(0-935699; 0-9701907; 0-9740190)* Orders Addr.: P.O. Box 1865, Bellevue, WA 98009 (SAN 696-2599) Tel 425-644-7185; Fax: 425-644-9274; Toll Free: 888-210-8216; Edit Addr.: 13256 Northup Way, No. 9, Bellevue, WA 98005
E-mail: liteinfo@illumin.com
Web site: http://www.illumin.com
Dist(s): **Baker & Taylor Bks.**
DeVorss & Co.
Follett Library Resources
Koen Pacific
New Leaf Distributing Co., Inc.
Partners/West
Quality Bks., Inc..

IM Pr., *(0-9654651; 0-9716911)* Orders Addr.: P.O. Box 5346, Takoma Park, MD 20913-5346 Tel 301-587-1202; Edit Addr.: 7214 Cedar Ave., Takoma Park, MD 20912 Do not confuse with companies with the same name in Cincinnati, OH, Fairfax Station, VA
E-mail: efaine@yahoo.com
Web site: http://www.takoma.com/ned/home.htm
Dist(s): **Book Clearing Hse..**

Image Imprint of Doubleday Publishing

Image Cascade Publishing, *(0-9639607; 1-930009; 1-59511)* 9557 N. Garden Ave., Fresno, CA 93720-4601 (SAN 253-2972) Tel 559-322-8747; Fax: 559-322-6369; Toll Free: 800-691-7779
E-mail: JoyCan@aol.com
Web site: http://www.imagecascade.com.

Image Comics, *(1-58240; 1-887279)* 1071 N. Batavia St., Suite A, Orange, CA 92867 Tel 714-288-0200; Fax: 714-288-2898
E-mail: brentimage@aol.com
Dist(s): **Diamond Book Distributors, Inc.**
Diamond Comic Distributors, Inc.
LPC Group
Trucatriche.

Image Maker Publishing Co., The, *(0-9644695)* 29417 Bluewater Rd., Malibu, CA 90265 Tel 310-457-4031; Fax: 310-457-5102
E-mail: imagemaker@netvip.com
Web site: http://www.malibu.org/imagemaker/.

Image Pr., Inc., *(1-891548)* Orders Addr.: P.O. Box 2407, Edmond, OK 73083-2407 Tel 405-844-6007; Fax: 405-348-5577; Edit Addr.: 247 N. Broadway, Suite 101, Edmond, OK 73034.

Images Pr., *(1-891577)* 27920 Roble Alto St., Los Altos Hills, CA 94022 (SAN 299-4844) Tel 650-948-9251; 650-948-8251; Fax: 650-941-6114 Do not confuse with companies with the same name in San Leandro, CA, New York, NY
E-mail: bugsmom2@aol.com
Dist(s): **Baker & Taylor Bks.**
Quality Bks., Inc..

Imagination Studio Imprint of Random Hse. Audio Publishing Group

Imaginative Publishing, LTD, *(0-9743335)* P.O. Box 150008, Fort Worth, TX 76108 Tel 817-246-6436; Toll Free: 877-246-6436
E-mail: publisher@imaginativepublishing.com
Web site: http://www.imaginativepublishing.com.

imaJen, Inc., 5530 Penn Ave., 1st Flr., Pittsburgh, PA 15206 Tel 412-441-4143; Fax: 412-441-4453.

ImaJinn Bks., *(1-893896)* P.O. Box 545, Canon City, CO 81215-0545 Toll Free: 877-625-3592
E-mail: orders@imajinnbooks.com
Web site: http://www.imajinnbooks.com.

Immanuel Pr., *(0-9659382)* Orders Addr.: P.O. Box 1083, Haleiwa, HI 96712 Tel 808-638-7193; Edit Addr.: 59-275 Kenui Rd., Haleiwa, HI 96712
E-mail: jbridgman@juno.com
Dist(s): **Booklines Hawaii, Ltd..**

†**Impact Pubs., Inc.,** *(0-915166; 1-886230)* P.O. Box 6016, Atascadero, CA 93422 (SAN 202-6864) Tel 805-466-5917; Fax: 805-466-5919; Toll Free: 800-246-7228; *Imprints:* Little Imp Books (Little Imp Books) Do not confuse with Impact Pubns. in Manassas Park, VA or Plantation, FL.
E-mail: info@impactpublishers.com
Web site: http://www.impactpublishers.com; *CIP.*

In Audio Imprint of Sound Room Pubs., Inc.

Incentive Pubns., Inc., *(0-86530; 0-913916)* 3835 Cleghorn Ave., Nashville, TN 37215 (SAN 203-8005) Tel 615-385-2934; Fax: 615-385-2967; Toll Free: 800-421-2830
E-mail: info@incentivepublications.com
Web site: http://www.incentivepublications.com.

Incentives For Learning, *(1-56872)* 111 Center Ave., Suite I, Pacheco, CA 94553 Tel 925-682-2428; Fax: 925-682-2645; Toll Free: 888-238-2379.

Incline Pr., *(0-9615161)* 2 Townsend St., Apt. 2-213, San Francisco, CA 94107-2025 (SAN 694-3853) Tel 415-284-0127.

Independence Pr. Imprint of Herald Publishing Hse.

Independent Pubs. Group, Subs. of Chicago Review Pr., 814 N. Franklin, Chicago, IL 60610 (SAN 202-0769) Tel 312-337-0747; Fax: 312-337-5985; Toll Free: 800-888-4741
E-mail: lreardon@ipgbook.com; usold@ipgbook.com
Web site: http://www.ipgbook.com.

Indian Trail Pr., *(0-9629284)* P.O. Box 55, Salado, TX 76571.

†**Indiana Univ. Pr.,** *(0-253)* 601 N. Morton St., Bloomington, IN 47404-3797 (SAN 202-5647) Fax: 812-855-7931; Toll Free: 800-842-6796
E-mail: iuporder@indiana.edu
Web site: http://www.Indiana.edu/~iupress
Dist(s): **Baker & Taylor International**
netLibrary, Inc.; *CIP.*

Individualized Education Systems/Poppy Ln. Publishing, *(0-938911)* Orders Addr.: P.O. Box 5136, Fresno, CA 93755 (SAN 661-8405) Tel 559-299-4639; Edit Addr.: 134 Poppy Ln., Clovis, CA 93612 (SAN 661-8413)
E-mail: Bette1234@aol.com
Dist(s): **American West Bks.**
Baker & Taylor Bks..

IndyPublish.com, *(1-58827; 1-4043; 1-4142)* P.O. Box 410186, Cambridge, MA 02141
E-mail: info@indypublish.com
Web site: http://www.indypublish.com
Dist(s): **NuvoMedia**
Replica Bks..

Infinity Plus One, LLC, *(1-58260)* 201 E. Ridgewood Ave., Ridgewood, NJ 07450 Tel 201-445-9631; Fax: 201-445-9632
E-mail: infinplus1@aol.com.

Infinity Publishing.com, *(0-9665678; 1-892896; 0-7414)* Div. of Buy Bks. on the Web.com, 519 W. Lancaster Ave., Haverford, PA 19041 Tel 610-520-2500; Fax: 610-519-0261; Toll Free: 877-289-2665
E-mail: info@buybooksontheweb.com.

Info-All Bk. Co., *(0-9617218)* 5 Old Well Ln., Dallas, PA 18612 (SAN 663-4087) Tel 717-288-9375.

Inheritance Pubns., *(0-921100)* P.O. Box 366, Pella, IA 50219 Tel 780-674-3949 (phone/fax); Toll Free: 800-563-3594 (phone/fax)
E-mail: inhpubl@telusplanet.net
Web site: http://www.telusplanet.net/public/inhpubl/webip/ip..

Ink & Feathers Comics, *(0-9664974)* Div. of Ink & Feathers Calligraphy, 202 E. Grove St., Streator, IL 61364 Tel 815-672-1171; Fax: 425-795-9686; *Imprints:* Side Show Comics (Side Show Comics)
E-mail: ifcomics@webtv.net
Dist(s): **Baker & Taylor Bks..**

Inka Dinka Ink Childrens Pr., *(0-939700)* Div. of HeBo, Inc., 4741 Guerley Rd., Cincinnati, OH 45238 (SAN 293-2814) Tel 513-471-0825; Fax: 513-251-7112
E-mail: iamix4@cinci.infi.net
Dist(s): **Baker & Taylor Bks..**

Inkwell, *(0-9627680; 1-887370)* Orders Addr.: P.O. Box 178, Dobbins, CA 95935-0178 (SAN 298-5918) Tel 530-692-1581; Toll Free: 800-242-8545; Edit Addr.: 14976 Fountain House Rd., Dobbins, CA 95935 Tel 916-692-1581 Do not confuse with Ink Well, Hermosa Beach, CA
E-mail: inkwell@oro.net
Web site: http://www.suresit.com/ca/i/inkwell.

Inkwell Productions, *(0-9658158; 0-9718155; 0-9728118)* 3370 N. Hayden Rd., No. 123-276, Scottsdale, AZ 85251 Toll Free: 888-324-2665
E-mail: info@inkwellproductions.com; inkwell productions@msn.com
Web site: http://www.inkwellproductions.com.

Innovative Kids, *(1-58476)* Div. of Innovative USA, 18 Ann St., Norwalk, CT 06854 Tel 203-838-6400; Fax: 203-855-5582; 203-852-7117; *Imprints:* IKIDS (IKIDS)
E-mail: info@innovativekids.com
Web site: http://www.innovativekids.com
Dist(s): **Chronicle Bks. LLC.**

Inquiring Voices Pr., *(0-9634637)* 100 Heritage Rd., Bloomington, IN 47408 (SAN 297-9292) Tel 812-336-6925; Fax: 812-333-1216
E-mail: ivpress@bluemarble.net
Web site: http://www.bluemarble.net/~ivpress/home.htm
Dist(s): **Baker & Taylor Bks.**
Partners Pubs. Group, Inc..

Inside-OUT Corp., *(1-929157)* 631 N. Stephanie St., PMB 239, Henderson, NV 89014-2633 Tel 702-396-9083; Fax: 702-396-2354
E-mail: bookmktg@aol.com.

Insight, *(0-9641035; 0-9703536)* 721 Hawthorne, Royal Oak, MI 48067 Tel 248-543-0997 (phone/fax) Do not confuse with Insight in Highland Park, IL, Canal Fulton, OH
E-mail: brenr@openadoptioninsight.org
Web site: http://www.openadoptioninsight.org.

Inspire Press, Inc., *(0-9741800)* P.O. Box 33241, Los Gatos, CA 95030 Tel 408-395-2003; Fax: 408-904-4662
E-mail: sharper@inspirepress.com
Web site: http://www.inspirepress.com.

Names

Inspired Ink Productions by Kapraun, *(0-9643313)* 36745 Hill St., Lower Salem, OH 45745 Tel 614-585-2706.

Institute for Human Potential & Social Development *See* **Order of the Legion of St. Michael**

Institute for the Achievement of Human Potential, *(0-936676; 0-944349)* Div. of Institutes for the Achievement of Human Potential, 8801 Stenton Ave., Wyndmoor, PA 19038 (SAN 215-7314) Tel 215-233-2050 (ext. 288)
E-mail: institutes@iahp.org; iahp@earthlink.net
Web site: http://www.iahp.org.

Instructional Fair * T S Dension Imprint of McGraw-Hill Children's Publishing

Interactive Knowledge *See* **netLibrary, Inc.**

Intercontinental Publishing, Inc., *(1-881164)* Orders Addr.: P.O. Box 7242, Fairfax Station, VA 22039 Tel 703-583-4800; Fax: 703-670-7825; Edit Addr.: 11681 Beacon Race Rd., Woodbridge, VA 22192
E-mail: icpub@worldnet.att.net
Web site: http://home.att.net/~icpub/index.html.

†Intercultural Pr., Inc., *(0-933662; 1-877864; 1-931930)* Div. of Nicholas Brealey Publishing, Ltd., P.O. Box 700, Yarmouth, ME 04096 (SAN 212-6699) Tel 207-846-5168; Fax: 207-846-5181; Toll Free: 866-372-2665
E-mail: books@interculturalpress.com
Web site: http://www.interculturalpress.com; *CIP.*

Interkids, *(0-9657928)* 100 Hunt Trail, Barrington, IL 60010-1709 Tel 847-382-7016; 847 382 7016; Fax: 847-382-7219
E-mail: interkids@earthlink.net
Dist(s): **Baker & Taylor Bks.**
Brodart Co..

Interlingua Foreign Language AudioBooks, *(1-58085)* Orders Addr.: P.O. Box 4175, Arlington, VA 22204-0175 Tel 703-575-7849; Fax: 703-575-8919; Toll Free: 800-336-4400; Edit Addr.: 838 S. Monroe, Arlington, VA 22204
E-mail: altech@pressroom.com
Web site: http://www.foreign-audio-books.com; http://www.russianaudio.com.

Interlink Publishing Group, Inc., *(0-940793; 1-56656)* 46 Crosby St., Northampton, MA 01060-1804 (SAN 664-8908) Tel 413-582-7054; Fax: 413-582-6731; Toll Free: 800-238-5465; *Imprints:* Crocodile Books (Crocodile Bks)
E-mail: info@interlinkbooks.com; editor@interlinkbooks.com
Web site: http://www.interlinkbooks.com.

†International Bk. Ctr., Inc., *(0-86685; 0-917062)* 2007 Laurel Dr., P.O. Box 295, Troy, MI 48099 (SAN 169-4014) Tel 248-879-8436; Fax: 810-254-7230
E-mail: ibc@ibcbooks.com
Web site: http://www.ibcbooks.com; *CIP.*

International Healing Foundation, Inc., *(0-9637058)* P.O. Box 901, Bowie, MD 20718 Tel 301-805-6111; Fax: 301-805-5155
E-mail: ihf90@aol.com.

International Language Centre, 1753 Connecticut Ave., NW, Washington, DC 20009 (SAN 209-1615) Tel 202-332-2894; Fax: 202-462-6657
E-mail: richard@newsinform.com; zisa@newsinform.com
Web site: http://www.newsinform.com.

International Law & Taxation Pubs., *(1-893713)* P.O. Box 025207, Miami, FL 33102-5207 Tel 407-650-2537 (phone/fax); Dept. PTY 2624, Unit C-102 1601 NW 97th Ave., Miami, FL 33172
E-mail: internationallaw@cyberhaven.com
Web site: http://
www.internationallawandtaxationpublishers.com.

International Learning Systems, Incorporated *See* **International Language Centre**

†International Polygonics, Ltd., *(0-930330; 1-55882)* P.O. Box 1563, New York, NY 10159 (SAN 211-0210) Tel 212-683-2914; Fax: 212-545-0429
Dist(s): **Independent Pubs. Group**; *CIP.*

†International Pubns. Service, *(0-8002)* Div. of Taylor & Francis, Inc., Orders Addr.: 325 Chestnut St., 8th Flr., Levittown, PA 19057-4700 Fax: 215-785-5515; Toll Free: 800-821-8312
E-mail: bkorders@tandfpa.com
Dist(s): **Taylor & Francis, Inc.**; *CIP.*

International Specialized Bk. Services, 920 NE 58th Ave., Suite 300, Portland, OR 97213-3786 (SAN 169-7129) Tel 503-287-3093; Fax: 503-280-8832; Toll Free: 800-944-6190
E-mail: info@isbs.com
Web site: http://www.isbs.com.

International Storytelling Press *See* **Storytelling World Pr.**

Interstellar Productions, Inc., *(0-9678580)* 1758 N. Park St., Suite B, Castle Rock, CO 80104 Fax: 303-688-7936; Toll Free: 800-806-0023; *Imprints:* I P I Toys (IPI Toys)
E-mail: renaten@ipitoys.com
Web site: http://www.ipitoys.com.

†InterVarsity Pr., *(0-8308; 0-87784)* Div. of InterVarsity Christian Fellowship of the USA, Orders Addr.: P.O. Box 1400, Downers Grove, IL 60515 (SAN 202-7089) Tel 630-734-4000; Fax: 630-734-4200; Toll Free: 800-843-9487 (orders); 800-843-1019 (customer service); 800-873-0143 (electronic ordering); 800-843-7225 (other depts.)
E-mail: mail@ivpress.com
Web site: http://www.ivpress.com
Dist(s): **Baker & Taylor Bks.**
CRC Pubns.
Riverside Bk. & Bible Resource; *CIP.*

Intervisual Bks., Inc., *(1-58117; 1-888443)* Orders Addr.: 12910 Culver Blvd., Suite C, Los Angeles, CA 90066-6709 Tel 310-302-0600; *Imprints:* Piggy Toes Press (Piggy Toes Pr)
E-mail: timperato@intervisualmedia.com
Web site: http://www.intervisualbooks.com.

Intes International (UK) Ltd. (GBR) *(0-9533178) Dist. by* **Diamond Book Dists.**

Intrigue Pr. Imprint of Corvus Publishing

Introspect Bks., *(1-890667)* Orders Addr.: P.O. Box 271615, Dallas, TX 75227 Tel 972-278-3265; Fax: 972-278-0306; Edit Addr.: 1521 Palm Valley Dr., Garland, TX 75043; *Imprints:* Hand-In-Hand Books (Hand-In-Hand Bks).

Ion Imagination Publishing, *(1-886184)* Div. of Ion Imagination Entertainment, Inc., Orders Addr.: P.O. Box 210943, Nashville, TN 37221-0943 (SAN 298-5411) Tel 615-646-3644; Fax: 615-646-6276; Toll Free: 800-335-8672; Edit Addr.: 133 Morton Mill Cir., Nashville, TN 37221
E-mail: flumpa@aol.com
Web site: http://www.flumpa.com
Dist(s): **Brodart Co.**
Professional Media Service Corp.
Quality Bks., Inc..

IPI Toys Imprint of Interstellar Productions, Inc.

ipicturebooks, LLC, *(1-58824; 1-59019; 1-59155; 1-59173)* 24 W. 25th St., No. 12, New York, NY 10010 Tel 212-645-9870; Fax: 212-645-9874
E-mail: aandrade@ipicturebooks.com
Web site: http://www.ipicturebooks.com
Dist(s): **Time Warner Bk. Group.**

IQRA International Educational Foundation, *(1-56316)* 7450 Skokie Blvd., Skokie, IL 60077-3374 Tel 847-673-4072; Fax: 847-673-4095; Toll Free: 800-521-4272
E-mail: kmohiuddin@iqra.org; pdc@iqra.org
Web site: http://www.iqra.org.

Ira Valley Ideas, *(0-9715874)* Orders Addr.: 112 Plain St., Rutland, VT 05701 Tel 802-235-2392
E-mail: ccf0005701@yahoo.com.

Irish American Bk. Co., Subs. of Roberts Rinehart Pubs., Inc., P.O. Box 666, Niwot, CO 80544-0666 Tel 303-652-2710; Fax: 303-652-2689; Toll Free: 800-452-7115
E-mail: irishbooks@aol.com
Web site: http://www.irishvillage.com.

Irish Bks. & Media, Inc., *(0-937702)* Orders Addr.: 1433 E. Franklin Ave., Suite 20, Minneapolis, MN 55404-2135 (SAN 111-8870) Tel 612-871-3505; Fax: 612-871-3358; Toll Free: 800-229-3505 Do not confuse with Irish Bks. in New York, NY
E-mail: Irishbook@aol.com
Web site: http://www.irishbook.com.

†Irvington Pubs., *(0-512; 0-8290; 0-8422; 0-89197)* Orders Addr.: P.O. Box 286, New York, NY 10276-0286 Fax: 212-861-0998; Toll Free Fax: 800-455-5520; Toll Free: 800-472-6037; *CIP.*

Irwin Professional Publishing Imprint of McGraw-Hill School Education Group

Isabel's, *(0-9629612)* 14 E. Gay St., Suite 400, Columbus, OH 43215-3413 Tel 614-224-0700; Fax: 614-224-0630.

Isha Enterprises, Inc., *(0-936981)* P.O. Box 25970, Scottsdale, AZ 85255 (SAN 658-7895) Tel 480-502-9454; Fax: 480-502-9456; Toll Free: 800-641-6015
E-mail: info@easygrammar.com
Web site: http://www.easygrammar.com.

Ishnuvu Publishing Co., *(0-9636906)* 963 Monroe Rd., Hattiesburg, MS 39401 Tel 601 583-2444
E-mail: ishnuvu@aol.com
Web site: http://members.aol.com/Ishnuvu/index.html.

ISIS Large Print Bks. (GBR) *(0-7531; 1-85089; 1-85695) Dist. by* **Transaction Pubs.**

Island Dog Pr., *(0-9648685)* 2 Quail Creek Ct., Greenville, SC 29615-4312.

Island Flowers, Inc., *(0-9637712)* 14000 Pines Blvd., Pembroke Pines, FL 33027-1504 Tel 954-431-3148.

Island Heritage Publishing, *(0-89610; 0-931548)* Div. of The Madden Corp., 94-411 Koaki St., Waipahu, HI 96797 (SAN 211-1403) Tel 808-564-8888; Fax: 808-564-8999; Toll Free: 800-468-2800
E-mail: hawaii4u@islandheritage.com
Web site: http://www.islandheritage.com/.

Island-Metro Pubns., Inc., *(0-9619832; 1-888465)* 75 Price Pkwy., Farmingdale, NY 11735 Tel 631-293-6600; Fax: 631-293-6614
E-mail: http://www.island-metro.com; info@island-metro.com.

Istra (FRA) *(2-01; 2-219) Dist. by* **Distribks Inc.**

Ithaca Hse., *(0-87886)* P.O. Box 4556, Ithaca, NY 14852 Tel 607-275-9658
E-mail: ithacahouse@juno.com.

iUniverse, Inc., *(0-9665514; 1-58348; 0-9668591; 1-893652; 0-595)* Orders Addr.: 2021 Pine Lake Rd., Suite 100, Lincoln, NE 68512 (SAN 254-9425) Tel 402-323-7800; Fax: 402-323-7824; Toll Free: 877-823-9235; *Imprints:* Writers Club Press (Writers Club Pr); Writer's Showcase Press (Writers Showcase); Backinprint.com (Backinprint); Authors Choice Press (Authors Choice Pr)
E-mail: pubservices@iuniverse.com; custservice@iuniverse.com
Web site: http://www.iUniverse.com.

iUniverse.com, Incorporated *See* **iUniverse, Inc.**

Ivy Bks. Imprint of Ballantine Bks.

Ivy Editorial Services, Inc., *(0-9667146)* 4 Susan Ct., Glen Cove, NY 11542 Tel 516-944-7340; Fax: 516-944-8663
E-mail: mspinter@aol.com.

J&M Publishing, *(0-9646590)* 2417 Valley View Rd., Narvon, PA 17555 Tel 610-286-5489 Do not confuse with companies with the same name in Lebanon, TN, Fayetteville, NC, Phoenix, AZ.

JK Publishing, *(0-945878)* 48 Janet Pl., Valley Stream, NY 11581-2819 (SAN 248-1642) Tel 516-375-7011
E-mail: kmarion@optonline.net.

J. Kid Productions, Ltd., *(0-9662670)* 10412 E. Weaver Cir., Englewood, CO 80111 Tel 303-850-7740 ; Fax: 303-850-7727; Toll Free: 888-790-4673
Dist(s): **BookWorld Services, Inc..**

Jackman Publishing, *(0-929985; 1-56509)* P.O. Box 1900, Orem, UT 84059 (SAN 250-9210) Tel 801-225-0859; Fax: 801-226-4100.

Jackson, Stephan L. & Assocs., *(1-880722)* 6322 Sovereign Dr., No. 110, San Antonio, TX 78229 Tel 210-340-5166; Fax: 210-340-4805; Toll Free: 800-367-5166.

Jade Ram Publishing, *(1-877721)* 3003 Wendy's Way, No. 9, Anchorage, AK 99517-1466 Tel 907-248-0979 ; Fax: 907-272-8432
E-mail: jaderam@alaska.net
Dist(s): **Publication Consultants**
Todd Communications.

Jadeda Pr., *(0-9672124)* 74 Main St., Framingham, MA 01702-2928
E-mail: efriedlander1@yahoo.com
Web site: http://www.mrsdigger.com.

Jalmar Pr., *(0-915190; 0-935266; 1-880396; 1-931061)* Subs. of B. L. Winch & Assocs., 24426 S. Main St., Suite 702, Carson, CA 90745 (SAN 113-3640) Tel 310-816-3085; Fax: 310-816-3092; Toll Free: 800-662-9662 (orders)
E-mail: jalmarpress@att.net
Web site: http://jalmarpress.com
Dist(s): **Winch, B. L. & Assocs.**
Baker & Taylor Bks.
Brodart Co..

JAM Imprint of Berkley Publishing Group

Jamestown, *(0-02; 0-07; 0-8092; 0-8442; 0-89061; 0-913327; 0-941263; 1-56943)* Div. of Glencoe/McGraw-Hill, Orders Addr.: P.O. Box 543, Blacklick, OH 43004-0543 Fax: 614-860-1877; Toll Free: 800-334-7344; Edit Addr.: P.O. Box 508, Columbus, OH 43216 Toll Free: 800-872-7323
Web site: jamestowneducation.com
Dist(s): **Libros Sin Fronteras**
McGraw-Hill Cos., The.

January Productions, Inc., *(0-87386; 0-934898)* P.O. Box 66, 116 Washington Ave., Hawthorne, NJ 07507 (SAN 222-822X) Tel 973-423-4666; Fax: 973-423-5569; Toll Free: 800-451-7450
E-mail: awpeller@worldnet.att.net
Web site: http://www.awpeller.com.

Janus Publishing Co. (GBR) *(1-85756) Dist. by* **Paul & Co Pubs.**

Names

Japanese American National Museum, *(1-881161)* 369 E. First St., Los Angeles, CA 90012 Tel 213-625-0414 ; Fax: 213-625-1770
Web site: http://www.janm.org
Dist(s): **RAM Pubns. & Distribution.**

Jason & Nordic Pubs., *(0-944727)* P.O. Box 441, Hollidaysburg, PA 16648 (SAN 244-9374) Tel 814-696-2920; Fax: 814-696-4250; *Imprints:* Turtle Books (Turtle Books)
E-mail: turtlbks@nb.net
Web site: http://www.jasonandnordic.com.

JayJo Bks., LLC, *(0-9639449; 1-891383)* Orders Addr.: P.O. Box 760, Plainview, NY 11803-0760 (SAN 178-5435) Tel 516-349-5520; Fax: 800-262-1886; Toll Free: 800-999-6884; Edit Addr.: 135 Dupont St., Plainview, NY 11803-0760
E-mail: jayjobook@guidancechannel.com
Web site: http://www.jayjo.com
Dist(s): **Quality Bks., Inc.**
Unique Bks., Inc..

Je Suis Derby Publishing, *(0-9627436)* Div. of Derby Corp., 535 Broadway, Revere, MA 02151 Tel 617-284-0903.

JeaMei Publishing, *(0-9717299)* 1444 E. Vine Ave., West Covina, CA 91791 Tel 213-944-3888; Fax: 626-918-5181
E-mail: aminah@earthlink.net
Web site: http://www.mtdumpling.com.

Jelinck, Donald A., *(0-9704607)* 1942 University Ave., Suite 206, Berkeley, CA 94704-1023 Tel 510-841-4787; Fax: 510-841-3651
E-mail: don@donjelinek.com
Web site: http://donjelinek.com.

Jermel Visuals, *(0-9649664)* 8 Saddle Hill Rd., Far Hills, NJ 07931-2204 Tel 908-879-8579; Fax: 908-879-7126.

Jersey Shore Pubns., *(0-9632906)* P.O. Box 176, Bay Head, NJ 08742-0176 Tel 732-892-1276; Fax: 732-892-3365
E-mail: JSVacation@aol.com
Web site: http://www.jerseyshorevacation.com
Dist(s): **Koen Bk. Distributors.**

Jessel Gallery, *(0-9660381)* 1019 Atlas Peak Rd., Napa, CA 94558 Tel 707-257-2350; Fax: 707-257-2396
Dist(s): **Baker & Taylor Bks..**

Jesuit Bks., *(0-913452)* 2300 S. Washington St., Tacoma, WA 98405 (SAN 201-0232) Tel 206-756-3266
Dist(s): **Baker & Taylor Bks.**
Quality Bks., Inc..

†Jewish Lights Publishing, *(1-58023; 1-879045)* Div. of LongHill Partners, Inc., Sunset Farm Offices, Rte. 4, Woodstock, VT 05091 (SAN 242-6439) Tel 802-457-4000; Fax: 802-457-4004; Toll Free: 800-962-4544 (orders)
E-mail: sales@jewishlights.com; everyone@longhillpartners.com
Web site: http://www.jewishlights.com
Dist(s): **Baker & Taylor Bks.**
Bookazine Co., Inc.
New Leaf Distributing Co., Inc.
Spring Arbor Distributors, Inc.; *CIP.*

†Jewish Pubn. Society, *(0-8276; 965-7157)* Orders Addr.: 22883 Quicksilver Dr., Dulles, VA 20166 (SAN 253-9446) Tel 703-661-1529; 703-661-1165; Fax: 703-661-1501; Toll Free: 800-355-1165; Edit Addr.: 2100 Arch St., 2nd Flr., Philadelphia, PA 19103 Tel 215-832-0601; Fax: 215-568-2017; Toll Free: 800-234-3151
E-mail: shirleyb@ix.netcom.com; marketing@jewishpub.org; www.jewishpub.org
Web site: http://www.jewishpub.org
Dist(s): **Gefen Bks.**; *CIP.*

Jimcin Recordings, *(1-55688)* Orders Addr.: P.O. Box 536, Portsmouth, RI 02871 (SAN 694-2377) Toll Free: 800-538-3034; Edit Addr.: 240 Bramans Ln., Portsmouth, RI 02871
E-mail: jimcin@jimcin.com
Web site: http://www.jimcin.com.

Jireh Pubs., *(0-9653197)* P.O. Box 99003, Norfolk, VA 23509-9003 Tel 757-558-4964; Fax: 757-558-4965 Do not confuse with companies with the same or similar name in West Monroe, LA , Baltimore, MD.
E-mail: MRossrodge@aol.com
Web site: http://www.jirehpublishers.com.

JMS Productions, *(1-889440)* Orders Addr.: P.O. Box 1936, New York, NY 10159 Tel 718-445-5340; Toll Free: 800-710-2030; Edit Addr.: 45-15 Colden St., No. 6A, Flushing, NY 11355.

JNMedia Bks. Imprint of JNMedia, Inc.

JNMedia, Inc., *(1-930128)* PMB 109 2124 Broadway, New York, NY 10023-1722 Fax: 916-404-6601; *Imprints:* JNMedia Books (JNMedia)
E-mail: jnmediany@aol.com
Web site: http://www.jnmedia.com.

Johnson, J LLC, *(0-9713224)* P.O. Box 910, Montrose, AL 36559 Tel 251-990-3358; Fax: 251-990-5966.

Johnson, Mabel Quality Paperbacks, *(0-9600838)* P.O. Box 7, Boring, OR 97009 (SAN 206-1015) Tel 503-663-3428.

Johnson, Michael Presentations, *(1-893672)* Rte. 1, Box 234, Idabel, OK 74745 Tel 580-286-7784; Fax: 580-286-7476
E-mail: michaelspeaks@msn.com.

Johnson, Zenobia M., *(0-9617411)* 327 Pompano Cir., Foster City, CA 94404-1903 (SAN 663-9739).

Johnston, Don Inc., *(1-893376; 1-58702; 1-4105)* Orders Addr.: 26799 W. Commerce Dr., Volo, IL 60073 Tel 847-740-0749; Fax: 847-740-7326; Toll Free: 800-999-4660
Web site: http://www.donjohnston.com.

Jomilt Pubns., *(0-9616076)* 329 W. Mt. Airy Ave., Philadelphia, PA 19119 (SAN 697-9939) Tel 215-750-4173.

Jonah Pr., *(0-929422)* P.O. Box 5473, Sherman Oaks, CA 91413 (SAN 249-4000) Tel 818-986-1809.

†Jonathan David Pubs., Inc., *(0-8246)* 68-22 Eliot Ave., Middle Village, NY 11379 (SAN 169-5274) Tel 718-456-8611; Fax: 718-894-2818
E-mail: jondavpub@aol.com
Web site: http://www.jdbooks.com; *CIP.*

†Jones, Bob Univ. Pr., *(0-89084; 1-57924; 1-59166)* 1700 Wade Hampton Blvd., Greenville, SC 29614 (SAN 223-7512) Tel 864-242-5731; Fax: 864-298-8398; Toll Free Fax: 800-525-8398; Toll Free: 800-845-5731
E-mail: bjup@bjup.com
Web site: http://www.bjup.com; *CIP.*

Joseph, Michael Imprint of Viking Penguin

JoshCo, LLC, *(0-9668355)* P.O. Box 23815, Knoxville, TX 37933-1815 Tel 865-675-6064
E-mail: joshcollc@aol.com
Web site: http://www.joshandfriends.com.

Joshua Morris Publishing, Incorporated *See* **Reader's Digest Children's Publishing, Inc.**

Journal Pubns., *(0-935676; 1-889971)* Orders Addr.: P.O. Box 9750, Glendale, CA 91226 (SAN 213-6287) ; Edit Addr.: 2663 Sausalito Ave., Carlsbad, CA 92008.

Jove Imprint of Berkley Publishing Group

Joy Enterprises, *(0-9639450)* 332 S. Queen St., Littlestown, PA 17340 Tel 717-359-7529 (phone/fax) Do not confuse with Joy Enterprises, Searcy, AR.

Joy Street Bks. Imprint of Little Brown & Co.

JTG of Nashville, *(0-938971; 1-884832)* Orders Addr.: P.O. Box 158116, Nashville, TN 37215 (SAN 630-3323) Fax: 615-665-9468; Toll Free: 800-222-2584
Dist(s): **Baker & Taylor Bks..**

Judaica Pr., Inc., The, *(0-910818; 1-880582; 1-932443)* 123 Ditmas Ave., Brooklyn, NY 11218 (SAN 204-9856) Tel 718-972-6200; Fax: 718-972-6204; Toll Free: 800-972-6201
E-mail: info@judaicapress.com
Web site: http://www.judaicapress.com.

†Judson Pr., *(0-8170)* Div. of American Baptist Churches, U.S.A., P.O. Box 851, Valley Forge, PA 19482-0851 (SAN 201-0348) Tel 610-768-2118; Fax: 610-768-2107; Toll Free: 800-331-1053
Web site: http://www.judsonpress.com
Dist(s): **Appalachian Bible Co.**
Riverside
Spring Arbor Distributors, Inc.; *CIP.*

Jump at the Sun Imprint of Hyperion Bks. for Children

Junebug Bks. Imprint of NewSouth, Inc.

Junior League of Charleston, South Carolina, Inc., *(0-9607854)* 51 Folly Rd., Charleston, SC 29407 (SAN 218-8031) Tel 843-763-5284; Fax: 843-763-1626
E-mail: office@jlcharleston.org
Web site: http://www.jlcharleston.org/.

Junior League of Philadelphia, Inc., *(0-9626959)* 215 S 16th St., Philadelphia, PA 19102 Tel 215-731-1446; Fax: 215-731-1978
E-mail: jlphila@atxmail.com
Web site: http://www.jphila.com.

Jupiter Pr., *(1-886645)* 77 S. Franklin St., Chagrin Falls, OH 44022 Tel 440-247-3616; Fax: 440-247-5431 Do not confuse with companies with the same name in Lake Bluff, IL, Syracuse, NY, Beverly Hills CA
E-mail: lundade@aol.com.

Just Good Vermont Products, *(0-9657986)* 633 Irish Settlement Rd., Underhill, VT 05489 Tel 802-899-3466; Fax: 802-899-5022.

Just Us Bks., Inc., *(0-940975)* 356 Glenwood Ave., East Orange, NJ 07107 (SAN 664-7413) Tel 973-676-4345; Fax: 973-677-7570
E-mail: JUSTUSBOOK@aol.com.

JUST-US Books *See* **Ike, J. Bks.**

Juventud, Editorial (ESP) *(84-261) Dist. by* **Continental Bk.**

Juventud, Editorial (ESP) *(84-261) Dist. by* **AIMS Intl.**

Juventud, Editorial (ESP) *(84-261) Dist. by* **Distribks Inc.**

KAC, Inc., *(0-9622353)* 3425 S. 94th Ave., Omaha, NE 68124 Tel 402-393-8537.

KCDI Publishing, *(0-9655719)* 674 E. Highway 80, Suite 303, Abilene, TX 79601 Tel 915-672-6476; Fax: 915-672-4202
Dist(s): **Hervey's Booklink & Cookbook Warehouse.**

K C Enterprise *See* **Wonder Kids Pubns.**

KRW International, Inc., *(0-9671611)* 9232 Eton Ave., Chatsworth, CA 91311 (SAN 254-6418) Tel 818-678-0000; Fax: 818-678-0005; Toll Free: 888-579-4685
E-mail: roni@krwintl.com.
Web site: http://www.quizm.com.

Kabel Pubs., *(0-930329; 1-57529)* 11225 Huntover Dr., Rockville, MD 20852-3613 (SAN 670-8323) Tel 301-468-6463 (phone/fax); Toll Free: 800-543-3167
E-mail: kabelcomp@erols.com
Web site: http://www.erols.com/kabelcomp/index2.html.

Kabouter Products, *(1-57909)* 1815 Highland Pl., Berkeley, CA 94709-1009 Tel 510-839-3931; Fax: 510-839-0954; Toll Free: 888-246-6637
Dist(s): **Bookpeople**
New Leaf Distributing Co., Inc.
Sunbelt Pubns., Inc..

Kaeden Bks. Imprint of Kaeden Corp.

Kaeden Corp., *(1-57874; 1-879835)* Orders Addr.: P.O. Box 16190, Rocky River, OH 44116 Tel 440-356-0030; Fax: 440-356-5081; Toll Free: 800-890-7323; Edit Addr.: 19915 Lake Rd., Rocky River, OH 44116; *Imprints:* Kaeden Books (Kaeden)
E-mail: books@kaeden.com
Web site: http://www.kaeden.com.

kahani.com, Inc., *(1-929981)* 31 Chase Ln., Ithaca, NY 14850
Web site: http://kahani.com.

Kalamvocas, Patricia Osborne, *(0-9648412)* 124 Woodridge Pl., Laurel, MD 20724-1801
E-mail: pattyok@prodigy.com.

Kalevala Bks., *(1-880954)* 160 Longridge Dr., Bloomingdale, IL 60108-1416.

†Kamehameha Schools Pr., *(0-87336)* 1887 Makuakane St., Honolulu, HI 96817 Tel 808-842-8719; Fax: 808-842-8895; Toll Free: 800-842-4682 (ext. 8719)
E-mail: kspress@ksbe.edu
Web site: http://www.ksbe.edu/pubs/KSPress/catalog.html
Dist(s): **Bess Pr., Inc.**
Booklines Hawaii, Ltd.
Island Heritage Publishing
Native Bks.; *CIP.*

Kamishibai for Kids, *(1-893533)* Orders Addr.: P.O. Box 629, New York, NY 10025 Tel 212-663-2471; Fax: 212-662-5836; Toll Free: 800-772-1228
E-mail: kamishi@cybernex.net
Web site: http://www.kamishibai.com.

Kane Pr., The, *(1-57565)* 240 W. 35th St., Suite 300, New York, NY 10001-2506 Tel 212-268-1435; Fax: 212-268-2044
E-mail: ndmattia@kanepress.com
Web site: http://www.kanepress.com
Dist(s): **Baker & Taylor Bks.**
Bookmen, Inc.
Booksource, The
Brodart Co..

†Kane/Miller Bk. Pubs., *(0-916291; 1-929132)* Orders Addr.: P.O. Box 8515, La Jolla, CA 92038 (SAN 295-8945) Tel 858-456-0540; Fax: 858-456-9641; Toll Free: 800-968-1930; *Imprints:* Cranky Nell Books (Cranky Nell Bks); Creative Nell (Creative Nell)
E-mail: kira@kanemiller.com
Web site: http://www.kanemiller.com; http://www.everyonepoops.com
Dist(s): **Cheng & Tsui Co.**
Distributors, The
Lectorum Pubns., Inc.; *CIP.*

Names

Kapa Hse. Pr., *(0-9637328)* Div. of Kapa Editorial Services, 1202 Lexington Ave., Suite 331, New York, NY 10028 Tel 212-288-7763; Fax: 212-439-6107; 212-288-7763
E-mail: pkalliopi@aol.com.

Kar-Ben Copies, Incorporated *See* **Kar-Ben Publishing**

†Kar-Ben Publishing, *(0-929371; 0-930494; 1-58013)* Div. of Lerner Publishing Group, 1251 Washington Ave., N, Minnapolis, MN 55401 (SAN 210-7511) Tel 612-332-3344; Toll Free Fax: 800-332-1132; Toll Free: 800-452-7236
E-mail: karben@aol.com
Web site: http://www.karben.com; *CIP.*

Karl Davidson Training & Development Company *See* **Team Effort Publishing Co.**

Karmichael Pr., *(0-9653966; 1-931770)* HC3, Box 155D, Port Saint Joe, FL 32456-9536 Tel 850-648-4488 (phone/fax); Toll Free: 888-443-9893
E-mail: books@karmichaelpress.com
Web site: http://www.karmichaelpress.com
Dist(s): **Baker & Taylor Bks.**
Book Wholesalers, Inc.
Brodart Co.
Follett Library Resources
Unique Bks., Inc..

Kate, Incorporated *See* **KAC, Inc.**

Kav Books, Incorporated *See* **Royal Fireworks Publishing Co.**

Kazi Pubns., Inc., *(0-933511; 0-935782; 1-56744)* 3023 W. Belmont Ave., Chicago, IL 60618 (SAN 162-3397) Tel 773-267-7001; Fax: 773-267-7002
E-mail: info@kazi.org
Web site: http://www.kazi.org.

Kehot Pubn. Society, *(0-8266)* Orders Addr.: 291 Kingston Ave., Brooklyn, NY 11213 Tel 718-778-0226; Fax: 718-778-4148; Toll Free: 877-463-7567 (877-4MERKOS); Edit Addr.: 770 Eastern Pkwy., Brooklyn, NY 11213 (SAN 220-7060) ; *Imprints:* Merkos L'Inyonei Chinuch (Merkos LInyonei Chinuch)
E-mail: kehot@juno.com; orders@kehotonline.com
Web site: http://www.kehotonline.com
Dist(s): **Baker & Taylor Bks.**
Bookazine Co., Inc..

Kelsey Enterprises Publishing *See* **Cheval International**

Kendall Green Pubns., 800 Florida Ave., NE, Washington, DC 20002-3695
Dist(s): **Gallaudet Univ. Pr..**

Kendall Publishing, *(0-9647633)* 6550 Delmonico Dr., No. 304, Colorado Springs, CO 80919 Tel 719-522-0880.

Kendall/Hunt Publishing Co., *(0-7872; 0-8403; 0-7575)* Orders Addr.: P.O. Box 1840, Dubuque, IA 52004-1840; Edit Addr.: 4050 Westmark Dr., Dubuque, IA 52002 (SAN 203-9184) Tel 563-589-1000; Fax: 563-589-1046; Toll Free Fax: 800-772-9165; Toll Free: 800-228-0810
E-mail: orders@kendallhunt.com; kmaiers@kendallhunt.com
Web site: http://www.kendallhunt.com.

Kennesaw Publishing, *(0-9664424)* 401 Old Mill Dr., Carrollton, GA 30117 Tel 770-830-0793; Fax: 770-830-9354
E-mail: kenpub@worldnet.att.net.

Kensington Bks. Imprint of Kensington Publishing Corp.

Kensington Publishing Corp., *(0-7860; 0-8184; 0-8217; 1-55817; 1-57566; 0-7582)* 850 Third Ave., New York, NY 10022-6222 Tel 212-407-1500; Fax: 212-935-0699; Toll Free: 800-221-2647; *Imprints:* Zebra Books (Zebra Kensgtn); Kensington Books (Knsington)
E-mail: jmclean@kensingtonbooks.com
Web site: http://www.kensingtonbooks.com
Dist(s): **Penguin Group (USA) Inc.**
Worldwide Media Service, Inc..

Kestrel Pubns., *(0-9628472)* 1811 Stonewood Dr., Dayton, OH 45432-4002 Tel 937-426-5110; Fax: 937-320-1832; Toll Free: 800-314-4678 (orders only)
E-mail: invisiblei@aol.com
Web site: http://www.invink.com
Dist(s): **Baker & Taylor Bks.**
Partners Pubs. Group, Inc..

Ketman Publishing *See* **Wooster Bk. Co., The**

Key Porter Bks. (CAN) *(0-88619; 0-919493; 0-919630; 1-55013; 1-55263; 1-85375; 1-55356) Dist. by* **Firefly Bks Limited.**

Khalifah's Booksellers & Associates *See* **Conquering Bks.**

Kid Galaxy, Incorporated *See* **Dolls Corp.**

Kids Can Pr., Ltd., *(0-919964; 0-921103; 1-55074; 1-55337)* 2250 Military Rd., Tonawanda, NY 14150 Toll Free Fax: 800-221-9985; Toll Free: 866-481-5827
E-mail: jcase@kidscan.com.

Kids Comfort, Inc., *(1-887453)* 2295 Rockledge Dr., NE, Keizer, OR 97303 Tel 503-390-3553.

Kidsbooks, Inc., *(0-942025; 1-56156; 1-58865)* Orders Addr.: 3535 W. Peterson Ave., Chicago, IL 60659 Tel 773-509-0707; Fax: 773-509-0404; Edit Addr.: 230 Fifth Ave., Suite 1710, New York, NY 10001 (SAN 666-3729) Tel 212-685-4444; Fax: 212-889-1122
E-mail: Dblau@kidsbooks.com
Web site: http://www.kidsbooks.com.

Kidz-Med, Inc., *(1-891359)* Orders Addr.: P.O. Box 490862, Miami, FL 33149-0862 Tel 305-361-6378; Fax: 305-361-6216; Edit Addr.: 450 Grapetree Dr., No. 311, Key Biscayne, FL 33149
E-mail: docbip@kidzmed.com
Web site: http://kidzmed.com
Dist(s): **Baker & Taylor Entertainment**
Medcom/Trainex
Professional Media Service Corp.
Quality Bks., Inc.
Silver Mine Video
Tapeworm Video Distributor, Inc.
Trademark Direct, Inc.
Unique Bks., Inc.
Veriad
Vide-O-Go/That's Infotainment.

Kimberlite Publishing Co., *(0-9632675)* 44091 Olive Ave., Hemet, CA 92544-2609 Tel 909-927-7726 Do not confuse with Kimberlite Publishing, Ventura, CA
E-mail: frumpypapa@yahoo.com.

Kimbo Educational, *(0-937124; 1-56346)* Div. of United Sound Arts, Inc., Orders Addr.: P.O. Box 477, Long Branch, NJ 07740 (SAN 630-1592) Tel 732-870-3340 (phone/fax); Toll Free: 800-631-2187; Edit Addr.: 10 N. Third Ave., Long Branch, NJ 07740
E-mail: kimboed@aol.com
Web site: http://www.kimboed.com
Dist(s): **Midwest Tape**
Rounder Kids Music Distribution.

Kindermusik International, *(0-945613; 1-931127; 1-58987)* Orders Addr.: P.O. Box 26575, Greensboro, NC 27415 (SAN 247-3747) Tel 336-273-3363; Fax: 336-273-2023; Toll Free: 800-628-5687; Edit Addr.: 6204 Corporate Park Dr., Browns Summit, NC 27214 (SAN 247-3755)
E-mail: info@kindermusik.com
Web site: http://www.kindermusik.com
Dist(s): **BookWorld Services, Inc..**

KinderWord, *(0-9642613)* 9218 Crownwood Rd., Ellicott City, MD 21042 Tel 410-750-3666
Dist(s): **Baker & Taylor Bks..**

Kindred Press *See* **Kindred Productions**

Kindred Productions, *(0-919797; 0-921788)* Orders Addr.: 315 S. Lincoln St., Hillsboro, KS 67063 Tel 316-947-3151; Fax: 316-947-3266; Toll Free: 800-545-7322
E-mail: kindred@mbconf.ca
Web site: http://www.mbconf.org/kindred.htm
Dist(s): **Spring Arbor Distributors, Inc..**

King RIT - ACKS Pubs., *(0-9714446)* 5584 Hwy 41 S., Oconto, WI 54153 Tel 920-834-3927
E-mail: thekings12@juno.com.

Kingfisher Imprint of Houghton Mifflin Co. Trade & Reference Div.

Kingsley, Jessica Pubs. (GBR) *(1-85302; 1-84310) Dist. by* **Taylor and Fran.**

Kitchen Sink Pr., Inc., *(0-87816; 1-56862; 1-879450)* Div. of Disappearing, Inc., 529 Belchertown Rd., Amherst, MA 01002-2705 (SAN 212-7784) Tel 413-586-9525; Fax: 413-586-7040
E-mail: service@deniskitchen.com
Web site: http://www.deniskitchen.com
Dist(s): **Baker & Taylor Bks.**
Bayside Entertainment Distribution
Capital City
Last Gasp Eco-Funnies, Inc..

Kiva Publishing, Inc., *(1-885772)* 21731 E. Buckskin Dr., Walnut, CA 91789 Tel 909-595-6833; Fax: 909-860-5424; Toll Free: 800-634-5482
E-mail: kivapub@aol.com
Web site: http://www.kivapub.com
Dist(s): **Baker & Taylor Bks.**
Bookpeople
Canyonlands Pubns.
New Leaf Distributing Co., Inc.
Quality Bks., Inc.
Treasure Chest Bks..

Klas, Nell, *(0-9628560)* 5685 Shadow Ridge Dr., Castro Valley, CA 94552 Tel 510-537-7706.

Klopp, Barbara Murray, *(0-9659428)* P.O. Box 147, Orr's Island, ME 04066 Tel 941-587-5064
E-mail: alexzig@midcoast.com
Web site: http://www.alexzig.com
Dist(s): **Magazines, Inc..**

Klutz, *(0-932592; 1-57054; 1-878257; 1-59174)* Div. of Scholastic, Inc., 455 Portage Ave., Palo Alto, CA 94306 (SAN 212-7539) Tel 650-857-0888; Fax: 650-857-9110
Web site: http://www.klutz.com
Dist(s): **Baker & Taylor Bks..**

†Kluwer Academic Pubs., *(0-412; 0-7923; 0-85200; 0-89838; 1-55608; 90-5576; 90-440; 1-4020)* Orders Addr.: P.O. Box 358, Hingham, MA 02018-0358 (SAN 662-0647) Tel 781-871-6600; Fax: 781-681-9045 (Customer Service); 781-871 6528; Edit Addr.: 101 Philip Dr. Assinippi Park, Norwell, MA 02061 (SAN 211-481X); a/o Kluwer Academic/Plenum Pubs., 233 Spring St., 7th Flr., New York, NY 10013-1522 Tel 212-620-8000; *Imprints:* Kluwer Academic/Human Science Press (Kluwer Acad Hman Sci)
E-mail: kluwer@wkap.com
Web site: http://www.wkap.nl
Dist(s): **Aspen Pubs., Inc.**
Lippincott Williams & Wilkins
netLibrary, Inc.; *CIP.*

Kluwer Academic/Human Science Pr. Imprint of Kluwer Academic Pubs.

†Knoll, Allen A. Pubs., *(0-9627297; 1-888310)* 200 W. Victoria St., Santa Barbara, CA 93101-3627 (SAN 299-0539) Tel 805-564-3377 (orders); Fax: 805-966-6657 (orders); Toll Free: 800-777-7623 (orders)
E-mail: bookinfo@knollpublishers.com
Web site: http://www.knollpublishers.com
Dist(s): **Baker & Taylor Bks.**
Brodart Co.; *CIP.*

†Knopf, Alfred A. Inc., *(0-375; 0-394; 0-676; 0-679)* Div. of The Knopf Publishing Group, Orders Addr.: 400 Hahn Rd., Westminster, MD 21157 Tel 410-848-1900; Toll Free Fax: 800-659-2436; Toll Free: 800-733-3000 (orders); Edit Addr.: 299 Park Ave., New York, NY 10171 (SAN 202-5825) Tel 212-751-2600; Fax: 212-572-2593; Toll Free: 800-726-0600
E-mail: customerservice@randomhouse.com
Web site: http://www.randomhouse.com/knopf
Dist(s): **Libros Sin Fronteras**; *CIP.*

Knopf Bks. for Young Readers Imprint of Random Hse. Children's Bks.

Knopf Publishing Group, *(0-375; 0-385; 1-4000)* Orders Addr.: 400 Hahn Rd., Westminster, MD 21157 Tel 410-848-1900; Toll Free: 800-726-0600; Edit Addr.: 299 Park Ave., New York, NY 10171; *Imprints:* Everyman's Library (Everymns Lib); Pantheon (Pantheon); Schocken (Schocken); Vintage (Vin Bks)
Dist(s): **Random Hse., Inc..**

Knowledge Adventure, Inc., *(1-56997)* Div. of Vivendi Universal Interactive, 6060 Center Dr., Los Angeles, CA 90045 Tel 310-649-8000.

Knowledge Kids Enterprises, Incorporated *See* **LeapFrog Enterprises, Inc.**

†Kodansha America, Inc., *(0-87011; 1-56836)* 575 Lexington Ave., 23rd Flr., New York, NY 10022-6102 (SAN 201-0526) Tel 917-322-6200; Fax: 212-935-6929; Toll Free: 800-451-7556
E-mail: Kabooks@aol.com; *CIP.*

Kolowalu Bk. Imprint of Univ. of Hawaii Pr.

Konecky & Konecky Imprint of Konecky, William S. Assocs., Inc.

Konecky, William S. Assocs., Inc., *(0-914427; 1-56852)* 72 Ayers Point Rd., Old Saybrook, CT 06475-4301 (SAN 663-2432) Tel 212-807-8230; Fax: 212-807-8239; *Imprints:* Konecky & Konecky (Konecky & Konecky).

Konemann, *(3-89508; 3-8290)* 137 W. 19th St., New York, NY 10011 Tel 212-367-8855; Fax: 212-367-8866; Toll Free: 888-317-8855
E-mail: mchin@konemann.com
Dist(s): **Bayside Entertainment Distribution**
Daedalus Bks.
Koen Bk. Distributors
Lectorum Pubns., Inc.
Mel Bay Pubns., Inc.
Trucatriche.

Kosciuszko Foundation, *(0-917004)* 15 E. 65th St., New York, NY 10021 (SAN 208-7251) Tel 212-734-2130; Fax: 212-628-4552; Toll Free: 800-287-9956
E-mail: thekf@pegasusnet.com
Web site: http://www.kosciuszkofoundation.org.

Names

Kramer, H.J. Inc., *(0-915811; 1-932073)* P.O. Box 1082, Tiburon, CA 94920 (SAN 294-0833) Fax: 415-435-5364; Toll Free: 800-972-6657; *Imprints:* Starseed Press (Starseed)
E-mail: hjkramer@jps.net
Web site: http://www.newworldlibrary.com
Dist(s): **Bookpeople**
New Leaf Distributing Co., Inc.
New World Library
Publishers Group West.

†Kregel Pubns., *(0-8254)* Div. of Kregel, Inc., Orders Addr.: P.O. Box 2607, Grand Rapids, MI 49501-2607 (SAN 206-9792) Tel 616-451-4775; Fax: 616-451-9330; Toll Free: 800-733-2607; Edit Addr.: 733 Wealthy St., SE., Grand Rapids, MI 49503-5553 (SAN 298-9115)
E-mail: kregelbooks@kregel.com
Web site: http://www.kregel.com
Dist(s): **Appalachian Bk. Distributors**
CRC Pubns.
FaithWorks
National Bk. Network
Riverside
Spring Arbor Distributors, Inc.; *CIP.*

Kripalu Pubns., *(0-940258)* Div. of Kripalu Ctr. for Yoga & Health, Box 793, Lenox, MA 01240 (SAN 217-5320) Tel 413-448-3168
Dist(s): **New Leaf Distributing Co., Inc..**

KrisPer Pubns., *(0-9660566)* 170 Hidden Valley Dr., Abilene, TX 79603 Tel 915-692-3811; Fax: 915-692-2116.

†Ktav Publishing Hse., Inc., *(0-87068; 0-88125)* Orders Addr.: P.O. Box 6249, Hoboken, NJ 07030 (SAN 201-0038) Tel 201-963-9524; Fax: 201-963-0102; Toll Free Fax: 800-626-7517 (orders); Edit Addr.: 900 Jefferson St., Hoboken, NJ 07030 (SAN 200-8866)
E-mail: orders@ktav.com; editor@ktav.com; staff@ktav.com
Web site: http://www.ktav.com
Dist(s): **Baker & Taylor Bks.**; *CIP.*

Kutie Kari Bks., Inc., *(1-884149)* 2461 Blueberry St., Inver Grove Heights, MN 55076 Tel 612-450-7427; Toll Free: 800-395-8843
E-mail: gharbo@garyharbo.com
Web site: http://www.garyharbo.com.

Kwela Bks. (ZAF) *(0-7957) Dist. by* **IPG Chicago.**

LCN, Inc., *(0-938934)* 6626 Silvermine Dr., No. 100, Austin, TX 78736-1703 (SAN 216-227X) Fax: 512-288-6452; Toll Free: 800-424-6291.

LNA Publishing, *(0-9653635)* 4939 Woods Edge Rd., Wilmington, NC 28409-3964.

L. T. Litho & Printing Company, Incorporated *See* **L.T. Publishing**

L.T. Publishing, *(1-879480)* 16811 Noyes Ave., Irvine, CA 92714 Tel 714-863-1340; Fax: 714-724-0732.

La Courte Echelle (CAN) *(0-920668; 2-89021) Dist. by* **Firefly Bks Limited.**

†La Leche League International, *(0-912500)* 1400 N. Meacham Rd., Schaumburg, IL 60173 (SAN 201-0585) Tel 847-519-7730; Fax: 847-519-0035
E-mail: llli@llli.org
Web site: http://www.lalecheleague.org; *CIP.*

Lacis Pubns., *(0-916896; 1-891656)* 3163 Adeline St., Berkeley, CA 94703 (SAN 202-9901) Tel 510-843-7178; Fax: 510-843-5018
E-mail: jules@lacis.com
Web site: http://www.lacis.com.

Ladybird Bks. Imprint of Penguin Group (USA) Inc.

Lamb, Wendy Imprint of Random Hse. Children's Bks.

Lambda Pubs., Inc., *(0-915361; 1-55774)* 3709 13th Ave., Brooklyn, NY 11218-3622 (SAN 291-0640) Tel 718-972-5449; Fax: 718-972-6307
E-mail: judaica@email.msn.com.

LaMear, Arline *See* **Lucky Cat Publishing**

Landmark Editions, Inc., *(0-933849)* P.O. Box 270169, Kansas City, MO 64127-2135 (SAN 692-6916) Tel 816-241-4919; Fax: 816-483-3755; Toll Free: 800-653-2665 (orders only); 1402 Kansas Ave., Kansas City, MO 64127
Web site: http://www.landmarkeditions.com
Dist(s): **Baker & Taylor Bks.**
Brodart Co.
Childswork/Childsplay.

Land's End Publishing, *(0-9709160)* Orders Addr.: P.O. Box 3066, Ocala, FL 34478 Tel 352-840-9562; Edit Addr.: 5801 NW 31st Ave., Ocala, FL 34475
E-mail: ayubu@aol.com.

Lane, Veronica Bks., *(0-9637597)* 513 Wilshire Blvd., No. 282, Santa Monica, CA 90401 (SAN 298-1157) Tel 310-315-9162; Fax: 310-315-9182; Toll Free: 800-651-1001.

†Lang, Peter Publishing, Inc., *(0-8204; 3-631)* Subs. of Verlag Peter Lang AG (SZ), 275 Seventh Ave., 28th Flr., New York, NY 10001-6708 (SAN 241-5534) Tel 212-647-7700; Fax: 212-647-7707; Toll Free: 800-770-5264
E-mail: patty@plang.com
Web site: http://www.peterlang.com; *CIP.*

LangMarc Publishing, *(1-880292)* Orders Addr.: P.O. Box 90488, Austin, TX 78709 (SAN 297-519X) Tel 512-394-0989; Fax: 512-394-0829; Toll Free: 800-864-1648 (orders only); Edit Addr.: 7500 Shadowridge Run, No. 28, Austin, TX 78749 Tel 512-394-0898; *Imprints:* North Sea Press (North Sea)
E-mail: langmarc@booksails.com
Web site: http://www.langmarc.com
Dist(s): **Baker & Taylor Bks.**
FaithWorks
Quality Bks., Inc.
Spring Arbor Distributors, Inc..

Lansing, Richard D. *See* **Purple Gorilla, LLC, The**

†Lantern Pr., Inc., Pubs., *(0-8313)* 6214 Wynfield Ct., Orlando, FL 32819 (SAN 201-0682) Tel 407-876-7720; Fax: 407-876-7758; *CIP.*

Lanton Haas Pr., *(0-9702482)* Orders Addr.: P.O. Box 29, Old Bethpage, NY 11804 Tel 516-367-3984; Fax: 516-367-6344; Edit Addr.: 37 Juneau Blvd., Woodbury, NY 11797
E-mail: appletreepress@aol.com.

†Laredo Publishing Co., Inc., *(1-56492)* 8907 Wilshire Blvd., No. 102, Beverly Hills, CA 90211 Tel 310-358-5288; Fax: 310-358-5282; Toll Free: 800-547-5113
E-mail: info@laredopublishing.com
Web site: http://www.laredopublishing.com; *CIP.*

†Larksdale, *(0-89896)* P.O. Box 801222, Houston, TX 77280 (SAN 220-0643) Tel 713-461-7200; Fax: 713-467-4770 (purchase orders); Toll Free: 877-461-7200; *Imprints:* Post Oak Press (Post Oak Pr); *CIP.*

†Larlin Corp., *(0-87419; 0-89783)* P.O. Box 1730, Marietta, GA 30061 (SAN 201-4432); *CIP.*

Larousse Kingfisher Chambers, Inc., *(0-7534; 1-85697; 970-22)* 215 Park Ave., S., New York, NY 10003 (SAN 297-7540) Tel 212-420-5800; Fax: 212-686-1082; 181 Ballardvale St., Wilmington, MA 01887
Web site: http://www.lkcpub.com
Dist(s): **Continental Bk. Co., Inc.**
Distribooks, Inc.
Giron Bks.
Lectorum Pubns., Inc.
Libros Sin Fronteras.

Last Gasp Eco-Funnies, Inc., *(0-86719)* Orders Addr.: P.O. Box 410067, San Francisco, CA 94141-0067 (SAN 216-8308); Edit Addr.: 777 Florida St., San Francisco, CA 94110-2025 (SAN 170-3242) Tel 415-824-6636; Fax: 415-824-1836; Toll Free: 800-366-5121
E-mail: lastgasp@hooked.net
Dist(s): **Bookpeople**
Publishers Group West
SPD-Small Pr. Distribution.

Latinarte, *(1-882161)* Orders Addr.: P.O. Box 1387, New York, NY 10159 Tel 212-714-7737.

Launch Pr., *(0-9613205; 1-877872)* P.O. Box 3050, Fairfax, VA 20855 (SAN 295-0154) Toll Free: 800-251-8336
Dist(s): **Self esteem shop II.**

Laurel Imprint of Dell Publishing

Laurel & Herbert, Inc., *(0-9619155)* P.O. Box 440266, Sugarloaf Shores, FL 33044 (SAN 243-4687) Tel 305-745-3506; Fax: 305-745-9070.

Laurel Leaf Imprint of Random Hse. Children's Bks.

Laurel Press *See* **Laurel & Herbert, Inc.**

Lavender Lady Pr., *(0-9639110)* P.O. Box 998, Sarasota, FL 34230-0998 Tel 941-629-7646; Fax: 941-629-4270.

Law, R.C. & Co., Inc., *(0-939925)* 4861 Chino Ave., Chino, CA 91710-5132 (SAN 200-609X) Tel 714-871-0940; Fax: 909-627-9475; Toll Free: 800-777-5292.

LB Bks. Imprint of Liberty Bell Productions

LCK Pr., *(1-891040)* Orders Addr.: P.O. Box 25011, Fort Wayne, IN 46895-5011 Tel 219-637-8520; Fax: 219-637-6317; Toll Free: 888-447-5747; Edit Addr.: 1607 Burningtree Ct., Fort Wayne, IN 46845.

LeapFrog Enterprises, Inc., *(1-58605; 1-932256; 1-59319)* 6401 Hollis St., Suite 150, Emeryville, CA 94608 Tel 510-420-5000; Fax: 510-420-5001; *Imprints:* LeapFrog School House (LeapSchHse)
Web site: http://www.leapfrogtoys.com.

LeapFrog Schl. Hse. Imprint of LeapFrog Enterprises, Inc.

Learn-Abouts, *(1-880038)* 8029 Renton Way, Sacramento, CA 95828 Tel 916-423-2499.

Learning Challenge, Inc., *(1-59203)* 36 Washington St., Wellesley, MA 02481 Tel 781-239-9900; Fax: 781-239-3273
Web site: http://www.learningchallenge.com.

Learning Crew, The, *(1-57812)* 571 W. 9320 S., Sandy, UT 84070 Tel 801-567-9792; Fax: 801-569-3094; Toll Free: 800-386-8673
E-mail: tlc@lgcy.com
Web site: http://www.learningcrew.com.

Learning Curve International, LLC, *(1-890647)* 314 W. Superior, 6th Flr., Chicago, IL 60610 Tel 312-470-7700; Fax: 312-470-9400; Toll Free: 800-704-8697
E-mail: jeff@lctmail.com
Web site: http://www.learningtoys.com; http://www.learningcurve.com.

Learning Horizons, Inc., *(1-58610)* Div. of American Greetings, One American Rd., Cleveland, OH 44144 Toll Free: 800-532-8876; *Imprints:* McClanahan Book (McClanahan Book)
E-mail: theresa.gamble@amgreetings.com
Web site: http://www.learninghorizons.com.

Learning Links, Inc., *(0-7675; 0-88122; 0-934048; 1-56982)* 2300 Marcus Ave., New Hyde Park, NY 11042 (SAN 241-3302) Tel 516-437-9071; Fax: 516-437-5392; Toll Free: 800-724-2616
Web site: http://www.learninglinks.com.

Learning Safari *See* **Pages, Inc.**

Leatherman, Diane, *(0-9665861)* P.O. Box 315, Cabin John, MD 20818-0315 Tel 301-229-1524
E-mail: diane.leatherman@prodigy.net
Web site: http://www.dianeleatherman.com.

Lectorum Pubns., Inc., *(0-9625162; 1-880507; 1-930332)* Subs. of Scholastic, Inc., 205 Chubb Ave., Lyndhurst, NJ 07071-3520 Tel 212-965-7322; Fax: 212-727-3035; Toll Free Fax: 877-532-8676; 877-532-8678; Toll Free: 800-345-5946
E-mail: info@lectorum.com
Web site: http://www.lectorum.com
Dist(s): **Libros Sin Fronteras.**

Lee & Low Bks., Inc., *(1-880000; 1-58430)* 95 Madison Ave., New York, NY 10016 Tel 212-779-4400 (General info./Editorial); Fax: 212-683-1894 (orders); Toll Free: 888-320-3395 (orders)
E-mail: info@leeandlow.com
Web site: http://www.leeandlow.com
Dist(s): **Lectorum Pubns., Inc..**

Lee Pubns., *(1-56297)* Div. of Stry-Lenkoff Co., Orders Addr.: P.O. Box 32120, Louisville, KY 40232 Tel 502-587-6804; Fax: 502-587-6822; Toll Free: 800-626-8247; Edit Addr.: 1100 W. Broadway, Louisville, KY 40232
Web site: http://www.leemagicpen.com.

Left Field Ink, *(0-9664737; 1-932431)* 3111 W. Burbank Blvd., No. 103, Burbank, CA 91505 (SAN 255-3082) Tel 818-558-5838; Fax: 818-558-1965; Toll Free: 800-768-6181; *Imprints:* Angel Gate (Angel Gate CA)
E-mail: dbishop@angelgatepress.com
Web site: http://www.leftfieldproduction.com; http://www.angelgatepress.com; http://www.prefabit.com; http://www.leftfieldink.com
Dist(s): **Diamond Comic Distributors, Inc..**

Left Field Productions *See* **Left Field Ink**

Legacy Hse., Inc., *(0-9608008)* Box 786, Orofino, ID 83544 (SAN 238-0684) Tel 208-476-5632 Do not confuse with Legacy Hse., Rescue, CA.

Legacy Pubns., *(0-933101)* Subs. of Pace Communications, Inc., Orders Addr.: 1301 Carolina, Greensboro, NC 27401 (SAN 662-2852) Tel 336-378-6065; Fax: 336-275-2864.

LegacyWords Publishing, *(0-934738; 1-56566)* 1214 Rugby Rd., Charlottesville, VA 22903-1237 (SAN 239-3948) Tel 434-984-1773; Fax: 434-977-1696
E-mail: frankt@tgmedia.com
Web site: http://www.legacywords.com
Dist(s): **Aviation Supplies & Academics, Inc..**

Lehua, Inc., *(0-9647491)* 931 University Ave., Suite 205, Honolulu, HI 96826
E-mail: lehua@ohia.com
Web site: http://www.lehuainc.com.

Leigh, Tina Illustrator, *(0-9715673)* P.O. Box 7, Higganum, CT 06441
E-mail: tleighillustrator@snet.net.

Names

Leisure Arts, Inc., *(0-942237; 1-57486)* Orders Addr.: P.O. Box 55595, Little Rock, AR 72215-5595 (SAN 666-9565) Tel 501-868-8800; Fax: 501-868-8937; Toll Free: 800-643-8030 (customer service); 800-526-5111 ; Edit Addr.: 5701 Ranch Dr., Little Rock, AR 72223 (SAN 666-9573) Tel 650-324-5586; Fax: 650-324-1532; Toll Free: 800-227-7346
E-mail: barker1@sunset.com
Web site: http://www.leisurearts.com.

Leisure Bks. Imprint of Dorchester Publishing Co., Inc.

Lem Publishing & Production, *(0-9612948)* Orders Addr.: P.O. Box 18045, Louisville, KY 40261 (SAN 291-2759) Tel 502-479-8020
E-mail: mary_meena@hotmail.com
Web site: http://www.bookstohave.com.

Lemonade Sundays, *(0-9647799)* Orders Addr.: P.O. Box 826, Mill Valley, CA 94942-0826 Tel 415-388-4829; Fax: 415-388-3579; Edit Addr.: 540 Browning St., Mill Valley, CA 94941
E-mail: dietzel@bigfoot.com
Web site:
http://members.tripod.com/~Dietzel/index.html
Dist(s): **Brush Dance, Inc.**
Children's Small Pr. Collection
Quality Bks., Inc..

Lems-Dworkin, Carol Pubs., *(0-9637048)* Orders Addr.: Box 1646, Evanston, IL 60204-1646 Tel 847-328-1029; Fax: 847-869-4239; Edit Addr.: 2305 Brown Ave., Evanston, IL 60201
E-mail: lemsdworkn@aol.com
Web site: http://members.aol.com lemsdworkn.

†Leonard, Hal Corp., *(0-634; 0-7935; 0-88188; 0-9607350; 1-56516)* Orders Addr.: P.O. Box 13819, Milwaukee, WI 53213-0819 Tel 414-774-3630; Fax: 414-774-3259; Toll Free: 800-524-4425; Edit Addr.: 7777 W. Bluemound Rd., Milwaukee, WI 53213 (SAN 239-250X)
E-mail: halinfo@halleonard.com
Web site: http://www.halleonard.com
Dist(s): **Giron Bks.**; *CIP.*

†Lerner Publishing Group, *(0-8225; 0-87614; 0-929371; 0-930494; 1-57505; 1-58013)* Orders Addr.: 1251 Washington Ave., N., Minneapolis, MN 55401 Toll Free Fax: 800-332-1132; Toll Free: 800-328-4929; *Imprints:* First Avenue Editions (First Ave Edns); Runestone Press (Runestone Pr); Lerner Publications (Lerner Publctns); Carolrhoda Books (Carolrhoda); LernerSports (LernerSports)
E-mail: custserve@lernerbook.com
Web site: http://www.lernerbooks.com;
http://www.karben.com; *CIP.*

Lerner Publishing Group, The *See* **Lerner Publishing Group**

Lerner Pubns. Imprint of Lerner Publishing Group

LernerSports Imprint of Lerner Publishing Group

Less Pr., *(0-9657367)* 100 Hannah Niles Way, Braintree, MA 02184-7261 Tel 781-848-0555.

Levin Family Publishing, *(0-9642777)* R.D. 4, Box 808, Green River Rd., Brattleboro, VT 05301 Tel 802-257-1482; Fax: 802-254-4670.

Levin, Hugh Lauter Assocs., *(0-88363)* 9 Burr Rd., Westport, CT 06880-4220 (SAN 201-6109)
E-mail: inquiries@hlla.com
Web site: http://www.hlla.com
Dist(s): **F&W Pubns., Inc.**
Publishers Group West.

Levine, Arthur A. Bks. Imprint of Scholastic, Inc.

Levinson Bks. Ltd. (GBR) *(1-86233; 1-899607) Dist. by* **Sterling.**

Levite of Apache Publishing, *(0-927562; 0-9618634)* 113 Hal Muldrow Dr., Norman, OK 73069-5268 (SAN 668-3983) Tel 405-366-6442.

LHA Bks., *(0-9656945)* Div. of Linda Hardy & Assocs., 16816 Second Ave., SW, Seattle, WA 98166 Tel 206-244-0339; Fax: 206-244-5574
E-mail: LHABooks@gte.net
Web site: http://www.home1.gte.net/lhabooks/ index.htm.

Liberty Bell Productions, *(1-890963)* 740 S. Burnside Ave. Apt. 117, Los Angeles, CA 90036-3890; *Imprints:* LB Books (LB Bks)
Dist(s): **APG Direct.**

Liberty Lines, *(0-9630669)* 404 Dublin Pike, Dublin, PA 18917 Tel 215-249-9030; Fax: 215-249-9130.

Librairie du Liban Pubns. (FRA) *Dist. by* **Intl Bk Ctr.**

Library of America, The, *(0-940450; 1-883011; 1-931082)* Div. of Literary Classics of the U. S., Inc., 14 E. 60th St., New York, NY 10022 (SAN 286-9918) Tel 212-308-3360; Fax: 212-750-8352
E-mail: info@loa.org
Web site: http://www.loa.org
Dist(s): **Penguin Group (USA) Inc..**

Libros de Ninos, *(0-9640533)* 1909 W. 27th St., Roswell, NM 88201-9737
Dist(s): **Booksource, The.**

Libros Sin Fronteras, P.O. Box 2085, Olympia, WA 98507 Tel 360-357-4332; Fax: 360-357-4964
E-mail: info@librossinfronteras.com
Web site: http://www.librossinfronteras.com.

Lickle Publishing, Inc., *(0-9650308; 1-890674)* 568 Island Dr., Palm Beach, FL 33480 Tel 561-881-0450; Fax: 561-881-0818; Toll Free: 888-454-2553
E-mail: wlickle@licklepub.com
Web site: http://www.licklepub.com.

Light & Life Communications, *(0-89367)* P.O. Box 535002, Indianapolis, IN 46253-5002 (SAN 206-8419) Tel 317-244-3660; Fax: 317-248-9055; Toll Free: 800-348-2513.

Light & Life Publishing Co., *(0-937032; 1-880971)* 4808 Park Glen Rd., Minneapolis, MN 55416 (SAN 213-8565) Tel 612-925-3888; Fax: 612-925-3918
E-mail: info@light-n-life.com
Web site: http://www.light-n-life.com.

Light Rain Communications, *(0-9639270)* 520 Third St., Harrisonburg, VA 22801 Tel 540-432-0485.

Light Technology Communication Services *See* **Light Technology Publishing**

Light Technology Publishing, *(0-929385; 1-891824)* Orders Addr.: P.O. Box 3870, Flagstaff, AZ 86003 (SAN 249-1389) Tel 520-526-1345; Fax: 520-714-1132; Toll Free: 800-450-0985; Edit Addr.: 4030 E. Huntington Dr., Flagstaff, AZ 86004; *Imprints:* Starchild Press (Strchld Pr)
E-mail: sedonajo@sedonajo.com
Web site: http://www.sedonajournal.com
Dist(s): **New Leaf Distributing Co., Inc..**

Light-Beams Publishing, *(0-9708104)* Orders Addr.: 10 Toon Ln., Lee, NH 03824 Tel 603-659-1300; Fax: 603-659-3399; Toll Free: 800-397-7641
E-mail: info@light-beams.com
Web site: http://www.lightbeams.com;
http://www.fairyhouses.com
Dist(s): **Baker & Taylor Bks.**
Book Wholesalers, Inc.
Brodart Co.
Koen Bk. Distributors
Library Video Co.
Midwest Tape.

Lighten Up Enterprises, *(1-879127)* P.O. Box 44516, Eden Prairie, MN 55344-1516 Tel 612-835-1882; Fax: 612-835-6540; Toll Free: 800-962-6082
Web site: http://www.lightenupinc.com
Dist(s): **Adventure Pubns., Inc..**

Lightning Rod Limited Imprint of Windstorm Creative Ltd.

Lightyear Entertainment, L.P., *(1-56896; 1-879496)* 434 Avenue Of The Americas. Flr. 6, New York, NY 10011-8411 Toll Free: 800-229-7867
E-mail: mail@lightyear.com
Web site: http://www.lightyear.com/
Dist(s): **Follett Media Distribution**
Warner Home Video, Inc..

Lightyear Pr. Imprint of Buccaneer Bks., Inc.

Liguori Pubns., *(0-7648; 0-89243)* One Liguori Dr., Liguori, MO 63057-9999 (SAN 202-6783) Tel 636-464-2500; Fax: 636-464-8449; Toll Free Fax: 800-325-9526; Toll Free: 800-325-9521 (orders)
E-mail: liguori@liguori.org; dcrosby@liguori.org
Web site: http://www.liguori.org
Dist(s): **ACTA Pubns.**
Baker & Taylor Bks..

Liko Publishing, *(0-9643781)* P.O. Box 673, Kealakekua, HI 96750 Tel 808-929-7542
Web site: http://www.21stcenturyhawaii.com/liko/
Dist(s): **Booklines Hawaii, Ltd.**
Native Bks..

Lilith & Co., *(0-9717860)* 31185 Blue Springs Rd., Meadowview, VA 24361-2441 Tel 276-475-5208
E-mail: pendragon@naxs.net
Web site: http://www.lilithandcompany.com.

Lily & Co. Publishing, *(1-929265)* P.O. Box 17382, Smithfield, RI 02917 Fax: 401-233-9623
E-mail: lilywriter@aol.com.

Limpid Butterfly Productions, The, *(0-9668781; 0-9709119)* P.O. Box 83942, San Diego, CA 92138 Fax: 858-679-4180; Toll Free: 800-837-7336
E-mail: booksbymaryo@hotmail.com;
look@limpidbutterfly.com
Web site: http://www.booksbymaryo.com;
http://www.limpidbutterfly.com
Dist(s): **Baker & Taylor Bks..**

Lincoln, Frances Ltd. (GBR) *(0-7112; 0-906459; 1-84507) Dist. by* **Publishers Group.**

Linden Pubs., *(0-89642; 0-7949)* 1750 N. Sycamore, Suite 305, Hollywood, CA 90028-8662 (SAN 206-7218) Tel 323-876-5190.

LinguiSystems, Inc., *(0-7606; 1-55999)* 3100 Fourth Ave., East Moline, IL 61244-9700 Tel 309-755-2300; Fax: 309-755-2377; Toll Free: 800-577-4555; 800-776-4332
E-mail: kmicka@linguisystems.com
Web site: http://www.linguisystems.com.

Linnet Bks. Imprint of Shoe String Pr., Inc.

†Lion Bks., *(0-87460)* 210 Nelson Rd., Scarsdale, NY 10583 (SAN 241-7529) Tel 914-725-2280; 914 725 3572; Fax: 914-725-3572; *CIP.*

†Lion Publishing, *(0-7459; 0-85648)* 4050 Lee Vance View, Colorado Springs, CO 80918-7102 (SAN 663-611X) Tel 719-536-0100; Toll Free: 800-437-4337
Web site: http://www.cookministries.com/
Dist(s): **Cook Communications Ministries**; *CIP.*

Lion Publishing PLC (GBR) *(0-7459; 0-85648) Dist. by* **Trafalgar.**

Lions & Tigers & Bears Publishing, Inc., *(1-893459)* 612 Hidden Valley Ln., Jefferson City, MO 65101 Tel 573-496-3600; Toll Free: 866-628-6463
Web site: http://www.MeAndUncleMike.com.

Lion's Paw Bks. Imprint of Coronet Bks. & Pubns.

LionX Publishing, *(0-9716085)* 705-2 E. Bidwell St., Suite No. 235, Folsom, CA 95630 (SAN 254-2021) Tel 916-984-0102; Fax: 916-984-3884
E-mail: info@lionxpublishing.com
Web site: http://www.lionxpublishing.com
Dist(s): **Biblio Distribution.**

Lippincott Imprint of Lippincott Williams & Wilkins

†Lippincott Williams & Wilkins, *(0-316; 0-397; 0-683; 0-7817; 0-8067; 0-8121; 0-88167; 0-89004; 0-89313; 0-89640; 0-911216; 1-881063; 4-260)* Orders Addr.: P.O. Box 1600, Hagerstown, MD 21741 Fax: 301-223-2400; Toll Free: 800-638-3030; Edit Addr.: 530 Walnut St., Philadelphia, PA 19106-3621 (SAN 201-0933) Tel 215-521-8300; Fax: 215-521-8902; Toll Free: 800-638-3030; 351 W. Camden St., Baltimore, MD 21201 Tel 410-528-4000; *Imprints:* Lippincott (Lippnctt)
E-mail: custserv@lww.com; orders@lww.com
Web site: http://www.lww.com
Dist(s): **Igaku-Shoin Medical Pubs.**; *CIP.*

Lippincott-Raven Publishers *See* **Lippincott Williams & Wilkins**

Listen U.S.A., *(0-88684)* Subs. of AMR Advanced Management Reports, P.O. Box 396, Greenwich, CT 06870 (SAN 695-4839) Tel 203-855-5525; Fax: 203-855-5526.

Listening Library Imprint of Random Hse. Audio Publishing Group

Literary Pubns., *(0-9617819; 1-930434)* Div. of Caswell Corp., Orders Addr.: P.O. Box 686, Avon, CT 06001-0686 (SAN 665-3197) Tel 860-677-8944; Fax: 860-676-2218; Toll Free: 800-203-7323; Edit Addr.: 34 Oak Bluff, Avon, CT 06001
E-mail: literarypub@aol.com
Web site: http://www.groundhounds.com.

Literate Ear, Inc., *(1-56544)* 8249 Fairview Rd., Elkins Park, PA 19117 Tel 215-635-4807; Fax: 215-635-4542; Toll Free: 800-777-8327.

Little Blue Works Imprint of Windstorm Creative Ltd.

†Little Brown & Co., *(0-316; 0-8212)* Div. of Time Warner Bk. Group, Orders Addr.: 3 Center Plaza, Boston, MA 02108-2084 (SAN 630-7248) Tel 617-227-0730; Toll Free Fax: 800-286-9471; Toll Free: 800-759-0190; Edit Addr.: Time & Life Bldg., 1271 Avenue of the Americas, New York, NY 10020 (SAN 200-2205) Tel 212-522-8700; Fax: 212-522-2067; Toll Free: 800-343-9204; *Imprints:* Joy Street Books (Joy St Bks); Back Bay (Back Bay)
E-mail: cust.service@littlebrown.com
Web site: http://www.littlebrown.com
Dist(s): **Continental Bk. Co., Inc.**
Hastings Bks.
Lectorum Pubns., Inc.
Rounder Kids Music Distribution
Beeler, Thomas T. Publisher
Thorndike Pr.
Time Warner Bk. Group
Warner Bks., Inc.; *CIP.*

Names

Little Brown Children's Bks., *(0-316; 0-8212)* Div. of Time Warner, Inc., 1271 Ave. of the Americas, New York, NY 10020 Tel 212-522-8700; Fax: 212-522-2067; Toll Free: 800-343-9204; 3 Center Plaza, Boston, NY 02108-2084 Tel 617-227-0730; Toll Free Fax: 800-286-9471; Toll Free: 800-759-0190; *Imprints:* Tingley, Megan Books (Megan Tingley Bks)
Web site: http://www.littlebrown.com
Dist(s): **Lectorum Pubns., Inc.**
Little Brown & Co.
Time Warner Bk. Group
Warner Bks., Inc..

Little Cajun Bks., *(0-931108)* Box 777, Loreauville, LA 70552 (SAN 212-5250) Tel 318-229-8455; Fax: 318-229-8457
E-mail: cajunmixes@aol.com
Web site: http://www.louisianacrawfishman.com.

Little City Bks., *(0-9652438)* 1033 Locust Ave., Charlottesville, VA 22901 Tel 804-295-3577; Toll Free: 800-373-5407.

Little Deer Pr., *(1-891360)* P.O. Box 183, Rainier, WA 98576 Tel 360-894-3459; Fax: 360-458-4399.

Little Egg Publishing Co., *(1-881669)* 9100 N. 55th St., Scottsdale, AZ 85253 Tel 602-443-1722; Fax: 602-443-8183.

Little Friend Pr., *(0-9641285; 1-890453)* P.O. Box 294, Scituate, MA 02066-0294 Toll Free: 800-617-3734
Dist(s): **Baker & Taylor Bks.**
Follett Library Resources
Koen Bk. Distributors
Quality Bks., Inc..

Little Imp Bks. Imprint of Impact Pubs., Inc.

Little Lochness Publishing, *(0-9654002)* 52 Durocher Terr., Poughkeepsie, NY 12603 Tel 914-473-7589.

Little Red Hen, *(0-9621669)* 412 Claremont Dr., Norman, OK 73069 (SAN 251-8457) Tel 405-329-0415.

Little Simon Imprint of Simon & Schuster Children's Publishing

Little Spirit Publishing, Inc., *(0-9619482)* 5410 Poncha Pass Ct., Colorado Springs, CO 80917 (SAN 244-9269) Tel 719-597-5733
E-mail: digthefun@canyoudigitgarden.com
Web site: http://www.canyoudigitgarden.com.

Little Tiger Pr., *(1-888444; 1-58431)* Div. of Futech Interactive Products, 39 S. La Salle St. Ste. 1410, Chicago, IL 60603-1706 Toll Free: 800-541-2205 Do not confuse Little Tiger Press in San Francisco, CA
E-mail: jody@futechsales.com
Dist(s): **Futech Educational Products, Inc.**
Lectorum Pubns., Inc..

Little Trucker Bks., *(1-892388)* P.O. Box 733, Hampstead, NC 28445 Tel 910-328-6281; Toll Free: 888-547-6281
Web site: http://www.littletruckerbooks.com.

Little Turtle Pr., *(0-9633574)* 6348 SE Morrison Ct., Portland, OR 97215-1948 Tel 503-221-1754 Do not confuse with Little Turtle Pubns., Omaha, NE.

Live Oak Media, *(0-87499; 0-941078; 1-59112; 1-59519)* Orders Addr.: P.O. Box 652, Pine Plains, NY 12567-0652 (SAN 217-3921) Tel 518-398-1010; Fax: 518-398-1070; Toll Free: 800-788-1121; Edit Addr.: P.O. Box 652, Pine Plains, NY 12567-0652 (SAN 669-1498)
E-mail: info@liveoakmedia.com
Web site: http://www.liveoakmedia.com
Dist(s): **BBC Audiobooks America**
Greathall Productions, Inc.
Lectorum Pubns., Inc.
Weston Woods Studios, Inc..

Living Water Pubns., *(0-9630534)* Orders Addr.: P.O. Box 13227, Edwardsville, KS 66113; Edit Addr.: 23 Beach, Edwardsville, KS 66113 Tel 913-441-6702 Do not confuse with Living Water Publications in Rockford, IL.

Livingston Pr., *(0-930501; 0-942979; 1-931982)* Univ. of West Alabama, Sta. 22, Livingston, AL 35470 Tel 205-652-3470; Fax: 205-652-3717; Toll Free: 800-959-3245 Do not confuse with Livingston Pr., Anaheim, CA
E-mail: jwt@uwa.edu
Web site: http://www.livingstonpress.uwa.edu.

L/L Research, *(0-945007)* Orders Addr.: P.O. Box 5195, Louisville, KY 40255-0195; Edit Addr.: 1504 Hobbs Park Rd., Louisville, KY 40223 (SAN 245-775X)
E-mail: carla@llresearch.org; jim@llresearch.org
Web site: http://www.llresearch.org
Dist(s): **New Leaf Distributing Co., Inc..**

Llama Bks., *(1-877778)* 821 Lenhardt Rd., Easley, SC 29640 Tel 864-859-8060; Fax: 864-855-9000.

Llewellyn Worldwide Ltd., *(0-7387; 0-87542; 1-56718; 1-892485)* 84 S. Wabasha St., Saint Paul, MN 55107 Tel 651-291-1970; Fax: 651-291-1908
Web site: http://www.llewellyn.com.

Lobster Cove Publishing Co., *(0-9669946)* c/o Bannon, 728 Washington St., Gloucester, MA 01930 Tel 978-281-5098; Fax: 978-524-3734
E-mail: kandk2@flash.net
Web site: http://www.gordon.edu/faculty/yonder_mountain.

Lobster Pr. (CAN) *(1-894222) Dist. by* **Publishers Group.**

Lobster Pr. (CAN) *(1-894222) Dist. by* **Advanced Global.**

Locust Hill Pr., *(0-933951; 0-9722289)* P.O. Box 260, West Cornwall, CT 06796 (SAN 693-0646) Tel 860-672-0060; Fax: 860-672-4968; 419 Main St., Goshen Tpke., West Cornwall, CT 06796
E-mail: locusthill@optonline.net.

Loder, Ann L., *(0-9636643)* 14 Hidden Valley Rd., Lafayette, CA 94549 Tel 925-284-5167
E-mail: murndal@aol.com
Web site: http://www.wenet.net/~rarimmer/Ann_Loder/author.html.

Lodestone Catalog, The, *(0-9642427; 1-57677)* Div. of Creative Audio Enterprises, Inc., 611 Empire Mill Rd., Bloomington, IN 47401 Tel 812-824-2400; Fax: 812-824-2401; Toll Free: 800-411-6463 (orders only)
E-mail: lodestone@lodestone-media.com
Web site: http://www.lodestone-media.com.

Logan, Tracy Pubns., *(0-9657524)* P.O. Box 734, Lindenhurst, NY 11757-0734 Tel 516-226-2724; Fax: 516-226-2904.

Logos Research Systems, Inc., *(1-57799)* 715 SE Fidalgo Ave., Oak Harbor, WA 98277-4049 Tel 360-679-6575; Fax: 360-675-8169; Toll Free: 800-875-6467
E-mail: info@logos.com
Web site: http://www.logos.com.

Lollipop Power Bks., *(0-914996)* Div. of Carolina Wren Pr., 120 Morris St., Durham, NC 27701 (SAN 206-9733) Tel 919-560-2738.

London Bridge, Div. of General Distribution Services, Orders Addr.: 4500 Witmer Industrial EST, Niagara Falls, NY 14305-1386 Toll Free: 800-805-1083.

London Circle Publishing, *(0-9667911; 1-930677)* Div. of Benicia Hse., 17315 Henning Ct., Weed, CA 96094 Tel 530-938-2527; Fax: 530-938-1756
E-mail: publisher@londoncircle.com
Web site: http://www.londoncircle.com.

Lone Pine Publishing, *(0-919433; 1-55105)* 1808 B St., NW, Suite 140, Auburn, WA 98001 Tel 425-204-5965; Fax: 425-204-6036; Toll Free Fax: 800-548-1169; Toll Free: 800-518-3541
E-mail: rtruppner@lonepinepublishing.com
Web site: http://www.lonepinepublishing.com
Dist(s): **American West Bks.**
Baker & Taylor Bks.
Bookmen, Inc.
Bookpeople
Koen Bk. Distributors
Partners Bk. Distributing, Inc.
Partners/West
Sunbelt Pubns., Inc..

Lone Star Bks., *(1-58907)* 4501 Forbes Blvd., Suite 200, Lanham, MD 20706 Toll Free Fax: 800-338-4550 ; Toll Free: 800-462-6420
Dist(s): **National Bk. Network.**

Lonejack Mountain Pr., *(0-9729101)* P.O. Box 28424, Bellingham, WA 98228-0424.

Long Hill Productions, Inc., *(0-9701450; 1-931179)* 6446 S. Western Ave., Clarendon Hills, IL 60514 (SAN 253-2883) Tel 630-920-8168; Fax: 630-920-8169
E-mail: info@long-hill.com
Web site: http://www.long-hill.com.

Long Wind Publishing, *(0-9658128; 1-892695)* 108 N. Depot Dr., Box 13024, Fort Pierce, FL 34950 Tel 561-595-0268; Fax: 561-595-6246
E-mail: LongWndPub@aol.com
Web site: http://www.longwindpub.com.

†Longman Publishing Group, *(0-13; 0-201; 0-321; 0-582; 0-8013; 1-74009)* Div. of Addison Wesley Longman, Inc., The Longman Bldg., 10 Bank St., White Plains, NY 10606-1951 (SAN 202-6856) Tel 914-993-5000; Fax: 914-997-8115 800-922-0579 (college, bkstores, customer service only)
E-mail: orders@mcp.com
Web site: http://store.awl.com
Dist(s): **Coronet Bks.**
Giron Bks.
Pearson Education
Trans-Atlantic Pubns., Inc.; *CIP.*

Longstreet Pr., Inc., *(0-929264; 1-56352)* Subs. of Cox Newspapers, Inc., 2140 Newmarket Pkwy., Suite 122, Marietta, GA 30067 (SAN 248-7640) Tel 770-980-1488; Fax: 770-859-9894; Toll Free: 800-927-1488
E-mail: rrichardson@longstreetpress.net
Dist(s): **National Bk. Network.**

Lookout Pr., *(1-882405)* Orders Addr.: 900 53rd St., Sacramento, CA 95819 Tel 916-456-6991.

Lorenz Bks. Imprint of Anness Publishing, Inc.

Lorimer, James & Co. (CAN) *(0-88862; 1-55028) Dist. by* **Orca Bk Pubs.**

Lorraine, A. Walter Imprint of Houghton Mifflin Co. Trade & Reference Div.

Los Andes Publishing Co., *(0-9637065; 1-57159)* P.O. Box 190, Chino Hills, CA 91709 Tel 626-810-9717; Toll Free: 800-532-8872
E-mail: losandes@losandes.com
Web site: http://www.losandes.com.

Los Arboles, *(0-941992)* Orders Addr.: P.O. Box 7000-54, Redondo Beach, CA 90277 (SAN 662-0752) ; Edit Addr.: 820 Calle de Arboles, Redondo Beach, CA 90277 (SAN 238-020X) Tel 310-375-0759
Dist(s): **Baker & Taylor Bks.**
New Leaf Distributing Co., Inc..

Lost Classics Bk. Co., *(0-9652735; 1-890623)* Orders Addr.: P.O. Box 1756, Fort Collins, CO 80522 Tel 970-493-3793 (Distribution Center); Toll Free Fax: 888-211-2665 (Wholesale, Libraries & Schools); Toll Free: 888-611-2665 (credit card orders only); Edit Addr.: P.O. Box 3429, Lake Wales, FL 33859-3429 Tel 863-676-1920; Fax: 863-676-1707; Toll Free: 888-611-2665
E-mail: lcbci@gte.net; lcbc@gte.net
Web site: http://lcbcbooks.com
Dist(s): **Applewood Bks.**
Consortium Bk. Sales & Distribution.

Lothian Bks. (AUS) *(0-85091; 0-7344) Dist. by* **Star Brght Bks.**

Lotus Pr., Inc., *(0-916418)* P.O. Box 21607, Detroit, MI 48221 Tel 313-861-1280; Fax: 313-861-4740 Do not confuse with companies with the same name or similar name in Westerville, OH, Lotus, CA, Bokeelia, FL, Brattleboro, VT, Tobyhanna, PA
E-mail: lotuspress@aol.com.

Love From the Sea, *(1-878291)* 11059 Trask Bridge Rd., Pecatonica, IL 61063
E-mail: DrCutburth@cs.com.

Love Publishing Co., *(1-892212)* Orders Addr.: P.O. Box 1358, Belmont, NC 28012-1358 Tel 704-829-9500; Fax: 704-829-9555; Edit Addr.: 28 Alice Ave., Belmont, NC 28012-1358 Do not confuse with companies with the same name in Indiantown, FL, Denver, CO, Bossier, LA.

Love Street Publishing, *(0-9658823)* Orders Addr.: P.O. Box 231, Medford, OR 97501-0016 Tel 541-608-7841 ; Edit Addr.: 406 W. Main St., Medford, OR 97501
E-mail: Bertolero9@aol.com.

†Lowell Hse., *(0-7373; 0-8092; 0-929923; 1-56565)* 2020 Avenue of the Stars, Suite 300, Los Angeles, CA 90067-4704 (SAN 250-863X) Tel 310-552-7555; Fax: 310-552-7573; *Imprints:* Roxbury Park (Roxbury Park)
Dist(s): **McGraw-Hill Trade**; *CIP.*

Lowell Hse. Juvenile, *(0-7373; 0-929923; 1-56565)* 2020 Avenue of the Stars, No. 300, Los Angeles, CA 90067 Tel 310-552-7555; Fax: 310-552-7573; *Imprints:* Roxbury Park Juvenile (Roxbury Pk Juvenile)
Web site: http://www.lowellh.com
Dist(s): **McGraw-Hill Trade.**

†Lowell Pr., The, Gallion Communications, *(0-913504; 0-932845)* P.O. Box 411877, Kansas City, MO 64141-1877 (SAN 207-0774) Tel 816-753-4545; Fax: 816-753-4057; Toll Free: 800-736-7660 Do not confuse with Lowell Pr. in Eugene, OR
E-mail: plowell@gri.net; *CIP.*

Lower Kuskokwim Schl. District, *(1-58084)* Orders Addr.: P.O. Box 305, Bethel, AK 99559 Tel 907-543-4928; Fax: 907-543-4935
E-mail: Joy_Shantz@fc.lksd-do.org; catalog@fc.lksd-do.org
Web site: http://www.lksd.org/catalog.

LRS, *(1-58118)* 14214 S. Figueroa St., Los Angeles, CA 90061-1034 Tel 310-354-2610; Fax: 310-354-2601; Toll Free: 800-255-5002
E-mail: lrsprint@aol.com
Web site: http://www.lrs-largeprint.com.

Luath Pr. Ltd. (GBR) *(0-946487; 1-84282) Dist. by* **Midpt Trade.**

Lubrecht & Cramer, Ltd., *(0-934454; 0-945345)* 18 E. Main St., Port Jervis, NY 12771; Edit Addr.: P.O. Box 3110, Port Jervis, NY 12771 (SAN 214-1256) Toll Free: 800-920-9334; 350 Fifth Ave., Suite 3304, New York, NY 10118-0069
E-mail: lubrecht@frontiernet.net; books@lubrechtcramer.com
Web site: http://www.lubrechtcramer.com.

Lucent Bks. Imprint of Gale Group

Lucky Cat Publishing, *(0-9720394)* 288 Franklin Ave., Astoria, OR 97103 Tel 503-338-6883
E-mail: cliff.arline@charter.net.

Lucky Pr., LLC, *(0-9676050; 0-9706377; 0-9713318)* 126 S. Maple St., Lancaster, OH 43130 Fax: 740-689-2951
E-mail: books@luckypress.com
Web site: http://www.luckypress.com; http://www.sleepy-dog.com
Dist(s): **National Bk. Network.**

Luft Publishing, *(0-9648936)* P.O. Box 72, Garland, NE 68360 Tel 402-588-2424.

Lumen Editions Imprint of Brookline Bks., Inc.

Luminary Media Group Imprint of Pine Orchard, Inc.

Luna, Rachel Nickerson *See* **Howard, Emma Bks.**

Lunchbox Pr., *(0-9678285)* 701 Greymoor Pl., Southlake, TX 76092 Tel 817-442-8930; Fax: 817-442-8985
E-mail: info@lunchboxpress.com
Web site: http://www.lunchboxpress.com
Dist(s): **Biblio Distribution**
National Bk. Network.

Luth & Assocs., *(0-9626153)* 5829 Tittabawassee Rd., Saginaw, MI 48604 Tel 517-792-9776.

Luthers, *(1-877633)* 1009 N. Dixie Freeway, New Smyrna Beach, FL 32168-6221 (SAN 200-3961) Tel 386-423-1600 (phone/fax)
E-mail: luthers@n-jcenter.com.

Lutherworth Pr., The (GBR) *(0-7188) Dist. by* **Parkwest Pubns.**

Luv-n-Hugs Bks., *(0-9658824)* 9733 Kent Ave., Montgomery, MN 56069 Tel 507-744-2027; Fax: 507-744-5210
E-mail: sherri@means.net
Web site: http://www.luvnhugsbooks.com.

Lyons Group, The *See* **Lyrick Studios**

Lyrick Publishing, *(1-57064; 1-58668)* Subs. of HIT Entertainment, 830 S. Greenville Ave., Allen, TX 75002 Tel 972-390-6794; Fax: 972-390-6030; Toll Free: 800-418-2371; *Imprints:* Big Red Chair Books (Big Red); Humongous Books (Humongous Bks); Barney Books (Barney Books)
E-mail: customerservice@HITEntertainment.com
Web site: http://www.HITEntertainment.com
Dist(s): **Lectorum Pubns., Inc..**

Lyrick Studios, *(0-7829; 0-89505; 0-913592; 1-55924; 1-57132)* Subs. of HIT Entertainment, 830 S. Greenville Ave., Allen, TX 75002 Tel 972-390-6002; 214-424-6630; Fax: 972-390-6030; Toll Free: 800-418-2371
E-mail: customerservice@HITEntertainment.com
Web site: http://www.HITEntertainment.com
Dist(s): **Midwest Tape**
Rounder Kids Music Distribution.

M.A.K. Pubns., Inc., *(1-882406)* 511 Deer Run Ct., Westerville, OH 43081-3248 Fax: 216-461-8139.

MDCT Publishing, *(0-9674491)* 5946 SW Cupola Dr., South Beach, OR 97366
E-mail: mdundy@teleport.com
Dist(s): **Partners/West.**

ME Media LLC, *(1-58925)* Orders Addr.: 1650 Bluegrass Lakes Pkwy., Alpharetta, GA 30004 Fax: 770-442-9742; Toll Free: 800-656-6479; Edit Addr.: 202 Old Ridgefield Rd., Wilton, CT 06897 (SAN 253-6382) Tel 203-834-0005; Fax: 203-834-0004; *Imprints:* Tiger Tales (Tiger Tales)
E-mail: etprial@tigertalesbooks.com
Web site: http://www.tigertalesbooks.com.

MNP Star Enterprises, *(0-938880)* P.O. Box 1552, Cupertino, CA 95015-1552 (SAN 215-9708).

M Q Pubns. (GBR) *(1-84072; 1-897954) Dist. by* **IPG Chicago.**

MAC Publishing, *(0-910223)* Div. of Claudja, Inc., PMB 346, 321 High School Rd. NE, Bainbridge Island, WA 98110 Tel 206-842-6303; Fax: 206-842-6235; Toll Free: 800-698-0148 (orders/inquiries)
E-mail: cblack@nwlink.com
Web site: http://www.claudiablack.com.

MacBride, E. J. Pubn., Inc., *(1-892511)* 129 W. 147th St., No. 20B, New York, NY 10039.

MacDonald Sward Publishing Co., *(0-945437)* RD 3, Box 104A, Greensburg, PA 15601 (SAN 247-1973) Tel 724-832-7767
Dist(s): **Amazon.Com**
Baker & Taylor Bks..

Mackinac Island State Park Commission *See* **Mackinac State Historic Parks**

Mackinac State Historic Parks, *(0-911872)* Orders Addr.: P.O. Box 873, Mackinaw City, MI 49701; Edit Addr.: 207 W. Sinclair, Mackinaw City, MI 49701 (SAN 202-5981) Tel 231-436-5564; Fax: 231-436-4210.

Macmillan Children's Bks. (GBR) *(0-330; 0-333) Dist. by* **Trans-Atl Phila.**

Macmillan Reference USA Imprint of Gale Group

Macmillan U.K. (GBR) *(0-333; 1-4050) Dist. by* **Trafalgar.**

Macmillan U.K. (GBR) *(0-333; 1-4050) Dist. by* **Trans-Atl Phila.**

Macmillan USA *See* **Alpha Bks.**

MacroPrintBooks Imprint of Science & Humanities Pr.

Madison Bks., Inc., *(0-8128; 0-8191; 0-911572; 1-56833; 1-879511)* Div. of Rowman & Littlefield Publishers, Inc., 200 Park Ave., S., Suite 1109, New York, NY 10003-1503 (SAN 246-7356) Tel 212-529-3888; Fax: 212-529-4223; Toll Free Fax: 800-338-4550; Toll Free: 800-462-6420; *Imprints:* Scarborough House (Scrbrough Hse)
Web site: http://www.univpress.com/
Dist(s): **National Bk. Network**
Rowman & Littlefield Pubs., Inc..

Madison, Dr. Ron *See* **Ned's Head Productions**

Mage Pubs., Inc., *(0-934211)* 1032 29th St., NW, Washington, DC 20007 (SAN 693-0476) Tel 202-342-1642; Fax: 202-342-9269; Toll Free: 800-962-0922 (orders only)
E-mail: info@mage.com
Web site: http://www.mage.com
Dist(s): **Baker & Taylor Bks..**

Magi Pubns. (GBR) *(1-85430; 1-870271) Dist. by* **Midpt Trade.**

Magic Attic Pr. Imprint of Millbrook Pr., Inc.

Magic Carpet Bks. Imprint of Harcourt Children's Bks.

Magic Carpet Rides Co., *(0-9658255)* P.O. Box 39748, Phoenix, AZ 85069-9748 Tel 602-978-2725 (phone/fax)
E-mail: daniel.mcrides@juno.com.

Magik Pubs., *(0-9626608)* 4321 Hempstead Tpke., Bethpage, NY 11714 Tel 516-731-5500; Fax: 516-735-1596.

Magination Pr. Imprint of American Psychological Assn.

Magnum Pr., *(0-9623698)* 901 Brett Dr., Edmond, OK 73013 Tel 405-359-4842; Fax: 405-282-2462
Dist(s): **Baker & Taylor Bks..**

Magnus Media Sales & Services, LLC *See* **Ann Arbor Media Group, LLC**

Magpie Pubns., *(0-936480)* P.O. Box 636, Alamo, CA 94507 (SAN 221-4091) Tel 925-838-9287 (phone/fax) ; Toll Free: 800-624-7435 (phone/fax)
Web site: http://www.pp.ph.ic.ac.uk/~magpie.

Majestic Publishing, *(0-9679065)* 1303 Hixson Pike, Suite A, Chattanooga, TN 37405 Tel 423-756-0102; Fax: 423-756-0144
E-mail: ellen1068@aol.com.

Makare Publishing Co., *(0-9655402)* P.O. Box 357171, Gainesville, FL 32635 Tel 352-333-3832; Fax: 352-333-3744
E-mail: makare@mindspring.com.

Make Believe Publishing, *(0-9675994)* Orders Addr.: P.O. Box 608817, Orlando, FL 32860-8817 Tel 407-599-4988; Fax: 407-599-4989; Toll Free: 800-509-5796; Edit Addr.: 1099 Henry Balch Dr., Orlando, FL 32810
E-mail: monte222@aol.com.

Makin' Do Enterprises, 628 Baker Pl. Rd., Lancaster, SC 29720 (SAN 277-7118) Tel 803-285-2888.

Malibu Bks. for Children, *(1-929084)* Div. of Malibu Films, Inc., 48 Broad St., No. 134, Red Bank, NJ 07701 Tel 732-933-0446 (phone/fax); Toll Free: 888-629-9947 (phone/fax)
E-mail: malibuinc@aol.com
Web site: http://www.malibu-kids.com.

Malvern Publishing Co., Ltd. (GBR) *(0-947993) Dist. by* **Brit Bk Co Inc.**

Manoa Pr., *(1-891839)* 2702 Menoa Rd., Honolulu, HI 96822 Tel 808-988-4904
E-mail: kauhua@lava.net
Dist(s): **Native Bks..**

Mantle Ministries, *(1-889128)* 228 Still Ridge, Bulverde, TX 78163 Tel 830-438-3777; Fax: 830-438-3370; Toll Free: 877-548-2327
E-mail: mantleministries@cs.com
Web site: http://www.mantlemin.com
Dist(s): **FaithWorks.**

Mantra Publishing, Ltd. (GBR) *(1-85269) Dist. by* **AIMS Intl.**

Maple Tree Pr. (CAN) *(0-919872; 0-920775; 1-895688; 1-894379) Dist. by* **Firefly Bks Limited.**

Marble House Editions, *(0-9677047)* 96-09 66th Ave., No. 1D, Rego Park, NY 11374 (SAN 253-6536) Tel 718-896-4186; Fax: 718-897-2818
E-mail: dougeliz@worldnet.att.net.

Marc Anthony Publishing, *(0-9635107)* Orders Addr.: P.O. Box 5610, Blue Jay, CA 92317 (SAN 297-8229) Tel 714-337-8911; Fax: 714-337-1571; Edit Addr.: 231 S. Fairway Dr., Blue Jay, CA 92317.

Marciel Publishing & Printing, *(1-879331)* W. 4914 Richland Ave., Spokane, WA 99204 Tel 509-838-0061 ; Toll Free: 800-729-2315; *Imprints:* Classic Publishing (Classc Pub).

MAR*CO Products, Inc., *(1-57543; 1-884063)* Orders Addr.: 1443 Old York Rd., Warminster, PA 18974 Tel 215-956-0313; Fax: 215-956-9041; Toll Free: 800-448-2197
E-mail: csfunk@marcoproducts.com; marcoproducts@comcast.net
Web site: http://www.store.yahoo.com/marcoproducts; http://www.marcoproducts.com.

Mariner Bks. Imprint of Houghton Mifflin Co. Trade & Reference Div.

Mariposa Printing & Publishing, Inc., *(0-933553)* 922 Baca St., Santa Fe, NM 87501 (SAN 691-8743) Tel 505-988-5582; Fax: 505-986-8774
Dist(s): **Continental Bk. Co., Inc..**

MarKel Pr., *(0-9621406)* Orders Addr.: P.O. Box 855, Marcola, OR 97454 (SAN 251-1886) Tel 541-933-2831; Edit Addr.: 94854 Kelso Ln., Marcola, OR 97454 (SAN 251-1894)
E-mail: mjkel@aol.com
Dist(s): **Baker & Taylor Bks..**

Marketing Directions, Inc., *(1-880218)* 615 Queen St., Southington, CT 06489 Tel 860-276-2452; Fax: 860-276-2453; Toll Free: 800-562-4357
E-mail: info@strongbooks.com
Web site: http://wwwstrongbooks.com.

Markins Enterprises, *(0-937729)* 2039 SE 45th Ave., Portland, OR 97215 (SAN 659-3224) Tel 503-235-1036.

Markowitz Publishing, *(0-9655890)* 769 Luakini St., Lahaina, HI 96761-1533.

MarLin Bks., *(0-9713839)* P.M.B. 444, 1001 S. Tenth, Suite G, McAllen, TX 78501 Tel 956-668-1516; Fax: 956-668-7580
E-mail: LMMR13@aol.com.

Marlowe & Co. Imprint of Avalon Publishing Group

Marsh, Carole Bks. Imprint of Gallopade International

Marsh Media, *(0-925159; 1-55942)* Div. of Marsh Film Enterprises, Inc., P.O. Box 8082, Shawnee Mission, KS 66208 Tel 816-523-1059; Fax: 816-333-7421; Toll Free: 800-821-3303 (for orders/customer service only)
E-mail: info@marshmedia.com
Web site: http://www.marshmedia.com
Dist(s): **Baker & Taylor Bks..**

Marsh Wind Pr., *(0-9642620)* Orders Addr.: P.O. Box 1596, Mount Pleasant, SC 29465 Tel 803-884-5957; Edit Addr.: 1180 Main Canal Dr., Mount Pleasant, SC 29464.

Marshfilm Enterprises, Incorporated *See* **Marsh Media**

Marsilio Pubs., *(0-941419; 1-56886)* 853 Broadway, Suite 600, New York, NY 10003 Tel 718-522-3982; *Imprints:* Eridanos Library (Eridanos Library)
Dist(s): **SPD-Small Pr. Distribution.**

Martin's *See* **Green Pastures Pr.**

Marvel Enterprises, *(0-7851; 0-87135; 0-939766; 0-9604146)* 10 E. 40th St. Flr. 9, New York, NY 10016-0201 (SAN 216-9088); *Imprints:* Marvel's Finest (Marvels Finest)
E-mail: mail@marvel.com
Web site: http://www.marvel.com
Dist(s): **Client Distribution Services.**

Marvel Entertainment Group, Incorporated *See* **Marvel Enterprises**

Marvel's Finest Imprint of Marvel Enterprises

Maryruth Bks., Inc., *(0-9713518; 0-9720295; 0-9746475)* 2938 Green Rd., Shaker Heights, OH 44122 Tel 216-491-9029; P.O. Box 221143, Beachwood, OH 44122 Tel 216-491-0261 (phone/fax)
E-mail: robcoulton@cs.com
Web site: http://www.maryruthbooks.com.

Names

Masquerade Bks., Inc., *(1-56333; 1-878320)* 801 Second Ave., New York, NY 10017 Tel 212-661-7878 ; Fax: 212-986-7355 Do not confuse with Masquerade Bks. Gardena, CA
E-mail: masqbks@aol.com
Web site: http://www.masqueradebooks.com
Dist(s): **Bookazine Co., Inc.**
Bookpeople.

Master Bks., *(0-89051)* P.O. Box 727, Green Forest, AR 72638-0727 (SAN 205-6119) Tel 870-438-5288; Fax: 870-438-5120; Toll Free: 800-999-3777
E-mail: nlp@newleafpress
Web site: http://www.masterbooks.net.

Mastery Education Corporation *See* **Charlesbridge Publishing, Inc.**

Masthof Pr., *(1-883294; 1-930353)* 219 Mill Rd., Morgantown, PA 19543-9701 Tel 610-286-0258; Fax: 610-286-6860
E-mail: mast@masthof.com
Web site: http://www.ponyinvestigators.com; http://www.masthof.com.

Maupin Hse. Publishing, *(0-929895)* Orders Addr.: P.O. Box 90148, Gainesville, FL 32607-0148 (SAN 250-7676) Tel 352-373-5588; Fax: 352-373-5546; Toll Free: 800-524-0634 (orders); Edit Addr.: 32 SW 42nd St., Gainesville, FL 32607 (SAN 250-7684); *Imprints:* Hoot Owl Books (Hoot Owl Bks)
E-mail: info@maupinhouse.com
Web site: http://www.maupinhouse.com.

Maval Medical Education *See* **Maval Publishing, Inc.**

Maval Publishing, Inc., *(1-884083; 1-59134)* Div. of Maval Printing Co., 567 Harrison St., Denver, CO 80206-4534 Tel 303-320-1835; Fax: 303-320-1546
E-mail: maval@maval.com
Web site: http://www.maval.com
Dist(s): **Majors Scientific Bks., Inc.**
Matthews Medical Bk. Co..

Maverick Bks., Inc., *(0-916941; 0-9608612; 1-59188)* Orders Addr.: Box 549, Perryton, TX 79070 (SAN 240-7183) Tel 806-435-7611; Fax: 806-435-2410; Edit Addr.: 402 S. Amherst, Suite 1, Perryton, TX 78070 Do not confuse with Maverick Books, Woodstock, NY
E-mail: hank1@ptsi.net
Web site: http://www.hankthecowdog.com
Dist(s): **Baker & Taylor Bks..**

Maximum Publishing Co., *(0-9740308)* 8405 Spinnaker Cove, Rowlett, TX 75088 Tel 972-412-0218 (phone/fax)
E-mail: mmorales@gisd.net.

Maxit Publishing, Inc., *(0-9700174; 0-9708904)* P.O. Box 680, Solvang, CA 93463 (SAN 253-6811) Tel 310-275-1000; 805-686-5100; Fax: 805-686-5102 (for orders, bills & invoices); Toll Free: 866-686-5100
E-mail: info@maxitpublishing.com; wsimon@maxitpublishing.com
Web site: http://www.maxitpublishing.com.

Mayhaven Publishing, *(1-878044; 1-932278)* Orders Addr.: P.O. Box 557, Mahomet, IL 61853 Tel 217-586-4493; Edit Addr.: 803 Buckthorn Cir., Mahomet, IL 61853
E-mail: mayhavenpublishing@mchsi.com
Web site: http://www.mayhavenpublishing.com
Dist(s): **Baker & Taylor Bks.**
Beyda & Assocs., Inc.
Booksource, The
Brodart Co.
Distributors, The
Forest Sales & Distributing Co.
Mumford Library Bks., Inc.
Quality Bks., Inc.
Unique Bks., Inc..

McClain Printing Co., *(0-87012)* P.O. Box 403, Parsons, WV 26287-0403 (SAN 203-9478) Tel 304-478-2881; Fax: 304-478-4658; Toll Free: 800-654-7179
E-mail: Mcclain@access.mountain.net
Web site: http://www.McClainPrinting.com.

McClanahan Bk. Imprint of Learning Horizons, Inc.

McClanahan Publishing Hse., Inc., *(0-913383)* P.O. Box 100, Kuttawa, KY 42055 (SAN 285-8371) Tel 270-388-9388; Fax: 270-388-6186; Toll Free: 800-544-6959
E-mail: books@kybooks.com
Web site: http://www.kybooks.com
Dist(s): **Barron's Bks.**
Partners Pubs. Group, Inc..

McClelland & Stewart/Tundra Bks., *(0-7710)* P.O. Box 1030, Plattsburgh, NY 12901 Tel 416-598-1114; Fax: 416-598-4002
E-mail: salesdept@mcclelland.com
Web site: http://www.mcclelland.com.

McDonald & Woodward Publishing Co., The, *(0-939923)* 431-B E. College St., Granville, OH 43023-1319 (SAN 663-6977) Tel 740-321-1140; Fax: 740-321-1141; Toll Free: 800-233-8787
E-mail: mwpubco@mwpubco.com
Web site: http://www.mwpubco.com.

McDonald, Diane, *(0-9721681)* P.O. Box 622, Sublette, IL 61367.

McDougal Littell Inc., *(0-395; 0-8123; 0-86609; 0-88343; 0-618)* Subs. of Houghton Mifflin Co., Orders Addr.: 1900 S. Batavia Ave., Geneva, IL 60134 Toll Free: 888-872-8380; Edit Addr.: P.O. Box 1667, Evanston, IL 60204 (SAN 202-2532) Toll Free: 800-462-6595 (customer service); 800-323-5435; 909 Davis St., Evanston, IL 60201 Tel 847-869-2300; Fax: 847-869-0841
Web site: http://www.mcdougallittell.com.

McElderry, Margaret K. Imprint of Simon & Schuster Children's Publishing

McGraw Publishing, Inc., *(1-930364; 1-930756; 1-931071; 0-9707093)* 51 Domingo Ave., Berkeley, CA 94702 Tel 510-644-9875; Fax: 281-340-2001; Toll Free: 866-815-2625; *Imprints:* Bookmice (Bookmic)
E-mail: info@eldoradobooks.org
Web site: http://www.eldoradobooks.org; http://www.mcgrawbooks.com.

McGraw-Hill Children's Publishing, *(0-7647; 0-7682; 0-7696; 0-86653; 0-88012; 1-56417; 1-56451; 1-56822; 1-57029; 1-57768; 0-7424; 1-58845)* Div. of The McGraw-Hill Education Group, 8787 Orion Pl., Columbus, OH 43240-4027 Toll Free Fax: 800-543-2690; Toll Free: 800-253-5469; 3195 Wilson Dr., NW., Grand Rapids, MI 49544 Tel 616-802-3000; *Imprints:* Cricket (Cricket); Instructional Fair * T S Dension (Instr Fair Dension); Fearon Teacher Aids (Fearon); Good Apple (GoodApple); Totline Publications (TotlineMc); Bedrick, Peter Books (Peter Bedrick); Mercer Mayer First Readers (Mercer Mayer); American Education Publishing (Am Educ Pubng); Gingham Dog Press (Gingham Dog)
E-mail: customer.service@mcgraw-hill.com
Web site: http://www.mhkids.com.

†McGraw-Hill Cos., The, *(0-02; 0-07)* 6480 Jimmy Carter Blvd., Norcross, GA 30071-1701 (SAN 254-881X) Tel 614-755-5637; Fax: 614-755-5611; Orders Addr.: 860 Taylor Station Rd., Blacklick, OH 43004-0545 (SAN 200-254X) Fax: 614-755-5645; Toll Free: 800-338-3987 (college); 800-525-5003 (subscriptions); 800-352-3566 (books - US/Canada orders); 800-722-4726 (orders & customer service); P.O. Box 545, Blacklick, OH 43004-0545 Fax: 614-759-3759; Toll Free: 877-833-5524
E-mail: customer.service@mcgraw-hill.com
Web site: http://www.ebooks.mcgraw-hill.com/; http://www.mcgraw-hill.com
Dist(s): **Libros Sin Fronteras**
McGraw-Hill Osborne
McGraw-Hill Primis Custom Publishing
Sams Technical Publishing, LLC; *CIP.*

McGraw-Hill Consumer Products *See* **McGraw-Hill Children's Publishing**

McGraw-Hill Higher Education, *(0-07)* Div. of the McGraw-Hill Cos., Orders Addr.: P.O. Box 545, Blacklick, OH 43004-0545 Toll Free: 800-338-3987; Edit Addr.: 1333 Burr Ridge Pkwy., Burr Ridge, IL 60521; *Imprints:* McGraw-Hill/Dushkin (Dshkn McG-Hill); McGraw-Hill Humanities, Social Sciences & World Languages (Mc-H Human Soc)
Web site: http://www.mhhe.com
Dist(s): **McGraw-Hill Cos., The.**

McGraw-Hill Humanities, Social Sciences & World Languages Imprint of McGraw-Hill Higher Education

McGraw-Hill Professional Book Group *See* **McGraw-Hill School Education Group**

McGraw-Hill School Education Group, *(0-07; 0-7602; 0-8306; 0-911314; 0-917253; 1-55738)* Div. of The McGraw-Hill Companies, Orders Addr.: P.O. Box 545, Blacklick, OH 43004-0545 Fax: 614-755-5645; Toll Free: 800-442-9685 (customer service); 800-722-4726 ; Edit Addr.: 8787 Orion Pl., Columbus, OH 43240 Tel 614-430-4000; c/o Grand Rapids Distribution Center, 3195 Wilson NW, Grand Rapids, MI 49544 (SAN 253-6420) Fax: 614-755-5611; *Imprints:* Irwin Professional Publishing (Irwn Prfssnl)
E-mail: customer.service@mcgraw-hill.com
Web site: http://www.pbg.mcgraw-hill.com/; http://www.accessmedbooks.com
Dist(s): **McGraw-Hill Cos., The**
Urban Land Institute
netLibrary, Inc..

McGraw-Hill Trade, *(0-07; 0-658; 0-8442)* Div. of McGraw-Hill Professional, Orders Addr.: P.O. Box 545, Blacklick, OH 43004-0545 Tel 800-722-4726; Fax: 614-755-5645; Edit Addr.: 2 Penn Plaza, New York, NY 10121 Tel 212-904-2000; *Imprints:* Passport Books (Passport Bks)
Web site: http://www.books.mcgraw-hill.com
Dist(s): **McGraw-Hill Cos., The.**

McGraw-Hill/Contemporary, *(0-658; 0-8092; 0-8325; 0-8442; 0-88499; 0-89061; 0-913327; 0-940279; 0-941263; 0-9630646; 1-56626; 1-56943; 1-57028)* Div. of McGraw-Hill Higher Education, 4255 W. Touhy Ave., Lincolnwood, IL 60712 (SAN 169-2208) Tel 847-679-5500; Fax: 847-679-2494; Toll Free Fax: 800-998-3103; Toll Free: 800-323-4900; *Imprints:* National Textbook Company (Natl Textbk Co)
E-mail: c_patton-vanbuskirk@mcgraw-hill.com; ntcpub@tribune.com
Web site: http://www.ntc-cb.com
Dist(s): **Continental Bk. Co., Inc.**
Giron Bks.
Libros Sin Fronteras
McGraw-Hill Cos., The
netLibrary, Inc..

McGraw-Hill/Dushkin Imprint of McGraw-Hill Higher Education

†McKay, David Co., Inc., *(0-679; 0-88326; 0-89440)* Subs. of Random Hse., Inc., Orders Addr.: 400 Hahn Rd., Westminster, MD 21157 Tel 410-848-1900; Toll Free: 800-733-3000 (orders only); Edit Addr.: 201 E. 50th St., MD 4-6, New York, NY 10022 (SAN 200-240X) Tel 212-751-2600; Fax: 212-872-8026
Dist(s): **Libros Sin Fronteras**; *CIP.*

McMurtrey, Martin A., *(0-9623961)* 808 Camden, San Antonio, TX 78215 Tel 210-223-9680.

Mcnarn Group, The, *(0-9678933)* 815 W. Pine St., Centralia, WA 98531 Tel 360-451-1384; Fax: 360-807-0221
E-mail: mcnarn@thoughtdairy.com; clytle@cen.quik.com
Web site: http://www.thoughtdairy.com/mcnarn.

McNutt, Nan & Assocs., *(0-9614534)* 12722 39th Ave., NE, Seattle, WA 98125 (SAN 692-3453) Tel 206-367-7789
Dist(s): **Sasquatch Bks..**

†Meadowbrook Pr., *(0-88166; 0-915658)* 5451 Smetana Dr., Minnetonka, MN 55343 (SAN 207-3404) Tel 612-930-1100; Fax: 612-930-1940; Toll Free: 800-338-2232
E-mail: mballard@meadowbrookpress.com
Web site: http://www.meadowbrookpress.com
Dist(s): **Simon & Schuster Children's Publishing**
Simon & Schuster, Inc.; *CIP.*

Meckley Publishing Co., *(1-892464)* P.O. Box 1251, Bowie, MD 20715-1251 Tel 301-262-2039; Fax: 410-741-1083; Toll Free: 800-383-2039
E-mail: kidgifts@puff.dsport.com.

Media Publishing, *(0-939644)* Div. of Trozzolo Resources, Inc., 802 Broadway St., Suite 300, Kansas City, MO 64105-1528 (SAN 216-6372) Tel 816-842-8111; Fax: 816-842-8188; Toll Free: 800-347-2665 Do not confuse with Media Publishing, Miami, FL
Dist(s): **Baker & Taylor Bks..**

Meena, Nicholas *See* **Lem Publishing & Production**

Melody Press *See* **Rufus Pr.**

Memory Lane Bks., *(0-9618951)* 14 Noon Dr., E., North Vernon, IN 47265 (SAN 242-9403) Tel 812-346-6985.

†Menasha Ridge Pr., Inc., *(0-89732)* 2000 First Ave., N., Suite 1400, Birmingham, AL 35203 (SAN 219-7294) Tel 205-322-0439; Fax: 205-326-1012; Toll Free: 800-247-9437
E-mail: info@menasharidge.com
Web site: http://www.menasharidge.com
Dist(s): **Globe Pequot Pr., The**; *CIP.*

Merced de Mendez, Ana T., *(0-9627442)* 404 Darien St., Villa Borinquen, Rio Piedras, PR 00920 Tel 809-783-1513.

Mercer Mayer First Readers Imprint of McGraw-Hill Children's Publishing

Mercier Pr., Ltd., The (IRL) *(0-85342; 1-85635; 1-86023) Dist. by* **Irish Bks Media.**

†Meredith Bks., *(0-696)* Div. of Meredith Corp., Orders Addr.: 1716 Locust St., LN-110, Des Moines, IA 50309-3023 (SAN 202-4055) Tel 515-284-2363; 515-284-2126 (sales); Fax: 515-284-3371; Toll Free: 800-678-8091; c/o Banta Packaging & Fulfillment, 1071 Willow Spring Rd., Harrisonburg, VA 22801 Tel 540-438-5185 Do not confuse with Meredith Pr. in Skaneateles, NY
E-mail: pmorgan@mdp.com
Web site: http://www.betterhomesandgardens.com; http://www.bhg.com; *CIP.*

Names

Meridian Hse., *(0-912339)* 6755 Mira Mesa Blvd., Suite 123-224, Dept. 224, San Diego, CA 92121 (SAN 265-1149) Tel 818-594-2610; *Imprints:* Beacon Hill Books (Beacon Hill Bks)
E-mail: meridianol@aol.com; velocityebooks@velocityebooks.com; meridianhouse@aol.com
Web site: http://members.aol.com/meridianol
Dist(s): **Baker & Taylor Bks.**
Brodart Co.
Coutts Library Service, Inc.
Distributors, The
New Leaf Distributing Co., Inc..

Merkos L'Inyonei Chinuch Imprint of Kehot Pubn. Society

Merriwell, Frank Inc., *(0-8373)* Subs. of National Learning Corp., 212 Michael Dr., Syosset, NY 11791 (SAN 209-259X) Tel 516-921-8888; Toll Free: 800-645-6337.

MesaView, Inc., *(1-58515)* 12 Teak Dr., Nashua, NH 03062 Tel 603-674-8755
E-mail: 991199@msn.com
Web site: http://www.mesaview.com.

Mesorah Pubns., Ltd., *(0-89906; 1-57819)* 4401 Second Ave., Brooklyn, NY 11232 (SAN 213-1269) Tel 718-921-9000; Fax: 718-680-1875; Toll Free: 800-637-6724
E-mail: info@artscroll.com
Web site: http://www.artscroll.com.

Mess Hall Writers, *(1-885531)* P.O. Box 1551, Jeffersonville, IN 47130 Tel 812-288-9888; Fax: 812-288-9695
E-mail: fooddudes2@aol.com.

MetroBooks Imprint of Friedman, Michael Publishing Group, Inc.

Meyer Enterprises *See* **Western New York Wares, Inc.**

Mi Tes Su, Inc., *(0-9660252)* Orders Addr.: P.O. Box 2551, Daytona Beach, FL 32115-2551 Tel 904-441-1428; Edit Addr.: 2441 Bellevue Ave., Daytona Beach, FL 32114.

†Micah Pubns., *(0-916288)* 255 Humphrey St., Marblehead, MA 01945 (SAN 209-1577) Tel 781-631-7601; Fax: 781-639-0772; Toll Free: 877-268-9963
E-mail: micah@micahbooks.com
Web site: http://www.micahbooks.com
Dist(s): **Book Publishing Co., The**
Jonathan David Pubs., Inc.; *CIP.*

Micah Publishing, *(1-889018)* 16727 Hutchinson Dr., Lakeville, MN 55044 Tel 612-953-4466; Fax: 612-953-4417 Do not confuse with companies with same name in Hartford, CT, Bridgeville, PA
Dist(s): **Baker & Taylor Bks.**
Koen Bk. Distributors.

Michael Neugebauer Bks. Imprint of North-South Bks., Inc.

MichaelsMind LLC, *(0-9704597; 1-932317)* 5600 Claire Rose Ln., Atlanta, GA 30327
E-mail: satiller@bellsouth.net
Web site: http://www.michaelsmind.com.

†Middle Atlantic Pr., *(0-912608; 0-9705804)* Orders Addr.: c/o Koen Book Distributors, P.O. Box 600, Moorestown, NJ 08057 (SAN 667-4534) Tel 856-235-4444; Fax: 856-727-6914; Toll Free Fax: 800-257-8481; Edit Addr.: 213 Austin Ave., Barrington, NJ 08007 Tel 856-547-4122
E-mail: tdoherty@koen.com; kbd@koen.com
Web site: http://www/koen.com/midat/index.html
Dist(s): **Koen Bk. Distributors;** *CIP.*

Mid-Peninsula Library Cooperative, *(0-933249)* 1525 Pyle Dr., Kingsford, MI 49802-1114 (SAN 692-3836) Tel 906-774-3005.

Midpoint Trade Bks., Inc., Orders Addr.: 1263 Southwest Blvd., Kansas City, KS 66103 (SAN 631-3736) Tel 913-831-2233; Fax: 913-362-7401; Toll Free: 800-742-6139 (consumer orders); Edit Addr.: 27 W. 20th St., No. 1102, New York, NY 10011 (SAN 631-1075) Tel 212-727-0190; Fax: 212-727-0195; P.O. Box 411037, Kansas City, MO 64141-1037 (SAN 253-8539) Tel 913-362-7400; Fax: 913-362-7401
E-mail: midpointny1@aol.com
Web site: http://midpt.com.

Midstates Publishing, *(0-929918)* 4820 Capital Ave. NE, Aberdeen, SD 57401-9685 (SAN 250-9741) Tel 605-225-5287.

Midwest European Pubns., 915 Foster St., Evanston, IL 60201 (SAN 169-1937) Tel 847-866-6289; Fax: 847-866-6290; Toll Free: 800-380-8919
E-mail: info@mep-eli.com
Web site: http://www.mep-eli.com.

Midwest Traditions, Inc., *(1-883953)* 3147 S. Pennsylvania Ave., Milwaukee, WI 53207 Tel 414-294-4319 (phone/fax); Toll Free: 800-736-9189; *Imprints:* Face to Face Books (Face to Face)
Dist(s): **Partners Pubs. Group, Inc..**

Milet Publishing, Ltd. (GBR) *(1-84059) Dist. by* **Consort Bk Sales.**

Milet Publishing, Ltd. (GBR) *(1-84059) Dist. by* **Pan Asian Pubns.**

Milkweed Editions, *(0-915943; 1-57131)* 1011 Washington Ave. S., Suite 300, Minneapolis, MN 55415-1246 (SAN 294-0671) Tel 612-332-3192; Fax: 612-215-2550; Toll Free: 800-520-6455
E-mail: market@milkweed.org
Web site: http://www.worldashome.org; http://www.milkweed.org
Dist(s): **Publishers Group West.**

†Millbrook Pr., Inc., *(0-7613; 1-56294; 1-878137; 1-878841)* Orders Addr.: 2 Old New Milford Rd., Dept. LS, Brookfield, CT 06804 (SAN 299-9390) Tel 203-740-2220; Fax: 203-740-2223; Toll Free: 800-462-4703; 800-568-2665 (electronically transmitted orders); *Imprints:* Copper Beech Books (Copper Beech Bks); Roaring Brook Press (Roaring Brook); Magic Attic Press (MagicAtPr); Twenty-First Century Books, Incorporated (TwentyFrstCent) Do not confuse with Mill Brook Pr., Highland Park, NJ
Web site: http://www.millbrookpress.com
Dist(s): **Simon & Schuster, Inc.;** *CIP.*

Mille Grazie Pr., *(0-9638843; 1-890887)* Orders Addr.: P.O. Box 92023, Santa Barbara, CA 93190 Tel 805-963-8408; Edit Addr.: 820 W. Victoria St., Suite A, Santa Barbara, CA 93101
E-mail: pobiz@mail.com
Dist(s): **SPD-Small Pr. Distribution.**

Miller-Marx, Kim, *(0-9644265)* 8125 Telegraph Rd., Bloomington, MN 55438 Tel 612-944-2155.

Milligan Bks., *(1-881524; 0-9719749; 0-9725941; 0-9742811)* 1425 W. Manchester Blvd., Suite C, Los Angeles, CA 90047 Tel 323-750-3592; Fax: 323-750-2886
E-mail: drrosie@aol.com
Web site: http://milliganbooks.com
Dist(s): **Baker & Taylor Bks..**

Milliken Publishing Co., *(0-7877; 0-88335; 1-55863)* 1100 Research Blvd., Saint Louis, MO 63132-0579 (SAN 205-8405) Tel 314-991-4220; Toll Free: 800-325-4136
Web site: http://www.millikenpub.com.

Millwood Publishing Imprint of Clark, Arthur H. Co.

Milly Molly Bks. (NZL) *(0-9582208; 1-877297; 1-86972) Dist. by* **Natl Bk Netwk.**

Milo Productions, *(1-882172)* Div. of Milo Productions, N69W15890 Eileen Ave., Menomonee Falls, WI 53051-5009.

†Minnesota Historical Society Pr., *(0-87351)* Orders Addr.: 11030 S. Langley Ave., Chicago, IL 60628 Toll Free Fax: 800-621-8476; Toll Free: 800-621-2736; Edit Addr.: 345 Kellogg Blvd., W., Saint Paul, MN 55102-1906 (SAN 202-6384) Tel 651-297-2221; Fax: 651-297-1345; Toll Free: 800-647-7827
E-mail: kevin.morrissey@mnhs.org
Web site: http://www.mnhs.org/mhspress
Dist(s): **Chicago Distribution Ctr.;** *CIP.*

Minnesota Humanities Commission, *(0-9629298; 1-931016)* 987 E. Ivy Ave., Saint Paul, MN 55106-2046 Tel 612-774-0105 (ext. 112); Fax: 651-774-0205
E-mail: leant@thinkmhc.org
Web site: http://www.thinkmhc.org
Dist(s): **Finney Co..**

Mirasol/Libros Juveniles Imprint of Farrar, Straus & Giroux

Miskin Publishing Group *See* **Tapestry Pr., Ltd.**

Mission City Pr., Inc., *(1-928749)* 312 Toddington Ct., Franklin, TN 37067 Tel 615-591-1007; Fax: 615-591-1006
E-mail: sandi@missioncitypress.com; missioncitypress@home.com
Web site: http://www.missioncitypress.com; http://www.alifeoffaith.com
Dist(s): **Zondervan.**

Mr. Padco Pubns., *(0-9615147)* Orders Addr.: P.O. Box 2111, Irwindale, CA 91706 (SAN 662-3069); Edit Addr.: 16850 Alcross St., Covina, CA 91722 (SAN 692-9052) Tel 626-966-3439.

Misty Mountain Publishing Co., *(0-9635083)* P.O. Box 111185, Anchorage, AK 99511 Fax: 907-278-2001; Toll Free: 800-750-8166
Dist(s): **Todd Communications.**

Mixx Entertainment, Inc., *(1-892213; 1-931514; 1-59182)* 5900 Wilshire Blvd., Suite 2000, Los Angeles, CA 90036 Tel 323-692-6700; Fax: 323-692-6701; *Imprints:* Mixx Special Editions (Mixx Special Edtns); Mixx Manga (Mixx Manga); Pocket Mixx (Pocket Mixx)
E-mail: info@tokyopop.com
Web site: http://www.tokyopop.com
Dist(s): **AU Media, Inc.**
Client Distribution Services
Diamond Book Distributors, Inc.
Middleman
SNAP! Entertainment.

Mixx Manga Imprint of Mixx Entertainment, Inc.

Mixx Special Editions Imprint of Mixx Entertainment, Inc.

Moanalua Gardens Foundation, *(1-882163)* 1352 Pineapple Pl., Honolulu, HI 96819 Tel 808-839-5334; Fax: 808-839-3658
E-mail: mgf@pixi.com
Web site: http://www.mgf-hawaii.com.

†Modern Curriculum Pr., *(0-7652; 0-8136; 0-87895)* Div. of Pearson Education, 4350 Equity Dr., Columbus, OH 43216 (SAN 206-6572) Fax: 614-771-7361 (credit card orders); Toll Free: 800-526-9907 (Customer Service)
Web site: http://www.pearsonlearning.com
Dist(s): **Lectorum Pubns., Inc.;** *CIP.*

Modern Library Imprint of Random House Adult Trade Publishing Group

Modern Publishing, *(0-7666; 0-87449; 1-56144)* Div. of Unisystems, Inc., 155 E. 55th St., New York, NY 10022 (SAN 253-2921) Tel 212-826-0850; Fax: 212-759-9096; *Imprints:* Honey Bear Books (Honey Bear Bks)
E-mail: info@modernpublishing.com; rvreeland@modernpublishing.com
Web site: http://www.modernpublishing.com
Dist(s): **Worldwide Media Service, Inc..**

Modern Signs Pr., Inc., *(0-916708)* Orders Addr.: P.O. Box 1181, Los Alamitos, CA 90720 (SAN 282-0056) Tel 562-493-4168; Toll Free: 800-572-7332; Edit Addr.: 10443 Los Alamitos Blvd., Los Alamitos, CA 90720 (SAN 282-0048) Tel 562-596-8548; Fax: 562-795-6614
E-mail: modsigns@aol.com
Web site: http://www.modsigns.com.

Moen, R.E., *(0-9614819)* 165 McIntosh Rd., La Crescent, MN 55947-1824 (SAN 693-0794) Tel 608-788-8753.

Mohawk River Pr., *(0-9662100)* Orders Addr.: P.O. Box 4095, Clifton Park, NY 12065-0850 Tel 518-383-2254; Fax: 518-373-8018; Edit Addr.: 57 Carriage Rd., Clifton Park, NY 12065
E-mail: Jimlabate@hotmail.com
Web site: http://www.mohawkriverpress.com.

Molino, Editorial (ESP) *(84-272) Dist. by* **Lectorum Pubns.**

Molino, Editorial (ESP) *(84-272) Dist. by* **AIMS Intl.**

Mom's Pride Enterprises, *(0-9720549)* 16521 N. 69th Dr., Peoria, AZ 85382 Tel 623-487-7589; Fax: 623-487-1504
E-mail: mrsb4kids@yahoo.com
Web site: http://www.mrsbstorytime.com.

Monday Morning Bks., Inc., *(0-912107; 1-57612; 1-878279)* Orders Addr.: P.O. Box 1680, Palo Alto, CA 94302 (SAN 264-7656) Tel 650-327-3374; Toll Free: 800-255-6049; Edit Addr.: 1111 Greenwood Ave., Palo Alto, CA 94301
E-mail: mmbooks@aol.com
Web site: http://www.mondaymorningbooks.com
Dist(s): **Quality Bks., Inc.**
Unique Bks., Inc..

Mondo Publishing, *(1-57255; 1-879531; 1-58653; 1-59034; 1-59336)* Div. of Music Plus, Inc., 980 Sixth Ave. of the Americas, New York, NY 10018 Toll Free Fax: 888-532-4492; Toll Free: 888-55-66636
Web site: http://www.mondopub.com.

Monkey Sisters, Incorporated, The *See* **Sussman, Ellen Educational Services**

Montemayor Pr., *(0-9674477; 1-932727)* P.O. Box 526, Millburn, NJ 07041 Tel 973-761-1341
E-mail: mail@montemayorpress.com
Web site: http://www.montemayorpress.com.

Monterey Home Video *See* **Monterey Media, Inc.**

Monterey Media, Inc., *(1-56994)* Div. of Monterey Media, Inc., 566 St. Charles Dr., Thousand Oaks, CA 91360-3901 Tel 805-494-7199; Fax: 805-496-6061; Toll Free: 800-424-2593; *Imprints:* Monterey SoundWorks (Monterey SoundWorks)
Web site: http://www.montereymedia.com
Dist(s): **Critics' Choice Video, Inc..**

Monterey Pacific Institute *See* **Monterey Pacific Pubs.**

Monterey Pacific Pubs., *(1-880710)* P.O. Box 1619, Bandon, OR 97411 Tel 650-994-6570; Fax: 650-994-6579
E-mail: ingram@uci.net
Dist(s): **Baker & Taylor Bks..**

Monterey SoundWorks Imprint of Monterey Media, Inc.

Montevista Pr., *(0-931551)* 3467 Pinehurst Ct., Bellingham, WA 98226-4170 (SAN 682-191X)
Dist(s): **Todd Communications.**

†Moody Pr., *(0-8024)* Div. of Moody Bible Institute, 820 N. LaSalle Blvd., Chicago, IL 60610 (SAN 202-5604) Tel 312-329-2102; Fax: 312-329-2019; Toll Free: 800-678-8812
Web site: http://www.moodypress.org
Dist(s): **Jones, Bob Univ. Pr.**; *CIP.*

Moon Mountain Publishing, Inc., *(0-9677929; 1-931659)* 80 Peachtree Rd., North Kingstown, RI 02852 Tel 401-884-6703; Fax: 401-884-7076; Toll Free: 800-353-5877
E-mail: hello@moonmountainpub.com
Web site: http://www.moonmountainpub.com
Dist(s): **National Bk. Network.**

Moons & Stars Publishing For Children, *(1-929063)* Div. of Moon Star Unlimited, Inc., P.O. Box 1763, Pasadena, TX 77506 Tel 713-473-7120; Fax: 713-473-1105.

Moore Bks., *(1-891635)* Orders Addr.: P.O. Box 324, Somerville, IN 47683 Tel 812-795-2502; Fax: 812-795-2665; Edit Addr.: 202 E. Illinois St., Somerville, IN 47683
E-mail: moorebooks@hotmail.com.

Moore Foundation, The, *(0-9713590)* Orders Addr.: P.O. Box 1, Camas, WA 98607 (SAN 631-5208) Tel 360-835-5500; Fax: 360-835-5392; Toll Free: 800-891-5255; Edit Addr.: 101 Moore Falls Rd., Washougal, WA 98671
E-mail: moorefnd@pacifier.com
Web site: http://www.moorefoundation.com.

Moore, Lonnie W. *See* **I & L Publishing**

Mora Art Studio, *(0-9671753)* Orders Addr.: P.O. Box 8494, Kansas City, MO 64114-0494 Tel 816-313-0370 ; Edit Addr.: 5309 Crisp Ave., Raytown, MO 64133
E-mail: eddy4art@yahoo.com; eddy@moraartstudio.com; info@moraartstudio.com
Web site: http://www.moraartstudio.com.

MoranoCo, Inc., *(0-9648855)* Orders Addr.: P.O. Box 4204, Metuchen, NJ 08840-4204 Tel 908-755-4473 (phone/fax); Edit Addr.: 16 Annette Dr., Edison, NJ 08820
E-mail: Marmoraro@aol.com
Web site: http://members.aol.com/marmorono.

†Morehouse Publishing, *(0-8192)* Orders Addr.: P.O. Box 1321, Harrisburg, PA 17105-1321 (SAN 202-6511) Tel 717-541-8130; Fax: 717-541-8128; Toll Free: 800-877-0012; Edit Addr.: 4775 Linglestown Rd., Harrisburg, PA 17112 Tel 717-541-8130; 717-236-0366; Fax: 717-541-8136
E-mail: morehouse@morehousegroup.com
Web site: http://www.morehousegroup.com; *CIP.*

Moreland Pr., Inc., *(0-9706677)* P.O. Box 15123, Clearwater, FL 33766-5123 Tel 813-891-0428
E-mail: janmahjong@aol.com; Morelandpress@aol.com
Web site: http://www.morelandpress.com
Dist(s): **Biblio Distribution**
Bookazine Co., Inc.
National Bk. Network.

Morganstern, Mimi, *(0-9700522)* 7235 Fairfax Dr., Tamarac, FL 33321-4308 Tel 954-720-3362; Toll Free: 800-484-8729 (code 0995)
E-mail: mmorganste@cs.com.

Moriarty, Timothy K., *(0-9650519)* 2120 SE Fourth St., Cape Coral, FL 33990-1413 Tel 941-772-2130.

†Morning Glory Pr., Inc., *(0-930934; 1-885356; 1-932538)* 6595 San Haroldo Way, Buena Park, CA 90620 (SAN 211-2558) Tel 714-828-1998; Fax: 714-828-2049; Toll Free: 888-612-8254 Do not confuse with Morning Glory Press in Nashua, NH
E-mail: jwl@morningglorypress.com
Web site: http://www.morningglorypress.com
Dist(s): **Independent Pubs. Group**; *CIP.*

Morris Publishing, *(0-7392; 0-9631249; 1-57502; 1-885591)* Subs. of Morris Pr. & Office Supplies, 3212 E. Hwy. 30, P.O. Box 2110, Kearney, NE 68847 Tel 308-236-7888; Fax: 308-237-0263; Toll Free: 800-650-7888 Do not confuse with companies with the same or similar name in Sarveta, PA, Plymouth Meeting, PA, Beecher City, IL, Urbana, IL, San Francisco, CA
E-mail: publish@morrispublishing.com; kimmyw414@yahoo.com; snowgers@mcn.org
Web site: http://morrispublishing.com.

Morrow, William & Co. Imprint of Morrow/Avon

Morrow/Avon, *(0-06; 0-380; 0-688)* Div. of HarperCollins General Bks. Grp., Orders Addr.: 1000 Keystone Industrial Pk., Scranton, PA 18512-4021 Toll Free Fax: 800-822-4090; Toll Free: 800-242-7737 ; Edit Addr.: 1350 Ave. of the Americas, New York, NY 10019 Tel 212-261-6788; Fax: 570-941-1599 (customer service); Toll Free: 800-242-7737 (orders); *Imprints:* Morrow, William & Company (Wm Morrow); Avon Books (Avon Bks); HarperTorch (HarpTorch); Eos (Eos); HarperEntertainment (HarpEntertain)
Web site: http://www.harpercollins.com/hc/
Dist(s): **HarperCollins Pubs.**
Lectorum Pubns., Inc..

Mosley, Marilyn C., *(0-9614850)* P.O. Box 1883, 13117 Burma Rd., SW, Vashon, WA 98070 (SAN 693-0972) Tel 206-567-4751.

Moss Portfolio, The, *(0-9665198)* 1 Poplar Grove Ln., Mathews, VA 23109 (SAN 630-4303) Tel 804-725-7378; Fax: 804-725-3040; Toll Free: 800-430-1320
E-mail: mossportfolio@ccsinc.com
Web site: http://www.p-buckley-moss.com.

Mother Courage Pr., *(0-941300)* 1533 Illinois, Racine, WI 53405 (SAN 239-4618) Tel 414-634-1047; Fax: 414-637-8242.

Mountain Bks. & Music, *(1-881650)* 4570 Mac Arthur Blvd., NW, Suite 104, Washington, DC 20007 Tel 202-338-7111; Fax: 202-338-0427.

†Mountain Pr. Publishing Co., Inc., *(0-87842)* Orders Addr.: P.O. Box 2399, Missoula, MT 59806-2399 (SAN 202-8832) Tel 406-728-1900; Fax: 406-728-1635; Toll Free: 800-234-5308; Edit Addr.: 1301 S. Third West, Missoula, MT 59801 (SAN 662-0868)
E-mail: johnargyle@aol.com; mtnpress@montana.com
Web site: http://www.mountainpresspublish.com
Dist(s): **Lone Pine Publishing**; *CIP.*

Mountain Top Historical Society, Inc., *(0-9624216)* Orders Addr.: P.O. Box 263, Haines Falls, NY 12436; Edit Addr.: Twilight Park-T2, Haines Falls, NY 12436 Tel 518-589-6191.

Mountaintop Bks., Inc., *(1-880679)* P.O. Box 705, Oxon Hill, MD 20750 Tel 301-505-2116 Do not confuse with Mountaintop Bks. in Glenwood, IA.

Mouse Works, *(0-7364; 1-57082)* Div. of Disney Bk. Publishing, Inc., A Walt Disney Co., 114 Fifth Ave., New York, NY 10011 (SAN 298-0797) Tel 212-633-4400; Fax: 212-633-4811
Web site: http://www.disneybooks.com.

†Moyer Bell, *(0-918825; 1-55921)* 549 Old North Rd., Kingston, RI 02881-1220 (SAN 630-1762) Tel 401-783-5480; Fax: 401-284-0959; Toll Free: 888-789-1945
E-mail: contact@moyerbellbooks.com
Web site: http://www.moyerbellbooks.com/
Dist(s): **Acorn Alliance**
Alliance Hse., Inc.
Client Distribution Services
Wittenborn Art Bks.; *CIP.*

Mozart Park Pr., *(0-9648262)* 2842 E. Devereaux, Philadelphia, PA 19149 Tel 215-289-3659.

Mr Do It All, Inc., *(0-9722038)* 2212 S. Chickasaw Trail, No. 220, Orlando, FL 32825 Toll Free: 800-425-9206
E-mail: info@planet-heller.com
Web site: http://www.planet-heller.com.

MSG Imprint of Simon & Schuster

MTV Imprint of Simon & Schuster

Muh-He-Con-Neew Pr., *(0-935790)* Affil. of Arvid E. Miller Memorial Library, Mohican Nation Reservation, N9136 Big Lake Rd., Gresham, WI 54128 Tel 715-787-4427
Dist(s): **Miller, Arvid E. Memorial Library Museum.**

Multicultural Pubns., *(0-9634932; 1-884242)* 936 Slosson St., Akron, OH 44320 Tel 330-865-9578; Fax: 330-734-0737; Toll Free: 800-238-0297
E-mail: multiculturalpub@prodigy.net
Web site: http://www.multiculturalpub.net
Dist(s): **Brodart Co.**
Follett Library Resources.

Multnomah Bks. Imprint of Multnomah Pubs., Inc.

Multnomah Pubs., Inc., *(0-88070; 0-930014; 0-945564; 1-57673; 1-885305; 1-58860; 1-59052)* Orders Addr.: P.O. Box 1720, Sisters, OR 97759 (SAN 247-123X) Tel 541-549-1144; Fax: 541-549-8048; Toll Free: 800-929-0910; Edit Addr.: 204 W. Adams, Sisters, OR 97759; *Imprints:* Multnomah Books (Multnomah Bks)
E-mail: djacobson@multnomahbooks.com
Web site: http://multnomahbooks.com
Dist(s): **Christian Bk. Distributors**
GL Services
Zondervan.

Munchweiler Pr., *(0-7940)* Orders Addr.: P.O. Box 2529, Victorville, CA 92393-2529 Tel 760-245-9215; Fax: 760-245-9418; Edit Addr.: 14217 Gale Dr., Victorville, CA 92393-2529 Tel 760-245-9215
E-mail: publisher@munchweilerpress.com
Web site: http://www.munchweilerpress.com.

Mundus Imprint of Ann Arbor Media Group, LLC

Murlin Pubns., *(1-892218)* P.O. Box 433, Orefield, PA 18069-0433
E-mail: party4@fast.net.

Murlin Publishing Company *See* **Murlin Pubns.**

Murray Pubns., *(0-9632132)* 4921 E. Stokes Ferry Rd., Hernando, FL 34442-2334 Tel 904-344-8394.

†Museum of Fine Arts, Boston, *(0-87846)* 465 Huntington Ave., Boston, MA 02115-4401 (SAN 202-2230) Tel 617-369-3438; Fax: 617-369-3459
E-mail: kmullins-mitchell@mfa.org
Web site: http://www.mfa.org
Dist(s): **Brown, David Bk. Co.**
Distributed Art Pubs./D.A.P.; *CIP.*

Museum of New Mexico Pr., *(0-89013)* Orders Addr.: 228 E. Palace Ave., Sante Fe, NM 87504-2087 (SAN 202-2575) Tel 505-827-6455
E-mail: dkosharek@oca.state.nm.us
Web site: http://www.mnmpress.org
Dist(s): **Univ. of New Mexico Pr..**

Music for Little People, Inc., *(1-56628; 1-877737)* 390 Lake Benbow Dr. No. C, Garberville, CA 95542 Tel 707-923-3991; Fax: 707-923-3241; Toll Free: 800-346-4445
Web site: http://www.mflp.com
Dist(s): **Bookpeople**
Educational Record Ctr., Inc.
Goldenrod Music, Inc.
Linden Tree Children's Records & Bks.
Music Design, Inc.
New Leaf Distributing Co., Inc.
Rounder Kids Music Distribution
Western Record Sales.

Music Resources International *See* **Kindermusik International**

MusicKit.COM, *(0-9713194)* 778 Western Dr., Point Richmond, CA 94801 Tel 510-237-5551; *Imprints:* MusicTales (MusicTales)
E-mail: kit@musickit.com
Web site: http://www.musickit.com
Dist(s): **Bookpeople.**

MusicTales Imprint of MusicKit.COM

Myers Publishing Company, The *See* **Myers, R.J. Publishing Co.**

Myers, R.J. Publishing Co., *(1-884108)* P.O. Box 70427, Washington, DC 20024 Tel 202-863-0056; Toll Free: 800-676-0256.

NAL, *(0-451; 0-452; 0-453; 0-525; 0-8015)* Div. of Penguin Putnam, Inc., Orders Addr.: 405 Murray Hill Pkwy., East Rutherford, NJ 07073 Toll Free: 800-788-6262 (individual consumer sales); 800-526-0275 (reseller sales); 800-631-8571 (reseller customer service); Edit Addr.: 375 Hudson St., New York, NY 10014-3657 Tel 212-366-2000; Fax: 212-366-2666; Toll Free: 800-331-4624 (Customer service); *Imprints:* Signet Books (Sig); Signet Classics (Sig Classics); ROC (ROC); Signet Vista (Sig Vista); Topaz (Topaz)
E-mail: online@penguinputnam.com
Web site: http://www.penguinputnam.com
Dist(s): **Penguin Group (USA) Inc..**

N A L/Dutton *See* **NAL**

NAPSAC Reproductions, *(0-934426; 1-932747)* Rte. 4, Box 646, Marble Hill, MO 63764 (SAN 222-4607) Tel 573-238-4846; Fax: 573-238-2010
E-mail: napsac@clas.net
Dist(s): **FaithWorks.**

NBM Publishing Co., *(0-918348; 1-56163)* Orders Addr.: 555 Eighth Ave., Suite 1202, New York, NY 10018-4312 (SAN 210-0835) Tel 212-643-5407; Fax: 212-643-1545; Toll Free: 800-886-1223; *Imprints:* Amerotica (Amerotica)
E-mail: catalog@nbmpublishing.com
Web site: http://www.nbmpub.com.

Nadja Publishing, *(0-9636335; 1-886234)* 31021 Hamilton Tr., Trabuco Canyon, CA 92679 Tel 714-858-9000; Fax: 714-858-3477; Toll Free: 800-795-9750
Dist(s): **APG Sales and Fulfillment.**

Names

Nags Head Art, Inc, *(0-9616344; 1-878405)* Orders Addr.: P. O. Drawer 1809, Nags Head, NC 27959 (SAN 200-9145) Tel 252-441-7480; Fax: 252-441-4842; Toll Free Fax: 800-246-7014; Toll Free: 800-541-2722; Edit Addr.: 7728 Virginia Dare Trail, Nags Head, NC 27959 (SAN 658-8107)
E-mail: suzannetate@yahoo.com
Web site: http://www.suzannetate.com
Dist(s): **Baker & Taylor Bks.**
Florida Classics Library
Koen Bk. Distributors
Mistco, Inc.
Weems & Plath, Inc..

Nana Banana Classics, *(1-886201)* Div. of Isy Productions, Inc., Orders Addr.: P.O. Box 7517, Greenwich, CT 06836 Tel 203-622-7544; Fax: 203-622-6717.

Nantucket Cobblestones, Ltd., *(0-9653674)* One Saint Matthews Dr., Barrington, NH 03825 Tel 603-942-9274.

Napa Valley Mustard Celebration, *(1-887534)* P.O. Box 464, Deer Park, CA 94576-0464 Tel 707-942-9762; Fax: 707-942-9606; Toll Free: 800-666-8782.

Napoleon Publishing/Rendezvous Pr. (CAN) *(0-929141; 1-894917) Dist. by* **Words Distrib.**

Narwhal Pr., Inc., *(1-886391)* 1590 Meeting St., Charleston, SC 29405 (SAN 298-6515) Tel 843-853-0510; Fax: 843-853-2528; Toll Free: 800-981-1943; *Imprints:* Shipwreck Press (Shipwreck Pr)
E-mail: shipwrx@bellsouth.net; shipwrex@aol.com
Web site: http://www.shipwrecks.com
Dist(s): **Baker & Taylor Bks.**
Sandlapper Publishing Co., Inc..

Nathan, Fernand (FRA) *(2-09) Dist. by* **Distribks Inc.**

National Assn. for Visually Handicapped, *(0-89064)* 3201 Balboa St., San Francisco, CA 94121 (SAN 202-0971) Tel 415-221-3201; Fax: 415-221-8754; 22 W. 21st St., 6th Flr., New York, NY 10010 (SAN 669-1870) Tel 212-889-3141
E-mail: staff@navh.org
Web site: http://www.navh.org.

National Bk. Network, Div. of Rowman & Littlefield Pubs., Inc., Orders Addr.: 15200 NBN Way, Blue Ridge Summit, PA 17214 (SAN 630-0065) Tel 717-794-3800; Fax: 717-794-3803; Toll Free Fax: 800-338-4550; Toll Free: 800-462-6420; a/o Les Petriw, 67 Mowat Ave., Suite 241, Toronto, ON M6P 3K3 Tel 416-534-1660; Fax: 416-534-3699; Edit Addr.: 4501 Forbes Blvd., Suite 200, Lanham, MD 20706 Tel 301-459-3366; Fax: 301-429-5747
E-mail: lpetriw@nbnbooks.com
Web site: http://www.nbnbooks.com.

National Braille Pr., *(0-939173)* Orders Addr.: 88 St. Stephen St., Boston, MA 02115 (SAN 273-0952) Tel 617-266-6160; Fax: 617-437-0456; Toll Free: 800-548-7323
E-mail: orders@nbp.org
Web site: http://www.nbp.org.

National Dance Education Organization, *(1-930798)* 4948 St. Elmo Ave., Suite 301, Bethesda, MD 20814-6013 Tel 301-657-2880; Fax: 301-657-2882
E-mail: ndeo@erols.com
Web site: http://www.ndeo.org.

National Family Resiliency Ctr., Inc., *(0-9729415)* 10632 Little Patuxent Pkwy., Suite 121, Columbia, MD 21044 Tel 410-740-9553; Fax: 301-596-1677
E-mail: info@divorceabc.com
Web site: http://www.divorceabc.com.

†National Geographic Society, *(0-7922; 0-87044)* 1145 17th St., NW, Washington, DC 20036 (SAN 202-8956) Tel 202-857-7000; Fax: 301-921-1575; Toll Free: 800-647-5463; 800-548-9797 (TTD users only)
Web site: http://nationalgeographic.com
Dist(s): **Andrews McMeel Publishing**
Follett Media Distribution
Lectorum Pubns., Inc.
Simon & Schuster Children's Publishing
Simon & Schuster, Inc.; *CIP.*

National Library of Poetry, *(1-56167)* 3600 Crondall Lane, Owening Mills, MD 21117 (SAN 631-1180) Tel 410-356-2000.

National Recording Co., Orders Addr.: P.O. Box 395, Glenview, IL 60025 (SAN 693-8175); Edit Addr.: 531 Pinar Dr., Orlando, FL 32825 Tel 407-282-3489.

National Textbook Co. Imprint of McGraw-Hill/ Contemporary

Native Sun Pubs., Inc., *(0-9625169; 1-879289)* Orders Addr.: P.O. Box 13394, Richmond, VA 23225 Tel 804-233-7768; Edit Addr.: 1021 Hioaks Rd., Richmond, VA 23225.

Natural Highs, *(0-9658526)* 72 Spring Lake Dr., San Antonio, TX 78248 Tel 210-408-7407; Fax: 210-408-7038
E-mail: RoBetW@aol.com.

Natural Science Industries, Ltd., *(1-878501)* 910 Orlando Ave., West Hempstead, NY 11552-3941 Tel 718-945-5400; Fax: 718-318-1194.

Naturegraph Pubs., Inc., *(0-87961; 0-911010)* Box 1047, 3543 Indian Creek Rd., Happy Camp, CA 96039 (SAN 202-8999) Tel 530-493-5353; Fax: 530-493-5240; Toll Free: 800-390-5353
E-mail: nature@sisqtel.net
Web site: http://www.naturegraph.com
Dist(s): **Gem Guides Bk. Co.**
New Leaf Distributing Co., Inc.
Sunbelt Pubns., Inc..

Nature's Nest Bks., *(1-930130)* 10139 NE Campbell Rd., Fayetteville, AR 72701 Fax: 501-443-0025; Toll Free: 888-464-2665
E-mail: naturesnestbooks@aol.com.

Nature's Shadows, *(1-890972)* 4422 Promesa Cir., San Diego, CA 92124-2313 Tel 760-480-0844.

†Nautical & Aviation Publishing Co. of America, Inc., The, *(0-933852; 1-877853)* 2055 Middleburg Ln., Mount Pleasant, SC 29464-4433 (SAN 213-3431) Tel 843-856-0561; Fax: 843-856-3164
E-mail: nauticalaviationpublishing@att.net
Web site: http://www.nauticalaviation.com; *CIP.*

Naxos AudioBooks Imprint of Naxos of America, Inc.

Naxos of America, Inc., *(962-634; 1-930838)* Div. of HNH International, Cambridge House, Suite 7 1260 N. Forest Rd., Williamsville, NY 14221 (SAN 253-407X) Tel 716-634-3215; Fax: 716-634-3051; *Imprints:* Naxos AudioBooks (Naxos AudioBooks)
E-mail: inquiries@naxosusa.com
Web site: http://www.naxosaudiobooks.com.

Ned's Head Productions, *(1-887206)* 307 State St., Apt. B3, Johnstown, PA 15905 (SAN 253-8059) Tel 814-255-6646 (phone/fax)
E-mail: drron@charter.net
Dist(s): **APG Sales and Fulfillment.**

Neema's Children Literature Assn., Inc., *(0-9740653)* Orders Addr.: P.O. Box 440073, Chicago, IL 60644-1937 Tel 773-378-0607; Fax: 773-378-0042; Edit Addr.: 5345 W. Ferdinand, Chicago, IL 60644-1937
E-mail: nclapub@aol.com.

Neff, Lisi A., *(0-9719396)* 6541 Fairland St., Alexandria, VA 22312 Tel 703-354-4376.

Neighborhood Pr. Publishing, *(0-9655340; 1-893108)* 459 Kingsley Ave., Suite H, Orange Park, FL 32073-4827 (SAN 253-8091) Tel 904-215-0150; Fax: 904-215-8885; Toll Free: 888-303-7958
E-mail: nppubs3@aol.com; Linda_Pryor@neighborhoodpress.com; nppubs@aol.com
Web site: http://www.members.aol.com/NPPubs/; http://neighborhoodpress.com.

Neighborhood Press Publishing Company *See* **Neighborhood Pr. Publishing**

Nellie Edge Resources, Inc., *(0-922053)* P.O. Box 12399, Salem, OR 97309-0399 (SAN 251-1045) Tel 503-399-0040; Fax: 503-399-0435; Toll Free: 800-523-4594.

†Nel-Mar Publishing, *(0-9615760; 1-877740)*
E-mail: Nelmar@gvtc.com
Dist(s): **Baker & Taylor Bks.**
Follett Library Resources; *CIP.*

†Nelson, Thomas Inc., *(0-7852; 0-8407; 0-8499; 0-86605; 0-89840; 0-918956; 1-4003)* Orders Addr.: P.O. Box 141000, Nashville, TN 37214-1000 (SAN 209-3820) Fax: 615-902-1866; Toll Free: 800-251-4000; Edit Addr.: 501 Nelson Pl., Nashville, TN 37214
E-mail: thomasnelson.com
Web site: http://www.thomasnelson.com
Dist(s): **Christian Bk. Distributors**
Twentieth Century Christian Bks.; *CIP.*

Nelson, Thomas Pubs., *(0-7852; 0-8407)* Div. of Thomas Nelson, Inc., Orders Addr.: P.O. Box 141000, Nashville, TN 37214-1000
Web site: http://ThomasNelsonPublishers.com
Dist(s): **Nelson, Thomas Inc.**
Vision Video.

Nelson, Tommy, *(0-7852; 0-8407; 0-8499; 1-4003)* Div. of Thomas Nelson, Inc., Orders Addr.: P.O. Box 141000, Nashville, TN 37214 Fax: 615-902-3330; Edit Addr.: 501 Nelson Pl., Nashville, TN 37214 Tel 615-889-9000; Toll Free: 800-251-4000
E-mail: mduncan@tommynelson.com
Web site: http://www.tommynelson.com
Dist(s): **CRC Pubns.**
Nelson, Thomas Inc.
Twentieth Century Christian Bks..

Neon Rose Productions Imprint of Smart Alternatives, Inc.

Nesak International, *(1-890095)* 14000 Military Trail, Suite 208A, Delray Beach, FL 33484-2630 Tel 561-638-9852; Fax: 561-638-9854
E-mail: nesak@ix.netcom.com
Web site: http://www.nesak.com.

Neshui Publishing, Inc., *(0-9652528; 1-931190)* 8029 Forsyth, Suite 204, Saint Louis, MO 63105 Tel 314-781-3808
E-mail: neshui62@hotmail.com
Web site: http://www.neshui.com
Dist(s): **Baker & Taylor Bks.**
Booksource, The
Raven West Coast Distribution.

netLibrary, Inc., *(0-585)* 4888 Pearl East Cir., Boulder, CO 80301 (SAN 253-9497) Tel 303-415-2548; Fax: 303-381-7000; 303-381-8999; Toll Free: 800-413-4557
E-mail: mgilbert@netlibrary.com
Web site: http://www.netlibrary.com
Dist(s): **ABC-CLIO, Inc..**

Network Publications *See* **ETR Assocs.**

Neumann Pr., The, *(0-911845; 1-930873)* 21892 Cty. 11, Long Prairie, MN 56347 (SAN 264-2425) Tel 320-732-6358; Fax: 320-732-3858; Toll Free: 800-746-2521
E-mail: asknp@lakes.com
Web site: http://www.neumannpress.com.

New Amsterdam Publishing, Incorporated *See* **Intercontinental Publishing, Inc.**

New Canaan Publishing Co., Inc., *(1-889658)* P.O. Box 752, New Canaan, CT 06840 Tel 203-966-3408; Toll Free: 800-705-5698
E-mail: djm@newcanaanpublishing.com
Web site: http://www.newcanaanpublishing.com
Dist(s): **FaithWorks.**

New Concepts Publishing, *(1-891020; 1-58608)* 5202 Humphreys Rd., Lake Park, GA 31636 Tel 229-257-0367; Fax: 229-219-1097
E-mail: ncp@newconceptspublishing.com
Web site: http://www.newconceptspublishing.com
Dist(s): **Baker & Taylor Bks..**

New Day Enterprises, Ltd., *(0-9675011)* 81 Park Ave., Arlington, MA 02476-5962 Tel 781-646-2929; Fax: 781-646-9292
E-mail: newday007@peoplepc.com.

New Day Pr., *(0-913678)* c/o Karamu Hse., 2355 E. 89th St., Cleveland, OH 44106 (SAN 279-2664) Tel 216-795-7070 (ext. 228); Fax: 216-795-7073 Do not confuse wtih New Day Press in Southlake, TX
E-mail: editor@newdaypress.com.

New Day Pubs., Philippines (PHL) *(971-10) Dist. by* **Book Bin.**

†New Directions Publishing Corp., *(0-8112)* 80 Eighth Ave., New York, NY 10011 (SAN 202-9081) Tel 212-255-0230; Fax: 212-255-0231; Toll Free: 800-233-4830
E-mail: nd@ndbooks.com
Web site: http://www.ndpublishing.com
Dist(s): **Continental Bk. Co., Inc.**
Norton, W. W. & Co., Inc.
SPD-Small Pr. Distribution; *CIP.*

†New England Pr., Inc., The, *(0-933050; 1-881535)* Orders Addr.: P.O. Box 575, Shelburne, VT 05482 (SAN 213-6376) Tel 802-863-2520; Fax: 802-863-1510
E-mail: nep@together.net
Web site: http://www.nepress.com; *CIP.*

New Era Pubns., Inc., *(0-939830)* P.O. Box 130109, Ann Arbor, MI 48113-0109 (SAN 111-8757) Tel 734-663-1929 Do not confuse with New Era Pubns. in Happy Camp, CA.

New Era Publishing Co., *(1-888086)* P.O. Box 60515, Pasadena, CA 91106-6515.

New Hope *See* **Woman's Missionary Union**

New Hope Imprint of Woman's Missionary Union

New Horizon Educational Services Pr., *(1-884197)* 7202 Foxtree Cove, Austin, TX 78750-7932 Tel 512-345-9502
E-mail: dale-bulla@pobox.com
Web site: http://www.pobox.com/~dale-bulla
Dist(s): **Brodart Co.**
Follett Library Resources
Hervey's Booklink & Cookbook Warehouse.

New Horizon Press *See* **New Horizon Educational Services Pr.**

Names

New Horizon Pr. Pubs., Inc., *(0-88282)* Orders Addr.: P.O. Box 669, Far Hills, NJ 07931 (SAN 677-119X) Tel 908-604-6311; Fax: 908-604-6330; Toll Free: 800-533-7978 (orders only); *Imprints:* Small Horizons (Small Horizons)
E-mail: nhp@newhorizonpressbooks.com
Web site: http://www.newhorizonpressbooks.com
Dist(s): **Kensington Publishing Corp..**

New Horizons Book Publishing Company *See* **World Citizens**

New Horizons Pr., *(0-9667770)* P.O. Box 2161, Leesburg, VA 20177-7545 Fax: 703-777-2695 Do not confuse with companies with the same name in Marietta, GA, Lake Mary, FL, Chico, CA, Ferrisburgh, VT..

New Horizons, Unlimited, *(0-9651804)* 484B Washington St., No. 238, Monterey, CA 93940 Tel 408-647-1527; Fax: 408-647-9493.

†New Jersey Historical Society, *(0-911020)* 52 Park Pl., Newark, NJ 07102-4302 (SAN 205-7131) Tel 973-596-8500; Fax: 973-596-6957; *CIP.*

New Readers Pr., *(0-88336; 1-56420)* Div. of Laubach Literacy International, Orders Addr.: P.O. Box 888, Syracuse, NY 13210 (SAN 202-1064) Fax: 315-422-6369; Toll Free: 800-448-8878; Edit Addr.: 1320 Jamesville Ave., Syracuse, NY 13210 Tel 315-422-9121
E-mail: nrp@laubach.org
Web site: http://www.newreaderspress.com
Dist(s): **CRC Pubns..**

†New Riders Publishing, *(0-7357; 0-934035; 1-56205; 1-57870)* Div. of Pearson Technology Group, 201 W. 103rd St., Indianapolis, IN 46290 Tel 317-581-3500; Fax: 317-581-4663; Toll Free: 800-428-5331 (orders) ; *Imprints:* Hayden (Hay)
Web site: http://www.newriders.com
Dist(s): **Alpha Bks.;** *CIP.*

New Rivers Pr., *(0-89823; 0-912284)* Minnesota State University, Moorhead, 1104 Seventh Ave. South, Moorhead, MN 56563 (SAN 202-9138) Tel 218-236-4681; Fax: 218-236-2236; Toll Free: 800-339-2011
E-mail: davisa@mnstate.edu
Web site: http://www.newriverspress.org
Dist(s): **Consortium Bk. Sales & Distribution**
SPD-Small Pr. Distribution.

†New Victoria Pubs., Inc., *(0-934678; 1-892281)* Orders Addr.: P.O. Box 27, Norwich, VT 05055 (SAN 212-1204) Tel 802-649-5297 (phone/fax); Toll Free: 800-326-5297 (phone/fax); Edit Addr.: 513 New Boston Rd., Norwich, VT 05055
E-mail: newvic@aol.com
Web site: http://www.newvictoria.com
Dist(s): **LPC Group;** *CIP.*

New World Enterprises, LLC *See* **A + Children's Bks. and Music**

Newbridge Communications, Incorporated *See* **Newbridge Educational Publishing**

Newbridge Educational Publishing, *(1-56784; 1-58273; 1-4007)* Div. of Haights Cross Communications, Orders Addr.: P.O. Box 5267, Clifton, NJ 07015 Tel 973-614-8763; Toll Free: 800-729-1463; Edit Addr.: 333 E. 38th St., 8th Flr., New York, NY 10016
E-mail: kristinl@newbridgeeducational.com
Web site: http://www.newbridgeeducational.com.

Newman, James A., *(0-9642980)* 1635 W. Hazelwood, Phoenix, AZ 85015 Tel 602-263-0017.

†Newmarket Pr., *(0-937858; 1-55704)* Div. of Newmarket Publishing & Communications Corp., 18 E. 48th St., New York, NY 10017 (SAN 217-2585) Tel 212-832-3575; Fax: 212-832-3629; Toll Free Fax: 800-458-6515 (trade orders); Toll Free: 800-233-4830 (trade orders)
E-mail: mailbox@newmarketpress.com
Web site: http://www.newmarketpress.com
Dist(s): **Norton, W. W. & Co., Inc.**
Worldwide Media Service, Inc.; *CIP.*

NewSound, LLC, 81 Demeritt Pl., Waterbury, VT 05676 Tel 802-244-7858; Fax: 802-244-1808; Toll Free: 800-342-0295 (wholesale orders)
E-mail: sales@newsoundmusic.com.

NewSouth, Inc., *(1-58838)* P.O. Box 1588, Montgomery, AL 36102-1588 Tel 334-834-3556; Fax: 334-834-3557; *Imprints:* Junebug Books (Junebug Bks)
E-mail: info@newsouthbooks.com
Web site: http://www.newsouthbooks.com.

NewStar Media, Inc., *(0-7871; 1-55800)* 8955 Beverly Blvd., Los Angeles, CA 90048 (SAN 297-2913) Tel 310-786-1600; Fax: 310-247-2924; Toll Free: 800-368-3007; *Imprints:* NewStar Press (NewStar Pr); Dove Audio (Dove Audio)
E-mail: customerservice@audiouniverse.com
Web site: http://www.newstarmedia.com; http://www.audiouniverse.com
Dist(s): **Lectorum Pubns., Inc.**
Landmark Audiobooks
Penguin Group (USA) Inc..

NewStar Pr. Imprint of NewStar Media, Inc.

Nibble Me Bks. Imprint of Playhouse Publishing

Nickel Pr., *(1-57122; 1-879424)* Div. of S.R. Jacobs & Assocs., 107 Knob Hill Pk. Dr., Reisterstown, MD 21136 Do not confuse with Nickel Press, Inc., Enterprise, AL.

Night Sky Bks., *(1-59014)* Div. of North-South Books, Inc., 11 E. 26th St., 17th Flr., New York, NY 10010 Tel 212-706-4545; Fax: 212-706-4546; Toll Free: 800-282-8257 Do not confuse with companies with the same name in Santa Fe, NM
E-mail: nightsky@northsouth.com
Web site: http://www.northsouth.com
Dist(s): **Chronicle Bks. LLC**
Lectorum Pubns., Inc..

Nightingale Rose Pubns., *(1-889755)* Div. of Nightingale Counseling Ctr., 16960 E. Bastanchury Rd., Suite J, Yorba Linda, CA 92886 Tel 714-993-5343; Fax: 714-993-3467; Toll Free: 800-943-5728
Web site: http://www.nightingalerose.com.

†Nilgiri Pr., *(0-915132; 1-888314; 1-58638)* Div. of the Blue Mountain Ctr. of Meditation, Orders Addr.: P.O. Box 256, Tomales, CA 94971-0256 (SAN 207-6853) Tel 707-878-2369; Fax: 707-878-2375; Toll Free: 800-475-2369 (orders)
E-mail: mailto:info@nilgiri.org; info@nilgiri.org
Web site: http://www.nilgiri.org
Dist(s): **Publishers Group West;** *CIP.*

Njoku, Scholastica Ibari, *(0-9617833)* Orders Addr.: P.O. Box 11557, Portland, OR 97211 (SAN 665-0724) ; Edit Addr.: 307 NE Holland, Portland, OR 97211 Tel 503-285-8160.

No Dead Lines *See* **Fithian Pr.**

No Exit Pr. (GBR) *(0-948353; 1-874061; 1-901982; 1-84243) Dist. by* **Trafalgar.**

NOA International, *(0-9644137)* P.O. Box 111092, Aurora, CO 80042-1092 Tel 303-755-1863; Fax: 303-369-5153.

Noble Endeaver, *(0-9700692)* P.O. Box 770, Prospect, KY 40059 Fax: 502-228-6771
E-mail: jilljacks@worldnet.att.net
Web site: http://www.jill1jackson.com.

Noble Publishing Assocs., *(0-923463; 1-56857)* 1300 NE 131st Cir., Vancouver, WA 98685 (SAN 251-656X) Tel 360-258-3119; Fax: 360-258-3122; Toll Free: 800-225-5259; 1311 NE 134th St., Suite 2A, Vancouver, WA 98685
E-mail: noblebooks@noblepublishing.com
Web site: http://www.noblepublishing.com.

Noguer y Caralt Editores, S. A. (ESP) *(84-217; 84-279) Dist. by* **Continental Bk.**

Noguer y Caralt Editores, S. A. (ESP) *(84-217; 84-279) Dist. by* **Lectorum Pubns.**

Norma S.A. (COL) *(958-04) Dist. by* **Lectorum Pubns.**

Norma S.A. (COL) *(958-04) Dist. by* **Distr Norma.**

North Bks., *(0-939495; 1-58287)* P.O. Box 1277, Wickford, RI 02852 (SAN 663-4052) Tel 401-294-3682; Fax: 401-294-9491.

North Carolina Wesleyan College Pr., *(0-933598)* 3400 N. Wesleyan Blvd., Rocky Mount, NC 27804 (SAN 238-6364) Tel 919-985-5153; Fax: 919-977-3701.

†North Country Bks., Inc., *(0-925168; 0-932052; 0-9601158; 1-59531)* 311 Turner St., Utica, NY 13501 (SAN 110-828X) Tel 315-735-4877
E-mail: ncbooks@adelphia.net; *CIP.*

North Country Pr., *(0-945980)* Div. of Maine Fulfillment Corp., R.R. 1, Box 1395, Unity, ME 04988 (SAN 247-9680) Tel 207-948-2208; Fax: 207-948-2717; Toll Free: 800-722-2169 Do not confuse with North Country Pr., White Cloud, MI
E-mail: ncp@uninet.net
Web site: http://www.midcoast.com/~ncp/.

North Point Pr. Imprint of Farrar, Straus & Giroux

North Pole Chronicles, *(0-9636442)* 7306 Park Ln., Dallas, TX 75225-2462 Tel 214-696-1717; Fax: 214-696-5288.

North Sea Pr. Imprint of LangMarc Publishing

North Star Publishing, *(0-9704437)* 1514 E. 19th Ave., Spokane, WA 99203 Tel 509-532-9566; Fax: 509-532-9568 Do not confuse with companies with the same name in Boulder, CO, Amherst, MA, Newport Beach, CA
E-mail: cmurphy@ior.com
Web site: http://www.ior.com/~cmurphy.

Northcountry Publishing Co., *(0-930366; 1-881794)* 1509 Fillmore St., Alexandria, MN 56308 (SAN 211-061X) Tel 320-763-3874.

Northland Press *See* **Northland Publishing**

Northland Pr., *(0-9620280)* Orders Addr.: P.O. Box 62, Boon, MI 49618-0062 (SAN 248-5818); Edit Addr.: 4198 S. 27th Rd., Cadillac, MI 49601 (SAN 248-5826).

†Northland Publishing, *(0-87358)* Orders Addr.: P.O. Box 1389, Flagstaff, AZ 86002-1389 Tel 928-774-5251; Fax: 928-774-0592; Toll Free Fax: 800-257-9082; Toll Free: 800-346-3257; *Imprints:* Rising Moon Books for Young Readers (Rising Moon Bks)
E-mail: info@northlandpub.com
Web site: http://www.northlandpub.com
Dist(s): **Lectorum Pubns., Inc.**
Libros Sin Fronteras; *CIP.*

†North-South Bks., Inc., *(0-7358; 1-55858; 1-58717)* 875 Sixth Ave., Suite 1901, New York, NY 10010 Tel 212-706-4545; Fax: 212-868-5951; *Imprints:* Ediciones Norte-Sur (Ediciones N-S); Michael Neugebauer Books (M Neugebauer Bks); Cheshire Studio Books (Cheshire Studio Bks)
E-mail: mnavarro@northsouth.com
Web site: http://www.northsouth.com
Dist(s): **Chronicle Bks. LLC**
Continental Bk. Co., Inc.
Lectorum Pubns., Inc.
Libros Sin Fronteras; *CIP.*

Northwest Monarch Pr., *(0-9626870)* Orders Addr.: P.O. Box 2593, Isabela, PR 00662-2005; Edit Addr.: 2223 Homer Ave., Bronx, NY 10473 Tel 718-585-6340.

Northwestern Publishing Hse., *(0-8100)* 2949 N. Mayfair Rd., Suite 200, Milwaukee, WI 53222 (SAN 206-7943) Tel 414-454-2100; Fax: 414-454-2170
E-mail: Therrian@nph.wels.net; kuehlt@nph.wels.net; johnsonr@nph.wels.net
Web site: http://www.nph.net.

Northwestern Univ. Pr., *(0-8101)* Orders Addr.: 11030 S. Langley Ave., Chicago, IL 60628 Tel 773-568-1550 ; Fax: 773-660-2235; Toll Free Fax: 800-621-8476; Toll Free: 800-621-2736; Edit Addr.: 625 Colfax St., Evanston, IL 60208-4210 (SAN 202-5787) Tel 847-491-5313; Fax: 847-491-8150
E-mail: nupress@northwestern.edu
Web site: http://www.nupress.northwestern.edu
Dist(s): **Univ. of Chicago Pr..**

Norton Family Office, *(0-9660139)* 225 Arizona Ave., Santa Monica, CA 90401 Tel 310-576-7700; Fax: 310-576-7701.

Norton Paperbacks Imprint of Norton, W. W. & Co., Inc.

Norton Pubs., Inc., Jeffrey /Audio-Forum, *(0-88432; 1-57970)* 96 Broad St., Guilford, CT 06437-2612 (SAN 213-957X) Tel 203-453-9794; Fax: 203-453-9774; Toll Free Fax: 888-453-4329; Toll Free: 800-243-1234
E-mail: info@audioforum.com
Web site: http://www.audioForum.com.

†Norton, W. W. & Co., Inc., *(0-393; 0-920256)* Orders Addr.: 800 Keystone Industrial Pk., Scranton, PA 18512 (SAN 157-1869) Tel 570-346-2020; Fax: 570-346-1442; Toll Free Fax: 800-548-6515; Toll Free: 800-233-4830 (book orders only); Edit Addr.: 500 Fifth Ave., New York, NY 10110-0017 (SAN 202-5795) Tel 212-354-5500; Fax: 212-869-0856; Toll Free: 800-223-2584; *Imprints:* Norton Paperbacks (Norton Paperbks)
E-mail: webmaster@wwnorton.com; Tworrell@wwnorton.com
Web site: http://www.wwnorton.com/trade; http://www.wwnorton.com
Dist(s): **Continental Bk. Co., Inc.**
Peoples Publishing Group, Inc., The
netLibrary, Inc.; *CIP.*

Nostalgia Pubns., *(0-9660599)* 2816 Lotus Hill Dr., Las Vegas, NV 89134 Tel 702-363-4534 (phone/fax).

Novel Units, Inc., *(1-56137; 1-58130)* Orders Addr.: P.O. Box 791610, San Antonio, TX 78279-1610 (SAN 253-9276) Tel 830-438-4262; Fax: 830-438-4263; Toll Free Fax: 877-688-3226; Toll Free: 800-688-3224
E-mail: novlunit@gvtc.com; editors@gvtc.com; ecslearn@gvtc.com
Web site: http://www.educyberstor.com
Dist(s): **Lectorum Pubns., Inc.**
Perma-Bound Bks..

Now Communications Co., *(0-940175)* 2511 Hartford Rd., Austin, TX 78703-2428 (SAN 664-3019).

Noware Bks., *(0-9656985; 1-893159)* Div. of Noware Productions, Inc., 140 Charles St., No. 16D, New York, NY 10014 Fax: 212-255-4458
E-mail: beckstein@hombeez.com
Web site: http://www.hombeez.com.

Noware Productions, Incorporated *See* **Noware Bks.**

NTC/Contemporary Publishing Company *See* **McGraw-Hill/Contemporary**

Numbers Unlimited, *(0-9654492)* P.O. Box 591, Alief, TX 77411-0591 Tel 713-495-7910.

O. M. Literature *See* **Gabriel Publishing**

O.T.S., *(0-9656252)* P.O. Box 17166, Sarasota, FL 34276 Tel 941-918-9215; Fax: 941-918-0265
E-mail: otsf@aol.com
Web site: http://www.otsf.org.

Oak Hill Bks., *(0-9616701)* Orders Addr.: P.O. Box . 5308, Coeur d' Alene, ID 83814 (SAN 661-3020) Tel 208-676-1845.

Oak Woods Media, *(0-88196)* P.O. Box 19127, Kalamazoo, MI 49019 (SAN 264-6285) Tel 616-375-5621; Fax: 616-375-7526
E-mail: oakwoods@net.link.net.

Oasis Audio, *(1-55536; 1-886463; 1-58926)* Div. of Domain Communications, 289 S. Main Pl., Carol Stream, IL 60188 Fax: 630-668-0158; Toll Free: 800-323-2500 (ext. 110)
E-mail: jelwell@oasisaudio.com; info@oasisaudio.com
Web site: http://www.oasisaudio.com
Dist(s): **Baker & Taylor Bks..**

O'Brien Pr., Ltd., The (IRL) *(0-86278; 0-905140; 0-9502046) Dist. by* **IPG Chicago.**

O'Brien Pr., Ltd., The (IRL) *(0-86278; 0-905140; 0-9502046) Dist. by* **Irish Amer Bk.**

Ocean Tree Bks., *(0-943734)* P.O. Box 1295, Santa Fe, NM 87504 (SAN 241-0478) Tel 505-983-1412; Fax: 505-983-0899
E-mail: oceantre@trail.com
Web site: http://www.oceantree.com
Dist(s): **Bookpeople**
New Leaf Distributing Co., Inc.
Treasure Chest Bks..

†Oceana Pubns., Inc., *(0-379)* 75 Main St., Dobbs Ferry, NY 10522-1601 (SAN 202-5744) Tel 914-693-8100; Fax: 914-693-0402; Toll Free: 800-831-0758
E-mail: orders@oceanalaw.com
Web site: http://www.oceanalaw.com*; CIP.*

O'Connor, Ilett K., *(0-9717003; 0-9725968)* 44 Garnet Pl., Elmont, NY 11003.

Odakai Books Imprint of Okpaku Communications Corp.

Odditeas, Inc., *(0-9702128)* P.O. Box 1155, Bluffton, SC 29910-1155 Fax: 843-757-7070
E-mail: tamelafleetwood@aol.com.

Oddo Publishing, Inc., *(0-87783)* Storybook Acres, Box 68, Fayetteville, GA 30214 (SAN 282-0757) Tel 770-461-7627.

Odyssey Classics Imprint of Harcourt Children's Bks.

Office Max, *(1-930503)* 416 Aspen St., Vandenberg AFB, CA 93437 Tel 805-734-0343 Do not confuse with Office Max in Dearborn, MI
E-mail: KHar934191@aol.com
Web site: http://hometown.aol.com/khar934191/myhomepage/index.

†Ohio Univ. Pr., *(0-8214)* Orders Addr.: 11030 S. Langley Ave., Chicago, IL 60628 Tel 773-568-1559; Fax: 773-660-2235; Toll Free Fax: 800-621-8476; Toll Free: 800-621-2736; Edit Addr.: Scott Quadrangle, Athens, OH 45701 (SAN 282-0773) Tel 740-593-1154; Fax: 740-593-4536
E-mail: gilbert@ohiou.edu
Web site: http://www.ohiou.edu/oupress/
Dist(s): **Univ. of Chicago Pr.**
netLibrary, Inc.*; CIP.*

O'Hollow Publishing, *(0-9669645)* Orders Addr.: P.O. Box 942, Price, UT 84501-0942 Tel 435-613-9413; Fax: 435-636-8272; Edit Addr.: 1010 W. 2060 N., Helper, UT 84526; *Imprints:* AlterLingo Books (AlterLingo)
E-mail: ohollow@afnetinc.com.

Okpaku Communications Corp., *(0-89388)* Div. of Third Pr. Review of Bks. Co., 222 Forest Ave., New Rochelle, NY 10804 (SAN 202-5701) Tel 914-632-2355; Fax: 914-632-2320; *Imprints:* Odakai Books (Odakai)
E-mail: okpaku@aol.com.

Old Alaska Today, *(0-9644491)* HC 33, Box 3191, Wasilla, AK 99654-9723 Tel 907-376-7323
Web site: http://www.mtaonline.net/~dustys
Dist(s): **News Group, The.**

Old Fort Niagara Assn., Inc., *(0-941967)* Orders Addr.: P.O. Box 169, Youngstown, NY 14174 (SAN 666-7783) Tel 716-745-7611; Fax: 716-745-9141; Edit Addr.: Ft. Niagara State Pk., Youngstown, NY 14174 (SAN 666-7791)
E-mail: ofn@oldfortniagara
Web site: http://www.oldfortniagara.org.

Old Hogan Publishing Co., *(0-9638851)* Orders Addr.: P.O. Box 91978, Tucson, AZ 85752 Tel 520-579-9321 ; Fax: 520-579-0502; Toll Free: 800-867-1506; Edit Addr.: 3600 W. Mesa Ridge Trail, Tucson, AZ 85742
E-mail: mgaraway@juno.com
Web site: http://www.oldhogan.com
Dist(s): **Hispanic Bks. Distributors & Pubs., Inc.**
Treasure Chest Bks..

Olde Springfield Shoppe *See* **Masthof Pr.**

Olivia & Hill Pr., The, *(0-934034)* Orders Addr.: P.O. Box 7396, Ann Arbor, MI 48107; Edit Addr.: 905 Olivia Ave., Ann Arbor, MI 48104 (SAN 212-923X) Tel 734-663-0235; Fax: 734-663-6590
E-mail: order@oliviahill.com
Web site: http://www.oliviahill.com.

Onion River Pr., *(0-9657144)* 21 Essex Way Ste. 106, Essex Jct, VT 05452-3386 Toll Free: 877-266-5722
E-mail: bookrack@together.net
Web site: http://www.onionriverpress.com.

Open Bk. Publishing Hse., *(0-9644142)* 1845 Balmore St. NW, North Canton, OH 44720-4903 Tel 330-497-3352; Fax: 330-497-3352; Toll Free: 800-238-0281
E-mail: molnarj@openbookph.com
Web site: http://www.openbookph.com.

Open Court Publishing Co., *(0-8126; 0-87548; 0-89688; 0-912050)* Div. of Carus Publishing Co., Orders Addr.: c/o Publishers Group West, 1700 Fourth St., Berkeley, CA 94710 Fax: 510-528-3444; Toll Free: 800-788-3123; Edit Addr.: 332 S. Michigan Ave., Suite 1100, Chicago, IL 60604-9968 Tel 312-939-1500; Fax: 312-939-8150; Toll Free: 800-815-2280
E-mail: opencourt@caruspub.com
Web site: http://www.opencourtbooks.com
Dist(s): **Publishers Group West.**

Open Hand Publishing, LLC, *(0-940880)* P.O. Box 20207, Greensboro, NC 27420 (SAN 219-6174) Tel 336-292-8585; Fax: 336-292-8588
E-mail: info@openhand.com
Web site: http://www.openhand.com
Dist(s): **Baker & Taylor Bks..**

†Open Horizons Publishing Co., *(0-912411)* 1200 S. Main St., Fairfield, IA 52556 (SAN 265-170X) Tel 641-472-6130; Fax: 641-472-1560; Toll Free: 800-796-6130
E-mail: orders@bookmarket.com; info@bookmarket.com
Web site: http://www.bookmarket.com; http://www.celebratetoday.com
Dist(s): **National Bk. Network***; CIP.*

Open Minds, Inc., *(1-888927)* P.O. Box 21325, Columbus, OH 43221-0325 Tel 614-486-4441; Fax: 614-486-6532 Do not confuse with companies with same or similar names in Gettysburg, PA, Honolulu, HI
E-mail: openmindsinc@msn.com
Web site: http://www.openmindsinc.com.

Open My World Publishing, *(0-941996)* P.O. Box 15011, San Diego, CA 92175 (SAN 238-602X) Tel 619-588-5389
Dist(s): **Cram, George F. Co., Inc.**
Perma-Bound Bks..

Open Vision Entertainment Corp., *(0-9721825)* 48 Summer St., Stoneham, MA 02180 Tel 781-438-7939 ; Fax: 781-438-8115
Web site: http://www.open-visions.com
Dist(s): **Fell, Frederick Pubs., Inc.**
FaithWorks.

Orbin Publishing, Ltd., *(0-9676205)* 118 Sunnymeadow Ln., Reisterstown, MD 21136 Tel 410-526-5210; Fax: 202-783-6947
E-mail: lgitomer@erols.com.

†Orbis Bks., *(0-88344; 1-57075)* Div. of The Catholic Foreign Mission Society of America, Inc., Orders Addr.: P.O. Box 308, Maryknoll, NY 10545-0308 (SAN 202-828X) Tel 914-941-7590 (ext. 2487); Fax: 914-945-0670; Toll Free: 800-258-5838
E-mail: orbisbooks@maryknoll.org
Web site: http://www.orbisbooks.com*; CIP.*

Orca Bk. Pubs., *(0-920501; 1-55143)* Orders Addr.: P.O. Box 468, Custer, WA 98240-0468 (SAN 630-9674) Tel 250-380-1229; Fax: 250-380-1892; Toll Free: 800-210-5277
E-mail: melanie@orcabook.com; mcolgan@orcabook.com
Web site: http://www.orcabook.com.

Orchard Bks. Imprint of Scholastic, Inc.

Orchid Isle Publishing Co., *(1-887916)* 131 Halai St., Hilo, HI 96720.

Order of the Legion of St. Michael, *(0-916843)* P.O. Box 184, Roscoe, SD 57471 (SAN 653-8762) Tel 605-287-4187; *Imprints:* Writers House Press (Writers Hse Pr)
E-mail: editor@writers-house-press.org; editor@stmchael-press.org
Web site: http://www.writers-house-press.org; http://www.stmichael-press.org.

†Oregon Historical Society Pr., *(0-87595)* 1200 SW Park Ave., Portland, OR 97205-2483 (SAN 202-8301) Tel 503-222-1741; Fax: 503-221-2035
E-mail: orhist@ohs.org
Web site: http://www.ohs.org
Dist(s): **Graphic Arts Ctr. Publishing Co.**
Univ. of Washington Pr.*; CIP.*

†Oregon State Univ. Pr., *(0-87071)* Oregon State Univ., 101 Waldo Hall, Corvallis, OR 97331 (SAN 202-8328) Tel 541-737-3166; Fax: 541-737-3170
E-mail: osu.press@oregonstate.edu
Web site: http://osu.orst.edu/dept/press
Dist(s): **American Society of Civil Engineers**
Univ. of Arizona Pr.*; CIP.*

Oresjozef Pubns., *(1-885566)* 167 Canton St., Randolph, MA 02368 Tel 781-961-5855; Toll Free: 617-851-0100
E-mail: ojozef@massed.net
Dist(s): **Educa Vision**
Haitiana Pubns., Inc..

Oriental Bk. Store, The, *(0-89986)* 1713 E. Colorado Blvd., Pasadena, CA 91106 (SAN 285-0818) Tel 626-577-2413.

Orion Publishing Group, Ltd. (GBR) *(0-575; 0-7528; 1-85797; 1-85881) Dist. by* **Trafalgar.**

Ortells, Alfredo Editorial S.L. (ESP) *(84-7189) Dist. by* **Continental Bk.**

Osage Bend Publishing Co., *(0-9626245; 1-58389)* 213 Belair Dr., Jefferson City, MO 65109 Tel 573-635-5580; Toll Free: 888-243-9772
E-mail: OBPC@Socket.net
Dist(s): **Follett Library Resources.**

Osborne Bks., *(0-9632817)* Orders Addr.: P.O. Box 902, Banning, CA 92220; Edit Addr.: P.O. Box 3126, Beaumont, CA 92223 Tel 909-849-2363.

Otter Creek Pr., Inc., *(1-890611)* 3154 Nautilus Rd., Middleburg, FL 32068 Tel 904-264-0465; Fax: 904-264-0465; Toll Free: 800-378-8163
E-mail: otterpress@aol.com; whill73528@aol.com
Web site: http://www.otterpress.com.

†Our Child Pr., *(0-9611872; 1-893516)* P.O. Box 74, Wayne, PA 19087-0074 (SAN 682-272X) Tel 610-964-0606; Fax: 610-964-0938
E-mail: ocp98@aol.com
Web site: http://www.members.aol.com/ocp98/index.html*; CIP.*

Our Kids Pubn., Inc., *(1-892089)* Orders Addr.: P.O. Box 59790, Chicago, IL 60659-0790 Tel 847-398-1041; Fax: 847-398-0058.

Our Sunday Visitor, Publishing Div., *(0-87973; 0-9707756; 1-931709; 1-59276)* 200 Noll Plaza, Huntington, IN 46750 (SAN 202-8344) Tel 260-356-8400; Fax: 260-359-9117; Toll Free: 800-348-2440
E-mail: osvbooks@osv.com
Web site: http://www.osv.com
Dist(s): **Baker & Taylor International**
Riverside
Spring Arbor Distributors, Inc..

Out of Our Mind, Incorporated *See* **Mora Art Studio**

Outlet Book Company, Incorporated *See* **Random Hse. Value Publishing**

Over the Rainbow Productions, *(0-9661330)* 1715 Rosedale, Suite B, Houston, TX 77004 Tel 713-523-1276; Fax: 713-526-0571
E-mail: apb3@prodigy.net
Web site: http://www.imneecie.com.

†Overlook Pr., The, *(0-87951; 1-58567; 1-59020)* 141 Wooster St., 4th Flr., New York, NY 10012 (SAN 202-8360) Tel 212-673-2210; Fax: 212-673-2296
Web site: http://www.overlookpress.com
Dist(s): **National Bk. Network**
Penguin Group (USA) Inc.*; CIP.*

Overmountain Pr., *(0-932807; 0-9644613; 1-57072)* P.O. Box 1261, Johnson City, TN 37605 (SAN 687-6641) Tel 423-926-2691; Fax: 423-232-1252; Toll Free: 800-992-2691 (orders only)
E-mail: beth@overmtn.com
Web site: http://www.silverdaggermysteries.com; http://www.overmountainpress.com.

Owen, Richard C. Pubs., Inc., *(0-913461; 1-57274; 1-878450)* P.O. Box 585, Katonah, NY 10536 (SAN 285-1814) Tel 914-232-3903; Fax: 914-232-3977; Toll Free: 800-336-5588 (orders)
Web site: http://www.RCOwen.com
Dist(s): **Lectorum Pubns., Inc..**

Owl Bks. Imprint of Holt, Henry & Co.

Ox Bow Pr., *(0-918024; 1-881987)* P.O. Box 4045, Woodbridge, CT 06525 (SAN 210-2501) Tel 203-387-5900; Fax: 203-387-0035
E-mail: oxbow@gte.net
Web site: http://www.oxbowpress-books.com.

Oxford Univ. Pr., Inc., *(0-19; 0-904147; 0-947946; 1-85221)* Orders Addr.: 2001 Evans Rd., Cary, NC 27513 (SAN 202-5892) Tel 919-677-0977 (general voice); Fax: 919-677-1303 (customer service); Toll Free: 800-445-9714 (customer service - inquiry); 800-451-7556 (customer service - orders); Edit Addr.: 198 Madison Ave., New York, NY 10016-4314 (SAN 202-5884) Tel 212-726-6000 (general voice); Fax: 212-726-6440 (general fax)
E-mail: orders@oup-usa.org; custserv@oup-usa.org
Web site: http://www.oup-usa.org
Dist(s): **netLibrary, Inc..**

Ozark Publishing, *(1-56763; 1-59381)* P.O. Box 228, Prairie Grove, AR 72753 (SAN 298-4318) Tel 214-649-0188; Fax: 501-846-2853; Toll Free: 800-321-5671
E-mail: srg304@aol.com
Web site: http://www.ozarkpublishing.com
Dist(s): **Central Programs**
Gumdrop Bks..

P&R Publishing, *(0-87552)* Orders Addr.: P.O. Box 817, Phillipsburg, NJ 08865-0817 (SAN 205-3918) Tel 908-454-0505; Fax: 908-859-2390; Toll Free: 800-631-0094 Do not confuse with P & R Publishing Co. in Sioux Center, IA
E-mail: tara@prpbooks.com
Web site: http://www.prpbooks.com
Dist(s): **CRC Pubns.**
Christian Literature Crusade, Inc..

PLC Publishing, *(0-9672309)* 6 Glaize View Dr., Town & Country, MO 63017-8410 Tel 314-878-7801.

Pacific Asia Pr., *(1-879600)* Div. of GreenShower Corp., 136 N. Grand Ave., Suite 222, West Covina, CA 91791-1728 Tel 626-575-3338; Fax: 626-527-9500; Toll Free: 800-537-4357
Web site: http://www.greenshower.com.

Pacific Greetings, *(0-9633493)* 65-1285 Puu Opelu Rd., Kamuela, HI 96743 Tel 808-885-4439 (phone/fax)
E-mail: hlhall@ilhawaii.net
Dist(s): **Booklines Hawaii, Ltd..**

Pacific Pr. Pubns., *(0-9678122)* 3260 Monument, Ann Arbor, MI 48108 Tel 734-975-1877 (phone/fax)
E-mail: hailstormx@aol.com.

†Pacific Pr. Publishing Assn., *(0-8163)* P.O. Box 5353, Nampa, ID 83653-5353 (SAN 202-8409) Tel 208-465-2500; Fax: 208-465-2531; Toll Free: 800-447-7377
E-mail: sanhin@pacificpress.com
Web site: http://www.AdventistBookCenter.com
Dist(s): **Riverside**
Spring Arbor Distributors, Inc.; *CIP.*

Pack, Denise Davis, *(0-9660637)* 112 Brookridge Dr., Hoganville, GA 30230 Tel 706-637-5654
E-mail: dPack@ravenet.com.

Padakami Pr., *(0-9628914)* 23 Dana St., Forty-Fort, Kingston, PA 18704 Tel 717-287-3668.

Page, Andrea, *(1-882183)* 5156 Highbury Cir., Sarasota, FL 34238-2797 (SAN 297-7869)
E-mail: andrea113@aol.com.

PageFree Publishing, Inc., *(1-929077; 1-930252; 1-58961)* 733 Howard St., Otsego, MI 49078 Tel 616-692-3926 (phone/fax); *Imprints:* Books OnScreen (Bks OnScreen)
E-mail: pagefreepublish@aol.com; publisher@pagefreepublishing.com
Web site: http://www.pagefreepublishing.com.

PageMill Pr., *(1-879290)* Div. of Circulus Publishing Group, Inc., 2716 Ninth St., Berkeley, CA 94710 Tel 510-848-3600; Fax: 510-848-1326
E-mail: rok27@aol.com
Dist(s): **FaithWorks.**

Pages, Inc., *(1-885885)* P.O. Box 3572, Dublin, OH 43016-0284; *Imprints:* Cornerstone Books (Cornerstone FL).

PAGES Publishing Group *See* **Darby Creek Publishing**

Pageturner Bks., *(0-9704678)* P.O. Box 171, Vineburg, CA 95487 Tel 707-933-8608; Fax: 707-938-0601
E-mail: pageturner@hotmail.com.

PageWorthy Bks., *(0-9652042)* P.O. Box 600095, Saint Paul, MN 55106 Tel 651-772-0864
Dist(s): **Bookmen, Inc..**

†Paideia Pubs., *(0-913993)* P.O. Box 343, Ashfield, MA 01330 (SAN 287-7511) Tel 413-628-3838
E-mail: products@edpsych.com; paideia@javanet.com
Web site: http://www.edpsych.com/; *CIP.*

Pajari Pr., *(0-9624315)* 11104 Snow Heights Blvd., NE, Albuquerque, NM 87112 Tel 505-299-7733.

Pajarito Pubns., *(0-918358)* 3412 Vista Grande Dr., NW, Albuquerque, NM 87120-1140 (SAN 209-8555) Tel 505-242-8075 Do not confuse with Pajarito Pr., Corrales, NM.

Palladium Bks., Inc., *(0-916211; 1-57457)* 12455 Universal Dr., Taylor, MI 48180-4077 (SAN 294-9504) Tel 734-946-2900; Fax: 734-946-1238
E-mail: palladiumbooks@palladiumbooks.com
Web site: http://www.PalladiumBooks.com.

Palmer Publications, Incorporated/Amherst Press *See* **Amherst Pr.**

Palmetto Conservation Foundation, *(0-9679016; 0-9745284)* Orders Addr.: P.O. Box 1984, Spartanburg, SC 29304 Toll Free: 800-416-8937; Edit Addr.: 187 N. Church St., Suite 802, Spartanburg, SC 29306
Web site: http://www.palmettoconservation.org
Dist(s): **Baker & Taylor Bks.**
Parnassus Bk. Distributors
Sandlapper Publishing Co., Inc..

Pam's Unique Technique, *(0-9638310)* 1601 Kesteven Rd., Winston-Salem, NC 27127.

Pan Asia Pubns. (USA), Inc., *(1-57227)* 29564 Union City Blvd., Union City, CA 94587 (SAN 173-685X) Tel 510-475-1185; Fax: 510-475-1489; Toll Free: 800-909-8088
E-mail: sales@panap.com
Web site: http://www.panap.com
Dist(s): **Lectorum Pubns., Inc..**

Pan Bks. Ltd. (GBR) *(0-330) Dist. by* **Trafalgar.**

Pangloss, Joseph Press *See* **Simon, Rachelle**

Pantheon Imprint of Knopf Publishing Group

PaPa Fuzz Pubns., *(1-928597)* 1408 W. Danny St., Claremore, OK 74017-8618
E-mail: papafuzzbk@aol.com.

Paper Posie, *(0-9707944)* 817 Vincente Way, Santa Barbara, CA 93105 Tel 805-569-2398; Fax: 805-563-0166; Toll Free: 800-360-1761
E-mail: paperposie@aol.com
Web site: http://www.paperposie.com.

PaperStar Imprint of Penguin Putnam Bks. for Young Readers

Parable Publishing House *See* **Barth Family Ministries**

Parachute Press, Incorporated *See* **Parachute Publishing, LLC**

Parachute Publishing, LLC, *(0-938753; 1-57351)* 156 Fifth Ave., New York, NY 10010 (SAN 661-5554) Tel 212-691-1421; Fax: 212-645-8769
E-mail: ppibooks@aol.com.

Paraclete Pr., Inc., *(0-941478; 1-55725)* Orders Addr.: P.O. Box 1568, Orleans, MA 02653 (SAN 282-1508) Tel 508-255-4685; Fax: 508-255-5705; Toll Free: 800-451-5006; Edit Addr.: 36 Southern Eagle Cartway, Brewster, MA 02631 (SAN 664-6239) Do not confuse with companies with the same or similar names in Indianapolis, IN, Pentwater, MI
E-mail: srmercy@paracletepress.com; miao@paracletepress.com
Web site: http://www.paracletepress.com.

†Paradigm Publishing, Inc., *(0-7638; 1-56118)* 300 York Ave., Saint Paul, MN 55101 Do not confuse with companies with the same or similar names in Oklahoma City, OK, Laguna Park, TX, Chicago, IL, Midvale, UT, Saint Cloud, FL, MacFarland, WI, LaPorte, CO; *CIP.*

Parallax Pr., *(0-938077; 1-888375)* Orders Addr.: P.O. Box 7355, Berkeley, CA 94707 (SAN 663-4494) Tel 510-525-0101; Fax: 510-525-7129; Toll Free: 800-863-5290; Edit Addr.: 850 Talbot Ave., Albany, CA 94706
E-mail: parallax@parallax.org
Web site: http://www.parallax.org
Dist(s): **SCB Distributors**
SPD-Small Pr. Distribution.

Pardy Chick Pubns., *(0-9705332)* 59-361 Wilinau Rd., Haleiwa, HI 96712-9654 Tel 808-638-8619
E-mail: dapardy@compuserve.com.

Pardy, DA *See* **Pardy Chick Pubns.**

†Parenting Pr., Inc., *(0-943990; 0-9602862; 1-884734)* Orders Addr.: P.O. Box 75267, Seattle, WA 98125 (SAN 215-6938) Tel 206-364-2900; Fax: 206-364-0702; Toll Free: 800-992-6657; Edit Addr.: 11065 Fifth Ave. NE, Suite F, Seattle, WA 98125 (SAN 699-5500)
E-mail: office@parentingpress.com
Web site: http://www.parentingpress.com
Dist(s): **Baker & Taylor Bks.**
Bookpeople
Brodart Co.
Follett Library Resources
Midwest Library Service; *CIP.*

Parkhurst Brook Pubs., *(0-9615664)* 303 Perrin Rd., Potsdam, NY 13676 (SAN 695-9121) Tel 315-265-9037
E-mail: mhcharle@northnet.org.

Parkway Pubs., Inc., *(0-9635752; 1-887905)* P.O. Box 3678, Boone, NC 28607 Tel 828-265-3993; Fax: 828-265-3993; Toll Free: 800-821-9155
E-mail: sales@parkwaypublishers.com; parkwaypub@hotmail.com
Web site: http://www.parkwaypublishers.com
Dist(s): **Baker & Taylor Bks..**

Parkwest Pubns., Inc., *(0-88186)* 451 Communipaw Ave., Jersey City, NJ 07304 (SAN 264-6846) Tel 201-432-3257; Fax: 201-432-3708
E-mail: parkwest@parkwestpubs.com; info@parkwestpubs.com
Web site: http://www.parkwestpubs.com.

Parragon, Inc., *(0-7525; 1-85813; 1-4054)* Div. of Parragon Publishing, 1250 Broadway, 24th Flr., New York, NY 10001 Tel 212-629-9773; Fax: 212-629-9756; *Imprints:* Bright Sparks (Bright Sparks)
Dist(s): **Central Programs.**

Parthian Bks. (GBR) *(0-9521558; 1-902638) Dist. by* **Dufour.**

Partners/West, 1901 Raymond Ave., SW, Suite C, Renton, WA 98055 (SAN 631-421X) Tel 425-227-8486; Fax: 425-204-1448; Toll Free: 800-563-2385.

Passeggiata Pr., *(1-57889)* 222 W B St., Pueblo, CO 81003-3404 Tel 719-544-1038; Fax: 719-544-7911
E-mail: Passeggiata@compuserve.com.

Passion Works, LLC, *(0-9708027)* 704 228th Ave., NE, No. 334, Sammamish, WA 98074 (SAN 253-6676) Tel 425-868-1281 (phone/fax)
E-mail: dchristiansen@passionworks.net
Web site: http://www.passionworks.net.

Passport Bks. Imprint of McGraw-Hill Trade

Pathways Publishing, *(1-58303)* P.O. Box 267, Hudson, MA 01749-0267 Toll Free: 888-333-7284 Do not confuse with Pathways Publishing Gulfport, MS
E-mail: sblair@pathwayspub.com
Web site: http://www.pathwayspub.com.

Patri Pubns., *(0-9645914)* P.O. Box 25184, Rochester, NY 14625 Tel 716-381-8746; Fax: 716-586-2093; *Imprints:* Stone Pine Books (Stone Pine Bks)
E-mail: patcosta@rochester.rr.com
Dist(s): **Baker & Taylor Bks.**
Brodart Co..

Patria Pr., Inc., *(1-882859)* 3842 Wolf Creek Cir., Carmel, IN 46033 (SAN 153-7504) Tel 317-844-6070 ; Fax: 317-844-8935; Toll Free: 877-736-7930
E-mail: info@patriapress.com
Web site: http://www.patriapress.com
Dist(s): **Independent Pubs. Group.**

Patty Cake Bks., *(0-9664794)* P.O. Box 852, Cotaro, AZ 85652-0852
E-mail: PattyCakeBooks@juno.com; jd-cromwell@juno.com.

Paul & Co. Pubs. Consortium, Inc., Div. of Independent Publishers Group, Orders Addr.: 814 N. Franklin St., Chicago, IL 60610 Tel 312-337-0747; Fax: 312-337-5985; Toll Free: 800-888-4741; Edit Addr.: P.O. Box 442, Concord, MA 01742 (SAN 630-5318)
E-mail: frontdesk@ipgbook.com
Web site: http://www.ipgbook.com
Dist(s): **Independent Pubs. Group.**

†Pauline Bks. & Media, *(0-8198)* 50 St. Paul's Ave., Boston, MA 02130-3491 (SAN 203-8900) Tel 617-522-8911; Fax: 617-524-8035; Toll Free: 800-876-4463 (orders only)
E-mail: jsmith@pauline.org; lilire@aol.com
Web site: http://www.PAULINE.org
Dist(s): **Alba Hse.**; *CIP.*

†**Paulist Pr.,** *(0-8091; 1-58768)* 997 MacArthur Blvd., Mahwah, NJ 07430-2096 (SAN 202-5159) Tel 201-825-7300 (ext. 232); Fax: 201-825-8345; Toll Free Fax: 800-836-3161; Toll Free: 800-218-1903 E-mail: info@paulistpress.com; mwhiton@paulistpress.com Web site: http://www.paulistpress.com *Dist(s):* **Baker & Taylor Bks. Bookazine Co., Inc. Riverside Spring Arbor Distributors, Inc.**; *CIP.*

Paupieres Publishing Co., *(0-944064)* P.O. Box 707, Houma, LA 70361-0707 (SAN 242-8334) Tel 504-876-9223.

Pavilion Bks., Ltd. (GBR) *(0-907516; 1-85145; 1-85793; 1-86205) Dist. by* **Trafalgar.**

Paw Prints Pr., *(1-58478)* Div. of Ceilidh, Inc., Orders Addr.: 2384 Tokay Ct., Paradise, CA 95969 (SAN 254-0932) Tel 530-876-8986; Fax: 530-876-8989; Toll Free: 888-999-2358 Do not confuse with Paw Prints Pr. in Sussex, NJ E-mail: pawprints@pawprintspress.com; pawprintsorders@pawprintspress.com Web site: http://www.pawprintspress.com *Dist(s):* **Baker & Taylor Bks. Book Wholesalers, Inc..**

Paws IV Publishing, *(0-934007)* P.O. Box 2364, Homer, AK 99603 (SAN 692-7890) Tel 907-235-7697 ; Fax: 907-235-7698; Toll Free: 800-807-7297 E-mail: pawsiv@ptialaska.net *Dist(s):* **Publishers Group West.**

Peaceful Village Publishing, *(0-9658061)* Orders Addr.: P.O. Box 7032, Snowmass Village, CO 81615 Tel 608-770-1441 Toll Free: 608-770-1441 E-mail: mfhumphrey@juno.com.

Peachtree Junior Imprint of Peachtree Pubs., Ltd.

†**Peachtree Pubs., Ltd.,** *(0-931948; 0-934601; 1-56145)* 1700 Chattahoochee Ave., Atlanta, GA 30318-2112 (SAN 212-1999) Tel 404-876-8761; Fax: 404-875-2578; Toll Free Fax: 800-875-8909; Toll Free: 800-241-0113; *Imprints:* Peachtree Junior (Peachtree); Freestone (Freestone) E-mail: peachtree@mindspring.com Web site: http://www.peachtree-online.com *Dist(s):* **Lectorum Pubns., Inc.**; *CIP.*

Peanut Butter Publishing, *(0-89716)* Div. of Classic Day Publishing LLC, 2100 Westlake Ave. N., Suite 106, Seattle, WA 98109 (SAN 212-7881) Tel 206-860-4900; Fax: 206-285-2800; Toll Free: 800-328-4348 E-mail: elliottwolf@classicdaypublishing.com Web site: http://www.classicdaypublishing.com *Dist(s):* **Todd Communications.**

Pearce-Evetts Publishing, *(0-936823)* 414 Foothills Rd., Greenville, SC 29617-7008 (SAN 699-9271) Tel 864-294-9494; Fax: 864-294-9696; Toll Free: 800-842-9571 E-mail: nicole@veenet.net Web site: http://www.tonjaweimer.com *Dist(s):* **Baker & Taylor Bks..**

Peartree, *(0-935343)* P.O. Box 14533, Clearwater, FL 33766 Tel 727-531-4973; Fax: 727-803-2667 E-mail: martree@aol.com *Dist(s):* **Amazon.Com Baker & Taylor Bks. Book Wholesalers, Inc. Brodart Co. Hamakor Judaica, Inc. Koen Bk. Distributors Ner Tamid Bk. Distributors Quality Bks., Inc..**

Peek-A-Bks., *(0-9700318)* PMB 234, 1669-2 Hollenbeck Ave., Sunnyvale, CA 94087 Tel 408-732-4535; Fax: 408-739-7231 E-mail: peekabooks@mindspring.com.

Peel Productions, Inc., *(0-939217)* P.O. Box 546-RRB, Columbus, NC 28722-0546 (SAN 662-6726) Tel 828-894-8838; Fax: 801-365-9898; Toll Free: 800-345-6665 (orders) E-mail: xwkmw0lrul001@sneakemail.com Web site: http://www.drawbooks.com; http://www.peelbooks.com *Dist(s):* **F&W Pubns., Inc. Midpoint Trade Bks., Inc. Pathway Bk. Service.**

Peepal Tree Pr., Ltd. (GBR) *(0-948833; 1-900715) Dist. by* **Paul & Co Pubs.**

Peerless Publishing, L.L.C., *(0-9666076)* Orders Addr.: P.O. Box 20466, Ferndale, MI 48220 Tel 248-542-1930; Fax: 248-542-3895; Edit Addr.: 414 W. Lewiston, Ferndale, MI 48220 E-mail: peerlesspublishing@ameritech.net Web site: http://www.spannet.org/peerless/index.html.

Pele Publishing, *(0-9651578)* Div. of Twiggs of Savannah, 241 Abercorn St., Savannah, GA 31404-4018 Tel 912-233-5526.

Pelham Bks. Imprint of Viking Penguin

Pelican Publishing, *(0-9655465)* 141 Hoyt Ave., Lowell, MA 01852 Tel 508-453-0129 Do not confuse with companies with the same or similar names in Dallas, TX, Gretna, LA E-mail: promo@pelicanpub.com; editorial@pelicanpub.com Web site: http://pelicanpub.com.

†**Pelican Publishing Co., Inc.,** *(0-88289; 0-911116; 1-56554; 1-58980)* Orders Addr.: P.O. Box 3110, Gretna, LA 70054 (SAN 212-0623) Tel 504-368-1175 ; Fax: 504-368-1195; Toll Free: 800-843-1724; 1000 Burmaster St., Gretna, LA 70053; *Imprints:* Firebird Press (Firebird Press) Do not confuse with companies with the same or similar names in Lowell, MA, Dallas, TX E-mail: promo@pelicanpub.com; Sales@pelicanpub.com Web site: http://www.bedandbreakfastguide.com; http://www.epelican.com; http://www.eirishbooks.com *Dist(s):* **Continental Bk. Co., Inc.**; *CIP.*

Pendulum Pr., Inc., *(0-87232; 0-88301)* Academic Bldg., Saw Mill Rd., West Haven, CT 06516 (SAN 202-8808) Tel 203-933-2551 Do not confuse with companies with same or similar names in Jacksonville, FL, Palm Coast, FL, Minneapolis, MN.

Penguin AudioBooks Imprint of Viking Penguin

Penguin Bks. Imprint of Viking Penguin

Penguin Bks. Imprint of Penguin Group (USA) Inc.

Penguin Bks., Ltd. (GBR) *(0-14) Dist. by* **Trafalgar.**

Penguin Classics Imprint of Viking Penguin

Penguin Group (USA) Inc., *(0-14)* Orders Addr.: 405 Murray Hill Pkwy., East Rutherford, NJ 07073-2136 (SAN 282-5074) Fax: 201-933-2903 (customer service); Toll Free Fax: 800-227-9604; Toll Free: 800-788-6262 (individual consumer sales); 800-526-0275 (reseller sales); 800-631-8571 (reseller customer service); Edit Addr.: 375 Hudson St., New York, NY 10014 Tel 212-366-2000; Fax: 212-366-2666; *Imprints:* Perigee Books (Perigee Bks); Coward-McCann (Coward); Sandcastle Books (Sandcastle Bks); Ace/Putnam (Ace-Putnam); Penguin Books (Penguin Bks); Ladybird Books (Ladybrd); Putnam Berkley Audio (Putnam Berkley Audio); Putnam & Grosset (Putnam & Grosset); Philomel (Philomel); G. P. Putnam's Sons (G P Putnam) E-mail: pmccarthy@penguinputnam.com Web site: http://www.penguinputnam.com *Dist(s):* **Viking Penguin.**

Penguin Putnam Bks. for Young Readers, *(0-448; 0-582; 0-7232; 0-7226; 1-59514)* Div. of Penguin Putnam, Inc., Orders Addr.: 405 Murray Hill Pkwy., East Rutherford, NJ 07073-2136 Toll Free Fax: 800-227-9604; Toll Free: 800-788-6262 (individual consumer sales); 800-631-8571 (reseller customer service); 800-526-0275 (reseller sales); Edit Addr.: 345 Hudson St., New York, NY 10014 Tel 212-366-2000; Fax: 212-366-2666; *Imprints:* Sandcastle Books (Sandcastle Bks); Viking (Viking); Putnam Berkley Audio (Putnam Berkley Audio); Dial Books for Young Readers (Dial Yng Read); Dutton Children's Books (Dutton Child); Fogelman, Phyllis Books (P Fogelman Bks); PaperStar (PapStar); Philomel (Philomel); Planet Dexter (Planet Dexter); Platt & Munk (Plat & Munk); Price Stern Sloan (Price Stern); Puffin Books (PuffinBks); G. P. Putnam's Sons (G P Putnam); Viking Children's Books (Viking Child); Warne, Frederick (F Warne); Dutton (Dutt); Grosset & Dunlap (G & D); Puffin-Alloy (Puffin-Alloy); Firebird (Firebird); Speak (Speak USA) E-mail: online@penguinputnam.com Web site: http://www.penguinputnam.com *Dist(s):* **Continental Bk. Co., Inc. Lectorum Pubns., Inc. Penguin Group (USA) Inc..**

Penguin Putnam, Incorporated *See* **Penguin Group (USA) Inc.**

Penguin/HighBridge, *(0-453)* 1000 Westgate Dr., Saint Paul, MN 55114 Tel 651-637-4722; Fax: 651-659-4495; Toll Free: 800-782-5756 (orders only) E-mail: highbridgeaudio@rivertrade.com Web site: http://www.penguinclassics.com/ *Dist(s):* **Landmark Audiobooks Penguin Group (USA) Inc..**

Peninsula Publishing, Inc., *(0-918146)* P.O. Box 412, Port Angeles, WA 98362 (SAN 210-1300) Tel 360-565-2285 Do not confuse with companies with the same name in Los Altos, CA, Palmetto, FL, Auburndale, FL.

Penny-Farthing Pr., Inc., *(0-9673683; 0-9719012)* 10370 Richmond Ave., Suite 980, Houston, TX 77042 Tel 713-780-0300; Fax: 713-780-4004; Toll Free: 800-926-comx (800-926-2669) E-mail: corp@pfpress.com Web site: http://www.pfpress.com *Dist(s):* **Baker & Taylor Bks. Diamond Book Distributors, Inc..**

PennyRoyal Bks., *(0-9654197)* Orders Addr.: P.O. Box 324, Royal Oak, MI 48068 Tel 248-548-4931; Fax: 248-548-5125; Toll Free: 800-247-6553; Edit Addr.: 1211 Irving, Royal Oaks, MI 48067 E-mail: Proyalbook@aol.com.

Pentland Pr., Inc., *(1-57197)* 5122 Bur Oak Cir., Raleigh, NC 27612 (SAN 298-5063) Tel 919-782-0281; Fax: 919-781-9042; Toll Free: 800-948-2786 E-mail: janetevans@mindspring.com Web site: http://www.pentlandpressusa.com *Dist(s):* **Baker & Taylor Bks. Midpoint Trade Bks., Inc..**

Penton Kids Imprint of Penton Overseas, Inc.

Penton Overseas, Inc., *(0-939001; 1-56015; 1-59125)* 2470 Impala Dr., Carlsbad, CA 92008 (SAN 631-0826) Tel 760-431-0060; Fax: 760-431-8110; Toll Free: 800-748-5804; *Imprints:* Penton Kids (Penton Kids) Web site: http://www.pentonoverseas.com.

Peoples Publishing Group, Inc., The, *(1-56256; 1-58984; 1-4138)* Orders Addr.: P.O. Box 513, Saddle Brook, NJ 07633 Tel 201-712-0090; Fax: 201-712-1534; Toll Free: 800-822-1080; Edit Addr.: 299 Market St., Saddle Brook, NJ 07663 E-mail: sales@peoplespublishing.com; customersupport@peoplespublishing.com; editorial@peoplespublishing.com; solvier@peoplespublishing.com Web site: http://www.peoplespublishing.com/.

Pepper Bird Publishing, *(1-56817)* Div. of The Pepper Bird Foundation, Orders Addr.: P.O. Box 1071, Williamsburg, VA 23187-1071 Tel 757-220-5761; Fax: 757-220-6711; Edit Addr.: 104 Kempe Dr., Williamsburg, VA 25188.

Pepper Vine Pr., *(0-9625777)* P.O. Box 2037, Granite Bay, CA 95746-2037 Tel 916-791-2237; Fax: 916-791-8463.

Peralt Montagut (ESP) *(84-87650; 84-86154; 84-8214) Dist. by* **imaJen.**

Perennial Imprint of HarperTrade

Perfection Form Company, The *See* **Perfection Learning Corp.**

Perfection Learning Corp., *(0-7807; 0-7891; 0-89598; 1-56312; 0-7569)* 1000 N. Second Ave., Logan, IA 51546 (SAN 221-0010) Tel 712-644-3553; Fax: 712-644-2122; Toll Free: 800-831-4190; *Imprints:* Covercraft (Covercraft) E-mail: rfetter@logan.phonline.com Web site: http://www.perfectionlearning.com.

Perigee Bks. Imprint of Berkley Publishing Group

Perigee Bks. Imprint of Penguin Group (USA) Inc.

Perinatal Loss *See* **Perinatal Loss**

Perinatal Loss, *(0-9615197; 0-9724241)* Div. of Metanoia Peace Community United Methodist Church, 2116 NE 18th Ave., Portland, OR 97212 (SAN 694-2911) Tel 503-284-7426; Fax: 503-282-8985 E-mail: grieving@tearsoup.com Web site: http://www.griefwatch.com *Dist(s):* **ACTA Pubns..**

PeriplusEdition Imprint of Tuttle Publishing

PeriWrinkle Productions, Inc., *(0-9635580)* 7542 Lamar Ct., Arvada, CO 80003-2846 Tel 303-620-9844 ; Fax: 303-446-2629.

Perma-Bound Bks., *(0-605; 0-7804; 0-8000; 0-8479)* Div. of Hertzberg-New Method, Inc., 617 E. Vandalia Rd., Jacksonville, IL 62650 (SAN 169-202X) Tel 217-243-5451; Fax: 217-243-7505; Toll Free Fax: 800-551-1169; Toll Free: 800-637-6581 (customer service) E-mail: books@permabound.com Web site: http://www.perma-bound.com.

Perry Heights Pr., *(0-9630181)* 610 Nod Hill Rd., Wilton, CT 06897-1305.

Perry Publishing, *(0-9626823; 0-9745812)* 9 Middle St., Hallowell, ME 04347 Tel 207-626-3242 Do not confuse with companies with the same name in Thompson Falls, MT Columbia, MD.

†**Persea Bks., Inc.,** *(0-89255)* 853 Broadway, Suite 604, New York, NY 10003 (SAN 212-8233) Tel 212-260-9256; Fax: 212-260-1902 E-mail: info@perseabooks.com Web site: http://www.perseabooks.com *Dist(s):* **Norton, W. W. & Co., Inc.**; *CIP.*

Names

Perspectives Pr., Inc., *(0-944934; 0-9609504)* P.O. Box 90318, Indianapolis, IN 46290-0318 (SAN 262-5059) Tel 317-872-3055
E-mail: ppress@iquest.net
Web site: http://www.perspectivespress.com
Dist(s): **Quality Bks., Inc..**

Peter Pauper Pr. Inc., *(0-88088; 1-59359)* 202 Mamaroneck Ave., Suite 400, White Plains, NY 10601 (SAN 204-9449) Tel 914-681-0144; Fax: 914-681-0389; Toll Free: 800-833-2311
E-mail: LBeilenson@peterpauper.com
Web site: http://www.peterpauper.com.

Peters, Tim & Co., Inc., *(1-879874)* Orders Addr.: P.O. Box 370, Peapack, NJ 07977 (SAN 254-9646) Tel 908-234-2050; Fax: 908-234-1961; Toll Free: 800-543-2230; Edit Addr.: 87 Main St., Peapack, NJ 07977
E-mail: tpc@biocomics.com
Web site: http://www.wellbook.com; http://www.biocomics.com; http://www.captainbio.com.

Peterson, George, *(0-9621320)* 7 Chapman Rd., Marlborough, CT 06447 (SAN 250-9822) Tel 860-295-0121.

Peterson Publishing Co., Inc., *(0-9709033)* 1574 Sherwood Dr., N., Mankato, MN 56003 Tel 507-625-4803 Do not confuse with Peterson Publishing Co. in Gunnison, CO.

Petra Publishing Corp., *(1-880015)* 4319 Scottsville Rd., Charlottesville, VA 22902-7800 Tel 804-244-3358 Do not confuse with companies with similar or same names in Fountain Hills, AZ, Berrien Springs,MI, Wilmington, OH.

Petrie Pr., *(0-9711638)* 9 Card Ave., Camden, NY 13316 Tel 315-245-2408
E-mail: lettiegus@aol.com
Dist(s): **North Country Bks., Inc..**

Petro Pals, Inc., *(0-9653562)* Div. of RobToy, Inc., Orders Addr.: P.O. Box 173, Old Greenwich, CT 06870-0173 Tel 203-637-5466; Fax: 203-637-8549; Edit Addr.: 177 Sound Beach Ave., Greenwich, CT 06870-0173
Dist(s): **Baker & Taylor Bks..**

Phillips, Robert B. Pub., *(0-9620577)* 389 Orchard Rd., Bakersville, NC 28705-8079 (SAN 249-1400).

Phillips, S.G. Inc., *(0-87599)* P.O. Box 416, Ghent, NY 12075 (SAN 293-3152) Tel 518-392-3068; Fax: 518-392-6493
E-mail: sgp@taconic.net.

Philomel Imprint of Penguin Group (USA) Inc.

Philomel Imprint of Penguin Putnam Bks. for Young Readers

†Philosophical Library, Inc., *(0-8022)* P.O. Box 1789, New York, NY 10010 (SAN 201-999X) Tel 212-886-1873; Fax: 212-873-6070
Dist(s): **Kensington Publishing Corp.**; *CIP.*

Piñata Books Imprint of Arte Publico Pr.

Picton Pr., *(0-89725; 0-912274; 0-929539; 0-9614281)* Div. of Picton Corp., P.O. Box 250, Rockport, ME 04856-0250 (SAN 249-6321) Tel 207-236-6565; Fax: 207-236-6713; *Imprints:* Cricketfield Press (Cricketfld Pr)
E-mail: sales@pictonpress.com
Web site: http://www.pictonpress.com.

Pictorial Legends, *(0-939031)* Subs. of Event Co., 435 Holland Ave., Los Angeles, CA 90042 (SAN 662-8486) Tel 213-254-4416
Dist(s): **Igram Pr..**

Picture Me Books, Incorporated *See* **Playhouse Publishing**

Picture Window Bks., *(1-4048)* 5115 Excelsior Blvd., Suite 232, Minneapolis, MN 55416 (SAN 254-8828) Toll Free Fax: 877-787-2746; Toll Free: 877-845-8392
E-mail: gbeer@capstone-press.com
Web site: http://www.picturewindowbooks.com.

Pieces of Learning, *(0-9623835; 1-880505; 1-931334)* Div. of Creative Learning Consultants, Inc., 1990 Market Rd., Marion, IL 62959 (SAN 298-461X) Tel 618-964-9426; Toll Free Fax: 800-844-0455; Toll Free: 800-729-5137
E-mail: polmarion@midamer.net
Web site: http://www.piecesoflearning.com
Dist(s): **Thinking Works.**

Pierce Harris Press Imprint of Vivisphere Publishing

Piggy Toes Pr. Imprint of Intervisual Bks., Inc.

Piglet Pr., Inc., *(1-886354)* Orders Addr.: P.O. Box 324, Issaquah, WA 98029-0324 Tel 206-392-2262; Fax: 206-313-0231; Edit Addr.: 2721 226th, SE, Issaquah, WA 98027
E-mail: piglet@piglet.com.

Pigtail Publishing, *(0-9677548)* 18 Banbury Dr., Westford, MA 01886-3518 Do not confuse with Pigtail Publishing, Coral Springs, FL.

Pilgrim Pr., The/United Church Pr., *(0-8298)* Div. of United Church Board for Homeland Ministries, Orders Addr.: 230 Sheldon Rd., Berea, OH 44017 Fax: 216-732-3713; Toll Free: 800-537-3394; Edit Addr.: 700 Prospect Ave. E., Cleveland, OH 44115-1100 Tel 216-736-3764; Fax: 216-736-2207
E-mail: ucpress@ucc.org; pilgrim@ucc.org
Web site: http://www.ucpress.com; http://www.pilgrimpress.com
Dist(s): **CRC Pubns.**
Women Ink.

Pine Hill Pr., Inc., *(1-57579)* 4000 W. 57th St., Sioux Falls, SD 57106 Tel 605-362-9200; Fax: 605-362-9222 Do not confuse with Pine Hill Pr., Lafayette, CA
E-mail: print@pinehillpress.com
Web site: http://www.pinehillpress.com
Dist(s): **BookWorld Services, Inc..**

Pine Orchard, Inc., *(0-9645727; 1-930580)* Orders Addr.: 1205 SE Professional Mall Blvd., Suite 112, Pullman, WA 99163 (SAN 253-4258) Tel 509-332-1520; Fax: 509-332-1035; Toll Free: 877-354-7433; *Imprints:* Luminary Media Group (Luminary Media)
E-mail: orders@pineorchard.com; pineorch@pineorchard.com
Web site: http://www.pineorchard.com
Dist(s): **Amazon.Com**
Baker & Taylor Bks.
Brodart Co..

Pine Orchard Press *See* **Pine Orchard, Inc.**

Pineapple Pr., Inc., *(0-910923; 1-56164)* P.O. Box 3889, Sarasota, FL 34230-3889 (SAN 285-0850) Tel 941-359-0886; Fax: 941-351-9988; Toll Free: 800-746-3275 Do not confuse with companies with same or similar names in Saint Johns, MI, Middletown, RI, Northampton, MA
E-mail: info@pineapplepress.com
Web site: http://www.pineapplepress.com
Dist(s): **American Wholesale Bk. Co.**
Baker & Taylor Bks..

Pinkston Publishing, *(0-9671708)* Orders Addr.: P.O. Box 1964, Rowlett, TX 75030-1964 Tel 972-816-3848 ; Edit Addr.: 7609 Dockside Dr., Rowlett, TX 75088 Tel 972-475-3923; Fax: 214-670-4980
E-mail: badge5591@cs.com
Dist(s): **Hervey's Booklink & Cookbook Warehouse.**

Pinnacle-Syatt Pubns., *(1-886580)* Div. of Pinnacle-Syatt Enterprises, 535 Calle Capistrano, San Marcos, CA 92069-8306 (SAN 299-1179) Tel 760-598-9896; Fax: 760-598-9897
E-mail: gwenevans@msn.com
Web site: http://www.pinnadesyatt.com.

Pinstripe Publishing, *(0-941973)* P.O. Box 711, Sedro Woolley, WA 98284 (SAN 666-2889) Tel 360-855-1416.

Pioneer Valley Educational Pr., Inc., *(1-58453)* P.O. Box 9375, North Amherst, MA 01059-9375 Tel 413-548-3906; Fax: 413-548-4914
E-mail: richard@pvep.com; dufresne@oitunix.oit.umass.edu
Web site: http://www.pvep.com.

Pippin Pr., *(0-945912)* Orders Addr.: P.O. Box 1347, New York, NY 10028 (SAN 247-8366) Tel 212-288-4920; Fax: 732-225-1562; Edit Addr.: 229 E. 85th St., New York, NY 10028.

Piqua Pr., Inc., *(1-880440)* P.O. Box 32230, Sarasota, FL 34239-0230 Tel 941-366-9143
E-mail: cls@piquapress.com
Web site: http://www.piquapress.com.

Pirate Publishing International, *(0-9674081)* 6323 St. Andrews Cir., No. 5, Fort Myers, FL 33919-1719 Tel 941-939-4845
E-mail: SuperK@juno.com
Dist(s): **Biblio Distribution.**

Pitspopany Pr., *(0-943706; 965-465; 1-930143; 1-932687)* Orders Addr.: 40 E. 78th St., Suite 16D, New York, NY 10021-1830 (SAN 238-373X) Tel 212-472-4959; Fax: 212-472-6253; Toll Free: 800-232-2931
E-mail: pitspop@netvision.net.il; popany@netvision.net.il; pitspopany@aol.com
Web site: http://www.pitspopany.com; http://www.devorapublishing.com
Dist(s): **Baker & Taylor Bks.**
Bookazine Co., Inc..

Pittman Pub., *(0-9615382)* Rte. 1, Box 255, Aulander, NC 27805 (SAN 695-4456) Tel 919-332-2511.

PJs Corner, *(0-9745615)* P.O. Box 8, Taft, CA 93268-8008 Fax: 661-770-8608; *Imprints:* Twiglet The Little Christmas Tree (Twiglet)
E-mail: pjscorner7@aol.com.

Plainsong Publishing, *(0-9709718)*
E-mail: dwhitejone@aol.com; dwhitejon@aol.com.

Planet Dexter Imprint of Penguin Putnam Bks. for Young Readers

Planeta Publishing Corp., *(0-9715256; 0-9719950)* 2057 NW 87th Ave., Miami, FL 33172 Tel 305-470-0016; 305-571-8400; Fax: 305-470-6267; Toll Free: 800-407-4770
E-mail: mnormanppc@aol.com
Web site: http://www.planetapublishing.com.

Platt & Munk Imprint of Penguin Putnam Bks. for Young Readers

†Platypus Bks., Ltd., *(0-930905)* 1315 Angelina, College Station, TX 77840-4854 (SAN 679-1727)
Dist(s): **Writers & Bks.**; *CIP.*

Platypus Media, L.L.C., *(0-9678020; 0-9700106; 1-930775)* Orders Addr.: 627 A St., NE, Washington, DC 20002 Tel 202-546-1674; Fax: 202-546-2356
E-mail: info@platypusmedia.com
Web site: http://www.platypusmedia.com.

Players Pr., Inc., *(0-88734)* P.O. Box 1132, Studio City, CA 91614-0132 (SAN 239-0213) Tel 818-789-4980
E-mail: Playerspress@att.net.

Playground Entertainment Marketing, *(1-893143)* 4529 Angeles Crest Hwy., No. 200, La Canada, CA 91011 Tel 818-790-0883; Fax: 818-790-0886.

Playhouse Publishing, *(1-57151; 1-878338)* 1566 Akron Peninsula Rd., Akron, OH 44313 Tel 330-762-6800; Fax: 330-762-2230; Toll Free: 800-762-6775; *Imprints:* Nibble Me Books (Nibble Me Bks)
E-mail: info@playhousepublishing.com
Web site: http://www.playhousepublishing.com; http://www.littlelucyandfriends.com; http://www.nibble-me-books.com
Dist(s): **Baker & Taylor Bks..**

Playmore, Inc., Pubs., *(0-86611; 1-59060)* 230 Fifth Ave., Suite 711, New York, NY 10001-7704 (SAN 219-340X) Tel 212-251-0600; Fax: 212-251-0966
E-mail: customerservice@playmorebooks.com.

†Pleasant Co. Pubns., *(0-937295; 1-56247; 1-58485; 1-59369)* Subs. of Mattel, Inc., Orders Addr.: P.O. Box 620991, Middleton, WI 53562-0991 Tel 608-836-4848; Toll Free Fax: 800-257-3865; Toll Free: 800-233-0264; Edit Addr.: 8400 Fairway Pl., Middleton, WI 53562-0998 (SAN 298-6337) Tel 608-836-4848; Fax: 608-831-7089; *Imprints:* American Girl (Amer Girl)
Web site: http://www.pleasantcopublications.com/
Dist(s): **American Wholesale Bk. Co.**
Anderson News Co.
Baker & Taylor Bks.
Brodart Co.
Follett Library Resources
Koen Bk. Distributors
Lectorum Pubns., Inc.
Levy Home Entertainment
Riverside
Spring Arbor Distributors, Inc.; *CIP.*

Pleiades Publishing, *(0-9662777)* Orders Addr.: P.O. Box 917, Captain Cook, HI 96704 Tel 808-322-1778; Fax: 808-322-1861; Edit Addr.: Aloha Theatre Bldg., Mamalahoa Hwy., Kainaliu, HI 96750 Do not confuse wtih companies with the same or similar name in Sandy, UT, Pittsford, NY
E-mail: hokukona@gfe.net.

Plume Imprint of Dutton/Plume

Pocahontas Pr., Inc., *(0-936015)* Orders Addr.: P.O. Box Drawer F, Blacksburg, VA 24063-1020 (SAN 630-124X) Tel 540-951-0467; Fax: 540-961-2847; Toll Free: 800-446-0467; Edit Addr.: 832 Hutcheson Dr., Blackburg, VA 24063-1020
E-mail: mchollim@vt.edu
Dist(s): **Baker & Taylor Bks.**
Coutts Library Service, Inc.
Koen Bk. Distributors
Quality Bks., Inc..

Pocket Imprint of Simon & Schuster

†Pocket Bks., *(0-671; 0-7432; 0-7434; 1-4165)* Div. of Simon & Schuster, Inc., Orders Addr.: 100 Front St., Riverside, NJ 08075 Toll Free Fax: 800-943-9831; Toll Free: 800-223-2336; Edit Addr.: 1230 Ave. of the Americas, New York, NY 10020 (SAN 202-5922) Tel 212-698-7000; *Imprints:* Archway Paperbacks (Archway)
E-mail: ssonline_feedback@simonsays.com
Web site: http://www.simonsays.com
Dist(s): **Simon & Schuster**
Thorndike Pr.; *CIP.*

Pocket Mixx Imprint of Mixx Entertainment, Inc.

Pocket of Sanity, *(0-9663019)* P.O. Box 5241, Fresno, CA 93755-5241 Tel 559-298-6181; Fax: 559-225-3670; Toll Free: 800-497-4909 (orders only)
E-mail: posanity@aol.com
Dist(s): **American West Bks..**

Pocket Paragon Imprint of Godine, David R. Pub.

Names

Pockets of Learning, *(1-888074; 1-58405)* Orders Addr.: 30 Cutler St., Suite 101, Warren, RI 02885 Tel 401-247-1991; Fax: 401-247-7860; Toll Free Fax: 800-370-1580; Toll Free: 800-635-2994
E-mail: pocketsofl@aol.com
Web site: http://www.pocketsoflearning.com.

Pockets Pr., *(1-881511)* 501 Creekwood Dr., Marietta, GA 30068 Tel 770-565-2492; Fax: 770-565-4925 Do not confuse with Pockets Press, Maryland Heights, MO.

Pohl, Linda Perelman, *(0-9625453)* 69 Forestview Ct., Williamsville, NY 14221 Tel 716-688-3838.

Polka Dot Pr. Corp., The, *(1-930248)* P.O. Box 471, Alpine, NJ 07620-0471 Tel 201-750-0372; Fax: 201-750-9372
E-mail: info@muffles.org.

Pollyanna Productions, *(0-945842)* Orders Addr.: P.O. Box 3222, Terre Haute, IN 47803; Edit Addr.: 4830 E. Poplar Dr., Terre Haute, IN 47803 (SAN 247-8285) Tel 812-877-3286; Toll Free: 800-257-3286
E-mail: polpr@aol.com
Dist(s): **Gryphon Hse., Inc..**

Polychrome Publishing Corp., *(1-879965)* 4509 N. Francisco, Chicago, IL 60625-3808 Tel 773-478-4455 ; Fax: 773-478-0786
E-mail: polypub@earthlink.net
Web site: http://www.home.earthlink.net/~polypub.

Polyglot Pr., Inc., *(1-931927; 1-4115)* 427 Queen St., Philadelphia, PA 19147 Tel 215-755-7559; Fax: 215-755-5569 Do not confuse with Polyglot Press in Fairfax, VA
E-mail: david@polyglotpress.com
Web site: http://www.polyglotpress.com.

Ponderosa Pr., *(0-9642244)* Orders Addr.: P.O. Box 278, Yosemite, CA 95389; Edit Addr.: 1 Flying Spur Rd., Yosemite, CA 95389 Tel 209-966-4863 Do not confuse with companies with the same name in Colorado Springs, CO, Fredericksburg, TX, Spokane, WA, Hackensack, MN, Riesel, TX.

Poolbeg Pr. (IRL) *(0-905169; 0-907085; 1-85371; 1-84223) Dist. by* **Dufour.**

Popular Pr. Imprint of Univ. of Wisconsin Pr.

Popular Pr., Inc., *(0-9642086)* 12555 Biscayne Blvd., No. 760, Miami, FL 33181 Tel 305-692-9284; Fax: 305-692-9039
Dist(s): **Koen Bk. Distributors.**

Portos Publishing Co., *(0-9663651)* Orders Addr.: P.O. Box 2009, Saratoga, CA 95070-0009 Tel 408-867-7946; Edit Addr.: 19375 Portos Ct., Saratoga, CA 95070.

Portraits West, *(0-9642639)* 93 Madera Dr., Lodi, CA 95240-0713 (SAN 298-3443) Tel 209-369-2113
Dist(s): **Baker & Taylor Bks.**
Bookmen, Inc..

Portunus Publishing Co., *(0-9641330; 1-886440)* 27875 Berwick Dr., Carmel, CA 93923 Tel 831-622-0604; Fax: 310-399-5644
E-mail: service@portunus.net
Dist(s): **Lectorum Pubns., Inc..**

Possibilities Unlimited, *(0-9711577)* 49 S. Kingsboro Ave., Gloversville, NY 12078 Tel 518-725-3565 Do not confuse with companies with the same or similar name in Oren, UT, Milford, CT
E-mail: arobbin1@nycap.rr.com.

Post Oak Pr. Imprint of Larksdale

Pota Pr., *(1-887963)* 112 Surfside Ave., Santa Cruz, CA 95060 Tel 831-423-4806 (phone/fax)
E-mail: jackpot@cruzio.com
Web site: http://www.cruzio.com/~nikan/index.htm.

Power for Kids Pr. Imprint of Rust Foundation for Literacy, Inc., The

PowerKids Pr. Imprint of Rosen Publishing Group, Inc., The

Praeger Pubs. Imprint of Greenwood Publishing Group, Inc.

Prairie Divide Productions, *(1-884610)* Orders Addr.: P.O. Box 129, 12526 Creedmore Lakes Rd., Red Feather Lakes, CO 80545 Tel 970-493-6593; Toll Free: 888-288-4841
E-mail: info@baltzbooks.com
Dist(s): **Baker & Taylor Bks.**
Book Wholesalers, Inc.
Brodart Co..

Prairie Lark Press *See* **SHARE-Pregnancy & Infant Loss Support, Inc.**

Prairie Paperbacks Imprint of Whitman, Albert & Co.

Precious Life Bks., Inc., *(1-889733)* Orders Addr.: P.O. Box 1948, Lewisburg, TN 37091 Tel 615-270-1921; Toll Free: 800-728-5945; Edit Addr.: 1448 New Columbia Hwy., Lewisburg, TN 37091.

Precious Resources, *(0-937836)* 349 S. Jackson St., Bluffton, OH 45817 (SAN 213-3512) Tel 419-358-0334
E-mail: precious@wcoil.com.

PremaNations Publishing, *(1-892176)* Div. of PremaNations, Inc., P.O. Box 321447, Cocoa Beach, FL 32932-1447 (SAN 299-5808) Tel 407-783-1867; Fax: 407-784-5372; Toll Free Fax: 877-372-4660; Toll Free: 877-372-4664
E-mail: Paradigm@PremaNations.com
Web site: http://www.PremaNations.com
Dist(s): **Baker & Taylor Bks.**
Bookpeople
New Leaf Distributing Co., Inc.
Quality Bks., Inc..

Premier Imprint of Ctr. Point Large Print

Premier Publishing *See* **Futech Interactive Products, Inc.**

Premium Pr. America, *(0-9637733; 1-887654)* Div. of Schnitzer Communications, Inc., Orders Addr.: P.O. Box 159015, Nashville, TN 37215-9015 Tel 615-256-8484; Fax: 615-256-8524; Toll Free: 800-891-7323; Edit Addr.: 2606 Eugenia Ave., Suite C, Nashville, TN 37211-2177
E-mail: bbsgcs@aol.com
Web site: http://www.premiumpress.com.

Prentice Hall, ESL Dept., *(0-13; 0-88345)* 240 Frisch Ct., Paramus, NJ 07652-5240 Tel 201-236-7000; Fax: 201-592-0904; Toll Free: 800-922-0579
Web site: http://vig.prenhall.com/
Dist(s): **Continental Bk. Co., Inc.**
Pearson Education.

†Prentice Hall PTR, *(0-13; 0-201; 0-672)* Div. of Pearson Technology Group, Orders Addr.: 200 Old Tappan Rd., Old Tappan, NJ 07675 Fax: 416-447-2819 (orders - Canada); Toll Free Fax: 800-445-6991 (government orders); 800-835-5327 (individual single copy orders - US); Toll Free: 800-567-3800 (orders - Canada); 800-282-0693 (individual single copy orders - US); 800-922-0579 (government orders); Edit Addr.: 240 Frisch Ct., Paramus, NJ 07652-5240
Web site: http://www.prenhall.com
Dist(s): **Cambridge Bk. Co.**
Continental Bk. Co., Inc.
IFSTA
Pearson Education
Penguin Group (USA) Inc.; *CIP.*

Prentice Hall (Schl. Div.), *(0-13)* Orders Addr.: 4350 Equity Dr., Columbus, OH 43216-2649 Fax: 614-771-7361; Toll Free: 800-848-9500; P.O. Box 2649, Columbus, OH 43216-2649; Edit Addr.: 160 Gould St. (Northeast Region), Needham Heights, MA 02194-2310 Tel 617-455-1300; 8445 Freeport Pkwy., Suite 400 (South Central Region), Irving, TX 75063 Tel 214-915-4255
Web site: http://www.phschool.com/.

Prentice-Hall *See* **Prentice Hall PTR**

Preproduction Pr. Imprint of Wood 'N Barnes

Presbyterian & Reformed Publishing Company *See* **P&R Publishing**

†Press Pacifica, Ltd., *(0-916630)* Orders Addr.: P.O. Box 47, Kailua, HI 96734 (SAN 249-292X) Tel 808-261-6594
Dist(s): **Booklines Hawaii, Ltd.**; *CIP.*

Preston-Speed Pubns., *(1-887159; 1-931587)* 51 Ridge Rd., Mill Hall, PA 17751 Tel 570-726-7844; Fax: 570-726-3547
E-mail: Preston@cub.kcnet.org
Web site: http://www.prestonspeed.com
Dist(s): **Greathall Productions, Inc..**

Prestwick Hse., Inc., *(1-58049)* Orders Addr.: P.O. Box 246, Cheswold, DE 19936 Tel 302-736-2665; Fax: 302-734-0549; Toll Free: 800-932-4593; Edit Addr.: 604 Forrest Ave., Dover, DE 19404
E-mail: books@prestwickhouse.com
Web site: http://www.prestwickhouse.com.

Price Stern Sloan Imprint of Penguin Putnam Bks. for Young Readers

Prickly Pr., *(1-893463)* 7911 W. 92nd Terr., Overland Park, KS 66212 Tel 913-648-2034 (phone/fax)
E-mail: ikesmith@kc.rr.com
Web site: http://www.readwest.com/flouncesmith.thm.

Priddy Bks. Imprint of St. Martin's Pr.

Pride & Imprints *See* **Windstorm Creative Ltd.**

Prima Lifestyles Imprint of Crown Publishing Group

Prime Crime Imprint of Berkley Publishing Group

Princess Publishing, *(1-883499)* 26 Princess Ave., Marlton, NJ 08053 Tel 609-983-3964 Do not confuse with companies with the same name in Portland, OR, Chesapeake, VA.

Prinit Pr., *(0-932970)* 211 NW Seventh St., Richmond, IN 47374-4051 (SAN 212-680X) Tel 765-966-7130; Fax: 765-966-7131; Toll Free: 800-478-4885
Web site: http://www.printpress.com.

Printwick Papers, *(0-9652076)* 980 Camino Dos Rios, Thousand Oaks, CA 91360-2302 Tel 805-499-6111; Fax: 805-499-7235; Toll Free: 800-869-9619.

Prism Pr., *(1-881602)* 117 Highland Ave., Edison, NJ 08817 Tel 732-572-6586 Do not confuse with companies with the same or similar name in Gladwin, MI, New York, NY, Baltimore, MD, Houston, TX, Dayton, NJ, Minneapolis, MN, Detroit, MI, Boulder, CO, West Hills, CA.

Proctor Pubns., *(1-882792; 1-928623)* Div. of Proctor Publications, LLC, Orders Addr.: P.O. Box 2498, Ann Arbor, MI 48106-2498 Tel 734-480-9900; Fax: 734-480-9811; Toll Free: 800-343-3034; Edit Addr.: 1832 Midvale, Ypsilanti, MI 48197
E-mail: dproctor9552@comcast.net
Web site: http://www.proctorpublications.com
Dist(s): **Baker & Taylor Bks.**
Follett Library Resources
Quality Bks., Inc.
Wayne State Univ. Pr..

Professional Business Consultant *See* **Milligan Bks.**

Profile Entertainment, Inc., *(0-88013; 0-931064; 0-934551)* 475 Park Ave., S., 8th Flr., New York, NY 10016 (SAN 212-1247) Tel 212-689-2830; Fax: 212-889-7933
E-mail: dee.erwine@starloggroup.com
Dist(s): **Kable News Co., Inc..**

Progeny Pr., *(1-58609)* Div of MG Publishers Group LLC, Orders Addr.: P.O. Box 223, Eau Claire, WI 54702-0223 Tel 715-838-0171; Fax: 715-836-0176; Toll Free: 877-776-4369; Edit Addr.: 202 S. Barstow, Eau Claire, WI 54701
E-mail: progeny@progenypress.com
Web site: http://www.progenypress.com.

†Prometheus Bks., Pubs., *(0-87975; 1-57392; 1-59102)* 59 John Glenn Dr., Amherst, NY 14228-2197 (SAN 202-0289) Tel 716-691-0133; Fax: 716-691-0137; Toll Free: 800-421-0351
E-mail: mhall@prometheusmail.com
Web site: http://www.prometheusbooks.com
Dist(s): **Paladin Pr.**; *CIP.*

Promise Land Pubs., *(0-9633091)* Orders Addr.: P.O. Box 110, Dalton, OH 44618-0110 (SAN 297-6749) Tel 216-828-2167; Edit Addr.: 310 Nickles St., Dalton, OH 44618
Dist(s): **Green Pastures Pr..**

Promise Pubns., *(0-9656498)* Orders Addr.: PMB 117 6632 Telegraph Rd., Bloomfield Hills, MI 48301-3013 Tel 248-865-9345; Fax: 248-538-0403 Do not confuse with Promise Pubns., Plano, TX
E-mail: sherea@realisticallyspeaking.net
Dist(s): **Baker & Taylor Bks..**

Prosperity Pr. Imprint of Clark, Arthur H. Co.

Providence Foundation, *(1-887456)* Orders Addr.: P.O. Box 6759, Charlottesville, VA 22906 Tel 804-978-4535 (phone/fax); Edit Addr.: 1084 Ramblewood Pl., Charlottesville, VA 22901
E-mail: provfdn@aol.com
Web site: http://www.providencefoundation.com.

Providence Hse. Pubs., *(1-57736; 1-881576)* 238 Seaboard Ln., Franklin, TN 37067 Tel 615-771-2020; Fax: 615-771-2002; Toll Free: 800-321-5692; *Imprints:* Hillsboro Press (Hillsboro Pr)
E-mail: books@providencehouse.com
Web site: http://www.providencehouse.com.

Provincetown Impressions *See* **Shank Painter Publishing Co.**

†Pruett Publishing Co., *(0-87108)* 7464 Arapahoe Rd., Suite A9, Boulder, CO 80303-1500 (SAN 205-4035) Tel 303-449-4919; Fax: 303-443-9019; Toll Free: 800-592-9727 (orders)
E-mail: pruettbks@aol.com
Web site: http://www.pruettpublishing.com; *CIP.*

P2 Educational Services, Inc., *(1-885964)* 4915 S. 146th Cir., Omaha, NE 68137-1402 Tel 712-727-3772.

Publicaciones Fher, S.A. (ESP) *(84-243) Dist. by* **AIMS Intl.**

Publication Consultants, *(0-9644809; 1-888125; 1-59433)* 7617 Highlander Dr., Anchorage, AK 99518 Tel 907-349-2424
E-mail: evan@alaskabooks.biz
Web site: http://www.alaskabooks.biz
Dist(s): **Baker & Taylor Bks.**
News Group, The
Partners/West
Todd Communications.

Names

Publications International, Ltd., *(0-7853; 0-88176; 1-56173; 1-4127)* 7373 N. Cicero Ave., Lincolnwood, IL 60712 (SAN 263-9823) Tel 847-676-3470; Fax: 847-676-3671
Web site: http://www.pilbooks.com
Dist(s): **Pan American Publishing, Inc.**
Penguin Group (USA) Inc.
Publishers Clearing Hse..

PublishAmerica, Inc., *(1-893162; 1-58851; 1-59129; 1-59286; 1-4137)* Div. of America Hse. Bk. Pubs., 230 E. Patrick St., Frederick, MD 21701 Tel 240-529-1030; Fax: 301-631-9073
Web site: http://www.publishamerica.com.

Publishers Group West, Subs. of Publishers Group Inc., 1700 Fourth St., Berkeley, CA 94710 (SAN 202-8522) Tel 510-528-1444; Fax: 510-528-3444; Toll Free: 800-788-3123; 800-788-3122 (electronic orders)
Web site: http://www.pgw.com.

Publishing Resources, Inc., *(0-89825)* Orders Addr.: P.O. Box 41307, Santurce, PR 00940 Tel 787-268-8080; Fax: 787-774-5781; Edit Addr.: 373 San Jorge St., 2nd Flr., Santurce, PR 00912 Do not confuse with Publishing Resources, Indianapolis, IN
Dist(s): **Irish Bks. & Media, Inc..**

Pueblo of Acoma Pr., *(0-915347)* P.O. Box 328, Acomita, NM 87034 (SAN 290-0386) Tel 505-552-6070.

Puffin Bks. Imprint of Viking Penguin

Puffin Bks. Imprint of Penguin Putnam Bks. for Young Readers

Puffin-Alloy Imprint of Penguin Putnam Bks. for Young Readers

Pug House Pr., *(0-9717900)* 250 E. Wynnewood Rd., No. E-13, Wynnewood, PA 19096
E-mail: amyunbounded@yahoo.com
Web site: http://www.amyunbounded.com.

Puget Sound Pr., *(0-9660092; 1-930809)* 6523 California Ave., SW, PMB 292, Seattle, WA 98136-1833 Tel 206-763-2415
Dist(s): **Baker & Taylor Bks.**
Partners/West
Quality Bks., Inc..

Pumpkin Patch Publishing, *(0-9646300; 0-9708400)* 4232 Riva De Tierra Ln., Las Vegas, NV 89135 Tel 815-765-0573
E-mail: sfiorello@lvcm.com; sfiorello@aol.com
Web site: http://www.pumpkinpatchpublishing.com.

Punking Pr., *(0-9641641)* 5980 Pease Rd., Williamson, NY 14589.

Puppetry in Practice, *(0-9720183)* 658 E. Seventh St., Brooklyn, NY 11218 Tel 718-854-0507; Fax: 718-854-1443
E-mail: tovaa@aol.com
Web site: http://www.puppetryinpractice.com.

Purple Chickie Pr., *(0-9674363)* 5049 Wornall Rd., No. AB, Kansas City, MO 64112 Tel 816-931-8093; Fax: 816-931-8094; *Imprints:* Rainy Day Books (Rainy Day)
E-mail: gammyK@aol.com.

Purple Cow, The, *(0-9656822)* 52 Melody Ln., Murphysboro, IL 62966 Tel 618-687-2050.

Purple Gorilla, LLC, The, *(0-9661844)* 393 Toilsome Hill Rd., Fairfield, CT 06825-1624 Tel 203-367-5040; Fax: 203-367-3459
E-mail: Purple_Gorilla@excite.com.

Purple Hse. Pr., *(1-930900)* Orders Addr.: P.O. Box 787, Cynthiana, KY 41031; Edit Addr.: 8138 US Hwy. 62 E., Cynthiana, KY 41031
E-mail: jimorgan@earthlink.net
Web site: http://www.purplehousepress.com.

Purple People, Inc., *(0-9707793)* P.O. Box 3194, Sedona, AZ 86340-3194 Tel 928-204-6400; Fax: 928-282-1662
E-mail: info@purplepeople.com
Web site: http://www.purplepeople.com.

PUSH Imprint of Scholastic, Inc.

Pussywillow Publishing Hse., *(0-934739)* 621 Leisure World, Mesa, AZ 85206-3153 (SAN 694-1702) Tel 480-641-9049; Fax: 480-854-1222
Dist(s): **Baker & Taylor Bks..**

Putnam & Grosset Imprint of Putnam Publishing Group, The

Putnam & Grosset Imprint of Penguin Group (USA) Inc.

Putnam Berkley Audio Imprint of Putnam Publishing Group, The

Putnam Berkley Audio Imprint of Penguin Group (USA) Inc.

Putnam Berkley Audio Imprint of Penguin Putnam Bks. for Young Readers

†Putnam Publishing Group, The, *(0-399; 0-698; 0-89828)* Div. of Penguin Putnam, Inc., Orders Addr.: 405 Murray Hill Pkwy., East Rutherford, NJ 07073-2136 Toll Free Fax: 800-227-9604; Toll Free: 800-788-6262 (individual consumer sales); 800-631-8571 (reseller customer service); 800-526-0275 (reseller sales); Edit Addr.: 375 Hudson St., New York, NY 10014 (SAN 202-5531) Tel 212-366-2000; Fax: 212-366-2643; *Imprints:* Coward-McCann (Coward); Sandcastle Books (Sandcastle Bks); Tuffy Books (Tuffy); Putnam Berkley Audio (Putnam Berkley Audio); Putnam & Grosset (Putnam & Grosset); Wee Sing Books (Wee Sing Bks); BlueHen Books (BlueHen)
E-mail: online@penguinputnam.com
Web site: http://www.penguinputnam.com
Dist(s): **Continental Bk. Co., Inc.**
Hastings Bks.
Lectorum Pubns., Inc.
Landmark Audiobooks
Penguin Group (USA) Inc.
Rounder Kids Music Distribution
Beeler, Thomas T. Publisher; *CIP.*

Pyrola Publishing, *(0-9618348)* P.O. Box 80961, Fairbanks, AK 99708 (SAN 667-3503) Tel 907-455-6469 (phone/fax)
E-mail: mshields@mosquitonet.com
Web site: http://www.maryshields.com
Dist(s): **Todd Communications.**

QDP Publishing, *(0-9647539)* Div. of W. Edmund Hood Writing Services, 126 Wadsworth Ave., Avon, NY 14414 Tel 716-226-8398.

Quail Ridge Pr., Inc., *(0-937552; 1-893062)* Orders Addr.: P.O. Box 123, Brandon, MS 39043 Tel 601-825-2063; Fax: 601-825-3091; Toll Free Fax: 800-864-1082; Toll Free: 800-343-1583
E-mail: info@quailridge.com
Web site: http://www.quailridge.com
Dist(s): **Gibson, Dot Pubns.**
Forest Sales & Distributing Co.
Partners Pubs. Group, Inc.
Southwest Cookbook Distributors.

Quaker Press of Friends General Conference, *(0-9620912; 1-888305)* 1216 Arch St., 2B, Philadelphia, PA 19107 (SAN 225-4484) Tel 215-561-1700; Fax: 215-561-0759; Toll Free: 800-966-4556
E-mail: barbarah@fgcquaker.org; bookstore@fgc.quaker.org
Web site: http://www.fgcquaker.org.

Quality Family Entertainment, Inc., *(1-884336)* 1133 Broadway, Suite 1520, New York, NY 10021 Tel 212-463-9623; Fax: 212-463-9626.

Quality Pubns., *(0-89137)* Div. of Quality Printing Co., Orders Addr.: 324 Mesquite, Abilene, TX 79601 (SAN 203-0071) Tel 915-677-6262; Fax: 915-677-1511; Toll Free: 800-359-7708
E-mail: publications@qpabilene.com
Web site: http://www.qpabilene.com.

Quarrier Pr., *(0-938985; 0-9646197; 1-891852)* 1416 Quarrier St., Charleston, WV 25301 Tel 304-342-1848 ; Fax: 304-343-0594; Toll Free: 888-982-7472
E-mail: wvbooks@ntelos.net
Dist(s): **Pictorial Histories Distribution.**

Quarter-Inch *See* **Quarter-Inch Publishing**

Quarter-Inch Publishing, *(0-9653422; 0-9740932)* 33255 Stoneman St., No. B, Lake Elsinore, CA 92530 Tel 909-609-3309; Fax: 909-609-3369
E-mail: quarteri@aol.com
Web site: http://www.quarterinchpublishing.com
Dist(s): **Sunbelt Pubns., Inc..**

Questar, Inc., *(0-927992; 1-56855; 1-59464)* Orders Addr.: P.O. Box 11345, Chicago, IL 60611-0345 Tel 312-266-9400; Fax: 312-266-9523; Toll Free: 800-544-8422; 800-633-5633 (orders only); Edit Addr.: 680 N. Lake Shore Dr., Suite 900, Chicago, IL 60611 (SAN 298-7368); 304 Park Ave., S., 11th Flr., New York, NY 10010 Tel 212-590-2470; Fax: 212-590-2472
E-mail: info@questar1.com; questarchi@aol.com
Web site: http://www.questar1.com
Dist(s): **Christian Bk. Distributors**
Explorations
Vision Video.

Questar Publishers, Incorporated *See* **Multnomah Pubs., Inc.**

Quiet Impact, Inc., *(0-9713749)* 140 Cherry St., No. 388, Hamilton, MT 59840 Fax: 406-363-5234
E-mail: elhamilton@quietimpact.com; elhamilton@character-in-action.com
Web site: http://www.character-in-action.com.

Quiet Vision Publishing, *(1-57646; 1-891595)* 12155 Mountain Shadow Rd., Sandy, UT 84092-5812 Tel 801-572-4018; Fax: 801-571-8625; Toll Free: 800-442-4018
E-mail: john@quietvision.com; info@quietvision.com
Web site: http://www.quietvision.com
Dist(s): **Baker & Taylor Bks.**
Sprout, Inc..

Quillpen, *(0-9673504)* 1520 Waverly Dr., Trenton, MI 48183 Tel 734-676-1285; Fax: 734-676-9822
E-mail: bfquillpen@msn.com.

R&M Publishing Co., *(0-936026)* P.O. Box 1276, Holly Hill, SC 29059 (SAN 213-6392) Tel 706-738-0360; Fax: 803-279-3080 Do not confuse with the same or similar name in Foresthill, CA, Las Vegas, NV, Minnetonka, MN
E-mail: Mackattack07319@cs.com.

RDR Bks., *(0-9636161; 1-57143)* 4456 Piedmont Ave., Oakland, CA 94611 Tel 510-595-0595; Fax: 510-595-0598; *Imprints:* Wetlands Press (Wetlands Pr)
E-mail: books@rdrbooks.com
Web site: http://www.rdrbooks.com
Dist(s): **Baker & Taylor Bks.**
Bookazine Co., Inc.
Bookpeople
Brodart Co.
Hervey's Booklink & Cookbook Warehouse
Koen Bk. Distributors
Koen Pacific
Partners Pubs. Group, Inc.
Partners/West
Quality Bks., Inc.
Sunbelt Pubns., Inc.
Unique Bks., Inc..

RHS Enterprises, *(0-914503)* Orders Addr.: P.O. Box 5779, Garden Grove, CA 92846-0779 (SAN 289-6699) Tel 714-892-9012; Edit Addr.: 11368 Matinicus Ct., Cypress, CA 90630 (SAN 241-936X)
Web site: http://www.copz.net/copza.18.htm.

R. N. M., Incorporated *See* **Onion River Pr.**

RRP Pubs., *(0-9607034)* 5 N. Bank St., Easton, PA 18042 (SAN 239-0264) Tel 610-252-1199.

Radiola Co., *(0-929541)* Div. of MediaBay, Inc., P.O. Box C, Sandy Hook, CT 06482 Toll Free: 800-243-0987.

Ragged Bears USA, *(1-929927)* Div. of Ragged Bears Publishing, Ltd., 413 Sixth Ave., Brooklyn, NY 11215-3310 Tel 718-768-3696; Fax: 718-369-0844
E-mail: publisher@raggedbears.com
Web site: http://www.raggedbears.com
Dist(s): **Chronicle Bks. LLC.**

Rain Bird, Incorporated *See* **Rain Bird Productions, Inc.**

Rain Bird Productions, Inc., *(1-879920)* 16 Judd Bridge Rd., Roxbury, CT 06783 Fax: 860-354-5852.

Rainbow Bks., Inc., *(0-935834; 1-56825)* P.O. Box 430, Highland City, FL 33846-0430 (SAN 213-5515) Tel 863-648-4420; Fax: 863-647-5951; Toll Free: 888-613-2665 (888-613-BOOK) Do not confuse with Rainbow Bks., Inc. in Amsterdam, NY
E-mail: RBIbooks@aol.com
Web site: http://www.rainbowbooksinc.com
Dist(s): **Baker & Taylor Bks.**
Book Clearing Hse..

Rainbow Bridge, *(0-9615210)* 823 Forest Ave., Palo Alto, CA 94301 (SAN 694-4132) Tel 415-321-7458
E-mail: garacon@pacbell.net.

Rainbow Hse. Publishing, *(1-893659)* Orders Addr.: P.O. Box 5360, Bridgeport, CT 06604; Edit Addr.: 690 W. Jackson Ave., Bridgeport, CT 06604 (SAN 299-8211) Tel 203-334-0646; Fax: 203-368-4012; Toll Free: 800-361-2609
E-mail: rainbow.house@snet.net
Web site: http://www.RainbowHousePublishing.com
Dist(s): **Baker & Taylor Bks.**
Quality Bks., Inc..

Rainbow Pr., *(0-943156)* 222 Edwards Dr., Fayetteville, NY 13066 (SAN 240-4354) Do not confuse with companies with the same name in Southampton, NY, Snover, MI, Sparta, NJ, Saco, ME, Boise, ID
Dist(s): **Baker & Taylor Bks..**

Rainbow Readers Publishing, *(1-888862)* Div. of Whirling Rainbow Productions, 1672 Edinburgh Ln., Aurora, IL 60504-6087 Toll Free: 888-280-4569
E-mail: katgibson@aol.com
Web site: http://www.zibberbibber.com; http://www.kathleengibson.com
Dist(s): **Baker & Taylor Bks.**
Professional Media Service Corp..

Raincoast Bk. Distribution (CAN) *(0-920417; 1-55192; 1-895714) Dist. by* **Publishers Group.**

Raincoast Bk. Distribution (CAN) *(0-920417; 1-55192; 1-895714) Dist. by* **Advanced Global.**

†Raintree Pubs., *(0-8114; 0-8172; 0-8393; 0-7398)* Div. of Harcourt, Inc., Orders Addr.: P.O. Box 26015, Austin, TX 78755 Toll Free Fax: 877-578-2638; Toll Free: 888-363-4266; Edit Addr.: 10801 N. Mopac Expressway, Bldg. 3, Austin, TX 78759 (SAN 658-1757) Tel 512-343-8227; Fax: 646-935-3713 Web site: http://www.raintreelibrary.com; *CIP.*

Raintree Steck-Vaughn Publishers *See* **Raintree Pubs.**

Rainy Day Bks. Imprint of Purple Chickie Pr.

Rairarubia Bks., *(0-9712206)* 1000 San Diego Rd., Santa Barbara, CA 93103 Fax: 805-966-4697 E-mail: raira@silcom.com Web site: http://www.rairarubia.com.

Ranch Hse. Pr., *(1-878438)* 2980 E. US Hwy. 160, Pagosa Springs, CO 81147-9741 (SAN 240-1126) Tel 970-264-2647.

†Rand McNally, *(0-528)* Orders Addr.: P.O. Box 7600, Chicago, IL 60680 Fax: 847-673-9935; Toll Free: 800-333-0136 (ext. 4771) E-mail: customerservice@randmcnally.com Web site: http://www.randmcnally.com *Dist(s):* **Bryant Altman Map, Inc.;** *CIP.*

Random House Adult Trade Publishing Group, *(0-375; 0-679; 0-8129; 1-4000)* Orders Addr.: 400 Hahn Rd., Westminster, MD 21157 Tel 410-848-1900 ; Toll Free: 800-726-0600; Edit Addr.: 299 Park Ave., New York, NY 10171 Tel 212-751-2600; Fax: 212-572-4949; Toll Free: 800-726-0600; *Imprints:* Modern Library (Mod Lib) *Dist(s):* **Libros Sin Fronteras**
Random Hse., Inc..

Random Hse. Audio Publishing Group, *(0-375; 0-553; 1-4000)* Div. of Random Hse., Diversified Pub. Group, Orders Addr.: 400 Hahn Rd., Westminster, MD 21157 (SAN 201-3975) Tel 410-848-1900; Toll Free: 800-726-0600; Edit Addr.: 1540 Broadway, New York, NY 10036; *Imprints:* Imagination Studio (ImaginStudio); RH Audio (Random AudioBks); Listening Library (Listening Lib) Web site: http://www.randomhouse.com/audio *Dist(s):* **Random Hse., Inc..**

Random Hse. Children's Bks., *(0-307; 0-375; 0-385; 0-394; 0-440; 0-676; 0-679; 1-58836; 1-4000)* Div. of Random Hse., Inc., Orders Addr.: 400 Hahn Rd., Westminster, MD 21157 Tel 410-848-1900; Toll Free: 800-726-0600; Edit Addr.: 1540 Broadway, New York, NY 10036 Tel 212-782-8491; Fax: 212-782-9577; Toll Free: 800-200-3552; *Imprints:* Delacorte Books for Young Readers (Delacorte Bks); Lamb, Wendy (Wendy Lamb); Fickling, David Books (D Fickling Bks); RH Para Ninos (ParaNinos); Dell Books for Young Readers (DBYR); Knopf Books for Young Readers (Knop); RH/Disney (RH Disney); Golden Books (Gold Bks); Random House Books for Young Readers (RHBYR); Bantam Books for Young Readers (BBYngRead); Doubleday Books for Young Readers (Doubleday Bk Yng); Yearling (Year); Dragonfly Books (Dragonfly Bks); Laurel Leaf (LaurelLeaf); Skylark (SkylarkRH); Starfire (Starfire); Sweet Valley (Sweet Valley) E-mail: kids@random.com; pmuller@randomhouse.com *Dist(s):* **Libros Sin Fronteras**
Random Hse., Inc..

Random House Home Video *See* **Random Hse. Video**

†Random Hse., Inc., *(0-307; 0-345; 0-375; 0-394; 0-553; 0-676; 0-679; 0-87665; 1-58836; 1-4000)* Div. of Bertelsmann AG, Orders Addr.: 400 Hahn Rd., Westminster, MD 21157 (SAN 202-5515) Tel 410-848-1900; Toll Free Fax: 800-659-2436; Toll Free: 800-726-0600 (customer service/orders); Edit Addr.: 1540 Broadway, New York, NY 10036 (SAN 202-5507) Tel 212-782-9000; Fax: 212-302-7985 E-mail: customerservice@randomhouse.com Web site: http://www.randomhouse.com *Dist(s):* **Giron Bks.**
Knopf, Alfred A. Inc.
Libros Sin Fronteras; *CIP.*

Random Hse. Information Group, *(0-375; 0-679; 1-4000)* Div. of Random Hse., Inc., Orders Addr.: 400 Hahn Rd., Westminster, MD 21157 Tel 410-848-1900; Toll Free: 800-726-0600; Edit Addr.: 280 Park Ave., New York, NY 10022 Tel 212-751-2600; Toll Free: 800-726-0600 E-mail: customerservice@randomhouse.com Web site: http://www.randomhouse.com/ *Dist(s):* **Bilingual Pubns. Co., The**
Libros Sin Fronteras
Random Hse., Inc..

Random House Reference & Information Publishing *See* **Random Hse. Information Group**

†Random Hse. Value Publishing, *(0-517; 0-609; 0-87000; 1-4000)* Div. of Random Hse., Diversified Pub. Group, Orders Addr.: 400 Hahn Rd., Westminster, MD 21157 Toll Free: 800-733-3000 (orders); 800-726-0600 (customer service, credit, electronic ordering dept.); Edit Addr.: 280 Park Ave., 11th Flr., New York, NY 10017 Tel 212-572-2400; *Imprints:* Gramercy (Gram) Web site: http://www.randomhouse.com *Dist(s):* **Random Hse., Inc.;** *CIP.*

Random Hse. Video, *(0-394; 0-679; 1-4000)* Orders Addr.: 400 Hahn Rd., Westminster, MD 21157 Tel 410-848-1900; Toll Free: 800-726-0600; Edit Addr.: 1540 Broadway, New York, NY 10036 Tel 212-782-9000 *Dist(s):* **Libros Sin Fronteras**
Random Hse., Inc..

Random Hse. Bks. for Young Readers Imprint of Random Hse. Children's Bks.

Random Hse. of Canada, Ltd. (CAN) *(0-09; 0-375; 0-394; 0-676; 0-679) Dist. by* **Random.**

Random Hse. UK, Ltd. (GBR) *(0-09; 0-224; 0-7126) Dist. by* **Trafalgar.**

Raphael, Morris Bks., *(0-9608866)* 1404 Bayou Side Dr., New Iberia, LA 70560 (SAN 241-0737) Tel 337-369-3220 *Dist(s):* **Cajun Country Distributors**
Forest Sales & Distributing Co..

Rascal Publishing, *(0-9671996)* HC 84 Box 50, Canyon City, OR 97820-9701 Tel 541-575-0545; Fax: 541-575-2915.

Raspberry Pr., Ltd., *(0-929568)* Orders Addr.: P.O. Box One, Dixon, IL 61021-0001 (SAN 250-2194) Tel 815-288-4910; Edit Addr.: 1989 Grand Detour Rd., Dixon, IL 61021 (SAN 250-2208) E-mail: raspberrypresslimited@yahoo.com *Dist(s):* **Baker & Taylor Bks.**
Brodart Co.
Quality Bks., Inc..

Ratna Pustak Bhandar (NPL) *Dist. by* **St Mut.**

Rattle OK Pubns., *(0-9626210; 1-883965)* Orders Addr.: P.O. Box 5614, Napa, CA 94581 (SAN 297-5475) Tel 707-253-9641; Edit Addr.: 296 Homewood Ave., Napa, CA 94558-5617 *Dist(s):* **Gryphon Hse., Inc..**

Ravan Pr. (ZMB) *(0-86975) Dist. by* **Ohio U Pr.**

Raven Productions, Inc.., *(0-9677057)* Orders Addr.: P.O. Box 188, Ely, MN 55731-0188 Tel 218-365-3375 ; Edit Addr.: 1575 Grant McMahon Blvd., Ely, MN 55731-0188 Do not confuse with companies with the same name in Venice, CA, Delta Junction, AK E-mail: astewartu@aol.com *Dist(s):* **Adventure Pubns., Inc..**

Raven Publishing *See* **Raven Publishing of Montana**

Raven Publishing of Montana, *(0-9714161)* Orders Addr.: P.O. Box 2885, Norris, MT 59745-2885 (SAN 254-5861) Tel 406-685-3545; Fax: 406-685-3599; Toll Free: 866-685-3545; Edit Addr.: 10 Cherry Creek Rd., Norris, MT 59745 Do not confuse with companies with the same or similar name in Bronx, NY, Pittsfield, MA E-mail: Janet@ravenpublishing.net Web site: http://www.ravenpublishing.net *Dist(s):* **Baker & Taylor Bks.**
Books West
Distributors, The
Quality Bks., Inc.
Wolverine Distributing, Inc..

Raven Rocks Pr., *(0-9615961)* 53650 Belmont Ridge, Beallsville, OH 43716 (SAN 696-5679) Tel 740-926-1481 (phone/fax) E-mail: jmrpress@1st.net.

Raven Tree Pr., LLC, *(0-9701107; 0-9720192; 0-9724973; 0-9741992)* 200 S. Washington St., Suite 306, Green Bay, WI 54301 (SAN 253-6005) Tel 920-438-1605; Fax: 920-438-1607; Toll Free: 877-256-0579 E-mail: amy@raventreepress.com; dawn@raventreepress.com Web site: http://www.raventreepress.com *Dist(s):* **Baker & Taylor Bks.**
FaithWorks
Follett Media Distribution.

Ravenstone Pr., *(0-9659712)* Orders Addr.: P.O. Box 1791, Manhattan, KS 66505-1791 Tel 785-776-0556; Fax: 785-776-0668; Edit Addr.: 804 Moro St., Manhattan, KS 66502 E-mail: raven@ravenstonepress.com Web site: http://www.ravenstonepress.com *Dist(s):* **Baker & Taylor Bks.**
Booksource, The.

Rayo Imprint of HarperTrade

Rays of Hope, *(0-9658766)* P.O. Box 336, Angwim, CA 94508 Tel 707-965-9400 E-mail: Romigram@aol.com.

Rayve Productions, Inc., *(1-877810)* Orders Addr.: P.O. Box 726, Windsor, CA 95492 (SAN 248-4250) Tel 707-838-6200; 707-544-7424 (phone/fax); Fax: 707-838-2220; Toll Free: 800-852-4890 E-mail: rayvepro@aol.com Web site: http://www.rayveproductions.com *Dist(s):* **Baker & Taylor Bks.**
Book Wholesalers, Inc.
Brodart Co.
Follett Library Resources
Majors, J. A. Co.
Quality Bks., Inc.
Sunbelt Pubns., Inc.
Unique Bks., Inc..

Read-A-Bol Group, The, *(0-938155)* Orders Addr.: 199 N. El Camino Real F-137, Encinitas, CA 92024 (SAN 242-1135); Edit Addr.: 301 Village Run, E., Encinitas, CA 92024 (SAN 659-8994) Tel 760-753-0663.

†Reader's Digest Assn., Inc., The, *(0-7621; 0-89577; 0-86438)* Orders Addr.: Reader's Digest Rd., Pleasantville, NY 10570 (SAN 282-2091) Toll Free: 800-334-9599 (Magazines); 800-463-8820 Web site: http://www.readersdigest.com *Dist(s):* **Leonard, Hal Corp.**
Penguin Group (USA) Inc.
Simon & Schuster, Inc.; *CIP.*

Reader's Digest Children's Bks. Imprint of Reader's Digest Children's Publishing, Inc.

Reader's Digest Children's Publishing, Inc., *(0-276; 0-7621; 0-88705; 0-88850; 0-89577; 1-57584; 1-57619; 0-7944)* Subs. of Reader's Digest Assn., Inc., Reader's Digest Rd., Pleasantville, NY 10570-7000 (SAN 283-2143) Tel 914-244-4800; Fax: 914-244-4841; *Imprints:* Reader's Digest Children's Books (RD Childrens); Reader's Digest Young Families, Incorporated (RDYF) Web site: http://www.readersdigestkids.com *Dist(s):* **Continental Bk. Co., Inc.**
Simon & Schuster Children's Publishing
Simon & Schuster, Inc..

Reader's Digest Young Families, Inc. Imprint of Reader's Digest Children's Publishing, Inc.

Reading Research Imprint of ARO Publishing Co.

Real Kids Real Adventures, *(1-928591)* Orders Addr.: P.O. Box 461572, 1102 Pyramid Dr., 1st Flr., Garland, TX 75040 Fax: 972-414-2839; Toll Free: 800-473-2538 E-mail: books@realkids.com Web site: http://www.realkids.com *Dist(s):* **BookMasters, Inc.**
Perfection Learning Corp..

Real Life Storybooks, *(1-882388)* 8370 Kentland Ave., West Hills, CA 91304 Tel 818-887-6431; Fax: 818-887-4541.

Rebecca Hse., *(0-945522)* 1550 California St., Suite 330, San Francisco, CA 94109 (SAN 247-1361) Tel 415-752-1453; Toll Free: 800-321-1912 (orders only) E-mail: Rebeccahse@aol.com *Dist(s):* **New Leaf Distributing Co., Inc..**

Reconciliation Pr. Imprint of Trinity Rivers Publishing, Inc.

Recorded Bks., LLC, *(0-7887; 1-55690; 1-84197; 1-4025)* 270 Skipjack Rd., Prince Frederick, MD 20678 (SAN 677-8887) Toll Free: 800-638-1304 E-mail: recordedbooks@recordedbooks.com Web site: http://www.recordedbooks.com.

Red Bird Publishing, *(0-9665072)* Div. of Darlene Trew Crist Writing & Editorial Services, 54 Church Ln., Wickford, RI 02852-5004 Tel 401-295-1356; Fax: 401-295-2793.

Red Carpet Publishing, *(0-9719657; 0-9722829)* P.O. Box 309, Noblesville, IN 46061-0309 (SAN 255-755X) Tel 317-847-9553; Fax: 317-773-5375 Web site: http://www.redcarpetpublishing.com.

†Red Crane Bks., Inc., *(1-878610)* Orders Addr.: P.O. Box 33590, Santa Fe, NM 87954; Edit Addr.: 2008 Rosina St., Suite C, Santa Fe, NM 87505 Tel 505-988-7070; Fax: 505-989-7476; Toll Free: 800-922-3392 E-mail: publish@redcrane.com Web site: http://www.redcrane.com *Dist(s):* **Consortium Bk. Sales & Distribution**
Continental Bk. Co., Inc.
Libros Sin Fronteras; *CIP.*

Red Fox Publishing Co., *(0-9677953)* 1839 NE 14th St., No. 615, Portland, OR 97212-4348 Tel 503-288-1007 Do not confuse with companies with the same or similar name in Belleuve, WA, Middletown, DE, Conifer, CO.

Names

†**Red Hen Pr.,** *(0-931093)* P.O. Box 454, Big Sur, CA 93920 (SAN 678-9420) Tel 831-667-2726 (phone/fax) Do not confuse with Red Hen Pr., Casa Grande, AZ
E-mail: HopeHen@aol.com
Dist(s): **Baker & Taylor Bks.**
Book Wholesalers, Inc.
Brodart Co.
Follett Library Resources; *CIP.*

Red Wagon Bks. Imprint of Harcourt Children's Bks.

Red Wolf Publications *See* **Red Wolf Publishing**

Red Wolf Publishing, *(0-9661687)* 2319 Merton, No. 3, Los Angeles, CA 90041 Tel 213-257-8559; Fax: 213-255-5900
E-mail: vozeta@loop.com.

Redbud Publishing Co., *(0-9720293)* P.O. Box 4402, Victoria, TX 77903-4402 Tel 361-572-8898 (phone/fax); 361-572-8881 (phone/fax) Do not confuse with Redbud Publishing Company in Tulsa, OK
E-mail: firebirds@cox-internet.com
Web site: http://www.redbudpublishing.com.

Redding Pr., *(0-9658879)* Orders Addr.: c/o Mary Mahony, P.O. Box 366, Belmont, MA 02178 Fax: 617-489-9476; Toll Free: 800-267-6012; Edit Addr.: 405 Concord Ave., Belmont, MA 02178
E-mail: msmahony@channel.com
Web site: http://www.channel.com/users/msmahony
Dist(s): **Baker & Taylor Bks.**
Koen Bk. Distributors
Quality Bks., Inc..

Redhawk Publishing, *(0-9641861)* 602 W. Pompa, Carlsbad, NM 88220
E-mail: rjr1095@hotmail.com
Web site: http://www.rwpbooks.bravepages.com
Dist(s): **Booksurge, LLC.**

Redleaf Pr., *(0-934140; 1-884834; 1-929610)* Div. of Resources for Child Caring, Inc., 450 N. Syndicate, Suite 5, Saint Paul, MN 55104 (SAN 212-8691) Tel 651-641-0305; Toll Free Fax: 800-641-0115; Toll Free: 800-423-8309
E-mail: jwurm@redleafpress.org; aholzman@redleafpress.org
Dist(s): **Consortium Bk. Sales & Distribution**
Gryphon Hse., Inc.
Lectorum Pubns., Inc..

Reef Publishing, *(0-9642652)* 1055 Neptune Ave., Leucadia, CA 92024 Tel 760-944-1300; Fax: 760-944-1188.

Reeve, Phyllis, *(0-9725590)* 829 Park Ln., Grosse Pointe Park, MI 48230 Tel 313-331-2378
E-mail: mpreeve@msn.com.

Regal Bks. Imprint of Gospel Light Pubns.

Regal Publications *See* **University Publishing Hse., Inc.**

Regina Pr., Malhame & Co., *(0-88271)* P.O. Box 608, Melville, NY 11747-0608 (SAN 203-0853) Tel 631-694-8600
E-mail: customerservice@malhame.com
Web site: http://www.malhame.com/.

Reivers Pr., *(0-9663764)* 3553 Eugene Pl., San Diego, CA 921166 Tel 619-584-1841.

Remember Productions *See* **JMS Productions**

Renaissance Bks. Imprint of St. Martin's Pr.

Replica Bks., *(0-7351)* Div. of Baker & Taylor, Orders Addr.: 1200 US Hwy., 22 E., Bridgewater, NJ 08807 Tel 908-541-7392; Fax: 908-541-7875; Toll Free: 800-775-1800; Edit Addr.: P.O. Box 6885, Bridgewater, NJ 08807-0885
E-mail: btinfo@baker-taylor.com.

†**Reprint Services Corp.,** *(0-7812; 0-932051)* P.O. Box 890820, Temecula, CA 92589-0820 (SAN 686-2640) Tel 909-296-3388; Fax: 909-767-0133; Toll Free: 800-273-6635
Web site: http://www.reprintservices.com; *CIP.*

Republic of Texas Pr. Imprint of Wordware Publishing, Inc.

Research Evaluation & Statistics *See* **Image Cascade Publishing**

Research Triangle Publishing, *(1-884570)* Orders Addr.: P.O. Box 1130, Fuquay Varina, NC 27526 Fax: 919-557-2161; Toll Free: 800-941-0020; Edit Addr.: 503 N. Ennis St., Fuquay Varina, NC 27526
E-mail: info@tripub.com
Web site: http://www.RTPWeb.com/BooksExpress.

†**Resource Pubns., Inc.,** *(0-89390)* 160 E. Virginia St., No. 290, San Jose, CA 95112-5876 (SAN 209-3081) Tel 408-286-8505; Fax: 408-287-8748; Toll Free: 888-273-7782 Do not confuse with Resource Pubns. in Los Angeles, CA
E-mail: info@rpinet.com
Web site: http://www.rpinet.com
Dist(s): **Empire Publishing Service**
Feldheim, Philipp Inc.; *CIP.*

Resources for Creative Teaching *See* **Nellie Edge Resources, Inc.**

Revelation I Publishing, *(1-890795)* P.O. Box 3, Antlers, OK 74523 Tel 405-298-6222.

†**Revell, Fleming H. Co.,** *(0-8007; 0-922066; 1-58743)* Div. of Baker Bk. Hse., Orders Addr.: P.O. Box 6287, Grand Rapids, MI 49516-6287 Toll Free Fax: 800-398-3111; Toll Free: 800-877-2665; Edit Addr.: 6030 E. Fulton, Ada, MI 49301 Tel 616-676-9185; Fax: 616-676-9573; *Imprints:* Spire (Spire)
E-mail: sharlow@bakerbooks.com
Web site: http://www.bakerbooks.com
Dist(s): **Baker Bk. Hse., Inc.**; *CIP.*

†**Review & Herald Publishing Assn.,** *(0-8127; 0-8280)* 55 W. Oak Ridge Dr., Hagerstown, MD 21740 (SAN 203-3798) Tel 301-393-3000
E-mail: Information@rhpa.org
Web site: http://www.reviewandherald.com/
Dist(s): **Spring Arbor Distributors, Inc.**; *CIP.*

RH Audio Imprint of Random Hse. Audio Publishing Group

RH Para Ninos Imprint of Random Hse. Children's Bks.

RH/Disney Imprint of Random Hse. Children's Bks.

Rhette Enterprises, Inc., *(0-9702319)* 3316 Shorewood Ave., Fort Gratiot, MI 48059 Tel 810-385-9416; Fax: 810-385-2304
E-mail: bobjan@futureone.com.

Rhino Entertainment, *(0-7379; 0-930589; 1-56826)* 10635 Santa Monica Blvd., Los Angeles, CA 90025-4900 (SAN 677-5454) Tel 310-474-4778; 888-622-9647; Fax: 310-441-6575
E-mail: drrhino@rhino.com
Web site: http://www.rhino.com.

Rhyme Tyme Pubns., *(0-9639486)* 2746 Danbury Dr., New Orleans, LA 70131-3848 (SAN 298-1343).

Ricara Features, *(0-911737)* Div. of Mohawk Nation Publishing Co., P.O. Box 664, Sanborn, NY 14132 (SAN 264-3472) Tel 519-445-2748; Fax: 519-445-1235
E-mail: ricara@attglobal.net
Dist(s): **Baker & Taylor Bks.**
Brodart Co.
Greenfield Review Literary Ctr., Inc..

Ridyl Publishing, *(1-889736)* 2118 Wilshire Blvd., Suite 467, Santa Monica, CA 90403 Tel 310-392-9544 ; Toll Free: 800-390-9920.

†**Rienner, Lynne Pubs., Inc.,** *(0-89410; 0-931477; 1-55587; 1-58826)* 1800 30th St., Suite 314, Boulder, CO 80301-1026 (SAN 683-1869) Tel 303-444-6684; Fax: 303-444-0824; *Imprints:* Three Continents (Three Contnts)
E-mail: sglover@rienner.com; questions@rienner.com; cservice@rienner.com
Web site: http://www.rienner.com
Dist(s): **Women Ink**; *CIP.*

Riley, Janeway, *(0-9637378)* 311 Garfield Ave., Eau Claire, WI 54701 Tel 715-834-1989
Dist(s): **Independent Pubs. Marketing.**

Rinehart, Roberts International Imprint of Rinehart, Roberts Pubs.

Rinehart, Roberts Pubs., *(0-911797; 0-943173; 1-57098; 1-57140; 1-879373; 1-58979)* Orders Addr.: 4720 Boston Way, Lanhan, MD 20706 Tel 301-459-3366; Toll Free Fax: 800-238-4650; Toll Free: 800-462-6420; Edit Addr.: c/o Rowman & Littlefield Publishing Group, 5360 Manhattan Cir., No. 101, Boulder, CO 80303 (SAN 264-3510) Tel 303-543-7835; *Imprints:* Rinehart, Roberts International (R Rinehart Intl)
E-mail: books@robertsrinehart.com
Web site: http://www.robertsrinehart.com
Dist(s): **National Bk. Network**
Rowman & Littlefield Pubs., Inc.
netLibrary, Inc..

Rip Off Pr., Inc., *(0-89620)* P.O. Box 4686, Auburn, CA 95604 (SAN 207-7671) Tel 530-885-8183; Fax: 530-885-8219; Toll Free: 800-468-2669
E-mail: ripoff@jps.net
Web site: http://www.ripoffpress.com.

Riplah Publishing, *(1-890830)* 2728 Country Green, Henderson, NV 89014 Tel 702-263-4993 (phone/fax)
E-mail: Riplah@aol.com
Web site: http://www.jumpkicks.com
Dist(s): **Origin Bk. Sales, Inc..**

Rising Eagle Pubs., *(0-9651559)* 13100 Shawnee Ln., 280G, Seal Beach, CA 90740 Tel 562-596-7566; Fax: 562-430-1097
E-mail: Risingeagle9@cs.com
Dist(s): **Baker & Taylor Bks.**
L-W Bk. Sales
Partners Pubs. Group, Inc..

Rising Moon Bks. for Young Readers Imprint of Northland Publishing

Rising Star Publishers *See* **WeWrite Corp.**

River City Publishing, *(0-913515; 0-9622815; 1-57966; 1-880216; 1-881320)* 1719 Mulberry St., Montgomery, AL 36106 (SAN 631-4910) Tel 334-265-6753; Fax: 334-265-8880; Toll Free: 877-408-7078; *Imprints:* Black Belt Press (Black Belt); Elliott & Clark (Elliott Clark) Do not confuse with companies with the same or similar names in Richland, WA, South Bend, IN
E-mail: sales@rivercitypublishing.com
Web site: http://www.rivercitypublishing.com.

River Road Pubns., Inc., *(0-938682)* 830 E. Savidge St., Spring Lake, MI 49456 (SAN 253-8172) Tel 616-842-6920; Fax: 616-842-0084; Toll Free: 800-373-8762
E-mail: socialstudies@riverroadpublications.com
Web site: http://www.riverroadpublications.com
Dist(s): **Partners Pubs. Group, Inc..**

River Walker Bks., *(0-9637288)* 3334 Wyandot St., Denver, CO 80211 Tel 303-480-5009.

Rivercity Pr. Imprint of Amereon, Ltd.

Rivercrest Industries, *(1-878908)* P.O. Box 771662, Houston, TX 77215-1662 Tel 281-565-3055; Fax: 281-565-3057
E-mail: info@rivercrestindustries.com
Web site: http://www.rivercrestindustries.com.

†**Rivercross Publishing, Inc.,** *(0-944957; 1-58141)* 6214 Wynfield Ct., Orlando, FL 32819 (SAN 245-6826) Tel 407-876-7720; Fax: 407-876-7758; Toll Free: 800-451-4522
E-mail: editor@rivercross.com
Web site: http://www.rivercross.com; *CIP.*

RiverMoon Bks., *(0-9647811)* Orders Addr.: P.O. Box 532, Stony Brook, NY 11790-0532 (SAN 298-8275) Tel 516-246-5881; Edit Addr.: 5 Beech Ln., Stony Brook, NY 11790 (SAN 298-8283).

RiverOak Publishing, *(1-58919)* Div. of Honor Bks., 2448 E. 81st St., Suite 4400, Tulsa, OK 74137-4322 Toll Free Fax: 877-663-1241; Toll Free: 800-493-2813
Dist(s): **Cook Communications Ministries.**

Riverpark Publishing Co., *(0-915029)* 3680 Little Rock Dr., Provo, UT 84604 (SAN 289-8217) Toll Free: 800-224-1606
E-mail: garyjoy@itsnet.com
Dist(s): **Baker & Taylor Bks..**

Riverside Editions Imprint of Houghton Mifflin Co.

Rivet Bks. Imprint of Feral Pr., Inc.

†**Rizzoli International Pubns., Inc.,** *(0-8478)* Subs. of RCS Rizzoli Editore Corp., 300 Park Ave., S., 3rd Flr., New York, NY 10010 (SAN 111-9192) Tel 212-387-3400; Fax: 212-387-3535
Dist(s): **Distributed Art Pubs./D.A.P.**
St. Martin's Pr.; *CIP.*

RKO Enterprises, *(0-9718034)* P.O. Box 117, LaGrange, IL 60525-0117
E-mail: oshea928@earthlink.net.

Roaring Brook Pr. Imprint of Millbrook Pr., Inc.

Robbie Dean Pr., *(0-9630608; 1-889743)* 2910 E. Eisenhower Pkwy., Ann Arbor, MI 48108 Tel 313-973-9511; Fax: 313-973-9475
E-mail: fairyha@aol.com.

Robinson Pubs., *(0-9718091)* P.O. Box 189, New London, NC 28127-0189 Tel 704-463-0213
E-mail: robinson@vnet.net
Web site: http://www.australiancowboy.com.

ROC Imprint of NAL

Rock Creek Pr., LLC, *(1-890826)* Orders Addr.: P.O. Box 4929, Springfield, MO 65808-4929; Edit Addr.: 1111 Bldg., Suite 2-100, 1111 S. Glenstone Ave., Springfield, MS 65808 Tel 417-887-9560
E-mail: gene3000@hotmail.com
Dist(s): **Baker & Taylor Bks..**

Rocking Horse Pr., *(0-932306)* 32 Ellise Rd., Storrs, CT 06268 (SAN 212-4467) Tel 860-429-1474.

Rocky Mountain West Co., *(1-891126)* P.O. Box 788, West Jordan, UT 84084-0459 Tel 801-567-9320.

Rocky River Pubs., LLC, *(0-944576)* P.O. Box 1679, Shepherdstown, WV 25443 (SAN 243-9409) Tel 304-876-2711; Fax: 304-263-2949; Toll Free: 800-343-0686
E-mail: rockyriv@intrepid.net
Web site: http://www.rockyriver.com
Dist(s): **Academic Bk. Ctr., Inc.**
Baker & Taylor Bks.
Follett Library Resources
Waldenbooks, Inc..

Rod & Staff Pubs., Inc., *(0-7399)* P.O. Box 3, 14193 Hwy. 172, Crockett, KY 41413 (SAN 206-7633) Tel 606-522-4348; Fax: 606-522-4896; Toll Free Fax: 800-643-1244.

Names

RoKarn Pubns., *(0-9625502)* Orders Addr.: P.O. Box 195, Nokesville, VA 22123 Toll Free: 800-869-0563; Edit Addr.: 8534 Stonewall Rd., Manassas, VA 22110 Tel 703-330-8249.

Ro-Land of Michigan *See* **Star Image Studio**

Roman, Inc., *(0-937739)* 555 Lawrence Ave., Roselle, IL 60172-1599 Fax: 630-529-1121; Toll Free: 800-729-7662
Web site: http://www.roman.com.

Ronald, George Pub., Ltd., *(0-85398)* 8325 17th St., N., Saint Petersburg, FL 33702-2843 (SAN 679-1859) ; 24 Gardiner Close Abingdon, Oxon, OX14 3YA Tel 01235 529137.

Ronan, Anne M. *See* **Polka Dot Pr. Corp., The**

Roscoe Village Foundation, Inc., *(1-880443)* 381 Hill St., Coshocton, OH 43812 Tel 614-622-7644; Fax: 614-622-2222.

Rose Window Pr., The, *(0-916634)* 16455 Tuba St., North Hills, CA 91343 (SAN 213-9510) Tel 818-360-3166.

†Rosen Publishing Group, Inc., The, *(0-8239; 1-4042)* a/o Dept. C234561, 29 E. 21st St., New York, NY 10010 (SAN 203-3720) Tel 212-777-3017; Fax: 212-777-0277; Toll Free: 800-237-9932; *Imprints:* PowerKids Press (PowerKids Pr)
E-mail: ginas@rosenpub.com
Web site: http://www.rosenpublishing.com
Dist(s): **Lectorum Pubns., Inc.**; *CIP.*

Rosholt Hse., *(0-910417)* 406 River Dr., Rosholt, WI 54473-9557 (SAN 260-1249) Tel 715-677-4722.

†Rossel Bks., *(0-940646)* Div. of R. C. C., Inc., 1228 Hardscrabble Rd., Chappaqua, NY 10514 Tel 914-238-3852; Toll Free: 800-221-2755 (orders only)
E-mail: srossel@rossel.net
Web site: http://www.rossel.net
Dist(s): **Behrman Hse., Inc.**; *CIP.*

Roundtable Publishing, *(0-915677)* P.O. Box 6488, Malibu, CA 90264-6488 (SAN 237-9260) Tel 310-457-8433 Do not confuse with Roundtable Publishing, Mesa, AZ
E-mail: joe@californiaunderwater.com.

Rourke Enterprises, Inc., *(0-86592)* Div. of Rourke Publishing Group, P.O. Box 3328, Vero Beach, FL 32964-3328 Tel 561-234-6001; Fax: 561-234-6622
E-mail: rourke@sunet.net
Web site: http://www.rourkepublishing.com.

Rourke Publishing, LLC, *(0-86592; 0-86593; 0-86625; 1-55916; 1-57103; 1-58952; 1-59515)* Orders Addr.: P.O. Box 3328, Vero Beach, FL 32963 Tel 561-234-6001; Fax: 561-234-6622; Toll Free: 800-394-7055
E-mail: rourke@rourkepublishing.com
Web site: http://www.rourkepublishing.com.

Rourke, Ray Publishing Company, Incorporated *See* **Rourke Enterprises, Inc.**

Roussan Pubs., Inc./Roussan Editeur, Inc. (CAN) *(1-896184; 2-921212; 2-9800915) Dist. by* **Orca Bk Pubs.**

†Routledge, *(0-04; 0-413; 0-415; 0-7100; 0-86861; 0-87830)* Mem. of Taylor & Frances Group, Orders Addr.: 7625 Empire Dr., Florence, KY 41042 Toll Free Fax: 800-248-4724 (orders, customer serv.); Toll Free: 800-634-7064 (orders, customer serv.); Edit Addr.: 29 W. 35th St., New York, NY 10001-2299 (SAN 213-196X) Tel 212-216-7800; Fax: 212-564-7854
E-mail: info@routledge-ny.com; cserve@routledge-ny.com
Web site: http://www.routledge-ny.com
Dist(s): **Taylor & Francis, Inc.**
Women Ink
netLibrary, Inc.; *CIP.*

Rowfant Pr., *(1-929731)* 2401 W. 27th St., N., Wichita, KS 67204 Tel 316-832-0309
E-mail: rowfant@hotmail.com
Web site: http://www.expage.com/RowfantPress
Dist(s): **Booksource, The.**

Rowohlt Taschenbuch Verlag GmbH (DEU) *(3-499) Dist. by* **Distribks Inc.**

Roxbury Park Imprint of Lowell Hse.

Roxbury Park Juvenile Imprint of Lowell Hse. Juvenile

Royal Fireworks Publishing Co., *(0-88092; 0-89824)* Orders Addr.: P.O. Box 399, Unionville, NY 10988 (SAN 240-2394) Tel 845-726-4444; Fax: 845-726-3824; Edit Addr.: 1 First Ave., Unionville, NY 10988
E-mail: rfpress@frontiernet.net
Dist(s): **Baker & Taylor Bks..**

R-Squared Press *See* **Insight**

rt Services International *See* **Art Services International**

Rufus Pr., *(0-9655349)* Orders Addr.: c/o Best Friends, P.O. Box 392, Kanab, UT 84741 Tel 435-644-2001; Fax: 435-644-2078.

Rundle, Vesta M., *(1-882672)* 2251 Fourth St., Charleston, IL 61920 Tel 217-345-2560
E-mail: vrundle@worthlink.net.

Runestone Pr. Imprint of Lerner Publishing Group

†Running Pr. Bk. Pubs., *(0-7624; 0-89471; 0-914294; 1-56138)* Div. of Perseus Books Group, 125 S. 22nd St., Philadelphia, PA 19103-4399 (SAN 204-5702) Tel 215-567-5080; Fax: 215-568-2919; Toll Free Fax: 800-453-2884; Toll Free: 800-345-5359 customer service; *Imprints:* Courage Books (Courage)
E-mail: support@runningpress.com
Web site: http://www.runningpress.com
Dist(s): **HarperCollins Pubs.**; *CIP.*

Rust Foundation for Literacy, Inc., The, *(1-885848)* 12021 Wilshire Blvd., No. 924, Los Angeles, CA 90025 Tel 818-386-1383; Fax: 818-784-1325; Toll Free: 800-676-9951; *Imprints:* Power for Kids Press (Power for Kids)
E-mail: PowerforKids@aol.com
Dist(s): **Penton Overseas, Inc..**

Rust, Patricia Productions *See* **Rust Foundation for Literacy, Inc., The**

†Rutgers Univ. Pr., *(0-8135)* 100 Joyce Kilmer Ave., Piscataway, NJ 08854-8099 (SAN 253-2115) Tel 732-445-7762; Fax: 732-445-7039; Toll Free Fax: 888-471-9014; Toll Free: 800-446-9323 (orders)
Web site: http://rutgerspress.rutgers.edu; *CIP.*

Rutledge Hill Pr., *(0-934395; 1-55853; 1-4016)* 501 Nelson Pl., Nashville, TN 37214 Tel 615-889-9000; 615-244-2700; Toll Free: 800-251-4000
E-mail: NelsonDirect@ThomasNelson.com
Web site: http://www.rutledgehillpress,com.

Rx Humor, *(0-9639002; 1-892157)* 2272 Vistamont Dr., Decatur, GA 30033 Tel 404-321-0126; Fax: 404-633-9198
E-mail: nshulma@emory.edu.

SBP Collaboratioin Works, *(1-889664)* 1414 Forest Ave. Apt. 16, Portland, ME 04103-1161.

S V E & Churchill Media, *(0-7932; 0-89290; 1-56357)* 6677 N. Northwest Hwy., Chicago, IL 60631-1304 (SAN 208-3930) Tel 773-775-9550; Fax: 773-775-5091; Toll Free Fax: 800-624-1678; Toll Free: 800-829-1900
E-mail: custserv@svemedia.com
Web site: http://www.svemedia.com
Dist(s): **Video Project, The**
Weston Woods Studios, Inc..

†SYDA Foundation, *(0-911307; 0-914602; 1-930939)* 371 Brickman Rd., South Fallsburg, NY 12779 (SAN 206-5649) Tel 845-434-2000 Toll Free Fax: 888-422-2339 (ordering); Toll Free: 888-422-3334 (ordering); P.O. Box 600, South Fallsburg, NY 12779 ; *Imprints:* Siddha Yoga Publication (Siddha Yoga Pubs)
Web site: http://www.siddhayoga.org
Dist(s): **Bookpeople**
New Leaf Distributing Co., Inc.
Words Distributing Co.; *CIP.*

S.A. Kokinos (ESP) *(84-88342) Dist. by* **Lectorum Pubns.**

Saddleback Publishing, Inc., *(1-56254)* Three Watson, Irvine, CA 92618-2716 Tel 949-860-2500; Fax: 949-860-2508; Toll Free: 800-637-8715
E-mail: info@sdlback.com
Web site: http://www.sdlback.com.

Sadlier, William H. Inc., *(0-8215; 0-87105)* 9 Pine St., New York, NY 10005-1002 (SAN 204-0948) Tel 212-227-2120; Fax: 212-312-6080; Toll Free: 800-221-5175; *Imprints:* Sadlier-Oxford (Sadlier-Oxford)
E-mail: customerservice@sadlier.com
Web site: http://www.sadlier.com.

Sadlier-Oxford Imprint of Sadlier, William H. Inc.

Sage, Joan, *(0-9669813)* 914 Kimball St., Philadelphia, PA 19147.

Saifer, Albert Pub., *(0-87556)* P.O. Box 7125, Watchung, NJ 07060 (SAN 204-7225).

Saint Martin's Griffin Imprint of St. Martin's Pr.

Saint Martin's Minotaur Imprint of St. Martin's Pr.

St. Mary's Pr., *(0-88489)* 702 Terrace Heights, Winona, MN 55987-1320 (SAN 203-073X) Tel 507-457-7900; Toll Free Fax: 800-344-9225; Toll Free: 800-533-8095
E-mail: smpress@smp.org
Web site: http://www.smp.org.

Saint Paul Books & Media *See* **Pauline Bks. & Media**

Salina Bookshelf, *(0-9644189; 1-893354)* 1254 W. University Ave., Suite 130, Flagstaff, AZ 86001 (SAN 253-0503) Tel 928-773-0066; Fax: 928-526-0386; Toll Free: 877-527-0070
E-mail: sales@salinabookshelf.com
Web site: http://www.salinabookshelf.com.

Salt Marsh Pubns., *(1-929202)* 163 Grand Oak Cir., Venice, FL 34292 Tel 941-484-9953; Toll Free: 888-441-2436
E-mail: smp@coastalnet.com
Dist(s): **Baker & Taylor Bks.**
Parnassus Bk. Distributors
Southern Bk. Service.

Samary Pr., *(0-9630798)* 201 E. Southern Ave., No. 24, Apache Junction, AZ 85219-3740; 675 W. Cotati Ave., Cotati, CA 94931 Tel 707-664-8598.

Sanctuary Pr., *(0-9676438)* 11566 S. Newman Rd., Maple City, MI 49664 Tel 616-228-4262 Do not confuse with companies with the same name in Lenoir, NC, Franklin, NC.

Sand & Silk, *(0-9617284)* Orders Addr.: P.O. Box 816, Calimesa, CA 92320-0816 (SAN 663-5210).

Sandcastle Bks. Imprint of Putnam Publishing Group, The

Sandcastle Bks. Imprint of Penguin Group (USA) Inc.

Sandcastle Bks. Imprint of Penguin Putnam Bks. for Young Readers

†Sandlapper Publishing Co., Inc., *(0-87844)* Orders Addr.: P.O. Box 730, Orangeburg, SC 29115 (SAN 203-2678) Toll Free Fax: 800-337-9420 (orders); Toll Free: 800-849-7263 (orders); Edit Addr.: 1281 Amelia St., NE., Orangeburg, SC 29116 Tel 803-533-1658; Fax: 803-534-5223
Dist(s): **Baker & Taylor Bks.**
Parnassus Bk. Distributors; *CIP.*

Sandpiper Pr., *(0-9658498)* Orders Addr.: P.O. Box 35145, Sarasota, FL 34278 Tel 941-926-9115; Fax: 941-927-7102; Toll Free: 800-557-5333 Do not confuse with companies with the same name in Saint Clair Shores, MI, Brookings, OR, Newport Beach, CA, Solana Beach, CA.

Sandstone Publishing, *(0-9621779)* 2710 Sunnyview Ln., Billings, MT 59102 Tel 406-656-5730.

Sandvik Publishing, *(1-58048; 1-881445)* Div. of Sandviks Bokforlag, Norway, 1 Pearl Buck Ct., Bristol, PA 19007 Tel 215-781-3614; Fax: 215-781-3610; Toll Free: 800-843-2445
E-mail: Nicole@sandvikpublishing.com; cust-serv@sandvikpublishing.com
Web site: http://www.sandviks.com.

Santa & Friends, *(1-880695)* 223 Woodville Rd., Falmouth, ME 04105 Tel 207-797-7752; Toll Free: 800-499-0440.

Santa Ines Pubns., *(0-9644386)* 330 W. Hwy 246, No. 232, Buellton, CA 93427 Tel 805-688-7862
E-mail: hernan@solvang.sbceo.k12.ca.us.

Santa's Publishing, *(0-9642311)* 668 Potomac Ct., San Jose, CA 95136 Tel 408-629-3051; Fax: 408-229-8092
E-mail: brucemcguy@hotmail.com
Web site: http://www.santasholidystore.com.

Santillana (COL) *(958-24) Dist. by* **Santillana.**

Santillana USA Publishing Co., Inc., *(0-88272; 1-56014; 1-58105; 84-294; 1-58986; 1-59437)* Div. of Grup Santillana De Ediciones, S.A., 2105 NW 86th Ave., Miami, FL 33122 (SAN 205-1133) Tel 305-591-9522; Fax: 305-591-9145; Toll Free Fax: 800-530-8099 (orders); Toll Free: 800-245-8584
E-mail: customerservice@santillanausa.com
Web site: http://www.santillanausa.com/
Dist(s): **Baker & Taylor Bks.**
Barnes & Noble, Inc.
Bilingual Pubns. Co., The
Continental Bk. Co., Inc.
Follett Library Resources
Lectorum Pubns., Inc.
Libros Sin Fronteras.

Saphrograph Corp., *(0-87557)* 5409 18th Ave., Brooklyn, NY 11204 (SAN 110-4128) Tel 718-331-1233; Fax: 718-331-8231.

Sasquatch Bks., *(0-912365; 1-57061)* 615 Second Ave., Suite 260, Seattle, WA 98104 (SAN 289-0208) Tel 206-467-4300 (ext 300); Fax: 206-467-4301; Toll Free: 800-775-0817
E-mail: books@sasquatchbooks.com
Web site: http://www.sasquatchbooks.com
Dist(s): **Publishers Group West.**

Sassy Cat Bks. Imprint of Briarwood Pubns.

Saulsman, Helen L., *(0-9663051)* 6455 Anita Dr., Dallas, TX 75214 Tel 214-826-5535; Fax: 972-216-7576.

Names

Savage Bks., *(0-9673000)* 7510 W. Sunset Blvd., Suite 277, Los Angeles, CA 90046-3418 Toll Free: 888-777-4631 Do not confuse with Savage Bks., in Honolulu, HI
E-mail: derek@savage1.com; michelangelo@hawaii.rr.com
Web site: http://SAVAGE1.com.

Savage, Derek Productions *See* **Savage Bks.**

Savage Parks Pr., *(0-9669130)* 25985 Genesee Trail Rd., K-322, Golden, CO 80401 Tel 303-778-1695; Fax: 303-526-1132
E-mail: nancy@nickelbuffalo.com
Web site: http://www.nickelbuffalo.com
Dist(s): **Baker & Taylor Bks.**
Biblio Distribution
Books West.

Scandia Pubs., *(0-937242)* Orders Addr.: 11594 Willamette Meridian NW, Silverdale, WA 98383 (SAN 282-2806) Tel 360-337-7688; Fax: 360-337-7602
E-mail: dorieerick@cs.com.

Scarborough Hse. Imprint of Madison Bks., Inc.

†Scarecrow Pr., Inc., *(0-8108; 1-57886)* Div. of Rowman & Littlefield Publishing Group, Orders Addr.: 15200 NBN Way, Box 191, Blue Ridge Summit, PA 17214 Tel 717-794-3800; Fax: 717-794-3803; Toll Free Fax: 800-338-4550; Toll Free: 800-462-6420; Edit Addr.: 4501 Forbes Blvd., Suite 200, Lanham, MD 20706-4310 (SAN 203-2651) Tel 301-459-3366; Fax: 301-429-5747
E-mail: custserv@rowman.com
Web site: http://www.scarecrowpress.com
Dist(s): **Rowman & Littlefield Pubs., Inc.**; *CIP.*

Scepter Pubs., Inc., *(0-933932; 1-889334; 1-59417)* Orders Addr.: P.O. Box 211, New York, NY 10018 Tel 212-354-0670; Fax: 212-354-0736; 914-632-5502; Toll Free: 800-322-8773; Edit Addr.: Eight W. 38th St., Suite 802, New York, NY 10018
E-mail: general@scepterpublishers.org; orders@scepterpublishers.org
Web site: http://www.scepterpublishers.org.

Scheewe, Susan Pubns., Inc., *(1-56770)* 13435 NE Whitaker Way, Portland, OR 97230 Tel 503-254-9100 ; Fax: 503-252-9508; Toll Free: 800-796-1953
E-mail: scheewepub@aol.com
Web site: http://www.painting-books.com.

Schiffer Publishing, Ltd., *(0-7643; 0-88740; 0-916838)* 4880 Lower Valley Rd., Atglen, PA 19310 (SAN 208-8428) Tel 610-593-1777; Fax: 610-593-2002
E-mail: schifferii@aol.com
Web site: http://www.schifferbooks.com.

Schlifer, Sherry, *(0-9700375)* 239 Ash Ln., Lafayette Hill, PA 19444-2101 Tel 610-828-6427
E-mail: sherbook@aol.com.

Schocken Imprint of Knopf Publishing Group

Schoenhof's Foreign Bks., Inc., *(0-87774)* Subs. of Editions Gallimard, 486 Green St., Cambridge, MA 02139 (SAN 212-0062) Tel 617-547-8855; Fax: 617-547-8551
E-mail: info@schoenhofs.com
Web site: http://www.schoenhofs.com
Dist(s): **Distribooks, Inc..**

†Scholarly Pr., Inc., *(0-403)* P.O. Box 160, Saint Clair Shores, MI 48080 (SAN 209-0473) Tel 810-231-3728 (phone/fax)
Dist(s): **North American Bk. Distributors**; *CIP.*

†Scholars' Facsimiles & Reprints, *(0-8201)* Subs. of Academic Resources Corp., 410 Lenawee Dr., Ann Arbor, MI 48104 (SAN 203-2627) Tel 734-741-0344
E-mail: nm320@columbia.edu; *CIP.*

Scholastic en Espanola Imprint of Scholastic, Inc.

†Scholastic, Inc., *(0-439; 0-590)* Orders Addr.: c/o HarperCollins, 1000 Keystone Industrial Pk., Scranton, PA 18512 Toll Free: 800-242-7737; Edit Addr.: 557 Broadway, New York, NY 10012-3999 (SAN 202-5442) Tel 212-343-6100; Fax: 212-343-6802; Toll Free: 800-325-6149 (customer service); *Imprints:* Cartwheel Books (Cartwheel); Scholastic Reference (Scholastic Ref); Blue Sky Press, The (Blue Sky Press); Levine, Arthur A. Books (A A Levine); Orchard Books (Orchard Bks); Scholastic Press (Scholastic Pr); Chicken House, The (Chick Hse); PUSH (PUSH); Scholastic en Espanola (Scholastic en Espanola); Scholastic Paperbacks (Schol Pbk); Sidekicks (Sidekicks); Tangerine Press (Tang Pr Sch)
Web site: http://www.scholastic.com; *CIP.*

Scholastic Library Publishing, *(0-516; 0-531)* 90 Old Sherman Tpke., Danbury, CT 06816 (SAN 253-8865) Tel 203-797-3500; Fax: 203-797-3657; Toll Free: 800-621-1115; *Imprints:* Children's Press (Childrens Pr); Watts, Franklin (Frank Watts)
E-mail: agraham@grolier.com
Web site: http://www.scholasticlibrary.com
Dist(s): **Lectorum Pubns., Inc..**

Scholastic Paperbacks Imprint of Scholastic, Inc.

Scholastic Pr. Imprint of Scholastic, Inc.

Scholastic Reference Imprint of Scholastic, Inc.

School Zone Publishing Co., *(0-88743; 0-938256; 1-58947)* P.O. Box 777, Grand Haven, MI 49417 (SAN 289-8314) Tel 616-846-5030; Fax: 616-846-6181; Toll Free Fax: 800-550-4618 (orders only); Toll Free: 800-253-0564; 1819 Industrial Dr., Grand Haven, MI 49417
E-mail: Bebb@schoolzone.com
Web site: http://www.schoolzone.com.

Schreiber Publishing, Inc., *(0-88400; 1-887563)* 51 Monroe St., Suite 101, Rockville, MD 20850 (SAN 298-6876) Tel 301-424-7737; Fax: 301-424-2336; Toll Free: 800-822-3213; *Imprints:* Shengold Books (Shengold Bks)
E-mail: spbooks@aol.com
Web site: http://www.schreibernet.com
Dist(s): **Baker & Taylor Bks.**
Fell, Frederick Pubs., Inc.
Libros Sin Fronteras
National Bk. Network
Quality Bks., Inc..

Science & Art Products, *(0-9634622)* 24861 Rotunde Mesa, Malibu, CA 90265 Tel 310-456-2496; Fax: 310-456-0728; Toll Free: 800-356-1733
Web site: http://www.scienceandart.com.

Science & Humanities Pr., *(1-888725)* Subs. of Banis & Assocs., Orders Addr.: P.O. Box 7151, Chesterfield, MO 63006-7151 (SAN 299-8459) Tel 636-394-4950; Fax: 636-394-1381; Edit Addr.: 1023 Stuyvesant Ln., Manchester, MO 63011-3601 Tel 636-394-4950; Fax: 636-394-1381; *Imprints:* MacroPrintBooks (MacroPrintBks)
E-mail: sales@sciencehumanitiespress.com; pub@macroprintbooks.com; banis@banis-associates.com
Web site: http://www.stressmyth.com; http://www.normajeanebook.com; http://www.route66book.com; http://www.accessible-travel.com; http://www.banis-associates.com; http://www.sciencehumanitiespress.com; http://www.macroprintbooks.com
Dist(s): **Beeler, Thomas T. Publisher.**

Scott, Carlton T. *See* **Ends of the Earth Books.com**

ScribbleBooks Co., The, *(0-9706406)* 18145 S. Lawndale, Homewood, IL 60430 Tel 708-957-7822; Fax: 708-957-5974
E-mail: mail@scribblebooks.com
Web site: http://www.scribblemonster.com.

Scribner Imprint of Simon & Schuster

Scribner Paper Fiction Imprint of Simon & Schuster

Scripts Publishing, *(1-889826)* Orders Addr.: 11450 NW 56th Dr., Unit 115, Coral Springs, FL 33076 Tel 954-341-8565; 954-346-8906; Fax: 954-753-6761
E-mail: AtaxiaBooks@aol.com
Web site: http://www.hometown.aol.com/pathamilto/myhomepage/profile.html.

Scripture Pr. Pubs., Inc., *(0-7814; 0-88207; 0-89693; 1-55513; 1-56476)* Div. of Cook Communications Ministries, 4050 Lee Vance View, Colorado Springs, CO 80918-7102 (SAN 222-9471) Tel 719-536-0100; Fax: 719-536-3269; Toll Free: 800-437-4337
Web site: http://www.chariotvictor.com
Dist(s): **BookWorld Services, Inc..**

†Scroll Pr., Inc., *(0-87592)* 2858 Valerie Ct., Merrick, NY 11566 (SAN 206-796X) Tel 516-379-4283; *CIP.*

Sea Challengers, Inc., *(0-930118)* Four Sommerset Rise, Skyline Forest, Monterey, CA 93940 (SAN 210-5446) Tel 831-373-6306; Fax: 831-373-4566
E-mail: seachall@aol.com
Dist(s): **Lectorum Pubns., Inc.**
Sunbelt Pubns., Inc..

Sea Critters, *(0-9665692)* Div. of Fashion Formulas by Ecoly, 9232 Eton Ave., Chatsworth, CA 91311 Tel 818-718-6982; Fax: 818-718-9353; Toll Free: 888-333-1277.

Sea Island Information Group, *(1-877610)* 11022 Belton St., Upper Marlboro, MD 20772-1402 Tel 301-350-1360.

Seabright Pr., *(0-9634359)* 33062 Sea Bright Dr., Dana Point, CA 92629 Tel 714-493-9713 Do not confuse with Seabright Pr., Santa Cruz, CA.

Seacoast Publishing, Inc., *(1-878561; 1-59421)* Orders Addr.: P.O. Box 26492, Birmingham, AL 35260 Tel 205-979-2909; Fax: 205-979-3706; Edit Addr.: 1149 Mountain Oaks Dr., Birmingham, AL 35226 Do not confuse with companies with the same name in Monterey, CA, East Hampton, NY
E-mail: seacoast@charter.net
Dist(s): **Booksource, The**
Hervey's Booklink & Cookbook Warehouse.

SeaScape Pr., Ltd., *(0-9669741)* 1010 Roble Ln., Santa Barbara, CA 93103-2046 (SAN 299-8386) Tel 805-965-4646; Fax: 805-963-8188; Toll Free: 800-929-2906
E-mail: seapress@aol.com
Web site: http://www.seascapepress.com.

SeaStar Bks., *(1-58717)* Div. of North-South Books, Inc., 11 E. 26th St., 17th Flr., New York, NY 10010 Tel 212-706-4545; Fax: 212-706-4546; Toll Free: 800-282-8257
E-mail: mbronzini@northsouth.com
Web site: http://www.northsouth.com
Dist(s): **Chronicle Bks. LLC**
Lectorum Pubns., Inc..

Second Story Pr. (CAN) *(0-921299; 0-929005; 1-896764) Dist. by* **Orca Bk Pubs.**

Secretaria de Educacion Publica (MEX) *(968-29; 970-18) Dist. by* **Santillana.**

Seedling Pubns., Inc., *(1-58323; 1-880612)* 4522 Indianola Ave., Columbus, OH 43214-2246 Tel 614-267-7333; Fax: 614-267-4205; Toll Free: 877-857-7333
E-mail: Sales@SeedlingPub.com
Web site: http://www.SeedlingPub.com.

Seesaw Music Corp., *(0-937205)* 2067 Broadway, New York, NY 10023 (SAN 658-6899) Tel 212-874-1200.

Separating Sickness Foundation *See* **Anoai Pr.**

Serpent's Tail Ltd. (GBR) *(1-85242) Dist. by* **Consort Bk Sales.**

Serres, Ediciones, S. L. (ESP) *(84-88061; 84-95040; 84-8488) Dist. by* **Lectorum Pubns.**

Serres, Ediciones, S. L. (ESP) *(84-88061; 84-95040; 84-8488) Dist. by* **Libros Fronteras.**

Shade Tree Bks., *(0-9617609)* 1200 Nelson Ct., Boulder City, NV 89005 (SAN 664-8614) Tel 702-293-2177 Do not confuse with Shade Tree Books in Huntington Beach, CA, Jonesboro, LA.

Shadow Mountain Imprint of Deseret Bk. Co.

ShadowPlay Pr., *(0-9638819)* P.O. Box 647, Forreston, IL 61030 Tel 815-938-3151; Fax: 815-371-1440
E-mail: sheilawelch@juno.com; ericwelch2@juno.com
Web site: http://www.shadowplay.userworld.com.

†Shambhala Pubns., Inc., *(0-87773; 1-56957; 1-57062; 1-59030)* Horticultural Hall, 300 Massachusetts Ave., Boston, MA 02115 (SAN 203-2481) Tel 617-424-0030; Fax: 617-236-1563
E-mail: editors@shambhala.com
Web site: http://www.shambhala.com
Dist(s): **Random Hse., Inc.**
Sounds True, Inc.; *CIP.*

Shamrock Hse., The, *(0-9702985)* 990 Forest Pond Ct., Marietta, GA 30068
E-mail: sales@shamrockpublishing.com
Web site: http://www.shamrockpublishing.com.

Shank Painter Publishing Co., *(0-9609814; 1-888959)* P.O. Box 720, North Eastham, MA 02651-0720 (SAN 264-3251) Tel 508-487-9169; Fax: 508-255-5184.

SHARE-Pregnancy & Infant Loss Support, Inc., *(0-918533)* 300 First Capitol Dr., Saint Charles, MO 63301-2893 (SAN 657-7113) Toll Free: 800-821-6819.

Sharp, Vera, *(0-9616987)* 1527 Blake Ave., Apt. No. 203, Glenwood Springs, CO 81601 (SAN 658-8360) Tel 970-945-4504.

Shaw Imprint of WaterBrook Pr.

Shaw & Co., *(0-944900)* 18 S. Mill Dr., Glastonbury, CT 06073 (SAN 245-6745) Tel 860-275-5000.

Shawangunk Pr., Inc., *(1-885482)* 8 Laurel Park Rd., Wappingers Falls, NY 12590 Tel 845-426-0657
Dist(s): **New Leaf Distributing Co., Inc..**

Sheer Bliss Communications, LLC, *(0-9679436)* P.O. Box 186, Newport, RI 02840 Fax: 401-848-2551
E-mail: gloria@wurman.com.

Shelf-Life Bks., *(1-880042)* Div. of M.A.P.S., Inc., 2132 Fordem, Madison, WI 53704-0599 Tel 608-244-7767; Fax: 608-244-8394.

Shengold Bks. Imprint of Schreiber Publishing, Inc.

Shen's Bks., *(1-885008)* 40951 Fremont Blvd., Fremont, CA 94538 (SAN 138-2926) Tel 510-668-1898; Fax: 510-668-1057; Toll Free: 800-456-6660
E-mail: info@shens.com
Web site: http://www.shens.com
Dist(s): **Bookpeople**
Lectorum Pubns., Inc.
Quality Bks., Inc..

Shipwreck Pr. Imprint of Narwhal Pr., Inc.

†Shoal Creek Pubs., *(0-88319)* Div. of Shearer Publishing, 406 Post Oak Rd., Fredericksburg, TX 78624 (SAN 203-2430) Tel 830-997-6529; Fax: 830-997-9752; Toll Free: 800-458-3808; *CIP.*

†Shoe String Pr., Inc., *(0-208)* 2 Linsley St., North Haven, CT 06473-2517 (SAN 213-2079) Tel 203-239-2702; Fax: 203-239-2568; *Imprints:* Linnet Books (Linnet Bks)
E-mail: books@shoestringpress.com
Web site: http://www.shoestringpress.com; *CIP.*

Shoe Tree Pr., Div. of F&W Pubns., Inc., 1507 Dana Ave., Cincinnati, OH 45207 Tel 513-531-2690; Fax: 513-531-4082; Toll Free Fax: 888-590-4082; Toll Free: 800-289-0963.

Shooting Star Publishing, *(0-615)* Div. of Primary Colors Inc., Orders Addr.: 3319 Greenfield Rd., PMB 310, Dearborn, MI 48120 Tel 313-865-1874; Fax: 313-865-1416
E-mail: yburton@primefun.com
Web site: http://www.primefun.com
Dist(s): **Baker & Taylor Bks..**

Shubert, Joseph L., *(0-9627015)* Rte. 27, P.O. Box 188, Kingfield, ME 04947 Tel 207-628-4626.

Shug' n Spice Pr., *(0-615)* Div. of Kaejae Entertainment, 304 Main Ave., No. 215, Norwalk, CT 06851
E-mail: kamichijackson@mail.com
Web site: http://www.shugandspice.com.

Shulsinger Sales, Inc., *(0-914080)* 50 Washington St., Brooklyn, NY 11201 (SAN 205-9851) Tel 718-852-0042; Fax: 718-935-9691; Toll Free: 800-548-0085
E-mail: uugam@aol.com.

Siddha Yoga Publication Imprint of SYDA Foundation

Side Show Comics Imprint of Ink & Feathers Comics

Sidekicks Imprint of Scholastic, Inc.

†Sierra Club Bks., *(0-375; 0-87156; 1-57805)* 85 Second St., San Francisco, CA 94105 (SAN 203-2406) Tel 415-977-5500; Fax: 415-977-5792
E-mail: information@sierraclub.org
Web site: http://www.sierraclub.org/books
Dist(s): **Univ. of California Pr.**; *CIP.*

Sierra Club Bks. for Children, *(0-87156; 1-57805)* Div. of Sierra Club Bks., 85 Second Street, San Francisco, CA 94105 Tel 415-977-5500; Fax: 415-977-5793
Web site: http://www.sierraclub.org/books
Dist(s): **Smith, Gibbs Pub..**

Sierra Oaks Publishing Co., *(0-940113)* P.O. Box 736, Newcastle, CA 95658-0736 (SAN 664-063X) Tel 916-663-1474; Fax: 916-663-1476
E-mail: sierraoak@aol.com
Web site: http://www.sierraoaks.com.

Sierra Raconteur Publishing, *(1-58365; 1-58582)* Orders Addr.: P.O. Box 452, Greenfield, IN 46140 Tel 317-462-0037; *Imprints:* Timeless Romance (Timeless Romance); Timeless Treasures (Timeless Treasures)
E-mail: LASoard@aol.com; LoriSoard@aol.com.

Sight & Sound International, Inc., *(0-88704)* 10101 Science Dr., Sturtevant, WI 53177-1757 (SAN 283-4065).

Sigmar (ARG) *(950-11) Dist. by* **Continental Bk.**

Signet Bks. Imprint of NAL

Signet Classics Imprint of NAL

Signet Vista Imprint of NAL

Silbert & Bress Pubns., *(0-89544)* P.O. Box 68, Mahopac, NY 10541 (SAN 210-5020) Tel 845-628-7910; Fax: 845-628-6027; Toll Free: 888-378-7664.

†Silver, Burdett & Ginn, Inc., *(0-382; 0-663)* Orders Addr.: P.O. Box 2500, Lebanon, IN 46052 Toll Free Fax: 800-841-8939; Toll Free: 800-552-2259; Edit Addr.: P.O. Box 480, Parsippany, NJ 07054 (SAN 204-5982); 108 Wilmot Rd., Suite 380, Midwest Div., Deerfield, IL 60015 (SAN 111-6517) Tel 708-945-1240
E-mail: customerservice@scottforesman.com
Web site: http://www.scottforesman.com/; *CIP.*

Silver Dolphin Bks. Imprint of Advantage Pubs. Group

Silver Dolphin Spanish Editions (MEX) *(970-718; 968-5308) Dist. by* **Publishers Group.**

Silver Elm Classic Imprint of Darby Creek Publishing

Silver Moon Pr., *(1-881889; 1-893110)* 160 Fifth Ave., Suite 622, New York, NY 10010-7003 Tel 212-242-6499; Fax: 212-242-6799; Toll Free: 800-874-3320
E-mail: mail@silvermoonpress.com
Web site: http://www.silvermoonpress.com.

Silver Rim Pr., *(1-878611)* 2759 Park Lake Dr., Boulder, CO 80301 Tel 303-666-4290 (phone/fax)
E-mail: Sybilset@aol.com.

Silver Seahorse Pr., *(0-9631798)* 2506 N. Clark St., Suite 320, Chicago, IL 60614 Tel 773-871-1772; Fax: 773-327-8978
E-mail: SeahorsePr@aol.com.

Silver Whistle Imprint of Harcourt Children's Bks.

Simon & Barklee, Inc./ExplorerMedia, *(0-9704661; 0-9714502)* 2280 E. Whidbey Shores Rd., Langley, WA 98260 Tel 360-730-2360; Fax: 360-730-2355; *Imprints:* Explorer Media (Explorer Media)
E-mail: cwsch@whidbey.com
Web site: http://simonandbarklee.com
Dist(s): **Baker & Taylor Bks.**
Quality Bks., Inc..

Simon & Schuster, *(0-671; 0-684; 0-689; 0-914676; 0-7432)* Div. of Simon & Schuster, Inc., Orders Addr.: 100 Front St., Riverside, NJ 08075 (SAN 200-2442) Toll Free Fax: 800-943-9831; Toll Free: 800-223-2348 (customer service); 800-223-2336 (ordering); Edit Addr.: 1230 Avenue of the Americas, New York, NY 10020 (SAN 200-2450) Tel 212-698-7000; Fax: 212-698-7007; Toll Free: 800-897-7650 (customer financial services); *Imprints:* Atria (Atria Bks); MSG (M S G); MTV (MTV Bks); Pocket (PB); Star Trek (Star Trek); Washington Square Press (Wash Sq Pr); Fireside (Fireside); Scribner (Scribner); Scribner Paper Fiction (ScriPapFic); Simon & Schuster (SimSchu); Touchstone (Touchstone)
E-mail: ssonline_feedback@simonsays.com; consumer.customerservice@simonandschuster.com
Web site: http://www.simonandschuster.com/ebooks; http://www.oasis.simonandschuster.com; http://www.simonsays.com
Dist(s): **Giron Bks.**
Libros Sin Fronteras
Simon & Schuster, Inc.
Thorndike Pr..

Simon & Schuster Imprint of Simon & Schuster

Simon & Schuster Audio, *(0-671; 0-7435)* Div. of Simon & Schuster New Media, Orders Addr.: 100 Front St., Riverside, NJ 08075 Toll Free Fax: 800-943-9831 (orders); Toll Free: 800-223-2336 (customer service); Edit Addr.: 1230 Avenue of the Americas, New York, NY 10020 Tel 212-698-7000; Fax: 212-698-2370; *Imprints:* Simon & Schuster Audioworks (Audioworks)
Web site: http://www.simonsays.com/subs/index.cfm?areaid=45
Dist(s): **Simon & Schuster, Inc..**

Simon & Schuster Audioworks Imprint of Simon & Schuster Audio

Simon & Schuster Bks. For Young Readers, *(0-689)* Div. of Simon & Schuster Children's Publishing, 1230 Avenue of the Americas, New York, NY 10020 Tel 212-698-7000; Fax: 212-698-7007
E-mail: ssonline_feedback@simonsays.com
Web site: http://www.SimonSaysKids.com.

Simon & Schuster Children's Publishing, *(0-02; 0-671; 0-684; 0-689; 0-7434)* Orders Addr.: 100 Front St., Riverside, NJ 08075 Toll Free Fax: 800-943-9831; Toll Free: 800-223-2336; Edit Addr.: 1230 Avenue of the Americas, New York, NY 10020 Tel 212-698-7200; *Imprints:* Aladdin (AlaChild); Aladdin Library (AlaLib); Atheneum (AthenSS); Atheneum/Anne Schwartz Books (Anne Schwart); Atheneum/Richard Jackson Books (Rich Jack); Little Simon (Little Simon); McElderry, Margaret K. (McElderry); Simon & Schuster Children's Publishing (SSChildren); Simon & Schuster/Paula Wiseman Books (Paula Wise); Simon Pulse (SPulse); Simon Spotlight (SSpot); Simon Spotlight/Nickelodeon (SiSpNick)
Web site: http://www.simonsays.com
Dist(s): **Simon & Schuster, Inc..**

Simon & Schuster Children's Publishing Imprint of Simon & Schuster Children's Publishing

Simon & Schuster Trade *See* **Simon & Schuster**

Simon & Schuster/Paula Wiseman Bks. Imprint of Simon & Schuster Children's Publishing

Simon Pulse Imprint of Simon & Schuster Children's Publishing

†Simon, Rachelle, *(0-934710)* 331 Vista Pacifica, Santa Barbara, CA 93109-2133 (SAN 213-9669) Tel 805-965-4259; Fax: 805-965-1959; *CIP.*

Simon Spotlight Imprint of Simon & Schuster Children's Publishing

Simon Spotlight/Nickelodeon Imprint of Simon & Schuster Children's Publishing

Simply Angels Creative Pr. & Design, *(0-9651678)* Orders Addr.: P.O. Box 644, Cambria, CA 93428 Tel 805-927-2824; Fax: 805-927-2825; Toll Free: 800-914-7577; Edit Addr.: 821 Cornwall St., Cambria, CA 93428
E-mail: starhall@aol.com
Web site: http://www.simplyangels.com.

Sir Fir Bks. & Music Imprint of Sir Fir Enterprises, LLC

Sir Fir Enterprises, LLC, *(0-9670160)* 1468 Shadowrock Heights, Marietta, GA 30062 Tel 770-565-7020; Fax: 770-565-6885; Toll Free: 877-565-7020; *Imprints:* Sir Fir Books & Music (Sir Fir Bks)
E-mail: rrwrites@mindspring.com
Web site: http://sirdouglasfir.com
Dist(s): **Baker & Taylor Bks.**
Quality Bks., Inc.
Unique Bks., Inc..

Sirius Entertainment, Inc., *(1-57989)* Orders Addr.: P.O. Box 834, Dover, NJ 07802 Tel 973-328-1455; Fax: 973-328-0774; Edit Addr.: 264 E. Blackwell St., Dover, NJ 07801
E-mail: sirent@aol.com
Dist(s): **Client Distribution Services.**

Sirken Pubns., *(0-9635483)* One White Lotus Rd., Brewster, NY 10509 Tel 914-279-9675
E-mail: msirken@aol.com.

Sistemas Tecnicos de Edicion, S.A. de C.V. (MEX) *(968-6579; 970-629) Dist. by* **AIMS Intl.**

Sisu Home Entertainment, Inc., *(1-56086; 1-884857)* 18 W. 27th St., 10th Flr., New York, NY 10001 Tel 212-779-1559; Fax: 212-779-7115; Toll Free Fax: 888-221-7478; Toll Free: 800-223-7478
E-mail: sisu@sisuent.com
Web site: http://www.sisuent.com.

Sisu Pr., *(0-9641573)* 2032 Western Rd., Iowa City, IA 52240 Tel 319-466-1660 Do not confuse with Sisu Press, Placerville, CO.

Sitare, Ltd., *(0-940178)* Orders Addr.: 1736 E. Charleston Blvd., Las Vegas, NV 89104-1952 (SAN 217-0833) Toll Free: 800-769-2120 (phone/fax)
E-mail: sitare@sbcglobal.net
Web site: http://
www.aaafivebuckbooksandposters.com.

SK Publications *See* **St Kitts Pr.**

Skandisk, Inc., *(0-9615394; 1-57534)* 6667 W. Old Shakopee Rd., Suite 109, Bloomington, MN 55438-2622 (SAN 695-4405) Tel 952-829-8998; Fax: 952-829-8992; Toll Free: 800-468-2424 (orders)
E-mail: lhamnes@skandisk.com; tomten@skandisk.com
Web site: http://www.skandisk.com
Dist(s): **Adventure Pubns., Inc..**

Skylark Imprint of Random Hse. Children's Bks.

Skylight Studios, *(0-9638756)* 165 White Oaks Rd., Williamstown, MA 01267-2257 Tel 413-663-9021.

Skyward Publishing Co., *(1-881554)* Div. of Paragon Media Corp., 17440 N. Dallas Pkwy., Suite 100, Dallas, TX 75287 (SAN 297-9705) Tel 972-490-8988
E-mail: george.burrell@paragonmediacorp.com
Web site: http://www.skywardpublishing.com
Dist(s): **Biblio Distribution**
Hervey's Booklink & Cookbook Warehouse.

Slator, Laraine, *(0-9707575)* 3170 Holiday Springs Blvd., Bldg. 6-103, Margate, FL 33063 Tel 954-346-2765
E-mail: LALO0926@aol.com.

Sleeping Bear Pr., *(1-57504; 1-886947; 1-58536)* Div. of Gale Group, Orders Addr.: P.O. Box 20, Chelsea, MI 48118 (SAN 253-8466) Tel 734-475-4411; Fax: 734-475-0787; Toll Free: 800-487-2323; Edit Addr.: 310 N. Main, Suite 300, Chelsea, MI 48118
E-mail: customerservice@sleepingbearpress.com
Web site: http://www.sleepingbearpress.com
Dist(s): **Baker & Taylor Bks.**
Keith Distributors
Partners Pubs. Group, Inc.
Southern Bk. Service
Urban Land Institute.

Sloane Pubns., *(0-9664248)* Orders Addr.: P.O. Box 7712, Portland, ME 04102 Tel 207-774-8733; Edit Addr.: 225 York St., Portland, ME 04102 Do not confuse with Sloane Pubns., Sun Lakes, AZ
E-mail: sloane@maine.rr.com.

Sloan/Manry Pubs., *(0-9622316)* 16809 Holbrook, Shaker Heights, OH 44120 Tel 216-752-1717.

SM Ediciones (ESP) *(84-348) Dist. by* **Continental Bk.**

Names

SM Ediciones (ESP) *(84-348) Dist. by* **AIMS Intl.**

SM Ediciones (ESP) *(84-348) Dist. by* **IBD Ltd.**

SM Ediciones (ESP) *(84-348) Dist. by* **Distribks Inc.**

Small Horizons Imprint of New Horizon Pr. Pubs., Inc.

Small Miracles Pr., *(0-9673794)* 972 Somerset Ln., York, PA 17403 Tel 717-845-9647 (phone/fax) Do not confuse with Small Miracles Pr, in Ojai, CA
E-mail: yopeggy@aol.com
Web site: http://www.goose.ycp.edu/~swojciec.

Small Planet Communications, Inc., *(0-9656211; 1-931376)* 15 Union St., Lawrence, MA 01840 Tel 978-794-2201; Fax: 978-794-8062; Toll Free: 800-475-9486 (orders only)
E-mail: planet@smplanet.com
Web site: http://www.PlanetBookClub.com/; http://www.smplanet.com.

Small Rain Pr., *(0-9655317)* Orders Addr.: P.O. Box 400, Lincoln, MA 01773 (SAN 299-3309) Tel 781-259-9656 (phone/fax); Edit Addr.: 63 Bedford Rd., Lincoln, MA 01773 (SAN 299-3317)
E-mail: info@smallrainpress.com.

Small Secrets Unlimted, Inc., *(0-9700943)* Div. of Dweebz, 17051 SE 272nd St., Suite 43, No. 22, Covington, WA 98042-4955 Tel 253-740-1314
E-mail: nllovejoy@dweebz.com
Web site: http://www.dweebz.com.

Smallfellow Pr. Imprint of Tallfellow Pr.

Smart Alec Toys Publishing, *(0-9670091)* P.O. Box 880, Andover, MA 01810 Tel 978-442-4892; Fax: 978-686-9444
E-mail: smatoys@aol.com
Web site: http://www.smartalectoys.com; http://www.marsmartians.com.

Smart Alternatives, Inc., *(0-9636140)* Orders Addr.: P.O. Box 5849, Austin, TX 78763 Tel 512-445-0602; Fax: 512-445-0210; Toll Free: 800-453-9226; Edit Addr.: 311 Le Grand Ave., Austin, TX 78704; *Imprints:* Neon Rose Productions (Neon Rose).

Smart Kids Publishing, *(1-891100)* 8403 Cliffridge Ln., La Jolla, CA 92037-2119 Tel 619-668-0570; Fax: 760-728-5309
Dist(s): **APG Sales and Fulfillment**
Penton Overseas, Inc..

Smarty Pants, *(1-55886)* 15104 Detroit Ave., Suite 2, Lakewood, OH 44107 (SAN 249-0110) Tel 216-221-5300; Fax: 216-221-5348 Do not confuse with Smarty Pants Books, Wynnewood, PA.

Smith & Kraus Pubs., Inc., *(0-9622722; 1-57525; 1-880399)* Orders Addr.: P.O. Box 127, Lyme, NH 03768 (SAN 255-1454) Tel 603-643-6431; 603-626-1510 (returns only); Fax: 603-643-1831; Toll Free: 800-895-4331
E-mail: sand@sover.net
Web site: http://www.smithkraus.com
Dist(s): **Baker & Taylor Bks..**

Smith, Florence B. *See* **Prickly Pr.**

†Smith, Gibbs Pub., *(0-87905; 1-58685)* Orders Addr.: P.O. Box 667, Layton, UT 84041 (SAN 201-9906) Toll Free Fax: 800-213-3023 (orders); Toll Free: 800-748-5439 (orders); Edit Addr.: 1877 E. Gentile St., Layton, UT 84040 Tel 801-544-9800; Fax: 801-546-8853
E-mail: info@gibbs-smith.com; text@gibbs-smith.com
Web site: http://www.gibbs-smith.com
Dist(s): **Athena Productions, Inc.;** *CIP.*

Smith Lane Pubs., *(0-9672639)* Orders Addr.: P.O. Box 54, Cotuit, MA 02635 Tel 508-420-9258; Fax: 508-420-1688; Toll Free: 888-338-6566; Edit Addr.: 215 Lewis Pond Rd., Cotuit, MA 02635
E-mail: SLPublishers@cs.com.

Smith, Peter Pub., Inc., *(0-8446)* Five Lexington Ave., Magnolia, MA 01930 (SAN 206-8885) Tel 978-525-3562; Fax: 978-525-3674.

Smith, W. H. Publishers, Incorporated *See* **Smithmark Pubs., Inc.**

Smithmark Pubs., Inc., *(0-7651; 0-8317)* Div. of US Media Holdings, 115 W. 18th St.. 5th Flr., New York, NY 10011-4113 (SAN 176-0912) Tel 212-519-1300; Fax: 212-519-1310; Toll Free: 800-932-0070 (customer service); Raritan Plaza 111, Fieldcrest Ave., Edison, NJ 08837 (SAN 658-1625) Tel 732-225-6499 (phone/fax); Toll Free Fax: 800-732-8688
Dist(s): **Continental Bk. Co., Inc..**

SMOOCH Imprint of Dorchester Publishing Co., Inc.

Smooth Stone Pr., *(0-9619401)* P.O. Box 19875, Saint Louis, MO 63144 (SAN 244-4259) Tel 314-968-2596
Dist(s): **Baker & Taylor Bks.**
Bookpeople
Koen Bk. Distributors
Midwest Library Service
New Leaf Distributing Co., Inc.
Nutri-Bks. Corp..

Snapping Turtle Pr., *(0-9642796; 1-888414)* 4064 W. Second St., Los Angeles, CA 90004 Fax: 213-383-5129.

Society for Visual Education, Incorporated *See* **S V E & Churchill Media**

Socks, Inc., *(0-9658267)* 250 W. 57th St., Suite 1517-13, New York, NY 10019 Tel 212-245-6980; Fax: 212-582-3627
E-mail: editorsatteambooks.com
Web site: http://teambooks.com.

SoftBook Pr., *(0-7410)* 900 Island Dr., Redwood City, CA 94065-5150
Web site: http://www.softbook.com.

SoftPlay, Inc., *(1-931312; 1-59292)* 3535 W. Peterson Ave., Chicago, IL 60659 Tel 773-509-0707; Fax: 773-509-0404
E-mail: sales@softplayforkids.com
Web site: http://www.softplayforkids.com.

Soho Pr., Inc., *(0-939149; 1-56947)* Orders Addr.: 16365 James Madison Hwy., Gordonsville, VA 22942 Tel 888-330-8477; Fax: 540-672-7600; Edit Addr.: 853 Broadway, New York, NY 10003 (SAN 662-5088) Tel 212-260-1900; Fax: 212-260-1902
E-mail: bdevendorf@sohopress.com
Web site: http://www.sohopress.com/
Dist(s): **Consortium Bk. Sales & Distribution.**

SolidGumboWorks, *(1-889851)* Orders Addr.: P.O. Box 41889, Philadelphia, PA 19101-1889 Tel 215-281-1040; Toll Free: 888-843-1084; Edit Addr.: 10825 E. Keswick Rd., Unit 241, Philadelphia, PA 19154.

Songs & Stories Children Love, *(0-934591)* 123 Valentine Ln., Yonkers, NY 10705 (SAN 694-0609) Tel 914-423-7045; Fax: 914-423-0722
E-mail: fdil@bestweb.net.

Sonny Boy Bks., *(0-9638863)* 109 E. 19th St., New York, NY 10003 Tel 212-473-1563
Dist(s): **Fotofolio, Inc..**

Sono Nis Pr. (CAN) *(0-919203; 0-919462; 0-9690282; 1-55039) Dist. by* **Orca Bk Pubs.**

Sonos Publishing, Incorporated *See* **Jackman Publishing**

Son-Rise Pubns. & Distribution Co., *(0-936369)* 51 Greenfield Rd., New Wilmington, PA 16142 (SAN 698-0031) Tel 724-946-9057; Fax: 724-946-8700; Toll Free: 800-358-0777
Web site: http://www.softspace.com/steelvalley; http://www.sonrisepublications.com
Dist(s): **Baker & Taylor Bks..**

Sonship Pr. Imprint of 21st Century Pr.

Sound Room Pubs., Inc., *(1-883049; 1-58472)* Orders Addr.: P.O. Box 3168, Falls Church, VA 22043 Tel 540-722-2535; Fax: 540-722-0903; Toll Free: 800-643-0295; Edit Addr.: 100 Weems Ln., Winchester, VA 22601; *Imprints:* Commuters Library (Commuters Library); In Audio (In Aud)
E-mail: commuterslib@worldnet.att.net
Web site: http://commuterslibrary
Dist(s): **Baker & Taylor Bks.**
Distributors, The
Follett Media Distribution.

Soundelux Audio Publishing, *(0-88142; 1-55935; 1-880690)* Div. of Soundelux Entertainment Group, 55 Mitchell Blvd., Suite 18, San Rafael, CA 94903-2010 Toll Free: 800-227-2020
E-mail: ibriggin@soundelux.com
Web site: http://www.soundelux.com/
Dist(s): **Landmark Audiobooks.**

Soundprints, *(0-924483; 1-56899; 1-931465; 1-59249)* Div. of Trudy Corp., 353 Main Ave., Norwalk, CT 06851 Tel 203 838 6009 Toll Free: 800-228-7839
Web site: http://www.soundprints.com.

Source Productions, Inc., *(1-883088)* Orders Addr.: P.O. Box 910, Redway, CA 95560 Tel 707-923-2136; Fax: 707-923-2137; Edit Addr.: 1271 Evergreen Rd., Suite 2, Redway, CA 95560 Do not confuse with Source Productions in Toluca Lake, CA
E-mail: Treehouse@asis.com.

South Asia Bks., *(0-8364; 0-88386)* P.O. Box 502, Columbia, MO 65205 (SAN 207-4044) Tel 573-474-0116; Fax: 573-474-8124
E-mail: sabooks@juno.com
Web site: http://www.southasiabooks.com.

Southern Ink Publishing, *(0-9648890)* Orders Addr.: P.O. Box 205, Schlater, MS 38952 Tel 601-658-2238; Fax: 601-658-4526; Toll Free: 800-787-1619.

Southern Tier Editions Imprint of Haworth Pr., Inc., The

Southwest Parks & Monuments Association *See* **Western National Parks Assn.**

Southwest Pubns., *(1-881260)* 3836 E. Dewberry, Mesa, AZ 85206 Tel 480-694-2821
E-mail: GOLD527@aol.com
Web site: http://www.members.aol.com/gold527.

Souvenir Pr. Ltd. (GBR) *(0-285) Dist. by* **IPG Chicago.**

Sovereign Grace Pubs., Inc., *(1-878442; 1-58960)* 4427 E. 200 N., Lafayette, IN 47905 (SAN 299-6847) Tel 765-429-4122; Fax: 765-429-4142; Toll Free: 800-447-9142 Do not confuse with Sovereign Grace Pubns., Lexington, KY
E-mail: jaygreenxx@iquest.net
Web site: http://www.sovgracepub.com.

Spanish Hse. Distributors, 1360 NW 88th Ave., Miami, FL 33172-3093 (SAN 169-1171) Tel 305-592-6136; Fax: 305-592-0087; Toll Free: 800-767-7726.

SpanPr., Inc., *(1-58045; 1-887578)* 5722 S. Flamingo Rd., Suite 277, Cooper City, FL 33330 Tel 305-592-7913; Fax: 305-477-5632; Toll Free: 800-585-8384
Dist(s): **Continental Bk. Co., Inc.**
Lectorum Pubns., Inc..

Sparklesoup Studios, Inc., *(0-9714776; 1-932379)* P.O. Box 142003, Irving, TX 75014
E-mail: sparklesoup@aol.com
Web site: http://www.sparklesoup.com.

Speak Imprint of Penguin Putnam Bks. for Young Readers

Special Kids Company, Incorporated *See* **Anythings Possible, Inc.**

Special Literature Pr., *(0-938594)* Orders Addr.: P.O. Box 55763, Indianapolis, IN 46205 (SAN 215-8175) Tel 317-253-6268 (phone/fax).

Spellbound Pubns., *(0-9653695)* P.O. Box 3278, Theodosia, MO 65761-9728
Dist(s): **New Leaf Distributing Co., Inc..**

Spinner Pubns., Inc., *(0-932027)* 164 William St., New Bedford, MA 02740-6022 (SAN 686-0826) Tel 508-994-4564; Fax: 508-994-6925; Toll Free: 800-292-6062
E-mail: spinner@spinnerpub.com
Web site: http://www.spinnerpub.com
Dist(s): **Baker & Taylor Bks..**

Spire Imprint of Revell, Fleming H. Co.

Spirit Bks., *(0-9644890)* 1603 S. Halsey, Harrisonville, MO 64701-0146 Tel 816-380-2493.

Spirit Pr., *(0-944296)* 1005 Granite Ridge Dr., Santa Cruz, CA 95065 (SAN 243-2544) Tel 408-426-7971 Do not confuse with companies with the same name in Porrtland, OR, Raleigh, NC
E-mail: klassoc@nc.rr.com.

Spiritseeker Publishing, Inc., *(0-9630419; 1-883064)* Orders Addr.: P.O. Box 2441, Fargo, ND 58108-2441 Tel 701-232-5966; Fax: 701-232-0633; Toll Free: 800-538-6415; Edit Addr.: 412 Eighth Ave., S., Fargo, ND 58103.

Spiritual Moon Publishing, Ltd., *(0-9654203)* 3487 Charleston Ct., Decatur, GA 30034 Tel 770-393-5935.

Spit & A Half *See* **Chiappetta, Joe**

Splash Imprint of Berkley Publishing Group

Spoken Arts, Inc., *(0-8045)* 8 Lawn Ave., New Rochelle, NY 10801-0100 (SAN 205-079X) Tel 914-633-4516; Toll Free: 800-326-4090
Web site: http://www.spokenartsmedia.com/Home.htm
Dist(s): **Follett Media Distribution**
Lectorum Pubns., Inc.
Weston Woods Studios, Inc..

Spoken Word, P.O. Box 1222, Simi Valley, CA 93062-1222 Do not confuse with Spoken Word in Washington, DC
Dist(s): **Baker & Taylor Bks..**

Sports Curriculum, *(1-884480)* Orders Addr.: P.O. Box 495, Santa Clara, CA 95052 Tel 408-243-9663; Edit Addr.: 841 N. Monroe St., San Jose, CA 95128
E-mail: scblitz@ix.netcom.com.

Spring Creek Pubns., *(0-945184)* Orders Addr.: P.O. Box 243, Rose Hill, KS 67133 (SAN 246-6309); Edit Addr.: 5810 S. Webb, Derby, KS 67037 (SAN 246-6317) Tel 316-788-2812 Do not confuse with companies with the same or similar name in Bozeman, MT, Payson, UT.

Spring Hse. Bks., *(1-892570)* Orders Addr.: P.O. Box 129, Wadmalaw Island, SC 29487 Tel 843-559-9307; Fax: 843-559-4759; Toll Free: 877-559-4759; Edit Addr.: 6697 Bears Bluff Rd., Wadmalaw Island, SC 29487
E-mail: springhouse@charleston.net.

Sprite Pr., *(0-9706654)* 5400 Mountville Rd., Glouster, OH 45732-9508 Tel 740-767-2470 (phone/fax)
E-mail: melduvall@aol.com.

Names

Square 1 Pubs., Inc., *(0-938961)* 6 Birch Hill Rd., Ballston Lake, NY 12019 (SAN 661-7271) Tel 518-877-4946; Fax: 518-877-0906; *Imprints:* Stamp Out Sheep Press (Stamp Out Sheep Pr)
E-mail: Mcreview@aol.com.

SRA/McGraw-Hill, *(0-02; 0-383)* Div. of The McGraw-Hill Education Group, Orders Addr.: 220 E. Daniel Dale Rd., DeSoto, TX 75115-2490 Fax: 972-228-1982; Toll Free: 800-843-8855; Edit Addr.: 8787 Orion Pl., Columbus, OH 43240-4027 Tel 614-430-6600; Fax: 614-430-6621; Toll Free: 800-468-5850
E-mail: sra@mcgraw-hill.com
Web site: http://www.mcgraw-hill.com/education/sra.html
Dist(s): **Libros Sin Fronteras**
Weston Woods Studios, Inc..

St Kitts Pr., *(0-9661879; 1-931206)* Div. of SK Pubns., Orders Addr.: P.O. Box 8173, Wichita, KS 67208 Tel 316-685-3201; Fax: 316-685-6650; Toll Free: 888-705-4887; Edit Addr.: 4200 E. 24th, Wichita, KS 67220 Do not confuse with SK Pubns., Northfield, OH
E-mail: stkitts@skpub.com
Web site: http://www.stkittspress.com
Dist(s): **Baker & Taylor Bks.**
Book Wholesalers, Inc.
Brodart Co.
Coutts Library Service, Inc.
Emery-Pratt Co.
Follett Library Resources.

St. Martin's Paperbacks Imprint of St. Martin's Pr.

†St. Martin's Pr., *(0-312; 0-8050; 0-940687; 0-9603648; 1-55927; 1-58063; 1-58238)* Div. of Holtzbrinck Publishers, Orders Addr.: 16365 James Madison Hwy., Gordonville, VA 22942 Tel 540-672-7600; Fax: 540-672-7540 (customer service) ; Toll Free Fax: 800-672-2054; Toll Free: 888-330-8477; Edit Addr.: 175 Fifth Ave., New York, NY 10010 (SAN 200-2132) Tel 212-726-0200 (College Div.); 212-674-5151 (Trade Div.); Fax: 212-686-9491 (College Div.); 212-674-3179 (Trade Div.); Toll Free: 800-470-4767 (College Div.); 800-221-7945 (Trade Div.); *Imprints:* Saint Martin's Griffin (St Martin Griffin); Saint Martin's Paperbacks (St Martins Paperbacks); Saint Martin's Minotaur (Minotaur); Golden Books Adult Publishing Group (Golden Adult); Priddy Books (Priddy); Renaissance Books (Rena Bks)
E-mail: webmaster@stmartins.com; enquiries@stmartins.com
Web site: http://www.smpcollege.com; http://www.stmartins.com
Dist(s): **Comag Marketing Group**
Holtzbrinck Pubs.
Libros Sin Fronteras; *CIP.*

Stabur Pr., Inc., *(0-941613)* P.O. Box 6191, Plymouth, MI 48170 (SAN 666-1777) Tel 734-451-9830; Fax: 734-451-9836; Toll Free: 888-222-6642
E-mail: calcomic@aol.com
Web site: http://www.calibercomics.com
Dist(s): **Diamond Book Distributors, Inc..**

Stage Harbor Pr., *(0-9676082)* Orders Addr.: P.O. Box 460, Orleans, MA 02653; Edit Addr.: 20 Salt Marsh Way, Eastham, MA 02642 Tel 508-945-9004 (phone/fax)
E-mail: SHP@thunderball.com
Web site: http://www.stageharbor.com.

Stamp Out Sheep Pr. Imprint of Square 1 Pubs., Inc.

†Standard Publishing, *(0-7847; 0-87239; 0-87403)* Div. of Standex International Corp., 8121 Hamilton Ave., Cincinnati, OH 45231-2323 (SAN 110-5515) Tel 513-931-4050; Fax: 513-931-0950; Toll Free Fax: 877-867-5751 (customer service); Toll Free: 800-543-1301; 800-543-1353 (customer service); *Imprints:* Bean Sprouts (Bean Sprouts) Do not confuse with Standard Publishing Corp., Boston, MA
E-mail: customerservice@standardpub.com; trolfes@standardpub.com
Web site: http://www.standardpub.com
Dist(s): **Twentieth Century Christian Bks.**; *CIP.*

Standard Publishing Company *See* **Standard Publishing**

Star Bright Bks., Inc., *(1-887734; 1-932065)* 42-26 28th St., Suite 2C, Long Island City, NY 11101 (SAN 254-5225) Tel 718-784-9112; Fax: 718-784-9012; Toll Free: 800-788-4439
E-mail: info@starbrightbooks.com
Web site: http://www.starbrightbooks.com
Dist(s): **Lectorum Pubns., Inc..**

Star Image Studio, *(0-9660959)* 11551 Four Towns Rd., Gillett, WI 54124-9537 Tel 920-855-6107; Fax: 920-855-2012
E-mail: starimage@ez-net.com
Dist(s): **Star Imaage Children's Bks.**
Bookstop, The.

Star Light Pr., *(1-879817)* 1811 S. First St., Austin, TX 78704-4299 Tel 512-441-0588; 512-441-0062 (phone/fax); *Imprints:* Bilingual (Bilingual)
E-mail: info@starlightpress.com
Web site: http://www.starlightpress.com
Dist(s): **Book Wholesalers, Inc.**
iLeon.

Star Pubns., *(0-932356)* 1211 W. 60th Terr., Kansas City, MO 64113 (SAN 212-4564) Tel 816-523-8228 Do not confuse with companies with the same name in Rancho Palos Verdes, CA, Orange Park, FL, San Jose, CA, Colorado Springs, CO.

Star Trek Imprint of Simon & Schuster

Starburst Company *See* **Starburst Pubs.**

Starburst Pubs., *(0-914984; 1-892016)* Orders Addr.: P.O. Box 4123, Lancaster, PA 17604 Tel 717-293-0939; Fax: 717-293-1945; Toll Free: 800-441-1456 (orders only)
E-mail: starburst@starburstpublishers.com
Web site: http://www.starburstpublishers.com
Dist(s): **Anchor Distributors**
Appalachian Bible Co.
Baker & Taylor Bks.
Brodart Co.
National Bk. Network
Nutri-Bks. Corp.
Quality Bks., Inc.
Riverside
Spring Arbor Distributors, Inc.
Unique Bks., Inc..

Starcatcher Pr., *(0-9700164)* 256 Tudor Cir., Ashland, OR 97520 Tel 541-488-4230; Fax: 541-488-4354
E-mail: starcatcherpress@aol.com; malcolm@wherewelive.com
Web site: http://www.starcatcherpress.com.

Starchild Pr. Imprint of Light Technology Publishing

Starfire Imprint of Random Hse. Children's Bks.

Starlog Group, Incorporated *See* **Profile Entertainment, Inc.**

Starscape Imprint of Doherty, Tom Assocs., LLC

Starseed Pr. Imprint of Kramer, H.J. Inc.

State Hse. Pr., *(0-938349; 1-880510)* Orders Addr.: P.O. Box 15247, Austin, TX 78761 (SAN 660-9651) Tel 512-759-2676; Fax: 512-846-2094; Toll Free: 800-421-3378; Edit Addr.: 111 East St., Hutto, TX 78634 (SAN 660-966X) Do not confuse with State House Publishing in Madison, WI
E-mail: statehousepress@aol.com
Dist(s): **Encino Pr..**

State Mutual Bk. & Periodical Service, Ltd., *(0-7855; 0-89771)* Orders Addr.: P.O. Box 1199, Bridgehampton, NY 11932-1199.

Steerforth Italia Imprint of Steerforth Pr.

Steerforth Pr., *(1-883642; 1-58642)* 105-106 Chelsea St., P.O. Box 70, South Royalton, VT 05068 Tel 802-763-2808; Fax: 802-763-2818; *Imprints:* Steerforth Italia (Steerforth Italia)
E-mail: helga@steerforth.com; info@steerforth.com
Web site: http://www.steerforth.com
Dist(s): **Publishers Group West.**

Steiner, Lili Pubns., *(1-891397)* 2160 Century Pk., E., No. 1508, Los Angeles, CA 90067 (SAN 299-4569) Tel 310-553-5520; Fax: 310-553-4340
E-mail: lilily@earthlink.net.

†SteinerBooks, Inc., *(0-8334; 0-88010; 0-89345; 0-910142; 1-58420; 1-85584; 0-9701097)* Orders Addr.: P.O. Box 960, Herndon, VA 20172-0960 Tel 703-661-1594 (orders); Fax: 702-661-1501; Toll Free Fax: 800-277-7947 (orders); Toll Free: 800-856-8664 (orders); Edit Addr.: P.O. Box 799, Great Barrington, MA 01230 Tel 413-528-8233; Fax: 413-528-8826; Fulfillment Addr.: 22883 Quicksilver Dr., Dulles, VA 20166 (SAN 253-9519) Tel 703-661-1529; Fax: 703-996-1010; *Imprints:* Bell Pond Books (Bell Pond)
E-mail: service@steinerbooks.org
Web site: http://www.lindisfarne.org; http://www.bellpondbooks.com; http://www.steinerbooks.org
Dist(s): **Bookpeople**
New Leaf Distributing Co., Inc.
Red Wheel/Weiser; *CIP.*

†Stemmer Hse. Pubs., Inc., *(0-88045; 0-916144)* 4 White Brook Rd., Gilsum, NH 03448 (SAN 207-9623) Tel 603-357-0236; Fax: 603-357-2073
E-mail: stemmerhouse@home.com
Web site: http://stemmer.com
Dist(s): **Pathway Bk. Service**; *CIP.*

Steppingstone Enterprises, Inc., *(0-939728)* 2108 S. University Dr. Park Place Plaza, Suite 103, Fargo, ND 58103 (SAN 216-7646).

Sterling House Publishing *See* **SterlingHouse Pubs., Inc.**

†Sterling Publishing Co., Inc., *(0-8069; 1-4027)* 387 Park Ave., S., New York, NY 10016-8810 (SAN 211-6324) Tel 212-532-7160; Fax: 212-213-2495; Toll Free Fax: 800-775-8736 (warehouse); *Imprints:* Sterling/Pinwheel (SterPin) Do not confuse with companies with similar names in Falls Church, VA, Fallbrook, CA, Lewisville, TX
E-mail: custservice@sterlingpub.com
Web site: http://www.sterlingpub.com; *CIP.*

Sterling Publishing Company, Incorporated *See* **Sterling Publishing Co., Inc.**

SterlingHouse Pubs., Inc., *(1-56315)* Div. of Lee Shore Agency, 7436 Washington Ave., Suite 200, Pittsburgh, PA 15218 Tel 412-271-8800; Fax: 412-271-8600; Toll Free: 888-542-2665
E-mail: info@sterlinghousepublisher.com
Web site: http://www.sterlinghousepublisher.com
Dist(s): **Fell, Frederick Pubs., Inc.**
Partners Pubs. Group, Inc..

Sterling/Pinwheel Imprint of Sterling Publishing Co., Inc.

Stevens & Shea Pubs., *(0-89550)* P.O. Box 794, Stockton, CA 95201 (SAN 206-3670) Tel 209-465-1880.

†Stevens, Gareth Inc., *(0-8368; 0-918831; 1-55532)* 330 W. Olive St., Suite 100, Milwaukee, WI 53212 (SAN 696-1592) Tel 414-332-3520; Fax: 414-332-3567; Toll Free: 800-542-2595
E-mail: info@gsinc.com
Dist(s): **Lectorum Pubns., Inc.**; *CIP.*

Stevens Publishing, *(0-9632054; 1-885529)* Orders Addr.: P.O. Box 160, Kila, MT 59920 Tel 406-756-0307; Fax: 406-257-5051; Edit Addr.: 1550 Rogers Ln. Rd., Kila, MT 59920 Do not confuse with Stevens Publishing Corp. in Waco, TX.

Stew & Rice Productions, *(0-9629842)* P.O. Box 272, Hakalau, HI 96710-0272 Tel 808-963-6422
E-mail: msakiko@aloha.net
Web site: http://www.aloha.net/~msakiko/books.html.

†Stewart, Tabori & Chang, *(0-941434; 0-941807; 1-55670; 1-899791; 1-58479)* Div. of Harry N. Abrams, Inc., 115 W. 18th St., 5th Flr., New York, NY 10011 (SAN 293-4000) Tel 212-519-1200; Fax: 212-519-1210
Dist(s): **Time Warner Bk. Group**; *CIP.*

Still Waters Pubs., *(0-9714276)* Orders Addr.: P.O. Box 615, Ellettsville, IN 47429 Tel 812-323-0625 Do not confuse with Still Water Publishers, Hobe Sound, FL
E-mail: stillwaterspublishers@yahoo.com
Web site: http://www.stillwaterspublishers.com.

Stillpoint Publishing, *(0-913299; 1-883478)* Div. of The Stillpoint Institute, Inc., Orders Addr.: P.O. Box 640, Walpole, NH 03608 (SAN 285-8630) Tel 603-756-9281; Fax: 603-756-9282; Toll Free: 800-847-4014 (credit card orders only)
E-mail: stillpoint@stillpoint.org
Web site: http://www.stillpoint.org
Dist(s): **Publishers Group West.**

Stirling, H. Publishing, *(0-9700757)* 43165 Ambro Cir., Banning, CA 92220 Tel 909-849-3774; Fax: 909-849-7344; Toll Free Fax: 800-454-3795; Toll Free: 800-814-8863.

Stoddard, Michael Eugene, *(0-9675924)* 536 S. Palm Dr., Brea, CA 92821-6641 Tel 626-821-3911; Fax: 714-990-5110
E-mail: webmaster@rockymesa.com
Web site: http://www.Rockymesa.com.

Stoecklein Publishing, *(0-922029; 1-931153)* Orders Addr.: Tenth St. Ctr., Suite A1, Ketchum, ID 83340; Edit Addr.: P.O. Box 856, Ketchum, ID 83340 (SAN 251-1002) Tel 208-726-5191; Fax: 208-726-9752; Toll Free: 800-727-5191
E-mail: drspub@micron.net
Dist(s): **Graphic Arts Ctr. Publishing Co.**
Sunbelt Pubns., Inc.
Western International, Inc..

Stone Pine Bks. Imprint of Patri Pubns.

Stone Studios, *(0-9619791)* 394 Fafnir, Kimberly, ID 83341 Tel 208-423-4355; Fax: 208-423-4334.

Stonehaven Pubs., *(0-937775)* Orders Addr.: P.O. Box 367, Lena, IL 61048 (SAN 659-347X); Edit Addr.: 602 Oak St., Lena, IL 61048 (SAN 659-3488) Tel 815-369-2823 Do not confuse with Stonehaven Pubs., Fort Worth, TX
E-mail: Shnash@aol.com.

Stoney Creek Pr., *(0-9700487)* 21022 Horsetree Cir., Trabuco Canyon, CA 92679 Tel 949-858-1561; P.O. Box 70, Trabuco Canyon, CA 92678 (SAN 253-4401) Tel 949-858-3021
E-mail: yod@cox.net; yod@home.com
Web site: http://www.firestories.com
Dist(s): **Baker & Taylor Bks.**
Partners/West
Quality Bks., Inc..

Story Reader, Inc., *(0-9720158; 0-9720651)* 5050 Quorum Dr., Suite 315, Dallas, TX 75240 Tel 214-415-9200; Fax: 972-620-0715
E-mail: admin@storyreaders.com
Web site: http://www.storyreaders.com.

Story Stuff, Inc., *(1-928811)* P.O. Box 501372, Indianapolis, IN 46250-6372 Fax: 317-913-1777
E-mail: jmferrone@storystuff.com
Web site: http://www.storystuff.com.

Story Teller, The, *(1-929098)* P.O. Box 1174, Sterling Heights, MI 48311-1174 Tel 810-977-0411 (phone/fax)
E-mail: storezby1@aol.com.

Storybook Pr. & Productions, *(1-887683)* 467 Central Park W., Apt. 6E, New York, NY 10025 Tel 212-975-2473; Toll Free: 800-779-4341
E-mail: storybookp@aol.com.

Storytellers Ink, Inc., *(0-9623072; 1-880812; 1-930767)* Orders Addr.: a/o Quinn Currie, P.O. Box 33398, Seattle, WA 98133-0398 Tel 206-365-8265; Fax: 206-363-0830 Do not confuse with Storytellers Ink, Inc. in Kansas City, MO
E-mail: publisher@storytellers-Ink.com
Web site: http://www.storytellers-ink.com.

Storytelling World Pr., *(1-884624)* 108 Oak Grove Blvd., Suite 201, Johnson City, TN 37601 Tel 423-542-8425; Fax: 423-929-4235.

Storytime Ink International, *(0-9628769)* P.O. Box 470505, Broadview Heights, OH 44147 Tel 440-838-4881
E-mail: storytimeink@att.net.

Storywriter Pr., *(0-9712952)* 330 Clayton Oaks Dr., Ellisville, MO 63011 Tel 636-391-6734
E-mail: storywriter@mindspring.com.

Straub Printing & Publishing *See* **Evergreen Pacific Publishing, Ltd.**

Strauss Consultants, 48 W. 25th St., 11th Flr., New York, NY 10010-2708 Toll Free Fax: 888-528-8273; Toll Free: 800-236-7918
E-mail: strausscon@aol.com.

Street Saint Pubns., *(0-615; 1-931090)* 441 Brighton Rd., Pacifica, CA 94044 Tel 650-355-4296
E-mail: lynnruth@pacbell.net
Web site: http://www.lynnruthmiller.com.

Streetlight Christian Comics Pubns., The, *(0-9644578)* Div. of The Streetlight Group, Orders Addr.: P.O. Box 35096, Phoenix, AZ 85069 Tel 602-955-1263.

Strode Pubs. Imprint of Circle Bk. Service, Inc.

Stuart, Jesse Foundation, The, *(0-945084; 1-931672)* Orders Addr.: P.O. Box 669, Ashland, KY 41105 (SAN 245-8837) Tel 606-326-1667; Fax: 606-325-2519; Edit Addr.: 1645 Winchester Ave., Ashland, KY 41101 (SAN 245-8845)
E-mail: jsf@inet99.net
Web site: http://www.jsfbooks.com.

Studio Five/Fourteen, *(1-891736)* Orders Addr.: P.O. Box 110254, Carrollton, TX 75011-0254 Tel 972-323-7357; Fax: 972-242-7456; Edit Addr.: 1203 Laguna Ct., Carrollton, TX 75006
Web site: http://www.artiebooks.com.

Studio 403, *(0-9633943)* 223 Boylton Ave., E., Seattle, WA 98102-5608 Tel 206-323-6764; Fax: 206-323-1701
E-mail: mark@studio403.com
Web site: http://www.sott.com/.

Studio Mouse LLC, *(1-59069)* 353 Main Ave., Norwalk, CT 06851 Tel 203-846-2274; Fax: 203-846-1776; Toll Free: 800-228-7839
E-mail: chelsea.shriver@soundprints.com.

Studio 17, *(0-9700777)* 17 Shakerag St., Mineral Point, WI 53565 Tel 608-987-3573
E-mail: mgrow@fammed.wisc.edu.

Stylewriter Pubns., *(0-9718288; 0-9721653; 0-9729411)* Div. of Stylewriter, Inc., 4395 N. Windsor Dr., Provo, UT 84604-6301 Fax: 801-997-8953; Toll Free: 866-802-7888
E-mail: customerservice@stylewriter-publications.com
Web site: http://www.stylewriter-publications.com/.

Sugar Ducky Bks., Inc., *(0-9727388)* P.O. Box 56954, Jacksonville, FL 32241-6954 (SAN 255-1403)
E-mail: service@sugarduckybooks.com
Web site: http://www.sugarduckybooks.com
Dist(s): **Independent Pubs. Group.**

Sugarene's Pr., *(0-9700186)* Orders Addr.: P.O. Box 11267, Elkins Park, PA 19020; Edit Addr.: 7807 Caversham Dr., Elkins Park, PA 19027 Tel 609-656-8141
E-mail: NBW1913@aol.com.

Sullwold, William S. Publishing, *(0-88492)* 18 Pearl St., Taunton, MA 02780 (SAN 203-1744) Tel 508-823-0924.

†Summit Publishing Group - Legacy Bks., *(0-9626219; 1-56530)* 3649 Conflans Rd., No. 103, Irving, TX 75061 (SAN 631-1253) Tel 972-399-8856 ; Fax: 972-313-9060 Do not confuse with Summit Publishing, Los Angeles, CA
E-mail: info@summitbooks.com
Web site: http://www.summitbooks.com
Dist(s): **BookWorld Services, Inc.**
Tapestry Pr.; *CIP.*

Sunbelt Media, Incorporated *See* **Eakin Pr.**

Sunburst Imprint of Farrar, Straus & Giroux

Sundance Publishing, *(0-7608; 0-88741; 0-940146; 1-56801)* Orders Addr.: P.O. Box 1326, Littleton, MA 01460 (SAN 169-3484) Tel 978-486-9201; Fax: 978-486-1053; Toll Free Fax: 800-456-2419; Toll Free: 800-343-8204 Do not confuse with Sundance Publishing, Inc., Patchogue, NY
E-mail: info@sundancepub.com
Web site: http://www.sundancepub.com/
Dist(s): **Lectorum Pubns., Inc..**

Sundog Publishing, *(0-9642662)* Div. of Sugarfoot Enterprises., 9040 Noble Cir., Anchorage, AK 99502 Tel 907-248-7595 Do not confuse with Sundog Publishing, Silver City, MN, Madison, WI.

Sunfleur Pubns., Inc., *(0-9653729)* 421 Westchester Rd., Statesville, NC 28677 Tel 704-873-5516; Fax: 704-873-3850
E-mail: hdarden@i-america.net
Web site: http://www.booksbyhunter.com
Dist(s): **Parnassus Bk. Distributors.**

Sunflower Publishing Company *See* **Sunfleur Pubns., Inc.**

Sunflower Univ. Pr., *(0-89745)* Subs. of Journal of the West, Inc., 1531 Yuma, Box 1009, Manhattan, KS 66505-1009 (SAN 218-5075) Tel 785-539-1888; Fax: 785-539-2233; Toll Free: 800-258-1232 (orders)
Web site: http://www.sunflower-univ-press.org.

Sunrise Bks., *(0-940652)* 1707 "E" St., Eureka, CA 95501 (SAN 665-7893) Tel 707-442-4004 (phone/fax) Do not confuse with with companies with the same name in Lebanon, VA, Lake Bluff, IL.

Sunrise Productions, *(0-9667129)* Orders Addr.: P.O. Box 1061, Marshfield, WI 54449; Edit Addr.: 202 S. Chestnut, Marshfield, WI 54449.

†Sunstone Pr., *(0-86534; 0-913270)* Orders Addr.: 239 Johnson St., Santa Fe, NM 87504-2321; Edit Addr.: P.O. Box 2321, Santa Fe, NM 87504-2321 (SAN 214-2090) Tel 505-988-4418; Fax: 505-988-1025; Toll Free: 800-243-5644 (orders only)
E-mail: jsmith@sunstonepress.com
Web site: http://www.sunstonepress.com
Dist(s): **Baker & Taylor Bks.**
Bookpeople
Brodart Co.
New Leaf Distributing Co., Inc.
Quality Bks., Inc.
Treasure Chest Bks.; *CIP.*

Super Bks. & Tapes, *(0-9650736)* P.O. Box 15703, Phoenix, AZ 85060-5703 Tel 602-840-2357
Dist(s): **SPI Bks..**

†Sussman, Ellen Educational Services, *(0-933606)* P.O. Box 945, Manchester, VT 05254 (SAN 212-7660) Tel 802-375-1266; Fax: 802-375-1219; Toll Free: 800-445-3892
E-mail: ellens@souer.net; *CIP.*

Suzy's Zoo, *(0-9643588; 0-9726147)* 9401 Waples St., Suite 150, San Diego, CA 92121-3909 (SAN 298-7481) Tel 858-452-9401; Fax: 858-452-2170; Toll Free: 800-777-4846
Web site: http://www.suzyszoo.com.

Swedenborg Foundation, Inc., *(0-87785)* 320 N. Church St., West Chester, PA 19380 (SAN 111-7920) Tel 610-430-3222; Fax: 610-430-7982; Toll Free: 800-355-3222 (customer service)
E-mail: info@swedenborg.com
Web site: http://www.Swedenborg.com
Dist(s): **Words Distributing Co..**

Sweet Dreams Bilingual Pubs., *(0-9673032)* 1515 University Dr., Suite 204-B, Coral Springs, FL 33071 Tel 954-255-2722; Fax: 954-255-2730
E-mail: librosbp@earthlink.net
Web site: http://www.bilingualpublishers.com.

Sweet Valley Imprint of Random Hse. Children's Bks.

Sweetgrass Communications, Inc., *(0-9632837)* Orders Addr.: P.O. Box 3221, Bismarck, ND 58502 Tel 701-223-0818; Fax: 701-223-8754; Toll Free: 800-247-0441; Edit Addr.: 2210 E. Broadway, Bismarck, ND 58501
Dist(s): **Saks News, Inc..**

Sweetlight Bks., *(0-9604462; 1-877714)* 16625 Heitman Rd., Cottonwood, CA 96022 (SAN 215-1154) Tel 916-529-5392
E-mail: swtlight@snowcrest.net
Web site: http://www.snowcrest.net/swtlight
Dist(s): **Baker & Taylor Bks.**
Bookpeople
New Leaf Distributing Co., Inc..

Sweetwater Pr., *(0-9615504)* P.O. Box 96, Ault, CO 80610-0096 (SAN 695-9199) Do not confuse with companies with similiar names in Raleigh, NC, Birmingham, AL,Miami FL, Little Rock AR
E-mail: rburgess@info2000.net
Web site: http://www.info2000.net/~rburgess/sweet1.htm.

Swift Learning Resources, *(0-944991; 1-56861)* Div. of Swift Printing Corp., 107 S. 1200 E., Lehi, UT 84043-1458 (SAN 245-6737) Toll Free: 800-292-2831
E-mail: swift@swift-net.com
Web site: http://www.swiftlearning.com.

Sybrell Publishing, *(0-9700599)* P.O. Box 554, Stone Mountain, GA 30086 Fax: 770-987-4093
E-mail: info@sybrell.com; sybrell@sybrell.com
Web site: http://www.sybrell.com.

Synaxis Pr., *(0-911523)* P.O. Box 689, Lynden, WA 98264 (SAN 685-4338) Tel 604-826-9336; Fax: 604-820-9758
Dist(s): **Oakwood Pubns..**

Syncopated Pr., *(0-9671978; 0-9717380)* P.O. Box 411, Plainwell, MI 49080 Tel 616-685-0470; Fax: 616-685-6765; Toll Free: 877-867-7737
E-mail: frontier@net-link.net
Web site: http://www.syncopatedpress.com.

†Syracuse Univ. Pr., *(0-8156)* 621 Skytop Rd., Suite 110, Syracuse, NY 13244-5290 (SAN 206-9776) Tel 315-443-2597; Fax: 315-443-5545
E-mail: supress@syr.edu
Web site: http://www.sumweb.syr.edu/su_press/
Dist(s): **Gryphon Hse., Inc.**
Music Sales Corp.
Penguin Group (USA) Inc.; *CIP.*

TBW Bks., *(0-931474)* P.O. Box 649, New Portland, ME 04954-0649 Tel 207-628-4399; Fax: 207-628-3399
E-mail: fiveduck@aol.com.

TEA Printers & Pubs., *(0-9642344)* 174 W. Meadow Rd., Rockland, ME 04841 Tel 207-594-7711 (phone/fax).

T E A Publishers *See* **TEA Printers & Pubs.**

T. E. Publishing, Inc., *(0-9722036)* P.O. Box 823, Bath, NY 14810 Tel 607-76-1307
E-mail: pcarlton@tepublishing.com.

TNT Bks., *(1-885227)* Orders Addr.: 3657 Cree Dr., Salt Lake City, UT 84120-2867 Fax: 801-968-8038
E-mail: twixom@msn.com
Dist(s): **Publishers & Distributors.**

TNT Publishing, *(0-9664727)* 4854 Country Cone Way, Powder Springs, GA 30127 Tel 770-943-7847 Do not confuse with TNT Publishing in Oakland, CA.

Tahoe Tourist Promotions, *(0-9626792)* Orders Addr.: P.O. Box 986, Kings Beach, CA 96143 Tel 916-546-3303; Fax: 916-546-8202; Edit Addr.: 8612 N. Lake Blvd., Kings Beach, CA 95719.

Tahrike Tarsile Quran, Inc., *(0-940368; 1-879402)* 80-08 51st Ave., Elmhurst, NY 11373 (SAN 658-1870) Tel 718-446-6472; Fax: 718-446-4370
E-mail: ttq@koranusa.org
Web site: http://www.koranusa.org
Dist(s): **Publishers Group West.**

Talented Tenth Literary Syndicate *See* **SolidGumboWorks**

Talewinds Imprint of Charlesbridge Publishing, Inc.

Talk Miramax Bks., *(0-7868)* Div. of Disney Bk. Publishing, Inc., A Walt Disney Co., 118 W. 20th St., New York, NY 10011-3602 Tel 212-830-5858
Dist(s): **Time Warner Bk. Group.**

Tallfellow Pr., *(0-9676061; 1-931290)* 1180 S. Beverly Dr., Suite 320, Los Angeles, CA 90035 Tel 310-203-3837; Fax: 310-203-3893; *Imprints:* Smallfellow Press (Smallfellow Pr)
E-mail: Tallfellow@pacbell.net
Web site: http://TallfellowPress
Dist(s): **SCB Distributors.**

Tangerine Pr. Imprint of Scholastic, Inc.

Tantor Media, Inc., *(1-4001)* 1315 Avenida De Verdes, San Clemente, CA 92672 (SAN 254-0509) Tel 949-481-2770; Fax: 949-481-2790
E-mail: kevin@tantor.com
Web site: http://www.tantor.com.

Tapestry Pr., Ltd., *(0-924234; 1-56888)* Orders Addr.: P.O. Box 1113, Acton, MA 01720 (SAN 252-2152) Tel 508-635-0251; Fax: 978-635-9393; Toll Free: 800-535-2007; Edit Addr.: 8 Jefferson Dr., Acton, MA 01720 Do not confuse with companies with the same or similar name in Arlington, TX, Springville, UT, Biloxi, MS.

†Taplinger Publishing Co., Inc., *(0-8008)* P.O. Box 175, Marlboro, NJ 07746 Tel 201-432-3257; Fax: 201-432-3708
E-mail: info@parkwestpubs.com
Web site: http://www.parkwestpubs.com/
Dist(s): **Parkwest Pubns., Inc.**; *CIP.*

Targum Pr., Inc., *(0-944070; 1-56871)* 22700 W. Eleven Mile Rd., Southfield, MI 48034 (SAN 242-8997) Tel 248-355-2266; Toll Free Fax: 888-298-9992
E-mail: targum@elronet.co.il
Web site: http://www.targum.com
Dist(s): **Feldheim, Philipp Inc..**

Tarpley Publishing, *(1-888479)* 1430 Nelson St., Apt. 316, Lakewood, CO 80215-4572.

Tarquin Pubns. (GBR) *(0-906212; 1-899618) Dist. by* **Parkwest Pubns.**

Tartan Tabby Pr., *(0-9659718)* 1157 S. Ravine St., Terre Haute, IN 47802 Tel 812-299-2754.

Tarvin, Kathy, *(0-9649170)* 4162 McLean Dr., Cincinnati, OH 45255 Tel 513-528-5442.

Tashmoo Pr., The, *(0-932384)* RFD Box 590, Vineyard Haven, MA 02568 (SAN 212-5706) Tel 508-693-3199.

Tattersall Pr., *(0-9639890)* Orders Addr.: P.O. Box 712, Elkhart, IN 46515-0712; Edit Addr.: 1920 Grant St., Elkhart, IN 46514 Tel 219-264-6692
Dist(s): **Winters Publishing.**

Tattoo Manufacturing, *(1-892800; 0-9678636; 0-9702195)* 3761 E. Technical Dr., Tuscon, AZ 85713-5343 Tel 520-584-0001; Fax: 520-747-1299; Toll Free: 800-747-8016; *Imprints:* Tattootles Books (Tattootles Bks)
E-mail: printexpression@aol.com
Web site: http://www.tattoosales.com.

Tattootles Bks. Imprint of Tattoo Manufacturing

†Taylor & Francis, Inc., *(0-335; 0-415; 0-8448; 0-85066; 0-89116; 0-903796; 0-905273; 1-56032; 1-85000)* Orders Addr.: 10650 Toebben Dr., Independence, KY 41051 Toll Free Fax: 800-248-4724; Toll Free: 800-634-7064; Edit Addr.: 325 Chestnut St., Philadelphia, PA 19106 (SAN 241-9246) Tel 215-625-8900; Fax: 215-625-2940; 29 W. 35th St., New York, NY 10001 Tel 212-216-7800; Fax: 212-564-7854
E-mail: info@taylorandfrancis.com
Web site: http://www.taylorandfrancis.com
Dist(s): **netLibrary, Inc.**; *CIP.*

Taylor Productions Imprint of GRM Assocs.

Tea Road Pr., *(0-9708666)* P.O. Box 16590, Boise, ID 83715 Tel 208-322-7239; Fax: 208-321-9539
E-mail: tearoad@aol.com
Web site: http://www.tearoadpress.com.

Teach My Children Pubns., *(0-9668891)* 258 Bahia Ln., E., Litchfield Park, AZ 85340-4728 Tel 602-935-0386
E-mail: oldbaha@goodnet.com.

Teach Services *See* **TEACH Services, Inc.**

TEACH Services, Inc., *(0-945383; 1-57258)* 254 Donovan Rd., Brushton, NY 12916 (SAN 246-9863) Tel 518-358-3494; Fax: 518-358-3028; Toll Free: 800-367-1844
E-mail: info@teachservicesinc.com
Web site: http://www.teachservicesinc.com.

Teacher Created Materials, Inc., *(0-87673; 1-55734; 1-57690; 0-7439)* 6421 Industry Way, Westminster, CA 92683-3608 (SAN 665-5270) Tel 714-891-7895; Fax: 714-892-0283; Toll Free: 800-662-4321
E-mail: ppulido@teachercreated.com
Web site: http://www.teachercreated.com.

Teaching, Inc., *(0-9614574; 1-881660)* P.O. Box 788, Edmonds, WA 98020 Tel 425-774-0755; Fax: 425-775-0755; Toll Free: 800-774-0755 (orders only).

Teaching Resource Ctr., *(1-56785)* P.O. Box 82777, San Diego, CA 92138-2777 Toll Free: 800-833-3389
E-mail: trc@trcabc.com.

Team Effort Publishing Co., *(0-9630884)* Orders Addr.: P.O. Box 5027, Huntsville, TX 77342 Toll Free: 800-289-5453; Edit Addr.: 427 Fish Hatchery Rd., Huntsville, TX 77342 Tel 409-295-5846.

Tecolote Pubns., *(0-938711)* Orders Addr.: 4918 Del Monte Ave., San Diego, CA 92107-3209 (SAN 661-5058) Tel 619-222-6066
E-mail: tecopubs@earthlink.com
Web site: http://www.tecolotepublications.com.

Teddy & Friends, *(0-9636154)* 4606 13th Pl., Vero Beach, FL 32966-2611.

Tegen, Katherine Bks. Imprint of HarperCollins Children's Bk. Group

Telcraft Bks., *(1-878893)* 388 S. Main St., No. 201, Akron, OH 44311 Tel 330-374-0658; Fax: 330-374-0713.

Tell Publications *See* **Telcraft Bks.**

Telstar, *(0-9624384; 1-878142)* 1098 Fort Rd., Benton Harbor, MI 49022 Tel 269-926-2226
E-mail: twocats@qtm.net.

Temco Publishing, *(1-889005)* 4338 Union Church Rd., Salisbury, MD 21804 Fax: 410-543-9316; Toll Free: 800-370-0250.

Temple, Ellen C. Publishing, Inc., *(0-936650)* 736 Crown Colony Dr., Suite 100, Lufkin, TX 75901 (SAN 215-1162) Tel 409-639-4707; Fax: 409-639-4716
E-mail: ectemple@icc.com
Dist(s): **Eakin Pr..**

Templeton Foundation Pr., *(1-890151; 1-932031)* Div. of John Templeton Foundation, 5 Radnor Corporate Ctr., Suite 120, Radnor, PA 19087 Tel 610-971-2670; Fax: 610-971-2672; Toll Free: 800-561-3367
E-mail: lbarrett@templeton.org; tfp@templetonpress.org
Web site: http://www.templetonpress.org
Dist(s): **Univ. of Chicago Pr..**

†Ten Speed Pr., *(0-89815; 0-913668; 1-58008)* Orders Addr.: P.O. Box 7123, Berkeley, CA 94707 (SAN 202-7674) Fax: 510-559-1629 (orders); Toll Free: 800-841-2665; 555 Richmond St., W. Suite 405, Box 702, Toronto, ON M5V 3B1 Tel 416-703-7775; Fax: 416-703-9992
E-mail: order@tenspeed.com; alan@tenspeed.ca; greg@tenspeed.com
Web site: http://www.tenspeed.com; *CIP.*

Tennedo Pubs., *(0-9638946)* 6315 Elwynne Dr., Cincinnati, OH 45236 Tel 513-791-3277
Web site: http://www.author.illustr.source.com.

Terk Bks. & Pubs., *(1-881690)* Orders Addr.: P.O. Box 160, Palos Heights, IL 60463; Edit Addr.: 8140 S. Scottsdale Ave., Chicago, IL 60652
E-mail: Terkbooks@aol.com.

Tern Bks. Imprint of Tern Bk. Co., Inc., The

Tern Bk. Co., Inc., The, *(0-9655782; 1-890309)* P.O. Box 720701, Orlando, FL 32872-0701 Tel 407-858-4869; Fax: 407-658-6320; Toll Free: 888-211-8376; *Imprints:* Tern Books (Tern Bks)
E-mail: photonat@idt.net
Web site: http://village.ios.com/~photonat
Dist(s): **Baker & Taylor Bks..**

Terra Nova Pr., *(0-944176)* 1309 Redwood Ln., Davis, CA 95616 (SAN 242-8741) Tel 916-753-1519; Fax: 916-753-6491.

Terrapin Pubns., *(0-9712942)* P.O. Box 323, Hastings-On-Hudson, NY 10706 Do not confuse with Terrapin Publishing in Roslindale, MA.

TexArt Services, Inc., *(0-935857)* P.O. Box 17423, San Antonio, TX 78217-0423 (SAN 696-0022) Tel 210-826-2889.

†Texas Christian Univ. Pr., *(0-87565; 0-912646)* P.O. Box 298300, Fort Worth, TX 76129 (SAN 202-7690) Tel 817-257-7822; Fax: 817-257-5075
E-mail: j.alter@tcu.edu; s.petty@tcu.edu
Web site: http://www.prs.tcu.edu/prs
Dist(s): **Texas A&M Univ. Pr.**; *CIP.*

Texas Instruments, Inc., *(0-89512)* Orders Addr.: P.O. Box 225558, Dallas, TX 75222-5558 Tel 972-293-5055; Fax: 972-293-5967.

Texas Review Pr., *(1-881515)* Div. of Sam Houston State Univ., English Dept., Sam Houston State Univ. English Dept., Box 2146, Huntsville, TX 77341-2146 Tel 936-294-1992; Fax: 936-294-1414
E-mail: eng_pdr@shsu.edu
Web site: http://www.tamu.edu/upress/TR/trgen.htm/
Dist(s): **Texas A&M Univ. Pr..**

†Texas Tech Univ. Pr., *(0-89672)* Affil. of Texas Tech Univ., Orders Addr.: P.O. Box 41037, Lubbock, TX 79409-1037 (SAN 218-5989) Tel 806-742-2982; Fax: 806-742-2979; Toll Free: 800-832-4042; Edit Addr.: 2903 Fourth St., Lubbock, TX 79409-1037
E-mail: ttup@ttu.edu
Web site: http://www.ttup.ttu.edu; *CIP.*

†Theatre Communications Group, Inc., *(0-88754; 0-913745; 0-930452; 0-948230; 1-55936; 1-84002; 1-85459; 1-870259; 1-899791)* 355 Lexington Ave., New York, NY 10017-6603 (SAN 210-9387) Tel 212-697-5230; Fax: 212-983-4847
Web site: http://www.tcg.org
Dist(s): **Consortium Bk. Sales & Distribution**; *CIP.*

Theodore Publishing, Inc., *(0-9653798)* Orders Addr.: P.O. Box 381812, Duncanville, TX 75138 Tel 972-298-0214 (phone/fax) Do not confuse with Theodore Publishing, Champaign, IL
E-mail: theodorepublishing@att.net
Web site: http://www.theodorepublishing.com
Dist(s): **Follett Library Resources**
Hervey's Booklink & Cookbook Warehouse.

Theytus Bks., Ltd. (CAN) *(0-919441; 1-894778) Dist. by* **Orca Bk Pubs.**

Third World Press, *(0-88378)* P.O. Box 19730, Chicago, IL 60619 (SAN 202-778X) Tel 773-651-0700; Fax: 773-651-7286
Web site: http://www.thirdworldpress.com.

Thomasson-Grant, Incorporated *See* **LegacyWords Publishing**

Thompson, Elizabeth, *(0-9619576)* 258 Basin Dr., No. N, Fort Lauderdale, FL 33308-5042 (SAN 245-4319) Tel 954-938-4468; Fax: 954-565-9991.

†Thorndike Pr., *(0-7838; 0-7862; 0-8161; 0-89621; 1-56054)* Div. of Gale Group, 295 Kennedy Memorial Dr., Waterville, ME 04901 Tel 207-859-1053; 207-859-1020; 207-859-1000; Toll Free Fax: 800-558-4676; Toll Free: 800-223-1244 (ext. 15); 800-877-4253 (customer resource ctr.)
E-mail: knobloch@galegroup.com; barb.littfield@galegroup.com
Web site: http://www.galegroup.com/thorndike; *CIP.*

Thornsbury Bailey & Brown, *(0-945253)* P.O. Box 5169, Arlington, VA 22205 (SAN 246-2192) Tel 703-532-2210.

Thornton Publishing, *(0-9670242; 0-9719597; 0-9723309; 1-932344)* 6834 S. University Blvd., No. 416, Littleton, CO 80122 Tel 303-794-8888; Fax: 720-863-2013 Do not confuse with companies with the same or similar names in New Iberia, LA, Forest Grove, OR, Burley, ID
E-mail: publisher@profitablepublishing.net
Web site: http://www.profitablepublishing.net.

Thorpe, F. A. Pubs. (GBR) *(0-7089; 0-85456) Dist. by* **Ulverscroft US.**

Thoth Publishing Co., *(0-9628067)* Orders Addr.: P.O. Box 11027, Springfield, MO 65808 Fax: 417-862-8207; Edit Addr.: 963 S. Delaware, Springfield, MO 65802 Tel 417-862-5520 Do not confuse with Thoth Publishing Company, West Hartford, CT.

Three Continents Imprint of Rienner, Lynne Pubs., Inc.

Three Pines Pr., *(0-9635247)* 2104 Brenner St., Saginaw, MI 48602 Tel 517-792-4989 Do not confuse with Three Pines Pr. in Cambridge, MA
E-mail: editor@threepinespress.com.

3 Pounds Pr., *(0-9675299)* Orders Addr.: PMB 329 25125 Santa Clara St., Hayward, CA 94544 Fax: 520-244-2599
E-mail: eddie@3pounds.com
Web site: http://www.3pounds.com.

Thriftecon Publications, *(1-880258)* 405 Ascot Ct., Knoxville, TN 37923-5807 Tel 423-539-9932
E-mail: RBreed4217@AOL.com.

Thunder & Ink, *(0-9623227)* P.O. Box 7014, Evanston, IL 60201
E-mail: Trb4320@ao.com.

Thunder Bay Pr. Imprint of Advantage Pubs. Group

Thunder Bay Pr., *(1-882376)* 2325 Jarco Dr., Holt, MI 48842 Tel 517-694-4616 Do not confuse with Thunder Bay Pr, San Diego, CA
E-mail: partnersbk@aol.com
Dist(s): **Partners Pubs. Group, Inc.**
Publishers Group West.

Thurman Hse., LLC, *(1-58989)* 5 Park Ctr. Ct., Suite 300, Owings Mills, MD 21117 Tel 410-902-9100; Fax: 410-902-7210
E-mail: thurmanhouse@ottenheimerpub.com.

Tidal Wave Productions *See* **Black, Judith Storyteller**

Tidewater Pubs. Imprint of Cornell Maritime Pr., Inc.

Tiffany Publishing Co., *(0-9616079)* 98 Puritan Ave., Worcester, MA 01604 (SAN 698-1321) Tel 508-756-1911.

Tiger Tales Imprint of ME Media LLC

Names

Tilbury Hse. Pubs., *(0-88448; 0-937966)* 2 Mechanic St., No. 3, Gardiner, ME 04345 Tel 207-582-1899; Fax: 207-582-8227; Toll Free: 800-582-1899 (orders) ; *Imprints:* Harpswell Press (Hrpswel Pr)
E-mail: tilbury@tilburyhouse.com; sbeach@tilburyhouse.com
Web site: http://www.tilburyhouse.com
Dist(s): **Lectorum Pubns., Inc..**

Timbertrails Imprint of Capstan Pubns.

Time Warner AudioBooks, *(1-57042; 1-58621; 1-59483)* Div. of Time Warner, Inc., 135 W. 50th St., 4th Flr., New York, NY 10020 Fax: 212-522-7994; *Imprints:* Warner Audio Video Entertainment (W A V E) (Warner Audio)
Web site: http://www.mytimewarneraudio.com
Dist(s): **Libros Sin Fronteras**
Landmark Audiobooks
Warner Bks., Inc..

Time Warner Bk. Group, *(0-446)* Orders Addr.: 3 Center Plaza, Boston, MA 02108 Toll Free Fax: 800-286-9471; Toll Free: 800-759-0190; Edit Addr.: 135 W. 50th St. Sports Illustrated Building, New York, NY 10020-1393 Tel 212-522-7381; Toll Free Fax: 800-477-5925
Web site: http://www.timewarner.com.

Timeless Romance Imprint of Sierra Raconteur Publishing

Timeless Treasures Imprint of Sierra Raconteur Publishing

Time-Life Custom Publishing *See* **Time-Life Inc.**

Time-Life Education, Inc., *(0-7054; 0-7370; 0-7835; 0-8094)* Orders Addr.: P.O. Box 85026, Richmond, VA 23285-5026 Toll Free Fax: 800-449-2011; Edit Addr.: 2000 Duke St., Alexandria, VA 22314 Tel 703-838-7000; Fax: 703-518-4124; Toll Free: 800-449-2010
E-mail: education@timelifecs.com
Web site: http://www.timelifeedu.com/
Dist(s): **Time Warner Bk. Group.**

†Time-Life, Inc., *(0-7835; 0-8094)* Div. of Time Warner Co., Orders Addr.: Three Center Plaza, Boston, MA 02108-2084 Toll Free Fax: 800-308-1083; 800-286-9471; Toll Free: 800-277-8844; 800-759-0190; Edit Addr.: 2000 Duke St., Alexandria, VA 22314 (SAN 202-7836) Tel 703-838-7000; Fax: 703-838-7090; Toll Free: 800-621-7026
Web site: http://timelifeedu.com
Dist(s): **Time Warner Bk. Group**
Time-Life Publishing Warehouse
Worldwide Media Service, Inc.; *CIP.*

Time-Life Inc., *(0-7054; 0-7370)* Div. of Time Warner, Inc., 2000 Duke St., Alexandria, VA 22314 Tel 703-838-7000; Fax: 703-838-7045
E-mail: jennifer_ward@time-inc.com.

T.I.M.M.-E. Co., Inc., *(0-9718232)* 230 E. 25th St, Suite 2E, New York, NY 10010
E-mail: tools4tolerance@aol.com
Web site: http://www.weareallthesameinside.com
Dist(s): **Bookazine Co., Inc..**

Tingley, J.R. Publishing, Inc., *(0-9660985)* 74 E. High St., Union City, PA 16438 Tel 814-438-2427; Fax: 814-438-1053.

Tingley, Megan Bks. Imprint of Little Brown Children's Bks.

Tiptoe Literary Service, *(0-937953)* 434 Sixth St., No. 206, Raymond, WA 98577-1804 (SAN 659-7971) Tel 360-942-4596
E-mail: ka7ton@arrl.net
Web site: http://www.willapabay.org/~anne.

Tiptoe Publishing *See* **Tiptoe Literary Service**

Titan Bks. Ltd. (GBR) *(0-907610; 1-84023; 1-85286; 1-900097) Dist. by* **Client Dist Srvs.**

Tiwinke Publishing, Inc., *(0-9660797)* Subs. of Oklahoma Corp., 1820 Seran Dr., Wewoka, OK 74884 Tel 405-382-7207; Fax: 405-257-3606.

Todd Communications, *(1-57833; 1-878100)* 203 W. 15th Ave., Suite 102, Anchorage, AK 99501 (SAN 298-6280) Tel 907-274-8633; Fax: 907-276-6858
E-mail: info@toddcom.com.

TOKYOPOP, Inc., *(1-892213; 1-931514; 1-59182; 1-59532)* Div. of Mixx Entertainment, Inc., 5900 Wilshire Blvd., Suite 2000, Los Angeles, CA 90036 Tel 323-692-6700; Fax: 323-692-6701
Dist(s): **Client Distribution Services.**

Tokyopop Press *See* **TOKYOPOP, Inc.**

Tomac Publishing, *(0-9638747)* 20 Ann St., Old Greenwich, CT 06870-2326 Tel 203-637-0341; 203 637 0341.

Tomato Enterprises, *(0-9617357)* P.O. Box 73892, Davis, CA 95617 (SAN 664-0427) Tel 530-750-1832; Fax: 530-759-9741
E-mail: leland@dcn.davis.ca.us.

Top Shelf Productions, *(1-891830; 961-90436)* Orders Addr.: P.O. Box 1282, Marietta, GA 30061-1282 Tel 770-425-0551; Fax: 770-427-6395; Edit Addr.: 1109 Grand Oaks Glen, Marietta, GA 30064 Tel 770-425-0551; Fax: 770-427-6395
E-mail: staros@bellsouth.net
Web site: http://www.topshelfcomix.com
Dist(s): **Diamond Book Distributors, Inc.**
Diamond Comic Distributors, Inc..

Topaz Imprint of NAL

Tor Bks. Imprint of Doherty, Tom Assocs., LLC

Tor Classics Imprint of Doherty, Tom Assocs., LLC

†Torah Aura Productions, *(0-933873; 1-891662)* 4423 Fruitland Ave., Los Angeles, CA 90058 (SAN 692-7025) Tel 323-585-7312; Fax: 323-585-0327; Toll Free: 800-238-6724
E-mail: jane@torahaura.com; *CIP.*

Torres, Eliseo & Sons, *(0-88303)* P.O. Box 2, Eastchester, NY 10709 (SAN 207-0235).

Tortuga Pr., *(1-889910)* PMB 181, 2777 Yulupa Ave., Santa Rosa, CA 95405 (SAN 299-1756) Tel 707-544-4720; Fax: 707-544-5609; Toll Free: 800-852-4890 (orders only)
E-mail: info@tortugapress.com
Web site: http://www.tortugapress.com
Dist(s): **Lectorum Pubns., Inc..**

Totline Pubns. Imprint of McGraw-Hill Children's Publishing

Tott Pubns., *(1-882225)* 513 Land Dr., Dayton, OH 45440 Tel 937-426-7638.

Touchstone Imprint of Simon & Schuster

Townsend, J.N. Publishing, *(0-9617426; 1-880158)* 4 Franklin St., Exeter, NH 03833 (SAN 630-303X) Tel 603-778-9883; Fax: 603-772-1980; Toll Free: 800-333-9883 (orders only)
E-mail: townsendpub@aol.com
Web site: http://www.jntownsendpublishing.com
Dist(s): **Hood, Alan C. & Co., Inc..**

Townsend Pr., *(0-944210; 1-59194)* 1038 Industrial Dr., West Berlin, NJ 08091-9164 (SAN 243-0444) Toll Free Fax: 800-225-8894; Toll Free: 800-772-6410
E-mail: townsendcs@aol.com
Web site: http://www.townsendpress.com.

Toy Box Productions, *(1-887729; 1-932332)* Div. of CRT, Custom Products, Inc., 7532 Hickory Hills Ct., Whites Creek, TN 37189 Tel 615-299-0822; 615-876-5490; Fax: 615-876-3931; Toll Free: 800-750-1511
E-mail: leeann@crttoybox.com
Dist(s): **Baker & Taylor Bks.**
Christian Bk. Distributors.

Toys 'n Things Press *See* **Redleaf Pr.**

Tradition Publishing Co., *(1-59187)* Orders Addr.: P.O. Box 370, Maple Plain, MN 55359
Dist(s): **Child's World, Inc..**

Trafalgar Square, *(0-943955; 1-57076)* Orders Addr.: P.O. Box 257, North Pomfret, VT 05053 (SAN 213-8859) Tel 802-457-1911; Fax: 802-457-1913; Toll Free: 800-423-4525; Edit Addr.: Howe Hill Rd., North Pomfret, VT 05053
E-mail: tsquare@sover.net
Web site: http://www.trafalgarsquarebooks.com.

Trail of Success Pubs., *(0-9632895)* 10803 Old Field Dr., Reston, VA 22091 Tel 703-758-2519.

Trails West Publishing, *(0-939729)* P.O. Box 8619, Santa Fe, NM 87504-8619 (SAN 663-7809) Tel 505-982-8058
Dist(s): **Cinco Puntos Pr.**
Continental Bk. Co., Inc..

†Transaction Pubs., *(0-7658; 0-87855; 0-88738; 1-56000; 1-4128)* 390 Campus Dr., Somerset, NJ 08873 (SAN 202-7941) Tel 732-445-2280; Fax: 732-445-3138; Toll Free: 888-999-6778
E-mail: orders@transactionpub.com; agarbie@transactionpub.com
Web site: http://www.transactionpub.com; *CIP.*

Transatlantic Arts, Inc., *(0-693)* P.O. Box 6086, Albuquerque, NM 87197 (SAN 202-7968) Tel 505-898-2289 Do not confuse with Trans-Atlantic Pubns., Inc., Philadelphia, PA.
E-mail: books@transatlantic.com
Web site: http://www.transatlantic.com/direct.

Trans-Atlantic Pubns., Inc., 311 Bainbridge St., Philadelphia, PA 19147 (SAN 694-0234) Tel 215-925-5083; Fax: 215-925-1912 Do not confuse with Transatlantic Arts, Inc., Albuquerque, NM
E-mail: order@transatlanticpub.com
Web site: http://www.transatlanticpub.com
Dist(s): **Baker & Taylor Bks..**

Transworld Publishers Ltd. (GBR) *(0-552) Dist. by* **Trafalgar.**

Treasure Bay, Inc., *(1-891327)* 17 Parkgrove Dr., South San Francisco, CA 94080 Tel 650-589-7980; Fax: 650-589-7927; Fulfillment Addr.: P.O. Box 2510, Novato, CA 94948 Tel 415-883-3530
E-mail: treasurebaybooks@yahoo.com.

Treasure Chest Bks., *(0-918080; 1-887896; 0-9700750)* Orders Addr.: P.O. Box 5250, Tucson, AZ 85703-0250 (SAN 209-3251) Tel 520-623-9558; Fax: 520-624-5888; Toll Free Fax: 800-715-5888; Toll Free: 800-969-9558; Edit Addr.: 451 N. Bonita Ave., Tucson, AZ 85745 Tel 602-623-9558
E-mail: info@treasurechestbooks.com; info@rionuevo.com
Web site: http://www.rionuevo.com/; http://www.treasurechestbooks.com
Dist(s): **Norton, W. W. & Co., Inc..**

Treasure Chest Publications *See* **Treasure Chest Bks.**

Trebloon Pubns., *(0-9715423)* P.O. Box 156, Lawrence, NY 11559 (SAN 254-1874) Fax: 516-432-8292; 12 Bayview Ave., Lawrence, NY 11559 Tel 516-432-8520
Web site: http://www.trebloon.com
Dist(s): **Baker & Taylor Bks..**

Treehouse Court Imprint of Dingles & Co.

Treeless Pr., *(1-58505)* 2887 College Ave., No. 1, Suite 295, Berkeley, CA 94705 Tel 510-848 6692
E-mail: admin@treelesspress.com; sgarthp@inkyfingers.com
Web site: http://www.treelesspress.com.

Trellis Publishing, Inc., *(0-9663281; 1-930650)* Orders Addr.: P.O. Box 16141, Duluth, MN 55816 (SAN 299-6669) Tel 715-399-0780; Fax: 715-399-0781; Toll Free: 800-513-0115; Edit Addr.: 9584 S. Foxboro-Chaffey Rd., Foxboro, WI 54836 (SAN 299-6677)
E-mail: trellis2@aol.com
Web site: http://www.trellispublishing.com
Dist(s): **Independent Pubs. Group.**

Trend Enterprises, Inc., *(1-889319; 1-58792)* Orders Addr.: P.O. Box 64073, Saint Paul, MN 55164 Tel 651-631-2850; Fax: 651-582-3500; Toll Free Fax: 800-845-4832; Toll Free: 800-328-5540; Edit Addr.: 300 Ninth Ave., SW, New Brighton, MN 55112
Web site: http://www.trendenterprises.com.

Tricycle Pr., *(1-58246; 1-883672)* Div. of Ten Speed Pr., Orders Addr.: P.O. Box 7123, Berkeley, CA 94707 Tel 510-559-1600; Fax: 510-559-1629
Web site: http://www.tenspeed.com
Dist(s): **Gryphon Hse., Inc.**
Ten Speed Pr.
Wolverine Distributing, Inc..

Trident Pr. International, *(1-58279; 1-888777; 1-86091)* Orders Addr.: 801 12th Ave., S., Suite 400, Naples, FL 34102 Tel 239-649-7077; Fax: 239-649-5832; Toll Free Fax: 800-494-4226; Toll Free: 800-593-3662; Edit Addr.: 395 W. Mayes St., Jackson, MO 39213
E-mail: tridentpress@worldnet.att.net
Web site: http://www.schoolbookzone.com; http://www.secondworldwar.net; http://www.trident-international.com.

Trinity Rivers Publishing, Inc., *(1-888565)* P.O. Box 209, Manassas, VA 20108-0209 Tel 703-330-3262 (phone/fax); *Imprints:* Reconciliation Press (Reconciliation Pr)
E-mail: publisher@trinityrivers.com
Web site: http://www.trinityrivers.com
Dist(s): **Follett Library Resources.**

Triple Exposure Publishing, Incorporated *See* **T. E. Publishing, Inc.**

Triune Bible Institute & Seminary *See* **Triune Biblical Univ.**

Triune Biblical Univ., *(1-55967)* Orders Addr.: P.O. Box 912, Kelso, WA 98626 (SAN 251-8120) Tel 360-577-0586; Fax: 360-578-2528; Edit Addr.: 1209 S. Third Ave., Kelso, WA 98626
E-mail: tbu@kalama.com; triunebiblical@kalama.com
Web site: http://triunebibleuni.uswestdex.com.

Tudor Pubs., Inc., *(0-936389)* 3109 Shady Lawn Dr., Greensboro, NC 27408 (SAN 697-3035) Tel 336-282-5907; Fax: 336-333-1099
E-mail: Eepfaff@aol.com
Dist(s): **Baker & Taylor Bks.**
Brodart Co..

Tuffy Bks. Imprint of Putnam Publishing Group, The

Tumbleweed Pr., *(0-938091)* 11503 Carrollwood Dr., Tampa, FL 33618 (SAN 659-705X) Tel 813-932-8487 Do nto confuse with Tumbleweed Press in Fuquay-Varina, NC .

Tundra Bks. of Northern New York, *(0-88776; 0-89541; 0-912766)* Affil. of Tundra Bks, Inc., P.O. Box 1030, Plattsburgh, NY 12901 Tel 416-598-4786; Fax: 416-598-0247
E-mail: mail@mcclelland.com
Web site: http://www.tundrabooks.com
Dist(s): **Baker & Taylor Bks.**
Bookmen, Inc.
Borders, Inc.
Brodart Co.
Random Hse., Inc..

Turley, Reid P., *(0-9651494)* 950 E. 140 N., Lindon, UT 84042 Tel 801-785-1176; Fax: 801-785-1078
E-mail: Reid_TurleyRSA@USA.com.

Turnage Publishing Co., Inc., *(1-880726)* 6737 Low Gap Rd., Blairsville, GA 30512 Tel 706-745-5125 (phone/fax)
E-mail: sturnage@peachnet.campuscwix.net.

Turtle Bks. Imprint of Jason & Nordic Pubs.

Turtle Bks., *(1-890515)* 866 United Nations Plaza, Suite 525, New York, NY 10017 Tel 212-644-2020; Fax: 212-223-4387
E-mail: turtlebook@aol.com
Web site: http://www.turtlebooks.com
Dist(s): **Lectorum Pubns., Inc.**
Publishers Group West.

Turtle Island Pr., Inc., *(1-889166)* 3104 E. Camelback Rd., Suite 614, Phoenix, AZ 85016 (SAN 299-5425) Tel 602-468-1141; Fax: 602-954-8560; Toll Free: 888-900-9699; *Imprints:* Dr. H Books (Dr H Books).

Turtleback Bks., *(0-606)* Orders Addr.: P.O. Box 14260, Madison, WI 53714-0260 Toll Free Fax: 800-828-0401; Toll Free: 800-448-8939; Edit Addr.: 2810 Crossroads Dr., Suite 2700, Madison, WI 5378-7942 Fax: 608-241-0666 Do not confuse with Turtleback Bks., Friday Harbor, WA. Turtleback Books are available only to schools and libraries. Not available to the retail market.
E-mail: turtleback@demco.com
Web site: http://www.turtlebackbooks.com/.

Tush People, The, *(0-9722514)* P.O. Box 950100, Mission Hills, CA 91395 Tel 661-298-2293; 818-897-1734; Fax: 818-899-4455
E-mail: dfav218@aol.com
Dist(s): **Biblio Distribution.**

Tusky Enterprises *See* **Tusky Pr., The**

Tusky Pr., The, *(1-879100)* 1733 Hutchinson Ln., Silver Spring, MD 20906 Tel 301-942-1904; Fax: 301-946-3944
E-mail: kg12@umail.umd.edu.

Tuttle Publishing, *(0-8048; 4-900737)* Orders Addr.: 364 Innovation Dr., North Clarendon, VT 05759-9436 Tel 802-773-8930; Fax: 802-773-6993; Toll Free Fax: 800-329-8885; Toll Free: 800-526-2778; Edit Addr.: 153 Milk St., 4th Flr., Boston, MA 02109 (SAN 213-2621) Tel 617-951-4080; Fax: 617-951-4045; Toll Free: 800) 247 1060; *Imprints:* Everyman's Classic Library in Paperback (Everyman's Classic Lib); PeriplusEdition (PeriplEdns)
E-mail: info@tuttlepublishing.com
Web site: http://www.tuttlemartialarts.com; http://www.tuttlepublishing.com
Dist(s): **Cheng & Tsui Co.**
Continental Bk. Co., Inc..

Twain's Huckleberry Press *See* **Huckleberry Pr.**

25th Century Pr., *(1-56721)* Div. of Rio Grande Technology, 100 E. Washington St., Suite 102, Charleston, WV 25301; 7102 Ilfield Rd., SW, Albuquerque, NM 87105 Tel 505-873-2220; Fax: 505-877-4443
E-mail: editor@25c.com.

21st Century Bks., Inc. Imprint of Millbrook Pr., Inc.

Twiglet The Little Christmas Tree Imprint of PJs Corner

Twin Pleasures Publishing Corp., *(0-9638629; 1-892228)* 8666 Moon Bay Cir., Indianapolis, IN 46236 Tel 317-823-7640; Fax: 317-823-7642; Toll Free: 800-894-6257.

Two Lives Publishing, *(0-9674468)* Orders Addr.: P.O. Box 736, Ridley Park, PA 19078; Edit Addr.: 508 N. Swarthmore Ave., No. 1, Ridley Park, PA 19078 Tel 610-532-2024; Fax: 610-532-2790; Toll Free Fax: 877-543-3812; Toll Free: 877-543-3899
E-mail: bcombs@TwoLives.com
Web site: http://www.TwoLives.com
Dist(s): **Baker & Taylor Bks.**
Book Wholesalers, Inc.
Bookpeople
Brodart Co.
Children's Library Services
Koen Bk. Distributors
Unique Bks., Inc..

Two Sisters Publishing, *(1-928659)* 8220 Sedona Sunrise Dr., Las Vegas, NV 89128-7909 Tel 702-363-8235; Fax: 702-363-7698.

Two-Can Imprint of Creative Publishing international, Inc.

Tyketoon Young Author Publishing Co., *(1-886210)* 7417 Douglas Ln., Fort Worth, TX 76180 Tel 817-581-2876.

Tympanon Productions, *(0-9639428)* 3047 Los Cerillos Dr., West Covina, CA 91791 Tel 909-612-5707; Fax: 909-612-5715.

†Tyndale Hse. Pubs., *(0-8423; 1-4143)* Orders Addr.: P.O. Box 80, Wheaton, IL 60189-0080 (SAN 206-7749) Tel 630-668-8310; Fax: 630-668-3245; Toll Free: 800-323-9400; Edit Addr.: 351 Executive Dr., Wheaton, IL 60188; *Imprints:* Tyndale Kids (Tyndale Kids)
Web site: http://www.tyndale.com
Dist(s): **Appalachian Bk. Distributors**
CRC Pubns.
Christian Bk. Distributors
Riverside
Spring Arbor Distributors, Inc.
Beeler, Thomas T. Publisher; *CIP.*

Tyndale Kids Imprint of Tyndale Hse. Pubs.

Typographeum, *(0-930126)* The Stone Cottage, 246 Bennington Rd., Francestown, NH 03043-3007 (SAN 211-3031) Tel 603-547-2425
E-mail: typographeum@surfglobal.net
Web site: http://www.abebooks.com/.

†UAHC Pr., *(0-8074)* 633 Third Ave., New York, NY 10017 (SAN 203-3291) Tel 212-650-4121; Fax: 212-650-4119; Toll Free: 888-489-8242
E-mail: rabrams@uahc.org; press@uahc.org
Web site: http://www.uahcpress.com; *CIP.*

U.S. Games Systems, Inc., *(0-88079; 0-913866; 1-57281)* 179 Ludlow St., Stamford, CT 06902 (SAN 158-6483) Tel 203-353-8400; Fax: 203-353-8431; Toll Free: 800-544-2637; *Imprints:* Cove Press (Cove Pr CT)
E-mail: usgames@aol.com
Web site: http://www.usgamesinc.com
Dist(s): **Bookpeople**
New Leaf Distributing Co., Inc..

UBASFILM, Ltd., *(0-9655666)* Orders Addr.: P.O. Box 1988, Lucerne Valley, CA 92356 Tel 760-247-2413; Fax: 760-961-1966; Edit Addr.: 28574 Sutter Rd., Lucerne Valley, CA 92356
E-mail: UBASFILM@aol.com.

UglyTown, *(0-9663473; 0-9724412)* 2148 1/2 W. Sunset Blvd., Suite 204, Los Angeles, CA 90026 Tel 213-484-8334; Fax: 213-484-8333
E-mail: mayorsoffice@uglytown.com
Web site: http://www.uglytown.com
Dist(s): **Words Distributing Co..**

UglyTown Productions *See* **UglyTown**

Ujamaa Enterprises, Inc., *(0-9639349)* 121 Underwood Rd., Oak Ridge, TN 37830 Tel 423-481-3607.

Ulverscroft Audio (U.S.A.), P.O. Box 1230, West Seneca, NY 14224-1230 Tel 716-674-4270; Fax: 716-674-4195; Toll Free: 800-955-9659
E-mail: sales@ulverscroftusa.com
Web site: http://www.ulverscroft.com/.

Ulverscroft Large Print Bks., Ltd., *(0-7089)* Div. of F. A Thorpe, Orders Addr.: P.O. Box 1230, West Seneca, NY 14224-1230; Edit Addr.: 1881 Ridge Rd., West Seneca, NY 14224-1230 (SAN 208-3035) Tel 716-674-4270; Fax: 716-674-4195; Toll Free: 800-955-9659
E-mail: enquiries@ulverscroft.co.uk
Web site: http://www.ulverscroft.co.uk.

Ulverscroft Soundings (U.S.A.) *See* **Ulverscroft Audio (U.S.A.)**

Umina, Lisa M., *(0-9718350)* P.O. Box 31844, Independence, OH 44131 Tel 216-642-0861 (phone/fax)
E-mail: lisa@halopublishing.com
Web site: http://www.halopublishing.com.

Under The Veil Pr., *(0-9653158)* P.O. Box 8441, Pittsburg, CA 94565-8441 Tel 510-439-4600; Fax: 925-691-1418; Toll Free: 800-724-5222
E-mail: Mcaulton11@hotmail.com.

†Unicorn Publishing Hse., Inc., The, *(0-88101)* 120 American Way, Morris Plains, NJ 07950 (SAN 240-4567) Tel 973-292-6861; Fax: 973-984-6194; *CIP.*

United Printing, *(0-9674002)* Orders Addr.: P.O. Box 936, Bismarck, ND 58502 Tel 701-223-0505; Fax: 701-223-5571; Edit Addr.: 117 W. Front Ave., Bismarck, ND 58502
E-mail: ealbers@nd-humanities.org
Web site: http://www.unitedprinting.com.

United Synagogue of America Bk. Service, *(0-8381)* Subs. of United Synagogue of America, 155 Fifth Ave., New York, NY 10010 (SAN 203-0551) Tel 212-533-7800
E-mail: booksvc@uscj.org
Web site: http://www.uscj.org/booksvc..

Unity Books & Multimedia Publishing (Unity School of Christianity) *See* **Unity Schl. of Christianity**

Unity Schl. of Christianity, *(0-87159)* Orders Addr.: 1901 NW Blue Pkwy., Unity Village, MO 64065-0001 (SAN 204-8817) Tel 816-524-3550; 816 251-3571 (ordering); Fax: 816-251-3551
E-mail: unity@unityworldhq.org
Web site: http://www.unityworldhq.org
Dist(s): **Bookpeople**
New Leaf Distributing Co., Inc..

Univ. of Queensland Pr. (AUS) *(0-7022) Dist. by* **Intl Spec Bk.**

Univ. of Western Australia Pr. (AUS) *(0-85564; 0-86422; 0-909751; 1-875560; 1-876268; 1-920694) Dist. by* **Intl Spec Bk.**

Universe Publishing, *(0-7893; 0-87663; 1-55550)* Div. of Rizzoli International Pubns., Inc., 300 Park Ave. S., 3rd Flr., New York, NY 10010 (SAN 202-537X) Tel 212-387-3400; Fax: 212-387-3444 Do not confuse with similar names in North Hollywood, CA, Englewood, NJ, Mendocino, CA
Dist(s): **Andrews McMeel Publishing**
Simon & Schuster, Inc.
St. Martin's Pr..

University Editions Imprint of Aegina Pr., Inc.

Univ. Editions, *(0-615; 0-9711659)* 1003 W. Centennial Dr., Peoria, IL 61614-2828 Tel 309-692-0621; Fax: 309-693-0628 Do not confuse with University Editions in Huntington, WV
E-mail: mikruc@aol.com
Web site: http://www.terrythetractor.com.

†Univ. of Alabama Pr., *(0-8173)* Orders Addr.: 11030 S. Langley, Chicago, IL 60628; Edit Addr.: P.O. Box 870380, Tuscaloosa, AL 35487-0380 (SAN 202-5272) Tel 205-348-5180; Fax: 205-348-9201
E-mail: jkramer@uapress.ua.edu; pjmcwill@uapress.ua.edu
Web site: http://www.uapress.ua.edu
Dist(s): **Univ. of Chicago Pr.**; *CIP.*

†Univ. of California Pr., *(0-520)* Orders Addr.: 1445 Lower Ferry Rd., Ewing, NJ 08618 Tel 609-883-1759 (Customer Service); Fax: 609-883-7413; Toll Free Fax: 800-999-1958 (U.S. & Canada); Toll Free: 800-777-4726 (U.S. & Canada); Edit Addr.: 2120 Berkeley Way, Berkeley, CA 94720 Tel 510-642-4247; 510-643-7154 (Journals); Fax: 510-643-7127; 510-642-1144 (Marketing); 510-642-9917 (Journals)
E-mail: orders@cpfs.pupress.princeton.edu; journals@ucop.edu; askucp@ucpress.edu
Web site: http://www.ucpress.edu
Dist(s): **California Princeton Fulfillment Services**; *CIP.*

†Univ. of Georgia Pr., *(0-8203)* 330 Research Dr., Suite B100, Athens, GA 30602-4901 (SAN 203-3054) Tel 706-369-6130; Fax: 706-369-6131
E-mail: books@ugapress.uga.edu
Web site: http://www.ugapress.uga.edu; http://www.uga.edu; *CIP.*

†Univ. of Hawaii Pr., *(0-8248; 0-87022)* Orders Addr.: 2840 Kolowalu St., Honolulu, HI 96822-1888 (SAN 202-5353) Tel 808-956-8255; Fax: 808-988-6052; *Imprints:* Kolowalu Book (Kolowalu Bk)
E-mail: uhpmkt@hawaii.edu; uhpbooks@hawaii.edu
Web site: http://www.uhpress.hawaii.edu; *CIP.*

Univ. of Idaho Pr., *(0-89301)* P.O. Box PO Box 1107, Moscow, ID 83844-1107 (SAN 208-905X) Tel 208-885-5939; Fax: 208-885-9059; Toll Free: 800-847-7377
E-mail: uipress@uidaho.edu; marys@uidaho.edu
Web site: http://www.uidaho.edu/~uipress; http://www.members.aol.com/sbeegel/hemrev.htm.

†Univ. of Minnesota Pr., *(0-8166)* Affil. of Univ. of Minnesota, 111 Third Ave. S., Suite 290, Minneapolis, MN 55401-2520 (SAN 213-2648) Tel 612-627-1970; Fax: 612-627-1980; Toll Free: 800-621-2736 (customer service only)
E-mail: ump@staff.tc.umn.edu
Web site: http://www.upress.umn.edu
Dist(s): **Chicago Distribution Ctr.**
Continental Bk. Co., Inc.
Univ. of Chicago Pr.; *CIP.*

†Univ. of Missouri Pr., *(0-8262)* 2910 LeMone Blvd., Columbia, MO 65201 (SAN 203-3143) Tel 573-882-7641; Fax: 573-884-4498; Toll Free: 800-828-1894 (orders only)
E-mail: order@ext.missouri.edu
Web site: http://www.system.missouri.edu/upress
Dist(s): **East-West Export Bks.**
netLibrary, Inc.; *CIP.*

Names

Vintage Imprint of Knopf Publishing Group

Vision Bks. International, *(1-56550)* 775 E. Blithedale Ave., No. 342, Mill Valley, CA 94941 (SAN 297-6447) Tel 415-383-0962; Fax: 415-383-4521
E-mail: publisher@vbipublishing.com
Web site: http://www.vbipublishing.com
Dist(s): **Baker & Taylor Bks.**
Brodart Co.
Quality Bks., Inc..

Vista Press Ventures, Incorporated *See* **Eaglemont Pr.**

Visual Evangels Publishing Co., *(0-915398)* 2129 W. Campbell Rd., No. 1118, Garland, TX 75044-2965 (SAN 212-002X).

Vital Issue Pr. Imprint of Huntington Hse. Pubs.

Vivisphere Publishing, *(1-892323; 1-58776)* Div. of Net Pub Corp., Orders Addr.: 2 Neptune Rd., Poughkeepsie, NY 12601 (SAN 253-441X) Tel 845-463-1100; Fax: 845-463-0018; Toll Free: 800-724-1100; *Imprints:* Pierce Harris Press (Pierce Harris Pr)
E-mail: cs@vivisphere.com
Web site: http://www.vivisphere.com.

Viz Comics Imprint of Viz Communications, Inc.

Viz Communications, Inc., *(0-929279; 1-56931; 1-59116)* Subs. of Shogakukan, Inc., 655 Bryant St., San Francisco, CA 94107-1612 (SAN 248-8604) Tel 415-546-7073; Fax: 415-546-7086; Toll Free: 800-788-3123 (Ext. 262 or 220); *Imprints:* Cadence Books (Cadence Bks); Viz Comics (Viz Comics)
E-mail: dallas@viz.com
Web site: http://www.viz.com
Dist(s): **Publishers Group West.**

†Volcano Pr., *(0-912078; 1-884244)* Orders Addr.: P.O. Box 270, Volcano, CA 95689 (SAN 220-0015) Tel 209-296-4991; Fax: 209-296-4995; Toll Free: 800-879-9636; Edit Addr.: 21496 National St., Volcano, CA 95689
E-mail: sales@volcanopress.com; info@volcanopress.com
Web site: http://www.volcanopress.com
Dist(s): **Baker & Taylor Bks.**
Bookpeople
New Leaf Distributing Co., Inc.
Quality Bks., Inc.; *CIP.*

Volo Imprint of Hyperion Bks. for Children

Voyage Publishing, *(0-9649454)* Div. of How it Works, Inc., P.O. Box 1386, Anacortes, WA 98221 Tel 360-293-3515; Fax: 360-293-2653; Toll Free: 800-664-6623
Dist(s): **Baker & Taylor Bks.**
Bookpeople
Brodart Co.
Follett Library Resources
New Leaf Distributing Co., Inc.
Quality Bks., Inc..

Voyager Bks./Libros Viajeros Imprint of Harcourt Children's Bks.

Voyageur Publishing Co., *(0-929146)* 2227 Belmont Blvd., Nashville, TN 37212 (SAN 248-6709) Tel 615-463-3179
E-mail: vikar@bellsouth.net
Dist(s): **Biblio Distribution.**

VR Pubns., *(0-9658334)* P.O. Box 1720, Higley, AZ 85236 (SAN 254-7570) Tel 480-905-0337; Fax: 480-596-4037
E-mail: vramospub@msn.com
Web site: http://www.users.uswest.net/~urpub.

VSP Bks. Imprint of Vacation Spot Publishing

WEB Publishing Co., *(0-9639014)* Orders Addr.: P.O. Box 528, Westminster, CO 80030-0528 Tel 303-426-1855; Fax: 303-428-1615; Edit Addr.: 2993 W. 81st Ave., Unit D, Westminster, CO 80030-4143
E-mail: wally@lawyernet.com
Dist(s): **Distributors, The.**

W.J. Fantasy, Inc., *(1-56021)* 955 Connecticut Ave., Bridgeport, CT 06607-1222 Tel 203-333-5212; Fax: 203-366-3826; Toll Free Fax: 800-200-3000; Toll Free: 800-222-7529
E-mail: wjfantasy@erols.com.

W M Books *See* **Sierra Raconteur Publishing**

W Publishing Group, *(0-8499; 0-87680)* Div. of Thomas Nelson, Inc., P.O. Box 141000, Nashville, TN 37214-1000 (SAN 203-283X) Tel 615-902-3400; Fax: 615-902-3200 Do not confuse with Word Publishing Co. in Greenville, MS
Web site: http://www.wordpublishing.com; http://www.thomasnelson.com
Dist(s): **Christian Bk. Distributors.**

W. W. Publishers, Incorporated *See* **Wonder Well Pubs.**

†Wadsworth, *(0-15; 0-314; 0-534; 0-8185; 0-8273; 1-4163)* Div. of Thomson Learning, Orders Addr.: 7625 Empire Dr., Florence, KY 41042-2978 (SAN 200-2663) Tel 859-525-2230; Toll Free: 800-354-9706 ; Edit Addr.: 10 Davis Dr., Belmont, CA 94002 (SAN 200-2213) Tel 650-595-2350; Fax: 606-592-9081
Web site: http://www.wadsworth.com; http://www.brookscole.com
Dist(s): **Thomson Learning**; *CIP.*

Wadsworth Publishing Company *See* **Wadsworth**

Wakefield Connection, The, *(0-9703632)* 5201 Kingston Pike, Suite 6-302, Knoxville, TN 37919-5026 Tel 865-546-5764
E-mail: rwferrin@esper.com
Web site: http://www.wakefieldconnection.com
Dist(s): **Independent Pubs. Group.**

Waking Light Pr., The, *(0-9605444)* P.O. Box 1329, Sparks, NV 89432 (SAN 215-983X) Tel 775-356-0216 (phone/fax).

†Waldman Hse. Pr., Inc., *(0-931674)* 525 N. Third St., Minneapolis, MN 55401 (SAN 295-0243) Tel 612-341-4044; Fax: 952-925-3626; Toll Free: 888-700-7333
E-mail: nedw@waldmanhouse.com
Dist(s): **Baker & Taylor Bks.**
Bookazine Co., Inc.
Bookmen, Inc.
Booksource, The
Distributors, The
Koen Bk. Distributors
Partners Pubs. Group, Inc.
Spring Arbor Distributors, Inc.; *CIP.*

†Walker & Co., *(0-8027)* 435 Hudson St., New York, NY 10014-3941 (SAN 202-5213) Tel 212-727-8300; Fax: 212-727-0984; Toll Free Fax: 800-218-9367; Toll Free: 800-289-2553 (orders)
E-mail: orders@walkerbooks.com
Web site: http://www.walkerbooks.com
Dist(s): **Beeler, Thomas T. Publisher**; *CIP.*

Walker Publishing Company *See* **Walker & Co.**

WallBuilders, Inc., *(0-925279; 1-932225)* Orders Addr.: P.O. Box 397, Aledo, TX 76008; Edit Addr.: 426 Circle Dr., Aledo, TX 76008 Tel 817-441-6044; Fax: 817-441-6866; Toll Free: 800-873-2845
Web site: http://www.wallbuilers.com
Dist(s): **Baker & Taylor Bks.**
Riverside
Spring Arbor Distributors, Inc..

Wallbuilders Press *See* **WallBuilders, Inc.**

Walt Disney Home Video, 3333 N. Pagosa Ct., Indianapolis, IN 46226 Tel 317-890-3030; Fax: 818-560-1930
Web site: http://disney.go.com/DisneyVideos/
Dist(s): **Buena Vista Home Video**
Critics' Choice Video, Inc.
Follett Media Distribution
Midwest Tape.

Walt Disney Records, *(0-7634; 1-55723)* Div. of Walt Disney Co., 3333 N. Pagosa Ct., Indianapolis, IN 46226 Tel 317-890-3030; Fax: 317-897-4614
Web site: http://disney.go.com/disneyrecords/index.html
Dist(s): **Rounder Kids Music Distribution.**

Waltsan Publishing, LLC, *(1-930430)* 5000 Barnett St., Fort Worth, TX 76103-2006 Tel 817-654-3099 (phone/fax)
E-mail: sandra@waltsan.com
Web site: http://www.waltsan.com.

Warbelow, Willy Lou, *(0-9618314)* P.O. Box 252, Tok, AK 99780 (SAN 667-2639) Tel 907-883-2881.

Warbranch Pr., Inc., *(0-9667114)* 329 Warbranch Rd., Central, SC 29630 Tel 864-654-4503; Fax: 864-654-0455
E-mail: kspalmer@aol.com.

Warehousing & Fulfillment Specialists, LLC (WFS, LLC), *(1-57102; 1-58029; 1-59093)* 1501 County Hospital Rd., Nashville, TN 37218 Toll Free Fax: 800-510-3650; Toll Free: 800-327-5113; *Imprints:* Eager Minds Press (Eager Minds)
E-mail: vhill@apgbooks.com
Web site: http://www.apgbooks.com
Dist(s): **APG Sales and Fulfillment.**

Waring, Shirley & Thomas Pubs., *(0-9622808)* 11 Mitchell Ln., Hanover, NH 03755 Tel 603-643-8331.

Warne, Frederick Imprint of Viking Penguin

Warne, Frederick Imprint of Penguin Putnam Bks. for Young Readers

Warner Audio Video Entertainment (WAVE) Imprint of Time Warner AudioBooks

†Warner Bks., Inc., *(0-445; 0-446)* Div. of Time Warner Bk. Group, Orders Addr.: c/o Little Brown & Co., 3 Center Plaza, Boston, MA 02108-2084 Fax: 800-286-9471; Toll Free: 800-759-0190; Edit Addr.: 1271 Avenue of the Americas, New York, NY 10020 (SAN 281-8892) Tel 212-522-7200; *Imprints:* Warner Vision (Warner Vision)
Web site: http://www.warnerbooks.com
Dist(s): **Lectorum Pubns., Inc.**
Libros Sin Fronteras
Little Brown & Co.
Perelandra, Ltd.
Beeler, Thomas T. Publisher
Thorndike Pr.
Time Warner Bk. Group; *CIP.*

Warner Bros. Pubns., *(0-7604; 0-7692; 0-87487; 0-89724; 0-89898; 0-910957; 0-913277; 1-55122; 1-57623; 0-7579)* Div. of AOL Time Warner, 15800 NW 48th Ave., Miami, FL 33014-6422 (SAN 203-0586) Tel 305-620-1500; Fax: 305-621-1094; Toll Free: 800-327-7643; 800-468-5010
Web site: http://warnerbrospub.com.

Warner Brothers Records, *(1-880528)* Div. of Creative Enterprises, 3300 Warner Blvd., Burbank, CA 91505 Tel 818-953-3467; Fax: 818-953-3797.

Warner Brothers Worldwide Publishing, *(1-890371)* Div. of Time Warner Entertainment Co., 4000 Warner Blvd., Bldg. 118, Burbank, CA 91522 Tel 626-979-8968; Fax: 626-979-8974.

Warner Vision Imprint of Warner Bks., Inc.

Warren Assocs., *(0-9643494)* 2491 Suncrest Ave., Eugene, OR 97405 Tel 541-683-9049.

Washington Expatriates Pr., *(0-9609062)* 127 7th St. SE, Washington, DC 20003 (SAN 241-2357) Tel 202-546-1020
Dist(s): **Barnes & Noble Bks.-Imports**
Borders, Inc..

Washington Square Pr. Imprint of Simon & Schuster

WaterBrook Pr., *(0-87788; 1-57856; 1-4000)* Div. of Random Hse., Inc., Orders Addr.: 400 Hahn Rd., Westminster, MD 21157 Tel 410-848-1900; Toll Free: 800-726-0600; Edit Addr.: 2375 Telstar Dr., Suite 160, Colorado Springs, CO 80920 (SAN 299-4682) Tel 719-590-4999; Fax: 719-590-8977; Toll Free Fax: 800-294-5686; Toll Free: 800-603-7051; *Imprints:* Shaw (ShawRH) Do not confuse with WaterBrook Pr., Great Falls, VA
Web site: randomhouse.com/waterbrook
Dist(s): **Random Hse., Inc..**

Watercress Pr., *(0-934955)* 111 Grotto Blvd., San Antonio, TX 78216-7131 (SAN 694-4116) Tel 210-344-5338; Fax: 210-320-9536
E-mail: ace@watercresspress.com
Web site: http://watercresspress.com.

Waterfront Bks., *(0-914525)* 85 Crescent Rd., Burlington, VT 05401 (SAN 289-6923) Tel 802-658-7477; Fax: 802-860-1368; Toll Free: 800-639-6063
Web site: http://www.waterfrontbooks.com/.

Watson-Guptill Bks. Imprint of Watson-Guptill Pubns., Inc.

†Watson-Guptill Pubns., Inc., *(0-8174; 0-8230)* Div. of VNU Business Media, Inc., 770 Broadway, New York, NY 10003 (SAN 282-5384); *Imprints:* Watson-Guptill Books (Watson-Guptill Bks)
E-mail: skerner@watsonguptill.com
Web site: http://www.watsonguptill.com; *CIP.*

Watts, Franklin Imprint of Scholastic Library Publishing

Way of Life Literature, *(1-58318)* 1701 Harns Rd., Oak Harbor, WA 98277 Tel 360-675-8311; Fax: 360-240-8347
E-mail: fbns@wayoflife.org
Web site: http://wayoflife.org/~dcloud.

†Wayne State Univ. Pr., *(0-8143)* Leonard N. Simons Bldg., 4809 Woodward Ave., Detroit, MI 48201-1309 (SAN 202-5221) Tel 313-577-6120; Fax: 313-577-6131; Toll Free: 800-978-7323 (customer orders); *Imprints:* Great Lakes Books (Great Lks Bks)
E-mail: j.stephenson@wayne.edu
Web site: http://wsupress.wayne.edu
Dist(s): **East-West Export Bks.**; *CIP.*

WayWord Publishing, *(0-9669647)* 12739 NE Shoreland Dr., Mequon, WI 53092 Tel 262-243-9460
E-mail: wayword@execpc.com.

Weaselsleeves Pr., *(1-878460)* Orders Addr.: P.O. Box 8187, Santa Fe, NM 87504; Edit Addr.: Las Dos Subdivision, Lot 27, Santa Fe, NM 87504 Tel 505-988-3871
Dist(s): **SPD-Small Pr. Distribution.**

Names

†Weatherhill, Inc., *(0-8348)* 41 Monroe Tpke., Trumbull, CT 06611-1315 (SAN 202-9529) Tel 203-459-5090; Fax: 203-459-5095; Toll Free: 800-437-7840
E-mail: weatherhill@weatherhill.com
Web site: http://www.weatherhill.com; *CIP.*

Weatherhill, John Incorporated *See* **Weatherhill, Inc.**

Wee Pr., *(0-9625005)* 800 S. 38th St., Terre Haute, IN 47803 Tel 812-234-6033.

Wee Sing Bks. Imprint of Putnam Publishing Group, The

Wee Smile Books *See* **Waking Light Pr., The**

Wee-Chee-Taw Publishing, *(0-9622632)* 4450 Phillips Dr., Wichita Falls, TX 76308 Tel 940-692-3791.

Wehmeyer, Betty Jean, *(1-892611)* 9315 Cobbleshire, Houston, TX 77037-2216 Tel 281-447-2400.

Weinberg, Michael Aron, *(0-9601014)* 17830 Sherman Way, Apt. 110, Reseda, CA 91335 (SAN 208-2314) Tel 818-996-8578
E-mail: egoldstone@iopener.net.

Welcome Rain Pubs., *(1-56649)* 532 LaGuardia Pl., No. 473, New York, NY 10012 (SAN 299-9528) Tel 212-889-0088; Fax: 212-889-0869
Dist(s): **National Bk. Network.**

Wellington Publishing, Inc., *(0-922984)* Orders Addr.: P.O. Box 14877, Chicago, IL 60614-0877 (SAN 251-7795) Tel 773-472-4820; Fax: 773-472-4924; Edit Addr.: 707 W. Junior Terr., Chicago, IL 60613 (SAN 251-7809)
E-mail: wellingt@interaccess.com.

Welty Pr., *(0-9632953)* 2101 E. Fourth St., Duluth, MN 55812 Tel 218-728-6928
E-mail: A1Snowman@aol.com.

Wesleyan Publishing Hse., *(0-89827)* 7990 Castleway Dr., Indianapolis, IN 46250-0434 (SAN 162-7104) Tel 317-570-5300; Fax: 317-570-5370; Toll Free Fax: 800-788-3535; Toll Free: 800-493-7539 (orders only)
E-mail: wph@wesleyan.org; wpg@wesleyan.org
Web site: http://www.wesleyan.org
Dist(s): **CRC Pubns..**

West Hill Pr., *(0-939775)* Orders Addr.: P.O. Box 221, Fitzwilliam, NH 03447 (SAN 663-7450) Tel 603-585-6883; Edit Addr.: Fisher Hill, Fitzwilliam, NH 03447 (SAN 663-7469).

West Winds Pr. Imprint of Graphic Arts Ctr. Publishing Co.

Westcliffe Pubs., *(0-929969; 0-942394; 1-56579)* Orders Addr.: P.O. Box 1261, Englewood, CO 80150 Tel 303-935-0900; Fax: 303-935-0903; Toll Free: 800-523-3692; Edit Addr.: 2650 S. Zuni St., Englewood, CO 80110-1145 (SAN 239-7528) Do not confuse with Westcliff Publications in Newport Beach, CA
E-mail: sales@westcliffepublishers.com
Web site: http://www.westcliffepublishers.com.

Western National Parks Assn., *(0-911408; 1-877856; 1-58369)* 12880 N. Vistoso Village Dr., Tucson, AZ 85737 (SAN 202-750X) Tel 520-622-1999; Fax: 520-623-9519
E-mail: dgallagher@wnpa.org; abby@wnpa.org
Web site: http://www.wnpa.org
Dist(s): **Many Feathers Bks. & Maps**
Sunbelt Pubns., Inc.
Treasure Chest Bks..

Western New York Wares, Inc., *(0-9620314; 1-879201)* Orders Addr.: P.O. Box 733, Buffalo, NY 14205 (SAN 248-6911) Tel 716-832-6088; Edit Addr.: 419 Parkside Ave., Buffalo, NY 14216 (SAN 248-692X) Tel 716-832-6088
E-mail: wnywares@gateway.net.

Western Printers, Inc., *(0-9710477)* 977 Garfield, Eugene, OR 97402 Tel 541-683-1188; Fax: 541-683-2701 Do not confuse with Western Printing Lewiston, ID
E-mail: westernprinters@mailcity.com.

Western Reflections Publishing Co., *(1-890437; 1-932738)* Orders Addr.: 219 Main St., Montrose, CO 81401 Tel 970-249-7180 Toll Free: 800-993-4490
Web site: http://www.westernreflectionspub.com
Dist(s): **Baker & Taylor Bks.**
Books West
Partners/West
Quality Bks., Inc.
Treasure Chest Bks..

†Westminster John Knox Pr., *(0-664; 0-8042)* Div. of Presbyterian Publishing Corp., Orders Addr.: 100 Witherspoon St., Louisville, KY 40202-1396 (SAN 202-9669) Tel 502-569-5058; 502-569-5052 (outside U.S. for ordering); Fax: 502-569-5113 (outside U.S. for faxed orders); Toll Free Fax: 800-541-5113 (toll-free U.S. faxed orders); Toll Free: 800-523-1631
E-mail: ppc@ctr.pcusa.org; BFalvey@ctr.pcus.org; SHardin@ctr.pcusa.org
Web site: http://www.wjk.org
Dist(s): **CRC Pubns.**
Presbyterian Publishing Corp.; *CIP.*

Weston Woods Studios, Inc., *(0-7882; 0-89719; 1-55592; 1-56008)* Div. of Scholastic, Inc,, 12 Oakwood Ave., Norwalk, CT 06850 (SAN 630-3838) Tel 203-226-3355; Fax: 203-845-0498; Toll Free: 800-290-7531; 800-243-5020 (customer service)
E-mail: Leighcorra@aol.com
Web site: http://www.scholastic.com
Dist(s): **Lectorum Pubns., Inc..**

Wetlands Pr. Imprint of RDR Bks.

WeWrite Corp., *(1-57635; 1-884987)* Orders Addr.: P.O. Box 498, Rochester, IL 62563 Tel 217-498-8458; Fax: 217-498-7524; Toll Free: 800-295-9037; Edit Addr.: 300 Pakey Rd., Springfield, IL 62707
E-mail: info@wewrite.net
Web site: http://www.wewrite.net
Dist(s): **Baker & Taylor Bks..**

Wheatmark, Inc., *(1-58736)* 610 E. Delano St., Suite 104, Tucson, AZ 85705 (SAN 253-1054) Tel 520-798-0888; Fax: 520-798-3394; Toll Free: 888-934-0888; *Imprints:* Hats Off Books (Hats Off Bks)
E-mail: editor@bookpublisher.com; orders@bookpublisher.com; shenrie@bookpublisher.com
Web site: http://www.bookpublisher.com
Dist(s): **Baker & Taylor Bks..**

Wheeler Publishing, Inc. Imprint of Gale Group

Whispering Coyote Imprint of Charlesbridge Publishing, Inc.

Whispering Oaks Pr., *(0-9652177)* 10801 Hickman Heights Rd., Kansas City, MO 64137-1945.

White Eagle Publishing Trust (GBR) *(0-85487) Dist. by* **DeVorss.**

White Mane Bks. Imprint of White Mane Publishing Co., Inc.

White Mane Publishing Co., Inc., *(0-942597; 1-57249)* Orders Addr.: P.O. Box 708, Shippensburg, PA 17257 (SAN 667-1926) Tel 717-532-2237; Fax: 717-532-6110; Toll Free: 888-948-6263; *Imprints:* Burd Street Press (Burd St Pr); WM Kids (WM Kids); White Mane Books (WM Books)
E-mail: marketing@whitemane.com
Web site: http://www.whitemane.com/.

White Wolf Publishing, Inc., *(0-9627790; 1-56504; 1-58846)* 1554 Litton Dr., Stone Mountain, GA 30083 (SAN 299-1349) Tel 404-292-1819; Fax: 678-382-3882; Toll Free: 800-454-9653; *Imprints:* Borealis (Borealis) Do not confuse with White Wolf Publishing, Cresson, TX
E-mail: dianez@white-wolf.com
Web site: http://www.white-wolf.com.

Whitecap Bks., Ltd. (CAN) *(0-920620; 0-921061; 0-921396; 1-55110; 1-895099; 1-55285) Dist. by* **Gr Arts Ctr Pub.**

†Whitman, Albert & Co., *(0-8075)* 6340 Oakton St., Morton Grove, IL 60053-2723 (SAN 201-2049) Tel 847-581-0033; Fax: 847-581-0039; Toll Free: 800-255-7675; *Imprints:* Prairie Paperbacks (Prairie Pbks)
E-mail: mail@awhitmanco.com
Web site: http://www.albertwhitman.com
Dist(s): **Lectorum Pubns., Inc.**; *CIP.*

Whitman Publishing LLC, *(0-937458; 1-930849; 0-7948)* Div. of Anderson Press Inc., Orders Addr.: 4001 Helton Dr., Florence, AL 35030 Tel 256-246-1166; Toll Free: 800-528-3992; Edit Addr.: 3101 Clairmont Rd., NE, Suite C, Atlanta, GA 30329 (SAN 253-522X) Tel 404-214-4300; Fax: 404-214-4391; Toll Free: 800-528-3992
E-mail: info@heharris.com
Web site: http://www.heharris.com.

Whyte Dove Pr., *(0-9708999)* P.O. Box 385, Quitman, TX 75783
E-mail: maykay@peoplescom.net.

†Wiener, Markus Pubs., Inc., *(0-910129; 1-55876)* 231 Nassau St., Princeton, NJ 08542 (SAN 282-5465) Tel 609-921-1141; Fax: 609-921-1140
E-mail: INFO@MARKUSWIENER.COM; PUBLISHER@MARKUSWIENER.COM
Web site: http://www.markuswiener.com; *CIP.*

Wilander Publishing Co., *(0-9628335)* Orders Addr.: P.O. Box 56121, Portland, OR 97238.

Wild Animal XPress, *(0-9708743)* P.O. Box 2461, Ramona, CA 92065-0942 Tel 619-462-1986; Fax: 619-462-1374
E-mail: wildanimalxpress@home.com.

Wildcat Pr., *(1-886902)* P.O. Box 607, Summit, NJ 07901 Tel 732-277-1038; Fax: 973-564-9768; Toll Free: 800-776-9763 Do not confuse with Wildcat Pr., in Beverly Hills, CA.

Wildflower Run, *(0-9667086)* Orders Addr.: P.O. Box 9656, College Station, TX 77842 Tel 979-764-0166
E-mail: atmgold@aol.com
Web site: http://www.aggiegoose.com.

Wildside Pr., *(1-880448; 1-58715; 1-59224)* Orders Addr.: P.O. Box 301, Holicong, PA 18928-0301 Tel 215-345-5645; Edit Addr.: 4355 Burnt House Hill Rd., Doylestown, PA 18901
E-mail: wildside@sff.net
Web site: http://www.wildsidepress.com
Dist(s): **Baker & Taylor Bks.**
Ingram Bk. Co.
NACSCORP, Inc..

WildWest Publishing, *(0-9721800)* P.O. Box 11658, Olympia, WA 98508
E-mail: clamityJan@aol.com
Web site: http://www.CalamityJan.com
Dist(s): **Biblio Distribution.**

†Wiley, John & Sons, Inc., *(0-02; 0-470; 0-471; 0-7645; 0-8260; 0-88422; 0-937721; 0-939246; 1-55828; 1-56561; 1-56884; 1-57313; 1-878058; 3-527)* Orders Addr.: 1 Wiley Dr., Somerset, NJ 08875-1272 Tel 732-469-4400; Fax: 732-302-2300; Toll Free: 800-225-5945 (orders); Edit Addr.: 111 River St., Hoboken, NJ 07030 (SAN 200-2272) Tel 201-748-6276 (Retail and Wholesale); 201-748-6000; Fax: 201-748-8641 (Retail and Wholesale); 201-748-6088; *Imprints:* Cliff Notes (Cliff)
E-mail: bookinfo@wiley.com; compbks@wiley.com
Web site: http://www.wiley.com; http://www.wiley.com/compbooks/; http://www.interscience.wiley.com
Dist(s): **American Society of Civil Engineers**
Aspen Pubs., Inc.
Peoples Publishing Group, Inc., The
Urban Land Institute
netLibrary, Inc.; *CIP.*

Will Hall Bks., *(0-9630310)* 611 Oliver Ave., Fayetteville, AR 72701 Tel 501-443-4403
Web site: http://www.willhallbooks.com.

Willard, John A., *(0-9612398)* 3119 Country Club Cir., Billings, MT 59102 (SAN 289-5323) Tel 406-259-1966.

Williams, David Park, *(1-886058)* 3465 La Salle St., Ann Arbor, MI 48108-2900 Tel 734-975-9059.

Williford Communications, *(1-890651)* 7608 Poplar Pike, Germantown, TN 38138 Tel 901-756-4661; Fax: 901-756-2429; Toll Free: 800-339-6778; *Imprints:* FamilyFinds (FamilyFinds)
E-mail: willifords@aol.com
Web site: http://www.willifordcommunications.com.

Willowisp Pr. Imprint of Darby Creek Publishing

WillowSpring Downs, *(0-9648525; 0-9742716)* 1582 N. Falcon, Hillsboro, KS 67063 Tel 620-367-8432; Fax: 620-367-8218; Toll Free: 888-551-0973
E-mail: willowspringdowns@juno.com
Dist(s): **Booksource, The.**

Wilshire Bk. Co., *(0-87980)* 12015 Sherman Rd., North Hollywood, CA 91605-3781 (SAN 168-9932) Tel 818-765-8579; Fax: 818-765-2922
E-mail: mpowers@mpowers.com
Web site: http://www.mpowers.com.

Wilshire House of Arkansas *See* **Ozark Publishing**

Winbush Publishing Co., *(1-880234)* 16821 Muirland St., Detroit, MI 48221 Tel 313-861-6590.

Windham Hill Productions, *(0-943885; 1-57442)* P.O. Box 5501, Beverly Hills, CA 90209-5501 Tel 650-329-0647.

Window Bks., *(1-889829)* Orders Addr.: 1011 Boren Ave., No. 199, Seattle, WA 98104 Tel 206-621-9129
E-mail: wndowbooks@aol.com
Web site: http://www.windowbooks.com.

WindSpirit Publishing, *(0-9643407)* 220 Compass Ave., Beachwood, NJ 08722-2919 Tel 732-240-6905; Fax: 732-240-7860
E-mail: windspiritpub@earthlink.net
Web site: http://www.windspiritpublishing.net
Dist(s): **Biblio Distribution.**

Names

Windstorm Creative Ltd., *(1-883573; 1-886383; 1-59092)* 7419 Ebbert Dr., SE, Port Orchard, WA 98367 (SAN 299-1330) Tel 360-769-7174 (phone/fax) ; *Imprints:* Little Blue Works (Little Blue); Lightning Rod Limited (Lightning Rod)
E-mail: wsc@windstormcreative.com
Web site: http://www.windstormcreative.com
Dist(s): **Alamo Square Distributors**
Baker & Taylor Bks.
Bookpeople.

Windswept Hse. Pubs., *(0-932433; 1-883650)* P.O. Box 159, Mount Desert, ME 04660 (SAN 687-4363) Tel 207-244-5027; Fax: 207-244-3369
E-mail: windswt@acadia.net
Web site: http://www.booknotes.com/windswept/.

Windward Bks. International, *(0-929155)* 191 Weston Rd., Lincoln, MA 01773 (SAN 248-5710) Tel 617-259-0423; Fax: 617-259-0288
E-mail: 103332.2702@compuserve.com.

Windword Pr., *(0-9642206)* 3109 Portman St., Keego Harbor, MI 48320-1208 Tel 248-682-5827; Fax: 248-851-0268; Toll Free: 800-718-5888 Do not confuse with Wind Word Pr. in Healdsburg, CA.

WinePress Publishing, *(0-9622413; 1-57921; 1-883893)* Orders Addr.: P.O. Box 428, Enumclaw, WA 98022 Tel 360-802-9758; Fax: 360-802-9992; Toll Free: 800-326-4674
E-mail: info@winepresspub.com; jhughes@winepresspub.com; adean@winepresspub.com
Web site: http://www.winepresspub.com
Dist(s): **Appalachian Bk. Distributors**
Baker & Taylor Bks.
Riverside
Spring Arbor Distributors, Inc..

Winslow Pr., *(1-890817; 1-58837)* Div. of Foundation for Concepts in Education, Inc., The, 115 E. 23rd St., 10th Flr., New York, NY 10010 Tel 212-254-2025; Fax: 212-254-1595; Toll Free: 800-617-3947
E-mail: winslow@winslowpress.com
Web site: http://www.winslowpress.com.

Winterthur, Henry Francis duPont Museum, Inc., *(0-912724)* Rte. 52, Winterthur, DE 19735 (SAN 205-5406) Tel 302-888-4600; Fax: 302-888-4950; Toll Free: 800-448-3883
E-mail: srandolph@winterthur.org
Web site: http://www.winterthur.org
Dist(s): **Univ. Pr. of New England**
Univ. of Tennessee Pr..

†Wisdom Pubns., *(0-86171)* 199 Elm St., Somerville, MA 02144 (SAN 246-022X) Tel 617-776-7416 (ext. 24); Fax: 617-776-7841; Toll Free Fax: 800-338-4550 (orders only); Toll Free: 800-462-6420 (orders only)
E-mail: marketing@wisdompubs.org
Web site: http://www.wisdompubs.org
Dist(s): **National Bk. Network**; *CIP.*

Wizard Works, *(0-9621543; 1-890692)* Orders Addr.: P.O. Box 1125, Homer, AK 99603-1125 Tel 907-235-8757 (phone/fax); Toll Free: 877-210-2665
E-mail: Wizard@xyz.net
Web site: http://www.xyz.net/~wizard.

Wizards of the Coast, *(0-7869; 1-57530; 1-880992; 0-7430)* Orders Addr.: P.O. Box 707, Renton, WA 98057-0709 Toll Free: 800-821-8028; Edit Addr.: 1801 Lind Ave., SW, Renton, WA 98055 (SAN 299-4410) Tel 425-226-6500
E-mail: angella@wizards.com
Web site: http://www.wizards.com
Dist(s): **Diamond Comic Distributors, Inc.**
Holtzbrinck Pubs.
Doherty, Tom Assocs., LLC.

WM Kids Imprint of White Mane Publishing Co., Inc.

Wolfhound Pr. (IRL) *(0-86327; 0-905473; 0-9503454)* *Dist. by* **Interlink Pub.**

Wolfhound Pr. (IRL) *(0-86327; 0-905473; 0-9503454)* *Dist. by* **Irish Amer Bk.**

Woman's Missionary Union, *(0-936625; 1-56309)* Orders Addr.: c/o Carol Causey, P.O. Box 830010, Birmingham, AL 35283-0010 (SAN 699-7015) Tel 205-991-8100; Fax: 205-995-4841; Toll Free: 800-968-7301; Edit Addr.: Hwy. 280 E., 100 Missionary Ridge, Birmingham, AL 35242-5235 (SAN 699-7023); *Imprints:* New Hope (New Hope)
E-mail: cwhite@wmu.org
Web site: http://www.wmu.com
Dist(s): **Broadman & Holman Pubs..**

Woman's Pr., The, *(0-9614878)* 600 F Cathedral Rd., No. 1107, Philadelphia, PA 19128-1933 (SAN 659-3631).

Women's Pr., Ltd., The (GBR) *(0-7043) Dist. by* **Trafalgar.**

Wonder Kids Pubns., *(1-56162)* Div. of KC Enterprise, P.O. Box 3485, Cerritos, CA 90703 Tel 562-404-4668 ; Fax: 562-404-8525.

Wonder Well Pubs., *(1-879567)* Div. of W.W. Pubs., Inc., 2100 Linwood Ave., Suite 3V, Fort Lee, NJ 07024-2937 Tel 201-592-6162; *Imprints:* Valeria Books (Valeria Bks)
Dist(s): **Baker & Taylor Bks.**
Brodart Co.
Lectorum Pubns., Inc..

Wonder Workshop, *(1-56919)* Div. of Stephens Group, Inc., 1123 Brookstone Blvd., Mount Juliet, TN 37122-3274 Toll Free: 800-627-6874.

Wood 'N Barnes, *(1-885473)* Div. of Jean Barnes Bks., 2717 NW 50th, Oklahoma City, OK 73112 (SAN 298-9433) Tel 405-942-6812; Fax: 405-946-4074; Toll Free: 800-678-0621; *Imprints:* Preproduction Press (PreProd Pr)
E-mail: wnb@barnesbooks.com
Web site: http://www.woodnbarnes.com.

†Woodbine Hse., *(0-933149; 1-890627)* 6510 Bells Mill Rd., Bethesda, MD 20817 (SAN 630-4052) Tel 301-897-3570; Fax: 301-897-5838
E-mail: info@woodbinehouse.com
Web site: http://www.woodbinehouse.com; *CIP.*

Woodmere Pr., *(0-942493)* 46 W. 94th St., New York, NY 10025 (SAN 678-3058) Tel 212-678-7839.

Woods Hole Historical Collection, *(0-9611374)* P.O. Box 185, Woods Hole, MA 02543 (SAN 283-1791) Tel 508-548-7270 (phone/fax)
E-mail: woods_hole_historical@hotmail.com
Web site: www.woodsholemuseum.org.

Woodsong Graphics, Inc., *(0-912661)* P.O. Box 304, Lahaska, PA 18931-0304 (SAN 282-8235) Tel 215-794-8321.

Wooster Bk. Co., The, *(1-888683; 1-59098)* 205 W. Liberty St., Wooster, OH 44691-4831 Tel 330-262-1688; Fax: 330-264-9753; Toll Free: 800-982-6651 (800-WUBook-1)
E-mail: mail@woosterbook.com
Web site: http://www.woosterbook.com.

Word Aflame Pr., *(0-912315; 0-932581; 1-56722; 0-7577)* Subs. of Pentecostal Publishing Hse., 8855 Dunn Rd., Hazelwood, MO 63042 (SAN 212-0046) Tel 314-837-7300; Fax: 314-837-6574
E-mail: pph@upci.org
Web site: http://www.upci.org/pph.

Word Play Pubns., *(0-9642922; 1-892847)* One Sutter St., San Francisco, CA 94104 Tel 415-397-3716; Fax: 415-291-8377
Web site: http://www.word-play.com
Dist(s): **Bookpeople**
Diamond Book Distributors, Inc.
Last Gasp Eco-Funnies, Inc.
Quality Bks., Inc.
Unique Bks., Inc..

Word Publishing *See* **W Publishing Group**

Word Wright International *See* **WordWright.biz, Inc.**

Words Distributing Co., *(0-914728)* Div. of Bookpeople, 7900 Edgewater Dr., Oakland, CA 94621 (SAN 154-7763) Tel 510-632-4700; Fax: 510-632-1281; Toll Free: 800-999-4650; 800-593-9673 (orders)
Dist(s): **Bookpeople.**

WordSHOP, Inc., *(0-9668469)* P.O. Box 236, Birdsboro, PA 19508-0236 Tel 610-582-7230.

Wordsworth Editions, Ltd. (GBR) *(1-85326; 1-84022) Dist. by* **Casemate Pubs.**

Wordsworth Editions, Ltd. (GBR) *(1-85326; 1-84022) Dist. by* **Advanced Global.**

†Wordware Publishing, Inc., *(0-915381; 1-55622; 0-556)* 2320 Los Rios Blvd., Suite 200, Plano, TX 75074-3557 (SAN 291-4786) Tel 972-423-0090; Fax: 972-881-9147; Toll Free: 800-229-4949 (orders); *Imprints:* Republic of Texas Press (Rep of TX Pr)
E-mail: info@wordware.com
Web site: http://www.wordware.com
Dist(s): **Hervey's Booklink & Cookbook Warehouse**
National Bk. Network
ibooks.com; *CIP.*

WordWright.biz, Inc., *(0-9700615; 0-9713832; 0-9717868; 1-932196)* P.O. Box 1785, Georgetown, TX 78627 Fax: 512-260-3080 (phone/fax)
E-mail: jnwriter@aol.com; snwriter@earthlink.net
Web site: http://www.wordwright.biz.

†Workman Publishing Co., Inc., *(0-7611; 0-89480; 0-911104; 1-56305)* 708 Broadway, New York, NY 10003 (SAN 203-2821) Tel 212-254-5900; Fax: 212-254-8098; Toll Free: 800-722-7202
E-mail: mged@workman.com
Web site: http://www.workmanweb.com; http://www.workman.com
Dist(s): **Worldwide Media Service, Inc.**; *CIP.*

Works of Hope Publishing, *(0-9712481)* 149 Eastern Ave., Gloucester, MA 01930 (SAN 254-041X) Tel 978-771-0777; Toll Free: 877-887-2828
E-mail: ElissaAmal@aol.com
Web site: http://www.worksofhope.com.

World Bk., Inc., *(0-7166)* Div. of Scott Fetzer Co., 233 N. Michigan, Suite 2000, Chicago, IL 60601 (SAN 201-4815) Tel 312-729-5800; Fax: 312-729-5614; 312-729-5600; Toll Free Fax: 888-690-4002 (Canadian orders); 800-433-9330 (US orders); Toll Free: 800-967-5325; 800-837-5365 (Canadian orders); 800-975-3250 (US orders)
Web site: http://www.worldbook.com.

World Citizens, *(0-932279)* 96 La Verne Ave., Mill Valley, CA 94941 (SAN 686-547X) Tel 415-380-8020 ; Toll Free: 800-247-6553 (orders only)
Dist(s): **Baker & Taylor Bks.**
BookMasters, Inc.
Bookpeople
Social Studies Schl. Service.

World of Learning Publishing *See* **Swift Learning Resources**

World Pr., Ltd., *(0-912171)* Div. of World News Syndicate, Ltd., P.O. Box 419, Hollywood, CA 90078 (SAN 276-9581) Tel 213-681-1629.

World Wide Distributors, Limited *See* **Island Heritage Publishing**

Worrywart Publishers *See* **WorryWart Publishing Co.**

WorryWart Publishing Co., *(1-881519)* Orders Addr.: P.O. Box 24911, Columbia, SC 29224-4911 Tel 803-699-0032; Fax: 803-699-0032 (ext. 51); Edit Addr.: 337 White Birch Cir., Columbia, SC 29223
E-mail: wworrywart@aol.com.

Wright Group, The, *(0-322; 0-7802; 0-940156; 1-55624; 1-55911; 1-4045)* Div. of The McGraw-Hill Education Group, 19201 120th Ave., NE, Suite 100, Bothell, WA 98011 Tel 425-486-8011; Fax: 425-486-6804; Toll Free Fax: 800-543-7323
Web site: http://www.wrightgroup.com/.

Wright Publishing, Inc., *(0-935087; 0-9652368)* Orders Addr.: P.O. Box 1956, Fayetteville, GA 30214 Tel 770-460-5525; Fax: 770-460-6426; Edit Addr.: 320 Devilla Trace, Fayetteville, GA 30214 (SAN 695-0507) Do not confuse with companies with same or similar name in Los Angeles, CA, Virgina Beach, VA, West Seneca, NY, Torrance, CA, New York , NY 09/27/02; dupe request (visa) send att: James Wright (prefix 0-935087) 10/01/02 Sent dupe 1st class JAZ
Dist(s): **Baker & Taylor Bks..**

Wright, Shirley L., *(0-9636377)* 28412 S. Hult Rd., Beavercreek, OR 97004 Tel 503-632-6815.

Wright/Monday Pr., *(0-9617597)* 214 James Thurber Ct., Falls Church, VA 22046 (SAN 664-8657) Tel 703-548-4930.

Write For You, *(0-9639678)* 16 Valley St., No. 44, Seattle, WA 98109 Tel 206-298-9409
E-mail: mi_lucien555.com@aol.

Write Team, The, *(0-9659001)* 16433 S. 18th St., Phoenix, AZ 85048 (SAN 299-6006) Tel 602-460-0099; Fax: 602-460-0098.

Write Together Publishing, *(1-930142; 1-931718)* 533 Inwood Dr., Nashville, TN 37211 Fax: 520-223-4850
E-mail: paul.clere@writetogether.com
Web site: http://www.writetogether.com.

Write World, Inc., *(0-9722173)* 3523 McKinney Ave., Suite 373, Dallas, TX 75204 (SAN 254-8445) Tel 214-521-0114; Fax: 214-599-9192
E-mail: writeworld@cs.com
Dist(s): **Baker & Taylor Bks.**
Ingram Bk. Co..

Writers & Readers Publishing, Inc., *(0-86316; 0-904613; 0-906386; 0-906495)* 457 Washington St., New York, NY 10013-1344 (SAN 665-813X) Tel 212-982-3158; Fax: 212-777-4924
Dist(s): **Publishers Group West.**

Writers Club Pr. Imprint of iUniverse, Inc.

Writers' Collective, The, *(0-9716734; 1-932133; 1-59411)* 780 Reservoir Ave., Suite 243, Cranston, RI 02910 Tel 401-785-4440
E-mail: factotum@writerscollective.org
Web site: http://www.writerscollective.org
Dist(s): **Baker & Taylor Bks..**

Writers Hse. Pr. Imprint of Order of the Legion of St. Michael

Writer's Ink. Studios, Inc., *(0-9704460)* P.O. Box 952, Windermere, FL 34786 Tel 407-876-3399; Fax: 270-964-5984; Toll Free: 888-229-9200
E-mail: writersinkstudios@cfl.rr.com; cat@brownbagbooks.com
Web site: http://www.brownbagbooks.com.

WHOLESALER & DISTRIBUTOR NAME INDEX

21st Century Antiques, Orders Addr.: P.O. Box 70, Hatfield, MA 01038 (SAN 110-8085); Edit Addr.: 11 1/2 Main St., Hatfield, MA 01038 (SAN 243-248X) Tel 413-247-9396.

21st Century Pubns., *(0-933278)* Orders Addr.: P.O. Box 702, Fairfield, IA 52556-0702 Tel 515-472-5105; Fax: 515-472-8443; Toll Free: 800-593-2665; Edit Addr.: 401 N. Fourth St., Fairfield, IA 52556 Do not confuse with Twenty First Century Pubns., Tolland, CT
E-mail: books21st@lisco.com
Web site: http://www.21stbooks.com.

3M Sportsman's Video Collection, 3M Ctr., Bldg. 223-4NE-05, Saint Paul, MN 55144-1000 (SAN 159-8929) Tel 612-733-7412; Fax: 612-736-7479; Toll Free: 800-940-8273 (orders only).

A & B Books, *See* **A & B Distributors & Pubs. Group**

A & B Distributors & Pubs. Group, *(1-881316; 1-886433)* Div. of A&B Distributors, 1000 Atlantic Ave., Brooklyn, NY 11238 (SAN 630-9216) Tel 718-783-7808; Fax: 718-783-7267; Toll Free: 877-542-6657; 146 Lawrence St., Brooklyn, NY 11201 (SAN 631-385X)
E-mail: maxtay@webspan.net.

A & M Church Supplies, 220 E. Genesee Ave., Saginaw, MI 48607-1228 (SAN 157-0145) Tel 517-753-4672; Fax: 517-753-4799; Toll Free: 800-345-4694.

A B C-Clio Information Services, *See* **ABC-CLIO, Inc.**

A B S Corporation, *See* **Budgetext**

A K J Book Fare, Incorporated, *See* **AKJ Educational Services, Inc.**

ABC-CLIO, Inc., *(0-87436; 0-903450; 1-57607; 1-85109)* 130 Cremona Dr., Santa Barbara, CA 93117 (SAN 301-5467) Tel 805-968-1911; Fax: 805-685-9685; Toll Free: 800-368-6868
E-mail: customerservice@abc-clio.com
Web site: http://www.abc-clio.com.

ABC'S Bk. Supply, Inc., 7319 W. Flagler St., Miami, FL 33144 Toll Free: 877-383-4240
E-mail: abcbooks@abcbooks.com.

Abel Love, Inc., Orders Addr.: P.O. Box 2250, Newport News, VA 23609 (SAN 158-4081) Tel 757-877-2939; Toll Free: 800-520-2939; Edit Addr.: 935 Lucas Creek Rd., Newport News, VA 23608 Fax: 804-877-2939.

Abingdon Pr., *(0-687)* Div. of United Methodist Publishing Hse., Orders Addr.: P.O. Box 801, Nashville, TN 37202-3919 (SAN 201-0054) Tel 615-749-6409; Fax: 615-749-6056; Toll Free Fax: 800-836-7802; Toll Free: 800-251-3320; Edit Addr.: 201 Eighth Ave., S., Nashville, TN 37202 (SAN 699-9956)
E-mail: info@abingdon.org
Web site: http://www.abingdonpress.com/.

Abrams & Co. Pubs., Inc., *(0-7664)* P.O. Box 10025, Waterbury, CT 06725 Tel 203-756-6562; Fax: 203-756-2895; Toll Free: 800-874-0029.

Academic Bk. Ctr., Inc., 5600 NE Hassalo St., Portland, OR 97213-3640 (SAN 169-7145) Tel 503-287-6657; Fax: 503-284-8859; Toll Free: 800-547-7704
E-mail: orders@acbc.com
Web site: http://www.abc.com.

Academic Bk. Services, Inc., 5490 Fulton Industrial Blvd., Atlanta, GA 30336 (SAN 631-0591) Tel 404-344-8317; Fax: 404-349-2127.

Academi-Text Medical Wholesalers, 333 N. Superior, Toledo, OH 43604 (SAN 135-2415) Tel 419-255-9755 ; Fax: 419-255-9606; Toll Free: 800-552-8398 (out of state).

Acorn Alliance, 549 Old North Rd., Kingston, RI 02881-1220 Tel 401-783-5480; Fax: 401-284-0959; Fulfillment Addr.: Client Distribution Services 193 Edwards Dr., Jackson, TN 38301 Toll Free Fax: 800-351-5073; Toll Free: 800-343-4499
E-mail: contact@moyerbellbooks.com
Web site: http://www.moyerbellbooks.com.

ACTA Pubns., *(0-87946; 0-914070; 0-915388)* 4848 N. Clark St., Chicago, IL 60640-4711 (SAN 204-7489) Tel 773-271-1030; Fax: 773-271-7399; Toll Free Fax: 800-397-0079; Toll Free: 800-397-2282
E-mail: acta@one.org.

Action Products International, Inc., 344 Cypress Rd., Ocala, FL 34472-3108 (SAN 630-8805) Tel 352-687-4961; Toll Free: 800-772-2846
E-mail: sales@apii.com.

Adams Bk. Co., Inc., 537 Sackett St., Brooklyn, NY 11217 (SAN 107-7171) Tel 718-875-5464; Fax: 718-852-3212; Toll Free: 800-221-0909
E-mail: sales@adamsbook.com
Web site: http://www.adamsbook.com.

Adams News, 1555 W. Galer St., Seattle, WA 98119 (SAN 169-8842) Tel 206-284-7617; Fax: 206-284-7599; Toll Free: 800-533-7617.

Adams, Robert Henry Fine Art, *(0-9713010)* 715 N. Franklin St., Chicago, IL 60610 (SAN 159-6918) Tel 312-642-8700; Fax: 312-642-8785
E-mail: info@adamsfineart.com
Web site: http://www.adamsfineart.com.

Addison-Wesley Longman, Inc., *(0-201; 0-321; 0-582; 0-673; 0-8013; 0-8053; 0-9654123)* Orders Addr.: 200 Old Tappan Rd., Old Tappan, NJ 07675 (SAN 299-4739) Toll Free: 800-922-0579; Edit Addr.: 75 Arlington St., Suite 300, Boston, MA 02116 (SAN 200-2000) Tel 617-848-7500; Toll Free: 800-447-2226
E-mail: pearsoned@eds.com; orderdeptnj@pearsoned.com
Web site: http://www.awl.com.

Addison-Wesley Publishing Company, Incorporated, *See* **Addison-Wesley Longman, Inc.**

Adelman, Joseph, 217-17 82nd Ave., Jamaica, NY 11427 (SAN 285-8002) Tel 212-465-1711.

Adler, Leo, P.O. Box 10308, Eugene, OR 97440-2308 (SAN 169-7021).

Adler's Foreign Bks., Inc., *(0-8417)* 915 Foster St., Evanston, IL 60201 (SAN 111-3089) Tel 847-864-0664; Fax: 847-864-0804; Toll Free: 800-235-3771
E-mail: info@afb-adlers.com
Web site: http://www.afb-adlers.com.

Advanced Global Distribution Services, 5880 Oberlin Dr., San Diego, CA 32121 Toll Free Fax: 800-499-3822; Toll Free: 800-284-3580.

Advanced Marketing Services, Incorporated, *See* **Advantage Pubs. Group**

Advantage Pubs. Group, *(0-934429; 1-57145; 1-59223)* 5880 Oberlin Dr., San Diego, CA 92121 (SAN 630-8090) Toll Free: 800-284-3580
E-mail: janetn@advmkt.com
Web site: http://www.advantagebooksonline.com; http://www.laurelglenbooks.com; http://www.thunderbaypress.com; http://www.bathroomreader.com; http://www.silverdolphinbooks.com.

Adventure Pubns., Inc., *(0-934860; 1-885061; 1-59193)* 820 Cleveland St., S., Cambridge, MN 55008 (SAN 212-7199) Tel 763-689-9800; Fax: 763-689-9039; Toll Free Fax: 877-725-0088; Toll Free: 800-678-7006
E-mail: orders@adventurepublications.net.

Advertising Specialties, Inc., 4920 River Rd., Pascagoula, MS 39567 (SAN 108-6316) Tel 601-769-7904
Web site: http://www.advmkt.com; http://www.advantagebooksonline.com.

Affiliated Bk. Distributor, Div. of North Shore Distributors, Inc., 1200 N. Branch St., Chicago, IL 60622 (SAN 169-2267).

Afro-American Bk. Distributor, 2537 Prospect, Houston, TX 77004 (SAN 169-8257).

Agencia de Publicaciones de Puerto Rico, GPO Box 4903, San Juan, PR 00936 (SAN 169-9296).

Agritech Publishing Group, Inc., Div. of Agritech Corp., 825 W. Samalayuca Dr., Tucson, AZ 85704-3912 (SAN 174-612X) Tel 520-544-2542.

AHA, Inc., *(0-918545)* P.O. Box 8405, Santa Cruz, CA 95061-8405 (SAN 295-5059) Tel 408-458-9119.

Aha Punana Leo, *(0-9645646; 1-58191; 1-890270)* 928 Nuuanu Ave., Suite 315, Honolulu, HI 96817-5193
E-mail: haawina@leoki.uhh.hawaii.edu
Web site: http://www.ahapunanaleo.org.

AIMS International Bks., Inc., *(0-922852)* 7709 Hamilton Ave., Cincinnati, OH 45231-3103 (SAN 630-270X) Tel 513-521-5590; Fax: 513-521-5592; Toll Free: 800-733-2067
E-mail: aimsbooks@fuse.net
Web site: http://www.aimsbooks.com.

A-K News Company, *See* **Aramark Magazine & Bk. Co.**

AK Pr. Distribution, *(1-873176; 1-902593)* 674-A 23rd St., Oakland, CA 94612-1163 (SAN 298-2234) Tel 510-208-1700; Fax: 510-208-1701
E-mail: akpress@akpress.org
Web site: http://www.akpress.org.

AKJ Educational Services, Inc., 5609-2A Fishers Ln., Rockville, MD 20852 (SAN 170-5431) Tel 301-770-4030; Fax: 301-770-2338; Toll Free: 800-770-2338
E-mail: info@akjedsvcs.com
Web site: http://www.akjedsvcs.com.

Alabama Bk. Store, Orders Addr.: P.O. Box 1279, Tuscaloosa, AL 35401-1626 Tel 205-758-4532; Fax: 205-758-5525; Toll Free: 800-382-2665 (orders only) ; Edit Addr.: 1015 University Blvd., Tuscaloosa, AL 35403-1279 (SAN 100-0063)
E-mail: ABS@AlabamaBook.com
Web site: http://www.AlabamaBook.com.

Alamo Square Distributors, P.O. Box 14543, San Francisco, CA 94114 Fax: 415-863-7456 E-mail: alamosqdist@earthlink.net.

Alba Hse., *(0-8189)* Div. of Society of St. Paul, 2187 Victory Blvd., Staten Island, NY 10314-6603 (SAN 201-2405) Tel 718-761-0047; Fax: 718-761-0057; 718-698-8390; Toll Free: 800-343-2522 E-mail: albabooks@aol.com Web site: http://www.albahouse.org.

Alexander News Company, *See* **Blue Ridge News Co.**

Alfonsi Enterprises, 8621 Gavinton Ct., Dublin, OH 43017-9615 (SAN 169-4227).

All America Distributors Corp., 8431 Melrose Pl., Los Angeles, CA 90069-5382 (SAN 168-972X) Tel 213-651-2650; Fax: 213-655-9452 E-mail: psi@loop.com.

Allentown News Agency, Inc., Orders Addr.: P.O. Box 446, Allentown, PA 18105; Edit Addr.: 719-723 Liberty St., Allentown, PA 18105 (SAN 169-7226) Tel 610-432-4441; Fax: 610-432-2708.

Alliance Hse., Inc., *(0-9665234)* 220 Ferris Ave., Suite 201, White Plains, NY 10603 Tel 914-328-5456; Fax: 914-946-1929 E-mail: alliancehs@aol.com.

Alonso Bk. & Periodical Services, Inc., 7670 Richmond Hwy., Alexandria, VA 22306 (SAN 170-7035) Tel 703-765-1211.

Alpen Bks, 3616 South Rd., Suite C-1, Mukilteo, WA 98275 Tel 425-290-8587; Fax: 425-290-9461.

Alpenbooks, *See* **Alpenbooks Pr.**

Alpenbooks Pr., *(0-9669795)* 3616 South Rd., C-1, Mukilteo, WA 98275 (SAN 113-5309) Tel 425-415-4560; Fax: 425-290-9461 E-mail: rkoch@alpenbooks.com Web site: http://www.alpenbooks.com.

Alpha & Omega Distributor, P.O. Box 36640, Colorado Springs, CO 80936-3664 (SAN 169-0515).

Alpha Bks., *(0-02; 0-672; 0-7357; 0-7897; 1-56761; 1-57595; 0-7431; 1-59257)* Div. of Pearson Technology Group, 201 W. 103rd St., Indianapolis, IN 46290 (SAN 219-6298) Tel 317-581-3500 Toll Free: 800-571-5840 (orders) Web site: http://www.idiotsguides.com.

Alpha Publishing, Inc., *(0-9717585)* P.O. Box 53788, Lafayette, LA 70505 Tel 337-237-7049; Fax: 337-237-7060; Toll Free: 800-749-4009 Do not confuse with companies with the same or similar name in Mamaroneck, NY, Mount Clair, CA, Louisville, KY, Pheonix, AZ, Annapolis, MD E-mail: joycedwyer@cs.com.

Alpine News Distributors, Div. of Mountain States Distributors, 0105 Marand Rd., Glenwood Springs, CO 81601 Tel 970-945-2269; Fax: 970-945-2260.

AMACOM, *(0-7612; 0-8144)* Orders Addr.: P.O. Box 169, Saranac Lake, NY 12983 (SAN 227-3578) Tel 518-891-5510; Fax: 518-891-2372; Toll Free: 800-250-5308 (orders & customer service); Edit Addr.: 1601 Broadway, New York, NY 10019-7420 (SAN 201-1670) Tel 212-586-8100; Fax: 212-903-8168 E-mail: cust_serv@amanet.org Web site: http://www.amacombooks.org.

Amarillo Periodical Distributors, P.O. Box 3823, Lubbock, TX 70404 (SAN 156-4986) Tel 806-745-6000.

Amato, Frank Pubns., Inc., *(0-936608; 0-941361; 0-9608744; 1-57188; 1-878175)* Orders Addr.: P.O. Box 82112, Portland, OR 97282 (SAN 214-3372) Tel 503-653-8108; Fax: 503-653-2766; Toll Free: 800-541-9498; Edit Addr.: 4040 SE Wister, Milwaukie, OR 97222 E-mail: wholesale@amatobooks.com; Lorraine@amatobooks.com Web site: http://www.amatobooks.com.

Amazon.Com, *(1-58060)* 1200 12th Ave. S., Suite 1200, Seattle, WA 98144 (SAN 179-4205) Tel 206-266-6817; Orders Addr.: P.O. Box 80387, Seattle, WA 98108-0387 (SAN 156-143X) Tel 206-622-2335; Fax: 206-622-2405; 1 Centerpoint Blvd., non-carton, New Castle, DE 19720 (SAN 155-3992); 1 Centerpoint Blvd., carton, New Castle, DE 19720 (SAN 156-1405); 520 S. Brandon, non-carton, Seattle, WA 98108 (SAN 152-6642); 520 S. Brandon, carton, Seattle, WA 98108 (SAN 156-1383); 1600 E. Newlands Dr., carton, Fernley, NV 89408 (SAN 156-5982); 1600 E. Newlands Dr., non-carton, Fernley, NV 89408 (SAN 156-6008); Edit Addr.: 520 Pike St., Seattle, WA 98101 (SAN 155-3984); P.O. Box 81226, Seattle, WA 98108-1226 E-mail: catalog-dept@amazon.com Web site: http://www.amazon.com.

Ambassador Bks. & Media, 42 Chasner St., Hempstead, NY 11550 (SAN 120-064X) Tel 516-489-4011; Fax: 516-489-5661; Toll Free: 800-431-8913 E-mail: ambassador@absbook.com Web site: http://www.absbook.com.

Ambassador Book Service, *See* **Ambassador Bks. & Media**

AMCAL, Inc., *(0-911855; 1-57624; 1-884358; 1-58625; 1-58913; 1-59282)* 2500 Bisso Ln., Bldg. 500, Concord, CA 94520 (SAN 263-9025) E-mail: amcal@amcalart.com Web site: http://www.amcalart.com.

American Bk. Ctr., Brooklyn Navy Yard, Bldg. 3, Brooklyn, NY 11205 (SAN 630-8821) Tel 718-834-0170.

American Buddhist Shim Gum Do Assn., Inc., *(0-9614427)* 203 Chestnut Hill Ave., Brighton, MA 02135 (SAN 113-2873) Tel 617-787-1506; Fax: 617-787-2708 E-mail: marystackhouse@shimgumdo.org Web site: http://www.shimgumdo.org.

American Business Systems, Inc., 315 Littleton Rd., Chelmsford, MA 01824 (SAN 264-8229) Tel 508-250-9600; Fax: 508-250-8027; Toll Free: 800-356-4034.

American Econo Clad, *See* **Sagebrush Corp.**

American Education Corp., The, *(0-87570; 1-58636)* 7506 N. Broadway, Suite 505, Oklahoma City, OK 73116-9016 (SAN 654-6250) Tel 405-840-6031; Fax: 405-848-3960; Toll Free: 800-222-2811 Web site: http://www.amered.com.

American Educational Computer, Incorporated, *See* **American Education Corp., The**

American International Distribution Corp., Orders Addr.: P.O. Box 80, Williston, VT 05495-0020 Tel 802-862-0095 (ext. 115); Fax: 802-864-7749; Toll Free: 800-426-4742; Edit Addr.: 50 Winter Sport Ln., Williston, VT 05495 (SAN 630-2238) Toll Free: 800-488-2665.

American Kennel Club Museum of the Dog, *(0-9615072)* 1721 S. Mason Rd., Saint Louis, MO 63131 (SAN 110-8751) Tel 314-821-3647; Fax: 314-821-7381.

American Magazine Service, *See* **Prebound Periodicals**

American Marketing & Publishing Company, *See* **Christian Publishing Network**

American Micro Media, 19 N. Broadway, Box 306, Red Hook, NY 12571 (SAN 653-9920) Tel 914-758-5567.

American Overseas Bk. Co., Inc., 550 Walnut St., Norwood, NJ 07648 (SAN 169-4863) Tel 201-767-7600; Fax: 201-784-0263 E-mail: books@aobc.com Web site: http://www.aobc.com.

American Society of Agronomy, *(0-89118)* 677 S. Segoe Rd., Madison, WI 53711-1086 (SAN 107-5683) Tel 608-273-8080; Fax: 608-273-2021 Web site: http://www.agronomy.org.

American Society of Civil Engineers, *(0-7844; 0-87262)* 1801 Alexander Bell Dr., Reston, VA 20191-4400 (SAN 204-7594) Tel 703-295-6300; Fax: 703-295-6211; Toll Free: 800-548-2723 E-mail: marketing@asce.org Web site: http://www.pubs.asce.org.

American West Bks., 1831 Industrial Way, No. 101, Sanger, CA 93657-9501 (SAN 630-8570) Toll Free: 800-497-4909 Do not confuse with American West Bks., Albuquerque, NM E-mail: JBM12@CSUFresno.edu.

American Wholesale Bk. Co., Subs. of Books-A-Million, Orders Addr.: 121 25th St., S., Birmingham, AL 35210 (SAN 631-7391) Tel 205-956-4151; Fax: 205-956-5530.

Americana Publishing, Inc., *(1-58807; 1-58943)* 303 San Mateo NE, Suite 104A, Albuquerque, NM 87108 Tel 505-265-6121 (ext. 171); Fax: 505-255-6189; Toll Free: 888-883-8203 (ext. 171) E-mail: editor@americanabooks.com Web site: http://www.americanabooks.com.

Americana Souvenirs & Gifts, *(1-890541)* 206 Hanover St., Gettysburg, PA 17325-1911 (SAN 169-7366) Toll Free: 800-692-7436.

America's Hobby Ctr., 146 W. 22nd St., New York, NY 10011 (SAN 111-0403) Tel 212-675-8922.

Ames News Agency, Inc., 2110 E. 13th St., Ames, IA 50010 (SAN 169-2550).

Amoskeag News Agency, 92 Allard Dr., Manchester, NH 03102 (SAN 169-4537) Tel 603-623-5343.

AMS Pr., Inc., *(0-404)* Brooklyn Navy Yard Bldg. 292, Suite 417, 63 Flushing Ave., New York, NY 11205 (SAN 106-6706) Tel 718-875-8100; Fax: 212-995-5413 Do not confuse with companies with the same or similar name in Los Angeles, CA, Pittsburgh, PA E-mail: amserve@earthlink.net.

Anchor Distributors, 30 Hunt Valley Cir., New Kensington, PA 15068 (SAN 631-077X) Tel 724-334-7000; Fax: 724-334-1200; Toll Free: 800-444-4484 E-mail: marketing@whitakerhouse.com.

Anderson News - Tacoma, 9914 32nd Ave., S., Lakewood, WA 98499 (SAN 108-1322) Tel 253-581-1940; Fax: 253-584-5941; Toll Free: 800-552-2000 (in Washington).

Anderson News Co., P.O. Box 386, Cloverdale, VA 24077-0386 (SAN 168-9223); 6355 N. Palafox St., Pensacola, FL 32503 (SAN 168-9363) Tel 904-477-0920; 2541 Westcott Blvd., Knoxville, TN 37931 Tel 423-966-7575; 3911 Volunteer Dr., Chattanooga, TN 37416 (SAN 169-7862) Tel 423-894-3945; 6301 Forbing Rd., Little Rock, AR 72219 Tel 501-562-7360; 3777 Hartsfield Rd., Tallahassee, FL 32303 Tel 904-575-8070; 1857 W. Grant, P.O. Box 5465, Tucson, AZ 85705 Tel 520-622-2831; 5184 Sullivan Gardens Pkwy., Kingsport, TN 37660-8104 (SAN 241-6131); 390 Exchange St., Box 1624, New Haven, CT 06506 (SAN 241-6158) Tel 203-777-5545; 5000 Moline St., Denver, CO 80239-2622 Tel 303-321-1111; 1709 N. East St., Flagstaff, AZ 86002 (SAN 168-9290) Tel 520-774-6171; Fax: 520-779-1958; 4935 Covington Way, Memphis, TN 38128; P.O. Box 22968, Chattanooga, TN 37422; P.O. Box 36003, Knoxville, TN 37930-6003; P.O. Box 280077, Memphis, TN 38168-0077; P.O. Box 6660, Pensacola, FL 32503 Do not confuse with Anderson News Company, Pinellas Park, FL.

Anderson News, LLC, 3840 Vineland Rd., Orlando, FL 32811-6427 (SAN 169-1201) Tel 407-841-8738; Fax: 407-839-4043; Toll Free: 800-338-3988; P.O. Box 616898, Orlando, FL 32811 E-mail: wigginsd@andersonnews.com.

Anderson-Austin News Co., LLC, 808 Newtown Cir., No. B, Lexington, KY 40511-1230 (SAN 169-2836) Tel 606-254-2765; Fax: 606-254-3328.

Andich Brothers News Company, *See* **Tobias News Co.**

Andrews McMeel Publishing, *(0-8362; 0-7407)* Orders Addr.: c/o Simon & Schuster, Inc., 100 Front St., Riverside, NJ 08075 Toll Free Fax: 800-943-9831; Toll Free: 800-943-9839 (Customer Service; 800-897-7650 (Credit Dept.); Edit Addr.: 4520 Main St., Kansas City, MO 64111-7701 (SAN 202-540X) Tel 816-932-6600; Fax: 816-932-6749; Toll Free: 800-851-8923 Web site: http://www.AndrewsMcMeel.com.

Andrzejewski's Marian Church Supply, *See* **A & M Church Supplies**

answers period, inc., *(0-917875)* Orders Addr.: P.O. Box 427, Goliad, TX 77963 (SAN 112-6431) Tel 361-645-2268; Toll Free: 800-852-4752 Web site: http://www.answersbook.com.

Anthracite News Company, *See* **Great Northern Distributors, Inc.**

Anthroposophic Press, Incorporated, *See* **SteinerBooks, Inc.**

Antiquarian Bookstore, The, 1070 Lafayette Rd., Portsmouth, NH 03801 (SAN 158-9938) Tel 603-436-7250.

Antique Collectors' Club, *(0-902028; 0-907462; 1-85149)* Orders Addr.: 91 Market St. Industrial Park, Wappingers Falls, NY 12590 (SAN 630-7787) Tel 845-297-0003; Fax: 845-297-0068; Toll Free: 800-252-5231 (orders) E-mail: info@antiquecc.com Web site: http://www.antiquecc.com; http://www.antiquecc.com.

AOAC International, *(0-935584)* 481 N. Frederick Ave. Suite 500, Gaithersburg, MD 20877-2417 (SAN 260-3411) Tel 301-924-7077; Fax: 301-924-7089; Toll Free: 800-379-2622 E-mail: aoac@aoac.org Web site: http://www.aoac.org.

AOL Time Warner Book Group, *See* **Time Warner Bk. Group**

A-One Bk. Distributors, Inc., 1121 Lincoln Ave., Unit 17, Holbrook, NY 11741-2264 (SAN 630-7981).

APG Direct, 3801 Carolina Ave., Richmond, VA 23222-2202.

APG Sales and Fulfillment, Div. of Warehousing and Fulfillment Specialists, LLC (WFS, LLC), 1501 County Hospital Rd., Nashville, TN 37218 (SAN 630-818X) Tel 615-254-2450; Fax: 615-254-2405; Toll Free: 800-327-5113
E-mail: sswift@agpbooks.com
Web site: http://www.apgbooks.com.

Apollo Bks., *(0-938290)* 91 Market St., Wappingers Falls, NY 12590-2333 (SAN 170-0928).

Apollo Library Bk. Supplier, 865 Kent Ln., Philadelphia, PA 19115 (SAN 159-8031).

Appalachian Bible Co., *(1-889049)* Orders Addr.: 522 Princeton Rd., Johnson City, TN 37605 (SAN 169-7889) Tel 423-282-9475; Fax: 423-282-9110; Toll Free: 800-289-2772; Edit Addr.: P.O. Box 1573, Johnson City, TN 37601
E-mail: appainc@aol.com.

Appalachian Bk. Distributors, Orders Addr.: 522 Princeton Rd., Johnson City, TN 37601 (SAN 630-7388) Tel 423-282-9475; Fax: 423-282-9110; Toll Free: 800-759-2779; Edit Addr.: 506 Princeton Rd., Johnson City, TN 37601.

Appalachian, Incorporated, *See* **Appalachian Bible Co.**

Apple Bk. Co., Div. of Scholastic Bk. Fairs, Inc., P.O. Box 217156, Charlotte, NC 28221-0156 Tel 704-596-6641; Fax: 704-599-1738; Toll Free: 800-331-1993; 5901 N. Northwoods Business Pkwy., Charlotte, NC 28269 (SAN 108-4569).

Applewood Bks., *(0-918222; 1-55709)* 128 The Great Rd., Bedford, MA 01730 (SAN 210-3419) Tel 781-271-0055; Fax: 781-271-0056; Toll Free: 800-277-5312
E-mail: applewood@awb.com
Web site: http://www.awb.com.

Arabic & Islamic Univ. Pr., 4263 Fountain Ave., Los Angeles, CA 90029 (SAN 107-6299) Tel 323-665-1000; Fax: 323-665-3107.

Aramark Magazine & Bk. Co., P.O. Box 25489, Oklahoma City, OK 73125 (SAN 169-6971) Tel 405-843-9383; Fax: 405-843-0379 Do not confuse with Aramark Magazine & Bk. Services, Inc., Norfolk, VA.

Aramark Magazine & Bk. Services, Inc., Box 2240, Norfolk, VA 23501 (SAN 169-8680) Do not confuse with Aramark Magazine & Book Co., Oklahoma City, OK.

Arbit Bks., Inc., *(0-930038)* 8050 N. Port Washington Rd., Milwaukee, WI 53217 (SAN 169-913X) Tel 414-352-4404.

Ardic Bk. Distributors, Inc., 331 High St., 2nd Flr., Burlington, NJ 08016-4411 (SAN 170-5415).

Argus International Corp., Subs. of ICS International Group, Skypark Business Pk., P.O. Box 4082, Irvine, CA 92716-4082 (SAN 681-9761) Tel 714-552-8494 (phone/fax).

Aries Pr., *(0-933646)* P.O. Box 30081, Chicago, IL 60630 (SAN 111-9168) Tel 312-725-8300.

Aries Productions, Inc., *(0-910035)* Orders Addr.: P.O. Box 29396, Sappington, MO 63126 (SAN 669-0009); Edit Addr.: 9633 Cinnabar Dr., Sappington, MO 63126 (SAN 241-2004) Tel 314-849-3722
E-mail: uspsisquad@aol.com
Web site: http://ww.ussisquad.com.

Arizona Periodicals, Inc., P.O. Box 5780, Yuma, AZ 85366-5780 Tel 520-782-1822.

Arkansas Bk. Co., 1207 E. Second St., Little Rock, AR 72202-2732 (SAN 168-9460) Tel 501-375-1184.

Arlington Card Co., Bk. Dept., 140 Gansett Ave., Cranston, RI 02910 (SAN 108-5794) Tel 401-942-3188.

Armstrong, J. B. News Agency, *See* **News Group, The**

Arnica Publishing, Inc., *(0-9726535; 0-9745686)* 620 SW Main, Suite 345, Portland, OR 97205 (SAN 255-0091) Tel 503-225-9900 (phone/fax); Toll Free: 800-323-6554 (orders)
E-mail: matt@arnicapublishing.com
Web site: http://arnicapublilshing.com.

Arrow, G. H. Co., P.O. Box 676, Bala Cynwyd, PA 19004 (SAN 111-3771) Tel 215-227-3211; Fax: 215-221-0631; Toll Free: 800-775-2776.

Arrowhead Magazine Co., Inc., P.O. Box 5947, San Bernardino, CA 92412 (SAN 169-0094) Tel 909-799-8294; Fax: 909-799-3774; 1055 Cooley Ave., San Bernardino, CA 92408 (SAN 249-2717) Tel 909-370-4420.

Ars Obscura, *(0-9623780)* P.O. Box 4424, Seattle, WA 98104-0424 (SAN 113-5368) Tel 206-324-9792.

Art Institute of Chicago, *(0-86559)* Orders Addr.: a/o Museum Shop Mail Order Dept., 1224 W. Van Buren, 3rd Flr., Chicago, IL 60607 Tel 312-563-5150; Fax: 312-563-1973 (attn: Museum Shop); Edit Addr.: 111 S. Michigan Ave., Chicago, IL 60603-6110 (SAN 204-479X) Tel 312-443-3540; Fax: 312-443-1334
Web site: http://www.artic.edu.

Artisan, *(1-57965; 1-885183)* Div. of Workman Publishing Co., Inc., 708 Broadway, New York, NY 10003 Tel 212-254-5900; Fax: 212-677-6692; Toll Free: 800-967-5630 Do not confuse with Artisan, Wheaton, IL
E-mail: artisan@workman.com.

Artisan House, *See* **Artisan**

Artisoft, Inc., *(0-927538)* 1 S. Church Ave., Suite 2200, Tucson, AZ 85745 (SAN 287-458X) Tel 520-670-7100; Fax: 520-670-7101; Toll Free: 800-233-5564.

ARVEST, P.O. Box 200248, Denver, CO 80220 (SAN 159-8694) Tel 303-388-8486; Fax: 303-355-4213; Toll Free: 800-739-0761
E-mail: copy@concentric.net.

ASM International, *(0-87170)* 9639 Kinsman Rd., Materials Park, OH 44073-0002 (SAN 204-7586) Tel 440-338-5151; Fax: 440-338-4634; Toll Free: 800-336-5152 (ext. 5900) Do not confuse with ASM International, Inc., Fort Lauderdale, FL
E-mail: Cust-Srv@asminternational.org
Web site: http://www.asminternational.org/.

Aspen Pubs., Inc., *(0-444; 0-7896; 0-8342; 0-87189; 0-87622; 0-89443; 0-912862)* Subs. of Wolters Kluwer Nv, Orders Addr.: 7210 McKinney Cir., Frederick, MD 21704 Fax: 301-417-7550; Toll Free Fax: 800-901-9075; Toll Free: 800-638-8437; 800-234-1660 (Customer Service); Edit Addr.: 1185 Avenue of the Americas, 37th Flr., New York, NY 10036 (SAN 203-4999) Tel 212-597-0200; Fax: 212-597-0338
E-mail: customer.service@aspenpubl.com
Web site: http://www.aspenpublishers.com.

Aspen West Publishing, *(0-9615390; 1-885348)* 8535 S. 700 W., Unit C, Sandy, UT 84070 (SAN 112-7993) Tel 801-565-1370; Fax: 801-565-1373; Toll Free: 800-222-9133 (orders only)
E-mail: kent@aspenwest.com
Web site: http://www.aspenwest.com.

Associated Publishers Group, *See* **APG Sales and Fulfillment**

Association of Official Analytical Chemists, *See* **AOAC International**

Astran, Inc., 591 SW Eighth St., Miami, FL 33130-3413 (SAN 169-1082) Tel 305-858-4300; Fax: 305-858-0405; Toll Free: 800-431-4957
Web site: http://www.astranbooks.com.

ATEXINC, Corp., *(0-9702332)* 13104 Canterbury Rd., Leawood, KS 66209 (SAN 631-774X) Tel 913-663-3703; Fax: 913-663-1881 Do not confuse with Atex, Inc., Bedford, MA
E-mail: atexinc@aol.com
Web site: http://www.atexinc.com.

Athena Productions, Inc., 5500 Collins Ave., No. 901, Miami Beach, FL 33140 Tel 305-868-8482; Fax: 305-868-8891.

Atlas News Co., Div. of Hudson News Co., P.O. Box 779, Boylston, MA 01505-0779 (SAN 169-3360).

Atlas Publishing Co., *(0-930575)* 1464 36th St., Ogden, UT 84403 (SAN 110-3873) Tel 801-627-1043.

AU Media, Inc., 3289 Lenworth Dr., Unit F, Mississauga, ON L4X 2H1 Tel 905-212-9719; Fax: 905-212-9720.

Audio Bk. Co., *(0-89926)* 125 N. Aspen Ave., Suite 2, Azusa, CA 91702 (SAN 158-1414) Fax: 626-969-6099; Toll Free: 800-423-8273
E-mail: sales@audiobookco.com
Web site: http://www.audiobookco.com.

Audio Language Studies, Incorporated, *See* **Durkin Hayes Publishing Ltd.**

Audubon Prints & Bks., 9720 Spring Ridge Ln., Vienna, VA 22182 (SAN 111-820X).

Augsburg Fortress Publishers, Publishing House of The Evangelical Lutheran Church in America, *See* **Augsburg Fortress, Pubs.**

Augsburg Fortress, Pubs., *(0-8006; 0-8066)* Orders Addr.: P.O. Box 1209, Minneapolis, MN 55440-1209 (SAN 169-4081) Tel 612-330-3300; Fax: 612-330-3455; Toll Free Fax: 800-722-7766; Toll Free: 800-328-4648 (orders only); Edit Addr.: 100 S. Fifth St., Suite 700, Minneapolis, MN 55402
E-mail: info@augsburgfortress.org; productinfo@augsburgfortress.org; subscriptions@augsburgfortress.org; customerservice@augsburgfortress.com
Web site: http://www.augsburgfortress.org.

Augusta News Co., 25 Second St., Apt. 124, Hallowell, ME 04347-1481 (SAN 169-3026).

Auromere, Inc., *(0-89744)* 2621 W. US Hwy. 12, Lodi, CA 95242-9200 (SAN 169-0043) Fax: 209-339-3715; Toll Free: 800-735-4691
E-mail: sasp@lodinet.com
Web site: http://www.auromere.com.

Austin Management Group, Orders Addr.: P.O. Box 3206, Paducah, KY 42002-3206 (SAN 135-3349); Edit Addr.: 1051 Husbands Rd., Paducah, KY 42003 (SAN 249-6844) Tel 502-442-1052.

Auto-Bound, Inc., 909 Marina Village Pkwy., No. 67B, Alameda, CA 94501-1048 (SAN 170-0782) Tel 510-521-8655; Fax: 510-521-8755; Toll Free: 800-523-5833.

Avanti Enterprises, Inc., 18901 Springfield, Flossmoor, IL 60422 (SAN 158-3727) Tel 708-799-6464; Fax: 708-799-8713; Toll Free: 800-799-6464.

Avenue Bks., 2270 Porter Way, Stockton, CA 95207-3339 (SAN 122-4158).

Avery BookStores, Inc., 308 Livingston St., Brooklyn, NY 11217 (SAN 169-510X).

Aviation Bk. Co., *(0-911720; 0-911721; 0-916413)* 7201 Perimeter Rd., S., No. C, Seattle, WA 98108-3812 (SAN 120-1530) Tel 206-767-5232; Fax: 206-763-3428; Toll Free: 800-423-2708
E-mail: sales@aviationbook.com.

Aviation Supplies & Academics, Inc., *(0-940732; 1-56027)* 7005 132nd Pl., SE, Newcastle, WA 98059-3153 (SAN 219-709X) Tel 425-235-1500; Fax: 425-235-0128; Toll Free: 800-272-2359
E-mail: asa@asa2fly.com
Web site: http://www.asa2fly.com.

Avonlea Bks., Inc., Orders Addr.: P.O. Box 74, White Plains, NY 10602-0074 (SAN 680-4446) Tel 914-946-5923; Fax: 914-761-3119; Toll Free: 800-423-0622
E-mail: avonlea@bushkin.com
Web site: http://www.bushkin.com.

B T P Distribution, 4135 Northgate Blvd., Suite 5, Sacramento, CA 95834-1226 (SAN 631-2489) Tel 916-567-2496; Fax: 916-441-6749.

Badger Bks., Inc., *(1-878569; 1-932542)* Orders Addr.: P.O. Box 192, Oregon, WI 53575 (SAN 297-9055) Tel 608-835-3638 (phone/fax); Toll Free: 800-928-2372; Edit Addr.: 350 Richards Rd., Oregon, WI 53575
E-mail: books@badgerbooks.com
Web site: http://www.badgerbooks.com.

Baggins Bks., 3560 Meridian St., Bellingham, WA 98225-1731 (SAN 156-501X) Do not confuse with Baggin's Books in Doylestown, PA.

Baker & Taylor Bks., *(0-8480)* Orders Addr.: Commerce Service Ctr., 251 Mt. Olive Church Rd., Commerce, GA 30599-9988 (SAN 169-1503) Tel 404-335-5000; Toll Free: 800-775-1800 (orders); 800-775-1200 (customer service); Reno Service Ctr., 1160 Trademark Dr., Reno, NV 89511 (SAN 169-4464) Tel 775-850-3800; Fax: 775-850-3826 (customer service); Toll Free Fax: 800-775-7480 (orders); Edit Addr.: National Sales Hdqtrs., 5 Lakepointe Plaza, Suite 500, 2709 Water Ridge Pkwy., Charlotte, NC 28217 (SAN 169-5606) Fax: 704-329-8989; Toll Free: 800-775-1800 (information) ; 1120 US Hwy. 22, E., Bridgewater, NJ 08807 (SAN 169-4901) Toll Free: 800-775-1500 (customer service) ; Momence Service Ctr., 5012 S. Gladiolus St., Momence, IL 60954-1799 (SAN 169-2100) Tel 815-472-2444 (international customers); Fax: 815-472-9886 (international customers); Toll Free: 800-775-2300 (customer service, academic libraries)
E-mail: btinfo@btol.com
Web site: http://www.btol.com.

Baker & Taylor Entertainment, Corporate Headquarters: 8140 N. Lehigh Ave., Morton Grove, IL 60053 (SAN 631-1156) Tel 847-965-8060; Fax: 847-965-8093; Toll Free: 800-775-2600; 7000 N. Austin Ave., Niles, IL 60714 (SAN 630-4311) Tel 847-647-0800; Fax: 847-647-7396; Toll Free: 800-775-2800; 1825 Monetary Ln., Suite 112, Carrollton, TX 75006 Tel 972-242-3098; Fax: 972-242-8375; Toll Free: 800-775-3300; 2501 SW 31st Ave., Pembroke Park, FL 33009 Tel 954-983-9055; Fax: 954-983-9350; Toll Free: 800-775-3400; 800-775-4300; 2150 Boggs Rd., Suite 640, Duluth, GA 30096 Tel 770-813-3253; Fax: 770-813-9460; Toll Free: 800-775-2600 (Orders only) ; 960 Turnpike St., Canton, MA 02021 Tel 781-821-2730; Fax: 781-821-1983; Toll Free: 800-775-2600; 3150 N. 24th St., Suite A210, Phoenix, AZ 85016 Tel 602-954-8558; Fax: 602-954-8870; Toll Free: 800-775-3300; 2709 Water Ridge Pkwy., Suite 500, Charlotte, NC 28217 Tel 704-329-9063; Fax: 704-329-9065; Toll Free: 800-775-2600; 8936 Comanche Ave., Chatsworth, CA 91311 Tel 818-886-0200; Fax: 818-886-0646; Toll Free:

800-775-4200; 3005 S. Parker Rd., Suite 318, Aurora, CO 80014 Tel 303-369-9229; Fax: 303-369-9669; Toll Free: 800-775-3300; Campbells Run Busn. Ctr., 100 Business Center Dr., Pittsburgh, PA 15205 Tel 412-787-8890; Fax: 412-787-0368; Toll Free: 800-775-2600; 5769 NE Columbia Blvd., Portland, OR 97218 Tel 503-249-8397; Fax: 503-282-5904; Toll Free: 800-775-3300; 1120 US Hwy. 22 E., Bridgewater, NJ 08807 Tel 908-541-7401; Fax: 908-541-7857; Toll Free: 800-775-2600
E-mail: info@btent.com
Web site: http://www.btent.com.

Baker & Taylor International, 1120 US Hwy. 22 E., Box 6885, Bridgewater, NJ 08807 (SAN 200-6804) Tel 908-541-7000; Fax: 908-729-4037.

Baker & Taylor Video, *See* **Baker & Taylor Entertainment**

Baker Bk. Hse., Inc., *(0-8007; 0-8010; 1-58558; 1-58743)* Orders Addr.: P.O. Box 6287, Grand Rapids, MI 49516-6287 Toll Free Fax: 800-398-3111 (orders only); Toll Free: 800-877-2665 (orders only); Edit Addr.: 6030 E. Fulton, Ada, MI 49301 Tel 616-676-9185; Fax: 616-676-9573
Web site: http://www.bakerbooks.com.

Ballantine Bks., *(0-345; 0-449; 0-8041; 0-87637; 1-4000)* Div. of Random Hse., Inc., Orders Addr.: 400 Hahn Rd., Westminster, MD 21157 Tel 410-848-1900; Toll Free Fax: 800-767-4465; Toll Free: 800-726-0600 (customer service); 800-733-3000 (orders); Edit Addr.: 1540 Broadway, 11th Flr., New York, NY 10036 (SAN 214-1175) Tel 212-782-9000; Fax: 212-940-7539; Toll Free: 800-733-3000
E-mail: bfi@randomnhouse.com; thenry@randomhouse.com
Web site: http://www.randomhouse.com.

Ballantine Publishing Group, *See* **Ballantine Bks.**

Balzekas Museum of Lithuanian Culture, 6500 S. Pulaski Rd., Chicago, IL 60629 (SAN 110-8522) Tel 773-582-6500; Fax: 773-582-5133.

Banner of Truth, The, *(0-85151)* Orders Addr.: P.O. Box 621, Carlisle, PA 17013 Tel 717-249-5747; Fax: 717-249-0604; Toll Free: 800-263-8085; Edit Addr.: 63 E. Louther St., Carlisle, PA 17013 (SAN 112-1553)
E-mail: info@banneroftruth.org
Web site: http://www.banneroftruth.co.uk.

Banyan Tree Bks., *(0-9604320)* 1963 El Dorado Ave., Berkeley, CA 94707 (SAN 207-3862) Fax: 510-524-2690
E-mail: banyan@uclink.berkeley.edu.

Barnes & Noble Bks.-Imports, *(0-389)* Div. of Rowman & Littlefield Pubs., Inc., 4720 Boston Way, Lanham, MD 20706 (SAN 206-7803) Tel 301-459-3366; Toll Free: 800-462-6420.

Barnes & Noble, Inc., *(0-7607; 0-88029; 1-4028)* 122 Fifth Ave., New York, NY 10011 (SAN 141-3651) Tel 212-633-3300
E-mail: staylor@bn.com.

Barnes&Noble.com, *(1-4005; 1-4006)* c/o Merch Accounts Payable/NR Dept., 76 Ninth Ave., 9th Flr., New York, NY 10011 (SAN 192-6551) Tel 212-414-6000
Web site: http://www.bn.com.

Barron's Bks., *(0-9722641)* 4704 Buckner Ln., Paducah, KY 42001-5352 Tel 270-443-1205
E-mail: bwhitey@webtv.net.

Basic Crafts Co., 6001 66th Ave., No. 10, Riverdale, MD 20737-1717 (SAN 169-5622) Toll Free: 800-847-4127 (outside New York).

Bay News, Inc., 3333 NW 35th Ave., Portland, OR 97210 Tel 503-219-3001; Fax: 503-241-1877.

Bayou Bks., 1005 Monroe St., Gretna, LA 70053 (SAN 120-1913) Tel 504-368-1171; Toll Free: 800-843-1724.

Bayside Distribution, *See* **Bayside Entertainment Distribution**

Bayside Entertainment Distribution, *(0-7691)* 885 Riverside Pkwy., West Sacramento, CA 95605 (SAN 631-1261) Tel 916-371-2800; Fax: 916-371-1995; Toll Free: 800-525-5709
E-mail: stecon@baysidedist.com.

BBC Audiobooks America, *(0-563; 0-7540; 0-7927; 0-89340; 1-55504)* Orders Addr.: P.O. Box 1450, Hampton, NH 03843-1450 (SAN 208-4864) Tel 603-926-8744; Fax: 603-929-3890; Toll Free: 800-621-0182; Edit Addr.: 1 Lafayette Rd., Hampton, NH 03843
E-mail: customerservice@bbcaudiobooksamerica.com
Web site: http://www.bbcaudiobooksamerica.com.

BCM Pubns., Inc., *(0-86508)* 237 Fairfield Ave., Upper Darby, PA 19082-2206 (SAN 211-7762) Tel 610-352-7177; Fax: 610-352-5561; Toll Free: 800-226-4685
E-mail: info@bcmintl.org; 103046.613@compuserve.com
Web site: http://www.bcmintl.org.

Beaver News Co., Inc., 230 W. Washington St., Rensselaer, IN 47978 (SAN 630-8864).

Beck's Bk. Store, 4520 N. Broadway, Chicago, IL 60640 (SAN 159-8139) Tel 773-784-7963; Fax: 773-784-0066
E-mail: rsvltrd@aol.com
Web site: http://www.aol.members/becks.html.

Beechwood Pubns., Inc., P.O. Box 1158, Kennett Square, PA 19348 (SAN 107-5853) Tel 610-444-5991 ; Fax: 215-566-4178.

Beekman Pubs., Inc., *(0-8464)* P.O. Box 888, Woodstock, NY 12498-0888 (SAN 170-1622) Tel 845-679-2300; Fax: 845-679-2301; Toll Free: 888-233-5626
E-mail: beekman@beekmanpublishers.com
Web site: http://www.beekmanpublishers.comw; http://www.beekman.net.

Beeler, Thomas T. Publisher, *(1-57490)* Orders Addr.: P.O. Box 659, Hampton Falls, NH 03844-0659; Edit Addr.: 22 King St., Hampton Falls, NH 03844-2414 Tel 603-772-1175; Fax: 603-778-9025; Toll Free: 800-818-7574
E-mail: tombeeler@hotmail.com
Web site: http://www.beelerpub.com.

Before Columbus Foundation, 655 13th St., Suite 300, The Raymond Hse., Oakland, CA 94612 (SAN 159-2955) Tel 510-268-9775.

Behrman Hse., Inc., *(0-87441)* 11 Edison Pl., Springfield, NJ 07081 (SAN 201-4459) Tel 973-379-7200; Fax: 973-379-7280; Toll Free: 800-221-2755
E-mail: webmaster@behrmanhouse.com
Web site: http://www.behrmanhouse.com.

Beijing Bk. Co., Inc., 701 E. Linden Ave., Linden, NJ 07036-2495 (SAN 169-5673) Tel 908-862-0909; Fax: 908-862-4201.

Bell Magazine, Orders Addr.: P.O. Box 1957, Monterey, CA 93940 (SAN 159-7221); Edit Addr.: 3 Justin Ct., Monterey, CA 93940 (SAN 169-0353) Tel 408-642-4668.

Benjamin News Group, P.O. Box 16147, Missoula, MT 59806 (SAN 631-6476) Tel 406-721-7801; Fax: 406-721-7802
E-mail: nypguy@dreamscape.com.

Bennett & Curran, Inc., *(1-879607)* 1545 W. Tufts Ave., Suite M, Englewood, CO 80110-5575 Tel 303-783-2255; Fax: 303-783-2256
E-mail: Jeff@bennettandcurran.com.

Bentley Pubs., *(0-8376)* 1734 Massachusetts Ave., Cambridge, MA 02138-1804 (SAN 213-9839) Tel 617-547-4170; Fax: 617-876-9235; Toll Free: 800-423-4595
E-mail: Sales@bentleypublishing.com
Web site: http://www.bentleypublishers.com.

Bentley, Robert Incorporated, Publishers, *See* **Bentley Pubs.**

Berkeley Educational Paperbacks, 2480 Bancroft Way, Berkeley, CA 94704 (SAN 168-9509) Tel 510-848-7907.

Berkley Publishing Group, *(0-425; 0-515)* Div. of Penguin Putnam, Inc., Orders Addr.: 405 Murray Hill Pkwy., East Rutherford, NJ 07073 Toll Free: 800-788-6262 (individual consumer sales); 800-847-5515 (orders); 800-631-8571 (customer service); Edit Addr.: 375 Hudson St., New York, NY 10014 (SAN 201-3991) Tel 212-366-2000; Fax: 212-366-2385
E-mail: online@penguinputnam.com
Web site: http://www.penguinputnam.com.

Bernan Assocs., *(0-400; 0-527; 0-89059)* Div. of Kraus Organization, The, Orders Addr.: 4611-F Assembly Dr., Lanham, MD 20706-4391 (SAN 169-3182) Tel 301-459-7666; Fax: 301-459-0056; Toll Free Fax: 800-865-3450; Toll Free: 800-274-4888
E-mail: order@bernan.com; query@bernan.com
Web site: http://www.bernan.com.

Bess Pr., Inc., *(0-935848; 1-57306; 1-880188)* 3565 Harding Ave., Honolulu, HI 96816 (SAN 239-4111) Tel 808-734-7159; Fax: 808-732-3627; Toll Free: 800-910-2377
E-mail: info@besspress.com
Web site: http://www.besspress.com.

Best Bk. Ctr., Inc., 1016 Ave. Ponce De Leon, San Juan, PR 00926 (SAN 132-4403) Tel 809-727-7945; Fax: 809-268-5022.

Best Continental Bk. Co., Inc., P.O. Box 615, Merrifield, VA 22116 (SAN 107-3737) Tel 703-280-1400.

Bethany Hse. Pubs., *(0-7642; 0-87123; 1-55661; 1-56179; 1-57778; 1-880089; 1-59066)* Div. of Baker Book House, Inc., Orders Addr.: P.O. Box 6287, Grand Rapids, MI 49516-6287 Toll Free: 800-877-2665; Edit Addr.: 11400 Hampshire Ave., S., Bloomington, MN 55438-2455 (SAN 201-4416) Tel 952-829-2500; Fax: 952-996-1393; Toll Free: 800-877-2665
E-mail: orders@bakerbooks.com
Web site: http://www.bethanyhouse.com.

Beyda & Assocs., Inc., 6943 Valjean Ave., Van Nuys, CA 91406 (SAN 169-0426) Tel 818-988-3102; Fax: 818-994-8724; Toll Free: 800-422-3932 (orders only)
E-mail: sales@beydabooks.com.

BHB International, Inc., Orders Addr.: 302 W. North 2nd St., Seneca, SC 29678 (SAN 631-0915) Tel 864-885-9444; Fax: 864-885-1090
E-mail: bhbbooks@aol.com
Web site: http://www.bhbinternational.com.

Biblio Distribution, Div. of National Book Network, Orders Addr.: 15200 NBN Way, Blue Ridge Summit, PA 17214 Toll Free Fax: 800-338-4550; Toll Free: 800-462-6420; Edit Addr.: 4501 Forbes Blvd., Suite 200, Lanham, MD 20706 (SAN 211-724X) Tel 301-459-3366; Fax: 301-429-5746
E-mail: custserv@nbnbooks.com
Web site: http://www.bibliodistribution.com.

Biblio Distribution Center, *See* **Biblio Distribution**

Biddy Bks., 1235 168 Model Rd., Manchester, TN 37355 (SAN 157-8561) Tel 931-728-6967.

Bilingual Educational Services, Inc., *(0-86624; 0-89075)* 2514 S. Grand Ave., Los Angeles, CA 90007 (SAN 218-4680) Tel 213-749-6213; Fax: 213-749-1820; Toll Free: 800-448-6032
E-mail: bes@besbooks.com; Sales@besbooks.com
Web site: http://www.besbooks.com.

Bilingual Pubns. Co., The, 270 Lafayette St., New York, NY 10012 (SAN 164-8993) Tel 212-431-3500; Fax: 212-431-3567 Do not confuse with Bilingual Pubns., in Denver, CO
E-mail: lindagoodman@juno.com.

Birdlegs Christian Apparel, P.O. Box 189, Duluth, GA 30136-0189 (SAN 631-3280) Toll Free: 800-545-0790.

Black Box Corp., 1000 Park Dr., Lawrence, PA 15055 (SAN 277-1985) Tel 412-746-5500; Fax: 412-746-0746.

Black Magazine Agency, Box 1018, Logansport, IN 46947 (SAN 107-0819) Tel 219-753-2429; Fax: 219-753-5480; Toll Free: 800-782-9787.

Blackburn News Agency, P.O. Box 1039, Kingsport, TN 37662 (SAN 169-7900).

Blackwell North America, *(0-913262; 0-916472; 0-946344)* Orders Addr.: 6024 SW Jean Rd., Bldg. G, Lake Oswego, OR 97034 (SAN 169-7048) Tel 503-684-1140; Fax: 503-639-2481; Toll Free: 800-547-6426 (in Oregon); Edit Addr.: 100 University Ct., Blackwood, NJ 08012 (SAN 169-4596) Tel 856-228-8900; Toll Free: 800-257-7341.

Blair, John F. Pub., *(0-89587; 0-910244)* 1406 Plaza Dr., Winston-Salem, NC 27103 (SAN 201-4319) Tel 336-768-1374; Fax: 336-768-9194; Toll Free: 800-222-9796
E-mail: blairpub@blairpub.com
Web site: http://www.blairpub.com.

Bloomington News Agency, P.O. Box 3757, Bloomington, IL 61702-3757 (SAN 169-1732).

Blue Cat, *(0-932679; 0-936200)* 469 Barbados, Walnut, CA 91789 (SAN 214-0322) Tel 909-594-3317.

Blue Feather Products, Inc., P.O. Box 2, Ashland, OR 97520 (SAN 630-8260) Tel 541-482-5268; Fax: 541-482-2338; Toll Free: 800-472-2487
E-mail: info@blue-feather.com
Web site: http://www.blue-feather.com.

Blue Mountain Arts Inc., *(0-88396; 1-58786)* Orders Addr.: P.O. Box 4549, Boulder, CO 80306 (SAN 299-9609) Tel 303-449-0536; 954-522-0055; Fax: 303-417-6496; 954-522-5330; Toll Free Fax: 800-256-1213; Toll Free: 800-473-2082
E-mail: ordersbma@mindspring.com.

Blue Mountain Arts (R) by SPS Studios, Incorporated, *See* **Blue Mountain Arts Inc.**

Blue Ridge News Co., 21 Westside Dr., No. B, Asheville, NC 28806-2846 (SAN 169-6335).

Blue Ridge News, Inc., 101 E. Patrick St., Frederick, MD 21701-5629 (SAN 169-3158) Tel 301-694-8440.

Boley International Subscription Agency, Inc., 1001 Fries Mill Rd., Blackwood, NJ 08012 (SAN 159-6225) Tel 609-629-2500.

Wholesalers & Distributors

Bollett Library Resources, 1340 Ridgeview Dr., McHenry, IL 60050 Tel 815-759-1700; Fax: 815-759-9552.

Bonneville News Co., 965 Beardsley Pl., Salt Lake City, UT 84119 Tel 801-972-5454; Fax: 801-972-1075; Toll Free: 800-748-5453.

Book Box, Inc., 3126 Purdue Ave., Los Angeles, CA 90066 (SAN 243-2285) Tel 310-391-2313.

Book Buy Back, 5150 Candlewood St., No. 6, Lakewood, CA 90712 (SAN 631-7251) Tel 562-461-9355; Fax: 562-461-9445.

Book Clearing Hse., 46 Purdy St., Harrison, NY 10528 (SAN 125-5169) Tel 914-835-0015; Fax: 914-835-0398; Toll Free: 800-431-1579 E-mail: bookch@aol.com; bchouse@delphi.com.

Book Co., The, 145 S. Glencoe St., Denver, CO 80222-1152 (SAN 200-2809).

Book Distribution Ctr., *(0-941722)* Div. of Free Islamic Literatures, Inc., Orders Addr.: P.O. Box 35844, Houston, TX 77235 (SAN 241-6395); Edit Addr.: P.O. Box 31669, Houston, TX 77231 (SAN 226-2770).

Book Distribution Ctr., Inc., Orders Addr.: P.O. Box 64631, Virginia Beach, VA 23467 (SAN 134-8019) Tel 757-456-0005; Fax: 757-552-0837; Edit Addr.: 4617 N. Witchduck Rd., Virginia Beach, VA 23455 (SAN 169-8672)
E-mail: sales@bookdist.com
Web site: http://www.bookdist.

Book Dynamics, Inc., *(0-9612440)* 18 Kennedy Blvd., East Brunswick, NJ 08816 (SAN 169-5649) Tel 732-545-5151; Fax: 732-545-5959; Toll Free: 800-441-4510.

Book Fairs of Covina, 1030 Bonita Ave., La Verne, CA 91750 (SAN 630-6225) Tel 909-593-0697; 1650 W. Orange Grove Ave., Pomona, CA 91768-2153 (SAN 299-2434).

Book Gallery, *(1-878382)* 632 S. Quincy Ave., Apt. 1, Tulsa, OK 74120-4635 (SAN 630-9321).

Book Home, The, 119 E. Dale St., Colorado Springs, CO 80903-4701 (SAN 249-3055) Tel 719-634-5885.

Book Hse., Inc., The, 208 W. Chicago St., Jonesville, MI 49250-0125 (SAN 169-3859) Tel 517-849-2117; Fax: 517-849-9716; Toll Free Fax: 800-858-9716; Toll Free: 800-248-1146
E-mail: bhinfo@thebookhouse.com.

Book Margins, Inc., 7100 Valley Green Rd., Fort Washington, PA 19034-2206 (SAN 106-7788) Tel 215-223-5300
E-mail: paul.gross@bookmargins.com
Web site: http://www.bookmargins.com.

Book Mart, The, 1153 E. Hyde Pk., Inglewood, CA 90302 (SAN 168-969X).

Book Publishing Co., The, *(0-913990; 1-57067; 0-9669317; 0-9673108)* P.O. Box 99, Summertown, TN 38483 (SAN 202-439X) Tel 931-964-3571; Fax: 931-964-3518; Toll Free: 888-260-8458 Do not confuse with Book Publishing Co., Seattle, WA
E-mail: bookpub@bookpubco.com
Web site: http://www.bookpubco.com.

Book Sales, Inc., *(0-7858; 0-89009; 1-55521)* Orders Addr.: 114 Northfield Ave., Edison, NJ 08837 (SAN 169-488X) Tel 732-225-0530; Fax: 212-779-6058; 732-225-2257; Toll Free: 800-526-7257; Edit Addr.: 276 Fifth Ave., Suite 206, New York, NY 10001 (SAN 299-4062) Tel 212-779-4972; Fax: 212-779-6058
E-mail: booksales@eclipse.net
Web site: http://www.booksales.com.

Book Service of Puerto Rico, 102 De Diego, Santurce, PR 00907 (SAN 169-9326) Tel 809-728-5000; Fax: 809-726-6131
E-mail: bellbook@coqui.net
Web site: http://home.coqui.net/bellbook.

Book Service Unlimited, P.O. Box 31108, Seattle, WA 98103-1108 (SAN 169-877X) Toll Free: 800-347-0042.

Book Services International, Orders Addr.: P.O. Box 1434-SMS, Fairfield, CT 06430 (SAN 157-9541) Tel 203-374-4939; Fax: 203-384-6099; Toll Free: 800-243-2790.

Book Shelf, The, 919 Central Ave., Fort Dodge, IA 50501 (SAN 169-2658) Tel 515-573-3535.

Book Travelers West, Orders Addr.: 9551 Landfall Dr., Huntington Beach, CA 92646 Tel 714-968-2301.

Book Warehouse, 5154 NW 165th St., Hialeah, FL 33014-6335.

Book Wholesalers, Inc., *(0-7587; 1-4046; 1-4131; 1-4155; 1-4156)* 1847 Mercer Rd., Lexington, KY 40511-1001 (SAN 135-5449) Toll Free: 800-888-4478
E-mail: jcarrico@bwibooks.com; nb
Web site: http://www.bwibooks.com.

Book World, 311 Sagamore Pkwy., N., Lafayette, IN 47904 (SAN 135-4051) Tel 765-448-1131 Do not confuse with companies with the same or similar name in Sun Lakes, AZ, Roanoke, VA
E-mail: fsjintl@pworld.net.ph.

Bookazine Co., Inc., 75 Hook Rd., Bayonne, NJ 07002 (SAN 169-5665) Tel 201-339-7777; Fax: 201-339-7778; Toll Free: 800-221-8112.

Booklegger, The, *(0-936421)* Orders Addr.: P.O. Box 2626, Grass Valley, CA 95945 (SAN 697-9548); Edit Addr.: 13100 Grass Valley Ave., Suite D, Grass Valley, CA 95945 (SAN 120-6125) Tel 530-272-1556 ; Fax: 530-272-2133; Toll Free Fax: 800-250-2199; Toll Free: 800-262-1556
E-mail: order@booklegger.com
Web site: http://www.booklegger.com/.

Bookline, Div. of Michiana News Service, Inc., 2232 S. 11th St., Niles, MI 49120 (SAN 169-3948) Tel 616-684-3013; Fax: 616-684-8740.

Booklines Hawaii, Ltd., *(1-929844; 1-58849)* 269 Pali'i St., Mililani, HI 96789 (SAN 630-6624) Tel 877-828-4852; Fax: 808-676-2031
E-mail: cynthiar@booklines.com
Web site: http://www.booklineshawaii.com.

Bookman Bks., 138 Elena St., Santa Fe, NM 87501 (SAN 630-933X) Tel 505-982-5964.

Bookmark, Inc., The, 14643 W. 95th St., Lenexa, KS 66215 (SAN 131-4017) Tel 913-894-1288; Fax: 913-894-1842; Toll Free: 800-642-1288.

BookMasters, Inc., *(0-917889)* Orders Addr.: P.O. Box 388, Mansfield, OH 44903 (SAN 631-3566) Tel 419-281-1802; Fax: 419-281-6883; Toll Free: 800-247-6553; 30 Amberwood Pkwy., Ashland, OH 44805 Fax: 419-281-6886 Do not confuse with BookMasters, Burleson, TX
E-mail: order@bookmaster.com; info@bookmasters.com
Web site: http://www.bookmasters.com.

Bookmen, Inc., Orders Addr.: 525 N. Third St., Minneapolis, MN 55401 (SAN 169-409X) Tel 612-359-5757; Fax: 612-341-2903; Toll Free Fax: 800-266-5636; Toll Free: 800-328-8411 (customer service)
Web site: http://www.bookmen.com.

Bookpeople, *(0-914728)* 7900 Edgewater Dr., Oakland, CA 94621 (SAN 168-9517) Tel 510-632-4700; Fax: 510-632-1281; Toll Free Fax: 800-999-4650
E-mail: custserv@bponline.com; bpeople@bponline.com
Web site: http://www.bponline.com.

Books & Research, Inc., 32 Main St., Hastings On Hudson, NY 10706-1602 (SAN 130-1101) Fax: 914-478-1315
E-mail: brinc@ix.netcom.com
Web site: http://www.books-and-research.com.

Books Nippan, *See* **Digital Manga Distribution**

Books to Grow On, 826 S. Aiken Ave., Pittsburgh, PA 15232 (SAN 128-438X); 210 S. Highland Ave., Pittsburgh, PA 15206 Fax: 412-621-5324.

Books West, 5757 Arapahoc Ave., Unit D2, Boulder, CO 80303 (SAN 631-4724) Tel 303-449-5995; Fax: 303-449-5951; Toll Free: 800-378-4188 Do not confuse with Books West, San Diego, CA
E-mail: wnack@rmi.net.

Booksellers Order Service, 828 S. Broadway, Tarrytown, NY 10591-5112 (SAN 106-5181) Tel 914-591-2665; Fax: 914-591-2720; Toll Free: 800-637-0037.

Booksmith Promotional Co., 100 Paterson Plank Rd., Jersey City, NJ 07307 (SAN 664-5364) Tel 201-659-2768; Fax: 201-659-3631.

Booksource, The, *(0-7383; 0-911891; 0-9641084; 1-890760)* 1230 Macklind Ave., Saint Louis, MO 63110-1432 (SAN 169-4324) Tel 314-647-0600; Fax: 314-647-2622; Toll Free: 800-444-0435
E-mail: vstadts@freewwweb.com
Web site: http://www.booksource.com.

Bookstop, The, 603 S. Military Ave., Green Bay, WI 54301 Tel 920-498-0008.

Booksurge, LLC, *(1-59109; 1-59457)* 5341 Dorchester Rd., Suite 16, North Charleston, SC 29418 (SAN 255-2132) Tel 843-579-0000; Fax: 843-577-7506; Toll Free: 866-308-6235
E-mail: editor@booksurge.com; info@imprintbooks.com
Web site: http://www.booksurge.com; http://www.imprintbooks.com.

BookWorld Distribution Services, Incorporated, *See* **BookWorld Services, Inc.**

BookWorld Services, Inc., *(1-884962)* 1933 Whitfield Pk. Loop, Sarasota, FL 34243 (SAN 173-0568) Tel 941-758-8094; Fax: 941-753-9396; Toll Free Fax: 800-777-2525; Toll Free: 800-444-2524 (orders only)
E-mail: central@bookworld.com; sales@bookworld.com
Web site: http://www.bookworld.com.

Bookworm, 14 Griffin St., Northport, ME 04849-4446 (SAN 170-8074).

Bookworm Bookfairs, 968 Farmington Ave., W., West Hartford, CT 06107 (SAN 156-5621).

Bookworm, The, 417 Monmouth Dr., Cherry Hill, NJ 08002 (SAN 120-9531) Tel 609-667-5884.

Borchardt, G. Inc., 136 E. 57th St., New York, NY 10022 (SAN 285-8614) Tel 212-753-5785; Fax: 212-838-6518.

Borders, Inc., 9910 N. By NE Blvd., Bldg. 4, Fishers, IN 46038 (SAN 152-5352); Plaza Las Americas, Space 497, 1st Flr. 525 F D Roosevelt Ave., Hato Rey, PR 00918 (SAN 193-2314); 455 Industrial Blvd., Suite E, La Vergne, TN 37086 (SAN 156-6474); Edit Addr.: 100 Phoenix Dr., Ann Arbor, MI 48108 (SAN 152-3546) Tel 734-477-1100; Fulfillment Addr.: a/o Fullfillment Center, 100 Phoenix Dr., Ann Arbor, MI 48108-2202 (SAN 197-0917).

Bound to Stay Bound Bks., *(0-9718238)* 1880 W. Morton Rd., Jacksonville, IL 62650 (SAN 169-1996) Toll Free Fax: 800-747-2872; Toll Free: 800-637-6586
Web site: http://www.btsb.com.

Bowers & Merena Galleries, Inc., *(0-943161)* Orders Addr.: P.O. Box 1224, Wolfeboro, NH 03894 (SAN 168-9746) Tel 603-569-5095; Fax: 603-569-5319; Toll Free: 800-222-5993; Edit Addr.: 61 S. Main St., Wolfeboro, NH 03894 (SAN 668-2561).

Boydell & Brewer, Inc., *(0-85115; 0-85991; 0-86193; 0-907239; 1-870252)* Div. of Boydell & Brewer, Ltd., 668 Mount Hope Ave., Rochester, NY 14620-2731 Tel 585-275-0419; Fax: 585-271-8778
E-mail: boydell@boydellusa.net
Web site: http://www.boydell.co.uk.

Brauninger News Co., Orders Addr.: Box 290, Trenton, NJ 08602-0290 (SAN 169-4936) Tel 609-396-1500; Fax: 609-394-2594
E-mail: philfriend@worldnet.att.net.

Breakfast Poems, 3424 Preston Ave., NW, Roanoke, VA 24012 Tel 540-366-5886 (phone/fax).

Bridge Pubns., Inc., *(0-88404; 1-57318; 1-4031)* 4751 Fountain Ave., Los Angeles, CA 90029 (SAN 208-3884) Tel 323-953-3320; Fax: 323-953-3328; Toll Free: 800-722-1733
E-mail: info@bridgepub.com
Web site: http://www.bridgepub.com; http://www.clearbodyclearmind.com.

Bright Horizons Specialty Distributors, Inc., 138 Springside Rd., Asheville, NC 28803 (SAN 110-4101) Tel 704-684-8840; Fax: 704-681-1790; Toll Free: 800-437-3959 (orders only).

Brisco Pubns., *(0-9603576)* P.O. Box 2161, Palos Verdes Peninsula, CA 90274 (SAN 133-0268) Tel 310-534-4943; Fax: 310-534-8437.

Broadman & Holman Pubs., *(0-8054; 0-87981; 1-55819; 1-58640; 0-8400)* Div. of LifeWay Christian Resources of the Southern Baptist Convention, 127 Ninth Ave., N., Nashville, TN 37234 (SAN 201-937X) Tel 615-251-2520; Fax: 615-251-5026 (Books Only); 615-251-2036 (Bibles Only); 615-251-2413 (Gifts/Supplies Only); Toll Free: 800-296-4036 (orders/returns); 800-251-3225; 800-725-5416
E-mail: broadmanholman@lifeway.com
Web site: http://www.broadmanholman.com.

Brodart Co., *(0-87272)* Orders Addr.: 500 Arch St., Williamsport, PA 17705 (SAN 169-7684) Tel 717-326-2461; 570-326-2461 (International); Fax: 570-326-1479; 519-759-1144 (Canada); Toll Free Fax: 800-999-6799; Toll Free: 800-233-8467 (US & Canada)
E-mail: bookinfo@brodart.com
Web site: http://www.brodart.com.

Brookes, Paul H. Publishing Co., *(0-933716; 1-55766)* Orders Addr.: P.O. Box 10624, Baltimore, MD 21285-0624 (SAN 212-730X) Tel 410-337-9580; Fax: 410-337-8539; Toll Free: 800-638-3775 (customer service/ordering/billing/fulfillment); Edit Addr.: 409 Washington Ave., Suite 500, Towson, MD 21204 (SAN 666-6485)
E-mail: custserv@brookespublishing.com
Web site: http://www.brookespublishing.com.

Brookings Institution Pr., *(0-8157)* 1775 Massachusetts Ave., NW, Washington, DC 20036-2188 (SAN 201-9396) Tel 202-797-6258; Fax: 202-797-6004; Toll Free: 800-275-1447
E-mail: brookinfo@brook.edu; bibooks@brook.edu
Web site: http://www.brookings.edu.

Brotherhood of Life, Inc., *(0-914732)* P.O. Box 46306, Las Vegas, NV 89114-6306 (SAN 111-3674) Fax: 702-319-5577
E-mail: brotherhoodoflife@hotmail.com
Web site: http://www.brotherhoodoflife.com.

Brunner News Agency, 217 Flanders Ave., P.O. Box 598, Lima, OH 45801 (SAN 169-6777) Tel 419-225-5826; Fax: 419-225-5537; Toll Free: 800-998-1727
E-mail: brunnews@aol.com
Web site: http://www.readmoreshallmark.com.

Brush Dance, Inc., *(1-891731; 1-931554; 1-59324)* 1 Simms St., San Rafael, CA 94941 (SAN 631-0710) Tel 415-259-0900; Fax: 415-259-0360; Toll Free: 800-531-7445
E-mail: jmalen@brushdance.com
Web site: http://www.brushdance.com.

Bryant Altman Map, Inc., Endicott St., Bldg. 26, Norwood, MA 02062 (SAN 630-2475) Tel 781-762-3339; Fax: 781-769-9080
E-mail: JPG63@aol.com.

Bryant-Altman Book & Map Distributors, *See* **Bryant Altman Map, Inc.**

Buckeye News Co., 6800 W. Central Ave., Suite F, Toledo, OH 43617-1157 (SAN 169-6874).

Budget Bk. Service, Inc., Div. of LDAP, Inc., 386 Park Ave. S., Suite 1913, New York, NY 10016-8804 (SAN 169-5762) Fax: 212-679-2247.

Budget Marketing, Inc., P.O. Box 1805, Des Moines, IA 50306 (SAN 285-8754).

Budgetext, Orders Addr.: P.O. Box 1487, Fayetteville, AR 72702 (SAN 111-3321) Tel 501-443-9205; Fax: 501-442-3064; Toll Free: 800-643-3432; Edit Addr.: 1936 N. Shiloh Dr., Fayetteville, AR 72704 (SAN 249-3330)
E-mail: wmorgan@absc.com; scaldwell@budgetext.com
Web site: http://www.budgetext.com.

Buena Vista Home Video, *(0-7888; 1-55890)* Div. of Walt Disney Studios, 500 S. Buena Vista St., Burbank, CA 91521-1120 (SAN 249-2342) Tel 818-560-4430; Fax: 818-972-2845; Toll Free: 800-723-4763
Web site: http://www.disney.com.

Burlington News Agency, Hercules Dr., P.O. Box 510, Colchester, VT 05446-0510 (SAN 169-8583) Tel 802-655-7000.

Burns News Agency, P.O. Box 1211, Rochester, NY 14603-1211 (SAN 169-5320).

BUSCA, Inc., *(0-9666196)* Orders Addr.: P.O. Box 854, Ithaca, NY 14851 (SAN 631-6514) Tel 607-546-4247 ; Fax: 607-546-4248; Edit Addr.: 5930 NYS Rte. 414, Hector, NY 14841 (SAN 631-6581)
E-mail: info@buscainc.com
Web site: http://www.buscainc.com.

Byrrd Enterprises, Inc., *(1-886715)* 1302 Lafayette Dr., Alexandria, VA 22308 (SAN 169-8605) Tel 703-765-5626; Fax: 703-768-4086; Toll Free: 800-628-0901
E-mail: byrrdbooks@aol.com.

C & B Bk. Hse., 21 Oak Ridge Rd., Monroe, CT 06468 (SAN 159-8279).

C & H News Co., P.O. Box 2768, Corpus Christi, TX 78403-2768 (SAN 169-8249).

Cajun Country Distributors, 8956 Trudeau Ave., Baton Rouge, LA 70806 (SAN 631-1733) Tel 504-924-1275.

Calico Subscription Co., P.O. Box 640337, San Jose, CA 95164-0337 (SAN 285-9173) Tel 408-432-8700; Fax: 408-432-8813; Toll Free: 800-952-2542.

California Princeton Fulfillment Services, 1445 Lower Ferry Rd., Ewing, NJ 08618 (SAN 630-639X) Tel 609-883-1759 (ext. 536); Toll Free: 800-777-4726
E-mail: donnaw@cpfs.pupress.princeton.edu.

Calvary Distribution, *(0-9676661; 0-9700218; 1-931667)* Div. of Calvary Chapel of Costa Mesa, 3232 W. MacArthur Blvd., Santa Ana, CA 92704 (SAN 631-7405) Tel 714-545-6548; Fax: 714-641-8201; Toll Free: 800-444-7664
E-mail: mail@calvaryd.org
Web site: http://www.calvaryd.org.

Cambridge Bk. Co., *(0-8428)* Div. of Simon & Schuster, Inc., 4350 Equity Dr., Box 249, Columbus, OH 43216 (SAN 169-5703) Toll Free: 800-238-5833
Web site: http://www.simonsays.com/.

Cambridge Univ. Pr., *(0-521; 0-511)* Orders Addr.: 100 Brook Hill Dr., West Nyack, NY 10994-2133 (SAN 281-3769) Tel 845-353-7500; Fax: 845-353-4141; Toll Free: 800-872-7423 (orders, returns, credit & accounting); 800-937-9600; Edit Addr.: 40 W. 20th St., New York, NY 10011-4211 (SAN 200-206X) Tel 212-924-3900; Fax: 212-691-3239
E-mail: orders@cup.org; information@cup.org; customer_service@cup.org
Web site: http://www.cup.org.

Canyonlands Pubns., *(0-9702595)* Orders Addr.: P.O. Box 16175, Bellemont, AZ 86015-6175 (SAN 114-3824) Tel 520-779-3888; Fax: 520-779-3778; Toll Free: 800-283-1983; Edit Addr.: 4860 N. Ken Morey, Bellemont, AZ 86015
E-mail: books@infomagic.com.

Cape News Co., P.O. Box 568680, Rockledge, FL 32955 Tel 407-636-5909.

Capital Business Systems, Div. of Capital Business Service, Orders Addr.: P.O. Box 2088, Napa, CA 94558 (SAN 698-3146) Tel 707-252-8844; Fax: 707-252-6368; Edit Addr.: 2033 First St., Napa, CA 94558.

Capital City, 2537 Daniels St., Madison, WI 53704-6772 (SAN 200-5328) Tel 608-223-2000; Fax: 608-223-2010.

Capital News Co., 961 Palmyra, Jackson, MS 39203 Tel 601-355-8341; Fax: 601-352-1343.

Capitol News Agency, P.O. Box 7886, Richmond, VA 23231 (SAN 249-2768); 5203 Hatcher St., Richmond, VA 23231-0271 Tel 804-222-7252.

Capper Pr., 1503 SW 42nd, Topeka, KS 66609 (SAN 285-8886) Tel 913-274-4324; Fax: 913-274-4305; Toll Free: 800-678-5779 (ext. 4324).

Cardinal Pubs. Group, 14 Lakeview Ct., Carmel, IN 46033 (SAN 631-7936) Tel 317-513-6104; Fax: 317-846-1557
E-mail: tdoherty@in.net.

Cards Bks. N Things, 1446 St., Rd. 2 West, La Porte, IN 46350 (SAN 159-8295).

Carolina Biological Supply Co., Pubns. Dept., *(0-89278)* 2700 York Rd., Burlington, NC 27215-3398 (SAN 249-2784) Tel 336-584-0381; Fax: 910-584-3399; Toll Free Fax: 800-222-7112; Toll Free: 800-334-5551
E-mail: carolina@carolina.com
Web site: http://www.carolina.com.

Carolina Cassette Distributors, Orders Addr.: P.O. Box 429, New Bern, NC 28560 (SAN 110-8395) Fax: 919-638-1291; Edit Addr.: 2600 Oaks Rd., New Bern, NC 28560 (SAN 659-2155) Tel 919-638-5583.

Carolina News Co., Orders Addr.: P.O. Box 10, Fayetteville, NC 28302; Edit Addr.: 245 Tillinghast St., Fayetteville, NC 28301 Tel 910-483-4135.

Cascade News, Inc., 1055 Commerce Ave., Longview, WA 98632 (SAN 169-8761) Tel 360-425-2450; Fax: 360-425-2451.

Casemate Pubs. & Bk. Distributors, LLC, *(0-9711709; 1-932033)* Orders Addr.: 2114 Darby Rd., 2nd Flr., Havertown, PA 19083 Tel 610-853-9131; Fax: 610-853-9146
E-mail: casemate@casematepublishing.com
Web site: http://www.casematepublishing.com.

Casino Distributors, Orders Addr.: P.O. Box 849, Pleasantville, NJ 08232 (SAN 169-457X) Tel 609-646-4165; Fax: 609-645-0152; Edit Addr.: 10 Canale Dr., Pleasantville, NJ 08234 (SAN 249-3276).

Casper Magazine Agency, P.O. Box 2340, Casper, WY 82602 (SAN 159-8325).

Cassette Book Company, *See* **Audio Bk. Co.**

Catholic Bookrack Service, 700 E. Elm St., La Grange, IL 60525 (SAN 169-2178) Tel 708-482-0044; Fax: 708-482-9644.

Catholic Literary Guild, Inc., 200 Hamilton Ave., White Plains, NY 10601 (SAN 285-8908) Tel 914-949-4444.

Catweasel Productions, *See* **Ars Obscura**

CBLS Pubs., *(1-878907; 1-59529)* 119 Brentwood St., Marietta, OH 45750 (SAN 169-5517) Tel 740-374-9458; Fax: 740-374-8029
E-mail: cbls@cbls.com
Web site: http://www.cbls.com.

CD Distributing, Inc., P.O. Box 4965, Missoula, MT 59806-4965 (SAN 169-4367) Fax: 406-454-0415.

Cedar Fort, Inc./CFI Distribution, *(0-934126; 1-55517)* 925 N. Main St., Springville, UT 84663-1051 (SAN 170-2858) Tel 801-489-4084; Fax: 801-489-1097; Toll Free Fax: 800-388-3727; Toll Free: 800-759-2665
E-mail: sales@cedarfort.com; cedarfort@cedarfort.com; editorial@cedarfort.com
Web site: http://www.cedarfort.com.

Cedar Graphics, *See* **Igram Pr.**

Centennial Pubns., 1400 Ash Dr., Fort Collins, CO 80521 (SAN 630-494X) Tel 970-493-2041 Do not confuse with Centennial Pubns., Grand Junction, CO.

Center for Applied Psychology, Incorporated, *See* **Childswork/Childsplay**

Central Arizona Distributing, 4932 W. Pasadena Ave., Glendale, AZ 85301 (SAN 170-6128) Tel 602-939-6511.

Central Illinois Periodicals, P.O. Box 3757, Bloomington, IL 61701 (SAN 630-8945) Tel 309-829-9405.

Central Kentucky News Distributing Company, *See* **Anderson-Austin News Co., LLC**

Central News of Sandusky, 5716 McCartney Rd., Sandusky, OH 44870-1538 (SAN 169-684X).

Central Programs, 802 N. 41st St., Bethany, MO 64424 Tel 660-425-7777.

Centralia News Co., 232 E. Broadway, Centralia, IL 62801 (SAN 159-8341) Tel 618-532-5601.

CentroLibros de Puerto Rico, Inc., Santa Rosa Unit, Bayamon, PR 00960 (SAN 631-1245) Tel 787-275-0460; Fax: 787-275-0360.

Century Bk. Distribution, 814 Boon, Traverse City, MI 49686 Tel 231-933-6405 (phone/fax).

Ceramic Book & Literature Service, *See* **CBLS Pubs.**

Chambers Kingfisher Graham Publishers, Incorporated, *See* **Larousse Kingfisher Chambers, Inc.**

Champaign-Urbana News Agency, Orders Addr.: P.O. Box 793, Champaign, IL 61824 (SAN 630-8953) Tel 217-351-7047; Edit Addr.: 503 Kenyon, Champaign, IL 61820.

Chelsea Green Publishing, *(0-930031; 1-890132; 1-931498; 88-86283)* Orders Addr.: P.O. Box 428, White River Junction, VT 05001 (SAN 669-7631) Tel 802-295-6300; Fax: 802-295-6444; Toll Free: 800-639-4099; Edit Addr.: 205 Gates-Briggs Bldg., Main St., White River Junction, VT 05001
Web site: http://www.chelseagreen.com.

Cheng & Tsui Co., *(0-646; 0-88727; 0-917056)* 25 West St., Boston, MA 02111-1213 (SAN 169-3387) Tel 617-988-2401; Fax: 617-426-3669
E-mail: service@cheng-tsui.com
Web site: http://www.cheng-tsui.com.

Chicago Distribution Ctr., 11030 S. Langley Ave., Chicago, IL 60628 (SAN 630-6047) Tel 773-568-1550 ; Fax: 773-660-2235; Toll Free: 800-621-2736; 800-621-8471 (credit & collections).

Chico News Agency, P.O. Box 690, Chico, CA 95927 (SAN 168-9533) Tel 530-895-1000; Fax: 530-895-0158.

Children's Bookfair Co., The, 700 E. Grand Ave., Chicago, IL 60611-3472 (SAN 630-6705) Tel 312-477-7323; 837 W. Altgeld St., Chicago, IL 60614 (SAN 630-6713).

Children's Library of Poetry, P.O. Box 831, Dearborn Heights, MI 48127 Tel 313-563-3030; Fax: 313-563-6888
E-mail: poetrylibrary@aol.com.

Children's Library Services, 860 Thimble Shoals Blvd., Newport News, VA 23606.

Child's World, Inc., *(0-89565; 0-913778; 1-56766; 1-59296)* Orders Addr.: P.O. Box 326, Chanhassen, MN 55317-0326 (SAN 211-0032) Tel 952-906-3939; Fax: 952-906-3940; Toll Free: 800-599-7323; Edit Addr.: 7081 W. 192nd Ave., Eden Prairie, MN 55346
E-mail: info@childsworld.com
Web site: http://www.childsworld.com.

Childswork/Childsplay, *(1-882732; 1-58815)* Div. of The Guidance Channel, Orders Addr.: P.O. Box 760, Plainview, NY 11803-0760 Tel 516-349-5520; Fax: 516-349-5521; Toll Free Fax: 800-262-1886; Toll Free: 800-962-1141; 135 Dupont St., Plainview, NY 11803-0760
E-mail: karens@at-risk.com; info@childswork.com
Web site: http://www.childswork.com.

China Bks. & Periodicals, Inc., *(0-8351)* 2929 24th St., San Francisco, CA 94110-4126 (SAN 145-0557) Tel 415-282-2994; Fax: 415-282-0994
E-mail: info@chinabooks.com
Web site: http://www.chinabooks.com.

China Cultural Ctr., 970 N. Broadway, Suite 103, Los Angeles, CA 90012 (SAN 111-8161) Tel 213-489-3827; Fax: 213-489-3080.

China House Gallery, China Institute in America, *See* **China Institute Gallery, China Institute in America**

China Institute Gallery, China Institute in America, *(0-9654270)* 125 E. 65th St., New York, NY 10021 (SAN 110-8743) Tel 212-744-8181; Fax: 212-628-4159
E-mail: gallery@chinainstitute.org
Web site: http://www.chinainstitute.org.

Chinese American Co., 44 Kneeland St., Boston, MA 02111 (SAN 159-7248) Fax: 617-451-2318.

Chivers North America, *See* **BBC Audiobooks America**

Christian Bk. Distributors, Orders Addr.: P.O. Box 7000, Peabody, MA 01961-7000 (SAN 630-5458) Tel 978-977-5000; Fax: 978-977-5010
Web site: http://www.christianbook.com.

Christian Distribtuion Services, Inc., 1230 Heil Quaker Blvd., Lavergne, TN 37086 Tel 615-793-5955; Fax: 615-793-5973.

Christian Literature Crusade, Inc., *(0-87508)* Div. of CLC Publications, Orders Addr.: P.O. Box 1449, Fort Washington, PA 19034-8449 Tel 215-542-1242; Fax: 215-542-7580; Toll Free: 800-659-1240; Edit Addr.: 701 Pennsylvania Ave., Fort Washington, PA 19034 (SAN 169-7358)
E-mail: joinclc@juno.com
Web site: http://www.clcusa.org.

Christian Printing Service, 4861 Chino Ave., Chino, CA 91710-5132 (SAN 108-2647) Tel 714-871-5200.

Christian Publishing Network, *(0-9628406)* P.O. Box 405, Tulsa, OK 74101 (SAN 631-2756) Tel 918-296-4673 (918-296-HOPE); Toll Free: 888-688-8125
E-mail: vpsales@olp.net.

Chronicle Bks. LLC, *(0-8118; 0-87701; 0-938491)* 85 Second St., San Francisco, CA 94105 (SAN 202-165X) Tel 415-537-4200; Fax: 415-537-4460; Toll Free Fax: 800-858-7787; Toll Free: 800-722-6657 (orders only)
E-mail: orders@chroniclebooks.com
Web site: http://www.chroniclebooks.com.

Church of Scientology Information Service-Pubns., *(0-915598)* c/o Bridge Pubns., Inc., 1414 N. Catalina, Los Angeles, CA 90029 (SAN 268-9774).

Church Richards Co., 10001 Roosevelt Rd., Westchester, IL 60154 (SAN 285-8975) Toll Free: 800-323-0227.

Cibolo Nature Ctr., P.O. Box 9, Boerne, TX 78006 Tel 830-249-4616.

Cinco Puntos Pr., *(0-938317)* 701 Texas Ave., El Paso, TX 79901 (SAN 661-0080) Tel 915-838-1625; Fax: 915-838-1635; Toll Free: 800-566-9072
E-mail: bbyrd@cincopuntos.com; leebyrd@cincopuntos.com
Web site: http://www.cincopuntos.com.

Circa Pubns., Inc., 415 Fifth Ave., Pelham, NY 10803-0408 (SAN 169-6122) Tel 914-738-5570; Toll Free: 800-582-5952 (orders only).

Circle Bk. Service, Inc., *(0-87397)* P.O. Box 626, Tomball, TX 77377 (SAN 158-2526) Tel 281-255-6824; Fax: 281-255-8158; Toll Free: 800-227-1591
E-mail: orders@circlebook.com
Web site: http://www.circlebook.com.

City News Agency, Orders Addr.: P.O. Box 561129, Charlotte, NC 28256-1129 (SAN 169-782X); Edit Addr.: P.O. Box 2069, Newark, OH 43055 (SAN 169-6947); 220 Cherry Ave., NE, Canton, OH 44702-1198 (SAN 169-6602); 303 E. Lasalle St., South Bend, IN 46617 (SAN 159-9992); 417 S. McKinnley, Harrisburg, IL 62946 (SAN 169-1961).

Clarks Out of Town News, 303 S. Andrews Ave., Fort Lauderdale, FL 33301 (SAN 159-8384) Tel 954-467-1543.

Classroom Reading Service, 10038 S. Pioneer Blvd., Santa Fe Springs, CA 90670 (SAN 131-3959) Tel 562-942-9501; Fax: 562-942-9370; Toll Free: 800-422-6657
E-mail: crsbooks@aol.com.

Client Distribution Services, 425 Madison Ave., New York, NY 10017 (SAN 631-760X) Tel 212-223-2969; Fax: 212-223-1504 Do not confuse with Client Distribution Services, Jackson, TN.
E-mail: skail@cds.aeneas.com; tflowers@cdsbooks.com
Web site: http://www.cdsbooks.com/.

Clover Bk. Service, 1220 S. Monroe St., Covingtons, LA 70433-3639 (SAN 106-472X) Tel 504-875-0038.

Cobblestone Publishing Co., *(0-382; 0-942389; 0-9607638)* Div. of Cricket Magazine Group, 30 Grove St., Suite C, Peterborough, NH 03458 (SAN 237-9937) Tel 603-924-7209; Fax: 603-924-7380; Toll Free: 800-821-0115
E-mail: custsvc@cobblestone.mv.com
Web site: http://www.cobblestonepub.com.

Coffman Pubns., *(0-9656315)* 8562 Calypso Ln., Gaithersburg, MD 20879 Tel 301-649-3820.

Cogan Bks., *(0-940688)* 15020 Desman Rd., La Mirada, CA 90638 (SAN 168-9649) Tel 714-523-0309 ; Fax: 714-523-0796; Toll Free: 800-733-3630.

Cole, Bill Enterprises, Inc., P.O. Box 60, Randolph, MA 02368-0060 (SAN 685-6373) Tel 617-986-2653.

Collector Bks., *(0-89145; 1-57432)* Div. of Schroeder Publishing Co., Inc., Orders Addr.: P.O. Box 3009, Paducah, KY 42003 (SAN 157-5368) Tel 270-898-6211; 270-898-7903; Fax: 270-898-8890; 270-898-1173; Toll Free: 800-626-5420 (orders only) ; Edit Addr.: 5801 Kentucky Dam Rd., Paducah, KY 42003 (SAN 200-7479)
E-mail: Info@collectorbooks.com; info@AQSquilt.com
Web site: http://www.AQSquilt.com; http://www.collectorbooks.com.

College Bk. Co. of California, Inc., 6590 Darrin Way, Cypress, CA 90630 (SAN 269-0802) Tel 714-894-4791.

Collegedale Distributors, *See* **Tree of Life Midwest**

Colonial Williamsburg Foundation, *(0-87935; 0-910412)* P.O. Box 3532, Williamsburg, VA 23187-3532 (SAN 128-4630) Fax: 757-565-8999 (orders only); Toll Free: 800-446-9240 (orders only)
Web site: http://www.colonialwilliamsburg.com.

Colorado Periodical Distributor, Inc., 1227 Pitkin St., Grand Junction, CO 81502 Tel 970-242-3865; Fax: 970-242-3760.

Columbia County News Agency, Inc., 135 Warren St., Hudson, NY 12534 (SAN 169-5339) Tel 518-828-1017.

Comag Marketing Group, 1790 Broadway, Suite 401, New York, NY 10019 (SAN 169-5800) Tel 212-841-8365; Fax: 212-977-9401.

Comics Hawaii Distributors, *See* **Hobbies Hawaii Distributors**

Common Ground Distributors, Inc., Orders Addr.: P.O. Box 25249, Asheville, NC 28813-1249 Toll Free: 800-654-0626; Edit Addr.: 115 Fairview Rd., Asheville, NC 28803-2307 (SAN 113-8006) Tel 828-274-5575; Fax: 828-274-1955
E-mail: orders@comground.com.

Communication Service Corporation, *See* **Gryphon Hse., Inc.**

Communications Plus USA, 2103 N. Decatur Rd., Suite 335, Decatur, GA 30033 (SAN 631-6735) Tel 404-727-7289.

Communications Technology, Inc., *(0-918232)* P.O. Box 209, Rindge, NH 03461 (SAN 159-8198) Tel 603-899-6957.

Computer & Technical Bks., 6338 Ranchview Ln., N., Osseo, MN 55311-3924 (SAN 630-8120).

Computer Book Service, *See* **Levy Home Entertainment**

Conde Nast Pubns., Inc., *(1-878494)* Four Times Sq., 20th Flr., New York, NY 10036 (SAN 285-905X) Tel 212-880-8800; Fax: 212-880-8289.

Consortium Bk. Sales & Distribution, Orders Addr.: 1045 Westgate Dr., Suite 90, Saint Paul, MN 55114-1065 (SAN 200-6049) Tel 651-221-9035; Fax: 651-221-0124; Toll Free: 800-283-3572 (orders)
E-mail: consortium@cbsd.com
Web site: http://www.cbsd.com.

Contemporary Arts Pr., *(0-931818)* Div. of La Mamelle, Inc., P.O. Box 3123, San Francisco, CA 94119-3123 (SAN 170-5423) Tel 415-282-0286.

Continental Bk. Co., Inc., *(0-9626800)* Eastern Div., 80-00 Cooper Ave., Bldg. No. 29, Glendale, NY 11385 (SAN 169-5436) Tel 718-326-0560; Fax: 718-326-4276; Toll Free: 800-364-0350; Western Div., 625 E. 70th Ave., No. 5, Denver, CO 80229 (SAN 630-2882) Tel 303-289-1761; Fax: 303-289-1764 Do not confuse with Continental Book Company, Denver, CO
E-mail: esl@continentalbook.com; bonjour@continentalbook.com; tag@continentalbook.com; hola@continentalbook.com
Web site: http://www.continentalbook.com.

Cook Communications Ministries, *(0-7459; 0-7814; 0-88207; 0-89191; 0-89693; 0-912692; 1-55513; 1-56476; 983-45027; 983-45018; 983-45031)* 4050 Lee Vance View, Colorado Springs, CO 80918 Tel 719-536-0100; Fax: 719-536-3269; Toll Free: 800-708-5550; 55 Woodslee Ave., Paris, ON N3L 3E5 Toll Free Fax: 800-461-8575; Toll Free: 800-263-2664 Do not confuse with Cook Communications Ministries International, same address
E-mail: bergerj@cookministries.org
Web site: http://www.cookministries.com.

Cookbooks by Morris Press, *See* **Morris Publishing**

Coos Bay Distributors, 131 N. Schoneman St., Coos Bay, OR 97420 (SAN 169-7064) Tel 541-888-5912.

Copper Island News, 1010 Wright St., Marquette, MI 49855-1834 (SAN 169-3824).

Cornerstone Publishing & Distribution, Inc., *(1-929281)* P.O. Box 490, Bountiful, UT 84011-0490 Tel 801-295-9451; Fax: 801-295-0196; Toll Free: 800-453-0812
E-mail: rrhopkins@utah-inter.net.

Coronet Bks., *(0-89563; 91-7916)* 311 Bainbridge St., Philadelphia, PA 19147 (SAN 210-6043) Tel 215-925-2762; Fax: 215-925-1912 Do not confuse with Coronet Bks. & Pubns., Eagle Point, OR
E-mail: rsmolin@ix.netcom.com; order@coronetbooks.com
Web site: http://www.coronetbooks.com.

Council Oak Bks., *(0-933031; 1-57178)* Orders Addr.: 2105 E. 15th St., Suite B, Tulsa, OK 74104 (SAN 689-5522) Toll Free: 800-247-8850 (orders only); Edit Addr.: 5806 S. Perkins Rd., Stillwater, OK 74074
E-mail: sdennison@counciloakbooks.com
Web site: http://www.counciloakbooks.com.

Country News Distributors, Div. of Bakers, Inc., P.O. Box 1258, Brattleboro, VT 05302-1258 (SAN 169-8575).

Countryside Bks., *(0-88453)* 2410 Northside Dr., Clearwater, FL 33761-2216 (SAN 107-4415) Tel 813-796-7337.

Coutts Library Service, Inc., 1823 Maryland Ave., Box 1000, Niagara Falls, NY 14302-1000 (SAN 169-5401) Tel 716-282-8627; Fax: 905-356-5064; Toll Free: 800-772-4304
E-mail: coutts@wizbang.coutts.on.ca.

Cove Distributors, 6325 Erdman Ave., Baltimore, MD 21205 (SAN 158-9814) Toll Free: 800-622-5656 (Orders).

Cowley Distributing, Inc., 732 Heisinger Rd., Jefferson City, MO 65109 (SAN 169-426X) Tel 573-636-6511; Fax: 573-636-6262; Toll Free: 800-346-5950 (orders).

Cox Subscriptions, Inc., 411 Marcia Dr., Goldsboro, NC 27530 (SAN 107-0061) Tel 919-735-1001; Fax: 919-734-3332; Toll Free: 800-553-8088.

CPG Publishing, Inc., *(1-931411)* Orders Addr.: c/o CPG Distribution, 7253 Grayson Rd., Harrisburg, PA 17111 Toll Free: 800-501-6883 (orders & customer service); Edit Addr.: P.O. Box 6142, New York, NY 10150 Tel 212-573-9180; Fax: 212-573-9181 Do not confuse with C P G Publishing Company in Gold Canyon, AZ
E-mail: cpgdistribution@juno.com.

Cram, George F. Co., Inc., *(0-87448)* 301 S. LaSalle St., P.O. Box 426, Indianapolis, IN 46201 (SAN 204-2630) Tel 317-635-5564; Fax: 317-635-2720; Toll Free: 800-227-4199
E-mail: cram-services@iquest.net.

CRC Pubns., *(0-930265; 0-933140; 1-56212)* 2850 Kalamazoo Ave., SE, Grand Rapids, MI 49560 (SAN 212-727X) Tel 616-224-0724; Fax: 616-224-0834; Toll Free Fax: 888-642-8606; Toll Free: 800-333-8300; P.O. Box 5070, Burlington, ON L7R 3Y8
E-mail: sales@crcpublications.org
Web site: http://www.crcpublications.org.

Creative Homeowner, *(0-932944; 1-58011; 1-880029)* Div. of Federal Marketing Corp., 24 Park Way, Upper Saddle River, NJ 07458-9960 (SAN 213-6627) Tel 201-934-7100; Fax: 201-934-7593; Toll Free: 800-631-7795
E-mail: info@creativehomeowner.com
Web site: http://www.creativehomeowner.com.

Creative Homeowner Press, *See* **Creative Homeowner**

Crescent Imports & Pubns., *(0-933127)* P.O. Box 7827, Ann Arbor, MI 48107-7827 (SAN 111-3976) Tel 734-665-3492; Fax: 734-677-1717; Toll Free: 800-521-9744
E-mail: crescentus@aol.com
Web site: http://www.crescentimports.com.

Crescent International, Inc., 2238 Otranto Rd., Charleston, SC 29418 (SAN 110-0777) Tel 803-797-6363; Fax: 803-797-6367.

Critics' Choice, *See* **Critics' Choice Video, Inc.**

Critics' Choice Video, Inc., *(1-932566)* 900 N Rohlwing Rd., Itasca, IL 60143 Tel 630-775-3300; Fax: 603-775-3340
Web site: http://www.ccvideo.com/.

Cromland, 1995 Highland Ave., Suite 200, Bethlehem, PA 18020 (SAN 254-6736) Tel 610-997-3000; Fax: 610-997-8880; Toll Free: 800-944-5554 (U.S. & Canada)
E-mail: info@cromland.com
Web site: http://www.cromland.com.

CrossLife Expressions, *(0-9636049; 1-57838)* Div. of Exchanged Life Ministries, Inc., 10610 E. Bethany Dr., Suite A, Aurora, CO 80014 (SAN 169-0590) Tel 303-750-0440; Fax: 303-750-1228; Toll Free: 800-750-6818
E-mail: info@crosslifebooks.com
Web site: http://www.crosslifebooks.com.

Crowley, Inc., 16120 U.S. Hwy. 19 N., Suite 220, Clearwater, FL 34624-6862 (SAN 285-9130) Tel 813-531-5889.

Crown Agents Service, Ltd., 3100 Massachusetts Ave., NW, Washington, DC 20008 (SAN 285-919X).

Cultural Hispana/Ameriketako Liburuak, Orders Addr.: P.O. Box 7729, Silver Spring, MD 20907 (SAN 159-2823); Edit Addr.: 1413 Crestridge Dr., Silver Spring, MD 20910 (SAN 249-3063) Tel 301-585-0134
E-mail: mokordo@erols.com
Web site: http://www.coloquio.com/libros.html.

Cybernetics Technology Corp., *(0-923458)* 1370 Port Washington Blvd., Port Washington, NY 11050-2628 (SAN 295-933X) Tel 516-883-7676.

Cypress Bk. Co., Inc., *(0-934643)* Subs. of China International Bk. Trading Corp., 3450 Third St., Unit 4B, San Francisco, CA 94124 (SAN 112-1162) Tel 415-821-3582; Fax: 415-821-3523; Toll Free: 800-383-1688
E-mail: sales@cypressbook.com; info@cypressbook.com; cypbook@pacbell.net
Web site: http://www.cypressbook.com.

D & H News Co., Inc., 79 Albany Post Rd., Montrose, NY 10548 (SAN 169-5533) Tel 914-737-3152.

Daedalus Bks., 9645 Gerwig Ln., Columbia, MD 21046-1520 (SAN 158-9202) Tel 410-309-2700
E-mail: tstock@daedalus-books.com; custserv@daedalus-books.com
Web site: http://www.daedalus-books.com.

Dakota News, Inc., 221 Petro Ave., Box 1310, Sioux Falls, SD 57101 (SAN 169-7854) Tel 605-336-3000; Fax: 605-336-7279; Toll Free: 800-658-5498.

Dakota West Bks., P.O. Box 9324, Rapid City, SD 57701 (SAN 630-351X) Tel 605-348-1075; Fax: 605-348-0615.

Darr Subscription Agency, P.O. Box 575, Louisburg, KS 66053-0575 (SAN 285-9149) Toll Free: 800-850-3741
E-mail: lgriff@midusa.net.

Dawson Subscription Service, *See* **Faxon Illinois Service Ctr.**

Day School Magazine Service, P.O. Box 262, Brooklyn, NY 11219 (SAN 285-9157) Tel 718-871-1486; Fax: 718-435-2342
E-mail: Elciv@juno.com.

De Vore Group/Carla Bks. & More, Orders Addr.: P.O. Box 10276, San Juan, PR 00922 (SAN 159-8309) Tel 809-721-7645; Fax: 809-722-9216; Edit Addr.: 1409 Ave. Ponce De Leon, San Juan, PR 00907-4023 (SAN 249-2776).

DeHoff Christian Bookstore, 749 NW Broad St., Murfreesboro, TN 37129 (SAN 184-4202) Tel 615-893-8322; Fax: 615-896-7447; Toll Free: 800-695-5385.

Dehoff Publications, *See* **DeHoff Christian Bookstore**

Delmar News Agency, Inc., P.O. Box 7169, Newark, DE 19714-7169 (SAN 169-0892) Tel 302-455-9922; Toll Free: 800-441-7025.

DeLong Subscription Agency, P.O. Box 806, Lafayette, IN 47902 (SAN 285-9246) Toll Free: 800-992-2092.

Deltiologists of America, *(0-913782)* P.O. Box 8, Norwood, PA 19074 (SAN 170-3072) Tel 610-485-8572.

Demco Media, Ltd., *(0-606)* Affil. of Demco, Inc., Orders Addr.: P.O. Box 14260, Madison, WI 53714-0260; Edit Addr.: 2810 Crossroads Dr., Suite 2700, Madison, WI 53718-7942 (SAN 111-1167) Fax: 608-241-0666; Toll Free Fax: 800-828-0401 (orders); Toll Free: 800-448-8939 (Turtleback customer orders/service) Demco Media titles are available only to schools and libraries. Not available to the retail market.
E-mail: mediacustserv@demco.com
Web site: http://www.demcomedia.com.

Derstine, Roy Bk. Co., 14 Birch Rd., Kinnelon, NJ 07405 (SAN 130-822X) Tel 973-838-1109.

DeRu's Fine Arts, *(0-939370)* 9100 E. Artesia Blvd., Bellflower, CA 90706 (SAN 159-3862) Tel 562-920-1312; Fax: 562-920-3077
E-mail: derusgal@aol.com.

Deseret Bk. Co., *(0-87579; 0-87747; 1-57345; 1-59038)* Div. of Deseret Management Corp., Orders Addr.: P.O. Box 30178, Salt Lake City, UT 84130 (SAN 150-763X) Tel 801-534-1515; 801-517-3165 (Wholesale Dept.); Fax: 801-517-3338; Toll Free: 800-453-3876; Edit Addr.: 40 E. South Temple, Salt Lake City, UT 84111
E-mail: dbwhsale@deseretbook.com; wholesale@deseretbook.com
Web site: http://www.deseretbook.com.

Desert News, 3242 S. Richey St., Tucson, AZ 85713 (SAN 114-3875) Tel 520-747-0428.

Desert News Co., 42257 6th St W., Suite 304, Lancaster, CA 93534-7163 (SAN 249-2849) Toll Free: 800-266-4571.

Devin-Adair Pubs., Inc., *(0-8159)* P.O. Box A, Old Greenwich, CT 06870 (SAN 112-062X) Tel 203-531-7755; Fax: 718-359-8568.

DeVorss & Co., *(0-87516)* Orders Addr.: P.O. Box 1389, Camarillo, CA 93011-1389 (SAN 168-9886) Tel 805-322-9011; Fax: 805-322-9010; Toll Free: 800-843-5743; Edit Addr.: 553 Constitution Ave., Camarillo, CA 93012
E-mail: service@devorss.com
Web site: http://www.devorss.com.

Diamond Book Distributors, Inc., 1966 Greenspring Dr., Suite 300, Timonium, MD 21093 (SAN 110-9502) Tel 410-560-7100; Fax: 410-560-7148; Toll Free: 800-452-6642
E-mail: service@diamondcomics.com; books@diamondcomics.com
Web site: http://www.diamondcomics.com.

Diamond Comic Distributors, Inc., *(1-59396)* Div. of Diamond Comic Distributors, Inc., 1966 Greenspring Dr., Suite 300, Timonium, MD 21093 Tel 410-560-7100; Fax: 410-560-2583; Toll Free: 800-452-6642
E-mail: wjanice@diamondcomics.com
Web site: http://www.diamondbookdistributors.com/.

Digital Manga Distribution, *(0-945814; 1-56970)* Div. of Digital Manga, Inc., 1123 Dominguez St., Unit K, Carson, CA 90746-3539 (SAN 111-817X) Tel 310-604-9701; Fax: 310-604-1134; Toll Free: 877-721-9701
E-mail: distribution@emanga.com
Web site: http://www.dmd-sales.com/.

Dillon Bk., Subs. of Harold Dillon, Inc., 460 S. Marion Pkwy., Apt. 851B, Denver, CO 80209-2508 (SAN 169-0493) Tel 303-442-5323; Toll Free: 800-525-0842.

Discount Bk. Distributors, 1854 Wallace School Rd., No. E, Charleston, SC 29407-4822 (SAN 107-2250) Tel 843-556-6582.

Distribooks, Inc., Div. of Midwest European Pubns., Inc., 8120 N. Ridgeway, Skokie, IL 60076 (SAN 630-9763) Tel 847-676-1596; Fax: 847-676-1195
E-mail: info@distribooks.com.

Distribuidora Escolar, Inc., 2250 SW 99th Ave., Miami, FL 00165-7569 (SAN 169-1104).

Distribuidora Norma, Inc., *(1-881700)* Div. of Carvajal International, Orders Addr.: P.O. Box 195040, Hato Rey, PR 00919-5040 Tel 809-788-5050 ; Fax: 809-788-7161; Edit Addr.: Carr 869 Km 1.5 Bo. Palmas, Royal Industrial, Catano, PR 00962
E-mail: normapr@caribe.net.

Distributed Art Pubs./D.A.P., *(1-881616; 1-891024)* Orders Addr.: a/o D.A.P. Book Distribution Ctr., 575 Prospect St., Lakewood, NJ 08701 Tel 732-363-5679; Toll Free: 800-338-2665; Edit Addr.: 155 Sixth Ave., 2nd Flr., New York, NY 10013-1507 (SAN 630-6446) Tel 212-627-1999; Fax: 212-627-9484
E-mail: dap@dapinc.com
Web site: http://www.artbook.com/.

Distribution Solutions Group, 1120 Rte. 22 E., Bridgewater, NJ 08807-0885 Toll Free: 866-374-4748.

Distributors International, Div. of Dennis-Landman Pubs., 1150 18th St., Santa Monica, CA 90403 (SAN 129-8089) Tel 310-828-0680
E-mail: info@moviecraft.com
Web site: http://www.moviecraft.com.

Distributors, The, *(0-942520)* 702 S. Michigan, South Bend, IN 46601 (SAN 169-2488) Tel 219-232-8500; Fax: 312-803-0887; Toll Free: 800-348-5200.

Divine, Inc., *(0-87305)* 15 Southwest Park, Westwood, MA 02090-1725 (SAN 159-8619) Tel 781-329-3350; Fax: 781-329-9875; Toll Free: 800-766-0039
E-mail: helpdesk@faxon.com; pubservices@faxon.com
Web site: http://www.faxon.com.

Dixie News Co., P.O. Box 561129, Charlotte, NC 28256-1129 (SAN 169-636X) Tel 704-376-0140; Fax: 704-335-8604; Toll Free: 800-532-1045.

D&J Bk. Distributors, *(1-883080)* 229-21B Merrick Blvd., Laurelton, NY 11413 (SAN 630-5091) Tel 718-949-5400; Fax: 718-949-6161; Toll Free: 800-446-4707.

Dog Museum, The, *See* **American Kennel Club Museum of the Dog**

Doherty, Tom Assocs., LLC, *(0-312; 0-7653; 0-8125)* Div. of Holtzbrinck Publishers, Orders Addr.: 16365 James Madison Hwy., Gordonsville, VA 22942-8501 Toll Free Fax: 800-672-2054; Toll Free: 888-330-8477; Edit Addr.: 175 Fifth Ave., New York, NY 10010 Tel 212-674-5151; Fax: 540-672-7540 (customer service).

Donars Spanish Bks., P.O. Box 808, Lafayette, CO 80026 (SAN 108-1586) Tel 303-666-9175; Toll Free: 800-552-3316
E-mail: donars@prolynx.com.

Downtown Bk. Ctr., Inc., *(0-941010)* 247 SE First St., Suites 236-237, Miami, FL 33131 (SAN 169-1112) Tel 305-377-9941
E-mail: raxdown@aol.com.

Dr. Leisure, *(0-9638802; 1-887471)* P.O. Box 1137, Kihei, HI 96753 Tel 808-879-4160
E-mail: drleisure@drleisure.com
Web site: http://www.drleisure.com.

Drown News Agency, P.O. Box 2080, Folsom, CA 95763-2080 (SAN 169-0450).

Dufour Editions, Inc., *(0-8023)* P.O. Box 7, Chester Springs, PA 19425-0007 (SAN 201-341X) Tel 610-458-5005; Fax: 610-458-7103; Toll Free: 800-869-5677
E-mail: dufour8023@aol.com; info@dufoureditions.com
Web site: http://go.to/Dufour; http://members.aol.com/Dufour8023/index.html.

Durkin Hayes Publishing Ltd., *(0-88625; 0-88646; 1-55204)* 2221 Niagara Falls Blvd., Niagara Falls, NY 14304-1696 (SAN 630-9518) Tel 716-731-9177; Fax: 716-731-9180; Toll Free: 800-962-5200
E-mail: info@dhaudio.com
Web site: http://www.dhaudio.com.

Duval News Co., Orders Addr.: P.O. Box 61297, Jacksonville, FL 32203 (SAN 169-1015); Edit Addr.: 5638 Commonwealth Ave., Jacksonville, FL 32205 (SAN 249-2865) Tel 904-783-2350.

Duval-Bibb Publishing Co., *(0-937713)* Div. of Mareeco Enterprises, Inc., Orders Addr.: 1808 B St. NW, Suite 140, Auburn, WA 98001 Toll Free Fax: 800-548-1169; Toll Free: 800-518-3541; P.O. Box 24168, Tampa, FL 33623-4168 (SAN 111-8641) Tel 813-281-0091; Fax: 813-282-0220
E-mail: reese.cop@gte.net
Web site: http://lonepinepublishing.com/ordering.

DUX Sales & Marketing, Orders Addr.: 209 A St., Penrose, CO 81240 Tel 719-372-0402.

Eagle Business Systems, *(0-928210)* P.O. Box 1240, El Toro, CA 92630-1240 (SAN 285-7510) Tel 714-859-9622.

Eagle Feather Trading Post, Inc., 168 W. 12th St., Ogden, UT 84404 (SAN 630-8996) Tel 801-393-3991 ; Fax: 801-745-0903; Toll Free: 800-547-3364 (orders only).

Eaglecrafts, Orders Addr.: 168 W. 12th St., Ogden, UT 84404 (SAN 630-6381) Tel 801-393-3991; Fax: 801-745-0903; Toll Free: 800-547-3364 (orders only)
E-mail: porsturbo@aol.com.

Eakin Pr., *(0-89015; 1-57168)* P.O. Drawer 90159, Austin, TX 78709-0159 (SAN 207-3633) Tel 512-288-1771; Fax: 512-288-1813; Toll Free: 800-880-8642
E-mail: sales@eakinpress.com; tom@eakinpress.com
Web site: http://www.eakinpress.com.

EAL Enterprises, Inc., Div. of Ambassador Bk. Service, 42 Chasner St., Hempstead, NY 11550 (SAN 169-6645) Toll Free: 800-431-8913.

East Kentucky News, Inc., 416 Teays Rd., Paintsville, KY 41240 (SAN 169-2879) Tel 606-789-8169.

East Texas Distributing, 7171 Grand Blvd., Houston, TX 77054 (SAN 169-8265) Tel 713-748-2520; Fax: 713-748-2504.

Eastern Bk. Co., Orders Addr.: P.O. Box 4540, Portland, ME 04112-4540 Fax: 207-774-0331; Toll Free Fax: 800-214-3895; Toll Free: 800-937-0331; Edit Addr.: 131 Middle St., Portland, ME 04112 (SAN 169-3050) Tel 207-774-0331
E-mail: info@ebc.com
Web site: http://www.ebc.com.

Eastern News Distributors, Subs. of Hearst Corp., 250 W. 55th St., New York, NY 10019 (SAN 169-5738) Tel 212-649-4484; Fax: 212-265-6239; Toll Free: 800-221-3148; 1 Media Way, 12406 Rte. 250, Milan, OH 44846-9705 (SAN 200-7711); 227 W. Trade St., Charlotte, NC 28202 (SAN 631-600X) Tel 704-348-8427
E-mail: enews@hearst.com.

Eastern Subscription Agency, 5413 Wynnefield Ave., Philadelphia, PA 19102 (SAN 285-9467) Tel 215-473-5309.

Easton News Co., 2601 Dearborn St., Easton, PA 18042 (SAN 169-7315).

Eastview Editions, *(0-89860)* P.O. Box 247, Bernardsville, NJ 07924 (SAN 169-4952) Tel 908-204-0535.

East-West Export Bks., c/o Univ. of Hawaii Pr., 2840 Kolowalu St., Honolulu, HI 96822 Tel 808-956-8830; Fax: 808-988-6052
E-mail: royden@hawaii.edu
Web site: http://www.2.hawaii.edu/uhpress/eweb.

Eastwind Bks. & Arts, Inc., 1435-A Stockton St., San Francisco, CA 94133 (SAN 127-3159) Tel 415-772-5888; Fax: 415-772-5885
E-mail: info@eastwindsf.com
Web site: http://www.eastwindsf.com.

Eau Claire News Co., Inc., 8100 Partridge Rd., Eau Claire, WI 54703-9646 (SAN 169-9059) Tel 715-835-5437.

EBS, Inc. Bk. Service, 290 Broadway, Lynbrook, NY 11563 (SAN 169-5487) Tel 516-593-1195; Fax: 516-596-2911.

EBSCO Subscription Services, 5724 Hwy. 280 E., Birmingham, AL 35242-6818 (SAN 285-9394) Tel 205-991-6000; Fax: 205-991-1479
E-mail: jacomo@ebsco.com
Web site: http://www.ebsco.com.

Econo-Clad Bks., *(0-613; 0-7857; 0-8085; 0-8335; 0-88103)* Div. of American Cos., Inc., Orders Addr.: P.O. Box 1777, Topeka, KS 66601 (SAN 169-2763) Tel 913-233-4252; Toll Free: 800-255-3502; Edit Addr.: 2101 N. Topeka Blvd., Topeka, KS 66608-1830 (SAN 249-2687)
E-mail: hkopperud@sagebrushcorp.com
Web site: http://www.sagebrushcorp.com.

Economical Wholesale Co., 6 King Philip Rd., Worcester, MA 01606 (SAN 169-3646).

EDC Publishing, *(0-7460; 0-88110; 1-58086; 0-7945)* Div. of Educational Development Corp., Orders Addr.: P.O. Box 470663, Tulsa, OK 74147-0663 (SAN 658-0505); Edit Addr.: 10302 E. 55th Pl., Tulsa, OK 74146-6515 (SAN 107-5322) Tel 918-622-4522; Fax: 918-665-7919; Toll Free: 800-475-4522
E-mail: edc@edcpub.com
Web site: http://www.edcpub.com.

Ediciones del Norte, *(0-910061)* P.O. Box 5130, Hanover, NH 03755 (SAN 241-2993).

Editorial Cernuda, Inc., 1040 27th Ave., SW, Miami, FL 33135 (SAN 158-8850) Tel 305-264-9400.

Educa Vision, *(1-881839; 1-58432)* 7550 NW 47th Ave., Coconut Creek, FL 33073 Tel 954-725-0701; Fax: 954-427-6739; Toll Free: 800-983-3822
E-mail: educa@aol.com
Web site: http://www.educavision.com.

Education Guide, Inc., *(0-914880)* P.O. Box 421, Randolph, MA 02368 (SAN 201-4580) Tel 617-376-0066; Fax: 617-376-0067.

Educational Bk. Distributors, P.O. Box 2510, Novato, CA 94948 (SAN 158-2259) Tel 415-883-3530; Fax: 415-883-4280; Toll Free: 800-761-5501
E-mail: PblshrSvcs@aol.com.

Educational Record Ctr., Inc., 3233 Burnt Mill Dr., Suite 100, Wilmington, NC 28403-2698 (SAN 630-592X) Tel 910-251-1235; Fax: 910-343-0311; Toll Free Fax: 888-438-1637; Toll Free: 800-438-1637
E-mail: info@erc-inc.com
Web site: http://www.erc-inc.com.

Edu-Tech Corp., The, 65 Bailey Rd., Fairfield, CT 06432 (SAN 157-5392) Tel 203-374-4212; Fax: 203-374-8050; Toll Free: 800-338-5463
E-mail: edutcorp@aoc.com.

Edward Weston Graphic, Incorporated, *See* **Weston, Edward Fine Arts**

El Qui-Jote Bk., Inc., 12651 Monarch, Houston, TX 77047 (SAN 107-8666) Tel 713-433-3388.

Elder's Bk. Store, 2115 Elliston Pl., Nashville, TN 37203 (SAN 112-6091) Tel 615-327-1867.

Elkins, C. J., 400 S. Beverly Dr. Suite 214, Beverly Hills, CA 90212 Toll Free: 800-769-2120
E-mail: sitare@zwallet.com; sitare@aol.com.

Ellis News Co., Affil. of L-S Distributors, 130 E. Grand Ave., South San Francisco, CA 94080 (SAN 169-0183) Tel 415-873-2094; Fax: 415-873-4222; Toll Free: 800-654-7040 (orders only).

ELS Educational Services, *(0-87789; 0-89285; 0-89318)* Orders Addr.: 200 Old Tappan Rd., Old Tappan, NJ 07675; Edit Addr.: 1357 Second St., Santa Monica, CA 90401-1102 (SAN 281-6326).

Elsevier, *(0-08; 0-444; 0-7204; 0-916086; 1-85617; 1-59278)* Orders Addr.: P.O. Box 945, New York, NY 10159-0945 (SAN 251-2564) Toll Free: 888-437-4636 ; 11830 Westline Industrial Dr., Saint Louis, MO 63146 (SAN 200-2108) Tel 314-453-7095 (Outside US); Toll Free Fax: 800-535-9935; Toll Free: 800-545-2522; 800-460-3110 (Outside US); Edit Addr.: 655 Ave. of the Americas, New York, NY 10010-5107 (SAN 200-2051) Tel 212-989-5800; Fax: 212-633-3680
E-mail: usinfo-f@elsevier.com; custserv@elsevier.com
Web site: http://www.elsevier.com.

Elsevier Science, *See* **Elsevier**

Emery-Pratt Co., Orders Addr.: 1966 W. Main St., Owosso, MI 48867-1397 (SAN 170-1401) Tel 989-723-5291; Fax: 989-723-4677; Toll Free Fax: 800-523-6379; Toll Free: 800-762-5683 (library orders only); 800-248-3887 (customer service only) Distributor to Libraries & Hospitals
E-mail: custserv@emery-pratt.com
Web site: http://www.emery-pratt.com.

Empire Comics, 375 Stone Rd., Rochester, NY 14616 (SAN 110-943X) Tel 716-442-0371; Fax: 716-442-7807
E-mail: empires@frontiernet.net.

Empire News of Jamestown, Foot Ave. & Extension St., Box 2029, Sta. A, Jamestown, NY 14702 (SAN 169-5371).

Empire Publishing Service, *(1-58690)* P.O. Box 1344, Studio City, CA 91614-0344 (SAN 630-5687) Tel 818-784-8918
E-mail: empirepubsvc@att.net.

Empire State News Corp., Orders Addr.: P.O. Box 1167, Buffalo, NY 14240-1167 Tel 716-681-1100; Fax: 716-681-1120; Toll Free: 800-414-6247; Edit Addr.: 2800 Walden Ave., Cheektowaga, NY 14225-4772 (SAN 169-5177)
Web site: http://www.esnc.com.

Encino Pr., *(0-88426)* 510 Baylor St., Austin, TX 78703 (SAN 201-3843) Tel 512-476-6821; Fax: 512-476-9393.

Entrepreneur Start a Business Store, 9114 River Look Ln., Fair Oaks, CA 95628-6565 (SAN 133-1485) Fax: 916-863-0361.

Epic Book Promotions, 914 Nolan Way, Chula Vista, CA 91911-2408 Tel 619-498-8547; Fax: 619-498-8540
E-mail: gvjack@pacbell.net.

Epson Mid-Atlantic, Subs. of Epson America, Inc., eight Neshaminy Interplex, Suite 319, Trerose, PA 19053 (SAN 285-7243) Tel 215-245-2180.

Eriksson Enterprises, 126 Sunset Dr., Farmington, UT 84025-3426 (SAN 110-5892).

ETD KroMar Temple, P.O. Box 535695, Grand Prairie, TX 75053-5625 (SAN 169-8435) Tel 254-778-5261; Fax: 254-778-5267.

European Bk. Co., Inc., 925 Larkin St., San Francisco, CA 94109 (SAN 169-0191) Tel 415-474-0626; Fax: 415-474-0630; Toll Free: 877-746-3666
E-mail: info@europeanbook.com.

European Press Service - PBD America Wholesalers, 30 Edison Dr., Wayne, NJ 07470-4713 (SAN 630-7825).

Evans Bk. Distribution & Pubs., Inc., *(0-9654884; 1-56684)* 895 W. 1700 S., Salt Lake City, UT 84104 Tel 801-975-1315; Fax: 801-975-1343; Toll Free: 877-655-2665.

Evans Book, *See* **Evans Bk. Distribution & Pubs., Inc.**

Events Unlimited, *See* **Internaturally, Inc.**

Ex Machina, *(0-944287)* Orders Addr.: P.O. Box 448, Sioux Falls, SD 57101 (SAN 243-3761) Tel 605-334-0869; Fax: 605-339-3219; Edit Addr.: 805 S. Sycamore, Sioux Falls, SD 57110-3180 (SAN 243-377X) Tel 605-334-0869
Web site: http://www.exmac.com.

Excaliber Publishing Co., *(1-881353)* 7954 W. Bury Ave., San Diego, CA 92126 (SAN 297-6412) Tel 619-695-3091; Fax: 619-695-3095.

Exciting Times, 17430C Crenshaw Blvd., Torrance, CA 90504 (SAN 114-4642) Tel 310-515-2676; Fax: 310-515-1382.

Executive Bks., *(0-937539)* Div. of Life Management Services, Inc., 206 W. Allen St., Mechanicsburg, PA 17055-6240 (SAN 156-5419) Tel 717-766-9499; Fax: 717-766-6565; Toll Free: 800-233-2665
E-mail: jason@executivebooks.com
Web site: http://www.executivebooks.com.

Explorations, 360 Interlocken Blvd., Suite 300, Broomfield, CO 80021 Toll Free Fax: 800-456-1139; Toll Free: 800-720-2114
E-mail: customerservice@gaiam.com
Web site: http://www.gaiam.com.

Faber & Faber, Inc., *(0-571)* Affil. of Farrar, Straus & Giroux, LLC, Orders Addr.: c/o Van Holtzbrinck Publishing Services, 16365 James Madison Hwy., Gordonsville, VA 22942 Fax: 540-572-7540; Toll Free: 888-330-8477; Edit Addr.: 19 Union Sq., W, New York, NY 10003-3304 (SAN 218-7256) Tel 212-741-6900; Fax: 212-633-9385.

Fairfield Bk. Service Co., 150 Margherita Lawn, Stratford, CT 06615 (SAN 131-0976) Tel 203-375-7607.

FaithWorks, Div. of National Book Network, Orders Addr.: 15200 NBN Way, Blue Ridge Summit, PA 17214 Toll Free: 877-323-4550; Edit Addr.: 9247 Hunterboro Dr., Brentwood, TN 37027 Tel 615-221-6442 (phone/fax) Do not confuse with Faithworks in Bronx NY
E-mail: custserv@faithworksonline.com
Web site: http://www.faithworksonline.com.

FaithWorks/NBN, *See* **FaithWorks**

Falk Bks. Inc., W.E., 7491 N. Federal Hwy., PMB 267, Boca Raton, FL 33487.

Falk, W. E., *See* **Falk Bks. Inc., W.E.**

Fall River News Co., Inc., 144 Robeson St., Fall River, MA 02720-4925 (SAN 169-3425) Tel 508-679-5266.

Family History World, P.O. Box 129, Tremonton, UT 84337 (SAN 159-673X) Fax: 801-250-6727; Toll Free: 800-377-6058
E-mail: genealogy@utahlinx.com
Web site: http://www.genealogical-institute.com.

Family Reading Service, 1601 N. Slappey Blvd., Albany, GA 31701-1431 (SAN 169-1376).

Fantagraphics Bks., *(0-930193; 1-56097)* 7563 Lake City Way, NE, Seattle, WA 98115 (SAN 251-5571) Tel 206-524-1967; Fax: 206-524-2104; Toll Free: 800-657-1100
E-mail: zura@fantagraphics.com; diva@eroscomix.com
Web site: http://www.fantagraphics.com; http://eroscomix.com.

Far West Bk. Service, 3515 NE Hassalo, Portland, OR 97232 (SAN 107-6760) Tel 503-234-7664; Fax: 503-231-0573; Toll Free: 800-964-9378.

Farrar, Straus & Giroux, *(0-374)* Div. of Holtzbrinck Publishers, Orders Addr.: c/o Holtzbrinck Publishers, 16365 James Madison Hwy., Gordonsville, VA 22942 Toll Free Fax: 800-672-2054; Toll Free: 888-330-8477; Edit Addr.: 19 Union Sq., W., New York, NY 10003 (SAN 206-782X) Tel 212-741-6900; Fax: 212-463-0641
E-mail: sales@fsgee.com; fsg.editorial@fsgee.com
Web site: http://www.fsbassociates.com/fsg/index.htm.

Faxon Company, The, *See* **Divine, Inc.**

Faxon Illinois Service Ctr., Affil. of Dawson Holdings PLC, 1001 W. Pines Rd., Oregon, IL 61061-9570 (SAN 286-0147) Tel 815-732-9001; Toll Free: 800-852-7404
E-mail: postmaster@dawson.com; sandy.nordman@dawson.com
Web site: http://www.faxon.com.

Fayette County News Agency, Orders Addr.: P.O. Box 993, Uniontown, PA 15401 Tel 724-437-1181; Edit Addr.: Cherry Tree Square 42 Matthew Dr., Uniontown, PA 15401 (SAN 169-765X).

FEC News Distributing, 2201 Fourth Ave., N., Lake Worth, FL 33461-3835 (SAN 169-1341) Tel 407-547-3000; Fax: 407-547-3080.

Feldheim, Philipp Inc., *(0-87306; 1-58330)* 202 Airport Executive Pk., Nanuet, NY 10954 (SAN 106-6307) Tel 845-356-2282; Fax: 845-425-1908; Toll Free: 800-237-7149
E-mail: mike613@netvision.net.il
Web site: http://www.feldheim.com.

Fell, Frederick Pubs., Inc., *(0-8119; 0-88391)* 2131 Hollywood Blvd., Suite 305, Hollywood, FL 33020-6750 Tel 954-925-0555; Fax: 954-925-5244
E-mail: info@fellpub.com
Web site: http://www.fellpub.com.

Fennell, Reginald F. Subscription Service, 1002 W. Michigan Ave., Jackson, MI 49202 (SAN 159-6071) Tel 517-782-3132; Fax: 517-782-1109.

FEP, A Booksource Co., 1230 Macklind Ave., Saint Louis, MO 63110 (SAN 169-1317) Tel 314-647-0600 ; Fax: 314-647-6850; Toll Free: 800-444-0435
Web site: http://www.booksource.com.

Fiddlecase Bks., HC 63 Box 104, East Alstead, NH 03602 (SAN 200-7495) Tel 603-835-7889.

Fiesta Bk. Co., *(0-88473)* P.O. Box 490641, Key Biscayne, FL 33149 (SAN 201-8470) Tel 305-858-4843.

Fiesta Publishing Corporation, *See* **Fiesta Bk. Co.**

Fine Assocs., One Farragut Sq., S., Washington, DC 20006 (SAN 169-0914) Tel 202-628-2609.

Finn News Agency, Inc., 4415 State Rd. 327, Auburn, IN 46706-9542 (SAN 169-2356).

Finney Co., *(0-912486)* 3943 Meadowbrook Rd., Minneapolis, MN 55426 (SAN 206-412X) Tel 952-938-9330; Fax: 952-938-7353; Toll Free: 800-846-7027
E-mail: feedback@finney-hobar.com
Web site: http://www.finney-hobar.com.

Fire Protection Publications, *See* **IFSTA**

Firebird Distributing, LLC, 1945 P St., Eureka, CA 95501-3007 (SAN 631-1229) Toll Free: 800-353-3575
E-mail: griffins@northcoast.com.; sales@firebirddistributing.com
Web site: http://www.firebirddistributing.com.

Firefly Bks., Ltd., *(0-920668; 1-55209; 1-895565; 1-896284; 1-55297)* 4 Daybreak Ln., Westport, CT 06880-2157
E-mail: service@fireflybooks.com
Web site: http://www.fireflybooks.com/.

Fischer, Carl LLC, *(0-8258)* Orders Addr.: 2480 Industrial Blvd., Paoli, PA 19301 Fax: 610-644-7110; Toll Free: 800-762-2328; Edit Addr.: 65 Bleeker St., New York, NY 10012-2420 (SAN 107-4245) Tel 212-772-0900; Fax: 212-477-6996; Toll Free: 800-762-2328
E-mail: cf-info@carlfischer.com
Web site: http://www.carlfischer.com.

Fish, Enrica Medical Bks., 814 Washington Ave., SE, Minneapolis, MN 55414 (SAN 157-8588) Tel 612-623-0707; Fax: 612-623-0539; Toll Free: 800-728-8398.

Flannery Co., 13123 Aerospace Dr., Victorville, CA 92394 (SAN 168-9754) Tel 760-246-8995; Fax: 760-246-8595; Toll Free: 800-456-3400.

Flannery, J. F. Company, *See* **Flannery Co.**

Fleming, Robert Hull Museum, *(0-934658)* Univ. of Vermont, 61 Colchester Ave., Burlington, VT 05405 (SAN 110-8824) Tel 802-656-2273; Fax: 802-656-8059
Web site: http://www.uvm.edu/~fleming/store/index.html.

Flora & Fauna Bks., P.O. Box 15718, Gainesville, FL 32604 (SAN 133-1221) Tel 352-373-5630; Fax: 352-373-3249
E-mail: ffbks@aol.com
Web site: http://www.ffbooks.com.

Florida Classics Library, *(0-912451)* P.O. Drawer 1657, Port Salerno, FL 34992-1657 (SAN 265-2404) Tel 561-546-9380 (orders); Fax: 561-546-7545 (orders).

Florida Schl. Bk. Depository, 1125 N. Ellis Rd., P.O. Box 6578, Jacksonville, FL 32236 (SAN 161-8423) Tel 904-781-7191; Fax: 904-781-3486; Toll Free: 800-447-7957.

Flury & Co., 322 First Ave S., Seattle, WA 98104 (SAN 107-5748) Tel 206-587-0260.

Fodor's Travel Guides, *See* **Fodor's Travel Pubns.**

Fodor's Travel Pubns., *(0-609; 0-676; 0-679; 0-7615; 1-878867; 1-4000)* Div. of Random Hse., Information Group, Orders Addr.: 400 Hahn Rd., Westminster, MD 21157 Tel 410-848-1900; Toll Free: 800-726-0600; Edit Addr.: 280 Park Ave., Tenth Flr., New York, NY 10017 Tel 212-572-8784; Fax: 212-572-2248
Web site: http://www.fodors.com.

Follett Audiovisual Resources, *See* **Follett Media Distribution**

Follett Educational Services, Orders Addr.: 1433 Internationale Pkwy., Woodridge, IL 60517 (SAN 631-7901) Tel 800-621-4272; Fax: 630-972-4673; Edit Addr.: 5563 S. Archer Ave., Chicago, IL 60638 (SAN 169-1899)
E-mail: mpetrou@fes.follett.com.

Follett Library Resources, *(0-329)* Div. of the Follett Corp., 1340 Ridgeview Dr., McHenry, IL 60050 (SAN 169-1902) Tel 815-759-1700; Toll Free: 800-435-6170.

Follett Media Distribution, 220 Exchange Dr., Suite A, Crystal Lake, IL 60014 (SAN 631-7316) Tel 815-455-1555; Fax: 815-455-7090; Toll Free: 888-281-1216.

Forest Hse. Publishing Co., Inc., *(1-56674; 1-878363)* P.O. Box 738, Lake Forest, IL 60045 Tel 847-295-8287; Fax: 847-295-8201; Toll Free: 800-394-7323
Web site: http://www.forest-house.com.

Forest Sales & Distributing Co., *(0-9712183)* 4157 Saint Louis St., New Orleans, LA 70119 (SAN 157-5511) Tel 504-486-3331; Fax: 504-486-6223; Toll Free: 800-347-2106
E-mail: tbooks2@juno.com.

Forsyth Travel Library, Inc., *(0-9614539)* 1750 E. 131st St., P.O. Box 480800, Kansas City, MO 64148-0800 (SAN 169-2755) Tel 816-942-9050; Fax: 816-942-6969; Toll Free: 800-367-7984 (orders only)
E-mail: forsyth@gvi.net
Web site: http://www.forsyth.com.

Fotofolio, Inc., *(1-881270; 1-58418)* 561 Broadway, New York, NY 10012-3918 (SAN 630-463X) Tel 212-226-0923; Fax: 212-226-0072
E-mail: contact@fotofolio.com; fotofolio@aol.com
Web site: http://www.fotofolio.com.

Franklin Bk. Co., Inc., 7804 Montgomery Ave., Elkins Park, PA 19027 (SAN 121-4160) Tel 215-635-5252; Fax: 215-635-6155
E-mail: service@franklinbook.com
Web site: http://www.franklinbook.com.

Franklin Readers Service, P.O. Box 662, Dunn Loring, VA 22027-0662 (SAN 285-9599).

Franklin Square Overseas, 17-19 Washington St., Tenafly, NJ 07670-2084 (SAN 285-9637) Tel 201-569-2500; Fax: 201-569-5141
E-mail: esstn@ebsco.com.

Fraser Publishing Co., *(0-87034; 0-918632)* Div. of Alvin Q. Garbanzo, Inc., Orders Addr.: P.O. Box 217, Flint Hill, VT 22747 (SAN 213-9537) Toll Free: 877-996-3336
E-mail: info@fraserbooks.com
Web site: http://www.fraserbooks.com.

Freihofer, A. G., 175 Fifth Ave., New York, NY 10010 (SAN 285-9602) Tel 272-460-7500; Fax: 272-473-6272.

French & European Pubns., Inc., *(0-320; 0-7859; 0-8288)* Rockefeller Ctr. Promenade, 610 Fifth Ave., New York, NY 10020-2497 (SAN 206-8109) Tel 212-581-8810; Fax: 212-265-1094
E-mail: frenchbookstore@aol.com
Web site: http://www.frencheuropean.com.

Friendly Hills Fellowship, *See* **Health and Growth Assocs.**

Fris News Co., 194 River Ave., Holland, MI 49423 (SAN 159-8643).

Frontline Communications, *See* **YWAM Publishing**

Fulcrum, Incorporated, *See* **Fulcrum Publishing**

Fulcrum Publishing, *(0-912347; 1-55591; 1-56373)* 16100 Table Mountain Pkwy., Suite 300, Golden, CO 80403 (SAN 200-2825) Tel 303-277-1623; Fax: 303-279-7111; Toll Free Fax: 800-726-7112; Toll Free: 800-992-2908
E-mail: dianneh@fulcrum-books.com
Web site: http://www.fulcrum-books.com; http://www.fulcrum-gardening.com.

Fulmont News Co., Affil. of Rubin Periodical Group, P.O. Box 1211, Rochester, NY 14603-1211 (SAN 169-5029) Tel 518-843-2421.

Fultz News Agency, 2008 Woodbrook, Denton, TX 76205 (SAN 169-8168).

Futech Educational Products, Inc., *(0-9627001; 1-889192)* 2999 N. 44th St., Suite 225, Phoenix, AZ 85018-7248 Tel 602-808-8765; Fax: 602-278-5667; Toll Free: 800-597-6278.

F&W Pubns., Inc., *(0-89134; 0-89879; 0-932620; 1-55870; 1-58180; 1-58297; 1-884910)* Orders Addr.: 4700 E. Galbraith Rd., Cincinnati, OH 45236 Tel 513-531-2690; Fax: 513-531-4082; Toll Free Fax: 888-590-4082; Toll Free: 800-289-0963; c/o AERO Fulfillment Services, 2800 Henkle Dr., Lebanon, OH 45036
E-mail: marcia.jones@fwpubs.com
Web site: http://www.fwpublications.com; http://www.artistsmagazine.com; http://www.artistsnetwork.com; http://www.davidandcharles.co.uk; http://www.krause.com; http://www.familytreemagazine.com; http://www.howdesign.com; http://www.idonline.com; http://www.memorymakersmagazine.com; http://www.popularwoodworking.com; http://www.writersdigest.com; http://www.writersmarket.com; http://www.writersonlineworkshops.com.

G A M Printers & Grace Christian Bookstore, *See* **GAM Pubn.**

Gabriel Resources, Orders Addr.: P.O. Box 1047, Waynesboro, GA 30830 Tel 706-554-1594; Fax: 706-554-7444; Toll Free: 800-732-6657 (8MORE-BOOKS); Edit Addr.: 129 Mobilization Dr., Waynesboro, GA 30830.

Galesburg News Agency, Inc., Five E. Simmons St., Galesburg, IL 61401 (SAN 169-1945).

Gallaudet Univ. Pr., *(0-913580; 0-930323; 1-56368)* 800 Florida Ave., NE, Washington, DC 20002-3695 (SAN 205-261X) Tel 202-651-5488; Fax: 202-651-5489; Toll Free Fax: 800-621-8476; Toll Free: 888-630-9347 (TTY)
E-mail: valencia.simmons@gallaudet.edu
Web site: http://www.gupress.gallaudet.edu/.

Galveston News Agency, P.O. Box 7608, San Antonio, TX 78207-0608 (SAN 169-8230).

GAM Pubn., P.O. Box 25, Sterling, VA 20167 (SAN 158-7218) Tel 703-450-4121; Fax: 703-450-5311.

Gamboge International, Inc., 18 Brittany Ave., Trumbull, CT 06611 (SAN 631-046X) Tel 203-261-2130; Fax: 203-452-0180
E-mail: gamboge@pcaet.com.

Gannon Distributing Co., *(0-88307)* 100 La Salle Cir., No. A, Santa Fe, NM 87505-6916 (SAN 201-5889).

Gardner's Bk. Service, 16461 N. 25th Ave., Phoenix, AZ 85023-3111 (SAN 106-9322) Tel 602-863-6000; Fax: 602-863-2400 (orders only); Toll Free: 800-851-6001 (orders only)
E-mail: gbsbooks@bgsbooks.com
Web site: http://www.gbsbooks.com.

Garrett Educational Corp., *(0-944483; 1-56074)* Orders Addr.: P.O. Box 1588, Ada, OK 74820 (SAN 169-6955) Tel 580-332-6884; Fax: 580-332-1560; Toll Free: 800-654-9366; Edit Addr.: 130 E. 13th St., Ada, OK 74820 (SAN 243-2722)
E-mail: mail@garrettbooks.com
Web site: http://www.garrettbooks.com.

Gasman News Agency, 2211 Third Ave., S., Escanaba, MI 49829 (SAN 169-3794).

Gefen Bks., *(0-86343; 965-229)* 12 New St., Hewlett, NY 11557-2012 Tel 516-295-2805; Fax: 516-295-2739; Toll Free: 800-477-5257
E-mail: gefenny@gefenpublishing.com
Web site: http://www.israelbooks.com.

Gem Guides Bk. Co., *(0-935182; 0-937799; 1-889786)* 315 Cloverleaf Dr., Suite F, Baldwin Park, CA 91706 (SAN 221-1637) Tel 626-855-1611; Fax: 626-855-1610
E-mail: gembooks@aol.com
Web site: http://www.gemguidesbooks.com.

Gemini Enterprises, P.O. Box 8251, Stockton, CA 95208 (SAN 128-1402).

Genealogical Sources, Unlimited, *(0-913857)* 407 Ascot Ct., Knoxville, TN 37923-5807 (SAN 170-8058) Tel 865-690-7831.

Genealogy Digest, 960 N. 400 E., North Salt Lake, UT 84054-1920 (SAN 110-389X); 420 S. 425 W., Bountiful, UT 84010 (SAN 243-2439).

General Medical Pubs., *(0-935236)* P.O. Box 210, Venice, CA 90294-0210 (SAN 215-689X) Tel 310-392-4911.

Generic Computer Products, Inc., *(0-918611)* P.O. Box 790, Marquette, MI 49855 (SAN 284-8856) Tel 906-226-7600; Fax: 906-226-8309.

Geographia Map Co., Inc., *(0-88433)* 231 Hackensack Plank Rd., Weehawken, NJ 07087 (SAN 132-5566) Tel 201-863-3866; Fax: 201-863-5977.

Gerold International Booksellers, Inc., 35-23 Utopia Pkwy., Flushing, NY 11358 (SAN 129-959X) Tel 718-358-4741; Fax: 718-358-3688.

Gibson, Dot Pubns., *(0-941162)* Orders Addr.: P.O. Box 117, Waycross, GA 31502-0117 (SAN 200-4143) Tel 912-285-2848; Fax: 912-285-0349; Toll Free: 800-336-8095; Edit Addr.: 383 Bonneyman Rd., Blackshear, GA 31516 (SAN 200-9676)
E-mail: info@dotgibson.com
Web site: http://www.dotgibson.com.

Gilmore-Howard, P.O. Box 1268, Arlington, TX 76004-1268 (SAN 157-485X).

Giron Bks., *(0-9741393)* 2130 W. 21st. St., Chicago, IL 60608-2608 Tel 773-847-3000; Fax: 773-847-9197; Toll Free: 800-405-4276
E-mail: isbn_san@gironbooks.com
Web site: http://www.gironbooks.com.

G-Jo Institute/Deer Haven Hills, Inc., *(0-916878)* Orders Addr.: P.O. Box 548, Columbus, NC 28722-0548 Tel 828-863-4660; Edit Addr.: P.O. Box 1460, Columbus, NC 28722-1460 (SAN 111-0004)
E-mail: office@g-jo.com
Web site: http://www.g-jo.com.

G-Jo Institute/Falkyn, Incorporated, *See* **G-Jo Institute/Deer Haven Hills, Inc.**

GL Services, 4588 Interstate Dr., Cincinnati, OH 45246 Tel 805-677-6815.

Global Engineering Documents-Latin America, 3909 NE 163rd St., Suite 110, North Miami Beach, FL 33160 (SAN 630-7868) Tel 305-944-1099; Fax: 305-944-1028
E-mail: global.csa@ihs.com.

Global Info Centres, *See* **Global Engineering Documents-Latin America**

Globe Pequot Pr., The, *(0-7627; 0-87106; 0-88742; 0-914788; 0-933469; 0-934802; 0-941130; 1-56440; 1-57034; 1-58574; 1-59228)* Div. of Morris Communications Corp., Orders Addr.: P.O. Box 480, Guilford, CT 06437-0480 (SAN 201-9892) Toll Free Fax: 800-820-2329 (in Connecticut); Toll Free: 800-243-0495 (24 hours); Edit Addr.: 246 Goose Ln., Guilford, CT 06437 Tel 203-458-4500; Fax: 203-458-4604
E-mail: info@globe-pequot.com; adessaint@globe-pequot.com
Web site: http://www.globe-pequot.com.

Goldberg, Louis Library Bk. Supplier, 45 Belvidere St., Nazareth, PA 18064 (SAN 169-7536) Tel 610-759-9458; Fax: 610-759-8134.

Goldenrod Music, Inc., 1310 Turner Rd., Lansing, MI 48906-4342 (SAN 630-5962) Tel 517-484-1777
E-mail: music@goldenrod.com
Web site: http://www.goldenrod.com.

Goldenrod/Horizon Distribution, *See* **Goldenrod Music, Inc.**

Goldman, S. Otzar Hasefarim, Inc., 125 Ditmas Ave., Brooklyn, NY 11218 (SAN 169-5770) Tel 718-972-6200; Fax: 718-972-6204; Toll Free: 800-972-6201.

Good News Magazine Distributors, 85 Crescent Ave., New Rochelle, NY 10801 (SAN 113-7271) Toll Free: 800-624-7257.

Gopher News Co., 420 First Ave., NW, Rochester, MN 55901 (SAN 169-4138) Tel 507-282-8641 (phone/fax).

Gopher News Company, *See* **St. Marie's Gopher News Co.**

Gospel Mission, Inc., Orders Addr.: P.O. Box 318, Choteau, MT 59422 (SAN 170-3196) Tel 406-466-2311; Edit Addr.: 316 First St., NW, Choteau, MT 59422 (SAN 243-2455).

Goyescas Corp. of Florida, 2155 NW 26th Ave., Miami, FL 33142 (SAN 169-1120).

Graham Services, Inc., 180 James Dr., E., Saint Rose, LA 70087-9481 (SAN 169-2895) Tel 504-467-5863; Fax: 504-464-6196; Toll Free: 800-457-7323 (in Los Angeles only)
E-mail: gsi@aol.com.

Granite Publishing & Distribution, LLC, *(1-890558; 1-930980; 1-932280)* 868 N. 1430 W., Orem, UT 84057 (SAN 631-0605) Tel 801-229-9023; Fax: 801-229-1924; Toll Free: 800-574-5779 Do not confuse with companies with same or similar names in Madison, WI, Columbus, NC
E-mail: granitepd@aol.com.

Graphic Arts Ctr. Publishing Co., *(0-88240; 0-912856; 0-932575; 1-55868)* Orders Addr.: P.O. Box 10306, Portland, OR 97296-0306 (SAN 201-6338) Tel 503-226-2402; Fax: 503-223-1410 (executive & editorial); Toll Free Fax: 800-355-9685 (sales office); Toll Free: 800-452-3032
E-mail: sales@gacpc.com
Web site: http://www.gacpc.com.

Great Lakes Reader's Service, Inc., Orders Addr.: P.O. Box 1078, Detroit, MI 48231 (SAN 285-9912) Tel 313-965-4577; Fax: 313-965-2445.

Great Northern Distributors, Inc., 634 South Ave., Rochester, NY 14620-1316 (SAN 169-7676) Tel 717-342-8159.

Great Outdoors Publishing Co., *(0-8200)* 4747 28th St., N., Saint Petersburg, FL 33714 (SAN 201-6273) Tel 727-525-6609; Fax: 727-527-4870; Toll Free: 800-869-6609
E-mail: FLBooks@aol.com
Web site: http://www.floridabook.com.

Greathall Productions, Inc., *(1-882513)* Orders Addr.: P.O. Box 5061, Charlottesville, VA 22905-5061 Tel 434-296-4288; Fax: 434-296-4490; Toll Free: 800-477-6234
E-mail: greathall@greathall.com
Web site: http://www.greathall.com.

Green Gate Bks., 6700 W. Chicago St., Chandler, AZ 85226 (SAN 169-6785) Tel 480-961-5176; Fax: 480-961-5256; Toll Free: 800-228-3816
E-mail: ggb@wcoil.com
Web site: http://www.greengatebooks.com.

Green Pastures Pr., *(0-9627643; 1-884377)* HC 67, Box 91-A, Mifflin, PA 17058 Tel 717-436-9115.

Greenfield Review Literary Ctr., Inc., *(0-87886; 0-912678)* 2 Middle Grove Rd., P.O. Box 308, Greenfield Center, NY 12833 (SAN 203-4506) Tel 518-583-1440; Fax: 518-583-9741
Web site: http://www.nativeauthors.com.

Grey Owl Indian Craft Co., Inc., 132-05 Merrick Blvd., P.O. Box 468, Jamaica, NY 11434 (SAN 132-9979) Tel 718-341-4000.

Grolier Americana, 1111 Crandon Blvd., Apt. C501, Key Biscayne, FL 33149-2734 (SAN 108-1764) Tel 305-551-6711.

Gryphon Hse., Inc., *(0-87659; 1-58904)* Orders Addr.: P.O. Box 207, Beltsville, MD 20704-0207 (SAN 169-3190) Tel 301-595-9500; Fax: 301-595-0051; Toll Free: 800-638-0928; Edit Addr.: 10726 Tucker St., Beltsville, MD 20705
E-mail: info@ghbooks.com
Web site: http://www.gryphonhouse.com.

Guardian Bk. Co., P.O. Box 202, Ottawa Lake, MI 49267-0202 (SAN 163-7355).

Gulf States Book Fairs, *See* **Gulf States Educational Bks.**

Gulf States Educational Bks., Orders Addr.: 368 Laurel Dr., Satsuma, AL 36572 (SAN 158-7870) Toll Free: 800-533-1189.

Gumdrop Bks., Div. of Central Programs, Inc., Orders Addr.: P.O. Box 505, Bethany, MO 64424 (SAN 631-4988) Tel 660-425-3923; Fax: 660-425-3970; Toll Free: 800-821-7199; Edit Addr.: 100 N. 16th St., Bethany, MO 64424 (SAN 131-0860)
E-mail: wecare@gumdropbooks.com
Web site: http://www.gumdropbooks.com.

Hagerstown News Distributors, *See* **Mid-States Distributors**

Haitiana Pubns., Inc., *(0-944987)* 22408 Linden Blvd., Cambria Heights, NY 11411-1725 (SAN 245-7059) Tel 718-978-6323; Fax: 718-978-6031
E-mail: haitiana@idt.net
Web site: http://idtnet/haitiana/.

Hale, Robert & Co., Inc., 1803 132nd Ave., NE, Suite 4, Bellevue, WA 98005 (SAN 200-6995) Tel 425-881-5212; Fax: 425-881-0731; Toll Free: 800-733-5330.

Ham Radio's Bookstore, *See* **Radio Bookstore**

Hamakor Judaica, Inc., 7777 Merrimac Ave., Niles, IL 60714 (SAN 169-1791) Tel 847-966-4040; Fax: 847-966-4033; Toll Free: 800-552-4088.

Hamel, Bernard H. Spanish Bk. Corp., 10977 Santa Monica Blvd., Los Angeles, CA 90025 (SAN 111-8862) Tel 310-475-0453; Fax: 310-473-6132
E-mail: spanish@primenet.com
Web site: http://www.BernardHamel.com; http://www.SpanishBooksUSA.com.

Hamilton News Co., Ltd., 41 Hamilton Ln., Glenmont, NY 12077 (SAN 169-5312) Tel 518-463-1135; Fax: 518-463-3154.

Hammond Publishing Co., Inc., *(1-883882)* P.O. Box 279, G7166 N. Saginaw St., Mount Morris, MI 48458 (SAN 185-142X) Tel 810-686-8881; Fax: 810-686-0561; Toll Free: 800-521-3440 (orders only)
E-mail: hammondpub@juno.com.

Hamon, Gerard Incorporated, *See* **Lafayette Bks.**

Handleman, 2050 S. Santa Cruz St., No. 1100, Anaheim, CA 92805-6816 (SAN 106-4886) Tel 626-912-8182.

Handler News Agency, P.O. Box 27007, Omaha, NE 68127-0007 (SAN 169-4405).

Harcourt Brace & Company, *See* **Harcourt Trade Pubs.**

Harcourt Trade Pubs., *(0-15)* Div. of Harcourt, Inc., Orders Addr.: 6277 Sea Harbor Dr., Orlando, FL 32887 (SAN 200-285X) Tel 619-699-6707; Toll Free Fax: 800-235-0256; Toll Free: 800-543-1918 (trade orders, inquiries, claims); Edit Addr.: 525 B St., Suite 1900, San Diego, CA 92101-4495 (SAN 200-2736) Tel 619-231-6616; 15 E. 26th St., 15th Flr., New York, NY 10010 Tel 212-592-1000
E-mail: apbcs@harcourtbrace.com
Web site: http://www.harcourtbooks.com.

Harness, Miller, 350 Page Rd., Washington, NC 27889-8753 (SAN 169-5789) Toll Free: 800-526-6310.

HarperCollins Pubs., *(0-00; 0-06; 0-688; 0-690; 0-694; 0-7322)* Div. of News Corp., Orders Addr.: 1000 Keystone Industrial Pk., Scranton, PA 18512-4621 (SAN 215-3742) Tel 570-941-1500; Toll Free Fax: 800-822-4090; Toll Free: 800-242-7737 (orders only) ; Edit Addr.: 10 E. 53rd St., New York, NY 10022-5299 (SAN 200-2086) Tel 212-207-7000
Web site: http://www.harpercollins.com.

Harrisburg News Co., 980 Briarsdale Rd., Harrisburg, PA 17109 (SAN 169-7420) Tel 717-561-8377; Fax: 717-561-1466
Web site: http://www.harrisburgnewsco.com.

Harrison Hse., Inc., *(0-89274; 1-57794)* Orders Addr.: P.O. Box 35035, Tulsa, OK 74153 (SAN 208-676X) Tel 918-494-5944; Fax: 918-494-3665; Toll Free: 800-888-4126; Edit Addr.: 2448 E. 81st St., Suite 4800, Tulsa, OK 74137
E-mail: iopordes@aidcvt.com; hh2@eaglemgmt.com
Web site: http://www.harrisonhouse.com.

Harry-Young Pubn. Services Agency, Inc., 6261 Manchester Blvd., Buena Park, CA 90621-2259 (SAN 110-8832).

Harvard Assocs., Inc., *(0-924346)* 10 Holworthy St., Cambridge, MA 02138 (SAN 170-2939) Tel 617-492-0660; Fax: 617-492-4610; Toll Free: 800-774-5646
E-mail: info@harvassoc.com
Web site: http://www.harvassoc.com.

Harvard Univ. Art Museums Shop, 32 Quincy St., Cambridge, MA 02138 (SAN 111-3372) Tel 617-495-8286; Fax: 617-495-9985
E-mail: appleyar@fas.harvard.edu
Web site: http://www.artmuseums.harvard.edu.

Harvest Distributors, *See* **ARVEST**

Hastings Bks., *(0-940846)* 116 N. Wayne Ave., Wayne, PA 19087 (SAN 205-048X).

Hawaiian Magazine Distributor, 3375 Koapaka St., No. D180, Honolulu, HI 98619-1865 (SAN 169-1619).

Health and Growth Assocs., *(0-9630266)* Orders Addr.: 28195 Fairview Ave., Hemet, CA 92544 Tel 909-927-1768; Fax: 909-927-1548
E-mail: flloomis@earthlink.net.

Health Communications, Inc., *(0-922352; 0-932194; 0-941405; 1-55874; 0-7573)* 3201 SW 15th St., Deerfield Beach, FL 33442-8157 (SAN 212-100X) Tel 954-360-0909; Fax: 954-360-0034; Toll Free: 800-851-9100 Do not confuse with Health Communications, Inc., Edison, NJ
E-mail: hci@hcibooks.com; terryy@hcibooks.com; lorig@hcibooks.com
Web site: http://www.hcibooks.com.

Hearst Distribution Group, Incorporated, Book Division, *See* **Comag Marketing Group**

Heartland Bk. Co., 10195 N. Lake Ave., Olathe, KS 66061 (SAN 631-2497) Tel 913-829-1784.

Heffernan Audio Visual, Orders Addr.: P.O. Box 5906, San Antonio, TX 78201-0906 Tel 210-732-4333; Fax: 210-732-5906; Edit Addr.: 2111 West Ave., San Antonio, TX 78201-2822 (SAN 166-8722)
E-mail: sales@heffernanav.com
Web site: http://www.heffernanav.com.

Heffernan School Supply, *See* **Heffernan Audio Visual**

Heimburger Hse. Publishing Co., *(0-911581)* 7236 W. Madison St., Forest Park, IL 60130 (SAN 264-0929) Tel 708-366-1973 (phone/fax)
E-mail: heimburgerhouse@heimburgerhouse.com
Web site: http://www.heimburgerhouse.com.

Heirloom Bible Pubs., Orders Addr.: P.O. Box 118, Wichita, KS 67201-0118 (SAN 630-2793) Fax: 316-267-1850; Toll Free: 800-676-2448; Edit Addr.: 9020 E. 35th St N., Wichita, KS 67226-2017.

Helix, 310 S. Racine St., Chicago, IL 60607 (SAN 111-915X) Tel 312-421-6000; Fax: 312-421-1586.

Herald Pr., *(0-8361)* Div. of Mennonite Publishing Hse., Inc., 616 Walnut Ave., Scottdale, PA 15683-1999 (SAN 202-2915) Tel 412-887-8500; 724-887-8500; Fax: 724-887-3111; Toll Free: 800-245-7894 (orders only) Do not confuse with Herald Pr., Charlotte, NC
E-mail: hp@mph.org
Web site: http://www.mph.org.

Herald Publishing Hse., *(0-8309)* P.O. Box 390, Independence, MO 64051-0390 Tel 816-521-3015; Fax: 816-521-3066; Toll Free: 800-767-8181; 1001W. Walnut St., Independence, MO 64051-0390 (SAN 111-7556)
E-mail: hhmark@heraldhouse.org
Web site: http://www.heraldhouse.org.

Heritage Bookstore, Orders Addr.: 2101 W. Chesterfield Blvd., Suite A101, Springfield, MO 65807-8672 (SAN 111-7696).

Hervey's Booklink & Cookbook Warehouse, P.O. Box 831870, Richardson, TX 75083 (SAN 630-9747).

Hi Jolly Library Service, 150 N. Gay St., Susanville, CA 96130-3902 (SAN 133-5944).

Hibel, Edna Studio, P.O. Box 9967, Riviera Beach, FL 33419 (SAN 111-1574) Tel 561-848-9640; Toll Free: 800-275-3426.

Hicks News Agency, Incorporated, *See* **NEWSouth Distributors**

Hill City News Agency, Inc., 3228 Odd Fellow Rd., Lynchburg, VA 24501 (SAN 169-8656) Tel 804-845-4231; Fax: 804-845-0864.

Hillsboro News, Orders Addr.: P.O. Box 25738, Tampa, FL 33622-5738 Tel 813-622-8087; Edit Addr.: 7002 Parke E. Blvd., Tampa, FL 33610.

Himber Bks., Div. of F. C. Himber & Son's, Inc., 1380 W. Second Ave., Eugene, OR 97402 Tel 541-686-8003 ; Toll Free: 800-888-5904.

Himber, F. C., *See* **Himber Bks.**

Hinrichs, E. Louis, P.O. Box 1090, Lompoc, CA 93438-1090 (SAN 133-1493) Tel 805-736-7512
E-mail: booklompoc@aol.com.

Historic Aviation Bks., 121 Fifth Ave., Suite 300, New Brighton, MN 55112 (SAN 129-5284) Tel 651-635-0100; Fax: 651-635-0700.

Historic Cherry Hill, *(0-943366)* 523 1/2 S. Pearl St., Albany, NY 12202 (SAN 110-8859) Tel 518-434-4791 ; Fax: 518-434-4806.

Hobbies Hawaii Distributors, 4420 Lawehana St., No. 3, Honolulu, HI 96818 (SAN 630-8619) Tel 808-423-0265; Fax: 808-423-1635.

Holiday Enterprises, Inc., 3328 US Hwy. 123, Rochester Bldg., Greenville, SC 29611 (SAN 169-779X) Tel 864-220-3161; Fax: 864-295-9757.

Holt, Henry & Co., *(0-03; 0-8050)* Div. of Holtzbrinck Publishers, Orders Addr.: 16365 James Madison Hwy., Gordonsville, VA 22942-8501 Toll Free Fax: 800-672-2054; Toll Free: 888-330-8477; Edit Addr.: 115 W. 18th St., 5th Flr., New York, NY 10011 (SAN 200-6472) Tel 212-886-9200; Fax: 540-672-7540 (customer service)
E-mail: info@hholt.com
Web site: http://www.henryholt.com.

Holtzbrinck Pubs., *(0-374)* Orders Addr.: 16365 James Madison Hwy., Gordonsville, VA 22942 (SAN 631-5011) Tel 540-672-7600; Fax: 540-672-7540 (Customer Service); 540-672-7664; Toll Free Fax: 800-672-2054 (Order Dept.); Toll Free: 888-330-8477 ; Edit Addr.: 175 Fifth Ave., New York, NY 10010 Tel 212-674-5151; Fax: 212-677-6487; Toll Free: 800-488-5233
E-mail: dean.athans.@hbpubny.com
Web site: http://www.vhpsva.com/bookseller/.

Holyoke News Co., Inc., 720 Main St., P.O. Box 990, Holyoke, MA 01041 (SAN 169-3468) Tel 413-534-4537; Fax: 413-538-7161; Toll Free: 800-628-8372
E-mail: sales@holyoke-news.com.

Homestead Bk., Inc., *(0-930180)* Orders Addr.: P.O. Box 31608, Seattle, WA 98103 (SAN 662-037X); Edit Addr.: 6101 22nd Ave., NW, Seattle, WA 98107 (SAN 169-8796) Tel 206-782-4532; Fax: 206-784-9328; Toll Free: 800-426-6777 (orders only)
Web site: http://www.homesteadbook.com.

Honor Bks., *(1-56292)* 2448 E. 81st St., Suite 4800, Tulsa, OK 74137-4285 (SAN 631-1687) Tel 918-523-5600; Fax: 918-496-3588; Toll Free: 800-678-2126 Do not confuse with Honor Bks., Rapid City, SD
E-mail: info@honorbooks.com
Web site: http://www.honorbooks.com/.

Hood, Alan C. & Co., Inc., *(0-911469)* P.O. Box 775, Chambersburg, PA 17201 (SAN 270-8221) Tel 717-267-0867; Fax: 717-267-0572.

Hotho & Co., 916 Norwood St., Fort Worth, TX 76107-2994 (SAN 169-8192) Tel 817-335-1833.

Houghton Mifflin Co., *(0-395; 0-87466; 0-9631591; 1-57630; 1-881527; 0-618)* 222 Berkeley St., Boston, MA 02116 (SAN 215-3793) Tel 617-351-5000
Web site: http://www.hmco.com.

Houghton Mifflin Co. Trade & Reference Div., *(0-395; 0-618)* Orders Addr.: 181 Ballardvalle St., Wilmington, MA 01887 Tel 978-661-1300; Toll Free: 800-225-3362; Edit Addr.: 222 Berkeley St., Boston, MA 02116 (SAN 200-2388) Tel 617-351-5000; Fax: 617-227-5409; 215 Park Ave., S., New York, NY 10003 Tel 212-420-5800; Fax: 212-420-5855
Web site: http://www.hmco.com/.

Houghton Mifflin Company (College Division), *See* **Houghton Mifflin Co. Trade & Reference Div.**

Houston Paperback Distributor, 4114 Gairloch Ln., Houston, TX 77025-2912 (SAN 169-8273).

Howell Pr., *(0-943231; 0-9616878; 1-57427)* 1713-2D Allied Ln., Charlottesville, VA 22903-5336 (SAN 661-6607) Tel 804-977-4006; Fax: 804-971-7204; Toll Free Fax: 888-971-7204; Toll Free: 800-868-4512
E-mail: custserv@howellpress.com
Web site: http://www.howellpress.com.

HPK Educational Resource Ctr., *(0-89895)* Div. of H. P. Koppelmann, Inc., 140 Van Block Ave., Hartford, CT 06141 (SAN 169-071X) Tel 860-549-6210; Toll Free: 800-243-7724.

Hubbard, P.O. Box 100, Defiance, OH 43512 (SAN 169-6726) Tel 419-784-4455; Fax: 419-782-1662; Toll Free: 800-582-0657
E-mail: hubbard@bright.net.

Hudson County News Co., 1305 Paterson Plank Rd., North Bergen, NJ 07047 (SAN 169-4782) Tel 201-867-3600.

Hudson Valley News Distributors, P.O. Box 1236, Newburgh, NY 12550 (SAN 169-6084) Tel 914-562-3399; Fax: 914-562-6010.

Humanics, Limited, *See* **Humanics Publishing Group**

Humanics Publishing Group, *(0-89334)* Orders Addr.: P.O. Box 7400, Atlanta, GA 30357-0400 (SAN 208-3833) Tel 561-533-6231; Fax: 404-874-1976; Toll Free: 888-874-8844 Do not confuse with Humanics ErgoSystems, Inc., Reseda, CA
E-mail: humanics@mindspring.com
Web site: http://www.humanicslearning.com; http://www.humanicsdealer.com; http://www.humanicspub.com.

Hyperion Pr., *(0-7868; 1-56282; 1-4013)* Div. of Disney Bk. Publishing, Inc., A Walt Disney Co., Orders Addr.: 3 Center Plaza, Boston, MA 02108 Toll Free: 800-759-0190; Edit Addr.: 77 W. 66th St., 11th Flr., New York, NY 10023-6298 Tel 212-456-0100; Fax: 212-456-0108
Web site: http://www.hyperionbooks.com.

Iaconi, Mariuccia Bk. Imports, *(0-9628720)* 970 Tennessee St., San Francisco, CA 94107 (SAN 161-1364) Tel 415-821-1216; Fax: 415-821-1596; Toll Free: 800-955-9577
E-mail: mibibook@ixnetcom.com
Web site: http://www.mibibook.com.

i.b.d., Ltd., *(0-88431)* 24 Hudson St., Kinderhook, NY 12106 (SAN 630-7779) Tel 518-758-1755; Fax: 518-758-6702
E-mail: lankhof@ibdltd.com
Web site: http://www.ibdltd.com.

ibooks.com, *(0-7561)* 804-C Rio Grande St., Austin, TX 78701-2220 Tel 512-478-2700; Fax: 512-478-0500
E-mail: kim@ibooks.com
Web site: http://www.ibooks.com/.

ICG Muse, Inc., 73 Spring St., Suite 206, New York, NY 10012 (SAN 631-7200) Tel 212-343-1119; Fax: 212-343-1116.

ID International Bk. Service, 126 Old Ridgefield Rd., Wilton, CT 06897-3017 (SAN 630-8074) Tel 203-834-2272; Fax: 203-762-9725
E-mail: orders@idintl.com.

Idaho News Agency, 2710 Julia St., Coeur D'Alene, ID 83814 (SAN 169-1651) Tel 208-664-3444.

Ideal Foreign Bks., Inc., 132-10 Hillside Ave., Richmond Hill, NY 11418 (SAN 169-6173) Tel 718-297-7477; Fax: 718-297-7645; Toll Free: 800-284-2490 (orders only).

IFSTA, *(0-87939)* Orders Addr.: c/o Oklahoma State Univ., Fire Protection Pubns., 930 N. Willis, Stillwater, OK 74078-8045 Tel 405-744-5723; Fax: 405-744-8204; Toll Free: 800-654-4055 (orders only)
Web site: http://www.ifsta.org/.

Ignatius Pr., *(0-89870; 1-58617)* Div. of Guadalupe Assocs., Inc., Orders Addr.: P.O. Box 1339, Fort Collins, CO 80522-1339 Tel 970-221-3920; Fax: 970-221-3964; Toll Free Fax: 800-278-3566; Toll Free: 800-651-1531 (credit card orders, no minimum, individual orders); 877-320-9276 (bookstore orders); Edit Addr.: 2515 McAllister St., San Francisco, CA 94118 (SAN 214-3887) Tel 415-387-2324; Fax: 415-387-0896
E-mail: info@ignatius.com
Web site: http://www.ignatius.com.

Igram Pr., *(0-911119; 1-930279)* 311 Parsons Dr., Hiawatha, IA 52233 (SAN 263-1709) Tel 319-393-3600; Fax: 319-393-3934; Toll Free: 800-393-2399
E-mail: clabarr@cedargraphicsinc.com.

iLeon, 535 Rte. 38, Suite 500, Cherry Hill, NJ 08002-2953 Tel 215-966-6090; Fax: 856-486-1843
E-mail: contact@ileon.com
Web site: http://ileon.com.

Illinois News Service, *See* **News Group - Illinois, The**

Image Processing Software, Inc., *(0-924507)* 6409 Appalachian Way, Madison, WI 53705 (SAN 265-5977) Tel 608-233-5033; 4414 Regent St., Madison, WI 53705 (SAN 249-3020).

Imperial News Co., Inc., 5131 Post Rd., Dublin, OH 43017-1160 (SAN 169-5509) Fax: 516-752-8515.

Imported Bks., Orders Addr.: St., Dallas, TX 75208 (SAN 169-8095) Tel 214-941-6497.

Incor Periodicals, 32150 Hwy. 34, Tangent, OR 97389-9704 (SAN 169-7072) Tel 541-926-8889; Fax: 541-926-9553.

Independent Institute, *(0-945999)* 100 Swan Way, Suite 200, Oakland, CA 94621-1428 (SAN 135-2938) Tel 510-632-1366; Fax: 510-568-6040; Toll Free: 800-927-8733
E-mail: info@indenpendent.org; orders@independent.org
Web site: http://www.independent.org.

Independent Magazine Co., 2970 N. Ontario St., Burbank, CA 91504-2016 (SAN 159-8783).

Independent Pubs. Group, Subs. of Chicago Review Pr., 814 N. Franklin, Chicago, IL 60610 (SAN 202-0769) Tel 312-337-0747; Fax: 312-337-5985; Toll Free: 800-888-4741
E-mail: lreardon@ipgbook.com; usold@ipgbook.com
Web site: http://www.ipgbook.com.

Independent Pubs. Marketing, 6824 Oaklawn Ave., Edina, MN 55435 (SAN 630-5725) Tel 612-920-9044 ; Fax: 612-920-7662; Toll Free: 800-669-9044
Web site: http://www.Stjohns.ipm.worldnet.att.net.

Indiana Periodicals, Inc., 2120 S. Meridian St., Indianapolis, IN 46225 (SAN 169-2380) Tel 317-786-1488; Fax: 317-782-4999.

Ingham Publishing, Inc., *(0-9611804; 1-891130)* Orders Addr.: P.O. Box 12642, Saint Petersburg, FL 33733-2642 Tel 813-343-4811; Fax: 813-381-2807; Edit Addr.: 5650 First Ave., N., Saint Petersburg, FL 33710 (SAN 112-8930)
E-mail: ftreflex@concentric.net.

Ingram Bk. Co., Subs. of Ingram Industries, Inc., Orders Addr.: 1 Ingram Blvd., P.O. Box 3006, La Vergne, TN 37086-1986 (SAN 169-7978) Tel 615-213-5000; Fax: 615-213-3976 (Electronic Orders); Toll Free Fax: 800-285-3296 (fax inquiry US & Canada); 800-876-0186 (orders); 877-663-5367 (Canadian orders); Toll Free: 800-937-8000 (orders only); 800-937-8200 (customer service US & Canada); 800-289-0687 (Canadian orders only customer service); 800-234-6737 (electronic orders US & Canada)) Do not confuse with Ingram Pr., Sacramento, CA
E-mail: customerservice@ingrambook.com; flashback@ingrambook.com; ics-sales@ingrambook.com
Web site: http://www.ingrambook.com.

Ingram Software, Subs. of Ingram Distribution Group, Inc., 1759 Wehrle, Williamsville, NY 14221 (SAN 285-760X) Toll Free: 800-828-7250; 900 W. Walnut Ave., Compton, CA 90220 (SAN 285-7073).

Inland Empire Periodicals, *See* **Incor Periodicals**

Integral Yoga Pubns., *(0-932040)* Satchidananda Ashram-Yogaville, Rte. 1, Box 1720, Buckingham, VA 23921 (SAN 285-0338) Tel 804-969-1706; Fax: 804-969-1463; Toll Free: 800-262-1008 (orders)
Web site: http://www.yogaville.org/pubs.html.

Interactive Knowledge, *See* **netLibrary, Inc.**

Interlink Publishing Group, Inc., *(0-940793; 1-56656)* 46 Crosby St., Northampton, MA 01060-1804 (SAN 664-8908) Tel 413-582-7054; Fax: 413-582-6731; Toll Free: 800-238-5465
E-mail: info@interlinkbooks.com; editor@interlinkbooks.com
Web site: http://www.interlinkbooks.com.

InterMountain Periodical Distributors, *See* **Majic Enterprises**

International Bks. & Tapes Supply, P.O. Box 5153, Long Island City, NY 11005 (SAN 631-6743) Tel 718-721-4246; Fax: 718-321-9004.

International Brecht Society, *(0-9623206)* c/o Marc Silberman, Univ. of Wisconsin, German Dept., 818 Van Hisc Hall, Madison, WI 53706 Tel 608-262-2192 ; Fax: 608-262-4747 Do not confuse with Pittsburgh, PA, AU.

International Historic Films, Inc., *(1-57299)* Orders Addr.: P.O. Box 29035, Chicago, IL 60629 Tel 773-927-2900; Fax: 773-927-9211; Edit Addr.: 3533 S. Archer Ave., Chicago, IL 60609
E-mail: info@ihffilm.com
Web site: http://historicvideo.com.

International Magazine Service, Div. of Periodical Pubs. Service Bureau, 1 N. Superior St., Sandusky, OH 44870 (SAN 285-9955) Tel 419-626-0623.

International Networking Assn., 4130 Citrus Ave., Suite 5, Rocklin, CA 95677 (SAN 631-1857).

International Periodical Distributors, 674 Via de la Valle, Suite 204, Solana Beach, CA 92075 (SAN 250-5290) Tel 619-481-5928; Toll Free: 800-999-1170; 800-228-5144 (in Canada).

International Publishers Marketing, Orders Addr.: 22883 Quicksilver Dr., Dulles, VA 20166 (SAN 253-3375) Toll Free: 800-758-3756; Edit Addr.: P.O. Box 605, Herndon, VA 20172-0605 Fax: 703-661-1501.

International Pubns. Service, *(0-8002)* Div. of Taylor & Francis, Inc., Orders Addr.: 325 Chestnut St., 8th Flr., Levittown, PA 19057-4700 Fax: 215-785-5515; Toll Free: 800-821-8312
E-mail: bkorders@tandfpa.com.

International Readers League, Div. of Periodical Pubs. Service Bureau, 1 N. Superior St., Sandusky, OH 44870 (SAN 285-9971) Tel 419-626-0633.

International Service Co., International Service Bldg., 333 Fourth Ave., Indialantic, FL 32903-4295 (SAN 169-5134) Tel 407-724-1443 (phone/fax).

International Specialized Bk. Services, 920 NE 58th Ave., Suite 300, Portland, OR 97213-3786 (SAN 169-7129) Tel 503-287-3093; Fax: 503-280-8832; Toll Free: 800-944-6190
E-mail: info@isbs.com
Web site: http://www.isbs.com.

International Thomson Publishing, *See* **Thomson Learning**

Internaturally, Inc., *(0-9636805)* Orders Addr.: P.O. Box 317, Newfoundland, NJ 07435 Tel 973-697-3552 ; Fax: 973-697-8313; Edit Addr.: 9 Deerhaven Ln., Newfoundland, NJ 07435
E-mail: naturally@internaturally.com
Web site: http://www.internaturally.com.

Internet Systems, Inc., Subs. of Internet Systems, Inc., 20250 Century Blvd., Germantown, MD 20874 (SAN 129-9611) Tel 301-540-5100; Fax: 301-540-5522; Toll Free: 800-638-8725
Web site: http://www.pwl.com/Internet.

Interstate Distributors, 199 Commander Shea Blvd., Quincy, MA 02171 (SAN 170-4885) Tel 617-328-9500; Toll Free: 800-365-6430.

Interstate Periodical Distributors, P.O. Box 2237, Madison, WI 53701 (SAN 169-9105) Tel 608-271-3600; Fax: 608-277-2410; Toll Free: 800-752-3131.

Intertech Bk. Services, Inc., 25971 Sarazen Dr., South Riding, VA 20152-1741 (SAN 630-5253).

Intrepid Group, Inc., The, 1331 Red Cedar Cir., Fort Collins, CO 80524 (SAN 631-5429) Tel 970-493-3793 ; Fax: 970-493-8781
E-mail: intrepid@fril.com.

Iowa & Illinois News, 8645 Northwest Blvd., Davenport, IA 52806-6418 (SAN 169-2607).

Iowa State Pr., *(0-8138)* 2121 S. State Ave., Ames, IA 50014-8300 (SAN 202-7194) Tel 515-292-0140; Fax: 515-292-3348
E-mail: orders@isupress.com
Web site: http://www.iowastatepress.com.

Iowa State University Press, *See* **Iowa State Pr.**

Irish American Bk. Co., Subs. of Roberts Rinehart Pubs., Inc., P.O. Box 666, Niwot, CO 80544-0666 Tel 303-652-2710; Fax: 303-652-2689; Toll Free: 800-452-7115
E-mail: irishbooks@aol.com
Web site: http://www.irishvillage.com.

Irish Bks. & Media, Inc., *(0-937702)* Orders Addr.: 1433 E. Franklin Ave., Suite 20, Minneapolis, MN 55404-2135 (SAN 111-8870) Tel 612-871-3505; Fax: 612-871-3358; Toll Free: 800-229-3505 Do not confuse with Irish Bks. in New York, NY
E-mail: Irishbook@aol.com
Web site: http://www.irishbook.com.

Ironside International Pubs., Inc., *(0-935554)* Orders Addr.: P.O. Box 55, Alexandria, VA 22313 (SAN 206-2380) Tel 703-684-6111; Fax: 703-683-5486; Edit Addr.: 3000 S. Eads St., Arlington, VA 22202 (SAN 663-656X).

Islamic Bk. Service, 1209 Cleburne, Hoston, TX 77004 (SAN 169-2453) Tel 713-528-1440; Fax: 713-528-1085.

Island Heritage Publishing, *(0-89610; 0-931548)* Div. of The Madden Corp., 94-411 Koaki St., Waipahu, HI 96797 (SAN 211-1403) Tel 808-564-8888; Fax: 808-564-8999; Toll Free: 800-468-2800
E-mail: hawaii4u@islandheritage.com
Web site: http://www.islandheritage.com/.

James & Law Co., Orders Addr.: P.O. Box 2468, Clarksburg, WV 26302-2468 (SAN 169-894X); Edit Addr.: Middletown Mall I-79 & U. S. 250, Fairmont, WV 26554 (SAN 169-8966) Tel 304-624-7401.

Janway, 11 Academy Rd., Cogan Station, PA 17728 (SAN 108-3708) Tel 717-494-1239; Fax: 717-494-1350; Toll Free: 800-877-5242.

Jeanies Classics, *(0-9609672)* Orders Addr.: 2123 Oxford St., Rockford, IL 61103 (SAN 271-7409); Edit Addr.: 2123 Oxford St., Rockford, IL 61103 (SAN 271-7395) Tel 815-968-4544.

Jean's Dulcimer Shop & Crying Creek Pubs., P.O. Box 8, Hwy. 32, Cosby, TN 37722 (SAN 249-9282) Tel 423-487-5543.

Jech Distributors, 674 Via De La Valle, No. 204, Solana Beach, CA 92075-2462 (SAN 107-0258) Tel 619-452-7251.

Jellyroll Productions, *See* **Osborne Enterprises Publishing**

Jende-Hagan, Incorporated, *See* **Renaissance Hse. Pubs.**

J&L Bk. Co., Orders Addr.: P.O. Box 13100, Spokane, WA 99213 (SAN 129-6817) Fax: 509-534-0152; 509-534-7713; Toll Free: 800-288-9756; Edit Addr.: 1710 Trent, Spokane, WA 99220 (SAN 243-2145).

Johnson News Agency, P.O. Box 9009, Moscow, ID 83843 (SAN 169-1678).

Johnson, Walter J. Inc., *(0-8472)* 1 New York Plaza 28th Flr., New York, NY 10004-1901 (SAN 209-1828).

Jonathan David Pubs., Inc., *(0-8246)* 68-22 Eliot Ave., Middle Village, NY 11379 (SAN 169-5274) Tel 718-456-8611; Fax: 718-894-2818
E-mail: jondavpub@aol.com
Web site: http://www.jdbooks.com.

Jones, Bob Univ. Pr., *(0-89084; 1-57924; 1-59166)* 1700 Wade Hampton Blvd., Greenville, SC 29614 (SAN 223-7512) Tel 864-242-5731; Fax: 864-298-8398; Toll Free Fax: 800-525-8398; Toll Free: 800-845-5731
E-mail: bjup@bjup.com
Web site: http://www.bjup.com.

Joseph Ruzicka, Incorporated, *See* **Southeast Library Bindery, Inc.**

Joshua Morris Publishing, Incorporated, *See* **Reader's Digest Children's Publishing, Inc.**

Joyce Media, Inc., *(0-917002)* P.O. Box 57, Acton, CA 93510 (SAN 208-7197) Tel 805-269-1169; Fax: 805-269-2139
E-mail: joycemed@pacbell.net
Web site: http://joycemedia.com.

Junior League of Greensboro Pubns., *(0-9605788)* 220 State St., Greensboro, NC 27408 (SAN 112-9597) Fax: 336-275-0677
E-mail: Jlgso@aol.com.

K. F. Enterprises, *See* **Production Assocs., Inc.**

K. M. R. Enterprises, *(0-9656379)* 5731 Pony Express Trail, Pollock Pines, CA 95726 (SAN 299-237X) Tel 530-644-1410.

Kable News Co., Inc., Subs. of AMREP Corp., 641 Lexington Ave., 6th Flr., New York, NY 10022 (SAN 169-5835) Tel 212-705-4600; Toll Free: 800-223-6640
E-mail: info@kable.com.

Kalispell News Agency, P.O. Box 4965, Missoula, MT 59806-4965 (SAN 169-4383) Toll Free: 800-955-1266.

Kamkin, Victor, 4956 Boiling Brook Pkwy., Rockville, MD 20852 Tel 301-881-5973; Fax: 301-881-1637; Toll Free: 800-852-6546; 925 Broadway, New York, NY 10010 (SAN 113-7395) Tel 212-673-0776; Fax: 212-673-2473.

Kane/Miller Bk. Pubs., *(0-916291; 1-929132)* Orders Addr.: P.O. Box 8515, La Jolla, CA 92038 (SAN 295-8945) Tel 858-456-0540; Fax: 858-456-9641; Toll Free: 800-968-1930
E-mail: kira@kanemiller.com
Web site: http://www.kanemiller.com; http://www.everyonepoops.com.

Kansas City Periodical Distributing, Orders Addr.: P.O. Box 14948, Lenexa, KS 66285-4948 (SAN 107-9433) ; Edit Addr.: 9605 Dice Ln., Lenexa, KS 66215 Tel 913-541-8600.

Kansas State Reading Circle, 715 W. Tenth St., C-170, Topeka, KS 66601 (SAN 169-2771).

Kaplan Press, Incorporated, *See* **PACT Hse. Publishing**

Kaybee Montessori, Inc., 7895-K Cessna Ave., Gaithersburg, MD 20879 (SAN 133-1256) Tel 301-963-2101; Fax: 301-963-2197; Toll Free: 800-732-9304.

Kazi Pubns., Inc., *(0-933511; 0-935782; 1-56744)* 3023 W. Belmont Ave., Chicago, IL 60618 (SAN 162-3397) Tel 773-267-7001; Fax: 773-267-7002
E-mail: info@kazi.org
Web site: http://www.kazi.org.

Keith Distributors, 1055 S. Ballenger Hwy., Flint, MI 48532 (SAN 112-6377) Tel 801-238-9104; 810-238-9104; Fax: 810-238-9028; Toll Free: 800-373-2366
E-mail: keithsbooks@juno.com.

Kendall Whaling Museum, *(0-937854)* 27 Everett St., P.O. Box 297, Sharon, MA 02067 (SAN 204-9783) Tel 781-784-5642; Fax: 781-784-0451; Toll Free: 800-927-1133 (orders)
Web site: http://www.kwm.org.

Kensington Publishing Corp., *(0-7860; 0-8184; 0-8217; 1-55817; 1-57566; 0-7582)* 850 Third Ave., New York, NY 10022-6222 Tel 212-407-1500; Fax: 212-935-0699; Toll Free: 800-221-2647
E-mail: jmclean@kensingtonbooks.com
Web site: http://www.kensingtonbooks.com.

Kent News Agency, Inc., P.O. Box 1828, Scottsbluff, NE 69363-1828 (SAN 169-4448) Tel 303-286-9694; 308-635-2225; Fax: 308-635-1563; Toll Free: 877-290-4740
E-mail: kentrob@prairieweb.com.

Keramos, P.O. Box 7500, Ann Arbor, MI 48107 (SAN 169-3670) Tel 313-439-1261.

Kerhulas News Co., P.O. Box 751, Union, SC 29379 (SAN 169-7838).

Ketab Corp., *(1-883819)* Orders Addr.: 1419 Westwood Blvd., Los Angeles, CA 90024 (SAN 107-7791) Tel 818-908-0808; Fax: 818-908-1457
E-mail: ketab@ketab.com
Web site: http://www.ketab.com.

Key Bk. Service, Inc., *(0-934636)* P.O. Box 1434, Fairfield, CT 06430 (SAN 169-0671) Tel 203-374-4939; Fax: 203-384-6099.

Kidsbooks, Inc., 220 Monroe Tpke., No. 560, Monroe, CT 06468-2247 (SAN 169-0795).

King Electronics Distributing, 1711 Southeastern Ave., Indianapolis, IN 46201-3990 (SAN 107-6795) Tel 317-639-1484; Fax: 317-639-4711.

Kinokuniya Bookstores of America Co., Ltd., 1581 Webster St., San Francisco, CA 94115 (SAN 121-8441) Tel 415-567-7625; Fax: 415-567-4109.

Kinokuniya Pubns. Service of New York, 10 W. 49th St., New York, NY 10020 (SAN 157-5414) Tel 212-765-1465; Fax: 212-307-5593
E-mail: kinokuniya@kinokuniya.com
Web site: http://www.kinokuniya.com.

Kirkbride, B.B. Bible Co., Inc., *(0-88707; 0-934854)* P.O. Box 606, Indianapolis, IN 46206-0606 (SAN 169-2372) Tel 317-633-1900; Fax: 317-633-1444; Toll Free: 800-428-4385
E-mail: hyperbible@aol.com
Web site: http://www.kirkbride.com.

Kitrick Management Co., Ltd., P.O. Box 15523, Cincinnati, OH 45215 (SAN 132-6236) Tel 513-782-2930; Fax: 513-782-2936
E-mail: bachb@aol.com.

Klein's Booklein, Orders Addr.: P.O. Box 968, Fowlerville, MI 48836 (SAN 631-3329) Tel 517-223-3964; Fax: 517-223-1314; Toll Free: 800-266-5534; Edit Addr.: One Klein Dr., Fowlerville, MI 48836 (SAN 631-3337).

Knopf, Alfred A. Inc., *(0-375; 0-394; 0-676; 0-679)* Div. of The Knopf Publishing Group, Orders Addr.: 400 Hahn Rd., Westminster, MD 21157 Tel 410-848-1900; Toll Free Fax: 800-659-2436; Toll Free: 800-733-3000 (orders); Edit Addr.: 299 Park Ave., New York, NY 10171 (SAN 202-5825) Tel 212-751-2600; Fax: 212-572-2593; Toll Free: 800-726-0600
E-mail: customerservice@randomhouse.com
Web site: http://www.randomhouse.com/knopf.

Koen Bk. Distributors, Orders Addr.: 10 Twosome Dr., P.O. Box 600, Moorestown, NJ 08057 (SAN 169-4642) Tel 609-235-4444; Fax: 609-727-6914; Toll Free Fax: 800-225-3840; Toll Free: 800-257-8481
E-mail: kbdinfo@koen.com
Web site: http://www.koen.com.

Koen Pacific, Orders Addr.: 18249 Olympic Ave., S., Tukwila, WA 98188-4722 (SAN 631-5593) Tel 206-575-7544; Fax: 206-575-7444; Toll Free: 800-995-4840
E-mail: info@koenpacific.com.

Kraus Reprint, *See* **Periodicals Service Co.**

Kurian, George Reference Bks., *(0-914746)* Orders Addr.: P.O. Box 519, Baldwin Place, NY 10505 (SAN 203-1981); Edit Addr.: 3689 Campbell Ct., Yorktown Heights, NY 10598 (SAN 110-6236) Tel 914-962-3287.

Kurtzman Bk. Sales Co., 17348 W. 12 Mile Rd., Southfield, MI 48076 (SAN 114-0787) Tel 248-557-7230; Fax: 248-557-8705; Toll Free: 800-869-0505.

Kuykendall's Pr., Bookstore Div., P.O. Box 627, Athens, AL 35612-0627 (SAN 168-9185) Tel 256-232-1754; Toll Free: 800-781-1754.

L L Company, *(0-937892)* 1647 Manning Ave., Los Angeles, CA 90024 (SAN 110-0009) Tel 310-615-0116; Fax: 310-640-6863; Toll Free: 800-473-3699
E-mail: wallacelab@aol.com.

La Belle News Agency, 814 University Blvd., Steubenville, OH 43952 (SAN 169-6858) Tel 740-282-9731.

La Cite French Bks., Div. of The La Cite Group, Inc., P.O. Box 64504, Los Angeles, CA 90064-0504 (SAN 168-9789)
E-mail: lacite@aol.com.

La Moderna Poesia, Inc., 5246 SW Eighth St., Miami, FL 33134 (SAN 169-1139) Tel 305-446-9884; Fax: 305-445-1635.

Lafayette Bks., P.O. Box 758, Mamaroneck, NY 10543-0758 (SAN 135-292X) Tel 914-833-0248.

Lakeport Distributors, Inc., 139 W. 18th St., P.O. Box 6195, Erie, PA 16501 (SAN 169-734X).

Lambert Bk. Hse., Inc., *(0-89315)* 4139 Parkway Dr., Florence, AL 35630-6347 (SAN 180-5169) Tel 205-764-4098; 256-974-1529 (orders ask Stan Johnson); Fax: 205-766-9200; Toll Free: 800-551-8511
E-mail: Info@lambertbookhouse.com.

Landmark Audiobooks, 4865 Sterling Dr., Boulder, CO 80301 Fax: 303-443-3775
Web site: http://www.landmarkaudio.com.

Landmark Bk. Co., *(0-929194)* 131 Hicks St., Brooklyn, NY 11201-2318 (SAN 169-5843).

Langenscheidt Pubs., Inc., *(0-88729; 3-468; 1-58573; 3-324)* Subs. of Langenscheidt KG, 46-35 54th Rd., Maspeth, NY 11378 (SAN 276-9441) Tel 718-784-0055 (ext. 108); Fax: 718-784-1216; Toll Free: 800-432-6277
E-mail: spohja@langenscheidt.com
Web site: http://www.langenscheidt.com; http://www.hagstrommap.com.

Larousse Kingfisher Chambers, Inc., *(0-7534; 1-85697; 970-22)* 215 Park Ave., S., New York, NY 10003 (SAN 297-7540) Tel 212-420-5800; Fax: 212-686-1082; 181 Ballardvale St., Wilmington, MA 01887
Web site: http://www.lkcpub.com.

Las Vegas News Agency, 2312 Silver Bluff Ct., Las Vegas, NV 89134-6092.

Lash Distributors, 7106 Geoffrey Way, Frederick, MD 21704 (SAN 169-3131).

Last Gasp Eco-Funnies, Inc., *(0-86719)* Orders Addr.: P.O. Box 410067, San Francisco, CA 94141-0067 (SAN 216-8308); Edit Addr.: 777 Florida St., San Francisco, CA 94110-2025 (SAN 170-3242) Tel 415-824-6636; Fax: 415-824-1836; Toll Free: 800-366-5121
E-mail: lastgasp@hooked.net.

Laster, Larry D. Old & Rare Bks., Prints & Maps, 2416 Maplewood Ave., Winston-Salem, NC 27103 (SAN 112-9600) Tel 336-724-7544; Fax: 336-724-9055.

Latcorp, Ltd., 10 Norden Ln., Huntington Station, NY 11746 (SAN 159-8910) Tel 516-271-0548; Fax: 516-549-8849.

Latin American Bk. Source, Inc., 289 Third Ave., Chula Vista, CA 91910 Tel 619-426-1226; Fax: 619-426-0212
Web site: http://www.latinbooks.com.

Latta, J. S. Incorporated, *See* **Latta's**

Latta's, 1502 Fourth Ave., P.O. Box 2668, Huntington, WV 25726 (SAN 169-8982) Fax: 304-525-5038; Toll Free: 800-624-3501.

LEA Bk. Distributors (Libros Espana y America), *(1-883110)* 170-23 83rd Ave., Jamaica Hills, NY 11432 (SAN 170-5407) Tel 718-291-9891; Fax: 718-291-9830
E-mail: leabook@idt.net
Web site: http://www.leabooks.com.

Learning Collection, The, 5180 Smith Rd., Suite B, Denver, CO 80216-4431 (SAN 630-8287) Tel 303-722-9843.

Lectorum Pubns., Inc., *(0-9625162; 1-880507; 1-930332)* Subs. of Scholastic, Inc., 205 Chubb Ave., Lyndhurst, NJ 07071-3520 Tel 212-965-7322; Fax: 212-727-3035; Toll Free Fax: 877-532-8676; 877-532-8678; Toll Free: 800-345-5946
E-mail: info@lectorum.com
Web site: http://www.lectorum.com.

Lee Bks., *(0-939818)* Div. of Lee S. Cole & Assocs., Inc., 524 San Anselmo Ave., No 215, San Anselmo, CA 94960-2614 (SAN 110-649X) Tel 415-456-4388; Fax: 415-456-7532; Toll Free: 800-828-3550 Do not confuse with other companies with the same or similar names in Jacksonville, FL, Columbia, SC
E-mail: lcs@lsc-associates.com
Web site: http://www.lsc-associates.com.

Leman Pubns., Inc., *(0-943721; 0-9602970)* Div. of Rodale Pr. Co., Box 4100, 741 Corporate Cir., Suite A, Golden, CO 80401-5622 (SAN 213-3415) Fax: 303-277-0370; Toll Free: 800-877-3775.

Leonard, Hal Corp., *(0-634; 0-7935; 0-88188; 0-9607350; 1-56516)* Orders Addr.: P.O. Box 13819, Milwaukee, WI 53213-0819 Tel 414-774-3630; Fax: 414-774-3259; Toll Free: 800-524-4425; Edit Addr.: 7777 W. Bluemound Rd., Milwaukee, WI 53213 (SAN 239-250X)
E-mail: halinfo@halleonard.com
Web site: http://www.halleonard.com.

Lerner Publishing Group, *(0-8225; 0-87614; 0-929371; 0-930494; 1-57505; 1-58013)* Orders Addr.: 1251 Washington Ave., N., Minneapolis, MN 55401 Toll Free Fax: 800-332-1132; Toll Free: 800-328-4929
E-mail: custserve@lernerbook.com
Web site: http://www.lernerbooks.com; http://www.karben.com.

Lerner Publishing Group, The, *See* **Lerner Publishing Group**

Levine, J. Religious Supplies, Five W. 30th St., New York, NY 10001 (SAN 169-5878) Tel 212-695-6888; Fax: 212-643-1044
E-mail: sales@levine.judica.com.

Levy, Charles Co., 1200 N. North Branch St., Chicago, IL 60622 (SAN 159-835X) Tel 312-440-4400.

Levy Home Entertainment, Div. of Charles Levy Co., 4201 Raymond Dr., Hillside, IL 60162 (SAN 176-2478) Tel 708-547-4400; 708-649-4158; Fax: 708-547-4503; Toll Free: 800-947-1967
E-mail: jsemeneck@levybooks.com.

Lewis, John W. Enterprises, 168 Perez St., P.O. Box 3375, Santurce, PR 00936 (SAN 169-9334) Tel 809-722-0104.

Liberation Distributors, *(0-89928)* P.O. Box 5341, Chicago, IL 60680 (SAN 169-880X) Tel 773-248-3442.

LibertyTree Press, *See* **Independent Institute**

Libraries Unlimited, Inc., *(0-313; 0-87287; 1-56308; 1-59158)* Div. of Greenwood Publishing Group, Orders Addr.: a/o Customer Service Group, Dept. 2229, P.O. Box 5007, Westport, CT 06881 Fax: 603-431-2214; Toll Free: 800-225-5800; Edit Addr.: 6931 S. Yosemite St., Englewood, CO 80112 Tel 303-770-1220; Fax: 303-220-8843
E-mail: lubooks@lu.com
Web site: http://www.lu.com.

Library & Educational Services, P.O. Box 146, Berrien Springs, MI 49103 Tel 616-695-1800; Fax: 616-695-8500
E-mail: libraryanded@juno.com.

Library Bk. Selection Service, P.O. Box 277, 2714 McGraw Dr., Bloomington, IL 61704 (SAN 169-1740) Tel 309-663-1411; Fax: 309-664-0059.

Library Video Co., *(1-4171)* P.O. Box 580, Wynnewood, PA 19096 (SAN 631-3205) Fax: 610-645-4050; Toll Free: 800-843-3620
E-mail: cs@libraryvideo.com
Web site: http://www.libraryvideo.com.

Libreria Bereana, 1825 San Alejandro, Urb San Ignacio, Rio Piedras, PR 00927-6819 (SAN 169-9288) Tel 809-764-6175.

Libros de Espana y America, *See* **LEA Bk. Distributors (Libros Espana y America)**

Libros Sin Fronteras, P.O. Box 2085, Olympia, WA 98507 Tel 360-357-4332; Fax: 360-357-4964
E-mail: info@librossinfronteras.com
Web site: http://www.librossinfronteras.com.

Light & Life Publishing Co., *(0-937032; 1-880971)* 4808 Park Glen Rd., Minneapolis, MN 55416 (SAN 213-8565) Tel 612-925-3888; Fax: 612-925-3918
E-mail: info@light-n-life.com
Web site: http://www.light-n-life.com.

Light Impressions Corp., *(0-87992)* Orders Addr.: P.O. Box 940, Rochester, NY 14603-0940 (SAN 169-619X) Toll Free Fax: 800-826-5539; Toll Free: 800-828-6216; Edit Addr.: P.O. Box 22708, Rochester, NY 14692-2708
Web site: http://www.lightimpresionsdirect.com.

Light Messages, 5216 Tahoe Dr., Durham, NC 27713
E-mail: books@lightmessages.com
Web site: http://www.lightmessages.com.

Lightning Source, Inc., 1246 Heil Quaker Blvd., LaVergne, TN 37086 (SAN 179-6976) Tel 615-213-4595; Fax: 615-213-4426.

Liguori Pubns., *(0-7648; 0-89243)* One Liguori Dr., Liguori, MO 63057-9999 (SAN 202-6783) Tel 636-464-2500; Fax: 636-464-8449; Toll Free Fax: 800-325-9526; Toll Free: 800-325-9521 (orders)
E-mail: liguori@liguori.org; dcrosby@liguori.org
Web site: http://www.liguori.org.

Likely Story Bookfairs, A, 7210 SW 57th Ave., Suite 207-A, South Miami, FL 33143 (SAN 631-1210) Tel 305-668-9183; Fax: 305-667-3323.

Lilly News Agency, P.O. Box 280077, Memphis, TN 38168-0077 (SAN 168-9452).

LIM Productions, LLC, *(1-929617)* 3553 Northdale St., NW, Uniontown, OH 44685-8004 Toll Free: 877-628-4532
E-mail: customerservice@limproductions.com
Web site: http://www.limproductions.com.

Limerock Bks., Inc., P.O. Box 57, New Canaan, CT 06840 (SAN 630-8708) Tel 203-322-5352; Fax: 203-322-2182 Do not confuse with Limerock Books, Thomaston, ME
E-mail: limerockbk@aol.com
Web site: http://www.netpocus.com/limerock.

Linden Tree Children's Records & Bks., 170 State St., Los Altos, CA 94022 (SAN 131-744X) Tel 415-949-3390; Fax: 415-949-0346.

Ling's International Bks., Orders Addr.: P.O. Box 82684, San Diego, CA 92138 (SAN 169-0116) Tel 619-292-8104; Fax: 619-292-8207; Edit Addr.: 3396 Via Cabo Verde., Escondido, CA 92029-7459.

Lippincott Williams & Wilkins, *(0-316; 0-397; 0-683; 0-7817; 0-8067; 0-8121; 0-88167; 0-89004; 0-89313; 0-89640; 0-911216; 1-881063; 4-260)* Orders Addr.: P.O. Box 1600, Hagerstown, MD 21741 Fax: 301-223-2400; Toll Free: 800-638-3030; Edit Addr.: 530 Walnut St., Philadelphia, PA 19106-3621 (SAN 201-0933) Tel 215-521-8300; Fax: 215-521-8902; Toll Free: 800-638-3030; 351 W. Camden St., Baltimore, MD 21201 Tel 410-528-4000; 345 Hudson St., 16th Flr., New York, NY 10014 Tel 212-886-1200 ; 16522 Hunters Green Pkwy., Hagerstown, MD 21740 Tel 301-223-2300; Fax: 301-223-2398; Toll Free: 800-638-3030
E-mail: custserv@lww.com; orders@lww.com
Web site: http://www.lww.com.

Lippincott-Raven Publishers, *See* **Lippincott Williams & Wilkins**

Literal Book Distributors: Books in Spanish, Orders Addr.: P.O. Box 7113, Langley Park, MD 20787; Edit Addr.: 7705 Georgia Ave. NW, Suite 102, Washington, DC 20012 (SAN 113-2784) Tel 202-723-8688; Fax: 202-882-6592; Toll Free: 800-366-8680.

Little Brown & Co., *(0-316; 0-8212)* Div. of Time Warner Bk. Group, Orders Addr.: 3 Center Plaza, Boston, MA 02108-2084 (SAN 630-7248) Tel 617-227-0730; Toll Free Fax: 800-286-9471; Toll Free: 800-759-0190; Edit Addr.: Time & Life Bldg., 1271 Avenue of the Americas, New York, NY 10020 (SAN 200-2205) Tel 212-522-8700; Fax: 212-522-2067; Toll Free: 800-343-9204
E-mail: cust.service@littlebrown.com
Web site: http://www.littlebrown.com.

Little Dania's Juvenile Promotions, Div. of Booksmith Promotional Co., 100 Paterson Plank Rd., Jersey City, NJ 07307 (SAN 169-5681) Tel 201-659-2317; Fax: 201-659-3631
E-mail: hochberga@aol.com.

Little Professor Bk. Ctrs., Inc., P.O. Box 3160, Ann Arbor, MI 48106-3160 (SAN 144-2503) Toll Free: 800-899-6232.

Login Fulfillment Services, *See* **LPC Group**

Lone Pine Publishing, *(0-919433; 1-55105)* 1808 B St., NW, Suite 140, Auburn, WA 98001 Tel 425-204-5965; Fax: 425-204-6036; Toll Free Fax: 800-548-1169; Toll Free: 800-518-3541
E-mail: rtruppner@lonepinepublishing.com
Web site: http://www.lonepinepublishing.com.

Lonely Planet Pubns., *(0-86442; 0-908086; 1-55992; 2-84070; 1-86450; 1-74059; 88-7063; 1-74104)* 150 Linden St., Oakland, CA 94607 (SAN 659-6541) Tel 510-893-8555; Fax: 510-893-8563; Toll Free: 800-275-8555 (orders, 9am - 5pm Pacific Time)
E-mail: gary.todoroff@lonelyplanet.com
Web site: http://www.lonelyplanet.com.

Long Beach Bks., Inc., P.O. Box 179, Long Beach, NY 11561-0179 (SAN 164-632X) Tel 718-471-5934.

Looseleaf Law Pubns., Inc., *(0-930137; 1-889031)* Orders Addr.: P.O. Box 650042, Fresh Meadows, NY 11365-0042 Tel 718-359-5559; Fax: 718-539-0941; Toll Free: 800-647-5547; Edit Addr.: 43-08 162nd St., Flushing, NY 11358 (SAN 135-0099)
E-mail: llawpub@erols.com
Web site: http://www.looseleaflaw.com.

Lord's Line, *(0-915952)* 1065 Lomita Blvd., No. 434, Harbor City, CA 90710-1944 (SAN 169-0051).

Lorimar Home Video, *See* **Warner Home Video, Inc.**

Los Angeles Mart, The, 1933 S. Broadway, Suite 665, Los Angeles, CA 90007 (SAN 168-9797) Tel 213-748-6449; Fax: 714-523-0796.

Louisville Distributors, *See* **United Magazine**

Louisville News Co., P.O. Box 36, Columbia, KY 42728 (SAN 169-281X) Tel 502-384-3444; Fax: 502-384-9324.

LPC Group, c/o CDS, 193 Edwards Dr., Jackson, TN 38305 (SAN 630-5644) Fax: 731-935-7731; 731-423-1973; Toll Free Fax: 800-351-5073; Toll Free: 800-343-4499
E-mail: lpc-info@lpcgroup.com
Web site: http://www.lpcgroup.com.

Ludington News Co., 1600 E. Grand Blvd., Detroit, MI 48211-3195 (SAN 169-3751) Tel 313-929-7600.

L-W Bk. Sales, 5243 S. Adams St., Marion, IN 46953 (SAN 630-6608) Tel 765-674-6450; Fax: 765-674-3503; Toll Free: 800-777-6450 E-mail: catalogs@lwbooks.com Web site: http://www.lwbooks.com.

L-W, Inc., *(0-89538)* P.O. Box 69, Gas City, IN 46933 (SAN 159-6292) Tel 765-674-6450; Fax: 765-674-3503; Toll Free: 800-777-6450 E-mail: catalogs@lwbooks.com; lwbooks@comteek.com Web site: http://www.lwbooks.com.

M & J Bk. Fair Service, 2307 Sherwood Cir., Minneapolis, MN 55431 (SAN 169-4030).

M & M News Agency, Orders Addr.: P.O. Box 1129, La Salle, IL 61301 (SAN 169-2062) Fax: 815-223-2828; Toll Free: 800-245-6247.

M L E S, *See* **Pathway Bk. Service**

Ma'ayan, *See* **WellSpring Bks.**

MacGregor News Agency, 1733 Industrial Park Dr., Mount Pleasant, MI 48858 (SAN 169-3921) Toll Free: 800-626-1982.

Macmillan USA, *See* **Alpha Bks.**

MacRae's Indian Bk. Distributor, 1605 Cole St., P.O. Box 652, Enumclaw, WA 98022 (SAN 157-5473) Tel 360-825-3737.

Madison Art Ctr., Inc., *(0-913883)* 211 State St., Madison, WI 53703 Tel 608-257-0158; Fax: 608-257-5722 E-mail: mac@itis.com Web site: http://www.madisonartcenter.org.

Magazine Distributors, Inc., 15 Sparks St., Plainville, CT 06062 (SAN 169-0817).

Magazines, Inc., 1135 Hammond St., Bangor, ME 04401 (SAN 169-3034) Tel 207-942-8237; Fax: 207-942-9226; Toll Free: 800-649-9224 (in Maine) E-mail: pam@mint.net.

Mahoning Valley Distributing Agency, Inc., 2556 Rush Blvd., Youngstown, OH 44507 Tel 330-788-6162; Fax: 330-788-9046.

Majic Enterprises, 313 E. Main St., Niles, MI 49120-2305 (SAN 169-8508).

Majors, J. A. Co., Orders Addr.: 1401 Lakeway Dr., Lewisville, TX 75057 (SAN 169-8117) Tel 972-353-1100; Fax: 972-353-1300; Toll Free: 800-633-1851 E-mail: dallas@majors.com Web site: http://www.majors.com.

Majors Scientific Bks., Inc., 1401 Lakeway Dr., Lewisville, TX 75057 Tel 972-353-1100; Fax: 972-353-1300; Toll Free: 800-633-1851 E-mail: dallas@majors.com Web site: http://www.majors.com.

Manchester News Co., Inc., P.O. Box 4838, Manchester, NH 03108-4838 (SAN 169-4480).

Manhattan Publishing Co., Div. of U.S. & Europe Bks., Inc., P.O. Box 850, Croton-on-Hudson, NY 10520 (SAN 113-7476) Tel 914-271-5194; Fax: 914-271-5856 Web site: http://www.manhattanpublishing.com.

Manitowoc News Agency, 907 S. Eighth St., Manitowoc, WI 54220 (SAN 159-9046).

Manning's Bks. & Prints, 580M Crespi Dr., Pacifica, CA 94044 (SAN 157-5384) Fax: 650-355-1851 E-mail: manningsbks@aol.com Web site: http://www.printsoldandrare.com.

Many Feathers Bks. & Maps, 2626 W. Indian School Rd., Phoenix, AZ 85017 (SAN 158-8877) Tel 602-266-1043; Toll Free: 800-279-7652.

Marco Bk. Distributors, *(0-88298)* P.O. Box 30108, Brooklyn, NY 11203-0108 (SAN 169-5142) Tel 718-774-0750; Fax: 718-774-0380; Toll Free: 800-842-4234.

MAR*CO Products, Inc., *(1-57543; 1-884063)* Orders Addr.: 1443 Old York Rd., Warminster, PA 18974 Tel 215-956-0313; Fax: 215-956-9041; Toll Free: 800-448-2197 E-mail: csfunk@marcoproducts.com; marcoproducts@comcast.net Web site: http://www.store.yahoo.com/marcoproducts; http://www.marcoproducts.com.

Marcus Wholesale, P.O. Box 1618, R49 E. Hwy. 4, Murphys, CA 95247 (SAN 185-0296).

Mardelva News Co., Inc., 8999 Ocean Hwy., Delmar, MD 21875 (SAN 169-3247) Tel 410-742-8613; Fax: 410-742-2616.

Marshall-Mangold Distribution Co., Inc., 4805 Nelson Ave., Baltimore, MD 21215-2507 (SAN 169-3115) Toll Free: 800-972-2665.

Martin's, *See* **Green Pastures Pr.**

Maruzen International Co., Ltd., 1200 Harbor Blvd., 10th Flr., Weehawken, NJ 07087 (SAN 630-6012) Tel 201-865-4400; Fax: 201-865-4845.

Marvin Law Bk., 11020 27th Ave., S., Burnsville, MN 55337 (SAN 163-898X) Tel 612-644-2236.

Matthews Medical Bk. Co., Four Sperry Rd., Fairfield, NJ 07004 (SAN 169-4316) Tel 973-276-7991; Fax: 973-276-7994.

Maughan, Graham, *See* **Maughan, Graham Publishing Co.**

Maughan, Graham Publishing Co., 50 E. 500, S., Provo, UT 84601-3203 (SAN 110-3903) Tel 801-377-3335; Toll Free: 800-234-3335.

Maus Tales, 77-490 Loma Vista, La Quinta, CA 92253 Fax: 760-564-6669 E-mail: maustales@aol.com.

Maverick Distributors, *(1-884646)* Orders Addr.: Drawer 7289, Bend, OR 97708 (SAN 298-3222) Tel 541-382-2728; Fax: 541-382-8444; Toll Free: 800-333-8046.

Maxwell Scientific International, Inc., *(0-8277)* Div. of Pergamon Pr., Inc., 1345 Ave. of the Americas, No. 1036C, New York, NY 10105-0302 (SAN 169-524X) Tel 914-592-9141.

MBI Distribution Services, *(0-7603; 0-87938; 0-912612; 1-85010)* Div. of MBI Publishing Co. LLC, Orders Addr.: 729 Prospect Ave., Osceola, WI 54020 (SAN 169-9164) Tel 715-294-3345; Fax: 715-294-4448; Toll Free: 800-458-0454; Edit Addr.: 380 Jackson St., Suite 200, Saint Paul, MN 55101-3885 Tel 651-287-5000; Fax: 651-287-5001 E-mail: mbibks@win.bright.net Web site: http://www.motorbooks.com.

MBS Textbook Exchange, Inc., Orders Addr.: 2711 W. Ash, Columbia, MO 65203-4613 (SAN 140-7015) Tel 573-445-2243; Fax: 573-446-5254; Toll Free: 800-325-0929 (orders); 800-325-0530 (customer service) Web site: http://www.mbsbooks.com.

McCaslin, Boyce, 3 Greenbriar Dr., Saint Louis, MO 63124-1819 (SAN 110-8298).

McCoy Church Goods, 1010 Howard Ave., San Mateo, CA 94401 (SAN 107-2315) Tel 415-342-0924.

McCrory's Books, *See* **McCrory's Wholesale Bks.**

McCrory's Wholesale Bks., Orders Addr.: P.O. Box 2032, Alexandria, LA 71301 (SAN 108-5999); Edit Addr.: 1808 Rapides Ave., Alexandria, LA 71301.

McGraw-Hill Cos., The, *(0-02; 0-07)* 6480 Jimmy Carter Blvd., Norcross, GA 30071-1701 (SAN 254-881X) Tel 614-755-5637; Fax: 614-755-5611; Orders Addr.: 860 Taylor Station Rd., Blacklick, OH 43004-0545 (SAN 200-254X) Fax: 614-755-5645; Toll Free: 800-338-3987 (college); 800-525-5003 (subscriptions); 800-352-3566 (books - US/Canada orders); 800-722-4726 (orders & customer service); P.O. Box 545, Blacklick, OH 43004-0545 Fax: 614-759-3759; Toll Free: 877-833-5524; a/o General Customer Service, P.O. Box 182604, Columbus, OH 43272 Fax: 614-759-3759; Toll Free: 877-833-5524 E-mail: customer.service@mcgraw-hill.com Web site: http://www.ebooks.mcgraw-hill.com/; http://www.mcgraw-hill.com.

McGraw-Hill Osborne, *(0-07; 0-88134; 0-931988)* Div. of The McGraw-Hill Professional, 2100 Powell St., 10th Flr., Emeryville, CA 94608 (SAN 274-3450) Tel 510-596-6600; Fax: 510-420-7740; Toll Free: 800-227-0900 E-mail: customer.service@mcgraw-hill.com Web site: http://www.osborne.com.

McGraw-Hill Primis Custom Publishing, *(0-390)* Div. of McGraw-Hill Higher Education, 148 Princeton-Hightstown Rd., Hightstown, NJ 08520-1450 Tel 609-426-5721; Toll Free: 800-962-9342.

McGraw-Hill Trade, *(0-07; 0-658; 0-8442)* Div. of McGraw-Hill Professional, Orders Addr.: P.O. Box 545, Blacklick, OH 43004-0545 Tel 800-722-4726; Fax: 614-755-5645; Edit Addr.: 2 Penn Plaza, New York, NY 10121 Tel 212-904-2000 Web site: http://www.books.mcgraw-hill.com.

McGraw-Hill/Contemporary, *(0-658; 0-8092; 0-8325; 0-8442; 0-88499; 0-89061; 0-913327; 0-940279; 0-941263; 0-9630646; 1-56626; 1-56943; 1-57028)* Div. of McGraw-Hill Higher Education, 4255 W. Touhy Ave., Lincolnwood, IL 60712 (SAN 169-2208) Tel 847-679-5500; Fax: 847-679-2494; Toll Free Fax: 800-998-3103; Toll Free: 800-323-4900 E-mail: c_patton-vanbuskirk@mcgraw-hill.com; ntcpub@tribune.com Web site: http://www.ntc-cb.com.

McKay, David Co., Inc., *(0-679; 0-88326; 0-89440)* Subs. of Random Hse., Inc., Orders Addr.: 400 Hahn Rd., Westminster, MD 21157 Tel 410-848-1900; Toll Free: 800-733-3000 (orders only); Edit Addr.: 201 E. 50th St., MD 4-6, New York, NY 10022 (SAN 200-240X) Tel 212-751-2600; Fax: 212-872-8026.

McKnight Sales Co., P.O. Box 4138, Pittsburgh, PA 15202 (SAN 169-7587) Tel 412-761-4443; Fax: 412-761-0122; Toll Free: 800-208-8078 E-mail: sales@mscmags.com Web site: http://www.mscmags.com.

McLemore, Hollern & Assocs., Orders Addr.: 3538 Maple Park Dr., Kingwood, TX 77339 Tel 281-360-5204.

Meany, P.D. Pubs., *(0-88835)* 825 E. Roosevelt Rd., Unit 447, Lombard, IL 60148 Tel 905-804-0512; Fax: 905-804-0513 E-mail: mbooks@interlog.com Web site: http://www.interlog.com/~mbooks/.

Medcom/Trainex, *(0-8463)* Orders Addr.: P.O. Box 6003, Cypress, CA 90630-0003 (SAN 205-4515) Fax: 714-898-4852; Toll Free: 800-877-1443 (customer service); Edit Addr.: 6060 Phyllis Dr., Cypress, CA 90630 Tel 714-891-1443 Web site: http://www.medcominc.com.

Medicina Biologica, 2937 NE Flanders St., Portland, OR 97232 (SAN 113-0226) Tel 503-287-6775; Fax: 503-235-3520 E-mail: med_bio@imagina.com.

Mel Bay Pubns., Inc., *(0-7866; 0-87166; 1-56222)* Orders Addr.: Four Industrial Dr., Pacific, MO 63069; Edit Addr.: P.O. Box 66, Pacific, MO 63069-0066 (SAN 657-3630) Tel 636-257-3970; Fax: 636-257-5062; Toll Free: 800-863-5229 E-mail: catalog@melbay.com; email@melbay.com Web site: http://www.melbay.com.

Melton Book Company, Incorporated, *See* **Nelson Direct**

Merced News Co., 1324 Coldwell Ave., Modesto, CA 95350-5702 (SAN 168-9894) Tel 209-722-5791.

Mercedes Book Distributors Corporation, *See* **Mercedes Distribution Ctr., Inc.**

Mercedes Distribution Ctr., Inc., Brooklyn Navy Yard, Bldg. No. 3, Brooklyn, NY 11205 (SAN 169-5150) Tel 718-522-7111; Fax: 718-935-9647; Toll Free: 800-339-4804 E-mail: contact@.mdist.com.

Merkos Pubns., 291 Kingston Ave., Brooklyn, NY 11213 (SAN 631-1040) Tel 718-778-0226; Fax: 718-778-4148.

Merry Thoughts, *(0-88230)* 364 Adams St., Bedford Hills, NY 10507 (SAN 169-5061) Tel 914-241-0447; Fax: 914-241-0247.

Metamorphosis Publishing Company, *See* **Metamorphous Pr., Inc.**

Metamorphous Pr., Inc., *(0-943920; 1-55552)* Orders Addr.: P.O. Box 10616, Portland, OR 97296-0616 (SAN 110-8786) Tel 503-228-4972; Fax: 503-223-9117; Toll Free: 800-937-7771 (orders only) ; Edit Addr.: 2950 NW 29th Ave., Portland, OR 97210 E-mail: metabooks@metamodels.com Web site: htp://www.metamodels.com.

Metro Systems, 3381 Stevens Creek Blvd., Suite 209, San Jose, CA 95117 (SAN 631-1016) Tel 408-247-4050; Fax: 408-247-4236.

Metropolitan News Co., 47-25 34th, Long Island City, NY 11101 (SAN 159-9089) Do not confuse with Metropolitan News Co. in Los Angeles, CA.

Meyer Enterprises, *See* **Western New York Wares, Inc.**

Miami Bks., Inc., 17842 State Rd. 9, Miami, FL 33162 (SAN 106-8997) Tel 305-652-3231.

Miami Valley News Agency, 2127 Old Troy Pike, Dayton, OH 45404 (SAN 169-6718) Fax: 513-233-8544; Toll Free: 800-791-5137.

Michiana News Service, 2232 S. 11th St., Niles, MI 49120 (SAN 110-5051) Tel 616-684-3013; Fax: 616-684-8740.

Michigan Church Supply, P.O. Box 279, Mount Morris, MI 48458-0279 (SAN 184-413X) Toll Free: 800-521-3440.

Michigan State Univ. Pr., *(0-87013; 0-937191)* 1405 S. Harrison Rd. Suite 25, East Lansing, MI 48823 (SAN 202-6295) Tel 517-355-9543; Fax: 517-432-2611 E-mail: msupress@msu.edu Web site: http://www.msupress.msu.edu.

Mickler's Bks., Inc., 61 Alafaya Woods Blvd., No. 197, Oviedo, FL 32765 Tel 407-365-8500; Toll Free Fax: 800-726-0585 E-mail: orders@micklers.com Web site: http://www.micklers.com.

Micklers Floridiana, Incorporated, *See* **Mickler's Bks., Inc.**

Microdistributors International, Inc., *(0-918025)* Subs. of Medcomp Technologies, Inc., 34 Maple Ave., P.O. Box 8, Armonk, NY 10504 (SAN 296-158X) Tel 914-273-6480.

Mid Penn Magazine Agency, 100 Eck Cir., Williamsport, PA 17701 (SAN 169-7692).

Mid South Manufacturing Agency, Incorporated, *See* **Mid-South Magazine Agency, Inc.**

Mid-Cal Periodical Distributors, P.O. Box 245230, Sacramento, CA 95824-5230 (SAN 169-0078).

Middleman, 619 Queen St., W., Toronto, ON M5V 2B7 Tel 416-203-2926; Fax: 416-504-9164.

Midpoint Trade Bks., Inc., Orders Addr.: 1263 Southwest Blvd., Kansas City, KS 66103 (SAN 631-3736) Tel 913-831-2233; Fax: 913-362-7401; Toll Free: 800-742-6139 (consumer orders); Edit Addr.: 27 W. 20th St., No. 1102, New York, NY 10011 (SAN 631-1075) Tel 212-727-0190; Fax: 212-727-0195; P.O. Box 411037, Kansas City, MO 64141-1037 (SAN 253-8539) Tel 913-362-7400; Fax: 913-362-7401
E-mail: midpointny1@aol.com
Web site: http://midpt.com.

Mid-South Magazine Agency, Inc., P.O. Box 4585, Jackson, MS 39296-4585 (SAN 286-0163) Toll Free: 800-748-9444.

Mid-State Periodicals, Inc., P.O. Box 3455, Quincy, IL 62305-3455 Tel 217-222-0833; Fax: 217-222-1256.

Mid-States Distributors, 1201 Sheffler Dr., Chambersburg, PA 17201 (SAN 169-3166) Tel 717-263-2413; Fax: 717-263-7289.

Midtown Auto Bks., 212 Burnet Ave., Syracuse, NY 13203 (SAN 169-6289).

Midwest European Pubns., 915 Foster St., Evanston, IL 60201 (SAN 169-1937) Tel 847-866-6289; Fax: 847-866-6290; Toll Free: 800-380-8919
E-mail: info@mep-eli.com
Web site: http://www.mep-eli.com.

Midwest Library Service, 11443 St. Charles Rock Rd., Bridgeton, MO 63044-2789 (SAN 169-4243) Tel 314-739-3100; Fax: 314-739-1326; Toll Free Fax: 800-962-1009; Toll Free: 800-325-8833
E-mail: hudson@midwestls.com.

Midwest Tape, Orders Addr.: P.O. Box 820, Holland, OH 43528-0820 (SAN 254-9913) Toll Free Fax: 800-444-6645; Toll Free: 800-875-2785
E-mail: randys@midwesttapes.com
Web site: http://www.midwesttapes.com.

MightyWords, Inc., *(1-58895; 0-7173; 1-4036)* 2850 Walsh Ave., Santa Clara, CA 95051 Tel 408-845-0100 ; Fax: 408-845-0425; Toll Free: 877-328-2724
Web site: http://www.mightywords.com.

Mightywords.com, *See* **MightyWords, Inc.**

Military History Assocs., 407B E. Sixth St., No. 200, Austin, TX 78701-3739 (SAN 111-7866).

Miller, Arvid E. Memorial Library Museum, N8510 Moh-He-Con-Nuck Rd., Bowker, WI 54416 Tel 715-793-4270.

Milligan News Co., Inc., 150 N. Autumn St., San Jose, CA 95110 (SAN 169-0272) Tel 408-286-7604; Fax: 408-298-0235; Toll Free: 800-873-2387.

Minerva Science Bookseller, Inc., 175 Fifth Ave., New York, NY 10010 (SAN 286-0171).

Mississippi Library Media & Supply Co., P.O. Box 108, Brandon, MS 39043-0108 (SAN 169-4189) Tel 601-824-1900; Fax: 601-824-1999; Toll Free: 800-257-7566 (in Mississippi).

Mistco, Inc., P.O. Box 694854, Miami, FL 33269 (SAN 630-8384) Tel 305-653-2003; Fax: 305-653-2037; Toll Free: 800-552-0446
E-mail: mistco@worldnet.att.net
Web site: http://www.mistco.com.

Mobile News Co., 1118 14th St., Tuscaloosa, AL 35401-3318 (SAN 168-924X) Tel 334-479-1435.

Modesto News Co., 1324 Coldwell Ave., Modesto, CA 95350-5702 (SAN 168-9908) Tel 209-577-5551.

Montfort Pubns., *(0-910984)* Div. of Montfort Missionaries, 26 S. Saxon Ave., Bay Shore, NY 11706-8993 (SAN 169-5053) Tel 631-665-0726; Fax: 631-665-4349
Web site: http://www.montfortmissionaries.com.

Mook & Blanchard, 546 S. Hofgaarden, La Puente, CA 91744 (SAN 168-9703) Tel 626-968-6424; Fax: 626-968-6877; Toll Free: 800-875-9911
E-mail: mookbook@ix.netcom.com
Web site: http://www.mookandblanchard.com.

Moon Over the Mountain Publishing Company, *See* **Leman Pubns., Inc.**

More, Thomas Assn., 205 W. Monroe St., 5th Flr., Chicago, IL 60606-5097 (SAN 169-1880) Tel 312-609-8880; Toll Free: 800-835-8965.

Morlock News Co., Inc., 496 Duanesburg Rd., Schenectady, NY 12306 (SAN 169-6246).

Morris Publishing, *(0-7392; 0-9631249; 1-57502; 1-885591)* Subs. of Morris Pr. & Office Supplies, 3212 E. Hwy. 30, P.O. Box 2110, Kearney, NE 68847 Tel 308-236-7888; Fax: 308-237-0263; Toll Free: 800-650-7888 Do not confuse with companies with the same or similar name in Sarveta, PA, Plymouth Meeting, PA, Beecher City, IL, Urbana, IL, San Francisco, CA
E-mail: publish@morrispublishing.com; kimmyw414@yahoo.com; snowgers@mcn.org
Web site: http://morrispublishing.com.

Moshy Brothers, Inc., 127 W. 25th St., New York, NY 10001 (SAN 169-5886) Tel 212-255-0613.

Mother Lode Distributing, 17890 Lime Rock Dr., Sonora, CA 95370-8707 (SAN 169-0361).

Motorbooks International Wholesalers & Distributors, *See* **MBI Distribution Services**

Mountain Maid, *See* **Light Messages**

Mountain States News Distributor, P.O. Drawer P, Fort Collins, CO 80522 Tel 970-221-2330; Fax: 970-221-1251.

Mountaineers Bks., The, *(0-89886; 0-916890; 0-938567; 1-59485)* Div. of Mountaineers, Orders Addr.: 1001 SW Klickitat Way, Suite 201, Seattle, WA 98134-1162 (SAN 212-8756) Tel 206-223-6303; Fax: 206-223-6306; Toll Free: 800-568-7604
E-mail: mbooks@mountaineersbooks.org
Web site: http://www.mountaineersbooks.org.

Moznaim Publishing Corp., *(0-940118; 1-885220)* 4304 12th Ave., Brooklyn, NY 11219 (SAN 214-4123) Tel 718-438-7680; Fax: 718-438-1305; Toll Free: 800-364-5118.

Mr. Paperback/Publishers News Co., 6030 Fostoria Ave., Findlay, OH 45840 (SAN 169-393X) Tel 419-424-6774; Fax: 419-420-1805; Toll Free: 800-872-0031.

M-S News Co., Inc., P.O. Box 13278, Wichita, KS 67213-0278 Fax: 316-267-5405.

Mullare News Agency, Inc., P.O. Box 578, Brockton, MA 02401 (SAN 169-3379) Tel 508-580-1000; Fax: 508-586-0968.

Multilingual Bks., Orders Addr.: P.O. Box 440632, Miami, FL 33144 (SAN 169-1155) Tel 305-471-9847 Do not confuse with Multilingual Bks., Seattle, WA.

Mumford Library Bks., Inc., 7847 Bayberry Rd., Jacksonville, FL 32256 (SAN 156-7721) Fax: 904-730-8913; Toll Free: 800-367-3927.

Mumford Library Book Sales, *See* **Mumford Library Bks., Inc.**

Murr's Library Service, 4045 E. Palm Ln., No. 5, Phoenix, AZ 85008-3116 (SAN 107-3222) Fax: 602-273-1217; Toll Free: 888-273-0279.

Music Design, Inc., 4650 N. Port Washington Rd., Milwaukee, WI 53212 (SAN 200-7649) Tel 414-961-8380; Fax: 414-961-8381; Toll Free: 800-862-7232
E-mail: order@musicdesign.com
Web site: http://www.musicdesign.com.

Music Sales Corp., *(0-7119; 0-8256)* Orders Addr.: 445 Bellvale Rd., P.O. Box 572, Chester, NY 10918 (SAN 662-0876) Tel 845-469-2271; Fax: 845-469-7544; Toll Free Fax: 800-345-6842; Toll Free: 800-431-7187; Edit Addr.: 257 Park Ave., S., 20th Flr., New York, NY 10010 (SAN 282-0277) Tel 212-254-2100; Fax: 212-254-2103
Web site: http://www.musicsales.com.

Musicart West, P.O. Box 1900, Orem, UT 84059-1900 (SAN 110-1250) Tel 801-225-0859; Toll Free: 800-950-1900 (orders only).

Mustard Seed Pubns., P.O. Box 1360, San Antonio, TX 78295 Tel 830-216-7244 Do not confuse with companies with the same name in PerryHall, MD, Clearwater, FL
E-mail: goodmarine@aol.com.

MVP Wholesales, 9301 W. Hwy. 290, No. D, Austin, TX 78736-7817 (SAN 630-9550) Tel 512-416-1452; Toll Free: 800-328-7931 (phone/fax).

NACSCORP, Inc., Subs. of National Assn. of College Stores, Orders Addr.: 528 E. Lorain St., Oberlin, OH 44074-1298 (SAN 134-2118) Tel 440-775-7777; Toll Free Fax: 800-344-5059; Toll Free: 800-321-3883 (orders only); 800-458-9303 (backorder status only); 800-334-9882 (support programs/technical support)
E-mail: service@nacscorp.com; orders@nacscorp.com
Web site: http://www.nacscorp.com.

Najarian Music Co., Inc., 269 Lexington St., Waltham, MA 02452 (SAN 169-3344) Tel 781-899-2200; Fax: 781-899-0838.

Napa Book Company, *See* **Napa Children's Bk. Co.**

Napa Children's Bk. Co., 1239 First St., Napa, CA 94559 (SAN 122-2732) Tel 707-224-3893; Fax: 707-224-1212.

National Assn. of the Deaf, *(0-913072)* 814 Thayer Ave., Silver Spring, MD 20910 (SAN 159-4974) Tel 301-587-6282; Fax: 301-587-4873
E-mail: sales@nad.org
Web site: http://www.nad.org.

National Bk. Co., Keystone Industrial Pk., Scranton, PA 18512 Tel 717-346-2020; Toll Free: 800-233-4830 Do not confuse with National Book Company, Portland, OR.

National Bk. Network, Div. of Rowman & Littlefield Pubs., Inc., Orders Addr.: 15200 NBN Way, Blue Ridge Summit, PA 17214 (SAN 630-0065) Tel 717-794-3800; Fax: 717-794-3803; Toll Free Fax: 800-338-4550; Toll Free: 800-462-6420; a/o Les Petriw, 67 Mowat Ave., Suite 241, Toronto, ON M6P 3K3 Tel 416-534-1660; Fax: 416-534-3699; Edit Addr.: 4501 Forbes Blvd., Suite 200, Lanham, MD 20706 Tel 301-459-3366; Fax: 301-429-5747
E-mail: lpetriw@nbnbooks.com
Web site: http://www.nbnbooks.com.

National Catholic Reading Distributor, 997 Macarthur Blvd., Mahwah, NJ 07430 (SAN 169-4855) Tel 201-825-7300; Fax: 201-825-8345; Toll Free: 800-218-1903
E-mail: paulistp@pipeline.com.

National Health Federation, Box 688, Monrovia, CA 91016 (SAN 227-9266) Tel 626-357-2181; Fax: 818-303-0642
E-mail: nhf@earthlink.net
Web site: http://www.healthfreedom.net.

National Learning Corp., *(0-8293; 0-8373)* 212 Michael Dr., Syosset, NY 11791 (SAN 206-8869) Tel 516-921-8888; Fax: 516-921-8743; Toll Free: 800-645-6337
E-mail: sales@passbooks.com.

National Magazine Service, Orders Addr.: P.O. Box 834, Mars, PA 16046 (SAN 169-7595); Edit Addr.: 535 Linden Way, Pittsburgh, PA 15202 Tel 412-898-0001.

National Organization Service, Inc., 4515 Fleur Dr., Suite 301, Des Moines, IA 50321-2369 (SAN 107-1548) Fax: 515-256-8028; Toll Free: 800-747-3032.

National Rifle Assn., *(0-935998)* a/o Office of the General Counsel, 11250 Waples Mill Rd., Fairfax, VA 22030 (SAN 213-859X) Tel 703-267-1269; Fax: 703-267-3985; Toll Free: 800-672-3888.

National Sales, Inc., 1818 W. 2300 South, Salt Lake City, UT 84119 (SAN 159-9127) Tel 801-972-2300; Fax: 801-972-2883.

National Technical Information Service, U.S. Dept. of Commerce, *(0-934213)* Orders Addr.: 5285 Port Royal Rd., Springfield, VA 22161 (SAN 205-7255) Tel 703-605-6000; Fax: 703-605-6900; Toll Free: 800-553-6847
E-mail: orders@ntis.gov; info@ntis.gov
Web site: http://wnc.fedworld.gov; http://www.ntis.gov.

National Video Resources, Inc., *(1-884188)* 73 Spring St., Suite 606, New York, NY 10012 Tel 212-274-8080; Fax: 212-274-8081
Web site: http://www.nvr.org.

Native Bks., P.O. Box 37095, Honolulu, HI 96837 (SAN 631-1121) Tel 808-845-8949; Fax: 808-847-6637; Toll Free: 800-887-7751.

Naval Institute Pr., *(0-87021; 1-55750; 1-59114)* Orders Addr.: 2062 Generals Hwy., Annapolis, MD 21401 (SAN 662-0930) Tel 410-268-6110; Fax: 410-571-1703; Toll Free: 800-233-8764; Edit Addr.: 291 Wood Rd., Beach Hall, Annapolis, MD 21402-5034 (SAN 202-9006)
E-mail: psappington@usni.org
Web site: http://www.navalinstitute.org.

Neighborhood Periodical Club, Inc., 653 Northland Blvd., Cincinnati, OH 45240-3215 (SAN 285-9262) Tel 513-851-8600; Fax: 513-851-8695.

Nelson Direct, P.O. Box 140300, Nashville, TN 37214 (SAN 169-8133) Toll Free: 800-441-0511 (sales); 800-933-9673
E-mail: csalazar@thomasnelson.com
Web site: http://www.nelsondirect.com.

Nelson News, Inc., P.O. Box 27007, Omaha, NE 68127-0007 (SAN 169-443X) Tel 402-734-3333; Fax: 402-731-0516.

Nelson, Thomas Inc., *(0-7852; 0-8407; 0-8499; 0-86605; 0-89840; 0-918956; 1-4003)* Orders Addr.: P.O. Box 141000, Nashville, TN 37214-1000 (SAN 209-3820) Fax: 615-902-1866; Toll Free: 800-251-4000; Edit Addr.: 501 Nelson Pl., Nashville, TN 37214
E-mail: thomasnelson.com
Web site: http://www.thomasnelson.com.

Wholesalers & Distributors

Nelson, Tommy, *(0-7852; 0-8407; 0-8499; 1-4003)* Div. of Thomas Nelson, Inc., Orders Addr.: P.O. Box 141000, Nashville, TN 37214 Fax: 615-902-3330; Edit Addr.: 501 Nelson Pl., Nashville, TN 37214 Tel 615-889-9000; Toll Free: 800-251-4000
E-mail: mduncan@tommynelson.com
Web site: http://www.tommynelson.com.

Ner Tamid Bk. Distributors, P.O. Box 10401, Riviera Beach, FL 33419-0401 (SAN 169-135X) Tel 561-686-9095.

Net Productions, 210 Elm Cir., Colorado Springs, CO 80906-3348 (SAN 159-9143).

netLibrary, Inc., *(0-585)* 4888 Pearl East Cir., Boulder, CO 80301 (SAN 253-9497) Tel 303-415-2548; Fax: 303-381-7000; 303-381-8999; Toll Free: 800-413-4557
E-mail: mgilbert@netlibrary.com
Web site: http://www.netlibrary.com.

New Alexandrian Bookstore, 110 N Cayuga St., Ithaca, NY 14850-4331 (SAN 159-4958) Tel 607-272-1163.

New Concepts Bks. & Tapes Distributors, Orders Addr.: P.O. Box 55068, Houston, TX 77255 (SAN 114-2682) Tel 713-465-7736; Fax: 713-465-7106; Toll Free: 800-842-4807; Edit Addr.: 9722 Pine Lake, Houston, TX 77055 (SAN 630-7531).

New England Bk. Reps., Orders Addr.: 35 Dalton Rd., Belmont, MA 02478 Tel 617-484-4659.

New England Bk. Service, Inc., 457 Pond Rd., North Ferrisburg, VT 05493 (SAN 170-0952) Tel 802-453-7637; Fax: 802-453-7642; Toll Free: 800-356-5772
E-mail: nebs@together.net.

New England Mobile Bk. Fair, 82 Needham St., P.O. Box 610159, Newton Highlands, MA 02461 (SAN 169-3530) Tel 617-527-5817; Fax: 617-527-0113.

New Era Pubns., Inc., *(0-939830)* P.O. Box 130109, Ann Arbor, MI 48113-0109 (SAN 111-8757) Tel 734-663-1929 Do not confuse with New Era Pubns. in Happy Camp, CA.

New Jersey Bk. Agency, Orders Addr.: P.O. Box 144, Morris Plains, NJ 07950 (SAN 106-861X) Tel 973-267-7093; Fax: 973-292-3177; Edit Addr.: 59 Leamoor Dr., Morris Plains, NJ 07950 (SAN 243-2307) Tel 973-267-7093; 908-204-9899.

New Jersey Bks., Inc., 59 Market St., Newark, NJ 07102 Tel 973-624-8070; Toll Free: 800-772-3678.

New Leaf Distributing Co., Inc., *(0-9627209)* Div. of Al-Wali Corp., 401 Thornton Rd., Lithia Springs, GA 30122-1557 (SAN 169-1449) Tel 770-948-7845; Fax: 770-944-2313; Toll Free Fax: 800-326-1066; Toll Free: 800-326-2665
E-mail: NewLeaf@NewLeaf-dist.com
Web site: http://www.NewLeaf-dist.com.

New Life Foundation, *(0-911203)* P.O. Box 2230, Pine, AZ 85544-2230 (SAN 170-3986) Tel 928-476-3224; Fax: 928-476-4743; Toll Free: 800-293-3377 (wholesale only)
E-mail: info@anewlife.org
Web site: http://www.anewlife.org.

New London News Co., 25 Westwood Ave., New London, CT 06320-2726 (SAN 169-0752).

New World Library, *(0-931432; 0-945934; 1-57731; 1-880032)* 14 Pamaron Way, Novato, CA 94949 (SAN 211-8777) Tel 415-884-2100; Fax: 415-884-2199; Toll Free: 800-972-6657 (retail orders only) Do not confuse with New World Library Publishing Co., Los Altos, CA
E-mail: escort@nwlib.com
Web site: http://www.newworldlibrary.com.

New World Pubns., Inc., *(1-878348)* 1861 Cornell Rd., Jacksonville, FL 32207 (SAN 298-4768) Tel 904-737-6558; Fax: 904-731-1188; Toll Free: 800-737-6558
E-mail: orders@fishid.com; eric@fishid.com
Web site: http://www.fishid.com.

New World Resource Ctr., 2600 W. Fullerton Ave., Chicago, IL 60647-3008 (SAN 169-1848).

New York Periodical Distributors, P.O. Box 29, Massena, NY 13662-0029 (SAN 169-6149).

Newborn Enterprises, Inc., P.O. Box 1713, Altoona, PA 16603 (SAN 169-7242) Tel 814-944-3593; Fax: 814-944-1881; Toll Free: 800-227-0285 (in Pennsylvania).

News Group - Illinois, The, 1301 SW Washington St., Peoria, IL 61602 (SAN 169-216X) Tel 309-673-4549; Fax: 309-673-8883.

News Group, The, 325 W. Potter Dr., Anchorage, AK 99518 (SAN 168-9274) Tel 907-563-3251; Fax: 907-261-8523 Do not confuse with companies with the same name in Columbus, SC, Winston-Salem, NC, Elizabeth, NC.

News Supply Co., 216 S. La Huerta Cir., Carlsbad, NM 88220-9620 (SAN 159-9151).

Newsdealers Supply Co., Inc., P.O. Box 3516, Tallahassee, FL 32315-3516.

NEWSouth Distributors, P.O. Box 61297, Jacksonville, FL 32236-1297 (SAN 159-8732).

Newsstand Distributors, 155 W. 14th St., Ogden, UT 84404 (SAN 169-8494) Fax: 810-621-7336; Toll Free: 800-283-6247; 800-231-4834 (in Utah).

Ng Hing Kee, 648 Jackson St., San Francisco, CA 94133 (SAN 107-1084) Tel 415-781-8330; Fax: 415-397-9766.

Niagara County News, 70 Nicholls St., Lockport, NY 14094 (SAN 169-541X) Tel 716-433-6466.

Noelke, Carl B., 529 Main, Box 563, La Crosse, WI 54602 (SAN 111-8315) Tel 608-782-8544.

Nonagon, 1556 Douglas Dr., El Cerrito, CA 94530 (SAN 654-0503) Tel 510-237-5290.

Nor-Cal News Co., 2040 Petaluma Blvd., P.O. Box 2508, Petaluma, CA 94953 (SAN 169-0035) Tel 707-763-2606; Fax: 707-763-3905.

North American Bk. Distributors, P.O. Box 510, Hamburg, MI 48139 (SAN 630-4680) Tel 810-231-3728.

North Carolina News Co., P.O. Box 1051, Durham, NC 27702-1051 Tel 919-682-5779.

North Carolina Schl. Bk. Depository, Inc., P.O. Box 950, Raleigh, NC 27602-0950 (SAN 169-6467) Tel 919-833-6615.

North Central Bk. Distributors, N57 W13636 Carmen Ave., Menomonee Falls, WI 53051 (SAN 173-5195) Tel 414-781-3299; Fax: 414-781-4432; Toll Free: 800-966-3299.

North Country Bks., Inc., *(0-925168; 0-932052; 0-9601158; 1-59531)* 311 Turner St., Utica, NY 13501 (SAN 110-828X) Tel 315-735-4877
E-mail: ncbooks@adelphia.net.

North Shore Distributors, 1200 N. Branch, Chicago, IL 60622 (SAN 169-2275).

North Shore News Co., Inc., 150 Blossom St., Lynn, MA 01902 (SAN 169-3492).

North Texas Periodicals, Inc., Orders Addr.: P.O. Box 3823, Lubbock, TX 79452 Tel 806-745-6000; Fax: 806-745-7028; Edit Addr.: 118 E. 70th St., Lubbock, TX 79404
E-mail: ntp@hts-online_net.

Northern News Co., P.O. Box 467, Petoskey, MI 49770-0467 (SAN 169-3964) Toll Free: 800-632-7138 (Michigan only).

Northern Schl. Supply Co., P.O. Box 2627, Fargo, ND 58108 (SAN 169-6548) Fax: 800-891-5836.

Northern Sun, 2916 E. Lake St., Minneapolis, MN 55406 (SAN 249-9290) Tel 612-729-2001; Fax: 612-729-0149; Toll Free: 800-258-8579.

Northern Sun Merchandising, *See* **Northern Sun**

Northwest News, 1560 NE First St., No. 13, Bend, OR 97701 (SAN 111-8587) Tel 541-382-6065; 3100 Merriman Rd., Medford, OR 97501 Tel 541-779-5225.

Northwest News Co., Inc., Orders Addr.: P.O. Box 4965, Missoula, MT 59806 (SAN 660-9406); Edit Addr.: 1701 Ranklin St., Missoula, MT 59802-1629 (SAN 169-4391) Tel 406-721-7801.

Norton News Agency, 801 Cedar Cross Rd., Dubuque, IA 52003-7735 (SAN 169-2631); 1467 Service Dr., Winona, MN 55987 (SAN 156-4889).

Norton, W. W. & Co., Inc., *(0-393; 0-920256)* Orders Addr.: 800 Keystone Industrial Pk., Scranton, PA 18512 (SAN 157-1869) Tel 570-346-2020; Fax: 570-346-1442; Toll Free Fax: 800-548-6515; Toll Free: 800-233-4830 (book orders only); Edit Addr.: 500 Fifth Ave., New York, NY 10110-0017 (SAN 202-5795) Tel 212-354-5500; Fax: 212-869-0856; Toll Free: 800-223-2584
E-mail: webmaster@wwnorton.com; Tworrell@wwnorton.com
Web site: http://www.wwnorton.com/trade; http://www.wwnorton.com.

NTC/Contemporary Publishing Company, *See* **McGraw-Hill/Contemporary**

Nueces News Agency, P.O. Box 2768, 209 N. Padre Island Dr., Corpus Christi, TX 78403 (SAN 169-8079).

Nueva Vida Distributors, 4300 Montana Ave., El Paso, TX 79903-4503 (SAN 107-8615) Tel 915-565-6215; Fax: 915-565-1722.

Nutri-Bks. Corp., Div. of Royal Pubns., Inc., 790 W. Tennessee Ave., P.O. Box 5793, Denver, CO 80223 Tel 303-778-8383; Fax: 303-744-9383; Toll Free: 800-279-2048 (orders only).

NuvoMedia, *(0-9673181)* 900 Island Dr. # 200, Redwood City, CA 94065-5150
E-mail: publish@nuvomedia.com
Web site: http://www.rocket-ebook.com.

Oak Knoll Pr., *(0-938768; 1-884718; 1-58456)* 310 Delaware St., New Castle, DE 19720 (SAN 216-2776) Tel 302-328-7232; Fax: 302-328-7274; Toll Free: 800-996-2556 Do not confuse with Oak Knoll Press in Hardy, VA
E-mail: oakknoll@oakknoll.com
Web site: http://www.oakknoll.com.

Oakwood Pubns., *(0-9618545; 1-879038; 1-891295)* Orders Addr.: P.O. Box 1128, Torrance, CA 90505 (SAN 668-1557) Tel 310-378-9245; Fax: 310-378-6782; Toll Free Fax: 800-903-4266; Toll Free: 800-747-9245; Edit Addr.: 3827 Bluff St., Torrance, CA 90505-6359 (SAN 668-1565)
E-mail: oakwoodpub@juno.com.

Ohio Periodical Distributors, P.O. Box 145449, Cincinnati, OH 45250-5449 (SAN 169-6904) Fax: 513-853-6245; Toll Free: 800-777-2216.

Oil City News Co., 112 Innis St., Oil City, PA 16301-2930 (SAN 169-7501).

Ollis Bk. Corp., Orders Addr.: P.O. Box 258, Steger, IL 60475 (SAN 658-1323); Edit Addr.: 28 E. 35th St., Steger, IL 60475 (SAN 169-2224) Tel 312-755-5151; Fax: 708-755-5153; Toll Free: 800-323-0343.

Olson News Agency, P.O. Box 129, Ishpeming, MI 49849 (SAN 169-3832).

Omnibooks, 456 Vista Del Mar Dr., Aptos, CA 95003-4832 (SAN 168-9487) Tel 408-688-4098; Toll Free: 800-626-6671.

Onondaga News Agency, 474 E. Brighton Ave., Syracuse, NY 13210 (SAN 169-6297) Tel 315-475-3121.

Options Unlimited, 550 Swan Creek Ct., Suwanee, GA 30174 (SAN 631-3949) Tel 770-237-3282 Do not confuse with Options Unlimited, Inc., Green Bay, WI.

Orange News Company, *See* **Anderson News, LLC**

Orbit Bks. Corp., 43 Timberline Dr., Poughkeepsie, NY 12603 (SAN 169-6157) Tel 914-462-5653; Fax: 914-462-8409.

Orca Bk. Pubs., *(0-920501; 1-55143)* Orders Addr.: P.O. Box 468, Custer, WA 98240-0468 (SAN 630-9674) Tel 250-380-1229; Fax: 250-380-1892; Toll Free: 800-210-5277
E-mail: melanie@orcabook.com; mcolgan@orcabook.com
Web site: http://www.orcabook.com.

Osborne Enterprises Publishing, *(0-932117)* P.O. Box 255, Port Townsend, WA 98368 (SAN 242-7567) Tel 360-385-1200; Fax: 360-385-6572; Toll Free: 800-246-3255 (orders only)
E-mail: jpo@olympus.net
Web site: http://www.jerryosborne.com.

Osborne/McGraw-Hill, *See* **McGraw-Hill Osborne**

Osiander Bk. Trade, 7483H Candlewood Rd., Hanover, MD 21076-3102 (SAN 130-0970).

Outbooks, Incorporated, *See* **Vistabooks**

Outdoorsman, The, Orders Addr.: P.O. Box 268, Boston, MA 02134 (SAN 169-3352).

Oxford Univ. Pr., Inc., *(0-19; 0-904147; 0-947946; 1-85221)* Orders Addr.: 2001 Evans Rd., Cary, NC 27513 (SAN 202-5892) Tel 919-677-0977 (general voice); Fax: 919-677-1303 (customer service); Toll Free: 800-445-9714 (customer service - inquiry); 800-451-7556 (customer service - orders); Edit Addr.: 198 Madison Ave., New York, NY 10016-4314 (SAN 202-5884) Tel 212-726-6000 (general voice); Fax: 212-726-6440 (general fax)
E-mail: orders@oup-usa.org; custserv@oup-usa.org
Web site: http://www.oup-usa.org.

Ozark Magazine Distributing, Incorporated, *See* **Ozark News Distributor, Inc.**

Ozark News Agency, Inc., P.O. Box 1150, Fayetteville, AR 72702.

Ozark News Distributor, Inc., 1630 N. Eldon, Springfield, MO 65803 (SAN 169-4332) Tel 417-862-9224; Fax: 417-862-6642; Toll Free: 800-743-0380.

P & G Wholesale, P.O. Box 1548, Fargo, ND 58102 (SAN 156-4536).

P. D. Music Headquarters, Inc., Orders Addr.: P.O. Box 252, New York, NY 10014 (SAN 282-5880) Tel 212-242-5322.

Pacific Learning, Inc., *(1-59055)* 15342 Graham St., Huntington Beach, CA 92649-1111 Fax: 714-895-5087; Toll Free: 800-279-0737
E-mail: rob.lang@pacificlearning.com
Web site: http://www.guidedreading.com.

Pacific Magazine-Bk. Wholesaler, 1515 NW 51st St., Seattle, WA 98107 (SAN 274-3884) Tel 206-789-5333.

Pacific Periodical Services, LLC, *See* **Anderson News - Tacoma**

Pacific Trade Group, 68-309 Crozier Dr., Waialua, HI 96791 (SAN 169-1635) Tel 808-636-2300; Fax: 808-636-2301.

PACT Hse. Publishing, *(0-88076)* Orders Addr.: P.O. Box 609, Lewisville, NC 27023 (SAN 239-9407) Tel 336-712-3244; Fax: 336-712-3243; Toll Free Fax: 800-452-7526 (International); Toll Free: 800-334-2014; Edit Addr.: 1310 Lewisville-Clemmons Rd., Lewisville, NC 27023 Do not confuse with Kaplan Pr. in Chicago, IL
E-mail: info@kaplanco.com
Web site: http://www.kaplanco.com.

Paladin Pr., *(0-87364; 1-58160; 1-891268)* Orders Addr.: c/o Gunbarrel Tech Ctr., 7077 Winchester Cir., Boulder, CO 80301 (SAN 662-1066) Tel 303-443-7250; Fax: 303-442-8741; Toll Free: 800-392-2400 (Credit Card Orders Only)
E-mail: sales@paladin-press.com; service@paladin-press.com; editorial@paladin-press.com
Web site: http://www.flying-machines.com; http://www.sycamoreisland.com; http:// www.paladin-press.com.

Palgrave, *See* **Palgrave Macmillan**

Palgrave Macmillan, *(0-312; 0-333; 1-4039)* Div. of Saint Martin's Press, LLC, Orders Addr.: 16365 James Madison Hwy., Gordonsville, VA 22942-8501 Toll Free Fax: 800-672-2054; Toll Free: 888-330-8477; Edit Addr.: 175 Fifth Ave., New York, NY 10010 Tel 212-982-9300; Fax: 212-777-6359; Toll Free: 800-221-7945
Web site: http://www.palgrave.com.

Palmer News Co., Inc., 1050 Republican, P.O. Box 1400, Topeka, KS 66601 Tel 913-234-6679; Fax: 913-234-6338.

Palmer News, Inc., 9605 Dice Ln., Lenexa, KS 66215 Tel 913-541-8600; Fax: 913-541-9413
E-mail: palmerco@oni.com.

Palmetto News Co., 200 Sunbelt Ct., Greer, SC 29650-9349.

Palmyra Publishing Co., *(0-9666627)* P.O. Box 1164, Sioux Falls, SD 57101-1164 Tel 605-330-2707; Fax: 605-330-6009
E-mail: alyajim@sd.cybernex.net.

Pan American Publishing, Inc., *(1-889867)* 420 E. Ohio St., Suite 4-F, Chicago, IL 60611-3355 (SAN 299-1977) Tel 773-404-7282.

Pan Asia Pubns. (USA), Inc., *(1-57227)* 29564 Union City Blvd., Union City, CA 94587 (SAN 173-685X) Tel 510-475-1185; Fax: 510-475-1489; Toll Free: 800-909-8088
E-mail: sales@panap.com
Web site: http://www.panap.com.

Paperback Books, Incorporated, *See* **Book Distribution Ctr., Inc.**

Paperbacks for Educators, *(0-9702376)* 426 W. Front St., Washington, MO 63090 (SAN 103-3379) Tel 636-239-1999; Fax: 636-239-4515; Toll Free Fax: 800-514-7323; Toll Free: 800-227-2591
E-mail: paperbacks@mail.usmo.com
Web site: http://www.any-book-in-print.com.

Parks & History Assn., *(1-887878)* 126 Raleigh St., SE, Washington, DC 20032 (SAN 122-4670) Tel 202-472-3083; Fax: 202-755-0469.

Parkwest Pubns., Inc., *(0-88186)* 451 Communipaw Ave., Jersey City, NJ 07304 (SAN 264-6846) Tel 201-432-3257; Fax: 201-432-3708
E-mail: parkwest@parkwestpubs.com; info@parkwestpubs.com
Web site: http://www.parkwestpubs.com.

Parliament News Co., Inc., P.O. Box 910, Santa Clarita, CA 91380-9010 (SAN 168-9924).

Parnassus Bk. Distributors, 200 Academy Way, Columbia, SC 29206-1445 (SAN 631-0680) Tel 803-782-7748; Toll Free: 800-782-7760.

Partners Bk. Distributing, Inc., Orders Addr.: P.O. Box 580, Holt, MI 48842; Edit Addr.: 2325 Jarco Dr., Holt, MI 48842 (SAN 630-4559) Tel 517-694-3205; Toll Free: 800-336-3137 (orders).

Partners Book Distributing, Incorporated, *See* **Partners Pubs. Group, Inc.**

Partners Pubs. Group, Inc., Orders Addr.: P.O. Box 580, Holt, MI 48842 Tel 517-694-3205; Fax: 517-694-0617; Toll Free: 800-336-3137; Edit Addr.: 2325 Jarco Dr., Holt, MI 48842 (SAN 631-3418).

Partners/West, 1901 Raymond Ave., SW, Suite C, Renton, WA 98055 (SAN 631-421X) Tel 425-227-8486; Fax: 425-204-1448; Toll Free: 800-563-2385.

Pathfinder Pr., *(0-87348; 0-913460)* Orders Addr.: P.O. Box 162767, Atlanta, GA 30321 Tel 404-769-0600; Fax: 707-667-1411; Edit Addr.: 4794 Clark Howell Hwy., Suite B-5, College Park, GA 30349; 545 E. Eighth Ave., New York, NY 10018 (SAN 202-5906) Do not confuse with companies with the same or similar names in Alameda, CA, Battle Ground, WA, Elicott City, MD
E-mail: orders@pathfinderpress.com
Web site: http://www.pathfinderpress.com.

Pathway Bk. Service, Div. of MLES, Inc., Orders Addr.: P.O. Box 89, Gilsum, NH 03448 Toll Free: 800-345-6665; Edit Addr.: 4 White Brook Rd., Gilsum, NH 03448 (SAN 170-0545) Tel 603-357-0236; Fax: 603-357-2073
E-mail: pbs@pathwaybook.com
Web site: http://www.pathwaybook.com.

Paul & Co. Pubs. Consortium, Inc., Div. of Independent Publishers Group, Orders Addr.: 814 N. Franklin St., Chicago, IL 60610 Tel 312-337-0747; Fax: 312-337-5985; Toll Free: 800-888-4741; Edit Addr.: P.O. Box 442, Concord, MA 01742 (SAN 630-5318)
E-mail: frontdesk@ipgbook.com
Web site: http://www.ipgbook.com.

Paulsen, G. Co., 27 Sheep Davis Rd., Pembroke, NH 03275 (SAN 169-4499) Tel 603-225-9787.

PBD, Inc., 1650 Bluegrass Lakes Pkwy., Alpharetta, GA 30004 (SAN 126-6039) Tel 770-442-8633; Fax: 770-442-9742
Web site: http://www.pbd.com.

PCI Educational Publishing, *(1-884074; 1-58804)* 12029 Warfield, San Antonio, TX 78216-3231 Tel 210-377-1999; Fax: 210-377-1121; Toll Free Fax: 888-259-8284; Toll Free: 800-594-4263
E-mail: lboulet@pcicatalog.com
Web site: http://www.pcicatalog.com.

Pearson Education, *(0-582)* Orders Addr.: 200 Old Tappan Rd., Old Tappan, NJ 07675 (SAN 200-2175) Tel 201-767-5152; Toll Free Fax: 800-922-0579; 800-445-6991; Toll Free: 800-428-5331; Edit Addr.: One Lake St., Upper Saddle River, NJ 07458 Tel 201-236-7000; Fax: 201-236-6549
E-mail: eugene.wang@pearsonptr.com; carole.wilkins@phschool.com; emily.mcgee@pearson.ed.com; joann.kebrdle@pearsoned.com
Web site: http://www.pearsoned.com.

Pee Dee News Co., 2321 Lawrens Cir., Florence, SC 29501-9408.

Pegram, Christine, 1901 Upper Cove Terr., Sarasota, FL 33581 (SAN 110-0254) Tel 941-921-2467.

Pekin News Agency, 1637 Monroe St., Madison, WI 53711-2021 (SAN 169-2151).

Pen Notes, Inc., *(0-939564)* 61 Bennington Ave., Freeport, NY 11520 (SAN 107-3621) Tel 516-868-5753; Fax: 516-868-8441
E-mail: pennotes@worldnet.att.net.

Penguin Group (USA) Inc., *(0-14)* Orders Addr.: 405 Murray Hill Pkwy., East Rutherford, NJ 07073-2136 (SAN 282-5074) Fax: 201-933-2903 (customer service); Toll Free Fax: 800-227-9604; Toll Free: 800-788-6262 (individual consumer sales); 800-526-0275 (reseller sales); 800-631-8571 (reseller customer service); Edit Addr.: 375 Hudson St., New York, NY 10014 Tel 212-366-2000; Fax: 212-366-2666
E-mail: pmccarthy@penguinputman.com
Web site: http://www.penguinputnam.com.

Penguin Putnam, Incorporated, *See* **Penguin Group (USA) Inc.**

Pen-Mar News Distributors, *See* **Americana Souvenirs & Gifts**

Penmarch Publishing, 3932 S. Willow Ave., Sioux Falls, SD 57105 Toll Free: 800-282-2399.

Penn News Co., 944 Franklin St., Johnstown, PA 15905 (SAN 169-7390).

Penton Overseas, Inc., *(0-939001; 1-56015; 1-59125)* 2470 Impala Dr., Carlsbad, CA 92008 (SAN 631-0826) Tel 760-431-0060; Fax: 760-431-8110; Toll Free: 800-748-5804
Web site: http://www.pentonoverseas.com.

Peoples Publishing Group, Inc., The, *(1-56256; 1-58984; 1-4138)* Orders Addr.: P.O. Box 513, Saddle Brook, NJ 07633 Tel 201-712-0090; Fax: 201-712-1534; Toll Free: 800-822-1080; Edit Addr.: 299 Market St., Saddle Brook, NJ 07663
E-mail: sales@peoplespublishing.com; customersupport@peoplespublishing.com; editorial@peoplespublishing.com; solvier@peoplespublishing.com
Web site: http://www.peoplespublishing.com/.

Perelandra, Ltd., *(0-927978; 0-9617713)* Orders Addr.: P.O. Box 3603, Warrenton, VA 20188 (SAN 665-0198) Tel 540-937-2153; Fax: 540-937-3360; Toll Free: 800-960-8806
E-mail: email@perelandra-ltd.com
Web site: http://www.perelandra-ltd.com.

Perfection Form Company, The, *See* **Perfection Learning Corp.**

Perfection Learning Corp., *(0-7807; 0-7891; 0-89598; 1-56312; 0-7569)* 1000 N. Second Ave., Logan, IA 51546 (SAN 221-0010) Tel 712-644-3553; Fax: 712-644-2122; Toll Free: 800-831-4190
E-mail: rfetter@logan.phonline.com
Web site: http://www.perfectionlearning.com.

Periodical Distributors, Incorporated, *See* **North Texas Periodicals, Inc.**

Periodical Marketing Services, 1065 Bloomfield Ave., Clifton, NJ 07012 (SAN 250-5304) Tel 201-342-6334.

Periodical Pubs. Service Bureau, One N. Superior St., Sandusky, OH 44870 (SAN 285-9351) Tel 419-626-0623.

Periodicals Service Co., *(0-527; 0-8115; 3-262; 3-601)* 11 Main St., Germantown, NY 12526 (SAN 164-8608) Tel 518-537-4700; Fax: 518-537-5899
E-mail: psc@backsets.com
Web site: http://www.backsets.com.

Perma-Bound Bks., *(0-605; 0-7804; 0-8000; 0-8479)* Div. of Hertzberg-New Method, Inc., 617 E. Vandalia Rd., Jacksonville, IL 62650 (SAN 169-202X) Tel 217-243-5451; Fax: 217-243-7505; Toll Free Fax: 800-551-1169; Toll Free: 800-637-6581 (customer service)
E-mail: books@permabound.com
Web site: http://www.perma-bound.com.

Perry Enterprises, *(0-941518)* 3907 N. Foothill Dr., Provo, UT 84604 (SAN 171-0281) Tel 801-226-1002.

Petterson Antiques, 201 King St., Charleston, SC 29401 (SAN 114-2399) Tel 803-723-5714.

Pictorial Histories Distribution, 1416 Quarrier St., Charleston, WV 25301 Tel 304-342-1848; Fax: 304-343-0594; Toll Free: 888-982-7472
E-mail: wvbooks@newwave.net.

Pittsfield News Co., Inc., 6 Westview Rd., Pittsfield, MA 01201 (SAN 124-2768) Tel 413-445-5682; Fax: 413-445-5683.

Plains Distribution Service, P.O. Box 931, Moorhead, MN 56561 (SAN 169-6556).

Planeta Publishing Corp., *(0-9715256; 0-9719950)* 2057 NW 87th Ave., Miami, FL 33172 Tel 305-470-0016; 305-571-8400; Fax: 305-470-6267; Toll Free: 800-407-4770
E-mail: mnormanppc@aol.com
Web site: http://www.planetapublishing.com.

Plath, C. North American Division of Litton Systems, Incorporated, *See* **Weems & Plath, Inc.**

Playskool, Inc., 200 Narragansett Pk. Dr., Pawtucket, RI 02862 (SAN 630-7264).

Plough Publishing Hse., The, *(0-87486)* Rte. 381 N., Farmington, PA 15437 (SAN 202-0092) Tel 724-329-1100; Fax: 724-329-0914; Toll Free: 800-521-8011
E-mail: plough@plough.com
Web site: http://www.plough.com.

PMG Bks. Ltd., 321 Nolan St., San Antonio, TX 78202 (SAN 631-3183) Tel 210-226-0772; Fax: 210-224-5194.

Pocket Bks., *(0-671; 0-7432; 0-7434; 1-4165)* Div. of Simon & Schuster, Inc., Orders Addr.: 100 Front St., Riverside, NJ 08075 Toll Free Fax: 800-943-9831; Toll Free: 800-223-2336; Edit Addr.: 1230 Ave. of the Americas, New York, NY 10020 (SAN 202-5922) Tel 212-698-7000
E-mail: ssonline_feedback@simonsays.com
Web site: http://www.simonsays.com.

Polybook Distributors, Orders Addr.: P.O. Box 109, Mount Vernon, NY 10550 Tel 914-664-1633; Fax: 904-428-3953; Edit Addr.: 22 S. Sixth Ave., Mount Vernon, NY 10550 (SAN 169-5568).

Pomona Valley News Agency, 10736 Fremont Ave., Ontario, CA 91762 (SAN 169-0019) Tel 909-591-3885.

Pop-M Company, *See* **Book Margins, Inc.**

Popular Subscription Service, P.O. Box 1566, Terre Haute, IN 47808 (SAN 285-9386) Tel 812-466-1258; Fax: 812-466-9443; Toll Free: 800-466-5038
E-mail: info@popularsubscriptionsvc.com
Web site: http://www.popularsubscriptionsvc.com.

Portland News Co., Orders Addr.: P.O. Box 6970, Scarborough, ME 04070-6970 (SAN 169-3093) Toll Free: 800-639-1708 (in Maine); Edit Addr.: 10 Southgate Rd., Scarborough, ME 04074 Tel 207-883-1300.

Portsmouth News Agency, 3051 Walnut St., Portsmouth, OH 45662 (SAN 169-6831).

Pratz News Agency, Orders Addr.: P.O. Box 892, Deming, NM 88030 (SAN 159-9275).

Prebound Periodicals, 2101 N. Topeka Blvd., Topeka, KS 66608 (SAN 285-8037) Tel 785-233-4252.

Premier Pubs., Inc., *(0-915665)* P.O. Box 330309, Fort Worth, TX 76163 (SAN 292-5966) Tel 817-293-7030 ; Fax: 817-293-3410.

Presbyterian Publishing Corp., *(0-664)* 100 Witherspoon St., Louisville, KY 40202-1396 Toll Free: 800-227-2872
E-mail: rpinotti@presbypub.com.

Printed Matter, Inc., *(0-89439)* 535 W. 22nd St., New York, NY 10011 (SAN 169-5924) Tel 212-925-0325; Fax: 212-925-0464
E-mail: dplatzker@printedmatter.org; staff@printedmatter.org
Web site: http://www.printedmatter.org.

Production Assocs., Inc., *(1-887120)* 1206 W. Collins Ave., Orange, CA 92867 Tel 714-771-6519; Fax: 714-771-2456; Toll Free: 800-535-8368
E-mail: mikec@production-associates.com
Web site: http://www.production-associates.com.

Proe & Proe, Orders Addr.: 3522 James St., Suite 212B, Syracuse, NY 13206 Tel 315-432-0474.

PRO-ED, Inc., *(0-88744; 0-89079; 0-933014; 0-936104; 0-944480; 1-4164)* 8700 Shoal Creek Blvd., Austin, TX 78757-6897 (SAN 222-1349) Tel 512-451-3246 Toll Free Fax: 800-737-1376; Toll Free: 800-897-3202; 800-828-1376
E-mail: ssmreker@proedinc.com
Web site: http://www.proedinc.com.

Professional Book Distributors, Incorporated, *See* **PBD, Inc.**

Professional Media Service Corp., 1160 Trademark Dr., Suite 109, Reno, NV 89511 (SAN 630-5776) Toll Free Fax: 800-253-8853; Toll Free: 800-223-7672.

Programming Concepts, Incorporated, *See* **PCI Educational Publishing**

Public Lands Interpretive Assn., *(1-879343)* 6501 Fourth St., NW, No. 1, Albuquerque, NM 87107-5800 (SAN 133-3119) Tel 505-345-9498; Fax: 505-344-1543.

Publication Consultants, *(0-9644809; 1-888125; 1-59433)* 7617 Highlander Dr., Anchorage, AK 99518 Tel 907-349-2424
E-mail: evan@alaskabooks.biz
Web site: http://www.alaskabooks.biz.

Publications Unlimited, 7512 Coconut Dr., Lake Worth, FL 33467-6511 (SAN 285-9432) Tel 407-434-4688.

Publishers Business Service, Inc., P.O. Box 25674, Chicago, IL 60625 (SAN 285-9459) Tel 312-561-5552.

Publishers Clearing Hse., 382 Channel Dr., Port Washington, NY 11050 (SAN 285-9440) Tel 516-883-5432.

Publishers Continental Sales Corp., 613 Franklin Sq., Michigan City, IN 46360 (SAN 285-9475) Tel 219-874-4245; Fax: 219-872-8961.

Publishers Group West, Subs. of Publishers Group Inc., 1700 Fourth St., Berkeley, CA 94710 (SAN 202-8522) Tel 510-528-1444; Fax: 510-528-3444; Toll Free: 800-788-3123; 800-788-3122 (electronic orders)
Web site: http://www.pgw.com.

Publishers Media, *(0-934064)* 1447 Valley View Rd., Glendale, CA 91202-1716 (SAN 159-6683) Tel 818-548-1998.

Publishers News Company, *See* **Mr. Paperback/ Publishers News Co.**

Publishers Services, Orders Addr.: P.O. Box 2510, Novato, CA 94948 (SAN 201-3037) Tel 415-883-3530 ; Fax: 415-883-4280.

Publishers Wholesale Assocs., Inc., Orders Addr.: P.O. Box 2078, Lancaster, PA 17608-2078 (SAN 630-7450) Fax: 717-397-9253; Edit Addr.: 231 N. Shippen St., Lancaster, PA 17608.

Pulley Learning Assocs., 210 Alpine Meadow Rd., Winchester, VA 22602-6701 (SAN 133-1434).

Purple Unicorn Bks., *(0-931998)* 1928 W. Kent Rd., Duluth, MN 55812-1154 (SAN 111-0071) Tel 218-525-4781 Do not confuse with Purple Unicorn in Augusta, ME.

Putnam Publishing Group, The, *(0-399; 0-698; 0-89828)* Div. of Penguin Putnam, Inc., Orders Addr.: 405 Murray Hill Pkwy., East Rutherford, NJ 07073-2136 Toll Free Fax: 800-227-9604; Toll Free: 800-788-6262 (individual consumer sales); 800-631-8571 (reseller customer service); 800-526-0275 (reseller sales); Edit Addr.: 375 Hudson St., New York, NY 10014 (SAN 202-5531) Tel 212-366-2000; Fax: 212-366-2643
E-mail: online@penguinputnam.com
Web site: http://www.penguinputnam.com.

Quality Bks., Inc., *(0-89196)* 1003 W. Pines Rd., Oregon, IL 61061-9680 (SAN 169-2127) Tel 815-732-4450; Fax: 815-732-4499; Toll Free: 800-323-4241 (libraries only)
E-mail: quality.books@dawson.com.

Quality Book Fairs, 110 W. Liberty St., Medina, OH 44256 (SAN 630-7752) Tel 330-725-6977; Fax: 330-723-5325.

Quality Schl. Plan, Inc., P.O. Box 10203, Des Moines, IA 50381-0001 (SAN 285-953X).

R & W Distribution, Inc., 87 Bright St., Jersey City, NJ 07302 (SAN 169-4723) Tel 201-333-1540; Fax: 201-333-1541
E-mail: rwmag@mail.idt.net.

Radio Bookstore, P.O. Box 209, Rindge, NH 03461-0209 (SAN 111-3496) Tel 603-899-6957 Do not confuse with Radio Bookstore Pr., Bellevue, WA.

Rainier News, Inc., 3400-D Industry Dr., E., Fife, WA 98424-1853 (SAN 169-8745) Toll Free: 800-843-2995 (in Washington).

RAM Pubns. & Distribution, *(0-9630785; 0-9703860)* Bergamot Sta., 2525 Michigan Ave., No. A2, Santa Monica, CA 90404 (SAN 298-2641) Tel 310-453-0043; Fax: 310-264-4888
E-mail: rampub@gte.net.

Random Hse., Inc., *(0-307; 0-345; 0-375; 0-394; 0-553; 0-676; 0-679; 0-87665; 1-58836; 1-4000)* Div. of Bertelsmann AG, Orders Addr.: 400 Hahn Rd., Westminster, MD 21157 (SAN 202-5515) Tel 410-848-1900; Toll Free Fax: 800-659-2436; Toll Free: 800-726-0600 (customer service/orders); Edit Addr.: 1540 Broadway, New York, NY 10036 (SAN 202-5507) Tel 212-782-9000; Fax: 212-302-7985
E-mail: customerservice@randomhouse.com
Web site: http://www.randomhouse.com.

Raven West Coast Distribution, 767 W. 18th St., Costa Mesa, CA 92627
E-mail: ken@ravenwcd.com.

Read News Agency, 2501 Greensboro Ave., Tuscaloosa, AL 35401-6520 Tel 205-752-3515.

Reader's Digest Children's Publishing, Inc., *(0-276; 0-7621; 0-88705; 0-88850; 0-89577; 1-57584; 1-57619; 0-7944)* Subs. of Reader's Digest Assn., Inc., Reader's Digest Rd., Pleasantville, NY 10570-7000 (SAN 283-2143) Tel 914-244-4800; Fax: 914-244-4841
Web site: http://www.readersdigestkids.com.

Readex Bk. Exchange, Box 1125, Carefree, AZ 85377 (SAN 159-9291).

Reading Circle, The, 1456 N. High St., Columbus, OH 43201-0458 (SAN 169-670X) Tel 614-299-9673; Fax: 614-299-1388.

Reading Peddler Bk. Fairs, 10580 3/4 W. Pico Blvd., Los Angeles, CA 90064 (SAN 157-9770) Tel 310-559-2665.

Readmor, Orders Addr.: P.O. Box 7264, Grand Rapids, MI 49508 (SAN 169-3875); Edit Addr.: 301 S. Rath Ave., Ludington, MI 49431 Tel 231-843-2537.

Readmore Academic Services, Orders Addr.: P.O. Box 1459, Blackwood, NJ 08012 (SAN 630-5741) Tel 609-227-1100; Fax: 609-227-8322; Toll Free: 800-645-6595; Edit Addr.: 700 Black Horse Pike, Suite 207, Blackwood, NJ 08012.

Readmore, Inc., 22 Cortlandt St., New York, NY 10007 (SAN 159-9313) Tel 212-349-5540; Fax: 212-233-0746; Toll Free: 800-221-3306.

Red Sea Pr., *(0-932415; 1-56902)* 11 Princess Rd., Suites D, E & F, Lawrenceville, NJ 08648 (SAN 630-1983) Tel 609-844-9583; Fax: 609-844-0198
E-mail: africawpress@nyo.com
Web site: http://www.africanworld.com/.

Red Wheel/Weiser, *(0-87728; 0-943233; 1-57324; 1-57863; 1-59003)* Div. of Weiser Bks., Orders Addr.: P.O. Box 612, York Beach, ME 03910-0612 Tel 207-363-4393; Fax: 207-363-5799; Toll Free Fax: 877-337-3309; Toll Free: 800-423-7087 (orders only)
E-mail: customerservice@redwheelweiser.com
Web site: http://www.redwheelweiser.com; http://www.weiserbooks.com.

Redwing Bk. Co., 44 Linden St., Brookline, MA 02445 (SAN 163-3597) Tel 617-738-4664; Fax: 617-738-4620; Toll Free: 800-873-3946
E-mail: bob@redwingbooks.com
Web site: http://www.redwingbooks.com.

Reference Bk. Ctr., 175 Fifth Ave., New York, NY 10010 (SAN 159-9356) Tel 212-677-2160; Fax: 212-533-0826.

Regent Bk. Co., Inc., Orders Addr.: P.O. Box 750, Lodi, NJ 07644-0750 Tel 973-574-7600; Fax: 973-574-7605; Toll Free: 800-999-9554; Edit Addr.: 25 Saddle River Ave., South Hackensack, NJ 07606 (SAN 169-4715)
E-mail: info@regentbook.com
Web site: http://www.regentbook.com.

Renaissance Hse. Pubs., *(0-935810; 0-939650; 1-55838)* Div. of Primer Pubs., 5738 N. Central Ave., Phoenix, AZ 85012 Tel 602-234-1574; Fax: 602-234-3062; Toll Free: 800-521-9221 (orders)
E-mail: bfessler@earthlink.net.

Replica Bks., *(0-7351)* Div. of Baker & Taylor, Orders Addr.: 1200 US Hwy., 22 E., Bridgewater, NJ 08807 Tel 908-541-7392; Fax: 908-541-7875; Toll Free: 800-775-1800; Edit Addr.: P.O. Box 6885, Bridgewater, NJ 08807-0885
E-mail: btinfo@baker-taylor.com.

Research Bks., Inc., 38 Academy St., P.O. Box 1507, Madison, CT 06443 Tel 203-245-3279; Fax: 203-245-1830
E-mail: info@researchbooks.com.

Resource Software International, Inc., *(0-87539)* Affil. of Datamatics Management, 330 New Brunswick Ave., Fords, NJ 08863 (SAN 264-8628) Tel 732-738-8500; Fax: 732-738-9603; Toll Free: 800-673-0366
E-mail: info@datamaticsinc.com
Web site: http://www.tc-1.com.

Rhinelander News Agency, 314 Courtney, Crescent Lake, WI 54501 (SAN 159-9372) Tel 715-362-6397.

Rhodes News Agency, *See* **Treasure Valley News**

Richardson's Bks., Inc., 2014 Lou Ellen Ln., Houston, TX 77018 (SAN 169-829X) Tel 713-688-2244; Fax: 713-688-8420; Toll Free: 800-392-8562.

Richardson's Educators, *See* **Richardson's Bks., Inc.**

Rio Grande Bk. Co., P.O. Box 2795, McAllen, TX 78502-2795 (SAN 169-8354).

Rishor News Co., Inc., 109 Mountain Laurel Dr., Butler, PA 16001-3921 (SAN 159-9402).

Rittenhouse Bk. Distributors, *(0-87381)* Orders Addr.: 511 Feheley Dr., King of Prussia, PA 19406 (SAN 213-4454) Tel 610-277-1414; Fax: 610-227-0390; Toll Free Fax: 800-223-7488; Toll Free: 800-345-6425
E-mail: alan.yockey@rittenhouse.com; joan.townshend@rittenhouse.com
Web site: http://www.rittenhouse.com.

Ritter Bk. Co., 7011 Foster Pl., Downers Grove, IL 60516-3446 (SAN 169-1856).

River Road Recipes Cookbook, 9523 Fenway Dr., Baton Rouge, LA 70809 (SAN 132-7852) Tel 504-924-0300 ; Fax: 504-927-2547; Toll Free: 800-204-1726.

Riverside, *(0-934298; 1-55518)* Orders Addr.: P.O. Box 370, Iowa Falls, IA 50126 (SAN 169-2666) Tel 641-648-4271; Toll Free: 800-922-9777 (Telemarketing); Edit Addr.: 636 S. Oak St., Iowa Falls, IA 50126 (SAN 631-2063) Toll Free Fax: 800-822-4271; Toll Free: 800-247-5111
E-mail: orders@riversideworld.com
Web site: http://www.riversideworld.com.

Riverside Bk. & Bible Resource, 1500 Riverside Dr., Iowa Falls, IA 50126 Tel 515-648-4801; Toll Free Fax: 800-822-4271; Toll Free: 800-247-5111.

Riverside World, *See* **Riverside**

Roadrunner Library Service, c/o Kerbs, 700 Highview Ave., Glen Ellyn, IL 60137-5504.

Roberts, F.M. Enterprises, *(0-912746)* P.O. Box 608, Dana Point, CA 92629-0608 (SAN 201-4688) Tel 714-493-1977; Fax: 714-493-7124.

Rockbottom Bks., Pentagon Towers, P.O. Box 398166, Minneapolis, MN 55439 (SAN 108-4402) Tel 612-831-2120.

Rockland Catskill, Inc., 26 Church St., Spring Valley, NY 10977 (SAN 169-6254) Tel 914-356-1222; Fax: 914-356-8415; Toll Free: 800-966-6247.

Rocky Mount News Agency, Two Great State Ln., Rocky Mount, NC 27801.

Rogue Valley News Agency, Inc., 550 Airport Rd., Medford, OR 97504-4156 (SAN 169-7137).

Rohr, Hans E., 76 State St., Newburyport, MA 01950-6616 (SAN 113-8804).

Roig Spanish Bks., 146 W. 29th St., No. 3W, New York, NY 10001-5303 (SAN 165-1021) Tel 212-695-6410; Fax: 212-695-6811
E-mail: roig@interport.net.

Rosenblum's, *See* **Rosenblum's World of Judaica, Inc.**

Rosenblum's World of Judaica, Inc., 2906 W. Devon Ave., Chicago, IL 60659 (SAN 169-1864) Tel 773-262-1700; Fax: 773-262-1930; Toll Free: 800-626-6536.

Rounder Kids Music Distribution, Orders Addr.: P.O. Box 516, Montpelier, VT 05602 (SAN 630-6675) Tel 802-223-5825; Fax: 802-223-5303; Toll Free: 800-223-6357; Edit Addr.: 79 River Rd., Montpelier, VT 05602
E-mail: Pauls@rounder.com.

Rowman & Littlefield Pubs., Inc., *(0-8476; 0-87471; 0-7425)* Div. of University Press of America, P.O. Box 191, Blue Ridge Summit, PA 17214-0191 Tel 717-794-3800; Fax: 717-794-3801; Orders Addr.: 15200 NBN Way, Blue Ridge Summit, PA 17214 Tel 717-794-3800; Fax: 717-794-3803; Toll Free Fax: 800-338-4550; Toll Free: 800-462-6420; 67 Mowat Ave., Suite 241, Toronto, ON M6K 3E3 Tel 416-534-1660; Fax: 416-534-3699; Edit Addr.: 4501 Forbes Blvd., Suite 200, Lanham, MD 20706 (SAN 203-3704) Tel 301-459-3366; Fax: 301-429-5747
E-mail: Rogers@univpress.com
Web site: http://www.rowmanlittlefield.com.

Rushmore News, Inc., 924 East St. Andrew, Rapid City, SD 57701 (SAN 169-7846) Tel 605-342-2617; Fax: 605-342-9091; Toll Free: 800-423-0501
E-mail: afreese911@aol.com.

Russell News Agency, Inc., P.O. Box 158, Sarasota, FL 33578 (SAN 169-1287).

Russica Bk. & Art Shop, Inc., 799 Broadway, New York, NY 10003 (SAN 165-1072) Tel 212-473-7480; Fax: 212-473-7486.

S & S News & Greeting, 5304 15th Ave., S., Minneapolis, MN 55417-1812 (SAN 159-9453) Tel 612-224-8227; Toll Free: 800-346-9892.

S & W Distributors, Inc., 1600-H E. Wendover Ave., Greensboro, NC 27405.

S. A. V. E. with Victor Hotho, *See* **S.A.V.E. Suzie & Vic Enterprises**

S V E & Churchill Media, *(0-7932; 0-89290; 1-56357)* 6677 N. Northwest Hwy., Chicago, IL 60631-1304 (SAN 208-3930) Tel 773-775-9550; Fax: 773-775-5091; Toll Free Fax: 800-624-1678; Toll Free: 800-829-1900
E-mail: custserv@svemedia.com
Web site: http://www.svemedia.com.

SAAN Corp., 189-01 Springfield Ave., Suite 201, Flossmoor, IL 60422 (SAN 631-0419) Tel 708-799-5225; Fax: 708-799-8713.

Saddleback Publishing, Inc., *(1-56254)* Three Watson, Irvine, CA 92618-2716 Tel 949-860-2500; Fax: 949-860-2508; Toll Free: 800-637-8715
E-mail: info@sdlback.com
Web site: http://www.sdlback.com.

Safari Museum Pr., 111 N. Lincoln Ave., Chanute, KS 66720 Tel 630-431-2730; Fax: 630-431-3848.

Sagebrush Corp., Orders Addr.: P.O. Box 1777, Topeka, KS 66601; Edit Addr.: 2101 N. Topeka Blvd., Topeka, KS 66601 (SAN 151-3478).

Sagebrush Pr., *(0-930704)* P.O. Box 87, Morongo Valley, CA 92256 (SAN 113-387X) Tel 760-363-7398 Do not confuse with companies with same name in Cedarville, CA, Salt Lake City, UT.

Saint Joe Distribution Center, *See* **American Bk. Ctr.**

Saks News, Inc., P.O. Box 1857, Bismarck, ND 58502 (SAN 169-653X).

Sams Technical Publishing, LLC, *(0-7906)* 9852 E. 30th St., Indianapolis, IN 46229 Toll Free Fax: 800-552-3910; Toll Free: 800-428-7267
E-mail: samstech@samswebsite.com
Web site: http://www.samswebsite.com.

San Diego Museum of Art, *(0-937108)* Orders Addr.: P.O. Box 122107, San Diego, CA 92112-2107 Tel 619-696-1970; Fax: 619-232-9367
Web site: http://www.sdmart.org.

San Franciscian a, *(0-934715)* P.O. Box 590955, San Francisco, CA 94159 (SAN 161-1607) Tel 415-751-7222.

San Val, Inc., 1230 Macklind Ave., Saint Louis, MO 63110-1432 (SAN 159-947X) Tel 314-644-6100; Fax: 314-647-0979; Toll Free: 800-458-8438
E-mail: sanval@misn.com
Web site: http://www.sanval.com.

Sandlapper Publishing Co., Inc., *(0-87844)* Orders Addr.: P.O. Box 730, Orangeburg, SC 29115 (SAN 203-2678) Toll Free Fax: 800-337-9420 (orders); Toll Free: 800-849-7263 (orders); Edit Addr.: 1281 Amelia St., NE., Orangeburg, SC 29116 Tel 803-533-1658; Fax: 803-534-5223.

Santa Barbara Botanic Garden, *(0-916436)* 1212 Mission Canyon Rd., Santa Barbara, CA 93105 (SAN 208-8398) Tel 805-682-4726; Fax: 805-563-0352.

Santa Barbara News Agency, 725 S. Kellogg Ave., Goleta, CA 93117-3806 (SAN 168-9665) Tel 805-564-5200.

Santa Monica Software, Inc., 30018 Zenith Point Rd., Malibu, CA 90265-4264 (SAN 630-6764) Tel 310-457-8381; Fax: 310-395-7635.

Santillana USA Publishing Co., Inc., *(0-88272; 1-56014; 1-58105; 84-294; 1-58986; 1-59437)* Div. of Grup Santillana De Ediciones, S.A., 2105 NW 86th Ave., Miami, FL 33122 (SAN 205-1133) Tel 305-591-9522; Fax: 305-591-9145; Toll Free Fax: 800-530-8099 (orders); Toll Free: 800-245-8584
E-mail: customerservice@santillanausa.com
Web site: http://www.santillanausa.com/.

Saphrograph Corp., *(0-87557)* 5409 18th Ave., Brooklyn, NY 11204 (SAN 110-4128) Tel 718-331-1233; Fax: 718-331-8231.

Sasquatch Bks., *(0-912365; 1-57061)* 615 Second Ave., Suite 260, Seattle, WA 98104 (SAN 289-0208) Tel 206-467-4300 (ext 300); Fax: 206-467-4301; Toll Free: 800-775-0817
E-mail: books@sasquatchbooks.com
Web site: http://www.sasquatchbooks.com.

Sathya Sai Bk. Ctr. of America, *(1-57836)* 305 W. First St., Tustin, CA 92780 (SAN 111-3542) Tel 714-669-0522; Fax: 714-669-9138
Web site: http://www.sathyasai.org/inform/tustin.html.

Saturday Shop, *(0-9613242)* P.O. Box 307, Clarksville, GA 30523 (SAN 295-5040) Tel 706-754-9200
E-mail: Saturdayshop@yahoo.com.

S.A.V.E. Suzie & Vic Enterprises, 303 N. Main, P.O. Box 30, Schulenburg, TX 78956 (SAN 630-6365) Tel 409-743-4145; Fax: 409-743-4147.

SCB Distributors, 15608 S. New Century Dr., Gardena, CA 90248-2129 (SAN 630-4818) Tel 310-532-9400; Fax: 310-532-7001; Toll Free: 800-729-6423 (orders only)
E-mail: aaron@scbdistributors.com; info@scbdistributors.com
Web site: http://www.scbdistributors.com.

Schmul Publishing Co., Inc., *(0-88019)* Orders Addr.: P.O. Box 716, Salem, OH 44460-0716 (SAN 180-2771) Tel 330-222-2249; Fax: 330-222-0001; Toll Free: 800-772-6657; Edit Addr.: 3583 Newgarden Rd., Salem, OH 44460
E-mail: spchale@valunet.com
Web site: http://www.wesleyanbooks.com.

Schoenhof's Foreign Bks., Inc., *(0-87774)* Subs. of Editions Gallimard, 486 Green St., Cambridge, MA 02139 (SAN 212-0062) Tel 617-547-8855; Fax: 617-547-8551
E-mail: info@schoenhofs.com
Web site: http://www.schoenhofs.com.

Scholar's Bookshelf, *(0-945726)* 110 Melrick Rd., Cranbury, NJ 08512 (SAN 110-8360) Tel 609-395-6933
E-mail: books@scholarsbookshelf.com
Web site: http://www.scholarsbookshelf.

Scholastic, Inc., *(0-439; 0-590)* Orders Addr.: c/o HarperCollins, 1000 Keystone Industrial Pk., Scranton, PA 18512 Toll Free: 800-242-7737; Edit Addr.: 557 Broadway, New York, NY 10012-3999 (SAN 202-5442) Tel 212-343-6100; Fax: 212-343-6802; Toll Free: 800-325-6149 (customer service)
Web site: http://www.scholastic.com.

Scholium International, Inc., *(0-333; 0-87936)* P.O. Box 1519, Port Washington, NY 11050-0306 (SAN 169-5282) Tel 516-767-7171; Fax: 516-944-9824
E-mail: info@scholium.com
Web site: http://www.scholium.com.

School Aid Co., *(0-87385)* 911 Colfax Dr., P.O. Box 123, Danville, IL 61832 (SAN 158-3719) Tel 217-442-6855; Toll Free: 800-447-2665.

School Aids, 9335 Interline Ave., Baton Rouge, LA 70809-1910 (SAN 169-2909) Tel 504-926-4498.

School Bk. Service, 3650 Coral Ridge Dr., Suite 112, Coral Springs, FL 33065-2559 (SAN 158-6963) Tel 954-341-7207; Fax: 954-341-7303; Toll Free: 800-228-7361
E-mail: compedge@ix.netcom.com.

School of Metaphysics, 163 Moonvalley Rd., Windyville, MO 65783 (SAN 159-5423) Tel 417-345-8411; Fax: 417-345-6668
E-mail: som@som.org
Web site: http://www.som.org.

Schroeder News Company, *See* **Merced News Co.**

Schroeder's Bk. Haven, 104 Michigan Ave., League City, TX 77573 (SAN 122-7998) Tel 281-332-5226; Fax: 281-332-1695; Toll Free: 800-894-5032
E-mail: schroedr@interloc.com.

Schulze News Co., 2451 Eastman Ave., Suite 13, Oxnard, CA 93030-5193 (SAN 169-0434) Tel 805-642-9759.

Schuylkill News Service, 1764 W. Market St., Pottsville, PA 17901 (SAN 159-9518) Tel 717-622-7510.

Schwartz Brothers, Inc., 822 Montgomery Ave., No. 204, Narberth, PA 19072-1937 (SAN 285-7529) Fax: 301-459-6418; Toll Free: 800-638-0243.

Schwarz, F. A. O., 500 Pierce St., Somerset, NJ 08873-1270 (SAN 170-8554).

Scientific & Medical Pubns. of France, Inc., 100 E. 42nd St., Suite 1510, New York, NY 10017 (SAN 169-5940) Tel 212-983-6278; Fax: 212-687-1407.

Seaboard Sub Agency, 44 S. Fulton St., Allentown, PA 18102 (SAN 285-9718) Tel 610-435-8174; Fax: 610-435-0290.

Selective Bks., Inc., *(0-912584)* P.O. Box 1140, Clearwater, FL 34617 (SAN 204-577X) Tel 813-447-0100.

Selective Publishers, Incorporated, *See* **Selective Bks., Inc.**

Self esteem shop II, *(0-9670949)* Div. of Self Esteem Shop, 32851 Woodward Ave., Royal Oak, MI 48073 Tel 248-554-9432; Fax: 248-549-0442
E-mail: info@selfesteemship.com
Web site: http://www.selfesteemshop.com.

Semler News Agency, Orders Addr.: P.O. Box 350, New Castle, PA 16101 (SAN 169-7471); Edit Addr.: P.O. Box 526, Morgantown, WV 26505 (SAN 169-8990).

Seneca News Agency, Box 631, Geneva, NY 14456 (SAN 169-5304) Tel 315-789-3551; Fax: 315-781-1015.

Sentai Distributors, 8839 Shirley Ave., Northridge, CA 91324 (SAN 168-8959) Tel 818-886-3113; Fax: 818-886-0423
Web site: http://www.plasticmodels.com.

Sepher-Hermon Pr., *(0-87203)* 1153 45th St., Brooklyn, NY 11219 (SAN 169-5959) Tel 718-972-9010; Fax: 718-972-6935.

Serendipity Couriers, Inc., 470 Du Bois St., San Rafael, CA 94901-3911 (SAN 169-0329) Tel 415-459-4000; Fax: 415-459-0833; Toll Free: 800-459-4005 (Bay area only)
E-mail: dipity@14.netcom.com.

Service News Co., 1306 N. 23rd St., Wilmington, NC 28406 (SAN 169-6491) Tel 910-762-0837; Fax: 910-762-9539; Toll Free: 800-552-8238; P.O. Box 5027, Macon, GA 31208; Pope's Island, Box D-629, New Bedford, MA 02742 (SAN 169-3514).

Seven Locks Pr., *(0-929765; 0-932020; 0-9615964; 1-931643)* 3100 W. Warner Ave., Suite 8, Santa Ana, CA 92704 (SAN 211-9781) Tel 714-545-2526; Fax: 714-545-1572; Toll Free: 800-354-5348
E-mail: sevenlocks@aol.com
Web site: http://sevenlockspress.com.

Shambhala Pubns., Inc., *(0-87773; 1-56957; 1-57062; 1-59030)* Horticultural Hall, 300 Massachusetts Ave., Boston, MA 02115 (SAN 203-2481) Tel 617-424-0030; Fax: 617-236-1563
E-mail: editors@shambhala.com
Web site: http://www.shambhala.com.

Sharon News Agency Co., 527 Silver St., Sharon, PA 16146 (SAN 169-7633).

Shea Bks., 1563 Solano Ave., Suite 206, Berkeley, CA 94707 (SAN 159-9720) Tel 510-528-5201; Fax: 510-528-4987.

Shelter Pubns., Inc., *(0-936070)* Orders Addr.: P.O. Box 279, Bolinas, CA 94924 (SAN 122-8463) Tel 415-868-0280; Fax: 415-868-9053; Toll Free: 800-307-0131; Edit Addr.: 285 Dogwood Rd, Bolinas, CA 94924
E-mail: shelter@shelterpub.com
Web site: http://www.shelterpub.com.

Shen's Bks., *(1-885008)* 40951 Fremont Blvd., Fremont, CA 94538 (SAN 138-2926) Tel 510-668-1898; Fax: 510-668-1057; Toll Free: 800-456-6660
E-mail: info@shens.com
Web site: http://www.shens.com.

Sheridan Hse., Inc., *(0-911378; 0-924486; 1-57409)* 145 Palisade St., Dobbs Ferry, NY 10522 (SAN 204-5915) Tel 914-693-2410; Fax: 914-693-0776; Toll Free: 888-743-7425 (orders only) Do not confuse with Sheridan House, Inc., in Ft. Lauderdale, FL
E-mail: Sheribks@aol.com
Web site: http://www.sheridanhouse.com.

Shinder's Book Company, *See* **Shinders Readmore Bookstore, Inc.**

Shinders Readmore Bookstore, Inc., 733 Hennepin Ave., Minneapolis, MN 55403 (SAN 125-6157) Tel 612-333-3628.

Shoppers Guide Pr., 706 N. Fifth, Alpine, TX 79830 (SAN 159-9550) Tel 915-837-7426.

Siena Library Co., 2101 Pennsylvania Ave., Suite 101, York, PA 17404 (SAN 631-2896) Tel 717-852-8712; Fax: 717-852-8554
E-mail: siena@cyberia.com; siena@blazenet.net.

Sierra News Co., 2136 Pony Express Ct., Stockton, CA 95215-7946 (SAN 169-4472).

Silky Way, Inc., 1227 38th Ave., San Francisco, CA 94122-1334 (SAN 169-3328).

Silver Bow News Distributing Co., Inc., 219 E. Park St., Butte, MT 59701 (SAN 169-4359) Tel 406-782-6995.

Silver, Burdett & Ginn, Inc., *(0-382; 0-663)* Orders Addr.: P.O. Box 2500, Lebanon, IN 46052 Toll Free Fax: 800-841-8939; Toll Free: 800-552-2259; Edit Addr.: P.O. Box 480, Parsippany, NJ 07054 (SAN 204-5982); 108 Wilmot Rd., Suite 380, Midwest Div., Deerfield, IL 60015 (SAN 111-6517) Tel 708-945-1240; 1925 Century Blvd. NE, Suite 14, Southeast Div., Atlanta, GA 30345 (SAN 111-6509); 8445 Freeport Pkwy., Suite 400, South Div., Irving, TX 75063 (SAN 108-0458) Tel 214-915-4200; 2001 The Alameda, West Div., San Jose, CA 95126 (SAN 111-6525) Tel 408-248-6854; 160 Gould St., East Div., Needham Heights, MA 02194-2310
E-mail: customerservice@scottforesman.com
Web site: http://www.scottforesman.com/.

Silver Mine Video, 6860 Canby Ave., Suite 117-118, Reseda, CA 91335 (SAN 631-6026) Tel 818-342-2880 ; Fax: 818-342-4029; Toll Free: 800-233-2880.

Simon & Schuster, *(0-671; 0-684; 0-689; 0-914676; 0-7432)* Div. of Simon & Schuster, Inc., Orders Addr.: 100 Front St., Riverside, NJ 08075 (SAN 200-2442) Toll Free Fax: 800-943-9831; Toll Free: 800-223-2348 (customer service); 800-223-2336 (ordering); Edit Addr.: 1230 Avenue of the Americas, New York, NY 10020 (SAN 200-2450) Tel 212-698-7000; Fax: 212-698-7007; Toll Free: 800-897-7650 (customer financial services)
E-mail: ssonline_feedback@simonsays.com; consumer.customerservice@simonandschuster.com
Web site: http://www.simonandschuster.com/ebooks; http://www.oasis.simonandschuster.com; http://www.simonsays.com.

Simon & Schuster Children's Publishing, *(0-02; 0-671; 0-684; 0-689; 0-7434)* Orders Addr.: 100 Front St., Riverside, NJ 08075 Toll Free Fax: 800-943-9831; Toll Free: 800-223-2336; Edit Addr.: 1230 Avenue of the Americas, New York, NY 10020 Tel 212-698-7200
Web site: http://www.simonsays.com.

Simon & Schuster, Inc., *(0-671)* Div. of Viacom Co., Orders Addr.: 100 Front St., Riverside, NJ 08075 Toll Free Fax: 800-943-9831; Toll Free: 800-223-2336 (orders); 800-223-2348 (customer service); Edit Addr.: 1230 Ave. of the Americas, New York, NY 10020.

Simon & Schuster Trade, *See* **Simon & Schuster**

Simon & Schuster Trade Paperbacks, *(0-684; 0-689)* Div. of Simon & Schuster Adult Publishing Group, Orders Addr.: 100 Front St., Riverside, NJ 08075 Toll Free Fax: 800-943-9831; Toll Free: 800-223-2336; Edit Addr.: 1230 Avenue of the Americas, New York, NY 10020 Tel 212-698-7000; Fax: 212-698-7007
Web site: http://www.simonandschuster.com.

Skandisk, Inc., *(0-9615394; 1-57534)* 6667 W. Old Shakopee Rd., Suite 109, Bloomington, MN 55438-2622 (SAN 695-4405) Tel 952-829-8998; Fax: 952-829-8992; Toll Free: 800-468-2424 (orders)
E-mail: lhamnes@skandisk.com; tomten@skandisk.com
Web site: http://www.skandisk.com.

S&L Sales Co., Inc., Orders Addr.: P.O. Box 2067, Waycross, GA 31502 (SAN 107-413X) Tel 912-283-0210; Fax: 912-283-0261; Toll Free: 800-243-3699 (orders only).

Slatner, Thomas & Co., Inc., 193 Palisade Ave., 3rd Flr., Jersey City, NJ 07036-1112 (SAN 130-9862) Tel 201-420-6700; Fax: 201-420-6787.

Slavica Pubs., *(0-89357)* c/o Indiana University, 2611 E. Tenth St., Bloomington, IN 47408-2618 (SAN 208-8576) Tel 812-856-4186; Fax: 812-856-4187
E-mail: slavica@indiana.edu
Web site: http://www.slavica.com.

Sleuth Pubns., Ltd., *(0-915341)* 3398 Washington, San Francisco, CA 94118 (SAN 130-9374) Tel 415-771-2689.

Small Press Distribution, *See* **SPD-Small Pr. Distribution**

Smith, Gibbs Pub., *(0-87905; 1-58685)* Orders Addr.: P.O. Box 667, Layton, UT 84041 (SAN 201-9906) Toll Free Fax: 800-213-3023 (orders); Toll Free: 800-748-5439 (orders); Edit Addr.: 1877 E. Gentile St., Layton, UT 84040 Tel 801-544-9800; Fax: 801-546-8853
E-mail: info@gibbs-smith.com; text@gibbs-smith.com
Web site: http://www.gibbs-smith.com.

Smith News Agency, 118 S. Mitchell St., Cadillac, MI 49601 (SAN 169-3727).

Smith, W. H. Publishers, Incorporated, *See* **Smithmark Pubs., Inc.**

Smithmark Pubs., Inc., *(0-7651; 0-8317)* Div. of US Media Holdings, 115 W. 18th St.. 5th Flr., New York, NY 10011-4113 (SAN 176-0912) Tel 212-519-1300; Fax: 212-519-1310; Toll Free: 800-932-0070 (customer service); Raritan Plaza 111, Fieldcrest Ave., Edison, NJ 08837 (SAN 658-1625) Tel 732-225-6499 (phone/fax); Toll Free Fax: 800-732-8688.

SNAP! Entertainment, 952 Queen St., W., Toronto, ON M6J 1G8 Tel 416-588-4006.

Snyder Magazine Agency, 3050 S. 9th Terr., Kansas City, KS 66103-2629 (SAN 285-9750).

Social Studies Schl. Service, *(1-56004)* 10200 Jefferson Blvd., P.O. Box 802, Culver City, CA 90232-0802 (SAN 168-9592) Tel 310-839-2436; Fax: 310-839-2249; Toll Free: 800-421-4246
E-mail: sssservice@aol.com
Web site: http://socialstudies.com.

Society for Visual Education, Incorporated, *See* **S V E & Churchill Media**

Sopris West, *(0-944584; 1-57035; 1-59318)* 4093 Specialty Pl., Longmont, CO 80401 (SAN 243-945X) Tel 303-651-2829; Fax: 303-776-5934; Toll Free: 800-547-6747 (orders only)
Web site: http://www.sopriswest.com.

Sort Card Co., The, 400 S. Summit View Dr., Fort Collins, CO 80524-1424 (SAN 159-9607).

Sounds True, Inc., *(1-56455; 1-59179)* 413 S. Arthur Ave., Boulder, CO 80027 Tel 303-665-3151; Fax: 303-665-5292; Toll Free: 800-333-9185
E-mail: traviss@soundstrue.com
Web site: http://www.soundstrue.com.

Source Bks., *(0-940147; 0-85650)* Orders Addr.: 204 E. 4th St., Suite O, Santa Ana, CA 92701 (SAN 248-2231) Tel 714-558-8944 (phone/fax); Toll Free: 800-695-4237 Do not confuse with Source Bks., Nashville, TN
E-mail: studio185@earthlink.net.

South Asia Bks., *(0-8364; 0-88386)* P.O. Box 502, Columbia, MO 65205 (SAN 207-4044) Tel 573-474-0116; Fax: 573-474-8124
E-mail: sabooks@juno.com
Web site: http://www.southasiabooks.com.

South Atlantic News, Orders Addr.: P.O. Box 61297, Jacksonville, FL 32236-1297; Edit Addr.: 1426 NE Eighth Ave., Ocala, FL 32678.

South Carolina Bookstore, Orders Addr.: P.O. Box 4767, West Columbia, SC 29171 (SAN 131-2294) Tel 803-796-8200; Fax: 803-794-6927; Toll Free: 800-845-8200; Edit Addr.: 523 Jasper St., West Columbia, SC 29169 (SAN 243-2390).

South Central Bks., Inc., 1106 S. Strong Blvd., McAlester, OK 74501-6952 (SAN 108-1144) Tel 405-275-4522; Toll Free: 800-548-9858.

South Eastern Bk. Co., Inc., 3333 Hwy. 641 N., P.O. Box 309, Murray, KY 42071 (SAN 630-4869) Tel 270-753-0732; Fax: 270-759-4742; Toll Free Fax: 800-433-6966 (orders); Toll Free: 800-626-3952 (orders)
E-mail: orders@sebook.com
Web site: http://www.sebook.com.

South Louisiana News Company, *See* **Southern Periodicals, Inc.**

Southeast Library Bindery, Inc., P.O. Box 35484, Greensboro, NC 27425-5484 (SAN 159-9445) Tel 336-931-0800
E-mail: 70304.3023@compuserve.com
Web site: http://www.webmasters.net/bookbinding/.

Southeast Periodical & Bk. Sales, Inc., 10100 NW 25th St., Box 520155-Biscayne Annex, Miami, FL 33152.

Southeastern Educational Toy & Bk. Distributors, Orders Addr.: P.O. Box 15129, Charlotte, NC 28211 (SAN 630-8104) Tel 704-364-6988; Edit Addr.: 4217 Park Rd., Charlotte, NC 28209 Tel 704-527-1921; Fax: 704-527-1653.

Southeastern Library Service, Subs. of Haskins Hse., P.O. Box 44, Gainesville, FL 32602-0044 (SAN 159-9615) Tel 352-372-3823.

Southern Bk. Service, *(0-9663836)* 5154 NW 165th St., Palmetto Lakes Industrial Pk., Hialeah, FL 33014-6335 (SAN 169-0981) Tel 305-624-4545; Fax: 305-621-0425; Toll Free: 800-766-3254
Web site: http://southernbooks.com.

Southern Cross Pubns., 1734 W. Roseberry Rd., P.O. Box 717, Donnelly, ID 83615 (SAN 110-8549) Tel 208-325-8606; Fax: 208-325-3400
E-mail: scp@cyberhighway.net
Web site: http://www.thoughtlines.com/southerncross/.

Southern Library Bindery Co., 2952 Sidco Dr., Nashville, TN 37204 (SAN 169-7986).

Southern Michigan News Co., 2571 Saradan, P.O. Box 908, Jackson, MI 49204 (SAN 169-3697) Tel 517-784-7163; Toll Free: 800-248-2213 (in Michigan); 800-828-2140.

Southern Periodicals, Inc., P.O. Box 407, Rayne, LA 70578-0407 (SAN 113-2520); 102 Industrial Dr., Rayne, LA 70578.

Southern Territory Assocs., Orders Addr.: 4508 64th St., Lubbock, TX 79414 Toll Free Fax: 800-799-9777; Toll Free: 800-331-7016.

Southern Tier News Co., P.O. Box 2128, Elmira Heights, NY 14903 (SAN 169-5223).

Southern Wisconsin News, 4838 N. County Rd. Y, Milton, WI 53563 (SAN 169-9121) Tel 608-756-2376 ; Fax: 608-756-2357.

Southwest Cookbook Distributors, Orders Addr.: P.O. Box 707, Bonham, TX 75418 (SAN 200-4925) Tel 903-583-8898; Fax: 903-583-2522; Toll Free: 800-725-8898 (orders); Edit Addr.: 1430 Texas Ave., Bonham, TX 75418 (SAN 630-8325).

Southwest Natural Cultural Heritage Association, *See* **Public Lands Interpretive Assn.**

Southwest News Co., Box 5465, Tucson, AZ 85704 (SAN 159-9631).

Southwestern Bk. Distributors, c/o Kerbs, 700 Highview Ave., Glen Ellyn, IL 60137-5504 (SAN 160-2373).

Sovereign News Company, *See* **Trans World News**

Spama, Inc., 78 Lake St., Jersey City, NJ 07306-3407 (SAN 169-5967).

Spanish & European Bookstore, Inc., 3102 Wilshire Blvd., Los Angeles, CA 90010 Tel 213-739-8899; Fax: 213-739-0087.

Spanish Bookstore-Wholesale, The, 10977 Santa Monica Blvd., Los Angeles, CA 90025-4538 (SAN 168-9835) Tel 310-475-0453; Fax: 310-473-6132
E-mail: BernardHamel@SpanishbooksUSA.com
Web site: http://www.BernardHamel.com.

Spanish Hse. Distributors, 1360 NW 88th Ave., Miami, FL 33172-3093 (SAN 169-1171) Tel 305-592-6136; Fax: 305-592-0087; Toll Free: 800-767-7726.

Spanishtech, Inc., Div. of Editor's Bureau, Ltd., P.O. Box 68, Westport, CT 06881 (SAN 289-9620) Tel 203-452-7655.

SPD-Small Pr. Distribution, *(0-914068)* 1341 Seventh St., Berkeley, CA 94710-1409 (SAN 204-5826) Tel 510-524-1668; Fax: 510-524-0852; Toll Free: 800-869-7553 (orders)
E-mail: orders@spdbooks.org
Web site: http://www.spdbooks.org.

Specialized Bk. Service, Inc., 307 Autumn Ridge Rd., Fairfield, CT 06432-1003 (SAN 166-9788) Tel 203-377-6510; Fax: 203-377-4792.

Specialty Bk. Services, 1150 N. San Francisco, Flagstaff, AZ 86001 (SAN 130-8114) Tel 520-779-7843.

Specialty Promotions, 6841 S. Cregier Ave., Chicago, IL 60649 (SAN 110-9987) Tel 773-493-6900.

Speedimpex U.S.A., Inc., 35-02 48th Ave., Long Island City, NY 11101-2421 (SAN 169-5479) Tel 718-392-7477; Fax: 718-361-0815
E-mail: nsalvatore@speedimpex.com
Web site: http://www.speedimpex.com.

Spencer Museum of Art, *(0-913689)* Affil. of Univ. of Kansas, Univ. of Kansas 1301 Mississippi St., Lawrence, KS 66045-7500 (SAN 111-347X) Tel 785-864-4710; Fax: 785-864-3112
E-mail: spencerart@ku.edu
Web site: http://www.ukans.edu/~sma.

SPI Bks., *(0-944007; 1-56171)* 99 Spring St., 3rd Flr., New York, NY 10012 Tel 212-431-5011; Fax: 212-431-8646
E-mail: ian@spibooks.com
Web site: http://www.spibooks.com.

Spring Arbor Distributors, Inc., Subs. of Ingram Industries Inc., 4271 Edison Ave., Chino, CA 91710; 7315 Innovation Blvd., Fort Wayne, IN 46818-1371; 201 Ingram Dr., Roseburg, OR 97470-7148; Newbury Rd., East Windsor, CT 06088; 25420 Weakley Rd., Petersburg, VA 23803; 11333 E. 53rd Ave., Denver, CO 80239-2108; Edit Addr.: 1 Ingram Blvd., La Vergne, TN 37086-1976 Fax: 615-213-5192; Toll Free: 800-395-4340; 800-395-7234 (customer service)
E-mail: orders@springarbor.com.

Springwater Bks., Orders Addr.: P.O. Box 194, Springwater, NY 14560-0194 (SAN 111-8900); Edit Addr.: Main St. & East Ave., Springwater, NY 14560-0194 (SAN 243-2412) Tel 716-669-2450.

Sprout, Inc., Orders Addr.: 430 Tenth Street, NW, Suite 007, Atlanta, GA 30318 Tel 404-892-9600; Fax: 404-881-1383.

Square Deal Records, 303 Higuera St., San Luis Obispo, CA 93401-4209 (SAN 170-6799) Tel 805-543-3636; Fax: 805-543-3938; Toll Free: 800-253-4114
E-mail: sdrsslo@aol.com.

St. Marie's Gopher News Co., 9000 Tenth Ave., N., Minneapolis, MN 55427 (SAN 169-4103) Tel 612-546-5300; Fax: 612-546-1487.

St. Martin's Pr., *(0-312; 0-8050; 0-940687; 0-9603648; 1-55927; 1-58063; 1-58238)* Div. of Holtzbrinck Publishers, Orders Addr.: 16365 James Madison Hwy., Gordonville, VA 22942 Tel 540-672-7600; Fax: 540-672-7540 (customer service); Toll Free Fax: 800-672-2054; Toll Free: 888-330-8477; Edit Addr.: 175 Fifth Ave., New York, NY 10010 (SAN 200-2132) Tel 212-726-0200 (College Div.); 212-674-5151 (Trade Div.); Fax: 212-686-9491 (College Div.); 212-674-3179 (Trade Div.); Toll Free: 800-470-4767 (College Div.); 800-221-7945 (Trade Div.)
E-mail: webmaster@stmartins.com; enquiries@stmartins.com
Web site: http://www.smpcollege.com; http://www.stmartins.com.

St. Mary Seminary Bookstore, 28700 Euclid Ave., Wyckliffe, OH 44092 (SAN 169-667X) Tel 216-943-7600.

Stackpole Bks., *(0-8117)* 5067 Ritter Rd., Mechanicsburg, PA 17055 (SAN 202-5396) Tel 717-796-0411; Fax: 717-796-0412
E-mail: sales@stackpolebooks.com
Web site: http://www.stackpolebooks.com.

Star Bright Bks., Inc., *(1-887734; 1-932065)* 42-26 28th St., Suite 2C, Long Island City, NY 11101 (SAN 254-5225) Tel 718-784-9112; Fax: 718-784-9012; Toll Free: 800-788-4439
E-mail: info@starbrightbooks.com
Web site: http://www.starbrightbooks.com.

Star Imaage Children's Bks., 11551 Four Towns Rd., Dept. 7, Gillett, WI 54124-9537 Tel 920-855-6107; Fax: 920-855-2012.

Starkmann Inc., 38 River St., Winchester, MA 01890 (SAN 126-6128) Tel 781-721-1537; Fax: 781-721-2825
E-mail: biggs@starkmann.co.uk.

Starmaster Co., 6911 Haverhill Dr., Knoxville, TN 37909 (SAN 108-1217) Tel 423-588-6661.

State Mutual Bk. & Periodical Service, Ltd., *(0-7855; 0-89771)* Orders Addr.: P.O. Box 1199, Bridgehampton, NY 11932-1199.

State News Agency, 2750 Griffith Rd., Winston Salem, NC 27103-6418 (SAN 169-6424).

SteinerBooks, Inc., *(0-8334; 0-88010; 0-89345; 0-910142; 1-58420; 1-85584; 0-9701097)* Orders Addr.: P.O. Box 960, Herndon, VA 20172-0960 Tel 703-661-1594 (orders); Fax: 702-661-1501; Toll Free Fax: 800-277-7947 (orders); Toll Free: 800-856-8664 (orders); Edit Addr.: P.O. Box 799, Great Barrington, MA 01230 Tel 413-528-8233; Fax: 413-528-8826; Fulfillment Addr.: 22883 Quicksilver Dr., Dulles, VA 20166 (SAN 253-9519) Tel 703-661-1529; Fax: 703-996-1010
E-mail: service@steinerbooks.org
Web site: http://www.lindisfarne.org; http://www.bellpondbooks.com; http://www.steinerbooks.org.

Sterling Publishing Co., Inc., *(0-8069; 1-4027)* 387 Park Ave., S., New York, NY 10016-8810 (SAN 211-6324) Tel 212-532-7160; Fax: 212-213-2495; Toll Free Fax: 800-775-8736 (warehouse) Do not confuse with companies with similar names in Falls Church, VA, Fallbrook, CA, Lewisville, TX
E-mail: custservice@sterlingpub.com
Web site: http://www.sterlingpub.com.

Sterling Publishing Company, Incorporated, *See* **Sterling Publishing Co., Inc.**

Stevens, Mark Industries, Div. of Christian World, Inc., 1215 N. Portland, Oklahoma City, OK 73107 (SAN 631-127X) Tel 405-948-1077; Fax: 405-948-1110; Toll Free: 800-654-6760.

Strauss Consultants, 48 W. 25th St., 11th Flr., New York, NY 10010-2708 Toll Free Fax: 888-528-8273; Toll Free: 800-236-7918
E-mail: strausscon@aol.com.

Streamwood Distribution, P.O. Box 91011, Mobile, AL 36691 Tel 334-665-0022; Fax: 334-665-0570.

Strelow, James C., 9440 El Blanco Ave., Fountain Valley, CA 92708 (SAN 132-4144) Tel 714-962-3697.

Subscription Acct., 84 Needham, Newton Highlands, MA 02161 (SAN 285-9424).

Subscription Hse., Inc., 209 Harvard St., Suite 407, Brookline, MA 02146-5005 (SAN 285-9343).

Subterranean Co., Orders Addr.: P.O. Box 160, Monroe, OR 97456 Tel 541-847-5274; Fax: 541-847-6018
E-mail: subco@clipper.net.

Success Education Assn., Box 175, Roanoke, VA 24002 (SAN 159-9690).

Sun Life, *(0-937930)* 2399 Cool Springs Rd., Thaxton, VA 24174 (SAN 240-8333) Tel 540-586-4898.

Sun News Company, *See* **Anderson News Co.**

Sunbelt Media, Incorporated, *See* **Eakin Pr.**

Sunbelt Pubns., Inc., *(0-916251; 0-932653; 0-9606704; 0-9620402)* 1250 Fayette St., El Cajon, CA 92020-1511 (SAN 630-0790) Tel 619-258-4911; Fax: 619-258-4916; Toll Free: 800-626-6579
E-mail: sunbeltpub@prodigy.net
Web site: http://www.sunbeltpub.com.

Sunburst Communications, Inc., *(0-7805; 0-911831; 1-55636; 1-55826)* 101 Castleton St., Pleasantville, NY 10570 (SAN 213-5620) Tel 914-747-3310; Toll Free: 800-431-1934
E-mail: webmaster@nysunburst.com
Web site: http://www.sunburst.com.

Sundance Publishing, *(0-7608; 0-88741; 0-940146; 1-56801)* Orders Addr.: P.O. Box 1326, Littleton, MA 01460 (SAN 169-3484) Tel 978-486-9201; Fax: 978-486-1053; Toll Free Fax: 800-456-2419; Toll Free: 800-343-8204 Do not confuse with Sundance Publishing, Inc., Patchogue, NY
E-mail: info@sundancepub.com
Web site: http://www.sundancepub.com/.

Sunset Bks./Sunset Publishing Corp., *(0-376)* 80 Willow Rd., Menlo Park, CA 94025-3691 Tel 650-321-3600; Fax: 650-324-1532; Toll Free: 800-227-7346 (except California); 800-321-0372 (in California)
Web site: http://sunsetbooks.com.

Sunshine Harbor, 825 Glen Arden Way, Altamonte Springs, FL 32701 (SAN 159-6640) Tel 407-339-0401.

Swedenborg Foundation, Inc., *(0-87785)* 320 N. Church St., West Chester, PA 19380 (SAN 111-7920) Tel 610-430-3222; Fax: 610-430-7982; Toll Free: 800-355-3222 (customer service)
E-mail: info@swedenborg.com
Web site: http://www.Swedenborg.com.

Swenson, Jim, 2610 Riverside Ln., NE, Rochester, MN 55901 (SAN 285-9505).

Swift News Agency, Orders Addr.: P.O. Box 160, Poncha Springs, CO 81242 (SAN 282-3810); Edit Addr.: 338 E. Hwy. 50, Poncha Springs, CO 81242 (SAN 169-0639).

Symmes Systems, *(0-916352)* 3977 Briarcliff Rd., NE, Atlanta, GA 30345-2647 (SAN 169-1465) Tel 404-876-7260.

T A Bookstore, *See* **Shea Bks.**

Tallahassee News Co., Inc., 3777 Hartsfield Rd., Tallahassee, FL 32303-1120.

Tapestry Pr., *(1-930819)* 3649 Conflans Rd., No. 103, Irving, TX 75061 Tel 972-399-8856; Fax: 972-313-9060 Do not confuse with companies with the same or similar name in Acton, MA, Springville, UT, Biloxi, MS
E-mail: info@tapestrypressinc.com
Web site: http://www.summitbooks.com.

Tapeworm Video Distributor, Inc., 27833 Avenue Hopkins, Unit 6, Valencia, CA 91355-3407 (SAN 630-8767) Tel 805-257-4904; Fax: 805-257-4820; Toll Free: 800-367-8437
E-mail: sales@tapeworm.com
Web site: http://www.tapeworm.com.

Tatnuck BookSeller, The, 335 Chandler St., Worcester, MA 01602-3402 (SAN 169-3654) Tel 508-756-7644.

Taylor & Francis, Inc., *(0-335; 0-415; 0-8448; 0-85066; 0-89116; 0-903796; 0-905273; 1-56032; 1-85000)* Orders Addr.: 10650 Toebben Dr., Independence, KY 41051 Toll Free Fax: 800-248-4724; Toll Free: 800-634-7064; Edit Addr.: 325 Chestnut St., Philadelphia, PA 19106 (SAN 241-9246) Tel 215-625-8900; Fax: 215-625-2940; 29 W. 35th St., New York, NY 10001 Tel 212-216-7800; Fax: 212-564-7854
E-mail: info@taylorandfrancis.com
Web site: http://www.taylorandfrancis.com.

TBN Enterprises, *See* **Ironside International Pubs., Inc.**

Technical Bk. Co., P.O. Box 25934, Los Angeles, CA 90025-8994 (SAN 168-9851) Toll Free: 800-233-5150.

Techno Mecca, Inc., 4412 W. Pico Blvd., 2nd Flr., Los Angeles, CA 90019 (SAN 631-7812) Tel 213-353-3900; Fax: 213-353-3910
E-mail: tjtj@tmecca.com
Web site: http://www.tmecca.com.

Temme Haus Pr., *(0-9727036)* 1784 Palm Ave., Stockton, CA 95205 (SAN 253-1925) Tel 209-463-5527.

Temple News Agency, *See* **ETD KroMar Temple**

Ten Speed Pr., *(0-89815; 0-913668; 1-58008)* Orders Addr.: P.O. Box 7123, Berkeley, CA 94707 (SAN 202-7674) Fax: 510-559-1629 (orders); Toll Free: 800-841-2665; 555 Richmond St., W. Suite 405, Box 702, Toronto, ON M5V 3B1 Tel 416-703-7775; Fax: 416-703-9992
E-mail: order@tenspeed.com; alan@tenspeed.ca; greg@tenspeed.com
Web site: http://www.tenspeed.com.

Territory Titles, 22 Camino Real, Sandia Park, NM 87047.

Tesla Bk. Co., *(0-914119; 0-9603536)* P.O. Box 121873, Chula Vista, CA 91912-6573 (SAN 241-8703) Tel 619-585-8487; Toll Free: 800-398-2056
E-mail: bfeuling@teslabook.com.

Texas A&M Univ. Pr., *(0-89096; 1-58544)* 4354 TAMU John H. Lindsey Bldg., Lewis St., College Station, TX 77843-4354 (SAN 658-1919) Tel 979-845-1436; Fax: 979-847-8752; Toll Free Fax: 888-617-2421 (orders); Toll Free: 800-826-8911 (orders)
E-mail: wjl@tampress.tamu.edu
Web site: http://www.tamu.edu/upress/.

Texas Art Supply, 2001 Montrose Blvd., Houston, TX 77006 (SAN 169-8303) Tel 713-526-5221; Fax: 713-524-7474; Toll Free: 800-888-9278
E-mail: info@texasart.com
Web site: http://www.texasart.com.

Texas Bk. Co., P.O. Box 212, Greenville, TX 75403 Fax: 903-454-2442; Toll Free: 800-527-1016
E-mail: monica@texasbook.com; diana@texasbook.com.

Texas Bookman, The, *(1-931040)* 2700 Lone Star Dr., Dallas, TX 75212-6209 (SAN 106-875X) Toll Free: 800-566-2665
E-mail: texas.bookman@halfpricebooks.com.

Texas Hill Country Cookbook, P.O. Box 126, Round Mountain, TX 78663 (SAN 110-831X) Tel 210-825-3242; Fax: 210-825-3244; Toll Free: 800-231-3553.

Texas Library Bk. Sales, 1408 West Koenig Lane, Austin, TX 78756 (SAN 169-8044) Tel 512-452-4140.

Thames Bk. Co., 1 Quarry Rd., Mystic, CT 06355-3200 (SAN 169-0760).

Thieme Medical Pubs., Inc., *(0-86577; 0-913258; 1-58890)* Subs. of Georg Thieme Verlag Stuttgart, 333 Seventh Ave., 5th Flr., New York, NY 10001 (SAN 169-5983) Tel 212-760-0888; Fax: 212-947-1112; Toll Free: 800-782-3488 (orders only)
E-mail: Info@Thieme.com; custserv@thieme.de
Web site: http://www.thieme.com.

Thieme-Stratton, Inc., *See* **Thieme Medical Pubs., Inc.**

Thinkers' Pr., Inc., *(0-938650; 1-888710)* Orders Addr.: P.O. Box 8, Davenport, IA 52805-0008 Tel 319-323-1226; Fax: 319-323-0511; Toll Free: 800-397-7117 (orders only); Edit Addr.: 1101 W. Fourth St., Davenport, IA 52802 (SAN 162-7759)
E-mail: tpi@chessco.com
Web site: http://www.chessco.com.

Thinking Works, Orders Addr.: P.O. Box 468, Saint Augustine, FL 32085-0468 Tel 904-824-0648; Fax: 904-824-8505; Toll Free: 800-633-3742 Do not confuse with Thinking Works!, Toledo, OH E-mail: thnkgwks@aug.com.

Thomas Brothers Maps, *(0-88130; 1-58174)* Div. of Rand McNally & Co., 17731 Cowan, Irvine, CA 92614 (SAN 158-8192) Fax: 949-757-1564; Toll Free: 800-899-6277 Web site: http://www.thomas.com.

Thompson Schl. Bk. Depository, Orders Addr.: P.O. Box 60160, Oklahoma City, OK 73146 (SAN 159-9747) Tel 405-525-9458; Fax: 405-524-5443; Edit Addr.: 39 NE 24th St., Oklahoma City, OK 73143.

Thomson Learning, 10650 Toebben Dr., Independence, KY 41051 (SAN 631-2144) Tel 859-525-6620; Fax: 859-525-0978; Toll Free: 800-347-7707 (customer service); 800-842-3636 (orders); a/o Customer Service, P.O. Box 6904, Florence, KY 41022-6904 Toll Free Fax: 800 487-8488; Toll Free: 800 354-9706 Web site: http://www.thomsonlearning.com.

Thomson, Linda, P.O. Box 1225, Orem, UT 84059-1225 (SAN 110-3881) Tel 801-226-0155; Fax: 801-226-0166; Toll Free: 800-226-0155.

Thorndike Pr., *(0-7838; 0-7862; 0-8161; 0-89621; 1-56054)* Div. of Gale Group, 295 Kennedy Memorial Dr., Waterville, ME 04901 Tel 207-859-1053; 207-859-1020; 207-859-1000; Toll Free Fax: 800-558-4676; Toll Free: 800-223-1244 (ext. 15); 800-877-4253 (customer resource ctr.) E-mail: knobloch@galegroup.com; barb.littfield@galegroup.com Web site: http://www.galegroup.com/thorndike.

Three Dimensional Publishing, *(1-877835)* 1015 Stirling Rd., Silver Spring, MD 20901 Tel 301-593-6450 E-mail: dexter@3dpublishing.com.

Tiffin News Agency, 1024 S. Bon Aire Ave., Tiffin, OH 44883-2553 (SAN 169-6866).

Tiger Bk. Distributors, Ltd., 328 S. Jefferson, Chicago, IL 60661 (SAN 631-0672) Tel 312-382-1160; Fax: 312-382-0323.

Time Warner Bk. Group, *(0-446)* Orders Addr.: 3 Center Plaza, Boston, MA 02108 Toll Free Fax: 800-286-9471; Toll Free: 800-759-0190; Edit Addr.: 135 W. 50th St. Sports Illustrated Building, New York, NY 10020-1393 Tel 212-522-7381; Toll Free Fax: 800-477-5925 Web site: http://www.timewarner.com.

Time-Life Publishing Warehouse, 5240 W. 76th, Indianapolis, IN 43268-4137 (SAN 631-1504) Fax: 717-348-6409; Toll Free: 800-277-8844 Web site: http://www.timelifecs.com; http://www.timelifeedu.com.

TIS, Inc., *(0-89917; 1-56581; 0-7421)* Orders Addr.: P.O. Box 669, Bloomington, IN 47402 Tel 812-332-3307; Fax: 812-331-7690; Toll Free: 800-367-4002; Edit Addr.: 5005 N. State Rd. 37 Business, Bloomington, IN 47404.

Titan Bookstore, P.O. Box 34080, Fullerton, CA 92634-9480 (SAN 106-4851).

Title Bks., Inc., 3013 Second Ave. S, Birmingham, AL 35233 (SAN 168-9207) Tel 205-324-2596.

Tobias News Co., 130 18th St., Rock Island, IL 61201 (SAN 169-2186) Tel 309-788-7517.

Todd Communications, *(1-57833; 1-878100)* 203 W. 15th Ave., Suite 102, Anchorage, AK 99501 (SAN 298-6280) Tel 907-274-8633; Fax: 907-276-6858 E-mail: info@toddcom.com.

Total Information, Inc., 844 Dewey Ave., Rochester, NY 14613 (SAN 123-7373) Tel 716-254-0621.

T.R. Bks., Orders Addr.: P.O. Box 310279, New Braunfels, TX 78131 (SAN 630-4885) Tel 830-625-2665; Fax: 830-620-0470; Toll Free: 800-659-4710; Edit Addr.: 822 N. Walnut Ave., New Braunfels, TX 78130 E-mail: trbooks@trbooks.com Web site: http://www.trbooks.com.

T.R. Trading Co., *See* **T.R. Bks.**

Tracor Technology Resources (TTR), Specialized Bk. Distributors, 1601 Research Blvd., Rockville, MD 20850 (SAN 169-3220) Tel 301-251-4970.

Trademark Direct, Inc., 14000 Rockland Rd., Libertyville, IL 60048 (SAN 631-6034) Tel 847-549-0040; Fax: 847-549-0115.

Trafalgar Square, *(0-943955; 1-57076)* Orders Addr.: P.O. Box 257, North Pomfret, VT 05053 (SAN 213-8859) Tel 802-457-1911; Fax: 802-457-1913; Toll Free: 800-423-4525; Edit Addr.: Howe Hill Rd., North Pomfret, VT 05053 E-mail: tsquare@sover.net Web site: http://www.trafalgarsquarebooks.com.

Trainex Press, *See* **Medcom/Trainex**

Trans World News, 3700 Kelley Ave., Cleveland, OH 44114-4533 (SAN 169-6688) Tel 216-391-4800; Fax: 216-391-9911; Toll Free: 800-321-9858.

Transamerican & Export News Co., 591 Camino de la Reina St., Suite 200, San Diego, CA 92108-3192 (SAN 169-0140) Tel 619-297-8065; Fax: 619-297-5353.

Trans-Atlantic Pubns., Inc., 311 Bainbridge St., Philadelphia, PA 19147 (SAN 694-0234) Tel 215-925-5083; Fax: 215-925-1912 Do not confuse with Transatlantic Arts, Inc., Albuquerque, NM E-mail: order@transatlanticpub.com Web site: http://www.transatlanticpub.com.

Traveler Restaurant, 741 Buckley Hwy., Union, CT 06076 (SAN 111-8218) Tel 860-684-4920.

Treasure Chest Bks., *(0-918080; 1-887896; 0-9700750)* Orders Addr.: P.O. Box 5250, Tucson, AZ 85703-0250 (SAN 209-3251) Tel 520-623-9558; Fax: 520-624-5888; Toll Free Fax: 800-715-5888; Toll Free: 800-969-9558; Edit Addr.: 451 N. Bonita Ave., Tucson, AZ 85745 Tel 602-623-9558 E-mail: info@treasurechestbooks.com; info@rionuevo.com Web site: http://www.rionuevo.com/; http://www.treasurechestbooks.com.

Treasure Chest Publications, *See* **Treasure Chest Bks.**

Treasure Valley News, 4242 S. Eagleson Rd. Ste. 108B, Boise, ID 83705-4985.

Tree Frog Trucking Co., 318 SW Taylor St., Portland, OR 97204 (SAN 169-7188) Tel 503-227-4760; Fax: 503-227-0829.

Tree of Life Midwest, P.O. Box 2629, Bloomington, IN 47402-2629 (SAN 169-7994) Toll Free: 800-999-4200.

Triangle News Co., Inc., 3498 Grand Ave., Pittsburgh, PA 15225 (SAN 169-7447).

Tri-County News Co., Inc., 1376 W. Main St., Santa Maria, CA 93458 (SAN 169-0345) Tel 805-925-6541; Fax: 805-925-3565 E-mail: trico2000@aol.com Web site: http://tri-countynews.com.

Tricycle Pr., *(1-58246; 1-883672)* Div. of Ten Speed Pr., Orders Addr.: P.O. Box 7123, Berkeley, CA 94707 Tel 510-559-1600; Fax: 510-559-1629 Web site: http://www.tenspeed.com.

Trinity Pr. International, *(1-56338)* Orders Addr.: P.O. Box 1321, Harrisburg, PA 17105-1321 Tel 717-541-8130; Fax: 717-671-5929; Toll Free: 800-877-0012; Edit Addr.: 4775 Linglestown Rd., Harrisburg, PA 17112 (SAN 253-8156) Fax: 717-541-8128 (administrative); 717-541-8136 (editorial) E-mail: trinity@morehousegroup.com Web site: http://www.trinitypressintl.com.

Tri-State News Agency, P.O. Box 778, Johnson City, TN 37601 (SAN 169-7897) Tel 423-926-8159; 604 Rolling Hills Dr., Johnson City, TN 37601 (SAN 282-4744).

Tri-State Periodicals, Inc., Orders Addr.: P.O. Box 1110, Evansville, IN 47706-1110 Tel 812-867-7416; Edit Addr.: 9844 Heddon Rd., Evansville, IN 47711 (SAN 241-7537) Tel 812-867-7419.

Trucatriche, Orders Addr.: 3800 Main St., Suite 8, Chula Vista, CA 91911 Tel 619-426-2690; Fax: 619-426-2695 E-mail: info@trucatriche.com.

Tulare County News, Box 831, Visalia, CA 93279 (SAN 169-0442) Tel 559-734-9206; Fax: 559-734-5732; Toll Free: 800-479-6006.

Turner Subscription Agency, Subs. of Dawson Holdings PLC, 1005 W Pines Rd., Oregon, IL 61061-9681 (SAN 107-7112) Tel 815-732-4476; Fax: 815-732-4489; Toll Free: 800-847-4201 E-mail: postmaster@dawson.com.

Tuttle Publishing, *(0-8048; 4-900737)* Orders Addr.: 364 Innovation Dr., North Clarendon, VT 05759-9436 Tel 802-773-8930; Fax: 802-773-6993; Toll Free Fax: 800-329-8885; Toll Free: 800-526-2778; Edit Addr.: 153 Milk St., 4th Flr., Boston, MA 02109 (SAN 213-2621) Tel 617-951-4080; Fax: 617-951-4045; Toll Free: 800) 247 1060 E-mail: info@tuttlepublishing.com Web site: http://www.tuttlemartialarts.com; http://www.tuttlepublishing.com.

Twentieth Century Christian Bks., *(0-89098)* 2809 Granny White Pike, Nashville, TN 37204 (SAN 206-2550) Tel 615-383-3842.

Twin City News Agency, Inc., P.O. Box 466, Lafayette, IN 47902-0466 Tel 765-742-1051.

Tyndale Hse. Pubs., *(0-8423; 1-4143)* Orders Addr.: P.O. Box 80, Wheaton, IL 60189-0080 (SAN 206-7749) Tel 630-668-8310; Fax: 630-668-3245; Toll Free: 800-323-9400; Edit Addr.: 351 Executive Dr., Wheaton, IL 60188 Web site: http://www.tyndale.com.

Typecase, The, 4041 W. Central Ave., Toledo, OH 43606.

Ubiquity Distributors, Inc., 607 Degraw St., Brooklyn, NY 11217 (SAN 200-7428) Tel 718-875-5491; Fax: 718-875-8047.

Ultra Bks., P.O. Box 945, Oakland, NJ 07436 (SAN 112-9074) Tel 201-337-8787.

Ulverscroft Large Print Bks., Ltd., *(0-7089)* Div. of F. A Thorpe, Orders Addr.: P.O. Box 1230, West Seneca, NY 14224-1230; Edit Addr.: 1881 Ridge Rd., West Seneca, NY 14224-1230 (SAN 208-3035) Tel 716-674-4270; Fax: 716-674-4195; Toll Free: 800-955-9659 E-mail: enquiries@ulverscroft.co.uk Web site: http://www.ulverscroft.co.uk.

Unarius Academy of Science Pubns., *(0-932642; 0-935097)* Orders Addr.: 145 S. Magnolia Ave., El Cajon, CA 92020-4522 (SAN 168-9614) Tel 619-444-7062; Fax: 619-444-9637; Toll Free: 800-475-7062 E-mail: uriel@unarius.org Web site: http://www.unarius.org.

Underground Railroad, The, 2769 Club House Rd., Mobile, AL 36605-4373 (SAN 630-7892) Tel 334-432-8811.

UNIPUB, *See* **Bernan Assocs.**

Unique Bks., Inc., 5010 Kemper Ave., Saint Louis, MO 63139 (SAN 630-0472) Tel 314-776-6695; Fax: 314-776-0841; Toll Free: 800-533-5446.

United Ad Label Company, Incorporated, *See* **Veriad**

United Magazine, Orders Addr.: P.O. Box 36, Columbia, KY 42728-0036 (SAN 169-2852) Tel 502-384-3444; Fax: 502-384-9324; Edit Addr.: 361 Industrial Park Rd., Louisville, KY 42728-0036 (SAN 250-3336).

United News Co., Inc., 111 Lake St., P.O. Box 3426, Bakersfield, CA 93305 (SAN 169-7579) Tel 805-323-7864.

United Society of Shakers, *(0-915836)* 707 Shaker Rd., New Gloucester, ME 04260 (SAN 158-619X) Tel 207-926-4597; Fax: 207-926-3559 E-mail: sdlshakers@aol.com Web site: http://www.shaker.lib.me.us.

United Subscription Service, 527 Third Ave., No. 284, New York, NY 10016-4100 (SAN 286-0104).

Univ. of Arizona Pr., *(0-8165)* 355 S. Euclid Ave., Suite 103, Tucson, AZ 85719 (SAN 205-468X) Tel 520-621-1441; Fax: 520-621-8899 E-mail: orders@uapress.arizona.edu Web site: http://www.uapress.arizona.edu.

Univ. of California Pr., *(0-520)* Orders Addr.: 1445 Lower Ferry Rd., Ewing, NJ 08618 Tel 609-883-1759 (Customer Service); Fax: 609-883-7413; Toll Free Fax: 800-999-1958 (U.S. & Canada); Toll Free: 800-777-4726 (U.S. & Canada); Edit Addr.: 2120 Berkeley Way, Berkeley, CA 94720 Tel 510-642-4247; 510-643-7154 (Journals); Fax: 510-643-7127; 510-642-1144 (Marketing); 510-642-9917 (Journals) E-mail: orders@cpfs.pupress.princeton.edu; journals@ucop.edu; askucp@ucpress.edu Web site: http://www.ucpress.edu.

Univ. of Chicago Pr., *(0-226; 0-89065; 0-943056; 1-892850)* Orders Addr.: 11030 S. Langley Ave., Chicago, IL 60628 (SAN 202-5280) Tel 773-568-1550 ; Fax: 773-660-2235; Toll Free Fax: 800-621-8476 (US & Canada); Toll Free: 800-621-2736 (US & Canada); Edit Addr.: 1427 E. 60th St., Chicago, IL 60637 (SAN 202-5299) Tel 773-702-7700; Fax: 773-702-9756 E-mail: general@press.uchicago.edu; kh@press.uchicago.edu Web site: http://www.press.uchicago.edu.

Univ. of Hawaii Pr., *(0-8248; 0-87022)* Orders Addr.: 2840 Kolowalu St., Honolulu, HI 96822-1888 (SAN 202-5353) Tel 808-956-8255; Fax: 808-988-6052 E-mail: uhpmkt@hawaii.edu; uhpbooks@hawaii.edu Web site: http://www.uhpress.hawaii.edu.

Univ. of Nebraska Pr., *(0-8032)* P.O. Box 880484, Lincoln, NE 68588-0484 (SAN 202-5337); 233 N. Eighth St., Lincoln, NE 68588-0255 Tel 402-472-3581 E-mail: pressmail@unl.edu Web site: http://www.nebraskapress.unl.edu.

Univ. of New Mexico Pr., *(0-8263)* 3721 Spirit Dr., SE, Albuquerque, NM 87106-5631 Tel 505-277-4810 (orders); Fax: 505-277-3350; Toll Free Fax: 800-622-8667; Toll Free: 800-249-7737 (orders only) ; Edit Addr.: 1720 Lomas Blvd., NE, Albuquerque, NM 87131-1591 (SAN 213-9588) Tel 505-277-2346; Fax: 505-277-9270
E-mail: unmpress@unm.edu
Web site: http://www.unmpress.com.

Univ. of Oklahoma Pr., *(0-8061)* Orders Addr.: 4100 28th Ave., NW, Norman, OK 73069-8218 (SAN 203-3194) Tel 405-325-2000; Fax: 405-364-5798; Toll Free: 800-627-7377; Edit Addr.: 1005 Asp Ave., Norman, OK 73019-6051 Fax: 405-325-4000
Web site: http://www.oupress.com.

Univ. of Tennessee Pr., *(0-87049; 1-57233)* Div. of Univ. of Tennessee & Member of Assn. of American Univ. Presses, Orders Addr.: 11030 S. Langley, Chicago, IL 60628 Tel 773-568-1550; Toll Free Fax: 800-621-8471; Toll Free: 800-621-2736 (orders only); Edit Addr.: 110 Conference Ctr. Bldg., Knoxville, TN 37996-0325 (SAN 212-9930) Tel 865-974-3321; Fax: 865-974-3724
E-mail: mcmillan@utpress.org; hannah@utpress.org
Web site: http//www.utpress.org.

Univ. of Texas Pr., *(0-292)* Orders Addr.: P.O. Box 7819, Austin, TX 78713-7819 (SAN 212-9876) Tel 512-471-7233; Fax: 512-320-0668; Toll Free: 800-252-3206; Edit Addr.: University of Texas at Austin, Austin, TX 78713-7819
E-mail: utpress@utpress.ppb.utexas.edu
Web site: http://www.utexas.edu/utpress.

Univ. of Washington Pr., *(0-295; 1-902716)* Orders Addr.: P.O. Box 50096, Seattle, WA 98145-5096 (SAN 212-2502); Edit Addr.: 1326 Fifth Ave., Suite 555, Seattle, WA 98101 Tel 206-543-8870; Fax: 206-685-3460; Toll Free Fax: 800-669-7993; Toll Free: 800-441-4115; 1126 N. 98th St., Seattle, WA 98103
E-mail: uwpord@u.washington.edu
Web site: http://www.washington.edu/uwpress.

Univ. Pr. of New England, *(0-87451; 0-915032; 1-58465)* Orders Addr.: 37 Lafayette St., Lebanon, NH 03766-1405 Tel 603-643-7100 (Sales Director); Toll Free: 800-421-1561; Edit Addr.: 23 S. Main St., Hanover, NH 03755-2048 (SAN 203-3283) Tel 603-448-1533; Fax: 603-643-1540
E-mail: University.Press@Dartmouth.edu
Web site: http://www.upne.com.

Univelt, Inc., *(0-87703; 0-912183)* Orders Addr.: P.O. Box 28130, San Diego, CA 92198-0130 (SAN 170-3099) Tel 760-746-4005; Fax: 760-746-3139; Edit Addr.: 740 Metcalf St., Suite 13, Escondido, CA 92025-1671 (SAN 658-2095)
E-mail: 76121.1532@compuserve.com
Web site: http://univelt.staigerland.com.

Universal Subscription Service, P.O. Box 35445, Houston, TX 77035 (SAN 287-4768).

University Bk. Service, Orders Addr.: P.O. Box 608, Grove City, OH 43123 (SAN 169-6912); Edit Addr.: 2297 Southwest Blvd., Suite A, Grove City, OH 43123 (SAN 282-4841) Toll Free: 800-634-4272.

Urban Land Institute, *(0-87420)* 1025 Thomas Jefferson St. NW, Suite 500 W., Washington, DC 20007-5201 (SAN 203-3399) Tel 202-624-7000; Fax: 202-624-7140; Toll Free: 800-321-5011
E-mail: bookstore@uli.org
Web site: http://www.ULI.ORG.

U.S. Games Systems, Inc., *(0-88079; 0-913866; 1-57281)* 179 Ludlow St., Stamford, CT 06902 (SAN 158-6483) Tel 203-353-8400; Fax: 203-353-8431; Toll Free: 800-544-2637
E-mail: usgames@aol.com
Web site: http://www.usgamesinc.com.

V H P S Holtzbrinck Publishers, *See* **Holtzbrinck Pubs.**

Val Publishing, 16 S. Terrace Ave., Mount Vernon, NY 10551 (SAN 107-6876) Tel 914-664-7077.

Valiant International Multi-Media Corp., 55 Ruta Ct., South Hackensack, NJ 07606 (SAN 652-8813) Tel 201-229-9800; Fax: 201-814-0418.

Valley Distributors, Inc., 2947 Felton Rd., Norristown, PA 19401 (SAN 169-7498) Tel 610-279-7650; Fax: 610-279-9093; Toll Free: 800-355-2665 (orders only).

Van Dyke News Agency, 2238 W. Pinedale Ave., Fresno, CA 93711-0453 (SAN 168-9630) Tel 209-291-7768; Fax: 209-291-7770.

Van Khoa Bks., 9200 Bolsa Ave., Suite 123, Westminster, CA 92683 (SAN 110-7534) Tel 714-892-0801
E-mail: vankhoa@vinet.com.

Verham News Corp., 75 Main St., West Lebanon, NH 03784 (SAN 169-4561) Fax: 603-298-8843.

Veriad, P.O. Box 2216, Brea, CA 92822 Tel 714-990-2700; Fax: 714-529-6310; Toll Free: 800-423-4643.

Victory Multimedia, *(0-9661850)* Div. of Victory Audio Video Services, Inc., 222 N. Sepulveda Blvd., No. 1306, El Segundo, CA 90245 (SAN 631-4112) Tel 310-416-9140; Fax: 310-416-9839
E-mail: sbvictory@juno.com.

Vida Life Publishers International, *See* **Vida Pubs.**

Vida Pubs., *(0-8297)* 8325 NW 53rd St., Suite 100, Miami, FL 33166 Tel 305-463-8432; Fax: 305-463-9329; Toll Free: 800-843-2548
E-mail: vidapubsales@harpercollins.com
Web site: http://www.editorialvida.com.

Video Project, The, 200 Estates Dr., Ben Lomond, CA 95005-9444 Toll Free: 800-475-2638
E-mail: videoproject@videoproject.org
Web site: http://www.videoproject.org.

Vide-O-Go/That's Infotainment, P.O. Box 2994, Princeton, NJ 08543-2994 (SAN 631-6042) Tel 609-716-1989; Fax: 609-716-1988; Toll Free: 800-323-8433
E-mail: videogo@aol.com
Web site: http://www.videogo.com.

Viking Penguin, *(0-14; 0-670)* Div. of Penguin Group (USA) Inc., Orders Addr.: 405 Murray Hill Pkwy, East Rutherford, NJ 07073 Toll Free: 800-788-6262 (individual consumer sales); 800-631-8571 (reseller customer service); 800-526-0275 (reseller sales); Edit Addr.: 375 Hudson St., New York, NY 10014-3657 (SAN 298-0258) Tel 212-366-2000; Fax: 212-366-2952; Toll Free: 800-331-4624
E-mail: publicity@warnerbooks.com
Web site: http://www.penguinputnam.com/.

Vinabind, P.O. Box 340, Steelville, MO 65565 (SAN 159-9828).

Vincennes News Agency, P.O. Box 1110, Evansville, IN 47706-1110 (SAN 169-2518).

Virginia Periodical Distributors, *See* **Aramark Magazine & Bk. Services, Inc.**

Vision Distributors, *(0-9626732)* Div. of Infinite Creations, Inc., Orders Addr.: P.O. Box 9839, Santa Fe, NM 87504 Tel 505-986-8221.

Vision Press, *See* **Vision Distributors**

Vision Video, *(1-56364)* Orders Addr.: P.O. Box 540, Worcester, PA 19490 Tel 610-584-3500; Fax: 610-584-4610; Toll Free: 800-523-0226; Edit Addr.: 2030 Wentz Church Rd., Worcester, PA 19490 (SAN 298-7392)
E-mail: info@gatewayfilms.com; info@visionvideo.com
Web site: http://www.gatewayfilms.com.

Vistabooks, *(0-89646)* 0637 Blue Ridge Rd., Silverthorne, CO 80498-8931 (SAN 211-0849) Tel 970-468-7673 (phone/fax)
E-mail: vistabooks@compuserve.com
Web site: http://www.vistabooks.com.

Vitality Distributors, 940 NW 51st Pl., Fort Lauderdale, FL 33309 (SAN 169-0973) Toll Free: 800-226-8482.

Vroman's, A. C., *(0-9639197)* 695 E. Colorado Blvd., Pasadena, CA 91101 (SAN 169-0027) Tel 626-449-5320; Fax: 626-792-7308.

WA Bk. Service, 26 Ranick Rd., Hauppauge, NY 11788 (SAN 107-2943) Tel 516-234-2255; Fax: 516-234-2268.

Wabash Valley News Agency, 2200 N. Curry Pike, No. 2, Bloomington, IN 47404-1486 (SAN 169-250X).

Waffle, O. G. Bk. Co. (The Bookhouse), P.O. Box 586, Marion, IA 52302 (SAN 112-8817) Tel 319-373-1832.

Waldenbooks Company, Incorporated, *See* **Waldenbooks, Inc.**

Waldenbooks, Inc., *(0-681)* Div. of Borders Group, Inc., a/o Calendar Orders, 455 Industrial Blvd., Ste. C, LaVergne, TN 37086 (SAN 179-3373); Orders Addr.: One Waldenbooks Dr., LaVergne, TN 37096; 11625 Venture, Mira Loma, CA 91752 Tel 909-361-4025; Edit Addr.: 100 Phoenix Dr., Ann Arbor, MI 48108-2202 (SAN 200-8858) Tel 734-477-1100
E-mail: customerservice@waldenbooks.com
Web site: http://www.waldenbooks.com; http://www.preferredreader.com.

Walker Art Ctr., *(0-935640)* Orders Addr.: 750 Vineland Pl., Minneapolis, MN 55403 (SAN 206-1880) Tel 612-375-7638; Fax: 612-375-7565
E-mail: lisa.middag@walkerart.org; paul.schumacher@walkerart.org.

Wallace's College Bk. Co., P.O. Box 689, Nicholasville, KY 40340-0689 (SAN 169-2844) Tel 606-255-0886; Fax: 606-259-9892; Toll Free Fax: 800-433-9329 (orders only); Toll Free: 800-354-9590 (orders only); 800-354-9500
E-mail: orders@wallaces.com.

Warner Bks., Inc., *(0-445; 0-446)* Div. of Time Warner Bk. Group, Orders Addr.: c/o Little Brown & Co., 3 Center Plaza, Boston, MA 02108-2084 Fax: 800-286-9471; Toll Free: 800-759-0190; Edit Addr.: 1271 Avenue of the Americas, New York, NY 10020 (SAN 281-8892) Tel 212-522-7200
Web site: http://www.warnerbooks.com.

Warner Home Video, Inc., *(0-7907; 1-55722)* Div. of Time Warner, Inc., 4000 Warner Blvd., Burbank, CA 91522 Tel 818-954-6000
Web site: http://www.warnerbros.com.

Warner Pr. Pubs., *(0-87162; 1-59317)* Orders Addr.: P.O. Box 2499, Anderson, IN 46018-2499 (SAN 691-4241) Tel 765-642-0256; Fax: 765-642-5652; Toll Free: 800-848-2464; Edit Addr.: 1200 E. Fifth St., Anderson, IN 46012 (SAN 111-8110) Tel 765-644-7721; Fax: 765-622-9511; Toll Free: 800-741-7721 (orders only)
Web site: http://www.choa.org.

Washington Bk. Distributors, 4930A Eisenhower Ave., Alexandria, VA 22304 (SAN 631-0095) Tel 703-212-9113; Fax: 703-212-9114; Toll Free: 800-699-9113
E-mail: zacwbd@prodigy.net
Web site: http://www.washingtonbk.com.

Washington Toy Co., 2163 28th Ave., San Francisco, CA 94116-1732 (SAN 107-1718).

Watson, W. R. & Staff, 150 Mariner Green Ct., Corte Madera, CA 94925 (SAN 286-0155) Tel 510-524-6156; Fax: 510-526-5023.

Watson-Guptill Pubns., Inc., *(0-8174; 0-8230)* Div. of VNU Business Media, Inc., 770 Broadway, New York, NY 10003 (SAN 282-5384)
E-mail: skerner@watsonguptill.com
Web site: http://www.watsonguptill.com.

Waubesa Press, *See* **Badger Bks., Inc.**

Waverly News Co., 17 State St., Newburyport, MA 01950 (SAN 169-3522).

Waymont Bk. Co., 136 Steuben St., Jersey City, NJ 07302 (SAN 630-768X) Tel 201-434-4268; Fax: 201-432-1293
E-mail: waymont@worldnet.att.net.

Wayne State Univ. Pr., *(0-8143)* Leonard N. Simons Bldg., 4809 Woodward Ave., Detroit, MI 48201-1309 (SAN 202-5221) Tel 313-577-6120; Fax: 313-577-6131; Toll Free: 800-978-7323 (customer orders)
E-mail: j.stephenson@wayne.edu
Web site: http://wsupress.wayne.edu.

Weatherhill, Inc., *(0-8348)* 41 Monroe Tpke., Trumbull, CT 06611-1315 (SAN 202-9529) Tel 203-459-5090; Fax: 203-459-5095; Toll Free: 800-437-7840
E-mail: weatherhill@weatherhill.com
Web site: http://www.weatherhill.com.

Weatherhill, John Incorporated, *See* **Weatherhill, Inc.**

Weems & Plath, Inc., *(1-878797)* 214 Eastern Ave., Annapolis, MD 21403 (SAN 630-9348) Tel 410-263-6700; Fax: 410-268-8713; Toll Free: 800-638-0428
E-mail: sales@weems-plath.com
Web site: http://www.weems-plath.com.

Weiner News Co., 1011 N. Frio, P.O. Box 7608, San Antonio, TX 78207 (SAN 169-8427) Tel 210-226-9333; Fax: 210-226-8679.

Weiser, Samuel Incorporated, *See* **Red Wheel/Weiser**

WellSpring Bks., P.O. Box 2765, Woburn, MA 01888-1465 (SAN 111-3399) Do not confuse with companies with the same or similar names in Albuquerque, NM, Ukiah, CA, Adelphia, NJ, Woburn, MA, Groton, VT.

Wenatchee News Agency, 434 Rock Island Rd., East Wenatchee, WA 98802-5360 (SAN 169-8885) Tel 509-662-3511.

West Texas News Co., Orders Addr.: 1214 Barranca, El Paso, TX 79935; Edit Addr.: P.O. Box 26488, El Paso, TX 79926 (SAN 169-8184) Tel 915-594-7586; Fax: 915-594-7589.

Westchester Pr., *(0-9671232)* 2132-J Crossing Way, High Point, NC 27262-8597
E-mail: westcpress@aol.com.

Western Book Distributors/Booksource, *See* **Western Booksource, Inc.**

Western Booksource, Inc., 4935 Metart Shwayn, Tillamook, OR 97141 (SAN 158-4332) Toll Free: 800-825-0100; 230 Fifth Ave., No. 1104, New York, NY 10001 Tel 212-889-9339; Fax: 212-889-9572.

Western International, Inc., *(0-9665194)* 1875 Oddie Blvd., Sparks, NV 89431-3559 (SAN 631-1695) Tel 775-359-4400; Fax: 775-359-4431; Toll Free: 800-634-6737.

Western Library Bks., 560 S. San Vicente Blvd., Los Angeles, CA 90048 (SAN 168-9878) Tel 213-653-8880.

Western Merchandisers, 2900 Airport Rd., Denton, TX 76207-2102 (SAN 156-4633).

Western Michigan News, *See* **Readmor**

Western New York Wares, Inc., *(0-9620314; 1-879201)* Orders Addr.: P.O. Box 733, Buffalo, NY 14205 (SAN 248-6911) Tel 716-832-6088; Edit Addr.: 419 Parkside Ave., Buffalo, NY 14216 (SAN 248-692X) Tel 716-832-6088
E-mail: wnywares@gateway.net.

Western Record Sales, 2991 Saint Andrews Rd., Fairfield, CA 94533-7839 (SAN 630-6667).

Western Reserve Historical Society, *(0-911704)* 10825 East Blvd., Cleveland, OH 44106 (SAN 110-8387) Tel 216-721-5722; Fax: 216-721-0645.

Weston, Edward Fine Arts, P.O. Box 3098, Chatsworth, CA 91313-3098 (SAN 168-9967) Tel 818-885-1044; Fax: 818-885-1021.

Weston Woods Studios, Inc., *(0-7882; 0-89719; 1-55592; 1-56008)* Div. of Scholastic, Inc., 12 Oakwood Ave., Norwalk, CT 06850 (SAN 630-3838) Tel 203-226-3355; Fax: 203-845-0498; Toll Free: 800-290-7531; 800-243-5020 (customer service)
E-mail: Leighcorra@aol.com
Web site: http://www.scholastic.com.

Westwater Bks., *(0-916370)* Div. of Belknap Photographic Services, Inc., P.O. Box 2560, Evergreen, CO 80437 (SAN 208-3698) Tel 303-674-5410; Fax: 303-670-0586; Toll Free: 800-628-1326.

Whatever Publishing, Incorporated, *See* **New World Library**

Whitaker Distributors, *See* **Anchor Distributors**

Whiting News Co., 1417 119th St., Whiting, IN 46394 (SAN 169-2542).

Whitlock & Co., 10001 Roosevelt Rd., Westchester, IL 60153 (SAN 285-9645).

Wholesale Distributors, P.O. Box 126, Burlington, IA 52601 (SAN 145-8051) Tel 319-753-1683; Fax: 319-753-5988; Toll Free: 800-272-1556.

Wickel, W. W. Co., Inc., 520 N. Exchange Ct., Aurora, IL 60504 (SAN 135-1230) Tel 630-820-0044; Fax: 630-820-0057; Toll Free: 800-728-0708.

Wieser Educational, Inc., 30085 Comercio, Santa Margarita, CA 92688 (SAN 630-7361) Tel 714-858-4920; Fax: 714-858-0209; Toll Free: 800-880-4433
E-mail: info@wieser-ed.com
Web site: http://www.wieser-ed.com.

Wilcor International Bk. Dept., 700 Broad St., Utica, NY 13501-1336 (SAN 107-7023) Tel 315-733-3542.

Wilcox & Follet Company, *See* **Follett Educational Services**

William Thomson, *See* **Thomson, Linda**

Williamson, Darcy, *See* **Southern Cross Pubns.**

Wilshire Bk. Co., *(0-87980)* 12015 Sherman Rd., North Hollywood, CA 91605-3781 (SAN 168-9932) Tel 818-765-8579; Fax: 818-765-2922
E-mail: mpowers@mpowers.com
Web site: http://www.mpowers.com.

Wilson & Sons, P.O. Box 996, Bellevue, WA 98009 (SAN 129-0010) Tel 425-392-1965
E-mail: dchief@seanst.com.

Winch, B. L. & Assocs., *(0-935266)* P.O. Box 1185, Torrance, CA 90505 (SAN 247-2716) Tel 310-816-3085; Fax: 310-816-3092; Toll Free: 800-662-9662 (orders only)
E-mail: czippi@att.net
Web site: http://www.ierc.com.

Windham County News Co., P.O. Box 8127, Brattleboro, VT 05304 (SAN 159-9917) Tel 802-254-2373.

Wine Appreciation Guild, Ltd., *(0-932664; 1-891267)* 360 Swift Ave., Unit 30, South San Francisco, CA 94080-6220 (SAN 169-0264) Tel 650-866-3020; Fax: 650-866-3513; Toll Free: 800-242-9462 (orders only)
E-mail: wineappreciation.com
Web site: http://www.wineappreciation.com.

Winebaum News, Inc., P.O. Box 1620, Raymond, NH 03077-3620 (SAN 169-4529).

Winters Publishing, *(0-9625329; 1-883651)* Orders Addr.: P.O. Box 501, Greensburg, IN 47240 (SAN 298-1645) Tel 812-663-4948 (phone/fax); Toll Free: 800-457-3230; Edit Addr.: 705 E. Washington, Greensburg, IN 47240 Do not confuse with Winters Publishing, Wichita, KS
E-mail: tmwinters@juno.com.

Wittenborn Art Bks., *(0-8150; 0-89648)* Orders Addr.: P.O. Box 2210, San Francisco, CA 94126 Toll Free: 800-660-6403; Edit Addr.: 1109 Geary Blvd., San Francisco, CA 94109 Tel 415-292-6500; Fax: 415-292-6594
E-mail: wittenborn@earthlink.net
Web site: http://www.art-books.com.

Wolper Sales Agency, Inc., 6 Centre Sq., Suite 302A, Easton, PA 18042-3606 (SAN 285-9785) Tel 610-559-9550; Fax: 610-559-9898.

Wolverine Distributing, Inc., *(0-941875)* P.O. Box 503, Powell, WY 82435 (SAN 666-1211) Tel 307-754-2948; Fax: 307-754-2968; Toll Free: 800-967-1633
E-mail: wolverine@tctwest.net.

Wolverine Gallery, *See* **Wolverine Distributing, Inc.**

Women Ink, 777 United Nations Plaza, New York, NY 10017 (SAN 630-8309) Tel 212-687-8633; Fax: 212-661-2704
E-mail: wink@womenink.org
Web site: http://www.womenink.org.

Woodbine Publishing Co., The, 15621 Chemical Ln., No. B, Huntington Beach, CA 92649 (SAN 114-4243) Tel 714-894-9080; Fax: 714-894-4949; Toll Free: 800-451-4788
Web site: http://www.safaripress.com.

Woodcrafters Lumber Sales, Inc., 212 NE Sixth Ave., Portland, OR 97232 (SAN 112-6075) Tel 503-231-0226; Toll Free: 800-777-3709.

Word for Today, The, *(0-936728; 1-931713)* Orders Addr.: P.O. Box 8000, Costa Mesa, CA 92628 (SAN 110-8379) Toll Free: 800-272-9673; Edit Addr.: 3232 W. MacArthur Blvd., Santa Ana, CA 92704 (SAN 214-2260) Tel 714-825-9673 Toll Free: 800-272-9637
E-mail: info@twft.com
Web site: http://www.twft.com.

Word of Life Distributors, 2717 W. Olympic Blvd., Suite 103, Los Angeles, CA 90006 (SAN 108-433X) Tel 213-382-4538; Fax: 213-382-1154; Toll Free: 800-347-7057.

Words Distributing Co., *(0-914728)* Div. of Bookpeople, 7900 Edgewater Dr., Oakland, CA 94621 (SAN 154-7763) Tel 510-632-4700; Fax: 510-632-1281; Toll Free: 800-999-4650; 800-593-9673 (orders).

Workman Publishing Co., Inc., *(0-7611; 0-89480; 0-911104; 1-56305)* 708 Broadway, New York, NY 10003 (SAN 203-2821) Tel 212-254-5900; Fax: 212-254-8098; Toll Free: 800-722-7202
E-mail: mged@workman.com
Web site: http://www.workmanweb.com; http://www.workman.com.

World Pubns., Inc., *(0-7669; 0-9640034; 1-57215; 0-7429; 1-4132)* Orders Addr.: P.O. Box 622, North Dighton, MA 02764; Edit Addr.: 455 Somerset Ave., Bldg. 2A, North Dighton, MA 02764 (SAN 631-7014) Tel 508-880-5555; Fax: 508-880-0469 Do not confuse with World Publications, Inc., Winter Park, FL
E-mail: sales@wrldpub.com
Web site: http://www.wrldpub.com/.

World Scientific Publishing Co., Inc., *(981-02; 9971-950; 981-238)* 1060 Main St., River Edge, NJ 07661 (SAN 241-9920) Tel 201-487-9655; Fax: 201-487-9656; Toll Free: 800-227-7562
Web site: http://www.worldscientific.com/index.cgi.

World Univ., *(0-941902)* P.O. Box 2470, Benson, AZ 85602 (SAN 239-7943) Tel 520-586-2985; Fax: 520-586-4764
E-mail: desertsanctuary@theriver.com
Web site: http://worlduniversity.org.

World Wide Distributors, Limited, *See* **Island Heritage Publishing**

World Wide Hunting Books, *See* **Woodbine Publishing Co., The**

World Wide Pubns., *(0-89066)* 1303 Hennepin Ave., Minneapolis, MN 55403-1780 (SAN 159-9941) Tel 612-338-0500; Fax: 612-338-3029; Toll Free: 800-788-0442.

World Wisdom Books, Incorporated, *See* **World Wisdom, Inc.**

World Wisdom, Inc., *(0-941532)* P.O. Box 2682, Bloomington, IN 47402-2682 (SAN 239-1406) Tel 812-333-4088 (ext. 32); Fax: 812-333-1642
E-mail: mknason@worldwisdom.com
Web site: http://www.worldwisdom.com.

Worldwide Media Service, Inc., Affil. of Hudson County News Agency, 30 Montgomery St., Jersey City, NJ 07302-3821 (SAN 630-4826) Tel 201-332-7100; Fax: 201-332-0265; Toll Free: 800-345-6478
Web site: http://www.americanmagazine.com.

Wright Bk./Educational, 2195 Owendale Dr., Dayton, OH 45439 (SAN 159-9968).

Writers & Bks., *(0-9618487)* 339 East Ave. Ste. 301, Rochester, NY 14604-2615 (SAN 156-9678).

Writers Pr., Inc., *(1-885101; 1-931041)* 2309 Mountainview Dr., Suite 185, Boise, ID 83706 Tel 208-327-0566; Fax: 208-327-3477; Toll Free: 800-574-1715 Do not confuse with companies with the same or similar name in Washington, DC, Victorville, CA
E-mail: publisher@writerspress.com; info@writerspress.com
Web site: http://www.writerspress.com.

Writer's Press Service, *See* **Writers Pr., Inc.**

Wybel Marketing Group, Orders Addr.: 213 W. Main St., Barrington, IL 60010 Tel 847-382-0384.

Wyoming Periodical Distributor, P.O. Box 2340, Casper, WY 82601 (SAN 169-9245).

X-S Bks., Inc., 81 Brookside Ave., Amsterdam, NY 12010-0740 (SAN 169-4634).

Yankee Bk. Peddler, Inc., 999 Maple St., Contoocook, NH 03229 (SAN 169-4510) Tel 603-746-3102; Fax: 603-746-5628; Toll Free: 800-258-3774
E-mail: ybp@office.ybp.com
Web site: http://www.ybp.com.

Yankee Paperback & Textbook Co., P.O. Box 18880, Tucson, AZ 85731 (SAN 112-1073) Tel 520-325-7229 (phone/fax); Toll Free: 800-340-2665 (in Arizona, California, Nevada, Colorado, New Mexico and Utah only).

Yankee Paperback Distributors, *See* **Yankee Paperback & Textbook Co.**

Ye Olde Genealogie Shoppe, *(0-932924; 1-878311)* Orders Addr.: P.O. Box 39128, Indianapolis, IN 46239 (SAN 200-7010) Tel 317-862-3330; Toll Free: 800-419-0200 (orders)
E-mail: yogs@iquest.net
Web site: www.yogs.com.

Yosemite Assn., *(0-939666; 1-930238)* Orders Addr.: P.O. Box 230, El Portal, CA 95318 (SAN 662-197X) Tel 209-379-2648; Fax: 209-379-2486; Edit Addr.: 5020 El Portal Rd., El Portal, CA 95318
E-mail: yose_yosemite_association@nps.gov
Web site: http://www.yosemite.org.

Young News, Inc., 1600 E. Grand Blvd., Detroit, MI 48211-3144 (SAN 169-3999) Fax: 517-753-7774.

Yuma News, Incorporated, *See* **Arizona Periodicals, Inc.**

YWAM Publishing, *(0-927545; 0-9615534; 1-57658)* Div. of Youth with a Mission International, Orders Addr.: P.O. Box 55787, Seattle, WA 98155 (SAN 695-8265) Tel 425-771-1153; Fax: 425-775-2383; Toll Free: 800-922-2143; Edit Addr.: 7825 230th St., SW, Edmonds, WA 98026 (SAN 248-4021)
E-mail: customerservice@ywampublishing.com
Web site: http://www.ywampublishing.com.

Zabel, C. & W. Co., Orders Addr.: P.O. Box 953, East Brunswick, NJ 08816-0953 (SAN 169-4731) Tel 732-254-1000; Fax: 732-254-0121; Edit Addr.: 24 Rebel Run Dr., East Brunswick, NJ 08816 (SAN 241-6441) Tel 201-947-3300.

Zeitlin Periodicals Co., Inc., 7917 Lark Meadow Ave., Las Vegas, NV 89131-4710 (SAN 160-8088).

Zondervan, *(0-310; 0-937336)* Subs. of HarperCollins US, c/o Zondervan, Order Processing-B36, 5300 Patterson Ave., SE, Grand Rapids, MI 49530 (SAN 203-2694) Tel 616-698-6900; Fax: 616-698-3439; Toll Free Fax: 800-934-6381 (fax orders); Toll Free: 800-727-1309 (orders & customer service)
E-mail: zprod@zph.com
Web site: http://www.zondervan.com.

Zondervan Publishing House, *See* **Zondervan**

Zubal, John T. Inc., *(0-939738)* 2969 W. 25th St., Cleveland, OH 44113 (SAN 165-5841) Tel 216-241-7640; Fax: 216-241-6966
Web site: http://www.zuba.com.